THE *ESPN* PRO FOOTBALL ENCYCLOPEDIA
FIRST EDITION

MONDAY NIGHT FOOTBALL

Date	Airtime (ET)	Match-up
Preseason		
Mon, 8/14	8:00PM	Oakland Raiders at Minnesota Vikings
Mon, 8/21	8:00PM	Dallas Cowboys at New Orleans Saints (Shreveport, LA)
Fri, 8/25	8:00PM	Pittsburgh Steelers at Philadelphia Eagles
Mon, 8/28	8:00PM	Green Bay Packers at Cincinnati Bengals
Regular Season		
9/11	7:00PM	Minnesota Vikings at Washington Redskins
	10:15PM	San Diego Chargers at Oakland Raiders
9/18	8:30PM	Pittsburgh Steelers at Jacksonville Jaguars
9/25	8:30PM	Atlanta Falcons at New Orleans Saints
10/2	8:30PM	Green Bay Packers at Philadelphia Eagles
10/9	8:30PM	Baltimore Ravens at Denver Broncos
10/16	8:30PM	Chicago Bears at Arizona Cardinals
10/23	8:30PM	N.Y. Giants at Dallas Cowboys
10/30	8:30PM	New England Patriots at Minnesota Vikings
11/6	8:30PM	Oakland Raiders at Seattle Seahawks
11/13	8:30PM	Tampa Bay Buccaneers at Carolina Panthers
11/20	8:30PM	N.Y. Giants at Jacksonville Jaguars
11/27	8:30PM	Green Bay Packers at Seattle Seahawks
12/4	8:30PM	Carolina Panthers at Philadelphia Eagles
12/11	8:30PM	Chicago Bears at St. Louis Rams
12/18	8:30PM	Cincinnati Bengals at Indianapolis Colts
12/25	8:30PM	N.Y. Jets at Miami Dolphins

Unless otherwise noted all telecasts air on Mondays.

All games will be distributed live (1) nationally, and (2) locally in the
home and away team markets via over-the-air syndication agreements.

THE ESPN PRO FOOTBALL ENCYCLOPEDIA
FIRST EDITION

EXECUTIVE EDITOR **GARY GILLETTE**
MANAGING EDITOR **MATT SILVERMAN**
EDITORS **PETE PALMER, KEN PULLIS, SEAN LAHMAN**
ASSOCIATE EDITORS **CHRIS KAHRL, TOD MAHER, GREG SPIRA**

STERLING PUBLISHING CO.,INC.
NEW YORK

Published by Sterling Publishing Co., Inc.
387 Park Avenue South, New York, NY 10016

Distributed in Canada by Sterling Publishing
c/o Canadian Manda Group, 165 Dufferin Street,
Toronto, Ontario, Canada M6K 3H6

Distributed in the United Kingdom by GMC Distribution Services,
Castle Place, 166 High Street, Lewes, East Sussex, England BN7 1XU

Distributed in Australia by Capricorn Link (Australia) Pty. Ltd.
P.O. Box 704, Windsor, NSW 2756, Australia

ISBN-13: 978-1-4027-4216-3
ISBN-10: 1-4027-4216-9

2 4 6 8 10 9 7 5 3 1

For information about custom editions, special sales, premium and
corporate purchases, please contact Sterling Special Sales
Department at 800-805-5489 or specialsales@sterlingpub.com

DEDICATION

This encyclopedia is dedicated to the members of the non-profit Professional Football Researchers Association (www.FootballResearch.com), unsung heroes in the quest to document the many missing portions of the history of the game.

ACKNOWLEDGMENTS

Any reference work of this magnitude, especially a first edition, depends on the contributions or expertise of dozens of people. The editors wish to alphabetically acknowledge those who helped in one way or another in the birth of this work:

Robbie Bohren, Ed Brickley, Bob Carroll, Ryall Carroll, Bill Ciminelli, Joe Cronin, Mark Dalton, Pete Fierle, Christie Gagnon Chuck Garrity, Jr., Steve Gietschier, Bob Gill, Greg Gladyszewski, Eric Goska, Todd Greanier, Mike Haim, Richard Hancock, Pat Hanlon, John Hendry, Tom Hoffman, John Hogrogian, Joe Horrigan, Stacey James, Rick Korch, Ann Kupferschmid, Jamie Lotze, Phil Lowry, Denny Lynch, Pete Moris, Terry Musolf, David Neft, Pete Newmann, David Pietrusza, Jack Reed, Bob Richardson, Beau Riffenburgh, Jim Saccomano, Dwight Spradlin, Ted Stafford, Steve Supanich, Melissa Thomas, John Troan T.J. Troup, John Turney, Nick Webster, Chris Willis, and Walt Wilson.

Special thanks to those colleagues who graciously agreed to blurb the encyclopedia: Allen Barra, Doug Drinen, King Kaufman, Warren Moon, Aaron Schatz, and John Thorn.

The editors cannot say enough about how pleasant it is to work with the good people at Sterling Publishing. Editorial Director Nathaniel Marunas provided exactly the kind of strong support and autonomy that writers and editors dream about but rarely ever get. The Sterling team that made this encyclopedia possible includes:

CEO Steve Riggio, for unwavering front-office support; Publisher Bruce Lubin, for canny management on the road and at home; Art Director Kevin Ullrich, for sketching out even the most difficult plays with style; Senior Designer Kevin Baier, for the snappy uniforms; Designer Michele Trombley, for taking care of the stuff printed in the corners of our helmets; Editorial Assistant Devorah Klein, for help with crucial fourth-down conversions; Managing Editor Maria Spano, for keeping the players on the move; and production manager Charlie Ryf, for his intimidating presence at the line of scrimmage.

Thanks also go to several people at ESPN—Sandy DeShong, Chris Raymond, Glen Waggoner, Eric Karabell, and Seth Wickersham—for their record-setting, not to mention extremely good-humored, efforts to get essential materials to the team during crunch time.

Kudos to the tremendous typesetting team at Scribe in Philadelphia, who once again proved that experience, expertise, patience, and hard work are a winning combination. David Rech and Andy Brown run the show there. Jeremy C. Ellis was the go-to guy—he never flinched at the hard work or pressing deadlines and never failed to do whatever was necessary to make this a better book.

Finally, we express our gratitude to our wives, who patiently keep our lives in balance while we work overtime to get everything done: Debbie Silverman, Vicki Gillette, Beth Palmer, Jennifer Pullis, and Heather Lahman.

CONTENTS

FOREWORD

Football statistics mean more now than ever. Thanks to fantasy football, fans reciting stats from the weekend's games surround every water cooler in America. Fans used to ask, "How about that comeback win by the Broncos?" Now it's, "Did you see Peyton Manning threw for 311 yards and four touchdowns? He's on my fantasy team."

From ESPN.com to ESPN Mobile, numbers are updated instantly and available with a click. So it's easy to find out how many yards Tom Brady passed for last week against the Dolphins. That's great, but it's also nice to put today's players in context. To put them in perspective. To see how they match up historically. That's why the *ESPN Pro Football Encyclopedia* is a heaven-sent gift to every NFL fan. It's a source of information. It's a source of conversation. The questions we have as pro football fans are endless, and now there's a place to find answers.

The NFL has grown so much—from the physical size of the players to the size of their contracts, from the Super Bowl having empty seats to billion-dollar television contracts—that it's easy to forget pieces of the game's past. Time has forgotten a lot of stars and a lot of records. Did you know that Deion Sanders isn't even among the top 20 in interceptions, but that Paul Krause is? Or that Paul Warfield led the league in touchdowns more times than Terrell Davis? Or that no Hall of Famer quarterback has a higher passer rating than Kurt Warner?

Sundays are more hyped—and scrutinized—than ever before. Player salaries are higher. Coaches are under more pressure not only to win but to win now. Rosters turn over every year, making it tougher to build a team. More fans pack the stadiums, and more money is dealt for television rights. The late, great Pete Rozelle dreamed of parity, and it's happening. Football just keeps getting bigger, and that's why the statistics are so important.

Flip through this book, you'll get every kind of record out there. Records for most games in a row with 300 yards passing, for most consecutive 1,000-yard rushing seasons, for MVP awards won, for wins, for losses. You'll get 10 pages alone on *Monday Night Football*. You can pack a lot of information into 1,472 pages. Check for yourself.

There are three records listed here that I think will never be touched, not with the way the game is played today.

The first is Brett Favre's record for consecutive starts by a quarterback: 221 (and counting). How amazing is this? Peyton Manning will have to make it through six more seasons uninterrupted just to tie Brett.

The second unbeatable record is the Dolphins' perfect 17–0 season in 1972. With parity, the salary cap and free agency, that record is safe. I guarantee it.

The final record I see standing forever is Don Shula's mark of 347 career wins. No one will coach as long as Shula did. There's too much pressure, too much impatience by owners.

But that's the beauty of the *ESPN Pro Football Encyclopedia*: it gives you a chance to enjoy those old records, and argue about them. It gives you a chance to remember what time forgot. It gives you a chance to spend a lot more time at the watercooler.

That's why if you're a football fan, this book is a must-have.

—Joe Theismann

INTRODUCTION

The NFL is midway through its ninth decade now, and the legends of yesteryear now appear in our minds in soft focus as the details of their greatness start to fade. Personal memories of the great two-way smash-mouth football stars of the first decades of the NFL are now the province of fewer and fewer fans. Records of the accomplishments and exploits of the founders and early stars of the NFL are virtually impossible to find now—short of a trip to the Hall of Fame in Canton, Ohio.

As time advances relentlessly, the importance of a football book of record grows with each passing day. The world needs a new football encyclopedia a lot more than it needs a good 5-cent cigar, another 5-buck cigar, another reality TV show, or another sports-talk radio show—and, most importantly, more than it needs another $60 football encyclopedia that would be published only every three years or so.

As any football fan with an interest in the sport's history can see, we have included a boatload of information and statistics about pro football never before available. Many of the basic player statistics were previously published in other encyclopedias, but it has been seven long years since anyone published a pro football encyclopedia of any sort. While *Total Football* was a terrific book, it cost a cool $60 in 1999, and it was out-of-date a year later.

The cold, hard fact is that publishers have viewed massive sports encyclopedias that cost $50 or more as dinosaurs for several years. Baseball, which unlike football, has a long, rich tradition of great encyclopedias, saw the last of these dinosaurs lumber off the playing field in 2004 with the publication of the eighth edition of *Total Baseball*—a book that came out in midseason and was obsolete within three months. That book was so expensive to print that the publisher lost money on every copy and couldn't afford to reprint it even when it sold out. People won't shell out $50 for a book anymore when so much information is available for free on the Web, and the economics of printing books that large make it impossible to update them annually.

In 2004, however, there was a breakthrough when Barnes & Noble published the first edition of what would become *The ESPN Baseball Encyclopedia*. More than 1,700 pages long and containing statistics for every player in baseball history—more stats than any other baseball encyclopedia ever—it boasted a retail price of only $25. This revolutionary new *Baseball Encyclopedia* was published

in paperback and designed from the start to be updated every year. Moreover, this new *Baseball Encyclopedia* was affordable enough for a fan to buy it every year. Remarkably, it was the first comprehensive baseball encyclopedia to be published for $25 in a quarter-century, and $25 in 1979 was worth a lot more than $25 is now.

Even though there are dozens of Websites out there in cyberspace that will give you career stats for all baseball players for free, the *ESPN Baseball Encyclopedia* has been a great success. The World Wide Web is a wonderful resource in many ways, for a multitude of reasons. Yet a Web page can be evanescent, and the unexpected treasure you find and bookmark today can show up in your browser as nothing but an "Error 404" message tomorrow. For this purpose, only a book will suffice.

Naturally, then, when we undertook to do a pro football encyclopedia, we modeled it on our baseball encyclopedia. First, we assembled an experienced editorial team with a vast amount of expertise in both football history as well as in publishing sports encyclopedias. Then we spent months designing the book to make it as readable as possible while still containing the maximum amount of information.

Finally, we undertook the hard work to fill an important gap in football's historical record. For the first time ever, you can now look up the starters at each position for every NFL team, dating back to 1920—which took an enormous amount of research. Using that new information, we compiled year-by-year height and weight data for regular players for the first time. And we have more information on football awards than ever before published.

So, until we can access all of this wealth of statistics and information on the Web while we're sprawled out in our backyard hammock, or sunning ourselves on the beach—or, more likely, while we're sitting in our easy chair, screaming at the TV as we watch the Big Game—we still need a good book to look this stuff up. The tiny screens on cell phones and other PDAs, even when they are Web-enabled, just don't cut it for serious reading.

Ultimately, the goal of this book is to entertain and edify the uncounted tens of millions of pro football fans, both diehard and casual, as well as the millions of avid fantasy football players. We've done the best job we can, and we hope you enjoy the fruits of our labor.

THE ESPN PRO FOOTBALL ENCYCLOPEDIA

THE HISTORY OF PRO FOOTBALL

In short, in life, as in a foot-ball game, the principle to follow is: Hit the line hard; don't foul and don't shirk, but hit the line hard. —Theodore Roosevelt, The Strenuous Life (1900)

The game of football as we know it came into being in Washington, D.C., at the White House. It was there in October 1905 that President Theodore Roosevelt insisted that the game's rules be revised. In 1905 alone, 18 young men were killed playing football. A century later, with 1.8 million playing football—plus a lot more padding—no college athletes were killed while playing football, although two high school players and one professional died as a direct result of the game in 2005.

Roosevelt supported football. According to the Teddy Roosevelt Association, 10 of his fellow Rough Riders in the Spanish-American War had listed "football player" as their occupation, and the President's son was a member of Harvard's freshman team, so he had an active interest in both keeping the game alive and making it safer. Roosevelt met with the three most important representatives of the game: Yale, Harvard, and Princeton. Today, the only chance anyone from these schools would have to sit in on a meeting of the most powerful representatives in football would be as a lawyer, policy maker, or president.

The representatives of the "Big Three" didn't leave the White House of a single mind to change the game. It took a brutal hit in that year's Harvard–Yale game, another meeting between Roosevelt and Harvard coach Bill Reid, and Yale coach Walter Camp reluctantly agreeing to major changes in the game his school dominated. The institution of the forward pass, 10 yards for a first down, and a 60-minute game—rules that most every American knows today—were radical ideas at the time.

Opening up the game kept players from bunching together dangerously in one area. The previous necessity for five yards for a first down and no other way to advance the ball made every play the equivalent of a goal-line stand. In a day when scoreless ties were not uncommon, increasing the number of yards required to maintain possession, offering a second option to move the ball (although the forward pass was still decades from becoming commonplace), and cutting down the number of minutes to inflict punishment (games had been 70 minutes long) went a long way to reducing injuries, fatal and otherwise. The professionals adhered to the collegiate rules, just as the early pros always followed what happened in college.

The first documented game called football in the United States had been played between Princeton and Rutgers on November 6, 1869. Rutgers won, 6–4, but don't think it was a touchdown against two safeties. Featuring 25 men to a side and rules that were essentially those of rugby, Rutgers won by being first to score six goals. Seven years later, as the game grew and adapted, the first rules of American football were written at a convention in Springfield, Massachusetts; the same city where 15 years later basketball would officially be born at the YMCA International Training School by James Naismith.

Football evolved away from rugby, with the ball snapped from center and only 11 men to a side. In 1882 Walter Camp pushed the concept of three downs to reach five yards, to keep teams from endlessly controlling the ball and boring the tar out of the patrons. (This innovation led to the field being lined so that it indeed resembled a gridiron.) Camp also designed the first prearranged plays and called signals. His 1888 rule that tackles could be made down to the knees, though, made the game more violent. The game's brutality is what led to the meeting with Roosevelt, but even by then the professionals had gotten the ball rolling.

Competitive athletic clubs in western Pennsylvania in the 1890s gave birth to the idea of professionalism in football. Baseball was well established as a major league sport and professional prizefighting was among the most popular sports in the country. Convention of the day made the upper class that inhabited many of these clubs aghast at the idea of paying athletes. Some of the better players were already receiving expenses for their efforts, though, and professionalism was beginning to lose some of its stigma. Or, at least, some of the

teams involved put up less of a stink to cover up their own practices that diverged from the "spirit of amateurism" that was more about class distinction than anything else. Those who liked to wager on the outcomes liked it more when there were better players on the field, with more at stake.

On November 12, 1892 the Alleghany Athletic Association openly paid William "Pudge" Heffelfinger $500 to play against Pittsburgh Athletic Club. Given the general shoddiness of football bookkeeping and record keeping that remained part of the game until after World War II, there were certainly others who were paid before then—and others who were paid that day—but the piece of paper that shows the AAA's expenses is justly called "pro football's birth certificate" by the Pro Football Hall of Fame. Heffelfinger, a former Yale player and a railroad office employee in Chicago, had balked at an initial offer of $250, but he wound up getting his price and scored the game's only touchdown—good for four points. The expense sheet showed that the club could afford it; the AAA still made a profit of $621 on the game. When the Amateur Athletic Union banned AAA from participation in 1897, the club, soon to fail due to dwindling membership, took the final step and went entirely professional.

In 1898 sportsman William C. Temple threw his hat into the ring. Temple had donated a cup given to winners of a National League postseason baseball series, and he naturally extended his interest to the gridiron. Temple paid the expenses of the entire Duquesnes Country and Athletic Club team, making him technically the first owner in pro football history. It was money well spent, too. The next year Duquesnes beat college teams at Washington & Jefferson, Penn State, and Bucknell. Bucknell featured a strong fullback and gifted kicker named Christy Mathewson, who would soon help elevate professional baseball above its vulgar and rowdy image. It would be several decades before professional football turned a similar corner.

A neighborhood group called the Morgan Athletic Club began playing on Chicago's South Side in 1898. Painting and decorating contractor Chris O'Brien purchased the club the next year and moved it to Normal Field, where they became known as the Normals and were acknowledged for their thriftiness. In 1901 O'Brien bought used jerseys from the University of Chicago. When someone commented on the faded maroon color, O'Brien replied cockily, "That's not maroon, it's Cardinal red!" That name has remained with the club through more than a century—except for suspensions of play in 1906–12 and again for World War I in 1918—through Racine Street and the franchise's later designation of Chicago, then to its later moves to St. Louis and Arizona. But that's too far ahead. The letters NFL hadn't even been put together when O'Brien bought his bargain jerseys.

THE FIRST NFL

The National Football League formed in 1902, and while it was football's first professional league, the only thing it shared with the modern NFL was its name. Mainly begun as a continuation of the war between the National and American leagues in baseball, the NFL fizzled out after a year. The league did introduce night football—Connie Mack's Philadelphia Athletics defeated the Kanaweola Athletic Club in Elmira, New York, 39–0—and an early two-sport star in Christy Mathewson, who played fullback for the Pittsburgh Stars until he was ordered not to risk injury by his full-time employers, the New York Giants baseball club.

The professional game moved west, to Ohio, where the town of Massillon's desire to beat Canton led to a team of ringers being brought in to finally end what had been a one-sided amateur rivalry. The one-upmanship in Ohio and the buildup of high-caliber professionals eventually led to charges of game-fixing in 1906. The mere rumor of a fix knocked down a crowd of 8,000 one week to fewer than 1,000 some 10 days later. The pro game evolved into lower pay for players, using mostly local fellows who worked during the

week. Interest in the Ohio League and the pro game in general was not the same until 1913.

The game itself underwent some changes in that span. In 1909 field goals were reduced from four points to three, and three years later the touchdown was upgraded from five points to six. Seven men were now required to be on the line and each game was divided into four 15-minute quarters. Pro football had evolved as well. George "Peggy" Parratt, who admitted he was a professional and lost his college standing at Case University, put together the Akron Indians, the best team in the pro football state. But in 1915 Jack Cusack signed Jim Thorpe to play for the Canton Bulldogs for the stunning sum of $250 per game. Thorpe, a football, baseball, and Olympic star unjustly stripped of his medals for being paid to play minor league baseball years before the 1912 Stockholm Games, was rightly considered the greatest athlete in the world. With Thorpe and former Carlisle Indian School teammate Pete Calac together in Canton, the Bulldogs won the Ohio League championship, and laid claim to being the best professional team in the country.

Thorpe's presence brought attention back to pro football, but the war in Europe, and America's late entry into it, sapped the professional ranks of manpower. Canton retained the title in 1917, but Greasy Neale's Dayton Triangles won in 1918 essentially because they were the only team able to play a full season. Even with people eager for entertainment after World War I, teams in Ohio lost money—including Ohio League champion Canton—because they plowed everything they had into paying the players. If they didn't pay top salaries, a competitor would, even an out-of-state one. It was time for a summit on the subject. Every team needed to abide by the same rules if most of the clubs were to survive. The heads of seven of these teams—owners would be too grand a term—met in August 1920 in a building that sold Hupmobiles, a company that would put out its last car in 1940. The football men gathered in the showroom would be hard-pressed for their enterprise to outlive the Hupmobile.

A larger group gathered there less than a month later to solve the common problem of trying to play football and not go broke. Among the men in the hot, crowded showroom were two major league outfielders, George Halas and Jim Thorpe, who were no longer in the major leagues. Thorpe, the biggest name there—by a mile—would be chosen the league's first president. The room was a mix of heat, optimism, and confusion. Because the Cardinals went by the name Racine—based on the street they played on—the team was listed in the minutes as being from Wisconsin. In a group of teams from places like Rock Island, Illinois, and Hammond, Indiana, as well as middling Ohio cities Akron, Dayton, and, don't forget, host Canton, it's easy to see how an out-of-the-way Wisconsin locale would fit right in with the American Professional Football Association.

It wasn't all small fish, but it was mostly rust belt. The first season included Cleveland, Detroit, Buffalo, and Rochester, in upstate New York, plus two Chicago teams—the Cardinals changed their designation to Chicago during the season to make things simpler for people from outside the city limits—and Columbus. Halas's squad was sponsored by starch manufacturer A.E. Staley and was based out of Decatur, closer to St. Louis than Chicago. From the start, Halas had big ideas for this little enterprise. The Staleys had more wins against league opponents than anyone else the first year, but the undefeated Akron Pros would be decreed champ after the first season. A full decade would pass before the championship was decided by game rather than by vote.

Halas took ownership of the team. After the first game of the 1921 season, he moved their home games from Staley Starch Works to a major league facility (Cubs Park, later known as Wrigley Field), which had been home to the failed Chicago Tigers a year before. Halas certainly would not fail. In fact, he used the league's loose rules to his advantage to snag the 1921 title from unsuspecting Buffalo. The All-Americans, thinking the season was over and the title won, believed a game with the Staleys was a mere exhibition. Halas took the win and ran, earning another win and a tie the next two weeks to claim the championship. The league's top offensive and defensive team had been Buffaloed.

The changing of his franchise's name to Bears—to fit the Cubs Park theme—resulted in the other owners considering his team a new franchise and turning several of his stars into free agents, but that was a rare case when Halas didn't get his way. He was the big draw in

a house of cards. Visitors had a real chance for a good gate at Cubs Park, while many of his competitors played in high school fields that held thousands less in towns with far fewer potential fans than Chicago. Halas took a disliking to Curly Lambeau right away and got Green Bay bounced from the league for hiring college players. Lambeau and the Packers quickly returned to the NFL, but the rivalry never relented.

GRANGE: SALVATION AND WAR
Halas secured the biggest star of the day, Red Grange, signing him after his final game in 1925 at his own alma mater, the University of Illinois. Joe Carr, the Columbus Panhandles manager who'd taken over the presidency from Thorpe in this renamed National Football League, stepped in to make sure teams did not grab future players while they were still enrolled in school, but the sage Carr would not interfere with the Galloping Ghost's mad dash around the country and across NFL fields.

Grange was the pro football stop in the Golden Age of Sport. Fans lined up around the block to see him, whether it was in Chicago for his debut on a snowy Thanksgiving Day, or a Saturday in Frankford, Pennsylvania, or a Wednesday in Providence, Rhode Island, which proved too small for Grange, so the game was switched to Braves Field in Boston. The stop that mattered most in the 19-game, 67-day barnstorming tour, though, was New York. The Giants had drawn 27,000 for their first home game at the Polo Grounds and had exceeded that total just once heading into the last home game of the year … against the Bears. It didn't matter that the Giants lost the game, or that they had a better record than the Bears that year, because the Bears' record didn't matter, either. What mattered was that 68,000 people jammed the Polo Grounds to see a pro football game. And those who couldn't get in or read about it in the newspaper were talking about the pro game. There were many dark days ahead, but the NFL was on the map, thanks to Red Grange. And very soon Grange was in another league all together.

Grange saw the crowds, too, and despite the kingly $3,000 per game and the large piece of the gate he received at every stop, Grange and his manager, C.C. Pyle, figured they could make even more if they owned a team. Rebuffed in an attempt to get a piece of the Bears in his next contract, Grange got the keys to Yankee Stadium and asked for a franchise. Although the likes of Halas and Lambeau both played for and ran their clubs, this was a different matter. In this case the star was calling the shots. The NFL, coerced by territorial Giants owner Tim Mara, said no. Then they watched nervously as Grange not only fielded his own team, but he also organized a league to play against him.

The NFL wasn't ready for a frontal assault. Having just achieved its first real victory thanks to Grange, the NFL was ill prepared to fight against him, but they were fortunate because the country wasn't ready for that much pro football. The American Football League had several stars lured from college and a few refugees from the NFL, but the crowds didn't come to see anyone but Grange. Only four of nine teams survived the season and the team with the most points and the most wins, Grange's New York Yankees, didn't even finish first. The Yankees were allowed in the NFL in 1927 with Grange a mere player, and a knee injury kept him from doing that until 1929.

The NFL's first decade was that of a binge league. It expanded out of control whenever there was a problem, and then pruned back to a manageable size, only to balloon up again. The number of teams in the league's first decade fluctuated from 14 the first year to 21 the next. To withstand the AFL in 1926, the NFL had bulged to 22 teams, the largest number it would have until the 1970 merger. By 1927 it was down to 12 clubs and in 1932, at the height of the Depression, the number stood at eight. The league grew stronger throughout, discontinuing the small town teams that had started the league and reasoning they'd done it for the greater good. The only town teams left in 1932 were the Green Bay Packers and the Portsmouth Spartans. The Packers managed to weather every storm that came their way, not to mention being one of the most accomplished throwing teams in the game with the excellent passer Lambeau teaching Arnie Herber. Since entering the league in 1930, Portsmouth was now the only team left from Ohio, the cradle of the pro game. They were also an excellent team and finished the 1932 season with a nearly identical

record to the Bears. With the Packers having lost to both clubs to end the season and with the Bears and Spartans having almost identical records, picking a champion was a thorny issue. Making these decisions hadn't gotten any easier in the last decade. The worst case was in 1925 when the Chicago Cardinals were declared champions over the Pottsville Maroons because the Maroons defied Carr and the league and played a game against a Notre Dame all-star team on the same day the Frankford Yellow Jackets had a game in the same territory. (The Maroons were expelled and then let back in lest they become part of Grange's AFL in 1926.)

But 1932 brought a different mindset. There was a way that could decide this and make money to boot by adding another game to the calendar: a championship game. The game would count in the regular standings, but it wouldn't be played like any game that had come before it. A blizzard that week forced the game inside to Chicago Stadium, where a field was marked off that was 20 yards short and several yards narrower than a regulation gridiron. The league improvised, and while the field had to recalibrated every time midfield was crossed, the 12,000 fans who would have been shivering at frozen Wrigley Field enjoyed the indoor spectacle, especially when the Bears won. Bronko Nagurski, the next bigger-than-life college star Halas had brought to town, passed to the great Grange in a play that stunned everyone. Nagurski took a few steps toward the line as if he was going to run, then he jumped up and threw a touchdown pass. Since passers had to be five yards behind the line of scrimmage, Portsmouth argued at the time—and through the winter—that it shouldn't have counted. The NFL did something it hadn't really done before. The next year it changed the rules to make passing easier; the league also voted to have a championship game every year. Change was coming to the game.

SUNDAYS IN PENNSYLVANIA
The lifting of the Sunday blue laws in Pennsylvania led to two teams from that state joining the league in 1933. Art Rooney brought in the Pittsburgh Pirates, and Bert Bell ushered in the Philadelphia Eagles. Along with George Preston Marshall, who'd founded the NFL's Boston Braves the year before, they were among the most influential men in league history. Each had a vastly different personality. Marshall was bombastic and liked to do things in a big way, and his way; Bell was a consensus builder who accomplished more from his home phone than an office full of lawyers, marketing, and publicity men ever could; and Rooney was a gambler whose patience and faith finally paid off some 40 years after he started. The 1933 season was also the last year the Spartans played in little Portsmouth before moving to Detroit, bringing a solid, if not always successful, franchise to that city after four earlier Motor City failures. It wasn't a time without hardships, certainly. The Cincinnati Reds also started in 1933 and were so bad and lost so much money the team was replaced by the St. Louis Gunners, an undermanned independent team. Hastily thrown into the NFL, the Gunners shut out Pittsburgh in their first game. That's how good Rooney's club was.

While Marshall became so fed up with lackluster fan support that he moved the 1936 NFL Championship Game from Boston to New York and then moved the franchise lock, stock, and barrel to Washington, the Pennsylvania clubs couldn't blame their fans for not coming and were grateful for those who stuck around. Bell came up with an idea that could help put his team, not to mention Rooney's, procure talent. The first NFL draft was held at the Ritz-Carlton Hotel in Philadelphia. There was only one problem. Many of the top college players didn't want to play in the NFL and they certainly didn't want to play for the Eagles or Steelers. None of Philadelphia's nine picks ever played in the NFL, including the first Heisman Trophy winner Jay Berwanger of the University of Chicago. The Steelers had three picks who actually became pros, but their first pick, Notre Dame quarterback Bill Shakespeare, didn't sign. There was money to be made for smart, enterprising young men with a college education, and the NFL of the 1930s wasn't the place to make it. While Halas traded for Berwanger and couldn't get him to play there, either, he hit it big at the first draft. His first pick, Joe Stydhahar of West Virginia, and his last choice, Dan Fortmann of Colgate, became Hall of Fame linemen and building blocks for the great Bears teams to come. Even with the failure to attract the best talent to the NFL the year of its institution,

the draft was an excellent idea that gave downtrodden teams hope for the future; even if the same people who made bad decisions on veteran players continued to perpetrate their sins in collecting rookie talent.

While pro football still needed to work on its image to get more college players—and fans—interested in the NFL, Halas was helping change the way the game looked on the field. His two best teams of the 1930s—the 13–0 squad in '34 and his 9–1–1 club in '37—lost in championship games. In the first, the Sneakers Game, Halas had been done him in when the Giants switched to sneakers on the icy field and ran all over the Bears in the fourth quarter. In the second, Washington's Slingin' Sammy Baugh had foiled Chicago with a record 358 yards through the air. When the third time came around, Halas would be ready. After a 7–3 loss to the Redskins in the ninth game of the 1940 season, and being called "crybabies" by Washington's Marshall, Halas brought in T-formation expert Clark Shaughnessy to teach his club the ins and outs of the system to spring on the Redskins in the rematch. Suffice to say, it worked. Since Halas was sure there were no crybabies on the other side of the field, he kept pouring it on until the scoreboard read 73–0, the biggest blowout in NFL history. It could have been higher: The Bears missed 4 extra points.

A year later the Bears again won the championship handily, but the priorities had changed. America had just entered the war—the first news of Pearl Harbor arrived at the same time as NFL games—and the type of enterprising, athletic leaders the armed forces needed were in every huddle in the NFL. Of the 638 men with NFL experience who served in World War II, 21 never made it back. Those who did return, found a different world.

As the war finally wound down in Europe and the Pacific, interest in the NFL remained strong. Although the Cleveland Rams, brought into the league in 1937, asked and received permission to suspend operations in 1943 because of the war, they resumed in 1944 and were NFL champions the year after that. Pittsburgh, renamed the Steelers in 1940, needed help to make it. The Eagles combined with them in 1943 (the "Steagles"), and then the Chicago Cardinals joined Pittsburgh the next year, earning the moniker "Carpets" and not winning a game. The manpower shortage forced the league to institute free substitution, allowing players to specialize on offense and defense rather than first teams and second teams that played both ways. (This trial would end when the war did, but it would come back in 1950, signaling the end of the two-way player.) Stars like Bronko Nagurski came back during the war while Green Bay's immortal pass-catcher Don Hutson and incomparable center Mel Hein continued lining up well into their 30s in an era when helmets weren't thick and careers weren't long.

Wealthy men in different cities wanted to make a go in this professional game. The NFL chose not to expand to the growing areas of the country in the West and South. In 1946 the NFL had the same number of teams (10) it had when the Rams entered the league nine years earlier. Only now there were eight other teams in a new league looking for a slice of the pro football pie.

AAFC SPELLS TROUBLE
The All-America Football Conference was a direct assault at the NFL's status quo. With newly re-christened civilians clamoring for diversions with the first free time they'd enjoyed in years, the time was ripe for a new venture—unlike the AFLs that had come and gone quickly in the past three decades. The NFL could not continue as it had been and changes were made immediately. Bert Bell replaced commissioner Elmer Layden, whose comment that the new league should "get a ball," turned into the AAFC's publicity campaign. Bell had sold the Eagles and was a minority owner with Rooney in Pittsburgh, but he gave that up to take over the league. The "togetherness" spirit of some of the owners who'd been around had helped keep new blood out; now it would have to keep the patient from bleeding too much at a critical time.

First, the Rams moved to Los Angeles. Owner Dan Reeves realized he could win championships and lose his shirt simultaneously in Cleveland. Second, Reeves did something on the West Coast that hadn't happened anywhere in the NFL since 1933: He signed African American players. Kenny Washington and Woody Strode were given contracts by the Rams after the issue was raised at a meeting

regarding opening up the Los Angeles Coliseum to pro football. Much as in baseball, an unwritten code had kept the game segregated. The early NFL, however, had several outstanding African American players, including Fritz Pollard, who served as player coach. Although Washington's Marshall received blame for the ban, it was a 10-team league and the others were complicit by their silence and inaction.

Cleveland's Paul Brown signed African Americans Marion Motley and Bill Willis, two of six Browns rookies who would end up in the Hall of Fame. Whether it was year-round coaching, scouting with near mathematical precision, extensive film study, or sending in plays through a Messenger Guard system, Brown was the first true modern coach as well as an old-school disciplinarian. Cleveland hit the ground running and the rest of the AAFC was pushed back like a tackling sled in a perfectly-executed Paul Brown drill. Cleveland dominated every facet of the league, winning all four league titles and averaging just one loss per season. Otto Graham brought Brown's game plan to fruition on the field in perhaps the most successful coach–quarterback tandem in NFL history. Graham played in a championship game in each of his 10 seasons with the Browns.

The AAFC had a team in Los Angeles, the Dons, owned by actor Don Ameche and several other well-heeled Hollywood types, but the league also brought the national sports to San Francisco for the first time. The 49ers seemed pure fun, while the Browns seemed to be all work. The results for each spoke for themselves. The 49ers were local, tapping a region that seemed to produce skilled players from area schools as if they were vineyards. Former Santa Clara coach Buck Shaw ran the second-best outfit in the league, but San Francisco was trapped in the same division as the Browns and didn't get to play them for the title until just days after a merger was announced. The Browns won and the league lost. Three teams were brought over and the four remaining clubs were flushed away. While threatened by the AAFC, the NFL was simply better established and more competitive. But they did not have the best team. That was the Browns.

Cleveland famously whipped two-time defending NFL champion Philadelphia—and Greasy Neale's innovative Eagle Defense—in its first game in the league in 1950. The Browns then won the NFL title in a classic match against the Rams. After losing the championship game three straight years—twice to the Lions—Graham led the Browns to wins in the title game his final two seasons. Though the Browns weren't the same without Automatic Otto, they still had their iconic leader and another Brown named Jim. The running back out of Syracuse immediately became the most dominant runner in the game, leading the NFL in rushing as a rookie and doubling the totals of the second-best rusher while averaging almost 6 yards per carry and 127 yards per game in his sophomore season. Jim Brown tore through defenses and scattered tacklers all over the field in a manner no one had seen before, and fans could now see it from their living room.

NFL games had long been on the radio, but football was not as suited to that medium as baseball, which could let a fan's imagination fill in the blanks on a summer evening. With just 12 games a year, and every one being important to a team's hopes of contention, football required more concentration to fans listening on the radio. Players were moving in many directions at once and even the best announcer couldn't possibly describe everything happening on a play. The best way to follow football was to watch it, and fans found that experts with cameras and access to different angles made the game more enjoyable to watch, all without leaving the comfort of home. Television was the perfect companion to the NFL. It was so good, in fact, the league had to put limits on it. The Rams broadcast every home game during the 1950 season and saw attendance plummet, giving the NFL all the ammunition it needed to install the blackout rule. Home games could not be shown on local television, a rule that was challenged in court and upheld. The rule actually created a new breed of diehard fans who traveled not to the stadium, but who would spend Sundays with friends outside the blackout zone or travel to Connecticut from New York and watch the game on TV at a hotel or bar. People going out of their way to watch pro football was a new idea, but was one that was just gathering steam.

The New York Giants, whose road games were broadcast throughout New York and New England had come a long way in the three decades since Red Grange had saved the fledgling team in the big market. With the club's baseball namesake having fled the city for California—along with the Brooklyn Dodgers—pro football became even more of a need for sports fans. The Mara family and Steve Owen, the team's coach for 22 seasons, had nurtured the fascination. Jim Lee Howell had big shoes to fill, and he filled them well. The Giants won their fourth NFL title in 1956, routing the rival Bears while again clad in sneakers. The Giants, now located at Yankee Stadium, had players like Charlie Conerly and Frank Gifford working under assistant Vince Lombardi on offense, plus an unstoppable defense featuring Sam Huff and Andy Robustelli under the tutelage of former Giant Tom Landry. They had become an eastern phenomenon and a national powerhouse.

The Baltimore Colts were more of a local thing, like Chesapeake Bay crabs. A team known as the Colts moved with the Browns and 49ers from the AAFC, but it was more about the market than the franchise. The Colts could barely compete in the AAFC and were drummed out of the NFL. The NFL still had a taste for Maryland, and Baltimoreans made it known they still hungered for a team, so the league gave the city another chance in 1953. Owner Carroll Rosenbloom brought in Browns assistant Weeb Ewbank the following year and the Colts moved up the standings. In 1956, the same years the Giants were ending an 18-year run without a title, the Colts were trying out this quarterback who'd come from semipro football: Johnny Unitas. Like Graham, Unitas was a born leader whose skills combined with those of breakout players Lenny Moore, Ray Berry, and Alan Ameche, made opponents feel queasy after a trip to Baltimore, and it wasn't from the seafood.

On December 28, 1958, the Colts, with their first division title, met the Giants at Yankee Stadium for the NFL title. The passion of these two clubs and their fans was beamed across the country on television, and the 45 million watching on NBC saw a finish unlike any other in the game's history. Unitas led the Colts to a tying field goal in the closing seconds, followed by the first sudden death in league history. Unitas led the Colts down the field once more in this newfangled fifth quarter and Ameche's 1-yard run not only won the first championship for the Colts, it put the NFL Championship Game on par with the World Series. Many found they liked it even more. A chilled afternoon in gray December deciding the championship, and doing it with a cold, calculated drive that decided things cleanly. The Giants wouldn't get last licks just because they were the home team. The best team won. In Baltimore the fans went crazy, jamming the streets awaiting their champions. They weren't the only ones watching, or waiting.

THE FOOLISH CLUB

With newfound interest in professional football as a result of television and the kinetic energy of the Colts and Giants, plus larger than life Paul Brown and Jim Brown in Cleveland, the NFL was showing signs of complacency and even arrogance. Just like after World War II, businessmen who wanted to start franchises in new territories were kept at arm's length. The All-America Football Conference had stretched the NFL, but in the end the AAFC brought the established league two excellent franchises in the Browns and 49ers, plus a crop of seasoned pros to fill out NFL rosters. A decade after the last AAFC game was played, the only new league being talked about was in baseball. While the Continental League eventually proved unsuccessful, it did spur expansion in the major leagues. Men of means who wanted to get involved in pro football hovered around the struggling Chicago Cardinals and lived in the hopes that their group would be chosen to bring the pro game to their city. The NFL was in no big hurry.

Lamar Hunt, the unassuming son of an oil billionaire, came up with the idea of taking a group of similarly frustrated men with capital and sporting ambitions and starting a new league. Hunt quickly found suitors in several desirable cities and plans were afoot for a new league. NFL commissioner Bert Bell, who knew how to even make enemies feel wanted, told Hunt he though a new league might be good for pro football. Bell died during an Eagles Steelers game not knowing how prophetic he was.

Pete Rozelle, Bell's compromise successor, took over in January 1960 with the American Football League ready to launch and the NFL having handed out expansion teams in Dallas, Hunt's hometown, and Minneapolis, one of the original AFL ownership groups poached by the NFL. The Cardinals were finally moving, to St. Louis, and the separate

drafts by the two leagues would become an annual battle of wills—and cash. It was a war, but the result was quite entertaining for football fans. The eight original AFL owners dubbed themselves the Foolish Club for following through on an idea that seemed destined to be as costly as it was precarious, but their venture proved to be a success.

Minneapolis was replaced by Oakland, mainly because Los Angeles Chargers owner Barron Hilton threatened to quit if he didn't get a West Coast club to pair up with. Hilton was also the first to relocate franchises—followed two years later by the Dallas Texans moving to Kansas City shortly after winning the AFL title—but the other owners gritted their teeth through losses on the field and in the wallet.

There were problems in the NFL office as well. Two of the league's biggest stars were found gambling on the NFL. Green Bay running back and the league's three-time leading scorer Paul Hornung and Detroit standout defensive tackle Alex Karras were suspended indefinitely. Yet they could, and did, apply for reinstatement after the 1963 season. Several Lions and even the coach, George Wilson, earned fines as well. The NFL took its lumps yet the league also showed what the punishment would be for future transgressors. Before the suspensions took effect, though, the NFL celebrated itself like never before. The league trumpeted its own history with the Pro Football Hall of Fame in Canton, Ohio, the place where the league had been born in the Hupmobile showroom 1920. The Hall of Fame was the exclusive home of NFL feats and tales—even after the 1970 merger it was another eight years before Lance Alworth became the first AFL player inducted—and it offered the perspective of time and success to tell those look-how-far-we've-come stories of the league's hand-to-mouth origins.

The AFL went over one million in attendance for the first time in 1962, but much of that was carried by Houston and San Diego, while Boston and New York drew almost half as many fans per game. New York was the AFL's weakest link, but Sonny Werblin replaced bumbling owner Harry Wismer in 1963, swapped the name Titans for Jets, and made immediate plans to become the football tenant in 1964 at state-of-the-art Shea Stadium, one of a number of multi-purpose stadiums in both leagues now coming off the drawing board and into production. Werblin scored the most significant blow in the two-league tussle by bringing Joe Namath to New York in 1965. Armed with Broadway Joe and a new TV contract with NBC—the network that had brought the game to the masses with the 1958 NFL Championship Game—the two leagues were suddenly on even ground. A protracted war would do neither side any good. Just like the National and American baseball leagues ended their war and started the wildly successful World Series in 1903, so the AFL and NFL joined together to bring about the even more popular Super Bowl after the 1966 season. Rozelle oversaw this new venture where all teams shared equally and stood on a level playing field financially. And it was good.

But it didn't start out perfect. The NFL representative in the first two title games between the leagues was the Green Bay Packers, the dominant team of the era, ruled with a mighty fist by Vince Lombardi. Lombardi's club came from the smallest market in either league, but he also knew they were the best and he wasn't afraid to say so. Green Bay dispatched both the Kansas City Chiefs and Oakland Raiders in the first two games. After winning five championships in nine seasons, after taking the NFL's most desolate outpost and transforming it into an indisputable power, and after becoming the face of professional football to the rabid masses, Lombardi retired. No one saw the shift that was coming.

Super Bowl III was to be a crowning of the heir to the NFL throne. Even with the icon of the past glory, Johnny Unitas, on the bench after an injury-plagued season, the Baltimore Colts still had quarterback Earl Morrall and the greatest young mind in the NFL, Don Shula, calling the shots. This contrived interleague rivalry, now officially called the Super Bowl, drew more attention each year, but the games were boring. Namath was anything but boring. The Jets, fulfilling Namath's guarantee, stunned the Colts in Super Bowl III. A year's passage led some to forget the enormity of the upset. What would little Kansas City do against powerful Minnesota? The Chiefs, having played amid the hoopla of the first Super Bowl against the Packers, were better prepared and made bigger plays than the heavily-favored Vikings. The game was a blowout going the other way. Despite the announced merger, the two leagues had been kept apart from each other in the regular season, like a newfound moon rock isolated to make sure it wouldn't contaminate anything. Now after four years, and a split in the big game, the two leagues would finally be one.

The Chiefs and Vikings played each other to open the first Sunday of the new two-conference NFL; Minnesota won. That first weekend of the season also saw the Steelers, Browns, and Colts playing for the AFC, the trio switching amid acrimony, feuds, and $3 million apiece. The Browns' first game in this brave new world came against the Jets on a Monday night, part of a radical programming idea to bring football into people's homes on a weeknight. Football as spectacle fit perfectly with the NFL's plans. The game had been stylized since 1962 by Ed Sabol, whose film of the 1962 NFL Championship Game was an instant hit with the league. Two years later Sabol's company was brought in-house as NFL Films, much like Rozelle had brought in NFL Properties to deal with merchandising the game. NFL Films produced a syndicated highlights show, with ever more spinoffs by Sabol and his enterprising son, Steve, to bring the NFL gospel into homes across the country, complete with the "Voice of God," John Facenda.

The schmaltzy but true TV movie *Brian's Song* about Bears great running back Gale Sayers and fullback Brian Piccolo moved men to tears as Billy Dee Williams portrayed Sayers and James Caan played the cancer-stricken Piccolo. The reaction to this movie inspired another true-life adaptation of a running back's life touched by cancer; this time it was the little brother of 1973 Heisman Trophy winner and Los Angeles Ram John Cappelletti. NFL stars in *The Longest Yard*, *M*A*S*H*, and *Blazing Saddles*, not to mention the scads of films starring Jim Brown, proved the players could act, but the made-for-TV tearjerkers showed that football had a heart. The league long-promoted the United Way among other charities and ran commercials starring players from different teams volunteering in the community. While not all orchestrated by the public relations genius Rozelle, it was all part of the image he wanted to convey. Football had long since passed baseball as the country's most popular sport, and the commissioner never looked back.

RUNNING BLUES

The amalgamation of the two leagues brought a sudden lessening of the aerial shows that the AFL had been famous for. In 1966, the year the merger was announced, eight AFL teams threw a total of 199 touchdown passes. In 1970, the first year of the merger, 14 AFC teams threw 199 touchdowns. Running the ball had never gone out of style, but now it was a way of life for the most successful teams in the game. The Dolphins became the first super power of the 1970s with a ball-control offense and a stifling—if nameless—defense. The Dolphins won 10 or more games in each of Don Shula's first six seasons after he jumped to Miami in 1970. His 1972 club became the only team to win every game, run through the playoffs, and win the Super Bowl. Shula did it with the first tandem 1,000-yard rushers in history; the Dolphins ran more and threw less than any AFC team. It was a successful combination.

In 1973 O.J. Simpson became the first running back to surpass 2,000 yards—and the only one to do it in a 14-game schedule—as the Bills improved by five games in the standings. Franco Harris, who surpassed 1,000 yards in seven of his first eight seasons, was a major part of Pittsburgh's resurgence as well. While the Dolphins, Bills, and Steelers all had quarterbacks who were dangerous and sure-handed receivers, a Bears running back named Walter Payton did not have such a luxury. Payton led the NFC in rushing attempts for four straight years, including a monster 1977 season when he finished with 1,852 yards and 16 total touchdowns, including a record-setting 275-yard rushing day against the first-place Vikings. Payton would retire as the game's all-time leading carrier and ground-gainer.

A great running game only carried a team so far. Besides a complimentary passing game, a defense that kept the other team off the field was an equally crucial component. And no team in the 1970s had a defense like the Steelers. Long a laughingstock of the NFL, the Steelers turned their fortunes around with the hiring of Chuck Noll as coach in 1969. Noll, a Messenger Guard under Paul Brown in the 1950s, was an assistant under Sid Gillman and Don Shula before getting his shot at a head coaching job. His first

Steelers team went 1–13, but the team began stockpiling great players from the draft: defensive linemen Joe Green and L.C. Greenwood in 1969; quarterback Terry Bradshaw and cornerback Mel Blount in 1970; linebacker Jack Ham in 1971; Harris in 1972; and the club's legendary draft in 1974 brought four future Hall of Famers in linebacker Jack Lambert, center Mike Webster, and receivers Lynn Swann and John Stallworth, not to mention a five-time Pro Bowler in Donnie Shell, signed by Pittsburgh after going undrafted that year. The Steelers won four Super Bowls in six years as the most dominant team of the post-merger era.

By 1974 the game was as popular as it had ever been, but the players wouldn't have known it from their paychecks. The merger had reduced bonuses and taken away any leverage for players. In 1974 the players went on strike for about six weeks, but the players returned to camp and the strike was lost. There was an alternative: the World Football Association. Launched by Gary Davidson, he had hoped it would be the equal of two other leagues he began: the American Basketball Association and the World Hockey Association. Both those leagues lasted far longer, applied much more pressure on the established leagues, and eventually had some franchises added to the existing basketball and hockey leagues. The WFL had none of these things going for it. Although it did help derail the Miami juggernaut when Larry Csonka, Jim Kiick, and Paul Warfield all left to join the Memphis Southmen. They didn't play long. The league folded after 12 games in 1975. It was less competition for NFL owners, but NFL players had one less option for employment to bid for their services.

The players soon had more work and two more teams. The arrival of the Tampa Bay Buccaneers and Seattle Seahawks in 1976 provided the first expansion teams since the Falcons, Saints, Dolphins, and Bengals were added in the late 1960s. The most marginal talent assembled in Tampa Bay, where the Bucs, originally an AFC West team, lost all 14 games. They switched with the Seahawks in the NFC in 1977, and only lost their first 12 games before finally winning. Two more games were added to the schedule in 1978, with a corresponding drop in the number of preseason exhibition games. The playoffs were also expanded, with a second wild card team being added from each conference.

That first extra AFC postseason berth went to the Houston Oilers, who had engineered a blockbuster trade to get the top pick in the 1978 draft. The Oilers selected Heisman Trophy winner Earl Campbell, a powerful running back from the University of Texas. With massive thighs and the ability to run over anything in his path, Campbell burst onto the scene, carrying the ball constantly and bringing the Oilers their greatest seasons since Houston played at Jeppesen Field in the mid-1960s. In another part of Texas, the Dallas Cowboys had enjoyed similar luck a year earlier after trading up in the draft and selecting Heisman Trophy winner Tony Dorsett. On a team already filled with offensive stars, plus the Doomsday Defense, Dorsett helped the Cowboys maintain their status as America's Team.

The NFL did something to help teams that didn't have future Hall of Fame running backs. Significant rules changes were implemented to help increase scoring, particularly in the passing game. Defenders were no longer allowed to make contact with receivers more than five yards beyond the line of scrimmage. Offensive linemen were helped by rules that allowed them to use open hands and extended arms for blocking. The results of these changes were immediately apparent. Four NFC quarterbacks threw for more than 3,000 yards, something that hadn't happened since 1973. Roger Staubach, 36, posted new career highs in touchdowns and passing yards while Fran Tarkenton of the Vikings led the NFL in attempts, completions, and yards in his final season. Saints quarterback Archie Manning and Jim Hart of the Cardinals also had prolific passing seasons, but their defenses gave up the passing yards just as quickly—the new rules worked both ways. That further made the word "parity" a reality.

After three decades in which the NFL grew in every way, the 1980s were a comedown. While the dynasties of the previous two decades had created an aura of bravado in the league, had given every other team someone to shoot for—even if unsuccessfully—the 1980s began with the Raiders looking to relocate even as they won the Super Bowl, setting off a 15-year period in which the Colts, Cardinals, Browns, Oilers, Rams, and the Raiders (again) all moved, while the Jets joined the Giants in slipping over to New Jersey while leaving "New York" on the stationary. The NFL fought the Raiders in their

move to Los Angeles, but Al Davis, the old AFL commissioner who never lost his contempt for Pete Rozelle or the old guard in the NFL, won in court. Even before the verdict was handed down, the Raiders were already playing at the Los Angeles Coliseum, putting together the first—and what would be the only—LA-based team to ever win a Super Bowl.

For all the heartache that the moving of teams like the Baltimore Colts and Oakland Raiders caused, in the end it was mainly tragic in those cities. As much as the NFL was tied together by a television contract that paid every team an equal amount and guaranteed a 60-40 split of every gate between home and visitor, life continued uninterrupted for the fans and teams in other cities. Until one day—September 26, 1982—when citizens in Oakland attended as many games as those in San Francisco. None.

The player's strike cut seven weeks from the schedule, and didn't resolve any long-term issues. Five years later another strike wiped out four weeks of the season. Replacement players took the field for three weeks during the season, much to the scorn of owners, coaches, and fans. While many coaching staffs caught up on their sleep during this odd month—and the concept of these so-called "scabs" was so jarring that many players crossed the picket lines, costing the union any chance at gaining anything—the Redskins made sure their club remained in good shape. Washington, which won the Super Bowl the season of the 1982 strike, beat three division rivals during the replacement period of the 1987 strike and was never challenged for the NFC East title. The Redskins won their second strike-season Super Bowl and offered no apologies.

There was still no agreement between players and management, but the problems in the NFL did not begin and end with labor vs. management. Drugs pervaded the game. Several big stars—including Pro Bowl running back Chuck Muncie and later Giants linebacker Lawrence Taylor—became deeply involved in cocaine. Others started using steroids. Football and steroids went hand in hand in the early 1980s. In a game with brutally short careers, where size and strength often make the difference at the line of scrimmage, the temptation for a physical advantage proved too great for many players. After close to a decade of use in the league, the NFL began testing for steroids in 1987, but players weren't suspended for violating the rules until 1989. The NFL began random, year-round testing in 1990. Steve Courson and Lyle Alzado later went public with their use of steroids during and blamed serious health problems on use of the substance.

The NFL also survived yet one more interloper: The United States Football League. The USFL did something the others hadn't tried, starting in the spring instead of the fall. The league began with 12 teams in 1983, mostly in NFL cities, with the idea of feeding off the insatiable football appetite of fans. The 18-game season started before baseball season and crowning a champion before the NFL training camps got going. The real competition between the leagues was for players. Herschel Walker, who was not considered eligible for the NFL draft because he was an underclassman, received the largest contract in pro football history to play at Giants Stadium—for the New Jersey Generals. George Allen, who hadn't coached in the NFL since 1977, was named head coach of the Chicago Blitz. The suggested salary cap was $1.2 million per club, but most clubs went way over that number and the USFL began with losses that continued to grow with the league. The USFL expanded to 16 teams in year two—with more Southern cities—and brought in rookies Jim Kelly, Steve Young, and Heisman Trophy winner Mike Rozier, while adding name veteran quarterbacks Doug Williams and Brian Sipe. The USFL had even bigger plans, announcing that the league would start playing in the fall in 1986 and filing a $1.69 billion antitrust suit against the NFL. The league never saw autumn of 1986. The USFL won in court, but a jury awarded the league $1, which trebled to $3.

The strikes, the drugs, the pressure of the USFL, wore down Pete Rozelle. His abrupt retirement in 1989 after 29 years stunned the football world. Then, just as in the meeting where he announced his news, the applause became deafening. Rozelle was hailed as the greatest sports commissioner ever, and any CEO in the country would be envious of the money and prestige he had brought to the game, the league, and to himself. Rozelle could finally relax; the fight was over, and he had won, decisively. No one could ever take his place, but someone would have to.

Paul Tagliabue, the league counsel who had slain several adversaries in court—he was actually given a crystal sword to celebrate the downfall of the USFL—was chosen as Rozelle's successor. But change was in the air in the NFL from California to Texas all the way to Germany. Al Davis drove many of the other owners nuts, but he did something no one else would: He hired an African American to coach his team. Art Shell, a Raiders offensive lineman in the 1970s with future NFL Players Association head Gene Upshaw, took over the club during the 1989 season. Although Fritz Pollard served as both a player and coach in the league's early days—unofficial segregation seeped in from 1934 to 1946—no NFL team had taken the step since the Hammond Pros last tried it in 1925. (Baseball saw its first African American manager, Frank Robinson, in 1975.) Jerry Jones bought the Cowboys and summarily dismissed Tom Landry, one of the most successful and upright men in the game's history. Cowboys president Tex Schramm, who'd been in Dallas since day one with Landry, left to take over the World League of American Football, a new spring venture by the NFL to bring football to Europe. Three of the 10 teams would be across the pond—London, Barcelona, and Frankfurt—and another would be in Montreal, heretofore the province of the Canadian Football League. The other teams were scattered through non-NFL markets in the South, plus a franchise in New York and another in California. Over time, the European fans grew to enjoy more than just the extra points, and the North American teams were dropped in favor of clubs like the Rhein Fire and Scottish Claymores. The league remained a solid training ground for young players—especially quarterbacks—who weren't ready for the NFL.

While the NFL survived three AFLs in the 1920s and 1930s, and merged with the fourth AFL in 1970, yet another AFL appeared in the 1980s: the Arena Football League. Played in the area of a professional hockey rink, the game started each year after the NFL season ended. Thus it fulfilled the longing of fans who needed football, any type of football, to get by. Although not as proficient at producing NFL-caliber pros as the Canadian Football League, the Arena league had several dozen alumni eventually reach the NFL. The AFL would spawn Kurt Warner—as well as gold helmets with goggles painted on them for his Iowa Barnstormers—a two-time NFL Most Valuable Player.

Cable network ESPN got a part of the NFL broadcast package in 1987, with national broadcasts of Sunday night games on the schedule for the first time. Already in love with football on its constant highlights show, *Sports Center*, ESPN burst at the seams with coverage and pregame programming for games it wasn't even broadcasting. Football obsession stretched far beyond the electric football, Super Toe, and hand-held computer games children devoured a generation earlier. Realistic video games kept fans thinking—and playing—NFL football before, during, and after the season. The growing obsession with the draft was fed by ESPN's live broadcast of the event and fans started playing general manager more and more with fantasy football.

BEST SERVED WITH RICE
On the field, the San Francisco 49ers had become the league's next dynasty. The Niners didn't win championships with the swift frequency of the Packers or the Steelers—more playoff games stoked different Super Bowl matchups—but quarterback Joe Montana and head coach Bill Walsh won three titles together, including two against different Cincinnati regimes. George Seifert took over for the retired Walsh and won another with Joe Montana at the helm. Back injuries made Montana's final years tumultuous despite the success. San Francisco had arguably the best quarterback in the game—the top "big-game quarterback," the pontificators extolled—but the 49ers also had the best backup quarterback in Steve Young. After losing consecutive championship games to the eventual Super Bowl champ Cowboys, Young finally beat Dallas and then set a Super Bowl record with 6 touchdown passes. The top receiver in history, Jerry Rice, was the favorite target of both Montana and Young (as well almost every other quarterback he played with in his record-obliterating 20 seasons). San Francisco's five championship were spread over two coaches, innumerable Pro Bowlers, and 15 seasons. The Buffalo Bills had their Super Bowl rise and fall between 49ers championships. The Bills reached the Super Bowl four straight times under coach Marv

Levy and a solid corps of veterans. The Bills lost each time in the midst of 13 straight Super Bowl victories by the NFC.

New stadiums popped up everywhere in the NFL, and sometimes the team that played there was as new as the stadium. While Los Angeles watched two teams move elsewhere, two new teams arrived in the relatively small markets of Jacksonville and Charlotte. (To widen the fan base, the Panthers simply called themselves Carolina and played their first season in Clemson, South Carolina, until the new stadium was ready.) All new stadiums, and several old ones, came with shiny new names that rarely reflected the city's history, geography, or even the owner's ego, but the facilities were instead named after phone companies, banks, web sites, and, yes, razor blades. Even in a league where change was expected and often embraced, this took some getting used to.

The strangest situation was in Cleveland, where Art Modell wrenched the Browns from a devoted fan base and placed them in Baltimore, which had never gotten over the sudden movement of the Colts a dozen years earlier. Shortly after Super Bowl XXX, the NFL agreed to launch a new franchise in Cleveland in 1999, one that would retain the Browns name, uniform, and records. Modell's team in Baltimore changed its name to Ravens while keeping the Browns' players and their spot in the AFC Central, but they would otherwise be treated like a new expansion franchise. The city of Cleveland also agreed to build a new venue to replace Cleveland Municipal Stadium, the Browns' only home for 50 seasons. Tagliabue, wary of backlash and any possible litigation, was creative in the lengths he went to appease cities divorced from their NFL teams. Houston, Baltimore, Cleveland, and St. Louis, which had lost teams, received other teams, even if it meant relocating from another city. Oakland even got a team back, although that was the same team that left in 1982. Still, Raiders fans picked up where they left off in their undying devotion to Al Davis and his silver and black.

This theory extended to the television networks as well. The NFL continued to command top dollar in television contracts. One of the reasons why was because they kept competition open. When one network weighed its ratings and ad revenues against rights fees in the billions and blinked, another network was there to readily take its place. First CBS dropped out after nearly four decades and was replaced by hungry Fox. When CBS's overall ratings plummeted, especially with the coveted young male demographic, they got back in the game and, coincidentally or not, climbed up the ratings ladder once more. NBC decided to put its energies and resources into the Olympics, but came back with the big-ticket, night-game package wrested from ABC—along with its announcers, Al Michaels and John Madden—while ESPN succeeded partner ABC on Monday nights. The Super Bowl likewise went from a rotation basis to the bidding process, the event suffering none of the ratings dips found in the regular season. While the number of Americans watching the game roughly doubled between the first game in 1967 and the 40th installment 2006, the 30-second ad rate went from $42,000 to $2.4 million. The league itself got into the game, so to speak, launching the NFL Network to hype itself further and adding selected games starting in 2006.

Helping stoke the league's ever-increasing finances were hints of the game's dynastic past, which manifest itself despite the turnover that went hand-in-hand with free agency in the salary cap era. The Green Bay Packers returned to the Super Bowl two straight years, solidifying their old-school values and rabid fan base with a Cheesehead in every pot. The Packers were denied a repeat by a better story: John Elway. The Denver quarterback, on the cusp of joining record-shattering Miami passer Dan Marino in having never won a Super Bowl (despite far more attempts by the Broncos), pulled out a win late in Super Bowl XXXII. Then the next year the Broncos won the Super Bowl again with an MVP performance by Elway, who soon retired a conquering hero. Just when it seemed that the relocated Rams, with Marshall Faulk, Kurt Warner, and a gang of unstoppable receivers, would start their own dynasty, the New England Patriots emerged with three Super Bowl wins in four. Two of those wins were decided on last-second field goals by Adam Vinatieri—set up with cool efficiency by quarterback Tom Brady—and the third came when Bill Belichick's vaunted defense held off a final Philadelphia drive. And just when the Patriots started to slip, it was back to the future with

a return to the dynasty of many fans' youth, the Pittsburgh Steelers, winning their first Super Bowl since the Terrible Towel was fresh.

Even with eight decades in the books, first-time issues came up that the NFL grappled to deal with. In the wake of attacks on New York's World Trade Center in September 2001, Tagliabue cancelled the weekend's games, as did NCAA football, Major League Baseball, and almost every other American sports organization. The greatest disappointment of the now-departed Rozelle's commissionership had been his failure to cancel games in the wake of John F. Kennedy's assassination in November 1963; this time the NFL got credit for acting first and also for lifting the TV blackout rule for a fearful public the first week back. The decision to push the games back, however, required rearranging the Super Bowl because there was no extra week in the schedule. Tagliabue finally brokered a deal with Ford dealers to move their convention to a week later in New Orleans. A devastating hurricane in that same city four years later created another first-time catastrophe for the NFL. Just two weeks before the start of the 2005 season, the Saints had to scramble to find a home. Trying to make the best of a grave situation that trivialized football, the Saints played home games in both Baton Rouge and San Antonio. But a decision to hold a Saints home game at Giants Stadium—against the Giants—made people angry (except Giants fans). Helping even less was Saints owner Tom Benson. Dissatisfied before Hurricane Katrina with his stadium and revenue situation, Benson made statements about moving the team while many citizens were already displaced and large parts of the Gulf Coast remained disaster areas. The fighting spirit of the region was displayed in a photograph of a refrigerator amid the rubble of a distressed city; spray-painted across the refrigerator it said, "Do Not Open. Benson inside." The city worked to rebuild the ravaged Superdome in time for the 2006 Saints season. No dates were set, however, for the next Super Bowl in a city that had hosted the game nine times.

The NFL had weathered catastrophes of all kinds, but a familiar one threatened the prosperity of a game that, despite two major strikes in a five-year span, had been uninterrupted by work stoppages longer than any of the other three major team sports. The most contentious part of the problem wasn't a management vs. player issue, but a potential owner against owner war that threatened the basis of the league's prosperity since the early days of Rozelle's reign. The game's senior owner, Wellington Mara, whose involvement traced back to when his father founded the Giants in 1925, recently died, and few of the old guard owners remained who could recall what it was like

for big-city teams like the Giants to say they'd take the same share of the pie as little Green Bay. These men had been replaced by a new generation raised in a corporate world where profits spoke louder than principles. Despite sharing TV money, the new or renovated stadiums in almost every city—for warm-weather and dome cities, Tagliabue had begun offering the incentive of hosting a Super Bowl if they followed the plan—created great disparities of wealth in the league. The growing divide between low-income and high-income teams was relative, of course. The bottom two teams, according to *Forbes* in 2005 were the Arizona Cardinals and the Minnesota Vikings. Their combined value and revenues barely topped that of the top club, Dan Snyder's Washington Redskins, a franchise worth $1.2 billion that brought in $287 million through income from things such as advertising and radio rights fees. In a league that had thrived on the notion that one team could beat another "on any given Sunday," how long could this hold true when one owner made twice what the other did? The concept of the New York Yankees and the Kansas City Royals, two 1970s rivals on opposite ends of the baseball spectrum with no road map back, didn't seem far fetched in the NFL if the long-term vision grew narrower.

Amid naysayers in the press and the furrowed brows of broadcasters drawn to sports in the first place by a passion for the NFL, owners from both sides of the fence put together a last-minute deal. A six-year extension of the collective bargaining agreement was approved just as the negotiating window was set to expire in March 2006. The new deal continued to maintain the salary cap and expanded it by enough to keep teams from having to immediately cut veterans because of salaries, while fixing labor costs through 2011. The biggest part of the deal, though, was revenue sharing. The top 15 teams would contribute to a pool to be shared by the bottom 17 revenue-generating teams. The wealthiest teams consented to this self-tax; the only two owners to vote no were the lower-income Bengals and Bills. Something that hard-liners like Snyder and Jones would seemingly never have done in business had occurred, for all intents and purposes, for the long-term good of the game. Tagliabue, employed by the league since 1969 and 17 years as commissioner, had seen enough to know that this was his opportunity to bow out on the highest possible note. With revenues of $5.8 billion in 2005, and 32 teams worth an average of $800 million each, the league was in good standing and had showed it was quite skilled at survival and adaptation on a constantly changing playing field.

FANTASY FOOTBALL

The first fantasy football league was founded by a group of Oakland sportswriters and Raiders employees in 1963. That first league was called the Greater Oakland Professional Pigskin Prognosticators League. The league received some publicity and inspired other leagues to form, but the time consuming nature of running such leagues limited the new "sport's" growth.

Fantasy football got a boost from the invention and popularization of rotisserie baseball in the 1980s. Rotisserie baseball received far more attention than did fantasy football as a result of the higher national media profile of its original participants, as well as the far greater importance that baseball fans already placed on their sport's statistics. The cottage fantasy sports industry that sprung up in response to the interest in fantasy baseball, however, quickly moved beyond one-trick pony status. In 1991, *Fantasy Baseball Magazine*, a struggling quarterly that had sprung up only two years before, published its first fantasy *football* cover. Statistical services which performed most of the challenging bookkeeping functions for fantasy leagues soon began serving both baseball and football fans.

In the mid-1990s the Internet quickly became an ideal home for these stats services as well as for the fantasy games themselves. The concurrent growth of football coverage on cable television and the launch of Sunday Ticket on DirecTV—which for the first time made every NFL game available to viewers who chose to subscribe—also were important factors that increased the popularity of fantasy football. The Internet was even more important to fantasy football than other fantasy sports, since football's more limited schedule makes both the sport itself and its fantasy version more popular to casual fans. By 1998 fantasy football had clearly passed fantasy baseball as the most popular fantasy sport, and estimates now have fantasy football being played by up to twice as many people as fantasy baseball.

Today, the NFL has embraced fantasy football. Fantasy football related content is said to account for over 30 percent of the traffic that hits NFL.com and the NFL's official team Websites. Fantasy games have become a huge business on the Web, with both NFL.com and the NFL Players Websites offering fantasy games, and with the league and its players union collecting millions of dollars in fees from the many Websites that offer their own games.

Many websites, including ESPN.com, have switched to an emphasis on free fantasy games in order to attract more of the millions of casual fantasy football players participating in the phenomenon. Current estimates say that 12–15 million fans participated in fantasy football during the 2005 season. More than 30 publications devoted to fantasy football will be published in 2006, with some titles reaching a circulation of 400,000. The fantasy sports industry as a whole, according to the Fantasy Sports Trade Association, is now a billion-dollar industry that is still growing.

In short, fantasy football—like the dominant NFL that it tracks—is the undisputed king of the fantasy sports universe.

THE GREATEST SEASONS FOR FANTASY

If you're a fan of fantasy football, you never forget that magical season. Remember when one-time stock boy Kurt Warner joined the Rams and led them to the Super Bowl? Or the year Priest Holmes moved to Kansas City from Baltimore and rushed his way to the top of the charts? Remember 49 touchdown passes in a single season? No way that can happen, right? Well, it did for you if you chose Peyton Manning in the 2004 fantasy draft.

Below are year-by-year lists of ESPN's top 20 fantasy players dating back to 1996, compliments of ESPN.com's Eric Karabell. What can they tell you about 2006? First, it pays to go with running backs early and often. A handful break out every season, but that doesn't mean such "veterans" as Steven Jackson, Cadillac Williams and Kevin Jones aren't worth a second look this fall. Hold off on picking a quarterback. There are always good values in the middle rounds. Daunte Culpepper, Drew Brees, and Jon Kitna should be bargains in '06. And finally, don't worry about the personality issues that dog wide receivers. Randy Moss? Terrell Owens? You're not having dinner with them; you just need them to make 15 touchdown catches.

And, hey, if you happen to see a stock boy with a great big arm, grab him. Everyone is still looking for the next Kurt Warner.

2005			2004			2003			2002			2001	
PLAYER	**PTS**		**PLAYER**	**PTS**		**PLAYER**	**PTS**		**PLAYER**	**PTS**		**PLAYER**	**PTS**
Shaun Alexander	361		Daunte Culpepper	366		Priest Holmes	371		Priest Holmes	370		Marshall Faulk	334
Larry Johnson	327		Peyton Manning	359		LaDainian Tomlinson	342		Ricky Williams	313		Kurt Warner	295
LaDainian Tomlinson	314		Shaun Alexander	300		Ahman Green	334		LaDainian Tomlinson	304		Jeff Garcia	294
Tiki Barber	303		Tiki Barber	294		Jamal Lewis	298		Rich Gannon	298		Priest Holmes	270
Edgerrin James	265		Donovan McNabb	291		Daunte Culpepper	281		Michael Vick	283		Rich Gannon	264
Carson Palmer	263		LaDainian Tomlinson	282		Clinton Portis	272		Daunte Culpepper	282		Steve McNair	259
Tom Brady	248		Curtis Martin	277		Peyton Manning	268		Clinton Portis	282		Donovan McNabb	259
Peyton Manning	241		Trent Green	257		Randy Moss	264		Shaun Alexander	269		Peyton Manning	256
Clinton Portis	238		Jake Plummer	255		Shaun Alexander	262		Deuce McAllister	263		Ahman Green	255
Steve Smith	236		Domanick Davis	252		Deuce McAllister	255		Peyton Manning	262		Brett Favre	255
Matt Hasselbeck	230		Edgerrin James	252		Trent Green	251		Charlie Garner	256		Aaron Brooks	255
Rudi Johnson	226		Brett Favre	250		Matt Hasselbeck	251		Steve McNair	253		Shaun Alexander	253
Eli Manning	222		Jake Delhomme	244		Torry Holt	241		Trent Green	253		Curtis Martin	243
LaMont Jordan	222		Corey Dillon	243		Steve McNair	235		Drew Bledsoe	252		Marvin Harrison	242
Jake Plummer	215		Aaron Brooks	241		Aaron Brooks	230		Tiki Barber	251		Terrell Owens	239
Michael Vick	214		Drew Brees	239		Fred Taylor	228		Aaron Brooks	247		Kordell Stewart	233
Drew Brees	209		Muhsin Muhammad	235		Jon Kitna	224		Jeff Garcia	246		Jay Fiedler	223
Trent Green	208		Marc Bulger	232		Jeff Garcia	223		Tom Brady	243		Corey Dillon	223
Kerry Collins	207		Tom Brady	223		Ricky Williams	222		Travis Henry	241		LaDainian Tomlinson	209
Drew Bledsoe	204		Michael Vick	218		Brett Favre	221		Marvin Harrison	239		David Boston	208

2000			1999			1998			1997			1996	
PLAYER	**PTS**		**PLAYER**	**PTS**		**PLAYER**	**PTS**		**PLAYER**	**PTS**		**PLAYER**	**PTS**
Marshall Faulk	374		Kurt Warner	317		Terrell Davis	355		Barry Sanders	315		Brett Favre	302
Daunte Culpepper	342		Marshall Faulk	310		Steve Young	355		Terrell Davis	293		Vinny Testaverde	277
Jeff Garcia	338		Edgerrin James	307		Jamal Anderson	307		Brett Favre	278		Terry Allen	276
Edgerrin James	327		Steve Beuerlein	297		Randall Cunningham	281		Kordell Stewart	275		Terrell Davis	268
Peyton Manning	297		Rich Gannon	254		Marshall Faulk	277		Jeff George	250		Mark Brunell	261
Rich Gannon	293		Peyton Manning	252		Fred Taylor	262		Dorsey Levens	246		Ricky Watters	253
Eddie George	285		Stephen Davis	251		Brett Favre	261		John Elway	242		John Elway	249
Donovan McNabb	282		Eddie George	245		Garrison Hearst	258		Steve McNair	241		Jeff Blake	249
Elvis Grbac	261		Marvin Harrison	236		Steve McNair	244		Drew Bledsoe	233		Curtis Martin	244
Mike Anderson	248		Brad Johnson	233		Vinny Testaverde	242		Steve Young	222		Drew Bledsoe	237
Robert Smith	244		Emmitt Smith	222		Emmitt Smith	236		Mark Brunell	222		Emmitt Smith	230
Fred Taylor	243		Randy Moss	220		Randy Moss	233		Jerome Bettis	219		Barry Sanders	229
Ahman Green	242		Doug Flutie	215		Antonio Freeman	226		Warren Moon	219		Jerome Bettis	213
Curtis Martin	236		Brett Favre	211		Chris Chandler	224		Abdul-Karim al-Jabbar	207		Michael Jackson	204
Ricky Watters	235		Dorsey Levens	210		Curtis Martin	216		Napoleon Kaufman	207		Tony Martin	201
Randy Moss	233		Charlie Garner	207		Trent Green	216		Rob Moore	206		Eddie George	198
Charlie Garner	232		Cris Carter	202		Ricky Watters	214		Corey Dillon	197		Steve Young	191
Mark Brunell	228		Curtis Martin	201		Robert Edwards	214		Antonio Freeman	195		Carl Pickens	190
Lamar Smith	223		Steve McNair	198		Jake Plummer	212		Marshall Faulk	194		Jeff Hostetler	188
Marvin Harrison	223		Jimmy Smith	197		Terrell Owens	202		Brad Johnson	194		Jerry Rice	186

Statistics are the lifeblood of sports historians. They provide an objective measure of athletic performance and detailed documentation for events that happened long ago. Unlike other sports, however, football statistics present several interesting challenges.

First, there is the unique nature of football itself. When a basketball player steps to the free-throw line, the success or failure of his shot rests entirely with him. A batter gets a hit or strikes out all by himself. Every action in football is a group effort. A runner relies on blockers. A quarterback needs a receiver to catch the ball. Defenders work in unison to stop a ball carrier. Very little of what happens on a football field is an individual effort. When we say that Jim Brown ran for 11 yards, we are assigning all of the credit for that play to one individual and ignoring the contributions of his teammates. Separating these contributions is not really possible in any scientific way, and thus we're left with only a partial picture.

Second, concerns the poor state of pro football's record keeping in its early years. From the beginning of the 20th century, baseball's American and National leagues had each refined a system for collecting statistics from its games. After every game, official scorers in each city sent detailed reports to centralized league offices, where day-by-day records were compiled and disseminated to the media. Professional football didn't have anything like that. Despite playing barely 8 percent of the games that the major leagues did, professional football was light years behind baseball in keeping track of what happened on the field. The National Football League didn't begin to keep any official statistics until 1932, and their early efforts were somewhat haphazard.

Third, and perhaps the most fundamental problem, has been a failure on the part of statisticians and record keepers to adequately answer the question "what should we keep track of?" Eighty-five years after the birth of the league, there still are no statistics to measure the performance of offensive linemen, and scant few pieces of data recorded for defensive players. More than 20,000 men have played in the National Football League (or the two leagues it has merged with, the All-America Football Conference and American Football League). Roughly 60 percent of those men were offensive linemen or defensive players, and by and large we have no data with which to measure their performance.

There are a number of basic statistics that the NFL simply does not include as part of its official record. Even though there are as many kickoffs as there are punts, the league has never kept track of kickoff distances or net yards on kickoffs for individuals. The passer has never gotten credit for yards gained on intercepted passes (for example, 25 passing yards for a throw intercepted 25 yards down the field), although a runner who makes a 20-yard run and then fumbles does get credit for the run. They do not count a loss on downs as a turnover, although it clearly is. The league does not keep track of blocked punt returns, or missed or blocked field goal returns, except for scoring plays in the box score.

THE HISTORICAL RECORD

Building the historical record for football has mostly been a retrospective process. The lack of contemporary record keeping in the league's early years has forced historians to reconstruct NFL playing statistics years after the fact, using sources that are sometimes riddled with errors and often incomplete.

Scoring plays for the period from 1920–32 were derived from contemporary newspaper game accounts. David Neft led the effort to reconstruct this data, and while the scoring statistics are complete, data in other statistical categories is fragmented. Barring the miraculous discovery of some previously unknown sources, the data from this period will never be complete.

New research by the Elias Sports Bureau in the late 1990s produced accurate data for the 1932 season for the first time, and the statistics for the rest of the 1930s were updated and improved. By the early 1940s, the statistical categories being recorded were quite similar to what we have today, and were reasonably accurate. In 1941 the NFL published its first Record Manual, containing a complete statistical accounting of the previous season. (This practice has continued each year to the present day.) Individual punting had been

introduced in 1939, punt and interception returns were added in 1941 and kickoff returns followed in 1942.

The main changes to NFL record keeping concern yards lost attempting to pass, or what is now call the quarterback sack. This was included in rushing yards up through 1946 (through 1949 for the AAFC). For 1947–48 the NFL kept sack plays separately and did not release the stats. Starting in 1949, yards lost were released and subtracted from gross passing yards to get a net figure. Times sacked were added for teams from 1961 and published for individual passers from 1969. Partial data from team media guides exist for 1960–68.

So when you look at rushing stats for passers in the 1940s, you have to keep this in mind. Sid Luckman has a career total of 204 rushes for minus-239 yards. What we have no way of knowing is how many of those rushing attempts were what we today would call sacks. We don't have the same problem with a modern passer. Troy Aikman shows 327 rushing attempts for 1,016 yards, plus 259 sacks for a loss of 1,748 yards. Combining these two categories together gives 586 rushes for minus-732 yards, about the same average as Luckman of minus-1 yard per carry. In Aikman's case, more data means a more accurate picture of his performance.

Individual sacks for defensive players began only in 1982, although some teams have unofficial data gathered from play-by-plays back into the 1960s. For 1960, the AFL also counted sacks as running plays, but did note them on the official score sheets. We have revised team and individual data not to include them. Lateral passes were kept separately from 1935–49 for teams and 1942–49 for players. After that, yards gained on laterals were included with the originating play.

Time of possession and third-down efficiency go back to 1981. Fourth-down efficiency started in 1984. The modern passer rating system was developed in 1973, although numbers can be calculated all the way back.

Safeties were not awarded to a particular player until 1942. Before then, all safeties were counted only for the team, although Tom Nash is credited with 2 during a single season, 1932. That remains a record.

When Elias merged the old AFL stats with the NFL's records, they made a few changes. The AFL counted blocked punt returns as regular punt returns, but the NFL did not, so these returns were subtracted from AFL players. The NFL counted blocked punts against the punter until 1978, and the AFL did not, so all AFL blocked punts were added to the AFL punter individual stats. The AFL counted returns of the free kick after a safety as punt returns, while the NFL has always counted them as kickoff returns. These remained as punt returns for AFL players.

The early AFL stats were not very accurate. The 1963 data had a great many changes made after the official figures were published. These changes have been accepted as official, although they were never actually listed separately. The only way to find them is to check current data in team media guides against the originally published numbers. The league never printed team defensive stats for that season in the official league guide, although there was a set published at the end of the season. We have managed to identify the game in which the offensive changes were made in almost every case and therefore modified the team defensive stats accordingly, although there are still a few small imbalances.

A turning point in NFL statistics came in 1973, when the NFL passer rating was developed. Before then, passers were ranked by adding the rank from four different categories: completion percentage, average gain, touchdown percentage and interception percentage, with the lowest number ranked first. Ratings of 1 for average performance and 2 for record performance were used, then multiplied by 100 and divided by 6, so an average passer would get a 67 rating. Average figures were 50 percent (completion percentage), 7 yards (average gain), 5 percent (touchdown percentage), and 5.5 percent (interception percentage). What the league did not do, however, was try to figure out exactly what each type of play was worth. It turns out the system is exactly proportional to taking yards gained, adding in a 20-yard bonus for each completion, an additional 80 yard bonus for each touchdown and, a 100-yard penalty for each interception. These bonuses and penalties were clearly in need of adjustment.

Under that system, if a quarterback completed a 90-yard pass from his own goal line to the opponent's 10, the passer would get 90 + 20, or 110 points. A 10-yard touchdown pass would be worth 10 + 20 + 80 or 110 yards also. The correct bonus for a touchdown pass is about 10 yards, because the yards are harder to come by near the other team's goal and the expected point total for a first and 10 on the opponent's 10 is only about 6 points. Scoring a touchdown raises this to 7, adding in about 10 extra yards. The proper penalty for an interception is about minus-40 or minus-45 yards, while there should be no bonus at all for completing a pass, the yards gained should take care of it.

Another feature of the system was that 2.375 points was the maximum in any one category. This was an arbitrary number that happened to be the value for a zero interception percentage, and obviously could not be exceeded. The other limits were 77.5 completion percentage, 12.5 average gain and 11.9 TD percentage, but in 1943, Sid Luckman had 28 touchdown passes in 202 attempts or 13.9 percent. His calculated passer rating was 107.6, but without the arbitrary limit on touchdown percentage, it would have been 114.2. Instead of being 12th all-time, that would be a record that stood for over 60 years, until Peyton Manning broke it with 121.1 in 2004. While derided by some as overly complicated and unfriendly to users, the rating system was a vast improvement to what had come before it.

A BRIEF HISTORY OF THE FOOTBALL ENCYCLOPEDIA

The first attempt at a football encyclopedia came after World War II. Sportswriter Roger Treat led a group of researchers in an effort to collect the scores of every game in league history and the name of each player who had taken the field for one of the NFL teams. That project took several years, culminating in the 1952 publication of *The Official National Football League Football Encyclopedia*. Published by the A.S. Barnes Company, it became known as the *Barnes Encyclopedia*. It became the gold standard for pro football reference for more than two decades, although none of its 17 editions contained team or individual playing statistics.

That innovation didn't come until 1974, with the publication of *The Sports Encyclopedia: Pro Football* by David Neft and Richard Cohen. For the first time, an encyclopedia presented not just the yearly rosters for each team but also the statistics for both individual players and the teams. A *New York Times* review of the book said it all with their headline: "Pro Football Reference Books: Finally a Good One." Five years later the first meeting of a group dedicated to the history of the game, the Pro Football Researchers Association, was held in Canton, Ohio; fittingly the birthplace of the pro game. The PFRA (www.footballresearch.com) would bring a level of concern for pro football records and research that had previously not existed among the public.

Neft & Cohen's encyclopedia was updated regularly over the next 25 years, though size constraints eventually led the editors to exclude or abbreviate data for seasons before 1960. It was the only pro football encyclopedia available until 1997, when two new entrants hit the market. Macmillan, the publishing house that had produced *The Baseball Encyclopedia* since 1969, came out with *The Pro Football Encyclopedia*, edited by Tod Maher and Bob Gill. At the same time, Harper Collins published *Total Football*, edited by Neft, John Thorn, Bob Carroll, and Michael Gershman. Both books presented, for the first time, individual playing statistics arranged alphabetically. Maher & Gil presented a series of registers with different sets of data—one for rushing, another for receiving, another for passing, and so on. *Total Football* presented all of a player's statistics under a single heading, although with many different configurations under individual player entries. *Total Football* most closely mirrored the model that baseball encyclopedias had been using since the 1960s. This encyclopedia, which published a second edition in 1999, bore the league's endorsement as the "Official Encyclopedia of the National Football League." *Total Football* also benefited from its collaboration with the Elias Sports Bureau, which serves as the league's official statistician. New research by Elias produced accurate data for the 1932 season for the first time, and the statistics for the rest of the 1930s were updated and improved.

The editors of *The 2006 ESPN Pro Football Encyclopedia* have built on the research of those four encyclopedia series. In fact, members of the staff for this book edited or contributed to each of those series, and have contributed significantly to the field of football research over the last 25 years.

Pete Palmer and Ken Pullis have spent years identifying and correcting errors in the official records by building an exhaustive database of game-by-game statistics. Palmer started his research in the early 1970s, while working as an editor for the Barnes Encyclopedia and serving as a member of the stat crew for the New England Patriots. The game stats were compiled by hand in those days, and inevitably, corrections were made to the official statistics after the data had been released. This led Palmer to examine the historical record, in search of scoring changes that hadn't made their way into the published statistics. He began to collect and computerize game-by-game team statistics and compare them to published year-end total for each club.

Tracking these discrepancies down usually required looking at the individual statistics, and that was data Pullis started compiling around the same time. The two collaborated to produce the most accurate statistical record ever compiled for professional football. By comparing individual stats from a game to team totals, comparing a player's game-by-game stats to his season totals, and comparing a team's season totals to a sum of its players totals, Palmer and Pullis uncovered and corrected thousands of changes and errors in the published game statistics.

Recent efforts to collect play-by-play data have yielded some new insights, as well. Sean Lahman has spearheaded an effort to computerize existing play-by-play accounts of NFL and AFL games back to 1960. The effort has led to the development of an analytical metric called "Total Adjusted Yards," which is included in this book's player register. In addition, game-by-game research has enabled us to publish for the first time a complete list of the actual regulars for each team at each position from the beginning of the two-platoon era in 1950.

AVAILABLE DATA

The following table summarizes the statistical data available for pro football, and the years in which it is available

Category	Team	Opponents	Individual
Points scored	1920–present	1920–present	1920–present
Touchdowns	1920–present	1920–present	1920–present
Field goals made	1920–present	1920–present	1920–present
Field goals attempted	1938–present	1941–present	1938–present
Field goals by distance	1966–present	Not kept	1966–present
PATs made	1920–present	1920–present	1920–present
PATs attempted	1920–present	1920–present	1939–present
Safeties	1920–present	1920–present	1942–present
Total first downs	1935–present	1941–present	N/A
First downs rush, pass, penalty	1941–present	1941–present	N/A
Third-down efficiency	1981–present	1981–present	N/A
Third-downs attempts/made	*1972–present	*1972–present	N/A

(Kept but not published 1970–71, some teams have unofficial data back to 1960)

Fourth-downs attempts/made	*1984–present	*1984–present	N/A

(Kept but not published 1982–83, some teams have unofficial data back to 1970)

Total yards gained	1932–present	1933–present	N/A
Rushing attempts	1932–present	1933–present	1932–present
Yards gained rushing	1932–present	1933–present	1932–present
Touchdowns rushing	1920–present	1920–present	1920–present

(Team rushing total included touchdowns on all types of returns up to 1946)

AVAILABLE DATA (CONT.)

Category	Team	Opponents	Individual
Passing attempts, completions	1932–present	1933–present	1932–present
Yards gained passing	1932–present	1933–present	1932–present
Times sacked	1961–present	1961–present	Defense 1982

(Some team have unofficial defensive data back into the 1960s)

Yards lost attempting to pass	1949–present	1949–present	Defense 1982

(Kept separately and not released 1947–48, included in rushing up to 1946)
(Individual data for passers in team section of league media book 1969–present)
(Kept but not published 1963–68, some teams have unofficial data back to 1960)

Touchdowns passing	1920–present	1920–present	1920–present
Passes had intercepted	1932–present	1933–present	1932–present
Passer rating system	Not calc.	Not calc.	1973–present
Laterals (attempts, completions, yards)	1935–1949	1942–1949	1942–1949

(Kept as part of whatever play was originally initiated for 1950–present)

Kickoffs	1948–1960	1948–1960	Not kept
Yards on kickoffs	Not kept	Not kept	Not kept
Punts	1939–present	1941–present	1939–present
Average distance of punts	1935–present	1941–present	1939–present
Net punting average	1943–1961, 1976–present		1943–1961

(Individual stats not inluding touchbacks 1943–45)

Punts had blocked	1943–present	*1969–present	1943–present
Punt returns	1941–present	1941–present	1941–present

AVAILABLE DATA (CONT.)

Category	Team	Opponents	Individual
Yards on punt returns	1935–present	1941–present	1941–present
Touchdowns on punt returns	1920–present	1920–present	1920–present
Kickoff returns	1941–present	1941–present	1941–present
Yards on kickoff returns	1940–present	1941–present	1941–present
Touchdowns on kickoff returns	1920–present	1920–present	1920–present
Interception returns	1935–present	1936–present	1941–present
Yards on interception returns	1940–present	1941–present	1941–present
Touchdowns on interception returns	1920–present	1920–present	1920–present
Penalties	1941–present	1941–present	N/A
Penalty yards	1935–present	1941–present	N/A
Fumbles	1935–present	1941–present	1945–present
Fumbles lost	1941–present	1935–present	1945–present
Yards on own fumbles	1945–present	Not kept	1945–present
Touchdowns on own fumbles	1920–present	1920–present	1920–present
Yards on opponent fumbles	1945–present	1948–1960	1945–present
Touchdowns on opponent fumbles	1920–present	1920–present	1920–present

(Yards on own fumbles and opponent fumbles combined in 1983)

Time of possession	1981–present	1981–present	N/A

*Not part of official statistics, but contained in the team section of the league media guide, which first came out after the 1969 season and was merged with the record manual after 1983.

THE PLAYER REGISTER

While professional football today has gotten itself onto the short list of dream occupations for almost every American boy, right there with fireman and police officer, pro football wasn't something players willingly owed up to in the early days of the league. College football was infinitely more respectable and acceptable than the pros, and young pro players often used fake names to protect their eligibility and earn cash while still in college. Johnny McNally took the name Johnny Blood after watching the film *Blood and Sand* in 1925 and ran with it all the way to the Pro Football Hall of Fame. In the list of 20,482 players to be found in this section, Johnny Blood is cross-referenced under both Johnny Blood and Johnny McNally. Likewise, Bobby Moore and Ahmad Rashad are also listed in two different places.

The names are one thing, but what about the statistics? Football is not as easily recorded as baseball, where the box score provides much of the essential information for a given game. For its first 12 seasons, little was tallied in the National Football League beyond touchdowns, field goals, and extra points. As a result, players during this time, even the great runners, ends, and passers of the day, have the same amount of information in the statistical section of their register entries as linemen. Since 1932, statistics have been kept in the areas modern fans are used to hearing about: rushing, receiving, and passing. Starting in 1932 rushing, passing, and receiving records were kept, but punts didn't get counted till 1939, punt and interception returns, and kickoff returns till 1941. Sacks became an official statistic only in 1982.

The editors of *The 2006 ESPN Pro Football Encyclopedia* have made the groundbreaking decision to publish different statistics in different registers. While Adam Vinatieri's biographical information is tracked in the Player Register, his career kicking statistics are found in the Kicking Register along with every other man who has ever booted a ball through the uprights. A third register, Defense and Specialists, provides the annual and career statistics of the top players in four different categories: interceptions, punts, returns (punts and kickoffs), and sacks. This way, the great players in each category appear side by side so the reader can easily compare the statistics of great ball hawks like Willie Davis and Deion Sanders without having to wade through all the players in history—much less all the other Davises and Sanders—most of whom never intercepted a pass in the NFL. The separate registers allows for comparing apples to apples and sacks to sacks.

Every player in pro football history is listed in the Player Register and each entry is broken into two parts: biographical information, which concerns a player's background, and statistical information, which deals with what he did on the field. In the separate registers you will find all 952 kickers who have recorded points. In the Defense and Specialist Register you will find the statistics for all 430 players with 20 or more interceptions, each of the 142 men who've punted 250 or more times, all 358 men with 75 or more kick or punt returns, and 112 pass rushers with 50 or more sacks. In addition, the 423 head coaches in NFL history have their own register.

BIOGRAPHICAL INFORMATION

Since every player appears in the Player Register, that is the starting point. Players are alphabetized in capital letters under the last name they used as professionals. That means the aforementioned JOHNNY BLOOD McNally, John Victor is listed directly before AL BLOODGOOD Elbert Lorraine. Full names are given next to use names. Bill Adams comes before Blue Adams and Bob Adams comes before Charlie Adams, although if arranged by their full given names rather than by their use name, the order would be much different. The editors of this book feel that if you're looking for Blue Adams, you shouldn't have to know that the Jacksonville and Tampa Bay defensive back is really named Daniel as you search through the 35 Adamses in the register. That's the kind of information you've opened up this book to learn. And since all 20,482 players in pro football history are listed in the Player Register, the more common names tend to have a lot of company. "Smith," for example, has 251 entries. The editors have been prudent in assigning nicknames as use names. Players who went by their use names and nicknames, such as Lou

"The Toe" Groza, are listed by their use name, first and middle name or initial (if any), followed by the nickname in quotation marks. The names are printed inside a black box to make them easier to locate.

Position is one of the most easily recognizable aspects of a player. The name may slip your mind, but if you're trying to remember a football player's name, the man's position will probably come to mind before the name—as likely will his team and the era in which he played. Position comes after name in the biographical line. A hyphen is used to differentiate between positions, with the position played most often appearing first. The game has changed a lot since 1920 and the 11 positions on the field at any time have accrued a lot of different names and meaning in those 85 years.

For pre-1950 positions, the same abbreviations are used on both offense and defense since the players generally played both ways. Here is an evolution of the position changes over the years, as they appear in this section:

1920–59

LE	Left End
LT	Left Tackle
LG	Left Guard
C	Center
RG	Right Guard
RT	Right Tackle
RE	Right End
QB	Quarterback
LH	Left Halfback
RH	Right Halfback
FB	Fullback
TB	Tailback (for Single Wing)
WB	Wingback (for Single Wing)
BB	Blocking Back (for Single Wing)

1960s

SE	Split End
TE	Tight End
HB	Halfback
FL	Flanker

1970s–Present

RB	Running Back
WR	Wide Receiver

The Steelers used the Single Wing until 1952. The same abbreviations were used for most of the offensive positions until the present, with a few changes. From the 1960s onward, the offense changed to split end and tight end and the halfbacks became halfback and flanker. For the 1970s, the halfback became a running back, while the split end and the flanker both became just wide receivers.

Starting in the 1950s forward all defensive backs are labeled DB. These were renamed cornerbacks and safeties in the 1960s. The DB was still used for the defensive backfield positions, but the following abbreviations were used for the other positions on defense:

1950s

LDE	Left Defensive End
LDT	Left Defensive Tackle
RDT	Right Defensive Tackle
LDE	Left defensive End
LLB	Left Linebacker
MLB	Middle Linebacker
RLB	Right Linebacker
MG	Middle Guard (in a 5–2 Defense)

1960s

LS	Left Safety
RS	Right Safety
CB	Cornerback

1970s–Present

NT	Nose Tackle (3–4 Defense)
LOLB	Left Outside Linebacker (3–4 Defense)
LILB	Left Inside Linebacker (3–4 Defense)
RILB	Right Inside Linebacker (3–4 Defense)
ROLB	Right Outside Linebacker (3–4 Defense)
LCB	Left Cornerback
RCB	Right Cornerback
SS	Strong Safety
FS	Free Safety

Some teams in the 1950s used a 5–2 defense, where the middle linebacker played on the line. Middle guard is used to refer to the defensive tackle who lined up over the center during this time period. The safeties became strong safety and free safeties. The only other change since then was if a team used a 3–4 defense, then they would have a nose tackle instead of left defensive tackle and a right defensive tackle and the linebackers would be right and left, outside and inside.

After the player's position comes his college. **None** means the player did not attend college, or else he is one of the very players in this book whose college is not known. In other cases, players attended more than one college; this information is given in the order the player attended the schools. Junior college is listed as **JC** and community college as **CC**. Since the names of college sometimes change over time, the editors have chosen the current name of the school for ease of understanding.

Next comes height and weight, the latter of which, of course, can fluctuate substantially over the course of a player's career. While one height and weight measurement is all there's room for in the register, the following charts show the average height and weight for the regulars at each position for every season.

TWO-WAY PLAYER HEIGHT AND WEIGHT BY POSITION

YEAR	E	HT(in)	WT	T	HT(in)	WT	G	HT(in)	WT	C	HT(in)	WT	B	HT(in)	WT
1920	29	71.2	180.2	27	71.4	205.7	33	71.6	198.3	18	71.6	197.3	69	69.9	179.7
1921	32	70.7	181.9	30	72.2	211.9	32	71.3	205.3	18	72.1	202.9	68	69.9	178.1
1922	35	70.7	183.2	34	72.1	214.7	37	71.7	205.8	18	71.9	202.3	85	69.8	182.8
1923	44	71.2	182.5	45	72	214.3	43	71.9	209.3	27	71.7	202.3	92	69.8	181.7
1924	42	71.4	185.5	44	72.1	216.3	42	72	207.1	18	72	199.8	97	70	179.8
1925	52	71.6	187.2	40	72.1	214.4	54	71.6	209.7	31	71.2	196.9	111	70	180.1
1926	51	71.5	187.9	56	71.8	215.3	61	71.8	210.8	29	71.1	198.4	130	69.8	179.4
1927	37	72.2	189.4	35	71.9	213.4	34	71.6	209.8	17	71.4	199.9	92	70.1	181.7
1928	25	72.4	192.9	32	72	214.4	22	71.7	212.9	16	72	201.3	70	70.2	182.4
1929	38	72.2	192.2	37	72.2	208.1	39	71.5	209.1	20	72.4	206.3	84	70.3	182.9
1930	35	72.4	192.1	35	72.7	216.3	43	72	211	25	72.6	208.6	90	70.4	185.3
1931	35	72.5	193.9	32	72.9	220.6	35	72	212.6	22	72.3	209.3	86	70.9	188.4
1932	31	72.8	197.8	26	73.2	220.2	29	71.9	218	18	72.7	208.6	64	71.6	193.7
1933	35	72.6	195.6	31	73.4	223.9	40	72	215.8	21	72.2	209.5	82	71.2	192.4
1934	35	72.9	198.8	34	73.7	225	44	71.7	218	21	72.6	214.5	84	71.3	192.7
1935	34	72.6	196.2	38	73.9	224	43	71.8	214.5	17	73.4	217.1	83	71.5	194.5
1936	39	72.6	194.4	38	74.3	225.6	45	71.5	212.2	17	73.6	211.3	85	71.5	194.7
1937	43	73.1	199.4	43	74.5	227.7	41	71.6	212.8	25	73.6	211.9	93	71.6	194.2
1938	49	73.2	198.2	50	74.2	227.6	42	71.4	215.8	27	73.4	212.7	109	71.6	195.3
1939	44	73.6	201	49	74.1	229.9	44	71.3	213.1	21	73.2	211.1	111	71.9	196
1940	53	73.7	202	56	74	228	44	71.7	214.3	23	73.6	211.9	110	72	195.7
1941	57	73.9	204.3	55	74	228.9	51	71.7	214.9	26	73.5	211.1	121	71.8	194.9
1942	50	73.7	202.3	49	74.1	231.8	44	71.7	212.2	27	72.8	208	112	71.9	195.1
1943	32	73.7	202.8	33	73.5	229.5	33	70.7	212.7	21	72.7	207.3	78	71.6	195.5
1944	45	73.6	203.2	47	73	229.1	40	70.9	213.4	21	72.9	210.3	99	71.3	192.1
1945	53	73.8	203.1	46	73.7	233.7	42	71.3	215.6	26	72.8	210.8	113	71.5	191.9
1946	102	73.8	205.5	95	74.4	234.5	86	71.7	215.9	60	73.1	211.5	221	71.5	193.2
1947	111	73.9	205.7	95	74.5	238.5	94	72	219	64	73	213.8	222	71.6	191.9
1948	111	73.7	204.4	94	74.6	239.2	88	72.3	220.6	71	73	216.1	243	71.8	192.6
1949	104	74	206	88	74.6	237.8	76	72.3	222.4	66	72.9	216.3	213	71.7	191.6

OFFENSIVE PLAYER HEIGHT AND WEIGHT BY POSITION

YEAR	E	HT(in)	WT	T	HT(in)	WT	G	HT(in)	WT	C	HT(in)	WT	B	HT(in)	WT	TE	HT(in)	WT	QB	HT(in)	WT
1950	28	74.3	204.3	28	74.8	236.7	29	72.7	222.6	14	74.4	227.5	45	71.8	195.7	—	—	—	17	72.8	190.2
1951	28	73.8	202.7	24	75	237.1	25	72.5	224.4	13	74.1	224.2	46	71.8	196.9	—	—	—	17	72.6	188.2
1952	26	73.8	201.2	26	74.7	239.9	25	73	226.8	12	74.6	228.9	45	71.9	197.4	—	—	—	18	72.5	190.8
1953	27	74.2	202.2	24	75.2	241.7	26	72.7	227.4	15	74.6	232.7	46	72	196.8	—	—	—	16	72.9	194.3
1954	28	74.1	202.6	24	75.1	242	26	73	229.1	12	74.8	230.2	41	72	199.3	—	—	—	16	73.1	196.6
1955	26	73.8	201.4	24	75.1	240.8	25	73.1	232.8	13	74.6	229	41	72.2	202.3	—	—	—	14	72.7	190.1
1956	28	73.8	200.9	24	75.2	243.5	25	73.2	234.6	12	74.4	233.3	44	72.1	200.3	—	—	—	19	72.5	192.2
1957	28	74.1	202.1	27	75	246.7	26	73.3	236	14	75.2	246	41	72.5	205.6	—	—	—	16	72.6	195.6
1958	27	73.9	201.5	27	75.2	248.8	28	73.3	235.3	13	74.9	239.7	40	72.6	205.1	—	—	—	17	72.8	194.8
1959	28	74	202.8	27	75.2	248.9	25	73.4	239.8	12	74.8	239.7	39	72.5	204.2	—	—	—	16	73.2	197.4
1960	42	73.7	201.2	44	75.5	250.3	46	73.2	238.9	22	74.8	241.3	55	72.3	204.3	24	74.6	212.1	25	73.2	195.4
1961	42	73.5	199.8	46	75.4	250.3	45	73.6	240.3	23	75	241.9	54	72.4	205.7	24	74.3	215.8	27	73	197.3
1962	44	73.3	198.1	46	75.5	252.3	47	73.8	242.7	23	74.8	242.7	56	72.7	209.4	23	75.1	223	26	73	197.2
1963	45	73.5	198	48	75.7	254.1	49	73.9	245.9	23	74.8	242.7	56	72.5	208.9	27	74.8	224.5	25	73.7	202
1964	46	73.2	196.1	50	75.7	255.2	47	74.3	247.5	25	74.8	243	55	72.6	210.2	27	74.9	225.6	28	73.7	201.6
1965	50	73.3	195.6	45	76	258.3	45	74.4	248.5	24	74.8	244.6	48	72.9	214.3	27	75	225.3	25	73.4	202.1
1966	49	73.5	198.9	49	76	258.2	51	74.6	249.5	25	74.6	244.4	56	72.8	212.2	28	75.3	225	29	73.7	202.6
1967	60	73.3	196.2	55	75.9	257.4	52	74.6	250.2	28	74.7	244.5	62	72.5	212.9	27	75.3	228.1	27	73.7	202.9
1968	58	73.2	195.9	53	76	258.2	53	74.7	250.1	26	74.8	244.9	63	72.6	211.9	30	75.6	229.5	32	73.6	202
1969	57	73.5	194.9	56	76.3	259.5	57	74.7	251.2	26	75.1	246.7	61	72.7	214.3	31	75.2	226.5	33	73.8	204.6
1970	60	73	192.6	53	76.2	259	58	74.8	252.9	27	75	246.9	61	72.6	213.5	29	75.5	230	31	73.7	203.2
1971	58	73.2	193.5	56	76.4	260.6	54	74.9	254.1	30	75.3	247.8	60	72.4	212.6	33	75.7	228.5	31	73.6	203.4
1972	60	73.4	193.9	52	76.5	259.7	56	74.8	252.4	28	75.1	246.6	58	72.6	213.1	28	75.7	229	32	74.1	206.9
1973	57	73.2	193.7	57	76.4	260.1	56	74.8	251.9	30	75.3	247.6	59	72.5	212.8	30	75.8	229.8	33	74.4	207.2
1974	55	73.1	193.6	53	76.3	261	60	75	253.5	27	75.3	248.9	59	72.3	211.4	28	75.6	229.6	32	74.1	205.6
1975	56	72.5	190.5	56	76.5	260.9	59	75	254.7	27	75.1	248	59	72	209.2	29	75.8	229.6	31	74.4	206.5
1976	63	72.2	188.9	63	76.8	262	64	75.1	256.6	29	75.1	249	65	72.3	209.8	30	75.6	229.6	35	74.2	205.5
1977	60	72.4	190.5	64	76.8	262.6	64	75.2	257.4	29	75	249.6	65	72.2	212.5	31	75.3	229.6	31	74.2	205.6
1978	61	72.5	190	65	76.7	262.8	59	75.1	257.6	31	75	251.1	72	72.3	212	35	75.1	230.1	33	74.5	205.6
1979	59	72.6	190.6	59	76.7	263.8	62	75.2	258	30	75.1	251.9	68	72.3	211	32	75.4	232.2	30	74.4	204.9
1980	62	72.7	191.6	65	76.7	264.8	64	75.1	259.1	29	75.1	251.5	72	72.1	211.1	35	75.3	233.9	32	74.5	207
1981	63	72.6	190.1	63	76.8	267.7	64	75.2	260.6	34	75	255.4	66	72	212.2	35	75.7	234.5	33	74.5	207
1982	56	72.6	189.3	57	77.1	270.2	56	75.5	262.5	28	75	257.3	55	72	212.1	32	76	237.2	29	74.6	206.4
1983	71	72.5	188.4	61	77.2	271.7	63	75.5	264.3	33	75.1	260.7	63	72	215	48	75.9	236	33	74.5	205.6

Offensive Player Height and Weight by Position (cont.)

YEAR	E	HT(IN)	WT	T	HT(IN)	WT	G	HT(IN)	WT	C	HT(IN)	WT	B	HT(IN)	WT	TE	HT(IN)	WT	QB	HT(IN)	WT
1984	63	72.4	186.5	66	76.9	275	65	75.6	267	32	75	261.8	59	71.8	214.1	49	75.8	237.1	37	74.7	206.9
1985	71	72.1	187	67	77.2	278.3	64	75.7	268.4	32	75.1	263.2	65	71.6	213.3	43	75.7	237.9	39	74.9	207.3
1986	65	72.3	187.2	67	77.3	282.4	63	75.9	272.6	34	75.2	266.1	68	71.6	214.5	40	75.6	238.1	38	74.9	208.1
1987	59	71.9	185.9	65	77.3	285.6	63	76	275.8	32	75.2	268.7	60	71.7	215	38	75.8	240.7	33	75.2	208.9
1988	66	72	187.4	60	77.3	287.8	67	75.8	279.3	33	75.3	272.2	66	71.7	215	40	75.8	242.6	38	75.1	210.3
1989	74	71.6	187.2	62	77.5	290.9	65	76	281.6	28	75.3	275.5	65	72.1	218.8	37	75.8	244.5	33	75.1	212.4
1990	71	71.6	186.9	64	77.3	292.7	61	75.8	285.8	31	75.3	278.1	59	72	218.9	40	75.1	242	32	75.1	212.8
1991	72	71.9	189	60	77.4	292.3	71	76.1	289.5	30	75.4	278.4	57	71.8	219.5	45	75.3	242.4	35	75.1	212.8
1992	75	72.1	189.9	63	77.5	294.4	64	76.1	291.5	30	75.2	281.8	55	72	222.3	44	75.5	246	34	75.2	216.1
1993	70	72.1	189.7	62	77.4	299.4	65	76.2	294.4	31	75.5	283.4	59	71.9	222.8	45	75.4	247.2	34	75.2	216.4
1994	66	72.2	191.5	67	77.4	301.5	65	76.1	297.6	30	75.5	286.2	65	71.7	224.1	47	75.5	249.4	35	75.1	215.1
1995	76	72.3	192.4	65	77.4	304.4	73	75.9	300.3	33	75.2	287.9	56	71.7	223.6	45	76	252.8	33	75.2	220.1
1996	81	72.4	194.3	71	77.4	305	73	76.1	303.9	36	75.1	290.4	65	71.9	226.3	51	75.7	251.2	35	75.3	219.7
1997	74	72.4	194.5	68	77.5	309.6	73	76.3	305.4	33	75.2	294.8	68	71.8	226.6	44	76.1	254.1	36	75.3	221.7
1998	70	72.6	196.5	67	77.4	310.4	73	76.1	308.6	32	75.2	293.5	62	71.8	228.5	42	76	254.2	39	75.1	218.8
1999	78	72.6	197.8	67	77.4	313.3	77	76.1	306.4	33	75.3	295.3	69	71.8	228.2	42	76.2	255.5	43	74.9	219.7
2000	77	72.6	198	72	77.5	314.4	65	76	307.6	37	75.1	299.7	66	71.9	230.7	52	76.2	254.7	42	75.1	222.1
2001	72	72.8	199.9	67	77.2	314.8	72	76.1	311.3	32	75.3	298.3	68	71.8	231.4	51	76.1	258.7	32	74.9	222.1
2002	79	72.7	200.1	77	77.3	316.2	75	75.9	313.5	35	75.2	298.3	62	71.6	229.9	53	75.9	257.1	41	74.8	222.5
2003	82	72.7	200.5	73	77.5	318.1	74	76	315.9	34	75.2	298.9	68	71.6	229.2	60	75.9	257.6	40	74.8	221.4
2004	86	72.9	200.9	75	77.5	318.4	81	75.8	313.4	35	75.2	297.9	65	71.5	228.3	57	75.9	257.2	38	75.1	223.3
2005	80	73.1	202.4	73	77.6	319.2	76	75.9	314	38	75.4	297.3	69	71.9	231.2	53	76	258.8	42	75	222.8

Defensive Player Height and Weight by Position

YEAR	DE	HT(IN)	WT	DT	HT(IN)	WT	LB	HT(IN)	WT	DB	HT(IN)	WT	P	HT(IN)	WT	K	HT(IN)	WT
1945	—	—	—	—	—	—	—	—	—	—	—	—	—	—	—	1	72	215
1946	—	—	—	—	—	—	—	—	—	—	—	—	—	—	—	—	—	—
1947	—	—	—	—	—	—	—	—	—	—	—	—	—	—	—	1	72	215
1948	—	—	—	—	—	—	—	—	—	—	—	—	—	—	—	1	72	215
1949	—	—	—	—	—	—	—	—	—	—	—	—	—	—	—	1	72	215
1950	28	74	213	38	74.4	241.9	32	72.5	214.2	48	71.8	184.5	—	—	—	—	—	—
1951	25	74.1	217.8	34	74.5	242.1	26	72.8	221.2	46	71.8	185.8	—	—	—	—	—	—
1952	27	74.5	221.1	36	74.8	243.6	26	72.8	216.8	47	71.9	187.2	—	—	—	—	—	—
1953	26	74.7	224.3	34	74.7	242	29	73	221.6	47	72.2	190.7	—	—	—	2	73	216
1954	26	74.7	223.8	33	74.6	248.8	27	73.3	222.8	49	72	189.5	—	—	—	1	72	215
1955	24	74.6	231.5	33	74.8	249.7	29	73.2	222.7	50	72.4	190.4	—	—	—	3	69.7	187
1956	26	74.7	231.3	31	74.7	249.5	33	73.2	223.5	53	72.4	190.3	—	—	—	3	72.7	212.7
1957	25	74.7	234.4	26	75	248.6	37	73.4	225.9	52	72.4	190.1	—	—	—	4	72.3	209.8
1958	25	74.7	239.7	24	75.1	252.4	40	73.4	226.4	52	72.5	190.5	—	—	—	4	73	214.8
1959	25	75.4	243.3	27	75	255.3	37	73.6	226.1	50	72.5	192	—	—	—	4	73	211.3
1960	45	75.2	242.4	43	75.1	257	66	73.5	226.1	87	72.5	191	1	71	175	5	72.8	211.8
1961	47	75.4	245.1	47	75.2	258.5	71	73.9	228.6	93	72.4	192.7	1	71	175	6	73	213.3
1962	46	75.6	246.5	47	75.4	260	71	73.9	229.1	92	72.3	191.7	2	71.5	181.5	5	72	209.4
1963	48	75.7	248.3	49	75.2	260.5	71	73.9	228.5	93	72.4	192.5	1	71	175	7	72	208.1
1964	46	75.9	249.3	45	75.5	260.4	72	74	227.8	98	72.3	192.6	3	72	186.3	11	72.4	206.7
1965	46	76	249.8	48	75.5	260.6	78	74	228.9	98	72.4	191.9	6	73.2	200	11	72.7	206.9
1966	51	76	250.9	53	75.8	261.8	80	74	228.3	103	72.4	191.9	7	73.6	204.3	15	71.8	199.6
1967	55	76.1	250.9	51	75.7	261.5	83	74	229.5	105	72.5	191.7	9	72.6	197	19	72.4	203.1
1968	57	76	252.6	58	75.9	261.4	85	74	229.2	112	72.5	192.5	10	73.1	202.1	23	72.3	197.7
1969	55	76.3	252.8	56	75.9	260.5	86	74.2	229.5	117	72.5	191.5	8	73.4	196.9	25	72.4	200
1970	58	76.2	253.2	55	76.1	261.3	89	74.2	230.3	112	72.8	192.1	13	73.7	198.1	25	72.1	200.7
1971	56	76.2	253.1	60	76.4	260.8	83	74.1	228.5	113	72.7	192.2	14	73.6	194.3	26	72.2	199.2
1972	56	76.1	253.1	56	76.2	258.5	89	74.1	229.3	115	72.6	190.9	15	74.1	197.9	30	72	196.6
1973	54	76.4	252.9	53	76.1	258.3	89	74.1	228.7	113	72.6	190.5	18	73.8	200.1	28	71.8	199.8
1974	57	76.4	252.9	51	76	258.3	92	74.2	229.3	115	72.6	190.7	23	73	196.8	31	71.8	197.7
1975	54	76.7	253.1	55	76	257.2	93	74.2	229.2	118	72.3	189	19	73.5	199.4	25	71.6	198.8
1976	63	76.7	253	63	75.8	257.9	94	74.3	229.1	123	72.4	190.3	22	73.8	201.5	30	71.3	193.3
1977	60	76.4	253.5	57	76	258.9	98	74.4	229	117	72.4	189.9	25	73.4	200.2	31	71.4	193.2
1978	62	76.5	254.5	53	76	259.5	105	74.3	227.8	125	72.3	189.2	25	73.2	197.4	32	71.4	190.1
1979	61	76.3	253.7	48	75.5	259	106	74.2	228.1	124	72.3	190.3	25	73.6	196.4	30	71.2	188
1980	59	76.5	254.3	47	75.4	258.7	114	74.4	227.5	130	72.2	190.4	25	73.3	196.1	30	71.4	188.9
1981	68	76.5	254.8	45	75.5	262.2	118	74.3	228.5	129	72.3	190.3	27	73.3	197.7	29	70.6	184.6
1982	57	76.5	257.8	37	75.6	261.2	103	74.5	228.6	112	72.2	190.0	26	73.7	198.6	28	71.1	186.6
1983	63	76.4	259.3	44	75.2	263.5	119	74.4	229.1	135	72.1	191.5	28	73.8	202.7	30	71.1	183.4
1984	64	76.6	262.3	39	75.2	264.4	126	74.4	229.7	132	72.1	191.2	27	73.8	201	32	71.1	183.4
1985	65	76.5	262.8	39	75.2	268.2	122	74.5	231.6	126	72.1	191.4	29	73.8	203.1	30	71	187.5
1986	61	76.5	264.9	43	75.4	270.3	117	74.5	232.8	133	72.2	191.6	31	73.2	198.7	31	70.9	186.8
1987	66	76.6	266.2	38	75.3	271.8	119	74.5	235.6	127	72.1	192.6	30	73.7	203.8	29	71.2	189
1988	70	76.5	270.7	37	75.3	275.1	124	74.5	236.7	130	72.1	193.4	30	73.5	204.5	32	71.1	188.6
1989	70	76.5	271.1	38	75.1	275.8	116	74.5	238.2	121	71.7	193.4	29	73.8	207.9	33	71.3	188.2
1990	66	76.4	271.5	45	75.2	278.9	116	74.4	238.8	132	71.7	193.1	28	73.8	210	31	71.5	192.5
1991	67	76.2	274.9	45	75.1	280.1	109	74.4	239.7	130	71.8	193.4	29	73.9	210.3	31	71.7	194
1992	65	76.2	276.4	51	75.3	285.4	113	74.4	240.9	132	71.7	194.4	31	73.8	210.4	31	71.7	194.6
1993	70	76.5	278.7	52	75.2	288.2	108	74.2	240.1	135	71.6	194.2	30	73.7	210.9	30	71.9	195.9
1994	63	76.3	276.6	60	75.2	291.6	99	74.1	241	124	71.5	194.3	29	74	211.4	30	71.8	193.3
1995	69	76.3	276.6	66	75.2	294.9	112	74	241.7	142	71.5	195.5	30	73.8	212	35	71.9	194.7
1996	74	76.4	274.6	66	75.3	295.6	106	74	242.7	138	71.6	196.7	29	74.1	214.2	32	72.3	198.9
1997	73	76.3	276.9	64	75.2	297.2	111	73.9	243	135	71.6	197.4	31	73.9	212.2	31	71.9	197
1998	69	76.2	277.6	62	75.3	298.7	106	74	242.1	145	71.5	197.1	30	74	212.2	31	72.1	196.4
1999	74	76.1	275.7	64	75.4	300.4	105	73.9	242.8	146	71.5	196.9	32	73.6	211.5	35	71.8	195.6
2000	68	76.1	277.3	67	75.2	300.5	108	73.9	242.9	140	71.7	198.7	31	73.9	212.9	37	71.9	199.7
2001	72	76.2	277	68	75.2	305.4	105	73.8	242.6	146	71.6	199.7	31	73.8	201.2	37	71.8	201.2
2002	72	76.1	277.6	68	75	306.4	113	73.8	242.3	157	71.7	200.1	34	73.9	212.3	40	71.9	202
2003	72	76	276.4	69	75.1	309.1	109	73.8	242.6	162	71.8	200.2	34	73.9	213.4	36	72	200.7
2004	73	76	276.8	70	74.8	305.7	115	73.8	242.6	160	71.7	199	32	74	210.8	37	72	200.4
2005	75	75.9	278.4	65	74.8	306.6	122	73.9	241.8	159	71.7	198.7	34	73.9	211.5	37	72.1	200.4

PLAYER'S ORIGIN

How a player originally entered the NFL is intriguing, but the crux of the matter is it can only occur with Shakespearean differentiation: by draft or not by draft. The amateur draft was instituted in 1936 and has undergone many incarnations (see separate section on the draft), but for the biographical line in the Player Register, it is represented simply by year and round. A player taken in the first round of the 1936 draft by the New York Giants will be listed as NYG: 1936, rnd 1. A player taken in the 30th round of the 1952 draft by the Philadelphia Eagles will be listed as Phi: 1952, rnd 30. If a player was not drafted, even if he played in the years before the NFL draft, no information is given. Draft information is given for players who played in the National Football League, All-America Football Conference, or American Football League. Other professional leagues are not included.

The player's birth date and birthplace is given by numerals after the abbreviation **B**. Likewise, his death and place of death are given after **D**. At the end of the biographical line is a piece of information available for a select few. Hall of Famers are designated with **HOF** and the year of entry into the shrine in Canton. In addition, if a player appears in one of the other registers, he will have the this indicated in brackets [**K** for Kicking Register, **I** for Interception, **P** for Punting, **R** for Kickoff and Punt Returns, **S** for Sacks, and **C** for Coach].

STATISTICAL INFORMATION

The second portion of each player's entry is the statistical section, the meat and potatoes of any sports encyclopedia. In the far left column is the year or years a player appeared in the league. This section only includes games played, so a man who does not get in a game, even if he is on the roster all season, is not included. This will appear as a gap in the player's record, especially in the case of backup quarterbacks stuck behind iron man starters.

Just as important as when a player played is the uniform he wore. The player's team appears next to the year in the register (see the book's inside back cover for a list of team codes). When players appear on more than one team in a season, each team is listed separately. If the player appeared in the AAFC and NFL, his career statistics for the AAFC are listed separately. AAFC teams are designated with **-A**. Statistics for players who appeared in both the NFL and AFL are treated the same both before and after the 1970 merger. AFL players for 1960–69 have -A in their team, but no separate AFL totals are computed.

There are several symbols that indicate whether a player appeared in postseason play or achieved recognition for his play during his career.

    †   Before the team name indicates postseason play.
    ★   After the team name indicates a player was listed on a recognized All-Pro first or second team and was on the Pro Bowl roster (the Pro Bowl began in 1939).
    ☆   Means the player was All-Pro only.
    ◇   Indicates Pro Bowl only.

Many hours of research for this book went into finding out who was a starter. The games column has two options. If a player appeared in 14 games and started 10, it will read 14 (10). If the player appeared in 14 games but did not start any of them, the column will simply read 14 (0). Zero starts are shown for 1920–49 and 1980–present. A blank means starts unknown. In the total line at the bottom of the column, career starts are also indicated; with zero if no known career starts were made. Games started are complete for 11 players per team per game for 1920–49 from Tod Maher. They are also complete for 1980–present for 22 players per team per game. For 1950–79, games started data is incomplete. Career totals may be incomplete for anyone who played in that period.

The positions column is used to differentiate between starters and reserves. The position is listed in this column only for regular starters, in which case the position is listed in caps. If the player is a highly-used sub, with roughly 5 games started, the position will be listed in lower case for the given season. Otherwise no position is listed. (Remember, the player's position, or positions, is given in the bio line as it applies to the player's full career.) Because of the way football is played, only about one-third of all players have ever been regulars.

Regulars were assigned one per position, 11 per team up through 1949, then 22 after that following the advent of two-platoon football. Two-platoon football was actually tried it in 1949 as an experiment, but 1950 is used as the starting point here. That was the first year the All-Pro teams had offensive and defensive parts. There was no set number needed to be a regular, just playing more than anyone else at that position. It was quite uncommon for a regular to have less than half the games started, and likewise to have more than half and not be a regular, although once in a while the regular might have only one-third of the starts because no one played more. The main criterion is games started, but this is complete back to 1980 only. For 1950–79 press guide bios were used. For 1920–49, Tod Maher's games started data was used from newspaper lineups. Sometimes a player would have hefty stats totals, but not many games started. In those cases the stats were used. The regulars have their positions in caps. Players who played a lot but were not regulars have a lower case position listed. This corresponds to roughly 5 games started when data is available, otherwise it is based on press guide information or stats. The starters were the ones who played the most at their position. There is only one starter per position (11 through 1949, 22 since). Subs had to have started at least one-third of the games, with best estimates made in the years where data is not available.

The other columns in the Player Register should be more familiar to most readers. The categories are as follows:

TEAM   Team-League (-A indicates AAFC and AFL)
G (GS, POS)   Games (Games Started, Position)
RUSH   Number of Carries
YD   Yards Gained on Ground
AVG (LG)   Yards Rushing Average (Longest Run)
TD   Touchdowns Rushing
REC   Touchdowns Receiving
YD   Yards Receiving
AVG (LG)   Average Yards per Catch (Longest Reception)
TD   Touchdowns Receiving
PASS   Passes Thrown
COMP   Passes Completed
PCT   Completion Percentage
YD   Yards Receiving
AVG (LG)   Average Yards per Pass (Longest Completion)
TD   Touchdown Passes
INT   Interceptions Thrown
SK   Times Sacked
YD   Yards Lost in Sacks
QBR   Quarterback Rating
KPR   Had a stat in the one of the other register categories. This includes kicking (**K**), punting (**P**), kickoff returns (**k**), punt returns (**p**), interception returns (**i**), or sacks (**s**), but the player may not have achieved the minimums to appear in these categories.
OTD   Other Touchdowns (i.e., not rushing or receiving). These could be on returns as mentioned above, or on fumble returns, blocked punt returns, field goal returns, or any touchdown that was not from the line of scrimmage via rush or pass
PTS   Points Scored
TAY   Total Adjusted Yards. This gives credit for yards and touchdowns from various methods. Touchdowns get a bonus of 10 yards. Since a team on the 1-yard line only averages about 6 points per time, rather than 7, you get an extra 10 yards for getting the ball over that final yard. For rushers it is Yards + 10 × TDs. Passing yards are split between the passer and receiver. So they each get Yards/2 + 5 × TDs. The passer gets an extra penalty of minus–40 × INTs. Returns are pegged to a slightly below average distance. Since it is relatively easy for a kick returner to pick up 20 yards on most kicks before the defense finds him, a formula is used where KRY stands for kick return yards. (Other formulas include PRY for punt return yards and INTY for interception return yards.) KRY – 15 × KR, PRY – 5 × PR and INTY – 5 × IR, and there is still a 10-yard bonus for each touchdown. Add them all up and you get TAY.

Dashes are used throughout the Player Register to indicate that the statistics do not apply to the player. For example, quarterbacks will generally have no receiving stats, so that portion of the table will have dashes for those categories.

Typical Game and Season Statistics

If you look at statistics from a typical game and a typical season since the early years of the NFL, you can quickly get a grasp on just how dramatically the game of football has changed. The biggest changes, of course, are in scoring—which was very low in the 1920s—and in passing, which steadily became more frequent as time went on.

Other interesting trends are also apparent. The interception rate was very high initially. In 1933 the ratio of completed passes to interceptions was almost 2 to 1, compared to today's value of 20 to 1. Some of that had to do with making the shape of the ball better suited to the passing game, but it is mostly due to experience and specialization. Rushing has remained relatively constant over the years. Field goal attempts and accuracy have improved considerably, though, helped by the introduction of kicking specialists and then the domination of soccer-style kickers, to the point where field goal percentage has just about doubled.

Looking at the averages, it's remarkable how much the passing side of the game improved. When the NFL initially developed their passer rating system, a typical mark was about 70. Now, however, the number is over 80, mainly due to more completions and less interceptions.

The tables below show statistics from a typical game for one team for each year, followed by statistics for a typical team for each season. (Note that, from 1935–40, the 1DR stats shown are actually total first downs and not just rushing first downs because passing first downs were not separately kept until 1941.)

Typical Game Statistics for Each Season

YEAR L	PTS	1DR	1DP	1PN	RA	RY	RTD	PA	PC	PY	PS	PSY	PTD	PI	PNT	PAV	PR	PRY	KR	KRY	IR	IRY	PN	PNY	FUM	FML	XPA	XPM	FGA	FGM
1921 N	10	—	—	—	—	—	—	—	—	—	—	—	—	—	—	—	—	—	—	—	—	—	—	—	—	—	—	—	—	0
1922 N	9	—	—	—	—	—	—	—	—	—	—	—	—	—	—	—	—	—	—	—	—	—	—	—	—	—	—	—	—	0
1923 N	8	—	—	—	—	—	—	—	—	—	—	—	—	—	—	—	—	—	—	—	—	—	—	—	—	—	—	—	—	0
1924 N	10	—	—	—	—	—	—	—	—	—	—	—	—	—	—	—	—	—	—	—	—	—	—	—	—	—	—	—	—	0
1925 N	9	—	—	—	—	—	—	—	—	—	—	—	—	—	—	—	—	—	—	—	—	—	—	—	—	—	—	—	—	0
1926 N	8	—	—	—	—	—	—	—	—	—	—	—	—	—	—	—	—	—	—	—	—	—	—	—	—	—	—	—	—	0
1927 N	9	—	—	—	—	—	—	—	—	—	—	—	—	—	—	—	—	—	—	—	—	—	—	—	—	—	—	—	—	0
1928 N	10	—	—	—	—	—	—	—	—	—	—	—	—	—	—	—	—	—	—	—	—	—	—	—	—	—	—	—	—	0
1929 N	10	—	—	—	—	—	—	—	—	—	—	—	—	—	—	—	—	—	—	—	—	—	—	—	—	—	—	—	—	0
1930 N	11	—	—	—	—	—	—	—	—	—	—	—	—	—	—	—	—	—	—	—	—	—	—	—	—	—	—	—	—	0
1931 N	10	—	—	—	—	—	—	—	—	—	—	—	—	—	—	—	—	—	—	—	—	—	—	—	—	—	—	—	—	0
1932 N	8	—	—	—	34	110	0.6	11	4	55	—	—	0.4	1.0	—	—	—	—	—	—	—	—	—	—	—	—	1.2	0.8	—	0.1
1933 N	10	—	—	—	36	121	0.6	14	5	78	—	—	0.5	2.2	—	—	—	—	—	—	—	—	—	—	—	—	1.3	1.0	—	0.3
1934 N	11	—	—	—	37	141	0.8	13	4	59	—	—	0.5	1.7	—	—	—	—	—	—	—	—	—	—	—	—	1.4	1.0	—	0.4
1935 N	11	9*	—	—	39	116	0.6	15	5	80	—	—	0.6	2.2	—	—	—	36	—	—	2	—	—	20	2.4	—	1.4	1.1	—	0.4
1936 N	12	11*	—	—	41	142	0.7	15	6	83	—	—	0.6	2.0	—	—	—	39	—	—	2	—	—	26	2.4	—	1.5	1.3	—	0.4
1937 N	13	10*	—	—	39	127	0.6	17	6	93	—	—	0.8	1.9	—	—	—	42	—	—	2	—	—	25	2.3	—	1.7	1.4	—	0.4
1938 N	13	11*	—	—	38	125	0.8	18	7	106	—	—	0.8	2.0	—	—	—	34	—	—	2	—	—	26	2.4	—	1.8	1.5	0.9	0.4
1939 N	15	11*	—	—	37	121	0.9	20	9	129	—	—	0.9	1.9	—	—	—	38	—	—	2	—	—	25	2.5	—	2.0	1.7	1.2	0.5
1940 N	15	11*	—	—	38	120	0.9	20	9	125	—	—	0.9	2.0	6	40	—	39	—	59	2	24	—	31	2.4	—	2.0	1.7	1.0	0.4
1941 N	16	6	4	1	37	117	1.0	20	9	122	—	—	0.9	2.0	6	41	3	41	3	64	2	28	4	38	2.3	1.1	2.2	1.9	1.1	0.4
1942 N	16	6	5	1	37	123	0.9	20	9	124	—	—	1.0	2.0	6	39	3	39	3	64	2	25	5	40	2.1	1.1	2.1	2.0	0.8	0.3
1943 N	19	6	5	1	37	118	1.1	22	10	141	—	—	1.4	2.3	6	38	3	36	3	70	2	29	5	45	2.3	0.9	2.7	2.5	0.9	0.2
1944 N	18	6	5	1	37	119	1.2	21	9	129	—	—	1.2	2.3	6	37	3	35	3	71	2	32	7	54	2.5	1.1	2.5	2.2	0.7	0.2
1945 N	18	6	5	1	36	123	1.3	21	10	144	—	—	1.1	1.9	5	38	3	34	3	69	2	26	6	57	2.8	1.1	2.5	2.3	0.8	0.3
1946 N	19	8	6	1	38	126	1.3	21	10	143	—	—	1.1	1.9	5	41	3	34	4	75	2	30	8	67	3.2	1.7	2.5	2.3	1.0	0.4
1946 A	20	6	4	1	35	120	1.1	20	10	135	—	—	1.2	1.7	5	41	3	41	4	80	2	25	4	33	3.3	1.6	2.6	2.5	0.9	0.4
1947 N	22	8	7	2	36	139	1.1	25	12	181	—	—	1.6	2.1	5	42	3	42	4	79	2	29	8	69	2.5	1.4	3.0	2.7	1.0	0.4
1947 A	21	7	5	1	35	151	1.3	21	10	148	—	—	1.3	1.5	4	41	3	35	4	87	1	24	4	31	2.8	1.3	2.9	2.6	1.0	0.4
1948 N	23	8	8	1	38	151	1.3	26	12	174	—	—	1.6	1.9	6	41	3	40	4	80	2	29	8	68	2.8	1.5	3.2	3.0	0.9	0.4
1948 A	23	8	6	1	35	162	1.4	25	12	177	—	—	1.5	1.7	5	41	3	37	4	78	2	24	6	48	2.6	1.2	3.1	2.9	0.7	0.3
1949 N	22	8	8	1	39	151	1.3	27	13	179	2	18	1.4	2.1	6	41	3	39	4	75	2	29	6	56	2.4	1.3	3.0	2.8	1.1	0.5
1949 A	21	7	5	1	36	153	1.4	23	11	166	—	—	1.2	1.7	5	40	3	36	3	74	2	23	5	40	2.9	1.6	2.9	2.8	0.9	0.4
1950 N	23	8	7	1	37	154	1.3	28	13	186	3	20	1.4	2.2	6	40	3	36	4	84	2	30	7	61	2.7	1.5	3.1	2.9	1.2	0.5
1951 N	22	9	8	2	38	152	1.2	27	13	184	3	21	1.4	2.0	6	40	3	31	4	79	2	26	7	59	2.2	1.3	2.8	2.7	1.3	0.7
1952 N	21	7	7	1	33	126	0.9	26	12	176	3	23	1.5	1.9	5	42	3	34	3	78	2	27	6	54	2.4	1.4	2.7	2.6	1.5	0.7
1953 N	22	8	8	1	33	134	1.2	30	14	193	2	19	1.3	2.1	6	41	4	21	4	85	2	30	6	49	2.5	1.4	2.7	2.6	1.6	0.8
1954 N	22	7	9	1	33	132	1.1	29	15	211	2	19	1.5	2.0	5	41	3	20	4	84	2	27	6	54	2.4	1.4	2.8	2.6	1.5	0.8
1955 N	21	8	8	1	37	147	1.2	27	13	176	2	16	1.3	1.8	5	41	3	19	4	82	2	23	5	46	2.3	1.5	2.7	2.5	1.7	0.8
1956 N	20	9	7	1	38	156	1.2	23	12	161	2	14	1.1	1.7	5	41	3	21	4	80	2	24	5	44	1.9	1.1	2.6	2.4	1.5	0.8
1957 N	20	7	8	1	36	140	1.1	23	12	172	2	18	1.2	1.6	5	41	3	18	3	78	2	24	5	47	2.2	1.3	2.5	2.3	1.7	0.9
1958 N	23	8	9	1	33	141	1.2	27	14	196	2	16	1.5	1.7	5	41	3	19	4	78	2	22	5	48	2.5	1.4	2.9	2.7	1.8	0.8
1959 N	21	8	8	1	34	144	1.1	26	13	187	2	17	1.4	1.5	5	43	3	20	3	70	2	20	4	41	2.3	1.3	2.7	2.6	1.7	0.8
1960 N	22	7	8	1	33	133	1.0	26	13	191	3	20	1.4	1.8	5	42	2	14	4	86	2	22	5	49	2.0	1.1	2.6	2.5	1.9	1.0
1960 A	24	7	10	2	30	125	1.2	33	16	218	2	20	1.7	2.0	5	38	2	17	4	92	2	22	5	48	2.4	1.3	3.0	2.8	1.9	0.8
1961 N	22	7	9	1	31	131	1.0	27	14	202	3	22	1.5	1.7	4	43	2	19	4	88	2	24	4	40	2.0	1.2	2.7	2.6	1.9	0.9
1961 A	24	6	9	1	29	115	1.2	32	15	217	3	22	1.6	2.1	5	41	2	19	4	85	2	31	5	47	2.2	1.2	2.9	2.8	1.9	0.8
1962 N	22	7	9	1	31	126	1.1	27	15	215	3	21	1.5	1.7	4	42	2	15	4	94	2	22	4	44	2.0	1.2	2.8	2.7	1.9	0.9
1962 A	23	6	9	1	29	126	1.0	31	15	210	2	20	1.6	2.2	5	40	2	15	4	93	2	28	5	48	2.0	1.1	2.7	2.5	2.0	1.1
1963 N	22	7	9	1	31	126	1.0	28	14	208	3	22	1.5	1.5	5	43	2	22	4	88	2	25	5	46	2.1	1.1	2.7	2.6	1.9	1.0
1963 A	23	6	10	1	27	113	1.0	32	15	224	3	25	1.7	1.9	5	41	2	22	4	96	2	25	5	47	1.9	1.1	2.8	2.7	1.9	0.9
1964 N	22	7	9	1	31	124	1.0	28	14	199	3	25	1.4	1.3	5	43	2	21	4	91	1	21	5	50	2.2	1.2	2.7	2.6	2.1	1.1
1964 A	23	6	10	1	28	110	0.9	33	16	236	3	24	1.7	2.1	5	41	2	23	4	95	2	32	5	44	1.9	1.0	2.7	2.6	2.0	1.1
1965 N	23	7	9	1	31	121	1.0	28	14	206	3	22	1.6	1.4	5	42	2	17	4	90	1	22	5	48	2.2	1.2	2.9	2.7	1.9	1.0
1965 A	21	6	9	1	29	109	0.8	33	15	208	2	19	1.5	1.8	5	43	2	23	4	88	2	26	5	52	1.8	1.0	2.4	2.4	2.3	1.2
1966 N	22	7	9	1	31	121	1.0	29	15	201	3	23	1.3	1.5	5	41	2	15	4	91	2	23	5	50	1.9	1.0	2.6	2.5	2.2	1.3
1966 A	23	6	9	1	29	116	0.9	32	15	215	2	18	1.6	1.7	5	41	2	18	4	93	2	24	5	48	1.7	0.9	2.6	2.5	2.2	1.1
1967 N	22	7	9	1	31	120	1.0	29	15	200	2	20	1.4	1.6	5	40	2	14	4	90	2	22	5	56	1.7	1.0	2.7	2.6	2.0	1.0
1967 A	23	6	9	1	29	116	0.9	31	15	206	3	23	1.5	1.8	5	42	3	24	4	88	2	30	5	48	1.8	0.9	2.6	2.6	2.1	1.1
1968 N	21	7	8	1	32	127	0.9	27	14	188	2	19	1.4	1.5	5	40	2	15	4	84	1	19	5	52	1.7	1.0	2.5	2.4	1.9	1.1
1968 A	22	6	9	1	32	126	1.0	29	14	199	2	22	1.4	1.6	6	42	3	24	4	83	2	24	5	49	1.8	1.0	2.5	2.5	2.2	1.3
1969 N	21	7	9	1	30	122	0.9	28	15	198	3	20	1.4	1.4	5	40	2	15	4	80	1	18	5	54	1.8	1.0	2.5	2.5	2.1	1.1
1969 A	21	6	9	1	30	122	0.9	29	14	200	2	21	1.4	1.7	5	42	2	19	4	83	2	26	5	54	1.7	1.0	2.3	2.3	2.3	1.3
1970 N	19	6	8	1	31	120	0.8	27	14	181	2	20	1.2	1.4	5	41	3	20	4	78	1	19	6	60	1.8	1.0	2.2	2.1	2.2	1.3
1971 N	19	7	8	1	32	130	0.9	26	13	174	2	18	1.1	1.5	5	41	2	17	4	84	1	22	5	54	2.1	1.1	2.2	2.2	2.2	1.3
1972 N	20	8	8	1	34	139	1.0	25	13	169	2	17	1.1	1.3	4	41	2	15	4	81	1	17	5	47	2.1	1.0	2.3	2.2	2.2	1.4
1973 N	19	8	7	1	36	144	0.9	24	13	159	2	18	1.0	1.3	5	41	2	20	3	78	1	19	5	47	2.3	1.1	2.1	2.1	2.4	1.5
1974 N	18	8	8	1	34	133	1.0	26	14	171	2	18	1.0	1.4	5	39	3	33	4	85	1	19	5	47	2.0	1.0	2.2	2.0	1.5	0.9
1975 N	21	8	9	1	36	145	1.1	27	14	183	2	20	1.2	1.5	5	40	3	28	4	91	1	21	6	52	2.2	1.1	2.5	2.3	1.6	1.0
1976 N	19	8	8	1	37	151	1.1	26	14	173	3	21	1.1	1.3	6	39	3	29	4	84	1	16	7	56	2.3	1.2	2.3	2.1	1.7	1.0
1977 N	17	8	8	1	37	144	0.9	25	13	162	2	20	1.0	1.4	6	38	3	28	4	75	1	20	6	56	2.1	1.1	2.1	1.9	1.6	0.9
1978 N	18	8	8	2	36	142	1.0	26	14	178	2	19	1.0	1.4	5	39	3	25	4	78	1	18	7	58	2.1	1.1	2.2	2.0	1.5	1.0
1979 N	20	8	9	2	34	136	1.1	29	16	199	2	19	1.2	1.3	5	39	3	21	4	81	1	19	6	54	2.0	1.1	2.4	2.2	1.6	1.0

Statistics from a Typical Game (cont.)

YEAR L	PTS	1DR	1DP	1PN	RA	RY	RTD	PA	PC	PY	PS	PSY	PTD	PI	PNT	PAV	PR	PRY	KR	KRY	IR	IRY	PN	PNY	FUM	FML	XPA	XPM	FGA	FGM
1980 N	20	7	10	1	32	128	1.0	31	17	214	2	18	1.4	1.4	5	40	3	22	4	78	1	17	6	53	1.9	0.9	2.5	2.3	1.7	1.1
1981 N	21	8	10	2	32	130	1.0	32	17	223	2	18	1.3	1.4	5	41	3	23	4	77	1	20	6	54	2.1	1.1	2.5	2.3	1.8	1.2
1982 N	20	7	10	1	31	118	0.9	31	18	221	3	21	1.4	1.4	5	41	3	22	4	78	1	16	6	51	2.1	1.0	2.4	2.2	1.8	1.2
1983 N	22	8	10	1	32	130	1.0	31	18	225	3	21	1.4	1.4	5	41	3	24	4	78	1	19	6	53	2.1	1.1	2.6	2.5	1.7	1.2
1984 N	21	7	11	1	31	124	0.9	32	18	228	3	22	1.4	1.3	5	41	3	23	4	77	1	19	6	54	2.0	1.0	2.5	2.4	1.8	1.3
1985 N	22	7	11	1	30	125	1.0	32	18	227	3	22	1.3	1.3	5	41	3	24	4	81	1	16	6	50	2.0	1.0	2.5	2.4	1.8	1.3
1986 N	21	7	11	2	30	119	0.9	32	18	226	3	20	1.3	1.3	5	40	3	22	4	75	1	15	6	52	2.0	1.0	2.4	2.3	1.8	1.2
1987 N	22	7	11	2	31	124	0.9	32	18	224	3	20	1.5	1.3	5	39	3	24	4	78	1	16	7	55	2.2	1.1	2.5	2.4	1.9	1.3
1988 N	20	7	10	1	30	121	0.9	32	17	218	2	17	1.2	1.2	5	40	3	21	4	75	1	15	6	51	1.8	0.9	2.3	2.2	1.8	1.3
1989 N	21	7	11	1	29	115	0.9	32	18	229	2	18	1.3	1.2	5	40	2	21	4	75	1	15	6	52	1.9	0.9	2.4	2.3	1.9	1.3
1990 N	20	6	10	1	28	114	0.8	30	17	211	2	17	1.3	1.1	4	40	2	19	4	70	1	14	6	48	1.8	0.9	2.3	2.2	1.8	1.3
1991 N	19	6	10	1	27	108	0.8	31	18	215	2	15	1.1	1.1	4	41	2	19	3	63	1	14	6	48	1.7	0.9	2.1	2.1	1.9	1.4
1992 N	19	6	10	1	27	111	0.7	30	17	205	3	18	1.2	1.2	5	42	2	20	3	60	1	18	6	48	1.7	0.9	2.1	2.1	1.7	1.3
1993 N	19	6	10	1	28	110	0.7	32	19	215	2	15	1.2	1.0	5	42	2	21	3	60	1	14	6	46	1.7	0.9	2.0	2.0	2.0	1.5
1994 N	20	6	11	1	28	104	0.8	34	20	227	2	14	1.3	1.1	5	42	2	21	4	87	1	15	6	52	1.6	0.8	2.1	2.0	2.0	1.4
1995 N	21	6	12	1	27	108	0.8	35	20	236	2	15	1.4	1.1	5	42	2	20	4	91	1	15	6	51	1.6	0.8	2.2	2.1	2.0	1.5
1996 N	20	6	11	2	28	109	0.8	33	19	222	2	15	1.3	1.1	5	43	2	24	4	88	1	15	7	53	1.6	0.8	2.1	2.0	1.9	1.5
1997 N	21	6	11	1	28	113	0.8	33	18	219	3	18	1.3	1.0	5	43	3	25	4	87	1	15	6	54	1.7	0.8	2.1	2.1	1.9	1.5
1998 N	21	6	10	2	28	113	0.8	32	18	221	3	16	1.4	1.1	5	42	2	24	4	86	1	15	7	58	1.5	0.7	2.2	2.1	1.9	1.5
1999 N	21	6	11	2	27	106	0.7	34	19	228	3	16	1.3	1.1	5	42	2	23	4	87	1	16	7	55	1.6	0.8	2.1	2.1	1.9	1.5
2000 N	21	6	11	2	28	113	0.8	33	19	222	2	15	1.3	1.1	5	42	2	23	4	90	1	14	6	53	1.6	0.8	2.1	2.1	1.8	1.5
2001 N	20	6	11	1	28	112	0.7	33	19	221	2	15	1.3	1.1	5	42	2	23	4	87	1	16	6	49	1.7	0.8	2.1	2.0	1.9	1.5
2002 N	22	6	11	2	28	116	0.9	34	20	227	2	15	1.4	1.0	5	41	2	21	4	94	1	15	7	54	1.6	0.8	2.3	2.2	1.9	1.4
2003 N	21	6	10	2	28	118	0.8	32	19	214	2	13	1.3	1.1	5	41	2	23	4	91	1	15	7	55	1.6	0.7	2.2	2.2	1.9	1.5
2004 N	21	6	11	2	28	117	0.8	32	19	225	2	15	1.4	1.0	5	42	2	20	4	91	1	16	7	57	1.6	0.7	2.3	2.3	1.7	1.4
2005 N	21	6	11	2	28	112	0.8	32	19	218	2	15	1.3	1.0	5	42	2	20	4	93	1	15	7	58	1.6	0.8	2.2	2.1	1.9	1.5

League Averages

YEAR LG	RY/A	COM%	GPY/A	TD%	INT%	NPY/A	PRAT	PRT	YD/PR	YD/KR	YD/IR	FUM%	XP%	FG%
1932 N	3.26	35.6	5.08	4.0	9.4	5.08	27.23	1.25	NA	NA	NA	NA	67.3	NA
1933 N	3.35	35.3	5.44	3.5	15.3	5.44	26.26	-1.08	NA	NA	NA	NA	79.3	NA
1934 N	3.82	31.4	4.43	3.5	12.8	4.43	18.79	-0.99	NA	NA	NA	NA	74.0	NA
1935 N	3.00	33.9	5.19	3.9	14.6	5.19	25.42	-0.99	NA	NA	NA	NA	77.5	NA
1936 N	3.45	36.5	5.41	4.0	13.0	5.41	28.93	-0.05	NA	NA	NA	NA	81.9	NA
1937 N	3.28	38.4	5.63	5.0	11.3	5.63	34.51	1.02	NA	NA	NA	NA	82.4	NA
1938 N	3.31	40.6	5.73	4.6	10.9	5.73	35.49	1.29	NA	NA	NA	NA	82.3	40.6
1939 N	3.26	42.5	6.33	4.4	9.3	6.33	39.74	2.57	NA	NA	NA	NA	82.1	38.8
1940 N	3.18	42.9	6.12	4.4	9.9	6.12	38.56	2.11	NA	NA	11.71	NA	85.1	39.6
1941 N	3.15	44.3	6.06	4.5	10.0	6.06	39.57	2.03	12.69	22:35	14.14	49.2	88.2	39.8
1942 N	3.34	43.8	6.05	4.8	9.7	6.05	40.25	2.15	12.15	21.96	12.69	50.0	92.8	35.5
1943 N	3.21	44.4	6.53	6.6	10.5	6.53	48.64	2.46	11.54	22.36	12.59	40.9	91.7	23.5
1944 N	3.20	42.9	6.11	5.5	11.1	6.11	42.14	1.69	11.59	21.74	13.62	44.6	87.6	33.3
1945 N	3.39	45.6	6.82	5.2	9.2	6.82	47.60	3.22	11.23	20.66	13.48	39.4	90.9	45.3
1946 N	3.32	44.8	6.72	5.4	9.1	6.72	47.64	3.18	11.79	21.02	15.60	52.1	92.8	42.7
1946 A	3.40	48.4	6.68	5.9	8.3	6.68	55.36	3.54	13.72	22.11	15.19	49.2	92.9	48.5
1947 N	3.90	47.0	7.25	6.3	8.4	7.25	57.57	4.11	12.92	19.99	13.99	54.5	92.4	44.5
1947 A	4.33	49.0	7.19	6.4	7.1	7.19	64.50	4.62	13.38	22.93	16.71	46.6	90.4	43.9
1948 N	4.00	48.1	6.70	6.3	7.4	6.70	60.00	3.98	12.06	21.14	14.75	55.2	93.4	40.9
1948 A	4.57	48.8	7.05	6.0	6.7	7.05	64.22	4.64	13.69	21.13	14.10	47.4	93.8	42.7
1949 N	3.89	46.6	6.55	5.1	7.5	5.46	53.88	3.66	11.91	21.11	13.90	53.8	94.4	45.6
1949 A	4.23	47.4	7.09	5.3	7.3	7.09	58.42	4.34	12.66	21.46	13.72	57.3	97.1	40.8
1950 N	4.16	46.6	6.74	5.1	8.0	5.49	52.88	3.67	11.14	22.57	13.71	56.4	93.9	44.2
1951 N	4.05	46.6	6.82	5.2	7.4	5.50	55.62	4.00	10.08	21.99	12.91	59.7	95.1	51.6
1952 N	3.82	46.7	6.80	5.6	7.3	5.30	57.72	4.09	10.24	22.57	14.23	58.2	94.6	43.8
1953 N	4.00	47.3	6.52	4.4	7.2	5.42	53.59	3.74	6.06	22.79	14.17	56.7	95.7	46.6
1954 N	3.98	50.4	7.18	5.0	6.9	6.02	61.72	4.55	5.82	21.80	13.26	58.4	95.7	53.6
1955 N	3.99	47.9	6.62	4.7	6.8	5.61	57.13	4.05	5.63	23.07	12.73	64.5	93.2	46.0
1956 N	4.11	50.5	7.08	4.9	7.3	6.02	59.62	4.28	6.73	22.59	14.18	59.9	94.1	51.1
1957 N	3.90	50.5	7.41	5.1	6.9	6.02	63.16	4.81	5.44	22.64	14.84	56.7	95.8	52.2
1958 N	4.23	49.4	7.16	5.3	6.2	6.12	65.29	4.93	5.74	22.32	13.11	57.5	95.6	46.9
1959 N	4.22	50.0	7.25	5.3	6.0	6.08	66.86	5.10	6.45	21.42	13.24	56.9	95.6	46.8
1960 N	4.08	50.2	7.23	5.4	6.7	5.91	64.18	4.77	6.72	21.80	12.73	54.3	96.8	56.2
1960 A	4.13	48.5	6.61	5.0	5.9	5.60	62.10	4.44	9.27	23.10	11.33	52.6	93.1	44.2
1961 N	4.22	52.1	7.48	5.4	6.3	6.08	68.51	5.20	9.46	23.38	14.42	57.4	97.0	48.1
1961 A	3.99	46.8	6.70	5.0	6.4	5.59	59.10	4.33	10.66	21.51	14.94	54.8	94.2	42.6
1962 N	4.07	53.3	7.85	5.6	6.1	6.48	72.59	5.68	8.20	23.70	13.41	59.8	95.4	49.5
1962 A	4.31	47.6	6.80	5.1	7.0	5.74	57.87	4.16	8.13	22.95	13.12	54.7	93.1	53.1
1963 N	4.05	51.5	7.52	5.6	5.6	6.15	71.74	5.57	9.37	23.40	15.94	55.3	95.0	49.6
1963 A	4.13	48.7	7.09	5.4	6.0	5.80	65.29	4.94	10.27	22.58	13.47	60.6	96.5	47.1
1964 N	4.00	51.4	7.16	5.1	4.8	5.64	71.69	5.50	9.13	23.35	15.39	54.3	95.1	53.1
1964 A	3.96	49.0	7.05	5.1	5.6	5.87	62.63	4.69	9.60	22.55	15.04	52.5	97.0	52.9
1965 N	3.92	51.3	7.46	5.7	5.1	6.08	73.51	5.72	7.81	23.22	15.85	53.8	95.6	53.8
1965 A	3.80	45.3	6.37	4.5	5.6	5.43	58.05	4.31	9.52	21.77	14.50	55.4	100.0	54.5
1966 N	3.90	51.6	6.91	4.6	5.2	5.59	67.44	5.03	6.34	22.06	14.89	54.3	96.3	55.7
1966 A	4.01	46.3	6.81	5.0	5.4	5.87	62.97	4.86	8.65	22.39	14.17	51.6	97.0	52.8
1967 N	3.92	51.0	6.94	5.0	5.7	5.75	66.65	4.89	6.08	22.58	13.45	56.6	96.9	49.2
1967 A	3.92	47.6	6.70	4.9	5.9	5.49	61.60	4.55	9.15	22.06	16.42	47.0	97.0	53.5
1968 N	4.02	51.6	7.02	5.1	5.5	5.77	68.65	5.08	7.06	21.32	12.79	59.8	95.1	55.6
1968 A	3.97	47.5	6.91	4.7	5.6	5.69	62.62	4.85	8.64	21.56	15.02	54.4	98.3	58.7
1969 N	4.00	52.6	6.99	5.1	4.9	5.76	71.60	5.29	6.38	21.67	12.63	55.3	97.7	52.7
1969 A	4.03	49.8	6.96	4.8	5.8	5.74	64.49	4.84	7.79	23.11	15.84	59.3	97.6	57.8
1970 N	3.83	51.1	6.73	4.4	5.2	5.51	65.55	4.82	7.36	22.06	13.37	56.1	96.9	59.4
1971 N	4.02	50.9	6.72	4.1	5.8	5.57	62.17	4.53	7.02	22.99	14.45	53.1	97.5	58.7
1972 N	4.14	51.7	6.82	4.5	5.3	5.66	66.32	4.87	7.14	23.06	13.12	48.4	96.5	61.1
1973 N	4.06	52.0	6.56	4.3	5.3	5.29	64.88	4.59	8.10	22.46	14.67	50.6	96.8	63.1
1974 N	3.88	52.5	6.49	3.9	5.2	5.35	64.22	4.54	9.79	22.17	13.91	49.0	90.6	60.6
1975 N	4.01	52.5	6.68	4.3	5.3	5.45	65.82	4.71	9.13	22.43	14.47	51.0	90.9	64.2
1976 N	4.08	52.2	6.63	4.2	4.8	5.28	67.01	4.87	9.03	21.44	12.96	55.0	89.8	59.5
1977 N	3.85	51.3	6.50	4.0	5.2	5.18	61.21	4.31	8.82	21.39	14.07	53.3	91.1	58.3
1978 N	3.95	53.1	6.73	4.0	5.4	5.54	65.01	4.69	8.38	21.38	12.96	52.0	92.0	63.1
1979 N	4.00	54.1	6.87	4.1	4.6	5.76	70.45	5.21	7.65	20.28	13.97	52.6	90.3	63.1
1980 N	3.97	56.2	7.00	4.4	4.6	5.96	73.74	5.38	8.29	19.92	12.25	48.2	94.0	63.6
1981 N	4.02	54.6	7.03	4.2	4.3	6.02	72.90	5.52	8.56	20.29	14.59	52.8	94.4	65.9
1982 N	3.82	56.4	7.02	4.0	4.4	5.84	73.43	5.44	8.13	20.09	11.87	50.0	93.9	68.2

League Averages (cont.)

YEAR LG	RY/A	COM%	GPY/A	TD%	INT%	NPY/A	PRAT	PRT	YD/PR	YD/KR	YD/IR	FUM%	XP%	FG%
1983 N	4.09	56.9	7.18	4.4	4.4	6.01	75.88	5.64	8.61	19.55	13.52	51.6	95.2	71.5
1984 N	4.02	56.4	7.14	4.3	4.1	5.90	76.12	5.73	8.63	19.81	14.58	49.0	96.3	71.7
1985 N	4.10	54.8	7.04	4.1	4.2	5.83	73.55	5.57	9.28	20.99	12.16	52.4	95.7	72.2
1986 N	3.94	55.4	6.99	4.1	4.0	5.88	74.13	5.59	8.58	19.75	11.62	47.4	96.0	68.6
1987 N	3.95	54.8	6.96	4.5	4.0	5.87	75.18	5.61	9.11	19.43	12.44	49.9	95.5	70.3
1988 N	4.01	54.3	6.91	3.9	3.9	5.93	72.91	5.54	8.49	19.95	12.39	50.0	95.6	71.7
1989 N	3.95	55.8	7.15	4.1	3.9	6.12	75.64	5.80	9.11	19.40	12.23	50.2	97.0	72.5
1990 N	4.10	56.0	7.01	4.3	3.6	5.98	77.35	5.83	8.43	19.13	12.98	50.6	96.4	74.4
1991 N	3.93	57.4	6.89	3.7	3.5	5.97	76.22	5.68	8.74	18.89	13.06	52.9	97.2	73.5
1992 N	4.03	57.5	6.86	3.8	3.9	5.78	75.26	5.51	9.15	19.42	15.41	51.4	97.7	72.6
1993 N	3.89	57.9	6.69	3.6	3.3	5.81	76.65	5.59	9.10	19.47	13.07	50.5	96.8	76.6
1994 N	3.72	58.0	6.77	3.9	3.1	5.98	78.44	5.74	8.94	21.22	14.36	49.5	98.8	78.9
1995 N	3.93	58.2	6.77	4.0	3.1	5.96	79.25	5.79	9.42	21.42	13.78	52.1	98.2	77.4
1996 N	3.85	57.6	6.68	3.9	3.4	5.83	76.85	5.54	10.04	21.97	12.91	48.6	98.6	80.0
1997 N	3.98	56.2	6.69	3.9	3.0	5.70	77.22	5.72	9.91	22.00	14.54	47.6	98.6	78.1
1998 N	3.99	56.6	6.85	4.2	3.3	5.89	78.25	5.80	10.00	22.27	13.83	48.6	98.3	79.6
1999 N	3.90	57.1	6.76	4.0	3.4	5.85	77.06	5.65	9.35	21.23	14.28	48.7	98.9	77.7
2000 N	4.08	58.2	6.75	3.9	3.3	5.85	78.08	5.67	9.98	21.92	13.23	51.9	99.1	79.7
2001 N	4.06	59.0	6.78	3.9	3.4	5.87	78.51	5.65	9.77	21.64	14.14	46.4	98.1	76.3
2002 N	4.22	59.6	6.72	4.0	3.1	5.88	80.44	5.75	9.53	21.78	14.28	50.1	98.5	77.5
2003 N	4.16	58.8	6.64	4.0	3.3	5.84	78.35	5.57	9.55	21.56	14.63	46.3	98.4	79.2
2004 N	4.14	59.8	7.05	4.5	3.2	6.14	82.83	6.06	8.60	21.69	15.75	47.9	99.2	80.8
2005 N	4.01	59.5	6.79	3.9	3.1	5.90	80.14	5.79	8.10	22.29	15.03	48.3	98.7	81.0

If you've reviewed all of the information in this introduction, you are now armed and ready to delve into the player stats themselves. After all, comparing Jim Brown to Walter Payton to Barry Sanders, and wrestling with questions like "Who was the greatest quarterback in NFL history?" is what this book is all about.

Abbey, Joe Joseph Reed, E, 6´1˝/202 lbs; Texas; North Texas; B3/21/1925 Denton, TX

YEAR	TEAM	G (GS, POS)	RUSH	YD	AVG (LG)	TD	REC	YD	AVG (LG)	TD	PASS	COMP	PCT	YD	AVG (LG)	TD	INT	SK	YD	QBR	KPR	OTD	PTS	TAY
1948	ChiB	12(1)	—	—	—	—	5	67	13.4(35)	0	—	—	—	—	—	—	—	—	—	—	—	—	0	34
1949	NYB	6(0)	—	—	—	—	8	110	13.8(48)	0	—	—	—	—	—	—	—	—	—	—	—	—	0	55
NFL	2	18(1)	—	—	—	—	13	177	13.6(48)	0	—	—	—	—	—	—	—	—	—	—	—	—	0	89

Abbott, Faye Lafayette, BB-FB-TB-QB-WB-E, 5´8˝/182 lbs; Syracuse; B8/16/1895 Clearport, OH, D1/21/1965 Dayton, OH **[KC]** **1921** Day 9 (6, bb), 6 **1922** Day 6 (1) **1923** Day 8 (8, BB), 6 **1924** Day 7 (5, BB) **1925** Day 8 (8, BB), 3 **1926** Day 6 (6, FB) **1927** Day 7 (4, TB) **1928** Day 5 (4), 3 **1929** Day 1 (1) **NFL** 57 (43), 18 [9 yrs]

Abbott, Vince Vincent Steven, K, 5´11˝/207 lbs; Washington; Cal State Fullerton; B5/31/1958 London, England **[K]** **1987** SD 12 (0) **1988** SD 11 (0) **NFL** 23 (0) [2 yrs]

Abbruzzi, Duke Louis John, HB-DB, 5´10˝/175 lbs; Rhode Island; B8/3/1917 Warren, RI, D12/6/1982 Newport, RI

YEAR	TEAM	G (GS, POS)	RUSH	YD	AVG (LG)	TD	REC	YD	AVG (LG)	TD	PASS	COMP	PCT	YD	AVG (LG)	TD	INT	SK	YD	QBR	KPR	OTD	PTS	TAY
1946	Bos	3(0)	6	26	4.3(10)	0	2	55	27.5(38)	0	1	1	100.0	11	11.0(11)	0	0	—	—	—	kp	—	0	82

Abdul-Jabbar, Karim Karim, aka Sharmin Shah and Abdul-Karim al-Jabbar, RB, 5´10˝/194 lbs; UCLA; 1996: Mia, rnd 3; B6/28/1974 Los Angeles, CA

YEAR	TEAM	G (GS, POS)	RUSH	YD	AVG (LG)	TD	REC	YD	AVG (LG)	TD	PASS	COMP	PCT	YD	AVG (LG)	TD	INT	SK	YD	QBR	KPR	OTD	PTS	TAY
1996	Mia	16(14, RB)	307	1116	3.6(29)	11	23	139	6.0(23)	0	0	0	0.0	0	0.0	0	0	1	3	—	—	—	66	1296
1997	†Mia	16(14, RB)	283	892	3.2(22)	**15**	29	261	9.0(36)	1	—	—	—	—	—	—	—	—	—	—	—	—	96	1178
1998	†Mia	15(15, RB)	270	960	3.6(45)	6	21	102	4.9(18)	0	—	—	—	—	—	—	—	—	—	—	—	—	36	1071
1999	Mia	3(3)	28	95	3.4(21)	1	4	25	6.3(14)	0	—	—	—	—	—	—	—	—	—	—	—	—	6	118
1999	Cle	10(6, rb)	115	350	3.0(12)	0	13	59	4.5(21)	1	—	—	—	—	—	—	—	—	—	—	—	—	6	385
2000	Ind	1(0)	1	-2	-2.0(-2)	0	—	—	—	—	—	—	—	—	—	—	—	—	—	—	—	—	0	-2
NFL	5	61(52)	1004	3411	3.4(45)	33	90	586	6.5(36)	2	0	0	0.0	0	0.0	0	0	1	3	—	—	—	210	4044

Abdullah, Hamza Hamza Muhammad, DB, 6´2˝/213 lbs; Washington State; 2005: TB, rnd 7; B8/20/1983 Pomona, CA **2005** Den 1 (0)

Abdullah, Khalid Khalid, LB, 6´2˝/227 lbs; Mars Hill; 2003: Cin, rnd 5; B3/6/1979 Jacksonville, FL **2003** Cin 16 (0)

Abdullah, Rabih Rabih Fard, RB, 6´0˝/220 lbs; Lehigh; B4/27/1975 Martinsville, VA

YEAR	TEAM	G (GS, POS)	RUSH	YD	AVG (LG)	TD	REC	YD	AVG (LG)	TD	PASS	COMP	PCT	YD	AVG (LG)	TD	INT	SK	YD	QBR	KPR	OTD	PTS	TAY
1999	TB	15(1)	5	12	2.4(10)	0	2	11	5.5(8)	0	—	—	—	—	—	—	—	—	—	—	—	—	0	18
2000	†TB	12(0)	16	70	4.4(19)	0	2	14	7.0(11)	0	—	—	—	—	—	—	—	—	—	—	k	—	0	78
2001	TB	16(0)	11	40	3.6(12)	0	2	26	13.0(14)	0	—	—	—	—	—	—	—	—	—	—	k	—	0	70
2002	ChiB	16(0)	—	—	—	—	—	—	—	—	—	—	—	—	—	—	—	—	—	—	k	—	0	47
2003	ChiB	15(0)	18	37	2.1(10)	0	8	55	6.9(17)	0	—	—	—	—	—	—	—	—	—	—	k	—	0	52
2004	†NE	9(0)	13	13	1.0(5)	1	1	9	9.0(9)	0	—	—	—	—	—	—	—	—	—	—	—	—	6	28
NFL	6	83(1)	63	172	2.7(19)	1	15	115	7.7(17)	0	—	—	—	—	—	—	—	—	—	—	k	—	6	292

Abdullah, Rahim Rahim Fahim, LB, 6´5˝/233 lbs; Clemson; 1999: Cle, rnd 2; B3/22/1976 Jacksonville, FL **1999** Cle 16 (13, LLB) **2000** Cle 13 (4) **NFL** 29 (17) [2 yrs]

Abel, Fred Fred K., BB-FB, 5´10˝/170 lbs; Washington; B7/17/1903 Lincoln, NE, D8/2/1980 Port Townsend, WA **1926** Mil 3 (1)

Abell, Bud Harry Everett, LB, 6´3˝/220 lbs; Missouri; 1964: KC, rnd 23/Dal, rnd 17; B12/21/1940 Kansas City, MO **1966**†KC-A 14 **1967** KC-A 14 **1968** KC-A 12 **NFL** 40 [3 yrs]

Abercrombie, Walter Walter Augustus, RB, 6´0˝/210 lbs; Baylor; 1982: Pit, rnd 1; B9/26/1959 Waco, TX

YEAR	TEAM	G (GS, POS)	RUSH	YD	AVG (LG)	TD	REC	YD	AVG (LG)	TD	PASS	COMP	PCT	YD	AVG (LG)	TD	INT	SK	YD	QBR	KPR	OTD	PTS	TAY
1982	†Pit	6(0)	21	100	4.8(34)	2	1	14	14.0(14)	0	—	—	—	—	—	—	—	—	—	—	k	—	12	161
1983	†Pit	15(13, RB)	112	446	4.0(50)	4	26	391	15.0(51)	3	—	—	—	—	—	—	—	—	—	—	—	—	42	697
1984	†Pit	14(7, rb)	145	610	4.2(31)	1	16	135	8.4(59)	0	—	—	—	—	—	—	—	—	—	—	—	—	6	688
1985	Pit	16(16, RB)	227	851	3.7(32)	7	24	209	8.7(27)	2	—	—	—	—	—	—	—	—	—	—	—	—	54	1036
1986	Pit	16(14, RB)	214	877	4.1(38)	6	47	395	8.4(27)	2	—	—	—	—	—	—	—	—	—	—	—	—	48	1145
1987	Pit	12(12, RB)	123	459	3.7(28)	2	24	209	8.7(24)	0	—	—	—	—	—	—	—	—	—	—	—	—	12	584
1988	†Phi	5(0)	5	14	2.8(5)	0	1	-2	-2.0(-2)	0	—	—	—	—	—	—	—	—	—	—	k	—	0	25
NFL	7	84(62)	847	3357	4.0(50)	22	139	1351	9.7(59)	7	—	—	—	—	—	—	—	—	—	—	k	—	174	4334

Aberson, Cliff Clifford Alexander, TB-DB, 6´0˝/195 lbs; none; B8/28/1921 Chicago, IL, D6/23/1973 Vallejo, CA

YEAR	TEAM	G (GS, POS)	RUSH	YD	AVG (LG)	TD	REC	YD	AVG (LG)	TD	PASS	COMP	PCT	YD	AVG (LG)	TD	INT	SK	YD	QBR	KPR	OTD	PTS	TAY
1946	GB	10(1)	48	161	3.4(13)	0	—	—	—	—	41	14	34.1	184	4.5(30)	0	5	—	—	—	ki	—	0	115

Abraham, Clifton Clifton Eugene, DB, 5´9˝/184 lbs; Florida State; 1995: TB, rnd 5; B12/9/1971 Dallas, TX **1995** TB 6 (0) **1996** ChiB 2 (0) **1997** Car 1 (0) **NFL** 9 (0) [3 yrs]

Abraham, Donnie Nathaniel Donnell, DB, 5´10˝/190 lbs; East Tennessee State; 1996: TB, rnd 3; B10/8/1973 Orangeburg, SC **[I]** **1996** TB 16 (12, RCB) **1997**†TB 16 (16, LCB) **1998** TB 13 (13, LCB) **1999**†TB 16 (16, LCB) **2000**†TB✧16 (16, LCB) **2001**†TB 15 (5, lcb) **2002**†NYJ 16 (16, LCB) **2003** NYJ 8 (2) **2004**†NYJ 16 (16, LCB) **NFL** 132 (112) [9 yrs]

Abraham, John John, DE, 6´4˝/256 lbs; South Carolina; 2000: NYJ, rnd 1; B5/6/1978 Timmonsville, SC **[S]** **2000** NYJ 6 (0) **2001**†NYJ★16 (15, RDE) **2002**†NYJ★16 (16, RDE) **2003** NYJ 7 (6, rde) **2004** NYJ✧12 (12, RDE) **2005** NYJ 16 (15, RDE) **NFL** 73 (64) [6 yrs]

Abraham, Robert Robert Eugene, LB, 6´1˝/228 lbs; North Carolina State; 1982: Hou, rnd 3; B7/13/1960 Myrtle Beach, SC **1982** Hou 9 (0) **1983** Hou 14 (13, RILB) **1984** Hou 16 (16, RILB) **1985** Hou 16 (15, RILB) **1986** Hou 16 (16, RILB) **1987** Hou 2 (0) **NFL** 73 (60) [6 yrs]

Abramowicz, Danny Daniel Stanley, E, 6´1˝/195 lbs; Xavier (OH); 1967: NO, rnd 17; B7/13/1945 Steubenville, OH

YEAR	TEAM	G (GS, POS)	RUSH	YD	AVG (LG)	TD	REC	YD	AVG (LG)	TD	PASS	COMP	PCT	YD	AVG (LG)	TD	INT	SK	YD	QBR	KPR	OTD	PTS	TAY
1967	NO	14(SE)	—	—	—	—	50	721	14.4(80)	6	—	—	—	—	—	—	—	—	—	—	—	—	36	391
1968	NO	14(FL)	2	27	13.5(18)	0	54	890	16.5(47)	7	—	—	—	—	—	—	—	—	—	—	—	—	42	507
1969	NO☆	14(FL)	3	61	20.3(28)	0	**73**	1015	13.9(49)	7	—	—	—	—	—	—	—	—	—	—	—	—	42	604
1970	NO	14(WR)	1	7	7.0(7)	0	55	906	16.5(48)	5	—	—	—	—	—	—	—	—	—	—	—	—	30	485
1971	NO	14(WR)	—	—	—	—	37	657	17.8(63)	5	—	—	—	—	—	—	—	—	—	—	p	—	30	349
1972	NO	13(WR)	—	—	—	—	38	668	17.6(51)	7	—	—	—	—	—	—	—	—	—	—	—	—	42	369
1973	NO	2	—	—	—	—	2	18	9.0(11)	0	—	—	—	—	—	—	—	—	—	—	—	—	0	9
1973	SF	12(11, WR)	—	—	—	—	35	442	12.6(54)	1	—	—	—	—	—	—	—	—	—	—	—	—	6	226
1974	SF	14(14, WR)	—	—	—	—	25	369	14.8(30)	1	1	1	100.0	41	41.0(41)	0	0	—	—	—	—	—	6	210
NFL	8	111(25)	6	95	15.8(28)	0	369	5686	15.4(80)	39	1	1	100.0	41	41.0(41)	0	0	—	—	—	p	—	234	3149

Abramowitz, Sid Sidney H., T, 6´6˝/280 lbs; Air Force; Tulsa; 1983: Bal, rnd 5; B5/21/1960 Culver City, CA **1983** Bal 14 (1) **1984**†Sea 4 (0) **1985** NYJ 1 (0) **1987** Ind 3 (3) **NFL** 22 (4) [4 yrs]

Abrams, Bobby Robert E., LB, 6´3˝/240 lbs; Michigan; B4/12/1967 Detroit, MI **1990**†NYG 16 (0) **1991** NYG 16 (2) **1992** Dal 4 (0) **1992** Cle 3 (0) **1992** NYG 1 (0) **1993** Dal 5 (0) **1993**†Min 4 (0) **1994**†Min 16 (0) **1995** NE 9 (1) **NFL** 74 (3) [6 yrs]

Abrams, Kevin Kevin R., DB, 5´8˝/175 lbs; Syracuse; 1997: Det, rnd 2; B2/28/1974 Tampa, FL **1997**†Det 15 (4) **1998** Det 16 (7, rcb) **1999** Det 1 (0) **NFL** 32 (11) [3 yrs]

Abrams, Nate Nathan, E, 5´4˝/145 lbs; none; B12/25/1897 Green Bay, WI, D4/30/1941 Green Bay, WI **1921** GB 1 (0), 6

Abramson, George George N., G-T, 5´7˝/198 lbs; Minnesota; B5/13/1903 Eveleth, MN, D3/15/1985 Beverly Hills, CA **[K]** **1925** GB☆10 (5, lg), 8

Abrell, Dick Richard Thompson, BB-WB, 5´10˝/172 lbs; Purdue; B5/18/1892 Linton, IN, D5/5/1973 West Orange, NJ **1920** Day 6 (0)

Abruzzese, Ray Raymond Louis, B, 6´1˝/194 lbs; Alabama; 1962: Buf, rnd 23/Bal, rnd 16; B10/27/1937 Philadelphia, PA **1962** Buf-A 12 (2) **1963**†Buf-A 14 (LS) **1964** Buf-A 9 **1965** NYJ-A 12 (RS) **1966** NYJ-A 14 (LS) **NFL** 61 (2) [5 yrs]

Abruzzino, Frank Frank Marion, BB-LB-C-G-E-WB-DB, 6´0˝/193 lbs; Colgate; B1/22/1908 Shinnston, WV, D6/13/1986 Fort Lauderdale, FL **1931** Bkn 14 (7, BB) **1933** Cin 9 (4) **NFL** 23 (11) [2 yrs]

Absher, Dick Richard Alfred, LB-K, 6´4˝/230 lbs; Maryland; 1967: Phi, rnd 5; B4/19/1944 Washington, DC **[K]** **1967** Was 1 **1967** Atl 1 **1968** Atl 10 **1969** NO 14 (MLB) **1970** NO 10 (MLB) **1971** NO 14 **1972** Phi 8 **NFL** 58 [6 yrs]

Ache, Steve Stephen J., LB, 6´3˝/229 lbs; Southwest Missouri State; B3/16/1962 Syracuse, NY **1987** Min 3 (0)

Achica, George George, DT, 6´5˝/260 lbs; USC; 1983: Bal, rnd 3; B12/19/1960 American Samoa **1985** Ind 4 (0)

Achiu, Sneeze Walter Tin Kit, WB-TB-E-BB, 5´8˝/169 lbs; Hawaii; Dayton; B8/3/1902 Honolulu, HI, D3/21/1989 Eugene, OR **1927** Day 7 (3) **1928** Day 4 (2) **NFL** 11 (5) [2 yrs]

Acker, Bill William Berry, NT, 6´3˝/255 lbs; Texas; 1980: SL, rnd 6; B11/7/1956 Freer, TX **1980** SL 16 (4) **1981** SL 8 (0) **1982** KC 3 (0) **1983** Buf 11 (0) **1984** Buf 15 (0) **1987** KC 2 (2) **NFL** 55 (6) [6 yrs]

Ackerman, Rick Richard Carl, NT-DT, 6´4˝/258 lbs; Memphis; B6/16/1959 La Grange, IL **1982**†SD 9 (1) **1983** SD 15 (13, NT) **1984** SD 9 (0) **1984**†LARd 6 (2) **1987** LARd 3 (2) **NFL** 42 (18) [4 yrs]

Ackerman, Tom Thomas Michael, G-C, 6´3˝/290 lbs; Eastern Washington; 1996: NO, rnd 5; B9/6/1972 Bellingham, WA **1996** NO 2 (0) **1997** NO 14 (0) **1998** NO 15 (10, C) **1999** NO 16 (8, LG) **2000**†NO 15 (0) **2001** NO 16 (0) **2002**†Ten 11 (3) **2003**†Ten 16 (0) **NFL** 105 (21) [8 yrs]

ACKS, RON Ronald William, LB, 6´2˝/214 lbs; Illinois; 1966: Min, rnd 4/NYJ, rnd 16; B10/3/1944 Herrin, IL **1968** Atl 1 **1969** Atl 14 **1970** Atl 8 **1971** Atl 14 (LLB) **1972** NE 14 (13, RLB) **1973** NE 14 (14, RLB) **1974** GB 13 **1975** GB 14 (1) **1976** GB 13 **NFL** 105 (28) [9 yrs]

ACORN, FRED Frederick Earl, DB, 5´10˝/185 lbs; Texas; 1984: TB, rnd 3; B3/17/1961 Rotan, TX **1984** TB 16 (1)

ADAMCHIK, ED Edward James, C, 6´2˝/235 lbs; Pittsburgh; 1963: NYG, rnd 12/Buf, rnd 21; B11/2/1941 Johnstown, PA **1965** NYG 2 **1965** Pit 2 **NFL** 4 [1 yr]

ADAMLE, MIKE Michael David, RB, 5´9˝/197 lbs; Northwestern; 1971: KC, rnd 5; B10/4/1949 Kent, OH

YEAR	TEAM	G(GS, POS)	RUSH	YD	AVG(LG)	TD	REC	YD	AVG(LG)	TD	PASS	COMP	PCT	YD	AVG(LG)	TD	INT	SK	YD	QBR	KPR	OTD	PTS	TAY
1971	†KC	8	13	43	3.3(15)	0	1	6	6.0(6)	1	—	—	—	—	—	—	—	—	—	—	k	—	6	95
1972	KC	14	73	303	4.2(19)	1	15	76	5.1(11)	0	—	—	—	—	—	—	—	—	—	—	k	—	6	416
1973	NYJ	14	67	264	3.9(36)	0	9	63	7.0(13)	0	—	—	—	—	—	—	—	—	—	—	k	—	0	300
1974	NYJ	12	28	93	3.3(21)	2	9	84	9.3(16)	0	—	—	—	—	—	—	—	—	—	—	k	—	12	142
1975	ChiB	14(7, rb)	94	353	3.8(21)	1	15	111	7.4(25)	0	2	2	100.0	57	28.5(44)	0	0	1	5	—	k	—	6	459
1976	ChiB	14	33	93	2.8(12)	0	4	28	7.0(12)	1	—	—	—	—	—	—	—	—	—	—	kp	—	8	123
NFL	6	76(7)	308	1149	3.7(36)	4	53	368	6.9(25)	2	2	2	100.0	57	28.5(44)	0	0	1	5	—	kp	—	38	1535

ADAMLE, TONY Anthony, LB-FB, 6´0˝/215 lbs; Ohio State; 1947: ChiB, rnd 12; B5/15/1924 Fairmont, WV, D10/7/2000 Kent, OH

YEAR	TEAM	G(GS, POS)	RUSH	YD	AVG(LG)	TD	REC	YD	AVG(LG)	TD	PASS	COMP	PCT	YD	AVG(LG)	TD	INT	SK	YD	QBR	KPR	OTD	PTS	TAY
1947	†Cle-A	14(1)	23	95	4.1	1	1	22	22.0(22)	0	—	—	—	—	—	—	—	—	—	—	ki	—	6	179
1948	†Cle-A	14(0)	17	88	5.2	1	—	—	—	—	—	—	—	—	—	—	—	—	—	—	—	—	6	98
1949	†Cle-A	12(2)	17	64	3.8	0	1	13	13.0(13)	0	—	—	—	—	—	—	—	—	—	—	i	—	0	93
AAFC	3	40(3)	57	247	4.3	2	2	35	17.5(22)	0	—	—	—	—	—	—	—	—	—	—	ki	—	12	370
1950	†Cle★	12(LLB)	3	8	2.7(3)	0	—	—	—	—	—	—	—	—	—	—	—	—	—	—	ki	—	0	13
1951	†Cle★	12(LLB)	—	—	—	—	—	—	—	—	—	—	—	—	—	—	—	—	—	—	i	—	0	7
1954	†Cle	11	—	—	—	—	—	—	—	—	—	—	—	—	—	—	—	—	—	—	—	—	—	—
NFL	3	35	3	8	2.7(3)	0	—	—	—	—	—	—	—	—	—	—	—	—	—	—	ki	—	0	20

ADAMS, ANTHONY Anthony, DT-NT, 6´/300 lbs; Penn State; 2003: SF, rnd 2; B6/18/1980 Detroit, MI **2003** SF 14 (1) **2004** SF 14 (12, LDT) **2005** SF 16 (16, NT) **NFL** 44 (29) [3 yrs]

ADAMS, BILL William Joseph, G-T, 6´2˝/255 lbs; Holy Cross; 1972: Mia, rnd 7; B2/4/1950 Lynn, MA **1972** Buf 6 **1974**†Buf 8 **1975** Buf 6 **1976** Buf 11 (1) **1977** Buf 9 **1978** Buf 6 **NFL** 46 (1) [6 yrs]

ADAMS, BLUE Daniel L., DB, 5´9˝/182 lbs; Cincinnati; 2003: Det, rnd 7; B10/15/1979 Miami, FL **2003** Jax 8 (0) **2005** TB 13 (0) **NFL** 21 (0) [2 yrs]

ADAMS, BOB Robert Bruce, TE-T, 6´2˝/225 lbs; Pacific; B8/15/1946 Stockton, CA

YEAR	TEAM	G(GS, POS)	RUSH	YD	AVG(LG)	TD	REC	YD	AVG(LG)	TD	PASS	COMP	PCT	YD	AVG(LG)	TD	INT	SK	YD	QBR	KPR	OTD	PTS	TAY
1969	Pit	14	—	—	—	—	6	80	13.3(19)	0	—	—	—	—	—	—	—	—	—	—	—	—	0	40
1970	Pit	14	—	—	—	—	3	36	12.0(17)	0	—	—	—	—	—	—	—	—	—	—	—	—	0	18
1971	Pit	14(TE)	—	—	—	—	20	160	8.0(21)	0	—	—	—	—	—	—	—	—	—	—	—	—	0	80
1973	NE	12(5, te)	2	7	3.5(4)	0	14	197	14.1(30)	0	—	—	—	—	—	—	—	—	—	—	—	—	0	106
1974	NE	13(7, te)	—	—	—	—	17	244	14.4(29)	0	—	—	—	—	—	—	—	—	—	—	—	—	0	122
1975	Den	2	—	—	—	—	—	—	—	—	—	—	—	—	—	—	—	—	—	—	—	—	—	—
1976	Atl	13	—	—	—	—	1	15	15.0(15)	0	—	—	—	—	—	—	—	—	—	—	k	—	0	14
NFL	7	82(12)	2	7	3.5(4)	0	61	732	12.0(30)	0	—	—	—	—	—	—	—	—	—	—	k	—	0	379

ADAMS, BRENT David Brent, T, 6´5˝/256 lbs; Tennessee-Chattanooga; 1975: Atl, rnd 8; B6/26/1952 Elberton, GA **1975** Atl 13 (LT) **1976** Atl 14 (14, LT) **1977** Atl 14 (LT) **NFL** 41 (14) [3 yrs]

ADAMS, CHARLIE Charlie, WR, 6´2˝/190 lbs; Hofstra; B10/23/1979 Camp Hill, PA **2003**†Den 4 (0) **2004**†Den 4 (0)

YEAR	TEAM	G(GS, POS)	RUSH	YD	AVG(LG)	TD	REC	YD	AVG(LG)	TD	PASS	COMP	PCT	YD	AVG(LG)	TD	INT	SK	YD	QBR	KPR	OTD	PTS	TAY
2005	†Den	16(2)	5	14	2.8(13)	0	21	203	9.7(21)	0	—	—	—	—	—	—	—	—	—	—	kp	—	0	237
NFL	3	24(2)	5	14	2.8(13)	0	21	203	9.7(21)	0	—	—	—	—	—	—	—	—	—	—	kp	—	0	269

ADAMS, CHET Chester Frank, aka Chester Frank Adamczyk, T-E-DT, 6´3˝/233 lbs; Ohio University; 1939: Cle, rnd 12; B10/24/1916 Cleveland, OH, D10/28/1990 Cleveland, OH **[K]** **1946**†Cle-A 14 (0) **1947**†Cle-A 13 (7, lt) **1948**†Cle-A 14 (0) **1949**†Buf-A 12 (0) **AAFC** 53 (7) [4 yrs]

1939 Cle 9 (5, LT) **1941** Cle★11 (11, LT) **1942** Cle★11 (11, LT) **1943** GB☆10 (6) **1950** NYY 12 (1)

YEAR	TEAM	G(GS, POS)	RUSH	YD	AVG(LG)	TD	REC	YD	AVG(LG)	TD	PASS	COMP	PCT	YD	AVG(LG)	TD	INT	SK	YD	QBR	KPR	OTD	PTS	TAY
1940	Cle☆	11(11, LT/le)	—	—	—	—	3	28	9.3	0	—	—	—	—	—	—	—	—	—	—	K	—	10	14
NFL	6	64(45)	—	—	—	—	3	28	9.3	0	—	—	—	—	—	—	—	—	—	—	K	—	108	14

ADAMS, CURTIS Curtis Ladonn, RB, 6´0˝/198 lbs; Central Michigan; 1985: SD, rnd 8; B4/30/1962 Muskegon, MI

YEAR	TEAM	G(GS, POS)	RUSH	YD	AVG(LG)	TD	REC	YD	AVG(LG)	TD	PASS	COMP	PCT	YD	AVG(LG)	TD	INT	SK	YD	QBR	KPR	OTD	PTS	TAY
1985	SD	1(0)	16	49	3.1(14)	1	1	12	12.0(12)	0	—	—	—	—	—	—	—	—	—	—	k	—	6	85
1986	SD	7(2)	118	366	3.1(22)	4	4	26	6.5(10)	0	—	—	—	—	—	—	—	—	—	—	k	—	24	444
1987	SD	12(4)	90	343	3.8(24)	1	4	38	9.5(21)	0	—	—	—	—	—	—	—	—	—	—	k	—	6	344
1988	SD	7(1)	38	149	3.9(14)	1	—	—	—	—	—	—	—	—	—	—	—	—	—	—	k	—	6	157
NFL	4	27(7)	262	907	3.5(24)	7	9	76	8.4(21)	0	—	—	—	—	—	—	—	—	—	—	k	—	42	1030

ADAMS, DAVID David Delaney, RB, 5´6˝/168 lbs; Arizona; 1987: Ind, rnd 12; B6/24/1964 Tucson, AZ

YEAR	TEAM	G(GS, POS)	RUSH	YD	AVG(LG)	TD	REC	YD	AVG(LG)	TD	PASS	COMP	PCT	YD	AVG(LG)	TD	INT	SK	YD	QBR	KPR	OTD	PTS	TAY
1987	Dal	3(0)	7	49	7.0(27)	1	1	8	8.0(8)	0	—	—	—	—	—	—	—	—	—	—	k	—	6	86

ADAMS, DOUG Douglas O., LB, 6´1˝/225 lbs; Ohio State; 1971: Den, rnd 7; B11/3/1949 Xenia, OH, D8/9/1997 Macon, OH **1971** Cin 11 **1972** Cin 14 **1973**†Cin 12 **1974** Cin 12 (MLB) **NFL** 49 [4 yrs]

ADAMS, EARNEST Earnest, LB, 6´3˝/226 lbs; Illinois; B3/12/1959 Fort Lauderdale, FL **1987** Det 3 (0)

ADAMS, FLOZELL Flozell Jootin 'The Hotel', T-G-TE, 6´7˝/335 lbs; Michigan State; 1998: Dal, rnd 2; B5/18/1975 Chicago, IL **1998**†Dal 16 (12, RG) **1999**†Dal 16 (16, LT) **2000** Dal 16 (16, LT) **2001** Dal 16 (16, LT) **2002** Dal 16 (16, LT) **2003**†Dal✧16 (16, LT) **2004** Dal✧16 (16, LT) **2005** Dal 6 (6, lt) **NFL** 118 (114) [8 yrs]

ADAMS, GEORGE George Wallace, RB, 6´1˝/225 lbs; Kentucky; 1985: NYG, rnd 1; B12/22/1962 Lexington, KY

YEAR	TEAM	G(GS, POS)	RUSH	YD	AVG(LG)	TD	REC	YD	AVG(LG)	TD	PASS	COMP	PCT	YD	AVG(LG)	TD	INT	SK	YD	QBR	KPR	OTD	PTS	TAY
1985	†NYG	16(0)	128	498	3.9(39)	2	31	389	12.5(70)	2	1	0	0.0	0	0.0	0	0	—	—	—	k	—	24	754
1987	NYG	12(7, FB)	61	169	2.8(14)	1	35	298	8.5(25)	1	—	—	—	—	—	—	—	—	—	—	k	—	12	364
1988	NYG	16(1)	29	76	2.6(15)	0	27	174	6.4(19)	0	—	—	—	—	—	—	—	—	—	—	—	—	0	163
1989	NYG	14(0)	9	29	3.2(8)	0	2	7	3.5(10)	0	—	—	—	—	—	—	—	—	—	—	—	—	0	33
1990	NE	16(7, fb)	28	111	4.0(13)	0	16	146	9.1(28)	1	—	—	—	—	—	—	—	—	—	—	k	—	6	181
1991	NE	2(1)	2	3	1.5(2)	0	—	—	—	—	—	—	—	—	—	—	—	—	—	—	—	—	0	3
NFL	6	76(16)	257	886	3.4(39)	3	111	1014	9.1(70)	4	1	0	0.0	0	0.0	0	0	—	—	—	k	—	42	1497

ADAMS, HENRY Henry, C, 6´1˝/190 lbs; Pittsburgh; B12/24/1915 California, PA **1939** ChiC 3 (1)

ADAMS, JOHN John William, T, 6´7˝/242 lbs; Notre Dame; 1945: Was, rnd 3; B9/22/1921 Charleston, AR, D8/20/1969 Bethesda, MD **1945**†Was☆10 (5, LT) **1946** Was☆11 (3) **1947** Was 10 (4) **1948** Was 12 (5, RT) **1949** Was 12 (9, RT) **NFL** 55 (26) [5 yrs]

ADAMS, JOHN John Albert, E-FB, 6´3˝/235 lbs; UCLA; Los Angeles State; 1959: ChiB, rnd 5; B11/28/1937 San Diego, CA, D8/8/1995 Helendale, CA

YEAR	TEAM	G(GS, POS)	RUSH	YD	AVG(LG)	TD	REC	YD	AVG(LG)	TD	PASS	COMP	PCT	YD	AVG(LG)	TD	INT	SK	YD	QBR	KPR	OTD	PTS	TAY
1959	ChiB	12	4	-13	-3.3(8)	0	—	—	—	—	—	—	—	—	—	—	—	—	—	—	—	—	0	-13
1960	ChiB	12	23	114	5.0(62)	0	2	-20	-10.0(0)	0	—	—	—	—	—	—	—	—	—	—	—	—	0	104
1961	ChiB	13	14	-2	-0.1(10)	1	5	80	16.0(36)	0	1	1	100.0	11	11.0(11)	0	0	—	—	—	P	—	6	54
1962	ChiB	14	—	—	—	—	5	111	22.2(59)	3	—	—	—	—	—	—	—	—	—	—	—	—	18	71
1963	LARm	13(TE)	—	—	—	—	9	93	10.3(19)	0	—	—	—	—	—	—	—	—	—	—	P	—	0	47
NFL	5	64	41	99	2.4(62)	1	21	264	12.6(59)	3	1	1	100.0	11	11.0(11)	0	0	—	—	—	P	—	24	262

ADAMS, JULIUS Julius Thomas, DE-DT, 6´3˝/270 lbs; Texas Southern; 1971: NE, rnd 2; B4/26/1948 Macon, GA **1971** NE 14 (11, RDT) **1972** NE 11 (11, LDE/ldt) **1973** NE 14 (14, RDT) **1974** NE 14 (14, RDE/lde) **1975** NE 9 (8, RDE) **1976**†NE 14 (14, RDE) **1977** NE 14 (14, RDE) **1978** NE 1 (1) **1979** NE 16 (2) **1980** NE✧16 (16, RDE) **1981** NE 16 (16, RDE) **1982**†NE 9 (9, RDE) **1983** NE 16 (16, RDE) **1984** NE 16 (1) **1985**†NE 16 (12, RDE) **1987** NE 10 (0) **NFL** 206 (159) [16 yrs]

ADAMS, KEITH Keith A., LB, 5´11˝/223 lbs; Clemson; 2001: Ten, rnd 7; B11/22/1979 Atlanta, GA **2001** Dal 4 (0) **2002** Dal 6 (5, mlb) **2002**†Phi 10 (0) **2003**†Phi 15 (0) **2004**†Phi 16 (2) **2005** Phi 16 (16, RLB) **NFL** 67 (23) [5 yrs]

ADAMS, MICHAEL Michael Glendale, DB, 5´9˝/195 lbs; Arkansas State; 1987: NO, rnd 3; B4/5/1964 Shelby, MS **1987**†NO 7 (3) **1988** NO 5 (0) **1989** Phx 3 (0) **NFL** 15 (3) [3 yrs]

ADAMS, MIKE Michael Christopher, WR, 5´11˝/185 lbs; Texas; 1997: Pit, rnd 7; B3/25/1974 Dallas, TX

YEAR	TEAM	G(GS, POS)	RUSH	YD	AVG(LG)	TD	REC	YD	AVG(LG)	TD	PASS	COMP	PCT	YD	AVG(LG)	TD	INT	SK	YD	QBR	KPR	OTD	PTS	TAY
1997	Pit	6(0)	—	—	—	—	1	39	39.0(39)	0	—	—	—	—	—	—	—	—	—	—	k	—	0	85

YEAR	TEAM	G(GS, POS)	RUSH	YD	AVG(LG)	TD	REC	YD	AVG(LG)	TD	PASS	COMP	PCT	YD	AVG(LG)	TD	INT	SK	YD	QBR	KPR	OTD	PTS	TAY

ADAMS, MIKE Michael Carl, DB, 5´10˝/195 lbs; Delaware; B3/24/1981 Paterson, NJ **2004** SF 8 (0) **2005** SF 14 (10, FS) **NFL** 22 (10) [2 yrs]

ADAMS, NEAL Howard O'Neal, E, 6´3˝/195 lbs; Arkansas; B1/21/1919 El Paso, AR, D10/27/1998 Sand Springs, OK

YEAR	TEAM	G(GS, POS)	RUSH	YD	AVG(LG)	TD	REC	YD	AVG(LG)	TD	PASS	COMP	PCT	YD	AVG(LG)	TD	INT	SK	YD	QBR	KPR	OTD	PTS	TAY
1942	NYG	11(11, LE)	—	—	—	—	6	87	14.5(24)	3	—	—	—	—	—	—	—	—	—	—	i	1	24	130
1943	NYG	8(8, LE)	—	—	—	—	8	65	8.1(17)	1	—	—	—	—	—	—	—	—	—	—	k	1	12	31
1944	†NYG	10(10, LE)	—	—	—	—	14	342	24.4(39)	1	—	—	—	—	—	—	—	—	—	—	k	—	6	175
1945	NYG	9(4)	—	—	—	—	—	—	—	—	—	—	—	—	—	—	—	—	—	—	—	—	—	—
NFL	4	38(33)	—	—	—	—	28	494	17.6(39)	5	—	—	—	—	—	—	—	—	—	—	ki	2	42	335
1946	Bkn-A	13(2)	—	—	—	—	15	225	15.0	2	—	—	—	—	—	—	—	—	—	—	—	—	12	123
1947	Bkn-A	1(0)	—	—	—	—	—	—	—	—	—	—	—	—	—	—	—	—	—	—	—	—	—	—
AAFC	2	14(2)	—	—	—	—	15	225	15.0(39)	2	—	—	—	—	—	—	—	—	—	—	—	—	12	123

ADAMS, PETE Peter Anthony, G, 6´4˝/260 lbs; USC; 1973: Cle, rnd 1; B5/4/1951 San Diego, CA **1974** Cle 12 (LG) **1976** Cle 13 (LG) **NFL** 25 [2 yrs]

ADAMS, SAM Samuel Edward, G-T, 6´3˝/256 lbs; Prairie View A&M; B9/20/1948 Jasper, TX **1972** NE 6 (1) **1973** NE 12 (7, LT) **1974** NE 14 (13, RG) **1975** NE 13 (13, RG) **1976**†NE 14 (14, RG) **1977** NE 14 (13, RG) **1978**†NE 16 (16, RG) **1979** NE 15 (13, RG) **1980** NE 15 (14, RG) **1981** NO 16 (16, RG) **NFL** 135 (120) [10 yrs]

ADAMS, SAM Samuel Aaron, DT-DE, 6´3˝/295 lbs; Texas A&M; 1994: Sea, rnd 1; B6/13/1973 Houston, TX **1994** Sea 12 (7, lde) **1995** Sea 16 (5, ldt) **1996** Sea 16 (15, LDT) **1997** Sea 16 (15, LDT) **1998** Sea 16 (11, LDT) **1999**†Sea 13 (13, LDT) **2000**†Bal★16 (16, LDT) **2001**†Bal★14 (14, LDT) **2002**†Oak 15 (14, LDT) **2003** Buf 15 (15, LDT) **2004** Buf✧16 (16, LDT) **2005** Buf 14 (9, LDT) **NFL** 179 (150) [12 yrs]

ADAMS, SCOTT Scott Alexander, G-T, 6´5˝/301 lbs; Georgia; B9/28/1966 Lake City, FL **1992**†Min 15 (0) **1993**†Min 15 (10, RG) **1994** NO 11 (0) **1995** ChiB 4 (0) **1996** TB 7 (2) **1997** Atl 6 (0) **NFL** 58 (12) [6 yrs]

ADAMS, STAN Stanley Earl, LB, 6´2˝/215 lbs; Memphis; B5/22/1960 Marion, AR **1984** LARd 4 (3)

ADAMS, STEFON Stefon Lee, DB, 5´10˝/189 lbs; East Carolina; 1985: LARd, rnd 3; B8/11/1963 High Point, NC **1986** LARd 16 (0) **1987** LARd 9 (0) **1988** LARd 14 (0) **1989** LARd 14 (0) **1990** Cle 10 (0) **1990**†Mia 2 (0) **NFL** 65 (0) [5 yrs]

ADAMS, THEO Theo P., T, 6´4˝/300 lbs; Hawaii; B4/24/1966 San Francisco, CA **1992** Sea 10 (0) **1993** TB 7 (0) **NFL** 17 (0) [2 yrs]

ADAMS, TOM Thomas Frank, WR, 6´5˝/215 lbs; Minnesota-Duluth; B4/26/1940 Keewatin, MN

YEAR	TEAM	G(GS, POS)	RUSH	YD	AVG(LG)	TD	REC	YD	AVG(LG)	TD	PASS	COMP	PCT	YD	AVG(LG)	TD	INT	SK	YD	QBR	KPR	OTD	PTS	TAY
1962	Min	6	—	—	—	—	3	51	17.0(32)	0	—	—	—	—	—	—	—	—	—	—	—	—	0	26

ADAMS, TONY Anthony Lee, QB, 6´0˝/198 lbs; Texas; Utah State; 1973: SD, rnd 14; B3/9/1950 San Antonio, TX

YEAR	TEAM	G(GS, POS)	RUSH	YD	AVG(LG)	TD	REC	YD	AVG(LG)	TD	PASS	COMP	PCT	YD	AVG(LG)	TD	INT	SK	YD	QBR	KPR	OTD	PTS	TAY
1975	KC	6(2)	8	42	5.3(16)	0	1	-7	-7.0(-7)	0	77	36	46.8	445	5.8(32)	2	4	11	85	—	—	—	0	111
1976	KC	14	5	46	9.2(21)	0	—	—	—	—	71	36	50.7	575	8.1(49)	3	4	9	79	—	—	—	0	189
1977	KC	14(3)	5	21	4.2(8)	0	—	—	—	—	92	47	51.1	691	7.5(63)	2	11	18	136	—	—	—	0	-64
1978	KC	16(2)	9	15	1.7(6)	0	—	—	—	—	79	44	55.7	415	5.3(26)	2	3	3	27	—	—	—	0	113
1987	Min	3(3)	11	31	2.8(12)	0	—	—	—	—	89	49	55.1	607	6.8(63)	3	5	18	120	—	—	—	0	150
NFL	5	53(10)	38	155	4.1(21)	0	1	-7	-7.0(-7)	0	408	212	52.0	2733	6.7(63)	12	27	59	447	—	—	—	0	498

ADAMS, VASHONE Vashone LaRey, DB, 5´10˝/197 lbs; Fort Hays State; Eastern Michigan; B9/12/1973 Aurora, CO **1995** Cle 8 (6, fs) **1996** Bal 16 (2) **1997** NO 5 (4) **NFL** 29 (12) [3 yrs]

ADAMS, VERLIN Verlin T., DE-T-G-E-LB, 6´0˝/205 lbs; Charleston (WV); 1943: NYG, rnd 31; B7/14/1918 Burnwell, KY, D4/30/1985 Charleston, WV **1943** NYG 4 (0) **1945** NYG 1 (0)

YEAR	TEAM	G(GS, POS)	RUSH	YD	AVG(LG)	TD	REC	YD	AVG(LG)	TD	PASS	COMP	PCT	YD	AVG(LG)	TD	INT	SK	YD	QBR	KPR	OTD	PTS	TAY
1944	†NYG	7(0)	—	—	—	—	1	12	12.0(12)	0	—	—	—	—	—	—	—	—	—	—	—	—	0	6
NFL	3	12(0)	—	—	—	—	1	12	12.0(12)	0	—	—	—	—	—	—	—	—	—	—	i	—	0	4

ADAMS, WILLIE Willie James, DE-LB, 6´2˝/235 lbs; New Mexico State; 1965: Was, rnd 11; B12/12/1941 Corpus Christi, TX **1965** Was 14 **1966** Was 14 **NFL** 28 [2 yrs]

ADAMS, WILLIS Willis Dean, WR, 6´2˝/194 lbs; Houston; 1979: Cle, rnd 1; B8/22/1956 Weimar, TX

YEAR	TEAM	G(GS, POS)	RUSH	YD	AVG(LG)	TD	REC	YD	AVG(LG)	TD	PASS	COMP	PCT	YD	AVG(LG)	TD	INT	SK	YD	QBR	KPR	OTD	PTS	TAY
1979	Cle	16	2	4	2.0(3)	0	1	6	6.0(6)	0	—	—	—	—	—	—	—	—	—	—	—	—	0	7
1980	†Cle	16(0)	2	7	3.5(15)	0	8	165	20.6(39)	0	—	—	—	—	—	—	—	—	—	—	—	—	0	90
1981	Cle	7(0)	—	—	—	—	1	24	24.0(24)	0	—	—	—	—	—	—	—	—	—	—	—	—	0	12
1982	Cle	1(0)	—	—	—	—	—	—	—	—	—	—	—	—	—	—	—	—	—	—	—	—	—	—
1983	Cle	16(6, wr)	1	2	2.0(2)	0	20	374	18.7(59)	2	—	—	—	—	—	—	—	—	—	—	—	—	12	199
1984	Cle	16(1)	—	—	—	—	21	261	12.4(24)	0	—	—	—	—	—	—	—	—	—	—	—	—	0	131
1985	Cle	3(3)	—	—	—	—	10	132	13.2(22)	0	—	—	—	—	—	—	—	—	—	—	—	—	0	66
NFL	7	75(10)	5	13	2.6(15)	0	61	962	15.8(59)	2	—	—	—	—	—	—	—	—	—	—	—	—	12	504

ADAMSON, KEN Kenneth Marshall, G, 6´2˝/235 lbs; Notre Dame; B10/12/1938 Phoenix, AZ **1960** Den-A☆14 (LG) **1961** Den-A★14 (LG) **1962** Den-A 4 **NFL** 32 [3 yrs]

ADDAMS, ABE Abraham Buchanan, DE, 6´2˝/220 lbs; Indiana; B7/12/1926 Louisville, KY **1949** Det 5 (0)

ADDERLEY, HERB Herbert A., DB, 6´0˝/205 lbs; Michigan State; 1961: GB, rnd 1/NYT, rnd 2; B6/8/1939 Philadelphia, PA; HOF 1980 **[RI]** **1961**†GB 14 (LCB) **1962**†GB☆14 (LCB) **1963** GB★14 (LCB) **1964** GB★13 (LCB) **1965**†GB★14 (LCB) **1966**†GB★14 (LCB) **1967**†GB★14 (LCB) **1968** GB☆14 (LCB) **1969** GB☆14 (LCB) **1970**†Dal 14 (LCB) **1971**†Dal 12 (LCB) **1972** Dal 13 (LCB) **NFL** 164 [12 yrs]

ADDISON, TOM Thomas Marion, LB, 6´2˝/230 lbs; South Carolina; 1958: Bal, rnd 12; B4/12/1936 Lancaster, SC **1960** Bos-A☆11 (LLB) **1961** Bos-A★14 (LLB) **1962** Bos-A★14 (LLB) **1963**†Bos-A★14 (LLB) **1964** Bos-A★14 (LLB) **1965** Bos-A 14 (LLB) **1966** Bos-A 14 (LLB) **1967** Bos-A 11 **NFL** 106 [8 yrs]

ADDUCI, NICK Nicholas Frank, LB, 5´10˝/207 lbs; Nebraska; B7/12/1929 Chicago, IL, D11/4/2005 Franfort, IL **1954** Was 10 (RLB) **1955** Was 12 **NFL** 22 [2 yrs]

ADICKES, JOHN John Matthew, C, 6´3˝/264 lbs; Baylor; 1987: Chi, rnd 6; B6/29/1964 Queens, NY **1987** ChiB 6 (0) **1988**†ChiB 16 (0) **1989** Min 1 (0) **NFL** 23 (0) [3 yrs]

ADICKES, MARK Mark Stephen, G, 6´4˝/278 lbs; Baylor; 1984: KC, rnd S1; B4/22/1961 Badconstadt, Germany **1986**†KC 15 (15, RG) **1988** KC 10 (10, RG) **1989** KC 16 (11, LG) **1990**†Was 8 (1) **1991**†Was 16 (0)

YEAR	TEAM	G(GS, POS)	RUSH	YD	AVG(LG)	TD	REC	YD	AVG(LG)	TD	PASS	COMP	PCT	YD	AVG(LG)	TD	INT	SK	YD	QBR	KPR	OTD	PTS	TAY
1987	KC	12(12, RG)	—	—	—	—	1	3	3.0(3)	1	—	—	—	—	—	—	—	—	—	—	—	—	6	7
NFL	6	77(49)	—	—	—	—	1	3	3.0(3)	1	—	—	—	—	—	—	—	—	—	—	—	—	6	7

ADKINS, BOB Robert Grant, BB-DE-G-LB, 6´1˝/213 lbs; Marshall; B2/17/1917 Letart, WV, D12/6/1997 Pleasant Valley, WV **[K]** **1941** GB 6 (0) **1945** GB 4 (0)

YEAR	TEAM	G(GS, POS)	RUSH	YD	AVG(LG)	TD	REC	YD	AVG(LG)	TD	PASS	COMP	PCT	YD	AVG(LG)	TD	INT	SK	YD	QBR	KPR	OTD	PTS	TAY
1940	GB	10(5, bb)	1	5	5.0(5)	0	4	73	18.3(55)	1	—	—	—	—	—	—	—	—	—	—	Ki	1	13	82
NFL	3	20(5)	1	5	5.0(5)	0	4	73	18.3(55)	1	—	—	—	—	—	—	—	—	—	—	Ki	1	16	151

ADKINS, KEVIN James Kevin, DB, 6´1˝/250 lbs; Oklahoma; B8/27/1965 Midwest City, OK **1987** KC 2 (0)

ADKINS, MARGENE Margene, WR, 5´10˝/183 lbs; Henderson J.C.; 1970: Dal, rnd 2; B4/30/1947 Fort Worth, TX **[R]**

YEAR	TEAM	G(GS, POS)	RUSH	YD	AVG(LG)	TD	REC	YD	AVG(LG)	TD	PASS	COMP	PCT	YD	AVG(LG)	TD	INT	SK	YD	QBR	KPR	OTD	PTS	TAY
1970	Dal	5	—	—	—	—	—	—	—	—	—	—	—	—	—	—	—	—	—	—	kp	—	0	68
1971	Dal	3	—	—	—	—	4	53	13.3(23)	0	—	—	—	—	—	—	—	—	—	—	p	—	0	12
1972	NO	14	—	—	—	—	9	96	10.7(38)	0	—	—	—	—	—	—	—	—	—	—	kp	—	0	388
1973	NYJ	13	—	—	—	—	6	109	18.2(29)	0	—	—	—	—	—	—	—	—	—	—	k	—	0	205
NFL	4	35	—	—	—	—	19	258	13.6(38)	0	—	—	—	—	—	—	—	—	—	—	kp	—	0	672

ADKINS, ROY Roy S., G, 5´7˝/180 lbs; Millikin; Bethany (WV); B10/5/1898 Bement, IL, D2/10/1975 Montclair, NJ **1920** Dec 4 (0)

ADKINS, SAM Samuel Alan, QB, 6´2˝/214 lbs; Wichita State; 1977: Sea, rnd 10; B5/21/1955 Van Nuys, CA

YEAR	TEAM	G(GS, POS)	RUSH	YD	AVG(LG)	TD	REC	YD	AVG(LG)	TD	PASS	COMP	PCT	YD	AVG(LG)	TD	INT	SK	YD	QBR	KPR	OTD	PTS	TAY
1977	Sea	1	3	6	2.0(4)	0	—	—	—	—	0	0	0.0	0	0.0	0	0	1	8	—	—	—	0	6
1979	Sea	3	2	11	5.5(9)	0	—	—	—	—	3	0	0.0	0	0.0	0	0	—	—	—	—	—	0	11
1980	Sea	4(0)	6	18	3.0(12)	0	—	—	—	—	23	10	43.5	136	5.9(22)	1	3	6	51	—	—	—	0	-29
1981	Sea	3(0)	3	28	9.3(13)	0	—	—	—	—	13	7	53.8	96	7.4(31)	1	1	2	14	—	—	—	0	41
NFL	4	11	14	63	4.5(13)	0	—	—	—	—	39	17	43.6	232	5.9(31)	2	4	9	73	—	—	—	0	29

AFFHOLTER, ERIK Erik Konrad, WR, 6´0˝/187 lbs; USC; 1989: Was, rnd 4; B4/10/1966 Detroit, MI

YEAR	TEAM	G(GS, POS)	RUSH	YD	AVG(LG)	TD	REC	YD	AVG(LG)	TD	PASS	COMP	PCT	YD	AVG(LG)	TD	INT	SK	YD	QBR	KPR	OTD	PTS	TAY
1991	GB	4(0)	—	—	—	—	7	68	9.7(20)	0	—	—	—	—	—	—	—	—	—	—	—	—	0	34

AFFLIS, DICK William Richard, T-DG-G, 6´0˝/251 lbs; Purdue; Nevada-Reno; 1951: GB, rnd 16; B6/27/1929 Lafayette, IN, D11/10/1991 Indianapolis, IN **1951** GB 12 (MG) **1952** GB 12 (LT) **1953** GB 12 (LT) **1954** GB 12 **NFL** 48 [4 yrs]

YEAR	TEAM	G(GS, POS)	RUSH	YD	AVG(LG)	TD	REC	YD	AVG(LG)	TD	PASS COMP	PCT	YD	AVG(LG)	TD	INT	SK	YD	QBR	KPR	OTD	PTS	TAY

AGAJANIAN, BEN Benjamin James, K, 6'0"/215 lbs; New Mexico; B8/28/1919 Santa Ana, CA **[K]** **1947** LAD-A 13 (2) **1948** LAD-A 13 (1) **AAFC** 26 (3) [2 yrs]

1945 Phi 1 (1) **1945** Pit 5 (1) **1949** NYG 12 (1) **1953** LARm 10 **1954** NYG 12 **1955** NYG 12 **1956**†NYG 10 **1957** NYG 12 **1960**†LAC-A 14 **1961** DalT-A 3 **1961**†GB 3 **1962** Oak-A 6 **1964** SD-A 3 **NFL** 103-(3) [11 yrs]

AGASE, ALEX Alexander Arrasi, LB-G, 5'10"/212 lbs; Purdue; Illinois; 1944: GB, rnd 8; B3/27/1922 Chicago, IL **1947** LAD-A 3 (1) **1947** ChiR-A 11 (11, RG) **1948**†Cle-A 13 (1) **1949**†Cle-A 11 (0) **AAFC** 38 (13) [3 yrs]

1950†Cle 11 (MLB) **1951**†Cle 11 (MLB) **1953** Bal 10 (RLB) **NFL** 32 [3 yrs]

AGE, LOUIS Louis Theodore, T, 6'7"/350 lbs; Louisiana-Lafayette; 1992: Chi, rnd 11; B2/1/1970 New Orleans, LA **1992** ChiB 6 (0)

AGEE, MEL Melvin, DE-DT, 6'5"/300 lbs; Illinois; 1991: Ind, rnd 6; B11/22/1968 Chicago, IL **1991** Ind 16 (2) **1992** Ind 1 (0) **1993** Atl 11 (7, lde) **1994** Atl 16 (6, ldt) **1995** Atl 10 (1) **NFL** 54 (16) [5 yrs]

AGEE, SAM Samuel Webster, FB, 6'1"/218 lbs; Vanderbilt; B10/21/1915 Courtland, AL

1938	ChiC	10(1)	48	178	3.7	1	2	5	2.5	0	2	2	100.0	27	13.5	0	0	—	—	—	—	6	204
1939	ChiC	11(4)	44	133	3.0	1	1	6	6.0(6)	0	3	0	0.0	0	0.0	0	0	—	—	—	—	6	146
NFL	2	21(5)	92	311	3.4	2	3	11	3.7(6)	0	5	2	40.0	27	5.4	0	0	—	—	—	—	12	350

AGEE, TOMMIE Thomas Lee, RB, 6'0"/225 lbs; Auburn; 1987: Sea, rnd 5; B2/22/1964 Chilton, AL

1988	†Sea	16(0)	1	2	2.0(2)	0	3	31	10.3(13)	0	1	0	0.0	0	0.0	0	1	—	—	—	—	0	-23
1989	KC	9(0)	1	3	3.0(3)	0	—	—	—	—	—	—	—	—	—	—	—	—	—	—	—	0	3
1990	Dal	16(11, FB)	53	213	4.0(28)	0	30	272	9.1(30)	1	—	—	—	—	—	—	—	—	—	—	—	6	354
1991	†Dal	16(0)	9	20	2.2(8)	1	7	43	6.1(9)	0	—	—	—	—	—	—	—	—	—	—	—	6	52
1992	†Dal	16(0)	16	54	3.4(10)	0	3	18	6.0(8)	0	—	—	—	—	—	—	—	—	—	—	—	0	63
1993	Dal	12(0)	6	13	2.2(6)	0	—	—	—	—	—	—	—	—	—	—	—	—	—	—	—	0	13
1994	†Dal	15(0)	5	4	0.8(3)	0	1	2	2.0(2)	0	—	—	—	—	—	—	—	—	—	—	—	0	5
NFL	7	100(11)	91	309	3.4(28)	1	44	366	8.3(30)	1	1	0	0.0	0	0.0	0	1	—	—	—	—	12	467

AGLER, BOB Robert, HB-DB-FB-LB, 6'1"/208 lbs; Otterbein; B3/13/1924 Columbus, OH; D9/16/2005 Westerville, OH

1948	LARm	8(0)	8	41	5.1(4)	0	—	—	—	—	—	—	—	—	—	—	—	—	—	—	—	0	41
1949	LARm	8(0)	4	7	1.8(4)	0	—	—	—	—	—	—	—	—	—	—	—	—	—	—	—	0	7
NFL	2	12	48	4.0(12)	0	—	—	—	—	—	—	—	—	—	—	—	—	—	—	—	—	0	48

AGNEW, RAY Raymond Mitchell, DT-DE, 6'3"/285 lbs; North Carolina State; 1990: NE, rnd 1; B12/9/1967 Winston-Salem, NC **1990** NE 12 (9, RDE) **1991** NE 13 (10, LDE) **1992** NE 14 (14, LDE) **1993** NE 16 (1) **1994**†NE 11 (3) **1995** NYG 16 (15, RDT) **1996** NYG 13 (2) **1997**†NYG 15 (0) **1998** SL 16 (12, LDT) **1999**†SL 16 (16, LDT) **2000**†SL 15 (15, LDT) **NFL** 157 (97) [11 yrs]

AGUIAR, LOUIE Louis Raymond, P, 6'2"/215 lbs; Utah State; B6/30/1966 Livermore, CA **[KP]** **1992** NYJ 16 (0) **1994**†KC 16 (0) **1995**†KC☆16 (0) **1996** KC 16 (0) **1998** KC 16 (0) **1999** GB 15 (0)

1991	†NYJ	16(0)	1	18	18.0(18)	0	—	—	—	—	—	—	—	—	—	—	—	—	—	KP	—	3	18
1993	NYJ	16(0)	3	-27	-9.0(5)	0	—	—	—	2	0	0.0	0	0.0	0	1	—	—	P	—	0	-67
1997	†KC	16(0)	2	11	5.5(6)	0	—	—	—	1	1	100.0	35	35.0(35)	0	0	—	—	P	—	0	29
2000	ChiB	9(0)	—	—	—	—	—	—	—	1	1	100.0	13	13.0(13)	0	0	—	—	P	—	0	7
NFL	10	152(0)	6	2	0.3(18)	0	—	—	—	4	2	50.0	48	12.0(35)	0	1	—	—	KP	—	3	-14

AGUIRRE, JOE Joseph A., E, 6'4"/225 lbs; St. Mary's (CA); 1941: Was, rnd 11; B10/17/1918 Rock Springs, WV **[K]**

1941	Was	10(1)	—	—	—	—	10	103	10.3(17)	2	—	—	—	—	—	—	—	—	K	—	26	62
1943	†Was☆	10(10, RE)	1	21	21.0(21)	0	37	420	11.4(44)	7	—	—	—	—	—	—	—	—	Kk	—	48	242
1944	Was☆	10(10, LE)	—	—	—	—	34	410	12.1(58)	4	—	—	—	—	—	—	—	—	KP	—	51	225
1945	†Was☆	10(9, LE)	—	—	—	—	16	189	11.8(28)	0	—	—	—	—	—	—	—	—	K	—	44	95
NFL	4	40(30)	1	21	21.0(21)	0	97	1122	11.6(58)	13	—	—	—	—	—	—	—	—	KPk	—	169	623
1946	LAD-A☆	14(9, LE)	2	-5	-2.5	0	14	246	17.6(68)	2	1	0	0.0	0	0.0	0	0	—	—	KP	—	55	128
1947	LAD-A	12(6, LE)	—	—	—	—	8	158	19.8(51)	4	—	—	—	—	—	—	—	—	—	—	24	99
1948	LAD-A	13(4, le)	—	—	—	—	38	599	15.8(67)	9	—	—	—	—	—	—	—	—	Kk	—	56	340
1949	LAD-A	4(0)	—	—	—	—	3	37	12.3	1	—	—	—	—	—	—	—	—	—	—	6	24
AAFC	4	43(19)	2	-5	-2.5(21)	0	63	1040	16.5(68)	16	1	0	0.0	0	0.0	0	0	—	—	KPk	—	141	590

AHANOTU, CHIDI Chidi Obioma, DE-DT, 6'2"/283 lbs; California; 1993: TB, rnd 6; B10/11/1970 Modesto, CA **1993** TB 16 (10, ldt/lde) **1994** TB 16 (16, LDE) **1995** TB 16 (15, LDE) **1996** TB 13 (13, LDE) **1997**†TB 16 (15, LDE) **1998** TB 4 (4) **1999**†TB 16 (15, LDE) **2000**†TB 16 (16, LDE) **2001**†SL 16 (16, LDE) **2002** Buf 16 (14, LDE) **2003** SF 16 (1) **2004** Mia 5 (0) **2004** TB 8 (5, rdt) **NFL** 174 (140) [12 yrs]

AHERN, DAN Daniel Francis, T, 6'2"/200 lbs; Georgetown (DC); B2/15/1898 Manchester, NH, D8/31/1963 Washington, DC **1921** Was 3 (2, RT)

AHRENS, DAVE David Iver, LB, 6'3"/238 lbs; Wisconsin; 1981: SL, rnd 6; B12/5/1958 Cedar Falls, IA **1981** SL 16 (10, MLB) **1982**†SL 9 (9, MLB) **1984** SL 16 (0) **1985** Ind 16 (0) **1986** Ind 16 (0, RILB) **1987**†Ind 12 (2) **1988** Det 8 (0) **1989** Mia 11 (8, lilb) **1990** Sea 10 (3)

| 1983 | SL | 16(5, mlb) | — | — | — | — | 1 | 4 | 4.0(4) | 0 | — | — | — | — | — | — | — | — | — | — | — | 0 | 2 |
| NFL | 10 | 130(47) | — | — | — | — | 1 | 4 | 4.0(4) | 0 | — | — | — | — | — | — | — | — | kpiS | 1 | 6 | 1 |

AIELLO, TONY Anthony Samuel, WB-BB, 5'6"/165 lbs; Youngstown State; B4/29/1921 Monongahela, PA **1944** Bkn 1 (0)

| 1944 | Det | 4(0) | 6 | 22 | 3.7(5) | 0 | — | — | — | — | — | — | — | — | — | — | — | — | p | — | 0 | 26 |
| NFL | 1 | 5(0) | 6 | 22 | 3.7(5) | 0 | — | — | — | — | — | — | — | — | — | — | — | — | — | — | 0 | 22 |

AIKEN, SAM Samuel, WR, 6'2"/204 lbs; North Carolina; 2003: Buf, rnd 4; B12/14/1980 Clinton, NC

2003	Buf	5(0)	—	—	—	—	3	35	11.7(19)	0	—	—	—	—	—	—	—	—	—	—	0	18
2004	Buf	16(0)	—	—	—	—	11	148	13.5(54)	0	—	—	—	—	—	—	—	—	—	—	0	74
2005	Buf	16(2)	—	—	—	—	4	57	14.3(22)	0	—	—	—	—	—	—	—	—	—	—	0	29
NFL	3	37(2)	—	—	—	—	18	240	13.3(54)	0	—	—	—	—	—	—	—	—	—	—	0	120

AIKENS, CARL Carl Kenneth, WR, 6'1"/185 lbs; Northern Illinois; B6/5/1962 Great Lakes, IL

| 1987 | LARd | 3 | 1 | 1.0(1) | 0 | 8 | 134 | 16.8(32) | 3 | — | — | — | — | — | — | — | — | — | — | — | 18 | 83 |

AIKMAN, TROY Troy Kenneth, QB, 6'4"/219 lbs; Oklahoma; UCLA; 1989: Dal, rnd 1; B11/21/1966 West Covina, CA; HOF 2006

1989	Dal	11(11, QB)	38	302	7.9(25)	0	1	-13	-13.0(-13)	0	293	155	52.9	1749	6.0(75)	9	18	19	155	55.7	—	0	495
1990	Dal	15(15, QB)	40	172	4.3(20)	1	—	—	—	399	226	56.6	2579	6.5(61)	11	18	39	288	66.6	—	6	807
1991	†Dal◇	12(12, QB)	16	5	0.3(9)	1	1	-6	-6.0(-6)	0	363	237	65.3	2754	7.6(61)	11	10	32	224	86.7	—	6	1044
1992	†Dal◇	16(16, QB)	37	105	2.8(19)	1	—	—	—	473	302	63.8	3445	7.3(87)	23	14	23	112	89.5	—	6	1393
1993	†Dal★	14(14, QB)	32	125	3.9(20)	0	—	—	—	392	271	69.1	3100	7.9(80)	15	6	26	153	99.0	—	6	1510
1994	†Dal★	14(14, QB)	30	62	2.1(13)	1	—	—	—	361	233	64.5	2676	7.4(90)	13	12	14	99	84.9	—	6	995
1995	†Dal★	16(16, QB)	21	32	1.5(12)	1	—	—	—	432	280	64.8	3304	7.6(50)	16	7	14	89	93.6	—	6	1494
1996	†Dal◇	15(15, QB)	35	42	1.2(10)	1	—	—	—	465	296	63.7	3126	6.7(61)	12	13	12	80.1	—	6	1155
1997	Dal	16(16, QB)	25	79	3.2(13)	0	—	—	—	518	292	56.4	3283	6.3(64)	19	12	33	269	78.0	—	6	1336
1998	†Dal	11(11, QB)	22	69	3.1(23)	2	—	—	—	315	187	59.4	2330	7.4(67)	12	5	9	58	88.5	—	12	1114
1999	†Dal	14(14, QB)	21	10	0.5(7)	1	—	—	—	442	263	59.5	2964	6.7(90)	17	12	19	130	81.1	—	6	1107
2000	Dal	11(11, QB)	10	13	1.3(5)	0	—	—	—	262	156	59.5	1632	6.2(48)	7	14	13	91	64.3	—	0	304
NFL	12	165(165)	327	1016	3.1(25)	9	2	-19	-9.5(-6)	0	4715	2898	61.5	32942	7.0(90)	165	141	259	1748	81.6	—	54	12753

AILINGER, JIM James Joseph, G, 5'11"/185 lbs; Buffalo; B7/10/1901 Buffalo, NY, D3/27/2001 Rochester, NY **1924** Buf 8 (0)

AIU, CHARLES Charles Kahoalii, G, 6'2"/251 lbs; Hawaii; B5/22/1954 Honolulu, HI **1976** SD 12 **1977** SD 14 (1) **1978** SD 6 **1978** Sea 1 **NFL** 33 (1) [3 yrs]

AKBAR, HAKIM Akmal Hakim, LB, 6'0"/222 lbs; San Diego State; 2001: NE, rnd 5; B8/11/1980 Riverside, CA **2001** NE 6 (0) **2002** SL 4 (0) **NFL** 10 (0) [2 yrs]

YEAR	TEAM	G(GS, POS)	RUSH	YD	AVG(LG)	TD	REC	YD	AVG(LG)	TD	PASS COMP	PCT	YD	AVG(LG)	TD	INT	SK	YD	QBR	KPR	OTD	PTS	TAY

AKERS, DAVID   David Roy, K, 5'10"/200 lbs; Louisville; B12/9/1974 Lexington, KY **[K]**   **1998** Was 1 (0)   **1999** Phi 16 (0)   **2001**†Phi★16 (0)   **2003**†Phi 16 (0)   **2004**†Phi★16 (0)
2005 Phi 12 (0)

YEAR	TEAM	G(GS, POS)	RUSH	YD	AVG(LG)	TD	...	KPR	OTD	PTS	TAY
2000	†Phi	16(0)	1	15	15.0(15)	0	—	K	—	121	15
2002	†Phi★	16(0)	1	10	10.0(10)	0	—	K	—	133	10
NFL	8	109(0)	2	25	12.5(15)	0	—	KP	—	689	25

AKIN, HAROLD   Harold Dwayne, T, 6'5"/260 lbs; Oklahoma State; 1967: SD, rnd 3; B1/11/1945 McAlester, OK   **1967** SD-A 3   **1968** SD-A 10   **NFL** 13 [2 yrs]

AKIN, LEN   Leonard Rosser, G-LB, 5'11"/207 lbs; Baylor; 1940: ChiB, rnd 7; B4/8/1916 McKinney, TX, D3/5/1987 Irving, TX   **1942**†ChiB 11 (1)

AKINS, AL   Albert George, HB-DB, 6'1"/199 lbs; Washington; Washington State; 1944: Cle, rnd 6; B6/13/1921 Spokane, WA, D8/29/1995 Reno, NV

YEAR	TEAM	G(GS)	RUSH	YD	AVG	TD	REC	YD	AVG(LG)	TD	KPR	OTD	PTS	TAY
1946	Cle-A	4(0)	5	42	8.4	—	—	—	—	—	ki	—	6	98
1947	Bkn-A	13(3)	15	79	5.3	1	6	101	16.8(60)	1	kpi	—	12	239
1948	Bkn-A	3(1)	4	-9	-2.3	0	2	1	0.5	0	—	—	0	-9
1948	†Buf-A	5(0)	—	—	—	—	1	11	11.0(11)	0	—	—	0	6
AAFC	3	25(4)	24	112	4.7	2	9	113	12.6(60)	1	kpi	—	18	334

AKINS, CHRIS   Christopher Drew, DB, 5'11"/200 lbs; Arkansas; Arkansas-Pine Bluff; 1999: GB, rnd 7; B11/29/1976 Little Rock, AR   **1999**†Dal 9 (0)   **2000** Dal 8 (0)   **2000** GB 2 (0)
2001 Cle 4 (0)   **2001** GB 11 (0)   **2002**†Cle 15 (0)   **2003**†NE 12 (0)   **NFL** 61 (0) [5 yrs]

AKINS, FRANK   Frank John, FB, 5'10"/208 lbs; Washington State; 1943: Was, rnd 30; B3/31/1919 John, MT, D7/6/1992 Redding, CA

YEAR	TEAM	G(GS)	RUSH	YD	AVG(LG)	TD	REC	YD	AVG(LG)	TD	KPR	OTD	PTS	TAY
1943	†Was	6(0)	10	25	2.5(11)	0	1	51	51.0(51)	0	P	—	0	51
1944	Was	6(1)	46	154	3.3(15)	1	5	27	5.4(9)	0	Pk	—	6	177
1945	†Was☆	10(2, FB)	147	797	5.4(45)	6	8	57	7.1(18)	0	k	—	36	892
1946	Was	6(2)	41	166	4.0(16)	0	2	15	7.5(8)	0	—	—	0	174
NFL	4	28(5)	244	1142	4.7(45)	7	16	150	9.4(51)	0	Pk	—	42	1292

AKIU, MIKE   Karl Michael, WR, 5'9"/182 lbs; Washington State; Hawaii; 1985: Hou, rnd 7; B2/12/1962 Kailua, HI

YEAR	TEAM	G(GS)	RUSH	YD	AVG	TD	REC	YD	AVG(LG)	TD	OTD	PTS	TAY
1985	Hou	9(0)	—	—	—	—	2	32	16.0(24)	0	1	6	16
1986	Hou	11(1)	—	—	—	—	4	67	16.8(27)	0	0	0	34
NFL	2	20(1)	—	—	—	—	6	99	16.5(27)	0	1	6	50

ALBAN, DICK   Richard Herbert, DB, 6'0"/193 lbs; Northwestern; 1952: Was, rnd 9; B6/17/1929 Hanover, PA **[I]**   **1952** Was 12 (DB)   **1953** Was 12 (DB)   **1954** Was◇12 (DB)
1955 Was☆12 (DB)   **1956** Pit 12 (DB)   **1957** Pit 12 (DB)   **1958** Pit 12 (DB)   **1959** Pit 12 (DB)   **NFL** 96 [8 yrs]

ALBANESE, DOM   Dominic, BB-E-FB, 5'9"/190 lbs; Ohio Dominican; B9/9/1903, D3/17/1992 Millersport, OH   **1925** Col 3 (1)

ALBANESE, VANNIE   Vincent Michelo, FB-DB-BB-LB, 6'0"/184 lbs; Syracuse; B12/2/1912 Syracuse, NY, D9/2/1984 Canandaigua, NY

YEAR	TEAM	G(GS)	RUSH	YD	AVG	TD	PASS COMP	PCT	YD	AVG(LG)	TD	INT	OTD	PTS	TAY
1937	Bkn	10(5, fb)	21	53	2.5	0	2	1	50.0	5	2.5(5)	0	0	—	0	56
1938	Bkn	8(0)	27	97	3.6	0	1	0	0.0	0	0.0	0	0	—	0	97
NFL	2	18(5)	48	150	3.1	0	3	1	33.3	5	1.7(5)	0	0	—	0	153

ALBERGHINI, TOM   Thomas Joseph, G, 5'10"/200 lbs; Holy Cross; 1943: Cle, rnd 13; B10/27/1920 Peabody, MA   **1945** Pit 1 (0)

ALBERT, FRANKIE   Frank Cullen, QB-DB, 5'10"/166 lbs; Stanford; 1942: ChiB, rnd 1; B1/27/1920 Chicago, IL, D9/4/2002 Palo Alto, CA **[KPC]**

YEAR	TEAM	G(GS, POS)	RUSH	YD	AVG	TD	REC	YD	AVG(LG)	TD	PASS COMP	PCT	YD	AVG(LG)	TD	INT	QBR	KPR	OTD	PTS	TAY
1946	SF-A☆	14(11, QB)	69	-10	-0.1	4	—	—	—	—	197	104	52.8	1404	7.1(54)	14	14	—	Pkp	—	24	257
1947	SF-A☆	14(9, QB)	46	179	3.9	5	—	—	—	—	242	128	52.9	1692	7.0(60)	18	15	—	KPk	—	30	573
1948	SF-A☆	14(9, QB)	69	349	5.1	8	1	1	1.0(1)	0	264	154	58.3	1990	7.5(59)	29	10	—	KP	—	49	1170
1949	†SF-A☆	12(9, QB)	35	249	7.1	3	—	—	—	—	260	129	49.6	1862	7.2(75)	27	16	—	KP	—	18	705
AAFC	4	54(38)	219	767	3.5	20	1	1	1.0(1)	0	963	515	53.5	6948	7.2(75)	88	55	83.4	KPkp	—	121	2705
1950	SF◇	12(QB)	53	272	5.1(42)	3	—	—	—	—	306	155	50.7	1767	5.8(43)	14	23	52.3	P	—	18	336
1951	SF	12(QB)	35	146	4.2(34)	3	—	—	—	—	166	90	54.2	1116	6.7(47)	5	10	60.2	P	—	18	359
1952	SF	12(qb)	22	87	4.0(20)	1	—	—	—	—	129	71	55.0	964	7.5(60)	8	10	67.5	P	—	6	219
NFL	3	36	110	505	4.6(42)	7	—	—	—	—	601	316	52.6	3847	6.4(75)	27	43	57.7	P	—	42	914

ALBERT, SERGIO   Sergio, K, 6'3"/195 lbs; Anahuac (Mexico); U.S. International; 1974: SL, rnd 8; B10/28/1951 Mexico City, Mexico   **1974**†SL 12

ALBERTS, TREV   Trev Kendall, LB, 6'4"/245 lbs; Nebraska; 1994: Ind, rnd 1; B8/8/1970 Cedar Falls, IA   **1994** Ind 5 (0)   **1995**†Ind 15 (3)   **1996** Ind 9 (4)   **NFL** 29 (7) [3 yrs]

ALBRECHT, ART   Arthur Walter, T-C-LB, 6'1"/203 lbs; Wisconsin; B2/24/1921 Manitowoc, WI, D2/1/2004 Manitowoc, WI   **1942** Pit 3 (0)   **1943** ChiC 5 (0)   **1944** Bos 6 (1)
NFL 14 (1) [3 yrs]

ALBRECHT, TED   Theodore Carl, T-G, 6'4"/253 lbs; California; 1977: Chi, rnd 1; B10/8/1954 Harvey, IL   **1977**†ChiB 14 (12, LT)   **1978** ChiB 15 (15, LT)   **1979**†ChiB 16 (16, LT)
1980 ChiB 16 (16, LT)   **1981** ChiB 16 (16, LT)   **NFL** 77 (75) [5 yrs]

ALBRIGHT, BILL   William Charles, G-T-DT, 6'1"/233 lbs; Wisconsin; 1951: NYG, rnd 20; B4/4/1929 Racine, WI   **1951** NYG 11   **1952** NYG 12   **1953** NYG 12   **1954** NYG 12
NFL 47 [4 yrs]

ALBRIGHT, ETHAN   Laurence Ethan, G-C-T, 6'5"/283 lbs; North Carolina; B5/1/1971 Greensboro, NC   **1995** Mia 10 (0)   **1996**†Buf 16 (0)   **1997** Buf 16 (0)   **1998** Buf 16 (0)
1999†Buf 16 (0)   **2000** Buf 16 (0)   **2001** Was 16 (0)   **2002** Was 16 (0)   **2003** Was 16 (0)   **2004** Was 16 (0)   **2005**†Was 16 (0)   **NFL** 170 (0) [11 yrs]

ALBRIGHT, IRA   Ira Ladol, NT-RB, 6'0"/285 lbs; Northeastern State (OK); B1/2/1959 Dallas, TX   **1987** Buf 3 (0)

ALBRITTON, VINCE   Vince Denader, DB, 6'2"/215 lbs; Washington; B7/23/1962 Oakland, CA   **1984** Dal 16 (0)   **1985**†Dal 7 (1)   **1986** Dal 16 (1)   **1987** Dal 11 (1)   **1988** Dal 6 (0)
1989 Dal 16 (16, SS)   **1990** Dal 8 (8, ss)   **1991** Dal 6 (0)   **NFL** 86 (27) [8 yrs]

ALDERMAN, GRADY   Grady Charles, T-G, 6'2"/247 lbs; Detroit Mercy; 1960: Det, rnd 10/DalT, rnd 2; B12/10/1938 Detroit, MI   **1960** Det 11   **1961** Min 14 (14, LT)
1962 Min 14 (14, LT)   **1963** Min◇14 (14, LT)   **1965** Min★13 (13, LT)   **1966** Min◇14 (14, LT)   **1967** Min◇14 (14, LT)   **1968**†Min 14 (14, LT)   **1969**†Min★14 (14, LT)
1970†Min 14 (11, LT)   **1971**†Min 13 (11, LT)   **1972** Min 14 (14, LT)   **1973**†Min 14 (14, LT)   **1974**†Min 13

YEAR	TEAM	G(GS, POS)	RUSH	YD	AVG(LG)	TD	...	KPR	OTD	PTS	TAY
1964	Min◇	14(14, LT)	0	22	(16)	0	—	—	—	0	22
NFL	15	204(175)	0	22	(16)	0	—	k	—	0	-8

ALDERTON, JOHN   John Reber, DE, 6'1"/200 lbs; Maryland; 1953: Pit, rnd 7; B9/5/1931   **1953** Pit 10

ALDRICH, KI   Charles Collins, C-LB-G, 6'0"/207 lbs; TCU; 1939: ChiC, rnd 1; B6/1/1916 Rogers, TX, D3/12/1983 Temple, TX **[K]**   **1939** ChiC★11 (10, C)   **1940** ChiC 11 (9, C)
1941 Was 11 (1)   **1942**†Was◇11 (10, C)   **1945**†Was☆6 (5, C)   **1946** Was 11 (10, C)   **1947** Was 12 (8, C)   **NFL** 73 (53) [7 yrs]

ALDRIDGE, ALLEN   Allen Ray, DE, 6'6"/250 lbs; Prairie View A&M; B4/27/1945 Eagle Lake, TX   **1971** Hou 13   **1972** Hou 8   **1974** Cle 14   **NFL** 35 [3 yrs]

ALDRIDGE, ALLEN   Allen Ray, LB, 6'1"/247 lbs; Houston; 1994: Den, rnd 2; B5/30/1972 Houston, TX   **1994** Den 16 (2)   **1995** Den 16 (12, RLB)   **1996**†Den 16 (16, MLB)
1997†Den 16 (15, RLB)   **1999**†Det 16 (14, LLB)   **2000** Det 16 (16, LLB)   **2001** Det 16 (16, LLB)   **NFL** 128 (104) [8 yrs]

ALDRIDGE, BENNIE   Bennie Leo, DB-HB, 6'0"/195 lbs; Oklahoma State; 1950: NYY, rnd 6; B10/24/1926 Velma, OK, D1956   **1951** NYY 12 (DB)   **1952** DalT 1   **1953** GB 8 (DB)

YEAR	TEAM	G(GS)	RUSH	YD	AVG(LG)	TD	REC	YD	AVG(LG)	TD	KPR	OTD	PTS	TAY
1950	NYY	11	16	69	4.3(35)	0	4	56	14.0(28)	0	pi	—	0	99
1952	SF	11	13	36	2.8(11)	0	4	22	5.5(16)	1	—	—	6	52
NFL	4	43	29	105	3.6(35)	0	8	78	9.8(28)	1	pi	—	6	233

ALDRIDGE, JERRY   Jerry Charles, RB, 6'2"/220 lbs; Angelo State (TX); 1979: SF, rnd 5; B9/17/1956 Jacksonville, TX   **1980** SF 1 (0)

ALDRIDGE, KEVIN   Kevin Lamar, DE, 6'1"/285 lbs; SMU; B3/3/1980 Palestine, TX   **2002** Ten 6 (0)

ALDRIDGE, LIONEL   Lionel, DE, 6'3"/254 lbs; Utah State; 1963: GB, rnd 4/Hou, rnd 6; B2/14/1941 Evergreen, LA, D2/12/1998 Shorewood, WI   **1963** GB 14 (RDE)
1964 GB☆14 (RDE)   **1965**†GB 14 (RDE)   **1966**†GB 13 (RDE)   **1967**†GB 12 (12, RDE)   **1968** GB 14 (RDE)   **1969** GB 14 (RDE)   **1970** GB 14 (RDE)   **1971** GB 14 (RDE)
1972 SD 14 (RDE)   **1973** SD 10 (RDE)   **NFL** 147 (12) [11 yrs]

ALDRIDGE, MELVIN   Melvin Keith, DB, 6'2"/195 lbs; Murray State; B7/22/1970 Pittsburgh, TX   **1993** Hou 1 (0)   **1995** Arz 2 (0)   **NFL** 3 (0) [2 yrs]

ALE, ARNOLD   Arnold Tauese, LB, 6'2"/234 lbs; Notre Dame; UCLA; B6/17/1970 San Pedro, CA   **1994** KC 3 (0)   **1996** SD 7 (0)   **NFL** 10 (0) [2 yrs]

ALEAGA, INK   Ink A., LB, 6'1"/225 lbs; Washington; B4/27/1973 Honolulu, HI   **1997** NO 3 (1)   **1998** NO 15 (3)   **1999** NO 8 (2)   **NFL** 26 (6) [3 yrs]

ALEX, KEITH   Hiram Keith, G, 6'4"/307 lbs; Texas A&M; 1992: Atl, rnd 9; B6/9/1969 Kountze, TX   **1993** Atl 14 (0)

ALEXAKOS, STEVE   Steven Theodore, G, 6'2"/250 lbs; San Jose State; 1969: Bos, rnd 9; B12/15/1946 Lowell, MA   **1970** Den 8 (1)   **1971** NYG 10   **NFL** 18 (1) [2 yrs]

YEAR	TEAM	G (GS, POS)	RUSH	YD	AVG(LG)	TD	REC	YD	AVG(LG)	TD	PASS	COMP	PCT	YD	AVG(LG)	TD	INT	SK	YD	QBR	KPR	OTD	PTS	TAY

ALEXANDER, BRENT Ronald Brent, DB, 5´11˝/189 lbs; Tennessee State; B7/10/1971 Gallatin, TN **[I]** **1994** Arz 16 (7, rcb) **1995** Arz 16 (13, FS) **1996** Arz 16 (15, FS) **1997** Arz 16 (15, FS) **1998** Car 16 (16, FS) **1999** Car 16 (16, SS) **2000** Pit 16 (16, FS) **2001**†Pit 16 (16, FS) **2002**†Pit 16 (16, FS) **2003** Pit 16 (16, FS) **2004** NYG 16 (16, FS/ss) **2005**†NYG 16 (16, FS) **NFL** 192 (178) [12 yrs]

ALEXANDER, BRUCE Bruce Edward, DB, 5´9˝/170 lbs; Stephen F. Austin State; B9/17/1965 Lufkin, TX **1989** Det 8 (1) **1990** Det 1 (0) **1991**†Det 9 (0) **1992**†Mia 12 (1) **1993** Mia 14 (0) **NFL** 44 (2) [5 yrs]

ALEXANDER, CHARLES Charles Fred, RB, 6´1˝/224 lbs; LSU; 1979: Cin, rnd 1; B7/28/1957 Galveston, TX

YEAR	TEAM	G (GS, POS)	RUSH	YD	AVG(LG)	TD	REC	YD	AVG(LG)	TD												OTD	PTS	TAY
1979	Cin	16	88	286	3.3(17)	1	11	91	8.3(13)	0	—	—	—	—	—	—	—	—	—	—	—	—	6	342
1980	Cin	16(16, RB)	169	702	4.2(37)	2	36	192	5.3(23)	0	—	—	—	—	—	—	—	—	—	—	—	—	12	818
1981	†Cin	15(14, RB)	98	292	3.0(16)	2	28	262	9.4(65)	1	—	—	—	—	—	—	—	—	—	—	—	—	18	448
1982	†Cin	9(9, RB)	64	207	3.2(18)	1	14	85	6.1(14)	1	—	—	—	—	—	—	—	—	—	—	—	—	12	265
1983	Cin	14(14, RB/fb)	153	523	3.4(12)	3	32	187	5.8(14)	0	—	—	—	—	—	—	—	—	—	—	—	—	18	647
1984	Cin	16(12, FB)	132	479	3.6(22)	2	29	203	7.0(22)	0	—	—	—	—	—	—	—	—	—	—	—	—	12	601
1985	Cin	16(5, fb)	44	156	3.5(18)	2	15	110	7.3(19)	0	—	—	—	—	—	—	—	—	—	—	—	—	12	231
NFL	7	102(70)	748	2645	3.5(37)	13	165	1130	6.8(65)	2	—	—	—	—	—	—	—	—	—	—	—	—	90	3350

ALEXANDER, DAN Daniel Lamarr, G-T, 6´4˝/260 lbs; LSU; 1977: NYJ, rnd 8; B6/17/1955 Houston, TX **1977** NYJ 14 (8, RG) **1978** NYJ 16 (16, RG) **1979** NYJ 16 (15, RG) **1980** NYJ 16 (15, RG) **1981**†NYJ 16 (16, RG) **1982**†NYJ 9 (9, RG) **1983** NYJ 16 (16, RG) **1984** NYJ 16 (16, RG) **1985**†NYJ☆16 (16, RG) **1986**†NYJ☆16 (16, RG) **1987** NYJ 12 (12, RT/rg) **1988** NYJ 14 (13, RG) **1989** NYJ 15 (14, RG) **NFL** 192 (182) [13 yrs]

ALEXANDER, DAN Daniel, RB, 6´0˝/257 lbs; Nebraska; 2001: Ten, rnd 6; B3/17/1978 Wentzville, MO **2001** Ten 7 (0) **2002** Jax 3 (0) **2003** SL 1 (0) **NFL** 11 (0) [3 yrs]

ALEXANDER, DAVID David Franklin, C-G-T, 6´3˝/275 lbs; Tulsa; 1987: Phi, rnd 5; B7/28/1964 Silver Spring, MD **1987** Phi 12 (0) **1988**†Phi 16 (12, LG) **1989**†Phi 16 (16, C) **1990**†Phi 16 (16, C) **1991** Phi 16 (16, C) **1992**†Phi 16 (16, C) **1993** Phi 16 (16, C) **1996** NYJ 7 (7, c)

| 1994 | Phi | 16(16, C) | — | — | — | — | 2 | 1 | 0.5(1) | 0 | — | — | — | — | — | — | — | — | — | — | — | — | 0 | 1 |
| NFL | 9 | 131(115) | — | — | — | — | 2 | 1 | 0.5(1) | 0 | — | — | — | — | — | — | — | — | — | — | k | — | 0 | -9 |

ALEXANDER, DERRICK Derrick Scott, WR, 6´2˝/195 lbs; Michigan; 1994: Cle, rnd 1; B11/6/1971 Detroit, MI

1994	†Cle	14(12, WR)	4	38	9.5(25)	0	48	828	17.3(81)	2	—	—	—	—	—	—	—	—	—	—	—	—	14	462
1995	Cle	14(2)	1	29	29.0(29)	0	15	216	14.4(40)	0	—	—	—	—	—	—	—	—	—	—	kp	1	6	328
1996	Bal	15(14, WR)	3	0	0.0(12)	0	62	1099	17.7(64)	9	—	—	—	—	—	—	—	—	—	—	kp	—	56	603
1997	Bal	15(13, WR)	1	0	0.0(0)	0	65	1009	15.5(92)	9	—	—	—	—	—	—	—	—	—	—	p	—	54	579
1998	KC	15(14, WR)	—	—	—	—	54	992	18.4(65)	4	—	—	—	—	—	—	—	—	—	—	—	—	24	516
1999	KC	16(15, WR)	2	82	41.0(82)	1	54	832	15.4(86)	2	—	—	—	—	—	—	—	—	—	—	—	—	18	518
2000	KC	16(16, WR)	3	45	15.0(26)	0	78	1391	17.8(81)	10	—	—	—	—	—	—	—	—	—	—	—	—	60	791
2001	KC	13(11, WR)	2	16	8.0(15)	0	27	470	17.4(46)	3	—	—	—	—	—	—	—	—	—	—	—	—	18	266
2002	Min	8(5, wr)	—	—	—	—	14	134	9.6(18)	1	—	—	—	—	—	—	—	—	—	—	—	—	6	72
NFL	9	126(102)	16	210	13.1(82)	1	417	6971	16.7(92)	40	—	—	—	—	—	—	—	—	—	—	kp	1	256	4134

ALEXANDER, DERRICK Derrick Laborn, DE, 6´4˝/277 lbs; Florida State; 1995: Min, rnd 1; B11/13/1973 Jacksonville, FL **1995** Min 15 (12, RDE) **1996**†Min 12 (9, RDE) **1997**†Min 14 (14, RDE) **1998**†Min 16 (16, LDE) **1999** Cle 16 (16, RDE) **NFL** 73 (67) [5 yrs]

ALEXANDER, DOC Joseph A., C-G-T-E, 5´11˝/220 lbs; Syracuse; B4/1/1898 Silver Creek, NY, D9/12/1975 New York, NY **[C]** **1921** Roc☆4 (4, C) **1922** Roc☆4 (4, C) **1924** Roc 2 (2) **1925** NYG 13 (12, C), 6 **1926** NYG 13 (11, LG), 12 **1927** NYG 4 (2), 6 **NFL** 40 (35), 24 [6 yrs]

ALEXANDER, ELIJAH Elijah Alfred, LB, 6´2˝/233 lbs; Kansas State; 1992: TB, rnd 10; B8/2/1970 Fort Worth, TX **1992** TB 12 (0) **1993**†Den 16 (0) **1994** Den 16 (16, RLB) **1995** Den 9 (8, LLB) **1996**†Ind 14 (3) **1997** Ind 13 (11, LLB) **1998** Ind 13 (9, RLB) **2000**†Oak 16 (16, RLB) **2001**†Oak 14 (13, RLB) **NFL** 123 (76) [9 yrs]

ALEXANDER, ERIC Eric, LB, 6´3˝/230 lbs; LSU; B2/8/1982 Tyler, TX **2004** NE 3 (0) **2005** NE 1 (0) **NFL** 4 (0) [2 yrs]

ALEXANDER, GLENN Glenn Elliott, WR, 6´3˝/205 lbs; Grambling State; 1970: Buf, rnd 3; B6/3/1947 New Orleans, LA

| 1970 | Buf | 13 | — | — | — | — | 4 | 51 | 12.8(16) | 0 | — | — | — | — | — | — | — | — | — | — | kp | — | 0 | 47 |

ALEXANDER, HAROLD Harold Donald, P, 6´2˝/224 lbs; Appalachian State; 1993: Atl, rnd 3; B10/20/1970 Pickens, SC

1993	Atl	16(0)	2	-7	-3.5(0)	0	—	—	—	—	—	—	—	—	—	—	—	—	—	P	—	0	-7
1994	Atl	15(0)	1	0	0.0(0)	0	—	—	—	—	—	—	—	—	—	—	—	—	—	P	—	0	0
NFL	2	31(0)	3	-7	-2.3	0	—	—	—	—	—	—	—	—	—	—	—	—	—	P	—	0	-7

ALEXANDER, JEFF Jeffrey O'Neal, RB, 6´0˝/232 lbs; Tulane; Southern (LA); B1/15/1965 Baton Rouge, LA **1992** Den 7 (0)

| 1989 | Den | 14(6, FB) | 45 | 146 | 3.2(11) | 2 | 8 | 84 | 10.5(28) | 0 | — | — | — | — | — | — | — | — | — | — | — | — | 12 | 208 |
| NFL | 2 | 21(6) | 45 | 146 | 3.2(11) | 2 | 8 | 84 | 10.5(28) | 0 | — | — | — | — | — | — | — | — | — | — | — | — | 12 | 208 |

ALEXANDER, JOHN John, T, 6´4˝/234 lbs; Rutgers; Fordham; B7/4/1896 New York, NY, D8/5/1986 Edison, NJ **1922** Mil 8 (7, RT) **1926** NYG☆9 (8, RT), 6 **NFL** 17 (15) [2 yrs]

ALEXANDER, JOHN John Wesley, DE, 6´2˝/250 lbs; Rutgers; 1977: Mia, rnd 11; B11/12/1955 Hattiesburg, MS **1977** Mia 4 **1978** Mia 8 **NFL** 12 [2 yrs]

ALEXANDER, KERMIT Kermit Joseph, DB, 5´11˝/187 lbs; UCLA; 1963: SF, rnd 1/Den, rnd 1; B1/4/1941 New Iberia, LA **[RI]** **1963** SF 14 (14, LCB) **1964** SF 14 (12, RS) **1965** SF 14 (14, RCB) **1966** SF 14 (14, RCB) **1967** SF 13 (13, RCB) **1968** SF★14 (14, RCB) **1969** SF 11 (10, RCB) **1970** LARm 14 (14, RCB) **1971** LARm 14 (14, SS) **1972** Phi 7 **1973** Phi 14 **NFL** 143 (114) [11 yrs]

ALEXANDER, KEVIN Kevin John, WR, 5´9˝/185 lbs; Utah State; B1/23/1975 Baton Rouge, LA

1996	NYG	4(0)	—	—	—	—	4	88	22.0(35)	0	—	—	—	—	—	—	—	—	—	k	—	0	41
1997	†NYG	14(8, WR)	—	—	—	—	18	276	15.3(40)	1	—	—	—	—	—	—	—	—	—	k	—	6	128
NFL	2	18(8)	—	—	—	—	22	364	16.5(40)	1	—	—	—	—	—	—	—	—	—	k	—	6	169

ALEXANDER, MIKE Michael Fitzgerald, WR, 6´3˝/195 lbs; Penn State; 1988: LARd, rnd 8; B3/19/1965 New York, NY

1989	LARd	16(0)	—	—	—	—	15	295	19.7(61)	1	—	—	—	—	—	—	—	—	—	—	—	6	153
1991	Buf	3(1)	—	—	—	—	1	7	7.0(7)	0	—	—	—	—	—	—	—	—	—	—	—	0	4
NFL	2	19(1)	—	—	—	—	16	302	18.9(61)	1	—	—	—	—	—	—	—	—	—	—	—	6	156

ALEXANDER, P.J. Patrick James, G, 6´4˝/297 lbs; Syracuse; B12/23/1978 Springfield, MA **2004**†Den 5 (0)

ALEXANDER, PATRISE Liyongo Patrise, LB, 6´1˝/244 lbs; Louisiana-Lafayette; B10/23/1972 Galveston, TX **1996** Was 16 (1) **1997** Was 16 (0) **1998** Was 1 (0) **NFL** 33 (1) [3 yrs]

ALEXANDER, RAY Vernest Raynard, WR, 6´4˝/195 lbs; Florida A&M; B1/8/1962 Miami, FL

1984	†Den	8(0)	—	—	—	—	8	132	16.5(41)	1	—	—	—	—	—	—	—	—	—	—	—	6	71
1988	Dal	16(11, WR)	—	—	—	—	54	788	14.6(50)	6	—	—	—	—	—	—	—	—	—	—	—	36	424
1989	Dal	2(0)	—	—	—	—	1	16	16.0(16)	0	—	—	—	—	—	—	—	—	—	—	—	0	8
NFL	3	26(11)	—	—	—	—	63	936	14.9(50)	7	—	—	—	—	—	—	—	—	—	—	—	42	503

ALEXANDER, ROBERT Robert Alan, RB, 6´0˝/185 lbs; West Virginia; 1981: LA, rnd 10; B4/21/1958 Charleston, WV

1982	LARm	9(0)	1	3	3.0(3)	0	1	-7	-7.0(-7)	0	—	—	—	—	—	—	—	—	—	k	—	0	19
1983	LARm	15(0)	7	28	4.0(15)	0	1	10	10.0(10)	0	—	—	—	—	—	—	—	—	—	k	—	0	60
NFL	2	24(0)	8	31	3.9(15)	0	2	3	1.5(10)	0	—	—	—	—	—	—	—	—	—	k	—	0	79

ALEXANDER, ROC Narond, DB, 6´0˝/193 lbs; Washington; B9/23/1981 Colorado Springs, CO **2004**†Den 16 (1) **2005** Den 10 (0) **NFL** 26 (1) [2 yrs]

ALEXANDER, ROGERS Rogers Bernard, LB, 6´3˝/222 lbs; Penn State; 1986: NYJ, rnd 4; B8/11/1964 Washington, DC **1986** NYJ 1 (0) **1987** NE 3 (2) **NFL** 4 (2) [2 yrs]

ALEXANDER, SHAUN Shaun, RB, 5´11˝/225 lbs; Alabama; 2000: Sea, rnd 1; B8/30/1977 Florence, KY

2000	Sea	16(1)	64	313	4.9(50)	2	5	41	8.2(18)	0	—	—	—	—	—	—	—	—	—	—	—	—	12	354
2001	Sea	16(12, RB)	309	1318	4.3(88)	14	44	343	7.8(28)	2	—	—	—	—	—	—	—	—	—	—	—	—	96	1640
2002	Sea	16(16, RB)	295	1175	4.0(58)	16	59	460	7.8(80)	2	—	—	—	—	—	—	—	—	—	—	—	—	108	1575
2003	†Sea◇	16(15, RB)	326	1435	4.4(55)	14	42	295	7.0(22)	2	—	—	—	—	—	—	—	—	—	—	—	—	96	1733
2004	†Sea★	16(16, RB)	353	1696	4.8(44)	16	23	170	7.4(24)	4	—	—	—	—	—	—	—	—	—	—	—	—	120	1961
2005	†Sea★	16(16, RB)	370	1880	5.1(88)	27	15	78	5.2(9)	1	—	—	—	—	—	—	—	—	—	—	—	—	168	2194
NFL	6	96(76)	1717	7817	4.6(88)	89	188	1387	7.4(80)	11	—	—	—	—	—	—	—	—	—	—	—	—	600	9456

ALEXANDER, STEPHEN — Stephen Todd, TE, 6´4˝/246 lbs; Oklahoma; 1998: Was, rnd 2; B11/7/1975 Chickasha, OK

YEAR	TEAM	G (GS, POS)	RUSH	YD	AVG(LG)	TD	REC	YD	AVG(LG)	TD	PASS	COMP	PCT	YD	AVG(LG)	TD	INT	SK	YD	QBR	KPR	OTD	PTS	TAY
1998	Was	15(5, te)	—	—	—	—	37	383	10.4(33)	4	—	—	—	—	—	—	—	—	—	—	—	—	24	212
1999	†Was	15(15, TE)	—	—	—	—	29	324	11.2(27)	3	—	—	—	—	—	—	—	—	—	—	—	—	18	177
2000	Was◇	16(16, TE)	—	—	—	—	47	510	10.9(30)	2	—	—	—	—	—	—	—	—	—	—	—	—	12	265
2001	Was	7(5, te)	—	—	—	—	9	85	9.4(21)	—	—	—	—	—	—	—	—	—	—	—	—	—	0	43
2002	SD	14(14, TE)	—	—	—	—	45	510	11.3(32)	1	—	—	—	—	—	—	—	—	—	—	—	—	6	260
2003	SD	3(0)	—	—	—	—	—	—	—	—	—	—	—	—	—	—	—	—	—	—	—	—	2	0
2004	Det	16(15, TE)	—	—	—	—	41	377	9.2(30)	1	—	—	—	—	—	—	—	—	—	—	—	—	6	194
2005	†Den	16(15, TE)	—	—	—	—	21	170	8.1(15)	1	—	—	—	—	—	—	—	—	—	—	—	—	6	90
NFL	8	102(85)	—	—	—	—	229	2359	10.3(33)	12	—	—	—	—	—	—	—	—	—	—	—	—	74	1240

ALEXANDER, VINCENT — Vincent Leon, RB, 5´10˝/205 lbs; Southern Mississippi; B3/11/1964 St. Tammany, LA

YEAR	TEAM	G (GS, POS)	RUSH	YD	AVG(LG)	TD	REC	YD	AVG(LG)	TD	PTS	TAY
1987	NO	1(0)	21	71	3.4(16)	1	2	15	7.5(10)	0	6	89

ALEXANDER, WILLIE — Willie James, DB, 6´2˝/194 lbs; Alcorn State; 1971: Hou, rnd 6; B9/21/1949 Montgomery, LA [I] 1971 Hou 14 (RCB) 1972 Hou 14 (LCB) 1973 Hou 11 (RCB) 1974 Hou 14 (LCB) 1975 Hou 14 (LCB) 1976 Hou 12 (LCB) 1977 Hou 14 (14, LCB) 1978†Hou 16 (16, LCB) 1979 Hou 13 NFL 122 (30) [9 yrs]

ALEXIS, ALTON — Alton, WR, 6´0˝/184 lbs; Tulane; 1980: Cin, rnd 11; B11/16/1957 New Iberia, LA 1980 Cin 1 (0)

ALEXIS, RICH — Rich, RB, 6´0˝/213 lbs; Washington; B3/6/1981 Coral Springs, FL, DJax 2005†Jax 2 (0)

ALFLEN, TED — Theodore Thomas, RB, 6´0˝/195 lbs; Springfield; B1/3/1947 Dunsmuir, CA 1969 Den-A 4

ALFONSE, JULIE — Julius, WB-TB-DB, 5´8˝/180 lbs; Minnesota; 1937: Cle, rnd 2; B10/12/1911 Cumberland, WI, D5/21/2000 Windsor, VT

YEAR	TEAM	G (GS, POS)	RUSH	YD	AVG(LG)	TD	REC	YD	AVG(LG)	TD	PASS	COMP	PCT	YD	AVG(LG)	TD	INT	SK	YD	QBR	KPR	OTD	PTS	TAY
1937	Cle	10(5, WB)	33	60	1.8	0	5	113	22.6	0	10	4	40.0	48	4.8	—	—	—	—	—	—	—	0	141
1938	Cle	10(6, WB)	16	16	1.0	0	2	47	23.5	0	2	2	100.0	19	9.5	0	0	—	—	—	—	2	12	49
NFL	2	20(11)	49	76	1.6	0	7	160	22.9	0	12	6	50.0	67	5.6	0	0	—	—	—	—	2	12	190

ALFORD, BRIAN — Brian Wayne, WR, 6´1˝/190 lbs; Purdue; 1998: NYG, rnd 3; B6/7/1975 Oak Park, MI

YEAR	TEAM	G (GS, POS)	RUSH	YD	AVG(LG)	TD	REC	YD	AVG(LG)	TD	PTS	TAY
1998	NYG	2(0)	—	—	—	—	1	11	11.0(11)	—	0	6
1999	NYG	2(0)	—	—	—	—	1	7	7.0(7)	1	6	9
NFL	2	4(0)	—	—	—	—	2	18	9.0(11)	1	6	14

ALFORD, BRUCE — Herbert Bruce, E-DB, 6´0˝/190 lbs; TCU; 1943: Phi, rnd 8; B9/12/1922 Waco, TX

YEAR	TEAM	G (GS, POS)	RUSH	YD	AVG(LG)	TD	REC	YD	AVG(LG)	TD	INT	SK	YD	QBR	KPR	OTD	PTS	TAY
1946	†NYY-A	13(10, RE)	—	—	—	—	13	173	13.3	—	—	—	—	—	k	—	0	134
1947	†NYY-A☆	13(13, RE)	—	—	—	—	20	298	14.9(52)	5	—	—	—	—	kpi	2	42	279
1948	NYY-A	14(10, RE)	—	—	—	—	32	578	18.1(57)	1	—	—	—	—	—	—	18	304
1949	†NYY-A	11(11, RE)	—	—	—	—	11	213	19.4	1	—	—	—	—	k	—	6	113
AAFC	4	51(44)	—	—	—	—	76	1262	16.6(57)	9	—	—	—	—	kpi	2	66	829
1950	NYY	12	—	—	—	—	1	14	14.0(14)	0	—	—	—	—	—	1	6	7
1951	NYY	12	—	—	—	—	4	65	16.3(59)	0	—	—	—	—	—	—	0	33
NFL	2	24	—	—	—	—	5	79	15.8(59)	0	—	—	—	—	—	1	6	40

ALFORD, BRUCE — Herbert Bruce, K, 6´0˝/190 lbs; TCU; 1967: Chi, rnd 5; B4/21/1945 Fort Worth, TX [K] 1967 Was 2 1968 Buf-A 11 1969 Buf-A 14 NFL 27 [3 yrs]

ALFORD, DARNELL — Darnell LaShawn, G, 6´4˝/328 lbs; Boston College; 2000: KC, rnd 6; B6/11/1977 Newark, NJ 2000 KC 1 (0) 2001 KC 2 (0) NFL 3 (0) [2 yrs]

ALFORD, GENE — Eugene Morris, WB-DB-BB-FB, 5´9˝/190 lbs; Sul Ross State; Texas Tech; B4/3/1905 Rising Star, TX, D12/1975 Ada, OK [K]

YEAR	TEAM	G (GS, POS)	RUSH	YD	AVG(LG)	TD	REC	YD	AVG(LG)	TD	PASS	COMP	PCT	YD	AVG(LG)	TD	INT	SK	YD	QBR	KPR	OTD	PTS	TAY
1931	Por	14(8, WB)	—	—	—	—	—	—	—	—	—	—	—	—	—	—	—	—	—	—	—	—	0	58
1932	Por	10(7, WB)	13	50	3.8	0	2	15	7.5	0	—	—	—	—	—	—	—	—	—	—	—	—	6	62
1933	Por	10(0)	18	59	3.3	0	2	76	38.0	1	6	0	0.0	0	0.0	0	1	—	—	—	—	—	0	7
1934	Cin	1(0)	2	7	3.5	0	—	—	—	—	—	—	—	—	—	—	—	—	—	—	—	—	0	7
1934	SL	3(1, WB)	7	20	2.9	0	1	7	7.0(7)	0	7	1	14.3	4	0.6(4)	0	1	—	—	—	K	—	6	-15
NFL	4	38(16)	40	136	3.4	1	5	98	19.6(7)	2	13	1	7.7	4	0.3(4)	0	2	—	—	—	K	—	24	127

ALFORD, LYNWOOD — Lynwood A., LB, 6´3˝/220 lbs; Syracuse; B8/22/1963 1987 NYJ 1 (0)

ALFORD, MIKE — Michael Deal, C, 6´3˝/230 lbs; Auburn; 1965: SL, rnd 14/KC, rnd 19; B6/19/1943 DeFuniak Springs, FL 1965 SL 13 1966 Det 12 NFL 25 [2 yrs]

ALFSON, WARREN — Warren Frank, G-LB, 6´0˝/198 lbs; Nebraska; 1941: Bkn, rnd 16; B5/10/1915 Wisner, NE, D6/4/2001 Wisner, NE 1941 Bkn 11 (11, LG)

ALIPATE, TUINEAU — Tuineau, LB, 6´1˝/245 lbs; Washington State; B8/21/1967, Tonga 1994 NYJ 8 (0) 1995 Min 16 (0) NFL 24 (0) [2 yrs]

ALLARD, DON — Donald J., QB, 6´1˝/188 lbs; Boston College; 1959: Was, rnd 1; B4/21/1936, D5/4/2002 Winchester, MA 1961 NYT-A 1 1962 Bos-A 4 NFL 5 [2 yrs]

ALLEGRE, RAUL — Raul Enrique, K, 5´9˝/165 lbs; Montana; Texas; B6/15/1959 Torreon, Mexico [K] 1983 Bal☆16 (0) 1984 Ind 12 (0) 1985 Ind 16 (0) 1986†NYG 13 (0) 1987 NYG 12 (0) 1988 NYG 6 (0) 1989†NYG 10 (0) 1990 NYG 3 (0) 1991 NYG 3 (0) 1991†NYJ 1 (0) NFL 92 (0) [9 yrs]

ALLEN, ANTHONY — Anthony Derrick, WR, 5´11˝/180 lbs; Washington; 1983: Atl, rnd 6; B6/29/1959 McComb, MS

YEAR	TEAM	G (GS, POS)	RUSH	YD	AVG(LG)	TD	REC	YD	AVG(LG)	TD	KPR	OTD	PTS	TAY
1985	Atl	16(2)	—	—	—	—	14	207	14.8(37)	2	kp	—	12	170
1986	Atl	5(2)	—	—	—	—	10	156	15.6(32)	2	p	—	12	88
1987	†Was	3(3)	—	—	—	—	13	337	25.9(88)	3	—	—	18	184
1988	Was	14(0)	—	—	—	—	5	48	9.6(18)	1	p	—	6	41
1989	SD	7(0)	—	—	—	—	2	19	9.5(11)	1	p	—	0	3
NFL	5	45(7)	—	—	—	—	44	767	17.4(88)	8	kp	—	48	485

ALLEN, BRIAN — Brian, RB, 5´9˝/205 lbs; Stanford; 2002: Ind, rnd 6; B4/20/1980 Ontario, CA 2003 Ind 4 (0)

ALLEN, BRIAN — Brian Lamar, LB, 6´0˝/232 lbs; Florida State; 2001: SL, rnd 3; B4/1/1978 Lake City, FL 2001 SL 3 (0) 2002 Car 16 (5, rlb) 2003†Car 14 (4) 2004 Car 14 (0) NFL 47 (9) [4 yrs]

ALLEN, BUDDY — Elihu, HB, 5´11˝/193 lbs; Utah State; 1960: Bos, rnd 1; B7/11/1937

YEAR	TEAM	G (GS, POS)	RUSH	YD	AVG(LG)	TD	REC	PTS	TAY
1961	Den-A	1	3	-4	-1.3(2)	0	—	0	-4

ALLEN, CARL — Carl Blanchard, RB-DB, 6´0˝/175 lbs; Ouachita Baptist; B6/25/1920 Haskell, OK, D7/3/1986 Portland, OR

YEAR	TEAM	G (GS, POS)	RUSH	YD	AVG(LG)	TD	REC	KPR	OTD	PTS	TAY
1948	Bkn-A	13(0)	1	9	9.0(9)	0	—	pi	1	6	66

ALLEN, CARL — Joseph Carl, DB, 6´0˝/185 lbs; Southern Mississippi; 1977: Cin, rnd 11; B12/21/1955 Hattiesburg, MS 1977 SL 14 (4) 1978 SL 15 (14, LCB) 1979 SL 15 (12, LCB) 1980 SL 16 (10, LCB) 1981 SL 10 (8, lcb) 1982†SL 9 (9, RCB) NFL 79 (57) [6 yrs]

ALLEN, CHUCK — Charles Richard, LB, 6´1˝/225 lbs; Washington; 1961: SD, rnd 28/LA, rnd 17; B9/7/1939 Cle Elum, WA [I] 1961 SD-A☆9 (MLB) 1962 SD-A☆14 (MLB) 1963†SD-A☆14 (MLB) 1964†SD-A★14 (RLB) 1965†SD-A 14 (MLB) 1966 SD-A 5 (mlb) 1967 SD-A 13 1968 SD-A 11 (MLB) 1969 SD-A 14 (MLB) 1970 Pit 14 (MLB) 1971 Pit 10 (MLB) 1972 Phi 12 (8, MLB) NFL 144 (8) [12 yrs]

ALLEN, DALVA — Dalva Ray, DE, 6´4˝/245 lbs; Houston; 1957: LA, rnd 23; B1/13/1935 Gonzales, TX 1960†Hou-A 14 (LDE) 1961†Hou-A 14 (LDE) 1962 Oak-A 14 (14, RDE) 1963 Oak-A☆14 (LDE) 1964 Oak-A 14 (LDE) NFL 70 (14) [5 yrs]

ALLEN, DAVID — David, RB, 5´9˝/195 lbs; Kansas State; B2/5/1978 Euless, TX [R]

YEAR	TEAM	G (GS, POS)	RUSH	YD	AVG(LG)	TD	REC	YD	AVG(LG)	TD	KPR	OTD	PTS	TAY
2003	Jax	14(0)	4	8	2.0(6)	0	6	60	10.0(31)	1	kp	—	6	448
2004	Jax	5(0)	—	—	—	—	2	8	4.0(5)	0	kp	—	0	118
2005	SL	4(0)	—	—	—	—	—	—	—	—	kp	—	0	130
NFL	3	23(0)	4	8	2.0(6)	0	8	68	8.5(31)	1	kp	—	6	696

ALLEN, DEREK — Derek Scott, G, 6´4˝/290 lbs; Illinois; B1/30/1971 Geneseo, IL 1995 NYG 1 (0)

ALLEN, DON — Donald Ray, FB, 6´0˝/200 lbs; Texas; B8/20/1939 Leon Co., TX

YEAR	TEAM	G (GS, POS)	RUSH	YD	AVG(LG)	TD	REC	YD	AVG(LG)	TD	KPR	PTS	TAY
1960	Den-A	10	30	18	0.6(4)	1	3	34	6.8(17)	0	k	6	42

ALLEN, DOUG — Douglas Ferguson, LB, 6´2˝/228 lbs; Penn State; 1974: Buf, rnd 2; B11/13/1951 Tampa, FL 1974†Buf 14 (8, LILB) 1975 Buf 14 (LILB) NFL 28 (8) [2 yrs]

ALLEN, DUANE — Duane Douglas, TE, 6´4˝/225 lbs; Mt.San Antonio J.C.; 1961: LA, rnd 9/1962: Den, rnd 33; B10/21/1937 Alhambra, CA, D5/7/2003 Pasadena, CA

YEAR	TEAM	G (GS, POS)	RUSH	YD	AVG(LG)	TD	REC	YD	AVG(LG)	TD	PTS	TAY
1961	LARm	10	—	—	—	—	2	80	40.0(48)	2	12	50
1962	LARm	7	—	—	—	—	3	90	30.0(43)	2	12	55

YEAR	TEAM	G (GS, POS)	RUSH	YD	AVG (LG)	TD	REC	YD	AVG (LG)	TD	PASS	COMP	PCT	YD	AVG (LG)	TD	INT	SK	YD	QBR	KPR	OTD	PTS	TAY
1963	LARm	7	—	—	—	—	—	—	—	—	—	—	—	—	—	—	—	—	—	—	—	—	—	—
1964	LARm	7	—	—	—	—	2	29	14.5(19)	1	—	—	—	—	—	—	—	—	—	—	—	—	6	20
1965	Pit	2	—	—	—	—	—	—	—	—	—	—	—	—	—	—	—	—	—	—	—	—	—	—
1966	ChiB	11	—	—	—	—	3	28	9.3(14)	0	—	—	—	—	—	—	—	—	—	—	—	—	0	14
1967	ChiB	5	—	—	—	—	—	—	—	—	—	—	—	—	—	—	—	—	—	—	—	—	—	—
NFL	7	49	—	—	—	—	10	227	22.7(48)	5	—	—	—	—	—	—	—	—	—	—	—	—	30	139

ALLEN, EARL Earl Edward, DB, 5´11˝/193 lbs; Michigan; Houston; B10/24/1961 Houston, TX **1987** Hou 1 (0)

ALLEN, ED Edmund Joseph, E, 5´8˝/175 lbs; Creighton; B6/5/1901 Dixon, IL, D2/20/1943 **1928** ChiC 2 (2)

ALLEN, EDDIE Edward Bostwic, FB-LB, 6´1˝/200 lbs; Pennsylvania; 1946: ChiB, rnd 11/1947: ChiR-A, rnd 7; B5/5/1920 Danville, NY

| 1947 | ChiB | 9(5, FB) | 12 | 16 | 1.3(7) | 0 | — | — | — | — | — | — | — | — | — | — | — | — | — | — | P | — | 0 | 16 |

ALLEN, EGYPT Egypt Tyrone, DB, 6´0˝/203 lbs; TCU; B7/28/1964 Dallas, TX **1987** ChiB 6 (3)

ALLEN, ERIC Eric Andre, DB, 5´10˝/184 lbs; Arizona State; 1988: Phi, rnd 2; B11/22/1965 San Diego, CA [I] **1988** Phi 16 (16, RCB) **1989**†Phi★15 (15, RCB)
1990†Phi 16 (15, RCB) **1991** Phi★16 (16, RCB) **1992**†Phi★16 (16, RCB) **1993** Phi★16 (16, RCB) **1994** Phi★16 (16, RCB) **1995** NO★16 (16, RCB) **1996** NO 16 (16, RCB)
1997 NO 16 (16, RCB) **1998** Oak 10 (10, RCB) **1999** Oak 16 (16, RCB) **2000**†Oak 16 (15, RCB) **2001** Oak 16 (15, RCB) **NFL** 217 (214) [14 yrs]

ALLEN, ERMAL Ermal Glen, QB-DB, 5´11˝/165 lbs; Kentucky; 1947: ChiR-A, rnd 10/ChiC, rnd 3; B12/25/1918 Kyles Ford, TN, D2/9/1988 Dallas, TX

| 1947 | †Cle-A | 12(0) | 7 | 11 | 1.6 | 0 | — | — | — | — | 13 | 4 | 30.8 | 88 | 6.8 | — | — | — | — | Ppi | — | 0 | 106 |

ALLEN, GARY Gary Eugene, RB, 5´10˝/183 lbs; Hawaii; 1982: Hou, rnd 6; B4/23/1960 Baldwin Park, CA **1983**†Dal 6 (0) **1984** Dal 16 (0)

1982	Hou	7(0)	2	2	1.0(9)	0	2	35	17.5(23)	1	—	—	—	—	—	—	—	—	—	—	k	—	6	92
1983	Hou	1(0)	1	5	5.0(5)	0	—	—	—	—	—	—	—	—	—	—	—	—	—	—	—	—	0	5
NFL	3	30(0)	3	7	2.3(9)	0	2	35	17.5(23)	1	—	—	—	—	—	—	—	—	—	—	kp	1	12	620

ALLEN, GEORGE George Robert, T, 6´7˝/270 lbs; West Texas A&M; 1966: Hou, rnd 4/Dal, rnd 17; B4/4/1944 Longview, TX **1966** Hou-A 9

ALLEN, GERRY Gerald, RB, 6´1˝/200 lbs; Nebraska-Omaha; 1966: Bal, rnd 8/NYJ, rnd 11; B6/26/1941 Canton, OH

1966	Bal	4	—	—	—	—	—	—	—	—	—	—	—	—	—	—	—	—	—	—	kp	—	0	3
1967	Was	11(FB)	77	262	3.4(30)	3	11	101	9.2(21)	1	—	—	—	—	—	—	—	—	—	—	k	—	24	346
1968	Was	11(HB)	123	399	3.2(20)	4	21	294	14.0(99)	1	—	—	—	—	—	—	—	—	—	—	—	—	30	591
1969	Was	2	1	3	3.0(3)	0	1	5	5.0(5)	0	—	—	—	—	—	—	—	—	—	—	—	—	0	6
NFL	4	28	201	664	3.3(30)	7	33	400	12.1(99)	2	—	—	—	—	—	—	—	—	—	—	kp	—	54	945

ALLEN, GRADY Grady Lynn, LB, 6´3˝/225 lbs; Texas A&M; B1/1/1946 St. Augustine, TX **1968** Atl 14 (LLB) **1969** Atl 14 (LLB) **1970** Atl 14 (LLB) **1971** Atl 3 **1972** Atl 14
NFL 59 [5 yrs]

ALLEN, GREG Gregory W., RB, 5´11˝/200 lbs; Florida State; 1985: Cle, rnd 2; B6/4/1963 Milton, FL

1985	Cle	7(0)	8	32	4.0(8)	0	—	—	—	—	—	—	—	—	—	—	—	—	—	—	k	—	0	21
1986	TB	2(0)	1	3	3.0(3)	0	—	—	—	—	—	—	—	—	—	—	—	—	—	—	k	—	0	9
NFL	2	9(0)	9	35	3.9(8)	0	—	—	—	—	—	—	—	—	—	—	—	—	—	—	k	—	0	30

ALLEN, HARVEY Harvey James, DB, 6´3˝/215 lbs; UNLV; B10/2/1964 **1987** Sea 2 (2)

ALLEN, IAN Ian Ramon, T, 6´4˝/310 lbs; Purdue; B7/22/1978 Newark, NJ **2002** NYG 3 (0) **2003** NYG 16 (11, RT) **2004** Phi 4 (0) **2005** Arz 2 (0) **NFL** 25 (11) [4 yrs]

ALLEN, JACKIE Jack Franklin, DB, 6´1˝/190 lbs; Baylor; 1969: Oak, rnd 6; B9/24/1947 Lawton, OK **1969** Oak-A 5 **1970** Buf 14 **1971** Buf 14 (FS) **1972** Phi 1 **NFL** 34 [4 yrs]

ALLEN, JAMES James, RB, 5´10˝/212 lbs; Oklahoma; B3/28/1975 Wynnewood, OK

1998	ChiB	6(2)	58	270	4.7(57)	1	8	77	9.6(33)	1	—	—	—	—	—	—	—	—	—	—	—	—	12	324
1999	ChiB	12(3)	32	119	3.7(13)	0	9	91	10.1(17)	0	—	—	—	—	—	—	—	—	—	—	—	—	0	165
2000	ChiB	16(15, RB)	290	1120	3.9(29)	2	39	291	7.5(26)	1	—	—	—	—	—	—	—	—	—	—	—	—	18	1291
2001	†ChiB	16(7, rb)	135	469	3.5(19)	1	30	203	6.8(34)	1	—	—	—	—	—	—	—	—	—	—	—	—	12	586
2002	Hou	16(5, rb)	155	519	3.3(32)	0	47	302	6.4(21)	0	2	1	50.0	5	2.5(5)	1	0	—	—	—	—	—	2	678
NFL	5	66(32)	670	2497	3.7(57)	4	133	964	7.2(34)	3	2	1	50.0	5	2.5(5)	1	0	—	—	—	—	—	44	3042

ALLEN, JAMES James Dshaune, LB, 6´2˝/240 lbs; Oregon State; 2002: NO, rnd 3; B11/11/1979 Portland, OR **2002** NO 14 (1) **2003** NO 15 (1) **2004** NO 16 (10, LLB)
2005 NO 3 (0) **NFL** 48 (12) [4 yrs]

ALLEN, JARED Jared Scot, DE, 6´6˝/265 lbs; Idaho State; 2004: KC, rnd 4; B4/3/1982 Los Gatos, CA **2004** KC 15 (10, RDE) **2005** KC 16 (15, RDE) **NFL** 31 (25) [2 yrs]

ALLEN, JEFF Jeffrey, DB, 5´11˝/190 lbs; California-Davis; 1980: Mia, rnd 8; B7/18/1957 Richmond, IN **1980** Mia 16 (0) **1982**†SD 9 (9, LCB) **NFL** 25 (9) [2 yrs]

ALLEN, JEFF Jeffery, DB, 5´11˝/190 lbs; Central Coll (IA); Iowa State; 1971: SL, rnd 13; B8/27/1948 Chicago, IL **1971** SL 1

ALLEN, JIMMY James Lee, DB, 6´2˝/194 lbs; Pierce Coll (CA); UCLA; 1974: Pit, rnd 4; B3/6/1952 Clearwater, FL [I] **1974**†Pit 14 (1) **1975**†Pit 14 **1976**†Pit 10 **1977**†Pit 12
1978 Det 14 (14, FS) **1979** Det 16 (14, SS) **1980** Det 15 (15, SS) **1981** Det 15 (15, FS) **NFL** 110 (59) [8 yrs]

ALLEN, JOHNNY John McKee, C-LB, 6´2˝/224 lbs; Purdue; 1955: Was, rnd 8; B6/4/1933 Monmouth, IL **1955** Was 12 **1956** Was 12 (C) **1957** Was 12 (c) **1958** Was 12 (RLB)
NFL 48 [4 yrs]

ALLEN, KENDERICK Kenderick, DT, 6´6˝/318 lbs; LSU; B9/14/1978 Bogalusa, LA **2003** NO 10 (1) **2004** NYG 5 (2) **2005**†NYG 14 (0) **NFL** 29 (3) [3 yrs]

ALLEN, KEVIN Kevin Eugene, T, 6´5˝/285 lbs; Indiana; 1985: Phi, rnd 1; B6/21/1963 Cincinnati, OH **1985** Phi 16 (4)

ALLEN, LARRY Larry Christopher, G-T, 6´3˝/325 lbs; Butte Coll (CA); Sonoma State; 1994: Dal, rnd 2; B11/27/1971 Los Angeles, CA **1994**†Dal 16 (10, RT) **1995**†Dal★16 (16, RG)
1996†Dal★16 (16, RG) **1997** Dal★16 (16, RG) **1998**†Dal★16 (16, LT) **1999**†Dal★11 (11, LG) **2000** Dal★16 (16, LG) **2001** Dal★16 (16, LG) **2002** Dal 5 (5, lg)
2003†Dal◇16 (16, LG) **2004** Dal◇16 (16, LG) **2005** Dal◇16 (16, LG) **NFL** 176 (170) [12 yrs]

ALLEN, LOU Louis Eugene, T, 6´3˝/215 lbs; Duke; 1950: Pit, rnd 5; B7/12/1924 Gadsden, AL **1950** Pit 12 (LT) **1951** Pit 12 (LT) **NFL** 24 [2 yrs]

ALLEN, LYNN Lynn, WB, Detroit Mercy; deceased **1920** Det 2 (0)

ALLEN, MARCUS Marcus LeMarr, RB, 6´2˝/210 lbs; USC; 1982: LARd, rnd 1; B3/26/1960 San Diego, CA; HOF 2003

1982	†LARd★	9(9, RB)	160	697	4.4(53)	11	38	401	10.6(51)	3	4	1	25.0	47	11.8(47)	0	0	—	—	—	—	—	84	1046
1983	†LARd	16(15, RB)	266	1014	3.8(19)	9	68	590	8.7(36)	2	7	4	57.1	111	15.9(43)	3	0	3	26	—	—	1	72	1480
1984	†LARd★	16(16, RB)	275	1168	4.2(52)	13	64	758	11.8(92)	5	4	1	25.0	38	9.5(38)	0	0	1	2	—	—	—	108	1721
1985	†LARd★	16(16, RB)	380	1759	4.6(61)	11	67	555	8.3(44)	3	2	1	50.0	16	8.0(16)	0	0	—	—	—	—	—	84	2170
1986	LARd★	13(10, RB)	208	759	3.6(20)	5	46	453	9.8(36)	2	—	—	—	—	—	—	—	—	—	—	—	—	42	1046
1987	LARd◇	12(12, RB)	200	754	3.8(44)	5	51	410	8.0(39)	0	2	1	50.0	23	11.5(23)	0	0	1	3	—	—	—	30	1021
1988	LARd	15(15, RB)	223	831	3.7(32)	7	34	303	8.9(30)	1	2	1	50.0	21	10.5(21)	0	0	1	1	—	—	—	48	1068
1989	LARd	8(5, rb)	69	293	4.2(15)	2	20	191	9.6(26)	0	—	—	—	—	—	—	—	—	—	—	—	—	12	409
1990	†LARd	16(15, RB)	179	682	3.8(28)	12	15	189	12.6(30)	1	1	0	0.0	0	—	0	0	—	—	—	—	—	78	862
1991	†LARd	8(2)	63	287	4.6(26)	2	15	131	8.7(25)	1	2	1	50.0	11	5.5(11)	1	0	—	—	—	—	—	12	383
1992	LARd	16	67	301	4.5(21)	2	28	277	9.9(40)	1	—	—	—	—	—	—	—	—	—	—	—	—	18	465
1993	†KC★	16(10, RB)	206	764	3.7(39)	12	34	238	7.0(18)	3	—	—	—	—	—	—	—	—	—	—	—	—	90	1018
1994	†KC	13(13, RB)	189	709	3.8(36)	7	42	349	8.3(38)	0	—	—	—	—	—	—	—	—	—	—	—	—	44	954
1995	†KC	16(15, RB)	207	890	4.3(38)	5	27	210	7.8(20)	0	—	—	—	—	—	—	—	—	—	—	—	—	30	1045
1996	KC	16(15, RB)	206	830	4.0(35)	9	27	270	10.0(59)	0	—	—	—	—	—	—	—	—	—	—	—	—	54	1055
1997	†KC	16(0)	124	505	4.1(30)	11	11	86	7.8(18)	0	2	2	100.0	15	7.5(14)	2	0	—	—	—	—	—	66	676
NFL	16	222(168)	3022	12243	4.1(61)	123	587	5411	9.2(92)	21	27	12	44.4	282	10.4(47)	6	1	6	32	—	—	1	872	16415

ALLEN, MARVIN Marvin Ray, RB, 5´10˝/215 lbs; Tulane; 1988: NE, rnd 11; B11/23/1965 Wichita Falls, TX

1988	NE	11(0)	7	40	5.7(12)	0	—	—	—	—	—	—	—	—	—	—	—	—	—	—	k	—	0	161
1989	NE	3(0)	11	51	4.6(18)	1	—	—	—	—	—	—	—	—	—	—	—	—	—	—	k	—	6	95
1990	NE	8(3)	63	237	3.8(29)	1	6	48	8.0(19)	0	—	—	—	—	—	—	—	—	—	—	k	—	6	274
1991	NE	15(0)	13	50	3.8(11)	0	1	9	9.0(9)	0	—	—	—	—	—	—	—	—	—	—	k	—	0	96
NFL	4	37(3)	94	378	4.0(29)	2	7	57	8.1(19)	0	—	—	—	—	—	—	—	—	—	—	k	—	12	626

Allen, Matt Matt, P, 6´2˝/246 lbs; Troy State; B10/23/1977 Montgomery, AL

YEAR	TEAM	G(GS, POS)	RUSH	YD	AVG(LG)	TD	REC	YD	AVG(LG)	TD	PASS	COMP	PCT	YD	AVG(LG)	TD	INT	SK	YD	QBR	KPR	OTD	PTS	TAY
2002	†NYG	14(0)	3	23	7.7(13)	0	—	—	—	—	—	—	—	—	—	—	—	—	—	—	P	—	0	23

Allen, Nate Nathaniel Sheraldton, DB, 5´10˝/170 lbs; Texas Southern; 1971: KC, rnd 11; B5/13/1948 Georgetown, SC **1971** KC 4 **1973** KC 14 (LCB) **1974** KC 12 (LCB) **1975** SF 14 (3) **1976†**Min 12 (11, RCB) **1977†**Min 14 **1978†**Min 16 **1979** Min 5 **1979** Det 3

YEAR	TEAM	G(GS, POS)	RUSH	YD	AVG(LG)	TD	REC	YD	AVG(LG)	TD	PASS	COMP	PCT	YD	AVG(LG)	TD	INT	SK	YD	QBR	KPR	OTD	PTS	TAY
1972	KC	14	—	—	—	—	1	20	20.0(20)	0	—	—	—	—	—	—	—	—	—	—	i	—	0	9
NFL	9	108(14)	—	—	—	—	1	20	20.0(20)	0	—	—	—	—	—	—	—	—	—	—	pi	2	12	114

Allen, Patrick Lloyd Patrick, DB, 5´10˝/180 lbs; Utah State; 1984: Hou, rnd 4; B8/26/1961 Seattle, WA **1984** Hou 16 (0) **1985** Hou 16 (16, RCB) **1986** Hou 16 (16, RCB) **1987†**Hou 11 (11, RCB) **1988†**Hou 15 (13, RCB) **1989†**Hou 16 (16, RCB) **1990†**Hou 16 (0) **NFL** 106 (72) [7 yrs]

Allen, Taje Taje LaQuane, DB, 5´10˝/185 lbs; Texas; 1997: SL, rnd 5; B11/6/1973 Lubbock, TX **1997** SL 14 (1) **1998** SL 16 (0) **1999†**SL 16 (2) **2000†**SL 11 (1) **2001** KC 16 (0) **2002** KC 6 (0) **NFL** 79 (4) [6 yrs]

Allen, Terry Terry Thomas, RB, 5´10˝/204 lbs; Clemson; 1990: Min, rnd 9; B2/21/1968 Commerce, GA

YEAR	TEAM	G(GS, POS)	RUSH	YD	AVG(LG)	TD	REC	YD	AVG(LG)	TD	PASS	COMP	PCT	YD	AVG(LG)	TD	INT	SK	YD	QBR	KPR	OTD	PTS	TAY
1991	Min	15(6, FB)	120	563	**4.7(55)**	2	6	49	8.2(21)	1	—	—	—	—	—	—	—	—	—	—	k	—	18	612
1992	†Min	16(16, RB)	266	1201	4.5(51)	13	49	478	9.8(36)	2	—	—	—	—	—	—	—	—	—	—	—	—	90	1580
1994	†Min☆	16(16, RB)	255	1031	4.0(45)	8	17	148	8.7(31)	0	—	—	—	—	—	—	—	—	—	—	—	—	50	1185
1995	Was☆	16(16, RB)	338	1309	3.9(28)	10	31	232	7.5(24)	1	—	—	—	—	—	—	—	—	—	—	—	—	66	1530
1996	Was★	16(16, RB)	347	1353	3.9(49)	**21**	32	194	6.1(28)	0	—	—	—	—	—	—	—	—	—	—	—	—	126	1660
1997	Was	10(10, RB)	210	724	3.4(34)	4	20	172	8.6(38)	1	—	—	—	—	—	—	—	—	—	—	—	—	30	855
1998	Was	10(10, RB)	148	700	4.7(45)	2	17	128	7.5(17)	0	—	—	—	—	—	—	—	—	—	—	—	—	12	784
1999	NE	16(13, RB)	254	896	3.5(39)	8	14	125	8.9(38)	1	—	—	—	—	—	—	—	—	—	—	—	—	54	1044
2000	†NO	4(3)	46	179	3.9(18)	2	1	7	7.0(7)	0	—	—	—	—	—	—	—	—	—	—	—	—	14	209
2001	†Bal	11(8, RB)	168	658	3.9(26)	3	17	68	4.0(11)	0	—	—	—	—	—	—	—	—	—	—	—	—	18	722
NFL	10	130(114)	2152	8614	4.0(55)	73	204	1601	7.8(38)	6	—	—	—	—	—	—	—	—	—	—	k	—	478	10180

Allen, Tremayne Tremayne Aubrey, TE, 6´2˝/234 lbs; Florida; B8/9/1974 Nashville, TN

YEAR	TEAM	G(GS, POS)	RUSH	YD	AVG(LG)	TD	REC	YD	AVG(LG)	TD	PASS	COMP	PCT	YD	AVG(LG)	TD	INT	SK	YD	QBR	KPR	OTD	PTS	TAY
1997	ChiB	2(0)	—	—	—	—	1	9	9.0(9)	0	—	—	—	—	—	—	—	—	—	—	—	—	0	5

Allen, Will Will D., DB, 5´10˝/196 lbs; Syracuse; 2001: NYG, rnd 1; B8/5/1978 Syracuse, NY **2001** NYG 13 (12, LCB) **2002†**NYG 15 (15, LCB) **2003** NYG 12 (12, LCB) **2004** NYG 16 (16, LCB) **2005†**NYG 16 (16, LCB) **NFL** 72 (71) [5 yrs]

Allen, Will Will, DB, 6´1˝/202 lbs; Ohio State; 2004: TB, rnd 4; B6/17/1982 Dayton, OH **2004** TB 16 (0) **2005†**TB 13 (8, fs) **NFL** 29 (8) [2 yrs]

Allerman, Kurt Kurt Daniel, LB, 6´3˝/222 lbs; Penn State; 1977: SL, rnd 3; B8/30/1955 Glen Ridge, NJ **1977** SL 14 **1978** SL 15 (9, RILB) **1979** SL 16 (11, RILB) **1980** GB 13 (11, RILB/lilb) **1981** GB 16 (0) **1982†**SL 9 (0) **1983** SL 16 (8, mlb) **1984** SL 16 (10, MLB) **1985** Det 10 (7, RILB) **NFL** 125 (56) [9 yrs]

Allert, Ty Ty Hunter, LB, 6´2˝/233 lbs; Texas; 1986: SD, rnd 4; B7/23/1963 Rosenberg, TX **1986** SD 16 (3) **1987** SD 3 (0) **1987** Phi 7 (0) **1988†**Phi 10 (0) **1989** Phi 7 (0) **1990** Den 7 (0) **1990** Sea 1 (0) **NFL** 51 (3) [5 yrs]

Alley, Don Donald Wayne, WR, 6´2˝/200 lbs; Adams State; 1967: Bal, rnd 16; B4/21/1945 Cheyenne, WY

YEAR	TEAM	G(GS, POS)	RUSH	YD	AVG(LG)	TD	REC	YD	AVG(LG)	TD	PASS	COMP	PCT	YD	AVG(LG)	TD	INT	SK	YD	QBR	KPR	OTD	PTS	TAY
1967	Bal	10	—	—	—	—	1	11	11.0(11)	0	—	—	—	—	—	—	—	—	—	—	—	—	0	6
1969	Pit	8	—	—	—	—	1	16	16.0(16)	0	—	—	—	—	—	—	—	—	—	—	—	—	0	8
NFL	2	18	—	—	—	—	2	27	13.5(16)	0	—	—	—	—	—	—	—	—	—	—	—	—	0	14

Allison, Henry Henry Henderson, G-T, 6´3˝/255 lbs; Coll. Of the Sequoias (CA); San Diego State; 1971: Phi, rnd 2; B2/11/1947 Stevenson, AL **1971** Phi 14 (LG) **1972** Phi 6 **1975** SL 14 **1976** SL 10 **1977** SL 8 **1977†**Den 3 **NFL** 55 [5 yrs]

Allison, Jim James Russell, RB, 6´0˝/215 lbs; El Camino Coll (CA); San Diego State; 1965: SD, rnd 12; B3/2/1943 Richmond, CA

YEAR	TEAM	G(GS, POS)	RUSH	YD	AVG(LG)	TD	REC	YD	AVG(LG)	TD	PASS	COMP	PCT	YD	AVG(LG)	TD	INT	SK	YD	QBR	KPR	OTD	PTS	TAY
1965	†SD-A	14	29	100	3.4(17)	0	8	109	13.6(44)	0	—	—	—	—	—	—	—	—	—	—	Pk	—	0	175
1966	SD-A	14	31	213	6.9(61)	2	12	99	8.3(20)	0	—	—	—	—	—	—	—	—	—	—	—	—	12	283
1967	SD-A	3	10	34	3.4(26)	0	—	—	—	—	—	—	—	—	—	—	—	—	—	—	—	—	0	34
1968	SD-A	12	23	31	1.3(6)	0	2	22	11.0(12)	0	1	1	100.0	23	23.0(23)	1	0	—	—	—	kp	—	0	75
NFL	4	43	93	378	4.1(61)	2	22	230	10.5(44)	0	1	1	100.0	23	23.0(23)	1	0	—	—	—	Pkp	—	12	566

Allison, Neely James Neely, E, 6´0˝/190 lbs; Texas A&M; B5/14/1902 Ballinger, TX, D2/21/1970 Houston, TX **1926** Buf 9 (7, LE), 6 **1927** Buf 2 (2) **1928** NYG 13 (13, LE) **NFL** 24 (22) [3 yrs]

Alliston, Buddy Vaughn Samuel, LB, 6´0˝/218 lbs; Mississippi; 1956: GB, rnd 15; B12/14/1933 Jackson, MS **1960** Den-A 11

Allman, Bob Robert M., E, 6´0˝/198 lbs; Michigan State; 1936: ChiB, rnd 4; B2/28/1913, D8/14/1995 Springfield, MI **1936** ChiB 1 (0)

Allred, Brian Brian McCray, DB, 5´10˝/175 lbs; Sacramento State; B3/16/1969 Washington, DC **1993** Sea 4 (0)

Allred, John John, TE, 6´4˝/249 lbs; USC; 1997: Chi, rnd 2; B9/9/1974 Del Mar, CA

YEAR	TEAM	G(GS, POS)	RUSH	YD	AVG(LG)	TD	REC	YD	AVG(LG)	TD	PASS	COMP	PCT	YD	AVG(LG)	TD	INT	SK	YD	QBR	KPR	OTD	PTS	TAY
1997	ChiB	15(4)	—	—	—	—	8	70	8.8(18)	0	—	—	—	—	—	—	—	—	—	—	k	—	0	26
1998	ChiB	4(0)	—	—	—	—	—	—	—	—	—	—	—	—	—	—	—	—	—	—	—	—	—	—
1999	ChiB	16(5, te)	—	—	—	—	13	102	7.8(26)	1	—	—	—	—	—	—	—	—	—	—	—	—	6	56
2000	ChiB	5(3)	—	—	—	—	9	109	12.1(25)	1	—	—	—	—	—	—	—	—	—	—	—	—	6	60
2002	†Pit	13(0)	—	—	—	—	—	—	—	—	—	—	—	—	—	—	—	—	—	—	k	—	0	-8
NFL	5	53(12)	—	—	—	—	30	281	9.4(26)	2	—	—	—	—	—	—	—	—	—	—	k	—	12	134

Allton, Joe Joseph J., T, 6´2˝/235 lbs; Oklahoma; B9/7/1920 Claremore, OK, D2/26/1989 Claremore, OK **1942** ChiC 11 (3)

Alm, Jeff Jeffrey Lawrence, DT, 6´6˝/284 lbs; Notre Dame; 1990: Hou, rnd 2; B3/31/1968 New York, NY, D12/14/1993 Houston, TX **1990†**Hou 16 (0) **1991†**Hou 12 (1) **1992** Hou 14 (7, RDT) **1993** Hou 2 (0) **NFL** 44 (8) [4 yrs]

Almodobar, Beau Beau, WR, 5´9˝/180 lbs; Norwich; B10/25/1962 **1987** NYG 2 (0)

Alphin, Gerald Gerald Alan, WR, 6´3˝/220 lbs; Kansas State; B5/21/1964 Portland, OR **1991** NO 5 (0)

YEAR	TEAM	G(GS, POS)	RUSH	YD	AVG(LG)	TD	REC	YD	AVG(LG)	TD	PASS	COMP	PCT	YD	AVG(LG)	TD	INT	SK	YD	QBR	KPR	OTD	PTS	TAY
1990	NO	11(0)	—	—	—	—	4	57	14.3(17)	0	—	—	—	—	—	—	—	—	—	—	—	—	0	29
NFL	2	16(0)	—	—	—	—	4	57	14.3(17)	0	—	—	—	—	—	—	—	—	—	—	—	—	0	29

Alston, Lyneal Lyneal, WR, 6´1˝/205 lbs; Southern Mississippi; B7/23/1964 Mobile, AL

YEAR	TEAM	G(GS, POS)	RUSH	YD	AVG(LG)	TD	REC	YD	AVG(LG)	TD	PASS	COMP	PCT	YD	AVG(LG)	TD	INT	SK	YD	QBR	KPR	OTD	PTS	TAY
1987	Pit	3(1)	—	—	—	—	3	84	28.0(42)	2	—	—	—	—	—	—	—	—	—	—	—	—	12	52

Alston, Mack Mack C., TE, 6´2˝/230 lbs; Maryland-Eastern Shore; 1970: Was, rnd 11; B4/27/1947 Georgetown, SC

YEAR	TEAM	G(GS, POS)	RUSH	YD	AVG(LG)	TD	REC	YD	AVG(LG)	TD	PASS	COMP	PCT	YD	AVG(LG)	TD	INT	SK	YD	QBR	KPR	OTD	PTS	TAY
1970	Was	8	—	—	—	—	—	—	—	—	—	—	—	—	—	—	—	—	—	—	—	—	—	—
1971	Was	12(7, te)	—	—	—	—	5	87	17.4(21)	0	—	—	—	—	—	—	—	—	—	—	—	—	0	44
1972	†Was	14	—	—	—	—	2	53	26.5(36)	0	—	—	—	—	—	—	—	—	—	—	—	—	0	27
1973	Hou	14(TE)	1	13	13.0(13)	0	19	195	10.3(39)	4	—	—	—	—	—	—	—	—	—	—	—	—	24	131
1974	Hou	13(TE)	1	-3	-3.0(-3)	0	17	249	14.6(33)	3	—	—	—	—	—	—	—	—	—	—	—	—	18	137
1975	Hou	13(TE)	—	—	—	—	18	165	9.2(26)	4	—	—	—	—	—	—	—	—	—	—	—	—	24	103
1976	Hou	14(TE)	—	—	—	—	19	174	9.2(29)	1	—	—	—	—	—	—	—	—	—	—	—	—	6	92
1977	†Bal	14	—	—	—	—	—	—	—	—	—	—	—	—	—	—	—	—	—	—	—	—	—	—
1978	Bal	16(13, TE)	—	—	—	—	18	210	11.7(23)	2	—	—	—	—	—	—	—	—	—	—	—	—	12	115
1979	Bal	14(4)	—	—	—	—	10	114	11.4(26)	1	—	—	—	—	—	—	—	—	—	—	—	—	6	62
1980	Bal	13(0)	—	—	—	—	—	—	—	—	—	—	—	—	—	—	—	—	—	—	—	—	—	—
NFL	11	145(24)	2	10	5.0(13)	0	108	1247	11.5(39)	15	—	—	—	—	—	—	—	—	—	—	—	—	90	709

Alston, O'Brien O'Brien Darwin, LB, 6´6˝/246 lbs; Maryland; 1988: Ind, rnd 10; B12/21/1965 New Haven, CT **1988** Ind 15 (11, LOLB) **1989** Ind 4 (4) **NFL** 19 (15) [2 yrs]

Alston, Richard Richard, WR, 6´0˝/213 lbs; East Carolina; B11/20/1980 Warrenton, NC **2004** Cle 9 (0)

Alstott, Mike Michael Joseph, RB, 6´1˝/248 lbs; Purdue; 1996: TB, rnd 2; B12/21/1973 Joliet, IL

YEAR	TEAM	G(GS, POS)	RUSH	YD	AVG(LG)	TD	REC	YD	AVG(LG)	TD	PASS	COMP	PCT	YD	AVG(LG)	TD	INT	SK	YD	QBR	KPR	OTD	PTS	TAY
1996	TB☆	16(16, FB)	96	377	3.9(39)	3	65	557	8.6(29)	3	—	—	—	—	—	—	—	—	—	—	k	—	36	700
1997	†TB★	15(15, FB)	176	665	3.8(47)	7	23	178	7.7(26)	3	—	—	—	—	—	—	—	—	—	—	k	—	60	824
1998	TB★	16(16, FB)	215	846	3.9(37)	8	22	152	6.9(26)	1	1	0	0.0	0	0.0	0	0	—	—	—	k	—	54	1000
1999	†TB★	16(16, FB)	242	949	3.9(30)	7	27	239	8.9(24)	2	—	—	—	—	—	—	—	—	—	—	k	—	54	1153
2000	†TB✧	13(13, FB)	131	465	3.5(20)	5	13	93	7.2(21)	0	1	0	0.0	0	0.0	0	0	—	—	—	—	—	30	562

YEAR	TEAM	G (GS, POS)	RUSH	YD	AVG (LG)	TD	REC	YD	AVG (LG)	TD	PASS	COMP	PCT	YD	AVG (LG)	TD	INT	SK	YD	QBR	KPR	OTD	PTS	TAY
2001	†TB✧	16 (16, FB)	165	680	4.1 (39)	10	35	231	6.6 (19)	1	—	—	—	—	—	—	—	—	—	—	—	—	70	901
2002	†TB✧	16 (9, FB)	146	548	3.8 (32)	5	35	242	6.9 (44)	2	—	—	—	—	—	—	—	—	—	—	—	—	42	729
2003	TB	4 (3)	27	77	2.9 (29)	2	10	83	8.3 (17)	0	—	—	—	—	—	—	—	—	—	—	—	—	12	139
2004	TB	14 (11, FB)	67	230	3.4 (32)	2	29	202	7.0 (20)	0	—	—	—	—	—	—	—	—	—	—	—	—	12	351
2005	†TB	16 (7, fb)	34	80	2.4 (9)	6	25	222	8.9 (24)	1	—	—	—	—	—	—	—	—	—	—	k	—	44	243
NFL	10	142 (122)	1299	4917	3.8 (47)	55	284	2199	7.7 (44)	13	2	0	0.0	0	0.0	0	0	—	—	—	k	—	414	6600

ALT, JOHN John Michael, T, 6´8˝/298 lbs; Iowa; 1984: KC, rnd 1; B5/30/1962 Stuttgart, Germany **1984** KC 15 (1) **1985** KC 13 (6, lt) **1986**†KC 7 (0) **1987** KC 9 (9, LT) **1988** KC 14 (13, LT) **1989** KC☆16 (16, LT) **1990**†KC☆16 (16, LT) **1991**†KC☆16 (16, LT) **1992**†KC✧16 (16, LT) **1993**†KC✧16 (16, LT) **1994**†KC 13 (13, LT) **1995**†KC 16 (16, LT) **1996** KC 12 (11, LT) **NFL** 179 (149) [13 yrs]

ALTHOFF, JIM James, DT, 6´3˝/278 lbs; Winona State; B9/27/1961 McHenry, IL **1987** ChiB 4 (3)

ALVAREZ, WILSON Wilson, K, 6´0˝/165 lbs; New Mexico Mil Inst; Coll. Of the Sequoias (CA); Southeastern Louisiana; B3/22/1957 Santa Cruz, Bolivia **[K]** **1981** Sea 4 (0)

ALVERS, STEVE Steven Dean, TE-C, 6´4˝/240 lbs; Taft Coll. (CA); Miami (Fl); 1979: NYG, rnd 7; B4/4/1957 Palm Beach, FL **1981**†Buf 16 (0) **1982** NYJ 3 (0) **NFL** 19 (0) [2 yrs]

ALVORD, STEVE Steven Lee, DT, 6´4˝/272 lbs; Washington; 1987: SL, rnd 8; B10/2/1964 Bellingham, WA **1987** SL 12 (6, RDT) **1988** Phx 15 (10, RDT) **NFL** 27 (16) [2 yrs]

ALWARD, TOM Thomas Lavern, G, 6´4˝/255 lbs; Nebraska; 1975: NYJ, rnd 6; B10/13/1952 Flint, MI **1976** TB 14 (9, RG)

ALWORTH, LANCE Lance Dwight 'Bambi', FL-WR, 6´0˝/184 lbs; Arkansas; 1962: Oak, rnd 2/SF, rnd 1; B8/3/1940 Houston, TX; HOF 1978

YEAR	TEAM	G (GS, POS)	RUSH	YD	AVG (LG)	TD	REC	YD	AVG (LG)	TD	PASS	COMP	PCT	YD	AVG (LG)	TD	INT	SK	YD	QBR	KPR	OTD	PTS	TAY
1962	SD-A	4	1	17	17.0 (17)	0	10	226	22.6 (67)	3	—	—	—	—	—	—	—	—	—	—	—	—	18	145
1963	†SD-A★	14 (FL)	2	14	7.0 (21)	0	61	1205	19.8 (85)	11	—	—	—	—	—	—	—	—	—	—	kp	—	66	803
1964	SD-A★	12 (FL)	3	60	20.0 (35)	2	61	1235	20.2 (82)	**13**	1	1	100.0	11	-11.0 (-11)	0	0	—	—	—	p	—	90	856
1965	†SD-A★	14 (FL)	3	-12	-4.0 (-1)	0	69	**1602**	**23.2 (85)**	**14**	—	—	—	—	—	—	—	—	—	—	—	—	84	859
1966	SD-A★	13 (FL)	3	10	3.3 (4)	0	**73**	**1383**	18.9 (78)	**13**	—	—	—	—	—	—	—	—	—	—	—	—	78	767
1967	SD-A★	11 (FL)	1	5	5.0 (5)	0	52	1010	19.4 (71)	9	1	0	0.0	0	0.0	0	0	—	—	—	—	—	54	555
1968	SD-A★	14 (FL)	3	18	6.0 (10)	0	**68**	**1312**	19.3 (80)	10	—	—	—	—	—	—	—	—	—	—	—	—	62	724
1969	SD-A★	14 (FL)	5	25	5.0 (16)	0	**64**	1003	15.7 (76)	4	—	—	—	—	—	—	—	—	—	—	—	—	24	547
1970	SD	14 (WR)	—	—	—	—	35	608	17.4 (80)	4	—	—	—	—	—	—	—	—	—	—	—	—	24	324
1971	†Dal	12 (11, WR)	2	-10	-5.0 (-4)	0	34	487	14.3 (26)	2	—	—	—	—	—	—	—	—	—	—	—	—	12	244
1972	†Dal	14 (7, WR)	1	2	2.0 (2)	0	15	195	13.0 (30)	2	—	—	—	—	—	—	—	—	—	—	—	—	12	110
NFL	11	136 (18)	24	129	5.4 (35)	2	542	10266	18.9 (85)	85	2	1	50.0	11	-5.5	0	0	—	—	—	kp	—	524	5932

ALZADO, LYLE Lyle Martin 'Darth Raider', DE-DT, 6´3˝/255 lbs; Yankton; 1971: Den, rnd 4; B4/3/1949 Brooklyn, NY, D5/14/1992 Portland, OR **1971** Den 12 (11, RDE) **1972** Den 14 (14, RDE) **1973** Den 14 (14, RDE) **1974** Den 14 (14, RDE) **1975** Den 14 (14, RDE) **1976** Den 1 (1) **1977**†Den★14 (14, RDE) **1978**†Den★16 (16, RDE) **1979** Cle☆15 (LDE) **1980**†Cle☆16 (15, RDE) **1981** Cle 15 (15, RDE) **1982**†LARd☆9 (9, RDE) **1983**†LARd 15 (15, RDE) **1984**†LARd 16 (16, RDE) **1985** LARd 11 (11, RDE) **NFL** 196 (179) [15 yrs]

AMANO, EUGENE Eugene, C, 6´4˝/315 lbs; Southeast Missouri State; 2004: Ten, rnd 7; B8/1/1982 San Pedro, CA **2004** Ten 15 (2) **2005** Ten 16 (0) **NFL** 31 (2) [2 yrs]

AMATO, KEN Kenneth Carlos, C, 6´2˝/245 lbs; Montana State; B5/18/1977, Puerto Rico **2003** Ten 16 (0) **2004** Ten 16 (0) **2005** Ten 7 (0) **NFL** 39 (0) [3 yrs]

AMBERG, JOHN John McCaslin, DB-HB, 5´11˝/195 lbs; Kansas; B3/6/1929 Johnson County, KS, D5/4/2004 Los Angeles County, CA

YEAR	TEAM	G (GS, POS)	RUSH	YD	AVG (LG)	TD	REC	YD	AVG (LG)	TD	PASS	COMP	PCT	YD	AVG (LG)	TD	INT	SK	YD	QBR	KPR	OTD	PTS	TAY
1951	NYG	12 (DB)	7	35	5.0 (8)	0	—	—	—	—	—	—	—	—	—	—	—	—	—	—	i	—	0	58
1952	NYG	12 (DB)	7	27	3.9 (9)	0	3	40	13.3 (18)	0	—	—	—	—	—	—	—	—	—	—	i	—	0	55
NFL	2	24	14	62	4.4 (9)	0	3	40	13.3 (18)	0	—	—	—	—	—	—	—	—	—	—	i	—	0	113

AMBROSE, ASHLEY Ashley Avery, DB, 5´11˝/190 lbs; Mississippi Valley State; 1992: Ind, rnd 2; B9/17/1970 New Orleans, LA **[I]** **1992** Ind 10 (2) **1993** Ind 14 (6, lcb) **1994** Ind 16 (4) **1995**†Ind 16 (0) **1996** Cin★16 (16, LCB) **1997** Cin 16 (16, LCB) **1998** Cin 15 (15, LCB) **1999** NO 16 (16, LCB) **2000** Atl 16 (16, RCB) **2001** Atl 16 (16, RCB) **2002**†Atl 16 (16, RCB) **2003** NO 16 (12, LCB) **2004** NO 9 (6, lcb) **NFL** 192 (141) [13 yrs]

AMBROSE, DICK Richard John, LB, 6´0˝/235 lbs; Virginia; 1975: Cle, rnd 12; B1/17/1953 New Rochelle, NY **1975** Cle 14 (10, MLB) **1976** Cle 10 (2) **1977** Cle 14 (14, MLB) **1978** Cle 16 (16, MLB) **1979** Cle 15 (14, MLB/lilb) **1980**†Cle 16 (16, RILB) **1981** Cle 16 (16, RILB) **1982**†Cle 9 (9, RILB) **1983** Cle 6 (6, lilb) **NFL** 116 (103) [9 yrs]

AMBROSE, JOHN John Vincent, C, 6´0˝/185 lbs; Catholic; B3/24/1910 Three Rivers, MA, D11/7/1995 Shrewsbury, MA **1932** Bkn 6 (2)

AMBROSE, WALT Walter L., G, 5´11˝/210 lbs; Carroll (WI); B8/7/1905 Portage, WI, deceased **1930** Por 1 (0)

AMECHE, ALAN Alan Dante 'The Horse', aka Lino Dante Ameche, FB, 6´0˝/218 lbs; Wisconsin; 1955: Bal, rnd 1; B6/1/1933 Kenosha, WI, D8/8/1988 Houston, TX

YEAR	TEAM	G (GS, POS)	RUSH	YD	AVG (LG)	TD	REC	YD	AVG (LG)	TD	PASS	COMP	PCT	YD	AVG (LG)	TD	INT	SK	YD	QBR	KPR	OTD	PTS	TAY
1955	Bal★	12 (FB)	**213**	**961**	4.5 (79)	**9**	27	141	5.2 (18)	0	—	—	—	—	—	—	—	—	—	—	k	—	54	**1122**
1956	Bal★	12 (FB)	178	858	4.8 (43)	8	26	189	7.3 (22)	0	—	—	—	—	—	—	—	—	—	—	k	—	48	1041
1957	Bal✧	12 (FB)	144	493	3.4 (49)	5	15	137	9.1 (40)	2	—	—	—	—	—	—	—	—	—	—	—	—	42	622
1958	†Bal★	12 (FB)	171	791	4.6 (28)	8	13	81	6.2 (18)	1	—	—	—	—	—	—	—	—	—	—	—	—	54	917
1959	†Bal☆	12 (FB)	178	679	3.8 (26)	7	13	129	9.9 (30)	1	—	—	—	—	—	—	—	—	—	—	—	—	48	819
1960	Bal	10 (FB)	80	263	3.3 (16)	3	7	56	8.0 (19)	0	—	—	—	—	—	—	—	—	—	—	—	—	18	321
NFL	6	70	964	4045	4.2 (79)	40	101	733	7.3 (40)	4	—	—	—	—	—	—	—	—	—	—	k	—	264	4840

AMERSON, GLEN Glen Douglas, DB, 6´1˝/186 lbs; Texas Tech; B11/24/1938 Munday, TX **1961** Phi 14

AMES, DAVE David Randolph, HB-DB, 6´0˝/185 lbs; Richmond; 1960: Bos, rnd 2/Pit, rnd 16; B1/16/1937 Portsmouth, VA **1961** NYT-A 5

YEAR	TEAM	G (GS, POS)	RUSH	YD	AVG (LG)	TD	REC	YD	AVG (LG)	TD	PASS	COMP	PCT	YD	AVG (LG)	TD	INT	SK	YD	QBR	KPR	OTD	PTS	TAY
1961	Den-A	7	19	114	6.0 (26)	0	6	20	3.3 (9)	0	—	—	—	—	—	—	—	—	—	—	kp	—	0	191
NFL	1	12	19	114	6.0 (26)	0	6	20	3.3 (9)	0	—	—	—	—	—	—	—	—	—	—	kpi	—	0	186

AMEY, OTIS Otis, WR, 5´10˝/197 lbs; Sacramento State; B12/4/1981 Union City, CA **2005** SF 11 (0)

AMEY, VINCENT Vincent Wayne, DE, 6´2˝/289 lbs; Arizona State; 1998: Oak, rnd 7; B2/9/1975 Los Angeles, CA **1998** Oak 4 (1)

AMMAN, RICHARD Richard Dale, DE-DT, 6´5˝/245 lbs; Florida State; 1972: Dal, rnd 10; B9/21/1950 Seattle, WA **1972** Bal 14 **1973** Bal 14 **NFL** 28 [2 yrs]

AMSLER, MARTY Charles Martin, DE, 6´5˝/255 lbs; Indiana; Evansville; 1965: Dal, rnd 18; B10/26/1942 Evansville, IN **1967** ChiB 14 (RDE) **1969** ChiB 11 **1970** Cin 3 **1970** GB 9 **NFL** 37 [3 yrs]

AMSTUTZ, JOE Gerald Joseph, C, 6´5˝/264 lbs; Indiana; 1957: Cle, rnd 6; B10/12/1934 Toledo, OH **1957** Cle 11 (c)

AMUNDSEN, NORM Norman Robert, G, 5´11˝/245 lbs; Wisconsin; 1955: GB, rnd 6; B9/28/1932 Chicago, IL **1957** GB 12

AMUNDSON, GEORGE George Arthur, RB, 6´3˝/215 lbs; Iowa State; 1973: Hou, rnd 1; B3/31/1951 Pendleton, OR

YEAR	TEAM	G (GS, POS)	RUSH	YD	AVG (LG)	TD	REC	YD	AVG (LG)	TD	PASS	COMP	PCT	YD	AVG (LG)	TD	INT	SK	YD	QBR	KPR	OTD	PTS	TAY
1973	Hou	9	15	56	3.7 (10)	0	7	60	8.6 (18)	0	—	—	—	—	—	—	—	—	—	—	—	—	0	86
1974	Hou	14	59	138	2.3 (11)	4	18	152	8.4 (29)	1	1	0	0.0	0	0.0	0	1	—	—	—	k	—	30	206
1975	Phi	6	—	—	—	—	—	—	—	—	—	—	—	—	—	—	—	—	—	—	—	—	—	—
NFL	3	29	74	194	2.6 (11)	4	25	212	8.5 (29)	1	1	0	0.0	0	0.0	0	1	—	—	—	k	—	30	292

ANANIS, VITO Vito Francis, HB-DB, 5´10˝/195 lbs; Boston College; B1/25/1915 Cambridge, MA, D9/3/1994 Wayland, MA

YEAR	TEAM	G (GS, POS)	RUSH	YD	AVG (LG)	TD	REC	YD	AVG (LG)	TD	PASS	COMP	PCT	YD	AVG (LG)	TD	INT	SK	YD	QBR	KPR	OTD	PTS	TAY
1945	Was	1 (1)	3	8	2.7 (5)	0	—	—	—	—	—	—	—	—	—	—	—	—	—	—	—	—	0	8

ANDABAKER, RUDY Rudolph Edward, G, 5´11˝/196 lbs; Pittsburgh; B8/1/1928 Donora, PA **1952** Pit 6 **1954** Pit 4 **NFL** 10 [2 yrs]

ANDERS, KIMBLE Kimble Lynard, RB, 5´11˝/225 lbs; Houston; B9/10/1966 Galveston, TX

YEAR	TEAM	G (GS, POS)	RUSH	YD	AVG (LG)	TD	REC	YD	AVG (LG)	TD	PASS	COMP	PCT	YD	AVG (LG)	TD	INT	SK	YD	QBR	KPR	OTD	PTS	TAY
1991	KC	2 (0)	—	—	—	—	2	30	15.0 (23)	0	—	—	—	—	—	—	—	—	—	—	—	—	0	15
1992	†KC	11 (2)	1	1	1.0 (1)	0	5	65	13.0 (28)	0	—	—	—	—	—	—	—	—	—	—	k	—	0	39
1993	†KC	16 (13, FB)	75	291	3.9 (18)	0	40	326	8.1 (27)	1	0	0	0.0	0	0.0	0	0	1	5	—	k	—	6	491
1994	†KC	16 (13, FB)	62	231	3.7 (19)	2	67	525	7.8 (30)	1	—	—	—	—	—	—	—	—	—	—	k	—	18	525
1995	†KC✧	16 (13, FB)	58	398	6.9 (44)	2	55	349	6.3 (28)	1	—	—	—	—	—	—	—	—	—	—	—	—	18	598
1996	KC✧	16 (15, FB)	54	201	3.7 (15)	2	60	529	8.8 (45)	2	—	—	—	—	—	—	—	—	—	—	k	—	24	503
1997	†KC✧	15 (14, FB)	79	397	5.0 (43)	0	59	453	7.7 (55)	2	—	—	—	—	—	—	—	—	—	—	k	—	12	619
1998	KC	16 (15, FB)	58	230	4.0 (20)	1	64	462	7.2 (29)	2	—	—	—	—	—	—	—	—	—	—	k	—	18	482
1999	KC	2 (2)	32	181	5.7 (46)	0	2	14	7.0 (9)	0	—	—	—	—	—	—	—	—	—	—	—	—	0	188
2000	KC	15 (7, RB)	76	331	4.4 (69)	2	15	76	5.1 (12)	0	—	—	—	—	—	—	—	—	—	—	k	—	12	388
NFL	10	125 (94)	495	2261	4.6 (69)	9	369	2829	7.7 (55)	9	0	0	0.0	0	0.0	0	0	1	5	—	k	—	108	3846

YEAR	TEAM	G (GS, POS)	RUSH	YD	AVG(LG)	TD	REC	YD	AVG(LG)	TD	PASS COMP	PCT	YD	AVG(LG)	TD	INT	SK	YD	QBR	KPR	OTD	PTS	TAY

ANDERSEN, JASON   Jason Allen, G, 6´6˝/319 lbs; Brigham Young; 1998: NE, rnd 7; B9/3/1975 Hayward, CA   **1999** NE 9 (1)   **2000** NE 7 (0)   **2002** KC 3 (0)   **NFL** 19 (1) [3 yrs]

ANDERSEN, MORTEN   Morten, K, 6´2˝/217 lbs; Michigan State; 1982: NO, rnd 4; B8/19/1960 Copenhagen, Denmark [K]   **1982** NO 8 (0)   **1983** NO 16 (0)   **1984** NO 16 (0)   **1985** NO★16 (0)   **1986** NO★16 (0)   **1987**†NO★12 (0)   **1988** NO★16 (0)   **1989** NO 16 (0)   **1990**†NO◇16 (0)   **1991**†NO 16 (0)   **1992**†NO★16 (0)   **1993** NO 16 (0)   **1994** NO 16 (0)   **1995**†Atl★16 (0)   **1996** Atl 16 (0)   **1997** Atl 16 (0)   **1998**†Atl 16 (0)   **1999** Atl 16 (0)   **2000** Atl 16 (0)   **2001** NYG 16 (0)   **2002** KC 14 (0)   **2003**†KC 16 (0)   **2004**†Min 16 (0)   **NFL** 354 (0) [23 yrs]

ANDERSEN, STAN   Stanley, T-E, 6´2˝/218 lbs; Stanford; 1940: ChiC, rnd 12; B9/14/1917 Portland, OR

1940	Cle	11 (5, lt)	—	—	—	—	—	—	—	—	—	—	—	—	—	—	—	—	—	—	—	0	10
1941	Cle	5 (3)	—	—	—	—	2	20	10.0 (12)	0	—	—	—	—	—	—	—	—	—	—	—	0	29
1941	Det	6 (3)	—	—	—	—	5	59	11.8 (24)	0	—	—	—	—	—	—	—	—	—	k	—	0	29
NFL	2	22 (11)	—	—	—	—	7	79	11.3 (24)	0	—	—	—	—	—	—	—	—	—	k	—	0	39

ANDERSON   WB, none; deceased   **1922** Ham 1 (0)

ANDERSON, ALEC   G, 5´8˝/166 lbs; Boston College; Holy Cross; Georgetown (DC); B6/17/1893, D11/14/1953   **1921** Was 1 (0)

ANDERSON, ALFRED   Alfred Anthony, RB, 6´1˝/219 lbs; Baylor; 1984: Min, rnd 3; B8/4/1961 Waco, TX

1984	Min	16 (14, FB)	201	773	3.8 (23)	2	17	102	6.0 (28)	1	7	3	42.9	95	13.6 (43)	2	1	2	8	—	k	—	18	1056
1985	Min	12 (6, fb)	50	121	2.4 (10)	2	16	175	10.9 (54)	1	—	—	—	—	—	—	—	—	—	—	—	—	30	254
1986	Min	16 (8, FB)	83	347	4.2 (29)	2	17	179	10.5 (37)	2	2	1	50.0	17	8.5 (17)	0	0	—	—	—	k	—	24	468
1987	†Min	10 (10, FB)	68	319	4.7 (27)	2	7	69	9.9 (22)	0	—	—	—	—	—	—	—	—	—	—	—	—	12	374
1988	†Min	16 (13, FB)	87	300	3.4 (18)	7	23	242	10.5 (19)	1	—	—	—	—	—	—	—	—	—	—	—	—	48	496
1989	†Min	11 (8, FB)	52	189	3.6 (14)	2	20	193	9.6 (18)	0	—	—	—	—	—	—	—	—	—	—	k	—	12	306
1990	Min	11 (6, FB)	59	207	3.5 (14)	2	13	80	6.2 (17)	0	—	—	—	—	—	—	—	—	—	—	k	—	12	266
1991	Min	16 (5, fb)	26	118	4.5 (19)	1	1	2	2.0 (2)	0	—	—	—	—	—	—	—	—	—	—	k	—	6	121
NFL	8	108 (70)	626	2374	3.8 (29)	22	114	1042	9.1 (54)	5	9	4	44.4	112	12.4 (43)	2	1	2	8	—	k	—	162	3339

ANDERSON, ANTHONY   Anthony Eugene, RB, 6´0˝/197 lbs; Temple; B9/27/1956 Wilmington, DE

1979	†Pit	16	18	118	6.6 (31)	1	—	—	—	—	—	—	—	—	—	—	—	—	—	—	k	—	6	133
1980	†Atl	16 (0)	6	5	0.8 (8)	0	—	—	—	—	—	—	—	—	—	—	—	—	—	—	k	—	0	-3
NFL	2	32	24	123	5.1 (31)	1	—	—	—	—	—	—	—	—	—	—	—	—	—	—	k	—	6	130

ANDERSON, ANTHONY   Anthony Ray, DB, 6´2˝/205 lbs; Grambling State; 1987: SD, rnd 10; B10/24/1964 Ruston, LA   **1987** SD 3 (0)

ANDERSON, ANTONIO   Antonio Kenneth, DT-DE, 6´6˝/311 lbs; Syracuse; 1997: Dal, rnd 4; B6/4/1973 Brooklyn, NY   **1997** Dal 16 (5, rdt)   **1998**†Dal 5 (0)   **NFL** 21 (5) [2 yrs]

ANDERSON, ARIC   Aric Howard, LB, 6´2˝/220 lbs; Millikin; B4/9/1965 Waverly, IA   **1987** GB 3 (0)

ANDERSON, ART   Arthur Anthony, T, 6´3˝/244 lbs; Idaho; B10/8/1936 Breckenridge, MN   **1961** ChiB 14 (RT)   **1963** Pit 13

| 1962 | ChiB | 14 (RT) | 1 | 7 | 7.0 (7) | 0 | — | — | — | — | — | — | — | — | — | — | — | — | — | — | — | — | 0 | 7 |
| **NFL** | 3 | 41 | 1 | 7 | 7.0 (7) | 0 | — | — | — | — | — | — | — | — | — | — | — | — | — | — | — | — | 0 | 7 |

ANDERSON, BENNIE   Bennie Tyron Lamar, G, 6´5˝/345 lbs; Tennessee State; B2/17/1977 St. Louis, MO   **2001**†Bal 16 (13, RG)   **2002** Bal 16 (16, RG)   **2003**†Bal 15 (15, RG)   **2004** Bal 16 (12, RG)   **2005** Buf 16 (15, LG)   **NFL** 79 (71) [5 yrs]

ANDERSON, BILL   William H., DE, 6´2˝/190 lbs; West Virginia; B1/6/1921 Triadelphia, WV, D4/1984 Wheeling, WV   **1945** Bos 6 (0)

ANDERSON, BILL   Walter William, E-TE, 6´3˝/211 lbs; Tennessee; 1958: Was, rnd 3; B7/16/1936 Hendersonville, NC

1958	Was	12 (8, LE)	—	—	—	—	18	396	22.0 (71)	2	—	—	—	—	—	—	—	—	—	—	—	—	12	208
1959	Was◇	11 (LE)	—	—	—	—	35	734	21.0 (70)	6	—	—	—	—	—	—	—	—	—	—	—	—	36	397
1960	Was◇	12 (SE)	1	6	6.0 (6)	0	38	488	12.8 (48)	3	—	—	—	—	—	—	—	—	—	—	—	—	18	265
1961	Was	14 (SE)	3	5	1.7 (13)	0	40	637	15.9 (42)	0	—	—	—	—	—	—	—	—	—	—	—	—	0	324
1962	Was	12 (SE)	—	—	—	—	23	386	16.8 (46)	2	—	—	—	—	—	—	—	—	—	—	P	—	12	203
1963	Was	13	—	—	—	—	14	288	20.6 (49)	1	1	0	0.0	0	0.0	0	1	—	—	—	—	—	6	109
1965	†GB	14	—	—	—	—	8	105	13.1 (27)	1	—	—	—	—	—	—	—	—	—	—	—	—	6	58
1966	†GB	10	—	—	—	—	2	14	7.0 (8)	0	—	—	—	—	—	—	—	—	—	—	—	—	0	7
NFL	8	98 (8)	4	11	2.8 (13)	0	178	3048	17.1 (71)	15	1	0	0.0	0	0.0	0	1	—	—	—	P	—	90	1570

ANDERSON, BILLY   William, DB-HB, 6´0˝/198 lbs; Compton CC (CA); 1953: ChiB, rnd 1; B3/3/1929 Los Angeles, CA

1953	ChiB	12 (DB)	—	—	—	—	3	33	11.0 (16)	0	—	—	—	—	—	—	—	—	—	Pkp	—	0	71
1954	ChiB	7	3	8	2.7 (6)	0	—	—	—	—	—	—	—	—	—	—	—	—	—	k	—	0	8
NFL	2	19	3	8	2.7 (6)	0	3	33	11.0 (16)	0	—	—	—	—	—	—	—	—	—	Pkp	—	0	79

ANDERSON, BILLY GUY   Billy Guy, QB, 6´1˝/195 lbs; Tulsa; 1965: Hou, rnd R11/LA, rnd 19; B2/17/1941 Palme, TX, D4/11/1996 Houston, TX   **1967**†Hou-A 8

ANDERSON, BOB   Robert Paul, HB, 6´2˝/215 lbs; Army; 1960: NYG, rnd 9; B3/31/1938 Elizabeth, NJ

| 1963 | NYG | 1 | 1 | -2 | -2.0 (-2) | 0 | — | — | — | — | — | — | — | — | — | — | — | — | — | — | — | 0 | -2 |

ANDERSON, BOBBY   Robert Conrad, RB, 6´0˝/208 lbs; Colorado; 1970: Den, rnd 1; B10/11/1947 Midland, MI

1970	Den	14	83	368	4.4 (27)	4	9	140	15.6 (37)	0	7	4	57.1	59	8.4 (25)	0	0	1	5	—	k	—	24	713
1971	Den	13 (13, FB)	139	533	3.8 (36)	3	37	353	9.5 (31)	1	3	1	33.3	48	16.0 (48)	0	0	1	6	—	k	—	24	836
1972	Den	9 (9, FB)	72	319	4.4 (40)	1	23	215	9.3 (40)	1	3	1	33.3	14	4.7 (14)	1	0	—	—	—	k	—	12	452
1973	Den	12	19	61	3.2 (11)	1	15	153	10.2 (29)	1	3	2	66.7	47	15.7 (28)	0	1	—	—	—	k	—	6	171
1975	NE	5	1	1	1.0 (1)	0	—	—	—	—	1	0	0.0	0	0.0	0	0	—	—	—	—	—	0	1
1975	Was	1	—	—	—	—	—	—	—	—	—	—	—	—	—	—	—	—	—	—	—	—	0	—
NFL	5	54 (22)	314	1282	4.1 (40)	9	84	861	10.3 (40)	2	17	8	47.1	168	9.9 (48)	1	0	2	11	—	k	—	66	2172

ANDERSON, BRAD   Bradley Stewart, WR, 6´2˝/198 lbs; Brigham Young; Arizona; 1984: Chi, rnd 8; B1/12/1961 Glendale, AZ

1984	†ChiB	13 (3)	—	—	—	—	3	77	25.7 (49)	1	—	—	—	—	—	—	—	—	—	—	—	—	6	44
1985	†ChiB	14 (0)	—	—	—	—	1	6	6.0 (6)	0	—	—	—	—	—	—	—	—	—	—	—	—	0	3
NFL	2	27 (3)	—	—	—	—	4	83	20.8 (49)	1	—	—	—	—	—	—	—	—	—	—	—	—	6	47

ANDERSON, BRUCE   Bruce Albert, DE-DT, 6´4˝/250 lbs; Willamette; 1966: LA, rnd 6; B1/18/1944 Coos Bay, OR   **1966** LARm 7   **1967** NYG 14   **1968** NYG 14 (RDE)   **1969** NYG 14 (LDE)   **1970** Was 10 (8, RDE)   **NFL** 59 (8) [5 yrs]

ANDERSON, BRYAN   Bryan Michael, G, 6´4˝/320 lbs; Pittsburgh; 2003: Chi, rnd 7; B3/30/1980 Philadelphia, PA   **2004** ChiB 4 (0)

ANDERSON, CHARLIE   Charles Edward, E, 6´0˝/230 lbs; Louisiana Tech; 1956: ChiC, rnd 15; B9/2/1933 Atlanta, AR   **1956** ChiC 2

ANDERSON, CHARLIE   Charlie Alexander, LB, 6´4˝/258 lbs; Mississippi; 2004: Hou, rnd 6; B12/8/1981 Jackson, MS   **2004** Hou 15 (0)   **2005** Hou 16 (0)   **NFL** 31 (0) [2 yrs]

ANDERSON, CHET   Chester Leonard, TE, 6´3˝/245 lbs; Minnesota; 1967: Pit, rnd 14; B3/14/1945 Duluth, MN

| 1967 | Pit | 14 | — | — | — | — | 8 | 141 | 17.6 (48) | 2 | — | — | — | — | — | — | — | — | — | — | — | — | 12 | 81 |

ANDERSON, CLIFF   Clifton Junior, E, 6´2˝/215 lbs; Indiana; 1952: ChiC, rnd 25; B11/25/1929 Cape May, NJ, D3/16/1979 Princess Anne, MD

1952	ChiC	12 (LE)	—	—	—	—	11	191	17.4 (30)	2	—	—	—	—	—	—	—	—	—	—	k	—	12	99
1953	ChiC	1	—	—	—	—	1	8	8.0 (8)	0	—	—	—	—	—	—	—	—	—	—	—	—	0	4
1953	NYG	8 (LE)	—	—	—	—	16	258	16.1 (32)	0	—	—	—	—	—	—	—	—	—	—	—	—	0	129
NFL	2	21	—	—	—	—	28	457	16.3 (32)	2	—	—	—	—	—	—	—	—	—	—	k	—	12	232

ANDERSON, COURTNEY   Courtney, TE, 6´7˝/270 lbs; San Jose State; 2004: Oak, rnd 7; B11/19/1980 Greenville, TX

2004	Oak	9 (4)	—	—	—	—	13	175	13.5 (28)	1	—	—	—	—	—	—	—	—	—	—	—	—	6	93
2005	Oak	14 (13, TE)	—	—	—	—	24	303	12.6 (36)	3	—	—	—	—	—	—	—	—	—	—	—	—	18	167
NFL	2	23 (17)	—	—	—	—	37	478	12.9 (36)	4	—	—	—	—	—	—	—	—	—	—	—	—	24	259

ANDERSON, CURTIS   Curtis Lee, DE-DT, 6´6˝/250 lbs; Central State (OH); 1979: Dal, rnd 5; B5/16/1957 Cincinnati, OH   **1979** KC 6

ANDERSON, CURTIS   Jerome Curtis, DB, 6´0˝/193 lbs; Pittsburgh; B9/29/1973 Lynchburg, VA   **1997** Jax 9 (0)

ANDERSON, DAMIEN Damien Ramone, RB, 5´11˝/212 lbs; Northwestern; B7/17/1979 Wilmington, IL

YEAR	TEAM	G(GS, POS)	RUSH	YD	AVG(LG)	TD	REC	YD	AVG(LG)	TD	PASS	COMP	PCT	YD	AVG(LG)	TD	INT	SK	YD	QBR	KPR	OTD	PTS	TAY
2002	Arz	10(1)	24	65	2.7(14)	0	3	36	12.0(12)	0	—	—	—	—	—	—	—	—	—	—	k	—	0	130
2003	Arz	16(0)	18	68	3.8(17)	0	6	36	6.0(11)	0	—	—	—	—	—	—	—	—	—	—	k	—	0	87
2004	Arz	4(0)	1	2	2.0(2)	0	—	—	—	—	—	—	—	—	—	—	—	—	—	—	—	—	0	2
2005	Arz	5(0)	2	7	3.5(6)	0	—	—	—	—	—	—	—	—	—	—	—	—	—	—	k	—	0	-1
NFL	4	35(1)	45	142	3.2(17)	0	9	72	8.0(12)	0	—	—	—	—	—	—	—	—	—	—	k	—	0	218

ANDERSON, DARREN Darren Hunter, DB, 5´10˝/185 lbs; Toledo; 1992: NE, rnd 4; B1/11/1969 Cincinnati, OH **1992** NE 1 (0) **1992** TB 1 (0) **1993** TB 14 (1) **1994**†KC 15 (1) **1995** KC 16 (0) **1996** KC 11 (3) **1997** KC 11 (0) **1998** Atl 5 (0) **NFL** 74 (5) [7 yrs]

ANDERSON, DICK Richard Paul, DB, 6´2˝/196 lbs; Colorado; 1968: Mia, rnd 3; B2/10/1946 Midland, MI **[I]** **1968** Mia-A 14 (13, RS/ls) **1970**†Mia 14 (13, SS) **1971**†Mia 14 (14, SS) **1972**†Mia★14 (13, FS) **1973**†Mia★14 (12, FS) **1974**†Mia★14 (14, SS) **1976** Mia 9 **1977** Mia 14

YEAR	TEAM	G(GS, POS)	RUSH	YD	AVG(LG)	TD	REC	YD	AVG(LG)	TD	PASS	COMP	PCT	YD	AVG(LG)	TD	INT	SK	YD	QBR	KPR	OTD	PTS	TAY
1969	Mia-A	14(14, RS)	—	—	—	—	1	8	8.0(8)	0	—	—	—	—	—	—	—	—	—	—	Ppi	—	0	117
NFL	9	121(93)	—	—	—	—	1	8	8.0(8)	0	—	—	—	—	—	—	—	—	—	—	Pkpi	4	24	759

ANDERSON, DICK Richard Joseph, T, 6´5˝/245 lbs; Ohio State; B1/26/1944 Massillon, OH **1967** NO 2

ANDERSON, DON Donald Cortez, DB, 5´10˝/196 lbs; Purdue; 1985: Ind, rnd 2; B7/8/1963 Detroit, MI **1985** Ind 5 (0) **1987** TB 11 (0) **NFL** 16 (0) [2 yrs]

ANDERSON, DONNY Garry Don, RB, 6´2˝/215 lbs; Texas Tech; 1965: GB, rnd 1/Hou, rnd R1; B5/16/1943 Borger, TX **[P]**

YEAR	TEAM	G(GS, POS)	RUSH	YD	AVG(LG)	TD	REC	YD	AVG(LG)	TD	PASS	COMP	PCT	YD	AVG(LG)	TD	INT	SK	YD	QBR	KPR	OTD	PTS	TAY
1966	†GB	14	25	104	4.2(15)	2	2	33	16.5(22)	0	—	—	—	—	—	—	—	—	—	—	Pkp	1	18	433
1967	†GB	14(hb)	97	402	4.1(40)	6	22	331	15.0(37)	3	2	1	50.0	19	9.5(19)	0	0	—	—	—	Pkp	—	54	766
1968	GB✧	14(HB)	170	761	4.5(42)	5	25	333	13.3(47)	1	3	1	33.3	12	4.0(12)	1	0	—	—	—	P	—	36	994
1969	GB	14(hb)	87	288	3.3(16)	1	14	308	22.0(51)	1	—	—	—	—	—	—	—	—	—	—	P	—	12	457
1970	GB	14(RB)	222	853	3.8(54)	5	36	414	11.5(34)	0	1	0	0.0	0	0.0	0	0	—	—	—	P	—	30	1110
1971	GB	14(RB)	186	757	4.1(31)	5	26	306	11.8(39)	1	4	2	50.0	9	2.3(5)	1	0	—	—	—	P	—	36	975
1972	SL	14(RB)	153	536	3.5(19)	4	28	298	10.6(56)	2	3	2	66.7	71	23.7(38)	0	0	—	—	—	P	—	36	771
1973	SL	14(RB)	167	679	4.1(54)	**10**	41	409	10.0(44)	3	—	—	—	—	—	—	—	—	—	—	—	—	78	999
1974	†SL	14(1)	90	316	3.5(16)	3	15	116	7.7(25)	3	—	—	—	—	—	—	—	—	—	—	—	—	36	419
NFL	9	126(1)	1197	4696	3.9(54)	41	209	2548	12.2(56)	14	13	6	46.2	111	8.5(38)	2	0	—	—	—	Pkp	1	336	6922

ANDERSON, DUNSTAN Dunstan Evrette, DE, 6´3˝/260 lbs; Tulsa; B12/31/1970 Fort Worth, TX, D5/31/2004 Fort Myers, FL **1994** Atl 1 (0) **1997** Mia 9 (1) **NFL** 10 (1) [2 yrs]

ANDERSON, DWAYNE Dwayne Everett, DB, 6´0˝/205 lbs; SMU; B12/7/1961 St. Louis, MD **1987** SL 1 (0)

ANDERSON, DWIGHT Dwight Orlando, DB, 5´10˝/180 lbs; South Dakota; B7/5/1981 Spanish Town, Jamaica **2004** SL 12 (0) **2005** SL 3 (0) **NFL** 15 (0) [2 yrs]

ANDERSON, EDDIE Edward Nicholas, E, 5´10˝/176 lbs; Notre Dame; B11/13/1900 Oskaloosa, IA, D4/26/1974 Clearwater, FL **1922** Roc 3 (3, RE) **1922** ChiC☆7 (5, RE) **1923** ChiC 11 (11, RE), 6 **1924** ChiC☆9 (9, RE) **1925** ChiC☆13 (12, RE), 6 **NFL** 43 (40), 12 [4 yrs]

ANDERSON, EDDIE Eddie Lee, DB, 6´1˝/210 lbs; Fort Valley State; 1986: Sea, rnd 6; B7/22/1963 Warner Robins, GA **1986** Sea 5 (0) **1987** LARd 13 (3) **1988** LARd 16 (5, fs) **1989** LARd 15 (10, FS) **1990**†LARd 16 (16, FS) **1991**†LARd 16 (16, FS) **1992** LARd 16 (16, FS) **1993**†LARd 16 (16, FS) **1994** LARd 14 (14, FS) **1995** Oak 14 (14, FS) **1996** Oak 7 (5, fs) **1997** Oak 11 (1) **NFL** 159 (116) [12 yrs]

ANDERSON, ERICK Erick Scott, LB, 6´1˝/240 lbs; Michigan; 1992: KC, rnd 7; B10/7/1968 Long Beach, CA **1993**†KC 8 (1) **1994** Was 2 (0) **NFL** 10 (1) [2 yrs]

ANDERSON, FLIPPER Willie Lee, WR, 6´0˝/175 lbs; UCLA; 1988: LARm, rnd 2; B3/7/1965 Paulsboro, NJ

YEAR	TEAM	G(GS, POS)	RUSH	YD	AVG(LG)	TD	REC	YD	AVG(LG)	TD	PASS	COMP	PCT	YD	AVG(LG)	TD	INT	SK	YD	QBR	KPR	OTD	PTS	TAY
1988	†LARm	16(1)	—	—	—	—	11	319	29.0(56)	0	—	—	—	—	—	—	—	—	—	—	—	—	0	160
1989	†LARm	16(13, WR)	1	-1	-1.0(-1)	0	44	1146	**26.0(78)**	5	—	—	—	—	—	—	—	—	—	—	—	—	30	597
1990	LARm	16(11, WR)	1	13	13.0(13)	0	51	1097	**21.5(55)**	4	—	—	—	—	—	—	—	—	—	—	—	—	24	582
1991	LARm	12(10, WR)	—	—	—	—	32	530	16.6(54)	1	—	—	—	—	—	—	—	—	—	—	—	—	6	270
1992	LARm	15(9, WR)	—	—	—	—	38	657	17.3(51)	7	—	—	—	—	—	—	—	—	—	—	k	—	42	358
1993	LARm	15(15, WR)	—	—	—	—	37	552	14.9(56)	4	—	—	—	—	—	—	—	—	—	—	—	—	24	296
1994	LARm	16(16, WR)	1	11	11.0(11)	0	46	945	20.5(72)	5	—	—	—	—	—	—	—	—	—	—	—	—	30	509
1995	Ind	2(2)	—	—	—	—	8	111	13.9(28)	2	—	—	—	—	—	—	—	—	—	—	—	—	12	66
1996	Was	2(0)	—	—	—	—	—	—	—	—	—	—	—	—	—	—	—	—	—	—	—	—	—	—
1997	Den	4(0)	—	—	—	—	—	—	—	—	—	—	—	—	—	—	—	—	—	—	—	—	—	—
NFL	10	114(77)	3	23	7.7(13)	0	267	5357	20.1(78)	28	—	—	—	—	—	—	—	—	—	—	k	—	168	2836

ANDERSON, FRED Fredell Lamont, DE-DT, 6´4˝/238 lbs; Oregon State; Prairie View A&M; B10/30/1954 Toppenish, WA **1978**†Pit 16 **1980** Sea 7 (1) **1981** Sea 14 (6, rde) **1982** Sea 1 (0) **NFL** 38 (7) [4 yrs]

ANDERSON, GARY Gary Allan, K, 5´11˝/193 lbs; Syracuse; 1982: Buf, rnd 7; B7/16/1959 Parys, South Africa **[K]** **1982**†Pit 9 (0) **1983**†Pit☆16 (0) **1984**†Pit★16 (0) **1985** Pit★16 (0) **1986** Pit 16 (0) **1987** Pit 12 (0) **1988** Pit 16 (0) **1989**†Pit 16 (0) **1990** Pit 16 (0) **1991** Pit 16 (0) **1992**†Pit 16 (0) **1993**†Pit★16 (0) **1995**†Phi 16 (0) **1996**†Phi 16 (0) **1997**†SF 16 (0) **1998**†Min★16 (0) **1999**†Min 16 (0) **2000**†Min 16 (0) **2001** Min 16 (0) **2002** Min 14 (0) **2003**†Ten 15 (0) **2004** Ten 15 (0)

YEAR	TEAM	G(GS, POS)	RUSH	YD	AVG(LG)	TD	REC	YD	AVG(LG)	TD	PASS	COMP	PCT	YD	AVG(LG)	TD	INT	SK	YD	QBR	KPR	OTD	PTS	TAY
1994	†Pit	16(0)	1	3	3.0(3)	0	—	—	—	—	—	—	—	—	—	—	—	—	—	—	K	—	104	3
NFL	23	353(0)	1	3	3.0(3)	0	—	—	—	—	—	—	—	—	—	—	—	—	—	—	K	—	2434	3

ANDERSON, GARY Gary Allan, G, 6´3˝/253 lbs; Stanford; 1977: Det, rnd 10; B9/22/1955 Fairfield, CA **1977** Det 13 (1) **1978** Det 1 (1) **1978** NO 2 **1980** Was 5 (1) **NFL** 21 (3) [3 yrs]

ANDERSON, GARY Gary Wayne, RB, 6´0˝/185 lbs; Arkansas; 1983: SD, rnd 1; B4/18/1961 Columbia, MO **[R]**

YEAR	TEAM	G(GS, POS)	RUSH	YD	AVG(LG)	TD	REC	YD	AVG(LG)	TD	PASS	COMP	PCT	YD	AVG(LG)	TD	INT	SK	YD	QBR	KPR	OTD	PTS	TAY
1985	SD	12(6, rb)	116	429	3.7(27)	4	35	422	12.1(52)	2	0	0	0.0	0	0.0	0	0	1	5	—	k	1	42	807
1986	SD✧	16(12, RB)	127	442	3.5(17)	1	80	871	10.9(65)	8	1	1	100.0	4	4.0(4)	1	0	—	—	—	kp	—	54	1159
1987	SD	12(7, RB)	80	260	3.3(25)	3	47	503	10.7(38)	2	—	—	—	—	—	—	—	—	—	—	k	—	30	655
1988	SD	14(13, RB)	225	1119	5.0(36)	3	32	182	5.7(20)	0	—	—	—	—	—	—	—	—	—	—	—	—	18	1240
1990	TB	16(13, RB)	166	646	3.9(22)	3	38	464	12.2(74)	2	—	—	—	—	—	—	—	—	—	—	k	—	30	951
1991	TB	16(5, rb)	72	263	3.7(64)	1	25	184	7.4(21)	0	—	—	—	—	—	—	—	—	—	—	k	—	6	498
1992	TB	15(4)	55	194	3.5(18)	1	34	284	8.4(34)	0	—	—	—	—	—	—	—	—	—	—	kp	—	6	490
1993	TB	4(0)	28	56	2.0(13)	0	11	89	8.1(28)	1	—	—	—	—	—	—	—	—	—	—	kp	—	6	135
1993	Det	6(1)	—	—	—	—	—	—	—	—	—	—	—	—	—	—	—	—	—	—	k	—	0	6
NFL	8	111(61)	869	3409	3.9(64)	16	302	2999	9.9(74)	15	1	1	100.0	4	4.0(4)	1	0	1	5	—	kp	1	192	5940

ANDERSON, HERBIE Herbert James, DB, 5´9˝/183 lbs; Texas A&M-Kingsville; 1991: Phx, rnd 10; B11/19/1968 Port Arthur, TX **1991** Hou 1 (0)

ANDERSON, HUNK Heartley William, G-C, 5´11˝/191 lbs; Notre Dame; B9/22/1898 Calumet, MI, D4/24/1978 West Palm Beach, FL **[C]** **1922** ChiB☆10 (10, LG) **1923** Cle 1 (1) **1923** ChiB 10 (9, LG) **1924** ChiB 10 (8, LG) **1925** ChiB 8 (4) **NFL** 39 (32) [4 yrs]

ANDERSON, JAMAL Jamal Sharif, RB, 5´11˝/237 lbs; Utah; 1994: Atl, rnd 7; B9/30/1972 Woodland Hills, CA

YEAR	TEAM	G(GS, POS)	RUSH	YD	AVG(LG)	TD	REC	YD	AVG(LG)	TD	PASS	COMP	PCT	YD	AVG(LG)	TD	INT	SK	YD	QBR	KPR	OTD	PTS	TAY
1994	Atl	3(0)	2	-1	-0.5(0)	0	—	—	—	—	—	—	—	—	—	—	—	—	—	—	k	—	0	-5
1995	†Atl	16(0)	39	161	4.1(13)	1	4	42	10.5(17)	0	—	—	—	—	—	—	—	—	—	—	k	—	6	373
1996	Atl	16(12, RB)	232	1055	4.5(32)	5	49	473	9.7(34)	1	—	—	—	—	—	—	—	—	—	—	k	—	36	1367
1997	Atl	16(15, RB)	290	1002	3.5(39)	7	29	284	9.8(47)	3	4	1	25.0	27	6.8(27)	1	1	—	—	—	—	—	60	1208
1998	†Atl★	16(16, RB)	**410**	**1846**	4.5(48)	**14**	27	319	11.8(27)	2	2	0	0.0	0	0.0	0	0	—	—	—	—	—	98	2156
1999	Atl	2(2)	19	59	3.1(20)	0	2	34	17.0(32)	0	—	—	—	—	—	—	—	—	—	—	—	—	0	76
2000	Atl	16(16, RB)	282	1024	3.6(42)	6	42	382	9.1(55)	0	—	—	—	—	—	—	—	—	—	—	—	—	38	1275
2001	Atl	3(3)	55	190	3.5(14)	1	3	111	37.0(**94**)	1	—	—	—	—	—	—	—	—	—	—	—	—	12	261
NFL	8	88(64)	1329	5336	4.0(48)	34	156	1645	10.5(94)	7	6	1	16.7	27	4.5(27)	1	1	—	—	—	k	—	250	6709

ANDERSON, JASON Jason, RB, 6´0˝/205 lbs; South Dakota; B4/29/1980 Palmdale, CA **2005** Hou 1 (0)

ANDERSON, JERRY Jerry O., DB, 5´11˝/198 lbs; Oklahoma; 1977: Cin, rnd 4; B10/27/1953 Murfreesboro, TN, D5/27/1989 Murfreesboro, TN **1977** Cin 14 **1978** TB 2 **NFL** 16 [2 yrs]

ANDERSON, JESSE Jesse Lemond, TE, 6´2˝/245 lbs; Mississippi State; 1990: TB, rnd 4; B7/26/1966 West Point, MS **1992** TB 1 (0) **1992** Pit 2 (0) **1993** NO 1 (0)

YEAR	TEAM	G(GS, POS)	RUSH	YD	AVG(LG)	TD	REC	YD	AVG(LG)	TD	PASS	COMP	PCT	YD	AVG(LG)	TD	INT	SK	YD	QBR	KPR	OTD	PTS	TAY
1990	TB	16(2)	—	—	—	—	5	77	15.4(52)	0	—	—	—	—	—	—	—	—	—	—	—	—	0	39
1991	TB	15(2)	—	—	—	—	6	73	12.2(34)	2	—	—	—	—	—	—	—	—	—	—	—	—	12	47
NFL	4	35(4)	—	—	—	—	11	150	13.6(52)	2	—	—	—	—	—	—	—	—	—	—	—	—	12	85

ANDERSON, JOHN Roger John, LB, 6´3˝/226 lbs; Michigan; 1978: GB, rnd 1; B2/14/1956 Waukesha, WI **[KI]** **1978** GB 13 (12, RLB) **1979** GB 7 (2) **1980** GB 9 (9, LOLB) **1981** GB 16 (16, LOLB) **1982**†GB 9 (9, LOLB) **1983** GB 16 (16, LOLB) **1984** GB 16 (16, LOLB) **1985** GB 16 (16, LOLB) **1986** GB 4 (4) **1987** GB 12 (12, LOLB) **1988** GB 14 (14, LOLB) **1989** GB 14 (14, LOLB) **NFL** 146 (140) [12 yrs]

ANDERSON, KEN Kenneth Allan, QB, 6´2˝/212 lbs; Augustana (IL); 1971: Cin, rnd 3; B2/15/1949 Batavia, NY

YEAR	TEAM	G (GS, POS)	RUSH	YD	AVG (LG)	TD	REC	YD	AVG (LG)	TD	PASS	COMP	PCT	YD	AVG (LG)	TD	INT	SK	YD	QBR	KPR	OTD	PTS	TAY
1971	Cin	11	22	125	5.7(16)	1	—	—	—	—	131	72	55.0	777	5.9(44)	5	4	23	159	72.6	—	—	6	389
1972	Cin	13(QB)	22	94	4.3(18)	3	—	—	—	—	301	171	56.8	1918	6.4(65)	7	7	18	155	74.0	—	—	18	838
1973	†Cin	14(QB)	26	97	3.7(17)	0	—	—	—	—	329	179	54.4	2428	7.4(78)	18	12	24	163	81.2	—	—	0	921
1974	Cin☆	13(QB)	43	314	7.3(20)	2	—	—	—	—	328	**213**	**64.9**	**2667**	**8.1(77)**	18	10	36	292	**95.7**	—	—	12	1358
1975	†Cin★	13(QB)	49	188	3.8(29)	2	—	—	—	—	**377**	**228**	60.5	**3169**	8.4(55)	21	11	32	247	**93.9**	—	—	12	1458
1976	Cin✧	14(QB)	31	134	4.3(25)	1	—	—	—	—	338	179	53.0	2367	7.0(85)	19	14	34	235	76.9	—	—	6	863
1977	Cin	14(QB)	26	128	4.9(17)	2	—	—	—	—	323	166	51.4	2145	6.6(**94**)	11	11	28	197	69.7	—	—	12	836
1978	Cin	12(QB)	29	167	5.8(16)	1	—	—	—	—	319	173	54.2	2219	7.0(57)	10	22	30	237	58.0	—	—	6	457
1979	Cin	15(QB)	28	235	8.4(21)	2	—	—	—	—	339	189	55.8	2340	6.9(73)	16	10	46	324	80.7	—	—	12	1105
1980	Cin	13(12, QB)	16	122	7.6(20)	0	—	—	—	—	275	166	60.4	1778	6.5(67)	6	13	24	174	66.9	—	—	0	521
1981	†Cin★	16(16, QB)	46	320	7.0(25)	1	—	—	—	—	479	300	**62.6**	3754	7.8(74)	29	10	25	140	**98.4**	—	—	6	**1952**
1982	†Cin★	9(9, QB)	25	85	3.4(12)	4	—	—	—	—	309	**218**	**70.6**	2495	8.1(56)	12	9	26	154	**95.3**	—	—	24	1073
1983	Cin	13(13, QB)	22	147	6.7(29)	1	—	—	—	—	297	198	**66.7**	2333	7.9(80)	12	13	25	187	85.6	—	—	6	864
1984	Cin	11(9, QB)	11	64	5.8(14)	0	—	—	—	—	275	175	63.6	2107	7.7(80)	10	12	24	191	81.0	—	—	0	688
1985	Cin	3(2)	1	0	0.0(0)	0	—	—	—	—	32	16	50.0	170	5.3(44)	2	0	2	16	—	—	—	0	95
1986	Cin	8(0)	—	—	—	—	—	—	—	—	23	11	47.8	171	7.4(43)	1	2	1	4	—	—	—	0	11
NFL	16	192(61)	397	2220	5.6(29)	20	—	—	—	—	4475	2654	59.3	32838	7.3(94)	197	160	398	2875	81.9	—	—	120	13424

ANDERSON, KEN Ken, DT, 6´3˝/310 lbs; Arkansas; B10/4/1975 Shreveport, LA **1999** ChiB 2 (0)

ANDERSON, KIM Kim Sherwood, DB, 5´11˝/183 lbs; Pasadena City Coll; Arizona State; 1979: Bal, rnd 3; B7/19/1957 Pasadena, CA **1980** Bal 16 (0) **1982** Bal 9 (2) **1983** Bal 16 (5, fs) **1984** Ind 1 (0)

YEAR	TEAM	G (GS, POS)	RUSH	YD	AVG (LG)	TD	REC	YD	AVG (LG)	TD	PASS	COMP	PCT	YD	AVG (LG)	TD	INT	SK	YD	QBR	KPR	OTD	PTS	TAY
1981	Bal	14(5, fs)	1	0	0.0(0)	0	—	—	—	—	—	—	—	—	—	—	—	—	—	—	kpi	—	0	133
NFL	5	56(12)	1	0	0.0	0	—	—	—	—	—	—	—	—	—	—	—	—	—	—	kpiS	1	6	326

ANDERSON, LARRY Lawrence Andrew, DB, 5´11˝/183 lbs; Louisiana Tech; 1978: Pit, rnd 4; B9/25/1956 West Monroe, LA **[R]** **1978**†Pit 16 (1) **1979**†Pit 16 **1980** Pit 4 (0) **1981** Pit 16 (0) **1982** Bal 9 (6, SS) **1983** Bal 9 (6, SS) **1984** Ind 12 (0) **NFL** 82 (13) [7 yrs]

ANDERSON, MARCUS Marcus James, WR, 5´11˝/178 lbs; Tulane; B6/12/1959 Port Arthur, TX

YEAR	TEAM	G (GS, POS)	RUSH	YD	AVG (LG)	TD	REC	YD	AVG (LG)	TD	PASS	COMP	PCT	YD	AVG (LG)	TD	INT	SK	YD	QBR	KPR	OTD	PTS	TAY
1981	ChiB	12(1)	—	—	—	—	9	243	27.0(85)	2	—	—	—	—	—	—	—	—	—	—	k	—	12	112

ANDERSON, MARQUES Marques Deon, DB, 5´11˝/212 lbs; UCLA; 2002: GB, rnd 3; B5/26/1979 Harbor City, CA **2002**†GB 14 (11, SS) **2003**†GB 16 (7, ss) **2004** Oak 14 (10, SS) **2005** Den 6 (0) **2005** SF 4 (0) **NFL** 54 (28) [4 yrs]

ANDERSON, MAX Max Arthur, RB, 5´8˝/180 lbs; Arizona State; 1968: Buf, rnd 5; B6/6/1945 Stockton, CA

YEAR	TEAM	G (GS, POS)	RUSH	YD	AVG (LG)	TD	REC	YD	AVG (LG)	TD	PASS	COMP	PCT	YD	AVG (LG)	TD	INT	SK	YD	QBR	KPR	OTD	PTS	TAY
1968	Buf-A	14(HB)	147	525	3.6(45)	2	22	140	6.4(23)	0	1	0	0.0	0	0.0	0	0	—	—	—	k	1	18	1011
1969	Buf-A	11	13	74	5.7(16)	1	7	65	9.3(22)	0	—	—	—	—	—	—	—	—	—	—	kp	—	6	190
NFL	2	25	160	599	3.7(45)	3	29	205	7.1(23)	0	1	0	0.0	0	0.0	0	0	—	—	—	kp	1	24	1201

ANDERSON, MEL Melvin Anthony, WR, 5´11˝/175 lbs; Minnesota; B8/29/1965 **1987** Pit 2 (0)

ANDERSON, MIKE Michael Moschello, RB, 6´0˝/230 lbs; Utah; 2000: Den, rnd 6; B9/21/1973 Winnsboro, SC

YEAR	TEAM	G (GS, POS)	RUSH	YD	AVG (LG)	TD	REC	YD	AVG (LG)	TD	PASS	COMP	PCT	YD	AVG (LG)	TD	INT	SK	YD	QBR	KPR	OTD	PTS	TAY
2000	†Den	16(12, RB)	297	1487	5.0(80)	**15**	23	169	7.3(18)	0	—	—	—	—	—	—	—	—	—	—	—	—	92	1722
2001	Den	16(7, rb)	175	678	3.9(62)	4	8	46	5.8(16)	0	—	—	—	—	—	—	—	—	—	—	—	—	26	741
2002	Den	15(12, FB)	84	386	4.6(32)	2	18	167	9.3(52)	2	—	—	—	—	—	—	—	—	—	—	k	—	24	509
2003	†Den	12(5, fb)	70	257	3.7(44)	3	12	53	4.4(18)	2	—	—	—	—	—	—	—	—	—	—	k	—	30	308
2005	†Den	15(15, RB)	239	1014	4.2(44)	12	18	212	11.8(66)	1	—	—	—	—	—	—	—	—	—	—	k	—	78	1248
NFL	5	74(51)	865	3822	4.4(80)	36	79	647	8.2(66)	5	—	—	—	—	—	—	—	—	—	—	k	—	250	4527

ANDERSON, NEAL Charles Neal, RB, 5´11˝/210 lbs; Florida; 1986: Chi, rnd 1; B8/14/1964 Graceville, FL

YEAR	TEAM	G (GS, POS)	RUSH	YD	AVG (LG)	TD	REC	YD	AVG (LG)	TD	PASS	COMP	PCT	YD	AVG (LG)	TD	INT	SK	YD	QBR	KPR	OTD	PTS	TAY
1986	†ChiB☆	14(1)	35	146	4.2(23)	0	4	80	20.0(58)	1	—	—	—	—	—	—	—	—	—	—	k	—	6	157
1987	ChiB	11(10, FB)	129	586	4.5(38)	3	47	467	9.9(59)	3	—	—	—	—	—	—	—	—	—	—	—	—	36	865
1988	†ChiB★	16(16, RB)	249	1106	4.4(80)	12	39	371	9.5(36)	0	1	0	0.0	0	0.0	0	0	—	—	—	—	—	72	1412
1989	ChiB★	16(16, RB)	274	1275	4.7(73)	11	50	434	8.7(49)	4	—	—	—	—	—	—	—	—	—	—	—	—	90	1622
1990	†ChiB★	15(14, RB)	260	1078	4.1(52)	10	42	484	11.5(50)	3	—	—	—	—	—	—	—	—	—	—	—	—	78	1435
1991	†ChiB✧	13(12, RB)	210	747	3.6(42)	6	47	368	7.8(26)	3	1	0	0.0	0	0.0	0	0	—	—	—	—	—	54	1006
1992	ChiB	16(11, RB)	156	582	3.7(49)	5	42	399	9.5(30)	6	—	—	—	—	—	—	—	—	—	—	—	—	66	862
1993	ChiB	15(11, RB)	202	646	3.2(45)	4	31	160	5.2(35)	0	1	0	0.0	0	0.0	0	0	—	—	—	—	—	24	766
NFL	8	116(91)	1515	6166	4.1(80)	51	302	2763	9.1(59)	20	3	0	0.0	0	0.0	0	0	—	—	—	k	—	426	8124

ANDERSON, OCKIE Oscar Carl, TB-BB-WB, 5´9˝/165 lbs; Colgate; B10/15/1894 Erie, PA, D1/25/1962 Buffalo, NY **1920** Buf 11 (6, TB) **1921** Buf 11 (11, TB), 42 **1922** Buf 7 (7, TB), 6 **NFL** 29 (24), 48 [3 yrs]

ANDERSON, OTTIS Ottis Jerome, RB, 6´2˝/220 lbs; Miami (FL); 1979: SL, rnd 1; B1/19/1957 West Palm Beach, FL

YEAR	TEAM	G (GS, POS)	RUSH	YD	AVG (LG)	TD	REC	YD	AVG (LG)	TD	PASS	COMP	PCT	YD	AVG (LG)	TD	INT	SK	YD	QBR	KPR	OTD	PTS	TAY
1979	SL★	16(16, RB)	331	1605	4.8(76)	8	41	308	7.5(28)	2	1	0	0.0	0	0.0	0	0	—	—	—	—	—	60	1849
1980	SL★	16(16, RB)	301	1352	4.5(52)	9	36	308	8.6(35)	0	—	—	—	—	—	—	—	—	—	—	—	—	54	1596
1981	SL	16(16, RB)	328	1376	4.2(28)	9	51	387	7.6(27)	0	—	—	—	—	—	—	—	—	—	—	—	—	54	1660
1982	†SL	8(8, RB)	145	587	4.0(64)	3	14	106	7.6(19)	0	—	—	—	—	—	—	—	—	—	—	—	—	18	670
1983	SL	15(15, RB)	296	1270	4.3(43)	5	54	459	8.5(40)	1	—	—	—	—	—	—	—	—	—	—	—	—	36	1555
1984	SL	15(15, RB)	289	1174	4.1(24)	6	70	611	8.7(57)	2	—	—	—	—	—	—	—	—	—	—	—	—	48	1550
1985	SL	9(8, RB)	117	479	4.1(38)	4	23	225	9.8(43)	0	—	—	—	—	—	—	—	—	—	—	—	—	24	632
1986	SL	4(3)	51	156	3.1(14)	2	10	91	9.1(19)	0	—	—	—	—	—	—	—	—	—	—	—	—	12	222
1986	†NYG	8(0)	24	81	3.4(16)	1	9	46	5.1(12)	0	—	—	—	—	—	—	—	—	—	—	—	—	6	114
1987	NYG	4(0)	2	6	3.0(4)	0	2	16	8.0(9)	0	—	—	—	—	—	—	—	—	—	—	—	—	0	14
1988	NYG	16(0)	65	208	3.2(11)	8	9	57	6.3(13)	0	—	—	—	—	—	—	—	—	—	—	—	—	48	317
1989	†NYG	16(16, RB)	325	1023	3.1(36)	14	28	268	9.6(26)	0	—	—	—	—	—	—	—	—	—	—	—	—	84	1297
1990	†NYG	16(11, RB)	225	784	3.5(28)	11	18	139	7.7(18)	0	—	—	—	—	—	—	—	—	—	—	—	—	66	964
1991	NYG	10(1)	53	141	2.7(9)	1	11	41	3.7(13)	0	—	—	—	—	—	—	—	—	—	—	—	—	6	172
1992	NYG	13(0)	10	31	3.1(6)	0	—	—	—	—	—	—	—	—	—	—	—	—	—	—	—	—	0	31
NFL	14	182(125)	2562	10273	4.0(76)	81	376	3062	8.1(57)	5	1	0	0.0	0	0.0	0	0	—	—	—	—	—	516	12639

ANDERSON, PAUL Paul Theodore, G, 6´0˝/200 lbs; Illinois; B2/6/1902 Rock Island, IL, D11/30/1970 Berryville, AR **1925** RI 1 (0)

ANDERSON, PRESTON Jerry Preston, DB, 6´1˝/183 lbs; Rice; 1974: Cle, rnd 16; B9/30/1951 Bonham, TX **1974** Cle 14

ANDERSON, RALPH Ralph M., E, 6´4˝/223 lbs; Santa Monica Coll (CA); Los Angeles State; 1958: ChiB, rnd 9; B1/1/1937 Long Beach, CA, D11/26/1960 Los Angeles, CA

YEAR	TEAM	G (GS, POS)	RUSH	YD	AVG (LG)	TD	REC	YD	AVG (LG)	TD	PASS	COMP	PCT	YD	AVG (LG)	TD	INT	SK	YD	QBR	KPR	OTD	PTS	TAY
1958	ChiB	12	—	—	—	—	11	177	16.1(30)	1	—	—	—	—	—	—	—	—	—	—	—	—	6	94
1960	LAC-A	10(SE)	—	—	—	—	44	614	14.0(46)	5	—	—	—	—	—	—	—	—	—	—	—	—	30	332
NFL	2	22	—	—	—	—	55	791	14.4(46)	6	—	—	—	—	—	—	—	—	—	—	—	—	36	426

ANDERSON, RALPH Ralph Edward, DB, 6´2˝/180 lbs; West Texas A&M; 1971: Pit, rnd 5; B4/3/1949 Dallas, TX **1971** Pit 7 **1972**†Pit 14 (FS) **1973** NE 13 (10, FS) **NFL** 34 (10) [3 yrs]

ANDERSON, RASHARD Rashard, DB, 6´2˝/204 lbs; Jackson State; 2000: Car, rnd 1; B6/14/1977 Forest, MS **2000** Car 12 (0) **2001** Car 15 (9, LCB) **NFL** 27 (9) [2 yrs]

ANDERSON, RICHIE Richard Darnoll, FB, 6´2˝/230 lbs; Penn State; 1993: NYJ, rnd 6; B9/13/1971 Sandy Spring, MD

YEAR	TEAM	G (GS, POS)	RUSH	YD	AVG (LG)	TD	REC	YD	AVG (LG)	TD	PASS	COMP	PCT	YD	AVG (LG)	TD	INT	SK	YD	QBR	KPR	OTD	PTS	TAY
1993	NYJ	7(0)	—	—	—	—	—	—	—	—	—	—	—	—	—	—	—	—	—	—	k	—	0	6
1994	NYJ	13(5, fb)	43	207	4.8(55)	1	25	212	8.5(27)	1	—	—	—	—	—	—	—	—	—	—	k	—	12	326
1995	NYJ	10(0)	5	17	3.4(10)	0	5	26	5.2(9)	0	1	0	0.0	0	0.0	0	0	—	—	—	—	—	0	30
1996	NYJ	16(13, FB)	47	150	3.2(11)	1	44	385	8.8(48)	0	—	—	—	—	—	—	—	—	—	—	—	—	6	353
1997	NYJ	16(3)	21	70	3.3(19)	0	26	150	5.8(19)	1	—	—	—	—	—	—	—	—	—	—	—	—	6	150

YEAR	TEAM	G (GS, POS)	RUSH	YD	AVG (LG)	TD	REC	YD	AVG (LG)	TD	PASS	COMP	PCT	YD	AVG (LG)	TD	INT	SK	YD	QBR	KPR	OTD	PTS	TAY
1998	†NYJ	8(1)	1	2	2.0(2)	0	3	12	4.0(7)	0	—	—	—	—	—	—	—	—	—	—	—	—	0	8
1999	NYJ	16(9, FB)	16	84	5.3(16)	0	29	302	10.4(29)	3	—	—	—	—	—	—	—	—	—	—	—	—	18	250
2000	NYJ◇	16(15, FB)	27	63	2.3(9)	0	88	853	9.7(41)	2	—	—	—	—	—	—	—	—	—	—	—	—	12	500
2001	†NYJ	16(16, FB)	26	102	3.9(12)	0	40	252	6.3(22)	2	—	—	—	—	—	—	—	—	—	—	—	—	12	238
2002	†NYJ	16(16, FB)	5	27	5.4(16)	0	45	257	5.7(15)	1	1	0	0.0	0	0.0	0	0	—	—	—	—	—	6	161
2003	†Dal	15(8, FB)	70	306	4.4(19)	4	69	493	7.1(37)	4	1	0	0.0	0	0.0	0	0	—	—	—	—	—	30	583
2004	Dal	12(4)	57	246	4.3(27)	1	26	207	8.0(28)	1	1	1	100.0	26	26.0(26)	1	0	—	—	—	—	—	6	378
NFL	12	161(90)	318	1274	4.0(55)	4	400	3149	7.9(48)	14	4	1	25.0	26	6.5(26)	1	0	—	—	—	k	—	108	2981

ANDERSON, RICKEY Rickey Recardo, RB, 6'1"/211 lbs; South Carolina State; 1978: SD, rnd 3; B3/21/1953 Kingsland, GA

YEAR	TEAM	G (GS, POS)	RUSH	YD	AVG (LG)	TD	REC	YD	AVG (LG)	TD	KPR	OTD	PTS	TAY
1978	SD	16	3	11	3.7(6)	0	1	-3	-3.0(-3)		k	—	0	3

ANDERSON, ROGER Roger Cole, DT-T, 6'5"/265 lbs; Virginia Union; 1964: NYG, rnd 7/SD, rnd 7; B11/11/1942 Bedford, VA **1964** NYG 11 (RT) **1965** NYG 8 **1967** NYG 4 **1968** NYG 14 (LDT) **NFL** 37 [4 yrs]

ANDERSON, RONNIE Ronnie Darrell, WR, 6'1"/189 lbs; Allegheny; B2/27/1974 Cleveland, OH

YEAR	TEAM	G (GS, POS)	REC	YD	AVG (LG)	TD	OTD	PTS	TAY
1998	Arz	4(0)	1	8	8.0(8)	0	—	0	4

ANDERSON, SCOTT Donald Scott, C, 6'4"/242 lbs; Missouri; 1974: Min, rnd 3; B2/13/1951 Benton, IL **1974**†Min 5 **1976** Min 2 **NFL** 7 [2 yrs]

ANDERSON, SCOTTY Scott, WR, 6'2"/191 lbs; Grambling State; 2001: Det, rnd 5; B11/24/1979 Jonesboro, LA

YEAR	TEAM	G (GS, POS)	REC	YD	AVG (LG)	TD	OTD	PTS	TAY
2001	Det	9(4)	12	211	17.6(69)	1	—	6	111
2002	Det	16(4)	25	322	12.9(34)	1	—	6	166
2003	Det	9(0)	17	325	19.1(72)	2	—	14	173
NFL	3	34(8)	54	858	15.9(72)	4	—	26	449

ANDERSON, STEVIE Stevie, WR, 6'5"/215 lbs; Grambling State; 1993: Phx, rnd 8; B5/12/1970 Monroe, LA

YEAR	TEAM	G (GS, POS)	REC	YD	AVG (LG)	TD	KPR	OTD	PTS	TAY
1994	NYJ	10(0)	9	90	10.0(17)	1	—	—	0	45
1995	Arz	6(0)	3	34	11.3(18)	1	k	—	10	24
1996	Arz	8(0)	4	64	16.0(19)	1	—	—	0	32
NFL	3	24(0)	16	188	11.8(19)	1	k	—	10	101

ANDERSON, STUART Stuart Noel, LB, 6'1"/238 lbs; Virginia; 1982: KC, rnd 4; B12/25/1959 Mathews, VA **1982**†Was 2 (0) **1983**†Was 16 (0) **1984** Was 2 (0) **1984** Cle 4 (0) **1985** Was 16 (0) **NFL** 40 (0) [4 yrs]

ANDERSON, SUGARFOOT Ezzret, E, 6'4"/215 lbs; Kentucky State; B2/10/1920 Nashville, AR

YEAR	TEAM	G (GS, POS)	RUSH	YD	AVG	TD	REC	YD	AVG	TD	OTD	PTS	TAY
1947	LAD-A	13(3)	3	24	8.0	0	11	126	11.5	1	—	6	92

ANDERSON, TAZ Tazwell Leigh, TE, 6'2"/220 lbs; Georgia Tech; 1960: Cle, rnd 7/DalT, rnd 2; B11/15/1938 Savannah, GA

YEAR	TEAM	G (GS, POS)	RUSH	YD	AVG (LG)	TD	REC	YD	AVG (LG)	TD	KPR	OTD	PTS	TAY
1961	SL	14(TE)	15	39	2.6(19)	1	22	399	18.1(78)	2	—	—	18	259
1962	SL	14(TE)	—	—	—		35	535	15.3(51)	3	k	—	18	274
1963	SL	5(te)	—	—	—		5	47	9.4(16)	0	—	—	0	24
1964	SL	13(TE)	—	—	—		7	60	8.6(13)	0	—	—	0	30
1966	Atl	8	—	—	—		10	195	19.5(62)	3	—	—	18	113
1967	Atl	8	—	—	—		8	99	12.4(21)	1	—	—	6	55
NFL	6	62	15	39	2.6(19)	1	87	1335	15.3(78)	9	k	—	60	753

ANDERSON, TERRY Terry C., WR, 5'9"/182 lbs; Bethune-Cookman; 1977: Mia, rnd 12; B1/10/1955 Eastover, SC **1978** Mia 4 **1980** SF 4 (0)

YEAR	TEAM	G (GS, POS)	RUSH	YD	AVG (LG)	TD	REC	YD	AVG (LG)	TD	KPR	OTD	PTS	TAY
1977	Mia	11	1	11	11.0(11)	0	—	—	—		kp	—	0	74
1978	Was	10	—	—	—		1	56	56.0(56)	0	kp	—	0	75
NFL	3	29	1	11	11.0(11)	0	1	56	56.0(56)	0	kp	—	0	215

ANDERSON, TIM Tim, DT, 6'4"/308 lbs; Ohio State; 2004: Buf, rnd 3; B11/22/1980 Fremont, OH **2004** Buf 3 (0) **2005** Buf 16 (12, RDT) **NFL** 19 (12) [2 yrs]

ANDERSON, VICKEY RAY Vickey Ray, RB, 6'0"/205 lbs; Oklahoma; B5/3/1956 Oklahoma City, OK

YEAR	TEAM	G (GS, POS)	RUSH	YD	AVG (LG)	TD	REC	YD	AVG (LG)	TD	OTD	PTS	TAY
1980	GB	7(0)	4	5	1.3(4)	0	2	2	1.0(2)	0	—	0	6

ANDERSON, WARREN Warren, WR, 6'2"/195 lbs; West Virginia State; 1977: Hou, rnd 4; B7/3/1955 Williamsburg, VA **1977** Hou 8 **1978** SL 2 **NFL** 10 [2 yrs]

ANDERSON, WILL Willard August, FB-BB-TB, 5'10"/173 lbs; Syracuse; B5/5/1897 Muskegon, MI, D4/24/1982 Hinsdale, IL **1923** Roc 1 (1) **1924** Roc 3 (2) **NFL** 4 (3) [2 yrs]

ANDERSON, WILLIAM William Tim, DB, 6'0"/205 lbs; Ohio State; 1971: SF, rnd 1; B8/1/1949 Colliers, WV **1975** SF 12 (2) **1976** Buf 3 **NFL** 15 (2) [2 yrs]

ANDERSON, WILLIE Willie Aaron, T, 6'5"/340 lbs; Auburn; 1996: Cin, rnd 1; B7/11/1975 Whistler, AL **1996** Cin 16 (10, LT) **1997** Cin 16 (16, RT) **1998** Cin 16 (16, RT) **1999** Cin 14 (14, RT) **2000** Cin 16 (16, RT) **2001** Cin 16 (16, RT) **2002** Cin 16 (16, RT) **2003** Cin★16 (16, RT) **2004** Cin★16 (16, RT) **2005**†Cin★16 (16, RT) **NFL** 158 (152) [10 yrs]

ANDERSON, WINNIE Winston Donley, E, 6'0"/185 lbs; Colgate; B11/10/1909 Charleston, WV, D11/11/1950 Columbus, OH

YEAR	TEAM	G (GS, POS)	REC	YD	AVG	TD	OTD	PTS	TAY
1936	NYG	5(1)	7	74	10.6	0	—	0	37

ANDOLSEK, ERIC Eric Thomas, G, 6'2"/254 lbs; LSU; 1988: Det, rnd 5; B8/22/1966 Thibodeaux, LA, D6/23/1992 Thibodeaux, LA **1988** Det 13 (0) **1989** Det 16 (16, LG) **1990** Det 16 (16, LG) **1991**†Det 16 (16, LG) **NFL** 61 (48) [4 yrs]

ANDRAKO, STEVE Stephen Francis, C-LB, 6'2"/210 lbs; Ohio State; 1940: Was, rnd 17; B9/11/1915 Braddock, PA, D11/30/1980 Half Moon Bay, CA **1940**†Was 5 (0)

ANDREW, TROY Troy Warden, C, 6'4"/305 lbs; Duke; B12/12/1977 Tamuning, Guam **2001**†Mia 8 (0)

ANDREWS, AL Alvin Wayne, LB, 6'3"/216 lbs; Laney Coll (CA); New Mexico State; B7/10/1945 Oakland, CA **1970** Buf 8 **1971** Buf 14 (rlb) **NFL** 22 [2 yrs]

ANDREWS, BILLY William Doughty, LB, 6'0"/220 lbs; Southeastern Louisiana; 1967: Cle, rnd 13; B6/14/1945 Clinton, LA **1967**†Cle 14 (rlb) **1968**†Cle 14 **1969**†Cle 14 **1970** Cle 14 (RLB) **1971**†Cle 14 (RLB) **1972**†Cle 14 (RLB) **1973** Cle 5 (mlb) **1974** Cle 11 **1975** SD 14 (6, rlb) **1976** KC 14 (14, LLB) **1977** KC 14 (LLB) **NFL** 142 (20) [11 yrs]

ANDREWS, GEORGE George Eldon, LB, 6'3"/226 lbs; Nebraska; 1979: LA, rnd 1; B11/28/1955 Omaha, NE **1980**†LARm 13 (7, rlb) **1981** LARm 15 (15, RLB) **1982** LARm 9 (9, RLB) **1983**†LARm 16 (16, ROLB) **1984** LARm 11 (11, ROLB)

YEAR	TEAM	G (GS, POS)	REC	YD	AVG (LG)	TD	QBR	OTD	PTS	TAY
1979	†LARm	16	1	2	2.0(2)	0	—	—	0	1
NFL	6	80(58)	1	2	2.0(2)	0	iS	—	0	18

ANDREWS, JABY J.B., WB-DB, /208 lbs; Texas-El Paso; B5/10/1912 Dallas, TX

YEAR	TEAM	G (GS, POS)	RUSH	YD	AVG	TD	PASS	COMP	PCT	YD	AVG	TD	INT	OTD	PTS	TAY
1934	SL	2(0)	10	52	5.2	0	19	8	42.1	97	5.1	0	1	—	0	61

ANDREWS, JOHN John Milton, TE-RB, 6'3"/227 lbs; Indiana; 1971: Bal, rnd 5; B11/2/1948 Indianapolis, IN

YEAR	TEAM	G (GS, POS)	RUSH	YD	AVG (LG)	TD	REC	YD	AVG (LG)	TD	KPR	OTD	PTS	TAY
1972	SD	1												
1973	Bal	8	—	—	—		1	1	1.0(1)	1	k	—	6	4
1974	Bal	14	5	6	1.2(4)	0	1	1	1.0(1)	0	k	—	0	9
NFL	3	23	5	6	1.2(4)	0	1	1	1.0(1)	1	k	—	6	13

ANDREWS, JOHN John V., DE-DT, 6'5"/251 lbs; Morgan State; 1973: Det, rnd 7; B11/7/1951 Detroit, MI **1975** Mia 14 (1) **1976** Mia 14 (4, RDE) **NFL** 28 (5) [2 yrs]

ANDREWS, MITCH Mitchell Dean, TE, 6'2"/239 lbs; LSU; B3/4/1964 Houma, LA

YEAR	TEAM	G (GS, POS)	REC	YD	AVG (LG)	TD	OTD	PTS	TAY
1987	†Den	8(3)	4	53	13.3(20)	0	—	0	27

ANDREWS, RICKY Richard Guy, LB, 6'2"/236 lbs; Washington; 1989: SD, rnd 10; B4/14/1966 Western Samoa **1990** Sea 15 (0)

ANDREWS, ROY Leroy B., G-T-BB-TB-E, 6'0"/226 lbs; Pittsburg State; B1898 Osage Township, KS, deceased [KC] **1923** SL 5 (4, RG) **1924** KC 8 (6, LT), 4 **1925** KC 7 (3), 4 **1926** KC 8 (1), 1 **1927** Cle 2 (0) **NFL** 30 [5 yrs]

ANDREWS, SHAWN Shawn, G-T, 6'4"/350 lbs; Arkansas; 2004: Phi, rnd 1; B12/25/1982 Camden, AR **2004** Phi 1 (1) **2005** Phi 16 (16, RG) **NFL** 17 (17) [2 yrs]

ANDREWS, STACY Stacy Dewayne, T, 6'4"/330 lbs; Mississippi; 2004: Cin, rnd 4; B6/2/1981 Camden, AR **2004** Cin 1 (0) **2005**†Cin 14 (0) **NFL** 15 (0) [2 yrs]

ANDREWS, TOM Thomas Edward, T-C, 6'4"/265 lbs; Louisville; 1984: Chi, rnd 4; B1/11/1962 Parma, OH **1984**†ChiB 7 (0) **1985**†ChiB 14 (0) **1987** Sea 2 (2) **NFL** 23 (2) [3 yrs]

ANDREWS, WILLIAM William L., RB, 6'0"/206 lbs; Auburn; 1979: Atl, rnd 3; B12/25/1955 Thomasville, GA

YEAR	TEAM	G (GS, POS)	RUSH	YD	AVG (LG)	TD	REC	YD	AVG (LG)	TD	OTD	PTS	TAY
1979	Atl	15(15, FB)	239	1023	4.3(23)	3	39	309	7.9(34)	2	—	30	1218
1980	†Atl★	16(16, FB)	265	1308	4.9(33)	4	51	456	8.9(26)	1	—	30	1581

YEAR	TEAM	G (GS, POS)	RUSH	YD	AVG (LG)	TD	REC	YD	AVG (LG)	TD	PASS	COMP	PCT	YD	AVG (LG)	TD	INT	SK	YD	QBR	KPR	OTD	PTS	TAY
1981	Atl★	16 (16, FB)	289	1301	4.5 (29)	10	81	735	9.1 (70)	2	—	—	—	—	—	—	—	—	—	—	—	—	72	1779
1982	†Atl★	9 (9, FB)	139	573	4.1 (19)	5	42	503	12.0 (**86**)	2	0	0	0.0	0	0.0	0	0	1	2	—	—	—	42	885
1983	Atl★	16 (16, RB)	331	1567	4.7 (27)	7	59	609	10.3 (40)	4	1	0	0.0	0	0.0	0	0	—	—	—	—	—	66	1962
1986	Atl	15 (0)	52	214	4.1 (13)	1	5	35	7.0 (14)	0	—	—	—	—	—	—	—	—	—	—	k	—	6	253
NFL	6	87 (72)	1315	5986	4.6 (33)	30	277	2647	9.6 (86)	11	1	0	0.0	0	0.0	0	0	1	2	—	k	—	246	7676

ANDRIE, GEORGE George Joseph, DE, 6´6˝/250 lbs; Marquette; 1962: Dal, rnd 6/SD, rnd 12; B4/20/1940 Grand Rapids, MI **1962** Dal 14 (RDE) **1963** Dal 12 (10, RDE) **1964** Dal 14 (LDE) **1965** Dal✧14 (RDE) **1966**†Dal★14 (RDE) **1967**†Dal★14 (RDE) **1968**†Dal★14 (RDE) **1969**†Dal★14 (RDE) **1970**†Dal 14 (RDE) **1971**†Dal 14 (RDE) **1972**†Dal 3 **NFL** 141 (10) [11 yrs]

ANDROS, PLATO Plato Gus, G-T-DG, 6´0˝/240 lbs; Oklahoma; B11/28/1921 Oklahoma City, OK **1947**†ChiC 12 (0) **1948**†ChiC 12 (9, LG) **1949** ChiC 12 (11, RT) **1950** ChiC 9 (4) **NFL** 45 (24) [4 yrs]

ANDRULEWICZ, TEDDY Theodore Stanislaus, WB, 5´11˝/175 lbs; Villanova; B1/1/1905 Mount Carmel, PA, D1/3/1996 Whitehall, PA **1930** Nwk 11 (4), 6

ANDRUS, LOU Louis John, LB, 6´6˝/230 lbs; Brigham Young; 1967: Den, rnd 11; B7/10/1943 Murray, UT **1967** Den-A 8

ANDRUS, SHELDON Sheldon James, DT, 6´2˝/271 lbs; Nicholls State; B10/5/1962 Lafayette, LA **1986** NO 1 (0) **1987** NO 3 (1) **NFL** 4 (1) [2 yrs]

ANDRUSKING, SIG Sigmond, G, 5´8˝/187 lbs; Detroit Mercy; B1914 Erie, PA **1937** Bkn 7 (1)

ANDRUSYSHYN, ZENON Zenon, P-K, 6´2˝/210 lbs; UCLA; 1970: Dal, rnd 9; B2/25/1947 Gunzburg, Germany

YEAR	TEAM	G (GS, POS)	RUSH	YD	AVG (LG)	TD	REC	YD	AVG (LG)	TD	PASS	COMP	PCT	YD	AVG (LG)	TD	INT	SK	YD	QBR	KPR	OTD	PTS	TAY
1978	KC	16	1	0	0.0 (0)	0	—	—	—	—	—	—	—	—	—	—	—	—	—	—	P	—	0	0

ANDRUZZI, JOE Joseph Dominic, G, 6´3˝/312 lbs; Southern Connecticut State; B8/23/1975 Brooklyn, NY **1998**†GB 15 (1) **1999** GB 8 (3) **2000** NE 11 (11, LG) **2001**†NE 16 (16, RG) **2002** NE 13 (13, RG) **2004**†NE 16 (16, LG) **2005** Cle 13 (13, LG)

YEAR	TEAM	G (GS, POS)	RUSH	YD	AVG (LG)	TD	REC	YD	AVG (LG)	TD	PASS	COMP	PCT	YD	AVG (LG)	TD	INT	SK	YD	QBR	KPR	OTD	PTS	TAY
2003	†NE	16 (16, RG)	—	—	—	—	1	0	0.0 (0)	0	—	—	—	—	—	—	—	—	—	—	—	—	0	0
NFL	8	108 (89)	—	—	—	—	1	0	0.0	0	—	—	—	—	—	—	—	—	—	—	—	—	0	0

ANE, CHARLIE Charlie Teetai, T-C, 6´2˝/260 lbs; USC; 1953: Det, rnd 4; B1/25/1931 Honolulu, HI **1953**†Det 12 (c) **1954**†Det 12 (RT) **1955** Det 12 (LT) **1956** Det★12 (C) **1957**†Det☆12 (RT) **1958** Det✧12 (RT/c)

YEAR	TEAM	G (GS, POS)	RUSH	YD	AVG (LG)	TD	REC	YD	AVG (LG)	TD	PASS	COMP	PCT	YD	AVG (LG)	TD	INT	SK	YD	QBR	KPR	OTD	PTS	TAY
1959	Det	11 (C)	0	10	(10)	0	—	—	—	—	—	—	—	—	—	—	—	—	—	—	—	—	0	10
NFL	7	83	0	10	(10)	0	—	—	—	—	—	—	—	—	—	—	—	—	—	—	k	—	0	14

ANE, CHARLIE Charlie Teetai, C, 6´1˝/233 lbs; Michigan State; B8/12/1952 Los Angeles, CA **1975** KC 14 **1976** KC 14 (1) **1977** KC 14 **1978** KC 16 **1979** KC 16 **1980** KC 16 (2) **1981** GB 15 (0) **NFL** 105 (3) [7 yrs]

ANELLI, MARK Mark Anthony, TE, 6´3˝/265 lbs; Wisconsin; 2002: SF, rnd 6; B6/5/1979 Addison, IL **2002** SF 2 (0)

ANGELO, JIM James Anthony, G, 6´3˝/275 lbs; Indiana (PA); B8/23/1963 Pittsburgh, PA **1987** Phi 1 (0)

ANGSMAN, ELMER Elmer Joseph, HB, 5´11˝/200 lbs; Notre Dame; 1946: ChiC, rnd 3; B12/11/1925 Chicago, IL, D4/11/2002 West Palm Beach, FL

YEAR	TEAM	G (GS, POS)	RUSH	YD	AVG (LG)	TD	REC	YD	AVG (LG)	TD	PASS	COMP	PCT	YD	AVG (LG)	TD	INT	SK	YD	QBR	KPR	OTD	PTS	TAY
1946	ChiC	11 (5, rh)	48	328	6.8 (61)	2	2	44	22.0 (38)	0	1	0	0.0	0	0.0	0	0	—	—	—	k	—	12	368
1947	†ChiC☆	12 (1, rh)	110	412	3.7 (18)	7	5	138	27.6 (52)	1	—	—	—	—	—	—	—	—	—	—	k	—	48	543
1948	†ChiC☆	12 (8, RH)	131	638	4.9 (72)	8	9	142	15.8 (38)	1	—	—	—	—	—	—	—	—	—	—	—	—	54	794
1949	ChiC☆	12 (12, RH)	125	674	5.4 (82)	6	5	57	11.4 (32)	0	1	0	0.0	0	0.0	0	0	—	—	—	k	—	36	754
1950	ChiC✧	12 (RH)	102	362	3.5 (21)	1	7	56	8.0 (20)	1	—	—	—	—	—	—	—	—	—	—	—	—	12	405
1951	ChiC	12 (RH)	121	380	3.1 (28)	3	9	195	21.7 (80)	1	—	—	—	—	—	—	—	—	—	—	k	—	24	534
1952	ChiC	12	46	114	2.5 (9)	0	4	22	5.5 (9)	1	—	—	—	—	—	—	—	—	—	—	—	—	6	130
NFL	7	83 (26)	683	2908	4.3 (82)	27	41	654	16.0 (80)	5	2	0	0.0	0	0.0	0	0	—	—	—	k	—	192	3527

ANGULO, RICHARD Richard, TE, 6´7˝/260 lbs; Western New Mexico; 2003: SL, rnd 7; B8/13/1980 Albuquerque, NM **2003** SL 5 (0)

YEAR	TEAM	G (GS, POS)	RUSH	YD	AVG (LG)	TD	REC	YD	AVG (LG)	TD	PASS	COMP	PCT	YD	AVG (LG)	TD	INT	SK	YD	QBR	KPR	OTD	PTS	TAY
2005	Min	2 (0)	—	—	—	—	1	11	11.0 (11)	0	—	—	—	—	—	—	—	—	—	—	—	—	0	6
NFL	2	7 (0)	—	—	—	—	1	11	11.0 (11)	0	—	—	—	—	—	—	—	—	—	—	—	—	0	6

ANKROM, SCOTT Scott Randall, WR, 6´1˝/194 lbs; TCU; 1989: Dal, rnd 12; B1/4/1966 San Antonio, TX **1989** Dal 10 (0)

ANNAN, DUNC Duncan Colin, TB-WB-FB-BB-T, 5´10˝/178 lbs; Brown; Chicago; B8/10/1895 Chicago, IL, D6/21/1981 Palm Beach, FL **[K]** **1920** ChiT 8 (4, TB) **1922** Tol 9 (7, WB), 31 **1923** Ham 2 (2) **1924** Ham 5 (5, TB) **1925** Ham 2 (2, TB) **1925** Akr 10 (7, WB), 6 **1926** Ham 3 (3, TB) **1926** Akr 4 (2) **NFL** 43 (32), 37 [6 yrs]

ANNO, SAM Samuel Scott-Griffin, LB, 6´2˝/236 lbs; USC; B1/26/1965 Silver Spring, MD **1987** LARm 3 (0) **1987**†Min 6 (0) **1988**†Min 13 (0) **1989** TB 16 (0) **1990** TB 16 (0) **1991** TB 16 (0) **1992**†SD 16 (0) **1993** SD 16 (0) **NFL** 102 (0) [7 yrs]

ANTHONY, CHARLES Charles Raymond, LB, 6´1˝/230 lbs; USC; 1974: SD, rnd 15; B7/10/1952 Houston, TX **1974** SD 13 (10, MLB)

ANTHONY, CORNELIUS Cornelius Armand, LB, 6´0˝/235 lbs; Texas A&M; B7/3/1978 Pinesville, LA **2002** SF 10 (0) **2003** SF 7 (0) **NFL** 17 (0) [2 yrs]

ANTHONY, REIDEL Reidel Clarence, WR, 5´11˝/178 lbs; Florida; 1997: TB, rnd 1; B10/20/1976 Pahokee, FL **[R]**

YEAR	TEAM	G (GS, POS)	RUSH	YD	AVG (LG)	TD	REC	YD	AVG (LG)	TD	PASS	COMP	PCT	YD	AVG (LG)	TD	INT	SK	YD	QBR	KPR	OTD	PTS	TAY
1997	†TB	16 (12, WR)	5	84	16.8 (26)	0	35	448	12.8 (38)	4	—	—	—	—	—	—	—	—	—	—	k	—	24	545
1998	TB	15 (13, WR)	4	43	10.8 (32)	0	51	708	13.9 (79)	7	—	—	—	—	—	—	—	—	—	—	k	—	44	860
1999	TB	13 (7, wr)	1	2	2.0 (2)	0	30	296	9.9 (30)	1	—	—	—	—	—	—	—	—	—	—	k	—	6	274
2000	†TB	16 (1)	—	—	—	—	15	232	15.5 (46)	4	—	—	—	—	—	—	—	—	—	—	k	—	24	179
2001	TB	13 (4)	3	22	7.3 (16)	0	13	162	12.5 (35)	0	—	—	—	—	—	—	—	—	—	—	p	—	0	100
NFL	5	73 (37)	13	151	11.6 (32)	0	144	1846	12.8 (79)	16	—	—	—	—	—	—	—	—	—	—	kp	—	98	1958

ANTHONY, TERRENCE Terrence Everett, DB, 5´10˝/183 lbs; Iowa State; 1987: Atl, rnd 9; B1/17/1965 East St. Louis, IL **1987** SL 1 (0)

ANTHONY, TERRY Terrence, WR, 6´0˝/200 lbs; Florida State; 1990: TB, rnd 11; B3/9/1968 Daytona Beach, FL **1990** TB 1 (0)

YEAR	TEAM	G (GS, POS)	RUSH	YD	AVG (LG)	TD	REC	YD	AVG (LG)	TD	PASS	COMP	PCT	YD	AVG (LG)	TD	INT	SK	YD	QBR	KPR	OTD	PTS	TAY
1991	TB	9 (0)	—	—	—	—	4	51	12.8 (14)	0	—	—	—	—	—	—	—	—	—	—	—	—	0	26
NFL	2	10 (0)	—	—	—	—	4	51	12.8 (14)	0	—	—	—	—	—	—	—	—	—	—	—	—	0	26

ANTHONY, TYRONE Edward Tyrone, RB, 5´11˝/212 lbs; North Carolina; 1984: NO, rnd 3; B3/3/1962 Winston-Salem, NC

YEAR	TEAM	G (GS, POS)	RUSH	YD	AVG (LG)	TD	REC	YD	AVG (LG)	TD	PASS	COMP	PCT	YD	AVG (LG)	TD	INT	SK	YD	QBR	KPR	OTD	PTS	TAY
1984	NO	15 (0)	20	105	5.3 (19)	1	12	113	9.4 (32)	0	—	—	—	—	—	—	—	—	—	—	k	—	6	332
1985	NO	16 (0)	17	65	3.8 (13)	0	28	185	6.6 (36)	0	—	—	—	—	—	—	—	—	—	—	k	—	0	289
NFL	2	31 (0)	37	170	4.6 (19)	1	40	298	7.4 (36)	0	—	—	—	—	—	—	—	—	—	—	k	—	6	620

ANTOINE, LIONEL Lionel Sylvester, T, 6´6˝/262 lbs; Southern Illinois; 1972: Chi, rnd 1; B8/31/1950 Biloxi, MS **1972** ChiB 5 **1973** ChiB 13 **1974** ChiB 14 (LT) **1975** ChiB 14 (LT) **1976** ChiB☆13 (8, LT) **1978** ChiB 9 (1) **NFL** 68 (9) [6 yrs]

ANTRUM, GLENN Glenn, WR, 5´11˝/175 lbs; Connecticut; B2/3/1966 Derby, CT **1989** NE 1 (0)

ANTWINE, HOUSTON Houston, DT-DE, 6´0˝/270 lbs; Southern Illinois; 1961: Hou, rnd 8/Det, rnd 3; B4/11/1939 Louise, MS **1961** Bos-A 14 **1962** Bos-A 14 (RDT) **1963**†Bos-A★14 (RDT) **1964** Bos-A★14 (RDT) **1965** Bos-A✧14 (RDT) **1966** Bos-A★14 (RDT) **1967** Bos-A★13 (RDT) **1968** Bos-A★14 (14, RDT) **1969** Bos-A☆14 (14, RDT) **1970** Bos 14 (14, RDE) **1971** NE 3 (3) **1972** Phi 14 (RDT) **NFL** 156 (45) [12 yrs]

APKE, STEVE Steven James, LB, 6´1˝/222 lbs; Pittsburgh; B8/3/1965 Cincinnati, OH **1987** Pit 3 (3)

APOLSKIS, CHUCK Charles Casimir, E, 6´2˝/207 lbs; DePaul; B12/18/1914 Cicero, IL, deceased **1938** ChiB 1 (0) **1939** ChiB 1 (0) **NFL** 2 (0) [2 yrs]

APOLSKIS, RAY Raymond Edward, C-G-LB, 5´11˝/206 lbs; Marquette; 1941: ChiC, rnd 5; B10/19/1918 Cicero, IL, D6/30/1960 San Mateo, CA **1941** ChiC✧11 (7, C) **1942** ChiC 11 (9, C) **1945** ChiC 5 (1) **1946** ChiC 6 (1) **1947**†ChiC 12 (5, rg) **1948**†ChiC 12 (1) **1949** ChiC 8 (1) **1950** ChiC 9 **NFL** 74 (25) [8 yrs]

APPLE, JIM James Dunbar, HB, 6´0˝/200 lbs; Upsala; B7/14/1938

YEAR	TEAM	G (GS, POS)	RUSH	YD	AVG (LG)	TD	REC	YD	AVG (LG)	TD	PASS	COMP	PCT	YD	AVG (LG)	TD	INT	SK	YD	QBR	KPR	OTD	PTS	TAY
1961	NYT-A	3	7	2	0.3 (7)	0	—	—	—	—	—	—	—	—	—	—	—	—	—	—	kp	—	0	5

APPLEGRAN, CLARENCE Clarence Oliver, G, 6´2˝/200 lbs; Illinois; B11/1893 Chicago, IL, D5/6/1960 Chicago, IL **1920** Det 4 (2, LG)

APPLETON, SCOTT Gordon Scott, DT-DE, 6´3˝/260 lbs; Texas; 1964: Hou, rnd 1/Dal, rnd 1; B2/20/1942 Brady, TX, D3/2/1992 Austin, TX **1964** Hou-A 14 (LDE/rdt) **1965** Hou-A 14 (ldt) **1966** Hou-A 14 **1967** SD-A 14 (14, RDT) **1968** SD-A 14 (14, RDT) **NFL** 70 (28) [5 yrs]

APSIT, MARGER Marger, BB-LB-DB-TB, 5´11˝/200 lbs; USC; B6/5/1909 Aurora, IL, D12/22/1988 Bakersfield, CA **1931** Fra 6 (0) **1931** Bkn 3 (1)

YEAR	TEAM	G (GS, POS)	RUSH	YD	AVG (LG)	TD	REC	YD	AVG (LG)	TD	PASS	COMP	PCT	YD	AVG (LG)	TD	INT	SK	YD	QBR	KPR	OTD	PTS	TAY
1932	GB	2 (0)	4	6	1.5	0	—	—	—	—	—	—	—	—	—	—	—	—	—	—	—	—	0	6
1933	Bos	12 (9, BB)	7	35	5.0	0	1	24	24.0 (24)	0	5	1	20.0	25	5.0 (25)	0	2	—	—	—	—	—	0	-21
NFL	3	23 (10)	11	41	3.7	0	1	24	24.0 (24)	0	5	1	20.0	25	5.0 (25)	0	2	—	—	—	—	—	0	-15

YEAR	TEAM	G(GS, POS)	RUSH	YD	AVG(LG)	TD	REC	YD	AVG(LG)	TD	PASS COMP	PCT	YD	AVG(LG)	TD	INT	SK	YD	QBR	KPR	OTD	PTS	TAY

APUNA, BEN Benjamin Calvin, LB, 6'1"/222 lbs; Arizona State; 1980: SL, rnd 7; B6/26/1957 Honolulu, HI **1980** NYG 10 (3)

ARAGUZ, LEO Leobardo Jaime, P, 5'11"/190 lbs; Stephen F. Austin State; B1/17/1970 Pharr, TX **[P]** **1999** Oak 16 (0) **2001** Det 3 (0) **2003** Min 2 (0) **2005** Sea 4 (0)

1996	Oak	3(0)	1	0	0.0(0)	0	—	—	—	—	—	—	—	—	—	—	—	—	P	—	0	0
1997	Oak	16(0)	1	0	0.0(0)	0	—	—	—	—	—	—	—	—	—	—	—	—	P	—	0	0
1998	Oak	16(0)	1	-12	-12.0(-12)	0	—	—	—	—	1	1	100.0	1	-1.0(-1)	0	0	—	—	P	—	0	-13
NFL	7	60(0)	3	-12	-4.0	0	—	—	—	—	1	1	100.0	1	-1.0(-1)	0	0	—	—	P	—	0	-13

ARAPOSTATHIS, EVAN Evan Anthony, P, 5'9"/160 lbs; Grossmont Coll (CA); Eastern Illinois; B10/30/1963 San Diego, CA

| 1986 | SL | 5(0) | — | — | — | — | — | — | — | — | 1 | 0 | 0.0 | 0 | 0.0 | 0 | — | — | — | P | — | 0 | 0 |

ARBANAS, FRED Frederick Vincent, TE, 6'3"/240 lbs; Michigan State; 1961: DalT, rnd 7/SL, rnd 2; B1/14/1939 Detroit, MI

1962	†DalT-A★	14(TE)	—	—	—	—	29	469	16.2(47)	6	—	—	—	—	—	—	—	—	—	—	—	36	265
1963	KC-A★	14(TE)	—	—	—	—	34	373	11.0(40)	6	—	—	—	—	—	—	—	—	—	—	—	36	217
1964	KC-A★	14(TE)	—	—	—	—	34	686	20.2(59)	8	—	—	—	—	—	—	—	—	—	—	—	48	383
1965	KC-A★	14(TE)	—	—	—	—	24	418	17.4(67)	4	—	—	—	—	—	—	—	—	—	—	—	24	229
1966	†KC-A☆	14(TE)	—	—	—	—	22	305	13.9(36)	4	—	—	—	—	—	—	—	—	—	—	—	26	173
1967	KC-A★	14(TE)	—	—	—	—	20	295	14.8(43)	5	—	—	—	—	—	—	—	—	—	—	—	30	173
1968	†KC-A	14(TE)	3	14	4.7(8)	0	11	189	17.2(48)	0	—	—	—	—	—	—	—	—	—	—	—	0	109
1969	†KC-A	14(TE)	1	1	1.0(1)	0	16	258	16.1(44)	0	—	—	—	—	—	—	—	—	—	—	—	0	130
1970	KC	6(TE)	—	—	—	—	8	108	13.5(26)	1	—	—	—	—	—	—	—	—	—	—	—	6	59
NFL	9	118	4	15	3.8(8)	0	198	3101	15.7(67)	34	—	—	—	—	—	—	—	—	—	—	—	206	1736

ARBUBAKRR, HASSON Hasson, DE, 6'4"/250 lbs; Pasadena City College (JC); Texas Tech; 1983: TB, rnd 9; B12/9/1960 Newark, NJ **1983** TB 16 (1) **1984** Min 4 (0) **NFL** 20 (1) [2 yrs]

ARBUCKLE, CHARLES Charles Edward, TE, 6'3"/248 lbs; UCLA; 1990: NO, rnd 5; B9/13/1968 Beaumont, TX

1992	Ind	16(3)	—	—	—	—	13	152	11.7(23)	1	—	—	—	—	—	—	—	—	—	—	—	6	81
1993	Ind	16(2)	—	—	—	—	15	90	6.0(23)	0	—	—	—	—	—	—	—	—	—	—	—	0	45
1994	Ind	7(0)	—	—	—	—	1	7	7.0(7)	0	—	—	—	—	—	—	—	—	—	—	—	0	4
1995	Ind	3(3)	—	—	—	—	4	33	8.3(12)	0	—	—	—	—	—	—	—	—	—	—	—	0	17
NFL	4	42(8)	—	—	—	—	33	282	8.5(23)	1	—	—	—	—	—	—	—	—	—	—	—	6	146

ARCHAMBEAU, LESTER Lester Milward, DE, 6'5"/275 lbs; Stanford; 1990: GB, rnd 7; B6/27/1967 Montville, NJ **1990** GB 4 (0) **1991** GB 16 (0) **1992** GB 16 (0) **1993** Atl 15 (11, RDE) **1994** Atl 16 (12, RDE) **1995**†Atl 16 (7, lde) **1996** Atl 15 (15, LDE) **1997** Atl 16 (16, LDE) **1998**†Atl 15 (15, LDE) **1999** Atl 15 (15, LDE) **2000**†Den 3 (0) **NFL** 147 (91) [11 yrs]

ARCHER, DAN Daniel G., G-T, 6'5"/245 lbs; Oregon; 1966: Oak, rnd R6; B9/29/1944 Grand Rapids, MI **1967**†Oak-A 14 **1968** Cin-A 8 **NFL** 22 [2 yrs]

ARCHER, DAVID David Mark, QB, 6'2"/207 lbs; Snow Coll (UT); Iowa State; B2/15/1962 Fayetteville, NC

1984	Atl	2(0)	6	38	6.3(12)	0	—	—	—	—	18	11	61.1	181	10.1(34)	1	1	7	45	—	—	0	94
1985	Atl	16(11, QB)	70	347	5.0(29)	2	—	—	—	—	312	161	51.6	1992	6.4(62)	7	17	43	312	56.5	—	12	718
1986	Atl	11(11, QB)	52	298	5.7(22)	0	—	—	—	—	294	150	51.0	2007	6.8(65)	10	9	34	249	71.6	—	0	992
1987	Atl	9(1)	2	8	4.0(7)	0	—	—	—	—	23	9	39.1	95	4.1(33)	0	2	3	24	—	—	0	-25
1988	Was	1(0)	3	1	0.3(4)	0	—	—	—	—	2	0	0.0	0	0.0	0	0	—	—	—	—	0	1
1989	SD	16(0)	2	14	7.0(14)	0	—	—	—	—	12	5	41.7	62	5.2(17)	0	1	2	12	—	—	0	5
NFL	6	55(23)	135	706	5.2(29)	2	—	—	—	—	661	336	50.8	4337	6.6(65)	18	30	89	642	61.9	—	12	1785

ARCHER, TROY James Troy, DT-DE, 6'4"/250 lbs; Colorado; 1976: NYG, rnd 1; B1/16/1955 Glendale, CA, D6/22/1979 North Bergen, NJ **1976** NYG 14 **1977** NYG 14 (14, RDT) **1978** NYG 10 (8, RDT) **NFL** 38 (22) [3 yrs]

ARCHIBALD, BEN Ben, T, 6'3"/320 lbs; Brigham Young; B8/26/1978 Tacoma, WA **2005** NO 6 (0)

ARCHIE, MIKE Michael Lamont, RB, 5'8"/205 lbs; Penn State; 1996: Hou, rnd 7; B10/14/1972 Sharon, PA **1996** Hou 2 (0) **1997** Ten 5 (0)

| 1998 | Ten | 16(0) | 6 | 24 | 4.0(20) | 1 | 5 | 25 | 5.0(7) | 0 | 2 | 1 | 50.0 | 18 | 9.0(18) | 1 | 0 | — | — | kp | — | 6 | 361 |
| NFL | 3 | 23(0) | 6 | 24 | 4.0(20) | 1 | 5 | 25 | 5.0(7) | 0 | 2 | 1 | 50.0 | 18 | 9.0(18) | 1 | 0 | — | — | kp | — | 6 | 349 |

ARCHOSKA, JULIE Julius, E, 5'11"/190 lbs; Syracuse; B3/13/1905 Lynn, MA, D3/18/1972 Lynn, MA **1930** SI 4 (1)

ARCHULETA, ADAM Adam Jason, DB, 6'0"/223 lbs; Arizona State; 2001: SL, rnd 1; B11/27/1977 Chandler, AZ **2001**†SL 13 (12, SS) **2002** SL 16 (16, SS) **2003**†SL 13 (13, SS) **2004**†SL 16 (14, SS) **2005** SL 14 (14, SS) **NFL** 72 (69) [5 yrs]

ARD, BILLY William Donovan, G, 6'3"/265 lbs; Wake Forest; 1981: NYG, rnd 8; B3/12/1959 East Orange, NJ **1981**†NYG 13 (6, lg) **1982** NYG 9 (9, LG) **1983** NYG 16 (16, LG) **1984** NYG 15 (15, LG) **1985**†NYG 16 (16, LG) **1986**†NYG 16 (16, LG) **1987** NYG 12 (12, LG) **1988** NYG 16 (16, LG) **1989** GB 15 (0) **1990** GB 15 (15, LG) **1991** GB 5 (2) **NFL** 148 (123) [11 yrs]

ARDIZZONE, TONY Anthony Allan, C, 6'3"/240 lbs; Northwestern; 1978: Det, rnd 6; B12/19/1956 La Grange, IL **1979**†ChiB 16

ARENA, TONY Anthony Gerald, C-LB, 6'0"/200 lbs; Michigan State; 1942: Det, rnd 13; B7/2/1918 Detroit, MI **1942** Det 1 (0)

ARENAS, JOE Lupe Joseph, HB-DB, 5'11"/180 lbs; Nebraska-Omaha; 1951: SF, rnd 8; B12/12/1925 Cedar Rapids, IA **[R]**

1951	SF	12	34	183	5.4(14)	3	1	12	12.0(12)	1	—	—	—	—	—	—	—	—	—	kp	—	24	618
1952	SF	12(LH)	44	183	4.2(14)	0	5	47	9.4(14)	1	1	0	0.0	0	0.0	0	—	—	—	kp	—	6	343
1953	SF	12(LH)	72	380	5.3(60)	6	10	113	11.3(38)	1	1	0	0.0	0	0.0	0	—	—	—	kpi	—	42	885
1954	SF	12(DB)	11	77	7.0(26)	0	2	12	6.0(12)	0	—	—	—	—	—	—	—	—	—	kpi	—	0	218
1955	SF	12(LH)	37	150	4.1(30)	0	13	255	19.6(53)	1	1	1	100.0	0	0.0	0	—	—	—	kpi	—	12	467
1956	SF	12(RH)	—	—	—	—	14	226	16.1(50)	1	—	—	—	—	—	—	—	—	—	kp	—	18	556
1957	†SF	12	5	14	2.8(7)	1	1	10	10.0(10)	0	3	3	100.0	92	30.7(33)	2	0	—	—	kp	—	6	337
NFL	7	84	203	987	4.9(60)	10	46	675	14.7(53)	6	6	3	50.0	92	15.3(33)	2	0	—	—	kpi	2	108	3423

ARENZ, ARNIE Arnold Henry, BB-LB, 6'2"/215 lbs; St. Louis; B10/13/1911 Flat River, MO, D1/31/1985 Olympia, WA

| 1934 | Bos | 3(0) | 4 | 11 | 2.8 | 0 | 2 | 8 | 4.0(8) | 0 | 8 | 1 | — | 8 | 1.6(8) | 0 | 1 | — | — | — | — | 0 | -17 |

ARGUS, BOB Robert Anthony, WB-FB-TB-BB, 5'10"/193 lbs; none; B1/21/1894 Hammondsport, NY, deceased **1920** Roc 10 (1, WB) **1921** Roc 5 (4, WB) **1922** Roc 5 (5, WB), 6 **1923** Roc 4 (4, WB) **1924** Roc 7 (5, FB) **1925** Roc 5 (3, FB) **NFL** 36 (22) [6 yrs]

ARIAIL, GUMP David William, E, 5'11"/205 lbs; Auburn; B12/29/1910 Birmingham, AL, D2/10/2001 Fayetteville, NC **1934** Bkn 1 (0) **1934** Cin 1 (1) **NFL** 2 (1) [1 yr]

ARIANS, JAKE Jacob Bruce, K, 5'11"/203 lbs; Alabama-Birmingham; B1/26/1978 Blacksburg, VA **[K]** **2001** Buf 10 (0)

ARIEY, MIKE Michael August, T, 6'5"/295 lbs; San Diego State; B3/12/1964 Bakersfield, CA **1989** GB 1 (0)

ARIRI, OBED Obed Chukwuma, K, 5'8"/170 lbs; Clemson; 1981: Bal, rnd 7; B4/7/1956 Owerri, Nigeria **[K]** **1984** TB 16 (0) **1987** Was 2 (0) **NFL** 18 (0) [2 yrs]

ARMOUR, JOJUAN JoJuan, DB, 5'11"/220 lbs; Miami (OH); 1999: Oak, rnd 7; B7/10/1976 Toledo, OH **1999** Cin 2 (0) **2000** Cin 4 (0) **2001** Cin 16 (11, SS) **2002** Cin 16 (8, SS) **NFL** 38 (19) [4 yrs]

ARMOUR, JUSTIN Justin Hugh, WR, 6'4"/210 lbs; Stanford; 1995: Buf, rnd 4; B1/1/1973 Colorado Springs, CO

1995	†Buf	15(9, WR)	4	-5	-1.3(6)	0	26	300	11.5(28)	3	1	0	0.0	0	0.0	0	—	—	—	—	—	18	160
1997	Phi	1(0)	—	—	—	—	—	—	—	—	—	—	—	—	—	—	—	—	—	—	—	—	—
1998	Den	8(0)	—	—	—	—	1	23	23.0(0)	0	—	—	—	—	—	—	—	—	—	—	—	0	12
1999	Bal	15(7, WR)	—	—	—	—	37	538	14.5(54)	4	—	—	—	—	—	—	—	—	—	—	—	24	289
NFL	4	39(16)	4	-5	-1.3(6)	0	64	861	13.5(54)	7	1	0	0.0	0	0.0	0	—	—	—	—	—	42	461

ARMOUR, PHIL Phillip, C, 6'3"/315 lbs; North Texas; B12/9/1976 Denton, TX **2000** Ind 3 (0)

ARMS, LOYD Lloyd, G, 6'1"/215 lbs; Oklahoma State; 1943: ChiB, rnd 14; B9/24/1919 Sulphur, OK, D6/18/1999 **1946** ChiC 8 (5, LG) **1947**†ChiC 12 (12, LG) **1948** ChiC 7 (2) **NFL** 27 (19) [3 yrs]

ARMSTEAD, JESSIE Jessie Willard, LB, 6'1"/237 lbs; Miami (FL); 1993: NYG, rnd 8; B10/26/1970 Dallas, TX **1993**†NYG 16 (0) **1994** NYG 16 (0) **1995** NYG 16 (2) **1996** NYG 16 (16, LLB) **1997**†NYG★16 (16, LLB) **1998** NYG★16 (16, LLB) **1999** NYG★16 (16, RLB) **2000**†NYG★16 (16, RLB) **2001** NYG✧16 (16, RLB) **2002** Was 16 (16, RLB) **2003** Was 16 (15, RLB) **NFL** 176 (129) [11 yrs]

YEAR	TEAM	G (GS, POS)	RUSH	YD	AVG (LG)	TD	REC	YD	AVG (LG)	TD	PASS	COMP	PCT	YD	AVG (LG)	TD	INT	SK	YD	QBR	KPR	OTD	PTS	TAY
ARMSTRONG, ADGER Adger, RB, 6´0˝/213 lbs; Texas A&M; B6/21/1957 Houston, TX																								
1980	†Hou	16(0)	—	—	—	—	—	—	—	—	—	—	—	—	—	—	—	—	—	—	—	—	—	—
1981	Hou	16(2)	31	146	4.7(18)	0	29	278	9.6(48)	1	—	—	—	—	—	—	—	—	—	—	k	—	6	281
1982	Hou	6(3)	8	15	1.9(5)	0	12	75	6.3(14)	0	—	—	—	—	—	—	—	—	—	—	—	—	0	53
1983	TB	11(5, fb)	7	30	4.3(7)	0	15	173	11.5(41)	2	—	—	—	—	—	—	—	—	—	—	k	—	12	122
1984	TB	15(9, fb)	10	34	3.4(9)	2	22	180	8.2(18)	3	—	—	—	—	—	—	—	—	—	—	—	—	30	159
1985	TB	16(0)	2	6	3.0(8)	0	2	4	2.0(3)	1	—	—	—	—	—	—	—	—	—	—	—	—	6	13
NFL	6	80(19)	58	231	4.0(18)	2	80	710	8.9(48)	7	—	—	—	—	—	—	—	—	—	—	k	—	54	627
ARMSTRONG, ANTONIO Antonio Donnell, aka Antonio Shorter, LB, 6´1˝/235 lbs; Texas A&M; 1995: SF, rnd 6; B10/15/1973 Houston, TX **1995** Mia 4 (0)																								
ARMSTRONG, BILL William Wright, G, 6´1˝/210 lbs; UCLA; B1920 **1943** Bkn 4 (0)																								
ARMSTRONG, BOB Robert Alva, T-G-C, 5´11˝/221 lbs; Rice; Missouri; B2/16/1909 Dallas, TX, D2/28/1990 San Antonio, TX **1931** Por 14 (3) **1932** Por 6 (5, LT) **NFL** 20 (8) [2 yrs]																								
ARMSTRONG, BRUCE Bruce Charles, T-G, 6´4˝/295 lbs; Louisville; 1987: NE, rnd 1; B9/7/1965 Miami, FL **1987** NE 12 (12, RT) **1988** NE☆16 (16, RT) **1989** NE☆16 (16, RT) **1990** NE★16 (16, LT) **1991** NE★16 (16, LT) **1992** NE 8 (8, LT) **1993** NE 16 (16, LT) **1994**†NE★16 (16, LT) **1995** NE★16 (16, LT) **1996**†NE★16 (16, LT) **1997**†NE✧16 (16, LT) **1998**†NE 16 (16, LT) **1999** NE 16 (16, LT) **2000** NE 16 (16, LT) **NFL** 212 (212) [14 yrs]																								
ARMSTRONG, CHARLIE Charles Andrew, DB-TB, 5´10˝/180 lbs; Mississippi College; 1941: ChiC, rnd 12; B4/20/1919 Hickory, MS, D7/20/2001 Meridian, MS																								
1946	Bkn-A	10(2)	22	78	3.5	0	—	—	—	—	21	9	42.9	126	6.0	1	2	—	—	—	Pkpi	—	0	225
ARMSTRONG, DERICK Derick, WR, 6´2˝/196 lbs; Arkansas-Monticello; B4/2/1979 Jasper, TX																								
2003	Hou	8(1)	—	—	—	—	7	75	10.7(18)	1	—	—	—	—	—	—	—	—	—	—	—	—	6	43
2004	Hou	14(1)	—	—	—	—	29	415	14.3(44)	1	—	—	—	—	—	—	—	—	—	—	—	—	6	213
2005	Hou	13(3)	—	—	—	—	9	115	12.8(28)	0	—	—	—	—	—	—	—	—	—	—	—	—	0	58
NFL	3	35(5)	—	—	—	—	45	605	13.4(44)	2	—	—	—	—	—	—	—	—	—	—	—	—	12	313
ARMSTRONG, GRAHAM Graham Leo, T, 6´4˝/230 lbs; John Carroll; B5/30/1918 Cleveland, OH, D1985, **[K]** **1941** Cle 7 (0) **1945** Cle 1 (0) **NFL** 8 (0) [2 yrs]																								
1947 Buf-A 14 (8, LT)																								
1948	†Buf-A	13(13, LT)	—	—	—	—	1	0	0.0	0	—	—	—	—	—	—	—	—	—	—	Kk	—	15	-6
AAFC	2	27(21)	—	—	—	—	1	0	0.0	0	—	—	—	—	—	—	—	—	—	—	Kk	—	23	-6
ARMSTRONG, HARVEY Harvey Lee, NT, 6´3˝/265 lbs; SMU; 1982: Phi, rnd 7; B12/29/1959 Houston, TX **1982** Phi 8 (0) **1983** Phi 16 (0) **1984** Phi 16 (0) **1986** Ind 16 (1) **1987**†Ind 11 (1) **1988** Ind 16 (1) **1989** Ind 16 (16, NT) **1990** Ind 12 (10, NT) **NFL** 111 (29) [8 yrs]																								
ARMSTRONG, JIMMY James Berton, DB, 5´8˝/166 lbs; Appalachian State; B6/18/1962 **1987** Dal 2 (2)																								
ARMSTRONG, 'JOHN John A., BB, 5´8˝/170 lbs; Dubuque; B1894, deceased **[KC]** **1923** RI 8 (7, BB), 12 **1924** RI 9 (5, BB), 7 **1925** RI 11 (8, BB), 31 **NFL** 28 (20), 50 [3 yrs]																								
ARMSTRONG, JOHN John Earl, DB, 5´9˝/190 lbs; Richmond; 1986: Min, rnd 11; B7/7/1963 Calhoun City, MS **1987** Buf 3 (2)																								
ARMSTRONG, NEILL Neill Ford, E-DB, 6´2˝/189 lbs; Oklahoma State; 1947: Phi, rnd 1/Bkn-A, rnd 1; B3/9/1926 Tishomingo, OK **[C]**																								
1947	†Phi	12(1)	—	—	—	—	17	197	11.6(46)	2	—	—	—	—	—	—	—	—	—	—	k	—	12	102
1948	†Phi	12(4)	—	—	—	—	24	325	13.5(33)	3	—	—	—	—	—	—	—	—	—	—	i	—	18	198
1949	†Phi	12(4)	—	—	—	—	24	271	11.3(45)	5	—	—	—	—	—	—	—	—	—	—	—	—	30	161
1950	Phi	12	—	—	—	—	8	124	15.5(36)	1	—	—	—	—	—	—	—	—	—	—	i	—	6	56
1951	Phi	6	—	—	—	—	3	44	14.7(18)	0	—	—	—	—	—	—	—	—	—	—	i	—	0	20
NFL	5	54(9)	—	—	—	—	76	961	12.6(46)	11	—	—	—	—	—	—	—	—	—	—	ki	—	66	536
ARMSTRONG, NORRIS Phillip Norris, T, 5´10˝/165 lbs; Centre; B9/15/1898 Fort Smith, AR, D10/11/1981 Danville, NY **1922** Mil 1 (0)																								
ARMSTRONG, OTIS Otis, RB, 5´10˝/196 lbs; Purdue; 1973: Den, rnd 1; B11/15/1950 Chicago, IL																								
1973	Den	14(1)	26	90	3.5(24)	0	2	43	21.5(36)	1	—	—	—	—	—	—	—	—	—	—	k	—	6	289
1974	Den★	14(14, FB/rb)	263	**1407**	**5.3**(**43**)	9	38	405	10.7(48)	3	—	—	—	—	—	—	—	—	—	—	k	—	72	**1861**
1975	Den	4(3)	31	155	5.0(33)	0	1	10	10.0(10)	0	—	—	—	—	—	—	—	—	—	—	—	—	0	160
1976	Den✧	14(14, RB)	247	1008	4.1(31)	5	39	457	11.7(36)	1	—	—	—	—	—	—	—	—	—	—	—	—	36	1292
1977	†Den	10(10, RB)	130	489	3.8(35)	4	18	128	7.1(20)	0	—	—	—	—	—	—	—	—	—	—	—	—	24	593
1978	†Den	16(9, RB)	112	381	3.4(20)	1	12	98	8.2(19)	1	—	—	—	—	—	—	—	—	—	—	—	—	12	445
1979	†Den	15(1)	108	453	4.2(26)	2	14	138	9.9(17)	1	—	—	—	—	—	—	—	—	—	—	k	—	18	553
1980	Den	9(6, rb)	106	470	4.4(20)	4	7	23	3.3(8)	0	—	—	—	—	—	—	—	—	—	—	—	—	24	522
NFL	8	96(58)	1023	4453	4.4(43)	25	131	1302	9.9(48)	7	—	—	—	—	—	—	—	—	—	—	k	—	192	5713
ARMSTRONG, QUINCY Carl Quince, C, 6´3˝/230 lbs; North Texas; 1951: NYG, rnd 26; B11/22/1928 Clyde, TX **1954** Cle 2																								
ARMSTRONG, RAY Ramon Lee, DT, 6´1˝/235 lbs; TCU; 1960: NYT, rnd 2/Phi, rnd 20; B10/6/1937 Ennis, TX **1960** Oak-A 14																								
ARMSTRONG, TRACE Raymond Lester, DE, 6´4˝/275 lbs; Arizona State; Florida; 1989: Chi, rnd 1; B10/5/1965 Bethesda, MD **[S]** **1989** ChiB 15 (14, LDE) **1990**†ChiB 16 (16, LDE) **1991**†ChiB 12 (12, LDE) **1992** ChiB 14 (14, LDE) **1993** ChiB 16 (16, LDE) **1994**†ChiB 15 (15, LDE) **1995**†Mia 15 (0) **1996** Mia 16 (9, LDE) **1997**†Mia 16 (16, LDE) **1998**†Mia 16 (0) **1999**†Mia 16 (2) **2000**†Mia★16 (0) **2001** Oak 3 (0) **2002**†Oak 15 (8, rde) **2003** Oak 10 (7, LDE) **NFL** 211 (129) [15 yrs]																								
ARMSTRONG, TYJI Tyji Donraphael, TE, 6´4˝/259 lbs; Iowa Central; Mississippi; 1992: TB, rnd 3; B10/3/1970 Inkster, MI																								
1992	TB	15(7, te)	—	—	—	—	7	138	19.7(81)	1	—	—	—	—	—	—	—	—	—	—	—	—	6	74
1993	TB	12(7, te)	2	5	2.5(4)	0	9	86	9.6(29)	1	—	—	—	—	—	—	—	—	—	—	—	—	6	53
1994	TB	16(9, te)	1	-1	-1.0(-1)	0	22	265	12.0(29)	1	—	—	—	—	—	—	—	—	—	—	k	—	6	128
1995	TB	16(3)	—	—	—	—	7	68	9.7(29)	0	—	—	—	—	—	—	—	—	—	—	k	—	0	25
1996	†Dal	16(7, te)	—	—	—	—	2	10	5.0(6)	0	—	—	—	—	—	—	—	—	—	—	—	—	0	5
1998	SL	12(0)	—	—	—	—	6	54	9.0(20)	0	—	—	—	—	—	—	—	—	—	—	—	—	0	27
NFL	6	87(33)	3	4	1.3(4)	0	53	621	11.7(81)	3	—	—	—	—	—	—	—	—	—	—	k	—	18	312
ARNDT, AL Alfred Herman, G, 5´11˝/205 lbs; South Dakota State; B7/15/1911 Comfrey, MN, deceased																								
1935	Pit	7(2)	1	21	21.0(21)	0	—	—	—	—	—	—	—	—	—	—	—	—	—	—	—	—	0	21
ARNDT, DICK Richard Lee, DT, 6´5˝/265 lbs; Stanford; Idaho; 1966: LA, rnd 5/Den, rnd R3; B3/12/1944 Bonners Ferry, ID **1967** Pit 14 **1968** Pit 3 **1969** Pit 3 **1970** Pit 14 **NFL** 34 [4 yrs]																								
ARNESON, JIM James Arnold, G-C, 6´3˝/247 lbs; Arizona; 1973: Dal, rnd 12; B1/7/1951 Iowa City, IA **1973**†Dal 12 **1974** Dal 14 **1975** Was 7 **NFL** 33 [3 yrs]																								
ARNESON, MARK Mark Edward, LB, 6´2˝/220 lbs; Arizona; 1972: SL, rnd 2; B9/9/1949 Iowa City, IA **1972** SL 14 (MLB) **1973** SL 14 (MLB) **1974**†SL 14 (11, MLB) **1975**†SL 14 (11, MLB) **1976** SL 14 (14, RLB) **1977** SL 14 (14, RLB) **1978** SL 16 (ROLB) **1979** SL 11 (ROLB) **1980** SL 16 (15, ROLB) **NFL** 127 (65) [9 yrs]																								
ARNETT, JON Jon Dwayne 'Jaguar Jon', HB-E, 5´11˝/197 lbs; USC; 1957: LA, rnd 1; B4/20/1935 Los Angeles, CA **[R]**																								
1957	LARm✧	12(lh)	86	347	4.0(68)	2	18	322	17.9(66)	3	—	—	—	—	—	—	—	—	—	—	kp	1	36	802
1958	LARm★	12(LH)	133	683	5.1(57)	6	35	494	14.1(75)	1	1	0	0.0	0	0.0	0	0	—	—	—	kp	—	42	1219
1959	LARm✧	12(LH)	73	371	5.1(80)	2	38	419	11.0(38)	1	5	1	20.0	13	2.6(13)	0	0	—	—	—	kp	1	24	831
1960	LARm✧	12(HB)	104	436	4.2(31)	2	29	226	7.8(24)	2	1	0	0.0	0	0.0	0	0	—	—	—	kp	—	24	750
1961	LARm★	14(HB)	158	609	3.9(26)	4	28	194	6.9(29)	0	13	3	23.1	47	3.6(20)	0	1	—	—	—	kp	1	30	1043
1962	LARm	10(HB)	76	238	3.1(40)	2	12	137	11.4(40)	0	5	3	60.0	28	5.6(15)	1	0	—	—	—	kp	—	12	427
1963	LARm	9(hb)	58	208	3.6(20)	1	15	119	7.9(41)	1	1	0	0.0	0	0.0	0	1	—	—	—	kp	—	12	344
1964	ChiB	14(HB)	119	400	3.4(21)	1	25	223	8.9(27)	2	4	0	0.0	0	0.0	0	0	—	—	—	kp	—	18	731
1965	ChiB	14	102	363	3.6(24)	5	12	114	9.5(30)	0	2	1	50.0	59	29.5(59)	1	0	—	—	—	kp	—	30	577
1966	ChiB	14	55	178	3.2(21)	1	10	42	4.2(11)	0	1	0	0.0	0	0.0	0	0	—	—	—	kp	—	6	201
NFL	10	123	964	3833	4.0(80)	26	222	2290	10.3(75)	10	33	8	24.2	147	4.5(59)	2	2	—	—	—	kp	3	234	6923
ARNOLD, DAVID David Paul, DB, 6´3˝/208 lbs; Michigan; 1989: Pit, rnd 5; B11/21/1966 Warren, OH **1989**†Pit 15 (0)																								
ARNOLD, JAHINE Jahine Amid, WR, 6´0˝/187 lbs; Fresno State; 1996: Pit, rnd 4; B6/19/1973 Rockville, CT **1998** Pit 3 (0) **1999** GB 1 (0)																								
1996	†Pit	9(0)	1	-3	-3.0(-3)	0	6	76	12.7(26)	0	—	—	—	—	—	—	—	—	—	—	kp	—	0	171
NFL	3	13(0)	1	-3	-3.0(-3)	0	6	76	12.7(26)	0	—	—	—	—	—	—	—	—	—	—	kp	—	0	203

YEAR	TEAM	G(GS, POS)	RUSH	YD	AVG(LG)	TD	REC	YD	AVG(LG)	TD	PASS COMP	PCT	YD	AVG(LG)	TD	INT	SK	YD	QBR	KPR	OTD	PTS	TAY

ARNOLD, JAY Jay Lawrence, HB-WB-DB-BB, 6´1˝/210 lbs; Texas; B9/9/1912 Rogers, TX, D4/8/1982 Houston, TX **[K]**

1937	Phi	10(6, WB)	5	7	1.4	0	8	142	17.8	0	—	—	—	—	—	—	—	—	—	—	—	0	78
1938	Phi	11(11, HB)	19	22	1.2	0	6	74	12.3(34)	2	—	—	—	—	—	—	—	—	—	K	2	27	79
1939	Phi	10(9, LH)	8	1	0.1	0	13	207	15.9(38)	1	—	—	—	—	—	—	—	—	—	P	1	12	110
1940	Phi	9(3)	3	9	3.0	0	7	145	20.7	0	—	—	—	—	—	—	—	—	—	i	—	0	81
1941	Pit	10(4)	2	4	2.0(4)	0	1	5	5.0(5)	0	—	—	—	—	—	—	—	—	—	i	—	0	2
NFL	5	50(33)	37	43	1.2(4)	0	35	573	16.4(38)	3	—	—	—	—	—	—	—	—	—	KPi	3	39	349

ARNOLD, JIM James Edward, P, 6´2˝/215 lbs; Vanderbilt; 1983: KC, rnd 5; B1/31/1961 Dalton, GA **[P]** **1983** KC 16 (0) **1985** KC 16 (0) **1986** Det 7 (0) **1987** Det★11 (0)
1989 Det 16 (0) **1990** Det 16 (0) **1992** Det 16 (0) **1993**†Det 16 (0) **1994** Mia 12 (0)

1984	KC☆	16(0)	1	0	0.0(0)	0	—	—	—	—	—	—	—	—	—	—	—	—	—	P	—	0	0
1988	Det★	16(0)	—	—	—	—	—	1	0	0.0	0	0.0	0	0	—	—	—	—	—	P	—	0	0
1991	†Det	16(0)	2	42	21.0(21)	0	—	—	—	—	—	—	—	—	—	—	—	—	—	P	—	0	42
NFL	12	174(0)	3	42	14.0(21)	0	—	1	0	0.0	0	0.0	0	0	—	—	—	—	—	P	—	0	42

ARNOLD, JOHN John Richard, WR, 5´10˝/175 lbs; Wyoming; B10/5/1955 Shizuoka, Japan **1979** Det 7 **1980** Det 10 (0) **NFL** 17 [2 yrs]

ARNOLD, LEFRANCIS LeFrancis, G, 6´3˝/245 lbs; Oregon; B11/24/1952 Los Angeles, CA **1974** Den 2

ARNOLD, WALT Walter Henslee, TE, 6´3˝/228 lbs; New Mexico; B8/31/1958 Galveston, TX

1980	†LARm	16(0)	—	—	—	—	5	75	15.0(33)	1	—	—	—	—	—	—	—	—	—	—	—	6	43
1981	LARm	16(9, TE)	—	—	—	—	20	212	10.6(24)	2	—	—	—	—	—	—	—	—	—	—	—	12	116
1982	Hou	9(0)	—	—	—	—	—	—	—	—	—	—	—	—	—	—	—	—	—	—	—	—	—
1983	Hou	13(1)	—	—	—	—	12	137	11.4(37)	1	—	—	—	—	—	—	—	—	—	—	—	6	74
1984	Was	4(0)	—	—	—	—	—	—	—	—	—	—	—	—	—	—	—	—	—	—	—	—	—
1984	KC	10(4)	—	—	—	—	11	95	8.6(15)	1	—	—	—	—	—	—	—	—	—	—	—	6	53
1985	KC	16(16, TE)	—	—	—	—	28	339	12.1(38)	1	—	—	—	—	—	—	—	—	—	k	—	6	154
1986	†KC	16(15, TE)	—	—	—	—	20	169	8.4(27)	1	—	—	—	—	—	—	—	—	—	—	1	12	90
1987	KC	5(4)	—	—	—	—	3	26	8.7(10)	0	—	—	—	—	—	—	—	—	—	—	—	0	13
NFL	8	105(49)	—	—	—	—	99	1053	10.6(38)	7	—	—	—	—	—	—	—	—	—	k	1	48	541

ARONSON, DOUG Douglas, G, 6´3˝/293 lbs; San Diego State; B8/14/1964 San Francisco, CA **1987** Cin 2 (0)

ARP, JOHN John Allen, T, 6´5˝/275 lbs; Lincoln (MO); B8/15/1965 **1987** ChiB 2 (1)

ARRINGTON, J.J. J.J., RB, 5´9˝/214 lbs; California; 2005: Arz, rnd 2; B1/23/1983 Rocky Mount, NC

| 2005 | Arz | 15(5, rb) | 112 | 370 | 3.3(32) | 2 | 25 | 139 | 5.6(15) | 0 | — | — | — | — | — | — | — | — | — | — | — | 12 | 460 |

ARRINGTON, LAVAR LaVar RaShad, LB, 6´3˝/253 lbs; Penn State; 2000: Was, rnd 1; B6/20/1978 Pittsburgh, PA **2000** Was 16 (11, RLB) **2001** Was★14 (14, LLB)
2002 Was★16 (16, LLB) **2003** Was★16 (16, LLB) **2004** Was 4 (2) **2005**†Was 12 (8, RLB) **NFL** 78 (67) [6 yrs]

ARRINGTON, RICK Richard Cameron, QB, 6´2˝/200 lbs; Georgia; Tulsa; B2/26/1947 Charlotte, NC

1970	Phi	6	4	33	8.3(15)	1	—	—	—	—	73	37	50.7	328	4.5(23)	1	3	2	19	—	—	—	6	92
1971	Phi	10	5	23	4.6(11)	0	—	—	—	—	118	55	46.6	576	4.9(65)	2	5	13	95	49.3	—	—	0	121
1972	Phi	1	1	2	2.0(2)	0	—	—	—	—	13	5	38.5	46	3.5(16)	0	1	4	28	—	—	—	0	-15
NFL	3	17	10	58	5.8(15)	1	—	—	—	—	204	97	47.5	950	4.7(65)	3	9	19	142	47.6	—	—	6	198

ARROBIO, CHUCK Charles Augustus, T, 6´4˝/250 lbs; USC; B7/9/1944 Los Angeles, CA **1966** Min 11

ARROWHEAD E, 5´7˝/160 lbs; none; deceased **1923** Oor 4 (3), 12

ARTERBURN, ELMER Elmer Forrest, DB, 5´10˝/175 lbs; Texas Tech; B6/15/1929 Drumright, OK **1954** ChiC 1

ARTHUR, GARY Gary Patrick, TE, 6´5˝/250 lbs; Miami (OH); 1970: NYJ, rnd 5; B1/9/1948 Dayton, OH **1970** NYJ 7

| 1971 | NYJ | 14 | — | — | — | — | 1 | 12 | 12.0(12) | 0 | — | — | — | — | — | — | — | — | — | — | — | 0 | 6 |
| NFL | 2 | 21 | — | — | — | — | 1 | 12 | 12.0(12) | 0 | — | — | — | — | — | — | — | — | — | — | — | 0 | 6 |

ARTHUR, MIKE Michael Scott, C, 6´3˝/280 lbs; Texas A&M; 1991: Cin, rnd 5; B5/7/1968 Minneapolis, MN **1991** Cin 7 (3) **1992** Cin 16 (13, C) **1993** NE 13 (11, C)
1994†NE 12 (11, C) **1995**†GB 11 (0) **1996** GB 5 (0) **NFL** 64 (38) [6 yrs]

ARTMAN, CORRIE Corwin Walter, T, 6´2˝/238 lbs; Stanford; B1/8/1907 Santa Monica, CA, D3/9/1970 Long Beach, CA **1931** NYG 12 (3) **1932** Bos 1 (1) **1933** Pit 10 (5, RT)
NFL 23 (9) [3 yrs]

ARTMORE, RODNEY Rodney Dwayne, DB, 6´0˝/210 lbs; Baylor; B6/14/1974 Galveston, TX **1999** GB 5 (0)

ARTOE, LEE Lee Robert Reno, T, 6´3˝/234 lbs; Santa Clara; California; 1940: ChiB, rnd 11; B3/2/1917 Tacoma, WA, D4/1/2005 Wilmette, IL **[K]** **1940**†ChiB★11 (7, RT)
1941†ChiB★11 (11, RT) **1942**†ChiB★11 (11, RT) **1945** ChiB☆9 (6, RT) **NFL** 42 (35) [4 yrs]

1946 LAD-A☆14 (13, RT) **1947** LAD-A 14 (6, RT) **1948**†Bal-A 14 (8, RT) **AAFC** 42 (27) [3 yrs]

ARVIE, HERMAN Herman Joseph, T, 6´4˝/312 lbs; Grambling State; 1993: Cle, rnd 5; B10/12/1970 Opelousas, LA **1993** Cle 16 (0) **1994**†Cle 16 (1) **1995** Cle 15 (2)

| 1996 | Bal | 14(1) | — | — | — | — | 1 | 1 | 1.0(1) | 1 | — | — | — | — | — | — | — | — | — | — | — | 6 | 6 |
| NFL | 4 | 61(4) | — | — | — | — | 1 | 1 | 1.0(1) | 1 | — | — | — | — | — | — | — | — | — | — | — | 6 | 6 |

ASAD, DOUG Douglas Samuel, TE, 6´2˝/205 lbs; Northwestern; B8/27/1938 Fairview Park, OH

1960	Oak-A	13	—	—	—	—	14	197	14.1(24)	1	—	—	—	—	—	—	—	—	—	k	—	6	125
1961	Oak-A	14(TE)	—	—	—	—	42	592	14.1(51)	2	—	—	—	—	—	—	—	—	—	k	—	12	301
NFL	2	27	—	—	—	—	56	789	14.1(51)	3	—	—	—	—	—	—	—	—	—	k	—	18	426

ASBURY, WILLIE William Wesley, RB, 6´1˝/226 lbs; Kent State; 1966: Atl, rnd 4; B2/22/1943 Crawfordsville, GA

1966	Pit	14(FB)	169	544	3.2(45)	7	19	228	12.0(37)	2	1	0.0	0	0.0	0	0	—	—	—	—	—	54	738
1967	Pit	12(FB)	80	315	3.9(73)	4	3	52	17.3(21)	0	—	—	—	—	—	—	—	—	—	—	—	24	381
1968	Pit	7	4	9	2.3(4)	0	3	27	9.0(16)	0	—	—	—	—	—	—	—	—	—	—	—	0	23
NFL	3	33	253	868	3.4(73)	11	25	307	12.3(37)	2	1	0.0	0	0.0	0	0	—	—	—	—	—	78	1142

ASCHBACHER, DARREL Darrel Godsil, G, 6´1˝/220 lbs; Boise State; Oregon; B6/2/1935 Prineville, OR **1959** Phi 11

ASCHENBRENNER, FRANK Francis Xavier, RB, 5´10˝/188 lbs; Marquette; North Carolina; Northwestern; 1947: Buf-A, rnd S/Pit, rnd 6; B7/12/1925 Heibuehl, Germany

| 1949 | ChiH-A | 6(0) | 8 | 14 | 1.8 | 0 | 2 | -4 | -2.0 | 0 | — | — | — | — | — | — | — | — | — | k | — | 0 | 17 |

ASH, JUDDY Julian Samuel, G, 6´2˝/205 lbs; Oregon State; B7/12/1900 San Francisco, CA, D10/30/1965 Newport, OR **1926** LA 2 (1)

ASHBAUGH, BILL William D., FB-WB, 5´10˝/175 lbs; Pittsburgh; B9/24/1899 Hartsville, NY, D7/1971 Olean, NY **1924** RI 1 (0) **1925** KC 1 (0) **NFL** 2 (0) [2 yrs]

ASHBURN, CLIFF Clifford L., G-T-E, 5´11˝/190 lbs; Nebraska; B11/21/1905 Tilden, NE, D11/9/1989 Scottsbluff, AZ **1929** NYG 13 (5, lg)

ASHE, RICHARD Richard Anthony, TE, 6´4˝/260 lbs; Humboldt State; B3/14/1967 Chicago, IL **1990** LARm 1 (0)

ASHER, BOB Robert Dabney, T-G, 6´5˝/250 lbs; Vanderbilt; 1970: Dal, rnd 2; B6/13/1948 Arlington, VA **1970**†Dal 6 **1972** ChiB 14 (RT) **1973** ChiB 13 (RT) **1974** ChiB 14 (RT)
1975 ChiB 11 (2) **NFL** 58 (2) [5 yrs]

ASHER, JAMIE James Allen, TE, 6´3˝/245 lbs; Louisville; 1995: Was, rnd 5; B10/31/1972 Indianapolis, IN

1995	Was	7(2)	—	—	—	—	14	172	12.3(20)	0	—	—	—	—	—	—	—	—	—	k	—	0	84
1996	Was	16(12, TE)	—	—	—	—	42	481	11.5(34)	4	—	—	—	—	—	—	—	—	—	k	—	24	259
1997	Was	16(13, TE)	—	—	—	—	49	474	9.7(24)	1	—	—	—	—	—	—	—	—	—	k	—	6	244
1998	Was	9(7, TE)	—	—	—	—	28	294	10.5(28)	0	—	—	—	—	—	—	—	—	—	k	—	0	140
NFL	4	48(34)	—	—	—	—	133	1421	10.7(34)	5	—	—	—	—	—	—	—	—	—	k	—	30	727

ASHLEY, WALKER LEE Walker Lee, LB, 6´0˝/234 lbs; Penn State; 1983: Min, rnd 3; B7/28/1960 Bayonne, NJ **1983** Min 15 (0) **1984** Min 15 (1) **1986** Min 16 (0) **1987**†Min 12 (0)
1988†Min 16 (0) **1989** KC 16 (15, LILB) **1990** Min 4 (0) **NFL** 94 (16) [7 yrs]

ASHMORE, DARRYL Darryl Allen, T, 6´7˝/310 lbs; Northwestern; 1992: LARm, rnd 7; B11/1/1969 Peoria, IL **1993** LARm 9 (7, rt) **1994** LARm 11 (3) **1995** SL 16 (15, RT)
1996 SL 6 (0) **1996** Was 5 (0) **1997** Was 11 (2) **1998** Oak 15 (4) **1999** Oak 16 (0) **2000**†Oak 16 (0) **2001**†Oak 14 (1) **NFL** 119 (34) [9 yrs]

YEAR	TEAM	G (GS, POS)	RUSH	YD	AVG (LG)	TD	REC	YD	AVG (LG)	TD	PASS	COMP	PCT	YD	AVG (LG)	TD	INT	SK	YD	QBR	KPR	OTD	PTS	TAY

Ashmore, Roger Marion Roger, T, 6´0˝/215 lbs; Gonzaga; B7/9/1899, IL, D2/26/1948 Aberdeen, WA [K] **1926** Mil 9 (9, RT), 2 **1927** Dul 9 (7, LT) **1928** GB☆13 (11, RT) **1929** GB 8 (4) **NFL** 39 (31) [4 yrs]

Ashton, Josh Joshua, RB, 6´1˝/205 lbs; Tulsa; 1971: NE, rnd 9; B8/24/1949 Eagle Lake, TX, D11/1/1993 Eagle Lake, TX

YEAR	TEAM	G (GS, POS)	RUSH	YD	AVG (LG)	TD	REC	YD	AVG (LG)	TD	PASS	COMP	PCT	YD	AVG (LG)	TD	INT	SK	YD	QBR	KPR	OTD	PTS	TAY
1972	NE	14 (12, FB)	128	546	4.3 (35)	3	22	207	9.4 (24)	1	—	—	—	—	—	—	—	—	—	—	k	—	24	769
1973	NE	12 (8, RB)	93	305	3.3 (34)	0	11	113	10.3 (51)	0	—	—	—	—	—	—	—	—	—	—	—	—	0	362
1974	NE	12	26	99	3.8 (22)	0	—	—	—	—	—	—	—	—	—	—	—	—	—	—	—	—	0	99
1975	†SL	2	10	44	4.4 (9)	0	—	—	—	—	—	—	—	—	—	—	—	—	—	—	—	—	0	44
NFL	4	40 (20)	257	994	3.9 (35)	3	33	320	9.7 (51)	1	—	—	—	—	—	—	—	—	—	—	k	—	24	1273

Ashworth, Tom Thomas F., T, 6´6˝/305 lbs; Colorado; B10/10/1977 Denver, CO **2002** NE 1 (0) **2003**†NE 16 (13, RT) **2004** NE 6 (6, rt)

YEAR	TEAM	G (GS, POS)	RUSH	YD	AVG (LG)	TD	REC	YD	AVG (LG)	TD	PASS	COMP	PCT	YD	AVG (LG)	TD	INT	SK	YD	QBR	KPR	OTD	PTS	TAY
2005	†NE	14 (11, RT)	—	—	—	—	1	1	1.0 (1)	1	—	—	—	—	—	—	—	—	—	—	—	—	6	6
NFL	4	37 (30)	—	—	—	—	1	1	1.0 (1)	1	—	—	—	—	—	—	—	—	—	—	—	—	6	6

Aska, Joe Joe, RB, 5´11˝/236 lbs; Central Oklahoma; 1995: Oak, rnd 3; B7/14/1972 St. Croix, Virgin Islands

YEAR	TEAM	G (GS, POS)	RUSH	YD	AVG (LG)	TD	REC	YD	AVG (LG)	TD	PASS	COMP	PCT	YD	AVG (LG)	TD	INT	SK	YD	QBR	KPR	OTD	PTS	TAY
1995	Oak	1 (0)	—	—	—	—	—	—	—	—	—	—	—	—	—	—	—	—	—	—	—	—	—	—
1996	Oak	15 (2)	62	326	5.3 (38)	1	8	63	7.9 (22)	0	—	—	—	—	—	—	—	—	—	—	k	—	6	370
1997	Oak	7 (0)	12	10	0.8 (4)	0	—	—	—	—	—	—	—	—	—	—	—	—	—	—	k	—	0	26
NFL	3	23 (2)	74	336	4.5 (38)	1	8	63	7.9 (22)	0	—	—	—	—	—	—	—	—	—	—	k	—	6	396

Askea, Mike Michael Vaughn, T, 6´4˝/260 lbs; Stanford; 1973: Den, rnd 7; B1/7/1951 Visalia, CA **1973** Den 4

Askew, B.J. Bobby DeAngelo, FB, 6´3˝/233 lbs; Michigan; 2003: NYJ, rnd 3; B8/19/1980 Cincinnati, OH

YEAR	TEAM	G (GS, POS)	RUSH	YD	AVG (LG)	TD	REC	YD	AVG (LG)	TD	PASS	COMP	PCT	YD	AVG (LG)	TD	INT	SK	YD	QBR	KPR	OTD	PTS	TAY
2003	NYJ	16 (0)	2	9	4.5 (6)	0	—	—	—	—	—	—	—	—	—	—	—	—	—	—	k	—	0	21
2004	†NYJ	16 (0)	6	23	3.8 (14)	0	2	12	6.0 (11)	0	—	—	—	—	—	—	—	—	—	—	k	—	0	17
2005	NYJ	10 (1)	13	59	4.5 (14)	0	1	11	11.0 (11)	0	—	—	—	—	—	—	—	—	—	—	—	—	0	65
NFL	3	42 (1)	21	91	4.3 (14)	0	3	23	7.7 (11)	0	—	—	—	—	—	—	—	—	—	—	k	—	0	103

Askew, Matthias Matthias, DT, 6´6˝/315 lbs; Michigan State; 2004: Cin, rnd 4; B7/1/1982 Fort Lauderdale, FL **2004** Cin 5 (0) **2005** Cin 1 (0) **NFL** 6 (0) [2 yrs]

Askson, Bert Bert, DE-TE, 6´3˝/223 lbs; Texas Southern; 1970: Pit, rnd 14; B12/16/1945 Houston, TX

YEAR	TEAM	G (GS, POS)	RUSH	YD	AVG (LG)	TD	REC	YD	AVG (LG)	TD	PASS	COMP	PCT	YD	AVG (LG)	TD	INT	SK	YD	QBR	KPR	OTD	PTS	TAY
1971	Pit	11	—	—	—	—	—	—	—	—	—	—	—	—	—	—	—	—	—	—	—	—	—	—
1973	NO	1	—	—	—	—	—	—	—	—	—	—	—	—	—	—	—	—	—	—	—	—	—	—
1975	GB	14	—	—	—	—	2	25	12.5 (18)	0	—	—	—	—	—	—	—	—	—	—	—	—	0	13
1976	GB	14	—	—	—	—	1	2	2.0 (2)	1	—	—	—	—	—	—	—	—	—	—	—	—	6	6
1977	GB	14	—	—	—	—	2	51	25.5 (34)	0	—	—	—	—	—	—	—	—	—	—	—	—	0	26
NFL	5	54	—	—	—	—	5	78	15.6 (34)	1	—	—	—	—	—	—	—	—	—	—	—	—	6	44

Asmus, Jim James Victor Daniel, K, 6´2˝/195 lbs; Hawaii; B12/2/1958 Meppal, Holland **1987** SF 3 (0)

Asomugha, Nnamdi Nnamdi, DB, 6´3˝/215 lbs; California; 2003: Oak, rnd 1; B7/6/1981 Lafayette, LA **2003** Oak 15 (1) **2004** Oak 16 (7, rcb) **2005** Oak 16 (16, LCB) **NFL** 47 (24) [3 yrs]

Aspatore, Ed Edward Charles, T-G, 6´1˝/220 lbs; Marquette; B6/23/1909 Fond du Lac, WI, D3/14/1986 Louisville, KY **1934** Cin 6 (1)

Asplundh, Les Lester, FB-BB-WB, 6´3˝/213 lbs; Swarthmore; B5/3/1901 Bryn Athyn, PA, D5/3/1984 Philadelphia, PA **1925** Buf 1 (0)

Atchason, Jack John Dean, E, 6´4˝/215 lbs; Western Illinois; 1960: DalT, rnd 1; B11/16/1936 Springfield, IL

YEAR	TEAM	G (GS, POS)	RUSH	YD	AVG (LG)	TD	REC	YD	AVG (LG)	TD	PASS	COMP	PCT	YD	AVG (LG)	TD	INT	SK	YD	QBR	KPR	OTD	PTS	TAY
1960	Bos-A	1	—	—	—	—	2	22	11.0 (14)	0	—	—	—	—	—	—	—	—	—	—	—	—	0	11
1960	Hou-A	2	—	—	—	—	3	26	8.7 (12)	1	—	—	—	—	—	—	—	—	—	—	—	—	6	18
NFL	1	3	—	—	—	—	5	48	9.6 (14)	1	—	—	—	—	—	—	—	—	—	—	—	—	6	29

Atcheson, Burl Burl M.K., E, none; B1902 Columbus, OH, deceased **1922** Col 1 (0)

Atessis, Bill William James, DE-DT, 6´3˝/240 lbs; Texas; 1971: Bal, rnd 2; B7/16/1949 Houston, TX **1971** NE 5

Athas, Pete Peter Garrett, DB-WR, 5´11˝/185 lbs; Tennessee; 1970: Dal, rnd 10; B9/15/1946 Hackensack, NJ [R] **1972** NYG 14 (LCB) **1973** NYG 14 (LCB) **1974** NYG 14 (LCB) **1975** Cle 6 (ss) **1975**†Min 5 **1976** NO 13

YEAR	TEAM	G (GS, POS)	RUSH	YD	AVG (LG)	TD	REC	YD	AVG (LG)	TD	PASS	COMP	PCT	YD	AVG (LG)	TD	INT	SK	YD	QBR	KPR	OTD	PTS	TAY
1971	NYG	13	1	3	3.0 (3)	0	—	—	—	—	—	—	—	—	—	—	—	—	—	—	pi	1	6	61
NFL	6	79	1	3	3.0 (3)	0	—	—	—	—	—	—	—	—	—	—	—	—	—	—	kpi	1	6	471

Atkeson, Dale Dale Wayne, FB, 6´2˝/211 lbs; none; B12/24/1930 Kansas City, MO

YEAR	TEAM	G (GS, POS)	RUSH	YD	AVG (LG)	TD	REC	YD	AVG (LG)	TD	PASS	COMP	PCT	YD	AVG (LG)	TD	INT	SK	YD	QBR	KPR	OTD	PTS	TAY
1954	Was	10 (fb)	68	176	2.6 (14)	2	4	75	18.8 (45)	0	—	—	—	—	—	—	—	—	—	—	kp	1	18	516
1955	Was	11 (FB)	77	300	3.9 (45)	1	9	81	9.0 (15)	1	—	—	—	—	—	—	—	—	—	—	k	—	12	402
1956	Was	5	63	163	2.6 (12)	1	6	28	4.7 (26)	0	—	—	—	—	—	—	—	—	—	—	kp	—	6	204
NFL	3	26	208	639	3.1 (45)	4	19	184	9.7 (45)	1	—	—	—	—	—	—	—	—	—	—	kp	1	36	1121

Atkins, Billy William Ellis, DB-HB, 6´1˝/196 lbs; Auburn; 1958: SF, rnd 5; B11/19/1934 Millport, AL, D11/5/1991 El Paso, TX [KI] **1959** SF 11 **1962** NYT-A 7 (LS) **1963** NYJ-A 2 **1963** Buf-A 1 **1964** Den-A 3

YEAR	TEAM	G (GS, POS)	RUSH	YD	AVG (LG)	TD	REC	YD	AVG (LG)	TD	PASS	COMP	PCT	YD	AVG (LG)	TD	INT	SK	YD	QBR	KPR	OTD	PTS	TAY
1958	SF	12 (DB)	1	5	5.0 (5)	0	—	—	—	—	—	—	—	—	—	—	—	—	—	—	Pi	—	0	6
1960	Buf-A	14 (LCB)	2	47	23.5 (36)	0	—	—	—	—	—	—	—	—	—	—	—	—	—	—	KPi	—	45	45
1961	Buf-A★	14 (RS)	2	87	43.5 (56)	1	—	—	—	—	—	—	—	—	—	—	—	—	—	—	KPpi	—	41	225
NFL	7	64	5	139	27.8 (56)	1	—	—	—	—	—	—	—	—	—	—	—	—	—	—	KPpi	—	86	286

Atkins, Bob Robert Lee, DB, 6´3˝/215 lbs; Grambling State; 1968: SL, rnd 2; B4/2/1946 Atlanta, GA **1968** SL 14 (LCB) **1969** SL 13 (rcb) **1970** Hou 14 **1971** Hou 12 **1972** Hou 14 **1973** Hou 5 (FS) **1974** Hou 14 (FS) **1975** Hou 14 (FS) **1976** Hou 14 **NFL** 114 [9 yrs]

Atkins, Corey Corey, LB, 6´0˝/235 lbs; South Carolina; B11/11/1976 Greenville, SC **2000** Atl 12 (0)

Atkins, Dave David Charles, RB, 6´1˝/205 lbs; Texas-El Paso; 1973: SF, rnd 8; B5/18/1949 Victoria, TX

YEAR	TEAM	G (GS, POS)	RUSH	YD	AVG (LG)	TD	REC	YD	AVG (LG)	TD	PASS	COMP	PCT	YD	AVG (LG)	TD	INT	SK	YD	QBR	KPR	OTD	PTS	TAY
1973	SF	5	4	19	4.8 (8)	1	1	-3	-3.0 (-3)	0	—	—	—	—	—	—	—	—	—	—	k	—	6	76
1974	SF	1	—	—	—	—	—	—	—	—	—	—	—	—	—	—	—	—	—	—	—	—	—	—
1975	SD	3	1	4	4.0 (4)	0	—	—	—	—	—	—	—	—	—	—	—	—	—	—	—	—	0	4
NFL	3	9	5	23	4.6 (8)	1	1	-3	-3.0 (-3)	0	—	—	—	—	—	—	—	—	—	—	k	—	6	80

Atkins, Doug Douglas Leon, DE, 6´8˝/257 lbs; Tennessee; 1953: Cle, rnd 1; B5/8/1930 Humboldt, TN; HOF 1982 **1953**†Cle 8 (lde) **1954**†Cle 12 (lde) **1955** ChiB 12 (RDE) **1956**†ChiB 6 (rde) **1957** ChiB★12 (RDE) **1958** ChiB★12 (RDE) **1959** ChiB★12 (RDE) **1960** ChiB★12 (RDE) **1961** ChiB★14 (RDE) **1962** ChiB★14 (RDE) **1963**†ChiB★14 (RDE) **1964** ChiB☆12 (RDE) **1965** ChiB★14 (RDE) **1966** ChiB 12 (RDE) **1967** NO 14 (LDE) **1968** NO☆11 (LDE) **1969** NO 14 (LDE) **NFL** 205 [17 yrs]

Atkins, Gene Gene Reynard, DB, 5´11˝/201 lbs; Florida A&M; 1987: NO, rnd 7; B11/22/1964 Tallahassee, FL [I] **1987**†NO 13 (5, ss) **1988** NO 16 (6, ss) **1989** NO 14 (12, SS) **1990**†NO 16 (16, FS) **1991**†NO 16 (16, FS) **1992**†NO 16 (16, FS) **1993** NO 16 (16, FS) **1994**†Mia 15 (15, FS) **1995**†Mia 16 (11, FS) **1996** Mia 5 (5, fs) **NFL** 143 (118) [10 yrs]

Atkins, George George Arthur, G, 6´1˝/210 lbs; Auburn; 1955: Det, rnd 15; B4/10/1932 Birmingham, AL **1955** Det 12

Atkins, James James Curtis, T, 6´6˝/306 lbs; Louisiana-Lafayette; B1/28/1970 Amite, LA **1994** Sea 4 (2) **1995** Sea 16 (16, LT) **1996** Sea 16 (16, LT) **1997** Sea 13 (3) **1999** Bal 2 (1) **2000** Det 2 (1)

YEAR	TEAM	G (GS, POS)	RUSH	YD	AVG (LG)	TD	REC	YD	AVG (LG)	TD	PASS	COMP	PCT	YD	AVG (LG)	TD	INT	SK	YD	QBR	KPR	OTD	PTS	TAY
1998	Bal	9 (6, lt)	—	—	—	—	1	0	0.0 (0)	0	—	—	—	—	—	—	—	—	—	—	—	—	0	0
NFL	7	62 (45)	—	—	—	—	1	0	0.0	0	—	—	—	—	—	—	—	—	—	—	—	—	0	0

Atkins, James James Hodges, DT, 6´5˝/325 lbs; Virginia Union; B6/23/1978 Brooklyn, NY **2003**†Ten 13 (4) **2004** SF 3 (0) **NFL** 16 (4) [2 yrs]

Atkins, Kelvin Kelvin Lamar, LB, 6´3˝/235 lbs; Illinois; 1982: TB, rnd 8; B7/3/1960 Orlando, FL **1983** ChiB 13 (0)

Atkins, Larry Larry Tabay, LB, 6´3˝/250 lbs; UCLA; 1999: KC, rnd 3; B7/21/1975 Santa Monica, CA **1999** KC 9 (0) **2000** KC 15 (0) **2001** KC 12 (0) **2002** KC 10 (0) **2003** Oak 3 (0) **NFL** 49 (0) [5 yrs]

Atkins, Pervis Pervis R., FL-HB-WR, 6´1˝/230 lbs; San Francisco State; New Mexico State; 1960: LA, rnd 3/Oak, rnd 2; B11/24/1935 Ruston, LA [R]

YEAR	TEAM	G (GS, POS)	RUSH	YD	AVG (LG)	TD	REC	YD	AVG (LG)	TD	PASS	COMP	PCT	YD	AVG (LG)	TD	INT	SK	YD	QBR	KPR	OTD	PTS	TAY
1961	LARm	14	5	19	3.8 (13)	0	5	67	13.4 (28)	0	—	—	—	—	—	—	—	—	—	—	k	—	0	70
1962	LARm	14 (FL)	7	19	2.7 (16)	0	35	393	11.2 (48)	1	—	—	—	—	—	—	—	—	—	—	kp	—	6	516
1963	LARm	14	5	11	2.2 (6)	0	14	174	12.4 (21)	1	—	—	—	—	—	—	—	—	—	—	kp	—	6	223
1964	Was	13	25	98	3.9 (17)	1	8	35	4.4 (10)	0	—	—	—	—	—	—	—	—	—	—	kp	—	6	308
1965	Was	4	18	44	2.4 (16)	0	1	0	0.0 (0)	0	—	—	—	—	—	—	—	—	—	—	kp	—	0	40

YEAR	TEAM	G (GS, POS)	RUSH	YD	AVG(LG)	TD	REC	YD	AVG(LG)	TD	PASS	COMP	PCT	YD	AVG(LG)	TD	INT	SK	YD	QBR	KPR	OTD	PTS	TAY
1965	Oak-A	5	—	—	—		1	6	6.0(6)		—	—	—	—	—	—	—	—	—	—		—	0	3
1966	Oak-A	14	14	10	0.7(9)	0	—	—	—		—	—	—	—	—	—	—	—	—	—	kp	—	0	191
NFL		6	78	74	201	2.7(17)	1	64	675	10.5(48)	2	—	—	—	—	—	—	—	—	—	kp	—	18	1350

ATKINS, STEVE Steven Elwood, RB, 6´0˝/216 lbs; Maryland; 1979: GB, rnd 2; B6/22/1956 Spotsylvania, VA

YEAR	TEAM	G (GS, POS)	RUSH	YD	AVG(LG)	TD	REC	YD	AVG(LG)	TD	…	KPR	OTD	PTS	TAY
1979	GB	7(1)	42	239	5.7(60)	1	10	89	8.9(19)	1			—	6	294
1980	GB	9(3)	67	216	3.2(16)	1	7	47	6.7(16)	1			—	12	255
1981	GB	3(0)	11	12	1.1(15)	0	1	2	2.0(2)	0			—	0	13
1981	Phi	1(0)	1	21	21.0(21)	0	—	—	—			k	—	0	21
NFL		3	20(4)	121	488	4.0(60)	2	18	138	7.7(19)	1	k	—	18	582

ATKINSON, AL Allen Edward, LB, 6´2˝/230 lbs; Villanova; 1965: Buf, rnd 3/Bal, rnd 6; B7/28/1943 Philadelphia, PA [I]   **1965** NYJ-A 14 (2)   **1966** NYJ-A 14 (14, MLB)
1967 NYJ-A 14 (MLB)   **1968**†NYJ-A★12 (MLB)   **1969**†NYJ-A 10 (MLB)   **1970** NYJ 14 (MLB)   **1971** NYJ 10 (MLB)   **1972** NYJ 13 (MLB)   **1973** NYJ 5   **1974** NYJ 14
NFL 120 (16) [10 yrs]

ATKINSON, FRANK Franklyn Rhem, DT, 6´3˝/240 lbs; Stanford; 1963: Pit, rnd 8; B12/13/1941   **1963** Pit 14 (LDT)   **1964** Den-A 3   **NFL** 17 [2 yrs]

ATKINSON, GEORGE George Henry 'Butch', DB, 6´0˝/180 lbs; Morris Brown; 1968: Oak, rnd 7; B1/4/1947 Savannah, GA [RI]   **1968**†Oak-A☆14 (6, lcb)   **1969**†Oak-A☆14 (12, LS)
1970†Oak 14 (14, SS)   **1971** Oak 14 (14, SS)   **1972**†Oak 14 (14, SS)   **1973** Oak 14 (13, SS)   **1974** Oak 14 (14, SS)   **1975** Oak 14 (14, SS)   **1976**†Oak☆14 (SS)
1977 Oak 12 (11, SS)   **1979** Den 6   **NFL** 144 (112) [11 yrs]

ATKINSON, JESS Jesse Gerald, K, 5´9˝/165 lbs; Maryland; B12/11/1961 Ann Arbor, MI [K]   **1985** SL 2 (0)   **1986**†Was 1 (0)   **1987** Was 1 (0)   **1988** Ind 1 (0)

YEAR	TEAM	G (GS, POS)	RUSH	YD	AVG(LG)	TD	…	KPR	OTD	PTS	TAY
1985	NYG	6(0)	1	14	14.0(14)	1		K	—	50	24
NFL		4	11(0)	1	14	14.0(14)	1	K	—	60	24

ATKINSON, RICKY Richard E., DB, 6´0˝/175 lbs; Southern Connecticut State; B8/28/1965 Middletown, CT   **1987** NE 1 (0)

ATOGWE, O.J. Oshiomogho, DB, 5´11˝/203 lbs; Stanford; 2005: SL, rnd 3; B6/23/1981 Windsor, Canada   **2005** SL 12 (0)

ATTACHE, REGGIE Reginald Edward, aka Laughing Gas, WB-FB, 5´7˝/195 lbs; Sherman ndian; B2/5/1894 Pechange Indian Reservation, CA, D6/22/1955 Pechange Indian Reservation, CA
1922 Oor 8 (6, WB)

ATTY, ALEX Alexander George, G, 5´8˝/216 lbs; West Virginia; 1939: Cle, rnd 18; B12/8/1916 Johnstown, PA, D5/2/1973 Pottsville, PA   **1939** Cle 3 (0)

ATWATER, STEVE Stephen Dennis, DB, 6´3˝/218 lbs; Arkansas; 1989: Den, rnd 1; B10/28/1966 Chicago, IL [I]   **1989** Den 16 (16, FS)   **1990** Den★15 (15, FS)
1991†Den★16 (16, FS)   **1992** Den★15 (15, FS)   **1993**†Den★16 (16, FS)   **1994** Den★14 (14, SS)   **1995** Den★16 (16, FS)   **1996**†Den★16 (16, FS)   **1997**†Den 15 (15, FS)
1998†Den✧16 (16, FS)   **1999** NYJ 12 (11, FS)   **NFL** 167 (166) [11 yrs]

ATWOOD, JOHN John Horton, HB-WB-DB, 5´11˝/195 lbs; Wisconsin; B1/27/1923 Janesville, WI

YEAR	TEAM	G (GS, POS)	RUSH	YD	AVG(LG)	TD	REC	YD	AVG(LG)	TD	…	KPR	OTD	PTS	TAY
1948	NYG	8(1)	9	6	0.7(9)	0	10	141	14.1(54)	1		kpi	—	6	102

AUDET, EARL Earl Toussaint, T, 6´2˝/252 lbs; Georgetown (DC); USC; 1944: Was, rnd 3; B5/14/1921 Providence, RI, D12/18/2002 Los Angeles, CA   **1945**†Was 10 (5, lt)
1946 LAD-A 13 (0)   **1947** LAD-A 14 (6, LT)   **1948** LAD-A 14 (14, RT)   **AAFC** 41 (20) [3 yrs]

AUDICK, DAN Daniel James Bartholomew, T-G, 6´3˝/252 lbs; Hawaii; 1977: Pit, rnd 4; B11/15/1954 San Bernardino, CA   **1977** SL 2   **1978** SD 1   **1979**†SD 16 (4)
1980†SD 15 (9, RT)   **1981**†SF 16 (16, LT)   **1982** SF 7 (2)   **1983** SL 12 (1)   **1984** SL 7 (1)   **NFL** 76 (33) [8 yrs]

AUER, HOWIE Howard Joseph, T, 6´1˝/205 lbs; Michigan; B1/9/1908 Detroit, MI, D11/12/1985 Venice, FL   **1933** Phi 2 (1)

AUER, JIM James Robert, DE, 6´7˝/275 lbs; Georgia; B1/4/1962 Philadelphia, PA   **1987** Phi 1 (0)

AUER, JOE Joseph, RB, 6´1˝/200 lbs; Miami (FL); Georgia Tech; 1963: KC, rnd 15/LA, rnd 5; B10/11/1941 Trenton, NJ

YEAR	TEAM	G (GS, POS)	RUSH	YD	AVG(LG)	TD	REC	YD	AVG(LG)	TD	…	KPR	OTD	PTS	TAY
1964	Buf-A	12(hb)	63	191	3.0(21)	2	11	166	15.1(43)	0		—	1	18	295
1965	Buf-A	5	3	19	6.3(14)	0	—	—	—			—	—	0	19
1966	Mia-A	14 (14, HB)	121	416	3.4(41)	4	22	263	12.0(27)	4		kp	1	54	970
1967	Mia-A	13(5, hb)	44	128	2.9(23)	1	18	218	12.1(68)	1		kp	—	18	380
1968	Atl	7	3	19	6.3(16)	0	—	—	—			k	—	0	20
NFL		5	51(19)	234	773	3.3(41)	7	51	647	12.7(68)	6	kp	2	90	1684

AUER, SCOTT Scott Eugene, G-T, 6´5˝/255 lbs; Michigan State; 1984: KC, rnd 9; B10/4/1961 Fort Wayne, IN   **1984** KC 16 (0)   **1985** KC 7 (6, lg)   **NFL** 23 (6) [2 yrs]

AUER, TODD Todd M., LB, 6´1˝/230 lbs; Western Illinois; B1/8/1965 Winona, MS   **1987** GB 3 (2)

AUGHTMAN, DOWE Lorenzo Dowe, DT, 6´2˝/260 lbs; Auburn; 1984: Dal, rnd 11; B1/28/1961 Brewton, AL   **1984** Dal 7 (0)

AUGUST, SKY Edward W., TB-WB, 5´10˝/180 lbs; Villanova; B8/5/1904 Mahanoy City, PA, D10/15/1993 Mahanoy City, PA   **1931** Pro 7 (1)

AUGUST, STEVE Steven Paul, T, 6´4˝/255 lbs; Tulsa; 1977: Sea, rnd 1; B9/4/1954 Jeannette, PA   **1977** Sea 6   **1978** Sea 14 (14, RT)   **1979** Sea 16 (16, RT)   **1980** Sea 16 (16, RT)
1982 Sea 8 (7, RT)   **1983**†Sea 15 (15, RT)   **1984** Sea 6 (6, rt)   **1984** Pit 5 (1)

YEAR	TEAM	G (GS, POS)	RUSH	YD	AVG(LG)	TD	REC	YD	AVG(LG)	TD	…	OTD	PTS	TAY
1981	Sea	16(16, RT)	—	—	—		1	9	9.0(9)	0			0	5
NFL		8	102(91)	—	—	—		1	9	9.0(9)	0		0	5

AUGUSTERFER, GENE Eugene Francis, BB-DB, 5´9˝/180 lbs; Catholic; B10/4/1914 Washington, DC, deceased   **1935** Pit 1 (0)

AUGUSTYNIAK, MIKE Michael Eugene, RB, 5´11˝/225 lbs; Purdue; B7/17/1956 Fort Wayne, IN

YEAR	TEAM	G (GS, POS)	RUSH	YD	AVG(LG)	TD	REC	YD	AVG(LG)	TD	…	OTD	PTS	TAY
1981	NYJ	10(8, FB)	85	339	4.0(12)	1	18	144	8.0(15)	0		—	6	421
1982	†NYJ	9(8, FB)	50	178	3.6(16)	4	24	189	7.9(15)	0		—	24	313
1983	NYJ	8(2)	18	50	2.8(6)	2	10	71	7.1(17)	0		—	18	111
NFL		3	27(18)	153	567	3.7(16)	7	52	404	7.8(17)	1	—	48	844

AULT, CHALMERS Chalmers Augustus, T, 5´9˝/195 lbs; West Virginia Wesleyan; B7/10/1900 Jacobsburg, OH, D5/18/1979 Buckhannon, WV   **1924** Cle 2 (0)   **1925** Cle 1 (1)
NFL 3 (1) [2 yrs]

AUPIU, DAVID Lotupue David, LB, 6´2˝/235 lbs; Brigham Young; B2/10/1961 Honolulu, HI   **1987** LARm 1 (0)

AUSTIN, BILL William Lee, G-T, 6´1˝/223 lbs; Oregon State; 1949: NYG, rnd 13/LAD-A, rnd 8; B10/18/1928 San Pedro, CA [C]   **1949** NYG 9 (4)   **1950**†NYG 12 (RG)
1953 NYG 12 (RG)   **1954** NYG✧11 (LG)   **1955** NYG☆12 (LG)   **1956**†NYG 8 (LG)   **1957** NYG 11   **NFL** 75 (4) [7 yrs]

AUSTIN, BILLY William Dominic, DB, 5´10˝/195 lbs; New Mexico; B3/8/1975 Washington, DC   **1998** Ind 1 (0)   **1999**†Ind 16 (0)   **2000**†Ind 16 (0)   **NFL** 33 (0) [3 yrs]

AUSTIN, CLIFF Clifford, RB, 6´0˝/203 lbs; Clemson; 1983: NO, rnd 3; B3/2/1960 Atlanta, GA

YEAR	TEAM	G (GS, POS)	RUSH	YD	AVG(LG)	TD	REC	YD	AVG(LG)	TD	…	KPR	OTD	PTS	TAY
1983	NO	11(0)	4	16	4.0(11)	0	2	25	12.5(18)	0		k	—	0	36
1984	Atl	15(0)	4	7	1.8(3)	0	—	—	—			k	—	0	24
1985	Atl	14(0)	20	110	5.5(17)	0	1	21	21.0(21)	0		k	1	6	384
1986	Atl	15(1)	62	280	4.5(22)	1	3	21	7.0(9)	0		k	—	6	316
1987	TB	3(2)	19	32	1.7(8)	1	5	51	10.2(20)	0			—	6	68
NFL		5	58(3)	109	445	4.1(22)	2	11	118	10.7(21)	1	k	1	18	826

AUSTIN, DARRELL Kenneth Darrell, G-C-T, 6´4˝/250 lbs; South Carolina; 1974: Den, rnd 16; B11/6/1951 Union, SC   **1975** NYJ 12   **1976** NYJ 11 (11, RG/c)   **1977** NYJ 9 (7, rg)
1978 NYJ 13   **1979**†TB 16   **1980** TB 8 (2)   **NFL** 69 (20) [6 yrs]

AUSTIN, ERIC Eric Dewayne, DB, 5´10˝/217 lbs; Jackson State; 1996: TB, rnd 4; B6/7/1973 Moss Point, MS   **1996** TB 2 (0)

AUSTIN, HISE Hise, DB, 6´4˝/191 lbs; Prairie View A&M; 1973: GB, rnd 8; B9/8/1950 Houston, TX   **1973** GB 9   **1975** KC 3   **NFL** 12 [2 yrs]

AUSTIN, JIM James L., E, 6´2˝/199 lbs; St. Mary's (CA); B9/10/1913 Omaha, NE, D10/1975 La Jolla, CA

YEAR	TEAM	G (GS, POS)	RUSH	YD	AVG(LG)	TD	REC	YD	AVG(LG)	TD	…	OTD	PTS	TAY
1937	Bkn	7(6, LE)	—	—	—		13	185	14.2				0	93
1938	Bkn	11(2)	—	—	—		14	180	12.9	1			6	95
1939	Det	10(1)	—	—	—		5	102	20.4	0			0	51
NFL		3	28(9)	—	—	—		32	467	14.6	1		6	239

AUSTIN, KENT Richard Kent, QB, 6´1˝/195 lbs; Mississippi; 1986: SL, rnd 12; B6/25/1963 Natick, MA

YEAR	TEAM	G (GS, POS)	RUSH	YD	AVG(LG)	TD	…	OTD	PTS	TAY
1986	SL	16(0)	1	0	0.0(0)	0		—	0	0

AUSTIN, OCIE Ocie Moore, DB, 6´3˝/200 lbs; Utah State; 1968: Bal, rnd 10; B1/8/1947 Norfolk, VA   **1968**†Bal 14   **1969** Bal 14   **1970** Pit 7 (FS)   **1971** Pit 14 (fs)   **NFL** 49 [4 yrs]

YEAR	TEAM	G(GS, POS)	RUSH	YD	AVG(LG)	TD	REC	YD	AVG(LG)	TD	PASS COMP	PCT	YD	AVG(LG)	TD	INT	SK	YD	QBR	KPR	OTD	PTS	TAY

AUSTIN, RAYMOND Raymond Demont, DB, 5´11˝/190 lbs; Tennessee; 1997: NYJ, rnd 5; B12/21/1974 Greensboro, NC **1997** NYJ 16 (0) **1998** ChiB 12 (0) **1999** ChiB 15 (0) **NFL** 43 (0) [3 yrs]

AUSTIN, REGGIE Reginald Antonio, DB, 5´9˝/185 lbs; Wake Forest; 2000: Chi, rnd 4; B1/21/1977 Atlanta, GA **2001** ChiB 9 (0) **2002** ChiB 9 (4) **NFL** 18 (4) [2 yrs]

AUTREY, BILLY William Rex, C, 6´3˝/220 lbs; Stephen F. Austin State; B1/17/1933 Ridge, TX **1953** ChiB 7

AUTRY, DARNELL Huntington Darnell, RB, 5´10˝/210 lbs; Northwestern; 1997: Chi, rnd 4; B6/19/1976 Wiesbaden, Germany

1997	ChiB	13(3)	112	319	2.8(17)	1	9	59	6.6(14)	0	—	—	—	—	—	—	—	—	—	—	—	8	359
2000	Phi	11(7, RB)	112	334	3.0(15)	3	24	275	11.5(37)	1	—	—	—	—	—	—	—	—	—	—	—	24	507
NFL	2	24(10)	224	653	2.9(17)	4	33	334	10.1(37)	1	—	—	—	—	—	—	—	—	—	—	—	32	865

AUTRY, HANK Melvin Henry, C, 6´3˝/240 lbs; Southern Mississippi; 1969: Hou, rnd 17; B5/2/1947 Hattiesburg, MS **1969**†Hou-A 14 **1970** Hou 14 **NFL** 28 [2 yrs]

AUZENNE, TROY Troy Anthony, T, 6´7˝/293 lbs; California; 1992: Chi, rnd 2; B6/26/1969 El Monte, CA **1992** ChiB 16 (16, LT) **1993** ChiB 11 (11, LT) **1994**†ChiB 11 (3) **1995** ChiB 11 (0) **1996**†Ind 12 (5, lt) **NFL** 61 (35) [5 yrs]

AVEDISIAN, CHUCK Charles Toros, G-LB, 5´9˝/203 lbs; Providence; B9/19/1917 West Hoboken, NJ, D8/26/1983 New Britain, CT **1942** NYG 10 (4) **1943**†NYG 10 (10, RG) **1944**†NYG 10 (5, rg) **NFL** 30 (19) [3 yrs]

AVELLINI, BOB Robert Hayden, QB, 6´2˝/208 lbs; Maryland; 1975: Chi, rnd 6; B8/28/1953 Queens, NY

1975	ChiB	8(4)	4	-3	-0.8(1)	1	—	—	—	—	126	67	53.2	942	7.5(57)	6	11	13	144	57.0	—	—	6	68
1976	ChiB	14(14, QB)	18	58	3.2(15)	1	—	—	—	—	271	118	43.5	1580	5.8(63)	8	15	24	225	49.4	—	—	6	298
1977	†ChiB	14(14, QB)	37	109	2.9(21)	1	—	—	—	—	293	154	52.6	2004	6.8(75)	11	18	23	200	61.3	—	—	6	456
1978	ChiB	13(12, QB)	34	54	1.6(10)	2	—	—	—	—	264	141	53.4	1718	6.5(61)	5	16	26	208	54.8	—	—	12	318
1979	ChiB	7(3)	3	10	3.3(5)	0	—	—	—	—	51	27	52.9	310	6.1(54)	2	3	8	58	—	—	—	0	55
1981	ChiB	9(0)	5	2	0.4(2)	0	—	—	—	—	32	15	46.9	185	5.8(72)	1	3	7	52	—	—	—	0	-21
1982	ChiB	2(2)	—	—	—	—	—	—	—	—	20	8	40.0	84	4.2(21)	0	0	4	31	—	—	—	0	42
1983	ChiB	2(0)	—	—	—	—	—	—	—	—	—	—	—	—	—	—	—	—	—	—	—	—	—	—
1984	ChiB	4(1)	3	-5	-1.7(0)	0	—	—	—	—	53	30	56.6	288	5.4(50)	0	3	6	43	—	—	—	0	19
NFL	9	73(50)	104	225	2.2(21)	5	—	—	—	—	1110	560	50.5	7111	6.4(75)	33	69	110	961	54.8	—	—	30	1236

AVENI, JOHN John Patrick, K-DE, 6´3˝/212 lbs; Indiana; 1959: ChiB, rnd 27; B3/17/1935 Glassboro, NJ, D1/20/2002 Philadelphia, PA **[K]** **1959** ChiB 12 **1960** ChiB 12

| 1961 | Was | 14 | — | — | — | — | 6 | 84 | 14.0(41) | 1 | 1 | 0 | 0.0 | 0 | 0.0 | 0 | 0 | — | — | — | K | — | 42 | 47 |
| NFL | 3 | 38 | — | — | — | — | 6 | 84 | 14.0(41) | 1 | 1 | 0 | 0.0 | 0 | 0.0 | 0 | 0 | — | — | — | K | — | 144 | 47 |

AVERNO, SISTO Sisto Joseph, LB-MG-G, 5´11˝/235 lbs; Muhlenberg; 1951: Cle, rnd 30; B5/12/1925 Paterson, NJ **1950** Bal 12 (3, MG) **1951** NYY 12 (LLB) **1952** DalT 12 (1, MG) **1953** Bal 12 (MLB) **1954** Bal 3 **NFL** 51 (4) [5 yrs]

AVERY, DON Donald Lee, T, 6´4˝/254 lbs; Alabama; USC; B2/10/1921 Los Angeles, CA **1946** Was 11 (2) **1947** Was 10 (4) **NFL** 21 (6) [2 yrs]

1948 LAD-A 1 (0)

AVERY, JIM James, TE, 6´2˝/235 lbs; Northern Illinois; B7/11/1944 Grand Rapids, MI **1966** Was 1

AVERY, JOHN John Edward, RB, 5´9˝/188 lbs; Mississippi; 1998: Mia, rnd 1; B1/11/1976 Richmond, VA

1998	†Mia	16(0)	143	503	3.5(44)	2	10	67	6.7(19)	1	—	—	—	—	—	—	—	—	—	k	—	18	1002
1999	Mia	1(0)	—	—	—	—	—	—	—	—	—	—	—	—	—	—	—	—	—	k	—	0	25
1999	Den	5(0)	5	21	4.2(11)	0	4	24	6.0(11)	0	—	—	—	—	—	—	—	—	—	k	—	0	65
2003	Min	6(0)	1	0	0.0(0)	0	2	24	12.0(13)	1	—	—	—	—	—	—	—	—	—	k	—	6	123
NFL	3	28(0)	149	524	3.5(44)	2	16	115	7.2(19)	2	—	—	—	—	—	—	—	—	—	k	—	24	1215

AVERY, KEN Kenneth William, LB, 6´0˝/227 lbs; Southern Mississippi; 1966: NYG, rnd 12/Bos, rnd R2; B5/23/1944 New York, NY **1967** NYG 13 (RLB) **1968** NYG 14 (RLB) **1969** Cin-A 14 **1970**†Cin 14 (RLB) **1971** Cin 14 (RLB) **1972** Cin 13 (RLB) **1973**†Cin 14 **1974** Cin 13 (mlb) **1975** KC 14 **NFL** 123 [9 yrs]

AVERY, STEVE Steven George, RB, 6´2˝/233 lbs; Northern Michigan; B8/18/1966 Milwaukee, WI **1989** Hou 1 (0) **1991** GB 1 (0) **1993**†Pit 0 (0)

1994	†Pit	14(1)	2	4	2.0(5)	0	1	2	2.0(2)	0	—	—	—	—	—	—	—	—	—	—	—	0	5
1995	Pit	11(2)	1	3	3.0(3)	0	11	82	7.5(18)	1	—	—	—	—	—	—	—	—	—	—	—	6	49
NFL	5	27(3)	3	7	2.3(5)	0	12	84	7.0(18)	1	—	—	—	—	—	—	—	—	—	—	—	6	54

AVEZZANO, JOE Joseph William, C, 6´2˝/235 lbs; Florida State; 1966: Bos, rnd R6; B11/17/1943 Yonkers, NY **1966** Bos-A 3

AVINGER, BUTCH Clarence Edmund, FB, 6´1˝/215 lbs; Alabama; 1951: Pit, rnd 1; B12/15/1928 Beatrice, AL

| 1953 | NYG | 12 | 5 | 6 | 1.2(5) | 0 | 2 | 8 | 4.0(4) | 0 | — | — | — | — | — | — | — | — | — | P | — | 0 | 10 |

AWALT, ROBERT Robert Mitchell, TE, 6´5˝/258 lbs; Nevada-Reno; San Diego State; 1987: SL, rnd 3; B4/9/1964 Landsthul, Germany

1987	SL☆	12(9, TE)	2	-9	-4.5(-1)	0	42	526	12.5(35)	6	—	—	—	—	—	—	—	—	—	—	—	36	284
1988	Phx	16(15, TE)	—	—	—	—	39	454	11.6(52)	4	—	—	—	—	—	—	—	—	—	—	—	24	247
1989	Phx	16(15, TE)	—	—	—	—	33	360	10.9(20)	0	1	0	0.0	0	0.0	0	1	—	—	—	—	—	0	140
1990	Dal	13(1)	—	—	—	—	13	133	10.2(25)	0	—	—	—	—	—	—	—	—	—	—	—	0	67
1991	†Dal	12(2)	—	—	—	—	5	57	11.4(20)	0	—	—	—	—	—	—	—	—	—	—	—	0	29
1992	†Buf	14(1)	—	—	—	—	4	34	8.5(10)	0	—	—	—	—	—	—	—	—	—	—	—	0	17
1993	Buf	12(1)	—	—	—	—	2	19	9.5(10)	0	—	—	—	—	—	—	—	—	—	—	—	0	10
NFL	7	95(44)	2	-9	-4.5(-1)	0	138	1583	11.5(52)	10	1	0	0.0	0	0.0	0	1	—	—	—	—	—	60	793

AWASOM, ADRIAN Adrian, DE, 6´5˝/275 lbs; North Texas; B10/25/1983 Fort Bend, TX **2005**†NYG 5 (0)

AYANBADEJO, BRENDON Oladele Brendon, LB, 6´1˝/230 lbs; UCLA; B9/6/1976 Chicago, IL **2003** Mia 16 (0) **2004** Mia 16 (2) **2005**†ChiB 16 (0) **NFL** 48 (2) [3 yrs]

AYANBADEJO, OBAFEMI Obafemi, RB, 6´2˝/235 lbs; San Diego State; B3/5/1975 Chicago, IL

1998	Min	1(0)	—	—	—	—	—	—	—	—	—	—	—	—	—	—	—	—	—	—	—	—	—
1999	Min	2(0)	—	—	—	—	—	—	—	—	—	—	—	—	—	—	—	—	—	—	—	—	—
1999	Bal	12(0)	—	—	—	—	1	2	2.0(2)	0	—	—	—	—	—	—	—	—	—	—	—	0	1
2000	Bal	8(4)	15	37	2.5(8)	1	23	168	7.3(26)	1	—	—	—	—	—	—	—	—	—	—	—	12	136
2001	†Bal	16(5, fb)	46	173	3.8(17)	1	24	121	5.0(18)	1	—	—	—	—	—	—	—	—	—	—	—	12	249
2003	Mia	16(2)	1	-2	-2.0(-2)	0	9	53	4.4(12)	0	—	—	—	—	—	—	—	—	—	—	—	0	25
2004	Arz	16(5, fb)	30	122	4.1(23)	3	19	171	9.0(21)	1	—	—	—	—	—	—	—	—	—	k	—	24	248
2005	Arz	16(2)	22	46	2.1(11)	0	34	231	6.8(18)	0	—	—	—	—	—	—	—	—	—	k	—	4	163
NFL	7	87(18)	114	376	3.3(23)	5	113	746	6.6(26)	3	—	—	—	—	—	—	—	—	—	k	—	52	820

AYDELETTE, BUDDY William Leslie, T, 6´4˝/256 lbs; Alabama; 1980: GB, rnd 7; B8/19/1956 Mobile, AL **1980** GB 9 (0) **1987** Pit 12 (5, lt) **NFL** 21 (5) [2 yrs]

AYERS, JOHN John Milton, G-T, 6´5˝/258 lbs; Texas; West Texas A&M; 1976: SF, rnd 8; B4/14/1953 Carrizo Springs, TX, D10/2/1995 Canyon, TX **1977** SF 14 (1) **1978** SF 16 (13, LT/lg) **1979** SF 16 (16, LG) **1980** SF 16 (16, LG) **1981**†SF 16 (16, LG) **1982** SF 8 (8, LG) **1983**†SF 16 (16, LG) **1984**†SF☆16 (16, LG) **1985**†SF☆16 (16, LG) **1986**†SF 14 (14, LG) **1987** Den 9 (5, rg) **NFL** 157 (137) [11 yrs]

AYERS, MARVIN Marvin Lee, DE, 6´5˝/265 lbs; SMU; Grambling State; B9/12/1963 Dallas, TX **1987** Phi 2 (1)

AYI, KOLE Bamikole Richard, LB, 6´1˝/231 lbs; Massachusetts; B9/27/1978 Ann Arbor, MI **2001** NE 1 (0) **2001** SL 6 (0) **2002** SL 6 (0) **NFL** 13 (0) [2 yrs]

AYODELE, AKIN Akinola James, LB, 6´2˝/251 lbs; Purdue; 2002: Jax, rnd 3; B9/17/1979 Dallas, TX **2002** Jax 16 (3) **2003** Jax 16 (16, LLB) **2004** Jax 16 (16, RLB) **2005**†Jax 16 (11, LLB) **NFL** 64 (46) [4 yrs]

AZELBY, JOE Joseph Kenneth, LB, 6´1˝/225 lbs; Harvard; 1984: Buf, rnd 10; B3/5/1962 New York, NY **1984** Buf 14 (0)

AZUMAH, JERRY Jerry, DB, 5´10˝/195 lbs; New Hampshire; 1999: Chi, rnd 5; B9/1/1977 Oklahoma City, OK **[R]** **1999** ChiB 16 (2) **2000** ChiB 14 (4) **2001**†ChiB 16 (5, lcb) **2002** ChiB 16 (16, RCB) **2003** ChiB★16 (13, RCB) **2004** ChiB 12 (8, RCB) **2005**†ChiB 15 (1) **NFL** 105 (49) [7 yrs]

BAAB, MIKE Michael James, C, 6´4˝/270 lbs; Texas; 1982: Cle, rnd 5; B12/6/1959 Fort Worth, TX **1982**†Cle 7 (0) **1983** Cle 15 (15, C) **1984** Cle 16 (16, C) **1986**†Cle 16 (16, C) **1987**†Cle 12 (12, C) **1988** NE 15 (12, C) **1989** NE 16 (16, C) **1990** Cle 16 (16, C) **1991** Cle 16 (16, C) **1992**†KC 2 (2)

| 1985 | †Cle | 16(16, C) | 1 | 0 | 0.0(0) | 0 | — | — | — | — | — | — | — | — | — | — | — | — | — | — | — | 0 | 0 |
| NFL | 11 | 147(137) | 1 | 0 | 0.0(0) | 0 | — | — | — | — | — | — | — | — | — | — | — | — | — | — | — | 0 | 0 |

YEAR	TEAM	G(GS, POS)	RUSH	YD	AVG(LG)	TD	REC	YD	AVG(LG)	TD	PASS	COMP	PCT	YD	AVG(LG)	TD	INT	SK	YD	QBR	KPR	OTD	PTS	TAY

BAACK, STEVE Steven William, NT-G-DE-DT, 6´4˝/264 lbs; Oregon; 1984: Det, rnd 3; B11/16/1960 Ames, IA **1984** Det 16 (0) **1985** Det 16 (1) **1986** Det 16 (0) **1987** Det 7 (0) **NFL** 55 (1) [4 yrs]

BAAS, DAVID David Andrew, G-C, 6´4˝/319 lbs; Michigan; 2005: SF, rnd 2; B12/28/1981 Sarasota, FL **2005** SF 13 (5, rg)

BABARTSKY, AL Albert John, T, 6´0˝/225 lbs; Fordham; 1938: ChiC, rnd 5; B4/19/1915 Shenandoah, PA, D12/29/2002 Kettering, OH **1938** ChiC 6 (6, RT) **1939** ChiC 11 (11, RT) **1941** ChiC 10 (8, RT) **1943**†ChiB 9 (0) **1944** ChiB 10 (5, LT) **1945** ChiB 8 (7, LT) **NFL** 54 (37) [6 yrs]

BABB, CHARLIE Charles David, DB, 6´0˝/190 lbs; Memphis; 1972: Mia, rnd 5; B2/4/1950 Sikeston, MO **1972**†Mia 14 **1973**†Mia 14 **1974**†Mia 14 **1975** Mia 14 (14, SS) **1976** Mia 14 (14, SS) **1977** Mia 6 (4) **1978**†Mia 16 (3) **1979** Mia 5 **NFL** 97 (35) [8 yrs]

BABB, GENE Eugene Walter, LB-FB, 6´3˝/216 lbs; Austin; 1957: SF, rnd 19; B12/27/1934 El Paso, TX

YEAR	TEAM	G(GS, POS)	RUSH	YD	AVG(LG)	TD	REC	YD	AVG(LG)	TD	PASS	COMP	PCT	YD	AVG(LG)	TD	INT	SK	YD	QBR	KPR	OTD	PTS	TAY
1957	†SF	12(FB)	102	330	3.2(19)	3	20	141	7.1(17)	0	—	—	—	—	—	—	—	—	—	—	k	—	18	416
1958	SF	12	7	9	1.3(4)	0	—	—	—	—	—	—	—	—	—	—	—	—	—	—	k	—	0	9
1960	Dal	10(5, fb)	39	115	2.9(12)	0	13	140	10.8(27)	1	—	—	—	—	—	—	—	—	—	—	k	—	6	191
1961	Dal	14(9, RLB)	—	—	—	—	—	—	—	—	—	—	—	—	—	—	—	—	—	—	k	—	0	4
1962	†Hou-A	14(MLB)	3	0	0.0(1)	0	—	—	—	—	—	—	—	—	—	—	—	—	—	—	i	1	6	31
1963	Hou-A	14(MLB)	1	7	7.0(7)	0	—	—	—	—	—	—	—	—	—	—	—	—	—	—	i	—	0	21
NFL	6	76(14)	152	461	3.0(19)	3	33	281	8.5(27)	1	—	—	—	—	—	—	—	—	—	—	ki	1	30	672

BABCOCK, HARRY Harry Lewis, E-DE, 6´2˝/193 lbs; Georgia; 1953: SF, rnd B1; B8/12/1930 West Nyack, NY

YEAR	TEAM	G(GS, POS)	RUSH	YD	AVG(LG)	TD	REC	YD	AVG(LG)	TD	PASS	COMP	PCT	YD	AVG(LG)	TD	INT	SK	YD	QBR	KPR	OTD	PTS	TAY
1953	SF	10	—	—	—	—	7	59	8.4(13)	0	—	—	—	—	—	—	—	—	—	—	k	—	0	3
1954	SF	12	—	—	—	—	6	91	15.2(33)	0	—	—	—	—	—	—	—	—	—	—	—	—	0	46
1955	SF	8	—	—	—	—	3	31	10.3(16)	0	—	—	—	—	—	—	—	—	—	—	—	—	0	16
NFL	3	30	—	—	—	—	16	181	11.3(33)	0	—	—	—	—	—	—	—	—	—	—	k	—	0	64

BABCOCK, SAM Samuel Lyle, WB-FB-BB, 5´6˝/168 lbs; Syracuse; B11/5/1901 Gray, IA, D7/28/1970 National City, CA **1926** Can 8 (3)

BABER, BILL William Franklin, TE, 6´3˝/255 lbs; Virginia; 2001: KC, rnd 5; B1/17/1979 Charlottesville, VA

YEAR	TEAM	G(GS, POS)	RUSH	YD	AVG(LG)	TD	REC	YD	AVG(LG)	TD	PASS	COMP	PCT	YD	AVG(LG)	TD	INT	SK	YD	QBR	KPR	OTD	PTS	TAY
2001	KC	1(0)	—	—	—	—	—	—	—	—	—	—	—	—	—	—	—	—	—	—	—	—	—	—
2002	KC	12(2)	—	—	—	—	2	10	5.0(7)	1	—	—	—	—	—	—	—	—	—	—	—	—	6	10
2003	†KC	16(0)	—	—	—	—	1	20	20.0(20)	0	—	—	—	—	—	—	—	—	—	—	—	—	0	10
2004	TB	1(0)	—	—	—	—	1	7	7.0(7)	0	—	—	—	—	—	—	—	—	—	—	—	—	0	4
NFL	4	30(2)	—	—	—	—	4	37	9.3(20)	1	—	—	—	—	—	—	—	—	—	—	—	—	6	24

BABERS, RODERICK Roderick Henri, DB, 5´9˝/190 lbs; Texas; 2003: NYG, rnd 4; B10/6/1980 Houston, TX **2003** Det 5 (0) **2004** Det 2 (0) **NFL** 7 (0) [2 yrs]

BABICH, BOB Robert, LB, 6´2˝/231 lbs; Miami (OH); 1969: SD, rnd 1; B5/5/1947 Youngstown, OH **1970** SD 14 (MLB) **1971** SD 14 (MLB) **1972** SD 14 (LLB) **1973** Cle 14 (MLB) **1974** Cle 14 (MLB) **1975** Cle 11 (11, RLB/mlb) **1976** Cle 14 (MLB) **1977** Cle 14 **1978** Cle 16 **NFL** 125 (11) [9 yrs]

BABIN, JASON Jason, LB-DE, 6´4˝/265 lbs; Western Michigan; 2004: Hou, rnd 1; B5/24/1980 Kalamazoo, MI **2004** Hou 16 (16, LOLB) **2005** Hou 12 (3) **NFL** 28 (19) [2 yrs]

BABINEAUX, JONATHAN Jonathan, DE-DT, 6´2˝/281 lbs; Iowa; 2005: Atl, rnd 2; B10/12/1981 Port Arthur, TX **2005** Atl 16 (6, RDE)

BABINEAUX, JORDAN Jordan, DB, 6´0˝/200 lbs; Southern Arkansas; B8/31/1982 Port Arthur, TX **2004**†Sea 6 (0) **2005**†Sea 16 (4) **NFL** 22 (4) [2 yrs]

BABINECZ, JOHN John Michael, LB, 6´1˝/222 lbs; Villanova; 1972: Dal, rnd 2; B7/27/1950 Pittsburgh, PA **1972**†Dal 14 **1973**†Dal 12 **1975** ChiB 14 (1) **NFL** 40 (1) [3 yrs]

BACCAGLIO, MARTY Martin H., DE, 6´3˝/245 lbs; San Jose State; 1967: SD, rnd 14; B9/28/1944 San Francisco, CA **1968** SD-A 9 **1968** Cin-A 3 **1969** Cin-A 14 **1970**†Cin 14 **NFL** 40 [3 yrs]

BACCHUS, CARL Robert Carl, E, 6´0˝/204 lbs; Missouri; B7/31/1904 Pine Bluff, AR, D3/2/1985 Kansas City, MO **1927** Cle☆10 (9, RE), 18 **1928** Det☆9 (8, RE), 24 **NFL** 19 (17), 42 [2 yrs]

BACHMAIER, JOE Joseph William, C-G-T-E, 5´9˝/175 lbs; none; B3/10/1895 Rochester, NY, D1/14/1974 Rochester, NY **1920** Roc 9 (1, C) **1921** Roc 4 (0) **1922** Roc 3 (1) **1923** Roc 1 (0) **1924** Roc 4 (0) **NFL** 21 (2) [5 yrs]

BACHMAN, JAY Jay Lance, C, 6´3˝/250 lbs; Cincinnati; 1967: GB, rnd 5; B12/8/1945 Hamilton, OH **1968** Den-A 6 **1969** Den-A 14 **1970** Den 11 (1) **1971** Den 14 **NFL** 45 (1) [4 yrs]

BACHMAN, TED Theodore Lewis, DB, 6´0˝/190 lbs; New Mexico State; B1/19/1952 Pensacola, FL **1976** Sea 5 **1976** Mia 8 **NFL** 13 [1 yr]

BACHOR, RIP Ludwig A., T, 6´0˝/215 lbs; Detroit Mercy; B12/10/1901 Calumet, MI, D12/11/1959 Lansing, MI **1928** Det 1 (1)

BACKNOR C, none; deceased **1921** Ton 1 (0)

BACKUS, JEFF Jeffrey Carl, T, 6´5˝/305 lbs; Michigan; 2001: Det, rnd 1; B9/21/1977 Midland, MI **2001** Det 16 (16, LT) **2002** Det 16 (16, LT) **2003** Det 16 (16, LT) **2004** Det 16 (16, LT) **2005** Det 16 (16, LT) **NFL** 80 (80) [5 yrs]

BACON, COY Lander McCoy, DE-DT, 6´4˝/270 lbs; Jackson State; B8/30/1942 Cadiz, KY **1968** LARm 7 **1969**†LARm 14 (13, RDT) **1970** LARm 14 (14, RDE) **1971** LARm☆14 (14, RDE) **1972** LARm★14 (14, RDE) **1973** SD 12 (RDE) **1974** SD 14 (14, RDE) **1975** SD 14 (RDE) **1976** Cin★14 (RDE) **1977** Cin★12 (RDE) **1978** Was 16 (14, RDE) **1979** Was 16 (14, RDE) **1980** Was 16 (15, RDE) **1981** Was 3 (3) **NFL** 180 (115) [14 yrs]

BACON, FRANK Francis William, WB-TB-E, 5´11˝/182 lbs; Wabash; B1/11/1894 South Bend, IN, D8/31/1977 Port Clinton, OH **1920** Day 9 (8, TB) **1921** Day 9 (6, TB), 36 **1922** Day 6 (6, WB), 6 **1923** Day 8 (7, WB) **1923** Akr 1 (1) **1924** Day 8 (8, RE), 6 **1925** Day 6 (5, WB) **NFL** 47 (41), 48 [6 yrs]

BACON, WAINE Waine, DB, 5´10˝/191 lbs; Alabama; 2003: Atl, rnd 6; B4/11/1979 Ft. Washington, MD **2004**†Ind 11 (0)

BADACZEWSKI, JOHN John Walter, G-DG, 6´1˝/239 lbs; Case Western Reserve; B1/27/1922 Johnstown, PA, D12/12/1999 **1946** Bos 11 (7, lg) **1947** Bos☆12 (12, RG) **1948** Bos 6 (0) **1948** ChiC 5 (0) **1949** Was 12 (7, RG) **1950** Was 12 **1951** Was 12 **1953** ChiB 12 (LG) **NFL** 82 (26) [7 yrs]

BADANJEK, RICK Richard Alan, RB, 5´8˝/217 lbs; Maryland; 1986: Was, rnd 7; B3/25/1962 Warren, OH **1986** Was 6 (0) **1988** Atl 6 (0)

YEAR	TEAM	G(GS, POS)	RUSH	YD	AVG(LG)	TD	REC	YD	AVG(LG)	TD	PASS	COMP	PCT	YD	AVG(LG)	TD	INT	SK	YD	QBR	KPR	OTD	PTS	TAY
1987	Atl	2(2)	29	87	3.0(31)	1	6	35	5.8(16)	0	—	—	—	—	—	—	—	—	—	—	k	—	6	112
NFL	3	14(2)	29	87	3.0(31)	1	6	35	5.8(16)	0	—	—	—	—	—	—	—	—	—	—	—	—	6	115

BADAR, RICHARD Richard Chester, QB, 6´1˝/190 lbs; Indiana; B3/8/1943 Cleveland, OH **1967** Pit 1

BADGER, BRAD Bradley Thomas, G-T, 6´4˝/320 lbs; Stanford; 1997: Was, rnd 5; B1/11/1975 Corvallis, OR **1997** Was 12 (1) **1998** Was 16 (16, LT/lg) **1999**†Was 14 (4) **2000**†Min 16 (0) **2001** Min 13 (12, LT) **2002**†Oak 7 (0) **2003** Oak 16 (11, lg/rg) **2004** Oak 16 (12, LG) **2005** Oak 16 (8, LG) **NFL** 126 (64) [9 yrs]

BADGRO, RED Morris Hiram, E-DE, 6´0˝/191 lbs; USC; B12/1/1902 Orillia, WA, D7/13/1998 Kent, WA; HOF 1981

YEAR	TEAM	G(GS, POS)	RUSH	YD	AVG(LG)	TD	REC	YD	AVG(LG)	TD	PASS	COMP	PCT	YD	AVG(LG)	TD	INT	SK	YD	QBR	KPR	OTD	PTS	TAY
1927	NYY	12(5, le)	—	—	—	—	—	—	—	—	—	—	—	—	—	—	—	—	—	—	—	—	—	—
1928	NYY	1(0)	—	—	—	—	—	—	—	—	—	—	—	—	—	—	—	—	—	—	—	—	—	—
1930	NYG☆	17(14, LE)	—	—	—	—	—	—	—	—	—	—	—	—	—	—	—	—	—	—	—	—	—	—
1931	NYG☆	13(11, LE)	—	—	—	—	—	—	—	—	—	—	—	—	—	—	—	—	—	—	—	—	—	—
1932	NYG	12(11, LE)	—	—	—	—	6	106	17.7	0	—	—	—	—	—	—	—	—	—	—	—	—	0	53
1933	†NYG☆	12(10, LE)	—	—	—	—	9	176	19.6	2	—	—	—	—	—	—	—	—	—	—	—	1	18	98
1934	NYG☆	13(13, LE)	—	—	—	—	**16**	206	12.9	1	—	—	—	—	—	—	—	—	—	—	—	—	6	108
1935	NYG	5(5, le)	—	—	—	—	1	13	13.0(13)	0	—	—	—	—	—	—	—	—	—	—	—	—	0	7
1936	Bkn	9(7, LE)	—	—	—	—	3	59	19.7	0	—	—	—	—	—	—	—	—	—	—	—	—	0	30
NFL	9	94(76)	—	—	—	—	35	560	16.0(13)	7	—	—	—	—	—	—	—	—	—	—	—	1	48	320

BAGARUS, STEVE Stephen Michael, HB-DB, 6´0˝/173 lbs; Notre Dame; B6/19/1919 South Bend, IN, D10/17/1981 Gaithersburg, MD

YEAR	TEAM	G(GS, POS)	RUSH	YD	AVG(LG)	TD	REC	YD	AVG(LG)	TD	PASS	COMP	PCT	YD	AVG(LG)	TD	INT	SK	YD	QBR	KPR	OTD	PTS	TAY
1945	†Was☆	10(8, LH)	39	154	3.9(18)	1	34	617	18.1(70)	5	—	—	—	—	—	—	—	—	—	—	kp	—	36	789
1946	Was☆	11(6, RH)	53	168	3.2(18)	0	31	438	14.1(51)	3	—	—	—	—	—	—	—	—	—	—	kpi	—	18	687
1947	LARm	2(0)	3	15	5.0(10)	0	—	—	—	—	—	—	—	—	—	—	—	—	—	—	kpi	—	0	45
1948	Was	5(0)	3	6	2.0(3)	0	15	100	6.7(14)	1	—	—	—	—	—	—	—	—	—	—	k	—	6	61
NFL	4	28(14)	98	343	3.5(18)	1	80	1155	14.4(70)	9	—	—	—	—	—	—	—	—	—	—	kpi	—	60	1582

BAGBY, HERM Herman, TB-WB-FB-BB, 5´9˝/175 lbs; Arkansas; B2/21/1903 Lake Village, AR, D2/29/1980 Lake Village, AR **1926** Bkn 8 (4, TB), 18 **1927** Cle 4 (0) **NFL** 12 (4) [2 yrs]

BAGDON, ED Edward, G-MG-LB, 5´10˝/204 lbs; Michigan State; 1950: ChiC, rnd 7; B4/30/1926 Dearborn, MI, D10/25/1990 Hesperia, CA **[K]** **1951** ChiC 12 (LG) **1952** Was 3

YEAR	TEAM	G(GS, POS)	RUSH	YD	AVG(LG)	TD	REC	YD	AVG(LG)	TD	PASS	COMP	PCT	YD	AVG(LG)	TD	INT	SK	YD	QBR	KPR	OTD	PTS	TAY
1950	ChiC	11(MG)	—	—	—	—	1	19	19.0(19)	0	—	—	—	—	—	—	—	—	—	—	k	—	0	6
NFL	3	26	—	—	—	—	1	19	19.0(19)	0	—	—	—	—	—	—	—	—	—	—	Kk	—	7	6

YEAR	TEAM	G(GS, POS)	RUSH	YD	AVG(LG)	TD	REC	YD	AVG(LG)	TD	PASS	COMP	PCT	YD	AVG(LG)	TD	INT	SK	YD	QBR	KPR	OTD	PTS	TAY
Baggett, Billy William Boyce, HB-DB, 5´11˝/175 lbs; LSU; 1951: LA, rnd 22; B6/2/1929 Greenville, TX																								
1952	DalT	11(1)	19	65	3.4(15)	0	3	41	13.7(27)	1	—	—	—	—	—	—	—	—	—	—	kpi	—	6	360
Baham, Curt Roy Curtis, DB, 5´11˝/180 lbs; Tulane; B3/2/1963 Covington, LA **1987** Sea 3 (0)																								
Bahan, Pete Leonard Finlan, BB-TB-FB, 5´9˝/165 lbs; Notre Dame; Detroit Mercy; B2/18/1898 Colegrove, PA, D5/1/1977 Fort Worth, TX **1923** Cle 7 (4, BB) **1923** Buf 2 (2) **NFL** 9 (6) [1 yr]																								
Bahnsen, Ken Kenneth Antone, FB, 5´10˝/200 lbs; North Texas; 1953: SF, rnd 21; B2/19/1930 Vinton, LA																								
1953	SF	7	1	1	1.0(1)	0	—	—	—	—	—	—	—	—	—	—	—	—	—	—	k	—	0	7
Bahr, Chris Christopher Kurt, K, 5´10˝/170 lbs; Penn State; 1976: Cin, rnd 2; B2/3/1953 State College, PA **[K]** **1976** Cin 14 **1977** Cin☆14 **1978** Cin 16 **1979** Cin 16 **1980**†Oak 16 (0) **1981** Oak 16 (0) **1982**†LARd 9 (0) **1983**†LARd 16 (0) **1984**†LARd 16 (0) **1985**†LARd 16 (0) **1986** LARd 16 (0) **1987** LARd 13 (0) **1988** LARd 16 (0) **1989** SD 16 (0) **NFL** 210 [14 yrs]																								
Bahr, Matt Matthew David, K, 5´10˝/175 lbs; Penn State; 1979: Pit, rnd 6; B7/6/1956 Philadelphia, PA **[K]** **1979**†Pit 16 **1980** Pit 16 (0) **1981** SF 4 (0) **1981** Cle 11 (0) **1982**†Cle 9 (0) **1983** Cle 16 (0) **1984** Cle 16 (0) **1985**†Cle 16 (0) **1986** Cle 12 (0) **1987**†Cle 3 (0) **1989**†Cle 16 (0) **1990**†NYG 13 (0) **1991** NYG 13 (0) **1992** NYG 12 (0) **1993** Phi 11 (0) **1993** NE 3 (0) **1994**†NE 16 (0) **1995** NE 16 (0)																								
1988	†Cle	16(0)	1	-8	-8.0(-8)	0	—	—	—	—	—	—	—	—	—	—	—	—	—	—	K	—	104	-8
NFL	17	235	1	-8	-8.0(-8)	0	—	—	—	—	—	—	—	—	—	—	—	—	—	—	KP	—	1422	-8
Bailey, Aaron Aaron Duane, WR, 5´10˝/185 lbs; Louisville; B10/24/1971 Ann Arbor, MI **[R]**																								
1994	Ind	13(0)	—	—	—	—	2	30	15.0(23)	0	—	—	—	—	—	—	—	—	—	—	—	—	0	15
1995	†Ind	15(3)	1	34	34.0(34)	0	21	379	18.0(45)	3	—	—	—	—	—	—	—	—	—	—	k	1	24	429
1996	†Ind	14(2)	—	—	—	—	18	302	16.8(40)	0	—	—	—	—	—	—	—	—	—	—	k	1	6	557
1997	Ind	13(4)	3	20	6.7(18)	0	26	329	12.7(22)	3	—	—	—	—	—	—	—	—	—	—	kp	—	18	595
1998	Ind	9(0)	—	—	—	—	—	—	—	—	—	—	—	—	—	—	—	—	—	—	kp	—	0	330
NFL	5	64(9)	4	54	13.5(34)	0	67	1040	15.5(45)	6	—	—	—	—	—	—	—	—	—	—	kp	2	48	1925
Bailey, Bill Edgar Lee, E-DE, 6´3˝/213 lbs; Duke; 1940: Bkn, rnd 4; B4/12/1916 Thomasville, NC, D4/9/1990 Winston-Salem, NC																								
1940	Bkn	10(1)	—	—	—	—	1	12	12.0(12)	0	—	—	—	—	—	—	—	—	—	—	—	—	0	6
1941	Bkn	5(0)	—	—	—	—	1	14	14.0(14)	0	—	—	—	—	—	—	—	—	—	—	—	—	0	7
NFL	2	15(1)	—	—	—	—	2	26	13.0(14)	0	—	—	—	—	—	—	—	—	—	—	—	—	0	13
Bailey, Boss Boss, LB, 6´3˝/233 lbs; Georgia; 2003: Det, rnd 2; B10/14/1979 Folkston, GA **2003** Det 16 (16, RLB) **2005** Det 11 (11, LLB) **NFL** 27 (27) [2 yrs]																								
Bailey, Byron Byron Ledare, HB, 5´10˝/192 lbs; Washington State; 1952: Det, rnd 25; B10/12/1930 Omaha, NE																								
1952	†Det	8	19	74	3.9(11)	2	2	28	14.0(24)	0	—	—	—	—	—	—	—	—	—	—	k	—	12	116
1953	GB	10	13	29	2.2(13)	0	8	119	14.9(50)	0	—	—	—	—	—	—	—	—	—	—	k	—	0	93
NFL	2	18	32	103	3.2(13)	2	10	147	14.7(50)	0	—	—	—	—	—	—	—	—	—	—	k	—	12	209
Bailey, Carlton Carlton Wilson, LB, 6´3˝/242 lbs; North Carolina; 1988: Buf, rnd 9; B12/15/1964 Baltimore, MD **1988**†Buf 6 (0) **1989**†Buf 16 (0) **1990**†Buf 16 (6, rilb) **1991**†Buf 16 (16, RILB) **1992**†Buf 16 (10, RILB) **1993**†NYG 16 (16, LILB) **1994** NYG 16 (11, MLB) **1995** Car 16 (14, RILB) **1996**†Car 16 (15, RILB) **1997** Car 8 (0) **NFL** 142 (88) [10 yrs]																								
Bailey, Champ Roland Champ, DB, 6´0˝/192 lbs; Georgia; 1999: Was, rnd 1; B6/22/1978 Folkston, GA **[I]** **1999**†Was 16 (16, LCB) **2001** Was✧16 (16, LCB) **2003** Was★16 (16, LCB) **2005**†Den★14 (14, LCB)																								
2000	Was★	16(16, LCB)	1	7	7.0(7)	1	3	78	26.0(42)	0	—	—	—	—	—	—	—	—	—	—	pi	—	6	139
2002	Was✧	16(16, LCB)	1	4	4.0(4)	0	—	—	—	—	—	—	—	—	—	—	—	—	—	—	kpi	—	0	111
2004	†Den★	16(16, LCB)	—	—	—	—	1	11	11.0(11)	0	—	—	—	—	—	—	—	—	—	—	i	—	0	-10
NFL	7	110(110)	2	11	5.5(7)	1	4	89	22.3(42)	0	—	—	—	—	—	—	—	—	—	—	kpiS	3	24	394
Bailey, Clarence Clarence J., RB, 5´11˝/220 lbs; Wesley; Hampton; B3/7/1963 Milford, DE																								
1987	Mia	3(1)	10	55	5.5(13)	0	—	—	—	—	—	—	—	—	—	—	—	—	—	—	—	—	0	55
Bailey, David David, DE, 6´4˝/240 lbs; Oklahoma State; B9/3/1965 Coatesville, PA **1990** Phi 13 (0)																								
Bailey, Don William Donald, C, 6´4˝/264 lbs; Miami (FL); 1983: Den, rnd 11; B3/24/1961 Miami, FL **1984** Ind 10 (0) **1985** Ind 10 (0) **NFL** 20 (0) [2 yrs]																								
Bailey, Edwin Edwin Raymond, G, 6´4˝/271 lbs; South Carolina State; 1981: Sea, rnd 5; B5/15/1959 Savannah, GA **1981** Sea 16 (16, LG) **1982** Sea 9 (9, LG) **1983**†Sea 16 (2) **1984**†Sea 12 (8, lg) **1985** Sea 16 (16, LG) **1987**†Sea 12 (12, LG) **1988**†Sea 16 (16, LG) **1989** Sea 16 (16, LG) **1990** Sea 11 (11, LG) **1991** Sea 3 (3)																								
1986	Sea	12(12, LG)	—	—	—	—	1	3	3.0(3)	0	—	—	—	—	—	—	—	—	—	—	—	—	0	2
NFL	11	139(121)	—	—	—	—	1	3	3.0(3)	0	—	—	—	—	—	—	—	—	—	—	—	—	0	2
Bailey, Elmer Elmer Francis, WR, 6´0˝/196 lbs; Lincoln (MO); Minnesota; 1980: Mia, rnd 4; B12/13/1957 Evanston, IL **1981**†Mia 16 (0) **1982** Bal 1 (0)																								
1980	Mia	14(0)	—	—	—	—	4	105	26.3(39)	0	—	—	—	—	—	—	—	—	—	—	—	—	0	53
NFL	3	31(0)	—	—	—	—	4	105	26.3(39)	0	—	—	—	—	—	—	—	—	—	—	—	—	0	53
Bailey, Eric Eric Renard, TE, 6´5˝/240 lbs; Kansas State; B5/12/1963 Fort Worth, TX																								
1987	Phi	3(3)	—	—	—	—	8	69	8.6(19)	0	—	—	—	—	—	—	—	—	—	—	—	—	0	35
Bailey, Harold Harold Craig, WR, 6´2˝/195 lbs; Oklahoma State; 1980: Hou, rnd 8; B4/12/1957 Houston, TX **1981** Hou 11 (0)																								
1982	Hou	9(8, WR)	1	13	13.0(13)	0	26	367	14.1(27)	0	—	—	—	—	—	—	—	—	—	—	—	—	0	197
NFL	2	20(8)	1	13	13.0(13)	0	26	367	14.1(27)	0	—	—	—	—	—	—	—	—	—	—	—	—	0	197
Bailey, Henry Henry Charles, WR, 5´8˝/176 lbs; UNLV; 1995: Pit, rnd 7; B2/28/1973 Suffolk, VA																								
1996	NYJ	8(0)	1	-4	-4.0(-4)	0	5	65	13.0(28)	0	—	—	—	—	—	—	—	—	—	—	k	—	0	139
Bailey, Howard Howard Henry, T, 6´0˝/205 lbs; Tennessee; B1/10/1912 Birmingham, AL, D8/1966 **1935** Phi 1 (0)																								
Bailey, Jim James Arrelaus, G, 6´2˝/215 lbs; West Virginia State; B1927 **1949** ChiH-A 7 (0)																								
Bailey, Jim James Randall, DT-DE, 6´4˝/253 lbs; Kansas; 1970: Bal, rnd 2; B6/9/1948 Kansas City, MO **1970** Bal 10 **1971**†Bal 13 **1972** Bal 14 (RDT) **1973** Bal 14 (LDT) **1974** Bal 14 (LDT) **1975** NYJ 14 (5, rde) **1976** Atl 7 (6, rdt) **1977** Atl 14 (LDT) **1978**†Atl 16 (LDT) **NFL** 116 (11) [9 yrs]																								
Bailey, Johnny Johnny Lee, RB, 5´8˝/190 lbs; Texas A&M-Kingsville; 1990: Chi, rnd 9; B3/17/1967 Houston, TX **[R]**																								
1990	†ChiB	16(1)	26	86	3.3(9)	0	—	—	—	—	1	1	100.0	22	22.0(22)	0	0	—	—	—	kp	1	6	344
1991	ChiB	14(0)	15	43	2.9(11)	1	—	—	—	—	—	—	—	—	—	—	—	—	—	—	kp	—	6	225
1992	Phx★	12(2)	52	233	4.5(15)	1	33	331	10.0(34)	1	—	—	—	—	—	—	—	—	—	—	kp	—	12	847
1993	Phx	13(0)	49	253	5.2(31)	1	32	243	7.6(30)	0	—	—	—	—	—	—	—	—	—	—	kp	1	12	736
1994	LARm	14(0)	11	35	3.2(9)	1	58	516	8.9(28)	0	—	—	—	—	—	—	—	—	—	—	kp	—	6	441
1995	SL	12(1)	36	182	5.1(17)	2	38	265	7.0(25)	0	—	—	—	—	—	—	—	—	—	—	kp	—	14	389
NFL	6	81(4)	189	832	4.4(31)	6	161	1355	8.4(34)	1	1	1	100.0	22	22.0(22)	0	0	—	—	—	kp	2	56	2981
Bailey, Karsten Karsten Mario, WR, 6´0˝/205 lbs; Auburn; 1999: Sea, rnd 3; B4/26/1977 Newnan, GA **1999** Sea 2 (0) **2003** GB 1 (0)																								
2000	Sea	9(0)	—	—	—	—	6	62	10.3(22)	1	—	—	—	—	—	—	—	—	—	—	—	—	6	36
2002	†GB	7(0)	—	—	—	—	3	26	8.7(10)	0	—	—	—	—	—	—	—	—	—	—	—	—	0	13
NFL	4	19(0)	—	—	—	—	9	88	9.8(22)	1	—	—	—	—	—	—	—	—	—	—	—	—	6	49
Bailey, Larry Lawrence, DT, 6´4˝/238 lbs; Pacific; 1974: Atl, rnd 9; B5/10/1952 San Mateo, CA **1974** Atl 1																								
Bailey, Mark Mark, RB, 6´3˝/237 lbs; California; Long Beach State; 1977: KC, rnd 4; B12/13/1954 Lynwood, CA																								
1977	KC	14(4)	66	266	4.0(37)	2	17	206	12.1(47)	1	—	—	—	—	—	—	—	—	—	—	k	—	18	395
1978	KC	13(5, fb)	83	298	3.6(17)	0	5	13	2.6(15)	0	—	—	—	—	—	—	—	—	—	—	—	—	0	305
NFL	2	27(9)	149	564	3.8(37)	2	22	219	10.0(47)	1	—	—	—	—	—	—	—	—	—	—	k	—	18	700
Bailey, Monk Claron Everett, DB, 6´2˝/180 lbs; Utah; B4/22/1938 Moab, UT **1964** SL 12 **1965** SL 11 (ls) **NFL** 23 [2 yrs]																								
Bailey, Robert Robin Martin Luther, DB, 5´9˝/176 lbs; Miami (FL); 1991: LARm, rnd 4; B9/3/1968 Barbados **1991** LARm 6 (0) **1992** LARm 16 (6, lcb) **1993** LARm 9 (3) **1994** LARm 16 (2) **1995** Was 4 (0) **1995**†Dal 9 (0) **1996** Mia 14 (0) **1997**†Det 15 (0) **1998** Det 16 (0) **1999**†Det 16 (11, LCB) **2000**†Bal 16 (0) **2001** Det 9 (0) **NFL** 146 (22) [11 yrs]																								

Bailey, Rodney Rodney Dwayne, DE, 6´3˝/306 lbs; Ohio State; 2001: Pit, rnd 6; B10/7/1979 Cleveland, OH **2001**†Pit 16 (1) **2002**†Pit 16 (0) **2003** Pit 16 (0) **2005**†Sea 8 (0) **NFL** 56 (1) [4 yrs]

Bailey, Russ Russell Brooks, C, 5´11˝/183 lbs; West Virginia; B10/17/1897 Weston, WV, D9/15/1949 Shawnee Hills, WV **1920** Akr 11 (9, C) **1921** Akr 12 (12, C) **NFL** 23 (21) [2 yrs]

Bailey, Stacey Stacey Dwayne, WR, 6´0˝/162 lbs; San Jose State; 1982: Atl, rnd 3; B2/10/1960 San Rafael, CA

YEAR	TEAM	G (GS, POS)	RUSH	YD	AVG (LG)	TD	REC	YD	AVG (LG)	TD	PASS	COMP	PCT	YD	AVG (LG)	TD	INT	SK	YD	QBR	KPR	OTD	PTS	TAY
1982	†Atl	5(0)	—	—	—	—	2	24	12.0(15)	1	—	—	—	—	—	—	—	—	—	—	—	—	6	17
1983	Atl	14(12, WR)	2	-5	-2.5(0)	0	55	881	16.0(53)	6	—	—	—	—	—	—	—	—	—	—	—	—	36	466
1984	Atl	16(16, WR)	—	—	—	—	67	1138	17.0(61)	6	—	—	—	—	—	—	—	—	—	—	—	—	36	599
1985	Atl	15(13, WR)	1	-3	-3.0(-3)	0	30	364	12.1(31)	0	—	—	—	—	—	—	—	—	—	—	—	—	0	179
1986	Atl	6(1)	1	6	6.0(6)	0	3	39	13.0(21)	0	—	—	—	—	—	—	—	—	—	—	—	—	0	26
1987	Atl	7(6, WR)	—	—	—	—	20	325	16.3(35)	3	—	—	—	—	—	—	—	—	—	—	—	—	18	178
1988	Atl	10(10, WR)	—	—	—	—	17	437	25.7(68)	2	—	—	—	—	—	—	—	—	—	—	—	—	12	229
1989	Atl	15(0)	—	—	—	—	8	170	21.3(41)	0	—	—	—	—	—	—	—	—	—	—	—	—	0	85
1990	Atl	3(1)	—	—	—	—	4	44	11.0(13)	0	—	—	—	—	—	—	—	—	—	—	—	—	0	22
NFL	9	91(59)	4	-2	-0.5(6)	0	206	3422	16.6(68)	18	—	—	—	—	—	—	—	—	—	—	—	—	108	1799

Bailey, Teddy William Theodore, RB, 6´1˝/225 lbs; Cincinnati; B8/12/1944 Cincinnati, OH **1967** Buf-A 1 **1969** Buf-A 2 **NFL** 3 [2 yrs]

Bailey, Thomas Thomas James, WR, 6´0˝/196 lbs; Auburn; B12/6/1971 Dallas, TX **1995** Cin 1 (0)

Bailey, Tom George Thomas, RB, 6´2˝/211 lbs; Florida State; 1971: Phi, rnd 10; B2/7/1949 Gainesville, FL

YEAR	TEAM	G (GS, POS)	RUSH	YD	AVG (LG)	TD	REC	YD	AVG (LG)	TD	PASS	COMP	PCT	YD	AVG (LG)	TD	INT	SK	YD	QBR	KPR	OTD	PTS	TAY
1971	Phi	13	23	41	1.8(7)	1	7	55	7.9(24)	0	—	—	—	—	—	—	—	—	—	—	—	—	6	79
1972	Phi	14	7	22	3.1(5)	0	5	32	6.4(9)	0	—	—	—	—	—	—	—	—	—	—	—	—	0	38
1973	Phi	12	20	91	4.6(15)	0	10	80	8.0(19)	1	—	—	—	—	—	—	—	—	—	—	k	—	6	124
1974	Phi	11	10	32	3.2(11)	0	6	27	4.5(15)	0	—	—	—	—	—	—	—	—	—	—	k	—	0	45
NFL	4	50	60	186	3.1(15)	1	28	194	6.9(24)	1	—	—	—	—	—	—	—	—	—	—	k	—	12	285

Bailey, Victor Victor, WR, 6´2˝/196 lbs; Texas-El Paso; Missouri; 1993: Phi, rnd 2; B7/3/1970 Fort Worth, TX

YEAR	TEAM	G (GS, POS)	RUSH	YD	AVG (LG)	TD	REC	YD	AVG (LG)	TD	PASS	COMP	PCT	YD	AVG (LG)	TD	INT	SK	YD	QBR	KPR	OTD	PTS	TAY
1993	Phi	16(10, WR)	—	—	—	—	41	545	13.3(58)	1	—	—	—	—	—	—	—	—	—	—	—	—	6	278
1994	Phi	16(0)	—	—	—	—	20	311	15.6(61)	1	—	—	—	—	—	—	—	—	—	—	p	—	6	161
1996	KC	2(0)	—	—	—	—	1	12	12.0(12)	0	—	—	—	—	—	—	—	—	—	—	—	—	0	6
NFL	3	34(10)	—	—	—	—	62	868	14.0(61)	2	—	—	—	—	—	—	—	—	—	—	p	—	12	444

Bain, Bill William Ernest, T-G, 6´4˝/279 lbs; Colorado; USC; 1975: GB, rnd 2; B8/9/1952 Los Angeles, CA **1975** GB 14 **1976** Den 14 (13, LT) **1978** Den 1 (1) **1979**†LARm 8 **1980**†LARm 16 (0) **1981** LARm 16 (3) **1982** LARm 9 (0) **1983**†LARm 16 (16, LT) **1984**†LARm☆16 (16, LT) **1985**†LARm 15 (6, lt) **1986** NYJ 4 (0) **1986**†NE 3 (0) **NFL** 132 (55) [11 yrs]

Baird, Bill William Arthur, DB-HB, 5´10˝/180 lbs; San Francisco State; B3/1/1939 Lindsay, CA **[RI]** **1963** NYJ-A 14 (RS) **1965** NYJ-A 14 (LCB) **1966** NYJ-A 14 (RCB) **1967** NYJ-A 14 (RS) **1968**†NYJ-A 14 (RS) **1969**†NYJ-A 14 (RS)

YEAR	TEAM	G (GS, POS)	RUSH	YD	AVG (LG)	TD	REC	YD	AVG (LG)	TD	PASS	COMP	PCT	YD	AVG (LG)	TD	INT	SK	YD	QBR	KPR	OTD	PTS	TAY
1964	NYJ-A	14(RS)	1	8	8.0(8)	0	—	—	—	—	—	—	—	—	—	—	—	—	—	—	kpi	1	6	263
NFL	7	98	1	8	8.0(8)	0	—	—	—	—	—	—	—	—	—	—	—	—	—	—	kpi	3	18	667

Baisi, Al Albert Frank, G, 6´0˝/217 lbs; West Virginia; B9/6/1917 Norton, WV, D4/15/2005 St. Paul, MN **1940**†ChiB✧7 (1) **1941**†ChiB✧9 (0) **1946** ChiB 4 (2) **1947** Phi 2 (0) **NFL** 22 (3) [4 yrs]

Bajema, Billy William, TE, 6´5˝/261 lbs; Oklahoma State; 2005: SF, rnd 7; B10/31/1982 Oklahoma City, OK

YEAR	TEAM	G (GS, POS)	RUSH	YD	AVG (LG)	TD	REC	YD	AVG (LG)	TD	PASS	COMP	PCT	YD	AVG (LG)	TD	INT	SK	YD	QBR	KPR	OTD	PTS	TAY
2005	SF	15(7, TE)	—	—	—	—	5	54	10.8(24)	0	—	—	—	—	—	—	—	—	—	—	—	—	0	27

Baker, Al James Albert London, DE, 6´6˝/265 lbs; Colorado State; 1978: Det, rnd 2; B12/9/1956 Jacksonville, FL **[S]** **1978** Det★16 (16, RDE) **1979** Det★16 (16, RDE) **1980** Det✧15 (15, RDE) **1981** Det 11 (11, RDE) **1982**†Det 9 (8, RDE) **1983** SL 16 (16, LDE) **1984** SL 15 (15, LDE) **1985** SL 16 (16, LDE) **1986** SL 16 (13, RDE) **1987**†Cle 12 (1) **1988**†Min 14 (4) **1989**†Cle 16 (16, LDE) **1990** Cle 9 (9, LDE) **NFL** 181 (156) [13 yrs]

Baker, Art Arthur Ray, FB, 6´0˝/220 lbs; Syracuse; 1961: Buf, rnd 3/Phi, rnd 1; B12/31/1937 Erie, PA

YEAR	TEAM	G (GS, POS)	RUSH	YD	AVG (LG)	TD	REC	YD	AVG (LG)	TD	PASS	COMP	PCT	YD	AVG (LG)	TD	INT	SK	YD	QBR	KPR	OTD	PTS	TAY
1961	Buf-A	14(FB)	152	498	3.3(35)	3	6	73	12.2(29)	0	—	—	—	—	—	—	—	—	—	—	k	—	18	666
1962	Buf-A	3	2	9	4.5(7)	0	3	12	4.0(9)	0	—	—	—	—	—	—	—	—	—	—	k	1	6	140
NFL	2	17	154	507	3.3(35)	3	9	85	9.4(29)	0	—	—	—	—	—	—	—	—	—	—	k	1	24	806

Baker, Bullet Roy Marlon, BB-WB-TB-HB, 5´8˝/180 lbs; Santa Clara; USC; B11/4/1900 Casper, WV, deceased **1927** NYY 14 (10, WB), 6 **1928** GB 11 (1) **1929** GB 2 (2) **1929** ChiC 4 (2) **1930** ChiC 10 (10, BB) **1931** SI 9 (3) **NFL** 50 (28), 6 [5 yrs]

Baker, Charles Charles Edward, LB, 6´2˝/226 lbs; New Mexico; 1980: SL, rnd 3; B9/26/1957 Mount Pleasant, TX **1980** SL 16 (1) **1981** SL 14 (8, rolb) **1982**†SL 9 (9, RLB) **1983** SL 16 (16, RLB) **1984** SL 9 (6, rlb) **1985** SL 15 (3) **1986** SL 16 (16, ROLB) **1987** SL 14 (3) **NFL** 109 (62) [8 yrs]

Baker, Chris Chris, TE, 6´3˝/258 lbs; Michigan State; 2002: NYJ, rnd 3; B11/18/1979 St. Albans, NY

YEAR	TEAM	G (GS, POS)	RUSH	YD	AVG (LG)	TD	REC	YD	AVG (LG)	TD	PASS	COMP	PCT	YD	AVG (LG)	TD	INT	SK	YD	QBR	KPR	OTD	PTS	TAY
2002	†NYJ	12(0)	—	—	—	—	2	14	7.0(10)	0	—	—	—	—	—	—	—	—	—	—	k	—	0	-15
2003	NYJ	16(0)	—	—	—	—	14	137	9.8(24)	0	—	—	—	—	—	—	—	—	—	—	k	—	0	45
2004	†NYJ	16(0)	—	—	—	—	18	182	10.1(23)	4	—	—	—	—	—	—	—	—	—	—	—	—	24	111
2005	NYJ	8(8, TE)	—	—	—	—	18	269	14.9(47)	1	—	—	—	—	—	—	—	—	—	—	k	—	6	121
NFL	4	52(8)	—	—	—	—	52	602	11.6(47)	5	—	—	—	—	—	—	—	—	—	—	k	—	30	261

Baker, Conway Conway Oscar, G-T, 5´11˝/228 lbs; Centenary; B9/9/1911 Marlin, TX, D5/28/1997 Shreveport, LA **[K]** **1936** ChiC 9 (7, LT) **1937** ChiC 6 (3) **1938** ChiC☆11 (4) **1939** ChiC 11 (2) **1940** ChiC 11 (5, lt) **1941** ChiC 10 (4) **1942** ChiC 11 (8, LG) **1943** ChiC 10 (8, LG) **1944** C-P 9 (7, LG) **1945** ChiC 8 (6, LG) **NFL** 96 (54) [10 yrs]

Baker, Dave David Lee, DB, 6´0˝/192 lbs; Oklahoma; 1959: SF, rnd 1; B7/30/1937 Coffeyville, KS, D9/4/2002 Norman, OK **[I]** **1959** SF✧12 (DB) **1960** SF☆12 (11, LS) **1961** SF☆14 (14, LS) **NFL** 38 (25) [3 yrs]

Baker, Ed Edward Everett, QB, 6´2˝/200 lbs; Lafayette; B5/29/1948 East Orange, NJ

YEAR	TEAM	G (GS, POS)	RUSH	YD	AVG (LG)	TD	REC	YD	AVG (LG)	TD	PASS	COMP	PCT	YD	AVG (LG)	TD	INT	SK	YD	QBR	KPR	OTD	PTS	TAY
1972	Hou	1	1	9	9.0(9)	0	—	—	—	—	10	4	40.0	47	4.7(18)	0	4	2	17	—	—	—	0	-128

Baker, Eugene Eugene Keith, WR, 6´2˝/183 lbs; Kent State; 1999: Atl, rnd 5; B3/18/1976 Monroeville, PA **2000** Atl 1 (0) **2003** Car 1 (0) **2004** Car 3 (0)

YEAR	TEAM	G (GS, POS)	RUSH	YD	AVG (LG)	TD	REC	YD	AVG (LG)	TD	PASS	COMP	PCT	YD	AVG (LG)	TD	INT	SK	YD	QBR	KPR	OTD	PTS	TAY
1999	Atl	3(1)	—	—	—	—	7	118	16.9(36)	0	—	—	—	—	—	—	—	—	—	—	—	—	0	59
NFL	4	8(1)	—	—	—	—	7	118	16.9(36)	0	—	—	—	—	—	—	—	—	—	—	kp	—	0	77

Baker, Frank Frank Louis, E, 6´2˝/182 lbs; Northwestern; B7/23/1909 Madison, WI, D9/14/1985 Richmond, CA **1931** GB 2 (2), 6

Baker, Jason Jason M., P, 6´1˝/201 lbs; Iowa; B5/17/1978 Fort Wayne, IN **[P]** **2002** SF 11 (0) **2002** Phi 2 (0) **2003**†KC 16 (0) **2004** KC 2 (0) **2004** Ind 4 (0) **2004**†Den 4 (0) **2005**†Car 16 (0)

YEAR	TEAM	G (GS, POS)	RUSH	YD	AVG (LG)	TD	REC	YD	AVG (LG)	TD	PASS	COMP	PCT	YD	AVG (LG)	TD	INT	SK	YD	QBR	KPR	OTD	PTS	TAY
2001	†SF	16(0)	1	0	0.0(0)	0	—	—	—	—	—	—	—	—	—	—	—	—	—	—	P	—	0	0
NFL	5	71(0)	1	0	0.0	0	—	—	—	—	—	—	—	—	—	—	—	—	—	—	P	—	0	0

Baker, Jerry Jerry Eugene, NT, 6´2˝/297 lbs; Tulane; B3/6/1960 Bartow, FL **1983**†Den 5 (0)

Baker, Jesse Jesse Lewis, DE, 6´5˝/269 lbs; Jacksonville State; 1979: Hou, rnd 2; B7/10/1957 Conyers, GA, D1/16/1999 Houston, TX **1979**†Hou 16 (2) **1980**†Hou 16 (4) **1981** Hou 16 (2) **1982** Hou 9 (9, RDE) **1983** Hou 16 (16, RDE) **1984** Hou 16 (16, RDE) **1985** Hou 16 (16, RDE) **1986** Dal 3 (0) **1986** Hou 11 (0) **1987**†Hou 9 (2) **NFL** 128 (67) [9 yrs]

Baker, John John Haywood, DE-DT-T, 6´6˝/279 lbs; North Carolina Central; 1958: LA, rnd 5; B6/10/1935 Raleigh, NC **1958** LARm 12 **1959** LARm 12 (ldt) **1960** LARm 12 **1961** LARm 13 **1962** Phi 7 (LDE) **1963** Pit 14 (RDE) **1964** Pit☆14 (RDE) **1965** Pit☆14 (RDE) **1966** Pit 7 **1967** Pit 13 **1968** Det 13 (LDE) **NFL** 131 [11 yrs]

Baker, John John, P, 6´3˝/223 lbs; North Texas; B4/22/1977 Brenham, TX **2000**†SL 15 (0)

YEAR	TEAM	G (GS, POS)	RUSH	YD	AVG (LG)	TD	REC	YD	AVG (LG)	TD	PASS	COMP	PCT	YD	AVG (LG)	TD	INT	SK	YD	QBR	KPR	OTD	PTS	TAY
2001	†SL	16(0)	1	0	0.0(0)	0	—	—	—	—	—	—	—	—	—	—	—	—	—	—	P	—	0	0
NFL	2	31(0)	1	0	0.0	0	—	—	—	—	—	—	—	—	—	—	—	—	—	—	P	—	0	0

Baker, John John Willey Alexander, DE, 6´5˝/260 lbs; Virginia Union; Norfolk State; 1964: GB, rnd 19; B8/15/1942 Detroit, MI **1970** NYG 14

Baker, Johnny John Hendrix, LB-DE, 6´3˝/230 lbs; Mississippi State; 1963: Hou, rnd 7/LA, rnd 3; B3/15/1941 Coy, AL **1963** Hou-A 6 **1965** Hou-A 7 (LLB) **1966** Hou-A☆14 (LLB) **1967** SD-A 10

YEAR	TEAM	G (GS, POS)	RUSH	YD	AVG (LG)	TD	REC	YD	AVG (LG)	TD	PASS	COMP	PCT	YD	AVG (LG)	TD	INT	SK	YD	QBR	KPR	OTD	PTS	TAY
1964	Hou-A	14(RLB)	—	—	—	—	2	18	9.0(10)	0	—	—	—	—	—	—	—	—	—	—	i	1	6	31
NFL	5	51	—	—	—	—	2	18	9.0(10)	0	—	—	—	—	—	—	—	—	—	—	i	1	6	26

YEAR	TEAM	G (GS, POS)	RUSH	YD	AVG(LG)	TD	REC	YD	AVG(LG)	TD	PASS	COMP	PCT	YD	AVG(LG)	TD	INT	SK	YD	QBR	KPR	OTD	PTS	TAY

BAKER, JON Jonathan, DG-LB-G, 6'2"/214 lbs; California; 1949: LARm, rnd 7/SF-A, rnd 12; B6/14/1923 San Francisco, CA, D11/26/1992 San Rafael, CA **1949** NYG 10 (2) **1950**†NYG 12 (MG) **1951** NYG★12 (MG) **1952** NYG★12 (MG) **NFL** 46 (2) [4 yrs]

BAKER, JON Jonathan David, K, 6'1"/185 lbs; Arizona State; B8/13/1972 Bakersfield, CA **1995** Dal 3 (0) **1999** KC 2 (0) **NFL** 5 (0) [2 yrs]

BAKER, KEITH Keith Loenard, WR, 5'10"/187 lbs; Texas A&M; Texas Southern; B6/4/1957 Dallas, TX

YEAR	TEAM	G (GS, POS)	RUSH	YD	AVG(LG)	TD	REC	YD	AVG(LG)	TD	KPR	OTD	PTS	TAY
1985	Phi	8(1)	—	—	—		2	25	12.5(20)	0	—	—	0	13

BAKER, LARRY Lawrence Joe, T, 6'2"/240 lbs; Bowling Green State; 1959: Cle, rnd 27; B3/9/1937 **1960** NYT-A 2

BAKER, MELVIN Melvin Clyde, WR, 6'0"/189 lbs; Texas Southern; 1974: Mia, rnd 8; B8/12/1950 Beaumont, TX

YEAR	TEAM	G (GS, POS)	RUSH	YD	AVG(LG)	TD	REC	YD	AVG(LG)	TD	KPR	OTD	PTS	TAY
1974	Mia	9	—	—	—		4	121	30.3(46)	2	k	—	12	78
1975	NO	2	1	21	21.0(21)	0	2	26	13.0(17)	0		—	0	34
1975	NE	1	—	—	—		—	—	—			—	—	
1975	SD	1	—	—	—		—	—	—			—	—	
1976	Hou	8	1	2	2.0(2)	0	3	32	10.7(14)	0	k	—	0	18
NFL	3	21	2	23	11.5(21)	0	9	179	19.9(46)	2	k	—	12	130

BAKER, MYRON Myron Tobias, LB, 6'1"/232 lbs; Louisiana Tech; 1993: Chi, rnd 4; B1/6/1971 Haughton, LA **1993** ChiB 16 (0) **1994** ChiB 16 (3) **1995** ChiB 16 (0) **1996**†Car 16 (0) **1997** Car 2 (0) **NFL** 66 (3) [5 yrs]

BAKER, RALPH Ralph Robert, LB, 6'3"/228 lbs; Penn State; 1964: NYJ, rnd 6/Pit, rnd 3; B8/25/1942 Lewistown, PA [K] **1964** NYJ-A 14 (LLB) **1965** NYJ-A 14 (LLB) **1966** NYJ-A 11 **1967** NYJ-A 14 (LLB) **1968**†NYJ-A 14 (LLB) **1969**†NYJ-A 11 (LLB) **1970** NYJ 14 (LLB) **1971** NYJ 12 (LLB) **1972** NYJ 10 (LLB) **1973** NYJ 14 (LLB) **1974** NYJ 14 (LLB) **NFL** 142 [11 yrs]

BAKER, RASHAD Rashad Steward, DB, 5'10"/198 lbs; Tennessee; B2/22/1982 Camden, NJ **2004** Buf 14 (3) **2005** Buf 14 (0) **NFL** 28 (3) [2 yrs]

BAKER, ROBERT Robert Cedrick, WR, 5'11"/200 lbs; Auburn; B5/14/1976 Gainesville, FL

YEAR	TEAM	G (GS, POS)	RUSH	YD	AVG(LG)	TD	REC	YD	AVG(LG)	TD	KPR	OTD	PTS	TAY
2002	Mia	10(0)	—	—	—		1	17	17.0(17)	0	p	—	0	29

BAKER, RON Ronald, G, 6'4"/260 lbs; Oklahoma State; 1977: Bal, rnd 10; B11/19/1954 Gary, IN **1978** Bal 16 **1979** Bal 16 (3) **1980**†Phi 16 (1) **1981**†Phi 16 (16, RG) **1982** Phi 9 (9, RG) **1983** Phi 16 (16, RG) **1984** Phi 16 (16, RG) **1985** Phi 15 (15, RG) **1986** Phi 16 (16, RG) **1987** Phi 10 (10, RG) **1988**†Phi 9 (7, rg) **NFL** 155 (109) [11 yrs]

BAKER, SAM Loris Hoskins, K-FB, 6'2"/217 lbs; Oregon State; 1952: LA, rnd 11; B11/12/1929 San Francisco, CA [KP]

YEAR	TEAM	G (GS, POS)	RUSH	YD	AVG(LG)	TD	REC	YD	AVG(LG)	TD	PASS	COMP	PCT	YD	AVG(LG)	TD	INT	KPR	OTD	PTS	TAY
1953	Was	11	17	72	4.2(32)	1	2	21	10.5(11)	0	—	—	—	—	—	—	—	Pk	—	6	144
1956	Was◇	12	25	117	4.7(32)	0	4	35	8.8(17)	0	—	—	—	—	—	—	—	KPp	—	67	130
1957	Was	12	2	23	11.5(12)	1	—	—	—		—	—	—	—	—	—	—	KP	—	77	33
1958	Was	12	—	—	—		—	—	—		—	—	—	—	—	—	—	KP	—	64	0
1959	Was	12	2	3	1.5(5)	0	—	—	—		—	—	—	—	—	—	—	KP	—	51	3
1960	Cle	12	1	-11	-11.0(-11)	0	—	—	—		—	—	—	—	—	—	—	KP	—	80	-11
1961	Cle	14	—	—	—		—	—	—		—	—	—	—	—	—	—	Pk	—	0	12
1962	Dal	14	—	—	—		—	—	—		1	0	0.0	0	0.0	0	0	KP	—	92	0
1963	Dal◇	14	1	15	15.0(15)	0	—	—	—		—	—	—	—	—	—	—	KP	—	65	15
1964	Phi	14	—	—	—		—	—	—		—	—	—	—	—	—	—	KP	—	84	0
1965	Phi	12	—	—	—		—	—	—		—	—	—	—	—	—	—	KP	—	65	0
1966	Phi☆	14	1	15	15.0(15)	0	—	—	—		—	—	—	—	—	—	—	KP	—	92	15
1967	Phi	14	—	—	—		—	—	—		—	—	—	—	—	—	—	KP	—	81	0
1968	Phi◇	14	—	—	—		1	3	3.0(3)	0	1	1	100.0	58	58.0(58)	1	0	KP	—	74	36
1969	Phi	14	—	—	—		—	—	—		—	—	—	—	—	—	—	K	—	79	0
NFL	15	195	49	234	4.8(32)	2	7	59	8.4(17)	0	2	1	50.0	58	29.0(58)	1	0	KPkp	—	977	376

BAKER, SHANNON Shannon Maurice, WR, 5'9"/185 lbs; Florida State; 1993: Atl, rnd 8; B7/20/1971 Bartow, FL

YEAR	TEAM	G (GS, POS)	RUSH	YD	AVG(LG)	TD	REC	YD	AVG(LG)	TD	OTD	PTS	TAY
1994	Ind	4(0)	—	—	—		2	15	7.5(10)	0	—	0	8

BAKER, STEPHEN Stephen Edward 'Touchdown Maker', WR, 5'8"/160 lbs; Fresno State; 1987: NYG, rnd 3; B8/30/1964 San Antonio, TX

YEAR	TEAM	G (GS, POS)	RUSH	YD	AVG(LG)	TD	REC	YD	AVG(LG)	TD	KPR	OTD	PTS	TAY
1987	NYG	12(5, WR)	1	18	18.0(18)	0	15	277	18.5(50)	2	p	—	12	168
1988	NYG	16(11, WR)	—	—	—		40	656	16.4(85)	7	p	—	42	372
1989	†NYG	15(4)	—	—	—		13	255	19.6(39)	2		—	12	138
1990	†NYG	16(8, WR)	1	3	3.0(3)	0	26	541	20.8(80)	4		—	24	294
1991	NYG	15(13, WR)	—	—	—		30	525	17.5(52)	4		—	24	283
1992	NYG	16(11, WR)	—	—	—		17	333	19.6(46)	2		—	12	177
NFL	6	90(52)	2	21	10.5(18)	0	141	2587	18.3(85)	21	p	—	126	1430

BAKER, TERRY Terry Wayne, QB, 6'3"/200 lbs; Oregon State; 1963: LA, rnd 1/SD, rnd 12; B5/5/1941 Pine River, MN

YEAR	TEAM	G (GS, POS)	RUSH	YD	AVG(LG)	TD	REC	YD	AVG(LG)	TD	PASS	COMP	PCT	YD	AVG(LG)	TD	INT	OTD	PTS	TAY
1963	LARm	4	9	46	5.1(12)	0	—	—	—		19	11	57.9	140	7.4(49)	0	4	—	0	-44
1964	LARm	5	24	82	3.4(12)	0	8	92	11.5(31)	0	1	0	0.0	0	0.0	0	0	—	0	128
1965	LARm	9	25	82	3.3(10)	1	22	210	9.5(38)	2	1	1	100.0	14	14.0(14)	0	0	—	18	214
NFL	3	18	58	210	3.6(18)	1	30	302	10.1(38)	2	21	12	57.1	154	7.3(49)	0	4	—	18	298

BAKER, TIM Timothy Charles, WR, 6'4"/208 lbs; Texas Tech; B10/23/1977 Amarillo, TX **2001** Pit 3 (0)

BAKER, TONY Vernon Anthony, RB, 5'11"/229 lbs; Iowa State; B2/16/1945 Fort Madison, IA, D8/9/1998 Mediapolis, IA

YEAR	TEAM	G (GS, POS)	RUSH	YD	AVG(LG)	TD	REC	YD	AVG(LG)	TD	OTD	PTS	TAY
1968	NO	1	4	2	0.5(3)	0	—	—	—		—	0	2
1969	NO◇	14(FB)	134	642	4.8(54)	1	34	352	10.4(35)	1	—	12	833
1970	NO	8(fb)	82	337	4.1(29)	1	12	47	3.9(11)	0	—	6	371
1971	NO	4	29	125	4.3(20)	0	6	44	7.3(29)	0	—	6	152
1971	Phi	5	17	49	2.9(13)	0	4	36	9.0(14)	0	—	0	67
1972	Phi	13(fb)	90	322	3.6(14)	0	16	114	7.1(14)	0	—	0	379
1973	†LARm	14	85	344	4.0(17)	7	—	—	—		—	42	414
1974	†LARm	14	53	135	2.5(13)	5	4	65	16.3(42)	0	—	30	218
1975	SD	13(1)	42	131	3.1(18)	1	6	27	4.5(7)	0	—	6	155
NFL	8	86(1)	536	2087	3.9(54)	15	82	685	8.4(42)	2	—	102	2590

BAKER, TONY Tony Ferrino, RB, 5'10"/182 lbs; East Carolina; 1986: Atl, rnd 10; B6/11/1964 High Point, NC

YEAR	TEAM	G (GS, POS)	RUSH	YD	AVG(LG)	TD	REC	YD	AVG(LG)	TD	KPR	OTD	PTS	TAY
1986	Atl	2(0)	1	3	3.0(3)	0	—	—	—			—	0	3
1986	Cle	2(0)	—	—	—		—	—	—			—	—	
1988	†Cle	4(0)	3	19	6.3(13)	0	—	—	—			—	0	19
1989	Phx	10(2)	20	31	1.5(6)	0	2	18	9.0(9)	0	k	—	0	120
NFL	3	18(2)	24	53	2.2(13)	0	2	18	9.0(9)	0	k	—	0	142

BAKER, WAYNE Wayne Mitchell, DT, 6'6"/270 lbs; Brigham Young; 1975: SF, rnd 3; B7/7/1953 Sandpoint, ID **1975** SF 14

BAKKEN, JIM James Leroy, K, 5'11"/200 lbs; Wisconsin; 1962: LA, rnd 7; B11/2/1940 Madison, WI [K] **1962** SL 8 **1963** SL 14 **1964** SL 14 **1966** SL 14 **1967** SL★14 **1968** SL☆14 **1969** SL 14 **1970** SL 14 **1971** SL 14 **1972** SL 14 **1973** SL 14 **1974**†SL☆14 **1976** SL★14 **1977** SL 14 **1978** SL 16

YEAR	TEAM	G (GS, POS)	RUSH	YD	AVG(LG)	TD	REC	YD	AVG(LG)	TD	PASS	COMP	PCT	YD	AVG(LG)	TD	INT	SK	YD	KPR	OTD	PTS	TAY
1965	SL◇	14	1	28	28.0(28)	0	—	—	—		—	—	—	—	—	—	—			KP	—	96	28
1975	†SL★	14	—	—	—		—	—	—		0	0	0.0	0	0.0	0	0	1	9	K	—	97	0
NFL	17	234	1	28	28.0(28)	0	—	—	—		0	0	0.0	0	0.0	0	0	1	9	KP	—	1380	28

BALASZ, FRANK Frank Steve, FB-LB-DB, 6'2"/212 lbs; Iowa; 1939: GB, rnd 18; B1/23/1918 Chicago, IL, deceased [K]

YEAR	TEAM	G (GS, POS)	RUSH	YD	AVG(LG)	TD	REC	YD	AVG(LG)	TD	PASS	COMP	PCT	YD	AVG(LG)	TD	INT	KPR	OTD	PTS	TAY
1939	†GB◇	5(0)	11	41	3.7	0	1	11	11.0(11)	0	—	—	—	—	—	—	—	P	—	0	47
1940	GB	7(1)	25	107	4.3	1	1	7	7.0(7)	0	1	0	0.0	0	0.0	0	1	i	—	6	87
1941	GB	1(0)	2	-1	-0.5(5)	0	—	—	—		—	—	—	—	—	—	—	K	—	1	-1
1941	ChiC	9(3)	21	82	3.9(30)	0	2	17	8.5(9)	0	—	—	—	—	—	—	—	Pk	—	0	17
1945	ChiC	2(0)	1	-1	-1.0(-1)	0	1	15	15.0(15)	0	—	—	—	—	—	—	—		—	0	7
NFL	4	24(4)	60	228	3.8(30)	1	5	50	10.0(15)	0	5	0	0.0	0	0.0	0	3	KPki	—	7	155

BALATTI, ED Edward T., E-DB, 6´1˝/195 lbs; none; B4/8/1924 Los Banos, CA, D8/27/1990 Novato, CA **[K]** **1948** SF-A 1 (0) **1948** NYY-A 2 (0) **1948**†Buf-A 7 (1)

YEAR	TEAM	G (GS, POS)	RUSH	YD	AVG (LG)	TD	REC	YD	AVG (LG)	TD	PASS	COMP	PCT	YD	AVG (LG)	TD	INT	SK	YD	QBR	KPR	OTD	PTS	TAY
1946	SF-A	14(0)	—	—	—	—	4	15	3.8	0	—	—	—	—	—	—	—	—	—	—	K	1	8	40
1947	SF-A	14(3)	—	—	—	—	8	98	12.3	1	—	—	—	—	—	—	—	—	—	—	Kkp	1	13	63
AAFC	3	38(4)	—	—	—	—	12	113	9.4	1	—	—	—	—	—	—	—	—	—	—	Kkp	2	21	103

BALDACCI, LOU Louis Granville, HB, 6´2˝/200 lbs; Michigan; 1956: Pit, rnd 10; B12/17/1934 Richmond, VA

YEAR	TEAM	G (GS, POS)	RUSH	YD	AVG (LG)	TD	REC	YD	AVG (LG)	TD	PASS	COMP	PCT	YD	AVG (LG)	TD	INT	SK	YD	QBR	KPR	OTD	PTS	TAY
1956	Pit	10	31	140	4.5(29)	0	5	62	12.4(22)	0	1	0	0.0	0	0.0	0	0	—	—	—	P	—	0	171

BALDASSIN, MIKE Michael Robert, LB, 6´1˝/218 lbs; Washington; B7/26/1955 Tacoma, WA **1977** SF 14 **1978** SF 16 **NFL** 30 [2 yrs]

BALDINGER, BRIAN Brian David, G-T-C, 6´4˝/278 lbs; Duke; B1/7/1960 Pittsburgh, PA **1982**†Dal 4 (0) **1983**†Dal 16 (0) **1984** Dal 16 (4) **1986** Dal 16 (0) **1987** Dal 3 (0) **1989** Ind 16 (3) **1990** Ind 16 (16, RT/rg) **1991** Ind 16 (14, C) **1992**†Phi 12 (3) **1993** Phi 12 (4)

YEAR	TEAM	G (GS, POS)	RUSH	YD	AVG (LG)	TD	REC	YD	AVG (LG)	TD	PASS	COMP	PCT	YD	AVG (LG)	TD	INT	SK	YD	QBR	KPR	OTD	PTS	TAY
1988	Ind	16(3)	—	—	—	—	1	37	37.0(37)	0	—	—	—	—	—	—	—	—	—	—	—	—	0	19
NFL	11	143(47)	—	—	—	—	1	37	37.0(37)	0	—	—	—	—	—	—	—	—	—	—	—	—	0	19

BALDINGER, GARY Gary Thomas, DE-NT, 6´3˝/264 lbs; Wake Forest; 1986: KC, rnd 9; B10/4/1963 Philadelphia, PA **1986** KC 5 (0) **1987** KC 7 (0) **1988** KC 11 (4) **1990** Ind 1 (0) **1990**†Buf 9 (0) **1991** Buf 7 (0) **1992** Buf 4 (0) **NFL** 44 (4) [6 yrs]

BALDINGER, RICH Richard L., G-T, 6´4˝/285 lbs; Wake Forest; 1982: NYG, rnd 10; B12/31/1959 Camp Lejeune, NC **1982** NYG 1 (0) **1983** NYG 2 (0) **1983** KC 6 (4) **1984** KC 14 (0) **1985** KC 16 (5, lg) **1986**†KC 16 (8, rt) **1987** KC 12 (11, LG) **1988** KC 14 (14, LG) **1989** KC 16 (8, lg) **1990**†KC 16 (16, RT) **1991**†KC 16 (15, RT) **1992**†KC 13 (11, RT) **1993** NE 15 (15, RG) **NFL** 157 (107) [12 yrs]

BALDISCHWILER, KARL John Karl, T, 6´5˝/265 lbs; Oklahoma; 1978: Mia, rnd 7; B1/19/1956 Okmulgee, OK **1978** Det 16 (15, LT) **1979** Det 16 (16, LT) **1980** Det 16 (16, LT) **1981** Det 16 (16, LT) **1982**†Det 9 (5, LT) **1983** Bal 14 (14, LT) **1985** Ind 16 (16, RT) **1986** Ind 15 (2) **NFL** 118 (100) [8 yrs]

BALDWIN, AL Alton, E-DB, 6´2˝/201 lbs; Arkansas; 1947: Buf-A, rnd 1/Bos, rnd 4; B3/21/1923 Hot Springs, AR, D5/23/1994 Hot Springs, AR **[K]**

YEAR	TEAM	G (GS, POS)	RUSH	YD	AVG (LG)	TD	REC	YD	AVG (LG)	TD	PASS	COMP	PCT	YD	AVG (LG)	TD	INT	SK	YD	QBR	KPR	OTD	PTS	TAY
1947	Buf-A	14(5, le)	—	—	—	—	25	468	18.7(59)	7	—	—	—	—	—	—	—	—	—	—	ki	—	42	340
1948	†Buf-A☆	13(13, LE)	—	—	—	—	54	916	17.0(58)	8	—	—	—	—	—	—	—	—	—	—	K	—	48	498
1949	†Buf-A☆	12(12, LE)	2	1	0.5	0	53	719	13.6	7	—	—	—	—	—	—	—	—	—	—	—	—	42	396
AAFC	3	39(30)	2	1	0.5	0	132	2103	15.9(59)	22	—	—	—	—	—	—	—	—	—	—	Kki	—	132	1234
1950	GB	12(LE/DB)	—	—	—	—	28	555	19.8(85)	3	—	—	—	—	—	—	—	—	—	—	i	—	18	303

BALDWIN, BOB Robert, FB, 6´1˝/225 lbs; Clemson; B7/7/1943 Baltimore, MD, D7/7/2002 Berlin, MD **1966** Bal 9

BALDWIN, BURR Burr Browning, E-DE, 6´1˝/197 lbs; UCLA; 1947: LAD-A, rnd 1/GB, rnd 3; B6/13/1922 Bakersfield, CA

YEAR	TEAM	G (GS, POS)	RUSH	YD	AVG (LG)	TD	REC	YD	AVG (LG)	TD	PASS	COMP	PCT	YD	AVG (LG)	TD	INT	SK	YD	QBR	KPR	OTD	PTS	TAY
1947	LAD-A	13(3)	—	—	—	—	12	275	22.9	1	—	—	—	—	—	—	—	—	—	—	—	—	6	143
1948	LAD-A	12(8, LE)	—	—	—	—	10	96	9.6	0	—	—	—	—	—	—	—	—	—	—	—	—	0	48
1949	LAD-A	9(8, LE)	1	1	1.0(1)	0	2	26	13.0	0	—	—	—	—	—	—	—	—	—	—	i	—	0	8
AAFC	3	34(19)	1	1	1.0(1)	0	24	397	16.5	1	—	—	—	—	—	—	—	—	—	—	i	—	6	199

BALDWIN, CLIFF Clifford William, TB-WB-BB, 5´9˝/170 lbs; none; B9/22/1900 Muncie, IN, D1/25/1979 Muncie, IN **1920** Mun 1 (0) **1921** Mun 2 (1, TB) **NFL** 3 (1) [2 yrs]

BALDWIN, DON Donald Wayne, DE, 6´3˝/263 lbs; Purdue; B7/9/1964 St. Charles, MO **1987** NYJ 8 (0)

BALDWIN, GEORGE George Whitfield Evans, E-T, 5´11˝/190 lbs; Virginia; B5/3/1902 Washington, DC, D6/13/1971 Neptune, NJ **1925** Cle 9 (4)

BALDWIN, JACK John David, C-LB, 6´3˝/223 lbs; Centenary; 1944: Bkn, rnd 24; B7/31/1921 Clyde, TX, D9/13/1989 Kerrville, TX **1946**†NYY-A 7 (3) **1947** NYY-A 2 (0) **1947** SF-A 3 (0) **1948**†Buf-A 3 (0) **AAFC** 15 (3) [3 yrs]

BALDWIN, KEITH Keith Manning, DE, 6´4˝/263 lbs; Texas A&M; 1982: Cle, rnd 2; B10/13/1960 Houston, TX **1982**†Cle 9 (1) **1983** Cle 16 (9, RDE) **1984** Cle 16 (16, RDE) **1985**†Cle 10 (0) **1987** SD 6 (1) **1988** SD 6 (1) **NFL** 63 (28) [6 yrs]

BALDWIN, RANDY Randy Chadwick, RB, 5´10˝/220 lbs; Mississippi; 1991: Min, rnd 4; B8/19/1967 Griffin, GA **[R]**

YEAR	TEAM	G (GS, POS)	RUSH	YD	AVG (LG)	TD	REC	YD	AVG (LG)	TD	PASS	COMP	PCT	YD	AVG (LG)	TD	INT	SK	YD	QBR	KPR	OTD	PTS	TAY
1991	Min	4(0)	—	—	—	—	—	—	—	—	—	—	—	—	—	—	—	—	—	—	k	—	0	-1
1992	Cle	15(0)	10	31	3.1(11)	0	2	30	15.0(20)	0	—	—	—	—	—	—	—	—	—	—	k	—	0	271
1993	Cle	14(0)	18	61	3.4(11)	0	1	5	5.0(5)	1	—	—	—	—	—	—	—	—	—	—	k	—	6	153
1994	†Cle	16(0)	23	78	3.4(16)	0	3	15	5.0(15)	0	—	—	—	—	—	—	—	—	—	—	k	1	6	429
1995	Car	7(2)	23	61	2.7(9)	0	—	—	—	—	—	—	—	—	—	—	—	—	—	—	k	—	0	167
1996	Bal	9(0)	—	—	—	—	—	—	—	—	—	—	—	—	—	—	—	—	—	—	k	—	0	105
NFL	6	65(2)	74	231	3.1(16)	0	6	50	8.3(20)	1	—	—	—	—	—	—	—	—	—	—	k	1	12	1123

BALDWIN, TOM Thomas Burke, NT-DT-DE, 6´4˝/274 lbs; Wisconsin; Tulsa; 1984: NYJ, rnd 9; B5/13/1961 Evergreen Park, IL, D5/1/2000 Naperville, IL **1984** NYJ 16 (2) **1985**†NYJ 16 (0) **1986**†NYJ 16 (6, nt) **1988** NYJ 16 (2) **NFL** 64 (10) [4 yrs]

BALL, DAVE David Stewart, DE, 6´6˝/275 lbs; UCLA; 2004: SD, rnd 5; B1/4/1981 Fairfield, CA **2004** SD 6 (0) **2005** SD 2 (0) **2005** NYJ 3 (0) **NFL** 11 (0) [2 yrs]

BALL, ERIC Eric Clinton, RB, 6´2˝/218 lbs; UCLA; 1989: Cin, rnd 2; B7/1/1966 Cleveland, OH **[R]**

YEAR	TEAM	G (GS, POS)	RUSH	YD	AVG (LG)	TD	REC	YD	AVG (LG)	TD	PASS	COMP	PCT	YD	AVG (LG)	TD	INT	SK	YD	QBR	KPR	OTD	PTS	TAY
1989	Cin	15(9, FB)	98	391	4.0(27)	3	6	44	7.3(15)	0	—	—	—	—	—	—	—	—	—	—	k	—	18	447
1990	†Cin	13(1)	22	72	3.3(15)	1	2	46	23.0(48)	1	—	—	—	—	—	—	—	—	—	—	k	—	12	236
1991	Cin	6(4)	10	21	2.1(10)	1	3	17	5.7(9)	0	—	—	—	—	—	—	—	—	—	—	k	—	6	107
1992	Cin	16(14, FB)	16	55	3.4(17)	2	6	66	11.0(35)	2	—	—	—	—	—	—	—	—	—	—	k	—	24	229
1993	Cin	15(1)	8	37	4.6(18)	1	4	39	9.8(24)	0	—	—	—	—	—	—	—	—	—	—	k	—	6	223
1994	Cin	16(0)	2	0	0.0(1)	0	1	4	4.0(4)	0	—	—	—	—	—	—	—	—	—	—	k	—	0	287
1995	Oak	16(0)	2	10	5.0(10)	0	—	—	—	—	—	—	—	—	—	—	—	—	—	—	—	—	0	10
NFL	7	97(29)	158	586	3.7(27)	8	22	216	9.8(48)	3	—	—	—	—	—	—	—	—	—	—	k	—	66	1538

BALL, JASON Jason, C, 6´2˝/301 lbs; New Hampshire; B3/21/1979 Fayetteville, NC **2002** SD 16 (13, C) **2003** SD 8 (8, C) **2004** SD 3 (2) **NFL** 27 (23) [3 yrs]

BALL, JERRY Jerry Lee 'Icebox', NT-DT, 6´1˝/312 lbs; SMU; 1987: Det, rnd 3; B12/15/1964 Beaumont, TX **1987** Det 12 (12, NT) **1988** Det 16 (16, NT) **1989** Det★16 (16, NT) **1990** Det★15 (15, NT) **1991** Det★13 (13, NT) **1992** Det 12 (12, NT) **1993** Cle 16 (7, ldt) **1994** LARd 16 (13, LDT) **1995** Oak 15 (15, LDT) **1996** Oak 16 (0) **1997**†Min 12 (6, ldt) **1998**†Min 16 (16, LDT) **1999** Cle 3 (3) **1999**†Min 13 (10, LDT) **NFL** 191 (154) [13 yrs]

BALL, LARRY Larry Lavern, LB, 6´6˝/232 lbs; Louisville; 1972: Mia, rnd 4; B9/27/1949 Iowa City, IA **1972**†Mia 10 **1973**†Mia 14 **1974**†Mia 14 **1975** Det 14 **1976** TB 13 **1977** Mia 8 **1978** Mia 6 **NFL** 79 [7 yrs]

BALL, MICHAEL Michael, DB, 6´0˝/216 lbs; Southern (LA); 1988: Ind, rnd 4; B8/5/1964 New Orleans, LA **1988** Ind 16 (0) **1989** Ind 16 (16, SS) **1990** Ind 16 (0) **1991** Ind 15 (14, SS) **1992** Ind 16 (0) **1993** Ind 5 (0) **NFL** 84 (30) [6 yrs]

BALL, SAM Samuel Davis, T, 6´4˝/250 lbs; Kentucky; 1966: Bal, rnd 1/NYJ, rnd 2; B6/1/1944 Henderson, KY **1966** Bal 7 **1967** Bal 14 (RT) **1968**†Bal 14 (RT) **1969** Bal 14 (RT) **1970**†Bal 12 **NFL** 61 [5 yrs]

BALLAGE, PAT Patrick Fitzgerald, DB, 6´1˝/202 lbs; Notre Dame; B4/8/1964 Fort Hood, TX **1986** Ind 2 (0) **1987** Ind 3 (1) **NFL** 5 (1) [2 yrs]

BALLARD, HOWARD Howard Louis, T, 6´6˝/325 lbs; Alabama A&M; 1987: Buf, rnd 11; B11/3/1963 Ashland, AL **1988**†Buf 16 (0) **1989**†Buf 16 (16, RT) **1990**†Buf☆16 (16, RT) **1991**†Buf☆16 (16, RT) **1992**†Buf★16 (16, RT) **1993**†Buf★16 (16, RT) **1994** Sea 16 (16, RT) **1995** Sea 16 (16, RT) **1996** Sea 16 (16, RT) **1997** Sea 10 (10, RT) **1998** Sea 16 (16, RT) **NFL** 170 (154) [11 yrs]

BALLARD, QUINTON Quinton McCoy, DT, 6´3˝/289 lbs; Elon; B11/18/1960 Ahoskie, NC **1983** Bal 15 (4)

BALLMAN, GARY Gary John, FL-TE-SE-WR, 6´1˝/215 lbs; Michigan State; 1962: Pit, rnd 8/Den, rnd 16; B7/6/1940 Detroit, MI, D5/20/2004 Aurora, CO

YEAR	TEAM	G (GS, POS)	RUSH	YD	AVG (LG)	TD	REC	YD	AVG (LG)	TD	PASS	COMP	PCT	YD	AVG (LG)	TD	INT	SK	YD	QBR	KPR	OTD	PTS	TAY
1962	Pit	3	3	7	2.3(3)	0	—	—	—	—	—	—	—	—	—	—	—	—	—	—	—	—	0	7
1963	Pit	14(FL)	8	59	7.4(18)	0	26	492	18.9(67)	5	—	—	—	—	—	—	—	—	—	—	k	1	36	708
1964	Pit★	13(FL)	11	43	3.9(11)	0	47	935	19.9(47)	7	1	0	0.0	0	0.0	0	1	—	—	—	k	—	42	682
1965	Pit✧	14(FL)	17	46	2.7(11)	3	40	859	21.5(87)	5	—	—	—	—	—	—	—	—	—	—	k	—	48	561
1966	Pit	13(FL)	—	—	—	—	41	663	16.2(79)	5	—	—	—	—	—	—	—	—	—	—	k	—	30	534
1967	Phi	12(FL)	1	17	17.0(17)	1	36	524	14.6(67)	6	—	—	—	—	—	—	—	—	—	—	k	—	42	332
1968	Phi	12(SE)	1	30	30.0(30)	0	30	341	11.4(55)	4	—	—	—	—	—	—	—	—	—	—	—	—	24	221
1969	Phi	14(TE)	—	—	—	—	31	492	15.9(80)	2	—	—	—	—	—	—	—	—	—	—	—	—	12	256
1970	Phi	14(8, TE)	—	—	—	—	47	601	12.8(26)	3	1	0	0.0	0	0.0	0	0	—	—	—	—	—	18	316
1971	Phi	6(6, TE)	—	—	—	—	13	238	18.3(57)	0	—	—	—	—	—	—	—	—	—	—	—	—	0	119
1972	Phi	8(4, te)	—	—	—	—	9	183	20.3(43)	0	—	—	—	—	—	—	—	—	—	—	—	—	0	92

YEAR	TEAM	G (GS, POS)	RUSH	YD	AVG(LG)	TD	REC	YD	AVG(LG)	TD	PASS	COMP	PCT	YD	AVG(LG)	TD	INT	SK	YD	QBR	KPR	OTD	PTS	TAY
1973	NYG	3	—	—	—	—	1	16	16.0(16)	0	—	—	—	—	—	—	—	—	—	—	—	0	8
1973	†Min	5	—	—	—	—	2	22	11.0(12)	0	—	—	—	—	—	—	—	—	—	—	—	0	11
NFL	12	131(18)	41	202	4.9(30)	4	323	5366	16.6(87)	37	2	0	0.0	0	0.0	0	1	—	—	—	k	1	252	3844

BALLOU, MIKE Mikell Randolph, LB, 6´3˝/238 lbs; UCLA; 1970: Bos, rnd 3; B9/11/1947 Los Angeles, CA **1970** Bos 14

BALOG, BOB Robert Steven, C-LB, 6´2˝/225 lbs; Georgia; Denver; B11/2/1924 **1949** Pit 7 (0) **1950** Pit 9 **NFL** 16 [2 yrs]

BALTZELL, VIC Victor Leroy, WB-DB, 5´11˝/205 lbs; Southwestern (KS); B6/20/1912 Soda Springs, ID, D4/25/1986 Omaha, NE

| 1935 | Bos | 2(0) | 1 | 0 | 0.0 | 0 | — | — | — | — | — | — | — | — | — | — | — | — | — | — | — | 0 | 0 |

BANAS, STEVE Stephen Peter, BB-DB, 5´0˝/190 lbs; Notre Dame; B4/30/1907 Bridgeport, CT, D5/10/1974 Gardena, CA

1935	Det	1(0)	3	0	0.0	0	—	—	—	—	—	—	—	—	—	—	—	—	—	—	—	0	0
1935	Phi	2(0)	5	3	0.6	0	—	—	—	—	2	0	0.0	0	0.0	0	0	—	—	—	—	0	3
NFL	1	3(0)	8	3	0.4	0	—	—	—	—	2	0	0.0	0	0.0	0	0	—	—	—	—	0	3

BANASZAK, JOHN John Arthur, DE-DT, 6´3˝/242 lbs; Eastern Michigan; B8/24/1950 Cleveland, OH **1975**†Pit 14 **1976**†Pit 13 (5, rde) **1977** Pit 8 **1978**†Pit 16 (15, RDT) **1979**†Pit 16 (16, RDE) **1980** Pit 12 (11, RDE) **1981** Pit 12 (12, RDE) **NFL** 91 (59) [7 yrs]

BANASZAK, PETE Peter Andrew, RB, 5´11˝/210 lbs; Miami (FL); 1966: Oak, rnd 5; B5/21/1944 Crivitz, WI

1966	Oak-A	14	4	18	4.5(7)	0	1	11	11.0(11)	0	—	—	—	—	—	—	—	—	—	—	—	0	24
1967	†Oak-A	10(fb)	68	376	5.5(47)	1	16	192	12.0(72)	1	—	—	—	—	—	—	—	—	—	—	—	12	487
1968	†Oak-A	13(11, HB)	91	362	4.0(43)	4	15	182	12.1(49)	1	1	0	0.0	0	0.0	0	1	—	—	—	—	30	458
1969	†Oak-A	12(4)	88	377	4.3(40)	0	17	119	7.0(10)	3	—	—	—	—	—	—	—	—	—	—	—	18	452
1970	†Oak	10	21	75	3.6(16)	2	1	2	2.0(2)	0	—	—	—	—	—	—	—	—	—	—	—	12	96
1971	Oak	14(14, RB)	137	563	4.1(30)	8	13	128	9.8(28)	0	—	—	—	—	—	—	—	—	—	—	k	48	692
1972	Oak	14	30	138	4.6(15)	1	9	63	7.0(16)	0	—	—	—	—	—	—	—	—	—	—	—	6	180
1973	†Oak	14	34	198	5.8(26)	0	6	31	5.2(9)	0	—	—	—	—	—	—	—	—	—	—	k	0	217
1974	†Oak	14(1)	80	272	3.4(20)	5	9	64	7.1(12)	0	—	—	—	—	—	—	—	—	—	—	k	30	371
1975	†Oak	14(rb)	187	672	3.6(27)	**16**	10	64	6.4(11)	0	—	—	—	—	—	—	—	—	—	—	k	96	858
1976	†Oak	14	114	370	3.2(15)	5	15	74	4.9(20)	0	—	—	—	—	—	—	—	—	—	—	k	30	450
1977	†Oak	14	67	214	3.2(11)	5	2	14	7.0(8)	0	—	—	—	—	—	—	—	—	—	—	k	30	285
1978	Oak	16	43	137	3.2(10)	0	7	78	11.1(20)	0	—	—	—	—	—	—	—	—	—	—	k	0	176
NFL	13	173(30)	964	3772	3.9(47)	47	121	1022	8.4(72)	5	1	0	0.0	0	0.0	0	1	—	—	—	k	—	312	4744

BANASZEK, CAS Casimir Joseph, T, 6´3˝/254 lbs; Northwestern; 1967: SF, rnd 1; B10/24/1945 Chicago, IL **1968** SF 14 (14, RT) **1969** SF 14 (14, RT) **1970**†SF☆13 (RT) **1971**†SF☆14 (14, RT) **1972**†SF 13 (13, RT) **1973** SF 9 (9, RT) **1974** SF 14 (14, RT) **1975** SF 14 (14, RT) **1976** SF 9 (8, RT) **1977** SF 6 **NFL** 120 (100) [10 yrs]

BANCROFT, HUGH Hugh Norman, E, none; B8/4/1894 Wetherfield Springs, NY, D10/31/1974 Dunedin, FL **1923** Roc 2 (1)

BANDISON, ROMEO Romeo, DT, 6´5˝/290 lbs; Oregon; 1994: Cle, rnd 3; B2/12/1971 The Hague, Netherlands **1995** Was 4 (0) **1996** Was 10 (0) **NFL** 14 (0) [2 yrs]

BANDUCCI, BRUNO Bruno, G, 5´11˝/216 lbs; Stanford; 1943: Phi, rnd 6; B11/11/1920 Tsingnano, Italy, D9/15/1985 Sonoma, CA **1946** SF-A☆14 (14, RG) **1947** SF-A☆10 (8, RG) **1948** SF-A 8 (0) **1949**†SF-A 12 (2) **AAFC** 44 (24) [4 yrs]
1944 Phi 10 (9, RG) **1945** Phi☆9 (8, RG) **1951** SF☆12 (RG) **1953** SF☆12 (RG) **1954** SF★11 (RG)

1950	SF	12(RG)	—	—	—	—	0	11	(11)	1	—	—	—	—	—	—	—	—	—	—	—	6	11
1952	SF☆	12(RG)	—	—	—	—	1	-4	-4.0(-4)	0	—	—	—	—	—	—	—	—	—	—	—	0	-2
NFL	7	78(17)	—	—	—	—	1	7.0(11)		1	—	—	—	—	—	—	—	—	—	—	k	6	-4

BANDURA, JOHN John Parker, E, 6´0˝/206 lbs; Louisiana-Lafayette; B8/7/1919 Hammond, IN, D5/25/1983 Hawthorne, CA **1943** Bkn 1 (0)

BANDY, DON Donald Stewart, G, 6´3˝/255 lbs; Tulsa; 1967: Was, rnd 6; B7/1/1945 South Gate, CA **1967** Was 14 **1968** Was 12 **NFL** 26 [2 yrs]

BANES, JOEY Bobby Joe, T, 6´7˝/282 lbs; Houston; 1990: Hou, rnd 11; B4/7/1967 Houston, TX **1990** Ind 1 (0)

BANET, HERB Herbert Charles, TB-HB-DB, 6´2˝/200 lbs; Manchester; B10/17/1913 Fort Wayne, IN, D3/12/2003 Fort Wayne, IN

| 1937 | GB | 7(2) | 9 | 29 | 3.2 | 0 | 1 | 6 | 6.0(6) | 0 | 7 | 1 | 14.3 | 2 | 0.3(2) | 0 | 2 | — | — | — | — | 0 | -47 |

BANFIELD, TONY James Anthony, DB, 6´1˝/185 lbs; Oklahoma State; B12/18/1937 Independence, KS [I] **1960**†Hou-A 11 **1961**†Hou-A☆14 (14, LCB) **1962**†Hou-A☆14 (14, LCB) **1963** Hou-A☆14 (LCB) **1965** Hou-A 14 (LCB) **NFL** 67 (28) [5 yrs]

BANGS, BEN Benton M., WB, 5´10˝/180 lbs; Washington State; B9/5/1893 Moscow, ID, D6/7/1970 Wenatchee, WA **1926** LA 1 (0)

BANJAVIC, EMIL Emil Thomas, WB-DB, 6´1˝/194 lbs; Arizona; 1942: Det, rnd 9; B9/19/1918 Staunton, IL, D12/1/1995 Las Vegas, NV

| 1942 | Det | 10(1) | 11 | 67 | 6.1(45) | 0 | 5 | 50 | 10.0(18) | 1 | — | — | — | — | — | — | — | — | — | — | Pkpi | 6 | 135 |

BANKER, TED Theodore William, G-C-T, 6´2˝/270 lbs; Southeast Missouri State; B2/17/1961 Belleville, IL **1984** NYJ 4 (0) **1985** NYJ 16 (4) **1986**†NYJ 16 (13, LG) **1987** NYJ 12 (9, LG) **1988** NYJ 11 (8, lg) **1989**†Cle 16 (16, LG) **NFL** 75 (50) [6 yrs]

BANKS, ANTONIO Antonio Dontral, DB, 5´10˝/203 lbs; Virginia Tech; 1997: Min, rnd 4; B3/12/1973 Ivor, VA **1998**†Min 4 (0) **1999**†Min 6 (1) **2000**†Min 14 (0) **NFL** 24 (1) [3 yrs]

BANKS, CARL Carl E., LB, 6´4˝/235 lbs; Michigan State; 1984: NYG, rnd 1; B8/29/1962 Flint, MI **1984**†NYG 16 (4) **1985**†NYG 12 (5, lolb) **1986**†NYG 16 (16, LOLB) **1987** NYG★12 (12, LOLB) **1988** NYG 14 (14, LOLB) **1990**†NYG 9 (8, LOLB) **1991** NYG 16 (15, LOLB) **1992** NYG 15 (15, LOLB) **1993** Was 15 (15, LLB) **1994**†Cle 16 (15, LLB) **1995** Cle 16 (16, LLB)

| 1989 | †NYG | 16(16, LOLB) | — | — | — | — | 1 | 22 | 22.0(22) | 1 | — | — | — | — | — | — | — | — | — | — | iS | 6 | 17 |
| **NFL** | 12 | 173(151) | — | — | — | — | 1 | 22 | 22.0(22) | 1 | — | — | — | — | — | — | — | — | — | — | iS | 1 | 12 | 32 |

BANKS, CHIP William, LB, 6´4˝/243 lbs; USC; 1982: Cle, rnd 1; B9/18/1959 Norman, OK **1982**†Cle★9 (9, LOLB) **1983** Cle★16 (16, LOLB) **1984** Cle 16 (16, LOLB) **1985**†Cle★16 (16, LOLB) **1986**†Cle★16 (16, LOLB) **1987** SD☆12 (12, ROLB) **1989** Ind 10 (10, LOLB) **1990** Ind 16 (16, LOLB) **1991** Ind 11 (9, LOLB) **1992** Ind 16 (16, LOLB) **NFL** 138 (136) [10 yrs]

BANKS, CHRIS Warren Christopher, G, 6´1˝/300 lbs; Kansas; 1996: Den, rnd 7; B4/4/1973 Lexington, MO **1998** Den 4 (0) **1999** Den 16 (1) **2000** Atl 8 (4) **NFL** 28 (5) [3 yrs]

BANKS, CHUCK Charles Edward, RB, 6´2˝/225 lbs; Ferrum; West Virginia Tech; 1986: Hou, rnd 12; B1/4/1964 Baltimore, MD

1986	Hou	13(3)	29	80	2.8(9)	0	7	71	10.1(17)	0	—	—	—	—	—	—	—	—	—	—	—	0	116
1987	Ind	3(1)	50	245	4.9(35)	0	9	50	5.6(18)	0	—	—	—	—	—	—	—	—	—	—	—	0	270
NFL	2	16(4)	79	325	4.1(35)	0	16	121	7.6(18)	0	—	—	—	—	—	—	—	—	—	—	—	0	386

BANKS, ESTES Estes McLeod, RB, 6´3˝/215 lbs; Colorado; 1967: Oak, rnd 8; B12/18/1945 Los Angeles, CA

1967	Oak-A	9	10	26	2.6(13)	0	—	—	—	—	—	—	—	—	—	—	—	—	—	—	—	0	26
1968	Cin-A	14	34	131	3.9(20)	0	4	15	3.8(13)	1	—	—	—	—	—	—	—	—	—	—	k	6	160
NFL	2	23	44	157	3.6(13)	1	4	15	3.8(13)	1	—	—	—	—	—	—	—	—	—	—	k	6	186

BANKS, FRED Frederick Bly, WR, 5´10˝/177 lbs; Chowan Coll (NC); Liberty; 1985: Cle, rnd 8; B5/26/1962 Columbus, GA

1985	†Cle	10(5, wr)	—	—	—	—	5	62	12.4(17)	2	—	—	—	—	—	—	—	—	—	—	—	12	41
1987	Mia	3(0)	—	—	—	—	1	10	10.0(10)	1	—	—	—	—	—	—	—	—	—	—	—	6	10
1988	Mia	11(2)	—	—	—	—	23	430	18.7(55)	2	—	—	—	—	—	—	—	—	—	—	—	12	225
1989	Mia	15(3)	—	—	—	—	30	520	17.3(61)	1	—	—	—	—	—	—	—	—	—	—	—	6	265
1990	Mia	8(1)	1	3	3.0(3)	0	13	131	10.1(23)	0	—	—	—	—	—	—	—	—	—	—	—	0	69
1991	Mia	7(0)	—	—	—	—	9	119	13.2(25)	1	—	—	—	—	—	—	—	—	—	—	—	6	65
1992	†Mia	16(0)	—	—	—	—	22	319	14.5(39)	3	—	—	—	—	—	—	—	—	—	—	—	18	175
1993	ChiB	2(0)	—	—	—	—	1	19	19.0(19)	0	—	—	—	—	—	—	—	—	—	—	—	0	10
1993	Mia	8(0)	—	—	—	—	1	26	26.0(26)	0	—	—	—	—	—	—	—	—	—	—	—	0	13
NFL	8	80(11)	1	3	3.0(3)	0	105	1636	15.6(61)	10	—	—	—	—	—	—	—	—	—	—	—	60	871

BANKS, GORDON Gordon Gerard, WR, 5´10˝/175 lbs; Stanford; B3/12/1958 Los Angeles, CA

1980	NO	7(0)	1	-5	-5.0(-5)	0	1	7	7.0(7)	0	—	—	—	—	—	—	—	—	—	—	—	0	-2
1981	NO	6(1)	—	—	—	—	2	18	9.0(12)	0	—	—	—	—	—	—	—	—	—	—	kp	0	-7
1985	†Dal	2(0)	1	-1	-1.0(-1)	0	—	—	—	—	—	—	—	—	—	—	—	—	—	—	p	0	11
1986	Dal	16(5, wr)	—	—	—	—	17	202	11.9(23)	0	—	—	—	—	—	—	—	—	—	—	kp	0	167

YEAR	TEAM	G(GS, POS)	RUSH	YD	AVG(LG)	TD	REC	YD	AVG(LG)	TD	PASS	COMP	PCT	YD	AVG(LG)	TD	INT	SK	YD	QBR	KPR	OTD	PTS	TAY
1987	Dal	5(4)	—	—	—	—	15	231	15.4(34)	1	—	—	—	—	—	—	—	—	—	—	p	—	6	129
NFL	5	36(10)	2	-6	-3.0(-1)	0	35	458	13.1(34)	1	—	—	—	—	—	—	—	—	—	—	kp	—	6	298

BANKS, MIKE Mike, TE, 6´4˝/262 lbs; Iowa State; 2002: Arz, rnd 7; B11/5/1979 Mason City, IA **2002** Arz 12 (0) **2003** Arz 6 (0) **NFL** 18 (0) [2 yrs]

BANKS, ROBERT Robert Nathan, DE, 6´5˝/259 lbs; Notre Dame; 1987: Hou, rnd 7; B12/10/1963 Williamsburg, VA **1988**†Hou 14 (0) **1989**†Cle 15 (15, RDE) **1990** Cle 15 (9, RDE) **NFL** 44 (24) [3 yrs]

BANKS, ROY Roy Fitzpatrick, WR, 5´10˝/190 lbs; Eastern Illinois; 1987: Ind, rnd 5; B11/29/1965 Detroit, MI **1987** Ind 1 (0) **1988** Ind 14 (0) **NFL** 15 (0) [2 yrs]

BANKS, TAVIAN Tavian Remond, RB, 5´9˝/203 lbs; Iowa; 1998: Jax, rnd 4; B2/17/1974 Bettendorf, IL

YEAR	TEAM	G(GS, POS)	RUSH	YD	AVG(LG)	TD	REC	YD	AVG(LG)	TD	PASS	COMP	PCT	YD	AVG(LG)	TD	INT	SK	YD	QBR	KPR	OTD	PTS	TAY
1998	†Jax	6(1)	26	140	5.4(51)	1	4	20	5.0(10)	0	—	—	—	—	—	—	—	—	—	—	k	—	6	218
1999	Jax	8(1)	23	82	3.6(21)	0	14	137	9.8(38)	0	—	—	—	—	—	—	—	—	—	—	k	—	0	154
NFL	2	14(2)	49	222	4.5(51)	1	18	157	8.7(38)	0	—	—	—	—	—	—	—	—	—	—	k	—	6	372

BANKS, TOM Thomas Sidney, C-G, 6´1˝/245 lbs; Auburn; 1970: SL, rnd 8; B8/20/1948 Birmingham, AL **1971** SL 9 (C) **1972** SL 14 (C) **1973** SL 14 (14, LG) **1974** SL 1 (1) **1975**†SL★14 (14, C) **1976** SL★14 (14, C) **1977** SL★14 (14, C) **1978** SL★16 (C) **1979** SL☆14 (C) **1980** SL 6 (6, rg) **NFL** 116 (63) [10 yrs]

BANKS, TONY Anthony Lamar, QB, 6´4˝/230 lbs; Michigan State; 1996: SL, rnd 2; B4/5/1973 San Diego, CA

YEAR	TEAM	G(GS, POS)	RUSH	YD	AVG(LG)	TD	REC	YD	AVG(LG)	TD	PASS	COMP	PCT	YD	AVG(LG)	TD	INT	SK	YD	QBR	KPR	OTD	PTS	TAY
1996	SL	14(13, QB)	61	212	3.5(22)	0	—	—	—	—	368	192	52.2	2544	6.9(77)	15	15	48	306	71.0	—	—	2	959
1997	SL	16(16, QB)	47	186	4.0(23)	1	—	—	—	—	487	252	51.7	3254	6.7(76)	14	13	43	317	71.5	—	—	6	1373
1998	SL	14(14, QB)	40	156	3.9(19)	3	—	—	—	—	408	241	59.1	2535	6.2(80)	7	14	41	237	68.6	—	—	20	929
1999	Bal	12(10, QB)	24	93	3.9(12)	0	—	—	—	—	320	169	52.8	2136	6.7(76)	17	8	33	190	81.2	—	—	0	926
2000	†Bal	11(8, qb)	19	57	3.0(10)	0	—	—	—	—	274	150	54.7	1578	5.8(53)	8	8	20	152	69.3	—	—	0	566
2001	Was	15(14, QB)	47	152	3.2(17)	2	—	—	—	—	370	198	53.5	2386	6.4(85)	10	10	29	173	71.3	—	—	12	1015
2003	Hou	7(3)	6	27	4.5(13)	0	—	—	—	—	102	61	59.8	693	6.8(46)	5	3	13	57	84.3	—	—	0	279
2004	Hou	5(0)	—	—	—	—	—	—	—	—	2	1	50.0	16	8.0(16)	0	0	—	—	—	—	—	0	8
2005	Hou	3(0)	2	-2	-1.0(-1)	0	—	—	—	—	25	14	56.0	173	6.9(31)	1	2	—	—	—	—	—	0	10
NFL	9	97(78)	246	881	3.6(23)	6	—	—	—	—	2356	1278	54.2	15315	6.5(85)	77	73	227	1432	72.4	—	—	40	6064

BANKS, WILLIE Willie Green, G, 6´2˝/250 lbs; Alcorn State; 1968: Was, rnd 6; B3/17/1946 Greenville, MS, D7/2/1989 Brentwood, MD **1968** Was 10 **1969** Was 9 **1970** NYG 5 **1973** NE 13 (1) **NFL** 37 (1) [4 yrs]

BANKSTON, MICHAEL Michael Kane, DE-NT-DT, 6´5˝/285 lbs; Sam Houston State; 1992: Phx, rnd 4; B3/12/1970 Eagle Lake, TX **1992** Phx 16 (6, NT) **1993** Phx 16 (12, LDE) **1994** Arz 16 (16, LDE) **1995** Arz 16 (16, LDE) **1996** Arz 16 (16, LDE) **1997** Arz 16 (16, LDE) **1998** Cin 16 (16, LDE) **1999** Cin 16 (9, RDE) **2000** Cin 16 (14, RDE/lde) **NFL** 144 (121) [9 yrs]

BANKSTON, WARREN Warren Stephen, RB-TE, 6´4˝/235 lbs; Tulane; 1969: Pit, rnd 2; B7/22/1947 Baton Rouge, LA

YEAR	TEAM	G(GS, POS)	RUSH	YD	AVG(LG)	TD	REC	YD	AVG(LG)	TD	PASS	COMP	PCT	YD	AVG(LG)	TD	INT	SK	YD	QBR	KPR	OTD	PTS	TAY
1969	Pit	14	62	259	4.2(15)	1	6	6	1.0(8)	0	—	—	—	—	—	—	—	—	—	—	k	—	6	301
1970	Pit	4	26	122	4.7(31)	2	7	30	4.3(20)	0	—	—	—	—	—	—	—	—	—	—	—	—	12	157
1971	Pit	14	70	274	3.9(30)	0	17	148	8.7(31)	0	—	—	—	—	—	—	—	—	—	—	k	—	0	349
1972	†Pit	7	7	20	2.9(11)	0	1	5	5.0(5)	0	—	—	—	—	—	—	—	—	—	—	k	—	0	28
1973	Oak	11	—	—	—	—	—	—	—	—	—	—	—	—	—	—	—	—	—	—	k	—	0	-3
1974	†Oak	14	1	6	6.0(6)	0	—	—	—	—	—	—	—	—	—	—	—	—	—	—	k	—	0	1
1975	†Oak	14	—	—	—	—	2	21	10.5(13)	1	—	—	—	—	—	—	—	—	—	—	k	—	6	20
1976	†Oak	14	1	3	3.0(3)	0	5	73	14.6(29)	1	—	—	—	—	—	—	—	—	—	—	k	—	6	42
1977	†Oak	14	—	—	—	—	—	—	—	—	—	—	—	—	—	—	—	—	—	—	k	—	0	-15
1978	Oak	8	—	—	—	—	—	—	—	—	—	—	—	—	—	—	—	—	—	—	—	—	—	—
NFL	10	114	167	684	4.1(31)	3	38	283	7.4(31)	2	—	—	—	—	—	—	—	—	—	—	k	—	30	879

BANNAN, JUSTIN Justin Lewis, DT, 6´3˝/305 lbs; Colorado; 2002: Buf, rnd 5; B4/18/1979 Sacramento, CA **2002** Buf 15 (0) **2003** Buf 14 (1) **2004** Buf 10 (0) **2005** Buf 16 (7, ldt) **NFL** 55 (8) [4 yrs]

BANNISTER, ALEX Alex, WR, 6´5˝/207 lbs; Eastern Kentucky; 2001: Sea, rnd 5; B4/23/1979 Cincinnati, OH

YEAR	TEAM	G(GS, POS)	RUSH	YD	AVG(LG)	TD	REC	YD	AVG(LG)	TD	PASS	COMP	PCT	YD	AVG(LG)	TD	INT	SK	YD	QBR	KPR	OTD	PTS	TAY
2001	Sea	16(0)	—	—	—	—	4	50	12.5(17)	0	—	—	—	—	—	—	—	—	—	—	—	1	6	25
2002	Sea	16(1)	—	—	—	—	—	—	—	—	—	—	—	—	—	—	—	—	—	—	—	—	0	0
2003	†Sea★	16(2)	—	—	—	—	3	61	20.3(31)	1	—	—	—	—	—	—	—	—	—	—	—	—	6	36
2004	Sea	7(1)	—	—	—	—	2	10	5.0(8)	0	—	—	—	—	—	—	—	—	—	—	—	—	0	5
2005	Sea	2(0)	—	—	—	—	—	—	—	—	—	—	—	—	—	—	—	—	—	—	—	—	—	—
NFL	5	57(4)	—	—	—	—	9	121	13.4(31)	1	—	—	—	—	—	—	—	—	—	—	—	1	12	66

BANNON, BRUCE Bruce Patrick, LB, 6´3˝/225 lbs; Penn State; 1973: NYJ, rnd 5; B3/11/1951 Rockaway, NJ **1973**†Mia 14 **1974**†Mia 14 **NFL** 28 [2 yrs]

BANONIS, VINCE Vincent Joseph, C-T-LB, 6´1˝/230 lbs; Detroit Mercy; 1942: ChiC, rnd 4; B4/9/1921 Detroit, MI **1942** ChiC 11 (5, rt) **1944** C-P 2 (0) **1946** ChiC☆11 (11, C) **1947**†ChiC☆12 (8, C) **1948**†ChiC☆12 (9, C) **1949** ChiC☆12 (5, c) **1950** ChiC 12 (4, c) **1951** Det 12 **1952**†Det 12 (C) **1953**†Det 12 (C) **NFL** 108 (42) [10 yrs]

BANSAVAGE, AL Albert Anthony, LB, 6´2˝/220 lbs; The Citadel; USC; 1960: Oak, rnd 2/Bal, rnd 6; B1/9/1938 Jersey City, NJ **1960**†LAC-A 3 **1961** Oak-A 14 **NFL** 17 [2 yrs]

BANTA, BRADFORD Dennis Bradford, TE-C, 6´6˝/253 lbs; USC; 1994: Ind, rnd 4; B12/14/1970 Baton Rouge, LA **1994** Ind 16 (0) **1996**†Ind 13 (0) **1997** Ind 15 (0) **1999**†Ind 16 (0) **2000** NYJ 16 (0) **2001** Det 16 (0) **2002** Det 16 (0) **2003** Det 13 (0) **2004** Buf 3 (0)

YEAR	TEAM	G(GS, POS)	RUSH	YD	AVG(LG)	TD	REC	YD	AVG(LG)	TD	PASS	COMP	PCT	YD	AVG(LG)	TD	INT	SK	YD	QBR	KPR	OTD	PTS	TAY
1995	†Ind	16(2)	—	—	—	—	1	6	6.0(6)	0	—	—	—	—	—	—	—	—	—	—	—	—	0	3
1998	Ind	16(0)	—	—	—	—	1	7	7.0(7)	0	—	—	—	—	—	—	—	—	—	—	—	—	0	4
NFL	11	156(2)	—	—	—	—	2	13	6.5(7)	0	—	—	—	—	—	—	—	—	—	—	—	—	0	7

BANTA, JACK Herbert Jack, HB, 5´11˝/191 lbs; USC; 1941; Was, rnd 12; B11/19/1917 Los Angeles, CA, D2/22/1977 Newport Beach, FL

YEAR	TEAM	G(GS, POS)	RUSH	YD	AVG(LG)	TD	REC	YD	AVG(LG)	TD	PASS	COMP	PCT	YD	AVG(LG)	TD	INT	SK	YD	QBR	KPR	OTD	PTS	TAY
1941	Was	1(0)	2	1	0.5(0)	0	—	—	—	—	—	—	—	—	—	—	—	—	—	—	—	—	0	1
1941	Phi	6(5, LH)	27	92	3.4(31)	1	2	42	21.0(37)	0	—	—	—	—	—	—	—	—	—	—	P	—	6	123
1944	Phi	7(2)	38	198	5.2(60)	3	1	8	8.0(8)	0	—	—	—	—	—	—	—	—	—	—	Pkpi	—	18	316
1945	Phi	5(1)	15	49	3.3(22)	1	1	10	10.0(10)	0	—	—	—	—	—	—	—	—	—	—	kp	—	6	125
1946	LARm	10(6, RH)	44	209	4.8(25)	0	8	81	10.1(32)	1	—	—	—	—	—	—	—	—	—	—	Pkpi	—	6	327
1947	LARm	12(8, RH)	40	193	4.8(23)	1	14	198	14.1(64)	0	—	—	—	—	—	—	—	—	—	—	Pkpi	—	6	334
1948	LARm	12(10, RH)	32	105	3.3(14)	0	4	34	8.5(14)	0	—	—	—	—	—	—	—	—	—	—	Pkp	—	0	160
NFL	6	53(32)	198	847	4.3(60)	6	30	373	12.4(64)	1	—	—	—	—	—	—	—	—	—	—	Pkpi	—	42	1386

BANTA-CAIN, TULLY Tully, LB, 6´2˝/254 lbs; California; 2003: NE, rnd 7; B8/28/1980 Mountain View, CA **2003**†NE 9 (0) **2004**†NE 16 (0) **2005**†NE 13 (0) **NFL** 38 (0) [3 yrs]

BARBARO, GARY Gary Wayne, DB, 6´4˝/203 lbs; Nicholls State; 1976: KC, rnd 3; B2/11/1954 New Orleans, LA **[I]** **1976** KC 14 (14, FS) **1977** KC 14 (14, FS) **1978** KC 16 (16, FS) **1979** KC 16 (16, FS) **1980** KC★16 (16, FS) **1981** KC★16 (16, FS) **1982** KC★9 (9, FS) **NFL** 101 (101) [7 yrs]

BARBAY, ROLAND Roland Anthony, NT, 6´4˝/250 lbs; LSU; 1987: Sea, rnd 7; B10/1/1964 New Orleans, LA **1987**†Sea 5 (0)

BARBEE, JOE Joseph Adams, DT, 6´3˝/250 lbs; Kent State; B8/30/1933 Cleveland, OH, D8/12/1969 Cleveland, OH **1960** Oak-A 1

BARBER, BEN Benjamin, T-G, 6´3˝/235 lbs; none; B4/8/1904, D9/1984 Greenville, SC **1925** Buf 9 (5, lt)

BARBER, BOB Robert J., DE, 6´3˝/240 lbs; Grambling State; 1975: Pit, rnd 2; B12/26/1951 Ferriday, LA **1976** GB 14 **1977** GB 14 (RDE) **1978** GB 16 **1979** GB 16 (rde) **NFL** 60 [4 yrs]

BARBER, CHRIS Christopher Edgar, DB, 6´0˝/187 lbs; North Carolina A&T; B1/15/1964 Fort Bragg, NC **1987** Cin 3 (3) **1989** Cin 8 (0) **1992** TB 3 (0) **NFL** 14 (3) [3 yrs]

BARBER, ERNIE Ernest C., C-LB, 6´1˝/225 lbs; San Francisco; B1/14/1915 Manteca, CA, D6/5/1989 Manteca, CA **1945** Was 3 (2)

BARBER, JIM James Patrick, T, 6´3˝/223 lbs; San Francisco; B7/21/1912 Murfreesboro, TN, D1/30/1998 Spokane, WA **1935** Bos 10 (1) **1936**†Bos 12 (9, RT) **1937**†Was 11 (10, RT) **1938** Was 11 (10, RT) **1939** Was☆10 (8, RT) **1940**†Was★11 (11, RT) **1941** Was 11 (10, RT) **NFL** 76 (59) [7 yrs]

BARBER, KANTROY Kantroy, RB, 6´0˝/243 lbs; Colorado; West Virginia; 1996: NE, rnd 4; B10/4/1973 Miami, FL **1999** Mia 2 (0)

BARBER, KURT Kurt, LB-DE, 6´4˝/245 lbs; USC; 1992: NYJ, rnd 2; B1/5/1969 Paducah, KY **1992** NYJ 16 (0) **1993** NYJ 13 (0) **1994** NYJ 15 (0) **1995** NYJ 6 (0) **NFL** 50 (0) [4 yrs]

YEAR	TEAM	G (GS, POS)	RUSH	YD	AVG(LG)	TD	REC	YD	AVG(LG)	TD	PASS COMP	PCT	YD	AVG(LG)	TD	INT	SK	YD	QBR	KPR	OTD	PTS	TAY

BARBER, MARION   Marion Sylvester, RB, 6′3″/224 lbs; Minnesota; 1981: NYJ, rnd 2; B12/6/1959 Fort Lauderdale, FL

1982	†NYJ	6(0)	8	24	3.0(4)	0	—	—	—	—	—	—	—	—	—	—	—	—	—	—	—	0	24
1983	NYJ	14(4)	15	77	5.1(13)	1	7	48	6.9(12)	1	—	—	—	—	—	—	—	—	—	k	—	12	110
1984	NYJ	14(5, FB)	31	148	4.8(18)	2	10	79	7.9(17)	0	—	—	—	—	—	—	—	—	—	—	—	12	208
1985	NYJ	8(1)	9	41	4.6(10)	0	3	46	15.3(22)	1	—	—	—	—	—	—	—	—	—	—	—	0	64
1986	†NYJ	15(0)	11	27	2.5(8)	0	5	36	7.2(16)	0	—	—	—	—	—	—	—	—	—	—	—	0	45
1987	NYJ	12(0)	—	—	—	—	—	—	—	—	—	—	—	—	—	—	—	—	—	k	—	0	-25
1988	NYJ	16(1)	—	—	—	—	—	—	—	—	—	—	—	—	—	—	—	—	—	k	—	0	-4
NFL	7	85(11)	74	317	4.3(18)	3	25	209	8.4(22)	1	—	—	—	—	—	—	—	—	—	k	—	24	422

BARBER, MARION   Marion, RB, 5′11″/221 lbs; Minnesota; 2005: Dal, rnd 4; B6/10/1983 Plymouth, MA

| 2005 | Dal | 13(2) | 138 | 538 | 3.9(28) | 5 | 18 | 115 | 6.4(21) | 0 | 0 | 0.0 | 0 | 0.0 | 0 | 0 | 1 | 3 | — | k | — | 30 | 659 |

BARBER, MARK   Mark Ernest, FB-LB, 5′11″/192 lbs; South Dakota State; B5/19/1915 Alpena, SD, D2/24/1975

| 1937 | Cle | 5(1) | 14 | 35 | 2.5 | 0 | — | — | — | — | 3 | 1 | 33.3 | 7 | 2.3(7) | 0 | 0 | — | — | — | — | 0 | 39 |

BARBER, MICHAEL   Michael Dale, WR, 5′10″/172 lbs; Marshall; 1989: SF, rnd 4; B6/19/1967 Winfield, WV

1989	SF	8(0)	—	—	—	—	—	—	—	—	—	—	—	—	—	—	—	—	—	—	—	—	—
1990	†Cin	16(1)	1	-13	-13.0(-13)	0	14	196	14.0(28)	1	—	—	—	—	—	—	—	—	—	k	—	6	89
1991	Cin	15(2)	—	—	—	—	23	255	11.1(42)	1	—	—	—	—	—	—	—	—	—	kp	—	6	130
1992	TB	2(0)	—	—	—	—	1	32	32.0(32)	0	—	—	—	—	—	—	—	—	—	—	—	0	16
NFL	4	41(3)	1	-13	-13.0(-13)	0	38	483	12.7(42)	2	—	—	—	—	—	—	—	—	—	kp	—	12	235

BARBER, MIKE   Michael Dwayne, TE, 6′3″/235 lbs; Louisiana Tech; 1976: Hou, rnd 2; B6/4/1953 Marshall, TX

1976	Hou	2	—	—	—	—	—	—	—	—	—	—	—	—	—	—	—	—	—	—	—	—	—
1977	Hou	13(10, TE)	—	—	—	—	9	94	10.4(23)	1	—	—	—	—	—	—	—	—	—	—	—	6	52
1978	†Hou	16(16, TE)	2	14	7.0(13)	0	32	513	16.0(72)	3	—	—	—	—	—	—	—	—	—	—	—	18	286
1979	Hou	15(15, TE)	2	4	2.0(6)	0	27	377	14.0(37)	3	—	—	—	—	—	—	—	—	—	—	—	18	208
1980	†Hou	16(16, TE)	1	1	1.0(1)	0	59	712	12.1(79)	5	—	—	—	—	—	—	—	—	—	k	—	30	379
1981	Hou	16(6, te)	—	—	—	—	13	190	14.6(35)	1	—	—	—	—	—	—	—	—	—	—	—	6	100
1982	LARm	9(3, TE)	—	—	—	—	18	166	9.2(21)	1	—	—	—	—	—	—	—	—	—	—	—	6	88
1983	†LARm☆	16(16, TE)	—	—	—	—	55	657	11.9(42)	3	—	—	—	—	—	—	—	—	—	—	—	18	344
1984	†LARm	11(2)	—	—	—	—	7	42	6.0(11)	0	—	—	—	—	—	—	—	—	—	—	—	0	21
1985	LARm	5(5, te)	—	—	—	—	1	29	29.0(29)	0	—	—	—	—	—	—	—	—	—	—	—	0	15
1985	Den	10(1)	—	—	—	—	1	8	8.0(8)	0	—	—	—	—	—	—	—	—	—	—	—	0	4
NFL	10	129(96)	5	19	3.8(13)	0	222	2788	12.6(79)	17	—	—	—	—	—	—	—	—	—	k	—	102	1495

BARBER, MIKE   Michael Lenard, LB, 6′0″/246 lbs; Clemson; B11/9/1971 Edgemoor, SC   **1995** Sea 2 (0)   **1996** Sea 13 (7, llb)   **1997** Sea 8 (2)   **1998** Ind 12 (6, MLB)   **1999**†Ind 16 (16, MLB)   **NFL** 51 (31) [5 yrs]

BARBER, RONDE   Jamael Oronde, DB, 5′10″/184 lbs; Virginia; 1997: TB, rnd 3; B4/7/1975 Roanoke, VA **[I]**   **1997**†TB 1 (0)   **1998** TB 16 (9, RCB)   **1999**†TB 16 (15, RCB)   **2000**†TB 16 (16, RCB)   **2001**†TB★16 (16, RCB)   **2002**†TB☆16 (16, RCB)   **2003** TB 16 (16, LCB/rcb)   **2004** TB★16 (16, RCB)   **2005**†TB★16 (16, RCB)   **NFL** 129 (120) [9 yrs]

BARBER, RUDY   Rudolph, LB, 6′1″/255 lbs; Bethune-Cookman; B12/24/1944 Auburndale, FL   **1968** Mia-A 2

BARBER, SHAWN   Steven William, LB, 6′2″/245 lbs; Richmond; 1998: Was, rnd 4; B1/14/1975 Richmond, VA   **1998** Was 16 (1)   **1999**†Was 16 (16, RLB)   **2000** Was 14 (14, LLB)   **2001** Was 3 (3)   **2002** Phi 16 (16, LLB)   **2003**†KC 16 (16, RLB)   **2004** KC 8 (8, RLB)   **2005** KC 3 (3)   **NFL** 92 (74) [8 yrs]

BARBER, STEW   Stewart Clair, T-LB-G, 6′2″/250 lbs; Penn State; 1961: Buf, rnd 4/Dal, rnd 3; B6/14/1939 Bradford, PA   **1961** Buf-A 14 (RLB)   **1962** Buf-A 14 (LT)   **1963**†Buf-A☆14 (LT)   **1964**†Buf-A 14 (LT)   **1965**†Buf-A 14 (LT)   **1966**†Buf-A 14 (LT)   **1967** Buf-A☆14 (14, LT/lg)   **1968** Buf-A☆14 (LT)   **1969** Buf-A 13 (lt)   **NFL** 125 (14) [9 yrs]

BARBER, TIKI   Atiim Kiambu, RB, 5′10″/200 lbs; Virginia; 1997: NYG, rnd 2; B4/7/1975 Roanoke, VA **[R]**

1997	†NYG	12(6, rb)	136	511	3.8(42)	3	34	299	8.8(29)	1	—	—	—	—	—	—	—	—	—	—	—	26	696
1998	NYG	16(4)	52	166	3.2(23)	0	42	348	8.3(87)	3	—	—	—	—	—	—	—	—	—	k	—	18	395
1999	NYG	16(1)	62	258	4.2(30)	0	66	609	9.2(56)	2	—	—	—	—	—	—	—	—	—	kp	—	18	955
2000	†NYG	16(12, RB)	213	1006	4.7(78)	8	70	719	10.3(36)	1	—	—	—	—	—	—	—	—	—	kp	1	54	1601
2001	†NYG☆	14(9, RB)	166	865	5.2(36)	4	72	577	8.0(44)	0	—	—	—	—	—	—	—	—	—	p	—	26	1342
2002	†NYG☆	16(15, RB)	304	1387	4.6(70)	11	69	597	8.7(38)	0	—	—	—	—	—	—	—	—	—	p	—	66	1796
2003	†NYG	16(16, RB)	278	1216	4.4(27)	2	69	461	6.7(36)	1	—	—	—	—	—	—	—	—	—	—	—	20	1472
2004	NYG★	16(14, RB)	322	1518	4.7(72)	13	52	578	11.1(62)	2	—	—	—	—	—	—	—	—	—	—	—	90	1947
2005	†NYG★	16(16, RB)	357	1860	5.2(95)	9	54	530	9.8(48)	2	1	0.0	0	0.0	0	0	0	0	—	—	—	68	**2225**
NFL	9	138(93)	1890	8787	4.6(95)	50	528	4718	8.9(87)	12	1	0.0	0	0.0	0	0	0	0	—	kp	1	386	12426

BARBOLAK, PETE   Peter M., T, 6′3″/235 lbs; Purdue; 1948: Pit, rnd 19/SF-A, rnd 20; B4/1/1926 Chicago, IL   **1949** Pit 10 (0)

BARBOUR, ELMER   Wesley Elmer, BB-LB, 6′1″/200 lbs; Wake Forest; 1945: NYG, rnd 1; B2/2/1919 Rocky Mount, NC, D2/10/1993 Norfolk, VA   **1945** NYG 3 (3)

BAREFIELD, JOHN   John Glen, LB, 6′2″/224 lbs; Texas A&M-Kingsville; 1978: SL, rnd 2; B3/23/1955 Victoria, TX   **1978** SL 9   **1979** SL 15   **1980** SL 6 (0)   **NFL** 30 [3 yrs]

BAREFOOT, KEN   Kenneth David, TE, 6′4″/230 lbs; Virginia Tech; 1968: Was, rnd 5; B10/11/1945 Portsmouth, VA   **1968** Was 8

BARFIELD, KEN   Kenneth Alfred, T-DT, 6′2″/238 lbs; Mississippi; 1952: Was, rnd 23; B7/19/1929 Sunnyside, GA, D9/24/2000 Jackson, MS   **1954** Was 8 (RT)

BARIL, ADRIAN   George Adrian, T-G, 5′11″/210 lbs; St. Thomas; B6/4/1898 Red Lake Falls, MN, D6/10/1961 Becker, MN   **1923** Min 9 (8, RT)   **1924** Min 5 (2)   **1925** Mil 2 (2)   **NFL** 16 (12) [3 yrs]

BARISICH, CARL   Carl John, DT-NT, 6′4″/258 lbs; Princeton; 1973: Cle, rnd 11; B7/12/1951 Jersey City, NJ   **1973** Cle 14   **1974** Cle 13 (3)   **1975** Cle 14   **1976** Sea 14 (6, rdt)   **1977** Mia 3   **1978**†Mia 16   **1979**†Mia 11   **1980** Mia 15 (0)   **1981** NYG 2 (0)   **NFL** 102 (9) [9 yrs]

BARKER, BRYAN   Bryan Christopher, P, 6′1″/202 lbs; Santa Clara; B6/28/1964 Jacksonville Beach, FL **[P]**   **1990**†KC 13 (0)   **1991**†KC 16 (0)   **1992**†KC 15 (0)   **1993**†KC 16 (0)   **1994** Phi 11 (0)   **1995** Jax 16 (0)   **1996**†Jax 16 (0)   **1998**†Jax 16 (0)   **2000** Jax 16 (0)   **2001** Was 16 (0)   **2002** Was 12 (0)   **2004**†GB 16 (0)   **2005** SL 11 (0)

1997	†Jax★	16(0)	1	0	0.0(0)	0	—	—	—	—	1	1	100.0	22	22.0(22)	0	0	—	—	P	—	0	11
1999	†Jax	16(0)	1	6	6.0(6)	0	—	—	—	—	—	—	—	—	—	—	—	—	—	P	—	0	6
2003	Was	16(0)	—	—	—	—	—	—	—	—	1	1	100.0	3	3.0(3)	0	0	—	—	P	—	0	2
NFL	16	238(0)	2	6	3.0(6)	0	—	—	—	—	2	2	100.0	25	12.5(22)	0	0	—	—	P	—	0	19

BARKER, DICK   Richard William, G, 5′9″/180 lbs; Iowa State; B1/6/1897 Sedalia, MO, D12/17/1964 State College, PA   **1921** ChiS 2 (0)   **1921** RI 3 (1)   **NFL** 5 (1) [1 yr]

BARKER, ED   Edward Ross, E, 6′3″/196 lbs; Washington State; 1953: LA, rnd 1; B5/31/1931 Dillon, MT

1953	Pit	6(LE)	—	—	—	—	17	172	10.1(22)	1	—	—	—	—	—	—	—	—	—	—	—	6	91
1954	Was	12(LE)	—	—	—	—	23	353	15.3(32)	3	—	—	—	—	—	—	—	—	—	—	—	18	192
NFL	2	18	—	—	—	—	40	525	13.1(32)	4	—	—	—	—	—	—	—	—	—	—	—	24	283

BARKER, HUB   Hubert Lyle, B-LB, 5′10″/193 lbs; Arkansas; B11/12/1918 Welch, OK, D4/6/1994 Tulsa, OK   **1942** NYG 1 (0)   **1943**†NYG 2 (0)   **1945** NYG 4 (0)

| 1944 | †NYG | 9(2) | 1 | 3 | 3.0(3) | 0 | 3 | 34 | 11.3(16) | 0 | — | — | — | — | — | — | — | — | — | — | — | 0 | 20 |
| NFL | 4 | — | 1 | 3 | 3.0(3) | 0 | 3 | 34 | 11.3(16) | 0 | — | — | — | — | — | — | — | — | — | — | — | 0 | 20 |

BARKER, LEO   Leonardo, LB, 6′2″/226 lbs; New Mexico State; 1984: Cin, rnd 7; B11/7/1959 Cristobal, Panama Canal Zone   **1984** Cin 16 (0)   **1985** Cin 16 (2)   **1986** Cin 16 (9, RILB)   **1987** Cin 12 (0)   **1988**†Cin 16 (1)   **1989** Cin 16 (0)   **1990**†Cin 14 (1)   **1991** Cin 16 (11, LILB)   **NFL** 122 (24) [8 yrs]

BARKER, ROY   Roy, DE-DT, 6′5″/287 lbs; North Carolina; 1992: Min, rnd 4; B2/14/1969 New York, NY   **1992**†Min 8 (0)   **1993**†Min 16 (16, LDE)   **1994**†Min 16 (15, LDE)   **1995** Min 16 (16, LDE)   **1996**†SF 16 (16, LDE)   **1997**†SF 13 (12, LDE)   **1998**†SF 16 (16, LDE)   **1999** Cle 12 (3)   **1999** GB 1 (0)   **2000** Min 4 (0)   **NFL** 118 (94) [9 yrs]

BARKER, TONY   Anthony Ray, LB, 6′2″/230 lbs; Rice; 1992: Was, rnd 10; B9/9/1968 Wichita, KS   **1992** Was 8 (2)

BARKMAN, RALPH   Ralph S., B, 5′8″/165 lbs; Schuylkill; B9/22/1907, NJ, D12/9/1998 Chester, NJ **[K]**   **1929** Ora 8 (4), 1

BARKSDALE, ROD   Rodney Dean, WR, 6′1″/189 lbs; Arizona; B9/8/1962 Los Angeles, CA

1986	LARd	16(15, WR)	—	—	—	—	18	434	24.1(57)	2	—	—	—	—	—	—	—	—	—	—	—	12	227
1987	Dal	12(1)	—	—	—	—	12	165	13.8(22)	1	—	—	—	—	—	—	—	—	—	—	—	6	88
NFL	2	28(16)	—	—	—	—	30	599	20.0(57)	3	—	—	—	—	—	—	—	—	—	—	—	18	315

YEAR	TEAM	G (GS, POS)	RUSH	YD	AVG (LG)	TD	REC	YD	AVG (LG)	TD	PASS COMP	PCT	YD	AVG (LG)	TD	INT	SK	YD	QBR	KPR	OTD	PTS	TAY

BARKUM, JEROME   Jerome Phillip, TE-WR, 6´3˝/218 lbs; Jackson State; 1972: NYJ, rnd 1; B7/18/1950 Gulfport, MS

1972	NYJ	14(1)	—	—	—	—	16	304	19.0(52)	2	—	—	—	—	—	—	—	—	—	k	—	12	147
1973	NYJ◇	14(14, WR)	1	2	2.0(2)	0	44	810	18.4(63)	6	—	—	—	—	—	—	—	—	—	—	—	36	437
1974	NYJ	14(14, WR)	1	2	2.0(2)	0	41	524	12.8(39)	3	—	—	—	—	—	—	—	—	—	—	—	18	279
1975	NYJ	13(13, WR)	1	-7	-7.0(-7)	0	36	549	15.3(56)	5	—	—	—	—	—	—	—	—	—	—	—	30	293
1976	NYJ	4(3)	—	—	—	—	5	54	10.8(25)	1	—	—	—	—	—	—	—	—	—	—	—	6	32
1977	NYJ	14(14, TE)	—	—	—	—	26	450	17.3(40)	6	—	—	—	—	—	—	—	—	—	—	—	36	255
1978	NYJ	16(16, TE)	—	—	—	—	28	391	14.0(27)	3	—	—	—	—	—	—	—	—	—	—	—	18	211
1979	NYJ	13(13, TE)	—	—	—	—	27	401	14.9(40)	4	—	—	—	—	—	—	—	—	—	—	—	24	221
1980	NYJ	16(11, TE)	—	—	—	—	13	244	18.8(28)	1	—	—	—	—	—	—	—	—	—	—	—	6	127
1981	†NYJ	16(16, TE)	—	—	—	—	39	495	12.7(40)	7	—	—	—	—	—	—	—	—	—	—	—	42	283
1982	†NYJ	9(8, TE)	—	—	—	—	19	182	9.6(29)	1	—	—	—	—	—	—	—	—	—	—	—	6	96
1983	NYJ	15(13, TE)	—	—	—	—	32	385	12.0(34)	1	—	—	—	—	—	—	—	—	—	—	—	6	198
NFL	12	158(136)	3	-3	-1.0(2)	0	326	4789	14.7(63)	40	—	—	—	—	—	—	—	—	—	k	—	240	2577

BARLE, LOU   Louis Peter, HB-QB, 6´1˝/205 lbs; Minnesota-Duluth; B6/23/1916 Gilbert, MN, D12/30/1996   **1938** Det 1 (0)

| 1939 | Cle | 3(0) | — | — | — | 2 | 16 | 8.0 | 0 | — | — | — | — | — | — | — | — | — | — | — | — | 0 | 8 |
| NFL | 2 | 4(0) | — | — | — | 2 | 16 | 8.0 | 0 | — | — | — | — | — | — | — | — | — | — | — | — | 0 | 8 |

BARLOW, COREY   Corey Antonio, DB, 5´9˝/182 lbs; Auburn; 1992: Phi, rnd 5; B11/1/1970 Atlanta, GA   **1993** Phi 10 (0)

BARLOW, KEVAN   Kevan C., RB, 6´1˝/238 lbs; Pittsburgh; 2001: SF, rnd 3; B1/7/1979 Pittsburgh, PA

2001	†SF	15(0)	125	512	4.1(25)	4	22	247	11.2(61)	1	—	—	—	—	—	—	—	—	—	—	—	30	681
2002	†SF	14(0)	145	675	4.7(35)	4	14	136	9.7(29)	1	—	—	—	—	—	—	—	—	—	—	—	30	788
2003	SF	16(4, rb)	201	1024	5.1(78)	6	35	307	8.8(48)	1	—	—	—	—	—	—	—	—	—	—	—	42	1243
2004	SF	15(14, RB)	244	822	3.4(60)	7	35	212	6.1(15)	0	—	—	—	—	—	—	—	—	—	—	—	42	998
2005	SF	12(12, RB)	176	581	3.3(29)	3	31	241	7.8(24)	0	—	—	—	—	—	—	—	—	—	—	—	18	732
NFL	5	72(30)	891	3614	4.1(78)	24	137	1143	8.3(61)	3	—	—	—	—	—	—	—	—	—	—	—	162	4441

BARLOW, REGGIE   Reggie Devon, WR, 6´0˝/190 lbs; Alabama State; 1996: Jax, rnd 4; B1/22/1973 Montgomery, AL **[R]**

1996	†Jax	7(0)	—	—	—	—	—	—	—	—	—	—	—	—	—	—	—	—	—	—	—	0	—
1997	†Jax	16(0)	—	—	—	—	5	74	14.8(29)	0	—	—	—	—	—	—	—	—	—	kp	1	6	396
1998	†Jax	16(2)	—	—	—	—	11	168	15.3(31)	0	—	—	—	—	—	—	—	—	—	kp	1	6	731
1999	†Jax	14(2)	—	—	—	—	16	202	12.6(31)	0	—	—	—	—	—	—	—	—	—	kp	1	6	446
2000	Jax	16(0)	—	—	—	—	1	28	28.0(28)	0	—	—	—	—	—	—	—	—	—	kp	—	0	128
2002	TB	2(1)	—	—	—	—	3	23	7.7(13)	0	—	—	—	—	—	—	—	—	—	—	—	0	12
2003	TB	11(0)	—	—	—	—	3	27	9.0(13)	1	—	—	—	—	—	—	—	—	—	kp	—	6	88
NFL	7	82(5)	—	—	—	—	39	522	13.4(31)	1	—	—	—	—	—	—	—	—	—	kp	3	24	1800

BARNA, GEORGE   George J., E, 6´1˝/198 lbs; Hobart; B3/23/1908, D11/24/1972 Royalton, NY   **1929** Fra 17 (13, RE), 6

BARNARD, BROOKS   Brooks Alexander, P, 6´2˝/188 lbs; Maryland; B11/4/1979 Arnold, MD   **2003** NE 1 (0)

BARNARD, CHARLES   William Charles, E, 6´2˝/190 lbs; Central Oklahoma; B3/3/1915 Ovalo, TX, D11/1968

| 1938 | †NYG◇ | 5(0) | — | — | — | — | 1 | 33 | 33.0(33) | 0 | — | — | — | — | — | — | — | — | — | — | — | 0 | 17 |

BARNDT, TOM   Thomas Allen, DT-NT-G-C, 6´3˝/301 lbs; Pittsburgh; 1995: KC, rnd 6; B3/14/1972 Mentor, OH   **1996** KC 13 (0) **1997** †KC 16 (1) **1998** KC 16 (16, NT)
1999 KC 16 (13, RDT) **2000** Cin 14 (5, rdt) **2001** NYJ 6 (1) **NFL** 81 (36) [6 yrs]

BARNES, AL   Allen Marvin, WR, 6´1˝/170 lbs; New Mexico State; B7/4/1949 Los Angeles, CA

1972	Det	9	—	—	—	—	4	58	14.5(17)	1	—	—	—	—	—	—	—	—	—	—	—	6	34
1973	Det	11	—	—	—	—	3	43	14.3(23)	1	—	—	—	—	—	—	—	—	—	k	—	6	12
NFL	2	20	—	—	—	—	7	101	14.4(23)	2	—	—	—	—	—	—	—	—	—	k	—	12	46

BARNES, BENNY   Benny Jewell, DB, 6´1˝/190 lbs; Stanford; B3/3/1951 Lufkin, TX   **1972** Dal 4 **1973** †Dal 14 **1975** †Dal 14 **1977** †Dal 14 (14, LCB) **1978** †Dal 14 (13, LCB)
1979 †Dal 15 (15, LCB) **1980** †Dal 11 (6, lcb) **1981** †Dal 16 (1) **1982** †Dal 9 (9, SS)

1974	Dal	14(3)	—	—	—	—	1	37	37.0(37)	0	—	—	—	—	—	—	—	—	—	—	—	0	19
1976	†Dal	14(14, LCB)	—	—	—	—	1	43	43.0(43)	0	—	—	—	—	—	—	—	—	—	i	—	0	40
NFL	11	139(75)	—	—	—	—	2	80	40.0(43)	0	—	—	—	—	—	—	—	—	—	iS	2	16	155

BARNES, BILLY RAY   William Ray, HB, 5´11˝/201 lbs; Wake Forest; 1957: Phi, rnd 2; B5/14/1935 Landis, NC

1957	Phi◇	12(LH)	143	529	3.7(41)	1	19	212	11.2(61)	1	1	0	0.0	0	0	0	—	—	—	—	—	12	650
1958	Phi◇	12(LH)	156	551	3.5(70)	7	35	423	12.1(33)	0	6	4	66.7	104	17.3(71)	3	0	—	—	—	—	42	900
1959	Phi◇	12(LH)	181	687	3.8(61)	7	32	314	9.8(47)	2	7	0	0.0	0	0	0	2	—	—	—	—	54	844
1960	†Phi	12(HB)	117	315	2.7(23)	4	19	132	6.9(16)	2	3	0	0.0	0	0	0	2	—	—	—	—	36	351
1961	Phi	12(HB)	92	309	3.4(43)	1	15	194	12.9(59)	3	—	—	—	—	—	—	—	—	—	—	—	24	431
1962	Was	10(LH)	159	492	3.1(32)	3	14	220	15.7(56)	0	4	3	75.0	48	12.0(22)	0	0	—	—	—	—	18	656
1963	Was	12(hb)	93	374	4.0(19)	5	15	256	17.1(54)	1	4	3	75.0	81	20.3(32)	1	0	—	—	—	p	—	36	598
1965	Min	14	48	148	3.1(18)	3	15	5.0(7)	0	—	—	—	—	—	—	—	—	—	—	k	—	0	148
1966	Min	2	5	16	3.2(4)	1	1	20	20.0(20)	0	—	—	—	—	—	—	—	—	—	—	—	6	36
NFL	9	98	994	3421	3.4(70)	29	153	1786	11.7(67)	9	25	10	40.0	233	9.3(71)	4	4	—	—	—	kp	—	228	4613

BARNES, BRANDON   Brandon Edward, LB, 6´2˝/240 lbs; Missouri; B6/12/1981 Sikeston, MO   **2004** Was 12 (0)

BARNES, BRUCE   Bruce Francis, P, 5´11˝/215 lbs; UCLA; 1973: NE, rnd 12; B6/21/1951 Coshocton, OH   **1973** NE 14 **1974** NE 9 **NFL** 23 [2 yrs]

BARNES, CHARLIE   Charles Edward, E, 6´5˝/230 lbs; Louisiana-Monroe; 1961: Buf, rnd 19/Was, rnd 8; B10/5/1939 Eudora, AR

| 1961 | DalT-A | 4 | — | — | — | — | 1 | 13 | 13.0(13) | 0 | — | — | — | — | — | — | — | — | — | — | — | 0 | 7 |

BARNES, DARIAN   Darian Durrell, FB, 6´2˝/250 lbs; Rutgers; Hampton; B2/28/1980 Toms River, NJ   **2002** †TB 6 (0) **2005** Mia 9 (5, fb)

2003	TB	14(0)	—	—	—	—	1	6	6.0(6)	0	—	—	—	—	—	—	—	—	—	—	—	0	3
2004	Dal	16(10, FB)	5	10	2.0(8)	0	10	59	5.9(14)	1	—	—	—	—	—	—	—	—	—	—	—	6	45
NFL	4	45(15)	5	10	2.0(8)	0	11	65	5.9(14)	1	—	—	—	—	—	—	—	—	—	—	—	6	48

BARNES, DERRICK   Derrick Carnelious, LB, 6´0˝/261 lbs; Oregon; B9/11/1974 Hattiesburg, MS   **1997** NO 1 (0)

BARNES, EARNEST   Earnest Earl, DE, 6´4˝/262 lbs; Mississippi State; B2/10/1961 Moss Point, MS   **1983** Bal 7 (1)

BARNES, EMERY   Emery Oakland, DE, 6´6˝/235 lbs; Oregon; 1954: GB, rnd 18; B12/15/1929 Hermiston, LA, D6/1/1998 Vancouver, Canada   **1956** GB 2

BARNES, ERICH   Erich Theodore, DB, 6´2˝/201 lbs; Purdue; 1958: ChiB, rnd 4; B7/4/1935 Elkhart, IN **[I]**   **1958** ChiB 12 (DB) **1959** ChiB★12 (DB) **1960** ChiB☆12 (RCB)
1962 NYG★14 (LCB) **1963** †NYG◇14 (LCB) **1964** NYG★14 (LCB) **1965** †Cle 14 (rcb) **1966** Cle☆14 (LCB) **1967** †Cle 13 (LCB/rcb) **1968** †Cle★14 (LCB) **1969** †Cle 14 (LCB)
1970 Cle 14 (LCB) **1971** Cle 2

| 1961 | †NYG★ | 14(LCB) | — | — | — | — | 2 | 74 | 37.0(62) | 1 | — | — | — | — | — | — | — | — | — | i | 2 | 18 | 222 |
| NFL | 14 | 177 | — | — | — | — | 2 | 74 | 37.0(62) | 1 | — | — | — | — | — | — | — | — | — | kpi | 9 | 60 | 705 |

BARNES, ERNIE   Ernest Eugene, G-T, 6´3˝/247 lbs; North Carolina Central; 1960: Bal, rnd 10; B7/15/1938 Durham, NC   **1960** NYT-A 5 **1961** †SD-A 10 **1962** SD-A 3
1964 Den-A 11

| 1963 | Den-A | 14(RG) | 0 | 2 | (2) | 0 | — | — | — | — | — | — | — | — | — | — | — | — | — | — | — | 0 | 2 |
| NFL | 5 | 43 | — | — | — | — | — | — | — | — | — | — | — | — | — | — | — | — | — | — | — | 0 | 2 |

BARNES, GARY   Gary Marshall, WR, 6´4˝/200 lbs; Clemson; 1962: GB, rnd 3/NYT, rnd 9; B9/13/1939 Fairfax, AL

1962	†GB	13	—	—	—	—	—	—	—	—	—	—	—	—	—	—	—	—	—	—	—	0	—
1963	Dal	12(3)	—	—	—	—	15	195	13.0(27)	0	—	—	—	—	—	—	—	—	—	—	—	0	98
1964	ChiB	13	—	—	—	—	4	61	15.3(33)	0	—	—	—	—	—	—	—	—	—	—	—	0	31
1966	Atl	9	—	—	—	—	12	173	14.4(52)	1	—	—	—	—	—	—	—	—	—	—	—	6	92
1967	Atl	13	—	—	—	—	10	154	15.4(44)	1	—	—	—	—	—	—	—	—	—	—	—	6	82
NFL	5	60(3)	—	—	—	—	41	583	14.2(52)	2	—	—	—	—	—	—	—	—	—	—	—	12	302

YEAR	TEAM	G(GS, POS)	RUSH	YD	AVG(LG)	TD	REC	YD	AVG(LG)	TD	PASS	COMP	PCT	YD	AVG(LG)	TD	INT	SK	YD	QBR	KPR	OTD	PTS	TAY

BARNES, JEFF   Jeffrey Keith, LB, 6´2˝/223 lbs; California; 1977: Oak, rnd 5; B3/1/1955 Philadelphia, PA   **1977**†Oak 14 (1)   **1978** Oak 16   **1979** Oak 16   **1980**†Oak 16 (6, rolb)
1981 Oak 15 (0)   **1982**†LARd 9 (0)   **1983** LARd 16 (0)   **1984** LARd 16 (5, lolb)   **1985** LARd 16 (1)   **1986** LARd 16 (0)   **1987** LARd 7 (0)   **NFL** 157 (13) [11 yrs]

BARNES, JOE   Joseph William, QB, 5´11˝/205 lbs; Texas Tech; 1974: Chi, rnd 13; B12/8/1951 Fort Worth, TX

| 1974 | ChiB | 3 | 1 | 19 | 19.0(19) | 0 | — | — | — | — | 9 | 2 | 22.2 | 29 | 3.2(24) | 0 | 1 | 3 | 30 | — | P | — | 0 | -7 |

BARNES, JOHNNIE   Johnnie Darnell, WR, 6´1˝/185 lbs; Hampton; 1992: SD, rnd 9; B7/21/1968 Suffolk, VA

1992	SD	1(0)	—	—	—		—	—	—		—													
1993	SD	14(0)	—	—	—		10	137	13.7(21)	0	—												0	69
1994	SD	11(0)	—	—	—		1	6	6.0(6)	0	—												0	3
1995	Pit	3(0)	—	—	—		3	48	16.0(25)	0	—												0	24
NFL	4	29(0)	—	—	—		14	191	13.6(25)	0	—												0	96

BARNES, KHALIF   Khalif, T, 6´6˝/305 lbs; Washington; 2005: Jax, rnd 2; B4/21/1982 San Diego, CA   **2005**†Jax 13 (12, LT)

BARNES, LARRY   Larry Edward, FB, 6´1˝/228 lbs; Colorado State; 1956: SF, rnd 7; B10/6/1931 Sterling, CO [K]   **1960** Oak-A 14

| 1957 | SF | 10 | 20 | 78 | 3.9(16) | 0 | 1 | 1 | 1.0(1) | 0 | 1 | 1 | 100.0 | 2 | -2.0(-2) | 0 | 0 | — | — | P | | — | 0 | 78 |
| NFL | 2 | 24 | 20 | 78 | 3.9(16) | 0 | 1 | 1 | 1.0(1) | 0 | 1 | 1 | 100.0 | 2 | -2.0(-2) | 0 | 0 | — | — | KP | | — | 55 | 78 |

BARNES, LARRY   Lawrence, RB, 5´11˝/220 lbs; Tennessee State; 1977: SD, rnd 6; B7/17/1954 Bessemer, AL

1977	SD	5	24	70	2.9(7)	0	1	10	10.0(10)	0	—											—	0	75
1978	SD	4	3	8	2.7(4)	0	2	13	6.5(7)	0	—											—	0	15
1978	SL	2	—	—	—		—	—	—		—												—	—
1978	†Phi	7	1	4	4.0(4)	1	—	—	—		—										k		6	6
1979	†Phi	16	25	74	3.0(21)	1	1	6	6.0(6)	0	—										k		6	95
NFL	3	34	53	156	2.9(21)	2	4	29	7.3(10)	0	—										k		12	191

BARNES, LEW   Lew Eric, WR, 5´8˝/163 lbs; Oregon; 1986: Chi, rnd 5; B12/27/1962 Long Beach, CA [R]   **1988** Atl 13 (0)   **1989** KC 2 (0)

| 1986 | †ChiB | 16(0) | — | — | — | | 4 | 54 | 13.5(14) | 0 | — | | | | | | | | | | kp | 1 | 6 | 283 |
| NFL | 3 | 31(0) | — | — | — | | 4 | 54 | 13.5(14) | 0 | — | | | | | | | | | | kp | 1 | 6 | 503 |

BARNES, LIONEL   Lionel, DE, 6´5˝/260 lbs; Louisiana-Monroe; 1999: SL, rnd 6; B4/19/1976 New Orleans, LA   **1999** SL 3 (0)   **2000** Ind 1 (0)   **2000** SL 1 (0)   **2001** Ind 6 (0)
2003 Jax 13 (0)   **2004** Jax 3 (3)   **NFL** 27 (3) [5 yrs]

BARNES, MARLON   Marlon, RB, 5´9˝/215 lbs; Colorado; B3/13/1976 Memphis, TN

| 2000 | ChiB | 13(0) | 15 | 81 | 5.4(20) | 0 | 1 | 7 | 7.0(7) | 0 | — | | | | | | | | | | | — | 0 | 85 |

BARNES, MIKE   Michael Howard, DB, 6´3˝/205 lbs; Texas-Arlington; 1967: SL, rnd 4; B12/30/1944 Denison, TX   **1967** SL 3   **1968** SL 14 (LS)   **NFL** 17 [2 yrs]

BARNES, MIKE   Michael Joseph, DT-DE, 6´6˝/255 lbs; Miami (FL); 1973: Bal, rnd 2; B12/24/1950 Pittsburgh, PA   **1973** Bal 14 (13, LDE)   **1974** Bal 11 (1)   **1975**†Bal 14 (14, LDT)
1976†Bal 14 (14, LDT)   **1977**†Bal★14 (14, LDT)   **1978** Bal 10 (10, LDT)   **1979** Bal 14 (14, LDT)   **1980** Bal 16 (15, LDT)   **1981** Bal 6 (2)   **NFL** 113 (97) [9 yrs]

BARNES, PAT   Patrick, QB, 6´3˝/215 lbs; California; B2/23/1975 Arlington Hts, IL   **1999** SF 1 (0)

BARNES, PETE   Peter G., LB, 6´1˝/239 lbs; Southern (LA); 1967: Hou, rnd 6; B8/31/1945 Keatchie, LA   **1967**†Hou-A 8   **1968** Hou-A 13   **1969** SD-A☆14 (RLB)   **1970** SD 14 (RLB)
1971 SD 14 (RLB)   **1972** SD 14   **1973** SL 12 (RLB)   **1974**†SL 14 (14, RLB)   **1975**†SL 14 (14, RLB)   **1976**†NE 13 (7, rolb)   **1977** NE 12 (11, ROLB)   **NFL** 142 (46) [11 yrs]

BARNES, RASHIDI   Rashidi, DB, 6´0˝/205 lbs; Colorado; 2000: Cle, rnd 7; B6/26/1978 Berkeley, CA   **2000** Cle 14 (0)

BARNES, REGGIE   Reginald Keith, LB, 6´1˝/235 lbs; Oklahoma; B10/23/1969 Arlington, TX   **1993**†Pit 16 (0)   **1995** Dal 7 (0)   **NFL** 23 (0) [2 yrs]

BARNES, RODRIGO   Rodrigo DeTriana, LB, 6´1˝/215 lbs; Rice; 1973: Dal, rnd 7; B2/10/1950 Waco, TX   **1973**†Dal 14   **1974** Dal 2   **1974** NE 5   **1975** NE 1   **1975** Mia 5   **1976**†Oak 5
NFL 32 [4 yrs]

BARNES, ROOSEVELT   Roosevelt, LB, 6´2˝/226 lbs; Purdue; 1982: Det, rnd 10; B8/3/1958 Fort Wayne, IN   **1982**†Det 9 (0)   **1983**†Det 16 (1)   **1984** Det 16 (0)   **1985** Det 16 (0)
NFL 57 (1) [4 yrs]

BARNES, TOMUR   Tomur, DB, 5´10˝/188 lbs; North Texas; B9/8/1970 McNair, TX   **1994** Hou 1 (0)   **1995** Hou 15 (0)   **1996** Hou 5 (0)   **1996** Min 2 (0)   **1996** Was 3 (0)
1997 Ten 3 (0)   **NFL** 29 (0) [4 yrs]

BARNES, WALT   Walter Lee 'Piggy', G, 6´1˝/238 lbs; LSU; B1/26/1918 Parkersburg, WV, D1/6/1998 Woodland Hills, CA   **1948** Phi 11 (0)   **1949**†Phi 12 (0)   **1950** Phi✧12
1951 Phi 12   **NFL** 47 [4 yrs]

BARNES, WALT   Walter Charles, DT-DE, 6´3˝/245 lbs; Nebraska; 1966: Was, rnd 2/KC, rnd 3; B1/19/1944 Chicago, IL   **1966** Was 14 (LDT)   **1967** Was 14 (LDT)   **1968** Was 14
1969 Den-A 9   **1970** Den 6   **1971** Den 4   **NFL** 61 [6 yrs]

BARNETT, BILL   William Perry, DE, 6´4˝/256 lbs; Nebraska; 1980: Mia, rnd 3; B5/10/1956 St. Paul, MN   **1980** Mia 16 (0)   **1981**†Mia 9 (2)   **1982** Mia 5 (5, rde)   **1983**†Mia 15 (0)
1984†Mia 16 (1)   **1985** Mia 16 (1)   **NFL** 77 (9) [6 yrs]

BARNETT, BUSTER   Buster, TE, 6´5˝/228 lbs; Jackson State; 1981: Buf, rnd 11; B11/24/1958 Macon, MS

1981	†Buf	16(0)	—	—	—		4	36	9.0(16)	1	—											—	6	23
1982	Buf	9(0)	—	—	—		4	39	9.8(22)	0	—											—	0	20
1983	Buf	15(1)	—	—	—		10	94	9.4(14)	0	—											—	0	47
1984	Buf	16(7, te)	—	—	—		8	67	8.4(18)	0	—											—	0	34
NFL	4	56(8)	—	—	—		26	236	9.1(22)	1	—											—	6	123

BARNETT, DEAN   Donald Dean, TE, 6´2˝/225 lbs; UNLV; B6/6/1957 Long Beach, CA   **1983** Den 8 (0)

BARNETT, DOUG   Douglas Shirl, DE, 6´3˝/250 lbs; Azusa Pacific; 1982: LARm, rnd 5; B4/12/1960 Montebello, CA   **1982** LARm 9 (0)   **1983** LARm 16 (0)   **1985** Was 2 (0)
1987 Atl 10 (0)   **NFL** 37 (0) [4 yrs]

BARNETT, FRED   Fred Lee, WR, 6´0˝/204 lbs; Arkansas State; 1990: Phi, rnd 3; B6/17/1966 Shelby, MS

1990	†Phi	16(11, WR)	2	13	6.5(12)	0	36	721	20.0(95)	8	—										k	—	48	419
1991	Phi	15(15, WR)	1	0	0.0(0)	0	62	948	15.3(75)	4	—											—	24	494
1992	†Phi✧	16(16, WR)	1	-15	-15.0(-15)	0	67	1083	16.2(71)	6	—											—	36	557
1993	Phi	4(4)	—	—	—		17	170	10.0(21)	0	—											—	0	85
1994	Phi	16(16, WR)	—	—	—		78	1127	14.4(54)	5	—											—	30	589
1995	†Phi	14(14, WR)	—	—	—		48	585	12.2(33)	5	—											—	32	318
1996	Mia	9(7, WR)	—	—	—		36	562	15.6(66)	3	—											—	18	296
1997	Mia	6(5, wr)	—	—	—		17	166	9.8(20)	1	—											—	6	88
NFL	8	96(88)	4	-2	-0.5(12)	0	361	5362	14.9(95)	32	—										k	—	194	2844

BARNETT, HARLON   Harlon T., DB, 5´11˝/200 lbs; Michigan State; 1990: Cle, rnd 4; B1/2/1967 Cincinnati, OH   **1990** Cle 6 (0)   **1991** Cle 16 (10, SS)   **1992** Cle 16 (0)
1993 NE 14 (12, FS)   **1994**†NE 16 (16, SS)   **1995** Min 15 (12, SS)   **1996**†Min 16 (4)   **NFL** 99 (54) [7 yrs]

BARNETT, NICK   Nicholas Alexander, LB, 6´2˝/240 lbs; Oregon State; 2003: GB, rnd 1; B5/27/1981 Fontana, CA   **2003**†GB 15 (15, MLB)   **2004**†GB 16 (16, MLB)
2005 GB 16 (16, MLB)   **NFL** 47 (47) [3 yrs]

BARNETT, OLIVER   Oliver Wesley, DE-DT, 6´3˝/288 lbs; Kentucky; 1990: Atl, rnd 3; B4/9/1966 Louisville, KY   **1990** Atl 15 (1)   **1991**†Atl 15 (2)   **1992** Atl 16 (7, rde)
1993†Buf 16 (6, lde)   **1994** Buf 16 (2)   **1995** SF 7 (0)   **NFL** 85 (18) [6 yrs]

BARNETT, SOLON   Solon Slade, T-G, 6´1˝/235 lbs; Southwestern (TX); Baylor; 1945: ChiC, rnd 14; B3/30/1921 New Willard, TX, D7/18/1998 Nacogdoches County, TX
1945 GB 4 (0)   **1946** GB 1 (1)   **NFL** 5 (1) [2 yrs]

BARNETT, STEVE   Jerry Stephen, T-G, 6´2˝/255 lbs; Oregon; 1963: Chi, rnd 2/SD, rnd 9; B6/3/1941 Sand Springs, OK   **1963**†ChiB 13   **1964** Was 14   **NFL** 27 [2 yrs]

BARNETT, TIM   Tim Andre, WR, 6´1˝/209 lbs; Jackson State; 1991: KC, rnd 3; B4/19/1968 Gunnison, MS

1991	†KC	16(9, WR)	—	—	—		41	564	13.8(63)	5	—											—	30	307
1992	†KC	12(9)	—	—	—		24	442	18.4(77)	4	—											—	24	241
1993	†KC	16(0)	1	3	3.0(3)	0	17	182	10.7(25)	1	—											—	6	99
NFL	3	44(12)	1	3	3.0(3)	0	82	1188	14.5(77)	10	—											—	60	647

YEAR	TEAM	G (GS, POS)	RUSH	YD	AVG(LG)	TD	REC	YD	AVG(LG)	TD	PASS	COMP	PCT	YD	AVG(LG)	TD	INT	SK	YD	QBR	KPR	OTD	PTS	TAY

BARNETT, TOM Thomas George, HB-DB, 5'11"/190 lbs; Purdue; 1959: Pit, rnd 8; B7/11/1937 Alliance, OH

YEAR	TEAM	G (GS, POS)	RUSH	YD	AVG(LG)	TD	REC	YD	AVG(LG)	TD	KPR	OTD	PTS	TAY
1959	Pit	12(RH)	75	238	3.2(19)	1	7	52	7.4(14)	1	k	—	12	273
1960	Pit	12	6	25	4.2(16)	0	—					k	—	0	25
NFL	2	24	81	263	3.2(19)	1	7	52	7.4(14)	1	k	—	12	298

BARNETT, TROY Troy Anthony, DE-DT, 6'5"/293 lbs; North Carolina; B5/24/1971 Jacksonville, NC **1994**†NE 14 (0) **1995** NE 16 (15, RDE) **1996** NE 1 (0) **1996** Was 3 (0)
NFL 34 (15) [3 yrs]

BARNETT, VINCENT Vincent Crawford, DB, 6'0"/200 lbs; Arkansas State; B2/19/1965 Mound Bayou, MS **1987** Cle 3 (0)

BARNEY, EPPIE Eppie, FL, 6'0"/201 lbs; Iowa State; 1967: Cle, rnd 3; B3/20/1944 Birmingham, AL, D1/21/2004

YEAR	TEAM	G (GS, POS)	RUSH	YD	AVG(LG)	TD	REC	YD	AVG(LG)	TD	KPR	OTD	PTS	TAY
1967	†Cle	14(fl)	—				1	3	3.0(3)	0	k	—	0	-3
1968	Cle	12(8, FL)	0	8	(8)	1	18	189	10.5(18)	1	k	—	12	118
NFL	2	26(8)	0	8	(8)	1	19	192	10.1(18)	1	k	—	12	115

BARNEY, LEM Lemuel Jackson, DB, 6'0"/188 lbs; Jackson State; 1967: Det, rnd 2; B9/8/1945 Gulfport, MS; HOF 1992 **[RI]** **1967** Det★14 (LCB) **1968** Det★14 (LCB) **1970**†Det☆13 (LCB) **1971** Det 9 (LCB) **1972** Det★14 (LCB) **1974** Det 13 (12, LCB) **1975** Det★10 (10, LCB) **1976** Det✧14 (14, LCB) **1977** Det 12 (RCB)

YEAR	TEAM	G (GS, POS)	RUSH	YD	AVG(LG)	TD	KPR	OTD	PTS	TAY
1969	Det★	13(LCB)	3	36	12.0(27)	0	Pkpi	1	6	327
1973	Det★	14(LCB)	2	9	4.5(7)	0	kpi	—	0	228
NFL	11	140(36)	5	45	9.0(27)	0	Pkpi	11	66	2063

BARNEY, MILTON Milton, WR, 5'9"/156 lbs; Alcorn State; B12/23/1963

YEAR	TEAM	G (GS, POS)	REC	YD	AVG(LG)	TD	KPR	OTD	PTS	TAY
1987	Atl	3(3)	10	175	17.5(32)	2	p	—	12	101

BARNHARDT, TOMMY John Thomas Ray, P, 6'2"/213 lbs; East Carolina; North Carolina; 1986: TB, rnd 9; B6/11/1963 Salisbury, NC **[P]**

YEAR	TEAM	G (GS, POS)	RUSH	YD	AVG(LG)	TD	PASS	COMP	PCT	YD	AVG(LG)	TD	INT	KPR	OTD	PTS	TAY
1987	NO	3(0)	1	-13	-13.0(-13)	0								P	—	0	-13
1987	†ChiB	2(0)	—											P	—	0	0
1988	Was	4(0)	—											P	—	0	0
1989	NO	11(0)	—											P	—	0	0
1990	†NO	16(0)	—											P	—	0	0
1991	†NO	16(0)	1	0	0.0(0)	0								P	—	0	0
1992	†NO	16(0)	4	-2	-0.5(12)	0								P	—	0	-2
1993	NO	16(0)	1	18	18.0(18)	0	1	1	100.0	7	7.0(7)	0	0	P	—	0	22
1994	NO	16(0)	1	21	21.0(21)	0	1	0	0.0	0	0.0	0	0	P	—	0	21
1995	Car	16(0)	—											P	—	0	0
1996	TB	16(0)	2	27	13.5(25)	0								P	—	0	27
1997	TB	6(0)	—				1	1	100.0	25	25.0(25)	0	0	P	—	0	13
1998	TB	16(0)	—											P	—	0	0
1999	NO	16(0)	1	4	4.0(4)	0								P	—	0	4
2000	Was	16(0)	1	11	11.0(11)	0								P	—	0	11
NFL	14	186(0)	12	66	5.5(25)	0	3	2	66.7	32	10.7(25)	0	0	P	—	0	82

BARNHART, DAN Daniel High, TB, 6'0"/200 lbs; St. Mary's (CA); Centenary; B6/27/1912 Chickasha, OK, D6/16/1965 Los Angeles County, CA

YEAR	TEAM	G (GS, POS)	RUSH	YD	AVG(LG)	TD	OTD	PTS	TAY
1934	Phi	1(0)	1	4	4.0(4)	0	—	0	7

BARNI, ROY Roy Bruno, DB, 5'11"/185 lbs; San Francisco; B2/15/1927 San Francisco, CA, D7/22/1957 San Francisco, CA **1952** ChiC 12 (DB) **1953** ChiC 8 **1954** Phi 10 (DB) **1955** Phi 4 **1955** Was 8 (DB) **1956** Was 12 (DB) **NFL** 54 [5 yrs]

BARNIKOW, EDDIE Edward John, FB, none; B12/18/1897 Meriden, CT, D12/1/1953 Schenectady, NY **1926** Har 2 (1)

BARNUM, LEN Leonard Warner, B, 6'0"/200 lbs; West Virginia Wesleyan; 1936: Pit, rnd 2; B9/18/1912 Parkersburg, WV, D11/24/1998 Columbia City, IN **[K]**

YEAR	TEAM	G (GS, POS)	RUSH	YD	AVG(LG)	TD	REC	YD	AVG(LG)	TD	PASS	COMP	PCT	YD	AVG(LG)	TD	INT	KPR	OTD	PTS	TAY
1938	†NYG	10(3)	35	97	2.8	1	3	37	12.3	0	6	1	16.7	45	7.5(45)	0	1	—		6	108
1939	†NYG	11(2)	91	237	2.6	2	3	50	16.7(17)	0	27	8	29.6	141	5.2	3	1	KP		24	328
1940	NYG	10(3)	48	128	2.7	0	1	15	15.0(15)	0	23	9	39.1	150	6.5	3	2	KPi		9	184
1941	Phi	11(8, QB)	35	64	1.8(20)	0	1	11	11.0(11)	0	55	19	34.5	260	4.7(33)	0	10	KPki		8	-178
1942	Phi	10(5, RH)	30	64	2.1(7)	0	3	54	18.0(32)	0	9	1	11.1	6	0.7(6)	0	1	KPki		16	100
NFL	5	52(21)	239	590	2.5(20)	3	11	167	15.2(32)	0	120	38	31.7	602	5.0(45)	6	15	KPkpi		63	542

BARNUM, PETE Robert LeRoy, B, 5'10"/195 lbs; West Virginia; B1901, PA, deceased **1926** Col 6 (5, TB), 6

BARNWELL, MALCOLM Malcolm, WR, 5'11"/184 lbs; Virginia Union; 1980: Oak, rnd 7; B6/28/1958 Charleston, SC

YEAR	TEAM	G (GS, POS)	RUSH	YD	AVG(LG)	TD	REC	YD	AVG(LG)	TD	KPR	OTD	PTS	TAY
1981	Oak	16(1)	—				9	190	21.1(61)	1	k	—	6	140
1982	†LARd	9(9, WR)	2	18	9.0(14)	0	23	387	16.8(52)	0		—	0	212
1983	†LARd	16(16, WR)	1	12	12.0(12)	0	35	513	14.7(41)	1		—	6	274
1984	†LARd	16(15, WR)	—				45	851	18.9(51)	2		—	12	436
1985	Was	7(2)	—				3	28	9.3(12)	0		—	0	14
1985	NO	2(0)	—										0	
NFL	5	66(43)	3	30	10.0(14)	0	115	1969	17.1(61)	4	k	—	24	1075

BARR, DAVE David Hoover, QB, 6'3"/210 lbs; California; 1995: Phi, rnd 4; B5/9/1972 Oakland, CA

YEAR	TEAM	G (GS, POS)	RUSH	YD	AVG(LG)	TD	PASS	COMP	PCT	YD	AVG(LG)	TD	INT	SK	YD	OTD	PTS	TAY
1995	SL	2(0)	1	5	5.0(5)	0	9	5	55.6	42	4.7(18)	0	0	1	4	—	0	26

BARR, SHORTY Wallace Andre, B, 5'8"/195 lbs; Wisconsin; B11/30/1897 Milwaukee, WI, D3/1980 Chenequa, WI **[C]** **1923** Rac 10 (9, BB), 6 **1924** Rac 9 (3) **1925** Mil 4 (4, BB)
1926 Rac 3 (0) **NFL** 26 (16), 6 [4 yrs]

BARR, TERRY Terry Albert, HB-DB-FL, 6'0"/189 lbs; Michigan; 1957: Det, rnd 3; B8/10/1935 Grand Rapids, MI

YEAR	TEAM	G (GS, POS)	RUSH	YD	AVG(LG)	TD	REC	YD	AVG(LG)	TD	PASS	COMP	PCT	YD	INT	KPR	OTD	PTS	TAY
1957	†Det	12(DB)	—													kpi	—	0	1
1958	Det☆	12(DB)	—													kpi	1	6	162
1959	Det	11(DB/lh)	5	57	11.4(37)	1	10	180	18.0(45)	0	1	0	0.0	0	0	kpi	—	6	292
1960	Det	12	17	74	4.4(19)	1	5	26	5.2(11)	1	1	0	0.0	0	0	kp	—	12	157
1961	Det	14(RH)	6	-8	-1.3(9)	0	40	630	15.8(61)	6							—	36	337
1962	Det	6	—				25	425	17.0(80)	3							—	18	228
1963	Det★	14(RH)	1	9	9.0(9)	0	66	1086	16.5(75)	13							—	78	617
1964	Det✧	14(RH)	2	31	15.5(19)	0	57	1030	18.1(58)	9	1	0	0.0	0	0		—	54	591
1965	Det	7(FL)	1	-12	-12.0(-12)	0	24	433	18.0(61)	3							—	18	220
NFL	9	102	32	151	4.7(37)	2	227	3810	16.8(80)	35						kpi	1	228	2604

BARRABEE, BOB Robert Sidney, E, 5'9"/190 lbs; NYU; B7/23/1905 Malden, MA, D6/1984 Elberon Park, NJ **1931** SI 10 (7, LE)

BARRAGAR, NATE Nathan R., C-G, 6'0"/212 lbs; USC; B6/3/1907, KS, D8/10/1985 Santa Monica, CA **1930** Min 8 (8, C) **1930** Fra☆5 (5, c) **1931** Fra 6 (5, C) **1931** GB☆7 (5, c)
1932 GB☆12 (8, C) **1934** GB☆12 (9, C) **1935** GB☆10 (5, C) **NFL** 60 (45) [5 yrs]

BARREL, NAPOLEON Napoleon Paul, C, 5'8"/200 lbs; Carlisle Indian; B12/25/1885 Richwood, MN, D12/1964, MI **1923** Oor 7 (5, c)

BARRETT, BOB Robert Patrick, E, 6'3"/200 lbs; Baldwin-Wallace; B11/18/1935 Cleveland, OH **1960** Buf-A 2

BARRETT, DAVE David Earl, RB, 6'0"/230 lbs; Houston; 1982: TB, rnd 4; B9/9/1959 Corpus Christi, TX **1982** TB 7 (0)

BARRETT, DAVID David, DB, 5'10"/208 lbs; Arkansas; 2000: Arz, rnd 4; B12/22/1977 Waterloo, IA **2000** Arz 16 (0) **2001** Arz 16 (9, LCB) **2002** Arz 14 (14, RCB)
2003 Arz 16 (16, RCB) **2004**†NYJ 16 (16, RCB) **2005** NYJ 13 (8, RCB) **NFL** 91 (63) [6 yrs]

BARRETT, EMMETT Emmett Edward, C, 6'2"/192 lbs; Portland; B11/7/1916 Sioux City, IA, D5/2/2005 Portland, OR **1942** NYG 10 (0)

BARRETT, JAN Jan M., E, 6'3"/226 lbs; Fresno State; 1963: GB, rnd 6/KC, rnd 9; B11/13/1938 Santa Barbara, CA, D10/7/1973 Bakersfield, CA

YEAR	TEAM	G (GS, POS)	REC	YD	AVG(LG)	TD	OTD	PTS	TAY
1963	GB	3							
1963	Oak-A	3	1	9	9.0(9)	0	—	0	5
1964	Oak-A	14	12	212	17.7(41)	2	—	12	116
NFL	2	20	13	221	10.7(41)	2	—	12	121

Barrett, Jean Jean Martin, T-G-C, 6´6˝/253 lbs; Tulsa; 1972: SF, rnd 2; B5/24/1951 Fort Worth, TX **1973** SF 14 **1974** SF 14 **1975** SF 9 (6, lg) **1976** SF 14 (14, LT) **1977** SF 14 (14, LT) **1979** SF 13 **1980** SF 15 (0) **NFL** 93 (34) [7 yrs]

Barrett, Jeff Warren Jefferson, E, 6´1˝/182 lbs; LSU; B2/8/1913 San Antonio, TX, D2/15/1970 Corpus Christi, TX

YEAR	TEAM	G (GS, POS)	RUSH	YD	AVG (LG)	TD	REC	YD	AVG (LG)	TD	PASS	COMP	PCT	YD	AVG (LG)	TD	INT	SK	YD	QBR	KPR	OTD	PTS	TAY
1936	Bkn	12 (3)	—	—	—	—	14	268	19.1	1	—	—	—	—	—	—	—	—	—	—	—	—	6	139
1937	Bkn	11 (9, RE)	1	8	8.0 (8)	0	20	461	**23.0**	3	—	—	—	—	—	—	—	—	—	—	—	—	18	254
1938	Bkn	11 (4)	2	3	1.5	0	13	205	15.8	2	—	—	—	—	—	—	—	—	—	—	—	—	12	116
NFL	3	34 (16)	3	11	3.7 (8)	0	47	934	19.9	6	—	—	—	—	—	—	—	—	—	—	—	—	36	508

Barrett, John John Patrick, C-T-E, 5´6˝/170 lbs; Detroit Mercy; B2/25/1899 Holyoke, MA, D9/1966 Detroit, MI **1924** Akr 5 (5, C), 6 **1925** Akr 8 (6, C) **1926** Det 11 (8, C), 6 **1927** Pot 5 (4) **1928** Det 5 (2) **NFL** 34 (25), 12 [5 yrs]

Barrett, Johnny John Francis, E-HB, 5´9˝/195 lbs; Washington & Lee; B8/29/1895, D3/1974 Montvale, NJ **1920** ChiT 6 (6, LE)

Barrett, Reggie Aaron Reginald, WR, 6´3˝/214 lbs; Texas-El Paso; 1991: Det, rnd 3; B8/14/1969 Corpus Christi, TX **1991** Det 2 (2)

YEAR	TEAM	G (GS, POS)	RUSH	YD	AVG (LG)	TD	REC	YD	AVG (LG)	TD	PASS	COMP	PCT	YD	AVG (LG)	TD	INT	SK	YD	QBR	KPR	OTD	PTS	TAY
1992	Det	8 (6, wr)	—	—	—	—	4	67	16.8 (24)	1	—	—	—	—	—	—	—	—	—	—	—	—	6	39
NFL	2	10 (8)	—	—	—	—	4	67	16.8 (24)	1	—	—	—	—	—	—	—	—	—	—	—	—	6	39

Barrie, Sebastian Sebastian J.L., DE-DT, 6´2˝/275 lbs; Prairie View A&M; Liberty; B5/26/1970 Dallas, TX **1992** GB 3 (0) **1994** Arz 10 (0) **1995**†SD 7 (0) **NFL** 20 (0) [3 yrs]

Barrington, Tom George Thomas, RB, 6´1˝/213 lbs; Ohio State; 1966: Was, rnd 3/KC, rnd 16; B1/29/1944 Lima, OH, D11/8/2002

YEAR	TEAM	G (GS, POS)	RUSH	YD	AVG (LG)	TD	REC	YD	AVG (LG)	TD	PASS	COMP	PCT	YD	AVG (LG)	TD	INT	SK	YD	QBR	KPR	OTD	PTS	TAY
1966	Was	6	10	37	3.7 (21)	0	2	23	11.5 (12)	0	1	0	0.0	0	0.0	0	0	—	—	—	k	—	0	58
1967	NO	14	34	121	3.6 (22)	0	4	50	12.5 (29)	0	2	0	0.0	0	0.0	0	0	—	—	—	k	—	0	154
1968	NO	14	45	111	2.5 (22)	0	9	33	3.7 (10)	1	6	2	33.3	42	7.0 (23)	0	0	—	—	—	—	—	6	154
1969	NO	11	7	33	4.7 (17)	1	4	42	10.5 (15)	0	2	1	50.0	15	7.5 (15)	0	0	1	0	—	kp	—	6	214
1970	NO	12 (RB)	72	228	3.2 (16)	2	22	130	5.9 (20)	0	—	—	—	—	—	—	—	—	—	—	k	—	12	352
NFL	5	57	168	530	3.2 (22)	3	41	278	6.8 (29)	1	11	3	27.3	57	5.2 (23)	0	0	1	0	—	kp	—	24	931

Barron, Alex Alex, T, 6´7˝/320 lbs; Florida State; 2005: SL, rnd 1; B9/28/1982 Orangeburg, SC **2005** SL 12 (11, RT)

Barron, Jim James Martin, T, 6´0˝/195 lbs; Georgetown (DC); B11/10/1890 South Boston, MA, D2/6/1936 Boston, MA **1921** Roc 4 (4, LT), 6

Barrow, Michael Michael Colvin, LB, 6´2˝/245 lbs; Miami (FL); 1993: Hou, rnd 2; B4/19/1970 Homestead, PA **1993**†Hou 16 (0) **1994** Hou 16 (16, RLB) **1995** Hou 13 (12, MLB) **1996** Hou 16 (16, RLB) **1997** Car 16 (16, LOLB) **1998** Car 16 (16, RILB) **1999** Car 16 (16, RLB) **2000**†NYG 15 (15, MLB) **2001** NYG 16 (16, MLB) **2002**†NYG 15 (14, MLB) **2003** NYG 16 (16, MLB) **2005** Dal 2 (0) **NFL** 173 (153) [12 yrs]

Barrows, Scott Scott Martin, G-C, 6´2˝/278 lbs; West Virginia; B3/31/1963 Marietta, OH **1986** Det 16 (4) **1987** Det 12 (10, LG) **1988** Det 16 (1) **NFL** 44 (15) [3 yrs]

Barry, Al Allan, G, 6´2˝/238 lbs; USC; 1953: GB, rnd 30; B12/24/1930 Beverly Hills, CA **1954** GB 12 (LG) **1957** GB 12 (LG) **1958**†NYG 12 (LG) **1959**†NYG 12 **1960**†LAC-A 5 **NFL** 53 [5 yrs]

Barry, Fred Frederick, DB, 5´10˝/184 lbs; Boston University; 1970: KC, rnd 8; B7/31/1948 Washington, PA **1970** Pit 9

Barry, Kevin Kevin Lee, T, 6´4˝/330 lbs; Arizona; B7/20/1979 Racine, WI **2002**†GB 14 (3) **2003**†GB 16 (1) **2004**†GB 13 (3) **2005** GB 16 (1) **NFL** 59 (8) [4 yrs]

Barry, Norm Norman Christopher, BB-HB, 5´10˝/170 lbs; Notre Dame; B12/25/1897 Chicago, IL, D10/13/1988 Chicago, IL **[C]** **1921** ChiC 3 (3) **1921** GB 8 (5, BB), 6 **1922** Mil 1 (0) **NFL** 12 (8) [2 yrs]

Barry, Odell Odell Carl, WR, 5´10˝/180 lbs; Findlay; 1964: Den, rnd 19; B10/10/1941 Memphis, TN

YEAR	TEAM	G (GS, POS)	RUSH	YD	AVG (LG)	TD	REC	YD	AVG (LG)	TD	PASS	COMP	PCT	YD	AVG (LG)	TD	INT	SK	YD	QBR	KPR	OTD	PTS	TAY
1964	Den-A	14	3	7	2.3 (11)	0	4	31	7.8 (13)	0	—	—	—	—	—	—	—	—	—	—	kp	1	6	642
1965	Den-A	12	2	19	9.5 (11)	0	2	11	5.5 (9)	0	—	—	—	—	—	—	—	—	—	—	kp	—	0	351
NFL	2	26	5	26	5.2 (11)	0	6	42	7.0 (13)	0	—	—	—	—	—	—	—	—	—	—	kp	1	6	992

Barry, Paul Paul F., FB-HB, 6´0˝/208 lbs; Tulsa; 1949: LA, rnd 13; B8/7/1926 El Paso, TX

YEAR	TEAM	G (GS, POS)	RUSH	YD	AVG (LG)	TD	REC	YD	AVG (LG)	TD	PASS	COMP	PCT	YD	AVG (LG)	TD	INT	SK	YD	QBR	KPR	OTD	PTS	TAY
1950	†LARm	12	50	231	4.6 (28)	2	7	122	17.4 (39)	0	—	—	—	—	—	—	—	—	—	—	—	—	12	312
1952	†LARm	6	3	-1	-0.3 (4)	0	2	43	21.5 (25)	1	—	—	—	—	—	—	—	—	—	—	—	—	6	26
1953	Was	12 (FB)	56	218	3.9 (22)	0	8	70	8.8 (18)	0	—	—	—	—	—	—	—	—	—	—	k	—	0	275
1954	ChiC	12	50	156	3.1 (26)	0	7	29	4.1 (26)	0	—	—	—	—	—	—	—	—	—	—	k	—	0	176
NFL	4	42	159	604	3.8 (28)	2	24	264	11.0 (39)	1	—	—	—	—	—	—	—	—	—	—	k	—	18	788

Barsha, John John F., aka Abraham Barshofsky, FB, Syracuse; B12/25/1898, Russia, D2/18/1976 New York, NY **1920** Roc 3 (0)

Bartalo, Steve Stephen James, RB, 5´9˝/200 lbs; Colorado State; 1987: TB, rnd 6; B7/15/1964 Limestone, ME

YEAR	TEAM	G (GS, POS)	RUSH	YD	AVG (LG)	TD	REC	YD	AVG (LG)	TD	PASS	COMP	PCT	YD	AVG (LG)	TD	INT	SK	YD	QBR	KPR	OTD	PTS	TAY
1987	TB	9 (0)	9	30	3.3 (6)	1	1	5	5.0 (5)	0	1	0	0.0	0	0.0	0	1	—	—	—	k	—	6	3

Bartee, William William Anthony, DB, 6´1˝/200 lbs; Oklahoma; 2000: KC, rnd 2; B6/25/1977 Daytona Beach, FL **2000** KC 16 (3) **2001** KC 16 (5, lcb) **2002** KC 14 (13, RCB) **2003**†KC 11 (1) **2004** KC 14 (9, RCB) **2005** KC 16 (0) **NFL** 87 (31) [6 yrs]

Bartell, Ronald Ronald, DB, 6´1˝/208 lbs; Howard; 2005: SL, rnd 2; B2/22/1982 Detroit, MI **2005** SL 10 (7, rcb)

Bartholomew, Brent Brent Robert, P, 6´2˝/220 lbs; Ohio State; 1999: Mia, rnd 6; B10/22/1976 Apopka, FL **1999** Mia 2 (0) **2000** ChiB 7 (0) **NFL** 9 (0) [2 yrs]

Bartholomew, Sam Samuel Wilson, FB, 5´11˝/188 lbs; Tennessee; 1940: Was, rnd 13; B4/10/1917 Charleston, WV, D2/15/1999 Johnson City, TN

YEAR	TEAM	G (GS, POS)	RUSH	YD	AVG (LG)	TD	REC	YD	AVG (LG)	TD	PASS	COMP	PCT	YD	AVG (LG)	TD	INT	SK	YD	QBR	KPR	OTD	PTS	TAY
1941	Phi	9 (2)	21	69	3.3 (10)	0	3	15	5.0 (7)	0	—	—	—	—	—	—	—	—	—	—	kpi	—	0	99

Bartkowski, Steve Steven Joseph, QB, 6´4˝/216 lbs; California; 1975: Atl, rnd 1; B11/12/1952 Des Moines, IA

YEAR	TEAM	G (GS, POS)	RUSH	YD	AVG (LG)	TD	REC	YD	AVG (LG)	TD	PASS	COMP	PCT	YD	AVG (LG)	TD	INT	SK	YD	QBR	KPR	OTD	PTS	TAY
1975	Atl	11 (11, QB)	14	15	1.1 (5)	2	—	—	—	—	255	115	45.1	1662	6.5 (68)	13	15	19	197	59.3	—	—	12	331
1976	Atl	5 (5, qb)	8	-10	-1.3 (2)	1	—	—	—	—	120	57	47.5	677	5.6 (50)	2	9	18	150	39.5	—	—	6	-12
1977	Atl	8 (7, QB)	18	13	0.7 (8)	0	—	—	—	—	136	64	47.1	796	5.9 (73)	5	13	29	296	38.4	—	—	0	-84
1978	†Atl	14 (13, QB)	33	60	1.8 (8)	2	—	—	—	—	369	187	50.7	2489	6.7 (71)	10	18	39	349	61.1	—	—	12	655
1979	Atl	14 (14, QB)	14	36	2.6 (18)	2	—	—	—	—	380	204	53.7	2505	6.6 (57)	17	20	39	286	67.3	—	—	12	594
1980	†Atl★	16 (16, QB)	25	35	1.4 (11)	2	—	—	—	—	463	257	55.5	3544	7.7 (81)	**31**	16	35	324	88.2	—	—	12	1342
1981	Atl✧	16 (16, QB)	11	2	0.2 (5)	0	—	—	—	—	533	297	55.7	3829	7.2 (70)	**30**	23	37	287	79.2	—	—	0	1147
1982	†Atl	9 (9, QB)	13	4	0.3 (10)	1	—	—	—	—	262	166	63.4	1905	7.3 (**86**)	8	11	20	177	77.9	—	—	6	567
1983	Atl	14 (14, QB)	16	38	2.4 (10)	1	—	—	—	—	432	274	63.4	3167	7.3 (76)	22	5	51	348	**97.6**	—	—	6	1542
1984	Atl	11 (11, QB)	15	34	2.3 (8)	0	—	—	—	—	269	181	**67.3**	2158	8.0 (61)	11	10	40	300	89.7	—	—	0	768
1985	Atl	5 (5, qb)	5	9	1.8 (5)	0	—	—	—	—	111	69	62.2	738	6.6 (62)	5	1	18	158	**92.8**	—	—	0	363
1986	LARm	6 (6, QB)	6	3	0.5 (7)	0	—	—	—	—	126	61	48.4	654	5.2 (42)	2	3	11	84	59.4	—	—	0	220
NFL	12	129 (127)	178	239	1.3 (18)	11	—	—	—	—	3456	1932	55.9	24124	7.0 (86)	156	144	356	2956	75.4	—	—	66	7431

Bartlett, Doug Douglas William, DT-DE, 6´2˝/239 lbs; Northern Illinois; 1987: LARm, rnd 4; B5/22/1963 Springfield, IL **1988** Phi 10 (0)

Bartlett, Earl Earl Elburn, HB, 6´0˝/200 lbs; Centre; B12/16/1908 Purcell, OK, D1/26/1987 Danville, KY **1939** Pit 1 (0)

Bartlewski, Rich Richard Stanley, TE, 6´5˝/250 lbs; Fresno State; B8/15/1967 Butler, PA **1990** LARd 4 (0) **1991** Atl 1 (0) **NFL** 5 (0) [2 yrs]

Bartley, Ephesians Ephesians Alexander, LB, 6´2˝/213 lbs; Florida; 1992: Phi, rnd 9; B8/9/1969 Jacksonville, FL **1992**†Phi 6 (0)

Barton, Don Donald Reed, HB, 5´11˝/175 lbs; Texas; B5/29/1930 Cisco, TX

YEAR	TEAM	G (GS, POS)	RUSH	YD	AVG (LG)	TD	REC	YD	AVG (LG)	TD	PASS	COMP	PCT	YD	AVG (LG)	TD	INT	SK	YD	QBR	KPR	OTD	PTS	TAY
1953	GB	5	7	40	5.7 (14)	0	2	51	25.5 (42)	1	—	—	—	—	—	—	—	—	—	—	kp	—	6	73

Barton, Eric Eric, LB, 6´2˝/245 lbs; Maryland; 1999: Oak, rnd 5; B9/29/1977 Fayetteville, NC **1999** Oak 16 (3) **2000** Oak 4 (0) **2001**†Oak 16 (1) **2002**†Oak 16 (16, RLB) **2003** Oak 16 (16, RLB) **2004**†NYJ 16 (15, RLB) **2005** NYJ 4 (3) **NFL** 88 (54) [7 yrs]

Barton, Greg Gregory Lee, QB, 6´2˝/195 lbs; Tulsa; 1968: Det, rnd 9; B7/14/1946 Denver, CO

YEAR	TEAM	G (GS, POS)	RUSH	YD	AVG (LG)	TD	REC	YD	AVG (LG)	TD	PASS	COMP	PCT	YD	AVG (LG)	TD	INT	SK	YD	QBR	KPR	OTD	PTS	TAY
1969	Det	1	—	—	—	—	—	—	—	—	1	0	0.0	0	0.0	0	0	—	—	—	—	—	0	0

Barton, Harris Harris Scott, T-G, 6´4˝/286 lbs; North Carolina; 1987: SF, rnd 1; B4/19/1964 Atlanta, GA **1987**†SF 12 (9, RT) **1988**†SF 16 (15, RT) **1989**†SF 16 (16, RT) **1990**†SF 16 (16, RG) **1991** SF 16 (16, RT) **1992**†SF☆13 (13, RT) **1993**†SF★15 (15, RT) **1994**†SF 9 (9, RT) **1995**†SF 12 (12, RT) **1996**†SF 13 (13, RT) **NFL** 138 (134) [10 yrs]

Barton, Jim James Edward, C, 6´5˝/250 lbs; Marshall; B6/12/1934 Kirbyville, PA **1960** DalT-A 14 (14, C) **1961** Den-A 14 (c) **1962** Den-A 14 (C) **NFL** 42 (14) [3 yrs]

Bartos, Hank Henry, G, 6´1˝/220 lbs; North Carolina; 1938: Was, rnd 12; B5/20/1913 Brooklyn, NY, D12/28/1987 **1938** Was 7 (0)

Bartos, Joe Joseph Stephen, DB-HB, 6´2˝/194 lbs; Navy; B11/18/1926 Lorain, OH, D3/11/1989 Bridgeport, CT

YEAR	TEAM	G (GS, POS)	RUSH	YD	AVG (LG)	TD	REC	YD	AVG (LG)	TD	PASS	COMP	PCT	YD	AVG (LG)	TD	INT	SK	YD	QBR	KPR	OTD	PTS	TAY
1950	Was	12 (DB)	9	36	4.0 (13)	0	—	—	—	—	—	—	—	—	—	—	—	—	—	—	—	—	0	36

Bartrum, Mike Michael Weldon, TE-C, 6´4˝/245 lbs; Marshall; B6/23/1970 Gallipolis, OH **1993**†KC 3 (0) **1995** GB 4 (0) **1997** NE 9 (0) **1998**†NE 16 (0) **2000**†Phi 16 (0) **2003**†Phi 16 (0)

YEAR	TEAM	G (GS, POS)	RUSH	YD	AVG (LG)	TD	REC	YD	AVG (LG)	TD	PASS	COMP	PCT	YD	AVG (LG)	TD	INT	SK	YD	QBR	KPR	OTD	PTS	TAY
1996	†NE	16 (0)	—	—	—	—	1	1	1.0 (1)	1	—	—	—	—	—	—	—	—	—	—	—	—	6	6
1999	NE	16 (0)	—	—	—	—	1	1	1.0 (1)	1	—	—	—	—	—	—	—	—	—	—	—	—	6	6
2001	†Phi	16 (0)	—	—	—	—	1	4	4.0 (4)	1	—	—	—	—	—	—	—	—	—	—	—	—	6	7
2002	†Phi	16 (0)	—	—	—	—	1	8	8.0 (8)	0	—	—	—	—	—	—	—	—	—	—	—	—	0	4
2004	†Phi	16 (0)	—	—	—	—	5	45	9.0 (17)	1	1	0	0.0	0	0.0	0	0	—	—	—	—	—	6	28
2005	Phi✧	16 (0)	—	—	—	—	2	6	3.0 (3)	2	—	—	—	—	—	—	—	—	—	—	—	—	12	13
NFL	12	160 (0)	—	—	—	—	11	65	5.9 (17)	6	1	0	0.0	0	0.0	0	0	—	—	—	—	—	36	63

Barwegan, Dick Richard James, G, 6´1˝/227 lbs; Purdue; 1945: Bkn, rnd 6; B12/25/1921 Chicago, IL, D9/3/1966 Baltimore, MD **1947**†NYY-A☆14 (14, RG) **1948**†Bal-A☆12 (12, LG) **1949** Bal-A☆12 (10, LG) **AAFC** 38 (36) [3 yrs]

1950†ChiB★11 (LG) **1951** ChiB★12 (LG) **1952** ChiB★11 (LG) **1953** Bal✧11 (LG) **1954** Bal 9 **NFL** 54 [5 yrs]

Barzilauskas, Carl Carl Joseph, DT, 6´6˝/271 lbs; Indiana; 1974: NYJ, rnd 1; B3/19/1951 Waterbury, CT **1974** NYJ 14 (LDT) **1975** NYJ 14 (14, LDT) **1976** NYJ 12 (LDT) **1977** NYJ 9 (LDT) **1978** GB 16 (RDT) **1979** GB 5 **NFL** 70 (14) [6 yrs]

Barzilauskas, Fritz Francis Daniel, G, 6´1˝/230 lbs; Holy Cross; Yale; 1947: Bos, rnd 1/Bkn-A, rnd 3; B6/13/1920 Waterbury, CT, D11/30/1990 North Haven, CT **1947** Bos 5 (1) **1948** Bos 12 (10, LG) **1949** NYB 12 (10, LG) **1951** NYG 7 **NFL** 36 (21) [4 yrs]

Basca, Nick Michael Martin, HB, 5´8˝/170 lbs; Villanova; B12/4/1916 Phoenixville, PA, D11/11/1944, France **[K]**

YEAR	TEAM	G (GS, POS)	RUSH	YD	AVG (LG)	TD	REC	YD	AVG (LG)	TD	PASS	COMP	PCT	YD	AVG (LG)	TD	INT	SK	YD	QBR	KPR	OTD	PTS	TAY
1941	Phi	11 (0)	15	44	2.9 (19)	1	2	45	22.5 (25)	0	4	0	0.0	0	0.0	0	1	—	—	—	KPkpi	—	18	59

Baschnagel, Brian Brian Dale, WR, 5´11˝/187 lbs; Ohio State; 1976: Chi, rnd 3; B1/8/1954 Kingston, NY **[R]**

YEAR	TEAM	G (GS, POS)	RUSH	YD	AVG (LG)	TD	REC	YD	AVG (LG)	TD	PASS	COMP	PCT	YD	AVG (LG)	TD	INT	SK	YD	QBR	KPR	OTD	PTS	TAY
1976	ChiB	14 (12, WR)	1	-12	-12.0 (-12)	0	13	226	17.4 (58)	0	—	—	—	—	—	—	—	—	—	—	kp	—	0	412
1977	ChiB	10 (4)	1	0	0.0 (0)	0	4	50	12.5 (25)	0	1	0	0.0	0	0.0	0	0	—	—	—	kp	1	6	286
1978	ChiB	16 (1)	2	0	0.0 (0)	0	2	29	14.5 (22)	0	—	—	—	—	—	—	—	—	—	—	kp	—	0	167
1979	†ChiB	16 (11, WR)	—	—	—	—	30	452	15.1 (54)	2	1	0	0.0	0	0.0	0	0	—	—	—	kp	—	12	316
1980	ChiB	16 (15, WR)	—	—	—	—	28	396	14.1 (37)	2	—	—	—	—	—	—	—	—	—	—	—	—	12	208
1981	ChiB	16 (15, WR)	1	10	10.0 (10)	0	34	554	16.3 (72)	3	1	1	100.0	18	18.0 (18)	0	0	—	—	—	kp	—	18	315
1982	ChiB	9 (9, WR)	—	—	—	—	12	194	16.2 (39)	2	1	0	0.0	0	0.0	0	0	—	—	—	—	—	12	107
1983	ChiB	16 (4)	2	2	1.0 (2)	0	5	70	14.0 (24)	0	—	—	—	—	—	—	—	—	—	—	k	—	0	34
1984	†ChiB	16 (1)	1	0	0.0 (0)	0	6	53	8.8 (17)	0	2	1	50.0	7	3.5 (7)	0	0	—	—	—	—	—	0	30
NFL	9	129 (72)	8	0	0.0 (10)	0	134	2024	15.1 (72)	9	6	2	33.3	25	4.2 (18)	0	0	—	—	—	kp	1	60	1875

Bashaw, Mose Moses J., T, 5´9˝/200 lbs; none; B1/1888, deceased **1920** Ham 7 (3, RT)

Bashir, Idrees Idrees, DB, 6´2˝/198 lbs; Memphis; 2001: Ind, rnd 2; B12/7/1978 Decatur, GA **2001** Ind 15 (15, FS) **2002**†Ind 14 (14, FS) **2003**†Ind 9 (9, FS) **2004**†Ind 13 (13, FS) **2005** Car 11 (0) **NFL** 62 (51) [5 yrs]

Basing, Myrt Myrton Nathan, B, 5´9˝/190 lbs; Lawrence; B10/29/1900 Appleton, WI, D4/29/1957 Colorado Springs, CO **1923** GB 9 (7, HB), 12 **1924** GB 11 (8, HB) **1925** GB 13 (10, FB), 36 **1926** GB 5 (3), 6 **1927** GB 3 (0) **NFL** 41 (28), 54 [5 yrs]

Basinger, Michael Michael, DE, 6´3˝/258 lbs; California-Riverside; B12/11/1951 Merced, CA **1974** GB 1

Baska, Rich Richard Paul, LB, 6´3˝/225 lbs; UCLA; B2/19/1952 Bismarck, ND **1976** Den 14 **1977** Den 4 **NFL** 18 [2 yrs]

Basnight, Michael Michael, RB, 6´1˝/235 lbs; North Carolina A&T; B9/3/1977 Norfolk, VA

YEAR	TEAM	G (GS, POS)	RUSH	YD	AVG (LG)	TD	REC	YD	AVG (LG)	TD	PASS	COMP	PCT	YD	AVG (LG)	TD	INT	SK	YD	QBR	KPR	OTD	PTS	TAY
1999	Cin	13 (1)	62	308	5.0 (46)	0	16	172	10.8 (47)	0	—	—	—	—	—	—	—	—	—	—	—	—	0	394

Basrak, Mike Michael J., C, 6´2˝/220 lbs; Duquesne; 1937: Pit, rnd 1; B11/23/1912 Bellaire, OH, D12/18/1973 Skokie, IL **1937** Pit☆10 (10, C) **1938** Pit☆5 (5, C) **NFL** 15 (15) [2 yrs]

Bass, Anthony Anthony Emmanole, DB, 6´1˝/192 lbs; Bethune-Cookman; B3/26/1975 St. Albans, WV **1998**†Min 3 (0) **1999**†Min 14 (3) **NFL** 17 (3) [2 yrs]

Bass, Bill William T., B, 5´10˝/180 lbs; Tennessee State; UNLV; B1922 Greensboro, NC

YEAR	TEAM	G (GS, POS)	RUSH	YD	AVG (LG)	TD	REC	YD	AVG (LG)	TD	PASS	COMP	PCT	YD	AVG (LG)	TD	INT	SK	YD	QBR	KPR	OTD	PTS	TAY
1947	ChiR-A	14 (3)	28	44	1.6	0	8	79	9.9	1	1	1	100.0	14	14.0 (14)	0	0	—	—	—	kpi	1	12	319

Bass, Dick Richard Lee, FB-HB, 5´10˝/197 lbs; Pacific; 1959: LA, rnd 1/1960: Hou, rnd 1; B3/15/1937 Georgetown, MS, D2/1/2006 Norwalk, CA

YEAR	TEAM	G (GS, POS)	RUSH	YD	AVG (LG)	TD	REC	YD	AVG (LG)	TD	PASS	COMP	PCT	YD	AVG (LG)	TD	INT	SK	YD	QBR	KPR	OTD	PTS	TAY
1960	LARm	12	31	153	4.9 (33)	0	13	92	7.1 (26)	0	—	—	—	—	—	—	—	—	—	—	kp	—	0	287
1961	LARm	14 (9, FB)	98	608	6.2 (73)	4	16	145	9.1 (37)	0	—	—	—	—	—	—	—	—	—	—	kp	1	30	1173
1962	LARm★	14 (FB)	196	1033	5.3 (57)	6	30	262	8.7 (33)	2	3	1	33.3	22	7.3 (22)	0	0	—	—	—	kp	—	48	1457
1963	LARm✧	12 (HB)	143	520	3.6 (51)	5	30	348	11.6 (53)	0	1	0	0.0	0	0.0	0	0	—	—	—	p	—	30	750
1964	LARm	9	72	342	4.8 (59)	2	9	83	9.2 (24)	0	—	—	—	—	—	—	—	—	—	—	kp	—	12	409
1965	LARm	12 (FB)	121	549	4.5 (49)	2	21	230	11.0 (36)	2	—	—	—	—	—	—	—	—	—	—	p	—	24	689
1966	LARm★	14 (FB)	248	1090	4.4 (50)	8	31	274	8.8 (40)	0	—	—	—	—	—	—	—	—	—	—	p	—	48	1307
1967	†LARm	14 (FB)	187	627	3.4 (27)	6	27	212	7.9 (30)	1	—	—	—	—	—	—	—	—	—	—	—	—	42	798
1968	LARm	10 (10, FB)	121	494	4.1 (20)	1	27	195	7.2 (28)	2	—	—	—	—	—	—	—	—	—	—	—	—	18	612
1969	LARm	1	1	1	1.0 (1)	0	—	—	—	—	—	—	—	—	—	—	—	—	—	—	—	—	0	1
NFL	10	112 (19)	1218	5417	4.4 (73)	34	204	1841	9.0 (53)	7	4	1	25.0	22	5.5 (22)	0	0	—	—	—	kp	1	252	7482

Bass, Don Donald Wayne, WR-TE, 6´2˝/219 lbs; Houston; 1978: Cin, rnd 3; B3/11/1956 Fort Worth, TX, D10/26/1989 Waxahachie, TX

YEAR	TEAM	G (GS, POS)	RUSH	YD	AVG (LG)	TD	REC	YD	AVG (LG)	TD	PASS	COMP	PCT	YD	AVG (LG)	TD	INT	SK	YD	QBR	KPR	OTD	PTS	TAY
1978	Cin	16 (TE)	1	-4	-4.0 (-4)	0	27	447	16.6 (51)	4	—	—	—	—	—	—	—	—	—	—	kp	1	30	266
1979	Cin	16 (WR)	4	35	8.8 (14)	0	58	724	12.5 (50)	3	—	—	—	—	—	—	—	—	—	—	—	—	18	412
1980	Cin	14 (12, WR)	—	—	—	—	32	409	12.8 (55)	6	—	—	—	—	—	—	—	—	—	—	—	—	36	235
1981	†Cin	6 (0)	1	9	9.0 (9)	0	—	—	—	—	—	—	—	—	—	—	—	—	—	—	—	—	0	9
1982	NO	3 (0)	—	—	—	—	—	—	—	—	—	—	—	—	—	—	—	—	—	—	—	—	0	0
NFL	5	55 (12)	6	40	6.7 (14)	0	117	1580	13.5 (55)	13	—	—	—	—	—	—	—	—	—	—	kp	1	84	921

Bass, Glenn Glenn Alden, SE-WR, 6´2˝/202 lbs; East Carolina; 1961: SD, rnd 23/SL, rnd 5; B4/12/1939 Wilson, NC

YEAR	TEAM	G (GS, POS)	RUSH	YD	AVG (LG)	TD	REC	YD	AVG (LG)	TD	PASS	COMP	PCT	YD	AVG (LG)	TD	INT	SK	YD	QBR	KPR	OTD	PTS	TAY
1961	Buf-A	14 (SE)	2	8	4.0 (16)	0	50	765	15.3 (76)	3	—	—	—	—	—	—	—	—	—	—	p	—	18	441
1962	Buf-A	14 (SE)	—	—	—	—	32	555	17.3 (76)	4	—	—	—	—	—	—	—	—	—	—	—	—	24	298
1963	†Buf-A	9	14	59	4.2 (9)	0	9	153	17.0 (74)	1	—	—	—	—	—	—	—	—	—	—	—	—	6	141
1964	†Buf-A	14 (WR)	—	—	—	—	43	897	20.9 (**94**)	7	—	—	—	—	—	—	—	—	—	—	—	—	42	484
1965	Buf-A	4	—	—	—	—	18	299	16.6 (38)	1	—	—	—	—	—	—	—	—	—	—	—	—	6	155
1966	†Buf-A	14	—	—	—	—	10	130	13.0 (19)	0	—	—	—	—	—	—	—	—	—	—	—	—	0	65
1967	Hou-A	7	—	—	—	—	5	42	8.4 (15)	1	—	—	—	—	—	—	—	—	—	—	—	—	6	26
1968	Hou-A	3	—	—	—	—	—	—	—	—	—	—	—	—	—	—	—	—	—	—	—	—	—	—
NFL	8	79	16	67	4.2 (16)	0	167	2841	17.0 (94)	17	—	—	—	—	—	—	—	—	—	—	p	—	102	1608

Bass, Mike Michael Thomas, DB, 6´0˝/190 lbs; Michigan; 1967: GB, rnd 12; B3/31/1945 Ypsilanti, MI **[I]** **1967** Det 2 **1969** Was 14 (RCB) **1970** Was 14 (14, RCB) **1971**†Was 14 (14, RCB) **1972**†Was 14 (14, RCB) **1973**†Was 14 (14, RCB) **1974**†Was☆14 (14, RCB) **1975** Was 14 (14, RCB) **NFL** 100 (84) [8 yrs]

Bass, Norm Norman Delaney, DB, 6´3˝/210 lbs; Pacific; B1/21/1939 Laurel, MS **1964** Den-A 1

Bass, Robert Robert Shawn, LB, 6´1˝/239 lbs; Miami (FL); B11/10/1970 Brooklyn, NY **1995** ChiB 2 (0)

Bassett, Henry Henry Herbert, T-G, 6´2˝/215 lbs; Nebraska; B9/1/1899 Atchison, KS, D2/1973 Tulsa, OK **1924** KC 7 (6, RT)

Bassett, Maurice Maurice LaFrancis, FB, 6´1˝/230 lbs; Langston; 1954: Cle, rnd 3; B4/26/1931 Chickasha, OK, D5/24/1991 Springfield, OH

YEAR	TEAM	G (GS, POS)	RUSH	YD	AVG (LG)	TD	REC	YD	AVG (LG)	TD	PASS	COMP	PCT	YD	AVG (LG)	TD	INT	SK	YD	QBR	KPR	OTD	PTS	TAY
1954	†Cle	12 (FB)	144	588	4.1 (22)	6	20	205	10.3 (33)	0	—	—	—	—	—	—	—	—	—	—	k	—	36	756
1955	†Cle	12 (fb)	38	174	4.6 (30)	3	9	83	9.2 (25)	0	—	—	—	—	—	—	—	—	—	—	k	—	18	292
1956	Cle	12 (fb)	41	129	3.1 (12)	1	4	29	7.3 (31)	1	—	—	—	—	—	—	—	—	—	—	—	—	12	159
NFL	3	36	223	891	4.0 (30)	10	33	317	9.6 (33)	1	—	—	—	—	—	—	—	—	—	—	k	—	66	1206

YEAR	TEAM	G (GS, POS)	RUSH	YD	AVG (LG)	TD	REC	YD	AVG (LG)	TD	PASS	COMP	PCT	YD	AVG (LG)	TD	INT	SK	YD	QBR	KPR	OTD	PTS	TAY
Bassi, Dick Richard Joseph, G, 5´11˝/214 lbs; Santa Clara; 1937: Was, rnd 4; B1/1/1915 San Luis Obispo, CA, D8/12/1973 San Francisco, CA **1938** ChiB 9 (0) **1939** ChiB 10 (1) **1940** Phi★11 (9, LG)																								
1941	Pit	11 (11, RG)	—	—	—	—	1	6	6.0 (6)	0	—	—	—	—	—	—	—	—	—	—	—	—	0	3
NFL	4	41 (21)	—	—	—	—	1	6	6.0 (6)	0	—	—	—	—	—	—	—	—	—	—	—	1	6	3
1946 SF-A 8 (8, LG) **1947** SF-A 8 (0) **AAFC** 41 (21) [4 yrs]																								
Bassman, Reds Herman, HB, 5´11˝/180 lbs; Ursinus; B2/25/1913 Philadelphia, PA																								
1936	Phi	8 (0)	4	19	4.8	0	2	38	19.0	0	3	1	33.3	3	1.0 (3)	0	1	—	—	—	—	—	0	-1
Baston, Bert Albert Pretson, E, 6´1˝/170 lbs; Minnesota; B12/3/1894 St. Louis Park, MN, D11/16/1979 St. Cloud, MN **1920** Cle 8 (7, LE)																								
Batch, Charlie Charles D'Donte, QB, 6´2˝/220 lbs; Eastern Michigan; 1998: Det, rnd 2; B12/5/1974 Pittsburgh, PA																								
1998	Det	12 (12, QB)	41	229	5.6 (17)	1	—	—	—	—	303	173	57.1	2178	7.2 (**98**)	11	6	37	222	83.5	—	—	6	1143
1999	Det	11 (10, QB)	28	87	3.1 (12)	2	—	—	—	—	270	151	55.9	1957	7.2 (74)	13	7	36	186	84.1	—	—	12	871
2000	Det	15 (15, QB)	44	199	4.5 (19)	2	—	—	—	—	412	221	53.6	2489	6.0 (59)	13	15	41	242	67.3	—	—	12	929
2001	Det	10 (9, QB)	12	45	3.8 (12)	0	—	—	—	—	341	198	58.1	2392	7.0 (76)	12	12	33	176	76.8	—	—	0	821
2003	Pit	4 (0)	1	11	11.0 (11)	0	—	—	—	—	8	4	50.0	47	5.9 (22)	0	0	1	2	—	—	—	0	35
2005	Pit	4 (2)	11	30	2.7 (15)	1	—	—	—	—	36	23	63.9	246	6.8 (43)	1	1	1	6	—	—	—	6	128
NFL	6	56 (48)	137	601	4.4 (19)	6	—	—	—	—	1370	770	56.2	9309	6.8 (98)	50	41	149	834	76.9	—	—	36	3926
Batchelor, Don Donald G., T, 6´3˝/225 lbs; Ohio Northern; Grove City; B6/15/1895 Hickville, OH, D9/24/1971 Grand Blanc, MI **1922** Can 1 (1) **1923** Tol 2 (2) **NFL** 3 (3) [2 yrs]																								
Bateman, Marv Marvin Fredrich, P, 6´4˝/213 lbs; Utah; 1972: Dal, rnd 3; B4/5/1950 Salt Lake City, UT **[KP]** **1972**†Dal 14 **1973**†Dal 13 **1974** Dal 2 **1974**†Buf 5 **1975** Buf 14 **1976** Buf☆14																								
1977	Buf	14	1	0	0.0 (0)	0	—	—	—	—	—	—	—	—	—	—	—	—	—	—	P	—	0	0
NFL	6	76	1	0	0.0	0	—	—	—	—	—	—	—	—	—	—	—	—	—	—	KP	—	1	0
Bates, Bill William Frederick, DB, 6´1˝/204 lbs; Tennessee; B6/6/1961 Knoxville, TN **1983**†Dal 16 (1) **1984** Dal★12 (2) **1985**†Dal 16 (2) **1986** Dal 15 (15, SS) **1987** Dal 12 (11, SS) **1988** Dal 16 (16, SS) **1991**†Dal 16 (0) **1992** Dal 5 (0) **1993**†Dal 16 (0) **1994**†Dal 15 (0) **1995**†Dal 16 (0) **1996**†Dal 14 (0) **1997** Dal 16 (0)																								
1989	Dal	16 (0)	1	0	0.0 (0)	0	—	—	—	—	—	—	—	—	—	—	—	—	—	—	i	—	0	13
1990	Dal	16 (0)	1	4	4.0 (4)	0	—	—	—	—	—	—	—	—	—	—	—	—	—	—	i	—	0	3
NFL	15	217 (47)	2	4	2.0 (4)	0	—	—	—	—	—	—	—	—	—	—	—	—	—	—	piS	—	0	98
Bates, D'Wayne D'Wayne Lavoris, WR, 6´2˝/212 lbs; Northwestern; 1999: Chi, rnd 3; B12/4/1975 Augusta, GA																								
1999	ChiB	7 (1)	—	—	—	—	2	19	9.5 (11)	0	—	—	—	—	—	—	—	—	—	—	—	—	0	10
2000	ChiB	5 (0)	1	-2	-2.0 (-2)	0	4	42	10.5 (18)	0	—	—	—	—	—	—	—	—	—	—	—	—	0	19
2001	†ChiB	11 (1)	—	—	—	—	9	160	17.8 (40)	1	—	—	—	—	—	—	—	—	—	—	—	—	6	85
2002	Min	14 (11, WR)	—	—	—	—	50	689	13.8 (59)	4	—	—	—	—	—	—	—	—	—	—	kp	—	24	438
2003	Min	10 (8, wr)	—	—	—	—	15	151	10.1 (18)	1	—	—	—	—	—	—	—	—	—	—	—	—	6	81
NFL	5	47 (21)	1	-2	-2.0 (-2)	0	80	1061	13.3 (59)	6	—	—	—	—	—	—	—	—	—	—	kp	—	36	632
Bates, Mario Mario Doniel, RB, 6´1˝/217 lbs; Arizona State; 1994: NO, rnd 2; B1/16/1973 Tucson, AZ																								
1994	NO	11 (7, rb)	151	579	3.8 (40)	6	8	62	7.8 (14)	0	—	—	—	—	—	—	—	—	—	—	k	—	36	675
1995	NO	16 (16, RB)	244	951	3.9 (66)	7	18	114	6.3 (26)	0	—	—	—	—	—	—	—	—	—	—	—	—	42	1078
1996	NO	14 (10, RB)	164	584	3.6 (33)	4	13	44	3.4 (15)	0	—	—	—	—	—	—	—	—	—	—	—	—	24	646
1997	NO	12 (7, RB)	119	440	3.7 (74)	4	5	42	8.4 (15)	0	1	1	100.0	21	21.0 (21)	1	0	—	—	—	—	—	24	517
1998	†Arz	16 (1)	60	165	2.8 (15)	6	1	14	14.0 (14)	0	—	—	—	—	—	—	—	—	—	—	—	—	36	232
1999	Arz	16 (2)	72	202	2.8 (16)	9	5	34	6.8 (18)	0	—	—	—	—	—	—	—	—	—	—	k	—	54	760
2000	Det	13 (0)	31	127	4.1 (23)	2	15	109	7.3 (17)	0	—	—	—	—	—	—	—	—	—	—	—	—	12	202
NFL	7	98 (43)	841	3048	3.6 (74)	38	65	419	6.4 (26)	0	1	1	100.0	21	21.0 (21)	1	0	—	—	—	k	—	228	4109
Bates, Michael Michael Dion, RB, 5´10˝/189 lbs; Arizona; 1992: Sea, rnd 6; B12/19/1969 Tucson, AZ **[R]** **1995** Cle 13 (0) **1996**†Car★14 (0) **1997** Car★16 (0) **1998** Car★14 (0) **2001** Was 16 (0) **2003** NYJ 8 (0) **2003**†Dal 1 (0)																								
1993	Sea	16 (1)	2	12	6.0 (6)	0	1	6	6.0 (6)	0	—	—	—	—	—	—	—	—	—	—	k	—	0	168
1994	Sea	15 (0)	2	-4	-2.0 (7)	0	5	112	22.4 (40)	1	—	—	—	—	—	—	—	—	—	—	k	—	6	175
1999	Car★	16 (0)	3	12	4.0 (12)	0	1	2	2.0 (2)	0	—	—	—	—	—	—	—	—	—	—	k	2	12	540
2000	Car★	16 (0)	5	13	2.6 (8)	0	5	38	7.6 (23)	0	—	—	—	—	—	—	—	—	—	—	kp	1	6	349
NFL	10	145 (1)	12	33	2.8 (12)	0	12	158	13.2 (40)	1	—	—	—	—	—	—	—	—	—	—	kp	5	36	3676
Bates, Patrick Patrick James, DB, 6´3˝/215 lbs; UCLA; Texas A&M; 1993: LARd, rnd 1; B11/27/1970 Galveston, TX **1993**†LARd 13 (0) **1994** LARd 16 (9, ss) **1996** Atl 15 (9, FS) **NFL** 44 (18) [3 yrs]																								
Bates, Solomon Solomon Augustus, LB, 6´1˝/243 lbs; Arizona State; 2003: Sea, rnd 4; B4/18/1982 Carver City, CA **2003** Sea 7 (0) **2004**†Sea 10 (3) **NFL** 17 (3) [2 yrs]																								
Bates, Ted Ted Douglas, LB, 6´3˝/219 lbs; Oregon State; 1959: ChiC, rnd 5; B9/22/1936 Baytown, TX **1959** ChiC 12 (MLB) **1960** SL 12 **1961** SL 14 (LLB) **1962** SL 8 **1963** NYJ-A 8 **NFL** 54 [5 yrs]																								
Batinski, Stan Stanley Charles, G-T, 5´10˝/215 lbs; Temple; B3/4/1917 Greenfield, MA, D1/29/1990 Greenfield, MA **1941** Det 8 (3) **1943** Det 7 (1) **1944** Det 9 (8, LT) **1945** Det☆10 (6, LG) **1946** Det 11 (10, LG) **1947** Det 12 (9, LG) **1948** Bos 12 (8, RG) **1949** NYB 12 (1) **NFL** 81 (46) [8 yrs]																								
Batiste, Michael Michael, G-T, 6´3˝/315 lbs; Tulane; B12/24/1970 Beaumont, TX **1995** Dal 2 (0) **1998** Was 6 (0) **NFL** 8 (0) [2 yrs]																								
Batorski, John John Michael, E, 6´2˝/238 lbs; Colgate; 1944: Was, rnd 18; B9/27/1920 Lackawanna, NY, D11/16/1982 Old Field, NY																								
1946	Buf-A	8 (2)	—	—	—	—	2	27	13.5	0	—	—	—	—	—	—	—	—	—	—	—	—	0	14
Battaglia, Marco Marco Antonio, TE, 6´3˝/250 lbs; Rutgers; 1996: Cin, rnd 2; B1/25/1973 Queens, NY																								
1996	Cin	16 (0)	—	—	—	—	8	79	9.9 (17)	0	—	—	—	—	—	—	—	—	—	—	k	—	0	33
1997	Cin	16 (0)	—	—	—	—	12	149	12.4 (34)	1	—	—	—	—	—	—	—	—	—	—	—	—	6	80
1998	Cin	16 (0)	—	—	—	—	10	47	4.7 (16)	1	—	—	—	—	—	—	—	—	—	—	k	—	6	19
1999	Cin	16 (0)	—	—	—	—	14	153	10.9 (30)	0	—	—	—	—	—	—	—	—	—	—	—	—	0	77
2000	Cin	16 (10, TE)	—	—	—	—	13	105	8.1 (15)	0	—	—	—	—	—	—	—	—	—	—	—	—	0	53
2001	Cin	8 (1)	—	—	—	—	13	118	9.1 (17)	0	—	—	—	—	—	—	—	—	—	—	—	—	0	59
2001	Was	3 (0)	—	—	—	—	1	9	9.0 (9)	0	—	—	—	—	—	—	—	—	—	—	—	—	0	5
2002	TB	2 (0)	—	—	—	—	—	—	—	—	—	—	—	—	—	—	—	—	—	—	—	—	—	—
2002	†Pit	1 (0)	—	—	—	—	—	—	—	—	—	—	—	—	—	—	—	—	—	—	—	—	—	—
2003	Car	2 (0)	—	—	—	—	—	—	—	—	—	—	—	—	—	—	—	—	—	—	—	—	—	—
NFL	8	96 (11)	—	—	—	—	71	660	9.3 (34)	2	—	—	—	—	—	—	—	—	—	—	k	—	12	323
Battaglia, Matt Matthew Martin, LB, 6´2˝/225 lbs; Louisville; B9/25/1965 Tallahassee, FL **1987** Phi 3 (2)																								
Batten, Pat Patrick Ward, FB, 6´2˝/225 lbs; Hardin-Simmons; 1964: Det, rnd 3/SD, rnd 7; B12/5/1941 Indianola, IA **1964** Det 3																								
Batteaux, Pat Patrick, WR, 6´0˝/195 lbs; TCU; B4/18/1978 Houston, TX																								
2001	SD	5 (0)	—	—	—	—	3	25	8.3 (17)	0	—	—	—	—	—	—	—	—	—	—	—	—	0	13
Battle, Arnaz Arnaz Jerome, WR, 6´1˝/217 lbs; Notre Dame; 2003: SF, rnd 6; B2/22/1980 Dallas, TX																								
2003	SF	8 (0)	2	14	7.0 (9)	0	—	—	—	—	—	—	—	—	—	—	—	—	—	—	k	—	0	27
2004	SF	14 (0)	2	5	2.5 (7)	0	8	143	17.9 (65)	0	—	—	—	—	—	—	—	—	—	—	kp	1	6	260
2005	SF	10 (8, wr)	8	11	1.4 (9)	0	32	363	11.3 (39)	3	2	2	100.0	27	13.5 (24)	0	0	—	—	—	—	—	18	221
NFL	3	32 (8)	12	30	2.5 (9)	0	40	506	12.6 (65)	3	2	2	100.0	27	13.5 (24)	0	0	—	—	—	kp	1	24	508
Battle, Jim James, G, 6´0˝/240 lbs; Southern Illinois; B2/20/1938 Bartow, FL **1963** Min 14																								
Battle, Jim James, T, 6´5˝/235 lbs; Southern (LA); 1966: Cle, rnd 6/Bos, rnd 7; B9/18/1941 Shreveport, LA **1966** Cle 6																								
Battle, Julian Julian, DB, 6´2˝/205 lbs; Tennessee; 2003: KC, rnd 3; B7/11/1981 Royal Palm Beach, FL **2003**†KC 14 (0) **2004** KC 12 (1) **NFL** 26 (1) [2 yrs]																								

YEAR	TEAM	G(GS, POS)	RUSH	YD	AVG(LG)	TD	REC	YD	AVG(LG)	TD	PASS	COMP	PCT	YD	AVG(LG)	TD	INT	SK	YD	QBR	KPR	OTD	PTS	TAY
Battle, Mike Michael Leonard, DB, 6´1˝/175 lbs; USC; 1969: NYJ, rnd 12; B7/9/1946 South Gate, CA **1969**†NYJ-A 14																								
1970	NYJ	14	—	—	—	—	1	2	2.0(2)	0	—	—	—	—	—	—	—	—	—	—	kp	—	0	314
NFL	2	28	—	—	—	—	1	2	2.0(2)	0	—	—	—	—	—	—	—	—	—	—	kpi	—	0	684
Battle, Ralph Ralph Keith, DB, 6´2˝/205 lbs; Jacksonville State; B6/15/1961 Huntsville, AL **1984** Cin 3 (0)																								
Battle, Ron Ronnie Jerome, TE, 6´3˝/220 lbs; North Texas; 1981: LA, rnd 7; B3/27/1959 Shreveport, LA **1981** LARm 4 (0)																								
1982	LARm.	9(0)	1	1	1.0(1)	0	2	62	31.0(51)	1	—	—	—	—	—	—	—	—	—	—	—	—	6	37
NFL	2	13(0)	1	1	1.0(1)	0	2	62	31.0(51)	1	—	—	—	—	—	—	—	—	—	—	—	—	6	37
Battles, Ainsley Ainsley Thomas, DB, 5´11˝/204 lbs; Vanderbilt; B11/6/1978 Lilburn, GA **2000** Pit 16 (2) **2001** Jax 13 (11, fs/ss) **2002** Jax 16 (4) **2004** Pit 1 (0) **NFL** 46 (17) [4 yrs]																								
Battles, Cliff Clifford Franklin, TB-FB-WB-DB, 6´1˝/195 lbs; West Virginia Wesleyan; B5/1/1910 Akron, OH, D4/28/1981 Clearwater, FL; HOF 1968 **[KC]**																								
1932	Bos☆	8(8, TB)	**148**	**576**	3.9	3	4	60	15.0	1	20	2	10.0	42	2.1	0	2	—	—	—	—	—	24	582
1933	Bos☆	12(11, TB)	136	737	**5.4**	3	11	185	16.8	0	21	5	23.8	65	3.1	0	3	—	—	—	K	1	27	**782**
1934	Bos☆	12(10, TB)	96	480	5.0	6	5	95	19.0	1	9	1	11.1	7	0.8(7)	0	0	—	—	—	K	—	43	596
1935	Bos☆	7(6, TB)	67	230	3.4	1	3	22	7.3	0	22	5	22.7	92	4.2	0	1	—	—	—	—	1	12	267
1936	†Bos☆	11(11, FB)	176	614	3.5	5	6	103	17.2	1	52	18	34.6	242	4.7	1	6	—	—	—	—	1	42	617
1937	†Was☆	10(8, tb)	**216**	**874**	4.0(75)	**5**	9	81	9.0	1	33	13	39.4	142	4.3	0	3	—	—	—	—	1	42	**931**
NFL	6	60(54)	839	3511	4.2(75)	23	38	546	14.4	4	157	44	28.0	590	3.8(7)	1	15	—	—	—	K	4	190	3774
Batton, Bobby Bobby Joe, RB, 5´11˝/185 lbs; UNLV; 1980: NYJ, rnd 7; B3/17/1957 Yazoo City, MS																								
1980	NYJ	8(0)	3	4	1.3(3)	0	—	—	—	—	—	—	—	—	—	—	—	—	—	—	—	—	0	4
Baty, Greg Gregory James, TE, 6´5˝/241 lbs; Stanford; 1986: NE, rnd 8; B8/28/1964 Hastings, MI																								
1986	†NE	16(7, te)	—	—	—	—	37	331	8.9(22)	2	—	—	—	—	—	—	—	—	—	—	—	—	12	176
1987	NE	5(0)	—	—	—	—	15	138	9.2(22)	2	—	—	—	—	—	—	—	—	—	—	—	—	12	79
1987	LARm	4(0)	—	—	—	—	3	37	12.3(20)	0	—	—	—	—	—	—	—	—	—	—	—	—	0	19
1988	Phx	1(0)	—	—	—	—	—	—	—	—	—	—	—	—	—	—	—	—	—	—	—	—	—	—
1990	†Mia	12(0)	—	—	—	—	—	—	—	—	—	—	—	—	—	—	—	—	—	—	—	—	0	0
1991	Mia	16(8, TE)	—	—	—	—	20	269	13.4(30)	1	—	—	—	—	—	—	—	—	—	—	—	—	6	140
1992	†Mia	16(0)	—	—	—	—	3	19	6.3(12)	1	—	—	—	—	—	—	—	—	—	—	—	—	6	15
1993	Mia	16(1)	—	—	—	—	5	78	15.6(32)	1	—	—	—	—	—	—	—	—	—	—	k	—	6	36
1994	†Mia	16(0)	—	—	—	—	2	11	5.5(8)	1	—	—	—	—	—	—	—	—	—	—	k	—	6	-5
NFL	8	102(16)	—	—	—	—	85	883	10.4(32)	8	—	—	—	—	—	—	—	—	—	—	k	—	48	459
Bauer, A.C. A.C., T, 6´2˝/210 lbs; none; B1900, deceased **1923** Rac 1 (1)																								
Bauer, Hank Henry John, RB, 5´10˝/200 lbs; California Lutheran; B7/15/1954 Scottsbluff, NE																								
1977	SD	13	4	4	1.0(3)	**0**	1	15	15.0(15)	1	—	—	—	—	—	—	—	—	—	—	—	—	6	17
1978	SD	16(4)	85	304	3.6(37)	8	10	78	7.8(14)	1	—	—	—	—	—	—	—	—	—	—	—	—	54	428
1979	†SD	16	22	28	1.3(6)	8	—	—	—	—	0	0	0.0	0	0.0	0	0	1	13	—	k	—	48	140
1980	†SD	16(0)	10	34	3.4(7)	1	—	—	—	—	—	—	—	—	—	—	—	—	—	—	k	—	6	51
1981	†SD	16(0)	2	7	3.5(4)	0	1	4	4.0(4)	1	—	—	—	—	—	—	—	—	—	—	kp	—	6	15
1982	†SD	9(0)	—	—	—	—	—	—	—	—	—	—	—	—	—	—	—	—	—	—	k	—	0	-6
NFL	6	86(4)	123	377	3.1(37)	17	12	97	8.1(15)	3	0	0	0.0	0	0.0	0	0	1	13	—	kp	—	120	645
Bauer, Herb Herbert Frank, E, 5´10˝/190 lbs; Baldwin-Wallace; B10/13/1906 Cleveland, OH, D7/30/1980 Ann Arbor, MI **1925** Cle 2 (1)																								
Bauer, John John Richard, T, 6´3˝/235 lbs; Illinois; 1954: Cle, rnd 1; B3/11/1932 Benton, IL **1954** NYG 2																								
Baugh, Sammy Samuel Adrian 'Slinging Sammy', QB-TB, 6´2˝/182 lbs; TCU; 1937: Was, rnd 1; B3/17/1914 Temple, TX; HOF 1963 **[KPIC]**																								
1937	†Was☆	11(5, TB)	86	240	2.8(41)	1	—	—	—	—	**171**	**81**	47.4	**1127**	6.6(59)	8	**14**	—	—	50.5	—	—	6	294
1938	Was★	9(3, TB)	21	35	1.7(9)	0	—	—	—	—	128	63	49.2	853	6.7(60)	5	11	—	—	48.1	—	—	0	47
1939	Was✧	9(1, tb)	14	46	3.3(13)	0	—	—	—	—	96	53	55.2	518	5.4(44)	6	9	—	—	52.3	P	—	0	-25
1940	†Was★	11(11, TB)	20	16	0.8(5)	0	—	—	—	—	177	111	**62.7**	**1367**	**7.7(81)**	**12**	10	—	—	**85.6**	Pi	—	0	429
1941	Was★	11(1, TB)	27	14	0.5(16)	0	—	—	—	—	193	106	54.9	1236	6.4(55)	10	**19**	—	—	52.2	Pi	—	0	-15
1942	†Was★	11(8, TB)	20	61	3.1(28)	1	—	—	—	—	225	132	**58.7**	1524	6.8(53)	16	11	—	—	82.5	Ppi	—	6	563
1943	†Was☆	10(7, TB)	19	-43	-2.3(4)	0	—	—	—	—	**239**	**133**	**55.6**	1754	7.3(72)	23	19	—	—	78.0	Ppi	—	0	249
1944	Was	8(4, qb)	19	-38	-2.0(17)	0	1	0	0.0(0)	0	146	82	56.2	849	5.8(71)	4	8	—	—	59.4	Ppi	—	0	91
1945	†Was☆	8(8, QB)	19	-71	-3.7(34)	0	—	—	—	—	182	**128**	**70.3**	1669	9.2(70)	11	4	—	—	**109.9**	KPi	—	1	753
1946	Was	11(2, QB)	18	-76	-4.2(13)	1	—	—	—	—	161	87	**54.0**	1163	7.2(51)	8	17	—	—	54.2	P	—	6	-125
1947	Was☆	12(1)	25	47	1.9(19)	2	—	—	—	—	**354**	**210**	**59.3**	**2938**	8.3(74)	**25**	15	—	—	**92.0**	P	—	12	1061
1948	Was☆	12(3, QB)	4	4	1.0(7)	1	—	—	—	—	**315**	**185**	**58.7**	**2599**	**8.3(86)**	22	**23**	—	—	78.3	—	—	6	504
1949	Was	12(8, QB)	13	67	5.2(17)	2	—	—	—	—	255	145	**56.9**	1903	7.5(76)	18	14	—	—	81.2	P	—	12	569
1950	Was	11(QB)	7	27	3.9(11)	1	—	—	—	—	166	90	54.2	1130	6.8(56)	10	11	—	—	68.1	P	—	6	212
1951	Was✧	12(QB)	11	-5	-0.5(7)	0	—	—	—	—	154	67	43.5	1104	7.2(53)	7	17	—	—	43.8	P	—	0	-98
1952	Was	7	1	1	1.0(1)	0	—	—	—	—	33	20	60.6	152	4.6(20)	2	1	—	—	—	P	—	0	47
NFL	16	165(62)	324	325	1.0(41)	9	1	0	0.0	0	2995	1693	56.5	21886	7.3(86)	187	203	—	—	72.2	KPpi	—	55	4553
Baugh, Tom Thomas Anthony, C, 6´3˝/274 lbs; Southern Illinois; 1986: KC, rnd 4; B12/1/1963 Chicago, IL **1986**†KC 5 (0) **1987** KC 12 (6, C) **1988** KC 12 (10, C) **1989**†Cle 16 (0) **NFL** 45 (16) [4 yrs]																								
Baughan, Maxie Maxie Calloway, LB, 6´1˝/227 lbs; Georgia Tech; 1960: Phi, rnd 2/Oak, rnd 1; B8/3/1938 Forkland, AL **1960**†Phi✧12 (12, RLB) **1961** Phi★14 (14, RLB) **1962** Phi 14 (14, RLB) **1963** Phi✧14 (14, RLB) **1964** Phi★14 (14, RLB) **1965** Phi★12 (12, RLB) **1966** LARm★14 (14, RLB) **1967**†LARm★14 (RLB) **1968** LARm★14 (14, RLB) **1969**†LARm★13 (13, RLB) **1970** LARm 10 (8, RLB) **1974** Was 2 **NFL** 147 (129) [12 yrs]																								
Baujan, Harry Harry Clifford, E, 5´8˝/170 lbs; Notre Dame; B5/24/1894 Beardstown, IL, D12/30/1976 Dayton, OH **1920** Cle 6 (5, RE) **1921** Cle 5 (3) **NFL** 11 (8) [2 yrs]																								
Bauman, Alf Alfred Ernest, DT-T, 6´2˝/228 lbs; Northwestern; 1942: Det, rnd 2; B1/3/1920 Chicago, IL, D3/2/1979 Pacifica, CA **1947** ChiR-A 3 (0) **1947**†Phi 2 (0) **1948** ChiB 5 (0) **1949** ChiB 12 (1) **1950**†ChiB 12 (RDT) **NFL** 31 (1) [3 yrs]																								
Bauman, Rashad Leddure Rashad, DB, 5´8˝/184 lbs; Oregon; 2002: Was, rnd 3; B5/7/1979 Tempe, AZ **2002** Was 16 (1) **2003** Was 12 (2) **2004** Cin 4 (0) **2005**†Cin 11 (1) **NFL** 43 (4) [4 yrs]																								
Baumann, Buddy Carl, T-G, 6´1˝/190 lbs; none; B1900, WI, deceased **1922** Rac 4 (1)																								
Baumann, Charlie Bruce Charles, K, 6´1˝/203 lbs; West Virginia; B8/25/1967 Erie, PA **[K]** **1991** Mia 2 (0) **1991** NE 7 (0) **1992** NE 16 (0) **NFL** 25 (0) [2 yrs]																								
Baumgardner, Joe Billy Joseph William, HB, 6´1˝/198 lbs; Texas; 1947: ChiB, rnd 28; B2/16/1925 Wheeler, TX **1948** Det 2 (0)																								
Baumgartner, Bill William R., E, 6´3˝/202 lbs; Minnesota; 1947: Mia-A, rnd 14/1943: ChiC, rnd 13; B4/17/1921 Duluth, MN, D9/1981 **1947** Bal-A 2 (0)																								
Baumgartner, Steve Steven John, DE-LB, 6´7˝/256 lbs; Purdue; 1973: NO, rnd 2; B3/26/1951 Chicago, IL **1973** NO 14 **1974** NO 14 **1975** NO 14 (14, RDE) **1976** NO 14 (13, RDE) **1977** NO 5 **1977** Hou 6 **1978**†Hou 16 **1979**†Hou 12 **NFL** 95 (27) [7 yrs]																								
Baumhower, Bob Robert Glenn, NT, 6´5˝/261 lbs; Alabama; 1977: Mia, rnd 2; B8/4/1955 Portsmouth, VA **1977** Mia 14 (14, NT) **1978**†Mia 16 (16, NT) **1979**†Mia★16 (16, NT) **1980** Mia 16 (16, NT) **1981**†Mia★16 (16, NT) **1982**†Mia★9 (8, NT) **1983**†Mia★16 (16, NT) **1984**†Mia★15 (15, NT) **1986** Mia 12 (12, NT) **NFL** 130 (129) [9 yrs]																								
Bausch, Frank Frank Joseph, C, 6´3˝/220 lbs; Kansas; B6/14/1908 Marion, SD, D4/6/1976 Wichita, KS **1935** Bos 10 (9, C) **1936**†Bos☆12 (11, C) **1937**†ChiB☆9 (7, C) **1938** ChiB☆11 (10, C) **1939** ChiB 11 (8, C) **1940**†ChiB✧10 (2) **1941** Phi 4 (4)																								
1934	Bos	11(7, C)	1	3	3.0(3)	0	—	—	—	—	—	—	—	—	—	—	—	—	—	—	—	—	0	3
NFL	8	78(58)	1	3	3.0(3)	0	—	—	—	—	—	—	—	—	—	—	—	—	—	—	—	—	0	3
Bausch, Jim James Aloysius Bernard, HB, 6´1˝/200 lbs; Wichita State; Kansas; B3/29/1906 Marion Junction, SD, D7/9/1974 Hot Springs, AR																								
1933	ChiC	2(1)	7	13	1.9	0	—	—	—	—	4	2	50.0	19	4.8	0	1	—	—	—	—	—	0	-18
1933	Cin	5(1)	29	57	2.0	0	—	—	—	—	22	4	18.2	41	1.9	0	2	—	—	—	—	—	0	-3
NFL	1	7(2)	36	70	1.9	0	—	—	—	—	26	6	23.1	60	2.3	0	3	—	—	—	—	—	0	-20

YEAR	TEAM	G (GS, POS)	RUSH	YD	AVG (LG)	TD	REC	YD	AVG (LG)	TD	PASS	COMP	PCT	YD	AVG (LG)	TD	INT	SK	YD	QBR	KPR	OTD	PTS	TAY

Bavaro, David David Anthony, LB, 6´0˝/234 lbs; Syracuse; 1990: Phx, rnd 9; B3/27/1967 Danvers, MA **1990** Phx 14 (0) **1991** Buf 2 (0) **1992**†Min 5 (0) **1993** NE 12 (0) **1994**†NE 9 (5, rilb) **NFL** 42 (5) [5 yrs]

Bavaro, Mark Mark Anthony, TE, 6´4˝/245 lbs; Notre Dame; 1985: NYG, rnd 4; B4/28/1963 Winthrop, MA

YEAR	TEAM	G (GS, POS)	RUSH	YD	AVG (LG)	TD	REC	YD	AVG (LG)	TD	PASS	COMP	PCT	YD	AVG (LG)	TD	INT	SK	YD	QBR	KPR	OTD	PTS	TAY
1985	†NYG	16 (16, TE)	—	—	—	—	37	511	13.8 (32)	4	—	—	—	—	—	—	—	—	—	—	—	—	24	276
1986	†NYG★	16 (15, TE)	—	—	—	—	66	1001	15.2 (41)	4	—	—	—	—	—	—	—	—	—	—	—	—	24	521
1987	NYG★	12 (12, TE)	—	—	—	—	55	867	15.8 (38)	8	—	—	—	—	—	—	—	—	—	—	k	—	48	475
1988	NYG	16 (15, TE)	—	—	—	—	53	672	12.7 (36)	4	—	—	—	—	—	—	—	—	—	—	—	—	24	356
1989	NYG	7 (7, te)	—	—	—	—	22	278	12.6 (29)	3	—	—	—	—	—	—	—	—	—	—	—	—	18	154
1990	†NYG	15 (15, TE)	—	—	—	—	33	393	11.9 (61)	5	—	—	—	—	—	—	—	—	—	—	—	—	30	222
1992	Cle	16 (16, TE)	—	—	—	—	25	315	12.6 (39)	2	—	—	—	—	—	—	—	—	—	—	—	—	12	168
1993	Phi	16 (16, TE)	—	—	—	—	43	481	11.2 (27)	6	—	—	—	—	—	—	—	—	—	—	—	—	36	271
1994	Phi	12 (11, TE)	—	—	—	—	17	215	12.6 (27)	3	—	—	—	—	—	—	—	—	—	—	—	—	18	123
NFL	9	126 (123)	—	—	—	—	351	4733	13.5 (61)	39	—	—	—	—	—	—	—	—	—	—	k	—	234	2563

Bawel, Bibbles Edward Raymond, DB, 6´1˝/185 lbs; Evansville; B11/21/1930 Boonville, IN

YEAR	TEAM	G (GS, POS)	RUSH	YD	AVG (LG)	TD	REC	YD	AVG (LG)	TD	PASS	COMP	PCT	YD	AVG (LG)	TD	INT	SK	YD	QBR	KPR	OTD	PTS	TAY
1952	Phi	12 (DB)	—	—	—	—	2	60	30.0 (52)	0	—	—	—	—	—	—	—	—	—	—	pi	1	6	212
1955	Phi	12 (DB)	—	—	—	—	1	6	6.0 (6)	0	—	—	—	—	—	—	—	—	—	—	kpi	2	12	152
1956	Phi	12	—	—	—	—	—	—	—	—	—	—	—	—	—	—	—	—	—	—	ki	—	0	38
NFL	3	36	—	—	—	—	3	66	22.0 (52)	0	—	—	—	—	—	—	—	—	—	—	kpi	3	18	402

Bax, Carl Carl William, G-T, 6´4˝/290 lbs; Missouri; 1989: TB, rnd 8; B1/5/1966 St. Charles, MO **1989** TB 6 (4) **1990** TB 9 (6, lg) **NFL** 15 (10) [2 yrs]

Baxley, Rob Robert R., T, 6´5˝/287 lbs; Iowa; 1992: Phx, rnd 11; B3/14/1969 Oswego, IL **1992** Phx 6 (0)

Baxter, Brad Herman Bradley, RB, 6´1˝/233 lbs; Alabama State; 1989: Min, rnd 11; B5/5/1967 Dothan, AL

YEAR	TEAM	G (GS, POS)	RUSH	YD	AVG (LG)	TD	REC	YD	AVG (LG)	TD	PASS	COMP	PCT	YD	AVG (LG)	TD	INT	SK	YD	QBR	KPR	OTD	PTS	TAY
1989	NYJ	1 (0)	—	—	—	—	—	—	—	—	—	—	—	—	—	—	—	—	—	—	—	—	—	—
1990	NYJ	16 (9, FB)	124	539	4.3 (28)	6	8	73	9.1 (22)	0	—	—	—	—	—	—	—	—	—	—	—	—	36	636
1991	†NYJ	16 (14, FB)	184	666	3.6 (31)	**11**	12	124	10.3 (34)	0	—	—	—	—	—	—	—	—	—	—	—	—	66	838
1992	NYJ	15 (15, FB)	152	698	4.6 (30)	6	4	32	8.0 (12)	0	—	—	—	—	—	—	—	—	—	—	—	—	36	774
1993	NYJ	16 (12, FB)	174	559	3.2 (16)	7	20	158	7.9 (24)	0	—	—	—	—	—	—	—	—	—	—	—	—	42	708
1994	NYJ	15 (9, FB)	60	170	2.8 (13)	4	10	40	4.0 (7)	0	—	—	—	—	—	—	—	—	—	—	—	—	24	230
1995	NYJ	15 (13, FB)	85	296	3.5 (26)	1	26	160	6.2 (20)	0	—	—	—	—	—	—	—	—	—	—	—	—	6	386
NFL	7	94 (72)	779	2928	3.8 (31)	35	80	587	7.3 (34)	0	—	—	—	—	—	—	—	—	—	—	—	—	210	3572

Baxter, Fred Frederick Denard, TE, 6´3˝/268 lbs; Auburn; 1993: NYJ, rnd 5; B6/14/1971 Brundidge, AL

YEAR	TEAM	G (GS, POS)	RUSH	YD	AVG (LG)	TD	REC	YD	AVG (LG)	TD	PASS	COMP	PCT	YD	AVG (LG)	TD	INT	SK	YD	QBR	KPR	OTD	PTS	TAY
1993	NYJ	7 (0)	—	—	—	—	3	48	16.0 (25)	1	—	—	—	—	—	—	—	—	—	—	—	—	6	29
1994	NYJ	11 (1)	—	—	—	—	3	11	3.7 (6)	1	—	—	—	—	—	—	—	—	—	—	k	—	6	16
1995	NYJ	15 (3)	—	—	—	—	18	222	12.3 (32)	1	—	—	—	—	—	—	—	—	—	—	k	—	6	62
1996	NYJ	16 (4)	—	—	—	—	7	114	16.3 (23)	0	—	—	—	—	—	—	—	—	—	—	—	—	0	57
1997	NYJ	16 (4)	—	—	—	—	27	276	10.2 (37)	3	—	—	—	—	—	—	—	—	—	—	k	—	18	138
1998	†NYJ	14 (2)	—	—	—	—	3	50	16.7 (23)	0	—	—	—	—	—	—	—	—	—	—	k	—	0	18
1999	NYJ	14 (8, TE)	—	—	—	—	8	66	8.3 (24)	2	—	—	—	—	—	—	—	—	—	—	—	—	12	43
2000	NYJ	9 (6, te)	—	—	—	—	4	22	5.5 (12)	2	—	—	—	—	—	—	—	—	—	—	k	—	12	21
2001	†ChiB	14 (14, TE)	—	—	—	—	22	148	6.7 (19)	2	—	—	—	—	—	—	—	—	—	—	—	—	12	84
2002	ChiB	5 (3)	—	—	—	—	5	51	10.2 (22)	0	—	—	—	—	—	—	—	—	—	—	—	—	0	26
2002	NE	1 (0)	—	—	—	—	—	—	—	—	—	—	—	—	—	—	—	—	—	—	—	—	—	—
2003	NE	12 (0)	—	—	—	—	—	—	—	—	—	—	—	—	—	—	—	—	—	—	—	—	—	—
NFL	11	134 (45)	—	—	—	—	100	1008	10.1 (37)	12	—	—	—	—	—	—	—	—	—	—	k	—	72	493

Baxter, Gary Gary Wayne, DB, 6´2˝/204 lbs; Baylor; 2001: Bal, rnd 2; B11/24/1978 Tyler, TX **2001**†Bal 6 (0) **2002** Bal 16 (14, RCB) **2003**†Bal 16 (16, FS/rcb) **2004** Bal 16 (16, RCB) **2005** Cle 5 (5, rcb) **NFL** 59 (51) [5 yrs]

Baxter, Jarrod Jarrod Anthony, FB, 6´1˝/245 lbs; New Mexico; 2002: Hou, rnd 5; B3/9/1979 Dayton, OH

YEAR	TEAM	G (GS, POS)	RUSH	YD	AVG (LG)	TD	REC	YD	AVG (LG)	TD	PASS	COMP	PCT	YD	AVG (LG)	TD	INT	SK	YD	QBR	KPR	OTD	PTS	TAY
2002	Hou	16 (10, FB)	7	14	2.0 (6)	0	5	33	6.6 (14)	1	—	—	—	—	—	—	—	—	—	—	k	—	6	40
2004	Hou	8 (1)	2	1	0.5 (1)	0	1	3	3.0 (3)	0	—	—	—	—	—	—	—	—	—	—	—	—	0	3
2005	Arz	8 (2)	—	—	—	—	1	4	4.0 (4)	0	—	—	—	—	—	—	—	—	—	—	—	—	0	2
NFL	3	32 (13)	9	15	1.7 (6)	0	7	40	5.7 (14)	1	—	—	—	—	—	—	—	—	—	—	k	—	6	44

Baxter, Jimmy James R., B, 5´7˝/173 lbs; Kenyon; B10/1892, OH, D7/26/1961 Toledo, OH **1923** Rac 1 (0) **1924** Ken 4 (0) **NFL** 5 (0) [2 yrs]

Baxter, Lloyd Lloyd Thomas, C, 6´2˝/210 lbs; Louisiana Tech; SMU; 1945: GB, rnd 24; B1/18/1923 Howe, TX **1948** GB 11 (0)

Bayless, Martin Martin Ashley, DB, 6´2˝/195 lbs; Bowling Green State; 1984: SL, rnd 4; B10/11/1962 Dayton, OH **1984** SL 3 (0) **1984** Buf 13 (1) **1985** Buf 12 (11, FS) **1986** Buf 16 (15, SS) **1987** SD 12 (11, SS) **1988** SD 15 (11, SS) **1989** SD 16 (16, SS) **1990** SD 14 (14, SS) **1991** SD 16 (13, SS) **1992**†KC 16 (16, SS) **1993**†KC 16 (10, SS) **1994** Was 16 (15, SS) **1995**†KC 12 (0) **1996** KC 16 (1) **NFL** 193 (134) [13 yrs]

Bayless, Rick Richard Allen, RB, 6´0˝/202 lbs; Iowa; B10/15/1964 Hugo, MN **1989** Min 1 (0)

Bayless, Tom Thomas McDowell, DT, 6´3˝/240 lbs; Purdue; 1970: NYJ, rnd 15; B12/17/1947 Knob Lick, MO **1970** NYJ 2

Bayley, John John Merrill, T, 5´11˝/180 lbs; Syracuse; B11/10/1903 Massena, NY, D4/5/1969 Massena, NY **1927** NYY 7 (3)

Baylor, John John Martin, DB, 6´0˝/203 lbs; Southern Mississippi; 1988: Ind, rnd 5; B3/5/1965 Meridian, MS **1989** Ind 16 (8, lcb) **1990** Ind 10 (0) **1991** Ind 16 (3) **1992** Ind 16 (15, SS) **1993** Ind 16 (11, SS) **NFL** 74 (37) [5 yrs]

Baylor, Raymond Raymond, DE, 6´5˝/263 lbs; Texas Southern; B3/7/1947 Houston, TX **1974** SD 1

Baylor, Tim Timothy, DB, 6´6˝/195 lbs; Morgan State; 1976: Bal, rnd 10; B3/23/1954 Washington, DC **1976**†Bal 14 **1977**†Bal 13 **1978** Bal 16 **1979** Min 16 **NFL** 59 [4 yrs]

Bayne, Chris Christopher Oliver, DB, 6´1˝/205 lbs; Fresno State; 1997: Atl, rnd 7; B3/22/1975 Riverside, CA **1997** Atl 13 (0) **1998**†Atl 10 (0) **NFL** 23 (0) [2 yrs]

Baynham, Craig Gordon Craig, HB, 6´1˝/204 lbs; Georgia Tech; 1966: Dal, rnd 12/Mia, rnd R9; B7/24/1944 Casper, WY

YEAR	TEAM	G (GS, POS)	RUSH	YD	AVG (LG)	TD	REC	YD	AVG (LG)	TD	PASS	COMP	PCT	YD	AVG (LG)	TD	INT	SK	YD	QBR	KPR	OTD	PTS	TAY
1967	†Dal	14	3	6	2.0 (3)	1	3	13	4.3 (17)	0	—	—	—	—	—	—	—	—	—	—	k	—	6	174
1968	†Dal	14 (8, HB)	103	438	4.3 (22)	5	29	380	13.1 (40)	3	1	0	0.0	0	0.0	0	0	—	—	—	k	—	48	938
1969	Dal	10	3	-2	-0.7 (2)	0	—	—	—	—	—	—	—	—	—	—	—	—	—	—	k	—	0	22
1970	ChiB	5	26	68	2.6 (9)	0	12	43	3.6 (13)	0	—	—	—	—	—	—	—	—	—	—	—	—	0	90
1972	SL	7	17	43	2.5 (11)	0	1	10	10.0 (10)	0	—	—	—	—	—	—	—	—	—	—	—	—	0	48
NFL	5	50 (8)	152	553	3.6 (22)	6	45	446	9.9 (40)	3	1	0	0.0	0	0.0	0	0	—	—	—	k	—	54	1271

Baysinger, Reaves Reaves Henry, E, 6´0˝/180 lbs; Syracuse; B2/22/1902 Akron, OH, D12/4/1994 Hilton, NY **1924** Roc 1 (1)

Baze, Winnie Winford Eason, B, 5´11˝/190 lbs; Schreiner College; Texas Tech; B7/14/1914 Robert Lee, TX

YEAR	TEAM	G (GS, POS)	RUSH	YD	AVG (LG)	TD	REC	YD	AVG (LG)	TD	PASS	COMP	PCT	YD	AVG (LG)	TD	INT	SK	YD	QBR	KPR	OTD	PTS	TAY
1937	Phi	10 (4)	3	14	4.7	0	1	2	2.0 (2)	0	3	0	0.0	0	0.0	0	0	—	—	—	—	—	0	15

Beach, Fred Fred Cantrell, G, /180 lbs; California; B2/8/1897, D9/24/1981 Loma Linda, CA **1926** LA 1 (0)

Beach, Pat Patrick Jesse, TE, 6´4˝/247 lbs; Washington State; 1982: Bal, rnd 6; B12/28/1959 Grants Pass, OR

YEAR	TEAM	G (GS, POS)	RUSH	YD	AVG (LG)	TD	REC	YD	AVG (LG)	TD	PASS	COMP	PCT	YD	AVG (LG)	TD	INT	SK	YD	QBR	KPR	OTD	PTS	TAY
1982	Bal	9 (1)	—	—	—	—	4	45	11.3 (17)	1	—	—	—	—	—	—	—	—	—	—	—	—	6	28
1983	Bal	16 (2)	—	—	—	—	5	56	11.2 (16)	1	—	—	—	—	—	—	—	—	—	—	k	—	6	18
1985	Ind	16 (16, TE)	—	—	—	—	36	376	10.4 (30)	6	—	—	—	—	—	—	—	—	—	—	—	—	36	218
1986	Ind	16 (16, TE)	—	—	—	—	25	265	10.6 (26)	1	—	—	—	—	—	—	—	—	—	—	—	—	6	138
1987	†Ind	12 (12, TE)	—	—	—	—	28	239	8.5 (16)	0	—	—	—	—	—	—	—	—	—	—	—	—	0	120
1988	Ind	16 (16, TE)	—	—	—	—	26	235	9.0 (23)	0	—	—	—	—	—	—	—	—	—	—	k	—	0	138
1989	Ind	16 (13, TE)	—	—	—	—	14	87	6.2 (17)	2	—	—	—	—	—	—	—	—	—	—	—	—	12	54
1990	Ind	12 (11, TE)	—	—	—	—	12	124	10.3 (21)	1	—	—	—	—	—	—	—	—	—	—	—	—	6	67
1991	Ind	16 (10, TE)	—	—	—	—	5	56	11.2 (26)	0	—	—	—	—	—	—	—	—	—	—	—	—	0	28
1992	†Phi	16 (7, te)	—	—	—	—	8	75	9.4 (16)	2	—	—	—	—	—	—	—	—	—	—	—	—	12	48

YEAR	TEAM	G (GS, POS)	RUSH	YD	AVG (LG)	TD	REC	YD	AVG (LG)	TD	PASS	COMP	PCT	YD	AVG (LG)	TD	INT	SK	YD	QBR	KPR	OTD	PTS	TAY
1993	Phx	15(0)	—	—	—	—	—	—	—	—	—	—	—	—	—	—	—	—	—	—	—	—	—	—
NFL	11	160(104)	—	—	—	—	163	1558	9.6(30)	14	—	—	—	—	—	—	—	—	—	—	k	—	84	854

BEACH, SANJAY Sanjay Ragiv, WR, 6´0˝/189 lbs; Colorado State; B2/21/1966 Clark AFB, Phillipines

YEAR	TEAM	G (GS, POS)	RUSH	YD	AVG (LG)	TD	REC	YD	AVG (LG)	TD	PASS	COMP	PCT	YD	AVG (LG)	TD	INT	SK	YD	QBR	KPR	OTD	PTS	TAY
1989	NYJ	1(0)	—	—	—	—	—	—	—	—	—	—	—	—	—	—	—	—	—	—	—	—	—	—
1991	SF	16(0)	—	—	—	—	4	43	10.8(20)	0	—	—	—	—	—	—	—	—	—	—	kp	—	0	32
1992	GB	16(11, WR)	—	—	—	—	17	122	7.2(20)	1	—	—	—	—	—	—	—	—	—	—	—	—	6	66
1993	†SF	9(0)	—	—	—	—	5	59	11.8(20)	1	—	—	—	—	—	—	—	—	—	—	—	—	6	35
NFL	4	42(11)	—	—	—	—	26	224	8.6(20)	2	—	—	—	—	—	—	—	—	—	—	kp	—	12	132

BEACH, WALTER Walter, DB-RB, 6´0˝/190 lbs; Central Michigan; 1960: Oak, rnd 2/NYG, rnd 15; B1/31/1935 Pontiac, MI **1961** Bos-A 12 **1963** Cle 1 **1964**†Cle 14 (RCB) **1965**†Cle 10 (RCB) **1966** Cle 5 (rcb)

YEAR	TEAM	G (GS, POS)	RUSH	YD	AVG (LG)	TD	REC	YD	AVG (LG)	TD	PASS	COMP	PCT	YD	AVG (LG)	TD	INT	SK	YD	QBR	KPR	OTD	PTS	TAY
1960	Bos-A	6	6	-4	-0.7(3)	0	9	132	14.7(51)	1	—	—	—	—	—	—	—	—	—	—	kp	—	6	124
NFL	6	48	6	-4	-0.7(3)	0	9	132	14.7(51)	1	—	—	—	—	—	—	—	—	—	—	kpi	1	12	232

BEAL, NORM Norman Lewis, DB, 5´11˝/170 lbs; Missouri; B6/16/1940 St. Louis, MO **1962** SL 7 (LS)

BEALLES, BILL William John, T, 6´7˝/290 lbs; Northern Illinois; Northen Iowa; B6/11/1963 Steubenville, OH **1987** Mia 3 (3)

BEALS, ALYN Alyn Richard, E-DE, 6´0˝/188 lbs; Santa Clara; 1943: ChiB, rnd 8; B4/27/1921 Marysville, CA, D8/11/1993 Redwood City, CA **[K]**

YEAR	TEAM	G (GS, POS)	RUSH	YD	AVG (LG)	TD	REC	YD	AVG (LG)	TD	PASS	COMP	PCT	YD	AVG (LG)	TD	INT	SK	YD	QBR	KPR	OTD	PTS	TAY
1946	SF-A☆	14(1, le)	2	-7	-3.5	0	**40**	586	14.6	**10**	—	—	—	—	—	—	—	—	—	—	K	—	61	336
1947	SF-A☆	13(9, RE)	5	48	9.6	0	47	655	13.9(54)	**10**	—	—	—	—	—	—	—	—	—	—	i	—	60	421
1948	SF-A☆	14(13, RE)	—	—	—	—	46	591	12.8	**14**	—	—	—	—	—	—	—	—	—	—	—	—	84	366
1949	†SF-A☆	12(8, RE)	4	32	8.0	0	44	678	15.4	**12**	—	—	—	—	—	—	—	—	—	—	K	—	**73**	431
AAFC	4	53(31)	11	73	6.6	0	177	2510	14.2(54)	46	—	—	—	—	—	—	—	—	—	—	Ki	—	278	1553
1950	SF	12(RE)	—	—	—	—	22	315	14.3(38)	3	—	—	—	—	—	—	—	—	—	—	—	—	18	173
1951	SF	12(re)	—	—	—	—	12	126	10.5(22)	0	—	—	—	—	—	—	—	—	—	—	—	—	0	63
NFL	2	24	—	—	—	—	34	441	13.0(54)	3	—	—	—	—	—	—	—	—	—	—	—	—	18	236

BEALS, SHAWN Shawn E., WR, 5´10˝/178 lbs; Idaho State; B8/16/1966 Walnut Creek, CA **1988** Phi 13 (0)

BEAMER, TIM Timothy Carl, DB, 5´11˝/190 lbs; Johnson C. Smith; Illinois; 1971: Buf, rnd 5; B4/6/1948 Galax, VA **1971** Buf 12

BEAMON, AUTRY Autry, DB, 6´1˝/190 lbs; Texas A&M-Commerce; 1975: Min, rnd 12; B11/12/1953 Terrell, TX **1975**†Min 14 **1976**†Min 14 **1977** Sea 14 (9, SS) **1978** Sea 16 (16, SS) **1979** Sea 15 (13, FS) **1980**†Cle 13 (0) **1981** Cle 14 (4) **NFL** 100 (42) [7 yrs]

BEAMON, WILLIE Willie, DB, 5´11˝/184 lbs; Northern Iowa; B6/14/1970 Belle Glade, FL **1993**†NYG 13 (0) **1994** NYG 15 (0) **1995** NYG 16 (0) **1996** NYG 5 (0) **NFL** 49 (0) [4 yrs]

BEAMS, BYRON Byron Donnell, T-DT, 6´6˝/248 lbs; Notre Dame; 1957: LA, rnd 20; B9/8/1929 Konowa, OK, D11/14/1992 **1959** Pit 6 **1960** Pit 3 **1961** Hou-A 7 **NFL** 16 [3 yrs]

BEAN, BUBBA Earnest Ray, RB, 5´11˝/195 lbs; Texas A&M; 1976: Atl, rnd 1; B1/26/1954 Kirbyville, TX

YEAR	TEAM	G (GS, POS)	RUSH	YD	AVG (LG)	TD	REC	YD	AVG (LG)	TD	PASS	COMP	PCT	YD	AVG (LG)	TD	INT	SK	YD	QBR	KPR	OTD	PTS	TAY
1976	Atl	14(4)	124	428	3.5(30)	2	16	148	9.3(50)	1	1	1	100.0	49	49.0(49)	1	0	—	—	—	k	—	18	565
1978	†Atl	15(15, FB)	193	707	3.7(25)	3	31	209	6.7(38)	1	1	0	0.0	0	0.0	0	1	—	—	—	—	—	24	807
1979	Atl	11(11, RB)	88	393	4.5(60)	1	12	137	11.4(49)	0	—	—	—	—	—	—	—	—	—	—	—	—	6	472
NFL	3	40(30)	405	1528	3.8(60)	6	59	494	8.4(50)	2	2	1	50.0	49	24.5(49)	1	1	—	—	—	k	—	48	1843

BEAN, ROBERT Robert D., DB, 5´11˝/178 lbs; Mississippi State; 2000: Cin, rnd 5; B1/6/1978 Atlanta, GA **2000** Cin 12 (4) **2001** Cin 15 (4) **2002** Jax 5 (0) **NFL** 32 (8) [3 yrs]

BEARD, ED Edward Leroy, LB, 6´1˝/226 lbs; Tennessee; 1964: SF, rnd 14/Oak, rnd 20; B12/9/1939 Fredericksburg, VA **1965** SF 12 **1966** SF 12 (12, MLB) **1967** SF 14 (14, MLB) **1968** SF 14 (14, MLB) **1969** SF 3 **1970**†SF 14 **1971**†SF 14 **1972**†SF 14 (mlb) **NFL** 97 (40) [8 yrs]

BEARD, TOM Thomas LeRoy, C, 6´6˝/280 lbs; Michigan State; 1971: Den, rnd 8; B6/10/1948 Findlay, OH **1972** Buf 12

BEASLEY, AARON Aaron Bruce, DB, 6´0˝/205 lbs; West Virginia; 1996: Jax, rnd 3; B7/7/1973 Pottstown, PA **[I]** **1996**†Jax 9 (7, LCB) **1997**†Jax 9 (7, lcb) **1998**†Jax 16 (15, LCB) **1999**†Jax 16 (16, RCB) **2000** Jax 14 (14, RCB) **2001** Jax 12 (12, RCB) **2002**†NYJ 15 (15, RCB) **2003** NYJ 16 (16, RCB) **2004**†Atl 14 (3) **NFL** 121 (105) [9 yrs]

BEASLEY, CHAD Thomas Chad, T, 6´5˝/300 lbs; Virginia Tech; 2002: Min, rnd 7; B11/13/1978 Upper St. Clair, PA **2003** Cle 8 (3)

BEASLEY, FRED Frederick Jerome, FB, 6´0˝/246 lbs; Auburn; 1998: SF, rnd 6; B9/18/1974 Montgomery, AL

YEAR	TEAM	G (GS, POS)	RUSH	YD	AVG (LG)	TD	REC	YD	AVG (LG)	TD	PASS	COMP	PCT	YD	AVG (LG)	TD	INT	SK	YD	QBR	KPR	OTD	PTS	TAY
1998	†SF	16(0)	—	—	—	—	1	11	11.0(11)	0	—	—	—	—	—	—	—	—	—	—	—	—	0	6
1999	SF	13(11, FB)	58	276	4.8(44)	4	32	282	8.8(24)	0	—	—	—	—	—	—	—	—	—	—	—	—	24	457
2000	SF	15(15, FB)	50	147	2.9(9)	3	31	233	7.5(34)	3	—	—	—	—	—	—	—	—	—	—	—	—	36	309
2001	†SF	15(12, FB)	23	73	3.2(16)	1	16	99	6.2(15)	0	—	—	—	—	—	—	—	—	—	—	—	—	6	133
2002	†SF☆	16(14, FB)	26	75	2.9(9)	0	22	152	6.9(25)	1	—	—	—	—	—	—	—	—	—	—	—	—	6	156
2003	SF★	16(11, FB)	17	24	1.4(5)	0	19	184	9.7(32)	1	—	—	—	—	—	—	—	—	—	—	—	—	6	121
2004	SF	14(10, FB)	9	15	1.7(4)	0	10	44	4.4(9)	0	—	—	—	—	—	—	—	—	—	—	—	—	0	37
2005	SF	9(7, FB)	—	—	—	—	2	12	6.0(6)	0	—	—	—	—	—	—	—	—	—	—	—	—	0	6
NFL	8	114(80)	183	610	3.3(44)	8	133	1017	7.6(34)	5	—	—	—	—	—	—	—	—	—	—	—	—	78	1224

BEASLEY, JOHN John H., G, 6´3˝/230 lbs; Earlham; B4/7/1897 Franklin, IN, D11/1964 Franklin, IN **1923** Day 5 (3, RG)

BEASLEY, JOHN John Walter, TE, 6´3˝/228 lbs; California; 1967: Min, rnd 8; B4/6/1945 Pasadena, CA

YEAR	TEAM	G (GS, POS)	RUSH	YD	AVG (LG)	TD	REC	YD	AVG (LG)	TD	PASS	COMP	PCT	YD	AVG (LG)	TD	INT	SK	YD	QBR	KPR	OTD	PTS	TAY
1967	Min	14	—	—	—	—	13	120	9.2(16)	4	—	—	—	—	—	—	—	—	—	—	—	—	24	80
1968	†Min	14(7, te)	—	—	—	—	23	289	12.6(20)	0	—	—	—	—	—	—	—	—	—	—	—	—	0	145
1969	†Min	14(12, TE)	—	—	—	—	33	361	10.9(32)	4	—	—	—	—	—	—	—	—	—	—	—	1	30	201
1970	†Min	14(14, TE)	—	—	—	—	17	237	13.9(40)	2	—	—	—	—	—	—	—	—	—	—	—	—	12	129
1972	Min	14(14, TE)	—	—	—	—	28	232	8.3(18)	1	—	—	—	—	—	—	—	—	—	—	—	—	6	121
1973	Min	5	—	—	—	—	1	3	3.0(0)	1	—	—	—	—	—	—	—	—	—	—	—	—	6	7
1973	NO	8(TE)	—	—	—	—	31	280	9.0(15)	1	—	—	—	—	—	—	—	—	—	—	—	—	6	145
1974	NO	14	—	—	—	—	5	85	17.0(30)	0	—	—	—	—	—	—	—	—	—	—	—	—	0	43
NFL	7	97(47)	—	—	—	—	151	1607	10.6(40)	13	—	—	—	—	—	—	—	—	—	—	—	1	84	869

BEASLEY, TERRY Terry Paul, WR, 5´11˝/186 lbs; Auburn; 1972: SF, rnd 1; B2/5/1950 Montgomery, AL

YEAR	TEAM	G (GS, POS)	RUSH	YD	AVG (LG)	TD	REC	YD	AVG (LG)	TD	PASS	COMP	PCT	YD	AVG (LG)	TD	INT	SK	YD	QBR	KPR	OTD	PTS	TAY
1972	SF	8	—	—	—	—	1	20	20.0(20)	0	—	—	—	—	—	—	—	—	—	—	—	—	0	10
1974	SF	13	1	-3	-3.0(-3)	0	17	253	14.9(68)	3	—	—	—	—	—	—	—	—	—	—	—	—	18	139
1975	SF	8(6, WR)	1	5	5.0(5)	0	20	297	14.9(28)	0	—	—	—	—	—	—	—	—	—	—	—	—	0	154
NFL	3	29(6)	2	2	1.0(5)	0	38	570	15.0(68)	3	—	—	—	—	—	—	—	—	—	—	—	—	18	302

BEASLEY, TOM Thomas Lynn, DE-DT, 6´5˝/253 lbs; Virginia Tech; 1977: Pit, rnd 3; B8/11/1954 Bluefield, WV **1978**†Pit 15 (2) **1979**†Pit 13 (5, lde) **1980** Pit 15 (4) **1981** Pit 13 (9, LDT) **1982** Pit 7 (7, RDE) **1983**†Pit 16 (14, RDE) **1984** Was 13 (3) **1985** Was 12 (0) **1986**†Was 1 (0) **NFL** 105 (44) [9 yrs]

BEATHARD, PETE Peter Frank, QB, 6´1˝/200 lbs; USC; 1964: KC, rnd 1/Det, rnd 1; B3/7/1942 Hermosa Beach, CA

YEAR	TEAM	G (GS, POS)	RUSH	YD	AVG (LG)	TD	REC	YD	AVG (LG)	TD	PASS	COMP	PCT	YD	AVG (LG)	TD	INT	SK	YD	QBR	KPR	OTD	PTS	TAY
1964	KC-A	14	4	43	10.8(41)	0	—	—	—	—	9	4	44.4	50	5.6(22)	1	2	—	—	—	—	—	0	-7
1965	KC-A	14(2)	25	138	5.5(26)	4	—	—	—	—	89	36	40.4	632	7.1(73)	1	6	—	—	—	—	—	26	259
1966	†KC-A	14	20	152	7.6(52)	1	—	—	—	—	90	39	43.3	578	6.4(77)	4	4	—	—	—	—	—	6	311
1967	KC-A	1	—	—	—	—	—	—	—	—	2	0	0.0	0	0.0	0	0	1	14	—	—	—	0	0
1967	†Hou-A	10(QB)	32	133	4.2(23)	1	—	—	—	—	229	94	41.0	1114	4.9(43)	9	14	14	111	44.2	—	—	6	185
1968	Hou-A	9(7, QB)	18	79	4.4(20)	2	—	—	—	—	223	105	47.1	1559	7.0(66)	7	16	14	150	51.0	—	—	12	274
1969	†Hou-A	12(QB)	19	89	4.7(16)	2	—	—	—	—	370	180	48.6	2455	6.6(86)	10	21	22	205	55.6	—	—	12	547
1970	SL	4	2	2	1.0(2)	0	—	—	—	—	17	7	41.2	114	6.7(58)	2	1	—	—	—	—	—	0	29
1971	SL	9(qb)	4	29	7.3(15)	0	—	—	—	—	141	60	42.6	1030	7.3(80)	6	12	6	46	46.7	—	—	0	94
1972	LARm	14	1	-1	-1.0(-1)	0	—	—	—	—	48	19	39.6	255	5.3(33)	1	7	4	34	—	—	—	0	-149
1973	KC	9	6	16	2.7(11)	1	—	—	—	—	64	31	48.4	389	6.1(44)	2	1	9	68	—	—	—	6	191
NFL	10	110(9)	131	680	5.2(52)	11	—	—	—	—	1282	575	44.9	8176	6.4(86)	43	84	70	628	49.9	—	—	68	1733

BEATTIE, BOB Robert Wetherson, T, 6´3˝/230 lbs; Princeton; B10/16/1902 New York, NY, D6/3/1983 Orangeburg, NY **1927** NYY 1 (0) **1929** Ora☆11 (10, RT) **1930** Nwk 5 (1) **NFL** 17 (11) [3 yrs]

YEAR	TEAM	G(GS, POS)	RUSH	YD	AVG(LG)	TD	REC	YD	AVG(LG)	TD	PASS	COMP	PCT	YD	AVG(LG)	TD	INT	SK	YD	QBR	KPR	OTD	PTS	TAY

BEATTY, CHUCK Charles, DB, 6´2˝/200 lbs; North Texas; 1969: Pit, rnd 7; B2/8/1946 Waxahachie, TX **1969** Pit 7 (LS) **1970** Pit 12 (SS) **1971** Pit 3 **1972** Pit 8 **1972** SL 4 **NFL** 34 [4 yrs]

BEATTY, ED Edward Marshall, C-LB, 6´3˝/229 lbs; Mississippi; 1954: LA, rnd 1; B4/6/1932 Clarksdale, MS **1955** SF 9 **1956** SF 12 (MLB) **1957** Pit 12 (C) **1958** Pit 12 (C) **1959** Pit 12 (C) **1960** Pit 12 (C) **1961** Pit 6 **1961** Was 5 **NFL** 80 [7 yrs]

BEAUCHAMP, AL Alfred, LB, 6´2˝/237 lbs; Southern (LA); 1968: Cin, rnd 5; B6/25/1944 Baton Rouge, LA **1968** Cin-A 14 (LLB) **1969** Cin-A 13 (LLB) **1970**†Cin 14 (LLB) **1971** Cin 14 (LLB) **1972** Cin 14 (LLB) **1973**†Cin 14 (LLB) **1974** Cin 14 (LLB) **1975**†Cin 14 (LLB) **1976** SL 14 **NFL** 125 [9 yrs]

BEAUCHAMP, JOE Joseph Scott, DB, 6´0˝/188 lbs; Iowa State; 1966: SD, rnd R6; B4/11/1944 Chicago, IL **[I]** **1966** SD-A 8 (rs) **1967** SD-A 14 (LCB) **1968** SD-A 14 (10, RS) **1969** SD-A 14 (rcb) **1970** SD 13 (RCB) **1971** SD 13 (RCB) **1972** SD 14 (LCB/fs) **1973** SD 9 (FS) **1974** SD 10 (10, FS) **1975** SD 8 (8, LCB) **NFL** 117 (28) [10 yrs]

BEAUDOIN, DOUG Douglas Lee, DB, 6´1˝/193 lbs; Minnesota; 1976: NE, rnd 9; B5/15/1954 Dickinson, ND **1976** NE 9 **1977** NE 11 **1978**†NE 15 (13, SS) **1979** NE 10 (8, SS) **1980** Mia 10 (0) **1981**†SD 4 (0) **NFL** 59 (21) [6 yrs]

BEAUFORD, CLAYTON Clayton Maurice, WR, 5´11˝/190 lbs; Auburn; 1985: Det, rnd 10; B3/1/1963 Palatka, FL **1987** Cle 1 (0)

BEAVER, JIM James Edward, DT, 6´1˝/235 lbs; Florida; 1961: Phi, rnd 8/1962: Buf, rnd 29; B5/18/1938 Miami, FL **1962** Phi 1

BEAVERS, AUBREY Aubrey Tod, LB, 6´3˝/234 lbs; Oklahoma; 1994: Mia, rnd 2; B8/30/1971 Houston, TX **1994**†Mia 16 (10, rlb) **1995**†Mia 16 (1) **1996** NYJ 7 (0) **NFL** 39 (11) [3 yrs]

BEAVERS, SCOTT Scott Travis, G, 6´4˝/277 lbs; Georgia Tech; B2/17/1967 Atlanta, GA **1990** Den 2 (0)

BEBAN, GARY Gary Joseph, QB, 6´1˝/195 lbs; UCLA; 1968: LA, rnd 2; B8/5/1946 San Francisco, CA **1969** Was 1

YEAR	TEAM	G(GS, POS)	RUSH	YD	AVG(LG)	TD	REC	YD	AVG(LG)	TD	PASS	COMP	PCT	YD	AVG(LG)	TD	INT	SK	YD	QBR	KPR	OTD	PTS	TAY
1968	Was	4	5	18	3.6(5)	0	1	12	12.0(12)	0	1	0	0.0	0	0.0	0	0	—	—	—	—	—	0	24
NFL	2	5	5	18	3.6(5)	0	1	12	12.0(12)	0	1	0	0.0	0	0.0	0	0	—	—	—	—	—	0	24

BEBOUT, NICK Nicholas, T, 6´5˝/261 lbs; Wyoming; 1973: Atl, rnd 6; B5/5/1951 Riverton, WY **1973** Atl 13 **1974** Atl 13 **1975** Atl 14 **1976** Sea 14 (13, LT) **1977** Sea 13 (12, LT) **1978** Sea 16 (16, LT) **1979** Sea 13 (13, LT) **1980** Min 1 (0) **NFL** 97 (54) [8 yrs]

BECH, BRETT Brett Lamar, WR, 6´1˝/184 lbs; LSU; B8/20/1971 Slidell, LA

YEAR	TEAM	G(GS, POS)	RUSH	YD	AVG(LG)	TD	REC	YD	AVG(LG)	TD	PASS	COMP	PCT	YD	AVG(LG)	TD	INT	SK	YD	QBR	KPR	OTD	PTS	TAY
1997	NO	10(0)	—	—	—	—	3	50	16.7(22)	0	—	—	—	—	—	—	—	—	—	—	k	—	0	27
1998	NO	16(0)	—	—	—	—	14	264	18.9(72)	3	—	—	—	—	—	—	—	—	—	—	k	—	18	152
1999	NO	8(0)	—	—	—	—	4	65	16.3(23)	1	—	—	—	—	—	—	—	—	—	—	k	—	8	35
NFL	3	34(0)	—	—	—	—	21	379	18.0(72)	4	—	—	—	—	—	—	—	—	—	—	k	—	26	214

BECHT, ANTHONY Anthony, TE, 6´5˝/272 lbs; West Virginia; 2000: NYJ, rnd 1; B8/8/1977 Media, PA

YEAR	TEAM	G(GS, POS)	RUSH	YD	AVG(LG)	TD	REC	YD	AVG(LG)	TD	PASS	COMP	PCT	YD	AVG(LG)	TD	INT	SK	YD	QBR	KPR	OTD	PTS	TAY
2000	NYJ	14(10, TE)	—	—	—	—	16	144	9.0(30)	2	—	—	—	—	—	—	—	—	—	—	k	—	12	52
2001	†NYJ	16(16, TE)	—	—	—	—	36	321	8.9(24)	5	—	—	—	—	—	—	—	—	—	—	—	—	30	186
2002	†NYJ	16(16, TE)	—	—	—	—	28	243	8.7(21)	5	—	—	—	—	—	—	—	—	—	—	—	—	32	147
2003	NYJ	16(16, TE)	—	—	—	—	40	356	8.9(29)	4	—	—	—	—	—	—	—	—	—	—	—	—	26	198
2004	†NYJ	16(16, TE)	—	—	—	—	13	100	7.7(19)	1	—	—	—	—	—	—	—	—	—	—	—	—	6	55
2005	†TB	16(16, TE)	—	—	—	—	16	112	7.0(17)	0	—	—	—	—	—	—	—	—	—	—	—	—	0	56
NFL	6	94(90)	—	—	—	—	149	1276	8.6(30)	17	—	—	—	—	—	—	—	—	—	—	k	—	106	693

BECHTOL, HUB Hubert E., E, 6´3˝/202 lbs; Texas; Texas Tech; 1947: Mia-A, rnd 2/Pit, rnd 1; B4/20/1926 Amarillo, TX **1949** Bal-A 12 (2)

YEAR	TEAM	G(GS, POS)	RUSH	YD	AVG(LG)	TD	REC	YD	AVG(LG)	TD	PASS	COMP	PCT	YD	AVG(LG)	TD	INT	SK	YD	QBR	KPR	OTD	PTS	TAY
1947	Bal-A	14(12, LE)	2	-1	-0.5	0	17	167	9.8	1	—	—	—	—	—	—	—	—	—	—	ki	—	6	88
1948	Bal-A	12(0)	—	—	—	—	2	25	12.5	0	—	—	—	—	—	—	—	—	—	—	—	—	0	17
AAFC	3	38(14)	2	-1	-0.5	0	19	192	10.1	1	—	—	—	—	—	—	—	—	—	—	ki	—	6	105

BECK, BRADEN Braden William, K, 6´2˝/200 lbs; Stanford; 1965: Hou, rnd 19; B1/12/1944 Oakland, CA **[K]** **1971** Hou 2

BECK, CARL Carl, T-G, 5´11˝/195 lbs; Bucknell; Lafayette; West Virginia; B1900 Harrisburg, PA, deceased **1921** Buf 6 (3)

BECK, CLARENCE Clarence R., T-G, 5´11˝/200 lbs; Penn State; B10/3/1894 Harrisburg, PA, D10/1970 Grampian, PA **1925** Pot 7 (3)

BECK, KEN Kenneth L., DT-DE, 6´2˝/245 lbs; Texas A&M; 1959: ChiC, rnd 4; B9/3/1935 Minden, LA **1959** GB 12 **1960**†GB 12 **NFL** 24 [2 yrs]

BECK, MARTY Martin J., B, 5´9˝/175 lbs; none; B1/2/1900 New York, NY, D6/15/1968 New York, NY **1921** Akr 8 (2) **1922** Akr 1 (1) **1924** Akr 1 (0) **1926** Akr 1 (0) **NFL** 11 (3) [4 yrs]

BECK, RAY Ray Merrill, G, 6´2˝/224 lbs; Georgia Tech; 1952: NYG, rnd 2; B3/7/1931 Bowden, GA **1952** NYG 12 (LG) **1955** NYG 12 **1956**†NYG 10 **1957** NYG 12 **NFL** 46 [4 yrs]

BECKER, DAVE David Paul, DB, 6´2˝/190 lbs; Iowa; 1979: Chi, rnd 12; B1/15/1957 Atlantic, IA **1980** ChiB 11 (0)

BECKER, DOUG Douglas James, LB, 6´0˝/220 lbs; Notre Dame; 1978: Pit, rnd 10; B6/27/1956 Hamilton, OH **1978** ChiB 1 **1978** Buf 8 **NFL** 9 [1 yr]

BECKER, JOHNNIE John W., T-G-B, 5´11˝/208 lbs; Dayton; Denison; B2/10/1903, D9/17/1947 **1926** Day 6 (1) **1927** Day 7 (7, RT) **1928** Day 5 (5, RT) **1929** Day 1 (0) **NFL** 19 (13) [4 yrs]

BECKER, KURT Kurt Frank, G, 6´5˝/271 lbs; Michigan; 1982: Chi, rnd 6; B12/22/1958 Aurora, IL **1982** ChiB 5 (0) **1983** ChiB 16 (14, RG) **1984**†ChiB 16 (16, RG) **1985** ChiB 3 (3) **1986**†ChiB 14 (1) **1987**†ChiB 12 (1) **1988**†ChiB 16 (0) **1989**†LARm 2 (0) **1990**†ChiB 10 (0) **NFL** 94 (35) [9 yrs]

BECKER, WAYLAND Wayland Herman, E, 6´0˝/198 lbs; Marquette; B11/2/1910 Soperton, WI, D12/1984 Lena, WI

YEAR	TEAM	G(GS, POS)	RUSH	YD	AVG(LG)	TD	REC	YD	AVG(LG)	TD	PASS	COMP	PCT	YD	AVG(LG)	TD	INT	SK	YD	QBR	KPR	OTD	PTS	TAY
1934	ChiB	2(1)	—	—	—	—	1	18	18.0(18)	0	—	—	—	—	—	—	—	—	—	—	—	—	0	9
1934	Bkn	9(8, RE)	—	—	—	—	3	28	9.3	0	—	—	—	—	—	—	—	—	—	—	—	—	0	14
1935	Bkn	11(6, re)	1	-3	-3.0(-3)	0	10	131	13.1	1	4	3	75.0	37	9.3	0	0	—	—	—	—	—	6	86
1936	GB	9(7, le)	—	—	—	—	5	66	13.2	1	—	—	—	—	—	—	—	—	—	—	—	—	6	38
1937	GB	10(6, le)	2	5	2.5	0	2	13	6.5(11)	0	—	—	—	—	—	—	—	—	—	—	—	—	0	12
1938	†GB	11(4)	—	—	—	—	7	166	23.7(49)	0	—	—	—	—	—	—	—	—	—	—	—	—	0	83
1939	Pit	2(1)	—	—	—	—	—	—	—	—	—	—	—	—	—	—	—	—	—	—	—	—	—	—
NFL	6	54(33)	3	2	0.7	0	28	422	15.1(49)	2	4	3	75.0	37	9.3	0	0	—	—	—	—	—	12	242

BECKETT, JACK John Wesley, T, 6´1˝/200 lbs; Oregon; B1/5/1892 Eight Mile, OR, D7/26/1981 San Diego, CA **1920** Buf 2 (1) **1922** Col 1 (1) **NFL** 3 (2) [2 yrs]

BECKETT, ROGERS Rogers, DB, 6´2˝/207 lbs; Marshall; 2000: SD, rnd 2; B1/31/1977 Apopka, FL **2000** SD 16 (3) **2001** SD 16 (16, FS) **2002** SD 16 (10, FS) **2003** Cin 16 (9, SS) **2004** Cin 7 (5, ss) **NFL** 71 (43) [5 yrs]

BECKHAM, TONY Antonio Dwight, DB, 6´1˝/187 lbs; Wisconsin-Stout; 2002: Ten, rnd 4; B10/1/1978 Gainesville, FL **2002**†Ten 14 (0) **2003**†Ten 16 (3) **2004** Ten 5 (1) **2005** Ten 15 (2) **NFL** 50 (6) [4 yrs]

BECKLES, IAN Ian Harold, G, 6´1˝/300 lbs; Indiana; 1990: TB, rnd 5; B7/20/1967 Montreal, Canada **1990** TB 16 (16, RG) **1991** TB 16 (16, RG) **1992** TB 11 (7, RG) **1993** TB 14 (14, RG) **1994** TB 16 (16, RG) **1995** TB 15 (15, RG) **1996** TB 14 (14, RG) **1997** Phi 9 (8, RG) **1998** Phi 16 (16, RG) **NFL** 127 (122) [9 yrs]

BECKLEY, ART Arthur K., B, 5´10˝/180 lbs; Michigan State; B9/1/1901, D1965, **[K]** **1926** Day 6 (5, TB), 3

BECKMAN, BRAD Bradley Scott, TE, 6´3˝/236 lbs; Nebraska-Omaha; 1988: Min, rnd 7; B12/31/1964 Lincoln, NE, D12/18/1989 Suwanee, GA **1988** NYG 9 (0)

YEAR	TEAM	G(GS, POS)	RUSH	YD	AVG(LG)	TD	REC	YD	AVG(LG)	TD	PASS	COMP	PCT	YD	AVG(LG)	TD	INT	SK	YD	QBR	KPR	OTD	PTS	TAY
1989	Atl	15(2)	—	—	—	—	11	102	9.3(21)	1	—	—	—	—	—	—	—	—	—	—	k	—	6	41
NFL	2	24(2)	—	—	—	—	11	102	9.3(21)	1	—	—	—	—	—	—	—	—	—	—	k	—	6	33

BECKMAN, ED Edwin Jay, TE, 6´4˝/229 lbs; Florida State; B1/2/1955 Key West, FL **1978** KC 16 **1980** KC 16 (0) **1981** KC 15 (0) **1982** KC 9 (0)

YEAR	TEAM	G(GS, POS)	RUSH	YD	AVG(LG)	TD	REC	YD	AVG(LG)	TD	PASS	COMP	PCT	YD	AVG(LG)	TD	INT	SK	YD	QBR	KPR	OTD	PTS	TAY
1977	KC	14(1)	—	—	—	—	1	3	3.0(3)	0	—	—	—	—	—	—	—	—	—	—	—	—	0	2
1979	KC	9(2)	—	—	—	—	2	21	10.5(12)	0	—	—	—	—	—	—	—	—	—	—	—	—	0	11
1983	KC	15(7, te)	—	—	—	—	13	130	10.0(20)	0	—	—	—	—	—	—	—	—	—	—	—	—	0	65
1984	KC	13(1)	—	—	—	—	7	44	6.3(9)	1	—	—	—	—	—	—	—	—	—	—	—	—	6	27
NFL	8	107(11)	—	—	—	—	23	198	8.6(20)	1	—	—	—	—	—	—	—	—	—	—	k	—	8	126

BECKMAN, TOM Thomas Clare, DE, 6´5˝/250 lbs; Michigan; 1972: SL, rnd 3; B9/21/1950 Saginaw, MI **1972** SL 2

BECKWITH, JOHN John C., HB, /150 lbs; none; B1895, OH, deceased **1920** Col 3 (0)

BEDELL, BRAD Brad, T, 6´4˝/306 lbs; Colorado; 2000: Cle, rnd 6; B2/12/1977 Arcadia, CA **2000** Cle 12 (0) **2001** Cle 15 (4) **2004** GB 4 (0) **NFL** 31 (4) [3 yrs]

BEDFORD, GENE William Eugene, E, 5´9˝/165 lbs; Centre; SMU; B12/2/1896 Dallas, TX, D10/6/1977 San Antonio, TX **1925** Roc 2 (2) **1926** Ham 1 (0) **NFL** 3 (2) [2 yrs]

YEAR	TEAM	G (GS, POS)	RUSH	YD	AVG (LG)	TD	REC	YD	AVG (LG)	TD	PASS	COMP	PCT	YD	AVG (LG)	TD	INT	SK	YD	QBR	KPR	OTD	PTS	TAY

BEDFORD, VANCE Vance Juano, DB, 5´11˝/170 lbs; Texas; 1982: SL, rnd 5; B8/20/1958 Beaumont, TX   **1982**†SL 0 (0)

BEDNARIK, CHUCK Charles Phillip 'Concrete Charlie', LB-C, 6´3˝/233 lbs; Pennsylvania; 1949: Phi, rnd B1/Bkn-A, rnd S1; B5/1/1925 Bethlehem, PA; HOF 1967 **[I]**
1949†Phi 10 (7, C) **1950** Phi★12 (RLB) **1951** Phi★12 (RLB) **1952** Phi★12 (RLB) **1953** Phi★12 (RLB) **1954** Phi★12 (C/RLB) **1955** Phi☆12 (RLB) **1956** Phi★12 (RLB)
1957 Phi★11 (LLB) **1958** Phi 12 (C) **1959** Phi 12 (C) **1960**†Phi★12 (C) **1961** Phi☆14 (C/llb) **1962** Phi 14 (MLB) **NFL** 169 (7) [14 yrs]

BEDNER, AL Albert Leon, G-T, 5´10˝/195 lbs; Lafayette; B7/9/1898 Wilkes-Barre, PA, D7/12/1988 Wilkes-Barre, PA   **1924** Fra 6 (0) **1925** NYG 9 (2) **1926** NYG 8 (0)
NFL 23 (2) [3 yrs]

BEDORE, TOM Thomas, G-LB, 5´11˝/193 lbs; Pepperdine; B11/17/1925 Faust, NY   **1944** Was 2 (0)

BEDSOLE, HAL Harold Jay, TE, 6´5˝/236 lbs; USC; 1964: Min, rnd 2/KC, rnd 8; B12/21/1941 Chicago, IL
1964	Min	14 (12, TE)	—	—	—	—	18	295	16.4 (43)	5	—	—	—	—	—	—	—	—	—	—	—	—	30	173
1965	Min	9	—	—	—	—	8	123	15.4 (36)	3	—	—	—	—	—	—	—	—	—	—	—	—	18	77
1966	Min	1	—	—	—	—	—	—	—	—	—	—	—	—	—	—	—	—	—	—	—	—	—	—
NFL		3	24 (12)	—	—	—	—	26	418	16.1 (43)	8	—	—	—	—	—	—	—	—	—	—	—	—	48	249

BEEBE, DON Donald Lee, WR, 5´11˝/185 lbs; Western Illinois; Aurora; Chadron State; 1989: Buf, rnd 3; B12/18/1964 Aurora, IL **[R]**
1989	†Buf	14 (0)	—	—	—	—	17	317	18.6 (63)	2	—	—	—	—	—	—	—	—	—	k	—	—	12	282
1990	Buf	12 (4)	1	23	23.0 (23)	0	11	221	20.1 (49)	1	—	—	—	—	—	—	—	—	—	k	—	—	6	168
1991	†Buf	11 (7, WR)	—	—	—	—	32	414	12.9 (34)	6	—	—	—	—	—	—	—	—	—	k	—	—	36	253
1992	†Buf	12 (8, WR)	1	-6	-6.0 (-6)	0	33	554	16.8 (65)	2	—	—	—	—	—	—	—	—	—	k	—	—	12	281
1993	†Buf	14 (14, WR)	—	—	—	—	31	504	16.3 (65)	3	—	—	—	—	—	—	—	—	—	k	—	—	18	277
1994	Buf	13 (11, WR)	2	11	5.5 (6)	0	40	527	13.2 (72)	4	—	—	—	—	—	—	—	—	—	k	—	—	24	345
1995	Car	14 (1)	—	—	—	—	14	152	10.9 (24)	1	—	—	—	—	—	—	—	—	—	k	—	—	6	161
1996	†GB	16 (6, wr)	—	—	—	—	39	699	17.9 (80)	4	—	—	—	—	—	—	—	—	—	k	2	—	36	558
1997	GB	10 (0)	—	—	—	—	2	28	14.0 (23)	0	—	—	—	—	—	—	—	—	—	k	—	—	0	58
NFL	9	116 (51)	4	28	7.0 (23)	0	219	3416	15.6 (80)	23	—	—	—	—	—	—	—	—	—	k	2	—	150	2381

BEEBE, KEITH William Keith, B, 5´9˝/180 lbs; Occidental; 1943: NYG, rnd 24; B3/16/1921 Anaheim, CA, D7/13/1998 Philadelphia, PA
| **1944** | NYG | 5 (0) | 8 | 12 | 1.5 (7) | 0 | — | — | — | — | 3 | 1 | 33.3 | 9 | 3.0 (9) | 0 | 1 | — | — | Pi | — | — | 0 | -13 |

BEECHAM, EARL Eral, RB, 5´8˝/180 lbs; Bucknell; B9/8/1965 Brooklyn, NY
| **1987** | NYG | 1 (0) | 5 | 22 | 4.4 (10) | 0 | — | — | — | — | — | — | — | — | — | — | — | — | — | k | — | — | 0 | 47 |

BEECHER, WILLIE William Wiegel, K, 5´10˝/170 lbs; Utah State; B4/14/1963 El Paso, TX **[K]**   **1987** Mia 3 (0)

BEEDE, FRANK Frank McNulty, G-C, 6´4˝/282 lbs; Panhandle State (OK); B5/1/1973 Antioch, CA   **1996** Sea 14 (2) **1997** Sea 16 (6, rg) **1999**†Sea 10 (0) **2000** Sea 7 (0)
NFL 47 (8) [4 yrs]

BEEKLEY, BRUCE Bruce Edward, LB, 6´2˝/225 lbs; Oregon; 1979: Atl, rnd 10; B12/15/1956 Cincinnati, OH   **1980** GB 15 (3)

BEEKLEY, FERRIS Ferris Eugene, B-G, 5´8˝/185 lbs; Miami (OH); B2/27/1897 Butler County, OH, D6/15/1986 Cincinnati, OH   **1921** Cin 2 (2, LH)

BEEMER, BOB Robert Lester, DE, 6´3˝/231 lbs; Toledo; B5/14/1963 Jackson, MI   **1987** Det 2 (0)

BEER, TOM Thomas John, TE-G, 6´4˝/235 lbs; Detroit Mercy; Houston; 1967: Den, rnd 2; B12/21/1944 Detroit, MI
1967	Den-A	14 (TE)	—	—	—	—	11	155	14.1 (29)	0	—	—	—	—	—	—	—	—	—	k	—	—	0	73
1968	Den-A	14 (TE)	—	—	—	—	20	276	13.8 (31)	1	—	—	—	—	—	—	—	—	—	—	—	—	6	143
1969	Den-A	9 (8, TE)	—	—	—	—	9	200	22.2 (48)	0	—	—	—	—	—	—	—	—	—	—	—	—	0	100
1970	Bos	14 (4)	—	—	—	—	11	150	13.6 (25)	0	—	—	—	—	—	—	—	—	—	—	—	—	0	64
1971	NE	14 (8, TE)	—	—	—	—	12	191	15.9 (31)	3	—	—	—	—	—	—	—	—	—	k	—	—	18	111
1972	NE	14	—	—	—	—	2	40	20.0 (21)	0	—	—	—	—	—	—	—	—	—	—	—	—	0	20
NFL	6	79 (20)	—	—	—	—	65	1012	15.6 (48)	4	—	—	—	—	—	—	—	—	—	k	—	—	24	510

BEER, TOM Thomas E., LB-RB, 6´1˝/221 lbs; Saginaw Valley State; Wayne State (MI); 1994: Det, rnd 7; B3/27/1969 Bay Port, MI   **1994** Det 9 (0) **1995**†Det 16 (0) **1996** Det 16 (1)
NFL 41 (1) [3 yrs]

BEESON, TERRY Terry Eugene, LB, 6´3˝/240 lbs; Kansas; 1977: Sea, rnd 2; B9/19/1955 Coffeyville, KS   **1977** Sea 14 (13, MLB) **1978** Sea 16 (16, MLB) **1979** Sea 16 (16, MLB)
1980 Sea 16 (16, MLB) **1981** Sea 15 (7, mlb) **1982** SF 5 (0) **NFL** 82 (68) [6 yrs]

BEHAN, CHARLIE Charles Edward, E, 6´3˝/195 lbs; Northern Illinois; B8/4/1920 Crystal Lake, IL, D5/18/1945 Okinawa
| **1942** | Det | 9 (0) | — | — | — | — | 4 | 63 | 15.8 (25) | 0 | — | — | — | — | — | — | — | — | — | — | — | — | 0 | 32 |

BEHMAN, BULL Russell K., T-G, 5´10˝/215 lbs; Lebanon Valley; Dickinson; B1/15/1900 Steelton, PA, D3/24/1950 Harrisburg, PA **[KC]**   **1924** Fra 14 (12, RG)
1925 Fra 16 (15, LT), 39 **1927** Fra 11 (11, RT) **1928** Fra☆16 (15, LT) **1929** Fra☆18 (15, LT) **1930** Fra 7 (1) **1931** Fra 8 (6, RT) **NFL** 90 (75) [7 yrs]

BEHNING, MARK Mark Gerald, T, 6´6˝/290 lbs; Nebraska; 1985: Pit, rnd 2; B9/26/1961 Alpena, MI   **1986** Pit 16 (1)

BEHRMAN, DAVE David Wesley, C-T, 6´5˝/260 lbs; Michigan State; 1963: Buf, rnd 1/Chi, rnd 1; B11/9/1941 Dowagiac, MI   **1963**†Buf-A 14 **1965** Buf-A◇14 (C) **1967** Den-A 11
NFL 39 [3 yrs]

BEIER, TOM Thomas Eugene, DB, 5´11˝/195 lbs; Detroit Mercy; Miami (FL); 1967: Mia, rnd 10; B6/23/1945 Fremont, OH   **1969** Mia-A 14 (7, LS)
| **1967** | Mia-A | 14 | — | — | — | — | 1 | 19 | 19.0 (19) | 0 | — | — | — | — | — | — | — | — | — | i | — | — | 0 | 12 |
| **NFL** | 2 | 28 (7) | — | — | — | — | 1 | 19 | 19.0 (19) | 0 | — | — | — | — | — | — | — | — | — | kpi | — | — | 0 | -6 |

BEIL, LARRY Lawrence J., T, 6´2˝/235 lbs; Portland; B8/31/1921, D1/1986   **1948** NYG 9 (0)

BEINOR, ED Joseph Edward, T-DE, 6´2˝/222 lbs; Notre Dame; 1939: Bkn, rnd 6; B11/16/1917 Harvey, IL, D1/6/1991 Edwardsville, IL   **1940** ChiC 11 (7, LT) **1941** ChiC 8 (3)
1941 Was 3 (0) **1942**†Was◇11 (3) **NFL** 33 (13) [3 yrs]

BEIRNE, JIM James Patrick, WR-TE, 6´2˝/206 lbs; Purdue; 1968: Hou, rnd 4; B10/15/1946 McKeesport, PA
1968	Hou-A	14 (WR)	1	3	3.0 (3)	0	31	474	15.3 (66)	4	—	—	—	—	—	—	—	—	—	—	—	—	24	260
1969	†Hou-A◇	14 (WR)	—	—	—	—	42	540	12.9 (37)	4	—	—	—	—	—	—	—	—	—	—	—	—	26	290
1970	Hou	14 (wr)	—	—	—	—	16	216	13.5 (25)	1	—	—	—	—	—	—	—	—	—	—	—	—	6	109
1971	Hou	14 (WR)	—	—	—	—	38	550	14.5 (40)	1	—	—	—	—	—	—	—	—	—	p	—	—	6	280
1972	Hou	10	—	—	—	—	7	95	13.6 (19)	1	—	—	—	—	—	—	—	—	—	—	—	—	6	53
1973	Hou	1	—	—	—	—	—	—	—	—	—	—	—	—	—	—	—	—	—	—	—	—	—	—
1974	SD	14	—	—	—	—	7	121	17.3 (26)	0	—	—	—	—	—	—	—	—	—	p	—	—	0	63
1975	Hou	6	—	—	—	—	1	15	15.0 (15)	0	—	—	—	—	—	—	—	—	—	—	—	—	0	8
1976	Hou	7	—	—	—	—	—	—	—	—	—	—	—	—	—	—	—	—	—	—	—	—	0	-3
NFL	9	94	1	3	3.0 (3)	0	142	2011	14.2 (66)	11	—	—	—	—	—	—	—	—	—	kp	—	—	68	1059

BEISEL, MONTY Monty Gene, LB, 6´3˝/254 lbs; Kansas State; 2001: KC, rnd 4; B8/20/1978 Douglass, KS   **2001** KC 16 (0) **2002** KC 16 (0) **2003**†KC 12 (0)
2004 KC 11 (9, mlb/rolb) **2005**†NE 15 (6, lilb) **NFL** 70 (15) [5 yrs]

BEISLER, RANDY Randall Lee, G-DT-DE-T, 6´5˝/250 lbs; Indiana; 1966: Phi, rnd 1; B10/24/1944 Gary, IN   **1966** Phi 14 (4) **1967** Phi 14 **1968** Phi 8 (8, LDT) **1969** SF 14
1970†SF 14 (LG) **1971**†SF 14 (14, LG) **1972**†SF 14 (14, LG) **1973** SF 14 (7, lg) **1974** SF 9 **1975** KC 3 (2) **NFL** 118 (49) [10 yrs]

BELANICH, BILL Frank William, T-E, 6´0˝/205 lbs; Dayton; B5/19/1903 Euclid, OH, D8/12/1960   **1927** Day 8 (8, LT), 6 **1928** Day 7 (7, LT) **1929** Day 4 (3, LT) **NFL** 19 (18) [3 yrs]

BELCHER, KEVIN Kevin, C-G, 6´3˝/270 lbs; Texas-El Paso; 1983: NYG, rnd 6; B2/23/1961 Detroit, MI, D6/28/2003 El Paso, TX   **1983** NYG 16 (0)
| **1984** | †NYG | 16 (16, C) | — | — | — | — | 1 | 4 | 4.0 (4) | 0 | — | — | — | — | — | — | — | — | — | — | — | — | 0 | 2 |
| **NFL** | 2 | 32 (16) | — | — | — | — | 1 | 4 | 4.0 (4) | 0 | — | — | — | — | — | — | — | — | — | — | — | — | 0 | 2 |

BELCHER, KEVIN Kevin Leander, T, 6´6˝/310 lbs; Wisconsin; 1985: LARd, rnd 7; B11/9/1961 Bridgeport, CT, D4/12/1997 Howard, WI   **1985** LARd 4 (0) **1987** Den 1 (1)
NFL 5 (1) [2 yrs]

BELDEN, BUNNY Charles C., B, 5´8˝/173 lbs; St. Mary's (CA); B12/7/1900 Chicago, IL, D11/1976 Skokie, IL   **1927** Dul 6 (1) **1930** ChiC 12 (7, TB), 18 **1931** ChiC 8 (0), 12
NFL 26 (8), 30 [3 yrs]

BELDING, LES Lester Coit, E-B, 5´11˝/195 lbs; Upper Iowa; Iowa; B12/5/1900 Mason City, IA, D1965   **1925** RI 1 (0)

YEAR	TEAM	G (GS, POS)	RUSH	YD	AVG (LG)	TD	REC	YD	AVG (LG)	TD	PASS COMP	PCT	YD	AVG (LG)	TD	INT	SK	YD	QBR	KPR	OTD	PTS	TAY

BELICHICK, STEVE Stephen Nicholas, FB, 5´9˝/190 lbs; Case Western Reserve; B1/7/1919 Monessen, PA, D11/19/2005 Annapolis, MD

| 1941 | Det | 6(3) | 28 | 118 | 4.2(11) | 2 | 1 | 13 | 13.0(13) | 0 | — | — | — | — | — | — | — | — | — | kpi | 1 | 18 | 253 |

BELIN, CHUCK Charles Edward, G, 6´2˝/305 lbs; Wisconsin; 1993: LARm, rnd 5; B10/27/1970 Milwaukee, WI **1994** LARm 14 (6, lg) **1995** SL 6 (0) **1996** SL 2 (0) **NFL** 22 (6) [3 yrs]

BELK, BILL William Arthur, DE-DT, 6´3˝/253 lbs; Maryland-Eastern Shore; 1968: SF, rnd 6; B2/19/1946 Lancaster, SC **1968** SF 10 (4) **1969** SF 14 (12, RDE) **1970**†SF 14 (RDE) **1971**†SF 8 **1972** SF 14 **1973** SF 13 **1974** SF 14 (LDT) **NFL** 87 (16) [7 yrs]

BELK, ROCKY Anthony Lovett, WR, 6´0˝/187 lbs; Miami (FL); 1983: Cle, rnd 7; B6/20/1960 Alexandria, VA

| 1983 | Cle | 10(0) | 1 | -5 | -5.0(-5) | 0 | 5 | 141 | 28.2(64) | 2 | — | — | — | — | — | — | — | — | — | — | 12 | 76 |

BELK, VENO Veno Luzon, TE, 6´3˝/233 lbs; Michigan State; B3/7/1963 Tifton, GA

| 1987 | Buf | 2(2) | — | — | — | — | 1 | 7 | 7.0(7) | 0 | — | — | — | — | — | — | — | — | — | — | 0 | 4 |

BELL, ALBERT Albert, WR, 6´0˝/170 lbs; Alabama; B4/23/1964 Birmingham, AL **1988** GB 5 (0)

BELL, ANTHONY Anthony Dewitt, LB, 6´3˝/235 lbs; Michigan State; 1986: SL, rnd 1; B7/2/1964 Miami, FL **1986** SL 16 (1) **1987** SL 12 (12, LLB) **1988** Phx 16 (16, LLB) **1989** Phx 16 (15, LLB) **1990** Phx 16 (16, LOLB) **1991**†Det 10 (0) **1992** LARd 16 (5, mlb) **NFL** 102 (65) [7 yrs]

BELL, BILL William Stephen, K, 6´0˝/192 lbs; Kansas; 1970: Atl, rnd 17; B12/9/1947 Fort Knox, KY [K] **1971** Atl 14 **1973** NE 3

| 1972 | Atl | 14 | 1 | -3 | -3.0(-3) | 0 | — | — | — | — | — | — | — | — | — | — | — | — | K | — | 79 | -3 |
| NFL | 3 | 31 | 1 | -3 | -3.0(-3) | 0 | — | — | — | — | — | — | — | — | — | — | — | — | KP | — | 154 | -3 |

BELL, BILLY Billy Ray, DB, 5´10˝/170 lbs; Lamar; B1/16/1961 Dayton, TX **1989** Hou 4 (0) **1991** KC 8 (1) **NFL** 12 (1) [2 yrs]

BELL, BOB Robert Francis, DT-DE, 6´4˝/250 lbs; Cincinnati; 1971: Det, rnd 1; B1/25/1948 Philadelphia, PA **1971** Det 14 **1972** Det 14 (RDT) **1973** Det 13 (RDT) **1974**†SL 9 **1975**†SL 14 (13, LDE) **1976** SL 14 (RDE) **1977** SL 7 **1978** SL 15 **NFL** 100 (13) [8 yrs]

BELL, BOBBY Robert Lee, LB-DE, 6´4˝/228 lbs; Minnesota; 1963: KC, rnd 7/Min, rnd 2; B6/17/1940 Shelby, NC; HOF 1983 [I] **1963** KC-A 14 (LDE) **1964** KC-A★14 (LDE) **1965** KC-A★14 (LLB) **1966**†KC-A★14 (LLB) **1967** KC-A★14 (LLB) **1968**†KC-A★14 (LLB) **1969**†KC★14 (LLB) **1970** KC★14 (LLB) **1971**†KC★14 (LLB) **1972** KC★14 (LLB) **1973** KC 14 (LLB) **1974** KC 14 (LLB) **NFL** 168 [12 yrs]

BELL, BOBBY Bobby Lee, LB, 6´3˝/217 lbs; Missouri; 1984: NYJ, rnd 4; B2/7/1962 St. Paul, MN **1984** NYJ 15 (2) **1987** ChiB 3 (3) **NFL** 18 (5) [2 yrs]

BELL, CARLOS Carlos R., TE, 6´5˝/238 lbs; Houston; 1971: NO, rnd 4; B9/21/1947 Clinton, OK **1971** NO 1

BELL, COLEMAN Coleman Bernard, TE, 6´2˝/243 lbs; Miami (FL); B4/22/1970 Tampa, FL

| 1995 | Was | 11(1) | — | — | — | — | 14 | 164 | 11.9(29) | 0 | — | — | — | — | — | — | — | — | — | — | 6 | 88 |

BELL, ED Edward, G-T, 6´1˝/227 lbs; Indiana; B9/20/1921 Chicago, IL, D12/6/1990 South Bend, IN **1946** Mia-A 7 (0) **1947** GB 11 (1) **1948** GB 12 (0) **1949** GB 12 (0) **NFL** 35 (1) [3 yrs]

BELL, EDDIE Edward B., DB-LB, 6´1˝/212 lbs; Pennsylvania; 1953: Phi, rnd 5; B3/25/1931 Philadelphia, PA **1955** Phi 12 (DB) **1956** Phi 12 (DB) **1957** Phi 12 (DB) **1958** Phi 12 (DB) **1960** NYT-A 14 (RLB) **NFL** 62 [5 yrs]

BELL, EDDIE Edward Allen, WR, 5´10˝/160 lbs; Idaho State; 1970: NYJ, rnd 9; B9/13/1946 Waco, TX

1970	NYJ	14	2	-7	-3.5(0)	0	21	246	11.7(26)	2	1	0	0.0	0	0.0	0	1	—	—	kp	—	12	100
1971	NYJ	14	—	—	—	—	5	110	22.0(31)	1	—	—	—	—	—	—	—	—	—	p	—	6	52
1972	NYJ	13(WR)	1	-5	-5.0(-5)	0	35	629	18.0(83)	2	—	—	—	—	—	—	—	—	—	—	12	320
1973	NYJ	13(WR)	—	—	—	—	24	319	13.3(38)	2	—	—	—	—	—	—	—	—	—	—	12	170
1974	NYJ	13	—	—	—	—	13	126	9.7(22)	1	—	—	—	—	—	—	—	—	—	—	6	68
1975	NYJ	14(WR)	—	—	—	—	20	344	17.2(38)	4	—	—	—	—	—	—	—	—	—	p	—	24	224
1976	SD	5	—	—	—	—	—	—	—	—	—	—	—	—	—	—	—	—	—	kp	—	0	-1
NFL	7	86	3	-12	-4.0	0	118	1774	15.0(83)	12	1	0	0.0	0	0.0	0	1	—	—	kp	—	72	932

BELL, GORDON Gordon Granville, RB, 5´9˝/180 lbs; Michigan; 1976: NYG, rnd 4; B12/25/1953 Troy, OH

1976	NYG	14	67	233	3.5(26)	2	25	198	7.9(20)	0	—	—	—	—	—	—	—	—	kp	—	12	430
1977	NYG	10	16	63	3.9(13)	0	4	33	8.3(12)	0	—	—	—	—	—	—	—	—	kp	—	0	130
1978	SL	6	7	23	3.3(9)	0	3	28	9.3(17)	0	—	—	—	—	—	—	—	—	kp	—	0	125
NFL	3	30	90	319	3.5(26)	2	32	259	8.1(20)	0	—	—	—	—	—	—	—	—	kp	—	12	685

BELL, GREG Gregory Leon, RB, 5´10˝/210 lbs; Notre Dame; 1984: Buf, rnd 1; B8/1/1962 Columbus, OH

1984	Buf◊	16(15, RB)	262	1100	4.2(85)	7	34	277	8.1(37)	1	—	—	—	—	—	—	—	—	—	k	—	48	1314
1985	Buf	16(15, FB/rb)	223	883	4.0(77)	8	58	.576	9.9(49)	1	1	0	0.0	0	0.0	0	—	—	—	—	54	1256
1986	Buf	6(6, rb)	90	377	4.2(42)	4	12	142	11.8(40)	2	—	—	—	—	—	—	—	—	—	—	36	498
1987	Buf	14	60	4.3(19)	0	4	37	9.3(12)	0	—	—	—	—	—	—	—	—	—	—	0	79
1987	LARm	2(1)	8	26	3.3(13)	0	5	59	11.8(32)	1	—	—	—	—	—	—	—	—	—	—	6	61
1988	†LARm	16(13, RB)	288	1212	4.2(44)	16	24	124	5.2(20)	0	—	—	—	—	—	—	—	—	—	—	108	1444
1989	†LARm	16(15, RB)	272	1137	4.2(47)	15	19	85	4.5(14)	0	—	—	—	—	—	—	—	—	—	—	90	1330
1990	†LARd	6(0)	47	164	3.5(21)	1	1	7	7.0(7)	0	—	—	—	—	—	—	—	—	—	—	6	178
NFL	7	80(67)	1204	4959	4.1(85)	51	157	1307	8.3(49)	7	1	0	0.0	0	0.0	0	—	—	—	k	—	348	6158

BELL, HENRY Henry, HB, 5´10˝/210 lbs; none; B1937

| 1960 | Den-A | 7(HB) | 43 | 238 | 5.5(69) | 2 | 2 | 13 | 6.5(11) | 0 | — | — | — | — | — | — | — | — | k | — | 0 | 275 |

BELL, JACOB Jacob, G, 6´5˝/300 lbs; Miami (OH); 2004: Ten, rnd 5; B3/2/1981 Cleveland, OH **2004** Ten 15 (14, LG) **2005** Ten 9 (1) **NFL** 24 (15) [2 yrs]

BELL, JASON Jason Dewande, DB, 6´0˝/182 lbs; UCLA; B4/1/1978 Long Beach, CA **2001** Dal 16 (0) **2002** Hou 13 (0) **2003** Hou 13 (0) **2004** Hou 9 (0) **2005** Hou 16 (0) **NFL** 67 (0) [5 yrs]

BELL, JERRY Gerald Alfred, TE, 6´5˝/230 lbs; Arizona State; 1982: TB, rnd 3; B3/7/1959 Derby, CT

1982	TB	9(1)	—	—	—	—	1	5	5.0(5)	0	—	—	—	—	—	—	—	—	—	—	0	3
1983	TB	16(6, te)	—	—	—	—	18	200	11.1(33)	1	—	—	—	—	—	—	—	—	—	—	6	105
1984	TB	16(11, TE)	—	—	—	—	29	397	13.7(27)	4	—	—	—	—	—	—	—	—	—	—	24	219
1985	TB	9(9, TE)	—	—	—	—	43	496	11.5(27)	2	—	—	—	—	—	—	—	—	—	—	12	258
1986	TB	10(3)	—	—	—	—	10	120	12.0(25)	0	—	—	—	—	—	—	—	—	—	—	0	60
NFL	5	60(30)	—	—	—	—	101	1218	12.1(33)	7	—	—	—	—	—	—	—	—	—	—	42	644

BELL, JOE Joseph, DE, 6´3˝/250 lbs; Norfolk State; B4/20/1956 **1979** Oak 1

BELL, KAY Kay Dee, T-G, 6´2˝/220 lbs; Washington State; 1937: Det, rnd 10; B10/14/1914 Hoquiam, WA, D10/27/1994 Redmond, WA **1937** ChiB 10 (1) **1942** NYG 11 (0) **NFL** 21 (1) [2 yrs]

BELL, KEN Kenneth Shawn, RB-WR, 5´10˝/190 lbs; Boston College; B11/16/1964 Greenwich, CT [R]

1986	†Den	16(0)	9	17	1.9(12)	0	2	10	5.0(7)	0	—	—	—	—	—	—	—	—	k	—	0	208
1987	†Den	12(1)	13	43	3.3(11)	0	1	8	8.0(8)	0	—	—	—	—	—	—	—	—	k	—	0	145
1988	Den	16(0)	9	36	4.0(6)	0	—	—	—	—	—	—	—	—	—	—	—	—	kp	—	0	257
1989	Den	15(0)	—	—	—	—	—	—	—	—	—	—	—	—	—	—	—	—	kp	—	0	190
NFL	4	59(1)	31	96	3.1(12)	0	3	18	6.0(0)	0	—	—	—	—	—	—	—	—	kp	—	0	800

BELL, KENDRELL Kendrell Alexander, LB, 6´1˝/254 lbs; Georgia; 2001: Pit, rnd 2; B7/2/1978 Augusta, GA **2001**†Pit★16 (16, RILB) **2002**†Pit 12 (12, LILB) **2003** Pit 16 (16, RILB) **2004** Pit 3 (0) **2005** KC 16 (14, ROLB) **NFL** 63 (58) [5 yrs]

BELL, KERWIN Kerwin Douglas, QB, 6´3˝/207 lbs; Florida; 1988: Mia, rnd 7; B6/15/1965 Live Oak, FL

| 1996 | Ind | 2(0) | 1 | -1 | -1.0(-1) | 0 | — | — | — | — | 5 | 5 | 100.0 | 75 | 15.0(30) | 1 | 0 | — | — | — | — | 0 | 42 |

BELL, KEVIN Kevin Abraham, WR, 5´10˝/180 lbs; Lamar; 1978: SD, rnd 12; B3/14/1955 Beaumont, TX **1978** NYJ 9

BELL, LEN Leonard Charles, DB, 5´11˝/201 lbs; Indiana; 1987: Cin, rnd 3; B3/14/1964 Rockford, IL **1987** Cin 1 (0)

YEAR	TEAM	G (GS, POS)	RUSH	YD	AVG (LG)	TD	REC	YD	AVG (LG)	TD	PASS COMP	PCT	YD	AVG (LG)	TD	INT	SK	YD	QBR	KPR	OTD	PTS	TAY

BELL, MARCUS Marcus, DT, 6'2"/339 lbs; Memphis; 2001: Arz, rnd 4; B6/1/1979 Memphis, TN **2001** Arz 13 (0) **2002** Arz 16 (4) **2003** Arz 13 (10, RDT) **2004** Det 16 (0) **2005** Det 15 (0) **NFL** 73 (14) [5 yrs]

BELL, MARCUS Marcus Udall, LB, 6'1"/245 lbs; Arizona; 2000: Sea, rnd 4; B7/19/1977 St. Johns, AZ **2000** Sea 16 (0) **2001** Sea 13 (0) **2002** Sea 16 (9, LLB) **NFL** 45 (9) [3 yrs]

BELL, MARK Mark Elvin, DE, 6'5"/241 lbs; Colorado State; 1979: Sea, rnd 4; B8/30/1957 Wichita, KS **1982** Sea 9 (1) **1983** Bal 7 (0) **1984** Ind 16 (0)

YEAR	TEAM	G (GS, POS)	RUSH	YD	AVG (LG)	TD	REC	YD	AVG (LG)	TD	KPR	OTD	PTS	TAY
1979	Sea	16(1)	—	—	—	—	2	20	10.0(16)	0			0	10
1980	Sea	16(0)	—	—	—	—	1	13	13.0(13)	0			0	7
NFL	5	64(2)	—	—	—	—	3	33	11.0(16)	0	S	—	0	17

BELL, MARK Mark Ricardo, WR, 5'9"/175 lbs; Colorado State; 1979: SL, rnd 5; B6/14/1957 Jamestown, OH **1981** SL 1 (1)

YEAR	TEAM	G (GS, POS)	RUSH	YD	AVG (LG)	TD	REC	YD	AVG (LG)	TD	KPR	OTD	PTS	TAY
1980	SL	11(0)	—	—	—	—	8	123	15.4(34)	0	p	—	0	152
NFL	2	12(1)	—	—	—	—	8	123	15.4(34)	0	p	—	0	62

BELL, MIKE Mike J., DE, 6'4"/255 lbs; Colorado State; 1979: KC, rnd 1; B8/30/1957 Wichita, KS **1979** KC 11 (4) **1980** KC 2 (2) **1981** KC 16 (16, RDE) **1982** KC 6 (5, RDE) **1983** KC 16 (16, RDE) **1984** KC 15 (14, RDE) **1985** KC 11 (11, RDE) **1987** KC 12 (12, RDE) **1988** KC 12 (12, RDE) **1989** KC 15 (6, rde) **1990**†KC 16 (2) **1991** KC 3 (0) **NFL** 135 (100) [12 yrs]

BELL, MYRON Myron Corey, DB, 5'11"/203 lbs; Michigan State; 1994: Pit, rnd 5; B9/15/1971 Toledo, OH **1994**†Pit 15 (0) **1995**†Pit 16 (9, SS) **1996**†Pit 16 (4) **1997**†Pit 16 (8, SS) **1998** Cin 16 (2) **1999** Cin 16 (16, SS) **2000** Pit 1 (0) **2001**†Pit 16 (1) **NFL** 112 (40) [8 yrs]

BELL, NICK H. Nickolas, RB, 6'2"/255 lbs; Iowa; 1991: LARd, rnd 2; B8/19/1968 Las Vegas, NV

YEAR	TEAM	G (GS, POS)	RUSH	YD	AVG (LG)	TD	REC	YD	AVG (LG)	TD	KPR	OTD	PTS	TAY
1991	†LARd	9(1)	78	307	3.9(15)	3	6	62	10.3(24)	0		—	18	368
1992	LARd	16(1)	81	366	4.5(66)	3	4	40	10.0(16)	0	k	—	18	417
1993	†LARd	10(3)	67	180	2.7(12)	1	11	111	10.1(24)	0		—	6	246
NFL	3	35(5)	226	853	3.8(66)	7	21	213	10.1(24)	0	k	—	42	1031

BELL, RICHARD Richard Aaron, RB, 6'0"/200 lbs; Nebraska; 1990: Pit, rnd 12; B5/3/1967 Los Angeles, CA

YEAR	TEAM	G (GS, POS)	RUSH	YD	AVG (LG)	TD	REC	YD	AVG (LG)	TD	KPR	OTD	PTS	TAY
1990	Pit	8(1)	5	18	3.6(12)	0	12	137	11.4(43)	1		—	6	92

BELL, RICK Richard Thomas, RB, 6'0"/205 lbs; St. John's (MN); B10/18/1960 St. Cloud, MN **1983** Min 14 (0)

BELL, RICKY Ricky Lynn, RB, 6'2"/220 lbs; USC; 1977: TB, rnd 1; B4/8/1955 Houston, TX, D11/28/1984 Inglewood, CA

YEAR	TEAM	G (GS, POS)	RUSH	YD	AVG (LG)	TD	REC	YD	AVG (LG)	TD	KPR	OTD	PTS	TAY
1977	TB	11(10, RB)	148	436	2.9(20)	1	11	88	8.0(23)	0		—	6	490
1978	TB	12(9, RB)	185	679	3.7(56)	6	15	122	8.1(22)	0		—	36	800
1979	†TB	16(16, FB)	283	1263	4.5(49)	7	25	248	9.9(26)	2		—	54	1467
1980	TB	14(12, FB)	174	599	3.4(40)	2	38	292	7.7(22)	1		—	18	770
1981	TB	7(3)	30	80	2.7(8)	0	8	92	11.5(22)	0		—	0	126
1982	SD	6	2	6	3.0(4)	0	—					—	0	1
NFL	6	64(50)	822	3063	3.7(56)	16	97	842	8.7(26)	3	k	—	114	3654

BELL, RICKY Richard, DB, 5'10"/194 lbs; North Carolina State; B10/2/1974 Columbia, SC **1996**†Jax 12 (0) **1997** ChiB 5 (0) **1998** ChiB 14 (0) **NFL** 31 (0) [3 yrs]

BELL, SHONN Jamara Riashonn, TE, 6'5"/240 lbs; Virginia Wise; B10/25/1974 Waynesboro, VA **1999** SF 2 (0)

BELL, TATUM Tatum, RB, 5'11"/190 lbs; Oklahoma State; 2004: Den, rnd 2; B3/2/1981 Dallas, TX

YEAR	TEAM	G (GS, POS)	RUSH	YD	AVG (LG)	TD	REC	YD	AVG (LG)	TD	KPR	OTD	PTS	TAY
2004	†Den	14(0)	75	396	5.3(29)	3	5	80	16.0(58)	0		—	18	466
2005	†Den	15(1, rb)	173	921	**5.3(68)**	8	18	104	5.8(14)	0		—	48	1053
NFL	2	29(1)	248	1317	5.3(68)	11	23	184	8.0(58)	0		—	66	1519

BELL, THEO Theopolis, WR, 6'0"/185 lbs; Arizona; 1976: Pit, rnd 4; B12/21/1953 Bakersfield, CA [R]

YEAR	TEAM	G (GS, POS)	RUSH	YD	AVG (LG)	TD	REC	YD	AVG (LG)	TD	KPR	OTD	PTS	TAY
1976	†Pit	13(1)	1	5	5.0(5)	0	3	43	14.3(19)	1	p	—	6	227
1978	†Pit	16	—	—	—	—	6	53	8.8(15)	1	p	—	6	79
1979	†Pit	13(1)	—	—	—	—	3	61	20.3(31)	0	p	—	0	184
1980	Pit	14(9, wr)	—	—	—	—	29	748	25.8(72)	2	kp	—	12	558
1981	†TB	16(9, WR)	1	7	7.0(7)	0	21	318	15.1(58)	2	p	—	12	173
1982	†TB	9(0)	—	—	—	—	15	203	13.5(25)	0	p	—	0	119
1983	TB	16(4)	—	—	—	—	25	410	16.4(52)	2	p	—	12	213
1984	TB	15(0)	—	—	—	—	22	350	15.9(29)	0	p	—	0	165
1985	TB	15(0)	—	—	—	—	12	189	15.8(24)	0		—	0	95
NFL	9	127(24)	2	12	6.0(7)	0	136	2375	17.5(72)	8	kp	—	48	1811

BELL, TODD Todd Anthony, DB-LB, 6'1"/207 lbs; Ohio State; 1981: Chi, rnd 4; B11/28/1958 Middletown, OH, D3/16/2005 Reynoldsburg, OH **1981** ChiB 16 (0) **1982** ChiB 9 (0) **1983** ChiB 15 (15, SS) **1984**†ChiB★16 (16, SS) **1986**†ChiB 15 (0) **1987**†ChiB 12 (11, SS) **1988** Phi 16 (16, RLB) **1989** Phi 4 (4) **NFL** 103 (62) [8 yrs]

BELL, TYRONE Tyrone Edward, DB, 6'2"/205 lbs; North Alabama; 1999: SD, rnd 6; B10/20/1974 West Point, MS **1999** GB 1 (0)

BELL, WILLIAM William, RB, 5'11"/214 lbs; Georgia Tech; B7/22/1971 Miami, FL

YEAR	TEAM	G (GS, POS)	RUSH	YD	AVG (LG)	TD	REC	YD	AVG (LG)	TD	KPR	OTD	PTS	TAY
1994	Was	8(0)									k	—	0	13
1995	Was	16(0)	4	13	3.3(5)	0					k	—	0	14
1996	Was	16(0)	—	—	—	—	3	23	7.7(12)	0	k	—	0	22
NFL	3	40(0)	4	13	3.3(5)	0	3	23	7.7(12)	0	k	—	0	49

BELL, YEREMIAH Yermiah Neavius, DB, 6'1"/200 lbs; Eastern Kentucky; 2003: Mia, rnd 6; B3/3/1978 Winchester, KY **2004** Mia 13 (0) **2005** Mia 16 (0) **NFL** 29 (0) [2 yrs]

BELLAMY, JAY John Jay, DB, 5'11"/200 lbs; Rutgers; B7/8/1972 Perth Amboy, NJ [I] **1994** Sea 3 (0) **1995** Sea 15 (0) **1996** Sea 16 (0) **1997** Sea 16 (7, ss) **1998** Sea 16 (16, SS) **1999**†Sea 16 (16, FS) **2000** Sea 16 (16, FS) **2001** NO 16 (16, FS) **2002** NO 16 (16, SS) **2003** NO 16 (16, SS) **2004** NO 16 (16, SS) **2005** NO 3 (3) **NFL** 165 (122) [12 yrs]

BELLAMY, MIKE Michael Sinclair, WR, 6'1"/195 lbs; Illinois; 1990: Phi, rnd 2; B6/28/1966 New York, NY **1990** Phi 6 (0)

BELLAMY, RONALD Ronald, WR, 6'0"/200 lbs; Michigan; B12/28/1981 New Orleans, LA

YEAR	TEAM	G (GS, POS)	RUSH	YD	AVG (LG)	TD	REC	YD	AVG (LG)	TD	KPR	OTD	PTS	TAY
2004	Mia	2(0)	—	—	—	—	1	8	8.0(8)	0			0	4

BELLAMY, VIC Victor K., DB, 6'1"/195 lbs; Syracuse; B6/1/1963 Philadelphia, PA **1987** Phi 3 (3)

BELLINGER, BOB Robert F., G, 5'11"/216 lbs; Gonzaga; B1/20/1913 Spokane, WA, D5/8/1955 Lansing, MI **1934** NYG 9 (2) **1935**†NYG 9 (8, RG) **NFL** 18 (10) [2 yrs]

BELLINGER, RODNEY Rodney Carwell, DB, 5'8"/186 lbs; Miami (FL); 1984: Buf, rnd 3; B6/4/1962 Miami, FL **1984** Buf 10 (2) **1985** Buf 16 (0) **1986** Buf 16 (9, LCB) **NFL** 42 (11) [3 yrs]

BELLINI, MARK Mark Joseph, WR, 5'11"/185 lbs; Brigham Young; 1987: Ind, rnd 7; B1/19/1964 San Leandro, CA

YEAR	TEAM	G (GS, POS)	RUSH	YD	AVG (LG)	TD	REC	YD	AVG (LG)	TD	KPR	OTD	PTS	TAY
1987	†Ind	10(1)	—	—	—	—	5	69	13.8(19)	0		—	0	35
1988	Ind	15(0)	—	—	—	—	5	64	12.8(25)	0		—	0	32
NFL	2	25(1)	—	—	—	—	10	133	13.3(25)	0		—	0	67

BELLINO, JOE Joseph Michael, HB, 5'9"/185 lbs; Navy; 1961: Bos, rnd 19/Was, rnd 17; B3/13/1938 Winchester, MA

YEAR	TEAM	G (GS, POS)	RUSH	YD	AVG (LG)	TD	REC	YD	AVG (LG)	TD	KPR	OTD	PTS	TAY
1965	Bos-A	10	24	49	2.0(10)	0	5	74	14.8(20)	0	k	—	0	119
1966	Bos-A	11	—	—	—	—	6	77	12.8(25)	1	kp	—	6	183
1967	Bos-A	14(1)	6	15	2.5(10)	0					kp	—	0	156
NFL	3	35(1)	30	64	2.1(10)	0	11	151	13.7(25)	1	kp	—	6	458

BELLISARI, GREG Greg Ernest, LB, 6'0"/236 lbs; Ohio State; B6/21/1975 Boca Raton, FL **1997**†TB 14 (0) **1998** TB 2 (0) **NFL** 16 (0) [2 yrs]

BELOTTI, GEORGE George D., C, 6'4"/250 lbs; USC; 1957: GB, rnd 8; B11/29/1934 Los Angeles, CA **1960**†Hou-A 14 (C) **1961** Hou-A 4 **1961** SD-A 2 **NFL** 20 [2 yrs]

BELSER, CEASAR Ceaser Edward, DB, 6'0"/205 lbs; Arkansas-Pine Bluff; 1966: Was, rnd 10; B9/13/1944 Montgomery, AL **1968**†KC-A 14 **1969**†KC-A 14 **1970** KC 14 **1971**†KC 14 **1974** SF 4 **NFL** 60 [5 yrs]

BELSER, JASON Jason Daks, DB, 5'9"/188 lbs; Oklahoma; 1992: Ind, rnd 8; B5/28/1970 Kansas City, MO **1992** Ind 16 (2) **1993** Ind 16 (16, FS/ss) **1994** Ind 13 (12, SS/fs) **1995**†Ind 16 (16, FS) **1996**†Ind 16 (16, FS) **1997** Ind 16 (16, FS) **1998** Ind 16 (16, FS/ss) **1999**†Ind 16 (16, FS) **2000**†Ind 16 (16, FS) **2001** KC 16 (0) **2002** KC 16 (8, fs) **NFL** 173 (134) [11 yrs]

YEAR	TEAM	G(GS,POS)	RUSH	YD	AVG(LG)	TD	REC	YD	AVG(LG)	TD	PASS	COMP	PCT	YD	AVG(LG)	TD	INT	SK	YD	QBR	KPR	OTD	PTS	TAY

BELTON, HORACE   Horace, RB, 5´8˝/200 lbs; Southeastern Louisiana; B7/16/1955 Baton Rouge, LA

1978	KC	16	24	79	3.3(8)	0	11	88	8.0(22)	0	—	—	—	—	—	—	—	—	—	—	k	—	0	215
1979	KC	16	44	134	3.0(12)	1	4	44	11.0(23)	0	—	—	—	—	—	—	—	—	—	—	k	—	6	299
1980	KC	14(3)	68	273	4.0(14)	2	5	94	18.8(55)	0	—	—	—	—	—	—	—	—	—	—	k	—	12	360
NFL	3	46(3)	136	486	3.6(14)	3	20	226	11.3(55)	0	—	—	—	—	—	—	—	—	—	—	k	—	18	874

BELTON, WILLIE   Willie Davis, RB, 5´11˝/207 lbs; Maryland-Eastern Shore; B12/12/1948 Greenville, SC, D12/5/1992 Greenville, NC

1971	Atl	14	56	237	4.2(16)	1	3	22	7.3(10)	0	—	—	—	—	—	—	—	—	—	—	kp	—	6	557
1972	Atl	14	10	20	2.0(8)	0	1	-1	-1.0(-1)	0	—	—	—	—	—	—	—	—	—	—	kp	—	0	171
1973	SL	3	—	—	—	—	—	—	—	—	—	—	—	—	—	—	—	—	—	—	kp	—	0	35
1974	SL	5	12	49	4.1(10)	0	—	—	—	—	—	—	—	—	—	—	—	—	—	—	kp	—	0	73
NFL	4	36	78	306	3.9(16)	1	4	21	5.3(10)	0	—	—	—	—	—	—	—	—	—	—	kp	—	6	836

BELWAY, BRIAN   Brian P., DE, 6´6˝/265 lbs; Calgary (Canada); B5/28/1963 Ottawa, Canada   **1987** LARd 1 (0)

BEMILLER, AL   Albert Delane, C-G-T, 6´3˝/243 lbs; Syracuse; 1961: Buf, rnd 7/SL, rnd 7; B4/18/1938 Hanover, PA   **1961** Buf-A 14 (14, C)   **1962** Buf-A 14 (14, C)
1963†Buf-A 14 (14, C)   **1964**†Buf-A 14 (14, RG)   **1965**†Buf-A◇14 (14, RG)   **1966**†Buf-A 14 (14, C)   **1967** Buf-A 14 (13, C/lt)   **1969** Buf-A 14 (C)

| 1968 | Buf-A | 14(14, C) | — | — | — | — | 1 | 0 | 0.0(0) | 0 | — | — | — | — | — | — | — | — | — | — | — | — | 0 | 0 |
| NFL | 9 | 126(111) | — | — | — | — | 1 | 0 | 0.0 | 0 | — | — | — | — | — | — | — | — | — | — | — | — | 0 | 0 |

BENDER, CAREY   Carey Wayne, RB, 5´8˝/185 lbs; Coe College; 1996 Buf 1 (0)

BENDER, WES   Wes Todd, RB, 5´10˝/242 lbs; USC; B8/2/1970 Van Nuys, CA

1994	LARd	9(0)	—	—	—	—	2	14	7.0(7)	0	—	—	—	—	—	—	—	—	—	—	—	—	0	7
1997	NO	11(0)	5	9	1.8(6)	0	—	—	—	—	—	—	—	—	—	—	—	—	—	—	—	—	0	9
NFL	2	20(0)	5	9	1.8(6)	0	2	14	7.0(7)	0	—	—	—	—	—	—	—	—	—	—	—	—	0	16

BENDROSS, JESSE   Jesse James, WR, 6´0˝/196 lbs; Alabama; 1984: SD, rnd 7; B7/19/1962 Hollywood, FL

1984	SD	16(0)	—	—	—	—	16	213	13.3(29)	0	—	—	—	—	—	—	—	—	—	—	—	—	0	107
1985	SD	16(2)	—	—	—	—	11	156	14.2(54)	2	—	—	—	—	—	—	—	—	—	—	k	—	12	75
1987	Phi	3(0)	—	—	—	—	—	—	—	—	—	—	—	—	—	—	—	—	—	—	—	—	0	—
NFL	3	35(2)	—	—	—	—	27	369	13.7(54)	2	—	—	—	—	—	—	—	—	—	—	k	—	12	182

BENEFIELD, DAVED   Daved, LB, 6´4˝/231 lbs; Cal State-Northridge; B2/16/1968 Los Angeles, CA   **1996**†SF 14 (0)

BENFATTI, LOU   Lewis Vincent, DT, 6´4˝/278 lbs; Penn State; 1994: NYJ, rnd 3; B3/9/1971 Green Pond, NJ   **1994** NYJ 7 (0)   **1995** NYJ 12 (0)   **NFL** 19 (0) [2 yrs]

BENGEN, BRANT   Brant Wayne, WR, 5´8˝/172 lbs; British Columbia; Idaho; B3/30/1964

| 1987 | Sea | 3(0) | — | — | — | — | 2 | 33 | 16.5(24) | 0 | — | — | — | — | — | — | — | — | — | — | k | — | 0 | 34 |

BENIRSCHKE, ROLF   Rolf Joachim, K, 6´0˝/171 lbs; California-Davis; 1977: Oak, rnd 12; B2/7/1955 Boston, MA **[K]**   **1977** SD 14   **1978** SD 15   **1979** SD 4   **1980**†SD 16 (0)
1981†SD 16 (0)   **1982**†SD★9 (0)   **1983** SD 16 (0)   **1984** SD 14 (0)   **1985** SD 1 (0)   **1986** SD 16 (0)   **NFL** 121 [10 yrs]

BENISH, DAN   Daniel James, DT, 6´5˝/273 lbs; Clemson; B11/21/1961 Youngstown, OH   **1983** Atl 16 (3)   **1984** Atl 15 (8, ldt)   **1985** Atl 16 (16, RDT)   **1986** Atl 5 (0)   **1987** Was 3 (3)
NFL 55 (30) [5 yrs]

BENJAMIN, BILL   William Joseph, LB, 6´3˝/226 lbs; San Jose State; B9/14/1958 Indianapolis, IN   **1987** Ind 2 (2)

BENJAMIN, GUY   Guy Emory, QB, 6´4˝/210 lbs; Stanford; 1978: Mia, rnd 2; B6/27/1955 Los Angeles, CA

1978	Mia	3	1	-2	-2.0(-2)	0	—	—	—	—	8	6	75.0	91	11.4(43)	1	1	—	—	—	—	—	0	9
1979	Mia	4	—	—	—	—	—	—	—	—	4	3	75.0	28	7.0(17)	0	0	1	10	—	—	—	0	14
1980	NO	2(0)	—	—	—	—	—	—	—	—	17	7	41.2	28	1.6(17)	0	1	—	—	—	—	—	0	-26
1981	SF	4(0)	1	1	1.0(1)	0	—	—	—	—	26	15	57.7	171	6.6(27)	1	1	3	30	—	—	—	0	52
1982	SF	2(0)	—	—	—	—	—	—	—	—	1	1	100.0	10	10.0(10)	0	0	—	—	—	—	—	0	5
1983	SF	4(0)	1	1	1.0(1)	0	—	—	—	—	12	7	58.3	111	9.3(73)	1	0	—	—	—	—	—	0	62
NFL	6	19	3	0	0.0(1)	0	—	—	—	—	68	39	57.4	439	6.5(73)	3	3	4	40	—	—	—	0	115

BENJAMIN, RYAN   Ryan Lamont, RB, 5´7˝/183 lbs; Pacific; B4/23/1970 Pixley, CA

| 1993 | Cin | 1(0) | 3 | 5 | 1.7(2) | 0 | 1 | 16 | 16.0(16) | 0 | — | — | — | — | — | — | — | — | — | — | k | — | 0 | 31 |

BENJAMIN, RYAN   Ryan Arthur, C, 6´1˝/242 lbs; South Florida; B11/11/1977 New Port Richey, FL   **2001** ChiB 1 (0)   **2002**†TB 10 (0)   **2003** TB 16 (0)   **NFL** 27 (0) [3 yrs]

BENJAMIN, TONY   Anthony Lee, RB, 6´3˝/225 lbs; Duke; 1977: Sea, rnd 6; B10/27/1955 Monessen, PA

1977	Sea	6	13	48	3.7(10)	0	4	27	6.8(9)	0	—	—	—	—	—	—	—	—	—	—	—	—	0	62
1978	Sea	6(1)	1	7	7.0(7)	0	1	9	9.0(9)	0	—	—	—	—	—	—	—	—	—	—	—	—	0	12
1979	Sea	16	5	13	2.6(8)	0	1	6	6.0(6)	0	—	—	—	—	—	—	—	—	—	—	k	—	0	19
NFL	3	28(1)	19	68	3.6(10)	0	6	42	7.0(9)	0	—	—	—	—	—	—	—	—	—	—	k	—	0	92

BENKERT, HEINIE   Henry Marvin, B, 5´9˝/168 lbs; Rutgers; B6/30/1901 Newark, NJ, D7/15/1972 Orange, NJ   **1925** NYG☆11 (10, WB)   **1926** Pot 8 (4)   **1929** Ora 8 (6, WB)
1930 Nwk 5 (4)   **NFL** 32 (24) [4 yrs]

BENNERS, FRED   Frederick Hagaman, QB, 6´3˝/195 lbs; University of the South (TN); SMU; 1951: NYG, rnd 8; B6/22/1930 Dallas, TX

| 1952 | NYG | 6 | 5 | 16 | 3.2(8) | 0 | — | — | — | — | 58 | 25 | 43.1 | 320 | 5.5(35) | 0 | 5 | — | — | — | — | — | 0 | -24 |

BENNETT, ANTOINE   Antoine, DB, 5´11˝/185 lbs; Florida A&M; 1991: Cin, rnd 12; B11/29/1967 Miami, FL   **1991** Cin 3 (0)   **1992** Cin 11 (2)   **NFL** 14 (2) [2 yrs]

BENNETT, BARRY   Barry Martin, DT-DE, 6´4˝/257 lbs; Concordia (MN); 1978: NO, rnd 3; B12/10/1955 St. Paul, MN   **1978** NO 16 (1)   **1979** NO 16 (14, LDT)   **1980** NO 15 (6, ldt)
1981 NO 3 (3)   **1982**†NYJ 7 (0)   **1983** NYJ 13 (0)   **1984** NYJ 15 (13, LDT)   **1985**†NYJ 16 (16, RDE)   **1986**†NYJ 16 (15, RDE)   **1987** NYJ 13 (11, RDE)   **1988** NYJ 1 (0)
1988 Min 1 (0)   **NFL** 132 (79) [11 yrs]

BENNETT, BEN   Ben, QB, 6´1˝/200 lbs; Duke; 1984: Atl, rnd 6; B5/5/1962 Greensboro, NC

| 1987 | Cin | 1(0) | 2 | 17 | 8.5(9) | 0 | — | — | — | — | 6 | 2 | 33.3 | 25 | 4.2(18) | 0 | 1 | — | — | — | — | — | 0 | -11 |

BENNETT, BRANDON   Brandon Purrell, RB, 5´11˝/220 lbs; South Carolina; B2/3/1973 Greenville, SC **[R]**

1998	Cin	14(1)	77	243	3.2(17)	2	8	153	19.1(55)	0	—	—	—	—	—	—	—	—	—	—	k	—	12	356
2000	Cin	16(0)	90	324	3.6(37)	3	19	168	8.8(25)	0	—	—	—	—	—	—	—	—	—	—	—	—	18	438
2001	Cin	16(1)	50	232	4.6(36)	0	20	150	7.5(15)	0	—	—	—	—	—	—	—	—	—	—	k	—	0	307
2002	Cin	12(0)	33	155	4.7(29)	0	18	109	6.1(15)	0	—	—	—	—	—	—	—	—	—	—	k	—	6	716
2003	Cin	16(0)	56	173	3.1(19)	0	25	176	7.0(16)	1	—	—	—	—	—	—	—	—	—	—	k	—	6	617
2004	Car	8(0)	6	17	2.8(11)	1	—	—	—	—	—	—	—	—	—	—	—	—	—	—	k	—	6	84
NFL	6	82(2)	312	1144	3.7(37)	6	90	756	8.4(55)	1	—	—	—	—	—	—	—	—	—	—	k	1	48	2517

BENNETT, CHARLES   Charles Anthony, DE, 6´5˝/257 lbs; Louisiana-Lafayette; 1985: Chi, rnd 7; B2/9/1963 Alligator, MS   **1987** Mia 3 (3)

BENNETT, CHUCK   Charles Henry, B, 5´9˝/193 lbs; Indiana; B8/9/1907 Linton, IN, D6/9/1973 Countryside, IL   **1930** Por 14 (12, TB), 42   **1931** Por 1 (0)

| 1933 | ChiC | 2(0) | 2 | -1 | -0.5 | 0 | — | — | — | — | — | — | — | — | — | — | — | — | — | — | — | — | 0 | -1 |
| NFL | 3 | 17(12) | 2 | -1 | -0.5 | 5 | — | — | — | — | — | — | — | — | — | — | — | — | — | — | — | 1 | 42 | 64 |

BENNETT, CORNELIUS   Cornelius O'Landa, LB, 6´2˝/237 lbs; Alabama; 1987: Ind, rnd 1; B8/25/1965 Birmingham, AL **[S]**   **1987** Buf 8 (7, LOLB)   **1988**†Buf 16 (16, LOLB)
1989†Buf☆12 (12, LOLB)   **1990**†Buf★16 (16, LOLB)   **1991**†Buf★16 (16, LOLB)   **1992**†Buf★15 (15, LOLB)   **1993**†Buf◇16 (16, LOLB)   **1994** Buf 16 (16, LOLB)
1995 Buf 14 (14, RILB)   **1996** Atl 13 (13, LLB)   **1997** Atl 16 (16, LLB)   **1998**†Atl 16 (16, LLB)   **1999** Ind 16 (16, LLB)   **2000**†Ind 16 (15, LLB)   **NFL** 206 (204) [14 yrs]

BENNETT, DARREN   Darren Leslie, P, 6´5˝/235 lbs; none; B1/9/1965 Sydney, Australia **[P]**   **1995**†SD★16 (0)   **1996** SD 16 (0)   **1997** SD 16 (0)   **1998** SD 16 (0)   **2000** SD★16 (0)
2001 SD 16 (0)   **2002** SD 16 (0)   **2004**†Min 15 (0)   **2005** Min 1 (0)

1999	SD	16(0)	1	0	0.0(0)	0	—	—	—	—	—	—	—	—	—	—	—	—	—	—	P	—	0	0
2003	SD	16(0)	—	—	—	—	—	—	—	—	1	0	0.0	0	0.0	0	0.0	—	—	—	P	—	0	0
NFL	11	160(0)	1	0	0.0	0	—	—	—	—	1	0	0.0	0	0.0	0	0.0	—	—	—	P	—	0	0

BENNETT, DONNELL   Donnell, RB, 6´0˝/242 lbs; Miami (FL); 1994: KC, rnd 2; B9/14/1972 Fort Lauderdale, FL

| 1994 | KC | 15(0) | 46 | 178 | 3.9(17) | 2 | 7 | 53 | 7.6(15) | 0 | — | — | — | — | — | — | — | — | — | — | k | — | 12 | 222 |
| 1995 | KC | 3(1) | 7 | 11 | 1.6(11) | 0 | 1 | 12 | 12.0(12) | 0 | — | — | — | — | — | — | — | — | — | — | — | — | 0 | 17 |

YEAR	TEAM	G(GS, POS)	RUSH	YD	AVG(LG)	TD	REC	YD	AVG(LG)	TD	PASS	COMP	PCT	YD	AVG(LG)	TD	INT	SK	YD	QBR	KPR	OTD	PTS	TAY
1996	KC	16(0)	36	166	4.6(34)	0	8	21	2.6(10)	0	—	—	—	—	—	—	—	—	—	—	—	—	0	177
1997	†KC	14(1)	94	369	3.9(14)	1	7	5	0.7(4)	0	—	—	—	—	—	—	—	—	—	—	—	—	6	382
1998	KC	16(10, RB)	148	527	3.6(26)	5	16	91	5.7(14)	1	—	—	—	—	—	—	—	—	—	—	—	—	36	628
1999	KC	15(1, rb)	161	627	3.9(44)	8	10	41	4.1(12)	0	—	—	—	—	—	—	—	—	—	—	—	—	48	734
2000	KC	7(2)	27	24	0.9(6)	1	2	17	8.5(13)	0	—	—	—	—	—	—	—	—	—	—	k	—	6	43
2001	Was	16(14, FB)	10	39	3.9(8)	0	15	112	7.5(30)	0	—	—	—	—	—	—	—	—	—	—	—	—	2	95
NFL	8	102(29)	529	1941	3.7(44)	17	66	352	5.3(30)	1	—	—	—	—	—	—	—	—	—	—	k	—	110	2295
BENNETT, DREW Andrew Russell, WR, 6´5˝/206 lbs; UCLA; B8/26/1978 Berkeley, CA																								
2001	Ten	14(1)	—	—	—	—	24	329	13.7(50)	1	—	—	—	—	—	—	—	—	—	—	k	—	8	166
2002	†Ten	16(7, wr)	—	—	—	—	33	478	14.5(53)	2	—	—	—	—	—	—	—	—	—	—	—	—	12	249
2003	†Ten	12(8, WR)	—	—	—	—	32	504	15.8(48)	4	1	1	100.0	14	14.0(14)	0	0	—	—	—	—	—	24	279
2004	Ten	16(16, WR)	1	12	12.0(12)	0	80	1247	15.6(48)	11	1	1	100.0	26	26.0(26)	1	0	—	—	—	k	—	66	686
2005	Ten	13(10, WR)	1	3	3.0(3)	0	58	738	12.7(55)	4	1	0	0.0	0	0.0	0	0	—	—	—	—	—	24	392
NFL	5	71(42)	2	15	7.5(12)	0	227	3296	14.5(55)	22	3	2	66.7	40	13.3(26)	1	0	—	—	—	k	—	134	1771
BENNETT, EDGAR Edgar, RB, 6´0˝/217 lbs; Florida State; 1992: GB, rnd 4; B2/15/1969 Jacksonville, FL																								
1992	GB	16(2)	61	214	3.5(18)	0	13	93	7.2(22)	0	—	—	—	—	—	—	—	—	—	—	k	—	0	290
1993	†GB	16(14, FB)	159	550	3.5(19)	9	59	457	7.7(39)	1	—	—	—	—	—	—	—	—	—	—	—	—	60	874
1994	†GB	16(15, FB)	178	623	3.5(39)	5	78	546	7.0(40)	4	—	—	—	—	—	—	—	—	—	—	—	—	54	966
1995	†GB	16(16, FB)	316	1067	3.4(23)	3	61	648	10.6(35)	4	—	—	—	—	—	—	—	—	—	—	—	—	42	1441
1996	†GB	16(15, RB)	222	899	4.0(23)	2	31	176	5.7(25)	1	—	—	—	—	—	—	—	—	—	—	—	—	22	1012
1998	ChiB	16(13, RB)	173	611	3.5(43)	2	28	209	7.5(31)	0	2	1	50.0	18	9.0(18)	1	0	—	—	—	—	—	12	750
1999	ChiB	16(1)	6	28	4.7(15)	0	14	116	8.3(34)	0	—	—	—	—	—	—	—	—	—	—	k	—	0	94
NFL	7	112(76)	1115	3992	3.6(43)	21	284	2245	7.9(40)	10	2	1	50.0	18	9.0(18)	1	0	—	—	—	k	—	190	5426
BENNETT, JUG Earl Clinton, G-LB, 5´8˝/188 lbs; Hardin-Simmons; 1943: GB, rnd 23; B2/27/1920 Skiatook, OK, D9/28/1992 Wichita Falls, TX **1946** GB 3 (0)																								
BENNETT, LEWIS Lewis Bonaparte, WR, 5´11˝/175 lbs; Florida A&M; B8/4/1963 Jacksonville, FL																								
1987	NYG	3(3)	—	—	—	—	10	184	18.4(46)	1	—	—	—	—	—	—	—	—	—	—	—	—	6	97
BENNETT, MICHAEL Michael, RB, 5´9˝/211 lbs; Wisconsin; 2001: Min, rnd 1; B8/13/1978 Milwaukee, WI																								
2001	Min	13(13, RB)	172	682	4.0(31)	2	29	226	7.8(80)	1	—	—	—	—	—	—	—	—	—	—	—	—	18	820
2002	Min✧	16(16, RB)	255	1296	5.1(85)	5	37	351	9.5(45)	1	—	—	—	—	—	—	—	—	—	—	—	—	36	1527
2003	Min	8(7, rb)	90	447	5.0(28)	1	12	132	11.0(40)	0	—	—	—	—	—	—	—	—	—	—	—	—	6	523
2004	†Min	11(7, RB)	70	276	3.9(25)	1	21	207	9.9(38)	1	—	—	—	—	—	—	—	—	—	—	—	—	12	395
2005	Min	16(6, rb)	126	473	3.8(61)	3	27	124	4.6(20)	2	—	—	—	—	—	—	—	—	—	—	—	—	30	575
NFL	5	64(49)	713	3174	4.5(85)	12	126	1040	8.3(80)	5	—	—	—	—	—	—	—	—	—	—	—	—	102	3839
BENNETT, MONTE Monte Lewis, NT-DE, 6´3˝/265 lbs; Kansas State; B4/27/1959 Sterling, KS **1981** NO 16 (6, nt) **1987** SD 3 (0) **NFL** 19 (6) [2 yrs]																								
BENNETT, PHIL Phillip, LB, 6´3˝/225 lbs; Miami (FL); 1957: Pit, rnd 19; B2/14/1935 **1960** Bos-A 2																								
BENNETT, ROY Roy Mitchell, DB, 6´2˝/195 lbs; Jackson State; B7/5/1961 Birmingham, AL **1988** SD 16 (2) **1989** SD 16 (0) **NFL** 32 (2) [2 yrs]																								
BENNETT, SEAN William Sean, RB, 6´1˝/230 lbs; Illinois; Evansville; Northwestern; 1999: NYG, rnd 4; B11/9/1975 Evansville, IN																								
1999	NYG	9(2)	29	126	4.3(40)	1	4	27	6.8(16)	0	—	—	—	—	—	—	—	—	—	—	—	—	6	150
2002	NYG	7(0)	—	—	—	—	5	37	7.4(10)	0	—	—	—	—	—	—	—	—	—	—	k	—	0	4
NFL	2	16(2)	29	126	4.3(40)	1	9	64	7.1(16)	0	—	—	—	—	—	—	—	—	—	—	k	—	6	153
BENNETT, SID Sydney Chisholm, T-G, 5´10˝/192 lbs; Northwestern; B2/2/1895 Geneva, IL, D12/30/1971 Elgin, IL **1920** ChiT 6 (4, RT) **1922** Mil 2 (2) **NFL** 8 (6) [2 yrs]																								
BENNETT, TOMMY Tommy, DB, 6´2˝/219 lbs; UCLA; B2/19/1973 Las Vegas, NV **1996** Arz 16 (1) **1997** Arz 13 (7, ss) **1998**†Arz 16 (16, SS) **1999** Arz 15 (15, SS) **2000** Arz 11 (0) **2001** Det 8 (1) **NFL** 79 (40) [6 yrs]																								
BENNETT, TONY Tony Lydell, DE-LB, 6´2˝/250 lbs; Mississippi; 1990: GB, rnd 1; B7/1/1967 Alligator, MS **[S]** **1990** GB 14 (0) **1991** GB 16 (16, ROLB) **1992** GB 16 (16, ROLB) **1993**†GB 10 (7, rolb) **1994** Ind 16 (15, RDE) **1995**†Ind 16 (16, RDE) **1996**†Ind 14 (13, RDE) **1997** Ind 6 (6, rde) **NFL** 108 (89) [8 yrs]																								
BENNETT, WOODY Woodrow, RB, 6´2˝/227 lbs; Miami (FL); B3/24/1955 York, PA																								
1979	NYJ	15	2	4	2.0(3)	1	1	9	9.0(9)	0	—	—	—	—	—	—	—	—	—	—	k	—	6	11
1980	NYJ	10(0)	3	13	4.3(19)	0	—	—	—	—	—	—	—	—	—	—	—	—	—	—	k	—	0	11
1980	Mia	4(3)	43	187	4.3(12)	0	3	26	8.7(19)	1	—	—	—	—	—	—	—	—	—	—	—	—	6	205
1981	Mia	3(3)	28	104	3.7(12)	0	4	22	5.5(10)	0	—	—	—	—	—	—	—	—	—	—	—	—	0	115
1982	†Mia	1(0)	9	15	1.7(5)	0	—	—	—	—	—	—	—	—	—	—	—	—	—	—	—	—	0	15
1983	†Mia	16(2)	49	197	4.0(25)	2	6	35	5.8(9)	0	—	—	—	—	—	—	—	—	—	—	k	—	12	226
1984	†Mia	16(9, FB)	144	606	4.2(23)	7	6	44	7.3(20)	1	—	—	—	—	—	—	—	—	—	—	—	—	48	703
1985	†Mia	16(13, FB)	54	256	4.7(17)	0	10	101	10.1(27)	1	—	—	—	—	—	—	—	—	—	—	—	—	6	312
1986	Mia	16(14, FB)	36	162	4.5(16)	0	4	33	8.3(13)	0	—	—	—	—	—	—	—	—	—	—	—	—	0	179
1987	Mia	12(11, FB)	25	102	4.1(18)	0	4	18	4.5(6)	0	—	—	—	—	—	—	—	—	—	—	—	—	0	111
1988	Mia	16(7, FB)	31	115	3.7(12)	0	2	16	8.0(12)	0	—	—	—	—	—	—	—	—	—	—	—	—	0	123
NFL	10	125(62)	424	1761	4.2(25)	10	40	304	7.6(27)	3	—	—	—	—	—	—	—	—	—	—	k	—	78	2009
BENSON, BRAD Bradley William, T-G-C, 6´3˝/262 lbs; Penn State; 1977: NE, rnd 8; B11/25/1955 Altoona, PA **1978** NYG 16 (5, rt) **1979** NYG 10 (10, LT) **1980** NYG 15 (14, LT) **1981**†NYG 11 (10, LT) **1982** NYG 9 (8, LT) **1983** NYG 16 (16, LT) **1984**†NYG 16 (16, RG/lt) **1985**†NYG 16 (16, LT) **1986**†NYG★16 (16, LT) **1987** NYG 12 (12, LT) **NFL** 137 (123) [10 yrs]																								
BENSON, CEDRIC Cedric Myron, RB, 5´10˝/222 lbs; Texas; 2005: Chi, rnd 1; B12/28/1982 Midland, TX																								
2005	ChiB	9(1)	67	272	4.1(36)	0	1	3	3.0(3)	0	—	—	—	—	—	—	—	—	—	—	—	—	0	274
BENSON, CHARLES Charles Henry, DE, 6´3˝/267 lbs; Baylor; 1983: Mia, rnd 3; B11/21/1960 Houston, TX **1983**†Mia 8 (0) **1984**†Mia 16 (0) **1985** Ind 1 (0) **1987** Det 3 (3) **NFL** 28 (3) [4 yrs]																								
BENSON, CLIFF Clifford Anthony, TE, 6´4˝/238 lbs; Purdue; 1984: Atl, rnd 5; B8/28/1961 Chicago, IL																								
1984	Atl	16(16, TE)	3	8	2.7(6)	0	26	244	9.4(30)	0	—	—	—	—	—	—	—	—	—	—	—	—	0	130
1985	Atl	16(14, TE)	—	—	—	—	10	37	3.7(6)	0	—	—	—	—	—	—	—	—	—	—	—	—	0	19
1987	Was	2(0)	—	—	—	—	—	—	—	—	—	—	—	—	—	—	—	—	—	—	—	—	—	—
1987	†NO	8(3)	—	—	—	—	2	11	5.5(6)	0	—	—	—	—	—	—	—	—	—	—	—	—	0	6
1988	NO	7(0)	—	—	—	—	1	5	5.0(5)	0	—	—	—	—	—	—	—	—	—	—	—	—	0	3
NFL	4	49(33)	3	8	2.7(6)	0	39	297	7.6(30)	0	—	—	—	—	—	—	—	—	—	—	—	—	0	157
BENSON, DARREN Darren, DT, 6´7˝/308 lbs; Trinity Valley CC (TX); 1995: Dal, rnd S3; B8/25/1974 Memphis, TN **1995**†Dal 6 (0) **1997** Dal 6 (0) **NFL** 12 (0) [2 yrs]																								
BENSON, DUANE Dean Duane, LB, 6´2˝/215 lbs; Hamline; 1967: Oak, rnd 11; B8/5/1945 Belmond, IA **1967**†Oak-A 8 **1968**†Oak-A 12 (6, llb) **1969**†Oak-A 14 **1970**†Oak 14 **1971** Oak 14 (5, rlb) **1972** Atl 14 **1973** Atl 14 **1974** Hou 13 (lolb) **1975** Hou 4 **1976** Hou 14 **NFL** 121 (11) [10 yrs]																								
BENSON, GEORGE George Nathan, B, 6´1˝/205 lbs; Northwestern; 1942: GB, rnd 19; B5/7/1919 Madison, IN, D8/24/2001 Cape Coral, FL																								
1947	Bkn-A	1(0)	2	5	2.5	0	—	—	—	—	—	—	—	—	—	—	—	—	—	—	—	—	0	5
BENSON, HARRY Harry Hartley, G, 5´10˝/218 lbs; Western Maryland; B10/7/1909 Baltimore, MD, D5/17/1943 Attu Island, AK **1935** Phi 6 (0)																								
BENSON, MITCHELL Mitchell Oswell, NT-DT, 6´4˝/302 lbs; TCU; 1989: Ind, rnd 3; B5/30/1967 Fort Worth, TX **1989** Ind 16 (0) **1990** Ind 9 (0) **1991** SD 16 (0) **NFL** 41 (0) [3 yrs]																								
BENSON, THOMAS Thomas Carl, LB, 6´2˝/238 lbs; Oklahoma; 1984: Atl, rnd 2; B9/6/1961 Ardmore, OK **1984** Atl 16 (0) **1985** Atl 16 (1) **1986** SD 16 (16, RILB) **1987** SD 11 (8, RILB) **1988** NE 12 (0) **1989** LARd 16 (16, LILB) **1990**†LARd 16 (16, RLB) **1991**†LARd 16 (14, RLB) **1992** LARd 1 (0) **NFL** 120 (71) [9 yrs]																								
BENSON, TROY Troy B., LB, 6´2˝/235 lbs; Pittsburgh; 1985: NYJ, rnd 5; B7/30/1963 Altoona, PA **1986**†NYJ 15 (1) **1987** NYJ 11 (11, LILB) **1988** NYJ 16 (16, LILB) **1989** NYJ 16 (15, LILB) **NFL** 58 (43) [4 yrs]																								

BENTLEY, ALBERT Albert Timothy, RB, 5´11˝/200 lbs; Miami (FL); 1984: Ind, rnd S2; B8/15/1960 Naples, FL [R]

YEAR	TEAM	G(GS, POS)	RUSH	YD	AVG(LG)	TD	REC	YD	AVG(LG)	TD	PASS	COMP	PCT	YD	AVG(LG)	TD	INT	SK	YD	QBR	KPR	OTD	PTS	TAY
1985	Ind	15(1)	54	288	5.3(26)	2	11	85	7.7(16)	0	1	1	100.0	6	6.0(6)	0	0	—	—	—	k	—	12	623
1986	Ind	12(3)	73	351	4.8(70)	3	25	230	9.2(38)	0	0	0	0.0	0	0.0	0	0	1	7	—	k	—	18	703
1987	†Ind	12(4)	142	631	4.4(17)	7	34	447	13.1(72)	2	—	—	—	—	—	—	—	—	—	—	k	—	54	1105
1988	Ind	16(2)	45	230	5.1(20)	2	26	252	9.7(21)	1	1	0	0.0	0	0.0	0	0	—	—	—	k	—	18	571
1989	Ind	16(8, FB)	75	299	4.0(22)	1	52	525	10.1(61)	3	1	0	0.0	0	0.0	0	0	—	—	—	k	1	30	660
1990	Ind	16(15, FB)	137	556	4.1(26)	4	71	664	9.4(73)	2	—	—	—	—	—	—	—	—	—	—	k	—	36	984
1991	Ind	1(0)	—	—	—	—	7	42	6.0(11)	0	—	—	—	—	—	—	—	—	—	—	—	—	0	21
1992	Pit	2(0)	—	—	—	—	—	—	—	—	—	—	—	—	—	—	—	—	—	—	k	—	0	2
NFL	8	90(33)	526	2355	4.5(70)	19	226	2245	9.9(73)	8	3	1	33.3	6	2.0(6)	0	0	1	7	—	k	1	168	4668

BENTLEY, KEVIN Kevin Kinte, LB, 6´1˝/245 lbs; Northwestern; 2002: Cle, rnd 4; B12/29/1979 Northridge, CA **2002**†Cle 12 (0) **2003** Cle 16 (14, LLB) **2004** Cle 16 (3) **2005**†Sea 15 (3) **NFL** 59 (20) [4 yrs]

BENTLEY, LECHARLES LeCharles Vernon, G-C, 6´2˝/299 lbs; Ohio State; 2002: NO, rnd 2; B11/7/1979 Cleveland, OH **2002** NO 14 (14, RG) **2003** NO✧13 (13, RG) **2004** NO 16 (16, C) **2005** NO✧14 (14, C) **NFL** 57 (57) [4 yrs]

BENTLEY, RAY Ray Russell, LB, 6´2˝/240 lbs; Central Michigan; B11/25/1960 Grand Rapids, MI **1986** Buf 13 (7, rilb) **1987** Buf 9 (4) **1988**†Buf 16 (16, RILB) **1989** Buf 15 (15, RILB) **1990**†Buf 16 (9, RILB) **1991**†Buf 16 (0) **1992** Cin 2 (2) **NFL** 87 (53) [7 yrs]

BENTLEY, SCOTT Scott L., K, 6´0˝/203 lbs; Florida State; B4/10/1974 Dallas, TX **[K]** **1997** Den 1 (0) **1997** Atl 2 (0) **1999** KC 2 (0) **2000** Den 1 (0) **2000** Was 6 (0) **NFL** 12 (0) [3 yrs]

BENTON, JIM James Warren, E, 6´3˝/200 lbs; Arkansas; 1938: Cle, rnd 2; B9/25/1916 Carthage, AR, D3/28/2001 Pine Bluff, AR

YEAR	TEAM	G(GS, POS)	RUSH	YD	AVG(LG)	TD	REC	YD	AVG(LG)	TD	PASS	COMP	PCT	YD	AVG(LG)	TD	INT	SK	YD	QBR	KPR	OTD	PTS	TAY
1938	Cle	11(9, LE)	—	—	—	—	21	418	19.9	5	—	—	—	—	—	—	—	—	—	—	—	1	36	234
1939	Cle★	11(11, LE)	7	19	2.7	0	27	388	14.4	**7**	—	—	—	—	—	—	—	—	—	—	—	1	48	248
1940	Cle	10(5, LE)	1	0	0.0	0	22	351	**16.0**	3	—	—	—	—	—	—	—	—	—	—	—	—	18	191
1942	Cle	9(7, LE)	—	—	—	—	23	345	15.0(45)	1	—	—	—	—	—	—	—	—	—	—	—	—	6	178
1943	†ChiB	9(7, LE)	—	—	—	—	13	235	18.1(55)	3	—	—	—	—	—	—	—	—	—	—	—	—	18	133
1944	Cle☆	10(4)	—	—	—	—	39	505	12.9(36)	6	—	—	—	—	—	—	—	—	—	—	k	1	42	257
1945	†Cle☆	9(4, LE)	—	—	—	—	45	**1067**	23.7(**84**)	8	—	—	—	—	—	—	—	—	—	—	k	—	48	545
1946	LARm☆	11(4)	—	—	—	—	**63**	**981**	15.6(57)	6	—	—	—	—	—	—	—	—	—	—	—	—	36	521
1947	LARm	11(4)	—	—	—	—	35	511	14.6(43)	6	—	—	—	—	—	—	—	—	—	—	—	—	36	286
NFL	9	91(55)	8	19	2.4	0	288	4801	16.7(84)	45	—	—	—	—	—	—	—	—	—	—	k	3	288	2590

BENTZ, CHRIS Christian, T, 6´4˝/215 lbs; Northern State; Montana; B12/20/1891, SD, D1/1981 Spokane, WA **1920** Det 2 (1)

BENTZ, ROMAN Roman Walter, G-T, 6´2˝/230 lbs; Tulane; 1943: Was, rnd 25; B9/1/1919 Iron Ridge, WI, D6/24/1996 Tomahawk, WI **1946**†NYY-A 12 (3) **1947**†NYY-A 13 (13, LG) **1948** NYY-A 5 (3) **1948** SF-A 4 (0) **AAFC** 34 (19) [3 yrs]

BENTZIN, AL Alfred Ernest, G, 6´0˝/188 lbs; Marquette; B3/7/1902 Watertown, WI, D1/1/1979 Watertown, WI **1924** Rac 10 (9, LG)

BENYOLA, GEORGE George, K, 5´10˝/195 lbs; Louisiana Tech; B9/17/1964 Perth Amboy, NJ **[K]** **1987** NYG 3 (0)

BENZ, EDDIE Edward G., aka Eddie Bentz, E, none; B2/1891, NY, D7/13/1971 Hamburg, NY **1922** Roc 1 (1)

BENZ, LARRY Larry Walker, DB, 5´11˝/185 lbs; Northwestern; B1/28/1941 Chattanooga, TN **1963** Cle 14 (14, LS) **1964**†Cle 13 (LS) **1965**†Cle 14 (RS) **NFL** 41 (14) [3 yrs]

BERCICH, BOB Robert Edward, DB, 6´1˝/198 lbs; Michigan State; 1960: LAC, rnd 1; B11/9/1936 Chicago, IL **1960** Dal 12 (6, LS) **1961** Dal 6 (6, LS) **NFL** 18 (12) [2 yrs]

BERCICH, PETE Peter James, LB, 6´1˝/240 lbs; Notre Dame; 1994: Min, rnd 7; B12/23/1971 Joliet, IL **1995** Min 9 (0) **1996**†Min 15 (1) **1997**†Min 16 (0) **1998**†Min 15 (1) **2000**†Min 2 (0) **NFL** 57 (2) [5 yrs]

BEREZNEY, PAUL Paul Lawrence, T, 6´2˝/220 lbs; Fordham; B9/25/1916 Jersey City, NJ, D3/29/1990 Columbus, GA **1942** GB 11 (11, RT) **1943** GB 10 (6, RT) **1944**†GB 10 (6, RT) **NFL** 31 (23) [3 yrs]

1946 Mia-A 1 (0)

BEREZNEY, PETE Peter John, T, 6´2˝/240 lbs; Notre Dame; 1946: Det, rnd 7; B11/14/1923 Jersey City, NJ **1947** LAD-A 12 (3) **1948**†Bal-A 13 (0) **AAFC** 25 (3) [2 yrs]

BERGEN, ADAM Adam, TE, 6´4˝/263 lbs; Lehigh; B9/3/1983 Seaford, NY

YEAR	TEAM	G(GS, POS)	RUSH	YD	AVG(LG)	TD	REC	YD	AVG(LG)	TD	PASS	COMP	PCT	YD	AVG(LG)	TD	INT	SK	YD	QBR	KPR	OTD	PTS	TAY
2005	Arz	16(10, TE)	—	—	—	—	28	270	9.6(32)	1	—	—	—	—	—	—	—	—	—	—	—	—	6	140

BERGER, JOE Joe, T, 6´5˝/290 lbs; Michigan Tech; 2005: Car, rnd 6; B5/25/1982 Fremont, MI **2005** Mia 3 (0)

BERGER, MITCH Mitchell Shannon, P, 6´4˝/220 lbs; Colorado; 1994: Phi, rnd 6; B6/24/1972 Kamloops, Canada **[P]** **1994** Phi 5 (0) **1996**†Min 16 (0) **1998**†Min 16 (0) **1999**†Min★16 (0) **2002** SL 16 (0) **2004** NO★16 (0) **2005** NO 16 (0)

YEAR	TEAM	G(GS, POS)	RUSH	YD	AVG(LG)	TD	REC	YD	AVG(LG)	TD	PASS	COMP	PCT	YD	AVG(LG)	TD	INT	SK	YD	QBR	KPR	OTD	PTS	TAY
1997	†Min	14(0)	1	0	0.0(0)	0	—	—	—	—	—	—	—	—	—	—	—	—	—	—	P	—	0	0
2000	†Min	16(0)	—	—	—	—	—	—	—	—	1	0	0.0	0	0.0	0	1	—	—	—	P	—	0	-40
2001	Min	12(0)	—	—	—	—	—	—	—	—	1	0	0.0	0	0.0	0	0	—	—	—	P	—	0	0
2003	NO	16(0)	—	—	—	—	—	—	—	—	1	0	0.0	0	0.0	0	0	—	—	—	P	—	0	0
NFL	11	159(0)	1	0	0.0	0	—	—	—	—	3	0	0.0	0	0.0	0	1	—	—	—	P	—	0	-40

BERGER, RON Ronald C., DT-DE, 6´8˝/290 lbs; Wayne State (NE); B9/30/1943 Detroit, MI **1969** Bos-A 7 (1) **1970** Bos 14 (12, RDT) **1971** NE 14 (6, ldt) **1972** NE 6 (3) **NFL** 41 (22) [4 yrs]

BERGERSON, GIL Charles Gilbert, G-T, 6´6˝/245 lbs; Oregon State; B7/19/1910 Veronia, OR, D9/18/1987 Corvallis, OR **1932** ChiB 13 (3) **1933** ChiB 2 (0) **1933** ChiC 8 (8, LG) **1935** Bkn 12 (7, LG) **1936** Bkn 5 (1) **NFL** 40 (19) [4 yrs]

BERGESON, ERIC Eric Scott, DB, 5´11˝/192 lbs; Brigham Young; B1/1/1966 Salt Lake City, UT **1990** Atl 13 (0)

BERGEY, BILL William Earl, LB, 6´4˝/243 lbs; Arkansas State; 1969: Cin, rnd 2; B2/9/1945 South Dayton, NY **[I]** **1969** Cin-A✧14 (MLB) **1970**†Cin 14 (MLB) **1971** Cin 14 (MLB) **1972** Cin 12 (MLB) **1973**†Cin 14 (MLB) **1974** Phi★14 (14, MLB) **1975** Phi☆14 (14, MLB) **1976** Phi★14 (14, MLB) **1977** Phi★14 (14, LILB) **1978**†Phi★16 (16, LILB) **1979** Phi 3 (3) **1980**†Phi☆16 (16, LILB) **NFL** 159 (91) [12 yrs]

BERGEY, BRUCE Bruce Gene, DE, 6´2˝/240 lbs; UCLA; 1971: KC, rnd 14; B8/8/1946 South Dayton, NY **1971** KC 6 **1971** Hou 1 **NFL** 7 [1 yr]

BERGOLD, SCOTT Scott M., T, 6´7˝/263 lbs; Wisconsin; 1985: SL, rnd 2; B11/19/1961 Milwaukee, WI **1985** SL 16 (0)

BERLIN, EDDIE Eddie, WR, 5´11˝/195 lbs; Northern Iowa; 2001: Ten, rnd 5; B1/14/1978 Urbandale, IA

YEAR	TEAM	G(GS, POS)	RUSH	YD	AVG(LG)	TD	REC	YD	AVG(LG)	TD	PASS	COMP	PCT	YD	AVG(LG)	TD	INT	SK	YD	QBR	KPR	OTD	PTS	TAY
2001	Ten	11(0)	—	—	—	—	2	28	14.0(19)	0	—	—	—	—	—	—	—	—	—	—	k	—	0	72
2002	†Ten	16(0)	—	—	—	—	1	14	14.0(14)	0	—	—	—	—	—	—	—	—	—	—	k	—	0	72
2003	Ten	14(0)	—	—	—	—	1	50	50.0(50)	1	—	—	—	—	—	—	—	—	—	—	k	—	6	43
2004	Ten	16(1)	—	—	—	—	20	278	13.9(31)	1	—	—	—	—	—	—	—	—	—	—	p	—	6	135
2005	†ChiB	5(0)	—	—	—	—	2	9	4.5(9)	0	—	—	—	—	—	—	—	—	—	—	—	—	0	5
NFL	5	62(1)	—	—	—	—	26	379	14.6(50)	2	—	—	—	—	—	—	—	—	—	—	kp	—	12	327

BERNARD, CHUCK Charles Joseph, C, 6´3˝/225 lbs; Michigan; B8/29/1911 Chicago, IL, D3/30/1962 Detroit, MI **1934** Det 10 (5, c)

BERNARD, DAVE David Edgar, LB-BB, 5´10˝/194 lbs; Mississippi; B9/26/1912 Jefferson, SD, D7/17/1973 Montgomery, AL **1945** Cle 7 (0)

YEAR	TEAM	G(GS, POS)	RUSH	YD	AVG(LG)	TD	REC	YD	AVG(LG)	TD	PASS	COMP	PCT	YD	AVG(LG)	TD	INT	SK	YD	QBR	KPR	OTD	PTS	TAY
1944	Cle	8(0)	1	6	6.0(6)	0	—	—	—	—	4	0	0.0	0	0.0	0	2	—	—	—	—	—	0	-74
NFL	2	15(0)	1	6	6.0(6)	0	—	—	—	—	4	0	0.0	0	0.0	0	2	—	—	—	—	—	0	-74

BERNARD, GEORGE George, G-T, none **1926** Rac 4 (3, RG)

BERNARD, KARL Gregory Karl, RB, 5´11˝/205 lbs; LSU; Louisiana-Lafayette; B10/12/1964 New Orleans, LA

YEAR	TEAM	G(GS, POS)	RUSH	YD	AVG(LG)	TD	REC	YD	AVG(LG)	TD	PASS	COMP	PCT	YD	AVG(LG)	TD	INT	SK	YD	QBR	KPR	OTD	PTS	TAY
1987	Det	8(3)	45	187	4.2(14)	2	13	91	7.0(12)	0	—	—	—	—	—	—	—	—	—	—	k	—	12	247

BERNARD, ROCKY Robert, DT, 6´3˝/293 lbs; Texas A&M; 2002: Sea, rnd 5; B4/19/1979 Baytown, TX **2002** Sea 16 (2) **2003** Sea 12 (0) **2004**†Sea 14 (1) **2005**†Sea 16 (6, rdt) **NFL** 58 (9) [4 yrs]

BERNARD, WALTER Walter Anton, DB, 6´2˝/200 lbs; New Mexico; B5/3/1978 San Diego, CA **2002** Sea 1 (0)

YEAR	TEAM	G (GS, POS)	RUSH	YD	AVG (LG)	TD	REC	YD	AVG (LG)	TD	PASS	COMP	PCT	YD	AVG (LG)	TD	INT	SK	YD	QBR	KPR	OTD	PTS	TAY
BERNARDI, FRANK Frank Dominic, DB-HB, 5´9˝/181 lbs; Colorado; 1955: ChiC, rnd 4; B6/17/1933 Highwood, IL																								
1955	ChiC	11	8	17	2.1(20)	0	4	77	19.3(39)	1	—	—	—	—	—	—	—	—	—	—	pi	—	6	142
1956	ChiC	12	14	4	0.3(7)	0	4	56	14.0(19)	0	—	—	—	—	—	—	—	—	—	—	kpi	1	6	207
1957	ChiC	12(DB)	1	4	4.0(4)	0	1	13	13.0(13)	0	1	0	0.0	0	0.0	0	0	—	—	—	pi	—	0	43
1960	Den-A	6(LCB)	—	—	—	—	—	—	—	—	—	—	—	—	—	—	—	—	—	—	—	—	—	—
NFL	4	41	23	25	1.1(20)	0	9	146	16.2(39)	1	1	0	0.0	0	0.0	0	0	—	—	—	kpi	1	12	391
BERNER, MIL Milford C., C, 6´2˝/204 lbs; Syracuse; B7/8/1906, D12/17/1993 Schaumburg, IL **1933** Cin 1 (0)																								
BERNET, ED Edward Nelson, E, 6´3˝/203 lbs; SMU; 1955: Pit, rnd 3; B10/24/1933 Dallas, TX																								
1955	Pit	12(LE)	—	—	—	—	22	276	12.5(38)	1	—	—	—	—	—	—	—	—	—	—	—	—	6	143
1960	DalT-A	9	—	—	—	—	4	49	12.3(15)	0	—	—	—	—	—	—	—	—	—	—	—	—	0	25
NFL	2	21	—	—	—	—	26	325	12.5(38)	1	—	—	—	—	—	—	—	—	—	—	—	—	6	168
BERNET, LEE Lee Anthony, T, 6´2˝/250 lbs; Wisconsin; B1/24/1944 Chicago, IL **1965** Den-A 12 **1966** Den-A 9 (RT) **NFL** 21 [2 yrs]																								
BERNHARDT, GEORGE George W., G, 5´10˝/213 lbs; Illinois; B6/15/1920, D12/1987 **1946** Bkn-A 14 (12, LG) **1947** Bkn-A 2 (2) **1948** Bkn-A 3 (2) **1948** ChiR-A 11 (8, RG) **AAFC** 30 (24) [3 yrs]																								
BERNHARDT, ROGER Roger Ernest, G, 6´4˝/244 lbs; Kansas; 1973: Pit, rnd 3; B10/14/1949 Lyons, NY **1974** NYJ 14 **1975** KC 4 (3) **NFL** 18 (3) [2 yrs]																								
BERNICH, KEN Kenneth Overton, LB, 6´2˝/250 lbs; Auburn; 1975: SD, rnd 4; B9/6/1951 Biloxi, MS **1975** NYJ 5																								
BERNOSKE, DAN Daniel Gabriel, G, 5´10˝/190 lbs; Indiana; B7/20/1905 Michigan City, IN, D6/29/1979 Indianapolis, IN **1926** Lou 2 (2, RG)																								
BERNS, BOBBY William Jennings, G-T, 6´1˝/200 lbs; Purdue; B12/10/1895 Linton, IN, D7/22/1980 Greenwood, IN **1920** Mun 1 (1, LT) **1922** Day 6 (6, LG) **1923** Day 8 (8, LG) **1924** Day 1 (0) **NFL** 16 (15) [4 yrs]																								
BERNS, RICK Richard Rickey, RB, 6´2˝/205 lbs; Nebraska; 1979: TB, rnd 3; B2/5/1956 Kadena AFB, Okinawa																								
1979	†TB	16(1)	23	102	4.4(16)	0	5	40	8.0(12)	0	—	—	—	—	—	—	—	—	—	—	k	—	0	113
1980	TB	16(2)	39	131	3.4(17)	0	1	6	6.0(6)	0	—	—	—	—	—	—	—	—	—	—	k	—	0	138
1982	†LARd	2(0)	—	—	—	—	—	—	—	—	—	—	—	—	—	—	—	—	—	—	—	—	—	—
1983	†LARd	16(0)	6	22	3.7(13)	0	—	—	—	—	—	—	—	—	—	—	—	—	—	—	—	—	0	22
NFL	4	50(3)	68	255	3.8(17)	0	6	46	7.7(12)	0	—	—	—	—	—	—	—	—	—	—	k	—	0	273
BERNSTEIN, JOE Joseph G., aka Joe Burten, FB-G-T, 6´0˝/210 lbs; LSU; Tulsa; B11/23/1893 Elmira, NY, D3/28/1967 Orange, NJ **1921** NYG 1 (0) **1923** RI 5 (3) **1924** RI 5 (2) **NFL** 11 (5) [3 yrs]																								
BERNSTINE, ROD Rod Earl, RB-TE, 6´3˝/238 lbs; Texas A&M; 1987: SD, rnd 1; B2/8/1965 Fairfield, CA																								
1987	SD	10(2)	1	9	9.0(9)	0	10	76	7.6(15)	1	—	—	—	—	—	—	—	—	—	—	k	—	6	50
1988	SD	14(13, TE)	2	7	3.5(5)	0	29	340	11.7(59)	0	—	—	—	—	—	—	—	—	—	—	—	—	0	177
1989	SD	5(0)	15	137	9.1(32)	1	21	222	10.6(36)	1	—	—	—	—	—	—	—	—	—	—	—	—	12	263
1990	SD	12(1)	124	589	4.8(40)	4	8	40	5.0(11)	0	—	—	—	—	—	—	—	—	—	—	—	—	24	649
1991	SD	13(8, RB)	159	766	4.8(63)	8	11	124	11.3(25)	0	1	1	100.0	11	11.0(11)	1	0	—	—	—	k	—	48	911
1992	†SD	9(1)	106	499	4.7(25)	4	12	86	7.2(16)	0	—	—	—	—	—	—	—	—	—	—	—	—	24	582
1993	Den	15(14, RB)	223	816	3.7(24)	4	44	372	8.5(41)	0	—	—	—	—	—	—	—	—	—	—	—	—	24	1042
1994	Den	3(3)	17	91	5.4(24)	0	9	70	7.8(16)	0	—	—	—	—	—	—	—	—	—	—	—	—	0	126
1995	Den	3(3)	23	76	3.3(18)	1	5	54	10.8(38)	0	—	—	—	—	—	—	—	—	—	—	—	—	6	113
NFL	9	84(45)	670	2990	4.5(63)	22	149	1384	9.3(59)	2	1	1	100.0	11	11.0(11)	1	0	—	—	—	k	—	144	3913
BERQUIST, JAY Jay Theodore John, G, 6´3˝/235 lbs; Nebraska; B7/30/1901 Loomis, NE, deceased **1924** KC 9 (9, LG) **1926** KC☆9 (9, LG) **1927** ChiC 1 (0) **NFL** 19 (18) [3 yrs]																								
BERRA, TIM Timothy Thomas, WR, 5´11˝/185 lbs; Massachusetts; 1974: Bal, rnd 17; B9/23/1951 Montclair, NJ **1974** Bal 14																								
BERRANG, ED Edward Patrick, DE-E, 6´2˝/206 lbs; Villanova; 1949: Was, rnd 5/NYY-A, rnd 13; B10/14/1922 Philadelphia, PA, D7/3/1992 Kensington, MD **1951** Was 2 **1951** Det 10 **1952** GB 1 **1952** Was 7																								
1949	Was	11(2)	—	—	—	—	1	5	5.0(5)	0	—	—	—	—	—	—	—	—	—	—	—	—	0	3
1950	Was	11(LDE)	—	—	—	—	1	14	14.0(14)	0	—	—	—	—	—	—	—	—	—	—	—	—	0	7
NFL	4	42(2)	—	—	—	—	2	19	9.5(14)	0	—	—	—	—	—	—	—	—	—	—	i	—	0	13
BERREHSEM, BILL William Stewart, T-E, 5´10˝/195 lbs; Washington & Jefferson; B4/25/1903, D11/6/1968 Baldwin, PA **1926** Col 6 (6, LT)																								
BERRIAN, BERNARD Bernard, WR, 6´1˝/190 lbs; Fresno State; 2004: Chi, rnd 3; B12/27/1980 Winton, CA																								
2004	ChiB	16(1)	8	28	3.5(25)	0	15	225	15.0(49)	2	—	—	—	—	—	—	—	—	—	—	kp	—	12	281
2005	†ChiB	11(2)	2	31	15.5(37)	0	13	246	18.9(54)	0	—	—	—	—	—	—	—	—	—	—	p	—	0	183
NFL	2	27(3)	10	59	5.9(37)	0	28	471	16.8(54)	2	—	—	—	—	—	—	—	—	—	—	kp	—	12	464
BERRY, BERTRAND Bertrand Demond, DE, 6´3˝/250 lbs; Notre Dame; 1997: Ind, rnd 3; B8/15/1975 Houston, TX **1997** Ind 10 (1) **1998** Ind 16 (12, RDE) **1999**†Ind 16 (0) **2001** Den 14 (0) **2002** Den 16 (1) **2003**†Den 16 (16, RDE) **2004** Arz★16 (16, RDE) **2005** Arz 8 (8, RDE) **NFL** 112 (54) [8 yrs]																								
BERRY, BOB Robert Chadwick, QB, 5´11˝/185 lbs; Oregon; 1964: Phi, rnd 11/Den, rnd 26; B3/10/1942 San Jose, CA																								
1965	Min	2	—	—	—	—	—	—	—	—	2	0	0.0	0	0.0	0	0	—	—	—	—	—	0	0
1966	Min	3	3	12	4.0(5)	0	—	—	—	—	37	13	35.1	215	5.8(52)	1	5	7	53	—	—	—	0	-76
1967	Min	2	—	—	—	—	—	—	—	—	7	3	42.9	43	6.1(21)	0	0	6	49	—	—	—	0	22
1968	Atl	10(7, QB)	26	139	5.3(45)	2	—	—	—	—	153	81	52.9	1433	9.4(66)	7	13	49	364	65.1	—	—	12	391
1969	Atl✧	7(QB)	20	68	3.4(30)	0	—	—	—	—	124	71	57.3	1087	8.8(88)	10	2	31	219	**106.5**	—	—	0	582
1970	Atl	12(QB)	13	60	4.6(16)	0	—	—	—	—	269	156	58.0	1806	6.7(51)	16	13	36	274	78.1	—	—	0	523
1971	Atl	11(QB)	19	31	1.6(9)	0	—	—	—	—	226	136	**60.2**	2005	8.9(84)	11	16	21	150	75.9	—	—	0	449
1972	Atl	14(QB)	24	86	3.6(16)	2	1	-9	-9.0(-9)	0	277	154	55.6	2158	**7.8**(**57**)	13	12	39	255	78.5	—	—	12	766
1973	Min	6	2	5	2.5(5)	0	—	—	—	—	24	10	41.7	121	5.0(30)	1	2	1	8	—	—	—	0	-10
1974	†Min	10	1	8	8.0(8)	0	—	—	—	—	48	34	70.8	305	6.4(21)	5	1	2	12	—	—	—	0	146
1975	†Min	1	1	0	0.0(0)	0	—	—	—	—	6	3	50.0	24	4.0(17)	0	0	1	9	—	—	—	0	12
NFL	11	78(7)	109	409	3.8(45)	4	1	-9	-9.0(-9)	0	1173	661	56.4	9197	7.8(88)	64	64	193	1393	77.2	—	—	24	2803
BERRY, CHARLIE Charles Francis, E, 6´0˝/185 lbs; Lafayette; B10/18/1902 Phillipsburg, NJ, D9/6/1972 Evanston, IL **[K]** **1925** Pot☆10 (9, LE), 74 **1926** Pot☆10 (7, LE), 18 **NFL** 20 (16), 92 [2 yrs]																								
BERRY, CONNIE MACK Connie Mack, E, 6´3˝/215 lbs; North Carolina State; B4/19/1915 Spartanburg, SC, D6/24/1980 Fayetteville, NC																								
1939	Det	3(0)	—	—	—	—	—	—	—	—	—	—	—	—	—	—	—	—	—	—	—	—	—	—
1940	GB	1(0)	—	—	—	—	1	17	17.0(17)	0	—	—	—	—	—	—	—	—	—	—	—	—	0	9
1940	Cle	3(0)	—	—	—	—	—	—	—	—	—	—	—	—	—	—	—	—	—	—	—	—	—	—
1942	ChiB	10(1)	—	—	—	—	4	29	7.3(16)	0	—	—	—	—	—	—	—	—	—	—	—	2	12	15
1943	†ChiB	10(2)	—	—	—	—	4	99	24.8(54)	2	—	—	—	—	—	—	—	—	—	—	—	—	12	60
1944	ChiB	10(7, LE)	—	—	—	—	21	378	**18.0**(**51**)	6	—	—	—	—	—	—	—	—	—	—	—	—	36	219
1945	ChiB	7(3)	—	—	—	—	12	202	16.8(51)	0	—	—	—	—	—	—	—	—	—	—	—	—	0	101
1946	ChiB	6(3)	—	—	—	—	4	58	14.5(21)	0	—	—	—	—	—	—	—	—	—	—	—	—	0	29
NFL	7	50(16)	—	—	—	—	46	783	17.0(54)	8	—	—	—	—	—	—	—	—	—	—	—	2	60	432
1947	ChiR-A	1(0)	—	—	—	—	—	—	—	—	—	—	—	—	—	—	—	—	—	—	—	—	—	—
BERRY, ED Edward J., DB, 5´10˝/183 lbs; Utah State; 1986: GB, rnd 7; B9/28/1963 San Francisco, CA **1986** GB 16 (0) **1987** SD 2 (1) **NFL** 18 (1) [2 yrs]																								
BERRY, GARY Gary John, DB, 5´11˝/193 lbs; Ohio State; 2000: GB, rnd 4; B10/24/1977 Worthington, OH **2000** GB 4 (0)																								
BERRY, GEORGE George W., G-T-C, 5´11˝/203 lbs; none; B2/18/1900 Milwaukee, WI, D3/25/1986 Half Moon Bay, CA **1922** Rac 2 (1) **1922** Ham 4 (4, RT) **1923** Ham 7 (7, LG) **1924** Ham 5 (4, LG) **1924** Akr☆3 (3) **1925** Akr 5 (4, RG), 6 **1926** Akr 8 (6, C) **1926** Ham 1 (0) **NFL** 35 (29) [5 yrs]																								
BERRY, GIL Gilbert Irwin, B, 5´10˝/178 lbs; Illinois; B3/21/1911 Lewistown, IL, D4/20/1974 Indianapolis, IN																								
1935	ChiC	6(2)	44	77	1.8	0	—	—	—	—	4	0	0.0	0	0.0	0	1	—	—	—	—	—	0	37
BERRY, HOWARD Joseph Howard, B, 5´11˝/165 lbs; Muhlenberg; Pennsylvania; B12/31/1894 Philadelphia, PA, D4/29/1976 Philadelphia, PA **[K]** **1921** Roc 4 (4, TB), 20																								

YEAR	TEAM	G (GS, POS)	RUSH	YD	AVG(LG)	TD	REC	YD	AVG(LG)	TD	PASS COMP	PCT	YD	AVG(LG)	TD	INT	SK	YD	QBR	KPR	OTD	PTS	TAY

BERRY, LATIN Latin Dafonso, DB, 5´10˝/196 lbs; Oregon; 1990: LARm, rnd 3; B1/13/1967 Lakeview Terrace, CA **1990** LARm 16 (0) **1991** Cle 15 (0) **1992** Cle 1 (0)
NFL 32 (0) [3 yrs]

BERRY, LOUIS Louis Albert, P, 6´0˝/193 lbs; Florida State; B7/21/1965 Hattiesburg, MS **1987** Atl 2 (0)

BERRY, RAY Raymond Lenn, LB, 6´2˝/227 lbs; Baylor; 1987: Min, rnd 2; B10/28/1963 Lovington, NM **1987**†Min 11 (0) **1988**†Min 15 (0) **1989**†Min 16 (10, LLB) **1990** Min 16 (3)
1991 Min 16 (16, MLB) **1992** Min 8 (0) **1993** Sea 7 (2) **NFL** 89 (31) [7 yrs]

BERRY, RAYMOND Raymond Emmett, E, 6´2˝/187 lbs; Schreiner College; SMU; 1954: Bal, rnd 20; B2/27/1933 Corpus Christi, TX; HOF 1973 [C]

1955	Bal	12	—	—	—	—	13	205	15.8(45)	0	—	—	—	—	—	—	—	—	—	k	—	0	100
1956	Bal	12(LE)	—	—	—	—	37	601	16.2(54)	2	—	—	—	—	—	—	—	—	—	—	—	12	311
1957	Bal☆	12(LE)	—	—	—	—	47	**800**	17.0(67)	6	—	—	—	—	—	—	—	—	—	—	—	36	430
1958	†Bal★	12(LE)	—	—	—	—	**56**	794	14.2(54)	**9**	—	—	—	—	—	—	—	—	—	—	—	54	442
1959	†Bal★	12(LE)	—	—	—	—	**66**	959	14.5(55)	**14**	—	—	—	—	—	—	—	—	—	—	—	84	550
1960	Bal☆	12(SE)	—	—	—	—	**74**	1298	17.5(70)	10	—	—	—	—	—	—	—	—	—	—	—	60	699
1961	Bal★	12(SE)	—	—	—	—	75	873	11.6(44)	0	—	—	—	—	—	—	—	—	—	—	—	0	437
1962	Bal	14(SE)	—	—	—	—	51	687	13.5(37)	3	—	—	—	—	—	—	—	—	—	—	—	18	359
1963	Bal☆	9(SE)	—	—	—	—	44	703	16.0(64)	3	—	—	—	—	—	—	—	—	—	—	—	18	367
1964	†Bal★	12(SE)	—	—	—	—	43	663	15.4(46)	6	—	—	—	—	—	—	—	—	—	—	—	36	362
1965	†Bal☆	14(SE)	—	—	—	—	58	739	12.7(40)	7	—	—	—	—	—	—	—	—	—	—	—	42	405
1966	Bal	14 (14, SE)	—	—	—	—	56	786	14.0(40)	7	—	—	—	—	—	—	—	—	—	—	—	42	428
1967	Bal	7(SE)	—	—	—	—	11	167	15.2(40)	1	—	—	—	—	—	—	—	—	—	—	—	6	89
NFL	13	154(14)	—	—	—	—	631	9275	14.7(70)	68	—	—	—	—	—	—	—	—	—	k	—	408	4975

BERRY, REGGIE Reginald Dennis, DB, 6´0˝/190 lbs; Long Beach State; B3/15/1950 Minneapolis, MN **1972** SD 9 **1973** SD 8 **1974** SD 13 **NFL** 30 [3 yrs]

BERRY, REX Charles Rex, DB-HB, 5´11˝/190 lbs; Brigham Young; 1951: SF, rnd 14; B9/9/1924 Moab, UT, D7/1/2005 Provo, UT [I] **1953** SF 12 (DB) **1954** SF 8 (DB)
1955 SF☆12 (DB) **1956** SF 12 (DB)

1951	SF	10	—	—	—	—	1	12	12.0(12)	0	—	—	—	—	—	—	—	—	—	i	—	0	63
1952	SF	12(DB)	1	7	7.0(7)	0	—	—	—	—	—	—	—	—	—	—	—	—	—	—	—	0	24
NFL	6	66	1	7	7.0(7)	0	1	12	12.0(12)	0	—	—	—	—	—	—	—	—	—	Pkpi	3	18	372

BERRY, ROYCE Royce Elmer, DE, 6´4˝/250 lbs; Houston; 1969: Cin, rnd 7; B4/14/1946 Odessa, TX **1969** Cin-A 13 (LDE) **1970**†Cin 14 (LDE) **1971** Cin 14 (LDE)
1972 Cin 14 (LDE) **1973**†Cin 14 (LDE) **1974** Cin 13 **1976** ChiB 12 (2) **NFL** 94 (2) [7 yrs]

BERRY, WAYNE Wayne Chandler, HB-DB, 6´0˝/175 lbs; Washington State; 1954: NYG, rnd 7; B8/2/1931 LaGrande, OR

| 1954 | NYG | 10 | 1 | 30 | 30.0(30) | 0 | — | — | — | — | — | — | — | — | — | — | — | — | — | — | — | 0 | 30 |

BERSCHET, MARV Marvin Walter, G-DE, 6´2˝/220 lbs; Illinois; 1952: Was, rnd 16; B12/28/1929 Arlington Heights, IL **1954** Was 12 (LG) **1955** Was 4 **NFL** 16 [2 yrs]

BERTAGNOLLI, LIBBY Libero Lorenz, G, 5´9˝/189 lbs; Washington-St. Louis; B11/13/1914 Benld, IL, D9/14/1992 Bloomington, IL **1942** ChiC 10 (2) **1945** ChiC 1 (0)
NFL 11 (2) [2 yrs]

BERTELLI, ANGELO Angelo Bortolo, QB, 6´1˝/190 lbs; Notre Dame; 1944: Bos, rnd 1; B6/18/1921 West Springfield, MA, D6/26/1999 Clifton, NJ [K]

1946	LAD-A	12(3, qb)	11	-16	-1.5	1	—	—	—	—	127	67	52.8	917	7.2	7	14	—	—	P	—	6	-73
1947	ChiR-A	1(0)	1	2	2.0(2)	0	—	—	—	—	7	2	28.6	5	-0.7	0	2	—	—	K	—	0	-81
1948	ChiR-A	3(2)	2	-1	-0.5	0	—	—	—	—	32	7	21.9	60	1.9	1	3	—	—	—	—	0	-86
AAFC	3	16(5)	14	-15	-1.1(2)	1	—	—	—	—	166	76	45.8	972	5.9	8	19	—	—	KP	—	6	-239

BERTELSEN, JIM James Allen, RB, 5´11˝/205 lbs; Texas; 1972: LA, rnd 2; B2/26/1950 St. Paul, MN

1972	LARm	14(8, RB)	123	581	4.7(42)	5	29	331	11.4(22)	1	—	—	—	—	—	—	—	—	—	kp	—	36	982
1973	†LARm◇	14(14, FB)	206	854	4.1(49)	4	19	267	14.1(44)	1	—	—	—	—	—	—	—	—	—	kp	—	30	1162
1974	†LARm	13(13, FB)	127	419	3.3(20)	2	20	175	8.8(19)	0	—	—	—	—	—	—	—	—	—	p	—	12	604
1975	LARm	13	116	457	3.9(19)	1	14	208	14.9(22)	0	—	—	—	—	—	—	—	—	—	kp	—	18	681
1976	†LARm	14	42	155	3.7(18)	2	6	33	5.5(10)	0	—	—	—	—	—	—	—	—	—	p	—	12	197
NFL	5	68(35)	614	2466	4.0(49)	16	88	1014	11.5(44)	2	—	—	—	—	—	—	—	—	—	kp	—	108	3624

BERTHUSEN, BILL William Scott, NT, 6´5˝/290 lbs; Iowa State; 1987: NYG, rnd 12; B6/26/1964 Grinnell, IA **1987** Cin 3 (3) **1987** NYG 1 (0) **NFL** 4 (3) [1 yr]

BERTI, TONY Charles Anton, T, 6´6˝/300 lbs; Colorado; 1995: SD, rnd 6; B6/21/1972 Rock Springs, WY **1995** SD 1 (0) **1996** SD 16 (14, RT) **1997** SD 16 (16, RT)
NFL 33 (30) [3 yrs]

BERTOGLIO, JIM James Emory, FB, 5´9˝/187 lbs; Creighton; B9/1/1905 Meaderville, MT, D1/14/1976 Salt Lake City, UT **1926** Col 7 (7, FB), 6

BERTON, SEAN Sean, TE, 6´4˝/272 lbs; West Virginia; North Carolina State; B10/31/1979 Columbia, SC

2003	Min	16(0)	—	—	—	—	—	—	—	—	—	—	—	—	—	—	—	—	—	k	—	0	-8
2004	†Min	14(7, TE)	—	—	—	—	9	78	8.7(14)	0	—	—	—	—	—	—	—	—	—	k	—	0	27
2005	NYG	14(0)	—	—	—	—	1	3	3.0(3)	0	—	—	—	—	—	—	—	—	—	—	—	0	2
NFL	3	44(7)	—	—	—	—	10	81	8.1(14)	0	—	—	—	—	—	—	—	—	—	k	—	0	21

BERTUCA, TONY Anthony Francis, LB, 6´2˝/225 lbs; Cal State-Chico; B1/4/1950 Chicago, IL **1974** Bal 14

BERWICK, ED Edward J., C-E, 6´0˝/185 lbs; Loyola (IL); B12/27/1904, D3/3/1977 High Island, TX **1926** Lou 4 (4, C)

BERZINSKI, WILL Willis John, HB, 6´2˝/195 lbs; Wisconsin-LaCrosse; 1956: LA, rnd 4; B7/18/1934 Arcadia, WI, D3/4/1994 Rochester, MN

| 1956 | Phi | 4 | 15 | 72 | 4.8(20) | 0 | 3 | 35 | 11.7(17) | 0 | — | — | — | — | — | — | — | — | — | — | — | 0 | 90 |

BESON, WARREN Warren L., C, 6´0˝/205 lbs; Minnesota; 1949: Bal-A, rnd 13/NYB, rnd 17; B11/16/1923 Minneapolis, MN, D10/25/1959 Northfield, MN **1949** Bal-A 3 (0)

BESS, GERALD Gerald D., DB, 6´0˝/188 lbs; Tuskegee; B5/24/1958 Pensacola, FL **1987** Buf 2 (1)

BESS, RUFUS Rufus T., DB, 5´9˝/184 lbs; South Carolina State; B9/13/1956 Hartsville, SC **1979** Oak 16 **1980**†Buf 16 (1) **1981**†Buf 16 (0) **1982**†Min 8 (0) **1983** Min 14 (6, lcb)
1984 Min 16 (13, RCB) **1985** Min 11 (11, RCB) **1986** Min 16 (0) **1987** Min 3 (2) **NFL** 116 (33) [9 yrs]

BESSILLIEU, DON Donald Andrew, DB, 6´1˝/200 lbs; Georgia Tech; 1979: Mia, rnd 5; B5/4/1956 Fort Benning, GA **1979**†Mia 16 **1980** Mia 16 (13, FS) **1981**†Mia 16 (6, fs)
1982†SL 3 (0) **1983** LARd 4 (0) **1985** LARd 4 (0) **NFL** 59 (19) [6 yrs]

BEST, ART Arthur Robie, RB, 6´1˝/205 lbs; Notre Dame; Kent State; 1977: LA, rnd 6; B3/18/1953 Camden, NJ

1977	†ChiB	14	6	20	3.3(6)	0	—	—	—	—	—	—	—	—	—	—	—	—	—	k	—	0	57
1978	ChiB	16	2	11	5.5(6)	0	—	—	—	—	—	—	—	—	—	—	—	—	—	—	—	0	11
1980	NYG	1(0)	—	—	—	—	—	—	—	—	—	—	—	—	—	—	—	—	—	—	—	—	—
NFL	3	31	8	31	3.9(6)	0	—	—	—	—	—	—	—	—	—	—	—	—	—	k	—	0	68

BEST, GREG Gregory Lee, DB, 5´10˝/185 lbs; Kansas State; B1/14/1960 New Brighton, PA **1983**†Pit 13 (0) **1984** Cle 5 (0) **NFL** 18 (0) [2 yrs]

BEST, KEITH Keith Alan, LB, 6´3˝/220 lbs; Kansas State; B8/21/1950 Canton, OH **1972** KC 6

BESTA, TEDDY Theodore, B, none; B9/25/1899 Chicago, IL, D7/1965 **1922** Ham 1 (1) **1924** Ham 2 (0) **NFL** 3 (1) [2 yrs]

BETHEA, ELVIN Elvin Lamont, DE, 6´2˝/260 lbs; North Carolina A&T; 1968: Hou, rnd 3; B3/1/1946 Trenton, NJ; HOF 2003 **1968** Hou-A 14 (14, RDE) **1969**†Hou-A★14 (14, RDE)
1970 Hou 14 (14, RDE) **1971** Hou★14 (14, RDE) **1972** Hou★14 (14, RDE) **1973** Hou★14 (14, RDE) **1974** Hou★14 (14, RDE) **1975** Hou★14 (14, RDE) **1976** Hou 14 (14, RDE)
1977 Hou 9 (9, RDE) **1978**†Hou★16 (16, RDE) **1979**†Hou★14 (14, RDE) **1980**†Hou★14 (14, RDE) **1981** Hou 15 (14, RDE) **1982** Hou 9 (0) **1983** Hou 7 (0) **NFL** 210 (191) [16 yrs]

BETHEA, LARRY Larry, DT-DE, 6´2˝/251 lbs; Michigan State; 1978: Dal, rnd 1; B7/21/1956 Florence, SC, D4/23/1987 Newport News, VA **1978**†Dal 16 **1979**†Dal 16 (2)
1980†Dal 11 (0) **1981**†Dal 16 (0) **1982**†Dal 8 (0) **1983** Dal 14 (0) **NFL** 81 (2) [6 yrs]

BETHUNE, BOBBY Bobby Wayne, DB, 5´11˝/190 lbs; Mississippi State; 1961: Chi, rnd 9; B12/10/1938 Leeds, AL **1962** SD-A 10 (RS)

BETHUNE, GEORGE George Edward, LB, 6´4˝/238 lbs; Alabama; 1989: LARm, rnd 7; B3/30/1967 Fort Walton Beach, FL **1989**†LARm 16 (0) **1990** LARm 16 (0) **NFL** 32 (0) [2 yrs]

BETTENCOURT, LARRY Lawrence Joseph, C, 5´11˝/205 lbs; St. Mary's (CA); B9/22/1905 Newark, NJ, D9/15/1978 New Orleans, LA **1933** GB 2 (1)

YEAR	TEAM	G (GS, POS)	RUSH	YD	AVG (LG)	TD	REC	YD	AVG (LG)	TD	PASS	COMP	PCT	YD	AVG (LG)	TD	INT	SK	YD	QBR	KPR	QTD	PTS	TAY

BETTERS, DOUG Douglas Lloyd, DE, 6´7˝/262 lbs; Montana; Nevada-Reno; 1978: Mia, rnd 6; B6/11/1956 Lincoln, NE **1978**†Mia 16 (6, rde) **1979**†Mia 16 (14, RDE) **1980** Mia 16 (16, RDE) **1981**†Mia 15 (15, LDE) **1982**†Mia 9 (7, LDE) **1983**†Mia★16 (16, LDE) **1984**†Mia 16 (16, LDE) **1985**†Mia 14 (14, LDE) **1986** Mia 16 (1) **1987** Mia 12 (0) **NFL** 146 (105) [10 yrs]

BETTERSON, JAMES James Thomas, RB, 6´0˝/210 lbs; North Carolina; 1976: Den, rnd 8; B8/20/1954 Blackshear, GA

YEAR	TEAM	G (GS, POS)	RUSH	YD	AVG (LG)	TD	REC	YD	AVG (LG)	TD	PASS	COMP	PCT	YD	AVG (LG)	TD	INT	SK	YD	QBR	KPR	QTD	PTS	TAY
1977	Phi	14(2)	62	233	3.8(17)	1	4	41	10.3(15)	0	—	—	—	—	—	—	—	—	—	—	k	—	6	262
1978	Phi	9	11	32	2.9(5)	0	2	8	4.0(5)	0	—	—	—	—	—	—	—	—	—	—	k	—	0	116
NFL	2	23(2)	73	265	3.6(17)	1	6	49	8.2(15)	0	—	—	—	—	—	—	—	—	—	—	k	—	6	378

BETTIGA, MIKE Michael John, WR, 6´3˝/193 lbs; Humboldt State; 1973: SF, rnd 15; B9/10/1950 Scotia, CA **1974** SF 10

BETTIS, JEROME Jerome Abram 'The Bus', RB, 5´11˝/252 lbs; Notre Dame; 1993: LARm, rnd 1; B2/16/1972 Detroit, MI

YEAR	TEAM	G (GS, POS)	RUSH	YD	AVG (LG)	TD	REC	YD	AVG (LG)	TD	PASS	COMP	PCT	YD	AVG (LG)	TD	INT	SK	YD	QBR	KPR	QTD	PTS	TAY
1993	LARm★	16(12, RB)	**294**	1429	4.9(71)	7	26	244	9.4(28)	0	—	—	—	—	—	—	—	—	—	—	—	—	42	1621
1994	LARm✧	16(16, RB)	319	1025	3.2(19)	3	31	293	9.5(34)	1	—	—	—	—	—	—	—	—	—	—	—	—	28	1207
1995	SL	15(13, RB)	183	637	3.5(41)	3	18	106	5.9(19)	0	—	—	—	—	—	—	—	—	—	—	—	—	18	720
1996	†Pit★	16(12, RB)	320	1431	4.5(50)	11	22	122	5.5(16)	0	—	—	—	—	—	—	—	—	—	—	—	—	66	1602
1997	†Pit★	15(15, RB)	**375**	1665	4.4(34)	7	15	110	7.3(19)	2	—	—	—	—	—	—	—	—	—	—	—	—	54	1800
1998	Pit	15(15, RB)	316	1185	3.8(42)	3	16	90	5.6(26)	0	—	—	—	—	—	—	—	—	—	—	—	—	18	1260
1999	Pit	16(16, RB)	299	1091	3.6(35)	7	21	110	5.2(17)	0	1	1	100.0	21	21.0(21)	1	0	—	—	—	—	—	42	1232
2000	Pit	16(16, RB)	355	1341	3.8(30)	8	13	97	7.5(25)	0	2	0	0.0	0	0.0	0	1	—	—	—	—	—	48	1430
2001	†Pit✧	11(11, RB)	225	1072	4.8(48)	4	8	48	6.0(16)	0	2	1	50.0	32	16.0(32)	1	0	—	—	—	—	—	24	1157
2002	†Pit	13(11, RB)	187	666	3.6(41)	9	7	57	8.1(15)	0	—	—	—	—	—	—	—	—	—	—	—	—	54	785
2003	Pit	16(10, RB)	246	811	3.3(21)	7	13	86	6.6(16)	0	—	—	—	—	—	—	—	—	—	—	—	—	44	924
2004	†Pit✧	15(6, RB)	250	941	3.8(29)	13	6	46	7.7(20)	0	1	1	100.0	10	10.0(10)	1	0	—	—	—	—	—	78	1104
2005	†Pit	12(0)	110	368	3.3(39)	9	4	40	10.0(16)	0	—	—	—	—	—	—	—	—	—	—	—	—	54	478
NFL	13	192(153)	3479	13662	3.9(71)	91	200	1449	7.2(34)	3	6	3	50.0	63	10.5(32)	3	1	—	—	—	—	—	570	15318

BETTIS, TOM William Thomas, LB, 6´2˝/228 lbs; Purdue; 1955: GB, rnd 1; B3/17/1933 Chicago, IL **[C]** **1955** GB 12 (LLB) **1956** GB 12 (LLB) **1957** GB 12 (LLB) **1958** GB 12 (LLB) **1959** GB 12 **1960** GB 12 **1961**†GB 12 **1962** Pit 11 **1963**†ChiB 14 **NFL** 109 [9 yrs]

BETTRIDGE, ED Edward N., LB, 6´1˝/235 lbs; Bowling Green State; B9/16/1940 Sandusky, OH **1964**†Cle 3

BETTRIDGE, JOHN John William, FB, 5´10˝/188 lbs; Ohio State; B3/19/1910 Sandusky, OH, D12/10/1975 Sandusky, OH

YEAR	TEAM	G (GS, POS)	RUSH	YD	AVG (LG)	TD	REC	YD	AVG (LG)	TD	PASS	COMP	PCT	YD	AVG (LG)	TD	INT	SK	YD	QBR	KPR	QTD	PTS	TAY
1937	ChiB	3(0)	1	0	0.0	0	—	—	—	—	—	—	—	—	—	—	—	—	—	—	—	—	0	0
1937	Cle	6(1)	21	35	1.7	0	1	17	17.0(17)	0	—	—	—	—	—	—	—	—	—	—	—	—	0	44
NFL	1	9(1)	22	35	1.6	0	1	17	17.0(17)	0	—	—	—	—	—	—	—	—	—	—	—	—	0	44

BETTS, LADELL Matthew, RB, 5´10˝/222 lbs; Iowa; 2002: Was, rnd 2; B8/27/1979 Blue Springs, MO **[R]**

YEAR	TEAM	G (GS, POS)	RUSH	YD	AVG (LG)	TD	REC	YD	AVG (LG)	TD	PASS	COMP	PCT	YD	AVG (LG)	TD	INT	SK	YD	QBR	KPR	QTD	PTS	TAY
2002	Was	11(0)	65	307	4.7(27)	1	12	154	12.8(40)	0	—	—	—	—	—	—	—	—	—	—	k	—	6	664
2003	Was	9(1)	77	255	3.3(13)	2	15	167	11.1(34)	0	—	—	—	—	—	—	—	—	—	—	k	—	12	373
2004	Was	16(1)	90	371	4.1(27)	1	15	108	7.2(20)	0	—	—	—	—	—	—	—	—	—	—	k	—	6	618
2005	†Was	12(0)	89	338	3.8(22)	1	10	78	7.8(26)	1	—	—	—	—	—	—	—	—	—	—	k	1	18	663
NFL	4	48(2)	321	1271	4.0(27)	5	52	507	9.8(40)	1	—	—	—	—	—	—	—	—	—	—	k	1	42	2318

BEUERLEIN, STEVE Stephen Taylor, QB, 6´3˝/220 lbs; Notre Dame; 1987: LARd, rnd 4; B3/7/1965 Hollywood, CA

YEAR	TEAM	G (GS, POS)	RUSH	YD	AVG (LG)	TD	REC	YD	AVG (LG)	TD	PASS	COMP	PCT	YD	AVG (LG)	TD	INT	SK	YD	QBR	KPR	QTD	PTS	TAY
1988	LARd	10(8, qb)	30	35	1.2(20)	0	1	21	21.0(21)	0	238	105	44.1	1643	6.9(57)	8	7	26	215	66.6	—	—	0	627
1989	LARd	10(7, qb)	16	39	2.4(10)	0	—	—	—	—	217	108	49.8	1677	7.7(67)	13	9	22	175	78.4	—	—	0	583
1991	†Dal	8(4)	7	-14	-2.0(-1)	0	—	—	—	—	137	68	49.6	909	6.6(66)	5	2	6	49	77.2	—	—	0	386
1992	†Dal	16(0)	4	-7	-1.8(-1)	0	—	—	—	—	18	12	66.7	152	8.4(27)	0	1	—	—	—	—	—	0	29
1993	Phx	16(14, QB)	22	45	2.0(20)	0	—	—	—	—	418	258	61.7	3164	7.6(65)	18	17	29	206	82.5	—	—	0	1037
1994	Arz	9(7, qb)	22	39	1.8(19)	1	—	—	—	—	255	130	51.0	1545	6.1(63)	5	9	20	129	61.6	—	—	6	487
1995	Jax	7(6, qb)	5	32	6.4(13)	0	—	—	—	—	142	71	50.0	952	6.7(71)	4	7	17	103	60.5	—	—	0	248
1996	Car	8(4)	12	17	1.4(13)	0	—	—	—	—	123	69	56.1	879	7.1(40)	8	2	18	136	93.5	—	—	0	417
1997	Car	7(3, qb)	4	32	8.0(20)	0	—	—	—	—	153	89	58.2	1032	6.7(52)	6	3	17	111	83.6	—	—	0	458
1998	Car	12(12, QB)	22	26	1.2(13)	0	—	—	—	—	343	216	63.0	2613	7.6(68)	17	12	44	251	88.2	—	—	0	938
1999	Car✧	16(16, QB)	27	124	4.6(16)	2	—	—	—	—	571	**343**	60.1	**4436**	7.8(88)	36	15	50	280	94.6	—	—	12	1942
2000	Car	16(16, QB)	44	106	2.4(15)	1	—	—	—	—	533	324	60.8	3730	7.0(54)	19	18	62	331	79.7	—	—	8	1356
2002	Den	8(3)	5	9	1.8(8)	1	—	—	—	—	117	68	58.1	925	7.9(52)	6	5	12	78	82.7	—	—	6	312
2003	Den	4(2)	5	13	2.6(7)	0	—	—	—	—	63	33	52.4	389	6.2(38)	2	5	9	60	—	—	—	0	18
NFL	14	147(102)	225	496	2.2(20)	5	1	21	21.0(21)	0	3328	1894	56.9	24046	7.2(88)	147	112	332	2124	80.3	—	—	32	8835

BEUTLER, TOM Thomas Joseph, LB, 6´1˝/234 lbs; Toledo; 1968: Cle, rnd 12; B9/29/1946 Bluffton, OH **1970** Cle 4 **1971**†Bal 4 **NFL** 8 [2 yrs]

BEVERLY, DAVID David Edward, P, 6´2˝/180 lbs; Auburn; B8/19/1950 Selma, AL **[P]**

YEAR	TEAM	G (GS, POS)	RUSH	YD	AVG (LG)	TD	REC	YD	AVG (LG)	TD	PASS	COMP	PCT	YD	AVG (LG)	TD	INT	SK	YD	QBR	KPR	QTD	PTS	TAY
1974	Hou	14	1	4	4.0(4)	0	—	—	—	—	—	—	—	—	—	—	—	—	—	—	P	—	0	4
1975	Hou	2	—	—	—	—	—	—	—	—	—	—	—	—	—	—	—	—	—	—	P	—	0	0
1975	GB	10	—	—	—	—	—	—	—	—	—	—	—	—	—	—	—	—	—	—	P	—	0	0
1976	GB	14	—	—	—	—	—	—	—	—	1	1	100.0	18	18.0(18)	0	0	—	—	—	P	—	0	9
1977	GB	14	2	-3	-1.5(0)	0	—	—	—	—	—	—	—	—	—	—	—	—	—	—	P	—	0	-3
1978	GB	16	1	0	0.0(0)	0	—	—	—	—	2	2	100.0	88	44.0(57)	0	0	—	—	—	P	—	0	44
1979	GB	16	—	—	—	—	—	—	—	—	2	1	50.0	23	11.5(23)	0	0	—	—	—	P	—	0	12
1980	GB	16(0)	6	21	3.5(11)	0	—	—	—	—	1	0	0.0	0	0.0	0	0	—	—	—	P	—	0	21
NFL	7	102	10	22	2.2(11)	0	—	—	—	—	6	4	66.7	129	21.5(57)	0	0	—	—	—	P	—	0	87

BEVERLY, DWIGHT Dwight Anthony, RB, 5´11˝/205 lbs; Illinois; 1984: Ind, rnd 6; B12/5/1961 Long Beach, CA

YEAR	TEAM	G (GS, POS)	RUSH	YD	AVG (LG)	TD	REC	YD	AVG (LG)	TD	PASS	COMP	PCT	YD	AVG (LG)	TD	INT	SK	YD	QBR	KPR	QTD	PTS	TAY
1987	NO	3(3)	62	217	3.5(25)	2	1	8	8.0(8)	0	—	—	—	—	—	—	—	—	—	—	k	—	12	242

BEVERLY, ED Edward Louis, WR, 5´11˝/172 lbs; Arizona State; 1973: SF, rnd 5; B9/27/1949 Harrisburg, PA **1973** SF 2

BEVERLY, ERIC Eric Raymonde, C-G, 6´3˝/300 lbs; Miami (OH); B3/28/1974 Cleveland, OH **1998** Det 16 (0) **1999** Det 16 (2) **2000** Det 16 (7, c) **2001** Det 16 (16, C) **2002** Det 15 (3) **2003** Det 13 (13, LG) **2004**†Atl 13 (3) **2005** Atl 16 (1) **NFL** 121 (45) [8 yrs]

BEVERLY, RANDY Randolph, DB, 5´11˝/190 lbs; Colorado State; B4/3/1944 Wildwood, NJ **1967** NYJ-A 14 (13, RCB) **1968**†NYJ-A 13 (RCB) **1969**†NYJ-A 13 (rcb) **1970** Bos 13 (3) **1971** NE 8 (2) **NFL** 61 (18) [5 yrs]

BEYERS, GEORGE George, B, /168 lbs; none; deceased **1921** Was 3 (1, WB)

BIAKABUTUKA, TIM Tshimanga, RB, 6´0˝/215 lbs; Michigan; 1996: Car, rnd 1; B1/24/1974 Kinshasa, Zaire

YEAR	TEAM	G (GS, POS)	RUSH	YD	AVG (LG)	TD	REC	YD	AVG (LG)	TD	PASS	COMP	PCT	YD	AVG (LG)	TD	INT	SK	YD	QBR	KPR	QTD	PTS	TAY
1996	Car	4(4)	71	229	3.2(17)	0	—	—	—	—	—	—	—	—	—	—	—	—	—	—	—	—	0	229
1997	Car	8(2)	75	299	4.0(26)	2	—	—	—	—	—	—	—	—	—	—	—	—	—	—	—	—	12	319
1998	Car	10(3)	101	427	4.2(41)	3	8	138	17.3(42)	1	—	—	—	—	—	—	—	—	—	—	—	—	24	531
1999	Car	11(11, RB)	138	718	5.2(67)	6	23	189	8.2(32)	0	—	—	—	—	—	—	—	—	—	—	—	—	36	873
2000	Car	12(11, RB)	173	627	3.6(43)	2	34	341	10.0(25)	2	—	—	—	—	—	—	—	—	—	—	—	—	24	828
2001	Car	5(4)	53	230	4.3(58)	1	12	121	10.1(47)	0	—	—	—	—	—	—	—	—	—	—	—	—	6	301
NFL	6	50(35)	611	2530	4.1(67)	14	77	789	10.2(47)	3	—	—	—	—	—	—	—	—	—	—	—	—	102	3080

BIANCHINI, FRANK Frank, RB, 5´8˝/190 lbs; Hofstra; B5/27/1961 **1987** NE 1 (0)

BIANCONE, JOHNNY John L., B, 5´6˝/165 lbs; Oregon State; B12/5/1911 Portland, OR, D9/6/1996 Portland, OR

YEAR	TEAM	G (GS, POS)	RUSH	YD	AVG (LG)	TD	REC	YD	AVG (LG)	TD	PASS	COMP	PCT	YD	AVG (LG)	TD	INT	SK	YD	QBR	KPR	QTD	PTS	TAY
1936	Bkn	5(1)	8	34	4.3	0	—	—	—	—	3	1	33.3	29	9.7(29)	0	0	—	—	—	—	—	0	49

BIASUCCI, DEAN Dean, K, 6´0˝/190 lbs; Western Carolina; B7/25/1962 Niagara Falls, NY **[K]** **1984** Ind 15 (0) **1986** Ind 16 (0) **1987**†Ind★12 (0) **1988** Ind☆16 (0) **1989** Ind 16 (0) **1990** Ind 16 (0) **1991** Ind 16 (0) **1992** Ind 16 (0) **1993** Ind 16 (0) **1994** Ind 16 (0) **1995** SL 8 (0) **NFL** 163 (0) [11 yrs]

BIBLA, MARTIN Martin John, G, 6´3˝/306 lbs; Miami (FL); 2002: Atl, rnd 4; B10/4/1979 Mountaintop, PA **2002**†Atl 10 (0) **2003** Atl 10 (2) **2004** Atl 11 (0) **NFL** 31 (2) [3 yrs]

BICKERSTAFF, ERIK Erik, RB, 6´0˝/230 lbs; Wisconsin; B7/25/1980 Birmingham, AL

YEAR	TEAM	G (GS, POS)	RUSH	YD	AVG (LG)	TD	REC	YD	AVG (LG)	TD	PASS	COMP	PCT	YD	AVG (LG)	TD	INT	SK	YD	QBR	KPR	QTD	PTS	TAY
2003	†Dal	4(0)	19	56	2.9(9)	1	—	—	—	—	—	—	—	—	—	—	—	—	—	—	k	—	6	60

YEAR	TEAM	G (GS, POS)	RUSH	YD	AVG (LG)	TD	REC	YD	AVG (LG)	TD	PASS	COMP	PCT	YD	AVG (LG)	TD	INT	SK	YD	QBR	KPR	OTD	PTS	TAY

Bickett, Duane Duane Clair, LB, 6´5˝/251 lbs; USC; 1985: Ind, rnd 1; B12/1/1962 Los Angeles, CA [S] **1985** Ind 16 (16, ROLB) **1986** Ind 16 (16, ROLB) **1987**†Ind★12 (12, ROLB) **1988** Ind☆16 (16, ROLB) **1989** Ind 16 (16, ROLB) **1990** Ind 15 (15, ROLB) **1991** Ind 16 (16, ROLB) **1992** Ind 15 (15, ROLB) **1993** Ind 15 (15, LLB) **1994** Sea 7 (1) **1995** Sea 13 (0) **1996**†Car 16 (0) **NFL** 173 (138) [12 yrs]

Bidwell, Josh Joshua John, P, 6´3˝/220 lbs; Oregon; 1999: GB, rnd 4; B3/13/1976 Roseburg, OR [P] **2000** GB 16 (0) **2001**†GB 16 (0) **2002**†GB 16 (0) **2003**†GB 16 (0) **2004** TB 16 (0) **2005**†TB★16 (0) **NFL** 96 (0) [6 yrs]

Bieberstein, Adolph Adolph Joseph, G, 5´10˝/205 lbs; Wisconsin; B12/17/1902 Phillips, WI, D12/31/1981 Madison, WI **1926** Rac 5 (5, LG) **1926** GB 1 (0) **NFL** 6 (5) [1 yr]

Biedermann, Leo Leo George, T, 6´7˝/254 lbs; California; 1978: Cle, rnd 12; B10/19/1955 Omaha, NE **1978** Cle 16

Biekert, Greg Gregory Scott, LB, 6´2˝/253 lbs; Colorado; 1993: LARd, rnd 7; B3/14/1969 Iowa City, IA **1993**†LARd 16 (0) **1994** LARd 16 (14, MLB) **1995** Oak 16 (14, MLB) **1996** Oak 16 (15, MLB) **1997** Oak 16 (16, MLB) **1998** Oak 16 (16, MLB) **1999** Oak 16 (16, MLB) **2000**†Oak 16 (16, MLB) **2001**†Oak 16 (16, MLB) **2002** Min 16 (16, MLB) **2003** Min 16 (16, MLB) **NFL** 176 (155) [11 yrs]

Bielski, Dick Richard Adam, E-FB, 6´1˝/224 lbs; Maryland; 1955: Phi, rnd 1; B9/7/1932 Maple Shade, NJ [K]

YEAR	TEAM	G (GS, POS)	RUSH	YD	AVG (LG)	TD	REC	YD	AVG (LG)	TD	PASS	COMP	PCT	YD	AVG (LG)	TD	INT	SK	YD	QBR	KPR	OTD	PTS	TAY
1955	Phi	12	28	67	2.4(8)	1	8	48	6.0(19)	0	—	—	—	—	—	—	—	—	—	—	K	—	56	101
1956	Phi	12	52	162	3.1(15)	1	8	63	7.9(17)	0	—	—	—	—	—	—	—	—	—	—	K	—	6	204
1957	Phi	12	—	—	—	—	8	81	10.1(19)	2	—	—	—	—	—	—	—	—	—	—	Kk	—	12	32
1958	Phi	12 (RE)	—	—	—	—	23	234	10.2(30)	1	—	—	—	—	—	—	—	—	—	—	k	—	6	113
1959	Phi	12	—	—	—	—	15	264	17.6(57)	1	—	—	—	—	—	—	—	—	—	—	K	—	6	137
1960	Dal	12	—	—	—	—	4	38	9.5(15)	1	—	—	—	—	—	—	—	—	—	—	k	—	6	13
1961	Dal✧	14 (TE)	—	—	—	—	26	377	14.5(28)	3	—	—	—	—	—	—	—	—	—	—	K	—	46	204
1962	Bal	14	—	—	—	—	15	200	13.3(22)	2	—	—	—	—	—	—	—	—	—	—	K	—	70	110
1963	Bal	14	—	—	—	—	—	—	—	—	—	—	—	—	—	—	—	—	—	—	k	—	0	-15
NFL	9	114	80	229	2.9(15)	2	107	1305	12.2(57)	10	—	—	—	—	—	—	—	—	—	—	Kk	—	208	898

Bienemann, Tom Thomas Jerome, DE-E-LB, 6´3˝/221 lbs; Drake; 1951: ChiC, rnd 11; B1/28/1928 Kenosha, WI, D10/5/1999 Kenosha, WI **1952** ChiC 12 (RDE) **1953** ChiC 12 (RDE) **1954** ChiC 11 (RDE) **1955** ChiC 10 (RDE) **1956** ChiC 8

YEAR	TEAM	G (GS, POS)	RUSH	YD	AVG (LG)	TD	REC	YD	AVG (LG)	TD	PASS	COMP	PCT	YD	AVG (LG)	TD	INT	SK	YD	QBR	KPR	OTD	PTS	TAY
1951	ChiC	12 (LDE)	—	—	—	—	1	8	8.0(8)	0	—	—	—	—	—	—	—	—	—	—	ki	—	0	8
NFL	6	65	—	—	—	—	1	8	8.0(8)	0	—	—	—	—	—	—	—	—	—	—	ki	—	0	3

Bieniemy, Eric Eric, RB, 5´7˝/207 lbs; Colorado; 1991: SD, rnd 2; B8/15/1969 New Orleans, LA [R]

YEAR	TEAM	G (GS, POS)	RUSH	YD	AVG (LG)	TD	REC	YD	AVG (LG)	TD	PASS	COMP	PCT	YD	AVG (LG)	TD	INT	SK	YD	QBR	KPR	OTD	PTS	TAY
1991	SD	15 (0)	3	17	5.7(15)	0	—	—	—	—	—	—	—	—	—	—	—	—	—	—	—	—	0	17
1992	†SD	15 (0)	74	264	3.6(21)	3	5	49	9.8(25)	0	—	—	—	—	—	—	—	—	—	—	kp	—	18	430
1993	SD	16 (0)	33	135	4.1(12)	1	1	0	0.0(0)	0	—	—	—	—	—	—	—	—	—	—	k	—	6	150
1994	†SD	16 (0)	73	295	4.0(36)	0	5	48	9.6(25)	0	—	—	—	—	—	—	—	—	—	—	—	—	0	319
1995	Cin	16 (1)	98	381	3.9(27)	3	43	424	9.9(33)	0	2	0	0.0	0	0.0	0	0	—	—	—	kp	—	18	683
1996	Cin	16 (0)	56	269	4.8(33)	2	32	272	8.5(42)	0	—	—	—	—	—	—	—	—	—	—	—	—	12	425
1997	Cin	16 (0)	21	97	4.6(20)	1	31	249	8.0(21)	0	—	—	—	—	—	—	—	—	—	—	k	1	12	521
1998	Cin	16 (0)	17	56	3.3(9)	0	27	153	5.7(15)	0	—	—	—	—	—	—	—	—	—	—	k	—	0	145
1999	Phi	16 (0)	12	75	6.3(28)	1	2	28	14.0(27)	0	—	—	—	—	—	—	—	—	—	—	k	—	6	159
NFL	9	142 (1)	387	1589	4.1(36)	11	146	1223	8.4(42)	0	2	0	0.0	0	0.0	0	0	—	—	—	kp	1	72	2848

Bierce, Scotty Bruce Wallace, E, 5´9˝/164 lbs; Akron; B9/3/1896 Kearney, NE, D4/26/1982 Valley City, OH [C] **1920** Akr 10 (6, RE) **1921** Akr 12 (12, RE), 12 **1922** Akr 4 (2), 12 **1923** Cle 7 (7, RE), 12 **1923** Buf 3 (2), 6 **1924** Cle 4 (3) **1925** Akr 8 (2) **NFL** 48 (34), 42 [6 yrs]

Bierria, Terreal Terreal, DB, 6´3˝/211 lbs; Georgia; 2002: Sea, rnd 4; B10/10/1980 Slidell, LA **2002** Sea 14 (0) **2004**†Sea 15 (12, SS) **NFL** 29 (12) [2 yrs]

Big Bear T, 6´4˝/215 lbs; none; deceased **1922** Oor 1 (1) **1923** Oor 5 (4) **NFL** 6 (5) [2 yrs]

Bigbee, Lyle Lyle Randolph, E, 6´0˝/180 lbs; Oregon; B8/22/1893 Sweet Home, OR, D8/5/1942 Portland, OR **1922** Mil 3 (1)

Bigby, Atari Atari, DB, 5´11˝/220 lbs; Central Florida; B9/19/1981 Miami, FL **2005** GB 1 (0)

Bigby, Keiron Keiron, WR, 5´10˝/177 lbs; Brown; B2/27/1966 **1987** Was 1 (0)

Biggs, Riley Riley Edgar, C, 6´2˝/230 lbs; Baylor; B3/24/1900 Montgomery County, PA, D11/24/1971 Liberty, TX **1926** NYG 3 (2) **1927** NYG 10 (3) **NFL** 13 (5) [2 yrs]

Biggs, Verlon Verlon Marion, DE, 6´4˝/275 lbs; Jackson State; 1965: NYJ, rnd 3; B3/16/1943 Moss Point, MS, D6/7/1994 Moss Point, MS **1965** NYJ-A☆14 (RDE) **1966** NYJ-A★14 (RDE) **1967** NYJ-A★14 (RDE) **1968**†NYJ-A✧13 (RDE) **1969**†NYJ-A 12 (RDE) **1970** NYJ 13 (RDE) **1971**†Was 13 (13, RDE) **1972**†Was☆14 (14, RDE) **1973**†Was 14 (14, RDE) **1974**†Was 14 (14, RDE) **NFL** 135 (55) [10 yrs]

Bighead, Jack John, DE-E, 6´3˝/215 lbs; Pepperdine; 1952: DalT, rnd 15; B4/23/1930 Beggs, OK, D4/28/1993 Parker, AZ **1955** LARm 2

YEAR	TEAM	G (GS, POS)	RUSH	YD	AVG (LG)	TD	REC	YD	AVG (LG)	TD	PASS	COMP	PCT	YD	AVG (LG)	TD	INT	SK	YD	QBR	KPR	OTD	PTS	TAY
1954	Bal	11	—	—	—	—	6	89	14.8(25)	0	—	—	—	—	—	—	—	—	—	—	—	—	0	45
NFL	2	13	—	—	—	—	6	89	14.8(25)	0	—	—	—	—	—	—	—	—	—	—	—	—	0	45

Bilbo, Jonathan Jonathan Payne, T-G, 6´0˝/195 lbs; Mississippi; B10/17/1914 Talisheek, LA, D2/27/2000 **1938** ChiC 8 (0) **1939** ChiC 1 (0) **NFL** 9 (0) [2 yrs]

Bilda, Dick Richard Francis, B, 6´2˝/210 lbs; Marquette; B5/17/1919 Milwaukee, WI, D11/29/1996

YEAR	TEAM	G (GS, POS)	RUSH	YD	AVG (LG)	TD	REC	YD	AVG (LG)	TD	PASS	COMP	PCT	YD	AVG (LG)	TD	INT	SK	YD	QBR	KPR	OTD	PTS	TAY
1944	GB	3 (0)	—	—	—	—	—	—	—	—	1	0	0.0	0	0.0	0	0	—	—	—	i	—	0	20

Biletnikoff, Fred Frederick S., WR-FL, 6´1˝/190 lbs; Florida State; 1965: Oak, rnd 2/Det, rnd 3; B2/23/1943 Erie, PA; HOF 1988

YEAR	TEAM	G (GS, POS)	RUSH	YD	AVG (LG)	TD	REC	YD	AVG (LG)	TD	PASS	COMP	PCT	YD	AVG (LG)	TD	INT	SK	YD	QBR	KPR	OTD	PTS	TAY
1965	Oak-A	14 (7, FL)	—	—	—	—	24	331	13.8(53)	0	—	—	—	—	—	—	—	—	—	—	—	—	0	166
1966	Oak-A	10 (FL)	—	—	—	—	17	272	16.0(78)	3	—	—	—	—	—	—	—	—	—	—	—	—	18	151
1967	†Oak-A✧	14 (fl)	—	—	—	—	40	876	**21.9(72)**	5	—	—	—	—	—	—	—	—	—	—	—	—	30	463
1968	†Oak-A	14 (14, FL)	—	—	—	—	61	1037	17.0(82)	6	—	—	—	—	—	—	—	—	—	—	—	1	42	549
1969	†Oak-A★	14 (14, FL)	—	—	—	—	54	837	15.5(53)	12	—	—	—	—	—	—	—	—	—	—	—	—	72	479
1970	†Oak★	14 (14, WR)	—	—	—	—	45	768	17.1(51)	7	—	—	—	—	—	—	—	—	—	—	—	—	42	419
1971	Oak★	14 (14, WR)	—	—	—	—	**61**	929	15.2(49)	9	—	—	—	—	—	—	—	—	—	—	—	—	54	510
1972	†Oak☆	14 (14, WR)	—	—	—	—	**58**	802	13.8(39)	7	—	—	—	—	—	—	—	—	—	—	—	—	42	436
1973	†Oak★	14 (14, WR)	—	—	—	—	48	660	13.8(32)	4	—	—	—	—	—	—	—	—	—	—	—	—	24	350
1974	†Oak★	14 (14, WR)	—	—	—	—	42	593	14.1(46)	7	—	—	—	—	—	—	—	—	—	—	—	—	42	332
1975	†Oak	11 (10, WR)	—	—	—	—	43	587	13.7(26)	2	—	—	—	—	—	—	—	—	—	—	—	—	12	304
1976	†Oak	13 (WR)	—	—	—	—	43	551	12.8(32)	7	—	—	—	—	—	—	—	—	—	—	—	—	42	311
1977	†Oak	14 (14, WR)	—	—	—	—	33	446	13.5(44)	5	—	—	—	—	—	—	—	—	—	—	—	—	30	248
1978	Oak	16 (2)	—	—	—	—	20	285	14.3(49)	2	—	—	—	—	—	—	—	—	—	—	—	—	12	153
NFL	14	190 (131)	—	—	—	—	589	8974	15.2(82)	76	—	—	—	—	—	—	—	—	—	—	—	1	462	4867

Billingsley, Ron Ronald Smith, DT-DE, 6´8˝/290 lbs; Wyoming; 1967: SD, rnd 1; B4/6/1945 Florence, AL **1967** SD-A 13 (RDE) **1968** SD-A 13 **1969** SD-A 9 (RDT) **1970** SD 9 (RDT) **1971** Hou 13 (RDT) **1972** Hou 4 **NFL** 61 [6 yrs]

Billman, John John Arthur, G-LB-T, 6´1˝/202 lbs; Minnesota; 1943: Phi, rnd 11; B12/1/1919 Minneapolis, MN **1946** Bkn-A 3 (0) **1947** ChiR-A 2 (1) **AAFC** 5 (1) [2 yrs]

Billock, Frank Francis, T, 6´0˝/230 lbs; St. Mary's (MN); B5/20/1912 Grand Rapids, MI, D10/1964 **1937** Pit 2 (1)

Billups, Lewis Lewis Kenneth, DB, 5´11˝/190 lbs; North Alabama; 1986: Cin, rnd 2; B10/10/1963 Tampa, FL, D4/9/1994 Orlando, FL **1986** Cin 12 (12, RCB) **1987** Cin 11 (11, RCB) **1988**†Cin 16 (16, LCB) **1989** Cin 16 (16, LCB) **1990**†Cin 15 (14, LCB) **1991** Cin 13 (7, lcb) **1992** GB 5 (4) **NFL** 88 (80) [7 yrs]

Billups, Terry Terry Michael, DB, 5´9˝/180 lbs; North Carolina; B2/9/1975 Wiesbaden, Germany **1998** Dal 1 (0) **1999** NE 2 (1) **NFL** 3 (1) [2 yrs]

Bingaman, Les Lester Alonza, DG-G, 6´3˝/272 lbs; Illinois; 1948: Det, rnd 3/Bkn-A, rnd 5; B2/3/1926 McKenzie, TN, D11/20/1970 Miami, FL **1948** Det 12 (0) **1949** Det 12 (1) **1950** Det☆12 (MG) **1951** Det★6 (MG) **1952**†Det☆12 (MG) **1953**†Det★12 (MG) **1954**†Det☆12 (MG) **NFL** 78 (1) [7 yrs]

Bingham, Craig Craig Marlon, LB, 6´2˝/218 lbs; Syracuse; 1982: Pit, rnd 6; B9/26/1959 Kingston, Jamaica **1982** Pit 6 (0) **1983**†Pit 12 (0) **1984**†Pit 11 (1) **1985** SD 8 (0) **1987** Pit 3 (3) **NFL** 40 (4) [5 yrs]

Bingham, Don Donald Dean, HB, 6´0˝/185 lbs; Sul Ross State; 1953: ChiB, rnd 7; B11/7/1929 Shattuck, OK

YEAR	TEAM	G (GS, POS)	RUSH	YD	AVG (LG)	TD	REC	YD	AVG (LG)	TD	PASS	COMP	PCT	YD	AVG (LG)	TD	INT	SK	YD	QBR	KPR	OTD	PTS	TAY
1956	†ChiB	12	7	36	5.1(12)	0	1	7	7.0(7)	0	—	—	—	—	—	—	—	—	—	—	kp	1	6	181

Bingham, Dwight Dwight Nottis, DE, 6´6˝/265 lbs; Mississippi; B8/5/1965 Kingston, Jamaica **1987** Atl 3 (0)

BINGHAM, GREGG Gregory Raleigh, LB, 6´1˝/227 lbs; Purdue; 1973: Hou, rnd 4; B3/13/1951 Evanston, IL **[I]** **1973** Hou 14 (14, MLB) **1974** Hou 14 (14, LILB) **1975** Hou 14 (14, RILB) **1976** Hou 14 (14, RILB) **1977** Hou 14 (14, RILB) **1978**†Hou 16 (16, RILB) **1979**†Hou 16 (16, LILB) **1980**†Hou 16 (16, RILB) **1981** Hou 16 (16, LILB) **1982** Hou 7 (7, LILB) **1983** Hou 16 (16, LILB) **1984** Hou 16 (16, LILB) **NFL** 173 (173) [12 yrs]

BINGHAM, GUY Guy Richard, C-G-T, 6´3˝/255 lbs; Montana; 1980: NYJ, rnd 10; B2/25/1958 Koiaumi Gumma Ken, Japan **1980** NYJ 16 (3) **1981**†NYJ 16 (0) **1982**†NYJ 7 (0) **1983** NYJ 16 (6, c) **1984** NYJ 16 (0) **1985**†NYJ 16 (3) **1986**†NYJ 16 (9, c) **1987** NYJ 12 (11, C) **1988** NYJ 10 (1) **1989** Atl 16 (0) **1990** Atl 16 (0) **1991**†Atl 13 (0) **1992**†Was 15 (0) **1993** Was 14 (0) **NFL** 199 (33) [14 yrs]

BINGHAM, RYON Ryon, DT, 6´3˝/303 lbs; Nebraska; 2004: SD, rnd 7; B6/6/1981 Sandy, UT **2005** SD 1 (0)

BINN, DAVID David Aaron, C, 6´3˝/245 lbs; California; B2/6/1972 San Mateo, CA **1994**†SD 16 (0) **1995**†SD 16 (0) **1996** SD 16 (0) **1997** SD 16 (0) **1998** SD 15 (0) **1999** SD 16 (0) **2000** SD 16 (0) **2001** SD 16 (0) **2002** SD 16 (0) **2003** SD 16 (0) **2004**†SD 16 (0) **2005** SD 16 (0) **NFL** 191 (0) [12 yrs]

BINOTTO, JOHN John, HB, 5´10˝/185 lbs; Duquesne; B11/24/1919 Lawrence, PA

YEAR	TEAM	G (GS, POS)	RUSH	YD	AVG (LG)	TD	REC	YD	AVG (LG)	TD	PASS	COMP	PCT	YD	AVG (LG)	TD	INT	SK	YD	QBR	KPR	OTD	PTS	TAY
1942	Pit	7(1)	16	57	3.6(30)	0	—	—	—	—	—	—	—	—	—	—	—	—	—	—	p	—	0	72
1942	Phi	2(0)	1	-10	-10.0(-10)	0	—	—	—	—	—	—	—	—	—	—	—	—	—	—	—	—	0	-10
NFL	1	9(1)	17	47	2.8(30)	0	—	—	—	—	—	—	—	—	—	—	—	—	—	—	p	—	0	62

BIODROWSKI, DENNIS Dennis James, G, 6´1˝/250 lbs; Memphis; 1962: SD, rnd 18; B6/27/1940 Gary, IN **1963** KC-A 2 **1964** KC-A 1 **1965** KC-A 6 **1966**†KC-A 14 **1967** KC-A 7 **NFL** 30 [5 yrs]

BIOLO, JOHN John Robert, G, 5´10˝/188 lbs; Lake Forest; B2/8/1916 Iron Mountain, MI, D2/4/2003 Green Bay, WI **1939** GB 1 (0)

BIRD, CORY Cory James, DB, 5´10˝/213 lbs; Virginia Tech; 2001: Ind, rnd 3; B8/10/1978 Atlantic City, NJ **2001** Ind 14 (0) **2002** Ind 6 (4) **2003**†Ind 12 (0) **2004**†Ind 13 (4) **NFL** 45 (8) [4 yrs]

BIRD, RODGER Rodger Paul, DB, 6´0˝/200 lbs; Kentucky; 1966: Oak, rnd 1; B7/2/1943 Corbin, KY **[R]** **1966** Oak-A 14 **1967**†Oak-A☆14 (RS) **1968**†Oak-A 10 (8, LS) **NFL** 38 (8) [3 yrs]

BIRD, STEVE Steven L., WR, 5´11˝/171 lbs; Eastern Kentucky; 1983: SL, rnd 5; B10/20/1960 Indianapolis, IN **1983** SL 14 (0) **1984** SL 8 (0) **1984** SD 1 (0) **NFL** 23 (0) [2 yrs]

BIRDEN, J.J. LaJourdain J., WR, 5´9˝/170 lbs; Oregon; 1988: Cle, rnd 8; B6/16/1965 Portland, OR

YEAR	TEAM	G (GS, POS)	RUSH	YD	AVG (LG)	TD	REC	YD	AVG (LG)	TD	PASS	COMP	PCT	YD	AVG (LG)	TD	INT	SK	YD	QBR	KPR	OTD	PTS	TAY
1990	†KC	11(0)	—	—	—	—	15	352	23.5(**90**)	3	—	—	—	—	—	—	—	—	—	—	kp	—	18	212
1991	†KC	15(0)	—	—	—	—	27	465	17.2(57)	2	—	—	—	—	—	—	—	—	—	—	—	—	12	243
1992	†KC	16(11, WR)	—	—	—	—	42	644	15.3(72)	3	—	—	—	—	—	—	—	—	—	—	p	—	18	337
1993	†KC	16(16, WR)	—	—	—	—	51	721	14.1(50)	2	—	—	—	—	—	—	—	—	—	—	p	—	12	389
1994	†KC	13(13, WR)	—	—	—	—	48	637	13.3(44)	4	—	—	—	—	—	—	—	—	—	—	—	—	26	339
1995	†Atl	10(10, WR)	—	—	—	—	31	303	9.8(24)	1	—	—	—	—	—	—	—	—	—	—	—	—	6	157
1996	Atl	12(12, WR)	—	—	—	—	30	319	10.6(57)	2	—	—	—	—	—	—	—	—	—	—	—	—	12	170
NFL	7	93(62)	—	—	—	—	244	3441	14.1(90)	17	—	—	—	—	—	—	—	—	—	—	kp	—	104	1845

BIRDSONG, CARL George Carlisle, P, 6´0˝/192 lbs; Southwestern Oklahoma State; B1/1/1959 Kaufman, TX **[P]**

YEAR	TEAM	G (GS, POS)	RUSH	YD	AVG (LG)	TD	REC	YD	AVG (LG)	TD	PASS	COMP	PCT	YD	AVG (LG)	TD	INT	SK	YD	QBR	KPR	OTD	PTS	TAY
1981	SL	16(0)	1	-2	-2.0(-2)	0	—	—	—	—	—	—	—	—	—	—	—	—	—	—	P	—	0	-2
1982	†SL☆	9(0)	—	—	—	—	—	—	—	—	—	—	—	—	—	—	—	—	—	—	P	—	0	0
1983	SL★	16(0)	—	—	—	—	—	—	—	—	1	1	100.0	11	11.0(11)	0	0	—	—	—	P	—	0	6
1984	SL	16(0)	—	—	—	—	—	—	—	—	—	—	—	—	—	—	—	—	—	—	P	—	0	0
1985	SL	16(0)	—	—	—	—	—	—	—	—	1	0	0.0	0	0.0	0	0	—	—	—	P	—	0	0
NFL	5	73(0)	1	-2	-2.0(-2)	0	—	—	—	—	2	1	50.0	11	5.5(11)	0	0	—	—	—	P	—	0	4

BIRDSONG, CRAIG Gary Craig, DB, 6´2˝/217 lbs; North Texas; B8/16/1964 Kaufman, TX **1987**†Hou 3 (0)

BIRDWELL, DAN Daniel Lee, DT-DE, 6´4˝/250 lbs; Houston; 1962: Oak, rnd 6/Det, rnd 5; B10/14/1940 Big Spring, TX, D2/14/1978 Huntington Beach, CA **[K]** **1962** Oak-A 14 **1963** Oak-A 10 **1964** Oak-A 14 (RDE) **1965** Oak-A 14 (ldt) **1966** Oak-A 14 (LDT) **1967**†Oak-A 14 (LDT) **1968**†Oak-A★14 (14, LDT) **1969** Oak-A 2 **NFL** 96 (14) [8 yrs]

BIRK, MATT Matthew Robert, C, 6´4˝/300 lbs; Harvard; 1998: Min, rnd 6; B7/23/1976 St. Paul, MN **1998**†Min 7 (0) **1999**†Min 15 (0) **2000**†Min★16 (16, C) **2001** Min✧16 (16, C) **2002** Min 16 (16, C) **2003** Min★16 (16, C) **2004**†Min✧12 (11, C) **NFL** 98 (75) [7 yrs]

BIRLEM, KEITH Keith, B-E, 5´11˝/198 lbs; San Jose State; B5/4/1915 San Jose, CA, D5/7/1943 Polebrook, U.K. **1939** Was 3 (0)

YEAR	TEAM	G (GS, POS)	RUSH	YD	AVG (LG)	TD	REC	YD	AVG (LG)	TD	PASS	COMP	PCT	YD	AVG (LG)	TD	INT	SK	YD	QBR	KPR	OTD	PTS	TAY
1939	ChiC	6(3)	—	—	—	—	2	17	8.5	0	—	—	—	—	—	—	—	—	—	—	—	—	0	9
NFL	1	9(3)	—	—	—	—	2	17	8.5	0	—	—	—	—	—	—	—	—	—	—	—	—	0	9

BIRNEY, TOM Thomas Francis, K, 6´4˝/220 lbs; Michigan State; B8/11/1956 Bellshill, Scotland **[K]** **1979** GB 6 **1980** GB 7 (0) **NFL** 13 [2 yrs]

BIRONAS, ROB Rob, K, 6´0˝/205 lbs; Georgia Southern; B1/29/1978 Louisville, **[K]** **2005** Ten 16 (0)

BISCAHA, JOE Joseph Daniel, E, 6´1˝/190 lbs; Richmond; 1959: NYG, rnd 27; B6/1/1937 Clifton, NJ **1960** Bos-A 1

YEAR	TEAM	G (GS, POS)	RUSH	YD	AVG (LG)	TD	REC	YD	AVG (LG)	TD	PASS	COMP	PCT	YD	AVG (LG)	TD	INT	SK	YD	QBR	KPR	OTD	PTS	TAY
1959	†NYG	8	—	—	—	—	1	5	5.0(5)	0	—	—	—	—	—	—	—	—	—	—	—	—	0	3
NFL	2	9	—	—	—	—	1	5	5.0(5)	0	—	—	—	—	—	—	—	—	—	—	—	—	0	3

BISHOP, BILL William Eugene, DT-T, 6´4˝/248 lbs; North Texas; 1952: ChiB, rnd 8; B5/8/1931 Borger, TX, D5/14/1998 Geneva, IL **1952** ChiB 12 (RDT) **1953** ChiB 12 (RDT) **1954** ChiB✧12 (RDT) **1955** ChiB 12 (RDT) **1956**†ChiB 12 (RDT) **1957** ChiB 11 (RDT) **1958** ChiB 12 (RDT) **1959** ChiB 12 (RDT) **1960** ChiB 12 **1961** Min 10 **NFL** 117 [10 yrs]

BISHOP, BLAINE Blaine Elwood, DB, 5´9˝/197 lbs; St. Joseph's (IN); Ball State; 1993: Hou, rnd 8; B7/24/1970 Indianapolis, IN **1993**†Hou 16 (2) **1994** Hou 16 (13, SS) **1995** Hou★16 (16, SS) **1996** Hou★15 (15, SS) **1997** Ten✧14 (14, SS) **1998** Ten 13 (13, SS) **1999**†Ten 15 (15, SS) **2000**†Ten★16 (16, SS) **2001** Ten 5 (4) **2002**†Phi 12 (12, SS) **NFL** 138 (120) [10 yrs]

BISHOP, DON Donald William, B, 6´2˝/209 lbs; Los Angeles C.C.; B7/1/1934 Los Angeles, CA, D11/13/1998 Chino, CA **[I]** **1959** Pit 2 **1959** ChiB 1 **1960** Dal 12 (RCB) **1961** Dal☆14 (RCB) **1962** Dal✧14 (RCB) **1963** Dal 13 (RCB) **1964** Dal 14 (7, RCB) **1965** Dal 14

YEAR	TEAM	G (GS, POS)	RUSH	YD	AVG (LG)	TD	REC	YD	AVG (LG)	TD	PASS	COMP	PCT	YD	AVG (LG)	TD	INT	SK	YD	QBR	KPR	OTD	PTS	TAY
1958	Pit	12	—	—	—	—	3	57	19.0(29)	0	—	—	—	—	—	—	—	—	—	—	—	—	0	29
NFL	8	96(7)	—	—	—	—	3	57	19.0(29)	0	—	—	—	—	—	—	—	—	—	—	pi	1	6	273

BISHOP, GREG Gregory Lawrence, G-T, 6´5˝/305 lbs; Pacific; 1993: NYG, rnd 4; B5/1/1971 Stockton, CA **1993**†NYG 8 (0) **1994** NYG 16 (1) **1995** NYG 16 (16, LG) **1996** NYG 16 (16, LT) **1997**†NYG 16 (16, LG) **1998** NYG 16 (16, LG) **1999** Atl 13 (2) **NFL** 101 (67) [7 yrs]

BISHOP, HAROLD Harold Lucius, TE, 6´4˝/254 lbs; LSU; 1994: TB, rnd 3; B4/8/1970 Boonville, MS

YEAR	TEAM	G (GS, POS)	RUSH	YD	AVG (LG)	TD	REC	YD	AVG (LG)	TD	PASS	COMP	PCT	YD	AVG (LG)	TD	INT	SK	YD	QBR	KPR	OTD	PTS	TAY
1994	TB	6(0)	—	—	—	—	—	—	—	—	—	—	—	—	—	—	—	—	—	—	—	—	—	—
1995	Cle	13(3)	—	—	—	—	16	135	8.4(21)	0	—	—	—	—	—	—	—	—	—	—	—	—	0	68
1996	Bal	8(2)	—	—	—	—	2	22	11.0(13)	0	—	—	—	—	—	—	—	—	—	—	—	—	0	11
1998	Pit	7(1)	—	—	—	—	1	4	4.0(4)	0	—	—	—	—	—	—	—	—	—	—	—	—	0	2
NFL	4	34(6)	—	—	—	—	19	161	8.5(21)	0	—	—	—	—	—	—	—	—	—	—	—	—	0	81

BISHOP, KEITH Keith Bryan, G-C, 6´3˝/260 lbs; Nebraska; Baylor; 1980: Den, rnd 6; B3/10/1957 San Diego, CA **1980** Den 16 (0) **1982** Den 9 (0) **1983**†Den 16 (16, LG) **1984**†Den 16 (14, LG) **1985** Den 14 (14, LG) **1986**†Den★16 (14, LG) **1987**†Den★12 (12, LG) **1988** Den 16 (10, LG) **1989**†Den 14 (7, lg) **NFL** 129 (87) [9 yrs]

BISHOP, MICHAEL Michael Paul, QB, 6´2˝/215 lbs; Kansas State; 1999: NE, rnd 7; B5/15/1976 Willis, TX

YEAR	TEAM	G (GS, POS)	RUSH	YD	AVG (LG)	TD	REC	YD	AVG (LG)	TD	PASS	COMP	PCT	YD	AVG (LG)	TD	INT	SK	YD	QBR	KPR	OTD	PTS	TAY
2000	NE	8(0)	7	-1	-0.1(2)	0	—	—	—	—	9	3	33.3	80	8.9(44)	1	1	—	—	—	—	—	0	4

BISHOP, RICHARD Richard Allen, DE-NT, 6´1˝/275 lbs; Louisville; 1974: Cin, rnd 5; B3/23/1950 Cleveland, OH **1976**†NE 14 **1977** NE 12 **1978**†NE 16 (15, RDE) **1979** NE 14 (14, RDE) **1980** NE 13 (5, lde) **1981** NE 16 (16, NT) **1982**†Mia 2 (0) **1983** LARm 2 (0) **NFL** 89 (50) [8 yrs]

BISHOP, SONNY Erwin Wilfred, G-T, 6´2˝/245 lbs; Fresno State; 1962: SD, rnd 11/Cle, rnd 18; B10/1/1939 Winner, SD **1962**†DalT-A 14 **1963** Oak-A 14 (RG) **1965** Hou-A☆14 (RG) **1966** Hou-A 14 (RG) **1967**†Hou-A 12 (RG) **1968** Hou-A✧14 (RG) **1969**†Hou-A☆14 (RG)

YEAR	TEAM	G (GS, POS)	RUSH	YD	AVG (LG)	TD	REC	YD	AVG (LG)	TD	PASS	COMP	PCT	YD	AVG (LG)	TD	INT	SK	YD	QBR	KPR	OTD	PTS	TAY
1964	Hou-A☆	14(RT)	—	—	—	—	1	0	0.0(0)	0	—	—	—	—	—	—	—	—	—	—	—	—	0	0
NFL	8	110	—	—	—	—	1	0	0.0	0	—	—	—	—	—	—	—	—	—	—	—	—	0	0

BISSELL, FRANK Franklin H.P., E, 6´1˝/180 lbs; Fordham; B8/5/1902 Oberlin, OH, D1/1/1983 Salina, KS **1925** Akr 8 (4, LE) **1926** Akr☆8 (8, RE) **NFL** 16 (12) [2 yrs]

BITTERLICH, DON Donald, K, 5´7˝/166 lbs; Temple; 1976: Sea, rnd 3; B1/5/1954 Westminster, PA **[K]** **1976** Sea 3

BIVINS, CHARLIE Charles Louis, HB-TE, 6´1˝/212 lbs; Morris Brown; 1960: Chi, rnd 7/Buf, rnd 1; B10/16/1938 Atlanta, GA, D3/11/1994, **[R]**

YEAR	TEAM	G (GS, POS)	RUSH	YD	AVG (LG)	TD	REC	YD	AVG (LG)	TD	PASS	COMP	PCT	YD	AVG (LG)	TD	INT	SK	YD	QBR	KPR	OTD	PTS	TAY
1960	ChiB	12	1	-11	-11.0(-11)	0	—	—	—	—	—	—	—	—	—	—	—	—	—	—	k	—	0	126
1961	ChiB	14	43	188	4.4(24)	1	4	-9	-2.3(4)	0	—	—	—	—	—	—	—	—	—	—	k	—	6	487
1962	ChiB	12	14	44	3.1(15)	1	3	52	17.3(28)	0	—	—	—	—	—	—	—	—	—	—	k	—	6	143

YEAR	TEAM	G (GS, POS)	RUSH	YD	AVG (LG)	TD	REC	YD	AVG (LG)	TD	PASS	COMP	PCT	YD	AVG (LG)	TD	INT	SK	YD	QBR	KPR	OTD	PTS	TAY
1963	†ChiB	14	44	104	2.4(17)	0	3	22	7.3(19)	0	—	—	—	—	—	—	—	—	—	—	k	—	0	125
1964	ChiB	11	29	92	3.2(17)	0	11	59	5.4(21)	1	—	—	—	—	—	—	—	—	—	—	k	—	6	225
1965	ChiB	14	—	—	—	—	4	108	27.0(52)	2	—	—	—	—	—	—	—	—	—	—	—	—	12	64
1966	ChiB	14	—	—	—	—	2	6	3.0(4)	0	—	—	—	—	—	—	—	—	—	—	—	—	0	3
1967	Pit	2	7	23	3.3(9)	1	1	24	24.0(24)	0	—	—	—	—	—	—	—	—	—	—	—	—	6	45
1967	Buf-A	9	15	58	3.9(43)	0	—	—	—	—	—	—	—	—	—	—	—	—	—	—	k	—	0	198
NFL	8	102	153	498	3.3(43)	3	28	262	9.4(52)	3	—	—	—	—	—	—	—	—	—	—	k	—	36	1415

Bizer, Herb Herbert D., E-FB, 5´11˝/205 lbs; Carroll (WI); B8/3/1906, WI, D12/4/1974 East Kingsford, MI **1929** Buf 9 (7, RE)

Bjork, Del Delbert Leonard, T, 6´1˝/218 lbs; Oregon; 1937: ChiB, rnd 6; B6/27/1914 Astoria, OR, D8/26/1988 Astoria, OR **1937**†ChiB 10 (4) **1938** ChiB✧10 (5, rt) **NFL** 20 (9) [2 yrs]

Bjorklund, Bob Robert John, C-LB-E, 6´2˝/225 lbs; Minnesota; 1941: Pit, rnd 20; B6/12/1918 Minneapolis, MN, D1/27/1994 Hopkins, MN **1941** Phi 7 (0)

Bjorklund, Hank John Henry, RB, 6´1˝/200 lbs; Princeton; 1972: NYJ, rnd 12; B6/5/1950 Glen Head, NY

YEAR	TEAM	G (GS, POS)	RUSH	YD	AVG (LG)	TD	REC	YD	AVG (LG)	TD	PASS	COMP	PCT	YD	AVG (LG)	TD	INT	SK	YD	QBR	KPR	OTD	PTS	TAY
1972	NYJ	7	15	42	2.8(10)	0	4	54	13.5(35)	0	—	—	—	—	—	—	—	—	—	—	k	—	0	114
1973	NYJ	10	22	72	3.3(14)	0	2	15	7.5(11)	0	—	—	—	—	—	—	—	—	—	—	k	—	0	120
1974	NYJ	13	23	57	2.5(12)	0	2	15	7.5(8)	0	—	—	—	—	—	—	—	—	—	—	k	—	0	78
NFL	3	30	60	171	2.8(14)	0	8	84	10.5(35)	0	—	—	—	—	—	—	—	—	—	—	k	—	0	311

Bjornson, Eric Eric Thomas, TE, 6´4˝/236 lbs; Washington; 1995: Dal, rnd 4; B12/15/1971 San Francisco, CA

YEAR	TEAM	G (GS, POS)	RUSH	YD	AVG (LG)	TD	REC	YD	AVG (LG)	TD	PASS	COMP	PCT	YD	AVG (LG)	TD	INT	SK	YD	QBR	KPR	OTD	PTS	TAY
1995	†Dal	14(1)	—	—	—	—	7	53	7.6(16)	0	—	—	—	—	—	—	—	—	—	—	—	—	0	27
1996	†Dal	14(10, TE)	—	—	—	—	48	388	8.1(25)	3	—	—	—	—	—	—	—	—	—	—	—	—	20	209
1997	Dal	14(14, TE)	—	—	—	—	47	442	9.4(32)	0	—	—	—	—	—	—	—	—	—	—	—	—	2	221
1998	†Dal	16(4)	1	7	7.0(7)	1	15	218	14.5(43)	1	—	—	—	—	—	—	—	—	—	—	—	—	12	131
1999	†Dal	16(6, te)	1	20	20.0(20)	1	10	131	13.1(32)	0	—	—	—	—	—	—	—	—	—	—	—	—	6	96
2000	NE	8(6, te)	—	—	—	—	20	152	7.6(19)	2	—	—	—	—	—	—	—	—	—	—	—	—	12	86
NFL	6	82(41)	2	27	13.5(20)	2	147	1384	9.4(43)	6	—	—	—	—	—	—	—	—	—	—	—	—	52	769

Black, Avion Avion Carlos, WR, 5´11˝/185 lbs; Tennessee State; 2000: Buf, rnd 4; B4/24/1977 Nashville, TN

YEAR	TEAM	G (GS, POS)	RUSH	YD	AVG (LG)	TD	REC	YD	AVG (LG)	TD	PASS	COMP	PCT	YD	AVG (LG)	TD	INT	SK	YD	QBR	KPR	OTD	PTS	TAY
2000	Buf	2(0)	—	—	—	—	—	—	—	—	—	—	—	—	—	—	—	—	—	—	k	—	0	30
2001	Buf	14(0)	—	—	—	—	8	90	11.3(25)	0	—	—	—	—	—	—	—	—	—	—	kp	—	0	197
2002	Hou	11(0)	—	—	—	—	6	52	8.7(14)	0	—	—	—	—	—	—	—	—	—	—	kp	1	6	323
NFL	3	27(0)	—	—	—	—	14	142	10.1(25)	0	—	—	—	—	—	—	—	—	—	—	kp	1	6	550

Black, Barry Barry, G, 6´2˝/280 lbs; Boise State; B3/7/1965 **1987** LARd 3 (2)

Black, Blondy John Thomas, B, 5´11˝/195 lbs; Mississippi State; 1943: Bkn, rnd 2; B8/20/1920 Philadelphia, MS, D5/4/2000 Madison, MS

YEAR	TEAM	G (GS, POS)	RUSH	YD	AVG (LG)	TD	REC	YD	AVG (LG)	TD	PASS	COMP	PCT	YD	AVG (LG)	TD	INT	SK	YD	QBR	KPR	OTD	PTS	TAY
1946	Buf-A	4(0)	1	10	10.0(10)	0	1	21	21.0(21)	0	—	—	—	—	—	—	—	—	—	—	pi	—	0	82
1947	Bal-A	5(0)	5	39	7.8	0	1	7	7.0(7)	0	—	—	—	—	—	—	—	—	—	—	—	—	0	43
AAFC	2	9(0)	6	49	8.2(10)	0	2	28	14.0(21)	0	—	—	—	—	—	—	—	—	—	—	pi	—	0	124

Black, Charlie Charles Terrece, E, 5´9˝/160 lbs; Kansas; B1/5/1901 Alton, IL, D12/14/1988 Citrus Heights, CA **1925** Dul 3 (1)

Black, James James, RB, 5´11˝/198 lbs; Akron; B4/3/1962 Lima, OH **1984** Cle 2 (0)

Black, James James R., DE, 6´4˝/280 lbs; South Carolina State; B11/4/1956 Xenia, OH **1987** KC 1 (0)

Black, Jordan Brian Jordan, T, 6´5˝/314 lbs; Notre Dame; 2003: KC, rnd 5; B1/28/1980 Garland, TX **2004** KC 16 (4) **2005** KC 16 (10, lt/rt) **NFL** 32 (14) [2 yrs]

Black, Mel Melvin, LB, 6´2˝/228 lbs; Eastern Illinois; B2/2/1962 New Haven, CT **1986** NE 3 (0) **1987** NE 3 (2) **NFL** 6 (2) [2 yrs]

Black, Mike Peter Michael, P, 6´1˝/197 lbs; Arizona State; 1983: Det, rnd 7; B1/18/1961 Glendale, CA **[P]**

YEAR	TEAM	G (GS, POS)	RUSH	YD	AVG (LG)	TD	REC	YD	AVG (LG)	TD	PASS	COMP	PCT	YD	AVG (LG)	TD	INT	SK	YD	QBR	KPR	OTD	PTS	TAY
1983	†Det	16(0)	2	-10	-5.0(0)	0	—	—	—	—	1	0	0.0	0	0.0	0	1	—	—	—	P	—	0	-50
1984	Det	16(0)	3	-6	-2.0(4)	0	—	—	—	—	—	—	—	—	—	—	—	—	—	—	P	—	0	-6
1985	Det	16(0)	1	0	0.0(0)	0	—	—	—	—	—	—	—	—	—	—	—	—	—	—	P	—	0	0
1986	Det	9(0)	1	-8	-8.0(-8)	0	—	—	—	—	—	—	—	—	—	—	—	—	—	—	P	—	0	-8
1987	Det	1(0)	1	0	0.0(0)	0	—	—	—	—	—	—	—	—	—	—	—	—	—	—	P	—	0	0
NFL	5	58(0)	8	-24	-3.0(4)	0	—	—	—	—	1	0	0.0	0	0.0	0	1	—	—	—	P	—	0	-64

Black, Mike Michael David, T, 6´4˝/285 lbs; Sacramento State; 1986: Sea, rnd 9; B8/24/1964 Auburn, CA **1986** Phi 1 (0) **1987** NYG 2 (2) **NFL** 3 (2) [2 yrs]

Black, Nathan Nathan Austin, WR, 6´0˝/190 lbs; Northwestern State (LA); B6/20/1978 Baton Rouge, LA **2002** Car 5 (0)

Black, Stan Stanley Ross, DB, 6´0˝/196 lbs; Mississippi State; 1977: SF, rnd 4; B11/12/1955 Greenville, MS **1977** SF 13

Black, Tim Timothy A., LB, 6´2˝/215 lbs; Baylor; 1977: Det, rnd 7; B1/3/1955 Midland, TX **1977** SL 4

Black, Todd Todd Mitchell, WR, 5´11˝/174 lbs; Concordia (MN); B4/12/1964 **1987** ChiB 1 (0)

Blackbear, Peter Coowee Scoorice, aka Bear Behind, E, 6´0˝/190 lbs; none; B10/11/1899, OK, D7/1976 Salina, OK **1923** Oor 2 (1)

Blackburn, Bill William Whitford, C, 6´6˝/228 lbs; Louisiana-Lafayette; Rice; 1944: ChiC, rnd 5; B2/5/1923 Weleetka, OK **1947**†ChiC 12 (4) **1948**†ChiC 12 (1) **1949** ChiC 12 (7, C) **1950** ChiC 12 (7, C)

YEAR	TEAM	G (GS, POS)	RUSH	YD	AVG (LG)	TD	REC	YD	AVG (LG)	TD	PASS	COMP	PCT	YD	AVG (LG)	TD	INT	SK	YD	QBR	KPR	OTD	PTS	TAY
1946	ChiC	11(1)	1	10	10.0(10)	0	—	—	—	—	—	—	—	—	—	—	—	—	—	—	Pi	1	8	51
NFL	5	59(20)	1	10	10.0(10)	0	—	—	—	—	—	—	—	—	—	—	—	—	—	—	Pkpi	4	26	154

Blackburn, Chase Chase, LB, 6´3˝/247 lbs; Akron; B6/10/1983 Marysville, OH **2005** NYG 15 (2)

Blackledge, Todd Todd Alan, QB, 6´3˝/225 lbs; Penn State; 1983: KC, rnd 1; B2/25/1961 Canton, OH

YEAR	TEAM	G (GS, POS)	RUSH	YD	AVG (LG)	TD	REC	YD	AVG (LG)	TD	PASS	COMP	PCT	YD	AVG (LG)	TD	INT	SK	YD	QBR	KPR	OTD	PTS	TAY
1983	KC	4(0)	1	0	0.0(0)	0	—	—	—	—	34	20	58.8	259	7.6(43)	3	0	4	50	—	—	—	0	145
1984	KC	11(8, qb)	18	102	5.7(26)	1	—	—	—	—	294	147	50.0	1707	5.8(46)	6	11	18	163	59.2	—	—	6	556
1985	KC	12(6, qb)	17	97	5.7(25)	0	—	—	—	—	172	86	50.0	1190	6.9(70)	6	14	15	112	50.3	—	—	0	162
1986	†KC	10(8, qb)	23	60	2.6(14)	0	—	—	—	—	211	96	45.5	1200	5.7(70)	10	6	25	192	67.6	—	—	0	470
1987	KC	3(2)	5	21	4.2(11)	0	—	—	—	—	31	15	48.4	154	5.0(19)	1	1	7	43	—	—	—	0	63
1988	Pit	3(3)	8	25	3.1(10)	1	—	—	—	—	79	38	48.1	494	6.3(34)	2	3	4	25	—	—	—	6	172
1989	Pit	3(2)	9	20	2.2(11)	0	—	—	—	—	60	22	36.7	282	4.7(30)	1	3	4	25	—	—	—	0	46
NFL	7	46(29)	81	325	4.0(26)	2	—	—	—	—	881	424	48.1	5286	6.0(70)	29	38	77	610	60.2	—	—	12	1613

Blacklock, Hugh Hugh M., T-C-G, 6´0˝/220 lbs; Michigan State; B1/1893 East Grand Rapids, MI, D5/18/1954 Grand Rapids, MI **[K]** **1920** Dec☆13 (8, RT) **1921** ChiS 11 (11, RT), 2 **1922** ChiB☆12 (11, RT) **1923** ChiB 4 (4) **1924** ChiB 11 (11, RT) **1925** ChiB 3 (1) **1926** Bkn 5 (5, RT) **NFL** 59 (51) [7 yrs]

Blackman, Ken Kenneth Blake, G, 6´6˝/320 lbs; Illinois; 1996: Cin, rnd 3; B11/8/1972 Brunswick, GA **1996** Cin 14 (10, RG) **1997** Cin 13 (13, RG) **1998** Cin 8 (8, RG) **NFL** 35 (31) [3 yrs]

Blackman, Stub Harold Lennon, FB, 5´11˝/195 lbs; Tulsa; B1/5/1908, D10/30/1994 Corsicana, TX **1930** ChiB 1 (0)

Blackmon, Don Donald Kirk, LB, 6´3˝/235 lbs; Tulsa; 1981: NE, rnd 4; B3/14/1958 Pompano, FL **1981** NE 16 (0) **1982**†NE 9 (9, ROLB) **1983** NE 15 (14, ROLB) **1984** NE 16 (16, ROLB) **1985**†NE 14 (14, ROLB) **1986**†NE☆15 (15, ROLB) **1987** NE 4 (0) **NFL** 89 (68) [7 yrs]

Blackmon, Harold Harold Gene, DB, 5´11˝/216 lbs; Northwestern; 2001: Sea, rnd 7; B5/20/1978 Chicago, IL **2001** Sea 2 (0) **2002** Sea 7 (0) **NFL** 9 (0) [2 yrs]

Blackmon, Robert Robert James, DB, 6´0˝/208 lbs; Baylor; 1990: Sea, rnd 2; B5/12/1967 Bay City, TX **1990** Sea 15 (5, ss) **1991** Sea 16 (16, SS) **1992** Sea 15 (15, SS) **1993** Sea 16 (16, SS) **1994** Sea 15 (15, SS) **1995** Sea☆13 (13, SS) **1996** Sea 16 (16, SS) **1997** Ind 14 (14, SS) **1998** Ind 15 (9, SS) **NFL** 135 (119) [9 yrs]

Blackmon, Roosevelt Roosevelt, DB, 6´1˝/185 lbs; Morris Brown; 1998: GB, rnd 4; B9/10/1974 Pahokee, FL **1998** GB 3 (0) **1998** Cin 12 (0) **1999** Cin 5 (3) **NFL** 20 (3) [2 yrs]

Blackmore, Richard Richard Earl, DB, 5´10˝/174 lbs; Mississippi State; B8/14/1956 Vicksburg, MS **1979**†Phi 16 **1980**†Phi 16 (0) **1981**†Phi 16 (3) **1982** Phi 9 (0) **1983**†SF 11 (1) **NFL** 68 (4) [5 yrs]

Blackshear, Jeff Jeffrey Leon, G, 6´6˝/323 lbs; Louisiana-Monroe; 1993: Sea, rnd 8; B3/29/1969 Fort Pierce, FL **1993** Sea 15 (2) **1994** Sea 16 (16, LG) **1995** Sea 16 (3) **1996** Bal 16 (12, RG) **1997** Bal 16 (16, RG) **1998** Bal 16 (16, RG) **1999** Bal 16 (16, RG) **2000** KC 16 (15, LG) **2002**†GB 1 (0) **NFL** 128 (96) [9 yrs]

Blackstock, Darryl Darryl Tyger, LB, 6´4˝/241 lbs; Virginia; 2005: Arz, rnd 3; B5/30/1983 Newport News, VA **2005** Arz 14 (1)

YEAR	TEAM	G(GS, POS)	RUSH	YD	AVG(LG)	TD	REC	YD	AVG(LG)	TD	PASS	COMP	PCT	YD	AVG(LG)	TD	INT	SK	YD	QBR	KPR	OTD	PTS	TAY

BLACKWELL, ALOIS — Alois Sterling, RB, 5'10"/195 lbs; Houston; 1978: Dal, rnd 4; B11/12/1954 Cuero, TX **1979** Dal 6

YEAR	TEAM	G(GS,POS)	RUSH	YD	AVG(LG)	TD	REC	YD	AVG(LG)	TD	...	KPR	OTD	PTS	TAY
1978	†Dal	13	9	37	4.1(13)	0	—	—	—	—	—	k	—	0	62
NFL	2	19	9	37	4.1(13)	0	—	—	—	—	—	k	—	0	37

BLACKWELL, HAL — Harold, HB-DB, 6'1"/205 lbs; South Carolina; B5/12/1919, D1/6/1994 Bronx, NY **1945** ChiC 2 (0)

BLACKWELL, KELLY — Kelly Reardon, TE, 6'1"/255 lbs; TCU; B2/13/1969 Blytheville, TX **1993** Dal 2 (0)

YEAR	TEAM	G(GS,POS)	REC	YD	AVG(LG)	TD	KPR	OTD	PTS	TAY
1992	ChiB	16(2)	5	54	10.8(18)	0	—	—	0	27
NFL	2	18(2)	5	54	10.8(18)	0	—	—	0	27

BLACKWELL, KORY — Kory, DB, 5'11"/185 lbs; Massachusetts; B8/3/1972 New York, NY **1998** NYG 5 (0)

BLACKWELL, WILL — William Herman, WR, 6'0"/185 lbs; San Diego State; 1997: Pit, rnd 2; B7/9/1975 Texarkana, TX [R]

YEAR	TEAM	G(GS,POS)	RUSH	YD	AVG(LG)	TD	REC	YD	AVG(LG)	TD	KPR	OTD	PTS	TAY
1997	†Pit	14(0)	2	14	7.0(11)	0	12	168	14.0(46)	1	kp	1	12	458
1998	Pit	16(2)	—	—	—	—	32	297	9.3(24)	1	kp	—	8	238
1999	Pit	11(1)	—	—	—	—	20	186	9.3(26)	0	kp	—	0	199
2000	Pit	5(0)	—	—	—	—	2	23	11.5(14)	0	k	1	6	153
2001	Pit	1(0)	—	—	—	—	1	8	8.0(8)	0	k	—	0	10
NFL	5	47(3)	2	14	7.0(11)	0	67	682	10.2(46)	2	kp	2	26	1057

BLACKWOOD, GLENN — Glenn Allen, DB, 6'0"/187 lbs; Texas; 1979: Mia, rnd 8; B2/23/1957 San Antonio, TX [I] **1979** Mia 11 **1980** Mia 16 (15, SS) **1981**†Mia 16 (16, SS) **1982**†Mia 9 (9, SS) **1983**†Mia 16 (16, SS) **1984** Mia 16 (16, SS) **1985** Mia 14 (14, SS) **1986** Mia 10 (10, SS) **1987** Mia 10 (10, SS) **NFL** 118 (106) [9 yrs]

BLACKWOOD, LYLE — Lyle Vernon, DB, 6'1"/190 lbs; TCU; 1973: Den, rnd 9; B5/2/1951 San Antonio, TX [I] **1973** Cin 7 **1974** Cin 13 (1) **1975** Cin 14 (2) **1977**†Bal☆14 (14, FS) **1978** Bal 16 (16, FS) **1979** Bal 16 (12, FS) **1980** Bal 11 (2) **1981** Mia 12 (10, FS) **1982**†Mia 9 (9, FS) **1983**†Mia 16 (16, FS) **1984**†Mia 16 (16, FS) **1985**†Mia 16 (0) **1986** Mia 5 (4)

YEAR	TEAM	G(GS,POS)	REC	YD	AVG(LG)	TD	KPR	OTD	PTS	TAY
1976	Sea	11	1	8	8.0(8)	0	kp	—	0	121
NFL	14	176(102)	1	8	8.0(8)	0	kpiS	2	12	515

BLADE, WILLIE — Willie, DT, 6'3"/315 lbs; Mississippi State; 2001: Dal, rnd 3; B2/7/1979 Warner Robins, GA **2003**†Dal 15 (14, LDT) **2004** Jax 5 (1) **NFL** 20 (15) [2 yrs]

BLADES, BENNIE — Horatio Benedict, DB, 6'0"/221 lbs; Miami (FL); 1988: Det, rnd 1; B9/3/1966 Fort Lauderdale, FL **1988** Det☆15 (14, SS) **1989** Det 16 (16, SS) **1990** Det 12 (12, FS) **1991**†Det★16 (16, FS) **1992** Det☆16 (16, FS) **1993** Det 4 (4) **1994**†Det 16 (16, FS) **1995**†Det 16 (16, SS) **1996** Det 15 (15, SS) **1997** Sea 10 (9, SS) **NFL** 136 (134) [10 yrs]

BLADES, BRIAN — Brian Keith, WR, 5'11"/189 lbs; Miami (FL); 1988: Sea, rnd 2; B7/24/1965 Fort Lauderdale, FL

YEAR	TEAM	G(GS,POS)	RUSH	YD	AVG(LG)	TD	REC	YD	AVG(LG)	TD	PASS	COMP	PCT	YD	AVG	TD	INT	SK	YD	QBR	KPR	OTD	PTS	TAY
1988	†Sea	16(7, WR)	5	24	4.8(12)	0	40	682	17.0(55)	8	0	0	0.0	—	—	0	0	1	0	—	—	—	48	405
1989	Sea★	16(14, WR)	1	3	3.0(3)	0	77	1063	13.8(60)	5	—	—	—	—	—	—	—	—	—	—	—	—	30	560
1990	Sea	16(16, WR)	3	19	6.3(12)	0	49	525	10.7(24)	3	—	—	—	—	—	—	—	—	—	—	—	—	18	297
1991	Sea	16(16, WR)	2	17	8.5(11)	0	70	1003	14.3(52)	2	—	—	—	—	—	—	—	—	—	—	—	—	12	529
1992	Sea	6(5, wr)	1	5	5.0(5)	0	19	256	13.5(37)	1	—	—	—	—	—	—	—	—	—	—	—	—	6	138
1993	Sea	16(16, WR)	5	52	10.4(26)	0	80	945	11.8(41)	3	—	—	—	—	—	—	—	—	—	—	—	—	18	540
1994	Sea	16(16, WR)	2	32	16.0(40)	0	81	1086	13.4(45)	4	—	—	—	—	—	—	—	—	—	—	—	—	26	595
1995	Sea	16(16, WR)	2	4	2.0(4)	0	77	1001	13.0(49)	4	—	—	—	—	—	—	—	—	—	—	—	—	24	525
1996	Sea	11(9, WR)	—	—	—	—	43	556	12.9(37)	2	—	—	—	—	—	—	—	—	—	—	—	—	12	288
1997	Sea	11(3)	—	—	—	—	30	319	10.6(27)	2	—	—	—	—	—	—	—	—	—	—	—	—	12	170
1998	Sea	16(6, WR)	—	—	—	—	15	184	12.3(47)	0	—	—	—	—	—	—	—	—	—	—	—	—	0	92
NFL	11	156(124)	21	156	7.4(40)	0	581	7620	13.1(80)	34	0	0	0.0	—	—	0	0	1	0	—	—	—	206	4136

BLADOS, BRIAN — Brian Timothy, T-G, 6'5"/300 lbs; North Carolina; 1984: Cin, rnd 1; B1/11/1962 Arlington, VA **1984** Cin 16 (14, LG) **1986** Cin 16 (8, RT) **1987** Cin 11 (4) **1988**†Cin 16 (1) **1989** Cin 13 (10, RT) **1990** Cin 4 (4) **1991** Cin 6 (3) **1991** Ind 7 (3) **1992** TB 2 (1)

YEAR	TEAM	G(GS,POS)	REC	YD	AVG(LG)	TD	OTD	PTS	TAY
1985	Cin	16(16, LG)	1	4	4.0(4)	0	—	0	2
NFL	9	107(63)	1	4	4.0(4)	0	—	0	2

BLAHAK, JOE — Joseph Phillip, DB, 5'9"/187 lbs; Nebraska; 1973: Hou, rnd 8; B8/29/1950 Columbia, NE **1973** Hou 12 (fs) **1974** Min 7 **1975**†Min 9 **1976** TB 2 (1) **1976**†NE 2 **1977** Min 12 **NFL** 44 (1) [5 yrs]

BLAILOCK, RUSS — William Russell, T-G, 5'10"/230 lbs; Baylor; B6/29/1902 McGregor, TX, D1/20/1972 Dallas, TX [K] **1923** Mil 12 (12, LT), 6 **1925** Akr 8 (5, lg), 5 **NFL** 20 (17), 11 [2 yrs]

BLAINE, ED — Edward Homer, G, 6'1"/240 lbs; Missouri; 1962: GB, rnd 2/NYT, rnd 4; B1/30/1940 Farmington, MO **1962**†GB 14 **1963** Phi 14 (13, LG) **1964** Phi☆14 (14, LG) **1965** Phi 14 (14, LG) **1966** Phi 14 (LG) **NFL** 70 (41) [5 yrs]

BLAIR, GEORGE — George Leroy, DB-K, 5'11"/195 lbs; Mississippi; 1960: LAC, rnd 2/NYG, rnd 6; B5/10/1938 Pascagoula, MS [K] **1961**†SD-A☆14 **1962** SD-A 14 **1963**†SD-A☆14 (LS) **1964** SD-A 4 **NFL** 46 [4 yrs]

BLAIR, MATT — Matthew Albert, LB, 6'5"/232 lbs; Iowa State; 1974: Min, rnd 2; B9/20/1950 Hilo, HI **1974**†Min 14 (6, llb) **1975** Min 14 **1976**†Min 14 (13, LLB) **1977**†Min 14 (13, LLB) **1978**†Min★16 (16, LLB) **1979** Min★16 (16, LLB) **1980** Min★14 (14, LLB) **1981** Min★16 (16, LOLB) **1982**†Min☆9 (9, LOLB) **1983** Min 16 (16, LOLB) **1984** Min 11 (9, LOLB) **1985** Min 6 (2) **NFL** 160 (130) [12 yrs]

BLAIR, MICHAEL — Michael Angelo Christopher, RB, 5'11"/245 lbs; Ball State; B11/26/1974 Chicago, IL

YEAR	TEAM	G(GS,POS)	RUSH	YD	AVG(LG)	TD	REC	YD	AVG(LG)	TD	OTD	PTS	TAY
1998	Cin	2(0)	1	4	4.0(4)	0	1	7	7.0(7)	0	—	0	8
1998	†GB	11(0)	2	3	1.5(2)	0	2	13	6.5(10)	0	—	0	10
NFL	1	13(0)	3	7	2.3(4)	0	3	20	6.7(10)	0	—	0	17

BLAIR, PAUL — Paul Kevin, T, 6'4"/295 lbs; Oklahoma State; 1986: Chi, rnd 4; B8/3/1963 Edmond, OK **1986** ChiB 14 (0) **1987**†ChiB 10 (2) **1990** Min 2 (0) **NFL** 26 (2) [3 yrs]

BLAIR, STANLEY — Stanley R., DB, 6'0"/190 lbs; Oklahoma State; Southeastern Oklahoma State; B7/12/1964 Pine Bluff, AR **1990** Phx 5 (0)

BLAIR, T.C. — Thomas Calvin, TE, 6'4"/220 lbs; Tulsa; 1974: Det, rnd 11; B8/4/1951 Ann Arbor, MI **1974** Det 11

BLAISE, KERLIN — Kerlin, G, 6'5"/315 lbs; Miami (FL); B12/25/1974 Orlando, FL **1999**†Det 16 (4) **2000** Det 12 (0) **2001** Det 6 (0) **2002** Det 2 (2) **2003** Det 2 (0) **NFL** 38 (6) [5 yrs]

BLAKE, JEFF — Jeffrey Bertrand, QB, 6'1"/223 lbs; East Carolina; 1992: NYJ, rnd 6; B12/4/1970 Daytona Beach, FL

YEAR	TEAM	G(GS,POS)	RUSH	YD	AVG(LG)	TD	PASS	COMP	PCT	YD	AVG(LG)	TD	INT	SK	YD	QBR	OTD	PTS	TAY
1992	NYJ	3(0)	2	-2	-1.0(1)	0	9	4	44.4	40	4.4(19)	0	1	2	7	—	—	0	-22
1994	Cin	10(9, QB)	37	204	5.5(16)	1	306	156	51.0	2154	7.0(76)	14	9	19	120	76.9	—	8	1001
1995	Cin◇	16(16, QB)	53	309	5.8(30)	2	567	326	57.5	3822	6.7(88)	28	17	24	152	82.1	—	14	1700
1996	Cin	16(16, QB)	72	317	4.4(18)	2	549	308	56.1	3624	6.6(61)	24	14	44	278	80.3	—	12	1709
1997	Cin	11(11, QB)	45	234	5.2(16)	3	317	184	58.0	2125	6.7(50)	8	7	39	244	77.6	—	18	1087
1998	Cin	8(2)	15	103	6.9(18)	0	93	51	54.8	739	7.9(67)	3	3	15	79	—	—	0	368
1999	Cin	14(12, QB)	63	332	5.3(16)	2	389	215	55.3	2670	6.9(76)	16	12	30	168	77.6	—	12	1287
2000	NO	11(11, QB)	57	243	4.3(20)	1	302	184	60.9	2025	6.7(49)	13	9	24	150	82.7	—	6	971
2001	NO	1(0)	1	-1	-1.0(-1)	0	0	0	0.0	0	0.0	0	0	0	0	—	—	0	-1
2002	Bal	11(10, QB)	39	106	2.7(17)	1	295	165	55.9	2084	7.1(77)	13	11	30	203	77.3	—	6	783
2003	Arz	13(13, QB)	30	177	5.9(19)	2	367	208	56.7	2247	6.1(71)	13	15	19	132	69.6	—	14	786
2004	Phi	3(0)	3	6	2.0(8)	0	37	18	48.6	126	3.4(21)	1	1	2	17	—	—	0	34
2005	ChiB	3(0)	1	-1	-1.0(-1)	0	9	8	88.9	55	6.1(17)	1	0	—	—	—	—	0	32
NFL	13	120(100)	418	2027	4.8(30)	14	3241	1827	56.4	21711	6.7(88)	134	99	248	1550	78.0	—	90	9733

BLAKE, RICKY — Ricky Darnell, RB, 6'2"/244 lbs; Alabama A&M; B7/15/1967 Fayetteville, TN

YEAR	TEAM	G(GS,POS)	RUSH	YD	AVG(LG)	TD	REC	YD	AVG(LG)	TD	OTD	PTS	TAY
1991	Dal	2(0)	15	80	5.3(30)	1	1	5	5.0(5)	0	—	6	93

BLAKE, TOM — Thomas Clinton, T, 6'2"/220 lbs; Tennessee; Cincinnati; B7/19/1927 Bushton, IL **1949** NYB 5 (0)

BLAKELY, ROBERT — Robert Ervin, WR, 6'0"/190 lbs; North Dakota State; B9/20/1959 St. Paul, MN **1982** KC 2 (0)

YEAR	TEAM	G (GS, POS)	RUSH	YD	AVG (LG)	TD	REC	YD	AVG (LG)	TD	PASS	COMP	PCT	YD	AVG (LG)	TD	INT	SK	YD	QBR	KPR	OTD	PTS	TAY
BLAKLEY, DWAYNE Dwayne David, TE, 6´4˝/257 lbs; Missouri; B8/10/1979 St. Joseph, MO																								
2004	†Atl	15(1)	—	—	—	—	4	35	8.8(13)	0	—	—	—	—	—	—	—	—	—	—	—	—	0	18
2005	Atl	16(1)	—	—	—	—	4	30	7.5(10)	1	—	—	—	—	—	—	—	—	—	—	—	—	6	20
NFL	2	31(2)	—	—	—	—	8	65	8.1(13)	1	—	—	—	—	—	—	—	—	—	—	—	—	6	38
BLANCHARD, CARY Robert Cary, K, 6´1˝/227 lbs; Oklahoma State; B11/5/1968 Fort Worth, TX **[K]** **1992** NYJ 11 (0) **1993** NYJ 16 (0) **1995**†Ind 12 (0) **1996**†Ind★16 (0) **1997** Ind 16 (0) **1998** Was 13 (0) **1999** NYG 10 (0) **2000** Arz 16 (0) **NFL** 110 (0) [8 yrs]																								
BLANCHARD, DICK Richard L., LB, 6´3˝/225 lbs; Tulsa; B1/17/1949 Waukesha, WI **1972** NE 14 (1)																								
BLANCHARD, TOM Thomas Richard, P, 6´0˝/190 lbs; Oregon; 1971: NYG, rnd 12; B5/28/1948 Grants Pass, OR **[P]**																								
1971	NYG	14	—	—	—	—	—	—	—	—	1	1	100.0	18	18.0(18)	0	0	—	—	—	P	—	0	9
1972	NYG	14	1	17	17.0(17)	0	—	—	—	—	1	0	0.0	0	0.0	0	0	—	—	—	P	—	0	17
1973	NYG	14	—	—	—	—	—	—	—	—	—	—	—	—	—	—	—	—	—	—	P	—	0	0
1974	NO	13	—	—	—	—	—	—	—	—	—	—	—	—	—	—	—	—	—	—	P	—	0	0
1975	NO	14	—	—	—	—	—	—	—	—	—	—	—	—	—	—	—	—	—	—	P	—	0	0
1976	NO	14	—	—	—	—	—	—	—	—	0	0	0.0	0	0.0	0	0	1	18	—	P	—	0	0
1977	NO	14	—	—	—	—	—	—	—	—	3	1	33.3	3	1.0(3)	1	1	—	—	—	P	—	0	-34
1978	NO	16	2	0	0.0(0)	0	—	—	—	—	—	—	—	—	—	—	—	—	—	—	P	—	0	0
1979	†TB	16	1	0	0.0(0)	0	—	—	—	—	—	—	—	—	—	—	—	—	—	—	P	—	0	0
1980	TB	16(0)	—	—	—	—	—	—	—	—	—	—	—	—	—	—	—	—	—	—	P	—	0	0
1981	TB	3(0)	1	0	0.0(0)	0	—	—	—	—	—	—	—	—	—	—	—	—	—	—	P	—	0	0
NFL	11	148	5	17	3.4(17)	0	—	—	—	—	5	2	40.0	21	4.2(18)	1	1	1	18	—	P	—	0	-8
BLAND, CARL Carl Nathaniel, WR, 5´11˝/182 lbs; Virginia Union; B8/17/1961 Fluvanna County, VA																								
1984	Det	3(0)	—	—	—	—	—	—	—	—	—	—	—	—	—	—	—	—	—	—	—	—	—	—
1985	Det	8(2)	—	—	—	—	12	157	13.1(24)	0	—	—	—	—	—	—	—	—	—	—	—	—	0	79
1986	Det	16(16, WR)	—	—	—	—	44	511	11.6(34)	2	—	—	—	—	—	—	—	—	—	—	k	—	12	290
1987	Det	10(0)	—	—	—	—	2	14	7.0(11)	1	—	—	—	—	—	—	—	—	—	—	kp	—	6	26
1988	Det	16(2)	1	4	4.0(4)	0	21	307	14.6(35)	2	—	—	—	—	—	—	—	—	—	—	kp	—	12	261
1989	GB	16(0)	—	—	—	—	11	164	14.9(46)	1	—	—	—	—	—	—	—	—	—	—	k	1	12	148
1990	GB	14(0)	—	—	—	—	—	—	—	—	—	—	—	—	—	—	—	—	—	—	k	—	0	-1
NFL	7	83(20)	1	4	4.0(4)	0	90	1153	12.8(46)	6	—	—	—	—	—	—	—	—	—	—	kp	1	42	802
BLAND, TONY Anthony, WR, 6´3˝/213 lbs; Florida A&M; B12/12/1972 St. Petersburg, FL **1997** Min 2 (0) **1998** Min 1 (0) **NFL** 3 (0) [2 yrs]																								
BLANDA, GEORGE George Frederick, QB, 6´2˝/215 lbs; Kentucky; 1949: ChiB, rnd 12/ChiH-A, rnd 2; B9/17/1927 Youngwood, PA; HOF 1981 **[K]**																								
1949	ChiB	12(2)	2	9	4.5(5)	1	—	—	—	—	21	9	42.9	197	9.4(44)	0	5	—	—	—	KP	—	27	-83
1950	Bal	1	—	—	—	—	—	—	—	—	—	—	—	—	—	—	—	—	—	—	—	—	—	—
1950	†ChiB	11	—	—	—	—	—	—	—	—	1	0	0.0	0	0.0	0	0	—	—	—	KP	—	18	0
1951	ChiB	12	—	—	—	—	—	—	—	—	—	—	—	—	—	—	—	—	—	—	Kki	—	44	-3
1952	ChiB	12(QB)	20	104	5.2(16)	1	—	—	—	—	131	47	35.9	664	5.1(59)	8	11	—	—	38.5	K	—	54	46
1953	ChiB	12(QB)	24	62	2.6(16)	0	0	7	(7)	0	**362**	**169**	46.7	2164	6.0(72)	14	23	—	—	52.3	K	—	48	298
1954	ChiB	8(QB)	19	41	2.2(19)	0	—	—	—	—	281	131	46.6	1929	6.9(76)	15	17	—	—	62.1	K	—	47	401
1955	ChiB	12	15	54	3.6(10)	2	—	—	—	—	97	42	43.3	459	4.7(51)	4	7	—	—	—	K	—	82	44
1956	†ChiB	12(qb)	6	47	7.8(17)	0	—	—	—	—	69	37	53.6	439	6.4(69)	7	4	—	—	—	KP	—	81	142
1957	ChiB	12	5	-5	-1.0(1)	1	—	—	—	—	19	8	42.1	65	3.4(13)	0	3	—	—	—	K	—	71	-83
1958	ChiB	12	—	—	—	—	—	—	—	—	7	2	28.6	19	2.7(12)	0	0	—	—	—	K	—	69	10
1960	†Hou-A	14(QB)	16	16	1.0(9)	4	—	—	—	—	363	169	46.6	2413	6.6(88)	24	22	—	—	65.4	K	—	115	503
1961	†Hou-A★	14(12, QB)	7	12	1.7(7)	0	1	-16	-16.0(-16)	0	362	187	51.7	**3330**	**9.2**(**80**)	**36**	22	—	—	**91.3**	K	—	112	969
1962	†Hou-A★	14(QB)	3	6	2.0(10)	0	—	—	—	—	418	197	47.1	2810	6.7(78)	27	**42**	—	—	51.3	K	—	81	-134
1963	Hou-A★	14(QB)	4	1	0.3(7)	0	—	—	—	—	**423**	**224**	53.0	**3003**	7.1(80)	24	**25**	—	—	70.1	K	—	66	623
1964	Hou-A	14(QB)	4	-2	-0.5(6)	0	0	-7	(-7)	0	**505**	**262**	51.9	3287	6.5(80)	17	**27**	—	—	61.4	K	—	76	643
1965	Hou-A	14(QB)	4	-6	-1.5(0)	0	—	—	—	—	**442**	**186**	42.1	2542	5.8(**95**)	20	**30**	—	—	47.9	K	—	61	165
1966	Hou-A☆	14(QB)	3	1	0.3(1)	0	—	—	—	—	271	122	45.0	1764	6.5(79)	17	21	—	—	55.3	K	—	87	128
1967	†Oak-A★	14	—	—	—	—	—	—	—	—	38	15	39.5	285	7.5(50)	3	3	—	—	—	K	—	**116**	38
1968	†Oak-A	14(1)	—	—	—	—	—	—	—	—	49	30	61.2	522	10.7(**94**)	6	2	—	—	—	K	—	117	211
1969	†Oak-A	14	1	0	0.0(0)	0	—	—	—	—	13	6	46.2	73	5.6(20)	2	1	1	4	—	K	—	105	7
1970	†Oak☆	14	2	4	2.0(4)	0	—	—	—	—	55	29	52.7	461	8.4(44)	6	5	4	37	—	K	—	84	65
1971	Oak	14	—	—	—	—	—	—	—	—	58	32	55.2	378	6.5(37)	4	6	2	26	—	K	—	86	-31
1972	†Oak	14	—	—	—	—	—	—	—	—	15	5	33.3	77	5.1(26)	1	0	2	19	—	K	—	95	44
1973	†Oak☆	14	—	—	—	—	—	—	—	—	—	—	—	—	—	—	—	—	—	—	K	—	100	0
1974	†Oak	14	—	—	—	—	—	—	—	—	4	1	25.0	28	7.0(28)	1	0	—	—	—	K	—	77	19
1975	†Oak	14	—	—	—	—	—	—	—	—	3	1	33.3	11	3.7(11)	0	1	3	8	—	K	—	83	-35
NFL	26	340(15)	135	344	2.5(19)	9	1	-16	-16.0(7)	0	4007	1911	47.7	26920	6.7(95)	236	277	12	94	60.6	KPki	—	2002	3983
BLANDIN, ERNIE Ernest Elmer, T-DT, 6´4˝/248 lbs; Tulane; 1942: Phi, rnd 5; B6/21/1919 Augusta, KS, D9/16/1968 Randallstown, MD **1946**†Cle-A 14 (5, lt) **1948**†Bal-A 14 (14, LT) **1949** Bal-A 10 (8, LT)																								
1947	†Cle-A	12(7, LT)	1	-6	-6.0(-6)	0	—	—	—	—	—	—	—	—	—	—	—	—	—	—	—	—	0	-6
AAFC	4	50(34)	1	-6	-6.0(-6)	0	—	—	—	—	—	—	—	—	—	—	—	—	—	—	—	—	0	-6
1953 Bal 9 (LT)																								
1950	Bal	12(11, LT)	—	—	—	—	1	16	16.0(16)	0	—	—	—	—	—	—	—	—	—	—	k	—	0	-6
NFL	2	21(11)	—	—	—	—	1	16	16.0(16)	0	—	—	—	—	—	—	—	—	—	—	—	—	0	8
BLANKENSHIP, BRIAN Brian Patrick, G, 6´1˝/286 lbs; Nebraska-Omaha; Nebraska; B4/7/1963 Omaha, NE **1987** Pit 13 (3) **1988** Pit 13 (12, LG) **1989** Pit 16 (7, rg) **1990** Pit 16 (13, LG) **1991** Pit 3 (3) **NFL** 61 (38) [5 yrs]																								
BLANKENSHIP, GREG Gregory, LB, 6´1˝/212 lbs; Cal State-Hayward; B3/24/1954 Vallejo, CA **1976** Oak 4 **1976**†Pit 6 **NFL** 10 [1 yr]																								
BLANKS, SID Sidney, RB, 6´1˝/200 lbs; Texas A&M-Kingsville; 1964: Hou, rnd 5/Chi, rnd 3; B4/29/1940 Del Rio, TX																								
1964	Hou-A★	14(HB)	145	756	5.2(91)	**6**	56	497	8.9(45)	1	1	1	100.0	8	8.0(8)	1	0	—	—	—	k	—	42	1151
1966	Hou-A	14(hb)	71	235	3.3(30)	0	19	234	12.3(42)	2	—	—	—	—	—	—	—	—	—	—	k	—	12	534
1967	†Hou-A	13	66	206	3.1(16)	1	11	93	8.5(39)	1	—	—	—	—	—	—	—	—	—	—	p	—	12	268
1968	Hou-A	14(HB)	63	169	2.7(10)	0	13	184	14.2(61)	0	—	—	—	—	—	—	—	—	—	—	p	—	0	330
1969	Bos-A	14	7	30	4.3(12)	0	2	16	8.0(13)	0	—	—	—	—	—	—	—	—	—	—	kp	—	0	64
1970	Bos	14	13	44	3.4(12)	0	5	49	9.8(18)	0	—	—	—	—	—	—	—	—	—	—	kp	—	0	154
NFL	6	83	365	1440	3.9(91)	7	106	1073	10.1(61)	4	1	1	100.0	8	8.0(8)	1	0	—	—	—	kp	—	66	2500
BLANTON, JERRY Gerald, LB, 6´1˝/231 lbs; Kentucky; 1978: Buf, rnd 11; B12/20/1956 Toledo, OH **1979** KC 16 **1980** KC 16 (3) **1981** KC 9 (9, LILB) **1982** KC 9 (9, LILB) **1983** KC 16 (16, LILB) **1984** KC 10 (9, lilb) **1985** KC 16 (3) **NFL** 92 (49) [7 yrs]																								
BLANTON, SCOTT Robert Scott, K, 6´2˝/221 lbs; Oklahoma; B7/1/1973 Norman, OK **[K]** **1996** Was 16 (0) **1997** Was 15 (0) **1998** Was 2 (0) **NFL** 33 (0) [3 yrs]																								
BLAYLOCK, ANTHONY Anthony Darius, DB, 5´10˝/190 lbs; Winston-Salem State; 1988: Cle, rnd 4; B2/21/1965 Raleigh, NC **1988** Cle 12 (0) **1989**†Cle 16 (1) **1990** Cle 16 (7, lcb) **1991** Cle 5 (1) **1991** SD 2 (0) **1992**†SD 11 (10, RCB) **1993** ChiB 9 (9, RCB) **NFL** 71 (28) [6 yrs]																								
BLAYLOCK, DERRICK Derrick DeShaun, RB, 5´9˝/205 lbs; Stephen F. Austin State; 2001: KC, rnd 5; B8/23/1979 Atlanta, TX																								
2002	KC	12(0)	16	72	4.5(16)	0	5	47	9.4(21)	0	—	—	—	—	—	—	—	—	—	—	k	—	0	100
2003	†KC	16(0)	22	112	5.1(25)	2	15	181	12.1(63)	1	—	—	—	—	—	—	—	—	—	—	k	—	18	245
2004	KC	12(5, rb)	118	539	4.6(24)	8	25	246	9.8(30)	1	—	—	—	—	—	—	—	—	—	—	k	—	54	754
2005	NYJ	7(1)	17	53	3.1(11)	0	3	17	5.7(10)	0	—	—	—	—	—	—	—	—	—	—	k	—	0	64
NFL	4	47(6)	173	776	4.5(25)	10	48	491	10.2(63)	2	—	—	—	—	—	—	—	—	—	—	k	—	72	1162
BLAZER, PHIL Philip Paul, G, 6´1˝/235 lbs; North Carolina; 1958: Det, rnd 8; B2/25/1936 **1960** Buf-A 14 (LG)																								

YEAR	TEAM	G (GS, POS)	RUSH	YD	AVG(LG)	TD	REC	YD	AVG(LG)	TD	PASS	COMP	PCT	YD	AVG(LG)	TD	INT	SK	YD	QBR	KPR	OTD	PTS	TAY

BLAZINE, TONY Anthony A., T, 6'0"/232 lbs; Illinois Wesleyan; B1/2/1912 Canton, IL, D7/3/1963 **1935** ChiC☆12 (8, LT) **1936** ChiC 11 (4) **1938** ChiC 11 (10, LT)
1939 ChiC◇11 (9, LT) **1940** ChiC 7 (7, RT) **1941**†NYG 10 (2)

| 1937 | ChiC | 11(6, LT) | — | — | — | | 1 | 2 | 2.0(2) | 0 | — | | — | — | — | — | | — | — | — | — | | — | 0 | 1 |
| NFL | 7 | 73(46) | — | — | — | | 1 | 2 | 2.0(2) | 0 | — | | — | — | — | — | | — | — | — | — | | 1 | 6 | 1 |

BLEAMER, JEFF Jeffrey Harrison, T-G, 6'4"/253 lbs; Penn State; 1975: Phi, rnd 8; B6/22/1953 Allentown, PA **1975** Phi 14 **1976** Phi 10 (1) **1977** NYJ 8 **NFL** 32 (1) [3 yrs]

BLEDSOE, CURTIS Curtis Kemp, RB, 5'11"/215 lbs; San Diego State; B3/19/1957 Odessa, TX

1981	KC	13(1)	20	65	3.3(13)	0	3	27	9.0(17)	0	—		—	—	—	—		—	—	k		—	0	106
1982	KC	3(0)	10	20	2.0(5)	0	1	5	5.0(5)	0	—		—	—	—	—		—	—			—	0	23
NFL	2	16(1)	30	85	2.8(13)	0	4	32	8.0(17)	0	—		—	—	—	—		—	—	k		—	0	128

BLEDSOE, DREW Drew McQueen, QB, 6'5"/238 lbs; Washington State; 1993: NE, rnd 1; B2/14/1972 Ellensburg, WA

1993	NE	13(12, QB)	32	82	2.6(15)	0	—		—	—		429	214	49.9	2494	5.8(54)	15	15	16	99	65.0	—		—	0	804
1994	†NE★	16(16, QB)	44	40	0.9(7)	0	—		—	—		**691**	**400**	57.9	**4555**	6.6(62)	25	**27**	22	139	73.6	—		—	0	1363
1995	NE	15(15, QB)	20	28	1.4(15)	0	1	-9	-9.0(-9)	0	**636**	323	50.8	3507	5.5(47)	13	16	23	170	63.7	—		—	0	1202
1996	†NE★	16(16, QB)	24	27	1.1(8)	0	—		—	—		**623**	**373**	59.9	4086	6.6(84)	27	15	30	190	83.7	—		—	0	1605
1997	†NE◇	16(16, QB)	28	55	2.0(8)	0	—		—	—		522	314	60.2	3706	7.1(76)	28	15	30	258	87.7	—		—	0	1448
1998	NE	14(14, QB)	28	44	1.6(10)	0	—		—	—		481	263	54.7	3633	7.6(**86**)	20	14	36	295	80.9	—		—	0	1401
1999	NE	16(16, QB)	42	101	2.4(25)	0	—		—	—		**539**	305	56.6	3985	7.4(68)	19	**21**	55	342	75.6	—		—	0	1349
2000	NE	16(16, QB)	47	158	3.4(16)	2	—		—	—		531	312	58.8	3291	6.2(59)	17	13	45	264	77.3	—		—	12	1389
2001	†NE	2(2)	5	18	3.6(8)	0	—		—	—		66	40	60.6	400	6.1(58)	2	2	5	21	—	—		—	0	148
2002	Buf◇	16(16, QB)	27	67	2.5(11)	2	—		—	—		610	375	61.5	4359	7.1(73)	24	15	54	369	86.0	—		—	12	1787
2003	Buf	16(16, QB)	24	29	1.2(11)	2	—		—	—		471	274	58.2	2860	6.1(54)	11	12	49	371	73.0	—		—	12	1054
2004	Buf	16(16, QB)	22	37	1.7(17)	0	—		—	—		450	256	56.9	2932	6.5(69)	20	16	37	215	76.6	—		—	0	963
2005	Dal	16(16, QB)	34	50	1.5(9)	2	—		—	—		499	300	60.1	3639	7.3(71)	23	17	49	295	83.7	—		—	12	1325
NFL	13	188(187)	377	736	2.0(25)	8	1	-9	-9.0(-9)	0	6548	3749	57.3	43447	6.6(86)	244	198	451	3028	77.3	—		—	48	15835

BLEEKER, MAL Malcolm S., G-C, 6'0"/205 lbs; Columbia; B1907 **1930** Bkn 3 (0)

BLEEKER, MEL Melvin Wallace, HB, 5'11"/189 lbs; USC; B8/20/1920 Los Angeles, CA, D4/24/1996 Mission Viejo, CA

1944	Phi	9(3)	60	315	5.3(37)	4	8	299	37.4(75)	4	—		—	—	—	—		—	—	pi		—	48	518
1945	Phi	4(4, RH)	50	167	3.3(20)	2	3	32	10.7(15)	0	—		—	—	—	—		—	—	p		—	12	220
1946	Phi	4(0)	6	-7	-1.2(6)	0	3	29	9.7(20)	0	—		—	—	—	—		—	—	—		—	0	8
1947	LARm	11(4)	23	111	4.8(35)	0	—		—	—		—		—	—	—	—		—	—	ki		1	6	111
NFL	4	28(11)	139	586	4.2(37)	6	14	360	25.7(75)	4	—		—	—	—	—		—	—	kpi		1	66	856

BLEICK, TOM Thomas Ward, DB, 6'2"/200 lbs; Georgia Tech; 1965: Bal, rnd 9/Hou, rnd R9; B3/21/1943 Talladega, AL **1966** Bal 7 **1967** Atl 2 **NFL** 9 [2 yrs]

BLEIER, BOB John Robert, QB, 6'3"/210 lbs; Richmond; B6/1/1964 Rochester, NY

| 1987 | NE | 3(2) | 5 | -5 | -1.0(1) | 1 | — | | — | — | | 39 | 14 | 35.9 | 181 | 4.6(35) | 1 | 1 | 3 | 28 | — | — | | — | 6 | 61 |

BLEIER, JOHNNY John L., B, /160 lbs; none; B8/25/1892, OH, D4/13/1981 Hyattsville, MD **1921** Was 3 (0)

BLEIER, ROCKY Robert Patrick, RB, 5'11"/210 lbs; Notre Dame; 1968: Pit, rnd 16; B3/5/1946 Appleton, WI

1968	Pit	10	6	39	6.5(21)	0	3	68	22.7(54)	0	—		—	—	—	—		—	—	kp		—	0	105
1971	Pit	6	—	—	—		—		—	—		—		—	—	—	—		—	—	kp		—	0	6
1972	†Pit	14	1	17	17.0(17)	0	—		—	—		—		—	—	—	—		—	—	kp		—	0	18
1973	†Pit	12	3	0	0.0(1)	0	—		—	—		—		—	—	—	—		—	—	kp		—	0	2
1974	†Pit	12(RB)	88	373	4.2(18)	2	7	87	12.4(24)	0	—		—	—	—	—		—	—	k		—	12	459
1975	†Pit	11(11, RB)	140	528	3.8(17)	2	15	65	4.3(13)	0	—		—	—	—	—		—	—	—		—	12	581
1976	†Pit	14(RB)	220	1036	4.7(28)	5	24	294	12.3(32)	0	—		—	—	—	—		—	—	—		—	30	1233
1977	†Pit	13(RB)	135	465	3.4(16)	4	18	161	8.9(30)	0	—		—	—	—	—		—	—	—		—	24	586
1978	†Pit	16(RB)	165	633	3.8(24)	5	17	168	9.9(32)	1	—		—	—	—	—		—	—	—		—	36	772
1979	†Pit	16(rb)	92	434	4.7(70)	4	31	277	8.9(28)	0	—		—	—	—	—		—	—	—		—	24	613
1980	Pit	16(6, RB)	78	340	4.4(19)	1	21	174	8.3(17)	1	—		—	—	—	—		—	—	—		—	12	442
NFL	11	140(17)	928	3865	4.2(70)	23	136	1294	9.5(54)	2	—		—	—	—	—		—	—	kp		—	150	4815

BLESSING, PAUL Paul Theodore, E, 6'4"/215 lbs; Nebraska-Kearney; B1/6/1919 Tilden, NE, D5/5/1990 Englewood, CO **1944** Det 8 (0)

BLEVINS, DARRIUS Darrius, WR, 6'2"/216 lbs; Memphis; B4/21/1976 Morristown, TN **2000** SL 5 (0)

BLEVINS, TONY Tony, DB, 6'0"/165 lbs; Kansas; B1/29/1975 Rockford, IL **1998** SF 2 (0) **1998** Ind 3 (0) **1999**†Ind 15 (1) **2000**†Ind 16 (1) **NFL** 36 (2) [3 yrs]

BLIGEN, DENNIS Dennis, RB, 5'11"/215 lbs; St. John's (NY); B3/3/1962 New York, NY

1984	NYJ	1(0)	—	—	—		—		—	—		—		—	—	—	—		—	—	—		—	—	—
1985	†NYJ	9(0)	22	107	4.9(28)	1	5	43	8.6(14)	0	—		—	—	—	—		—	—	—		—	6	139
1986	NYJ	4(2)	20	65	3.3(10)	1	2	6	3.0(4)	0	—		—	—	—	—		—	—	—		—	6	78
1986	TB	1(0)	—	—	—		—		—	—		—		—	—	—	—		—	—	—		—	—	—
1987	NYJ	6(2)	31	128	4.1(15)	1	11	81	7.4(19)	0	—		—	—	—	—		—	—	—		—	6	179
NFL	4	21(4)	73	300	4.1(28)	3	18	130	7.2(19)	0	—		—	—	—	—		—	—	—		—	18	395

BLINKA, STAN Stanley John, LB, 6'2"/230 lbs; Sam Houston State; 1979: NYJ, rnd 5; B4/29/1957 Columbus, OH **1979** NYJ 16 (16, MLB) **1980** NYJ 16 (16, MLB)
1981†NYJ 16 (16, MLB) **1982**†NYJ 8 (8, MLB) **1983** NYJ 16 (2) **NFL** 72 (58) [5 yrs]

BLISS, HARRY Harold W., B, 5'8"/155 lbs; Ohio State; B6/17/1897, D5/1967 Shelby, OH [K] **1921** Col 9 (8, BB), 1

BLISS, HOMER Homer Clisson, G, 5'11"/195 lbs; Washington & Jefferson; B8/16/1904, D4/1970 Detroit, MI **1928** ChiC 1 (0)

BLOEDORN, GREG Gregory S., C, 6'6"/278 lbs; Cornell; B11/15/1972 Elmhurst, IL **1997** Sea 2 (0) **1999** Sea 9 (0) **NFL** 11 (0) [2 yrs]

BLONDIN, TOM Thomas Albert, G, 6'0"/195 lbs; West Virginia Wesleyan; B10/25/1910 Marietta, OH, D12/15/1978 Parkersburg, WV **1933** Cin 3 (0)

BLOOD, JOHNNY John Victor, aka John McNally, TB-HB-WB-BB-DB, 6'1"/188 lbs; Wisconsin-River Falls; St. John's(MN); Notre Dame; B11/27/1903 New Richmond, WI, D11/28/1985 Palm Springs, CA; HOF 1963 [KC]
1925 Mil 6 (5, WB) **1926** Dul 13 (7, TB), 6 **1927** Dul 9 (8, TB), 6 **1928** Pot 10 (8, TB), 19 **1929** GB☆12 (9, HB), 30 **1930** GB☆10 (3), 30 **1931** GB☆14 (6, TB), 84

1932	GB	13(3)	37	130	3.5	0	14	168	12.0	3	0		0.0	0	0.0	0		0	—	—		1	24	239
1933	GB	9(3)	14	41	2.9	0	9	215	26.9(38)	3	2		0.0	0	0.0	0		0	—	K		0	19	164
1934	Pit	5(1)	3	3	1.0	0	1	10	10.0(10)	0	1		0.0	0	0.0	0		0	—	—		0	0	8
1935	GB	9(4, HB)	42	115	2.7	0	25	404	16.2(70)	3	33	11	33.3	164	5.0	0	3	—	—		1	24	304
1936	†GB	8(3)	13	65	5.0	0	7	147	21.0(46)	2	6	3	50.0	20	3.3	1	0	—	K		1	19	174
1937	Pit	9(2)	9	37	4.1	0	10	168	16.8	4	25	10	40.0	115	4.6	1	2	—	K		1	30	134
1938	Pit	10(4, BB)	2	-5	-2.5	0	2	5	2.5	0	—		—	—	—	—		—	—	K		0	0	-3
NFL	14	137(66)	120	386	3.2	5	67	1117	16.7(70)	37	70	24	34.3	299	4.3	4	5	—	K		7	297	1219

BLOODGOOD, AL Elbert Lorraine, B, 5'8"/153 lbs; DePauw; Nebraska; B9/5/1901 Beatrice, NE, D1947, [K] **1925** KC 6 (4, BB), 7 **1926** KC☆11 (10, BB), 47 **1927** Cle 10 (1), 45
1928 NYG 5 (1), 6 **1930** GB 3 (0) **NFL** 35 (16), 105 [5 yrs]

BLOUNT, ALVIN Alvin Wilbert, RB, 5'9"/197 lbs; Maryland; 1987: Dal, rnd 9; B2/12/1965 Washington, DC

| 1987 | Dal | 2(2) | 46 | 125 | 2.7(15) | 3 | 1 | 5 | 5.0(5) | 0 | — | | — | — | — | — | | — | — | — | | — | 18 | 158 |

BLOUNT, ED Edward Cleo, QB, 6'0"/195 lbs; Washington State; B2/26/1964 Los Angeles, CA

| 1987 | SF | 1(0) | 1 | 0 | 0.0(0) | 0 | — | | — | — | | — | | — | — | — | — | | — | — | — | | — | 0 | 0 |

BLOUNT, ERIC Eric Lamont, WR, 5'9"/192 lbs; North Carolina; 1992: Phx, rnd 8; B9/22/1970 Ayden, NC

1992	Phx	4(0)	1	-1	-1.0(-1)	0	3	18	6.0(18)	0	—		—	—	—	—		—	—	kp		—	0	130
1993	Phx	6(0)	5	28	5.6(7)	1	5	36	7.2(9)	0	—		—	—	—	—		—	—	kp		—	6	144
NFL	2	10(0)	6	27	4.5(7)	1	8	54	6.8(18)	0	—		—	—	—	—		—	—	kp		—	6	274

YEAR	TEAM	G(GS, POS)	RUSH	YD	AVG(LG)	TD	REC	YD	AVG(LG)	TD	PASS	COMP	PCT	YD	AVG(LG)	TD	INT	SK	YD	QBR	KPR	OTD	PTS	TAY

BLOUNT, JEB   John Eugene, QB, 6´3˝/200 lbs; Tulsa; 1976: Oak, rnd 2; B7/12/1954 Tyler, TX

| 1977 | TB | 5(4) | 5 | 26 | 5.2(12) | 0 | — | — | — | — | 89 | 37 | 41.6 | 522 | 5.9(56) | 0 | 7 | 18 | 164 | — | — | — | 0 | 7 |

BLOUNT, LAMAR   Lloyd Lamar, E-B, 6´1˝/190 lbs; Duke; Mississippi State; 1944: NYG, rnd 2; B4/11/1920 Decatur, MS

1946	Mia-A	12(6, RE)	—	—	—	—	13	218	16.8	1	—	—	—	—	—	—	—	—	—	—	—	—	6	114
1947	Buf-A	5(0)	3	7	2.3	0	8	148	18.5	0	—	—	—	—	—	—	—	—	—	—	—	—	0	81
1947	Bal-A	5(3)	1	-2	-2.0(-2)	0	—	—	—	—	—	—	—	—	—	—	—	—	—	—	—	—	0	-2
AAFC	2	22(9)	4	5	1.3	0	21	366	17.4	1	—	—	—	—	—	—	—	—	—	—	—	—	6	193

BLOUNT, MEL   Melvin Cornell, DB, 6´3˝/205 lbs; Southern (LA); 1970: Pit, rnd 3; B4/10/1948 Vidalia, GA; HOF 1989 **[I]**   **1970** Pit 14 (9, LCB)   **1971** Pit 14 (9, RCB)   **1972**†Pit 14 (14, RCB)   **1973**†Pit 14 (14, RCB)   **1974**†Pit 13 (13, RCB)   **1975**†Pit☆14 (14, RCB)   **1976**†Pit★14 (14, RCB)   **1977**☆Pit☆14 (13, RCB)   **1978**†Pit★16 (16, RCB)   **1979**†Pit★16 (16, RCB)   **1980** Pit 16 (16, RCB)   **1981** Pit★16 (16, RCB)   **1982**†Pit 9 (9, RCB)   **1983**†Pit 16 (16, RCB)   **NFL** 200 (189) [14 yrs]

BLOUNT, TONY   Anthony Urban, DB, 6´1˝/195 lbs; Virginia; 1980: NYG, rnd 5; B11/5/1958 Atlanta, GA   **1980** NYG 3 (0)

BLOZIS, AL   Alfred Charles, T, 6´6˝/250 lbs; Georgetown (DC); 1942: NYG, rnd 5; B1/5/1919 Garfield, NJ, D1/31/1945 Colmar, France   **1942** NYG✧11 (11, RT)   **1944**†NYG 2 (2)

| 1943 | †NYG☆ | 10(10, RT) | — | — | — | — | 1 | 15 | 15.0(15) | 0 | — | — | — | — | — | — | — | — | — | — | — | — | 6 | 8 |
| NFL | 3 | 23(23) | — | — | — | — | 1 | 15 | 15.0(15) | 0 | — | — | — | — | — | — | — | — | — | — | — | — | 6 | 8 |

BLUE, FORREST   Forrest Murrell, C, 6´6˝/261 lbs; Auburn; 1968: SF, rnd 1; B9/7/1944 Marfa, TX   **1968** SF 14   **1969** SF 14 (14, C)   **1970**†SF 14 (14, C)   **1971**†SF★14 (14, C)   **1972**†SF★14 (14, C)   **1973** SF★14 (14, C)   **1974** SF★12 (12, C)   **1975** Bal 11   **1976**†Bal 14   **1977**†Bal 14   **1978** Bal 13   **NFL** 148 (82) [11 yrs]

BLUE, LUTHER   Luther, WR, 5´11˝/185 lbs; Iowa State; 1977: Det, rnd 4; B10/21/1954 Valdosta, GA

1977	Det	14	1	-6	-6.0(-6)	0	8	90	11.3(21)	1	—	—	—	—	—	—	—	—	—	—	kp	—	6	48
1978	Det	16(15, WR)	5	9	1.8(10)	0	31	350	11.3(26)	2	—	—	—	—	—	—	—	—	—	—	kp	—	12	283
1979	Det	9	1	-8	-8.0(-8)	0	8	102	12.8(26)	1	—	—	—	—	—	—	—	—	—	—	k	—	6	59
1980	Phi	3(0)	—	—	—	—	—	—	—	—	—	—	—	—	—	—	—	—	—	—	k	—	0	1
NFL	4	42(15)	7	-5	-0.7(10)	0	47	542	11.5(26)	4	—	—	—	—	—	—	—	—	—	—	kp	—	24	391

BLUE, TONY   Anthony Allen, DB, 5´9˝/185 lbs; UNLV; B9/19/1964 Inglewood, CA   **1987** Sea 3 (0)

BLUMENSTOCK, JIM   James A., FB, 5´11˝/190 lbs; Fordham; 1942: NYG, rnd 21; B4/28/1918 Rutherford, NJ, D7/31/1963 Passaic, NJ

| 1947 | NYG | 10(3) | 54 | 168 | 3.1(25) | 2 | 4 | 15 | 3.8(24) | 0 | 8 | 4 | 50.0 | 48 | 6.0(19) | 0 | 1 | — | — | — | kp | — | 12 | 230 |

BLUMER, HERB   Herbert George, E-G-T, 6´1˝/200 lbs; Missouri; B3/7/1900 St. Louis, MO, D4/13/1987 Danville, CA   **1925** ChiC 10 (6, le), 12   **1926** ChiC 12 (12, LE)   **1927** ChiC 9 (4)   **1928** ChiC 6 (6, LE)   **1929** ChiC☆10 (9, RG)   **1930** ChiC 11 (9, RG)   **1933** ChiC 1 (1)   **NFL** 59 (47) [7 yrs]

BLUNDIN, MATT   Matthew Brent, QB, 6´3˝/233 lbs; Virginia; 1992: KC, rnd 2; B3/7/1969 Darby, PA

1993	KC	1(0)	—	—	—	—	—	—	—	—	3	1	33.3	2	0.7(2)	0	0	—	—	—	—	—	0	1
1994	KC	1(0)	—	—	—	—	—	—	—	—	5	1	20.0	13	2.6(13)	0	1	—	—	—	—	—	0	-34
1997	Det	1(0)	—	—	—	—	—	—	—	—	1	0	0.0	0	0.0	0	1	—	—	—	—	—	0	-40
NFL	3	3(0)	—	—	—	—	—	—	—	—	9	2	22.2	15	1.7(13)	0	2	—	—	—	—	—	0	-73

BLY, DRE'   Donald Andre, DB, 5´9˝/185 lbs; North Carolina; 1999: SL, rnd 2; B5/22/1977 Chesapeake, VA **[I]**   **1999**†SL 16 (2)   **2000**†SL 16 (3)   **2001**†SL 16 (4)   **2002** SL 16 (16, RCB)   **2003** Det★14 (14, RCB)   **2004** Det✧13 (13, RCB)   **2005** Det 12 (11, RCB)   **NFL** 103 (63) [7 yrs]

BLYE, RONNIE   Ronald Jerry, aka Ronald Jerry Biley, RB, 6´1˝/202 lbs; Notre Dame; Florida A&M; B12/29/1943 Clearwater, FL

1968	NYG	13	53	243	4.6(17)	1	10	91	9.1(23)	0	—	—	—	—	—	—	—	—	—	—	k	—	6	508
1969	Phi	14	8	25	3.1(11)	0	2	-6	-3.0(1)	0	—	—	—	—	—	—	—	—	—	—	k	—	0	107
NFL	2	27	61	268	4.4(17)	1	12	85	7.1(23)	0	—	—	—	—	—	—	—	—	—	—	k	—	6	615

BOADWAY, STEVE   Steven Troy, LB, 6´4˝/240 lbs; Arizona; B6/20/1962 Bakersfield, CA   **1987** Det 2 (0)

BOARD, DWAINE   Dwaine P., DE, 6´5˝/248 lbs; North Carolina A&T; 1979: Pit, rnd 5; B11/29/1956 Union Hall, VA   **1979** SF 16 (5, rde)   **1980** SF 3 (3)   **1981**†SF 16 (11, RDE)   **1982** SF 1 (1)   **1983**†SF 16 (13, RDE)   **1984**†SF 16 (16, RDE)   **1985**†SF 16 (16, RDE)   **1986**†SF 16 (15, RDE)   **1987**†SF 14 (12, RDE)   **1988** SF 3 (0)   **1988** NO 4 (0)   **NFL** 121 (92) [10 yrs]

BOATNER, MACK   Mark Ernest, RB, 6´0˝/220 lbs; Southeastern Louisiana; 1982: Mia, rnd 9; B10/4/1958 White Castle, LA   **1986** TB 7 (0)

BOATSWAIN, HARRY   Harry Kwane, G-T, 6´4˝/310 lbs; New Haven; 1991: SF, rnd 5; B6/26/1969 Brooklyn, NY, D8/8/2005 Brooklyn, NY   **1992**†SF 16 (2)   **1993**†SF 16 (2)   **1994**†SF 13 (4)   **1995**†Phi 13 (7, rg)   **1996** NYJ 16 (4)   **NFL** 74 (19) [5 yrs]

BOATWRIGHT, BON   Bon Lovell, DT, 6´5˝/262 lbs; Oklahoma State; 1974: SD, rnd 8; B10/28/1951 Henderson, TX   **1974** SD 10

BOB, ADAM   Adam, LB, 6´2˝/240 lbs; Texas A&M; 1989: NYJ, rnd 10; B10/30/1967 Milwaukee, WI   **1989** NYJ 5 (0)

BOBADASH, E.   E., E, none; deceased   **1922** Oor 1 (0)

BOBER, CHRIS   Chris, C, 6´5˝/310 lbs; Nebraska-Omaha; B12/24/1976 Omaha, NE   **2001** NYG 16 (0)   **2002**†NYG 15 (15, C)   **2003** NYG 16 (16, C)   **2004** KC 12 (2)   **2005** KC 16 (2)   **NFL** 75 (35) [5 yrs]

BOBO, HUBERT   Hubert Lee, LB, 6´0˝/220 lbs; Ohio State; 1957: Phi, rnd 13; B7/2/1934 Athens, OH   **1960** LAC-A 3   **1961** NYT-A 14 (MLB)   **1962** NYT-A 14 (MLB)   **NFL** 31 [3 yrs]

BOBO, ORLANDO   Orlando, G, 6´3˝/301 lbs; Louisiana-Monroe; B2/9/1974 West Point, MS   **1997**†Min 5 (0)   **1998** Min 4 (0)   **2000** Bal 7 (0)   **2001**†Bal 12 (0)

| 1999 | Cle | 9(1) | — | — | — | — | 1 | 3 | 3.0(3) | 0 | — | — | — | — | — | — | — | — | — | — | — | — | 0 | 2 |
| NFL | 5 | 37(1) | — | — | — | — | 1 | 3 | 3.0(3) | 0 | — | — | — | — | — | — | — | — | — | — | k | — | 0 | -3 |

BOCK, JOE   Joseph Alan, C, 6´4˝/256 lbs; Virginia; B7/21/1959 Rochester, NY   **1987** SL 1 (0)   **1987** Buf 1 (0)   **NFL** 2 (0) [1 yr]

BOCK, JOHN   John Matthew, C-G, 6´3˝/290 lbs; Louisville; Indiana State; B2/11/1971 Chicago, IL   **1995** NYJ 10 (7, c)   **1996** Mia 2 (0)   **1997**†Mia 14 (3)   **1998**†Mia 16 (6, lg)   **1999** Mia 7 (0)   **2000** Mia 6 (1)   **NFL** 55 (17) [6 yrs]

BOCK, WAYNE   Wayne R., DT, 6´4˝/265 lbs; Illinois; 1957: ChiC, rnd 5; B5/28/1934 Third River Township, MN   **1957** ChiC 4

BOCKWOLDT, COLBY   Colby, LB, 6´1˝/225 lbs; Brigham Young; 2004: NO, rnd 7; B4/14/1981 Ogden, UT   **2004** NO 16 (7, rlb)   **2005** NO 16 (16, RLB)   **NFL** 32 (23) [2 yrs]

BODDEN, LEIGH   Leigh Edmond, DB, 6´1˝/195 lbs; Duquesne; B9/24/1981 Hyattsville, MD   **2003** Cle 13 (1)   **2004** Cle 8 (1)   **2005** Cle 13 (11, RCB)   **NFL** 34 (13) [3 yrs]

BODDIE, TONY   Dominec Leanthony, RB, 5´11˝/195 lbs; Montana State; B11/11/1960 Portsmith, WA

1986	Den	1(0)	1	2	2.0(2)	0	—	—	—	—	—	—	—	—	—	—	—	—	—	—	—	—	0	2
1987	†Den	5(0)	3	7	2.3(4)	1	9	85	9.4(26)	0	—	—	—	—	—	—	—	—	—	—	—	—	6	60
NFL	2	6(0)	4	9	2.3(4)	1	9	85	9.4(26)	0	—	—	—	—	—	—	—	—	—	—	—	—	6	62

BODEN, LYNN   Lynn Ray, G-T, 6´3˝/270 lbs; South Dakota State; 1975: Det, rnd 1; B6/5/1953 Stromburg, NE   **1975** Det 14 (12, LG)   **1976** Det 14 (8, LG)   **1977** Det 13 (13, RG)   **1978** Det 16 (16, RG)   **1979** ChiB 10   **NFL** 67 (49) [5 yrs]

BODENGER, MAURY   Morris, G, 5´10˝/214 lbs; Tulane; B7/31/1909 New Orleans, LA, D2/9/1960 Cleveland, OH   **1931** Por 13 (13, LG)   **1932** Por☆12 (10, LG)   **1933** Por 11 (9, LG)   **1934** Det 12 (10, LG)   **NFL** 48 (42) [4 yrs]

BODIE, PING   M. Risso, FB, none; B5/10/1897, Italy, D12/14/1981 Stockton, CA   **1921** ChiC 1 (0)

BODY, PATRICK   Patrick, DB, 6´2˝/201 lbs; Toledo; B1/17/1982 Pittsburgh, PA   **2005** Cin 6 (0)

BOEDEKER, BILL   William Henry, HB, 5´11˝/192 lbs; DePaul; B3/7/1924 Milwaukee, WI

1946	ChiR-A	12(1)	6	8	1.3	0	5	82	16.4	1	—	—	—	—	—	—	—	—	—	—	kpi	—	6	148
1947	Cle-A	12(3)	31	194	6.3	4	8	175	21.9	1	—	—	—	—	—	—	—	—	—	—	kp	—	30	437
1948	†Cle-A	14(3)	78	254	3.3	3	13	237	18.2	2	—	—	—	—	—	—	—	—	—	—	kp	—	30	412
1949	Cle-A	12(7, LH)	50	269	5.4	1	11	371	33.7	2	—	—	—	—	—	—	—	—	—	—	k	—	18	529
AAFC	4	50(14)	165	725	4.4	8	37	865	23.4	6	—	—	—	—	—	—	—	—	—	—	kpi	—	84	1525
1950	GB	9	8	16	2.0(8)	0	1	10	10.0(10)	0	—	—	—	—	—	—	—	—	—	—	kp	—	0	50
1950	Phi	1	—	—	—	—	—	—	—	—	—	—	—	—	—	—	—	—	—	—	—	—	0	—
NFL	1	10	8	16	2.0(8)	0	1	10	10.0(10)	0	—	—	—	—	—	—	—	—	—	—	—	—	0	21

BOEKE, JIM   James Frederick, T, 6´5˝/255 lbs; Heidelberg; 1960: LA, rnd 19/Bos, rnd 2; B9/11/1938 Akron, OH   **1960** LARm 12 (LT)   **1961** LARm 14 (LT)   **1962** LARm 14   **1963** LARm 14   **1964** Dal 14   **1965** Dal 14 (14, LT)   **1966**†Dal 10 (10, LT)   **1967**†Dal 14   **1968** NO 13   **NFL** 119 (24) [9 yrs]

YEAR	TEAM	G(GS, POS)	RUSH	YD	AVG(LG)	TD	REC	YD	AVG(LG)	TD	PASS COMP	PCT	YD	AVG(LG)	TD	INT	SK	YD	QBR	KPR	OTD	PTS	TAY

BOENSCH, FRED   Frederick Macmilian, G-LB, 6´4˝/228 lbs; California; Stanford; 1944: Cle, rnd 9; B9/27/1920 Portland, OR, D4/20/2000 Redwood City, CA   **1947** Was 12 (8, RG)
1948 Was 12 (11, RG)   **NFL** 24 (19) [2 yrs]

BOERIGTER, MARC   Marc Robert, WR, 6´3˝/220 lbs; Hastings; B5/4/1978 Hastings, NE

YEAR	TEAM	G(GS, POS)					REC	YD	AVG(LG)	TD										KPR		PTS	TAY
2002	KC	16(2)	—	—	—	—	20	420	21.0(99)	8	—	—	—	—	—	—	—	—	—	—	—	48	250
2003	†KC	15(0)	—	—	—	—	11	158	14.4(30)	0	—	—	—	—	—	—	—	—	—	k	—	0	108
2005	KC	10(0)	—	—	—	—	8	119	14.9(38)	0	—	—	—	—	—	—	—	—	—	—	—	2	60
NFL	3	41(2)	—	—	—	—	39	697	17.9(99)	8	—	—	—	—	—	—	—	—	—	k	—	50	418

BOERIO, CHUCK   Charles, LB, 6´0˝/205 lbs; Illinois; 1952: GB, rnd 20; B3/9/1930 Kincaid, IL   **1952** GB 1

BOETTCHER, CHAMP   Raymond Edward, B, 5´10˝/193 lbs; Lawrence; B9/18/1900 Reeseville, WI, D12/20/1965 Watertown, WI   **1926** Rac 4 (1)

BOGGAN, REX   Rex Reed, DT, 6´3˝/245 lbs; Mississippi; 1952: NYG, rnd 20; B3/27/1930 Tupelo, MS, D12/8/1985 Spartanburg, SC   **1955** NYG 11 (RDT)

BOGGS, MARK   Mark Allen, T, 6´5˝/301 lbs; Ball State; B5/7/1964 Kankakee, IL   **1987** Ind 1 (0)

BOGLE, PHIL   Phil, G-T, 6´2˝/332 lbs; New Haven; B9/27/1979 Spring Valley, NY   **2003** SD 15 (13, RG)

BOGUE, GEORGE   George Richardson, FB, 6´0˝/210 lbs; Stanford; B2/10/1906 Omaha, NE, D10/13/1972 Pasadena, CA [K]   **1930** ChiC 4 (3), 1   **1930** Nwk 3 (3)   **NFL** 7 (6) [1 yr]

BOHANNON, FRED   Frederick Jerome, DB, 6´0˝/201 lbs; Mississippi Valley State; B5/31/1958 Birmingham, AL, D2/8/1999 Birmingham, AL   **1982** †Pit 7 (0)

BOHLING, DEWEY   Dewey, HB, 5´11˝/190 lbs; Hardin-Simmons; 1959: Pit, rnd 13; B8/22/1938 Hebron, NE

1960	NYT-A	14(HB)	123	431	3.5(49)	2	30	268	8.9(15)	4	5	0	0.0	0	0.0	0	0	—	0	—	—	36	605
1961	NYT-A	5	13	19	1.5(9)	0	3	34	11.3(27)	0	—	—	—	—	—	—	—	—	—	—	—	0	36
1961	Buf-A	7	42	134	3.2(18)	2	10	183	18.3(41)	1	1	0	0.0	0	0.0	0	0	—	0	kp	—	18	327
NFL	2	26	178	584	3.3(49)	4	43	485	11.3(41)	5	6	0	0.0	0	0.0	0	0	—	0	kp	—	54	968

BOHLINGER, ROB   Robert Paul, T, 6´8˝/310 lbs; Wyoming; B6/14/1975 Minneapolis, MN   **1998** Car 13 (1)

BOHLMANN, FRANK   Frank Henry, G, 5´11˝/212 lbs; Marquette; B1/26/1917 Milwaukee, WI, D10/24/1999 Aurora, CO   **1942** ChiC 5 (0)

BOHM, RON   Ronald Leland, DT, 6´3˝/250 lbs; Illinois; B9/3/1964 Princeton, IL   **1987** SL 3 (3)

BOHOVICH, REED   George Reed, G-T, 6´1˝/260 lbs; Lehigh; 1962: NYG, rnd 9/NYT, rnd 19; B11/18/1941 Buffalo, NY   **1962** †NYG 10

BOHREN, KARL   Karl W., B, 5´8˝/180 lbs; Pittsburgh; B5/26/1902, D3/11/1987 Jefferson, PA   **1927** Buf 3 (2)

BOIMAN, ROCKY   Rocky Michael, LB, 6´4˝/236 lbs; Notre Dame; 2002: Ten, rnd 4; B1/24/1980 Cincinnati, OH   **2002** Ten 16 (0)   **2003** †Ten 16 (2)   **2004** Ten 7 (6, LLB)
2005 Ten 15 (2)   **NFL** 54 (10) [4 yrs]

BOJOVIC, NOVO   Novo, K, 5´10˝/172 lbs; Central Michigan; B11/2/1959 Titograd, Yugoslavia [K]   **1985** SL 6 (0)

BOKAMPER, KIM   Kim E., DE-LB, 6´6˝/245 lbs; Concordia (MN); San Jose State; 1976: Mia, rnd 1; B9/25/1954 San Diego, CA   **1977** Mia 14 (14, LOLB)   **1978** †Mia 16 (16, LOLB)
1979 †Mia◊14 (13, LOLB)   **1980** Mia 16 (16, LOLB)   **1981** Mia 16 (1)   **1982** †Mia 9 (6, RDE)   **1983** †Mia 15 (15, RDE)   **1984** †Mia 11 (10, RDE)   **1985** †Mia 16 (12, RDE)
NFL 127 (103) [9 yrs]

BOLAN, GEORGE   George Henry, FB, 5´11˝/203 lbs; Purdue; B4/1897 Lake Forest, IL, D1/17/1940 Lake Forest, IL   **1921** ChiS 5 (1)   **1922** ChiB 10 (6, FB), 12   **1923** ChiB 10 (7, fb)
1924 ChiB 1 (0)   **NFL** 26 (14) [4 yrs]

BOLCAR, NED   Ned Francis, LB, 6´1˝/240 lbs; Notre Dame; 1990: Sea, rnd 6; B1/12/1967 Phillipsburg, NJ   **1990** Sea 5 (0)   **1991** Mia 8 (0)   **NFL** 13 (0) [2 yrs]

BOLDEN, GARY   Gary, DT, 6´1˝/275 lbs; Southwestern Oklahoma State; B2/13/1962 Clinton, OK   **1987** Phi 2 (0)

BOLDEN, JURAN   Juran T., DB, 6´2˝/207 lbs; Mississippi Delta C.C.; 1996: Atl, rnd 4; B6/27/1974 Washington, DC   **1996** Atl 9 (0)   **1997** Atl 14 (1)   **1998** Atl 3 (0)   **1998** GB 3 (0)
1998 Car 6 (0)   **1999** KC 7 (0)   **2002** Atl 14 (6, lcb)   **2003** Atl 8 (8, LCB)   **2004** Jax 13 (0)   **2005** †TB 16 (2)   **NFL** 93 (17) [8 yrs]

BOLDEN, LEROY   Leroy, HB, 5´8˝/170 lbs; Michigan State; 1955: Cle, rnd 6; B8/24/1932 Wabash, AR

1958	†Cle	11	15	55	3.7(15)	0	—	—	—	—	—	—	—	—	—	—	—	—	—	k	1	6	217
1959	Cle	12	4	11	2.8(9)	0	—	—	—	—	—	—	—	—	—	—	—	—	—	k	—	0	46
NFL	2	23	19	66	3.5(15)	0	—	—	—	—	—	—	—	—	—	—	—	—	—	k	1	6	263

BOLDEN, RICKEY   Rickey Allen, T-TE-G, 6´6˝/274 lbs; SMU; 1984: Cle, rnd 4; B9/8/1961 Dallas, TX   **1985** †Cle 16 (9, lt/rg)   **1986** †Cle 7 (5, lt)   **1987** Cle 5 (5, lt)   **1989** †Cle 6 (3)

1984	Cle	12(9, TE)	—	—	—	—	1	19	19.0(19)	0	—	—	—	—	—	—	—	—	—	—	—	0	10
1988	†Cle	16(3)	—	—	—	—	1	3	3.0(3)	1	—	—	—	—	—	—	—	—	—	—	—	6	6
NFL	6	62(34)	—	—	—	—	2	22	11.0(19)	1	—	—	—	—	—	—	—	—	—	—	—	6	16

BOLDIN, ANQUAN   Anquan, WR, 6´1˝/218 lbs; Florida State; 2003: Arz, rnd 2; B10/3/1980 Pahokee, FL

2003	Arz◊	16(16, WR)	5	40	8.0(23)	0	101	1377	13.6(71)	8	0	0	0.0	0	0	0	1	—	—	p	—	48	759
2004	Arz	10(9, WR)	1	3	3.0(3)	0	56	623	11.1(31)	1	—	—	—	—	—	—	—	—	—	p	—	6	320
2005	Arz	14(14, WR)	12	45	3.8(11)	0	102	1402	13.7(54)	7	1	0	0.0	0	0.0	0	0	—	—	p	—	44	781
NFL	3	40(39)	18	88	4.9(23)	0	259	3402	13.1(71)	16	2	0	0.0	0	0.0	0	1	—	—	p	—	98	1859

BOLDT, CHASE   Stephen Chase, B, 5´7˝/145 lbs; none; B5/7/1900 Louisville, KY, D5/16/1973 Louisville, KY   **1921** Lou 2 (2, TB)   **1922** Lou 4 (4, BB), 6   **1923** Lou 2 (1)
NFL 8 (7) [3 yrs]

BOLEY, MICHAEL   Michael, LB, 6´2˝/228 lbs; Southern Mississippi; 2005: Atl, rnd 5; B8/24/1982 Athens, AL   **2005** Atl 16 (11, LLB)

BOLIN, BOOKIE   Treva Gene, G, 6´2˝/240 lbs; Mississippi; 1962: NYG, rnd 5/DalT, rnd 14; B6/17/1940 Hamilton, AL   **1962** †NYG 9   **1963** †NYG 13 (RG)   **1964** NYG 14 (RG)
1965 NYG 14 (RG)   **1966** NYG 14 (RG)   **1967** NYG 13 (RG)   **1968** †Min 6   **1969** Min 6   **NFL** 89 [8 yrs]

BOLINGER, RUSS   Russell Dean, G-T, 6´5˝/255 lbs; California-Riverside; Long Beach State; 1976: Det, rnd 3; B9/10/1954 Wichita, KS   **1976** Det 12 (7, lg)   **1977** Det 14 (14, LG)
1980 Det 16 (15, RG)   **1981** Det 16 (16, RG)   **1982** †Det 9 (5, RG)   **1983** LARm 16 (1)   **1984** LARm 16 (0)   **1985** LARm 6 (2)

| 1979 | Det | 16(16, RG) | — | — | — | — | 1 | -1 | -1.0(-1) | 0 | — | — | — | — | — | — | — | — | — | — | — | 0 | -1 |
| NFL | 9 | 121(76) | — | — | — | — | 1 | -1 | -1.0(-1) | 0 | — | — | — | — | — | — | — | — | — | — | — | 0 | -1 |

BOLKOVAC, NICK   Nicholas Frank, DT-T, 6´1˝/230 lbs; Pittsburgh; 1951: Was, rnd 30; B3/20/1928 McKees Rocks, PA [K]   **1953** Pit 12   **1954** Pit 5   **NFL** 17 [2 yrs]

BOLL, DON   Donald Elroy, T-G, 6´2˝/270 lbs; Nebraska; 1953: Was, rnd 4; B7/16/1927 Scribner, NE, D12/29/2001 West Point, NE   **1953** Was 12 (12, LT)   **1954** Was 12 (12, LT)
1955 Was 12 (12, LT)   **1956** Was 12 (12, LT)   **1957** Was 12 (12, LT)   **1958** Was 9 (9, LT)   **1959** Was 12 (12, LG)   **1960** NYG 11   **NFL** 92 (81) [8 yrs]

BOLLER, KYLE   Kyle Bryan, QB, 6´3˝/220 lbs; California; 2003: Bal, rnd 1; B6/17/1981 Burbank, CA

2003	Bal	11(9, QB)	30	62	2.1(15)	0	—	—	—	—	224	116	51.8	1260	5.6(73)	7	9	17	92	62.4 P	—	0	367
2004	Bal	16(16, QB)	53	189	3.6(19)	1	—	—	—	—	464	258	55.6	2559	5.5(57)	13	11	35	247	70.9 —	—	6	1104
2005	Bal	9(9, QB)	23	66	2.9(9)	1	—	—	—	—	293	171	58.4	1799	6.1(47)	11	12	23	146	71.8 —	—	6	551
NFL	3	36(34)	106	317	3.0(19)	2	—	—	—	—	981	545	55.6	5618	5.7(73)	31	32	75	485	69.2 P	—	12	2021

BOLLINGER, BRIAN   Brian Reid, G, 6´5˝/285 lbs; North Carolina; 1992: SF, rnd 3; B11/21/1968 Indialantic, FL   **1992** †SF 16 (0)   **1993** †SF 16 (0)   **1994** SF 7 (0)   **NFL** 39 (0) [3 yrs]

BOLLINGER, BROOKS   Brooks, QB, 6´0˝/205 lbs; Wisconsin; 2003: NYJ, rnd 6; B11/15/1979 Grand Forks, ND

2004	NYJ	1(0)	1	2	2.0(2)	0	—	—	—	—	9	5	55.6	60	6.7(26)	0	0	1	8	—	—	0	32
2005	NYJ	11(9, QB)	35	135	3.9(15)	0	—	—	—	—	266	150	56.4	1558	5.9(60)	7	6	32	193	72.9 —	—	0	709
NFL	2	12(9)	36	137	3.8(15)	0	—	—	—	—	275	155	56.4	1618	5.9(60)	7	6	33	201	73.0 —	—	0	741

BOLLINGER, EDDIE   Edward Ebbert, T, 6´1˝/215 lbs; Bucknell; B7/9/1906 Nothlumberland, PA, D7/14/1984 Lancaster, PA   **1930** Fra 4 (2)

BOLTON, ANDY   Andrew, RB, 6´1˝/205 lbs; Fisk; 1976: Sea, rnd 4; B5/23/1954 Memphis, TN

1976	Sea	5(2)	13	44	3.4(22)	0	—	—	—	—	—	—	—	—	—	—	—	—	—	k	—	0	99
1976	Det	7	2	27	13.5(22)	0	—	—	—	—	—	—	—	—	—	—	—	—	—	—	—	0	27
1977	Det	14	3	4	1.3(2)	0	1	6	6.0(6)	0	—	—	—	—	—	—	—	—	—	k	—	0	3
1978	Det	6	2	5	2.5(3)	0	—	—	—	—	—	—	—	—	—	—	—	—	—	—	—	0	5
NFL	3	32(2)	20	80	4.0(22)	0	1	6	6.0(6)	0	—	—	—	—	—	—	—	—	—	k	—	0	134

BOLTON, HARRY   Harry, T, 6´3˝/280 lbs; Oklahoma State; B3/24/1919 Gray Horse, OK, D7/1986 Fairfax, OK   **1944** Det 1 (0)

YEAR	TEAM	G(GS, POS)	RUSH	YD	AVG(LG)	TD	REC	YD	AVG(LG)	TD	PASS COMP	PCT	YD	AVG(LG)	TD	INT	SK	YD	QBR	KPR	OTD	PTS	TAY

BOLTON, RON Ronald Clifton, DB, 6´2˝/180 lbs; Norfolk State; 1972: NE, rnd 5; B4/16/1950 Petersburg, VA **[I]**   **1972** NE 14 (4)   **1973** NE 14 (14, RCB)   **1974** NE 14 (14, RCB)
1975 NE 13 (13, RCB)   **1976** Cle 14 (12, RCB)   **1977** Cle 14 (5, lcb)   **1978** Cle 10 (8, lcb)   **1979** Cle 16 (16, LCB)   **1980**†Cle 16 (16, LCB)   **1981** Cle 16 (16, LCB)   **1982**†Cle 4 (2)
NFL 145 (120) [11 yrs]

BOLTON, SCOTT Scott Allen, WR, 6´0˝/188 lbs; Auburn; 1988: GB, rnd 12; B1/4/1965 Mobile, AL

| **1988** | GB | 4(0) | — | — | — | — | 2 | 33 | 16.5(18) | 0 | — | — | — | — | — | — | — | — | — | — | — | 0 | 17 |

BOMAR, LYNN Robert Lynn, E, 6´1˝/210 lbs; Vanderbilt; B1/21/1901 Gallatin, TN, D6/11/1964 Nashville, TN   **1925** NYG☆12 (12, RE), 18   **1926** NYG 8 (7, RE), 12
NFL 20 (19), 30 [2 yrs]

BONADIES, JACK John A., G-T, /208 lbs; none; B12/2/1892 Perticara, Italy, D10/13/1965 Hartford, CT   **1926** Har 5 (0)

BOND, CHUCK Charles Eishmel, T, 6´2˝/236 lbs; Washington; 1937: Was, rnd 5; B11/5/1914 Fairland, WA, D9/24/1989 Puyallup, WA   **1937**†Was 11 (0)   **1938** Was 11 (1)
NFL 22 (1) [2 yrs]

BOND, JIM James D., G, 5´9˝/200 lbs; Pittsburgh; B2/1894 Pittsburgh, PA, deceased   **1926** Bkn 2 (2)

BOND, RINK Randall Earl, B, 5´10˝/200 lbs; Washington; B6/3/1917 Fairland, WA   **1938** Was 1 (0)

| **1939** | Pit | 11(11, BB) | 1 | 4 | 4.0(4) | 0 | — | — | — | — | — | — | — | — | — | — | — | — | — | — | — | 0 | 4 |
| **NFL** | 2 | 12(11) | 1 | 4 | 4.0(4) | 0 | — | — | — | — | — | — | — | — | — | — | — | — | — | — | — | 0 | 4 |

BONDURANT, BOURBON Bourbon Patch, T-E, 6´1˝/202 lbs; DePauw; B2/18/1898 Brandenburg, KY, D9/4/1971 Scottsdale, AZ **[K]**   **1921** Evv 5 (5, LT), 6   **1922** ChiB 1 (0)
1922 Evv 2 (2, LT)   **NFL** 8 (7) [2 yrs]

BONE, WARREN Warren James, DE, 6´4˝/260 lbs; Texas Southern; B11/4/1964 Fairfield, AL   **1987** GB 1 (0)

BONELLI, ERNIE Ernest Bernard, B, 5´11˝/194 lbs; Pittsburgh; B7/27/1919 Russellton, PA

1945	ChiC	7(2)	32	93	2.9(22)	0	3	9	3.0(7)	0	—	—	—	—	—	—	—	—	—	kpi	—	0	153
1946	Pit	3(0)	6	7	1.2(4)	0	1	26	26.0(26)	0	—	—	—	—	—	—	—	—	—	—	—	0	20
NFL	2	10(2)	38	100	2.6(22)	0	4	35	8.8(26)	0	—	—	—	—	—	—	—	—	—	kpi	—	0	173

BONHAM, SHANE Steven Shane, DT, 6´2˝/272 lbs; Air Force; Tennessee; 1994: Det, rnd 3; B10/18/1970 Fairbanks, AK   **1994**†Det 15 (1)   **1995**†Det 16 (0)   **1996** Det 15 (2)
1997 Det 16 (0)   **1998**†SF 8 (0)   **1999** SF 3 (0)   **1999**†Ind 3 (0)   **NFL** 76 (3) [6 yrs]

BONIOL, CHRIS Christopher Donald, K, 5´11˝/169 lbs; Louisiana Tech; B12/9/1971 Alexandria, LA **[K]**   **1994**†Dal 16 (0)   **1995**†Dal 16 (0)   **1996**†Dal☆16 (0)   **1997** Phi 16 (0)
1998 Phi 16 (0)   **1999** ChiB 10 (0)   **NFL** 90 (0) [6 yrs]

BONNER, BRIAN Brian, LB, 6´2˝/225 lbs; Wisconsin; Minnesota; 1988: SF, rnd 9; B10/9/1965 Minneapolis, MN   **1989** Was 6 (0)

BONNER, GLEN Glen Lee, RB, 6´2˝/202 lbs; Washington; B5/5/1952 Bremerton, WA

1974	SD	12(3)	66	199	3.0(12)	3	11	101	9.2(22)	1	—	—	—	—	—	—	—	—	—	—	—	24	285
1975	SD	10(1)	28	120	4.3(12)	0	2	8	4.0(5)	0	—	—	—	—	—	—	—	—	—	—	—	0	124
NFL	2	22(4)	94	319	3.4(12)	3	13	109	8.4(22)	1	—	—	—	—	—	—	—	—	—	—	—	24	409

BONNER, MELVIN Melvin, WR, 6´3˝/207 lbs; Baylor; 1993: Den, rnd 6; B2/18/1970 Hempstead, TX   **1993** Den 3 (0)

BONNESS, RIK Richard Kyes, LB, 6´3˝/220 lbs; Nebraska; 1976: Oak, rnd 3; B3/20/1954 Borger, TX   **1976**†Oak 14   **1977** TB 13   **1978** TB 16 (2)   **1979**†TB 16   **NFL** 59 (2) [4 yrs]

BONO, STEVE Steven Christopher, QB, 6´4˝/215 lbs; UCLA; 1985: Min, rnd 6; B5/11/1962 Norristown, PA

1985	Min	1(0)	—	—	—	—	—	—	—	—	10	1	10.0	5	0.5(5)	0	0	2	13	—	—	0	3
1986	Min	1(0)	—	—	—	—	—	—	—	—	1	1	100.0	3	3.0(3)	0	0	—	—	—	—	0	2
1987	Pit	3(3)	8	27	3.4(23)	1	1	2	2.0(2)	—	74	34	45.9	438	5.9(57)	5	2	6	30	—	—	6	202
1988	Pit	2(0)	—	—	—	—	—	—	—	—	35	10	28.6	110	3.1(15)	1	2	1	8	—	—	0	-20
1989	SF	1(0)	—	—	—	—	—	—	—	—	5	4	80.0	62	12.4(45)	1	0	—	—	—	—	0	36
1991	SF	9(6, qb)	17	46	2.7(18)	0	—	—	—	—	237	141	59.5	1617	6.8(78)	11	4	11	91	88.5	—	—	0	750
1992	†SF	16(0)	15	23	1.5(19)	0	—	—	—	—	56	36	64.3	463	8.3(36)	2	2	2	14	—	—	0	185
1993	†SF	8(0)	12	14	1.2(10)	1	—	—	—	—	61	39	63.9	416	6.8(33)	0	1	4	18	—	—	6	192
1994	KC	7(2)	4	-1	-0.3(2)	0	—	—	—	—	117	66	56.4	796	6.8(62)	4	4	—	—	—	—	0	257
1995	†KC◇	16(16, QB)	28	113	4.0(76)	5	—	—	—	—	520	293	56.3	3121	6.0(60)	21	10	21	158	79.5	—	30	1429
1996	KC	14(13, QB)	26	27	1.0(17)	0	—	—	—	—	438	235	53.7	2572	5.9(69)	12	13	22	161	68.0	—	0	853
1997	GB	2(0)	3	-3	-1.0(-1)	0	—	—	—	—	10	5	50.0	29	2.9(14)	0	0	1	15	—	—	0	12
1998	SL	6(2)	10	13	1.3(7)	0	—	—	—	—	136	69	50.7	807	5.9(47)	5	4	6	57	—	—	2	282
1999	Car	2(0)	2	-2	-1.0(-1)	0	—	—	—	—	1	0	0.0	0	0.0	0	0	—	—	—	—	0	-2
NFL	14	88(42)	125	257	2.1(76)	7	2	4	2.0(2)	0	1701	934	54.9	10439	6.1(78)	62	42	76	565	75.3	—	44	4178

BONOWITZ, ELLIOTT Elliott, G-B-T-E, 6´1˝/190 lbs; Wilmington (DE); B1903, deceased   **1923** Col 6 (0)   **1924** Day 8 (6, LG)   **1925** Day 6 (4, LG)   **NFL** 20 (10) [3 yrs]

BOOKER, FRED Fred, DB, 5´9˝/199 lbs; LSU; B6/4/1978 Independence, LA   **2005** NO 12 (0)

BOOKER, MARTY Marty Montez, WR, 6´0˝/212 lbs; Louisiana-Monroe; 1999: Chi, rnd 3; B7/31/1976 Marrero, LA

1999	ChiB	9(4)	1	8	8.0(8)	0	19	219	11.5(57)	3	—	—	—	—	—	—	—	—	—	—	—	18	133
2000	ChiB	15(7, wr)	2	-1	-0.5(5)	0	47	490	10.4(41)	2	—	—	—	—	—	—	—	—	—	—	—	12	254
2001	†ChiB	16(16, WR)	4	8	2.0(13)	0	100	1071	10.7(60)	8	2	1	50.0	34	17.0(34)	1	0	—	—	—	—	48	606
2002	ChiB◇	16(16, WR)	—	—	—	—	97	1189	12.3(54)	6	5	1	20.0	44	8.8(44)	1	0	—	—	—	—	36	652
2003	ChiB	13(13, WR)	3	-7	-2.3(1)	0	52	715	13.8(61)	4	—	—	—	—	—	—	—	—	—	—	—	24	371
2004	Mia	15(15, WR)	1	-8	-8.0(-8)	0	50	638	12.8(45)	1	1	1	100.0	48	48.0(48)	0	0	—	—	—	—	6	340
2005	Mia	15(11, WR)	—	—	—	—	39˚	686	17.6(60)	3	1	0	0.0	0	0.0	0	0	—	—	—	—	18	358
NFL	7	99(82)	11	0	0.0(13)	0	404	5008	12.4(66)	27	9	3	33.3	126	14.0(48)	2	0	—	—	—	—	162	2712

BOOKER, MICHAEL Michael Allen, DB, 6´2˝/203 lbs; Nebraska; 1997: Atl, rnd 1; B4/27/1975 Oceanside, CA   **1997** Atl 15 (2)   **1998**†Atl 14 (6, rcb)   **1999** Atl 13 (1)   **2000**†Ten 15 (1)
2001 Ten 16 (0)   **NFL** 73 (10) [5 yrs]

BOOKER, VAUGHN Vaughn Jamel, DE, 6´5˝/290 lbs; Cincinnati; B2/24/1968 Cincinnati, OH   **1994**†KC 13 (0)   **1995**†KC 16 (10, LDE)   **1996** KC 14 (12, RDE)
1997†KC 13 (13, LDE)   **1998**†GB 16 (4)   **1999** GB 14 (14, LDE)   **2000** Cin 9 (9, LDE)   **2001** Cin 14 (13, LDE)   **2002** Cin 6 (5, lde)   **NFL** 115 (80) [9 yrs]

BOOKMAN, JOHNNY John Dolan, DB, 5´11˝/182 lbs; Miami (FL); 1957: NYG, rnd 8; B9/6/1932 Baton Rouge, LA, D10/23/1995 Baton Rouge, LA   **1957** NYG 11   **1960** DalT-A☆14
1961 NYT-A 8 (LCB)   **NFL** 33 [3 yrs]

BOOKOUT, BILLY Billy Paul, DB, 5´11˝/180 lbs; Oklahoma; Austin; B1/1/1932 Choice, TX   **1955** GB 12 (DB)   **1956** GB 7 (DB)   **NFL** 19 [2 yrs]

BOOKS, BOB Robert C., FB, 5´11˝/190 lbs; Dickinson; B1902, deceased   **1926** Fra 4 (0)

BOONE, ALFONSO Alfonso D., DT, 6´4˝/328 lbs; Mt.San Antonio J.C.; 2000: Det, rnd 7; B1/11/1976 Saginaw, MI   **2001**†ChiB 11 (0)   **2002** ChiB 16 (5, ldt)   **2003** ChiB 16 (6, ldt)
2004 ChiB 12 (2)   **2005**†ChiB 16 (1)   **NFL** 71 (14) [5 yrs]

BOONE, DAVE Humphrey David, DE, 6´3˝/248 lbs; Eastern Michigan; 1974: Min, rnd 11; B10/30/1951 Detroit, MI, D3/19/2005 Point Roberts, WA   **1974** Min 5

BOONE, GREG Gregory Joel, RB, 5´9˝/196 lbs; Duke; B1/8/1962 Aberdeen, MA

| **1987** | TB | 2(0) | 1 | 2 | 2.0(2) | 0 | — | — | — | — | — | — | — | — | — | — | — | — | — | — | — | 0 | 2 |

BOONE, J.R. J.R., E-HB, 5´8˝/162 lbs; Tulsa; 1948: ChiB, rnd 22; B7/29/1921 Clinton, OK

1948	ChiB	11(1)	48	266	5.5(40)	5	10	143	14.3(38)	2	1	1	100.0	4	4.0(4)	0	0	—	—	—	kpi	—	42	490
1949	ChiB	12(1)	35	111	3.2(22)	0	14	336	24.0(43)	3	—	—	—	—	—	—	—	—	—	pi	—	18	410
1950	†ChiB	10	13	15	1.2(7)	0	8	139	17.4(31)	0	—	—	—	—	—	—	—	—	—	p	—	0	215
1951	ChiB	10	3	9	3.0(6)	0	6	117	19.5(24)	0	—	—	—	—	—	—	—	—	—	p	—	0	111
1952	SF	12(le)	24	72	3.0(12)	0	25	461	18.4(53)	1	—	—	—	—	—	—	—	—	—	p	—	6	319
1953	GB	8	7	24	3.4(24)	0	6	55	9.2(18)	1	1	1	100.0	2	-2.0(-4)	0	0	—	—	—	—	—	6	55
NFL	6	63(2)	130	497	3.8(40)	5	69	1251	18.1(53)	7	2	2	100.0	4	1.0(4)	0	0	—	—	—	kpi	—	72	1598

BOONE, JACK Robert Lee, B, 5´11˝/175 lbs; Elon; B5/28/1916 Roanoke Rapids, NC, D2/6/1984 Greenville, NC

| **1942** | Cle | 2(0) | 3 | -1 | -0.3(3) | 0 | 2 | 58 | 29.0(34) | 1 | — | — | — | — | — | — | — | — | — | pi | — | 6 | 32 |

BOOSE, DORIAN Dorian Alexander, DE, 6´5˝/292 lbs; Washington State; 1998: NYJ, rnd 2; B1/29/1974 Frankfurt, Germany **1998** NYJ 12 (0) **1999** NYJ 12 (0) **2000** NYJ 9 (0) **2001** Was 10 (2) **NFL** 43 (2) [4 yrs]

BOOTH, CLARENCE Clarence E., T, 6´0˝/223 lbs; SMU; 1943: ChiC, rnd 18; B9/4/1919 Childress, TX **1943** ChiC 6 (0) **1944** C-P 5 (0) **NFL** 11 (0) [2 yrs]

BOOTH, DICK Richard Thomas, B, 6´1˝/190 lbs; Case Western Reserve; B7/13/1918 Newell, WV

YEAR	TEAM	G(GS, POS)	RUSH	YD	AVG(LG)	TD	REC	YD	AVG(LG)	TD	PASS	COMP	PCT	YD	AVG(LG)	TD	INT	SK	YD	QBR	KPR	OTD	PTS	TAY
1941	Det	11(5, WB)	29	80	2.8(17)	1	7	103	14.7(36)	0	8	5	62.5	135	16.9(71)	2	1	—	—	—	Pki	—	6	254
1945	Det	4(0)	4	20	5.0(9)	0	3	90	30.0(54)	1	—	—	—	—	—	—	—	—	—	—	kp	—	6	79
NFL	2	15(5)	33	100	3.0(17)	1	10	193	19.3(54)	1	8	5	62.5	135	16.9(71)	2	1	—	—	—	Pkpi	—	12	333

BOOTH, ISSAC Isaac Ramoun, DB, 6´5˝/193 lbs; California; 1994: Cle, rnd 5; B2/24/1968 Indianapolis, IN **1994**†Cle 16 (1) **1995** Cle 9 (1) **1996** Bal 11 (3) **NFL** 36 (5) [3 yrs]

BOOTY, JOHN John Fitzgerald, DB, 6´0˝/185 lbs; TCU; 1988: NYJ, rnd 10; B10/9/1965 Deberry, TX **1988** NYJ 16 (0) **1989** NYJ 9 (1) **1990** NYJ 13 (1) **1991** Phi 13 (1) **1992**†Phi 16 (11, LCB/fs) **1993** Phx 12 (12, SS) **1994** NYG 16 (9, fs)

YEAR	TEAM	G(GS, POS)	RUSH	YD	AVG(LG)	TD	REC	YD	AVG(LG)	TD	PASS	COMP	PCT	YD	AVG(LG)	TD	INT	SK	YD	QBR	KPR	OTD	PTS	TAY
1995	TB	7(2)	—	—	—	—	1	48	48.0(48)	0	—	—	—	—	—	—	—	—	—	—	i	—	0	40
NFL	8	102(37)	—	—	—	—	1	48	48.0(48)	0	—	—	—	—	—	—	—	—	—	—	kiS	—	0	149

BOOZER, EMERSON Emerson, RB, 5´11˝/195 lbs; Maryland-Eastern Shore; 1966: NYJ, rnd 6/Pit, rnd 7; B7/4/1943 Augusta, GA

YEAR	TEAM	G(GS, POS)	RUSH	YD	AVG(LG)	TD	REC	YD	AVG(LG)	TD	PASS	COMP	PCT	YD	AVG(LG)	TD	INT	SK	YD	QBR	KPR	OTD	PTS	TAY
1966	NYJ-A✧	14(HB)	97	455	4.7(54)	5	8	133	16.6(26)	0	—	—	—	—	—	—	—	—	—	—	k	1	36	851
1967	NYJ-A☆	8(HB)	119	442	3.7(48)	**10**	12	205	17.1(49)	3	—	—	—	—	—	—	—	—	—	—	k	—	78	708
1968	†NYJ-A✧	12(HB)	143	441	3.1(33)	5	12	101	8.4(23)	0	—	—	—	—	—	—	—	—	—	—	—	—	30	542
1969	†NYJ-A	14(HB)	130	604	4.6(50)	4	20	222	11.1(29)	0	—	—	—	—	—	—	—	—	—	—	—	—	24	755
1970	NYJ	10(FB)	139	581	4.2(27)	5	28	258	9.2(33)	0	—	—	—	—	—	—	—	—	—	—	—	—	30	760
1971	NYJ	14(RB)	188	618	3.3(19)	5	11	120	10.9(36)	1	—	—	—	—	—	—	—	—	—	—	—	—	36	733
1972	NYJ	11(RB)	120	549	4.6(37)	11	11	142	12.9(49)	3	—	—	—	—	—	—	—	—	—	—	—	—	84	745
1973	NYJ	13(RB)	182	831	4.6(52)	3	22	130	5.9(15)	3	—	—	—	—	—	—	—	—	—	—	—	—	36	941
1974	NYJ	13(RB)	153	563	3.7(20)	4	14	161	11.5(29)	1	—	—	—	—	—	—	—	—	—	—	—	—	30	689
1975	NYJ	9(4)	20	51	2.6(8)	0	1	16	16.0(16)	1	—	—	—	—	—	—	—	—	—	—	—	—	6	64
NFL	10	118(4)	1291	5135	4.0(54)	52	139	1488	10.7(49)	12	—	—	—	—	—	—	—	—	—	—	k	1	390	6786

BORAK, FRED Fred Aloisius, DE, 6´1˝/195 lbs; Creighton; B5/4/1913 Kenosha, WI, D4/1966 **1938** GB 1 (0)

BORCHARDT, JON Jon L., G-T, 6´5˝/260 lbs; Montana State; 1979: Buf, rnd 3; B8/13/1957 Minneapolis, MN **1979** Buf 16 **1980** Buf 16 (0) **1981**†Buf 16 (9, LG) **1982** Buf 9 (9, RG) **1983** Buf 16 (16, RG) **1984** Buf 16 (16, RG) **1985** Sea 13 (1) **1986** Sea 16 (4) **1987**†Sea 12 (0) **NFL** 130 (55) [9 yrs]

BORCKY, DENNIS Dennis Michael, NT, 6´4˝/285 lbs; Memphis; B9/14/1964 Chester, PA **1987** NYG 2 (2)

BORDANO, CHRIS Chris, LB, 6´1˝/241 lbs; SMU; 1998: NO, rnd 6; B12/30/1974 San Antonio, TX **1998** NO 16 (6, mlb) **1999** NO 15 (12, MLB) **2000** Atl 2 (0) **NFL** 33 (18) [3 yrs]

BORDELON, BEN Benjamin Gerald, T, 6´5˝/301 lbs; LSU; B4/9/1974 Mathews, LA **1997** SD 16 (2)

BORDELON, KEN Kenneth Patrick, LB, 6´4˝/228 lbs; LSU; 1976: LA, rnd 5; B8/26/1954 New Orleans, LA **1976** NO 12 **1977** NO 14 **1979** NO 16 (14, LLB) **1980** NO 16 (14, LLB) **1981** NO 15 (3) **1982** NO 9 (0) **NFL** 82 (31) [6 yrs]

BORDEN, LES Lester Dewis, E-DE, 6´0˝/185 lbs; Fordham; B4/8/1910 Everett, MA, D5/19/1981 Gulph Mills, PA **1935** NYG 1 (0)

BORDEN, NATE Nathaniel, DE, 6´0˝/234 lbs; Indiana; 1955: GB, rnd 25; B9/22/1932 Detroit, MI, D9/30/1992 Las Vegas, NV **1955** GB 12 (RDE) **1956** GB 12 (RDE) **1957** GB 9 (RDE) **1958** GB 12 (LDE) **1959** GB 12 **1960** Dal 12 (LDE) **1961** Dal 14 (RDE) **1962** Buf-A 9 (lde) **NFL** 92 [8 yrs]

BORDERS, NATE Nathan Wayne, DB, 5´10˝/190 lbs; Indiana; B6/11/1963 Ellwood City, PA **1987** Cin 3 (0)

BORELLI, NICK Nicholas Charles, B, 5´10˝/175 lbs; Muhlenberg; B3/2/1905 Cliffside Park, NJ, D12/12/1992 Cliffside Park, NJ **1930** Nwk 10 (6, WB)

BORGELLA, JOCELYN Jocelyn Kenza, DB, 5´10˝/180 lbs; Cincinnati; 1994: Det, rnd 6; B8/26/1971 Nassau, Bahamas **1994** Det 4 (0) **1996** Det 11 (0) **NFL** 15 (0) [2 yrs]

BORGOGNONE, DIRK Dirk Ronald, K, 6´2˝/221 lbs; Tennessee; Pacific; B1/9/1968 Elko, NV **1995** GB 2 (0)

BORLAND, KYLE Kyle Craig, LB, 6´3˝/232 lbs; Wisconsin; B7/5/1961 Denison, IA **1987** LARm 2 (2)

BORRESEN, RICH Richard David, TE, 6´5˝/252 lbs; Northwestern; B3/16/1964 Queens, NY **1987** Dal 3 (3)

BORTON, JOHN John Robert, QB, 6´0˝/208 lbs; Ohio State; 1955: Cle, rnd 13; B12/14/1932 Alliance, OH, D4/8/2002 Massillon, OH

YEAR	TEAM	G(GS, POS)	RUSH	YD	AVG(LG)	TD	REC	YD	AVG(LG)	TD	PASS	COMP	PCT	YD	AVG(LG)	TD	INT	SK	YD	QBR	KPR	OTD	PTS	TAY
1957	Cle	5	—	—	—	—	—	—	—	—	6	3	50.0	22	3.7(8)	0	1	—	—	—	—	—	0	-29

BORTZ, MARK Mark Steven, G, 6´6˝/282 lbs; Iowa; 1983: Chi, rnd 8; B2/12/1961 Pardeeville, WI **1983** ChiB 16 (0) **1984**†ChiB 15 (15, LG) **1985**†ChiB 16 (16, LG) **1987**†ChiB 12 (12, LG) **1988**†ChiB✧16 (16, LG) **1989** ChiB 16 (16, LG) **1990**†ChiB★16 (16, LG) **1991**†ChiB 9 (9, LG) **1992** ChiB 12 (12, LG) **1993** ChiB 16 (16, LG) **1994**†ChiB 12 (12, LG)

YEAR	TEAM	G(GS, POS)	RUSH	YD	AVG(LG)	TD	REC	YD	AVG(LG)	TD	PASS	COMP	PCT	YD	AVG(LG)	TD	INT	SK	YD	QBR	KPR	OTD	PTS	TAY
1986	†ChiB	15(15, LG)	—	—	—	—	1	8	8.0(8)	0	—	—	—	—	—	—	—	—	—	—	—	—	0	4
NFL	12	171(155)	—	—	—	—	1	8	8.0(8)	0	—	—	—	—	—	—	—	—	—	—	—	—	0	4

BORUM, JARVIS Jarvis, T, 6´7˝/324 lbs; North Carolina State; B9/16/1978 Columbia, SC **2001** Arz 1 (1)

BORYLA, MIKE Michael Jay, QB, 6´3˝/200 lbs; Stanford; 1974: Cin, rnd 4; B3/6/1951 Rockville Centre, NY

YEAR	TEAM	G(GS, POS)	RUSH	YD	AVG(LG)	TD	REC	YD	AVG(LG)	TD	PASS	COMP	PCT	YD	AVG(LG)	TD	INT	SK	YD	QBR	KPR	OTD	PTS	TAY
1974	Phi	4(3)	6	25	4.2(11)	0	—	—	—	—	102	60	58.8	580	5.7(29)	5	3	4	39	78.9	—	—	0	220
1975	Phi✧	7(5, qb)	8	33	4.1(11)	0	—	—	—	—	166	87	52.4	996	6.0(46)	6	12	12	69	52.7	—	—	0	81
1976	Phi	11(QB)	29	166	5.7(22)	2	—	—	—	—	246	123	50.0	1247	5.1(48)	9	14	29	235	53.4	—	—	12	295
1978	TB	1(1)	—	—	—	—	—	—	—	—	5	2	40.0	15	3.0(18)	0	0	4	57	—	—	—	0	8
NFL	4	23(9)	43	224	5.2(22)	2	—	—	—	—	519	272	52.4	2838	5.5(48)	20	29	49	400	58.1	—	—	12	603

BOSA, JOHN John Wilfred, DE, 6´4˝/270 lbs; Boston College; 1987: Mia, rnd 1; B1/10/1964 Keene, NH **1987** Mia 12 (12, RDE) **1988** Mia 6 (6, rde) **1989** Mia 13 (3) **NFL** 31 (21) [3 yrs]

BOSARGE, WAYNE Wade, DB, 5´10˝/175 lbs; Tulsa; B9/14/1955 Bayou La Batre, AL **1977** Mia 5 **1977** NO 5 **NFL** 10 [1 yr]

BOSCH, FRANK Frank William, DT-DE, 6´4˝/255 lbs; Colorado; 1968: Was, rnd 17; B10/24/1945 Bremerton, WA **1968** Was 14 **1969** Was 14 (rdt) **1970** Was 11 (6, rde/ldt) **NFL** 39 (6) [3 yrs]

BOSCHETTI, RYAN Ryan S., DT, 6´4˝/295 lbs; UCLA; B10/7/1981 Belmont, CA **2004** Was 3 (1) **2005**†Was 13 (1) **NFL** 16 (2) [2 yrs]

BOSDETT, JOHN John Alfred, E, none; B11/4/1895 Cook County, IL, D9/19/1980 Oklahoma City, OK **1920** ChiT 6 (1)

BOSELLI, TONY Don Anthony, T, 6´7˝/324 lbs; USC; 1995: Jax, rnd 1; B4/17/1972 Modesto, CA **1995** Jax 13 (12, LT) **1996**†Jax★16 (16, LT) **1997**†Jax★12 (12, LT) **1998**†Jax★15 (15, LT) **1999** Jax★16 (16, LT) **2000** Jax✧16 (16, LT) **2001** Jax 3 (3) **NFL** 91 (90) [7 yrs]

BOSLEY, BRUCE Bruce Lee, C-G-DE, 6´2˝/241 lbs; West Virginia; 1956: SF, rnd 2; B11/5/1933 Fresno, CA, D4/26/1995 San Francisco, CA **1956** SF 12 (LDE) **1957**†SF 6 **1958** SF 12 (LG) **1959** SF☆12 (LG) **1960** SF★12 (12, LG) **1961** SF☆12 (12, LG) **1962** SF 13 (9, C) **1963** SF 14 (9, C) **1964** SF 14 (14, C) **1965** SF✧14 (14, C) **1966** SF★14 (14, C) **1967** SF✧14 (14, C) **1968** SF 14 (14, C) **1969** Atl 12 (C) **NFL** 175 (112) [14 yrs]

BOSLEY, KEITH Keith, T, 6´5˝/320 lbs; Eastern Kentucky; B6/19/1963 Richmond, KY **1987** Cle 3 (2)

BOSO, CAP Casper N., TE, 6´4˝/232 lbs; Illinois; 1986: Pit, rnd 8; B9/10/1962 Kansas City, MO

YEAR	TEAM	G(GS, POS)	RUSH	YD	AVG(LG)	TD	REC	YD	AVG(LG)	TD	PASS	COMP	PCT	YD	AVG(LG)	TD	INT	SK	YD	QBR	KPR	OTD	PTS	TAY
1986	SL	2(0)	—	—	—	—	—	—	—	—	—	—	—	—	—	—	—	—	—	—	—	—	—	—
1987	†ChiB	12(0)	—	—	—	—	17	188	11.1(31)	2	—	—	—	—	—	—	—	—	—	—	—	—	12	104
1988	†ChiB	6(0)	—	—	—	—	6	50	8.3(15)	0	—	—	—	—	—	—	—	—	—	—	—	—	0	25
1989	ChiB	16(0)	—	—	—	—	17	182	10.7(43)	1	—	—	—	—	—	—	—	—	—	—	—	—	6	96
1990	ChiB	13(1)	—	—	—	—	11	135	12.3(25)	1	—	—	—	—	—	—	—	—	—	—	—	—	6	73
1991	ChiB	6(1)	—	—	—	—	3	36	12.0(22)	0	—	—	—	—	—	—	—	—	—	—	—	—	0	18
NFL	6	55(2)	—	—	—	—	54	591	10.9(43)	4	—	—	—	—	—	—	—	—	—	—	—	—	24	316

BOSSELER, DON Donald John, FB, 6´1˝/212 lbs; Miami (FL); 1957: Was, rnd 1; B1/24/1936 Weathersfield, NY

YEAR	TEAM	G(GS, POS)	RUSH	YD	AVG(LG)	TD	REC	YD	AVG(LG)	TD	PASS	COMP	PCT	YD	AVG(LG)	TD	INT	SK	YD	QBR	KPR	OTD	PTS	TAY
1957	Was☆	12(FB)	167	673	4.0(28)	7	19	152	8.0(25)	0	—	—	—	—	—	—	—	—	—	—	—	—	42	819
1958	Was	10(fb)	109	475	4.4(23)	4	14	101	7.2(28)	0	—	—	—	—	—	—	—	—	—	—	p	—	24	563
1959	Was✧	12(FB)	119	644	5.4(41)	3	11	47	4.3(10)	0	1	0	0.0	0	0.0	0	0	—	—	—	—	—	18	698
1960	Was	11(FB)	109	428	3.9(29)	2	13	86	6.6(50)	0	—	—	—	—	—	—	—	—	—	—	—	—	12	491
1961	Was	12(FB)	77	220	2.9(16)	2	16	94	5.9(18)	1	—	—	—	—	—	—	—	—	—	—	—	—	18	292

YEAR	TEAM	G(GS, POS)	RUSH	YD	AVG(LG)	TD	REC	YD	AVG(LG)	TD	PASS	COMP	PCT	YD	AVG(LG)	TD	INT	SK	YD	QBR	KPR	OTD	PTS	TAY
1962	Was	14(FB)	93	336	3.6(15)	2	32	258	8.1(35)	0	—	—	—	—	—	—	—	—	—	—	—	—	12	485
1963	Was	14(FB)	79	290	3.7(18)	2	25	289	11.6(61)	0	—	—	—	—	—	—	—	—	—	—	—	—	12	455
1964	Was	11	22	46	2.1(9)	0	6	56	9.3(18)	0	—	—	—	—	—	—	—	—	—	—	—	—	0	74
NFL	8	96	775	3112	4.0(41)	22	136	1083	8.0(61)	1	1	0	0.0	0	0.0	0	0	—	—	—	p	—	138	3876

Bostic, James James Edward, RB, 5´11˝/230 lbs; Auburn; 1994: LARm, rnd 3; B3/13/1972 Fort Lauderdale, FL **1998** Phi 2 (0)

YEAR	TEAM	G(GS, POS)	RUSH	YD	AVG(LG)	TD	REC	YD	AVG(LG)	TD	PASS	COMP	PCT	YD	AVG(LG)	TD	INT	SK	YD	QBR	KPR	OTD	PTS	TAY
1999	Phi	9(0)	5	19	3.8(5)	0	5	8	1.6(7)	0	—	—	—	—	—	—	—	—	—	—	—	—	0	23
NFL	2	11(0)	5	19	3.8(5)	0	5	8	1.6(7)	0	—	—	—	—	—	—	—	—	—	—	—	—	0	23

Bostic, Jason Jason Devon, DB, 5´9˝/190 lbs; Georgia Tech; B6/30/1976 Lauderhill, FL **1999** Phi 1 (0) **2000**†Phi 16 (0) **2002** Buf 14 (0) **NFL** 31 (0) [3 yrs]

Bostic, Jeff Jeff Lynn, C, 6´2˝/268 lbs; Clemson; B9/18/1958 Greensboro, NC **1980** Was 16 (0) **1982**†Was 9 (9, C) **1983**†Was★16 (16, C) **1984** Was 8 (8, C) **1985** Was 10 (6, c) **1986**†Was 16 (16, C) **1987**†Was 12 (5, c) **1988** Was 13 (11, C) **1989** Was 16 (16, C) **1990**†Was 16 (16, C) **1991**†Was 16 (16, C) **1992** Was 4 (4) **1993** Was 16 (10, C)

YEAR	TEAM	G(GS, POS)	RUSH	YD	AVG(LG)	TD	REC	YD	AVG(LG)	TD	PASS	COMP	PCT	YD	AVG(LG)	TD	INT	SK	YD	QBR	KPR	OTD	PTS	TAY
1981	Was	16(16, C)	—	—	—	—	1	-4	-4.0(-4)	0	—	—	—	—	—	—	—	—	—	—	—	—	0	-2
NFL	14	184(149)	—	—	—	—	1	-4	-4.0(-4)	0	—	—	—	—	—	—	—	—	—	—	—	—	0	-2

Bostic, Joe Joe Earl, G-T, 6´3˝/265 lbs; Clemson; 1979: SL, rnd 3; B4/20/1957 Greensboro, NC **1979** SL 16 (14, RT) **1980** SL 16 (15, RG/lg) **1981** SL 14 (14, RG) **1982**†SL 8 (8, RG) **1983** SL 14 (14, RG) **1984** SL 16 (16, RG) **1985** SL 16 (16, RG) **1986** SL 13 (13, RG) **1987** SL 9 (4) **1988** Phx 10 (1) **NFL** 132 (115) [10 yrs]

Bostic, John Jonathan Earl, DB, 5´10˝/176 lbs; Bethune-Cookman; 1985: KC, rnd 6; B10/6/1962 Titusville, FL **1985** Det 13 (0) **1986** Det 13 (0) **1987** Det 3 (1) **NFL** 29 (1) [3 yrs]

Bostic, Keith William Keith, DB, 6´1˝/216 lbs; Michigan; 1983: Hou, rnd 2; B1/17/1961 Ann Arbor, MI **1983** Hou 16 (12, SS) **1984** Hou 16 (16, SS) **1985** Hou 16 (16, SS) **1986** Hou 16 (16, SS) **1987**†Hou★12 (12, SS) **1988**†Hou 16 (16, SS) **1990** Cle 4 (0) **NFL** 96 (88) [7 yrs]

Bostick, Lew Lewis Townley, G-T, 6´0˝/197 lbs; Alabama; 1939: Cle, rnd 9; B10/3/1916 Birmingham, AL, D10/18/1999, **[K]** **1939** Cle 7 (2) **1942** Cle 1 (0) **NFL** 8 (2) [2 yrs]

Boston, David David, WR, 6´2˝/240 lbs; Ohio State; 1999: Arz, rnd 1; B8/19/1978 Houston, TX

YEAR	TEAM	G(GS, POS)	RUSH	YD	AVG(LG)	TD	REC	YD	AVG(LG)	TD	PASS	COMP	PCT	YD	AVG(LG)	TD	INT	SK	YD	QBR	KPR	OTD	PTS	TAY
1999	Arz	16(8, wr)	5	0	0.0(7)	0	40	473	11.8(43)	2	—	—	—	—	—	—	—	—	—	—	p	—	12	274
2000	Arz	16(16, WR)	3	9	3.0(24)	0	71	1156	16.3(70)	7	—	—	—	—	—	—	—	—	—	—	—	—	42	622
2001	Arz★	16(16, WR)	5	35	7.0(17)	0	98	**1598**	16.3(61)	8	—	—	—	—	—	—	—	—	—	—	—	—	48	874
2002	Arz	8(8, wr)	2	29	14.5(22)	0	32	512	16.0(34)	1	—	—	—	—	—	—	—	—	—	—	—	—	6	290
2003	SD	14(14, WR)	3	18	6.0(13)	0	70	880	12.6(46)	7	—	—	—	—	—	—	—	—	—	—	—	—	44	493
2005	Mia	5(0)	—	—	—	—	4	80	20.0(54)	0	—	—	—	—	—	—	—	—	—	—	—	—	0	40
NFL	6	75(62)	18	91	5.1(24)	0	315	4699	14.9(70)	25	—	—	—	—	—	—	—	—	—	—	p	—	152	2593

Boston, McKinley McKinley, DE-LB, 6´2˝/250 lbs; Minnesota; 1968: NYG, rnd 15; B11/5/1945 Elizabeth City, NC **1968** NYG 13 **1969** NYG 14 (6, lde) **NFL** 27 (6) [2 yrs]

Boswell, Ben Benjamin, T, 6´0˝/245 lbs; TCU; B3/4/1910 Fort Worth, TX, D5/1981 Momence, IL **1933** Por 1 (0) **1934** Bos 11 (6, RT) **NFL** 12 (6) [2 yrs]

Bosworth, Brian Brian Keith 'The Boz', LB, 6´2˝/248 lbs; Oklahoma; 1987: Sea, rnd S1; B3/9/1965 Oklahoma City, OK **1987**†Sea 12 (12, RILB) **1988** Sea 10 (10, LILB) **1989** Sea 2 (2) **NFL** 24 (24) [3 yrs]

Botchan, Ron Ronald Leslie, LB, 6´1˝/238 lbs; Occidental; B2/15/1935 Brooklyn, NY **1960**†LAC-A 14 **1961**†Hou-A 14 **NFL** 28 [2 yrs]

Botkin, Kirk Kirk Randal, TE, 6´3˝/245 lbs; Arkansas; B3/19/1971 Baytown, TX

YEAR	TEAM	G(GS, POS)	RUSH	YD	AVG(LG)	TD	REC	YD	AVG(LG)	TD	PASS	COMP	PCT	YD	AVG(LG)	TD	INT	SK	YD	QBR	KPR	OTD	PTS	TAY
1994	NO	3(0)	—	—	—	—	—	—	—	—	—	—	—	—	—	—	—	—	—	—	—	—	—	—
1995	NO	16(0)	—	—	—	—	1	8	8.0(8)	0	—	—	—	—	—	—	—	—	—	—	—	—	0	4
1996	†Pit	16(0)	—	—	—	—	4	36	9.0(17)	0	—	—	—	—	—	—	—	—	—	—	—	—	0	18
1997	†Pit	13(1)	—	—	—	—	1	11	11.0(11)	0	—	—	—	—	—	—	—	—	—	—	—	—	0	6
NFL	4	48(1)	—	—	—	—	6	55	9.2(17)	0	—	—	—	—	—	—	—	—	—	—	—	—	0	28

Boucher, Scott Scott Allen, G, 6´3˝/260 lbs; Louisiana-Monroe; B9/15/1958 Houston, TX **1987** Hou 2 (0)

Boudreaux, Jim James Lee, T-DE, 6´4˝/260 lbs; Louisiana Tech; 1966: Bos, rnd 2/Cle, rnd 13; B4/15/1945 Ville Platte, LA **1966** Bos-A 4 **1967** Bos-A 5 **1968** Bos-A 3 **NFL** 12 [3 yrs]

Bouggess, Lee Lee Edward, RB, 6´2˝/210 lbs; Louisville; 1970: Phi, rnd 3; B1/18/1948 Louisville, KY

YEAR	TEAM	G(GS, POS)	RUSH	YD	AVG(LG)	TD	REC	YD	AVG(LG)	TD	PASS	COMP	PCT	YD	AVG(LG)	TD	INT	SK	YD	QBR	KPR	OTD	PTS	TAY
1970	Phi	14(FB)	159	401	2.5(20)	2	50	401	8.0(34)	2	1	0	0.0	0	0.0	0	0	—	—	—	—	—	24	632
1971	Phi	10(FB)	97	262	2.7(26)	2	24	170	7.1(27)	1	—	—	—	—	—	—	—	—	—	—	—	—	18	372
1973	Phi	8	15	34	2.3(11)	1	4	18	4.5(6)	0	—	—	—	—	—	—	—	—	—	—	—	—	6	53
NFL	3	32	271	697	2.6(26)	5	78	589	7.6(34)	3	1	0	0.0	0	0.0	0	0	—	—	—	—	—	48	1057

Bouie, Kevin Kevin Lamont, RB, 6´1˝/230 lbs; Mississippi State; 1995: Phi, rnd 7; B8/18/1971 Pahokee, FL **1996** SD 1 (0)

YEAR	TEAM	G(GS, POS)	RUSH	YD	AVG(LG)	TD	REC	YD	AVG(LG)	TD	PASS	COMP	PCT	YD	AVG(LG)	TD	INT	SK	YD	QBR	KPR	OTD	PTS	TAY
1997	Arz	5(0)	11	26	2.4(6)	0	—	—	—	—	—	—	—	—	—	—	—	—	—	—	k	—	0	72
NFL	2	6(0)	11	26	2.4(6)	0	—	—	—	—	—	—	—	—	—	—	—	—	—	—	—	—	0	26

Bouie, Tony Tony Vanderson, DB, 5´10˝/188 lbs; Arizona; B8/7/1972 New Orleans, LA **1995** TB 9 (3) **1996** TB 16 (0) **1998** TB 16 (0)

YEAR	TEAM	G(GS, POS)	RUSH	YD	AVG(LG)	TD	REC	YD	AVG(LG)	TD	PASS	COMP	PCT	YD	AVG(LG)	TD	INT	SK	YD	QBR	KPR	OTD	PTS	TAY
1997	†TB	16(1)	—	—	—	—	1	25	25.0(25)	0	—	—	—	—	—	—	—	—	—	—	—	—	0	13
NFL	4	57(4)	—	—	—	—	1	25	25.0(25)	0	—	—	—	—	—	—	—	—	—	—	i	—	0	27

Bouley, Gil Gilbert J., T-DT, 6´2˝/235 lbs; Boston College; 1944: Cle, rnd 3; B11/15/1921 Plainfield, CT, D2/8/2006 Boston, MA **1945**†Cle 6 (6, RT) **1946** LARm 11 (11, RT) **1949**†LARm 12 (6, rt)

YEAR	TEAM	G(GS, POS)	RUSH	YD	AVG(LG)	TD	REC	YD	AVG(LG)	TD	PASS	COMP	PCT	YD	AVG(LG)	TD	INT	SK	YD	QBR	KPR	OTD	PTS	TAY
1947	LARm☆	12(10, RT)	—	—	—	—	1	15	15.0(15)	0	—	—	—	—	—	—	—	—	—	—	p	1	6	27
1948	LARm☆	12(12, RT)	—	—	—	—	1	15	15.0(15)	0	—	—	—	—	—	—	—	—	—	—	k	—	0	1
1950	†LARm	11(RDT)	—	—	—	—	1	11	11.0(11)	0	—	—	—	—	—	—	—	—	—	—	—	—	0	6
NFL	6	64(45)	—	—	—	—	3	41	13.7(15)	0	—	—	—	—	—	—	—	—	—	—	kp	1	6	33

Boulware, Michael Michael, DB-LB, 6´3˝/220 lbs; Florida State; 2004: Sea, rnd 2; B9/17/1981 Columbia, SC **2004**†Sea 16 (4) **2005**†Sea 16 (16, SS) **NFL** 32 (20) [2 yrs]

Boulware, Peter Peter Nicholas, LB-DE, 6´4˝/255 lbs; Florida State; 1997: Bal, rnd 1; B12/18/1974 Columbia, SC **[S]** **1997** Bal 16 (16, LLB) **1998** Bal✧16 (16, LLB) **1999** Bal★16 (11, LLB) **2000**†Bal 16 (15, LLB) **2001**†Bal 16 (14, LLB/rde) **2002** Bal✧16 (16, ROLB) **2003** Bal✧15 (14, ROLB) **2005** Bal 15 (0) **NFL** 126 (102) [8 yrs]

Bouman, Todd Todd, QB, 6´2˝/229 lbs; St. Cloud State; B8/1/1972 Ruthton, MN

YEAR	TEAM	G(GS, POS)	RUSH	YD	AVG(LG)	TD	REC	YD	AVG(LG)	TD	PASS	COMP	PCT	YD	AVG(LG)	TD	INT	SK	YD	QBR	KPR	OTD	PTS	TAY
2001	Min	5(3)	9	61	6.8(21)	0	—	—	—	—	89	51	57.3	795	8.9(80)	8	4	4	27	—	—	—	0	339
2002	Min	1(0)	1	9	9.0(9)	0	—	—	—	—	6	3	50.0	85	14.2(48)	0	0	2	22	—	—	—	0	52
2003	NO	4(0)	3	1	0.3(2)	0	—	—	—	—	13	7	53.8	81	6.2(19)	1	0	2	8	—	—	—	0	47
2004	NO	16(0)	—	—	—	—	—	—	—	—	—	—	—	—	—	—	—	—	—	—	—	—	—	—
2005	NO	16(3)	8	15	1.9(6)	0	—	—	—	—	122	68	55.7	722	5.9(43)	2	7	8	59	54.7	—	—	0	106
NFL	5	42(6)	21	86	4.1(21)	0	—	—	—	—	230	129	56.1	1683	7.3(80)	11	11	16	116	75.3	—	—	0	543

Boures, Emil Emil Nicholas, T-C-G, 6´1˝/259 lbs; Pittsburgh; 1982: Pit, rnd 7; B1/29/1960 Bridgeport, PA **1982** Pit 5 (1) **1983**†Pit 16 (3) **1984** Pit 8 (6, lt) **1985** Pit 6 (4) **NFL** 35 (14) [4 yrs]

Boutte, Marc Marc Anthony, DT, 6´4˝/307 lbs; LSU; 1992: LARm, rnd 3; B7/25/1969 Lake Charles, LA **1992** LARm 16 (15, LDT) **1993** LARm 16 (16, LDT) **1994** Was 9 (3) **1995** Was 16 (16, LDT) **1996** Was 10 (10, LDT) **1997** Was 16 (14, RDT) **1998** Was 13 (1) **1999** Was 6 (0) **NFL** 102 (75) [8 yrs]

Boutwell, Leon Leon A., B, 5´7˝/188 lbs; Carlisle Indian; B10/3/1892 Orr, ND, D10/4/1969 Mechanicsburg, OH **1922** Oor 8 (8, BB) **1923** Oor 7 (4) **NFL** 15 (12) [2 yrs]

Boutwell, Tommy Thomas Mitchell, WR-QB, 6´2˝/200 lbs; Southern Mississippi; 1969: Cle, rnd 13; B12/31/1946 Bluffton, OH

YEAR	TEAM	G(GS, POS)	RUSH	YD	AVG(LG)	TD	REC	YD	AVG(LG)	TD	PASS	COMP	PCT	YD	AVG(LG)	TD	INT	SK	YD	QBR	KPR	OTD	PTS	TAY
1969	Mia-A	5	—	—	—	—	4	29	7.3(12)	0	—	—	—	—	—	—	—	—	—	—	—	—	0	15

Bouwens, Shawn Shawn, G, 6´5˝/293 lbs; Nebraska Wesleyan; 1990: NE, rnd 9; B5/25/1968 Lincoln, NE **1991**†Det 16 (0) **1992** Det 16 (16, LG) **1993**†Det 15 (1) **1994**†Det 16 (16, LG) **1995** Jax 10 (9, LG) **NFL** 73 (42) [5 yrs]

Bouyer, Willie Willie Louis, WR, 6´3˝/200 lbs; Michigan State; B9/24/1966 Detroit, MI

YEAR	TEAM	G(GS, POS)	RUSH	YD	AVG(LG)	TD	REC	YD	AVG(LG)	TD	PASS	COMP	PCT	YD	AVG(LG)	TD	INT	SK	YD	QBR	KPR	OTD	PTS	TAY
1989	Sea	1(0)	—	—	—	—	1	9	9.0(9)	0	—	—	—	—	—	—	—	—	—	—	—	—	0	5

Bouza, Matt Matthew Kyle, WR, 6´3˝/211 lbs; California; B4/8/1958 San Jose, CA

YEAR	TEAM	G(GS, POS)	RUSH	YD	AVG(LG)	TD	REC	YD	AVG(LG)	TD	PASS	COMP	PCT	YD	AVG(LG)	TD	INT	SK	YD	QBR	KPR	OTD	PTS	TAY
1981	SF	1(0)	—	—	—	—	—	—	—	—	—	—	—	—	—	—	—	—	—	—	—	—	—	—
1982	Bal	9(9, WR)	—	—	—	—	22	287	13.0(34)	2	—	—	—	—	—	—	—	—	—	—	kp	—	12	130

YEAR	TEAM	G(GS, POS)	RUSH	YD	AVG(LG)	TD	REC	YD	AVG(LG)	TD	PASS	COMP	PCT	YD	AVG(LG)	TD	INT	SK	YD	QBR	KPR	OTD	PTS	TAY
1983	Bal	11(11, WR)	—	—	—	—	25	385	15.4(26)	0	—	—	—	—	—	—	—	—	—	—	k	—	0	174
1984	Ind	16(4)	—	—	—	—	22	270	12.3(22)	0	—	—	—	—	—	—	—	—	—	—	p	—	0	137
1985	Ind	12(5, wr)	—	—	—	—	27	381	14.1(40)	2	—	—	—	—	—	—	—	—	—	—	—	—	12	201
1986	Ind	16(14, WR)	1	12	12.0(12)	0	71	830	11.7(33)	5	—	—	—	—	—	—	—	—	—	—	—	—	30	452
1987	†Ind	12(12, WR)	—	—	—	—	42	569	13.5(44)	4	—	—	—	—	—	—	—	—	—	—	—	—	24	305
1988	Ind	15(5, wr)	—	—	—	—	25	342	13.7(28)	4	—	—	—	—	—	—	—	—	—	—	—	—	24	191
1989	Ind	2(0)	—	—	—	—	—	—	—	—	—	—	—	—	—	—	—	—	—	—	—	—	—	—
NFL	9	94(60)	1	12	12.0(12)	0	234	3064	13.1(44)	17	—	—	—	—	—	—	—	—	—	—	kp	—	102	1588

Bova, Tony Anthony J., E-B, 6´1˝/190 lbs; St. Francis (PA); B8/21/1917 Pittsburgh, PA, D10/16/1973 O'Hara Township, PA

YEAR	TEAM	G(GS, POS)	RUSH	YD	AVG(LG)	TD	REC	YD	AVG(LG)	TD	PASS	COMP	PCT	YD	AVG(LG)	TD	INT	SK	YD	QBR	KPR	OTD	PTS	TAY
1942	Pit	11(10, LE)	—	—	—	—	3	37	12.3(17)	0	—	—	—	—	—	—	—	—	—	—	ki	—	0	17
1943	P-P	10(6, LE)	1	11	11.0(11)	0	17	419	24.6(51)	5	—	—	—	—	—	—	—	—	—	—	—	—	30	246
1944	C-P	9(8, LE)	14	-22	-1.6(3)	0	19	287	15.1(46)	2	30	6	20.0	96	3.2(34)	0	1	—	—	—	—	—	12	140
1945	Pit	10(5, HB)	6	11	1.8(5)	0	15	215	14.3(52)	0	1	0	0.0	0	0.0	0	0	—	—	—	k	—	0	128
1946	Pit	11(0)	—	—	—	—	6	171	28.5(37)	0	—	—	—	—	—	—	—	—	—	—	—	—	0	86
1947	Pit	10(0)	—	—	—	—	—	—	—	—	—	—	—	—	—	—	—	—	—	—	k	—	2	1
NFL	6	61(29)	21	0	0.0(11)	0	60	1129	18.8(52)	7	31	6	19.4	96	3.1(34)	0	1	—	—	—	ki	—	44	616

Bove, Peter Peter Anthony, G, 5´10˝/187 lbs; Holy Cross; B9/21/1906, VT, D6/11/1974 St. Croix, Virgin Islands **1930** Nwk 3 (1)

Bowdell, Gordon Gordon Bennett, WR, 6´2˝/203 lbs; Michigan State; 1971: Bal, rnd 7; B10/9/1948 Detroit, MI

YEAR	TEAM	G(GS, POS)	RUSH	YD	AVG(LG)	TD	REC	YD	AVG(LG)	TD	PASS	COMP	PCT	YD	AVG(LG)	TD	INT	SK	YD	QBR	KPR	OTD	PTS	TAY
1971	Den	2	—	—	—	—	1	19	19.0(19)	0	—	—	—	—	—	—	—	—	—	—	—	—	0	10

Bowden, Joe Joseph Tarrod, LB, 5´11˝/230 lbs; Oklahoma; 1992: Hou, rnd 5; B2/25/1970 Dallas, TX **1992**†Hou 14 (0) **1993**†Hou 16 (6, rlb) **1994** Hou 14 (1) **1995** Hou 16 (14, RLB) **1996** Hou 16 (16, LLB) **1997** Ten 16 (16, LLB) **1998** Ten 16 (16, MLB) **1999**†Ten 15 (15, RLB) **2000** Dal 16 (0) **NFL** 139 (84) [9 yrs]

Bowdoin, Jim James L., G, 6´1˝/227 lbs; Alabama; B1/15/1904 Coffee Springs, AL, D5/11/1969 Chickasaw, AL **1928** GB 11 (7, LG) **1929** GB 12 (11, RG) **1930** GB 9 (9, RG) **1931** GB 13 (11, RG) **1932** Bkn 6 (5, RG) **1932** NYG 6 (4) **1933** Por 7 (2) **1934** Bkn 11 (1) **NFL** 75 (50) [7 yrs]

Bowen, Ken Kenneth Edgar, LB, 6´1˝/220 lbs; East Tennessee State; B11/15/1962 Columbus, GA **1987** Atl 1 (0)

Bowen, Matt Matthew Sean, DB, 6´1˝/207 lbs; Iowa; 2000: SL, rnd 6; B11/12/1976 Glen Ellyn, IL **2000**†SL 16 (2) **2001** SL 1 (0) **2001**†GB 5 (0) **2002**†GB 16 (6, ss) **2003** Was 16 (16, FS) **2004** Was 5 (5, ss) **2005**†Was 13 (1) **NFL** 72 (30) [6 yrs]

Bowens, David David Walter, DE, 6´3˝/260 lbs; Michigan; Western Illinois; 1999: Den, rnd 5; B7/3/1977 Denver, CO **1999** Den 16 (0) **2000** GB 14 (0) **2001**†Mia 8 (0) **2002** Mia 14 (0) **2003** Mia 4 (0) **2004** Mia 16 (15, LDE) **2005** Mia 16 (0) **NFL** 88 (15) [7 yrs]

Bowens, Tim Timothy L., DT, 6´4˝/325 lbs; Mississippi; 1994: Mia, rnd 1; B2/7/1973 Okolona, MS **1994**†Mia☆16 (15, LDT) **1995**†Mia 16 (16, LDT) **1996** Mia 16 (16, RDT) **1997**†Mia 16 (16, LDT) **1998**†Mia✧16 (16, LDT) **1999**†Mia 16 (15, LDT) **2000**†Mia 15 (15, LDT) **2001**†Mia 15 (15, LDT) **2002** Mia✧16 (16, LDT) **2003** Mia 13 (13, LDT) **2004** Mia 2 (2) **NFL** 157 (155) [11 yrs]

Bower, Phil James Philip, B, 5´8˝/160 lbs; Middlebury; Dartmouth; B10/22/1894 Richmond, VA, D7/17/1975 Vergennes, VT **1921** Cle 5 (3)

Bowers, Andy Andrew Wyant Wayne, DE, 6´5˝/283 lbs; Utah; B2/22/1976 Salt Lake City, UT **2001** Arz 1 (1)

Bowers, Bill William James, DB, 6´0˝/198 lbs; USC; B10/31/1928 Kansas City, MO **1954** LARm 8

Bowers, R.J. Raymond Keith, RB, 6´0˝/250 lbs; Grove City; B2/10/1974 Honolulu, HI

YEAR	TEAM	G(GS, POS)	RUSH	YD	AVG(LG)	TD	REC	YD	AVG(LG)	TD	PASS	COMP	PCT	YD	AVG(LG)	TD	INT	SK	YD	QBR	KPR	OTD	PTS	TAY
2001	Pit	3(0)	18	84	4.7(21)	1	1	0	0.0(0)	0	—	—	—	—	—	—	—	—	—	—	—	—	6	94
2002	Cle	4(0)	—	—	—	—	—	—	—	—	—	—	—	—	—	—	—	—	—	—	—	—	—	—
2003	Cle	1(0)	—	—	—	—	1	2	2.0(2)	1	—	—	—	—	—	—	—	—	—	—	—	—	6	6
NFL	3	8(0)	18	84	4.7(21)	1	2	2	1.0(2)	1	—	—	—	—	—	—	—	—	—	—	—	—	12	100

Bowers, Sam Samuel Tyrone, TE, 6´4˝/250 lbs; Tennessee State; Fordham; B12/22/1957 White Plains, NY

YEAR	TEAM	G(GS, POS)	RUSH	YD	AVG(LG)	TD	REC	YD	AVG(LG)	TD	PASS	COMP	PCT	YD	AVG(LG)	TD	INT	SK	YD	QBR	KPR	OTD	PTS	TAY
1987	ChiB	3(0)	—	—	—	—	1	6	6.0(6)	0	—	—	—	—	—	—	—	—	—	—	—	—	0	3

Bowick, Tony Vantorio Bernard, NT, 6´2˝/265 lbs; Tennessee-Chattanooga; 1989: Atl, rnd 12; B10/3/1966 Dothan, AL **1989** Atl 12 (0)

Bowie, Larry Lawrence Glen, G, 6´2˝/245 lbs; Purdue; 1962: Min, rnd 6/DalT, rnd 8; B10/13/1939 Pike, WV **1962** Min 14 **1963** Min 14 (14, RG) **1964** Min 14 (14, RG) **1965** Min 14 (14, RG) **1966** Min 14 **1967** Min 14 (14, RG) **1968** Min 8 (8, RG) **NFL** 92 (64) [7 yrs]

Bowie, Larry Larry Darnell, RB, 6´0˝/249 lbs; Georgia; B3/21/1973 Anniston, AL

YEAR	TEAM	G(GS, POS)	RUSH	YD	AVG(LG)	TD	REC	YD	AVG(LG)	TD	PASS	COMP	PCT	YD	AVG(LG)	TD	INT	SK	YD	QBR	KPR	OTD	PTS	TAY
1996	Was	3(0)	—	—	—	—	3	17	5.7(8)	0	—	—	—	—	—	—	—	—	—	—	—	—	0	9
1997	Was	15(13, FB)	28	100	3.6(18)	2	34	388	11.4(39)	2	—	—	—	—	—	—	—	—	—	—	k	—	24	324
1998	Was	5(4)	4	8	2.0(4)	0	7	53	7.6(17)	1	—	—	—	—	—	—	—	—	—	—	—	—	6	40
1999	Was	2(0)	—	—	—	—	—	—	—	—	—	—	—	—	—	—	—	—	—	—	k	—	0	-15
NFL	4	25(17)	32	108	3.4(18)	2	44	458	10.4(39)	3	—	—	—	—	—	—	—	—	—	—	k	—	30	357

Bowles, Todd Todd Robert, DB, 6´2˝/203 lbs; Temple; B11/18/1963 Elizabeth, NJ **1986**†Was 15 (2) **1987**†Was 12 (12, FS) **1988** Was 16 (16, FS) **1989** Was 16 (16, FS) **1990**†Was 16 (16, FS) **1991** SF 16 (14, FS) **1992**†Was 16 (4) **1993** Was 10 (2) **NFL** 117 (82) [8 yrs]

Bowling, Andy Andrew Walter, LB, 6´2˝/235 lbs; Virginia Tech; 1967: SL, rnd 4; B9/25/1945 Lynchburg, VA **1967** Atl 6

Bowman, Barry Barry D., P, 5´11˝/190 lbs; Louisiana Tech; B12/18/1964 **1987** Sea 1 (0)

Bowman, Bill William Ekron, FB, 6´2˝/215 lbs; William & Mary; 1954: Det, rnd 3; B9/22/1931 Birmingham, AL

YEAR	TEAM	G(GS, POS)	RUSH	YD	AVG(LG)	TD	REC	YD	AVG(LG)	TD	PASS	COMP	PCT	YD	AVG(LG)	TD	INT	SK	YD	QBR	KPR	OTD	PTS	TAY
1954	†Det☆	12(FB)	96	397	4.1(61)	2	34	288	8.5(66)	2	—	—	—	—	—	—	—	—	—	—	k	1	30	669
1956	Det	6	20	84	4.2(13)	1	5	34	6.8(18)	1	—	—	—	—	—	—	—	—	—	—	k	—	12	125
1957	Pit	5	28	76	2.7(13)	0	11	107	9.7(21)	0	—	—	—	—	—	—	—	—	—	—	—	—	0	130
NFL	3	23	144	557	3.9(61)	3	50	429	8.6(66)	3	—	—	—	—	—	—	—	—	—	—	k	1	42	924

Bowman, Jim James Edwin, DB, 6´2˝/210 lbs; Central Michigan; 1985: NE, rnd 2; B10/26/1963 Cadillac, MI **1985**†NE 16 (0) **1986**†NE 16 (1) **1987** NE 12 (8, SS) **1988** NE 16 (1) **1989** NE 13 (2) **NFL** 73 (12) [5 yrs]

Bowman, Ken Kenneth Brian, C, 6´3˝/230 lbs; Wisconsin; 1964: GB, rnd 8/NYJ, rnd 10; B12/15/1942 Milan, IL **1964** GB 14 (c) **1965**†GB 14 (C) **1966**†GB 4 **1967**†GB 13 (C) **1968** GB 14 (C) **1969** GB 12 (C) **1970** GB 10 (C) **1971** GB 14 (C) **1972**†GB 14 (C) **1973** GB 14 (C) **NFL** 123 [10 yrs]

Bowman, Kevin Kevin Gerard, WR, 6´3˝/205 lbs; Colorado; San Jose State; B2/23/1962 Sacramento, CA

YEAR	TEAM	G(GS, POS)	RUSH	YD	AVG(LG)	TD	REC	YD	AVG(LG)	TD	PASS	COMP	PCT	YD	AVG(LG)	TD	INT	SK	YD	QBR	KPR	OTD	PTS	TAY
1987	Phi	3(3)	—	—	—	—	6	127	21.2(62)	1	—	—	—	—	—	—	—	—	—	—	kp	—	6	140

Bowman, Steve Steven Ellis, HB, 6´0˝/195 lbs; Alabama; 1966: NYG, rnd 15/Oak, rnd 20; B11/30/1944 Pascagoula, MS **1966** NYG 4

Bownes, Fabien Fabien Alfranso, WR, 5´11˝/185 lbs; Western Illinois; B2/29/1972 Aurora, IL **1995** ChiB 1 (0) **2000** Sea 16 (0) **2001** Sea 16 (0)

YEAR	TEAM	G(GS, POS)	RUSH	YD	AVG(LG)	TD	REC	YD	AVG(LG)	TD	PASS	COMP	PCT	YD	AVG(LG)	TD	INT	SK	YD	QBR	KPR	OTD	PTS	TAY
1997	ChiB	16(0)	—	—	—	—	12	146	12.2(21)	0	—	—	—	—	—	—	—	—	—	—	k	—	0	184
1998	ChiB	16(0)	—	—	—	—	5	69	13.8(44)	1	—	—	—	—	—	—	—	—	—	—	k	—	6	44
1999	†Sea	15(0)	1	-14	-14.0(-14)	0	4	68	17.0(49)	1	—	—	—	—	—	—	—	—	—	—	k	—	6	35
NFL	6	80(0)	1	-14	-14.0(-14)	0	21	283	13.5(49)	2	—	—	—	—	—	—	—	—	—	—	k	—	12	301

Bowser, Arda Arda Crawford, B, 6´2˝/210 lbs; Bethany (WV); Bucknell; B1/9/1899 Danville, PA, D9/7/1996 Winter Park, FL **[K]** **1922** Can 5 (0), 14 **1923** Cle 3 (2) **NFL** 8 (2) [2 yrs]

Bowser, Charles Charles Emanuel, LB, 6´3˝/231 lbs; Duke; 1982: Mia, rnd 4; B10/2/1959 Plymouth, NC **1982**†Mia 9 (0) **1983**†Mia 16 (16, ROLB) **1984**†Mia 15 (15, ROLB) **1985** Mia 2 (2) **NFL** 42 (33) [4 yrs]

Bowyer, Walt Walter Nathaniel, DE, 6´4˝/254 lbs; Arizona State; 1983: Den, rnd 10; B9/8/1960 Pittsburgh, PA **1983**†Den 14 (3) **1984**†Den 16 (1) **1987**†Den 15 (3) **1988** Den 16 (11, LDE) **NFL** 61 (18) [4 yrs]

Box, Cloyce Cloyce Kennedy, E-HB, 6´4˝/220 lbs; Louisiana Tech; West Texas A&M; 1948: Was, rnd 20; B8/24/1923 Hamilton, TX, D10/24/1993 Frisco, TX

YEAR	TEAM	G(GS, POS)	RUSH	YD	AVG(LG)	TD	REC	YD	AVG(LG)	TD	PASS	COMP	PCT	YD	AVG(LG)	TD	INT	SK	YD	QBR	KPR	OTD	PTS	TAY
1949	Det	10(5, rh)	30	62	2.1(11)	0	15	276	18.4(43)	4	—	—	—	—	—	—	—	—	—	—	k	—	24	225
1950	Det★	12(LE)	—	—	—	—	50	1009	20.2(82)	11	—	—	—	—	—	—	—	—	—	—	—	—	66	560
1952	†Det★	12(LE)	—	—	—	—	42	924	22.0(77)	**15**	—	—	—	—	—	—	—	—	—	—	—	—	90	537
1953	†Det	12(LE)	—	—	—	—	16	403	25.2(**97**)	2	—	—	—	—	—	—	—	—	—	—	—	—	12	212

YEAR	TEAM	G (GS, POS)	RUSH	YD	AVG (LG)	TD	REC	YD	AVG (LG)	TD	PASS	COMP	PCT	YD	AVG (LG)	TD	INT	SK	YD	QBR	KPR	OTD	PTS	TAY
1954	†Det	11	1	20	20.0(20)	0	6	53	8.8(14)	0	—	—	—	—	—	—	—	—	—	—	—	—	0	47
NFL	5	57(5)	31	82	2.6(20)	0	129	2665	20.7(97)	32	—	—	—	—	—	—	—	—	—	—	k	—	192	1580

Boyarsky, Jerry Gerard Mark Joseph, NT, 6´3˝/290 lbs; Pittsburgh; 1981: NO, rnd 5; B5/15/1959 Scranton, PA **1981** NO 11 (7, NT) **1982**†Cin 2 (0) **1983** Cin 15 (14, NT) **1984** Cin 15 (0) **1985** Cin 16 (0) **1986** Buf 10 (0) **1986** GB 2 (0) **1987** GB 12 (8, NT) **1988** GB 2 (2) **1989** GB 13 (0) **NFL** 98 (31) [9 yrs]

Boyd, Bill Walter Alvin, B, 5´11˝/175 lbs; Westminster (MO); B1907 Louisiana, MO **1930** ChiC 12 (2), 12 **1931** ChiC 4 (0) **NFL** 16 (2) [2 yrs]

Boyd, Bob Robert B., E-DB, 6´2˝/201 lbs; Loyola Marymount; B3/7/1928 Riverside, CA

YEAR	TEAM	G (GS, POS)	RUSH	YD	AVG (LG)	TD	REC	YD	AVG (LG)	TD	PASS	COMP	PCT	YD	AVG (LG)	TD	INT	SK	YD	QBR	KPR	OTD	PTS	TAY
1950	†LARm	12	1	-2	-2.0(-2)	0	9	220	24.4(72)	4	—	—	—	—	—	—	—	—	—	—	—	—	24	128
1951	†LARm	12	—	—	—	—	9	128	14.2(28)	1	—	—	—	—	—	—	—	—	—	—	i	—	6	62
1953	LARm	12(RE)	—	—	—	—	24	548	**22.8(70)**	4	—	—	—	—	—	—	—	—	—	—	kpi	—	24	322
1954	LARm★	12(RE)	—	—	—	—	53	**1212**	22.9(80)	6	—	—	—	—	—	—	—	—	—	—	—	—	36	636
1955	†LARm	7(FL)	—	—	—	—	22	383	17.4(74)	3	—	—	—	—	—	—	—	—	—	—	—	—	18	207
1956	LARm	12(FL)	1	-7	-7.0(-7)	0	30	586	19.5(61)	7	—	—	—	—	—	—	—	—	—	—	k	—	42	323
1957	LARm	12(FL)	—	—	—	—	29	534	18.4(51)	3	—	—	—	—	—	—	—	—	—	—	—	—	18	282
NFL	7	79	2	-9	-4.5(-2)	0	176	3611	20.5(80)	28	—	—	—	—	—	—	—	—	—	—	kpi	—	168	1960

Boyd, Bobby Robert Dean, DB, 5´11˝/195 lbs; Oklahoma; 1960: Bal, rnd 10/LAC, rnd 1; B12/3/1937 Garland, TX **[I]** **1960** Bal 11 (LCB) **1963** Bal 12 (LCB) **1965**†Bal☆14 (LCB) **1966** Bal☆14 (14, LCB) **1967** Bal☆14 (LCB) **1968**†Bal★14 (LCB)

YEAR	TEAM	G (GS, POS)	RUSH	YD	AVG (LG)	TD	REC	YD	AVG (LG)	TD	PASS	COMP	PCT	YD	AVG (LG)	TD	INT	SK	YD	QBR	KPR	OTD	PTS	TAY
1961	Bal	14(LCB)	—	—	—	—	—	—	—	—	1	0	0.0	0	0.0	0	0	—	—	—	pi	—	0	73
1962	Bal	14(LCB)	2	13	6.5(15)	0	—	—	—	—	—	—	—	—	—	—	—	—	—	—	pi	—	0	149
1964	†Bal★	14(LCB)	1	25	25.0(25)	0	—	—	—	—	—	—	—	—	—	—	—	—	—	—	ki	—	0	150
NFL	9	121(14)	3	38	12.7(25)	0	—	—	—	—	1	0	0.0	0	0.0	0	0	—	—	—	kpi	5	30	863

Boyd, Brent Brent Varner, G, 6´3˝/268 lbs; UCLA; 1980: Min, rnd 3; B3/23/1957 Downey, CA **1980**†Min 16 (9, lg) **1981** Min 3 (3) **1982** Min 4 (0) **1983** Min 16 (1) **1985** Min 15 (14, LG) **1986** Min 5 (0) **NFL** 59 (27) [6 yrs]

Boyd, Danny Daniel Edward, K, 6´0˝/213 lbs; LSU; B6/1/1978 Bradenton, FL **[K]** **2002** Jax 4 (0)

Boyd, Dennis Dennis James, DT-DE-T-C, 6´6˝/255 lbs; Oregon State; 1977: Sea, rnd 3; B11/5/1955 Washington, DC **1977** Sea 14 (5, rdt) **1978** Sea 16 (16, LDT) **1979** Sea 11 (4) **1982** Sea 2 (2)

YEAR	TEAM	G (GS, POS)	RUSH	YD	AVG (LG)	TD	REC	YD	AVG (LG)	TD	PASS	COMP	PCT	YD	AVG (LG)	TD	INT	SK	YD	QBR	KPR	OTD	PTS	TAY
1981	Sea	16(0)	—	—	—	—	1	3	3.0(3)	1	—	—	—	—	—	—	—	—	—	—	—	—	6	7
NFL	5	59(27)	—	—	—	—	1	3	3.0(3)	1	—	—	—	—	—	—	—	—	—	—	k	—	6	-3

Boyd, Elmo Elmo David, WR, 6´0˝/188 lbs; Eastern Kentucky; 1977: SF, rnd 3; B6/15/1954 Muleshoe, TX **1978** GB 2

YEAR	TEAM	G (GS, POS)	RUSH	YD	AVG (LG)	TD	REC	YD	AVG (LG)	TD	PASS	COMP	PCT	YD	AVG (LG)	TD	INT	SK	YD	QBR	KPR	OTD	PTS	TAY
1978	SF	9(5, wr)	—	—	—	—	9	115	12.8(32)	1	—	—	—	—	—	—	—	—	—	—	—	—	6	63
NFL	1	11(5)	—	—	—	—	9	115	12.8(32)	1	—	—	—	—	—	—	—	—	—	—	—	—	6	63

Boyd, Greg Gregory Earl, DE, 6´6˝/274 lbs; San Diego State; 1976: NE, rnd 6; B9/15/1952 Merced, CA **1977** NE 13 **1978** NE 10 **1980** Den 16 (0) **1981** Den 15 (0) **1982** Den 9 (0) **1983** GB 12 (1) **1984** SF 2 (0) **1984** LARd 5 (0) **NFL** 82 (1) [7 yrs]

Boyd, Greg Gregory Paul, DB, 6´2˝/201 lbs; Arizona; 1973: Mia, rnd 14; B12/30/1950 Scottsdale, AZ **1973** NE 2 **1974** NO 4 **NFL** 6 [2 yrs]

Boyd, James James Aaron, DB, 5´11˝/207 lbs; Penn State; 2001: Jax, rnd 3; B10/17/1977 Norfolk, VA **2001** Jax 16 (0) **2002** Jax 10 (0) **NFL** 26 (0) [2 yrs]

Boyd, Jerome Jerome Anthony, LB, 6´2˝/225 lbs; Oregon State; B9/18/1961 Los Angeles, CA **1983** Sea 5 (0)

Boyd, LaVell LaVell, WR, 6´3˝/218 lbs; Louisville; B9/12/1976 Louisville, KY **2000** Cin 2 (0)

Boyd, Malik Malik A., DB, 5´10˝/175 lbs; Southern (LA); B11/5/1970 Houston, TX **1994**†Min 16 (1)

Boyd, Sam Sam Bradford, E, 6´2˝/190 lbs; Baylor; 1939: Pit, rnd 6; B8/12/1914 Rockwall, TX, D6/8/2001 Granbury, TX **1940** Pit 3 (0)

YEAR	TEAM	G (GS, POS)	RUSH	YD	AVG (LG)	TD	REC	YD	AVG (LG)	TD	PASS	COMP	PCT	YD	AVG (LG)	TD	INT	SK	YD	QBR	KPR	OTD	PTS	TAY
1939	Pit	11(4)	—	—	—	—	21	423	20.1	2	—	—	—	—	—	—	—	—	—	—	—	—	12	222
NFL	2	14(4)	—	—	—	—	21	423	20.1	2	—	—	—	—	—	—	—	—	—	—	—	—	12	222

Boyd, Sean Sean Lefell, DB, 6´2˝/206 lbs; North Carolina; 1996: Min, rnd 5; B12/19/1972 Gastonia, NC **1996** Atl 2 (0)

Boyd, Stephen Stephen Gerard, LB, 6´0˝/247 lbs; Boston College; 1995: Det, rnd 5; B8/22/1972 Valley Stream, NY **1995**†Det 16 (0) **1996** Det 8 (5, rlb) **1997**†Det 16 (16, MLB) **1998** Det 13 (13, MLB) **1999**†Det✧14 (14, MLB) **2000** Det★15 (15, MLB) **2001** Det 4 (4) **NFL** 86 (67) [7 yrs]

Boyd, Thomas Thomas Barton, LB, 6´3˝/210 lbs; Alabama; 1982: GB, rnd 8; B11/24/1959 Huntsville, AL **1987** Det 4 (3)

Boyd, Tommie Tommie Leeshay, WR, 6´0˝/195 lbs; Toledo; B12/21/1971 Lansing, MI

YEAR	TEAM	G (GS, POS)	RUSH	YD	AVG (LG)	TD	REC	YD	AVG (LG)	TD	PASS	COMP	PCT	YD	AVG (LG)	TD	INT	SK	YD	QBR	KPR	OTD	PTS	TAY
1997	†Det	16(1)	—	—	—	—	10	142	14.2(32)	0	—	—	—	—	—	—	—	—	—	—	—	—	0	71
1998	Det	9(0)	—	—	—	—	4	52	13.0(19)	1	—	—	—	—	—	—	—	—	—	—	kp	—	6	65
NFL	2	25(1)	—	—	—	—	14	194	13.9(32)	1	—	—	—	—	—	—	—	—	—	—	kp	—	6	136

Boyda, Mike Michael Bartholomew, LB-FB, 6´1˝/205 lbs; Washington & Lee; 1949: NYB, rnd 5; B11/28/1921 Jenners, PA, D7/16/1984 Overland Park, KS

YEAR	TEAM	G (GS, POS)	RUSH	YD	AVG (LG)	TD	REC	YD	AVG (LG)	TD	PASS	COMP	PCT	YD	AVG (LG)	TD	INT	SK	YD	QBR	KPR	OTD	PTS	TAY
1949	NYB	9(0)	—	—	—	—	—	—	—	—	1	0	0.0	0	0.0	0	0	—	—	—	Pi	—	0	20

Boydston, Max Max Ray, E, 6´2˝/210 lbs; Oklahoma; 1955: ChiC, rnd 1; B1/22/1932 Ardmore, OK, D12/12/1998 Muskogee, OK

YEAR	TEAM	G (GS, POS)	RUSH	YD	AVG (LG)	TD	REC	YD	AVG (LG)	TD	PASS	COMP	PCT	YD	AVG (LG)	TD	INT	SK	YD	QBR	KPR	OTD	PTS	TAY
1955	ChiC	9	—	—	—	—	3	79	26.3(67)	1	—	—	—	—	—	—	—	—	—	—	—	—	6	45
1956	ChiC	12	—	—	—	—	6	116	19.3(39)	2	—	—	—	—	—	—	—	—	—	—	—	—	12	68
1957	ChiC	12	—	—	—	—	14	193	13.8(33)	0	—	—	—	—	—	—	—	—	—	—	—	—	0	97
1958	ChiC	10	—	—	—	—	3	42	14.0(25)	1	—	—	—	—	—	—	—	—	—	—	—	—	6	26
1960	DalT-A	14(te)	—	—	—	—	29	357	12.3(25)	3	—	—	—	—	—	—	—	—	—	—	—	—	18	194
1961	DalT-A	11(TE)	—	—	—	—	12	167	13.9(24)	1	—	—	—	—	—	—	—	—	—	—	—	—	6	89
1962	Oak-A	14(TE)	—	—	—	—	30	374	12.5(58)	0	—	—	—	—	—	—	—	—	—	—	—	—	0	187
NFL	7	82	—	—	—	—	97	1328	13.7(67)	8	—	—	—	—	—	—	—	—	—	—	—	—	48	704

Boyer, Brant Brant T., LB, 6´1˝/240 lbs; Arizona; 1994: Mia, rnd 6; B6/27/1971 Ogden, UT **1994**†Mia 14 (0) **1995** Jax 2 (0) **1996**†Jax 12 (0) **1997**†Jax 16 (2) **1998** Jax 11 (0) **1999**†Jax 16 (0) **2000** Jax 12 (5, RLB) **2001** Cle 16 (1) **2002**†Cle 16 (1)

YEAR	TEAM	G (GS, POS)	RUSH	YD	AVG (LG)	TD	REC	YD	AVG (LG)	TD	PASS	COMP	PCT	YD	AVG (LG)	TD	INT	SK	YD	QBR	KPR	OTD	PTS	TAY
2003	Cle	15(7, rlb)	1	7	7.0(7)	0	—	—	—	—	1	0	0.0	0	0.0	0	0	—	—	—	i	—	0	6
NFL	10	130(16)	1	7	7.0(7)	0	—	—	—	—	1	0	0.0	0	0.0	0	0	—	—	—	iS	—	0	11

Boyer, Mark Mark Hearn, TE-RB-WR, 6´4˝/233 lbs; USC; 1985: Ind, rnd 9; B9/16/1962 Huntington Beach, CA

YEAR	TEAM	G (GS, POS)	RUSH	YD	AVG (LG)	TD	REC	YD	AVG (LG)	TD	PASS	COMP	PCT	YD	AVG (LG)	TD	INT	SK	YD	QBR	KPR	OTD	PTS	TAY
1985	Ind	16(6, wr)	—	—	—	—	25	274	11.0(33)	0	—	—	—	—	—	—	—	—	—	—	—	—	0	137
1986	Ind	16(7, RB)	—	—	—	—	22	237	10.8(38)	1	—	—	—	—	—	—	—	—	—	—	—	—	6	124
1987	†Ind	7(6, TE)	—	—	—	—	10	73	7.3(15)	0	—	—	—	—	—	—	—	—	—	—	—	—	0	37
1988	Ind	16(13, TE)	—	—	—	—	27	256	9.5(24)	2	—	—	—	—	—	—	—	—	—	—	—	—	12	138
1989	Ind	16(5, te)	—	—	—	—	11	58	5.3(15)	2	—	—	—	—	—	—	—	—	—	—	—	—	12	39
1990	NYJ	16(16, TE)	—	—	—	—	40	334	8.4(25)	1	—	—	—	—	—	—	—	—	—	—	k	—	6	171
1991	†NYJ	11(10, TE)	—	—	—	—	16	153	9.6(22)	0	—	—	—	—	—	—	—	—	—	—	k	—	0	62
1992	NYJ	16(16, TE)	—	—	—	—	19	149	7.8(23)	0	—	—	—	—	—	—	—	—	—	—	—	—	0	75
NFL	8	114(79)	—	—	—	—	170	1534	9.0(38)	6	—	—	—	—	—	—	—	—	—	—	k	—	36	781

Boyer, Verdi Verdi Emerson, G, 5´10˝/185 lbs; UCLA; B9/2/1911 San Francisco, CA, D5/27/2003 Pasadena, CA **1936** Bkn 11 (4)

Boyett, Lon Lon, TE, 6´6˝/240 lbs; Cal State-Northridge; B12/24/1953 Lancaster, CA **1978** SF 3

Boyette, Garland Garland Dean, LB-DE, 6´1˝/238 lbs; Grambling State; B3/22/1940 Rayville, LA **1962** SL 14 (MLB) **1963** SL 9 **1966** Hou-A 14 (rde) **1967**†Hou-A 14 (MLB) **1968** Hou-A✧14 (MLB) **1969**†Hou-A✧14 (MLB) **1970** Hou 13 (MLB) **1971** Hou 14 (MLB) **1972** Hou 14 (mlb) **NFL** 120 [9 yrs]

Boykin, Deral Deral Lamont, DB, 5´11˝/198 lbs; Louisville; 1993: LARm, rnd 6; B9/2/1970 Kent, OH **1993** LARm 16 (0) **1994** Was 12 (0) **1995** Jax 5 (0) **1996**†Phi 10 (0) **NFL** 43 (0) [4 yrs]

Boykin, Greg Gregory, RB, 6´0˝/225 lbs; Northwestern; 1977: NO, rnd 7; B12/8/1953 Ravenna, OH

YEAR	TEAM	G (GS, POS)	RUSH	YD	AVG (LG)	TD	REC	YD	AVG (LG)	TD	PASS	COMP	PCT	YD	AVG (LG)	TD	INT	SK	YD	QBR	KPR	OTD	PTS	TAY
1977	NO	14	5	-9	-1.8(4)	0	3	21	7.0(9)	0	—	—	—	—	—	—	—	—	—	—	k	—	0	3
1978	SF	16(8, FB)	102	361	3.5(23)	2	19	112	5.9(22)	0	—	—	—	—	—	—	—	—	—	—	k	—	12	429
NFL	2	30(8)	107	352	3.3(23)	2	22	133	6.0(22)	0	—	—	—	—	—	—	—	—	—	—	k	—	12	432

YEAR	TEAM	G (GS, POS)	RUSH	YD	AVG(LG)	TD	REC	YD	AVG(LG)	TD	PASS COMP	PCT	YD	AVG(LG)	TD	INT	SK	YD	QBR	KPR	OTD	PTS	TAY

BOYLAN, JIM James Owen, WR, 6´1˝/185 lbs; Washington State; B3/19/1939 Washington, DC
| 1963 | Min | 3 | — | — | — | — | 6 | 78 | 13.0(19) | 1 | — | — | — | — | — | — | — | — | — | — | — | 6 | 44 |

BOYLE, JIM James Robert, T, 6´5˝/270 lbs; Tulane; 1984: Mia, rnd 9; B7/27/1961 Cincinnati, OH **1988** Pit 6 (0)
| 1987 | Pit | 3(3) | — | — | — | — | 1 | 0 | 0.0(0) | 0 | — | — | — | — | — | — | — | — | — | — | — | 0 | 0 |
| NFL | 2 | 9(3) | — | — | — | — | — | — | — | — | — | — | — | — | — | — | — | — | — | k | — | 0 | 4 |

BOYLE, KNUCKLES William, T, 5´11˝/232 lbs; Albright; B1909 **1934** NYG 1 (0)

BOYNTON, BENNY Ben Lee, B, 5´9˝/170 lbs; Williams; B12/6/1898 Waco, TX, D1/23/1963 Dallas, TX **[K]** **1921** Roc 3 (3), 23 **1921** Was☆2 (2, TB), 9 **1922** Roc☆1 (1) **1924** Roc 1 (1) **1924** Buf☆9 (9, BB), 59 **NFL** 16 (16), 91 [3 yrs]

BOYNTON, GEORGE George Douglas, DB, 5´11˝/190 lbs; Eastern New Mexico; Texas A&M-Commerce; 1960: Bal, rnd 16; B7/6/1937 Los Angeles, CA **1962** Oak-A 3

BOYNTON, JOHN John Alden, T, 6´4˝/255 lbs; Tennessee; 1968: Mia, rnd 7; B3/28/1946 Pikeville, TN **1969** Mia-A 14

BRAASE, ORDELL Ordell Wayne, DE, 6´4˝/245 lbs; South Dakota; 1954: Bal, rnd 14; B3/13/1932 Mitchell, SD **1957** Bal 12 **1958**†Bal 12 **1959**†Bal 12 **1960** Bal☆12 (RDE) **1961** Bal 13 (RDE) **1962** Bal 14 (RDE) **1963** Bal 14 (RDE) **1964**†Bal 14 (RDE) **1965**†Bal☆12 (RDE) **1966** Bal★14 (14, RDE) **1967** Bal★14 (RDE) **1968**†Bal 14 (RDE) **NFL** 157 (14) [12 yrs]

BRAATZ, TOM Thomas Myron, LB-E, 6´1˝/216 lbs; Marquette; 1955: Was, rnd 14; B5/12/1933 Kenosha, WI **1958** Was 3 **1958** LARm 1 **1959** Was 12 (RLB) **1960** Dal 12
| 1957 | Was | 10 | — | — | — | — | 2 | 52 | 26.0(37) | 0 | — | — | — | — | — | — | — | — | — | — | — | 0 | 26 |
| NFL | 4 | 38 | — | — | — | — | 2 | 52 | 26.0(37) | 0 | — | — | — | — | — | — | — | — | ki | — | 0 | 30 |

BRABHAM, CARY Cary, DB, 6´0˝/195 lbs; SMU; B8/11/1970 Longview, TX **1994** LARd 7 (0)

BRABHAM, DANNY Daniel Edward, LB, 6´4˝/235 lbs; Arkansas; 1963: Hou, rnd 1/SL, rnd 3; B2/25/1941 Magnolia, MS **1963** Hou-A 14 **1964** Hou-A 13 (LLB) **1965** Hou-A 14 (RLB) **1966** Hou-A 3 **1967** Hou-A 12 **1968** Cin-A 9 **NFL** 65 [6 yrs]

BRACE, BILL George Wells, G-C, 6´0˝/180 lbs; Brown; B11/19/1895 Sheridan, NY, D1/7/1972 Jamestown, NY **1920** Buf 10 (6, LG) **1921** Buf 11 (11, LG) **1922** Buf 10 (7, LG) **NFL** 31 (24) [3 yrs]

BRACELIN, GREG Gregory Lee, LB, 6´1˝/214 lbs; California; 1980: Den, rnd 9; B4/16/1957 Lawrence, KS **1980** Den 12 (0) **1981** Oak 15 (0) **1982** Bal 9 (6, ROLB) **1983** Bal 16 (16, LOLB) **1984** NFL 68 (29) [5 yrs]

BRACKEN, DON Donald Craig, P, 6´1˝/214 lbs; Michigan; B2/16/1962 Coalinga, CA **[P]** **1985** GB 7 (0) **1986** GB 13 (0) **1987** GB 12 (0) **1988** GB 16 (0) **1989** GB 16 (0) **1990** GB 16 (0) **1992** LARm 16 (0) **1993** LARm 3 (0) **NFL** 99 (0) [8 yrs]

BRACKENS, TONY Tony Lynn, DE, 6´4˝/267 lbs; Texas; 1996: Jax, rnd 2; B12/26/1974 Fairfield, TX **[S]** **1996** Jax 16 (1) **1997**†Jax 15 (3) **1998**†Jax 12 (8, rde) **1999**†Jax★16 (15, RDE) **2000** Jax 16 (16, RDE) **2001** Jax 12 (12, RDE) **2002** Jax 5 (5, rde) **2003** Jax 15 (15, LDE) **NFL** 107 (75) [8 yrs]

BRACKETT, GARY Gary, LB, 5´11˝/235 lbs; Rutgers; B5/23/1980 Glassboro, NJ **2003**†Ind 16 (0) **2004**†Ind 15 (1) **2005**†Ind 16 (16, MLB) **NFL** 47 (17) [3 yrs]

BRACKETT, M.L. M.L., DE-DT-LB, 6´5˝/248 lbs; Auburn; 1956: ChiB, rnd 2; B7/4/1933 Elowah County, AL **1956**†ChiB 12 **1957** ChiB 8 **1958**†NYG 12 **NFL** 32 [3 yrs]

BRACKINS, CHARLIE Charles, QB, 6´2˝/202 lbs; Prairie View A&M; 1955: GB, rnd 16; B1/12/1932 Dallas, TX
| 1955 | GB | 7 | — | — | — | — | 2 | 0 | 0.0 | 0 | 0 | 0.0 | 0 | 0 | — | — | — | — | — | — | — | 0 | 0 |

BRADEN, DAVID David Thomas, G-LB, 6´0˝/210 lbs; Marquette; B9/27/1917 Milwaukee, WI, D8/2/1980 Milwaukee, WI **1945** ChiC 1 (0)

BRADFORD, COREY Corey Lamont, WR, 6´1˝/197 lbs; Jackson State; 1998: GB, rnd 5; B12/8/1975 Baton Rouge, LA
1998	†GB	8(0)	—	—	—	—	3	27	9.0(18)	0	—	—	—	—	—	—	—	—	—	k	—	0	17
1999	GB	16(2)	—	—	—	—	37	637	17.2(74)	5	—	—	—	—	—	—	—	—	—	—	—	32	344
2000	GB	2(2)	—	—	—	—	—	—	—	—	—	—	—	—	—	—	—	—	—	—	—	—	—
2001	†GB	16(6, wr)	—	—	—	—	31	526	17.0(56)	2	—	—	—	—	—	—	—	—	—	—	—	12	273
2002	Hou	16(16, WR)	2	-11	-5.5(0)	0	45	697	15.5(81)	6	—	—	—	—	—	—	—	—	—	—	—	36	368
2003	Hou	16(6, wr)	—	—	—	—	24	460	19.2(78)	4	—	—	—	—	—	—	—	—	—	—	—	24	250
2004	Hou	15(10, WR)	—	—	—	—	27	399	14.8(47)	3	—	—	—	—	—	—	—	—	—	—	—	18	215
2005	Hou	16(6, wr)	1	-2	-2.0(-2)	0	34	436	12.8(50)	5	—	—	—	—	—	—	—	—	—	—	—	32	241
NFL	8	105(48)	3	-13	-4.3	0	201	3182	15.8(81)	25	—	—	—	—	—	—	—	—	—	k	—	154	1706

BRADFORD, PAUL Paul, DB, 5´9˝/185 lbs; Portland State; 1997: SD, rnd 5; B4/20/1974 East Palo Alto, CA **1997** SD 15 (4)

BRADFORD, RONNIE Ronnie Lee, DB, 5´10˝/188 lbs; Colorado; 1993: Mia, rnd 4; B10/1/1970 Minot, ND **1993**†Den 10 (3) **1994** Den 12 (1) **1995** Den 4 (0) **1996** Arz 15 (11, RCB) **1997** Atl 16 (15, RCB) **1998**†Atl 14 (10, RCB) **1999** Atl 16 (16, RCB) **2000** Atl 16 (15, FS) **2001** Atl 14 (14, FS) **2002** Min 16 (15, FS) **NFL** 133 (100) [10 yrs]

BRADFUTE, BYRON Byron Gilbert, T, 6´3˝/243 lbs; Southern Mississippi; 1960: LAC, rnd 1; B12/12/1937 Beeville, TX **1960** Dal 12 **1961** Dal 5 **NFL** 17 [2 yrs]

BRADLEY, BILL William Calvin, DB, 5´11˝/190 lbs; Texas; 1969: Phi, rnd 3; B1/24/1947 Palestine, TX **[RI]** **1971** Phi★14 (FS) **1972** Phi★14 (FS) **1974** Phi☆14 (FS) **1975** Phi 14 (FS) **1976** Phi 14 (FS) **1977** SL 4 (1)
1969	Phi	14	1	5	5.0(5)	0	—	—	—	1	0	0.0	0	0	—	—	—	—	Pkpi	1	6	259
1970	Phi	12	1	14	14.0(14)	0	—	—	—	0	0	0.0	0	0	—	—	—	—	P	—	0	14
1973	Phi★	14(FS)	1	0	0.0(0)	0	—	—	—	0	0	0.0	0	0	—	—	—	—	Ppi	—	0	67
NFL	9	114(1)	3	19	6.3(14)	0	—	—	—	1	0	0.0	0	0	—	—	—	—	Pkpi	1	6	897

BRADLEY, CARLOS Carlos Humberto, LB, 6´0˝/224 lbs; Wake Forest; 1981: SD, rnd 11; B4/27/1960 Philadelphia, PA **1981** SD 8 (0) **1982**†SD 9 (0) **1983** SD 16 (0) **1984** SD 8 (1) **1985** SD 10 (2) **1987** Phi 3 (1) **NFL** 54 (4) [6 yrs]

BRADLEY, CHUCK Charles John, TE, 6´6˝/243 lbs; Oregon; 1973: Mia, rnd 2; B10/13/1950 Hinsdale, IL **1977** SD 1 **1977**†ChiB 7
1975	SD	4	—	—	—	—	1	42	42.0(42)	0	—	—	—	—	—	—	—	—	—	—	—	0	21
1976	SD	7	—	—	—	—	1	7	7.0(7)	0	—	—	—	—	—	—	—	—	—	—	—	0	4
NFL	3	19	—	—	—	—	2	49	24.5(42)	0	—	—	—	—	—	—	—	—	—	—	—	0	25

BRADLEY, CHUCK Charles Warren, T, 6´5˝/296 lbs; Kentucky; 1993: Hou, rnd 6; B4/9/1970 Covington, KY **1993** Cin 1 (0)

BRADLEY, DANNY Daniel Louis, RB, 5´9˝/175 lbs; Oklahoma; 1985: LARm, rnd 7; B3/2/1963 Pine Bluff, AR
| 1987 | Det | 3(1) | — | — | — | — | 7 | 50 | 7.1(14) | 2 | — | — | — | — | — | — | — | — | — | kp | — | 12 | 81 |

BRADLEY, DAVE David Earl, G, 6´4˝/245 lbs; Penn State; 1969: GB, rnd 2; B2/13/1947 Burnham, PA **1969** GB 4 **1970** GB 4 **1971** GB 7 **1972** SL 1 **NFL** 16 [4 yrs]

BRADLEY, ED Edward William, G, 6´0˝/212 lbs; Wake Forest; 1950: ChiB, rnd 16; B9/16/1926 Stratford, CT **1950**†ChiB 4 **1952** ChiB 8 **NFL** 12 [2 yrs]

BRADLEY, ED Edward William, LB, 6´2˝/239 lbs; Wake Forest; 1972: Pit, rnd 4; B4/22/1950 Bridgeport, CT **1972**†Pit 12 **1973**†Pit 14 **1974**†Pit 10 **1975**†Pit 13 **1976** Sea 14 (14, MLB) **1977** SF 14 **1978** SF 16 (16, RLB) **NFL** 93 (30) [7 yrs]

BRADLEY, FREDDIE Freddie Lee, RB, 5´10˝/208 lbs; Arkansas; Sonoma State; 1996: SD, rnd 7; B6/12/1970 Helena, AR
| 1996 | SD | 10(1) | 32 | 109 | 3.4(17) | 0 | 1 | 20 | 20.0(20) | 0 | — | — | — | — | — | — | — | — | — | — | — | 0 | 119 |

BRADLEY, HAL Harold Willard, G, /185 lbs; Iowa; B9/27/1905, KS, deceased **1928** ChiC 2 (1)

BRADLEY, HAL Eugene Hal, E, 6´4˝/205 lbs; Elon; B11/23/1913 Winston-Salem, NC, D6/14/1981 Durham, NC
1938	Was	7(1)	—	—	—	—	1	14	14.0(14)	0	—	—	—	—	—	—	—	—	—	—	—	0	7
1939	Was	1(1)	—	—	—	—	—	—	—	—	—	—	—	—	—	—	—	—	—	—	—	—	—
1939	ChiC	3(0)	—	—	—	—	3	29	9.7	0	—	—	—	—	—	—	—	—	—	—	—	0	15
NFL	2	11(1)	—	—	—	—	4	43	10.8(14)	0	—	—	—	—	—	—	—	—	—	—	—	0	22

BRADLEY, HAROLD Harold William, G, 6´2˝/230 lbs; Iowa; B10/13/1929 Chicago, IL **1954**†Cle 12 (RG) **1955**†Cle 11 (RG) **1956** Cle 12 (rg) **1958** Phi 12 (12, LG) **NFL** 47 (12) [4 yrs]

BRADLEY, HENRY Henry Averson, NT-DT, 6´2˝/261 lbs; Alcorn State; 1978: SD, rnd 9; B9/4/1953 St. Joseph, LA **1979** Cle 5 **1980**†Cle 16 (16, NT) **1981** Cle 16 (16, NT) **1982**†Cle 6 (5, NT) **NFL** 43 (37) [4 yrs]

BRADLEY, JON Jon, DT, 6´1˝/302 lbs; Arkansas State; B1/13/1981 Barton, AR **2004** TB 6 (0) **2005** TB 13 (0) **NFL** 19 (0) [2 yrs]

BRADLEY, LUTHER Luther Alexander, DB, 6´2˝/195 lbs; Notre Dame; 1978: Det, rnd 1; B5/7/1955 Florence, SC **1978** Det 16 (16, RCB) **1979** Det 16 (16, RCB) **1980** Det 8 (4) **1981** Det 16 (0) **NFL** 56 (36) [4 yrs]

BRADLEY, MARK Mark, WR, 6´1˝/201 lbs; Oklahoma; 2005: Chi, rnd 2; B1/29/1982 Pine Bluff, AR

YEAR	TEAM	G (GS, POS)	RUSH	YD	AVG (LG)	TD	REC	YD	AVG (LG)	TD	PASS	COMP	PCT	YD	AVG (LG)	TD	INT	SK	YD	QBR	KPR	OTD	PTS	TAY
2005	ChiB	7(4)	—	—	—	—	18	230	12.8(54)	0	—	—	—	—	—	—	—	—	—	—	k	—	0	125

BRADLEY, MELVIN Melvin, LB, 6´2˝/282 lbs; Arkansas; 1999: Arz, rnd 6; B8/15/1976 Barton, AR **1999** Arz 1 (0)

BRADLEY, STEVE Steven, QB, 6´2˝/216 lbs; Valparaiso; Indiana; 1986: Cin, rnd 12; B7/16/1963

YEAR	TEAM	G (GS, POS)	RUSH	YD	AVG (LG)	TD	REC	YD	AVG (LG)	TD	PASS	COMP	PCT	YD	AVG (LG)	TD	INT	SK	YD	QBR	KPR	OTD	PTS	TAY
1987	ChiB	1(1)	1	-3	-3.0(-3)	0	—	—	—	—	18	6	33.3	77	4.3(18)	2	3	3	24	—	—	—	0	-75

BRADSHAW, CHARLIE Charles Marvin, T, 6´6˝/255 lbs; Baylor; 1957: LA, rnd 8; B3/13/1936 Waco, TX, D1/23/2002 Plano, TX **1958** LARm 12 **1959** LARm 12 (RT) **1960** LARm 12 (RT) **1961** Pit 12 (LT) **1962** Pit 14 (LT) **1963** Pit★14 (LT) **1964** Pit★14 (LT) **1965** Pit 14 (LT) **1966** Pit 14 (LT) **1967** Det 14 (RT) **1968** Det 13 (RT) **NFL** 145 [11 yrs]

BRADSHAW, CRAIG William Craig, QB, 6´5˝/215 lbs; Louisiana Tech; Utah State; 1980: Hou, rnd 7; B8/14/1957 Shreveport, LA **1980** Hou 2 (0)

BRADSHAW, JIM James W., WB, 5´6˝/150 lbs; Illinois; UNLV; B6/23/1898 Greene County, MO, D7/6/1987 Monterey, CA **1924** KC 1 (0)

BRADSHAW, JIM James Alfred, DB, 6´2˝/205 lbs; Tennessee-Chattanooga; 1963: Pit, rnd 18/Bos, rnd 20; B1/13/1939 St. Clairsville, OH **1963** Pit 14 **1964** Pit 14 (LS) **1965** Pit 12 (LS) **1966** Pit 9 **1967** Pit 13 **NFL** 62 [5 yrs]

BRADSHAW, MORRIS Morris, WR, 6´1˝/195 lbs; Ohio State; 1974: Oak, rnd 4; B10/19/1952 Highland, IL

YEAR	TEAM	G (GS, POS)	RUSH	YD	AVG (LG)	TD	REC	YD	AVG (LG)	TD	PASS	COMP	PCT	YD	AVG (LG)	TD	INT	SK	YD	QBR	KPR	OTD	PTS	TAY
1974	Oak	12	—	—	—	—	—	—	—	—	—	—	—	—	—	—	—	—	—	—	k	—	0	-15
1975	†Oak	14	1	-5	-5.0(-5)	0	7	180	25.7(48)	4	—	—	—	—	—	—	—	—	—	—	—	—	24	105
1976	†Oak	14	1	4	4.0(4)	0	1	25	25.0(25)	1	—	—	—	—	—	—	—	—	—	—	—	—	6	22
1977	†Oak	14(1)	—	—	—	—	5	90	18.0(28)	0	—	—	—	—	—	—	—	—	—	—	—	—	0	45
1978	Oak	16(14, WR)	1	5	5.0(5)	0	40	552	13.8(44)	2	—	—	—	—	—	—	—	—	—	—	—	—	12	291
1979	Oak	3(3)	—	—	—	—	3	28	9.3(12)	0	—	—	—	—	—	—	—	—	—	—	—	—	0	14
1980	†Oak	16(0)	—	—	—	—	6	132	22.0(45)	1	—	—	—	—	—	—	—	—	—	—	—	—	6	71
1981	Oak	15(8, WR)	—	—	—	—	22	298	13.5(29)	3	—	—	—	—	—	—	—	—	—	—	—	—	18	164
1982	NE	8(5, WR)	—	—	—	—	6	111	18.5(48)	1	—	—	—	—	—	—	—	—	—	—	—	—	6	61
NFL	9	112(31)	3	4	1.3(5)	0	90	1416	15.7(48)	12	—	—	—	—	—	—	—	—	—	—	k	—	72	757

BRADSHAW, TERRY Terry Paxton 'The Blond Bomber', QB, 6´3˝/215 lbs; Louisiana Tech; 1970: Pit, rnd 1; B9/2/1948 Shreveport, LA; HOF 1989

YEAR	TEAM	G (GS, POS)	RUSH	YD	AVG (LG)	TD	REC	YD	AVG (LG)	TD	PASS	COMP	PCT	YD	AVG (LG)	TD	INT	SK	YD	QBR	KPR	OTD	PTS	TAY
1970	Pit	13(8, QB)	32	233	7.3(22)	1	—	—	—	—	218	83	38.1	1410	6.5(**87**)	6	**24**	25	242	30.4	P	—	6	18
1971	Pit	14(13, QB)	53	247	4.7(39)	5	—	—	—	—	373	203	54.4	2259	6.1(49)	13	22	33	287	59.7	—	—	30	612
1972	†Pit	14(14, QB)	58	346	6.0(20)	7	—	—	—	—	308	147	47.7	1887	6.1(78)	12	12	29	237	64.1	—	—	42	940
1973	†Pit	10(9, QB)	34	145	4.3(21)	3	—	—	—	—	180	89	49.4	1183	6.6(67)	10	15	24	186	54.5	—	—	18	217
1974	†Pit	8(7, QB)	34	224	6.6(34)	2	—	—	—	—	148	67	45.3	785	5.3(56)	7	8	10	104	55.2	—	—	12	352
1975	†Pit★	14(14, QB)	35	210	6.0(27)	3	—	—	—	—	286	165	57.7	2055	7.2(59)	18	9	31	290	88.0	—	—	18	998
1976	†Pit	10(8, QB)	31	219	7.1(17)	3	—	—	—	—	192	92	47.9	1177	6.1(50)	10	9	16	164	65.4	—	—	18	528
1977	†Pit	14(14, QB)	31	171	5.5(26)	3	—	—	—	—	314	162	51.6	2523	**8.0**(**65**)	17	19	26	235	71.4	—	—	18	788
1978	†Pit★	16(16, QB)	32	93	2.9(17)	1	0	1	(1)	0	368	207	56.3	2915	**7.9**(**70**)	**28**	20	21	222	**84.7**	—	—	6	901
1979	†Pit★	16(16, QB)	21	83	4.0(28)	0	—	—	—	—	472	259	54.9	3724	7.9(65)	26	25	24	196	77.0	—	—	0	1075
1980	Pit	15(15, QB)	36	111	3.1(18)	2	—	—	—	—	424	218	51.4	3339	7.9(68)	24	22	33	245	75.0	P	—	12	1041
1981	Pit	14(14, QB)	38	162	4.3(16)	2	—	—	—	—	370	201	54.3	2887	7.8(90)	22	14	17	155	83.9	—	—	12	1176
1982	†Pit	9(9, QB)	8	10	1.3(6)	0	—	—	—	—	240	127	52.9	1768	7.4(74)	**17**	11	18	131	81.4	—	—	0	539
1983	Pit	1(1)	1	3	3.0(3)	0	—	—	—	—	8	5	62.5	77	9.6(24)	2	0	—	—	—	—	—	0	52
NFL	14	168(158)	444	2257	5.1(39)	32	0	1	(1)	0	3901	2025	51.9	27989	7.2(90)	212	210	307	2694	70.9	P	—	192	9232

BRADSHAW, WES Wesley Walker, B, 5´8˝/175 lbs; Trinity (TX); Baylor; B11/26/1897 Athens, TX, D4/10/1960 Athens, TX **1924** Rl 7 (3) **1926** Buf 1 (0) **NFL** 8 (3) [2 yrs]

BRADY, DONNY Donald Maynard, DB, 6´2˝/195 lbs; Wisconsin; B11/26/1973 North Bellmore, NY **1995** Cle 2 (0) **1996** Bal 16 (13, RCB) **1997** Bal 16 (5, rcb) **1998** Bal 13 (0) **NFL** 47 (18) [4 yrs]

BRADY, ED Ed John, LB, 6´2˝/238 lbs; Illinois; 1984: LARm, rnd 8; B6/17/1962 Morris, IL **1984**†LARm 16 (0) **1985**†LARm 16 (0) **1986** Cin 16 (0) **1987** Cin 12 (0) **1988**†Cin 16 (0) **1989** Cin 16 (0) **1990**†Cin 16 (0) **1991** Cin 16 (0) **1992** TB 16 (0) **1993** TB 16 (0) **1994** TB 16 (0) **1995** TB 16 (0) **NFL** 188 (0) [12 yrs]

BRADY, JEFF Jeffrey Thomas, LB, 6´1˝/235 lbs; Kentucky; 1991: Pit, rnd 12; B11/9/1968 Cincinnati, OH **1991** Pit 16 (0) **1992** GB 8 (0) **1993** LARm 6 (0) **1993** SD 3 (0) **1994** TB 16 (0) **1995** Min 16 (7, mlb) **1996**†Min 16 (16, MLB) **1997**†Min 15 (14, MLB) **1998** Car 16 (16, LILB) **1999** Ind 3 (0) **NFL** 115 (53) [9 yrs]

BRADY, KERRY Kerry Patrick, K, 6´1˝/205 lbs; Hawaii; B8/27/1963 Vancouver, WA **[K]** **1987** Dal 1 (0) **1988** Ind 2 (0) **1989** Buf 3 (0) **NFL** 6 (0) [3 yrs]

BRADY, KYLE Kyle James, TE, 6´6˝/278 lbs; Penn State; 1995: NYJ, rnd 1; B1/14/1972 New Cumberland, PA

YEAR	TEAM	G (GS, POS)	RUSH	YD	AVG (LG)	TD	REC	YD	AVG (LG)	TD	PASS	COMP	PCT	YD	AVG (LG)	TD	INT	SK	YD	QBR	KPR	OTD	PTS	TAY
1995	NYJ	15(11, TE)	—	—	—	—	26	252	9.7(29)	2	—	—	—	—	—	—	—	—	—	—	k	—	12	131
1996	NYJ	16(16, TE)	—	—	—	—	15	144	9.6(25)	1	—	—	—	—	—	—	—	—	—	—	k	—	8	73
1997	NYJ	16(14, TE)	—	—	—	—	22	238	10.8(24)	2	—	—	—	—	—	—	—	—	—	—	—	—	12	129
1998	†NYJ	16(16, TE)	—	—	—	—	30	315	10.5(35)	5	—	—	—	—	—	—	—	—	—	—	k	—	30	188
1999	†Jax	13(12, TE)	—	—	—	—	32	346	10.8(30)	1	—	—	—	—	—	—	—	—	—	—	—	—	8	178
2000	Jax	16(15, TE)	—	—	—	—	64	729	11.4(36)	3	—	—	—	—	—	—	—	—	—	—	—	—	20	380
2001	Jax	16(16, TE)	—	—	—	—	36	386	10.7(20)	2	—	—	—	—	—	—	—	—	—	—	—	—	12	203
2002	Jax	16(16, TE)	—	—	—	—	43	461	10.7(42)	4	—	—	—	—	—	—	—	—	—	—	—	—	24	251
2003	Jax	16(14, TE)	—	—	—	—	29	281	9.7(26)	1	—	—	—	—	—	—	—	—	—	—	k	—	6	141
2004	Jax	11(8, TE)	—	—	—	—	14	103	7.4(21)	1	—	—	—	—	—	—	—	—	—	—	k	—	6	57
2005	†Jax	16(14, TE)	—	—	—	—	18	157	8.7(33)	1	—	—	—	—	—	—	—	—	—	—	k	—	6	93
NFL	11	167(152)	—	—	—	—	329	3412	10.4(42)	23	—	—	—	—	—	—	—	—	—	—	k	—	144	1821

BRADY, PAT Patrick Thomas, QB-K, 6´1˝/195 lbs; Bradley; Nevada-Reno; 1952: NYG, rnd 13; B9/7/1926 Seattle, WA

YEAR	TEAM	G (GS, POS)	RUSH	YD	AVG (LG)	TD	REC	YD	AVG (LG)	TD	PASS	COMP	PCT	YD	AVG (LG)	TD	INT	SK	YD	QBR	KPR	OTD	PTS	TAY
1952	Pit	12	—	—	—	—	—	—	—	—	3	1	33.3	14	4.7(14)	0	0	—	—	—	P	—	0	7
1953	Pit	12	—	—	—	—	—	—	—	—	1	0	0.0	0	0.0	0	0	—	—	—	P	—	0	0
1954	Pit	12	—	—	—	—	—	—	—	—	—	—	—	—	—	—	—	—	—	—	P	—	0	0
NFL	3	36	—	—	—	—	—	—	—	—	4	1	25.0	14	3.5(14)	0	0	—	—	—	P	—	0	7

BRADY, PHILIP Phillip Alonzo, DB, 6´3˝/210 lbs; Brigham Young; B4/22/1943 Tempe, AZ **1969** Den-A 4

BRADY, RICKEY Rickey Lee, TE, 6´4˝/246 lbs; Oklahoma; 1994: LARm, rnd 6; B11/19/1970 Oklahoma City, OK **1994** LARm 1 (0)

BRADY, TOM Thomas Edward Patrick, QB, 6´4˝/225 lbs; Michigan; 2000: NE, rnd 6; B8/3/1977 San Mateo, CA

YEAR	TEAM	G (GS, POS)	RUSH	YD	AVG (LG)	TD	REC	YD	AVG (LG)	TD	PASS	COMP	PCT	YD	AVG (LG)	TD	INT	SK	YD	QBR	KPR	OTD	PTS	TAY
2000	NE	1(0)	—	—	—	—	—	—	—	—	3	1	33.3	6	2.0(6)	0	0	—	—	—	—	—	0	3
2001	†NE✧	15(14, QB)	36	43	1.2(12)	0	1	23	23.0(23)	0	413	264	63.9	2843	6.9(**91**)	18	12	41	216	86.5	—	—	0	1086
2002	NE	16(16, QB)	42	110	2.6(15)	1	—	—	—	—	601	373	62.1	3764	6.3(49)	**28**	14	31	190	85.7	—	—	6	1582
2003	†NE	16(16, QB)	42	63	1.5(11)	1	—	—	—	—	527	317	60.2	3620	6.9(82)	23	12	32	219	85.9	P	—	6	1518
2004	†NE✧	16(16, QB)	43	28	0.7(10)	0	—	—	—	—	474	288	60.8	3692	7.8(50)	28	14	26	162	92.6	—	—	0	1454
2005	†NE★	16(16, QB)	27	89	3.3(15)	1	—	—	—	—	530	334	63.0	**4110**	7.8(71)	26	14	26	188	92.3	—	—	6	1724
NFL	6	80(78)	190	333	1.8(15)	3	1	23	23.0(23)	0	2548	1577	61.9	18035	7.1(91)	123	66	156	975	88.5	P	—	18	7367

BRAGG, MIKE Michael Edward, P, 5´11˝/186 lbs; Richmond; 1968: Was, rnd 5; B9/26/1946 Richmond, VA **[KP]** **1971**†Was 14 **1972**†Was 14 **1973**†Was 14 **1974**†Was 14 **1975** Was 14 **1976**†Was 14 **1977** Was 14 **1979** Was 16 **1980** Bal 16 (0)

YEAR	TEAM	G (GS, POS)	RUSH	YD	AVG (LG)	TD	REC	YD	AVG (LG)	TD	PASS	COMP	PCT	YD	AVG (LG)	TD	INT	SK	YD	QBR	KPR	OTD	PTS	TAY
1968	Was	14	1	-3	-3.0(-3)	0	—	—	—	—	—	—	—	—	—	—	—	—	—	—	P	—	0	-3
1969	Was	14	1	3	3.0(3)	0	—	—	—	—	—	—	—	—	—	—	—	—	—	—	P	—	0	3
1970	Was	14	2	25	12.5(40)	0	—	—	—	—	1	0	0.0	0	0.0	0	0	—	—	—	P	—	0	25
1978	Was	16	—	—	—	—	—	—	—	—	2	2	100.0	69	34.5(56)	0	0	—	—	—	P	—	0	35
NFL	13	188	4	25	6.3(40)	0	—	—	—	—	3	2	66.7	69	23.0(56)	0	0	—	—	—	KP	—	10	60

BRAGGS, BYRON Byron Charles, DE, 6´4˝/290 lbs; Alabama; 1981: GB, rnd 5; B10/10/1959 Montgomery, AL **1981** GB 16 (0) **1982**†GB 9 (0) **1983** GB 16 (14, LDE) **1984** TB 14 (0) **NFL** 55 (14) [4 yrs]

YEAR	TEAM	G(GS, POS)	RUSH	YD	AVG(LG)	TD	REC	YD	AVG(LG)	TD	PASS	COMP	PCT	YD	AVG(LG)	TD	INT	SK	YD	QBR	KPR	OTD	PTS	TAY

BRAGGS, STEPHEN Stephen, DB, 5´9˝/178 lbs; Texas; 1987: Cle, rnd 6; B8/29/1965 Houston, TX **1987**†Cle 12 (0) **1988**†Cle 16 (1) **1989** Cle 7 (0) **1990** Cle 15 (2) **1991** Cle 16 (10, rcb) **1992**†Mia 6 (0) **1993** Mia 11 (5, fs) **NFL** 83 (18) [7 yrs]

BRAGONIER, DENNIS Dennis John, DB, 6´0˝/186 lbs; Stanford; B Hayward, CA **1974** SF 2

BRAHAM, RICH Richard Lee, C-G, 6´4˝/305 lbs; West Virginia; 1994: Arz, rnd 3; B11/6/1970 Morgantown, WV **1994** Cin 3 (0) **1996** Cin 16 (16, LG) **1997** Cin 16 (16, LG) **1998** Cin 12 (12, LG) **1999** Cin 16 (16, C) **2000** Cin 9 (9, C) **2001** Cin 16 (16, C) **2002** Cin 15 (15, C) **2003** Cin 16 (15, C) **2004** Cin 10 (10, C) **2005**†Cin 15 (15, C) **NFL** 144 (140) [11 yrs]

BRAHANEY, TOM Thomas Frank, C, 6´2˝/245 lbs; Oklahoma; 1973: SL, rnd 5; B10/23/1951 Midland, TX **1973** SL 14 **1974**†SL 14 (13, C) **1975**†SL 14 (2) **1976** SL 14 **1977** SL 14 **1978** SL 16 **1979** SL 16 (4) **1980** SL 16 (16, C) **1981** SL 16 (14, C) **NFL** 134 (49) [9 yrs]

BRAHM, LARRY Lawrence, G, 5´10˝/204 lbs; Temple; B8/12/1916 Bayonne, NJ, D6/16/1959 Yonkers, NY **1942** Cle 10 (0)

BRAIDWOOD, CHUCK Charles G., E, 6´0˝/199 lbs; Loyola (IL); Tennessee-Chattanooga; B10/15/1903, D1/8/1945 South Pacific **1930** Por 10 (2) **1931** Cle☆8 (8, RE) **1932** ChiC 1 (0)

YEAR	TEAM	G(GS, POS)	RUSH	YD	AVG(LG)	TD	REC	YD	AVG(LG)	TD	PASS	COMP	PCT	YD	AVG(LG)	TD	INT	SK	YD	QBR	KPR	OTD	PTS	TAY
1933	Cin	6(2)	—	—	—	—	2	29	14.5	0	—	—	—	—	—	—	—	—	—	—	—	—	0	15
NFL	4	25(12)	—	—	—	—	2	29	14.5	0	—	—	—	—	—	—	—	—	—	—	—	—	0	15

BRAMAN, ART Arthur H., T, 5´11˝/215 lbs; Yale; B8/4/1897 Torrington, CT, D8/12/1967 Carmel Highlands, CA **1922** Rac 8 (8, LT) **1923** Rac 6 (5, LT) **NFL** 14 (13) [2 yrs]

BRAMLETT, DON Donald Kirk, DT, 6´2˝/270 lbs; Memphis; B10/5/1962 Memphis, TN **1987** Min 3 (1)

BRAMLETT, JOHN John Cameron, LB, 6´1˝/220 lbs; Memphis; B7/7/1941 Memphis, TN **1965** Den-A☆14 (RLB) **1966** Den-A★14 (RLB) **1967** Mia-A✧14 (10, RLB) **1968** Mia-A 13 (10, RLB) **1969** Bos-A 12 (12, RLB) **1970** Bos 12 (11, RLB) **1971** Atl 7 **NFL** 86 (43) [7 yrs]

BRAMMER, MARK Mark Dewitt, TE, 6´3˝/238 lbs; Michigan State; 1980: Buf, rnd 3; B5/3/1958 Traverse City, MI

YEAR	TEAM	G(GS, POS)	RUSH	YD	AVG(LG)	TD	REC	YD	AVG(LG)	TD	PASS	COMP	PCT	YD	AVG(LG)	TD	INT	SK	YD	QBR	KPR	OTD	PTS	TAY
1980	†Buf	16(5, te)	1	8	8.0(8)	0	26	283	10.9(36)	4	—	—	—	—	—	—	—	—	—	—	—	—	24	170
1981	†Buf	16(16, TE)	2	17	8.5(11)	0	33	365	11.1(24)	2	—	—	—	—	—	—	—	—	—	—	—	—	12	210
1982	Buf	9(9, TE)	—	—	—	—	25	225	9.0(22)	2	—	—	—	—	—	—	—	—	—	—	—	—	12	123
1983	Buf	12(12, TE)	—	—	—	—	25	215	8.6(21)	2	—	—	—	—	—	—	—	—	—	—	—	—	12	118
1984	Buf	12(1)	—	—	—	—	7	49	7.0(12)	0	—	—	—	—	—	—	—	—	—	—	—	—	0	25
NFL	5	65(43)	3	25	8.3(11)	0	116	1137	9.8(36)	10	—	—	—	—	—	—	—	—	—	—	—	—	60	644

BRANCATO, GEORGE George, HB-DB, 5´9˝/177 lbs; LSU; B5/27/1931 Brooklyn, NY

YEAR	TEAM	G(GS, POS)	RUSH	YD	AVG(LG)	TD	REC	YD	AVG(LG)	TD	PASS	COMP	PCT	YD	AVG(LG)	TD	INT	SK	YD	QBR	KPR	OTD	PTS	TAY
1954	ChiC	5	2	26	13.0(18)	0	3	28	9.3(22)	0	—	—	—	—	—	—	—	—	—	—	—	—	0	40

BRANCH, BRUCE Bruce Lamont, DB, 5´11˝/189 lbs; Penn State; B9/14/1978 Queens, NY **2002** Was 1 (0)

BRANCH, CALVIN Calvin Stanley, DB, 5´11˝/195 lbs; Iowa State; Colorado State; 1997: Oak, rnd 6; B5/8/1974 Versailles, KY **1997** Oak 6 (0) **1998** Oak 16 (0) **1999** Oak 16 (1) **2000**†Oak 16 (0) **2005** Oak 6 (0) **NFL** 60 (1) [5 yrs]

BRANCH, CLIFF Clifford, WR, 5´11˝/170 lbs; Colorado; 1972: Oak, rnd 4; B8/1/1948 Houston, TX

YEAR	TEAM	G(GS, POS)	RUSH	YD	AVG(LG)	TD	REC	YD	AVG(LG)	TD	PASS	COMP	PCT	YD	AVG(LG)	TD	INT	SK	YD	QBR	KPR	OTD	PTS	TAY
1972	†Oak	14(1)	1	5	5.0(5)	0	3	41	13.7(19)	0	—	—	—	—	—	—	—	—	—	—	kp	—	0	43
1973	†Oak	13	—	—	—	—	19	290	15.3(54)	3	—	—	—	—	—	—	—	—	—	—	—	—	18	160
1974	†Oak★	14(14, WR)	—	—	—	—	60	**1092**	18.2(67)	**13**	—	—	—	—	—	—	—	—	—	—	—	—	78	611
1975	†Oak★	14(14, WR)	2	18	9.0(15)	0	51	893	17.5(53)	9	—	—	—	—	—	—	—	—	—	—	—	—	54	510
1976	†Oak★	14(WR)	3	12	4.0(10)	0	46	1111	24.2(**88**)	**12**	—	—	—	—	—	—	—	—	—	—	—	—	72	628
1977	†Oak★	13(13, WR)	—	—	—	—	33	540	16.4(43)	6	—	—	—	—	—	—	—	—	—	—	—	—	36	300
1978	Oak	16(16, WR)	—	—	—	—	49	709	14.5(41)	1	—	—	—	—	—	—	—	—	—	—	—	—	6	360
1979	Oak	14(13, WR)	1	4	4.0(4)	0	59	844	14.3(66)	6	—	—	—	—	—	—	—	—	—	—	—	—	36	456
1980	†Oak	16(15, WR)	1	1	1.0(1)	0	44	858	19.5(**86**)	7	—	—	—	—	—	—	—	—	—	—	—	—	42	465
1981	Oak	16(15, WR)	—	—	—	—	41	635	15.5(53)	1	—	—	—	—	—	—	—	—	—	—	—	—	6	323
1982	†LARd	9(9, WR)	2	10	5.0(7)	0	30	575	19.2(51)	4	—	—	—	—	—	—	—	—	—	—	—	—	24	318
1983	†LARd	12(12, WR)	1	20	20.0(20)	0	39	696	17.8(**99**)	5	—	—	—	—	—	—	—	—	—	—	—	—	30	393
1984	†LARd	14(14, WR)	—	—	—	—	27	401	14.9(47)	0	—	—	—	—	—	—	—	—	—	—	—	—	0	201
1985	LARd	4(0)	—	—	—	—	—	—	—	—	—	—	—	—	—	—	—	—	—	—	—	—	—	—
NFL	14	183(136)	11	70	6.4(20)	0	501	8685	17.3(99)	67	—	—	—	—	—	—	—	—	—	—	kp	—	402	4765

BRANCH, COLIN Colin Leander, DB, 6´0˝/203 lbs; Stanford; 2003: Car, rnd 4; B3/2/1980 Cincinnati, OH **2003**†Car 16 (0) **2004** Car 16 (15, FS) **NFL** 32 (15) [2 yrs]

BRANCH, DEION Anthony, WR, 5´9˝/193 lbs; Louisville; 2002: NE, rnd 2; B7/18/1979 Albany, GA

YEAR	TEAM	G(GS, POS)	RUSH	YD	AVG(LG)	TD	REC	YD	AVG(LG)	TD	PASS	COMP	PCT	YD	AVG(LG)	TD	INT	SK	YD	QBR	KPR	OTD	PTS	TAY
2002	NE	13(7, wr)	2	0	0.0(4)	0	43	489	11.4(49)	2	—	—	—	—	—	—	—	—	—	—	kp	—	12	626
2003	†NE	15(12, WR)	1	11	11.0(11)	0	57	803	14.1(66)	3	—	—	—	—	—	—	—	—	—	—	p	—	18	434
2004	†NE	9(9, WR)	—	—	—	—	35	454	13.0(26)	4	—	—	—	—	—	—	—	—	—	—	p	—	24	242
2005	†NE	16(15, WR)	—	—	—	—	78	998	12.8(51)	5	—	—	—	—	—	—	—	—	—	—	—	—	30	524
NFL	4	53(43)	3	11	3.7(11)	0	213	2744	12.9(66)	14	—	—	—	—	—	—	—	—	—	—	kp	—	84	1825

BRANCH, MEL Melvin Leroy, DE, 6´2˝/230 lbs; LSU; 1960: Den, rnd 2/SF, rnd 10; B2/15/1937 Leesville, LA **1960** DalT-A☆14 (RDE) **1961** DalT-A✧14 (RDE) **1962**†DalT-A★14 (RDE) **1963** KC-A★14 (RDE) **1964** KC-A 14 (RDE) **1965** KC-A 14 (RDE) **1966** Mia-A 14 **1967** Mia-A 14 (14, RDE) **1968** Mia-A 14 (7, rde) **NFL** 126 (21) [9 yrs]

BRANCH, REGGIE Reginald Elroy, RB, 5´11˝/232 lbs; West Virginia State; East Carolina; B10/22/1962 Sanford, FL **1985** Was 8 (0) **1986**†Was 1 (0) **1988** Was 7 (0) **1989** Was 10 (0)

YEAR	TEAM	G(GS, POS)	RUSH	YD	AVG(LG)	TD	REC	YD	AVG(LG)	TD	PASS	COMP	PCT	YD	AVG(LG)	TD	INT	SK	YD	QBR	KPR	OTD	PTS	TAY
1987	†Was	12(0)	4	9	2.3(3)	1	—	—	—	—	—	—	—	—	—	—	—	—	—	—	k	—	6	20
NFL	5	38(0)	4	9	2.3(3)	1	—	—	—	—	—	—	—	—	—	—	—	—	—	—	k	—	6	11

BRANDAU, ART Arthur Albert, C-G, 6´2˝/210 lbs; Tennessee; 1945: Pit, rnd 10; B6/23/1922 Baltimore, MD, D1/8/2001 Lewes, DE **1945** Pit 1 (0) **1946** Pit 5 (0) **NFL** 6 (0) [2 yrs]

BRANDAU, BUTCH Arthur Frank, B, /192 lbs; none; B12/5/1897, D7/1973 Detroit, MI **1921** Det 4 (2)

BRANDENBURG, DAN Daniel James, LB, 6´2˝/240 lbs; Indiana State; 1996: Buf, rnd 7; B2/16/1973 Rensselaer, IN **1997** Buf 12 (0) **1998**†Buf 16 (1) **1999**†Buf 14 (0) **NFL** 42 (1) [3 yrs]

BRANDES, JOHN John Wesley, TE, 6´2˝/249 lbs; Cameron; B4/2/1964 Fort Riley, KS **1988** Ind 16 (0) **1989** Ind 16 (0) **1990**†Was 16 (0) **1991**†Was 16 (0) **1992** Was 1 (0) **1992** NYG 4 (0) **1993**†SF 9 (0)

YEAR	TEAM	G(GS, POS)	RUSH	YD	AVG(LG)	TD	REC	YD	AVG(LG)	TD	PASS	COMP	PCT	YD	AVG(LG)	TD	INT	SK	YD	QBR	KPR	OTD	PTS	TAY
1987	†Ind	12(2)	—	—	—	—	5	35	7.0(13)	0	—	—	—	—	—	—	—	—	—	—	—	—	0	18
NFL	7	90(2)	—	—	—	—	5	35	7.0(13)	0	—	—	—	—	—	—	—	—	—	—	k	—	0	13

BRANDON, DAVID David Sherrod, LB, 6´4˝/234 lbs; Memphis; 1987: Buf, rnd 3; B2/9/1965 Memphis, TN **1987** SD 8 (1) **1988** SD 8 (1) **1989** SD 13 (0) **1991** Cle 16 (8, llb) **1992** Cle 16 (15, LLB) **1993** Cle 6 (3) **1993** Sea 7 (0) **1994** Sea 13 (0) **1995**†SD 15 (1) **1996** Atl 16 (2) **1997** Atl 4 (4) **NFL** 122 (35) [10 yrs]

BRANDON, MICHAEL Michael Breon, DE, 6´4˝/290 lbs; Florida; 1992: Ind, rnd 12; B7/30/1968 Perry, FL **1993** Ind 15 (0) **1994** Arz 1 (0) **1995**†SF 11 (0) **1996** SF 4 (0) **NFL** 31 (0) [4 yrs]

BRANDON, SAM Samuel Terrill, DB, 6´2˝/200 lbs; UNLV; 2002: Den, rnd 4; B7/5/1979 Toledo, OH **2002** Den 16 (2) **2003**†Den 16 (10, fs) **2004**†Den 9 (0) **2005** Den 14 (0) **NFL** 55 (12) [4 yrs]

BRANDT, DAVID David James, C-G, 6´4˝/309 lbs; Michigan; B9/25/1977 Grand Rapids, MI **2001** Was 13 (1) **2004** SD 3 (0) **NFL** 16 (1) [2 yrs]

BRANDT, JIM James Richard, DB-HB, 6´1˝/205 lbs; St. Thomas; 1951: Pit, rnd 12; B5/19/1929 Fargo, ND

YEAR	TEAM	G(GS, POS)	RUSH	YD	AVG(LG)	TD	REC	YD	AVG(LG)	TD	PASS	COMP	PCT	YD	AVG(LG)	TD	INT	SK	YD	QBR	KPR	OTD	PTS	TAY
1952	Pit	9	—	—	—	—	—	—	—	—	—	—	—	—	—	—	—	—	—	—	k	—	0	9
1953	Pit	12(DB)	42	106	2.5(9)	3	2	15	7.5(11)	0	1	0	0.0	0	0.0	0	0	—	—	—	kp	—	18	193
1954	Pit	12	19	82	4.3(20)	1	1	9	9.0(9)	0	—	—	—	—	—	—	—	—	—	—	—	—	6	97
NFL	3	33	61	188	3.1(20)	4	3	24	8.0(11)	0	1	0	0.0	0	0.0	0	0	—	—	—	kp	—	24	298

BRANEY, SPEED Joseph P., aka Joseph P. Breheney, G-T, 6´0˝/188 lbs; Syracuse; Fordham; B8/29/1892 Johnston, RI, D12/1/1949 Providence, RI **1925** Pro 6 (0) **1926** Pro 7 (4) **NFL** 13 (4) [2 yrs]

BRANNAN, SOLOMON Solomon Embra, DB-HB, 6´1˝/188 lbs; Morris Brown; B9/5/1942 Savannah, GA **1965** KC-A 10 **1966** KC-A 3 **1967** NYJ-A 12 **NFL** 25 [3 yrs]

BRANNON, ROBERT Robert Lee, DE, 6´7˝/245 lbs; Kent State; Arkansas; B3/26/1961 Charleston, SC **1987** Cle 1 (0) **1987** NO 1 (0) **NFL** 2 (0) [1 yr]

BRANON, PHIL Phillip James, T, 6´0˝/200 lbs; Holy Cross; B9/27/1898 Fairbanks, VT, D11/20/1970 Montego Bay, Jamaica **1925** Cle 1 (0)

Branstetter, Kent Kent Wayne, T, 6´3˝/260 lbs; Houston; 1972: NO, rnd 9; B2/3/1949 Galveston, TX **1973** GB 9

Brantley, Chris Christopher Charles, WR, 5´10˝/180 lbs; Rutgers; 1994: LARm, rnd 4; B12/12/1970 Rahway, NJ

YEAR	TEAM	G (GS, POS)	RUSH	YD	AVG (LG)	TD	REC	YD	AVG (LG)	TD	PASS	COMP	PCT	YD	AVG (LG)	TD	INT	SK	YD	QBR	KPR	OTD	PTS	TAY
1994	LARm	13(0)	—	—	—	—	4	29	7.3(10)	0	—	—	—	—	—	—	—	—	—	—	kp	—	0	63
1996	Buf	9(0)	—	—	—	—	5	47	9.4(22)	1	—	—	—	—	—	—	—	—	—	—	—	—	6	29
NFL	2	22(0)	—	—	—	—	9	76	8.4(22)	1	—	—	—	—	—	—	—	—	—	—	kp	—	6	91

Brantley, John John Phillip, LB, 6´2˝/243 lbs; Georgia; 1988: Hou, rnd 12; B10/23/1965 Ocala, FL **1989** Hou 8 (0) **1992**†Was 12 (2) **NFL** 20 (2) [2 yrs]

Brantley, Scot Scot Eugene, LB, 6´1˝/230 lbs; Florida; 1980: TB, rnd 3; B2/24/1958 Chester, SC **1980** TB 16 (0) **1981**†TB 16 (0) **1982**†TB 9 (9, RILB) **1983** TB 16 (15, RILB) **1984** TB 16 (16, RILB) **1985** TB 13 (13, RILB) **1986** TB 16 (16, RILB) **1987** TB 12 (2) **NFL** 114 (71) [8 yrs]

Branton, Gene Rheugene James, WR, 6´4˝/223 lbs; Texas Southern; 1983: TB, rnd 6; B11/23/1960 Tampa, FL **1983** TB 1 (0) **1985** TB 3 (0) **NFL** 4 (0) [2 yrs]

Bratkowski, Zeke° Edmund Raymond, QB, 6´2˝/210 lbs; Georgia; 1953: ChiB, rnd 2; B10/20/1931 Danville, IL

YEAR	TEAM	G (GS, POS)	RUSH	YD	AVG (LG)	TD	REC	YD	AVG (LG)	TD	PASS	COMP	PCT	YD	AVG (LG)	TD	INT	SK	YD	QBR	KPR	OTD	PTS	TAY
1954	ChiB	12(4, qb)	15	35	2.3(19)	1	—	—	—	—	130	67	51.5	1087	8.4(71)	8	17	—	—	60.8	P	—	6	-52
1957	ChiB	12	12	83	6.9(24)	0	—	—	—	—	80	37	46.3	527	6.6(44)	1	9	—	—	—	P	—	0	-9
1958	ChiB	12	3	0	0.0(2)	0	—	—	—	—	90	41	45.6	571	6.3(67)	7	6	—	—	—	P	—	0	81
1959	ChiB	12	7	86	12.3(41)	0	—	—	—	—	62	31	50.0	403	6.5(36)	2	5	—	—	—	—	—	0	98
1960	ChiB	11(qb)	8	20	2.5(10)	0	—	—	—	—	175	87	49.7	1051	6.0(59)	6	21	—	—	40.4	P	—	0	-265
1961	LARm	13(QB)	12	36	3.0(16)	3	—	—	—	—	230	124	53.9	1547	6.7(84)	8	13	—	—	63.1	P	—	18	360
1962	LARm	13(QB)	7	14	2.0(11)	0	—	—	—	—	219	110	50.2	1541	7.0(80)	9	16	—	—	56.5	—	—	0	190
1963	LARm	4	3	-1	-0.3(1)	0	—	—	—	—	82	45	54.9	471	5.7(42)	3	6	—	—	—	—	—	0	10
1963	GB	2	1	-2	-2.0(-2)	0	—	—	—	—	11	4	36.4	96	8.7(64)	1	3	—	—	—	—	—	0	-69
1964	GB	5	2	0	0.0(0)	0	—	—	—	—	36	19	52.8	277	7.7(33)	1	1	5	46	—	—	—	0	104
1965	†GB	6	4	-1	-0.3(1)	0	—	—	—	—	48	21	43.8	348	7.3(80)	3	4	8	79	—	—	—	0	28
1966	†GB	8	4	7	1.8(4)	0	—	—	—	—	64	36	56.3	569	8.9(74)	4	2	5	46	—	—	—	0	232
1967	†GB	6	5	6	1.2(4)	0	—	—	—	—	94	53	56.4	724	7.7(86)	5	9	6	64	—	—	—	0	33
1968	GB	10	8	24	3.0(13)	0	—	—	—	—	126	68	54.0	835	6.6(72)	3	7	11	107	59.5	—	—	0	177
1971	GB	6	1	1	1.0(1)	1	—	—	—	—	37	19	51.4	298	8.1(50)	4	3	1	12	—	—	—	6	60
NFL	14	132(4)	92	308	3.3(41)	5	—	—	—	—	1484	762	51.3	10345	7.0(86)	65	122	36	354	54.3	P	—	30	976

Bratt, Eddie Edwin, E, /190 lbs; none; B3/6/1898 Foreston, MN, D9/23/1970 Minneapolis, MN **1924** Dul 1 (0)

Bratton, Jason Jason Edward, RB, 6´1˝/252 lbs; Grambling State; B10/19/1972 Longview, TX

YEAR	TEAM	G (GS, POS)	RUSH	YD	AVG (LG)	TD	REC	YD	AVG (LG)	TD	PASS	COMP	PCT	YD	AVG (LG)	TD	INT	SK	YD	QBR	KPR	OTD	PTS	TAY
1996	Buf	2(0)	4	8	2.0(5)	0	—	—	—	—	—	—	—	—	—	—	—	—	—	—	—	—	0	8

Bratton, Mel Melvin Torrance, RB, 6´1˝/225 lbs; Miami (FL); 1989: Den, rnd 7; B2/2/1965 Miami, FL

YEAR	TEAM	G (GS, POS)	RUSH	YD	AVG (LG)	TD	REC	YD	AVG (LG)	TD	PASS	COMP	PCT	YD	AVG (LG)	TD	INT	SK	YD	QBR	KPR	OTD	PTS	TAY
1989	†Den	16(3)	30	108	3.6(9)	1	10	69	6.9(17)	3	—	—	—	—	—	—	—	—	—	—	k	—	24	157
1990	Den	16(3)	27	82	3.0(10)	3	29	276	9.5(63)	1	—	—	—	—	—	—	—	—	—	—	k	—	24	247
NFL	2	32(6)	57	190	3.3(10)	4	39	345	8.8(63)	4	—	—	—	—	—	—	—	—	—	—	k	—	48	404

Bratzke, Chad Chad Allen, DE, 6´5˝/270 lbs; Eastern Kentucky; 1994: NYG, rnd 5; B9/15/1971 Waukegan, IL **[S]** **1994** NYG 2 (0) **1995** NYG 6 (0) **1996** NYG 16 (16, RDE) **1997** NYG 10 (10, RDE) **1998** NYG 16 (16, RDE) **1999**†Ind 16 (16, RDE) **2000**†Ind 16 (16, RDE) **2001** Ind 15 (15, RDE) **2002**†Ind 16 (16, LDE) **2003**†Ind 16 (3) **NFL** 129 (108) [10 yrs]

Bravo, Alex Alexander, DB, 6´0˝/190 lbs; Cal Poly-San Luis Obispo; 1954: LA, rnd 9; B7/27/1930 Tucson, AZ **1957** LARm 12 **1958** LARm 3 **1960** Oak-A 14 (LS) **1961** Oak-A 14 (RS) **NFL** 43 [4 yrs]

Bravyak, Jack John, DE, 6´3˝/255 lbs; Temple; B9/10/1959 **1987** Buf 1 (0)

Brawley, Ed Edward Michael, G, 5´9˝/175 lbs; Holy Cross; B7/17/1888 Boston, MA, D5/1/1956 Peabody, MA **1921** NYG 1 (0) **1921** Cle 5 (3) **NFL** 6 (3) [1 yr]

Braxton, David David Harold, LB, 6´2˝/240 lbs; Wake Forest; 1989: Min, rnd 2; B5/25/1965 Omaha, NE **1989**†Min 3 (0) **1990** Min 1 (0) **1990** Phx 11 (0) **1991** Phx 16 (2) **1992** Phx 15 (2) **1993** Phx 16 (0) **1994** Cin 9 (0) **NFL** 71 (4) [6 yrs]

Braxton, Hezekiah Hezekiah Ezekial, FB, 6´2˝/227 lbs; Virginia Union; 1961: SD, rnd 12; B4/11/1936 Baltimore, MD **1963** Buf-A 1

YEAR	TEAM	G (GS, POS)	RUSH	YD	AVG (LG)	TD	REC	YD	AVG (LG)	TD	PASS	COMP	PCT	YD	AVG (LG)	TD	INT	SK	YD	QBR	KPR	OTD	PTS	TAY
1962	SD-A	8	17	35	2.1(15)	1	4	17	4.3(6)	0	—	—	—	—	—	—	—	—	—	—	p	—	8	49
NFL	2	9	17	35	2.1(15)	1	4	17	4.3(6)	0	—	—	—	—	—	—	—	—	—	—	—	—	8	54

Braxton, Jim James Robert, RB, 6´1˝/243 lbs; West Virginia; 1971: Buf, rnd 3; B5/23/1949 Vanderbilt, PA, D7/28/1986 Buffalo, NY

YEAR	TEAM	G (GS, POS)	RUSH	YD	AVG (LG)	TD	REC	YD	AVG (LG)	TD	PASS	COMP	PCT	YD	AVG (LG)	TD	INT	SK	YD	QBR	KPR	OTD	PTS	TAY
1971	Buf	13	21	84	4.0(14)	0	18	141	7.8(25)	0	3	1	33.3	49	16.3(49)	0	0	—	—	—	k	—	0	194
1972	Buf	14(FB)	116	453	3.9(21)	5	24	232	9.7(25)	1	—	—	—	—	—	—	—	—	—	—	k	—	36	621
1973	Buf	6(fb)	108	494	4.6(36)	4	6	101	16.8(37)	0	—	—	—	—	—	—	—	—	—	—	k	—	24	570
1974	†Buf	12(FB)	146	543	3.7(21)	4	18	171	9.5(15)	0	—	—	—	—	—	—	—	—	—	—	—	—	24	669
1975	Buf	14(FB)	186	823	4.4(29)	9	26	282	10.8(32)	4	—	—	—	—	—	—	—	—	—	—	—	—	78	1074
1976	Buf	1	1	0	0.0(0)	0	—	—	—	—	—	—	—	—	—	—	—	—	—	—	—	—	0	0
1977	Buf	14(14, FB)	113	372	3.3(12)	1	43	461	10.7(27)	1	—	—	—	—	—	—	—	—	—	—	—	—	12	618
1978	Buf	6	30	73	2.4(5)	0	5	38	7.6(12)	0	—	—	—	—	—	—	—	—	—	—	—	—	0	92
1978	†Mia	10(2)	20	48	2.4(15)	2	4	47	11.8(19)	0	—	—	—	—	—	—	—	—	—	—	—	—	12	92
NFL	8	90(16)	741	2890	3.9(36)	25	144	1473	10.2(37)	6	3	1	33.3	49	16.3(49)	0	0	—	—	—	k	—	186	3928

Braxton, Tyrone Tyrone Scott, DB, 5´11˝/185 lbs; North Dakota State; 1987: Den, rnd 12; B12/17/1964 Madison, WI **[I]** **1987**†Den 2 (0) **1988** Den 16 (0) **1989**†Den 16 (16, LCB) **1990** Den 3 (2) **1991**†Den 16 (15, LCB) **1992** Den 16 (14, LCB) **1993**†Den 16 (16, LCB) **1994**†Mia 16 (0) **1995** Den 16 (16, SS) **1996**†Den★16 (16, SS) **1997**†Den 16 (16, SS) **1998**†Den 16 (6, ss) **1999** Den 16 (15, SS) **NFL** 181 (132) [13 yrs]

Bray, Maury Andrew Maurice, T, 6´2˝/220 lbs; SMU; B8/27/1909 Paducah, KY, D12/9/1966 Tahoka, TX **1935** Pit 12 (1) **1936** Pit 12 (4) **NFL** 24 (5) [2 yrs]

Bray, Ray Raymond Robert, G-DG, 6´0˝/237 lbs; Western Michigan; North Carolina; 1939: ChiB, rnd 9; B2/1/1917 Caspian, MI, D12/26/1993 Mesa, AZ **1939** ChiB 11 (0) **1940** ChiB✧6 (1) **1941**†ChiB✧11 (7, RG) **1942**†ChiB 11 (10, RG) **1946**†ChiB☆10 (5, rg) **1947** ChiB 12 (8, RG) **1948** ChiB☆12 (10, RG) **1949** ChiB✧12 (11, RG) **1950**†ChiB★12 (RG) **1951** ChiB✧12 (MG) **1952** GB 12 **NFL** 121 (52) [11 yrs]

Brayton, Tyler Tyler, DE, 6´6˝/280 lbs; Colorado; 2003: Oak, rnd 1; B11/20/1979 Richland, WA **2003** Oak 16 (16, RDE) **2004** Oak 15 (15, LDE) **2005** Oak 16 (3) **NFL** 47 (34) [3 yrs]

Brazell, Carl Carl L., B, 5´10˝/195 lbs; Baylor; B7/20/1917, D5/30/1978 Zanesville, OH

YEAR	TEAM	G (GS, POS)	RUSH	YD	AVG (LG)	TD	REC	YD	AVG (LG)	TD	PASS	COMP	PCT	YD	AVG (LG)	TD	INT	SK	YD	QBR	KPR	OTD	PTS	TAY
1938	Cle	11(8, BB)	4	14	3.5	0	7	100	14.3	0	—	—	—	—	—	—	—	—	—	—	—	—	0	64

Braziel, Larry Lawrence, DB, 6´0˝/188 lbs; USC; 1979: Bal, rnd 5; B9/25/1954 Fort Worth, TX **1979** Bal 16 (9, RCB) **1980** Bal 15 (15, RCB) **1981** Bal 16 (16, RCB) **1982**†Cle 6 (0) **1983** Cle 13 (7, LCB) **1984** Cle 13 (1) **1985**†Cle 16 (0) **NFL** 95 (48) [7 yrs]

Brazile, Robert Robert Lorenzo, LB, 6´4˝/241 lbs; Jackson State; 1975: Hou, rnd 1; B2/7/1953 Mobile, AL **1975** Hou☆14 (14, ROLB) **1976** Hou★14 (14, ROLB) **1977** Hou★14 (14, ROLB) **1978**†Hou★16 (16, ROLB) **1979**†Hou★16 (16, ROLB) **1980**†Hou★16 (16, ROLB) **1981** Hou★16 (16, ROLB) **1982** Hou★9 (9, ROLB) **1983** Hou 16 (16, ROLB) **1984** Hou 16 (16, ROLB) **NFL** 147 (147) [10 yrs]

Brazinsky, Sam Samuel Joseph, C, 6´1˝/215 lbs; Villanova; B1/9/1921 Kulpmont, PA, D5/12/2003 Manville, NJ **1946** Buf-A 5 (0)

Brazley, Carl Carl Eugene, DB, 6´0˝/180 lbs; Western Kentucky; B9/5/1957 Louisville, KY **1987** SD 2 (2)

Brazzell, Chris Chris, WR, 6´2˝/193 lbs; Angelo State (TX); B5/22/1976 Alice, TX

YEAR	TEAM	G (GS, POS)	RUSH	YD	AVG (LG)	TD	REC	YD	AVG (LG)	TD	PASS	COMP	PCT	YD	AVG (LG)	TD	INT	SK	YD	QBR	KPR	OTD	PTS	TAY
1999	†Dal	5(0)	—	—	—	—	5	114	22.8(53)	0	—	—	—	—	—	—	—	—	—	—	—	—	0	57
2000	Dal	9(0)	—	—	—	—	2	12	6.0(10)	0	—	—	—	—	—	—	—	—	—	—	—	—	0	6
NFL	2	14(0)	—	—	—	—	7	126	18.0(53)	0	—	—	—	—	—	—	—	—	—	—	—	—	0	63

Breaux, Don Donald Carl, QB, 6´1˝/205 lbs; McNeese State; B8/3/1940 Jennings, LA

YEAR	TEAM	G (GS, POS)	RUSH	YD	AVG (LG)	TD	REC	YD	AVG (LG)	TD	PASS	COMP	PCT	YD	AVG (LG)	TD	INT	SK	YD	QBR	KPR	OTD	PTS	TAY
1963	Den-A	9(qb)	11	50	4.5(15)	0	—	—	—	—	138	70	50.7	935	6.8(71)	7	6	—	—	71.4	—	—	0	313
1965	†SD-A	14	1	-1	-1.0(-1)	0	—	—	—	—	43	22	51.2	404	9.4(66)	2	4	—	—	—	—	—	0	51
NFL	2	23	12	49	4.1(15)	0	—	—	—	—	181	92	50.8	1339	7.4(71)	9	10	—	—	68.8	—	—	0	364

Bredde, Bill William M., DB-HB, 6´1˝/195 lbs; Oklahoma State; 1954: ChiC, rnd 4; B12/31/1932 Yuma, AZ

YEAR	TEAM	G (GS, POS)	RUSH	YD	AVG (LG)	TD	REC	YD	AVG (LG)	TD	PASS	COMP	PCT	YD	AVG (LG)	TD	INT	SK	YD	QBR	KPR	OTD	PTS	TAY
1954	ChiC	12(DB)	13	57	4.4(14)	1	3	44	14.7(27)	0	—	—	—	—	—	—	—	—	—	—	ki	—	6	127

YEAR	TEAM	G(GS, POS)	RUSH	YD	AVG(LG)	TD	REC	YD	AVG(LG)	TD	PASS COMP	PCT	YD	AVG(LG)	TD	INT	SK	YD	QBR	KPR	OTD	PTS	TAY

BREDICE, JOHN John Joseph, E, 6'1"/213 lbs; Boston University; 1956: Phi, rnd 9; B6/23/1934 Waterbury, CT

| 1956 | Phi | 12(RE) | — | — | — | — | 10 | 146 | 14.6(40) | 1 | — | — | — | — | — | — | — | — | — | — | — | 6 | 78 |

BREDING, ED Edward Vincent, LB, 6'4"/235 lbs; Texas A&M; 1967: Was, rnd 15; B11/3/1944 Billings, MT   **1967** Was 14 (5, mlb)   **1968** Was 14 (MLB)   **NFL** 28 (5) [2 yrs]

BREECH, JIM James Thomas, K, 5'6"/161 lbs; California; 1978: Det, rnd 8; B4/11/1956 Sacramento, CA **[K]**   **1979** Oak 16   **1980** Cin 4 (0)   **1981**†Cin 16 (0)   **1982**†Cin 9 (0)   **1983** Cin 16 (0)   **1984** Cin 16 (0)   **1985** Cin 16 (0)   **1986** Cin 16 (0)   **1987** Cin 12 (0)   **1988**†Cin 16 (0)   **1989** Cin 12 (0)   **1990**†Cin 16 (0)   **1991** Cin 16 (0)

| 1992 | Cin | 16(0) | — | — | — | — | — | — | — | — | 1 | 1 | 100.0 | 12 | 12.0(12) | 0 | 0 | — | — | — | K | — | 88 | 6 |
| NFL | 14 | 197 | — | — | — | — | — | — | — | — | 1 | 1 | 100.0 | 12 | 12.0(12) | 0 | 0 | — | — | — | KP | — | 1246 | 6 |

BREEDEN, BILL William John, B, 6'1"/210 lbs; Oklahoma; 1937: Pit, rnd 3; B11/7/1913 Haskell, OK, D12/16/1982 Dallas, TX

| 1937 | Pit | 9(3) | 10 | 25 | 2.5 | 0 | 6 | 59 | 9.8 | 0 | — | — | — | — | — | — | — | — | — | — | — | 0 | 55 |

BREEDEN, LOUIS Louis Everett, DB, 5'11"/185 lbs; North Carolina Central; 1977: Cin, rnd 7; B10/26/1953 Hamlet, NC **[I]**   **1978** Cin 16 (LCB)   **1979** Cin 10 (LCB)   **1980** Cin 16 (5, lcb)   **1981**†Cin 16 (16, LCB)   **1982**†Cin☆6 (6, LCB)   **1983** Cin 14 (13, LCB)   **1984** Cin 16 (15, LCB)   **1985** Cin 16 (16, LCB)   **1986** Cin 16 (16, LCB)   **1987** Cin 8 (2)   **NFL** 134 (89) [10 yrs]

BREEDLOVE, KEVIN Kevin, G-T, 6'3"/315 lbs; Georgia; B6/25/1980 Arlington, TX   **2003** SD 1 (0)

BREEDLOVE, ROD Rodney Winston, LB, 6'2"/230 lbs; Maryland; 1960: SF, rnd 3/LAC, rnd 1; B3/10/1938 Cumberland, MS   **1960** Was 11   **1961** Was 11 (RLB)   **1962** Was★14 (RLB)   **1963** Was 14 (RLB)   **1964** Was 12 (RLB)   **1965** Pit 14   **1966** Pit 11   **1967** Pit 14   **NFL** 101 [8 yrs]

BREEN, ADRIAN Adrian Owen, QB, 6'4"/183 lbs; Morehead State; B1/11/1965 New York, NY

| 1987 | Cin | 2(1) | 6 | 18 | 3.0(9) | 0 | — | — | — | — | 8 | 3 | 37.5 | 9 | 1.1(6) | 1 | 0 | 3 | 18 | — | — | 0 | 28 |

BREEN, GENE Joseph Eugene, LB, 6'2"/230 lbs; Virginia Tech; 1963: GB, rnd 15/SD, rnd 16; B6/21/1941 Crafton, PA   **1964** GB 6   **1965** Pit 14 (RLB)   **1966** Pit 2   **1967**†LARm 7   **1968** LARm 3   **NFL** 32 [5 yrs]

BREES, DREW Drew Christopher, QB, 6'0"/221 lbs; Purdue; 2001: SD, rnd 2; B1/15/1979 Austin, TX

2001	SD	1(0)	2	18	9.0(13)	0	—	—	—	—	27	15	55.6	221	8.2(40)	1	0	2	12	180	—	0	134
2002	SD	16(16, QB)	38	130	3.4(15)	1	—	—	—	—	526	320	60.8	3284	6.2(52)	17	16	24	180	76.9	—	6	1227
2003	SD	11(11, QB)	21	84	4.0(18)	0	1	21	21.0(21)	0	356	205	57.6	2108	5.9(68)	11	15	21	178	67.5	—	6	609
2004	†SD◇	15(15, QB)	53	85	1.6(22)	2	1	38	38.0(38)	0	400	262	65.5	3159	7.9(79)	27	7	18	131	104.8	—	12	1559
2005	SD	16(16, QB)	21	49	2.3(9)	1	—	—	—	—	500	323	64.6	3576	7.2(54)	24	15	27	223	89.2	—	6	1367
NFL	5	59(58)	135	366	2.7(22)	4	2	59	29.5(38)	1	1809	1125	62.2	12348	6.8(79)	80	53	92	724	84.9	—	30	4895

BREGEL, JEFF Jeffrey Bryan, G, 6'4"/280 lbs; USC; 1987: SF, rnd 2; B5/1/1964 Redondo Beach, CA   **1987** SF 5 (0)   **1988** SF 13 (6)   **1989** SF 3 (3)   **NFL** 21 (3) [3 yrs]

BREITENSTEIN, BOB Robert Corr, T-G, 6'3"/265 lbs; Tulsa; 1965: Den, rnd 5/Was, rnd 2; B4/8/1943 Buenos Aires, Argentina   **1965** Den-A 14 (LT)   **1966** Den-A 14 (LT)   **1967** Den-A 2   **1967** Min 11 (7, rt)   **1969** Atl 10   **1970** Atl 7   **NFL** 58 (7) [5 yrs]

BRENKERT, WAYNE Wayne Dewey, B, 5'11"/170 lbs; Washington & Jefferson; B3/5/1898 Highland Park, MI, D8/1/1979 Eustis, FL **[C]**   **1923** Akr 7 (6, TB), 12   **1924** Akr 8 (8, BB), 18   **NFL** 15 (14), 30 [2 yrs]

BRENNAN, BRIAN Brian Michael, WR, 5'9"/178 lbs; Boston College; 1984: Cle, rnd 4; B2/15/1962 Bloomfield, MI

1984	Cle	15(4)	—	—	—	—	35	455	13.0(52)	3	—	—	—	—	—	—	—	—	—	—	p	—	18	317
1985	†Cle	12(10, WR)	—	—	—	—	32	487	15.2(57)	0	1	1	100.0	33	33.0(33)	1	0	—	—	—	p	1	6	333
1986	†Cle	16(0)	—	—	—	—	55	838	15.2(57)	6	1	1	100.0	35	35.0(35)	0	0	—	—	—	—	1	42	467
1987	†Cle	13(1)	—	—	—	—	43	607	14.1(53)	6	—	—	—	—	—	—	—	—	—	—	—	—	36	334
1988	†Cle	16(1)	—	—	—	—	46	579	12.6(33)	1	—	—	—	—	—	—	—	—	—	—	—	—	6	295
1989	†Cle	14(2)	—	—	—	—	28	289	10.3(38)	0	—	—	—	—	—	—	—	—	—	—	—	—	0	145
1990	Cle	16(5, wr)	—	—	—	—	45	568	12.6(28)	2	—	—	—	—	—	—	—	—	—	—	p	—	12	321
1991	Cle	15(3)	—	—	—	—	31	325	10.5(30)	1	—	—	—	—	—	—	—	—	—	—	p	—	6	169
1992	Cin	9(0)	—	—	—	—	16	166	10.4(21)	1	—	—	—	—	—	—	—	—	—	—	—	—	6	88
1992	†SD	6(0)	—	—	—	—	3	22	7.3(12)	0	—	—	—	—	—	—	—	—	—	—	kp	—	0	4
NFL	9	132(26)	—	—	—	—	334	4336	13.0(57)	20	2	2	100.0	68	34.0(35)	1	0	—	—	—	kp	2	132	2470

BRENNAN, JOHN John Carter, G, 6'1"/204 lbs; Michigan; 1939: GB, rnd 19; B9/28/1914 Racine, WI, D3/1975   **1939** GB 2 (0)

BRENNAN, LEO Leo Francis, T, 6'0"/210 lbs; Holy Cross; B9/19/1919 Boston, MA   **1942** Phi 11 (2)

BRENNAN, MATT Matthew William, B, 6'1"/190 lbs; Villanova; Fordham; Lafayette; B10/3/1897 Stamford, CT, D1/3/1963, PA **[K]**   **1925** NYG 6 (3), 3   **1926** Bkn 10 (9, BB), 11   **NFL** 16 (12), 14 [2 yrs]

BRENNAN, MIKE Michael Sean, T, 6'5"/274 lbs; Notre Dame; 1990: Cin, rnd 4; B3/22/1967 Los Angeles, CA   **1990**†Cin 16 (0)   **1991** Cin 3 (0)   **NFL** 19 (0) [2 yrs]

BRENNAN, PHIL Phillip, E, 5'11"/165 lbs; Loyola (IL); B8/20/1902, D9/24/1994 Park Ridge, IL   **1930** Nwk 1 (0)

BRENNAN, WILLIS Willis, G-T, 6'0"/214 lbs; none; B2/12/1893 Chicago, IL, deceased   **1920** ChiC 9 (5, RT)   **1921** ChiC 6 (5, lg)   **1922** ChiC 8 (4)   **1923** ChiC 10 (8, RG)   **1924** ChiC 10 (9, LT), 6   **1925** ChiC 13 (12, RG)   **1926** ChiC☆11 (11, RG)   **1927** ChiC 11 (11, RG)   **NFL** 78 (65) [8 yrs]

BRENNER, AL Allen Ray, DB, 6'1"/200 lbs; Michigan State; 1969: NYG, rnd 7; B11/13/1947 Benton Harbor, MI   **1969** NYG 6   **1970** NYG 1   **NFL** 7 [2 yrs]

BRENNER, HOBY Hoby F.J., TE, 6'4"/240 lbs; USC; 1981: NO, rnd 3; B6/2/1959 Linwood, CA

1981	NO	9(1)	—	—	—	—	7	143	20.4(34)	0	—	—	—	—	—	—	—	—	—	—	—	0	72
1982	NO	8(8, TE)	—	—	—	—	16	171	10.7(25)	0	—	—	—	—	—	—	—	—	—	—	—	0	86
1983	NO	16(16, TE)	—	—	—	—	41	574	14.0(38)	3	—	—	—	—	—	—	—	—	—	—	—	18	302
1984	NO	16(16, TE)	—	—	—	—	28	554	19.8(57)	6	—	—	—	—	—	—	—	—	—	—	—	36	307
1985	NO	16(16, TE)	—	—	—	—	42	652	15.5(30)	3	—	—	—	—	—	—	—	—	—	—	—	18	341
1986	NO	15(12, TE)	—	—	—	—	18	286	15.9(34)	0	—	—	—	—	—	—	—	—	—	—	—	0	143
1987	†NO◇	12(10, TE)	—	—	—	—	20	280	14.0(29)	2	—	—	—	—	—	—	—	—	—	—	—	12	150
1988	NO	10(8, TE)	—	—	—	—	5	67	13.4(24)	0	—	—	—	—	—	—	—	—	—	—	—	0	34
1989	NO	16(16, TE)	—	—	—	—	34	398	11.7(30)	4	—	—	—	—	—	—	—	—	—	—	—	24	219
1990	†NO	16(16, TE)	—	—	—	—	17	213	12.5(31)	2	—	—	—	—	—	—	—	—	—	—	—	12	117
1991	†NO	16(16, TE)	—	—	—	—	16	179	11.2(21)	0	—	—	—	—	—	—	—	—	—	—	—	0	90
1992	†NO	15(13, TE)	—	—	—	—	12	161	13.4(23)	0	—	—	—	—	—	—	—	—	—	—	—	0	81
1993	NO	10(9, TE)	—	—	—	—	11	171	15.5(27)	1	—	—	—	—	—	—	—	—	—	—	—	6	91
NFL	13	175(157)	—	—	—	—	267	3849	14.4(57)	21	—	—	—	—	—	—	—	—	—	—	—	126	2030

BRENNER, RAY Raymond, WB, 5'5"/145 lbs; none; B3/18/1898 East Greenville, OH, D6/14/1975 Massillon, OH   **1925** Can 2 (0)

BRETHAUER, MONTE Monte Leon, DB-E, 6'1"/178 lbs; Oregon; 1953: Bal, rnd 24; B4/8/1931 Portland, OR, D10/14/1994 Portland, OR   **1955** Bal 12

| 1953 | Bal | 12 | — | — | — | — | 10 | 133 | 13.3(25) | 0 | — | — | — | — | — | — | — | — | — | i | — | 0 | 79 |
| NFL | 2 | 24 | — | — | — | — | 10 | 133 | 13.3(25) | 0 | — | — | — | — | — | — | — | — | — | Pi | — | 0 | 79 |

BRETT, JEEP Edwin Darragh, E-DE, 6'2"/205 lbs; Washington State; 1936: ChiC, rnd 4; B3/20/1914 Lewiston, ID, D5/7/1989 Edmonds, WA

1936	ChiC	1(0)	—	—	—	—	—	—	—	—	—	—	—	—	—	—	—	—	—	—	—	—	—
1936	Pit	8(4)	—	—	—	—	7	139	19.9	0	—	—	—	—	—	—	—	—	—	—	—	0	70
1937	Pit	10(7, LE)	—	—	—	—	8	135	16.9	1	—	—	—	—	—	—	—	—	—	—	—	6	73
NFL	2	19(11)	—	—	—	—	15	274	18.3	—	—	—	—	—	—	—	—	—	—	—	—	6	142

BRETTSCHNEIDER, CARL Carl Eugene, LB, 6'1"/223 lbs; Iowa State; B12/2/1931 Dundee, IL   **1956** ChiC 12 (LLB)   **1957** ChiC 12 (LLB)   **1958** ChiC 10 (LLB)   **1959** ChiC 12 (LLB)   **1960** Det 12 (LLB)   **1961** Det 12 (LLB)   **1962** Det☆14 (LLB)   **1963** Det 5   **NFL** 89 [8 yrs]

BREUNIG, BOB Robert Paul, LB, 6'7"/226 lbs; Arizona State; 1975: Dal, rnd 3; B7/4/1953 Inglewood, CA   **1976**†Dal 14 (14, LLB)   **1977**†Dal 14 (14, MLB)   **1978**†Dal 16 (16, MLB)   **1979**†Dal★16 (16, MLB)   **1980**†Dal 16 (16, MLB)   **1981**†Dal 16 (16, MLB)   **1982**†Dal☆9 (9, MLB)   **1983**†Dal☆16 (16, MLB)   **1984** Dal 8 (8, MLB)

| 1975 | †Dal | 10 | — | — | — | — | 1 | 21 | 21.0(21) | 0 | — | — | — | — | — | — | — | — | — | — | k | — | 0 | -7 |
| NFL | 10 | 135(125) | — | — | — | — | 1 | 21 | 21.0(21) | 0 | — | — | — | — | — | — | — | — | — | — | kiS | — | 0 | 9 |

BREW, DORIAN Dorian Culbert, DB, 5'10"/182 lbs; Kansas; 1996: Mia, rnd 3; B7/19/1974 St. Louis, MO   **1996** Bal 7 (0)   **1997** Bal 3 (0)   **1997** SD 6 (0)   **NFL** 16 (0) [2 yrs]

BREWER, BILLY Billy Ervin, DB, 6'0"/190 lbs; Mississippi; 1960: Bos, rnd 2; B10/8/1934 Columbus, MS   **1960** Was 11 (RS)

YEAR	TEAM	G (GS, POS)	RUSH	YD	AVG(LG)	TD	REC	YD	AVG(LG)	TD	PASS	COMP	PCT	YD	AVG(LG)	TD	INT	SK	YD	QBR	KPR	OTD	PTS	TAY

BREWER, CHRIS Christopher, RB, 6´1˝/203 lbs; Arizona; 1984: Den, rnd 9; B1/23/1962 Denver, CO

YEAR	TEAM	G (GS, POS)	RUSH	YD	AVG(LG)	TD	REC	YD	AVG(LG)	TD	…	PTS	TAY
1984	Den	13(0)	10	28	2.8(8)	0	2	20	10.0(16)	0	—	0	38
1987	ChiB	3(1)	24	55	2.3(16)	2	5	56	11.2(19)	1	—	18	108
NFL 2		16(1)	34	83	2.4(16)	2	7	76	10.9(19)	1	—	18	146

BREWER, DEWELL Dewell Lerome, RB, 5´8˝/210 lbs; Oklahoma; B5/22/1970 Lawton, OK **1994** Ind 16 (0)

BREWER, JACK Jack, DB, 6´0˝/190 lbs; SMU; Minnesota; B1/8/1979 Fort Worth, TX **2002** Min 15 (1) **2003** Min 6 (0) **2004** NYG 13 (0) **2005** Phi 6 (0) **NFL** 40 (1) [4 yrs]

BREWER, JOHN John Mills, TB-WB, 6´0˝/185 lbs; Georgia Tech; B4/6/1906 Griffin, GA, D5/2/1980 New Port Richey, FL **1929** Day 6 (3, TB)

BREWER, JOHN John Edward, FB, 6´4˝/230 lbs; Louisville; 1952: Phi, rnd 28; B8/26/1928 Twin Branch, WV, D7/28/1983 Louisville, KY

YEAR	TEAM	G (GS, POS)	RUSH	YD	AVG(LG)	TD	REC	YD	AVG(LG)	TD	…	PTS	TAY
1952	Phi	12(fb)	50	188	3.8(71)	2	5	19	3.8(12)	0	—	12	218
1953	Phi	6	17	85	5.0(19)	1	4	43	10.8(16)	0	—	6	117
NFL 2		18	67	273	4.1(71)	3	9	62	6.9(16)	0	—	18	334

BREWER, JOHNNY Johnny Lee, TE-LB-DE, 6´4˝/230 lbs; Mississippi; 1960: Cle, rnd 4/Oak, rnd 2; B3/8/1937 Vicksburg, MS **1961** Cle 14 **1966** Cle◇14 (RLB) **1967** Cle 14 (RLB)
1968 NO 14 (RLB) **1969** NO 14 (RLB) **1970** NO 9

YEAR	TEAM	G (GS, POS)	RUSH	YD	AVG(LG)	TD	REC	YD	AVG(LG)	TD	…	KPR	OTD	PTS	TAY
1962	Cle	14(TE)	—	—	—	—	22	290	13.2(37)	2	—			12	155
1963	Cle	14(TE)	—	—	—	—	29	454	15.7(55)	0	—			0	227
1964	Cle	14(TE)	—	—	—	—	25	338	13.5(41)	3	—			18	184
1965	Cle	14(TE)	—	—	—	—	13	174	13.4(25)	1	—			6	92
NFL 10		135	—	—	—	—	89	1256	14.1(55)	6	—	ki	1	42	715

BREWER, SEAN Sean, TE, 6´4˝/255 lbs; San Jose State; 2001: Cin, rnd 3; B10/5/1977 Riverside, CA **2002** Cin 3 (2) **2003** Atl 9 (0) **NFL** 12 (2) [2 yrs]

BREWER, UNTZ Edward Brooke, HB, 5´6˝/160 lbs; Maryland; B11/21/1894 Washington, DC, D2/11/1970 Rockville, MD [C] **1922** Akr 8 (4), 6

BREWINGTON, JIM James Wilson, T, 6´6˝/280 lbs; North Carolina Central; 1961: GB, rnd 17; B2/25/1939 Greenville, NC **1961** Oak-A 14

BREWSTER, PETE Darrell Burton, E, 6´3˝/210 lbs; Purdue; 1952: ChiC, rnd 2; B9/1/1930 Adams City, IN

YEAR	TEAM	G (GS, POS)	RUSH	YD	AVG(LG)	TD	REC	YD	AVG(LG)	TD	…	KPR	PTS	TAY
1952	†Cle	12(RE)	—	—	—	—	4	117	29.3(47)	1	—	k	6	60
1953	†Cle	12(12, LE)	—	—	—	—	32	632	19.8(45)	4	—		24	336
1954	†Cle	12(12, LE)	—	—	—	—	42	676	16.1(57)	4	—		24	358
1955	†Cle◇	12(12, LE)	—	—	—	—	34	622	18.3(41)	6	—		36	341
1956	Cle★	12(12, LE)	—	—	—	—	28	417	14.9(41)	1	—		6	214
1957	†Cle☆	12(LE)	—	—	—	—	30	614	20.5(56)	2	—		12	317
1958	†Cle	11(LE)	—	—	—	—	16	294	18.4(38)	1	—		6	152
1959	Pit	9(LE)	—	—	—	—	22	360	16.4(42)	2	—		12	190
1960	Pit	12	—	—	—	—	2	26	13.0(18)	0	—		0	13
NFL 9		104(48)	67	—	—	—	210	3758	17.9(57)	21	—	k	126	1980

BREWSTER, WALT Walter Southgate, T, 6´1˝/195 lbs; West Virginia; B11/11/1907 Lewisburg, WV, D5/1957 **1929** Buf 8 (7, RT)

BREZINA, BOBBY Robert Paul, HB, 6´0˝/200 lbs; Houston; 1963: GB, rnd 20; B4/28/1941 Sinton, TX **1963** Hou-A 1

BREZINA, GREG Gregory, LB, 6´0˝/226 lbs; Houston; 1968: Atl, rnd 11; B1/7/1946 Sinton, TX **1968** Atl 10 (1) **1972** Atl 14 (RLB) **1973** Atl 14 (RLB) **1974** Atl 14 (RLB)
1975 Atl 14 (RLB) **1976** Atl 11 (11, RLB) **1977** Atl 14 (RLB) **1978**†Atl 16 (RLB) **1979** Atl 16 (RLB)

YEAR	TEAM	G (GS, POS)	RUSH	YD	AVG(LG)	TD	REC	YD	AVG(LG)	TD	…	KPR	PTS	TAY
1969	Atl◇	14(RLB)	—	—	—	—	1	9	9.0(9)	0	—	i	0	2
1971	Atl	14(RLB)	—	—	—	—	1	3	3.0(3)	0	—	i	0	9
NFL 11		151(12)	—	—	—	—	2	12	6.0(9)	0	—	i	0	41

BRIAN, BILL William Lawson, T-C-LB, 6´2˝/210 lbs; Gonzaga; B10/12/1912 Lincoln, NE **1936** Phi 11 (3)

YEAR	TEAM	G (GS, POS)	RUSH	YD	AVG(LG)	TD	…	PTS	TAY
1935	Phi	9(5, RT)	1	2	2.0(2)	0	—	0	2
NFL 2		20(8)	1	2	2.0(2)	0	—	0	2

BRIAN, HARRY Harold William, aka Harry Hite, B, 6´0˝/180 lbs; Grove City; B9/25/1896 Lincoln, NE, D3/14/1985 Fort Worth, TX **1926** Har 4 (4), 6

BRIANTE, FRANK Francis Xavier, B, 5´10˝/185 lbs; NYU; B3/5/1905 White Plains, NY, D5/26/1996 White Plains, NY **1929** SI 9 (7, FB), 6 **1930** Nwk 4 (3, FB), 6
NFL 13 (10), 12 [2 yrs]

BRICE, ALUNDIS Alundis Marcell, DB, 5´10˝/178 lbs; Mississippi; 1995: Dal, rnd 4; B5/1/1970 Brookhaven, MA **1995**†Dal 11 (1) **1996** Dal 14 (1) **NFL** 25 (2) [2 yrs]

BRICE, WILL William Jamison, P, 6´4˝/227 lbs; Virginia; B10/24/1974 Lancaster, SC **1997** SL 6 (0) **1999** Cin 11 (0) **NFL** 17 (0) [2 yrs]

BRICK, SHIRLEY Shirley Eclipse, E, 5´8˝/165 lbs; Rice; B6/1898 San Antonio, TX, D1/3/1929 Salamanca, NY **1920** Buf 1 (0)

BRICKLEY, GEORGE George Vincent, B, 5´10˝/190 lbs; Trinity (CT); B7/19/1894 Everett, MA, D2/23/1947 Everett, MA **1920** Cle 5 (4, TB) **1921** NYG 2 (2, TB) **NFL** 7 (6) [2 yrs]

BRIDGES, JEREMY Jeremy, G-T, 6´4˝/301 lbs; Southern Mississippi; 2003: Phi, rnd 6; B4/19/1980 Fort Wayne, IN **2004** Arz 14 (8, rg) **2005** Arz 7 (3) **NFL** 21 (11) [2 yrs]

BRIDGFORD, LANE Lane, B, 5´10˝/180 lbs; Knox; B8/11/1898 Joy, IL, D7/12/1973 Los Angeles, CA **1921** RI 5 (4, TB) **1922** RI 3 (1) **NFL** 8 (5) [2 yrs]

BRIEHL, TOM Thomas Michael, LB, 6´3˝/247 lbs; Stanford; 1985: Hou, rnd 4; B9/8/1962 Phoenix, AZ **1985** Hou 16 (0) **1987** Hou 3 (3) **NFL** 19 (3) [2 yrs]

BRIEN, DOUG Douglas Robert Zachariah, K, 6´0˝/180 lbs; California; 1994: SF, rnd 3; B11/24/1970 Bloomfield, NJ [K] **1994**†SF 16 (0) **1995** SF 6 (0) **1995** NO 8 (0)
1996 NO 16 (0) **1997** NO 16 (0) **1998** NO 16 (0) **1999** NO 16 (0) **2000**†NO 16 (0) **2001** Ind 1 (0) **2001** TB 2 (0) **2002** Min 6 (0) **2003** NYJ 16 (0) **2004**†NYJ 16 (0)
2005 ChiB 3 (0) **NFL** 154 (0) [12 yrs]

BRIGANCE, O.J. Orenthal James, LB, 6´0˝/236 lbs; Rice; B9/29/1969 Houston, TX **1996** Mia 12 (0) **1997**†Mia 16 (0) **1998**†Mia 16 (0) **1999**†Mia 16 (0) **2000**†Bal 16 (0)
2001†SL 8 (0) **2002** NE 1 (0) **2002** SL 13 (0) **NFL** 98 (0) [7 yrs]

BRIGGS, BILL William John, DE, 6´3˝/245 lbs; Iowa; 1966: NYG, rnd 5; B12/25/1943 Sanford, NC **1966** Was 9 **1967** Was 14 **NFL** 23 [2 yrs]

BRIGGS, BOB Robert Louis, FB, 6´1˝/228 lbs; Central Oklahoma; 1965: Was, rnd 10; B1/12/1941 Amarillo, TX

YEAR	TEAM	G (GS, POS)	RUSH	YD	AVG(LG)	TD	REC	YD	AVG(LG)	TD	…	KPR	PTS	TAY
1965	Was	7	6	10	1.7(6)	0	3	40	13.3(31)	0	—	k	0	8

BRIGGS, BOB Robert James, DE-DT, 6´4˝/258 lbs; Heidelberg; 1967: SF, rnd 9; B4/28/1945 Toledo, OH, D5/5/1997 Sanibel Island, FL **1968** SD-A 14 **1969** SD-A 14 (LDE)
1970 SD 10 (LDT) **1971**†Cle 14 **1972**†Cle 13 (RDE) **1973** Cle 12 **1974** KC 7 **NFL** 84 [7 yrs]

BRIGGS, GREGG Gregg, DB, 6´3˝/214 lbs; Arkansas-Pine Bluff; Texas Southern; 1992: Dal, rnd 5; B10/19/1968 Meadville, MS **1995**†Dal 11 (0) **1996** ChiB 14 (0) **1997** Min 14 (0)
1998†Min 0 (0) **NFL** 39 (0) [4 yrs]

BRIGGS, LANCE Lance Marell, LB, 6´1˝/245 lbs; Arizona; 2003: Chi, rnd 3; B11/12/1980 Sacramento, CA **2003** ChiB 16 (13, LLB) **2004** ChiB 16 (16, RLB)
2005†ChiB★16 (16, RLB) **NFL** 48 (45) [3 yrs]

BRIGGS, PAUL Paul Leonard, T, 6´4˝/248 lbs; Colorado; 1944: Det, rnd 7; B4/18/1920 Providence, RI **1948** Det 12 (2)

BRIGGS, WALTER Walter Robert, QB, 6´1˝/205 lbs; Montclair State; B8/6/1965 Elmira, NY

YEAR	TEAM	G (GS, POS)	RUSH	YD	AVG(LG)	TD	REC	YD	AVG	TD	PASS	COMP	PCT	YD	AVG(LG)	TD	INT	SK	…	OTD	PTS	TAY
1987	NYJ	1(0)	1	4	4.0(4)	0	—	—	—	—	2	0	0.0	0	0.0	0	1	—	—	—	0	-36

BRIGHAM, HI Haven Alva, G, 5´11˝/185 lbs; Ohio State; B7/13/1892 Toledo, OH, D10/6/1987 Toledo, OH **1920** Col 3 (1)

BRIGHAM, JEREMY Jeremy Paul, TE, 6´6˝/255 lbs; Washington; 1998: Oak, rnd 5; B3/22/1975 Boston, MA

YEAR	TEAM	G (GS, POS)	RUSH	YD	AVG(LG)	TD	REC	YD	AVG(LG)	TD	…	PTS	TAY
1998	Oak	2(0)	—	—	—	—	—	—	—	—	—	0	—
1999	Oak	16(2)	—	—	—	—	8	108	13.5(29)	0	—	0	54
2000	†Oak	15(3)	—	—	—	—	13	107	8.2(19)	2	—	12	64
2001	†Oak	14(3)	—	—	—	—	12	85	7.1(17)	1	—	6	48
2002	†Oak	0(0)	—	—	—	—	—	—	—	—	—	0	0
NFL 5		47(8)	—	—	—	—	33	300	9.1(29)	3	—	18	165

BRIGHT, ANTHONY Anthony Leonard, WR, 6´1˝/170 lbs; Valencia CC (FL); B3/28/1977 Starke, FL **2002** Car 1 (0)

BRIGHT, GREG Gregory Keith, DB, 6´0˝/208 lbs; Morehead State; 1980: Cin, rnd 9; B8/2/1957 Fort Campbell, KY **1980** Cin 16 (16, SS) **1981** Cin 4 (2) **NFL** 20 (18) [2 yrs]

YEAR	TEAM	G (GS, POS)	RUSH	YD	AVG(LG)	TD	REC	YD	AVG(LG)	TD	PASS COMP	PCT	YD	AVG(LG)	TD	INT	SK	YD	QBR	KPR	OTD	PTS	TAY

BRIGHT, LEON   Leon, RB, 5´9˝/192 lbs; Florida State; B5/19/1955 Starke, FL **[R]**

1981	†NYG	15(1)	51	197	3.9(25)	2	28	291	10.4(36)	0	—	—	—	—	—	—	—	—	—	kp	—	12	619
1982	NYG	8(0)	1	5	5.0(5)	0	2	19	9.5(13)	0	—	—	—	—	—	—	—	—	—	kp	—	0	167
1983	NYG	7(0)	1	2	2.0(2)	0	2	33	16.5(19)	0	—	—	—	—	—	—	—	—	—	kp	—	0	211
1984	TB	12(0)	—	—	—	—	—	—	—	—	—	—	—	—	—	—	—	—	—	kp	—	0	121
1985	TB	8(0)	—	—	—	—	—	—	—	—	—	—	—	—	—	—	—	—	—	kp	—	0	112
NFL	5	50(1)	53	204	3.8(25)	2	32	343	10.7(36)	0	—	—	—	—	—	—	—	—	—	kp	—	12	1229

BRIGHTFUL, LAMONT   Lamont Eugene, DB, 5´10˝/160 lbs; Eastern Washington; 2002: Bal, rnd 6; B1/29/1979 Oak Harbor, WA   **2002** Bal 12 (0)   **2003**†Bal 16 (0)   **2004** Mia 2 (0)
NFL 30 (0) [3 yrs]

BRILL, HAL   Harold Edwin, TB, 5´10˝/175 lbs; Wichita State; B3/26/1914, D9/20/1980 Wichita, KS   **1939** Det 2 (0)

BRILZ, DARRICK   Darrick Joseph, C-G, 6´3˝/287 lbs; Oregon State; B2/14/1964 Richmond, CA   **1987** Was 7 (4)   **1988** SD 14 (0)   **1989** Sea 14 (0)   **1990** Sea 16 (5, lg)
1991 Sea 16 (7, lg)   **1992** Sea 16 (16, RG)   **1993** Sea 16 (16, LG)   **1994** Cin 15 (15, C)   **1995** Cin 16 (16, C)   **1996** Cin 13 (13, C)   **1997** Cin 16 (16, C)   **1998** Cin 16 (16, C)
NFL 175 (124) [12 yrs]

BRIM, JAMES   James Hamilton, WR, 6´3˝/187 lbs; Wake Forest; B2/28/1963 Mount Airy, NC

| 1987 | Min | 3(3) | 2 | 36 | 18.0(38) | 1 | 18 | 282 | 15.7(63) | 2 | — | — | — | — | — | — | — | — | — | — | — | 18 | 197 |

BRIM, MICHAEL   Michael Anthony, DB, 6´0˝/192 lbs; Virginia Union; 1988: Phx, rnd 4; B1/23/1966 Danville, VA, D4/19/2005 Richmond, VA   **1988** Phx 4 (0)   **1989** Det 2 (0)
1989†Min 7 (0)   **1990** Min 16 (3)   **1991**†NYJ 16 (12, LCB)   **1992** NYJ 16 (16, LCB)   **1993** Cin 16 (16, LCB)   **1994** Cin 16 (16, LCB)   **1995** Cin 1 (0)   **NFL** 94 (63) [8 yrs]

BRINDLEY, WALT   Walter C., B, 5´8˝/153 lbs; Drake; B5/24/1895, D8/13/1959   **1921** RI 2 (0)   **1922** RI 3 (1)   **NFL** 5 (1) [2 yrs]

BRINK, LARRY   Lawrence Raymond, DE-E, 6´5˝/236 lbs; Northern Illinois; 1948: LA, rnd 17; B9/12/1923 Milaca, MN   **1949** LARm 11 (1)   **1950**†LARm✧12 (LDE)
1951†LARm★12 (LDE)   **1952** LARm☆12 (LDE)   **1953** LARm☆12 (LDE)   **1954** ChiB 12 (LDE)

| 1948 | LARm | 11(0) | 1 | -3 | -3.0(-3) | 0 | 4 | 36 | 9.0(18) | 0 | — | — | — | — | — | — | — | — | — | — | — | 0 | 15 |
| NFL | 7 | 82(1) | 1 | -3 | -3.0(-3) | 0 | 4 | 36 | 9.0(18) | 0 | — | — | — | — | — | — | — | — | — | i | 1 | 8 | 10 |

BRINKLEY, LESTER   Lester L., DE, 6´6˝/270 lbs; Mississippi; B5/13/1965 Ruleville, MS, D7/11/2002 Houston, TX   **1990** Dal 6 (0)

BRINKMAN, CHARLIE   Charles William, WR, 6´2˝/208 lbs; Louisville; B5/26/1949 Cincinnati, OH   **1972** Cle 1

BRINSON, DANA   Dana Demore, WR, 5´9˝/167 lbs; Nebraska; 1989: SD, rnd 8; B4/10/1965 Valdosta, GA

| 1989 | SD | 10(0) | 17 | 64 | 3.8(9) | 0 | 12 | 71 | 5.9(11) | 0 | — | — | — | — | — | — | — | — | — | p | — | 0 | 157 |

BRINSON, LARRY   Lawrence Sylvester, RB, 6´2˝/214 lbs; Florida; B6/6/1954 Opa-Locka, FL

1977	†Dal	14	8	28	3.5(20)	1	—	—	—	—	—	—	—	—	—	—	—	—	—	k	—	6	192
1978	†Dal	10	18	96	5.3(39)	2	—	—	—	—	—	—	—	—	—	—	—	—	—	k	—	12	119
1979	†Dal	14	14	48	3.4(10)	0	—	—	—	—	—	—	—	—	—	—	—	—	—	k	—	0	41
1980	Sea	7(0)	16	57	3.6(22)	1	1	9	9.0(9)	0	—	—	—	—	—	—	—	—	—	—	—	6	72
NFL	4	45	56	229	4.1(39)	4	1	9	9.0(9)	0	—	—	—	—	—	—	—	—	—	k	—	24	424

BRISBY, VINCENT   Vincent Cole, WR, 6´3˝/190 lbs; Louisiana-Monroe; 1993: NE, rnd 2; B1/25/1971 Houston, TX

1993	NE	16(12, WR)	—	—	—	—	45	626	13.9(39)	2	—	—	—	—	—	—	—	—	—	—	—	12	323
1994	†NE	14(11, WR)	—	—	—	—	58	904	15.6(43)	5	—	—	—	—	—	—	—	—	—	—	—	30	477
1995	NE	16(16, WR)	—	—	—	—	66	974	14.8(72)	3	—	—	—	—	—	—	—	—	—	—	—	18	502
1996	†NE	3(0)	—	—	—	—	—	—	—	—	—	—	—	—	—	—	—	—	—	—	—	—	—
1997	†NE	16(4)	—	—	—	—	23	276	12.0(31)	2	—	—	—	—	—	—	—	—	—	—	—	12	148
1998	NE	6(1)	—	—	—	—	7	96	13.7(27)	2	—	—	—	—	—	—	—	—	—	—	—	12	58
1999	NE	12(1)	—	—	—	—	18	266	14.8(40)	0	—	—	—	—	—	—	—	—	—	—	—	0	133
2000	NYJ	3(1)	—	—	—	—	4	60	15.0(19)	0	—	—	—	—	—	—	—	—	—	—	—	0	30
NFL	8	86(46)	—	—	—	—	221	3202	14.5(72)	14	—	—	—	—	—	—	—	—	—	—	—	84	1671

BRISCOE, MARLIN   Marlin Oliver, WR-QB-FL, 5´11˝/178 lbs; Nebraska-Omaha; 1968: Den, rnd 14; B9/10/1945 Oakland, CA

1968	Den-A	11(QB)	41	308	7.5(34)	3	—	—	—	—	224	93	41.5	1589	7.1(66)	14	13	—	—	62.9	—	—	18	683
1969	Buf-A	13(FL)	—	—	—	—	32	532	16.6(50)	5	1	0	0.0	0	0.0	0	1	—	—	—	—	—	30	251
1970	Buf★	14(WR)	3	19	6.3(11)	0	57	1036	18.2(48)	8	—	—	—	—	—	—	—	—	—	—	—	—	48	577
1971	Buf	14(WR)	—	—	—	—	44	603	13.7(75)	5	2	1	50.0	36	18.0(36)	0	0	—	—	—	—	—	30	345
1972	†Mia	10	—	—	—	—	16	279	17.4(51)	4	3	3	100.0	72	24.0(26)	0	0	—	—	—	k	—	24	181
1973	†Mia	14(14, WR)	2	-5	-2.5(2)	0	30	447	14.9(53)	2	1	0	0.0	0	0.0	0	0	—	—	—	—	—	12	229
1974	Mia	4	1	17	17.0(17)	0	11	132	12.0(20)	1	1	0	0.0	0	0.0	0	0	1	0	—	—	—	6	88
1975	SD	3	—	—	—	—	2	25	12.5(14)	0	—	—	—	—	—	—	—	—	—	—	—	—	0	13
1975	Det	8(7, WR)	2	-3	-1.5(6)	0	22	347	15.8(59)	4	2	0	0.0	0	0.0	0	0	0	0	—	—	—	24	191
1976	†NE	14(5, wr)	—	—	—	—	10	136	13.6(21)	1	0	0	0.0	0	0.0	0	0	1	9	—	—	—	6	73
NFL	9	105(26)	49	336	6.9(34)	3	224	3537	15.8(75)	30	233	97	41.6	1697	7.3(66)	14	14	2	20	62.1	k	—	198	2628

BRISTER, BUBBY   Walter Andrew, QB, 6´3˝/205 lbs; Tulane; Louisiana-Monroe; 1986: Pit, rnd 3; B8/15/1962 Alexandria, LA

1986	Pit	2(2)	6	10	1.7(9)	1	—	—	—	—	60	21	35.0	291	4.8(58)	0	2	6	57	—	—	—	6	86
1987	Pit	2(0)	—	—	—	—	—	—	—	—	12	4	33.3	20	1.7(10)	0	3	2	14	—	—	—	0	-110
1988	Pit	13(13, QB)	45	209	4.6(20)	6	—	—	—	—	370	175	47.3	2634	7.1(**89**)	11	14	36	292	65.3	—	—	36	1081
1989	†Pit	14(14, QB)	27	25	0.9(15)	0	1	-10	-10.0(-10)	0	342	187	54.7	2365	6.9(79)	9	10	45	452	73.1	—	—	0	848
1990	Pit	16(16, QB)	25	64	2.6(11)	0	—	—	—	—	387	223	57.6	2725	7.0(**90**)	20	14	28	213	81.6	—	—	0	967
1991	Pit	8(8, qb)	11	17	1.5(8)	0	—	—	—	—	190	103	54.2	1350	7.1(65)	9	9	15	145	72.9	—	—	0	377
1992	Pit	6(4)	10	16	1.6(8)	0	—	—	—	—	116	63	54.3	719	6.2(42)	2	5	13	88	61.0	—	—	0	186
1993	Phi	10(8, QB)	20	39	2.0(13)	0	—	—	—	—	309	181	58.6	1905	6.2(58)	14	5	19	148	84.9	—	—	0	862
1994	Phi	7(2)	1	7	7.0(7)	0	—	—	—	—	76	51	67.1	507	6.7(53)	2	1	5	39	—	—	—	0	231
1995	NYJ	9(4, qb)	16	18	1.1(7)	0	1	2	2.0(2)	0	170	93	54.7	726	4.3(32)	4	8	16	122	53.7	—	—	0	82
1997	†Den	1(0)	4	2	0.5(2)	0	—	—	—	—	9	6	66.7	48	5.3(15)	0	0	—	—	—	—	—	0	26
1998	†Den	7(4)	19	102	5.4(38)	0	—	—	—	—	131	78	59.5	986	7.5(48)	10	3	7	49	99.0	—	—	6	535
1999	Den	2(0)	2	17	8.5(17)	0	—	—	—	—	20	12	60.0	87	4.3(11)	0	3	—	—	—	—	—	0	-60
2000	†Min	2(0)	5	20	4.0(12)	0	—	—	—	—	20	10	50.0	82	4.1(20)	0	1	1	6	—	—	—	0	21
NFL	14	99(75)	191	546	2.9(38)	8	2	-8	-4.0(2)	0	2212	1207	54.6	14445	6.5(90)	81	78	193	1625	72.3	—	—	48	5130

BRISTER, WILLIE   Willie Jerry, TE, 6´4˝/236 lbs; Southern (LA); 1974: NYJ, rnd 15; B1/28/1952 Tylertown, MS

1974	NYJ	12	—	—	—	—	5	90	18.0(32)	0	—	—	—	—	—	—	—	—	—	—	—	—	0	45
1975	NYJ	12(1)	—	—	—	—	1	3	3.0(3)	0	—	—	—	—	—	—	—	—	—	—	1	6	2
NFL	2	24(1)	—	—	—	—	6	93	15.5(32)	0	—	—	—	—	—	—	—	—	—	—	1	6	47

BRISTOR, JOHN   John Rollins, DB, 6´0˝/188 lbs; California (PA); Waynesburg; B11/25/1955 Waynesburg, PA   **1979** SF 1

BRISTOW, OBIE   Jessie Gordon, B, 6´2˝/210 lbs; Central Oklahoma; Oklahoma; B4/17/1900 Pryor, OK, D12/22/1969 Big Spring, TX   **1925** KC 8 (7, WB)   **1925** Cle 1 (0)
1926 KC 8 (8, TB)   **NFL** 17 (15) [2 yrs]

BRITO, GENE   Genaro Herman, DE-E, 6´1˝/226 lbs; Loyola Marymount; 1951: Was, rnd 17; B10/23/1925 Los Angeles, CA, D6/8/1965 Duarte, CA   **1955** Was★12 (LDE)
1956 Was★12 (LDE)   **1957** Was★12 (LDE)   **1958** Was★12 (LDE)   **1959** LARm 2   **1960** LARm✧11 (LDE)

1951	Was	12(RE)	—	—	—	—	24	313	13.0(38)	0	—	—	—	—	—	—	—	—	—	—	k	—	0	136
1952	Was	12(RE)	—	—	—	—	21	270	12.9(28)	2	—	—	—	—	—	—	—	—	—	—	k	—	12	120
1953	Was✧	12(LDE)	—	—	—	—	2	35	17.5(24)	0	—	—	—	—	—	—	—	—	—	—	k	—	0	9
NFL	9	97	—	—	—	—	47	618	13.1(38)	2	—	—	—	—	—	—	—	—	—	—	ki	—	12	265

BRITT, CHARLEY   Charles William, DB, 6´2˝/180 lbs; Georgia; 1960: LA, rnd 3/Den, rnd 1; B3/20/1938 Augusta, GA, D10/2/1981, GA   **1960** LARm 12 (RCB)   **1961** LARm 11
1962 LARm 11 (RS)   **1963** LARm 10   **1964** Min 5   **NFL** 49 [5 yrs]

YEAR	TEAM	G(GS, POS)	RUSH	YD	AVG(LG)	TD	REC	YD	AVG(LG)	TD	PASS	COMP	PCT	YD	AVG(LG)	TD	INT	SK	YD	QBR	KPR	OTD	PTS	TAY

BRITT, EDDIE Edward Joseph, TB-DB-FB, 6´2˝/205 lbs; Holy Cross; B7/19/1912 Lexington, MA, D11/21/1978 Pelham, NH

1936	†Bos	10(5, TB)	72	180	2.5	0	6	106	17.7	0	44	18	40.9	294	6.7	3	5	—	—	—	—	—	0	195
1937	Was	4(0)	7	21	3.0	0	—	—	—	—	—	—	—	—	—	—	—	—	—	—	—	—	0	21
1938	Bkn	1(0)	—	—	—	—	—	—	—	—	—	—	—	—	—	—	—	—	—	—	—	—		
NFL	3	15(5)	79	201	2.5	0	6	106	17.7	0	44	18	40.9	294	6.7	3	5	—	—	—	—	—	0	216

BRITT, JAMES James Earl, DB, 6´0˝/185 lbs; LSU; 1983: Atl, rnd 2; B9/12/1960 Minden, LA **1983** Atl 14 (8, FS) **1984** Atl 16 (16, RCB) **1985** Atl 2 (2) **1986** Atl 16 (2) **1987** Atl 12 (0) **NFL** 60 (28) [5 yrs]

BRITT, JESSIE Jessie Loftin, WR, 6´4˝/198 lbs; North Carolina A&T; B3/3/1963 Suffolk, VA **1986** Pit 8 (0)

BRITT, MAURICE Maury Lee, E, 6´4˝/210 lbs; Arkansas; 1941: Det, rnd 13; B6/29/1919 Carlisle, AR, D11/26/1995 Little Rock, AR

| 1941 | Det | 9(0) | — | — | — | — | 1 | 45 | 45.0(45) | — | — | — | — | — | — | — | — | — | — | — | — | — | 6 | 28 |

BRITT, OSCAR Oscar Lee, G, 5´11˝/193 lbs; Mississippi; 1943: Was, rnd 14; B6/18/1919 Brookhaven, MS, D12/13/1992 Ontario, CA **1946** Was 1 (0)

BRITT, RALPH James Ralph, TE, 6´3˝/240 lbs; North Carolina State; B3/18/1965 Goldsboro, NC **1987** Pit 3 (0)

BRITT, RANKIN Alton Rankin, E, 6´2˝/205 lbs; Texas A&M; 1939: Phi, rnd 9; B7/3/1913, D1/1979 Waco, TX **1939** Phi 1 (0)

BRITTENUM, JON Jon Roger, QB, 6´0˝/185 lbs; Arkansas; 1966: Mia, rnd R8; B5/27/1944 Brinkley, AR

| 1968 | SD-A | 14 | 2 | -4 | -2.0(0) | 0 | — | — | — | — | 17 | 9 | 52.9 | 125 | 7.4(22) | 1 | 1 | 7 | 63 | — | — | — | 0 | 24 |

BRITTON, EARL Earl Tanner, B, 6´3˝/212 lbs; Illinois; B7/15/1903 Elgin, IL, D10/24/1973 Elgin, IL **[K]** **1925** ChiB 5 (0) **1926** Bkn 3 (2) **1927** Day 8 (7, FB), 3 **1927** Fra 6 (5, fb) **1928** Day 7 (7, FB) **1929** ChiC 2 (1) **NFL** 31 (22) [5 yrs]

BROADHURST, MAX Arthur, T, 6´0˝/220 lbs; none; B8/9/1886, WI, D10/1964, OR **1920** Day 1 (0)

BROADLEY, KARL Karl T., G, 6´4˝/250 lbs; Bethany (WV); B11/10/1895 Fort Worth, TX, D4/13/1967 St. Petersburg, FL **1925** Cle 4 (3)

BROADNAX, JERRY Gerald Lee, TE, 6´2˝/225 lbs; Southern (LA); B8/19/1951 Dallas, TX

| 1974 | Hou | 8 | — | — | — | — | 3 | 69 | 23.0(42) | 0 | — | — | — | — | — | — | — | — | — | — | — | — | 0 | 35 |

BROADSTONE, MARION Marion Glenn, T-G, 6´2˝/210 lbs; Nebraska; B6/24/1906 Pender, NE, D4/10/1972 San Jose, CA **1931** NYG 3 (1)

BROCK, CHARLEY Charles Jacob, C-HB-FB, 6´2˝/207 lbs; Nebraska; 1939: GB, rnd 3; B3/15/1916 Columbus, NE, D5/25/1987 Green Bay, WI **[I]** **1939** GB❖10 (1) **1940** GB★11 (4, C) **1941** GB 11 (3, HB) **1942** GB❖11 (4, fb) **1943** GB☆6 (6, C) **1944** GB☆10 (6, C) **1945** GB☆10 (6, C) **1946** GB❖11 (11, C) **1947** GB 12 (6, C) **NFL** 92 (47) [9 yrs]

BROCK, CLYDE Clyde, T, 6´5˝/268 lbs; Utah State; 1962: Chi, rnd 2/Hou, rnd 8; B8/30/1940 Los Angeles, CA **1962** Dal 14 **1963** Dal 4 **1963** SF 6 **NFL** 24 [2 yrs]

BROCK, DIETER Ralph Dieter, QB, 6´0˝/195 lbs; Jacksonville State; Auburn; B2/12/1951 Birmingham, AL

| 1985 | †LARm | 15(15, QB) | 20 | 38 | 1.9(13) | 0 | — | — | — | — | 365 | 218 | 59.7 | 2658 | 7.3(64) | 16 | 13 | 51 | 351 | 82.0 | — | — | 0 | 927 |

BROCK, FRED Fred, WR, 5´11˝/181 lbs; Southern Mississippi; B11/15/1974 Montgomery, AL

1997	Arz	2(0)	—	—	—	—	1	29	29.0(29)	0	—	—	—	—	—	—	—	—	—	—	—	—	0	15
1998	†Arz	12(0)	—	—	—	—	2	12	6.0(7)	0	—	—	—	—	—	—	—	—	—	—	—	—	0	6
NFL	2	14(0)	—	—	—	—	3	41	13.7(29)	0	—	—	—	—	—	—	—	—	—	—	—	—	0	21

BROCK, LOU James Lewis, B, 6´0˝/195 lbs; Purdue; 1940: GB, rnd 3; B12/9/1917 Stafford, KS, D5/7/1989 Stafford, KS **[K]**

1940	GB	11(4, HB)	18	60	3.3	0	5	97	19.4(33)	0	2	0	0.0	0	0.0	0	0	—	—	Pi	—	0	200	
1941	GB	11(4)	14	44	3.1(14)	0	22	307	14.0(36)	2	—	—	—	—	—	—	—	—	—	Pkpi	—	12	313	
1942	GB	11(4)	95	237	2.5(24)	2	20	139	6.9(29)	1	—	—	—	—	—	—	—	—	—	KPkpi	—	20	444	
1943	GB	10(8, HB)	45	67	1.5(9)	2	4	57	14.3(32)	1	22	9	40.9	274	12.5(86)	3	1	—	—	Pkp	—	18	360	
1944	†GB	5(5, HB)	36	200	5.6(42)	3	4	74	18.5(52)	2	21	5	23.8	94	4.5(48)	2	0	—	—	Pkp	—	30	361	
1945	GB	10(4)	46	196	4.3(28)	3	4	87	21.8(46)	0	22	5	22.7	151	6.9(50)	2	3	—	—	kpi	—	18	267	
NFL	6	58(29)	254	804	3.2(42)	10	59	761	12.9(52)	6	67	19	28.4	519	7.7(86)	7	4	—	—	KPkpi	—	98	1943	

BROCK, LOU Louis Clark, DB, 5´10˝/175 lbs; USC; 1987: SD, rnd 2; B5/8/1964 Chicago, IL **1987** SD 1 (0) **1988** Sea 1 (0) **1988** Det 2 (0) **NFL** 4 (0) [2 yrs]

BROCK, MATT Matthew Lee, DE-DT, 6´5˝/300 lbs; Oregon; 1989: GB, rnd 3; B1/14/1966 Ogden, UT **1989** GB 7 (0) **1990** GB 16 (16, LDE) **1991** GB 16 (16, LDE) **1992** GB 16 (16, LDE) **1993** †GB 16 (13, RDE) **1994** †GB 5 (0) **1995** NYJ 16 (15, RDT) **1996** NYJ 16 (16, RDT) **NFL** 108 (92) [8 yrs]

BROCK, PETE Peter Anthony, C-T-G, 6´5˝/267 lbs; Colorado; 1976: NE, rnd 1; B7/14/1954 Portland, OR **1977** NE 14 (4) **1978** †NE 15 **1979** NE 16 (7, lt) **1980** NE 16 (0) **1981** NE 16 (16, C) **1982** †NE 9 (9, C) **1983** NE 13 (13, C) **1984** NE 12 (12, C) **1985** NE 9 (8, C) **1986** †NE 16 (16, C) **1987** NE 4 (3)

| 1976 | †NE | 14 | — | — | — | — | 1 | 6 | 6.0(6) | 1 | — | — | — | — | — | — | — | — | — | — | — | — | 6 | 8 |
| NFL | 12 | 154(88) | — | — | — | — | 1 | 6 | 6.0(6) | 1 | — | — | — | — | — | — | — | — | — | — | — | — | 6 | 8 |

BROCK, RAHEEM Raheem Fukwan, DE, 6´4˝/274 lbs; Temple; 2002: Phi, rnd 7; B6/10/1978 Newark, NJ **2002** Ind 13 (6, lde) **2003** †Ind 16 (16, LDE) **2004** Ind 16 (16, LDE) **2005** †Ind 16 (16, LDE) **NFL** 61 (54) [4 yrs]

BROCK, STAN Stanley James, T, 6´6˝/295 lbs; Colorado; 1980: NO, rnd 1; B6/8/1953 Portland, OR **1980** NO 16 (12, RT) **1981** NO 16 (16, RT) **1982** NO 9 (9, RT) **1983** NO 16 (16, RT) **1984** NO 14 (14, RT) **1985** NO 16 (16, RT) **1986** NO 16 (16, RT) **1987** †NO 12 (12, RT) **1988** NO 7 (7, RT) **1989** NO 16 (16, RT) **1990** †NO 16 (16, RT) **1991** †NO 16 (16, RT) **1992** †NO 16 (16, RT) **1993** SD 16 (16, RT) **1994** †SD 16 (16, RT) **1995** †SD 9 (9, RT) **NFL** 234 (223) [16 yrs]

BROCK, WILLIE William, C, 6´3˝/250 lbs; Colorado; 1978: KC, rnd 12; B9/20/1955 Portland, OR **1978** Det 4

BROCKERMEYER, BLAKE Blake Weeks, T, 6´4˝/295 lbs; Texas; 1995: Car, rnd 1; B4/11/1973 Fort Worth, TX **1995** Car 16 (16, LT) **1996** †Car 12 (12, LT/rt) **1997** Car 16 (13, LT) **1998** Car 14 (14, LT) **1999** ChiB 15 (14, LT) **2000** ChiB 15 (14, LT) **2001** †ChiB 16 (16, LT) **2002** Den 16 (1) **2003** †Den 16 (2) **NFL** 136 (103) [9 yrs]

BROCKHAUS, JEFF Jeffrey Jerome, K, 6´2˝/218 lbs; Missouri; B4/15/1959 Fort Lauderdale, FL **[K]** **1987** SF 3 (0)

BROCKINGTON, JOHN John Stanley, RB, 6´1˝/225 lbs; Ohio State; 1971: GB, rnd 1; B9/7/1948 Brooklyn, NY

1971	GB★	14(FB)	216	1105	5.1(52)	4	14	98	7.0(29)	1	—	—	—	—	—	—	—	—	—	—	—	—	30	1199
1972	†GB★	14(FB)	274	1027	3.7(30)	8	19	243	12.8(48)	1	—	—	—	—	—	—	—	—	—	—	—	—	54	1234
1973	GB★	14(FB)	265	1144	4.3(53)	3	16	128	8.0(37)	0	1	0	0.0	0	0.0	0	0	—	—	—	—	—	18	1238
1974	GB	14(FB)	266	883	3.3(33)	5	43	314	7.3(29)	0	—	—	—	—	—	—	—	—	—	—	—	—	30	1090
1975	GB	14(FB)	144	434	3.0(19)	7	33	242	7.3(21)	1	—	—	—	—	—	—	—	—	—	—	—	—	48	630
1976	GB	14(9, FB)	117	406	3.5(29)	2	11	49	4.5(20)	0	—	—	—	—	—	—	—	—	—	—	—	—	12	451
1977	GB	1	11	25	2.3(8)	0	2	1	0.5(6)	0	—	—	—	—	—	—	—	—	—	—	—	—	0	26
1977	KC	10(FB)	54	161	3.0(12)	1	19	222	11.7(48)	1	—	—	—	—	—	—	—	—	—	—	—	—	12	287
NFL	7	95(9)	1347	5185	3.8(53)	30	157	1297	8.3(48)	4	1	0	0.0	0	0.0	0	0	—	—	—	—	—	204	6154

BRODA, HAL Harold Albert, E, 6´1˝/180 lbs; Brown; B7/27/1905 Canton, OH, D2/13/1989 Canton, OH **1927** Cle 3 (2)

BRODHEAD, BOB Robert Edgar, QB, 6´2˝/207 lbs; Duke; 1958: Cle, rnd 12; B12/20/1936 Kittanning, PA

| 1960 | Buf-A | 4 | 15 | 100 | 6.7(19) | 0 | — | — | — | — | 25 | 7 | 28.0 | 75 | 3.0(18) | 0 | 3 | — | — | — | — | — | 2 | 18 |

BRODIE, JOHN John Riley, QB, 6´1˝/198 lbs; Stanford; 1957: SF, rnd 1; B8/14/1935 Menlo Park, CA

1957	SF	5	2	0	0.0(0)	0	—	—	—	—	21	11	52.4	160	7.6(28)	2	3	—	—	—	—	—	0	-30
1958	SF	12(qb)	11	-12	-1.1(6)	1	—	—	—	—	172	103	59.9	1224	7.1(61)	6	13	—	—	61.8	—	—	6	120
1959	SF	12	5	6	1.2(6)	0	—	—	—	—	64	30	46.9	354	5.5(34)	2	7	—	—	—	—	—	0	-87
1960	SF	11(8, QB)	18	171	9.5(30)	1	—	—	—	—	207	103	49.8	1111	5.4(65)	6	9	—	—	57.5	—	—	6	407
1961	SF	14(12, QB)	28	90	3.2(29)	1	—	—	—	—	283	155	54.8	2588	9.1(70)	14	12	—	—	84.7	—	—	12	994
1962	SF	14(14, QB)	37	258	7.0(21)	4	—	—	—	—	304	175	57.6	2272	7.5(80)	18	16	—	—	79.0	—	—	24	884
1963	SF	3(3)	7	63	9.0(24)	0	—	—	—	—	61	30	49.2	367	6.0(44)	3	4	—	—	—	—	—	0	102
1964	SF	14(12, QB)	27	135	5.0(38)	2	—	—	—	—	392	193	49.2	2498	6.4(63)	14	16	—	—	64.6	—	—	12	834
1965	SF★	13(13, QB)	15	60	4.0(13)	1	—	—	—	—	391	242	61.9	3112	8.0(59)	30	16	—	—	95.3	—	—	6	1136
1966	SF	14(13, QB)	5	18	3.6(7)	3	—	—	—	—	427	232	54.3	2810	6.6(63)	16	22	—	—	65.8	—	—	18	653
1967	SF	14(10, QB)	20	147	7.3(15)	1	—	—	—	—	349	168	48.1	2013	5.8(63)	11	16	—	—	57.6	—	—	6	579
1968	SF	14(14, QB)	18	71	3.9(15)	1	—	—	—	—	404	234	57.9	3020	7.5(65)	22	21	—	—	78.0	—	—	0	851
1969	SF	13(5, qb)	11	62	5.6(15)	1	—	—	—	—	347	194	55.9	2405	6.9(80)	16	15	16	134	74.9	—	—	0	745

YEAR	TEAM	G(GS, POS)	RUSH	YD	AVG(LG)	TD	REC	YD	AVG(LG)	TD	PASS	COMP	PCT	YD	AVG(LG)	TD	INT	SK	YD	QBR	KPR	OTD	PTS	TAY
1970	†SF★	14(14, QB)	9	29	3.2(12)	2	—	—	—	—	378	223	59.0	2941	7.8(79)	24	10	8	67	93.8	—	—	12	1240
1971	†SF	14(14, QB)	14	45	3.2(12)	3	—	—	—	—	387	208	53.7	2642	6.8(71)	18	24	11	111	65.0	—	—	18	526
1972	†SF	6	3	8	2.7(4)	1	—	—	—	—	110	70	63.6	905	8.2(53)	9	8	8	39	—	—	—	6	196
1973	SF	14(6, QB)	5	16	3.2(14)	1	—	—	—	—	194	98	50.5	1126	5.8(66)	3	12	4	29	47.7	—	—	6	124
NFL	17	201(138)	235	1167	5.0(38)	22	—	—	—	—	4491	2469	55.0	31548	7.0(83)	214	224	47	380	72.3	—	—	132	9271

BRODNAX, J.W.   John Willis, FB, 6′0″/208 lbs; LSU; 1959: Pit, rnd 15; B3/6/1936

| 1960 | Den-A | 14 | 15 | 18 | 1.2(7) | 0 | 5 | 39 | 7.8(42) | 1 | — | — | — | — | — | — | — | — | — | — | k | — | 6 | 85 |

BRODNICKI, CHUCK   Charles T., G, 6′2″/218 lbs; Villanova; B11/2/1908, D8/1986 Chicago, IL   **1934** Bkn 1 (0)

BROHM, JEFF   Jeffrey Scott, QB, 6′1″/205 lbs; Louisville; B4/24/1971 Louisville, KY

1996	†SF	3(0)	16	43	2.7(22)	0	—	—	—	—	34	21	61.8	189	5.6(49)	1	0	2	10	—	—	—	0	143
1997	†SF	5(0)	4	11	2.8(10)	0	—	—	—	—	24	16	66.7	164	6.8(21)	0	1	5	37	—	—	—	0	53
NFL	2	8(0)	20	54	2.7(22)	0	—	—	—	—	58	37	63.8	353	6.1(49)	1	1	7	47	—	—	—	0	196

BROKER, FRED   Frederick, T, 5′9″/175 lbs; Carlisle Indian; B1/17/1893, D12/1971 Park Rapids, MN   **1922** Oor 11 (0)

BRONSON, BEN   Ben, WR, 5′9″/159 lbs; Baylor; B9/9/1972 Jasper, TX   **1995** Ind 9 (0)

BRONSON, JOHN   John, TE, 6′3″/260 lbs; Penn State; B7/8/1982 Kent, WA   **2005** Arz 1 (0)

BRONSON, ZACK   Robert Zack, DB, 6′1″/204 lbs; McNeese State; B1/28/1974 Jasper, TX   **1997**†SF 16 (0)   **1998**†SF 11 (1)   **1999** SF 15 (2)   **2000** SF 9 (7, FS)   **2001**†SF 16 (16, FS)   **2002**†SF 5 (5, fs)   **2003** SF 12 (12, FS)   **NFL** 84 (43) [7 yrs]

BROOKER, TOMMY   William Thomas, E-K, 6′2″/235 lbs; Alabama; 1962: DalT, rnd 17/Was, rnd 16; B10/31/1939 Demopolis, AL [K]   **1964** KC-A◇14   **1965** KC-A 14   **1966** KC-A 4

1962	†DalT-A	14	—	—	—	—	4	138	34.5(92)	3	—	—	—	—	—	—	—	—	—	—	K	—	87	84
1963	KC-A	9	—	—	—	—	2	32	16.0(16)	0	—	—	—	—	—	—	—	—	—	—	K	—	38	16
NFL	5	55	—	—	—	—	6	170	28.3(92)	3	—	—	—	—	—	—	—	—	—	—	K	—	290	100

BROOKING, KEITH   Keith Howard, LB, 6′2″/245 lbs; Georgia Tech; 1998: Atl, rnd 1; B10/30/1975 Senoia, GA   **1998**†Atl 15 (0)   **1999** Atl 13 (13, RLB)   **2000** Atl 5 (5, llb)   **2001** Atl◇16 (16, MLB)   **2002**†Atl◇16 (16, LILB)   **2003** Atl◇16 (16, LILB)   **2004**†Atl◇16 (16, LLB)   **2005** Atl◇16 (16, MLB)   **NFL** 113 (98) [8 yrs]

BROOKINS, JASON   Jason Arnaz, RB, 6′0″/235 lbs; Lane; B1/5/1976 Mexico, MO

| 2001 | †Bal | 12(3, rb) | 151 | 551 | 3.6(25) | 5 | 6 | 45 | 7.5(15) | 0 | — | — | — | — | — | — | — | — | — | — | k | — | 30 | 632 |

BROOKINS, MITCHELL   Mitchell Eugene, WR, 5′11″/196 lbs; Illinois; 1984: Buf, rnd 4; B12/10/1960 Chicago, IL

1984	Buf	16(0)	2	27	13.5(16)	0	18	318	17.7(70)	1	—	—	—	—	—	—	—	—	—	—	—	—	6	191
1985	Buf	5(1)	—	—	—	—	3	71	23.7(46)	0	—	—	—	—	—	—	—	—	—	—	k	—	0	98
NFL	2	21(1)	2	27	13.5(16)	0	21	389	18.5(70)	1	—	—	—	—	—	—	—	—	—	—	k	—	6	289

BROOKS, AARON   Aaron Lafette, QB, 6′4″/205 lbs; Virginia; 1999: GB, rnd 4; B3/24/1976 Newport News, VA

2000	†NO	8(5, qb)	41	170	4.1(29)	2	—	—	—	—	194	113	58.2	1514	7.8(53)	9	6	15	94	—	—	—	12	752
2001	NO	16(16, QB)	80	358	4.5(26)	1	—	—	—	—	558	312	55.9	3832	6.9(63)	26	22	50	330	76.4	—	—	6	1534
2002	NO	16(16, QB)	62	253	4.1(21)	2	—	—	—	—	528	283	53.6	3572	6.8(64)	27	15	36	236	80.1	—	—	16	1594
2003	NO	16(16, QB)	54	175	3.2(15)	2	—	—	—	—	518	306	59.1	3546	6.8(76)	24	8	34	195	88.8	—	—	12	1768
2004	NO	16(16, QB)	58	173	3.0(15)	4	1	1	1.0(1)	0	542	309	57.0	3810	7.0(57)	21	16	41	223	79.5	—	—	24	1584
2005	NO	13(13, QB)	45	281	6.2(22)	2	—	—	—	—	431	240	55.7	2882	6.7(66)	13	17	33	202	70.0	—	—	12	1127
NFL	6	85(82)	340	1410	4.1(29)	13	1	1	1.0(1)	0	2771	1563	56.4	19156	6.9(76)	120	84	209	1280	79.7	—	—	82	8359

BROOKS, AHMAD   Ahmad Drushane, DB, 5′8″/180 lbs; Texas; B3/13/1980 Abilene, TX   **2002** Buf 6 (2)

BROOKS, BARRETT   Barrett Charles, T, 6′4″/312 lbs; Kansas State; 1995: Phi, rnd 2; B5/5/1972 St. Louis, MO   **1995**†Phi 16 (16, LT)   **1996**†Phi 16 (15, LT)   **1997** Phi 16 (14, RT)   **1998** Phi 16 (1)   **1999**†Det 16 (12, RT)   **2000** Det 15 (4)   **2002** GB 2 (0)   **2004** Pit 5 (0)   **2005**†Pit 16 (0)   **NFL** 118 (62) [9 yrs]

BROOKS, BILL   William, WR, 6′0″/188 lbs; Boston University; 1986: ind, rnd 4; B4/6/1964 Boston, MA

1986	Ind	16(12, WR)	4	5	1.3(12)	0	65	1131	17.4(84)	8	—	—	—	—	—	—	—	—	—	kp	—	48	685
1987	†Ind	12(12, WR)	2	-2	-1.0(1)	0	51	722	14.2(52)	3	—	—	—	—	—	—	—	—	—	p	—	18	400
1988	Ind	16(16, WR)	5	62	12.4(38)	0	54	867	16.1(53)	3	—	—	—	—	—	—	—	—	—	p	—	18	511
1989	Ind	16(16, WR)	2	-3	-1.5(0)	0	63	919	14.6(55)	4	—	—	—	—	—	—	—	—	—	—	—	24	477
1990	Ind	16(16, WR)	—	—	—	—	62	823	13.3(75)	5	—	—	—	—	—	—	—	—	—	—	—	30	437
1991	Ind	16(16, WR)	—	—	—	—	72	888	12.3(46)	4	—	—	—	—	—	—	—	—	—	—	—	24	464
1992	Ind	14(10, WR)	2	14	7.0(8)	0	44	468	10.6(29)	1	—	—	—	—	—	—	—	—	—	—	—	6	253
1993	†Buf	16(13, WR)	3	30	10.0(15)	0	60	714	11.9(32)	5	—	—	—	—	—	—	—	—	—	p	—	30	410
1994	Buf	16(9, WR)	—	—	—	—	42	482	11.5(32)	2	—	—	—	—	—	—	—	—	—	—	—	12	251
1995	†Buf	15(10, WR)	3	7	2.3(9)	0	53	763	14.4(51)	11	—	—	—	—	—	—	—	—	—	p	—	66	449
1996	Was	16(2)	—	—	—	—	17	224	13.2(31)	0	—	—	—	—	—	—	—	—	—	—	—	0	112
NFL	11	169(132)	21	113	5.4(38)	0	583	8001	13.7(84)	46	—	—	—	—	—	—	—	—	—	kp	—	276	4447

BROOKS, BILLY   William McKinley, WR, 6′3″/204 lbs; Oklahoma; 1976: Cin, rnd 1; B8/20/1953 Houston, TX

1976	Cin	12(8, WR)	1	-13	-13.0(-13)	0	16	191	11.9(25)	0	—	—	—	—	—	—	—	—	—	—	—	0	83
1977	Cin	14(9, WR)	2	-4	-2.0(4)	0	39	772	19.8(94)	4	—	—	—	—	—	—	—	—	—	—	—	24	402
1978	Cin	15(12, WR)	—	—	—	—	30	506	16.9(45)	2	—	—	—	—	—	—	—	—	—	—	—	12	263
1979	Cin	4(4)	—	—	—	—	8	214	26.8(73)	1	—	—	—	—	—	—	—	—	—	—	—	6	112
1981	SD	7(0)	—	—	—	—	1	21	21.0(21)	0	—	—	—	—	—	—	—	—	—	—	—	0	11
1981	Hou	3(0)	—	—	—	—	2	16	8.0(16)	0	—	—	—	—	—	—	—	—	—	—	—	0	8
NFL	5	55(33)	3	-17	-5.7(4)	0	96	1720	17.9(94)	7	—	—	—	—	—	—	—	—	—	—	—	42	878

BROOKS, BOB   Robert Arthur, FB, 6′0″/215 lbs; Ohio University; 1961: NYT, rnd 21/Det, rnd 9; B5/3/1938

| 1961 | NYT-A | 14 | 15 | 55 | 3.7(9) | 0 | — | — | — | — | — | — | — | — | — | — | — | — | — | — | k | — | 0 | 46 |

BROOKS, BOBBY   Bobby Daniel, DB, 6′1″/195 lbs; Bishop; 1974: NYG, rnd 11; B2/24/1951 Dallas, TX   **1974** NYG 14   **1975** NYG 14 (LCB)   **1976** NYG 4   **NFL** 32 [3 yrs]

BROOKS, BOBBY   Robert, LB, 6′2″/240 lbs; Fresno State; B3/3/1976 Vallejo, CA   **1999** Oak 1 (0)   **2000**†Oak 16 (0)   **2001**†Oak 16 (0)   **2002** Jax 3 (0)   **NFL** 36 [4 yrs]

BROOKS, BUCKY   William Eldridge, DB, 6′0″/192 lbs; North Carolina; 1994: Buf, rnd 2; B1/22/1971 Raleigh, NC   **1994** Buf 3 (0)   **1996**†GB 2 (0)   **1996**†Jax 6 (1)   **1997** Jax 3 (0)   **1997** GB 3 (0)   **1997** KC 3 (0)   **1998** KC 6 (0)   **1998** Oak 6 (0)   **NFL** 32 (1) [4 yrs]

BROOKS, BUD   William, G, 6′0″/210 lbs; Arkansas; 1955: Det, rnd 5; B9/6/1930 Wynne, AR, D4/19/2005 Richmond, VA   **1955** Det 1

BROOKS, CARLOS   Carlos, DB, 6′0″/200 lbs; Bowling Green State; B5/8/1971 Hamilton, OH   **1995** Arz 7 (0)

BROOKS, CHET   Terrance Donnell, DB, 5′11″/191 lbs; Texas A&M; 1988: SF, rnd 11; B1/1/1966 Midland, TX   **1988** SF 10 (0)   **1989**†SF 15 (15, SS)   **1990** SF 8 (8, SS)   **NFL** 33 (23) [3 yrs]

BROOKS, CLIFF   Clifford, DB, 6′1″/190 lbs; Tennessee State; 1972: Cle, rnd 2; B6/21/1949 Pineland, TX   **1972**†Cle 14   **1973** Cle 14 (rcb)   **1974** Cle 13 (rcb)   **1975** Phi 14   **1976** Phi 1   **1976** NYJ 1   **1976** Buf 1   **NFL** 58 [5 yrs]

BROOKS, DERRICK   Derrick Dewan, LB, 6′0″/235 lbs; Florida State; 1995: TB, rnd 1; B4/18/1973 Pensacola, FL [I]   **1995** TB 16 (13, RLB)   **1996** TB 16 (16, RLB)   **1997**†TB★16 (16, RLB)   **1998** TB★16 (16, RLB)   **1999**†TB★16 (16, RLB)   **2000**†TB★16 (16, RLB)   **2001**†TB★16 (16, RLB)   **2002**†TB★16 (16, RLB)   **2003** TB★16 (16, RLB)   **2004** TB★16 (16, RLB)   **2005**†TB★16 (16, RLB)   **NFL** 176 (173) [11 yrs]

BROOKS, ETHAN   Ethan Barbier, T, 6′6″/310 lbs; Williams; 1996: Atl, rnd 7; B4/27/1972 Hartford, CT   **1996** Atl 2 (0)   **1998** SL 15 (0)   **2000** Arz 14 (3)   **2002** Bal 15 (13, RT)   **2003**†Bal 15 (3)   **2004** Bal 14 (7, lt)   **2005** Dal 1 (0)   **NFL** 76 (26) [7 yrs]

BROOKS, GREG   Greg, DB, 5′11″/177 lbs; Southern Mississippi; 2004: Cin, rnd 6; B12/16/1980 Harvey, LA   **2005** Cin 11 (0)

BROOKS, JAMAL   Jamal, LB, 6′2″/240 lbs; Hampton; B11/9/1976 Los Angeles, CA   **2001** Dal 16 (1)

Brooks, James James Robert, RB, 5´10˝/180 lbs; Auburn; 1981: SD, rnd 1; B12/28/1958 Warner Robins, GA **[R]**

YEAR	TEAM	G(GS, POS)	RUSH	YD	AVG(LG)	TD	REC	YD	AVG(LG)	TD	PASS	COMP	PCT	YD	AVG(LG)	TD	INT	SK	YD	QBR	KPR	OTD	PTS	TAY
1981	†SD	14(2)	109	525	4.8(28)	3	46	329	7.2(29)	3	—	—	—	—	—	—	—	—	—	—	kp	—	36	1264
1982	†SD	9(0)	87	430	4.9(48)	6	13	66	5.1(12)	0	—	—	—	—	—	—	—	—	—	—	kp	—	36	855
1983	SD	15(5, rb)	127	516	4.1(61)	3	25	215	8.6(36)	0	—	—	—	—	—	—	—	—	—	—	kp	—	18	828
1984	Cin	15(11, RB)	103	396	3.8(33)	2	34	268	7.9(27)	2	—	—	—	—	—	—	—	—	—	—	k	—	24	599
1985	Cin	16(16, RB)	192	929	4.8(39)	7	55	576	10.5(57)	5	1	1	100.0	8	8.0(8)	1	0	—	—	—	k	—	72	1314
1986	Cin★	16(16, RB)	205	1087	**5.3**(**56**)	5	54	686	12.7(54)	4	1	0	0.0	0	0.0	0	0	—	—	—	—	—	54	1500
1987	Cin	9(7, RB)	94	290	3.1(18)	1	22	272	12.4(46)	2	—	—	—	—	—	—	—	—	—	—	k	—	18	458
1988	†Cin★	15(15, RB)	182	931	5.1(51)	8	29	287	9.9(28)	6	—	—	—	—	—	—	—	—	—	—	k	—	84	1164
1989	Cin★	16(14, RB)	221	1239	**5.6**(**65**)	7	37	306	8.3(25)	2	—	—	—	—	—	—	—	—	—	—	—	—	54	1472
1990	†Cin★	16(15, RB)	195	1004	5.1(56)	5	26	269	10.3(35)	4	—	—	—	—	—	—	—	—	—	—	—	—	54	1209
1991	Cin	15(12, RB)	152	571	3.8(25)	2	40	348	8.7(40)	2	—	—	—	—	—	—	—	—	—	—	k	—	24	800
1992	Cle	4(2)	13	38	2.9(13)	0	2	-1	-0.5(4)	0	—	—	—	—	—	—	—	—	—	—	—	—	0	38
1992	TB	2(0)	5	6	1.2(4)	0	—	—	—	—	—	—	—	—	—	—	—	—	—	—	k	—	0	10
NFL	12	162(115)	1685	7962	4.7(65)	49	383	3621	9.5(57)	30	2	1	50.0	8	4.0(8)	1	0	—	—	—	kp	—	474	11509

Brooks, Jermaine Jermaine, DT, 6´3˝/285 lbs; Arkansas; B4/11/1979 Pasadena, CA **2003**†Dal 1 (0)

Brooks, Jon Jonathan, LB, 6´2˝/215 lbs; Clemson; 1979: Det, rnd 4; B6/22/1957 Saluda, SC **1979** Det 15 **1980** Atl 4 (0) **1980** SL 1 (0) **NFL** 20 [2 yrs]

Brooks, Kevin Kevin Craig, DT-DE, 6´6˝/277 lbs; Michigan; 1985: Dal, rnd 1; B2/9/1963 Detroit, MI **1985** Dal 11 (0) **1986** Dal 9 (0) **1987** Dal 13 (12, LDT) **1988** Dal 15 (14, LDT) **1989** Det 15 (15, RDE) **1990** Det 6 (4) **NFL** 69 (45) [6 yrs]

Brooks, Larry Larry Lee, DT, 6´3˝/255 lbs; Virginia State; 1972: LA, rnd 14; B6/10/1950 Prince George, VA **1972** LARm 8 (7, RDT) **1973**†LARm 14 (14, LDT) **1974**†LARm☆13 (13, LDT) **1975** LARm 8 (8, LDT) **1976**†LARm★14 (14, LDT) **1977**†LARm★14 (14, LDT) **1978**†LARm★14 (14, LDT) **1979**†LARm★16 (16, LDT) **1980**†LARm★16 (14, LDT) **1981** LARm 8 (8, RDT) **1982** LARm 6 (0) **NFL** 131 (122) [11 yrs]

Brooks, Lee Leonard Leo, DT, 6´5˝/261 lbs; Texas; 1970: Hou, rnd 2; B12/7/1947 Shidler, OK, D4/4/2002 **1970** Hou 13 **1971** Hou 11 **1972** Hou 12 (RDT) **1973** SL 13 (5, ldt) **1974**†SL 14 (13, LDT) **1975** SL 8 **1976** SL✧8 **NFL** 79 (18) [7 yrs]

Brooks, Macey Barry Macey, WR, 6´5˝/212 lbs; James Madison; B2/2/1975 Hampton, VA

YEAR	TEAM	G(GS, POS)	RUSH	YD	AVG(LG)	TD	REC	YD	AVG(LG)	TD	PASS	COMP	PCT	YD	AVG(LG)	TD	INT	SK	YD	QBR	KPR	OTD	PTS	TAY
1999	ChiB	9(2)	1	7	7.0(7)	0	14	160	11.4(30)	0	—	—	—	—	—	—	—	—	—	—	—	—	0	87
2000	ChiB	16(3)	—	—	—	—	26	216	8.3(27)	0	—	—	—	—	—	—	—	—	—	—	—	—	0	108
NFL	2	25(5)	1	7	7.0(7)	0	40	376	9.4(30)	0	—	—	—	—	—	—	—	—	—	—	—	—	0	195

Brooks, Michael Michael, LB, 6´1˝/236 lbs; LSU; 1987: Den, rnd 3; B10/2/1964 Ruston, LA **1987**†Den 12 (0) **1988** Den 16 (4) **1989**†Den 16 (16, ROLB) **1990** Den 16 (16, ROLB) **1991**†Den 14 (14, ROLB) **1992** Den✧15 (14, RILB) **1993**†NYG☆13 (13, RILB) **1994** NYG 16 (16, LLB) **1995** NYG 16 (16, MLB) **1996** Det 4 (4) **NFL** 138 (113) [10 yrs]

Brooks, Michael Michael Antonio, DB, 6´0˝/195 lbs; North Carolina State; B3/12/1967 Greensboro, NC **1989** SD 1 (0) **1990** SD 1 (0) **1990** Dal 3 (0) **NFL** 5 (0) [2 yrs]

Brooks, Perry Perry, DT, 6´3˝/264 lbs; Southern (LA); 1976: NE, rnd 7; B12/4/1954 Bogalusa, LA **1978** Was 16 (2) **1979** Was 12 **1980** Was 12 (7, RDT) **1981** Was 15 (12, RDT) **1982**†Was 5 (5, RDT) **1983**†Was 16 (0) **1984**†Was 16 (1) **NFL** 92 (27) [7 yrs]

Brooks, Reggie Reginald Arthur, RB, 5´8˝/209 lbs; Notre Dame; 1993: Was, rnd 2; B1/19/1971 Tulsa, OK

YEAR	TEAM	G(GS, POS)	RUSH	YD	AVG(LG)	TD	REC	YD	AVG(LG)	TD	PASS	COMP	PCT	YD	AVG(LG)	TD	INT	SK	YD	QBR	KPR	OTD	PTS	TAY
1993	Was	16(11, RB)	223	1063	4.8(85)	3	21	186	8.9(43)	0	—	—	—	—	—	—	—	—	—	—	k	—	18	1183
1994	Was	12(5, rb)	100	297	3.0(15)	2	13	68	5.2(16)	0	—	—	—	—	—	—	—	—	—	—	—	—	12	351
1995	Was	1(0)	2	-2	-1.0(-1)	0	—	—	—	—	—	—	—	—	—	—	—	—	—	—	—	—	0	-2
1996	TB	11(4)	112	368	3.3(56)	2	3	13	4.3(9)	0	—	—	—	—	—	—	—	—	—	—	—	—	12	395
NFL	4	40(20)	437	1726	3.9(85)	7	37	267	7.2(43)	0	—	—	—	—	—	—	—	—	—	—	k	—	42	1927

Brooks, Robert Robert Darren, WR, 6´0˝/177 lbs; South Carolina; 1992: GB, rnd 3; B6/23/1970 Greenwood, SC

YEAR	TEAM	G(GS, POS)	RUSH	YD	AVG(LG)	TD	REC	YD	AVG(LG)	TD	PASS	COMP	PCT	YD	AVG(LG)	TD	INT	SK	YD	QBR	KPR	OTD	PTS	TAY
1992	GB	16(1)	2	14	7.0(8)	0	12	126	10.5(18)	1	—	—	—	—	—	—	—	—	—	—	kp	—	6	197
1993	†GB	14(0)	3	17	5.7(21)	0	20	180	9.0(25)	0	—	—	—	—	—	—	—	—	—	—	kp	1	6	438
1994	†GB	16(16, WR)	1	0	0.0(0)	0	58	648	11.2(35)	4	—	—	—	—	—	—	—	—	—	—	kp	2	36	641
1995	†GB	16(15, WR)	4	21	5.3(21)	0	102	1497	14.7(**99**)	13	—	—	—	—	—	—	—	—	—	—	k	—	78	848
1996	GB	7(7, WR)	4	2	0.5(6)	0	23	344	15.0(38)	4	—	—	—	—	—	—	—	—	—	—	—	—	24	194
1997	†GB	15(15, WR)	2	19	9.5(15)	0	60	1010	**16.8**(**48**)	7	—	—	—	—	—	—	—	—	—	—	—	—	42	559
1998	†GB	12(12, WR)	1	2	2.0(2)	0	31	420	13.5(30)	3	—	—	—	—	—	—	—	—	—	—	—	—	18	227
2000	Den	4(0)	—	—	—	—	3	51	17.0(25)	0	—	—	—	—	—	—	—	—	—	—	—	—	0	26
NFL	8	100(66)	17	75	4.4(21)	0	309	4276	13.8(99)	32	—	—	—	—	—	—	—	—	—	—	kp	3	210	3129

Brooks, Rodregis Rodregis Antonio, DB, 5´9˝/184 lbs; Alabama-Birmingham; 2000: Ind, rnd 7; B8/30/1978 Alexander City, AL **2001** Ind 5 (0)

Brooks, Steve Steven Edward, TE, 6´5˝/245 lbs; Occidental; B6/2/1971 Ventura, CA **1996** Det 1 (0)

Brooks, Tony Raymond Anthony, RB, 6´0˝/230 lbs; Holy Cross (IN); Notre Dame; 1992: Phi, rnd 4; B8/17/1969 Tulsa, OK **1992** Phi 5 (0)

Brookshier, Tom Thomas Jefferson, DB, 6´0˝/196 lbs; Colorado; 1953: Phi, rnd 10; B12/16/1931 Roswell, NM **[I]** **1953** Phi 11 (DB) **1956** Phi 11 (DB) **1957** Phi 12 (DB) **1958** Phi 11 (DB) **1959** Phi★12 (DB) **1960**†Phi★12 (RCB) **1961** Phi 7 (RCB) **NFL** 76 [7 yrs]

Brophy, Jay James Jay, LB, 6´3˝/233 lbs; Miami (FL); 1984: Mia, rnd 2; B7/27/1960 Akron, OH **1984**†Mia 11 (5, lilb) **1985**†Mia 16 (6, lilb) **1986** Mia 4 (0) **1987** NYJ 3 (3) **NFL** 34 (14) [4 yrs]

Brosky, Al Alfred Edward, DB, 5´11˝/175 lbs; Illinois; 1951: LA, rnd 27; B6/9/1930 Chicago, IL **1954** ChiC 9 (DB)

Bross, Mal Matthew A., B, 5´9˝/170 lbs; Gonzaga; B12/7/1903, D2/8/1989 Seattle, WA **1927** GB 2 (1)

Brostek, Bern Bern Orion, C-G, 6´3˝/300 lbs; Washington; 1990: LARm, rnd 1; B9/11/1966 Honolulu, HI **1990** LARm 16 (2) **1991** LARm 14 (8, LG) **1992** LARm 16 (16, C) **1993** LARm 16 (16, C) **1994** LARm 11 (10, C) **1995** SL 16 (16, C) **1996** SL 16 (16, C) **1997** SL 1 (1) **NFL** 106 (85) [8 yrs]

Brotzki, Bob Robert John, T, 6´5˝/281 lbs; Syracuse; 1986: Ind, rnd 9; B12/24/1962 Sandusky, OH **1986** Ind 2 (0) **1987** Ind 11 (0) **1988** Ind 1 (0) **1988** Dal 4 (0) **NFL** 18 (0) [3 yrs]

Broughton, Luther Luther Rashard, TE, 6´2˝/248 lbs; Furman; 1997: Phi, rnd 5; B11/30/1974 Charleston, SC

YEAR	TEAM	G(GS, POS)	RUSH	YD	AVG(LG)	TD	REC	YD	AVG(LG)	TD	PASS	COMP	PCT	YD	AVG(LG)	TD	INT	SK	YD	QBR	KPR	OTD	PTS	TAY
1998	Car	16(4)	—	—	—	—	6	142	23.7(68)	1	—	—	—	—	—	—	—	—	—	—	—	—	6	76
1999	Phi	16(3)	—	—	—	—	26	295	11.3(33)	4	—	—	—	—	—	—	—	—	—	—	k	—	24	158
2000	†Phi	15(1)	—	—	—	—	12	104	8.7(21)	0	—	—	—	—	—	—	—	—	—	—	k	—	0	57
2001	Car	15(0)	—	—	—	—	2	22	11.0(13)	0	—	—	—	—	—	—	—	—	—	—	k	—	0	12
NFL	4	62(8)	—	—	—	—	46	563	12.2(68)	5	—	—	—	—	—	—	—	—	—	—	k	—	30	303

Broughton, Nehemiah Nehemiah, FB, 5´11˝/250 lbs; The Citadel; 2005: Was, rnd 7; B11/4/1982 North Charleston, SC

YEAR	TEAM	G(GS, POS)	RUSH	YD	AVG(LG)	TD	REC	YD	AVG(LG)	TD	PASS	COMP	PCT	YD	AVG(LG)	TD	INT	SK	YD	QBR	KPR	OTD	PTS	TAY
2005	Was	4(0)	1	3	3.0(3)	0	—	—	—	—	—	—	—	—	—	—	—	—	—	—	k	—	0	-7

Broughton, Walter Walter Craig, WR, 5´10˝/180 lbs; Jacksonville State; B10/20/1962 Brewton, AL

YEAR	TEAM	G(GS, POS)	RUSH	YD	AVG(LG)	TD	REC	YD	AVG(LG)	TD	PASS	COMP	PCT	YD	AVG(LG)	TD	INT	SK	YD	QBR	KPR	OTD	PTS	TAY
1986	Buf	8(0)	1	-6	-6.0(-6)	0	3	71	23.7(57)	0	—	—	—	—	—	—	—	—	—	—	kp	—	0	101
1987	Buf	9(0)	—	—	—	—	5	90	18.0(39)	1	—	—	—	—	—	—	—	—	—	—	—	—	6	50
1988	Buf	1(0)	—	—	—	—	—	—	—	—	—	—	—	—	—	—	—	—	—	—	—	—	—	—
NFL	3	18(0)	1	-6	-6.0(-6)	0	8	161	20.1(57)	1	—	—	—	—	—	—	—	—	—	—	kp	—	6	151

Broughton, Willie Willie Lee, DT-NT, 6´5˝/285 lbs; Miami (FL); 1985: Ind, rnd 4; B9/9/1964 Fort Pierce, FL **1985** Ind 15 (1) **1986** Ind 15 (8, NT) **1989** Dal 16 (14, RDT/ldt) **1990** Dal 4 (0) **1992** LARd 16 (8, LDT) **1993**†LARd 15 (0) **1995** NO 16 (11, LDT) **1996** NO 14 (5, rdt) **NFL** 111 (47) [8 yrs]

Broussard, Fred Frederick E., C, 6´3˝/235 lbs; Texas A&M; Northwestern State (LA); 1955: Pit, rnd 4; B4/29/1933 **1955** Pit 6 (c) **1955** NYG 1 **1960** Den-A 1 **NFL** 8 [2 yrs]

Broussard, Jamall Jamall, WR, 5´9˝/172 lbs; Texas Tech; San Jose State; B8/19/1981 Nederland, TX **2004** Car 8 (0)

Broussard, Steve John Steven, P, 6´0˝/200 lbs; Auburn; Southern Mississippi; B7/19/1947 McComb, MS **1975** GB 4

Broussard, Steve Steven Nelson, RB-WR, 5´7˝/201 lbs; Washington State; 1990: Atl, rnd 1; B2/22/1967 Los Angeles, CA **[R]**

YEAR	TEAM	G(GS, POS)	RUSH	YD	AVG(LG)	TD	REC	YD	AVG(LG)	TD	PASS	COMP	PCT	YD	AVG(LG)	TD	INT	SK	YD	QBR	KPR	OTD	PTS	TAY
1990	Atl	13(10, RB)	126	454	3.6(50)	4	24	160	6.7(18)	0	—	—	—	—	—	—	—	—	—	—	k	—	24	574
1991	Atl	14(5, rb)	99	449	4.5(36)	4	12	120	10.0(25)	1	—	—	—	—	—	—	—	—	—	—	—	—	30	554

YEAR	TEAM	G (GS, POS)	RUSH	YD	AVG(LG)	TD	REC	YD	AVG(LG)	TD	PASS	COMP	PCT	YD	AVG(LG)	TD	INT	SK	YD	QBR	KPR	OTD	PTS	TAY
1992	Atl	15(1)	84	363	4.3(27)	1	11	96	8.7(24)	1	—	—	—	—	—	—	—	—	—	—	—	—	12	426
1993	Atl	8(0)	39	206	5.3(26)	1	1	4	4.0(4)	0	—	—	—	—	—	—	—	—	—	—	—	—	6	218
1994	Cin	13(3)	94	403	4.3(37)	0	1	0	0.0	0	0.0			0	0		—	—	—	k	—	14	542
1995	Sea	15(1)	46	222	4.8(21)	1	10	94	9.4(25)	0	—	—	—	—	—	—	—	—	—	k	—	6	698
1996	Sea	12(0)	15	106	7.1(26)	1	6	26	4.3(9)	0	—	—	—	—	—	—	—	—	—	k	—	6	463
1997	Sea	16(1)	70	418	6.0(77)	5	24	143	6.0(20)	1	—	—	—	—	—	—	—	—	—	k	—	36	871
1998	Sea	15(0)	5	4	0.8(3)	0	4	21	5.3(16)	0	—	—	—	—	—	—	—	—	—	k	1	6	371
NFL	9	121(21)	578	2625	4.5(77)	19	126	882	7.0(25)	3	1	0	0.0	0	0.0	0	0	—	—	—	k	1	140	4716

BROVELLI, ANGELO Angelo Augustine, B, 6´0˝/193 lbs; St. Mary's (CA); B8/21/1910 Porterville, CA, D8/5/1995 Acampo, CA **[K]**

YEAR	TEAM	G (GS, POS)	RUSH	YD	AVG	TD	REC	YD	AVG	TD	PASS	COMP	PCT	YD	AVG	TD	INT					OTD	PTS	TAY
1933	Pit	8(8, TB)	60	236	3.9	2	6	137	22.8	0	25	8	32.0	114	4.6	0	3	—	—	—	K	—	13	262
1934	Pit	5(5, FB)	37	112	3.0	1	—	—	—	0								—	—	—	K	—	6	122
NFL	2	13(13)	97	348	3.6	3	6	137	22.8	0	25	8	32.0	114	4.6	0	3	—	—	—	K	—	19	384

BROWN, A.B. Anthony James, RB, 5´9˝/210 lbs; Pittsburgh; West Virginia; 1989: NYJ, rnd 8; B12/4/1965 Salem, NJ

1989	NYJ	16(0)	12	63	5.3(17)	0	4	10	2.5(6)	0	—	—	—	—	—	—	—	—	—	—	—	0	68
1990	NYJ	1(0)	1	8	8.0(8)	0	—	—	—	0	—	—	—	—	—	—	—	—	—	—	—	0	56
1991	†NYJ	9(0)	3	4	1.3(2)	1	—	—	—	0	—	—	—	—	—	—	—	—	—	k	—	6	-36
1992	NYJ	7(1)	24	42	1.8(9)	0	4	30	7.5(20)	0	—	—	—	—	—	—	—	—	—	—	—	0	57
NFL	4	33(1)	40	117	2.9(17)	1	8	40	5.0(20)	0	—	—	—	—	—	—	—	—	—	k	—	6	145

BROWN, AARON Aaron Lewis, DE, 6´5˝/255 lbs; Minnesota; 1966: KC, rnd 1; B11/16/1943 Port Arthur, TX, deceased **1966**†KC-A 14 **1968**†KC-A 14 (RDE)
1969†KC-A☆14 (RDE) **1970** KC☆11 (RDE) **1971**†KC☆13 (RDE) **1972** KC 12 **1973** GB 8 **1974** GB 2 **NFL** 88 [8 yrs]

BROWN, AARON Aaron Cedric, LB, 6´2˝/235 lbs; Ohio State; 1978: TB, rnd 10; B1/13/1956 Warren, OH **1978** TB 16 **1979**†TB 12 (1) **1980** TB 16 (1) **1985** Phi 7 (0)
1986 Atl 16 (0) **1987** Atl 6 (1) **NFL** 73 (3) [6 yrs]

BROWN, ALEX Alex James, DE, 6´3˝/272 lbs; Florida; 2002: Chi, rnd 4; B6/4/1979 Jasper, FL **2002** ChiB 15 (9, RDE) **2003** ChiB 16 (16, RDE) **2004** ChiB 16 (16, RDE)
2005†ChiB 16 (16, RDE) **NFL** 63 (57) [4 yrs]

BROWN, ALLEN Allen, TE, 6´5˝/235 lbs; Mississippi; 1965: GB, rnd 3/SD, rnd 3; B3/2/1943 Natchez, MS **1966**†GB 5

| 1967 | GB | 14 | — | — | — | 3 | 43 | 14.3(17) | 0 | — | — | — | — | — | — | — | — | — | k | — | 0 | 20 |
| NFL | 2 | 19 | — | — | — | 3 | 43 | 14.3(17) | 0 | — | — | — | — | — | — | — | — | — | — | — | 0 | 22 |

BROWN, ANDRE Andre Lamont, WR, 6´3˝/210 lbs; Miami (FL); B8/21/1966 Chicago, IL

1989	Mia	16(0)	—	—	—	24	410	17.1(48)	5	—	—	—	—	—	—	—	—	—	k	—	30	209
1990	Mia	6(0)	—	—	—	3	49	16.3(24)	0	—	—	—	—	—	—	—	—	—	k	—	0	25
NFL	2	22(0)	—	—	—	27	459	17.0(48)	5	—	—	—	—	—	—	—	—	—	k	—	30	234

BROWN, ANTHONY Anthony Quantrell, T-G, 6´5˝/315 lbs; Utah; B11/6/1972 Okinawa, Japan **1995** Cin 7 (1) **1996** Cin 7 (0) **1997** Cin 6 (0) **1998** Cin 16 (5, rg)
1999 Pit 16 (11, RT) **NFL** 52 (17) [5 yrs]

BROWN, ANTONIO Antonio Duval, WR, 5´10˝/175 lbs; West Virginia; B3/3/1978 Miami, FL

2003	Buf	16(0)	1	17	17.0(17)	0	—	—	—	0	—	—	—	—	—	—	—	—	kp	—	0	329
2004	Was	3(0)	—	—	—	0	—	—	—	0	—	—	—	—	—	—	—	—	kp	—	0	90
2005	†Was	7(0)	2	7	3.5(4)	0	—	—	—	0	—	—	—	—	—	—	—	—	kp	1	6	169
NFL	3	26(0)	3	24	8.0(17)	0	—	—	—	0	—	—	—	—	—	—	—	—	kp	1	6	588

BROWN, ARNOLD Arnold Lee, DB, 5´11˝/185 lbs; North Carolina Central; 1985: Sea, rnd 5; B8/27/1962 Wilmington, NC **1985** Det 7 (0) **1987** Sea 2 (0) **NFL** 9 (0) [2 yrs]

BROWN, BARRY Joseph Barry, TE-LB, 6´3˝/230 lbs; Florida; 1965: Bal, rnd 19/Den, rnd R4; B4/17/1943 Boston, MA **1966** Bal 10 **1967** Bal 14 **1968** NYG 12

1969	Bos-A	7(2)	—	—	—	6	69	11.5(15)	0	—	—	—	—	—	—	—	—	—	—	—	0	35
1970	Bos	14(10, TE)	—	—	—	15	145	9.7(22)	0	—	—	—	—	—	—	—	—	—	k	—	0	58
NFL	5	57(12)	—	—	—	21	214	10.2(22)	0	—	—	—	—	—	—	—	—	—	ki	—	0	78

BROWN, BILL William Lewis, BB-QB-DB, 6´0˝/202 lbs; Texas Tech; B6/1/1917 McKeesport, PA

1943	Bkn	5(0)	—	—	—	4	42	10.5(19)	0	—	—	—	—	—	—	—	—	—	—	—	0	21
1944	Bkn	10(6, BB)	4	10	2.5(3)	0	2	10	5.0(8)	0	3	1	33.3	11	3.7(11)	0	0	—	—	—	kpi	—	0	25
NFL	2	15(6)	4	10	2.5(3)	0	6	52	8.7(19)	0	3	1	33.3	11	3.7(11)	0	0	—	—	—	kpi	—	0	46

BROWN, BILL William Dorsey, RB, 5´11˝/228 lbs; Illinois; 1961: Chi, rnd 2/NYT, rnd 6; B6/29/1938 Mendota, IL

1961	ChiB	14	22	81	3.7(20)	0	2	6	3.0(13)	0	—	—	—	—	—	—	—	—	—	k	—	0	78
1962	Min	14	34	103	3.0(15)	0	10	124	12.4(29)	1	—	—	—	—	—	—	—	—	—	—	—	6	170
1963	Min	14(13, FB)	128	445	3.5(21)	5	17	109	6.4(30)	2	—	—	—	—	—	—	—	—	—	k	1	48	630
1964	Min★	14(14, FB)	226	866	3.8(48)	7	48	703	14.6(64)	9	—	—	—	—	—	—	—	—	—	k	—	96	1326
1965	Min★	14(12, FB)	160	699	4.4(40)	6	41	503	12.3(47)	1	—	—	—	—	—	—	—	—	—	—	—	42	1016
1966	Min	14(14, FB)	251	829	3.3(33)	6	37	359	9.7(56)	0	1	0	0.0	0	0.0	0	0	—	—	—	—	—	36	1069
1967	Min◊	14(14, FB)	185	610	3.3(29)	5	22	263	12.0(43)	0	—	—	—	—	—	—	—	—	—	—	—	30	792
1968	†Min★	14(14, FB)	222	805	3.6(32)	11	31	329	10.6(57)	3	1	1	100.0	3	3.0(3)	0	—	—	—	—	—	—	84	1096
1969	†Min	12(12, FB)	126	430	3.4(30)	3	21	183	8.7(27)	0	—	—	—	—	—	—	—	—	—	—	—	18	552
1970	†Min	14(12, FB)	101	324	3.2(18)	0	15	149	9.9(17)	2	—	—	—	—	—	—	—	—	—	—	—	12	409
1971	†Min	14(8, fb)	46	136	3.0(23)	2	10	94	9.4(36)	0	—	—	—	—	—	—	—	—	—	—	—	12	203
1972	Min	14	82	263	3.2(19)	4	22	298	13.5(76)	4	—	—	—	—	—	—	—	—	—	k	—	48	464
1973	†Min	14	47	206	4.4(21)	3	5	22	4.4(7)	1	—	—	—	—	—	—	—	—	—	k	—	24	242
1974	†Min	14	19	41	2.2(11)	0	5	41	8.2(21)	0	—	—	—	—	—	—	—	—	—	k	—	0	36
NFL	14	194(113)	1649	5838	3.5(48)	52	286	3183	11.1(76)	23	2	1	50.0	3	1.5(3)	0	0	—	—	—	k	1	456	8079

BROWN, BILL William Evans, LB, 6´1˝/230 lbs; Bridgeport; Syracuse; 1957: ChiB, rnd 9; B4/25/1936, D4/18/1989 Hempstead, NY **1960** Bos-A 14 (MLB)

BROWN, BOB Robert Stanford, T, 6´4˝/280 lbs; Nebraska; 1964: Phi, rnd 1; B12/8/1941 Cleveland, OH; HOF 2004 **1964** Phi☆14 (14, RT) **1965** Phi★14 (14, RT)
1966 Phi☆14 (14, RT) **1967** Phi☆ 8 (8, RT) **1968** Phi★14 (RT) **1969**†LARm★14 (14, RT) **1970** LARm★14 (14, RT) **1971** Oak★10 (10, RT) **1972**†Oak☆14 (14, RT)
1973 Oak 10 (8, RT) **NFL** 126 (110) [10 yrs]

BROWN, BOBBY Braynard Ontawyn, WR, 6´2˝/197 lbs; Notre Dame; B3/26/1977 Fort Lauderdale, FL

| 2000 | Cle | 6(0) | — | — | — | 2 | 14 | 7.0(8) | 0 | — | — | — | — | — | — | — | — | — | — | — | 0 | 7 |

BROWN, BOOKER Booker Taylor, T-G, 6´2˝/257 lbs; USC; 1974: Hou, rnd 6; B9/25/1952 Desson, MS **1975** SD 11 (7, lt) **1977** SD 6 (1) **NFL** 17 (8) [2 yrs]

BROWN, BOYD Boyd, TE, 6´4˝/222 lbs; Alcorn State; 1974: Den, rnd 17; B5/24/1952 Crosby, MS **1974** Den 14 **1976** Den 14 **1977** NYG 6

| 1975 | Den | 12 | — | — | — | 1 | 14 | 14.0(14) | 0 | — | — | — | — | — | — | — | — | — | — | — | 0 | 7 |
| NFL | 4 | 46 | — | — | — | 1 | 14 | 14.0(14) | 0 | — | — | — | — | — | — | — | — | — | — | — | 0 | 14 |

BROWN, BUD Charles Lee, DB, 6´0˝/194 lbs; Southern Mississippi; 1984: Mia, rnd 11; B4/19/1961 DeKalb, MS **1984**†Mia 16 (0) **1985**†Mia 16 (16, FS) **1986** Mia 16 (15, FS)
1987 Mia 9 (7, FS) **1988** Mia 16 (3) **NFL** 73 (41) [5 yrs]

BROWN, BUDDY William Brightie, G, 6´1˝/220 lbs; Arkansas; 1951: Was, rnd 19; B10/19/1926 Wynne, AR, D2/23/2004 Marble Falls, TX **1951** Was 12 **1952** Was 12 (RG)
1953 GB 11 (RG) **1954** GB 12 (12, RG) **1955** GB 12 (12, RG) **1956** GB 12 (RG) **NFL** 71 (24) [6 yrs]

BROWN, C.C. Ceandris Nehemiah, DB, 6´2˝/210 lbs; Louisiana-Lafayette; 2005: Hou, rnd 6; B1/27/1983 Greenwood, MS **2005** Hou 16 (13, SS/fs)

BROWN, CARLOS Carlos Allen, QB, 6´3˝/210 lbs; Pacific; 1975: GB, rnd 12; B7/31/1952 Shreveport, LA

1975	GB	13	—	—	—	—	—	—	4	3	75.0	63	15.8(27)	1	0	—	—	—	—	—	0	37
1976	GB	13(3)	12	49	4.1(21)	0	—	—	—	74	26	35.1	333	4.5(47)	2	6	10	66	—	—	—	0	-15
NFL	2	26(3)	12	49	4.1(21)	0	—	—	—	78	29	37.2	396	5.1(47)	3	6	10	66	—	—	—	0	22

BROWN, CEDRIC Cedric Wallace, DB, 6´1˝/199 lbs; Kent State; 1976: Oak, rnd 12; B5/6/1954 Columbus, OH **[I]** **1976** TB 1 **1977** TB 14 (14, FS) **1978** TB 14 (13, FS)
1979†TB 16 (15, FS) **1980** TB 13 (13, FS) **1981**†TB 16 (15, FS) **1982** TB 9 (9, FS) **1983** TB 8 (7, fs) **1984** TB 9 (8, fs) **NFL** 100 (95) [9 yrs]

BROWN, CEDRICK Cedrick David, DB, 5´10˝/178 lbs; Washington State; B9/6/1964 Compton, CA **1987** Phi 12 (0)

Brown, Chad Chadwick Everett, LB, 6´2˝/245 lbs; Colorado; 1993: Pit, rnd 2; B7/12/1970 Altadena, CA [S] **1993**†Pit 16 (9, RILB) **1994**†Pit 16 (16, RILB) **1995**†Pit 10 (10, RILB) **1996**†Pit★14 (14, ROLB) **1997** Sea 15 (15, RLB) **1998** Sea★16 (16, RLB) **1999**†Sea✧15 (15, RLB) **2000** Sea 16 (16, RLB) **2001** Sea 16 (16, RLB) **2002** Sea 8 (8, RLB) **2003**†Sea 14 (13, RLB) **2004**†Sea 7 (7, RLB) **2005**†NE 15 (5, rilb) **NFL** 178 (160) [13 yrs]

Brown, Chad Chadrick Chico, DE, 6´7˝/265 lbs; Mississippi; 1993: Phx, rnd 8; B7/9/1971 Thomasville, GA **1993** Phx 5 (0) **1994** Arz 8 (2) **1995** Arz 5 (4) **NFL** 18 (6) [3 yrs]

Brown, Charles Charles Edwin, T, 6´4˝/245 lbs; Houston; B8/1/1936 **1962** Oak-A 14 (LT)

Brown, Charlie Charles, WR, 5´10˝/182 lbs; South Carolina State; 1981: Was, rnd 8; B10/29/1958 Charleston, SC

YEAR	TEAM	G (GS, POS)	RUSH	YD	AVG (LG)	TD	REC	YD	AVG (LG)	TD	PASS	COMP	PCT	YD	AVG (LG)	TD	INT	SK	YD	QBR	KPR	OTD	PTS	TAY
1982	†Was★	9 (9, WR)	—	—	—	—	32	690	**21.6** (**78**)	**8**	—	—	—	—	—	—	—	—	—	—	—	—	48	385
1983	†Was★	15 (14, WR)	4	53	13.3 (17)	0	**78**	1225	15.7 (75)	8	—	—	—	—	—	—	—	—	—	—	—	—	48	706
1984	†Was	9 (4)	—	—	—	—	18	200	11.1 (36)	3	—	—	—	—	—	—	—	—	—	—	—	—	18	115
1985	Atl	13 (9, WR)	—	—	—	—	24	412	17.2 (48)	2	—	—	—	—	—	—	—	—	—	—	—	—	12	216
1986	Atl	16 (15, WR)	—	—	—	—	63	918	14.6 (42)	4	—	—	—	—	—	—	—	—	—	—	—	—	24	479
1987	Atl	6 (0)	—	—	—	—	5	103	20.6 (23)	0	—	—	—	—	—	—	—	—	—	—	—	—	0	52
NFL	6	68 (51)	4	53	13.3 (17)	0	220	3548	16.1 (78)	25	—	—	—	—	—	—	—	—	—	—	—	—	150	1952

Brown, Charlie Charles Edward, DB-HB, 6´2˝/220 lbs; Syracuse; 1966: Chi, rnd 2/SD, rnd 4; B9/13/1942 Heflin, AL **1966** ChiB 14 **1967** ChiB 8

YEAR	TEAM	G (GS, POS)	RUSH	YD	AVG (LG)	TD	REC	YD	AVG (LG)	TD	PASS	COMP	PCT	YD	AVG (LG)	TD	INT	SK	YD	QBR	KPR	OTD	PTS	TAY
1968	Buf-A	8	3	39	13.0 (27)	0	—	—	—	—	—	—	—	—	—	—	—	—	—	—	k	—	0	133
NFL	3	30	3	39	13.0 (27)	0	—	—	—	—	—	—	—	—	—	—	—	—	—	—	ki	—	0	183

Brown, Charlie Charles Kelly, WR, 6´2˝/195 lbs; Northern Arizona; 1970: Det, rnd 14; B10/13/1948 Oakland, CA

YEAR	TEAM	G (GS, POS)	RUSH	YD	AVG (LG)	TD	REC	YD	AVG (LG)	TD	PASS	COMP	PCT	YD	AVG (LG)	TD	INT	SK	YD	QBR	KPR	OTD	PTS	TAY
1970	Det	14	—	—	—	—	2	38	19.0 (23)	0	—	—	—	—	—	—	—	—	—	—	—	—	0	19

Brown, Charlie Charles Robert, RB, 5´10˝/195 lbs; Missouri; 1967: NO, rnd 10; B10/16/1945 Jefferson City, MO **1968** NO 3

YEAR	TEAM	G (GS, POS)	RUSH	YD	AVG (LG)	TD	REC	YD	AVG (LG)	TD	PASS	COMP	PCT	YD	AVG (LG)	TD	INT	SK	YD	QBR	KPR	OTD	PTS	TAY
1967	NO	3	8	16	2.0 (7)	2	3	23	7.7 (9)	0	—	—	—	—	—	—	—	—	—	—	kp	—	12	62
NFL	2	6	8	16	2.0 (7)	2	3	23	7.7 (9)	0	—	—	—	—	—	—	—	—	—	—	kp	1	18	109

Brown, Chris Christopher, T, 6´1˝/295 lbs; New York Tech; Lamar; B7/16/1963 **1987** NYJ 1 (0)

Brown, Chris Christopher Rajean, RB, 6´3˝/219 lbs; Colorado; 2003: Ten, rnd 3; B4/17/1981 Winfield, IL

YEAR	TEAM	G (GS, POS)	RUSH	YD	AVG (LG)	TD	REC	YD	AVG (LG)	TD	PASS	COMP	PCT	YD	AVG (LG)	TD	INT	SK	YD	QBR	KPR	OTD	PTS	TAY
2003	†Ten	11 (0)	56	221	3.9 (28)	0	8	61	7.6 (11)	0	—	—	—	—	—	—	—	—	—	—	—	—	0	252
2004	Ten	11 (11, RB)	220	1067	4.8 (52)	6	20	147	7.3 (21)	0	—	—	—	—	—	—	—	—	—	—	—	—	36	1201
2005	Ten	15 (14, RB)	224	851	3.8 (38)	5	25	327	13.1 (57)	2	—	—	—	—	—	—	—	—	—	—	—	—	42	1075
NFL	3	37 (25)	500	2139	4.3 (52)	11	53	535	10.1 (57)	2	—	—	—	—	—	—	—	—	—	—	—	—	78	2527

Brown, Chris Christopher Duke, DB, 6´0˝/200 lbs; Notre Dame; 1984: Pit, rnd 6; B4/11/1962 Owensboro, KY **1984**†Pit 16 (4) **1985** Pit 6 (0) **NFL** 22 (4) [2 yrs]

Brown, Chris Christopher Dannell, DB, 6´1˝/195 lbs; Alabama-Birmingham; B5/9/1978 Atlanta, GA **2003** Jax 4 (0)

Brown, Chuck Charles Edwin, C-G, 6´1˝/235 lbs; Houston; B3/15/1957 Houston, TX **1979** SL 4

Brown, Clay Clayton Lee, TE, 6´3˝/223 lbs; Brigham Young; 1981: Den, rnd 2; B9/20/1958 Los Angeles, CA **1982** Atl 1 (0) **1983** Den 3 (0) **NFL** 4 (0) [2 yrs]

Brown, Cornell Cornell Desmond, LB, 6´0˝/240 lbs; Virginia Tech; 1997: Bal, rnd 6; B3/15/1975 Englewood, NJ **1997** Bal 16 (1) **1998** Bal 16 (1) **1999** Bal 16 (5, llb) **2000**†Bal 15 (1) **2002** Bal 16 (14, LOLB) **2003**†Bal 16 (3) **2004** Bal 13 (0) **NFL** 108 (25) [7 yrs]

Brown, Corwin Corwin Alan, DB, 6´1˝/200 lbs; Michigan; 1993: NE, rnd 4; B4/25/1970 Chicago, IL **1993** NE 15 (12, SS) **1994**†NE 16 (0) **1995** NE 16 (2) **1996**†NE 14 (0) **1998**†NYJ 16 (1) **1999** Det 13 (1) **2000** Det 14 (4)

YEAR	TEAM	G (GS, POS)	RUSH	YD	AVG (LG)	TD	REC	YD	AVG (LG)	TD	PASS	COMP	PCT	YD	AVG (LG)	TD	INT	SK	YD	QBR	KPR	OTD	PTS	TAY
1997	NYJ	16 (0)	—	—	—	—	1	26	26.0 (26)	0	—	—	—	—	—	—	—	—	—	—	—	—	0	13
NFL	8	120 (20)	—	—	—	—	1	26	26.0 (26)	0	—	—	—	—	—	—	—	—	—	—	iS	1	6	10

Brown, Courtney Courtney Lanair, DE, 6´4˝/280 lbs; Penn State; 2000: Cle, rnd 1; B2/14/1978 Charleston, SC **2000** Cle 16 (16, LDE) **2001** Cle 5 (5, rde) **2002** Cle 11 (11, RDE) **2003** Cle 13 (13, LDE) **2004** Cle 2 (2) **2005**†Den 14 (13, LDE) **NFL** 61 (60) [6 yrs]

Brown, Curtis Curtis Jerome, RB, 5´10˝/203 lbs; Missouri; 1977: Buf, rnd 3; B12/7/1954 St. Louis, MO

YEAR	TEAM	G (GS, POS)	RUSH	YD	AVG (LG)	TD	REC	YD	AVG (LG)	TD	PASS	COMP	PCT	YD	AVG (LG)	TD	INT	SK	YD	QBR	KPR	OTD	PTS	TAY
1977	Buf	7	8	34	4.3 (9)	0	5	20	4.0 (12)	1	—	—	—	—	—	—	—	—	—	—	k	—	6	70
1978	Buf	15 (10, FB)	128	591	4.6 (58)	4	18	130	7.2 (31)	0	—	—	—	—	—	—	—	—	—	—	kp	1	30	874
1979	Buf	15 (15, FB)	172	574	3.3 (25)	1	39	401	10.3 (**84**)	3	—	—	—	—	—	—	—	—	—	—	k	—	24	797
1980	†Buf	16 (16, FB)	153	559	3.7 (34)	3	27	137	5.1 (20)	0	—	—	—	—	—	—	—	—	—	—	k	—	18	689
1981	†Buf	14 (8, FB)	62	226	3.6 (13)	0	7	46	6.6 (10)	1	—	—	—	—	—	—	—	—	—	—	k	—	6	289
1982	Buf	9 (3)	41	187	4.6 (19)	0	6	38	6.3 (28)	0	—	—	—	—	—	—	—	—	—	—	k	—	0	208
1983	Hou	2 (0)	3	0	0.0 (1)	1	—	—	—	—	—	—	—	—	—	—	—	—	—	—	—	—	6	10
NFL	7	78 (52)	567	2171	3.8 (58)	9	102	772	7.6 (84)	5	—	—	—	—	—	—	—	—	—	—	kp	1	90	2936

Brown, Cyron Cyron DeAndre, DE, 6´5˝/265 lbs; Illinois; Western Illinois; B6/28/1975 Chicago, IL **1998** Den 4 (0) **1999** Den 7 (0) **NFL** 11 (0) [2 yrs]

Brown, Dan Daniel Joseph, DE, 6´1˝/200 lbs; Villanova; 1950: Was, rnd 11; B8/26/1925 Philadelphia, PA, D6/17/1995 Havertown, PA **1950** Was 11 (RDE)

Brown, Dante Dante, RB, 6´1˝/218 lbs; Memphis; B7/28/1980 Cincinnati, OH

YEAR	TEAM	G (GS, POS)	RUSH	YD	AVG (LG)	TD	REC	YD	AVG (LG)	TD	PASS	COMP	PCT	YD	AVG (LG)	TD	INT	SK	YD	QBR	KPR	OTD	PTS	TAY
2004	Pit	1 (0)	1	2	2.0 (2)	0	—	—	—	—	—	—	—	—	—	—	—	—	—	—	—	—	0	2

Brown, Dave David Alexander, WB-FB-HB, 5´11˝/190 lbs; Alabama; 1943: NYG, rnd 25; B2/14/1920 Birmingham, AL, D8/18/2000 Keystone Heights, FL

YEAR	TEAM	G (GS, POS)	RUSH	YD	AVG (LG)	TD	REC	YD	AVG (LG)	TD	PASS	COMP	PCT	YD	AVG (LG)	TD	INT	SK	YD	QBR	KPR	OTD	PTS	TAY
1943	†NYG	10 (4, fb)	32	131	4.1 (14)	0	5	29	5.8 (12)	0	—	—	—	—	—	—	—	—	—	—	pi	—	0	251
1946	†NYG	7 (5, wb)	9	5	0.6 (8)	0	—	—	—	—	—	—	—	—	—	—	—	—	—	—	p	—	0	0
1947	NYG	7 (6, wb)	6	5	0.8 (3)	0	1	5	5.0 (5)	0	—	—	—	—	—	—	—	—	—	—	kp	—	0	25
NFL	3	24 (15)	47	141	3.0 (14)	0	6	34	5.7 (12)	0	—	—	—	—	—	—	—	—	—	—	kpi	—	0	275

Brown, Dave David Steven, DB, 6´1˝/190 lbs; Michigan; 1975: Pit, rnd 1; B1/16/1953 Akron, OH, D1/10/2006 Lubbock, TX [I] **1975**†Pit 13 **1976** Sea 14 (14, FS) **1977** Sea 14 (14, RCB) **1978** Sea 16 (16, RCB) **1979** Sea 16 (16, RCB) **1980** Sea 16 (16, RCB) **1981** Sea 10 (10, RCB) **1982** Sea 9 (9, RCB) **1983**†Sea 16 (16, RCB) **1984**†Sea★16 (16, RCB) **1985** Sea☆16 (16, RCB) **1986** Sea 16 (16, RCB) **1987** GB 12 (12, RCB) **1988** GB 16 (16, RCB) **1989** GB 16 (16, RCB) **NFL** 216 (203) [15 yrs]

Brown, Dave David Dwayne, LB, 6´2˝/215 lbs; Miami (OH); B1/17/1964 Dayton, OH **1987** Phi 1 (0)

Brown, Dave David Michael, QB, 6´5˝/220 lbs; Duke; 1992: NYG, rnd S1; B2/25/1970 Summit, NJ

YEAR	TEAM	G (GS, POS)	RUSH	YD	AVG (LG)	TD	REC	YD	AVG (LG)	TD	PASS	COMP	PCT	YD	AVG (LG)	TD	INT	SK	YD	QBR	KPR	OTD	PTS	TAY
1992	NYG	2 (0)	2	-1	-0.5 (1)	0	—	—	—	—	7	4	57.1	21	3.0 (8)	0	0	4	19	—	—	—	0	10
1993	†NYG	1 (0)	3	-4	-1.3 (-1)	0	—	—	—	—	—	—	—	—	—	—	—	—	—	—	—	—	0	-4
1994	NYG	15 (15, QB)	60	196	3.3 (21)	2	—	—	—	—	350	201	57.4	2536	7.2 (53)	12	16	42	248	72.5	P	—	12	904
1995	NYG	16 (16, QB)	45	228	5.1 (23)	4	—	—	—	—	456	254	55.7	2814	6.2 (57)	11	10	44	206	73.1	P	—	24	1330
1996	NYG	16 (16, QB)	50	170	3.4 (18)	0	—	—	—	—	398	214	53.8	2412	6.1 (37)	12	20	49	276	61.3	—	—	0	636
1997	NYG	7 (6, qb)	17	29	1.7 (7)	1	—	—	—	—	180	93	51.7	1023	5.7 (62)	5	3	13	67	—	—	—	6	456
1998	Arz	1 (0)	1	2	2.0 (2)	0	—	—	—	—	5	2	40.0	31	6.2 (19)	0	0	1	6	—	—	—	0	18
1999	Arz	8 (5, qb)	13	49	3.8 (10)	0	—	—	—	—	169	84	49.7	944	5.6 (71)	2	6	18	130	—	—	—	0	291
2000	Arz	6 (2)	1	0	0.0 (0)	0	—	—	—	—	69	40	58.0	467	6.8 (44)	2	3	10	53	—	—	—	0	124
2001	Arz	1 (0)	—	—	—	—	—	—	—	—	—	—	—	—	—	—	—	—	—	—	—	—	—	—
NFL	10	73 (60)	192	669	3.5 (23)	7	—	—	—	—	1634	892	54.6	10248	6.3 (71)	44	58	181	1005	67.9	P	—	42	3763

Brown, Dean Dean Venor, DB, 5´10˝/175 lbs; Fort Valley State; B11/6/1945 McDonough, GA **1969**†Cle 5 **1970** Mia 5 **NFL** 10 [2 yrs]

Brown, DeAuntae DeAuntae, DB, 5´11˝/195 lbs; Central State (OH); 1997: Phi, rnd 7; B4/28/1974 Detroit, MI **1997** Phi 1 (0)

Brown, Dee Dadrian L., RB, 5´10˝/209 lbs; Syracuse; 2001: Car, rnd 6; B5/12/1978 Clearwater, FL **2003** Pit 1 (0) **2004** Cle 5 (0)

YEAR	TEAM	G (GS, POS)	RUSH	YD	AVG (LG)	TD	REC	YD	AVG (LG)	TD	PASS	COMP	PCT	YD	AVG (LG)	TD	INT	SK	YD	QBR	KPR	OTD	PTS	TAY
2002	Car	14 (3)	102	360	3.5 (24)	4	17	86	5.1 (15)	1	1	0	0.0	0	0.0	0	1	—	—	—	k	—	30	466
2005	KC	8 (0)	7	21	3.0 (7)	0	3	23	7.7 (9)	1	—	—	—	—	—	—	—	—	—	—	—	—	6	38
NFL	4	28 (3)	109	381	3.5 (24)	4	20	109	5.4 (15)	2	1	0	0.0	0	0.0	0	1	—	—	—	k	—	36	552

Brown, Delvin Delvin Jaquin, DB, 5´11˝/202 lbs; Miami (FL); B9/17/1979 Miami, FL **2001** Jax 5 (0)

Brown, Dennis Dennis Trammel, DE, 6´4˝/290 lbs; Washington; 1990: SF, rnd 2; B11/6/1967 Los Angeles, CA **1990**†SF 15 (0) **1991** SF 16 (4) **1992**†SF 16 (3) **1993**†SF 16 (16, LDE) **1994**†SF 16 (14, LDE) **1995**†SF 16 (16, LDE) **1996**†SF 14 (0) **NFL** 109 (53) [7 yrs]

YEAR	TEAM	G (GS, POS)	RUSH	YD	AVG (LG)	TD	REC	YD	AVG (LG)	TD	PASS	COMP	PCT	YD	AVG (LG)	TD	INT	SK	YD	QBR	KPR	OTD	PTS	TAY

BROWN, DEREK Derek Darnell, RB, 5'9"/201 lbs; Nebraska; 1993: NO, rnd 4; B4/15/1971 Banning, CA

YEAR	TEAM	G (GS, POS)	RUSH	YD	AVG (LG)	TD	REC	YD	AVG (LG)	TD	KPR	OTD	PTS	TAY
1993	NO	13(12, RB)	180	705	3.9(60)	2	21	170	8.1(19)	1	k	—	18	828
1994	NO	16(9, RB)	146	489	3.3(16)	3	44	428	9.7(37)	1	k	—	24	726
1995	NO	16(0)	49	159	3.2(35)	1	35	266	7.6(19)	1	k	—	12	307
1996	NO	11(0)	13	30	2.3(12)	0	8	54	6.8(14)	0	k	—	0	52
NFL	4	56(21)	388	1383	3.6(60)	6	108	918	8.5(37)	3	k	—	54	1913

BROWN, DEREK Derek Vernon, TE, 6'6"/259 lbs; Notre Dame; 1992: NYG, rnd 1; B3/31/1970 Fairfax, VA

YEAR	TEAM	G (GS, POS)	REC	YD	AVG (LG)	TD	KPR	OTD	PTS	TAY
1992	NYG	16(7, te)	4	31	7.8(9)	0			0	16
1993	†NYG	16(0)	7	56	8.0(14)	0			0	28
1994	NYG	13(0)	—	—	—	—	k		0	-14
1996	†Jax	16(14, TE)	17	141	8.3(16)	0			0	71
1997	Jax	13(8, te)	8	84	10.5(21)	1			6	47
1998	Oak	16(4)	7	89	12.7(27)	0			0	45
1999	Arz	15(0)	—	—	—	—			—	—
NFL	7	105(33)	43	401	9.3(27)	1	k		6	192

BROWN, DON Donald Albert, HB, 6'1"/205 lbs; Houston; 1959: LA, rnd 2; B8/30/1937 Dayton, TX **1960** Hou-A 3

BROWN, DON Donald Colby, T, 6'6"/262 lbs; Santa Clara; B4/12/1959 San Jose, CA **1983** SD 13 (0)

BROWN, DONALD Donald, DB, 5'11"/189 lbs; Oklahoma; Maryland; 1986: SD, rnd 5; B11/28/1963 Annapolis, MD **1986** SD 13 (7, RCB) **1986** Mia 2 (0) **1987** NYG 3 (3) NFL 18 (10) [2 yrs]

BROWN, DOUG Douglas Gordon, DT, 6'7"/290 lbs; Simon Fraser; B9/29/1974 Coquitlam, Canada **1998** Was 10 (8, RDT) **1999**†Was 10 (0) NFL 20 (8) [2 yrs]

BROWN, DOUG Douglas Pat, DT, 6'4"/250 lbs; Fresno State; 1960: LA, rnd 12/DalT, rnd 2; B5/31/1938 Long Beach, CA **1962** LARm 1 **1964** Oak-A 12 NFL 13 [2 yrs]

BROWN, ED Charles Edward, QB, 6'2"/200 lbs; San Francisco; 1952: ChiB, rnd 6; B10/26/1928 San Luis Obispo, CA [KP]

YEAR	TEAM	G (GS, POS)	RUSH	YD	AVG (LG)	TD	REC	YD	AVG (LG)	TD	PASS	COMP	PCT	YD	AVG (LG)	TD	INT	SK	YD	QBR	KPR	OTD	PTS	TAY
1954	ChiB	12	9	36	4.0(18)	0	—	—			17	10	58.8	283	16.6(69)	3	1	—	—	—	Pi	—	0	166
1955	ChiB	12(QB)	43	203	4.7(32)	2	—	—			164	85	51.8	1307	8.0(86)	9	10	—	—	71.4	P	—	12	522
1956	†ChiB◇	12(QB)	40	164	4.1(31)	1	—	—			168	96	**57.1**	1667	**9.9(70)**	11	12	—	—	**83.1**	P	1	12	583
1957	ChiB	12(QB)	31	129	4.2(31)	1	—	—			185	84	45.4	1321	7.1(74)	6	16	—	—	44.4	P	—	6	190
1958	ChiB	12(QB)	32	94	2.9(28)	3	—	—			218	102	46.8	1418	6.5(79)	10	17	—	—	51.0	P	—	18	203
1959	ChiB	12(QB)	33	108	3.3(46)	1	—	—			247	125	50.6	1881	7.6(88)	13	10	—	—	76.7	P	—	6	724
1960	ChiB	12(QB)	19	89	4.7(38)	2	1	-6	-6.0(-6)	0	149	59	39.6	1079	7.2(91)	7	11	—	—	50.2	P	—	12	241
1961	ChiB	14	13	18	1.4(13)	0	—	—			98	46	46.9	742	7.6(84)	4	11	—	—		KP	—	4	-31
1962	Pit	14	2	-8	-4.0(-2)	0	—	—			84	43	51.2	726	8.6(50)	5	6	—	—		P	—	0	140
1963	Pit	14(QB)	15	20	1.3(7)	2	—	—			362	168	46.4	2982	8.2(85)	21	20	—	—	71.4	P	—	12	836
1964	Pit	14(QB)	26	110	4.2(22)	2	—	—			272	121	44.5	1990	7.3(54)	12	19	—	—	55.2	P	—	12	425
1965	Pit	13	1	-1	-1.0(-1)	0	—	—			18	7	38.9	123	6.8(39)	0	5	—	—	—	P	—	0	-140
1965	Bal	1	1	-2	-2.0(-2)	0	—	—			5	3	60.0	81	16.2(68)	1	0	3	24	—	P	—	0	44
NFL	12	154	265	960	3.6(46)	14	1	-6	-6.0(-6)	0	1987	949	47.8	15600	7.9(91)	102	138	3	24	62.8	KPi	—	94	3900

BROWN, EDDIE Paul Edward, DB, 5'11"/187 lbs; Tennessee; 1974: Cle, rnd 8; B2/19/1952 Jasper, TN [R] **1974** Cle 13 **1975** Cle 3 **1975** Was 11 **1976**†Was★14 **1977** Was★14 **1978** LARm 1 **1979**†LARm 16 (5, fs) NFL 72 (5) [6 yrs]

BROWN, EDDIE Eddie Lee, WR, 6'0"/185 lbs; Miami (FL); 1985: Cin, rnd 1; B12/18/1962 Miami, FL

YEAR	TEAM	G (GS, POS)	RUSH	YD	AVG (LG)	TD	REC	YD	AVG (LG)	TD	PASS	COMP	PCT	YD	AVG (LG)	TD	INT	SK	YD	QBR	KPR	OTD	PTS	TAY
1985	Cin	16(16, WR)	14	129	9.2(35)	0	53	942	17.8(68)	8	0	0	0.0	0	0.0	0	0	1	6	—	k	—	48	631
1986	Cin	16(16, WR)	8	32	4.0(17)	0	58	964	16.6(57)	4	—											—	24	534
1987	Cin	12(12, WR)	1	0	0.0(0)	0	44	608	13.8(47)	3	—											—	18	319
1988	†Cin★	16(16, WR)	1	-5	-5.0(-5)	0	53	**1273**	**24.0(86)**	9	—										p	—	54	675
1989	Cin	15(15, WR)	—	—			52	814	15.7(46)	6	—											—	36	437
1990	†Cin	14(12, WR)	—	—			44	706	16.0(50)	**9**	—											—	54	398
1991	Cin	13(12, WR)	1	8	8.0(8)	0	59	827	14.0(53)	2	—											—	12	432
NFL	7	102(99)	25	164	6.6(35)	0	363	6134	16.9(86)	41	0	0	0.0	0	0.0	0	0	1	6	—	kp	—	246	3425

BROWN, ELTON Elton Gillett, G, 6'5"/329 lbs; Virginia; 2005: Arz, rnd 4; B5/22/1982 Hampton, VA **2005** Arz 9 (9, RG)

BROWN, ERIC Eric, WR, 6'2"/180 lbs; Tulsa; B9/7/1964

YEAR	TEAM	G (GS, POS)	REC	YD	AVG (LG)	TD	OTD	PTS	TAY
1987	KC	2(1)	5	69	13.8(23)	0	—	0	35

BROWN, ERIC Eric Jon, DB, 6'1"/210 lbs; Mississippi State; 1998: Den, rnd 2; B3/20/1975 San Antonio, TX **1998** Den 11 (10, SS) **1999** Den 10 (10, FS) **2000**†Den 16 (16, FS) **2001** Den 16 (16, FS) **2002** Hou 15 (15, SS) **2003** Hou 16 (16, SS) **2004** Hou 13 (4) NFL 97 (87) [7 yrs]

BROWN, ERIC Eric, DB, 5'11"/177 lbs; Savannah State; B4/12/1967 **1989** Dal 1 (0)

BROWN, ERNIE Ernest Davis, DE, 6'3"/295 lbs; Syracuse; B3/14/1971 Pittsburgh, PA **1999** Pit 3 (0)

BROWN, FAKHIR Fakhir Hamin, DB, 5'11"/192 lbs; Grambling State; B9/21/1977 Detroit, MI **1999** SD 9 (3) **2000** SD 9 (8, LCB) **2002** NO 12 (0) **2003** NO 16 (0) **2004** NO 16 (10, RCB) **2005** NO 12 (4) NFL 74 (25) [6 yrs]

BROWN, FRED W. Frederick, G, 6'2"/195 lbs; NYU; B12/9/1905, D7/3/1973 Brooklyn, NY **1930** SI 7 (1)

BROWN, FRED Frederick, HB, 5'11"/185 lbs; Georgia; 1961: Buf, rnd 6; B12/22/1938 Atlanta, GA

YEAR	TEAM	G (GS, POS)	RUSH	YD	AVG (LG)	TD	REC	YD	AVG (LG)	TD	KPR	OTD	PTS	TAY
1961	Buf-A	5	53	192	3.6(13)	1	1	11	11.0(11)	0	kp	1	12	297
1963	Buf-A	4	6	18	3.0(8)	1	3	7	2.3(7)	0	k	—	6	42
NFL	2	9	59	210	3.6(13)	2	4	18	4.5(11)	0	kp	1	18	338

BROWN, FRED Fred Richert, LB-TE, 6'4"/240 lbs; Miami (FL); 1965: LA, rnd 3/Bos, rnd 8; B5/4/1943 Honolulu, HI **1965** LARm 14 **1967** Phi 13 (3) **1968** Phi 7

YEAR	TEAM	G (GS, POS)	REC	YD	AVG (LG)	TD	KPR	OTD	PTS	TAY
1969	Phi	6	1	20	20.0(20)	0		—	0	10
NFL	4	40(3)	1	20	20.0(20)	0	ki	—	0	31

BROWN, GARY Gary Leroy, RB, 5'11"/230 lbs; Penn State; 1991: Hou, rnd 8; B7/1/1969 Williamsport, PA

YEAR	TEAM	G (GS, POS)	RUSH	YD	AVG (LG)	TD	REC	YD	AVG (LG)	TD	KPR	OTD	PTS	TAY
1991	†Hou	11(0)	8	85	10.6(39)	1	2	1	0.5(4)	0	k	—	6	81
1992	†Hou	16(0)	19	87	4.6(26)	1	1	5	5.0(5)	0	k	—	6	100
1993	†Hou	16(8, RB)	195	1002	**5.1(26)**	6	21	240	11.4(38)	2	k	—	48	1191
1994	Hou	12(8, rb)	169	648	3.8(18)	4	18	194	10.8(24)	1		—	30	790
1995	Hou	10(4)	86	293	3.4(21)	0	6	16	2.7(7)	0		—	0	301
1997	SD	15(14, RB)	253	945	3.7(32)	4	21	137	6.5(27)	0		—	24	1054
1998	NYG	16(11, RB)	247	1063	4.3(45)	5	13	36	2.8(12)	0		—	30	1131
1999	NYG	3(2)	55	177	3.2(28)	0	2	2	1.0(1)	0		—	0	178
NFL	8	99(47)	1032	4300	4.2(45)	21	84	631	7.5(38)	3	k	—	144	4825

BROWN, GARY Gary Lee, T, 6'4"/307 lbs; Georgia Tech; 1994: Pit, rnd 5; B6/25/1971 Amityville, NY **1994** GB 1 (0) **1995**†GB 16 (16, lt) **1996** GB 8 (5, lt) NFL 25 (5) [3 yrs]

BROWN, GEORGE George T., T, /190 lbs; none; B7/13/1894 Millport, OH, D3/24/1973 Youngstown, OH **1923** Akr 3 (3)

BROWN, GEORGE George William, G-DG, 6'2"/222 lbs; TCU; 1949: Pit, rnd 8; B9/23/1923 Boyd, TX **1949**†NYY-A 8 (0)
1950 NYY 12

BROWN, GILBERT Gilbert Jesse 'The Gravedigger', DT, 6'2"/340 lbs; Kansas; 1993: Min, rnd 3; B2/22/1971 Detroit, MI **1993**†GB 2 (0) **1994** GB 13 (1) **1995**†GB 13 (7, rdt) **1996**†GB 16 (16, LDT) **1997** GB 12 (12, LDT) **1998** GB 16 (16, LDT) **1999** GB 16 (15, LDT) **2001**†GB 11 (11, LDT) **2002** GB 12 (11, LDT) **2003** GB 14 (14, LDT) NFL 125 (103) [10 yrs]

BROWN, GORDON Gordon S., RB, 5'11"/220 lbs; Tulsa; B3/19/1963 Philadelphia, PA

YEAR	TEAM	G (GS, POS)	RUSH	YD	AVG (LG)	TD	OTD	PTS	TAY
1987	Ind	3(0)	19	85	4.5(18)	1	—	6	95

BROWN, GREG Gregory Lee, DE-DT, 6'5"/254 lbs; Kansas State; Eastern Illinois; B1/5/1957 Washington, DC [S] **1981**†Phi 16 (0) **1982** Phi 9 (0) **1983** Phi 16 (5, rde) **1984** Phi 16 (16, RDE) **1985** Phi 16 (16, RDE) **1986** Phi 16 (15, RDE) **1987** Atl 12 (5, lde) **1988** Atl 16 (1) NFL 117 (58) [8 yrs]

YEAR	TEAM	G (GS, POS)	RUSH	YD	AVG(LG)	TD	REC	YD	AVG(LG)	TD	PASS	COMP	PCT	YD	AVG(LG)	TD	INT	SK	YD	QBR	KPR	OTD	PTS	TAY

BROWN, GUY   Guy, LB, 6´4˝/223 lbs; Houston; 1977: Dal, rnd 4; B6/1/1955 Palestine, TX   **1977**†Dal 14 (1)   **1978**†Dal 15   **1979**†Dal 15   **1980**†Dal 16 (0)   **1981**†Dal 16 (6, llb) **1982**†Dal 9 (8, RLB)   **NFL** 85 (15) [6 yrs]

BROWN, HARDY   Hardy, LB-DB-FB, 6´0˝/193 lbs; SMU; Tulsa; 1947: NYG, rnd 12; B5/8/1924 Quanah, TX, D11/8/1991 Stockton, CA **[K]**   **1950** Was 8 (RLB)   **1950** Bal 4 **1951** SF☆12 (MLB)   **1952** SF★12 (MLB)   **1953** SF 12 (MLB)   **1954** SF 11 (LLB)   **1955** SF 12 (RLB)   **1956** ChiC 8   **1960** Den-A 13 (MLB)   **NFL** 92 [8 yrs]

1948	Bkn-A	11(4)	6	23	3.8	1	3	36	12.0	1	—	—	—	—	—	—	—	—	—	—	Ki	—	37	51
1949	ChiH-A	12(1)	1	2	2.0(2)	0	1	10	10.0(10)	0	—	—	—	—	—	—	—	—	—	—	Pi	—	0	51
AAFC	2	23(5)	7	25	3.6(2)	1	4	46	11.5(10)	1	—	—	—	—	—	—	—	—	—	—	KPi	—	37	102

BROWN, HOWIE   Howard Kenneth, G-T-DT, 5´11˝/215 lbs; Indiana; 1946: GB, rnd 22/1947: Mia-A, rnd 18; B1/26/1922 Dayton, OH, D4/4/1975 Bloomington, IL   **1948** Det 12 (12, LG) **1949** Det 12 (10, RT)   **1950** Det 12   **NFL** 36 (22) [3 yrs]

BROWN, IVORY LEE   Ivory Lee, RB, 6´2˝/245 lbs; Arkansas-Pine Bluff; 1991: Phx, rnd 7; B8/17/1969 Palestine, TX

| 1992 | Phx | 7(5, rb) | 68 | 194 | 2.9(13) | 2 | 7 | 54 | 7.7(18) | 0 | — | — | — | — | — | — | — | — | — | — | — | — | 12 | 241 |

BROWN, J.B.   James Harold, DB, 6´0˝/193 lbs; Maryland; 1989: Mia, rnd 12; B1/5/1967 Washington, DC   **1989** Mia 16 (0)   **1990**†Mia 16 (16, RCB)   **1991** Mia 15 (11, RCB) **1992**†Mia 16 (16, RCB)   **1993** Mia 16 (16, RCB)   **1994** Mia 16 (16, RCB)   **1995**†Mia 13 (12, RCB)   **1996** Mia 14 (1)   **1997** Pit 13 (0)   **1998**†Arz 15 (6, RCB)   **1999**†Det 13 (3) **2000** Det 3 (0)   **NFL** 166 (97) [12 yrs]

BROWN, JACK   John Roman, C-G-T, 6´0˝/191 lbs; Dayton; B10/24/1902 Dayton, OH, D11/25/1987 Dayton, OH   **1926** Day 2 (0)   **1927** Day 3 (0)   **1928** Day 5 (0)   **1929** Day 6 (0) **NFL** 16 (0) [4 yrs]

BROWN, JAMES   James Lamont, T, 6´6˝/330 lbs; Virginia State; 1992: Dal, rnd 3; B11/30/1970 Philadelphia, PA   **1993** NYJ 14 (1)   **1994** NYJ 16 (6, rt)   **1995** NYJ 14 (12, RT) **1996** Mia 16 (16, RT)   **1997**†Mia 16 (16, RT)   **1998**†Mia 16 (16, RT)   **1999** Mia 15 (14, RT)   **2000** Cle 7 (5, rt)   **NFL** 114 (86) [8 yrs]

BROWN, JAMIE   Jamie Sheppard, T, 6´8˝/320 lbs; Florida A&M; 1995: Den, rnd 4; B4/24/1972 Miami, FL   **1995** Den 6 (0)   **1996**†Den 12 (2)   **1997** Den 11 (2)   **1998** SF 8 (5, lt) **1999** Was 1 (0)   **NFL** 38 (9) [5 yrs]

BROWN, JAMMAL   Jammal F., T, 6´6˝/313 lbs; Oklahoma; 2005: NO, rnd 1; B3/30/1981 El Paso, TX   **2005** NO 13 (13, RT)

BROWN, JASON   J.W. Jason, C, 6´3˝/313 lbs; North Carolina; 2005: Bal, rnd 4; B5/5/1983 Henderson, NC   **2005** Bal 6 (1)

BROWN, JEROME   Jerome, DT, 6´2˝/292 lbs; Miami (FL); 1987: Phi, rnd 1; B2/4/1965 Brooksville, FL, D6/25/1992 Brooksville, FL   **1987** Phi 12 (8, RDT)   **1988**†Phi 16 (15, RDT) **1989**†Phi☆16 (16, RDT)   **1990**†Phi★16 (15, RDT)   **1991** Phi☆16 (11, RDT)   **NFL** 76 (65) [5 yrs]

BROWN, JESSE   Jesse J., TB, 5´10˝/180 lbs; Pittsburgh; B11/6/1902, D11/1987 Ellwood City, PA   **1926** Pot 14 (11, TB)

BROWN, JIM   James Nathaniel, FB, 6´2˝/232 lbs; Syracuse; 1957: Cle, rnd 1; B2/17/1936 St. Simons Island, GA; HOF 1971

1957	†Cle★	12(12, FB)	202	**942**	4.7(69)	9	16	55	3.4(12)	1	—	—	—	—	—	—	—	—	—	—	k	—	60	**1111**
1958	†Cle★	12(12, FB)	**257**	**1527**	5.9(65)	17	16	138	8.6(46)	1	—	—	—	—	—	—	—	—	—	—	k	—	108	**1800**
1959	Cle★	12(12, FB)	**290**	**1329**	4.6(70)	14	24	190	7.9(25)	0	—	—	—	—	—	—	—	—	—	—	k	—	84	**1592**
1960	Cle★	12(12, FB)	215	1257	5.8(71)	9	19	204	10.7(37)	2	—	—	—	—	—	—	—	—	—	—	k	—	66	**1549**
1961	Cle★	14(14, FB)	**305**	**1408**	4.6(38)	8	46	459	10.0(77)	2	3	1	33.3	37	12.3(37)	1	0	—	—	—	k	—	60	**1771**
1962	Cle★	14(14, FB)	230	996	4.3(31)	13	47	517	11.0(53)	5	2	1	50.0	28	14.0(28)	0	0	—	—	—	k	—	108	1424
1963	Cle★	14(14, FB)	291	**1863**	**6.4(80)**	12	24	268	11.2(83)	3	4	0	0.0	0	0	0	0	1	8	—	—	—	90	**2132**
1964	†Cle★	14(14, FB)	280	1446	5.2(71)	7	36	340	9.4(40)	2	1	1	100.0	13	13.0(13)	1	0	—	—	—	k	—	54	**1708**
1965	†Cle★	14(14, FB)	289	1544	5.3(67)	17	34	328	9.6(32)	4	2	1	50.0	39	19.5(39)	1	0	—	—	—	k	—	126	**1923**
NFL	9	118(118)	2359	12312	5.2(80)	106	262	2499	9.5(83)	20	12	4	33.3	117	9.8(39)	3	0	1	8	—	k	—	756	15008

BROWN, JOE   Joe, DT, 6´6˝/288 lbs; Ohio State; B3/5/1977 Columbus, OH   **2001** Sea 2 (0)

BROWN, JOHN   John Edward, LB-C, 6´4˝/230 lbs; North Carolina Central; B4/9/1922 Belen, MS   **1947** LAD-A 14 (2)   **1948** LAD-A 14 (0)   **1949** LAD-A 12 (3)   **AAFC** 40 (5) [3 yrs]

BROWN, JOHN   John Calvin, T, 6´2˝/248 lbs; Syracuse; 1961: Cle, rnd 4; B6/9/1939 Camden, NJ   **1962** Cle 14   **1963** Cle 14 (14, RT)   **1964**†Cle 11   **1965**†Cle 14   **1966** Cle 14 (rt) **1967** Pit 13 (RT)   **1968** Pit 14 (RT)   **1969** Pit 14 (RT)   **1970** Pit 14 (RT)   **1971** Pit 14 (RT)   **NFL** 136 (14) [10 yrs]

BROWN, JONATHAN   Jonathan Bernard, DE, 6´4˝/270 lbs; Tennessee; 1998: GB, rnd 3; B11/28/1975 Chickasha, OK   **1998** GB 4 (0)   **2001** SL 3 (0)   **NFL** 7 (0) [2 yrs]

BROWN, JOSH   Joshua, K, 6´0˝/202 lbs; Nebraska; 2003: Sea, rnd 7; B4/29/1979 Tulsa, OK **[K]**   **2003**†Sea 16 (0)   **2004**†Sea 16 (0)   **2005**†Sea 16 (0)   **NFL** 48 (0) [3 yrs]

BROWN, KEN   Kenneth J., RB, 5´10˝/203 lbs; none; B11/8/1945 Holdenville, OK, D1/11/2001 Oklahoma City, OK

1970	Cle	11	1	-8	-8.0(-8)	0	—	—	—	—	—	—	—	—	—	—	—	—	—	—	k	—	0	6
1971	†Cle	10	11	47	4.3(17)	0	—	—	—	—	—	—	—	—	—	—	—	—	—	—	k	—	0	152
1972	†Cle	14	32	114	3.6(14)	2	5	64	12.8(19)	0	—	—	—	—	—	—	—	—	—	—	k	—	12	339
1973	Cle	14(FB)	161	537	3.3(17)	0	22	187	8.5(46)	0	—	—	—	—	—	—	—	—	—	—	—	—	0	631
1974	Cle	14(rb)	125	458	3.7(27)	4	29	194	6.7(19)	2	—	—	—	—	—	—	—	—	—	—	k	—	36	599
1975	Cle	14	16	45	2.8(8)	1	2	23	11.5(17)	0	—	—	—	—	—	—	—	—	—	—	k	—	6	88
NFL	6	77	346	1193	3.4(27)	7	58	468	8.1(46)	2	—	—	—	—	—	—	—	—	—	—	k	—	54	1814

BROWN, KEN   Kenneth Bernard, WR, 5´8˝/175 lbs; Southern Arkansas; B3/10/1965 Monroe, LA   **1987** Cin 3 (3)

BROWN, KEN   Kenneth Anderson, LB, 6´1˝/235 lbs; Virginia Tech; 1995: Den, rnd 4; B5/9/1971 Wiesbaden, Germany   **1995** Den 2 (0)

BROWN, KEN   Kenneth Eugene, C, 6´1˝/245 lbs; New Mexico; B4/19/1954 Saginaw, MI   **1979**†Den 16   **1980** GB 1 (0)   **NFL** 17 [2 yrs]

BROWN, KEVIN   Kevin Don, P, 6´2˝/178 lbs; West Texas A&M; B1/11/1963 Panhandle, TX

| 1987 | ChiB | 3(0) | 1 | 0 | 0.0(0) | 0 | — | — | — | — | — | — | — | — | — | — | — | — | — | — | P | — | 0 | 0 |

BROWN, KRIS   Kristopher Clayton, K, 5´11˝/206 lbs; Nebraska; 1999: Pit, rnd 7; B12/23/1976 Southlake, TX **[K]**   **1999** Pit 16 (0)   **2000** Pit 16 (0)   **2002** Hou 16 (0)   **2003** Hou 16 (0) **2004** Hou 16 (0)

2001	†Pit	16(0)	1	6	6.0(6)	0	—	—	—	—	—	—	—	—	—	—	—	—	—	—	KP	—	124	6
2005	Hou	16(0)	1	4	4.0(4)	0	—	—	—	—	—	—	—	—	—	—	—	—	—	—	K	—	102	4
NFL	7	112(0)	2	10	5.0(6)	0	—	—	—	—	—	—	—	—	—	—	—	—	—	—	KP	—	675	10

BROWN, LANCE   Lance Allen, DB, 6´2˝/200 lbs; Indiana; 1995: Pit, rnd 5; B2/2/1972 Jacksonville, FL   **1995** Arz 11 (5, RCB)   **1996** Arz 1 (0)   **1998** Pit 16 (0)   **1999** Pit 16 (0) **2001** Buf 14 (1)   **NFL** 58 (6) [5 yrs]

BROWN, LARON   Laron Gregg, WR, 5´9˝/172 lbs; Tennessee; Texas; 1987: Was, rnd 11; B11/10/1963 Dayton, OH

| 1987 | Den | 3(1) | — | — | — | — | 4 | 40 | 10.0(18) | 0 | — | — | — | — | — | — | — | — | — | — | k | — | 0 | 32 |

BROWN, LARRY   Lawrence, T-TE, 6´4˝/246 lbs; Kansas; 1971: Pit, rnd 5; B6/16/1949 Jacksonville, FL   **1977**†Pit 14 (14, RT)   **1978**†Pit 8 (5, rt)   **1980** Pit 16 (16, RT) **1981** Pit 14 (14, RT)   **1982**†Pit◇8 (8, RT)   **1983**†Pit 8 (8, rt)   **1984** Pit 7 (7, RT)

1971	Pit	13	—	—	—	—	1	3	3.0(3)	1	—	—	—	—	—	—	—	—	—	—	—	—	6	7
1972	†Pit	9	—	—	—	—	1	13	13.0(13)	1	—	—	—	—	—	—	—	—	—	—	—	—	6	12
1973	†Pit	14(1)	—	—	—	—	5	88	17.6(45)	0	—	—	—	—	—	—	—	—	—	—	—	—	0	44
1974	†Pit	14(12, TE)	—	—	—	—	17	190	11.2(35)	1	—	—	—	—	—	—	—	—	—	—	—	—	6	100
1975	†Pit	14(13, TE)	—	—	—	—	16	244	15.3(27)	1	—	—	—	—	—	—	—	—	—	—	—	—	6	127
1976	†Pit	13(8, TE)	—	—	—	—	7	97	13.9(35)	0	—	—	—	—	—	—	—	—	—	—	—	—	0	49
1979	†Pit	15(14, RT)	—	—	—	—	1	1	1.0(1)	1	—	—	—	—	—	—	—	—	—	—	—	—	6	6
NFL	14	167(120)	—	—	—	—	48	636	13.3(45)	5	—	—	—	—	—	—	—	—	—	—	—	—	30	343

BROWN, LARRY   Larry, DB, 5´11˝/186 lbs; TCU; 1991: Dal, rnd 12; B11/30/1969 Miami, FL   **1991**†Dal 16 (13, RCB)   **1992**†Dal 16 (15, RCB)   **1993**†Dal 16 (16, RCB) **1994**†Dal 15 (15, RCB)   **1995**†Dal 16 (15, RCB)   **1996** Oak 8 (1)   **1997** Oak 4 (0)   **1998** Dal 4 (0)   **NFL** 95 (75) [8 yrs]

BROWN, LARRY   Larry Donell, T, 6´5˝/260 lbs; Miami (FL); 1978: KC, rnd 9; B6/4/1955 Jacksonville, FL   **1978** KC 1   **1979** KC 4   **NFL** 5 [2 yrs]

BROWN, LARRY   Lawrence, WR, 5´11˝/180 lbs; Mankato State; B9/4/1963 Miami, FL   **1987** Min 1 (0)

BROWN, LARRY   Larry Lovette, TE, 6´4˝/280 lbs; Georgia; B9/1/1976 Decatur, GA   **1999**†Ten 9 (0)

BROWN, LARRY   Lawrence, RB, 5´11˝/195 lbs; Kansas State; 1969: Was, rnd 8; B9/19/1947 Clairton, PA

| 1969 | Was◇ | 14(HB) | 202 | 888 | 4.4(57) | 4 | 34 | 302 | 8.9(31) | 0 | — | — | — | — | — | — | — | — | — | — | — | — | 24 | 1079 |
| 1970 | Was★ | 13(13, RB) | 237 | **1125** | 4.7(75) | 5 | 37 | 341 | 9.2(66) | 2 | — | — | — | — | — | — | — | — | — | — | — | — | 42 | 1356 |

YEAR	TEAM	G (GS, POS)	RUSH	YD	AVG (LG)	TD	REC	YD	AVG (LG)	TD	PASS	COMP	PCT	YD	AVG (LG)	TD	INT	SK	YD	QBR	KPR	OTD	PTS	TAY
1971	†Was★	13(13, RB)	**253**	948	3.7(34)	4	16	176	11.0(36)	2	—	—	—	—	—	—	—	—	—	—	—	—	36	1086
1972	†Was★	12(12, RB)	285	**1216**	4.3(38)	8	32	473	14.8(89)	4	—	—	—	—	—	—	—	—	—	—	—	—	72	**1553**
1973	†Was	14(14, RB)	**273**	860	3.2(27)	8	40	482	12.1(64)	6	—	—	—	—	—	—	—	—	—	—	—	—	84	1211
1974	†Was	11(11, RB)	163	430	2.6(16)	3	37	388	10.5(34)	4	1	1	100.0	16	16.0(16)	0	0	—	—	—	—	—	42	682
1975	Was	14(8, rb)	97	352	3.6(43)	3	25	225	9.0(39)	2	—	—	—	—	—	—	—	—	—	—	—	—	30	505
1976	†Was	11	20	56	2.8(11)	0	17	98	5.8(15)	0	—	—	—	—	—	—	—	—	—	—	—	—	0	105
NFL	8	102(71)	1530	5875	3.8(75)	35	238	2485	10.4(89)	20	1	1	100.0	16	16.0(16)	0	0	—	—	—	—	—	330	7576

BROWN, LOMAS Lomas, T, 6´4˝/282 lbs; Florida; 1985: Det, rnd 1; B3/30/1963 Miami, FL **1985** Det 16 (16, LT) **1986** Det 16 (16, LT) **1987** Det 11 (11, LT) **1988** Det 16 (16, LT) **1990** Det★16 (16, LT) **1991**†Det★15 (15, LT) **1992** Det★16 (16, LT) **1993**†Det✧11 (11, LT) **1994**†Det★16 (16, LT) **1995**†Det★15 (14, LT) **1996** Arz★16 (16, LT) **1997** Arz 14 (14, LT) **1998**†Arz 16 (16, LT) **1999** Cle 10 (10, LT) **2000**†NYG 16 (16, LT) **2001** NYG 16 (16, LT) **2002**†TB 11 (0)

YEAR	TEAM	G (GS, POS)	RUSH	YD	AVG (LG)	TD	REC	YD	AVG (LG)	TD	PASS	COMP	PCT	YD	AVG (LG)	TD	INT	SK	YD	QBR	KPR	OTD	PTS	TAY
1989	Det☆	16(16, LT)	1	3	3.0(3)	0	—	—	—	—	—	—	—	—	—	—	—	—	—	—	—	—	0	3
NFL	18	263(251)	1	3	3.0(3)	0	—	—	—	—	—	—	—	—	—	—	—	—	—	—	—	—	0	3

BROWN, MARC Marc Stacy, WR, 6´2˝/195 lbs; Towson State; B5/7/1961 Nyack, NY

YEAR	TEAM	G (GS, POS)	RUSH	YD	AVG (LG)	TD	REC	YD	AVG (LG)	TD	PASS	COMP	PCT	YD	AVG (LG)	TD	INT	SK	YD	QBR	KPR	OTD	PTS	TAY
1987	Buf	3(0)	—	—	—	—	9	120	13.3(30)	1	—	—	—	—	—	—	—	—	—	—	k	—	6	70

BROWN, MARK Marc Anthony, LB, 6´2˝/230 lbs; Purdue; 1983: Mia, rnd 9; B7/18/1961 New Brunswick, NJ **1983**†Mia 14 (1) **1984**†Mia 16 (9, RILB) **1985**†Mia 15 (15, RILB) **1986** Mia 14 (11, ROLB) **1987** Mia 12 (12, ROLB) **1988** Mia 13 (12, LILB) **1989** Det 6 (3) **1990** Det 15 (0) **1991** Det 2 (0) **NFL** 107 (63) [9 yrs]

BROWN, MARK Mark, LB, 6´0˝/238 lbs; Auburn; B5/19/1980 Paterson, NJ **2003** NYJ 1 (0) **2004**†NYJ 12 (5, llb) **2005** NYJ 15 (11, RLB) **NFL** 28 (16) [3 yrs]

BROWN, MARV Marvin Clifford, HB, 5´8˝/150 lbs; Tarleton State; Texas A&M-Commerce; 1953: Det, rnd 25; B8/15/1930 Marshall, TX

YEAR	TEAM	G (GS, POS)	RUSH	YD	AVG (LG)	TD	REC	YD	AVG (LG)	TD	PASS	COMP	PCT	YD	AVG (LG)	TD	INT	SK	YD	QBR	KPR	OTD	PTS	TAY
1957	Det	4	2	6	3.0(3)	0	—	—	—	—	—	—	—	—	—	—	—	—	—	—	kp	—	0	23

BROWN, MATT Matthew, HB, 5´10˝/170 lbs; Syracuse; deceased **1920** Akr 1 (0)

BROWN, MICHAEL Michael, LB, 5´10˝/220 lbs; Louisville; B1/16/1980 Louisville, KY **2004** Was 2 (0)

BROWN, MIKE Mike, DB, 5´10˝/212 lbs; Nebraska; 2000: Chi, rnd 2; B2/13/1978 Scottsdale, AZ **2000** ChiB 16 (16, FS) **2001**†ChiB☆16 (16, FS) **2002** ChiB 16 (15, FS) **2003** ChiB 16 (16, FS) **2004** ChiB 2 (2) **2005**†ChiB★12 (12, SS) **NFL** 78 (77) [6 yrs]

BROWN, MILFORD Milford, G, 6´4˝/320 lbs; Florida State; 2002: Hou, rnd S6; B8/15/1980 Montgomery, AL **2003** Hou 3 (2) **2004** Hou 2 (2) **2005** Hou 13 (12, LG) **NFL** 18 (16) [3 yrs]

BROWN, MONTY Montague N.Gai, LB, 6´0˝/238 lbs; Ferris State; B4/13/1970 Bridgeport, MI **1993**†Buf 13 (0) **1994** Buf 3 (0) **1995**†Buf 16 (6, lilb) **1996** NE 11 (7, llb) **NFL** 43 (13) [4 yrs]

BROWN, NA Na Orlando, WR, 6´0˝/196 lbs; North Carolina; 1999: Phi, rnd 4; B2/22/1977 Reidsville, NC

YEAR	TEAM	G (GS, POS)	RUSH	YD	AVG (LG)	TD	REC	YD	AVG (LG)	TD	PASS	COMP	PCT	YD	AVG (LG)	TD	INT	SK	YD	QBR	KPR	OTD	PTS	TAY
1999	Phi	12(5, wr)	—	—	—	—	18	188	10.4(27)	1	—	—	—	—	—	—	—	—	—	—	p	—	6	99
2000	†Phi	14(2)	—	—	—	—	9	80	8.9(18)	1	—	—	—	—	—	—	—	—	—	—	—	—	6	45
2001	†Phi	16(2)	—	—	—	—	7	95	13.6(18)	0	—	—	—	—	—	—	—	—	—	—	p	—	0	53
NFL	3	42(9)	—	—	—	—	34	363	10.7(27)	2	—	—	—	—	—	—	—	—	—	—	p	—	12	197

BROWN, NORRIS Willie Norris, TE, 6´3˝/220 lbs; Georgia; 1983: Min, rnd 8; B7/10/1961 Laurens, SC **1983** Min 2 (0)

BROWN, OMAR Omar Lamont, DB, 5´10˝/200 lbs; North Carolina; 1998: Atl, rnd 4; B3/28/1975 York, PA **1998** Atl 2 (0) **1999** Atl 13 (0) **NFL** 15 (0) [2 yrs]

BROWN, ORLANDO Orlando Claude, T, 6´7˝/360 lbs; Central State (OH); South Carolina State; B12/12/1970 Washington, DC **1994**†Cle 14 (8, rt) **1995** Cle 16 (16, RT) **1996** Bal 16 (16, RT) **1997** Bal 16 (16, RT) **1998** Bal 13 (13, RT) **1999** Cle 15 (15, RT) **2003**†Bal 16 (13, RT) **2004** Bal 14 (13, RT) **2005** Bal 9 (9, RT) **NFL** 129 (119) [9 yrs]

BROWN, OTTO Otto, DB, 6´1˝/188 lbs; Prairie View A&M; B1/12/1947 Tallahassee, FL **1969**†Dal 14 **1970** NYG 13 **1971** NYG 12 (LCB) **1972** NYG 13 **1973** NYG 11 **NFL** 63 [5 yrs]

BROWN, PETE Samuel Morris, C-LB, 6´2˝/210 lbs; Georgia Tech; 1953: SF, rnd 10; B12/19/1930 Rossville, GA, D9/4/2001 Atlanta, GA **1953** SF 12

YEAR	TEAM	G (GS, POS)	RUSH	YD	AVG (LG)	TD	REC	YD	AVG (LG)	TD	PASS	COMP	PCT	YD	AVG (LG)	TD	INT	SK	YD	QBR	KPR	OTD	PTS	TAY
1954	SF	12	1	-6	-6.0(-6)	0	—	—	—	—	1	1	100.0	19	19.0(19)	0	0	—	—	—	Pi	—	0	46
NFL	2	24	1	-6	-6.0(-6)	0	—	—	—	—	1	1	100.0	19	19.0(19)	0	0	—	—	—	—	—	0	4

BROWN, PRESTON Preston Neville, WR, 5´10˝/184 lbs; Vanderbilt; 1980: NE, rnd 6; B3/2/1958 Nashville, TN **1980** NE 5 (0) **1983** NYJ 16 (0) **1984** Cle 2 (0)

YEAR	TEAM	G (GS, POS)	RUSH	YD	AVG (LG)	TD	REC	YD	AVG (LG)	TD	PASS	COMP	PCT	YD	AVG (LG)	TD	INT	SK	YD	QBR	KPR	OTD	PTS	TAY
1982	†NE	9(4)	—	—	—	—	4	114	28.5(41)	1	—	—	—	—	—	—	—	—	—	—	—	—	6	62
NFL	4	32(4)	—	—	—	—	4	114	28.5(41)	1	—	—	—	—	—	—	—	—	—	—	kp	—	6	301

BROWN, RALPH Ralph, DB, 5´10˝/185 lbs; Nebraska; 2000: NYG, rnd 5; B9/16/1978 Hacienda Heights, CA **2000** NYG 2 (0) **2001** NYG 8 (0) **2002**†NYG 16 (2) **2003** NYG 11 (7, rcb) **2004**†Min 12 (0) **2005** Min 16 (0) **NFL** 65 (9) [6 yrs]

BROWN, RAY Raymond Lloyd, DB-QB, 6´2˝/195 lbs; Mississippi; 1958: Bal, rnd 5; B9/7/1936 Clarksdale, MS

YEAR	TEAM	G (GS, POS)	RUSH	YD	AVG (LG)	TD	REC	YD	AVG (LG)	TD	PASS	COMP	PCT	YD	AVG (LG)	TD	INT	SK	YD	QBR	KPR	OTD	PTS	TAY
1958	†Bal	12(12, DB)	1	-9	-9.0(-9)	0	—	—	—	—	2	1	50.0	1	-0.5(-1)	0	0	—	—	—	Pi	—	0	100
1959	†Bal	12(DB)	2	4	2.0(3)	0	—	—	—	—	4	1	25.0	14	3.5(14)	0	0	—	—	—	Pi	—	0	75
1960	Bal	12	2	25	12.5(23)	0	—	—	—	—	13	6	46.2	65	5.0(21)	1	0	—	—	—	P	—	0	63
NFL	3	36(12)	5	20	4.0(23)	0	—	—	—	—	19	8	42.1	78	4.1(21)	1	0	—	—	—	Pi	—	0	237

BROWN, RAY Raymond Madison, DB, 6´1˝/208 lbs; West Texas A&M; 1971: Atl, rnd 6; B1/12/1949 Fort Worth, TX **[I]** **1971** Atl 10 (FS) **1972** Atl 14 (SS) **1973** Atl 14 (SS) **1974** Atl☆14 (SS) **1975** Atl 14 (FS) **1976** Atl 14 (14, SS) **1977** Atl 14 (SS) **1978** NO 16 (16, SS) **1979** NO 12 (12, SS) **1980** NO 15 (9, SS) **NFL** 137 (51) [10 yrs]

BROWN, RAY Leonard Ray, G-T, 6´5˝/318 lbs; Memphis; Arkansas State; 1986: SL, rnd 8; B12/12/1962 Marion, AR **1986** SL 11 (4) **1987** SL 7 (3) **1988** Phx 15 (1) **1989** Was 7 (0) **1990**†Was 0 (0) **1992**†Was 16 (8, lg) **1993** Was 16 (14, LG) **1994** Was 16 (16, LG) **1995** Was 16 (16, LG) **1996**†SF 16 (16, LG) **1997**†SF 15 (15, LG) **1998**†SF 16 (16, LG) **1999** SF 16 (16, LG) **2000** SF 16 (16, LG) **2001**†SF★16 (16, LG) **2002** Det 16 (16, RG) **2003** Det 16 (16, RG) **2004** Was 16 (14, RT) **2005**†Was 15 (2) **NFL** 262 (205) [19 yrs]

BROWN, RAY Raynard Albert, WR, 5´9˝/185 lbs; South Carolina; 1987: Det, rnd 10; B7/25/1965 Bronx, NY **1987** SF 1 (0)

BROWN, REGGIE Reginald Van, RB, 5´11˝/211 lbs; Oregon; 1982: Atl, rnd 4; B3/12/1960 Dendron, VA **1982**†Atl 8 (0) **1983** Atl 2 (0)

YEAR	TEAM	G (GS, POS)	RUSH	YD	AVG (LG)	TD	REC	YD	AVG (LG)	TD	PASS	COMP	PCT	YD	AVG (LG)	TD	INT	SK	YD	QBR	KPR	OTD	PTS	TAY
1987	Phi	3(3)	39	136	3.5(23)	0	8	53	6.6(14)	0	—	—	—	—	—	—	—	—	—	—	k	—	0	168
NFL	3	13(3)	39	136	3.5(23)	0	8	53	6.6(14)	0	—	—	—	—	—	—	—	—	—	—	k	—	0	274

BROWN, REGGIE Reggie, WR, 6´1˝/197 lbs; Georgia; 2005: Phi, rnd 2; B1/13/1981 Carrollton, GA

YEAR	TEAM	G (GS, POS)	RUSH	YD	AVG (LG)	TD	REC	YD	AVG (LG)	TD	PASS	COMP	PCT	YD	AVG (LG)	TD	INT	SK	YD	QBR	KPR	OTD	PTS	TAY
2005	Phi	16(11, WR)	1	5	5.0(5)	0	43	571	13.3(56)	4	—	—	—	—	—	—	—	—	—	—	—	—	24	311

BROWN, REGGIE Reginald Alonzo, WR, 6´1˝/195 lbs; Alabama State; B5/5/1970 Miami, FL

YEAR	TEAM	G (GS, POS)	RUSH	YD	AVG (LG)	TD	REC	YD	AVG (LG)	TD	PASS	COMP	PCT	YD	AVG (LG)	TD	INT	SK	YD	QBR	KPR	OTD	PTS	TAY
1993	Hou	4(0)	—	—	—	—	2	30	15.0(26)	0	—	—	—	—	—	—	—	—	—	—	—	—	0	15
1994	Hou	4(0)	—	—	—	—	4	34	8.5(11)	0	—	—	—	—	—	—	—	—	—	—	—	—	2	17
NFL	2	8(0)	—	—	—	—	6	64	10.7(26)	0	—	—	—	—	—	—	—	—	—	—	—	—	2	32

BROWN, REGGIE Reginald Dwayne, LB, 6´2˝/241 lbs; Texas A&M; 1996: Det, rnd 1; B9/28/1974 Austin, TX **1996** Det 10 (10, RLB) **1997** Det 16 (16, RLB) **NFL** 26 (26) [2 yrs]

BROWN, REGGIE Regilyn DeWayne, RB, 6´0˝/244 lbs; Fresno State; 1996: Sea, rnd 3; B6/26/1973 Highland Park, MI

YEAR	TEAM	G (GS, POS)	RUSH	YD	AVG (LG)	TD	REC	YD	AVG (LG)	TD	PASS	COMP	PCT	YD	AVG (LG)	TD	INT	SK	YD	QBR	KPR	OTD	PTS	TAY
1996	Sea	7(0)	—	—	—	—	—	—	—	—	—	—	—	—	—	—	—	—	—	—	k	—	0	-9
1997	Sea	11(0)	—	—	—	—	—	—	—	—	—	—	—	—	—	—	—	—	—	—	k	—	0	1
1998	Sea	15(1)	1	2	2.0(2)	0	—	—	—	—	—	—	—	—	—	—	—	—	—	—	k	—	0	-14
1999	†Sea	16(8, FB)	14	38	2.7(9)	0	34	228	6.7(26)	1	—	—	—	—	—	—	—	—	—	—	—	—	6	157
2000	Sea	12(1)	3	6	2.0(3)	0	2	9	4.5(6)	0	—	—	—	—	—	—	—	—	—	—	k	—	0	-1
NFL	5	61(10)	18	46	2.6(9)	0	36	237	6.6(26)	1	—	—	—	—	—	—	—	—	—	—	k	—	6	135

BROWN, RICHARD Richard McClure, C, 6´1˝/220 lbs; Iowa; B5/27/1907 Waverly, IA **1930** Por 11 (8, C)

BROWN, RICHARD Richard Solomon, LB, 6´3˝/240 lbs; San Diego State; B9/21/1965 Western Samoa **1987** LARm 8 (0) **1989** LARm 13 (2) **1990** SD 11 (0) **1991** Cle 16 (12, MLB) **1992** Cle 10 (0) **1994**†Min 3 (0) **1995** Min 16 (0) **1996**†Min 14 (0) **NFL** 91 (14) [8 yrs]

BROWN, ROBERT Robert Lee, DE, 6´2˝/268 lbs; Chowan Coll. (NC); Virginia Tech; 1982: GB, rnd 4; B5/21/1960 Edenton, NC **1982**†GB 8 (0) **1983** GB 16 (0) **1984** GB 16 (0) **1985** GB 16 (4) **1986** GB 16 (16, RDE) **1987** GB 12 (12, RDE) **1988** GB 16 (16, RDE) **1989** GB 16 (16, RDE/lde) **1990** GB 16 (16, RDE) **1991** GB 16 (16, RDE) **1992** GB 16 (16, RDE) **NFL** 164 (112) [11 yrs]

BROWN, ROBERT Robert Earl, TE, 6´2˝/225 lbs; Alcorn State; B1/1/1943 Pace, MS

YEAR	TEAM	G (GS, POS)	RUSH	YD	AVG (LG)	TD	REC	YD	AVG (LG)	TD	PASS	COMP	PCT	YD	AVG (LG)	TD	INT	SK	YD	QBR	KPR	OTD	PTS	TAY
1969	SL	12	—	—	—	—	—	—	—	—	—	—	—	—	—	—	—	—	—	—	—	—	—	—
1970	SL	14	1	8	8.0(8)	0	—	—	—	—	—	—	—	—	—	—	—	—	—	—	—	—	0	8
1971	†Min	8	—	—	—	—	6	141	23.5(48)	0	—	—	—	—	—	—	—	—	—	—	—	—	0	71
1972	NO	14	—	—	—	—	11	175	15.9(34)	1	—	—	—	—	—	—	—	—	—	—	—	—	6	93
1973	NO	5(te)	—	—	—	—	11	132	12.0(26)	0	—	—	—	—	—	—	—	—	—	—	—	—	0	66
NFL	5	53	1	8	8.0(8)	0	28	448	16.0(48)	1	—	—	—	—	—	—	—	—	—	—	—	—	6	237

BROWN, ROBERT Robert Eddie, DT-DE, 6´5˝/260 lbs; Arkansas-Pine Bluff; 1964: SF, rnd 13/Den, rnd 1; B2/22/1940 Bonita, LA, D12/10/1998 Memphis, TN **1966** GB 14 **1967**†GB 14 **1968** GB 6 **1969** GB 14 (rdt) **1970** GB 14 (LDT/lde) **1971** GB☆14 (RDT) **1972**†GB★14 (RDT) **1973** GB 14 (RDT) **1974** SD 14 (13, RDT) **1975**†Cin 14 (LDT) **1976** Cin 14 (LDT) **NFL** 146 (13) [11 yrs]

BROWN, ROGER Roger Lee, DT, 6´5˝/300 lbs; Maryland-Eastern Shore; 1960: Det, rnd 4/NYT, rnd 2; B5/1/1937 Surrey County, VA **1960** Det 12 (RDT) **1961** Det☆14 (RDT) **1962** Det★14 (RDT) **1963** Det★14 (RDT) **1964** Det★14 (RDT) **1965** Det★14 (RDT) **1966** Det★14 (RDT) **1967**†LARm✧14 (RDT) **1968** LARm 14 (14, RDT) **1969**†LARm 14 **NFL** 138 (14) [10 yrs]

BROWN, ROGER Roger, DB, 6´0˝/196 lbs; Virginia Tech; 1990: GB, rnd 8; B12/16/1966 Baltimore, MD **1990**†NYG 5 (0) **1991** NYG 16 (1) **1992** NE 16 (3) **NFL** 37 (4) [3 yrs]

BROWN, RON Ronald, LB, 6´4˝/225 lbs; USC; 1987: SD, rnd 8; B4/28/1964 Oroville, CA **1987** LARd 3 (0) **1988** LARd 16 (0) **NFL** 19 (0) [2 yrs]

BROWN, RON Ronald James, WR, 5´11˝/181 lbs; Arizona State; 1983: Cle, rnd 2; B3/31/1961 Los Angeles, CA **[R]**

YEAR	TEAM	G (GS, POS)	RUSH	YD	AVG (LG)	TD	REC	YD	AVG (LG)	TD	PASS	COMP	PCT	YD	AVG (LG)	TD	INT	SK	YD	QBR	KPR	OTD	PTS	TAY
1984	†LARm	16(0)	2	25	12.5(16)	0	23	478	20.8(54)	4	—	—	—	—	—	—	—	—	—	—	—	—	24	284
1985	†LARm★	13(9, WR)	2	13	6.5(9)	0	14	215	15.4(43)	3	—	—	—	—	—	—	—	—	—	—	k	3	36	664
1986	LARm	14(12, WR)	4	5	1.3(11)	0	25	396	15.8(65)	3	—	—	—	—	—	—	—	—	—	—	k	—	18	472
1987	LARm	12(11, WR)	2	22	11.0(11)	0	26	521	20.0(52)	2	—	—	—	—	—	—	—	—	—	—	k	1	18	479
1988	†LARm	7(0)	3	24	8.0(13)	0	2	16	8.0(10)	0	—	—	—	—	—	—	—	—	—	—	k	—	0	148
1989	†LARm	16(0)	6	27	4.5(12)	0	5	113	22.6(39)	1	—	—	—	—	—	—	—	—	—	—	k	—	6	352
1990	†LARd	16(0)	—	—	—	—	—	—	—	—	—	—	—	—	—	—	—	—	—	—	k	—	0	125
1991	LARm	6(0)	2	11	5.5(11)	0	3	52	17.3(21)	0	—	—	—	—	—	—	—	—	—	—	k	—	0	113
NFL	8	100(32)	21	127	6.0(16)	0	98	1791	18.3(65)	13	—	—	—	—	—	—	—	—	—	—	k	4	102	2636

BROWN, RON Ronald William, WR, 5´10˝/186 lbs; Colorado; 1986: NYG, rnd 6; B1/11/1963 Queens, NY

YEAR	TEAM	G (GS, POS)	RUSH	YD	AVG (LG)	TD	REC	YD	AVG (LG)	TD	PASS	COMP	PCT	YD	AVG (LG)	TD	INT	SK	YD	QBR	KPR	OTD	PTS	TAY
1987	SL	3(0)	1	9	9.0(9)	0	2	16	8.0(9)	0	—	—	—	—	—	—	—	—	—	—	k	—	0	42

BROWN, RONNIE Ronnie, RB, 6´0˝/233 lbs; Auburn; 2005: Mia, rnd 1; B12/12/1981 Rome, GA

YEAR	TEAM	G (GS, POS)	RUSH	YD	AVG (LG)	TD	REC	YD	AVG (LG)	TD	PASS	COMP	PCT	YD	AVG (LG)	TD	INT	SK	YD	QBR	KPR	OTD	PTS	TAY
2005	Mia	15(14, RB)	207	907	4.4(65)	4	32	232	7.3(38)	1	—	—	—	—	—	—	—	—	—	—	—	—	30	1068

BROWN, ROSEY Roosevelt, T, 6´3˝/255 lbs; Morgan State; 1953: NYG, rnd 27; B10/20/1932 Charlottesville, VA, D6/9/2004 Columbus, NJ; HOF 1975 **1953** NYG 12 (LT) **1954** NYG 12 (LT) **1955** NYG✧12 (LT) **1956** NYG★12 (LT) **1957** NYG★12 (LT) **1958** NYG★11 (LT) **1959** NYG★12 (LT) **1960** NYG★12 (LT) **1961** NYG☆14 (LT) **1962** NYG★13 (LT) **1963** NYG☆13 (LT) **1964** NYG✧13 (LT) **1965** NYG★14 (LT) **NFL** 162 [13 yrs]

BROWN, RUBEN Ruben Parnell, G, 6´3˝/300 lbs; Pittsburgh; 1995: Buf, rnd 1; B2/13/1972 Englewood, NJ **1995**†Buf 16 (16, LG) **1996**†Buf✧14 (14, LG) **1997** Buf✧16 (16, LG) **1998** Buf★13 (13, LG) **1999**†Buf★14 (14, LG) **2000** Buf★16 (16, LG) **2001** Buf✧16 (16, LG) **2003** Buf✧15 (15, LG) **2004** ChiB 9 (9, LG) **2005**†ChiB 12 (12, LG)

YEAR	TEAM	G (GS, POS)	RUSH	YD	AVG (LG)	TD	REC	YD	AVG (LG)	TD	PASS	COMP	PCT	YD	AVG (LG)	TD	INT	SK	YD	QBR	KPR	OTD	PTS	TAY
2002	Buf★	16(16, LG)	—	—	—	—	1	-6	-6.0(-6)	0	—	—	—	—	—	—	—	—	—	—	—	—	0	-3
NFL	11	157(157)	—	—	—	—	1	-6	-6.0(-6)	0	—	—	—	—	—	—	—	—	—	—	—	—	0	-3

BROWN, RUFUS Rufus Benard, G, 6´2˝/295 lbs; Florida A&M; B6/19/1962 Bartow, FL **1987** TB 2 (0)

BROWN, RUFUS Rufus, DB, 5´9˝/188 lbs; Florida State; B7/18/1980 San Antonio, TX **2004** Was 1 (0)

BROWN, RUSH Rush, DT-NT-DE, 6´2˝/257 lbs; Ball State; 1980: SL, rnd 10; B6/27/1954 Laurinburg, NC **1980** SL 16 (10, NT) **1981** SL 16 (13, RDT) **1982**†SL 9 (9, RDT) **1983** SL 6 (1) **NFL** 47 (33) [4 yrs]

BROWN, SELWYN Selwyn G., DB, 5´11˝/205 lbs; Miami (FL); B9/28/1965 St. Petersburg, FL **1988** TB 4 (0)

BROWN, SHELDON Sheldon Dion, DB, 5´10˝/196 lbs; South Carolina; 2002: Phi, rnd 2; B3/19/1979 Lancaster, SC **2002**†Phi 16 (0) **2003**†Phi 16 (3) **2004**†Phi 16 (16, RCB) **2005** Phi 16 (16, RCB) **NFL** 64 (35) [4 yrs]

BROWN, SIDNEY Sidney Louis, DB, 6´0˝/186 lbs; Oklahoma; 1977: NE, rnd 3; B1/27/1956 New Orleans, LA **1978**†NE 16

BROWN, SONNY Clifton D., DB, 6´2˝/200 lbs; Oklahoma; B11/12/1963 Tinker AFB, OK **1987** Hou 2 (0)

BROWN, STAN Byron Stanley, WR, 5´11˝/185 lbs; Purdue; 1971: Cle, rnd 5; B8/4/1949 Martinez, CA **1971**†Cle 6

BROWN, STEVE Steven Douglas, DB, 5´11˝/189 lbs; Oregon; 1983: Hou, rnd 3; B5/20/1960 Sacramento, CA **1983** Hou 16 (10, LCB) **1984** Hou 16 (16, LCB) **1985** Hou 15 (14, LCB) **1986** Hou 16 (16, LCB) **1987**†Hou 10 (10, LCB) **1988**†Hou 14 (14, LCB) **1989**†Hou 16 (16, LCB) **1990** Hou 16 (0) **NFL** 119 (96) [8 yrs]

BROWN, TED Thomas Edward, RB, 5´10˝/206 lbs; North Carolina State; 1979: Min, rnd 1; B2/15/1957 High Point, NC

YEAR	TEAM	G (GS, POS)	RUSH	YD	AVG (LG)	TD	REC	YD	AVG (LG)	TD	PASS	COMP	PCT	YD	AVG (LG)	TD	INT	SK	YD	QBR	KPR	OTD	PTS	TAY
1979	Min	14(9, FB)	130	551	4.2(34)	1	31	197	6.4(35)	0	—	—	—	—	—	—	—	—	—	—	k	—	6	726
1980	†Min	16(16, FB)	219	912	4.2(55)	8	62	623	10.0(67)	2	—	—	—	—	—	—	—	—	—	—	—	—	60	1314
1981	Min	16(16, FB)	274	1063	3.9(34)	6	83	694	8.4(63)	2	1	0	0.0	0	0.0	0	1	—	—	—	—	—	48	1440
1982	†Min	8(8, FB)	120	515	4.3(30)	1	31	207	6.7(29)	2	—	—	—	—	—	—	—	—	—	—	—	—	18	639
1983	Min	10(8, FB)	120	476	4.0(43)	10	41	357	8.7(25)	1	—	—	—	—	—	—	—	—	—	—	—	—	66	760
1984	Min	13(9, RB)	98	442	4.5(19)	3	46	349	7.6(35)	3	—	—	—	—	—	—	—	—	—	—	—	—	36	662
1985	Min	14(9, FB)	93	336	3.6(30)	7	30	291	9.7(54)	3	—	—	—	—	—	—	—	—	—	—	k	—	60	559
1986	Min	13(0)	63	251	4.0(60)	4	15	132	8.8(20)	0	—	—	—	—	—	—	—	—	—	—	k	—	24	345
NFL	8	104(75)	1117	4546	4.1(60)	40	339	2850	8.4(67)	13	1	0	0.0	0	0.0	0	1	—	—	—	k	—	318	6442

BROWN, TERRY Terry Lynn, DB, 6´0˝/205 lbs; Oklahoma State; 1969: SL, rnd 3; B1/9/1947 Walters, OK **1970** SL 10 **1972** Min 8 **1973**†Min 14 **1974**†Min 14 **1975**†Min 13 (12, SS) **1976** Cle 12 (ss)

YEAR	TEAM	G (GS, POS)	RUSH	YD	AVG (LG)	TD	REC	YD	AVG (LG)	TD	PASS	COMP	PCT	YD	AVG (LG)	TD	INT	SK	YD	QBR	KPR	OTD	PTS	TAY
1969	SL	14	—	—	—	—	1	7	7.0(7)	0	—	—	—	—	—	—	—	—	—	—	kpi	—	0	124
NFL	7	85(12)	—	—	—	—	1	7	7.0(7)	0	—	—	—	—	—	—	—	—	—	—	kpi	2	12	241

BROWN, THEOTIS Theotis, RB, 6´2˝/225 lbs; UCLA; 1979: SL, rnd 2; B4/20/1957 Chicago, IL

YEAR	TEAM	G (GS, POS)	RUSH	YD	AVG (LG)	TD	REC	YD	AVG (LG)	TD	PASS	COMP	PCT	YD	AVG (LG)	TD	INT	SK	YD	QBR	KPR	OTD	PTS	TAY
1979	SL	16(1)	73	318	4.4(30)	7	25	191	7.6(19)	0	—	—	—	—	—	—	—	—	—	—	—	—	42	484
1980	SL	16(0)	40	186	4.7(19)	1	21	290	13.8(63)	1	—	—	—	—	—	—	—	—	—	—	k	—	12	342
1981	SL	4(3)	15	52	3.5(11)	2	4	60	15.0(28)	0	—	—	—	—	—	—	—	—	—	—	—	—	12	102
1981	Sea	10(6, rb)	141	531	3.8(43)	6	25	268	10.7(51)	0	—	—	—	—	—	—	—	—	—	—	—	—	36	725
1982	Sea	9(0)	53	141	2.7(17)	2	12	95	7.9(18)	0	—	—	—	—	—	—	—	—	—	—	k	—	12	212
1983	Sea	3(0)	6	14	2.3(6)	0	—	—	—	—	—	—	—	—	—	—	—	—	—	—	—	—	0	14
1983	KC	12(9, FB)	124	467	3.8(49)	8	47	418	8.9(53)	2	1	1	100.0	11	11.0(11)	0	0	—	—	—	k	—	60	848
1984	KC	14(7, FB)	97	337	3.5(25)	4	38	236	6.2(17)	0	—	—	—	—	—	—	—	—	—	—	—	—	24	495
NFL	6	84(26)	549	2046	3.7(49)	30	172	1558	9.1(63)	3	1	1	100.0	11	11.0(11)	0	0	—	—	—	k	—	198	3221

BROWN, THOMAS Thomas Wayne, DE-NT, 6´4˝/247 lbs; Baylor; 1980: Phi, rnd 11; B7/8/1957 Galveston, TX **1980**†Phi 16 (0) **1981** Cle 16 (4) **1983** Cle 16 (0) **NFL** 48 (4) [3 yrs]

BROWN, TIM Timothy Donell, WR, 6´0˝/195 lbs; Notre Dame; 1988: LARd, rnd 1; B7/22/1966 Dallas, TX **[R]**

YEAR	TEAM	G (GS, POS)	RUSH	YD	AVG (LG)	TD	REC	YD	AVG (LG)	TD	PASS	COMP	PCT	YD	AVG (LG)	TD	INT	SK	YD	QBR	KPR	OTD	PTS	TAY
1988	LARd★	16(9, WR)	14	50	3.6(12)	1	43	725	16.9(65)	5	—	—	—	—	—	—	—	—	—	—	kp	1	42	1140
1989	LARd	1(1)	—	—	—	—	1	8	8.0(8)	0	—	—	—	—	—	—	—	—	—	—	kp	—	0	45
1990	†LARd	16(0)	—	—	—	—	18	265	14.7(51)	3	—	—	—	—	—	—	—	—	—	—	p	—	18	273
1991	†LARd★	16(1)	5	16	3.2(9)	0	36	554	15.4(78)	5	—	—	—	—	—	—	—	—	—	—	kp	1	36	527
1992	LARd	15(12, WR)	3	-4	-1.3(3)	0	49	693	14.1(68)	7	—	—	—	—	—	—	—	—	—	—	kp	—	42	560
1993	†LARd★	16(16, WR)	2	7	3.5(14)	0	80	**1180**	14.8(71)	7	—	—	—	—	—	—	—	—	—	—	p	1	48	907
1994	LARd★	16(16, WR)	—	—	—	—	89	**1309**	14.7(77)	9	—	—	—	—	—	—	—	—	—	—	p	—	54	987
1995	Oak★	16(16, WR)	—	—	—	—	89	**1342**	15.1(80)	10	—	—	—	—	—	—	—	—	—	—	p	—	60	905
1996	Oak★	16(16, WR)	6	35	5.8(15)	0	90	1104	12.3(42)	9	—	—	—	—	—	—	—	—	—	—	kp	—	54	753
1997	Oak★	16(16, WR)	5	19	3.8(12)	0	**104**	**1408**	13.5(59)	5	—	—	—	—	—	—	—	—	—	—	k	—	32	740
1998	Oak	16(16, WR)	1	-7	-7.0(-7)	0	81	1012	12.5(49)	9	—	—	—	—	—	—	—	—	—	—	p	—	54	552
1999	Oak✧	16(16, WR)	1	4	4.0(4)	0	90	1344	14.9(47)	6	—	—	—	—	—	—	—	—	—	—	—	—	36	706

YEAR TEAM	G (GS, POS)	RUSH	YD	AVG (LG)	TD	REC	YD	AVG (LG)	TD	PASS	COMP	PCT	YD	AVG (LG)	TD	INT	SK	YD	QBR	KPR	OTD	PTS	TAY
2000 †Oak	16 (16, WR)	3	12	4.0 (7)	0	76	1128	14.8 (45)	11	—	—	—	—	—	—	—	—	—	—	—	—	66	631
2001 †Oak✧	16 (16, WR)	4	39	9.8 (19)	0	91	1165	12.8 (46)	9	—	—	—	—	—	—	—	—	—	—	p	1	60	758
2002 †Oak	16 (16, WR)	6	19	3.2 (9)	0	81	930	11.5 (45)	2	—	—	—	—	—	—	—	—	—	—	p	—	12	499
2003 Oak	16 (15, WR)	—	—	—	—	52	567	10.9 (36)	2	—	—	—	—	—	—	—	—	—	—	—	—	12	294
2004 TB	15 (4)	—	—	—	—	24	200	8.3 (21)	1	—	—	—	—	—	—	—	—	—	—	p	—	6	123
NFL 17	255 (202)	50	190	3.8 (19)	1	1094	14934	13.7 (80)	100	—	—	—	—	—	—	—	—	—	—	kp	4	632	10397

BROWN, TIMMY Thomas Allen, RB, 5´11˝/198 lbs; Ball State; 1959: GB, rnd 27; B5/24/1937 Knightstown, IN **[R]**

YEAR TEAM	G (GS, POS)	RUSH	YD	AVG (LG)	TD	REC	YD	AVG (LG)	TD	PASS	COMP	PCT	YD	AVG (LG)	TD	INT	SK	YD	QBR	KPR	OTD	PTS	TAY
1959 GB	1	—	—	—	—	—	—	—	—	—	—	—	—	—	—	—	—	—	—	—	—	—	—
1960 †Phi	12	9	35	3.9 (13)	2	9	247	27.4 (71)	2	—	—	—	—	—	—	—	—	—	—	kp	—	24	316
1961 Phi	13	50	338	6.8 (47)	1	14	264	18.9 (65)	2	—	—	—	—	—	—	—	—	—	—	kp	2	30	971
1962 Phi✧	14 (HB)	137	545	4.0 (61)	5	52	849	16.3 (82)	6	—	—	—	—	—	—	—	—	—	—	kp	2	78	1492
1963 Phi★	14 (HB)	192	841	4.4 (34)	6	36	487	13.5 (80)	4	3	1	33.3	11	3.7 (11)	1	1	—	—	—	kp	1	66	1667
1964 Phi	10 (HB)	90	356	4.0 (36)	5	15	244	16.3 (87)	5	2	0	0.0	0	0.0	0	1	—	—	—	kp	—	60	801
1965 Phi★	13 (HB)	158	861	**5.4** (**54**)	6	50	682	13.6 (45)	3	1	0	0.0	0	0.0	0	0	—	—	—	kp	—	54	1271
1966 Phi☆	13 (HB)	161	548	3.4 (24)	3	33	371	11.2 (39)	3	—	—	—	—	—	—	—	—	—	—	kp	2	48	1056
1967 Phi	7	53	179	3.4 (13)	1	22	202	9.2 (41)	1	—	—	—	—	—	—	—	—	—	—	k	—	12	401
1968 †Bal	11	39	159	4.1 (10)	2	4	53	13.3 (18)	0	—	—	—	—	—	—	—	—	—	—	kp	—	12	324
NFL 10	108	889	3862	4.3 (61)	31	235	3399	14.5 (87)	26	6	1	16.7	11	1.8 (11)	1	2	—	—	—	kp	7	384	8297

BROWN, TOM Thomas McClaren, E, 6´2˝/216 lbs; William & Mary; B5/22/1921 Pittsburgh, PA

YEAR TEAM	G (GS, POS)	RUSH	YD	AVG (LG)	TD	REC	YD	AVG (LG)	TD	PASS	COMP	PCT	YD	AVG (LG)	TD	INT	SK	YD	QBR	KPR	OTD	PTS	TAY
1942 Pit	9 (0)	—	—	—	—	4	69	17.3 (30)	0	—	—	—	—	—	—	—	—	—	—	—	1	6	35

BROWN, TOM Thomas William, DB, 6´1˝/192 lbs; Maryland; 1963: GB, rnd 2/Buf, rnd 3; B12/12/1940 Laureldale, PA **1964** GB 14 (LS) **1965**†GB 14 (RS) **1966**†GB 14 (RS) **1967**†GB 14 (LS) **1968** GB 14 (LS) **1969** Was 1 **NFL** 71 [6 yrs]

BROWN, TOM Thomas Martin, RB, 6´1˝/223 lbs; Pittsburgh; 1987: Mia, rnd 7; B11/20/1964 Ridgway, PA

YEAR TEAM	G (GS, POS)	RUSH	YD	AVG (LG)	TD	REC	YD	AVG (LG)	TD	PASS	COMP	PCT	YD	AVG (LG)	TD	INT	SK	YD	QBR	KPR	OTD	PTS	TAY
1987 Mia	1 (0)	3	3	1.0 (3)	0	1	6	6.0 (6)	0	—	—	—	—	—	—	—	—	—	—	—	—	0	6
1989 Mia	9 (7, FB)	13	26	2.0 (6)	0	13	117	9.0 (23)	0	—	—	—	—	—	—	—	—	—	—	—	—	0	85
NFL 2	10 (7)	16	29	1.8 (6)	0	14	123	8.8 (23)	0	—	—	—	—	—	—	—	—	—	—	—	—	0	91

BROWN, TOM Thomas William, WR, 6´4˝/190 lbs; Augustana (SD); B12/24/1963 Princeton, MN **1987** Cin 2 (0)

BROWN, TONY Anthony Brester, T, 6´5˝/285 lbs; Pittsburgh; B7/11/1964 Stamford, CT **1987** Buf 2 (2)

BROWN, TONY Anthony Lamar, DB, 5´9˝/183 lbs; Fresno State; 1992: Hou, rnd 5; B5/15/1970 Bangkok, Thailand **1992**†Hou 12 (1) **1993**†Hou 16 (0) **1994** Sea 13 (5, lcb) **1995** Sea 16 (0) **NFL** 57 (6) [4 yrs]

BROWN, TONY Tony Anthony, DT, 6´2˝/283 lbs; Memphis; B9/29/1980 Chattanooga, TN **2004** SF 16 (4)

BROWN, TRAVIS Travis Martin, QB, 6´3˝/215 lbs; Northern Arizona; B7/17/1977 Phoenix, AZ

YEAR TEAM	G (GS, POS)	RUSH	YD	AVG (LG)	TD	REC	YD	AVG (LG)	TD	PASS	COMP	PCT	YD	AVG (LG)	TD	INT	SK	YD	QBR	KPR	OTD	PTS	TAY
2000 Sea	1 (0)	—	—	—	—	—	—	—	—	1	0	0.0	0	0.0	0	0	—	—	—	—	—	0	0
2001 Buf	1 (0)	1	10	10.0 (10)	0	—	—	—	—	33	15	45.5	201	6.1 (34)	1	2	1	2	—	—	—	0	36
2003 Buf	2 (0)	1	5	5.0 (5)	0	—	—	—	—	18	14	77.8	160	8.9 (28)	0	1	1	7	—	—	—	0	45
NFL 3	4 (0)	2	15	7.5 (10)	0	—	—	—	—	52	29	55.8	361	6.9 (34)	1	3	2	9	—	—	—	0	81

BROWN, TROY Troy Fitzgerald, WR, 5´10˝/196 lbs; Marshall; 1993: NE, rnd 8; B7/2/1971 Barnwell, SC **[R]**

YEAR TEAM	G (GS, POS)	RUSH	YD	AVG (LG)	TD	REC	YD	AVG (LG)	TD	PASS	COMP	PCT	YD	AVG (LG)	TD	INT	SK	YD	QBR	KPR	OTD	PTS	TAY
1993 NE	12 (0)	—	—	—	—	2	22	11.0 (14)	0	—	—	—	—	—	—	—	—	—	—	kp	—	0	128
1994 †NE	9 (0)	—	—	—	—	—	—	—	—	—	—	—	—	—	—	—	—	—	—	kp	—	0	81
1995 NE	16 (0)	—	—	—	—	14	159	11.4 (31)	0	—	—	—	—	—	—	—	—	—	—	k	1	6	287
1996 †NE	16 (0)	—	—	—	—	21	222	10.6 (38)	0	—	—	—	—	—	—	—	—	—	—	k	—	0	310
1997 †NE	16 (6, wr)	1	-18	-18.0 (-18)	0	41	607	14.8 (67)	6	—	—	—	—	—	—	—	—	—	—	—	—	36	316
1998 †NE	10 (0)	—	—	—	—	23	346	15.0 (52)	1	—	—	—	—	—	—	—	—	—	—	p	—	6	318
1999 NE	13 (1)	—	—	—	—	36	471	13.1 (37)	1	1	0	0.0	0	0.0	0	0	—	—	—	kp	—	6	607
2000 NE	16 (15, WR)	6	46	7.7 (35)	0	83	944	11.4 (44)	4	—	—	—	—	—	—	—	—	—	—	kp	1	30	842
2001 †NE★	16 (13, WR)	11	91	8.3 (31)	0	101	1199	11.9 (60)	5	—	—	—	—	—	—	—	—	—	—	kp	2	42	1002
2002 NE	14 (13, WR)	3	14	4.7 (21)	0	97	890	9.2 (38)	3	—	—	—	—	—	—	—	—	—	—	p	—	20	529
2003 †NE	12 (10, WR)	6	27	4.5 (11)	0	40	472	11.8 (82)	4	—	—	—	—	—	—	—	—	—	—	p	—	24	431
2004 †NE	12 (0)	—	—	—	—	17	184	10.8 (22)	1	—	—	—	—	—	—	—	—	—	—	pi	—	6	127
2005 †NE	13 (3)	—	—	—	—	39	466	11.9 (71)	2	—	—	—	—	—	—	—	—	—	—	p	—	12	238
NFL 13	175 (61)	27	160	5.9 (35)	0	514	5982	11.6 (82)	27	1	0	0.0	0	0.0	0	0	—	—	—	kpi	4	188	5214

BROWN, TYRONE Tyrone Barry, WR, 5´11˝/168 lbs; Toledo; B1/3/1973 Cincinnati, OH

YEAR TEAM	G (GS, POS)	RUSH	YD	AVG (LG)	TD	REC	YD	AVG (LG)	TD	PASS	COMP	PCT	YD	AVG (LG)	TD	INT	SK	YD	QBR	KPR	OTD	PTS	TAY
1995 †Atl	6 (5, wr)	—	—	—	—	17	198	11.6 (26)	0	—	—	—	—	—	—	—	—	—	—	—	—	0	99
1996 Atl	9 (3)	—	—	—	—	28	325	11.6 (38)	1	—	—	—	—	—	—	—	—	—	—	—	—	6	168
NFL 2	15 (8)	—	—	—	—	45	523	11.6 (38)	1	—	—	—	—	—	—	—	—	—	—	—	—	6	267

BROWN, VINCENT Vincent Bernard, LB, 6´2˝/245 lbs; Mississippi Valley State; 1988: NE, rnd 2; B1/9/1965 Atlanta, GA **1988** NE 16 (3) **1989** NE 14 (10, RILB) **1990** NE 16 (14, LOLB) **1991** NE☆16 (15, RILB) **1992** NE☆13 (13, LILB) **1993** NE☆16 (16, LILB) **1994**†NE 16 (16, LILB) **1995** NE 16 (16, LILB) **NFL** 123 (103) [8 yrs]

BROWN, WILBERT Wilbert Lemon, G, 6´2˝/320 lbs; Houston; B5/9/1977 Texarkana, TX **1999** SD 5 (0) **2002** Was 14 (9, RG) **2003**†NE 1 (0) **NFL** 20 (9) [3 yrs]

°**BROWN, WILLIE** William Ferdie, DB, 6´1˝/195 lbs; Grambling State; B12/2/1940 Yazoo City, MS; HOF 1984 **[I]** **1963** Den-A 8 (lcb) **1964** Den-A★14 (LCB) **1965** Den-A★14 (LCB) **1966** Den-A☆14 (LCB) **1967**†Oak-A★14 (RCB) **1968**†Oak-A★14 (14, RCB) **1969**†Oak-A★14 (14, RCB) **1970**†Oak★8 (7, rcb) **1971** Oak★14 (14, RCB) **1972**†Oak★14 (14, RCB) **1973**†Oak★14 (14, RCB) **1974** Oak☆9 (9, RCB) **1975**†Oak 12 (12, RCB) **1976**†Oak 14 (RCB) **1977**†Oak 14 (14, RCB) **1978** Oak 13 (2) **NFL** 204 (114) [16 yrs]

BROWN, WILLIE Willie F., WR-HB, 6´0˝/188 lbs; USC; 1964: LA, rnd 3/SD, rnd 6; B3/21/1942 Tuscaloosa, AL

YEAR TEAM	G (GS, POS)	RUSH	YD	AVG (LG)	TD	REC	YD	AVG (LG)	TD	PASS	COMP	PCT	YD	AVG (LG)	TD	INT	SK	YD	QBR	KPR	OTD	PTS	TAY
1964 LARm	9	—	—	—	—	1	19	19.0 (19)	0	—	—	—	—	—	—	—	—	—	—	kp	—	0	45
1965 LARm	14	44	133	3.0 (19)	0	4	91	22.8 (37)	1	—	—	—	—	—	—	—	—	—	—	kp	—	6	457
1966 Phi	7	—	—	—	—	—	—	—	—	—	—	—	—	—	—	—	—	—	—	kp	—	0	-28
NFL 3	30	44	133	3.0 (19)	0	5	110	22.0 (37)	1	—	—	—	—	—	—	—	—	—	—	kp	—	6	473

BROWNE, GORDIE Gordon Wayland, T, 6´5˝/265 lbs; Boston College; 1974: NYJ, rnd 2; B12/5/1951 Franklin, MA **1974** NYJ 10 **1975** NYJ 13 **NFL** 23 [2 yrs]

BROWNE, JIM James Christopher, RB, 6´1˝/215 lbs; Northwestern; Boston College; B3/16/1962 Pontiac, MI

YEAR TEAM	G (GS, POS)	RUSH	YD	AVG (LG)	TD	REC	YD	AVG (LG)	TD	PASS	COMP	PCT	YD	AVG (LG)	TD	INT	SK	YD	QBR	KPR	OTD	PTS	TAY
1987 LARd	2 (1)	2	1	0.5 (2)	0	2	8	4.0 (5)	0	—	—	—	—	—	—	—	—	—	—	—	—	0	5

BROWNER, JIM Jimmie Lee, DB, 6´1˝/209 lbs; Notre Dame; 1979: Cin, rnd 12; B12/4/1955 Warren, OH **1979** Cin 16 **1980** Cin 2 (0) **NFL** 18 [2 yrs]

BROWNER, JOEY Joey Matthew, DB, 6´2˝/221 lbs; USC; 1983: Min, rnd 1; B5/15/1960 Warren, OH **[I]** **1983** Min 16 (1) **1984** Min 16 (8, lcb) **1985** Min★16 (16, SS) **1986** Min✧16 (16, SS) **1987**†Min★12 (12, SS) **1988**†Min★16 (16, SS) **1989**†Min★16 (16, SS) **1990** Min★16 (16, SS) **1991** Min 14 (14, SS) **1992** TB 7 (2) **NFL** 145 (117) [10 yrs]

BROWNER, KEITH Keith Tellus, LB, 6´6˝/245 lbs; USC; 1984: TB, rnd 2; B1/24/1962 Warren, OH **1984** TB 16 (10, LOLB) **1985** TB 16 (5, lolb) **1986** TB 15 (13, LOLB) **1987** SF 1 (1) **1987** LARd 1 (0) **1988** SD 16 (15, LOLB) **NFL** 65 (44) [5 yrs]

BROWNER, ROSS Ross Dean, DE, 6´3˝/262 lbs; Notre Dame; 1978: Cin, rnd 1; B3/22/1954 Warren, OH **[K]** **1978** Cin 11 (RDE) **1979** Cin 16 (16, RDE) **1980** Cin 15 (15, RDE) **1981**†Cin 16 (16, RDE) **1982**†Cin 9 (9, RDE) **1983** Cin 12 (9, RDE) **1984** Cin 16 (16, RDE) **1985** Cin 16 (16, RDE) **1986** Cin 16 (15, RDE) **1987** GB 11 (2) **NFL** 138 (114) [10 yrs]

BROWNING, CHARLIE Charles A., HB, 6´2˝/200 lbs; Washington; 1965: NYJ, rnd 17/Pit, rnd 7; B7/28/1943 **1965** NYJ-A 1

BROWNING, DAVE David Scott, DE, 6´5˝/245 lbs; Washington; 1978: Oak, rnd 2; B8/18/1956 Spokane, WA **1978** Oak 12 (7, RDE) **1979** Oak 16 (16, RDE) **1980**†Oak 16 (16, RDE) **1981** Oak 16 (16, RDE) **1982** LARd 5 (4) **1983** NE 12 (0) **NFL** 77 (59) [6 yrs]

BROWNING, GREGG Gregg, E, 6´0˝/190 lbs; Denver; 1945: Pit, rnd 6; B1/12/1922 Trinidad, CO

YEAR TEAM	G (GS, POS)	RUSH	YD	AVG (LG)	TD	REC	YD	AVG (LG)	TD	PASS	COMP	PCT	YD	AVG (LG)	TD	INT	SK	YD	QBR	KPR	OTD	PTS	TAY
1947 NYG	3 (0)	—	—	—	—	1	12	12.0 (12)	0	—	—	—	—	—	—	—	—	—	—	—	—	0	6

BROWNING, JOHN John Edward, DT-DE, 6´4˝/297 lbs; West Virginia; 1996: KC, rnd 3; B9/30/1973 Miami, FL **1996** KC 13 (2) **1997**†KC 14 (13, RDE) **1998** KC 8 (8, lde) **2000** KC 16 (16, RDT/lde) **2001** KC 6 (6, ldt) **2002** KC 16 (16, LDT) **2003**†KC 16 (16, LDT) **2004** KC 16 (7, ldt) **2005** KC 16 (12, LDT) **NFL** 121 (96) [9 yrs]

BROWNLEE, CLAUDE Claude, DT, 6´4˝/265 lbs; Benedictine; 1966: Bal, rnd 10; B4/8/1944 Columbus, GA **1967** Mia-A 3

YEAR	TEAM	G (GS, POS)	RUSH	YD	AVG(LG)	TD	REC	YD	AVG(LG)	TD	PASS	COMP	PCT	YD	AVG(LG)	TD	INT	SK	YD	QBR	KPR	OTD	PTS	TAY

BROWNLOW, DARRICK Darrick Dewayne, LB, 5'10"/237 lbs; Illinois; 1991: Dal, rnd 5; B12/28/1968 Indianapolis, IN **1991**†Dal 16 (0) **1992** TB 16 (4, MLB) **1993** TB 15 (0)
1994†Dal 16 (0) **1995** Was 16 (0) **1996** Was 16 (0) **NFL** 95 (4) [6 yrs]

BROYLES, JAMES James, G, 6'4"/319 lbs; Southwest Missouri State; B5/18/1978 Hammond, IN **2002** SL 1 (0)

BRUBAKER, DICK Carl Richard, E-DE, 6'0"/202 lbs; Ohio Wesleyan; Ohio State; 1955: ChiC, rnd 15; B1/2/1932 Cleveland, OH, D6/14/1978

1955	ChiC	10	—	—	—	—	6	125	20.8(43)	0	—	—	—	—	—	—	—	—	—	—	—	—	0	63
1957	ChiC	3	—	—	—	—	—	—	—	—	—	—	—	—	—	—	—	—	—	—	—	—	—	—
1960	Buf-A	9	—	—	—	—	7	75	10.7(17)	1	—	—	—	—	—	—	—	—	—	—	—	—	6	43
NFL	3	22	—	—	—	—	13	200	15.4(43)	1	—	—	—	—	—	—	—	—	—	—	—	—	6	105

BRUCE, ARLAND Arland R., WR, 5'10"/193 lbs; Minnesota; B11/23/1977 Olathe, KS **2003** SF 2 (0)

BRUCE, AUNDRAY Aundray, LB-TE-DE, 6'5"/265 lbs; Auburn; 1988: Atl, rnd 1; B4/30/1966 Montgomery, AL **1988** Atl 16 (16, LOLB) **1989** Atl 16 (13, LOLB) **1990** Atl 16 (3)
1992 LARd 16 (4) **1993**†LARd 16 (0) **1994** Oak 14 (0) **1995** Oak 16 (0) **1997** Oak 10 (3) **1998** Oak 1 (0)

| 1991 | †Atl | 14 (3) | — | — | — | — | 1 | 11 | 11.0(11) | 0 | — | — | — | — | — | — | — | — | — | — | — | — | 0 | 6 |
| NFL | 11 | 151 (42) | — | — | — | — | 1 | 11 | 11.0(11) | 0 | — | — | — | — | — | — | — | — | — | — | kiS | 1 | 6 | 7 |

BRUCE, GAIL Gail Robert, DE-E, 6'1"/206 lbs; Washington; 1946: Pit, rnd 30; B9/29/1923 Puyallup, WA, D8/23/1998 Santa Maria, CA **[K]**

1948	SF-A	14 (0)	1	1	1.0(1)	0	5	49	9.8		—	—	—	—	—	—	—	—	—	—	—	—	0	26
1949	†SF-A	12 (4)	—	—	—	—	1	9	9.0(9)		—	—	—	—	—	—	—	—	—	—	ki	—	0	-3
AAFC	2	26 (4)	1	1	1.0(1)	0	6	58	9.7(9)	0	—	—	—	—	—	—	—	—	—	—	ki	—	0	23
1950	SF	12 (RDE)	—	—	—	—	1	10	10.0(10)	0	—	—	—	—	—	—	—	—	—	—	i	—	0	4
1951	SF	12 (RDE)	—	—	—	—	—	—	—	—	—	—	—	—	—	—	—	—	—	—	K	—	1	0
NFL	2	24	—	—	—	—	1	10	10.0(10)	0	—	—	—	—	—	—	—	—	—	—	Ki	—	1	4

BRUCE, ISAAC Isaac Isidore, WR, 6'0"/188 lbs; Memphis; 1994: LARm, rnd 2; B11/10/1972 Fort Lauderdale, FL

1994	LARm	12 (0)	1	2	2.0(2)	0	21	272	13.0(34)	3	—	—	—	—	—	—	—	—	—	—	—	—	18	153
1995	SL☆	16 (16, WR)	3	17	5.7(12)	0	119	1781	15.0(72)	13	—	—	—	—	—	—	—	—	—	—	—	—	80	1025
1996	SL★	16 (16, WR)	1	4	4.0(4)	0	84	1338	15.9(70)	7	2	1	50.0	15	7.5(15)	0	1	—	—	—	—	—	42	676
1997	SL	12 (12, WR)	—	—	—	—	56	815	14.6(59)	5	—	—	—	—	—	—	—	—	—	—	—	—	30	433
1998	SL	5 (5, wr)	1	30	30.0(30)	0	32	457	14.3(80)	1	—	—	—	—	—	—	—	—	—	—	—	—	6	264
1999	†SL★	16 (16, WR)	5	32	6.4(11)	0	77	1165	15.1(60)	12	—	—	—	—	—	—	—	—	—	—	—	—	74	675
2000	†SL◇	16 (16, WR)	1	11	11.0(11)	0	87	1471	16.9(78)	9	—	—	—	—	—	—	—	—	—	—	—	—	54	792
2001	†SL◇	16 (16, WR)	4	23	5.8(10)	0	64	1106	17.3(51)	6	—	—	—	—	—	—	—	—	—	—	—	—	36	606
2002	SL	16 (16, WR)	3	18	6.0(13)	0	79	1075	13.6(34)	7	—	—	—	—	—	—	—	—	—	—	—	—	42	591
2003	†SL	15 (15, WR)	2	17	8.5(14)	0	69	981	14.2(41)	5	2	2	100.0	66	33.0(41)	0	0	—	—	—	—	—	30	566
2004	†SL	16 (16, WR)	—	—	—	—	89	1292	14.5(56)	6	1	0	0.0	0	0.0	0	0	—	—	—	—	—	36	676
2005	SL	11 (10, WR)	—	—	—	—	36	525	14.6(46)	3	—	—	—	—	—	—	—	—	—	—	—	—	18	278
NFL	12	167 (154)	21	154	7.3(30)	0	813	12278	15.1(80)	77	6	3	50.0	81	13.5(41)	0	1	—	—	—	—	—	466	6731

BRUCKNER, LES Leslie Charles, FB, 6'1"/195 lbs; Michigan State; B4/16/1918 Milan, MI **1945** ChiC 2 (0)

BRUCKNER, NICK Nicholas P., WR, 5'11"/185 lbs; Syracuse; B5/19/1961 Queens, NY **1983** NYJ 7 (0) **1985** NYJ 9 (0)

| 1984 | NYJ | 16 (0) | — | — | — | — | 1 | 11 | 11.0(11) | 0 | — | — | — | — | — | — | — | — | — | — | kp | — | 0 | 23 |
| NFL | 3 | 32 (0) | — | — | — | — | 1 | 11 | 11.0(11) | 0 | — | — | — | — | — | — | — | — | — | — | — | — | 0 | 6 |

BRUDER, DOC Woodruff Harlan, B, 5'11"/178 lbs; Pittsburgh; West Virginia; B2/5/1901 Houston, TX, D11/13/1952 Houston, TX **[K]** **1925** Buf 6 (4), 6 **1925** Fra 5 (1), 2
1926 Fra 13 (8, wb), 19 **NFL** 24 (13), 27 [2 yrs]

BRUDER, HANK Henry George, B, 6'0"/199 lbs; Northwestern; B11/22/1907 Pekin, IL, D6/29/1970 Mattoon, IL **[K]**

1931	GB	13 (6, HB)	—	—	—	—	—	—	—	—	—	—	—	—	—	—	—	—	—	—	—	—	—	—
1932	GB	14 (5, WB)	75	209	2.8	2	8	143	17.9	2	4	1	25.0	23	5.8(23)	0	1	—	—	—	—	—	24	282
1933	GB	9 (7, tb)	77	250	3.2	2	4	69	17.3(40)	0	7	3	42.9	14	2.0	0	—	—	—	—	—	—	—	12	312
1934	GB	13 (9, BB)	48	106	2.2	1	7	104	14.9	1	6	2	33.3	22	3.7	0	0	—	—	—	K	—	1	22	194
1935	GB	10 (7, bb)	44	158	3.6	0	4	67	16.8(30)	0	1	1	100.0	17	17.0(17)	0	—	—	—	—	—	—	1	6	210
1936	†GB	11 (9, BB)	4	-7	-1.8	0	2	25	12.5(23)	0	—	—	—	—	—	—	—	—	—	—	—	—	0	6
1937	GB	10 (6, BB)	15	56	3.7	1	—	—	—	—	6	0	0.0	0	—	0	—	—	—	—	—	—	—	6	-14
1938	†GB	8 (1)	2	6	3.0	0	2	14	7.0	0	—	—	—	—	—	—	—	—	—	—	—	—	0	13
1939	†GB◇	10 (2)	—	—	—	—	4	65	16.3(22)	1	—	—	—	—	—	—	—	—	—	—	—	—	6	38
1940	Pit	8 (7, BB)	—	—	—	—	5	49	9.8	0	—	—	—	—	—	—	—	—	—	—	—	—	0	25
NFL	10	106 (59)	265	778	2.9	7	36	536	14.9(40)	6	24	7	29.2	76	3.2(23)	1	3	—	—	—	K	—	2	94	1089

BRUDZINSKI, BOB Robert Louis, LB, 6'4"/230 lbs; Ohio State; 1977: LA, rnd 1; B1/1/1955 Fremont, OH **1977**†LARm 14 (7, LLB) **1978**†LARm 16 (10, RLB)
1979†LARm 16 (16, RLB) **1980** LARm 9 (8, RLB) **1981**†Mia 16 (16, LOLB) **1982** Mia 9 (9, LOLB) **1983**†Mia 16 (16, LOLB) **1984**†Mia 16 (16, LOLB) **1985**†Mia 14 (13, LOLB)
1986 Mia 16 (16, LOLB) **1987** Mia 12 (8, LOLB) **1988** Mia 16 (16, LOLB) **1989** Mia 10 (0) **NFL** 180 (135) [13 yrs]

BRUECKMAN, CHARLIE Charles William, LB, 6'2"/223 lbs; Pittsburgh; 1957: SF, rnd 5; B11/23/1935 McKees Rocks, PA **1958** Was 9 **1960** LAC-A 14 **NFL** 23 [2 yrs]

BRUENER, MARK Mark Frederick, TE, 6'4"/260 lbs; Washington; 1995: Pit, rnd 1; B9/16/1972 Olympia, WA

1995	†Pit	16 (13, TE)	—	—	—	—	26	238	9.2(29)	3	—	—	—	—	—	—	—	—	—	—	k	—	18	123
1996	Pit	12 (12, TE)	—	—	—	—	12	141	11.8(36)	0	—	—	—	—	—	—	—	—	—	—	—	—	2	71
1997	†Pit	16 (16, TE)	—	—	—	—	18	117	6.5(18)	6	—	—	—	—	—	—	—	—	—	—	—	—	36	89
1998	Pit	16 (16, TE)	—	—	—	—	19	157	8.3(20)	2	—	—	—	—	—	—	—	—	—	—	—	—	12	82
1999	Pit	14 (14, TE)	—	—	—	—	18	176	9.8(29)	0	—	—	—	—	—	—	—	—	—	—	—	—	0	88
2000	Pit	16 (16, TE)	—	—	—	—	17	192	11.3(30)	3	—	—	—	—	—	—	—	—	—	—	—	—	18	111
2001	Pit	9 (9, TE)	—	—	—	—	12	98	8.2(21)	0	—	—	—	—	—	—	—	—	—	—	—	—	0	49
2002	Pit	12 (12, TE)	—	—	—	—	13	66	5.1(10)	1	—	—	—	—	—	—	—	—	—	—	—	—	6	38
2003	Pit	14 (0)	—	—	—	—	2	12	6.0(11)	1	—	—	—	—	—	—	—	—	—	—	—	—	6	11
2004	Hou	16 (11, TE)	—	—	—	—	4	52	13.0(27)	0	—	—	—	—	—	—	—	—	—	—	—	—	0	26
2005	Hou	16 (15, TE)	—	—	—	—	2	22	11.0(19)	0	—	—	—	—	—	—	—	—	—	—	k	—	0	7
NFL	11	157 (134)	—	—	—	—	143	1271	8.9(36)	16	—	—	—	—	—	—	—	—	—	—	k	—	98	694

BRUER, BOB Robert Anthony, TE, 6'5"/235 lbs; Mankato State; 1975: Hou, rnd 9; B5/22/1953 Madison, WI

1979	SF	16 (4)	5	-4	-0.8(6)	0	26	254	9.8(19)	1	—	—	—	—	—	—	—	—	—	—	k	—	6	133
1980	SF	1 (0)	—	—	—	—	—	—	—	—	—	—	—	—	—	—	—	—	—	—	—	—	—	—
1980	†Min	12 (0)	—	—	—	—	—	—	—	—	—	—	—	—	—	—	—	—	—	—	k	—	0	-10
1981	Min	15 (0)	—	—	—	—	7	38	5.4(10)	3	—	—	—	—	—	—	—	—	—	—	—	—	18	34
1982	Min	8 (2)	—	—	—	—	8	102	12.8(24)	1	—	—	—	—	—	—	—	—	—	—	—	—	12	61
1983	Min	16 (10, TE)	—	—	—	—	31	315	10.2(26)	2	—	—	—	—	—	—	—	—	—	—	—	—	12	168
NFL	5	68 (16)	5	-4	-0.8(6)	0	72	709	9.8(26)	8	—	—	—	—	—	—	—	—	—	—	k	—	48	386

BRUGGERS, BOB Robert Eugene, LB, 6'1"/230 lbs; Minnesota; B4/20/1944 Lincoln, NE **1966** Mia-A 14 **1967** Mia-A 4 (1) **1968** Mia-A 6 **1968** SD-A 5 **1969** SD-A 12
1970 SD 13 **1971** SD 3 **NFL** 57 (1) [6 yrs]

BRUHIN, JOHN John Glenn, G, 6'3"/280 lbs; Tennessee; 1988: TB, rnd 4; B12/9/1964 Knoxville, TN **1988** TB 16 (6, rg) **1989** TB 9 (8, RG) **1990** TB 14 (1) **1991** TB 10 (6, lg)
NFL 49 (21) [4 yrs]

BRUMBAUGH, BOYD Urban Boyd, B, 5'11"/195 lbs; Duquesne; 1938: Bkn, rnd 1; B8/24/1915 Springdale, PA, D4/5/1988 Homestead, FL

1938	Bkn	7 (3)	45	191	4.2	0	1	5	5.0(5)	1	—	—	—	—	—	—	—	—	—	—	—	—	6	199
1939	Bkn	5 (1)	25	61	2.4	0	1	5	5.0(5)	0	—	—	—	—	—	—	—	—	—	—	—	—	0	64
1939	Pit	6 (4)	86	282	3.3	2	4	90	22.5	1	7	3	42.9	121	17.3(17)	2	1	—	—	—	P	—	18	383
1940	Pit	8 (4)	32	79	2.5	0	1	0	0.0	0	7	2	28.6	46	6.6	0	1	—	—	—	P	—	0	62
1941	Pit	10 (7, TB)	68	114	1.7(8)	2	1	1	1.0(1)	0	41	13	31.7	260	6.3(72)	2	8	—	—	—	kp	—	12	86
NFL	4	36 (19)	256	727	2.8(8)	4	8	101	12.6(5)	2	55	18	31.6	427	7.5(72)	4	10	—	—	—	Pkp	—	36	792

BRUMBAUGH, CARL Carl Lowry, B, 5´10˝/170 lbs; Ohio State; Florida; B9/22/1906 West Milton, OH, D10/25/1969 West Milton, OH **[K]**

YEAR	TEAM	G (GS, POS)	RUSH	YD	AVG (LG)	TD	REC	YD	AVG (LG)	TD	PASS	COMP	PCT	YD	AVG (LG)	TD	INT	SK	YD	QBR	KPR	OTD	PTS	TAY
1930	ChiB	14 (12, QB)	—	—	—	—	—	—	—	—	—	—	—	—	—	—	—	—	—	—	—	—	—	—
1931	ChiB☆	12 (9, QB)	—	—	—	—	—	—	—	—	—	—	—	—	—	—	—	—	—	—	—	—	—	—
1932	ChiB	13 (0)	17	14	0.8	0	9	129	14.3	0	7	3	42.9	71	10.1	0	0	—	—	—	—	—	0	114
1933	†ChiB	13 (9, QB)	20	39	2.0	0	5	82	16.4	0	29	8	27.6	101	3.5	1	6	—	—	—	—	—	0	-105
1934	†ChiB	13 (12, QB)	7	-9	-1.3	0	5	84	16.8	2	35	8	22.9	232	6.6	2	2	—	—	—	K	—	14	89
1936	ChiB	12 (3)	9	-1	-0.1	0	5	39	7.8	2	28	8	28.6	140	5.0	3	3	—	—	—	—	—	12	-7
1937	Cle	4 (3)	2	8	4.0	0	—	—	—	—	2	1	50.0	20	10.0 (20)	0	0	—	—	—	—	—	0	18
1937	Bkn	5 (1)	5	-11	-2.2	0	—	—	—	—	16	4	25.0	67	4.2	0	3	—	—	—	—	—	0	-98
1937	ChiB	1 (0)	—	—	—	—	—	—	—	—	—	—	—	—	—	—	—	—	—	—	—	—	—	—
1938	ChiB	9 (0)	3	-15	-5.0	0	1	23	23.0 (23)	0	4	2	50.0	25	6.3	0	0	—	—	—	—	—	0	9
NFL	8	96 (49)	63	25	0.4	1	25	357	14.3 (23)	4	121	34	28.1	656	5.4 (20)	9	14	—	—	—	K	—	39	47

BRUMBAUGH, JUSTIN Justin Jay, BB-TB, 6´0˝/205 lbs; Bucknell; B3/2/1905 Springdale, PA, D7/3/1951 Rochester, MN **1931** Fra 6 (6, BB)

BRUMFIELD, JACK Jackson Louis, DE, 6´2˝/215 lbs; Southern Mississippi; B5/1/1931 Franklinton, LA **1954** SF 12 (RDE)

BRUMFIELD, JIM James I., RB, 6´1˝/195 lbs; Indiana State; 1970: NO, rnd 10; B9/4/1947 Osyka, MS **1971** Pit 14

BRUMFIELD, SCOTT Scott Wheeler, G-T, 6´8˝/321 lbs; Brigham Young; B8/19/1970 Salt Lake City, UT **1993** Cin 16 (7, rg) **1994** Cin 2 (0) **1995** Cin 13 (11, LG) **1996** Cin 9 (8, rg) **1997** Cin 15 (3) **NFL** 55 (29) [5 yrs]

BRUMLEY, BOB Robert Lee, WB, 6´0˝/200 lbs; Rice; 1942: Cle, rnd 8; B9/24/1919

YEAR	TEAM	G (GS, POS)	RUSH	YD	AVG (LG)	TD	REC	YD	AVG (LG)	TD	PASS	COMP	PCT	YD	AVG (LG)	TD	INT	SK	YD	QBR	KPR	OTD	PTS	TAY
1945	Det	1 (0)	5	18	3.6 (4)	0	2	27	13.5 (29)	0	—	—	—	—	—	—	—	—	—	—	—	—	0	32

BRUMM, DON Donald Dwain, DE, 6´3˝/245 lbs; Purdue; 1963: SL, rnd 1/KC, rnd 3; B10/4/1941 Chicago Heights, IL **1963** SL 11 (RDE) **1964** SL 14 (RDE) **1965** SL 14 (RDE) **1966** SL 14 (RDE) **1967** SL 10 (RDE) **1968** SL✧14 (LDE) **1969** SL 4 **1970** Phi 7 **1971** Phi 9 **1972** SL 14 (LDE) **NFL** 111 [10 yrs]

BRUMM, FRED Frederick, T-C, Union (NY); B11/1887 Tonawanda, NY, deceased **1921** Ton 1 (0)

BRUMM, ROMAN Roman Henry, E-T-C-G, 6´0˝/182 lbs; Wisconsin-LaCrosse; Wisconsin-Eau Claire; Wisconsin; B3/5/1898 Madison, WI, D9/2/1981 Los Angeles County, CA **1924** Rac 9 (9, LE) **1925** Mil 5 (5, LT) **1926** Rac 4 (2, C) **NFL** 18 (16) [3 yrs]

BRUNDAGE, DEWEY Jean Dewey, DE, 6´3˝/210 lbs; Brigham Young; 1954: Det, rnd 22; B10/1/1931 Alhambra, CA **1954** Pit 11 (LDE)

BRUNDIGE, BILL William Glenn, DT-DE, 6´5˝/270 lbs; Colorado; 1970: Was, rnd 2; B11/13/1948 Holyoke, CO **1970** Was 14 (14, RDT) **1971**†Was 14 **1972**†Was 11 (10, LDT) **1973**†Was 14 (12, LDT) **1974**†Was 14 (13, LDT) **1975** Was 14 (13, LDT) **1976**†Was 14 (6, ldt/rde) **1977** Was 12 (6, ldt) **NFL** 107 (74) [8 yrs]

BRUNE, LARRY Lawrence Dee, DB, 6´2˝/202 lbs; Rice; 1976: Min, rnd 7; B5/4/1953 San Diego, CA **1980**†Min 16 (0)

BRUNELL, MARK Mark Allen, QB, 6´1˝/217 lbs; Washington; 1993: GB, rnd 5; B9/17/1970 Los Angeles, CA

YEAR	TEAM	G (GS, POS)	RUSH	YD	AVG (LG)	TD	REC	YD	AVG (LG)	TD	PASS	COMP	PCT	YD	AVG (LG)	TD	INT	SK	YD	QBR	KPR	OTD	PTS	TAY
1994	†GB	2 (0)	6	7	1.2 (5)	1	—	—	—	—	27	12	44.4	95	3.5 (25)	0	0	2	16	—	—	—	6	65
1995	Jax	13 (10, QB)	67	480	7.2 (27)	4	—	—	—	—	346	201	58.1	2168	6.3 (45)	15	7	39	238	82.6	—	—	24	1399
1996	†Jax✧	16 (16, QB)	80	396	4.9 (33)	3	—	—	—	—	557	353	**63.4**	**4367**	**7.8** (**62**)	19	**20**	50	257	84.0	—	—	22	**1905**
1997	†Jax✧	14 (14, QB)	48	257	5.4 (15)	2	—	—	—	—	435	264	60.7	3281	7.5 (75)	18	7	33	189	91.2	—	—	12	1728
1998	†Jax	13 (13, QB)	49	192	3.9 (18)	0	—	—	—	—	354	208	58.8	2601	7.3 (78)	20	9	28	172	89.9	—	—	0	1233
1999	†Jax✧	15 (15, QB)	47	208	4.4 (15)	1	—	—	—	—	441	259	58.7	3060	6.9 (62)	14	9	29	174	82.0	—	—	8	1458
2000	Jax	16 (16, QB)	48	236	4.9 (16)	2	—	—	—	—	512	311	60.7	3640	7.1 (67)	20	14	54	289	84.0	—	—	12	1616
2001	Jax	15 (15, QB)	39	224	5.7 (38)	1	—	—	—	—	473	289	61.1	3309	7.0 (44)	19	13	57	387	84.1	—	—	6	1464
2002	Jax	15 (15, QB)	43	207	4.8 (27)	0	—	—	—	—	416	245	58.9	2788	6.7 (79)	17	7	34	210	85.7	—	—	0	1406
2003	Jax	3 (3)	8	19	2.4 (12)	1	—	—	—	—	82	54	65.9	484	5.9 (65)	2	0	9	46	—	—	—	6	281
2004	Was	9 (9, QB)	19	62	3.3 (21)	0	—	—	—	—	237	118	49.8	1194	5.0 (49)	7	6	15	105	63.9	—	—	0	454
2005	†Was	16 (15, QB)	42	111	2.6 (25)	0	—	—	—	—	454	262	57.7	3050	6.7 (78)	23	10	27	213	85.9	—	—	0	1351
NFL	12	147 (141)	496	2399	4.8 (38)	15	—	—	—	—	4334	2576	59.4	30037	6.9 (79)	174	102	377	2296	84.1	—	—	96	14358

BRUNELLI, SAM Samuel Aldino, T-G, 6´2˝/270 lbs; Colorado State; B12/13/1943 Fort Morgan, CO **1966** Den-A 2 **1967** Den-A 12 (LT) **1968** Den-A 14 (LT) **1969** Den-A 14 (14, LT) **1970** Den 13 (12, LT) **1971** Den 5 (4) **NFL** 60 (30) [6 yrs]

BRUNET, BOB Robert Paul, RB, 6´1˝/205 lbs; Louisiana Tech; 1968: Was, rnd 7; B7/29/1946 Larose, LA

YEAR	TEAM	G (GS, POS)	RUSH	YD	AVG (LG)	TD	REC	YD	AVG (LG)	TD	PASS	COMP	PCT	YD	AVG (LG)	TD	INT	SK	YD	QBR	KPR	OTD	PTS	TAY
1968	Was	7 (fb)	71	227	3.2 (15)	0	18	160	8.9 (39)	1	—	—	—	—	—	—	—	—	—	—	—	—	6	312
1970	Was	6	9	37	4.1 (11)	0	3	28	9.3 (14)	0	—	—	—	—	—	—	—	—	—	—	—	—	0	51
1971	†Was	7	10	27	2.7 (5)	0	2	4	2.0 (5)	0	—	—	—	—	—	—	—	—	—	—	—	—	0	29
1972	†Was	14 (1)	30	82	2.7 (18)	2	1	8	8.0 (8)	0	—	—	—	—	—	—	—	—	—	—	k	—	12	176
1973	†Was	14	2	4	2.0 (3)	0	—	—	—	—	—	—	—	—	—	—	—	—	—	—	—	—	0	4
1975	Was	14	6	23	3.8 (11)	1	—	—	—	—	—	—	—	—	—	—	—	—	—	—	k	—	6	41
1976	†Was	14	—	—	—	—	—	—	—	—	—	—	—	—	—	—	—	—	—	—	k	—	0	25
1977	Was	5	3	6	2.0 (3)	0	—	—	—	—	—	—	—	—	—	—	—	—	—	—	k	—	0	16
NFL	8	81 (1)	131	406	3.1 (18)	3	24	200	8.3 (39)	1	—	—	—	—	—	—	—	—	—	—	k	—	24	654

BRUNEY, FRED Frederick Karl, DB, 5´10˝/184 lbs; Ohio State; 1953: Cle, rnd 3; B12/30/1931 Martins Ferry, OH **[C]** **1953** SF 12 (SS) **1956** SF 5 **1956** Pit 5 **1957** Pit 12 (DB) **1958** LARm 3 **1960** Bos-A☆12 (LS) **1961** Bos-A✧14 (RS) **1962** Bos-A✧14 **NFL** 77 [7 yrs]

BRUNKLACHER, AUSTIN N. Austin, G, /193 lbs; none; B1898, KY, deceased **1921** Lou 1 (1) **1922** Lou 4 (2, LG) **1923** Lou 2 (2, LG) **NFL** 7 (5) [3 yrs]

BRUNNER, SCOTT Scott Lee, QB, 6´5˝/206 lbs; Delaware; 1980: NYG, rnd 6; B3/24/1957 Sellersville, PA

YEAR	TEAM	G (GS, POS)	RUSH	YD	AVG (LG)	TD	REC	YD	AVG (LG)	TD	PASS	COMP	PCT	YD	AVG (LG)	TD	INT	SK	YD	QBR	KPR	OTD	PTS	TAY
1980	NYG	16 (3)	10	18	1.8 (12)	0	—	—	—	—	112	52	46.4	610	5.4 (50)	4	6	10	76	—	—	—	0	103
1981	†NYG	16 (6, qb)	14	20	1.4 (23)	0	—	—	—	—	190	79	41.6	978	5.1 (43)	5	11	9	67	—	—	—	0	94
1982	NYG	9 (9, QB)	19	27	1.4 (10)	1	—	—	—	—	298	161	54.0	2017	6.8 (47)	10	9	17	130	73.9	—	—	6	736
1983	NYG	16 (12, QB)	26	64	2.5 (12)	0	—	—	—	—	386	190	49.2	2516	6.5 (62)	9	22	31	218	54.3	—	—	0	487
1985	SL	16 (0)	3	8	2.7 (8)	0	—	—	—	—	60	30	50.0	336	5.6 (40)	1	6	4	27	—	—	—	0	-59
NFL	5	73 (30)	72	137	1.9 (23)	1	—	—	—	—	1046	512	48.9	6457	6.2 (62)	29	54	71	518	56.3	—	—	6	1361

BRUNO, DAVE David, P, 6´1˝/235 lbs; Moriane Valley CC (IL); B3/19/1963 Chicago, IL **1987** Min 2 (0)

BRUNO, JOHN John Currie, P, 6´2˝/190 lbs; Penn State; 1987: SL, rnd 5; B9/10/1964 Jeannette, PA, D4/13/1992 Pittsburgh, PA **1987** Pit 3 (0)

BRUNSON, LARRY Lawrence Rudolph, WR, 5´11˝/180 lbs; Mesa; Colorado; 1972: Den, rnd 11; B8/11/1949 Little Rock, AR **[R]**

YEAR	TEAM	G (GS, POS)	RUSH	YD	AVG (LG)	TD	REC	YD	AVG (LG)	TD	PASS	COMP	PCT	YD	AVG (LG)	TD	INT	SK	YD	QBR	KPR	OTD	PTS	TAY
1974	KC	14	5	-33	-6.6 (0)	0	22	374	17.0 (84)	2	—	—	—	—	—	—	—	—	—	—	kp	—	12	280
1975	KC	14 (WR)	2	89	44.5 (65)	0	23	398	17.3 (36)	2	—	—	—	—	—	—	—	—	—	—	kp	—	12	290
1976	KC	14 (14, WR)	3	-1	-0.3 (5)	0	33	656	19.9 (57)	1	—	—	—	—	—	—	—	—	—	—	p	—	6	564
1977	KC	11 (WR)	2	8	4.0 (11)	0	20	295	14.8 (63)	0	—	—	—	—	—	—	—	—	—	—	kp	—	0	215
1978	Oak	2	—	—	—	—	—	—	—	—	—	—	—	—	—	—	—	—	—	—	k	—	0	64
1979	Oak	11	—	—	—	—	5	49	9.8 (17)	1	—	—	—	—	—	—	—	—	—	—	kp	—	6	214
1980	Den	13 (0)	—	—	—	—	1	15	15.0 (15)	0	—	—	—	—	—	—	—	—	—	—	kp	—	0	333
NFL	7	79 (14)	12	63	5.3 (65)	0	104	1787	17.2 (84)	6	—	—	—	—	—	—	—	—	—	—	kp	—	36	1959

BRUNSON, MIKE Michael Sanders, RB, 6´1˝/190 lbs; Mesa; Arizona State; 1970: Atl, rnd 11; B7/30/1947 Little Rock, AR

YEAR	TEAM	G (GS, POS)	RUSH	YD	AVG (LG)	TD	REC	YD	AVG (LG)	TD	PASS	COMP	PCT	YD	AVG (LG)	TD	INT	SK	YD	QBR	KPR	OTD	PTS	TAY
1970	Atl	8	1	9	9.0 (9)	0	—	—	—	—	—	—	—	—	—	—	—	—	—	—	k	—	0	3

BRUNSWICK G, 5´10˝/182 lbs; none; D **1920** Ham 1 (0)

BRUPBACHER, ROSS Ross Alan, LB, 6´3˝/215 lbs; Texas A&M; 1970: Chi, rnd 4; B4/7/1948 Lafayette, LA **1970** ChiB 14 **1971** ChiB 14 (RLB) **1972** ChiB 14 (RLB) **1976** ChiB 14 (12, LLB) **NFL** 56 (12) [4 yrs]

BRUSCHI, TEDY Tedy Lacap, LB, 6´1˝/247 lbs; Arizona; 1996: NE, rnd 3; B6/9/1973 San Francisco, CA **1996**†NE 16 (0) **1997**†NE 16 (1) **1998**†NE 16 (7, rlb) **1999** NE 14 (14, RLB) **2000** NE 16 (16, ROLB) **2001**†NE 15 (9, MLB) **2002** NE 11 (9, mlb) **2003**†NE☆16 (16, MLB) **2004**†NE★16 (16, RILB) **2005**†NE 9 (9, LILB) **NFL** 145 (97) [10 yrs]

BRUTLEY, DARYON Daryon Marquee, DB, 5´11˝/187 lbs; Northern Iowa; B5/31/1979 Eufaula, AL **2003** Phi 1 (0)

BRUTZ, JIM James Charles, T, 6´0˝/230 lbs; Notre Dame; B2/12/1919 Niles, OH, D11/5/2000, OH **1946** ChiR-A 14 (3) **1948** ChiR-A 9 (8, LT) **AAFC** 23 (11) [2 yrs]

YEAR	TEAM	G (GS, POS)	RUSH	YD	AVG(LG)	TD	REC	YD	AVG(LG)	TD	PASS	COMP	PCT	YD	AVG(LG)	TD	INT	SK	YD	QBR	KPR	OTD	PTS	TAY

BRYAN, BILL   William Kirby, C-G, 6´2˝/251 lbs; Duke; 1977: Den, rnd 4; B6/21/1955 Burlington, NC   **1977** Den 1   **1978**†Den 13 (12, C)   **1979**†Den 16 (16, C)   **1980** Den 16 (16, C)   **1981** Den 14 (14, C)   **1982** Den 9 (9, C)   **1983**†Den 16 (16, C)   **1984**†Den 16 (16, C)   **1985** Den☆16 (16, C)   **1986**†Den 16 (16, C)   **1987** Den 4 (4)   **1988** Den 16 (16, C)   **NFL** 153 (151) [12 yrs]

BRYAN, JOHNNY   John Frederick, B, 5´8˝/170 lbs; Dartmouth; Chicago; B2/28/1897 Chicago, IL, D7/1/1966 Fort Collins, CO [C]   **1922** ChiC 10 (3)   **1923** ChiB 12 (12, QB), 24   **1924** ChiB 11 (3), 18   **1925** ChiB 6 (2), 6   **1925** Mil 5 (5, TB)   **1926** Mil 9 (7, TB), 6   **1926** ChiB 3 (1)   **1927** ChiB 1 (1)   **NFL** 57 (34), 54 [6 yrs]

BRYAN, RICK   Rick Don, DE-DT-NT-LB, 6´4˝/265 lbs; Oklahoma; 1984: Atl, rnd 1; B3/20/1962 Tulsa, OK [K]   **1984** Atl 16 (16, RDT)   **1985** Atl 16 (16, LDE)   **1986** Atl☆16 (16, RDE)   **1987** Atl 9 (9, RDE)   **1988** Atl 16 (15, RDE)   **1989** Atl 2 (2)   **1990** Atl 16 (5, nt)   **1991**†Atl 16 (12, LDE)   **1993** Atl 2 (2)   **NFL** 109 (93) [9 yrs]

BRYAN, STEVE   Steven Ray, DE-NT-LB, 6´2˝/256 lbs; Oklahoma; 1987: Chi, rnd 5; B5/6/1964 Wagoner, OK   **1987** Den 4 (3)   **1988** Den 8 (0)   **NFL** 12 (3) [2 yrs]

BRYAN, WALTER   Walter Dean, DB-HB, 6´1˝/185 lbs; Tarleton State; Texas Tech; 1955: Bal, rnd 9; B12/23/1933 Olney, TX

| 1955 | Bal | 10 | | 2 | 4 | 2.0(8) | 0 | — | — | — | — | — | — | — | — | — | — | i | — | — | — | 0 | 3 |

BRYANT, ANTHONY   Anthony, DT, 6´3˝/336 lbs; Alabama; 2005: TB, rnd 6; B11/6/1981 Newbern, AL   **2005** TB 4 (0)

BRYANT, ANTONIO   Antonio, WR, 6´1˝/192 lbs; Pittsburgh; 2002: Dal, rnd 2; B3/9/1981 Miami, FL

2002	Dal	16(15, WR)	6	40	6.7(24)	0	44	733	16.7(78)	6	—	—	—	—	—	—	—	—	—	—	—	36	437
2003	†Dal	16(5, wr)	2	0	0.0(2)	0	39	550	14.1(54)	2	—	—	—	—	—	—	—	—	—	—	—	12	285
2004	Dal	5(1)	—	—	—	—	16	266	16.6(48)	0	—	—	—	—	—	—	—	—	—	—	—	0	133
2004	Cle	10(7, WR)	—	—	—	—	42	546	13.0(55)	4	—	—	—	—	—	—	—	—	—	—	—	24	293
2005	Cle	16(15, WR)	1	3	3.0(3)	0	69	1009	14.6(54)	4	—	—	—	—	—	—	—	—	—	—	—	24	528
NFL	4	63(43)	9	43	4.8(24)	0	210	3104	14.8(78)	16	—	—	—	—	—	—	—	—	—	—	—	96	1675

BRYANT, BENO   Wilson, RB, 5´9˝/175 lbs; Washington; B1/1/1971 Los Angeles, CA

| 1994 | Sea | 2(0) | 1 | 6 | 6.0(6) | 0 | — | — | — | — | — | — | — | — | — | — | — | — | — | kp | — | 0 | 63 |

BRYANT, BILL   William, DB, 5´11˝/195 lbs; Grambling State; 1974: Cin, rnd 6; B2/24/1951 Shreveport, LA   **1976** NYG 14 (4, LCB)   **1977** NYG 14 (4, LCB)   **1978** NYG 11   **1978**†Phi 3   **NFL** 42 (8) [3 yrs]

BRYANT, BOB   Robert R., T, 6´3˝/226 lbs; Texas Tech; B6/14/1918 Frederick, OK, D11/3/2000 Oklahoma City, OK   **1946** SF-A 14 (3, lt)   **1947** SF-A 14 (14, LT)   **1948** SF-A 14 (14, LT)   **1949** SF-A 5 (5, lt)   **AAFC** 47 (36) [4 yrs]

BRYANT, BOB   Robert E., E, 6´5˝/230 lbs; Texas; B5/19/1937

| 1960 | DalT-A | 10(TE) | — | — | — | — | 5 | 43 | 8.6(17) | 0 | — | — | — | — | — | — | — | — | — | — | — | 0 | 22 |

BRYANT, BOBBY   Bobby Lee, DB, 6´1˝/170 lbs; South Carolina; 1967: Min, rnd 7; B1/24/1944 Macon, GA [I]   **1968**†Min 14   **1969** Min☆10 (10, RCB)   **1970**†Min 11 (10, LCB)   **1971** Min 13   **1972** Min 14 (14, RCB)   **1973**†Min☆14 (14, RCB)   **1974** Min 1   **1975**†Min★14 (14, RCB)   **1976**†Min◇12 (3)   **1977**†Min 14 (14, RCB)   **1978**†Min 16 (16, RCB)   **1979**†Min 14 (14, RCB)   **1980**†Min 14 (12, RCB)   **NFL** 161 (121) [13 yrs]

BRYANT, CHARLIE   Charles Limar, RB, 6´0˝/207 lbs; Allen; 1966: SL, rnd 9; B3/7/1941 Lake View, SC, D10/19/2001 Florence, SC

1966	SL	4	5	31	6.2(18)	0	—	—	—	—	—	—	—	—	—	—	—	—	k	—	0	71
1967	SL	14	3	16	5.3(8)	0	—	—	—	—	—	—	—	—	—	—	—	—	k	—	0	130
1968	Atl	2	9	29	3.2(7)	0	1	11	11.0(11)	0	—	—	—	—	—	—	—	—	k	—	0	72
1969	Atl	14	50	246	4.9(41)	0	2	15	7.5(9)	0	—	—	—	—	—	—	—	—	k	—	0	346
NFL	4	34	67	322	4.8(41)	0	2	8.7(11)	0	—	—	—	—	—	—	—	—	—	k	—	0	618

BRYANT, CHUCK   Charles S., E, 6´2˝/220 lbs; Ohio State; 1962: SL, rnd 3/SD, rnd 13; B9/12/1940   **1962** SL 13

BRYANT, CULLEN   William Cullen, RB, 6´1˝/234 lbs; Colorado; 1973: LA, rnd 2; B5/20/1951 Fort Sill, OK

1973	†LARm	13	—	—	—	—	—	—	—	—	—	—	—	—	—	—	—	—	k	1	6	184
1974	†LARm	14	10	24	2.4(7)	0	2	14	7.0(8)	0	—	—	—	—	—	—	—	—	kp	1	6	399
1975	†LARm	14(13, FB)	117	467	4.0(18)	2	20	229	11.4(31)	0	—	—	—	—	—	—	—	—	kp	—	12	739
1976	†LARm☆	14	21	64	3.0(12)	2	2	28	14.0(25)	0	—	—	—	—	—	—	—	—	kp	1	18	503
1977	†LARm	14	6	42	7.0(24)	0	4	28	7.0(14)	0	—	—	—	—	—	—	—	—	kp	—	0	102
1978	†LARm	16(9, RB)	178	658	3.7(26)	7	8	76	9.5(37)	0	—	—	—	—	—	—	—	—	p	—	42	778
1979	†LARm	16(16, FB)	177	619	3.5(15)	5	31	227	7.3(24)	0	—	—	—	—	—	—	—	—	—	—	30	783
1980	†LARm	16(16, FB)	183	807	4.4(20)	3	53	386	7.3(25)	3	—	—	—	—	—	—	—	—	—	—	36	1045
1981	LARm	13(12, FB)	109	436	4.0(20)	1	22	160	7.3(39)	0	—	—	—	—	—	—	—	—	—	—	6	526
1982	LARm	1(0)	—	—	—	—	—	—	—	—	—	—	—	—	—	—	—	—	—	—	—	2
1983	†Sea	10(3)	27	87	3.2(9)	0	3	8	2.7(3)	0	—	—	—	—	—	—	—	—	—	—	0	91
1984	†Sea	9(2)	20	58	2.9(8)	0	3	20	6.7(11)	0	—	—	—	—	—	—	—	—	k	—	0	76
1987	LARm	3(0)	1	2	2.0(2)	0	—	—	—	—	—	—	—	—	—	—	—	—	—	—	0	2
NFL	13	153(71)	849	3264	3.8(26)	20	148	1176	7.9(39)	3	—	—	—	—	—	—	—	—	kp	3	156	5227

BRYANT, DOMINGO   Domingo Garcia, DB, 6´4˝/178 lbs; Texas A&M; 1986: Pit, rnd 6; B12/8/1963 Nacogdoches, TX   **1987**†Hou 13 (3)   **1988**†Hou 14 (3)   **NFL** 27 (3) [2 yrs]

BRYANT, FERNANDO   Fernando Antoneiyo, DB, 5´10˝/174 lbs; Alabama; 1999: Jax, rnd 1; B3/26/1977 Albany, GA   **1999**†Jax 16 (16, LCB)   **2000** Jax 14 (14, LCB)   **2001** Jax 10 (9, LCB)   **2002** Jax 16 (16, LCB)   **2003** Jax 16 (16, LCB)   **2004** Det 10 (10, LCB)   **2005** Det 2 (2)   **NFL** 84 (83) [7 yrs]

BRYANT, HUBIE   Hubert Lavann, WR, 5´10˝/170 lbs; Minnesota; B2/10/1946 Pittsburgh, PA

1970	Pit	14(wr)	3	25	8.3(24)	0	8	154	19.3(63)	0	—	—	—	—	—	—	—	—	p	—	0	76
1971	NE	11(2)	4	1	0.3(1)	0	14	212	15.1(48)	1	—	—	—	—	—	—	—	—	kp	—	6	188
1972	NE	2	—	—	—	—	—	—	—	—	—	—	—	—	—	—	—	—	—	—	0	—
NFL	3	27(2)	7	26	3.7(24)	0	22	366	16.6(63)	1	—	—	—	—	—	—	—	—	kp	—	6	264

BRYANT, JEFF   Jeffrey Dwight, DE-DT, 6´5˝/276 lbs; Clemson; 1982: Sea, rnd 1; B5/22/1960 Atlanta, GA [S]   **1982** Sea 9 (9, RDE)   **1983**†Sea 16 (16, RDE)   **1984**†Sea☆16 (16, RDE)   **1985** Sea 16 (16, RDE)   **1986** Sea 12 (12, RDE)   **1987** Sea 12 (12, RDE)   **1988**†Sea 16 (12, RDE)   **1989** Sea 15 (15, RDE)   **1990** Sea 15 (14, RDT)   **1991** Sea 16 (14, LDT)   **1992** Sea 16 (16, LDE)   **1993** Sea 16 (15, LDE)   **NFL** 175 (167) [12 yrs]

BRYANT, JIM   James Gorman, BB-WB, 5´6˝/156 lbs; George Washington; Pennsylvania; B7/12/1894 Toronto, Canada, D4/18/1972 Sacramento, CA   **1920** Cle 3 (3, BB)

BRYANT, JUNIOR   Edward Ethan, DT-DE, 6´4˝/278 lbs; Notre Dame; B1/16/1971 Omaha, NE   **1995**†SF 16 (4)   **1996**†SF 16 (1)   **1997** SF 16 (3)   **1998**†SF 16 (16, RDT)   **1999** SF 16 (16, RDT/lde)   **2000** SF 3 (3)   **NFL** 83 (43) [6 yrs]

BRYANT, KELVIN   Kelvin Leroy, RB, 6´2˝/195 lbs; North Carolina; 1983: Was, rnd 7; B9/26/1960 Tarboro, NC

1986	†Was	10(0)	69	258	3.7(22)	4	43	449	10.4(60)	3	—	—	—	—	—	—	—	—	—	—	42	538
1987	†Was	11(1)	77	406	5.3(28)	1	43	490	11.4(39)	5	1	0	0.0	0	0.0	0	0	0	—	—	36	686
1988	Was	10(4)	108	498	4.6(25)	1	42	447	10.6(47)	5	—	—	—	—	—	—	—	—	—	—	36	757
1990	Was	15(0)	6	24	4.0(12)	0	26	248	9.5(37)	1	—	—	—	—	—	—	—	—	—	—	6	153
NFL	4	46(5)	260	1186	4.6(28)	6	154	1634	10.6(47)	14	1	0	0.0	0	0.0	0	0	0	—	—	120	2133

BRYANT, MATT   Matt, K, 5´9˝/200 lbs; Baylor; B5/29/1975 Orange, TX [K]   **2002**†NYG 16 (0)   **2003** NYG 11 (0)   **2004** Ind 1 (0)   **2004** Mia 3 (0)   **2005**†TB 15 (0)   **NFL** 46 (0) [4 yrs]

BRYANT, RODERICK   Roderick, DB, 6´1˝/185 lbs; Idaho; B2/17/1981 Washington, DC   **2004** NYJ 13 (0)

BRYANT, ROMBY   Romby, WR, 6´1˝/181 lbs; Tulsa; B12/21/1979 Oklahoma City, OK   **2005** Atl 3 (0)

BRYANT, STEVE   Stephen Theodore, WR, 6´2˝/195 lbs; Purdue; 1982: Hou, rnd 4; B10/10/1959 Los Angeles, CA

1982	Hou	7(0)	—	—	—	—	—	—	—	—	—	—	—	—	—	—	—	—	—	—	—	0	—
1983	Hou	16(6, wr)	—	—	—	—	16	211	13.2(26)	0	1	1	100.0	24	24.0(24)	1	0	—	—	—	—	0	123
1984	Hou	14(3)	—	—	—	—	19	278	14.6(28)	0	—	—	—	—	—	—	—	—	—	—	—	0	139
1985	Hou	4(0)	—	—	—	—	—	—	—	—	—	—	—	—	—	—	—	—	—	—	—	0	—
1987	Ind	1(0)	—	—	—	—	1	12	12.0(12)	0	—	—	—	—	—	—	—	—	—	—	—	0	6
NFL	5	42(9)	—	—	—	—	36	501	13.9(28)	0	1	1	100.0	24	24.0(24)	1	0	—	—	—	—	0	268

BRYANT, TIM   Timothy, LB, 6´1˝/217 lbs; Vanderbilt; Southern Mississippi; B5/5/1962 Nashville, TN   **1987** Min 1 (0)

BRYANT, TONY   Tony, DE, 6´6˝/275 lbs; Florida State; 1999: Oak, rnd 2; B9/3/1976 Marathon, FL   **1999** Oak 10 (0)   **2000**†Oak 16 (16, LDE)   **2001**†Oak 16 (16, RDE)   **2002** Oak 8 (8, RDE)   **2004** NO 16 (0)   **2005** NO 16 (1)   **NFL** 82 (41) [6 yrs]

Bryant, Trent Trent Baron, DB, 5´10˝/180 lbs; Arkansas; 1981: Bal, rnd 10; B8/14/1959 Arkadelphia, AR **1981** Was 4 (0) **1982** KC 9 (1) **1983** KC 16 (2) **1987** KC 3 (2) **NFL** 32 (5) [4 yrs]

Bryant, Warren Warren, T, 6´6˝/273 lbs; Kentucky; 1977: Atl, rnd 1; B11/11/1955 Miami, FL **1977** Atl 14 (14, RT) **1978** Atl 13 (11, RT) **1979** Atl 16 (16, RT) **1980**†Atl 16 (16, RT) **1981** Atl 11 (10, RT) **1982**†Atl 9 (9, RT) **1983** Atl 16 (16, RT) **1984** Atl 4 (0) **1984**†LARd 5 (0) **NFL** 104 (92) [8 yrs]

Bryant, Waymond Waymond, LB, 6´4˝/236 lbs; Tennessee State; 1974: Chi, rnd 1; B7/28/1952 Dallas, TX **1974** ChiB 13 (mlb) **1975** ChiB 13 (13, RLB/mlb) **1976** ChiB 14 (RLB) **1977**†ChiB 13 (12, RLB) **NFL** 53 (25) [4 yrs]

Bryant, Wendell Wendell, DT, 6´5˝/303 lbs; Wisconsin; 2002: Arz, rnd 1; B9/12/1980 St. Louis, MO **2002** Arz 14 (4) **2003** Arz 12 (5, ldt) **2004** Arz 3 (0) **NFL** 29 (9) [3 yrs]

Bryson, Shawn Adrian Shawn, RB, 6´1˝/228 lbs; Tennessee; 1999: Buf, rnd 3; B11/20/1976 Franklin, NC

YEAR	TEAM	G (GS, POS)	RUSH	YD	AVG (LG)	TD	REC	YD	AVG (LG)	TD	PASS	COMP	PCT	YD	AVG (LG)	TD	INT	SK	YD	QBR	KPR	OTD	PTS	TAY
2000	Buf	16(7, rb)	161	591	3.7(24)	0	32	271	8.5(32)	2	—	—	—	—	—	—	—	—	—	—	k	—	14	739
2001	Buf	15(3)	80	341	4.3(68)	2	9	59	6.6(23)	0	—	—	—	—	—	—	—	—	—	—	k	—	12	450
2002	Buf	6(0)	13	35	2.7(10)	0	1	9	9.0(9)	0	—	—	—	—	—	—	—	—	—	—	k	—	0	43
2003	Det	16(13, RB)	158	606	3.8(39)	3	54	340	6.3(26)	0	—	—	—	—	—	—	—	—	—	—	—	—	18	806
2004	Det	16(1)	50	264	5.3(28)	0	44	322	7.3(30)	0	—	—	—	—	—	—	—	—	—	—	k	—	0	422
2005	Det	16(2)	64	306	4.8(77)	1	37	284	7.7(63)	0	—	—	—	—	—	—	—	—	—	—	k	—	6	453
NFL	6	85(26)	526	2143	4.1(77)	6	177	1285	7.3(63)	2	—	—	—	—	—	—	—	—	—	—	k	—	50	2912

Brzezinski, Doug Douglas Gregory, G, 6´4˝/305 lbs; Boston College; 1999: Phi, rnd 3; B3/11/1976 Livonia, MI **1999** Phi 16 (16, LG) **2000**†Phi 16 (0) **2001**†Phi 16 (1) **2002**†Phi 16 (5, lg) **2003** Car 1 (0) **2004** Car 8 (8, rg) **NFL** 73 (30) [6 yrs]

Bua, Tony Anthony, LB, 5´11˝/218 lbs; Arkansas; 2004: Mia, rnd 5; B2/11/1980 River Ridge, LA **2004** Mia 7 (0)

Buben, Mark Mark, DE-NT, 6´3˝/260 lbs; Tufts; B3/23/1957 Auburn, MA **1979** NE 16 **1981** NE 16 (4) **1982** Cle 3 (0) **NFL** 35 (4) [3 yrs]

Bucchianeri, Mike Amadeo Roger, G, 5´10˝/212 lbs; Indiana; B1/9/1917 Van Voorhis, PA, D2/19/1992 Ocala, FL **1941** GB 1 (0) **1944** GB 8 (1) **1945** GB 5 (0) **NFL** 14 (1) [3 yrs]

Bucek, Ray Felix A., G-LB, 6´0˝/186 lbs; Texas A&M; 1943: Pit, rnd 19; B1/31/1922 Schulenburg, TX, D8/13/1965 Cape Giradeau, MO **1946** Pit 11 (11, RG)

Buchanan, Buck Junious, DT, 6´7˝/270 lbs; Grambling State; 1963: KC, rnd 1/NYG, rnd 19; B9/10/1940 Gainesville, AL, D7/16/1992 Kansas City, MO; HOF 1990 **1963** KC-A 14 (LDT) **1964** KC-A★14 (RDT) **1965** KC-A★14 (RDT) **1966**†KC-A★14 (RDT) **1967** KC-A★14 (RDT) **1968**†KC-A★14 (RDT) **1969**†KC-A★14 (RDT) **1970** KC★14 (RDT) **1971**†KC★14 (RDT) **1972** KC 14 (RDT) **1973** KC 14 (RDT) **1974** KC 14 (RDT) **1975** KC 14 (RDT) **NFL** 182 [13 yrs]

Buchanan, Charles Charles Harrison, DE, 6´3˝/245 lbs; Tennessee State; 1987: Pit, rnd 8; B9/20/1964 Memphis, TN **1988** Cle 9 (0)

Buchanan, Ray Raymond Louis, DB, 5´9˝/186 lbs; Louisville; 1993: Ind, rnd 3; B9/29/1971 Chicago, IL **[I]** **1993** Ind 16 (5, fs) **1994** Ind☆16 (16, FS/lcb) **1995**†Ind 16 (16, LCB) **1996**†Ind 13 (13, LCB) **1997** Atl 16 (16, LCB) **1998**†Atl★16 (16, LCB) **1999** Atl 16 (16, LCB) **2000** Atl 16 (16, LCB) **2001** Atl 16 (16, LCB) **2002**†Atl 12 (11, LCB) **2003** Atl 15 (8, lcb) **2004** Oak 16 (16, FS) **NFL** 184 (165) [12 yrs]

Buchanan, Richard Richard Lawrence, WR, 5´10˝/178 lbs; Northwestern; B5/8/1969 Chicago, IL **1993** LARm 5 (0)

YEAR	TEAM	G (GS, POS)	RUSH	YD	AVG (LG)	TD	REC	YD	AVG (LG)	TD	PASS	COMP	PCT	YD	AVG (LG)	TD	INT	SK	YD	QBR	KPR	OTD	PTS	TAY
1994	LARm	3(0)	—	—	—	—	5	60	12.0(18)	0	—	—	—	—	—	—	—	—	—	—	—	—	0	30
NFL	2	8(0)	—	—	—	—	5	60	12.0(18)	0	—	—	—	—	—	—	—	—	—	—	p	—	0	31

Buchanan, Steve Stephen, BB-TB, 5´8˝/160 lbs; Miami (OH); B3/4/1903, D11/21/1992 Dayton, OH **1929** Day 6 (5, BB)

Buchanan, Tim Timothy, LB, 6´1˝/230 lbs; Arizona State; Hawaii; 1969: Cin, rnd 8; B5/26/1946 Pasadena, CA **1969** Cin-A 14

Buchanon, Phillip Phillip Darren, DB, 5´10˝/185 lbs; Miami (FL); 2002: Oak, rnd 1; B9/19/1980 Fort Myers, FL **[R]** **2002** Oak 6 (2) **2003** Oak 16 (10, RCB) **2004** Oak 14 (14, LCB) **2005** Hou 10 (6, lcb) **NFL** 46 (32) [4 yrs]

Buchanon, Willie Willie James, DB, 6´0˝/190 lbs; San Diego State; 1972: GB, rnd 1; B11/4/1950 Oceanside, CA **[I]** **1972**†GB 14 (14, LCB) **1973** GB✧6 (6, lcb) **1974** GB✧14 (14, LCB) **1975** GB 2 (2) **1976** GB 14 (14, LCB) **1977** GB 14 (14, LCB) **1978** GB★16 (16, LCB) **1979**†SD 16 (16, LCB) **1980**†SD 16 (16, LCB) **1981**†SD 16 (16, LCB) **1982**†SD 9 (1) **NFL** 137 (129) [11 yrs]

Bucher, Bill William George, E, 5´10˝/180 lbs; Clarkson; B4/23/1903, D5/29/1976 Detroit, MI **1925** Det 1 (1)

Bucher, Frank Frank H., E, 5´11˝/190 lbs; Detroit Mercy; B12/19/1900 Fairport, NY, D3/20/1971 Brighton, MI **1925** Pot 10 (9, RE), 12 **1926** Pot 13 (12, RE) **NFL** 23 (21) [2 yrs]

Buck, Cub Howard, T, 6´0˝/259 lbs; Wisconsin; B8/7/1892 Eau Claire County, WI, D6/14/1966 Rock Island, IL **[K]** **1920** Can☆11 (8, LT) **1921** GB 6 (6, RT) **1922** GB 10 (10, LT), 6 **1923** GB 10 (10, LT), 23 **1924** GB 11 (11, LT), 17 **1925** GB 12 (12, LT), 8 **NFL** 60 (57), 54 [6 yrs]

Buck, Jason Jason Ogden, DE-DT, 6´5˝/268 lbs; Brigham Young; 1987: Cin, rnd 1; B7/27/1963 Moses Lake, WA **1987** Cin 12 (0) **1988**†Cin 16 (0) **1989** Cin 16 (16, RDE) **1990**†Cin 16 (6, rde) **1991**†Was 8 (1) **1992**†Was 16 (5, ldt) **1993** Was 13 (3) **NFL** 97 (31) [7 yrs]

Buck, Mike Mike Eric, QB, 6´3˝/227 lbs; Maine; 1990: NO, rnd 6; B4/22/1967 Long Island, NY

YEAR	TEAM	G (GS, POS)	RUSH	YD	AVG (LG)	TD	REC	YD	AVG (LG)	TD	PASS	COMP	PCT	YD	AVG (LG)	TD	INT	SK	YD	QBR	KPR	OTD	PTS	TAY
1991	NO	2(0)	—	—	—	—	—	—	—	—	2	1	50.0	61	30.5(61)	0	1	—	—	—	—	—	0	-10
1992	NO	2(0)	3	-4	-1.3(-1)	0	—	—	—	—	4	2	50.0	10	2.5(10)	0	0	—	—	—	—	—	0	1
1993	NO	4(1)	1	0	0.0(0)	0	—	—	—	—	54	32	59.3	448	8.3(63)	4	3	3	17	—	—	—	0	124
1995	Arz	4(0)	1	0	0.0(0)	0	—	—	—	—	32	20	62.5	271	8.5(28)	1	0	2	10	—	—	—	0	141
NFL	4	12(1)	5	-4	-0.8	0	—	—	—	—	92	55	59.8	790	8.6(63)	5	4	5	27	—	—	—	0	256

Buck, Vince Vincent Lamont, DB, 6´0˝/198 lbs; Central State (OH); 1990: NO, rnd 2; B1/12/1968 Owensboro, KY **1990**†NO 16 (1) **1991** NO 13 (13, LCB) **1992**†NO 10 (5, lcb) **1993** NO 16 (16, LCB) **1994** NO 16 (16, FS) **1995** NO 13 (13, FS) **NFL** 84 (64) [6 yrs]

Buckey, Don Donald, WR, 5´11˝/180 lbs; North Carolina State; 1976: NYJ, rnd 12; B11/9/1953 Akron, OH

YEAR	TEAM	G (GS, POS)	RUSH	YD	AVG (LG)	TD	REC	YD	AVG (LG)	TD	PASS	COMP	PCT	YD	AVG (LG)	TD	INT	SK	YD	QBR	KPR	OTD	PTS	TAY
1976	NYJ	4	—	—	—	—	5	36	7.2(14)	0	—	—	—	—	—	—	—	—	—	—	—	—	0	18

Buckey, Jeff Jeffrey Michael, G, 6´5˝/305 lbs; Stanford; 1996: Mia, rnd 7; B8/7/1974 Bakersfield, CA **1996** Mia 15 (1) **1997**†Mia 16 (12, LG) **1998** Mia 7 (0) **1999** SF 7 (0) **NFL** 45 (13) [4 yrs]

Buckeye, Garland Garland Maiers, G-C, 6´0˝/238 lbs; none; B10/16/1897 Heron Lake, MN, D11/14/1975 Stone Lake, WI **1920** ChiT 6 (3, RG) **1921** ChiC 5 (5, RG) **1922** ChiC 11 (11, RG) **1923** ChiC 10 (7, rg) **1924** ChiC 8 (7, RG) **NFL** 40 (33) [5 yrs]

Buckhalter, Correll Correll, RB, 6´0˝/222 lbs; Nebraska; 2001: Phi, rnd 4; B10/6/1978 Collins, MS

YEAR	TEAM	G (GS, POS)	RUSH	YD	AVG (LG)	TD	REC	YD	AVG (LG)	TD	PASS	COMP	PCT	YD	AVG (LG)	TD	INT	SK	YD	QBR	KPR	OTD	PTS	TAY
2001	†Phi	15(6, rb)	129	586	4.5(48)	2	13	130	10.0(26)	0	—	—	—	—	—	—	—	—	—	—	k	—	12	684
2003	†Phi	15(5, rb)	126	542	4.3(64)	8	10	133	13.3(27)	1	—	—	—	—	—	—	—	—	—	—	—	—	54	694
NFL	2	30(11)	255	1128	4.4(64)	10	23	263	11.4(27)	1	—	—	—	—	—	—	—	—	—	—	k	—	66	1378

Buckler, Bill William Earl, G-T-E, 6´0˝/238 lbs; Alabama; B4/29/1901 St. Paul, MN, D6/20/1979 Wood River, IL **[K]** **1926** ChiB☆15 (15, LG), 1 **1927** ChiB 12 (11, LG) **1928** ChiB 13 (8, LG) **1931** ChiB 13 (8, RG) **1932** ChiB 14 (6, rg), 1 **1933** ChiB 11 (3) **NFL** 78 (51), 2 [6 yrs]

Bucklew, Phil Phillip Hinkle, E, 6´1˝/205 lbs; Xavier (OH); B12/18/1914 Columbus, OH, D12/30/1992 Fairfax, VA

YEAR	TEAM	G (GS, POS)	RUSH	YD	AVG (LG)	TD	REC	YD	AVG (LG)	TD	PASS	COMP	PCT	YD	AVG (LG)	TD	INT	SK	YD	QBR	KPR	OTD	PTS	TAY
1937	Cle	11(9, LE)	—	—	—	—	3	51	17.0	0	—	—	—	—	—	—	—	—	—	—	—	—	0	26
1938	Cle	1(0)	—	—	—	—	1	14	14.0(14)	0	—	—	—	—	—	—	—	—	—	—	—	—	0	7
NFL	2	12(9)	—	—	—	—	4	65	16.3(14)	0	—	—	—	—	—	—	—	—	—	—	—	—	0	33

Buckley, Curtis Curtis LaDonn, DB-WR, 6´0˝/186 lbs; Texas A&M-Commerce; B9/25/1970 Oakdale, CA **1993** TB 10 (2) **1994** TB 13 (0) **1995** TB 15 (0) **1996**†SF 15 (0) **1997**†SF 15 (0) **1998** SF 8 (0) **1998** NYG 6 (0) **1999**†Was 7 (0) **NFL** 89 (2) [7 yrs]

Buckley, Marcus Marcus Wayne, LB, 6´3˝/240 lbs; Texas A&M; 1993: NYG, rnd 3; B2/3/1971 Fort Worth, TX **1993**†NYG 16 (2) **1994** NYG 16 (1) **1995** NYG 16 (5, rlb) **1996** NYG 15 (2) **1997**†NYG 12 (3) **1998** NYG 14 (12, RLB) **1999** NYG 12 (0) **NFL** 101 (25) [7 yrs]

Buckley, Ralph Ralph Joseph, BB-HB, 5´8˝/175 lbs; Fordham; B3/18/1907 Meriden, CT, D7/13/1979 Dunedin, FL **1930** SI 7 (5, BB), 6

Buckley, Terrell Douglas Terrell, DB, 5´10˝/180 lbs; Florida State; 1992: GB, rnd 1; B6/7/1971 Pascagoula, MS **[RI]** **1992** GB 14 (12, LCB) **1993**†GB 16 (16, LCB) **1994**†GB 16 (16, LCB) **1995**†Mia 16 (4) **1996** Mia 16 (16, LCB) **1997**†Mia 16 (16, LCB) **1998**†Mia 16 (16, LCB) **1999**†Mia 16 (11, LCB) **2000**†Den 16 (16, RCB) **2001**†NE 15 (1) **2002** NE 16 (2) **2003** Mia 16 (5, cb) **2004**†NYJ 16 (0) **2005**†NYG 4 (0) **NFL** 209 (131) [14 yrs]

Bucklin, Ted Theodore Henry, FB-G, 6´0˝/199 lbs; Idaho; B3/9/1903 Idaho Falls, ID, D10/20/1945 Idaho Falls, ID **1927** ChiC 9 (9, FB), 6 **1931** NYG 5 (0) **NFL** 14 (9) [2 yrs]

Buckman, Tom Thomas Harry, TE, 6´4˝/230 lbs; Texas A&M; 1969: GB, rnd 12; B3/7/1947 Fort Worth, TX

YEAR	TEAM	G (GS, POS)	RUSH	YD	AVG (LG)	TD	REC	YD	AVG (LG)	TD	PASS	COMP	PCT	YD	AVG (LG)	TD	INT	SK	YD	QBR	KPR	OTD	PTS	TAY
1969	Den-A	7(1)	—	—	—	—	4	48	12.0(20)	1	—	—	—	—	—	—	—	—	—	—	—	—	6	29

YEAR	TEAM	G(GS, POS)	RUSH	YD	AVG(LG)	TD	REC	YD	AVG(LG)	TD	PASS	COMP	PCT	YD	AVG(LG)	TD	INT	SK	YD	QBR	KPR	OTD	PTS	TAY

BUCKNER, BRENTSON Brentson Andre, DT-DE-NT, 6´2˝/305 lbs; Clemson; 1994: Pit, rnd 2; B9/30/1971 Columbus, GA **1994**†Pit 13 (5, rde) **1995**†Pit 16 (16, LDE/nt) **1996**†Pit 15 (14, LDE) **1997** Cin 14 (5, nt) **1998**†SF 13 (0) **1999** SF 16 (6, rdt) **2000** SF 16 (16, RDT) **2001** Car 16 (10, LDT) **2002** Car 12 (12, LDT) **2003**†Car 12 (12, LDT) **2004** Car 15 (15, LDT) **2005**†Car 16 (16, LDT) **NFL** 174 (127) [12 yrs]

BUCZKOWSKI, BOB John Robert, DE, 6´5˝/260 lbs; Pittsburgh; 1986: LARd, rnd 1; B5/5/1964 Pittsburgh, PA **1987** LARd 2 (0) **1989** Phx 4 (0) **1990** Cle 15 (3) **NFL** 21 (3) [3 yrs]

BUDA, CARL Carl Joseph, G, 5´11˝/220 lbs; Creighton; Tulsa; 1944: Pit, rnd 11; B2/22/1919 Omaha, NE, D6/22/1994 Omaha, NE **1945** Pit 3 (0)

BUDD, FRANK Francis Joseph, WR, 5´10˝/187 lbs; Villanova; 1962: Phi, rnd 7; B7/20/1939 Long Branch, NJ

YEAR	TEAM	G(GS, POS)	RUSH	YD	AVG(LG)	TD	REC	YD	AVG(LG)	TD	PASS	COMP	PCT	YD	AVG(LG)	TD	INT	SK	YD	QBR	KPR	OTD	PTS	TAY
1962	Phi	13	—	—	—	—	5	130	26.0(49)	1	—	—	—	—	—	—	—	—	—	—	—	—	6	70
1963	Was	14	—	—	—	—	5	106	21.2(50)	0	—	—	—	—	—	—	—	—	—	—	k	—	0	155
NFL	2	27	—	—	—	—	10	236	23.6(50)	1	—	—	—	—	—	—	—	—	—	—	k	—	6	225

BUDD, JOHNNY John Walter, T-G, 5´11˝/246 lbs; Lafayette; B1/14/1899 Newton, NJ, D12/26/1963 Fountain Hill, PA **[K]** **1926** Fra☆17 (15, RT), 30 **1927** Pot 13 (10, RG) **1928** Pot 10 (10, LT), 3 **NFL** 40 (35), 33 [3 yrs]

BUDDE, BRAD Brad Edward, G, 6´4˝/262 lbs; USC; 1980: KC, rnd 1; B5/9/1959 Detroit, MI **1980** KC 16 (3) **1981** KC 16 (16, LG) **1982** KC 9 (9, LG) **1983** KC 12 (12, LG) **1984** KC 16 (16, LG) **1985** KC 7 (7, LG) **1986**†KC 16 (16, LG) **NFL** 92 (79) [7 yrs]

BUDDE, ED Edward Leon, G, 6´5˝/265 lbs; Michigan State; 1963: KC, rnd 1/Phi, rnd 1; B11/2/1940 Highland Park, MI **1963** KC-A✧14 **1964** KC-A 14 (LG) **1965** KC-A 14 (LG) **1966**†KC-A★14 (LG) **1967** KC-A★14 (LG) **1968**†KC-A★14 (LG) **1969**†KC-A★14 (LG) **1970** KC★14 (LG) **1971**†KC★14 (LG) **1972** KC 13 (LG) **1973** KC 12 (LG) **1974** KC 14 (LG) **1975** KC 1 (1) **1976** KC 11 **NFL** 177 (1) [14 yrs]

BUDKA, FRANK Frank Charles, DB, 6´0˝/194 lbs; Notre Dame; 1964: Chi, rnd 4; B3/20/1942 Cleveland, OH **1964** LARm 14 (2)

BUDNESS, BILL William Walter, LB, 6´2˝/218 lbs; Boston University; 1964: Oak, rnd 4; B1/30/1943 Chicopee, MA **1964** Oak-A 9 (LLB) **1965** Oak-A 14 (mlb) **1966** Oak-A 14 (MLB) **1967**†Oak-A 13 **1968**†Oak-A 14 **1969**†Oak-A 14 **1970**†Oak 14 (5, mlb) **NFL** 92 (5) [7 yrs]

BUDREWICZ, TOM Thomas Paul, G, 6´2˝/245 lbs; Brown; 1960: NYT, rnd 2/Chi, rnd 12; B5/27/1938 Greenfield, MA **1961** NYT-A 2

BUEHLER, GEORGE George Siegrist, G, 6´2˝/260 lbs; Stanford; 1969: Oak, rnd 2; B8/10/1947 Whittier, CA **1969**†Oak-A 2 **1970**†Oak 14 **1971** Oak 14 (14, RG) **1972**†Oak 14 (14, RG) **1973**†Oak 14 (14, RG) **1974**†Oak 14 (14, RG) **1975**†Oak 14 (14, RG) **1976**†Oak 14 (RG) **1977**†Oak 14 (14, RG) **1978** Oak 1 **1978** Cle 11 (2) **1979** Cle 11 **NFL** 137 (86) [11 yrs]

BUENNING, DAN Dan, G, 6´4˝/320 lbs; Wisconsin; 2005: TB, rnd 4; B10/26/1981 Green Bay, WI **2005**†TB 16 (16, LG)

BUETOW, BART Barton Max, T, 6´5˝/250 lbs; Minnesota; 1972: Min, rnd 3; B10/28/1950 Minneapolis, MN **1973** NYG 7 **1976**†Min 2 **NFL** 9 [2 yrs]

BUFFALO, TED William Francis, T-E-G, 6´0˝/190 lbs; Haskell Indian; B11/5/1901, WI, D8/19/1969 Washburn, WI **1923** Oor 9 (6, LT), 6

BUFFINGTON, HARRY Harry Webster, G, 6´0˝/206 lbs; Oklahoma State; B8/27/1919 Pryor, OK, D11/19/2003 Lubbock, TX **1942** NYG 9 (8, RG) **1946** Bkn-A 12 (10, RG) **1947** Bkn-A 14 (14, RG) **1948** Bkn-A 10 (1) **AAFC** 36 (25) [3 yrs]

BUFFONE, DOUG Douglas John, LB, 6´3˝/230 lbs; Louisville; 1966: Chi, rnd 4/SD, rnd 8; B6/27/1944 Yatesboro, PA **[I]** **1966** ChiB 14 **1967** ChiB 14 (LLB) **1968** ChiB 14 (LLB) **1969** ChiB 14 (LLB) **1970** ChiB 14 (LLB) **1972** ChiB 14 (LLB) **1973** ChiB 14 (LLB) **1974** ChiB 14 (LLB) **1975** ChiB 14 (LLB) **1976** ChiB 2 **1977**†ChiB 13 (LLB) **1978** ChiB 15 (15, LLB)

YEAR	TEAM	G(GS, POS)	RUSH	YD	AVG(LG)	TD	REC	YD	AVG(LG)	TD	PASS	COMP	PCT	YD	AVG(LG)	TD	INT	SK	YD	QBR	KPR	OTD	PTS	TAY
1971	ChiB	14(LLB)	1	19	19.0(19)	0	—	—	—	—	—	—	—	—	—	—	—	—	—	—	i	—	0	36
1979	†ChiB	16	1	14	14.0(14)	0	1	22	22.0(22)	0	—	—	—	—	—	—	—	—	—	—	i	—	0	26
NFL	14	186(15)	2	33	16.5(19)	0	1	22	22.0(22)	0	—	—	—	—	—	—	—	—	—	—	i	1	6	135

BUFORD, MAURY Maury Anthony, P, 6´1˝/191 lbs; Texas Tech; 1982: SD, rnd 8; B2/18/1960 Mount Pleasant, TX **[P]**

YEAR	TEAM	G(GS, POS)	RUSH	YD	AVG(LG)	TD	REC	YD	AVG(LG)	TD	PASS	COMP	PCT	YD	AVG(LG)	TD	INT	SK	YD	QBR	KPR	OTD	PTS	TAY
1982	†SD	9(0)	—	—	—	—	—	—	—	—	—	—	—	—	—	—	—	—	—	—	P	—	0	0
1983	SD	16(0)	—	—	—	—	—	—	—	—	1	0	0.0	0	0.0	0	0	—	—	—	P	—	0	0
1984	SD	16(0)	—	—	—	—	—	—	—	—	—	—	—	—	—	—	—	—	—	—	P	—	0	0
1985	†ChiB	16(0)	—	—	—	—	—	—	—	—	1	1	100.0	5	5.0(5)	0	0	—	—	—	P	—	0	3
1986	†ChiB	16(0)	1	-13	-13.0(-13)	0	—	—	—	—	—	—	—	—	—	—	—	—	—	—	P	—	0	-13
1988	NYG	15(0)	—	—	—	—	—	—	—	—	—	—	—	—	—	—	—	—	—	—	P	—	0	0
1989	ChiB	16(0)	1	6	6.0(6)	0	—	—	—	—	—	—	—	—	—	—	—	—	—	—	P	—	0	6
1990	†ChiB	16(0)	1	-9	-9.0(-9)	0	—	—	—	—	—	—	—	—	—	—	—	—	—	—	P	—	0	-9
1991	†ChiB	16(0)	—	—	—	—	—	—	—	—	—	—	—	—	—	—	—	—	—	—	P	—	0	0
NFL	9	136(0)	3	-16	-5.3(6)	0	—	—	—	—	2	1	50.0	5	2.5(5)	0	0	—	—	—	P	—	0	-14

BUFORD, TONY Anthony D., LB, 6´2˝/222 lbs; Tulsa; B4/21/1964 St. Louis, MO **1987** SL 2 (1)

BUGENHAGEN, GARY Gary Alan, G-T, 6´2˝/240 lbs; Syracuse; 1967: Buf, rnd 4; B2/6/1945 Buffalo, NY **1967** Buf-A 14 **1970** Bos 10 (6, lg) **NFL** 24 (6) [2 yrs]

BUGGS, DANNY Daniel, WR, 6´2˝/188 lbs; West Virginia; 1975: NYG, rnd 3; B4/22/1953 Duluth, GA

YEAR	TEAM	G(GS, POS)	RUSH	YD	AVG(LG)	TD	REC	YD	AVG(LG)	TD	PASS	COMP	PCT	YD	AVG(LG)	TD	INT	SK	YD	QBR	KPR	OTD	PTS	TAY
1975	NYG	14	1	0	0.0(0)	0	—	—	—	—	—	—	—	—	—	—	—	—	—	—	kp	—	0	111
1976	NYG	5	—	—	—	—	—	—	—	—	—	—	—	—	—	—	—	—	—	—	—	—	—	—
1976	†Was	6	—	—	—	—	2	25	12.5(13)	0	—	—	—	—	—	—	—	—	—	—	—	—	0	13
1977	Was	14(7, wr)	—	—	—	—	26	341	13.1(45)	1	—	—	—	—	—	—	—	—	—	—	—	—	6	193
1978	Was	13(11, WR)	—	—	—	—	36	575	16.0(63)	2	—	—	—	—	—	—	—	—	—	—	—	—	12	298
1979	Was	16(16, WR)	—	—	—	—	46	631	13.7(45)	1	—	—	—	—	—	—	—	—	—	—	—	—	6	321
NFL	5	68(34)	1	0	0.0	0	110	1572	14.3(63)	4	—	—	—	—	—	—	—	—	—	—	kp	—	24	934

BUHLER, LARRY Lawrence Abraham, B, 6´2˝/210 lbs; Minnesota; 1939: GB, rnd 1; B5/28/1917 Mountain Lake, MN, D8/21/1990 Rochester, MN

YEAR	TEAM	G(GS, POS)	RUSH	YD	AVG(LG)	TD	REC	YD	AVG(LG)	TD	PASS	COMP	PCT	YD	AVG(LG)	TD	INT	SK	YD	QBR	KPR	OTD	PTS	TAY
1939	†GB✧	3(1)	5	3	0.6	0	—	—	—	—	—	—	—	—	—	—	—	—	—	—	—	—	0	3
1940	GB	7(2)	36	118	3.3	0	—	—	—	—	—	—	—	—	—	—	—	—	—	—	i	—	0	166
1941	†GB	11(7, BB)	—	—	—	—	—	—	—	—	—	—	—	—	—	—	—	—	—	—	k	—	0	-5
NFL	3	21(10)	41	121	3.0	0	—	—	—	—	—	—	—	—	—	—	—	—	—	—	ki	—	0	164

BUIE, DREW Leslie Drew, WR, 6´0˝/185 lbs; Catawba; 1969: Oak, rnd 9; B7/12/1947 Council, NC

YEAR	TEAM	G(GS, POS)	RUSH	YD	AVG(LG)	TD	REC	YD	AVG(LG)	TD	PASS	COMP	PCT	YD	AVG(LG)	TD	INT	SK	YD	QBR	KPR	OTD	PTS	TAY
1969	†Oak-A	14	—	—	—	—	1	37	37.0(37)	0	—	—	—	—	—	—	—	—	—	—	—	—	0	19
1970	†Oak	14	—	—	—	—	2	52	26.0(33)	0	—	—	—	—	—	—	—	—	—	—	—	—	0	26
1971	Oak	14(6, wr)	2	32	16.0(24)	0	5	133	26.6(63)	2	—	—	—	—	—	—	—	—	—	—	—	—	12	109
1972	Cin	4	—	—	—	—	1	5	5.0(5)	0	—	—	—	—	—	—	—	—	—	—	—	—	0	3
NFL	4	46(6)	2	32	16.0(24)	0	9	227	25.2(63)	2	—	—	—	—	—	—	—	—	—	—	—	—	12	156

BUIVID, RAY Raymond Vincent, B, 6´1˝/195 lbs; Marquette; 1937: ChiC, rnd 1; B8/15/1915 Sheboygan, WI, D7/5/1972 Cherry Hill, NJ

YEAR	TEAM	G(GS, POS)	RUSH	YD	AVG(LG)	TD	REC	YD	AVG(LG)	TD	PASS	COMP	PCT	YD	AVG(LG)	TD	INT	SK	YD	QBR	KPR	OTD	PTS	TAY
1937	†ChiB	6(0)	19	24	1.3	0	1	4	4.0(4)	1	35	17	48.6	205	5.9	6	2	—	—	—	—	—	6	84
1938	ChiB	11(6, qb)	32	65	2.0	0	1	8	8.0(8)	0	48	17	35.4	295	6.1	5	2	—	—	—	—	—	0	162
NFL	2	17(6)	51	89	1.7	0	2	12	6.0(8)	1	83	34	41.0	500	6.0	11	4	—	—	—	—	—	6	245

BUJNOCH, GLENN Glenn David, G, 6´5˝/260 lbs; Texas A&M; 1976: Cin, rnd 2; B12/20/1953 Houston, TX **1976** Cin 14 **1978** Cin 16 (16, LG) **1979** Cin 15 (15, LG) **1980** Cin 16 (16, LG) **1981** Cin 6 (5, lg) **1982**†Cin 9 (0) **1983** TB 6 (2) **1984** TB 8 (3)

YEAR	TEAM	G(GS, POS)	RUSH	YD	AVG(LG)	TD	REC	YD	AVG(LG)	TD	PASS	COMP	PCT	YD	AVG(LG)	TD	INT	SK	YD	QBR	KPR	OTD	PTS	TAY
1977	Cin	13(13, LG)	1	4	4.0(4)	1	—	—	—	—	—	—	—	—	—	—	—	—	—	—	—	—	6	14
NFL	9	103(70)	1	4	4.0(4)	1	—	—	—	—	—	—	—	—	—	—	—	—	—	—	—	—	6	14

BUKANT, JOE Joseph, B, 6´0˝/216 lbs; Washington-St. Louis; 1938: Phi, rnd 3; B10/31/1915 Divernon, IL

YEAR	TEAM	G(GS, POS)	RUSH	YD	AVG(LG)	TD	REC	YD	AVG(LG)	TD	PASS	COMP	PCT	YD	AVG(LG)	TD	INT	SK	YD	QBR	KPR	OTD	PTS	TAY
1938	Phi	11(1)	48	119	2.5	0	—	—	—	—	1	1	100.0	14	14.0(14)	0	0	—	—	—	—	—	0	126
1939	Phi	11(3)	59	136	2.3	3	—	—	—	—	1	0	0.0	0	0.0	0	0	—	—	—	P	—	18	166
1940	Phi	11(4, LH)	18	50	2.8	1	1	13	13.0(13)	0	—	—	—	—	—	—	—	—	—	—	Pi	—	6	72
1942	ChiC	10(3)	17	34	2.0(15)	0	—	—	—	—	15	4	26.7	56	3.7(20)	0	2	—	—	—	—	—	0	-18
1943	ChiC	8(7, tb)	42	87	2.1(10)	0	1	0	0.0(0)	0	40	14	35.0	109	2.7(15)	1	5	—	—	—	P	—	0	-54
NFL	5	51(18)	184	426	2.3(15)	4	2	13	6.5(13)	0	57	19	33.3	179	3.1(20)	1	7	—	—	—	Pi	—	24	292

BUKATY, FRED Frederick Francis, FB, 5´11˝/195 lbs; Kansas; B2/13/1936 Kansas City, KS

YEAR	TEAM	G(GS, POS)	RUSH	YD	AVG(LG)	TD	REC	YD	AVG(LG)	TD	PASS	COMP	PCT	YD	AVG(LG)	TD	INT	SK	YD	QBR	KPR	OTD	PTS	TAY
1961	Den-A	14(FB)	76	187	2.5(45)	5	14	94	6.7(13)	0	—	—	—	—	—	—	—	—	—	—	k	—	32	280

BUKICH, RUDY Rudolph Andrew, QB, 6´1˝/195 lbs; Iowa; USC; 1953: LA, rnd 2; B3/15/1932 St. Louis, MO

YEAR	TEAM	G (GS, POS)	RUSH	YD	AVG (LG)	TD	REC	YD	AVG (LG)	TD	PASS	COMP	PCT	YD	AVG (LG)	TD	INT	SK	YD	QBR	KPR	OTD	PTS	TAY
1953	LARm	8	14	28	2.0(17)	1	—	—	—	—	32	14	43.8	169	5.3(30)	0	3	—	—	—	—	—	6	3
1956	LARm	3	1	8	8.0(8)	0	—	—	—	—	23	10	43.5	130	5.7(34)	1	3	—	—	—	—	—	0	-42
1957	Was	7	8	-2	-0.3(16)	0	—	—	—	—	28	6	21.4	103	3.7(35)	0	3	—	—	—	—	—	0	-71
1958	Was	3	1	23	23.0(23)	0	—	—	—	—	22	8	36.4	166	7.5(37)	1	1	—	—	—	—	—	0	71
1958	ChiB	1	1	-7	-7.0(-7)	0	—	—	—	—	1	0	0.0	0	0.0	0	0	—	—	—	—	—	0	-7
1959	ChiB	5	1	0	0.0(0)	0	—	—	—	—	—	—	—	—	—	—	—	—	—	—	—	—	0	0
1960	Pit	12	3	-8	-2.7(0)	0	—	—	—	—	51	25	49.0	358	7.0(51)	2	3	—	—	—	—	—	0	61
1961	Pit	11(qb)	14	4	0.3(12)	2	—	—	—	—	156	89	57.1	1253	8.0(88)	11	16	—	—	—	—	—	12	66
1962	ChiB	5	—	—	—	—	—	—	—	—	13	3	23.1	79	6.1(65)	1	4	—	—	—	—	—	0	-116
1963	ChiB	6	7	1	0.1(2)	1	—	—	—	—	43	29	67.4	369	8.6(44)	3	2	—	—	—	—	—	6	131
1964	ChiB	9(qb)	12	28	2.3(12)	0	—	—	—	—	160	99	**61.9**	1099	6.9(63)	12	7	—	—	—	—	—	0	358
1965	ChiB☆	14(QB)	28	33	1.2(24)	3	—	—	—	—	312	176	56.4	2641	8.5(80)	20	9	25	214	93.7	—	—	18	1124
1966	ChiB	14(QB)	18	14	0.8(12)	2	—	—	—	—	309	147	47.6	1858	6.0(80)	10	21	26	211	49.3	—	—	12	173
1967	ChiB	3	4	-13	-3.3(2)	0	—	—	—	—	33	18	54.5	185	5.6(30)	0	2	5	42	—	—	—	0	-1
1968	ChiB	2	—	—	—	—	—	—	—	—	7	2	28.6	23	3.3(13)	0	0	3	21	—	—	—	0	12
NFL	14	103	112	109	1.0(24)	9	—	—	—	—	1190	626	52.6	8433	7.1(88)	61	74	59	488	66.6	—	—	54	1761

BUKSAR, GEORGE George Benjamin, LB-FB, 6´0˝/206 lbs; Purdue; San Francisco; 1949: LA, rnd 10; B8/12/1926 St. Joseph, MI **[K]**

YEAR	TEAM	G (GS, POS)	RUSH	YD	AVG (LG)	TD	REC	YD	AVG (LG)	TD	PASS	COMP	PCT	YD	AVG (LG)	TD	INT	SK	YD	QBR	KPR	OTD	PTS	TAY
1949	ChiH-A	6(0)	13	16	1.2	1	—	—	—	—	1	0	0.0	0	0.0	0	0	—	—	—	—	—	6	26
1950	Bal	9(2, LLB)	12	44	3.7(25)	0	2	2	1.0(2)	0	—	—	—	—	—	—	—	—	—	—	i	—	0	94
1951	Was	11(RLB)	—	—	—	—	—	—	—	—	—	—	—	—	—	—	—	—	—	—	kpi	—	0	6
1952	Was	10(RLB)	3	3	1.0(3)	0	2	3	1.5(3)	0	—	—	—	—	—	—	—	—	—	—	Kk	—	24	-13
NFL	3	30(2)	15	47	3.1(25)	0	4	5	1.3(3)	0	—	—	—	—	—	—	—	—	—	—	Kkpi	—	24	88

BULAICH, NORM Norman Batton, RB, 6´1˝/218 lbs; TCU; 1970: Bal, rnd 1; B12/25/1946 Galveston, TX

YEAR	TEAM	G (GS, POS)	RUSH	YD	AVG (LG)	TD	REC	YD	AVG (LG)	TD	PASS	COMP	PCT	YD	AVG (LG)	TD	INT	SK	YD	QBR	KPR	OTD	PTS	TAY
1970	†Bal	12(RB)	139	426	3.1(15)	3	11	123	11.2(20)	0	—	—	—	—	—	—	—	—	—	—	—	—	18	518
1971	Bal★	13(FB)	152	741	4.9(67)	8	25	229	9.2(30)	2	—	—	—	—	—	—	—	—	—	—	—	—	60	946
1972	Bal	6	27	109	4.0(18)	1	9	55	6.1(10)	0	—	—	—	—	—	—	—	—	—	—	k	—	6	194
1973	Phi	14(FB)	106	436	4.1(20)	1	42	403	9.6(80)	3	—	—	—	—	—	—	—	—	—	—	—	—	24	663
1974	Phi	11(8, FB)	50	152	3.0(13)	0	28	204	7.3(26)	0	—	—	—	—	—	—	—	—	—	—	—	—	0	254
1975	Mia	14	78	309	4.0(30)	5	32	276	8.6(59)	5	—	—	—	—	—	—	—	—	—	—	—	—	60	522
1976	Mia	11(6, fb)	122	540	4.4(35)	4	28	151	5.4(25)	0	—	—	—	—	—	—	—	—	—	—	—	—	24	656
1977	Mia	14(7, FB)	91	416	4.6(29)	4	25	180	7.2(14)	0	—	—	—	—	—	—	—	—	—	—	—	—	24	546
1978	†Mia	16(3)	40	196	4.9(63)	2	16	92	5.8(22)	0	—	—	—	—	—	—	—	—	—	—	—	—	12	262
1979	Mia	9	9	37	4.1(9)	2	8	53	6.6(13)	1	—	—	—	—	—	—	—	—	—	—	—	—	18	89
NFL	10	120(24)	814	3362	4.1(67)	30	224	1766	7.9(80)	11	—	—	—	—	—	—	—	—	—	—	k	—	246	4647

BULAND, WALT Walter, T-G, 6´1˝/213 lbs; none; B1892, MN, deceased **1920** RI 5 (3, RT) **1921** RI 6 (3, RT) **1924** GB 1 (1) **1924** RI 5 (4) **1926** Dul 2 (1) **NFL** 19 (12) [4 yrs]

BULGER, CHET Chester Noyes, T, 6´3˝/260 lbs; Auburn; B9/18/1917 Rumford, ME **[K]** **1942** ChiC 5 (5, RT) **1943** ChiC☆10 (10, RT) **1944** C-P 10 (7, RT) **1945** ChiC☆10 (7, RT) **1946** ChiC 6 (1) **1947**†ChiC 12 (10, LT) **1948**†ChiC☆12 (12, LT) **1949** ChiC 9 (0) **1950** Det 12 **NFL** 86 (52) [9 yrs]

BULGER, MARC Marc Robert, QB, 6´3˝/215 lbs; West Virginia; 2000: NO, rnd 6; B4/5/1977 Pittsburgh, PA

YEAR	TEAM	G (GS, POS)	RUSH	YD	AVG (LG)	TD	REC	YD	AVG (LG)	TD	PASS	COMP	PCT	YD	AVG (LG)	TD	INT	SK	YD	QBR	KPR	OTD	PTS	TAY
2002	SL	7(7, QB)	12	-13	-1.1(1)	1	1	3	3.0(3)	0	214	138	64.5	1826	**8.5(58)**	14	6	12	102	**101.5**	—	—	6	742
2003	†SL✧	15(15, QB)	29	75	2.6(28)	4	—	—	—	—	532	336	63.2	**3845**	7.2(48)	22	**22**	37	288	81.4	—	—	24	1268
2004	†SL	14(14, QB)	19	89	4.7(19)	3	—	—	—	—	485	321	66.2	3964	8.2(56)	21	14	41	302	93.7	—	—	18	1646
2005	SL	8(8, QB)	9	29	3.2(9)	0	1	1	1.0(1)	0	287	192	66.9	2297	**8.0(57)**	14	9	26	188	94.4	—	—	0	888
NFL	4	44(44)	69	180	2.6(28)	8	2	4	2.0(3)	0	1518	987	65.0	11932	7.9(58)	71	51	116	880	90.6	—	—	48	4543

BULL, RONNIE Ronald David, RB, 6´0˝/200 lbs; Baylor; 1962: Chi, rnd 1/DalT, rnd 1; B2/2/1940 Kingsville, TX

YEAR	TEAM	G (GS, POS)	RUSH	YD	AVG (LG)	TD	REC	YD	AVG (LG)	TD	PASS	COMP	PCT	YD	AVG (LG)	TD	INT	SK	YD	QBR	KPR	OTD	PTS	TAY
1962	ChiB	14(HB)	113	363	3.2(24)	1	31	331	10.7(52)	0	3	0	0.0	0	0.0	0	0	—	—	—	k	—	6	639
1963	†ChiB	13(hb)	117	404	3.5(18)	1	19	132	6.9(44)	2	3	0	0.0	0	0.0	0	0	—	—	—	k	—	18	490
1964	ChiB	13(FB)	86	320	3.7(50)	1	15	35	2.3(9)	0	3	1	33.3	13	4.3(13)	0	0	—	—	—	k	—	6	368
1965	ChiB	13(FB)	91	417	4.6(33)	3	16	186	11.6(41)	1	3	2	66.7	63	21.0(54)	0	0	—	—	—	—	—	24	577
1966	ChiB	14(FB)	100	318	3.2(13)	0	20	174	8.7(28)	0	1	1	100.0	21	21.0(21)	0	0	—	—	—	—	—	0	416
1967	ChiB	12	61	176	2.9(11)	0	18	250	13.9(63)	1	—	—	—	—	—	—	—	—	—	—	—	—	6	306
1968	ChiB	13(FB)	107	472	4.4(24)	3	17	145	8.5(24)	0	1	0	0.0	0	0.0	0	0	—	—	—	—	—	18	575
1969	ChiB	6(FB)	44	187	4.3(16)	0	14	91	6.5(17)	0	1	0	0.0	0	0.0	0	0	—	—	—	—	—	0	233
1970	ChiB	12(FB)	68	214	3.1(28)	0	13	60	4.6(17)	0	4	2	50.0	46	11.5(34)	1	1	—	—	—	—	—	0	232
1971	Phi	13(RB)	94	351	3.7(39)	0	9	75	8.3(15)	1	1	1	100.0	15	15.0(15)	0	0	—	—	—	—	—	6	401
NFL	10	123	881	3222	3.7(50)	9	172	1479	8.6(63)	5	20	7	35.0	158	7.9(54)	1	1	—	—	—	k	—	84	4235

BULL, SCOTT John Scott, QB, 6´5˝/211 lbs; Arkansas; 1976: SF, rnd 6; B6/8/1953 Camden, AR

YEAR	TEAM	G (GS, POS)	RUSH	YD	AVG (LG)	TD	REC	YD	AVG (LG)	TD	PASS	COMP	PCT	YD	AVG (LG)	TD	INT	SK	YD	QBR	KPR	OTD	PTS	TAY
1976	SF	14(2)	15	66	4.4(18)	2	—	—	—	—	48	21	43.8	252	5.3(30)	2	4	5	44	—	—	—	12	62
1977	SF	6	5	20	4.0(8)	0	—	—	—	—	24	7	29.2	89	3.7(26)	0	2	6	47	—	—	—	0	-16
1978	SF	16(5, qb)	29	100	3.4(15)	1	—	—	—	—	121	48	39.7	651	5.4(48)	1	11	22	160	—	—	—	6	1
NFL	3	36(7)	49	186	3.8(18)	3	—	—	—	—	193	76	39.4	992	5.1(48)	3	17	33	251	—	—	—	18	47

BULLARD, COURTLAND Courtland, LB, 6´3˝/240 lbs; Ohio State; 2002: SL, rnd 5; B9/2/1978 Miami, FL **2002** SL 11 (1) **2003** SL 9 (0) **NFL** 20 (1) [2 yrs]

BULLARD, KENDRICKE Kendricke Bernard, WR, 6´1˝/183 lbs; Arkansas State; B4/30/1972 San Diego, CA **1996**†Jax 12 (0)

BULLARD, LOUIS Louis Eugene, T, 6´6˝/265 lbs; Jackson State; 1978: Sea, rnd 5; B5/6/1956 Hernando, MS **1978** Sea 16 **1979** Sea 3 (2) **1980** Sea 16 (13, LT) **NFL** 35 (15) [3 yrs]

BULLMAN, GALE Delmar Gale, E, 6´0˝/182 lbs; West Virginia Wesleyan; B8/18/1901 Lesterville, WV, D6/24/1977 Rolla, MO **1925** Col 3 (3)

BULLOCKS, AMOS Amos Lee, HB, 6´1˝/202 lbs; Southern Illinois; 1962: Dal, rnd 20/Buf, rnd 10; B2/7/1939 Chicago, IL

YEAR	TEAM	G (GS, POS)	RUSH	YD	AVG (LG)	TD	REC	YD	AVG (LG)	TD	PASS	COMP	PCT	YD	AVG (LG)	TD	INT	SK	YD	QBR	KPR	OTD	PTS	TAY
1962	Dal	11	33	196	5.9(73)	2	3	46	15.3(22)	1	—	—	—	—	—	—	—	—	—	—	k	—	18	299
1963	Dal	14(3)	96	341	3.6(17)	2	7	70	10.0(22)	0	—	—	—	—	—	—	—	—	—	—	k	—	12	564
1964	Dal	1	—	—	—	—	—	—	—	—	—	—	—	—	—	—	—	—	—	—	k	—	0	4
1966	Pit	8	29	83	2.9(13)	1	5	64	12.8(18)	1	1	0	0.0	0	0.0	0	0	—	—	—	—	—	12	130
NFL	4	34(3)	158	620	3.9(73)	5	15	180	12.0(22)	2	1	0	0.0	0	0.0	0	0	—	—	—	k	—	42	997

BULLOCKS, JOSH Joshua, DB, 6´0˝/207 lbs; Nebraska; 2005: NO, rnd 2; B2/28/1983 Chattanooga, TN **2005** NO 16 (13, FS)

BULLOUGH, CHUCK Charles George, LB, 6´1˝/238 lbs; Michigan State; 1992: Phi, rnd 8; B3/3/1969 Lansing, MI **1993** Mia 3 (0) **1994** Mia 1 (1) **NFL** 4 (1) [2 yrs]

BULLOUGH, HANK Henry Charles, G-LB, 6´0˝/230 lbs; Michigan State; 1955: GB, rnd 5; B1/24/1934 Scranton, PA **[C]** **1955** GB 12 **1958** GB 8 **NFL** 20 [2 yrs]

BULLUCK, BRIAN Brian Jay, LB, 6´3˝/236 lbs; North Carolina State; B10/29/1965 Roanoke Rapids, NC **1987** Ind 2 (1)

BULLUCK, KEITH Keith J., LB, 6´3˝/235 lbs; Syracuse; 2000: Ten, rnd 1; B4/4/1977 Suffern, NY **2000**†Ten 16 (1) **2001** Ten 15 (3) **2002**†Ten☆16 (16, RLB) **2003**†Ten★16 (16, RLB) **2004** Ten 16 (16, RLB) **2005** Ten 16 (16, RLB) **NFL** 95 (68) [6 yrs]

BULMAN, TIM Tim, DT, 6´3˝/294 lbs; Boston College; B10/31/1982 Milton, MA **2005** Arz 8 (1)

BULTMAN, ART Arthur Frank, C-LB-T, 6´2˝/201 lbs; Indiana; Marquette; B9/16/1907 Green Bay, WI, D2/1967 **1931** Bkn 12 (9, C) **1932** GB 13 (6, c) **1933** GB 13 (9, C) **1934** GB 11 (4) **NFL** 49 (28) [4 yrs]

BUMGARDNER, MAX Max Andrew, DE, 6´2˝/190 lbs; Texas; 1948: ChiB, rnd 1/1947: SF-A, rnd 20; B5/13/1923 Wichita Falls, TX, D4/12/2005 Greenville, TX **1948** Det 11 (2)

BUMGARDNER, REX Rex Keith, HB-DB, 5´11˝/193 lbs; West Virginia; B9/6/1923 Clarksburg, WV, D6/1/1998 Clarksburg, WV

YEAR	TEAM	G (GS, POS)	RUSH	YD	AVG (LG)	TD	REC	YD	AVG (LG)	TD	PASS	COMP	PCT	YD	AVG (LG)	TD	INT	SK	YD	QBR	KPR	OTD	PTS	TAY
1948	†Buf-A	13(3)	14	82	5.9	0	1	63	63.0(63)	0	—	—	—	—	—	—	—	—	—	—	kpi	2	12	393
1949	†Buf-A	10(8, RH)	101	391	3.9	1	7	168	24.0	4	—	—	—	—	—	—	—	—	—	—	kp	—	30	548
AAFC	2	23(11)	115	473	4.1	1	8	231	28.9(63)	4	—	—	—	—	—	—	—	—	—	—	kpi	2	42	941

YEAR	TEAM	G(GS, POS)	RUSH	YD	AVG(LG)	TD	REC	YD	AVG(LG)	TD	PASS	COMP	PCT	YD	AVG(LG)	TD	INT	SK	YD	QBR	KPR	OTD	PTS	TAY
1950	†Cle	10(LH)	67	231	3.4(26)	2	9	112	12.4(25)	1	—	—	—	—	—	—	—	—	—	—	—	—	18	312
1951	†Cle	10(lh)	45	126	2.8(20)	1	5	61	12.2(19)	1	—	—	—	—	—	—	—	—	—	—	k	—	12	202
1952	†Cle	11(lh)	9	38	4.2(24)	0	—	—	—	—	—	—	—	—	—	—	—	—	—	—	kpi	—	0	79
NFL	3	31	121	395	3.3(26)	3	14	173	12.4(63)	2	—	—	—	—	—	—	—	—	—	—	kpi	—	30	593

BUNCH, DEREK   Derek Carl, LB, 6´3˝/215 lbs; Michigan State; B10/28/1961 Fort Sill, OK   **1987** Was 3 (0)

BUNCH, JARROD   Jarrod Glenn, FB, 6´2˝/250 lbs; Michigan; 1991: NYG, rnd 1; B8/9/1968 Ashtabula, OH

1991	NYG	16(1)	1	0	0.0(0)	0	2	8	4.0(6)	0	—	—	—	—	—	—	—	—	—	—	—	—	0	4
1992	NYG	16(13, FB)	104	501	4.8(37)	3	11	50	4.5(13)	1	—	—	—	—	—	—	—	—	—	—	k	—	24	558
1993	†NYG	13(8, FB)	33	128	3.9(13)	2	13	98	7.5(15)	1	—	—	—	—	—	—	—	—	—	—	—	—	18	202
1994	LARd	3(0)	—	—	—	—	—	—	—	—	—	—	—	—	—	—	—	—	—	—	—	—	—	—
NFL	4	48(22)	138	629	4.6(37)	5	26	156	6.0(15)	5	—	—	—	—	—	—	—	—	—	—	k	—	42	764

BUNCOM, FRANK   Frank James, LB, 6´2˝/235 lbs; USC; 1962: SD, rnd 6; B11/2/1939 Shreveport, LA, D9/14/1969 Cincinnati, OH   **1962** SD-A 14   **1963** SD-A 14   **1964**†SD-A★14 (14, MLB)   **1965**†SD-A★14 (14, RLB)   **1966** SD-A☆14 (14, RLB)   **1967** SD-A★14 (RLB)   **1968** Cin-A☆12 (RLB)   **NFL** 96 (42) [7 yrs]

BUNDRA, MIKE   Michael P., DT, 6´3˝/255 lbs; USC; 1962: Det, rnd 6; B6/24/1939 Coplay, PA   **1962** Det 12   **1963** Det 14   **1964** Min 4   **1964** Cle 9   **1965** NYG 9 (RDT)   **NFL** 48 [4 yrs]

BUNDREN, JIM   Jim G., G, 6´3˝/303 lbs; Clemson; B10/6/1974 Wilmington, DE   **1999** Cle 16 (1)   **2000** Cle 11 (9, LG)   **NFL** 27 (10) [2 yrs]

BUNGARDA, KEN   Kestutis John, T, 6´6˝/270 lbs; Missouri; 1979: Cin, rnd 11; B1/25/1957 Hartford, CT   **1980** SF 15 (0)

BUNTING, JOHN   John Stephen, LB, 6´1˝/220 lbs; North Carolina; 1972: Phi, rnd 10; B7/15/1950 Portland, ME   **1972** Phi 14 (3)   **1973** Phi 7 (7, rlb)   **1974** Phi 14 (12, RLB)   **1975** Phi 14 (14, RLB)   **1976** Phi 14 (14, RLB)   **1977** Phi 14 (14, LLB)   **1978** Phi 6 (6, lolb)   **1979**†Phi 15 (15, LLB)   **1980**†Phi 16 (16, LOLB)   **1981**†Phi 9 (8, LOLB)   **1982** Phi 9 (9, LOLB)   **NFL** 132 (118) [11 yrs]

BUNYAN, JOHN   John J., G-C, 5´10˝/215 lbs; NYU; B1906   **1929** SI 5 (5, rg)   **1930** SI 11 (9, RG)   **1932** SI 6 (6, LG)   **1932** Bkn 1 (0)   **NFL** 23 (20) [3 yrs]

BUNZ, DAN   Daniel, LB, 6´4˝/226 lbs; California-Riverside; Long Beach State; 1978: SF, rnd 1; B10/7/1955 Roseville, CA   **1978** SF 16 (16, MLB)   **1979** SF 14 (12, MLB)   **1980** SF 16 (9, MLB/lilb)   **1981**†SF 14 (8, LILB)   **1982** SF 1 (1)   **1983**†SF 9 (0)   **1984**†SF 16 (16, LOLB)   **1985** Det 2 (0)   **NFL** 88 (62) [8 yrs]

BUONICONTI, NICK   Nicholas Anthony, LB, 5´11˝/220 lbs; Notre Dame; 1962: Bos, rnd 13; B12/15/1940 Springfield, MA; HOF 2001 [I]   **1962** Bos-A☆14 (MLB)   **1963**†Bos-A★14 (MLB)   **1964** Bos-A★14 (MLB)   **1965** Bos-A★14 (MLB)   **1966** Bos-A★14 (MLB)   **1967** Bos-A 13 (MLB)   **1968** Bos-A☆8 (8, MLB)   **1969** Mia-A 13 (13, MLB)   **1970**†Mia-A 14 (14, MLB)   **1971** Mia 14 (14, MLB)   **1972**†Mia★14 (14, MLB)   **1973**†Mia 13 (13, MLB)   **1974**†Mia 13 (13, MLB)   **1976** Mia 11   **NFL** 183 (89) [14 yrs]

BURBAGE, CORNELL   Cornell Rodney, WR, 5´10˝/186 lbs; Kentucky; B2/22/1965 Lexington, KY

1987	Dal	3(2)	—	—	—	—	7	168	24.0(77)	2	—	—	—	—	—	—	—	—	—	—	p	—	12	98
1988	Dal	10(0)	—	—	—	—	2	50	25.0(41)	0	—	—	—	—	—	—	—	—	—	—	k	—	0	173
1989	Dal	10(1)	—	—	—	—	17	134	7.9(15)	0	—	—	—	—	—	—	—	—	—	—	kp	—	0	67
NFL	3	23(3)	—	—	—	—	26	352	13.5(77)	2	—	—	—	—	—	—	—	—	—	—	kp	—	12	338

BURCH, JERRY   Gerald Thomas, WR-P, 6´1˝/195 lbs; Georgia Tech; 1961: Oak, rnd 13/Min, rnd 6; B12/13/1939

| 1961 | Oak-A | 14 | — | — | — | — | 18 | 235 | 13.1(54) | 1 | — | — | — | — | — | — | — | — | — | — | P | — | 6 | 123 |

BURCHFIELD, DON   Donald Lee, TE, 6´3˝/233 lbs; Ball State; 1971: NO, rnd 13; B3/17/1949 Indianapolis, IN

| 1971 | NO | 14 | — | — | — | — | 3 | 36 | 12.0(16) | 0 | — | — | — | — | — | — | — | — | — | — | k | — | 0 | 8 |

BURDICK, LLOYD   Lloyd Sumner, T, 6´4˝/248 lbs; Illinois; B8/8/1908 Assumption, IL, D8/9/1945 Michigan, ND   **1931** ChiB 9 (7, RT)   **1932** ChiB 13 (12, RT)   **1933** Cin 10 (9, RT)   **NFL** 32 (28) [3 yrs]

BURFORD, CHRIS   Christopher William, SE-WR, 6´3˝/220 lbs; Stanford; 1960: DalT, rnd 1/Cle, rnd 9; B1/31/1938 Oakland, CA

1960	DalT-A	14(SE)	—	—	—	—	46	789	17.2(57)	5	—	—	—	—	—	—	—	—	—	—	—	—	30	420
1961	DalT-A✧	14(SE)	1	-13	-13.0(-13)	0	51	850	16.7(54)	5	—	—	—	—	—	—	—	—	—	—	—	—	30	437
1962	DalT-A☆	11(SE)	1	13	13.0(13)	0	45	645	14.3(49)	12	—	—	—	—	—	—	—	—	—	—	—	—	72	396
1963	KC-A	14(SE)	1	10	10.0(10)	0	68	824	12.1(69)	9	—	—	—	—	—	—	—	—	—	—	—	—	56	467
1964	KC-A	12(SE)	—	—	—	—	51	675	13.2(55)	7	—	—	—	—	—	—	—	—	—	—	—	—	42	373
1965	KC-A	11(SE)	—	—	—	—	47	575	12.2(57)	6	—	—	—	—	—	—	—	—	—	—	—	—	36	318
1966	†KC-A	14(SE)	—	—	—	—	58	758	13.1(38)	8	—	—	—	—	—	—	—	—	—	—	—	—	48	419
1967	KC-A	13(SE)	—	—	—	—	25	389	15.6(55)	3	—	—	—	—	—	—	—	—	—	—	—	—	18	210
NFL	8	103	3	10	3.3(13)	0	391	5505	14.1(69)	55	—	—	—	—	—	—	—	—	—	—	—	—	332	3038

BURGEIS, GLEN   Murl Glenn, T, 6´1˝/218 lbs; Tulsa; 1945: ChiB, rnd 7; B10/7/1921 Ballard, TX, D6/1/1998 Flint, TX   **1945** ChiB 3 (1)

BURGER, TODD   Todd Richard, G, 6´3˝/303 lbs; Penn State; B3/20/1970 Clark, NJ   **1994**†ChiB 4 (0)   **1995** ChiB 16 (1)   **1996** ChiB 11 (8, RG)   **1997** ChiB 15 (15, RG)   **1998**†NYJ 16 (16, LG)   **NFL** 62 (40) [5 yrs]

BURGESS, CHARLIE   Charles, LB, 6´0˝/230 lbs; Carson-Newman; B12/29/1962   **1987** NYG 2 (0)

BURGESS, DERRICK   Derrick Lee, DE-LB, 6´2˝/266 lbs; Mississippi; 2001: Phi, rnd 3; B8/12/1978 Lake City, SC   **2001**†Phi 16 (4)   **2002** Phi 1 (0)   **2004**†Phi 12 (11, RDE)   **2005** Oak★16 (12, RDE)   **NFL** 45 (27) [4 yrs]

BURGESS, FERNANZA   Fernanza, WR, 6´1˝/210 lbs; Morris Brown; B3/6/1960 Miami, FL   **1984** Mia 3 (0)   **1984** NYJ 11 (0)   **NFL** 14 (0) [1 yr]

BURGESS, JAMES   James Paul, LB, 6´0˝/230 lbs; Miami (FL); B3/31/1974 Miami, FL   **1997** SD 15 (4)   **1998** SD 16 (0)   **NFL** 31 (4) [2 yrs]

BURGESS, MARVELL   Marvell, DB, 6´3˝/195 lbs; Henderson State; B10/7/1965 Miami, FL   **1987** Mia 1 (0)

BURGESS, RONNIE   Ronald K., DB, 5´11˝/174 lbs; Wake Forest; 1985: GB, rnd 10; B3/7/1963 Sumter, SC   **1985** GB 7 (0)

BURGIN, AL   Albert E., G, 6´0˝/200 lbs; none; B4/13/1894 Toledo, OH, D7/28/1978 San Francisco, CA   **1922** Tol 1 (1)

BURGMEIER, TED   Ted Joseph, DB, 5´10˝/185 lbs; Notre Dame; 1978: Mia, rnd 5; B11/8/1955 Dubuque, IA   **1978** KC 8 (2)

BURGNER, EARL   Earl William, BB-WB, 5´6˝/165 lbs; Wittenberg; B5/19/1900 Akron, OH, D1/11/1970 Dayton, OH   **1923** Day 2 (1)

BURK, ADRIAN   Adrian Matthew, QB, 6´2˝/190 lbs; Baylor; 1950: Bal, rnd 1; B12/14/1927 Mexia, TX, D7/28/2003 Houston, TX **[P]**

1950	Bal	12(3, qb)	11	19	1.7(10)	1	—	—	—	—	119	43	36.1	798	6.7(69)	6	12	—	—	37.4	P	—	6	-22
1951	Phi	12(QB)	28	12	0.4(11)	1	—	—	—	—	218	92	42.2	1329	6.1(53)	14	**23**	—	—	44.5	P	—	6	-164
1952	Phi	12(qb)	7	28	4.0(12)	0	—	—	—	—	82	37	45.1	561	6.8(84)	4	5	—	—	—	P	—	0	129
1953	Phi	10(qb)	8	54	6.8(32)	3	—	—	—	—	119	56	47.1	788	6.6(61)	4	9	—	—	48.6	P	—	18	138
1954	Phi✧	12(QB)	15	18	1.2(15)	0	—	—	—	—	231	123	53.2	1740	7.5(84)	**23**	17	—	—	**80.4**	P	—	0	323
1955	Phi✧	12(QB)	36	132	3.7(30)	2	—	—	—	—	228	110	48.2	1359	6.0(57)	9	17	—	—	49.2	P	—	12	197
1956	Phi	12	17	61	3.6(11)	0	—	—	—	—	82	39	47.6	426	5.2(40)	1	6	—	—	—	P	—	0	39
NFL	7	82(3)	122	324	2.7(32)	7	—	—	—	—	1079	500	46.3	7001	6.5(84)	61	89	—	—	52.2	P	—	42	640

BURK, SCOTT   Marshall Scott, DB, 6´2˝/193 lbs; Oklahoma State; 1979: Cin, rnd 9; B8/2/1956 Houston, TX   **1979** Cin 16

BURKE, ANTHONY   Anthony Howard, DT, 6´3˝/262 lbs; Minnesota; B9/2/1964 Kankakee, IL   **1987** SL 1 (0)

BURKE, CHICK   Charles Francis, WB, 5´9˝/166 lbs; Dartmouth; B9/30/1901 Natick, MA, D5/20/1973 Keene, NH   **1925** Pro 5 (2)

BURKE, DON   Donald, LB-G, 6´0˝/235 lbs; USC; 1950: SF, rnd 12; B2/7/1926 Chico, CA   **1950** SF 6   **1951** SF 9   **1952** SF 12 (RLB)   **1953** SF 10   **1954** SF 2   **NFL** 39 [5 yrs]

BURKE, JOE   Joseph Richard, RB, 6´0˝/200 lbs; Rutgers; B2/9/1961 Albany, NY   **1987** NYJ 2 (0)

BURKE, JOHN   John Richard, TE-WR, 6´3˝/248 lbs; Virginia Tech; 1994: NE, rnd 4; B9/7/1971 Elizabeth, NJ

1994	†NE	16(6, wr)	—	—	—	—	9	86	9.6(17)	0	—	—	—	—	—	—	—	—	—	—	k	—	0	9
1995	NE	16(4)	—	—	—	—	15	136	9.1(21)	0	—	—	—	—	—	—	—	—	—	—	k	—	0	60
1996	†NE	11(2)	—	—	—	—	1	19	19.0(19)	0	—	—	—	—	—	—	—	—	—	—	k	—	0	10
1997	NYJ	7(1)	—	—	—	—	—	—	—	—	—	—	—	—	—	—	—	—	—	—	—	—	—	—
1998	SD	10(6, te)	—	—	—	—	3	32	10.7(17)	0	—	—	—	—	—	—	—	—	—	—	k	—	0	6
NFL	5	60(19)	—	—	—	—	28	273	9.8(21)	0	—	—	—	—	—	—	—	—	—	—	k	—	0	85

YEAR	TEAM	G (GS, POS)	RUSH	YD	AVG (LG)	TD	REC	YD	AVG (LG)	TD	PASS	COMP	PCT	YD	AVG (LG)	TD	INT	SK	YD	QBR	KPR	OTD	PTS	TAY

BURKE, MARK Mark, DB, 6´1˝/175 lbs; West Virginia; B6/10/1954 Marietta, OH **1976** Phi 1

BURKE, MIKE Michael Dennis, P, 5´10˝/188 lbs; Oregon State; Miami (FL); B7/28/1950 Sacramento, CA **[K]**

YEAR	TEAM	G	REC	YD	AVG	PASS	PCT	AVG	KPR	PTS	TAY
1974	†LARm	8	1	0	0.0	0	0.0	0 0	KP	1	0

BURKE, RANDY Randall William, WR, 6´2˝/190 lbs; Kentucky; 1977: Bal, rnd 1; B5/26/1955 Miami, FL

YEAR	TEAM	G (GS)	REC	YD	AVG (LG)	TD	KPR	PTS	TAY
1978	Bal	15	—	—	—	—	kp	2	-18
1979	Bal	16 (2)	6	151	25.2 (59)	0		0	76
1980	Bal	10 (0)	14	185	13.2 (19)	3		18	108
1981	Bal	16 (1)	10	153	15.3 (24)	0	kp	0	77
NFL	4	57 (3)	30	489	16.3 (59)	3	kp	20	242

BURKE, TOM Thomas, DE, 6´3˝/275 lbs; Wisconsin; 1999: Arz, rnd 3; B10/12/1976 Poplar, WI **1999** Arz 16 (3) **2000** Arz 2 (0) **2001** Arz 12 (9, RDE) **2002** Arz 6 (0) **NFL** 36 (12) [4 yrs]

BURKE, VERN Vernon Eugene, SE-TE, 6´4˝/215 lbs; Oregon State; 1963: SF, rnd 5/Oak, rnd 15; B4/30/1941 San Luis Obispo, CA

YEAR	TEAM	G	REC	YD	AVG (LG)	TD	PTS	TAY
1965	SF	3	2	38	19.0 (27)	1	6	24
1966	Atl	14 (SE)	28	348	12.4 (45)	1	6	179
1967	NO	7	8	84	10.5 (21)	0	0	42
NFL	3	24	38	470	12.4 (45)	2	12	245

BURKETT, CHRIS Chris, WR, 6´4˝/205 lbs; Jackson State; 1985: Buf, rnd 2; B8/21/1962 Laurel, MS

YEAR	TEAM	G (GS, POS)	RUSH	YD	AVG (LG)	TD	REC	YD	AVG (LG)	TD	OTD	PTS	TAY
1985	Buf	16 (1)	—	—	—		21	371	17.7 (38)	0		0	186
1986	Buf	14 (10, WR)	—	—	—		34	778	**22.9 (84)**	4		24	409
1987	Buf☆	12 (12, WR)	—	—	—		56	765	13.7 (47)	4		24	403
1988	†Buf	11 (8, wr)	—	—	—		23	354	15.4 (34)	1		6	182
1989	Buf	2 (2)	—	—	—		3	20	6.7 (9)	0		0	10
1989	NYJ	13 (3)	1	-4	-4.0 (-4)	0	21	278	13.2 (50)	1		6	140
1990	NYJ	16 (4)	—	—	—		14	204	14.6 (46)	0		0	102
1991	†NYJ	15 (1)	1	-2	-2.0 (-2)	0	23	327	14.2 (50)	4	1	30	182
1992	NYJ	16 (5, wr)	—	—	—		57	724	12.7 (37)	1		6	367
1993	NYJ	16 (16, WR)	—	—	—		40	531	13.3 (77)	4		24	286
NFL	9	131 (62)	2	-6	-3.0 (-2)	0	292	4352	14.9 (84)	19	1	120	2265

BURKETT, JACKIE Walter Jackson, LB-C, 6´4˝/230 lbs; Auburn; 1959: Bal, rnd 1/1960: NYT, rnd 1; B12/16/1936 Thorsby, AL **1961** Bal 14 (LLB) **1962** Bal 14 (9, MLB) **1963** Bal 14 (LLB) **1964**†Bal 12 (1) **1965** Bal 11 **1966** Bal 14 (llb) **1967** NO 14 (RLB) **1968** Dal 3 **1969**†Dal 11 **1970** NO 14 (RLB) **NFL** 121 (10) [10 yrs]

BURKETT, JEFF Jefferson Davis, E-DB, 6´1˝/190 lbs; LSU; B7/15/1921 Hattiesburg, MS, D10/24/1947 Bryce Canyon, UT

YEAR	TEAM	G (GS)	RUSH	YD	AVG (LG)	TD	REC	YD	AVG (LG)	TD	KPR	PTS	TAY
1947	ChiC	3 (0)	1	11	11.0 (11)	0	2	44	22.0 (21)	1	Pi	6	58

BURKS, DIALLEO Diaello, WR, 6´2˝/181 lbs; Eastern Kentucky; B7/7/1974 La Grange, GA **2000** Car 1 (0)

BURKS, JOE Joseph, C, 5´10˝/171 lbs; Washington State; B7/8/1899, D11/1969 Chicago, IL **1926** Mil 9 (8, C)

BURKS, RANDY Randall James, WR, 5´11˝/170 lbs; Southeastern Oklahoma State; Oklahoma State; 1976: SL, rnd 8; B8/22/1953 Idabel, OK

YEAR	TEAM	G	REC	YD	AVG (LG)	TD	PTS	TAY
1976	ChiB	1	1	55	55.0 (55)	1	6	33

BURKS, RAYMOND Raymond Charles, LB, 6´3˝/217 lbs; UCLA; 1977: KC, rnd 12; B3/9/1955 Gardena, CA

YEAR	TEAM	G	REC	YD	AVG (LG)	TD	KPR	PTS	TAY
1977	KC	13	1	51	51.0 (51)	0	k	0	51

BURKS, SHAWN Shawn Spencer, LB, 6´1˝/230 lbs; LSU; B2/10/1963 Baton Rouge, LA **1986**†Was 15 (0)

BURKS, STEVE Steven Bruce, WR, 6´5˝/211 lbs; Arkansas State; 1975: NE, rnd 4; B8/6/1953 Little Rock, AR

YEAR	TEAM	G (GS)	RUSH	YD	AVG (LG)	TD	REC	YD	AVG (LG)	TD	KPR	PTS	TAY
1975	NE	13	—	—	—		6	158	26.3 (76)	0	k	0	84
1976	†NE	8 (1)	1	2	2.0 (2)	0	2	27	13.5 (17)	0		0	16
1977	NE	13	—	—	—		5	79	15.8 (22)	0		0	40
NFL	3	34 (1)	1	2	2.0 (2)	0	13	264	20.3 (76)	0	k	0	139

BURL, ALEX Alexander, HB, 5´10˝/185 lbs; Colorado State; 1954: ChiC, rnd 30; B8/8/1931 Warren, AR

YEAR	TEAM	G	RUSH	YD	AVG (LG)	TD	REC	YD	AVG (LG)	TD	KPR	PTS	TAY
1956	ChiC	8	1	2	2.0 (2)	0	2	24	12.0 (19)	1	k	0	33

BURLESON, JOHN John Charles, T-G, 6´2˝/237 lbs; SMU; B8/21/1909 Albany, TX, D10/6/1983 Abilene, TX **1933** Por 1 (0) **1933** Pit 3 (0) **1933** Cin 2 (0) **NFL** 6 (0) [1 yr]

BURLESON, NATE Nate, WR, 6´0˝/192 lbs; Nevada-Reno; 2003: Min, rnd 3; B8/19/1981 Seattle, WA

YEAR	TEAM	G (GS, POS)	RUSH	YD	AVG (LG)	TD	REC	YD	AVG (LG)	TD	KPR	OTD	PTS	TAY
2003	Min	16 (9, WR)	—	—	—		29	455	15.7 (52)		p		12	233
2004	†Min	16 (15, WR)	6	49	8.2 (11)	0	68	1006	14.8 (68)	9	kp	1	62	717
2005	Min	12 (9, WR)	2	-6	-3.0 (-2)	0	30	328	10.9 (20)	1	p		6	159
NFL	3	44 (33)	8	43	5.4 (11)		127	1789	14.1 (68)	12	kp	1	80	1109

BURLEY, GARY Gary Steven, DE-DT, 6´3˝/272 lbs; Pittsburgh; 1975: Cin, rnd 3; B12/8/1952 Urbancrest, OH **1976** Cin 14 (LDE) **1977** Cin 14 (LDE) **1978** Cin 16 (LDE) **1979** Cin 16 (LDE) **1980** Cin 11 (0) **1981**†Cin 16 (3) **1982** Cin 4 (0) **1983** Cin 14 (0) **1984** Atl 12 (8, LDT) **NFL** 117 (11) [9 yrs]

BURMAN, GEORGE George Robert, C-G-T, 6´3˝/255 lbs; Northwestern; 1964: Chi, rnd 15; B12/1/1942 Chicago, IL **1964** ChiB 14 (5, c) **1967**†LARm 14 **1968** LARm 1 **1969**†LARm 14 **1970** LARm 14 **1971**†Was 14 **1972**†Was 14 **NFL** 85 (5) [7 yrs]

BURMEISTER, DANNY Daniel Joseph, DB, 6´2˝/201 lbs; North Carolina; B9/13/1963 **1987** Was 3 (0)

BURMEISTER, FORREST Forrest Barth, G-T, 6´4˝/215 lbs; Purdue; B8/18/1913 Davenport, IA, D12/5/1997 **1937** Cle 11 (8, LG) **1938** Cle 1 (0) **NFL** 12 (8) [2 yrs]

BURNELL, MAX Herman Joseph, B, 5´11˝/180 lbs; Notre Dame; B5/7/1915 Escambia, MI, D10/20/2004 Rockwall, TX **1944** ChiB 2 (0)

BURNETT, BOBBY Robert Clell, RB, 6´3˝/210 lbs; Arkansas; 1966: Buf, rnd 4/Chi, rnd 10; B1/4/1943 Clinton, AR

YEAR	TEAM	G (GS, POS)	RUSH	YD	AVG (LG)	TD	REC	YD	AVG (LG)	TD	PTS	TAY
1966	†Buf-A★	14 (HB)	187	766	4.1 (32)	4	34	419	12.3 (48)	4	48	1036
1967	Buf-A	8	45	96	2.1 (18)	0	11	114	10.4 (38)	0	0	153
1969	Den-A	3	5	9	1.8 (5)	0	—	—	—		0	9
NFL	3	25	237	871	3.7 (32)	4	45	533	11.8 (48)	4	48	1198

BURNETT, CHESTER Chester Dean, LB, 5´10˝/230 lbs; Arizona; 1998: Min, rnd 7; B4/15/1975 Denver, CO **1998** Was 5 (0) **2000** Cle 7 (0) **NFL** 12 (0) [2 yrs]

BURNETT, DALE Dale, B, 6´1˝/187 lbs; Emporia State; B1/23/1909 Larned, KS, D4/17/1997 Emporia, KS **[K]**

YEAR	TEAM	G (GS, POS)	RUSH	YD	AVG (LG)	TD	REC	YD	AVG (LG)	TD	PASS	COMP	PCT	YD	AVG (LG)	TD	INT	KPR	OTD	PTS	TAY
1930	NYG	14 (8, fb)	—	—	—		—	—	—											—	—
1931	NYG	14 (8, wb)	—	—	—		—	—	—											—	—
1932	NYG	12 (8, WB)	28	75	2.7	0	11	125	11.4	1										6	143
1933	NYG	14 (12, WB)	17	34	2.0	0	12	212	17.7	3	1	0	0.0	0			0		1	24	165
1934	†NYG	10 (9, WB)	4	6	1.5	0	10	166	16.6	2										12	99
1935	NYG	8 (7, WB)	6	32	5.3	0	12	209	17.4	4									2	36	157
1936	NYG	12 (10, WB)	10	0	0.0	0	16	246	15.4	3										18	138
1937	NYG	9 (2)	7	4	0.6	0	10	121	12.1	1										6	70
1938	†NYG◇	11 (0)	6	13	2.2	0	13	145	11.2	1										6	91
1939	†NYG	11 (0)	1	3	3.0 (3)	0	8	86	10.8	0										0	46
NFL	10	115 (64)	79	167	2.1 (3)	5	92	1310	14.2	19	1	0	0.0	0				K	3	166	977

BURNETT, KEVIN Kevin Bradley, LB, 6´3˝/237 lbs; Tennessee; 2005: Dal, rnd 2; B12/24/1982 Englewood, CA **2005** Dal 13 (0)

BURNETT, LEN Leonard Everett, DB, 6´1˝/195 lbs; Oregon; B8/29/1939 San Diego, CA **1961** Pit 4

BURNETT, RAY James Raymond, HB, Arkansas Tech; Central Arkansas; B1/29/1914 New Hope, AR, D7/19/1996 North Little Rock, AR

YEAR	TEAM	G (GS)	RUSH	YD	AVG (LG)	TD	PASS	COMP	PCT	YD	AVG (LG)	TD	INT	PTS	TAY
1938	ChiC	1 (0)	1	-10	-10.0 (-10)	0	2	1	50.0	19	9.5 (19)	0	0	0	-1

BURNETT, ROB Robert Barry, DE, 6´4˝/265 lbs; Syracuse; 1990: Cle, rnd 5; B8/27/1967 East Orange, NJ **[S]** **1990** Cle 16 (6, lde) **1991** Cle 13 (8, LDE) **1992** Cle 16 (16, LDE) **1993** Cle 16 (16, LDE) **1994**†Cle★ 16 (16, LDE) **1995** Cle 16 (16, LDE) **1996** Bal 6 (6, lde) **1997** Bal 15 (15, LDE) **1998** Bal 16 (16, LDE) **1999** Bal 16 (16, LDE) **2000**†Bal☆ 16 (16, LDE) **2001** Bal 13 (13, LDE) **2002** Mia 15 (0) **2003** Mia 12 (0) **NFL** 202 (160) [14 yrs]

YEAR	TEAM	G (GS, POS)	RUSH	YD	AVG(LG)	TD	REC	YD	AVG(LG)	TD	PASS COMP	PCT	YD	AVG(LG)	TD	INT	SK	YD	QBR	KPR	OTD	PTS	TAY

BURNETT, VICTOR Victor, DE, 6´5˝/250 lbs; Texas Tech; Fresno State; B10/5/1962 Los Angeles, CA **1987** SL 3 (0)

BURNETTE, DAVE David Lynn, T, 6´6˝/278 lbs; Central Arkansas; Arkansas; 1985: Ind, rnd 12; B3/24/1961 Parkin, AR **1987** Dal 1 (0)

BURNETTE, REGGIE Reginald, LB, 6´2˝/240 lbs; Houston; 1991: GB, rnd 7; B10/4/1968 Rayville, LA **1991** GB 3 (0) **1992** TB 15 (2) **1993** TB 5 (2) **NFL** 23 (4) [3 yrs]

BURNETTE, TOM Thomas Denmark, BB, 6´1˝/194 lbs; North Carolina; 1938: rnd 8; B7/29/1915 Fremont, NC, D9/9/1994 Martinsville, VA **[K]** **1938** Phi 5 (0)

| 1938 | Pit | 6(1) | 1 | 0 | | 0 | 1 | 3 | 3.0(3) | 0 | 1 | 0 | 0.0 | | 0 | 0 | 0 | — | — | K | — | 0 | 2 |
| **NFL** | 1 | 14(1) | 1 | 0 | 0.0 | 0 | 1 | 3 | 3.0(3) | 0 | 1 | 0 | 0.0 | 0 | 0 | 0 | 0 | — | — | K | — | 0 | 2 |

BURNHAM, LEM Lemuel, DE, 6´4˝/236 lbs; U.S. International; 1974: KC, rnd 15; B8/30/1947 Winter Haven, FL **1977** Phi 14 **1978** Phi 15 **1979**†Phi 16 **NFL** 45 [3 yrs]

BURNHAM, STANLEY Stanley, TB-BB, 5´10˝/175 lbs; Harvard; B3/2/1897 Ipswich, MA, D7/10/1949 **1925** Fra 5 (2)

BURNHAM, TIM Timothy Scott, TB-BB, 6´5˝/250 lbs; Washington; B5/6/1963 Redding, CA **1987** Sea 3 (3)

BURNINE, HANK Harold Henry, E, 6´2˝/188 lbs; Missouri; 1955: NYG, rnd 12; B11/9/1932 Henrietta, MO

1956	NYG	3	—	—	—	—	—	—	—	—	—	—	—	—	—	—	—	—	—	—	—	—	—
1956	Phi	7	—	—	—	—	10	208	20.8(52)	2	—	—	—	—	—	—	—	—	—	—	—	12	114
1957	Phi	7	—	—	—	—	7	63	9.0(16)	0	—	—	—	—	—	—	—	—	—	—	—	0	32
NFL	2	17	—	—	—	—	17	271	15.9(52)	2	—	—	—	—	—	—	—	—	—	—	—	12	146

BURNS, CURRY Curry, DB, 6´0˝/216 lbs; Louisville; 2003: Hou, rnd 7; B2/12/1981 Miami, FL **2003** Hou 1 (0) **2004** NYG 8 (2) **NFL** 9 (2) [2 yrs]

BURNS, ED Edward Joseph, QB, 6´3˝/210 lbs; Nebraska; B12/7/1954 Council Bluffs, IA **1979** NO 16 **1980** NO 2 (0) **NFL** 18 [2 yrs]

BURNS, JASON Jason, RB, 5´7˝/196 lbs; Wisconsin; B11/27/1972 Chicago, IL

| 1995 | Cin | 1(0) | 1 | 1 | 1.0(1) | 0 | — | — | — | — | — | — | — | — | — | — | — | — | — | — | — | 0 | 1 |

BURNS, JOE Joe Frank, RB, 5´9˝/215 lbs; Georgia Tech; B9/15/1979 Thomasville, GA

2002	Buf	10(0)	5	7	1.4(6)	0	—	—	—	—	—	—	—	—	—	—	—	—	—	k	—	0	27
2003	Buf	16(1)	39	113	2.9(12)	0	7	62	8.9(14)	0	—	—	—	—	—	—	—	—	—	k	—	0	146
2004	Buf	16(0)	20	73	3.7(21)	0	1	7	7.0(7)	0	—	—	—	—	—	—	—	—	—	k	—	0	77
2005	Buf	16(0)					1	19	19.0(19)	1	—	—	—	—	—	—	—	—	—	k	—	6	16
NFL	4	58(1)	64	193	3.0(21)	0	9	88	9.8(19)	1	—	—	—	—	—	—	—	—	—	k	—	6	265

BURNS, KEITH Keith Bernard, LB, 6´2˝/235 lbs; Oklahoma State; 1994: Den, rnd 7; B5/16/1972 Greeleyville, SC **1994** Den 11 (1) **1995** Den 16 (0) **1996**†Den 16 (0) **1997**†Den 16 (0) **1998**†Den 16 (0) **1999** ChiB 15 (0) **2000**†Den 13 (0) **2001** Den 16 (0) **2002** Den 16 (1) **2003**†Den 16 (0) **2004** TB 16 (0) **2005**†Den 15 (1) **NFL** 182 (3) [12 yrs]

BURNS, LAMONT Lamont Antonio, G, 6´4˝/300 lbs; East Carolina; 1997: NYJ, rnd 5; B3/16/1974 Greensboro, NC **1997** NYJ 4 (3)

BURNS, LEON Leon Keith, RB, 6´2˝/228 lbs; Long Beach State; 1971: SD, rnd 11; B9/15/1940 Oakland, CA, D12/22/1984 Los Angeles, CA

1971	SD	14	61	223	3.7(25)	1	3	22	7.3(10)	0	—	—	—	—	—	—	—	—	—	k	—	6	233
1972	SL	14(FB)	26	69	2.7(9)	2	6	24	4.0(12)	0	—	—	—	—	—	—	—	—	—	k	—	12	93
NFL	2	28	87	292	3.4(25)	3	9	46	5.1(12)	0	—	—	—	—	—	—	—	—	—	k	—	18	326

BURNS, MIKE Michael Wayne, DB, 6´0˝/181 lbs; USC; 1977: SF, rnd 6; B4/6/1954 Oakland, CA **1977** SF 14 **1978** Det 15 (11, SS) **NFL** 29 (11) [2 yrs]

BURNS, ROBERT Robert Henry, RB, 6´3˝/212 lbs; Georgia; 1974: NYJ, rnd 9; B1/12/1952 Tampa, FL

| 1974 | NYJ | 14 | 40 | 158 | 4.0(12) | 0 | 11 | 83 | 7.5(18) | 1 | — | — | — | — | — | — | — | — | — | k | — | 6 | 212 |

BURNSIDE, GEORGE George Harrison, BB, 5´9˝/160 lbs; Wisconsin; South Dakota; B1/21/1899 Oconto Falls, WI, D11/1962, WA **1926** Rac 2 (2)

BURRELL, CLINTON Clinton Blane, DB, 6´1˝/192 lbs; LSU; 1979: Cle, rnd 6; B9/4/1956 Franklin, LA **1979** Cle 16 **1980**†Cle 15 (13, RCB) **1981** Cle 2 (2) **1982**†Cle 9 (9, SS) **1983** Cle 12 (11, SS) **1984** Cle 13 (0) **NFL** 67 (35) [6 yrs]

BURRELL, GEORGE George Reed, DB, 5´10˝/180 lbs; Pennsylvania; B1/1/1948 Camden, NJ **1969** Den-A 14 (7, RS)

BURRELL, JOHN Johnny Buster, WR, 6´3˝/185 lbs; Rice; 1962: SF, rnd 7/DalT, rnd 25; B11/22/1940 Fort Worth, TX

1962	Pit	14	6	38	6.3(18)	0	8	193	24.1(42)	0	—	—	—	—	—	—	—	—	—	—	—	0	135
1963	Pit	14	—	—	—	—	2	27	13.5(14)	0	—	—	—	—	—	—	—	—	—	—	—	0	14
1964	Pit	14	—	—	—	—	6	113	18.8(43)	0	—	—	—	—	—	—	—	—	—	k	—	0	27
1966	Was	4	—	—	—	—	1	9	9.0(9)	0	—	—	—	—	—	—	—	—	—	—	—	0	5
1967	Was	10	—	—	—	—	9	95	10.6(23)	0	—	—	—	—	—	—	—	—	—	k	—	0	35
NFL	5	56	6	38	6.3(18)	0	26	437	16.8(43)	0	—	—	—	—	—	—	—	—	—	k	—	0	214

BURRELL, ODE Ode, RB-WR-P, 6´0˝/190 lbs; Mississippi State; 1964: Hou, rnd 4/GB, rnd 3; B9/15/1939 Goodman, MS

1964	Hou-A	7	8	10	1.3(5)	0	5	73	14.6(36)	0	—	—	—	—	—	—	—	—	—	kp	1	6	246
1965	Hou-A★	14(HB)	130	528	4.1(63)	3	55	650	11.8(52)	4	—	—	—	—	—	—	—	—	—	kp	—	46	1009
1966	Hou-A	14(HB)	122	406	3.3(45)	0	33	400	12.1(34)	5	1	1	100.0	9	9.0(9)	0	0	—	—	kp	—	30	675
1967	†Hou-A	10(WR)	3	-3	-1.0(2)	0	12	193	16.1(39)	0	—	—	—	—	—	—	—	—	—	p	—	0	94
1968	Hou-A	1	—	—	—	—	2	35	17.5(33)	0	—	—	—	—	—	—	—	—	—	kp	—	0	74
1969	†Hou-A	13	41	147	3.6(19)	0	5	28	5.6(8)	0	—	—	—	—	—	—	—	—	—	Pkp	—	0	188
NFL	6	59	304	1088	3.6(63)	3	112	1379	12.3(52)	9	1	1	100.0	9	9.0(9)	0	0	—	—	Pkp	1	82	2284

BURRESS, PLAXICO Plaxico, WR, 6´5˝/226 lbs; Michigan State; 2000: Pit, rnd 1; B8/12/1977 Norfolk, VA

2000	Pit	12(8, WR)	—	—	—	—	22	273	12.4(39)	0	—	—	—	—	—	—	—	—	—	—	—	0	137
2001	†Pit	16(16, WR)	—	—	—	—	66	1008	15.3(43)	6	—	—	—	—	—	—	—	—	—	—	—	36	534
2002	†Pit	16(15, WR)	—	—	—	—	78	1325	17.0(62)	7	—	—	—	—	—	—	—	—	—	—	—	44	698
2003	Pit	16(16, WR)	1	-7	-7.0(-7)	0	60	860	14.3(47)	4	—	—	—	—	—	—	—	—	—	—	—	24	443
2004	†Pit	11(11, WR)	—	—	—	—	35	698	19.9(48)	5	—	—	—	—	—	—	—	—	—	—	—	30	374
2005	†NYG	16(15, WR)	—	—	—	—	76	1214	16.0(78)	7	—	—	—	—	—	—	—	—	—	—	—	42	642
NFL	6	87(81)	1	-7	-7.0(-7)	0	337	5378	16.0(78)	29	—	—	—	—	—	—	—	—	—	—	—	176	2827

BURRIS, BO James England, DB, 6´3˝/195 lbs; Houston; 1967: NO, rnd 2; B10/16/1944 Luling, TX **1967** NO 14 **1968** NO 14 (LS) **1969** NO 12 **NFL** 40 [3 yrs]

BURRIS, BUDDY Paul Buddy, G-LB, 5´11˝/215 lbs; Tulsa; Oklahoma; 1947: GB, rnd 5/Bkn-A, rnd 9; B1/20/1923 Rogers County, OK **1949** GB 10 (0) **1950** GB 12 (LG) **1951** GB 7 (LG) **NFL** 29 [3 yrs]

BURRIS, HENRY Henry Armand, QB, 6´0˝/195 lbs; Temple; B6/4/1975 Fort Smith, AR

| 2002 | ChiB | 6(1) | 15 | 104 | 6.9(17) | 0 | — | — | — | 51 | 18 | 35.3 | 207 | 4.1(45) | 3 | 5 | — | — | — | — | — | 0 | 23 |

BURRIS, JEFF Jeffrey Lamar, DB, 6´0˝/190 lbs; Notre Dame; 1994: Buf, rnd 1; B6/7/1972 Rock Hill, SC **[R]** **1994** Buf 16 (0) **1995** Buf 9 (9, LCB) **1996**†Buf 15 (15, LCB) **1997** Buf 14 (14, LCB) **1998** Ind 14 (14, LCB) **1999**†Ind 16 (16, LCB) **2000**†Ind 16 (16, LCB) **2001** Ind 15 (15, LCB) **2002** Cin 16 (12, LCB) **2003** Cin 13 (8, lcb) **NFL** 144 (119) [10 yrs]

BURROUGH, JOHN John Leslie, DE-DT, 6´5˝/275 lbs; Washington State; Wyoming; 1995: Atl, rnd 7; B5/17/1972 Laramie, WY **1995**†Atl 16 (0) **1996** Atl 16 (1) **1997** Atl 16 (1) **1998**†Atl 16 (3) **1999**†Min 10 (2) **2000**†Min 14 (6, lde) **2002** SL 1 (0) **NFL** 89 (13) [7 yrs]

BURROUGH, KEN Kenneth Othell 'Double Zero', WR, 6´3˝/215 lbs; Texas Southern; 1970: NO, rnd 1; B7/14/1948 Jacksonville, FL

1970	NO	12	1	4	4.0(4)	0	13	196	15.1(35)	2	—	—	—	—	—	—	—	—	—	k	—	12	185
1971	Hou	13	—	—	—	—	25	370	14.8(62)	1	—	—	—	—	—	—	—	—	—	k	—	6	227
1972	Hou	14(WR)	—	—	—	—	26	521	20.0(80)	4	—	—	—	—	—	—	—	—	—	—	—	24	281
1973	Hou	14(WR)	5	38	7.6(34)	0	43	577	13.4(49)	2	—	—	—	—	—	—	—	—	—	—	—	18	347
1974	Hou	11(WR)	1	0	0.0(0)	0	36	492	13.7(51)	2	—	—	—	—	—	—	—	—	—	—	—	12	256
1975	Hou◇	14(WR)	—	—	—	—	53	**1063**	20.1(77)	8	—	—	—	—	—	—	—	—	—	—	—	48	572
1976	Hou	14(WR)	3	22	7.3(12)	0	51	932	18.3(69)	7	—	—	—	—	—	—	—	—	—	—	—	42	523
1977	Hou★	14(WR)	4	10	2.5(28)	0	43	**816**	19.0(85)	8	1	0	0.0	0	0.0(0)	0	0	—	—	—	—	48	458
1978	†Hou	16(WR)	3	-11	-3.7(1)	0	47	624	13.3(44)	2	1	0	0.0	0	0.0(0)	0	0	—	—	—	—	12	311
1979	†Hou	16(WR)	—	—	—	—	40	752	18.8(55)	6	—	—	—	—	—	—	—	—	—	—	—	36	406
1980	Hou	2(0)	—	—	—	—	4	91	22.8(54)	0	—	—	—	—	—	—	—	—	—	—	—	0	46

YEAR	TEAM	G (GS, POS)	RUSH	YD	AVG(LG)	TD	REC	YD	AVG(LG)	TD	PASS COMP	PCT	YD	AVG(LG)	TD	INT	SK	YD	QBR	KPR	OTD	PTS	TAY
1981	Hou	16(16, WR)	—	—	—	—	40	668	16.7(71)	7	—	—	—	—	—	—	—	—	—	—	—	42	369
NFL	12	156(16)	17	63	3.7(34)	1	421	7102	16.9(85)	49	3	0	0.0	0	0.0	0	0	—	—	—	k	—	300	3979

BURROUGHS, DERRICK Derrick D'wayne, DB, 6'1"/180 lbs; Memphis; 1985: Buf, rnd 1; B5/18/1962 Mobile, AL **1985** Buf 14 (8, LCB) **1986** Buf 15 (5, lcb) **1987** Buf 12 (12, RCB) **1988**†Buf 14 (13, LCB) **1989** Buf 3 (3) **NFL** 58 (41) [5 yrs]

BURROUGHS, DON Donald Edward, DB, 6'4"/190 lbs; Colorado State; B8/19/1931 Los Angeles, CA [I] **1955**†LARm 12 (DB) **1956** LARm 12 (DB) **1957** LARm 12 (DB) **1958** LARm 12 (DB) **1959** LARm 10 (DB) **1960**†Phi☆12 (LS) **1961** Phi☆13 (LS) **1962** Phi☆12 (RS) **1963** Phi 13 (RS) **1964** Phi 14 (RS) **NFL** 122 [10 yrs]

BURROUGHS, JIM James Edward, DB, 6'1"/190 lbs; Michigan State; 1982: Bal, rnd 3; B1/21/1958 Pahokee, FL **1982** Bal 8 (5, LCB) **1983** Bal 16 (16, LCB) **1984** Ind 6 (5, lcb) **NFL** 30 (26) [3 yrs]

BURROUGHS, SAMMIE Sammie Lee, LB, 6'0"/227 lbs; Portland State; B6/21/1973 Pomona, CA **1996**†Ind 16 (1) **1997** Ind 16 (1) **NFL** 32 (2) [2 yrs]

BURROW, CURTIS Curtis D., K, 5'11"/185 lbs; Central Arkansas; B12/11/1962 Brinkley, AR [K] **1988** GB 1 (0)

BURROW, JIM James Arthur, DB, 5'11"/181 lbs; Nebraska; 1976: GB, rnd 8; B11/29/1953 Hampton, VA **1976** GB 3

BURROW, KEN Kenneth Robert, WR, 6'0"/190 lbs; Utah State; San Diego State; 1971: Atl, rnd 2; B3/29/1948 Richmond, CA

1971	Atl	14(WR)	1	5	5.0(5)	0	33	741	22.5(84)	6	—	—	—	—	—	—	—	—	—	—	—	36	406
1972	Atl	14(WR)	3	3	1.0(8)	0	29	492	17.0(40)	5	—	—	—	—	—	—	—	—	—	—	—	30	274
1973	Atl	9	2	17	8.5(9)	0	31	567	18.3(57)	7	—	—	—	—	—	—	—	—	—	—	—	42	336
1974	Atl	14(WR)	—	—	—	—	34	545	16.0(48)	1	—	—	—	—	—	—	—	—	—	—	—	6	278
1975	Atl	13(WR)	—	—	—	—	25	323	12.9(23)	2	—	—	—	—	—	—	—	—	—	—	—	12	172
NFL	5	64	6	25	4.2(9)	0	152	2668	17.6(84)	21	—	—	—	—	—	—	—	—	—	—	—	126	1464

BURRUS, HARRY Harry Clifton, B-E, 6'1"/195 lbs; Hardin-Simmons; 1942: ChiB, rnd 6; B4/6/1921 Slaton, TX, D9/20/2004 Winter Haven, FL [K]

1946	†NYY-A	11(3)	1	3	3.0(3)	0	10	251	25.1	1	—	—	—	—	—	—	—	—	—	i	—	6	161
1947	†NYY-A	14(5, wb)	1	5	5.0(5)	0	8	192	24.0	2	—	—	—	—	—	—	—	—	—	i	—	12	117
1948	ChiR-A	1(0)	—	—	—	—	2	60	30.0	0	—	—	—	—	—	—	—	—	—	K	—	2	30
1948	Bkn-A	12(1)	1	-3	-3.0(-3)	0	8	167	20.9	1	—	—	—	—	—	—	—	—	—	i	—	6	153
AAFC	3	38(9)	3	5	1.7(5)	0	28	670	23.9	4	—	—	—	—	—	—	—	—	—	Ki	—	26	460

BURRUSS, LLOYD Lloyd Earl, DB, 6'0"/204 lbs; Maryland; 1981: KC, rnd 3; B10/31/1957 Charlottesville, VA [I] **1981** KC 16 (14, SS) **1982** KC 9 (9, SS) **1983** KC 12 (12, SS) **1984** KC 16 (16, SS) **1985** KC 15 (14, SS) **1986**†KC★15 (13, SS) **1987** KC 11 (11, SS) **1988** KC☆10 (9, SS) **1989** KC 9 (1) **1990**†KC 16 (1) **1991**†KC 16 (3) **NFL** 145 (103) [11 yrs]

BURSE, TONY Tony Lee, RB, 6'0"/220 lbs; Middle Tennessee State; 1987: Sea, rnd 12; B4/4/1965 Lafayette, GA

| 1987 | †Sea | 12(0) | 7 | 36 | 5.1(16) | 0 | — | — | — | — | — | — | — | — | — | — | — | — | — | k | — | 0 | 22 |

BURSON, JIMMY James Oertell, DB, 6'0"/175 lbs; Auburn; 1963: SL, rnd 11/Hou, rnd 8; B10/13/1940 La Grange, GA **1963** SL 1 **1964** SL 14 (RCB) **1965** SL 12 (RCB) **1966** SL 11 (LCB/rcb) **1967** SL 13 (RCB) **1968** Atl 14 (RCB) **NFL** 65 [6 yrs]

BURT, HAL Harold Alan, G, 5'10"/175 lbs; Kansas; B9/11/1900 Eureka, KS, D4/7/1979 Kerrville, TX **1924** Cle 2 (2)

BURT, JIM James P., NT-DT, 6'1"/260 lbs; Miami (FL); B6/7/1959 Buffalo, NY **1981**†NYG 13 (0) **1982** NYG 4 (2) **1983** NYG 7 (6, nt) **1984**†NYG 16 (15, NT) **1985**†NYG 16 (15, NT) **1986**†NYG★13 (13, NT) **1987** NYG 8 (8, NT) **1988** NYG 16 (11, NT) **1989**†SF 8 (3) **1990**†SF 13 (3) **1991** SF 4 (1) **NFL** 118 (77) [11 yrs]

BURT, RUSS Russell Edward, WB-FB, 5'8"/170 lbs; Canisius; B12/15/1900 Buffalo, NY, D4/7/1978 Orlando, FL [K] **1924** Buf 1 (0), 7 **1925** Buf 1 (0) **NFL** 2 (0) [2 yrs]

BURTON, AL Albert, DE, 6'5"/267 lbs; Bethune-Cookman; B3/30/1952 Daytona Beach, FL **1976** Hou 12 (lde) **1977** Hou 6 **NFL** 18 [2 yrs]

BURTON, DEREK Derek, T, 6'2"/270 lbs; Oklahoma State; B8/10/1963 Seattle, WA **1987** Min 3 (3)

BURTON, JAMES James Terrell, DB, 5'9"/184 lbs; Hawaii; Fresno State; 1994: KC, rnd 5; B4/27/1971 Torrance, CA **1994**†ChiB 13 (1) **1995** ChiB 11 (2) **1996** ChiB 16 (3) **1997** ChiB 5 (1) **NFL** 45 (7) [4 yrs]

BURTON, KENDRICK Kendrick Duran, DE, 6'5"/288 lbs; Alabama; 1996: Hou, rnd 4; B9/7/1973 Decatur, AL **1996** Hou 4 (2)

BURTON, LARRY Lawrence Godfrey, WR, 6'1"/192 lbs; Purdue; 1975: NO, rnd 1; B12/15/1951 Northampton, VA

1975	NO	13(11, WR)	2	8	4.0(5)	0	16	305	19.1(71)	2	—	—	—	—	—	—	—	—	—	—	—	12	171
1976	NO	14(12, WR)	3	-4	-1.3(4)	0	18	297	16.5(69)	2	—	—	—	—	—	—	—	—	—	—	—	12	155
1977	NO	1(1)	—	—	—	—	1	13	13.0(13)	0	—	—	—	—	—	—	—	—	—	—	—	0	7
1978	SD	3	—	—	—	—	5	127	25.4(55)	1	—	—	—	—	—	—	—	—	—	—	—	18	79
1979	†SD	12	—	—	—	—	4	62	15.5(23)	0	—	—	—	—	—	—	—	—	—	—	—	0	31
NFL	5	43(24)	5	4	0.8(5)	0	44	804	18.3(71)	7	—	—	—	—	—	—	—	—	—	—	—	42	441

BURTON, LEON Walter Leon, HB, 5'9"/172 lbs; Arizona State; 1958: SF, rnd 8; B3/13/1935 Flint, MI

| 1960 | NYT-A | 14 | 16 | 119 | 7.4(30) | 1 | 3 | 8 | 2.7(8) | 0 | — | — | — | — | — | — | — | — | — | kp | 2 | 18 | 598 |

BURTON, LEONARD Leonard Bernard, C, 6'3"/275 lbs; South Carolina; 1986: Buf, rnd 3; B6/18/1964 Memphis, TN **1986** Buf 14 (0) **1987** Buf 12 (3) **1988**†Buf 16 (4) **1989**†Buf 16 (0) **1992** Det 2 (2) **NFL** 60 (9) [5 yrs]

BURTON, LYLE Lyle Ralph, G-T-FB, 6'1"/195 lbs; DePauw; B5/21/1900 Sullivan, IL, D2/8/1962 Peoria, IL **1924** Ham 1 (0) **1925** RI 7 (6, RG) **NFL** 8 (6) [2 yrs]

BURTON, RON Ronald Eugene, HB, 5'10"/190 lbs; Northwestern; 1960: Bos, rnd 1/Phi, rnd 1; B7/25/1936 Springfield, OH, D9/13/2003 Boston, MA

1960	Bos-A	13(hb)	66	280	4.2(77)	1	21	196	9.3(35)	0	—	—	—	—	—	—	—	—	—	kp	—	6	484
1961	Bos-A	14(HB)	82	260	3.2(43)	2	13	115	8.8(45)	0	1	0	0.0	0	—	0	1	—	—	kp	1	18	572
1962	Bos-A	14(HB)	134	548	4.1(59)	2	40	461	11.5(69)	4	—	—	—	—	—	—	—	—	—	kp	1	42	879
1963	†Bos-A	0	—	—	—	—	—	—	—	—	—	—	—	—	—	—	—	—	—	—	—	0	0
1964	Bos-A	14(HB)	102	340	3.3(33)	3	27	306	11.3(59)	2	—	—	—	—	—	—	—	—	—	kp	—	30	582
1965	Bos-A	14	45	108	2.4(22)	1	10	127	12.7(73)	2	—	—	—	—	—	—	—	—	—	kp	—	18	261
NFL	6	69	429	1536	3.6(77)	9	111	1205	10.9(73)	8	1	0	0.0	0	—	0	1	—	—	kp	2	114	2777

BURTON, RON Ronald Leon, LB, 6'1"/250 lbs; North Carolina; B5/2/1964 Richmond, VA **1987** Dal 12 (2) **1988** Dal 16 (15, LLB) **1989** Dal 6 (3) **1989** Phx 10 (0) **1990** LARd 5 (0) **NFL** 49 (20) [4 yrs]

BURTON, SHANE Franklin Shane, DE-DT, 6'6"/305 lbs; Tennessee; 1996: Mia, rnd 5; B1/18/1974 Logan, WV **1996** Mia 16 (8, lde) **1997**†Mia 16 (4) **1998**†Mia 15 (0) **1999** ChiB 15 (0) **2000** NYJ 16 (16, RDE) **2001**†NYJ 15 (13, LDT) **2002** Car 16 (4) **2003**†Car 16 (4) **NFL** 125 (49) [8 yrs]

BUSBY, SHERRILL Sherrill, DE, 6'2"/200 lbs; Troy State; B6/17/1916 Florala, AL, D6/26/1986 Pensacola, FL **1940** Bkn 2 (0)

BUSCH, ELMER Elmer Eugene, G-C, 5'10"/200 lbs; Sherman Indian; Carlisle Indian; B1890, CA, D1/14/1949 Menocino County, CA **1922** Oor 9 (9, RG)

BUSCH, MIKE Michael Paul, QB, 6'4"/214 lbs; Idaho State; South Dakota State; B2/8/1962 Huron, SD

| 1987 | NYG | 2(1) | — | — | — | — | — | — | — | — | 47 | 17 | 36.2 | 278 | 5.9(63) | 3 | 2 | 7 | 72 | — | — | 0 | 74 |

BUSH, BLAIR Blair Walter, C, 6'3"/268 lbs; Washington; 1978: Cin, rnd 1; B11/25/1956 Fort Hood, TX **1978** Cin 16 (16, C) **1979** Cin 12 (12, C) **1980** Cin 16 (13, C) **1981** Cin 16 (16, C) **1982**†Cin 8 (8, C) **1983**†Sea 16 (14, C) **1984**†Sea 16 (16, C) **1985** Sea 16 (16, C) **1986** Sea 7 (7, C) **1987** Sea 11 (11, C) **1988**†Sea 16 (14, C) **1989** GB 16 (16, 0) **1990** GB 16 (0) **1992** LARm 16 (0) **1993** LARm 16 (0) **1994** LARm 16 (0) **NFL** 246 (161) [17 yrs]

BUSH, DEVIN Devin Marquese, DB, 5'11"/210 lbs; Florida State; 1995: Atl, rnd 1; B7/3/1973 Miami, FL **1995**†Atl 11 (5, fs) **1996** Atl 16 (15, SS) **1997** Atl 16 (16, FS) **1998**†Atl 13 (0) **1999**†SL 16 (7, fs) **2000**†SL 13 (12, SS) **2001** Cle 16 (7, fs) **2002** Cle 15 (9, FS) **NFL** 116 (71) [8 yrs]

BUSH, FRANK Frank Everett, LB, 6'1"/218 lbs; North Carolina State; 1985: Hou, rnd 5; B1/10/1963 Athens, GA **1985** Hou 16 (11, ROLB) **1986** Hou 3 (3) **NFL** 19 (14) [2 yrs]

BUSH, LEWIS Lewis Fitzgerald, LB, 6'2"/245 lbs; Washington State; 1993: SD, rnd 4; B12/21/1969 Atlanta, GA **1993** SD 16 (0) **1994**†SD 16 (0) **1995**†SD 16 (15, LLB) **1996** SD 16 (16, LLB) **1997** SD 14 (13, MLB/llb) **1998** SD 10 (10, LLB) **1999** SD 16 (14, LLB) **2000** KC 16 (8, LLB) **2001** KC 12 (11, LLB) **2002** KC 9 (5, lolb) **NFL** 141 (92) [10 yrs]

BUSH, RAY Raymond M., E, 5'8"/180 lbs; Loyola (IL); B1903, deceased **1926** Lou 4 (4, RE)

BUSH, STEVE Steven Jack, TE, 6'3"/280 lbs; Arizona State; B7/4/1974 Paradise Valley, AZ

| 1997 | Cin | 16(0) | — | — | — | — | — | — | — | — | — | — | — | — | — | — | — | — | — | — | — | 0 | — |
| 1998 | Cin | 12(2) | — | — | — | — | 4 | 39 | 9.8(18) | 0 | — | — | — | — | — | — | — | — | — | — | — | 0 | 20 |

YEAR	TEAM	G (GS, POS)	RUSH	YD	AVG (LG)	TD	REC	YD	AVG (LG)	TD	PASS	COMP	PCT	YD	AVG (LG)	TD	INT	SK	YD	QBR	KPR	OTD	PTS	TAY
1999	Cin	13(0)	—	—	—	—	1	4	4.0(4)	0	—	—	—	—	—	—	—	—	—	—	—	—	0	2
2000	Cin	16(0)	—	—	—	—	3	39	13.0(18)	0	—	—	—	—	—	—	—	—	—	—	k	—	0	-8
2001	Arz	9(7, TE)	—	—	—	—	8	80	10.0(16)	0	—	—	—	—	—	—	—	—	—	—	k	—	0	34
2002	Arz	16(12, TE)	—	—	—	—	19	121	6.4(13)	1	—	—	—	—	—	—	—	—	—	—	k	—	6	60
2003	Arz	16(4)	—	—	—	—	11	71	6.5(14)	1	—	—	—	—	—	—	—	—	—	—	—	—	6	41
2004	SF	5(2)	—	—	—	—	2	10	5.0(6)	1	—	—	—	—	—	—	—	—	—	—	—	—	6	10
2005	SF	15(2)	—	—	—	—	3	21	7.0(10)	0	—	—	—	—	—	—	—	—	—	—	—	—	0	11
NFL	9	118(29)	—	—	—	—	51	385	7.5(18)	3	—	—	—	—	—	—	—	—	—	—	k	—	18	169

BUSHBY, TOM Thomas Bateman, TB-WB, 5´10˝/200 lbs; Kansas State; B12/30/1911 Munden, KS, D10/1983 Northridge, CA **1935** Phi 2 (0)

YEAR	TEAM	G (GS, POS)	RUSH	YD	AVG (LG)	TD	REC	YD	AVG (LG)	TD	PASS	COMP	PCT	YD	AVG (LG)	TD	INT	SK	YD	QBR	KPR	OTD	PTS	TAY
1934	Cin	6(4, TB)	7	9	1.3	0	1	4	4.0(4)	0	—	—	—	—	—	—	—	—	—	—	—	—	0	11
NFL	2	8(4)	7	9	1.3	0	1	4	4.0(4)	0	—	—	—	—	—	—	—	—	—	—	—	—	0	11

BUSICH, SAM Samuel, E, 6´3˝/189 lbs; Ohio State; B11/17/1913 Lorain, OH, D2/1/1991, **[K]**

YEAR	TEAM	G (GS, POS)	RUSH	YD	AVG (LG)	TD	REC	YD	AVG (LG)	TD	PASS	COMP	PCT	YD	AVG (LG)	TD	INT	SK	YD	QBR	KPR	OTD	PTS	TAY
1936	†Bos	11(0)	—	—	—	—	6	57	9.5	1	—	—	—	—	—	—	—	—	—	—	K	—	10	34
1937	Cle	10(8, RE)	—	—	—	—	13	136	10.5	0	—	—	—	—	—	—	—	—	—	—	—	—	0	68
1943	Det	1(0)	—	—	—	—	—	—	—	—	—	—	—	—	—	—	—	—	—	—	K	—	1	0
NFL	3	22(8)	—	—	—	—	19	193	10.2	1	—	—	—	—	—	—	—	—	—	—	K	—	11	102

BUSICK, STEVE Steven Ray, LB, 6´4˝/227 lbs; USC; 1981: Den, rnd 7; B12/10/1958 Los Angeles, CA **1981** Den 16 (0) **1982** Den 9 (0) **1983**†Den 16 (15, RILB) **1984**†Den 16 (16, RILB) **1985** Den 16 (16, RILB) **1986** LARm 4 (1) **1987** SD 1 (0) **NFL** 78 (48) [7 yrs]

BUSLER, RAY Raymond Albert, T, 6´1˝/222 lbs; Marquette; B1/16/1914 Watertown, WI, D10/9/1969 Granite City, IL **1940** ChiC 11 (0) **1941** ChiC 8 (2) **1945** ChiC 1 (0) **NFL** 20 (2) [3 yrs]

BUSS, ART Arthur T., T, 6´3˝/219 lbs; Michigan State; B7/14/1911 St. Joseph, MI, D3/23/1998 Chelsea, MI **1934**†ChiB 13 (2) **1935** ChiB 9 (9, LT) **1936** Phi 12 (12, LT) **1937** Phi 11 (11, LT) **NFL** 45 (34) [4 yrs]

BUSSELL, GERRY Gerald Wheeler, DB, 6´0˝/190 lbs; Georgia Tech; 1965: Den, rnd 9/Cle, rnd 2; B9/7/1943 Middlesboro, KY **1965** Den-A 6

BUSSEY, BARNEY Barney Albert, DB-LB, 6´0˝/215 lbs; South Carolina State; 1984: Cin, rnd 5; B5/20/1962 Lincolnton, GA **1986** Cin 16 (0) **1987** Cin 12 (1) **1988**†Cin 16 (0) **1989** Cin 16 (1) **1990**†Cin 16 (5, ss) **1991** Cin 12 (7, fs) **1992** Cin 16 (4) **1993** TB 16 (7, RLB) **1994** TB 16 (15, RLB) **1995** TB 8 (5, ss) **NFL** 144 (45) [10 yrs]

BUSSEY, DEXTER Dexter Manley, RB, 6´1˝/195 lbs; Oklahoma; Texas-Arlington; 1974: Det, rnd 3; B3/11/1952 Dallas, TX

YEAR	TEAM	G (GS, POS)	RUSH	YD	AVG (LG)	TD	REC	YD	AVG (LG)	TD	PASS	COMP	PCT	YD	AVG (LG)	TD	INT	SK	YD	QBR	KPR	OTD	PTS	TAY
1974	Det	11	9	22	2.4(9)	0	4	24	6.0(8)	0	—	—	—	—	—	—	—	—	—	—	k	—	0	18
1975	Det	13(13, FB)	157	696	4.4(32)	2	14	175	12.5(65)	2	—	—	—	—	—	—	—	—	—	—	k	—	24	822
1976	Det	14(14, RB)	196	858	4.4(46)	3	28	218	7.8(27)	0	—	—	—	—	—	—	—	—	—	—	k	—	18	996
1977	Det	8(4)	85	338	4.0(31)	4	11	116	10.5(39)	1	—	—	—	—	—	—	—	—	—	—	—	—	30	441
1978	Det	16(16, RB)	225	924	4.1(36)	5	31	275	8.9(18)	1	—	—	—	—	—	—	—	—	—	—	—	—	36	1117
1979	Det	16(10, RB)	144	625	4.3(38)	1	15	102	6.8(22)	0	—	—	—	—	—	—	—	—	—	—	—	—	6	686
1980	Det	16(16, FB)	145	720	**5.0(40)**	3	39	364	9.3(30)	0	—	—	—	—	—	—	—	—	—	—	—	—	18	932
1981	Det	16(15, FB)	105	446	4.2(23)	0	18	92	5.1(16)	0	—	—	—	—	—	—	—	—	—	—	—	—	0	492
1982	†Det	9(6, FB)	48	136	2.8(10)	0	16	138	8.6(21)	0	—	—	—	—	—	—	—	—	—	—	—	—	0	205
1983	†Det	15(3)	57	249	4.4(26)	0	8	49	6.1(14)	1	—	—	—	—	—	—	—	—	—	—	—	—	6	279
1984	Det	16(3)	32	91	2.8(18)	0	9	63	7.0(19)	0	—	—	—	—	—	—	—	—	—	—	—	—	0	123
NFL	11	150(100)	1203	5105	4.2(46)	18	193	1616	8.4(65)	5	—	—	—	—	—	—	—	—	—	—	k	—	138	6109

BUSSEY, YOUNG Ruey Young, QB, 5´9˝/184 lbs; LSU; 1940: ChiB, rnd 20; B10/4/1917 Timpson, TX, D1/7/1945 Lingayen Gulf, Phillipines

YEAR	TEAM	G (GS, POS)	RUSH	YD	AVG (LG)	TD	REC	YD	AVG (LG)	TD	PASS	COMP	PCT	YD	AVG (LG)	TD	INT	SK	YD	QBR	KPR	OTD	PTS	TAY
1941	†ChiB✧	10(0)	13	-27	-2.1(16)	0	—	—	—	—	40	13	32.5	353	8.8(48)	5	3	—	—	—	Ppi	—	0	85

BUTCHER, PAUL Paul Martin, LB, 6´0˝/230 lbs; Wayne State (MI); B11/8/1963 Detroit, MI **1986** Det 12 (0) **1987** Det 12 (0) **1988** Det 16 (0) **1989**†LARm 0 (0) **1990** LARm 16 (1) **1991** LARm 16 (3) **1992** LARm 1 (1) **1993** Ind 16 (0) **1994** Ind 13 (0) **1995** Car 16 (0) **1996** Oak 16 (0) **NFL** 134 (5) [11 yrs]

BUTCHER, WENDELL Wendell Ralph, B, 6´1˝/197 lbs; Gustavus Adolphus; B3/28/1914 Worthington, MN, D12/18/1988 Memphis, TN

YEAR	TEAM	G (GS, POS)	RUSH	YD	AVG (LG)	TD	REC	YD	AVG (LG)	TD	PASS	COMP	PCT	YD	AVG (LG)	TD	INT	SK	YD	QBR	KPR	OTD	PTS	TAY
1938	Bkn	9(3)	30	99	3.3	1	3	44	14.7	0	—	—	—	—	—	—	—	—	—	—	—	—	6	131
1939	Bkn	10(5, BB)	2	2	1.0	0	9	73	8.1	0	—	—	—	—	—	—	—	—	—	—	—	—	0	39
1940	Bkn	5(0)	—	—	—	—	2	21	10.5	0	—	—	—	—	—	—	—	—	—	—	—	—	0	11
1941	Bkn	9(1)	1	2	2.0(2)	0	—	—	—	—	—	—	—	—	—	—	—	—	—	—	—	—	0	2
1942	Bkn	11(8, BB)	—	—	—	—	1	16	16.0(16)	0	—	—	—	—	—	—	—	—	—	—	—	—	0	8
NFL	5	44(17)	33	103	3.1(2)	1	15	154	10.3(16)	0	—	—	—	—	—	—	—	—	—	—	—	—	6	190

BUTKUS, CARL Carl John, G-T, 6´1˝/245 lbs; George Washington; B12/26/1922 Scranton, PA, D8/3/1978 Washington, DC **1948** NYY-A 4 (1)

1948 Was 9 (0) **1949** NYG 11 (7, LG) **NFL** 20 (7) [1 yr]

BUTKUS, DICK Richard Marvin, LB, 6´3˝/245 lbs; Illinois; 1965: Chi, rnd 1/Den, rnd 2; B12/9/1942 Chicago, IL; HOF 1979 **[Kl]** **1965** ChiB★14 (MLB) **1966** ChiB★14 (MLB) **1967** ChiB★14 (MLB) **1968** ChiB★13 (MLB) **1969** ChiB★13 (MLB) **1970** ChiB★14 (MLB) **1971** ChiB★14 (MLB) **1973** ChiB 9 (MLB)

YEAR	TEAM	G (GS, POS)	RUSH	YD	AVG (LG)	TD	REC	YD	AVG (LG)	TD	PASS	COMP	PCT	YD	AVG (LG)	TD	INT	SK	YD	QBR	KPR	OTD	PTS	TAY
1972	ChiB★	14(MLB)	1	28	28.0(28)	0	—	—	—	—	—	—	—	—	—	—	—	—	—	—	Kki	—	1	37
NFL	9	119	1	28	28.0(28)	0	—	—	—	—	—	—	—	—	—	—	—	—	—	—	Kki	1	10	24

BUTLER, BILL William R., DB-HB, 5´10˝/189 lbs; Tennessee-Chattanooga; 1959: GB, rnd 19; B7/10/1937 Berlin, WI **[R]** **1960** Dal 12 (RS) **1961** Pit 10 (LS) **1962** Min 14 (12, RS)

YEAR	TEAM	G (GS, POS)	RUSH	YD	AVG (LG)	TD	REC	YD	AVG (LG)	TD	PASS	COMP	PCT	YD	AVG (LG)	TD	INT	SK	YD	QBR	KPR	OTD	PTS	TAY
1959	GB	11	7	49	7.0(16)	0	1	-2	-2.0(-2)	0	—	—	—	—	—	—	—	—	—	—	kp	1	6	288
1963	Min	14	17	48	2.8(11)	0	4	39	9.8(19)	0	—	—	—	—	—	—	—	—	—	—	kp	1	6	411
1964	Min	14	5	11	2.2(6)	0	1	58	58.0(58)	0	—	—	—	—	—	—	—	—	—	—	kpi	—	0	298
NFL	6	75(12)	29	108	3.7(16)	0	6	95	15.8(58)	0	—	—	—	—	—	—	—	—	—	—	kpi	4	24	1655

BUTLER, BILL William Edward, RB, 6´0˝/218 lbs; Kansas State; 1972: NO, rnd 5; B8/12/1950 Leaksville, NC

YEAR	TEAM	G (GS, POS)	RUSH	YD	AVG (LG)	TD	REC	YD	AVG (LG)	TD	PASS	COMP	PCT	YD	AVG (LG)	TD	INT	SK	YD	QBR	KPR	OTD	PTS	TAY
1972	NO	14(FB)	54	233	4.3(27)	0	25	226	9.0(21)	2	—	—	—	—	—	—	—	—	—	—	k	—	12	355
1973	NO	13(fb)	87	348	4.0(19)	1	19	125	6.6(16)	2	—	—	—	—	—	—	—	—	—	—	—	—	18	431
1974	NO	14	21	74	3.5(10)	0	2	3	1.5(2)	0	—	—	—	—	—	—	—	—	—	—	k	—	0	73
NFL	3	41	162	655	4.0(27)	1	46	354	7.7(21)	4	—	—	—	—	—	—	—	—	—	—	k	—	30	858

BUTLER, BILL William M., LB, 6´4˝/226 lbs; Cal State-Northridge; B8/4/1947 Los Angeles, CA **1970** Den 14

BUTLER, BOB Robert Douglas, G, 6´1˝/230 lbs; Kentucky; 1962: Phi, rnd 9; B10/27/1940 Madisonville, KY **1962** Phi 3 **1963** NYJ-A 1 **NFL** 4 [2 yrs]

BUTLER, BOBBY Robert Calvin, DB, 5´11˝/174 lbs; Florida State; 1981: Atl, rnd 1; B5/28/1959 Boynton Beach, FL **[I]** **1981** Atl 16 (16, LCB) **1982**†Atl 9 (9, LCB) **1983** Atl 16 (16, LCB) **1984** Atl 15 (15, LCB) **1985** Atl 16 (16, LCB) **1986** Atl 7 (7, LCB) **1987** Atl 12 (12, LCB) **1988** Atl 16 (16, LCB) **1989** Atl 16 (11, LCB) **1990** Atl 16 (6, lcb) **1991**†Atl 15 (2) **1992** Atl 15 (0) **NFL** 169 (126) [12 yrs]

BUTLER, CANNONBALL James, RB, 5´9˝/194 lbs; Edward Waters; 1965: Pit, rnd 14; B5/4/1943 Quincy, FL **[R]**

YEAR	TEAM	G (GS, POS)	RUSH	YD	AVG (LG)	TD	REC	YD	AVG (LG)	TD	PASS	COMP	PCT	YD	AVG (LG)	TD	INT	SK	YD	QBR	KPR	OTD	PTS	TAY
1965	Pit	14	46	108	2.3(12)	0	9	117	13.0(43)	1	—	—	—	—	—	—	—	—	—	—	k	—	6	306
1966	Pit	14	46	114	2.5(19)	2	4	93	23.3(66)	1	—	—	—	—	—	—	—	—	—	—	k	1	24	395
1967	Pit	11(hb)	90	293	3.3(24)	0	4	23	5.8(13)	0	—	—	—	—	—	—	—	—	—	—	k	—	0	378
1968	Atl	12(FB)	94	365	3.9(60)	2	15	127	8.5(31)	0	—	—	—	—	—	—	—	—	—	—	k	—	12	693
1969	Atl✧	14(FB)	163	655	4.0(39)	3	17	297	17.5(65)	2	—	—	—	—	—	—	—	—	—	—	k	—	30	1054
1970	Atl	14(FB)	166	636	3.8(33)	0	24	151	6.3(25)	1	—	—	—	—	—	—	—	—	—	—	k	—	6	791
1971	Atl	13(FB)	186	594	3.2(19)	2	15	143	9.5(27)	2	—	—	—	—	—	—	—	—	—	—	k	—	24	873
1972	SL	5	6	3	0.5(5)	0	1	8	8.0(8)	0	—	—	—	—	—	—	—	—	—	—	k	—	0	32
NFL	8	97	797	2768	3.5(60)	9	89	959	10.8(66)	7	—	—	—	—	—	—	—	—	—	—	k	1	102	4519

BUTLER, CHUCK Charles Wallace, LB, 6´0˝/220 lbs; Utah State; Boise State; B12/18/1961 New Haven, CT **1984** Sea 8 (0)

BUTLER, DAVE David Michael, LB, 6´4˝/225 lbs; Notre Dame; B7/17/1965 Ridgewood, NJ **1987** Cle 1 (0)

BUTLER, DUANE Duane M., DB, 6´1˝/211 lbs; Eastern Michigan; Illinois State; B11/29/1973 Trotwood, OH **1997**†Min 3 (0) **1998**†Min 14 (0) **NFL** 17 (0) [2 yrs]

BUTLER, FRANK Frank John, C-LB-T, 6´3˝/230 lbs; Notre Dame; Michigan State; B5/3/1909 Bloomington, IL, D11/1979 Greenwood, IL **1934** GB 3 (1) **1935** GB 6 (4) **1936**†GB 9 (5, c) **1938**†GB 8 (1) **NFL** 26 (11) [4 yrs]

YEAR	TEAM	G (GS, POS)	RUSH	YD	AVG (LG)	TD	REC	YD	AVG (LG)	TD	PASS COMP	PCT	YD	AVG (LG)	TD	INT	SK	YD	QBR	KPR	OTD	PTS	TAY

BUTLER, GARY   Gary Bernard, TE, 6´3˝/235 lbs; Rice; 1973: KC, rnd 2; B1/11/1951 Houston, TX

1973	KC	14	2	10	5.0(9)	0	8	124	15.5(48)	2	—	—	—	—	—	—	—	—	—	—	—	12	82
1975	ChiB	8	—	—	—	—	—	—	—	—	—	—	—	—	—	—	—	—	—	—	—	—	—
1977	TB	3	—	—	—	—	1	21	21.0(21)	0	—	—	—	—	—	—	—	—	—	—	—	0	11
NFL	3	25	2	10	5.0(9)	0	9	145	16.1(48)	2	—	—	—	—	—	—	—	—	—	—	—	12	93

BUTLER, HILLARY   Hillary, LB, 6´2˝/240 lbs; Washington; B1/5/1971 San Francisco, CA   **1998** Sea 7 (0)

BUTLER, JACK   John Bradshaw, DB, 6´1˝/200 lbs; St. Bonaventure; B11/12/1927 Pittsburgh, PA [I]   **1951** Pit 12 (DB)   **1955** Pit✧12 (DB)   **1957** Pit★12 (DB)   **1958** Pit★12 (DB)
1959 Pit☆7 (DB)

1952	Pit	12(DB)	—	—	—	—	3	37	12.3(20)	2	—	—	—	—	—	—	—	—	—	i	—	12	162
1953	Pit	12(DB)	—	—	—	—	2	43	21.5(33)	1	—	—	—	—	—	—	—	—	—	pi	1	12	139
1954	Pit	12(DB)	—	—	—	—	1	12	12.0(12)	0	—	—	—	—	—	—	—	—	—	i	2	12	81
1956	Pit★	12(DB)	—	—	—	—	1	10	10.0(10)	1	—	—	—	—	—	—	—	—	—	i	1	12	93
NFL	9	103	—	—	—	—	7	102	14.6(33)	4	—	—	—	—	—	—	—	—	—	pi	5	54	680

BUTLER, JAMES   James, DB, 6´3˝/210 lbs; Georgia Tech; B9/7/1982 Bainbridge, GA   **2005**†NYG 16 (1)

BUTLER, JERAMETRIUS   Jerametrius Tarell, DB, 5´10˝/181 lbs; Kansas State; 2001: SL, rnd 5; B11/28/1978 Dallas, TX   **2001**†SL 16 (0)   **2002** SL 9 (0)   **2003**†SL 16 (15, LCB)
2004†SL 16 (16, LCB)   **NFL** 57 (31) [4 yrs]

BUTLER, JERRY   Jerry O'Dell, WR, 6´0˝/178 lbs; Clemson; 1979: Buf, rnd 1; B10/17/1957 Ware Shoals, SC

1979	Buf	13(13, WR)	2	13	6.5(12)	0	48	834	17.4(75)	4	—	—	—	—	—	—	—	—	—	—	—	24	450
1980	†Buf★	16(16, WR)	1	18	18.0(18)	0	57	832	14.6(69)	6	—	—	—	—	—	—	—	—	—	—	—	36	464
1981	†Buf	16(16, WR)	1	1	1.0(1)	0	55	842	15.3(67)	8	—	—	—	—	—	—	—	—	—	—	—	48	462
1982	Buf	7(7, WR)	—	—	—	—	26	336	12.9(47)	4	—	—	—	—	—	—	—	—	—	—	—	24	188
1983	Buf	9(9, WR)	—	—	—	—	36	385	10.7(25)	3	—	—	—	—	—	—	—	—	—	—	—	18	208
1985	Buf	16(13, WR)	—	—	—	—	41	770	18.8(60)	2	—	—	—	—	—	—	—	—	—	—	—	12	395
1986	Buf	11(6, wr)	—	—	—	—	15	302	20.1(53)	2	—	—	—	—	—	—	—	—	—	—	—	12	161
NFL	7	88(80)	4	32	8.0(18)	0	278	4301	15.5(75)	29	—	—	—	—	—	—	—	—	—	—	—	174	2328

BUTLER, JERRY   Jerry Kenneth, RB, 5´11˝/193 lbs; East Tennessee State; B12/7/1961 Smyrna, TN

| 1987 | Atl | 1(0) | 1 | 1 | 1.0(1) | 0 | 2 | 7 | 3.5(4) | 0 | — | — | — | — | — | — | — | — | — | kp | — | 0 | 3 |

BUTLER, JOHN   John Damon, DB, 6´1˝/200 lbs; Principia; B4/13/1965 San Diego, CA   **1987** SF 3 (0)

BUTLER, JOHNNY   John William, HB-TB, 5´10˝/185 lbs; Tennessee; 1942: Pit, rnd 7; B9/10/1918 Knoxville, TN, D4/1963

1943	P-P	10(9, LH)	87	362	4.2(69)	3	3	63	21.0(37)	0	13	6	46.2	84	6.5(26)	0	1	—	—	—	Pkp	—	18	471
1944	C-P	3(3)	20	48	2.4(14)	0	3	109	36.3(67)	2	—	—	—	—	—	—	—	—	—	—	kpi	—	12	158
1944	Bkn	6(3, TB)	40	46	1.1(0)	0	—	—	—	—	23	8	34.8	107	4.7(30)	0	1	—	—	—	Ppi	—	0	102
1945	Phi	7(0)	21	61	2.9(18)	1	2	14	7.0(9)	0	—	—	—	—	—	—	—	—	—	—	ki	—	6	111
NFL	3	26(15)	168	517	3.1(69)	4	8	186	23.3(67)	2	36	14	38.9	191	5.3(30)	0	2	—	—	—	Pkpi	—	36	841

BUTLER, KEITH   John Keith, LB, 6´4˝/230 lbs; Memphis; 1978: Sea, rnd 2; B5/16/1956 Anniston, AL   **1978** Sea 16 (14, RLB)   **1979** Sea 14 (14, RLB)   **1980** Sea 16 (16, RLB)
1981 Sea 16 (16, RLB)   **1982** Sea 8 (8, RLB)   **1983**†Sea 16 (16, RILB)   **1984**†Sea 16 (16, RILB)   **1985** Sea 16 (16, RILB)   **1986** Sea 16 (16, RILB)   **1987**†Sea 12 (0)
NFL 146 (132) [10 yrs]

BUTLER, KELLY   Kelly Don, T-TE, 6´6˝/290 lbs; Purdue; 2004: Det, rnd 6; B7/24/1982 Grand Rapids, MI   **2005** Det 16 (16, RT)

BUTLER, KEVIN   Kevin Gregory, K, 6´0˝/215 lbs; Georgia; 1985: Chi, rnd 4; B7/24/1962 Savannah, GA [K]   **1985**†ChiB☆16 (0)   **1986**†ChiB 16 (0)   **1987**†ChiB 12 (0)
1988†ChiB 16 (0)   **1989** ChiB☆16 (0)   **1990**†ChiB 16 (0)   **1991**†ChiB 16 (0)   **1992** ChiB 16 (0)   **1993** ChiB 16 (0)   **1994**†ChiB 15 (0)   **1995** ChiB 16 (0)   **1996** Arz 7 (0)
1997 Arz 6 (0)   **NFL** 184 (0) [13 yrs]

BUTLER, LEROY   LeRoy, DB, 6´0˝/197 lbs; Florida State; 1990: GB, rnd 2; B7/19/1968 Jacksonville, FL [I]   **1990** GB 16 (0)   **1991** GB 16 (16, RCB)   **1992** GB 15 (15, SS)
1993†GB★16 (16, SS)   **1994**†GB 13 (13, SS)   **1995**†GB 16 (16, SS)   **1996**†GB★16 (16, SS)   **1997**†GB★16 (16, SS)   **1998**†GB★16 (16, SS)   **1999** GB 16 (16, SS)
2000 GB 16 (16, SS)   **2001** GB 9 (9, SS)   **NFL** 181 (165) [12 yrs]

BUTLER, MIKE   Michael Anthony, DE, 6´5˝/265 lbs; Kansas; 1977: GB, rnd 1; B4/4/1954 Washington, DC   **1977** GB 14 (14, LDE)   **1978** GB 16 (16, LDE)   **1979** GB 14 (14, LDE)
1980 GB 16 (16, LDE)   **1981** GB☆16 (16, LDE)   **1982**†GB 9 (9, LDE)   **1985** GB 10 (2)   **NFL** 95 (87) [7 yrs]

BUTLER, RAY   Raymond Leonard, WR, 6´3˝/200 lbs; USC; 1980: Bal, rnd 4; B6/28/1956 Port Lavaca, TX

1980	Bal	16(16, WR)	—	—	—	—	34	574	16.9(42)	2	—	—	—	—	—	—	—	—	—	—	—	12	297
1981	Bal	16(16, WR)	—	—	—	—	46	832	18.1(67)	9	—	—	—	—	—	—	—	—	—	—	—	54	461
1982	Bal	9(9, WR)	3	10	3.3(10)	0	17	268	15.8(53)	2	—	—	—	—	—	—	—	—	—	—	—	12	154
1983	Bal	11(7, WR)	—	—	—	—	10	207	20.7(60)	3	—	—	—	—	—	—	—	—	—	—	—	18	119
1984	Ind	16(15, WR)	—	—	—	—	43	664	15.4(74)	6	—	—	—	—	—	—	—	—	—	—	—	36	362
1985	Ind	11(9, WR)	1	-1	-1.0(-1)	0	19	345	18.2(72)	2	—	—	—	—	—	—	—	—	—	—	—	12	182
1985	Sea	2(0)	—	—	—	—	—	—	—	—	—	—	—	—	—	—	—	—	—	—	—	—	—
1986	Sea	16(0)	—	—	—	—	19	351	18.5(67)	4	—	—	—	—	—	—	—	—	—	—	—	24	196
1987	†Sea	12(3)	—	—	—	—	33	465	14.1(40)	5	—	—	—	—	—	—	—	—	—	—	—	30	258
1988	†Sea	11(5, wr)	—	—	—	—	18	242	13.4(46)	4	—	—	—	—	—	—	—	—	—	—	—	24	141
NFL	9	120(80)	4	9	2.3(10)	0	239	3948	16.5(74)	37	—	—	—	—	—	—	—	—	—	—	—	222	2168

BUTLER, ROBB   Robb, DB, 6´0˝/217 lbs; Robert Morris; B9/14/1981 Pittsburgh, PA   **2004**†SD 5 (0)

BUTLER, SKIP   William Foster, K, 6´1˝/201 lbs; Texas-Arlington; 1970: GB, rnd 4; B10/21/1947 Gladewater, TX [K]   **1971** NO 2   **1971** NYG 1   **1972** Hou 13   **1973** Hou 14
1974 Hou 14   **1975** Hou 14   **1977** Hou 1

| 1976 | Hou | 14 | 1 | 0 | 0.0(0) | 0 | — | — | — | — | — | — | — | — | — | — | — | — | — | KP | — | 72 | 0 |
| NFL | 7 | 73 | 1 | 0 | 0.0(0) | 0 | — | — | — | — | — | — | — | — | — | — | — | — | — | KP | — | 340 | 0 |

BUTLER, SOL   Edward Solomon, WB-BB-HB, 5´8˝/185 lbs; Dubuque; B7/26/1897, OK, D11/6/1988 Chicago, IL   **1923** RI 3 (0)   **1923** Ham 3 (0)   **1924** Ham 5 (4, WB), 6
1924 Akr 1 (1), 6   **1925** Ham 2 (2)   **1926** Can 8 (5, bb)   **1926** Ham 1 (1)   **NFL** 23 (13), 12 [4 yrs]

BUTLER, TERRY   Terry, RB, 6´1˝/200 lbs; Villanova; B8/2/1982 Syracuse, NY   **2005** NYJ 1 (0)

BUTSKO, HARRY   Harry, LB, 6´3˝/225 lbs; Maryland; 1963: Was, rnd 15/SD, rnd 27; B2/2/1941 Pottsville, PA   **1963** Was 4

BUTTLE, GREG   Gregory Ellis, LB, 6´3˝/235 lbs; Penn State; 1976: NYJ, rnd 3; B6/20/1954 Atlantic City, NJ   **1977** NYJ 13 (13, LLB)   **1978** NYJ 8 (8, lolb)   **1979** NYJ 16 (16, LLB)
1980 NYJ 14 (14, LLB)   **1981**†NYJ 15 (14, LLB)   **1982**†NYJ 7 (7, LLB)   **1983** NYJ 9 (8, LLB)   **1984** NYJ 14 (13, LLB)

| 1976 | NYJ | 14(14, LLB) | 1 | 26 | 26.0(26) | 0 | — | — | — | — | — | — | — | — | — | — | — | — | — | i | 1 | 6 | 36 |
| NFL | 9 | 110(107) | 1 | 26 | 26.0(26) | 0 | — | — | — | — | — | — | — | — | — | — | — | — | — | iS | 3 | 20 | 176 |

BUTTS, EDDIE   Edward Carmack, TB-BB-WB, /190 lbs; Cal State-Chico; B8/18/1903, deceased   **1929** ChiC 9 (5, tb)

BUTTS, MARION   Marion Stevenson, RB, 6´1˝/248 lbs; Northeastern Oklahoma A&M; Florida State; 1989: SD, rnd 7; B8/1/1966 Sylvester, GA

1989	SD	15(5, rb)	170	683	4.0(50)	9	7	21	3.0(8)	0	—	—	—	—	—	—	—	—	—	—	—	54	784
1990	SD★	14(13, RB)	265	1225	4.6(52)	8	16	117	7.3(26)	0	—	—	—	—	—	—	—	—	—	—	—	48	1364
1991	SD✧	16(8, rb)	193	834	4.3(44)	6	10	91	9.1(46)	1	—	—	—	—	—	—	—	—	—	k	—	42	930
1992	†SD	15(14, RB)	218	809	3.7(22)	4	9	73	8.1(22)	0	—	—	—	—	—	—	—	—	—	—	—	24	886
1993	SD	16(16, RB)	185	746	4.0(27)	4	15	105	7.0(23)	0	—	—	—	—	—	—	—	—	—	—	—	24	839
1994	NE	16(15, RB)	243	703	2.9(26)	8	9	54	6.0(15)	0	—	—	—	—	—	—	—	—	—	—	—	48	810
1995	Hou	12(2)	71	185	2.6(9)	4	2	10	5.0(10)	0	—	—	—	—	—	—	—	—	—	k	—	24	214
NFL	7	104(73)	1345	5185	3.9(52)	43	68	471	6.9(46)	1	—	—	—	—	—	—	—	—	—	k	—	264	5825

BUTZ, DAVE   David Roy, DT-DE, 6´7˝/291 lbs; Purdue; 1973: SL, rnd 1; B6/23/1950 Lafayette, AL   **1973** SL 12 (10, LDE)   **1974** SL 1 (1)   **1975** Was 14 (1)   **1976**†Was 14 (8, LDT)
1977 Was 12 (7, LDT)   **1978** Was 16 (16, LDT)   **1979** Was☆15 (14, LDT)   **1980** Was 16 (16, LDT)   **1981** Was 16 (16, LDT)   **1982**†Was 9 (9, LDT)   **1983**†Was★16 (16, LDT)
1984†Was☆15 (15, LDT)   **1985** Was 16 (16, LDT)   **1986**†Was 16 (16, LDT)   **1987**†Was 12 (12, LDT)   **1988** Was 16 (16, LDT)   **NFL** 216 (189) [16 yrs]

YEAR	TEAM	G(GS, POS)	RUSH	YD	AVG(LG)	TD	REC	YD	AVG(LG)	TD	PASS	COMP	PCT	YD	AVG(LG)	TD	INT	SK	YD	QBR	KPR	OTD	PTS	TAY

BUZIN, RICH Richard Lawrence, T, 6´5˝/255 lbs; Penn State; 1968: NYG, rnd 2; B1/25/1946 Youngstown, OH **1968** NYG 14 **1969** NYG 14 (RT) **1970** NYG 14 (RT) **1971** LARm 5 **1972** ChiB 2 **NFL** 49 [5 yrs]

BUZYNISKI, BERNARD Bernard, LB, 6´3˝/228 lbs; Holy Cross; B5/3/1938 Lockport, NY **1960** Buf-A 14

BYARS, KEITH Keith Alan, RB-TE, 6´1˝/245 lbs; Ohio State; 1986: Phi, rnd 1; B10/14/1963 Dayton, OH

YEAR	TEAM	G(GS, POS)	RUSH	YD	AVG(LG)	TD	REC	YD	AVG(LG)	TD	PASS	COMP	PCT	YD	AVG(LG)	TD	INT	SK	YD	QBR	KPR	OTD	PTS	TAY
1986	Phi	16(8, RB)	177	577	3.3(32)	1	11	44	4.0(17)	0	2	1	50.0	55	27.5(55)	1	0	1	7	—	k	—	6	659
1987	Phi	10(8, RB)	116	426	3.7(30)	3	21	177	8.4(30)	1	—	—	—	—	—	—	—	—	—	—	—	—	24	550
1988	†Phi	16(16, RB)	152	517	3.4(52)	6	72	705	9.8(37)	4	2	0	0.0	0	0.0	0	0	—	—	—	k	—	60	940
1989	†Phi	16(15, RB)	133	452	3.4(16)	5	68	721	10.6(60)	0	—	—	—	—	—	—	—	—	—	—	k	—	30	875
1990	†Phi☆	16(15, RB)	37	141	3.8(23)	0	81	819	10.1(54)	3	4	4	100.0	53	13.3(18)	4	0	—	—	—	—	—	18	612
1991	Phi	16(16, FB)	94	383	4.1(28)	1	62	564	9.1(37)	3	2	0	0.0	0	0.0	0	1	—	—	—	—	—	24	650
1992	†Phi	15(15, TE/fb)	41	176	4.3(23)	1	56	502	9.0(46)	2	1	0	0.0	0	0.0	0	0	—	—	—	—	—	18	447
1993	Mia✧	16(16, FB)	64	269	4.2(77)	3	61	613	10.0(27)	3	2	1	50.0	11	5.5(11)	1	0	—	—	—	—	—	36	631
1994	Mia	9(9, FB)	19	64	3.4(12)	2	49	418	8.5(34)	5	—	—	—	—	—	—	—	—	—	—	—	—	42	318
1995	†Mia	16(16, FB)	15	44	2.9(15)	1	51	362	7.1(26)	2	—	—	—	—	—	—	—	—	—	—	—	—	18	245
1996	Mia	4(4)	—	—	—	—	5	40	8.0(16)	0	—	—	—	—	—	—	—	—	—	—	—	—	0	20
1996	†NE	10(6, te)	2	2	1.0(3)	0	27	249	9.2(27)	2	—	—	—	—	—	—	—	—	—	—	—	—	14	137
1997	†NE	16(8, FB)	11	24	2.2(5)	0	20	189	9.4(51)	3	—	—	—	—	—	—	—	—	—	—	—	—	18	134
1998	†NYJ	13(9, FB)	4	34	8.5(13)	0	26	258	9.9(29)	3	—	—	—	—	—	—	—	—	—	—	—	—	18	178
NFL	13	189(161)	865	3109	3.6(77)	23	610	5661	9.3(60)	31	13	6	46.2	119	9.2(55)	6	1	1	7	—	k	—	326	6393

BYAS, RICK Richard Reese, DB, 5´9˝/180 lbs; Eastern Michigan; Wayne State (MI); B10/19/1950 Detroit, MI **1974** Atl 14 **1975** Atl 14 **1976** Atl 14 **1977** Atl 14 (RCB) **1978**†Atl 16 (RCB) **1979** Atl 16 (RCB) **1980**†Atl 15 (0) **NFL** 103 [7 yrs]

BYERS, KEN Kenneth Vernon, G, 6´1˝/240 lbs; Cincinnati; 1962: NYG, rnd 7/Bos, rnd 16; B4/6/1940 Logan, OH **1962**†NYG 14 **1963**†NYG 14 **1964** NYG 8 **1964** Min 6 (2) **1965** Min 14 **NFL** 56 (2) [4 yrs]

BYERS, SCOTT Norman Scott, DB, 5´11˝/170 lbs; Long Beach State; B7/3/1958 Bayonne, NJ **1984** SD 6 (0)

BYKOWSKI, FRANK Frank Peter, G, 6´0˝/205 lbs; Purdue; 1940: Pit, rnd 6; B3/24/1915 South Bend, IN, D4/1/1985 Bradenton, FL **1940** Pit 1 (0)

BYLER, JOSEPH Joseph Edward, T, 6´5˝/240 lbs; Nebraska; B8/25/1922 Republican City, NE, D5/5/1994 Des Moines, IA **1946** NYG 7 (0)

BYNER, EARNEST Earnest Alexander, RB, 5´10˝/215 lbs; East Carolina; 1984: Cle, rnd 10; B9/15/1962 Milledgeville, GA

YEAR	TEAM	G(GS, POS)	RUSH	YD	AVG(LG)	TD	REC	YD	AVG(LG)	TD	PASS	COMP	PCT	YD	AVG(LG)	TD	INT	SK	YD	QBR	KPR	OTD	PTS	TAY
1984	Cle	16(3)	72	426	5.9(54)	2	11	118	10.7(26)	0	—	—	—	—	—	—	—	—	—	—	k	1	18	590
1985	†Cle	16(13, RB)	244	1002	4.1(36)	8	45	460	10.2(31)	2	—	—	—	—	—	—	—	—	—	—	—	—	60	1322
1986	†Cle	7(7, rb)	94	277	2.9(37)	2	37	328	8.9(40)	2	—	—	—	—	—	—	—	—	—	—	—	—	24	471
1987	†Cle☆	12(12, RB)	105	432	4.1(21)	8	52	552	10.6(37)	2	—	—	—	—	—	—	—	—	—	—	k	—	60	785
1988	†Cle	16(16, RB)	157	576	3.7(27)	3	59	576	9.8(39)	2	—	—	—	—	—	—	—	—	—	—	—	—	30	904
1989	Was	16(13, RB/fb)	134	580	4.3(24)	7	54	458	8.5(27)	2	1	0	0.0	0	0.0	0	0	—	—	—	—	—	54	889
1990	†Was★	16(16, RB)	**297**	1219	4.1(22)	6	31	279	9.0(19)	1	2	1	50.0	31	15.5(31)	1	0	—	—	—	—	—	42	1444
1991	†Was★	16(16, RB)	274	1048	3.8(32)	5	34	308	9.1(31)	0	4	1	25.0	18	4.5(18)	1	0	—	—	—	—	—	30	1266
1992	†Was	16(16, RB)	262	998	3.8(23)	6	39	338	8.7(29)	1	3	1	33.3	41	13.7(41)	1	0	—	—	—	—	—	42	1258
1993	Was	16(3)	23	105	4.6(16)	1	27	194	7.2(20)	0	—	—	—	—	—	—	—	—	—	—	—	—	6	212
1994	†Cle	16(1)	75	219	2.9(15)	2	11	102	9.3(30)	0	—	—	—	—	—	—	—	—	—	—	—	—	12	290
1995	Cle	16(2)	115	432	3.8(23)	2	61	494	8.1(29)	2	—	—	—	—	—	—	—	—	—	—	k	—	24	732
1996	Bal	16(8, RB)	159	634	4.0(42)	4	30	270	9.0(40)	1	—	—	—	—	—	—	—	—	—	—	k	—	30	815
1997	Bal	16(6, rb)	84	313	3.7(19)	0	21	128	6.1(17)	0	—	—	—	—	—	—	—	—	—	—	k	—	2	362
NFL	14	211(132)	2095	8261	3.9(54)	56	512	4605	9.0(40)	15	10	3	30.0	90	9.0(41)	3	0	—	—	—	k	1	434	11340

BY'NOT'E, BUTLER Butler, RB, 5´9˝/190 lbs; Ohio State; 1994: Den, rnd 7; B9/29/1972 St. Louis, MO **1994** Den 9 (0) **1995** Car 7 (0) **NFL** 16 (0) [2 yrs]

BYNUM, KENNY Kenneth Bernard, RB, 5´11˝/191 lbs; South Carolina State; 1997: SD, rnd 5; B5/29/1974 Gainesville, FL **[R]**

YEAR	TEAM	G(GS, POS)	RUSH	YD	AVG(LG)	TD	REC	YD	AVG(LG)	TD	PASS	COMP	PCT	YD	AVG(LG)	TD	INT	SK	YD	QBR	KPR	OTD	PTS	TAY
1997	SD	13(0)	30	97	3.2(19)	0	2	4	2.0(3)	0	—	—	—	—	—	—	—	—	—	—	k	—	0	343
1998	SD	10(0)	11	23	2.1(14)	0	4	27	6.8(12)	0	—	—	—	—	—	—	—	—	—	—	k	—	0	97
1999	SD	16(5, rb)	92	287	3.1(25)	1	16	209	13.1(80)	2	—	—	—	—	—	—	—	—	—	—	k	—	18	638
2000	SD	14(0)	7	26	3.7(9)	0	2	13	6.5(7)	0	—	—	—	—	—	—	—	—	—	—	k	—	0	80
NFL	4	53(5)	140	433	3.1(25)	1	24	253	10.5(80)	2	—	—	—	—	—	—	—	—	—	—	k	—	18	1157

BYNUM, REGGIE Reginald Deshain, WR, 6´1˝/185 lbs; Oregon State; 1986: Buf, rnd 9; B2/10/1964 Greenville, MS

YEAR	TEAM	G(GS, POS)	RUSH	YD	AVG(LG)	TD	REC	YD	AVG(LG)	TD	PASS	COMP	PCT	YD	AVG(LG)	TD	INT	SK	YD	QBR	KPR	OTD	PTS	TAY
1987	Buf	1(1)	—	—	—	—	2	24	12.0(17)	0	—	—	—	—	—	—	—	—	—	—	—	—	0	12

BYRD, BORIS Boris Kaelin, DB, 6´0˝/210 lbs; Austin Peay State; B4/15/1962 Warren County, KY **1987** NYG 3 (0)

BYRD, BUTCH George Edward, DB, 6´0˝/211 lbs; Boston University; 1964: Buf, rnd 4; B9/20/1941 Watervliet, NY **[RI]** **1964**†Buf-A★14 (14, RCB) **1965**†Buf-A★14 (14, RCB) **1966**†Buf-A★14 (14, RCB) **1967** Buf-A 14 (14, RCB) **1968** Buf-A★14 (14, RCB) **1969** Buf-A★14 (RCB) **1970** Buf 14 (RCB) **1971** Den 14 **NFL** 112 (70) [8 yrs]

BYRD, DARRYL Darryl Terrence, LB, 6´1˝/220 lbs; Illinois; B9/3/1960 San Diego, CA **1983**†LARd 16 (0) **1984**†LARd 16 (1) **1987** LARd 3 (0) **NFL** 35 (1) [3 yrs]

BYRD, DENNIS Dennis Wayne, DE, 6´4˝/260 lbs; North Carolina State; 1968: Bos, rnd 1; B8/31/1946 Lincolnton, NC **1968** Bos-A 14 (14, LDE)

BYRD, DENNIS Dennis DeWayne, DT-DE, 6´5˝/270 lbs; Tulsa; 1989: NYJ, rnd 2; B10/5/1966 Oklahoma City, OK **1989** NYJ 16 (0) **1990** NYJ 16 (16, RDT) **1991**†NYJ 16 (16, RDT) **1992** NYJ 9 (8, lde) **NFL** 57 (40) [4 yrs]

BYRD, GILL Gill Arnette, DB, 5´11˝/195 lbs; San Jose State; 1983: SD, rnd 1; B2/20/1961 San Francisco, CA **[I]** **1983** SD 14 (12, LCB) **1984** SD 13 (13, LCB) **1985** SD 16 (16, SS) **1986** SD 15 (14, FS/rcb) **1987** SD 12 (12, RCB) **1988** SD 16 (16, RCB) **1989** SD☆16 (16, LCB) **1990** SD☆16 (16, LCB) **1991** SD★15 (15, LCB) **1992**†SD☆16 (16, LCB) **NFL** 149 (146) [10 yrs]

BYRD, ISAAC Isaac, WR, 6´1˝/188 lbs; Kansas; 1997: KC, rnd 6; B11/16/1974 St. Louis, MO

YEAR	TEAM	G(GS, POS)	RUSH	YD	AVG(LG)	TD	REC	YD	AVG(LG)	TD	PASS	COMP	PCT	YD	AVG(LG)	TD	INT	SK	YD	QBR	KPR	OTD	PTS	TAY
1997	Ten	2(0)	—	—	—	—	—	—	—	—	—	—	—	—	—	—	—	—	—	—	—	—	—	—
1998	Ten	4(3)	—	—	—	—	6	71	11.8(18)	0	—	—	—	—	—	—	—	—	—	—	—	—	0	36
1999	†Ten	12(6, wr)	—	—	—	—	14	261	18.6(65)	2	—	—	—	—	—	—	—	—	—	—	kp	—	12	125
2000	Car	15(4)	—	—	—	—	22	241	11.0(34)	2	—	—	—	—	—	—	—	—	—	—	kp	—	12	173
2001	Car	15(5, wr)	1	-2	-2.0(-2)	0	37	492	13.3(42)	1	—	—	—	—	—	—	—	—	—	—	kp	—	6	355
2002	Car	13(3)	1	0	0.0(0)	0	14	164	11.7(31)	1	—	—	—	—	—	—	—	—	—	—	kp	—	6	178
NFL	6	61(21)	2	-2	-1.0	0	93	1229	13.2(65)	6	—	—	—	—	—	—	—	—	—	—	kp	—	36	866

BYRD, ISRAEL Israel Fabian, DB, 5´11˝/184 lbs; Utah State; B2/1/1971 St. Louis, MO **1994** NO 3 (0) **1995** NO 4 (0) **NFL** 7 (0) [2 yrs]

BYRD, MAC MacArthur N., LB, 6´0˝/215 lbs; USC; B4/28/1942 Woodville, MS, D1/22/2004 Sacramento, CA **1965** LARm 2

BYRD, RICHARD Richard Ellen, DE-NT, 6´3˝/264 lbs; Southern Mississippi; 1985: Hou, rnd 2; B3/20/1962 Natchez, MS **1985** Hou 15 (0) **1986** Hou 16 (16, RDE) **1987**†Hou 12 (11, RDE) **1988**†Hou 16 (7, nt) **1989**†Hou 16 (8, RDE) **NFL** 75 (42) [5 yrs]

BYRD, SYLVESTER Sylvester Carl, TE, 6´2˝/225 lbs; Kansas; B5/1/1963 Kansas City, KS

YEAR	TEAM	G(GS, POS)	RUSH	YD	AVG(LG)	TD	REC	YD	AVG(LG)	TD	PASS	COMP	PCT	YD	AVG(LG)	TD	INT	SK	YD	QBR	KPR	OTD	PTS	TAY
1987	Atl	3(2)	—	—	—	—	7	125	17.9(33)	0	—	—	—	—	—	—	—	—	—	—	—	—	0	63

BYRDSONG, SHAWN Rodrick Shawn, DB, 5´10˝/188 lbs; Mississippi State; B10/2/1979 Longview, TX **2002** Bal 1 (0)

BYRNE, BILL William Joseph, G, 6´0˝/240 lbs; Boston College; 1962: Phi, rnd 4; B11/19/1940 New York, NY **1963** Phi 12

BYRUM, CARL Carl Edward, RB, 6´0˝/232 lbs; Mississippi Valley State; 1986: Buf, rnd 5; B6/29/1963 Olive Branch, MS

YEAR	TEAM	G(GS, POS)	RUSH	YD	AVG(LG)	TD	REC	YD	AVG(LG)	TD	PASS	COMP	PCT	YD	AVG(LG)	TD	INT	SK	YD	QBR	KPR	OTD	PTS	TAY
1986	Buf	13(3)	38	156	4.1(18)	0	13	104	8.0(17)	1	—	—	—	—	—	—	—	—	—	—	—	—	6	213
1987	Buf	13(8, FB)	66	280	4.2(30)	0	3	23	7.7(20)	0	—	—	—	—	—	—	—	—	—	—	—	—	0	292
1988	†Buf	15(1)	28	91	3.3(11)	0	2	0	0.0(3)	0	—	—	—	—	—	—	—	—	—	—	k	—	0	70
NFL	3	41(12)	132	527	4.0(30)	0	18	127	7.1(20)	1	—	—	—	—	—	—	—	—	—	—	k	—	6	575

YEAR	TEAM	G (GS, POS)	RUSH	YD	AVG(LG)	TD	REC	YD	AVG(LG)	TD	PASS COMP	PCT	YD	AVG(LG)	TD	INT	SK	YD	QBR	KPR	OTD	PTS	TAY

CABRAL, BRIAN   Kealilhaaheo Brian David, aka Brian David Kealilhaaheo, LB, 6´1˝/233 lbs; Colorado; 1978: Atl, rnd 4; B6/23/1956 Fort Benning, GA   **1979** Atl 3   **1980** GB 7 (0)
1981 ChiB 16 (4)   **1982** ChiB 8 (0)   **1983** ChiB 16 (4)   **1985**†ChiB 1 (0)   **1986** ChiB 3 (0)

| 1984 | †ChiB | 16 (0) | — | — | — | | 1 | 7 | 7.0 (7) | 0 | — | | — | — | — | — | — | — | | | | 0 | 4 |
| NFL | 8 | 70 (8) | — | — | — | | 1 | 7 | 7.0 (7) | 0 | — | | — | — | — | — | — | — | | kS | | 0 | -16 |

CABRELLI, LARRY   Lawrence Andrew, E-DB, 5´11˝/194 lbs; Colgate; B3/28/1917 Newark, NJ, D6/5/1974 Bryn Mawr, PA

1941	Phi	7 (2)	—	—	—		4	90	22.5 (50)	1	—		—	—	—	—	—	—				6	50
1942	Phi	11 (11, LE)	—	—	—		15	229	15.3 (29)	1	—		—	—	—	—	—	—				6	120
1943	P-P	10 (9, RE)	—	—	—		12	199	16.6 (49)	1	—		—	—	—	—	—	—		i	1	12	134
1944	Phi	9 (9, RE)	1	-2	-2.0 (-2)	0	14	169	12.1 (30)	1	—		—	—	—	—	—	—				6	88
1945	Phi	10 (8, RE)	—	—	—		15	140	9.3 (19)	0	—		—	—	—	—	—	—		ki		0	61
1946	Phi	8 (6, RE)	—	—	—		8	98	12.3 (38)	1	—		—	—	—	—	—	—				6	54
1947	†Phi	6 (0)	—	—	—		—	—	—		—		—	—	—	—	—	—					
NFL	7	61 (45)	1	-2	-2.0 (-2)	0	68	925	13.6 (50)	5	—		—	—	—	—	—	—		ki	1	36	506

CABRINHA, AUGIE   August Hermenglide, WB, 5´9˝/170 lbs; Dayton; B4/13/1902 Honolulu, HI, D3/8/1979 Honolulu, HI   **1927** Day 3 (1)

CADDEL, ERNIE   Ernest Wiley, WB, 6´2˝/199 lbs; Stanford; B3/12/1911 Granite, OK, D3/28/1992 Roseville, CA

1933	Por	11 (10, WB)	70	286	4.1	2	6	107	17.8	**3**	—		—	—	—	—	—	—				30	375
1934	Det	12 (12, WB)	105	528	5.0	4	9	127	14.1	1	13	5	38.5	106	8.2	1	1	—			1	36	665
1935	†Det☆	12 (10, WB)	87	450	**5.2**	**6**	10	171	17.1	1	4	4	66.7	169	28.2	2	1	—				36	**650**
1936	Det☆	11 (8, WB)	91	580	**6.4**	4	19	150	7.9	1	4	1	25.0	30	7.5 (30)	0	2	—				30	635
1937	Det☆	11 (11, WB)	76	429	**5.6**	3	9	80	8.9	0	4	0	0.0	0	0.0	0	0	—				18	499
1938	Det	7 (4)	14	38	2.7	1	1	6	6.0	0	2	2	100.0	45	22.5	0	0	—				6	74
NFL	6	64 (55)	443	2311	5.2	20	54	641	11.9 (6)	5	29	12	41.4	350	12.1 (30)	3	4	—			1	156	2897

CADE, EDDIE   Eddie Ray, DB, 6´1˝/206 lbs; Arizona State; B8/4/1973 Casa Grande, AZ   **1995** NE 10 (0)

CADE, MOSSY   Tomories, DB, 6´1˝/197 lbs; Texas; 1984: SD, rnd 1; B12/26/1961 Casa Grande, AZ   **1985** GB 14 (3)   **1986** GB 16 (16, RCB)   **NFL** 30 (19) [2 yrs]

CADIGAN, DAVE   David Patrick, G-T, 6´4˝/285 lbs; USC; 1988: NYJ, rnd 1; B4/6/1965 Needham, MA   **1988** NYJ 5 (4)   **1989** NYJ 13 (4)   **1990** NYJ 5 (5, RG)   **1991** NYJ 15 (10, LG)
1992 NYJ 15 (12, LG)   **1993** NYJ 16 (16, LG)   **1994** Cin 13 (13, LG)   **NFL** 82 (64) [7 yrs]

CADILE, JIM   James Dee, G-T, 6´4˝/240 lbs; San Jose State; 1962: Chi, rnd 4/Oak, rnd 22; B7/16/1940 San Jose, CA   **1962** ChiB 4   **1963**†ChiB 13   **1964** ChiB 14 (14, RG)
1965 ChiB 14 (14, RG)   **1966** ChiB 14 (14, RG)   **1967** ChiB 10 (RG)   **1968** ChiB 14 (RG)   **1969** ChiB 14 (RG)   **1970** ChiB 12 (RG)   **1971** ChiB 13 (RG)   **1972** ChiB 6
NFL 128 (42) [11 yrs]

CADREZ, GLENN   Glenn E., LB, 6´3˝/240 lbs; Houston; 1992: NYJ, rnd 6; B1/2/1970 El Centro, CA   **1992** NYJ 16 (0)   **1993** NYJ 16 (0)   **1994** NYJ 16 (0)   **1995** NYJ 1 (0)
1995 Den 10 (7, llb)   **1996**†Den 16 (0)   **1997**†Den 16 (0)   **1998**†Den 16 (15, MLB)   **1999** Den 16 (15, RLB)   **2000**†Den 16 (3)   **2001** KC 16 (5, lolb)   **2002** KC 12 (1)
NFL 167 (46) [11 yrs]

CADWELL, JOHN   John, G, 6´3˝/230 lbs; Oregon State; B9/16/1930 Oakland, CA   **1961** DalT-A 4

CAESAR, IVAN   Ivan Orsen, LB, 6´1˝/241 lbs; Boston College; 1991: Min, rnd 11; B1/7/1967 St. Thomas, Virgin Islands   **1991** Min 14 (2)

CAFEGO, GEORGE   George, FB-QB-HB, 5´10˝/169 lbs; Tennessee; 1940: ChiC, rnd 1; B8/30/1915 Whipple, WV, D2/9/1998 Knoxville, TN

1940	Bkn	10 (4)	41	109	2.7	0	9	105	11.7	0	17	7	41.2	105	6.2	1	2	—	—	—	P	0	139
1943	Bkn	5 (3)	19	-46	-2.4 (0)	0	—	—	—		36	17	47.2	209	5.8 (36)	0	3	—	—	—	Pkp	0	-16
1943	†Was	4 (3)	15	34	2.3 (20)	0	—	—	—		9	5	55.6	49	5.4 (0)	1	0	—	—	—	Pkp	0	123
1944	Bos	9 (5, FB)	61	31	0.5 (17)	1	2	8	4.0 (4)	0	73	35	47.9	454	6.2 (50)	3	7	—	—	—	Pkpi	6	73
1945	Bos	7 (5, QB)	19	-51	-2.7 (3)	0	2	20	10.0 (15)	0	26	13	50.0	149	5.7 (29)	0	4	—	—	—	Pkpi	6	-118
NFL	4	35 (20)	155	77	0.5 (20)	1	13	133	10.2 (15)	0	161	77	47.8	966	6.0 (50)	5	16	—	—	—	Pkpi	6	202

CAFFEY, LEE ROY   Lee Roy, LB, 6´4˝/240 lbs; Texas A&M; 1963: Phi, rnd 7/Hou, rnd 4; B6/3/1941 Thorndale, TX, D1/18/1994 Houston, TX   **1963** Phi 14 (LLB)   **1964** GB 14 (RLB)
1965†GB✧14 (RLB)   **1966**†GB☆14 (RLB)   **1967** GB 13 (RLB)   **1968** GB 14 (RLB)   **1969** GB 14 (RLB)   **1970** ChiB 14 (RLB)   **1971**†Dal 6   **1972** SD 12   **NFL** 129 [10 yrs]

CAGLE, CHRIS   Christian Keener, B, 5´10˝/174 lbs; Louisiana-Lafayette; Army; B5/1/1905 De Ridder, LA, D12/23/1942 Queens, NY

1930	NYG	4 (2)	—	—	—		—	—	—		—		—	—	—	—	—	—					
1931	NYG	14 (7, FB)	—	—	—		—	—	—		—		—	—	—	—	—	—					
1932	NYG	10 (7, FB)	73	205	2.8	1	8	135	16.9	2	7	3	42.9	68	9.7	0	1	—			1	24	297
1933	Bkn	10 (6, tb)	49	135	2.8	0	5	59	11.8	0	74	31	41.9	457	6.2	2	10	—				0	3
1934	Bkn	10 (4, TB)	22	51	2.3	0	—	—	—		60	14	23.3	224	3.7	3	7	—				0	-102
NFL	5	48 (26)	144	391	2.7	2	13	194	14.9	2	141	48	34.0	749	5.3	6	18	—			1	30	213

CAGLE, JIM   James Colquitt, DT, 6´5˝/255 lbs; Georgia; 1974: Phi, rnd 5; B1/15/1952 Jacksonville, FL   **1974** Phi 14

CAGLE, JOHN   John Link, DE, 6´3˝/260 lbs; Clemson; 1969: Bos, rnd 14; B3/26/1947 Anderson, SC   **1969** Bos-A 6 (1)

CAHILL, BILL   William Blackburn, DB, 5´11˝/180 lbs; Washington; 1973: NO, rnd 7; B5/5/1951 Bellevue, WA   **1973** Buf 5   **1974**†Buf 14   **NFL** 19 [2 yrs]

CAHILL, DAVE   David Allen, DT-DE, 6´3˝/245 lbs; Northern Arizona; B7/26/1942 Stanley, WI   **1966** Phi 14 (2)   **1967**†LARm 14   **1969** Atl 11 (RDT)   **NFL** 39 (2) [3 yrs]

CAHILL, DENNY   William Dennis, G, /225 lbs; none; deceased   **1920** Roc 2 (0)

CAHILL, RONNIE   Ronald Maurice, TB, 5´8˝/170 lbs; Holy Cross; B4/24/1915 Leominster, MA, D9/6/1992 Leominster, MA

| 1943 | ChiC | 10 (2, TB) | 62 | -11 | -0.2 (25) | 0 | — | — | — | | 109 | 50 | 45.9 | 608 | 5.6 (67) | 3 | 21 | — | | 33.1 | Pkp | 0 | -507 |

CAHOON, TINY   Ivan Wells, T, 6´2˝/235 lbs; Montana; Gonzaga; B5/22/1900 Baraboo, WI, D2/3/1973 Concord, CA   **1926** GB 11 (10, LT)   **1927** GB 8 (8, LT), 6   **1928** GB 10 (7, lt)
1929 GB 2 (2)   **NFL** 31 (27) [4 yrs]

CAIN, J.V.   James Victor, TE-WR, 6´4˝/224 lbs; Colorado; 1974: SL, rnd 1; B7/22/1951 Houston, TX, D7/22/1979 St. Charles, MO

1974	†SL	14 (3)	—	—	—		13	152	11.7 (40)	1	—		—	—	—	—	—	—		k		6	71
1975	†SL	14 (7, te)	—	—	—		12	134	11.2 (18)	1	—		—	—	—	—	—	—				6	72
1976	SL	14 (14, TE)	—	—	—		26	400	15.4 (34)	5	—		—	—	—	—	—	—				30	225
1977	SL	13 (13, TE)	—	—	—		25	328	13.1 (38)	2	—		—	—	—	—	—	—				12	174
NFL	4	55 (37)	—	—	—		76	1014	13.3 (40)	9	—		—	—	—	—	—	—		k		54	542

CAIN, JEREMY   Jeremy Robert, LB, 6´1˝/231 lbs; Massachusetts; B4/24/1980 Boynton Beach, FL   **2004** ChiB 5 (0)   **2005** ChiB 3 (0)   **NFL** 8 (0) [2 yrs]

CAIN, JIM   James Edgar, DE-E, 6´1˝/202 lbs; Alabama; 1949: ChiC, rnd 7/ChiH-A, rnd 8; B10/1/1927 Eudora, AR, D10/5/2001   **1949** ChiC 12 (0)   **1953**†Det 12 (LDE)
1954†Det 12 (RDE)   **1955** Det 12 (RDE)

| 1950 | Det | 12 (RDE) | — | — | — | | 1 | 8 | 8.0 (8) | 0 | — | | — | — | — | — | — | — | | k | 1 | 6 | -1 |
| NFL | 5 | 60 | — | — | — | | 1 | 8 | 8.0 (8) | 0 | — | | — | — | — | — | — | — | | k | 1 | 6 | -1 |

CAIN, JOE   Joseph Harrison, LB, 6´1˝/242 lbs; Stanford; Oregon Tech; 1988: Min, rnd 8; B6/11/1965 Los Angeles, CA   **1989** Sea 9 (0)   **1990** Sea 16 (5, rlb)   **1991** Sea 16 (0)
1992 Sea 16 (8, llb)   **1993** ChiB 15 (15, LLB)   **1994**†ChiB 16 (15, LLB)   **1995** ChiB 16 (16, MLB)   **1996** ChiB 16 (15, LLB)   **1997** Sea 11 (0)   **NFL** 131 (74) [9 yrs]

CAIN, LYNN   Lynn Dwight, RB, 6´1˝/205 lbs; USC; 1979: Atl, rnd 4; B10/16/1955 Los Angeles, CA

1979	Atl	10 (2)	63	295	4.7 (35)	2	15	181	12.1 (28)	0	—		—	—	—	—	—	—		k		24	460
1980	†Atl	16 (16, RB)	235	914	3.9 (37)	8	24	223	9.3 (30)	1	—		—	—	—	—	—	—				54	1111
1981	Atl	16 (16, RB)	156	542	3.5 (35)	4	55	421	7.7 (28)	2	—		—	—	—	—	—	—				36	803
1982	†Atl	9 (9, RB)	54	173	3.2 (8)	1	13	101	7.8 (17)	1	—		—	—	—	—	—	—				12	239
1983	Atl	16 (0)	19	63	3.3 (10)	1	3	24	8.0 (11)	0	—		—	—	—	—	—	—		k		6	120
1984	Atl	15 (2)	77	276	3.6 (31)	3	12	87	7.3 (18)	0	—		—	—	—	—	—	—				18	350
1985	LARm	7 (1)	11	46	4.2 (9)	0	5	24	4.8 (13)	0	—		—	—	—	—	—	—		k		0	83
NFL	7	89 (46)	615	2309	3.8 (37)	19	127	1061	8.4 (30)	6	—		—	—	—	—	—	—		k		150	3164

CAIN, PATRICK   Patrick James, C-G, 6´2˝/260 lbs; Cal Poly-Pomona; Wichita State; B10/1/1962 Denver, CO   **1987** Det 3 (2)

CALAC, PETE   Peter, B-E, 5´10˝/190 lbs; Carlisle Indian; West Virginia Wesleyan; B5/13/1892 Valley Center, CA, D1/13/1968 Canton, OH   **1920** Can 13 (8, FB)
1921 Cle 8 (8, FB), 18   **1921** Was 1 (1)   **1922** Oor 9 (9, RE), 12   **1923** Oor 10 (9, RE), 6   **1924** Buf 11 (10, FB), 12   **1925** Can 7 (7, FB)   **1926** Can 10 (7, FB)   **NFL** 69 (59), 48 [7 yrs]

YEAR	TEAM	G (GS, POS)	RUSH	YD	AVG (LG)	TD	REC	YD	AVG (LG)	TD	PASS	COMP	PCT	YD	AVG (LG)	TD	INT	SK	YD	QBR	KPR	OTD	PTS	TAY

Calahan, Jeremy Jeremy, DT, 6´3˝/295 lbs; Rice; B7/7/1983 Austin, TX **2005** SL 1 (0)

Calcagni, Ralph Ralph Cleo, T, 6´3˝/230 lbs; Cornell; Pennsylvania; 1944: Bos, rnd 31; B2/6/1922 Smithton, PA, D8/29/1948 Meadville, PA **1946** Bos 11 (5, RT) **1947**†Pit 9 (0) **NFL** 20 (5) [2 yrs]

Caldwell, Alan Alan Lorenzo, DB, 6´0˝/176 lbs; North Carolina; B5/22/1956 Winston-Salem, NC **1979** NYG 16

Caldwell, Bruce Bruce, TB-FB, 6´0˝/190 lbs; Brown; Yale; B2/8/1906 Ashton, RI, D2/15/1959 New Haven, CT **[K]** **1928** NYG 10 (6, TB), 9

Caldwell, Bryan Bryan Craig, DE, 6´4˝/248 lbs; Arizona State; 1983: Dal, rnd 3; B5/6/1960 Oakland, CA **1984** Hou 8 (0)

Caldwell, Darryl Darryl, TB-FB, 6´5˝/245 lbs; Tennessee State; B2/2/1960 Birmingham, AL **1983** Buf 14 (0)

Caldwell, David David Anthony, NT, 6´1˝/261 lbs; TCU; B2/28/1965 Bay City, TX **1987** GB 3 (3)

Caldwell, Knute Harold Paul, aka Knute Cauldwell, T, 6´1˝/210 lbs; Wabash; B1/1897 Rockville, IN, deceased **[K]** **1925** Akr 5 (5, LT), 5 **1926** Akr 7 (7, LT) **NFL** 12 (12) [2 yrs]

Caldwell, Mike Mike Isiah, LB, 6´2˝/235 lbs; Middle Tennessee State; 1993: Cle, rnd 3; B8/31/1971 Oak Ridge, TN **1993** Cle 15 (1) **1994**†Cle 16 (1) **1995** Cle 16 (6, rlb) **1996** Bal 9 (9, RILB) **1997** Arz 16 (0) **1998** Phi 16 (8, llb) **1999** Phi 14 (2) **2000**†Phi 16 (3) **2001**†Phi 16 (16, LLB) **2002** ChiB 16 (3) **2003** Car 9 (0) **NFL** 159 (49) [11 yrs]

Caldwell, Mike Michael Todd, WR, 6´2˝/200 lbs; California; B3/28/1971 Cleveland, OH **1995** SF 2 (0)

YEAR	TEAM	G (GS, POS)	RUSH	YD	AVG (LG)	TD	REC	YD	AVG (LG)	TD	PASS	COMP	PCT	YD	AVG (LG)	TD	INT	SK	YD	QBR	KPR	OTD	PTS	TAY
1996	†SF	1(0)	—	—	—	—	2	9	4.5(8)	0	—	—	—	—	—	—	—	—	—	—		—	0	5
NFL	2	3(0)	—	—	—	—	2	9	4.5(8)	0	—	—	—	—	—	—	—	—	—	—	k	—	0	15

Caldwell, Ravin Ravin, LB, 6´3˝/233 lbs; Arkansas; 1986: Was, rnd 5; B8/4/1963 Port Arthur, TX **1987**†Was 12 (0) **1988** Was 16 (1) **1989** Was 15 (13, LLB) **1990**†Was 16 (0) **1991**†Was 16 (0) **1992** Was 4 (0) **1993**†SF 0 (0) **NFL** 79 (14) [7 yrs]

Caldwell, Reche Donald Reche, WR, 5´11˝/194 lbs; Florida; 2002: SD, rnd 2; B3/28/1979 Tampa, FL

YEAR	TEAM	G (GS, POS)	RUSH	YD	AVG (LG)	TD	REC	YD	AVG (LG)	TD	PASS	COMP	PCT	YD	AVG (LG)	TD	INT	SK	YD	QBR	KPR	OTD	PTS	TAY
2002	SD	16(2)	2	9	4.5(6)	0	22	208	9.5(26)	3	1	1	100.0	20	20.0(20)	0	0	—	—	—	kp	—	20	211
2003	SD	9(4)	5	39	7.8(14)	0	8	80	10.0(15)	0	—	—	—	—	—	—	—	—	—	—	—	—	0	79
2004	SD	6(6, wr)	4	45	11.3(20)	0	18	310	17.2(58)	3	—	—	—	—	—	—	—	—	—	—	—	—	18	215
2005	SD	16(2)	2	10	5.0(7)	0	28	352	12.6(43)	1	—	—	—	—	—	—	—	—	—	—	k	—	6	245
NFL	4	47(14)	13	103	7.9(20)	0	76	950	12.5(58)	7	1	1	100.0	20	20.0(20)	0	0	—	—	—	kp	—	44	750

Caldwell, Scott Craig Scott, RB, 5´10˝/196 lbs; Texas-Arlington; 1985: Det, rnd 8; B2/8/1963 Dallas, TX

YEAR	TEAM	G (GS, POS)	RUSH	YD	AVG (LG)	TD	REC	YD	AVG (LG)	TD	PASS	COMP	PCT	YD	AVG (LG)	TD	INT	SK	YD	QBR	KPR	OTD	PTS	TAY
1987	Den	3(1)	16	53	3.3(7)	0	4	34	8.5(14)	0	—	—	—	—	—	—	—	—	—	—	—	—	0	70

Caldwell, Tony Anthony L., LB, 6´1˝/225 lbs; Washington; 1983: LARd, rnd 3; B4/1/1961 Los Angeles, CA **1983**†LARd 16 (0) **1984**†LARd 16 (0) **1985** LARd 3 (0) **1987** Sea 1 (1) **NFL** 36 (1) [4 yrs]

Caleb, Jamie Jamie, HB-FB, 6´1˝/210 lbs; Grambling State; 1959: Cle, rnd 16; B10/29/1936 Calhoun, LA

YEAR	TEAM	G (GS, POS)	RUSH	YD	AVG (LG)	TD	REC	YD	AVG (LG)	TD	PASS	COMP	PCT	YD	AVG (LG)	TD	INT	SK	YD	QBR	KPR	OTD	PTS	TAY
1960	Cle	12	8	60	7.5(30)	1	5	-18	-3.6(2)	0	—	—	—	—	—	—	—	—	—	—	k	—	6	76
1961	Min	10	3	11	3.7(4)	0	2	-8	-4.0(5)	0	1	0	0.0	0	0.0	0	0	—	—	—	kp	—	0	184
1965	Cle	5	—	—	—	—	—	—	—	—	—	—	—	—	—	—	—	—	—	—	—	—	—	—
NFL	3	27	11	71	6.5(30)	1	7	-26	-3.7(5)	0	1	0	0.0	0	0.0	0	0	—	—	—	kp	—	6	260

Calhoun, Don Donald Clevester, RB, 6´0˝/206 lbs; Kansas State; 1974: Buf, rnd 10; B4/29/1952 Muskogee, OK

YEAR	TEAM	G (GS, POS)	RUSH	YD	AVG (LG)	TD	REC	YD	AVG (LG)	TD	PASS	COMP	PCT	YD	AVG (LG)	TD	INT	SK	YD	QBR	KPR	OTD	PTS	TAY
1974	†Buf	14(1)	21	88	4.2(15)	0	2	10	5.0(7)	0	—	—	—	—	—	—	—	—	—	—	k	—	0	93
1975	Buf	6	19	80	4.2(11)	0	—	—	—	—	—	—	—	—	—	—	—	—	—	—	—	—	0	80
1975	NE	5(1)	23	104	4.5(38)	1	5	111	22.2(62)	1	—	—	—	—	—	—	—	—	—	—	k	—	12	177
1976	†NE	14(3)	129	721	**5.6(54)**	1	12	56	4.7(12)	0	—	—	—	—	—	—	—	—	—	—	k	—	6	807
1977	NE	14(14, RB)	198	727	3.7(25)	4	13	152	11.7(47)	0	—	—	—	—	—	—	—	—	—	—	—	—	24	843
1978	NE	14(2)	76	391	5.1(73)	1	3	29	9.7(15)	0	—	—	—	—	—	—	—	—	—	—	—	—	6	416
1979	NE	16(6, fb)	137	456	3.3(29)	5	15	66	4.4(14)	1	—	—	—	—	—	—	—	—	—	—	—	—	36	544
1980	NE	16(16, FB)	200	787	3.9(22)	9	27	129	4.8(12)	0	—	—	—	—	—	—	—	—	—	—	—	—	54	942
1981	NE	14(7, fb)	57	205	3.6(33)	2	7	71	10.1(20)	0	—	—	—	—	—	—	—	—	—	—	k	—	12	269
1982	Phi	1(0)	—	—	—	—	—	—	—	—	—	—	—	—	—	—	—	—	—	—	—	—	—	—
NFL	9	114(50)	860	3559	4.1(73)	23	84	624	7.4(62)	2	—	—	—	—	—	—	—	—	—	—	k	—	150	4169

Calhoun, Eric Eric V., T-G, 5´9˝/210 lbs; Denison; B8/1/1900, D9/23/1974 South Euclid, OH **1926** Day 6 (6, LT)

Calhoun, Mike Michael Edward, DT-DE, 6´4˝/260 lbs; Notre Dame; 1979: Dal, rnd 10; B5/6/1957 Youngstown, OH **1980** TB 3 (0) **1980** SF 4 (0) **NFL** 7 (0) [1 yr]

Calhoun, Rick James Rickey, RB, 5´7˝/190 lbs; Cal State-Fullerton; 1987: Det, rnd 9; B5/30/1963 Montgomery, AL

YEAR	TEAM	G (GS, POS)	RUSH	YD	AVG (LG)	TD	REC	YD	AVG (LG)	TD	PASS	COMP	PCT	YD	AVG (LG)	TD	INT	SK	YD	QBR	KPR	OTD	PTS	TAY
1987	LARd	3(0)	7	36	5.1(18)	0	1	17	17.0(17)	0	—	—	—	—	—	—	—	—	—	—	kp	1	6	189

Calicchio, Lonny Lawrence Robert, P, 6´3˝/249 lbs; Mississippi; B10/24/1972 Plantation, FL **1997** Phi 2 (0)

Calico, Tyrone Tyrone Bernard, WR, 6´4˝/223 lbs; Middle Tennessee State; 2003: Ten, rnd 2; B11/9/1980 Millington, TN

YEAR	TEAM	G (GS, POS)	RUSH	YD	AVG (LG)	TD	REC	YD	AVG (LG)	TD	PASS	COMP	PCT	YD	AVG (LG)	TD	INT	SK	YD	QBR	KPR	OTD	PTS	TAY
2003	†Ten	14(2)	1	5	5.0(5)	0	18	297	16.5(45)	4	—	—	—	—	—	—	—	—	—	—	—	—	26	174
2004	Ten	1(0)	—	—	—	—	2	13	6.5(9)	0	—	—	—	—	—	—	—	—	—	—	—	—	0	7
2005	Ten	12(6, wr)	—	—	—	—	22	191	8.7(18)	0	—	—	—	—	—	—	—	—	—	—	—	—	0	96
NFL	3	27(8)	1	5	5.0(5)	0	42	501	11.9(45)	4	—	—	—	—	—	—	—	—	—	—	—	—	26	276

Caliguire, Dean Dean Patrick, G-C, 6´2˝/280 lbs; Pittsburgh; 1990: SF, rnd 4; B3/2/1967 Pittsburgh, PA **1991** SF 2 (0) **1991** Pit 7 (0) **NFL** 9 (0) [1 yr]

Call, Jack John Arthur, HB, 6´1˝/200 lbs; Colgate; 1957: Bal, rnd 13; B7/30/1935 Cortland, NY

YEAR	TEAM	G (GS, POS)	RUSH	YD	AVG (LG)	TD	REC	YD	AVG (LG)	TD	PASS	COMP	PCT	YD	AVG (LG)	TD	INT	SK	YD	QBR	KPR	OTD	PTS	TAY
1957	Bal	12	33	145	4.4(24)	0	4	18	4.5(8)	0	—	—	—	—	—	—	—	—	—	—	k	—	0	273
1958	†Bal	12	37	154	4.2(35)	0	4	28	7.0(12)	0	—	—	—	—	—	—	—	—	—	—	k	—	0	186
1959	Pit	4	3	9	3.0(4)	0	1	0	0.0(0)	0	—	—	—	—	—	—	—	—	—	—	k	—	0	65
NFL	3	28	73	308	4.2(35)	0	9	46	5.1(12)	0	—	—	—	—	—	—	—	—	—	—	k	—	0	524

Call, Kevin Kevin Bradley, T, 6´7˝/302 lbs; Colorado State; 1984: Ind, rnd 5; B11/13/1961 Boulder, CO **1984** Ind 15 (0) **1985** Ind 14 (0) **1986** Ind 16 (16, RT) **1987**†Ind 12 (12, RT) **1988** Ind 8 (4) **1989** Ind 15 (15, RT) **1990** Ind 8 (8, rt) **1991** Ind 16 (16, RT) **1992** Ind 16 (16, RT) **1993** Ind 10 (0) **NFL** 130 (87) [10 yrs]

Callahan, Bill William Timothy, DB, 6´0˝/200 lbs; Pittsburgh; 1986: Pit, rnd 4; B4/11/1964 Natrona Heights, PA **1987** Buf 1 (1)

Callahan, Bob Robert Francis, C-LB, 6´0˝/205 lbs; Missouri; Michigan; 1947: ChiC, rnd 31; B9/26/1923 St. Louis, MO **1948** Buf-A 7 (0)

Callahan, Dan Dan Earl, G, 6´0˝/230 lbs; Wooster; B7/11/1938 Akron, OH **1960** NYT-A 9

Callahan, Jim James Ross, TB, 5´11˝/185 lbs; Texas Tech; Texas; 1944: Bkn, rnd 2; B12/19/1920 El Paso, TX, D3/27/1978 El Paso, TX

YEAR	TEAM	G (GS, POS)	RUSH	YD	AVG (LG)	TD	REC	YD	AVG (LG)	TD	PASS	COMP	PCT	YD	AVG (LG)	TD	INT	SK	YD	QBR	KPR	OTD	PTS	TAY
1946	Det	9(7, tb)	52	86	1.7(40)	2	—	—	—	—	67	22	32.8	359	5.4(56)	2	7	—	—	—	Pkpi	—	12	109

Calland, Lee Arthur Lee, DB, 6´0˝/190 lbs; Louisville; B9/14/1941 Louisville, KY **1963** Min 14 (14, LCB) **1964** Min 1 **1965** Min 5 **1966** Atl 14 (14, RCB) **1967** Atl 14 (RCB) **1968** Atl 7 **1969** ChiB 4 **1969** Pit 8 **1970** Pit 14 (RCB) **1971** Pit 13 (rcb) **1972** Pit 7 **NFL** 101 (28) [10 yrs]

Callicutt, Ken Kenneth Byron, RB, 6´0˝/190 lbs; Clemson; B8/20/1955 Chester, SC

YEAR	TEAM	G (GS, POS)	RUSH	YD	AVG (LG)	TD	REC	YD	AVG (LG)	TD	PASS	COMP	PCT	YD	AVG (LG)	TD	INT	SK	YD	QBR	KPR	OTD	PTS	TAY
1978	Det	13	—	—	—	—	—	—	—	—	—	—	—	—	—	—	—	—	—	—	k	—	0	-18
1979	Det	16	3	6	2.0(10)	0	2	16	8.0(11)	0	—	—	—	—	—	—	—	—	—	—	kp	—	0	65
1980	Det	13(0)	—	—	—	—	1	19	19.0(19)	0	—	—	—	—	—	—	—	—	—	—	kp	—	0	66
1981	Det	16(0)	—	—	—	—	2	24	12.0(16)	0	—	—	—	—	—	—	—	—	—	—	k	—	0	5
1982	Det	8(0)	—	—	—	—	—	—	—	—	—	—	—	—	—	—	—	—	—	—	—	—	—	—
NFL	5	66	3	6	2.0(10)	0	5	59	11.8(19)	0	—	—	—	—	—	—	—	—	—	—	kp	—	0	118

Calligaro, Len Leonard John, BB-LB, 5´11˝/190 lbs; Wisconsin; B6/4/1921 Hurley, WI

YEAR	TEAM	G (GS, POS)	RUSH	YD	AVG (LG)	TD	REC	YD	AVG (LG)	TD	PASS	COMP	PCT	YD	AVG (LG)	TD	INT	SK	YD	QBR	KPR	OTD	PTS	TAY
1944	†NYG	10(6, BB)	3	4	1.3(3)	1	2	11	5.5(10)	0	—	—	—	—	—	—	—	—	—	—	—	—	6	20

Callihan, Bill William Earl, B-T, 6´3˝/217 lbs; Nebraska; 1939: Det, rnd 9; B5/15/1916 Paxton, NE, D8/23/1986 Columbus, NE **[K]**

YEAR	TEAM	G (GS, POS)	RUSH	YD	AVG (LG)	TD	REC	YD	AVG (LG)	TD	PASS	COMP	PCT	YD	AVG (LG)	TD	INT	SK	YD	QBR	KPR	OTD	PTS	TAY
1940	Det	10(1)	—	—	—	—	4	42	10.5	0	—	—	—	—	—	—	—	—	—	—	i	—	0	29
1941	Det	11(6, BB)	—	—	—	—	4	34	8.5(22)	0	—	—	—	—	—	—	—	—	—	—	—	—	0	17
1942	Det	11(10, BB)	—	—	—	—	4	48	12.0(17)	0	1	0	0.0	0	0.0	0	1	—	—	—	Pi	—	0	-2
1943	Det	10(4, bb)	5	17	3.4(6)	1	8	108	13.5(40)	3	2	0	0.0	0	0.0	0	1	—	—	—	pi	—	24	53

YEAR	TEAM	G (GS, POS)	RUSH	YD	AVG (LG)	TD	REC	YD	AVG (LG)	TD	PASS	COMP	PCT	YD	AVG (LG)	TD	INT	SK	YD	QBR	KPR	OTD	PTS	TAY
1944	Det	10 (10, BB)	1	3	3.0 (3)	0	8	67	8.4 (21)	0	—	—	—	—	—	—	—	—	—	—	k	—	0	38
1945	Det	10 (10, LT)	27	85	3.1 (16)	0	4	88	22.0 (29)	1	5	3	60.0	34	6.8 (15)	1	2	—	—	—	Ki	—	31	74
NFL	6	62 (41)	33	105	3.2 (16)	1	32	387	12.1 (40)	4	8	3	37.5	34	4.3 (15)	1	4	—	—	—	KPkpi	—	55	209

CALLOWAY, CHRIS Christopher Fitzpatrick, WR, 5´10˝/188 lbs; Michigan; 1990: Pit, rnd 4; B3/29/1968 Chicago, IL

YEAR	TEAM	G (GS, POS)	RUSH	YD	AVG (LG)	TD	REC	YD	AVG (LG)	TD	PASS	COMP	PCT	YD	AVG (LG)	TD	INT	SK	YD	QBR	KPR	OTD	PTS	TAY
1990	Pit	16 (2)	—	—	—	—	10	124	12.4 (20)	1	—	—	—	—	—	—	—	—	—	—	—	—	6	67
1991	Pit	12 (0)	—	—	—	—	15	254	16.9 (33)	1	—	—	—	—	—	—	—	—	—	—	—	—	6	132
1992	NYG	16 (1)	—	—	—	—	27	335	12.4 (28)	1	—	—	—	—	—	—	—	—	—	—	k	—	6	172
1993	†NYG	16 (9, WR)	—	—	—	—	35	513	14.7 (47)	3	—	—	—	—	—	—	—	—	—	—	k	—	18	271
1994	NYG	16 (14, WR)	8	77	9.6 (20)	0	43	666	15.5 (51)	2	—	—	—	—	—	—	—	—	—	—	—	—	12	420
1995	NYG	16 (15, WR)	2	-9	-4.5 (-3)	0	56	796	14.2 (49)	3	—	—	—	—	—	—	—	—	—	—	—	—	18	404
1996	NYG	16 (15, WR)	1	2	2.0 (2)	0	53	739	13.9 (36)	4	—	—	—	—	—	—	—	—	—	—	—	—	24	392
1997	†NYG	16 (16, WR)	1	-1	-1.0 (-1)	0	58	849	14.6 (68)	8	—	—	—	—	—	—	—	—	—	—	—	—	48	464
1998	NYG	16 (16, WR)	—	—	—	—	62	812	13.1 (36)	6	—	—	—	—	—	—	—	—	—	—	—	—	36	436
1999	Atl	11 (6, wr)	—	—	—	—	22	314	14.3 (33)	1	—	—	—	—	—	—	—	—	—	—	—	—	6	162
2000	NE	7 (2)	—	—	—	—	5	95	19.0 (28)	0	—	—	—	—	—	—	—	—	—	—	—	—	0	48
NFL	11	158 (96)	12	69	5.8 (20)	0	386	5497	14.2 (68)	30	—	—	—	—	—	—	—	—	—	—	k	—	180	2966

CALLOWAY, ERNIE Ernest Henry, DT-DE, 6´6˝/255 lbs; Texas Southern; 1969: Phi, rnd 2; B1/1/1948 Orlando, FL **1969** Phi 14 (RDT) **1970** Phi 14 (LDE) **1971** Phi 14 (8, RDT) **1972** Phi 5 **NFL** 47 (8) [4 yrs]

CALMUS, ROCKY Rocky Ayres, LB, 6´3˝/238 lbs; Oklahoma; 2002: Ten, rnd 3; B8/1/1979 Tulsa, OK **2002** Ten 13 (1) **2003** Ten 10 (9, MLB) **2004** Ten 4 (3) **NFL** 27 (13) [3 yrs]

CALVELLI, TONY Anthony T., C-G, 5´10˝/189 lbs; Stanford; 1939: Det, rnd 11; B7/16/1915 Stockton, CA, deceased **1939** Det 7 (0) **1940** Det 11 (6, C) **NFL** 18 (6) [2 yrs]

1947 SF-A 13 (1)

CALVIN, TOM Thomas Marvin, HB, 6´0˝/200 lbs; Alabama; 1951: Pit, rnd 25; B6/13/1926 Athens, AL

YEAR	TEAM	G (GS, POS)	RUSH	YD	AVG (LG)	TD	REC	YD	AVG (LG)	TD	PASS	COMP	PCT	YD	AVG (LG)	TD	INT	SK	YD	QBR	KPR	OTD	PTS	TAY
1952	Pit	12	7	14	2.0 (11)	0	2	4	2.0 (6)	0	—	—	—	—	—	—	—	—	—	—	kp	—	0	63
1953	Pit	10	13	65	5.0 (15)	0	4	28	7.0 (16)	0	—	—	—	—	—	—	—	—	—	—	—	—	0	79
1954	Pit	6	12	57	4.8 (8)	0	1	19	19.0 (19)	0	—	—	—	—	—	—	—	—	—	—	k	—	0	67
1955	Pit	2	—	—	—	—	—	—	—	—	—	—	—	—	—	—	—	—	—	—	—	—	—	—
NFL	4	30	32	136	4.3 (15)	0	7	51	7.3 (19)	0	—	—	—	—	—	—	—	—	—	—	kp	—	0	209

CAMARILLO, RICH Richard Jon, P, 5´11˝/202 lbs; Washington; B11/29/1959 Whittier, CA **[KP]** **1981** NE 9 (0) **1982**†NE☆9 (0) **1983** NE★16 (0) **1984** NE 7 (0) **1985**†NE 16 (0) **1986**†NE 16 (0) **1988** LARm 9 (0) **1992** Phx★15 (0) **1996** Oak 1 (0)

YEAR	TEAM	G (GS, POS)	RUSH	YD	AVG (LG)	TD	REC	YD	AVG (LG)	TD	PASS	COMP	PCT	YD	AVG (LG)	TD	INT	SK	YD	QBR	KPR	OTD	PTS	TAY
1987	NE	12 (0)	1	0	0.0 (0)	0	—	—	—	—	—	—	—	—	—	—	—	—	—	—	P	—	0	0
1989	Phx★	15 (0)	—	—	—	—	—	—	—	—	1	1	100.0	0	0.0 (0)	0	0	—	—	—	P	—	0	0
1990	Phx☆	16 (0)	1	-11	-11.0 (-11)	0	—	—	—	—	—	—	—	—	—	—	—	—	—	—	P	—	0	-11
1991	Phx★	16 (0)	—	—	—	—	—	—	—	—	1	0	0.0	0	0.0	0	0	—	—	—	P	—	0	0
1993	Phx★	16 (0)	1	0	0.0 (0)	0	—	—	—	—	—	—	—	—	—	—	—	—	—	—	P	—	0	0
1994	Hou	16 (0)	—	—	—	—	—	—	—	—	1	0	0.0	0	0.0	0	0	—	—	—	P	—	0	0
1995	Hou	16 (0)	—	—	—	—	—	—	—	—	1	0	0.0	0	0.0	0	0	—	—	—	P	—	0	0
NFL	16	205 (0)	3	-11	-3.7	0	—	—	—	—	4	1	25.0	0	0.0	0	0	—	—	—	KP	—	0	-11

CAMBAL, DENNIS Dennis Hayden, TE, 6´2˝/225 lbs; William & Mary; 1972: Oak, rnd 14; B1/27/1949 Waltham, MA **1973** NYJ 8

CAMERON, GLENN Glenn Scott, LB, 6´2˝/225 lbs; Florida; 1975: Cin, rnd 1; B2/21/1953 Miami, FL **1975**†Cin 14 **1976** Cin 14 **1977** Cin 14 **1978** Cin 15 (LLB) **1979** Cin 15 **1980** Cin 14 (14, RILB) **1981**†Cin 16 (16, RILB) **1982**†Cin 9 (9, RILB) **1983** Cin 16 (16, RILB) **1984** Cin 16 (14, RILB) **1985** Cin 16 (15, RILB) **NFL** 159 (84) [11 yrs]

CAMERON, JACK Jack Lyndon, WR, 6´0˝/182 lbs; Winston-Salem State; B11/5/1961 Durham, NC

YEAR	TEAM	G (GS, POS)	RUSH	YD	AVG (LG)	TD	REC	YD	AVG (LG)	TD	PASS	COMP	PCT	YD	AVG (LG)	TD	INT	SK	YD	QBR	KPR	OTD	PTS	TAY
1984	†ChiB	16 (1)	—	—	—	—	1	13	13.0 (13)	0	—	—	—	—	—	—	—	—	—	—	k	—	0	102

CAMERON, JOHN John James, G, /175 lbs; Kalamazoo; Central Michigan; B7/13/1900, deceased **1926** Det 8 (2)

CAMERON, PAUL Paul Leslie, DB, 6´0˝/185 lbs; UCLA; 1954: Pit, rnd 8; B10/4/1932 Burbank, CA **1954** Pit 12 (DB)

CAMP, JIM James Vernon, QB, 6´0˝/162 lbs; Randolph-Macon; North Carolina; 1948: Bkn-A, rnd 12/ChiC, rnd 8; B8/8/1924 Union, SC, D1/31/2002 Durham, NC

YEAR	TEAM	G (GS, POS)	RUSH	YD	AVG (LG)	TD	REC	YD	AVG (LG)	TD	PASS	COMP	PCT	YD	AVG (LG)	TD	INT	SK	YD	QBR	KPR	OTD	PTS	TAY
1948	Bkn-A	12 (3)	8	43	5.4	0	1	43	43.0 (43)	0	—	—	—	—	—	—	—	—	—	—	ki	—	0	126

CAMP, REGGIE Reginald Louis, DE, 6´4˝/274 lbs; California; 1983: Cle, rnd 3; B2/28/1961 San Francisco, CA **1983** Cle 16 (16, LDE) **1984** Cle 16 (16, LDE) **1985**†Cle 16 (16, LDE) **1986**†Cle 16 (16, LDE) **1987**†Cle 6 (5, lde) **1988** Atl 4 (0) **NFL** 74 (69) [6 yrs]

CAMPANA, AL Albert Louis, DB-HB, 5´11˝/180 lbs; Youngstown State; B2/25/1926 Hubbard, OH

YEAR	TEAM	G (GS, POS)	RUSH	YD	AVG (LG)	TD	REC	YD	AVG (LG)	TD	PASS	COMP	PCT	YD	AVG (LG)	TD	INT	SK	YD	QBR	KPR	OTD	PTS	TAY
1950	†ChiB	9	45	134	3.0 (23)	1	5	58	11.6 (30)	0	—	—	—	—	—	—	—	—	—	—	ki	—	6	162
1951	ChiB	2	2	3	1.5 (3)	0	—	—	—	—	—	—	—	—	—	—	—	—	—	—	—	—	0	3
1952	ChiB	12 (DB)	9	14	1.6 (6)	0	1	3	3.0 (3)	0	—	—	—	—	—	—	—	—	—	—	—	—	0	16
1953	ChiC	8	2	-5	-2.5 (0)	0	—	—	—	—	—	—	—	—	—	—	—	—	—	—	k	—	0	6
NFL	4	31	58	146	2.5 (23)	1	6	61	10.2 (30)	0	—	—	—	—	—	—	—	—	—	—	ki	—	6	187

CAMPANELLA, JOE Joseph Arthur, LB-DT-T, 6´2˝/242 lbs; Ohio State; 1952: Cle, rnd 3; B9/3/1930 Cleveland, OH, D2/15/1967 Baltimore, MD **1952** DalT 12 (2, RDT) **1953** Bal 12 **1954** Bal 12 (MLB) **1955** Bal 11 (MLB) **1956** Bal 10 (MLB) **1957** Bal 11 **NFL** 68 (2) [6 yrs]

CAMPBELL, ARNOLD Arnold Rene, DE, 6´3˝/260 lbs; Alcorn State; B11/13/1962 Charleston, MS **1987** Buf 3 (0)

CAMPBELL, BILL William Roscoe, T-LB-C-DB, 6´0˝/195 lbs; Oklahoma; 1943: ChiC, rnd 17; B8/6/1920 Pawhuska, OK, D10/1974 **1945** ChiC 6 (2) **1946** ChiC 11 (7, rt) **1947**†ChiC 4 (1) **1948** ChiC 7 (2) **1949** ChiC 6 (0) **1949** NYB 4 (0) **NFL** 38 (12) [5 yrs]

CAMPBELL, BOB Robert Thomas, WR, 6´0˝/195 lbs; Penn State; 1969: Pit, rnd 4; B4/18/1947 Johnson City, NY

YEAR	TEAM	G (GS, POS)	RUSH	YD	AVG (LG)	TD	REC	YD	AVG (LG)	TD	PASS	COMP	PCT	YD	AVG (LG)	TD	INT	SK	YD	QBR	KPR	OTD	PTS	TAY
1969	Pit	14	1	5	5.0 (5)	0	1	32	32.0 (32)	0	—	—	—	—	—	—	—	—	—	—	kp	—	0	146

CAMPBELL, CARTER Carter Bradford, DE-LB, 6´4˝/240 lbs; Weber State; 1970: SF, rnd 8; B9/29/1947 Mobile, AL **1970** SF 1 **1971** Den 14 (2) **1972** NYG 14 **1973** NYG 14 (LDE) **NFL** 43 (2) [4 yrs]

CAMPBELL, DANIEL Daniel Allen, TE, 6´5˝/263 lbs; Texas A&M; 1999: NYG, rnd 3; B4/13/1976 Clifton, TX

YEAR	TEAM	G (GS, POS)	RUSH	YD	AVG (LG)	TD	REC	YD	AVG (LG)	TD	PASS	COMP	PCT	YD	AVG (LG)	TD	INT	SK	YD	QBR	KPR	OTD	PTS	TAY
1999	NYG	12 (1)	—	—	—	—	—	—	—	—	—	—	—	—	—	—	—	—	—	—	—	—	—	—
2000	†NYG	16 (5, te)	—	—	—	—	8	46	5.8 (13)	3	—	—	—	—	—	—	—	—	—	—	—	—	18	38
2001	NYG	16 (13, TE)	—	—	—	—	13	148	11.4 (25)	1	—	—	—	—	—	—	—	—	—	—	k	—	6	57
2002	†NYG	16 (16, TE)	—	—	—	—	22	175	8.0 (27)	1	—	—	—	—	—	—	—	—	—	—	k	—	6	69
2003	†Dal	16 (16, TE)	—	—	—	—	20	195	9.8 (23)	1	—	—	—	—	—	—	—	—	—	—	—	—	6	103
2004	Dal	3 (2)	—	—	—	—	2	16	8.0 (9)	0	—	—	—	—	—	—	—	—	—	—	—	—	0	8
2005	Dal	16 (12, TE)	—	—	—	—	3	24	8.0 (18)	1	—	—	—	—	—	—	—	—	—	—	k	—	6	16
NFL	7	95 (65)	—	—	—	—	68	604	8.9 (27)	7	—	—	—	—	—	—	—	—	—	—	k	—	42	290

CAMPBELL, DICK Raymond Richard, LB, 6´1˝/227 lbs; Marquette; 1958: Pit, rnd 10; B7/17/1935 Green Bay, WI **1958** Pit 12 **1959** Pit 12 **1960** Pit 12 (MLB) **NFL** 36 [3 yrs]

CAMPBELL, DON Donald C., T, 6´0˝/225 lbs; Carnegie Mellon; B11/25/1916, D9/1/1991 Philadelphia, PA **1939** Pit 11 (6, LT) **1940** Pit 11 (6, LT) **NFL** 22 (12) [2 yrs]

CAMPBELL, EARL Earl Christian 'Tyler Rose', RB, 5´11˝/232 lbs; Texas; 1978: Hou, rnd 1; B3/29/1955 Tyler, TX; HOF 1991

YEAR	TEAM	G (GS, POS)	RUSH	YD	AVG (LG)	TD	REC	YD	AVG (LG)	TD	PASS	COMP	PCT	YD	AVG (LG)	TD	INT	SK	YD	QBR	KPR	OTD	PTS	TAY
1978	†Hou★	15 (14, RB)	302	**1450**	4.8 (81)	13	12	48	4.0 (20)	0	—	—	—	—	—	—	—	—	—	—	—	—	78	**1604**
1979	†Hou★	16 (16, RB)	**368**	**1697**	4.6 (61)	**19**	16	94	5.9 (46)	0	—	—	—	—	—	—	—	—	—	—	—	—	114	**1934**
1980	†Hou★	15 (15, RB)	**373**	**1934**	**5.2 (55)**	**13**	11	47	4.3 (10)	0	2	1	50.0	57	28.5 (57)	1	0	—	—	—	—	—	78	**2121**
1981	Hou★	16 (16, RB)	**361**	**1376**	3.8 (43)	10	36	156	4.3 (17)	0	—	—	—	—	—	—	—	—	—	—	—	—	60	1554
1982	Hou	9 (9, RB)	157	538	3.4 (22)	2	18	130	7.2 (46)	0	1	0	0.0	0	0.0	0	1	—	—	—	—	—	12	583
1983	Hou✧	14 (14, RB)	322	1301	4.0 (42)	12	19	216	11.4 (66)	0	—	—	—	—	—	—	—	—	—	—	—	—	72	1529
1984	Hou	6 (6, rb)	96	278	2.9 (22)	4	3	27	9.0 (15)	0	—	—	—	—	—	—	—	—	—	—	—	—	24	332
1984	NO	8 (0)	50	190	3.8 (19)	0	—	—	—	—	—	—	—	—	—	—	—	—	—	—	—	—	0	190
1985	NO	16 (13, RB)	158	643	4.1 (45)	1	6	88	14.7 (39)	0	—	—	—	—	—	—	—	—	—	—	—	—	6	697
NFL	8	115 (103)	2187	9407	4.3 (81)	74	121	806	6.7 (66)	0	3	1	33.3	57	19.0 (57)	1	1	—	—	—	—	—	444	10544

YEAR	TEAM	G (GS, POS)	RUSH	YD	AVG (LG)	TD	REC	YD	AVG (LG)	TD	PASS	COMP	PCT	YD	AVG (LG)	TD	INT	SK	YD	QBR	KPR	OTD	PTS	TAY

CAMPBELL, GARY Gary Kalani, LB, 6´1˝/218 lbs; Colorado; 1976: Pit, rnd 10; B3/4/1952 Honolulu, HI **1977**†ChiB 14 (2) **1978** ChiB 16 (16, RLB) **1979**†ChiB 16 (16, RLB) **1980** ChiB 16 (16, RLB) **1981** ChiB 16 (16, RLB) **1982** ChiB 9 (9, RLB) **1983** ChiB 6 (4) **NFL** 93 (79) [7 yrs]

CAMPBELL, GLENN Glenn Rex, E, 5´11˝/199 lbs; Emporia State; B4/20/1904 Thayer, KS, D9/16/1973 Topeka, KS

YEAR	TEAM	G (GS, POS)	RUSH	YD	AVG (LG)	TD	REC	YD	AVG (LG)	TD	PASS	COMP	PCT	YD	AVG (LG)	TD	INT	SK	YD	QBR	KPR	OTD	PTS	TAY
1929	NYG	15 (6, re)	—	—	—	—	—	—	—	—	—	—	—	—	—	—	—	—	—	—	—	—	—	—
1930	NYG	17 (16, RE)	—	—	—	—	—	—	—	—	—	—	—	—	—	—	—	—	—	—	—	—	—	—
1931	NYG	14 (4)	—	—	—	—	—	—	—	—	—	—	—	—	—	—	—	—	—	—	—	—	—	—
1932	NYG	10 (2)	—	—	—	—	5	44	8.8	0	—	—	—	—	—	—	—	—	—	—	—	—	0	22
1933	†NYG	12 (6, re)	—	—	—	—	8	129	16.1	1	—	—	—	—	—	—	—	—	—	—	—	—	6	70
1935	Phi	1 (0)	—	—	—	—	1	2	2.0 (2)	0	—	—	—	—	—	—	—	—	—	—	—	—	0	1
1935	Pit	1 (0)	1	6	6.0 (6)	0	—	—	—	—	5	2	40.0	38	7.6	0	0	—	—	—	—	—	0	25
NFL	6	70 (34)	1	6	6.0 (6)	0	14	175	12.5 (2)	6	5	2	40.0	38	7.6	0	0	—	—	—	—	2	48	143

CAMPBELL, JACK John Carter, T, 6´5˝/277 lbs; USC; Utah; 1982: Sea, rnd 6; B12/16/1958 Los Angeles, CA **1982** Sea 1 (0)

CAMPBELL, JEFF Jeff, WR, 5´8˝/167 lbs; Colorado; 1990: Det, rnd 5; B3/26/1968 Denver, CO

YEAR	TEAM	G (GS, POS)	RUSH	YD	AVG (LG)	TD	REC	YD	AVG (LG)	TD	PASS	COMP	PCT	YD	AVG (LG)	TD	INT	SK	YD	QBR	KPR	OTD	PTS	TAY
1990	Det	16 (8, WR)	—	—	—	—	19	236	12.4 (51)	2	—	—	—	—	—	—	—	—	—	—	kp	—	12	181
1991	Det	14 (1)	—	—	—	—	2	49	24.5 (28)	0	—	—	—	—	—	—	—	—	—	—	k	—	0	-26
1992	Det	12 (0)	—	—	—	—	8	155	19.4 (78)	1	—	—	—	—	—	—	—	—	—	—	kp	—	6	84
1993	Det	10 (0)	—	—	—	—	7	55	7.9 (12)	0	—	—	—	—	—	—	—	—	—	—	—	—	0	28
1994	Den	16 (1)	2	6	3.0 (6)	0	1	22	22.0 (22)	1	—	—	—	—	—	—	—	—	—	—	k	—	6	1
NFL	5	68 (10)	2	6	3.0 (6)	0	37	517	14.0 (78)	4	—	—	—	—	—	—	—	—	—	—	kp	—	24	268

CAMPBELL, JESSE Jesse Gilbert, DB, 6´1˝/211 lbs; North Carolina State; 1991: Phi, rnd 2; B4/11/1969 Washington, DC **1992** NYG 11 (0) **1993**†NYG 16 (0) **1994** NYG 14 (10, FS) **1995** NYG 16 (16, SS) **1996** NYG 16 (16, SS) **1997** Was 16 (16, SS) **1998** Was 3 (3) **NFL** 92 (61) [7 yrs]

CAMPBELL, JIM James Ray, LB, 6´2˝/232 lbs; West Texas A&M; 1968: SD, rnd 14; B1/16/1946 Coleman, TX **1969** SD-A 1

CAMPBELL, JOE Joseph Patrick, DE-NT, 6´6˝/254 lbs; Maryland; 1977: NO, rnd 1; B5/8/1955 Wilmington, DE **1977** NO 14 (6, rde) **1978** NO 16 (16, RDE) **1979** NO 10 **1980** NO 5 (0) **1980**†Oak 10 (0) **1981** Oak 3 (0) **1981**†TB 7 (0) **NFL** 65 (22) [5 yrs]

CAMPBELL, JOE Joseph, DE, 6´4˝/245 lbs; New Mexico State; 1988: SD, rnd 4; B12/28/1966 Chandler, AZ **1988** SD 16 (0) **1989** SD 9 (0) **NFL** 25 (0) [2 yrs]

CAMPBELL, JOHN John William, LB, 6´3˝/225 lbs; Minnesota; 1963: Min, rnd 11/KC, rnd 5; B10/7/1938 Wadena, MN **1963** Min 14 **1964** Min 14 **1965** Pit 14 (LLB) **1966** Pit☆13 (LLB) **1967** Pit 14 (LLB) **1968** Pit 8 **1969** Pit 3 **1969** Bal 8 **NFL** 88 [7 yrs]

CAMPBELL, KELLY Kelly, WR, 5´10˝/173 lbs; Georgia Tech; B7/23/1980 Atlanta, GA

YEAR	TEAM	G (GS, POS)	RUSH	YD	AVG (LG)	TD	REC	YD	AVG (LG)	TD	PASS	COMP	PCT	YD	AVG (LG)	TD	INT	SK	YD	QBR	KPR	OTD	PTS	TAY
2002	Min	6 (2)	1	11	11.0 (11)	0	13	176	13.5 (32)	3	—	—	—	—	—	—	—	—	—	—	—	—	18	114
2003	Min	15 (6, WR)	10	71	7.1 (19)	0	25	522	20.9 (72)	4	—	—	—	—	—	—	—	—	—	—	k	—	24	378
2004	†Min	16 (3)	3	4	1.3 (16)	0	19	364	19.2 (61)	1	—	—	—	—	—	—	—	—	—	—	k	—	6	426
NFL	3	37 (11)	14	86	6.1 (19)	0	57	1062	18.6 (72)	8	—	—	—	—	—	—	—	—	—	—	k	—	48	918

CAMPBELL, KEN Kenneth, E, 6´1˝/213 lbs; West Chester; B1939 **1960** NYT-A 1

CAMPBELL, KHARY Khary, LB, 6´1˝/230 lbs; Bowling Green State; B4/4/1979 Brooklyn, NY **2002**†NYJ 9 (0) **2003** NYJ 4 (0) **2004** Was 9 (0) **2005**†Was 15 (0) **NFL** 37 (0) [4 yrs]

CAMPBELL, LAMAR Lamar, DB, 5´11˝/182 lbs; Wisconsin; B8/29/1976 Chester, PA **1998** Det 12 (0) **1999**†Det 15 (2) **2000** Det 16 (2) **2001** Det 12 (12, SS/fs) **2002** Det 9 (2) **NFL** 64 (18) [5 yrs]

CAMPBELL, LEON Leon, FB, 6´0˝/199 lbs; Arkansas; 1950: Bal, rnd 2; B7/1/1927 Bauxite, AR, D9/2/2002 Little Rock, AR

YEAR	TEAM	G (GS, POS)	RUSH	YD	AVG (LG)	TD	REC	YD	AVG (LG)	TD	PASS	COMP	PCT	YD	AVG (LG)	TD	INT	SK	YD	QBR	KPR	OTD	PTS	TAY
1950	Bal	3 (2)	20	93	4.7 (14)	0	1	5	5.0 (5)	0	—	—	—	—	—	—	—	—	—	—	—	—	0	96
1952	ChiB	8	24	76	3.2 (18)	0	2	1	0.5 (3)	0	—	—	—	—	—	—	—	—	—	—	k	1	6	163
1953	ChiB	12	22	130	5.9 (39)	0	5	74	14.8 (47)	0	—	—	—	—	—	—	—	—	—	—	k	—	0	337
1954	ChiB	6	18	38	2.1 (24)	0	3	0	0.0 (2)	0	—	—	—	—	—	—	—	—	—	—	k	—	0	70
1955	Pit	12	18	42	2.3 (27)	0	9	76	8.4 (36)	0	—	—	—	—	—	—	—	—	—	—	k	—	0	153
NFL	5	41 (2)	102	379	3.7 (39)	0	20	156	7.8 (47)	0	—	—	—	—	—	—	—	—	—	—	k	1	6	818

CAMPBELL, MARION Francis Marion, DE-DT-MG-G-T, 6´3˝/250 lbs; Georgia; 1952: SF, rnd 4; B5/25/1929 Chester, SC **[C]** **1954** SF 12 (RDT) **1955** SF 11 (RDT) **1956** Phi 12 (MG) **1957** Phi 10 **1958** Phi 11 (RDE) **1959** Phi✧12 (RG) **1960**†Phi★12 (RDE) **1961** Phi 14 (RDE) **NFL** 94 [8 yrs]

CAMPBELL, MARK Mark Joseph, TE, 6´6˝/255 lbs; Michigan; B12/6/1975 Clawson, MI

YEAR	TEAM	G (GS, POS)	RUSH	YD	AVG (LG)	TD	REC	YD	AVG (LG)	TD	PASS	COMP	PCT	YD	AVG (LG)	TD	INT	SK	YD	QBR	KPR	OTD	PTS	TAY
1999	Cle	14 (4)	—	—	—	—	9	131	14.6 (21)	0	—	—	—	—	—	—	—	—	—	—	k	—	0	49
2000	Cle	16 (10, TE)	—	—	—	—	12	80	6.7 (17)	1	—	—	—	—	—	—	—	—	—	—	k	—	6	30
2002	†Cle	16 (16, TE)	—	—	—	—	25	179	7.2 (26)	3	—	—	—	—	—	—	—	—	—	—	k	—	18	96
2003	Buf	16 (11, TE)	—	—	—	—	34	339	10.0 (31)	1	—	—	—	—	—	—	—	—	—	—	—	—	6	175
2004	Buf	12 (12, TE)	—	—	—	—	17	203	11.9 (27)	5	—	—	—	—	—	—	—	—	—	—	—	—	30	127
2005	Buf	14 (10, TE)	—	—	—	—	19	139	7.3 (27)	0	—	—	—	—	—	—	—	—	—	—	—	—	0	70
NFL	6	88 (63)	—	—	—	—	116	1071	9.2 (31)	10	—	—	—	—	—	—	—	—	—	—	k	—	60	545

CAMPBELL, MARK Mark Anthony, DT, 6´1˝/290 lbs; Florida; 1996: Den, rnd 3; B9/12/1972 Jamaica **1997** Arz 5 (0)

CAMPBELL, MATT Matthew Thomas, G-T-TE, 6´4˝/284 lbs; South Carolina; B7/14/1972 North Augusta, SC **1996**†Car 9 (8, lt/lg) **1997** Car 16 (14, LG) **1998** Car 10 (10, lg) **1999** Car 10 (10, LG) **2000** Car 14 (14, LG) **2001** Was 11 (5, rg)

YEAR	TEAM	G (GS, POS)	RUSH	YD	AVG (LG)	TD	REC	YD	AVG (LG)	TD	PASS	COMP	PCT	YD	AVG (LG)	TD	INT	SK	YD	QBR	KPR	OTD	PTS	TAY
1995	Car	10 (1)	—	—	—	—	3	32	10.7 (12)	0	—	—	—	—	—	—	—	—	—	—	—	—	0	16
NFL	7	80 (62)	—	—	—	—	3	32	10.7 (12)	0	—	—	—	—	—	—	—	—	—	—	—	—	0	16

CAMPBELL, MIKE Michael Linwood, RB, 5´11˝/200 lbs; Lenoir-Rhyne; 1967: SL, rnd 6; B5/29/1945 Altavista, VA

YEAR	TEAM	G (GS, POS)	RUSH	YD	AVG (LG)	TD	REC	YD	AVG (LG)	TD	PASS	COMP	PCT	YD	AVG (LG)	TD	INT	SK	YD	QBR	KPR	OTD	PTS	TAY
1968	Det	3	7	24	3.4 (5)	0	2	15	7.5 (9)	0	—	—	—	—	—	—	—	—	—	—	—	—	0	32

CAMPBELL, MILT Milton Gray, HB, 6´3˝/217 lbs; Indiana; 1957: Cle, rnd 5; B12/9/1933 Plainfield, NJ

YEAR	TEAM	G (GS, POS)	RUSH	YD	AVG (LG)	TD	REC	YD	AVG (LG)	TD	PASS	COMP	PCT	YD	AVG (LG)	TD	INT	SK	YD	QBR	KPR	OTD	PTS	TAY
1957	†Cle	9	7	23	3.3 (14)	0	1	25	25.0 (25)	1	1	0	0.0	0	0.0	0	0	—	—	—	k	—	6	139

CAMPBELL, RICH Richard Delano, QB, 6´4˝/224 lbs; California; 1981: GB, rnd 1; B12/22/1958 Miami, FL **1982**†GB 1 (0) **1983** GB 1 (0)

YEAR	TEAM	G (GS, POS)	RUSH	YD	AVG (LG)	TD	REC	YD	AVG (LG)	TD	PASS	COMP	PCT	YD	AVG (LG)	TD	INT	SK	YD	QBR	KPR	OTD	PTS	TAY
1981	GB	2 (0)	—	—	—	—	—	—	—	—	30	15	50.0	168	5.6 (27)	0	4	2	11	—	—	—	0	-76
1984	GB	3 (0)	2	2	1.0 (5)	0	—	—	—	—	38	16	42.1	218	5.7 (43)	3	5	5	46	—	—	—	0	-74
NFL	4	7 (0)	2	2	1.0 (5)	0	—	—	—	—	68	31	45.6	386	5.7 (43)	3	9	7	57	—	—	—	0	-150

CAMPBELL, RUSS Russell Lee, TE, 6´5˝/259 lbs; Kansas State; 1992: Pit, rnd 7; B4/2/1969 Columbus, OH **1992** Pit 7 (0)

CAMPBELL, SCOTT Robert Scott, QB, 6´0˝/196 lbs; Purdue; 1984: Pit, rnd 7; B4/15/1962 Hershey, PA

YEAR	TEAM	G (GS, POS)	RUSH	YD	AVG (LG)	TD	REC	YD	AVG (LG)	TD	PASS	COMP	PCT	YD	AVG (LG)	TD	INT	SK	YD	QBR	KPR	OTD	PTS	TAY
1984	Pit	5 (0)	3	-5	-1.7 (0)	0	—	—	—	—	15	8	53.3	109	7.3 (25)	1	1	—	—	—	—	—	0	15
1985	Pit	16 (2)	9	28	3.1 (14)	0	—	—	—	—	96	43	44.8	612	6.4 (51)	4	6	10	60	—	—	—	0	114
1986	Pit	3 (0)	—	—	—	—	—	—	—	—	4	0	0.0	0	0.0	0	0	1	5	—	—	—	0	0
1986	Atl	1 (0)	1	7	7.0 (7)	0	—	—	—	—	3	1	33.3	7	2.3 (7)	0	0	1	9	—	—	—	0	11
1987	Atl	12 (9, QB)	21	102	4.9 (24)	2	—	—	—	—	260	136	52.3	1728	6.6 (44)	11	14	25	178	65.0	—	—	12	481
1989	Atl	1 (0)	—	—	—	—	—	—	—	—	—	—	—	—	—	—	—	—	—	—	—	—	—	—
1990	Atl	7 (2)	9	38	4.2 (20)	0	—	—	—	—	76	36	47.4	527	6.9 (70)	3	4	9	55	—	—	—	0	157
NFL	6	45 (13)	43	170	4.0 (24)	2	—	—	—	—	454	224	49.3	2983	6.6 (70)	19	25	46	307	61.6	—	—	12	777

CAMPBELL, SONNY Thee Arthur, RB, 5´11˝/192 lbs; Northern Arizona; B3/5/1948 Marana, AZ

YEAR	TEAM	G (GS, POS)	RUSH	YD	AVG (LG)	TD	REC	YD	AVG (LG)	TD	PASS	COMP	PCT	YD	AVG (LG)	TD	INT	SK	YD	QBR	KPR	OTD	PTS	TAY
1970	Atl	11	28	116	4.1 (15)	2	7	92	13.1 (27)	0	—	—	—	—	—	—	—	—	—	—	k	—	12	262
1971	Atl	14	29	79	2.7 (8)	0	3	40	13.3 (29)	0	—	—	—	—	—	—	—	—	—	—	k	—	0	134
NFL	2	25	57	195	3.4 (15)	2	10	132	13.2 (29)	0	—	—	—	—	—	—	—	—	—	—	k	—	12	396

CAMPBELL, STAN Stanley Hugh, G, 6´0˝/226 lbs; Iowa State; 1952: Det, rnd 18; B8/26/1930 Hastings, NE, D3/14/2005 Elgin, IL **1952**†Det 3 **1955** Det 7 **1956** Det 7 **1957**†Det 12 (RG) **1958** Det 12 (RG) **1959** Phi 12 (12) **1960**†Phi 12 (RG) **1961** Phi 13 (RG) **1962** Oak-A 14 (LG) **NFL** 92 (12) [9 yrs]

CAMPBELL, TOMMY George Thomas, DB, 6´0˝/188 lbs; Iowa State; 1973: Atl, rnd 7; B12/30/1947 New York, NY **1976** Phi 14 (2)

CAMPBELL, WOODY Woodrow Lamar, RB, 5´10˝/204 lbs; Northwestern; 1967: Hou, rnd 10; B9/26/1944 Mount Pleasant, FL

YEAR	TEAM	G (GS, POS)	RUSH	YD	AVG (LG)	TD	REC	YD	AVG (LG)	TD	PASS	COMP	PCT	YD	AVG (LG)	TD	INT	SK	YD	QBR	KPR	OTD	PTS	TAY
1967	†Hou-A✧	14(HB)	110	511	4.6(42)	4	17	136	8.0(32)	2	1	0	0.0	0	0.0	0	0	—	—	—	k	—	36	633
1968	Hou-A	14(hb)	115	436	3.8(37)	6	21	234	11.1(39)	0	—	—	—	—	—	—	—	—	—	—	—	—	36	613
1969	†Hou-A	4	28	98	3.5(10)	1	7	82	11.7(37)	0	—	—	—	—	—	—	—	—	—	—	—	—	6	149
1970	Hou	6(rb)	59	189	3.2(28)	1	15	78	5.2(10)	0	—	—	—	—	—	—	—	—	—	—	—	—	6	238
1971	Hou	12(RB)	96	259	2.7(18)	1	20	179	8.9(24)	0	2	2	100.0	34	17.0(20)	2	0	—	—	—	—	—	6	386
NFL	5	50	408	1493	3.7(42)	13	80	709	8.9(39)	2	3	2	66.7	34	11.3(20)	2	0	—	—	—	k	—	90	2019

CAMPEN, JAMES James Frederick, C, 6´3˝/269 lbs; Tulane; B6/11/1964 Sacramento, CA **1987** NO 3 (3) **1988** NO 3 (0) **1989** GB 15 (1) **1990** GB 16 (16, C) **1991** GB 13 (13, C) **1992** GB 13 (13, C) **1993** GB 4 (4) **NFL** 67 (50) [7 yrs]

CAMPFIELD, BILLY William, RB, 5´11˝/200 lbs; Kansas; 1978: Phi, rnd 11; B8/20/1956 Las Vegas, NV

YEAR	TEAM	G (GS, POS)	RUSH	YD	AVG (LG)	TD	REC	YD	AVG (LG)	TD	PASS	COMP	PCT	YD	AVG (LG)	TD	INT	SK	YD	QBR	KPR	OTD	PTS	TAY
1978	†Phi	16(2)	61	247	4.0(50)	0	15	101	6.7(25)	0	—	—	—	—	—	—	—	—	—	—	k	—	0	396
1979	†Phi	16	30	165	5.5(40)	3	16	115	7.2(17)	0	—	—	—	—	—	—	—	—	—	—	k	1	24	409
1980	†Phi	15(0)	44	120	2.7(9)	1	26	275	10.6(50)	2	—	—	—	—	—	—	—	—	—	—	k	—	18	428
1981	†Phi	16(0)	31	115	3.7(13)	1	36	326	9.1(29)	3	—	—	—	—	—	—	—	—	—	—	k	—	24	346
1982	Phi	6(0)	1	2	2.0(2)	0	14	141	10.1(24)	1	—	—	—	—	—	—	—	—	—	—	k	—	6	78
1983	NYG	4(0)	2	21	10.5(13)	0	1	12	12.0(12)	0	—	—	—	—	—	—	—	—	—	—	k	—	0	46
NFL	6	73(2)	169	670	4.0(50)	5	108	970	9.0(50)	6	—	—	—	—	—	—	—	—	—	—	k	1	72	1701

CAMPIGLIO, BOB Robert Fulton, B, 6´1˝/183 lbs; West Liberty State; B1908 Milton, PA

YEAR	TEAM	G (GS, POS)	RUSH	YD	AVG (LG)	TD	REC	YD	AVG (LG)	TD	PASS	COMP	PCT	YD	AVG (LG)	TD	INT	SK	YD	QBR	KPR	OTD	PTS	TAY
1932	SI☆	11(5, TB)	104	504	**4.8**	2	3	59	19.7(26)	1	20	7	35.0	109	5.4	0	0	—	—	—	—	—	18	613
1933	Bos	6(1)	10	30	3.0	0	—	—	—	—	1	0	0.0	0	0.0	0	1	—	—	—	—	—	0	-10
NFL	2	17(6)	114	534	4.7	2	3	59	19.7(26)	1	21	7	33.3	109	5.2	0	1	—	—	—	—	—	18	603

CAMPION, T.J. Thomas J., T, 6´2˝/235 lbs; Southeastern Louisiana; 1947: Phi, rnd 19; B11/14/1918, D2/8/1996 Louisville, KY **1947** Phi 5 (0)

CAMPOFREDA, NICK Nicholas William, C-T, 6´1˝/240 lbs; Western Maryland; B1/14/1914 Baltimore, MD, D5/23/1959 Towson, MD **1944** Was 3 (3)

CAMPORA, DON Don Carlo, T-DT, 6´3˝/268 lbs; Pacific; 1950: SF, rnd 2; B8/30/1927 Trenton, UT, D6/5/1978 San Bernardino, CA **1950** SF 12 (LT) **1952** SF 8 **1953** Was 5 **NFL** 25 [3 yrs]

CAMPOS, ALAN Alan Raul, LB, 6´3˝/236 lbs; Louisville; 1996: Dal, rnd 5; B3/3/1973 Miami, FL **1996**†Dal 15 (0)

CANADA, LARRY Lawrence L., RB, 6´2˝/233 lbs; Wisconsin; B12/16/1954 Chicago, IL

YEAR	TEAM	G (GS, POS)	RUSH	YD	AVG (LG)	TD	REC	YD	AVG (LG)	TD	PASS	COMP	PCT	YD	AVG (LG)	TD	INT	SK	YD	QBR	KPR	OTD	PTS	TAY
1978	†Den	16	79	365	4.6(47)	3	6	37	6.2(12)	0	—	—	—	—	—	—	—	—	—	—	—	—	18	414
1979	†Den	16	36	143	4.0(17)	0	3	36	12.0(15)	0	—	—	—	—	—	—	—	—	—	—	k	—	0	147
1981	Den	16(0)	33	113	3.4(11)	3	3	37	12.3(20)	1	—	—	—	—	—	—	—	—	—	—	k	—	24	156
NFL	3	48	148	621	4.2(47)	6	12	110	9.2(20)	1	—	—	—	—	—	—	—	—	—	—	k	—	42	716

CANADEO, TONY Anthony Robert 'The Gray Ghost of Gonzaga', HB-TB-FB-DB, 5´11˝/190 lbs; Gonzaga; 1941: GB, rnd 9; B5/5/1919 Chicago, IL, D11/29/2003 Green Bay, WI; HOF 1974 **[R]**

YEAR	TEAM	G (GS, POS)	RUSH	YD	AVG (LG)	TD	REC	YD	AVG (LG)	TD	PASS	COMP	PCT	YD	AVG (LG)	TD	INT	SK	YD	QBR	KPR	OTD	PTS	TAY
1941	†GB	9(4)	43	137	3.2(16)	3	—	—	—	—	16	4	25.0	54	3.4(18)	2	0	—	—	—	Pkpi	—	18	280
1942	GB	11(5, tb)	89	272	3.1(50)	3	10	66	6.6(15)	0	59	24	40.7	310	5.3(36)	3	4	—	—	—	Pkpi	—	18	463
1943	GB☆	10(8, TB)	94	489	5.2(35)	3	3	31	10.3(13)	2	129	56	43.4	875	6.8(51)	9	12	—	—	51.0	Pkpi	—	30	697
1944	GB	3(0)	31	149	4.8(34)	0	1	12	12.0(12)	0	20	9	45.0	89	4.4(17)	0	0	—	—	—	Pkp	—	0	196
1946	GB	11(5, TB)	122	476	3.9(27)	0	2	25	12.5(15)	0	27	7	25.9	189	7.0(51)	1	3	—	—	—	kpi	—	0	605
1947	GB	12(6, LH)	103	464	4.5(35)	2	—	—	—	—	8	3	37.5	101	12.6(38)	1	1	—	—	—	kp	—	12	648
1948	GB☆	12(9, LH)	123	589	4.8(49)	4	9	81	9.0(32)	0	8	2	25.0	24	3.0(15)	0	0	—	—	—	Pkpi	—	24	759
1949	GB☆	12(12, LH)	208	1052	5.1(54)	4	3	-2	-0.7(3)	0	—	—	—	—	—	—	—	—	—	—	k	—	24	1081
1950	GB	12(FB)	93	247	2.7(15)	4	10	54	5.4(20)	0	—	—	—	—	—	—	—	—	—	—	kp	—	24	528
1951	GB	12(LH)	54	131	2.4(15)	1	22	226	10.3(46)	2	—	—	—	—	—	—	—	—	—	—	k	—	18	305
1952	GB	12(LH)	65	191	2.9(35)	2	9	86	9.6(21)	1	1	0	0.0	0	0.0	0	0	—	—	—	kp	—	18	290
NFL	11	116(49)	1025	4197	4.1(54)	26	69	579	8.4(46)	5	268	105	39.2	1642	6.1(51)	16	20	—	—	49.1	Pkpi	—	186	5851

CANADY, JIM James Maurice, B, 5´10˝/178 lbs; Texas; 1947: ChiB, rnd 5/Mia-A, rnd 17; B1/14/1926 Austin, TX

YEAR	TEAM	G (GS, POS)	RUSH	YD	AVG (LG)	TD	REC	YD	AVG (LG)	TD	PASS	COMP	PCT	YD	AVG (LG)	TD	INT	SK	YD	QBR	KPR	OTD	PTS	TAY
1948	ChiB	3(0)	2	8	4.0(6)	0	—	—	—	—	—	—	—	—	—	—	—	—	—	—	p	—	0	40
1949	ChiB	5(0)	—	—	—	—	—	—	—	—	—	—	—	—	—	—	—	—	—	—	i	—	0	7
1949	NYB	7(1)	23	91	4.0(46)	0	5	80	16.0(26)	0	—	—	—	—	—	—	—	—	—	—	kpi	—	0	256
NFL	2	15(1)	25	99	4.0(46)	0	5	80	16.0(26)	0	—	—	—	—	—	—	—	—	—	—	kpi	—	0	303

CANALE, JUSTIN Justin Dominic, G, 6´2˝/250 lbs; Mississippi State; 1965: Bos, rnd 6/Cle, rnd 12; B4/11/1943 Memphis, TN **[K]** **1965** Bos-A 14 **1966** Bos-A 14 **1967** Bos-A 14 **1969** Cin-A 8

YEAR	TEAM	G (GS, POS)	RUSH	YD	AVG (LG)	TD	REC	YD	AVG (LG)	TD	PASS	COMP	PCT	YD	AVG (LG)	TD	INT	SK	YD	QBR	KPR	OTD	PTS	TAY
1968	Bos-A	14(13, LG)	—	—	—	—	1	0	0.0(0)	0	—	—	—	—	—	—	—	—	—	—	—	—	0	0
NFL	5	64(13)	—	—	—	—	1	0	0.0	0	—	—	—	—	—	—	—	—	—	—	Kk	—	1	-30

CANALE, ROCCO Rocco P., T-G, 5´11˝/240 lbs; Boston College; 1943: Phi, rnd 9; B5/1/1917 Boston, MA, D11/1/1995 Watertown, NY **1943** P-P 5 (0) **1944** Phi 9 (1) **1945** Phi 3 (0) **1946** Bos 11 (6, RG) **1947** Bos 10 (5, lt) **NFL** 38 (12) [5 yrs]

CANALE, WHIT John Whitfield, DE-DT, 6´3˝/245 lbs; Tennessee; 1965: Pit, rnd 17; B12/27/1941 Sarasota, FL **1966** Mia-A 3 **1968** Bos-A 13 **NFL** 16 [2 yrs]

CANCIK, PHIL Phillip, LB, 6´1˝/228 lbs; Northern Arizona; B4/19/1957 South Bend, IN **1980** NYG 5 (2) **1981** KC 16 (1) **NFL** 21 (3) [2 yrs]

CANIDATE, TRUNG Trung Jered, RB, 5´11˝/205 lbs; Arizona; 2000: SL, rnd 1; B3/3/1977 Phoenix, AZ

YEAR	TEAM	G (GS, POS)	RUSH	YD	AVG (LG)	TD	REC	YD	AVG (LG)	TD	PASS	COMP	PCT	YD	AVG (LG)	TD	INT	SK	YD	QBR	KPR	OTD	PTS	TAY
2000	SL	3(0)	3	6	2.0(3)	0	1	4	4.0(4)	0	—	—	—	—	—	—	—	—	—	—	—	—	0	8
2001	†SL	16(2)	78	441	5.7(45)	6	17	154	9.1(29)	0	—	—	—	—	—	—	—	—	—	—	k	—	36	786
2002	SL	16(1)	17	48	2.8(22)	0	4	31	7.8(13)	0	—	—	—	—	—	—	—	—	—	—	k	—	0	156
2003	Was	11(10, RB)	142	600	4.2(38)	1	10	71	7.1(25)	1	—	—	—	—	—	—	—	—	—	—	—	—	12	651
NFL	4	46(13)	240	1095	4.6(45)	7	32	260	8.1(29)	1	—	—	—	—	—	—	—	—	—	—	k	—	48	1600

CANLEY, SHELDON Sheldon Lavell, RB, 5´9˝/195 lbs; San Jose State; 1991: SF, rnd 7; B4/19/1968 Santa Barbara, CA

YEAR	TEAM	G (GS, POS)	RUSH	YD	AVG (LG)	TD	REC	YD	AVG (LG)	TD	PASS	COMP	PCT	YD	AVG (LG)	TD	INT	SK	YD	QBR	KPR	OTD	PTS	TAY
1992	NYJ	1(0)	4	9	2.3(4)	0	—	—	—	—	—	—	—	—	—	—	—	—	—	—	—	—	0	9

CANNADY, JOHN John Hanley, LB-C, 6´2˝/227 lbs; Indiana; 1947: NYG, rnd 3; B5/9/1923 Charleston, SC, D9/28/2002 Charleston, SC **1948** NYG 12 (12, C) **1949** NYG 12 (1) **1950**†NYG✧11 (RLB) **1951** NYG☆12 (RLB) **1952** NYG✧12 (RLB) **1953** NYG 12 (MLB) **1954** NYG 10 (RLB)

YEAR	TEAM	G (GS, POS)	RUSH	YD	AVG (LG)	TD	REC	YD	AVG (LG)	TD	PASS	COMP	PCT	YD	AVG (LG)	TD	INT	SK	YD	QBR	KPR	OTD	PTS	TAY
1947	NYG☆	11(6, c)	1	14	14.0(14)	0	—	—	—	—	—	—	—	—	—	—	—	—	—	—	i	—	0	9
NFL	8	92(19)	1	14	14.0(14)	0	—	—	—	—	—	—	—	—	—	—	—	—	—	—	i	—	0	147

CANNAMELA, PAT Patterson N., LB, 6´0˝/195 lbs; USC; 1952: DalT, rnd 11; B4/27/1929 New London, CT, D1/28/1973 Hollywood, CA **[K]** **1952** DalT 12 (LLB)

CANNAVA, AL Anthony Louis, HB-DB, 5´10˝/180 lbs; Notre Dame; Boston College; B5/24/1924 Boston, MA

YEAR	TEAM	G (GS, POS)	RUSH	YD	AVG (LG)	TD	REC	YD	AVG (LG)	TD	PASS	COMP	PCT	YD	AVG (LG)	TD	INT	SK	YD	QBR	KPR	OTD	PTS	TAY
1950	GB	1	1	2	2.0(2)	0	1	28	28.0(28)	0	—	—	—	—	—	—	—	—	—	—	kp	—	0	10

CANNAVINO, JOE Joseph Patrick, DB, 5´11˝/185 lbs; Ohio State; 1960: Oak, rnd 2/1957: Bal, rnd 16; B1/20/1935 Cleveland, OH **1960** Oak-A☆14 (RCB) **1961** Oak-A 14 (LS) **1962** Buf-A 4 **NFL** 32 [3 yrs]

CANNELLA, JOHN John Matthew, G-C-LB-T, 6´1˝/199 lbs; Fordham; B2/8/1908 New York, NY, D10/31/1996 Glen Cove, NY **1933**†NYG 9 (1) **1934** NYG 2 (0) **NFL** 11 (1) [2 yrs]

CANNIDA, JAMES James Thomas, DT, 6´2˝/275 lbs; Nevada-Reno; 1998: TB, rnd 6; B1/3/1975 Savannah, GA **1998** TB 10 (0) **1999** TB 2 (0) **2000**†TB 16 (0) **2001** TB 12 (2) **2002**†Ind 10 (7, rdt) **NFL** 50 (9) [5 yrs]

CANNON, BILLY William Abb, TE-HB-FB, 6´1˝/207 lbs; LSU; 1960: Hou, rnd 1/LA, rnd 1; B8/2/1937 Philadelphia, MS

YEAR	TEAM	G (GS, POS)	RUSH	YD	AVG (LG)	TD	REC	YD	AVG (LG)	TD	PASS	COMP	PCT	YD	AVG (LG)	TD	INT	SK	YD	QBR	KPR	OTD	PTS	TAY
1960	†Hou-A☆	14(HB)	152	644	4.2(39)	1	15	187	12.5(88)	5	3	0	0.0	0	0.0	0	0	—	—	—	kp	1	42	1005
1961	†Hou-A★	14(HB)	200	**948**	**4.7(61)**	6	43	586	13.6(78)	9	5	0	0.0	0	0.0	0	1	—	—	—	kp	—	90	**1500**
1962	†Hou-A	14(HB)	147	474	3.2(64)	7	32	451	14.1(60)	6	3	2	66.7	46	15.3(40)	1	0	—	—	—	k	—	80	1000
1963	Hou-A	6	13	45	3.5(12)	0	5	39	7.8(12)	0	1	0	0.0	0	0.0	0	0	—	—	—	k	—	0	74
1964	Oak-A	14(FB)	89	338	3.8(34)	3	37	454	12.3(40)	5	—	—	—	—	—	—	—	—	—	—	k	—	48	823
1965	Oak-A	10(TE)	—	—	—	—	7	127	18.1(36)	0	—	—	—	—	—	—	—	—	—	—	—	—	0	64
1966	Oak-A	14(TE)	—	—	—	—	14	436	31.1(75)	2	—	—	—	—	—	—	—	—	—	—	p	—	12	235
1967	†Oak-A☆	14(TE)	—	—	—	—	32	629	19.7(64)	10	—	—	—	—	—	—	—	—	—	—	—	—	60	365

YEAR	TEAM	G (GS, POS)	RUSH	YD	AVG (LG)	TD	REC	YD	AVG (LG)	TD	PASS	COMP	PCT	YD	AVG (LG)	TD	INT	SK	YD	QBR	KPR	OTD	PTS	TAY
1968	†Oak-A☆	14 (13, TE)	—	—	—	—	23	360	15.7 (48)	6	—	—	—	—	—	—	—	—	—	—	—	—	36	210
1969	†Oak-A✧	13 (11, TE)	—	—	—	—	21	262	12.5 (53)	2	—	—	—	—	—	—	—	—	—	—	—	—	12	141
1970	KC	6	1	6	6.0 (6)	0	7	125	17.9 (45)	2	—	—	—	—	—	—	—	—	—	—	—	—	12	79
NFL	11	133 (24)	602	2455	4.1 (64)	17	236	3656	15.5 (88)	47	12	2	16.7	46	3.8 (40)	1	1	—	—	—	kp	1	392	5493

CANNON, BILLY William Abb, LB, 6´4˝/231 lbs; Texas A&M; 1984: Dal, rnd 1; B10/8/1961 Baton Rouge, LA **1984** Dal 8 (0)

CANNON, JOHN John Raymond, DE-NT, 6´5˝/260 lbs; William & Mary; 1982: TB, rnd 3; B7/30/1960 Long Branch, NJ **1982**†TB 9 (0) **1983** TB 14 (11, LDE) **1984** TB 16 (16, LDE) **1985** TB 16 (16, LDE) **1986** TB 9 (8, lde) **1987** TB 11 (11, LDE) **1988** TB 16 (3) **1989** TB 16 (3) **1990** TB 15 (5, rde) **NFL** 122 (73) [9 yrs]

CANNON, MARK Mark Maida, C, 6´3˝/258 lbs; Texas-Arlington; 1984: GB, rnd 11; B6/14/1962 Whittier, CA **1984** GB 16 (0) **1985** GB 16 (16, C) **1986** GB 7 (7, c) **1987** GB 12 (12, C) **1988** GB 16 (16, C) **1989** GB 1 (0) **1989** KC 11 (0) **1991** Ind 4 (0) **NFL** 83 (51) [7 yrs]

CANTOR, LEO° Leo, B, 6´0˝/195 lbs; UCLA; B2/28/1919 Chicago, IL, D6/4/1995 San Fernando, CA

YEAR	TEAM	G (GS, POS)	RUSH	YD	AVG (LG)	TD	REC	YD	AVG (LG)	TD	PASS	COMP	PCT	YD	AVG (LG)	TD	INT	SK	YD	QBR	KPR	OTD	PTS	TAY
1942	NYG	10 (1)	67	124	1.9 (18)	2	—	—	—	—	29	12	41.4	155	5.3 (35)	1	1	—	—	—	Pkpi	—	12	276
1945	ChiC	10 (8, LH)	83	291	3.5 (18)	5	15	159	10.6 (33)	0	18	3	16.7	116	6.4 (62)	0	4	—	—	—	Pkpi	—	30	431
NFL	2	20 (9)	150	415	2.8 (18)	7	15	159	10.6 (33)	0	47	15	31.9	271	5.8 (62)	1	5	—	—	—	Pkpi	—	42	706

CANTRELL, BARRY Barry, P, 6´1˝/195 lbs; Fordham; B11/2/1976 Margate, FL **2000** Dal 2 (0)

CANTU, ROLANDO Rolando, T, 6´5˝/361 lbs; none; B2/25/1981 Monterey, Mexico **2005** Arz 1 (0)

CANTY, CHRIS Christopher Shawn Patrick, DB, 5´9˝/185 lbs; Kansas State; 1997: NE, rnd 1; B3/30/1976 Voorhees, NJ **1997**†NE 16 (1) **1998**†NE 16 (9, RCB) **1999**†Sea 14 (1) **2000** Sea 12 (1) **2000**†NO 3 (0) **NFL** 61 (12) [4 yrs]

CANTY, CHRIS Christopher Lee, DE, 6´7˝/286 lbs; Virginia; 2005: Dal, rnd 4; B11/10/1982 Bronx, NY **2005** Dal 16 (2)

CAPECE, BILL William George, K, 5´7˝/170 lbs; Florida State; 1981: Hou, rnd 12; B4/1/1959 Miami, FL **[K]** **1981**†TB 13 (0) **1982**†TB 9 (0) **1983** TB 15 (0) **NFL** 37 (0) [3 yrs]

CAPERS, JAMES James O., LB, 6´4˝/232 lbs; Central Michigan; B6/14/1959 Kalamazoo, MI **1987** Cle 3 (0)

CAPERS, WAYNE Wayne Erwin, WR, 6´2˝/198 lbs; Kansas; 1983: Pit, rnd 2; B5/17/1961 Miami, FL

YEAR	TEAM	G (GS, POS)	RUSH	YD	AVG (LG)	TD	REC	YD	AVG (LG)	TD	PASS	COMP	PCT	YD	AVG (LG)	TD	INT	SK	YD	QBR	KPR	OTD	PTS	TAY
1983	†Pit	11 (4)	—	—	—	—	10	185	18.5 (36)	1	—	—	—	—	—	—	—	—	—	—	—	—	6	98
1984	†Pit	16 (0)	1	-3	-3.0 (-3)	0	7	81	11.6 (19)	0	—	—	—	—	—	—	—	—	—	—	—	—	0	38
1985	Ind	14 (10, WR)	3	18	6.0 (20)	1	25	438	17.5 (80)	4	—	—	—	—	—	—	—	—	—	—	—	—	30	267
1986	Ind	6 (3)	1	11	11.0 (11)	0	9	118	13.1 (27)	0	—	—	—	—	—	—	—	—	—	—	—	—	0	70
NFL	4	47 (17)	5	26	5.2 (20)	1	51	822	16.1 (80)	5	—	—	—	—	—	—	—	—	—	—	—	—	36	472

CAPONE, WARREN Warren Samuel, LB, 6´1˝/218 lbs; LSU; B8/14/1951 Baton Rouge, LA **1975**†Dal 5 **1976** NO 7 **NFL** 12 [2 yrs]

CAPP, DICK Richard Francis, TE-LB, 6´4˝/240 lbs; Boston College; 1966: Bos, rnd 17; B4/9/1942 Portland, ME **1967**†GB 2 **1968** Pit 14 **NFL** 16 [2 yrs]

CAPPADONA, BOB Robert Joseph, RB, 6´1˝/225 lbs; Notre Dame; Northeastern; 1965: Bos, rnd R3/SF, rnd 10; B12/13/1942 Watertown, MA

YEAR	TEAM	G (GS, POS)	RUSH	YD	AVG (LG)	TD	REC	YD	AVG (LG)	TD	PASS	COMP	PCT	YD	AVG (LG)	TD	INT	SK	YD	QBR	KPR	OTD	PTS	TAY
1966	Bos-A	14	22	88	4.0 (13)	1	—	—	—	—	—	—	—	—	—	—	—	—	—	—	k	—	8	99
1967	Bos-A	13	28	100	3.6 (11)	0	6	104	17.3 (42)	1	—	—	—	—	—	—	—	—	—	—	k	—	6	138
1968	Buf-A	14 (fb)	73	272	3.7 (33)	1	18	92	5.1 (21)	2	—	—	—	—	—	—	—	—	—	—	—	—	20	338
NFL	3	41	123	460	3.7 (33)	2	24	196	8.2 (42)	3	—	—	—	—	—	—	—	—	—	—	k	—	34	575

CAPPELLETTI, GINO Gino Raymond Michael, FL-SE-DB-WR-K, 6´0˝/190 lbs; Minnesota; B3/26/1934 Keewatin, MN **[K]**

YEAR	TEAM	G (GS, POS)	RUSH	YD	AVG (LG)	TD	REC	YD	AVG (LG)	TD	PASS	COMP	PCT	YD	AVG (LG)	TD	INT	SK	YD	QBR	KPR	OTD	PTS	TAY
1960	Bos-A	14 (RCB)	—	—	—	—	1	28	28.0 (28)	0	—	—	—	—	—	—	—	—	—	—	Kkpi	—	60	100
1961	Bos-A★	14 (SE)	—	—	—	—	45	768	17.1 (53)	8	1	1	100.0	27	27.0 (27)	1	0	—	—	—	K	—	**147**	443
1962	Bos-A	14 (SE)	1	-5	-5.0 (-5)	0	34	479	14.1 (40)	5	—	—	—	—	—	—	—	—	—	—	K	—	128	260
1963	†Bos-A★	14 (SE)	1	2	2.0 (2)	0	34	493	14.5 (38)	2	—	—	—	—	—	—	—	—	—	—	K	—	**113**	259
1964	Bos-A★	14 (FL)	1	7	7.0 (7)	0	49	865	17.7 (58)	7	0	0	0.0	0	0.0	0	0	1	11	—	K	—	**155**	475
1965	Bos-A✧	14 (FL)	—	—	—	—	37	680	18.4 (57)	9	—	—	—	—	—	—	—	—	—	—	K	—	**132**	385
1966	Bos-A★	14 (FL)	—	—	—	—	43	676	15.7 (63)	6	—	—	—	—	—	—	—	—	—	—	K	—	**119**	368
1967	Bos-A	14 (FL)	—	—	—	—	35	397	11.3 (35)	3	—	—	—	—	—	—	—	—	—	—	K	—	95	214
1968	Bos-A	14 (2)	1	2	2.0 (2)	0	13	182	14.0 (30)	2	—	—	—	—	—	—	—	—	—	—	K	—	83	103
1969	Bos-A	14	—	—	—	—	1	21	21.0 (21)	0	—	—	—	—	—	—	—	—	—	—	K	—	68	11
1970	Bos	13	—	—	—	—	—	—	—	—	—	—	—	—	—	—	—	—	—	—	K	—	30	0
NFL	11	153 (2)	4	6	1.5 (7)	0	292	4589	15.7 (63)	42	1	1	100.0	27	27.0 (27)	1	0	1	11	—	Kkpi	—	1130	2615

CAPPELLETTI, JOHN John Raymond, RB, 6´1˝/215 lbs; Penn State; 1974: LA, rnd 1; B8/9/1952 Philadelphia, PA

YEAR	TEAM	G (GS, POS)	RUSH	YD	AVG (LG)	TD	REC	YD	AVG (LG)	TD	PASS	COMP	PCT	YD	AVG (LG)	TD	INT	SK	YD	QBR	KPR	OTD	PTS	TAY
1974	†LARm	14 (1)	55	198	3.6 (20)	0	6	35	5.8 (9)	0	—	—	—	—	—	—	—	—	—	—	k	—	0	203
1975	†LARm	13	48	158	3.3 (30)	6	—	—	—	—	—	—	—	—	—	—	—	—	—	—	k	—	36	212
1976	†LARm	14 (14, FB)	177	688	3.9 (38)	1	30	302	10.1 (32)	1	—	—	—	—	—	—	—	—	—	—	—	—	12	854
1977	†LARm	14 (14, FB)	178	598	3.4 (15)	5	28	228	8.1 (25)	1	—	—	—	—	—	—	—	—	—	—	—	—	36	767
1978	†LARm	14 (14, FB)	174	604	3.5 (26)	3	41	382	9.3 (37)	1	—	—	—	—	—	—	—	—	—	—	—	—	24	830
1980	†SD	10 (8, FB)	101	364	3.6 (46)	5	13	112	8.6 (12)	0	—	—	—	—	—	—	—	—	—	—	k	—	30	455
1981	†SD	16 (5, fb)	68	254	3.7 (30)	4	10	126	12.6 (25)	1	—	—	—	—	—	—	—	—	—	—	—	—	30	362
1982	†SD	9 (6, FB)	22	82	3.7 (17)	0	7	48	6.9 (22)	0	—	—	—	—	—	—	—	—	—	—	—	—	0	106
1983	SD	1 (0)	1	5	5.0 (5)	0	—	—	—	—	—	—	—	—	—	—	—	—	—	—	—	—	0	5
NFL	9	105 (62)	824	2951	3.6 (46)	24	135	1233	9.1 (37)	4	—	—	—	—	—	—	—	—	—	—	k	—	168	3794

CAPPLEMAN, BILL George William, QB, 6´3˝/210 lbs; Florida State; 1970: Min, rnd 2; B3/12/1947 Brooksville, FL

YEAR	TEAM	G (GS, POS)	RUSH	YD	AVG (LG)	TD	REC	YD	AVG (LG)	TD	PASS	COMP	PCT	YD	AVG (LG)	TD	INT	SK	YD	QBR	KPR	OTD	PTS	TAY
1970	Min	1	—	—	—	—	—	—	—	—	7	4	57.1	49	7.0 (26)	0	0	—	—	—	—	—	0	25
1973	Det	7	1	-2	-2.0 (-2)	0	—	—	—	—	11	5	45.5	33	3.0 (8)	0	1	—	—	—	—	—	0	-26
NFL	2	8	1	-2	-2.0 (-2)	0	—	—	—	—	18	9	50.0	82	4.6 (26)	0	1	—	—	—	—	—	0	-1

CAPPS, BILL Thomas Wilburn, T-G, 6´1˝/233 lbs; East Central (OK); B6/23/1904 Coalville, OK, D2/9/1979 Weatherford, OK **1929** Fra 5 (4) **1930** Fra 9 (6, rt) **1930** Min 1 (1) **NFL** 15 (11) [2 yrs]

CAPRIA, CARL Carl Daniel, DB, 6´3˝/185 lbs; Purdue; 1974: Det, rnd 5; B6/8/1952 Bronx, NY **1974** Det 12 **1975** NYJ 1 **NFL** 13 [2 yrs]

CAPRON, RALPH Ralph Earl, WB, 5´11˝/165 lbs; Minnesota; B6/16/1889 Minneapolis, MN, D9/18/1980 Los Angeles, CA **1920** ChiT 1 (1)

CAPUZZI, JIM Camillo James, DB-QB, 6´0˝/190 lbs; Marquette; Cincinnati; B3/12/1932 Niles, OH **1955** GB 2 **1956** GB 7 **NFL** 9 [2 yrs]

CARA, MAC Dominic Anthony, E, 5´10˝/193 lbs; North Carolina State; 1937: Was, rnd 10; B11/11/1914 Reggie di Calabria, Italy, D4/16/1993 Steubenville, OH

YEAR	TEAM	G (GS, POS)	RUSH	YD	AVG (LG)	TD	REC	YD	AVG (LG)	TD	PASS	COMP	PCT	YD	AVG (LG)	TD	INT	SK	YD	QBR	KPR	OTD	PTS	TAY
1937	Pit	10 (4)	—	—	—	—	2	36	18.0	0	—	—	—	—	—	—	—	—	—	—	—	—	0	18
1938	Pit	9 (3)	1	-1	-1.0 (-1)	0	4	18	4.5	0	—	—	—	—	—	—	—	—	—	—	—	—	0	8
NFL	2	19 (7)	1	-1	-1.0 (-1)	0	6	54	9.0	0	—	—	—	—	—	—	—	—	—	—	—	—	0	26

CARANCI, ROLAND Roland, T, 6´2˝/214 lbs; Colorado; B3/4/1921 Marshall, CO, D2/26/1998 Arlington Heights, IL **1944** NYG 2 (0)

CARANO, GLENN Glenn Thomas, QB, 6´3˝/201 lbs; UNLV; 1977: Dal, rnd 2; B11/18/1955 San Pedro, CA **1978** Dal 2 **1979** Dal 3 **1982**†Dal 7 (0) **1983**†Dal 16 (0)

YEAR	TEAM	G (GS, POS)	RUSH	YD	AVG (LG)	TD	REC	YD	AVG (LG)	TD	PASS	COMP	PCT	YD	AVG (LG)	TD	INT	SK	YD	QBR	KPR	OTD	PTS	TAY
1980	†Dal	3 (0)	4	6	1.5 (5)	0	—	—	—	—	12	5	41.7	69	5.8 (25)	2	0	1	0	—	—	—	0	51
1981	†Dal	5 (1)	8	9	1.1 (11)	0	—	—	—	—	45	16	35.6	235	5.2 (55)	1	1	1	11	—	—	—	0	92
NFL	6	36 (1)	12	15	1.3 (11)	0	—	—	—	—	57	21	36.8	304	5.3 (55)	3	1	2	11	—	—	—	0	142

CARAPELLA, AL Alfred Richard, DT-MG-T-LB, 6´0˝/235 lbs; Miami (FL); 1951: SF, rnd 5; B4/26/1927 Tuckahoe, NY **1951** SF 12 (RDT) **1952** SF 12 (RDT) **1953** SF 12 (RDT) **1954** SF✧12 (MG) **1955** SF 12 (MG) **NFL** 60 [5 yrs]

CARAVELLO, JOE Joseph John, TE, 6´3˝/270 lbs; Tulane; B6/6/1963 Santa Monica, CA

YEAR	TEAM	G (GS, POS)	RUSH	YD	AVG (LG)	TD	REC	YD	AVG (LG)	TD	PASS	COMP	PCT	YD	AVG (LG)	TD	INT	SK	YD	QBR	KPR	OTD	PTS	TAY
1987	Was	11 (5, te)	—	—	—	—	2	29	14.5 (22)	0	—	—	—	—	—	—	—	—	—	—	—	—	0	15
1988	Was	12 (6, te)	—	—	—	—	2	15	7.5 (8)	0	—	—	—	—	—	—	—	—	—	—	—	—	0	8
1989	SD	12 (9, TE)	1	0	0.0 (0)	0	10	95	9.5 (37)	0	—	—	—	—	—	—	—	—	—	—	—	—	0	48
1990	SD	7 (7, TE)	—	—	—	—	2	21	10.5 (17)	1	—	—	—	—	—	—	—	—	—	—	—	—	6	16
NFL	4	42 (27)	1	0	0.0	0	16	160	10.0 (37)	1	—	—	—	—	—	—	—	—	—	—	—	—	6	85

YEAR	TEAM	G(GS, POS)	RUSH	YD	AVG(LG)	TD	REC	YD	AVG(LG)	TD	PASS	COMP	PCT	YD	AVG(LG)	TD	INT	SK	YD	QBR	KPR	OTD	PTS	TAY
CARBERRY, GLENN Glen Michael, E, 6´0˝/190 lbs; Army; Notre Dame; B4/10/1896 Ames, IA, D2/19/1976 Bronx, NY **1923** Buf☆10 (10, LE) **1924** Buf 2 (2) **1925** Cle 1 (1) **NFL** 13 (13) [3 yrs]																								
CARD, HARPER J. Harper, T, 6´1˝/183 lbs; none; B1903, deceased **1921** Lou 1 (1, RT) **1922** Lou 4 (4, LT) **NFL** 5 (5) [2 yrs]																								
CARDARELLI, CARL Carlo, C, 5´9˝/170 lbs; none; B9/8/1895 Akron, OH, D8/11/1969 San Jose, CA **1924** Akr 2 (0) **1925** Cle 1 (0) **NFL** 3 (0) [2 yrs]																								
CARDINAL, FRED Frederick, B, 5´11˝/220 lbs; Notre Dame; Baldwin-Wallace; B2/12/1925 Dover, OH, D2/5/2004 Barberton, OH **1947** NYY-A 1 (0)																								
CARDWELL, JOE Joseph Thomas, T-DE, 6´3˝/235 lbs; Duke; B1/31/1912 Montgomery, AL, D7/6/1957 Norfolk, VA **1937** Pit 7 (3) **1938** Pit 11 (7, LT) **NFL** 18 (10) [2 yrs]																								
CARDWELL, JOHN John R., HB, 5´9˝/170 lbs; none; B7/28/1893, D5/13/1974 Wilmington, DE **1923** SL 2 (1)																								
CARDWELL, LLOYD Lloyd Raymond, WB-DB-FB, 6´2˝/195 lbs; Nebraska; 1937: Det, rnd 1; B4/19/1913 Republic, KS, D11/9/1997 Omaha, NE																								
1937	Det	9(0)	36	181	5.0	0	3	51	17.0(45)	1	—	—	—	—	—	—	—	—	—	—	—	—	6	212
1938	Det★	10(6, WB)	73	294	4.0	4	9	138	15.3	1	1	1	100.0	35	35.0(35)	0	0	—	—	—	—	—	30	426
1939	Det☆	10(8, WB)	29	141	4.9	1	13	250	19.2	2	—	—	—	—	—	—	—	—	—	—	—	—	18	286
1940	Det☆	10(8, WB)	48	186	3.9	2	20	349	17.5	1	1	0	0.0	0	0.0	0	0	—	—	—	i	—	18	383
1941	Det	4(2)	10	19	1.9(12)	0	—	—	—	—	—	—	—	—	—	—	—	—	—	—	kp	—	0	36
1942	Det	7(2)	6	78	13.0(80)	1	5	135	27.0(51)	0	—	—	—	—	—	—	—	—	—	—	kpi	—	6	219
1943	Det	7(2)	3	6	2.0(2)	0	1	9	9.0(9)	0	—	—	—	—	—	—	—	—	—	—	kp	—	0	33
NFL	7	57(28)	205	905	4.4(80)	8	51	932	18.3(51)	5	2	1	50.0	35	17.5(35)	0	0	—	—	—	kpi	—	78	1593
CAREY, BOB Robert Winfield, E, 6´5˝/219 lbs; Michigan State; 1952: LA, rnd 1; B2/8/1930 Charlevoix, MI, D10/25/1988 Cincinnati, OH **[K]**																								
1952	†LARm	12	—	—	—	—	36	539	15.0(61)	1	—	—	—	—	—	—	—	—	—	—	K	1	12	275
1954	LARm	2	—	—	—	—	5	49	9.8(13)	0	—	—	—	—	—	—	—	—	—	—	K	—	5	25
1956	LARm	7	—	—	—	—	5	60	12.0(18)	1	—	—	—	—	—	—	—	—	—	—	—	—	6	35
1958	ChiB	11	—	—	—	—	1	15	15.0(15)	0	—	—	—	—	—	—	—	—	—	—	—	—	0	8
NFL	4	32	—	—	—	—	47	663	14.1(61)	2	—	—	—	—	—	—	—	—	—	—	K	1	23	342
CAREY, BRIAN Brian Richard, WR, 6´0˝/200 lbs; American International; B11/6/1963 Woburn, MA **1987** NE 2 (0)																								
CAREY, JOE Joseph, G-T, 6´2˝/195 lbs; Illinois Tech; B11/1895 Chicago, IL, D7/22/1962 **1920** ChiC 7 (3) **1921** GB 6 (4, LG) **NFL** 13 (7) [2 yrs]																								
CAREY, RICHARD Richard Andre, DB, 5´9˝/185 lbs; Idaho; B5/6/1968 Seattle, WA **1989** Cin 7 (0) **1990** Cin 3 (0) **NFL** 10 (0) [2 yrs]																								
CAREY, VERNON Vernon A., T-G, 6´5˝/363 lbs; Miami (FL); 2004: Mia, rnd 1; B7/13/1981 Miami, FL **2004** Mia 14 (2) **2005** Mia 16 (14, RT) **NFL** 30 (16) [2 yrs]																								
CARL, HARLAND Harland Irvin, HB, 6´0˝/195 lbs; Wisconsin; 1953: ChiB, rnd 14; B10/1/1931 Greenwood, WI																								
1956	ChiB	9	29	66	2.3(12)	1	2	31	15.5(20)	0	—	—	—	—	—	—	—	—	—	—	k	—	6	134
CARLISLE, COOPER Cooper Morrison, G-T, 6´5˝/295 lbs; Florida; 2000: Den, rnd 4; B8/11/1977 Greenville, MS **2000**†Den 14 (0) **2001** Den 16 (0) **2002** Den 1 (0) **2004**†Den 16 (4) **2005**†Den 16 (16, RG)																								
2003	†Den	16(2)	—	—	—	—	1	6	6.0(6)	1	—	—	—	—	—	—	—	—	—	—	—	—	6	8
NFL	6	79(22)	—	—	—	—	1	6	6.0(6)	1	—	—	—	—	—	—	—	—	—	—	—	—	6	8
CARLSON, CODY Matthew Cody, QB, 6´3˝/202 lbs; Baylor; 1987: Hou, rnd 3; B11/5/1963 Dallas, TX																								
1988	Hou	6(5, qb)	12	36	3.0(10)	1	—	—	—	—	112	52	46.4	775	6.9(51)	4	6	10	72	—	—	—	6	214
1989	Hou	6(0)	3	-3	-1.0(0)	0	—	—	—	—	31	15	48.4	155	5.0(23)	0	1	2	20	—	—	—	0	35
1990	†Hou	6(1)	11	52	4.7(16)	0	—	—	—	—	55	37	67.3	383	7.0(53)	4	2	3	15	—	—	—	0	184
1991	Hou	3(0)	4	-3	-0.8(0)	0	—	—	—	—	12	7	58.3	114	9.5(68)	1	0	1	9	—	—	—	0	59
1992	Hou	11(6, qb)	27	77	2.9(13)	1	—	—	—	—	227	149	**65.6**	1710	7.5(65)	9	11	15	90	81.2	—	—	6	547
1993	Hou	8(2)	14	41	2.9(10)	2	—	—	—	—	90	51	56.7	605	6.7(47)	2	4	8	53	—	—	—	12	214
1994	Hou	5(5, qb)	10	17	1.7(6)	0	—	—	—	—	132	59	44.7	727	5.5(81)	1	4	15	115	—	—	—	0	226
NFL	7	45(19)	81	217	2.7(16)	4	—	—	—	—	659	370	56.1	4469	6.8(81)	21	28	54	374	70.0	—	—	24	1477
CARLSON, DEAN Dean Paul, QB, 6´3˝/210 lbs; Iowa State; 1972: KC, rnd 7; B8/1/1950 Rushford, MN																								
1974	KC	1	2	17	8.5(11)	0	—	—	—	—	15	7	46.7	116	7.7(34)	0	1	2	13	—	—	—	0	35
CARLSON, HAL Harold Erwin, G, 6´3˝/220 lbs; Northwestern; DePaul; B1/22/1915 Chicago, IL, D6/6/1981 Scottsdale, IL **1937** ChiC 1 (0)																								
CARLSON, IRV Irvin G., WB-TB, 5´8˝/170 lbs; St. John's (MN); Wisconsin; B8/1896 St. Cloud, MN, deceased **1924** Ken 2 (2)																								
CARLSON, JEFF Jeffrey Allen, QB, 6´3˝/215 lbs; Weber State; 1989: LARm, rnd 4; B5/23/1966 Long Beach, CA																								
1990	TB	1(0)	1	0	0.0(0)	0	—	—	—	—	—	—	—	—	—	—	—	—	—	—	—	—	0	0
1991	TB	3(1)	5	25	5.0(11)	0	—	—	—	—	65	31	47.7	404	6.2(36)	1	6	11	73	—	—	—	0	-8
1992	NE	3(2)	11	32	2.9(7)	0	—	—	—	—	49	18	36.7	232	4.7(40)	1	3	3	21	—	—	—	0	33
NFL	3	7(3)	17	57	3.4(11)	0	—	—	—	—	114	49	43.0	636	5.6(40)	2	9	14	94	—	—	—	0	25
CARLSON, MARK Mark, T, 6´6˝/284 lbs; Southern Connecticut State; B6/6/1963 Milford, CT **1987** Was 3 (3)																								
CARLSON, OKE Eugene, T-G-C, 6´0˝/206 lbs; none; B12/10/1897, D4/1977 Butte Lake, MN **1924** Dul 4 (0) **1925** Dul 3 (3, RT) **1926** Dul 11 (9, LG) **NFL** 18 (12) [3 yrs]																								
CARLSON, ROY Roy Harold, E-G, 5´9˝/178 lbs; Bradley; B5/8/1906 Chicago, IL, D9/10/1984 Phoenix, AZ **1928** ChiB 10 (3), 6 **1929** Day 6 (4, LE) **NFL** 16 (7) [2 yrs]																								
CARLSON, WES Wesley C., G-T, 6´1˝/210 lbs; Detroit Mercy; B7/24/1901, MI, D7/12/1989 Benton Harbor, MI **1926** GB 4 (2)																								
CARLSON, ZUCK Jules Ed, G-T-C-LB, 6´0˝/208 lbs; Oregon State; B11/12/1904 Isaca, ID, D1/21/1986 Chicago, IL **1929** ChiB 14 (9, LG) **1930** ChiB☆13 (8, LG) **1931** ChiB☆11 (8, LG) **1932** ChiB☆13 (12, LG) **1933** ChiB☆11 (11, LG) **1934** ChiB☆12 (10, LG) **1935** ChiB 12 (5, lg) **1936** ChiB 9 (4) **NFL** 95 (67) [8 yrs]																								
CARLTON, DARRYL Darryl Marvin, T, 6´6˝/271 lbs; Tampa; 1975: Mia, rnd 1; B6/24/1953 Bartow, FL, D4/28/1994 **1975** Mia 14 (1) **1976** Mia 14 (8, RT) **1977** TB 14 (13, RT) **1978** TB 13 (12, RT) **1979** TB 16 (2) **NFL** 71 (36) [5 yrs]																								
CARLTON, WRAY Linwood Wray, HB-FB, 6´2˝/225 lbs; Duke; 1959: Phi, rnd 3; B6/18/1937 Wallace, NC																								
1960	Buf-A☆	14(FB)	137	533	3.9(54)	7	29	477	16.4(70)	4	—	—	—	—	—	—	—	—	—	—	—	—	66	862
1961	Buf-A	14(HB)	101	311	3.1(27)	4	17	193	11.4(22)	0	2	0	0.0	0	0.0	0	0	—	—	—	k	—	24	448
1962	Buf-A	11(hb)	94	530	**5.6(51)**	2	7	54	7.7(25)	0	—	—	—	—	—	—	—	—	—	—	—	—	12	577
1963	Buf-A	4	29	125	4.3(19)	0	1	9	9.0(9)	0	—	—	—	—	—	—	—	—	—	—	—	—	0	130
1964	†Buf-A	4	39	114	2.9(11)	1	2	23	11.5(17)	0	—	—	—	—	—	—	—	—	—	—	—	—	6	136
1965	†Buf-A	14(HB)	156	592	3.8(80)	**6**	24	196	8.2(23)	1	—	—	—	—	—	—	—	—	—	—	—	—	42	755
1966	†Buf-A★	14(FB)	156	696	4.5(23)	6	21	280	13.3(55)	0	—	—	—	—	—	—	—	—	—	—	—	—	36	896
1967	Buf-A	12(FB)	107	467	4.4(21)	3	9	97	10.8(24)	0	—	—	—	—	—	—	—	—	—	—	—	—	18	546
NFL	8	87	819	3368	4.1(80)	29	110	1329	12.1(70)	5	2	0	0.0	0	0.0	0	0	—	—	—	k	—	204	4348
CARMAN, CHARLIE William Charlies, G, 5´10˝/215 lbs; Vanderbilt; B1/6/1897, D11/1975 McAllen, TX **1920** Det 1 (0) **1921** Det 6 (3, LG) **NFL** 7 (3) [2 yrs]																								
CARMAN, ED Edmund Ralph, E-T, 5´11˝/199 lbs; Purdue; B1/21/1894 Joliet, IL, D4/9/1964 West Lafayette, IN **[K]** **1922** Ham 6 (6, RE) **1925** Buf 1 (0) **1925** Ham 5 (2), 1 **NFL** 12 (8) [2 yrs]																								
CARMAN, JON Jonathan Daniel, T, 6´7˝/335 lbs; Georgia Tech; B1/14/1976 Sterling, VA **2000** Buf 3 (0) **2001** Buf 9 (2) **NFL** 12 (2) [2 yrs]																								
CARMICHAEL, AL Albert Reinhold, HB, 6´1˝/200 lbs; USC; 1953: GB, rnd 1; B11/10/1928 Boston, MA **[R]**																								
1953	GB	12(RH)	49	199	4.1(41)	1	12	131	10.9(52)	0	—	—	—	—	—	—	—	—	—	—	kp	—	6	625
1954	GB	10(RH)	33	130	3.9(23)	0	18	251	13.9(45)	0	—	—	—	—	—	—	—	—	—	—	kp	—	0	485
1955	GB	10	6	45	7.5(20)	0	16	222	13.9(32)	1	—	—	—	—	—	—	—	—	—	—	kp	1	12	418
1956	GB	12(RH)	32	199	6.2(35)	0	13	180	13.8(63)	1	—	—	—	—	—	—	—	—	—	—	kp	1	12	796
1957	GB	12	37	118	3.2(10)	1	13	184	14.2(39)	0	—	—	—	—	—	—	—	—	—	—	kp	—	6	510
1958	GB	12	9	21	2.3(8)	0	3	26	8.7(14)	1	—	—	—	—	—	—	—	—	—	—	kp	—	6	296
1960	Den-A	10	41	211	5.1(47)	2	32	616	19.3(59)	5	1	1	100.0	26	26.0(26)	0	0	—	—	—	kp	—	42	854
1961	Den-A	6	15	24	1.6(8)	0	5	23	4.6(14)	0	—	—	—	—	—	—	—	—	—	—	kp	—	0	129
NFL	8	84	222	947	4.3(47)	4	112	1633	14.6(63)	8	1	1	100.0	26	26.0(26)	0	0	—	—	—	kp	2	84	4112

YEAR	TEAM	G (GS, POS)	RUSH	YD	AVG (LG)	TD	REC	YD	AVG (LG)	TD	PASS	COMP	PCT	YD	AVG (LG)	TD	INT	SK	YD	QBR	KPR	OTD	PTS	TAY

CARMICHAEL, HAROLD Lee Harold, WR-TE, 6´8˝/225 lbs; Southern (LA); 1971: Phi, rnd 7; B9/22/1949 Jacksonville, FL

1971	Phi	9(6, te)	—	—	—	—	20	288	14.4(50)	2				—	—	—					—	—	0	144
1972	Phi	13(5, wr)	—	—	—	—	20	276	13.8(54)	2				—	—	—					—	—	12	148
1973	Phi★	14(14, WR)	3	42	14.0(23)	0	67	1116	16.7(73)	9				—	—	—					—	—	54	645
1974	Phi☆	14(14, WR)	2	-6	-3.0(-1)	0	56	649	11.6(39)	8	1	0	0.0	0	0.0	0					—	—	48	359
1975	Phi	14(13, WR)	1	6	6.0(6)	0	49	639	13.0(62)	7				—	—	—					—	—	42	361
1976	Phi	14(14, WR)	—	—	—	—	42	503	12.0(24)	5	2	0	0.0	0	0.0	0					—	—	30	277
1977	Phi☆	14(14, WR)	—	—	—	—	46	665	14.5(50)	7				—	—	—					—	—	42	368
1978	†Phi★	16(16, WR)	1	21	21.0(21)	0	55	1072	19.5(56)	8				—	—	—					—	—	48	597
1979	†Phi★	16(16, WR)	1	0	0.0(0)	0	52	872	16.8(50)	11				—	—	—					—	—	66	491
1980	†Phi★	16(16, WR)	—	—	—	—	48	815	17.0(56)	9				—	—	—					—	—	54	453
1981	†Phi	16(16, WR)	1	1	1.0(1)	0	61	1028	16.9(85)	6				—	—	—					—	—	36	545
1982	Phi	9(8, WR)	—	—	—	—	35	540	15.4(46)	4				—	—	—					—	—	24	290
1983	Phi	15(11, WR)	—	—	—	—	38	515	13.6(35)	3	1	1	100.0	45	45.0(45)	1	0				—	—	18	300
1984	Dal	2(0)	—	—	—	—	1	7	7.0(7)	0				—	—	—					—	—	0	4
NFL	14	182(163)	9	64	7.1(23)	0	590	8985	15.2(85)	79	4	1	25.0	45	11.3(45)	1	0				—	—	474	4979

CARMICHAEL, PAUL Paul Harold, HB, 6´0˝/200 lbs; El Camino College (JC); B8/28/1944 Inglewood, CA **1965** Den-A 3

CARNELLY, RAY Raymond Harry, HB, 6´2˝/190 lbs; Carnegie Mellon; 1939: Bkn, rnd 14; B8/11/1916 Beaver Falls, PA, D11/14/2002 Orange, TX **[K]**

| 1939 | Bkn | 9(3) | 15 | 64 | 4.3 | 0 | 1 | 5 | 5.0(5) | 0 | 14 | 3 | 21.4 | 35 | 2.5 | 0 | 3 | | | | K | — | 0 | -36 |

CARNEY, ART Arthur Gerald, G-E, 6´2˝/230 lbs; Navy; B9/23/1900 New York, NY, D3/24/1962 Bronxville, NY **1925** NYG☆9 (8, LG) **1926** NYG 8 (7, re) **NFL** 17 (15) [2 yrs]

CARNEY, CHUCK Charles Roslyn, T-G, 6´1˝/190 lbs; Illinois; B8/25/1900 Chicago, IL, D9/5/1984 Manchester, MA **1922** Col 3 (1)

CARNEY, JOHN John Michael, K, 5´11˝/180 lbs; Notre Dame; B4/20/1964 Hartford, CT **[K]** **1988** TB 4 (0) **1989** TB 1 (0) **1990** LARm 1 (0) **1990** SD☆12 (0) **1991** SD 16 (0) **1992**†SD 16 (0) **1993** SD 16 (0) **1994**†SD★16 (0) **1995**†SD 16 (0) **1996** SD 16 (0) **1997** SD 4 (0) **1998** SD 16 (0) **1999** SD 16 (0) **2000** SD 16 (0) **2002** NO 16 (0) **2004** NO 16 (0) **2005** NO 16 (0)

2001	NO	15(0)	1	-1	-1.0(-1)	0	—	—	—	—				—	—	—					K	—	113	-1
2003	NO	16(0)	1	3	3.0(3)	0	—	—	—	—				—	—	—					K	—	102	3
NFL	18	245(0)	2	2	1.0(3)	0	—	—	—	—				—	—	—					KP	—	1634	2

CAROLAN, BRETT Brett H., TE, 6´3˝/241 lbs; Washington State; B3/16/1971 San Rafael, CA

1994	SF	5(0)	—	—	—	—	2	10	5.0(6)	0				—	—	—						—	0	5
1995	SF	14(0)	—	—	—	—	1	3	3.0(3)	0				—	—	—						—	0	2
1996	Mia	6(2)	—	—	—	—	4	48	12.0(21)	1				—	—	—						—	6	29
NFL	3	25(2)	—	—	—	—	7	61	8.7(21)	1				—	—	—						—	6	36

CAROLAN, REGGIE Reginald Howard, TE, 6´6˝/236 lbs; Idaho; 1961: SD, rnd 17/LA, rnd 8; B10/25/1939 San Rafael, CA, D1/2/1983 San Rafael, CA

1962	SD-A◇	14	—	—	—	—	3	39	13.0(18)	1				—	—	—						—	6	25
1963	SD-A	4	—	—	—	—	—	—	—	—				—	—	—						—	0	
1964	KC-A	6	—	—	—	—	3	54	18.0(25)	1				—	—	—						—	6	32
1965	KC-A	14	—	—	—	—	6	65	10.8(14)	0				—	—	—						—	2	33
1966	†KC-A	14	—	—	—	—	7	154	22.0(45)	3				—	—	—						—	18	92
1967	KC-A	14	—	—	—	—	2	26	13.0(23)	0				—	—	—					Pk	—	2	0
1968	†KC-A	14	—	—	—	—	2	26	13.0(19)	0				—	—	—					P	—	0	13
NFL	7	80	—	—	—	—	23	364	15.8(45)	5				—	—	—					Pk	—	34	194

CAROLINE, J.C. James C., DB-HB, 6´0˝/185 lbs; Illinois; 1956: ChiB, rnd 7; B1/17/1933 Warrenton, GA **[I]** **1959** ChiB 12 (DB) **1960** ChiB 12 (LCB) **1961** ChiB 14 (LCB) **1962** ChiB 14 (LCB) **1963**†ChiB 14 **1964** ChiB 14 **1965** ChiB 2

1956	†ChiB★	12(DB)	34	141	4.1(26)	2	—	—	—	—				—	—	—					kpi	2	24	354
1957	ChiB	12(DB)	1	1	1.0(1)	0	1	33	33.0(33)	0				—	—	—					kpi	—	0	37
1958	ChiB	12(db/rh)	33	121	3.7(19)	0	5	78	15.6(58)	1				—	—	—					k	—	6	198
NFL	10	118	68	263	3.9(26)	2	6	111	18.5(58)	1				—	—	—					kpi	3	36	710

CAROLLO, JOE Joseph Paul, T, 6´2˝/265 lbs; Notre Dame; 1962: LA, rnd 2/DalT, rnd 18; B3/25/1940 Wyandotte, MI **1962** LARm 13 (LT) **1963** LARm 14 (LT) **1964** LARm 14 (LT) **1965** LARm 14 (LT) **1966** LARm 14 (14, LT) **1967**†LARm 14 (14, LT) **1968** LARm◇14 (14, LT) **1969** Phi 14 (RT) **1970** Phi 14 (RT) **1971** LARm 11 **1972**†Cle 2 **1973** Cle 12 **NFL** 150 (42) [12 yrs]

CARON, ROGER Roger Eugene, T, 6´5˝/282 lbs; Harvard; 1985: Ind, rnd 5; B6/3/1962 Boston, MA **1985** Ind 7 (1) **1986** Ind 3 (0) **NFL** 10 (1) [2 yrs]

CAROTHERS, DON Donald E., E, 6´5˝/225 lbs; Bradley; 1957: ChiC, rnd 10; B5/13/1934 Moline, IL

| 1960 | Den-A | 3 | — | — | — | — | 2 | 25 | 12.5(20) | 0 | | | | — | — | — | | | | | | — | 0 | 13 |

CARPE, JOE Joseph A., T-E-C, 6´0˝/197 lbs; Millikin; B1/23/1903 Westville, IL, D11/3/1977 Quincy, MA **1926** Fra 6 (1) **1927** Pot 4 (1) **1928** Pot 9 (7, RT) **1929** Bos 6 (6, LT) **1933** Phi 2 (1) **NFL** 27 (16) [5 yrs]

CARPENTER, BRIAN Brian Milton, DB, 5´10˝/167 lbs; Michigan; 1982: Dal, rnd 4; B11/27/1960 Flint, MI **1982** NYG 4 (0) **1983**†Was 15 (0) **1984** Was 3 (0) **1984** Buf 13 (10, LCB) **NFL** 35 (10) [3 yrs]

CARPENTER, DWAINE Dwaine L., DB, 6´1˝/203 lbs; North Carolina A&T; B11/4/1976 Pinehurst, NC **2003** SF 15 (2) **2004** SF 15 (6, lcb) **2005** SF 2 (0) **2005** SL 1 (0) **NFL** 33 (8) [3 yrs]

CARPENTER, JACK Jack Chrisman, T, 6´0˝/240 lbs; Columbia; Missouri; Michigan; 1947: Cle-A, rnd 3/1944: ChiC, rnd 15; B7/29/1923 Kansas City, MO, D10/16/2005 Honolulu, HI **1947** Buf-A 13 (2) **1948**†Buf-A 12 (5, rt) **1949**†SF-A 3 (0)

| 1949 | Buf-A | 8(7, LT) | — | — | — | — | 2 | 20 | 10.0 | 0 | | | | — | — | — | | | | | | — | 0 | 10 |
| AAFC | 3 | 36(14) | — | — | — | — | 2 | 20 | 10.0 | 0 | | | | — | — | — | | | | | | — | 0 | 10 |

CARPENTER, KEION Keion Eric, DB, 5´11˝/205 lbs; Virginia Tech; B10/31/1977 Baltimore, MD **1999**†Buf 10 (0) **2000** Buf 12 (12, FS) **2001** Buf 15 (10, FS) **2002**†Atl 16 (16, FS) **2003** Atl 15 (8, fs) **2005** Atl 15 (15, SS) **NFL** 83 (61) [6 yrs]

CARPENTER, KEN Kenneth Leroy, HB-FL, 6´0˝/195 lbs; Oregon State; 1950: Cle, rnd 1; B2/26/1926 Seaside, OR

1950	†Cle	12(lh)	35	181	5.2(21)	1	5	45	9.0(16)	0	1	0	0.0	0	0.0	0	1				kp	—	6	235
1951	†Cle◇	11(LH)	85	402	4.7(30)	4	12	183	15.3(45)	2				—	—	—					kp	—	36	708
1952	†Cle	8(LH)	72	408	5.7(37)	3	16	136	8.5(41)	1				—	—	—					kp	1	30	679
1953	†Cle	12(LH)	46	216	4.2(30)	3	9	109	12.1(32)	2				—	—	—					kp	—	30	387
1960	Den-A	6(fl)	4	13	3.3(9)	0	29	350	12.1(36)	1				—	—	—					kp	—	6	193
NFL	5	49	242	1199	5.0(61)	11	71	823	11.6(45)	6	1	0	0.0	0	0.0	0	1				kp	1	108	2201

CARPENTER, LEW Lewis Glenn, HB-FB, 6´1˝/220 lbs; Arkansas; 1953: Det, rnd 8; B1/12/1932 Hayti, MO

1953	†Det	12	7	24	3.4(12)	0	—	—	—	—				—	—	—					ki	1	6	154
1954	†Det	11(LH)	104	476	4.6(60)	3	16	145	9.1(23)	2				—	—	—					k	—	30	605
1955	Det	12(LH)	137	543	4.0(49)	6	44	312	7.1(34)	2				—	—	—					k	—	48	787
1957	†Cle	10(lh)	83	315	3.8(55)	4	5	65	13.0(21)	0				—	—	—					k	—	24	397
1958	†Cle	12(lh)	73	308	4.2(30)	2	5	47	9.4(18)	0				—	—	—					k	—	12	355
1959	GB	12	60	322	5.4(55)	1	5	47	9.4(23)	0				—	—	—					kp	—	6	450
1960	†GB	12	1	24	24.0(24)	0	1	21	21.0(21)	0				—	—	—					kp	—	0	118
1961	†GB	14	1	5	5.0(5)	0	3	29	9.7(16)	0				—	—	—					p	—	0	120
1962	†GB	14	—	—	—	—	7	104	14.9(22)	0				—	—	—						—	0	52
1963	GB	14	2	8	4.0(5)	0	1	12	12.0(12)	0				—	—	—						—	0	52
NFL	10	123	468	2025	4.3(60)	16	87	782	9.0(34)	4				—	—	—					kpi	1	126	3049

CARPENTER, PRESTON Verda Preston, E-HB, 6´2˝/190 lbs; Arkansas; 1956: Cle, rnd 1; B1/24/1934 Hayti, MO

1956	Cle☆	12(LH)	188	756	4.0(30)	0	16	124	7.8(34)	0				—	—	—					kp	—	0	987
1957	†Cle	12(RE)	3	86	28.7(39)	1	27	398	14.7(33)	2				—	—	—						—	18	305
1958	†Cle	12(RE)	3	2	0.7(22)	0	29	474	16.3(74)	1				—	—	—						—	6	244

YEAR	TEAM	G(GS, POS)	RUSH	YD	AVG(LG)	TD	REC	YD	AVG(LG)	TD	PASS	COMP	PCT	YD	AVG(LG)	TD	INT	SK	YD	QBR	KPR	OTD	PTS	TAY
1959	Cle	12(LE)	1	4	4.0(4)	0	24	372	15.5(43)	2	—	—	—	—	—	—	—	—	—	—	—	—	12	200
1960	Pit	12(TE)	17	36	2.1(20)	0	29	495	17.1(70)	2	2	1	50.0	2	1.0(2)	0	0	—	—	—	kp	—	12	455
1961	Pit	13(TE)	7	9	1.3(13)	0	33	460	13.9(40)	4	—	—	—	—	—	—	—	—	—	—	p	—	24	262
1962	Pit★	13(TE)	1	-3	-3.0(-3)	0	36	492	13.7(43)	4	—	—	—	—	—	—	—	—	—	—	kp	—	24	351
1963	Pit	14	1	-3	-3.0(-3)	0	17	233	13.7(28)	1	—	—	—	—	—	—	—	—	—	—	p	—	6	119
1964	Was	14(TE)	1	7	7.0(7)	0	31	466	15.0(39)	3	1	0	0.0	0	0.0	0	0	—	—	—	p	—	18	264
1965	Was	9(TE)	—	—	—	—	23	298	13.0(36)	0	—	—	—	—	—	—	—	—	—	—	—	—	0	149
1966	Was	1	—	—	—	—	3	31	10.3(17)	0	—	—	—	—	—	—	—	—	—	—	—	—	0	16
1966	Min	12(12, TE)	1	-10	-10.0(-10)	0	27	487	18.0(52)	4	—	—	—	—	—	—	—	—	—	—	—	—	24	254
1967	Mia-A	13	—	—	—	—	10	127	12.7(42)	0	—	—	—	—	—	—	—	—	—	—	k	—	0	106
NFL	12	149(12)	223	884	4.0(39)	1	305	4457	14.6(74)	23	3	1	33.3	2	0.7(2)	0	0	—	—	—	kp	—	144	3710

Carpenter, Rob Robert Joseph, RB, 6´1˝/224 lbs; Miami (OH); 1977: Hou, rnd 3; B4/20/1955 Lancaster, OH

YEAR	TEAM	G(GS, POS)	RUSH	YD	AVG(LG)	TD	REC	YD	AVG(LG)	TD	PASS	COMP	PCT	YD	AVG(LG)	TD	INT	SK	YD	QBR	KPR	OTD	PTS	TAY
1977	Hou	11(7, FB)	144	652	4.5(77)	1	23	156	6.8(27)	0	—	—	—	—	—	—	—	—	—	—	—	—	6	740
1978	Hou	11	82	348	4.2(20)	5	17	150	8.8(37)	0	—	—	—	—	—	—	—	—	—	—	k	—	30	469
1979	†Hou	16	92	355	3.9(13)	3	16	116	7.3(22)	1	—	—	—	—	—	—	—	—	—	—	k	—	24	452
1980	†Hou	15(1)	97	359	3.7(46)	3	43	346	8.0(25)	0	—	—	—	—	—	—	—	—	—	—	k	—	18	554
1981	Hou	4(4)	18	74	4.1(20)	0	13	80	6.2(33)	1	—	—	—	—	—	—	—	—	—	—	—	—	6	119
1981	†NYG	10(8, FB)	190	748	3.9(35)	5	24	201	8.4(37)	0	—	—	—	—	—	—	—	—	—	—	—	—	30	899
1982	NYG	5(5, FB)	67	204	3.0(23)	1	7	29	4.1(11)	0	—	—	—	—	—	—	—	—	—	—	—	—	6	229
1983	NYG	10(10, FB)	170	624	3.7(37)	4	26	258	9.9(38)	2	—	—	—	—	—	—	—	—	—	—	—	—	36	803
1984	†NYG	16(16, FB)	250	795	3.2(22)	7	26	209	8.0(19)	1	—	—	—	—	—	—	—	—	—	—	—	—	48	975
1985	†NYG	14(10, FB)	60	201	3.3(46)	0	20	162	8.1(23)	0	—	—	—	—	—	—	—	—	—	—	—	—	0	282
1986	LARm	6(0)	2	3	1.5(3)	0	—	—	—	—	—	—	—	—	—	—	—	—	—	—	k	—	0	-8
NFL	10	118(61)	1172	4363	3.7(77)	29	215	1707	7.9(38)	5	—	—	—	—	—	—	—	—	—	—	k	—	204	5513

Carpenter, Rob Robert Gordon, WR, 6´2˝/190 lbs; Notre Dame; Syracuse; 1991: Cin, rnd 4; B8/1/1968 Amityville, NY

YEAR	TEAM	G(GS, POS)	RUSH	YD	AVG(LG)	TD	REC	YD	AVG(LG)	TD	PASS	COMP	PCT	YD	AVG(LG)	TD	INT	SK	YD	QBR	KPR	OTD	PTS	TAY
1991	NE	9(1)	—	—	—	—	3	45	15.0(23)	0	—	—	—	—	—	—	—	—	—	—	—	—	0	23
1992	NYJ	16(0)	1	2	2.0(2)	0	13	161	12.4(51)	1	1	0	0.0	0	0.0	0	0	—	—	—	p	—	6	156
1993	NYJ	16(0)	—	—	—	—	6	83	13.8(18)	0	—	—	—	—	—	—	—	—	—	—	—	—	0	42
1994	NYJ	3(0)	—	—	—	—	—	—	—	—	—	—	—	—	—	—	—	—	—	—	—	—	—	—
1995	†Phi	16(4)	—	—	—	—	29	318	11.0(29)	0	—	—	—	—	—	—	—	—	—	—	p	—	0	178
NFL	5	60(5)	1	2	2.0(2)	0	51	607	11.9(51)	1	1	0	0.0	0	0.0	0	0	—	—	—	p	—	6	398

Carpenter, Ron Ronald Nelson, DT-DE, 6´4˝/261 lbs; North Carolina State; 1970: Cin, rnd 2; B6/24/1948 High Point, NC **1970**†Cin 14 (RDE) **1971** Cin 14 (RDE) **1972** Cin 14 **1973**†Cin 13 (RDT) **1974** Cin 14 (RDT) **1975**†Cin 14 (RDT) **1976** Cin 14 (RDT) **NFL** 97 [7 yrs]

Carpenter, Ron Ronald Allen, DB, 6´1˝/189 lbs; Miami (OH); B1/20/1970 Cincinnati, OH **1993** Min 7 (0) **1993** Cin 6 (0) **1995** NYJ 13 (4) **1996** NYJ 2 (0) **1998** SL 6 (0) **1999**†SL 11 (0) **NFL** 45 (4) [5 yrs]

Carpenter, Ron Ronnie Dean, LB, 6´2˝/230 lbs; Texas A&M; 1964: SD, rnd 12; B9/2/1941 Marshall, TX **1964**†SD-A 12 (LLB) **1965**†SD-A 6 **NFL** 18 [2 yrs]

Carpenter, Steve Steven, DB, 6´2˝/195 lbs; Western Illinois; B1/22/1958 Staunton, IL **1980** NYJ 3 (0) **1981** SL 1 (0) **NFL** 4 (0) [2 yrs]

Carr, Carl Carl Edward, LB, 6´3˝/230 lbs; North Carolina; 1986: NYJ, rnd 10; B3/26/1964 South Boston, VA **1987** Det 3 (3)

Carr, Charley Henry Clytus, B, 5´10˝/175 lbs; Western Michigan; B1/21/1904 Otsego, MI, D11/1/1976 Marshall, MI **1926** Ham 2 (0)

Carr, Chetti Chester L., DB, 5´9˝/185 lbs; Central Oklahoma; Northwestern Oklahoma State; B1/1/1963 Enid, OK **1987** LARd 2 (0)

Carr, Chris Chris, DB, 5´10˝/180 lbs; Boise State; B4/30/1983 Reno, NV **2005** Oak 16 (0)

Carr, David David, QB, 6´3˝/233 lbs; Fresno State; 2002: Hou, rnd 1; B7/21/1979 Bakersfield, CA

YEAR	TEAM	G(GS, POS)	RUSH	YD	AVG(LG)	TD	REC	YD	AVG(LG)	TD	PASS	COMP	PCT	YD	AVG(LG)	TD	INT	SK	YD	QBR	KPR	OTD	PTS	TAY
2002	Hou	16(16, QB)	59	282	4.8(20)	3	—	—	—	—	444	233	52.5	2592	5.8(81)	9	15	76	411	62.8	—	—	18	1053
2003	Hou	12(11, QB)	27	151	5.6(36)	2	—	—	—	—	295	167	56.6	2013	6.8(78)	9	13	15	90	69.5	—	—	12	703
2004	Hou	16(16, QB)	73	299	4.1(24)	0	—	—	—	—	466	285	61.2	3531	7.6(69)	16	14	49	301	83.5	—	—	0	1585
2005	Hou	16(16, QB)	56	308	5.5(20)	1	—	—	—	—	423	256	60.5	2488	5.9(53)	14	11	68	424	77.2	—	—	6	1192
NFL	4	60(59)	215	1040	4.8(36)	6	—	—	—	—	1628	941	57.8	10624	6.5(81)	48	53	208	1226	73.7	—	—	36	4532

Carr, Earl Earl, RB, 6´0˝/224 lbs; Florida; 1978: SL, rnd 5; B1/22/1955 Tallahassee, FL

YEAR	TEAM	G(GS, POS)	RUSH	YD	AVG(LG)	TD	REC	YD	AVG(LG)	TD	PASS	COMP	PCT	YD	AVG(LG)	TD	INT	SK	YD	QBR	KPR	OTD	PTS	TAY
1978	SF	14	1	2	2.0(2)	0	—	—	—	—	—	—	—	—	—	—	—	—	—	—	—	—	0	2
1979	Phi	1	1	-1	-1.0(-1)	0	1	2	2.0(2)	0	—	—	—	—	—	—	—	—	—	—	—	—	0	0
NFL	2	15	2	1	0.5(2)	0	1	2	2.0(2)	0	—	—	—	—	—	—	—	—	—	—	—	—	0	2

Carr, Eddie Edwin Forest, DB-HB, 6´0˝/185 lbs; none; B4/27/1923

YEAR	TEAM	G(GS, POS)	RUSH	YD	AVG(LG)	TD	REC	YD	AVG(LG)	TD	PASS	COMP	PCT	YD	AVG(LG)	TD	INT	SK	YD	QBR	KPR	OTD	PTS	TAY
1947	SF-A	10(0)	11	42	3.8	0	4	41	10.3	0	—	—	—	—	—	—	—	—	—	—	kpi	—	0	139
1948	SF-A	13(1)	14	121	8.6	1	3	40	13.3	0	—	—	—	—	—	—	—	—	—	—	ki	1	12	271
1949	SF-A	7(2)	19	120	6.3	2	7	165	23.6	3	—	—	—	—	—	—	—	—	—	—	pi	2	42	301
AAFC	3	30(3)	44	283	6.4	3	14	246	17.6	3	—	—	—	—	—	—	—	—	—	—	kpi	3	54	710

Carr, Fred Freddie Alton, LB, 6´5˝/238 lbs; Texas-El Paso; 1968: GB, rnd 1; B8/19/1946 Phoenix, AZ **1968** GB 14 **1969** GB 14 **1970** GB★14 (14, RLB) **1971** GB 14 (14, RLB) **1972**†GB★14 (14, RLB) **1973** GB 14 (14, RLB) **1974** GB☆14 (14, RLB) **1975** GB★14 (14, RLB) **1976** GB☆14 (14, RLB) **1977** GB 14 (14, RLB) **NFL** 140 (112) [10 yrs]

Carr, Gregg Gregg Kevin, LB, 6´2˝/219 lbs; Auburn; 1985: Pit, rnd 6; B3/31/1962 Birmingham, AL **1985** Pit 16 (2) **1986** Pit 16 (0) **1987** Pit 12 (0) **1988** Pit 13 (5, rolb) **NFL** 57 (7) [4 yrs]

Carr, Harlan Harlan Bradley, WB-QB, 5´10˝/165 lbs; Syracuse; B4/30/1903 Union Springs, NY, D10/24/1970 Auburn, NY **1927** Buf 5 (5, WB), 6 **1927** Pot 5 (4), 12 **NFL** 10 (9), 18 [1 yr]

Carr, Henry Henry Joseph, DB, 6´3˝/190 lbs; Arizona State; 1965: NYG, rnd 4/KC, rnd R3; B11/27/1942 Detroit, MI **1965** NYG 14 (LS) **1966** NYG 14 (RS) **1967** NYG 9 (RCB) **NFL** 37 [3 yrs]

Carr, Jimmy James Henry, DB-LB-HB, 6´1˝/206 lbs; Charleston (WV); B3/25/1933 Kayford, WV **1957** ChiC 6 **1959** Phi 12 (DB) **1960**†Phi 10 (LCB) **1961** Phi 13 (LCB) **1962** Phi 14 (LS) **1963** Phi 14 (LS) **1964** Was 14 **1965** Was 13

YEAR	TEAM	G(GS, POS)	RUSH	YD	AVG(LG)	TD	REC	YD	AVG(LG)	TD	PASS	COMP	PCT	YD	AVG(LG)	TD	INT	SK	YD	QBR	KPR	OTD	PTS	TAY
1955	ChiC	12	30	115	3.8(41)	0	9	157	17.4(59)	0	—	—	—	—	—	—	—	—	—	—	kp	—	0	222
NFL	9	108	30	115	3.8(41)	0	9	157	17.4(59)	0	—	—	—	—	—	—	—	—	—	—	kpi	1	6	312

Carr, Levert Levert F., T-G-DT, 6´2˝/273 lbs; North Central; B6/30/1944 Birmingham, AL **1969** SD-A 7 **1970** Buf 7 **1971** Buf 14 (rg) **1972** Hou 14 (RT) **1973** Hou 13 (rt) **NFL** 55 [5 yrs]

Carr, Lydell Lydell, RB, 6´1˝/226 lbs; Oklahoma; 1988: NO, rnd 4; B5/27/1965 Enid, OK **1989** Phx 5 (0)

Carr, Paul Paul Howard, DB-LB, 6´0˝/205 lbs; Houston; 1953: SF, rnd 7; B9/4/1931 Los Angeles, CA **1955** SF 10 **1956** SF 12 (DB) **1957**†SF 8 **NFL** 30 [3 yrs]

Carr, Reggie Reginald S., DE, 6´3˝/300 lbs; Jackson State; B2/17/1963 Meridian, MS **1987** NYG 3 (3)

Carr, Roger Roger Dale, WR, 6´3˝/200 lbs; Louisiana Tech; 1974: Bal, rnd 1; B7/1/1952 Seminole, OK

YEAR	TEAM	G(GS, POS)	RUSH	YD	AVG(LG)	TD	REC	YD	AVG(LG)	TD	PASS	COMP	PCT	YD	AVG(LG)	TD	INT	SK	YD	QBR	KPR	OTD	PTS	TAY
1974	Bal	11(8, WR)	—	—	—	—	21	405	19.3(57)	0	—	—	—	—	—	—	—	—	—	—	—	—	0	203
1975	†Bal	14(14, WR)	—	—	—	—	23	517	22.5(90)	2	—	—	—	—	—	—	—	—	—	—	—	—	12	269
1976	†Bal★	14(14, WR)	—	—	—	—	43	**1112**	**25.9(79)**	11	—	—	—	—	—	—	—	—	—	—	—	—	66	611
1977	Bal	7	—	—	—	—	11	199	18.1(45)	1	—	—	—	—	—	—	—	—	—	—	—	—	6	105
1978	Bal	16(16, WR)	—	—	—	—	30	629	21.0(78)	6	—	—	—	—	—	—	—	—	—	—	—	—	36	345
1979	Bal	9(9, WR)	—	—	—	—	27	400	14.8(37)	1	—	—	—	—	—	—	—	—	—	—	—	—	6	205
1980	Bal	16(16, WR)	1	-8	-8.0(-8)	0	61	924	15.1(43)	5	—	—	—	—	—	—	—	—	—	—	—	—	30	479
1981	Bal	15(15, WR)	—	—	—	—	38	584	15.4(43)	3	—	—	—	—	—	—	—	—	—	—	—	—	18	307
1982	Sea	9(0)	—	—	—	—	15	265	17.7(50)	2	—	—	—	—	—	—	—	—	—	—	—	—	12	143
1983	SD	4(0)	—	—	—	—	2	36	18.0(23)	0	—	—	—	—	—	—	—	—	—	—	—	—	0	18
NFL	10	115(92)	1	-8	-8.0(-8)	0	271	5071	18.7(90)	31	—	—	—	—	—	—	—	—	—	—	—	—	186	2683

Carr, Tom Thomas Winther, DT, 6´4˝/264 lbs; Morgan State; 1966: Bal, rnd 20; B4/6/1942 Philadelphia, PA **1968** NO 4

YEAR	TEAM	G(GS, POS)	RUSH	YD	AVG(LG)	TD	REC	YD	AVG(LG)	TD	PASS	COMP	PCT	YD	AVG(LG)	TD	INT	SK	YD	QBR	KPR	OTD	PTS	TAY

Carreker, Alphonso Alphonso, DE, 6´6˝/268 lbs; Florida State; 1984: GB, rnd 1; B5/25/1962 Columbus, OH **1984** GB 14 (14, LDE) **1985** GB 16 (10, LDE) **1986** GB 16 (16, LDE) **1987** GB 12 (12, LDE) **1988** GB 14 (11, LDE) **1989**†Den 16 (16, LDE) **1991** Den 6 (1) **NFL** 94 (80) [7 yrs]

Carreker, Vince Vincent Lewis, DB, 6´0˝/183 lbs; Central State (OH); Cincinnati; B8/21/1963 Columbus, OH **1987** Cle 2 (0)

Carrell, Duane Duane Blore, P, 5´10˝/185 lbs; Florida State; B10/3/1949 Washington, DC **[P]**

YEAR	TEAM	G(GS, POS)	RUSH	YD	AVG(LG)	TD	REC	YD	AVG(LG)	TD	PASS	COMP	PCT	YD	AVG(LG)	TD	INT	SK	YD	QBR	KPR	OTD	PTS	TAY
1974	Dal	7	—	—	—	—	—	—	—	—	1	1	100.0	37	37.0(37)	0	0	—	—	—	P	—	0	19
1975	†LARm	14	—	—	—	—	—	—	—	—	—	—	—	—	—	—	—	—	—	—	P	—	0	0
1976	NYJ	14	2	0	0.0(0)	0	—	—	—	—	—	—	—	—	—	—	—	—	—	—	P	—	0	0
1977	NYJ	2	2	-15	-7.5(0)	0	—	—	—	—	—	—	—	—	—	—	—	—	—	—	P	—	0	-15
1977	SL	10	—	—	—	—	—	—	—	—	—	—	—	—	—	—	—	—	—	—	P	—	0	0
NFL	4	47	4	-15	-3.8	0	—	—	—	—	1	1	100.0	37	37.0(37)	0	0	—	—	—	P	—	0	4

Carrell, John John, LB, 6´3˝/227 lbs; Texas Tech; 1965: Oak, rnd R7/Pit, rnd 15; B12/19/1942 Amarillo, TX **1966** Hou-A 6

Carrier, Mark John Mark, WR, 6´0˝/186 lbs; Nicholls State; 1987: TB, rnd 3; B10/28/1965 Lafayette, LA

YEAR	TEAM	G(GS, POS)	RUSH	YD	AVG(LG)	TD	REC	YD	AVG(LG)	TD	PASS	COMP	PCT	YD	AVG(LG)	TD	INT	SK	YD	QBR	KPR	OTD	PTS	TAY
1987	TB	10(5, WR)	—	—	—	—	26	423	16.3(38)	3	—	—	—	—	—	—	—	—	—	—	k	—	18	212
1988	TB	16(16, WR)	—	—	—	—	57	970	17.0(59)	5	—	—	—	—	—	—	—	—	—	—	—	—	30	510
1989	TB★	16(15, WR)	—	—	—	—	86	1422	16.5(78)	9	—	—	—	—	—	—	—	—	—	—	—	—	54	756
1990	TB	16(16, WR)	—	—	—	—	49	813	16.6(68)	4	—	—	—	—	—	—	—	—	—	—	—	—	24	427
1991	TB	16(16, WR)	—	—	—	—	47	698	14.9(35)	2	—	—	—	—	—	—	—	—	—	—	—	—	12	359
1992	TB	14(12, WR)	—	—	—	—	56	692	12.4(40)	4	—	—	—	—	—	—	—	—	—	—	—	—	24	366
1993	Cle	16(16, WR)	4	26	6.5(15)	1	43	746	17.3(55)	3	—	—	—	—	—	—	—	—	—	—	p	1	30	496
1994	†Cle	16(6, wr)	1	14	14.0(14)	1	29	452	15.6(43)	5	—	—	—	—	—	—	—	—	—	—	p	—	36	342
1995	Car	16(15, WR)	3	-4	-1.3(4)	0	66	1002	15.2(66)	3	—	—	—	—	—	—	—	—	—	—	p	—	18	507
1996	†Car	16(15, WR)	—	—	—	—	58	808	13.9(39)	6	—	—	—	—	—	—	—	—	—	—	—	—	36	434
1997	Car	9(6, WR)	—	—	—	—	33	436	13.2(36)	2	—	—	—	—	—	—	—	—	—	—	—	—	12	228
1998	Car	16(1)	—	—	—	—	19	301	15.8(42)	2	—	—	—	—	—	—	—	—	—	—	—	—	12	161
NFL	12	177(139)	8	36	4.5(15)	2	569	8763	15.4(78)	48	—	—	—	—	—	—	—	—	—	—	kp	1	306	4797

Carrier, Mark Mark Anthony, DB, 6´1˝/192 lbs; USC; 1990: Chi, rnd 1; B4/28/1968 Lake Charles, LA **[I]** **1990**†ChiB★16 (16, FS) **1991**†ChiB★16 (16, FS) **1992** ChiB 16 (14, FS) **1993** ChiB✧16 (16, FS) **1994**†ChiB☆16 (15, FS) **1995** ChiB 16 (15, FS) **1996** ChiB 13 (13, FS) **1997**†Det 16 (16, FS) **1998** Det 13 (13, FS) **1999**†Det 15 (15, FS) **2000** Was 15 (15, FS) **NFL** 168 (164) [11 yrs]

Carrington, Darren Darren Russell, DB, 6´2˝/200 lbs; Northern Arizona; 1989: Den, rnd 5; B10/10/1966 Bronx, NY **[I]** **1989**†Den 16 (0) **1990** Det 12 (0) **1991** SD 16 (1) **1992**†SD 16 (4) **1993** SD 16 (14, SS) **1994**†SD 16 (16, SS) **1995** Jax 6 (2) **1996** Oak 15 (10, FS) **NFL** 113 (47) [8 yrs]

Carrington, Ed Edward Codrington, TE, 6´4˝/225 lbs; Virginia; 1967: Hou, rnd 7; B9/1/1944 Beaumont, TX **1968** Hou-A 1 **1969**†Hou-A 14 **NFL** 15 [2 yrs]

Carroccio, Russ Russell B., G-T-DT-DG, 6´1˝/235 lbs; Virginia; B4/28/1931, D6/28/1994 Wayne, NJ **1954** NYG 9 **1955** NYG 5 **1955** Phi 7 **NFL** 21 [2 yrs]

Carroll, Ahmad Ahmad, DB, 5´11˝/190 lbs; Arkansas; 2004: GB, rnd 1; B8/4/1983 Atlanta, GA **2004**†GB 14 (11, LCB) **2005** GB 16 (16, LCB) **NFL** 30 (27) [2 yrs]

Carroll, Bart Bart J., T, 5´11˝/180 lbs; Colgate; B12/29/1893 Massena, NY, D4/1/1967 Schenectady, NY **1920** Roc 2 (1, LT)

Carroll, Bird Elmer Ellsworth, E, 5´8˝/185 lbs; Washington & Jefferson; B7/25/1896 Scottsdale, PA, D8/6/1982 Winter Park, FL **[K]** **1921** Can 6 (5), 6 **1922** Can☆12 (10, RE), 7 **1923** Can☆9 (8, RE), 13 **1925** Can 7 (6, RE) **NFL** 34 (29), 26 [4 yrs]

Carroll, Gene Henry Eugene, E-G, 5´10˝/190 lbs; Marietta; Waynesburg; B10/16/1896 St. Marys, WV, D2/17/1968 West Chester, PA **1922** Col 4 (2)

Carroll, Herman Herman, DE, 6´4˝/265 lbs; Mississippi State; 1994: NO, rnd 5; B6/20/1971 Natchez, MS **1994** NO 4 (0)

Carroll, Jay Jay Timothy, TE, 6´4˝/230 lbs; Minnesota; 1984: TB, rnd 7; B11/8/1961 Winona, MN

YEAR	TEAM	G(GS, POS)	RUSH	YD	AVG(LG)	TD	REC	YD	AVG(LG)	TD	PASS	COMP	PCT	YD	AVG(LG)	TD	INT	SK	YD	QBR	KPR	OTD	PTS	TAY
1984	TB	16(2)	—	—	—	—	5	50	10.0(17)	1	—	—	—	—	—	—	—	—	—	—	—	—	6	30
1985	Min	15(0)	—	—	—	—	1	8	8.0(8)	0	—	—	—	—	—	—	—	—	—	—	—	—	0	4
NFL	2	31(2)	—	—	—	—	6	58	9.7(17)	1	—	—	—	—	—	—	—	—	—	—	—	—	6	34

Carroll, Jim James Samuel, LB, 6´2˝/230 lbs; Notre Dame; 1965: NYG, rnd 12; B5/6/1943 Jonesboro, AR **1965** NYG 14 (LLB) **1966** NYG 1 **1966** Was 12 **1967** Was 14 (LLB) **1968** Was 14 **1969** NYJ-A 6 **NFL** 61 [5 yrs]

Carroll, Joe Joseph Walker, LB, 6´1˝/220 lbs; Pittsburgh; 1972: Oak, rnd 11; B5/29/1950 Warren, OH **1972**†Oak 13 **1973**†Oak 9 **NFL** 22 [2 yrs]

Carroll, Leo Leo H., DE, 6´7˝/250 lbs; Tulsa; San Diego State; 1967: Atl, rnd 2; B2/16/1944 Alhambra, CA **1968** GB 6 **1969** Was 14 (LDE) **1970** Was 7 (lde/rde) **NFL** 27 [3 yrs]

Carroll, Ronnie Ronald Dean, G, 6´2˝/265 lbs; Arkansas; Sam Houston State; 1973: Buf, rnd 12; B4/11/1949 Galveston, TX **1974** Hou 14

Carroll, Travis Travis C., LB, 6´4˝/240 lbs; Alabama; Florida; B10/26/1978 Jacksonville, FL **2002** NO 6 (0) **2003** NO 1 (0) **2003** Hou 4 (0) **NFL** 11 (0) [2 yrs]

Carroll, Victor Victor E., T-C-G, 6´3˝/235 lbs; Nevada-Reno; B11/9/1912 Alhambra, CA, D7/6/1986 Mission Viejo, CA **1936**†Bos 5 (1) **1937**†Was 10 (2) **1938** Was 10 (6, C) **1939** Was 11 (3) **1940**†Was 11 (4) **1942** Was✧6 (0) **1943**†NYG 10 (0) **1944**†NYG 10 (9, RT) **1945** NYG 2 (2) **1946**†NYG 6 (1)

YEAR	TEAM	G(GS, POS)	RUSH	YD	AVG(LG)	TD	REC	YD	AVG(LG)	TD	PASS	COMP	PCT	YD	AVG(LG)	TD	INT	SK	YD	QBR	KPR	OTD	PTS	TAY
1941	Was	10(0)	—	—	—	—	1	31	31.0(31)	0	—	—	—	—	—	—	—	—	—	—	i	1	6	54
1947	NYG	11(1)	—	—	—	—	7	123	17.6(29)	2	—	—	—	—	—	—	—	—	—	—	i	—	12	98
NFL	12	102(29)	—	—	—	—	8	154	19.3(31)	2	—	—	—	—	—	—	—	—	—	—	kpi	3	32	193

Carroll, Wesley Wesley Byron, WR, 6´0˝/183 lbs; Miami (FL); 1991: NO, rnd 2; B9/6/1967 Cleveland, OH

YEAR	TEAM	G(GS, POS)	RUSH	YD	AVG(LG)	TD	REC	YD	AVG(LG)	TD	PASS	COMP	PCT	YD	AVG(LG)	TD	INT	SK	YD	QBR	KPR	OTD	PTS	TAY
1991	†NO	12(0)	—	—	—	—	18	184	10.2(31)	1	—	—	—	—	—	—	—	—	—	—	—	—	6	97
1992	†NO	16(5, wr)	—	—	—	—	18	292	16.2(72)	2	—	—	—	—	—	—	—	—	—	—	—	—	12	156
1993	Cin	12(0)	—	—	—	—	6	81	13.5(28)	0	—	—	—	—	—	—	—	—	—	—	—	—	0	41
NFL	3	40(5)	—	—	—	—	42	557	13.3(72)	3	—	—	—	—	—	—	—	—	—	—	—	—	18	294

Carruth, Paul Ott Paul Ott, RB, 6´1˝/220 lbs; Alabama; B7/22/1961 Hattiesburg, MS

YEAR	TEAM	G(GS, POS)	RUSH	YD	AVG(LG)	TD	REC	YD	AVG(LG)	TD	PASS	COMP	PCT	YD	AVG(LG)	TD	INT	SK	YD	QBR	KPR	OTD	PTS	TAY
1986	GB	16(12, FB)	81	308	3.8(42)	2	24	134	5.6(19)	2	—	—	—	—	—	—	—	—	—	—	k	—	24	385
1987	GB	12(5, rb)	64	192	3.0(23)	3	10	78	7.8(19)	1	1	1	100.0	3	3.0(3)	1	0	—	—	—	k	—	24	266
1988	GB	15(4)	49	114	2.3(14)	0	24	211	8.8(31)	0	2	0	0.0	0	0.0	0	0	—	—	—	—	—	0	220
1989	KC	2(1)	—	—	—	—	1	3	3.0(3)	0	—	—	—	—	—	—	—	—	—	—	—	—	0	2
NFL	4	45(22)	194	614	3.2(42)	5	59	426	7.2(31)	3	3	1	33.3	3	1.0(3)	1	0	—	—	—	k	—	48	872

Carruth, Rae Rae Lamar, WR, 5´11˝/194 lbs; Colorado; 1997: Car, rnd 1; B1/20/1974 Sacramento, CA

YEAR	TEAM	G(GS, POS)	RUSH	YD	AVG(LG)	TD	REC	YD	AVG(LG)	TD	PASS	COMP	PCT	YD	AVG(LG)	TD	INT	SK	YD	QBR	KPR	OTD	PTS	TAY
1997	Car	15(14, WR)	6	23	3.8(6)	0	44	545	12.4(52)	4	—	—	—	—	—	—	—	—	—	—	—	—	24	316
1998	Car	2(1)	—	—	—	—	4	59	14.8(47)	0	—	—	—	—	—	—	—	—	—	—	—	—	0	30
1999	Car	5(5, wr)	1	4	4.0(4)	0	14	200	14.3(43)	0	—	—	—	—	—	—	—	—	—	—	—	—	0	104
NFL	3	22(20)	7	27	3.9(6)	0	62	804	13.0(52)	4	—	—	—	—	—	—	—	—	—	—	—	—	24	449

Carson, Carlos Carlos Andre, WR, 5´11˝/180 lbs; LSU; 1980: KC, rnd 5; B12/28/1958 Lake Worth, FL

YEAR	TEAM	G(GS, POS)	RUSH	YD	AVG(LG)	TD	REC	YD	AVG(LG)	TD	PASS	COMP	PCT	YD	AVG(LG)	TD	INT	SK	YD	QBR	KPR	OTD	PTS	TAY
1980	KC	16(1)	2	41	20.5(37)	0	5	68	13.6(32)	0	—	—	—	—	—	—	—	—	—	—	k	—	0	392
1981	KC	5(1)	1	-1	-1.0(-1)	0	7	179	25.6(53)	1	—	—	—	—	—	—	—	—	—	—	k	—	6	171
1982	KC	9(7, WR)	—	—	—	—	27	494	18.3(51)	2	—	—	—	—	—	—	—	—	—	—	—	—	12	257
1983	KC☆	16(16, WR)	2	20	10.0(18)	0	80	**1351**	16.9(50)	7	1	1	100.0	48	48.0(48)	1	0	—	—	—	k	—	42	757
1984	KC	16(16, WR)	1	-8	-8.0(-8)	0	57	1078	18.9(57)	4	—	—	—	—	—	—	—	—	—	—	k	—	24	538
1985	KC	15(14, WR)	3	25	8.3(13)	0	47	843	17.9(37)	4	—	—	—	—	—	—	—	—	—	—	—	—	24	467
1986	†KC	10(7, WR)	—	—	—	—	21	497	23.7(70)	4	—	—	—	—	—	—	—	—	—	—	k	—	24	282
1987	KC★	12(12, WR)	1	-7	-7.0(-7)	0	55	**1044**	19.0(81)	7	—	—	—	—	—	—	—	—	—	—	—	—	42	550
1988	KC	14(14, WR)	1	1	1.0(1)	0	46	711	15.5(80)	3	—	—	—	—	—	—	—	—	—	—	—	—	18	372
1989	KC	7(3)	—	—	—	—	7	95	13.6(28)	1	—	—	—	—	—	—	—	—	—	—	—	—	6	53
1989	Phi	6(1)	1	-9	-9.0(-9)	0	1	12	12.0(12)	0	—	—	—	—	—	—	—	—	—	—	—	—	0	-3
NFL	10	126(92)	12	62	5.2(37)	0	353	6372	18.1(81)	33	1	1	100.0	48	48.0(48)	1	0	—	—	—	k	—	198	3833

YEAR	TEAM	G (GS, POS)	RUSH	YD	AVG (LG)	TD	REC	YD	AVG (LG)	TD	PASS	COMP	PCT	YD	AVG (LG)	TD	INT	SK	YD	QBR	KPR	OTD	PTS	TAY

CARSON, HARRY Harold Donald, LB, 6´2˝/237 lbs; South Carolina State; 1976: NYG, rnd 4; B11/26/1953 Florence, SC; HOF 2006 **1976** NYG 12 (7, MLB)
1977 NYG 14 (14, MLB) **1978** NYG★16 (16, MLB) **1979** NYG★16 (RILB) **1980** NYG 8 (7, RILB) **1981**†NYG★16 (16, RILB) **1982** NYG☆9 (9, RILB) **1983** NYG 10 (10, RILB)
1984†NYG☆16 (16, RILB) **1985**†NYG★16 (16, RILB) **1987** NYG☆12 (12, RILB) **1988** NYG 12 (10, RILB)

| 1986 | †NYG★ | 16(16, RILB) | — | — | — | — | 1 | 13 | 13.0(13) | 1 | — | — | — | — | — | — | — | — | — | — | iS | — | 6 | 27 |
| NFL | 13 | 173(149) | — | — | — | — | 1 | 13 | 13.0(13) | 1 | — | — | — | — | — | — | — | — | — | — | kiS | 1 | 12 | 159 |

CARSON, HOWARD Hueland Howard, LB, 6´2˝/233 lbs; Howard Payne; B2/11/1957 Hico, TX **1981** LARm 10 (0) **1982** LARm 2 (2) **1983**†LARm 16 (0) **NFL** 28 (2) [3 yrs]

CARSON, JOHN John Richard, E, 6´3˝/202 lbs; Georgia; 1953: Cle, rnd 15; B1/31/1930 Atlanta, GA

1954	Was	12	—	—	—	—	12	139	11.6(42)	0	—	—	—	—	—	—	—	—	—	—	—	—	0	70
1955	Was	12(LE)	—	—	—	—	23	443	19.3(51)	3	—	—	—	—	—	—	—	—	—	—	—	—	18	237
1956	Was☆	12(LE)	—	—	—	—	39	504	12.9(26)	3	—	—	—	—	—	—	—	—	—	—	—	—	18	267
1957	Was★	12(LE)	—	—	—	—	34	583	17.1(38)	3	—	—	—	—	—	—	—	—	—	—	—	—	18	307
1958	Was	4	—	—	—	—	14	244	17.4(28)	2	—	—	—	—	—	—	—	—	—	—	—	—	12	132
1959	Was	5	—	—	—	—	6	74	12.3(17)	0	—	—	—	—	—	—	—	—	—	—	—	—	0	37
1960	†Hou-A	14(TE)	—	—	—	—	45	604	13.4(47)	4	—	—	—	—	—	—	—	—	—	—	—	—	24	322
NFL	7	71	—	—	—	—	173	2591	15.0(51)	15	—	—	—	—	—	—	—	—	—	—	—	—	90	1371

CARSON, KERN Kern, HB, 6´1˝/200 lbs; San Diego State; 1963: Den, rnd 29/Bal, rnd 17; B1/29/1941 Hope, AR **1965** SD-A 3

| 1965 | NYJ-A | 10 | 7 | 25 | 3.6(15) | 2 | — | — | — | — | — | — | — | — | — | — | — | — | — | — | kp | — | 12 | 148 |
| NFL | 1 | 13 | 7 | 25 | 3.6(15) | 2 | — | — | — | — | — | — | — | — | — | — | — | — | — | — | kp | — | 12 | 147 |

CARSON, LEONARD Leonardo Tremayne, DT, 6´2˝/305 lbs; Auburn; 2000: SD, rnd 4; B2/11/1977 Mobile, AL **2000** SD 4 (0) **2001** SD 16 (13, LDT) **2002** SD 16 (6, ldt)
2003 Dal 8 (0) **2003** SD 5 (0) **2004** Dal 15 (15, LDT) **NFL** 64 (34) [5 yrs]

CARSON, MALCOLM Malcolm Darryl, G, 6´2˝/260 lbs; Tennessee-Chattanooga; B11/1/1959 Birmingham, AL **1984** Min 1 (0)

CARSTENS, JORDAN Jordan Lee, DT, 6´5˝/300 lbs; Iowa State; B1/22/1981 Carroll, IA **2004** Car 12 (1) **2005**†Car 16 (15, RDT) **NFL** 28 (16) [2 yrs]

CARSWELL, DWAYNE Dwayne, TE, 6´3˝/260 lbs; Liberty; B1/18/1972 Jacksonville, FL

1994	Den	4(0)	—	—	—	—	—	—	—	—	—	—	—	—	—	—	—	—	—	—	k	—	0	-15
1995	Den	9(2)	—	—	—	—	3	37	12.3(23)	0	—	—	—	—	—	—	—	—	—	—	—	—	0	19
1996	†Den	16(2)	—	—	—	—	15	85	5.7(11)	0	—	—	—	—	—	—	—	—	—	—	—	—	0	43
1997	†Den	16(3)	—	—	—	—	12	96	8.0(24)	1	—	—	—	—	—	—	—	—	—	—	—	—	6	53
1998	†Den	16(1)	—	—	—	—	4	51	12.8(15)	0	—	—	—	—	—	—	—	—	—	—	—	—	0	26
1999	Den	16(11, TE)	—	—	—	—	24	201	8.4(20)	2	—	—	—	—	—	—	—	—	—	—	—	—	12	111
2000	†Den	16(16, TE)	—	—	—	—	49	495	10.1(43)	3	—	—	—	—	—	—	—	—	—	—	k	—	18	248
2001	Den◊	16(16, TE)	—	—	—	—	34	299	8.8(25)	4	—	—	—	—	—	—	—	—	—	—	—	—	26	170
2002	Den	16(7, te)	—	—	—	—	21	189	9.0(19)	1	—	—	—	—	—	—	—	—	—	—	k	—	6	84
2003	†Den	16(10, TE)	—	—	—	—	6	53	8.8(19)	.1	—	—	—	—	—	—	—	—	—	—	—	—	6	32
2004	†Den	15(14, TE)	—	—	—	—	22	198	9.0(20)	1	—	—	—	—	—	—	—	—	—	—	—	—	6	104
2005	Den	7(0)	—	—	—	—	2	3	1.5(2)	2	—	—	—	—	—	—	—	—	—	—	k	—	12	-4
NFL	12	163(82)	—	—	—	—	192	1707	8.9(43)	15	—	—	—	—	—	—	—	—	—	—	k	—	92	868

CARSWELL, ROBERT Robert Lee, DB, 5´11˝/215 lbs; Clemson; 2001: SD, rnd 7; B10/26/1978 Gary, IN **2001** SD 16 (0) **2002** SD 2 (0) **NFL** 18 (0) [2 yrs]

CARTER, ALEX Alexander, DE, 6´3˝/255 lbs; Tennessee State; B9/6/1963 Miami, FL **1987** Cle 3 (1)

CARTER, ALLEN Wayne Allen, RB, 5´11˝/208 lbs; USC; 1975: NE, rnd 4; B12/12/1952 Pomona, CA **1976** NE 1

| 1975 | NE | 14 | 22 | 95 | 4.3(19) | 0 | 2 | 39 | 19.5(26) | 0 | — | — | — | — | — | — | — | — | — | — | k | 1 | 6 | 524 |
| NFL | 2 | 15 | 22 | 95 | 4.3(19) | 0 | 2 | 39 | 19.5(26) | 0 | — | — | — | — | — | — | — | — | — | — | k | 1 | 6 | 528 |

CARTER, ANDRE Andre, DE-LB, 6´4˝/265 lbs; California; 2001: SF, rnd 1; B5/12/1979 Denver, CO **2001**†SF 15 (15, LDE) **2002**†SF 16 (16, LDE) **2003** SF 15 (15, RDE)
2004 SF 7 (6, RDE) **2005** SF 16 (14, ROLB) **NFL** 69 (66) [5 yrs]

CARTER, ANTHONY Anthony, WR, 5´11˝/168 lbs; Michigan; 1983: Mia, rnd 12; B9/17/1960 Riviera Beach, FL

1985	Min	16(15, WR)	—	—	—	—	43	821	19.1(57)	8	—	—	—	—	—	—	—	—	—	—	p	—	48	523
1986	Min	12(10, WR)	1	12	12.0(12)	0	38	686	18.1(60)	7	—	—	—	—	—	—	—	—	—	—	p	—	42	390
1987	†Min★	12 (11, WR)	—	—	—	—	38	922	24.3(73)	7	—	—	—	—	—	—	—	—	—	—	p	—	42	521
1988	†Min★	16(16, WR)	4	41	10.3(21)	0	72	1225	17.0(67)	6	—	—	—	—	—	—	—	—	—	—	kp	—	36	667
1989	†Min	16(16, WR)	3	18	6.0(17)	0	65	1066	16.4(50)	4	—	—	—	—	—	—	—	—	—	—	kp	—	24	572
1990	Min	15(14, WR)	3	16	5.3(11)	0	70	1008	14.4(56)	8	—	—	—	—	—	—	—	—	—	—	p	—	48	560
1991	Min	15(15, WR)	13	117	9.0(32)	1	51	553	10.8(46)	5	—	—	—	—	—	—	—	—	—	—	—	—	36	429
1992	†Min	16(14, WR)	16	66	4.1(14)	1	41	580	14.1(54)	2	1	0	0.0	0	0.0	0	—	—	—	—	—	—	18	376
1993	†Min	15(14, WR)	7	19	2.7(9)	0	60	775	12.9(39)	5	—	—	—	—	—	—	—	—	—	—	—	—	30	432
1994	†Det	4(1)	—	—	—	—	8	97	12.1(18)	3	—	—	—	—	—	—	—	—	—	—	—	—	18	64
1995	Det	3(0)	—	—	—	—	—	—	—	—	—	—	—	—	—	—	—	—	—	—	kp	—	0	14
NFL	11	140(126)	47	289	6.1(32)	2	486	7733	15.9(73)	55	1	0	0.0	0	0.0	0	—	—	—	—	kp	—	342	4546

CARTER, BERNARD Edward Bernard, LB, 6´3˝/238 lbs; East Carolina; 1994: TB, rnd 6; B8/22/1971 Tallahassee, FL **1995** Jax 5 (0)

CARTER, BLANCHARD Blanchard, T, 6´4˝/250 lbs; UNLV; 1977: Bal, rnd 7; B6/3/1955 Stockton, CA **1977** TB 13

CARTER, CARL Carl Anthony, DB, 5´11˝/180 lbs; Texas Tech; 1986: SL, rnd 4; B3/7/1964 Fort Worth, TX **1986** SL 14 (4) **1987** SL 12 (12, LCB) **1988** Phx 16 (16, LCB)
1989 Phx 15 (15, RCB) **1990**†Cin 15 (11, RCB) **1991** TB 11 (10, RCB) **1992** GB 7 (1) **NFL** 90 (69) [7 yrs]

CARTER, CHRIS Christopher Cary, DB, 6´1˝/201 lbs; Texas; 1997: NE, rnd 3; B9/27/1974 Tyler, TX **1997**†NE 16 (0) **1998**†NE 16 (0) **1999** NE 15 (15, FS) **2000** Cin 16 (10, SS)
2001 Cin 16 (4) **2002** Hou 13 (0) **NFL** 92 (29) [6 yrs]

CARTER, CRIS Christopher D., WR, 6´3˝/202 lbs; Ohio State; 1987: Phi, rnd S4; B11/25/1965 Troy, OH

1987	Phi	9(0)	—	—	—	—	5	84	16.8(25)	2	1	0	0.0	0	0.0	0	—	—	—	—	k	—	12	113
1988	†Phi	16(16, WR)	1	1	1.0(1)	0	39	761	19.5(80)	6	—	—	—	—	—	—	—	—	—	—	—	1	42	412
1989	†Phi	16(15, WR)	2	16	8.0(11)	0	45	605	13.4(42)	11	—	—	—	—	—	—	—	—	—	—	—	—	66	374
1990	Min	16(5, wr)	2	6	3.0(8)	0	27	413	15.3(78)	3	—	—	—	—	—	—	—	—	—	—	—	—	18	228
1991	Min	16(16, WR)	—	—	—	—	72	962	13.4(50)	5	—	—	—	—	—	—	—	—	—	—	—	—	30	506
1992	†Min	12(12, WR)	5	15	3.0(6)	0	53	681	12.8(44)	6	—	—	—	—	—	—	—	—	—	—	—	—	36	386
1993	†Min◊	16(16, WR)	—	—	—	—	86	1071	12.5(58)	9	—	—	—	—	—	—	—	—	—	—	—	—	54	581
1994	†Min★	16(16, WR)	—	—	—	—	122	1256	10.3(65)	7	—	—	—	—	—	—	—	—	—	—	—	—	46	663
1995	Min★	16(16, WR)	1	0	0.0(0)	0	122	1371	11.2(60)	17	—	—	—	—	—	—	—	—	—	—	—	—	102	771
1996	†Min★	16(16, WR)	—	—	—	—	96	1163	12.1(43)	10	—	—	—	—	—	—	—	—	—	—	k	—	60	620
1997	†Min★	16(16, WR)	—	—	—	—	89	1069	12.0(43)	13	—	—	—	—	—	—	—	—	—	—	—	—	84	600
1998	†Min◊	16(16, WR)	1	-1	-1.0(-1)	0	78	1011	13.0(54)	12	—	—	—	—	—	—	—	—	—	—	—	—	72	565
1999	†Min★	16(16, WR)	—	—	—	—	90	1241	13.8(68)	13	—	—	—	—	—	—	—	—	—	—	—	—	78	686
2000	†Min◊	16(16, WR)	—	—	—	—	96	1274	13.3(53)	9	—	—	—	—	—	—	—	—	—	—	—	—	54	682
2001	Min	16(16, WR)	1	4	4.0(4)	0	73	871	11.9(52)	6	—	—	—	—	—	—	—	—	—	—	—	—	36	470
2002	Mia	5(1)	—	—	—	—	8	66	8.3(15)	1	—	—	—	—	—	—	—	—	—	—	—	—	6	38
NFL	16	234(209)	13	41	3.2(11)	0	1101	13899	12.6(80)	130	1	0	0.0	0	0.0	0	—	—	—	—	k	1	796	7690

CARTER, DALE Dale Lavelle, DB, 6´1˝/194 lbs; Tennessee; 1992: KC, rnd 1; B11/28/1969 Covington, GA [RI] **1992**†KC 16 (9, RCB) **1994**†KC★16 (16, RCB)
1995†KC★16 (14, LCB) **1997**†KC★16 (15, LCB) **1998** KC 11 (9, lcb) **1999** Den 14 (14, RCB) **2001** Min 8 (8, LCB) **2002** NO 7 (7, lcb) **2003** NO 8 (8, lcb) **2005** Bal 15 (2)

1993	†KC	15(11, RCB)	1	2	2.0(2)	0	—	—	—	—	—	—	—	—	—	—	—	—	—	—	pi	—	0	109
1996	KC★	14(14, LCB)	1	3	3.0(3)	0	6	89	14.8(46)	1	—	—	—	—	—	—	—	—	—	—	pi	—	6	63
NFL	12	156(127)	2	5	2.5(3)	0	6	89	14.8(46)	1	—	—	—	—	—	—	—	—	—	—	kpiS	3	24	618

CARTER, DARYL Daryl, LB, 6´2˝/222 lbs; Wisconsin; B2/24/1975 Milwaukee, WI **1997** ChiB 1 (0)

CARTER, DAVID David C., C-G, 6´2˝/250 lbs; Western Kentucky; 1977: Hou, rnd 6; B11/27/1953 Vincennes, IN **1977** Hou 14 **1978**†Hou 16 **1979**†Hou 16 (2) **1980**†Hou 16 (4) **1981** Hou 16 (13, C) **1982** Hou 9 (9, C) **1983** Hou 16 (16, C) **1984** Hou 7 (0) **1984** NO 7 (0) **1985** NO 4 (0) **NFL** 121 (44) [9 yrs]

CARTER, DEXTER Dexter Anthony, RB, 5´9˝/170 lbs; Florida State; 1990: SF, rnd 1; B9/15/1967 Baxley, GA **[R]**

YEAR	TEAM	G (GS, POS)	RUSH	YD	AVG (LG)	TD	REC	YD	AVG (LG)	TD	PASS	COMP	PCT	YD	AVG (LG)	TD	INT	SK	YD	QBR	KPR	OTD	PTS	TAY
1990	†SF	16 (5, rb)	114	460	4.0 (74)	1	25	217	8.7 (26)	0	—	—	—	—	—	—	—	—	—	—	k	—	6	747
1991	SF	16 (14, RB)	85	379	4.5 (53)	2	23	253	11.0 (26)	1	—	—	—	—	—	—	—	—	—	—	k	1	24	825
1992	SF	3 (0)	4	9	2.3 (6)	0	1	43	43.0 (43)	1	—	—	—	—	—	—	—	—	—	—	k	—	6	61
1993	†SF	16 (0)	10	72	7.2 (50)	1	3	40	13.3 (14)	0	—	—	—	—	—	—	—	—	—	—	kp	1	12	472
1994	†SF	16 (0)	8	34	4.3 (18)	0	7	99	14.1 (44)	0	—	—	—	—	—	—	—	—	—	—	kp	1	6	610
1995	NYJ	10 (0)	—	—	—	—	1	0	0.0 (0)	0	—	—	—	—	—	—	—	—	—	—	kp	—	0	250
1995	†SF	7 (0)	7	22	3.1 (15)	0	1	4	4.0 (4)	0	—	—	—	—	—	—	—	—	—	—	kp	1	6	330
1996	†SF	16 (0)	19	66	3.5 (18)	1	—	—	—	—	—	—	—	—	—	—	—	—	—	—	kp	—	6	507
NFL	7	100 (19)	247	1042	4.2 (74)	5	61	656	10.8 (44)	2	—	—	—	—	—	—	—	—	—	—	kp	4	66	3800

CARTER, DREW Drew, WR, 6´3˝/200 lbs; Ohio State; 2004: Car, rnd 5; B9/5/1981 Solon, OH

YEAR	TEAM	G (GS, POS)	RUSH	YD	AVG (LG)	TD	REC	YD	AVG (LG)	TD	PASS	COMP	PCT	YD	AVG (LG)	TD	INT	SK	YD	QBR	KPR	OTD	PTS	TAY
2005	†Car	3 (0)	—	—	—	—	5	103	20.6 (40)	1	—	—	—	—	—	—	—	—	—	—	—	—	6	57

CARTER, DYSHOD Dyshod Vontae, DB, 5´10˝/195 lbs; Kansas State; B6/18/1978 Denver, CO **2001** Cle 5 (0) **2004** Arz 6 (0) **2004** Cle 5 (0) **2005** Arz 3 (0) **NFL** 19 (0) [3 yrs]

CARTER, GERALD Gerald Louis, WR, 6´1˝/190 lbs; Texas A&M; 1980: TB, rnd 9; B6/19/1957 Bryan, TX

YEAR	TEAM	G (GS, POS)	RUSH	YD	AVG (LG)	TD	REC	YD	AVG (LG)	TD	PASS	COMP	PCT	YD	AVG (LG)	TD	INT	SK	YD	QBR	KPR	OTD	PTS	TAY
1980	NYJ	3 (0)	—	—	—	—	—	—	—	—	—	—	—	—	—	—	—	—	—	—	k	—	0	-3
1981	†TB	16 (0)	—	—	—	—	1	10	10.0 (10)	0	—	—	—	—	—	—	—	—	—	—	—	—	0	5
1982	†TB	9 (0)	—	—	—	—	10	140	14.0 (27)	0	—	—	—	—	—	—	—	—	—	—	—	—	0	70
1983	TB	16 (9, WR)	1	0	0.0 (0)	0	48	694	14.5 (56)	2	—	—	—	—	—	—	—	—	—	—	—	—	12	357
1984	TB	16 (9, WR)	1	16	16.0 (16)	0	60	816	13.6 (74)	5	—	—	—	—	—	—	—	—	—	—	—	—	30	449
1985	TB	16 (16, WR)	1	13	13.0 (13)	0	40	557	13.9 (40)	3	—	—	—	—	—	—	—	—	—	—	—	—	18	307
1986	TB	15 (15, WR)	1	-5	-5.0 (-5)	0	42	640	15.2 (46)	2	—	—	—	—	—	—	—	—	—	—	—	—	12	325
1987	TB	12 (12, WR)	—	—	—	—	38	586	15.4 (57)	5	—	—	—	—	—	—	—	—	—	—	—	—	30	318
NFL	8	103 (61)	4	24	6.0 (16)	0	239	3443	14.4 (74)	17	—	—	—	—	—	—	—	—	—	—	k	—	102	1828

CARTER, JEROME Jerome, DB, 5´11˝/219 lbs; Florida State; 2005: SL, rnd 4; B10/25/1982 Lake City, FL **2005** SL 14 (2)

CARTER, JIM James Charles, LB-G, 6´3˝/235 lbs; Minnesota; 1970: GB, rnd 3; B10/18/1948 St. Paul, MN **1970** GB 11 (LLB) **1971** GB 13 (MLB) **1972**†GB☆14 (MLB) **1973** GB✧14 (MLB) **1974** GB 14 (MLB) **1975** GB 12 (MLB) **1977** GB 14 (MLB) **1978** GB 14 **NFL** 106 [8 yrs]

CARTER, JIMMIE Jimmie Renerd, LB, 6´1˝/220 lbs; New Mexico; 1984: Det, rnd 7; B7/26/1961 Weimar, TX **1987** SL 1 (0)

CARTER, JOE William Joseph, E, 6´1˝/201 lbs; Austin; SMU; B7/23/1910 Dalhart, TX **[K]**

YEAR	TEAM	G (GS, POS)	RUSH	YD	AVG (LG)	TD	REC	YD	AVG (LG)	TD	PASS	COMP	PCT	YD	AVG (LG)	TD	INT	SK	YD	QBR	KPR	OTD	PTS	TAY
1933	Phi	9 (8, RE)	—	—	—	—	5	109	21.8	2	—	—	—	—	—	—	—	—	—	—	K	—	13	65
1934	Phi	11 (10, RE)	—	—	—	—	**16**	238	14.9	4	—	—	—	—	—	—	—	—	—	—	—	—	24	139
1935	Phi	11 (11, RE)	7	19	2.7	0	11	260	23.6	2	—	—	—	—	—	—	—	—	—	—	—	—	12	159
1936	Phi☆	9 (9, RE)	—	—	—	—	4	42	10.5	1	—	—	—	—	—	—	—	—	—	—	—	—	6	26
1937	Phi	10 (8, RE)	—	—	—	—	15	282	18.8 (86)	3	—	—	—	—	—	—	—	—	—	—	—	—	18	156
1938	Phi★	11 (11, RE)	—	—	—	—	27	386	14.3	7	—	—	—	—	—	—	—	—	—	—	—	1	48	228
1939	Phi✧	11 (11, RE)	1	4	4.0 (4)	0	24	292	12.2	2	—	—	—	—	—	—	—	—	—	—	—	—	12	160
1940	Phi	6 (4)	1	-3	-3.0 (-3)	0	12	201	16.8	0	—	—	—	—	—	—	—	—	—	—	—	—	0	98
1942	GB	11 (5, RE)	—	—	—	—	2	19	9.5 (10)	1	—	—	—	—	—	—	—	—	—	—	—	—	6	15
1944	Bkn	10 (9, RE)	—	—	—	—	13	143	11.0 (45)	0	—	—	—	—	—	—	—	—	—	—	P	—	0	72
1945	ChiC	10 (4)	—	—	—	—	3	17	5.7 (10)	0	—	—	—	—	—	—	—	—	—	—	k	—	0	38
NFL	11	109 (90)	9	20	2.2 (4)	0	132	1989	15.1 (86)	22	—	—	—	—	—	—	—	—	—	—	KPk	1	139	1154

CARTER, JOE Joseph Thomas, RB, 5´11˝/198 lbs; Alabama; 1984: Mia, rnd 4; B6/23/1962 Starkville, MS

YEAR	TEAM	G (GS, POS)	RUSH	YD	AVG (LG)	TD	REC	YD	AVG (LG)	TD	PASS	COMP	PCT	YD	AVG (LG)	TD	INT	SK	YD	QBR	KPR	OTD	PTS	TAY
1984	†Mia	13 (2)	100	495	**4.9** (**35**)	1	8	53	6.6 (15)	0	—	—	—	—	—	—	—	—	—	—	—	—	6	532
1985	†Mia	10 (0)	14	76	5.4 (19)	0	2	7	3.5 (4)	0	—	—	—	—	—	—	—	—	—	—	k	—	0	102
1986	Mia	7 (0)	4	18	4.5 (9)	0	1	6	6.0 (6)	0	—	—	—	—	—	—	—	—	—	—	k	—	0	19
NFL	3	30 (2)	118	589	5.0 (35)	1	11	66	6.0 (15)	0	—	—	—	—	—	—	—	—	—	—	k	—	6	652

CARTER, JON Jon Stacy, DT, 6´4˝/273 lbs; Pittsburgh; 1988: NYG, rnd 5; B3/12/1965 Los Angeles, CA **1989** Dal 13 (0)

CARTER, JONATHAN Jonathan, WR, 6´0˝/180 lbs; Troy State; 2001: NYG, rnd 5; B3/20/1979 Anniston, AL **2001** NYG 2 (0) **2002** NYG 1 (0)

YEAR	TEAM	G (GS, POS)	RUSH	YD	AVG (LG)	TD	REC	YD	AVG (LG)	TD	PASS	COMP	PCT	YD	AVG (LG)	TD	INT	SK	YD	QBR	KPR	OTD	PTS	TAY
2003	NYJ	9 (0)	—	—	—	—	4	93	23.3 (62)	1	—	—	—	—	—	—	—	—	—	—	k	1	12	309
2004	†NYJ	13 (1)	—	—	—	—	10	173	17.3 (46)	1	—	—	—	—	—	—	—	—	—	—	k	—	6	211
NFL	4	25 (1)	—	—	—	—	14	266	19.0 (62)	2	—	—	—	—	—	—	—	—	—	—	k	1	18	553

CARTER, KENT Kent Alexander, LB, 6´3˝/235 lbs; USC; 1972: SL, rnd 17; B5/25/1950 Los Angeles, CA **1974** NE 2

CARTER, KERRY Kerry, RB, 6´1˝/238 lbs; Stanford; B12/19/1980 Port of Spain, Trinidad

YEAR	TEAM	G (GS, POS)	RUSH	YD	AVG (LG)	TD	REC	YD	AVG (LG)	TD	PASS	COMP	PCT	YD	AVG (LG)	TD	INT	SK	YD	QBR	KPR	OTD	PTS	TAY
2003	†Sea	16 (0)	3	-2	-0.7 (1)	0	—	—	—	—	—	—	—	—	—	—	—	—	—	—	k	—	0	63
2004	†Sea	16 (0)	4	15	3.8 (6)	0	—	—	—	—	—	—	—	—	—	—	—	—	—	—	k	—	0	148
NFL	2	32 (0)	7	13	1.9 (6)	0	—	—	—	—	—	—	—	—	—	—	—	—	—	—	k	—	0	211

CARTER, KEVIN Kevin Louis, DE-DT, 6´5˝/290 lbs; Florida; 1995: SL, rnd 1; B9/21/1973 Miami, FL **[S]** **1995** SL 16 (16, LDE) **1996** SL 16 (16, LDE) **1997** SL 16 (16, LDE) **1998** SL 16 (16, LDE) **1999**†SL★16 (16, LDE) **2000**†SL 16 (13, LDE) **2001** Ten 16 (16, LDE) **2002**†Ten✧16 (16, LDE) **2003**†Ten 16 (16, LDE) **2004** Ten 16 (16, LDT) **2005** Mia 16 (16, LDE) **NFL** 176 (173) [11 yrs]

CARTER, KI-JANA Kenneth Leonard, RB, 5´10˝/222 lbs; Penn State; 1995: Cin, rnd 1; B9/12/1973 Westerville, OH

YEAR	TEAM	G (GS, POS)	RUSH	YD	AVG (LG)	TD	REC	YD	AVG (LG)	TD	PASS	COMP	PCT	YD	AVG (LG)	TD	INT	SK	YD	QBR	KPR	OTD	PTS	TAY
1996	Cin	16 (4)	91	264	2.9 (31)	8	22	169	7.7 (20)	1	—	—	—	—	—	—	—	—	—	—	—	—	54	434
1997	Cin	15 (10, rb)	128	464	3.6 (79)	7	21	157	7.5 (35)	0	1	0	0.0	0	0.0	0	0	—	—	—	k	—	42	607
1998	Cin	1 (0)	2	4	2.0 (4)	0	6	25	4.2 (8)	0	—	—	—	—	—	—	—	—	—	—	—	—	0	17
1999	Cin	3 (0)	6	15	2.5 (8)	1	3	24	8.0 (11)	0	—	—	—	—	—	—	—	—	—	—	—	—	6	37
2001	Was	14 (0)	63	308	4.9 (30)	3	13	83	6.4 (15)	0	—	—	—	—	—	—	—	—	—	—	k	—	18	371
2003	NO	8 (0)	19	72	3.8 (31)	1	1	11	11.0 (11)	0	—	—	—	—	—	—	—	—	—	—	—	—	6	88
2004	NO	2 (0)	10	17	1.7 (8)	0	—	—	—	—	—	—	—	—	—	—	—	—	—	—	—	—	0	17
NFL	7	59 (14)	319	1144	3.6 (79)	20	66	469	7.1 (35)	1	1	0	0.0	0	0.0	0	0	—	—	—	k	—	126	1569

CARTER, LOUIS Louis Edward, RB, 5´11˝/207 lbs; Maryland; 1975: Oak, rnd 3; B2/6/1953 Laurel, MD

YEAR	TEAM	G (GS, POS)	RUSH	YD	AVG (LG)	TD	REC	YD	AVG (LG)	TD	PASS	COMP	PCT	YD	AVG (LG)	TD	INT	SK	YD	QBR	KPR	OTD	PTS	TAY
1975	Oak	8	11	27	2.5 (11)	0	2	39	19.5 (22)	0	—	—	—	—	—	—	—	—	—	—	k	—	0	45
1976	TB	14 (8, RB)	171	521	3.0 (26)	1	20	135	6.8 (19)	0	5	2	40.0	24	4.8 (23)	1	0	—	—	—	k	—	6	691
1977	TB	14 (1)	59	117	2.0 (20)	2	10	65	6.5 (19)	0	2	0	0.0	0	0.0	0	0	—	—	—	—	—	12	170
1978	TB	16	81	275	3.4 (17)	1	19	139	7.3 (17)	0	5	2	40.0	87	17.4 (66)	0	0	—	—	—	k	—	6	405
NFL	4	52 (9)	322	940	2.9 (26)	4	51	378	7.4 (22)	0	12	4	33.3	111	9.3 (66)	1	0	—	—	—	k	—	24	1310

CARTER, M.L. Milton Louis, DB, 5´9˝/173 lbs; Cal State-Fullerton; San Jose State; B12/9/1955 Beaufort, SC **1979** KC 16 (rcb) **1980** KC 7 (2) **1981** KC 10 (0) **NFL** 33 (2) [3 yrs]

CARTER, MARTY Marty LaVincent, DB, 6´1˝/209 lbs; Middle Tennessee State; 1991: TB, rnd 8; B12/17/1969 La Grange, GA **1991** TB 14 (11, FS) **1992** TB 16 (16, SS) **1993** TB 16 (14, SS) **1995** ChiB 16 (16, SS) **1996** ChiB 16 (16, SS) **1997** ChiB 15 (15, SS) **1998** ChiB 16 (16, SS) **1999** Atl 11 (11, SS) **2000** Atl 16 (16, SS) **2001** Atl 5 (5, ss) **2001** Det 4 (1)

YEAR	TEAM	G (GS, POS)	RUSH	YD	AVG (LG)	TD	REC	YD	AVG (LG)	TD	PASS	COMP	PCT	YD	AVG (LG)	TD	INT	SK	YD	QBR	KPR	OTD	PTS	TAY
1994	TB	16 (14, SS)	—	—	—	—	1	21	21.0 (21)	0	—	—	—	—	—	—	—	—	—	—	kS	—	0	-5
NFL	11	161 (151)	—	—	—	—	1	21	21.0 (21)	0	—	—	—	—	—	—	—	—	—	—	kiS	—	0	9

CARTER, MICHAEL Michael D'Andrea, NT, 6´2˝/285 lbs; SMU; 1984: SF, rnd 5; B10/29/1960 Dallas, TX **1984**†SF 16 (0) **1985**†SF★12 (9, NT) **1986**†SF☆15 (13, NT) **1987**†SF★12 (12, NT) **1988**†SF★16 (16, NT) **1989**†SF 8 (8, NT) **1990**†SF 15 (13, NT) **1991** SF 15 (15, NT) **1992**†SF 12 (11, NT) **NFL** 121 (97) [9 yrs]

CARTER, MIKE Michael Norman, WR, 6´1˝/210 lbs; Sacramento State; 1970: GB, rnd 15; B2/18/1948 Little Rock, AR **1970** GB 2

YEAR	TEAM	G (GS, POS)	RUSH	YD	AVG (LG)	TD	REC	YD	AVG (LG)	TD	PASS	COMP	PCT	YD	AVG (LG)	TD	INT	SK	YD	QBR	KPR	OTD	PTS	TAY
1972	SD	5	1	25	25.0 (25)	0	2	24	12.0 (14)	0	—	—	—	—	—	—	—	—	—	—	—	—	0	37
NFL	2	7	1	25	25.0 (25)	0	2	24	12.0 (14)	0	—	—	—	—	—	—	—	—	—	—	—	—	0	37

Carter, Pat Wendell Patrick, TE, 6´4˝/256 lbs; Florida State; 1988: Det, rnd 2; B8/1/1966 Sarasota, FL

YEAR	TEAM	G (GS, POS)	RUSH	YD	AVG (LG)	TD	REC	YD	AVG (LG)	TD	PASS	COMP	PCT	YD	AVG (LG)	TD	INT	SK	YD	QBR	KPR	OTD	PTS	TAY
1988	Det	15(14, TE)	—	—	—	—	13	145	11.2(31)	0	—	—	—	—	—	—	—	—	—	—	—	—	0	73
1989	†LARm	16(0)	—	—	—	—	—	—	—	—	—	—	—	—	—	—	—	—	—	—	—	—	—	—
1990	LARm	16(4)	—	—	—	—	8	58	7.3(16)	0	—	—	—	—	—	—	—	—	—	—	—	—	0	29
1991	LARm	16(5, te)	—	—	—	—	8	69	8.6(18)	2	—	—	—	—	—	—	—	—	—	—	k	—	12	48
1992	LARm	16(16, TE)	—	—	—	—	20	232	11.6(25)	3	—	—	—	—	—	—	—	—	—	—	—	—	18	131
1993	LARm	11(10, TE)	—	—	—	—	14	166	11.9(38)	1	—	—	—	—	—	—	—	—	—	—	—	—	6	88
1994	Hou	16(12, TE)	—	—	—	—	11	74	6.7(19)	1	—	—	—	—	—	—	—	—	—	—	—	—	6	42
1995	SL	16(5, te)	—	—	—	—	—	—	—	—	—	—	—	—	—	—	—	—	—	—	—	—	—	—
1996	Arz	16(16, TE)	—	—	—	—	26	329	12.7(36)	1	—	—	—	—	—	—	—	—	—	—	—	—	6	170
1997	Arz	16(10, TE)	—	—	—	—	7	44	6.3(15)	1	—	—	—	—	—	—	—	—	—	—	—	—	6	27
NFL	10	154(92)	—	—	—	—	107	1117	10.4(38)	9	—	—	—	—	—	—	—	—	—	—	k	—	54	607

Carter, Perry Perry Lynn, DB, 6´0˝/194 lbs; Southern Mississippi; 1994: Arz, rnd 4; B8/5/1971 McComb, MS **1995**†KC 2 (0) **1996** Oak 4 (0) **1997** Oak 16 (7, rcb) **1998** Oak 6 (0) **NFL** 28 (7) [4 yrs]

Carter, Quincy Quincy, QB, 6´2˝/213 lbs; Georgia; 2001: Dal, rnd 2; B10/13/1977 Decatur, GA

YEAR	TEAM	G (GS, POS)	RUSH	YD	AVG (LG)	TD	REC	YD	AVG (LG)	TD	PASS	COMP	PCT	YD	AVG (LG)	TD	INT	SK	YD	QBR	KPR	OTD	PTS	TAY
2001	Dal	8(8, QB)	45	150	3.3(17)	1	—	—	—	—	176	90	51.1	1072	6.1(64)	5	7	12	56	—	—	—	6	441
2002	Dal	7(7, qb)	27	91	3.4(16)	0	—	—	—	—	221	125	56.6	1465	6.6(80)	7	8	19	130	—	—	—	0	539
2003	†Dal	16(16, QB)	68	257	3.8(19)	2	—	—	—	—	505	292	57.8	3302	6.5(64)	17	21	37	185	71.4	—	—	12	1173
2004	NYJ	7(3)	12	20	1.7(9)	0	—	—	—	—	58	35	60.3	498	8.6(69)	3	1	12	70	—	—	—	0	244
NFL	4	38(34)	152	518	3.4(19)	3	—	—	—	—	960	542	56.5	6337	6.6(80)	32	37	80	441	71.7	—	—	18	2397

Carter, Rodney Rodney Carl, RB, 6´0˝/218 lbs; Purdue; 1986: Pit, rnd 7; B10/30/1964 Elizabeth, NJ

YEAR	TEAM	G (GS, POS)	RUSH	YD	AVG (LG)	TD	REC	YD	AVG (LG)	TD	PASS	COMP	PCT	YD	AVG (LG)	TD	INT	SK	YD	QBR	KPR	OTD	PTS	TAY
1987	Pit	11(2)	5	12	2.4(4)	0	16	180	11.3(26)	3	—	—	—	—	—	—	—	—	—	—	—	—	18	117
1988	Pit	14(1)	36	216	6.0(64)	3	32	363	11.3(33)	2	3	2	66.7	56	18.7(40)	0	0	—	—	—	—	—	30	466
1989	Pit	15(0)	11	16	1.5(7)	1	38	267	7.0(22)	3	1	1	100.0	15	15.0(15)	0	0	2	7	—	—	—	24	182
NFL	3	40(3)	52	244	4.7(64)	4	86	810	9.4(33)	8	4	3	75.0	71	17.8(40)	0	0	2	7	—	—	—	72	765

Carter, Ross Roscoe Challis, G-C, 6´0˝/200 lbs; Oregon; 1936: ChiC, rnd 8; B3/10/1914 Republic, MO, D6/16/2002 Eugene, OR **1936** ChiC 10 (0) **1937** ChiC 11 (11, RG) **1938** ChiC☆11 (10, RG) **1939** ChiC 10 (9, RG) **NFL** 42 (30) [4 yrs]

Carter, Rubin Rubin, NT-DT, 6´0˝/256 lbs; Miami (FL); 1975: Den, rnd 5; B12/12/1952 Pompano Beach, FL **1975** Den 14 (8, ldt) **1976** Den 14 (14, NT/ldt) **1977**†Den☆14 (14, NT) **1978**†Den 16 (16, NT) **1979**†Den 15 (15, NT) **1980** Den 16 (16, NT) **1981** Den 16 (16, NT) **1982** Den 9 (7, NT) **1983**†Den 16 (15, NT) **1984**†Den 15 (15, NT) **1985** Den 16 (16, NT) **1986** Den 5 (2) **NFL** 166 (154) [12 yrs]

Carter, Russell Russell Edmonds, DB, 6´2˝/195 lbs; SMU; 1984: NYJ, rnd 1; B2/10/1962 Philadelphia, PA **1984** NYJ 11 (8, rcb) **1985**†NYJ 8 (8, RCB) **1986**†NYJ 13 (13, RCB) **1987** NYJ 8 (6, rcb) **1988** LARd 15 (12, SS) **1989** LARd 9 (0) **NFL** 64 (47) [6 yrs]

Carter, Steve Stephen Edward, WR, 5´10˝/170 lbs; Albany State (GA); B9/12/1962 New York, NY

YEAR	TEAM	G (GS, POS)	RUSH	YD	AVG (LG)	TD	REC	YD	AVG (LG)	TD	PASS	COMP	PCT	YD	AVG (LG)	TD	INT	SK	YD	QBR	KPR	OTD	PTS	TAY
1987	TB	3(1)	—	—	—	—	1	12	12.0(12)	0	—	—	—	—	—	—	—	—	—	—	—	—	0	6

Carter, Tim Timothy M., WR, 6´0˝/200 lbs; Auburn; 2002: NYG, rnd 2; B9/21/1979 Atlanta, GA

YEAR	TEAM	G (GS, POS)	RUSH	YD	AVG (LG)	TD	REC	YD	AVG (LG)	TD	PASS	COMP	PCT	YD	AVG (LG)	TD	INT	SK	YD	QBR	KPR	OTD	PTS	TAY
2002	NYG	5(0)	3	28	9.3(13)	0	2	37	18.5(27)	0	—	—	—	—	—	—	—	—	—	—	k	—	0	50
2003	NYG	12(2)	—	—	—	—	26	309	11.9(30)	0	—	—	—	—	—	—	—	—	—	—	k	—	0	149
2004	NYG	5(0)	2	23	11.5(15)	0	12	182	15.2(38)	1	—	—	—	—	—	—	—	—	—	—	—	—	6	119
2005	NYG	15(1)	6	46	7.7(22)	0	10	186	18.6(44)	0	—	—	—	—	—	—	—	—	—	—	—	—	0	139
NFL	4	37(3)	11	97	8.8(22)	0	50	714	14.3(44)	1	—	—	—	—	—	—	—	—	—	—	k	—	6	456

Carter, Tim Timothy Jerome, DB, 6´0˝/183 lbs; Tulane; B7/15/1978 Tallahassee, FL **2001** NO 2 (0)

Carter, Tom Thomas, DB, 6´0˝/185 lbs; Notre Dame; 1993: Was, rnd 1; B9/5/1972 St. Petersburg, FL **[I]** **1993** Was 14 (11, LCB) **1994** Was 16 (16, LCB) **1995** Was 16 (16, LCB) **1996** Was 16 (16, LCB) **1997** ChiB 16 (16, LCB) **1998** ChiB 4 (4) **1999** ChiB 12 (6, rcb) **1999** Cin 2 (2) **2000** Cin 16 (11, LCB) **2001** Cin 6 (0) **NFL** 118 (98) [9 yrs]

Carter, Tony Antonio Marcus, RB, 6´0˝/230 lbs; Minnesota; B8/23/1972 Columbus, OH

YEAR	TEAM	G (GS, POS)	RUSH	YD	AVG (LG)	TD	REC	YD	AVG (LG)	TD	PASS	COMP	PCT	YD	AVG (LG)	TD	INT	SK	YD	QBR	KPR	OTD	PTS	TAY
1994	†ChiB	14(0)	—	—	—	—	1	24	24.0(24)	0	—	—	—	—	—	—	—	—	—	—	k	—	0	21
1995	ChiB	16(11, FB)	10	34	3.4(7)	0	40	329	8.2(27)	1	—	—	—	—	—	—	—	—	—	—	k	—	6	183
1996	ChiB	16(11, FB)	11	43	3.9(23)	0	41	233	5.7(29)	0	—	—	—	—	—	—	—	—	—	—	—	—	0	160
1997	ChiB	16(10, FB)	9	56	6.2(16)	0	24	152	6.3(19)	0	—	—	—	—	—	—	—	—	—	—	k	—	0	136
1998	†NE	11(7, FB)	2	3	1.5(3)	0	18	166	9.2(49)	0	—	—	—	—	—	—	—	—	—	—	—	—	0	86
1999	NE	16(14, FB)	6	26	4.3(9)	0	20	108	5.4(20)	0	—	—	—	—	—	—	—	—	—	—	—	—	0	80
2000	NE	16(6, FB)	37	90	2.4(9)	2	9	73	8.1(21)	0	—	—	—	—	—	—	—	—	—	—	k	—	12	148
2001	Den	16(6, fb)	1	4	4.0(4)	0	11	83	7.5(17)	0	—	—	—	—	—	—	—	—	—	—	k	—	0	60
2002	GB	12(0)	—	—	—	—	—	—	—	—	—	—	—	—	—	—	—	—	—	—	kp	—	0	7
NFL	9	133(65)	76	256	3.4(23)	2	164	1168	7.1(49)	1	—	—	—	—	—	—	—	—	—	—	kp	—	18	879

Carter, Tyrone Tyrone, DB, 5´8˝/190 lbs; Minnesota; 2000: Min, rnd 4; B3/31/1976 Fort Lauderdale, FL **2000**†Min 15 (7, fs) **2001** Min 15 (7, fs) **2002** Min 16 (7, rcb) **2003** NYJ 16 (10, FS) **2004**†Pit 9 (0) **2005**†Pit 16 (0) **NFL** 87 (31) [6 yrs]

Carter, Virgil Virgil R., QB, 6´1˝/192 lbs; Brigham Young; 1967: Chi, rnd 6; B11/9/1945 Anabella, UT **[K]**

YEAR	TEAM	G (GS, POS)	RUSH	YD	AVG (LG)	TD	REC	YD	AVG (LG)	TD	PASS	COMP	PCT	YD	AVG (LG)	TD	INT	SK	YD	QBR	KPR	OTD	PTS	TAY
1968	ChiB	7(5, qb)	48	265	5.5(31)	4	—	—	—	—	122	55	45.1	769	6.3(50)	4	5	6	45	—	—	—	24	510
1969	ChiB	3	4	19	4.8(11)	0	—	—	—	—	71	36	50.7	343	4.8(41)	2	5	3	20	—	—	—	0	1
1970	†Cin	13(QB)	34	246	7.2(73)	2	—	—	—	—	278	143	51.4	1647	5.9(56)	9	9	21	154	66.9	—	—	12	775
1971	Cin	10(QB)	8	42	5.3(19)	0	—	—	—	—	222	138	**62.2**	1624	7.3(**90**)	10	7	13	122	86.2	K	—	1	624
1972	Cin	10	12	57	4.8(14)	2	—	—	—	—	82	47	57.3	579	7.1(36)	3	4	6	37	—	—	—	12	222
1975	SD	1(1)	2	11	5.5(9)	0	—	—	—	—	5	3	60.0	24	4.8(11)	0	1	1	10	—	—	—	0	-17
1976	ChiB	8	1	0	0.0(0)	0	—	—	—	—	5	3	60.0	77	15.4(55)	1	0	—	—	—	—	—	0	44
NFL	7	52(6)	109	640	5.9(73)	8	—	—	—	—	785	425	54.1	5063	6.4(90)	29	31	50	388	69.9	K	—	49	2157

Carter, Walter Walter Burke, DE, 6´4˝/276 lbs; Florida State; 1980: Oak, rnd 10; B12/19/1957 Richmond, VA **1987** TB 2 (1)

Carter, Willie Willie Lee, HB-DB, 5´11˝/198 lbs; Tennessee State; B2/23/1931 Louisville, KY, D6/6/1986 Louisville, KY

YEAR	TEAM	G (GS, POS)	RUSH	YD	AVG (LG)	TD	REC	YD	AVG (LG)	TD	PASS	COMP	PCT	YD	AVG (LG)	TD	INT	SK	YD	QBR	KPR	OTD	PTS	TAY
1953	ChiC	8	2	-3	-1.5(2)	0	—	—	—	—	—	—	—	—	—	—	—	—	—	—	kp	—	0	55

Carthen, Jason Jason, LB, 6´3˝/255 lbs; Ohio University; B11/16/1970 Toledo, OH **1993** NE 5 (0) **1994** NE 1 (0) **NFL** 6 (0) [2 yrs]

Carthens, Milt Milton, T, 6´4˝/305 lbs; Michigan; B10/22/1960 **1987** Ind 1 (0)

Carthon, Maurice Maurice, RB, 6´1˝/225 lbs; Arkansas State; B4/24/1961 Chicago, IL

YEAR	TEAM	G (GS, POS)	RUSH	YD	AVG (LG)	TD	REC	YD	AVG (LG)	TD	PASS	COMP	PCT	YD	AVG (LG)	TD	INT	SK	YD	QBR	KPR	OTD	PTS	TAY
1985	†NYG	16(6, rb)	27	70	2.6(12)	0	8	81	10.1(22)	0	—	—	—	—	—	—	—	—	—	—	—	—	0	111
1986	†NYG	16(16, FB)	72	260	3.6(12)	0	16	67	4.2(10)	0	—	—	—	—	—	—	—	—	—	—	—	—	0	294
1987	NYG	11(5, fb)	26	60	2.3(10)	0	8	71	8.9(25)	0	—	—	—	—	—	—	—	—	—	—	—	—	0	96
1988	NYG	16(14, FB)	46	146	3.2(8)	2	19	194	10.2(24)	1	—	—	—	—	—	—	—	—	—	—	—	—	18	268
1989	†NYG	16(10, FB)	57	153	2.7(18)	0	15	132	8.8(18)	0	—	—	—	—	—	—	—	—	—	—	—	—	0	219
1990	†NYG	16(13, FB)	36	143	4.0(12)	0	14	151	10.8(63)	0	—	—	—	—	—	—	—	—	—	—	—	—	0	219
1991	NYG	16(8, FB)	32	109	3.4(10)	0	7	39	5.6(9)	0	—	—	—	—	—	—	—	—	—	—	—	—	0	129
1992	Ind	16(5, fb)	4	9	2.3(5)	0	3	10	3.3(6)	0	—	—	—	—	—	—	—	—	—	—	—	—	0	14
NFL	8	123(77)	300	950	3.2(18)	2	90	745	8.3(63)	1	—	—	—	—	—	—	—	—	—	—	—	—	18	1348

Carthon, Ran Ran, RB, 6´0˝/218 lbs; Florida; B2/10/1981 Osceola, AR

YEAR	TEAM	G (GS, POS)	RUSH	YD	AVG (LG)	TD	REC	YD	AVG (LG)	TD	PASS	COMP	PCT	YD	AVG (LG)	TD	INT	SK	YD	QBR	KPR	OTD	PTS	TAY
2005	Ind	6(0)	13	18	1.4(7)	1	1	10	10.0(10)	0	—	—	—	—	—	—	—	—	—	—	k	—	6	50

Carton, Charlie Charles Peter, E-T-G-C, 5´10˝/195 lbs; Holy Cross; B3/6/1901 Philadelphia, PA, D6/9/1951 Queens, NY **1925** Fra 13 (8, le), 6

Cartwright, Rock Rock, FB, 5´7˝/223 lbs; Kansas State; 2002: Was, rnd 7; B12/3/1979 Conroe, TX

YEAR	TEAM	G (GS, POS)	RUSH	YD	AVG (LG)	TD	REC	YD	AVG (LG)	TD	PASS	COMP	PCT	YD	AVG (LG)	TD	INT	SK	YD	QBR	KPR	OTD	PTS	TAY
2002	Was	16(0)	3	22	7.3(20)	0	11	121	11.0(22)	1	—	—	—	—	—	—	—	—	—	—	k	—	6	107
2003	Was	15(3)	107	411	3.8(22)	4	18	176	9.8(40)	0	—	—	—	—	—	—	—	—	—	—	k	—	24	535

YEAR	TEAM	G (GS, POS)	RUSH	YD	AVG (LG)	TD	REC	YD	AVG (LG)	TD	PASS	COMP	PCT	YD	AVG (LG)	TD	INT	SK	YD	QBR	KPR	OTD	PTS	TAY
2004	Was	13(0)	2	0	0.0(2)	0	—	—	—	—	—	—	—	—	—	—	—	—	—	—	—	—	0	0
2005	†Was	16(0)	27	199	7.4(52)	2	2	23	11.5(17)	0	—	—	—	—	—	—	—	—	—	—	k	—	12	253
NFL	4	60(3)	139	632	4.5(52)	6	31	320	10.3(40)	1	—	—	—	—	—	—	—	—	—	—	k	—	42	894

CARTY, JOHNDALE Johndale Edward, DB, 6´0˝/196 lbs; Utah State; 1999: Atl, rnd 4; B8/27/1977 Miami, FL **1999** Atl 14 (0) **2000** Atl 15 (0) **2001** Atl 16 (2) **2002**†Atl 16 (1) **NFL** 61 (3) [4 yrs]

CARVER, DALE Dale Keith, LB, 6´2˝/225 lbs; Georgia; B3/5/1961 Melbourne, FL **1983** Cle 16 (0)

CARVER, MEL Melvin, RB, 5´11˝/221 lbs; UNLV; B7/14/1959 Pensacola, FL

YEAR	TEAM	G (GS, POS)	RUSH	YD	AVG (LG)	TD	REC	YD	AVG (LG)	TD	PASS	COMP	PCT	YD	AVG (LG)	TD	INT	SK	YD	QBR	KPR	OTD	PTS	TAY
1982	†TB	9(1)	70	229	3.3(13)	1	4	46	11.5(24)	1	—	—	—	—	—	—	—	—	—	—	k	—	12	284
1983	TB	16(9, RB)	114	348	3.1(16)	0	32	262	8.2(20)	1	—	—	—	—	—	—	—	—	—	—	k	—	6	478
1984	TB	5(1)	11	44	4.0(12)	0	3	27	9.0(12)	0	—	—	—	—	—	—	—	—	—	—	—	—	0	58
1985	TB	2(0)	—	—	—	—	—	—	—	—	—	—	—	—	—	—	—	—	—	—	—	—	—	—
1987	Ind	1(0)	2	3	1.5(3)	0	—	—	—	—	—	—	—	—	—	—	—	—	—	—	—	—	0	3
NFL	5	33(11)	197	624	3.2(16)	1	39	335	8.6(24)	2	—	—	—	—	—	—	—	—	—	—	k	—	18	823

CARVER, SHANTE Shante Ebony, DE, 6´5˝/250 lbs; Arizona State; 1994: Dal, rnd 1; B2/12/1971 Stockton, CA **1994** Dal 10 (0) **1995**†Dal 16 (3) **1996**†Dal 10 (7, RDE) **1997** Dal 16 (16, RDE) **NFL** 52 (26) [4 yrs]

CARWELL, LARRY Lawrence Neil, DB, 6´1˝/188 lbs; Iowa State; 1967: Hou, rnd 3; B8/5/1944 Vada, GA, D1/10/1984 Bahamas **1967** Hou-A 9 **1968** Hou-A 14 (RCB) **1969** Bos-A 13 (13, LCB) **1970** Bos 10 (9, LCB) **1971** NE 14 (11, LCB) **1972** NE 14 (14, LCB) **NFL** 74 (47) [6 yrs]

CASANEGA, KEN Kenneth Thomas, QB-DB-HB, 5´11˝/175 lbs; Santa Clara; 1942: Pit, rnd 3; B2/18/1921, CA **1948** SF-A 1 (0)

YEAR	TEAM	G (GS, POS)	RUSH	YD	AVG (LG)	TD	REC	YD	AVG (LG)	TD	PASS	COMP	PCT	YD	AVG (LG)	TD	INT	SK	YD	QBR	KPR	OTD	PTS	TAY
1946	SF-A	14(5, qb)	29	90	3.1	1	5	102	20.4	1	—	—	—	—	—	—	—	—	—	—	kpi	—	12	436
AAFC	2	15(5)	29	90	3.1	1	5	102	20.4	1	—	—	—	—	—	—	—	—	—	—	—	—	12	156

CASANOVA, TOMMY Thomas Henry, DB, 6´2˝/202 lbs; LSU; 1972: Cin, rnd 2; B8/29/1950 New Orleans, LA **[R]** **1972** Cin☆14 (FS) **1973**†Cin 10 (FS) **1974** Cin✧14 (FS) **1975**†Cin☆11 (SS) **1976** Cin★11 (SS)

YEAR	TEAM	G (GS, POS)	RUSH	YD	AVG (LG)	TD	REC	YD	AVG (LG)	TD	PASS	COMP	PCT	YD	AVG (LG)	TD	INT	SK	YD	QBR	KPR	OTD	PTS	TAY
1977	Cin★	11(SS)	1	20	20.0(20)	0	—	—	—	—	—	—	—	—	—	—	—	—	—	—	pi	—	0	16
NFL	6	71	1	20	20.0(20)	0	—	—	—	—	—	—	—	—	—	—	—	—	—	—	kpi	4	24	622

CASARES, RICK Ricardo Jose, FB, 6´2˝/226 lbs; Florida; 1954: ChiB, rnd 2; B7/4/1931 Tampa, FL

YEAR	TEAM	G (GS, POS)	RUSH	YD	AVG (LG)	TD	REC	YD	AVG (LG)	TD	PASS	COMP	PCT	YD	AVG (LG)	TD	INT	SK	YD	QBR	KPR	OTD	PTS	TAY
1955	ChiB★	12(FB)	125	672	**5.4(81)**	4	16	136	8.5(29)	1	3	2	66.7	27	9.0(23)	1	1	—	—	—	—	—	30	764
1956	†ChiB★	12(FB)	**234**	**1126**	4.8(68)	**12**	23	203	8.8(33)	2	3	0	0.0	0	0.0	0	1	—	—	—	Pk	—	84	**1368**
1957	ChiB★	12(FB)	**204**	700	3.4(25)	6	25	225	9.0(43)	0	2	1	50.0	32	16.0(32)	0	0	—	—	—	Pk	—	36	874
1958	ChiB★	12(FB)	176	651	3.7(64)	2	32	290	9.1(50)	1	4	1	25.0	13	3.3(13)	1	0	—	—	—	—	—	18	833
1959	ChiB✧	12(FB)	177	699	3.9(47)	10	27	273	10.1(43)	2	1	0	0.0	0	0.0	0	1	—	—	—	P	—	72	906
1960	ChiB	12(FB)	160	566	3.5(35)	5	8	64	8.0(21)	0	—	—	—	—	—	—	—	—	—	—	P	—	30	648
1961	ChiB	13(FB)	135	588	4.4(23)	8	8	69	8.6(31)	0	—	—	—	—	—	—	—	—	—	—	—	—	48	703
1962	ChiB	13(fb)	75	255	3.4(18)	2	10	71	7.1(24)	1	2	1	50.0	35	17.5(35)	1	0	—	—	—	—	—	18	338
1963	ChiB	10	65	277	4.3(30)	0	19	94	4.9(25)	1	—	—	—	—	—	—	—	—	—	—	k	—	6	317
1964	ChiB	13	35	123	3.5(28)	0	14	113	8.1(51)	2	—	—	—	—	—	—	—	—	—	—	—	—	12	190
1965	Was	3	2	5	2.5(3)	0	1	5	5.0(5)	0	—	—	—	—	—	—	—	—	—	—	—	—	0	8
1966	Mia-A	6	43	135	3.1(10)	0	8	45	5.6(20)	1	—	—	—	—	—	—	—	—	—	—	—	—	6	163
NFL	12	130	1431	5797	4.1(81)	49	191	1588	8.3(51)	11	15	5	33.3	107	7.1(35)	3	3	—	—	—	Pk	—	360	7108

CASCADDEN, CHAD Chad Stevens, LB, 6´1˝/235 lbs; Wisconsin; B5/14/1972 Chippewa Falls, WI **1995** NYJ 12 (0) **1996** NYJ 16 (8, rlb) **1997** NYJ 15 (0) **1998**†NYJ 13 (4) **1999** NYJ 4 (0) **NFL** 60 (12) [5 yrs]

CASE, ERNIE Ernest Francis, QB-DB, 5´10˝/170 lbs; UCLA; 1947: Mia-A, rnd S/GB, rnd 1; B11/23/1919 Case, TX, D12/13/1995 Palos Verde Estates, CA **[K]**

YEAR	TEAM	G (GS, POS)	RUSH	YD	AVG (LG)	TD	REC	YD	AVG (LG)	TD	PASS	COMP	PCT	YD	AVG (LG)	TD	INT	SK	YD	QBR	KPR	OTD	PTS	TAY
1947	Bal-A	14(10, qb)	1	0	0.0	0	—	—	—	—	11	4	36.4	49	4.5	0	1	—	—	—	KPkpi	—	4	83

CASE, FRANK Francis, DE, 6´4˝/243 lbs; Penn State; 1981: KC, rnd 11; B8/14/1958 Jacksonville, NC **1981** KC 7 (0)

CASE, PETE Ronald Lee, G, 6´3˝/245 lbs; Georgia; 1962: Phi, rnd 2/Hou, rnd 3; B12/27/1940 Dayton, OH **1962** Phi 14 (rg) **1963** Phi 12 (RG) **1964** Phi 14 (rg) **1965** NYG 14 (LG) **1966** NYG 14 (LG) **1968** NYG☆14 (LG) **1969** NYG 14 (LG) **1970** NYG 7

YEAR	TEAM	G (GS, POS)	RUSH	YD	AVG (LG)	TD	REC	YD	AVG (LG)	TD	PASS	COMP	PCT	YD	AVG (LG)	TD	INT	SK	YD	QBR	KPR	OTD	PTS	TAY
1967	NYG	14(LG)	0	16	(16)	0	—	—	—	—	—	—	—	—	—	—	—	—	—	—	—	—	0	16
NFL	9	117	0	16	(16)	0	—	—	—	—	—	—	—	—	—	—	—	—	—	—	—	—	0	16

CASE, SCOTT Jeffrey Scott, DB, 6´1˝/188 lbs; Northeastern Oklahoma A&M; Oklahoma; 1984: Atl, rnd 2; B5/17/1962 Waynoka, OK **[I]** **1984** Atl 16 (0) **1985** Atl 14 (13, SS) **1986** Atl 16 (15, RCB) **1987** Atl 11 (10, RCB) **1988** Atl★16 (15, RCB) **1989** Atl 14 (8, rcb) **1990** Atl 16 (16, FS) **1991**†Atl 16 (16, FS) **1992** Atl 12 (11, FS) **1993** Atl 16 (16, FS) **1994** Atl 15 (3) **1995**†Dal 16 (1) **NFL** 178 (124) [12 yrs]

CASE, STONEY Stoney Jarrod, QB, 6´3˝/204 lbs; New Mexico; 1995: Arz, rnd 3; B7/7/1972 Odessa, TX

YEAR	TEAM	G (GS, POS)	RUSH	YD	AVG (LG)	TD	REC	YD	AVG (LG)	TD	PASS	COMP	PCT	YD	AVG (LG)	TD	INT	SK	YD	QBR	KPR	OTD	PTS	TAY
1995	Arz	2(0)	1	4	4.0(4)	0	—	—	—	—	2	1	50.0	19	9.5(19)	0	1	—	—	—	—	—	0	-27
1997	Arz	3(1)	7	8	1.1(3)	1	—	—	—	—	55	29	52.7	316	5.7(30)	0	2	10	89	—	—	—	6	96
1999	Bal	10(4, qb)	36	141	3.9(28)	3	—	—	—	—	170	77	45.3	988	5.8(54)	3	8	17	116	—	—	—	18	360
2000	Det	5(1)	16	117	7.3(27)	1	—	—	—	—	91	56	61.5	503	5.5(40)	1	4	12	75	—	—	—	6	224
NFL	4	20(6)	60	270	4.5(28)	5	—	—	—	—	318	163	51.3	1826	5.7(54)	4	15	39	280	—	—	—	30	653

CASEY, ALVRO Alvro E., aka Running Wolf, T, 6´0˝/215 lbs; Haskell Indian; Northeastern Oklahoma; B3/29/1903 Muskogee, OK, D10/22/1971 Big Spring, TX **1926** Akr 4 (4, RT)

CASEY, BERNIE Bernard Terry, HB-FL-TE-WR, 6´4˝/215 lbs; Bowling Green State; 1961: SF, rnd 1/NYT, rnd 9; B6/8/1939 Wyco, WV

YEAR	TEAM	G (GS, POS)	RUSH	YD	AVG (LG)	TD	REC	YD	AVG (LG)	TD	PASS	COMP	PCT	YD	AVG (LG)	TD	INT	SK	YD	QBR	KPR	OTD	PTS	TAY
1961	SF	12	—	—	—	—	10	185	18.5(51)	1	—	—	—	—	—	—	—	—	—	—	—	—	6	98
1962	SF	13(11, RH/te)	—	—	—	—	53	819	15.5(48)	6	—	—	—	—	—	—	—	—	—	—	—	—	36	440
1963	SF	14(10, RH)	—	—	—	—	47	762	16.2(68)	7	—	—	—	—	—	—	—	—	—	—	—	—	42	416
1964	SF	13(13, RH/lh)	—	—	—	—	58	808	13.9(63)	4	—	—	—	—	—	—	—	—	—	—	—	—	24	424
1965	SF	14(14, RH)	—	—	—	—	59	765	13.0(59)	8	—	—	—	—	—	—	—	—	—	—	—	—	48	423
1966	SF	13(13, FL)	1	23	23.0(23)	0	50	669	13.4(32)	1	—	—	—	—	—	—	—	—	—	—	—	—	6	363
1967	†LARm✧	14(FL)	—	—	—	—	53	871	16.4(57)	8	—	—	—	—	—	—	—	—	—	—	—	—	48	476
1968	LARm	12(11, FL)	—	—	—	—	29	565	19.5(55)	5	—	—	—	—	—	—	—	—	—	—	—	—	30	308
NFL	8	105(72)	1	23	23.0(23)	0	359	5444	15.2(68)	40	—	—	—	—	—	—	—	—	—	—	—	—	240	2945

CASEY, EDDIE Edward Lawrence, WB, 5´10˝/161 lbs; Harvard; B5/16/1894 Natick, MA, D7/26/1966 Boston, MA **[C]** **1920** Buf 1 (0)

CASEY, PETE Albert R., WB-HB, /180 lbs; none; B12/2/1895 Potosi, MO, D8/25/1976 St. Louis, MO **1923** SL 7 (7, WB), 12

CASEY, TIM Timothy Michael, LB, 6´1˝/225 lbs; Oregon; B2/29/1944 Portland, OR **1969** ChiB 3 **1969** Den-A 2 **NFL** 5 [1 yr]

CASEY, TOM Thomas Ray, TB-DB, 5´11˝/175 lbs; Hampton; B7/30/1924 Wellsville, OH

YEAR	TEAM	G (GS, POS)	RUSH	YD	AVG (LG)	TD	REC	YD	AVG (LG)	TD	PASS	COMP	PCT	YD	AVG (LG)	TD	INT	SK	YD	QBR	KPR	OTD	PTS	TAY
1948	NYY-A	11(0)	18	75	4.2	0	—	—	—	—	5	2	40.0	31	6.2	1	0	—	—	—	Pkp	1	6	355

CASH, ANTOINE Antoine, LB, 6´1˝/223 lbs; Southern Mississippi; B3/5/1982 Anguilla, MS **2005** Atl 3 (0)

CASH, CHRIS Chris, DB, 5´11˝/170 lbs; USC; 2002: Det, rnd 6; B7/13/1980 Stockton, CA **2002** Det 16 (12, RCB) **2004** Det 11 (5, lcb) **2005** Atl 3 (0) **NFL** 30 (17) [3 yrs]

CASH, JOHN John Lewis, DE, 6´3˝/240 lbs; Allen; B8/5/1936 Brunswick, GA **1961** Den-A 14 (LDE) **1962** Den-A 14 (RDE) **NFL** 28 [2 yrs]

CASH, KEITH Keith Lowell, TE, 6´4˝/242 lbs; Texas; 1991: Was, rnd 7; B8/7/1969 San Antonio, TX

YEAR	TEAM	G (GS, POS)	RUSH	YD	AVG (LG)	TD	REC	YD	AVG (LG)	TD	PASS	COMP	PCT	YD	AVG (LG)	TD	INT	SK	YD	QBR	KPR	OTD	PTS	TAY
1991	Pit	5(0)	—	—	—	—	7	90	12.9(20)	1	—	—	—	—	—	—	—	—	—	—	p	—	6	51
1992	†KC	15(8, te)	—	—	—	—	12	113	9.4(19)	2	—	—	—	—	—	—	—	—	—	—	k	—	12	88
1993	†KC	15(0)	1	0	0.0(0)	0	24	242	10.1(24)	4	—	—	—	—	—	—	—	—	—	—	—	—	24	141
1994	†KC	6(5, te)	—	—	—	—	19	192	10.1(31)	2	—	—	—	—	—	—	—	—	—	—	—	—	12	106
1995	†KC	14(14, TE)	—	—	—	—	42	419	10.0(38)	1	—	—	—	—	—	—	—	—	—	—	—	—	6	215
1996	KC	9(5, te)	—	—	—	—	14	80	5.7(20)	0	—	—	—	—	—	—	—	—	—	—	—	—	0	40
NFL	6	64(32)	1	0	0.0	0	118	1136	9.6(38)	10	—	—	—	—	—	—	—	—	—	—	kp	—	60	640

YEAR	TEAM	G(GS, POS)	RUSH	YD	AVG(LG)	TD	REC	YD	AVG(LG)	TD	PASS COMP	PCT	YD	AVG(LG)	TD	INT	SK	YD	QBR	KPR	OTD	PTS	TAY
CASH, KERRY Kerry Lenard, TE, 6´4˝/245 lbs; Texas; 1991: Ind, rnd 5; B8/7/1969 San Antonio, TX																						
1991	Ind	4(2)	—	—	—	—	1	18	18.0(18)	0	—	—	—	—	—	—	—	—	—	—	—	0	9
1992	Ind	16(16, TE)	—	—	—	—	43	521	12.1(41)	3	—	—	—	—	—	—	—	—	—	—	—	18	276
1993	Ind	16(14, TE)	—	—	—	—	43	402	9.3(37)	3	—	—	—	—	—	—	—	—	—	k	—	18	212
1994	Ind	16(16, TE)	—	—	—	—	16	190	11.9(24)	1	—	—	—	—	—	—	—	—	—	—	—	6	100
1995	Oak	16(10, TE)	—	—	—	—	25	254	10.2(23)	2	—	—	—	—	—	—	—	—	—	—	—	12	137
1996	ChiB	3(2)	—	—	—	—	4	42	10.5(14)	0	—	—	—	—	—	—	—	—	—	—	—	0	21
NFL	6	71(60)	—	—	—	—	132	1427	10.8(41)	9	—	—	—	—	—	—	—	—	—	k	—	54	755
CASH, RICK Richard Francis, DE-DT, 6´5˝/248 lbs; Missouri; Truman State; 1968: GB, rnd 10; B7/1/1945 St. Louis, MO **1968** Atl 14 (RDE) **1969**†LARm 14 **1970** LARm 8																						
1972 NE 14 (13, RDT) **1973** NE 14 (14, RDE) **NFL** 64 (27) [5 yrs]																						
CASILLAS, TONY Tony Steven, DT-NT, 6´3˝/278 lbs; Oklahoma; 1986: Atl, rnd 1; B10/26/1963 Tulsa, OK **1986** Atl 16 (16, NT) **1987** Atl 9 (9, NT) **1988** Atl 16 (16, NT)																						
1989 Atl☆16 (16, NT) **1990** Atl 9 (0) **1991**†Dal 16 (16, LDT) **1992**†Dal 15 (15, LDT) **1993**†Dal 15 (14, LDT) **1994** NYJ 13 (11, RDT) **1995** NYJ 11 (5, LDT) **1996**†Dal 16 (3)																						
1997 Dal 15 (14, LDT) **NFL** 167 (135) [12 yrs]																						
CASNER, KEN Kenneth Wayne, DT, 6´2˝/245 lbs; Baylor; 1952: LA, rnd 4; B1/23/1930 Fort Scott, KS **1952** LARm 11																						
CASON, AVEION Aveion Marquet, RB, 5´10˝/204 lbs; Illinois State; B7/12/1979 St. Petersburg, FL																						
2001	SL	1(0)	11	31	2.8(19)	0	4	32	8.0(9)	0	—	—	—	—	—	—	—	—	—	—	—	0	47
2001	Det	5(0)	—	—	—	—	—	—	—	—	—	—	—	—	—	—	—	—	—	k	—	0	13
2002	Det	10(3)	26	107	4.1(40)	0	19	288	15.2(37)	2	—	—	—	—	—	—	—	—	—	k	—	12	279
2003	Dal	10(0)	40	220	5.5(63)	2	17	142	8.4(28)	0	1	1	100.0	37	37.0(37)	0	0	—	—	—	k	—	12	336
2004	†SL	3(0)	—	—	—	—	—	—	—	—	—	—	—	—	—	—	—	—	—	k	—	0	100
2005	SL	2(0)	10	65	6.5(14)	1	1	11	11.0(11)	0	—	—	—	—	—	—	—	—	—	k	—	6	99
NFL	31(3)	87	423	4.9(63)	3	41	473	11.5(37)	2	1	1	100.0	37	37.0(37)	0	0	—	—	—	k	—	30	873
CASON, JIM James Allnut, DB-HB, 6´0˝/171 lbs; LSU; 1948: SF-A, rnd 3/ChiC, rnd 7; B7/25/1927 Sondheimer, LA [I]																						
1948	SF-A	13(5, rh)	20	146	7.3(59)	2	4	99	24.8	1	—	—	—	—	—	—	—	—	—	kpi	—	18	503
1949	†SF-A☆	12(6, lh)	21	70	3.3	1	5	38	7.6	0	2	1	50.0	38	19.0(38)	1	0	—	—	—	kpi	—	6	558
AAFC	2	25(11)	41	216	5.3(59)	3	9	137	15.2	1	2	1	50.0	38	19.0(38)	1	0	—	—	—	kpi	—	24	1061
1950	SF	9(LH)	38	129	3.4(24)	1	30	374	12.5(43)	3	—	—	—	—	—	—	—	—	—	kpi	—	24	494
1951	SF◇	12(SS)	1	5	5.0(5)	0	1	8	8.0(8)	0	—	—	—	—	—	—	—	—	—	kpi	1	6	222
1952	SF	10(SS)	—	—	—	—	—	—	—	—	—	—	—	—	—	—	—	—	—	i	—	0	-6
1954	SF◇	9(DB)	2	1	0.5(3)	0	—	—	—	—	13	7	53.8	40	3.1(25)	0	1	—	—	—	—	—	0	-19
1955	†LARm	12(DB)	—	—	—	—	—	—	—	—	—	—	—	—	—	—	—	—	—	i	1	6	26
1956	LARm	12(DB)	—	—	—	—	—	—	—	—	—	—	—	—	—	—	—	—	—	i	—	0	43
NFL	6	64	41	135	3.3(59)	1	31	382	12.3(43)	3	13	7	53.8	40	3.1(38)	0	1	—	—	—	kpi	2	36	760
CASON, WENDELL Wendell B., DB, 5´11˝/191 lbs; Oregon; B1/22/1963 Lakewood, CA **1985** Atl 14 (14, RCB) **1986** Atl 16 (6, ss) **1987** Atl 3 (2) **NFL** 33 (22) [3 yrs]																						
CASPER, CY Charles Andrew, B, 6´0˝/190 lbs; TCU; B5/28/1912 Memphis, TN, D3/7/1968 Fort Worth, TX																						
1934	GB	1(0)	4	19	4.8	—	—	—	—	—	—	—	—	—	—	—	—	—	—	—	—	0	19
1934	SL	3(1)	23	80	3.5	0	5	70	14.0	0	4	1	25.0	29	7.3(29)	0	0	—	—	—	—	1	0	130
1935	Pit	9(4)	56	102	1.8	1	5	94	18.8	1	4	1	25.0	3	0.8(3)	0	0	—	—	—	—	1	18	166
NFL	2	13(5)	83	201	2.4	1	10	164	16.4	1	8	2	25.0	32	4.0(29)	0	0	—	—	—	—	1	18	314
CASPER, DAVE David John 'Ghost', TE, 6´4˝/240 lbs; Notre Dame; 1974: Oak, rnd 2; B9/26/1951 Bemidji, MN; HOF 2002																						
1974	†Oak	14	—	—	—	—	4	26	6.5(17)	3	—	—	—	—	—	—	—	—	—	—	—	18	28
1975	†Oak	14	—	—	—	—	5	71	14.2(20)	1	—	—	—	—	—	—	—	—	—	—	—	6	41
1976	†Oak★	13(13, TE)	1	5	5.0(5)	0	53	691	13.0(30)	10	—	—	—	—	—	—	—	—	—	—	—	60	401
1977	†Oak★	14(14, TE)	—	—	—	—	48	584	12.2(27)	6	—	—	—	—	—	—	—	—	—	—	—	36	322
1978	Oak★	16(16, TE)	1	5	5.0(5)	0	62	852	13.7(44)	9	1	0	0.0	0	0.0	0	0	—	—	—	—	1	60	476
1979	Oak★	15(12, TE)	—	—	—	—	57	771	13.5(42)	3	—	—	—	—	—	—	—	—	—	—	—	18	401
1980	Oak	6(6, te)	—	—	—	—	22	270	12.3(35)	1	—	—	—	—	—	—	—	—	—	—	—	6	140
1980	†Hou◇	10(9, te)	2	8	4.0(6)	0	34	526	15.5(43)	3	—	—	—	—	—	—	—	—	—	—	—	18	286
1981	Hou	16(10, TE)	—	—	—	—	33	572	17.3(52)	3	—	—	—	—	—	—	—	—	—	—	—	48	326
1982	Hou	9(9, TE)	2	9	4.5(8)	0	36	573	15.9(38)	6	—	—	—	—	—	—	—	—	—	—	—	36	326
1983	Hou	3(2)	—	—	—	—	7	79	11.3(17)	0	—	—	—	—	—	—	—	—	—	—	—	0	40
1983	Min	10(9, te)	—	—	—	—	13	172	13.2(34)	0	—	—	—	—	—	—	—	—	—	—	—	0	86
1984	†LARd	7(0)	—	—	—	—	4	29	7.3(13)	2	—	—	—	—	—	—	—	—	—	—	—	12	25
NFL	11	147(100)	6	27	4.5(8)	0	378	5216	13.8(52)	52	1	0	0.0	0	0.0	0	0	—	—	—	—	1	318	2895
CASSADY, CRAIG Craig Howard, DB, 5´11˝/175 lbs; Ohio State; 1976: NO, rnd 8; B12/21/1953 Columbus, OH **1977** NO 12 (3)																						
CASSADY, HOWARD Howard Albert 'Hopalong', HB-SE-FL, 5´10˝/183 lbs; Ohio State; 1956: Det, rnd 1; B3/2/1934 Columbus, OH [R]																						
1956	Det	12(LH)	97	413	4.3(33)	0	9	83	9.2(21)	0	2	0	0.0	0	0.0	0	1	—	—	—	kp	—	0	575
1957	†Det	12(RH)	73	250	3.4(57)	3	25	325	13.0(48)	3	—	—	—	—	—	—	—	—	—	k	—	36	540
1958	Det	10(RH)	45	198	4.4(33)	0	23	406	17.7(81)	7	—	—	—	—	—	—	—	—	—	kp	—	42	461
1959	Det	12(RH)	52	203	3.9(18)	1	15	316	21.1(59)	4	—	—	—	—	—	—	—	—	—	kp	—	30	443
1960	Det	12(RH)	17	28	1.6(16)	1	20	238	11.9(40)	1	—	—	—	—	—	—	—	—	—	kp	—	12	204
1961	Det.	14	31	131	4.2(14)	1	5	45	9.0(76)	1	1	0	0.0	0	0.0	0	0	—	—	—	kp	—	12	240
1962	Cle	5	—	—	—	—	—	—	—	—	—	—	—	—	—	—	—	—	—	kp	—	0	95
1962	Phi	5(se)	1	6	6.0(6)	0	14	188	13.4(47)	2	—	—	—	—	—	—	—	—	—	kp	—	12	146
1963	Det	2	—	—	—	—	—	—	—	—	—	—	—	—	—	—	—	—	—	p	—	0	2
NFL	8	84	316	1229	3.9(57)	6	111	1601	14.4(81)	18	3	0	0.0	0	0.0	0	2	—	—	—	kp	—	144	2705
CASSARA, FRANK Frank, FB-LB, 6´0˝/215 lbs; St. Mary's (CA); B3/22/1928 San Fernando, CA																						
1954	SF	6	3	17	5.7(10)	0	1	12	12.0(12)	0	—	—	—	—	—	—	—	—	—	—	—	0	23
CASSEL, MATT Matt, QB, 6´5˝/230 lbs; Southern California; 2005: NE, rnd 7; B5/17/1982 Northridge, CA																						
2005	†NE	2(0)	6	12	2.0(9)	0	—	—	—	—	24	13	54.2	183	7.6(36)	2	1	1	1	—	—	—	0	74
CASSESE, TOM Thomas Lee, DB-HB, 6´1˝/198 lbs; C.W. Post; 1967: Den, rnd 8; B4/7/1946 Queens, NY																						
1967	Den-A	14(LS)	1	5	5.0(5)	0	—	—	—	—	—	—	—	—	—	—	—	—	—	kpi	—	0	27
CASSIANO, DICK Richard Peter, B, 5´11˝/175 lbs; Pittsburgh; 1940: GB, rnd 6; B10/7/1917 Albany, NY, D5/28/1980 Guilderland, NY																						
1940	Bkn	10(1)	35	84	2.4	0	2	67	33.5(44)	2	30	9	30.0	128	4.3	1	2	—	—	—	—	—	12	117
CASSIDY BB; none; deceased **1921** Ton 1 (0)																						
CASSIDY, RON Ronald Gene, WR, 6´0˝/184 lbs; Utah State; 1979: GB, rnd 8; B7/23/1957 Ventura, CA																						
1979	GB	8	—	—	—	—	6	102	17.0(23)	0	—	—	—	—	—	—	—	—	—	—	—	0	51
1980	GB	15(1)	—	—	—	—	5	109	21.8(43)	0	—	—	—	—	—	—	—	—	—	p	—	0	109
1981	GB	10(0)	—	—	—	—	1	6	6.0(6)	0	—	—	—	—	—	—	—	—	—	—	—	0	-7
1983	GB	12(0)	—	—	—	—	—	—	—	—	—	—	—	—	—	—	—	—	—	—	—	0	0
1984	GB	15(0)	—	—	—	—	2	16	8.0(9)	0	—	—	—	—	—	—	—	—	—	p	—	0	8
NFL	5	60(1)	—	—	—	—	14	233	16.6(43)	0	—	—	—	—	—	—	—	—	—	p	—	0	161
CASSIDY, WALT Walter E., E, 5´10˝/200 lbs; Detroit Mercy; B12/16/1899, D10/24/1974 Cleveland, OH **1924** Ken 5 (5, LE)																						
CASTEEL, MIKE Miles Webster, B, 5´11˝/175 lbs; Kalamazoo; B12/30/1895 Elmira, NY, D3/27/1977 Phoenix, AZ **1922** RI 6 (2), 6																						
CASTER, RICH Richard C., TE-WR, 6´5˝/228 lbs; Jackson State; 1970: NYJ, rnd 2; B10/16/1948 Mobile, AL																						
1970	NYJ	14	—	—	—	—	19	393	20.7(72)	3	—	—	—	—	—	—	—	—	—	k	—	18	197
1971	NYJ	14(WR)	2	10	5.0(17)	0	26	454	17.5(57)	2	—	—	—	—	—	—	—	—	—	—	—	36	267

YEAR	TEAM	G (GS, POS)	RUSH	YD	AVG (LG)	TD	REC	YD	AVG (LG)	TD	PASS	COMP	PCT	YD	AVG (LG)	TD	INT	SK	YD	QBR	KPR	OTD	PTS	TAY
1972	NYJ★	14 (TE)	2	6	3.0(6)	0	39	833	21.4(80)	10	—	—	—	—	—	—	—	—	—	—	—	—	60	473
1973	NYJ	14 (TE)	1	-9	-9.0(-9)	0	35	593	16.9(49)	4	—	—	—	—	—	—	—	—	—	—	—	—	24	308
1974	NYJ★	13 (TE)	—	—	—	—	38	745	19.6(89)	7	—	—	—	—	—	—	—	—	—	—	—	—	42	408
1975	NYJ★	14 (TE)	—	—	—	—	47	820	17.4(91)	4	—	—	—	—	—	—	—	—	—	—	—	—	24	430
1976	NYJ	14 (TE)	6	73	12.2(60)	0	31	391	12.6(41)	1	—	—	—	—	—	—	—	—	—	—	—	—	6	274
1977	NYJ	10 (WR)	2	-15	-7.5(-6)	0	10	205	20.5(58)	1	—	—	—	—	—	—	—	—	—	—	—	—	6	93
1978	†Hou	14 (wr)	5	32	6.4(11)	0	20	316	15.8(47)	5	—	—	—	—	—	—	—	—	—	—	—	—	30	215
1979	†Hou	16 (WR)	4	25	6.3(10)	0	18	239	13.3(36)	1	—	—	—	—	—	—	—	—	—	—	k	—	6	135
1980	†Hou	16 (1)	—	—	—	—	27	341	12.6(68)	3	—	—	—	—	—	—	—	—	—	—	—	—	18	186
1981	NO	4 (0)	1	-3	-3.0(-3)	0	7	108	15.4(31)	0	—	—	—	—	—	—	—	—	—	—	—	—	0	51
1981	Was	3 (1)	—	—	—	—	5	77	15.4(26)	0	—	—	—	—	—	—	—	—	—	—	—	—	0	39
1982	†Was	1 (0)	—	—	—	—	—	—	—	—	—	—	—	—	—	—	—	—	—	—	—	—		
NFL	13	161 (2)	23	119	5.2(60)	0	322	5515	17.1(91)	45	—	—	—	—	—	—	—	—	—	—	k	—	270	3072

CASTETE, JESSE   Jesse Joseph, DB, 5′11″/180 lbs; McNeese State; 1956: ChiB, rnd 24; B9/3/1933 St.Landry, LA   **1956** ChiB 8   **1956** LARm 3   **1957** LARm 11   **NFL** 22 [2 yrs]

CASTIGLIA, JIM   James Vincent, FB, 5′11″/208 lbs; Georgetown (DC); 1941: Pit, rnd 22; B9/30/1918 Passaic, NJ

YEAR	TEAM	G (GS, POS)	RUSH	YD	AVG (LG)	TD	REC	YD	AVG (LG)	TD	PASS	COMP	PCT	YD	AVG (LG)	TD	INT	SK	YD	QBR	KPR	OTD	PTS	TAY
1947	Bal-A	2 (2)	9	18	2.0	0	1	10	10.0(10)	0	—	—	—	—	—	—	—	—	—	—	—	1	6	23
1941	Phi	11 (6, FB)	60	183	3.1(47)	4	4	24	6.0(11)	0	7	0	0.0	0	0.0	0	1	—	—	ki	—	24	284
1945	Phi	1 (1)	13	29	2.2(6)	0	—	—	—	—	—	—	—	—	—	—	—	—	—	—	—	0	29
1946	Phi	11 (2)	39	87	2.2(14)	1	11	51	4.6(23)	0	—	—	—	—	—	—	—	—	—	k	—	6	125
1947	Was	7 (0, fb)	104	426	4.1(33)	5	11	88	8.0(25)	0	—	—	—	—	—	—	—	—	—	k	—	30	515
1948	Was	10 (1)	97	330	3.4(16)	0	7	73	10.4(32)	2	—	—	—	—	—	—	—	—	—	k	—	12	380
NFL	5	40 (10)	313	1055	3.4(47)	10	33	236	7.2(32)	2	7	0	0.0	0	0.0	0	1	—	—	ki	—	72	1332

CASTILLE, JEREMIAH   Jeremiah, DB, 5′10″/175 lbs; Alabama; 1983: TB, rnd 3; B1/15/1961 Columbus, GA   **1983** TB 15 (7, lcb)   **1984** TB 16 (16, LCB)   **1985** TB 16 (16, LCB)   **1986** TB 13 (6, lcb)   **1987**†Den 11 (0)   **1988** Den 16 (15, RCB)   **NFL** 87 (60) [6 yrs]

CASTILLO, LUIS   Luis Alberto, DE-DT, 6′3″/306 lbs; Northwestern; 2005: SD, rnd 1; B8/4/1983 Garfield, NJ   **2005** SD 16 (15, LDE)

CASTLE, ERIC   Eric Dean, DB, 6′3″/212 lbs; Oregon; 1993: SD, rnd 6; B3/15/1970 Longview, WA   **1993** SD 5 (0)   **1994**†SD 16 (1)   **1995**†SD 16 (0)   **1996** SD 16 (0)   **NFL** 53 (1) [4 yrs]

CASTON, TOBY   Sebastian Tobias, LB, 6′1″/235 lbs; LSU; 1987: Hou, rnd 6; B7/17/1965 Monroe, LA, D10/2/1994 Dallas, TX   **1987** Hou 6 (0)   **1988**†Hou 16 (0)   **1989** Det 16 (0)   **1990** Det 12 (4)   **1991**†Det 16 (0)   **1992** Det 15 (0)   **1993**†Det 9 (0)   **NFL** 90 (4) [7 yrs]

CASTOR, CHRIS   Christopher David, WR, 6′0″/170 lbs; Duke; 1983: Sea, rnd 5; B8/13/1960 Burlington, NC   **1983**†Sea 8 (0)

YEAR	TEAM	G (GS, POS)	RUSH	YD	AVG (LG)	TD	REC	YD	AVG (LG)	TD	PASS	COMP	PCT	YD	AVG (LG)	TD	INT	SK	YD	QBR	KPR	OTD	PTS	TAY
1984	Sea	15 (0)	—	—	—	—	8	89	11.1(21)	0	—	—	—	—	—	—	—	—	—	—	—	—	0	45
NFL	2	23 (0)	—	—	—	—	8	89	11.1(21)	0	—	—	—	—	—	—	—	—	—	—	—	—	0	45

CATALANO, TONY   Anthony Emil, G, none; B4/13/1895 Indianapolis, IN, D7/25/1980 Boise, ID   **1920** Ham 1 (0)

CATANHO, ALCIDES   Alcides, LB, 6′4″/230 lbs; Rutgers; B1/20/1972 Elizabeth, NJ   **1995** NE 12 (0)   **1996** Was 15 (0)   **NFL** 27 (0) [2 yrs]

CATANO, MARK   Mark R., NT, 6′3″/265 lbs; Valdosta State; B1/26/1962 Yonkers, NY   **1984**†Pit 16 (0)   **1985** Pit 15 (6, nt)   **1986** Buf 1 (0)   **NFL** 32 (6) [3 yrs]

CATCHINGS, TONEY   Toney Bruce, LB, 6′3″/236 lbs; Cincinnati; B8/11/1965 Jackson, MS   **1987** Cin 3 (0)

CATER, GREG   Gregory Wayne, P, 6′0″/191 lbs; Tennessee-Chattanooga; 1980: Buf, rnd 10; B4/17/1957 La Grange, GA [P]   **1981**†Buf 16 (0)   **1982** Buf 9 (0)   **1983** Buf 16 (0)   **1986** SL 11 (0)

YEAR	TEAM	G (GS, POS)	RUSH	YD	AVG (LG)	TD	REC	YD	AVG (LG)	TD	PASS	COMP	PCT	YD	AVG (LG)	TD	INT	SK	YD	QBR	KPR	OTD	PTS	TAY
1980	†Buf	16 (0)	2	-10	-5.0(-1)	0	—	—	—	—	1	1	100.0	15	15.0(15)	0	0	—	—	P	—	—	0	-3
1987	SL	9 (0)	2	3	1.5(11)	0	—	—	—	—	—	—	—	—	—	—	—	—	—	P	—	—	0	3
NFL	6	77 (0)	4	-7	-1.8(11)	0	—	—	—	—	1	1	100.0	15	15.0(15)	0	0	—	—	P	—	—	0	1

CATERBONE, MIKE   Michael Thomas, WR, 5′11″/175 lbs; Franklin & Marshall; B2/17/1962 Lancaster, PA

YEAR	TEAM	G (GS, POS)	RUSH	YD	AVG (LG)	TD	REC	YD	AVG (LG)	TD	PASS	COMP	PCT	YD	AVG (LG)	TD	INT	SK	YD	QBR	KPR	OTD	PTS	TAY
1987	Mia	3 (1)	—	—	—	—	2	46	23.0(30)	0	—	—	—	—	—	—	—	—	—	p	—	—	0	56

CATERBONE, THOMAS   Thomas Paul, DB, 5′8″/175 lbs; Franklin & Marshall; B6/29/1964 Lancaster, PA   **1987** Phi 2 (0)

CATHCART, ROYAL   Royal Jenesen, HB, 6′0″/185 lbs; California-Santa Barbara; B4/8/1926 Canute, OK

YEAR	TEAM	G (GS, POS)	RUSH	YD	AVG (LG)	TD	REC	YD	AVG (LG)	TD	PASS	COMP	PCT	YD	AVG (LG)	TD	INT	SK	YD	QBR	KPR	OTD	PTS	TAY
1950	SF	2	3	5	1.7(3)	0	—	—	—	—	—	—	—	—	—	—	—	—	—	—	—	—	0	5

CATHCART, SAM   Samuel Woodrow, DB-HB, 6′0″/175 lbs; California-Santa Barbara; B7/7/1924 Canute, OK

YEAR	TEAM	G (GS, POS)	RUSH	YD	AVG (LG)	TD	REC	YD	AVG (LG)	TD	PASS	COMP	PCT	YD	AVG (LG)	TD	INT	SK	YD	QBR	KPR	OTD	PTS	TAY
1949	†SF-A	12 (0)	69	412	6.0(57)	1	12	182	15.2(72)	0	—	—	—	—	—	—	—	—	—	kpi	—	6	757
1950	SF	12 (DB/lh)	33	76	2.3(17)	0	7	99	14.1(24)	0	—	—	—	—	—	—	—	—	—	kpi	—	0	390
1952	SF	12	6	21	3.5(7)	0	2	15	7.5(13)	0	1	0	0.0	0	0.0	0	1	—	—	kpi	—	0	61
NFL	2	24	39	97	2.5(57)	0	9	114	12.7(72)	0	1	0	0.0	0	0.0	0	1	—	—	kpi	—	0	450

CATLIN, TOM   Thomas Allen, LB-C, 6′1″/213 lbs; Oklahoma; 1953: Bal, rnd 4; B9/8/1931 Ponca City, OK   **1953**†Cle 12 (llb)   **1954**†Cle☆11 (LLB)   **1957**†Cle 4   **1958**†Cle 12   **1959** Phi 12 (RLB)   **NFL** 51 [5 yrs]

CATO, DARYL   Ralph Daryl, C-LB, 6′2″/195 lbs; Arkansas; B1/8/1920 Lonoke, AR, D10/3/1970

YEAR	TEAM	G (GS, POS)	RUSH	YD	AVG (LG)	TD	REC	YD	AVG (LG)	TD	PASS	COMP	PCT	YD	AVG (LG)	TD	INT	SK	YD	QBR	KPR	OTD	PTS	TAY
1946	Mia-A	12 (3)	0	3	(3)	0	—	—	—	—	—	—	—	—	—	—	—	—	—	i	—	0	27

CAVALLI, CARMEN   Carmen Anthony, DE, 6′4″/245 lbs; Richmond; 1960: Oak, rnd 1; B6/11/1937 Philadelphia, PA   **1960** Oak-A 14 (LDE)

CAVANAUGH, MATT   Matthew Andrew, QB, 6′2″/212 lbs; Pittsburgh; 1978: NE, rnd 2; B10/27/1956 Youngstown, OH

YEAR	TEAM	G (GS, POS)	RUSH	YD	AVG (LG)	TD	REC	YD	AVG (LG)	TD	PASS	COMP	PCT	YD	AVG (LG)	TD	INT	SK	YD	QBR	KPR	OTD	PTS	TAY
1979	NE	13	1	-2	-2.0(-2)	0	—	—	—	—	1	1	100.0	10	10.0(10)	0	0	—	—	—	—	—	0	3
1980	NE	16 (4)	19	97	5.1(22)	0	—	—	—	—	105	63	60.0	885	8.4(40)	9	5	8	62	—	—	—	0	385
1981	NE	16 (8, QB)	17	92	5.4(11)	3	1	9	9.0(9)	0	219	115	52.5	1633	7.5(65)	5	13	19	137	—	—	—	18	448
1982	†NE	7 (3)	2	3	1.5(3)	0	—	—	—	—	60	27	45.0	490	8.2(75)	5	5	7	86	—	—	—	0	73
1983	SF	5 (0)	1	8	8.0(8)	0	—	—	—	—	—	—	—	—	—	—	—	—	—	—	—	—	0	8
1984	†SF	8 (1)	4	-11	-2.8(-1)	0	—	—	—	—	61	33	54.1	449	7.4(51)	4	0	5	40	—	—	—	0	234
1985	†SF	16 (1)	4	5	1.3(13)	0	—	—	—	—	54	28	51.9	334	6.2(41)	1	1	7	53	—	—	—	0	137
1986	Phi	10 (2)	9	26	2.9(11)	0	—	—	—	—	58	28	48.3	397	6.8(49)	2	4	9	56	—	—	—	0	75
1987	Phi	3 (0)	1	-2	-2.0(-2)	0	—	—	—	—	—	—	—	—	—	—	—	—	—	—	—	—	0	-2
1988	Phi	5 (0)	—	—	—	—	—	—	—	—	16	7	43.8	101	6.3(42)	1	1	—	—	—	—	—	0	16
1989	†Phi	9 (0)	2	-3	-1.5(0)	0	—	—	—	—	5	3	60.0	33	6.6(13)	1	1	—	—	—	—	—	0	-22
1990	†NYG	0 (0)	—	—	—	—	—	—	—	—	—	—	—	—	—	—	—	—	—	—	—	—	0	0
1991	NYG	4 (0)	—	—	—	—	—	—	—	—	—	—	—	—	—	—	—	—	—	—	—	—		
NFL	13	112 (19)	60	213	3.6(22)	3	1	9	9.0(9)	0	579	305	52.7	4332	7.5(75)	28	30	55	434	71.7	—	—	18	1354

CAVENESS, RONNIE   Ronald Glen, LB, 6′1″/225 lbs; Arkansas; 1965: KC, rnd 2/LA, rnd 9; B3/6/1943 Houston, TX   **1965** KC-A 7   **1966** Hou-A 14 (mlb)   **1967**†Hou-A 14   **1968** Hou-A 11   **NFL** 46 [4 yrs]

CAVER, JIM   James, DB, 5′9″/175 lbs; Missouri; B9/28/1960 Birmingham, AL   **1983** Det 2 (0)

CAVER, QUINTON   Quinton Tyrone, LB, 6′4″/241 lbs; Arkansas; 2001: Phi, rnd 2; B8/22/1978 Anniston, AL   **2001**†Phi 11 (0)   **2002** Phi 5 (0)   **2002** KC 1 (0)   **2003**†KC 12 (0)   **2004** KC 16 (4)   **2005** Dal 8 (0)   **NFL** 53 (4) [5 yrs]

CAVIL, BEN   Ben Anthony, G, 6′2″/310 lbs; Oklahoma; B1/31/1972 Galveston, TX   **1997** Bal 15 (8, LG)   **1998** Bal 16 (6, lg)   **NFL** 31 (14) [2 yrs]

CAVIL, KWAME   Kwame, WR, 6′2″/202 lbs; Texas; B5/3/1979 Waco, TX

YEAR	TEAM	G (GS, POS)	RUSH	YD	AVG (LG)	TD	REC	YD	AVG (LG)	TD	PASS	COMP	PCT	YD	AVG (LG)	TD	INT	SK	YD	QBR	KPR	OTD	PTS	TAY
2000	Buf	16 (0)	—	—	—	—	4	66	16.5(39)	0	—	—	—	—	—	—	—	—	—	k	—	0	19

CAVNESS, GRADY   Grady Crayton, DB, 5′11″/187 lbs; Texas-El Paso; 1969: Den, rnd 2; B3/1/1947 Houston, TX   **1969** Den-A 14 (14, LCB)   **1970** Atl 4   **NFL** 18 (14) [2 yrs]

CAVOSIE, JOHN   John Clement, B-E, 6′0″/207 lbs; Wisconsin; Butler; B1/6/1908 Shenandoah, PA, D3/16/1995 Indianapolis, IN [K]

YEAR	TEAM	G (GS, POS)	RUSH	YD	AVG (LG)	TD	REC	YD	AVG (LG)	TD	PASS	COMP	PCT	YD	AVG (LG)	TD	INT	SK	YD	QBR	KPR	OTD	PTS	TAY
1931	Por	13 (3)																						
1932	Por	11 (7, FB)	62	184	3.0	2	—	—	—	—	12	5	41.7	66	5.5	2	0	—	—	—	—	1	18	257

YEAR	TEAM	G(GS, POS)	RUSH	YD	AVG(LG)	TD	REC	YD	AVG(LG)	TD	PASS	COMP	PCT	YD	AVG(LG)	TD	INT	SK	YD	QBR	KPR	OTD	PTS	TAY
1933	Por	9(8, LE)	7	8	1.1	0	6	148	24.7(45)	1	3	1	33.3	8	2.7(8)	0	0	—	—	—	K	—	10	91
NFL	3	33(18)	69	192	2.8	2	6	148	24.7(45)	1	15	6	40.0	74	4.9(8)	2	0	—	—	—	K	1	28	348

CAYLOR, LOWELL Lowell Howard, DB, 6´3˝/205 lbs; Miami (OH); 1963: Chi, rnd 16/NYJ, rnd 24; B6/17/1941 Dayton, OH **1964**†Cle 13

CAYWOOD, LES Lester Leroy, G-T, 6´0˝/230 lbs; St. John's (NY); B8/18/1903 Sapulpa, OK, D2/4/1986 Oakwood, OK **1926** Buf 6 (6, LT) **1927** Pot 5 (3) **1927** NYG 1 (0) **1927** Cle 2 (1) **1928** Det 9 (9, LG) **1929** NYG 12 (11, RG/lg) **1930** NYG 16 (8, LG), 6 **1931** ChiC 1 (0) **1931** NYG 11 (10, RG) **1932** NYG 7 (5, rg) **1932** Bkn 1 (0) **1933** Cin 10 (10, RG) **1934** Cin 8 (6, LG) **NFL** 89 (69) [9 yrs]

CEARING, LLOYD Lloyd, B, /185 lbs; Valparaiso; B11/3/1900 Monon, IN, deceased **1922** Ham 6 (6, TB) **1923** Ham 7 (5, WB) **NFL** 13 (11) [2 yrs]

CEASER, CURTIS Curtis, WR, 6´2˝/190 lbs; Grambling State; 1995: NYJ, rnd 7; B8/11/1972 Lincoln, NE **1995** NYJ 4 (0)

CECIL, CHUCK Charles Douglas, DB, 6´0˝/185 lbs; Arizona; 1988: GB, rnd 4; B11/8/1964 Red Bluff, CA **1988** GB 16 (2) **1989** GB 9 (0) **1990** GB 9 (8, FS) **1991** GB 16 (16, FS) **1992** GB★16 (16, FS) **1993** Phx 15 (7, fs) **1995** Hou 14 (12, FS) **NFL** 95 (61) [7 yrs]

CEFALO, JIMMY James Cameron, WR, 5´11˝/190 lbs; Penn State; 1978: Mia, rnd 3; B10/5/1955 Pittston, PA

YEAR	TEAM	G(GS, POS)	RUSH	YD	AVG(LG)	TD	REC	YD	AVG(LG)	TD	PASS	COMP	PCT	YD	AVG(LG)	TD	INT	SK	YD	QBR	KPR	OTD	PTS	TAY
1978	†Mia	16(1)	—	—	—	—	6	145	24.2(43)	3	—	—	—	—	—	—	—	—	—	—	kp	—	18	190
1979	†Mia	16(3)	—	—	—	—	12	223	18.6(30)	3	—	—	—	—	—	—	—	—	—	—	p	—	18	127
1980	Mia	16(4)	—	—	—	—	11	199	18.1(52)	1	—	—	—	—	—	—	—	—	—	—	—	—	6	105
1981	†Mia	16(6, wr)	—	—	—	—	29	631	21.8(69)	3	—	—	—	—	—	—	—	—	—	—	—	—	18	331
1982	†Mia	9(9, WR)	—	—	—	—	17	356	20.9(46)	1	—	—	—	—	—	—	—	—	—	—	—	—	6	183
1983	Mia	1(1)	—	—	—	—	—	—	—	—	—	—	—	—	—	—	—	—	—	—	—	—	—	—
1984	†Mia	16(0)	—	—	—	—	18	185	10.3(25)	2	—	—	—	—	—	—	—	—	—	—	—	—	12	103
NFL	7	90(24)	—	—	—	—	93	1739	18.7(69)	13	—	—	—	—	—	—	—	—	—	—	kp	—	78	1037

CELERI, BOB Robert Lavern, QB, 5´10˝/180 lbs; California; 1950: SF, rnd 10; B6/1/1927 Fort Bragg, CA, D3/9/1975 Buffalo, NY

YEAR	TEAM	G(GS, POS)	RUSH	YD	AVG(LG)	TD	REC	YD	AVG(LG)	TD	PASS	COMP	PCT	YD	AVG(LG)	TD	INT	SK	YD	QBR	KPR	OTD	PTS	TAY
1951	NYY	11(QB)	36	107	3.0(17)	0	2	71	35.5(51)	1	238	102	42.9	1797	7.6(75)	12	15	—	—	59.8	P	—	6	506
1952	DalT	8(4, qb)	17	135	7.9(31)	0	4	37	9.3(13)	1	75	31	41.3	490	6.5(78)	3	3	—	—	—	P	—	6	299
NFL	2	19(4)	53	242	4.6(31)	0	6	108	18.0(51)	2	313	133	42.5	2287	7.3(78)	15	18	—	—	60.0	P	—	12	805

CELESTIN, OLIVER Oliver, DB, 6´0˝/207 lbs; Texas Southern; B2/25/1981 New Orleans, LA **2004**†NYJ 8 (0) **2005** NYJ 12 (0) **NFL** 20 (0) [2 yrs]

CELOTTO, MARIO Mario Raymond, LB, 6´3˝/228 lbs; USC; 1978: Buf, rnd 7; B8/23/1956 Los Angeles, CA **1978** Buf 4 **1980**†Oak 11 (0) **1981** Oak 7 (0) **1981** LARm 3 (0) **NFL** 25 [3 yrs]

CEMORE, TONY Anthony Salvatore, G, 6´0˝/210 lbs; Creighton; B8/8/1917 Omaha, NE, D3/28/1981 Omaha, NE **1941** Phi 10 (1)

CENCI, JOHN John Richard, C, 6´0˝/215 lbs; Pittsburgh; B1/4/1934 Pittsburgh, PA **1956** Pit 7

CENTERS, LARRY Larry Eugene, FB, 6´0˝/225 lbs; Stephen F. Austin State; 1990: Phx, rnd 5; B6/1/1968 Tatum, TX

YEAR	TEAM	G(GS, POS)	RUSH	YD	AVG(LG)	TD	REC	YD	AVG(LG)	TD	PASS	COMP	PCT	YD	AVG(LG)	TD	INT	SK	YD	QBR	KPR	OTD	PTS	TAY
1990	Phx	6(0)	—	—	—	—	—	—	—	—	—	—	—	—	—	—	—	—	—	—	k	—	0	32
1991	Phx	9(2)	14	44	3.1(8)	0	19	176	9.3(23)	0	—	—	—	—	—	—	—	—	—	—	kp	—	0	227
1992	Phx	16(1)	37	139	3.8(28)	0	50	417	8.3(26)	2	—	—	—	—	—	—	—	—	—	—	—	—	12	358
1993	Phx	16(9, FB)	25	152	6.1(33)	0	66	603	9.1(29)	3	—	—	—	—	—	—	—	—	—	—	—	—	18	469
1994	Arz	16(5, fb)	115	336	2.9(17)	5	77	647	8.4(36)	2	—	—	—	—	—	—	—	—	—	—	—	—	42	720
1995	Arz✧	16(10, FB)	78	254	3.3(20)	2	101	962	9.5(32)	2	1	0	0.0	0	0.0	0	1	—	—	—	k	—	24	725
1996	Arz★	16(14, FB)	116	425	3.7(24)	2	99	766	7.7(39)	7	—	—	—	—	—	—	—	—	—	—	—	—	54	863
1997	Arz	15(14, FB)	101	276	2.7(14)	1	54	409	7.6(29)	1	—	—	—	—	—	—	—	—	—	—	—	—	12	496
1998	†Arz	16(12, FB)	31	110	3.5(14)	0	69	559	8.1(54)	2	—	—	—	—	—	—	—	—	—	—	—	—	12	400
1999	†Was	16(12, FB)	13	51	3.9(12)	0	69	544	7.9(33)	3	—	—	—	—	—	—	—	—	—	—	—	—	18	338
2000	Was	15(5, fb)	19	103	5.4(14)	0	81	600	7.4(26)	3	—	—	—	—	—	—	—	—	—	—	—	—	18	418
2001	Buf✧	16(13, FB)	34	160	4.7(50)	2	80	620	7.8(26)	2	—	—	—	—	—	—	—	—	—	—	—	—	24	500
2002	Buf	16(7, FB)	11	56	5.1(13)	2	43	388	9.0(25)	0	—	—	—	—	—	—	—	—	—	—	—	—	12	270
2003	†NE	9(3)	21	82	3.9(13)	0	19	106	5.6(14)	1	—	—	—	—	—	—	—	—	—	—	—	—	6	140
NFL	14	198(107)	615	2188	3.6(50)	14	827	6797	8.2(54)	28	1	0	0.0	0	0.0	0	1	—	—	—	kp	—	252	5954

CEPHOUS, FRANK Frank, RB, 5´10˝/205 lbs; UCLA; 1984: NYG, rnd 11; B7/4/1961 Philadelphia, PA

YEAR	TEAM	G(GS, POS)	RUSH	YD	AVG(LG)	TD	REC	YD	AVG(LG)	TD	PASS	COMP	PCT	YD	AVG(LG)	TD	INT	SK	YD	QBR	KPR	OTD	PTS	TAY
1984	†NYG	16(0)	3	2	0.7(2)	0	—	—	—	—	—	—	—	—	—	—	—	—	—	—	k	—	0	45

CEPPETELLI, GENE Eugene C., C, 6´2˝/245 lbs; Villanova; B7/28/1942 Sudbury, Canada **1968** Phi 14 (C) **1969** Phi 7 **1969** NYG 6 **NFL** 27 [2 yrs]

CERCONE, MATT Matthew Anthony, TE, 6´5˝/252 lbs; Arizona State; B11/30/1975 Bakersfield, CA **2000** Min 2 (0) **2002** Min 3 (0) **NFL** 5 (0) [2 yrs]

CERESINO, GORDY Gordon Joseph, LB, 6´0˝/224 lbs; Stanford; B10/26/1957 Thunder Bay, Canada **1979** SF 16

CERNE, JOE Joseph, C, 6´2˝/240 lbs; Northwestern; 1965: SF, rnd 2/KC, rnd 9; B4/26/1942 Chrnomlj, Yugoslavia **1965** SF 11 **1966** SF 14 **1967** SF 14 **1968** Atl 6 **NFL** 45 [4 yrs]

CERQUA, MARQ Marq Vincent, LB, 6´2˝/223 lbs; Furman; Carson-Newman; B4/3/1977 Miami, FL **2001** TB 3 (0) **2002** ChiB 2 (0) **NFL** 5 (0) [2 yrs]

CESAIRE, JACQUES Jacques, DE-DT, 6´2˝/295 lbs; Southern Connecticut State; B8/30/1980 Worcester, MA **2003** SD 4 (0) **2004**†SD 16 (12, LDE) **2005** SD 16 (5, rde) **NFL** 36 (17) [3 yrs]

CESARE, WILLIAM William Joseph, DB, 5´11˝/190 lbs; Memphis; Miami (FL); B6/2/1955 New York, NY **1978** TB 10 **1979**†TB 16 **1980** Mia 2 (0) **1981**†TB 16 (0) **1982**†Det 2 (0) **NFL** 46 [5 yrs]

CESARIO, SAL Salvatore J., T, 6´4˝/255 lbs; Cal Poly-San Luis Obispo; 1986: NYJ, rnd 12; B7/4/1963 Stockton, CA **1987** Dal 3 (3)

CHADWICK, JEFF Jeffrey Allan, WR, 6´3˝/190 lbs; Grand Valley State; B12/16/1960 Detroit, MI

YEAR	TEAM	G(GS, POS)	RUSH	YD	AVG(LG)	TD	REC	YD	AVG(LG)	TD	PASS	COMP	PCT	YD	AVG(LG)	TD	INT	SK	YD	QBR	KPR	OTD	PTS	TAY
1983	†Det	16(4)	—	—	—	—	40	617	15.4(45)	4	—	—	—	—	—	—	—	—	—	—	—	—	24	329
1984	Det	16(3)	1	12	12.0(12)	1	37	540	14.6(46)	2	—	—	—	—	—	—	—	—	—	—	—	—	18	302
1985	Det	7(5, wr)	—	—	—	—	25	478	19.1(56)	3	—	—	—	—	—	—	—	—	—	—	—	—	18	254
1986	Det	15(15, WR)	—	—	—	—	53	995	18.8(73)	5	—	—	—	—	—	—	—	—	—	—	—	—	30	523
1987	Det	8(8, WR)	1	-6	-6.0(-6)	0	30	416	13.9(36)	0	—	—	—	—	—	—	—	—	—	—	—	—	0	202
1988	Det	10(8, WR)	—	—	—	—	20	304	15.2(32)	3	—	—	—	—	—	—	—	—	—	—	—	—	18	167
1989	Det	1(1)	—	—	—	—	1	9	9.0(9)	0	—	—	—	—	—	—	—	—	—	—	—	—	0	5
1989	Sea	11(0)	—	—	—	—	8	95	11.9(19)	0	—	—	—	—	—	—	—	—	—	—	—	—	0	48
1990	Sea	16(0)	1	-3	-3.0(-3)	0	27	478	17.7(54)	4	—	—	—	—	—	—	—	—	—	—	—	—	24	256
1991	Sea	12(0)	—	—	—	—	22	255	11.6(29)	3	—	—	—	—	—	—	—	—	—	—	—	—	18	143
1992	LARm	14(2)	—	—	—	—	29	362	12.5(27)	3	—	—	—	—	—	—	—	—	—	—	—	—	18	196
NFL	10	126(46)	3	3	1.0(12)	1	292	4549	15.6(73)	27	—	—	—	—	—	—	—	—	—	—	—	—	168	2423

CHAFFEY, PAT Patrick Lowell, RB, 6´1˝/220 lbs; Oregon State; 1990: Chi, rnd 5; B4/19/1967 McMinnville, OR

YEAR	TEAM	G(GS, POS)	RUSH	YD	AVG(LG)	TD	REC	YD	AVG(LG)	TD	PASS	COMP	PCT	YD	AVG(LG)	TD	INT	SK	YD	QBR	KPR	OTD	PTS	TAY
1991	†Atl	14(2)	29	127	4.4(27)	1	—	—	—	—	—	—	—	—	—	—	—	—	—	—	k	—	6	136
1992	NYJ	14(0)	27	186	6.9(32)	1	7	56	8.0(14)	0	—	—	—	—	—	—	—	—	—	—	—	—	6	224
1993	NYJ	3(0)	5	17	3.4(7)	0	4	55	13.8(20)	1	—	—	—	—	—	—	—	—	—	—	—	—	6	50
NFL	3	31(2)	61	330	5.4(32)	2	11	111	10.1(20)	1	—	—	—	—	—	—	—	—	—	—	k	—	18	410

CHALENSKI, MIKE Michael Alan, DE-DT, 6´5˝/279 lbs; Pittsburgh; UCLA; B1/28/1970 Elizabeth, NJ **1993** Phi 15 (0) **1995** Phi 9 (0) **1996** NYJ 15 (7, rde) **1997**†Mia 8 (0) **1998** Det 8 (0) **NFL** 55 (7) [5 yrs]

CHALMERS, GEORGE George B., C, 6´0˝/196 lbs; NYU; B10/19/1908 Los Angeles, CA, D8/7/1988 Los Angeles, CA **1933** Bkn 7 (0)

CHAMBERLAIN, BYRON Byron Daniel, TE, 6´1˝/250 lbs; Missouri; Wayne State (NE); 1995: Den, rnd 7; B10/17/1971 Honolulu, HI

YEAR	TEAM	G(GS, POS)	RUSH	YD	AVG(LG)	TD	REC	YD	AVG(LG)	TD	PASS	COMP	PCT	YD	AVG(LG)	TD	INT	SK	YD	QBR	KPR	OTD	PTS	TAY
1995	Den	5(0)	—	—	—	—	1	11	11.0(11)	0	—	—	—	—	—	—	—	—	—	—	—	—	0	6
1996	†Den	11(0)	—	—	—	—	12	129	10.8(17)	0	—	—	—	—	—	—	—	—	—	—	k	—	0	69
1997	†Den	10(0)	—	—	—	—	2	18	9.0(9)	0	—	—	—	—	—	—	—	—	—	—	k	—	0	7
1998	†Den	16(0)	—	—	—	—	3	35	11.7(16)	0	—	—	—	—	—	—	—	—	—	—	—	—	0	18
1999	Den	16(0)	—	—	—	—	32	488	15.3(**88**)	2	—	—	—	—	—	—	—	—	—	—	—	—	12	254
2000	†Den	15(0)	—	—	—	—	22	283	12.9(38)	1	—	—	—	—	—	—	—	—	—	—	k	—	6	142

YEAR	TEAM	G (GS, POS)	RUSH	YD	AVG (LG)	TD	REC	YD	AVG (LG)	TD	PASS	COMP	PCT	YD	AVG (LG)	TD	INT	SK	YD	QBR	KPR	OTD	PTS	TAY
2001	Min◇	16 (15, TE)	—	—	—	—	57	666	11.7 (47)	3	—	—	—	—	—	—	—	—	—	—	—	—	18	348
2002	Min	13 (9, TE)	—	—	—	—	34	389	11.4 (61)	0	—	—	—	—	—	—	—	—	—	—	—	—	0	195
2003	Was	4 (1)	—	—	—	—	4	29	7.3 (15)	0	—	—	—	—	—	—	—	—	—	—	—	—	0	15
NFL	9	106 (25)	—	—	—	—	167	2048	12.3 (88)	6	—	—	—	—	—	—	—	—	—	—	k	—	36	1051

Chamberlain, Dan Daniel, E-HB, 6´3˝/200 lbs; Sacramento State; 1959: Det, rnd 25; B8/26/1937 Grand Rapids, MI

YEAR	TEAM	G (GS, POS)	RUSH	YD	AVG (LG)	TD	REC	YD	AVG (LG)	TD	PASS	COMP	PCT	YD	AVG (LG)	TD	INT	SK	YD	QBR	KPR	OTD	PTS	TAY
1960	Buf-A	12 (SE)	—	—	—	—	17	279	16.4 (49)	4	—	—	—	—	—	—	—	—	—	—	k	—	24	169
1961	Buf-A	3	—	—	—	—	1	16	16.0 (16)	0	—	—	—	—	—	—	—	—	—	—	—	—	0	8
NFL	2	15	—	—	—	—	18	295	16.4 (49)	4	—	—	—	—	—	—	—	—	—	—	k	—	24	177

Chamberlain, Garth Garth G., G, 6´0˝/215 lbs; Brigham Young; 1942: Pit, rnd 17; B5/20/1920 Alton, UT, D12/21/1988 Chandler, AZ **1945** Pit 3 (0)

Chamberlin, Frank Frank Jacob, LB, 6´1˝/235 lbs; Boston College; 2000: Ten, rnd 5; B1/2/1978 Mahwah, NJ **2000**†Ten 12 (0) **2001** Ten 16 (0) **2002**†Ten 15 (3) **2003** Cin 5 (0) **2005** Hou 9 (0) **NFL** 57 (3) [5 yrs]

Chamberlin, Guy Berlin Guy, E-WB, 6´2˝/196 lbs; Nebraska Wesleyan; Nebraska; B1/16/1894 Blue Springs, NE, D4/4/1967 Lincoln, NE; HOF 1965 **[C]** **1920** Dec☆12 (8, LE) **1921** ChiS 11 (11, LE), 18 **1922** Can☆12 (11, LE), 42 **1923** Can☆11 (10, LE), 12 **1924** Cle☆9 (7, LE), 12 **1925** Fra 14 (12, LE), 12 **1926** Fra 17 (8, le), 6 **1927** ChiC 6 (1) **NFL** 92 (68), 102 [8 yrs]

Chambers, Bill William Joseph, G, 6´2˝/230 lbs; Alabama; Georgia Tech; UCLA; 1945: Phi, rnd 13; B1923 **1948** NYY-A 13 (2) **1949**†NYY-A 12 (0) **AAFC** 25 (2) [2 yrs]

Chambers, Chris Chris J., WR, 5´11˝/210 lbs; Wisconsin; 2001: Mia, rnd 2; B8/12/1978 Cleveland, OH

YEAR	TEAM	G (GS, POS)	RUSH	YD	AVG (LG)	TD	REC	YD	AVG (LG)	TD	PASS	COMP	PCT	YD	AVG (LG)	TD	INT	SK	YD	QBR	KPR	OTD	PTS	TAY
2001	Mia	16 (7, wr)	1	-11	-11.0 (-11)	0	48	883	**18.4** (**74**)	7	—	—	—	—	—	—	—	—	—	—	k	—	42	737
2002	Mia	15 (15, WR)	6	78	13.0 (45)	0	52	734	14.1 (59)	3	—	—	—	—	—	—	—	—	—	—	—	—	18	460
2003	Mia	16 (16, WR)	4	30	7.5 (12)	0	64	963	15.0 (57)	**11**	—	—	—	—	—	—	—	—	—	—	—	—	66	567
2004	Mia	15 (15, WR)	9	76	8.4 (24)	0	69	898	13.0 (76)	7	—	—	—	—	—	—	—	—	—	—	—	—	44	560
2005	Mia◇	16 (16, WR)	12	92	7.7 (61)	0	82	1118	13.6 (77)	11	—	—	—	—	—	—	—	—	—	—	—	—	66	706
NFL	5	78 (69)	32	265	8.3 (61)	0	315	4596	14.6 (77)	39	—	—	—	—	—	—	—	—	—	—	k	—	236	3029

Chambers, Kirk Kirk, T, 6´7˝/307 lbs; Stanford; 2004: Cle, rnd 6; B3/19/1979 Provo, UT **2004** Cle 6 (0) **2005** Cle 15 (0) **NFL** 21 (0) [2 yrs]

Chambers, Rusty Russell Francis, LB, 6´1˝/218 lbs; Tulane; B11/10/1953 Amite, LA, D7/1/1981 Hammond, LA **1975** NO 12 **1976** NO 4 (1) **1976** Mia 10 **1977** Mia 14 (2) **1978**†Mia 16 (15, RILB) **1979**†Mia 16 (16, RILB) **1980** Mia 16 (12, LILB) **NFL** 88 (46) [6 yrs]

Chambers, Wally Wallace Hassim, DT-DE, 6´6˝/250 lbs; Eastern Kentucky; 1973: Chi, rnd 1; B5/15/1951 Phenix City, AL **1973** ChiB◇14 (14, RDT) **1974** ChiB☆14 (14, RDT) **1975** ChiB★14 (14, RDT) **1976** ChiB★14 (13, RDT) **1977** ChiB 4 (1) **1978** TB 12 (2) **1979**†TB 16 (16, LDE) **NFL** 88 (74) [7 yrs]

Chamblee, Al Aldric Doran, LB, 6´1˝/240 lbs; Virginia Tech; 1991: TB, rnd 12; B11/17/1968 Virginia Beach, VA **1991** TB 9 (0) **1992** TB 13 (3) **NFL** 22 (3) [2 yrs]

Chamblin, Corey Corey Jermaine, DB, 5´10˝/189 lbs; Tennessee Tech; B5/29/1977 Birmingham, AL **1999**†Jax 11 (0)

Champagne, Ed Edward J., T-DT, 6´3˝/236 lbs; LSU; 1947: LA, rnd 18; B12/4/1922 New Orleans, LA, D6/15/2003 Raleigh, NC **1947** LARm 4 (0) **1948** LARm 12 (0) **1949**†LARm 12 (7, RT)

YEAR	TEAM	G (GS, POS)	RUSH	YD	AVG (LG)	TD	REC	YD	AVG (LG)	TD	PASS	COMP	PCT	YD	AVG (LG)	TD	INT	SK	YD	QBR	KPR	OTD	PTS	TAY
1950	†LARm	11 (LDT)	—	—	—	—	4	52	13.0 (21)	1	—	—	—	—	—	—	—	—	—	—	—	—	6	31
NFL	4	39 (7)	—	—	—	—	4	52	13.0 (21)	1	—	—	—	—	—	—	—	—	—	—	—	—	6	31

Champion, Jim James Henry, LB-T-DT, 6´0˝/238 lbs; Mississippi State; 1950: NYY, rnd 18; B1/11/1926 Tillatoba, MS **1950** NYY 7 **1951** NYY 12 (RLB) **NFL** 19 [2 yrs]

Chancey, Robert Robert Dewayne, RB, 6´0˝/250 lbs; none; B9/7/1972 Macon, AL

YEAR	TEAM	G (GS, POS)	RUSH	YD	AVG (LG)	TD	REC	YD	AVG (LG)	TD	PASS	COMP	PCT	YD	AVG (LG)	TD	INT	SK	YD	QBR	KPR	OTD	PTS	TAY
1997	SD	6 (0)	—	—	—	—	—	—	—	—	—	—	—	—	—	—	—	—	—	—	—	—	—	—
1998	ChiB	16 (1)	29	122	4.2 (14)	2	11	102	9.3 (15)	0	—	—	—	—	—	—	—	—	—	—	k	—	12	181
1999	Dal	1 (0)	14	57	4.1 (11)	0	—	—	—	—	—	—	—	—	—	—	—	—	—	—	—	—	0	57
2000	SD	4 (3)	42	141	3.4 (14)	2	1	6	6.0 (6)	0	1	0	0.0	0	0.0	0	0	—	—	—	—	—	12	164
NFL	4	27 (4)	85	320	3.8 (14)	4	12	108	9.0 (15)	0	1	0	0.0	0	0.0	0	0	—	—	—	k	—	24	402

Chandler, Al Albert Morris, TE, 6´2˝/233 lbs; Oklahoma; 1973: Cin, rnd 2; B11/18/1950 Oklahoma City, OK

YEAR	TEAM	G (GS, POS)	RUSH	YD	AVG (LG)	TD	REC	YD	AVG (LG)	TD	PASS	COMP	PCT	YD	AVG (LG)	TD	INT	SK	YD	QBR	KPR	OTD	PTS	TAY
1973	†Cin	13	—	—	—	—	—	—	—	—	—	—	—	—	—	—	—	—	—	—	—	—	—	—
1974	Cin	14	—	—	—	—	1	9	9.0 (9)	0	—	—	—	—	—	—	—	—	—	—	—	—	0	5
1976	†NE	14 (3)	—	—	—	—	5	49	9.8 (29)	3	—	—	—	—	—	—	—	—	—	—	—	—	18	40
1977	NE	14 (3)	—	—	—	—	7	68	9.7 (16)	0	—	—	—	—	—	—	—	—	—	—	—	—	0	34
1978	NE	4	—	—	—	—	—	—	—	—	—	—	—	—	—	—	—	—	—	—	—	—	—	—
1978	SL	11 (TE)	—	—	—	—	16	190	11.9 (47)	4	—	—	—	—	—	—	—	—	—	—	—	—	24	115
1979	SL	8	—	—	—	—	5	49	9.8 (28)	2	—	—	—	—	—	—	—	—	—	—	—	—	12	35
1979	NE	7	—	—	—	—	1	2	2.0 (2)	0	—	—	—	—	—	—	—	—	—	—	—	—	0	1
NFL	6	85 (6)	—	—	—	—	35	367	10.5 (47)	9	—	—	—	—	—	—	—	—	—	—	—	—	54	229

Chandler, Bob Robert Donald, WR, 6´0˝/180 lbs; USC; 1971: Buf, rnd 7; B4/24/1949 Long Beach, CA, D1/27/1995 Los Angeles, CA **[K]**

YEAR	TEAM	G (GS, POS)	RUSH	YD	AVG (LG)	TD	REC	YD	AVG (LG)	TD	PASS	COMP	PCT	YD	AVG (LG)	TD	INT	SK	YD	QBR	KPR	OTD	PTS	TAY
1971	Buf	13	—	—	—	—	5	60	12.0 (20)	0	—	—	—	—	—	—	—	—	—	—	—	—	0	30
1972	Buf	14 (WR)	3	27	9.0 (16)	0	33	528	16.0 (43)	5	—	—	—	—	—	—	—	—	—	—	—	—	30	316
1973	Buf	14 (WR)	5	-14	-2.8 (18)	0	30	427	14.2 (37)	3	1	0	0.0	0	0.0	0	0	—	—	—	Kp	—	19	210
1974	†Buf	14	—	—	—	—	7	88	12.6 (21)	1	—	—	—	—	—	—	—	—	—	—	—	—	6	49
1975	Buf☆	14 (13, WR)	2	5	2.5 (5)	0	55	746	13.6 (35)	6	—	—	—	—	—	—	—	—	—	—	—	—	36	408
1976	Buf	14 (14, WR)	1	0	0.0 (0)	0	61	824	13.5 (58)	10	—	—	—	—	—	—	—	—	—	—	—	—	60	462
1977	Buf☆	14 (WR)	—	—	—	—	60	745	12.4 (31)	4	—	—	—	—	—	—	—	—	—	—	—	—	24	393
1978	Buf	16 (WR)	—	—	—	—	44	581	13.2 (44)	5	—	—	—	—	—	—	—	—	—	—	—	—	30	316
1979	Buf	3	—	—	—	—	—	—	—	—	—	—	—	—	—	—	—	—	—	—	—	—	—	—
1980	†Oak	16 (16, WR)	—	—	—	—	49	786	16.0 (56)	10	—	—	—	—	—	—	—	—	—	—	—	—	60	443
1981	Oak	11 (7, wr)	—	—	—	—	26	458	17.6 (45)	4	—	—	—	—	—	—	—	—	—	—	—	—	24	249
1982	LARd	2 (0)	—	—	—	—	—	—	—	—	—	—	—	—	—	—	—	—	—	—	—	—	—	—
NFL	12	145 (50)	11	18	1.6 (18)	0	370	5243	14.2 (58)	48	1	0	0.0	0	0.0	0	0	—	—	—	Kp	—	289	2875

Chandler, Chris Christopher Mark, QB, 6´4˝/224 lbs; Washington; 1988: Ind, rnd 3; B10/12/1965 Everett, WA

YEAR	TEAM	G (GS, POS)	RUSH	YD	AVG (LG)	TD	REC	YD	AVG (LG)	TD	PASS	COMP	PCT	YD	AVG (LG)	TD	INT	SK	YD	QBR	KPR	OTD	PTS	TAY
1988	Ind	15 (13, QB)	46	139	3.0 (29)	3	—	—	—	—	233	129	55.4	1619	6.9 (54)	8	12	18	128	—	—	—	18	539
1989	Ind	3 (3)	7	57	8.1 (23)	1	—	—	—	—	80	39	48.8	537	6.7 (82)	2	3	3	17	—	—	—	6	226
1990	TB	7 (3)	13	71	5.5 (18)	1	—	—	—	—	83	42	50.6	464	5.6 (68)	1	6	15	103	—	—	—	6	78
1991	TB	6 (3)	18	79	4.4 (12)	0	—	—	—	—	104	53	51.0	557	5.4 (35)	4	8	10	76	—	—	—	0	58
1991	Phx	3 (2)	8	32	4.0 (12)	0	—	—	—	—	50	25	50.0	289	5.8 (45)	1	2	7	58	—	—	—	0	102
1992	Phx	15 (13, QB)	36	149	4.1 (18)	1	—	—	—	—	413	245	59.3	2832	6.9 (72)	15	15	29	226	77.1	—	—	6	1050
1993	Phx	4 (2)	3	2	0.7 (1)	0	—	—	—	—	103	52	50.5	471	4.6 (27)	3	2	4	25	—	—	—	0	173
1994	LARm	12 (6, qb)	18	61	3.4 (22)	1	—	—	—	—	176	108	61.4	1352	7.7 (72)	7	2	7	46	—	—	—	6	702
1995	Hou	13 (13, QB)	28	58	2.1 (9)	2	—	—	—	—	356	225	63.2	2460	6.9 (76)	17	10	21	173	87.8	—	—	14	993
1996	Hou	12 (12, QB)	28	113	4.0 (16)	0	—	—	—	—	320	184	57.5	2099	6.6 (63)	16	11	25	153	79.7	—	—	0	803
1997	Atl◇	14 (14, QB)	43	158	3.7 (19)	0	—	—	—	—	342	202	59.1	2692	7.9 (56)	20	7	39	261	95.1	—	—	0	1324
1998	†Atl◇	14 (14, QB)	36	121	3.4 (19)	2	1	22	22.0 (22)	0	327	190	58.1	3154	**9.6** (**78**)	25	12	45	283	100.9	—	—	12	1374
1999	Atl	12 (12, QB)	16	57	3.6 (14)	1	—	—	—	—	307	174	56.7	2339	7.6 (60)	16	11	32	230	83.5	—	—	6	877
2000	Atl	14 (13, QB)	21	60	2.9 (16)	0	1	-4	-4.0 (-4)	0	331	192	58.0	2236	6.8 (55)	10	12	40	251	73.5	—	—	0	746
2001	Atl	14 (14, QB)	25	84	3.4 (22)	0	—	—	—	—	365	223	61.1	2847	7.8 (**94**)	16	14	41	261	84.1	—	—	0	1028
2002	ChiB	9 (7, qb)	10	32	3.2 (14)	0	—	—	—	—	161	103	64.0	1023	6.4 (76)	4	4	23	144	—	—	—	0	404
2003	ChiB	8 (6, qb)	14	35	2.5 (11)	0	—	—	—	—	192	107	55.7	1050	5.5 (37)	3	7	14	101	61.3	—	—	2	295
2004	SL	5 (2)	1	2	2.0 (2)	0	—	—	—	—	62	35	56.5	463	7.5 (75)	2	8	7	54	—	—	—	0	-77
NFL	17	180 (152)	371	1310	3.5 (29)	12	2	18	9.0 (22)	0	4005	2328	58.1	28484	7.1 (94)	170	146	380	2590	79.1	—	—	76	10691

Chandler, Don Donald Gene 'Babe', FB-P-K, 6´2˝/215 lbs; Florida; 1956: NYG, rnd 5; B9/5/1934 Council Bluffs, IA **[KP]**

YEAR	TEAM	G (GS, POS)	RUSH	YD	AVG (LG)	TD	REC	YD	AVG (LG)	TD	PASS	COMP	PCT	YD	AVG (LG)	TD	INT	SK	YD	QBR	KPR	OTD	PTS	TAY
1956	†NYG	12	1	7	7.0 (7)	0	1	5	5.0 (5)	0	—	—	—	—	—	—	—	—	—	—	KP	—	3	10
1957	NYG	12	1	2	2.0 (2)	0	—	—	—	—	2	2	100.0	40	20.0 (27)	0	0	—	—	—	P	—	0	22
1958	†NYG	12	1	15	15.0 (15)	0	—	—	—	—	1	1	100.0	27	27.0 (27)	0	0	—	—	—	P	—	0	29

YEAR	TEAM	G (GS, POS)	RUSH	YD	AVG (LG)	TD	REC	YD	AVG (LG)	TD	PASS	COMP	PCT	YD	AVG (LG)	TD	INT	SK	YD	QBR	KPR	OTD	PTS	TAY
1959	†NYG	12	1	24	24.0(24)	0	—	—	—	—	—	—	—	—	—	—	—	—	—	—	KP	—	2	24
1960	NYG	8	2	19	9.5(24)	0	—	—	—	—	—	—	—	—	—	—	—	—	—	—	P	—	0	19
1961	†NYG	14	3	30	10.0(30)	0	—	—	—	—	—	—	—	—	—	—	—	—	—	—	P	—	0	30
1962	†NYG	14	1	-11	-11.0(-11)	0	—	—	—	—	—	—	—	—	—	—	—	—	—	—	KP	—	104	-11
1963	†NYG	14	1	0	0.0(0)	0	—	—	—	—	—	—	—	—	—	—	—	—	—	—	KP	—	**106**	0
1964	NYG☆	14	—	—	—	—	—	—	—	—	—	—	—	—	—	—	—	—	—	—	KP	—	54	0
1965	†GB☆	14	1	27	27.0(27)	0	—	—	—	—	—	—	—	—	—	—	—	—	—	—	KP	—	88	27
1966	†GB	14	1	33	33.0(33)	0	—	—	—	—	—	—	—	—	—	—	—	—	—	—	KP	—	77	33
1967	†GB★	14	—	—	—	—	—	—	—	—	—	—	—	—	—	—	—	—	—	—	KP	—	96	0
NFL	12	154	13	146	11.2(33)	0	1	5	5.0(5)	0	3	3	100.0	67	22.3(27)	0	0	—	—	—	KP	—	530	182

Chandler, Edgar Edgar Thomas, LB, 6´3˝/225 lbs; Georgia; 1968: Buf, rnd 4; B8/31/1946 Cedartown, GA, D10/17/1992 Rome, GA **1968** Buf-A 13 **1969** Buf-A 14 (llb) **1970** Buf 14 (MLB) **1971** Buf 14 (MLB) **1972** Buf 1 **1973** NE 12 (11, MLB) **NFL** 68 (11) [6 yrs]

Chandler, Jeff Jeffrey Robin, K, 6´2˝/218 lbs; Florida; 2002: SF, rnd 4; B6/18/1979 Jacksonville, FL **[K]** **2002**†SF 6 (0) **2003** SF 2 (0) **2004** Car 2 (0) **2004** Was 3 (0) **NFL** 13 (0) [3 yrs]

Chandler, Karl Karl Victor, C-G, 6´5˝/250 lbs; Princeton; B2/15/1952 Delaware County, PA **1974** NYG 14 (4) **1975** NYG 14 (4, lg) **1976** NYG 12 (11, C) **1977** NYG 14 (10, C) **1978** Det 11 **1979** Det 1 **NFL** 66 (29) [6 yrs]

Chandler, Thornton Thornton Greene, TE, 6´5˝/243 lbs; Florida A&M; Alabama; 1986: Dal, rnd 6; B11/27/1963 Jacksonville, FL

YEAR	TEAM	G (GS, POS)	RUSH	YD	AVG (LG)	TD	REC	YD	AVG (LG)	TD	PASS	COMP	PCT	YD	AVG (LG)	TD	INT	SK	YD	QBR	KPR	OTD	PTS	TAY
1986	Dal	15(1)	—	—	—	—	6	57	9.5(15)	2	—	—	—	—	—	—	—	—	—	—	—	—	12	39
1987	Dal	12(1)	—	—	—	—	5	25	5.0(9)	1	—	—	—	—	—	—	—	—	—	—	k	—	6	10
1988	Dal	16(12, TE)	—	—	—	—	18	186	10.3(29)	1	—	—	—	—	—	—	—	—	—	—	—	—	6	98
1989	Dal	6(0)	—	—	—	—	—	—	—	—	—	—	—	—	—	—	—	—	—	—	k	—	0	-7
NFL	4	49(14)	—	—	—	—	29	268	9.2(29)	4	—	—	—	—	—	—	—	—	—	—	k	—	24	139

Chandler, Wes Wesley Sandy, WR, 6´0˝/196 lbs; Florida; 1978: NO, rnd 1; B8/22/1956 New Smyrna Beach, FL

YEAR	TEAM	G (GS, POS)	RUSH	YD	AVG (LG)	TD	REC	YD	AVG (LG)	TD	PASS	COMP	PCT	YD	AVG (LG)	TD	INT	SK	YD	QBR	KPR	OTD	PTS	TAY
1978	NO	16(5, wr)	2	10	5.0(10)	0	35	472	13.5(58)	2	—	—	—	—	—	—	—	—	—	—	kp	—	12	599
1979	NO★	16(16, WR)	—	—	—	—	65	1069	16.4(**85**)	6	—	—	—	—	—	—	—	—	—	—	Pkp	—	36	594
1980	NO	16(16, WR)	1	9	9.0(9)	0	65	975	15.0(50)	6	1	1	100.0	43	43.0(43)	0	0	1	10	—	p	—	36	544
1981	NO	4(4)	—	—	—	—	17	285	16.8(39)	1	—	—	—	—	—	—	—	—	—	—	—	—	6	148
1981	†SD	12(11, WR)	5	-1	-0.2(9)	0	52	857	16.5(51)	5	2	0	0.0	0	0.0	0	0	—	—	—	kp	—	30	512
1982	†SD★	8(8, WR)	5	32	6.4(21)	0	49	**1032**	**21.1(66)**	**9**	—	—	—	—	—	—	—	—	—	—	p	—	54	593
1983	SD✧	16(14, WR)	2	25	12.5(23)	0	58	845	14.6(44)	5	0	0	0.0	0	0.0	0	0	1	3	—	p	—	30	459
1984	SD	15(15, WR)	—	—	—	—	52	708	13.6(63)	6	—	—	—	—	—	—	—	—	—	—	p	—	36	384
1985	SD✧	15(13, WR)	1	9	9.0(9)	0	67	1199	17.9(75)	10	—	—	—	—	—	—	—	—	—	—	—	—	60	659
1986	SD	16(14, WR)	—	—	—	—	56	874	15.6(40)	4	—	—	—	—	—	—	—	—	—	—	Pkp	—	24	451
1987	SD	12(11, WR)	—	—	—	—	39	617	15.8(27)	2	—	—	—	—	—	—	—	—	—	—	—	—	12	319
1988	SF	4(4)	—	—	—	—	4	33	8.3(9)	0	—	—	—	—	—	—	—	—	—	—	p	—	0	15
NFL	11	150(131)	16	84	5.3(23)	0	559	8966	16.0(85)	56	3	1	33.3	43	14.3(43)	0	0	2	13	—	Pkp	—	336	5274

Chandnois, Lynn Lynn Everett, HB-WB-TB, 6´2˝/198 lbs; Michigan State; 1950: Pit, rnd 1; B2/24/1925 Fayette, MI **[R]**

YEAR	TEAM	G (GS, POS)	RUSH	YD	AVG (LG)	TD	REC	YD	AVG (LG)	TD	PASS	COMP	PCT	YD	AVG (LG)	TD	INT	SK	YD	QBR	KPR	OTD	PTS	TAY
1950	Pit	12(WB)	71	216	3.0(17)	0	7	158	22.6(51)	0	6	1	16.7	5	0.8(5)	0	2	—	—	—	kp	—	0	407
1951	Pit	12(WB)	108	332	3.1(34)	2	28	440	15.7(55)	4	43	16	37.2	256	6.0(49)	2	4	—	—	—	kp	—	36	775
1952	Pit✧	12(RH)	97	298	3.1(25)	1	28	370	13.2(48)	2	2	0	0.0	0	0.0	0	0	—	—	—	kp	2	30	893
1953	Pit✧	12(RH)	123	470	3.8(38)	3	43	412	9.6(55)	0	3	1	33.3	11	3.7(11)	0	0	—	—	—	kp	1	24	988
1954	Pit	11	45	147	3.3(15)	1	22	176	8.0(23)	0	3	1	33.3	13	4.3(13)	0	0	—	—	—	kp	—	6	285
1955	Pit	8(RH)	105	353	3.4(23)	5	27	385	14.3(36)	0	1	0	0.0	0	0.0	0	1	—	—	—	k	—	30	644
1956	Pit	5(rh)	44	118	2.7(28)	4	7	71	10.1(17)	1	1	0	0.0	0	0.0	0	0	—	—	—	k	—	30	370
NFL	7	72	593	1934	3.3(38)	16	162	2012	12.4(55)	7	59	19	32.2	285	4.8(49)	2	7	—	—	—	kp	3	156	4360

Chanoine, Roger Roger, T, 6´4˝/305 lbs; Temple; B9/11/1976 Newark, NJ **1999** Cle 1 (0) **2000** Cle 7 (0) **2001** Cle 16 (16, RT) **2002** Cle 9 (2) **NFL** 33 (18) [4 yrs]

Chantiles, Tom Thomas James, T, 6´0˝/220 lbs; USC; B7/2/1916 York, PA, D1/19/1999 Laguna Beach, CA **1942** Det 2 (0)

Chapman, Clarence Clarence Earl, DB, 5´10˝/185 lbs; Eastern Michigan; 1976: Oak, rnd 7; B12/10/1953 Detroit, MI **1976** NO 1 **1977** NO 14 (14, RCB) **1978** NO 14 (14, LCB) **1979** NO 16 (15, LCB) **1980** NO 12 (10, LCB) **1981** Cin 5 (0) **1985** Det 3 (0) **NFL** 65 (53) [7 yrs]

Chapman, Doug Doug, RB, 5´10˝/213 lbs; Marshall; 2000: Min, rnd 3; B8/22/1977 Chesterfield, VA

YEAR	TEAM	G (GS, POS)	RUSH	YD	AVG (LG)	TD	REC	YD	AVG (LG)	TD	PASS	COMP	PCT	YD	AVG (LG)	TD	INT	SK	YD	QBR	KPR	OTD	PTS	TAY
2001	Min	16(3)	63	195	3.1(19)	0	16	135	8.4(38)	1	—	—	—	—	—	—	—	—	—	—	—	—	6	268
2002	Min	6(0)	12	89	7.4(27)	0	—	—	—	—	—	—	—	—	—	—	—	—	—	—	k	—	0	149
2003	Min	4(0)	15	33	2.2(6)	0	1	8	8.0(8)	0	—	—	—	—	—	—	—	—	—	—	k	—	0	28
NFL	3	26(3)	90	317	3.5(27)	0	17	143	8.4(38)	1	—	—	—	—	—	—	—	—	—	—	k	—	6	445

Chapman, Gil Gil, WR, 5´9˝/180 lbs; Michigan; 1975: Buf, rnd 7; B8/23/1953 Elizabeth, NJ

YEAR	TEAM	G (GS, POS)	RUSH	YD	AVG (LG)	TD	REC	YD	AVG (LG)	TD	PASS	COMP	PCT	YD	AVG (LG)	TD	INT	SK	YD	QBR	KPR	OTD	PTS	TAY
1975	NO	9	—	—	—	—	1	7	7.0(8)	0	—	—	—	—	—	—	—	—	—	—	kp	—	0	320

Chapman, Kory Kory, RB, 6´1˝/202 lbs; Jacksonville State; B7/13/1980 Batesville, MS **2005** Ind 3 (0)

Chapman, Lamar Lamar, DB, 6´0˝/186 lbs; Kansas State; 2000: Cle, rnd 5; B11/6/1976 Liberal, KS **2000** Cle 7 (0) **2001** Cle 1 (0) **NFL** 8 (0) [2 yrs]

Chapman, Mike Michael George, C-G, 6´4˝/250 lbs; Texas; B2/10/1961 Laredo, TX **1984** Atl 4 (0)

Chapman, Ted Edward Arthur, DE, 6´3˝/260 lbs; Maryland; B4/5/1964 Philadelphia, PA **1987** LARd 2 (1)

Chappell, Leo Leonidas Marion, aka Leon Shappell, G, 6´2˝/205 lbs; none; B12/24/1898 Neota, IL, D5/28/1978 Carmel Valley, CA **1920** ChiC 8 (6, RG) **1921** ChiC 1 (0) **NFL** 9 (6) [2 yrs]

Chapple, Dave David T., P, 6´0˝/184 lbs; California-Santa Barbara; 1969: SF, rnd 10; B3/30/1947 Arcadia, CA **1971** Buf 1 **1972** LARm★14 **1974** LARm 6 **1974** NE 5

YEAR	TEAM	G (GS, POS)	RUSH	YD	AVG (LG)	TD	REC	YD	AVG (LG)	TD	PASS	COMP	PCT	YD	AVG (LG)	TD	INT	SK	YD	QBR	KPR	OTD	PTS	TAY
1973	†LARm	14	1	0	0.0(0)	0	—	—	—	—	—	—	—	—	—	—	—	—	—	—	P	—	0	0
NFL	4	40	1	0	0.0	0	—	—	—	—	—	—	—	—	—	—	—	—	—	—	P	—	0	0

Chapple, Jack John Louis, LB, 6´1˝/225 lbs; Stanford; 1965: SF, rnd 3/KC, rnd 2; B7/23/1943 Daytona Beach, FL, D10/19/1979 Palo Alto, CA **1965** SF 14 (6, rlb)

Chappuis, Bob Robert Richard, TB-DB, 6´0˝/190 lbs; Michigan; 1947: Cle-A, rnd 1/Det, rnd 5; B2/24/1923 Toledo, OH

YEAR	TEAM	G (GS, POS)	RUSH	YD	AVG (LG)	TD	REC	YD	AVG (LG)	TD	PASS	COMP	PCT	YD	AVG (LG)	TD	INT	SK	YD	QBR	KPR	OTD	PTS	TAY
1948	Bkn-A	13(6, TB)	52	310	6.0	1	—	—	—	—	213	100	46.9	1402	6.6	8	15	—	—	—	kp	—	6	474
1949	ChiH-A	6(0)	4	13	3.3	0	—	—	—	—	14	2	14.3	40	2.9	0	4	—	—	—	—	—	0	-127
AAFC	2	19(6)	56	323	5.8	1	—	—	—	—	227	102	44.9	1442	6.4	8	19	—	—	—	kp	—	6	347

Chapura, Dick Richard Harry, DT, 6´3˝/277 lbs; Missouri; 1987: Chi, rnd 10; B6/15/1964 Sarasota, FL **1987** ChiB 2 (0) **1988**†ChiB 15 (0) **1989** ChiB 16 (3) **1990**†Phi 7 (0) **1990** Phx 3 (0) **NFL** 43 (3) [4 yrs]

Charles, John John James, DB, 6´0˝/205 lbs; Purdue; 1967: Bos, rnd 1; B5/9/1944 Newark, NJ **1967** Bos-A 14 (RCB) **1968** Bos-A 12 (11, LS) **1969** Bos-A 13 (13, LS) **1970** Min 8 **1971** Hou 14 (FS) **1972** Hou 13 (FS) **1973** Hou 4 **1974** Hou 1 **NFL** 79 (24) [8 yrs]

Charles, Mike Michael William, NT-DE-DT, 6´4˝/292 lbs; Syracuse; 1983: Mia, rnd 2; B9/23/1962 Newark, NJ **1983**†Mia 16 (3) **1984**†Mia 10 (6, rde) **1985**†Mia 16 (16, NT) **1986** Mia 9 (4) **1987** SD 11 (10, NT) **1988** SD 16 (14, NT) **1989** SD 6 (1) **1990** LARd 10 (0) **1991** LARm 7 (4) **NFL** 101 (58) [9 yrs]

Charles, Win Winston Holt, B, 5´9˝/160 lbs; William & Mary; B1904, D1/29/1949 **1928** Day 5 (4, TB)

Charlton, Clifford Clifford Tyrone, LB, 6´3˝/240 lbs; Florida; 1988: Cle, rnd 1; B2/16/1965 Tallahassee, FL **1988**†Cle 16 (1) **1989**†Cle 15 (0) **NFL** 31 (1) [2 yrs]

Charlton, Ike Isaac C., DB, 5´11˝/199 lbs; Virginia Tech; 2000: Sea, rnd 2; B10/6/1977 Orlando, FL **2000** Sea 16 (0) **2001** Sea 15 (1) **2002** Jax 15 (0) **2003** NYG 7 (2) **NFL** 53 (3) [4 yrs]

Charon, Carl Carl Henry, DB, 5´10˝/202 lbs; Michigan State; 1962: Was, rnd 18; B3/17/1940 Boyne City, MI **1962** Buf-A 14 (RS) **1963**†Buf-A 12 **NFL** 26 [2 yrs]

Charpier, Len Leonard Louis, FB, 5´10˝/235 lbs; Illinois; B2/17/1897 Washington Heights, IL, D10/3/1947 Chicago, IL **1920** ChiC 1 (1)

Chase, Ben Benjamin Semple, G, 6´3˝/235 lbs; Navy; B3/18/1923 Bisbee, AZ, D3/6/1998 Poway, CA **1947** Det 11 (0)

YEAR	TEAM	G (GS, POS)	RUSH	YD	AVG(LG)	TD	REC	YD	AVG(LG)	TD	PASS COMP	PCT	YD	AVG(LG)	TD	INT	SK	YD	QBR	KPR	OTD	PTS	TAY

CHASE, MARTIN Cecil Martin, DT, 6´2˝/310 lbs; Oklahoma; 1998: Bal, rnd 5; B12/19/1974 Lawton, OK **1999** Bal 3 (0) **2000**†NO 9 (0) **2001** NO 16 (3) **2002** NO 13 (1) **2003** Was 13 (2) **2005** Jax 1 (0) **NFL** 55 (6) [6 yrs]

CHASE, RALPH Ralph E., T, 6´3˝/219 lbs; Pittsburgh; B12/19/1902, D10/24/1989 Gillett, PA **1926** Ham 1 (0) **1926** Akr 4 (3) **NFL** 5 (3) [1 yr]

CHATHAM, MATT Matthew, LB, 6´4˝/250 lbs; South Dakota; B6/28/1977 Sioux City, IA **2000** NE 6 (0) **2001**†NE 11 (0) **2002** NE 13 (0) **2003**†NE 16 (4) **2004**†NE 5 (0) **2005**†NE 15 (0) **NFL** 66 (4) [6 yrs]

CHATMAN, ANTONIO Antonio Taveras, WR, 5´9˝/177 lbs; Cincinnati; B2/12/1979 Jackson, AL **[R]**

2003	†GB	16 (0)	—	—	—	—	—	—	—	—	—	—	—	—	—	—	—	—	—	kp	—	0	376
2004	†GB	16 (2)	4	36	9.0 (18)	0	22	246	11.2 (21)	1	—	—	—	—	—	—	—	—	—	kp	—	6	439
2005	GB	16 (3)	8	34	4.3 (11)	0	49	549	11.2 (25)	4	—	—	—	—	—	—	—	—	—	kp	1	30	511
NFL	3	48 (5)	12	70	5.8 (18)	0	71	795	11.2 (25)	5	—	—	—	—	—	—	—	—	—	kp	1	36	1326

CHATMAN, CLIFF Clifford, RB, 6´2˝/225 lbs; Oklahoma; Central Oklahoma; 1981: NYG, rnd 4; B3/13/1959 Clinton, OK

| 1982 | NYG | 6 (3) | 22 | 80 | 3.6 (13) | 2 | 1 | 13 | 13.0 (13) | 0 | — | — | — | — | — | — | — | — | — | — | — | 12 | 107 |

CHATMAN, JESSE Jesse, RB, 5´8˝/215 lbs; Eastern Washington; B9/22/1979 Houston, TX

2002	SD	10 (0)	6	19	3.2 (11)	0	3	44	14.7 (25)	0	—	—	—	—	—	—	—	—	—	—	—	0	41
2003	SD	16 (0)	8	17	2.1 (6)	0	5	54	10.8 (23)	0	—	—	—	—	—	—	—	—	k	—	—	0	45
2004	†SD	15 (0)	65	392	6.0 (52)	3	2	17	8.5 (17)	0	—	—	—	—	—	—	—	—	k	—	—	18	460
NFL	3	41 (0)	79	428	5.4 (52)	3	10	115	11.5 (25)	0	—	—	—	—	—	—	—	—	k	—	—	18	546

CHATMAN, RICKY Ricky Lynn, LB, 6´2˝/230 lbs; LSU; B1/4/1962 Jonesboro, LA **1987** Ind 3 (0)

CHAVEZ, LAZ Lazarus Emmanuel, LB, 6´0˝/220 lbs; Iona; B12/20/1963 Port Chester, NY **1987** Mia 3 (0)

CHAVIS, EDDIE Edward L., WR, 6´0˝/182 lbs; Montclair State; B7/12/1963 Plainfield, NJ

| 1987 | Mia | 3 (1) | — | — | — | — | 7 | 108 | 15.4 (27) | 0 | — | — | — | — | — | — | — | — | — | — | — | 0 | 54 |

CHAVOUS, BARNEY Barney Lewis, DE-DT, 6´3˝/252 lbs; South Carolina State; 1973: Den, rnd 2; B3/22/1951 Aiken, SC **1973** Den 14 (14, RDT) **1974** Den 14 (14, LDE) **1975** Den 9 (9, LDE) **1976** Den 14 (14, LDE) **1977**†Den 13 (11, LDE) **1978**†Den 16 (16, LDE) **1979**†Den 16 (16, LDE) **1980** Den 16 (16, LDE) **1981** Den 16 (16, LDE) **1982** Den 9 (9, LDE) **1983**†Den 15 (13, LDE) **1984**†Den 15 (15, LDE) **1985** Den 16 (16, LDE) **NFL** 183 (178) [13 yrs]

CHAVOUS, COREY Corey, DB, 6´1˝/205 lbs; Vanderbilt; 1998: Arz, rnd 2; B1/15/1976 Aiken, SC **1998**†Arz 16 (5, rcb) **1999** Arz 15 (4) **2000** Arz 16 (1) **2001** Arz 14 (14, RCB) **2002** Min 16 (16, SS/lcb) **2003** Min✧16 (16, SS) **2004** Min 16 (16, SS) **2005** Min 16 (16, SS) **NFL** 125 (88) [8 yrs]

CHEATHAM, ERNIE Ernest Clifford, DT, 6´4˝/255 lbs; Loyola Marymount; 1951: Pit, rnd 21; B7/26/1929 Long Beach, CA **1954** Pit 4 **1954** Bal 2 **NFL** 6 [1 yr]

CHEATHAM, LLOYD Hilliard Lloyd, B, 6´2˝/211 lbs; Auburn; 1942: ChiC, rnd 2; B3/20/1919 Nantes, OK, D6/11/1989 Charlotte, NC

1942	ChiC	11 (3)	1	1	1.0 (1)	0	6	29	4.8 (11)	1	—	—	—	—	—	—	—	—	—	kpi	—	6	44
1946	†NYY-A	13 (7, BB)	3	2	0.7	0	4	54	13.5 (15)	1	—	—	—	—	—	—	—	—	—	kpi	—	6	45
1947	†NYY-A	14 (10, BB)	1	-2	-2.0 (-2)	0	4	124	31.0 (70)	2	—	—	—	—	—	—	—	—	—	k	—	12	70
1948	NYY-A	12 (9, BB)	2	1	0.5	0	7	76	10.9 (50)	0	—	—	—	—	—	—	—	—	—	k	—	0	42
AAFC	3	39 (26)	6	1	0.2 (1)	0	15	254	16.9 (70)	3	—	—	—	—	—	—	—	—	—	kpi	—	18	157

CHECKAYE, COONIE Severin Joseph, BB, 5´9˝/185 lbs; none; B1/6/1893 Muncie, IN, D11/18/1970 Muncie, IN **[C]** **1920** Mun 1 (1, BB) **1921** Mun 2 (1, BB) **NFL** 3 (2) [2 yrs]

CHEEK, LOUIS Louis Ray, T-G, 6´6˝/295 lbs; Texas A&M; 1988: Mia, rnd 8; B10/6/1964 Galveston, TX **1988** Mia 15 (0) **1989** Mia 13 (1) **1990** Dal 4 (0) **1990**†Phi 1 (1) **1991** GB 12 (9, LT) **NFL** 45 (11) [4 yrs]

CHEEK, RICHARD Richard, G, 6´3˝/266 lbs; Auburn; 1970: Buf, rnd 8; B1/19/1948 Panama City, FL **1970** Buf 14 (LG)

CHEEK, STEPHEN Stephen Andrew, P, 6´4˝/205 lbs; Humboldt State; B4/18/1977 Westfield, NJ

| 2004 | KC | 12 (0) | 1 | 0 | 0.0 (0) | 0 | — | — | — | — | — | — | — | — | — | — | — | — | — | P | — | 0 | 0 |

CHEEKS, B.W. Will, HB, 6´1˝/229 lbs; Texas Southern; B8/1/1941 Hearne, TX **1965** Hou-A 2

CHEEVER, MICHAEL Michael John, C, 6´4˝/293 lbs; Georgia Tech; 1996: Jax, rnd 2; B6/24/1973 Newnan, GA **1996**†Jax 11 (2) **1997** Jax 6 (4) **NFL** 17 (6) [2 yrs]

CHELF, DONALD Donald Richard, T-G, 6´3˝/235 lbs; Iowa; 1954: Bal, rnd 12; B3/25/1933 West Liberty, IA **1960** Buf-A 14 (RT) **1961** Buf-A 14 **NFL** 28 [2 yrs]

CHENOWETH, RED Fred Myer, WB-TB, 5´6˝/150 lbs; West Virginia; B8/26/1893 Fairmont, WV, D6/24/1965 Weston, WV **1921** Lou 1 (1, WB)

CHERNE, HAROLD Harold Thomas, T-G, 6´0˝/230 lbs; DePaul; B3/7/1907 La Salle, IL, D1/31/1983 Salinas, CA **1933** Bos 4 (0)

CHEROKE, GEORGE George, G, 5´9˝/195 lbs; Ohio State; B1/2/1921 Jenners, PA **1946** Cle-A 14 (0)

CHERRY, BILL William Kimble, C-G, 6´4˝/275 lbs; Middle Tennessee State; B1/5/1961 Deland, FL **1986** GB 16 (1) **1987** GB 12 (0) **NFL** 28 (1) [2 yrs]

CHERRY, DERON Deron Leigh, DB, 5´11˝/197 lbs; Rutgers; B9/12/1959 Riverside, NJ **[I]** **1981** KC 13 (0) **1982** KC 7 (0) **1983** KC✧16 (16, FS) **1984** KC★16 (16, FS) **1985** KC★16 (16, FS) **1986**†KC★16 (16, FS) **1987** KC★8 (8, FS) **1988** KC★16 (16, FS) **1989** KC☆15 (15, FS) **1990**†KC 9 (6, fs) **1991** KC 16 (15, FS) **NFL** 148 (124) [11 yrs]

CHERRY, ED Edgar Franklin, FB, 6´0˝/208 lbs; Hardin-Simmons; 1938: ChiC, rnd 7; B7/16/1913 Wellington, TX, D11/11/1985 San Angelo, TX

1938	ChiC	2 (0)	6	18	3.0	0	—	—	—	—	—	—	—	—	—	—	—	—	—	—	—	0	18
1939	ChiC	4 (1)	10	30	3.0	0	—	—	—	—	—	—	—	—	—	—	—	—	—	—	—	0	30
1939	Pit	2 (0)	—	—	—	—	—	—	—	—	—	—	—	—	—	—	—	—	—	—	—	—	—
NFL	3	8 (1)	16	48	3.0	0	—	—	—	—	—	—	—	—	—	—	—	—	—	—	—	0	48

CHERRY, JE'ROD Je'Rod L., DB, 6´1˝/210 lbs; California; 1996: NO, rnd 2; B5/30/1973 Charlotte, NC **1996** NO 13 (0) **1997** NO 16 (0) **1998** NO 14 (0) **1999** NO 16 (0) **2000**†Phi 13 (0) **2001** NE 16 (0) **2002** NE 16 (0) **2003**†NE 11 (0) **2004**†NE 12 (0) **NFL** 127 (0) [9 yrs]

CHERRY, MIKE Mike, QB, 6´3˝/226 lbs; Arkansas; Murray State; 1997: NYG, rnd 6; B12/15/1973 Texarkana, AR

1997	NYG	1 (0)	1	-2	-2.0 (-2)	0	—	—	—	—	—	—	—	—	—	—	—	—	—	—	—	0	-2
1998	NYG	1 (0)	3	-3	-1.0 (-1)	0	—	—	—	—	1	0	0.0	0	0.0	0	0	1	9	—	—	0	-3
NFL	2	2 (0)	4	-5	-1.3 (-1)	0	—	—	—	—	1	0	0.0	0	0.0	0	0	1	9	—	—	0	-5

CHERRY, RAPHEL Raphel Jerome, DB, 6´0˝/194 lbs; Hawaii; 1985: Was, rnd 5; B12/19/1961 Little Rock, AR **1987** Det 10 (10, FS) **1988** Det 16 (3)

| 1985 | Was | 16 (6, ss) | — | — | — | — | 1 | 11 | 11.0 (11) | 0 | — | — | — | — | — | — | — | — | — | kpi | — | 0 | 21 |
| NFL | 3 | 42 (19) | — | — | — | — | 1 | 11 | 11.0 (11) | 0 | — | — | — | — | — | — | — | — | — | kpi | — | 0 | 8 |

CHERRY, STAN Stanley D., LB, 6´5˝/200 lbs; Morgan State; B11/2/1950 Baltimore, MS, D2/10/1993 Baltimore, MD **1973** Bal 3

CHERRY, TONY Anthony Earl, RB, 5´7˝/187 lbs; Oregon; 1986: SF, rnd 9; B2/8/1963 Tripoli, Libya

1986	SF	5 (0)	11	42	3.8 (10)	0	—	—	—	—	—	—	—	—	—	—	—	—	—	k	—	0	41
1987	SF	1 (0)	13	65	5.0 (16)	1	—	—	—	—	—	—	—	—	—	—	—	—	—	—	—	6	75
NFL	2	6 (1)	24	107	4.5 (16)	1	—	—	—	—	—	—	—	—	—	—	—	—	—	k	—	6	116

CHERUNDOLO, CHUCK Charles James, C-LB, 6´1˝/215 lbs; Penn State; B8/8/1916 Old Forge, PA **1937** Cle 11 (9, C) **1938** Cle✧11 (10, C) **1939** Cle 10 (3) **1940** Phi 11 (5, c) **1941** Pit✧11 (9, C) **1942** Pit★11 (11, C) **1945** Pit 6 (5, C) **1946** Pit 11 (11, C) **1947**†Pit★12 (12, C) **1948** Pit 12 (6, C) **NFL** 106 (81) [10 yrs]

CHESBRO, RED Marcel Marcus, G, 5´11˝/190 lbs; Colgate; 1938: Cle, rnd 7; B8/22/1914 Brookfield, NY, D4/11/1970 Hamilton, NY **1938** Cle 8 (2)

CHESLEY, AL Albert Cornell, LB, 6´3˝/240 lbs; Pittsburgh; 1979: Phi, rnd 11; B8/23/1957 Washington, DC **1979**†Phi 16 **1980**†Phi 16 (0) **1981**†Phi 16 (16, LILB) **1982** Phi 4 (0) **1982** ChiB 4 (2) **NFL** 56 (18) [4 yrs]

CHESLEY, FRANK Francis Michael, LB, 6´3˝/219 lbs; Wyoming; 1978: NO, rnd 6; B7/14/1955 Washington, DC **1978** GB 1

CHESLEY, JOHN John Kenneth, TE, 6´5˝/225 lbs; Oklahoma State; 1984: Mia, rnd 10; B7/2/1962 Washington, DC **1984** Mia 1 (0)

CHESNEY, CHET Chester Anton, C-LB, 6´2˝/227 lbs; DePaul; B3/9/1916 Chicago, IL, D9/20/1986 Marco Island, FL **1939** ChiB 7 (1) **1940** ChiB✧3 (0) **NFL** 10 (1) [2 yrs]

CHESSER, GEORGE George Allen, RB-P, 6´2˝/220 lbs; Mississippi; Delta State; B9/11/1942 Starkville, MS

1966	Mia-A	14	16	74	4.6 (19)	0	1	4	4.0 (4)	0	—	—	—	—	—	—	—	—	—	P	—	0	76
1967	Mia-A	4	2	3	1.5 (2)	0	—	—	—	—	—	—	—	—	—	—	—	—	—	—	—	0	3
NFL	2	18	18	77	4.3 (19)	0	1	4	4.0 (4)	0	—	—	—	—	—	—	—	—	—	P	—	0	79

YEAR	TEAM	G (GS, POS)	RUSH	YD	AVG (LG)	TD	REC	YD	AVG (LG)	TD	PASS	COMP	PCT	YD	AVG (LG)	TD	INT	SK	YD	QBR	KPR	OTD	PTS	TAY
CHESSON, WES Wesley Merritt, WR, 6´2˝/195 lbs; Duke; 1971: Atl, rnd 7; B1/15/1949 Edenton, NC																								
1971	Atl	14(WR)	1	-4	-4.0(-4)	0	20	224	11.2(24)	0	—	—	—	—	—	—	—	—	—	—	—	—	0	108
1972	Atl	13(WR)	—	—	—	—	18	338	18.8(46)	1	—	—	—	—	—	—	—	—	—	—	k	—	6	159
1973	Atl	2	—	—	—	—	2	36	18.0(20)	1	—	—	—	—	—	—	—	—	—	—	—	—	6	23
1973	Phi	2	—	—	—	—	—	—	—	—	—	—	—	—	—	—	—	—	—	—	—	—	—	—
1974	Phi	12	—	—	—	—	—	—	—	—	—	—	—	—	—	—	—	—	—	—	k	—	0	-14
NFL	4	43	1	-4	-4.0(-4)	0	40	598	14.9(46)	2	—	—	—	—	—	—	—	—	—	—	k	—	12	276
CHESTER, LARRY Larry Travis, DT, 6´2˝/325 lbs; Temple; B10/17/1975 Hammond, LA **1998** Ind 14 (2) **1999**†Ind 16 (8, ldt) **2000**†Ind 16 (0) **2001** Car 11 (5, rdt) **2002** Mia 16 (16, RDT) **2003** Mia 15 (15, RDT) **2004** Mia 2 (2) **NFL** 90 (48) [7 yrs]																								
CHESTER, RAYMOND Raymond Thomas, TE, 6´3˝/232 lbs; Morgan State; 1970: Oak, rnd 1; B6/28/1948 Cambridge, MD																								
1970	†Oak★	14(13, TE)	—	—	—	—	42	556	13.2(43)	7	—	—	—	—	—	—	—	—	—	—	—	—	42	313
1971	Oak★	14(14, TE)	3	5	1.7(6)	0	28	442	15.8(67)	7	—	—	—	—	—	—	—	—	—	—	—	—	42	261
1972	†Oak★	13(10, TE)	1	3	3.0(3)	0	34	576	16.9(68)	8	—	—	—	—	—	—	—	—	—	—	—	—	48	331
1973	Bal	13(TE)	1	1	1.0(1)	0	18	181	10.1(40)	1	—	—	—	—	—	—	—	—	—	—	—	—	6	97
1974	Bal	14(TE)	—	—	—	—	37	461	12.5(45)	1	—	—	—	—	—	—	—	—	—	—	—	—	6	236
1975	†Bal	14(TE)	—	—	—	—	38	457	12.0(32)	3	—	—	—	—	—	—	—	—	—	—	—	—	18	244
1976	†Bal	14(14, TE)	—	—	—	—	24	467	19.5(40)	3	—	—	—	—	—	—	—	—	—	—	—	—	18	249
1977	†Bal	14(14, TE)	—	—	—	—	31	556	17.9(78)	3	—	—	—	—	—	—	—	—	—	—	—	—	18	293
1978	Oak	16	—	—	—	—	13	146	11.2(27)	2	—	—	—	—	—	—	—	—	—	—	k	—	12	80
1979	Oak★	14(13, TE)	—	—	—	—	58	712	12.3(39)	8	—	—	—	—	—	—	—	—	—	—	—	—	48	396
1980	†Oak	16(10, TE)	—	—	—	—	28	366	13.1(47)	4	—	—	—	—	—	—	—	—	—	—	—	—	24	203
1981	Oak	16(5, te)	—	—	—	—	13	93	7.2(15)	1	—	—	—	—	—	—	—	—	—	—	—	—	6	52
NFL	12	172(93)	5	9	1.8(6)	0	364	5013	13.8(78)	48	—	—	—	—	—	—	—	—	—	—	k	—	288	2753
CHETTI, JOE Joseph Salvatore, RB, 5´9˝/205 lbs; C.W. Post; B11/19/1963 Bay Shore, NY																								
1987	Buf	2(0)	—	—	—	—	1	9	9.0(9)	0	—	—	—	—	—	—	—	—	—	—	—	—	0	5
CHEVERKO, GEORGE George Francis, B, 6´1˝/197 lbs; Fordham; 1944: Cle, rnd 7; B7/29/1920 Beaver Meadows, PA, D11/1977																								
1947	NYG	9(1)	19	63	3.3(20)	0	17	300	17.6(62)	3	—	—	—	—	—	—	—	—	—	—	kpi	—	18	360
1948	NYG	8(5, lh)	3	10	3.3(6)	0	1	41	41.0(41)	0	—	—	—	—	—	—	—	—	—	—	kpi	—	0	185
1948	Was	2(1)	—	—	—	—	—	—	—	—	—	—	—	—	—	—	—	—	—	—	i	—	0	19
NFL	2	19(7)	22	73	3.3(20)	0	18	341	18.9(62)	3	—	—	—	—	—	—	—	—	—	—	kpi	—	18	564
CHEVRIER, RANDY Randy Robert, DT, 6´2˝/291 lbs; McGill; 2001: Jax, rnd 7; B6/6/1976 St. Leonard, Canada **2001** Dal 8 (0) **2001** Cin 5 (0) **NFL** 13 (0) [1 yr]																								
CHEYUNSKI, JIM James Michael, LB, 6´1˝/225 lbs; Syracuse; 1968: Bos, rnd 12; B12/29/1945 Bridgewater, MA **1968** Bos-A 13 (4) **1969** Bos-A 14 (14, MLB) **1970** Bos 11 (11, MLB) **1971** NE 14 (14, MLB) **1972** NE 14 (11, MLB) **1973** Buf 13 (MLB) **1974**†Buf 14 (RILB) **1975**†Bal 14 (8, MLB) **1976**†Bal 14 (MLB) **NFL** 121 (62) [9 yrs]																								
CHIAVERINI, DARRIN Darrin, WR, 6´2˝/210 lbs; Colorado; 1999: Cle, rnd 5; B10/12/1977 Orange County, CA																								
1999	Cle	16(8, WR)	—	—	—	—	44	487	11.1(28)	4	—	—	—	—	—	—	—	—	—	—	k	—	24	269
2000	Cle	10(2)	—	—	—	—	8	68	8.5(18)	1	—	—	—	—	—	—	—	—	—	—	—	—	6	39
2001	Dal	16(0)	1	3	3.0(3)	0	10	107	10.7(21)	2	—	—	—	—	—	—	—	—	—	—	—	—	12	67
2002	†Atl	7(0)	—	—	—	—	—	—	—	—	—	—	—	—	—	—	—	—	—	—	—	—	—	—
NFL	4	49(10)	1	3	3.0(3)	0	62	662	10.7(28)	7	—	—	—	—	—	—	—	—	—	—	k	—	42	374
CHICKEN, FRED Fred S., TB, 5´10˝/185 lbs; none; B4/5/1888 Minneapolis, MN, D11/24/1968 La Crosse, WI **1920** RI 6 (5, TB)																								
CHICKERNEO, JOHN John Louis, B-LB, 6´1˝/205 lbs; Pittsburgh; 1939: NYG, rnd 2; B3/13/1917 Gary, IN, D10/3/1995 Deerfield, IL **1942** NYG 4 (4)																								
CHICKILLO, NICK Nicholas Angelo, LB-G, 5´11˝/220 lbs; Miami (FL); 1953: ChiC, rnd 15; B10/17/1930 Scranton, PA **1953** ChiC 12 (LLB)																								
CHICKILLO, TONY Anthony Paul, NT-DE-G, 6´3˝/262 lbs; Miami (FL); 1983: TB, rnd 5; B7/8/1960 Miami, FL **1984** SD 1 (0) **1985** SD 4 (1) **1987** NYJ 2 (1) **NFL** 7 (2) [3 yrs]																								
CHILDRESS, BRANDON Brandon, WR, 5´10˝/185 lbs; Ohio State; B3/31/1982 Warrensville Heights, OH																								
2005	NE	1(0)	—	—	—	—	3	32	10.7(21)	0	—	—	—	—	—	—	—	—	—	—	—	—	0	16
CHILDRESS, FREDDIE Freddie Lee, G-T, 6´4˝/331 lbs; Arkansas; 1989: Cin, rnd 2; B9/17/1966 Little Rock, AR **1991** NE 15 (1) **1992** Cle 16 (0) **NFL** 31 (1) [2 yrs]																								
CHILDRESS, JOE Joseph, HB-FB-FL, 6´0˝/202 lbs; Auburn; 1956: ChiC, rnd 1; B10/26/1933 Robertsdale, AL, D5/5/1986 Kingwood, TX																								
1956	ChiC	11	43	203	4.7(30)	0	6	82	13.7(34)	1	—	—	—	—	—	—	—	—	—	—	k	—	6	234
1957	ChiC	12(RH)	41	168	4.1(39)	1	10	146	14.6(28)	0	2	1	50.0	43	21.5(43)	0	1	—	—	—	—	—	6	233
1958	ChiC	10(RH)	50	170	3.4(30)	0	35	406	11.6(26)	4	1	0	0.0	0	0.0	0	0	—	—	—	—	—	24	393
1959	ChiC	9	30	59	2.0(9)	0	4	73	18.3(52)	1	—	—	—	—	—	—	—	—	—	—	—	—	6	101
1960	SL	12(FL)	34	240	7.1(28)	0	11	202	18.4(52)	2	—	—	—	—	—	—	—	—	—	—	—	—	12	351
1962	SL	14(hb)	37	162	4.4(15)	0	15	207	13.8(42)	1	—	—	—	—	—	—	—	—	—	—	k	—	6	245
1963	SL	14(FB)	174	701	4.0(28)	2	25	354	14.2(78)	2	—	—	—	—	—	—	—	—	—	—	—	—	24	908
1964	SL	9(HB)	102	413	4.0(17)	0	12	203	16.9(46)	2	—	—	—	—	—	—	—	—	—	—	—	—	12	525
1965	SL	5(fb)	19	94	4.9(13)	0	3	27	9.0(10)	0	—	—	—	—	—	—	—	—	—	—	—	—	0	108
NFL	9	96	530	2210	4.2(39)	3	121	1700	14.0(78)	13	3	1	33.3	43	14.3(43)	0	1	—	—	—	k	—	96	3096
CHILDRESS, O.J. Orin J., LB, 6´1˝/244 lbs; Clemson; 1999: NYG, rnd 7; B12/6/1975 Hermitage, TN **1999** NYG 4 (0)																								
CHILDRESS, RAY Raymond Clay, DT-DE, 6´6˝/272 lbs; Texas A&M; 1985: Hou, rnd 1; B10/20/1962 Memphis, TN **[S]** **1985** Hou 16 (16, LDE) **1986** Hou 16 (16, LDE) **1987**†Hou 13 (13, LDE) **1988**†Hou★16 (16, LDE) **1989** Hou☆14 (14, LDE) **1990**†Hou★16 (16, LDT) **1991**†Hou★15 (15, LDT) **1992**†Hou★16 (16, LDT) **1993**†Hou★16 (16, LDT) **1994** Hou 16 (16, LDT) **1995** Hou 6 (6, ldt) **1996**†Dal 3 (0) **NFL** 163 (160) [12 yrs]																								
CHILDS, CLARENCE Clarence Norris, DB-HB, 5´11˝/186 lbs; Florida A&M; 1961: Bos, rnd 20; B1/13/1938 Lakeland, FL **[R]** **1965** NYG 14 **1966** NYG 14 (RCB) **1967** NYG 14 **1968** ChiB 4																								
1964	NYG	13	40	102	2.6(19)	0	11	97	8.8(24)	0	—	—	—	—	—	—	—	—	—	—	kp	1	6	648
NFL	5	59	40	102	2.6(19)	0	11	97	8.8(24)	0	—	—	—	—	—	—	—	—	—	—	kpi	2	12	1647
CHILDS, HENRY Henry, TE, 6´2˝/223 lbs; Kansas State; 1974: Atl, rnd 5; B4/16/1951 Thomasville, GA																								
1974	Atl	6	—	—	—	—	—	—	—	—	—	—	—	—	—	—	—	—	—	—	k	—	0	-15
1974	NO	1	—	—	—	—	—	—	—	—	—	—	—	—	—	—	—	—	—	—	—	—	—	—
1975	NO	14	—	—	—	—	10	179	17.9(38)	0	—	—	—	—	—	—	—	—	—	—	—	—	0	90
1976	NO	14(11, TE)	1	16	16.0(16)	1	26	349	13.4(46)	3	—	—	—	—	—	—	—	—	—	—	k	—	24	207
1977	NO	13(10, TE)	—	—	—	—	33	518	15.7(59)	**9**	—	—	—	—	—	—	—	—	—	—	—	—	54	304
1978	NO☆	16(16, TE)	2	-4	-2.0(-1)	0	53	869	16.4(52)	4	—	—	—	—	—	—	—	—	—	—	—	—	24	451
1979	NO★	16(16, TE)	—	—	—	—	51	846	16.6(51)	5	—	—	—	—	—	—	—	—	—	—	—	—	30	448
1980	NO	13(6, te)	—	—	—	—	34	463	13.6(30)	6	—	—	—	—	—	—	—	—	—	—	—	—	36	262
1981	LARm	7(7, te)	1	0	0.0(0)	0	12	145	12.1(39)	1	—	—	—	—	—	—	—	—	—	—	—	—	6	78
1984	GB	3(2)	—	—	—	—	4	32	8.0(17)	0	—	—	—	—	—	—	—	—	—	—	—	—	0	16
NFL	9	103(68)	4	12	3.0(16)	1	223	3401	15.3(59)	28	—	—	—	—	—	—	—	—	—	—	k	—	174	1839
CHILDS, JIMMY James Joe, WR, 6´2˝/194 lbs; Cal Poly-San Luis Obispo; 1978: SL, rnd 4; B8/9/1956 El Dorado, AR																								
1978	SL	8	—	—	—	—	4	50	12.5(23)	1	—	—	—	—	—	—	—	—	—	—	k	—	6	47
1979	SL	13	—	—	—	—	8	93	11.6(22)	0	—	—	—	—	—	—	—	—	—	—	—	—	0	47
NFL	2	21	—	—	—	—	12	143	11.9(23)	1	—	—	—	—	—	—	—	—	—	—	k	—	6	94
CHILDS, RON Ron Lee, LB, 5´11˝/212 lbs; Washington State; B9/18/1971 Kennewick, WA **1995** NO 9 (0)																								
CHILLAR, BRANDON Brandon Oneil, LB, 6´3˝/230 lbs; UCLA; 2004: SL, rnd 4; B10/21/1982 Los Angeles, CA **2004**†SL 16 (5, llb) **2005** SL 16 (7, rlb) **NFL** 32 (12) [2 yrs]																								

YEAR	TEAM	G (GS, POS)	RUSH	YD	AVG (LG)	TD	REC	YD	AVG (LG)	TD	PASS COMP	PCT	YD	AVG (LG)	TD	INT	SK	YD	QBR	KPR	OTD	PTS	TAY

CHILTON, GENE Gene Allan, C-T, 6´3˝/281 lbs; Texas; 1986: SL, rnd 3; B3/27/1964 Houston, TX **1986** SL 16 (7, c) **1987** SL 11 (0) **1989** KC 16 (0) **1990** NE 4 (3)
1992 NE 16 (16, C)

| 1991 | NE | 16 (16, C) | 1 | 0 | 0.0 (0) | 0 | — | — | — | — | — | — | — | — | — | — | — | — | — | — | — | 0 | 0 |
| NFL | 6 | 79 (42) | 1 | 0 | 0.0 (0) | 0 | — | — | — | — | — | — | — | — | — | — | — | — | — | — | — | 0 | 0 |

CHIPLEY, BILL William Allen, E-DB, 6´3˝/199 lbs; Clemson; Washington & Lee; 1947: Bos, rnd 8/Buf-A, rnd 14; B7/2/1920 Lynchburg, VA, D12/27/2002 Lookout Mountain, TN

1947	Bos	6 (2)	1	3	3.0 (3)	0	5	105	21.0 (40)	1	—	—	—	—	—	—	—	—	—	—	—	6	61
1948	Bos	12 (1)	—	—	—	—	13	131	10.1 (22)	1	—	—	—	—	—	—	—	—	—	i	1	12	118
1949	NYB	12 (9, LE)	—	—	—	—	57	631	11.1 (69)	2	—	—	—	—	—	—	—	—	—	k	—	12	318
NFL	3	30 (12)	1	3	3.0 (3)	0	75	867	11.6 (69)	4	—	—	—	—	—	—	—	—	—	ki	1	30	496

CHIRICO, JOHN John J., RB, 6´0˝/220 lbs; Columbia; B8/15/1965 Brooklyn, NY

| 1987 | NYJ | 3 (1) | 12 | 22 | 1.8 (4) | 1 | 4 | 18 | 4.5 (8) | 0 | — | — | — | — | — | — | — | — | — | — | — | 6 | 41 |

CHISICK, ANDY Andrew Bernard, C, 6´1˝/207 lbs; Villanova; 1940: ChiC, rnd 7; B6/10/1916 Sagamore, PA, D3/13/1986 Somerset, KY **1940** ChiC 11 (2) **1941** ChiC 11 (4)
NFL 22 (6) [2 yrs]

CHLEBEK, ED Edward, QB, 5´11˝/175 lbs; Western Michigan; B2/9/1940

| 1963 | NYJ-A | 2 | — | — | — | — | — | — | — | — | 4 | 2 | 50.0 | 5 | 1.3 (4) | 0 | 0 | — | — | — | — | 0 | 3 |

CHMURA, MARK Mark William, TE, 6´5˝/248 lbs; Boston College; 1992: GB, rnd 6; B2/22/1969 Deerfield, MA

1993	†GB	14 (0)	—	—	—	—	2	13	6.5 (7)	0	—	—	—	—	—	—	—	—	—	k	—	0	-9
1994	†GB	14 (4)	—	—	—	—	14	165	11.8 (27)	0	—	—	—	—	—	—	—	—	—	—	—	0	83
1995	†GB★	16 (15, TE)	—	—	—	—	54	679	12.6 (33)	7	—	—	—	—	—	—	—	—	—	—	—	44	375
1996	†GB	13 (13, TE)	—	—	—	—	28	370	13.2 (29)	0	—	—	—	—	—	—	—	—	—	—	—	0	185
1997	†GB◇	15 (14, TE)	—	—	—	—	38	417	11.0 (32)	6	—	—	—	—	—	—	—	—	—	—	—	36	239
1998	†GB★	15 (14, TE)	—	—	—	—	47	554	11.8 (25)	4	—	—	—	—	—	—	—	—	—	—	—	24	297
1999	GB	2 (1)	—	—	—	—	5	55	11.0 (16)	0	—	—	—	—	—	—	—	—	—	—	—	0	28
NFL	7	89 (62)	—	—	—	—	188	2253	12.0 (33)	17	—	—	—	—	—	—	—	—	—	k	—	104	1197

CHOATE, BOB Robert M., G, 6´1˝/225 lbs; Haskell Indian; B12/2/1893 Pryor, OK, D7/13/1985 Antioch, CA **1924** KC 1 (0)

CHOATE, PUTT Mark Putnam, LB, 6´0˝/225 lbs; SMU; B12/11/1956 Big Spring, TX **1987** GB 2 (2)

CHOBOIAN, MAX Max John, QB, 6´4˝/215 lbs; Oregon; Cal State-Northridge; B3/17/1942 Tulare, CA, D1/2/1977 Fresno, CA

| 1966 | Den-A | 14 (qb) | 21 | 45 | 2.1 (12) | 2 | — | — | — | — | 163 | 82 | 50.3 | 1110 | 6.8 (79) | 4 | 12 | — | — | 49.9 | — | 12 | 160 |

CHOMA, JOHN John Gregory, G-C-T, 6´5˝/261 lbs; Virginia; 1978: SD, rnd 5; B2/9/1955 Cleveland, OH **1981**†SF 14 (0) **1982** SF 7 (0) **1983** SF 6 (0) **NFL** 27 (0) [3 yrs]

CHOMYSZAK, STEVE Stephen John, DT-DE, 6´6˝/265 lbs; Syracuse; 1966: NYJ, rnd 12; B2/27/1944 Johnson City, NY, D1/25/1988 Johnson City, NY **1966** NYJ-A 2 **1968** Cin-A 10
1969 Cin-A 14 (RDE) **1970**†Cin 14 (RDT) **1971** Cin 14 (RDT) **1972** Cin 13 (RDT) **1973**†Cin 12 **NFL** 79 [7 yrs]

CHORAK, JASON Jason, DE, 6´4˝/256 lbs; Washington; 1998: SL, rnd 7; B9/23/1974 Vashon, WA **1998** Ind 8 (0)

CHOROVICH, DICK Richard Milan, DT-T, 6´4˝/260 lbs; Miami (OH); 1955: Bal, rnd 12; B11/29/1933 St. Clairsville, OH, D7/15/1997 St. Clairsville, OH **1955** Bal 11 **1956** Bal 3
1960†LAC-A☆14 (RDT) **NFL** 28 [3 yrs]

CHRAPE, JOSEPH Joseph, G-T, /210 lbs; Hibbing CC (MN); B1910, MN **1929** Min 9 (8, RG)

CHREBET, WAYNE Wayne John, WR, 5´10˝/188 lbs; Hofstra; B8/14/1973 Garfield, NJ

1995	NYJ	16 (16, WR)	1	1	1.0 (1)	0	66	726	11.0 (32)	4	—	—	—	—	—	—	—	—	—	—	—	24	384
1996	NYJ	16 (9, WR)	—	—	—	—	84	909	10.8 (44)	3	—	—	—	—	—	—	—	—	—	p	—	18	469
1997	NYJ	16 (1)	—	—	—	—	58	799	13.8 (70)	3	—	—	—	—	—	—	—	—	—	k	—	18	405
1998	†NYJ	16 (15, WR)	—	—	—	—	75	1083	14.4 (63)	8	—	—	—	—	—	—	—	—	—	—	—	48	582
1999	NYJ	11 (11, WR)	—	—	—	—	48	631	13.1 (50)	3	—	—	—	—	—	—	—	—	—	—	—	18	331
2000	NYJ	16 (16, WR)	3	-3	-1.0 (8)	0	69	937	13.6 (50)	8	—	—	—	—	—	—	—	—	—	—	—	48	506
2001	†NYJ	15 (15, WR)	—	—	—	—	56	750	13.4 (36)	1	—	—	—	—	—	—	—	—	—	—	—	6	380
2002	†NYJ	15 (15, WR)	—	—	—	—	51	691	13.5 (37)	9	1	0	0.0	0	0	0	0	—	—	—	—	54	391
2003	NYJ	7 (5, wr)	—	—	—	—	27	289	10.7 (29)	1	—	—	—	—	—	—	—	—	—	—	—	6	150
2004	†NYJ	16 (1)	—	—	—	—	31	397	12.8 (35)	1	—	—	—	—	—	—	—	—	—	—	—	6	204
2005	NYJ	8 (0)	—	—	—	—	15	153	10.2 (20)	0	—	—	—	—	—	—	—	—	—	—	—	0	77
NFL	11	152 (104)	4	-2	-0.5 (8)	0	580	7365	12.7 (70)	41	1	0	0.0	0	0	0	0	—	—	kp	—	246	3875

CHRISTENSEN, ERIK Erik Robert, DE, 6´3˝/235 lbs; Richmond; 1955: Was, rnd 7; B10/30/1931 Elizabeth, NJ **1956** Was 2

CHRISTENSEN, FRANK Frank Langdon, B-T, 6´1˝/199 lbs; Utah; B6/1/1910 Salt Lake City, UT, D9/6/2001 Salt Lake City, UT **[K]**

1934	Det	11 (9, FB)	96	304	3.2	2	1	43	43.0 (43)	0	8	3	37.5	23	2.9	0	0	—	—	—	—	12	357
1935	Det	12 (12, BB)	11	6	0.5	0	5	57	11.4	1	21	6	28.6	92	4.4	0	3	—	—	K	—	8	-35
1936	Det	11 (7, BB)	2	-2	-1.0	0	2	58	29.0	1	6	2	33.3	22	3.7	0	1	—	—	—	—	6	3
1937	Det	8 (4, rt)	—	—	—	—	—	—	—	—	—	—	—	—	—	—	—	—	—	—	—	—	—
NFL	4	42 (32)	109	308	2.8	2	8	158	19.8 (43)	2	35	11	31.4	137	3.9	0	4	—	—	K	—	26	326

CHRISTENSEN, GEORGE George Washington, T-G, 6´2˝/238 lbs; Oregon; B12/13/1909 Pendleton, OR, D7/1/1968 Detroit, MI **1931** Por☆14 (13, RT) **1932** Por☆12 (12, RT)
1933 Por☆11 (11, RT) **1934** Det☆13 (13, RT) **1935** Det☆12 (10, RT) **1936** Det☆12 (7, RT) **1937** Det 10 (5) **1938** Det 11 (3) **NFL** 95 (74) [8 yrs]

CHRISTENSEN, JEFF Jeffrey Bruce, QB, 6´3˝/202 lbs; Eastern Illinois; 1983: Cin, rnd 5; B1/8/1960 Gibson City, IL

1983	Cin	1 (0)	1	-2	-2.0 (-2)	0	—	—	—	—	—	—	—	—	—	—	—	—	—	—	—	0	-2
1987	Cle	3 (2)	11	41	3.7 (15)	0	—	—	—	—	58	24	41.4	297	5.1 (34)	1	3	5	37	—	—	—	0	75
NFL	2	4 (2)	12	39	3.3 (15)	0	—	—	—	—	58	24	41.4	297	5.1 (34)	1	3	5	37	—	—	—	0	73

CHRISTENSEN, KOESTER Koester L., E, 5´10˝/195 lbs; Michigan State; B1905, D1946 **1930** Por 1 (0)

CHRISTENSEN, TODD Todd Jay, TE-FB, 6´3˝/230 lbs; Brigham Young; 1978: Dal, rnd 2; B8/3/1956 Bellefonte, PA

1979	NYG	1	—	—	—	—	—	—	—	—	—	—	—	—	—	—	—	—	—	—	—	—	0	0
1979	Oak	12	—	—	—	—	—	—	—	—	—	—	—	—	—	—	—	—	—	—	—	—	0	-5
1980	Oak	16 (0)	—	—	—	—	—	—	—	—	0	0	0.0	0	0.0	0	0	1	7	—	k	1	6	-5
1981	Oak	16 (0)	—	—	—	—	8	115	14.4 (30)	2	—	—	—	—	—	—	—	—	—	—	k	—	12	62
1982	LARd	9 (9, TE)	1	-6	-6.0 (-6)	0	42	510	12.1 (50)	4	—	—	—	—	—	—	—	—	—	—	—	24	269
1983	LARd★	16 (16, TE)	—	—	—	—	92	1247	13.6 (45)	12	—	—	—	—	—	—	—	—	—	—	—	72	684
1984	LARd★	16 (16, TE)	—	—	—	—	80	1007	12.6 (38)	7	—	—	—	—	—	—	—	—	—	—	—	42	539
1985	LARd★	16 (16, TE)	—	—	—	—	82	987	12.0 (48)	6	—	—	—	—	—	—	—	—	—	—	—	36	524
1986	LARd★	16 (16, TE)	—	—	—	—	95	1153	12.1 (55)	8	—	—	—	—	—	—	—	—	—	—	—	48	617
1987	LARd★	12 (12, TE)	—	—	—	—	47	663	14.1 (33)	2	—	—	—	—	—	—	—	—	—	—	—	12	342
1988	LARd	7 (5, te)	—	—	—	—	15	190	12.7 (22)	0	—	—	—	—	—	—	—	—	—	—	—	0	95
NFL	10	137 (90)	1	-6	-6.0 (-6)	0	461	5872	12.7 (55)	41	0	0	0.0	0	0.0	0	0	1	7	—	k	1	252	3124

CHRISTENSON, BRAD Brandon Wade, TE, 6´1˝/256 lbs; Northwestern Oklahoma State; B5/10/1977 Garland, TX **2002**†Oak 0 (0)

CHRISTIAN, BOB Robert Douglas, RB, 5´11˝/226 lbs; Northwestern; 1991: Atl, rnd 12; B11/14/1968 St. Louis, MO

1992	ChiB	2 (0)	—	—	—	—	—	—	—	—	—	—	—	—	—	—	—	—	—	—	—	—	0	0
1993	ChiB	14 (1)	8	19	2.4 (12)	0	16	160	10.0 (36)	0	—	—	—	—	—	—	—	—	—	—	—	0	99
1994	ChiB	12 (0)	7	29	4.1 (8)	0	2	30	15.0 (21)	0	—	—	—	—	—	—	—	—	—	—	—	0	44
1995	Car	14 (12, FB)	41	158	3.9 (17)	0	29	255	8.8 (23)	1	—	—	—	—	—	—	—	—	—	—	—	8	291
1997	Atl	16 (12, FB)	7	8	1.1 (3)	0	22	154	7.0 (19)	1	—	—	—	—	—	—	—	—	—	—	—	6	90
1998	Atl	14 (10, FB)	8	21	2.6 (6)	2	19	214	11.3 (39)	1	—	—	—	—	—	—	—	—	—	—	—	18	153
1999	Atl	16 (14, FB)	38	174	4.6 (33)	5	40	354	8.9 (36)	2	—	—	—	—	—	—	—	—	—	—	—	42	411
2000	Atl	16 (14, FB)	9	19	2.1 (7)	0	44	315	7.2 (19)	0	—	—	—	—	—	—	—	—	—	—	—	0	177
2001	Atl	16 (8, fb)	44	284	6.5 (53)	2	45	392	8.7 (42)	1	—	—	—	—	—	—	—	—	—	—	—	24	510

YEAR	TEAM	G (GS, POS)	RUSH	YD	AVG(LG)	TD	REC	YD	AVG(LG)	TD	PASS	COMP	PCT	YD	AVG(LG)	TD	INT	SK	YD	QBR	KPR	OTD	PTS	TAY
2002	Atl	15(10, FB)	31	119	3.8(16)	3	13	174	13.4(55)	0	—	—	—	—	—	—	—	—	—	—	—	—	18	236
NFL	10	135(81)	193	831	4.3(53)	12	230	2048	8.9(55)	7	—	—	—	—	—	—	—	—	—	—	—	—	116	2010

CHRISTIANSEN, BOB   Robert Scott, DT, 6´4˝/230 lbs; UCLA; 1972: LA, rnd 5; B5/8/1949 Marshalltown, IA   **1972** Buf 4

CHRISTIANSEN, JACK   John LeRoy, DB, 6´1˝/205 lbs; Colorado State; 1951: Det, rnd 6; B12/20/1928 Sublette, KS, D6/29/1986 Stanford, CA; HOF 1970 [RIC]   **1951** Det 12 (DB)
1954†Det★11 (DB)   **1955** Det★9 (DB)   **1956** Det★12 (DB)   **1957**†Det★12 (DB)   **1958** Det 10 (db)

1952	†Det☆	11(DB)	—	—	—	—	2	3	—	—	32	10.7(11)	—	—	—	—	—	—	—	—	—	kpi	2	24	657
1953	†Det★	12(DB)	0	-5	(-5)	0	—	—	—	—	—	—	—	—	—	—	—	—	—	—	—	kpi	1	6	198
NFL	8	89	19	143	7.5(65)	2	3	32	10.7(11)	0	—	—	—	—	—	—	—	—	—	—	—	kpi	11	78	1879

CHRISTIANSEN, MARTY   Martin Alexander, FB, 6´0˝/200 lbs; Minnesota; 1940: ChiC, rnd 5; B4/23/1916 Minneapolis, MN, D3/29/1999 Minneapolis, MN

| 1940 | ChiC | 6(1) | 32 | 71 | 2.2 | 1 | — | — | — | — | — | — | — | — | — | — | — | — | — | — | — | — | 6 | 81 |

CHRISTIANSON, OSCAR   Oscar C., E-TB, 5´10˝/186 lbs; none; B4/2/1899, MN, D5/19/1972 St. Anthony, MN   **1921** Min 4 (3, LE), 6   **1922** Min 4 (3, LE)   **1923** Min 6 (3)
1924 Min 6 (4, RE)   **NFL** 20 (13) [4 yrs]

CHRISTIE, STEVE   Geoffrey Stephen, K, 6´0˝/195 lbs; William & Mary; B11/13/1967 Hamilton, Canada [K]   **1990** TB☆16 (0)   **1991** TB 16 (0)   **1992**†Buf 16 (0)   **1993**†Buf 16 (0)
1994 Buf 16 (0)   **1995**†Buf 16 (0)   **1996**†Buf 16 (0)   **1997** Buf 16 (0)   **1998**†Buf 16 (0)   **1999**†Buf 16 (0)   **2000** Buf 16 (0)   **2001** SD 5 (0)   **2002** SD 16 (0)   **2003** SD 16 (0)
2004 NYG 16 (0)   **NFL** 229 (0) [15 yrs]

CHRISTMAN, FLOYD   Floyd F., B, 5´11˝/180 lbs; Thiel; B10/14/1902 Greenville, PA, D1/24/1971 Rock Creek, OH   **1925** Buf 9 (8, FB), 6

CHRISTMAN, PAUL   Paul Joseph, QB, 6´0˝/210 lbs; Missouri; 1941: ChiC, rnd 2; B3/5/1918 St. Louis, MO, D3/2/1970 Lake Forest, IL

1945	ChiC	8(3, QB)	30	-34	-1.1(9)	1	—	—	—	—	219	89	40.6	1147	5.2(70)	5	12	—	—	—	k	—	6	124
1946	ChiC☆	11(3, QB)	28	-61	-2.2(6)	3	—	—	—	—	229	100	43.7	1656	7.2(82)	13	18	—	54.8	—	—	—	18	142
1947	†ChiC☆	12(8, QB)	8	11	1.4(3)	2	—	—	—	—	301	138	45.8	2191	7.3(80)	17	22	—	59.0	—	—	—	12	332
1948	ChiC	7(2, qb)	8	6	0.8(5)	1	—	—	—	—	114	51	44.7	740	6.5(71)	5	4	—	66.4	—	—	—	6	251
1949	ChiC	12(7, QB)	4	34	8.5(22)	0	—	—	—	—	151	75	49.7	1015	6.7(50)	11	13	—	59.9	—	—	—	0	77
1950	GB	11(qb)	7	18	2.6(4)	0	—	—	—	—	126	51	40.5	545	4.3(44)	7	7	—	49.2	—	—	—	6	56
NFL	6	61(23)	85	-26	-0.3(22)	8	—	—	—	—	1140	504	44.2	7294	6.4(82)	58	76	—	54.8	k	—	48	980

CHRISTOPHER, HERB   Herbert, DB, 5´10˝/195 lbs; Morris Brown; B4/7/1954 Thomasville, GA   **1979** KC 9 (6, ss)   **1980** KC 16 (16, SS)   **1981** KC 16 (2)   **1982** KC 9 (0)
NFL 50 (24) [4 yrs]

CHRISTOPHERSON, JIM   James Monroe, LB-K, 6´0˝/218 lbs; Concordia (MN); B2/17/1938 Wadena, MN [K]   **1962** Min 14

CHRISTOPHERSON, RYAN   Ryan Ray, RB, 5´11˝/237 lbs; Wyoming; 1995: Jax, rnd 5; B7/26/1972 Sioux Falls, SD   **1996** Jax 2 (0)   **1996** Arz 6 (0)

| 1995 | Jax | 11(0) | 16 | 16 | 1.0(10) | 1 | 1 | -1 | -1.0(-1) | 0 | — | — | — | — | — | — | — | — | — | — | — | — | 6 | 26 |
| NFL | 2 | 19(0) | 16 | 16 | 1.0(10) | 1 | 1 | -1 | -1.0(-1) | 0 | — | — | — | — | — | — | — | — | — | — | — | — | 6 | 26 |

CHRISTY, DICK   Richard Joseph, HB, 5´10˝/191 lbs; North Carolina State; 1958: GB, rnd 3; B11/24/1935 Philadelphia, PA, D8/7/1966 Chester, PA [R]

1958	Pit	12	38	101	2.7(19)	0	7	73	10.4(26)	0	—	—	—	—	—	—	—	—	—	—	kp	—	0	350
1960	Bos-A	13(HB)	78	363	4.7(48)	3	26	268	10.3(53)	2	11	6	54.5	94	8.5(39)	2	2	—	—	kp	—	30	804
1961	NYT-A	14(HB)	81	180	2.2(16)	2	29	521	18.0(68)	1	1	0	0.0	0	0.0(0)	0	0	—	—	kp	2	30	914
1962	NYT-A✧	14(HB)	114	535	4.7(47)	3	62	538	8.7(41)	3	6	0	0.0	0	0.0(0)	0	0	—	—	kp	2	48	1298
1963	NYJ-A	11(HB)	26	88	3.4(13)	1	8	73	9.1(13)	0	—	—	—	—	—	—	—	—	—	kp	—	6	361
NFL	5	64	337	1267	3.8(48)	9	132	1473	11.2(68)	6	18	6	33.3	94	5.2(39)	2	2	—	—	kp	4	114	3726

CHRISTY, EARL   Earl Oliver, HB-DB, 5´10˝/195 lbs; Maryland-Eastern Shore; B3/19/1943 Perryman, MD   **1966** NYJ-A 6   **1967** NYJ-A 10   **1968**†NYJ-A 14   **NFL** 30 [3 yrs]

CHRISTY, GREG   Gregory Alan, T, 6´4˝/285 lbs; Pittsburgh; B4/29/1962 Natrona Heights, PA   **1985** Buf 7 (0)

CHRISTY, JEFF   Jeffrey Allen, C, 6´3˝/284 lbs; Pittsburgh; 1992: Phx, rnd 4; B2/3/1969 Natrona Heights, PA   **1993**†Min 9 (0)   **1994**†Min 16 (16, C)   **1995** Min 16 (16, C)
1996†Min 16 (16, C)   **1997** Min 12 (12, C)   **1998**†Min★16 (16, C)   **1999**†Min★16 (16, C)   **2000**†TB✧ 16 (16, C)   **2001** TB 15 (15, C)   **2002**†TB 16 (16, C)   **NFL** 148 (139) [10 yrs]

CHRYPLEWICZ, PETE   Peter Gerald, TE, 6´5˝/253 lbs; Notre Dame; 1997: Det, rnd 5; B4/27/1974 Detroit, MI

1997	Det	10(0)	—	—	—	—	3	27	9.0(12)	1	—	—	—	—	—	—	—	—	—	—	—	—	6	19
1998	Det	16(2)	—	—	—	—	4	20	5.0(8)	2	—	—	—	—	—	—	—	—	—	—	—	—	12	20
1999	Det	11(1)	—	—	—	—	2	18	9.0(13)	0	—	—	—	—	—	—	—	—	—	—	—	—	0	9
NFL	3	37(3)	—	—	—	—	9	65	7.2(13)	3	—	—	—	—	—	—	—	—	—	—	—	—	18	48

CHUKWURAH, PATRICK   Patrick, LB, 6´1˝/250 lbs; Wyoming; 2001: Min, rnd 5; B3/1/1979 Nigeria   **2001** Min 16 (3)   **2002** Min 11 (2)   **2004**†Den 14 (0)   **2005**†Den 14 (0)
NFL 55 (5) [4 yrs]

CHUNG, EUGENE   Von Eugene, G-T, 6´4˝/301 lbs; Virginia Tech; 1992: NE, rnd 1; B6/14/1969 Prince George Co., MD   **1992** NE 15 (14, RG/rt)   **1993** NE 16 (16, LG)   **1994** NE 3 (0)
1995 Jax 11 (0)   **1997** Ind 10 (0)   **NFL** 55 (30) [5 yrs]

CHURCHMAN, RICKY   Richard Cecil, DB, 6´1˝/195 lbs; Texas; 1980: SF, rnd 4; B3/14/1958 Pearland, TX   **1980** SF 16 (15, SS)   **1981** SF 3 (0)   **NFL** 19 (15) [2 yrs]

CHURCHWELL, DON   Dennis Hanson, DT-T, 6´1˝/253 lbs; Mississippi; 1959: Bal, rnd 5/1960: Oak, rnd 2; B5/11/1936 Leakesville, MS   **1959** Was 10 (RDT)   **1960** Oak-A 1
NFL 11 [2 yrs]

CHUY, DON   Donald John, G, 6´0˝/260 lbs; Clemson; 1963: LA, rnd 5/Hou, rnd 5; B7/20/1941 Newark, NJ   **1963** LARm 14 (RG)   **1964** LARm 12 (RG)   **1965** LARm 11 (LG)
1966 LARm 9   **1967**†LARm 14 (4)   **1968** LARm 14   **1969** Phi 8 (rg)   **NFL** 82 (4) [7 yrs]

CIBULAS, JOE   Joseph James, T, 6´0˝/220 lbs; Duquesne; 1943: Pit, rnd 25; B5/31/1921 Whitney, PA, D5/15/1998 Pittsburgh, PA   **1945** Pit 5 (0)

CICCOLELLA, MIKE   Michael Eugene, LB, 6´0˝/225 lbs; Dayton; 1965: NYG, rnd 18/SD, rnd R12; B10/19/1943 Follansbee, WV   **1966** NYG 14 (MLB)   **1967** NYG 7   **1968** NYG 14
NFL 35 [3 yrs]

CICCONE, BEN   Benjamin M., C, 5´10˝/197 lbs; Duquesne; B10/10/1909 New Castle, PA, D7/7/1990 New Castle, PA   **1935** Pit 12 (6, C)   **1942** ChiC 2 (0)

| 1934 | Pit | 11(0) | 1 | -5 | -5.0(-5) | 0 | — | — | — | — | — | — | — | — | — | — | — | — | — | — | — | — | 0 | -5 |
| NFL | 3 | 25(6) | 1 | -5 | -5.0(-5) | 0 | — | — | — | — | — | — | — | — | — | — | — | — | — | — | — | — | 0 | -5 |

CICHOWSKI, CHICK   Eugene Walker, DB, 6´0˝/195 lbs; Indiana; 1957: Pit, rnd 21; B5/20/1934 Chicago, IL   **1958** Was 1   **1959** Was 1   **1957** Pit 12   **NFL** 14 [3 yrs]

CICHOWSKI, TOM   Thomas John, T, 6´4˝/250 lbs; Maryland; 1966: Oak, rnd R2/GB, rnd 2; B6/13/1944 New Britain, CT   **1967** Den-A 11 (RT)   **1968** Den-A 2   **NFL** 13 [2 yrs]

CIESLAK, BRAD   Brad, TE, 6´3˝/262 lbs; Northern Illinois; B7/1/1982 Long Grove, IL   **2005** Buf 2 (0)

CIFELLI, GUS   August Blaze, T, 6´4˝/244 lbs; Notre Dame; 1950: Det, rnd 19; B2/3/1926 Philadelphia, PA   **1950** Det 12 (RT)   **1951** Det 12 (RT)   **1952**†Det 12 (RT)
1953 GB 12 (RT)   **1954** Phi 7   **NFL** 60 [5 yrs]

CIFERS, BOB   Robert Gale, HB, 5´11˝/201 lbs; Tennessee; 1944: Det, rnd 2; B9/5/1920 Church Hill, TN, D7/1/2001 Nashville, TN

1946	Det	11(2)	8	18	2.3(6)	0	4	178	44.5(70)	4	6	2	33.3	24	4.0(26)	0	1	—	—	Pp	—	24	97
1947	†Pit	10(4)	87	356	4.1(41)	0	3	58	19.3(37)	0	3	2	66.7	28	9.3(22)	0	0	—	—	Pki	—	0	426
1948	Pit	12(7, HB)	112	361	3.2(21)	1	4	55	13.8(29)	0	4	0	0.0	0	0.0(0)	0	1	—	—	Pkp	—	6	472
1949	GB	9(1)	23	52	2.3(19)	0	1	5	5.0(5)	0	—	—	—	—	—	—	—	—	—	P	—	0	55
NFL	4	42(14)	230	787	3.4(41)	1	12	296	24.7(70)	4	13	4	30.8	52	4.0(26)	0	2	—	—	Pkpi	—	30	1049

CIFERS, ED   Edward C., E, 6´2˝/227 lbs; Tennessee; 1941: Was, rnd 6; B7/18/1916 Church Hill, TN, D7/19/2005 Knoxville, TN

1941	Was	11(9, RE)	—	—	—	—	10	94	9.4(19)	1	—	—	—	—	—	—	—	—	—	—	—	—	6	52
1942	†Was★	11(9, RE)	—	—	—	—	18	196	10.9(19)	1	—	—	—	—	—	—	—	—	—	—	k	2	18	73
1946	Was	11(8, RE)	—	—	—	—	6	61	10.2(14)	0	—	—	—	—	—	—	—	—	—	—	—	—	0	31
1947	ChiB	11(3)	—	—	—	—	3	48	16.0(22)	1	—	—	—	—	—	—	—	—	—	—	ki	1	12	57
1948	ChiB☆	12(6, RE)	1	5	5.0(5)	0	—	—	—	—	—	—	—	—	—	—	—	—	—	—	—	—	0	5
NFL	5	56(35)	1	5	5.0(5)	0	37	399	10.8(22)	3	—	—	—	—	—	—	—	—	—	—	ki	3	36	218

CINDRICH, RALPH   Ralph Edward, LB, 6´1˝/228 lbs; Pittsburgh; 1972: Atl, rnd 5; B10/29/1949 Washington, PA   **1972** NE 12 (3)   **1973** Hou 13 (llb)   **1974** Hou 6   **1974** Den 1
1975 Hou 4   **NFL** 36 (3) [4 yrs]

YEAR	TEAM	G (GS, POS)	RUSH	YD	AVG(LG)	TD	REC	YD	AVG(LG)	TD	PASS COMP	PCT	YD	AVG(LG)	TD	INT	SK	YD	QBR	KPR	OTD	PTS	TAY

CIPA, LARRY   Lawrence Andre, QB, 6´3˝/209 lbs; Michigan; 1974: NO, rnd 15; B10/5/1951 Detroit, MI

1974	NO	4	12	35	2.9(15)	1	—	—	—	—	55	20	36.4	242	4.4(30)	0	0	4	36	—	—	—	6	166
1975	NO	4	6	2	0.3(3)	0	—	—	—	—	37	14	37.8	182	4.9(28)	1	3	3	14	—	—	—	0	-22
NFL	2	8	18	37	2.1(15)	1	—	—	—	—	92	34	37.0	424	4.6(30)	1	3	7	50	—	—	—	6	144

CISOWSKI, STEVE   Steven James, T, 6´5˝/275 lbs; Santa Clara; 1986: NYG, rnd 8; B1/16/1963 Campbell, CA   **1987** Dal 3 (3)

CIURCIU, VINNY   Vincenzo, LB, 5´11˝/235 lbs; Boston College; B5/2/1980 Hackensack, NJ   **2003** TB 8 (0)   **2003**†Car 2 (0)   **2004** Car 16 (4)   **2005**†Car 15 (1)   **NFL** 41 (5) [3 yrs]

CIVILETTO, FRANK   Frank Jerry, WB, 5´9˝/180 lbs; Case Western Reserve; Springfield; B9/11/1900 Buffalo, NY, D2/9/1970 Cleveland Heights, OH   **1923** Cle 4 (3)

CLABO, NEIL   William Neil, P, 6´2˝/200 lbs; Tennessee; 1975: Min, rnd 10; B11/18/1952 Miami Beach, FL   **1975**†Min☆14   **1976**†Min 13   **1977**†Min 14   **NFL** 41 [3 yrs]

CLACK, DARRYL   Darryl Earl, RB, 5´10˝/219 lbs; Arizona State; 1986: Dal, rnd 2; B10/29/1963 San Antonio, TX [R]

1986	Dal	16(0)	4	19	4.8(8)	0	1	18	18.0(18)	0	—	—	—	—	—	—	—	—	—	—	k	—	0	164
1987	Dal	12(0)	—	—	—	—	—	—	—	—	—	—	—	—	—	—	—	—	—	—	k	—	0	200
1988	Dal	15(0)	11	54	4.9(17)	0	17	126	7.4(18)	1	—	—	—	—	—	—	—	—	—	—	k	—	6	332
1989	Dal	8(1)	14	40	2.9(17)	2	4	69	17.3(44)	0	—	—	—	—	—	—	—	—	—	—	k	—	12	106
NFL	4	51(1)	29	113	3.9(17)	2	22	213	9.7(44)	1	—	—	—	—	—	—	—	—	—	—	k	—	18	802

CLACK, JIM   James Thomas, C-G, 6´3˝/250 lbs; Wake Forest; B10/26/1947 Rocky Mount, NC, D4/7/2006 Greensboro, NC   **1971** Pit 14 (c)   **1972**†Pit 14   **1973**†Pit 12 (c)   **1974**†Pit 13 (lg)   **1975**†Pit 14 (14, LG)   **1976**†Pit 11 (RG)   **1977**†Pit 14 (14, RG)   **1978** NYG☆16 (16, C)   **1979** NYG☆16 (16, C)   **1980** NYG 16 (16, C)   **1981**†NYG 6 (6, c)   **NFL** 146 (82) [11 yrs]

CLAGO, WALT   Walter, E, 6´0˝/195 lbs; Detroit Mercy; B6/1899 Detroit, MI, deceased   **1921** Det 6 (6, LE)   **1922** RI 7 (5, RE)   **NFL** 13 (11) [2 yrs]

CLAIBORNE, CHRIS   Chris, LB, 6´3˝/259 lbs; USC; 1999: Det, rnd 1; B7/26/1978 Oceanside, CA   **1999**†Det 15 (13, RLB)   **2000** Det 16 (14, RLB)   **2001** Det 16 (16, MLB)   **2002** Det 16 (15, MLB)   **2003** Min 12 (12, RLB)   **2004**†Min 12 (12, MLB)   **2005** SL 14 (7, MLB)   **NFL** 101 (89) [7 yrs]

CLAIBORNE, ROBERT   Robert Cardell, WR, 5´10˝/175 lbs; San Diego State; 1990: Det, rnd 12; B7/10/1967 New Orleans, LA

1992	SD	9(0)	—	—	—	—	1	15	15.0(15)	0	—	—	—	—	—	—	—	—	—	—	—	—	0	8
1993	TB	5(0)	—	—	—	—	5	61	12.2(16)	0	—	—	—	—	—	—	—	—	—	—	kp	—	0	30
NFL	2	14(0)	—	—	—	—	6	76	12.7(16)	0	—	—	—	—	—	—	—	—	—	—	kp	—	0	37

CLAIR, FRANK   Frank James, E, 6´1˝/204 lbs; Ohio State; B5/12/1917 Hamilton, OH

| 1941 | Was | 10(1) | — | — | — | — | 2 | 12 | 6.0(9) | 0 | — | — | — | — | — | — | — | — | — | — | — | — | 0 | 6 |

CLAITT, RICKEY   Rickey, RB, 5´10˝/206 lbs; Bethune-Cookman; B4/12/1957 Sylvester, GA

1980	Was	15(1)	57	215	3.8(16)	1	3	34	11.3(26)	1	—	—	—	—	—	—	—	—	—	—	k	—	12	235
1981	Was	13(0)	3	19	6.3(11)	0	—	—	—	—	—	—	—	—	—	—	—	—	—	—	k	—	0	18
NFL	2	28(1)	60	234	3.9(16)	1	3	34	11.3(26)	1	—	—	—	—	—	—	—	—	—	—	k	—	12	253

CLANCY, JACK   John David, SE-WR, 6´2˝/195 lbs; Michigan; 1966: Mia, rnd R3/SL, rnd 5; B6/18/1944 Humboldt, IA

1967	Mia-A◇	14(9, SE)	3	-4	-1.3(2)	0	67	868	13.0(44)	2	1	1	100.0	17	17.0(17)	0	0	—	—	—	—	—	12	449
1969	Mia-A	8(7, SE)	—	—	—	—	21	289	13.8(50)	1	—	—	—	—	—	—	—	—	—	—	—	—	6	150
1970	GB	14(WR)	—	—	—	—	16	244	15.3(33)	2	—	—	—	—	—	—	—	—	—	—	—	—	12	132
NFL	3	36(16)	3	-4	-1.3(2)	0	104	1401	13.5(50)	5	1	1	100.0	17	17.0(17)	0	0	—	—	—	—	—	30	730

CLANCY, KENDRICK   Lakendrick Tridel, DT, 6´1˝/292 lbs; Mississippi; 2000: Pit, rnd 3; B9/17/1978 Tuscaloosa, AL   **2000** Pit 9 (0)   **2001** Pit 16 (4)   **2002**†Pit 7 (0)   **2003** Pit 12 (0)   **2004**†Pit 8 (0)   **2005**†NYG 16 (15, LDT)   **NFL** 68 (19) [6 yrs]

CLANCY, SAM   Sam, DE-DT, 6´7˝/288 lbs; Pittsburgh; 1982: Sea, rnd 11; B5/29/1958 Pittsburgh, PA   **1983**†Sea 13 (0)   **1985** Cle 14 (0)   **1986**†Cle 16 (1)   **1987** Cle 13 (8, LDE)   **1988**†Cle 16 (12, LDE)   **1989** Ind 16 (0)   **1990** Ind 16 (8, rde)   **1991** Ind 16 (1)   **1992** Ind 16 (9, lde)   **1993** Ind 16 (8, LDT)   **NFL** 152 (47) [10 yrs]

CLANCY, SEAN   Sean Matthew, LB, 6´4˝/218 lbs; Amherst; 1978: Mia, rnd 8; B10/22/1956 Manhasset, NY   **1978**†Mia 16   **1979** SL 10   **NFL** 26 [2 yrs]

CLANCY, STU   Stuart Joseph, B, 5´10˝/189 lbs; Holy Cross; B6/6/1906 Branford, CT, D9/24/1965 Branford, CT

1930	Nwk	2(1)	—	—	—	—	—	—	—	—	—	—	—	—	—	—	—	—	—	—	—	—	—	—
1931	SI	11(4)	—	—	—	—	—	—	—	—	—	—	—	—	—	—	—	—	—	—	—	—	—	—
1932	SI	9(2)	18	25	1.4	0	1	15	15.0(15)	0	13	2	15.4	45	3.5	0	4	—	—	—	—	—	0	-105
1932	NYG	3(0)	36	156	4.3	0	3	43	14.3(40)	1	—	—	—	—	—	—	—	—	—	—	—	—	6	183
1933	†NYG	11(3)	44	136	3.1	2	14	7.0	—	0	3	1	33.3	35	11.7(35)	0	0	—	—	—	—	—	12	181
1934	NYG	9(1)	17	60	3.5	0	—	—	—	—	—	—	—	—	—	—	—	—	—	—	—	—	0	60
1935	NYG	5(0)	13	32	2.5	1	—	—	—	—	—	—	—	—	—	—	—	—	—	—	—	—	6	42
NFL	6	50(11)	128	409	3.2	4	6	72	12.0(40)	1	16	3	18.8	80	5.0(35)	0	4	—	—	—	—	—	30	370

CLANTON, CHUCK   Cleveland Edward, DB, 5´11˝/192 lbs; Auburn; 1984: GB, rnd S2; B7/15/1962 Richmond, VA   **1985** GB 3 (0)

CLAPHAN, SAM   Samuel Jack, T-G, 6´6˝/285 lbs; Oklahoma; 1979: Cle, rnd 2; B10/10/1956 Tahlequah, OK, D11/26/2001 Siloam Springs, AR   **1981**†SD 16 (0)   **1982**†SD 2 (0)   **1983** SD 16 (0)   **1984** SD 16 (16, LT)   **1985** SD 12 (12, RT)   **1986** SD 16 (14, LG)   **1987** SD 9 (4)   **NFL** 87 (46) [7 yrs]

CLARIDGE, DENNIS   Dennis Bert, QB, 6´2˝/220 lbs; Nebraska; 1963: GB, rnd 3/Oak, rnd 26; B8/18/1941 Phoenix, AZ

1965	GB	1	2	-3	-1.5(1)	0	—	—	—	—	1	1	100.0	13	13.0(13)	0	0	—	—	—	—	—	0	4
1966	Atl	7	5	15	3.0(12)	0	—	—	—	—	70	40	57.1	471	6.7(62)	2	9	77	—	—	—	—	0	181
NFL	2	8	7	12	1.7(12)	0	—	—	—	—	71	41	57.7	484	6.8(62)	2	2	9	77	—	—	—	0	184

CLARIDGE, TRAVIS   Travis, G-T, 6´5˝/300 lbs; USC; 2000: Atl, rnd 2; B3/23/1978 Detroit, MI, D2/28/2006 Las Vegas, NV   **2000** Atl 16 (16, RG)   **2001** Atl 14 (11, RG)   **2002**†Atl 16 (16, LG)   **2003** Atl 6 (6, lg)   **NFL** 52 (49) [4 yrs]

CLARK, AL   Al, DB, 6´0˝/185 lbs; Grambling State; Northern Arizona; Eastern Michigan; 1971: Det, rnd 3; B2/29/1948 Bogalusa, LA   **1971** Det 9   **1972** LARm 14 (6, LCB)   **1973**†LARm 14   **1974** LARm 14 (4)   **1975** LARm 4 (4)   **1976** Phi 14 (13, RCB)   **NFL** 69 (27) [6 yrs]

CLARK, ALGY   Myers Arden, B, 5´10˝/190 lbs; Ohio State; B1904, OH [KC]   **1930** Bkn 10 (1)   **1931** Cle 8 (8, BB), 12   **1934** Phi 3 (0)

1932	Bos	9(1)	—	—	—	—	1	25	25.0(25)	0	—	—	—	—	—	—	—	—	—	—	—	1	6	13
1933	Cin	10(7, BB)	6	13	2.2	0	5	82	16.4	0	4	2	50.0	13	3.3	0	1	—	—	—	—	K	—	15	21
1934	Cin	7(6, BB)	1	0	0.0	0	2	18	9.0	0	10	4	40.0	28	2.8	0	2	—	—	—	—	K	—	3	-57
NFL	5	47(23)	7	13	1.9	0	8	125	15.6(25)	0	14	6	42.9	41	2.9	0	3	—	—	—	—	K	1	36	-9

CLARK, ALLAN   Allan Vincent, RB, 5´10˝/186 lbs; Northern Arizona; 1979: NE, rnd 10; B6/8/1957 Grand Rapids, MN   **1982** Buf 1 (0)   **1982**†GB 5 (0)

1979	NE	16	19	84	4.4(19)	0	2	35	17.5(20)	0	—	—	—	—	—	—	—	—	—	—	k	—	12	383
1980	NE	11(0)	9	56	6.2(15)	1	—	—	—	—	—	—	—	—	—	—	—	—	—	—	k	1	12	42
NFL	3	33	28	140	5.0(19)	1	2	35	17.5(20)	0	—	—	—	—	—	—	—	—	—	—	k	1	24	440

CLARK, BABE   Otho, FB-C-T, none; deceased   **1920** Roc 8 (0)

CLARK, BERNARD   Bernard, LB, 6´2˝/248 lbs; Miami (FL); 1990: Cin, rnd 3; B1/12/1967 Tampa, FL   **1990**†Cin 14 (0)   **1991** Sea 2 (0)   **1991** Cin 12 (0)   **NFL** 28 (0) [2 yrs]

CLARK, BERYL   Beryl Leon, B, 5´11˝/170 lbs; Oklahoma; 1940: ChiC, rnd 16; B10/13/1917 Cherokee, OK, D1/15/2000 Cherokee, OK [K]

| 1940 | ChiC | 9(3) | 39 | 9 | 0.2 | 0 | 1 | 20 | 20.0(20) | 0 | 58 | 25 | 43.1 | 316 | 5.4 | 0 | — | — | — | — | KPi | — | 3 | -5 |

CLARK, BILL   William, G-C, 6´1˝/190 lbs; none; deceased   **1920** ChiC 3 (2)

CLARK, BILL   William D., G, 5´11˝/194 lbs; none; B8/12/1891, TN, D1/31/1973 Cleveland, OH   **1920** Day 2 (0)

CLARK, BOOBIE   Charles Lee, RB, 6´2˝/245 lbs; Bethune-Cookman; 1973: Cin, rnd 12; B11/8/1950 Jacksonville, FL, D10/25/1988 Jacksonville, FL

1973	†Cin	14(FB)	254	988	3.9(26)	8	45	347	7.7(39)	0	—	—	—	—	—	—	—	—	—	—	—	—	48	1242
1974	Cin	8(FB)	99	312	3.2(22)	6	23	194	8.4(23)	1	—	—	—	—	—	—	—	—	—	—	—	—	36	464
1975	†Cin	14(FB)	167	594	3.6(17)	4	42	334	8.0(27)	0	—	—	—	—	—	—	—	—	—	—	—	—	24	801
1976	Cin	13(FB)	151	671	4.4(24)	7	23	158	6.9(15)	1	—	—	—	—	—	—	—	—	—	—	—	—	48	825
1977	Cin	10	68	226	3.3(10)	1	7	33	4.7(11)	0	—	—	—	—	—	—	—	—	—	—	—	—	6	253
1978	Cin	14(fb)	40	187	4.7(20)	0	11	73	6.6(26)	0	—	—	—	—	—	—	—	—	—	—	k	—	0	220
1979	†Hou	15	22	51	2.3(7)	0	6	58	9.7(38)	0	—	—	—	—	—	—	—	—	—	—	—	—	0	80

YEAR	TEAM	G(GS, POS)	RUSH	YD	AVG(LG)	TD	REC	YD	AVG(LG)	TD	PASS	COMP	PCT	YD	AVG(LG)	TD	INT	SK	YD	QBR	KPR	OTD	PTS	TAY
1980	†Hou	6(0)	1	3	3.0(3)	0	—	—	—	—	—	—	—	—	—	—	—	—	—	—	—	—	0	3
NFL	8	94	802	3032	3.8(26)	25	157	1197	7.6(39)	2	—	—	—	—	—	—	—	—	—	—	k	—	162	3887

CLARK, BRET Bret, DB, 6´3˝/198 lbs; Nebraska; 1985: LARd, rnd 7; B2/24/1961 Nebraska City, NE **1987** Atl 1 (1) **1988** Atl 12 (11, FS)

YEAR	TEAM	G(GS, POS)	RUSH	YD	AVG(LG)	TD	REC	YD	AVG(LG)	TD	PASS	COMP	PCT	YD	AVG(LG)	TD	INT	SK	YD	QBR	KPR	OTD	PTS	TAY
1986	Atl	16(16, FS)	2	8	4.0(6)	0	—	—	—	—	—	—	—	—	—	—	—	—	—	—	iS	—	0	77
NFL	3	29(28)	2	8	4.0(6)	0	—	—	—	—	—	—	—	—	—	—	—	—	—	—	iS	—	0	97

CLARK, BRIAN Brian Matthew, K, 6´2˝/190 lbs; Florida; 1982: NE, rnd 10; B6/28/1958 Canton, OH **1982** TB 1 (0)

CLARK, BRUCE Bruce, DE-DT, 6´3˝/273 lbs; Penn State; 1980: GB, rnd 1; B3/31/1958 New Castle, PA **1982** NO 9 (9, LDE) **1983** NO 15 (15, LDE) **1984** NO✧15 (15, LDE) **1985** NO 16 (16, LDE) **1986** NO 16 (16, LDE) **1987**†NO☆15 (15, LDE) **1988** NO 16 (2) **1989** KC 11 (0) **NFL** 113 (88) [8 yrs]

CLARK, BRYAN Monte Bryan, QB, 6´2˝/198 lbs; Michigan State; 1982: SF, rnd 9; B7/27/1960 Redwood City, CA **1984** Cin 1 (0)

CLARK, CHARLIE Charles Arthur, G, 5´10˝/205 lbs; Harvard; B2/15/1898 Somerville, MA, D5/31/1960 New York, NY **1924** ChiC 4 (2)

CLARK, DALLAS Dallas Dean, TE, 6´3˝/257 lbs; Iowa; 2003: Ind, rnd 1; B6/12/1979 Livermore, IA

YEAR	TEAM	G(GS, POS)	RUSH	YD	AVG(LG)	TD	REC	YD	AVG(LG)	TD	PASS	COMP	PCT	YD	AVG(LG)	TD	INT	SK	YD	QBR	KPR	OTD	PTS	TAY
2003	†Ind	10(10, TE)	—	—	—	—	29	340	11.7(42)	1	—	—	—	—	—	—	—	—	—	—	—	—	6	175
2004	†Ind	15(13, TE)	—	—	—	—	25	423	16.9(80)	5	—	—	—	—	—	—	—	—	—	—	—	—	30	237
2005	†Ind	15(14, TE)	—	—	—	—	37	488	13.2(56)	4	—	—	—	—	—	—	—	—	—	—	—	—	24	264
NFL	3	40(37)	—	—	—	—	91	1251	13.7(80)	10	—	—	—	—	—	—	—	—	—	—	—	—	60	676

CLARK, DAN Dan Lee, LB, 6´2˝/233 lbs; San Jose State; B5/21/1964 Toma, Japan **1987** LARm 1 (0)

CLARK, DANNY Daniel, LB, 6´2˝/248 lbs; Illinois; 2000: Jax, rnd 7; B5/9/1977 Blue Island, IL **2000** Jax 16 (0) **2001** Jax 13 (3) **2002** Jax 16 (16, LLB) **2003** Jax 16 (9, RLB) **2004** Oak 16 (16, MLB) **2005** Oak 16 (15, RLB) **NFL** 93 (59) [6 yrs]

CLARK, DARIUS Darius, DB, 5´10˝/210 lbs; Duke; B4/13/1977 Tampa, FL **2001** Den 7 (0)

CLARK, DARRYL Darryl Wade, RB, 5´11˝/204 lbs; Texas; B8/9/1961 Houston, TX

YEAR	TEAM	G(GS, POS)	RUSH	YD	AVG(LG)	TD	REC	YD	AVG(LG)	TD	PASS	COMP	PCT	YD	AVG(LG)	TD	INT	SK	YD	QBR	KPR	OTD	PTS	TAY
1987	ChiB	3(0)	5	11	2.2(5)	0	—	—	—	—	—	—	—	—	—	—	—	—	—	—	—	—	0	11

CLARK, DERRICK Derrick, RB, 6´1˝/235 lbs; Florida State; Evangel (MO); B5/4/1971 Apopka, FL

YEAR	TEAM	G(GS, POS)	RUSH	YD	AVG(LG)	TD	REC	YD	AVG(LG)	TD	PASS	COMP	PCT	YD	AVG(LG)	TD	INT	SK	YD	QBR	KPR	OTD	PTS	TAY
1994	Den	16(4)	56	168	3.0(12)	3	9	47	5.2(10)	0	—	—	—	—	—	—	—	—	—	—	k	—	18	211

CLARK, DESMOND Desmond Darice, TE, 6´3˝/255 lbs; Wake Forest; 1999: Den, rnd 6; B4/20/1977 Bartow, FL

YEAR	TEAM	G(GS, POS)	RUSH	YD	AVG(LG)	TD	REC	YD	AVG(LG)	TD	PASS	COMP	PCT	YD	AVG(LG)	TD	INT	SK	YD	QBR	KPR	OTD	PTS	TAY
1999	Den	9(0)	—	—	—	—	1	5	5.0(5)	0	—	—	—	—	—	—	—	—	—	—	—	—	0	3
2000	†Den	16(2)	—	—	—	—	27	339	12.6(44)	3	—	—	—	—	—	—	—	—	—	—	—	—	18	185
2001	Den	16(4)	—	—	—	—	51	566	11.1(39)	6	—	—	—	—	—	—	—	—	—	—	k	—	36	309
2002	Mia	11(0)	—	—	—	—	2	42	21.0(26)	0	—	—	—	—	—	—	—	—	—	—	—	—	0	21
2003	ChiB	15(15, TE)	—	—	—	—	44	433	9.8(31)	2	—	—	—	—	—	—	—	—	—	—	—	—	12	227
2004	ChiB	15(13, TE)	—	—	—	—	24	282	11.8(31)	1	—	—	—	—	—	—	—	—	—	—	—	—	6	146
2005	†ChiB	16(16, TE)	—	—	—	—	24	229	9.5(31)	2	—	—	—	—	—	—	—	—	—	—	—	—	12	125
NFL	7	98(50)	—	—	—	—	173	1896	11.0(44)	14	—	—	—	—	—	—	—	—	—	—	k	—	84	1014

CLARK, DEXTER Dexter Dewayne, DB, 6´0˝/190 lbs; Toledo; B5/5/1964 Dermott, AR **1987** Det 2 (0)

CLARK, DON Donald Rex, G-LB, 5´11˝/197 lbs; USC; B12/22/1923 Shurdan, IA, D8/6/1989 Huntington Beach, CA **1948** SF-A 14 (14, LG) **1949** SF-A 12 (10, LG) **AAFC** 26 (24) [2 yrs]

CLARK, DUTCH Earl Harry, TB-DB, 6´0˝/185 lbs; Colorado College; B10/11/1906 Fowler, CO, D8/5/1978 Canon City, CO; HOF 1963 **[KC]**

YEAR	TEAM	G(GS, POS)	RUSH	YD	AVG(LG)	TD	REC	YD	AVG(LG)	TD	PASS	COMP	PCT	YD	AVG(LG)	TD	INT	SK	YD	QBR	KPR	OTD	PTS	TAY
1931	Por☆	11(7, tb)	—	—	—	—	—	—	—	—	—	—	—	—	—	—	—	—	—	—	—	—	—	—
1932	Por☆	11(9, TB)	137	461	3.4	3	10	107	10.7	3	52	17	32.7	272	5.2	2	8	—	—	—	K	—	**55**	386
1934	Det☆	12(10, TB)	123	763	6.2	**8**	6	72	12.0	0	50	23	46.0	383	7.7	0	3	—	—	—	K	—	73	951
1935	†Det☆	12(6, TB)	120	427	3.6	4	9	124	13.8	2	26	11	42.3	133	5.1	2	4	—	—	—	K	—	**55**	456
1936	Det☆	12(6,.TB)	123	628	5.1	**7**	1	5	5.0(5)	0	71	38	53.5	467	6.6	4	6	—	—	—	K	—	**73**	714
1937	Det☆	11(11, TB)	96	468	4.9	**5**	2	33	16.5(23)	1	39	19	48.7	202	5.2	1	3	—	—	—	K	—	45	526
1938	Det	6(0)	7	25	3.6	0	—	—	—	—	12	6	50.0	50	4.2	1	2	—	—	—	K	—	8	-25
NFL	7	75(49)	606	2772	4.6	36	28	341	12.2(23)	6	250	114	45.6	1507	6.0	11	26	—	—	—	K	—	369	3101

CLARK, DWIGHT Dwight Edward, WR, 6´4˝/212 lbs; Clemson; 1979: SF, rnd 10; B1/8/1957 Kinston, NC

YEAR	TEAM	G(GS, POS)	RUSH	YD	AVG(LG)	TD	REC	YD	AVG(LG)	TD	PASS	COMP	PCT	YD	AVG(LG)	TD	INT	SK	YD	QBR	KPR	OTD	PTS	TAY
1979	SF	16(3)	—	—	—	—	18	232	12.9(30)	0	—	—	—	—	—	—	—	—	—	—	—	—	0	116
1980	SF	16(12, WR)	—	—	—	—	82	991	12.1(71)	8	—	—	—	—	—	—	—	—	—	—	—	—	48	536
1981	†SF★	16(16, WR)	3	32	10.7(18)	0	**85**	1105	13.0(78)	4	1	0	0.0	0	0.0	0	0	—	—	—	—	—	24	605
1982	SF★	9(8, WR)	—	—	—	—	**60**	**913**	15.2(51)	5	—	—	—	—	—	—	—	—	—	—	—	—	30	482
1983	SF	16(13, WR)	3	18	6.0(9)	0	70	840	12.0(46)	8	1	0	0.0	0	0.0	0	0	—	—	—	—	—	48	478
1984	†SF	16(14, WR)	—	—	—	—	52	880	16.9(80)	6	1	0	0.0	0	0.0	0	0	—	—	—	—	—	36	470
1985	†SF	16(14, WR)	—	—	—	—	54	705	13.1(49)	10	—	—	—	—	—	—	—	—	—	—	—	—	60	403
1986	†SF	16(14, WR)	—	—	—	—	61	794	13.0(45)	2	—	—	—	—	—	—	—	—	—	—	—	—	12	407
1987	†SF	13(4)	—	—	—	—	24	290	12.1(40)	5	—	—	—	—	—	—	—	—	—	—	—	—	30	170
NFL	9	134(98)	6	50	8.3(18)	0	506	6750	13.3(80)	48	3	0	0.0	0	0.0	0	0	—	—	—	—	—	288	3665

CLARK, ERNIE Ernest Robert, LB, 6´1˝/220 lbs; Michigan State; 1963: Det, rnd 13; B8/11/1937 Arcadia, FL **1963** Det 14 **1964** Det 14 (LLB) **1965** Det 14 (LLB) **1966** Det 14 (MLB) **1967** Det 12 (LLB) **1968** SL 14 (llb) **NFL** 82 [6 yrs]

CLARK, GAIL Gail Allen, LB, 6´2˝/226 lbs; Michigan State; 1973: Pit, rnd 4; B4/14/1951 Bellefontaine, OH **1973** ChiB 11 **1974** NE 8 **NFL** 19 [2 yrs]

CLARK, GARY Gary C., WR, 5´9˝/173 lbs; James Madison; 1984: Was, rnd S2; B5/1/1962 Radford, VA

YEAR	TEAM	G(GS, POS)	RUSH	YD	AVG(LG)	TD	REC	YD	AVG(LG)	TD	PASS	COMP	PCT	YD	AVG(LG)	TD	INT	SK	YD	QBR	KPR	OTD	PTS	TAY
1985	Was	16(10, WR)	2	10	5.0(7)	0	72	926	12.9(55)	5	—	—	—	—	—	—	—	—	—	—	p	—	30	498
1986	†Was★	15(15, WR)	—	—	—	—	74	1265	17.1(55)	7	—	—	—	—	—	—	—	—	—	—	p	—	42	677
1987	†Was★	12(11, WR)	1	0	0.0(0)	0	56	1066	19.0(84)	7	—	—	—	—	—	—	—	—	—	—	—	—	42	568
1988	Was	16(13, WR)	2	6	3.0(4)	0	59	892	15.1(60)	7	—	—	—	—	—	—	—	—	—	—	p	—	42	495
1989	Was	15(12, WR)	2	19	9.5(11)	0	79	1229	15.6(80)	9	—	—	—	—	—	—	—	—	—	—	—	—	54	679
1990	†Was★	16(16, WR)	1	1	1.0(1)	0	75	1112	14.8(53)	8	—	—	—	—	—	—	—	—	—	—	—	—	48	597
1991	†Was★	16(16, WR)	1	0	0.0(0)	0	70	1340	19.1(82)	10	—	—	—	—	—	—	—	—	—	—	—	—	60	720
1992	†Was	16(14, WR)	2	18	9.0(12)	0	64	912	14.3(47)	5	—	—	—	—	—	—	—	—	—	—	—	—	30	499
1993	Phx	14(10, WR)	—	—	—	—	63	818	13.0(55)	4	—	—	—	—	—	—	—	—	—	—	—	—	24	429
1994	Arz	15(2)	—	—	—	—	50	771	15.4(45)	1	—	—	—	—	—	—	—	—	—	—	—	—	6	391
1995	†Mia	16(0)	—	—	—	—	37	525	14.2(42)	2	—	—	—	—	—	—	—	—	—	—	—	—	12	273
NFL	11	167(119)	11	54	4.9(12)	0	699	10856	15.5(84)	65	—	—	—	—	—	—	—	—	—	—	p	—	390	5824

CLARK, GREG Gregory Klondike, LB, 6´0˝/228 lbs; Arizona State; 1988: Chi, rnd 12; B3/5/1965 Los Angeles, CA **1988**†ChiB 15 (0) **1989** Mia 16 (4) **1990** LARm 11 (0) **1991** GB 2 (0) **1991** SD 14 (0) **1992** Sea 12 (0) **NFL** 70 (4) [5 yrs]

CLARK, GREG Gregory Jay, TE, 6´4˝/251 lbs; Stanford; 1997: SF, rnd 3; B4/7/1972 Bountiful, UT

YEAR	TEAM	G(GS, POS)	RUSH	YD	AVG(LG)	TD	REC	YD	AVG(LG)	TD	PASS	COMP	PCT	YD	AVG(LG)	TD	INT	SK	YD	QBR	KPR	OTD	PTS	TAY
1997	†SF	15(4)	—	—	—	—	8	96	12.0(23)	1	—	—	—	—	—	—	—	—	—	—	—	—	6	53
1998	†SF	13(8, TE)	—	—	—	—	12	124	10.3(23)	1	—	—	—	—	—	—	—	—	—	—	—	—	8	67
1999	SF	12(11, TE)	—	—	—	—	34	347	10.2(24)	0	—	—	—	—	—	—	—	—	—	—	—	—	0	174
2000	SF	15(15, TE)	—	—	—	—	38	342	9.0(34)	2	—	—	—	—	—	—	—	—	—	—	—	—	12	181
NFL	4	55(38)	—	—	—	—	92	909	9.9(34)	4	—	—	—	—	—	—	—	—	—	—	—	—	26	475

CLARK, HAL Harold E., E-B, 5´10˝/195 lbs; none; B10/25/1893, NY, D7/9/1973 Rochester, NY **1920** Roc 8 (1, RE) **1922** Roc 3 (1) **1923** Roc 4 (3, RE), 6 **1924** Roc 7 (5, RE) **1925** Roc 5 (2) **NFL** 27 (12) [5 yrs]

CLARK, HERMAN Herman Pikea, G-MG-LB, 6´3˝/256 lbs; Oregon State; 1952: ChiB, rnd 4; B11/30/1930 Honolulu, HI, D11/9/1989 Molokai, HI **1952** ChiB 12 (MG) **1954** ChiB 5 **1955** ChiB☆11 (LG) **1956**†ChiB☆12 (LG) **1957** ChiB 12 (LG) **NFL** 52 [5 yrs]

YEAR	TEAM	G(GS, POS)	RUSH	YD	AVG(LG)	TD	REC	YD	AVG(LG)	TD	PASS COMP	PCT	YD	AVG(LG)	TD	INT	SK	YD	QBR	KPR	OTD	PTS	TAY

CLARK, HOWARD   Howard Morris, TE, 6'2"/215 lbs; Tennessee-Chattanooga; B8/23/1935 Dalton, GA

YEAR	TEAM	G(GS, POS)	REC	YD	AVG(LG)	TD	PTS	TAY
1960	†LAC-A☆	13(TE)	27	431	16.0(50)	0	0	216
1961	SD-A	10(TE)	11	182	16.5(33)	0	0	91
NFL	2	23	38	613	16.1(50)	0	0	307

CLARK, JAMES   James A., B, 5'9"/170 lbs; Pittsburgh; B1909, deceased

YEAR	TEAM	G(GS, POS)	RUSH	YD	AVG	TD	REC	YD	AVG(LG)	TD	PASS	COMP	PCT	YD	AVG	TD	PTS	TAY
1933	Pit	10(5, HB)	76	192	2.5	0											0	192
1934	Pit	9(3)	31	84	2.7	0	1	28	28.0(28)	1	1	0	0.0	0	0.0	0	6	103
NFL	2	19(8)	107	276	2.6	0	1	28	28.0(28)	1	1	0	0.0	0	0.0	0	6	295

CLARK, JESSIE   Jessie Lee, RB, 6'0"/231 lbs; Arkansas; Louisiana Tech; 1983: GB, rnd 7; B1/3/1960 Thebes, AR

YEAR	TEAM	G(GS, POS)	RUSH	YD	AVG(LG)	TD	REC	YD	AVG(LG)	TD	KPR	PTS	TAY
1983	GB	16(0)	71	328	4.6(42)	0	18	279	15.5(75)	0		6	473
1984	GB	11(10, FB)	87	375	4.3(43)	4	29	234	8.1(20)	2		36	542
1985	GB	16(14, FB)	147	633	4.3(80)	5	24	252	10.5(55)	2		42	819
1986	GB	5(1)	18	41	2.3(9)	0	6	41	6.8(12)	0		0	62
1987	GB	12(10, FB)	56	211	3.8(57)	0	22	119	5.4(19)	0		6	276
1988	Det	5(0)											
1988	Phx	4(0)									k	0	-20
1989	Phx	11(0)	10	42	4.2(9)	0					k	0	27
1989	Min	3(0)	10	57	5.7(14)	0	2	14	7.0(12)	0	k	0	55
1990	Min	5(3)	16	49	3.1(11)	0	1	4	4.0(4)	0	k	0	51
NFL	8	88(38)	415	1736	4.2(80)	9	102	943	9.2(75)	6	k	90	2284

CLARK, JIM   James Kalaeone, T-G-DT-LB, 6'1"/230 lbs; Oregon State; 1952: Was, rnd 5; B7/18/1929 Honolulu, HI   **1952** Was 12   **1953** Was 12 (RT)   **NFL** 24 [2 yrs]

CLARK, JON   Jon, T, 6'6"/345 lbs; Temple; 1996: Chi, rnd 6; B4/11/1973 Philadelphia, PA   **1996** ChiB 1 (0)   **1997** ChiB 1 (0)   **1998**†Arz 6 (0)   **1999** Arz 2 (0)   **NFL** 10 (0) [4 yrs]

CLARK, KELVIN   Kelvin Wayne, T-G, 6'3"/260 lbs; Nebraska; 1979: Den, rnd 1; B1/30/1956 Odessa, TX   **1979**†Den 15   **1980** Den 14 (5, rt)   **1981** Den 16 (5)   **1982** NO 9 (0)   **1983** NO 16 (0)   **1984** NO 16 (15, LT/rg)   **1985** NO 2 (2)   **NFL** 88 (25) [7 yrs]

CLARK, KEN   Kenneth Lawrence, P, 6'2"/197 lbs; St. Mary's (Canada); B5/26/1948 Southampton, England

YEAR	TEAM	G(GS, POS)	RUSH	YD	AVG(LG)	PASS	COMP	PCT	YD	AVG(LG)	TD	INT	QBR	PTS	TAY
1979	†LARm	16	1	3	3.0(3)	2	2	100.0	32	16.0(30)	0	0	P	0	19

CLARK, KEN   Kenneth R., TE-RB, 5'9"/201 lbs; Nebraska; 1990: Ind, rnd 8; B6/11/1966 Evergreen, AL

YEAR	TEAM	G(GS, POS)	RUSH	YD	AVG(LG)	TD	REC	YD	AVG(LG)	TD	KPR	PTS	TAY
1990	Ind	5(3)	7	10	1.4(11)	0	5	23	4.6(11)	0		0	22
1991	Ind	16(7, TE)	114	366	3.2(25)	0	33	245	7.4(23)	0		0	489
1992	Ind	13(2)	40	134	3.3(13)	0	5	46	9.2(17)	0	k	0	166
NFL	3	34(12)	161	510	3.2(25)	0	43	314	7.3(23)	0	k	0	676

CLARK, KENNY   Kenny, WR, 6'1"/217 lbs; Central Florida; B5/14/1978 Gainesville, FL   **2003** Min 1 (0)

CLARK, KEVIN   Kevin Randall, DB, 5'10"/185 lbs; San Jose State; B6/8/1964 Sacramento, CA   **1987**†Den 11 (3)   **1988** Den 3 (0)   **1990** Den 8 (0)   **1991** Den 4 (0)   **NFL** 26 (3) [4 yrs]

CLARK, LEROY   Leroy Darnell, P, 5'11"/202 lbs; Prairie View A&M; B1/16/1950 College Station, TX   **1976** Hou 1

CLARK, LOUIS   Louis Steven, WR, 6'0"/193 lbs; Mississippi State; 1987: Sea, rnd 10; B7/3/1964 Shannon, MS

YEAR	TEAM	G(GS, POS)	REC	YD	AVG(LG)	TD	KPR	PTS	TAY
1987	Sea	2(0)							
1988	†Sea	7(0)	1	20	20.0(20)	1		6	15
1989	Sea	16(6, wr)	25	260	10.4(28)	1	k	6	151
1990	Sea	4(0)							
1991	Sea	16(0)	21	228	10.9(24)	2		12	124
1992	Sea	10(10, WR)	20	290	14.5(33)	1		6	150
NFL	6	55(16)	67	798	11.9(33)	6	k	30	440

CLARK, MARIO   Mario Sean, DB, 6'2"/194 lbs; Oregon; 1976: Buf, rnd 1; B3/29/1954 Pasadena, CA [I]   **1976** Buf 14 (14, LCB)   **1977** Buf 14 (13, LCB)   **1978** Buf 16 (16, LCB)   **1979** Buf 16 (16, LCB)   **1980**†Buf 16 (15, LCB)   **1981**†Buf☆16 (16, LCB)   **1982** Buf 9 (9, LCB)   **1983** Buf 14 (14, LCB)   **1984** SF 11 (6, lcb)   **NFL** 126 (119) [9 yrs]

CLARK, MIKE   Michael Vincent, K, 6'1"/205 lbs; Texas A&M; B11/7/1940 Marshall, TX; D7/24/2002 Dallas, TX [K]   **1963** Phi 14   **1964** Pit 14   **1965** Pit 14   **1966** Pit◇14   **1968**†Dal 14   **1969**†Dal 14   **1970**†Dal 14   **1971**†Dal 12   **1973** Dal 4

YEAR	TEAM	G(GS, POS)	PASS	COMP	PCT	YD	AVG	TD	INT	KPR	PTS	TAY
1967	Pit	14	1	0	0.0	0	0.0	0	0	K	71	0
NFL	10	128	1	0	0.0	0	0.0	0	0	K	724	0

CLARK, MIKE   Michael Hugh, DE, 6'4"/253 lbs; Florida; 1981: LA, rnd 7; B3/30/1959 Dothan, AL   **1981** Was 5 (0)   **1982** SF 6 (0)   **1987** TB 3 (3)   **NFL** 14 (3) [3 yrs]

CLARK, MONTE   Monte Dale, T-DT-DE, 6'6"/265 lbs; USC; 1959: SF, rnd 4; B1/24/1937 Fillmore, CA [C]   **1959** SF 12 (RDT)   **1960** SF 12 (7, RDT/lde)   **1961** SF 12 (8, RDT)   **1962** Dal 14 (10, RT)   **1963** Cle 8   **1964**†Cle 14 (RT)   **1965**†Cle 14 (14, RT)   **1966** Cle 12 (RT/lt)   **1967**†Cle 13 (RT)   **1968**†Cle 14 (RT)   **1969**†Cle 14 (RT)   **NFL** 139 (39) [11 yrs]

CLARK, PHIL   Philip Eugene, DB, 6'3"/208 lbs; Northwestern; 1967: Dal, rnd 3; B4/28/1945 Burlington, KY   **1967**†Dal 11   **1968**†Dal 12   **1969**†Dal 14 (RCB)   **1970** ChiB 13 (SS)   **1971** NE 2   **NFL** 52 [5 yrs]

CLARK, POTS   Alfred F., HB, 5'7"/180 lbs; UNLV; B12/11/1900, D9/18/1973 Ontario, CA   **1927** Fra 1 (0)   **1927** Dul 6 (4)   **NFL** 7 (4) [1 yr]

CLARK, RANDY   Randall Byron, C-T-G, 6'3"/260 lbs; Northern Illinois; 1980: Chi, rnd 8; B7/27/1957 Chicago, IL   **1980** SL 8 (0)   **1981** SL 16 (0)   **1982**†SL 9 (0)   **1983** SL 14 (13, C)   **1984** SL☆16 (16, C)   **1985** SL 16 (16, C)   **1986** SL 12 (10, C)   **1987** Atl 3 (3)   **NFL** 94 (58) [8 yrs]

CLARK, RANDY   Randall Charles, DB, 6'0"/195 lbs; Florida; 1984: KC, rnd 8; B2/18/1962 Marshall, MI   **1984** TB 2 (0)

CLARK, REGGIE   Reggie Boice, LB, 6'2"/238 lbs; North Carolina; B10/17/1967 Charlotte, NC   **1994** Pit 5 (0)   **1995** Jax 5 (0)   **1996** Jax 5 (0)   **NFL** 15 (0) [3 yrs]

CLARK, RICO   Rico Cornell, DB, 5'10"/181 lbs; Louisville; B6/6/1974 Atlanta, GA   **1997** Ind 4 (2)   **1998** Ind 16 (0)   **1999** Cin 8 (1)   **1999** NE 1 (0)   **NFL** 29 (3) [3 yrs]

CLARK, ROBERT   Robert James, WR, 5'11"/175 lbs; North Carolina Central; 1987: NO, rnd 10; B8/6/1965 Brooklyn, NY

YEAR	TEAM	G(GS, POS)	REC	YD	AVG(LG)	TD	KPR	PTS	TAY
1987	NO	2(0)	3	38	12.7(14)	0		0	19
1988	NO	16(0)	19	245	12.9(21)	2		12	133
1989	Det	16(16, WR)	41	748	18.2(69)	2		12	384
1990	Det	16(15, WR)	52	914	17.6(57)	8		48	497
1991	†Det	14(14, WR)	47	640	13.6(68)	6	k	36	335
1992	Mia	3(0)	3	59	19.7(45)	0		0	30
NFL	6	67(45)	165	2644	16.0(69)	18	k	108	1397

CLARK, RYAN   Ryan Terry, DB, 5'11"/200 lbs; LSU; B10/12/1979 Marrero, LA   **2002** NYG 6 (0)   **2003** NYG 16 (4)   **2004** Was 15 (11, SS)   **2005**†Was 13 (13, SS)   **NFL** 50 (28) [4 yrs]

CLARK, SEDRIC   Sedric C., LB, 6'2"/245 lbs; Tulsa; 1996: Oak, rnd 7; B1/28/1973 Missouri City, TX   **1996** Bal 6 (0)

CLARK, SPARK   Michael Keith, RB, 5'7"/182 lbs; Akron; B5/22/1965 Jackson, MS   **1987** Pit 1 (0)

CLARK, STEVE   Steven, DB, 6'2"/190 lbs; Liberty; B12/14/1962 Arlington, VA   **1987** Buf 3 (1)

CLARK, STEVE   Steven Dion, DE, 6'5"/258 lbs; Kansas State; 1981: NE, rnd 5; B10/29/1959 Chattanooga, TN   **1981** NE 7 (0)

CLARK, STEVE   Stephen Spence, G-NT, 6'4"/255 lbs; Utah; 1982: Mia, rnd 9; B8/2/1960 Salt Lake City, UT   **1982** Mia 2 (0)   **1983** Mia 11 (0)   **1984**†Mia 12 (0)   **1985**†Mia 16 (5, rg)   **NFL** 41 (5) [4 yrs]

CLARK, TORIN   Torin, DB, 6'1"/175 lbs; West Virginia State; B12/31/1963   **1987** TB 2 (2)

CLARK, VINNIE   Vincent Eugene, DB, 6'0"/202 lbs; Ohio State; 1991: GB, rnd 1; B1/22/1969 Cincinnati, OH   **1991** GB 16 (4)   **1992** GB 16 (11, RCB)   **1993** Atl 15 (9, rcb)   **1994** Atl 11 (11, LCB)   **1994** NO 5 (4)   **1995** Jax 16 (16, LCB)   **1996** Jax 4 (4)   **NFL** 83 (59) [6 yrs]

CLARK, WAYNE   Wayne Joseph, E, 6'3"/210 lbs; Utah; B4/13/1918 Los Angeles, CA, deceased

YEAR	TEAM	G(GS, POS)	REC	YD	AVG(LG)	TD	PTS	TAY
1944	Det	8(0)	2	27	13.5(19)	0	0	14

Clark, Wayne Wayne Maurice, QB, 6´2˝/203 lbs; U.S. International; 1970: SD, rnd 8; B5/30/1947 Oskaloosa, IA

YEAR	TEAM	G (GS, POS)	RUSH	YD	AVG (LG)	TD	REC	YD	AVG (LG)	TD	PASS	COMP	PCT	YD	AVG (LG)	TD	INT	SK	YD	QBR	KPR	OTD	PTS	TAY
1970	SD	1	—	—	—	—	—	—	—	—	2	1	50.0	48	24.0(48)	0	0	—	—	—	—	—	0	24
1972	SD	13	2	-8	-4.0(3)	0	—	—	—	—	6	2	33.3	67	11.2(62)	0	2	2	9	—	—	—	0	-55
1973	SD	11(4)	13	86	6.6(16)	0	—	—	—	—	90	40	44.4	532	5.9(54)	0	9	9	96	—	—	—	0	-8
1974	Cin	14	1	8	8.0(8)	1	—	—	—	—	22	9	40.9	98	4.5(19)	0	3	1	1	—	—	—	6	-53
1975	KC	1	—	—	—	—	—	—	—	—	—	—	—	—	—	—	—	—	—	—	—	—	0	0
NFL	5	40(4)	16	86	5.4(16)	1	—	—	—	—	120	52	43.3	745	6.2(62)	0	14	12	106	—	—	—	6	-92

Clark, Willie Willie Calvin, DB, 5´10˝/186 lbs; Notre Dame; 1994: SD, rnd 3; B1/6/1972 New Haven, CT **1994**†SD 6 (0) **1995**†SD 16 (2) **1996** SD 16 (4) **1997** Phi 16 (2) **1998** SD 5 (0) **NFL** 59 (8) [5 yrs]

Clarke, Adrien Adrien, G, 6´5˝/330 lbs; Ohio State; 2004: Phi, rnd 7; B3/26/1981 Shaker Heights, OH **2005** Phi 13 (4)

Clarke, Frank Frank Delano, E, 6´1˝/215 lbs; Colorado; 1956: Cle, rnd 5; B2/7/1934 Beloit, WI

YEAR	TEAM	G (GS, POS)	RUSH	YD	AVG (LG)	TD	REC	YD	AVG (LG)	TD	PASS	COMP	PCT	YD	AVG (LG)	TD	INT	SK	YD	QBR	KPR	OTD	PTS	TAY
1957	†Cle	12	—	—	—	—	4	77	19.3(43)	0	—	—	—	—	—	—	—	—	—	—	k	—	0	31
1958	†Cle	12	—	—	—	—	3	91	30.3(34)	0	—	—	—	—	—	—	—	—	—	—	—	—	0	46
1959	Cle	12	—	—	—	—	3	44	14.7(20)	0	—	—	—	—	—	—	—	—	—	—	—	—	0	22
1960	Dal	8	1	-6	-6.0(-6)	0	9	290	32.2(76)	3	—	—	—	—	—	—	—	—	—	—	—	—	18	154
1961	Dal	14(FL)	—	—	—	—	41	919	**22.4**(**80**)	9	—	—	—	—	—	—	—	—	—	—	—	—	54	505
1962	Dal	12(FL)	—	—	—	—	47	1043	**22.2**(**66**)	**14**	—	—	—	—	—	—	—	—	—	—	—	—	84	592
1963	Dal	14(FL)	1	12	12.0(12)	0	43	833	19.4(75)	10	—	—	—	—	—	—	—	—	—	—	—	—	60	479
1964	Dal☆	14(FL)	10	46	4.6(21)	0	65	973	15.0(49)	5	1	0	0.0	0	0.0	0	0	—	—	—	—	—	30	558
1965	Dal	14(TE)	8	58	7.3(21)	0	41	682	16.6(53)	4	—	—	—	—	—	—	—	—	—	—	—	—	24	419
1966	†Dal	14	8	49	6.1(26)	0	26	355	13.7(33)	4	—	—	—	—	—	—	—	—	—	—	—	—	24	247
1967	†Dal	14	4	72	18.0(56)	1	9	119	13.2(23)	1	—	—	—	—	—	—	—	—	—	—	—	—	12	147
NFL	11	140	32	231	7.2(56)	1	291	5426	18.6(80)	50	1	0	0.0	0	0.0	0	0	—	—	—	k	—	306	3196

Clarke, Fred Fred, E, none; deceased **1920** Roc 1 (0)

Clarke, Hagood Hagood, DB, 6´0˝/205 lbs; Florida; 1964: Buf, rnd 18/SF, rnd 7; B6/14/1942 Atlanta, GA **1964**†Buf-A 14 (ls) **1965**†Buf-A✧14 (LS) **1966**†Buf-A☆14 (LS) **1967** Buf-A 11 (4) **1968** Buf-A 14 **NFL** 67 (4) [5 yrs]

Clarke, Harry Harry Charles, HB-DB, 6´0˝/186 lbs; West Virginia; 1940: ChiB, rnd 13; B12/1/1916 Cumberland, MD, D12/31/2005 Morgantown, WV **[K]**

YEAR	TEAM	G (GS, POS)	RUSH	YD	AVG (LG)	TD	REC	YD	AVG (LG)	TD	PASS	COMP	PCT	YD	AVG (LG)	TD	INT	SK	YD	QBR	KPR	OTD	PTS	TAY
1940	†ChiB✧	11(0)	56	258	4.6	2	3	80	26.7	0	3	0	0.0	0	0.0	0	2	—	—	—	Pi	1	18	290
1941	†ChiB✧	10(3)	28	122	4.4(15)	0	2	61	30.5(38)	0	—	—	—	—	—	—	—	—	—	—	Kkpi	—	1	324
1942	†ChiB	10(7, LH)	58	273	4.7(26)	4	6	131	21.8(49)	2	—	—	—	—	—	—	—	—	—	—	kp	—	36	524
1943	†ChiB☆	10(10, LH)	120	556	4.6(20)	2	23	535	**23.3**(**52**)	7	1	0	0.0	0	0.0	0	1	—	—	—	kpi	1	60	**1085**
NFL	4	41(20)	262	1209	4.6(26)	8	34	807	23.7(52)	9	4	0	0.0	0	0.0	0	3	—	—	—	KPkpi	2	115	2222
1946	LAD-A	14(2)	62	250	4.0	0	10	123	12.3(71)	2	—	—	—	—	—	—	—	—	—	—	kpi	—	12	351
1947	LAD-A	12(3)	44	173	3.9	2	3	54	18.0	0	—	—	—	—	—	—	—	—	—	—	kp	—	12	348
1948	LAD-A	2(2)	6	22	3.7	0	3	19	6.3	0	—	—	—	—	—	—	—	—	—	—	kp	—	0	45
1948	ChiR-A	5(2)	16	57	3.6	0	1	19	19.0(19)	0	—	—	—	—	—	—	—	—	—	—	kp	—	0	107
AAFC	3	33(9)	128	502	3.9(26)	2	17	215	12.6(71)	2	—	—	—	—	—	—	—	—	—	—	kpi	—	24	850

Clarke, Ken Kenneth Maurice, NT-DT, 6´2˝/268 lbs; Syracuse; B8/28/1956 Savannah, GA **1978**†Phi 16 **1979**†Phi 16 **1980**†Phi 16 (0) **1981**†Phi 16 (0) **1982** Phi 9 (9, NT) **1983** Phi 16 (16, NT) **1984** Phi 16 (16, NT) **1985** Phi 16 (16, NT) **1986** Phi 16 (16, LDT) **1987** Phi 11 (10, LDT) **1988**†Sea 16 (1) **1989**†Min 11 (0) **1990** Min 12 (10, RDT) **1991** Min 16 (16, LDT) **NFL** 203 (110) [14 yrs]

Clarke, Leon Leon T., E-FL, 6´4˝/232 lbs; USC; 1956: LA, rnd 2; B1/10/1933 Los Angeles, CA

YEAR	TEAM	G (GS, POS)	RUSH	YD	AVG (LG)	TD	REC	YD	AVG (LG)	TD	PASS	COMP	PCT	YD	AVG (LG)	TD	INT	SK	YD	QBR	KPR	OTD	PTS	TAY
1956	LARm✧	12(RE)	—	—	—	—	36	650	18.1(60)	4	—	—	—	—	—	—	—	—	—	—	—	—	24	345
1957	LARm	9(RE)	1	-4	-4.0(-4)	0	23	442	19.2(70)	4	—	—	—	—	—	—	—	—	—	—	—	—	24	237
1958	LARm	11	—	—	—	—	18	135	7.5(17)	4	—	—	—	—	—	—	—	—	—	—	—	1	30	88
1959	LARm	11	—	—	—	—	29	453	15.6(60)	0	—	—	—	—	—	—	—	—	—	—	—	—	0	227
1960	Cle	9(fl)	—	—	—	—	11	184	16.7(86)	4	—	—	—	—	—	—	—	—	—	—	—	—	24	112
1961	Cle	13	—	—	—	—	11	211	19.2(41)	2	—	—	—	—	—	—	—	—	—	—	—	—	12	116
1962	Cle	11(te)	—	—	—	—	10	106	10.6(22)	0	—	—	—	—	—	—	—	—	—	—	—	—	0	53
1963	Min	3	—	—	—	—	3	34	11.3(14)	0	—	—	—	—	—	—	—	—	—	—	—	—	0	17
NFL	8	79	1	-4	-4.0(-4)	0	141	2215	15.7(86)	18	—	—	—	—	—	—	—	—	—	—	—	1	114	1194

Clarke, Phil Phil, LB, 6´0˝/241 lbs; Pittsburgh; B1/9/1977 Miami, FL **1999** NO 8 (3) **2000**†NO 14 (4) **2001** NO 13 (0) **NFL** 35 (7) [3 yrs]

Clarkin, Bill William C., T-G, 5´10˝/210 lbs; none; B9/11/1898 Hartford, CT, D12/7/1982 Altoona, FL **1929** Ora 5 (1)

Clarks, Conrad Conrad, DB, 5´10˝/200 lbs; Louisiana-Monroe; B4/21/1969 Franklin, LA **1995**†Ind 5 (0)

Clarkson, Stu Stuart Lenox, LB-C, 6´2˝/217 lbs; Texas A&M-Kingsville; 1942: ChiB, rnd 22; B7/4/1919 Corpus Christi, TX, D10/25/1957 Hitchcock, TX **1942** ChiB 7 (0) **1946**†ChiB 11 (2) **1947** ChiB 12 (3) **1948** ChiB 10 (1) **1949** ChiB 12 (0) **1950**†ChiB 11 (LLB) **1951** ChiB 11 (RLB) **NFL** 74 (6) [7 yrs]

Clasby, Bob Robert James, DT-DE, 6´5˝/260 lbs; Notre Dame; 1983: Sea, rnd 9; B9/28/1960 Detroit, MI **1986** SL 16 (10, LDE) **1987** SL 12 (12, LDT) **1988** Phx 16 (16, LDT) **1989** Phx 4 (4) **1990** Phx 1 (1) **NFL** 49 (43) [5 yrs]

Clatt, Corwin Corwin Samuel, FB, 6´0˝/210 lbs; Notre Dame; 1945: ChiC, rnd 6; B2/5/1924 West Des Moines, IA, D6/2/1997 Peoria, IL **1949** ChiC 12 (0)

YEAR	TEAM	G (GS, POS)	RUSH	YD	AVG (LG)	TD	REC	YD	AVG (LG)	TD	PASS	COMP	PCT	YD	AVG (LG)	TD	INT	SK	YD	QBR	KPR	OTD	PTS	TAY
1948	†ChiC	12(4)	6	38	6.3(26)	0	—	—	—	—	—	—	—	—	—	—	—	—	—	—	i	—	0	53
NFL	2	24(4)	6	38	6.3(26)	0	—	—	—	—	—	—	—	—	—	—	—	—	—	—	pi	—	0	99

Clatterbuck, Bob Robert Dean, QB, 6´3˝/195 lbs; Houston; 1954: NYG, rnd 27; B7/3/1932 Columbia, MD, D Hurricane, UT

YEAR	TEAM	G (GS, POS)	RUSH	YD	AVG (LG)	TD	REC	YD	AVG (LG)	TD	PASS	COMP	PCT	YD	AVG (LG)	TD	INT	SK	YD	QBR	KPR	OTD	PTS	TAY
1954	NYG	10(qb)	19	-21	-1.1(3)	1	—	—	—	—	101	50	49.5	781	7.7(72)	6	7	—	—	—	—	—	6	130
1955	NYG	3	1	-3	-3.0(-3)	0	—	—	—	—	16	6	37.5	46	2.9(14)	0	0	—	—	—	—	—	0	20
1956	NYG	2	—	—	—	—	—	—	—	—	7	4	57.1	54	7.7(21)	0	1	—	—	—	—	—	0	-13
1957	NYG	1	3	3	1.0(3)	0	—	—	—	—	2	2	100.0	39	19.5(28)	1	0	—	—	—	—	—	0	28
1960	LAC-A	2(2)	3	11	3.7(9)	0	—	—	—	—	23	15	65.2	112	4.9(19)	1	1	—	—	—	—	—	0	32
NFL	5	18(2)	26	-10	-0.4(9)	1	—	—	—	—	149	77	51.7	1032	6.9(72)	8	9	—	—	—	—	—	6	196

Clauss, Jared Jared, DT, 6´5˝/280 lbs; Iowa; 2004: Ten, rnd 7; B4/7/1981 West Des Moines, IA **2004** Ten 14 (1) **2005** Ten 15 (1) **NFL** 29 (2) [2 yrs]

Clavelle, Shannon Shannon Lynn, DE, 6´2˝/287 lbs; Colorado; 1995: Buf, rnd 6; B10/12/1973 Lafayette, LA **1995**†GB 1 (0) **1996** GB 8 (0) **1997** GB 6 (0) **1997** KC 1 (0) **NFL** 16 (0) [3 yrs]

Claxton, Ben Ben, G, 6´2˝/301 lbs; Mississippi; 2003: Den, rnd 5; B7/30/1980 Dublin, GA **2005** Atl 2 (0)

Clay, Billy William Frank, DB, 6´1˝/195 lbs; Mississippi; 1966: Was, rnd 4/Den, rnd 5; B4/26/1944 Oxford, MS **1966** Was 6

Clay, Boyd Boyd Davis, T, 6´1˝/220 lbs; Tennessee; 1940: Cle, rnd 11; B5/6/1915 Hohenwald, TN, D6/22/1978 Mt. Juliet, TN **[K]** **1940** Cle 11 (5, rt) **1941** Cle 11 (0) **1942** Cle 8 (0) **1944** Cle 4 (0) **NFL** 34 (5) [4 yrs]

Clay, Hayward Hayward John, TE, 6´3˝/260 lbs; Texas A&M; 1996: SL, rnd 6; B7/5/1973 Snyder, TX

YEAR	TEAM	G (GS, POS)	RUSH	YD	AVG (LG)	TD	REC	YD	AVG (LG)	TD	PASS	COMP	PCT	YD	AVG (LG)	TD	INT	SK	YD	QBR	KPR	OTD	PTS	TAY
1996	SL	11(4)	—	—	—	—	4	51	12.8(34)	0	—	—	—	—	—	—	—	—	—	—	—	—	0	26
1998	†Dal	3(2)	—	—	—	—	1	27	27.0(27)	0	—	—	—	—	—	—	—	—	—	—	—	—	0	14
NFL	2	14(6)	—	—	—	—	5	78	15.6(34)	0	—	—	—	—	—	—	—	—	—	—	—	—	0	39

Clay, John John Gregory, T, 6´5˝/300 lbs; Missouri; 1987: LARd, rnd 1; B5/1/1964 St. Louis, MO **1987** LARd 10 (9, RT) **1988** SD 2 (1) **NFL** 12 (10) [2 yrs]

Clay, Ozzie Ozzie, WR, 6´0˝/190 lbs; Iowa State; 1964: Was, rnd 17; B9/10/1941 Hickory, NC, D3/10/2005 Washington, DC **1964** Was 14

Clay, Randy Oscar Randall, HB-DB, 6´0˝/188 lbs; Texas; 1950: NYG, rnd 3; B5/30/1928 Pampa, TX **[K]**

YEAR	TEAM	G (GS, POS)	RUSH	YD	AVG (LG)	TD	REC	YD	AVG (LG)	TD	PASS	COMP	PCT	YD	AVG (LG)	TD	INT	SK	YD	QBR	KPR	OTD	PTS	TAY
1950	†NYG	12(RH)	74	254	3.4(56)	2	7	69	9.9(16)	0	—	—	—	—	—	—	—	—	—	—	Kki	—	15	351
1953	NYG	12(DB)	16	26	1.6(6)	0	5	51	10.2(33)	1	—	—	—	—	—	—	—	—	—	—	Kki	—	32	74
NFL	2	24	90	280	3.1(56)	2	12	120	10.0(33)	1	—	—	—	—	—	—	—	—	—	—	Kki	—	47	424

Clay, Roy Roy Harvey, WB-DB, 6´0˝/185 lbs; Colorado State; 1944: NYG, rnd 8; B1/10/1920, D4/18/1996 Watsonville, CA **1944** NYG 1 (0)

YEAR	TEAM	G (GS, POS)	RUSH	YD	AVG(LG)	TD	REC	YD	AVG(LG)	TD	PASS	COMP	PCT	YD	AVG(LG)	TD	INT	SK	YD	QBR	KPR	OTD	PTS	TAY

CLAY, WALT   Walter Earl, B, 5´11˝/196 lbs; Colorado; 1946: NYG, rnd 10; B1/8/1924 Erie, CO

1946	ChiR-A	13(2)	65	283	4.4	1	4	48	12.0	0	27	12	44.4	140	5.2	2	3	—	—	—	Pkpi	—	6	362
1947	ChiR-A	3(0)	—	—	—	—	—	—	—	—	—	—	—	—	—	—	—	—	—	—	—	—	0	0
1947	LAD-A	8(0)	9	42	4.7	0	1	52	52.0	0	—	—	—	—	—	—	—	—	—	—	i	—	0	83
1948	LAD-A	13(8, fb)	86	293	3.4	3	10	118	11.8	1	—	—	—	—	—	—	—	—	—	—	ki	—	24	398
1949	LAD-A	10(1)	9	34	3.8	0	—	—	—	—	1	1	100.0	8	8.0(8)	0	0	—	—	—	—	—	0	38
AAFC	4	47(11)	169	652	3.9	4	15	218	14.5	1	28	13	46.4	148	5.3(8)	2	3	—	—	—	Pkpi	—	30	881

CLAY, WILLIE   Willie James, DB, 5´10˝/193 lbs; Georgia Tech; 1992: Det, rnd 8; B9/5/1970 Pittsburgh, PA [I]   **1992** Det 6 (0)   **1993**†Det 16 (1)   **1994**†Det 16 (16, SS)   **1995**†Det 16 (16, SS)   **1996**†NE 16 (15, FS)   **1997**†NE 16 (16, FS)   **1998**†NE 16 (16, FS)   **1999** NO 16 (10, FS)   **NFL** 118 (90) [8 yrs]

CLAYBORN, RAYMOND   Raymond Dean, DB, 6´0˝/186 lbs; Texas; 1977: NE, rnd 1; B1/2/1955 Fort Worth, TX [I]   **1977** NE☆14 (2)   **1978**†NE 16 (16, LCB)   **1979** NE 16 (16, LCB)   **1980** NE 16 (16, LCB)   **1981** NE 16 (16, LCB)   **1982**†NE 9 (9, RCB)   **1983** NE★16 (16, RCB)   **1984** NE 16 (16, RCB)   **1985**†NE★16 (16, RCB)   **1986**†NE★16 (16, RCB)   **1987** NE 10 (10, RCB)   **1988** NE 16 (16, RCB)   **1989** NE 14 (14, RCB)   **1990** Cle 1 (1)   **NFL** 208 (196) [15 yrs]

CLAYBROOKS, DeVONE   Natravis DeVone, DT, 6´3˝/292 lbs; East Carolina; B9/15/1977 Martinsville, VA   **2002**†TB 2 (0)   **2003** SF 3 (0)   **2004** Dal 8 (0)   **NFL** 13 (0) [3 yrs]

CLAYBROOKS, FELIPE   Felipe A., DE, 6´5˝/275 lbs; Georgia Tech; B1/22/1978 Decatur, GA   **2001** Cle 4 (0)   **2003** Cle 7 (0)   **NFL** 11 (0) [2 yrs]

CLAYPOOL, RALPH   Ralph LeClair, C, 5´9˝/191 lbs; Purdue; B12/15/1898 Blue Grass, IA, D11/17/1969 St. Louis, MO   **1925** ChiC☆13 (12, C)   **1926** ChiC☆11 (10, C)   **1927** ChiC 2 (2)   **1928** ChiC 4 (4, C)   **NFL** 30 (28) [4 yrs]

CLAYTON, CAREY   Carey Arthur, C, 6´3˝/285 lbs; Texas-El Paso; B8/31/1977 Dyersburg, TN   **2001** SD 1 (0)

CLAYTON, HARVEY   Harvey Jerome, DB, 5´9˝/179 lbs; Florida State; B4/4/1961 Kendall, FL   **1983**†Pit 14 (0)   **1984**†Pit 14 (0)   **1985** Pit 14 (14, RCB)   **1986** Pit 15 (12, RCB)   **1987** NYG 2 (0)   **NFL** 59 (26) [5 yrs]

CLAYTON, MARK   Mark Gregory, WR, 5´9˝/177 lbs; Louisville; 1983: Mia, rnd 8; B4/8/1961 Indianapolis, IN

1983	†Mia	14(0)	2	9	4.5(9)	0	6	114	19.0(39)	1	1	1	100.0	48	48.0(48)	1	0	—	—	—	kp	1	12	307
1984	†Mia★	15(15, WR)	3	35	11.7(30)	0	73	1389	19.0(65)	18	1	0	0.0	0	0.0	0	1	1	8	—	kp	—	108	804
1985	†Mia★	16(16, WR)	1	10	10.0(10)	0	70	996	14.2(45)	4	0	0	0.0	0	0.0	0	0	1	7	—	p	—	24	532
1986	Mia◇	15(14, WR)	2	33	16.5(22)	0	60	1150	19.2(68)	10	—	—	—	—	—	—	—	—	—	—	p	—	60	653
1987	Mia	12(12, WR)	2	8	4.0(4)	0	46	776	16.9(43)	7	—	—	—	—	—	—	—	—	—	—	—	—	42	431
1988	Mia★	16(16, WR)	1	4	4.0(4)	0	86	1129	13.1(45)	14	—	—	—	—	—	—	—	—	—	—	—	—	84	639
1989	Mia	15(15, WR)	3	9	3.0(11)	0	64	1011	15.8(78)	9	—	—	—	—	—	—	—	—	—	—	—	—	54	560
1990	†Mia	10(10, WR)	—	—	—	—	32	406	12.7(43)	3	—	—	—	—	—	—	—	—	—	—	—	—	18	218
1991	Mia◇	16(16, WR)	—	—	—	—	70	1053	15.0(43)	12	—	—	—	—	—	—	—	—	—	—	—	—	72	587
1992	†Mia	13(13, WR)	—	—	—	—	43	619	14.4(44)	3	—	—	—	—	—	—	—	—	—	—	—	—	18	325
1993	†GB	16(15, WR)	—	—	—	—	32	331	10.3(32)	3	—	—	—	—	—	—	—	—	—	—	—	—	18	181
NFL	11	158(142)	14	108	7.7(30)	0	582	8974	15.4(78)	84	2	1	50.0	48	24.0(48)	1	1	2	15	—	kp	1	510	5234

CLAYTON, MARK   Mark, WR, 5´10˝/193 lbs; Oklahoma; 2005: Bal, rnd 1; B7/2/1982 Oklahoma City, OK

| 2005 | Bal | 14(10, WR) | 8 | 33 | 4.1(11) | 0 | 44 | 471 | 10.7(47) | 2 | 0 | 0 | 0.0 | 0 | 0.0 | 0 | 0 | — | — | — | p | — | 18 | 289 |

CLAYTON, MICHAEL   Michael Rashard, WR, 6´4˝/197 lbs; LSU; 2004: TB, rnd 1; B10/13/1982 Baton Rouge, LA

2004	TB	16(13, WR)	5	30	6.0(15)	0	80	1193	14.9(75)	7	—	—	—	—	—	—	—	—	—	—	p	—	42	659
2005	TB	14(10, WR)	1	2	2.0(2)	0	32	372	11.6(41)	0	—	—	—	—	—	—	—	—	—	—	p	—	0	188
NFL	2	30(23)	6	32	5.3(15)	0	112	1565	14.0(75)	7	—	—	—	—	—	—	—	—	—	—	p	—	42	847

CLAYTON, RALPH   Ralph Darrell, WR-FB, 6´3˝/222 lbs; Michigan; 1980: NYJ, rnd 2; B9/29/1958 Highland Park, MI   **1981** SL 7 (0)

CLAYTON, STAN   Stanley David, G-T, 6´3˝/265 lbs; Penn State; 1988: Atl, rnd 10; B1/31/1965 Philadelphia, PA   **1988** Atl 2 (2)   **1989** Atl 13 (9, LG)   **1990** NE 11 (3)   **NFL** 26 (14) [3 yrs]

CLEARY, PAUL   Paul Hanson, E-DE, 6´1˝/196 lbs; USC; 1948: ChiR-A, rnd 4/Det, rnd 10; B2/7/1922 North Loop, NE, D1/9/1996 South Laguna, CA   **1949** ChiH-A 10 (0)

| 1948 | NYY-A | 13(0) | — | — | — | 4 | 37 | 9.3 | 0 | — | — | — | — | — | — | — | — | — | — | — | k | — | 0 | 12 |
| AAFC | 2 | 23(0) | — | — | — | 4 | 37 | 9.3 | 0 | — | — | — | — | — | — | — | — | — | — | — | — | — | 0 | 19 |

CLEELAND, CAM   Cameron Ross, TE, 6´4˝/272 lbs; Washington; 1998: NO, rnd 2; B8/15/1975 Sedro-Woolley, WA

1998	NO	16(16, TE)	—	—	—	—	54	684	12.7(53)	6	—	—	—	—	—	—	—	—	—	—	—	—	36	372
1999	NO	11(8, TE)	—	—	—	—	26	325	12.5(31)	1	—	—	—	—	—	—	—	—	—	—	—	—	8	168
2001	NO	9(7, TE)	—	—	—	—	13	138	10.6(19)	4	—	—	—	—	—	—	—	—	—	—	—	—	24	89
2002	NE	12(1)	—	—	—	—	16	112	7.0(22)	1	—	—	—	—	—	—	—	—	—	—	—	—	6	61
2003	†SL	16(10, TE)	2	-5	-2.5(0)	0	10	145	14.5(29)	0	—	—	—	—	—	—	—	—	—	—	—	—	0	68
2004	†SL	16(9, TE)	1	-2	-2.0(-2)	0	7	57	8.1(15)	0	—	—	—	—	—	—	—	—	—	—	—	—	0	27
2005	SL	9(3)	—	—	—	—	5	17	3.4(9)	1	—	—	—	—	—	—	—	—	—	—	—	—	6	14
NFL	7	89(54)	3	-7	-2.3	0	131	1478	11.3(53)	13	—	—	—	—	—	—	—	—	—	—	—	—	80	797

CLEMENS, BOB   Robert William, FB, 6´1˝/208 lbs; Pittsburgh; 1961: Bal, rnd 10/1962: Hou, rnd 30; B8/27/1939 North Braddock, PA

| 1962 | Bal | 9 | 2 | 9 | 4.5(6) | 0 | — | — | — | — | — | — | — | — | — | — | — | — | — | — | — | — | 0 | 9 |

CLEMENS, BOB   Robert Norwood, FB, 6´2˝/200 lbs; Georgia; 1955: GB, rnd 7; B8/3/1933 Scottsboro, AL   **1955** GB 2

CLEMENS, CAL   Charles Calvin, BB, 6´1˝/195 lbs; USC; B7/7/1909 Oklahoma City, OK, D5/1966, **[K]**

| 1936 | †GB | 9(3) | 3 | -8 | -2.7 | 0 | 1 | 18 | 18.0(18) | 0 | 1 | 0 | 0.0 | 0 | 0.0 | 0 | 0 | — | — | — | K | — | 1 | 1 |

CLEMENT, ALEX   Alexander Mitchell, WB, 5´10˝/170 lbs; Williams; B2/11/1904 Plymouth, MA, D1/13/1970 Plymouth, MA   **1925** Fra 4 (1)

CLEMENT, ANTHONY   Anthony, T, 6´8˝/333 lbs; Louisiana-Lafayette; 1998: Arz, rnd 2; B4/10/1976 Lafayette, LA   **1998** Arz 1 (0)   **1999** Arz 16 (14, RT)   **2000** Arz 16 (16, RT)   **2001** Arz 16 (16, RT)   **2002** Arz 1 (0)   **2003** Arz 16 (16, RT)   **2004** Arz 16 (7, rt)   **2005** SF 14 (6, lt)   **NFL** 96 (75) [8 yrs]

CLEMENT, HENRY   Henry Littlefield, TE, 6´3˝/195 lbs; North Carolina; 1961: Pit, rnd 11; B6/15/1939 New York, NY

| 1961 | Pit | 14 | — | — | — | — | 5 | 65 | 13.0(9) | 0 | — | — | — | — | — | — | — | — | — | — | — | — | 0 | 33 |

CLEMENT, JOHNNY   John Louis, TB, 6´0˝/189 lbs; SMU; 1941: ChiC, rnd 4; B10/31/1919 Stonebluff, OK, D12/1969

1941	ChiC	9(4, tb)	61	94	1.5(25)	1	—	—	—	—	100	48	48.0	690	6.9(76)	3	7	—	—	51.7	Pkp	—	6	244
1946	Pit	11(0)	43	60	1.4(13)	1	1	22	22.0(22)	0	47	16	34.0	345	7.3(52)	1	3	—	—	—	Pkp	—	6	171
1947	†Pit☆	10(4, TB)	129	670	5.2(43)	4	1	6	6.0(6)	0	123	52	42.3	1004	8.2(68)	7	9	—	—	59.8	k	—	24	899
1948	Pit	5(1)	67	261	3.9(28)	2	—	—	—	—	58	18	31.0	281	4.8(39)	3	7	—	—	—	—	—	12	157
NFL	4	35(9)	300	1085	3.6(43)	8	2	28	14.0(22)	0	328	134	40.9	2320	7.1(76)	14	26	—	—	46.8	Pkp	—	48	1470
1949	ChiH-A☆	12(0, tb)	106	388	3.7	5	—	—	—	—	114	58	50.9	906	7.9	6	13	—	—	—	—	—	30	401

CLEMENTS, CHASE   George Chase, T, 6´2˝/205 lbs; Washington & Jefferson; B12/31/1901, D8/8/1971 Toledo, OH   **1925** Akr 2 (2)   **1925** Cle 1 (0)   **NFL** 3 (2) [1 yr]

CLEMENTS, CHUCK   Chad, QB, 6´3˝/214 lbs; Houston; 1997: NYJ, rnd 6; B9/29/1973 Kingsville, TX

| 1997 | NYJ | 1(0) | 2 | -3 | -1.5(-1) | 0 | — | — | — | — | — | — | — | — | — | — | — | — | — | — | — | — | 0 | -3 |

CLEMENTS, NATE   Nathan D., DB, 6´0˝/209 lbs; Ohio State; 2001: Buf, rnd 1; B12/12/1979 Shaker Heights, OH [I]   **2001** Buf 16 (11, RCB)   **2002** Buf 16 (16, RCB)   **2003** Buf 16 (16, RCB)   **2004** Buf◇16 (16, RCB)   **2005** Buf 16 (16, RCB)   **NFL** 80 (75) [5 yrs]

CLEMENTS, TOM   Thomas Albert, QB, 6´0˝/183 lbs; Notre Dame; B6/18/1953 McKees Rocks, PA

| 1980 | KC | 1(0) | 2 | 0 | 0.0(0) | 0 | — | — | — | — | 12 | 7 | 58.3 | 77 | 6.4(18) | 0 | 0 | 3 | 30 | — | — | — | 0 | 39 |

CLEMENTS, VINCE   Vincent Anthony, RB, 6´3˝/210 lbs; Connecticut; 1971: Min, rnd 4; B1/4/1949 Southington, CT

1972	NYG	4	46	221	4.8(19)	0	9	118	13.1(39)	0	—	—	—	—	—	—	—	—	—	—	—	—	0	280
1973	NYG	12	57	214	3.8(11)	1	15	129	8.6(16)	1	—	—	—	—	—	—	—	—	—	—	—	—	12	294
NFL	2	16	103	435	4.2(19)	1	24	247	10.3(39)	1	—	—	—	—	—	—	—	—	—	—	—	—	12	574

CLEMONS, CHARLIE   Charlie Fitzgerald, LB, 6´2˝/250 lbs; Georgia; B7/4/1972 Griffin, GA   **1997** SL 5 (0)   **1998** SL 16 (0)   **1999**†SL 16 (0)   **2001** NO 16 (15, MLB)   **2002** NO 16 (14, MLB)   **2003** Hou 9 (8, ROLB)   **NFL** 78 (37) [6 yrs]

CLEMONS, CHRIS   Chris, LB, 6´3˝/234 lbs; Georgia; B10/30/1981 Griffin, GA   **2004** Was 6 (0)   **2005** Was 14 (1)   **NFL** 20 (1) [2 yrs]

YEAR	TEAM	G (GS, POS)	RUSH	YD	AVG (LG)	TD	REC	YD	AVG (LG)	TD	PASS	COMP	PCT	YD	AVG (LG)	TD	INT	SK	YD	QBR	KPR	OTD	PTS	TAY

CLEMONS, CRAIG Craig Lynn, DB, 5′11″/195 lbs; Iowa; 1972: Chi, rnd 1; B6/1/1949 Sidney, OH **1972** ChiB 14 **1973** ChiB 14 (SS) **1974** ChiB 14 (SS) **1975** ChiB 14 (FS) **1976** ChiB 14 (FS) **1977**†ChiB 12 **NFL** 82 [6 yrs]

CLEMONS, DUANE Duane Anthony, DE, 6′5″/275 lbs; California; 1996: Min, rnd 1; B5/23/1974 Riverside, CA [S] **1996** Min 13 (0) **1997**†Min 13 (3) **1998** Min 16 (3) **1999**†Min 16 (9, lde) **2000** KC 12 (12, RDE) **2001** KC 16 (15, RDE) **2002** KC 16 (16, RDE) **2003** Cin 16 (13, LDE) **2004** Cin 14 (14, LDE) **2005** Cin 10 (0) **NFL** 142 (85) [10 yrs]

CLEMONS, MICHAEL Michael Lutrell, RB, 5′5″/166 lbs; William & Mary; 1987: KC, rnd 8; B1/15/1965 Clearwater, FL

| 1987 | KC | 8(0) | | 2 | 7 | 3.5(7) | 0 | — | — | — | — | — | — | — | — | — | — | — | — | — | kp | — | 0 | 62 |

CLEMONS, NIC Nic, DE, 6′6″/298 lbs; Georgia; B2/3/1980 Griffin, GA **2005**†Was 8 (0)

CLEMONS, RAY Norville Raymond, G, 6′0″/215 lbs; Central Oklahoma; B6/4/1912, D12/11/1980 Detroit, MI

| 1939 | Det | 6(0) | — | — | — | — | 1 | 5 | 5.0(5) | 0 | — | — | — | — | — | — | — | — | — | P | — | 0 | 3 |

CLEMONS, RAY Raymond Gordon, G, 5′10″/220 lbs; St. Mary's (CA); B4/2/1921 Roseville, CA, D12/27/2005 Sacramento, CA **1947** GB 9 (1)

CLEMONS, TOPPER Orman Wendell, RB, 5′11″/205 lbs; Wake Forest; 1986: Dal, rnd 8; B9/16/1963 Riverside, NJ

| 1987 | Phi | 3(0) | | 3 | 0 | 0.0(3) | 0 | 1 | 13 | 13.0(13) | 1 | — | — | — | — | — | — | — | — | — | k | — | 6 | -4 |

CLENDENEN, MIKE Michael Dean, K, 5′11″/191 lbs; Houston; B6/12/1963 Dallas, TX [K] **1987** Den 3 (0)

CLEVE, AINER Ainer Martin, B-E, 5′9″/175 lbs; none; B11/27/1897 Minneapolis, MN, D3/23/1990 Edina, MN **1921** Min 3 (1) **1922** Min 4 (3, WB), 6 **1923** Min 8 (6, TB), 6 **1924** Min 4 (3, WB) **NFL** 19 (13), 12 [4 yrs]

CLEVELAND, GREG Gregory Leon, NT, 6′5″/295 lbs; Florida; B8/19/1964 Winter Park, FL **1987** Mia 2 (0)

CLIFTON, CHAD Jeffrey Chad, T, 6′5″/330 lbs; Tennessee; 2000: GB, rnd 2; B6/26/1976 Martin, TN **2000** GB 13 (10, LT) **2001**†GB 14 (13, LT) **2002** GB 10 (9, lt) **2003**†GB 16 (16, LT) **2004**†GB 16 (16, LT) **2005** GB 16 (16, LT) **NFL** 85 (80) [6 yrs]

CLIFTON, GREGORY Gregory, WR, 5′11″/175 lbs; Johnson C. Smith; VMI; B2/6/1968 Charlotte, NC

| 1993 | Was | 2(0) | — | — | — | — | 1 | 75 | 7.5(10) | 0 | — | — | — | — | — | — | — | — | — | — | — | — | 0 | 8 |

CLIFTON, KYLE Ronald Kyle, LB, 6′4″/236 lbs; TCU; 1984: NYJ, rnd 3; B8/23/1962 Olney, TX **1984** NYJ 16 (9, MLB) **1985**†NYJ 16 (16, LILB) **1986**†NYJ☆16 (16, LILB) **1987** NYJ 12 (8, RILB) **1988** NYJ 16 (15, RILB) **1989** NYJ 16 (16, RILB) **1990** NYJ 16 (16, MLB) **1991**†NYJ 16 (16, MLB) **1992** NYJ 16 (16, MLB) **1993** NYJ 16 (16, MLB) **1994** NYJ 16 (5, mlb) **1995** NYJ 16 (0) **1996** NYJ 16 (0) **NFL** 204 (149) [13 yrs]

CLIME, BEN Benjamin Sidney, G-E-WB, 5′11″/190 lbs; Swarthmore; B10/14/1891 Philadelphia, PA, D1/13/1973 Fort Lauderdale, FL **1920** Roc 6 (0) **1921** Roc 1 (0) **NFL** 7 (0) [2 yrs]

CLINE, DOUG Charles Douglas, LB-FB, 6′2″/230 lbs; Clemson; 1960: Hou, rnd 1/NYG, rnd 14; B3/22/1938 Valdese, NC, D10/10/1995 Rutherford College, NC **1961**†Hou-A 14 (LLB) **1962**†Hou-A☆14 (LLB) **1963** Hou-A☆14 (LLB) **1964** Hou-A 14 (MLB) **1965** Hou-A 14 (MLB) **1966** Hou-A 9 (MLB) **1966** SD-A 2

| 1960 | †Hou-A | 14 (LLB) | | 37 | 105 | 2.8(19) | 2 | 4 | 15 | 3.8(10) | 0 | — | — | — | — | — | — | — | — | — | k | — | 12 | 130 |
| NFL | 7 | | | 37 | 105 | 2.8(19) | 2 | 4 | 15 | 3.8(10) | 0 | — | — | — | — | — | — | — | — | — | ki | 3 | 32 | 181 |

CLINE, JACKIE Jackie Wayne, DE-NT, 6′5″/279 lbs; Alabama; B3/13/1960 Kansas City, MO **1987** Pit 1 (0) **1987** Mia 7 (0) **1988** Mia 14 (9, RDE) **1989** Mia 15 (2) **1990** Det 5 (0) **NFL** 42 (11) [4 yrs]

CLINE, OLLIE Oliver Monroe, FB, 6′0″/200 lbs; Ohio State; 1948: Cle-A, rnd 3/ChiB, rnd 14; B12/31/1925 Mount Vernon, OH, D5/12/2001 Springfield, OH

1948	†Cle-A	11(0)		29	124	4.4			—	—	—	—	—	—	—	—	—	—	—	—	k	—	0	139
1949	†Buf-A	11(11, FB)		125	518	4.1	3	15	110	7.3	0	—	—	—	—	—	—	—	—	—	k	—	18	609
AAFC	2	22(11)		154	647	4.2	3	15	110	7.3	0	—	—	—	—	—	—	—	—	—	k	—	18	748
1950	Det	10(FB)		69	227	3.3(14)	2	7	18	2.6(25)	0	—	—	—	—	—	—	—	—	—	k	—	12	261
1951	Det	12		3	15	5.0(10)	0	—	—	—	—	—	—	—	—	—	—	—	—	—	k	—	0	18
1952	†Det	8		13	36	2.8(8)	1	2	45	22.5(30)	0	—	—	—	—	—	—	—	—	—	k	—	6	69
1953	†Det	12(FB)		42	169	4.0(31)	0	10	126	12.6(28)	1	—	—	—	—	—	—	—	—	—	k	—	6	222
NFL	4	42		127	447	3.5(41)	3	19	189	9.9(30)	1	—	—	—	—	—	—	—	—	—	k	—	24	570

CLINE, TONY Anthony Francis, DE, 6′3″/244 lbs; Miami (FL); 1970: Oak, rnd 4; B7/25/1948 Michigan, IN **1970**†Oak 14 (12, LDE) **1971** Oak 13 (6, lde) **1972**†Oak 14 (14, LDE) **1973**†Oak 14 (11, RDE) **1974**†Oak 5 (1) **1975**†Oak 12 (12, LDE) **1976** SF 7 (2)

| 1977 | SF | 14 | — | — | — | — | 1 | 15 | 15.0(15) | 0 | — | — | — | — | — | — | — | — | — | — | — | 0 | 8 |
| NFL | 8 | 93(58) | — | — | — | — | 1 | 15 | 15.0(15) | 0 | — | — | — | — | — | — | — | — | — | i | — | 0 | 4 |

CLINE, TONY Amthony Francis, TE, 6′4″/247 lbs; Stanford; 1995: Buf, rnd 4; B11/24/1971 Davis, CA

1995	†Buf	16(1)	—	—	—	—	8	64	8.0(17)	0	—	—	—	—	—	—	—	—	—	—	k	—	0	28
1996	†Buf	16(7, TE)	—	—	—	—	19	117	6.2(15)	1	—	—	—	—	—	—	—	—	—	—	k	—	6	64
1997	Buf	10(1)	—	—	—	—	1	29	29.0(29)	0	—	—	—	—	—	—	—	—	—	—	k	—	0	-1
1999	Pit	2(0)	—	—	—	—	—	—	—	—	—	—	—	—	—	—	—	—	—	—	k	—	0	-22
1999	SF	8(0)	—	—	—	—	4	45	11.3(30)	0	—	—	—	—	—	—	—	—	—	—	—	—	0	23
NFL	4	52(9)	—	—	—	—	32	255	8.0(30)	1	—	—	—	—	—	—	—	—	—	—	k	—	6	92

CLINKSCALE, DEXTOR Frederick Dextor, DB, 5′11″/192 lbs; South Carolina State; B4/13/1958 Greenville, SC **1980**†Dal 16 (0) **1982**†Dal 9 (0) **1983**†Dal 15 (15, SS) **1984** Dal 15 (15, SS) **1985**†Dal 16 (16, SS) **1986** Ind 5 (0) **NFL** 76 (46) [6 yrs]

CLINKSCALES, JOEY William Joseph, WR, 6′0″/199 lbs; Tennessee; 1987: Pit, rnd 9; B5/21/1964 Asheville, NC **1988** Pit 4 (0) **1988** TB 3 (0)

| 1987 | Pit | 7(3) | — | — | — | — | 13 | 240 | 18.5(57) | 1 | — | — | — | — | — | — | — | — | — | — | — | — | 6 | 125 |
| NFL | 2 | 14(3) | — | — | — | — | 13 | 240 | 18.5(57) | 1 | — | — | — | — | — | — | — | — | — | — | — | — | 6 | 125 |

CLINTON, CHARLES Charles, DB, 5′8″/170 lbs; San Jose State; B1/29/1962 **1987** Hou 2 (0)

CLOUD, JACK Jack Martin, LB-FB, 5′10″/220 lbs; William & Mary; 1950: GB, rnd 6; B1/1/1925 Britton, OK

1950	GB	9		18	52	2.9(13)	3	3	19	6.3(13)	0	—	—	—	—	—	—	—	—	—	—	—	18	92
1951	GB	4		29	61	2.1(19)	1	3	16	5.3(6)	1	—	—	—	—	—	—	—	—	—	—	—	12	84
1952	Was	8		7	21	3.0(5)	0	—	—	—	—	—	—	—	—	—	—	—	—	—	k	—	0	24
1953	Was	12(RLB)		3	7	2.3(5)	0	—	—	—	—	—	—	—	—	—	—	—	—	—	ki	1	6	54
NFL	4	33		57	141	2.5(19)	4	6	35	5.8(13)	1	—	—	—	—	—	—	—	—	—	ki	1	36	254

CLOUD, MIKE Michael Alexander, RB, 5′10″/205 lbs; Boston College; 1999: KC, rnd 2; B7/1/1975 Charleston, SC

1999	KC	11(0)		35	128	3.7(14)	0	3	25	8.3(12)	0	—	—	—	—	—	—	—	—	—	k	—	0	139
2000	KC	16(4)		30	84	2.8(15)	1	2	16	8.0(13)	0	—	—	—	—	—	—	—	—	—	k	1	12	341
2001	KC	15(0)		7	54	7.7(16)	1	—	—	—	—	—	—	—	—	—	—	—	—	—	—	—	6	118
2002	KC	14(2)		49	115	2.3(9)	2	6	48	8.0(13)	0	—	—	—	—	—	—	—	—	—	—	—	12	159
2003	NE	5(1)		27	118	4.4(42)	5	1	8	8.0(8)	0	—	—	—	—	—	—	—	—	—	k	—	30	180
2004	NYG	10(0)		21	90	4.3(26)	3	1	8	8.0(8)	0	—	—	—	—	—	—	—	—	—	k	—	18	177
2005	NE	6(0)		23	59	2.6(15)	0	—	—	—	—	—	—	—	—	—	—	—	—	—	k	—	0	59
2005	†NYG	1		0	0	0.0(0)	0	—	—	—	—	—	—	—	—	—	—	—	—	—	—	—	0	0
NFL	7	78(7)		193	648	3.4(42)	12	13	100	7.7(13)	0	—	—	—	—	—	—	—	—	—	k	1	78	1172

CLOUTIER, DAVE David Lee, DB, 6′0″/195 lbs; South Carolina; Maine; 1962: Dal, rnd 18; B11/22/1938 Gardiner, ME **1964** Bos-A 12

CLOW, HERBERT Herbert W., FB, 5′4″/160 lbs; Wisconsin-Superior; B5/7/1899, MN, D11/24/1977 Duluth, MN **1924** Dul 1 (0)

CLOWES, JOHN John Alexander, T-G-DT, 6′1″/240 lbs; William & Mary; B12/15/1921 Williamsburg, VA, D2/13/1978 Norfolk, VA **1948** Bkn-A 14 (8, LT) **1949** ChiH-A 12 (0) **AAFC** 26 (8) [2 yrs]

1950 NYY 11 **1951** NYY 12 (LG) **NFL** 23 [2 yrs]

CLUNE, DON Donald Andrew, WR, 6′3″/195 lbs; Pennsylvania; 1974: NYG, rnd 5; B7/31/1952 Havertown, PA

1974	NYG	4																						
1975	NYG	14	—	—	—	—	5	97	19.4(41)	0	—	—	—	—	—	—	—	—	—	—	—	—	0	49
1976	Sea	10(1)	—	—	—	—	4	67	16.8(27)	0	—	—	—	—	—	—	—	—	—	—	—	—	0	34
NFL	3	28(1)	—	—	—	—	9	164	18.2(41)	0	—	—	—	—	—	—	—	—	—	—	—	—	0	82

COADY, RICH Richard Joseph, C-TE, 6´3˝/245 lbs; Memphis; 1968: Chi, rnd 11; B12/17/1944 Chicago, IL **1971** ChiB 14 (C) **1972** ChiB 14 (C) **1973** ChiB 14 (C) **1974** ChiB 11 (C)

YEAR	TEAM	G (GS, POS)	RUSH	YD	AVG (LG)	TD	REC	YD	AVG (LG)	TD	PASS	COMP	PCT	YD	AVG (LG)	TD	INT	SK	YD	QBR	KPR	OTD	PTS	TAY
1970	ChiB	14 (TE)	—	—	—	—	6	44	7.3 (14)	1	—	—	—	—	—	—	—	—	—	—	—	—	6	27
NFL	5	67	—	—	—	—	6	44	7.3 (14)	1	—	—	—	—	—	—	—	—	—	—	—	—	6	27

COADY, RICH Richard Joseph, DB, 6´1˝/210 lbs; Texas A&M; 1999: SL, rnd 3; B1/26/1976 Dallas, TX **1999**†SL 16 (0) **2000** SL 12 (2) **2001** SL 12 (2) **2002**†Ten 14 (2) **2003**†SL 13 (5, ss) **2004**†SL 16 (5, fs) **NFL** 83 (16) [6 yrs]

COAKER, JOHN John F., T-G, none; B10/22/1902, NY, D2/1982 **1924** Roc 5 (2)

COAKLEY, DEXTER William Dexter, LB, 5´10˝/236 lbs; Appalachian State; 1997: Dal, rnd 3; B10/20/1972 Charleston, SC **1997** Dal 16 (16, RLB) **1998**†Dal 16 (16, RLB) **1999**†Dal✧16 (16, RLB) **2001** Dal✧15 (15, RLB) **2002** Dal 16 (16, RLB) **2003**†Dal✧16 (16, RLB) **2005** SL 12 (9, RLB)

YEAR	TEAM	G (GS, POS)	RUSH	YD	AVG (LG)	TD	REC	YD	AVG (LG)	TD	PASS	COMP	PCT	YD	AVG (LG)	TD	INT	SK	YD	QBR	KPR	OTD	PTS	TAY
2000	Dal	16 (16, RLB)	1	26	26.0 (26)	0	—	—	—	—	—	—	—	—	—	—	—	—	—	—	—	—	0	26
2004	Dal	16 (16, RLB)	1	33	33.0 (33)	0	—	—	—	—	—	—	—	—	—	—	—	—	—	—	—	—	0	33
NFL	9	139 (136)	2	59	29.5 (33)	0	—	—	—	—	—	—	—	—	—	—	—	—	—	—	kiS	5	30	306

COAN, BERT Elroy Bert, HB, 6´5˝/220 lbs; TCU; Kansas; 1962: Oak, rnd 14/Was, rnd 7; B7/2/1940 Timpson, TX

YEAR	TEAM	G (GS, POS)	RUSH	YD	AVG (LG)	TD	REC	YD	AVG (LG)	TD	PASS	COMP	PCT	YD	AVG (LG)	TD	INT	SK	YD	QBR	KPR	OTD	PTS	TAY
1962	SD-A	4	12	10	0.8 (8)	0	1	52	52.0 (52)	0	—	—	—	—	—	—	—	—	—	—	k	—	0	37
1963	KC-A	8	18	100	5.6 (51)	0	2	35	17.5 (31)	0	—	—	—	—	—	—	—	—	—	—	—	—	0	118
1964	KC-A	8	11	56	5.1 (37)	2	2	8	4.0 (4)	0	—	—	—	—	—	—	—	—	—	—	k	—	12	129
1965	KC-A	14	45	137	3.0 (21)	1	9	85	9.4 (23)	2	—	—	—	—	—	—	—	—	—	—	k	—	18	394
1966	†KC-A	14	96	521	5.4 (57)	7	18	131	7.3 (20)	2	1	1	100.0	18	18.0 (18)	1	0	—	—	—	k	—	54	688
1967	KC-A	12	63	275	4.4 (38)	4	5	41	8.2 (24)	0	—	—	—	—	—	—	—	—	—	—	k	—	24	350
1968	†KC-A	12	40	160	4.0 (24)	1	2	15	7.5 (12)	0	—	—	—	—	—	—	—	—	—	—	k	—	6	203
NFL	7	72	285	1259	4.4 (57)	15	39	367	9.4 (52)	4	1	1	100.0	18	18.0 (18)	1	0	—	—	—	k	—	114	1917

COATES, BEN Ben Terence, TE, 6´5˝/245 lbs; Livingstone; 1991: NE, rnd 5; B8/16/1969 Greenwood, SC

YEAR	TEAM	G (GS, POS)	RUSH	YD	AVG (LG)	TD	REC	YD	AVG (LG)	TD	PASS	COMP	PCT	YD	AVG (LG)	TD	INT	SK	YD	QBR	KPR	OTD	PTS	TAY
1991	NE	16 (2)	1	-6	-6.0 (-6)	0	10	95	9.5 (17)	1	—	—	—	—	—	—	—	—	—	—	k	—	6	38
1992	NE	16 (2)	1	2	2.0 (2)	0	20	171	8.6 (22)	3	—	—	—	—	—	—	—	—	—	—	—	—	18	103
1993	NE	16 (10, TE)	—	—	—	—	53	659	12.4 (54)	8	—	—	—	—	—	—	—	—	—	—	—	—	48	370
1994	†NE★	16 (16, TE)	1	0	0.0 (0)	0	**96**	1174	12.2 (62)	7	—	—	—	—	—	—	—	—	—	—	—	—	42	622
1995	NE★	16 (15, TE)	—	—	—	—	84	915	10.9 (35)	6	—	—	—	—	—	—	—	—	—	—	—	—	36	488
1996	†NE★	16 (15, TE)	—	—	—	—	62	682	11.0 (84)	9	—	—	—	—	—	—	—	—	—	—	—	—	56	386
1997	†NE✧	16 (16, TE)	—	—	—	—	66	737	11.2 (35)	8	—	—	—	—	—	—	—	—	—	—	k	—	48	414
1998	†NE★	14 (14, TE)	—	—	—	—	67	668	10.0 (33)	6	—	—	—	—	—	—	—	—	—	—	—	—	36	364
1999	NE	16 (15, TE)	—	—	—	—	32	370	11.6 (27)	2	—	—	—	—	—	—	—	—	—	—	—	—	12	195
2000	†Bal	16 (8, te)	—	—	—	—	9	84	9.3 (28)	0	—	—	—	—	—	—	—	—	—	—	—	—	2	42
NFL	10	158 (113)	3	-4	-1.3 (2)	0	499	5555	11.1 (84)	50	—	—	—	—	—	—	—	—	—	—	k	—	304	3020

COATES, RAY Raymond Jerald, HB-DB, 6´1˝/195 lbs; LSU; 1948: NYG, rnd 8/Buf-A, rnd 17; B5/8/1924 New Orleans, LA

YEAR	TEAM	G (GS, POS)	RUSH	YD	AVG (LG)	TD	REC	YD	AVG (LG)	TD	PASS	COMP	PCT	YD	AVG (LG)	TD	INT	SK	YD	QBR	KPR	OTD	PTS	TAY
1948	NYG	9 (0)	50	176	3.5 (18)	3	—	—	—	—	2	1	50.0	26	13.0 (26)	1	0	—	—	—	k	—	18	241
1949	NYG	12 (2)	27	55	2.0 (11)	0	8	152	19.0 (51)	1	—	—	—	—	—	—	—	—	—	—	pi	—	6	190
NFL	2	21 (2)	77	231	3.0 (18)	3	8	152	19.0 (51)	1	2	1	50.0	26	13.0 (26)	1	0	—	—	—	kpi	—	24	431

COATES, SHERROD Sherrod, LB, 6´2˝/225 lbs; Western Kentucky; B12/22/1978 Boynton Beach, FL **2003** Cle 16 (0) **2004** Cle 5 (0) **NFL** 21 (0) [2 yrs]

COBB, ALF Alfred R., G-T, 5´11˝/210 lbs; Syracuse; B6/7/1892 Athol, MA, D9/7/1974 West Hartford, CT **1920** Akr☆11 (9, RG) **1921** Akr 1 (0) **1925** Cle 9 (7, lt) **NFL** 21 (16) [3 yrs]

COBB, DEANDRA DeAndra, RB, 5´10˝/196 lbs; Michigan State; 2005: Atl, rnd 6; B5/18/1981 Las Vegas, NV **2005** Atl 3 (0)

COBB, GARRY Gary Wilbert, LB, 6´2˝/227 lbs; USC; 1979: Dal, rnd 9; B3/16/1957 Carthage, NC **1979** Det 8 **1980** Det 16 (0) **1983**†Det 15 (15, LLB) **1984** Det 16 (16, LLB) **1985** Phi 16 (16, ROLB) **1986** Phi 16 (16, LLB) **1987** Phi 12 (7, RLB) **1988** Dal 16 (14, RLB) **1989** Dal 3 (0)

YEAR	TEAM	G (GS, POS)	RUSH	YD	AVG (LG)	TD	REC	YD	AVG (LG)	TD	PASS	COMP	PCT	YD	AVG (LG)	TD	INT	SK	YD	QBR	KPR	OTD	PTS	TAY
1981	Det	16 (16, LLB)	—	—	—	—	1	19	19.0 (19)	0	—	—	—	—	—	—	—	—	—	—	i	—	0	27
1982	†Det	6 (6, LLB)	—	—	—	—	1	25	25.0 (25)	0	—	—	—	—	—	—	—	—	—	—	i	—	0	15
NFL	11	140 (106)	—	—	—	—	2	44	22.0 (25)	0	—	—	—	—	—	—	—	—	—	—	iS	—	0	38

COBB, MARVIN Marvin Lawrence, DB, 6´0˝/189 lbs; USC; 1975: Cin, rnd 11; B8/6/1953 Detroit, MI **1975**†Cin 13 **1976** Cin 14 (FS) **1978** Cin 16 (SS) **1979** Cin 14 (SS) **1980** Pit 6 (0) **1980** Min 2 (0)

YEAR	TEAM	G (GS, POS)	RUSH	YD	AVG (LG)	TD	REC	YD	AVG (LG)	TD	PASS	COMP	PCT	YD	AVG (LG)	TD	INT	SK	YD	QBR	KPR	OTD	PTS	TAY
1977	Cin	14 (FS)	1	0	0.0 (0)	0	—	—	—	—	1	0	0.0	0	0.0	0	0	—	—	—	kpi	—	0	26
NFL	6	79	1	0	0.0	0	—	—	—	—	1	0	0.0	0	0.0	0	0	—	—	—	kpi	1	6	187

COBB, MIKE Michael, TE, 6´5˝/244 lbs; Michigan State; 1977: Cin, rnd 1; B12/10/1955 Youngstown, OH

YEAR	TEAM	G (GS, POS)	RUSH	YD	AVG (LG)	TD	REC	YD	AVG (LG)	TD	PASS	COMP	PCT	YD	AVG (LG)	TD	INT	SK	YD	QBR	KPR	OTD	PTS	TAY
1977	Cin	13	—	—	—	—	—	—	—	—	—	—	—	—	—	—	—	—	—	—	—	—	—	—
1978	ChiB	13	—	—	—	—	1	7	7.0 (7)	0	—	—	—	—	—	—	—	—	—	—	—	—	0	4
1979	†ChiB	16 (15, TE)	—	—	—	—	6	91	15.2 (38)	0	—	—	—	—	—	—	—	—	—	—	—	—	0	46
1980	ChiB	4 (3)	—	—	—	—	2	16	8.0 (9)	0	—	—	—	—	—	—	—	—	—	—	—	—	0	8
1981	ChiB	16 (1)	—	—	—	—	2	20	10.0 (11)	0	—	—	—	—	—	—	—	—	—	—	—	—	0	10
NFL	5	62 (19)	—	—	—	—	11	134	12.2 (38)	0	—	—	—	—	—	—	—	—	—	—	—	—	0	67

COBB, REGGIE Reginald John, RB, 6´1˝/212 lbs; Tennessee; 1990: TB, rnd 2; B7/7/1968 Knoxville, TN

YEAR	TEAM	G (GS, POS)	RUSH	YD	AVG (LG)	TD	REC	YD	AVG (LG)	TD	PASS	COMP	PCT	YD	AVG (LG)	TD	INT	SK	YD	QBR	KPR	OTD	PTS	TAY
1990	TB	16 (13, FB)	151	480	3.2 (17)	2	39	299	7.7 (17)	0	—	—	—	—	—	—	—	—	—	—	k	—	12	708
1991	TB	16 (11, RB)	196	752	3.8 (59)	7	15	111	7.4 (21)	0	—	—	—	—	—	—	—	—	—	—	k	—	42	863
1992	TB	16 (13, RB)	310	1171	3.8 (25)	9	21	156	7.4 (27)	0	—	—	—	—	—	—	—	—	—	—	—	—	54	1339
1993	TB	12 (10, RB)	221	658	3.0 (16)	3	9	61	6.8 (19)	1	—	—	—	—	—	—	—	—	—	—	—	—	24	724
1994	†GB	16 (13, RB)	153	579	3.8 (30)	3	35	299	8.5 (37)	1	—	—	—	—	—	—	—	—	—	—	—	—	24	764
1995	Jax	1 (0)	9	18	2.0 (5)	0	—	—	—	—	—	—	—	—	—	—	—	—	—	—	—	—	0	18
1996	NYJ	15 (0)	25	85	3.4 (9)	1	4	23	5.8 (12)	0	—	—	—	—	—	—	—	—	—	—	k	—	6	250
NFL	7	92 (60)	1065	3743	3.5 (59)	25	123	949	7.7 (37)	2	—	—	—	—	—	—	—	—	—	—	k	—	162	4664

COBB, ROBERT Robert Lewis, DE, 6´4˝/248 lbs; Cincinnati; Arizona; 1981: LA, rnd 3; B10/12/1957 Cincinnati, OH **1981** LARm 6 (0) **1982** TB 3 (0) **1984** Min 2 (1) **NFL** 11 (1) [3 yrs]

COBB, TOM Thomas, T-G, 5´11˝/250 lbs; St. John's (NY); B11/29/1903, D12/1978 East Prairie, MO **1926** KC 11 (11, LT) **1927** Cle 12 (12, LT) **1928** Det 9 (7, LT) **1931** ChiC 5 (1) **NFL** 37 (31) [4 yrs]

COBB, TREVOR Trevor Sebastian, RB, 5´9˝/209 lbs; Rice; B11/20/1970 Houston, TX **1994** ChiB 1 (0)

COBBINS, LYRON Lyrron Duryea, LB, 5´11˝/240 lbs; Notre Dame; B9/17/1974 Kansas City, KS **1997** Arz 6 (0)

COBBLE, ERIC Eric Neal, RB, 5´10˝/205 lbs; Southwest Texas State; B4/11/1964

YEAR	TEAM	G (GS, POS)	RUSH	YD	AVG (LG)	TD	REC	YD	AVG (LG)	TD	PASS	COMP	PCT	YD	AVG (LG)	TD	INT	SK	YD	QBR	KPR	OTD	PTS	TAY
1987	Hou	3 (0)	9	23	2.6 (12)	0	—	—	—	—	—	—	—	—	—	—	—	—	—	—	—	—	0	23

COBBS, CEDRIC Cedric, RB, 6´1˝/225 lbs; Arkansas; 2004: NE, rnd 4; B1/9/1981 Little Rock, AR

YEAR	TEAM	G (GS, POS)	RUSH	YD	AVG (LG)	TD	REC	YD	AVG (LG)	TD	PASS	COMP	PCT	YD	AVG (LG)	TD	INT	SK	YD	QBR	KPR	OTD	PTS	TAY
2004	NE	3 (0)	22	50	2.3 (13)	0	—	—	—	—	—	—	—	—	—	—	—	—	—	—	—	—	0	50

COBBS, DUFFY Robert S., DB, 5´11˝/178 lbs; Penn State; B1/17/1964 **1987** NE 3 (0)

COBOURNE, AVON Avon, RB, 5´8˝/205 lbs; West Virginia; B3/6/1979 Camden, NJ

YEAR	TEAM	G (GS, POS)	RUSH	YD	AVG (LG)	TD	REC	YD	AVG (LG)	TD	PASS	COMP	PCT	YD	AVG (LG)	TD	INT	SK	YD	QBR	KPR	OTD	PTS	TAY
2003	Det	7 (0)	10	27	2.7 (19)	0	4	30	7.5 (13)	0	—	—	—	—	—	—	—	—	—	—	k	—	0	60

COCHRAN, ANTONIO Antonio Desez, DE, 6´4˝/299 lbs; Georgia; 1999: Sea, rnd 4; B6/21/1976 Montezuma, GA **1999** Sea 4 (0) **2000** Sea 15 (0) **2001** Sea 16 (2) **2002** Sea 16 (16, RDE) **2003**†Sea 15 (7, LDE) **2004**†Sea 16 (7, rde) **2005** Arz 3 (0) **NFL** 85 (32) [7 yrs]

COCHRAN, LEON Leon Thomas, FB, 6´0˝/209 lbs; Auburn; B4/13/1924 Birmingham, AL

YEAR	TEAM	G (GS, POS)	RUSH	YD	AVG (LG)	TD	REC	YD	AVG (LG)	TD	PASS	COMP	PCT	YD	AVG (LG)	TD	INT	SK	YD	QBR	KPR	OTD	PTS	TAY
1949	Was	11 (2)	34	135	4.0 (16)	1	7	82	11.7 (22)	0	—	—	—	—	—	—	—	—	—	—	—	—	6	186

COCHRAN, MARK Mark Donald, T, 6´5˝/284 lbs; Baylor; 1986: Hou, rnd 11; B5/6/1963 Pasadena, CA **1987** SF 3 (3)

COCHRAN, MOOSE Stuart W., E, 6´0˝/195 lbs; Chicago; B6/6/1897 Wheaton, IL, D5/10/1979 Wheaton, IL **1922** Mil 2 (0)

YEAR	TEAM	G (GS, POS)	RUSH	YD	AVG(LG)	TD	REC	YD	AVG(LG)	TD	PASS COMP	PCT	YD	AVG(LG)	TD	INT	SK	YD	QBR	KPR	OTD	PTS	TAY

COCHRAN, RED John Thomas, QB-FB-HB, 6´0˝/190 lbs; Wake Forest; 1944: ChiC, rnd 8/1947: Buf-A, rnd S; B8/2/1922 Fairfield, AL, D9/5/2004 Green Bay, WI

1947	†ChiC	12(3)	14	36	2.6(9)	1	1	7	7.0(7)	1	1	0	0	0.0	0	0	0	—	—	Pkpi	—	12	220
1948	†ChiC	12(5, qb)	3	15	5.0(9)	0	—	—	—	—	1	0	0	0.0	0	0	0	—	—	Pkpi	—	0	164
1949	ChiC	12(0)	20	87	4.3(22)	1	7	107	15.3(33)	1	1	0	0	0.0	0	0	0	—	—	Pkp	2	24	551
NFL	3	36(8)	37	138	3.7(22)	2	8	114	14.3(33)	2	2	0	0	0.0	0	0	0	—	—	Pkpi	2	36	934

COCKRELL, GENE Eugene Oliver, T-DE, 6´4˝/247 lbs; Oklahoma; Hardin-Simmons; 1957: Cle, rnd 28; B1/10/1934 Pampa, TX   **1960** NYT-A 14 (RT)   **1961** NYT-A 14 (RT)
1962 NYT-A 14 (RT)   **NFL** 42 [3 yrs]

COCKROFT, DON Donald Lee, K, 6´2˝/195 lbs; Adams State; 1967: Cle, rnd 3; B2/6/1945 Cheyenne, WY [KP]   **1968**†Cle 14   **1969**†Cle 14   **1970** Cle 14   **1972**†Cle☆14
1977 Cle 14   **1978** Cle☆16   **1979** Cle 16   **1980**†Cle 16 (0)

1971	†Cle	14	1	12	12.0(12)	0	—	—	—	—	—	—	—	—	—	—	—	—	—	KP	—	79	12
1973	Cle	14	1	-3	-3.0(-3)	0	—	—	—	—	—	—	—	—	—	—	—	—	—	KP	—	90	-3
1974	Cle	14	—	—	—	—	—	—	—	—	1	1	100.0	27	27.0(27)	0	0	0	—	—	KP	—	71	14
1975	Cle	14	—	—	—	—	—	—	—	—	2	2	100.0	0	0.0(1)	0	0	0	—	—	KP	—	72	0
1976	Cle	14	—	—	—	—	—	—	—	—	1	0	0.0	0	0.0	0	0	0	—	—	KP	—	72	0
NFL	13	188	2	9	4.5(12)	0	—	—	—	—	4	3	75.0	27	6.8(27)	0	0	0	—	—	KP	—	1080	23

COCOZZO, JOE Joseph Raymond, G, 6´4˝/300 lbs; Michigan; 1993: SD, rnd 3; B8/7/1970 Mechanicville, NY   **1993** SD 16 (5, rg)   **1994**†SD 13 (13, LG)   **1995**†SD 16 (7, rg)
1996 SD 16 (11, RG)   **1997** SD 16 (12, LG)   **NFL** 77 (48) [5 yrs]

COCROFT, SHERMAN Sherman Carlson, DB, 6´1˝/195 lbs; San Jose State; B8/29/1961 Watsonville, CA   **1985** KC 16 (0)   **1986** KC 16 (0)   **1987** KC 12 (1)   **1988**†Buf 13 (0)
1989 TB 10 (2)   **NFL** 67 (3) [5 yrs]

CODER, RON Ronald William, G-T, 6´4˝/250 lbs; Penn State; 1976: Pit, rnd 3; B5/24/1954 Savannah, GA   **1976** Sea 13   **1977** Sea 14 (14, RG)   **1979** Sea 15 (5, rg)   **1980** SL 11 (2)
NFL 53 (21) [4 yrs]

CODIE, NAKIA Nakia, DB, 6´2˝/208 lbs; Baylor; B1/20/1976 Cleburne, TX   **2000** Pit 6 (0)

CODY, BILL William Eugene, LB, 6´2˝/230 lbs; Auburn; 1966: Det, rnd 5/NYJ, rnd 15; B8/2/1944 Greenwood, MS   **1966** Det 1   **1967** NO 9   **1968** NO 14   **1969** NO 3   **1970** NO 14
1972 Phi 11   **NFL** 52 [6 yrs]

CODY, ED Edward Joseph, FB, 5´10˝/191 lbs; Purdue; 1946: GB, rnd 5/1947: LAD-A, rnd 16; B2/27/1923 Newington, CT [K]

1947	GB	10(0)	56	263	4.7(32)	2	1	2	2.0(2)	0	—	—	—	—	—	—	—	—	—	kp	—	12	423
1948	GB	10(0)	26	58	2.2(10)	0	—	—	—	—	—	—	—	—	—	—	—	—	—	Kk	—	11	59
1949	ChiB	8(0)	11	25	2.3(11)	0	—	—	—	—	—	—	—	—	—	—	—	—	—	kpi	1	6	135
1950	†ChiB	10	—	—	—	—	—	—	—	—	—	—	—	—	—	—	—	—	—	—	—	0	0
NFL	4	38	93	346	3.7(32)	2	1	2	2.0(2)	0	—	—	—	—	—	—	—	—	—	Kkpi	1	29	617

CODY, MAC Maclin, WR, 5´11˝/182 lbs; Memphis; B8/7/1972 St. Louis, MO

1999	Arz	13(0)	—	—	—	—	6	60	10.0(16)	1	—	—	—	—	—	—	—	—	—	kp	—	6	264
2000	Arz	15(1)	—	—	—	—	17	212	12.5(24)	0	—	—	—	—	—	—	—	—	—	kp	—	0	176
NFL	2	28(1)	—	—	—	—	23	272	11.8(24)	1	—	—	—	—	—	—	—	—	—	kp	—	6	440

CODY, SHAUN Shaun, DT, 6´4˝/292 lbs; USC; 2005: Det, rnd 2; B1/22/1983 Whittier, CA   **2005** Det 16 (2)

CODY, TAY Tay, DB, 5´9˝/180 lbs; Florida State; 2001: SD, rnd 3; B10/6/1977 Colquitt, GA   **2001** SD 14 (11, LCB)   **2002** SD 4 (0)   **2003** SD 1 (0)   **NFL** 19 (11) [3 yrs]

COFALL, STAN Stanley Bingham, WB-TB, 5´11˝/190 lbs; Notre Dame; B5/5/1894 Cleveland, OH; D9/21/1961 Cleveland, OH [C]   **1920** Cle 3 (3, WB)

COFER, JOE Joseph Louis, DB, 6´0˝/200 lbs; Tennessee; B3/5/1963 Knoxville, TN   **1987** Was 3 (1)

COFER, MIKE James Michael, K, 6´1˝/195 lbs; North Carolina State; B2/19/1964 Columbia, SC [K]   **1987** NO 2 (0)   **1988**†SF 16 (0)   **1989**†SF☆16 (0)   **1990**†SF 16 (0)
1991 SF 16 (0)   **1992**†SF 16 (0)   **1993**†SF 16 (0)   **1995** Ind 4 (0)   **NFL** 102 (0) [8 yrs]

COFER, MIKE Michael Lynn, LB-DE, 6´5˝/245 lbs; Tennessee; 1983: Det, rnd 3; B4/7/1960 Knoxville, TN [S]   **1983**†Det 16 (6, rde)   **1984** Det 16 (16, LDE)   **1985** Det 7 (7, rolb)
1986 Det 16 (15, ROLB)   **1987** Det 11 (11, ROLB)   **1988** Det★16 (16, ROLB)   **1989** Det 15 (7, ROLB)   **1990** Det☆16 (16, ROLB)   **1991** Det 2 (2)   **1992** Det 8 (8, ROLB)
NFL 123 (104) [10 yrs]

COFFEE, PAT James Lilburn, TB, 5´11˝/183 lbs; LSU; B8/3/1915 Deann, AR, D1/25/1986 Baton Rouge, LA

1937	ChiC	9(4, tb)	55	157	2.9	1	—	—	—	—	119	52	43.7	824	6.9(97)	4	11	—	40.0	—	—	6	159
1938	ChiC	10(1)	40	169	4.2	2	—	—	—	—	39	16	41.0	200	5.1	0	4	—	—	—	—	12	129
NFL	2	19(5)	95	326	3.4	3	—	—	—	—	158	68	43.0	1024	6.5(97)	4	15	—	33.8	—	—	18	288

COFFEY, DONALD Donald Eugene, WR, 6´4˝/190 lbs; Memphis; 1961: SD, rnd 25/SF, rnd 12; B8/16/1939 Burnsville, NC   **1963** Den-A 3

COFFEY, JUNIOR Junior Lee, RB, 6´2˝/215 lbs; Washington; 1965: GB, rnd 7/Hou, rnd 16; B3/21/1942 Kyle, TX

1965	†GB	13	3	12	4.0(10)	0	—	—	—	—	—	—	—	—	—	—	—	—	—	k	—	0	6
1966	Atl	14(HB)	199	722	3.6(37)	4	15	182	12.1(46)	1	—	—	—	—	—	—	—	—	—	k	—	30	861
1967	Atl	14(HB)	180	722	4.0(20)	4	30	196	6.5(22)	1	—	—	—	—	—	—	—	—	—	—	—	30	865
1969	Atl	6	49	168	3.4(19)	1	8	64	8.0(19)	2	—	—	—	—	—	—	—	—	—	—	—	18	220
1969	NYG	6	82	343	4.2(20)	1	6	25	4.2(22)	1	—	—	—	—	—	—	—	—	—	—	—	12	371
1971	NYG	6	22	70	3.2(10)	0	5	20	4.0(11)	0	—	—	—	—	—	—	—	—	—	—	—	0	80
NFL	5	59	535	2037	3.8(37)	10	64	487	7.6(46)	5	—	—	—	—	—	—	—	—	—	k	—	90	2403

COFFEY, KEN Kenneth Eugene, DB, 6´0˝/193 lbs; Southwest Texas State; 1982: Was, rnd 9; B7/11/1960 Rantoul, IL   **1983**†Was 13 (4)   **1984**†Was 12 (10, SS)
1986†Was 16 (9, SS)   **NFL** 41 (23) [3 yrs]

COFFEY, WAYNE Wayne Everett, WR, 5´7˝/158 lbs; Southwest Texas State; B5/30/1964 Rantoul, IL

| 1987 | NE | 3(2) | — | — | — | — | 3 | 66 | 22.0(35) | 0 | — | — | — | — | — | — | — | — | — | — | — | 0 | 33 |

COFFIELD, RANDY Randall Steven, LB, 6´4˝/215 lbs; Florida State; 1976: Sea, rnd 10; B12/12/1953 Miami, FL   **1976** Sea 13   **1978** NYG 2   **1979** NYG 9   **NFL** 24 [3 yrs]

COFFMAN, PAUL Paul Randolph, TE, 6´3˝/222 lbs; Kansas State; B3/29/1956 St. Louis, MO

1978	GB	16	—	—	—	—	—	—	—	—	—	—	—	—	—	—	—	—	—	—	—	—	—
1979	GB	16(16, TE)	—	—	—	—	56	711	12.7(78)	4	—	—	—	—	—	—	—	—	—	—	—	24	376
1980	GB	16(16, TE)	1	3	3.0(3)	0	42	496	11.8(25)	3	—	—	—	—	—	—	—	—	—	—	—	18	266
1981	GB	16(16, TE)	—	—	—	—	55	687	12.5(29)	4	—	—	—	—	—	—	—	—	—	k	—	24	396
1982	†GB◇	9(9, TE)	—	—	—	—	23	287	12.5(42)	2	—	—	—	—	—	—	—	—	—	—	—	12	154
1983	GB★	16(16, TE)	—	—	—	—	54	814	15.1(74)	11	—	—	—	—	—	—	—	—	—	—	—	66	462
1984	GB★	14(13, TE)	—	—	—	—	43	562	13.1(44)	9	—	—	—	—	—	—	—	—	—	—	—	54	326
1985	GB	16(16, TE)	—	—	—	—	49	666	13.6(32)	6	—	—	—	—	—	—	—	—	—	—	—	36	363
1986	†KC	15(0)	—	—	—	—	12	75	6.3(10)	2	—	—	—	—	—	—	—	—	—	—	—	12	48
1987	KC	12(1)	—	—	—	—	5	42	8.4(13)	1	—	—	—	—	—	—	—	—	—	—	—	6	26
1988	Min	8(0)	—	—	—	—	—	—	—	—	—	—	—	—	—	—	—	—	—	—	—	—	—
NFL	11	154(103)	1	3	3.0(3)	0	339	4340	12.8(78)	42	—	—	—	—	—	—	—	—	—	k	—	252	2415

COFIELD, TIM Tim Lee, LB, 6´2˝/243 lbs; Elizabeth City State; B5/18/1963 Murfreesboro, NC   **1986**†KC 15 (15, ROLB)   **1987** KC 12 (5, rolb)   **1988** KC 16 (15, ROLB)
1989 NYJ 6 (2)   **1989**†Buf 5 (0)   **NFL** 54 (37) [4 yrs]

COGDILL, GAIL Gail Ross, SE-WR, 6´3˝/200 lbs; Washington State; 1960: Det, rnd 6/DalT, rnd 1; B4/7/1937 Worland, WY

1960	Det◇	12(SE)	—	—	—	—	43	642	14.9(63)	1	—	—	—	—	—	—	—	—	—	—	—	6	326
1961	Det	14(SE)	—	—	—	—	45	956	21.2(84)	6	—	—	—	—	—	—	—	—	—	—	—	36	508
1962	Det★	14(SE)	1	2	2.0(2)	0	53	991	18.7(72)	7	—	—	—	—	—	—	—	—	—	k	1	48	522
1963	Det★	14(SE)	—	—	—	—	48	945	19.7(70)	10	—	—	—	—	—	—	—	—	—	—	—	60	523
1964	Det☆	11(SE)	1	-4	-4.0(-4)	0	45	665	14.8(57)	2	—	—	—	—	—	—	—	—	—	—	1	18	339
1965	Det	9(SE)	—	—	—	—	20	247	12.4(33)	1	—	—	—	—	—	—	—	—	—	—	—	0	124
1966	Det	14(SE)	—	—	—	—	47	411	8.7(21)	1	—	—	—	—	—	—	—	—	—	—	—	6	211
1967	Det	14(se)	—	—	—	—	21	322	15.3(52)	1	—	—	—	—	—	—	—	—	—	—	—	6	166

YEAR	TEAM	G (GS, POS)	RUSH	YD	AVG (LG)	TD	REC	YD	AVG (LG)	TD	PASS	COMP	PCT	YD	AVG (LG)	TD	INT	SK	YD	QBR	KPR	OTD	PTS	TAY
1968	Det	3	—	—	—	—	3	42	14.0(20)	0	—	—	—	—	—	—	—	—	—	—	—	—	0	21
1968	†Bal	5	—	—	—	—	—	—	—	—	—	—	—	—	—	—	—	—	—	—	—	—	—	—
1969	Atl	13(SE)	—	—	—	—	24	374	15.6(52)	5	—	—	—	—	—	—	—	—	—	—	—	—	30	212
1970	Atl	6	—	—	—	—	7	101	14.4(30)	1	—	—	—	—	—	—	—	—	—	—	—	—	6	56
NFL	11	127	2	-2	-1.0(2)	0	356	5696	16.0(84)	34	—	—	—	—	—	—	—	—	—	—	k	2	216	3005

COGHILL, GEORGE George, DB, 6´0˝/210 lbs; Wake Forest; B3/30/1970 Fredericksburg, VA **1998**†Den 9 (0) **1999** Den 13 (5, ss) **2000**†Den 16 (0) **2001** Den 16 (0) **NFL** 54 (5) [4 yrs]

COHEN, ABE Abraham, G, 6´0˝/230 lbs; Tennessee-Chattanooga; 1955: NYG, rnd 26; B3/23/1933 **1960** Bos-A 14

COHEN, DUSTIN Dustin Will, LB, 6´3˝/236 lbs; Miami (OH); B12/22/1976 Cincinnati, OH **2000**†SL 0 (0) **2001**†SL 4 (0) **NFL** 4 (0) [2 yrs]

COIA, ANGELO Angelo Anthony, SE-WR, 6´3˝/195 lbs; USC; 1960: Chi, rnd 20/NYT, rnd 1; B4/21/1938 Philadelphia, PA

YEAR	TEAM	G (GS, POS)	RUSH	YD	AVG (LG)	TD	REC	YD	AVG (LG)	TD	PASS	COMP	PCT	YD	AVG (LG)	TD	INT	SK	YD	QBR	KPR	OTD	PTS	TAY
1960	ChiB	12(10, SE)	3	-4	-1.3(25)	0	25	478	19.1(59)	4	—	—	—	—	—	—	—	—	—	—	p	—	24	247
1961	ChiB	11	—	—	—	—	12	249	20.8(64)	3	—	—	—	—	—	—	—	—	—	—	—	—	18	140
1962	ChiB	9	—	—	—	—	22	361	16.4(71)	4	—	—	—	—	—	—	—	—	—	—	—	—	24	201
1963	†ChiB	12	2	2	1.0(4)	0	11	116	10.5(18)	1	—	—	—	—	—	—	—	—	—	—	—	—	6	65
1964	Was	14(SE)	—	—	—	—	29	500	17.2(80)	5	—	—	—	—	—	—	—	—	—	—	—	—	30	275
1965	Was	13(se)	—	—	—	—	18	240	13.3(45)	3	—	—	—	—	—	—	—	—	—	—	—	—	18	135
1966	Atl	6	—	—	—	—	4	93	23.3(39)	0	—	—	—	—	—	—	—	—	—	—	—	—	0	47
NFL	7	77(10)	5	-2	-0.4(25)	0	121	2037	16.8(80)	20	—	—	—	—	—	—	—	—	—	—	p	—	120	1109

COKELEY, WILL Will Harlin, LB, 6´2˝/220 lbs; Kansas State; B12/6/1960 Topeka, KS **1987** Buf 3 (3)

COLAHAN, JACK John Roland, T, 6´3˝/212 lbs; Colorado Mines; B2/5/1905, MN, D7/2/1973 Las Vegas, NV **1928** NYY 2 (1)

COLAVITO, STEVE Steven Michael, LB, 6´0˝/225 lbs; Wesley; Wake Forest; B8/9/1951 New York, NY **1975** Phi 4

COLBERT, DANNY Danny Joel, DB, 5´11˝/175 lbs; TCU; Tulsa; 1974: SD, rnd 9; B12/15/1950 Corsicana, TX **1974** SD 6 **1975** SD 13 (6, lcb) **1976** SD 13 (9, LCB) **NFL** 32 (15) [3 yrs]

COLBERT, DARRELL Darrell Ray, WR, 5´10˝/174 lbs; Texas Southern; B11/16/1964 Beaumont, TX

YEAR	TEAM	G (GS, POS)	RUSH	YD	AVG (LG)	TD	REC	YD	AVG (LG)	TD	PASS	COMP	PCT	YD	AVG (LG)	TD	INT	SK	YD	QBR	KPR	OTD	PTS	TAY
1987	KC	12(0)	—	—	—	—	3	21	7.0(9)	0	—	—	—	—	—	—	—	—	—	—	kp	—	0	20
1988	KC	3(0)	—	—	—	—	1	-3	-3.0(-3)	0	—	—	—	—	—	—	—	—	—	—	—	—	0	-2
NFL	2	15(0)	—	—	—	—	4	18	4.5(9)	0	—	—	—	—	—	—	—	—	—	—	kp	—	0	18

COLBERT, KEARY Keary, WR, 6´2˝/210 lbs; USC; 2004: Car, rnd 2; B5/21/1982 Oxnard, CA

YEAR	TEAM	G (GS, POS)	RUSH	YD	AVG (LG)	TD	REC	YD	AVG (LG)	TD	PASS	COMP	PCT	YD	AVG (LG)	TD	INT	SK	YD	QBR	KPR	OTD	PTS	TAY
2004	Car	15(15, WR)	—	—	—	—	47	754	16.0(63)	5	—	—	—	—	—	—	—	—	—	—	k	—	32	402
2005	†Car	16(16, WR)	1	6	6.0(6)	0	25	282	11.3(42)	2	—	—	—	—	—	—	—	—	—	—	—	—	12	157
NFL	2	31(31)	1	6	6.0(6)	0	72	1036	14.4(63)	7	—	—	—	—	—	—	—	—	—	—	k	—	44	559

COLBERT, LEWIS Lewis Welton, P, 5´11˝/182 lbs; Auburn; 1986: KC, rnd 8; B8/23/1963 Phenix City, AL **1986**†KC 16 (0) **1987** KC 2 (0) **1989** SD 2 (0) **NFL** 20 (0) [3 yrs]

COLBERT, RONDY Rondy Estes, DB, 5´9˝/185 lbs; Lamar; 1975: NYG, rnd 17; B1/7/1954 Corsicana, TX **1975** NYG 14 **1976** NYG 14 (2) **1977** SL 4 **NFL** 32 (2) [3 yrs]

COLCHICO, DANIEL Daniel Memetta, DE, 6´5˝/245 lbs; San Jose State; 1959: SF, rnd 7/1960: Bos, rnd 1; B5/27/1935 Berkeley, CA **1960** SF 12 (11, LDE) **1961** SF 14 (14, LDE) **1962** SF 14 (14, LDE) **1963** SF 14 (14, LDE) **1964** SF 12 (11, LDE) **1965** SF 1 **1969** NO 9 **NFL** 76 (64) [7 yrs]

COLCLOUGH, JIM James Michael, E, 6´0˝/185 lbs; Boston College; 1959: Was, rnd 30; B3/31/1936 Medford, MA, D5/16/2004 Boston, MA

YEAR	TEAM	G (GS, POS)	RUSH	YD	AVG (LG)	TD	REC	YD	AVG (LG)	TD	PASS	COMP	PCT	YD	AVG (LG)	TD	INT	SK	YD	QBR	KPR	OTD	PTS	TAY
1960	Bos-A	14(FL)	—	—	—	—	49	666	13.6(61)	9	—	—	—	—	—	—	—	—	—	—	—	—	54	378
1961	Bos-A	14(FL)	3	37	12.3(16)	0	42	757	18.0(58)	9	—	—	—	—	—	—	—	—	—	—	—	—	54	461
1962	Bos-A✧	14(FL)	1	14	14.0(14)	0	40	868	**21.7(78)**	10	—	—	—	—	—	—	—	—	—	—	—	—	60	498
1963	†Bos-A	14(FL)	—	—	—	—	42	693	16.5(56)	3	—	—	—	—	—	—	—	—	—	—	—	—	18	362
1964	Bos-A	14(fl)	—	—	—	—	32	657	20.5(59)	5	—	—	—	—	—	—	—	—	—	—	—	—	34	354
1965	Bos-A	14(SE)	—	—	—	—	40	677	16.9(41)	3	—	—	—	—	—	—	—	—	—	—	—	—	18	354
1966	Bos-A	14	—	—	—	—	16	284	17.8(32)	0	—	—	—	—	—	—	—	—	—	—	k	—	0	129
1967	Bos-A	14	—	—	—	—	14	263	18.8(52)	0	—	—	—	—	—	—	—	—	—	—	—	—	0	132
1968	Bos-A	14(4)	—	—	—	—	8	136	17.0(44)	0	—	—	—	—	—	—	—	—	—	—	—	—	0	68
NFL	9	126(4)	4	51	12.8(16)	0	283	5001	17.7(78)	39	—	—	—	—	—	—	—	—	—	—	k	—	238	2734

COLCLOUGH, RICARDO Ricardo Sanchez, DB, 5´10˝/186 lbs; Tusculum; 2004: Pit, rnd 2; B4/18/1982 Sumter, SC **2004**†Pit 16 (0) **2005**†Pit 14 (0) **NFL** 30 (0) [2 yrs]

COLE, CHRIS Charles Christopher, WR, 6´0˝/195 lbs; Texas A&M; 2000: Den, rnd 3; B11/12/1977 Orange, TX **[R]**

YEAR	TEAM	G (GS, POS)	RUSH	YD	AVG (LG)	TD	REC	YD	AVG (LG)	TD	PASS	COMP	PCT	YD	AVG (LG)	TD	INT	SK	YD	QBR	KPR	OTD	PTS	TAY
2000	Den	8(0)	—	—	—	—	—	—	—	—	—	—	—	—	—	—	—	—	—	—	k	—	0	99
2001	Den	16(1)	—	—	—	—	9	128	14.2(21)	0	—	—	—	—	—	—	—	—	—	—	k	—	0	471
2003	Den	11(0)	2	8	4.0(8)	0	3	36	12.0(18)	0	—	—	—	—	—	—	—	—	—	—	k	—	0	290
NFL	3	35(1)	2	8	4.0(8)	0	12	164	13.7(21)	0	—	—	—	—	—	—	—	—	—	—	k	—	0	860

COLE, COLIN Colin, DT, 6´2˝/299 lbs; Iowa; B6/24/1980 Toronto, Canada **2004** GB 3 (1) **2005** GB 16 (4) **NFL** 19 (5) [2 yrs]

COLE, EDDIE Edward Lee, LB, 6´2˝/235 lbs; Mississippi; 1979: Det, rnd 11; B12/16/1956 Clarkside, MS **1979** Det 15 (2) **1980** Det 13 (0) **NFL** 28 (2) [2 yrs]

COLE, EMERSON Emerson Elvin, FB-DB-LB, 6´2˝/215 lbs; Toledo; 1950: Cle, rnd 12; B12/10/1927 Carrier Mills, IL **1952** Cle 6 **1952** ChiB 1

YEAR	TEAM	G (GS, POS)	RUSH	YD	AVG (LG)	TD	REC	YD	AVG (LG)	TD	PASS	COMP	PCT	YD	AVG (LG)	TD	INT	SK	YD	QBR	KPR	OTD	PTS	TAY
1950	†Cle	12(fb)	26	105	4.0(16)	0	—	—	—	—	—	—	—	—	—	—	—	—	—	—	k	—	0	112
1951	†Cle	12(fb)	46	252	5.5(23)	1	4	30	7.5(17)	0	—	—	—	—	—	—	—	—	—	—	k	—	6	275
NFL	3	31	72	357	5.0(23)	1	4	30	7.5(17)	0	—	—	—	—	—	—	—	—	—	—	k	—	6	411

COLE, FRED Frederick Michael, G, 6´0˝/226 lbs; Maryland; 1959: ChiB, rnd 6; B6/14/1937 Newark, NJ **1960**†LAC-A 14 (RG)

COLE, JOHN John, FB, 5´9˝/197 lbs; St. Joseph's (PA); B1915, deceased **[K]**

YEAR	TEAM	G (GS, POS)	RUSH	YD	AVG (LG)	TD	REC	YD	AVG (LG)	TD	PASS	COMP	PCT	YD	AVG (LG)	TD	INT	SK	YD	QBR	KPR	OTD	PTS	TAY
1938	Phi	11(0)	1	4	4.0(4)	0	2	9	4.5	0	—	—	—	—	—	—	—	—	—	—	—	—	0	9
1940	Phi	7(1)	26	75	2.9	0	2	11	5.5	0	—	—	—	—	—	—	—	—	—	—	KP	—	6	81
NFL	2	18(1)	27	79	2.9(4)	0	4	20	5.0	0	—	—	—	—	—	—	—	—	—	—	KP	—	6	89

COLE, LARRY Lawrence Rudolph, DE-DT, 6´5˝/252 lbs; Air Force; Hawaii; 1968: Dal, rnd 16; B11/15/1946 Clarkfield, MN **1968**†Dal 14 (10, LDE) **1969**†Dal 14 (LDE) **1970**†Dal 10 (10, LDE) **1971**†Dal 14 (LDE) **1972**†Dal 9 (7, LDE) **1973**†Dal 14 (LDE) **1974** Dal 14 (LDE) **1975**†Dal 13 (8, RDT) **1976**†Dal 14 (8, RDT) **1977**†Dal 12 **1978**†Dal 16 (3) **1979**†Dal 16 (16, LDE/ldt) **1980**†Dal 16 (16, LDT) **NFL** 176 (78) [13 yrs]

COLE, LEE Leatris, DB, 5´11˝/188 lbs; Arizona State; B6/25/1974 Riverside, CA **1996** Hou 2 (0)

COLE, LINZY Linzy, WR, 5´11˝/172 lbs; TCU; 1970: Chi, rnd 9; B4/21/1948 Dallas, TX **1971** Hou 14 **1972** Hou 2 **1972** Buf 8

YEAR	TEAM	G (GS, POS)	RUSH	YD	AVG (LG)	TD	REC	YD	AVG (LG)	TD	PASS	COMP	PCT	YD	AVG (LG)	TD	INT	SK	YD	QBR	KPR	OTD	PTS	TAY
1970	ChiB	7	—	—	—	—	3	47	15.7(34)	0	—	—	—	—	—	—	—	—	—	—	p	—	0	37
NFL	3	31	—	—	—	—	3	47	15.7(34)	0	—	—	—	—	—	—	—	—	—	—	kp	—	0	614

COLE, PETE Garth Peter, G-T, 5´11˝/222 lbs; Trinity (TX); B5/5/1916 Stamford, TX, D9/7/1971 **1937** NYG 2 (0) **1938**†NYG✧9 (1) **1939**†NYG 10 (0) **1940** NYG 9 (0) **NFL** 30 (1) [4 yrs]

COLE, ROBIN Robin, LB-DE, 6´2˝/220 lbs; New Mexico; 1977: Pit, rnd 1; B9/11/1955 Los Angeles, CA **1977**†Pit 8 **1978**†Pit 16 (8, rlb) **1979**†Pit 13 (8, rlb) **1980** Pit 14 (12, RLB) **1981** Pit 14 (13, RLB) **1982**†Pit 9 (9, ROLB) **1983**†Pit 16 (16, ROLB) **1984**†Pit★16 (16, RILB) **1985** Pit 16 (16, RILB) **1986** Pit 16 (16, RILB) **1987** Pit 12 (12, RILB) **1988** NYJ 16 (4) **NFL** 166 (130) [12 yrs]

COLE, TERRY Terry Phillip, RB, 6´2˝/220 lbs; Indiana; 1968: Bal, rnd 9; B7/7/1945 Dallas, TX, D11/11/2005 Indianapolis, IN

YEAR	TEAM	G (GS, POS)	RUSH	YD	AVG (LG)	TD	REC	YD	AVG (LG)	TD	PASS	COMP	PCT	YD	AVG (LG)	TD	INT	SK	YD	QBR	KPR	OTD	PTS	TAY
1968	†Bal	14	104	418	4.0(21)	3	13	75	5.8(18)	0	—	—	—	—	—	—	—	—	—	—	k	—	18	534
1969	Bal	9(fb)	73	204	2.8(27)	2	9	65	7.2(18)	1	—	—	—	—	—	—	—	—	—	—	—	—	18	262
1970	Pit	10	9	8	0.9(6)	0	3	31	10.3(20)	0	—	—	—	—	—	—	—	—	—	—	—	—	0	24
1971	†Mia	4	3	11	3.7(4)	0	—	—	—	—	—	—	—	—	—	—	—	—	—	—	—	—	0	11
NFL	4	37	189	641	3.4(27)	5	25	171	6.8(20)	1	—	—	—	—	—	—	—	—	—	—	k	—	36	830

COLE, TRENT Trent, DE-LB, 6´2˝/257 lbs; Cincinnati; 2005: Phi, rnd 5; B10/5/1982 Xenia, OH **2005** Phi 15 (7, rde)

YEAR	TEAM	G(GS, POS)	RUSH	YD	AVG(LG)	TD	REC	YD	AVG(LG)	TD	PASS	COMP	PCT	YD	AVG(LG)	TD	INT	SK	YD	QBR	KPR	OTD	PTS	TAY
COLELLA, TOM	Thomas Anthony, HB-TB, 6´0˝/187 lbs; Canisius; 1942: Det, rnd 7; B7/3/1918 Albion, NY, D5/15/1992 Hamburg, NY **[KI]**																							
1942	Det	9(2)	23	51	2.2(34)	0	—	—	—	—	41	18	43.9	178	4.3(23)	0	4	—	—	—	Pkpi	—	0	3
1943	Det	8(0)	15	24	1.6(18)	0	1	-1	-1.0(-1)	0	31	11	35.5	103	3.3(21)	0	4	—	—	—	Pp	—	0	-84
1944	Cle	10(8, TB)	53	208	3.9(75)	2	2	64	32.0(54)	1	75	27	36.0	336	4.5(25)	4	10	—	—	—	KPkpi	—	21	222
1945	Cle	10(1)	46	224	4.9(30)	2	7	64	9.1(20)	2	1	0	0.0	0	0.0	0	0	—	—	—	kp	—	24	325
NFL	4	37(11)	137	507	3.7(75)	4	10	127	12.7(54)	3	148	56	37.8	617	4.2(25)	4	18	—	—	—	KPkpi	—	45	466
1946	†Cle-A	14(2)	30	118	3.9(50)	2	1	12	12.0(12)	1	—	—	—	—	—	—	—	—	—	—	Pkpi	—	18	355
1947	†Cle-A	14(7, LH)	11	77	7.0	1	4	63	15.8(18)	1	—	—	—	—	—	—	—	—	—	—	Pkpi	2	24	330
1948	†Cle-A	13(2)	14	60	4.3	1	1	7	7.0(7)	0	—	—	—	—	—	—	—	—	—	—	Ppi	—	6	133
1949	Buf-A	11(0)	7	-9	-1.3	0	2	6	3.0	0	—	—	—	—	—	—	—	—	—	—	—	—	0	47
AAFC	4	52(11)	62	246	4.0(75)	4	8	88	11.0(54)	2	—	—	—	—	—	—	—	—	—	—	Pkpi	2	48	864
COLEMAN, AL	Alvin M., DB, 6´1˝/183 lbs; Jackson State; Tennessee State; 1967: Min, rnd 4; B12/27/1944 Gulfport, MS **1967** Min 2 **1969** Cin-A 14 (LS) **1970**†Cin 11 (fs) **1971** Cin 4 **1972** Phi 12 **1973** Phi 14 **NFL** 57 [6 yrs]																							
COLEMAN, ANDRE	Andre Clintonian, WR, 5´9˝/165 lbs; Kansas State; 1994: SD, rnd 3; B9/19/1972 Charlotte, NC **[R]** **1994**†SD☆13 (0) **1997** Sea 2 (0) **1997**†Pit 8 (0)																							
1995	†SD☆	15(0)	—	—	—	—	3	67	22.3(41)	0	—	—	—	—	—	—	—	—	—	—	kp	3	18	731
1996	SD	16(10, WR)	2	0	0.0(7)	0	36	486	13.5(50)	2	—	—	—	—	—	—	—	—	—	—	k	—	12	638
1998	Pit	4(0)	—	—	—	—	4	49	12.3(13)	1	—	—	—	—	—	—	—	—	—	—	p	—	6	33
NFL	5	58(10)	2	0	0.0(7)	0	43	602	14.0(50)	3	—	—	—	—	—	—	—	—	—	—	kp	5	48	2106
COLEMAN, ANTHONY	Anthony Quinn, DB, 6´0˝/185 lbs; Baylor; B8/20/1964 Henderson, TX **1987** Dal 3 (0)																							
COLEMAN, BEN	Benjamin Leon, G-T, 6´5˝/330 lbs; Wake Forest; 1993: Phx, rnd 2; B5/18/1971 South Hill, VT **1993** Phx 12 (0) **1994** Arz 15 (13, RG/lt) **1995** Arz 3 (0) **1995** Jax 10 (5, rg) **1996**†Jax 16 (16, LG) **1997**†Jax 16 (16, LG) **1998**†Jax 16 (16, LG) **1999**†Jax 16 (12, LG) **2000** SD 16 (16, LT) **2001** Was 15 (10, RG) **NFL** 135 (104) [9 yrs]																							
COLEMAN, CHARLES	Charles Edward, TE, 6´4˝/222 lbs; Alcorn State; B9/16/1963 Kokomo, MS																							
1987	NYG	3(0)	—	—	—	—	1	5	5.0(5)	1	—	—	—	—	—	—	—	—	—	—	k	—	0	8
COLEMAN, CHRIS	Chris, WR, 6´0˝/202 lbs; North Carolina State; B5/8/1977 Shelby, NC **2000**†Ten 13 (0)																							
2001	Ten	16(0)	—	—	—	—	1	19	19.0(19)	0	—	—	—	—	—	—	—	—	—	—	k	—	0	96
NFL	2	29(0)	—	—	—	—	1	19	19.0(19)	0	—	—	—	—	—	—	—	—	—	—	k	—	0	120
COLEMAN, CLARENCE	Clarence, WR, 5´10˝/193 lbs; Ferris State; B6/4/1980 Miami, FL																							
2003	Buf	14(0)	—	—	—	—	8	69	8.6(12)	0	—	—	—	—	—	—	—	—	—	—	—	—	0	35
COLEMAN, COSEY	Cosey Clinton, G, 6´4˝/322 lbs; Tennessee; 2000: TB, rnd 2; B10/27/1978 Clarkston, GA **2000** TB 8 (0) **2001**†TB 16 (16, RG) **2002**†TB 15 (15, RG) **2005** Cle 14 (14, RG)																							
2003	TB	16(16, RG)	—	—	—	—	0	0	(1)	0	—	—	—	—	—	—	—	—	—	—	—	—	0	1
2004	TB	16(16, RG)	—	—	—	—	1	4	4.0(4)	0	—	—	—	—	—	—	—	—	—	—	—	—	0	2
NFL	6	85(77)	—	—	—	—	1	5	5.0(4)	0	—	—	—	—	—	—	—	—	—	—	—	—	0	3
COLEMAN, DAN	Daniel, DE, 6´4˝/249 lbs; Murray State; B8/14/1962 Lansing, MI **1987** Min 3 (1)																							
COLEMAN, DENNIS	Dennis Franklin, LB, 6´4˝/225 lbs; Mississippi; 1971: Mia, rnd 6; B12/19/1948 Aberdeen, MS **1971** NE 9																							
COLEMAN, DON	Donald Alvin, LB, 6´2˝/222 lbs; Michigan; 1974: NO, rnd 16; B1/11/1952 Toledo, OH **1974** NO 14 **1975** NO 13 (LLB) **NFL** 27 [2 yrs]																							
COLEMAN, ERIC	Eric Gerard, DB, 6´0˝/190 lbs; Wyoming; 1989: NE, rnd 2; B12/27/1966 Denver, CO **1989** NE 8 (0) **1990** NE 7 (0) **NFL** 15 (0) [2 yrs]																							
COLEMAN, ERIK	Erik James, DB, 5´10˝/200 lbs; Washington State; 2004: NYJ, rnd 5; B5/6/1982 Sacramento, CA **2004**†NYJ 16 (16, FS) **2005** NYJ 16 (16, SS) **NFL** 32 (32) [2 yrs]																							
COLEMAN, FRED	Frederick, TE, 6´4˝/240 lbs; Louisiana-Monroe; 1976: Buf, rnd 5; B6/26/1953 Greenville, MS **1976** Buf 7																							
COLEMAN, FRED	Fred Dewayne, WR, 6´0˝/190 lbs; Washington; 1998: Buf, rnd 6; B1/31/1975 Tyler, TX **2002** NE 1 (0)																							
2001	†NE	8(0)	—	—	—	—	2	50	25.0(46)	0	—	—	—	—	—	—	—	—	—	—	—	—	0	25
NFL	2	9(0)	—	—	—	—	2	50	25.0(46)	0	—	—	—	—	—	—	—	—	—	—	—	—	0	25
COLEMAN, GREG	Gregory Jerome, P, 6´0˝/185 lbs; Florida A&M; 1976: Cin, rnd 14; B9/9/1954 Jacksonville, FL **[P]**																							
1977	Cle	14	1	-3	-3.0(-3)	0	—	—	—	—	—	—	—	—	—	—	—	—	—	—	P	—	0	-3
1978	†Min	9	2	22	11.0(17)	0	—	—	—	—	—	—	—	—	—	—	—	—	—	—	P	—	0	22
1979	Min	16	—	—	—	—	—	—	—	—	—	—	—	—	—	—	—	—	—	—	P	—	0	0
1980	†Min	16(0)	—	—	—	—	—	—	—	—	—	—	—	—	—	—	—	—	—	—	P	—	0	0
1981	Min	15(0)	—	—	—	—	—	—	—	—	—	—	—	—	—	—	—	—	—	—	P	—	0	0
1982	†Min	9(0)	1	15	15.0(15)	0	—	—	—	—	—	—	—	—	—	—	—	—	—	—	P	—	0	15
1983	Min	16(0)	1	-9	-9.0(-9)	0	—	—	—	—	—	—	—	—	—	—	—	—	—	—	P	—	0	-9
1984	Min	16(0)	2	11	5.5(13)	0	—	—	—	—	1	0	0.0	0	0.0	0	0	0	0	—	P	—	0	11
1985	Min	16(0)	2	0	0.0(0)	0	—	—	—	—	—	—	—	—	—	—	—	—	—	—	P	—	0	0
1986	Min	16(0)	2	46	23.0(30)	0	—	—	—	—	—	—	—	—	—	—	—	—	—	—	P	—	0	46
1987	Min	9(0)	—	—	—	—	—	—	—	—	—	—	—	—	—	—	—	—	—	—	P	—	0	0
1988	Was	10(0)	2	-13	-6.5(0)	0	—	—	—	—	1	0	0.0	0	0.0	0	0	0	0	—	P	—	0	-13
NFL	12	162	13	69	5.3(30)	0	—	—	—	—	2	0	0.0	0	0.0	0	0	0	0	—	P	—	0	69
COLEMAN, HERB	Herbert Edward, C-G, 6´0˝/200 lbs; Notre Dame; 1945: Bos, rnd 12; B6/18/1923 Chester, WV, D1/1/1985 Northville, MI **1946** ChiR-A 14 (12, C) **1947** ChiR-A 13 (4) **1948** ChiR-A 9 (8, rg) **1948** Bal-A 1 (0) **AAFC** 37 (24) [3 yrs]																							
COLEMAN, KaRON	KaRon, RB, 5´7˝/198 lbs; Stephen F. Austin State; B5/22/1978 Missouri City, TX																							
2000	†Den	9(0)	54	183	3.4(24)	1	1	5	5.0(5)	0	—	—	—	—	—	—	—	—	—	—	—	6	196
2001	Den	4(0)	4	17	4.3(8)	0	6	45	7.5(9)	0	—	—	—	—	—	—	—	—	—	—	—	0	40
2002	Den	2(0)	—	—	—	—	—	—	—	—	—	—	—	—	—	—	—	—	—	—	k	—	0	-9
NFL	3	15(0)	58	200	3.4(24)	1	7	50	7.1(9)	0	—	—	—	—	—	—	—	—	—	—	k	—	6	226
COLEMAN, KENYON	Kenyon Octavia, DE, 6´5˝/285 lbs; UCLA; 2002: Oak, rnd 5; B4/10/1979 Fontana, CA **2002** Oak 1 (0) **2003** Dal 16 (0) **2004** Dal 12 (0) **2005** Dal 12 (5, lde) **NFL** 41 (5) [4 yrs]																							
COLEMAN, KEO	Keombani M., LB, 6´1˝/255 lbs; Mississippi State; 1992: NYJ, rnd 4; B5/1/1970 Los Angeles, CA **1992** NYJ 6 (0) **1993** GB 12 (2) **NFL** 18 (2) [2 yrs]																							
COLEMAN, LEONARD	Leonard David, DB, 6´2˝/203 lbs; Vanderbilt; 1984: Ind, rnd 1; B1/30/1962 Boynton Beach, FL **1985** Ind 12 (0) **1986** Ind 16 (16, LCB) **1987** Ind 4 (0) **1988** SD 16 (0) **1989** SD 1 (0) **NFL** 49 (16) [5 yrs]																							
COLEMAN, LINCOLN	Lincoln Cales, FB, 6´1˝/249 lbs; Notre Dame; Baylor; B8/12/1969 Dallas, TX																							
1993	†Dal	7(0)	34	132	3.9(16)	2	4	24	6.0(10)	0	—	—	—	—	—	—	—	—	—	—	—	12	164
1994	Dal	11(0)	64	180	2.8(13)	1	8	46	5.8(14)	0	—	—	—	—	—	—	—	—	—	—	—	6	213
NFL	2	18(0)	98	312	3.2(16)	3	12	70	5.8(14)	0	—	—	—	—	—	—	—	—	—	—	—	18	377
COLEMAN, MARCO	Marco Darnell, DE-LB, 6´3˝/286 lbs; Georgia Tech; 1992: Mia, rnd 1; B12/18/1969 Dayton, OH **[S]** **1992**†Mia 16 (15, LOLB/rde) **1993** Mia 15 (15, RDE) **1994**†Mia 16 (16, RDE) **1995**†Mia 16 (16, RDE) **1996** SD 16 (16, RDE) **1997** SD 16 (16, RDE) **1998** SD 16 (16, RDE) **1999**†Was 16 (16, RDE) **2000** Was◇16 (16, RDE) **2001** Was 12 (12, LDE) **2002** Jax 16 (16, LDE) **2003**†Phi 13 (0) **2004**†Den 16 (16, LDE) **2005**†Den 7 (0) **NFL** 207 (185) [14 yrs]																							
COLEMAN, MARCUS	Marcus Le'Shan, DB, 6´2˝/210 lbs; Texas Tech; 1996: NYJ, rnd 5; B5/24/1974 Dallas, TX **[I]** **1996** NYJ 13 (4) **1997** NYJ 16 (2) **1998**†NYJ 14 (0) **1999** NYJ 16 (10, RCB) **2001**†NYJ 16 (16, RCB) **2002** Hou 16 (16, RCB) **2004** Hou 12 (12, FS) **2005** Hou 15 (11, FS)																							
2000	NYJ	16(16, RCB)	—	—	—	—	1	45	45.0(45)	1	—	—	—	—	—	—	—	—	—	—	i	—	8	14
2003	Hou	15(15, RCB)	—	—	—	—	1	6	6.0(6)	0	—	—	—	—	—	—	—	—	—	—	i	—	0	63
NFL	10	149(102)	—	—	—	—	2	51	25.5(45)	1	—	—	—	—	—	—	—	—	—	—	i	2	20	402

YEAR	TEAM	G(GS,POS)	RUSH	YD	AVG(LG)	TD	REC	YD	AVG(LG)	TD	PASS COMP	PCT	YD	AVG(LG)	TD	INT	SK	YD	QBR	KPR	OTD	PTS	TAY

COLLINS, TODD Todd Steven, QB, 6´4˝/225 lbs; Michigan; 1995: Buf, rnd 2; B11/5/1971 Walpole, MA

1995	Buf	7(1)	9	23	2.6(10)	0	—	—	—	—	29	14	48.3	112	3.9(18)	0	1	6	43	—	—	—	0	39
1996	†Buf	7(3)	21	43	2.0(10)	0	—	—	—	—	99	55	55.6	739	7.5(95)	4	5	11	53	—	—	—	0	233
1997	Buf	14(13, QB)	30	77	2.6(11)	0	—	—	—	—	391	215	55.0	2367	6.1(77)	12	13	39	278	69.5	—	—	0	801
2001	KC	1(0)	2	6	3.0(7)	0	—	—	—	—	4	3	75.0	40	10.0(26)	0	0	—	—	—	—	—	0	26
2002	KC	3(0)	1	7	7.0(7)	0	—	—	—	—	6	5	83.3	73	12.2(29)	1	0	—	—	—	—	—	0	49
2003	KC	5(0)	8	-7	-0.9(0)	0	—	—	—	—	12	9	75.0	74	6.2(20)	0	0	—	—	—	—	—	0	30
2004	KC	2(0)	1	4	4.0(4)	0	—	—	—	—	5	1	20.0	42	8.4(42)	0	0	—	—	—	—	—	0	25
2005	KC	2(0)	2	-2	-1.0(-1)	0	—	—	—	—	—	—	—	—	—	—	—	—	—	—	—	—	0	-2
NFL	8	41(17)	74	151	2.0(11)	0	—	—	—	—	546	302	55.3	3447	6.3(95)	17	19	56	374	70.4	—	—	0	1200

COLLINS, TODD Todd Franklin, LB, 6´2˝/248 lbs; Georgia; Tennessee; Carson-Newman; 1992: NE, rnd 3; B5/27/1970 New Market, TN **1992** NE 10 (1) **1993** NE 16 (12, RILB) **1994** NE 7 (7, RILB) **1996**†NE 16 (9, LLB) **1997** NE 15 (15, RLB) **1998** NE 12 (10, RLB) **1999**†SL 16 (13, RLB) **2000**†SL 14 (11, RLB) **NFL** 106 (77) [8 yrs]

COLLINS, TONY Anthony, RB, 5´11˝/208 lbs; East Carolina; 1981: NE, rnd 2; B5/27/1959 Sanford, FL

1981	NE	16(11, RB)	204	873	4.3(29)	7	26	232	8.9(22)	0	1	—	0.0	0	0.0	0	0	—	—	—	kp	—	42	1247
1982	†NE	9(9, RB)	164	632	3.9(54)	1	19	187	9.8(33)	2	—	—	—	—	—	—	—	—	—	—	—	—	18	746
1983	NE★	16(16, RB)	219	1049	4.8(54)	10	27	257	9.5(20)	0	—	—	—	—	—	—	—	—	—	—	—	—	60	1278
1984	NE	16(5, rb)	138	550	4.0(21)	5	16	100	6.3(19)	0	—	—	—	—	—	—	—	—	—	—	k	—	30	819
1985	NE	16(16, RB)	163	657	4.0(28)	3	52	549	10.6(49)	4	—	—	—	—	—	—	—	—	—	—	—	—	30	972
1986	†NE	16(15, RB)	156	412	2.6(17)	3	77	684	8.9(49)	5	—	—	—	—	—	—	—	—	—	—	—	—	48	809
1987	NE	13(11, RB)	147	474	3.2(19)	3	44	347	7.9(29)	3	—	—	—	—	—	—	—	—	—	—	k	—	36	696
1990	Mia	1(0)	—	—	—	—	—	—	—	—	—	—	—	—	—	—	—	—	—	—	k	—	0	0
NFL	8	103(83)	1191	4647	3.9(54)	32	261	2356	9.0(49)	12	1	0	0.0	0	0.0	0	0	—	—	—	kp	—	264	6565

COLLINS, TRENT Trent John, DB, 6´1˝/187 lbs; San Diego State; B5/18/1961 New Orleans, LA **1987** NYJ 3 (3)

COLLINSWORTH, CRIS Anthony Cris, WR, 6´5˝/192 lbs; Florida; 1981: Cin, rnd 2; B1/27/1959 Dayton, OH

1981	†Cin★	16(16, WR)	—	—	—	—	67	1009	15.1(74)	8	—	—	—	—	—	—	—	—	—	—	—	—	48	545
1982	†Cin★	9(9, WR)	1	-11	-11.0(-11)	0	49	700	14.3(50)	1	—	—	—	—	—	—	—	—	—	—	—	—	6	344
1983	Cin★	14(14, WR)	2	2	1.0(8)	0	66	1130	17.1(63)	5	—	—	—	—	—	—	—	—	—	—	—	—	30	592
1984	Cin	15(14, WR)	1	7	7.0(7)	0	64	989	15.5(57)	6	—	—	—	—	—	—	—	—	—	—	—	—	36	532
1985	Cin☆	16(16, WR)	1	3	3.0(3)	0	65	1125	17.3(71)	5	1	0	0.0	0	0.0	0	0	—	—	—	—	—	30	551
1986	Cin	16(15, WR)	2	-16	-8.0(-6)	0	62	1024	16.5(46)	10	—	—	—	—	—	—	—	—	—	—	—	—	60	546
1987	Cin	8(6, WR)	—	—	—	—	31	494	15.9(53)	0	—	—	—	—	—	—	—	—	—	—	—	—	0	247
1988	†Cin	13(0)	—	—	—	—	13	227	17.5(36)	1	—	—	—	—	—	—	—	—	—	—	—	—	6	119
NFL	8	107(90)	7	-15	-2.1(8)	0	417	6698	16.1(74)	36	1	0	0.0	0	0.0	0	1	—	—	—	—	—	216	3474

COLLONS, FERRIC Ferric Jason, DE, 6´7˝/290 lbs; California; B12/4/1969 Belleville, IL **1995** NE 16 (4) **1996**†NE 15 (5, lde) **1997** NE 5 (5, lde) **1998**†NE 14 (11, LDE) **1999** NE 14 (0) **NFL** 64 (25) [5 yrs]

COLMAN, DOUG Douglass Clayton, LB, 6´2˝/250 lbs; Nebraska; 1996: NYG, rnd 6; B6/4/1973 Somers Point, NJ **1996** NYG 13 (0) **1997**†NYG 14 (0) **1998** NYG 16 (0) **1999**†Ten 16 (0) **2000** Cle 6 (0) **NFL** 64 (0) [5 yrs]

COLMAN, WAYNE Wayne Charles, LB, 6´2˝/230 lbs; Temple; B4/13/1946 Ventnor, NJ **1968** Phi 14 **1969** Phi 5 **1969** NO 4 **1970** NO 14 (llb) **1971** NO 14 (RLB) **1972** NO 14 (RLB) **1973** NO 12 (RLB) **1974** NO 14 (RLB) **1976** NO 7 **NFL** 98 [8 yrs]

COLMER, MICKEY John Francis, B, 6´2˝/219 lbs; Miramonte J.C.; B10/23/1918 Redondo Beach, CA, D7/20/2000 Redondo Beach, CA

1946	Bkn-A	12(6, WB)	46	155	3.4	0	22	327	14.9	1	—	—	—	—	—	—	—	—	—	—	kpi	—	6	317
1947	Bkn-A	14(10, FB)	152	578	3.8	9	18	190	10.6	1	3	1	33.3	20	6.7(20)	0	0	—	—	—	Pk	—	60	810
1948	Bkn-A☆	14(11, FB)	164	704	4.3	6	21	372	17.7(78)	4	1	0	0.0	0	0.0	0	0	—	—	—	Pk	—	60	1013
1949	NYY-A	8(2)	36	100	2.8	0	2	10	5.0	0	1	0	0.0	0	0.0	0	0	—	—	—	Pk	—	0	106
AAFC	4	48(29)	398	1537	3.9	15	63	899	14.3(78)	6	5	1	20.0	20	4.0(20)	0	0	—	—	—	Pkpi	—	126	2246

COLO, DON Donald Richard, DT, 6´3˝/252 lbs; Brown; 1950: Bal, rnd 3; B1/5/1925 East Bridgewater, MA **1950** Bal 12 (1, LDT) **1951** NYY 12 (RDT) **1952** DalT 4 **1953**†Cle✩12 (LDT) **1954**†Cle★12 (RDT) **1955**†Cle★12 (RDT) **1956** Cle☆12 (rdt) **1957**†Cle☆12 (RDT) **1958**†Cle★12 (RDT) **NFL** 100 (1) [9 yrs]

COLOMBO, MARC Marc Edward, T, 6´7˝/320 lbs; Boston College; 2002: Chi, rnd 1; B10/8/1978 Bridgewater, MA **2002** ChiB 10 (5, lt) **2004** ChiB 8 (2) **2005** ChiB 1 (0) **2005** Dal 4 (0) **NFL** 23 (7) [3 yrs]

COLON, HARRY Harry, DB, 6´0˝/203 lbs; Missouri; 1991: NE, rnd 8; B2/14/1969 Kansas City, KS **1991** NE 16 (14, SS) **1992** Det 16 (16, FS) **1993**†Det 15 (11, FS) **1994**†Det 16 (0) **1995** Jax 16 (16, SS) **1997** Det 8 (4) **NFL** 87 (45) [6 yrs]

COLORITO, TONY Anthony Ivor, NT, 6´5˝/260 lbs; USC; 1986: Den, rnd 5; B9/8/1964 Brooklyn, NY **1986**†Den 15 (0)

COLQUITT, CRAIG Joseph Craig, P, 6´1˝/182 lbs; Tennessee; 1978: Pit, rnd 3; B6/9/1954 Knoxville, TN [P] **1978**†Pit 16 **1979**†Pit 16 **1983**†Pit 16 (0) **1987** Ind 1 (0)

1980	Pit	16(0)	1	17	17.0(17)	0	—	—	—	—	—	—	—	—	—	—	—	—	—	P	—	—	0	17
1981	Pit	16(0)	1	8	8.0(8)	0	—	—	—	—	—	—	—	—	—	—	—	—	—	P	—	—	0	8
1984	†Pit	16(0)	1	0	0.0(9)	0	—	—	—	—	—	—	—	—	—	—	—	—	—	P	—	—	0	0
NFL	7	97	3	25	8.3(17)	0	—	—	—	—	—	—	—	—	—	—	—	—	—	P	—	—	0	25

COLQUITT, DUSTIN Dustin Farr, P, 6´2˝/211 lbs; Tennessee; 2005: KC, rnd 3; B5/6/1982 Knoxville, TN **2005** KC 16 (0)

COLQUITT, JIMMY James Michael, P, 6´4˝/209 lbs; Tennessee; B1/17/1963 Knoxville, TN **1985** Sea 2 (0)

COLSTON, TIM Timothy Maurice, NT, 6´0˝/275 lbs; Kansas State; B12/18/1973 Tampa, FL **1996** Car 2 (0)

COLTER, JEFF Jeffrey, DB, 5´10˝/171 lbs; Kansas; B4/23/1961 Tucson, AZ **1984** Min 16 (0) **1987** KC 1 (0) **NFL** 17 (0) [2 yrs]

COLTERYAHN, LLOYD Lloyd Kenneth, E, 6´2˝/220 lbs; Maryland; 1953: Pit, rnd 4; B8/26/1931 Brentwood, PA

1954	Bal	12(LE)	—	—	—	—	30	384	12.8(21)	0	—	—	—	—	—	—	—	—	—	—	—	—	0	192
1955	Bal	12(LE)	—	—	—	—	21	251	12.0(22)	3	—	—	—	—	—	—	—	—	—	—	—	—	18	141
1956	Bal	3	—	—	—	—	3	29	9.7(16)	0	—	—	—	—	—	—	—	—	—	—	—	—	0	15
NFL	3	27	—	—	—	—	54	664	12.3(22)	3	—	—	—	—	—	—	—	—	—	—	—	—	18	347

COLTON, GEORGE George Curtis, G, 6´4˝/279 lbs; Maryland; 1986: NE, rnd 9; B7/28/1963 Lindenhurst, NY **1987** NE 3 (3)

COLVIN, JIM James R., DT-DE-G, 6´3˝/252 lbs; Houston; 1960: Bal, rnd 8/Den, rnd 2; B11/30/1937 Monahans, TX **1960** Bal 12 (2) **1961** Bal 13 **1962** Bal 14 (14, LDT) **1963** Bal 14 (14, LDT) **1964** Dal 14 (14, LDT) **1965** Dal 14 (14, LDT) **1966**†Dal 14 (14, LDT) **1967** NYG 8 **NFL** 103 (72) [8 yrs]

COLVIN, ROSEVELT Rosevelt, LB, 6´3˝/250 lbs; Purdue; 1999: Chi, rnd 4; B9/5/1977 Indianapolis, IN **1999** ChiB 11 (0) **2000** ChiB 13 (8, llb) **2001**†ChiB 16 (13, LLB) **2002** ChiB 15 (15, LLB) **2003** NE 2 (2) **2005**†NE 16 (11, RLB) **NFL** 90 (50) [7 yrs]

COLZIE, NEAL Cornelius Connie, DB, 6´2˝/200 lbs; Ohio State; 1975: Oak, rnd 1; B2/28/1954 Fitzgerald, GA, D8/19/2001 South Miami, FL [RI] **1975**†Oak 3 (2) **1976**†Oak 14 (1) **1977**†Oak 13 (3) **1978** Oak 16 **1979**†Mia 16 (16, FS) **1980** TB 16 (1) **1981**†TB 16 (16, SS) **1982**†TB☆9 (9, SS) **1983** TB 5 (3) **NFL** 118 (51) [9 yrs]

COMBS, BILL Lloyd William, E-DB, 5´11˝/183 lbs; Purdue; B6/29/1920 Holder, IL, D10/27/1998 West Lafayette, IN

| 1942 | Phi | 10(0) | — | — | — | — | 4 | 44 | 11.0(19) | 1 | — | — | — | — | — | — | — | — | — | — | — | — | 6 | 27 |

COMBS, CHRIS Christopher Allen, TE-T, 6´4˝/238 lbs; New Mexico; 1980: Hou, rnd 4; B3/17/1958 San Diego, CA

1980	SL	16(0)	—	—	—	—	2	52	26.0(38)	1	—	—	—	—	—	—	—	—	—	—	—	—	6	31
1981	SL	16(2)	—	—	—	—	5	54	10.8(13)	0	—	—	—	—	—	—	—	—	—	—	—	—	0	27
NFL	2	32(2)	—	—	—	—	7	106	15.1(38)	1	—	—	—	—	—	—	—	—	—	—	—	—	6	58

COMBS, CHRIS Christopher Brandon, DE, 6´4˝/284 lbs; Duke; 2000: Pit, rnd 6; B12/15/1976 Roanoke, VA **2000** Pit 6 (0) **2001** Pit 2 (0) **2002** Jax 2 (0) **NFL** 10 (0) [3 yrs]

COMBS, DEREK Derek Alan, DB, 6´0˝/185 lbs; Ohio State; 2001: Oak, rnd 7; B2/28/1979 Columbus, OH **2002** Oak 4 (0) **2003** GB 8 (0) **NFL** 12 (0) [2 yrs]

COMEAUX, DARREN Darren, LB, 6´1˝/227 lbs; Arizona State; B4/15/1960 San Diego, CA **1982** Den 3 (0) **1983**†Den 14 (0) **1984**†Den 16 (0) **1985** Den 11 (0) **1986**†Den 16 (0) **1987**†SF 8 (0) **1988** Sea 9 (6, lilb) **1989** Sea 16 (13, LILB) **1990** Sea 9 (9, MLB) **1991** Sea 16 (11, MLB) **NFL** 118 (39) [10 yrs]

COMELLA, GREG Greg, FB, 6´1˝/248 lbs; Stanford; B7/29/1975 Wellesley, MA

YEAR	TEAM	G (GS, POS)	RUSH	YD	AVG (LG)	TD	REC	YD	AVG (LG)	TD	PASS	COMP	PCT	YD	AVG (LG)	TD	INT	SK	YD	QBR	KPR	OTD	PTS	TAY
1998	NYG	16(0)	1	6	6.0(6)	0	1	3	3.0(3)	0	—	—	—	—	—	—	—	—	—	—	k	—	0	5
1999	NYG	16(3)	1	0	0.0(0)	0	8	39	4.9(26)	0	—	—	—	—	—	—	—	—	—	—	k	—	0	21
2000	†NYG	16(12, FB)	10	45	4.5(16)	0	36	274	7.6(25)	0	—	—	—	—	—	—	—	—	—	—	kp	—	0	167
2001	NYG	16(13, FB)	4	15	3.8(9)	0	39	253	6.5(26)	1	—	—	—	—	—	—	—	—	—	—	—	—	6	147
2002	Ten	12(7, fb)	1	0	0.0(0)	0	10	70	7.0(17)	0	—	—	—	—	—	—	—	—	—	—	—	—	0	35
2003	Hou	5(0)	—	—	—	—	—	—	—	—	—	—	—	—	—	—	—	—	—	—	—	—	—	—
2004	TB	7(0)	—	—	—	—	1	12	12.0(12)	0	—	—	—	—	—	—	—	—	—	—	k	—	0	11
NFL	7	88(35)	17	66	3.9(16)	0	95	651	6.9(26)	1	—	—	—	—	—	—	—	—	—	—	kp	—	6	385

COMER, HOOK John S., FB, /180 lbs; none; B10/1898 Cass Township, OH, deceased **1926** Can 1 (1)

COMER, MARTY Martin F., DE-E, 6´0˝/203 lbs; Tulane; 1943: Bkn, rnd 5; B10/28/1917 Indianapolis, IN, D3/22/1998 New Orleans, LA

YEAR	TEAM	G (GS, POS)	RUSH	YD	AVG (LG)	TD	REC	YD	AVG (LG)	TD	PASS	COMP	PCT	YD	AVG (LG)	TD	INT	SK	YD	QBR	KPR	OTD	PTS	TAY
1946	Buf-A	6(3)	—	—	—	—	2	17	8.5	0	—	—	—	—	—	—	—	—	—	—	—	1	6	9
1947	Buf-A	14(2)	—	—	—	—	2	75	37.5	1	—	—	—	—	—	—	—	—	—	—	—	—	6	43
1948	Buf-A	7(4)	—	—	—	—	5	66	13.2	1	—	—	—	—	—	—	—	—	—	—	—	—	6	38
AAFC	3	27(9)	—	—	—	—	9	158	17.6	2	—	—	—	—	—	—	—	—	—	—	—	1	18	89

COMIER, ULYSSES Adonis, FB, 5´10˝/195 lbs; none; B1905, deceased **1929** Buf 3 (1)

COMMISA, VINCE Vincent John, G, 5´9˝/190 lbs; Notre Dame; B11/1/1921 Newark, NJ, D3/5/1990 Orange, NJ **1944** Bos 1 (0)

COMMISKEY, CHUCK Charles Edward, G, 6´4˝/290 lbs; Mississippi; 1981: Phi, rnd 9; B3/28/1958 Killeen, TX **1986** NO 16 (10, RG) **1987**†NO 12 (4) **1988** NO 6 (0) **NFL** 34 (14) [3 yrs]

COMP, IRV Irving Henry, B, 6´2˝/204 lbs; Benedictine; 1943: GB, rnd 3; B5/17/1919 Milwaukee, WI, D7/11/1989 Woodruff, WI **[I]**

YEAR	TEAM	G (GS, POS)	RUSH	YD	AVG (LG)	TD	REC	YD	AVG (LG)	TD	PASS	COMP	PCT	YD	AVG (LG)	TD	INT	SK	YD	QBR	KPR	OTD	PTS	TAY
1943	GB	9(2, tb)	77	182	2.4(27)	3	—	—	—	—	92	46	50.0	662	7.2(79)	7	4	—	—	—	Pkpi	1	24	563
1944	†GB	10(8, TB)	52	134	2.6(28)	2	2	16	8.0(11)	1	**177**	80	45.2	**1159**	6.5(55)	12	**21**	—	—	50.0	kpi	—	18	18
1945	GB	9(7, TB)	57	92	1.6(18)	1	1	50	50.0(50)	1	106	44	41.5	865	8.2(75)	7	11	—	—	53.1	kpi	1	18	278
1946	GB	11(2, tb)	61	62	1.0(29)	1	—	—	—	—	94	27	28.7	333	3.5(35)	1	8	—	—	—	ki	—	6	-35
1947	GB	12(1)	5	46	9.2(34)	0	—	—	—	—	1	0	0.0	0	0.0	0	1	—	—	—	pi	—	0	36
1948	GB	11(1)	3	3	1.0(2)	0	—	—	—	—	49	16	32.7	335	6.8(50)	1	7	—	—	—	pi	—	0	-24
1949	GB	7(0)	—	—	—	—	—	—	—	—	—	—	—	—	—	—	—	—	—	—	i	—	0	9
NFL	7	69(21)	255	519	2.0(34)	7	3	66	22.0(50)	2	519	213	41.0	3354	6.5(79)	28	52	—	—	41.6	Pkpi	2	66	845

COMPAGNO, TONY Anthony, FB, 5´11˝/199 lbs; St. Mary's (CA); 1943: Pit, rnd 21; B1/29/1921 Daly City, CA, D4/8/1971 San Mateo, CA

YEAR	TEAM	G (GS, POS)	RUSH	YD	AVG (LG)	TD	REC	YD	AVG (LG)	TD	PASS	COMP	PCT	YD	AVG (LG)	TD	INT	SK	YD	QBR	KPR	OTD	PTS	TAY
1946	Pit	10(8, FB)	67	217	3.2(23)	1	8	101	12.6(36)	0	—	—	—	—	—	—	—	—	—	—	ki	—	6	325
1947	†Pit	12(4)	34	126	3.7(13)	2	9	190	21.1(39)	1	—	—	—	—	—	—	—	—	—	—	ki	2	30	411
1948	Pit	12(1)	24	101	4.2(20)	0	1	4	4.0(4)	0	—	—	—	—	—	—	—	—	—	—	pi	1	6	258
NFL	3	34(13)	125	444	3.6(23)	3	18	295	16.4(39)	1	—	—	—	—	—	—	—	—	—	—	kpi	3	42	994

COMPTON, CHUCK Charles, DB, 5´10˝/190 lbs; Boise State; B1/13/1965 Atwater, CA **1987** GB 2 (0)

COMPTON, DICK Richard Lee, SE-B, 6´2˝/190 lbs; McMurry; B4/16/1940 Colorado City, TX

YEAR	TEAM	G (GS, POS)	RUSH	YD	AVG (LG)	TD	REC	YD	AVG (LG)	TD	PASS	COMP	PCT	YD	AVG (LG)	TD	INT	SK	YD	QBR	KPR	OTD	PTS	TAY
1962	Det	10	1	3	3.0(3)	0	—	—	—	—	—	—	—	—	—	—	—	—	—	—	—	—	0	3
1963	Det	13	—	—	—	—	2	41	20.5(22)	0	—	—	—	—	—	—	—	—	—	—	Pkpi	—	0	38
1964	Det	12	3	2	0.7(4)	0	—	—	—	—	—	—	—	—	—	—	—	—	—	—	—	—	0	44
1965	Hou-A	3	1	2	2.0(2)	0	3	140	46.7(**95**)	2	—	—	—	—	—	—	—	—	—	—	k	—	12	90
1967	Pit	12(SE)	1	1	1.0(1)	0	42	507	12.1(40)	1	—	—	—	—	—	—	—	—	—	—	—	—	6	260
1968	Pit	7	—	—	—	—	5	45	9.0(14)	1	—	—	—	—	—	—	—	—	—	—	—	—	6	28
NFL	6	57	6	8	1.3(4)	0	52	733	14.1(95)	4	—	—	—	—	—	—	—	—	—	—	Pkpi	—	24	462

COMPTON, MIKE Michael Eugene, G-C, 6´6˝/310 lbs; West Virginia; 1993: Det, rnd 3; B9/18/1970 Richlands, VA **1993** Det 8 (0) **1994** Det 2 (0) **1995**†Det 16 (7, lg) **1996** Det 15 (15, LG) **1997**†Det 16 (16, LG) **1998** Det 16 (16, LG) **1999**†Det 15 (15, C) **2000** Det 16 (16, C/lg) **2001**†NE 16 (16, LG) **2002** NE 16 (16, LG) **2003** NE 2 (2) **2004** Jax 13 (0) **NFL** 151 (119) [12 yrs]

COMPTON, OGDEN Ogden Bingham, QB, 6´1˝/180 lbs; Hardin-Simmons; B8/25/1932 Ithaca, NY

YEAR	TEAM	G (GS, POS)	RUSH	YD	AVG (LG)	TD	REC	YD	AVG (LG)	TD	PASS	COMP	PCT	YD	AVG (LG)	TD	INT	SK	YD	QBR	KPR	OTD	PTS	TAY
1955	ChiC	9	6	-8	-1.3(5)	0	—	—	—	—	61	22	36.1	339	5.6(**98**)	1	6	—	—	—	—	—	0	-74

COMSTOCK, ED Elwyn C., G-T, 6´2˝/208 lbs; West Virginia Wesleyan; Washington-St. Louis; B7/12/1903, D8/1980 Belle Meade, NJ **1929** Buf 8 (7, RG) **1930** Bkn 6 (0) **1931** SI 9 (3) **NFL** 23 (10) [3 yrs]

COMSTOCK, RUDY Rudolph S., G-T, 5´10˝/209 lbs; Georgetown (DC); B9/23/1900, OK, D11/1975 Penn Yan, NY **1923** Can☆12 (11, LG) **1924** Cle 9 (9, LG) **1925** Can 8 (7, RG/lg) **1926** Fra☆17 (16, RG) **1927** Fra 18 (18, LG) **1928** Fra 16 (16, RG) **1929** Fra 17 (15, RG) **1930** NYG☆15 (11, RG) **1931** GB 14 (7, lg) **1932** GB 13 (10, lg) **1933** GB 13 (7, RG) **NFL** 152 (127) [11 yrs]

CONATY, BILL William Buckley, C, 6´2˝/306 lbs; Virginia Tech; B3/8/1973 Baltimore, MD **1997** Buf 1 (0) **1998**†Buf 15 (1) **1999**†Buf 7 (1) **2000** Buf 16 (0) **2001** Buf 16 (16, C) **2002** Buf 11 (0) **2004** Min 8 (0) **NFL** 74 (18) [7 yrs]

CONCANNON, JACK John Joseph, QB, 6´3˝/205 lbs; Boston College; 1964: Phi, rnd 2/Bos, rnd 1; B2/25/1943 Boston, MA, D11/28/2005 Newton, MA

YEAR	TEAM	G (GS, POS)	RUSH	YD	AVG (LG)	TD	REC	YD	AVG (LG)	TD	PASS	COMP	PCT	YD	AVG (LG)	TD	INT	SK	YD	QBR	KPR	OTD	PTS	TAY
1964	Phi	4	16	134	8.4(29)	1	—	—	—	—	23	12	52.2	199	8.7(38)	2	1	7	47	—	—	—	6	214
1965	Phi	3	9	104	11.6(38)	0	—	—	—	—	29	12	41.4	176	6.1(34)	1	3	3	42	—	—	—	0	77
1966	Phi	11	25	195	7.8(29)	2	1	7	7.0(7)	0	51	21	41.2	262	5.1(44)	1	4	3	22	—	p	—	12	188
1967	ChiB	13(QB)	67	279	4.2(31)	3	—	—	—	—	186	92	49.5	1260	6.8(93)	6	14	19	168	50.9	—	—	18	409
1968	ChiB	7(QB)	28	104	3.7(16)	2	—	—	—	—	143	71	49.7	715	5.0(51)	5	9	9	72	49.7	—	—	12	147
1969	ChiB	14(qb)	22	62	2.8(30)	1	—	—	—	—	160	87	54.4	783	4.9(38)	4	8	14	104	55.3	—	—	6	164
1970	ChiB	14(QB)	42	136	3.2(16)	2	—	—	—	—	385	194	50.4	2130	5.5(69)	16	18	24	206	61.5	—	—	12	581
1971	ChiB	3	5	5	1.0(2)	0	—	—	—	—	77	42	54.5	334	4.3(28)	0	3	8	61	—	—	—	0	52
1974	GB	14	3	7	2.3(6)	1	—	—	—	—	54	28	51.9	381	7.1(56)	1	3	3	21	—	—	—	6	93
1975	Det	7	—	—	—	—	—	—	—	—	2	1	50.0	30	15.0(30)	0	0	1	9	—	—	—	0	15
NFL	10	90	217	1026	4.7(38)	12	1	7	7.0(7)	0	1110	560	50.5	6270	5.6(93)	36	63	91	752	54.8	p	—	72	1938

CONCANNON, RICK Ernest Raymond, G-T, 6´0˝/217 lbs; NYU; B1/12/1908 Waltham, MA, D6/17/1986 Bradenton, FL **1932** SI 1 (0) **1934** Bos 10 (3) **1935** Bos 11 (6, LG) **1936** Bos 3 (0) **NFL** 25 (9) [4 yrs]

CONDIT, MERL Merlyn Edwin, HB, 5´11˝/187 lbs; West Virginia; Carnegie Mellon; 1940: Cle, rnd 2; B3/21/1917 Belle Vernon, PA, D10/18/1992 Wexford, PA **[K]**

YEAR	TEAM	G (GS, POS)	RUSH	YD	AVG (LG)	TD	REC	YD	AVG (LG)	TD	PASS	COMP	PCT	YD	AVG (LG)	TD	INT	SK	YD	QBR	KPR	OTD	PTS	TAY
1940	Pit✧	10(2)	52	205	3.9	0	4	30	7.5	1	15	2	13.3	33	2.2	0	2	—	—	—	Pi	—	6	159
1941	Bkn	11(11, HB)	91	357	3.9(41)	4	5	32	6.4(21)	0	6	1	16.7	3	0.5(3)	0	1	—	—	—	KPkpi	—	41	452
1942	Bkn★	11(11, HB)	129	647	5.0(63)	2	9	111	12.3(56)	0	17	5	29.4	27	1.6(14)	0	2	—	—	—	KPkpi	1	37	910
1943	Bkn	8(7, HB)	67	190	2.8(25)	1	7	101	14.4(65)	1	6	0	0.0	0	0.0	0	1	—	—	—	KPkpi	—	12	316
1945	†Was	5(0)	36	173	4.8(41)	3	3	16	5.3(12)	0	—	—	—	—	—	—	—	—	—	—	K	—	19	211
1946	Pit	9(8, HB)	46	141	3.1(23)	1	4	33	8.3(23)	0	4	2	50.0	89	22.3(80)	1	0	—	—	—	Kkp	—	10	207
NFL	6	54(39)	421	1713	4.1(63)	11	32	323	10.1(65)	2	48	10	20.8	152	3.2(80)	1	6	—	—	—	KPkpi	1	125	2254

CONDO, JON Jon, LB, 6´3˝/244 lbs; Maryland; B8/26/1981 Phillipsburg, PA **2005** Dal 3 (0)

CONDON, TOM Thomas Joseph, G, 6´3˝/255 lbs; Boston College; 1974: KC, rnd 10; B10/26/1952 Derby, CT **1974** KC 14 **1975** KC 9 (9, RG) **1976** KC 14 (13, RG) **1977** KC 14 (14, RG) **1978** KC 16 (16, RG) **1979** KC 16 (16, RG) **1980** KC 16 (16, RG) **1981** KC 16 (16, RG) **1982** KC 7 (7, RG) **1983** KC 9 (8, RG) **1984** KC 16 (16, RG) **1985** NE 1 (0) **NFL** 148 (131) [12 yrs]

CONDREN, GLEN Glen Paige, DT-DE, 6´4˝/251 lbs; Oklahoma; 1964: NYG, rnd 11/NYJ, rnd 19; B6/10/1942 Fort Smith, AR **1965** NYG 8 **1966** NYG 13 **1967** NYG 13 (RDE) **1969** Atl 9 **1970** Atl 14 (RDT) **1971** Atl 12 (RDT) **1972** Atl 10 **NFL** 79 [7 yrs]

CONE, FRED Fred, FB-K, 5´11˝/199 lbs; Clemson; 1951: GB, rnd 3; B6/21/1926 Pine Apple, AL **[K]**

YEAR	TEAM	G (GS, POS)	RUSH	YD	AVG (LG)	TD	REC	YD	AVG (LG)	TD	PASS	COMP	PCT	YD	AVG (LG)	TD	INT	SK	YD	QBR	KPR	OTD	PTS	TAY
1951	GB	12(FB)	56	190	3.4(16)	1	28	315	11.3(49)	0	—	—	—	—	—	—	—	—	—	—	KPk	—	50	363
1952	GB	10(FB)	70	276	3.9(30)	2	8	98	12.3(37)	1	—	—	—	—	—	—	—	—	—	—	Kk	—	53	343
1953	GB	12(FB)	92	301	3.3(41)	5	18	165	9.2(30)	1	—	—	—	—	—	—	—	—	—	—	K	—	74	439
1954	GB	12	15	18	1.2(11)	0	4	19	4.8(13)	0	—	—	—	—	—	—	—	—	—	—	Kk	—	54	35

YEAR	TEAM	G (GS, POS)	RUSH	YD	AVG(LG)	TD	REC	YD	AVG(LG)	TD	PASS COMP	PCT	YD	AVG(LG)	TD	INT	SK	YD	QBR	KPR	OTD	PTS	TAY

COLLINS, TODD   Todd Steven, QB, 6´4˝/225 lbs; Michigan; 1995: Buf, rnd 2; B11/5/1971 Walpole, MA

YEAR	TEAM	G (GS, POS)	RUSH	YD	AVG(LG)	TD	REC	YD	AVG(LG)	TD	PASS COMP	PCT	YD	AVG(LG)	TD	INT	SK	YD	QBR	KPR	OTD	PTS	TAY
1995	Buf	7(1)	9	23	2.6(10)	0	—	—	—	—	29 14	48.3	112	3.9(18)	0	1	6	43	—	—	—	0	39
1996	†Buf	7(3)	21	43	2.0(10)	0	—	—	—	—	99 55	55.6	739	7.5(95)	4	5	11	53	—	—	—	0	233
1997	Buf	14(13, QB)	30	77	2.6(11)	0	—	—	—	—	391 215	55.0	2367	6.1(77)	12	13	39	278	69.5	—	—	0	801
2001	KC	1(0)	2	6	3.0(7)	0	—	—	—	—	4 3	75.0	40	10.0(26)	0	0	0	—	—	—	—	0	26
2002	KC	3(0)	1	7	7.0(7)	0	—	—	—	—	6 5	83.3	73	12.2(29)	1	0	0	—	—	—	—	0	49
2003	KC	5(0)	8	-7	-0.9(0)	0	—	—	—	—	12 9	75.0	74	6.2(20)	0	0	0	—	—	—	—	0	30
2004	KC	2(0)	1	4	4.0(4)	0	—	—	—	—	5 1	20.0	42	8.4(42)	0	0	0	—	—	—	—	0	25
2005	KC	2(0)	2	-2	-1.0(-1)	0	—	—	—	—	—	—	—	—	—	—	—	—	—	—	—	0	-2
NFL	8	41(17)	74	151	2.0(11)	0	—	—	—	—	546 302	55.3	3447	6.3(95)	17	19	56	374	70.4	—	—	0	1200

COLLINS, TODD   Todd Franklin, LB, 6´2˝/248 lbs; Georgia; Tennessee; Carson-Newman; 1992: NE, rnd 5; B5/27/1970 New Market, TN   **1992** NE 10 (0)   **1993** NE 16 (12, RILB) **1994** NE 7 (7, RILB) **1996**†NE 16 (15, RLB) **1997**†NE 15 (15, RLB) **1998** NE 12 (10, RLB) **1999**†SL 16 (13, RLB) **2000**†SL 14 (11, RLB)   **NFL** 106 (77) [8 yrs]

COLLINS, TONY   Anthony, RB, 5´11˝/208 lbs; East Carolina; 1981: NE, rnd 2; B5/27/1959 Sanford, FL

YEAR	TEAM	G (GS, POS)	RUSH	YD	AVG(LG)	TD	REC	YD	AVG(LG)	TD	PASS COMP	PCT	YD	AVG(LG)	TD	INT	SK	YD	QBR	KPR	OTD	PTS	TAY
1981	NE	16(11, RB)	204	873	4.3(29)	7	26	232	8.9(22)	0	1	0.0	0	0.0	0	0	—	—	kp	—	42	1247
1982	†NE	9(9, RB)	164	632	3.9(54)	1	19	187	9.8(33)	2	—	—	—	—	—	—	—	—	—	—	18	746
1983	NE★	16(16, RB)	219	1049	4.8(50)	10	27	257	9.5(20)	0	—	—	—	—	—	—	—	—	—	—	60	1278
1984	NE	16(5, rb)	138	550	4.0(21)	5	16	100	6.3(19)	0	—	—	—	—	—	—	—	—	k	—	30	819
1985	†NE	16(16, RB)	163	657	4.0(28)	3	52	549	10.6(49)	2	—	—	—	—	—	—	—	—	—	—	30	972
1986	†NE	16(15, RB)	156	412	2.6(17)	3	77	684	8.9(49)	5	—	—	—	—	—	—	—	—	—	—	48	809
1987	NE	13(11, RB)	147	474	3.2(19)	3	44	347	7.9(29)	3	—	—	—	—	—	—	—	—	k	—	36	696
1990	Mia	1(0)	—	—	—	—	—	—	—	—	—	—	—	—	—	—	—	—	k	—	0	0
NFL	8	103(83)	1191	4647	3.9(54)	32	261	2356	9.0(49)	12	1	0.0	0	0.0	0	0	—	—	kp	—	264	6565

COLLINS, TRENT   Trent John, DB, 6´1˝/187 lbs; San Diego State; B5/18/1961 New Orleans, LA   **1987** NYJ 3 (3)

COLLINSWORTH, CRIS   Anthony Cris, WR, 6´5˝/192 lbs; Florida; 1981: Cin, rnd 2; B1/27/1959 Dayton, OH

YEAR	TEAM	G (GS, POS)	RUSH	YD	AVG(LG)	TD	REC	YD	AVG(LG)	TD	PASS COMP	PCT	YD	AVG(LG)	TD	INT	SK	YD	QBR	KPR	OTD	PTS	TAY
1981	†Cin★	16(16, WR)	—	—	—	—	67	1009	15.1(74)	8	—	—	—	—	—	—	—	—	—	—	48	545
1982	†Cin★	9(9, WR)	1	-11	-11.0(-11)	0	49	700	14.3(50)	1	—	—	—	—	—	—	—	—	—	—	6	344
1983	Cin★	14(14, WR)	2	2	1.0(8)	0	66	1130	17.1(63)	5	—	—	—	—	—	—	—	—	—	—	30	592
1984	Cin	15(14, WR)	1	7	7.0(7)	0	64	989	15.5(57)	6	—	—	—	—	—	—	—	—	—	—	36	532
1985	Cin☆	16(16, WR)	1	3	3.0(3)	0	65	1125	17.3(71)	5	1	0.0	0	0.0	0	0	—	—	—	—	30	551
1986	Cin	16(15, WR)	2	-16	-8.0(-6)	0	62	1024	16.5(46)	10	—	—	—	—	—	—	—	—	—	—	60	546
1987	Cin	8(6, WR)	—	—	—	—	31	494	15.9(53)	0	—	—	—	—	—	—	—	—	—	—	0	247
1988	†Cin	13(0)	—	—	—	—	13	227	17.5(36)	1	—	—	—	—	—	—	—	—	—	—	6	119
NFL	8	107(90)	7	-15	-2.1(8)	0	417	6698	16.1(74)	36	1	0.0	0	0.0	0	0	—	—	—	—	216	3474

COLLONS, FERRIC   Ferric Jason, DE, 6´7˝/290 lbs; California; B12/4/1969 Belleville, IL   **1995** NE 16 (4) **1996**†NE 15 (5, lde) **1997** NE 5 (5, lde) **1998**†NE 14 (11, LDE) **1999** NE 14 (0)   **NFL** 64 (25) [5 yrs]

COLMAN, DOUG   Douglass Clayton, LB, 6´2˝/250 lbs; Nebraska; 1996: NYG, rnd 6; B6/4/1973 Somers Point, NJ   **1996** NYG 13 (0) **1997**†NYG 14 (0) **1998** NYG 16 (0) **1999** Ten 16 (0) **2000** Cle 5 (0)   **NFL** 64 (0) [5 yrs]

COLMAN, WAYNE   Wayne Charles, LB, 6´2˝/230 lbs; Temple; B4/13/1946 Ventnor, NJ   **1968** Phi 14 **1969** Phi 5 **1969** NO 4 **1970** NO 14 (llb) **1971** NO 14 (RLB) **1972** NO 14 (RLB) **1973** NO 12 (RLB) **1974** NO 14 (RLB) **1976** NO 7   **NFL** 98 [8 yrs]

COLMER, MICKEY   John Francis, B, 6´2˝/219 lbs; Miramonte J.C.; B10/23/1918 Redondo Beach, CA, D7/20/2000 Redondo Beach, CA

YEAR	TEAM	G (GS, POS)	RUSH	YD	AVG(LG)	TD	REC	YD	AVG(LG)	TD	PASS COMP	PCT	YD	AVG(LG)	TD	INT	SK	YD	QBR	KPR	OTD	PTS	TAY
1946	Bkn-A	12(6, WB)	46	155	3.4	0	22	327	14.9	1	—	—	—	—	—	—	—	—	kpi	—	6	317
1947	Bkn-A	14(10, FB)	152	578	3.8	9	18	190	10.6	1	3	33.3	20	6.7(20)	0	0	—	—	Pk	—	60	810
1948	Bkn-A☆	14(11, FB)	164	704	4.3	6	21	372	17.7(78)	4	1	0.0	0	0.0	0	0	—	—	Pk	—	60	1013
1949	NYY-A	8(2)	36	100	2.8	0	2	10	5.0	0	1	0.0	0	0.0	0	0	—	—	Pk	—	0	106
AAFC	4	48(29)	398	1537	3.9	15	63	899	14.3(78)	6	5	1	20.0	20	4.0(20)	0	0	—	—	Pkpi	—	126	2246

COLO, DON   Donald Richard, DT, 6´3˝/252 lbs; Brown; 1950: Bal, rnd 3; B1/5/1925 East Bridgewater, MA   **1950** Bal 12 (1, LDT) **1951** NYY 12 (RDT) **1952** DalT 4 **1953**†Cle☆12 (LDT) **1954**†Cle★12 (RDT) **1955**†Cle★12 (RDT) **1956** Cle☆12 (rdt) **1957**†Cle☆12 (RDT) **1958**†Cle★12 (RDT)   **NFL** 100 (1) [9 yrs]

COLOMBO, MARC   Marc Edward, T, 6´7˝/320 lbs; Boston College; 2002: Chi, rnd 1; B10/8/1978 Bridgewater, MA   **2002** ChiB 10 (5, lt) **2004** ChiB 8 (2) **2005** ChiB 1 (0) **2005** Dal 4 (0)   **NFL** 23 (7) [3 yrs]

COLON, HARRY   Harry, DB, 6´0˝/203 lbs; Missouri; 1991: NE, rnd 8; B2/14/1969 Kansas City, KS   **1991** NE 16 (14, SS) **1992** Det 16 (0) **1993**†Det 15 (11, FS) **1994**†Det 16 (0) **1995** Jax 16 (16, SS) **1997** Det 8 (4)   **NFL** 87 (45) [6 yrs]

COLORITO, TONY   Anthony Ivor, NT, 6´5˝/260 lbs; USC; 1986: Den, rnd 5; B9/8/1964 Brooklyn, NY   **1986**†Den 15 (0)

COLQUITT, CRAIG   Joseph Craig, P, 6´1˝/182 lbs; Tennessee; 1978: Pit, rnd 3; B6/9/1954 Knoxville, TN [P]   **1978**†Pit 16 **1979**†Pit 16 **1983**†Pit 16 (0) **1987** Ind 1 (0)

YEAR	TEAM	G (GS, POS)	RUSH	YD	AVG(LG)	TD	REC	YD	AVG(LG)	TD	PASS COMP	PCT	YD	AVG(LG)	TD	INT	SK	YD	QBR	KPR	OTD	PTS	TAY
1980	Pit	16(0)	1	17	17.0(17)	0	—	—	—	—	—	—	—	—	—	—	—	—	P	—	0	17
1981	Pit	16(0)	1	8	8.0(8)	0	—	—	—	—	—	—	—	—	—	—	—	—	P	—	0	8
1984	†Pit	16(0)	1	0	0.0(9)	0	—	—	—	—	—	—	—	—	—	—	—	—	P	—	0	0
NFL	7	97	3	25	8.3(17)	0	—	—	—	—	—	—	—	—	—	—	—	—	P	—	0	25

COLQUITT, DUSTIN   Dustin Farr, P, 6´2˝/211 lbs; Tennessee; 2005: KC, rnd 3; B5/6/1982 Knoxville, TN   **2005** KC 16 (0)

COLQUITT, JIMMY   James Michael, P, 6´4˝/209 lbs; Tennessee; B1/17/1963 Knoxville, TN   **1985** Sea 2 (0)

COLSTON, TIM   Timothy Maurice, NT, 6´0˝/275 lbs; Kansas State; B12/18/1973 Tampa, FL   **1996** Car 2 (0)

COLTER, JEFF   Jeffrey, DB, 5´10˝/171 lbs; Kansas; B4/23/1961 Tucson, AZ   **1984** Min 16 (0) **1987** KC 1 (0)   **NFL** 17 (0) [2 yrs]

COLTERYAHN, LLOYD   Lloyd Kenneth, E, 6´2˝/220 lbs; Maryland; 1953: Pit, rnd 4; B8/26/1931 Brentwood, PA

YEAR	TEAM	G (GS, POS)	RUSH	YD	AVG(LG)	TD	REC	YD	AVG(LG)	TD	PASS COMP	PCT	YD	AVG(LG)	TD	INT	SK	YD	QBR	KPR	OTD	PTS	TAY
1954	Bal	12(LE)	—	—	—	—	30	384	12.8(21)	0	—	—	—	—	—	—	—	—	—	—	0	192
1955	Bal	12(LE)	—	—	—	—	21	251	12.0(22)	3	—	—	—	—	—	—	—	—	—	—	18	141
1956	Bal	3	—	—	—	—	3	29	9.7(16)	0	—	—	—	—	—	—	—	—	—	—	0	15
NFL	3	27	—	—	—	—	54	664	12.3(22)	3	—	—	—	—	—	—	—	—	—	—	18	347

COLTON, GEORGE   George Curtis, G, 6´4˝/279 lbs; Maryland; 1986: NE, rnd 9; B7/28/1963 Lindenhurst, NY   **1987** NE 3 (3)

COLVIN, JIM   James R., DT-DE-G, 6´3˝/252 lbs; Houston; 1960: Bal, rnd 8/Den, rnd 2; B11/30/1937 Monahans, TX   **1960** Bal 12 (2) **1961** Bal 13 **1962** Bal 14 (14, LDT) **1963** Bal 14 (14, LDT) **1964** Dal 14 (14, LDT) **1965** Dal 14 (14, LDT) **1966**†Dal 14 (14, LDT) **1967** NYG 8   **NFL** 103 (72) [8 yrs]

COLVIN, ROSEVELT   Rosevelt, LB, 6´3˝/250 lbs; Purdue; 1999: Chi, rnd 4; B9/5/1977 Indianapolis, IN   **1999** ChiB 11 (0) **2000** ChiB 13 (8, llb) **2001**†ChiB 16 (13, LLB) **2002** ChiB 15 (15, RLB) **2003** NE 2 (2) **2004**†NE 16 (1) **2005** NE 16 (11, RLB)   **NFL** 90 (50) [7 yrs]

COLZIE, NEAL   Cornelius Connie, DB, 6´2˝/200 lbs; Ohio State; 1975: Oak, rnd 1; B2/28/1954 Fitzgerald, GA, D8/19/2001 South Miami, FL [RI]   **1975**†Oak 14 (2) **1976**†Oak 14 (1) **1977**†Oak 13 (3) **1978** Oak 16 **1979**†Mia 16 (16, FS) **1980** TB 16 (1) **1981**†TB 16 (16, SS) **1982**†TB☆9 (9, SS) **1983** TB 5 (3)   **NFL** 118 (51) [9 yrs]

COMBS, BILL   Lloyd William, E-DB, 5´11˝/183 lbs; Purdue; B6/29/1920 Holder, IL, D10/27/1998 West Lafayette, IN

YEAR	TEAM	G (GS, POS)	RUSH	YD	AVG(LG)	TD	REC	YD	AVG(LG)	TD	PASS COMP	PCT	YD	AVG(LG)	TD	INT	SK	YD	QBR	KPR	OTD	PTS	TAY
1942	Phi	10(0)	—	—	—	—	4	44	11.0(19)	1	—	—	—	—	—	—	—	—	—	—	6	27

COMBS, CHRIS   Christopher Allen, TE-T, 6´4˝/238 lbs; New Mexico; 1980: Hou, rnd 4; B3/17/1958 San Diego, CA

YEAR	TEAM	G (GS, POS)	RUSH	YD	AVG(LG)	TD	REC	YD	AVG(LG)	TD	PASS COMP	PCT	YD	AVG(LG)	TD	INT	SK	YD	QBR	KPR	OTD	PTS	TAY
1980	SL	16(0)	—	—	—	—	2	52	26.0(38)	1	—	—	—	—	—	—	—	—	—	—	6	31
1981	SL	16(2)	—	—	—	—	5	54	10.8(13)	0	—	—	—	—	—	—	—	—	—	—	0	27
NFL	2	32(2)	—	—	—	—	7	106	15.1(38)	1	—	—	—	—	—	—	—	—	—	—	6	58

COMBS, CHRIS   Christopher Brandon, DE, 6´4˝/284 lbs; Duke; 2000: Pit, rnd 6; B12/15/1976 Roanoke, VA   **2000** Pit 6 (0) **2001** Pit 2 (0) **2002** Jax 2 (0)   **NFL** 10 (0) [3 yrs]

COMBS, DEREK   Derek Alan, DB, 6´0˝/185 lbs; Ohio State; 2001: Oak, rnd 7; B2/28/1979 Columbus, OH   **2002** Oak 4 (0) **2003** GB 8 (0)   **NFL** 12 (0) [2 yrs]

COMEAUX, DARREN   Darren, LB, 6´1˝/227 lbs; Arizona State; B4/15/1960 San Diego, CA   **1982** Den 3 (0) **1983**†Den 14 (0) **1984**†Den 16 (0) **1985** Den 11 (0) **1986**†Den 16 (0) **1987**†SF 8 (0) **1988**†Sea 9 (6, lilb) **1989** Sea 16 (13, LILB) **1990** Sea 9 (9, MLB) **1991** Sea 16 (11, MLB)   **NFL** 118 (39) [10 yrs]

YEAR	TEAM	G (GS, POS)	RUSH	YD	AVG (LG)	TD	REC	YD	AVG (LG)	TD	PASS	COMP	PCT	YD	AVG (LG)	TD	INT	SK	YD	QBR	KPR	OTD	PTS	TAY

COMELLA, GREG   Greg, FB, 6´1˝/248 lbs; Stanford; B7/29/1975 Wellesley, MA

1998	NYG	16(0)	1	6	6.0(6)	0	3	3.0(3)		0	—	—	—	—	—	—	—	—	—	k	—	0	5
1999	NYG	16(3)	1	0	0.0(0)	0	8	39	4.9(26)	0	—	—	—	—	—	—	—	—	—	k	—	0	21
2000	†NYG	16(12, FB)	10	45	4.5(16)	0	36	274	7.6(25)	0	—	—	—	—	—	—	—	—	—	kp	—	0	167
2001	NYG	16(13, FB)	4	15	3.8(9)	0	39	253	6.5(26)	1	—	—	—	—	—	—	—	—	—	—	—	6	147
2002	Ten	12(7, fb)	1	0	0.0(0)	0	10	70	7.0(17)	0	—	—	—	—	—	—	—	—	—	—	—	0	35
2003	Hou	5(0)	—	—	—	—	—	—	—	—	—	—	—	—	—	—	—	—	—	—	—	—	—
2004	TB	7(0)	—	—	—	—	1	12	12.0(12)	0	—	—	—	—	—	—	—	—	—	k	—	0	11
NFL	7	88(35)	17	66	3.9(16)	0	95	651	6.9(26)	1	—	—	—	—	—	—	—	—	—	kp	—	6	385

COMER, HOOK   John S., FB, /180 lbs; none; B10/1898 Cass Township, OH, deceased   **1926** Can 1 (1)

COMER, MARTY   Martin F., DE-E, 6´0˝/203 lbs; Tulane; 1943: Bkn, rnd 5; B10/28/1917 Indianapolis, IN, D3/22/1998 New Orleans, LA

1946	Buf-A	6(3)	—	—	—	—	2	17	8.5	0	—	—	—	—	—	—	—	—	—	—	1	6	9
1947	Buf-A	14(2)	—	—	—	—	2	75	37.5	1	—	—	—	—	—	—	—	—	—	—	—	6	43
1948	Buf-A	7(4)	—	—	—	—	5	66	13.2	1	—	—	—	—	—	—	—	—	—	—	—	6	38
AAFC	3	27(9)	—	—	—	—	9	158	17.6	2	—	—	—	—	—	—	—	—	—	—	1	18	89

COMIER, ULYSSES   Adonis, FB, 5´10˝/195 lbs; none; B1905, deceased   **1929** Buf 3 (1)

COMMISA, VINCE   Vincent John, G, 5´9˝/190 lbs; Notre Dame; B11/1/1921 Newark, NJ, D3/5/1990 Orange, NJ   **1944** Bos 1 (0)

COMMISKEY, CHUCK   Charles Edward, G, 6´4˝/290 lbs; Mississippi; 1981: Phi, rnd 9; B3/28/1958 Killeen, TX   **1986** NO 16 (10, RG)   **1987**†NO 12 (4)   **1988** NO 6 (0)
NFL 34 (14) [3 yrs]

COMP, IRV   Irving Henry, B, 6´2˝/204 lbs; Benedictine; 1943: GB, rnd 3; B5/17/1919 Milwaukee, WI, D7/11/1989 Woodruff, WI [I]

1943	GB	9(2, tb)	77	182	2.4(27)	3	—	—	—	—	92	46	50.0	662	7.2(79)	7	4	—	—	—	Pkpi	1	20	563
1944	†GB	10(8, TB)	52	134	2.6(28)	2	2	16	8.0(11)	1	177	80	45.2	1159	6.5(55)	12	21	—	50.0	kpi	—	18	18
1945	GB	9(7, TB)	57	92	1.6(18)	1	1	50	50.0(50)	1	106	44	41.5	865	8.2(75)	7	11	—	53.1	kpi	1	18	278
1946	GB	11(2, tb)	61	62	1.0(29)	1	—	—	—	—	94	27	28.7	333	3.5(35)	1	8	—	—	ki	—	6	-35
1947	GB	12(1)	5	46	9.2(34)	0	—	—	—	—	1	0	0.0	0	0.0	0	1	—	—	pi	—	0	36
1948	GB	11(1)	3	3	1.0(2)	0	—	—	—	—	49	16	32.7	335	6.8(50)	0	7	—	—	pi	—	0	-24
1949	GB	7(0)	—	—	—	—	—	—	—	—	—	—	—	—	—	—	—	—	—	i	—	0	9
NFL	7	69(21)	255	519	2.0(34)	7	3	66	22.0(50)	2	519	213	41.0	3354	6.5(79)	28	52	—	41.6	Pkpi	2	66	845

COMPAGNO, TONY   Anthony, FB, 5´11˝/199 lbs; St. Mary's (CA); 1943: Pit, rnd 21; B1/29/1921 Daly City, CA, D4/8/1971 San Mateo, CA

1946	Pit	10(8, FB)	67	217	3.2(23)	1	8	101	12.6(36)	0	—	—	—	—	—	—	—	—	—	ki	—	6	325
1947	†Pit	12(4)	34	126	3.7(12)	2	9	190	21.1(39)	1	—	—	—	—	—	—	—	—	—	ki	2	30	411
1948	Pit	12(1)	24	101	4.2(20)	0	1	4	4.0(4)	0	—	—	—	—	—	—	—	—	—	pi	1	6	258
NFL	3	34(13)	125	444	3.6(23)	3	18	295	16.4(39)	1	—	—	—	—	—	—	—	—	—	kpi	3	42	994

COMPTON, CHUCK   Charles, DB, 5´10˝/190 lbs; Boise State; B1/13/1965 Atwater, CA   **1987** GB 2 (0)

COMPTON, DICK   Richard Lee, SE-B, 6´2˝/190 lbs; McMurry; B4/16/1940 Colorado City, TX

1962	Det	10	1	3	3.0(3)	0	—	—	—	—	—	—	—	—	—	—	—	—	—	—	—	0	3
1963	Det	13	—	—	—	—	2	41	20.5(22)	0	—	—	—	—	—	—	—	—	—	Pkpi	—	0	38
1964	Det	12	3	2	0.7(4)	0	—	—	—	—	—	—	—	—	—	—	—	—	—	—	—	0	44
1965	Hou-A	3	1	2	2.0(2)	0	3	140	46.7(95)	2	—	—	—	—	—	—	—	—	—	k	—	12	90
1967	Pit	12(SE)	1	1	1.0(1)	0	42	507	12.1(40)	1	—	—	—	—	—	—	—	—	—	pi	—	6	260
1968	Pit	7	—	—	—	—	5	45	9.0(14)	1	—	—	—	—	—	—	—	—	—	—	—	6	28
NFL	6	57	6	8	1.3(4)	0	52	733	14.1(95)	4	—	—	—	—	—	—	—	—	—	Pkpi	—	24	462

COMPTON, MIKE   Michael Eugene, G-C, 6´6˝/310 lbs; West Virginia; 1993: Det, rnd 3; B9/18/1970 Richlands, VA   **1993** Det 8 (0)   **1994** Det 2 (0)   **1995**†Det 16 (7, lg)
1996 Det 15 (15, LG)   **1997**†Det 16 (16, LG)   **1998** Det 16 (16, LG)   **1999**†Det 15 (15, C)   **2000** Det 16 (16, C/lg)   **2001**†NE 16 (16, LG)   **2002** NE 16 (16, LG)   **2003** NE 2 (2)
2004 Jax 13 (0)   NFL 151 (119) [12 yrs]

COMPTON, OGDEN   Ogden Bingham, QB, 6´1˝/180 lbs; Hardin-Simmons; B8/25/1932 Ithaca, NY

| 1955 | ChiC | 9 | 6 | -8 | -1.3(5) | 0 | — | — | — | — | 61 | 22 | 36.1 | 339 | 5.6(98) | 1 | 6 | — | — | — | — | 0 | -74 |

COMSTOCK, ED   Elwyn C., G-T, 6´2˝/208 lbs; West Virginia Wesleyan; Washington-St. Louis; B7/12/1903, D8/1980 Belle Meade, NJ   **1929** Buf 8 (7, RG)   **1930** Bkn 6 (0)
1931 SI 9 (3)   NFL 23 (10) [3 yrs]

COMSTOCK, RUDY   Rudolph S., G-T, 5´10˝/209 lbs; Georgetown (DC); B9/23/1900, OK, D11/1975 Penn Yan, NY   **1923** Can☆12 (11, LG)   **1924** Cle 9 (9, LG)   **1925** Can 8 (7, RG/
lg)   **1926** Fra☆17 (16, RG)   **1927** Fra 18 (18, LG)   **1928** Fra 16 (16, RG)   **1929** Fra 17 (15, RG)   **1930** NYG☆15 (11, RG)   **1931** GB 14 (7, lg)   **1932** GB 13 (10, lg)   **1933** GB 13 (7, RG)

CONATY, BILL   William Buckley, C, 6´2˝/... ...inia Tech; B3/8/1973 Baltimore, MD   **1997** Buf 1 (0)   **1998**†Buf 15 (1)   **1999**†Buf 7 (1)   **2000** Buf 16 (0)   **2001** Buf 16 (16, C)
2002 Buf 11 (0)   **2004** Min 8 (0)   NFL 74 (18) [7 yrs]

CONCANNON, JACK   John Joseph, QB, 6´3˝/205 lbs; Bosto... ...ge; 1964: Phi, rnd 2/Bos, rnd 1; B2/25/1943 Boston, MA, D11/28/2005 Newton, MA

1964	Phi	4	16	134	8.4(29)	—	—	—	23	12	52.2	199	8.7(38)	2	1	7	47	—	—	6	214
1965	Phi	3	9	104	11.6(38)	0	—	—	—	29	12	41.4	176	6.1(34)	1	3	3	42	—	—	0	77
1966	Phi	11	25	195	7.8(29)	2	1	...(7)	0	51	21	41.2	262	5.1(44)	1	4	3	22	—	p	12	188
1967	ChiB	13(QB)	67	279	4.2(31)	3	—	—	—	186	92	49.5	1260	6.8(93)	6	14	19	168	50.9	—	18	409
1968	ChiB	7(QB)	28	104	3.7(16)	2	—	—	...13	71	49.7	715	5.0(51)	5	9	9	72	49.7	—	12	147
1969	ChiB	14(qb)	22	62	2.8(30)	1	—	—	...87	54.4	783	4.9(38)	4	8	14	104	55.3	—	6	164
1970	ChiB	14(QB)	42	136	3.2(16)	2	—	—	...50.4	2130	5.5(69)	16	18	24	206	61.5	—	12	581
1971	ChiB	3	5	5	1.0(2)	0	—	—	—	...234	4.3(28)	0	3	8	61	—	—	0	52
1974	GB	14	3	7	2.3(6)	1	—	—	—	54	...981	7.1(56)	1	3	3	21	—	—	6	93
1975	Det	3	—	—	—	—	—	—	2	30	15.0(30)	0	1	0	9	—	—	0	15
NFL	10	90	217	1026	4.7(38)	12	1	7	7.0(7)	0	1110	560	...6270	5.6(93)	36	63	91	752	54.8	p	72	1938

CONCANNON, RICK   Ernest Raymond, G-T, 6´0˝/217 lbs; NYU; B1/12/1908 Waltham, MA, D6/17/1986 Bradenton, FL   **1932** SI 1 (0)   **1934** Bos 10 (3)   **1935** Bos 11 (6, LG)
1936 Bos 3 (0)   NFL 25 (9) [4 yrs]

CONDIT, MERL   Merlyn Edwin, HB, 5´11˝/187 lbs; West Virginia; Carnegie Mellon; 1940: Cle, rnd 2; B3/21/1917 Belle Vernon, PA, D10/18/1992 Wexford, PA [K]

1940	Pit✧	10(2)	52	205	3.9	0	4	30	7.5	1	15	2	13.3	33	2.2	0	2	—	—	Pi	—	6	159
1941	Bkn	11(11, HB)	91	357	3.9(41)	4	5	32	6.4(21)	0	6	1	16.7	3	0.5(3)	0	1	—	—	KPkpi	—	41	452
1942	Bkn★	11(11, HB)	129	647	5.0(63)	2	9	111	12.3(56)	0	17	5	29.4	27	1.6(14)	0	2	—	—	KPkpi	1	37	910
1943	Bkn	8(7, HB)	67	190	2.8(25)	1	7	101	14.4(65)	1	6	0	0.0	0	0.0	0	1	—	—	KPpi	—	12	316
1945	†Was	5(0)	36	173	4.8(41)	3	3	16	5.3(12)	0	—	—	—	—	—	—	—	—	—	K	—	19	211
1946	Pit	9(8, HB)	46	141	3.1(23)	1	4	33	8.3(23)	0	4	2	50.0	89	22.3(80)	1	0	—	—	Kkp	—	10	207
NFL	54(39)	421	1713	4.1(63)	12	33	323	10.1(65)	2	48	10	20.8	152	3.2(80)	1	6	—	—	KPkpi	1	125	2254

CONDO, JON   Jon, LB, 6´3˝/244 lbs; Maryland; B8/26/1981 Phillipsburg, PA   **2005** Dal 3 (0)

CONDON, TOM   Thomas Joseph, G, 6´3˝/255 lbs; Boston College; 1974: KC, rnd 10; B10/26/1952 Derby, CT   **1974** KC 14   **1975** KC 9 (9, RG)   **1976** KC 14 (13, RG)
1977 KC 14 (14, RG)   **1978** KC 16 (16, RG)   **1979** KC 16 (16, RG)   **1980** KC 16 (16, RG)   **1981** KC 16 (16, RG)   **1982** KC 7 (7, RG)   **1983** KC 9 (8, RG)   **1984** KC 16 (16, RG)
1985 NE 1 (0)   NFL 148 (131) [12 yrs]

CONDREN, GLEN   Glen Paige, DT-DE, 6´4˝/251 lbs; Oklahoma; 1964: NYG, rnd 11/NYJ, rnd 19; B6/10/1942 Fort Smith, AR   **1965** NYG 8   **1966** NYG 13   **1967** NYG 13 (RDE)
1969 Atl 9   **1970** Atl 14 (RDT)   **1971** Atl 12 (RDT)   **1972** NFL 79 [7 yrs]

CONE, FRED   Fred, FB-K, 5´11˝/199 lbs; Clemson; 1951: GB, rnd 3; B6/21/1926 Pine Apple, AL [K]

1951	GB	12(FB)	56	190	3.4(16)	1	28	315	11.3(49)	0	—	—	—	—	—	—	—	—	—	KPk	—	50	363
1952	GB	10(FB)	70	276	3.9(30)	2	8	98	12.3(37)	1	—	—	—	—	—	—	—	—	—	Kk	—	53	343
1953	GB	12(FB)	92	301	3.3(41)	5	18	165	9.2(30)	1	—	—	—	—	—	—	—	—	—	K	—	74	439
1954	GB	12	15	18	1.2(11)	0	4	19	4.8(13)	0	—	—	—	—	—	—	—	—	—	Kk	—	54	35

YEAR	TEAM	G (GS, POS)	RUSH	YD	AVG (LG)	TD	REC	YD	AVG (LG)	TD	PASS	COMP	PCT	YD	AVG (LG)	TD	INT	SK	YD	QBR	KPR	OTD	PTS	TAY
1955	GB	12	12	25	2.1 (14)	0	1	7	7.0 (7)	0	—	—	—	—	—	—	—	—	—	—	K	—	78	29
1956	GB	12 (fb)	49	211	4.3 (21)	2	12	218	18.2 (69)	2	—	—	—	—	—	—	—	—	—	—	K	—	72	350
1957	GB	12	53	135	2.5 (26)	2	4	30	7.5 (10)	0	—	—	—	—	—	—	—	—	—	—	Kk	—	74	178
1960	Dal	12	—	—	—	—	—	—	—	—	—	—	—	—	—	—	—	—	—	—	K	—	39	0
NFL	8	94	347	1156	3.3 (41)	12	75	852	11.4 (69)	4	—	—	—	—	—	—	—	—	—	—	KPk	—	494	1735

CONERLY, CHARLIE Charles Albert, QB, 6´1˝/185 lbs; Mississippi; 1945: Was, rnd 13/1947: Bkn-A, rnd 2; B9/19/1921 Clarksdale, MS, D2/13/1996 Memphis, TN **[K]**

YEAR	TEAM	G (GS, POS)	RUSH	YD	AVG (LG)	TD	REC	YD	AVG (LG)	TD	PASS	COMP	PCT	YD	AVG (LG)	TD	INT	SK	YD	QBR	KPR	OTD	PTS	TAY
1948	NYG	12 (4, QB)	40	160	4.0 (40)	5	—	—	—	—	299	162	54.2	2175	7.3 (65)	22	13	—	—	84.0	Pk	—	30	900
1949	NYG	12 (11, QB)	23	42	1.8 (7)	0	—	—	—	—	305	152	49.8	2138	7.0 (**85**)	17	20	—	—	64.1	P	—	0	396
1950	†NYG✧	11 (QB)	23	22	1.0 (14)	1	—	—	—	—	132	56	42.4	1000	7.6 (43)	8	7	—	—	67.1	P	—	6	292
1951	NYG	12 (QB)	17	65	3.8 (18)	1	—	—	—	—	189	93	49.2	1277	6.8 (69)	10	22	—	—	49.3	P	—	6	-117
1952	NYG	11 (QB)	27	115	4.3 (33)	0	—	—	—	—	169	82	48.5	1090	6.4 (70)	13	10	—	—	70.4	K	—	2	325
1953	NYG	12 (QB)	24	91	3.8 (24)	0	—	—	—	—	303	143	47.2	1711	5.6 (60)	13	**25**	—	—	44.9	—	—	0	12
1954	NYG	10 (QB)	24	107	4.5 (24)	1	—	—	—	—	210	103	49.0	1439	6.9 (68)	17	11	—	—	76.7	K	—	7	482
1955	NYG	12 (QB)	12	10	0.8 (12)	0	—	—	—	—	202	98	48.5	1310	6.5 (71)	13	13	—	—	64.2	K	—	1	210
1956	†NYG★	12 (QB)	11	11	1.0 (8)	0	—	—	—	—	174	90	51.7	1143	6.6 (48)	10	7	—	—	75.0	P	—	0	353
1957	NYG☆	12 (QB)	15	24	1.6 (13)	1	—	—	—	—	232	128	55.2	1712	7.4 (70)	11	11	—	—	74.9	—	—	6	505
1958	†NYG	10 (QB)	12	-17	-1.4 (11)	0	—	—	—	—	184	88	47.8	1199	6.5 (44)	10	9	—	—	66.8	—	—	0	273
1959	†NYG☆	10 (QB)	15	38	2.5 (10)	1	—	—	—	—	194	113	58.2	1706	**8.8** (**77**)	14	4	—	—	**102.7**	—	—	6	811
1960	NYG	12 (QB)	14	1	0.1 (17)	0	—	—	—	—	134	66	49.3	954	7.1 (70)	8	7	—	—	70.9	P	—	0	238
1961	†NYG	13	13	16	1.2 (9)	0	—	—	—	—	106	44	41.5	634	6.0 (37)	7	8	—	—	52.2	—	—	0	48
NFL	14	161 (15)	270	685	2.5 (40)	10	—	—	—	—	2833	1418	50.1	19488	6.9 (85)	173	167	—	—	68.2	KPk	—	64	4726

CONGER, MEL Melvin Reese, DE-E, 6´2˝/225 lbs; Georgia; B6/4/1919 Atlanta, GA, D7/21/1996 Atlanta, GA **1947** Bkn-A 2 (0)

YEAR	TEAM	G (GS, POS)	RUSH	YD	AVG (LG)	TD	REC	YD	AVG (LG)	TD	PASS	COMP	PCT	YD	AVG (LG)	TD	INT	SK	YD	QBR	KPR	OTD	PTS	TAY
1946	NYY-A	7 (0)	—	—	—	—	3	61	20.3	0	—	—	—	—	—	—	—	—	—	—	—	—	0	31
AAFC	2	9 (0)	—	—	—	—	3	61	20.3	0	—	—	—	—	—	—	—	—	—	—	—	—	0	31

CONJAR, LARRY Lawrence Wayne, RB, 6´1˝/214 lbs; Notre Dame; 1967: Cle, rnd 2; B10/28/1945 Harrisburg, PA

YEAR	TEAM	G (GS, POS)	RUSH	YD	AVG (LG)	TD	REC	YD	AVG (LG)	TD	PASS	COMP	PCT	YD	AVG (LG)	TD	INT	SK	YD	QBR	KPR	OTD	PTS	TAY
1967	†Cle	12 (fb)	20	78	3.9 (16)	0	6	68	11.3 (27)	0	—	—	—	—	—	—	—	—	—	—	—	—	0	112
1968	Phi	14	8	21	2.6 (6)	0	—	—	—	—	—	—	—	—	—	—	—	—	—	—	—	—	2	21
1969	Bal	6	1	0	0.0 (0)	0	—	—	—	—	—	—	—	—	—	—	—	—	—	—	—	—	0	0
1970	Bal	3	1	3	3.0 (3)	0	—	—	—	—	—	—	—	—	—	—	—	—	—	—	—	—	0	3
NFL	4	35	30	102	3.4 (16)	0	6	68	11.3 (27)	0	—	—	—	—	—	—	—	—	—	—	—	—	2	136

CONKLIN, CARY Cary Lee, QB, 6´4˝/220 lbs; Washington; 1990: Was, rnd 4; B2/29/1968 Yakima, WA

YEAR	TEAM	G (GS, POS)	RUSH	YD	AVG (LG)	TD	REC	YD	AVG (LG)	TD	PASS	COMP	PCT	YD	AVG (LG)	TD	INT	SK	YD	QBR	KPR	OTD	PTS	TAY
1992	Was	1 (0)	3	-4	-1.3 (-1)	0	—	—	—	—	2	2	100.0	16	8.0 (10)	1	0	—	—	—	—	—	0	9
1993	Was	2 (2)	2	-2	-1.0 (-1)	0	—	—	—	—	87	46	52.9	496	5.7 (34)	4	3	8	45	—	—	—	0	146
1995	SF	4 (0)	—	—	—	—	—	—	—	—	12	4	33.3	48	4.0 (28)	0	0	2	20	—	—	—	0	24
NFL	3	7 (2)	5	-6	-1.2 (-1)	0	—	—	—	—	101	52	51.5	560	5.5 (34)	5	3	10	65	—	—	—	0	179

CONKRIGHT, BILL William Franklin, C-LB-E-DE, 6´1˝/203 lbs; Oklahoma; 1937: ChiB, rnd 5; B4/17/1914 Beggs, OK, D10/27/1980 Houston, TX **[C]** **1937**†ChiB 8 (1) **1939** Cle 11 (8, C) **1940** Cle 2 (2) **1941** Cle 11 (7, C) **1942** Cle 11 (8, C) **1943** Bkn 7 (4) **1943** Was 2 (0) **1944** Cle 1 (0)

YEAR	TEAM	G (GS, POS)	RUSH	YD	AVG (LG)	TD	REC	YD	AVG (LG)	TD	PASS	COMP	PCT	YD	AVG (LG)	TD	INT	SK	YD	QBR	KPR	OTD	PTS	TAY
1938	ChiB	9 (0)	—	—	—	—	1	2	2.0 (2)	1	—	—	—	—	—	—	—	—	—	—	—	—	6	6
NFL	8	62 (30)	—	—	—	—	1	2	2.0 (2)	1	—	—	—	—	—	—	—	—	—	—	i	—	6	3

CONLAN, SHANE Shane Patrick, LB, 6´3˝/235 lbs; Penn State; 1987: Buf, rnd 1; B3/4/1964 Frewsburg, NY **1987** Buf☆12 (12, LILB/lolb) **1988**†Buf★13 (13, LILB) **1989**†Buf✧10 (9, lilb) **1990**†Buf★16 (16, LILB) **1991**†Buf 16 (15, LILB) **1992**†Buf 13 (12, LILB) **1993** LARm 12 (11, MLB) **1994** LARm 15 (15, MLB) **1995** SL 13 (11, MLB) **NFL** 120 (114) [9 yrs]

CONLEE, GERRY Gerry Russell, C, 5´11˝/203 lbs; St. Mary's (CA); B8/22/1914 Porterville, CA, D7/16/2005 El Cajon, CA **1938** Cle 8 (2) **1943** Det 10 (2) **NFL** 18 (4) [2 yrs]

1946 SF-A 10 (2) **1947** SF-A 13 (1) **AAFC** 23 (3) [2 yrs]

CONLEY, JOHN John, T-G, 5´11˝/205 lbs; none; B1890, deceased **1922** Col 6 (4) **1926** Col 4 (2) **NFL** 10 (6) [2 yrs]

CONLEY, STEVE Stephen Craig, LB-RB, 6´2˝/225 lbs; Kansas; 1972: Cin, rnd 7; B3/9/1949 Chicago, IL **1972** SL 7

YEAR	TEAM	G (GS, POS)	RUSH	YD	AVG (LG)	TD	REC	YD	AVG (LG)	TD	PASS	COMP	PCT	YD	AVG (LG)	TD	INT	SK	YD	QBR	KPR	OTD	PTS	TAY
1972	Cin	1	3	8	2.7 (5)	0	—	—	—	—	—	—	—	—	—	—	—	—	—	—	—	—	0	8
NFL	1	8	3	8	2.7 (5)	0	—	—	—	—	—	—	—	—	—	—	—	—	—	—	—	—	0	8

CONLEY, STEVE Stephen, LB, 6´5˝/235 lbs; Arkansas; 1996: Pit, rnd 3; B1/18/1972 Chicago, IL **1996** Pit 2 (0) **1997**†Pit 16 (0) **1998** Ind 1 (0) **1998** Pit 2 (0) **NFL** 21 (0) [3 yrs]

CONLIN, CHRIS Christopher Howard, G, 6´4˝/290 lbs; Penn State; 1987: Mia, rnd 5; B6/7/1965 Philadelphia, PA **1987** Mia 3 (0) **1990** Ind 16 (0) **1991** Ind 8 (2) **NFL** 27 (2) [3 yrs]

CONLIN, RAY Raymond Mario, DT, 6´2˝/258 lbs; Ohio State; B6/7/1962 Philadelphia, PA **1987** Phi 1 (1)

CONN, DICK Richard Raymond, DB, 6´0˝/185 lbs; Georgia; B1/9/1951 Louisville, KY **1974**†Pit 12 **1975** NE 3 (1) **1976**†NE 13 (1) **1977** NE 14 **1978**†NE 15 **1979** NE 1 **NFL** 58 (2) [6 yrs]

CONN, TUFFY George Washington, B, 5´6˝/155 lbs; Oregon State; B2/22/1895 Helron, IL, D8/2/1973 Laguna Beach, CA **1920** Akr 3 (0) **1920** Cle 6 (3) **NFL** 9 (3) [1 yr]

CONNAUGHTON, BABE Harry Aloysius, G, 6´2˝/285 lbs; Georgetown (DC); B6/6/1905 Philadelphia, PA, D8/11/1969 Braham, MN **1927** Fra 16 (16, RG)

CONNELL, ALBERT Albert Gene Anthony, WR, 6´0˝/179 lbs; Texas A&M; 1997: Was, rnd 4; B5/13/1974 Fort Lauderdale, FL

YEAR	TEAM	G (GS, POS)	RUSH	YD	AVG (LG)	TD	REC	YD	AVG (LG)	TD	PASS	COMP	PCT	YD	AVG (LG)	TD	INT	SK	YD	QBR	KPR	OTD	PTS	TAY
1997	Was	5 (1)	1	3	3.0 (3)	0	9	138	15.3 (41)	2	—	—	—	—	—	—	—	—	—	—	—	—	12	82
1998	Was	14 (5, wr)	—	—	—	—	28	451	16.1 (61)	2	—	—	—	—	—	—	—	—	—	—	—	—	12	236
1999	†Was	15 (14, WR)	1	8	8.0 (8)	0	62	1132	18.3 (62)	7	—	—	—	—	—	—	—	—	—	—	—	—	42	609
2000	Was	16 (13, WR)	—	—	—	—	39	762	19.5 (77)	3	—	—	—	—	—	—	—	—	—	—	—	—	18	396
2001	NO	11 (1)	1	6	6.0 (6)	0	12	191	15.9 (46)	2	—	—	—	—	—	—	—	—	—	—	—	—	12	112
NFL	5	61 (34)	3	17	5.7 (8)	0	150	2674	17.8 (77)	16	—	—	—	—	—	—	—	—	—	—	—	—	96	1434

CONNELL, BILL William Joseph, WB, /181 lbs; none; B10/19/1893 Rochester, NY, D3/1/1976 Canandaigua, NY **1920** Roc 1 (0)

CONNELL, MIKE Michael C., P, 6´1˝/200 lbs; Cincinnati; 1978: SF, rnd 10; B3/15/1956 Sharon, PA **[P]** **1978** SF 16 **1980** Was 16 (0)

YEAR	TEAM	G (GS, POS)	RUSH	YD	AVG (LG)	TD	REC	YD	AVG (LG)	TD	PASS	COMP	PCT	YD	AVG (LG)	TD	INT	SK	YD	QBR	KPR	OTD	PTS	TAY
1981	Was	16 (0)	1	0	0.0 (0)	0	—	—	—	—	—	—	—	—	—	—	—	—	—	—	P	—	0	0
NFL	3	48	1	0	0.0	0	—	—	—	—	—	—	—	—	—	—	—	—	—	—	P	—	0	0

CONNELL, WARD Ward Thomas, B-E, 5´10˝/173 lbs; Notre Dame; B5/1899 Menomonee Falls, WI, deceased **1926** ChiC 2 (0)

CONNELLY, MIKE Michael James, C-G-T, 6´4˝/247 lbs; Washington State; Utah State; 1960: Buf, rnd 1; B10/16/1935 Monrovia, CA **1960** Dal 12 **1961** Dal 14 (C) **1962** Dal 14 (C) **1963** Dal 14 (C) **1964** Dal 14 (C) **1965** Dal 10 **1966**†Dal 14 **1967**†Dal 14 (14, C) **1968** Pit 14 **NFL** 120 (14) [9 yrs]

CONNER, CLYDE Clyde Raymond, E, 6´2˝/193 lbs; Pacific; B5/18/1933 Tuttle, OK

YEAR	TEAM	G (GS, POS)	RUSH	YD	AVG (LG)	TD	REC	YD	AVG (LG)	TD	PASS	COMP	PCT	YD	AVG (LG)	TD	INT	SK	YD	QBR	KPR	OTD	PTS	TAY
1956	SF	12 (le)	—	—	—	—	22	362	16.5 (49)	1	—	—	—	—	—	—	—	—	—	—	—	—	6	186
1957	†SF☆	8 (LE)	—	—	—	—	30	412	13.7 (41)	4	—	—	—	—	—	—	—	—	—	—	—	—	24	226
1958	SF	12 (LE)	—	—	—	—	49	512	10.4 (26)	5	—	—	—	—	—	—	—	—	—	—	—	—	30	281
1959	SF	9 (LE)	—	—	—	—	13	162	12.5 (37)	1	—	—	—	—	—	—	—	—	—	—	—	—	6	86
1960	SF	10 (10, SE)	—	—	—	—	38	531	14.0 (65)	2	—	—	—	—	—	—	—	—	—	—	—	—	12	276
1961	SF	5 (5, se)	—	—	—	—	11	177	16.1 (45)	1	—	—	—	—	—	—	—	—	—	—	—	—	6	94
1962	SF	13 (10, SE)	—	—	—	—	24	240	10.0 (18)	4	—	—	—	—	—	—	—	—	—	—	—	—	24	140
1963	SF	11 (9, SE)	—	—	—	—	16	247	15.4 (42)	0	—	—	—	—	—	—	—	—	—	—	—	—	0	124
NFL	8	80 (34)	—	—	—	—	203	2643	13.0 (65)	18	—	—	—	—	—	—	—	—	—	—	—	—	108	1412

CONNER, DARION Darion, LB, 6´2˝/250 lbs; Jackson State; 1990: Atl, rnd 2; B9/28/1967 Macon, MS **1990** Atl 16 (7, ROLB) **1991**†Atl 15 (14, ROLB) **1992** Atl 16 (16, ROLB) **1993** Atl 14 (10, RLB) **1994** NO 16 (13, LOLB) **1995** Car 16 (16, ROLB) **1996**†Phi 7 (0) **1997** Phi 14 (0) **NFL** 114 (76) [8 yrs]

CONNERS, DAN Daniel Joseph, LB, 6´2˝/230 lbs; Miami (FL); 1964: Oak, rnd 2/Chi, rnd 5; B2/6/1941 St. Mary's, PA **1964** Oak-A 5 **1965** Oak-A 14 **1966** Oak-A✧14 (mlb) **1967**†Oak-A★14 (MLB) **1968**†Oak-A★14 (14, MLB) **1969**†Oak-A☆14 (14, MLB) **1970**†Oak 10 (9, MLB) **1971** Oak 14 (14, MLB) **1972**†Oak 14 (9, MLB) **1973**†Oak 14 (14, MLB) **1974**†Oak 14 (14, MLB) **NFL** 141 (88) [11 yrs]

CONNOLLY, DANIEL Daniel, G, 6´4˝/311 lbs; Southeast Missouri State; B9/2/1982 St. Louis, MO **2005**†Jax 4 (0)

YEAR	TEAM	G (GS, POS)	RUSH	YD	AVG(LG)	TD	REC	YD	AVG(LG)	TD	PASS	COMP	PCT	YD	AVG(LG)	TD	INT	SK	YD	QBR	KPR	OTD	PTS	TAY

CONNOLLY, HARRY Harry William, TB, 5´11˝/190 lbs; Boston College; 1943: Pit, rnd 5; B7/16/1920 Norwalk, CT, D1/14/2006 New Bedford, MA

| 1946 | Bkn-A | 3(2) | 8 | 18 | 2.3 | 0 | — | — | — | 8 | 2 | 25.0 | 29 | 3.6 | 0 | 1 | — | — | — | kp | — | 0 | 5 |

CONNOLLY, TED Theodore William, G, 6´3˝/240 lbs; Santa Clara; Tulsa; 1954: SF, rnd 9; B12/5/1931 Oakland, CA **1954** SF 12 **1956** SF 5 **1957** SF 10 (RG) **1958** SF 12 (RG) **1959** SF 12 (RG) **1960** SF 4 **1961** SF✧14 (12, RG) **1962** SF☆13 (11, RG) **1963** Cle 10 **NFL** 92 (23) [9 yrs]

CONNOR, BILL William Joseph, G-T, 6´1˝/240 lbs; Rhode Island; Providence; Catholic; B4/8/1899 Providence, RI, D12/14/1980 Norwich, CT **1929** Bos 7 (3) **1930** Nwk 1 (0) **NFL** 8 (3) [2 yrs]

CONNOR, DUTCH Stafford Joseph, aka Stanislaus Josef Koszarek, B, 6´0˝/190 lbs; New Hampshire; B4/16/1894 Poland, D11/24/1978 Alamo Heights, TX **[K]** **1925** Pro 3 (3), 2 **1926** Bkn 1 (0) **NFL** 4 (3) [2 yrs]

CONNOR, GEORGE George Leo, T-LB-DT-G, 6´3˝/240 lbs; Holy Cross; Notre Dame; 1946: NYG, rnd 1; B1/21/1925 Chicago, IL, D3/31/2003 Evanston, IL; HOF 1975 **1948** ChiB 11 (5, lt) **1951** ChiB★12 (LT/LLB) **1952** ChiB★12 (LT/RLB) **1954** ChiB☆8 (RLB) **1955** ChiB☆12

1949	ChiB☆	12(6, LT)	—	—	—		3	51	17.0(25)	0	—	—	—	—	—	—	—	—	—		—	—	0	26
1950	†ChiB★	11(LT)	—	—	—		1	21	21.0(21)	0	—	—	—	—	—	—	—	—	—	i	—	—	0	23
1953	ChiB★	12(LT)	—	—	—		1	17	17.0(17)	0	—	—	—	—	—	—	—	—	—	k	—	—	0	15
NFL		8	90(11)	—	—	—		5	89	17.8(25)	0	—	—	—	—	—	—	—	—	ki	—	1	6	77

CONNORS, HAM Hamilton C., E, /190 lbs; none; B2/22/1898 Pittsburgh, PA, D2/27/1967 East Rochester, NY **1925** Roc 1 (1)

CONNOT, SCOTT Scott, DB, 6´3˝/216 lbs; South Dakota State; B6/24/1981 Spencer, NE **2004** KC 2 (0)

CONOLY, ZUEHL William Zuehl, G, 6´0˝/227 lbs; Southwestern (TX); Texas; 1943: Phi, rnd 10; B9/13/1920 San Antonio, TX **1946** ChiC 9 (0)

CONOVER, FRANK Frank, DT, 6´5˝/317 lbs; Syracuse; 1991: Cle, rnd 8; B4/6/1968 Manalapan, NJ **1991** Cle 4 (1)

CONOVER, LARRY Lamer S.G., C, 5´10˝/190 lbs; Penn State; B3/1894 Atlantic City, NJ, D8/4/1955 Atlantic City, NJ **[K]** **1921** Can 1 (1) **1923** Can☆12 (12, C), 1 **1925** Cle 11 (11, C) **NFL** 24 (24) [3 yrs]

CONOVER, SCOTT Kelsey Scott, T-G, 6´4˝/276 lbs; Purdue; 1991: Det, rnd 5; B9/27/1968 Neptune, NJ **1991**†Det 16 (3) **1992** Det 15 (15, RT) **1993** Det 1 (0) **1995**†Det 14 (2) **1996** Det 10 (7, rg)

| 1994 | Det | 11(0) | — | — | — | | 1 | 1 | 1.0(1) | 1 | — | — | — | — | — | — | — | — | — | | — | — | 6 | 6 |
| NFL | | 6 | 67(27) | — | — | — | | 1 | 1 | 1.0(1) | 1 | — | — | — | — | — | — | — | — | | — | — | 6 | 6 |

CONRAD, BOBBY JOE Robert Joseph, FL-DB-HB-WR-K, 6´2˝/194 lbs; Texas A&M; 1958: NYG, rnd 5; B11/17/1935 Clifton, TX **[K]**

1958	ChiC	12(DB)	—	—	—		—	—	—		—	—	—	—	—	—	—	—	—	Kkpi	—	51	78
1959	ChiC	12(RH)	74	328	4.4(56)	2	14	142	10.1(25)	3	3	2	66.7	82	27.3(52)	1	1	—	—	Kkp	1	84	621
1960	SL	12	23	91	4.0(33)	0	7	103	14.7(24)	0	—	—	—	—	—	—	—	—	—	Kkp	—	34	347
1961	SL	14(FL)	20	22	1.1(7)	0	30	499	16.6(50)	2	1	1	100.0	5	5.0(5)	0	0	—	—	Kkp	1	22	385
1962	SL	14(FL)	—	—	—		62	954	15.4(72)	4	—	—	—	—	—	—	—	—	—	Kp	—	24	497
1963	SL☆	14(FL)	1	0	0.0(0)	0	73	967	13.2(48)	10	—	—	—	—	—	—	—	—	—	p	—	60	530
1964	SL★	14(FL)	—	—	—		61	780	12.8(53)	4	—	—	—	—	—	—	—	—	—	k	—	36	431
1965	SL	14(FL)	—	—	—		58	909	15.7(71)	5	—	—	—	—	—	—	—	—	—		—	30	480
1966	SL	14(FL)	—	—	—		34	388	11.4(40)	2	—	—	—	—	—	—	—	—	—		—	12	204
1967	SL	14(FL)	—	—	—		47	637	13.6(53)	2	—	—	—	—	—	—	—	—	—		—	12	329
1968	SL	14(FL)	—	—	—		32	449	14.0(80)	4	—	—	—	—	—	—	—	—	—		—	24	245
1969	†Dal	8	—	—	—		4	74	18.5(34)	0	—	—	—	—	—	—	—	—	—		—	0	37
NFL		12	156	118	441	3.7(56)	2	422	5902	14.0(80)	38	4	3	75.0	87	21.8(52)	1	1	—	—	Kkpi	2	389	4182

CONRAD, CHRIS Christopher Lee, T, 6´6˝/301 lbs; Fresno State; 1998: Pit, rnd 3; B5/27/1975 Fullerton, CA **1998** Pit 6 (1) **1999** Pit 11 (3) **NFL** 17 (4) [2 yrs]

CONRAD, J.R. James Robert, G, 6´4˝/300 lbs; Oklahoma; 1996: NE, rnd 7; B2/2/1974 Fairland, OK **1997** NYJ 12 (1)

CONRAD, MARTY Martin Henry, C-G-E, 6´1˝/240 lbs; Kalamazoo; B11/30/1895, deceased **1922** Tol 8 (8, C) **1923** Tol 8 (8, C) **1924** Ken 3 (3, C) **1925** Akr 3 (1) **NFL** 22 (20) [4 yrs]

CONSIDINE, SEAN Sean, DB, 6´1˝/206 lbs; Iowa; 2005: Phi, rnd 4; B10/28/1981 Byron, IL **2005** Phi 6 (0)

CONSTANTINE, IRV C. Irving, HB, 5´9˝/200 lbs; Syracuse; B1/18/1907 New York, NY, D5/14/1966 New Hyde Park, NY **1931** SI 1 (0)

CONTI, ENIO Enio Edward, G, 5´11˝/204 lbs; Arkansas; Bucknell; B2/15/1913 Naples, Italy, D5/22/2005 Tallahassee, FL **1942** Phi✧11 (10, RG) **1943** P-P 10 (1) **1944** Phi 8 (5, LG) **1945** Phi 2 (1)

| 1941 | Phi | 9(8, LG) | 1 | -1 | -1.0(-1) | 0 | — | — | — | — | — | — | — | — | — | — | — | — | — | | — | 0 | -1 |
| NFL | | 5 | 40(25) | 1 | -1 | -1.0(-1) | 0 | — | — | — | — | — | — | — | — | — | — | — | — | i | — | 0 | -6 |

CONTOULIS, JOHN John James, DT, 6´5˝/260 lbs; Connecticut; 1962: Min, rnd 16/1963: NYJ, rnd 4; B10/9/1940 New London, CT **1964** NYG 12

CONTZ, BILL William, T, 6´5˝/268 lbs; Penn State; 1983: Cle, rnd 5; B12/5/1961 Belle Vernon, PA **1983** Cle 16 (0) **1984** Cle 15 (9, RT) **1985** Cle 4 (0) **1986** Cle 1 (0) **1986** NO 13 (13, LT) **1987** NO 3 (0) **1988** NO 11 (3) **NFL** 63 (25) [6 yrs]

CONWAY, BRETT Brett Alan, K, 6´2˝/208 lbs; Penn State; 1997: GB, rnd 3; B3/8/1975 Atlanta, GA **[K]** **1998** Was 6 (0) **2000** Was 2 (0) **2000** Oak 1 (0) **2000** NYJ 1 (0) **2001** Was 16 (0) **2002** Was 1 (0) **2003** NYG 5 (0) **2003** Cle 3 (0)

| 1999 | †Was | 16(0) | — | — | — | | — | — | — | — | 1 | 0 | 0.0 | 0 | 0.0 | 0 | 0 | — | — | K | — | 115 | 0 |
| NFL | | 6 | 51(0) | — | — | — | | — | — | — | — | 1 | 0 | 0.0 | 0 | 0.0 | 0 | 0 | — | — | KP | — | 299 | 0 |

CONWAY, CURTIS Curtis LaMont, WR, 6´1˝/196 lbs; USC; 1993: Chi, rnd 1; B1/13/1971 Los Angeles, CA

1993	ChiB	16(7, WR)	5	44	8.8(18)	0	19	231	12.2(38)	2	—	—	—	—	—	—	—	—	—	k	—	12	305
1994	†ChiB	13(12, WR)	6	31	5.2(12)	0	39	546	14.0(85)	2	1	1	100.0	23	23.0(23)	1	0	—	—	kp	—	14	432
1995	ChiB	16(16, WR)	5	77	15.4(20)	0	62	1037	16.7(76)	12	1	0	0.0	0	0.0	0	0	—	—		—	72	656
1996	ChiB	16(16, WR)	8	50	6.3(19)	0	81	1049	13.0(58)	7	1	1	100.0	33	33.0(33)	1	0	—	—		—	42	631
1997	ChiB	7(7, wr)	3	17	5.7(10)	0	30	476	15.9(55)	1	1	0	0.0	0	0.0	0	0	—	—		—	6	260
1998	ChiB	15(15, WR)	5	48	9.6(29)	0	54	733	13.6(47)	3	1	0	0.0	0	0.0	0	0	—	—		—	18	430
1999	ChiB	9(8, WR)	1	-2	-2.0(-2)	0	44	426	9.7(30)	4	—	—	—	—	—	—	—	—	—		—	24	231
2000	SD	14(14, WR)	3	31	10.3(13)	0	53	712	13.4(68)	5	—	—	—	—	—	—	—	—	—		—	30	412
2001	SD	16(16, WR)	7	116	16.6(67)	1	71	1125	15.8(72)	6	—	—	—	—	—	—	—	—	—		—	42	719
2002	SD	13(13, WR)	7	53	7.6(22)	2	57	852	14.9(52)	5	—	—	—	—	—	—	—	—	—		—	42	524
2003	NYJ	16(15, WR)	—	—	—		46	640	13.9(45)	2	—	—	—	—	—	—	—	—	—		—	12	330
2004	SF	16(5, wr)	—	—	—		40	403	10.6(37)	3	—	—	—	—	—	—	—	—	—		—	20	217
NFL		12	167(144)	50	465	9.3(67)	3	594	8230	13.9(85)	52	5	2	40.0	56	11.2(33)	2	0	—	—	kp	—	334	5144

CONWAY, DAVE David Alexander, K, 6´0˝/195 lbs; Texas; 1967: SD, rnd 7; B1/6/1945 Baytown, TX **[K]** **1971** GB 1

CONWELL, ERNIE Ernest Harold, TE, 6´2˝/265 lbs; Washington; 1996: SL, rnd 2; B8/17/1972 Renton, WA

1996	SL	10(8, TE)	—	—	—		15	164	10.9(26)	0	—	—	—	—	—	—	—	—	—		—	0	82
1997	SL	16(16, TE)	—	—	—		38	404	10.6(46)	4	—	—	—	—	—	—	—	—	—		—	24	222
1998	SL	7(7, te)	—	—	—		15	105	7.0(13)	0	—	—	—	—	—	—	—	—	—		—	0	53
1999	†SL	3(0)	—	—	—		1	11	11.0(11)	0	—	—	—	—	—	—	—	—	—		—	0	6
2000	†SL	16(1)	2	23	11.5(17)	0	5	40	8.0(17)	0	—	—	—	—	—	—	—	—	—		—	0	43
2001	†SL☆	16(13, TE)	7	28	4.0(13)	1	38	431	11.3(47)	4	—	—	—	—	—	—	—	—	—		—	30	274
2002	SL	16(10, TE)	6	30	5.0(15)	1	34	419	12.3(52)	2	—	—	—	—	—	—	—	—	—		—	18	260
2003	NO	16(10, TE)	—	—	—		26	290	11.2(32)	2	—	—	—	—	—	—	—	—	—		—	12	155
2004	NO	16(10, TE)	—	—	—		10	102	10.2(28)	1	—	—	—	—	—	—	—	—	—		—	6	56
2005	NO	9(9, TE)	—	—	—		13	165	12.7(31)	1	—	—	—	—	—	—	—	—	—		—	6	88
NFL		10	119(84)	15	81	5.4(17)	2	195	2131	10.9(52)	14	—	—	—	—	—	—	—	—	—		—	96	1237

CONWELL, JOE Joseph Stanislaus, T, 6´5˝/280 lbs; North Carolina; 1984: SF, rnd S2; B2/24/1961 Philadelphia, PA **1986** Phi 16 (9, rt) **1987** Phi 12 (12, RT) **NFL** 28 (21) [2 yrs]

YEAR	TEAM	G(GS, POS)	RUSH	YD	AVG(LG)	TD	REC	YD	AVG(LG)	TD	PASS	COMP	PCT	YD	AVG(LG)	TD	INT	SK	YD	QBR	KPR	OTD	PTS	TAY

CONZELMAN, JIMMY James Good, BB-TB-HB-E, 6´0˝/175 lbs; Washington-St. Louis; B3/6/1898 St. Louis, MO, D7/31/1970 St. Louis, MO; HOF 1964 **[KC]** **1920** Dec 11 (3) **1921** RI 7 (6, BB), 15 **1922** RI 7 (6, BB), 48 **1922** Mil 3 (3) **1923** Mil☆12 (12, BB), 26 **1924** Mil 13 (13, TB), 6 **1925** Det☆12 (9, TB), 18 **1926** Det 12 (4), 13 **1927** Pro 14 (6, bb), 24 **1928** Pro 4 (3), 13 **1929** Pro 9 (2), 6 **NFL** 104 (67), 169 [10 yrs]

COOK, ANTHONY Anthony Andrew, DE-DT, 6´3˝/295 lbs; South Carolina State; 1995: Hou, rnd 2; B5/30/1972 Bennettsville, SC **1995** Hou 10 (4) **1996** Hou 12 (11, LDE) **1997** Ten 16 (16, LDE) **1998** Ten 13 (3) **1999**†Was 16 (7, lde) **NFL** 67 (41) [5 yrs]

COOK, CHARLES Charles McKinley, DE, 6´3˝/255 lbs; Miami (FL); B5/13/1959 Gainesville, FL **1983** NYG 4 (0)

COOK, CLAIR Clair, WB-HB, 5´9˝/170 lbs; none; B1/7/1909, D11/1983 Bellaire, MI **1928** Day 4 (2, WB)

COOK, DAMION Damion Lamar, G-T, 6´5˝/335 lbs; Bethune-Cookman; B4/16/1979 Nashville, TN **2002** Bal 3 (0) **2003** Bal 1 (0) **2004** Bal 9 (0) **2004** Cle 6 (6, rg) **NFL** 19 (6) [3 yrs]

COOK, DAVE David Fouts, B, 6´2˝/203 lbs; Illinois; B1/1/1912 Elgin, IL, D12/19/1949 St. Louis, MO **[K]**

YEAR	TEAM	G(GS, POS)	RUSH	YD	AVG(LG)	TD	REC	YD	AVG(LG)	TD	PASS	COMP	PCT	YD	AVG(LG)	TD	INT	SK	YD	QBR	KPR	OTD	PTS	TAY
1934	ChiC	9(9, WB)	23	112	4.9	0	2	9	4.5	0	—	—	—	—	—	—	—	—	—	—	K	—	4	117
1935	ChiC	10(5, wb)	31	121	3.9	1	—	—	—	—	1	1	100.0	7	7.0(7)	0	0	—	—	—	—	—	6	135
1936	ChiC	2(2)	3	15	5.0	0	1	2	2.0(2)	0	—	—	—	—	—	—	—	—	—	—	—	—	0	16
1936	Bkn	3(0)	7	9	1.3	0	—	—	—	—	—	—	—	—	—	—	—	—	—	—	—	—	0	9
NFL	3	24(16)	64	257	4.0	1	3	11	3.7(2)	0	1	1	100.0	7	7.0(7)	0	0	—	—	—	K	—	10	276

COOK, ED Edward Joseph, T-G, 6´2˝/245 lbs; Notre Dame; B6/29/1932 Philadelphia, PA **1958** ChiC 8 **1959** ChiC 12 (lg) **1960** SL 11 (LT) **1961** SL 14 (LT) **1962** SL 7 (LT) **1963** SL 13 (LG) **1964** SL 14 **1965** SL 14 **1966** Atl 14 (14, LG) **1967** Atl 4 **NFL** 111 (14) [10 yrs]

COOK, FRED Frederick Harrison, DE, 6´4˝/244 lbs; Southern Mississippi; 1974: Bal, rnd 2; B4/15/1952 Pascagoula, MS **1974** Bal 14 (14, LDE) **1975**†Bal 14 (14, LDE) **1976**†Bal☆14 (14, LDE) **1977**†Bal☆14 (14, LDE) **1978** Bal 16 (16, LDE) **1979** Bal 16 (16, LDE) **1980** Bal 16 (16, LDE) **NFL** 104 (104) [7 yrs]

COOK, GENE Eugene, E, 6´3˝/215 lbs; Toledo; 1958: GB, rnd 13; B1/11/1934 Greenfield, TN

YEAR	TEAM	G(GS, POS)	RUSH	YD	AVG(LG)	TD	REC	YD	AVG(LG)	TD	PASS	COMP	PCT	YD	AVG(LG)	TD	INT	SK	YD	QBR	KPR	OTD	PTS	TAY
1959	Det	1	—	—	—	—	1	43	43.0(43)	0	—	—	—	—	—	—	—	—	—	—	—	—	0	22

COOK, GREG Gregory Lynn, QB, 6´4˝/220 lbs; Cincinnati; 1969: Cin, rnd 1; B11/20/1946 Dayton, OH

YEAR	TEAM	G(GS, POS)	RUSH	YD	AVG(LG)	TD	REC	YD	AVG(LG)	TD	PASS	COMP	PCT	YD	AVG(LG)	TD	INT	SK	YD	QBR	KPR	OTD	PTS	TAY
1969	Cin-A	11(QB)	25	148	5.9(30)	1	—	—	—	—	197	106	53.8	1854	**9.4**(**78**)	15	11	29	195	**88.3**	—	—	6	720
1973	Cin	1	—	—	—	—	—	—	—	—	3	1	33.3	11	3.7(11)	0	0	—	—	—	—	—	0	6
NFL	2	12	25	148	5.9(30)	1	—	—	—	—	200	107	53.5	1865	9.3(78)	15	11	29	195	87.6	—	—	6	726

COOK, JAMEEL Jameel A., FB, 5´10˝/237 lbs; Illinois; 2001: TB, rnd 6; B2/8/1979 Miami, FL

YEAR	TEAM	G(GS, POS)	RUSH	YD	AVG(LG)	TD	REC	YD	AVG(LG)	TD	PASS	COMP	PCT	YD	AVG(LG)	TD	INT	SK	YD	QBR	KPR	OTD	PTS	TAY
2001	†TB	16(3)	2	2	1.0(2)	0	17	89	5.2(16)	0	—	—	—	—	—	—	—	—	—	—	—	—	0	47
2002	†TB	14(1)	—	—	—	—	4	43	10.8(14)	0	—	—	—	—	—	—	—	—	—	—	—	—	0	22
2003	TB	14(8, FB)	1	-1	-1.0(-1)	0	20	120	6.0(19)	1	—	—	—	—	—	—	—	—	—	—	—	—	6	64
2004	TB	12(5, fb)	—	—	—	—	7	44	6.3(9)	1	—	—	—	—	—	—	—	—	—	—	—	—	6	27
2005	†TB	16(0)	—	—	—	—	7	43	6.1(11)	1	—	—	—	—	—	—	—	—	—	—	—	—	6	27
NFL	5	72(17)	3	1	0.3(2)	0	55	339	6.2(19)	3	—	—	—	—	—	—	—	—	—	—	—	—	18	186

COOK, JAMES James C., G, 6´3˝/220 lbs; Notre Dame; B11/27/1888 Green Bay, WI, D8/21/1979 Green Bay, WI **1921** GB 2 (1)

COOK, KELLY Kelly Edward, RB, 5´11˝/225 lbs; Oklahoma State; B8/20/1962 Cushing, OK

YEAR	TEAM	G(GS, POS)	RUSH	YD	AVG(LG)	TD	REC	YD	AVG(LG)	TD	PASS	COMP	PCT	YD	AVG(LG)	TD	INT	SK	YD	QBR	KPR	OTD	PTS	TAY
1987	GB	11(0)	2	3	1.5(2)	0	—	—	—	—	—	—	—	—	—	—	—	—	—	—	k	—	0	0

COOK, LEON Leon Spencer, T, 6´0˝/245 lbs; Northwestern; B3/27/1920 Enid, OK, D5/1983 Minneapolis, MN **1942** Phi 2 (0)

COOK, MARV Marvin Eugene, TE, 6´4˝/234 lbs; Iowa; 1989: NE, rnd 3; B2/24/1966 Iowa City, IA

YEAR	TEAM	G(GS, POS)	RUSH	YD	AVG(LG)	TD	REC	YD	AVG(LG)	TD	PASS	COMP	PCT	YD	AVG(LG)	TD	INT	SK	YD	QBR	KPR	OTD	PTS	TAY
1989	NE	16(0)	—	—	—	—	3	13	4.3(5)	0	—	—	—	—	—	—	—	—	—	—	—	—	0	7
1990	NE	16(16, TE)	—	—	—	—	51	455	8.9(35)	5	—	—	—	—	—	—	—	—	—	—	—	—	30	253
1991	NE★	16(16, TE)	—	—	—	—	82	808	9.9(49)	3	—	—	—	—	—	—	—	—	—	—	—	—	18	419
1992	NE✧	16(15, TE)	—	—	—	—	52	413	7.9(27)	2	—	—	—	—	—	—	—	—	—	—	—	—	12	217
1993	NE	16(12, TE)	—	—	—	—	22	154	7.0(17)	1	—	—	—	—	—	—	—	—	—	—	k	—	6	75
1994	†ChiB	16(8, TE)	—	—	—	—	21	212	10.1(34)	1	—	—	—	—	—	—	—	—	—	—	—	—	6	111
1995	SL	16(10, TE)	—	—	—	—	26	135	5.2(16)	1	—	—	—	—	—	—	—	—	—	—	—	—	6	73
NFL	7	112(77)	—	—	—	—	257	2190	8.5(49)	13	—	—	—	—	—	—	—	—	—	—	k	—	78	1153

COOK, RASHARD Rashard Jermaine, DB, 5´11˝/205 lbs; USC; 1999: Chi, rnd 6; B4/18/1977 San Diego, CA **1999** Phi 13 (0) **2000**†Phi 14 (0) **2001**†Phi 16 (3) **2002** Phi 4 (0) **NFL** 47 (3) [4 yrs]

COOK, TED Theodore Walter, E-DB, 6´2˝/195 lbs; Alabama; 1944: Bkn, rnd 22; B2/6/1922 Birmingham, AL, D5/2/1990 Birmingham, AL

YEAR	TEAM	G(GS, POS)	RUSH	YD	AVG(LG)	TD	REC	YD	AVG(LG)	TD	PASS	COMP	PCT	YD	AVG(LG)	TD	INT	SK	YD	QBR	KPR	OTD	PTS	TAY
1947	Det	11(5, le)	—	—	—	—	7	111	15.9(29)	1	—	—	—	—	—	—	—	—	—	—	kpi	—	6	40
1948	GB	12(5, le)	—	—	—	—	13	156	12.0(23)	0	—	—	—	—	—	—	—	—	—	—	pi	—	0	137
1949	GB	11(4)	—	—	—	—	25	442	17.7(50)	1	—	—	—	—	—	—	—	—	—	—	ki	—	6	245
1950	GB	12(RE)	—	—	—	—	16	182	11.4(21)	3	—	—	—	—	—	—	—	—	—	—	—	—	18	106
NFL	4	46(14)	—	—	—	—	61	891	14.6(50)	5	—	—	—	—	—	—	—	—	—	—	kpi	—	30	528

COOK, TOI Toi Fitzgerald, DB, 5´11˝/188 lbs; Stanford; 1987: NO, rnd 8; B12/3/1964 Chicago, IL **[I]** **1987** NO 7 (0) **1988** NO 16 (0) **1990**†NO 16 (16, RCB) **1991** NO 14 (14, RCB) **1992**†NO 16 (15, LCB) **1993** NO 16 (16, RCB) **1994**†SF 16 (2) **1995** SF 2 (0) **1996**†Car 15 (0) **1997** Car 16 (0)

YEAR	TEAM	G(GS, POS)	RUSH	YD	AVG(LG)	TD	REC	YD	AVG(LG)	TD	PASS	COMP	PCT	YD	AVG(LG)	TD	INT	SK	YD	QBR	KPR	OTD	PTS	TAY
1989	NO	16(14, RCB)	—	—	—	—	1	8	8.0(8)	0	—	—	—	—	—	—	—	—	—	—	iS	1	6	80
NFL	11	150(77)	—	—	—	—	1	8	8.0(8)	0	—	—	—	—	—	—	—	—	—	—	piS	2	12	248

COOKE, BILL William Morrill, DT-DE-T, 6´5˝/249 lbs; Connecticut; Massachusetts; 1975: GB, rnd 10; B2/26/1951 Lowell, MA **1975** GB 5 **1976** SF 9 **1977** SF 14 **1978** Sea 4 (3) **1978** Det 12 **1979** Sea 15 **1980** Sea 16 (3) **NFL** 75 (6) [6 yrs]

COOKE, ED Edward Grey, DE-LB, 6´4˝/250 lbs; Maryland; 1958: ChiB, rnd 3; B5/3/1935 Pilot Mountain, NC **1958** ChiB 3 **1958** Phi 7 **1959**†Bal 4 **1960** NYT-A 11 **1961** NYT-A 14 (LLB) **1962** NYT-A 14 (LLB) **1963** NYJ-A 9 **1964** Den-A 14 (RDE) **1965** Den-A 14 (LDE) **1966** Mia-A✧14 (13, LDE) **1967** Mia-A 13 (12, LDE) **NFL** 117 (25) [10 yrs]

COOKS, JOHNIE Johnie Earl, LB, 6´4˝/247 lbs; Mississippi State; 1982: Bal, rnd 1; B11/23/1958 Leland, MS **1982** Bal 9 (8, LILB) **1983** Bal 16 (11, LILB) **1984** Ind 16 (13, LOLB) **1985** Ind 16 (16, LOLB) **1986** Ind 15 (15, LOLB) **1987**†Ind 10 (10, LOLB) **1988** Ind 1 (1) **1988** NYG 13 (3) **1989** NYG 16 (13, RILB) **1990**†NYG 14 (6, lolb) **1991** Cle 2 (0) **NFL** 128 (96) [10 yrs]

COOKS, KERRY Kerry George, DB, 5´11˝/204 lbs; Iowa; 1998: Min, rnd 5; B3/28/1974 Dallas, TX **1998** GB 9 (0)

COOKS, RAYFORD Rayford Earrl, DE, 6´3˝/245 lbs; North Texas; B8/25/1962 Dallas, TX **1987** Hou 10 (1)

COOKS, TERRENCE Terrence Kenneth, LB, 6´0˝/230 lbs; Nicholls State; B10/25/1966 New Orleans, LA **1989** NE 3 (0)

COOLBAUGH, BOB Irwin Robert, FL-WR, 6´4˝/200 lbs; Richmond; 1961: Oak, rnd 15/Was, rnd 12; B7/5/1939 Kingston, PA

YEAR	TEAM	G(GS, POS)	RUSH	YD	AVG(LG)	TD	REC	YD	AVG(LG)	TD	PASS	COMP	PCT	YD	AVG(LG)	TD	INT	SK	YD	QBR	KPR	OTD	PTS	TAY
1961	Oak-A	14(FL)	—	—	—	—	32	435	13.6(46)	4	—	—	—	—	—	—	—	—	—	—	k	—	26	238

COOLEY, CHRIS Chris, TE, 6´4˝/252 lbs; Utah State; 2004: Was, rnd 3; B7/11/1982 Powell, WY

YEAR	TEAM	G(GS, POS)	RUSH	YD	AVG(LG)	TD	REC	YD	AVG(LG)	TD	PASS	COMP	PCT	YD	AVG(LG)	TD	INT	SK	YD	QBR	KPR	OTD	PTS	TAY
2004	Was	16(9, TE)	—	—	—	—	37	314	8.5(31)	6	—	—	—	—	—	—	—	—	—	—	—	—	36	187
2005	†Was☆	16(16, TE)	—	—	—	—	71	774	10.9(32)	7	—	—	—	—	—	—	—	—	—	—	—	—	42	422
NFL	2	32(25)	—	—	—	—	108	1088	10.1(32)	13	—	—	—	—	—	—	—	—	—	—	—	—	78	609

COOMBS, LARRY Lawrence Mahlon, G-C, 6´4˝/260 lbs; Idaho; B8/9/1957 Arcata, CA **1980** NO 1 (0)

COOMBS, TOM Thomas Barton, TE, 6´3˝/236 lbs; Puget Sound; Idaho; 1982: NYJ, rnd 7; B5/31/1959 Eureka, CA **1982**†NYJ 3 (0)

YEAR	TEAM	G(GS, POS)	RUSH	YD	AVG(LG)	TD	REC	YD	AVG(LG)	TD	PASS	COMP	PCT	YD	AVG(LG)	TD	INT	SK	YD	QBR	KPR	OTD	PTS	TAY
1983	NYJ	12(1)	—	—	—	—	1	1	1.0(1)	0	—	—	—	—	—	—	—	—	—	—	—	—	0	1
NFL	2	15(1)	—	—	—	—	1	1	1.0(1)	0	—	—	—	—	—	—	—	—	—	—	—	—	0	1

COOMER, JOE Joseph David, T-G, 6´6˝/281 lbs; Austin; B9/11/1918 Greenville, TX, D10/18/1979 Whitehouse, TX **1941** Pit✧10 (6, LT) **1945** Pit 9 (5, lt) **1946** Pit 7 (3) **1947**†ChiC 12 (1) **1948**†ChiC 12 (0) **1949** ChiC 12 (2) **NFL** 62 (17) [6 yrs]

COON, TY Edward Howard, G, 6´0˝/215 lbs; North Carolina State; 1940: Bkn, rnd 7; B7/26/1915 White Plains, NY, D1/9/1992 Watertown, CT **1940** Bkn 9 (0)

COONEY, MARK Mark Joseph, LB, 6´4˝/230 lbs; Colorado; 1974: GB, rnd 16; B6/2/1951 Denver, CO **1974** GB 13

YEAR	TEAM	G(GS, POS)	RUSH	YD	AVG(LG)	TD	REC	YD	AVG(LG)	TD	PASS COMP	PCT	YD	AVG(LG)	TD	INT	SK	YD	QBR	KPR	OTD	PTS	TAY

COONS, ROB   Robert Allan, TE, 6´5˝/249 lbs; Pittsburgh; B9/18/1969 Brea, CA

1995	Buf	4(0)	—	—	—	—	3	28	9.3(13)	0	—	—	—	—	—	—	—	—	—	—	—	0	14
1996	†Buf	16(0)	—	—	—	—	1	12	12.0(12)	0	—	—	—	—	—	—	—	—	—	—	—	0	6
1997	Buf	12(0)	—	—	—	—	—	—	—	—	—	—	—	—	—	—	—	—	—	k	—	0	-3
NFL	3	32(0)	—	—	—	—	4	40	10.0(13)	0	—	—	—	—	—	—	—	—	—	k	—	0	17

COOPER, ADRIAN   Adrian, TE, 6´5˝/255 lbs; Oklahoma; 1991: Pit, rnd 4; B4/27/1968 Denver, CO

1991	Pit	16(8, te)	—	—	—	—	11	147	13.4(47)	2	—	—	—	—	—	—	—	—	—	—	—	12	84
1992	†Pit	16(15, TE)	—	—	—	—	16	197	12.3(27)	3	—	—	—	—	—	—	—	—	—	k	—	18	107
1993	†Pit	14(3)	—	—	—	—	9	112	12.4(38)	0	—	—	—	—	—	—	—	—	—	k	—	0	43
1994	Min	12(11, TE)	—	—	—	—	32	363	11.3(34)	0	—	—	—	—	—	—	—	—	—	—	—	0	182
1995	Min	13(13, TE)	—	—	—	—	18	207	11.5(41)	0	—	—	—	—	—	—	—	—	—	—	—	0	104
1996	†SF	6(0)	—	—	—	—	1	11	11.0(11)	0	—	—	—	—	—	—	—	—	—	—	—	0	6
NFL	6	77(50)	—	—	—	—	87	1037	11.9(47)	5	—	—	—	—	—	—	—	—	—	k	—	30	524

COOPER, ANDRE   Andre Damon, WR, 6´2˝/210 lbs; Florida State; B6/21/1975 Camden, SC

| 1999 | Den | 10(1) | — | — | — | — | 9 | 98 | 10.9(21) | 0 | — | — | — | — | — | — | — | — | — | — | — | 0 | 49 |

COOPER, BERT   Bertram Genard, LB, 6´1˝/242 lbs; Florida State; 1975: NYJ, rnd 12; B8/24/1952 Tallahassee, FL   **1976** TB 12 (3)

COOPER, BILL   William Albert, FB-LB, 6´3˝/215 lbs; Muskingum; 1961: SF, rnd 3/Den, rnd 14; B7/12/1939 Carrollton, OH   **1963** SF 14   **1964** SF 2

1961	SF	12	8	17	2.1(6)	1	—	—	—	—	—	—	—	—	—	—	—	—	—	k	—	6	26
1962	SF	10	2	-2	-1.0(2)	0	—	—	—	—	—	—	—	—	—	—	—	—	—	k	—	0	0
NFL	4	38	10	15	1.5(6)	1	—	—	—	—	—	—	—	—	—	—	—	—	—	k	—	6	4

COOPER, BUD   William Gordon, B, 6´1˝/204 lbs; Penn State; B4/14/1913 Buffalo, NY, D8/11/1998 Dallas, PA

| 1937 | Cle | 5(2) | 19 | 45 | 2.4 | 0 | 1 | 14 | 14.0(14) | 0 | 5 | 2 | 40.0 | 21 | 4.2 | 0 | 1 | — | — | — | — | 0 | 23 |

COOPER, CHRIS   Chris, DT-DE, 6´5˝/275 lbs; Nebraska-Omaha; 2001: Oak, rnd 6; B12/27/1977 Lincoln, NE   **2001**†Oak 12 (1)   **2002**†Oak 16 (1)   **2003** Oak 16 (9, LDT)   **2004** Dal 2 (0)   **2004** SF 8 (2)   **NFL** 54 (13) [4 yrs]

COOPER, DEKE   John Delvicchio, DB, 6´3˝/215 lbs; Notre Dame; B10/18/1977 Swainsboro, GA   **2002** Car 10 (0)   **2003** Jax 14 (10, FS)   **2004** Jax 16 (12, SS)   **2005**†Jax 16 (12, SS)   **NFL** 56 (22) [4 yrs]

COOPER, EARL   Marion Earl, RB-TE, 6´2˝/227 lbs; Rice; 1980: SF, rnd 1; B9/17/1957 Giddings, TX

1980	SF	16(16, FB)	171	720	4.2(47)	5	83	567	6.8(66)	4	—	—	—	—	—	—	—	—	—	—	—	54	1074
1981	†SF	16(11, FB)	98	330	3.4(23)	1	51	477	9.4(50)	0	—	—	—	—	—	—	—	—	—	—	—	6	579
1982	SF	9(5, FB)	24	77	3.2(9)	0	19	153	8.1(20)	1	—	—	—	—	—	—	—	—	—	—	—	6	159
1983	†SF	16(0)	—	—	—	—	15	207	13.8(73)	3	—	—	—	—	—	—	—	—	—	k	—	18	119
1984	†SF	16(8, TE)	3	13	4.3(7)	0	41	459	11.2(26)	4	—	—	—	—	—	—	—	—	—	k	—	24	248
1985	SF	15(0)	2	12	6.0(14)	0	4	45	11.3(20)	0	—	—	—	—	—	—	—	—	—	—	—	0	35
1986	LARd	5(0)	—	—	—	—	—	—	—	—	—	—	—	—	—	—	—	—	—	—	—	—	—
NFL	7	93(40)	298	1152	3.9(47)	6	213	1908	9.0(73)	12	—	—	—	—	—	—	—	—	—	k	—	108	2211

COOPER, EVAN   Evan, DB, 5´11˝/185 lbs; Michigan; 1984: Phi, rnd 4; B6/25/1962 Miami, FL **[R]**   **1984** Phi 16 (0)   **1985** Phi 16 (0)   **1986** Phi 16 (13, RCB)   **1987** Phi 12 (1)   **1988** Atl 9 (0)   **1989** Atl 16 (13, SS)   **NFL** 85 (27) [6 yrs]

COOPER, GEORGE   George Junious, LB, 6´2˝/225 lbs; Michigan State; B12/24/1958 Detroit, MI   **1987**†SF 10 (2)

COOPER, HAL   Harold W., G, 5´10˝/207 lbs; Detroit Mercy; B1914, deceased   **1937** Det 7 (1)

COOPER, JARROD   Jarrod Alexander, DB, 6´0˝/210 lbs; Kansas State; 2001: Car, rnd 5; B3/31/1978 Akron, OH   **2001** Car 16 (0)   **2002** Car 6 (0)   **2003**†Car 12 (0)   **2004** Car 6 (0)   **2004** Oak 9 (0)   **2005** Oak 16 (10, SS)   **NFL** 65 (10) [5 yrs]

COOPER, JIM   James Paul, C-LB, 6´0˝/205 lbs; TCU; North Texas; 1948: Pit, rnd 8; B6/28/1924 Colorado City, TX   **1948** Bkn-A 1 (0)

COOPER, JIM   James Albert, T-C-G, 6´5˝/262 lbs; Temple; 1977: Dal, rnd 6; B9/28/1955 Philadelphia, PA   **1977**†Dal 14   **1978**†Dal 14 (2)   **1979**†Dal 15 (11, RT)   **1980**†Dal 15 (15, RT)   **1981**†Dal 16 (16, RT)   **1982**†Dal 9 (9, RT)   **1983**†Dal 16 (15, RT)   **1984** Dal 7 (7, RT)   **1985**†Dal 15 (15, RT)   **1986** Dal 12 (9, rt)   **NFL** 133 (99) [10 yrs]

COOPER, JOE   Joseph Donald, K, 5´10˝/175 lbs; California; B10/30/1960 Fresno, CA **[K]**   **1986** NYG 2 (0)

| 1984 | Hou | 7(0) | 1 | -2 | -2.0(-2) | 0 | — | — | — | — | — | — | — | — | — | — | — | — | — | K | — | 46 | -2 |
| NFL | 2 | 9(0) | 1 | -2 | -2.0(-2) | 0 | — | — | — | — | — | — | — | — | — | — | — | — | — | K | — | 56 | -2 |

COOPER, JOSH   Joshua Martez, DE, 6´3˝/261 lbs; Mississippi; B12/5/1980 Marietta, GA   **2004** SF 1 (0)

COOPER, KEN   Kenneth Rousseau, G, 6´1˝/205 lbs; Vanderbilt; 1949: GB, rnd 15; B2/26/1923 Rogersville, AL   **1949** Bal-A 12 (5, rg)

1950 Bal 12 (8, RG)

COOPER, LOUIS   Alexander Louis, LB, 6´2˝/240 lbs; Western Carolina; 1985: Sea, rnd 11; B8/5/1963 Marion, SC   **1985** KC 8 (0)   **1986**†KC 16 (13, LOLB)   **1987** KC 12 (6, LOLB)   **1988** KC 11 (4)   **1989** KC 16 (0)   **1990**†KC 16 (0)   **1991** Mia 12 (0)   **1993** Phi 11 (0)   **NFL** 102 (23) [8 yrs]

COOPER, MARK   Mark Samuel, G-T, 6´5˝/270 lbs; Miami (FL); 1983: Den, rnd 2; B2/14/1960 Camden, NJ   **1983**†Den 10 (2)   **1984** Den 15 (4)   **1986**†Den 8 (4)   **1987** Den 5 (0)   **1987** TB 4 (2)   **1988** TB 15 (0)   **1989** TB 6 (5, rg)

| 1985 | Den | 15(2) | — | — | — | — | 1 | 13 | 13.0(13) | 0 | — | — | — | — | — | — | — | — | — | — | — | 0 | 7 |
| NFL | 7 | 78(19) | — | — | — | — | 1 | 13 | 13.0(13) | 0 | — | — | — | — | — | — | — | — | — | — | — | 0 | 7 |

COOPER, MARQUIS   Marquis, LB, 6´4˝/215 lbs; Washington; 2004: TB, rnd 3; B3/11/1982 Mesa, AZ   **2004** TB 14 (0)   **2005**†TB 12 (0)   **NFL** 26 (0) [2 yrs]

COOPER, NORM   Norman Tellons, C-LB, 6´4˝/210 lbs; Samford; B8/8/1913 Rogersville, AL, D12/26/1994 Birmingham, AL   **1937** Bkn 10 (5, c)   **1938** Bkn 10 (1)   **NFL** 20 (6) [2 yrs]

COOPER, RAFAEL   Rafael, RB, 5´11˝/205 lbs; Minnesota; Louisville; B1/8/1975 Detroit, MI

| 2002 | Det | 5(0) | 12 | 57 | 4.8(18) | 0 | 4 | 4 | 4.0(4) | 0 | — | — | — | — | — | — | — | — | — | k | — | 0 | 99 |

COOPER, REGGIE   Reginald John, LB, 6´2˝/214 lbs; Nebraska; B7/11/1968 Bogalusa, LA   **1991**†Dal 2 (0)

COOPER, RICHARD   Richard Warren, T, 6´5˝/290 lbs; Tennessee; B11/1/1964 Memphis, TN   **1990** NO 2 (1)   **1991**†NO 15 (11, LT)   **1993** NO 16 (16, LT)   **1994** NO 14 (14, RT)   **1995** NO 14 (14, RT)   **1996**†Phi 16 (16, RT)   **1998** Phi 15 (15, RT)

| 1992 | †NO | 16(16, LT) | — | — | — | — | 0 | 20 | (20) | 0 | — | — | — | — | — | — | — | — | — | — | — | 0 | 10 |
| NFL | 8 | 108(103) | — | — | — | — | 0 | 20 | (20) | 0 | — | — | — | — | — | — | — | — | — | — | — | 0 | 10 |

COOPER, SAM   Samuel VanVoorhis, T, 6´0˝/200 lbs; Geneva; B2/1/1909 Venetia, PA, D8/22/1998 Green Tree, PA   **1933** Pit 1 (0)

COOPER, STEPHEN   Stephen, LB, 6´1˝/235 lbs; Maine; B6/19/1979 Wareham, MA   **2003** SD 16 (0)   **2004**†SD 16 (2)   **2005** SD 16 (2)   **NFL** 48 (4) [3 yrs]

COOPER, THURLOW   Sheldon Thurlow, TE-DE, 6´5˝/228 lbs; Maine; 1956: Cle, rnd 16; B3/18/1933 Augusta, ME **[K]**

1960	NYT-A	13(TE)	—	—	—	—	9	161	17.9(38)	3	—	—	—	—	—	—	—	—	—	k	—	20	81
1961	NYT-A	14(TE)	—	—	—	—	15	208	13.9(35)	4	—	—	—	—	—	—	—	—	—	Kk	—	24	109
1962	NYT-A	14(TE)	—	—	—	—	12	122	10.2(25)	1	—	—	—	—	—	—	—	—	—	k	—	8	54
NFL	3	41	—	—	—	—	36	491	13.6(38)	8	—	—	—	—	—	—	—	—	—	Kk	—	52	244

COPE, FRANK   Francis Wallace, T, 6´2˝/225 lbs; Santa Clara; B11/19/1915 Anaconda, MT, D10/8/1990 San Jose, CA   **1938**†NYG✧9 (0)   **1939**†NYG 11 (8, LT)   **1940** NYG★11 (8, LT)   **1941**†NYG 11 (0)   **1942** NYG 11 (11, LT)   **1943**†NYG✩10 (10, LT)   **1944**†NYG✩10 (10, LT)   **1945** NYG✩9 (8, LT)   **1946**†NYG✩11 (4)   **1947** NYG 5 (2)   **NFL** 98 (61) [10 yrs]

COPE, JIM   James Charles, LB, 6´1˝/235 lbs; Ohio State; 1975: Cle, rnd 5; B6/23/1953 Oil City, PA   **1976** Atl 6

COPELAND, ANTHONY   Anthony Lamar, LB, 6´2˝/250 lbs; Wichita State; Louisville; B4/14/1963   **1987** Was 3 (0)

COPELAND, DANNY   Danny Lamar, DB, 6´2˝/210 lbs; Eastern Kentucky; 1988: Cle, rnd 9; B1/24/1966 Camilla, GA   **1989** KC 16 (0)   **1990**†KC 14 (0)   **1991** Was 16 (14, SS)   **1992**†Was 13 (13, SS)   **1993** Was 14 (14, SS)   **NFL** 73 (41) [5 yrs]

COPELAND, HORACE   Horace Cornellius, WR, 6´3˝/200 lbs; Miami (FL); 1993: TB, rnd 4; B1/2/1971 Orlando, FL

| 1993 | TB | 14(8, WR) | 3 | 34 | 11.3(22) | 0 | 30 | 633 | 21.1(67) | 4 | — | — | — | — | — | — | — | — | — | — | — | 24 | 371 |
| 1994 | TB | 16(2) | — | — | — | — | 17 | 308 | 18.1(65) | 0 | — | — | — | — | — | — | — | — | — | — | — | 2 | 154 |

YEAR	TEAM	G(GS, POS)	RUSH	YD	AVG(LG)	TD	REC	YD	AVG(LG)	TD	PASS	COMP	PCT	YD	AVG(LG)	TD	INT	SK	YD	QBR	KPR	OTD	PTS	TAY
1995	TB	15(7, wr)	—	—	—	—	35	605	17.3(64)	2	—	—	—	—	—	—	—	—	—	—	—	—	12	313
1997	†TB	13(11, WR)	—	—	—	—	33	431	13.1(49)	1	—	—	—	—	—	—	—	—	—	—	—	—	6	221
1998	Mia	2(0)	—	—	—	—	—	—	—	—	—	—	—	—	—	—	—	—	—	—	—	—	—	—
NFL	5	60(28)	3	34	11.3(22)	0	115	1977	17.2(67)	7	—	—	—	—	—	—	—	—	—	—	—	—	44	1058

Copeland, Jim Wyatte James, C-G, 6´3˝/243 lbs; Virginia; 1967: Cle, rnd 10; B3/5/1945 Charlottesville, VA **1967**†Cle 14 **1968**†Cle 14 **1969**†Cle 8 **1970** Cle 14 **1971**†Cle 14 (c) **1972** Cle 1 **1973** Cle 14 (c) **1974** Cle 2 **NFL** 81 [8 yrs]

Copeland, John John Anthony, DE-DT-NT, 6´3˝/285 lbs; Alabama; 1993: Cin, rnd 1; B9/20/1970 Lanett, AL **1993** Cin 14 (14, LDE) **1994** Cin 12 (12, LDE) **1995** Cin 16 (16, LDE) **1996** Cin 13 (13, LDE) **1997** Cin 15 (15, LDE) **1998** Cin 5 (0) **1999** Cin 16 (16, LDE) **2000** Cin 16 (16, RDT/rde) **NFL** 107 (102) [8 yrs]

Copeland, Ron Ronald Wayne, WR, 6´5˝/196 lbs; UCLA; 1969: Chi, rnd 7; B10/3/1946 Los Angeles, CA, D5/22/1975 Walnut, CA **1969** ChiB 6

Copeland, Russell Russell Samoan, WR, 6´0˝/200 lbs; Memphis; 1993: Buf, rnd 4; B11/14/1971 Tupelo, MS

YEAR	TEAM	G(GS, POS)	RUSH	YD	AVG(LG)	TD	REC	YD	AVG(LG)	TD	PASS	COMP	PCT	YD	AVG(LG)	TD	INT	SK	YD	QBR	KPR	OTD	PTS	TAY
1993	†Buf	16(2)	—	—	—	—	13	242	18.6(60)	0	—	—	—	—	—	—	—	—	—	—	kp	1	6	326
1994	Buf	15(4)	1	-7	-7.0(-7)	0	21	255	12.1(35)	1	—	—	—	—	—	—	—	—	—	—	kp	—	6	184
1995	†Buf	16(15, WR)	1	-1	-1.0(-1)	0	42	646	15.4(77)	1	—	—	—	—	—	—	—	—	—	—	p	—	6	325
1996	†Buf	11(0)	—	—	—	—	7	85	12.1(31)	0	—	—	—	—	—	—	—	—	—	—	kp	—	0	138
1998	Phi	11(0)	—	—	—	—	18	221	12.3(20)	0	—	—	—	—	—	—	—	—	—	—	k	—	0	118
1998	GB	3(1)	—	—	—	—	2	11	5.5(12)	0	—	—	—	—	—	—	—	—	—	—	—	—	0	6
NFL	5	72(22)	2	-8	-4.0(-1)	0	103	1460	14.2(77)	2	—	—	—	—	—	—	—	—	—	—	kp	1	18	1095

Copley, Charlie Charles Francis, T-E, 5´9˝/191 lbs; Muhlenberg; Missouri-Rolla; B9/1887 Mahanoy City, PA, D5/29/1944 Reading, PA **[K]** **1920** Akr 11 (9, RT) **1921** Akr 12 (11, RT), 10 **1922** Akr 3 (2) **1922** Mil 4 (3), 1 **NFL** 30 (25), 11 [3 yrs]

Coppage, Al Alton Minor, E, 6´1˝/195 lbs; Oklahoma; 1940: ChiC, rnd 13; B2/8/1916 Pilot Point, TX, D1/9/1992 Hollis, OK

YEAR	TEAM	G(GS, POS)	RUSH	YD	AVG(LG)	TD	REC	YD	AVG(LG)	TD	PASS	COMP	PCT	YD	AVG(LG)	TD	INT	SK	YD	QBR	KPR	OTD	PTS	TAY
1940	ChiC	11(7, RE)	—	—	—	—	15	163	10.9(41)	1	—	—	—	—	—	—	—	—	—	—	—	—	6	87
1941	ChiC	9(2)	—	—	—	—	8	117	14.6(40)	0	—	—	—	—	—	—	—	—	—	—	—	—	0	59
1942	ChiC	11(5, re)	—	—	—	—	20	196	9.8(32)	0	—	—	—	—	—	—	—	—	—	—	k	—	0	94
NFL	3	31(14)	—	—	—	—	43	476	11.1(41)	1	—	—	—	—	—	—	—	—	—	—	k	—	6	239
1946	Cle-A	14(1)	—	—	—	—	2	34	17.0	0	—	—	—	—	—	—	—	—	—	—	—	—	0	17
1947	Buf-A	13(10, RE)	—	—	—	—	20	226	11.3	2	—	—	—	—	—	—	—	—	—	—	k	—	12	121
AAFC	2	27(11)	—	—	—	—	22	260	11.8(41)	2	—	—	—	—	—	—	—	—	—	—	k	—	12	138

Coppens, Gus August Richard, T, 6´5˝/270 lbs; UCLA; 1978: LA, rnd 12; B2/7/1955 Lynwood, CA **1979** NYG 9

Copper, Terrance Terrance, WR, 6´0˝/204 lbs; East Carolina; B3/12/1982 Washington, NC

YEAR	TEAM	G(GS, POS)	RUSH	YD	AVG(LG)	TD	REC	YD	AVG(LG)	TD	PASS	COMP	PCT	YD	AVG(LG)	TD	INT	SK	YD	QBR	KPR	OTD	PTS	TAY
2004	Dal	10(0)	1	-1	-1.0(-1)	0	7	84	12.0(22)	1	—	—	—	—	—	—	—	—	—	—	k	—	6	113
2005	Dal	16(0)	—	—	—	—	1	5	5.0(5)	0	—	—	—	—	—	—	—	—	—	—	k	—	0	5
NFL	2	26(0)	1	-1	-1.0(-1)	0	8	89	11.1(22)	1	—	—	—	—	—	—	—	—	—	—	k	—	6	118

Corbett, George George Burdette, B, 5´9˝/179 lbs; Millikin; B6/14/1908 Dix, IL, D10/11/1990 Springfield, IL **[K]**

YEAR	TEAM	G(GS, POS)	RUSH	YD	AVG(LG)	TD	REC	YD	AVG(LG)	TD	PASS	COMP	PCT	YD	AVG(LG)	TD	INT	SK	YD	QBR	KPR	OTD	PTS	TAY
1932	ChiB	12(1)	52	178	3.4	0	7	164	23.4	1	3	2	66.7	61	20.3(**36**)	0	0	—	—	—	K	—	7	296
1933	†ChiB	6(3)	25	54	2.2	0	—	—	—	—	12	4	33.3	31	2.6(9)	0	2	—	—	—	—	—	0	-11
1934	ChiB	7(2)	30	119	4.0	0	1	2	2.0(2)	0	3	1	33.3	36	12.0(36)	1	0	—	—	—	—	—	0	143
1935	ChiB	4(0)	9	0	0.0	0	2	5	2.5	0	7	1	14.3	9	1.3(9)	0	0	—	—	—	K	—	3	7
1936	ChiB	9(0)	13	45	3.5	0	3	69	23.0	1	13	5	38.5	64	4.9	0	1	—	—	—	—	—	6	77
1937	ChiB	1(0)	—	—	—	—	—	—	—	—	—	—	—	—	—	—	—	—	—	—	—	—	—	—
1938	ChiB	7(3)	7	29	4.1	0	1	10	10.0(10)	0	9	3	33.3	32	3.6	1	3	—	—	—	—	1	6	-55
NFL	7	46(9)	136	425	3.1	0	14	250	17.9(10)	2	47	16	34.0	233	5.0(36)	2	6	—	—	—	K	1	22	457

Corbett, Jim James B., TE, 6´4˝/218 lbs; Pittsburgh; 1977: Cin, rnd 7; B2/22/1955 Brockton, MA

YEAR	TEAM	G(GS, POS)	RUSH	YD	AVG(LG)	TD	REC	YD	AVG(LG)	TD	PASS	COMP	PCT	YD	AVG(LG)	TD	INT	SK	YD	QBR	KPR	OTD	PTS	TAY
1977	Cin	14	1	-1	-1.0(-1)	0	7	127	18.1(47)	1	—	—	—	—	—	—	—	—	—	—	—	—	6	68
1978	Cin	16	—	—	—	—	12	187	15.6(51)	0	—	—	—	—	—	—	—	—	—	—	k	—	0	94
1979	Cin	10	—	—	—	—	3	34	11.3(15)	0	—	—	—	—	—	—	—	—	—	—	—	—	0	17
1980	Cin	4(0)	—	—	—	—	3	28	9.3(12)	0	—	—	—	—	—	—	—	—	—	—	—	—	0	14
NFL	4	44	1	-1	-1.0(-1)	0	25	376	15.0(51)	1	—	—	—	—	—	—	—	—	—	—	k	—	6	192

Corbett, Steve Stephen Paul, G, 6´4˝/250 lbs; Boston College; 1974: NE, rnd 2; B8/11/1951 Dover, NH **1975** NE 14

Corbitt, Don Donald Oliver, C, 6´4˝/224 lbs; Arizona; 1948: Was, rnd 28; B4/1/1924 Creston, IA, D9/3/1993 Phoenix, AZ **1948** Was 3 (0)

Corbo, Tom Thomas Joseph, G, 5´11˝/210 lbs; Duquesne; B1/11/1918 Altoona, PA, D4/19/2000 Kirtland, OH **1944** Cle 10 (6, RG)

Corcoran, Bunny Arthur Andrew, E-B, 5´11˝/185 lbs; Georgetown (DC); Fordham; B11/23/1894 Boston, MA, D7/27/1958 Chelsea, MA **1920** Can 11 (1) **1921** Akr 1 (1) **1921** Cle 8 (8, LE), 6 **1922** Akr 9 (9, RE) **1923** Buf 1 (1) **NFL** 30 (20), 6 [4 yrs]

Corcoran, Jack John Walton, C-G, /180 lbs; St. Thomas; St. Louis; B6/13/1904 St. Paul, MN, D1/8/1987 Encinitas, CA **1930** Min 5 (3)

Corcoran, King James Sean Patrick, QB, 6´0˝/200 lbs; Maryland; B7/6/1943 Jersey City, NJ

YEAR	TEAM	G(GS, POS)	RUSH	YD	AVG(LG)	TD	REC	YD	AVG(LG)	TD	PASS	COMP	PCT	YD	AVG(LG)	TD	INT	SK	YD	QBR	KPR	OTD	PTS	TAY
1968	Bos-A	2(1)	1	-1	-1.0(-1)	0	—	—	—	—	7	3	42.9	33	4.7(14)	0	2	1	10	—	—	—	0	-65

Cordileone, Lou Louis Anthony, DT-DE-G, 6´1˝/250 lbs; Clemson; 1960: NYG, rnd 1/Buf, rnd 1; B8/4/1937 Jersey City, NJ **1960** NYG 11 **1961** SF 12 **1962** LARm 2 **1962** Pit 12 **1963** Pit 14 **1967** NO 11 **1968** NO 13 **NFL** 75 [6 yrs]

Cordill, Olie Oliver James, WB-HB-P, 6´2˝/190 lbs; Rice; 1940: Cle, rnd 1; B4/28/1916 Big Spring, TX, D11/14/1988 Spicewood, TX

YEAR	TEAM	G(GS, POS)	RUSH	YD	AVG(LG)	TD	REC	YD	AVG(LG)	TD	PASS	COMP	PCT	YD	AVG(LG)	TD	INT	SK	YD	QBR	KPR	OTD	PTS	TAY
1940	Cle✧	10(7, WB)	24	73	3.0	0	14	158	11.3(26)	2	—	—	—	—	—	—	—	—	—	—	Pi	—	12	159

Cordill, Ollie Oliver James, DB-P-E, 6´3˝/185 lbs; Memphis; 1965: Hou, rnd R4/Cle, rnd 11; B6/20/1943 Houston, TX **1967** SD-A 3 **1968** Atl 1 **1969** NO 12 **NFL** 16 [3 yrs]

Cordovano, Sam Samuel S., G, 5´11˝/185 lbs; Georgetown (DC); B12/10/1906 Adams, PA, D7/13/1995 Hilton Head, SC **1930** Nwk 9 (5, lg)

Corey, Walt Walter Martin, LB, 6´2˝/240 lbs; Miami (FL); B5/9/1938 Latrobe, PA **1960** DalT-A 14 (LLB) **1962**†DalT-A 14 (RLB) **1963** KC-A✧12 (RLB) **1964** KC-A 13 (RLB) **1965** KC-A 7 **1966**†KC-A 9 **NFL** 69 [6 yrs]

Corgan, Chuck Charles Howard, B-E, 6´0˝/183 lbs; Arkansas; B12/4/1902 Wagoner, OK, D6/13/1928 Wagoner, OK **[K]** **1924** KC 9 (9, BB), 26 **1925** KC 2 (2), 6 **1926** Har 7 (7, BB) **1926** KC 1 (0) **1927** NYG 11 (11, LE) **NFL** 30 (29), 32 [4 yrs]

Corgan, Mike Michael Henry, FB, 5´10˝/188 lbs; Notre Dame; B10/26/1918 Olongopo, Phillipines, D5/28/1989 Lincoln, NE

YEAR	TEAM	G(GS, POS)	RUSH	YD	AVG(LG)	TD	REC	YD	AVG(LG)	TD	PASS	COMP	PCT	YD	AVG(LG)	TD	INT	SK	YD	QBR	KPR	OTD	PTS	TAY
1943	Det	4(1)	5	14	2.8(8)	0	1	9	9.0(9)	0	—	—	—	—	—	—	—	—	—	—	—	—	0	19

Corker, John John B., LB, 6´5˝/240 lbs; Oklahoma State; 1980: Hou, rnd 5; B12/29/1958 Miami, FL **1980**†Hou 16 (0) **1981** Hou 11 (0) **1982** Hou 3 (0) **1988** GB 2 (0) **NFL** 32 (0) [4 yrs]

Corley, Anthony Anthony George, RB, 6´0˝/210 lbs; UNLV; B8/10/1960 Reno, NV **1985** SD 4 (0)

YEAR	TEAM	G(GS, POS)	RUSH	YD	AVG(LG)	TD	REC	YD	AVG(LG)	TD	PASS	COMP	PCT	YD	AVG(LG)	TD	INT	SK	YD	QBR	KPR	OTD	PTS	TAY
1984	†Pit	14(0)	18	89	4.9(23)	0	—	—	—	—	—	—	—	—	—	—	—	—	—	—	k	—	0	89
NFL	2	18(0)	18	89	4.9(23)	0	—	—	—	—	—	—	—	—	—	—	—	—	—	—	—	—	0	89

Corley, Bert Elbert Ellis, C, 6´2˝/210 lbs; Mississippi State; 1947: Buf-A, rnd 6/1944: NYG, rnd 14; B9/9/1920 Okolona, MS, D9/22/1988 Tupelo, MS **1947** Buf-A 13 (4) **1948** Bal-A 9 (8, C) **AAFC** 22 (12) [2 yrs]

Corley, Chris Christopher Ramon, TE, 6´4˝/285 lbs; South Carolina; B10/24/1963 Columbia, SC **1987** Sea 1 (0)

Cormier, Joe Joseph Daily, LB, 6´6˝/230 lbs; USC; 1986: Min, rnd 10; B5/3/1963 Los Angeles, CA **1987** LARd 2 (1)

Corn, Joe Joseph Huey, HB, 5´6˝/168 lbs; none; B10/5/1923 Honolulu, HI, D7/27/2001 Waianae, HI

YEAR	TEAM	G(GS, POS)	RUSH	YD	AVG(LG)	TD	REC	YD	AVG(LG)	TD	PASS	COMP	PCT	YD	AVG(LG)	TD	INT	SK	YD	QBR	KPR	OTD	PTS	TAY
1948	LARm	9(0)	11	27	2.5(6)	0	—	—	—	—	—	—	—	—	—	—	—	—	—	—	kp	—	0	93

Cornelison, Jerry Jerry G., T, 6´4˝/250 lbs; SMU; 1958: Cle, rnd 16; B9/13/1936 Dallas, TX **1960** DalT-A☆14 (RT) **1961** DalT-A☆14 (RT) **1962**†DalT-A✧14 **1964** KC-A 14 **1965** KC-A 14 **NFL** 70 [5 yrs]

Cornelius, Charles Charles Edward, DB, 5´9˝/176 lbs; Bethune-Cookman; B7/27/1952 Boynton Beach, FL **1977** Mia 13 **1978**†Mia 16 **1979** SF 16 (14, LCB) **1980** SF 16 (6, lcb) **NFL** 61 (20) [4 yrs]

CORNELL, BO Robert Paul, LB-RB, 6´2˝/220 lbs; Washington; 1971: Cle, rnd 2; B3/7/1949 Seattle, WA **1974**†Buf 14 (LOLB) **1975** Buf 14 (11, ROLB) **1976** Buf 14 (1) **1977** Buf 12

YEAR	TEAM	G(GS, POS)	RUSH	YD	AVG(LG)	TD	REC	YD	AVG(LG)	TD	PASS	COMP	PCT	YD	AVG(LG)	TD	INT	SK	YD	QBR	KPR	OTD	PTS	TAY
1971	†Cle	14	11	12	1.1(6)	0	1	18	18.0(18)	0	—	—	—	—	—	—	—	—	—	—	k	—	0	25
1972	†Cle	14	7	8	1.1(7)	0	2	7	3.5(5)	0	—	—	—	—	—	—	—	—	—	—	—	—	0	12
1973	Buf	14	4	13	3.3(7)	0	—	—	—	—	—	—	—	—	—	—	—	—	—	—	k	—	0	0
NFL	7	96(12)	22	33	1.5(7)	0	3	25	8.3(18)	0	—	—	—	—	—	—	—	—	—	—	k	1	6	32

CORNELSON, MARTIN Martin Shaw, C, 6´1˝/230 lbs; North Carolina State; B6/4/1961 Clinton, SC **1987** NYJ 3 (0)

CORNISH, FRANK Frank Edgar, DT, 6´4˝/282 lbs; Grambling State; 1965: Chi, rnd 11/KC, rnd R2; B6/20/1944 New Orleans, LA **1966** ChiB 14 **1967** ChiB 14 (LDT) **1968** ChiB 13 **1969** ChiB 14 (LDT) **1970**†Cin 1 **1970**†Mia 11 **1971** Mia 10 **1972** Buf 6 **NFL** 83 [7 yrs]

CORNISH, FRANK Frank Edgar, C-G, 6´4˝/287 lbs; UCLA; 1990: SD, rnd 6; B9/24/1967 Chicago, IL **1990** SD 16 (16, C) **1991** SD 16 (0) **1992**†Dal 11 (2) **1993**†Dal 14 (3) **1994** Min 7 (0) **1994**†Dal 0 (0) **1995** Jax 3 (0) **1995**†Phi 2 (0) **NFL** 69 (21) [6 yrs]

CORNSWEET, AL Albert Charles, FB, 5´7˝/180 lbs; Brown; B7/16/1906 Cleveland, OH, D10/16/1991 Falls Church, VA **[C]** **1931** Cle 4 (3)

CORNWELL, FRED Frederick Keith, TE, 6´6˝/236 lbs; USC; 1984: Dal, rnd 3; B8/7/1961 Osborne, KS

YEAR	TEAM	G(GS, POS)	RUSH	YD	AVG(LG)	TD	REC	YD	AVG(LG)	TD	PASS	COMP	PCT	YD	AVG(LG)	TD	INT	SK	YD	QBR	KPR	OTD	PTS	TAY
1984	Dal	14(1)	—	—	—	—	2	23	11.5(13)	1	—	—	—	—	—	—	—	—	—	—	—	—	6	17
1985	†Dal	16(1)	—	—	—	—	6	77	12.8(32)	1	—	—	—	—	—	—	—	—	—	—	—	—	6	44
NFL	2	30(2)	—	—	—	—	8	100	12.5(32)	2	—	—	—	—	—	—	—	—	—	—	—	—	12	60

CORONADO, BOB Robert H., WR, 6´2˝/195 lbs; Pacific; 1959: ChiB, rnd 10; B5/22/1936 Vallejo, CA

YEAR	TEAM	G(GS, POS)	RUSH	YD	AVG(LG)	TD	REC	YD	AVG(LG)	TD	PASS	COMP	PCT	YD	AVG(LG)	TD	INT	SK	YD	QBR	KPR	OTD	PTS	TAY
1961	Pit	5	1	-7	-7.0(-7)	0	3	32	10.7(14)	0	—	—	—	—	—	—	—	—	—	—	—	—	0	9

CORRAL, FRANK John Frank, K, 6´2˝/224 lbs; UCLA; 1978: LA, rnd 3; B6/16/1955 Chihuahua, Mexico **[K]** **1978**†LARm★16 **1979**†LARm 16 **1980**†LARm 16 (0)

YEAR	TEAM	G(GS, POS)	RUSH	YD	AVG(LG)	TD	REC	YD	AVG(LG)	TD	PASS	COMP	PCT	YD	AVG(LG)	TD	INT	SK	YD	QBR	KPR	OTD	PTS	TAY
1981	LARm	16(0)	—	—	—	—	—	—	—	—	1	0	0.0	0	0.0	0	0	—	—	—	KP	—	87	0
NFL	4	64	—	—	—	—	—	—	—	—	1	0	0.0	0	0.0	0	0	—	—	—	KP	—	379	0

CORREAL, CHUCK Charles Alan, C, 6´3˝/247 lbs; Penn State; 1979: Phi, rnd 8; B5/17/1956 Uniontown, PA **1980**†Atl 16 (0)

CORRINGTON, KIP Kip Alan, DB, 6´0˝/175 lbs; Texas A&M; 1988: Det, rnd 9; B4/12/1965 Ames, IA **1989**†Den 16 (0) **1990** Den 16 (1) **NFL** 32 (1) [2 yrs]

CORSETTI, RICO Enrico S., LB, 6´1˝/225 lbs; Bates; B1/13/1963 Newton, MA **1987** NE 2 (0)

CORTEMEGLIA, CHRIS Christopher, WB, 6´0˝/210 lbs; SMU; B9/21/1903 Bryan, TX, D3/14/1989 Houston, TX **1927** Fra 2 (0)

CORTES, JULIO Julio Ceaser, LB, 6´0˝/226 lbs; Miami (FL); B8/13/1962 New York, NY **1987** Sea 3 (3)

CORTEZ, BRUCE Bruce Ford, DB, 6´0˝/175 lbs; Missouri Southern State; Parsons; 1967: NO, rnd 16; B10/29/1945 Carthage, MO **1967** NO 1

CORTEZ, JOSE Jose Antonio, K, 5´11˝/200 lbs; Oregon State; B5/27/1975 San Vincente, El Salvador **[K]** **1999** NYG 1 (0) **2001**†SF 16 (0) **2002** SF 10 (0) **2002** Was 4 (0) **2003** Min 2 (0) **2004**†Min 8 (0) **2005** Dal 7 (0) **2005** Phi 4 (0) **2005** SF 1 (0) **2005**†Ind 2 (0) **NFL** 55 (0) [6 yrs]

CORVINO, ANTHONY Anthony, G-T, 6´1˝/262 lbs; Southern Connecticut State; B9/15/1965 **1987** NYJ 2 (0)

CORYATT, QUENTIN Quentin John, LB, 6´3˝/250 lbs; Texas A&M; 1992: Ind, rnd 1; B8/1/1970 St. Croix, Virgin Islands **1992** Ind 7 (7, lilb) **1993** Ind 16 (16, MLB) **1994** Ind 16 (15, RLB) **1995**†Ind 16 (16, RLB) **1996** Ind 8 (7, rlb) **1997** Ind 15 (15, RLB) **1999** Dal 4 (1) **NFL** 82 (77) [7 yrs]

CORZINE, RED Lester Howard, FB-BB, 5´11˝/213 lbs; Davis & Elkins; B1/19/1909 Balcolm, IL, D7/26/2003 Oceanside, CA

YEAR	TEAM	G(GS, POS)	RUSH	YD	AVG(LG)	TD	REC	YD	AVG(LG)	TD	PASS	COMP	PCT	YD	AVG(LG)	TD	INT	SK	YD	QBR	KPR	OTD	PTS	TAY
1933	Cin	9(7, FB)	100	239	2.4	1	2	38	19.0(36)	0	7	4	57.1	47	6.7	0	1	—	—	—	—	—	6	252
1934	Cin	8(8, FB)	58	162	2.8	0	2	22	11.0	0	11	5	45.5	33	3.0	0	2	—	—	—	—	—	0	110
1934	SL	2(1)	4	5	1.3	1	—	—	—	—	—	—	—	—	—	—	—	—	—	—	—	—	6	15
1935	†NYG	11(7, BB)	32	105	3.3	0	—	—	—	—	—	—	—	—	—	—	—	—	—	—	—	1	6	105
1936	NYG	10(3)	7	12	1.7	0	1	36	36.0(36)	1	—	—	—	—	—	—	—	—	—	—	—	—	6	35
1937	NYG	11(10, BB)	8	23	2.9	0	9	75	8.3(23)	1	1	0	0.0	0	0.0	0	0	—	—	—	—	—	6	66
NFL	5	51(36)	209	546	2.6	2	14	171	12.2(36)	2	19	9	47.4	80	4.2	0	3	—	—	—	—	1	30	582

COSBIE, DOUG Douglas Durant, TE, 6´6˝/236 lbs; Holy Cross; Santa Clara; 1979: Dal, rnd 3; B3/27/1956 Palo Alto, CA

YEAR	TEAM	G(GS, POS)	RUSH	YD	AVG(LG)	TD	REC	YD	AVG(LG)	TD	PASS	COMP	PCT	YD	AVG(LG)	TD	INT	SK	YD	QBR	KPR	OTD	PTS	TAY
1979	†Dal	16(1)	—	—	—	—	5	36	7.2(12)	0	—	—	—	—	—	—	—	—	—	—	—	—	0	18
1980	†Dal	16(0)	—	—	—	—	2	11	5.5(6)	1	—	—	—	—	—	—	—	—	—	—	k	—	6	9
1981	†Dal	16(0)	4	33	8.3(15)	0	17	225	13.2(28)	5	—	—	—	—	—	—	—	—	—	—	k	—	30	156
1982	†Dal	9(9, TE)	1	-2	-2.0(-2)	0	30	441	14.7(45)	4	—	—	—	—	—	—	—	—	—	—	k	—	24	228
1983	†Dal✧	16(16, TE)	—	—	—	—	46	588	12.8(61)	6	—	—	—	—	—	—	—	—	—	—	k	—	36	311
1984	Dal★	16(16, TE)	—	—	—	—	60	789	13.1(36)	4	—	—	—	—	—	—	—	—	—	—	—	—	24	415
1985	†Dal★	16(16, TE)	—	—	—	—	64	793	12.4(42)	6	—	—	—	—	—	—	—	—	—	—	—	—	36	427
1986	Dal	16(15, TE)	1	9	9.0(9)	0	28	312	11.1(22)	1	—	—	—	—	—	—	—	—	—	—	—	—	6	170
1987	Dal	12(12, TE)	1	-5	-5.0(-5)	0	36	421	11.7(30)	3	—	—	—	—	—	—	—	—	—	—	—	—	18	221
1988	Dal	11(4)	—	—	—	—	12	112	9.3(21)	0	—	—	—	—	—	—	—	—	—	—	—	—	0	56
NFL	10	144(89)	7	35	5.0(15)	0	300	3728	12.4(61)	30	—	—	—	—	—	—	—	—	—	—	k	—	180	2008

COSGROVE, THOMAS Thomas, HB, 5´11˝/175 lbs; none

YEAR	TEAM	G(GS, POS)	RUSH	YD	AVG(LG)	TD	REC	YD	AVG(LG)	TD	PASS	COMP	PCT	YD	AVG(LG)	TD	INT	SK	YD	QBR	KPR	OTD	PTS	TAY
1935	Pit	1(0)	3	18	6.0	0	—	—	—	—	—	—	—	—	—	—	—	—	—	—	—	—	0	18

COSLET, BRUCE Bruce Noel, TE, 6´4˝/227 lbs; Pacific; B8/5/1946 Oakdale, CA **[C]**

YEAR	TEAM	G(GS, POS)	RUSH	YD	AVG(LG)	TD	REC	YD	AVG(LG)	TD	PASS	COMP	PCT	YD	AVG(LG)	TD	INT	SK	YD	QBR	KPR	OTD	PTS	TAY
1969	Cin-A	8	—	—	—	—	1	39	39.0(39)	1	—	—	—	—	—	—	—	—	—	—	—	—	6	25
1970	†Cin	14	—	—	—	—	8	98	12.3(24)	1	—	—	—	—	—	—	—	—	—	—	—	—	6	54
1971	Cin	14(te)	—	—	—	—	21	356	17.0(71)	4	—	—	—	—	—	—	—	—	—	—	—	—	24	198
1972	Cin	10	—	—	—	—	5	48	9.6(17)	1	—	—	—	—	—	—	—	—	—	—	—	—	6	29
1973	†Cin	13	—	—	—	—	9	123	13.7(18)	0	—	—	—	—	—	—	—	—	—	—	k	—	0	47
1974	Cin	14	—	—	—	—	2	24	12.0(18)	0	—	—	—	—	—	—	—	—	—	—	—	—	0	12
1975	†Cin	14	1	1	1.0(1)	0	10	117	11.7(18)	0	—	—	—	—	—	—	—	—	—	—	—	—	0	60
1976	Cin	14	—	—	—	—	5	73	14.6(32)	2	—	—	—	—	—	—	—	—	—	—	—	—	12	47
NFL	8	101	1	1	1.0(1)	0	61	878	14.4(71)	9	—	—	—	—	—	—	—	—	—	—	k	—	54	470

COSNER, DON Donald Stewart, WB, 6´2˝/200 lbs; Montana State; B2/16/1917 Malta, MT **1939** ChiC 1 (0)

COSS, ERIC Eric, C, 6´3˝/270 lbs; Temple; B6/12/1963, D **1987** NYJ 3 (3)

COSTA, DAVE David Joseph, DT-DE, 6´2˝/250 lbs; Utah; 1963: Oak, rnd 7/LA, rnd 3; B10/27/1941 Yonkers, NY **1963** Oak-A✧14 (RDT) **1964** Oak-A 14 (RDT) **1965** Oak-A 14 (RDT) **1966**†Buf-A☆14 **1967** Den-A★14 (RDT) **1968** Den-A★14 (RDT) **1969** Den-A★14 (14, RDT) **1970** Den 14 (14, RDT) **1971** Den 14 (14, LDT) **1972** SD 14 (RDT) **1973** SD 14 (14, RDT) **1974**†Buf 14 **NFL** 168 (56) [12 yrs]

COSTA, DAVE David C., T, 6´5˝/307 lbs; Wisconsin; B9/8/1978 Ellwood City, PA **2001**†SF 14 (0)

COSTA, PAUL Sebastian Paul, TE-T, 6´6˝/268 lbs; Notre Dame; 1964: KC, rnd 14/GB, rnd 4; B12/7/1941 Yonkers, NY **1969** Buf-A 14 (RT) **1970** Buf 14 (RT) **1971** Buf 11 (rt) **1972** Buf 9

YEAR	TEAM	G(GS, POS)	RUSH	YD	AVG(LG)	TD	REC	YD	AVG(LG)	TD	PASS	COMP	PCT	YD	AVG(LG)	TD	INT	SK	YD	QBR	KPR	OTD	PTS	TAY
1965	†Buf-A✧	10(TE)	—	—	—	—	21	401	19.1(46)	0	—	—	—	—	—	—	—	—	—	—	—	—	0	201
1966	†Buf-A✧	14(14, TE)	0	1	(1)	0	27	400	14.8(50)	3	—	—	—	—	—	—	—	—	—	—	—	—	18	216
1967	Buf-A	14(14, TE)	—	—	—	—	39	726	18.6(63)	2	—	—	—	—	—	—	—	—	—	—	—	—	12	373
1968	Buf-A	14(TE)	2	11	5.5(6)	1	15	172	11.5(27)	1	—	—	—	—	—	—	—	—	—	—	k	—	12	105
NFL	8	100(28)	2	12	6.0(6)	1	102	1699	16.7(63)	6	—	—	—	—	—	—	—	—	—	—	k	—	42	880

COSTELLO, BRAD Brad, P, 6´0˝/231 lbs; Michigan State; Boston University; B12/12/1974 Moorestown, NJ **1999** Cin 5 (0)

YEAR	TEAM	G(GS, POS)	RUSH	YD	AVG(LG)	TD	REC	YD	AVG(LG)	TD	PASS	COMP	PCT	YD	AVG(LG)	TD	INT	SK	YD	QBR	KPR	OTD	PTS	TAY
1998	Cin	3(0)	1	0	0.0(0)	0	—	—	—	—	—	—	—	—	—	—	—	—	—	—	P	—	0	0
NFL	2	8(0)	1	0	0.0	0	—	—	—	—	—	—	—	—	—	—	—	—	—	—	P	—	0	0

COSTELLO, JOE Joseph Patrick, DE, 6´3˝/245 lbs; Central Connecticut State; B6/1/1960 New York, NY **1986** Atl 14 (0) **1987** Atl 9 (4) **1988** Atl 6 (0) **1989** LARd 2 (0) **NFL** 31 (4) [4 yrs]

COSTELLO, TOM Thomas Francis, LB, 6´4˝/220 lbs; Dayton; Miami (FL); B5/23/1941 Queens, NY **1964** NYG 2 **1965** NYG 8 **NFL** 10 [2 yrs]

YEAR	TEAM	G (GS, POS)	RUSH	YD	AVG(LG)	TD	REC	YD	AVG(LG)	TD	PASS	COMP	PCT	YD	AVG(LG)	TD	INT	SK	YD	QBR	KPR	OTD	PTS	TAY

COSTELLO, VINCE Vincent, LB, 6´0˝/230 lbs; Ohio University; B8/4/1932 Dellroy, OH [I] **1957**†Cle 12 (MLB) **1958**†Cle 12 (MLB) **1959** Cle 12 (MLB) **1960** Cle 12 (MLB) **1961** Cle 14 (LLB) **1962** Cle 13 (MLB) **1963** Cle 14 (MLB) **1964**†Cle 14 (MLB) **1965**†Cle 13 (MLB) **1967** NYG 14 (14, MLB) **1968** NYG 2

| 1966 | Cle | 14 (MLB) | — | — | — | — | 1 | -7 | -7.0(-7) | 0 | — | — | — | — | — | — | — | — | — | — | i | — | 0 | -9 |
| NFL | 12 | 146 (14) | — | — | — | — | 1 | -7 | -7.0(-7) | 0 | — | — | — | — | — | — | — | — | — | — | i | 2 | 12 | 186 |

COSTER, JOE Howard Owen, T, 5´10˝/175 lbs; Western Maryland; Maryland; B11/24/1895, D8/20/1966 **1921** Was 1 (0)

COSTICT, RAY Ray Charles, LB, 6´0˝/217 lbs; Mississippi State; 1977: NE, rnd 11; B3/19/1955 Moss Point, MS **1977** NE 14 (2) **1978**†NE 16 (3) **1979** NE 16 (1) **NFL** 46 (6) [3 yrs]

COSTON, ZED Fred Monroe, C, 6´2˝/222 lbs; Texas A&M; 1939: Phi, rnd 5; B7/12/1915 Dallas, TX, D3/23/2003 **1939** Phi 1 (0)

COTA, CHAD Chad Garrett, DB, 6´1˝/198 lbs; Oregon; 1995: Car, rnd 7; B8/8/1971 Ashland, OR **1995** Car 16 (0) **1996**†Car 16 (2) **1997** Car 16 (16, SS) **1998** NO 16 (16, SS) **1999**†Ind 15 (15, SS) **2000**†Ind 16 (16, SS) **2001** Ind 16 (16, SS) **2002** SL 14 (1) **NFL** 125 (82) [8 yrs]

COTCHERY, JERRICHO Jerricho, WR, 6´1˝/200 lbs; North Carolina State; 2004: NYJ, rnd 4; B6/16/1982 Birmingham, AL

2004	†NYJ	12 (0)	—	—	—	—	6	60	10.0(18)	0	—	—	—	—	—	—	—	—	—	—	k	1	6	207
2005	NYJ	16 (1)	1	4	4.0(4)	0	19	251	13.2(45)	0	—	—	—	—	—	—	—	—	—	—	kp	—	0	242
NFL	2	28 (1)	1	4	4.0(4)	0	25	311	12.4(45)	0	—	—	—	—	—	—	—	—	—	—	kp	1	6	449

COTHRAN, JEFF Jeffrey Lance, FB, 6´1˝/249 lbs; Ohio State; 1994: Cin, rnd 3; B6/28/1971 Middletown, OH

1994	Cin	14 (4)	26	85	3.3(13)	0	4	24	6.0(8)	1	—	—	—	—	—	—	—	—	—	—	—	—	6	102
1995	Cin	14 (13, FB)	16	62	3.9(15)	0	8	44	5.5(15)	0	—	—	—	—	—	—	—	—	—	—	—	—	0	84
1996	Cin	11 (11, FB)	15	44	2.9(9)	1	7	49	7.0(14)	0	—	—	—	—	—	—	—	—	—	—	k	—	6	75
NFL	3	39 (28)	57	191	3.4(15)	1	19	117	6.2(15)	1	—	—	—	—	—	—	—	—	—	—	k	—	12	261

COTHREN, PAIGE Jennings Paige, K, 5´11˝/201 lbs; Mississippi; 1957: LA, rnd 22; B7/12/1935 Natchez, MS [K] **1957** LARm 12 **1958** LARm 12 **1959** Phi 7 **NFL** 31 [3 yrs]

COTNEY, MARK John Mark, DB, 6´0˝/204 lbs; New Mexico Highlands; Cameron; 1975: Hou, rnd 7; B6/26/1952 Altus, OK **1975** Hou 14 (3) **1976** TB 14 (13, SS) **1977** TB 14 (12, SS) **1978** TB 16 (15, SS) **1979**†TB 16 (15, SS) **1980** TB 16 (16, SS) **1982**†TB 9 (0) **1983** TB 12 (12, SS) **1984** TB 16 (9, SS) **NFL** 127 (95) [9 yrs]

COTTON, BARNEY Barney T., G, 6´5˝/264 lbs; Nebraska; 1979: Cin, rnd 3; B9/30/1956 Omaha, NE **1979** Cin 13 **1980** SL 16 (9, LG) **1981** SL 16 (2) **NFL** 45 (11) [3 yrs]

COTTON, CRAIG Craig Lee, TE, 6´5˝/216 lbs; Youngstown State; 1969: SD, rnd 8; B7/7/1947 Elizabeth, PA

1969	Det	13	—	—	—	—	—	—	—	—	—	—	—	—	—	—	—	—	—	—	—	—	—	—
1970	†Det	14	—	—	—	—	1	6	6.0(6)	0	—	—	—	—	—	—	—	—	—	—	—	—	0	3
1971	Det	14	—	—	—	—	6	88	14.7(34)	0	—	—	—	—	—	—	—	—	—	—	k	—	0	33
1972	Det	14	—	—	—	—	8	129	16.1(35)	1	—	—	—	—	—	—	—	—	—	—	—	—	6	70
1973	ChiB	13 (TE)	—	—	—	—	13	186	14.3(63)	0	—	—	—	—	—	—	—	—	—	—	k	—	0	78
1975	SD	9	—	—	—	—	—	—	—	—	—	—	—	—	—	—	—	—	—	—	—	—	—	—
NFL	6	77	—	—	—	—	28	409	14.6(63)	1	—	—	—	—	—	—	—	—	—	—	k	—	6	184

COTTON, FEST Fest, DT, 6´2˝/255 lbs; Dayton; B10/18/1949 Macon, MS **1972** Cle 3

COTTON, FORREST Forrest George, T, 6´1˝/195 lbs; Notre Dame; B1/14/1901 Elgin, IL, D3/6/1967 Kansas City, MO **1923** RI 8 (7, LT) **1925** RI 8 (5, lt) **NFL** 16 (12) [2 yrs]

COTTON, KENYON Timothy, RB, 6´0˝/255 lbs; Louisiana-Lafayette; B2/23/1974 Bossier City, LA

1997	Bal	15 (0)	2	2	1.0(1)	1	—	—	—	—	—	—	—	—	—	—	—	—	—	—	—	—	6	12
1998	Bal	12 (0)	2	8	4.0(7)	0	—	—	—	—	—	—	—	—	—	—	—	—	—	—	k	—	0	11
NFL	2	27 (0)	4	10	2.5(7)	1	—	—	—	—	—	—	—	—	—	—	—	—	—	—	k	—	6	23

COTTON, MARCUS Marcus Glenn, LB, 6´3˝/225 lbs; USC; 1988: Atl, rnd 2; B8/11/1966 Los Angeles, CA **1988** Atl 11 (5, rolb) **1989** Atl 16 (1) **1990** Atl 7 (1) **1990** Cle 7 (0) **1991** Sea 3 (0) **NFL** 44 (7) [4 yrs]

COTTON, RUSS James Russell, QB, 6´2˝/196 lbs; Texas-El Paso; 1941: Pit, rnd 13; B5/24/1915 Palestine, TX

| 1942 | Pit | 11 (0) | — | — | — | — | 2 | 58 | 29.0(41) | 0 | — | — | — | — | — | — | — | — | — | — | i | — | 0 | 24 |

COTTRELL, BILL William Henry, T-G-C, 6´4˝/255 lbs; Delaware Valley; B9/18/1944 Chester, PA **1967** Det 14 (10, LT) **1968** Det 14 **1969** Det 14 **1970**†Det 10 **1972** Den 11 **NFL** 63 (10) [5 yrs]

COTTRELL, DANA Dana Robert, LB, 6´3˝/234 lbs; Syracuse; B1/11/1974 Boston, MA **1998**†NE 2 (0)

COTTRELL, TED Theodore John, LB, 6´2˝/233 lbs; Delaware Valley; 1969: Atl, rnd 7; B6/13/1947 Chester, PA **1969** Atl 10 **1970** Atl 14 **NFL** 24 [2 yrs]

COUCH, TIM Timothy Scott, QB, 6´4˝/220 lbs; Kentucky; 1999: Cle, rnd 1; B7/31/1977 Hyden, KY

1999	Cle	15 (14, QB)	40	267	6.7(40)	1	—	—	—	—	399	223	55.9	2447	6.1(78)	15	13	56	359	73.2	—	—	8	1056
2000	Cle	7 (7, qb)	12	45	3.8(31)	0	—	—	—	—	215	137	63.7	1483	6.9(79)	7	9	10	78	77.3	—	—	0	462
2001	Cle	16 (16, QB)	38	128	3.4(15)	0	1	-10	-10.0(-10)	0	454	272	59.9	3040	6.7(78)	17	21	51	353	73.1	—	—	0	888
2002	Cle	14 (14, QB)	23	77	3.3(14)	0	—	—	—	—	443	273	61.6	2842	6.4(78)	18	18	30	213	76.8	—	—	0	868
2003	Cle	10 (8, qb)	11	39	3.5(17)	1	—	—	-3	-3.0(-3)	0	203	120	59.1	1319	6.5(71)	7	6	19	116	77.6	—	6	502
NFL	5	62 (59)	124	556	4.5(40)	2	2	-13	-6.5(-3)	0	1714	1025	59.8	11131	6.5(79)	64	67	166	1119	75.1	—	14	3775

COUGHLIN, DANNY Daniel Martin, WB, 5´9˝/175 lbs; St. Thomas; Notre Dame; B6/1897 Fairbault, MN, deceased **1923** Min 2 (2)

COUGHLIN, FRANK Francis Edward, T, 6´3˝/220 lbs; Notre Dame; B2/28/1896 Chicago, IL, D9/8/1951 Indianapolis, IN [C] **1921** RI 3 (3) **1921** Det 2 (1) **1921** GB 5 (5, LT) **NFL** 10 (9) [1 yr]

COULTER, TEX DeWitt Echoles, T-C-E, 6´4˝/250 lbs; Texas A&M; Cornell; Army; 1947: ChiC, rnd 1; B10/26/1924 Fort Worth, TX **1946**†NYG 9 (7, LT) **1948** NYG☆12 (5, lt) **1949** NYG 12 (11, C) **1951** NYG★12 (LT)

1947	NYG	12 (12, LE)	—	—	—	8	107	13.4(47)	1	—	—	—	—	—	—	—	—	—	—	k	—	6	45
1952	NYG★	12 (LT)	—	—	—	1	9	9.0(9)	0	—	—	—	—	—	—	—	—	—	—	—	—	0	5
NFL	6	69 (35)	—	—	—	9	116	12.9(47)	1	—	—	—	—	—	—	—	—	—	—	k	—	6	46

COUNTS, JOHNNY John E., HB, 5´10˝/170 lbs; Illinois; 1962: NYT, rnd 24; B2/28/1939 Mount Pleasant, NY, D2/21/2004 Newburgh, NY **1963** NYG 3

| 1962 | †NYG | 14 | 14 | 55 | 3.9(23) | 0 | 4 | 62 | 15.5(24) | 0 | — | — | — | — | — | — | — | — | — | — | kp | 1 | 6 | 483 |
| NFL | 2 | 17 | 14 | 55 | 3.9(23) | 0 | 4 | 62 | 15.5(24) | 0 | — | — | — | — | — | — | — | — | — | — | kp | 1 | 6 | 515 |

COUPPEE, AL Albert Wallace, G-B, 6´0˝/225 lbs; Iowa; 1942: Was, rnd 22; B6/4/1920 Council Bluffs, IA, D7/3/1998 Laguna Hills, CA

| 1946 | Was | 7 (1) | 3 | 22 | 7.3(17) | 0 | — | — | — | — | — | — | — | — | — | — | — | — | — | — | — | — | 0 | 22 |

COURSON, STEVE Stephen Paul, G, 6´1˝/274 lbs; South Carolina; 1977: Pit, rnd 5; B10/1/1955 Philadelphia, PA, D11/10/2005 Henry Clay Township, PA **1978**†Pit 16 (1) **1979**†Pit 16 (8, RG) **1980** Pit 8 (6, rg) **1981** Pit 16 (16, RG) **1982**†Pit 8 (8, RG) **1983**†Pit 9 (9, RG) **1984** TB 14 (12, LG) **1985** TB 16 (13, LG) **NFL** 103 (73) [8 yrs]

COURTNEY, GERRY Gerald L., TB, 6´0˝/195 lbs; Syracuse; B3/2/1918 Tulsa, OK, D12/1963

| 1942 | Bkn | 5 (0) | 8 | 12 | 1.5(11) | 1 | — | — | — | — | 0 | 4 | 1 | 25.0 | 14 | 3.5(14) | 0 | 2 | — | — | — | i | — | 6 | -24 |

COURTNEY, MATT Matthew Carter, DB, 5´11˝/194 lbs; Idaho State; B12/21/1961 Greeley, CO **1987** SF 3 (3)

COURVILLE, VINCE Vincent Eric, WR, 5´9˝/170 lbs; Texas Southern; Rice; B12/5/1959 Galveston, TX **1987** Dal 2 (0)

COUSIN, TERRY Terry Sean, DB, 5´9˝/181 lbs; South Carolina; B4/11/1975 Miami, FL **1997** ChiB 6 (0) **1998** ChiB 16 (12, LCB) **1999** ChiB 16 (9, RCB) **2000** Atl 15 (0) **2001**†Mia 16 (2) **2002** Car 16 (16, LCB) **2003**†Car 13 (13, LCB) **2004** NYG 16 (5, fs) **2005**†Jax 16 (5, cb) **NFL** 130 (62) [9 yrs]

COUSINEAU, TOM Thomas Michael, LB, 6´3˝/225 lbs; Ohio State; 1979: Buf, rnd 1; B5/6/1957 Fairview Park, OH **1982**†Cle 9 (8, LILB) **1983** Cle☆16 (16, RILB) **1984** Cle☆16 (16, RILB) **1985** Cle 16 (15, RILB) **1986** SF 4 (3) **1987** SF 4 (3) **NFL** 66 (59) [6 yrs]

COUSINO, BRAD Bradley Gene, LB, 6´0˝/218 lbs; Miami (OH); B4/5/1953 Toledo, OH **1975** Cin 14 **1976** NYG 6 **1977**†Pit 3 **NFL** 23 [3 yrs]

COUTRE, LARRY Lawrence Edward, HB, 5´10˝/175 lbs; Notre Dame; 1950: GB, rnd 4; B4/11/1928 Chicago, IL

1950	GB	12	41	283	6.9(53)	1	17	206	12.1(77)	2	—	—	—	—	—	—	—	—	—	—	—	—	18	406
1953	GB	7	22	39	1.8(8)	0	1	-4	-4.0(-4)	0	—	—	—	—	—	—	—	—	—	—	kp	—	0	44
1953	Bal	3	—	—	—	—	—	—	—	—	—	—	—	—	—	—	—	—	—	—	kp	—	0	149
NFL	2	22	63	322	5.1(53)	1	18	202	11.2(77)	2	—	—	—	—	—	—	—	—	—	—	kp	—	18	599

YEAR	TEAM	G (GS, POS)	RUSH	YD	AVG(LG)	TD	REC	YD	AVG(LG)	TD	PASS COMP	PCT	YD	AVG(LG)	TD	INT	SK	YD	QBR	KPR	OTD	PTS	TAY

COVERT, JIMBO James Paul, T, 6´4˝/277 lbs; Pittsburgh; 1983: Chi, rnd 1; B3/22/1960 Conway, PA **1983** ChiB 16 (16, LT) **1984**†ChiB 16 (16, LT) **1985**†ChiB★15 (15, LT) **1986**†ChiB★16 (16, LT) **1987**†ChiB☆9 (9, LT) **1988**†ChiB 9 (8, lt) **1989** ChiB 15 (15, LT) **1990**†ChiB☆15 (15, LT) **NFL** 111 (110) [8 yrs]

COVINGTON, DAMIEN Damien Emere, LB, 5´11˝/236 lbs; North Carolina State; 1995: Buf, rnd 3; B12/4/1972 Berlin, NJ, D11/29/2002 Lindenwold, NJ **1995**†Buf 12 (1) **1996**†Buf 9 (2) **1997** Buf 8 (8, RILB) **NFL** 29 (11) [3 yrs]

COVINGTON, JAIME Jaime A., RB, 6´1˝/234 lbs; Syracuse; 1985: Min, rnd 9; B12/12/1962 Flushing, NY

| 1987 | NYG | 2(0) | 4 | 0 | 0.0(2) | 0 | 1 | 9 | 9.0(9) | 0 | — | — | — | — | — | — | — | — | — | — | — | 0 | 5 |

COVINGTON, JOHN John Shaft, DB, 6´0˝/198 lbs; Notre Dame; 1994: Ind, rnd 5; B4/22/1972 Winter Haven, FL **1994** Ind 3 (0)

COVINGTON, SCOTT Scott, QB, 6´2˝/217 lbs; Miami (FL); 1999: Cin, rnd 7; B1/17/1976 Laguna Niguel, CA

1999	Cin	3(0)	2	-4	-2.0(-2)	0	—	—	—	—	5	4	80.0	23	4.6(8)	0	0	—	—	—	—	0	8
2002	SL	1(1)	—	—	—	—	—	—	—	—	5	2	40.0	7	1.4(4)	0	0	2	16	—	—	0	4
NFL	2	4(1)	2	-4	-2.0(-2)	0	—	—	—	—	10	6	60.0	30	3.0(8)	0	0	2	16	—	—	0	11

COVINGTON, TONY Anthony Lawrence, DB, 5´11˝/192 lbs; Virginia; 1991: TB, rnd 4; B12/26/1967 Winston-Salem, NC **1991** TB 16 (12, SS) **1992** TB 1 (1) **1994** TB 14 (2) **1995** Sea 11 (0) **NFL** 42 (15) [4 yrs]

COWAN, BOB Robert George, B, 5´11˝/185 lbs; Indiana; 1947: Cle-A, rnd 4/1945: ChiC, rnd 12; B1/2/1923 Fort Wayne, IN, D1/20/2004 Fort Wayne, IN

1947	Cle-A	10(1)	38	181	4.8	2	5	60	12.0	1	—	—	—	—	—	—	—	—	—	k	—	18	246
1948	†Cle-A	14(11, RH)	33	99	3.0	1	15	265	17.7	4	—	—	—	—	—	—	—	—	—	k	—	30	270
1949	Bal-A	9(0)	1	0	0.0	0	1	26	26.0(26)	5	—	—	—	—	—	—	—	—	—	i	—	0	15
AAFC	3	33(12)	72	280	3.9	3	21	351	16.7(26)	5	—	—	—	—	—	—	—	—	—	k	—	48	531

COWAN, CHARLEY Charles Edward, T-G, 6´4˝/264 lbs; New Mexico Highlands; 1961: LA, rnd 4/Den, rnd 5; B6/19/1938 Braeholm, WV, D4/29/1998 Whittier, CA **1961** LARm 14 (LG) **1962** LARm 14 (LG) **1963** LARm 14 (LG) **1964** LARm 14 (LG) **1965** LARm 13 (RT) **1966** LARm 14 (14, RT) **1967**†LARm★14 (14, RT) **1968** LARm★13 (13, RT) **1969**†LARm★14 (14, LT) **1970** LARm◊14 (14, LT) **1971** LARm★14 (14, LT) **1972** LARm 13 (13, LT) **1973**†LARm☆14 (14, LT) **1974**†LARm 14 (13, LT)

| 1975 | LARm | 13(13, LT) | — | — | — | 1 | 1 | 1.0(1) | 0 | — | — | — | — | — | — | — | — | — | — | — | — | 0 | 1 |
| NFL | 15 | 206(136) | — | — | — | 1 | 1 | 1.0(1) | 0 | — | — | — | — | — | — | — | — | — | — | k | — | 0 | -30 |

COWAN, LARRY Lawrence Donnell, RB, 5´11˝/194 lbs; Jackson State; 1982: Mia, rnd 7; B7/11/1960 Mobile, AL **1982**†NE 6 (0)

| 1982 | Mia | 2(0) | 1 | 3 | 3.0(3) | 0 | — | — | — | — | — | — | — | — | — | — | — | — | — | — | — | 0 | 3 |
| NFL | 1 | 8(0) | 1 | 3 | 3.0(3) | 0 | — | — | — | — | — | — | — | — | — | — | — | — | — | — | — | 0 | 3 |

COWAN, LES Leslie Lowden, DT-E, 6´5˝/235 lbs; McMurry; 1950: LA, rnd 9; B12/24/1925 Stamford, TX, D3/9/1979 Weatherford, TX **1951** ChiB 9 (RDT)

COWART, SAM Samuel, LB, 6´2˝/245 lbs; Florida State; 1998: Buf, rnd 2; B2/26/1975 Jacksonville, FL **1998**†Buf 16 (11, RILB) **1999**†Buf 16 (16, RILB) **2000** Buf★12 (12, RILB) **2001** Buf 1 (1) **2002**†NYJ 16 (16, RLB) **2003** NYJ 15 (15, RLB) **2004**†NYJ 9 (2) **2005** Min 15 (14, MLB) **NFL** 100 (87) [8 yrs]

COWHER, BILL William Laird, LB, 6´3˝/225 lbs; North Carolina State; B5/8/1957 Pittsburgh, PA **[C]** **1980**†Cle 16 (2) **1982**†Cle 9 (2) **1983** Phi 16 (0) **1984** Phi 4 (0) **NFL** 45 (4) [4 yrs]

COWHIG, GERRY Gerard Finbar, LB-FB-DB, 6´2˝/215 lbs; Notre Dame; 1945: Cle, rnd 6/1947: Cle-A, rnd 2; B7/5/1921 Boston, MA, D12/6/1995 Van Nuys, CA

1947	LARm	8(4)	25	104	4.2(21)	0	—	—	—	—	—	—	—	—	—	—	—	—	ki	—	0	98
1948	LARm	12(3)	46	206	4.5(14)	2	3	18	6.0(9)	0	—	—	—	—	—	—	—	—	kpi	—	12	225
1949	†LARm	11(1)	10	32	3.2(8)	1	—	—	—	—	—	—	—	—	—	—	—	—	ki	1	12	84
1950	ChiC	12(LLB)	—	—	—	—	—	—	—	—	—	—	—	—	—	—	—	—	—	—	—	—	—
1951	Phi	11	—	—	—	—	—	—	—	—	—	—	—	—	—	—	—	—	k	1	6	-3
NFL	5	54(8)	81	342	4.2(21)	3	3	18	6.0(9)	0	—	—	—	—	—	—	—	—	kpi	2	30	404

COWLINGS, AL Allen G., DE-DT-LB, 6´5˝/255 lbs; USC; 1970: Buf, rnd 1; B6/16/1947 San Francisco, CA **1970** Buf 13 (RDE) **1971** Buf 14 (LDE) **1972** Buf 14 (RDE) **1973** Hou 14 (LDT) **1974** Hou 14 (LOLB) **1975**†LARm 5 **1976** Sea 1 **1977**†LARm 14 **1979** SF 12 **NFL** 101 [9 yrs]

COWNE, JOHN John Kendall, C, 6´2˝/245 lbs; Virginia Tech; B5/23/1962 Fairfax, VA **1987** Was 3 (0)

COWSETTE, DELBERT Delbert Ray, DT, 6´1˝/287 lbs; Maryland; 2000: Was, rnd 7; B9/3/1977 Cleveland, OH **2001** Was 16 (0) **2002** Was 16 (0) **NFL** 32 (0) [2 yrs]

COX, AARON Aaron Dion, WR, 5´9˝/174 lbs; Arizona State; 1988: LARm, rnd 1; B3/13/1965 Los Angeles, CA

1988	†LARm	16(15, WR)	—	—	—	—	28	590	21.1(69)	5	—	—	—	—	—	—	—	—	—	—	30	320
1989	†LARm	16(3)	—	—	—	—	20	340	17.0(51)	3	—	—	—	—	—	—	—	—	—	—	18	185
1990	LARm	14(1)	—	—	—	—	17	266	15.6(32)	0	—	—	—	—	—	—	—	—	—	—	0	133
1991	LARm	15(5, wr)	—	—	—	—	15	216	14.4(39)	0	—	—	—	—	—	—	—	—	—	—	0	108
1992	LARm	10(4)	—	—	—	—	18	261	14.5(49)	0	—	—	—	—	—	—	—	—	—	—	0	131
1993	Ind	11(0)	—	—	—	—	4	59	14.8(24)	0	—	—	—	—	—	—	—	—	—	—	0	30
NFL	6	82(28)	—	—	—	—	102	1732	17.0(69)	8	—	—	—	—	—	—	—	—	—	—	48	906

COX, ARTHUR Arthur Dean, TE, 6´3˝/262 lbs; Texas Southern; B2/5/1961 Plant City, FL

1983	Atl	16(9, TE)	—	—	—	—	9	83	9.2(19)	1	—	—	—	—	—	—	—	—	—	—	6	47
1984	Atl	16(16, TE)	—	—	—	—	34	329	9.7(23)	3	—	—	—	—	—	—	—	—	—	—	18	180
1985	Atl	16(16, TE)	—	—	—	—	33	454	13.8(62)	2	—	—	—	—	—	—	—	—	—	—	12	237
1986	Atl	16(15, TE)	—	—	—	—	24	301	12.5(49)	1	—	—	—	—	—	—	—	—	—	—	6	156
1987	Atl	12(10, TE)	—	—	—	—	11	101	9.2(19)	0	—	—	—	—	—	—	—	—	k	—	0	47
1988	SD	16(16, TE)	—	—	—	—	18	144	8.0(20)	0	—	—	—	—	—	—	—	—	—	—	0	72
1989	SD	16(16, TE)	—	—	—	—	22	200	9.1(24)	2	—	—	—	—	—	—	—	—	—	—	12	110
1990	SD	16(14, TE)	—	—	—	—	14	93	6.6(12)	1	—	—	—	—	—	—	—	—	—	—	6	52
1991	SD	8(8, TE)	—	—	—	—	5	53	10.6(19)	0	—	—	—	—	—	—	—	—	—	—	0	27
1991	Mia	2(0)	—	—	—	—	—	—	—	—	—	—	—	—	—	—	—	—	—	—	—	—	—
1991	Cle	3(0)	—	—	—	—	—	—	—	—	—	—	—	—	—	—	—	—	—	—	—	—	—
NFL	9	137(120)	—	—	—	—	170	1758	10.3(62)	10	—	—	—	—	—	—	—	—	k	—	60	925

COX, BILLY John William, DE-DB-HB-E, 6´3˝/189 lbs; Duke; 1951: Was, rnd 8; B6/17/1929 Brandon, TX

1951	Was	10	2	7	3.5(5)	0	—	—	—	—	—	—	—	—	—	—	—	—	Pi	—	0	-3
1952	Was	12(LDE)	3	-1	-0.3(14)	0	2	19	9.5(13)	0	—	—	—	—	—	—	—	—	Pi	—	0	37
1955	Was	4	—	—	—	—	5	71	14.2(28)	0	—	—	—	—	—	—	—	—	—	—	0	36
NFL	3	26	5	6	1.2(14)	0	7	90	12.9(28)	0	—	—	—	—	—	—	—	—	Pi	—	0	69

COX, BRYAN Bryan Keith, LB, 6´4˝/250 lbs; Western Illinois; 1991: Mia, rnd 5; B2/17/1968 St. Louis, MO **[S]** **1991** Mia 13 (13, ROLB) **1992**†Mia☆16 (16, ROLB) **1993** Mia 16 (16, RLB) **1994**†Mia★16 (16, MLB) **1995**†Mia★16 (16, MLB) **1996** ChiB 9 (9, MLB) **1997** ChiB 16 (15, MLB) **1998**†NYJ 16 (10, RLB) **1999** NYJ 12 (11, LILB) **2000** NYJ 15 (15, LILB) **2002** NO 9 (1)

| 2001 | †NE | 11(7, llb) | — | — | — | — | 1 | 7 | 7.0(7) | 0 | — | — | — | — | — | — | — | — | — | — | 0 | 4 |
| NFL | 12 | 165(145) | — | — | — | — | 1 | 7 | 7.0(7) | 0 | — | — | — | — | — | — | — | — | kiS | 2 | 14 | 58 |

COX, CUROME Curome, DB, 6´1˝/199 lbs; Maryland; B2/28/1981 Washington, DC **2005**†Den 13 (1)

COX, FRED Frederick William, K, 5´11˝/200 lbs; Pittsburgh; 1961: Cle, rnd 8/NYT, rnd 28; B12/11/1938 Monongahela, PA **[K]** **1963** Min 14 **1964** Min 14 **1965** Min 14 **1966** Min 14 **1967** Min 14 **1968**†Min☆14 **1969**†Min☆14 **1971**†Min☆14 **1972** Min 14 **1973**†Min 14 **1974**†Min 14 **1975**†Min 14 **1976**†Min 14 **1977**†Min 14

| 1970 | †Min★ | 14 | — | — | — | — | 1 | 1 | 100.0 | 1 | -1.0(-1) | 0 | 0 | — | — | K | — | 125 | -1 |
| NFL | 15 | 210 | — | — | — | — | 1 | 1 | 100.0 | 1 | -1.0(-1) | 0 | 0 | — | — | KP | — | 1365 | -1 |

COX, GREG Gregory Mark, DB, 6´0˝/223 lbs; San Jose State; B1/6/1965 Niagara Falls, NY **1988**†SF 15 (0) **1989**†NYG 16 (0) **1990** SF 13 (0) **1991** SF 11 (0) **NFL** 55 (0) [4 yrs]

COX, JIM James Ellingson, G-LB, 6´1˝/208 lbs; California; Stanford; 1944: GB, rnd 21; B9/6/1920 St. Louis, MO **1948** SF-A 14 (0)

COX, JIM James Allen, TE, 6´3˝/230 lbs; Miami (FL); 1968: Mia, rnd 2; B12/21/1946 Baltimore, MD

| 1968 | Mia-A | 13 | — | — | — | — | 11 | 147 | 13.4(30) | 0 | — | — | — | — | — | — | — | — | — | — | 0 | 115 |

COX, LARRY Lawrence Donald, DT, 6´3˝/255 lbs; Abilene Christian; 1966: Den, rnd 10; B11/12/1943 Anson, TX **1966** Den-A 11 (RDT) **1967** Den-A 13 **1968** Den-A 9 **NFL** 33 [3 yrs]

YEAR	TEAM	G(GS, POS)	RUSH	YD	AVG(LG)	TD	REC	YD	AVG(LG)	TD	PASS COMP	PCT	YD	AVG(LG)	TD	INT	SK	YD	QBR	KPR	°OTD	PTS	TAY

COX, NORM   Norman Lawrence, QB-TB, 6′2″/210 lbs; TCU; B9/22/1925 Stamford, TX

1946	ChiR-A	3(0)	1	12	12.0(12)	0	—	—	—	—	—	—	—	—	—	—	—	—	—	—	0	12
1947	ChiR-A	2(0)	1	-3	-3.0(-3)	0	—	—	—	—	2	1	50.0	9	4.5(9)	0	0	—	—	—	0	2
AAFC	2	5(0)	2	9	4.5(12)	0	—	—	—	—	2	1	50.0	9	4.5(9)	0	0	—	—	—	0	14

COX, RENARD   Renard, DB, 6′0″/191 lbs; Maryland; B3/3/1978 Richmond, VA   **2001** Jax 5 (0)

COX, RON   Ronald Eugene, LB, 6′2″/235 lbs; Fresno State; 1990: Chi, rnd 2; B2/27/1968 Fresno, CA   **1990**†ChiB 13 (0)   **1991** ChiB 6 (0)   **1992** ChiB 16 (3)   **1993** ChiB 16 (2)
1994†ChiB 15 (3)   **1995** ChiB 16 (13, RLB)   **1996**†GB 16 (1)   **1997** ChiB 15 (13, LLB)   **NFL** 113 (35) [8 yrs]

COX, STEVE   Stephen Everett, P-K, 6′4″/195 lbs; Tulsa; Arkansas; 1981: Cle, rnd 5; B5/11/1958 Shreveport, LA **[KP]**   **1981** Cle 16 (0)   **1983** Cle 7 (0)   **1986**†Was☆16 (0)
1987†Was 12 (0)   **1988** Was 1 (0)

1982	†Cle	9(0)	2	-11	-5.5(0)	0	—	—	—	—	—	—	—	—	—	—	—	—	—	KP	0	-11
1984	Cle	16(0)	—	—	—	—	—	—	—	—	1	1	100.0	16	16.0(16)	0	0	—	—	KP	3	8
1985	Was	12(0)	—	—	—	—	—	—	—	—	1	1	100.0	11	11.0(11)	0	0	—	—	KP	0	6
NFL	8	89(0)	2	-11	-5.5	0	—	—	—	—	2	2	100.0	27	13.5(16)	0	0	—	—	KP	21	3

COX, TOM   Thomas Franklin, DB, 6′5″/260 lbs; USC; B12/4/1962 Xenia, OH   **1987** LARm 3 (0)

COX, TORRIE   Torrie Twan, DB, 5′9″/181 lbs; Pittsburgh; 2003: TB, rnd 6; B10/29/1980 Miami, FL   **2004** TB 10 (0)   **2005**†TB 15 (0)   **NFL** 25 (0) [2 yrs]

COYLE, ERIC   Eric, C, 6′3″/260 lbs; Colorado; B10/26/1963 Longmont, CO   **1987** Was 3 (3)

COYLE, ROSS   Charles Ross, DB, 6′3″/195 lbs; Oklahoma; 1959: LA, rnd 20; B3/23/1937 Marlow, OK   **1961** LARm 13

CRABB, CLAUDE   Claude Clarence, DB-WR, 6′1″/192 lbs; Colorado; 1962: Was, rnd 19/Buf, rnd 27; B3/8/1940 Monterey, CA   **1962** Was 13 (LCB)   **1963** Was 13 (LS)
1967†LARm 14   **1968** LARm 3

1964	Phi	13	—	—	—	—	1	14	14.0(14)	0	—	—	—	—	—	—	—	—	—	—	0	7
1965	Phi	10	—	—	—	—	2	41	20.5(27)	0	—	—	—	—	—	—	—	—	—	—	0	21
1966	LARm	14(1)	—	—	—	—	1	47	47.0(47)	0	—	—	—	—	—	—	—	—	—	—	0	24
NFL	7	80(1)	—	—	—	—	4	102	25.5(47)	0	—	—	—	—	—	—	—	—	—	pi	1	6	141

CRABLE, BOB   Robert Edward, LB, 6′3″/228 lbs; Notre Dame; 1982: NYJ, rnd 1; B9/22/1959 Cincinnati, OH   **1982**†NYJ 9 (2)   **1983** NYJ 14 (11, MLB)   **1984** NYJ 5 (2)
1985†NYJ 10 (2)   **1986**†NYJ 16 (15, ROLB)   **1987** NYJ 12 (11, ROLB)   **NFL** 66 (43) [6 yrs]

CRABTREE, CLEM   Clem Gurley, T-G, 6′3″/225 lbs; Wake Forest; B11/11/1918 Durham, NC, D1/1981   **1940** Det 9 (0)   **1941** Det 9 (3)   **NFL** 18 (3) [2 yrs]

CRABTREE, CLYDE   Clyde, B, 5′8″/160 lbs; Northwestern; Florida; B11/3/1905 Altoona, IA, D4/21/1994 South Miami, FL   **1930** Fra 14 (7, BB), 12   **1930** Min 1 (0)   **NFL** 15 (7) [1 yr]

CRABTREE, ERIC   Eric Leslie, WR-SE-FL-DB, 6′0″/185 lbs; Pittsburgh; 1966: Den, rnd 13/Bal, rnd 11; B11/3/1944 Monessen, PA

1966	Den-A	14	—	—	—	—	1	38	38.0(38)	0	—	—	—	—	—	—	—	—	—	k	0	73
1967	Den-A	14(SE)	2	2	1.0(6)	0	46	716	15.6(76)	5	—	—	—	—	—	—	—	—	—	kp	30	410
1968	Den-A	14(FL)	—	—	—	—	35	601	17.2(72)	5	—	—	—	—	—	—	—	—	—	k	30	341
1969	Cin-A	14(SE)	—	—	—	—	40	855	21.4(73)	7	—	—	—	—	—	—	—	—	—		42	463
1970	Cin	14(WR)	3	23	7.7(16)	0	19	231	12.2(29)	2	—	—	—	—	—	—	—	—	—		12	-149
1971	Cin	7(WR)	1	1	1.0(1)	0	14	102	7.3(22)	2	—	—	—	—	—	—	—	—	—		12	62
1971	NE	6(4)	2	11	5.5(18)	0	9	120	13.3(31)	1	—	—	—	—	—	—	—	—	—		6	76
NFL	6	83(4)	8	37	4.6(18)	0	164	2663	16.2(76)	22	—	—	—	—	—	—	—	—	—	kp	132	1573

CRADDOCK, NATE   Nathaniel, FB, 6′1″/220 lbs; Parsons; 1963: Bos, rnd 22; B12/3/1940 Des Moines, IA

| 1963 | Bal | 3 | 1 | 1 | 1.0(1) | 0 | — | — | — | — | — | — | — | — | — | — | — | — | — | — | 0 | 1 |

CRAFT, DONNIE   Donald Joseph, RB, 6′0″/206 lbs; Louisville; 1982: Hou, rnd 12; B11/19/1959 Panama City, FL

1982	Hou	9(2)	18	42	2.3(10)	3	23	230	10.0(49)	1	—	—	—	—	—	—	—	—	—	—	24	192
1983	Hou	15(2)	55	147	2.7(8)	0	12	99	8.3(14)	0	—	—	—	—	—	—	—	—	—	—	0	197
1984	Hou	1(0)	—	—	—	—	—	—	—	—	—	—	—	—	—	—	—	—	—	—	0	0
NFL	3	25(4)	73	189	2.6(10)	3	35	329	9.4(49)	1	—	—	—	—	—	—	—	—	—	—	24	389

CRAFT, JASON   Jason Donnell Andre, DB, 5′10″/176 lbs; Colorado State; 1999: Jax, rnd 5; B2/13/1976 Denver, CO   **1999**†Jax 16 (0)   **2000** Jax 16 (3)   **2001** Jax 16 (8, lcb)
2002 Jax 16 (16, RCB)   **2003** Jax 6 (6, rcb)   **2004** NO 14 (0)   **2005** NO 16 (4)   **NFL** 100 (37) [7 yrs]

CRAFT, RUSS   William Russell, DB-HB, 5′9″/178 lbs; Alabama; 1943: Phi, rnd 15; B10/15/1919 McEwen, TN **[I]**

1946	Phi	9(1)	27	108	4.0(24)	0	4	48	12.0(35)	0	—	—	—	—	—	—	—	—	—	kpi	0	275
1947	†Phi	10(4)	5	-1	-0.2(4)	0	2	66	33.0(34)	1	—	—	—	—	—	—	—	—	—	pi	6	32
1948	†Phi	12(4)	13	67	5.2(23)	0	4	138	34.5(70)	2	—	—	—	—	—	—	—	—	—	p	12	163
1949	†Phi	10(2)	11	5	0.5(6)	0	1	37	37.0(37)	0	—	—	—	—	—	—	—	—	—	pi	1	6	71
1950	Phi	12(DB)	8	52	6.5(19)	0	1	14	14.0(14)	0	—	—	—	—	—	—	—	—	—	kpi	1	6	299
1951	Phi◊	12(DB)	—	—	—	—	—	—	—	—	—	—	—	—	—	—	—	—	—	kpi	0	64
1952	Phi◊	12(DB)	—	—	—	—	—	—	—	—	—	—	—	—	—	—	—	—	—	ki	1	6	40
1953	Phi	12(DB)	—	—	—	—	—	—	—	—	—	—	—	—	—	—	—	—	—	i	0	26
1954	Pit	11(DB)	—	—	—	—	—	—	—	—	—	—	—	—	—	—	—	—	—	i	1	6	115
NFL	9	100(9)	64	231	3.6(24)	0	12	303	25.3(70)	3	—	—	—	—	—	—	—	—	—	kpi	4	42	1085

CRAFTS, JERRY   Jerry Wayne, T-G, 6′5″/343 lbs; Oklahoma; Louisville; 1991: Ind, rnd 11; B1/6/1968 Tulsa, OK   **1992** Buf 6 (0)   **1993**†Buf 16 (0)   **1994** Buf 16 (7, rt)
1997 Phi 15 (6, rg)   **1998** Phi 1 (0)   **NFL** 54 (13) [5 yrs]

CRAIG, CLARK   Clark Western, E, 5′9″/180 lbs; Oklahoma Baptist; Pennsylvania; B6/19/1902 Shawnee, OK, D11/28/1977 Shawnee, OK   **1925** Fra 2 (2)

CRAIG, DAMEYUNE   Dameyune Vashon, QB, 6′1″/200 lbs; Auburn; B4/19/1974 Mobile, AL

2000	Car	4(0)	2	4	2.0(5)	0	2	4	2.0(4)	0	—	—	—	—	—	—	—	—	—	—	0	6
2001	Car	2(0)	3	20	6.7(13)	0	—	—	—	—	8	4	50.0	34	4.3(18)	0	0	2	15	—	0	37
NFL	6	6(0)	5	24	4.8(13)	0	2	4	2.0(4)	0	8	4	50.0	34	4.3(18)	0	0	2	15	—	0	43

CRAIG, DOBIE   Dobie, FL-WR-HB, 6′5″/200 lbs; Baylor; Howard Payne; B2/14/1938 El Campo, TX

1962	Oak-A	14(11, FL)	1	8	8.0(8)	0	27	492	18.2(46)	4	—	—	—	—	—	—	—	—	—	—	24	274
1963	Oak-A	12(fl)	—	—	—	—	7	196	28.0(**93**)	2	—	—	—	—	—	—	—	—	—	—	12	108
1964	Hou-A	7	—	—	—	—	4	46	11.5(25)	1	—	—	—	—	—	—	—	—	—	—	6	28
NFL	3	33(11)	1	8	8.0(8)	0	38	734	19.3(93)	7	—	—	—	—	—	—	—	—	—	—	42	410

CRAIG, LARRY   Lawrence Gantt, B-E, 6′1″/211 lbs; South Carolina; 1939: GB, rnd 6; B6/27/1916 Six Mile, SC, D5/31/1992 Ninety Six, SC

1939	†GB★	11(8, BB)	2	6	3.0	0	3	44	14.7(28)	0	—	—	—	—	—	—	—	—	—	—	0	28
1940	GB	11(5, BB)	3	9	3.0	0	6	67	11.2(24)	0	—	—	—	—	—	—	—	—	—	i	0	38
1941	†GB◊	11(4, bb)	1	1	1.0(1)	0	2	13	6.5(12)	0	—	—	—	—	—	—	—	—	—	—	0	8
1942	GB◊	11(5, BB)	2	0	0.0(4)	0	—	—	—	—	—	—	—	—	—	—	—	—	—	k	0	-6
1943	GB	10(10, BB)	1	3	3.0(3)	0	—	—	—	—	—	—	—	—	—	—	—	—	—	—	0	3
1944	†GB	10(8, BB)	—	—	—	—	2	17	8.5(9)	0	—	—	—	—	—	—	—	—	—	ki	0	26
1945	GB	10(9, BB)	—	—	—	—	—	—	—	—	—	—	—	—	—	—	—	—	—	k	1	6	44
1946	GB	11(11, BB)	1	-3	-3.0(-3)	0	—	—	—	—	—	—	—	—	—	—	—	—	—	k	0	-15
1947	GB☆	12(6, le)	—	—	—	—	1	14	14.0(14)	0	—	—	—	—	—	—	—	—	—	—	0	7
1948	GB	12(5, LE)	—	—	—	—	—	—	—	—	—	—	—	—	—	—	—	—	—	—	0	0
1949	GB	12(5, LE)	—	—	—	—	—	—	—	—	—	—	—	—	—	—	—	—	—	—	0	0
NFL	11	121(76)	10	16	1.6(4)	0	14	155	11.1(28)	0	—	—	—	—	—	—	—	—	—	ki	1	6	84

CRAIG, NEAL   Cornelius, DB, 6′1″/191 lbs; Fisk; 1971: Cin, rnd 7; B4/21/1948 Cincinnati, OH   **1971** Cin 12 (ss)   **1972** Cin 14 (SS)   **1973**†Cin 14 (SS)   **1974**†Buf 14 (SS)
1976 Cle 14 (SS)

| 1975 | Cle | 11(FS) | — | — | — | — | 1 | 1 | 1.0(1) | 0 | — | — | — | — | — | — | — | — | — | i | 0 | -5 |
| NFL | 6 | 79 | — | — | — | — | 1 | 1 | 1.0(1) | 0 | — | — | — | — | — | — | — | — | — | ki | 2 | 12 | 157 |

YEAR	TEAM	G(GS, POS)	RUSH	YD	AVG(LG)	TD	REC	YD	AVG(LG)	TD	PASS COMP	PCT	YD	AVG(LG)	TD	INT	SK	YD	QBR	KPR	OTD	PTS	TAY

CRAIG, PACO Francisco Luis, WR, 5´10˝/173 lbs; UCLA; 1988: Det, rnd 10; B2/2/1965 Santa Maria, CA

| 1988 | Det | 8(0) | — | — | — | — | 2 | 29 | 14.5(18) | 0 | | | | | | | | | | — | | 0 | 15 |

CRAIG, REGGIE Reginald Mark, WR, 6´1˝/187 lbs; Arkansas; B6/10/1953 Baytown, TX **1976** KC 1 **1977** Buf 4

1975	KC	.14	—	—	—	—	1	10	10.0(10)	0										kp		0	101
1977	Cle	5	—	—	—	—	1	5	5.0(5)	0										p		0	-3
NFL	3	24	—	—	—	—	2	15	7.5(10)	0										kp		0	114

CRAIG, ROGER Roger Timothy, RB, 6´0˝/222 lbs; Nebraska; 1983: SF, rnd 2; B7/10/1960 Davenport, IA

1983	†SF	16(13, FB)	176	725	4.1(71)	8	48	427	8.9(23)	4												72	1039
1984	†SF	16(16, FB)	155	649	4.2(28)	7	71	675	9.5(64)	3												60	1072
1985	†SF★	16(16, FB)	214	1050	4.9(62)	9	92	1016	11.0(73)	6												90	1678
1986	†SF	16(15, FB)	204	830	4.1(25)	7	81	624	7.7(48)	0												42	1212
1987	†SF★	14(14, RB/fb)	215	815	3.8(25)	3	66	492	7.5(35)	1												24	1096
1988	†SF★	16(15, RB)	310	1502	4.8(46)	9	76	534	7.0(22)	1										k		60	1866
1989	†SF★	16(16, RB)	271	1054	3.9(27)	6	49	473	9.7(44)	1												42	1356
1990	†SF	11(11, RB)	141	439	3.1(26)	1	25	201	8.0(31)	0												6	550
1991	LARd	15(13, RB)	162	590	3.6(15)	1	17	136	8.0(20)	0												6	668
1992	†Min	15(1)	105	416	4.0(21)	4	22	164	7.5(22)	0												24	538
1993	†Min	14(3)	38	119	3.1(11)	1	19	169	8.9(31)	1										k		12	215
NFL	11	165(133)	1991	8189	4.1(71)	56	566	4911	8.7(73)	17										k		438	11288

CRAIG, STEVE Steven Arthur, TE, 6´3˝/231 lbs; Northwestern; 1974: Min, rnd 3; B3/13/1951 Akron, OH

1974	†Min	14	—	—	—	—	4	26	6.5(10)	1												6	18
1975	†Min	14(1)	—	—	—	—	6	68	11.3(17)	0												0	.34
1976	†Min	14	—	—	—	—	3	33	11.0(17)	0												0	17
1977	†Min	14	—	—	—	—	1	14	14.0(14)	0												0	7
1978	†Min	16	—	—	—	—	4	31	7.8(9)	0										k		0	1
NFL	5	72(1)	—	—	—	—	18	172	9.6(17)	1										k		6	76

CRAIN, MILT Thomas Milton, FB, 6´2˝/225 lbs; Baylor; 1943: Pit, rnd 15; B12/25/1921 San Antonio, TX, D12/13/2000 Houston, TX

| 1944 | Bos | 10(4) | 26 | 78 | 3.0(8) | 0 | 1 | 16 | 16.0(16) | 0 | | | | | | | | | | Pkpi | | 0 | 84 |

CRAKES, JOE Joseph Henry, E, 6´1˝/205 lbs; South Dakota; B12/29/1907 Platte, SD, D3/23/1976 Victorville, CA **1932** ChiC 1 (0)

| 1933 | Cin | 9(4) | — | — | — | — | 4 | 40 | 10.0 | 0 | 1 | 0 | 0.0 | 0 | 0 | 0 | — | — | | | | 0 | 20 |
| NFL | 2 | 10(4) | — | — | — | — | 4 | 40 | 10.0 | 0 | 1 | 0 | 0.0 | 0 | 0 | 0 | — | — | | | | 0 | 20 |

CRAMER, CARL Carl, B, 5´11˝/184 lbs; Hamline; B12/20/1897 Winnebago, MN, D2/1978 Canal Fulton, OH **[K]** **1920** Cle 7 (4, FB) **1921** Akr 11 (11, WB), 31 **1922** Akr 10 (10, WB), 36 **1923** Akr 7 (7, WB) **1924** Akr 8 (7, FB), 9 **1925** Akr 5 (1) **1926** Akr 8 (8, FB) **NFL** 56 (48), 76 [7 yrs]

CRAMER, CASEY Casey R., RB, 6´2˝/235 lbs; Dartmouth; 2004: TB, rnd 7; B1/5/1982 Middleton, WI **2004** Car 6 (1) **2005**†Car 1 (0) **NFL** 7 (1) [2 yrs]

CRANE, DENNIS Dennis Walter, DT-T, 6´7˝/260 lbs; USC; 1968: Was, rnd 4; B2/23/1945 San Bernardino, CA **1968** Was 14 (14, LDT) **1969** Was 10 (LDT) **1970** NYG 9 **NFL** 33 (14) [3 yrs]

CRANE, GARY Gary Don, LB, 6´5˝/230 lbs; Arkansas State; 1969: Den, rnd 14; B5/19/1946 Dexter, MO **1969** Den-A 6

CRANE, PAUL Paul Edward, LB-C, 6´3˝/212 lbs; Alabama; B1/29/1944 Pascagoula, MS **1966** NYJ-A 14 (LLB) **1967** NYJ-A 11 **1968**†NYJ-A 13 **1969**†NYJ-A 14 (llb) **1970** NYJ 14 **1971** NYJ 14 **1972** NYJ 8 **NFL** 88 [7 yrs]

CRANGLE, JACK Walter Francis, B, 6´1˝/200 lbs; Illinois; B6/8/1899 Onarga, IL, D9/1/1944 Independence, MO **1923** ChiC☆9 (8, FB), 18

CRANGLE, MIKE Michael, DE, 6´4˝/243 lbs; Cincinnati; Tennessee-Martin; 1972: NO, rnd 4; B2/3/1947 Chicago, IL **1972** NO 13

CRASS, BILL William Arthur, FB, 6´0˝/205 lbs; LSU; B6/9/1911 Childress, TX, D5/27/1996 Pasadena, CA

| 1937 | ChiC | 3(0) | 5 | 8 | 1.6 | 0 | — | — | — | — | 1 | 0 | 0.0 | 0 | 0 | 0 | — | — | | | | 0 | 8 |

CRAVEN, BILL William Moten, DB, 5´11˝/190 lbs; Harvard; B12/18/1951 Ranson, WV **1976** Cle 13

CRAVER, AARON Aaron LaRenze, RB, 6´0˝/218 lbs; Fresno State; 1991: Mia, rnd 3; B12/18/1968 Los Angeles, CA

1991	Mia	14(0)	20	58	2.9(7)	1	8	67	8.4(25)	0										k		6	237
1992	†Mia	6(0)	3	9	3.0(8)	0	—	—	—	—										k		0	63
1994	†Mia	8(0)	6	43	7.2(19)	0	24	237	9.9(28)	0												2	162
1995	Den	16(10, FB)	73	333	4.6(23)	5	43	369	8.6(32)	1										k		36	518
1996	†Den	15(15, FB)	59	232	3.9(28)	2	39	297	7.6(39)	1	1	0	0.0	0	0	0	—	—		k		18	406
1997	SD	15(5, fb)	20	71	3.6(22)	0	4	26	6.5(20)	0										k		0	107
1998	NO	16(10, FB)	45	180	4.0(25)	2	33	214	6.5(49)	2	1	0	0.0	0	0	0	—	—		k	1	30	434
1999	NO	13(10, FB)	17	40	2.4(8)	0	19	154	8.1(29)	0										k		0	105
NFL	8	103(50)	243	966	4.0(28)	10	170	1364	8.0(49)	4	2	0	0.0	0	0	0	—	—		k	1	92	2030

CRAVER, KEYUO Keyou Boderek, DB, 5´10˝/195 lbs; Nebraska; 2002: NO, rnd 4; B8/22/1980 Dallas, TX **2002** NO 10 (1) **2003** NO 12 (0) **NFL** 22 (1) [2 yrs]

CRAWFORD, BILL William, G, 6´2˝/235 lbs; British Columbia; B7/17/1937, Canada **1960** NYG 4

CRAWFORD, CASEY Casey Stuart, TE, 6´6˝/255 lbs; Virginia; B8/1/1977 Washington, DC

2000	Car	8(0)	—	—	—	—	4	47	11.8(16)	1												6	29
2001	Car	3(1)	—	—	—	—	1	10	10.0(10)	0											1	6	-2
2002	TB	4(0)	—	—	—	—	—	—	—	—										k		0	0
NFL	3	15(1)	—	—	—	—	5	57	11.4(16)	1										k	1	12	27

CRAWFORD, CHARLES Charles, RB, 6´2˝/235 lbs; Oklahoma State; 1986: Phi, rnd S7; B3/8/1964 Bristow, OK **1987** Phi 2 (0)

| 1986 | Phi | 16(5, rb) | 28 | 88 | 3.1(15) | 1 | — | — | — | — | | | | | | | | | | k | | 6 | 190 |
| NFL | 2 | 18(5) | 28 | 88 | 3.1(15) | 1 | — | — | — | — | | | | | | | | | | k | | 6 | 190 |

CRAWFORD, DENNY Denver Junior, G-T, 6´0˝/190 lbs; Tennessee; 1947: GB, rnd 15; B6/16/1921 Kingsport, TN, D8/14/2005 Kingsport, TN **1948** NYY-A 8 (6, LG)

CRAWFORD, DERRICK Derrick Lorwenzo, WR, 5´10˝/185 lbs; Memphis; 1984: SF, rnd S1; B9/3/1960 Memphis, TN

| 1986 | †SF | 10(0) | — | — | — | — | 5 | 70 | 14.0(42) | 0 | | | | | | | | | | kp | | 0 | 85 |

CRAWFORD, ED Edward Slater, DB-E, 6´3˝/185 lbs; Mississippi; 1956: NYG, rnd 13; B7/25/1934 Corinth, MS

| 1957 | NYG | 12 | — | — | — | — | 2 | 40 | 20.0(27) | 0 | | | | | | | | | | ki | | 0 | 26 |

CRAWFORD, ELBERT Elbert, G-C, 6´3˝/280 lbs; Arkansas; 1990: LARm, rnd 8; B6/20/1966 Chicago, IL **1990** NE 14 (0) **1991** NE 16 (16, LG) **NFL** 30 (16) [2 yrs]

CRAWFORD, FRED Frederick Eugene, E-DE-T, 6´2˝/200 lbs; Duke; B7/27/1910 Waynesville, NC, D3/5/1974 Tallahassee, FL

| 1935 | ChiB | 6(0) | — | — | — | — | 1 | 10 | 10.0(10) | 0 | | | | | | | | | | | | 0 | 5 |

CRAWFORD, HILTON Hilton, DB, 6´2˝/195 lbs; Grambling State; 1969: SF, rnd 9; B2/2/1945 Converse, LA **1969** Buf-A 7

CRAWFORD, JIM James Lee, HB-FB, 6´1˝/205 lbs; Wyoming; 1957: Pit, rnd 14; B8/26/1935 Greybull, WY **[K]**

1960	Bos-A	14(fb)	51	238	4.7(39)	2	10	92	9.2(40)	0										K		14	304
1961	Bos-A	10	41	148	3.6(34)	0	9	85	9.4(25)	0												0	191
1962	Bos-A	14(hb)	139	459	3.3(22)	2	22	224	10.2(44)	2										k		26	595
1963	†Bos-A	14(HB)	71	233	3.3(19)	1	10	89	8.9(28)	0	2	2	100.0	27	13.5(15)	0	0	0	—	—		6	301
1964	Bos-A	2	—	—	—	—	1	11	11.0(11)	0												0	6
NFL	5	54	302	1078	3.6(39)	5	52	501	9.6(44)	2	2	2	100.0	27	13.5(15)	0	0	0	—	Kk		46	1396

CRAWFORD, KEITH Keith LaCharles, WR-DB, 6´2˝/188 lbs; Howard Payne; B11/21/1970 Palestine, TX **1995**†GB 13 (0) **1996** SL 16 (1) **1998** KC 8 (0)

| 1993 | †NYG | 7(0) | — | — | — | — | 1 | 6 | 6.0(6) | 0 | | | | | | | | | | | | 0 | 3 |
| 1997 | SL | 15(2) | 2 | 32 | 16.0(23) | 0 | 11 | 232 | 21.1(69) | 0 | | | | | | | | | | | | 0 | 148 |

YEAR	TEAM	G(GS, POS)	RUSH	YD	AVG(LG)	TD	REC	YD	AVG(LG)	TD	PASS	COMP	PCT	YD	AVG(LG)	TD	INT	SK	YD	QBR	KPR	OTD	PTS	TAY
1999	GB	3(0)	—	—	—	—	1	14	14.0(14)	0	—	—	—	—	—	—	—	—	—	—	—	—	0	7
NFL	6	62(3)	2	32	16.0(23)	0	13	252	19.4(69)	0	—	—	—	—	—	—	—	—	—	—	k	—	0	145

CRAWFORD, KEN   Kenneth James, B, 5´11˝/185 lbs; Miami (OH); B9/1898 Woodstock, CA, D3/9/1957   **1920** Akr 7 (1) **1921** Ham 1 (0) **1921** Cin 3 (3, RH) **1923** Day 1 (0) **1925** Ham 1 (1) **NFL** 13 (5) [4 yrs]

CRAWFORD, MIKE   Michael Gerald, RB, 5´10˝/215 lbs; Arizona State; 1986: TB, rnd 12; B1/3/1964 San Fernando, CA   **1987** Cle 3 (0)

CRAWFORD, MIKE   Michael Joseph, LB, 6´1˝/238 lbs; UNLV; 1997: Mia, rnd 6; B10/29/1974 Reno, NV   **1997**†Mia 7 (0)

CRAWFORD, MUSH   Walter Charles, T-G, 6´0˝/200 lbs; Beloit; Lake Forest; Illinois; B12/23/1898 Waukegan, IL, D10/27/1966 Roanoke, VA   **1925** ChiB 3 (0) **1927** NYY 9 (7, lt) **NFL** 12 (7) [2 yrs]

CRAWFORD, RUFUS   Rufus, RB, 5´10˝/180 lbs; Virginia State; B5/21/1955 Gastonia, NC

| 1978 | Sea | 16 | 8 | 19 | 2.4(11) | 0 | 4 | 25 | 6.3(8) | 0 | — | — | — | — | — | — | — | — | — | kp | — | 0 | 450 |

CRAWFORD, TIM   Timothy, LB, 6´4˝/245 lbs; Texas Tech; 1986: NYJ, rnd 3; B12/17/1962 Houston, TX   **1987** Cle 3 (3)

CRAWFORD, VERNON   Vernon Dean, LB, 6´4˝/245 lbs; Florida State; 1997: NE, rnd 5; B6/25/1974 Texas City, TX   **1997** NE 16 (0) **1998**†NE 16 (1) **1999** NE 9 (0) **NFL** 41 (1) [3 yrs]

CRAYNE, DICK   Richard Cherry, FB, 6´0˝/205 lbs; Iowa; 1936: Bkn, rnd 1; B4/24/1913 West Chester, IA, D8/1985 Le Mars, IA [K]

1936	Bkn	12(12, FB)	64	203	3.2	1	1	32	32.0(32)	0	2	1	50.0	52	26.0(52)	0	0	—	—	—	K	—	7	255
1937	Bkn	10(4)	47	135	2.9	0	1	4	4.0(4)	0	4	2	50.0	20	5.0	0	0	—	—	—	K	—	3	147
NFL	2	22(16)	111	338	3.0	1	2	36	18.0(32)	0	6	3	50.0	72	12.0(52)	0	0	—	—	—	K	—	10	402

CRAYTON, PATRICK   Patrick, WR, 6´1˝/205 lbs; Northwestern Oklahoma State; 2004: Dal, rnd 7; B4/7/1979 De Soto, TX

2004	Dal	8(0)	—	—	—	—	12	162	13.5(39)	1	1	0	0.0	0	0.0	0	0	—	—	—	p	—	6	60
2005	Dal	11(0)	1	0	0.0(0)	0	22	341	15.5(63)	2	—	—	—	—	—	—	—	—	—	—	p	—	12	232
NFL	2	19(0)	1	0	0.0(0)	0	34	503	14.8(63)	3	1	0	0.0	0	0.0	0	0	—	—	—	p	—	18	292

CRECION, GABE   Gabriel John, TE, 6´5˝/255 lbs; UCLA; B7/9/1977 West Hills, CA   **2004** SF 1 (0)

CREECH, BOB   Robert Edwin, LB, 6´3˝/236 lbs; TCU; 1971: Phi, rnd 14; B1/26/1949 Corpus Christi, TX   **1971** Phi 3 **1972** Phi 13 (RLB) **1973** NO 2 **NFL** 18 [3 yrs]

CREEKMUR, LOU   Louis, T-G-DG-DT, 6´4˝/246 lbs; William & Mary; 1948: Phi, rnd 26/LAD-A, rnd 28; B1/22/1927 Hopelawn, NJ; HOF 1996   **1950** Det◇12 (LG) **1951** Det★12 (LG) **1952**†Det★12 (LT) **1953**†Det★12 (LT) **1954**†Det★12 (LT) **1955** Det★12 (MG) **1956** Det★12 (LT) **1957**†Det★12 (LT) **1958** Det★12 (LT) **1959** Det 8 (LT) **NFL** 116 [10 yrs]

CREGAR, BILL   William Osmund, G-LB, 5´11˝/195 lbs; Holy Cross; 1947: Pit, rnd 18; B5/2/1925 Newark, NJ   **1947**†Pit 11 (0) **1948** Pit 12 (6, RG) **NFL** 23 (6) [2 yrs]

CREIGHTON, MILAN   Milan Standish, E, 6´0˝/190 lbs; Arkansas; B1/21/1908 Gothenburg, NE [C]

1931	ChiC	9(5, LE)	—	—	—	—	—	—	—	—	—	—	—	—	—	—	—	—	—	—	—	12	0
1932	ChiC	10(9, LE)	—	—	—	—	5	74	14.8	—	—	—	—	—	—	—	—	—	—	—	—	0	37
1933	ChiC	11(8, LE)	—	—	—	—	7	80	11.4	—	—	—	—	—	—	—	—	—	—	—	—	0	40
1934	ChiC	9(8, LE)	1	12	12.0(12)	0	6	84	14.0	0	—	—	—	—	—	—	—	—	—	—	—	0	54
1935	ChiC	8(1)	—	—	—	—	1	8	8.0(8)	0	—	—	—	—	—	—	—	—	—	—	—	0	4
1936	ChiC	6(6, LE)	—	—	—	—	—	—	—	—	—	—	—	—	—	—	—	—	—	—	—	—	—
1937	ChiC	2(0)	—	—	—	—	—	—	—	—	—	—	—	—	—	—	—	—	—	—	—	—	—
NFL	7	55(37)	1	12	12.0(12)	0	19	246	12.9(8)	—	—	—	—	—	—	—	—	—	—	—	—	12	135

CREMER, TED   Theodore Roosevelt, E-DE, 6´2˝/209 lbs; Auburn; B3/16/1919 Corbin, KY, D11/20/1980 Birmingham, AL   **1948** Det 4 (0) **1948** GB 3 (0)

1946	Det	11(9, LE)	—	—	—	—	15	179	11.9(39)	—	—	—	—	—	—	—	—	—	—	—	—	0	90
1947	Det	12(10, RE)	—	—	—	—	13	117	9.0(32)	1	—	—	—	—	—	—	—	—	—	—	—	6	64
NFL	3	30(19)	—	—	—	—	28	296	10.6(39)	1	—	—	—	—	—	—	—	—	—	—	—	6	153

CRENNEL, CARL   Carl Lee, LB, 6´1˝/230 lbs; West Virginia; 1970: Pit, rnd 9; B9/14/1948 Lynchburg, VA   **1970** Pit 3

CRENSHAW, LEON   Leon, DT, 6´7˝/280 lbs; Tuskegee; B7/14/1943 Greenville, AL   **1968** GB 10

CRENSHAW, WILLIS   Willis Clarence, RB, 6´2˝/230 lbs; Kansas State; 1963: SL, rnd 9/Buf, rnd 26; B7/16/1941 St. Louis, MO

1964	SL	14	60	297	4.9(49)	1	8	58	7.3(19)	0	—	—	—	—	—	—	—	—	—	—	k	—	6	481
1965	SL	14(FB)	127	437	3.4(27)	0	23	232	10.1(78)	1	—	—	—	—	—	—	—	—	—	—	k	—	6	551
1966	SL	14(FB)	94	360	3.8(33)	0	15	46	3.1(19)	0	—	—	—	—	—	—	—	—	—	—	k	—	0	383
1967	SL	14	44	149	3.4(23)	0	6	30	5.0(12)	0	—	—	—	—	—	—	—	—	—	—	k	—	0	148
1968	SL	14(FB)	203	813	4.0(66)	6	23	232	10.1(42)	1	—	—	—	—	—	—	—	—	—	—	k	—	42	1008
1969	SL	14(fb)	55	172	3.1(26)	3	11	94	8.5(31)	0	—	—	—	—	—	—	—	—	—	—	k	—	18	223
1970	Den	12(12, FB)	69	200	2.9(25)	5	18	105	5.8(39)	1	—	—	—	—	—	—	—	—	—	—	—	—	36	308
NFL	7	96(12)	652	2428	3.7(66)	15	104	797	7.7(78)	3	—	—	—	—	—	—	—	—	—	—	k	—	108	3102

CRESPINO, BOBBY   Robert, SE-TE, 6´5˝/225 lbs; Mississippi; 1961: Cle, rnd 1/Oak, rnd 6; B1/11/1938 Duncan, MS

1961	Cle	13(se)	—	—	—	—	2	62	31.0(49)	1	—	—	—	—	—	—	—	—	—	—	—	6	36
1962	Cle	14	—	—	—	—	2	13	6.5(9)	0	—	—	—	—	—	—	—	—	—	—	—	0	7
1963	Cle	14	—	—	—	—	2	22	11.0(18)	1	—	—	—	—	—	—	—	—	—	—	—	6	16
1964	NYG	13	—	—	—	—	12	165	13.8(27)	0	—	—	—	—	—	—	—	—	—	—	—	0	83
1965	NYG	14	—	—	—	—	7	57	8.1(15)	4	—	—	—	—	—	—	—	—	—	—	—	24	49
1966	NYG	14	—	—	—	—	16	167	10.4(19)	2	—	—	—	—	—	—	—	—	—	—	—	12	94
1967	NYG	14	—	—	—	—	10	125	12.5(24)	1	—	—	—	—	—	—	—	—	—	—	k	—	6	60
1968	NYG	11	—	—	—	—	7	130	18.6(43)	0	—	—	—	—	—	—	—	—	—	—	—	0	65
NFL	8	107	—	—	—	—	58	741	12.8(49)	9	—	—	—	—	—	—	—	—	—	—	k	—	54	408

CRESWELL, SMILEY   Smiley Lawrence, DE, 6´4˝/251 lbs; Michigan State; 1983: NE, rnd 5; B12/11/1959 Everett, WA   **1985** Phi 3 (0) **1985**†NE 0 (0) **NFL** 3 (0) [1 yr]

CREWS, RON   Ronald Edward, NT-DE, 6´4˝/256 lbs; Notre Dame; UNLV; 1980: Cle, rnd 4; B10/9/1956 Springfield, IL   **1980**†Cle 16 (0)

CREWS, TERRY   Terry Alan, LB, 6´2˝/245 lbs; Western Michigan; 1991: LARm, rnd 11; B7/30/1968 Flint, MI   **1991** LARm 6 (0) **1993** SD 10 (0) **1995** Was 16 (0) **NFL** 32 (0) [3 yrs]

CRIBBS, JAMES   James Clark, DE, 6´3˝/269 lbs; Memphis; 1989: Det, rnd 12; B7/10/1966 Memphis, TN   **1989** Det 7 (0)

CRIBBS, JOE   Joe Stanier, RB, 5´11˝/190 lbs; Auburn; 1980: Buf, rnd 2; B1/5/1958 Sulligent, AL

1980	†Buf★	16(16, RB)	306	1185	3.9(48)	11	52	415	8.0(21)	1	1	1	100.0	13	13.0(13)	0	0	—	—	—	kp	—	72	1532
1981	†Buf★	15(15, RB)	257	1097	4.3(35)	3	40	603	15.1(45)	7	1	1	100.0	9	9.0(9)	1	0	—	—	—	—	—	60	1473
1982	†Buf	7(6, RB)	134	633	4.7(62)	3	13	99	7.6(31)	0	1	0	0.0	0	0.0	0	0	—	—	—	—	—	18	673
1983	†Buf★	16(16, RB)	263	1131	4.3(45)	3	57	524	9.2(33)	7	2	1	50.0	3	1.5(3)	0	0	—	—	—	—	—	60	1460
1985	Buf	10(5, RB)	122	399	3.3(16)	1	18	142	7.9(32)	0	—	—	—	—	—	—	—	—	—	—	—	6	480
1986	†SF	14(10, RB)	152	590	3.9(19)	4	35	346	9.9(33)	0	—	—	—	—	—	—	—	—	—	—	—	30	813
1987	†SF	11(2)	70	300	4.3(20)	1	9	70	7.8(16)	0	—	—	—	—	—	—	—	—	—	—	k	1	12	487
1988	Ind	1(0)	—	—	—	—	—	—	—	—	—	—	—	—	—	—	—	—	—	—	—	0	
1988	Mia	12(0)	5	21	4.2(11)	0	—	—	—	—	—	—	—	—	—	—	—	—	—	—	k	—	0	269
NFL	8	102(70)	1309	5356	4.1(62)	27	224	2199	9.8(65)	15	5	3	60.0	25	5.0(13)	1	1	—	—	—	kp	1	258	7186

CRIBBS, JOSH   Joshua, WR, 6´1˝/192 lbs; Kent State; B6/9/1983 Upper Marlboro, MD

| 2005 | Cle | 14(0) | — | — | — | — | 7 | 70 | 7.0(17) | 0 | — | — | — | — | — | — | — | — | — | — | kp | 1 | 6 | 433 |

CRIMMINS, BERNIE   Bernard Anthony, G-HB-FB, 5´11˝/195 lbs; Notre Dame; B4/14/1919 Louisville, KY, D3/19/1993 West Lafayette, IN   **1945** GB 6 (0)

CRISLER, HAL   Harold James, E, 6´4˝/215 lbs; San Jose State; Iowa State; B12/31/1923 Richmond, CA, D11/2/1987 Santa Clara County, CA

1946	Bos	11(8, RE)	4	6	1.5(6)	0	32	385	12.0(62)	5	—	—	—	—	—	—	—	—	—	—	k	—	30	216
1947	Bos	10(1)	—	—	—	—	25	363	14.5(49)	2	—	—	—	—	—	—	—	—	—	—	—	12	192
1948	Was	11(1)	—	—	—	—	33	599	18.2(79)	6	—	—	—	—	—	—	—	—	—	pi	—	36	382
1949	Was	11(7, LE)	—	—	—	—	26	388	14.9(47)	4	—	—	—	—	—	—	—	—	—	—	—	24	214

YEAR	TEAM	G(GS, POS)	RUSH	YD	AVG(LG)	TD	REC	YD	AVG(LG)	TD	PASS	COMP	PCT	YD	AVG(LG)	TD	INT	SK	YD	QBR	KPR	OTD	PTS	TAY
1950	Bal	10(5, RE)	—	—	—	—	19	307	16.2(62)	5	—	—	—	—	—	—	—	—	—	—	—	—	30	179
NFL	5	53(22)	4	6	1.5(6)	0	135	2042	15.1(79)	22	—	—	—	—	—	—	—	—	—	—	kpi	—	132	1181

CRISMAN, JOEL Joel Devere, G, 6´5˝/302 lbs; USC; B2/3/1971 Cherokee, IA **1996** TB 9 (0)

CRISS, SHADWICK Shadwick Leon, DB, 5´11˝/184 lbs; Missouri; B1/11/1976 Sherman, TX **2000** Jax 3 (0)

CRISSY, CRIS William Robert, DB, 5´11˝/195 lbs; Princeton; 1981: NE, rnd 12; B2/3/1959 Penn Yan, NY **1981** Was 1 (0)

CRIST, CHUCK Charles Thomas, DB, 6´2˝/205 lbs; Penn State; B1/16/1951 Salamanca, NY **[I]** **1972** NYG 14 **1973** NYG 14 **1974** NYG 13 (SS) **1975** NO 8 **1976** NO 14 (14, SS) **1977** NO 14 (SS) **1978** SF 15 (15, SS/fs) **NFL** 92 (29) [7 yrs]

CRISWELL, JEFF Jeffrey L., T-G, 6´7˝/291 lbs; Graceland College (IA); B3/7/1964 Grinnell, IA **1987** Ind 3 (3) **1988** NYJ 15 (12, LT) **1989** NYJ 16 (16, LT) **1990** NYJ 16 (16, LT) **1991**†NYJ 16 (16, LT) **1992** NYJ 14 (13, LT) **1993** NYJ 16 (16, LT) **1994** NYJ 15 (15, LT) **1995**†KC 15 (4) **1996** KC 15 (5, lt) **1997**†KC 16 (16, LT) **1998** KC 14 (14, LT) **NFL** 171 (146) [12 yrs]

CRISWELL, KIRBY Kirby Lynn, LB-DE, 6´5˝/238 lbs; Kansas; 1980: Cin, rnd 2; B8/31/1957 Grinnell, IA **1980** SL 4 (0) **1981** SL 2 (0) **NFL** 6 (0) [2 yrs]

CRISWELL, RAY Ray Alan, P, 6´0˝/192 lbs; Florida; 1986: Phi, rnd 5; B8/16/1963 Lake City, FL **[K]**

YEAR	TEAM	G(GS, POS)	RUSH	YD	AVG(LG)	TD	REC	YD	AVG(LG)	TD	PASS	COMP	PCT	YD	AVG(LG)	TD	INT	SK	YD	QBR	KPR	OTD	PTS	TAY
1987	TB	3(0)	1	0	0.0(0)	0	—	—	—	—	—	—	—	—	—	—	—	—	—	—	P	—	0	0
1988	TB	16(0)	2	0	0.0(0)	0	—	—	—	—	—	—	—	—	—	—	—	—	—	—	KP	—	1	0
NFL	2	19(0)	3	0	0.0	0	—	—	—	—	—	—	—	—	—	—	—	—	—	—	KP	—	1	0

CRITCHFIELD, HANK Henry Brown, C, 5´10˝/207 lbs; Wooster; B6/14/1905 Columbus, OH, D7/29/1980 Wooster, OH **1931** Cle 9 (9, C)

CRITCHFIELD, LARRY Lawrence K., G, 5´11˝/195 lbs; Grove City; B1/6/1908 Ursina, PA, D6/30/1965 Confluence, PA **1933** Pit 11 (10, LG)

CRITER, KEN Kenneth William, LB, 6´0˝/225 lbs; Wisconsin; B2/17/1947 Fond du Lac, WI **1969** Den-A 14 **1970** Den 14 (1) **1971** Den 11 **1972** Den 8 **1973** Den 14 **1974** Den 14 **NFL** 75 (1) [6 yrs]

CRITTENDEN, RAY Raymond C., WR, 6´1˝/192 lbs; Virginia Tech; B3/1/1970 Washington, DC

YEAR	TEAM	G(GS, POS)	RUSH	YD	AVG(LG)	TD	REC	YD	AVG(LG)	TD	PASS	COMP	PCT	YD	AVG(LG)	TD	INT	SK	YD	QBR	KPR	OTD	PTS	TAY
1993	NE	16(2)	1	-3	-3.0(-3)	0	16	293	18.3(44)	1	—	—	—	—	—	—	—	—	—	—	kp	—	6	309
1994	†NE	16(2)	—	—	—	—	28	379	13.5(32)	3	—	—	—	—	—	—	—	—	—	—	kp	—	18	365
1997	SD	2(0)	—	—	—	—	—	—	—	—	—	—	—	—	—	—	—	—	—	—	—	—	—	—
NFL	3	34(4)	1	-3	-3.0(-3)	0	44	672	15.3(44)	4	—	—	—	—	—	—	—	—	—	—	kp	—	24	673

CRITTENDON, JACK Jack, E, 6´1˝/190 lbs; Wayne State (MI); B8/9/1930 Ferndale, MI, D2/2/1993 Toronto, Canada **[K]**

YEAR	TEAM	G(GS, POS)	RUSH	YD	AVG(LG)	TD	REC	YD	AVG(LG)	TD	PASS	COMP	PCT	YD	AVG(LG)	TD	INT	SK	YD	QBR	KPR	OTD	PTS	TAY
1954	ChiC	10	—	—	—	—	5	48	9.6(15)	0	—	—	—	—	—	—	—	—	—	—	K	—	0	24

CROCICCHIA, JIM James Francis, QB, 6´2˝/209 lbs; Pennsylvania; B2/19/1964 Waterbury, CT

YEAR	TEAM	G(GS, POS)	RUSH	YD	AVG(LG)	TD	REC	YD	AVG(LG)	TD	PASS	COMP	PCT	YD	AVG(LG)	TD	INT	SK	YD	QBR	KPR	OTD	PTS	TAY
1987	NYG	1(1)	4	5	1.3(7)	0	—	—	—	—	15	6	40.0	89	5.9(46)	1	0	2	17	—	—	—	0	55

CROCKER, CHRIS Christopher Alan, DB, 5´11˝/194 lbs; Marshall; 2003: Cle, rnd 3; B3/9/1980 Chesapeake, VA **2003** Cle 16 (1) **2004** Cle 12 (5, fs) **2005** Cle 16 (16, SS) **NFL** 44 (22) [3 yrs]

CROCKETT, BOBBY Robert Paul, SE-WR, 6´3˝/200 lbs; Arkansas; 1966: Buf, rnd 10/NYG, rnd 19; B4/3/1943 Briggsville, AR

YEAR	TEAM	G(GS, POS)	RUSH	YD	AVG(LG)	TD	REC	YD	AVG(LG)	TD	PASS	COMP	PCT	YD	AVG(LG)	TD	INT	SK	YD	QBR	KPR	OTD	PTS	TAY
1966	†Buf-A	14(12, SE)	—	—	—	—	31	533	17.2(53)	3	—	—	—	—	—	—	—	—	—	—	—	—	18	282
1968	Buf-A	9	—	—	—	—	6	76	12.7(23)	0	—	—	—	—	—	—	—	—	—	—	—	—	0	38
1969	Buf-A	5	—	—	—	—	4	50	12.5(19)	0	—	—	—	—	—	—	—	—	—	—	—	—	0	25
NFL	3	28(12)	—	—	—	—	41	659	16.1(53)	3	—	—	—	—	—	—	—	—	—	—	—	—	18	345

CROCKETT, HENRI Henri Woodrau, LB, 6´2˝/240 lbs; Florida State; 1997: Atl, rnd 4; B10/28/1974 Pompano Beach, FL **1997** Atl 16 (10, RLB) **1998**†Atl 10 (10, RLB) **1999** Atl 16 (14, LLB) **2000** Atl 15 (12, RLB) **2001** Atl 16 (15, RLB) **2002** Min 14 (11, RLB) **2003** Min 16 (15, LLB) **NFL** 103 (87) [7 yrs]

CROCKETT, MONTE Monte Julius, HB-TE, 6´4˝/218 lbs; New Mexico Highlands; B7/14/1938 Talcott, WV

YEAR	TEAM	G(GS, POS)	RUSH	YD	AVG(LG)	TD	REC	YD	AVG(LG)	TD	PASS	COMP	PCT	YD	AVG(LG)	TD	INT	SK	YD	QBR	KPR	OTD	PTS	TAY
1960	Buf-A	14	—	—	—	—	14	173	12.4(41)	1	—	—	—	—	—	—	—	—	—	—	p	—	6	92
1961	Buf-A	14	—	—	—	—	20	325	16.3(51)	0	—	—	—	—	—	—	—	—	—	—	k	—	0	148
1962	Buf-A	12(HB)	—	—	—	—	1	14	14.0(14)	0	—	—	—	—	—	—	—	—	—	—	—	—	0	7
NFL	3	40	—	—	—	—	35	512	14.6(51)	1	—	—	—	—	—	—	—	—	—	—	kp	—	6	246

CROCKETT, RAY Donald Ray, DB, 5´10˝/185 lbs; Baylor; 1989: Det, rnd 4; B1/5/1967 Dallas, TX **[I]** **1989** Det 16 (0) **1990** Det 16 (6, lcb) **1991**†Det 16 (16, LCB) **1992** Det 15 (15, LCB) **1993** Det 16 (16, LCB) **1994** Den 14 (14, RCB) **1995** Den 16 (16, LCB) **1996**†Den 15 (15, LCB) **1997**†Den 16 (16, LCB) **1998**†Den 16 (16, LCB) **1999** Den 16 (16, LCB) **2000**†Den 13 (11, LCB) **2001** KC 14 (12, LCB) **2002** KC 15 (5, rcb) **NFL** 214 (174) [14 yrs]

CROCKETT, WILLIS Willis Robert, LB, 6´3˝/234 lbs; Georgia Tech; 1989: Dal, rnd 5; B8/25/1966 Douglas, GA **1990** Dal 13 (0)

CROCKETT, ZACK Zachary Theopolis, FB, 6´2˝/240 lbs; Florida State; 1995: Ind, rnd 3; B12/2/1972 Pompano Beach, FL

YEAR	TEAM	G(GS, POS)	RUSH	YD	AVG(LG)	TD	REC	YD	AVG(LG)	TD	PASS	COMP	PCT	YD	AVG(LG)	TD	INT	SK	YD	QBR	KPR	OTD	PTS	TAY
1995	†Ind	16(0)	1	0	0.0(0)	0	2	35	17.5(19)	0	—	—	—	—	—	—	—	—	—	—	—	—	0	18
1996	Ind	5(5, fb)	31	164	5.3(25)	0	11	96	8.7(32)	1	—	—	—	—	—	—	—	—	—	—	—	—	6	217
1997	Ind	16(11, FB)	95	300	3.2(20)	1	15	112	7.5(19)	0	—	—	—	—	—	—	—	—	—	—	—	—	6	366
1998	Ind	2(1)	2	5	2.5(5)	0	1	1	1.0(1)	0	—	—	—	—	—	—	—	—	—	—	—	—	0	6
1998	†Jax	10(1)	—	—	—	—	1	4	4.0(4)	0	—	—	—	—	—	—	—	—	—	—	—	—	0	2
1999	Oak	13(1)	45	91	2.0(7)	4	8	56	7.0(12)	1	—	—	—	—	—	—	—	—	—	—	—	—	30	164
2000	†Oak	16(4)	43	130	3.0(11)	7	10	62	6.2(15)	0	—	—	—	—	—	—	—	—	—	—	—	—	42	231
2001	†Oak	16(0)	57	145	2.5(10)	6	2	10	5.0(8)	0	—	—	—	—	—	—	—	—	—	—	—	—	36	210
2002	†Oak	16(0)	40	118	3.0(33)	8	—	—	—	—	—	—	—	—	—	—	—	—	—	—	—	—	48	198
2003	Oak	16(7, FB)	48	145	3.0(44)	7	7	53	7.6(16)	0	—	—	—	—	—	—	—	—	—	—	—	—	42	242
2004	Oak	16(9, FB)	48	232	4.8(47)	2	16	87	5.4(11)	0	—	—	—	—	—	—	—	—	—	—	—	—	12	296
2005	Oak	16(9, FB)	60	208	3.5(24)	1	13	111	8.5(23)	0	—	—	—	—	—	—	—	—	—	—	—	—	6	274
NFL	11	158(48)	470	1538	3.3(47)	36	86	627	7.3(32)	2	—	—	—	—	—	—	—	—	—	—	—	—	228	2222

CROEL, MIKE Michael Stephen, LB-DE, 6´3˝/238 lbs; Nebraska; 1991: Den, rnd 1; B6/6/1969 Detroit, MI **1991**†Den 13 (10, RILB) **1992** Den 16 (16, LOLB) **1993**†Den 16 (16, LOLB) **1994** Den 13 (12, LLB) **1995** NYG 16 (14, LLB) **1996** Bal 16 (16, LOLB) **1998** Sea 12 (0) **NFL** 102 (84) [7 yrs]

CROFT, ABE Abraham, E, 6´0˝/183 lbs; SMU; 1944: ChiB, rnd 5; B3/12/1920 Houston, TX, D12/2/1972 Houston, TX

YEAR	TEAM	G(GS, POS)	RUSH	YD	AVG(LG)	TD	REC	YD	AVG(LG)	TD	PASS	COMP	PCT	YD	AVG(LG)	TD	INT	SK	YD	QBR	KPR	OTD	PTS	TAY
1944	ChiB	10(0)	—	—	—	—	9	140	15.6(67)	2	—	—	—	—	—	—	—	—	—	—	i	—	12	94
1945	ChiB	1(0)	—	—	—	—	2	12	6.0(10)	0	—	—	—	—	—	—	—	—	—	—	—	—	0	6
NFL	2	11(0)	—	—	—	—	11	152	13.8(67)	2	—	—	—	—	—	—	—	—	—	—	i	—	12	100

CROFT, DON Donald Thomas, DT, 6´4˝/254 lbs; Texas-El Paso; 1972: Bal, rnd 5; B1/7/1949 Temple, TX **1972** Buf 14 (LDT) **1974** Buf 6 **1975** Buf 13 **1976** Det 1 **NFL** 34 [4 yrs]

CROFT, LEE Leland Reynolds, G-T, 6´1˝/190 lbs; Wisconsin-Platteville; B11/5/1898 Mineral Point, WI, D1/28/1984 Odessa, TX **1924** Rac 1 (1)

CROFT, TINY Milburn Russell, T, 6´3˝/287 lbs; Alabama; Ripon; 1942: Was, rnd 20; B11/7/1920 Chicago, IL, D1/22/1977 St. Germain, WI **1942** GB 7 (0) **1943** GB 4 (0) **1944**†GB 10 (7, LT) **1945** GB 9 (2) **1946** GB 11 (2) **1947** GB 10 (0) **NFL** 51 (11) [6 yrs]

CROFT, WIN Winfield Scott, G, 5´11˝/235 lbs; Utah; B2/28/1910 Cowley, WV, D7/8/1993 Gallup, NM **1935** Bkn 11 (5, lg) **1936** Pit 9 (1) **NFL** 20 (6) [2 yrs]

CROFTCHECK, DON Donald Anthony, G-LB, 6´2˝/230 lbs; Indiana; 1965: Was, rnd 8/KC, rnd 17; B9/12/1942 Allison, PA **1965** Was 14 (LG) **1966** Was 12 **1967** ChiB 9 **NFL** 35 [3 yrs]

CROMWELL, NOLAN Nolan Neil, DB, 6´1˝/200 lbs; Kansas; 1977: LA, rnd 2; B1/30/1955 Smith Center, KS **[KI]**

YEAR	TEAM	G(GS, POS)	RUSH	YD	AVG(LG)	TD	REC	YD	AVG(LG)	TD	PASS	COMP	PCT	YD	AVG(LG)	TD	INT	SK	YD	QBR	KPR	OTD	PTS	TAY
1977	†LARm	14	—	—	—	—	—	—	—	—	—	—	—	—	—	—	—	—	—	—	—	—	0	0
1978	†LARm	16	1	16	16.0(16)	1	—	—	—	—	—	—	—	—	—	—	—	—	—	—	pi	1	12	55
1979	†LARm	16(16, FS/lcb)	1	5	5.0(5)	1	—	—	—	—	—	—	—	—	—	—	—	—	—	—	i	—	6	99
1980	†LARm★	16(16, FS)	2	0	0.0(0)	0	—	—	—	—	1	0	0.0	0	0.0	0	0	—	—	—	Kpi	1	7	110
1981	LARm★	16(16, FS)	1	17	17.0(17)	0	—	—	—	—	—	—	—	—	—	—	—	—	—	—	i	—	0	86
1982	LARm★	9(9, FS)	1	17	17.0(17)	1	—	—	—	—	—	—	—	—	—	—	—	—	—	—	i	—	6	45
1983	†LARm★	16(16, SS)	1	0	0.0(0)	0	—	—	—	—	—	—	—	—	—	—	—	—	—	—	i	1	6	71
1984	LARm	11(11, SS)	—	—	—	—	—	—	—	—	—	—	—	—	—	—	—	—	—	—	i	1	6	49
1985	†LARm	16(16, SS)	—	—	—	—	—	—	—	—	—	—	—	—	—	—	—	—	—	—	kiS	—	0	-17
1986	†LARm	16(16, SS)	—	—	—	—	—	—	—	—	—	—	—	—	—	—	—	—	—	—	i	1	6	86

YEAR	TEAM	G (GS, POS)	RUSH	YD	AVG(LG)	TD	REC	YD	AVG(LG)	TD	PASS COMP	PCT	YD	AVG(LG)	TD	INT	SK	YD	QBR	KPR	OTD	PTS	TAY
1987	LARm	15(8, FS)	—	—	—	—	—	—	—	—	—	—	—	—	—	—	—	—	—	iS	—	0	18
NFL	11	161(124)	7	55	7.9(17)	3	—	—	—	—	1	0	0.0	0	0.0	0	0	—	—	KkpiS	5	49	602

CRONAN, PETE Peter Joseph, LB, 6´2˝/238 lbs; Boston College; 1977: Sea, rnd 2; B1/13/1955 Bourne, MA   **1977** Sea 14 (1)   **1978** Sea 15 (1)   **1979** Sea 16 (1)   **1981** Sea 5 (0)
1981 Was 10 (2)   **1982†**Was 7 (0)   **1983†**Was 16 (0)   **1984†**Was 3 (0)   **1985** Was 4 (0)   **NFL** 90 (5) [8 yrs]

CRONIN, BILL William, B-E, 5´10˝/183 lbs; Boston College; B4/18/1901, D4/1948   **1927** Pro 9 (3), 6   **1928** Pro 9 (1, WB)   **1929** Pro 10 (7, le)   **NFL** 28 (11) [3 yrs]

CRONIN, BILL William F., TE, 6´5˝/231 lbs; Boston College; 1965: Oak, rnd 15; B11/20/1943 Lawrence, MA   **1965** Phi 2

| 1966 | Mia-A | 14 | — | — | — | — | 7 | 83 | 11.9(25) | 1 | — | — | — | — | — | — | — | — | — | — | — | 6 | 47 |
| NFL | 2 | 16 | — | — | — | — | 7 | 83 | 11.9(25) | 1 | — | — | — | — | — | — | — | — | — | — | — | 6 | 47 |

CRONIN, FRITZ Francis B., E-G, 5´11˝/182 lbs; St. Mary's (MN); B6/20/1905 Lake City, MN, D3/1969 Manchester, NH   **1927** Dul 8 (6, RE)

CRONIN, GENE Eugene Edward, DE-LB-G, 6´2˝/229 lbs; Pacific; 1956: Det, rnd 7; B11/20/1933 Spalding, NE   **1956** Det 12 (rde)   **1957†**Det 12 (12, RDE)   **1958** Det 12 (12, RDE)
1959 Det 12 (12)   **1960** Dal 11 (RLB)   **1961** Was 14   **1962** Was 14   **NFL** 87 (36) [7 yrs]

CRONIN, JACK John Patrick, B, 5´11˝/178 lbs; Boston College; B5/3/1903 Hingham, MA, D1/18/1993 Jupiter, FL   **1927** Pro 12 (3), 6   **1928** Pro 8 (5), 18   **1929** Pro 12 (5, wb), 6
1930 Pro 10 (3)   **NFL** 42 (16), 30 [4 yrs]

CRONIN, JERRY Jeremiah George, E, 6´0˝/198 lbs; Rutgers; B12/12/1909 New York, NY, D7/1984 Huntington, NY   **1932** Bkn 4 (1)

CRONIN, TOMMY Thomas V., HB, 5´9˝/170 lbs; Loras; Marquette; B4/29/1896 Janesville, WI, D4/24/1964 Janesville, WI   **1922** GB 5 (1), 6

CRONKHITE, DOC Henry Oliver, E, 6´5˝/210 lbs; Kansas State; B3/10/1911, D12/26/1949 Wichita, KS

| 1934 | Bkn | 6(2) | — | — | — | — | 1 | 3 | 3.0(3) | 0 | — | — | — | — | — | — | — | — | — | — | — | 0 | 2 |

CROOK, AL Alfred John, C-G-T, 5´10˝/190 lbs; Washington & Jefferson; B11/20/1897 Detroit, MO, D2/17/1958   **1925** Det 8 (6, c)   **1926** Det 8 (4)   **NFL** 16 (10) [2 yrs]

CROOM, COREY Corey Vincent, RB, 5´11˝/208 lbs; Ball State; B5/22/1971 Sandusky, OH

1993	NE	14(1)	60	198	3.3(22)	1	8	92	11.5(21)	0	—	—	—	—	—	—	—	—	—	—	—	6	254
1994	†NE	16(0)	—	—	—	—	—	—	—	—	—	—	—	—	—	—	—	—	—	k	—	0	22
1995	NE	13(1)	13	54	4.2(12)	0	1	8	8.0(8)	0	—	—	—	—	—	—	—	—	—	—	—	0	58
NFL	3	43(2)	73	252	3.5(22)	1	9	100	11.1(21)	0	—	—	—	—	—	—	—	—	—	k	—	6	334

CROOM, LARRY Larry Lewis, RB, 5´10˝/205 lbs; UNLV; B10/29/1981 Long Beach, CA

| 2004 | Arz | 6(1) | 29 | 76 | 2.6(20) | 0 | 2 | 16 | 8.0(8) | 0 | — | — | — | — | — | — | — | — | — | k | — | 0 | 158 |

CROOM, SYLVESTER Sylvester J., C, 6´0˝/235 lbs; Alabama; B9/25/1954 Tuscaloosa, AL   **1975** NO 1

CROOMS, CHRIS Christopher Dale, DB, 6´2˝/211 lbs; Texas A&M; 1992: LARm, rnd 5; B2/4/1969 Houston, TX   **1992** LARm 16 (0)

CROPPER, MARSHALL Marshall Joseph, WR, 6´4˝/200 lbs; Maryland-Eastern Shore; B4/1/1944 Wattsville, VA

1967	Pit	7	—	—	—	—	1	11	11.0(11)	0	—	—	—	—	—	—	—	—	—	—	—	0	6
1968	Pit	5	—	—	—	—	4	54	13.5(17)	0	—	—	—	—	—	—	—	—	—	k	—	0	35
1969	Pit	4	—	—	—	—	9	116	12.9(19)	0	—	—	—	—	—	—	—	—	—	—	—	0	58
NFL	3	16	—	—	—	—	14	181	12.9(19)	0	—	—	—	—	—	—	—	—	—	k	—	0	99

CROSBY, CLEVELAND Cleveland Pittsburgh, DE, 6´5˝/250 lbs; Purdue; Arizona; 1980: Cle, rnd 2; B4/3/1956 West Point, MS   **1982** Bal 9 (0)

CROSBY, CLIFTON Clifton, DB, 5´10˝/179 lbs; Maryland; B9/17/1974 Erie, PA   **1999** SL 1 (0)   **2001** Ind 14 (0)   **2002†**Ind 16 (0)   **2003†**Ind 14 (0)   **NFL** 45 (0) [4 yrs]

CROSBY, PHILLIP Phillip Jermaine, FB, 6´0˝/242 lbs; Tennessee; B11/5/1976 Bessemer City, NC

2001	Buf	16(2)	—	—	—	—	2	16	8.0(9)	0	—	—	—	—	—	—	—	—	—	—	—	0	8
2002	Buf	16(4)	—	—	—	—	4	33	8.3(11)	0	—	—	—	—	—	—	—	—	—	k	—	0	17
2003	Buf	3(0)	—	—	—	—	—	—	—	—	—	—	—	—	—	—	—	—	—	—	—	0	0
NFL	3	35(6)	—	—	—	—	6	49	8.2(11)	0	—	—	—	—	—	—	—	—	—	k	—	0	25

CROSBY, RON Ronald, LB, 6´3˝/224 lbs; Penn State; 1977: Det, rnd 5; B3/2/1955 McKeesport, PA   **1978** NO 14   **1979** NYJ 12   **1980** NYJ 16 (16, RLB)   **1981†**NYJ 16 (3)
1982†NYJ 9 (0).

| 1983 | NYJ | 16(1) | 1 | 5 | 5.0(5) | 0 | — | — | — | — | — | — | — | — | — | — | — | — | — | — | — | 0 | 5 |
| NFL | 6 | 83(20) | 1 | 5 | 5.0(5) | 0 | — | — | — | — | — | — | — | — | — | — | — | — | — | i | — | 0 | 42 |

CROSBY, STEVE Steven Kent, RB, 5´11˝/205 lbs; Kansas State; Fort Hays State; 1974: NYG, rnd 17; B7/3/1950 Great Bend, KS

1974	NYG	9	14	55	3.9(10)	0	2	44	22.0(44)	0	—	—	—	—	—	—	—	—	—	Pk	—	0	94
1975	NYG	4	—	—	—	—	—	—	—	—	—	—	—	—	—	—	—	—	—	Pk	—	0	-1
1976	NYG	2	1	-1	-1.0(-1)	0	—	—	—	—	—	—	—	—	—	—	—	—	—	—	—	0	-1
NFL	3	15	15	54	3.6(10)	0	2	44	22.0(44)	0	—	—	—	—	—	—	—	—	—	Pk	—	0	92

CROSS, BILLY William Jarrel, HB, 5´6˝/151 lbs; West Texas A&M; 1951: ChiC, rnd 24; B5/3/1929 Fry, TX

1951	ChiC	12(LH)	53	283	5.3(39)	3	18	322	17.9(80)	3	—	—	—	—	—	—	—	—	—	p	—	36	493
1952	ChiC	12(LH)	71	347	4.9(45)	2	17	234	13.8(56)	2	—	—	—	—	—	—	—	—	—	kp	—	24	600
1953	ChiC	12(RH)	51	196	3.8(56)	1	17	285	16.8(51)	1	—	—	—	—	—	—	—	—	—	kp	—	12	406
NFL	3	36	175	826	4.7(56)	6	52	841	16.2(80)	6	—	—	—	—	—	—	—	—	—	kp	—	72	1499

CROSS, BOBBY Robert Joe, T-DT, 6´4˝/240 lbs; Stephen F. Austin State; 1952: ChiB, rnd 9; B4/4/1931 Ranger, TX, D6/18/1989 Kilgore, TX   **1952** ChiB 12   **1954** LARm 12 (LT)
1955†LARm 12 (LT)   **1956** SF 12 (LT)   **1957†**SF 12 (RT)   **1958** ChiC 12 (LT)   **1959** ChiC 11   **1960** Bos-A 4   **NFL** 87 (8 yrs]

CROSS, HOWARD Howard Edward, TE, 6´5˝/260 lbs; Alabama; 1989: NYG, rnd 6; B8/8/1967 Huntsville, AL

1989	†NYG	16(4)	—	—	—	—	6	107	17.8(27)	1	—	—	—	—	—	—	—	—	—	—	—	6	59
1990	†NYG	16(8, te)	—	—	—	—	8	106	13.3(21)	0	—	—	—	—	—	—	—	—	—	k	—	0	48
1991	NYG	16(16, TE)	—	—	—	—	20	283	14.1(30)	2	—	—	—	—	—	—	—	—	—	—	—	12	148
1992	NYG	16(16, TE)	—	—	—	—	27	357	13.2(29)	2	—	—	—	—	—	—	—	—	—	—	—	12	189
1993	†NYG	16(16, TE)	—	—	—	—	21	272	13.0(32)	5	—	—	—	—	—	—	—	—	—	k	—	30	146
1994	NYG	16(16, TE)	—	—	—	—	31	364	11.7(40)	4	—	—	—	—	—	—	—	—	—	—	—	24	202
1995	NYG	15(15, TE)	—	—	—	—	18	197	10.9(26)	0	—	—	—	—	—	—	—	—	—	—	—	0	99
1996	NYG	16(16, TE)	—	—	—	—	22	178	8.1(19)	1	—	—	—	—	—	—	—	—	—	—	—	6	94
1997	†NYG	16(16, TE)	—	—	—	—	21	150	7.1(26)	2	—	—	—	—	—	—	—	—	—	—	—	12	85
1998	NYG	16(16, TE)	—	—	—	—	13	90	6.9(22)	0	—	—	—	—	—	—	—	—	—	—	—	0	45
1999	NYG	16(15, TE)	—	—	—	—	9	55	6.1(12)	0	—	—	—	—	—	—	—	—	—	—	—	0	28
2000	†NYG	16(11, TE)	—	—	—	—	4	30	7.5(18)	0	—	—	—	—	—	—	—	—	—	—	—	0	15
2001	NYG	16(6, te)	—	—	—	—	1	5	5.0(5)	0	—	—	—	—	—	—	—	—	—	—	—	0	3
NFL	13	207(171)	—	—	—	—	201	2194	10.9(40)	17	—	—	—	—	—	—	—	—	—	k	—	102	1158

CROSS, IRV Irvin Acie, DB, 6´2˝/195 lbs; Northwestern; 1961: Phi, rnd 7; B7/27/1939 Hammond, IN [I]   **1961** Phi 13 (rcb)   **1962** Phi 14 (RCB)   **1963** Phi 14 (RCB)
1964 Phi✧14 (RCB)   **1965** Phi✧14 (RCB)   **1966** LARm 14 (RCB)   **1967†**LARm 14 (RCB)   **1968** LARm 14 (14, RCB)   **1969** Phi 14 (RCB)   **NFL** 125 (14) [9 yrs]

CROSS, JEFF Jeffrey Alan, DE, 6´4˝/280 lbs; Missouri; 1988: Mia, rnd 9; B3/25/1966 Riverside, CA [S]   **1988** Mia 16 (1)   **1989** Mia 16 (16, RDE)   **1990†**Mia★16 (16, RDE)
1991 Mia 16 (16, RDE)   **1992†**Mia 16 (16, RDE/lde)   **1993** Mia 16 (16, LDE)   **1994†**Mia 13 (10, LDE)   **1995†**Mia 16 (16, LDE)   **NFL** 125 (107) [8 yrs]

CROSS, JUSTIN Justin Allen, T, 6´6˝/263 lbs; Western State (CO); 1981: Buf, rnd 10; B4/29/1959 Montreal, Canada   **1982** Buf 9 (0)   **1983** Buf 15 (13, RT)   **1984** Buf 7 (0)
1985 Buf 3 (0)   **1986** Buf 10 (1)   **NFL** 44 (16) [5 yrs]

CROSS, RANDY Randall Laureat, G-C, 6´3˝/259 lbs; UCLA; 1976: SF, rnd 2; B4/25/1954 Brooklyn, NY   **1976** SF 14 (10, C)   **1977** SF 14 (14, C)   **1978** SF 9 (9, C)
1979 SF 16 (16, RG)   **1980** SF✩16 (16, RG)   **1981†**SF★16 (16, RG)   **1982** SF✧9 (8, RG)   **1983†**SF 16 (16, RG)   **1984†**SF★16 (16, RG)   **1985** SF✩15 (15, RG)
1986†SF✩16 (16, RG)   **1987** SF✩12 (12, C)   **1988†**SF 16 (16, C)   **NFL** 185 (180) [13 yrs]

CROSSAN, DAVE David Henry, C, 6´4˝/245 lbs; Maryland; 1963: Phi, rnd 3/Den, rnd 16; B6/8/1940 Philadelphia, PA   **1965** Was 14   **1966** Was 14   **1967** Was 11   **1968** Was 14
1969 Was 6   **NFL** 59 [5 yrs]

YEAR	TEAM	G(GS, POS)	RUSH	YD	AVG(LG)	TD	REC	YD	AVG(LG)	TD	PASS COMP	PCT	YD	AVG(LG)	TD	INT	SK	YD	QBR	KPR	OTD	PTS	TAY

CROSSWHITE, LEON   Leon Mac, RB, 6´2˝/215 lbs; Oklahoma; 1973: Det, rnd 2; B4/28/1951 Hennessey, OK

1973	Det	7	.11	30	2.7(5)	0	1	4	4.0(4)	0	—	—	—	—	—	—	—	—	—	—	—	—	6	42
1974	Det	14(1)	12	49	4.1(9)	1	3	31	10.3(13)	0	—	—	—	—	—	—	—	—	—	k	—	—	6	71
NFL	2	21(1)	23	79	3.4(9)	2	4	35	8.8(13)	0	—	—	—	—	—	—	—	—	—	k	—	—	12	113

CROSTON, DAVE   David Charles, T, 6´5˝/280 lbs; Iowa; 1987: GB, rnd 3; B11/10/1963 Sioux City, IA   **1988** GB 16 (1)

CROTTY, JIM   James Richard, DB, 6´1˝/190 lbs; Notre Dame; 1960: Was, rnd 12/DalT, rnd 1; B3/31/1938 Storm Lake, IA   **1960** Was 9   **1961** Was 5   **1961** Buf-A 5   **1962** Buf-A 3   **NFL** 22 [3 yrs]

CROUCH, BILLY   William Butler, C, 6´1˝/187 lbs; Davidson; B11/4/1898 Moorestown, TN, D2/23/1934 Washington, DC   **1921** Was 3 (3, C)

CROUCH, TERRY   Terry Wayne, G, 6´2˝/278 lbs; Oklahoma; 1982: Bal, rnd 5; B7/6/1959 Dallas, TX   **1982** Bal 9 (6, LG)

CROUDIP, DAVID   David Rodney, DB, 5´8˝/183 lbs; San Diego State; B1/25/1958 Indianapolis, IN, D10/10/1988 Duluth, GA   **1984**†LARm 16 (0)   **1985** SD 2 (0)   **1985** Atl 11 (0)   **1986** Atl 15 (7, lcb)   **1987** Atl 12 (2)   **1988** Atl 6 (0)   **NFL** 62 (9) [5 yrs]

CROUSE, RAY   Marlon Ray, RB, 5´11˝/214 lbs; UNLV; B3/16/1959 Oakland, CA

| 1984 | GB | 16(0) | 53 | 169 | 3.2(14) | 0 | 9 | 93 | 10.3(25) | 1 | — | — | — | — | — | — | — | — | — | — | — | — | 6 | 221 |

CROUTHAMEL, JAKE   John Jacob, HB, 6´0˝/195 lbs; Dartmouth; 1960: LAC, rnd 1; B6/27/1938 Perkasie, PA

| 1960 | Bos-A | 2 | 4 | 16 | 4.0(6) | 0 | — | — | — | — | — | — | — | — | — | — | — | — | — | k | — | — | 0 | 13 |

CROW, AL   Albert Lee, DT, 6´7˝/260 lbs; William & Mary; 1955: NYG, rnd 28; B8/20/1932   **1960** Bos-A 3

CROW, JOHN DAVID   John David, HB-TE-FB, 6´2˝/220 lbs; Texas A&M; 1958: ChiC, rnd 1; B7/8/1935 Marion, LA

1958	ChiC	7(rh)	52	221	4.3(83)	2	20	362	18.1(91)	3	1	0	0.0	0	0.0	0	1	—	—	—	k	1	36	452
1959	ChiC★	12(LH)	140	666	4.8(73)	3	27	328	12.1(36)	4	—	—	—	—	—	—	—	—	—	—	k	—	42	990
1960	SL★	12(HB)	183	1071	**5.9(57)**	6	25	462	18.5(52)	6	3	18	9	50.0	247	13.7(52)	2	1	—	—	—	—	54	1471
1961	SL	8	48	192	4.0(17)	1	20	306	15.3(31)	3	14	4	28.6	76	5.4(32)	1	1	—	—	—	—	—	24	373
1962	SL★	14(HB)	192	751	3.9(35)	14	23	246	10.7(53)	3	20	12	60.0	241	12.1(57)	0	0	—	—	—	p	—	102	1146
1963	SL	3	9	34	3.8(9)	0	—	—	—	—	3	2	66.7	27	9.0(17)	0	0	—	—	—	—	—	0	53
1964	SL	13(FB)	163	554	3.4(57)	7	23	257	11.2(22)	1	1	0	0.0	0	0	0	0	—	—	—	—	—	48	758
1965	SF◇	14(13, LH)	132	514	3.9(30)	2	28	493	17.6(54)	7	4	2	50.0	61	15.3(45)	1	1	—	—	—	—	—	54	811
1966	SF	14(14, HB)	121	477	3.9(31)	1	30	341	11.4(54)	3	4	2	50.0	61	15.3(46)	0	1	—	—	—	—	—	24	663
1967	SF	14(14, HB)	113	479	4.2(39)	2	31	373	12.0(53)	3	5	2	40.0	46	9.2(25)	0	0	—	—	—	—	—	30	724
1968	SF	14(14, TE)	4	4	1.0(3)	0	31	531	17.1(54)	5	—	—	—	—	—	—	—	—	—	—	—	—	30	295
NFL	11	125(55)	1157	4963	4.3(83)	38	258	3699	14.3(91)	35	70	33	47.1	759	10.8(57)	5	5	—	—	—	kp	1	444	7733

CROW, LINDON   Lindon Oscar, DB, 6´1˝/195 lbs; USC; 1955: ChiC, rnd 2; B4/4/1933 Denison, TX **[I]**   **1955** ChiC 12 (DB)   **1956** ChiC★12 (DB)   **1957** ChiC◇12 (DB)   **1958**†NYG 12 (db)   **1959**†NYG★12 (DB)   **1960** NYG 12 (LCB)   **1961** LARm 14 (LS)   **1962** LARm 14 (LS)   **1963** LARm 14 (LS)   **1964** LARm 9   **NFL** 123 [10 yrs]

CROW, ORIEN   John Orien, C, 6´2˝/220 lbs; Haskell Indian; B9/7/1912 Salem, MO   **1933** Bos 11 (9, C)

| 1934 | Bos | 11(5, c) | — | — | — | — | 2 | 20 | 10.0 | 0 | — | — | — | — | — | — | — | — | — | — | — | — | 0 | 10 |
| NFL | 2 | 22(14) | — | — | — | — | 2 | 20 | 10.0 | 0 | — | — | — | — | — | — | — | — | — | — | — | — | 0 | 10 |

CROW, WAYNE   Charles Wayne, HB-DB, 6´1˝/205 lbs; California; 1960: SL, rnd 8; B5/5/1938 Coolidge, AZ

1960	Oak-A	14(RS)	—	—	—	—	—	—	—	—	—	—	—	—	—	—	—	—	—	Pi	—	—	0	30
1961	Oak-A	14(HB)	119	490	4.1(62)	2	17	105	6.2(22)	0	10	6	60.0	165	16.5(46)	0	0	—	—	—	P	—	14	645
1962	Buf-A	14	110	589	5.4(52)	1	8	80	10.0(25)	1	4	2	50.0	16	4.0(10)	0	1	—	—	—	P	—	12	612
1963	Buf-A	5	6	6	1.0(7)	0	5	69	13.8(28)	0	—	—	—	—	—	—	—	—	—	P	—	—	0	41
NFL	4	47	235	1085	4.6(62)	3	30	254	8.5(28)	1	14	8	57.1	181	12.9(46)	0	1	—	—	—	Pi	—	26	1328

CROWDER, CHANNING   Randolph Channing, LB, 6´2˝/247 lbs; Florida; 2005: Mia, rnd 3; B12/2/1983 State College, PA   **2005** Mia 16 (13, RLB)

CROWDER, EARL   Earl Franklin, BB, 6´0˝/198 lbs; Oklahoma; 1939: ChiC, rnd 10; B1/21/1915 Cherokee, OK, D2/6/1984 Cherokee, OK

1939	ChiC	6(1)	6	-5	-0.8	0	2	59	29.5	0	7	2	28.6	6	0.9	0	0	—	—	—	—	—	0	28
1940	Cle	3(0)	—	—	—	—	2	33	16.5	0	—	—	—	—	—	—	—	—	—	—	—	—	0	17
NFL	2	9(1)	6	-5	-0.8	0	4	92	23.0	0	7	2	28.6	6	0.9	0	0	—	—	—	—	—	0	44

CROWDER, RANDY   Randolph Channing, DT-NT-DE, 6´2˝/242 lbs; Penn State; 1974: Mia, rnd 6; B7/30/1953 Sharon, PA   **1974**†Mia 12   **1975** Mia 13 (11, LDT)   **1976** Mia 14 (14, LDT)   **1978** TB 14   **1979**†TB 16 (8, NT)   **1980** TB 2 (2)   **NFL** 71 (35) [6 yrs]

CROWE, LARRY   Larry Darnell, RB, 6´1˝/198 lbs; Texas Southern; 1971: Pit, rnd 8; B1/18/1950 Diana, TX   **1975** Atl 5

| 1972 | Phi | 1 | 1 | 2 | 2.0(2) | 0 | — | — | — | — | — | — | — | — | — | — | — | — | — | — | — | — | 0 | 2 |
| NFL | 2 | 6 | 1 | 2 | 2.0(2) | 0 | — | — | — | — | — | — | — | — | — | — | — | — | — | — | — | — | 0 | 2 |

CROWE, PAUL   Paul James, B, 6´1˝/190 lbs; St. Mary's (CA); B10/23/1924 Chino, CA, D12/13/1989 Butte County, CA

1948	SF-A	14(0)	12	65	5.4	0	16	(16)	1	—	—	—	—	—	—	—	—	—	—	kpi	1	12	124
1949	SF-A	2(1)	2	0	0.0	0	—	—	—	—	—	—	—	—	—	—	—	—	—	—	—	0	0
1949	LAD-A	7(0)	1	2	2.0(2)	0	—	—	—	—	—	—	—	—	—	—	—	—	—	pi	1	6	88
AAFC	2	23(1)	15	67	4.5(2)	0	16	(16)	1	—	—	—	—	—	—	—	—	—	—	kpi	2	18	212
1951	NYY	9(DB)	—	—	—	—	3	20	6.7(10)	0	—	—	—	—	—	—	—	—	—	i	—	0	10

CROWELL, ANGELO   Angelo Delvonne, LB, 6´1˝/235 lbs; Virginia; 2003: Buf, rnd 3; B8/16/1981 Forsyth County, NC   **2003** Buf 6 (0)   **2004** Buf 16 (0)   **2005** Buf 15 (13, RLB)   **NFL** 37 (13) [3 yrs]

CROWELL, GERMANE   Germane L., WR, 6´3˝/213 lbs; Virginia; 1998: Det, rnd 2; B9/13/1976 Winston-Salem, NC

1998	Det	14(2)	1	35	35.0(35)	0	25	464	18.6(68)	3	—	—	—	—	—	—	—	—	—	—	—	18	282
1999	†Det	16(15, WR)	5	38	7.6(20)	0	81	1338	16.5(77)	7	—	—	—	—	—	—	—	—	—	—	—	44	742
2000	Det	9(7, wr)	1	12	12.0(12)	0	34	430	12.6(50)	3	—	—	—	—	—	—	—	—	—	—	—	18	242
2001	Det	5(4)	1	6	6.0(6)	0	22	289	13.1(46)	2	—	—	—	—	—	—	—	—	—	—	—	12	161
2002	Det	10(5, wr)	—	—	—	—	22	201	9.1(22)	1	—	—	—	—	—	—	—	—	—	—	—	6	106
NFL	5	54(33)	8	91	11.4(35)	0	184	2722	14.8(77)	16	—	—	—	—	—	—	—	—	—	—	—	98	1532

CROWELL, ODIS   Odis Leonard, T, 6´2˝/220 lbs; Hardin-Simmons; B10/7/1914 Matador, TX   **1947** SF-A 2 (0)

CROWL, BERNIE   Richard Bernard, G-C, 5´10˝/185 lbs; Rutgers; B3/25/1908 Brooklyn, NY, D11/12/1998 Vernon, CT   **1930** Bkn 2 (0)

CROWLEY, JIM   James Harold, TB-HB, 5´9˝/165 lbs; Notre Dame; B9/10/1902 Chicago, IL, D1/15/1986 Scranton, PA **[C]**   **1925** GB 2 (0), 6   **1925** Pro 1 (0)   **NFL** 3 (0) [1 yr]

CROWLEY, JOE   Joseph A., E-DB, 6´0˝/194 lbs; Dartmouth; B4/6/1919 Brighton, MA, D12/1985 Yonkers, NY

1944	Bos	9(9, RE)	1	10	10.0(10)	0	13	279	21.5(67)	3	—	—	—	—	—	—	—	—	—	i	—	18	165
1945	Bos	9(3)	—	—	—	—	1	12	12.0(12)	0	—	—	—	—	—	—	—	—	—	i	—	0	46
NFL	2	18(12)	1	10	10.0(10)	0	14	291	20.8(67)	3	—	—	—	—	—	—	—	—	—	i	—	18	211

CROWTHER, RAE   Rae, E, 5´11˝/175 lbs; Penn State; Colgate; B12/11/1902 Rosemont, PA, D11/3/1980 Haddonfield, NJ   **1925** Fra☆19 (17, RE), 18   **1926** Fra 14 (13, RE)   **NFL** 33 (30) [2 yrs]

CROWTHER, SAVILLE   Saville Evans, G-T, 6´1˝/220 lbs; Penn State; Colgate; B7/10/1901 Rosemont, PA, D7/8/1962 Philadelphia, PA   **1925** Fra 2 (2)

CROYLE, PHIL   Philip Gordon, LB, 6´3˝/223 lbs; California; 1971: Hou, rnd 7; B10/30/1947 Great Lakes, IL   **1971** Hou 14   **1972** Hou 12 (RLB)   **1973** Hou 1   **1973** Buf 5   **NFL** 32 [3 yrs]

CRUDUP, DERRICK   Derrick, DB-RB, 6´2˝/220 lbs; Florida; Oklahoma; 1988: LARd, rnd 7; B2/15/1965 Delray Beach, FL   **1989** LARd 4 (0)   **1991**†LARd 16 (0)   **NFL** 20 (0) [2 yrs]

CRUM, BOB   Robert Harvey, DE, 6´5˝/240 lbs; Arizona; 1973: Cle, rnd 3; B6/28/1951 Mesa, AZ   **1974**†SL 14

CRUMP, DWAYNE   Dwayne Anthony, DB, 5´11˝/180 lbs; Fresno State; 1973: SL, rnd 6; B8/9/1950 Madera, CA   **1973** SL 14 (LCB)   **1974**†SL 14   **1975**†SL 14 (3)   **1976** SL 13   **NFL** 55 (3) [4 yrs]

CRUMP, GEORGE   George Stanley, DE, 6´4˝/260 lbs; East Carolina; 1982: NE, rnd 4; B7/22/1959 Portsmouth, VA   **1982**†NE 9 (0)

YEAR	TEAM	G (GS, POS)	RUSH	YD	AVG(LG)	TD	REC	YD	AVG(LG)	TD	PASS COMP	PCT	YD	AVG(LG)	TD	INT	SK	YD	QBR	KPR	OTD	PTS	TAY

CRUMP, HARRY Harry M., FB, 6´1˝/205 lbs; Boston College; B6/18/1940 Framingham, MA

| 1963 | †Bos-A | 14 | 49 | 120 | 2.4(21) | 5 | 6 | 46 | 7.7(12) | 0 | — | — | — | — | — | — | — | — | — | k | — | 30 | 181 |

CRUMPLER, ALGE Algernon Darius, TE, 6´2˝/262 lbs; North Carolina; 2001: Atl, rnd 2; B12/23/1977 Greenville, NC

2001	Atl	16(12, TE)	—	—	—	—	25	330	13.2(57)	3	—	—	—	—	—	—	—	—	—	k	—	18	167
2002	†Atl	16(9, TE)	—	—	—	—	36	455	12.6(33)	5	—	—	—	—	—	—	—	—	—	k	—	30	247
2003	Atl★	16(16, TE)	—	—	—	—	44	552	12.5(63)	3	—	—	—	—	—	—	—	—	—	—	—	18	291
2004	†Atl◇	14(14, TE)	—	—	—	—	48	774	16.1(49)	6	—	—	—	—	—	—	—	—	—	—	—	36	417
2005	Atl◇	16(16, TE)	—	—	—	—	65	877	13.5(48)	5	—	—	—	—	—	—	—	—	—	—	—	32	464
NFL	5	78(67)	—	—	—	—	218	2988	13.7(63)	22	—	—	—	—	—	—	—	—	—	k	—	134	1585

CRUMPLER, CARLESTER Carlester, TE, 6´6˝/260 lbs; East Carolina; 1994: Sea, rnd 7; B9/5/1971 Greenville, NC

1994	Sea	9(4)	—	—	—	—	2	19	9.5(12)	0	—	—	—	—	—	—	—	—	—	—	—	0	10
1995	Sea	16(7, te)	—	—	—	—	23	254	11.0(24)	1	—	—	—	—	—	—	—	—	—	—	—	6	132
1996	Sea	16(7, te)	—	—	—	—	26	258	9.9(26)	1	—	—	—	—	—	—	—	—	—	—	—	0	129
1997	Sea	15(12, TE)	—	—	—	—	31	361	11.6(30)	1	—	—	—	—	—	—	—	—	—	—	—	6	186
1998	Sea	11(1)	—	—	—	—	6	52	8.7(16)	1	—	—	—	—	—	—	—	—	—	—	—	6	31
1999	†Min	11(1)	—	—	—	—	2	35	17.5(31)	1	—	—	—	—	—	—	—	—	—	—	—	6	23
NFL	6	78(32)	—	—	—	—	90	979	10.9(31)	4	—	—	—	—	—	—	—	—	—	—	—	24	510

CRUSAN, DOUG Douglas Gordon, T, 6´5˝/250 lbs; Indiana; 1968: Mia, rnd 1; B7/26/1946 Monessen, PA **1968** Mia-A 14 (8, LT) **1969** Mia-A 14 (14, LT) **1970**†Mia 14 (14, LT) **1971**†Mia 14 (14, LT) **1972**†Mia 11 (10, LT) **1973**†Mia 14 **1974** Mia 1 **NFL** 82 (60) [7 yrs]

CRUTCHER, TOMMY Thomas Joe, LB, 6´3˝/229 lbs; TCU; 1964: GB, rnd 3/KC, rnd 11; B8/10/1941 McKinney, TX, D2/16/2002 McAllen, TX **1965**†GB 14 **1966**†GB 14 **1967**†GB 14 **1968** NYG 14 (LLB) **1969** NYG 14 (RLB) **1971** GB 12 **1972** GB 12

| 1964 | GB | 14 | 1 | 5 | 5.0(5) | 0 | — | — | — | — | — | — | — | — | — | — | — | — | — | k | — | 0 | 29 |
| NFL | 8 | 108 | 1 | 5 | 5.0(5) | 0 | — | — | — | — | — | — | — | — | — | — | — | — | — | ki | — | 0 | 44 |

CRUTCHFIELD, BUDDY Buddy, DB, 6´0˝/196 lbs; North Carolina Central; B3/7/1976 Raleigh, NC **1998** Was 2 (0) **1999** NYJ 4 (0) **NFL** 6 (0) [2 yrs]

CRUTCHFIELD, DARREL Darrel, DB, 6´0˝/177 lbs; Clemson; B2/26/1979 San Diego, CA **2001** Phi 4 (0)

CRUTCHFIELD, DWAYNE Dwayne A., RB, 6´0˝/235 lbs; Iowa State; 1982: NYJ, rnd 3; B9/30/1959 Cincinnati, OH

1982	†NYJ	6(0)	22	78	3.5(8)	1	—	—	—	—	—	—	—	—	—	—	—	—	—	—	—	6	88
1983	NYJ	11(8, FB)	137	571	4.2(17)	3	19	133	7.0(15)	0	—	—	—	—	—	—	—	—	—	—	—	18	668
1983	Hou	2(0)	3	7	2.3(5)	0	—	—	—	—	—	—	—	—	—	—	—	—	—	—	—	0	7
1984	†LARm	15(0)	73	337	4.6(36)	1	2	11	5.5(7)	1	—	—	—	—	—	—	—	—	—	k	—	12	363
NFL	3	34(8)	235	993	4.2(36)	5	21	144	6.9(15)	1	—	—	—	—	—	—	—	—	—	k	—	36	1125

CRUZ, RONNIE Ronnie, RB, 6´0˝/237 lbs; Northern State; B6/11/1981 Lakeport, CA

| 2005 | KC | 14(0) | — | — | — | — | 1 | 15 | 15.0(15) | 0 | — | — | — | — | — | — | — | — | — | — | — | 0 | 8 |

CRYDER, BOB Robert Joseph, T-G, 6´4˝/275 lbs; Alabama; 1978: NE, rnd 1; B9/7/1956 East St. Louis, IL **1978** NE 5 **1979** NE 16 (2) **1980** NE 16 (2) **1981** NE 15 (15, RG) **1982**†NE 9 (3) **1983** NE 14 (14, RT) **1984**†Sea 16 (10, RT) **1985** Sea 15 (14, RT) **1986** Sea 1 (0) **NFL** 107 (60) [9 yrs]

CSONKA, LARRY Lawrence Richard 'Zonk', RB, 6´3˝/237 lbs; Syracuse; 1968: Mia, rnd 1; B12/25/1946 Stow, OH; HOF 1987

1968	Mia-A	11(11, FB)	138	540	3.9(40)	6	11	118	10.7(65)	1	—	—	—	—	—	—	—	—	—	—	—	42	664
1969	Mia-A	11(11, FB)	131	566	4.3(54)	2	21	183	8.7(42)	1	—	—	—	—	—	—	—	—	—	—	—	18	683
1970	†Mia★	14(14, FB)	193	874	4.5(53)	6	11	94	8.5(54)	0	—	—	—	—	—	—	—	—	—	—	—	36	981
1971	†Mia★	14(14, FB)	195	1051	5.4(28)	7	13	113	8.7(25)	1	—	—	—	—	—	—	—	—	—	—	—	48	1183
1972	†Mia★	14(14, FB)	213	1117	5.2(45)	6	5	48	9.6(14)	0	—	—	—	—	—	—	—	—	—	—	—	36	1201
1973	†Mia★	14(14, FB)	219	1003	4.6(25)	5	7	22	3.1(9)	0	—	—	—	—	—	—	—	—	—	—	—	30	1064
1974	†Mia◇	12(12, FB)	197	749	3.8(24)	9	7	35	5.0(11)	0	—	—	—	—	—	—	—	—	—	—	—	54	857
1976	NYG	12(12, FB)	160	569	3.6(13)	4	6	39	6.5(14)	0	—	—	—	—	—	—	—	—	—	—	—	24	629
1977	NYG	14(14, FB)	134	464	3.5(15)	1	2	20	10.0(12)	0	—	—	—	—	—	—	—	—	—	—	—	6	484
1978	NYG	14(13, FB)	91	311	3.4(12)	6	7	73	10.4(23)	0	—	—	—	—	—	—	—	—	—	—	—	36	408
1979	†Mia	16(16, FB)	220	837	3.8(22)	12	16	75	4.7(18)	1	—	—	—	—	—	—	—	—	—	—	—	78	1000
NFL	11	146(145)	1891	8081	4.3(54)	64	106	820	7.7(65)	4	—	—	—	—	—	—	—	—	—	—	—	408	9151

CUBA, PAUL Paul J., T, 6´0˝/212 lbs; Pittsburgh; B6/12/1908 New Castle, PA, D8/12/1990 New Castle, PA **1933** Phi 9 (8, LT) **1934** Phi 10 (10, LT) **1935** Phi 10 (8, LT) **NFL** 29 (26) [3 yrs]

CUDZIK, WALT Walter Jacob, C-LB, 6´2˝/231 lbs; Purdue; 1954: Was, rnd 18; B2/21/1932 Chicago, IL, D12/11/2005 Gulf Shores, AL **[K]** **1954** Was 1 **1961** Bos-A 14 (C) **1962** Bos-A 14 (C) **1963**†Bos-A 14 (C) **1964**†Buf-A 14 (C)

| 1960 | Bos-A☆ | 14(C) | — | — | — | — | 1 | 11 | 11.0(11) | 0 | — | — | — | — | — | — | — | — | — | K | — | 0 | 6 |
| NFL | 6 | 71 | — | — | — | — | 1 | 11 | 11.0(11) | 0 | — | — | — | — | — | — | — | — | — | Kk | — | 0 | -10 |

CUFF, WARD Ward Lloyd, WB-QB-HB, 6´1˝/192 lbs; Marquette; 1937: NYG, rnd 4; B8/12/1913 Redwood Falls, MN, D12/24/2002 Vallejo, CA **[K]**

1937	NYG	11(9, WB)	4	32	8.0	2	5	117	23.4	2	—	—	—	—	—	—	—	—	—	K	—	30	121
1938	†NYG★	11(11, WB)	18	38	2.1	0	8	114	14.3	1	—	—	—	—	—	—	—	—	—	K	1	45	110
1939	†NYG★	9(8, WB)	23	102	4.4	0	10	83	8.3	2	—	—	—	—	—	—	—	—	—	K	—	39	154
1940	NYG	8(8, WB)	15	86	5.7	1	13	220	16.9	1	—	—	—	—	—	—	—	—	—	Ki	—	36	217
1941	†NYG★	11(10, WB)	28	157	5.6(37)	0	19	317	16.7(42)	2	—	—	—	—	—	—	—	—	—	Kkpi	—	46	479
1942	†NYG★	11(10, WB)	38	189	5.0(15)	0	16	267	16.7(35)	2	—	—	—	—	—	—	—	—	—	Kkpi	—	39	438
1943	†NYG☆	10(10, WB)	80	523	**6.5(65)**	3	7	52	7.4(17)	0	1	0	0.0	0	0	0	0	0	—	Kkpi	—	53	659
1944	†NYG☆	10(9, WB)	76	425	5.6(29)	0	11	135	12.3(23)	2	—	—	—	—	—	—	—	—	—	Kkpi	—	17	617
1945	NYG	11(9, WB)	48	214	4.5(25)	0	12	172	14.3(34)	0	—	—	—	—	—	—	—	—	—	kpi	—	0	429
1946	ChiC	10(7, qb)	13	78	6.0(26)	1	5	82	16.4(39)	1	—	—	—	—	—	—	—	—	—	Kp	—	55	148
1947	GB	10(0)	1	7	7.0(7)	0	—	—	—	—	—	—	—	—	—	—	—	—	—	K	—	51	7
NFL	11	110(87)	344	1851	5.4(65)	7	106	1559	14.7(41)	13	1	0	0.0	0	0	0	0	0	—	Kkpi	1	411	3377

CULBREATH, JIM James Clifford, RB, 6´0˝/209 lbs; Oklahoma; 1977: GB, rnd 10; B10/21/1952 Yeadon, PA

1977	GB	13	12	53	4.4(18)	0	2	6	3.0(5)	0	—	—	—	—	—	—	—	—	—	k	—	0	63
1978	GB	12	30	92	3.1(15)	0	7	78	11.1(19)	0	—	—	—	—	—	—	—	—	—	k	—	0	129
1979	GB	4	5	8	1.6(6)	0	—	—	—	—	—	—	—	—	—	—	—	—	—	—	—	0	8
1980	Phi	2(0)	1	3	3.0(3)	0	—	—	—	—	—	—	—	—	—	—	—	—	—	—	—	0	3
1980	NYG	1(0)	—	—	—	—	—	—	—	—	—	—	—	—	—	—	—	—	—	—	—		
NFL	4	32	48	156	3.3(18)	0	9	84	9.3(19)	0	—	—	—	—	—	—	—	—	—	k	—	0	203

CULLARS, WILLIE Willie Edward, DE, 6´5˝/250 lbs; Kansas State; 1974: Phi, rnd 7; B8/4/1951 Washington, GA **1974** Phi 13

CULLEN, DAVID David Emerson, G, 5´10˝/230 lbs; Geneva; B3/18/1905 Freedom, PA, D5/15/1982 Butler, PA **1931** Cle 2 (1)

CULLITY, DAVE David Richard, T, 6´7˝/275 lbs; Utah; B6/15/1964 La Mirada, CA **1989** SF 2 (0)

CULLOM, JIM James Henry, G, 5´11˝/235 lbs; California; 1950: Was, rnd 17; B11/5/1925 Healdsburg, CA, D3/4/1998 Oakland, CA **1951** NYY 2

CULLORS, DERRICK Derrick Shane, RB, 6´0˝/195 lbs; TCU; Murray State; B12/26/1972 Dallas, TX

1997	†NE	15(1)	22	101	4.6(24)	0	2	8	4.0(6)	0	—	—	—	—	—	—	—	—	—	k	1	6	276
1998	†NE	16(0)	18	48	2.7(15)	0	14	146	10.4(43)	1	—	—	—	—	—	—	—	—	—	k	—	6	536
NFL	2	31(1)	40	149	3.7(24)	0	16	154	9.6(43)	1	—	—	—	—	—	—	—	—	—	k	1	12	812

CULP, CURLEY Curley, DT-NT-G, 6´2˝/265 lbs; Arizona State; 1968: Den, rnd 2; B3/10/1946 Yuma, AZ **1968**†KC-A 9 **1969**†KC-A☆14 (LDT) **1970** KC 14 (LDT) **1971**†KC★14 (LDT) **1972** KC 14 (LDT) **1973** KC 13 (LDT) **1974** KC 4 **1974** Hou 8 (LDT) **1975** Hou★14 (NT) **1976** Hou★14 (NT) **1977** Hou★14 (NT) **1978**†Hou★16 (NT) **1979**†Hou☆16 (NT) **1980** Hou 5 (5, nt) **1980** Det 2 (2) **1981** Det 2 (2) **NFL** 179 (7) [14 yrs]

CULPEPPER, BRAD John Broward, DT, 6´1˝/275 lbs; Florida; 1992: Min, rnd 10; B5/8/1969 Tallahassee, FL **1992** Min 11 (2) **1993**†Min 15 (0) **1994** TB 16 (15, LDT/rdt) **1995** TB 16 (4) **1996** TB 13 (13, LDT) **1997**†TB 16 (16, LDT) **1998** TB 16 (16, LDT) **1999**†TB 16 (16, LDT) **2000** ChiB 12 (1) **NFL** 131 (83) [9 yrs]

CULPEPPER, DAUNTE Daunte, QB, 6´4˝/264 lbs; Central Florida; 1999: Min, rnd 1; B1/28/1977 Ocala, FL

YEAR	TEAM	G(GS, POS)	RUSH	YD	AVG(LG)	TD	REC	YD	AVG(LG)	TD	PASS	COMP	PCT	YD	AVG(LG)	TD	INT	SK	YD	QBR	KPR	OTD	PTS	TAY
1999	Min	1(0)	3	6	2.0(9)	0	—	—	—	—	—	—	—	—	—	—	—	—	—	—	—	—	0	6
2000	†Min★	16(16, QB)	89	470	5.3(27)	7	—	—	—	—	474	297	62.7	3937	8.3(78)	**33**	16	34	181	98.0	—	—	42	2034
2001	Min	11(11, QB)	71	416	5.9(34)	5	1	0	0.0(0)	0	366	235	64.2	2612	7.1(57)	14	13	33	186	83.3	—	—	34	1322
2002	Min	16(16, QB)	106	609	5.7(38)	10	—	—	—	—	549	333	60.7	3853	7.0(61)	18	**23**	47	244	75.3	—	—	62	1806
2003	Min✧	14(14, QB)	73	422	5.8(42)	4	—	—	—	—	454	295	65.0	3479	**7.7(59)**	25	11	37	196	96.4	—	—	24	1887
2004	†Min★	16(16, QB)	88	406	4.6(16)	2	—	—	—	—	**548**	**379**	69.2	**4717**	**8.6(82)**	**39**	11	46	238	**110.9**	—	—	14	**2540**
2005	Min	7(7, qb)	24	147	6.1(18)	1	—	—	—	—	216	139	64.4	1564	7.2(68)	6	12	31	169	72.0	—	—	6	489
NFL	7	81(80)	454	2476	5.5(42)	29	1	0	0.0	0	2607	1678	64.4	20162	7.7(82)	135	86	228	1214	91.5	—	—	182	10082

CULPEPPER, ED Robert Edward, DT, 6´1˝/255 lbs; Alabama; 1955: GB, rnd 9; B1/21/1934 Bradenton, FL **1958** ChiC 11 (RDT) **1959** ChiC 11 (LDT) **1960** SL 10 **1961** Min 14 (14, RDT) **1962**†Hou-A 14 (LDT) **1963** Hou-A 14 **NFL** 74 (14) [6 yrs]

CULPEPPER, WILLIE Willie James, WR, 5´11˝/155 lbs; Louisiana-Lafayette; B3/27/1967 Jacksonville, FL **1992** TB 3 (0)

CULVER, AL Alvin Sager, T, 6´2˝/245 lbs; Notre Dame; B6/11/1908 Wilmette, IL, D2/7/1982 Plymouth, IN **1932** ChiB 3 (0) **1932** GB 1 (1) **NFL** 4 (1) [1 yr]

CULVER, FRANK Franklin Z., C-E, 5´11˝/175 lbs; Syracuse; B4/24/1897 Toledo, OH, D1/13/1969 Yonkers, NY **1923** Buf 12 (12, C) **1924** Buf 8 (8, C) **1924** Roc 1 (1) **1925** Can☆8 (8, LE) **NFL** 29 (29) [3 yrs]

CULVER, RODNEY Rodney Dwayne, RB, 5´9˝/224 lbs; Notre Dame; 1992: Ind, rnd 4; B12/23/1969 Detroit, MI, D5/11/1996 Dade County, FL

YEAR	TEAM	G(GS, POS)	RUSH	YD	AVG(LG)	TD	REC	YD	AVG(LG)	TD	PASS	COMP	PCT	YD	AVG(LG)	TD	INT	SK	YD	QBR	KPR	OTD	PTS	TAY
1992	Ind	16(2)	121	321	2.7(36)	7	26	210	8.1(27)	2	—	—	—	—	—	—	—	—	—	—	—	—	54	506
1993	Ind	16(1)	65	150	2.3(9)	3	11	112	10.2(26)	1	—	—	—	—	—	—	—	—	—	—	k	1	30	247
1994	†SD	3(0)	8	63	7.9(22)	0	—	—	—	—	—	—	—	—	—	—	—	—	—	—	—	—	0	63
1995	SD	8(2)	47	155	3.3(17)	3	5	21	4.2(12)	0	—	—	—	—	—	—	—	—	—	—	—	—	18	196
NFL	4	43(5)	241	689	2.9(36)	13	42	343	8.2(27)	3	—	—	—	—	—	—	—	—	—	—	k	1	102	1012

CUMBY, GEORGE George Edward, LB, 6´0˝/220 lbs; Oklahoma; 1980: GB, rnd 1; B7/5/1956 Gorman, TX **1980** GB 9 (2) **1981** GB 16 (16, RILB) **1982**†GB☆9 (9, RILB) **1983** GB 15 (14, RILB) **1984** GB 16 (16, RILB) **1985** GB 15 (1) **1986** Buf 11 (8, RILB) **1987** Phi 1 (0) **NFL** 92 (66) [8 yrs]

CUMISKEY, FRANK Frank Steven, E, 6´2˝/205 lbs; Ohio State; B7/24/1911 Youngstown, OH, D7/16/1982 Sun City, AZ

YEAR	TEAM	G(GS, POS)	RUSH	YD	AVG(LG)	TD	REC	YD	AVG(LG)	TD	PASS	COMP	PCT	YD	AVG(LG)	TD	INT	SK	YD	QBR	KPR	OTD	PTS	TAY
1937	Bkn	9(2)	—	—	—	—	5	50	10.0	0	—	—	—	—	—	—	—	—	—	—	—	—	0	25

CUMMINGS, ED Edward Arthur, LB, 6´3˝/232 lbs; Stanford; B6/29/1941 Anaconda, MT **1964** NYJ-A 11 **1965** Den-A 14 (mlb) **NFL** 25 [2 yrs]

CUMMINGS, JOE Joe Edward, LB, 6´2˝/242 lbs; Wyoming; B6/8/1974 Missoula, MT **1996** SD 3 (0) **1998**†Buf 9 (2) **1999**†Buf 16 (2) **NFL** 28 (4) [3 yrs]

CUMMINGS, MACK Mack, WR, 6´0˝/195 lbs; East Tennessee State; B3/3/1959 Gainesville, FL **1987** NYG 1 (0)

CUNDIFF, BILLY Bill, K, 6´1˝/201 lbs; Drake; B3/30/1980 Valley Center, CA **[K]** **2002** Dal 16 (0) **2003**†Dal 15 (0) **2004** Dal 16 (0) **2005** Dal 6 (0) **NFL** 53 (0) [4 yrs]

CUNEO, ERNIE Ernest L., G, 5´9˝/192 lbs; Penn State; Columbia; B5/27/1905 Carlstadt, NJ, D3/1/1988 Arlington, VA **1929** Ora 12 (11, LG) **1930** Bkn 6 (0) **NFL** 18 (11) [2 yrs]

CUNNINGHAM, BENNIE Bennie Lee, TE, 6´5˝/254 lbs; Clemson; 1976: Pit, rnd 1; B12/23/1954 Laurens, SC

YEAR	TEAM	G(GS, POS)	RUSH	YD	AVG(LG)	TD	REC	YD	AVG(LG)	TD	PASS	COMP	PCT	YD	AVG(LG)	TD	INT	SK	YD	QBR	KPR	OTD	PTS	TAY
1976	†Pit	12	—	—	—	—	5	49	9.8(20)	1	—	—	—	—	—	—	—	—	—	—	—	—	6	30
1977	†Pit	12(10, TE)	—	—	—	—	20	347	17.4(43)	2	—	—	—	—	—	—	—	—	—	—	—	—	12	184
1978	Pit	6(6, te)	—	—	—	—	16	321	20.1(48)	2	—	—	—	—	—	—	—	—	—	—	—	—	12	171
1979	†Pit	15(8, TE)	—	—	—	—	36	512	14.2(28)	4	—	—	—	—	—	—	—	—	—	—	—	—	24	276
1980	Pit	15(1)	—	—	—	—	18	232	12.9(35)	2	—	—	—	—	—	—	—	—	—	—	—	—	12	126
1981	Pit	15(15, TE)	—	—	—	—	41	574	14.0(30)	3	—	—	—	—	—	—	—	—	—	—	—	—	18	302
1982	†Pit	9(9, TE)	—	—	—	—	21	277	13.2(31)	2	—	—	—	—	—	—	—	—	—	—	—	—	12	149
1983	†Pit	16(16, TE)	—	—	—	—	35	442	12.6(29)	3	—	—	—	—	—	—	—	—	—	—	—	—	18	236
1984	†Pit	7(4)	—	—	—	—	4	64	16.0(29)	1	—	—	—	—	—	—	—	—	—	—	—	—	6	37
1985	Pit	11(11, TE)	—	—	—	—	6	61	10.2(17)	0	—	—	—	—	—	—	—	—	—	—	—	—	0	31
NFL	10	118(80)	—	—	—	—	202	2879	14.3(48)	20	—	—	—	—	—	—	—	—	—	—	—	—	120	1540

CUNNINGHAM, CARL Carl Madison, LB, 6´4˝/230 lbs; Houston; 1967: Den, rnd 4; B7/23/1944 Houston, TX **1967** Den-A 13 (LLB) **1968** Den-A 14 (LLB) **1969** Den-A 14 (14, LLB) **1970** Den 14 (14, LLB) **1971** NO 13 **NFL** 68 (28) [5 yrs]

CUNNINGHAM, COOKIE Harold Brewer, E, 6´3˝/210 lbs; Ohio State; B2/4/1905 Mount Vernon, OH, D11/3/1995 Leesburg, FL **1927** Cle 5 (5, LE) **1929** ChiB 11 (11, LE) **1931** SI 10 (7, le) **NFL** 26 (23) [3 yrs]

CUNNINGHAM, DICK Richard Karekin, T-LB, 6´3˝/245 lbs; Arkansas; 1966: Buf, rnd R4/Det, rnd 9; B10/12/1944 Boston, MA **1967** Buf-A 14 (rt) **1968** Buf-A 14 (RT) **1970** Buf 14 **1971** Buf 5 **1972** Buf 9 **1973** Phi 9 **1973** Hou 1 **NFL** 66 [6 yrs]

CUNNINGHAM, DOUG Julian Douglas, RB, 6´0˝/200 lbs; Mississippi; 1967: SF, rnd 6; B9/14/1945 Louisville, MS

YEAR	TEAM	G(GS, POS)	RUSH	YD	AVG(LG)	TD	REC	YD	AVG(LG)	TD	PASS	COMP	PCT	YD	AVG(LG)	TD	INT	SK	YD	QBR	KPR	OTD	PTS	TAY
1967	SF	14	43	212	4.9(64)	2	13	121	9.3(29)	0	—	—	—	—	—	—	—	—	—	—	kp	—	12	768
1968	SF	10	6	7	1.2(5)	0	2	25	12.5(16)	0	—	—	—	—	—	—	—	—	—	—	k	—	0	96
1969	SF	14(13, HB)	147	541	3.7(33)	3	51	484	9.5(58)	0	3	3	100.0	48	16.0(31)	1	0	—	—	—	kp	—	18	922
1970	†SF	12(RB)	128	443	3.5(25)	3	35	209	6.0(29)	0	—	—	—	—	—	—	—	—	—	—	—	—	18	578
1971	†SF	14	25	98	3.9(14)	1	19	188	9.9(28)	0	—	—	—	—	—	—	—	—	—	—	k	—	6	233
1972	SF	4	8	32	4.0(12)	0	—	—	—	—	—	—	—	—	—	—	—	—	—	—	—	—	0	32
1973	SF	14	44	165	3.8(12)	1	15	118	7.9(23)	0	—	—	—	—	—	—	—	—	—	—	k	—	6	287
1974	†Was	2	5	17	3.4(5)	0	2	26	13.0(18)	0	—	—	—	—	—	—	—	—	—	—	—	—	0	30
NFL	8	84(13)	406	1515	3.7(64)	10	137	1171	8.5(58)	0	3	3	100.0	48	16.0(31)	1	0	—	—	—	kp	—	60	2945

CUNNINGHAM, DOUGLAS Douglas Scott, WR, 6´3˝/195 lbs; Rice; B11/14/1955 San Antonio, TX

YEAR	TEAM	G(GS, POS)	RUSH	YD	AVG(LG)	TD	REC	YD	AVG(LG)	TD	PASS	COMP	PCT	YD	AVG(LG)	TD	INT	SK	YD	QBR	KPR	OTD	PTS	TAY
1979	Min	6	—	—	—	—	5	50	10.0(15)	0	—	—	—	—	—	—	—	—	—	—	—	—	0	25

CUNNINGHAM, ED Edward Patrick, C-G, 6´3˝/290 lbs; Washington; 1992: Phx, rnd 3; B8/14/1969 Washington, DC **1992** Phx 10 (5, c) **1993** Phx 15 (15, C) **1994** Arz 16 (16, C) **1995** Arz 9 (8, C) **1996** Sea 11 (3) **NFL** 61 (47) [5 yrs]

CUNNINGHAM, ERIC Eric Allan, G, 6´3˝/257 lbs; Penn State; 1979: NYJ, rnd 4; B3/16/1957 Akron, OH, D1/22/1995 New Haven, CT **1979** NYJ 11 (1) **1980** NYJ 6 (0) **NFL** 17 (1) [2 yrs]

CUNNINGHAM, JAY Jay, DB, 5´10˝/185 lbs; Bowling Green State; 1965: Bos, rnd 14; B10/9/1943 Youngstown, OH **1965** Bos-A 14 **1966** Bos-A 14 (1) **1967** Bos-A 12 (1) **NFL** 40 (2) [3 yrs]

CUNNINGHAM, JIM James Walter, FB, 6´0˝/224 lbs; Pittsburgh; 1961: Was, rnd 3/NYT, rnd 14; B3/11/1939 Connellsville, PA

YEAR	TEAM	G(GS, POS)	RUSH	YD	AVG(LG)	TD	REC	YD	AVG(LG)	TD	PASS	COMP	PCT	YD	AVG(LG)	TD	INT	SK	YD	QBR	KPR	OTD	PTS	TAY
1961	Was	14(fb)	69	160	2.3(19)	1	12	90	7.5(17)	1	—	—	—	—	—	—	—	—	—	—	Pk	—	12	240
1962	Was	14	35	144	4.1(27)	1	6	43	7.2(23)	1	—	—	—	—	—	—	—	—	—	—	k	—	12	205
1963	Was	14	16	33	2.1(7)	1	8	86	10.8(19)	0	—	—	—	—	—	—	—	—	—	—	k	—	6	92
NFL	3	42	120	337	2.8(27)	3	26	219	8.4(23)	2	—	—	—	—	—	—	—	—	—	—	Pk	—	30	537

CUNNINGHAM, LEON Horace Leon, LB-C, 6´3˝/215 lbs; South Carolina; 1955: Det, rnd 8; B8/19/1931, D4/5/1987 Leon, AR **1955** Det 8

CUNNINGHAM, RANDALL Randall, QB, 6´4˝/212 lbs; UNLV; 1985: Phi, rnd 2; B3/27/1963 Santa Barbara, CA

YEAR	TEAM	G(GS, POS)	RUSH	YD	AVG(LG)	TD	REC	YD	AVG(LG)	TD	PASS	COMP	PCT	YD	AVG(LG)	TD	INT	SK	YD	QBR	KPR	OTD	PTS	TAY
1985	Phi	6(4)	29	205	7.1(37)	0	—	—	—	—	81	34	42.0	548	6.8(69)	1	8	20	150	—	—	—	0	164
1986	Phi	15(5, qb)	66	540	8.2(20)	5	—	—	—	—	209	111	53.1	1391	6.7(75)	8	7	72	489	—	P	—	30	1046
1987	Phi	12(12, QB)	76	505	**6.6(45)**	3	1	-3	-3.0(-3)	0	406	223	54.9	2786	6.9(70)	23	12	54	380	83.0	—	—	18	1562
1988	†Phi★	16(16, QB)	93	624	**6.7(33)**	6	—	—	—	—	**560**	301	53.8	3808	6.8(80)	24	16	57	442	77.6	P	—	36	**2068**
1989	†Phi✧	16(16, QB)	104	621	**6.0(51)**	4	—	—	—	—	532	290	54.5	3400	6.4(66)	21	15	45	343	75.5	P	—	24	1866
1990	†Phi★	16(16, QB)	118	942	**8.0(52)**	5	—	—	—	—	465	271	58.3	3466	7.5(**95**)	**30**	13	49	431	91.6	—	—	30	**2355**
1991	Phi	1(1)	—	—	—	—	—	—	—	—	4	1	25.0	19	4.8(19)	0	0	2	16	—	—	—	0	10
1992	†Phi☆	15(15, QB)	87	549	**6.3(30)**	5	—	—	—	—	384	233	60.7	2775	7.2(75)	19	11	60	437	87.3	—	—	30	1642
1993	Phi	4(4)	18	110	6.1(26)	1	—	—	—	—	110	76	69.1	850	7.7(80)	5	5	7	33	—	—	—	6	370
1994	Phi	14(14, QB)	65	288	4.4(22)	3	—	—	—	—	490	265	54.1	3229	6.6(**93**)	16	13	43	333	74.4	P	—	18	1493
1995	†Phi	7(4)	21	98	4.7(20)	0	—	—	—	—	121	69	57.0	605	5.0(33)	3	5	13	79	—	—	—	0	216
1997	†Min	6(3)	19	127	6.7(28)	0	—	—	—	—	88	44	50.0	501	5.7(34)	6	4	7	60	—	P	—	0	248

YEAR	TEAM	G (GS, POS)	RUSH	YD	AVG (LG)	TD	REC	YD	AVG (LG)	TD	PASS	COMP	PCT	YD	AVG (LG)	TD	INT	SK	YD	QBR	KPR	OTD	PTS	TAY
1998	†Min★	15(14, QB)	32	132	4.1(22)	1	1	-3	-3.0(-3)	0	425	259	60.9	3704	8.7(67)	34	10	20	132	**106.0**	—	—	8	1763
1999	†Min	6(6, qb)	10	58	5.8(14)	0	—	—	—	—	200	124	62.0	1475	7.4(61)	8	9	15	101	—	—	—	0	476
2000	Dal	6(3)	23	89	3.9(19)	1	—	—	—	—	125	74	59.2	849	6.8(76)	6	4	8	45	—	—	—	6	394
2001	Bal	6(2)	14	40	2.9(15)	1	—	—	—	—	89	54	60.7	573	6.4(30)	3	2	12	66	—	—	—	6	272
NFL	16	161(135)	775	4928	6.4(52)	35	2	-6	-3.0(-3)	0	4289	2429	56.6	29979	7.0(95)	207	134	484	3537	81.5	P	—	212	15940

CUNNINGHAM, RICHIE Richard Anthony, K, 5´10˝/167 lbs; Louisiana-Lafayette; B8/18/1970 Houma, LA **[K]** **1997** Dal☆16 (0) **1998**†Dal 16 (0) **1999** Dal 12 (0) **1999** Car 3 (0) **2000** Car 4 (0) **2002** Jax 1 (0) **NFL** 52 (0) [5 yrs]

CUNNINGHAM, RICK Patrick Dante Ross, T, 6´7˝/311 lbs; Texas A&M; 1990: Ind, rnd 4; B1/4/1967 Los Angeles, CA **1990** Ind 2 (0) **1992** Phx 8 (6, rt) **1993** Phx 16 (16, RT) **1994** Arz 11 (10, RT) **1995** Min 11 (1) **1997** Oak 7 (0) **1998** Oak 12 (0)

YEAR	TEAM	G (GS, POS)	RUSH	YD	AVG (LG)	TD	REC	YD	AVG (LG)	TD	PASS	COMP	PCT	YD	AVG (LG)	TD	INT	SK	YD	QBR	KPR	OTD	PTS	TAY
1996	Oak	13(0)	—	—	—	—	1	3	3.0(3)	1	—	—	—	—	—	—	—	—	—	—	—	—	6	7
NFL	8	80(33)	—	—	—	—	1	3	3.0(3)	1	—	—	—	—	—	—	—	—	—	—	—	—	6	7

CUNNINGHAM, SAM Samuel Lewis 'Bam', RB, 6´3˝/226 lbs; USC; 1973: NE, rnd 1; B8/15/1950 Santa Barbara, CA

YEAR	TEAM	G (GS, POS)	RUSH	YD	AVG (LG)	TD	REC	YD	AVG (LG)	TD	PASS	COMP	PCT	YD	AVG (LG)	TD	INT	SK	YD	QBR	KPR	OTD	PTS	TAY
1973	NE	14(10, FB)	155	516	3.3(25)	4	15	144	9.6(34)	1	—	—	—	—	—	—	—	—	—	—	—	—	30	633
1974	NE☆	10(10, FB)	166	811	4.9(75)	9	22	214	9.7(37)	2	—	—	—	—	—	—	—	—	—	—	—	—	66	1018
1975	NE	13(13, FB)	169	666	3.9(17)	6	32	253	7.9(24)	2	—	—	—	—	—	—	—	—	—	—	—	—	48	863
1976	†NE	11(11, FB)	172	824	4.8(24)	3	27	299	11.1(41)	0	—	—	—	—	—	—	—	—	—	—	—	—	18	1004
1977	NE	14(14, FB)	270	1015	3.8(31)	4	42	370	8.8(35)	1	—	—	—	—	—	—	—	—	—	—	—	—	30	1245
1978	†NE★	16(14, FB)	199	768	3.9(52)	8	31	297	9.6(31)	0	—	—	—	—	—	—	—	—	—	—	—	—	48	997
1979	NE	12(12, FB)	159	563	3.5(27)	5	29	236	8.1(20)	0	—	—	—	—	—	—	—	—	—	—	—	—	30	731
1981	NE	11(8, FB)	86	269	3.1(12)	4	12	92	7.7(12)	0	—	—	—	—	—	—	—	—	—	—	—	—	24	355
1982	NE	6(2)	9	21	2.3(4)	0	—	—	—	—	—	—	—	—	—	—	—	—	—	—	—	—	0	21
NFL	9	107(94)	1385	5453	3.9(75)	43	210	1905	9.1(41)	6	—	—	—	—	—	—	—	—	—	—	—	—	294	6866

CUNNINGHAM, T.J. Anthony, DB, 6´0˝/191 lbs; Colorado; 1996: Sea, rnd 6; B10/24/1972 Aurora, CO **1996** Sea 9 (0)

CUOZZO, GARY Gary Samuel, QB, 6´0˝/195 lbs; Virginia; B4/26/1941 Montclair, NJ

YEAR	TEAM	G (GS, POS)	RUSH	YD	AVG (LG)	TD	REC	YD	AVG (LG)	TD	PASS	COMP	PCT	YD	AVG (LG)	TD	INT	SK	YD	QBR	KPR	OTD	PTS	TAY
1963	Bal	5	3	26	8.7(26)	0	—	—	—	—	17	10	58.8	104	6.1(23)	0	0	2	19	—	—	—	0	78
1964	Bal	9	7	-2	-0.3(10)	0	—	—	—	—	36	15	41.7	163	4.5(22)	2	3	2	19	—	—	—	0	-31
1965	Bal	7(qb)	6	8	1.3(10)	0	—	—	—	—	105	54	51.4	700	6.7(44)	7	4	10	73	—	—	—	0	233
1966	Bal	7	1	9	9.0(9)	0	—	—	—	—	50	26	52.0	424	8.5(69)	4	2	8	82	—	—	—	0	161
1967	NO	13(QB)	19	43	2.3(10)	1	—	—	—	—	260	134	51.5	1562	6.0(49)	7	12	33	236	59.8	—	—	6	389
1968	Min	4	1	4	4.0(4)	0	—	—	—	—	33	24	72.7	297	9.0(31)	1	0	4	32	—	—	—	0	158
1969	†Min	9	3	-4	-1.3(2)	0	—	—	—	—	98	49	50.0	693	7.1(50)	4	5	6	54	—	—	—	0	163
1970	†Min	12(12, QB)	17	61	3.6(15)	0	—	—	—	—	257	128	49.8	1720	6.7(72)	7	10	23	161	64.3	—	—	0	556
1971	†Min	8(8, QB)	15	24	1.6(9)	0	—	—	—	—	168	75	44.6	842	5.0(52)	6	8	13	97	52.2	—	—	0	155
1972	SL	8(QB)	4	7	1.8(9)	0	—	—	—	—	158	69	43.7	897	5.7(68)	5	11	13	89	43.7	—	—	0	41
NFL	10	82(20)	76	176	2.3(26)	1	—	—	—	—	1182	584	49.4	7402	6.3(72)	43	55	114	862	62.1	—	—	6	1902

CUPP, KEITH Keith Eric, T, 6´6˝/301 lbs; Findlay; B6/20/1964 Lima, OH **1987** Cin 3 (3)

CUPPOLETTI, BREE Randolph Bruno, G, 5´10˝/200 lbs; Oregon; B6/19/1910 Virginia, MN, D9/21/1960 Virginia, MN **1934** ChiC 11 (5, lg) **1936** ChiC☆12 (12, LG) **1937** ChiC 10 (7, LG) **1938** ChiC 11 (8, LG) **1939** Phi 10 (8, RG)

YEAR	TEAM	G (GS, POS)	RUSH	YD	AVG (LG)	TD	REC	YD	AVG (LG)	TD	PASS	COMP	PCT	YD	AVG (LG)	TD	INT	SK	YD	QBR	KPR	OTD	PTS	TAY
1935	ChiC☆	12(11, LG)	1	9	9.0	0	—	—	—	—	—	—	—	—	—	—	—	—	—	—	—	—	0	9
NFL	6	66(51)	1	9	9.0	0	—	—	—	—	—	—	—	—	—	—	—	—	—	—	—	—	0	9

CURCHIN, JEFF Jeff Mansfield, T-G, 6´7˝/260 lbs; Florida State; 1970: Chi, rnd 6; B12/17/1947 Binghamton, NY **1970** ChiB 14 **1971** ChiB 12 **1972** Buf 1 **NFL** 27 [3 yrs]

CURCILLO, TONY Anthony, DB-HB, 6´1˝/200 lbs; Ohio State; 1953: ChiC, rnd 6; B5/27/1931 Long Branch, NJ

YEAR	TEAM	G (GS, POS)	RUSH	YD	AVG (LG)	TD	REC	YD	AVG (LG)	TD	PASS	COMP	PCT	YD	AVG (LG)	TD	INT	SK	YD	QBR	KPR	OTD	PTS	TAY
1953	ChiC	12(DB)	8	29	3.6(12)	0	—	—	—	—	—	—	—	—	—	—	—	—	—	—	Kr	—	0	27

CURCIO, MIKE Michael A., LB, 6´1˝/237 lbs; Temple; 1980: Phi, rnd 8; B1/24/1957 Hudson, NY **1981**†Phi 16 (0) **1982** Phi 5 (0) **1983** GB 13 (0) **NFL** 34 (0) [3 yrs]

CURE, ARMAND Armand Arthur, B, 6´0˝/198 lbs; Rhode Island; B8/1/1919 New Bedford, MA, D12/5/2003 Long Beach, CA

YEAR	TEAM	G (GS, POS)	RUSH	YD	AVG (LG)	TD	REC	YD	AVG (LG)	TD	PASS	COMP	PCT	YD	AVG (LG)	TD	INT	SK	YD	QBR	KPR	OTD	PTS	TAY
1947	Bal-A	1(0)	2	-1	-0.5	0	—	—	—	—	—	—	—	—	—	—	—	—	—	—	—	—	0	-1

CURETON, WILL Will, QB, 6´3˝/200 lbs; Texas A&M-Commerce; B12/2/1950 Meridian, TX

YEAR	TEAM	G (GS, POS)	RUSH	YD	AVG (LG)	TD	REC	YD	AVG (LG)	TD	PASS	COMP	PCT	YD	AVG (LG)	TD	INT	SK	YD	QBR	KPR	OTD	PTS	TAY
1975	Cle	1	1	1	1.0(1)	0	—	—	—	—	32	10	31.3	95	3.0(16)	1	1	2	21	—	—	—	0	14

CURLEY, AUGUST August Onorato, LB, 6´3˝/226 lbs; USC; 1983: Det, rnd 4; B1/24/1960 Little Rock, AR **1983** Det 10 (0) **1984** Det 8 (0) **1985** Det 16 (14, LILB) **1986** Det 4 (0) **NFL** 38 (14) [4 yrs]

CURLEY, DAN Daniel Lawrence, FB, 6´4˝/254 lbs; Eastern Washington; 2003: SL, rnd 5; B4/25/1978 Tacoma, WA **2003** SL 1 (0)

CURRAN, HARRY Harry Ambrose, HB-WB, 5´10˝/180 lbs; Massachusetts; B6/2/1894 Marlboro, MA, D6/28/1976 South Pasadena, FL **1920** ChiC 9 (5, RH) **1921** ChiC 1 (0) **NFL** 10 (5) [2 yrs]

CURRAN, PAT Patrick Michael, TE-TB, 6´4˝/238 lbs; Iowa State; Lakeland; 1969: LA, rnd 6; B9/21/1945 Milwaukee, WI **[K]**

YEAR	TEAM	G (GS, POS)	RUSH	YD	AVG (LG)	TD	REC	YD	AVG (LG)	TD	PASS	COMP	PCT	YD	AVG (LG)	TD	INT	SK	YD	QBR	KPR	OTD	PTS	TAY
1969	†LARm	1	—	—	—	—	—	—	—	—	—	—	—	—	—	—	—	—	—	—	k	—	0	-2
1970	LARm	14(1)	25	92	3.7(11)	0	3	25	8.3(14)	0	2	0	0.0	0	0.0	0	1	—	—	—	k	1	6	71
1971	LARm	14	—	—	—	—	1	2	2.0(2)	1	—	—	—	—	—	—	—	—	—	—	k	—	6	-4
1972	LARm	10	—	—	—	—	—	—	—	—	—	—	—	—	—	—	—	—	—	—	k	—	0	-23
1973	†LARm	14	—	—	—	—	5	56	11.2(27)	1	—	—	—	—	—	—	—	—	—	—	k	—	6	42
1974	†LARm	13	—	—	—	—	—	—	—	—	—	—	—	—	—	—	—	—	—	—	k	—	0	1
1975	SD	14(14, TE)	3	21	7.0(12)	0	45	619	13.8(39)	0	—	—	—	—	—	—	—	—	—	—	Kk	—	1	314
1976	SD	14(14, TE)	1	12	12.0(12)	0	33	349	10.6(29)	1	—	—	—	—	—	—	—	—	—	—	—	—	6	192
1977	SD	14(5, te)	1	2	2.0(2)	0	10	123	12.3(20)	0	—	—	—	—	—	—	—	—	—	—	—	—	0	64
1978	SD	14	—	—	—	—	9	92	10.2(20)	2	—	—	—	—	—	—	—	—	—	—	—	—	12	56
NFL	10	122(34)	30	127	4.2(12)	0	106	1266	11.9(39)	5	2	0	0.0	0	0.0	0	1	—	—	—	Kk	1	37	709

CURRAN, WILLIAM William Martin, WR, 5´10˝/175 lbs; UCLA; B12/30/1959 Inglewood, CA

YEAR	TEAM	G (GS, POS)	RUSH	YD	AVG (LG)	TD	REC	YD	AVG (LG)	TD	PASS	COMP	PCT	YD	AVG (LG)	TD	INT	SK	YD	QBR	KPR	OTD	PTS	TAY
1982	†Atl	7(0)	—	—	—	—	—	—	—	—	—	—	—	—	—	—	—	—	—	—	—	—	—	—
1983	Atl	16(0)	—	—	—	—	1	15	15.0(15)	0	—	—	—	—	—	—	—	—	—	—	k	—	0	4
1984	Atl	14(0)	—	—	—	—	1	7	7.0(7)	0	—	—	—	—	—	—	—	—	—	—	kp	—	0	34
NFL	3	37(0)	—	—	—	—	2	22	11.0(15)	0	—	—	—	—	—	—	—	—	—	—	kp	—	0	37

CURRENT, MIKE Michael Wayne, T, 6´5˝/274 lbs; Ohio State; 1967: Den, rnd 3; B9/17/1945 Lima, OH **1967** Den-A 3 **1967** Mia-A 1 **1968** Den-A 14 (RT) **1969** Den-A✧14 (14, RT) **1970** Den 14 (14, RT) **1971** Den 14 (14, RT) **1972** Den 14 (14, RT) **1973** Den 14 (14, RT) **1974** Den 14 (14, RT) **1975** Den 7 (7, RT) **1976** TB 14 (14, RT) **1977** Mia 14 (14, RT) **1978**†Mia 16 (15, RT) **1979**†Mia 16 (16, RT) **NFL** 169 (150) [13 yrs]

CURRIE, DAN Daniel George, LB, 6´3˝/235 lbs; Michigan State; 1958: GB, rnd 1; B6/27/1935 Detroit, MI **1958** GB 12 **1959** GB 12 (LLB) **1960**†GB✧12 (LLB) **1961**†GB☆12 (LLB) **1962**†GB☆14 (LLB) **1963** GB☆14 (LLB) **1964** GB 14 **1965** LARm 14 (RLB) **1966** LARm 14 **NFL** 118 [9 yrs]

CURRIE, HERSCHEL Herschel Lamont, DB, 6´0˝/190 lbs; Oregon State; B9/8/1965 Chicago, IL **1994** Arz 1 (0)

CURRIER, BILL William Frank, DB, 6´0˝/196 lbs; South Carolina; 1977: Hou, rnd 9; B1/5/1955 Glen Burnie, MD **1977** Hou 14 (11, SS) **1978**†Hou 14 (11, SS) **1979**†Hou 16 **1980** NE 16 (0) **1981**†NYG 16 (14, SS) **1982** NYG 9 (9, SS) **1983** NYG 15 (15, SS) **1984**†NYG 9 (8, SS) **1985** NYG 2 (2) **NFL** 111 (70) [9 yrs]

CURRIVAN, DON Donald F., E, 6´0˝/193 lbs; Boston College; 1943: ChiC, rnd 3; B3/6/1920 Mansfield, MA, D5/16/1956 Hyannis, MA

YEAR	TEAM	G (GS, POS)	RUSH	YD	AVG (LG)	TD	REC	YD	AVG (LG)	TD	PASS	COMP	PCT	YD	AVG (LG)	TD	INT	SK	YD	QBR	KPR	OTD	PTS	TAY
1943	ChiC	7(7, RE)	—	—	—	—	5	79	15.8(34)	1	—	—	—	—	—	—	—	—	—	—	—	1	12	45
1944	C-P	10(0)	—	—	—	—	7	163	23.3(72)	2	—	—	—	—	—	—	—	—	—	—	k	—	12	91
1945	Bos	10(5, RE)	—	—	—	—	16	397	24.8(80)	4	—	—	—	—	—	—	—	—	—	—	k	—	24	207
1946	Bos	11(3)	—	—	—	—	11	262	23.8(60)	4	—	—	—	—	—	—	—	—	—	—	kp	—	24	167
1947	Bos	12(3)	—	—	—	—	24	782	**32.6**(**78**)	9	—	—	—	—	—	—	—	—	—	—	i	1	60	431
1948	Bos	3(0)	—	—	—	—	2	29	14.5(0)	0	—	—	—	—	—	—	—	—	—	—	—	—	0	15
1948	LARm	10(2)	1	-4	-4.0(-4)	0	10	189	18.9(58)	3	—	—	—	—	—	—	—	—	—	—	—	1	24	106

YEAR	TEAM	G (GS, POS)	RUSH	YD	AVG(LG)	TD	REC	YD	AVG(LG)	TD	PASS COMP	PCT	YD	AVG(LG)	TD	INT	SK	YD	QBR	KPR	OTD	PTS	TAY
1949	†LARm	12 (0)	—	—	—	—	3	78	26.0(40)	1	—	—	—	—	—	—	—	—	—	i		6	50
NFL	7	75 (20)	1	-4	-4.0(-4)	0	78	1979	25.4(80)	24	—	—	—	—	—	—	—	—	—	kpi	3	162	1110

CURRY, BILL William Alexander, C-LB, 6´3˝/235 lbs; Georgia Tech; 1964: GB, rnd 20/Oak, rnd 23; B10/21/1942 College Park, GA **1965**†GB 14 **1966**†GB 14 (C) **1967** Bal 11 **1968**†Bal 14 (C) **1969** Bal☆14 (C) **1970**†Bal 14 (C) **1971**†Bal★14 (C) **1972** Bal◇14 (C) **1973** Hou 4 **1974**†LARm 10 **NFL** 123 [10 yrs]

CURRY, BUDDY George Jessel, LB, 6´4˝/224 lbs; North Carolina; 1980: Atl, rnd 2; B6/4/1958 Greenville, NC **1980**†Atl☆16 (16, RILB) **1981** Atl 16 (16, RILB) **1982**†Atl☆9 (9, RILB) **1983** Atl 16 (16, RLB) **1984** Atl 16 (16, MLB) **1985** Atl 16 (14, MLB) **1986** Atl 16 (16, LILB) **1987** Atl 4 (4, LILB) **NFL** 109 (107) [8 yrs]

CURRY, CLARENCE Clarence, DB, 6´1˝/190 lbs; Villanova; B12/7/1981 Rochester, MI **2004** Arz 1 (0)

CURRY, CRAIG Craig Anthony, DB, 6´0˝/187 lbs; Texas; 1984: Ind, rnd 4; B7/20/1961 Houston, TX **1984** TB 5 (0) **1985** TB 16 (7, ss) **1986** TB 16 (10, FS) **1987** Ind 3 (0) **NFL** 40 (17) [4 yrs]

CURRY, DEMARCUS DeMarcus Jerrell, T, 6´5˝/332 lbs; Auburn; B4/30/1975 Columbus, GA **2001** TB 3 (0)

CURRY, DONTE Donte, LB, 6´1˝/233 lbs; Morris Brown; B7/22/1978 Savannah, GA **2001** Was 8 (0) **2002** Det 16 (10, RLB) **2003** Det 11 (0) **2004** Det 12 (0) **2005** Det 13 (2) **NFL** 60 (12) [5 yrs]

CURRY, ERIC Eric Felece, DE, 6´5˝/270 lbs; Alabama; 1993: TB, rnd 1; B2/3/1970 Thomasville, GA **1993** TB 10 (10, RDE) **1994** TB 15 (14, RDE) **1995** TB 16 (16, RDE) **1996** TB 12 (3) **1997** TB 6 (1) **1998** Jax 11 (0) **1999** Jax 5 (0) **NFL** 75 (44) [7 yrs]

CURRY, IVORY Ivory, DB, 5´11˝/185 lbs; Florida; B2/6/1961 Miami, FL, D8/22/1989 Brandon, FL **1987** TB 3 (2)

CURRY, JULIUS Julius Justin, DB, 6´0˝/195 lbs; Michigan; B5/17/1979 Detroit, MI **2003** Det 3 (0)

CURRY, RONALD Ronald Antonio, WR, 6´2˝/220 lbs; North Carolina; 2002: Oak, rnd 7; B5/28/1979 Hampton, VA

YEAR	TEAM	G (GS, POS)	RUSH	YD	AVG(LG)	TD	REC	YD	AVG(LG)	TD	PASS COMP	PCT	YD	AVG(LG)	TD	INT	SK	YD	QBR	KPR	OTD	PTS	TAY
2002	Oak	1 (0)	—	—	—	—	—	—	—	—	—	—	—	—	—	—	—	—	—			0	23
2003	Oak	16 (2)	1	0	0.0(0)	0	5	31	6.2(16)	0	—	—	—	—	—	—	—	—	k			0	16
2004	Oak	12 (3)	1	-3	-3.0(-3)	0	50	679	13.6(63)	6	1	0	0.0	0	0.0	0	0	0	k		36	370
2005	Oak	2 (0)	—	—	—	—	2	12	6.0(8)	0	—	—	—	—	—	—	—	—				0	6
NFL	4	31 (5)	2	-3	-1.5	0	57	722	12.7(63)	6	1	0	0.0	0	0.0	0	0	0	k		36	414

CURRY, ROY Roy, WR, 6´1˝/185 lbs; Jackson State; 1963: Pit, rnd 12; B11/9/1939

YEAR	TEAM	G (GS, POS)	RUSH	YD	AVG(LG)	TD	REC	YD	AVG(LG)	TD										KPR	OTD	PTS	TAY
1963	Pit	6	—	—	—	—	1	31	31.0(31)	1	—	—	—	—	—	—	—	—	—	k		6	33

CURRY, SCOTT Scott Richard, T, 6´5˝/300 lbs; Montana; 1999: GB, rnd 6; B12/25/1975 Conrad, MT **1999** GB 5 (1)

CURRY, SHANE Shane Clifton, DE, 6´5˝/270 lbs; Georgia Tech; Miami (FL); 1991: Ind, rnd 2; B4/7/1968 Cincinnati, OH, D5/3/1992 Cincinnati, OH **1991** Ind 9 (0)

CURTIN, DON Don William, BB, 5´8˝/155 lbs; Marquette; B1902 Woodville, WI, deceased [K] **1926** Mil 3 (2), 7 **1926** Rac 1 (0) **NFL** 4 (2) [1 yr]

CURTIS, BOBBY Robert Waymon, LB, 6´3˝/235 lbs; The Citadel; Jackson State; Savannah State; B10/23/1964 Macon, GA **1987** Was 3 (3)

CURTIS, CANUTE Canute, LB, 6´2˝/250 lbs; West Virginia; 1997: Cin, rnd 6; B8/4/1974 Amityville, NY **1997** Cin 3 (0) **1998** Cin 5 (0) **1999** Cin 15 (0) **2000** Cin 15 (0) **2001** Cin 16 (4) **2002** Cin 16 (11, LLB) **NFL** 70 (15) [6 yrs]

CURTIS, ISAAC Isaac Fischer, WR, 6´1˝/192 lbs; California; San Diego State; 1973: Cin, rnd 1; B10/20/1950 Santa Ana, CA

YEAR	TEAM	G (GS, POS)	RUSH	YD	AVG(LG)	TD	REC	YD	AVG(LG)	TD										KPR	OTD	PTS	TAY
1973	†Cin★	14 (WR)	2	-11	-5.5(1)	0	45	843	18.7(77)	9	—	—	—	—	—	—	—	—	↧			54	456
1974	†Cin★	14 (WR)	8	62	7.8(20)	0	30	633	21.1(77)	10	—	—	—	—	—	—	—	—				60	429
1975	†Cin★	14 (WR)	6	-9	-1.5(14)	0	44	934	21.2(55)	7	—	—	—	—	—	—	—	—				42	493
1976	Cin★	14 (WR)	3	29	9.7(19)	0	41	766	18.7(85)	6	—	—	—	—	—	—	—	—				36	442
1977	Cin	8 (WR)	—	—	—	—	20	338	16.9(54)	2	—	—	—	—	—	—	—	—				12	179
1978	Cin	16 (WR)	1	1	1.0(1)	0	47	737	15.7(57)	3	—	—	—	—	—	—	—	—				18	385
1979	Cin	16 (WR)	2	-11	-5.5(-4)	0	32	605	18.9(67)	8	—	—	—	—	—	—	—	—				48	332
1980	Cin	15 (13, WR)	—	—	—	—	43	610	14.2(67)	3	—	—	—	—	—	—	—	—				18	320
1981	†Cin	15 (14, WR)	—	—	—	—	37	609	16.5(68)	2	—	—	—	—	—	—	—	—				12	315
1982	†Cin	9 (9, WR)	3	15	5.0(8)	0	23	320	13.9(45)	1	—	—	—	—	—	—	—	—				6	180
1983	Cin	16 (16, WR)	—	—	—	—	42	571	13.6(80)	2	—	—	—	—	—	—	—	—				12	296
1984	Cin	16 (13, WR)	—	—	—	—	12	135	11.3(22)	0	—	—	—	—	—	—	—	—				0	68
NFL	12	167 (65)	25	76	3.0(20)	0	416	7101	17.1(85)	53	—	—	—	—	—	—	—	—				318	3892

CURTIS, KEVIN Kevin Deevon, WR, 5´11˝/186 lbs; Utah State; 2003: SL, rnd 3; B7/17/1978 Murray, UT

YEAR	TEAM	G (GS, POS)	RUSH	YD	AVG(LG)	TD	REC	YD	AVG(LG)	TD										KPR	OTD	PTS	TAY
2003	SL	4 (1)	—	—	—	—	4	13	3.3(8)	0	—	—	—	—	—	—	—	—				0	7
2004	†SL	15 (0)	3	24	8.0(15)	0	32	421	13.2(41)	2	—	—	—	—	—	—	—	—				14	245
2005	SL	16 (9, WR)	1	5	5.0(5)	1	60	801	13.4(83)	6	—	—	—	—	—	—	—	—				42	446
NFL	3	35 (10)	4	29	7.3(15)	1	96	1235	12.9(83)	8	—	—	—	—	—	—	—	—				56	697

CURTIS, MIKE James Michael 'Mad Dog', LB-FB, 6´3˝/232 lbs; Duke; 1965: Bal, rnd 1/KC, rnd 3; B3/27/1943 Washington, DC [I] **1966** Bal 12 (7, LLB) **1967** Bal 3 **1968**†Bal 14 (LLB) **1969** Bal☆14 (MLB) **1970**†Bal 14 (MLB) **1971**†Bal★13 (MLB) **1972** Bal (MLB) **1973** Bal 7 (MLB) **1974** Bal★14 (MLB) **1975** Bal 6 (6, mlb) **1976** Sea 14 (14, RLB) **1977** Was 14 (10, RLB) **1978** Was 13 (2)

YEAR	TEAM	G (GS, POS)	RUSH	YD	AVG(LG)	TD	REC	YD	AVG(LG)	TD										KPR	OTD	PTS	TAY
1965	†Bal	14	6	1	0.2(4)	0	1	5	5.0(5)	0	—	—	—	—	—	—	—	—	k			0	-17
NFL	14	166 (39)	6	1	0.2(4)	0	1	5	5.0(5)	0	—	—	—	—	—	—	—	—	ki		3	18	187

CURTIS, SCOTT Alston Scott, LB, 6´1˝/230 lbs; New Hampshire; B12/26/1964 Burlington, VT **1988** Phi 16 (0) **1989**†Den 16 (0) **1990** Den 9 (1) **NFL** 41 (1) [3 yrs]

CURTIS, TOM Thomas Newton, DB, 6´1˝/196 lbs; Michigan; 1970: Bal, rnd 14; B11/1/1947 Cleveland, OH **1970** Bal 10 **1971**†Bal 14 **NFL** 24 [2 yrs]

CURTIS, TRAVIS Travis Fenner, DB, 5´10˝/180 lbs; West Virginia; B9/27/1965 Washington, DC **1987** SL 12 (1) **1988** Phx 12 (0) **1988** Was 1 (0) **1989**†Min 16 (11, FS) **1990** NYJ 14 (3) **1991** Was 1 (0) **NFL** 56 (15) [5 yrs]

CURZON, HARRY Harry M., B-E, 6´0˝/195 lbs; none; B11/12/1894 Champaign, IL, D4/25/1966 Coral Gables, FL **1925** Buf 5 (2), 6 **1925** Ham 4 (3) **1926** Lou 1 (1) **1926** Ham 4 (4, WB) **1928** ChiC 1 (0) **NFL** 15 (10), 6 [3 yrs]

CUSHING, MATT Matt Jay, TE, 6´4˝/255 lbs; Illinois; B7/2/1975 Chicago, IL

YEAR	TEAM	G (GS, POS)	RUSH	YD	AVG(LG)	TD	REC	YD	AVG(LG)	TD										KPR	OTD	PTS	TAY
1999	Pit	7 (1)	—	—	—	—	2	29	14.5(22)	0	—	—	—	—	—	—	—	—				0	15
2000	Pit	7 (1)	—	—	—	—	4	17	4.3(5)	0	—	—	—	—	—	—	—	—				0	9
2001	†Pit	13 (3)	—	—	—	—	5	24	4.8(9)	1	—	—	—	—	—	—	—	—				6	17
2002	†Pit	6 (0)	—	—	—	—	1	4	4.0(4)	0	—	—	—	—	—	—	—	—				0	2
2003	Pit	4 (0)	—	—	—	—	—	—	—	—	—	—	—	—	—	—	—	—				—	—
2004	†Pit	16 (0)	—	—	—	—	1	17	17.0(17)	0	—	—	—	—	—	—	—	—	k			0	9
NFL	6	53 (5)	—	—	—	—	13	91	7.0(22)	1	—	—	—	—	—	—	—	—	k			6	51

CUSICK, PETER Peter Martin, NT, 6´1˝/255 lbs; Ohio State; 1975: NE, rnd 3; B10/27/1952 San Bernardino, CA **1975** NE 13

CUTHBERT, RANDY Randy Alan, RB, 6´2˝/225 lbs; Duke; B1/16/1970 Lansdale, PA **1994** Pit 1 (0)

YEAR	TEAM	G (GS, POS)	RUSH	YD	AVG(LG)	TD	REC	YD	AVG(LG)	TD										KPR	OTD	PTS	TAY
1993	†Pit	10 (0)	1	7	7.0(7)	0	1	3	3.0(3)	0	—	—	—	—	—	—	—	—				0	9
NFL	2	11 (0)	1	7	7.0(7)	0	1	3	3.0(3)	0	—	—	—	—	—	—	—	—				0	9

CUTLER, HARRY Harry G., T, 6´2˝/190 lbs; none; B9/13/1893, D4/24/1964 Dayton, OH **1920** Day 7 (3, LT)

CUTSINGER, GARY Gary Leon, DE, 6´5˝/245 lbs; Oklahoma State; 1962: Hou, rnd 4/GB, rnd 7; B2/4/1940 Perry, OK **1962**†Hou-A 14 (LDE) **1963** Hou-A 14 (LDE) **1964** Hou-A 14. **1965** Hou-A 14 (LDE) **1966** Hou-A 14 (LDE) **1968** Hou-A 14 **NFL** 84 [6 yrs]

CVERCKO, ANDY Andrew Bertram, G, 6´1˝/243 lbs; Northwestern; 1959: GB, rnd 5; B11/6/1937 Campbell, OH **1960**†GB 12 **1961** Dal 11 (10, LG) **1962** Dal 14 (LG) **1963** Cle 2 **1963** Was 8 **NFL** 47 (10) [4 yrs]

CYRE, HECTOR Hector J., T-G-E, 6´2˝/215 lbs; Gonzaga; B10/25/1901, D8/5/1971 Langley, WA **1926** GB 10 (6, lt) **1928** NYY 3 (1) **NFL** 13 (7) [2 yrs]

CZAROBSKI, ZIGGY Zygmont Peter, aka Sigismunt Peter Czarobski, T, 6´0˝/230 lbs; Notre Dame; 1945: ChiC, rnd 7; B9/13/1922 Chicago, IL, D7/1/1984 Chicago, IL **1948** ChiR-A 14 (3) **1949** ChiH-A 12 (12, RT) **AAFC** 26 (15) [2 yrs]

YEAR	TEAM	G(GS, POS)	RUSH	YD	AVG(LG)	TD	REC	YD	AVG(LG)	TD	PASS	COMP	PCT	YD	AVG(LG)	TD	INT	SK	YD	QBR	KPR	OTD	PTS	TAY

DAANEN, JERRY   Jerome Theodore, WR, 6´0˝/190 lbs; Miami (FL); 1968: SL, rnd 8; B12/15/1944 Green Bay, WI

1968	SL	14(2)	—	—	—	—	4	35	8.8(15)	0	—	—	—	—	—	—	—	—	—	—	—	—	0	18
1969	SL	9	—	—	—	—	2	12	6.0(7)	0	—	—	—	—	—	—	—	—	—	—	—	—	0	6
1970	SL	14	—	—	—	—	2	31	15.5(22)	0	—	—	—	—	—	—	—	—	—	—	—	—	0	16
NFL	3	37(2)	—	—	—	—	8	78	9.8(22)	0	—	—	—	—	—	—	—	—	—	—	—	—	0	39

DABNEY, CARLTON   Carlton Roland, DT, 6´3˝/259 lbs; Morgan State; 1968: Atl, rnd 2; B1/26/1947 Richmond, VA   **1968** Atl 14 (14, RDT)

DACH, CARSON   Carson Eliot, C, 6´1˝/253 lbs; Eastern Michigan; B9/29/1980 Flint, MI   **2003** NYG 16 (0)

DADDIO, BILL   Louis William, E, 5´11˝/207 lbs; Pittsburgh; 1939: ChiC, rnd 5; B4/26/1916 Meadville, PA, D7/5/1989 Mount Lebanon, PA **[K]**

1941	ChiC	11(3)	—	—	—	—	5	39	7.8(14)	0	—	—	—	—	—	—	—	—	—	—	K	—	20	20
1942	ChiC	11(10, LE)	—	—	—	—	11	108	9.8(23)	0	—	—	—	—	—	—	—	—	—	—	Ki	—	29	58
NFL	2	22(13)	—	—	—	—	16	147	9.2(23)	1	—	—	—	—	—	—	—	—	—	—	Ki	—	49	78
1946	Buf-A	3(1)	—	—	—	—	—	—	—	—	—	—	—	—	—	—	—	—	—	—	K	—	3	0

D'ADDIO, DAVE   David John, RB, 6´2˝/235 lbs; Maryland; 1984: Det, rnd 4; B7/13/1961 Newark, NJ

| 1984 | Det | 16(2) | 7 | 46 | 6.6(14) | 0 | 1 | 12 | 12.0(12) | 0 | — | — | — | — | — | — | — | — | — | — | — | — | 0 | 37 |

DADMUN, HARRIE   Harrie Holland, G-T, 6´0˝/235 lbs; Tufts; Harvard; B6/25/1894 Cambridge, MA, D9/11/1980 Concord, MN   **1920** Can☆2 (2)   **1921** NYG 1 (1, LG)   **NFL** 3 (3) [2 yrs]

DAFFER, TED   Terrell Edwin, DE, 6´0˝/198 lbs; Tennessee; 1952: ChiB, rnd 21; B9/24/1929 Norfolk, VA   **1954** ChiB 12

DAFNEY, BERNARD   Bernard Eugene, G-T, 6´5˝/324 lbs; Tennessee; 1992: Hou, rnd 9; B11/1/1968 Los Angeles, CA, D1/11/2006 Conyers, GA   **1992** Min 2 (0)   **1993**†Min 16 (4)   **1994**†Min 16 (16, RG)   **1995** Arz 11 (8, rg)   **1996**†Pit 14 (1)   **1997** Bal 1 (0)   **NFL** 60 (29) [6 yrs]

DaGATA, FRED   Frederick Albert, FB, 5´10˝/187 lbs; Boston College; Providence; B4/4/1908 Fall River, MA, D5/1/1980 Fall River, MA   **1931** Pro 1 (0)

D'AGOSTINO, FRANK   Francis Joseph, G-T, 6´1˝/245 lbs; Auburn; 1956: Phi, rnd 2; B3/11/1934 Philadelphia, PA, deceased   **1956** Phi 12   **1960** NYT-A 2   **NFL** 14 [2 yrs]

D'AGOSTINO, LOU   Louis, FB, 6´0˝/235 lbs; Hofstra; Rhode Island; B12/12/1973 Brooklyn, NY   **1996** NYJ 9 (0)

DAHL, BOB   Robert Allen, G-T, 6´5˝/318 lbs; Notre Dame; 1991: Cin, rnd 3; B1/15/1968 Chicago, IL   **1992** Cle 9 (9, LG)   **1993** Cle 16 (16, RG)   **1994**†Cle 15 (15, RG)   **1995** Cle 16 (16, RG)   **1996** Was☆15 (15, RG)   **1997** Was 11 (9, rg)   **NFL** 82 (80) [6 yrs]

DAHLGREN, GEORGE   George Arthur, G-T, 5´10˝/200 lbs; Wisconsin-LaCrosse; Beloit; B4/17/1887 La Crosse, WI, D1/6/1940 Chicago, IL   **1924** Ken 4 (4, LG)   **1925** RI 1 (0)   **1925** Ham 3 (2, LG)   **1926** Ham 2 (2, LT)   **NFL** 10 (8) [3 yrs]

DAHMS, TOM   Thomas G., T, 6´5˝/242 lbs; San Diego State; B4/19/1927 San Diego, CA, D11/30/1988 Orange County, CA   **1951**†LARm 12 (RT)   **1952**†LARm 12 (RT)   **1953** LARm 12 (RT)   **1954** LARm 12   **1955** GB 12 (RT)   **1956** ChiC 12 (LT)   **1957** SF 8   **NFL** 80 [7 yrs]

DAIGLE, ANTHONY   Anthony John, RB, 5´10˝/203 lbs; Arizona State; Fresno State; 1994: KC, rnd 6; B4/5/1970 San Francisco, CA   **1994** Pit 1 (0)

DAILEY, CASEY   Casey, LB, 6´3˝/249 lbs; Northwestern; 1998: NYJ, rnd 5; B6/11/1975 LaVerne, CA   **1999** NYJ 6 (0)

DAILEY, TED   Theodore E., E, 5´9˝/170 lbs; Pittsburgh; B9/25/1908 Phillipsburg, NJ, D10/3/1992 Syracuse, NY

| 1933 | Pit | 10(4) | 1 | 1 | 1.0(1) | 0 | 7 | 66 | 9.4 | 0 | — | — | — | — | — | — | — | — | — | — | — | — | 0 | 34 |

DALBY, DAVE   David Merle, C, 6´3˝/247 lbs; UCLA; 1972: Oak, rnd 4; B10/19/1950 Alexandria, MN, D8/30/2002 Dana Point, CA   **1972**†Oak 14   **1973**†Oak 14   **1974**†Oak 14   **1975**†Oak 14 (14, C)   **1976**†Oak 14 (C)   **1977**†Oak◊14 (14, C)   **1978** Oak 16 (16, C)   **1980**†Oak 14 (14, C)   **1981** Oak 16 (7, c)   **1982**†LARd 9 (9, C)   **1983**†LARd 16 (16, C)   **1984**†LARd 16 (14, C)   **1985**†LARd 16 (2)

| 1979 | Oak | 16(15, C) | — | — | — | — | 1 | 1 | 1.0(1) | 0 | — | — | — | — | — | — | — | — | — | — | — | — | 0 | 1 |
| NFL | 14 | 205(121) | — | — | — | — | 1 | 1 | 1.0(1) | 0 | — | — | — | — | — | — | — | — | — | — | — | — | 0 | 1 |

DALE, CARROLL   Carroll Wayne, WR-TE-FL, 6´2˝/200 lbs; Virginia Tech; 1960: LA, rnd 8; B4/24/1938 Wise, VA

1960	LARm	12(TE)	—	—	—	—	19	336	17.7(63)	3	—	—	—	—	—	—	—	—	—	—	—	—	18	183
1961	LARm	14(TE)	—	—	—	—	35	561	16.0(68)	2	—	—	—	—	—	—	—	—	—	—	—	—	12	291
1962	LARm	14(TE)	—	—	—	—	29	584	20.1(80)	3	—	—	—	—	—	—	—	—	—	—	—	—	18	307
1963	LARm	12(FL)	1	12	12.0(12)	0	34	638	18.8(66)	7	—	—	—	—	—	—	—	—	—	—	—	—	42	366
1964	LARm	13	—	—	—	—	32	544	17.0(44)	2	—	—	—	—	—	—	—	—	—	—	—	—	12	282
1965	†GB	13(FL)	—	—	—	—	20	382	19.1(77)	2	—	—	—	—	—	—	—	—	—	—	—	—	12	201
1966	†GB	14(TE)	—	—	—	—	37	876	23.7(83)	7	—	—	—	—	—	—	—	—	—	—	—	—	42	473
1967	†GB	13(FL)	1	9	9.0(9)	0	35	738	21.1(86)	5	—	—	—	—	—	—	—	—	—	—	—	—	30	403
1968	GB★	14(FL)	—	—	—	—	42	818	19.5(63)	8	—	—	—	—	—	—	—	—	—	—	—	—	48	449
1969	GB◊	14(WR)	—	—	—	—	45	879	19.5(48)	6	—	—	—	—	—	—	—	—	—	—	—	—	36	470
1970	GB◊	14(WR)	2	9	4.5(8)	0	49	814	16.6(89)	2	—	—	—	—	—	—	—	—	—	—	—	—	24	319
1971	GB	14(WR)	—	—	—	—	31	598	19.3(77)	4	—	—	—	—	—	—	—	—	—	—	—	—	6	164
1972	†GB	14(WR)	—	—	—	—	16	317	19.8(48)	1	—	—	—	—	—	—	—	—	—	—	—	—	0	96
1973	†Min	13(12, WR)	—	—	—	—	14	192	13.7(40)	0	—	—	—	—	—	—	—	—	—	—	—	—	312	4429
NFL	14	189(12)	4	30	7.5(12)	0	438	8277	18.9(89)	52	—	—	—	—	—	—	—	—	—	—	—	—	312	4429

DALE, JEFFERY   Jeffery Dwayne, DB, 6´3˝/211 lbs; LSU; 1985: SD, rnd 2; B10/6/1962 Pineville, LA   **1985** SD 16 (16, FS)   **1986** SD 16 (16, SS)   **1988** SD 10 (2)   **NFL** 42 (34) [3 yrs]

DALE, ROLAND   Roland Hall, DE, 6´3˝/210 lbs; Mississippi; B10/30/1927 Magee, MS   **1950** Was 11 (rde)

DALEY, BILL   William Edward, FB-DB-LB, 6´2˝/210 lbs; DePaul; Michigan; Minnesota; Columbia; 1943: Pit, rnd 1; B9/16/1919 Melrose, MN

1946	Bkn-A	2(1)	7	25	3.6	0	2	-5	-2.5	0	—	—	—	—	—	—	—	—	—	—	k	—	0	18
1946	Mia-A	1(0)	38	5.4	0	—	—	—	—	—	—	—	—	—	—	—	—	—	—	—	—	—	0	38
1947	ChiR-A	14(12, FB)	121	447	3.7	4	12	116	9.7	0	6	3	50.0	70	11.7	1	1	—	—	—	kp	—	24	583
1948	NYY-A	7(0)	40	102	2.6	1	4	31	7.8	0	—	—	—	—	—	—	—	—	—	—	Pk	—	6	156
AAFC	3	24(13)	175	612	3.5	5	18	142	7.9	0	6	3	50.0	70	11.7	1	1	—	—	—	Pkp	—	30	794

DALLAFIOR, KEN   Kenneth Ray, G-T-C, 6´4˝/276 lbs; Minnesota; 1982: Pit, rnd 5; B8/26/1959 Royal Oak, MI   **1985** SD 3 (0)   **1986** SD 12 (1)   **1987** SD 9 (0)   **1988** SD 13 (13, LT)   **1989** Det 16 (11, RG)   **1990** Det 16 (15, RG)   **1991**†Det 6 (5, rg)   **1992** Det 12 (12, RG)   **NFL** 87 (57) [8 yrs]

DALLY, DILLY   Dilly, G, none   **1926** Har 6 (3)

DALMAN, CHRIS   Chris William, C-G, 6´3˝/287 lbs; Stanford; 1993: SF, rnd 6; B3/15/1970 Salinas, CA   **1993**†SF 15 (0)   **1994**†SF 16 (4)   **1996**†SF 16 (16, RG)   **1997**†SF 13 (13, C)   **1998**†SF 15 (15, C)   **1999** SF 15 (15, C)

| 1995 | †SF | 15(1) | — | — | — | — | 1 | -1 | -1.0(-1) | 0 | — | — | — | — | — | — | — | — | — | — | k | — | 0 | -17 |
| NFL | 7 | 105(64) | — | — | — | — | 1 | -1 | -1.0(-1) | 0 | — | — | — | — | — | — | — | — | — | — | k | — | 0 | -17 |

D'ALONZO, PETE   Peter Joseph, FB, 5´10˝/210 lbs; Villanova; 1951: Det, rnd 4; B5/26/1929 Orange, NJ, D12/27/2001 Budd Lake, NJ

1951	Det	12	2	11	5.5(7)	0	—	—	—	—	—	—	—	—	—	—	—	—	—	—	—	—	0	11
1952	Det	4	5	7	1.4(3)	0	2	4	2.0(10)	0	—	—	—	—	—	—	—	—	—	—	—	—	0	9
NFL	2	16	7	18	2.6(7)	0	2	4	2.0(10)	0	—	—	—	—	—	—	—	—	—	—	—	—	0	20

DALRYMPLE, SLATS   Robert Hew, C, 6´2˝/210 lbs; Indiana; Wabash; B7/15/1896 Nelsonville, OH, D5/23/1978 Dublin, GA   **1922** Evv 1 (1)

DALTON, ANTICO   Antico, LB, 6´1˝/240 lbs; Hampton; 1999: Min, rnd 6; B12/31/1975 Eden, NC   **1999** Min 2 (0)   **2000** NE 3 (0)   **NFL** 5 (0) [2 yrs]

DALTON, LIONAL   Lional Deshawn, DT, 6´1˝/315 lbs; Eastern Michigan; B2/21/1975 Detroit, MI   **1998** Bal 2 (0)   **1999** Bal 16 (2)   **2000**†Bal 16 (1)   **2001**†Bal 16 (3)   **2002** Den 16 (13, LDT)   **2003** Was 12 (9, RDT)   **2004** KC 16 (14, RDT)   **NFL** 110 (55) [8 yrs]

DALTON, MOXIE   Maurice Jack, B, 5´6˝/165 lbs; Carroll (WI); Loras; B9/1894 Janesville, WI, D2/9/1954   **1922** Rac 5 (2)

DALTON, OAKLEY   Oakley, DT, 6´6˝/285 lbs; Jackson State; 1977: NO, rnd 12; B7/18/1952 Welch, WV   **1977** NO 1

DALUISO, BRAD   Bradley William, K, 6´2˝/215 lbs; San Diego State; UCLA; B12/31/1967 San Diego, CA **[K]**   **1991** Atl 2 (0)   **1991**†Buf 14 (0)   **1992** Den 16 (0)   **1993**†NYG 15 (0)   **1994** NYG 16 (0)   **1995** NYG 16 (0)   **1996** NYG 16 (0)   **1997**†NYG 16 (0)   **1998** NYG 16 (0)   **1999** NYG 6 (0)   **2000**†NYG 14 (0)   **2001** Oak 1 (0)   **NFL** 148 (0) [11 yrs]

D'AMATO, MIKE   Michael Anthony, DB, 6´2˝/205 lbs; Hofstra; 1968: NYJ, rnd 10; B3/3/1943 Brooklyn, NY   **1968**†NYJ-A 13

DAMIANI, FRANK   Francis Anthony, T, 6´1˝/225 lbs; Manhattan; B7/27/1922 Carnegie, PA   **1944** NYG 4 (0)

YEAR	TEAM	G(GS, POS)	RUSH	YD	AVG(LG)	TD	REC	YD	AVG(LG)	TD	PASS	COMP	PCT	YD	AVG(LG)	TD	INT	SK	YD	QBR	KPR	OTD	PTS	TAY

DAMKROGER, MAURY Maurice Albert, LB, 6´2˝/230 lbs; Nebraska; 1974: NE, rnd 7; B1/8/1952 Cambridge, NE **1974** NE 11 **1975** NE 2 **NFL** 13 [2 yrs]

DAMORE, JOHN John Lawrence, C-G, 6´0˝/228 lbs; Northwestern; 1955: NYG, rnd 13; B10/20/1933 Riverside, IL **1957** ChiB 4 **1959** ChiB 8 **NFL** 12 [2 yrs]

DANCEWICZ, BOLEY Francis Joseph, QB-DB, 5´10˝/187 lbs; Notre Dame; 1946: Bos, rnd 1; B10/3/1924 Lynn, MA, D6/26/1985 Boston, MA

1946	Bos	8(1)	14	81	5.8(41)	0	—	—	—	—	34	13	38.2	162	4.8(45)	1	6	—	—	—	i	—	0	-74
1947	Bos	12(1, QB)	47	145	3.1(41)	1	—	—	—	—	169	66	39.1	1203	7.1(69)	11	18	—	—	46.4	P	—	6	92
1948	Bos	3(0)	4	3	0.8(2)	1	—	—	—	—	35	17	48.6	186	5.3(33)	0	5	—	—	—	—	—	6	-94
NFL	3	23(2)	65	229	3.5(41)	2	—	—	—	—	238	96	40.3	1551	6.5(69)	12	29	—	—	40.1	Pi	—	12	-77

DANEHE, DICK Richard Michael, T, 6´2˝/235 lbs; USC; B9/10/1920 Memphis, TN **1948** LAD-A 5 (0)

| 1947 | LAD-A | 11(4, rt) | — | — | — | 0 | 8 | (8) | 0 | — | — | — | — | — | — | — | — | — | — | — | — | — | 0 | 4 |
| AAFC | 2 | 16(4) | — | — | — | 0 | 8 | (8) | 0 | — | — | — | — | — | — | — | — | — | — | — | — | — | 0 | 4 |

DANELO, JOE Joseph Peter, K, 5´9˝/166 lbs; Washington State; 1975: Mia, rnd 10; B9/2/1953 Spokane, WA [K] **1975** GB 12 **1976** NYG 14 **1977** NYG 14 **1978** NYG 16 **1980** NYG 16 (0) **1981**†NYG 16 (0) **1982** NYG 9 (0) **1983** Buf 14 (0) **1984** Buf 9 (0)

| 1979 | NYG | 16 | — | — | — | — | 1 | 1 | 1.0(1) | 0 | — | — | — | — | — | — | — | — | — | — | K | — | 55 | 1 |
| NFL | 10 | 136 | — | — | — | — | 1 | 1 | 1.0(1) | 0 | — | — | — | — | — | — | — | — | — | — | K | — | 639 | 1 |

DANENHAUER, BILL William Adolph, DE, 6´5˝/245 lbs; Emporia State; 1956: Bal, rnd 17; B6/3/1934 Clay Center, KS **1960** Den-A 4 **1960** Bos-A 3 **NFL** 7 [1 yr]

DANENHAUER, ELDON Eldon Voss, T, 6´5˝/245 lbs; Emporia State; Pittsburg State; B10/4/1935 Clay Center, KS **1960** Den-A 14 (RT) **1961** Den-A 14 (RT) **1962** Den-A★14 (RT) **1963** Den-A☆9 (RT) **1964** Den-A☆14 (RT) **1965** Den-A★14 (RT) **NFL** 79 [6 yrs]

DANEY, GEORGE George Anthony, G, 6´4˝/240 lbs; Detroit Mercy; Texas-El Paso; 1968: KC, rnd 1; B2/2/1946 Washington, PA, D2/15/1990 Raytown, MO **1968**†KC-A 14 **1969**†KC-A 14 **1970** KC 14 **1971**†KC 14 **1972** KC 14 **1973** KC 14 **1974** KC 13 (RG) **NFL** 97 [7 yrs]

DANIEL, EUGENE Eugene, DB, 5´11˝/178 lbs; LSU; 1984: Ind, rnd 8; B5/4/1961 Baton Rouge, LA [I] **1984** Ind 15 (14, RCB) **1985** Ind 16 (16, RCB) **1986** Ind 15 (15, RCB) **1987**†Ind 12 (11, RCB) **1988** Ind 16 (15, RCB) **1989** Ind 15 (14, RCB) **1990** Ind 15 (15, RCB) **1991** Ind 16 (16, RCB) **1992** Ind 14 (13, RCB) **1993** Ind 16 (16, RCB) **1994** Ind 16 (15, RCB) **1995**†Ind 16 (16, RCB) **1996**†Ind 16 (9, RCB) **1997** Bal 9 (6, rcb) **NFL** 207 (191) [14 yrs]

DANIEL, KENNY Kenneth Ray, DB, 5´10˝/180 lbs; San Jose State; B6/1/1960 Martinez, CA **1984**†NYG 15 (1) **1986** Ind 15 (2) **1987** Ind 2 (0) **NFL** 32 (3) [3 yrs]

DANIEL, WILLIE William Paul, DB, 5´11˝/190 lbs; Mississippi State; B11/10/1937 New Albany, MS **1961** Pit 14 (RS) **1962** Pit 13 (RS) **1963** Pit 13 **1964** Pit 14 (RS) **1965** Pit 9 (RS) **1966** Pit 12 **1967**†LARm 14 (2) **1968** LARm 14 **1969** LARm 10 **NFL** 113 (2) [9 yrs]

DANIELL, AVERELL Averell Edward, T, 6´3˝/215 lbs; Pittsburgh; 1937: GB, rnd 2; B11/6/1914 Pittsburgh, PA, D1/26/1999 Pittsburgh, PA **1937** GB 5 (1) **1937** Bkn 4 (2) **NFL** 9 (3) [1 yr]

DANIELL, JIM James Laughlin, T, 6´2˝/230 lbs; Ohio State; 1942: ChiB, rnd 12; B4/10/1918 Pittsburgh, PA, D12/13/1983 Pittsburgh, PA **1945** ChiB 7 (5, lt) **1946** Cle-A 14 (9, LT)

DANIELS, CALVIN Calvin Richard, LB, 6´3˝/236 lbs; North Carolina; 1982: KC, rnd 2; B12/26/1958 Morehead City, NC **1982** KC 9 (0) **1983** KC 16 (1) **1984** KC 16 (16, ROLB) **1985** KC 16 (16, LOLB) **1986**†Was 13 (10, LLB) **NFL** 70 (43) [5 yrs]

DANIELS, CLEM Clemon C., HB-DB, 6´1˝/220 lbs; Prairie View A&M; B7/9/1937 McKinney, TX

1960	DalT-A	14	1	-2	-2.0(-2)	0	—	—	—	—	—	—	—	—	—	—	—	—	—	—	kpi	—	0	74
1961	Oak-A	14	31	154	5.0(39)	2	13	150	11.5(30)	0	—	—	—	—	—	—	—	—	—	—	kp	—	12	339
1962	Oak-A	14(HB)	161	766	4.8(72)	7	24	318	13.3(74)	1	1	0	0.0	0	0.0	0	0	—	—	—	k	—	48	1170
1963	Oak-A★	14(HB)	215	**1099**	5.1(74)	3	30	685	**22.8**(73)	5	1	1	100.0	10	10.0(10)	0	0	—	—	—	—	—	48	**1502**
1964	Oak-A★	14(HB)	173	824	4.8(42)	6	42	696	16.6(60)	6	1	0	0.0	0	0.0	0	0	—	—	—	k	—	48	1239
1965	Oak-A★	14(HB)	219	884	4.0(57)	5	36	568	15.8(69)	7	2	1	100.0	95	47.5(53)	0	0	—	—	—	—	—	72	**1301**
1966	Oak-A★	14(HB)	204	801	3.9(64)	7	40	652	16.3(68)	3	3	0	0.0	0	0.0	0	1	—	—	—	—	—	60	1172
1967	Oak-A	9(HB)	130	575	4.4(52)	4	16	222	13.9(40)	2	1	1	100.0	28	28.0(28)	0	0	—	—	—	k	—	36	750
1968	SF	9	12	37	3.1(11)	0	2	23	11.5(16)	0	—	—	—	—	—	—	—	—	—	—	k	—	0	105
NFL	9	110	1146	5138	4.5(74)	30	203	3314	16.3(74)	24	9	4	44.4	133	14.8(53)	0	1	—	—	—	kpi	—	324	7651

DANIELS, DAVE David Lee, DT, 6´3˝/245 lbs; Florida A&M; 1965: Hou, rnd R6/Chi, rnd 13; B4/5/1941 East Palatka, FL **1966** Oak-A 14

DANIELS, DAVID David, WR, 6´1˝/190 lbs; Penn State; 1991: Sea, rnd 3; B9/16/1969 Sarasota, FL

1991	Sea	16(0)	—	—	—	—	4	38	9.5(19)	0	—	—	—	—	—	—	—	—	—	—	—	—	0	19
1992	Sea	13(1)	—	—	—	—	5	99	19.8(57)	0	—	—	—	—	—	—	—	—	—	—	—	—	0	50
NFL	2	29(1)	—	—	—	—	9	137	15.2(57)	0	—	—	—	—	—	—	—	—	—	—	—	—	0	69

DANIELS, DEXTER Dexter Lavista, LB, 6´1˝/241 lbs; Florida; 1996: Bal, rnd 6; B12/8/1973 Valdosta, GA **1996** Bal 4 (0)

DANIELS, DICK Richard Bernard, DB, 5´9˝/180 lbs; Pacific (OR); B10/19/1944 Portland, OR **1966**†Dal 4 **1967**†Dal 14 **1968**†Dal 14 (8, rs) **1969** ChiB 8 (RS) **1970** ChiB 13 (FS) **NFL** 53 (8) [5 yrs]

DANIELS, JACK Jack, TB, /135 lbs; none; B1909, MI, deceased **1925** Mil 1 (0)

DANIELS, JEROME Jerome Alvonne, G-T, 6´5˝/350 lbs; Northeastern; 1997: Mia, rnd 4; B9/13/1974 Hartford, CT **1998** Arz 8 (5, lg)

DANIELS, LeSHUN LeShun, G, 6´1˝/304 lbs; Ohio State; B5/30/1974 Warren, OH **1997** Min 1 (0)

DANIELS, PHILLIP Phillip Bernard, DE, 6´5˝/285 lbs; Georgia; 1996: Sea, rnd 4; B3/4/1973 Donalsonville, GA [S] **1996** Sea 15 (0) **1997** Sea 13 (10, RDE) **1998** Sea 16 (15, RDE) **1999**†Sea 16 (16, RDE) **2000** ChiB 14 (14, RDE) **2001**†ChiB 16 (16, RDE) **2002** ChiB 13 (13, LDE) **2003** ChiB 16 (16, LDE) **2004** Was 5 (5, rde) **2005**†Was 16 (16, RDE) **NFL** 140 (121) [10 yrs]

DANIELS, TRAVIS Travis Antwon, DB, 6´2˝/194 lbs; LSU; 2005: Mia, rnd 4; B9/8/1982 Hollywood, FL **2005** Mia 16 (14, LCB)

DANIELSON, GARY Gary Dennis, QB, 6´2˝/195 lbs; Purdue; B9/10/1951 Detroit, MI

1976	Det	1																						
1977	Det	13(2)	7	62	8.9(16)	0	—	—	—	—	100	42	42.0	445	4.4(61)	1	5	9	64	—	—	—	0	90
1978	Det	16(11, QB)	22	93	4.2(25)	0	—	—	—	—	351	199	56.7	2294	6.5(47)	18	17	25	237	73.5	—	—	0	650
1980	Det	16(16, QB)	48	232	4.8(33)	2	—	—	—	—	417	244	58.5	3223	7.7(87)	13	11	44	338	82.4	—	—	12	1489
1981	Det	6(4)	9	23	2.6(11)	2	—	—	—	—	96	56	58.3	784	8.2(45)	3	5	12	84	—	—	—	12	250
1982	Det	8(5, QB)	23	92	4.0(16)	0	—	—	—	—	197	100	50.8	1343	6.8(70)	10	**14**	19	145	—	—	—	0	254
1983	†Det	10(0)	6	8	1.3(8)	0	—	—	—	—	113	59	52.2	720	6.4(54)	7	4	8	68	—	—	—	0	243
1984	Det	15(14, QB)	41	218	5.3(40)	3	1	22	22.0(22)	0	410	252	61.5	3076	7.5(77)	17	15	41	335	83.1	—	—	24	1287
1985	Cle	8(6, qb)	25	126	5.0(28)	0	—	—	—	—	163	97	59.5	1274	7.8(72)	8	6	17	128	—	—	—	0	563
1987	Cle	6(1)	1	0	0.0(0)	0	—	—	—	—	33	25	75.8	281	8.5(23)	4	0	2	4	—	—	—	0	161
1988	Cle	2(1)	4	3	0.8(5)	0	—	—	—	—	52	31	59.6	324	6.2(26)	0	1	6	43	—	—	—	0	125
NFL	11	101(60)	186	857	4.6(40)	7	1	22	22.0(22)	0	1932	1105	57.2	13764	7.1(87)	81	78	183	1446	76.6	—	—	48	5110

DANJEAN, ERNIE Ernest Joseph, LB, 6´0˝/230 lbs; Auburn; 1957: GB, rnd 19; B3/5/1934 New Orleans, LA **1957** GB 12

DANMEIER, RICK Richard Craig, K, 6´0˝/194 lbs; Sioux Falls; B4/8/1952 St. Paul, MN [K] **1977** Min 1 **1978**†Min 16 **1979** Min 16 **1980**†Min 16 (0) **1981** Min 16 (0) **1982**†Min 9 (0) **NFL** 74 [6 yrs]

DANOWSKI, ED Edward Frank, B, 6´1˝/198 lbs; Fordham; B9/30/1911 Jamesport, NY, D2/1/1997 East Patchogue, NY

1934	†NYG	8(3)	75	248	3.3(11)	0	—	—	—	—	32	15	46.9	230	7.2	2	3	—	—	—	—	—	0	253
1935	†NYG☆	12(8, TB)	130	335	2.6(7)	2	—	—	—	—	**113**	**57**	50.4	794	7.0	**10**	9	—	—	**69.7**	—	—	12	442
1936	NYG	12(5, TB)	91	259	2.8(13)	0	—	—	—	—	104	47	45.2	515	5.0	5	10	—	—	36.8	—	—	6	142
1937	NYG☆	11(7, TB)	66	95	1.4(9)	1	—	—	—	—	134	66	**49.3**	814	6.1	8	5	—	—	**72.8**	—	—	6	352
1938	†NYG★	11(8, TB)	48	215	4.5(32)	1	—	—	—	—	129	70	**54.3**	848	6.6	7	8	—	—	**66.9**	—	—	6	364
1939	NYG	11(8, TB)	25	21	0.8(7)	0	—	—	—	—	101	42	41.6	437	4.3	3	6	—	—	39.9	P	—	0	15
1941	NYG	6(0)	—	—	—	—	1	12	12.0(12)	0	24	12	50.0	179	7.5(65)	2	3	—	—	—	—	—	0	-15
NFL	7	71(40)	435	1173	2.7(32)	4	1	12	12.0(12)	0	637	309	48.5	3817	6.0(65)	37	44	—	—	58.1	P	—	24	1553

DANSBY, KARLOS Karlos, LB, 6´5˝/235 lbs; Auburn; 2004: Arz, rnd 2; B11/3/1981 Birmingham, AL **2004** Arz 15 (11, LLB) **2005** Arz 15 (15, LLB) **NFL** 30 (26) [2 yrs]

YEAR	TEAM	G (GS, POS)	RUSH	YD	AVG(LG)	TD	REC	YD	AVG(LG)	TD	PASS COMP	PCT	YD	AVG(LG)	TD	INT	SK	YD	QBR	KPR	OTD	PTS	TAY

DANTZLER, WOODROW   Woodrow, RB, 5´10˝/209 lbs; Clemson; B10/4/1979 Orangeburg, SC   **2002** Dal 5 (0)

| 2003 | Atl | 9(0) | 8 | 21 | 2.6(12) | 1 | — | — | — | — | 1 | 0 | 0.0 | 0 | 0.0 | 0 | 0 | 1 | 5 | — | kp | — | 6 | 63 |
| NFL | 2 | 14(0) | 8 | 21 | 2.6(12) | 1 | — | — | — | — | 1 | 0 | 0.0 | 0 | 0.0 | 0 | 0 | 1 | 5 | — | kp | 1 | 12 | 270 |

DANZIGER, FRED   Frederick W., FB, 5´11˝/175 lbs; Michigan State; B1/12/1906 Detroit, MI, D10/18/1948 Dearborn, MI   **1931** Cle 1 (0)

DaPRATO, NENO   Neno Joseph, FB, 5´10˝/185 lbs; Michigan State; B1/14/1893 Iron Mountain, MI, D4/29/1984 Parkesburg, PA   **1921** Det 6 (5, FB)

DAR DAR, KIRBY   Kirby David, WR, 5´9˝/185 lbs; Syracuse; B3/27/1972 Morgan City, LA   **1995**†Mia 1 (0)   **1996** Mia 11 (0)   **1998** Mia 2 (0)   **NFL** 14 (0) [3 yrs]

DARBY, AL   Alvis Russell, TE, 6´5˝/221 lbs; Florida; 1976: Sea, rnd 6; B9/14/1954 Miami, FL   **1976** Sea 1   **1976** Hou 2   **1978** TB 6 (1)   **NFL** 9 (1) [2 yrs]

DARBY, BYRON   Byron Keith, DE-NT, 6´4˝/260 lbs; USC; 1983: Phi, rnd 5; B6/4/1960 Los Angeles, CA   **1983** Phi 16 (0)   **1984** Phi 16 (0)   **1985** Phi 10 (1)   **1987**†Ind 12 (4)   **1988** Ind 16 (1)   **1989** Det 1 (0)

| 1986 | Phi | 16(7, LDE) | — | — | — | — | 2 | 16 | 8.0(13) | 0 | — | — | — | — | — | — | — | — | — | S | — | 0 | 8 |
| NFL | 7 | 87(13) | — | — | — | — | 2 | 16 | 8.0(13) | 0 | — | — | — | — | — | — | — | — | — | kS | — | 0 | -19 |

DARBY, CHARTRIC   Chartric Terrell, DT, 6´0˝/270 lbs; South Carolina State; B10/22/1975 North, SC   **2001** TB 13 (0)   **2002**†TB 16 (6, ldt)   **2003** TB 16 (1)   **2004** TB 16 (16, LDT)   **2005**†Sea 14 (14, LDT)   **NFL** 75 (37) [5 yrs]

DARBY, MATT   Matthew Lamont, DB, 6´2˝/200 lbs; UCLA; 1992: Buf, rnd 5; B11/19/1968 Virginia Beach, VA   **1992**†Buf 16 (1)   **1993**†Buf 16 (3)   **1994** Buf 16 (16, FS)   **1995**†Buf 7 (3)   **1996** Arz 15 (15, SS)   **1997** Arz 11 (7, SS)   **NFL** 81 (45) [6 yrs]

DARBY, PAUL   Paul Willie, WR, 5´10˝/192 lbs; Southwest Texas State; 1979: NYJ, rnd 12; B10/22/1956 Austin, TX   **1979** NYJ 15

| 1980 | NYJ | 8(0) | 1 | 15 | 15.0(15) | 0 | 3 | 48 | 16.0(20) | 1 | — | — | — | — | — | — | — | — | — | k | — | 6 | 78 |
| NFL | 2 | 23 | 1 | 15 | 15.0(15) | 0 | 3 | 48 | 16.0(20) | 1 | — | — | — | — | — | — | — | — | — | kp | — | 6 | 73 |

DARCHE, JEAN-PHILLIPE   Jean-Phillipe, C, 6´0˝/246 lbs; McGill; B2/28/1975 Montreal, Canada   **2000** Sea 16 (0)   **2001** Sea 16 (0)   **2002** Sea 16 (0)   **2003**†Sea 16 (0)   **2004**†Sea 16 (0)   **2005**†Sea 16 (0)   **NFL** 96 (0) [6 yrs]

DARDAR, RAMSEY   James Ramsey, DT-G-T, 6´2˝/264 lbs; LSU; 1983: SL, rnd 3; B10/3/1959 Cecilia, LA   **1984** SL 16 (6, rdt)

DARDEN, THOM   Thomas Vincent, DB, 6´2˝/195 lbs; Michigan; 1972: Cle, rnd 1; B8/28/1950 Sandusky, OH [I]   **1972**†Cle 14 (SS/fs)   **1973** Cle 11 (FS)   **1974** Cle 14 (FS)   **1976** Cle☆14 (14, FS)   **1977** Cle 14 (14, FS)   **1978** Cle★16 (16, FS)   **1979** Cle☆16 (16, FS)   **1980**†Cle 16 (10, FS)   **NFL** 128 (56) [9 yrs]

DARDEN, TONY   Tony Dwayne, DB, 5´11˝/193 lbs; Texas Tech; 1998: Min, rnd 7; B8/11/1975 Baton Rouge, LA   **2000** SD 16 (3)

DARILEK, TREY   Trey Keith, G, 6´6˝/290 lbs; Texas-El Paso; 2004: Phi, rnd 4; B4/23/1981 San Antonio, TX   **2004** Phi 3 (0)   **2005** Phi 15 (0)   **NFL** 18 (0) [2 yrs]

DARIUS, DONOVIN   Donovin Lee, DB, 6´1˝/225 lbs; Syracuse; 1998: Jax, rnd 1; B8/12/1975 Camden, NJ   **1998**†Jax 14 (14, SS)   **1999**†Jax 16 (16, SS)   **2000** Jax 16 (16, SS)   **2001** Jax 11 (11, SS)   **2002** Jax 14 (14, SS)   **2003** Jax 16 (16, SS)   **2004** Jax 16 (16, SS)   **2005** Jax 2 (2)   **NFL** 105 (105) [8 yrs]

DARKINS, CHRIS   Christopher Oji, DB, 6´0˝/205 lbs; Minnesota; 1996: GB, rnd 4; B4/30/1974 San Francisco, CA   **1997**†GB 14 (0)

DARLING, BOOB   Bernard Edward, C, 6´1˝/206 lbs; Wisconsin; Ripon: Beloit; B11/18/1903 Winnebago County, WI, D3/5/1968 Green Bay, WI   **1927** GB 1 (0)   **1928** GB 7 (1)   **1929** GB 11 (7, C)   **1930** GB 13 (7, C)   **1931** GB 4 (1)   **NFL** 36 (16) [5 yrs]

DARLING, DEVARD   Devard, WR, 6´1˝/213 lbs; Florida State; Washington State; 2004: Bal, rnd 3; B4/16/1982 Bahamas   **2005** Bal 10 (0)

| 2004 | Bal | 3(0) | — | — | — | — | 2 | 5 | 2.5(4) | 0 | — | — | — | — | — | — | — | — | — | — | — | 0 | 3 |
| NFL | 2 | 13(0) | — | — | — | — | 2 | 5 | 2.5(4) | 0 | — | — | — | — | — | — | — | — | — | — | — | 0 | 3 |

DARLING, JAMES   James Jackson, LB, 6´1˝/247 lbs; Washington State; 1997: Phi, rnd 2; B12/29/1974 Denver, CO   **1997** Phi 16 (6, llb)   **1998** Phi 12 (8, LLB)   **1999** Phi 15 (10, LLB)   **2000**†Phi 16 (0)   **2001**†NYJ 16 (0)   **2002**†NYJ 16 (0)   **2003** Arz 16 (0)   **2004** Arz 15 (15, RLB)   **2005** Arz 14 (14, MLB)   **NFL** 136 (53) [9 yrs]

DARNALL, BILL   William Carlyle, WR, 6´2˝/197 lbs; North Carolina; 1966: Mia, rnd R6; B4/21/1944 Washington, DC

1968	Mia-A	11	—	—	—	—	2	25	12.5(13)	—	—	—	—	—	—	—	—	—	—	—	—	0	13
1969	Mia-A	2	—	—	—	—	1	13	13.0(13)	—	—	—	—	—	—	—	—	—	—	—	—	0	7
NFL	2	13	—	—	—	—	3	38	12.7(13)	0	—	—	—	—	—	—	—	—	—	—	—	0	19

DARNS, PHIL   Phillip, DE, 6´3˝/245 lbs; Mississippi Valley State; B7/27/1959 Tampa, FL   **1984** TB 2 (0)

DARRAGH, DAN   Daniel Meyer, QB, 6´3˝/196 lbs; William & Mary; 1968: Buf, rnd 13; B11/28/1946 Pittsburgh, PA

1968	Buf-A	11(7, QB)	13	11	0.8(8)	0	—	—	—	—	215	92	42.8	917	4.3(41)	3	14	—	—	33.0	—	—	0	-76
1969	Buf-A	3	6	14	2.3(8)	0	—	—	—	—	52	24	46.2	365	7.0(53)	1	6	11	103	—	—	—	0	-39
1970	Buf	3	1	26	26.0(26)	0	—	—	—	—	29	11	37.9	71	2.4(19)	0	2	5	36	—	—	—	0	-19
NFL	3	17(7)	20	51	2.6(26)	0	—	—	—	—	296	127	42.9	1353	4.6(53)	4	22	16	139	30.4	—	—	0	-133

DARRE, BERNIE   Bernard John, G, 6´2˝/230 lbs; Tulane; 1960: Was, rnd 15/Den, rnd 1; B11/8/1939 New Orleans, LA   **1961** Was 12

DARRINGTON, CHRIS   Chris, WR, 5´10˝/180 lbs; Weber State; B7/13/1964

| 1987 | Hou | 3(0) | — | — | — | — | 1 | 38 | 38.0(38) | 0 | — | — | — | — | — | — | — | — | — | — | — | 0 | 19 |

DARROW, BARRY   Barry Wayne, T, 6´7˝/260 lbs; Western Montana; Montana; 1973: SD, rnd 17; B6/27/1950 Peoria, IL   **1974** Cle 13   **1975** Cle 14 (9, rt)   **1976** Cle 14 (RT)   **1977** Cle 14 (12, RT)   **1978** Cle 16 (14, RT)   **NFL** 71 (35) [5 yrs]

DARWIN, MATT   Matthew Wayne, T-C, 6´4˝/268 lbs; Texas A&M; 1986: Phi, rnd 4; B3/11/1963 Houston, TX   **1986** Phi 16 (10, C)   **1987** Phi 12 (12, LT)   **1988**†Phi 16 (16, LT)   **1989** Phi 15 (12, LT)   **1990** Phi 2 (2)   **NFL** 61 (52) [5 yrs]

DASTILLUNG, DANE   Harry, G-T, 6´0˝/190 lbs; Marietta; Xavier (OH); B4/2/1897 Cincinnati, OH, D11/30/1982 Cincinnati, OH   **1921** Cin 4 (3, LG)

DAUGHERTY, BOB   Robert J., HB, 6´1˝/210 lbs; Tulsa; 1964: SF, rnd 8/SD, rnd 16; B10/4/1942   **1966** SF 4

DAUGHERTY, DICK   Richard Lee, LB-C, 6´1˝/219 lbs; Oregon; 1951: LA, rnd 18; B3/31/1929 Moundsville, WV   **1951**†LARm 12 (LG)   **1952**†LARm 12 (LG)   **1953** LARm 12   **1956** LARm 12 (C)   **1957** LARm★9 (RLB)   **1958** LARm 12 (RLB)   **NFL** 69 [6 yrs]

DAUGHERTY, RON   Ronald, WR, 6´3˝/185 lbs; Northeastern Illinois; B3/17/1958 Chicago, IL

| 1987 | Min | 3(0) | — | — | — | — | 2 | 21 | 10.5(13) | 0 | — | — | — | — | — | — | — | — | — | — | — | 0 | 11 |

DAUGHERTY, RUSS   Russell S., WB, 5´10˝/175 lbs; Illinois; B1/31/1902 Streator, IL, D3/1971 Sierra Madre, CA [C]   **1927** Fra 2 (1)

DAUKAS, LOU   Louis James, C, 6´0˝/203 lbs; Cornell; B7/4/1921 Nashua, NH, D7/22/2005 Glastonbury, CT   **1947** Bkn-A 4 (0)

DAUKAS, NICK   Nicholas James, T, 6´4˝/225 lbs; Dartmouth; 1944: Phi, rnd 28; B12/11/1922 Nashua, NH, D2/25/2003 Middletown, CT   **1947** Bkn-A 7 (1)

| 1946 | Bkn-A | 8(1) | — | — | — | — | 2 | 19 | 9.5 | 0 | — | — | — | — | — | — | — | — | — | i | — | 0 | 10 |
| AAFC | 2 | 15(2) | — | — | — | — | 2 | 19 | 9.5 | 0 | — | — | — | — | — | — | — | — | — | — | — | 0 | 10 |

DAUM, MITCH   Mitchell, TE, 6´5˝/250 lbs; Wyoming; B11/13/1963 Kimball, NE   **1987** Hou 2 (0)

DAUM, RED   Carl V., E-B, 5´7˝/166 lbs; Akron; B9/18/1898 Akron, OH, D6/30/1959 Akron, OH   **1922** Akr 9 (5, LE), 12   **1923** Akr 7 (5, LE)   **1924** Akr 8 (8, LE)   **1925** Akr 5 (4), 6   **1926** Akr 8 (8, LE)   **NFL** 37 (30), 18 [5 yrs]

DAVENPORT, CHARLES   Charles Donald, WR, 6´3˝/210 lbs; North Carolina State; 1992: Pit, rnd 4; B11/22/1968 Fayetteville, NC

1992	†Pit	15(1)	—	—	—	—	9	136	15.1(31)	0	—	—	—	—	—	—	—	—	—	—	1	6	68
1993	†Pit	16(0)	—	—	—	—	4	51	12.8(19)	0	—	—	—	—	—	—	—	—	—	—	—	0	26
1994	Pit	7(0)	—	—	—	—	—	—	—	—	—	—	—	—	—	—	—	—	—	—	—	0	—
NFL	3	38(1)	—	—	—	—	13	187	14.4(31)	0	—	—	—	—	—	—	—	—	—	—	1	6	94

DAVENPORT, JOE   Joe Dean, TE, 6´6˝/268 lbs; Arkansas; B10/29/1976 Springdale, AR

2001	Ind	3(0)	—	—	—	—	—	—	—	—	—	—	—	—	—	—	—	—	—	—	—	0	—
2002	†Ind	10(7, te)	—	—	—	—	8	70	8.8(22)	0	—	—	—	—	—	—	—	—	—	—	—	0	35
2003	†Ind	16(2)	—	—	—	—	3	23	7.7(9)	0	—	—	—	—	—	—	—	—	—	—	—	0	12
NFL	3	29(9)	—	—	—	—	11	93	8.5(22)	0	—	—	—	—	—	—	—	—	—	—	—	0	47

DAVENPORT, NAJEH   Najeh Trenadious Montae, RB, 6´1˝/245 lbs; Miami (FL); 2002: GB, rnd 4; B2/8/1979 Raleigh, NC

2002	GB	8(0)	39	184	4.7(43)	1	5	33	6.6(15)	0	—	—	—	—	—	—	—	—	—	—	k	—	6	251
2003	†GB	15(0)	77	420	5.5(76)	2	6	38	6.3(12)	0	—	—	—	—	—	—	—	—	—	—	k	—	12	724
2004	†GB	11(1)	71	359	5.1(40)	2	4	33	8.3(12)	0	—	—	—	—	—	—	—	—	—	—	k	—	12	472

YEAR	TEAM	G (GS, POS)	RUSH	YD	AVG (LG)	TD	REC	YD	AVG (LG)	TD	PASS	COMP	PCT	YD	AVG (LG)	TD	INT	SK	YD	QBR	KPR	OTD	PTS	TAY
2005	GB	5 (1)	30	105	3.5 (24)	2	2	3	1.5 (2)	0	—	—	—	—	—	—	—	—	—	—	k	—	12	166
NFL	4	39 (2)	217	1068	4.9 (76)	7	17	107	6.3 (13)	0	—	—	—	—	—	—	—	—	—	—	k	—	42	1612

DAVENPORT, RON Ronald Donovan, RB, 6´2˝/230 lbs; Louisville; 1985: Mia, rnd 6; B12/22/1962 Summerset, Bermuda

YEAR	TEAM	G (GS, POS)	RUSH	YD	AVG (LG)	TD	REC	YD	AVG (LG)	TD	PASS	COMP	PCT	YD	AVG (LG)	TD	INT	SK	YD	QBR	KPR	OTD	PTS	TAY
1985	†Mia	16 (1)	98	370	3.8 (33)	**11**	13	74	5.7 (17)	2	—	—	—	—	—	—	—	—	—	—	—	—	78	527
1986	Mia	16 (2)	75	314	4.2 (35)	0	20	177	8.9 (27)	1	—	—	—	—	—	—	—	—	—	—	k	—	6	453
1987	Mia	10 (1)	32	114	3.6 (27)	1	27	249	9.2 (29)	1	—	—	—	—	—	—	—	—	—	—	—	—	12	254
1988	Mia	16 (5, fb)	55	273	5.0 (64)	0	30	282	9.4 (27)	0	—	—	—	—	—	—	—	—	—	—	k	—	0	425
1989	Mia	9 (3)	14	56	4.0 (9)	1	3	19	6.3 (9)	0	—	—	—	—	—	—	—	—	—	—	k	—	6	80
NFL	5	67 (12)	274	1127	4.1 (64)	13	93	801	8.6 (29)	4	—	—	—	—	—	—	—	—	—	—	k	—	102	1738

DAVENPORT, WAYNE Wayne, HB, /187 lbs; Hardin-Simmons; B12/16/1906 San Saba, TX, D4/27/2001 San Angelo, TX **1931** GB 2 (1)

DAVEY, DON Donald Vincent, DT-DE, 6´4˝/273 lbs; Wisconsin; 1991: GB, rnd 3; B4/8/1968 Scottsville, NY **1991** GB 16 (0) **1992** GB 9 (0) **1993**†GB 9 (0) **1994**†GB 16 (2) **1995** Jax 16 (16, RDT) **1996**†Jax 16 (12, LDT) **1997** Jax 10 (10, RDT) **NFL** 92 (40) [7 yrs]

DAVEY, ROHAN Rohan St. Patrick, QB, 6´2˝/245 lbs; LSU; 2002: NE, rnd 4; B4/14/1978 Clarendon, Jamaica

YEAR	TEAM	G (GS, POS)	RUSH	YD	AVG (LG)	TD	REC	YD	AVG (LG)	TD	PASS	COMP	PCT	YD	AVG (LG)	TD	INT	SK	YD	QBR	KPR	OTD	PTS	TAY
2002	NE	2 (0)	2	-4	-2.0 (-2)	0	—	—	—	—	2	1	50.0	3	1.5 (3)	0	0	—	—	—	—	—	0	-3
2003	NE	1 (0)	—	—	—	—	—	—	—	—	7	3	42.9	31	4.4 (16)	0	0	—	—	—	—	—	0	16
2004	NE	4 (0)	4	-1	-0.3 (3)	0	—	—	—	—	10	4	40.0	54	5.4 (20)	0	0	—	—	—	—	—	0	26
NFL	3	7 (0)	6	-5	-0.8 (3)	0	—	—	—	—	19	8	42.1	88	4.6 (20)	0	0	—	—	—	—	—	0	39

DAVID, BOB Robert Joseph, G, 6´0˝/219 lbs; Notre Dame; Villanova; 1947: LA, rnd 27; B1/15/1921 Blue Island, FL **1947** LARm 8 (0) **1948** LARm 3 (1) **NFL** 11 (1) [2 yrs]

1948 ChiR-A 4 (0)

DAVID, JASON Jason Aeron Walter, DB, 5´8˝/165 lbs; Washington State; 2004: Ind, rnd 4; B6/12/1982 Covina, CA **2004**†Ind 16 (11, RCB) **2005**†Ind 16 (16, CB) **NFL** 32 (27) [2 yrs]

DAVID, JIM James Theodore, DB, 5´11˝/178 lbs; Colorado State; 1952: Det, rnd 22; B12/2/1927 Florence, SC **[I]** **1952**†Det 12 (DB) **1953**†Det 12 (DB) **1954**†Det★12 (DB) **1955** Det★12 (DB) **1956** Det★12 (DB) **1957**†Det★12 (DB) **1958** Det★12 (DB) **1959** Det✧12 (DB) **NFL** 96 [8 yrs]

DAVID, STAN Stanley Chaunce, LB, 6´3˝/210 lbs; Texas Tech; 1984: Buf, rnd 7; B2/17/1962 North Platte, NE **1984** Buf 16 (3)

DAVIDDS-GARRIDO, NORBERT Norberto, aka Norberto Garrido Jr., T, 6´6˝/315 lbs; USC; 1996: Car, rnd 4; B10/4/1972 La Puente, CA **1996**†Car 12 (8, RT) **1997** Car 15 (15, RT) **1998** Car 16 (16, RT) **1999** Car 16 (0) **2000** Arz 9 (2) **NFL** 68 (41) [5 yrs]

DAVIDSON, BEN Benjamin Earl, DE-DT, 6´8˝/275 lbs; Washington; 1961: NYG, rnd 4; B6/14/1940 Los Angeles, CA **1961**†GB 14 **1962** Was 14 **1963** Was 14 **1964** Oak-A 12 (rde) **1965** Oak-A☆14 (RDE) **1966** Oak-A★14 (14, RDE) **1967**†Oak-A★14 (RDE) **1968**†Oak-A✧14 (14, RDE) **1969**†Oak-A 14 (14, RDE) **1970**†Oak 14 (14, RDE) **1971** Oak 14 (14, RDE) **NFL** 152 (70) [11 yrs]

DAVIDSON, BILL William A., B-E, 6´0˝/182 lbs; Temple; B6/15/1915 Pittsburgh, PA, D8/1970

YEAR	TEAM	G (GS, POS)	RUSH	YD	AVG (LG)	TD	REC	YD	AVG (LG)	TD	PASS	COMP	PCT	YD	AVG (LG)	TD	INT	SK	YD	QBR	KPR	OTD	PTS	TAY
1937	Pit	11 (10, HB)	101	293	2.9	1	4	169	42.3	2	24	8	33.3	81	3.4	0	5	—	—	—	—	1	24	248
1938	Pit	10 (2)	33	52	1.6	0	12	229	19.1	0	2	2	100.0	10	5.0	0	0	—	—	—	—	—	0	172
1939	Pit	7 (2)	21	27	1.3	0	6	27	4.5	0	7	1	14.3	8	1.1 (8)	0	0	—	—	—	—	—	0	45
NFL	3	28 (14)	155	372	2.4	1	22	425	19.3	2	33	11	33.3	99	3.0 (8)	0	5	—	—	—	—	1	24	464

DAVIDSON, CHY Chy, WR, 5´11˝/175 lbs; Rhode Island; 1981: NE, rnd S11; B5/9/1959 Queens Village, NY **1984** NYJ 3 (0) **1985** NYJ 1 (0) **NFL** 4 (0) [2 yrs]

DAVIDSON, COTTON Francis Marion, QB, 6´1˝/182 lbs; Baylor; 1954: Bal, rnd 1; B11/30/1931 Gatesville, TX **[KP]**

YEAR	TEAM	G (GS, POS)	RUSH	YD	AVG (LG)	TD	REC	YD	AVG (LG)	TD	PASS	COMP	PCT	YD	AVG (LG)	TD	INT	SK	YD	QBR	KPR	OTD	PTS	TAY
1954	Bal	12	11	31	2.8 (15)	0	—	—	—	—	64	28	43.8	309	4.8 (29)	0	5	—	—	—	P	—	0	-15
1957	Bal	12	—	—	—	—	—	—	—	—	2	0	0.0	0	0.0	0	1	—	—	—	Pk	—	0	-36
1960	DalT-A	14 (14, QB)	14	36	2.6 (7)	1	1	-1	-1.0 (-1)	0	379	179	47.2	2474	6.5 (74)	15	16	—	—	64.2	KP	—	16	718
1961	DalT-A✧	14 (12, QB)	21	123	5.9 (40)	1	—	—	—	—	330	151	45.8	2445	7.4 (71)	17	23	—	—	59.2	KP	—	26	521
1962	DalT-A	1	—	—	—	—	—	—	—	—	—	—	—	—	—	—	—	—	—	—	P	—	0	0
1962	Oak-A	13 (QB)	25	54	2.2 (19)	3	—	—	—	—	321	119	37.1	1977	6.2 (90)	7	23	—	—	36.1	KP	—	25	188
1963	Oak-A✧	14 (qb)	23	133	5.8 (18)	4	—	—	—	—	194	77	39.7	1276	6.6 (73)	11	10	—	—	60.0	—	—	24	466
1964	Oak-A	14 (qb)	29	167	5.8 (33)	2	—	—	—	—	320	155	48.4	2497	7.8 (60)	21	19	—	—	72.1	—	—	12	781
1965	Oak-A	2	—	—	—	—	—	—	—	—	1	1	100.0	8	8.0 (8)	0	0	—	—	—	—	—	0	4
1966	Oak-A	14 (qb)	6	-11	-1.8 (5)	0	—	—	—	—	139	59	42.4	770	5.5 (51)	2	11	—	—	32.4	—	—	0	-56
1968	Oak-A	1	—	—	—	—	—	—	—	—	2	1	50.0	4	2.0 (4)	0	0	—	—	—	—	—	0	2
NFL	10	111 (26)	129	533	4.1 (40)	11	1	-1	-1.0 (-1)	0	1752	770	43.9	11760	6.7 (90)	73	108	—	—	54.9	KPk	—	103	2572

DAVIDSON, GREG Gregory Merle, C, 6´2˝/250 lbs; North Texas; B4/24/1958 Independence, IA **1980**†Hou 14 (0) **1981** Hou 16 (0) **1982** Hou 9 (0) **NFL** 39 (0) [3 yrs]

DAVIDSON, JEFF Jeffrey John, G-T, 6´5˝/309 lbs; Ohio State; 1990: Den, rnd 5; B10/3/1967 Akron, OH **1990** Den 12 (0) **1991**†Den 16 (14, LT) **1992** Den 16 (16, LG) **NFL** 44 (30) [3 yrs]

DAVIDSON, JOE Joseph Burl, G-C, 6´0˝/200 lbs; Colgate; Oklahoma State; B1/24/1903 Durand, MI, D5/14/1982 Dallas, TX **1928** ChiC 6 (5, RG) **1930** Nwk 6 (3) **NFL** 12 (8) [2 yrs]

DAVIDSON, KENNY Kenneth Darnell, DE, 6´5˝/272 lbs; LSU; 1990: Pit, rnd 2; B8/17/1967 Shreveport, LA **1990** Pit 14 (0) **1991** Pit 13 (1) **1992**†Pit 16 (13, LDE) **1993**†Pit 16 (9, LDE) **1994** Hou 16 (16, LDE) **1995** Hou 15 (12, LDE) **1996** Cin 3 (1) **NFL** 93 (52) [7 yrs]

DAVIDSON, PETE Peter Stewart, DT, 6´5˝/255 lbs; The Citadel; 1960: LAC, rnd 1; B1/25/1937 Dayton, OH **1960** Hou-A 1

DAVIS, ANDRA Andra Raynard, LB, 6´1˝/255 lbs; Florida; 2002: Cle, rnd 5; B12/23/1978 Live Oak, FL **2002**†Cle 16 (0) **2003** Cle 16 (16, MLB) **2004** Cle 11 (11, MLB) **2005** Cle 16 (16, LILB) **NFL** 59 (43) [4 yrs]

DAVIS, ANDRE Andre, DT, 6´3˝/330 lbs; Southern (LA); B10/7/1975 Baton Rouge, LA **1996** Jax 2 (0)

DAVIS, ANDRE' Andre' N., WR, 6´1˝/195 lbs; Virginia Tech; 2002: Cle, rnd 2; B6/12/1979 Niskayuna, NY **[R]**

YEAR	TEAM	G (GS, POS)	RUSH	YD	AVG (LG)	TD	REC	YD	AVG (LG)	TD	PASS	COMP	PCT	YD	AVG (LG)	TD	INT	SK	YD	QBR	KPR	OTD	PTS	TAY
2002	†Cle	16 (4)	3	7	2.3 (9)	0	37	420	11.4 (31)	6	—	—	—	—	—	—	—	—	—	—	kp	1	42	573
2003	Cle	16 (8, WR)	5	28	5.6 (7)	0	40	576	14.4 (49)	5	—	—	—	—	—	—	—	—	—	—	kp	—	30	576
2004	Cle	7 (7, wr)	1	-3	-3.0 (-3)	0	16	416	26.0 (**99**)	2	—	—	—	—	—	—	—	—	—	—	—	—	12	215
2005	†NE	9 (4)	—	—	—	—	9	190	21.1 (60)	1	—	—	—	—	—	—	—	—	—	—	k	—	6	163
NFL	4	48 (23)	9	32	3.6 (9)	0	102	1602	15.7 (99)	14	—	—	—	—	—	—	—	—	—	—	kp	1	90	1527

DAVIS, ANDY Andrew Nathan, DB, 6´0˝/188 lbs; George Washington; 1952: Was, rnd 2; B7/28/1927 Indianapolis, IN **1952** Was 6 (DB)

DAVIS, ANTHONY Anthony, RB, 5´10˝/190 lbs; USC; 1975: NYJ, rnd 2; B9/8/1952 Huntsville, TX

YEAR	TEAM	G (GS, POS)	RUSH	YD	AVG (LG)	TD	REC	YD	AVG (LG)	TD	PASS	COMP	PCT	YD	AVG (LG)	TD	INT	SK	YD	QBR	KPR	OTD	PTS	TAY
1977	TB	11	95	297	3.1 (35)	1	8	91	11.4 (30)	0	—	—	—	—	—	—	—	—	—	—	k	—	6	405
1978	Hou	2	—	—	—	—	—	—	—	—	—	—	—	—	—	—	—	—	—	—	k	—	0	38
1978	†LARm	2	3	7	2.3 (4)	0	—	—	—	—	—	—	—	—	—	—	—	—	—	—	—	—	0	7
NFL	2	15	98	304	3.1 (35)	1	8	91	11.4 (30)	0	—	—	—	—	—	—	—	—	—	—	k	—	6	450

DAVIS, ANTHONY Anthony Darvise, LB, 6´0˝/235 lbs; Utah; 1992: Hou, rnd 11; B3/7/1969 Pasco, WA **1993** Sea 10 (0) **1994**†KC 5 (0) **1995**†KC 16 (2) **1996** KC 16 (15, ROLB) **1997**†KC 15 (15, ROLB) **1998** KC 16 (16, ROLB) **1999** GB 14 (1) **2000**†Bal 14 (0) **NFL** 106 (49) [8 yrs]

DAVIS, ANTHONY Anthony Sherrod, T, 6´4˝/322 lbs; Virginia Tech; B3/27/1980 Paterson, NJ **2004** TB 2 (0) **2005**†TB 16 (16, LT) **NFL** 18 (16) [2 yrs]

DAVIS, ANTONE Antone Eugene, T-G, 6´4˝/330 lbs; Tennessee; 1991: Phi, rnd 1; B2/28/1967 Sweetwater, TX **1991** Phi 16 (15, RT) **1992**†Phi 15 (15, RT) **1993** Phi 16 (16, RT) **1994** Phi 16 (14, LG) **1995**†Phi 15 (14, RT) **1996** Atl 16 (10, RT) **1997** Atl 3 (3) **NFL** 97 (87) [7 yrs]

DAVIS, ART Arthur Ganong, DB-HB, 6´1˝/195 lbs; Mississippi State; 1956: Pit, rnd 1; B11/29/1934 Clarksdale, MS

YEAR	TEAM	G (GS, POS)	RUSH	YD	AVG (LG)	TD	REC	YD	AVG (LG)	TD	PASS	COMP	PCT	YD	AVG (LG)	TD	INT	SK	YD	QBR	KPR	OTD	PTS	TAY
1956	Pit	9 (DB)	5	6	1.2 (9)	0	1	9	9.0 (9)	0	—	—	—	—	—	—	—	—	—	—	p	—	0	1

DAVIS, BEN Benjamin Frank, DB, 5´11˝/180 lbs; Defiance; 1967: Cle, rnd 17; B10/30/1945 Birmingham, AL **1967**†Cle 14 (lcb) **1968**†Cle☆14 (RCB) **1969** Cle 1 **1970** Cle 7 (rcb) **1971**†Cle 12 (RCB) **1972**†Cle✧14 (RCB) **1973** Cle 13 (RCB) **1974** Det 9 (3) **1975** Det 11 (3) **1976** Det 14 **NFL** 109 (6) [10 yrs]

DAVIS, BILL William Dorris, T, 6´1˝/234 lbs; Texas Tech; 1940: ChiC, rnd 11; B11/10/1916 Grapevine, TX, D11/8/1994 Addison, TX **1940** ChiC 10 (3) **1941** ChiC 10 (5, LT) **1943** Bkn 8 (1) **NFL** 28 (9) [3 yrs]

1946 Mia-A 12 (5, rt)

YEAR	TEAM	G (GS, POS)	RUSH	YD	AVG(LG)	TD	REC	YD	AVG(LG)	TD	PASS COMP	PCT	YD	AVG(LG)	TD	INT	SK	YD	QBR	KPR	OTD	PTS	TAY

DAVIS, BILLY William Augusta, WR, 6´1˝/205 lbs; Pittsburgh; B7/6/1972 El Paso, TX

1995	†Dal	16(0)	—	—	—	—	—	—	—	—	—	—	—	—	—	—	—	—	—	—	—	—	—
1996	†Dal	13(0)	—	—	—	—	—	—	—	—	—	—	—	—	—	—	—	—	—	—	—	—	—
1997	Dal	16(0)	—	—	—	—	3	33	11.0(12)	0	—	—	—	—	—	—	—	—	—	—	—	0	17
1998	†Dal	16(11, WR)	4	15	3.8(8)	0	39	691	17.7(80)	3	—	—	—	—	—	—	—	—	—	k	—	18	371
1999	Bal	16(0)	—	—	—	—	6	121	20.2(73)	0	—	—	—	—	—	—	—	—	—	—	—	0	61
2000	†Bal	16(1)	—	—	—	—	3	62	20.7(28)	0	—	—	—	—	—	—	—	—	—	—	—	0	31
NFL	6	93(12)	4	15	3.8(8)	0	51	907	17.8(80)	3	—	—	—	—	—	—	—	—	—	k	—	18	479

DAVIS, BILLY William Henry, LB, 6´4˝/210 lbs; Clemson; B12/6/1961 Alexandria, VA   **1984** SL 1 (0)

DAVIS, BOB James Robert, HB-FB-QB-P, 6´1˝/180 lbs; Kentucky; B5/4/1914 Greenup, KY, D7/1969, FL **[K]**

1938	Cle	8(3, fb)	22	100	4.5	0	3	31	10.3	0	24 6	25.0	49	2.0	0	2	—	—	—	K	—	0	60
1942	Phi	10(6, LH)	43	207	4.8(44)	2	6	93	15.5(48)	1	—	—	—	—	—	—	—	—	—	kpi	—	18	343
1944	Bos	10(10, QB)	95	363	3.8(80)	1	19	97	5.1(23)	0	18 8	44.4	88	4.9(25)	1	2	—	—	—	Pkpi	—	6	627
1945	Bos	10(9, RH)	29	91	3.1(12)	0	9	56	6.2(29)	0	10 5	50.0	73	7.3(23)	3	0	—	—	—	Pkpi	—	0	249
1946	Bos	11(5, lh)	41	143	3.5(21)	0	10	150	15.0(37)	1	1 1	100.0	7	7.0(7)	0	0	—	—	—	kpi	—	6	403
NFL	5	49(33)	230	904	3.9(80)	3	47	427	9.1(48)	2	53 20	37.7	217	4.1(25)	4	4	—	—	—	KPkpi	—	30	1680

DAVIS, BOB Robert Ellersie, QB, 6´2˝/205 lbs; Virginia; 1967: Hou, rnd 2; B9/15/1945 Neptune, NJ

1967	Hou-A	2(1)	5	32	6.4(10)	0	—	—	—	—	19 9	47.4	71	3.7(17)	0	2	2	10	—	—	—	0	-13
1968	Hou-A	6(3)	15	91	6.1(20)	1	—	—	—	—	86 33	38.4	441	5.1(53)	0	6	6	72	—	—	—	6	82
1969	Hou-A	2	3	2	0.7(4)	0	—	—	—	—	42 25	59.5	223	5.3(22)	2	4	3	32	—	—	—	0	-37
1970	NYJ	1	2	11	5.5(10)	0	—	—	—	—	17 6	35.3	66	3.9(16)	0	0	—	—	—	—	—	0	44
1971	NYJ	13(QB)	18	154	8.6(24)	1	—	—	—	—	121 49	40.5	624	5.2(44)	10	8	14	92	—	—	—	6	206
1972	NYJ	14	6	32	5.3(20)	0	—	—	—	—	22 10	45.5	114	5.2(35)	2	1	6	52	—	—	—	0	59
1973	NO	2	3	10	3.3(7)	0	—	—	—	—	17 5	29.4	14	0.8(14)	0	2	5	36	—	—	—	0	-63
NFL	7	40(4)	52	332	6.4(24)	2	—	—	—	—	324 137	42.3	1553	4.8(53)	14	23	36	294	—	—	—	12	279

DAVIS, BOB Robert Billingsley, E-DE, 5´11˝/192 lbs; Penn State; B9/26/1921 Monongahela, PA, D11/16/1998 Pleasant HillS, PA

1946	Pit	11(11, RE)	—	—	—	—	1	13	13.0(13)	0	—	—	—	—	—	—	—	—	—	—	1	6	7
1947	†Pit	11(11, RE)	—	—	—	—	5	145	29.0(44)	0	—	—	—	—	—	—	—	—	—	k	—	0	61
1948	Pit	12(4)	—	—	—	—	2	14	7.0(11)	0	—	—	—	—	—	—	—	—	—	k	—	0	0
1949	Pit	11(0)	—	—	—	—	—	—	—	—	—	—	—	—	—	—	—	—	—	—	—	0	0
1950	Pit	10	—	—	—	—	—	—	—	—	—	—	—	—	—	—	—	—	—	—	—	0	0
NFL	5	55(26)	—	—	—	—	8	172	21.5(44)	0	—	—	—	—	—	—	—	—	—	k	1	6	67

DAVIS, BOB Robert Thomas, T, 6´4˝/235 lbs; Georgia Tech; 1947: NYG, rnd 6/Buf-A, rnd 2; B5/3/1927 Columbus, GA   **1948** Bos 12 (0)

DAVIS, BRAD Bradford Timothy, RB, 5´10˝/204 lbs; LSU; 1975: Atl, rnd 9; B2/9/1953 Hammond, LA   **1975** Atl 3   **1976** Atl 1   **NFL** 4 [2 yrs]

DAVIS, BRIAN Brian Wesely, DB, 6´2˝/190 lbs; Nebraska; 1987: Was, rnd 2; B8/31/1963 Phoenix, AZ   **1987**†Was 7 (0)   **1988** Was 9 (6, lcb)   **1989** Was 15 (9, LCB)   **1990** Was 7 (0)   **1991** Sea 16 (2)   **1992** Sea 13 (0)   **1993** SD 11 (0)   **1994** Min 9 (0)   **NFL** 87 (17) [8 yrs]

DAVIS, BRUCE Bruce Edward, WR, 5´8˝/160 lbs; Baylor; 1984: Cle, rnd 2; B2/25/1963 Dallas, TX

| 1984 | Cle | 14(1) | 1 | 6 | 6.0(6) | 0 | 7 | 119 | 17.0(43) | 2 | — | — | — | — | — | — | — | — | — | k | — | 12 | 175 |

DAVIS, BRUCE Bruce Edward, T-G, 6´6˝/287 lbs; UCLA; 1979: Oak, rnd 11; B6/21/1956 Rutherfordton, NC   **1979** Oak 12   **1980**†Oak 16 (0)   **1981** Oak 16 (0)   **1982**†LARd 9 (9, LT)   **1983**†LARd 16 (16, LT)   **1984**†LARd 16 (15, LT)   **1985**†LARd 16 (16, LT)   **1986** LARd 16 (16, LT)   **1987** LARd 4 (4)   **1987**†Hou 7 (7, LT)   **1988**†Hou 16 (16, LT)   **1989**†Hou 16 (16, LT)   **NFL** 160 (115) [11 yrs]

DAVIS, BUDDY Arthur E., T, 6´2˝/235 lbs; Alabama State; B12/19/1929 Montgomery, AL, D11/18/1987 Montgomery, AL   **1953** ChiB 2   **1954** ChiB 1   **NFL** 3 [2 yrs]

DAVIS, BUTCH John Charles, DB, 5´11˝/183 lbs; Missouri; 1970: Chi, rnd 12; B7/3/1948 La Jolla, CA   **1970** ChiB 10

DAVIS, CAREY Carey Alexander, RB, 5´10˝/225 lbs; Illinois; B3/27/1981 St. Louis, MO   **2004** Ind 1 (0)   **2004**†Atl 0 (0)   **NFL** 1 (0) [1 yr]

DAVIS, CARL Carl Lewis, E-T-G, 6´0˝/194 lbs; Michigan; West Virginia; B5/19/1903 Charleston, WV, D10/14/1959 Charleston, WV   **1927** Fra 8 (3)

DAVIS, CHARLES Charles Mack, DT-NT, 6´1˝/269 lbs; TCU; 1974: Pit, rnd 9; B11/17/1951 Wortham, TX   **1974**†Pit 14   **1975**†SL 14 (12, LDT)   **1976** SL 14 (14, LDT)   **1977** SL 14 (LDT)   **1978** SL 1   **1979** SL 16 (NT)   **1980** Hou 1 (0)   **NFL** 74 (26) [7 yrs]

DAVIS, CHARLIE Charles Douglas, RB, 5´11˝/200 lbs; Colorado; 1974: Cin, rnd 2; B1/16/1952 West Columbia, TX

1974	Cin	14(RB)	72	375	5.2(29)	0	19	171	9.0(32)	0	—	—	—	—	—	—	—	—	—	k	—	0	524
1976	TB	6(4)	41	107	2.6(13)	1	3	32	10.7(23)	0	—	—	—	—	—	—	—	—	—	k	—	6	146
NFL	2	20(4)	113	482	4.3(29)	1	22	203	9.2(32)	0	—	—	—	—	—	—	—	—	—	k	—	6	670

DAVIS, CHAUNCEY Chauncey, DE, 6´1˝/258 lbs; Florida State; 2005: Atl, rnd 4; B1/27/1983 Auburndale, FL   **2005** Atl 16 (5, rde)

DAVIS, CHRIS Christopher Weldon, LB, 6´1˝/225 lbs; Purdue; San Diego State; B7/26/1963 Rahway, NJ   **1987** NYG 3 (2)

DAVIS, CHRIS Christopher Michael, FB, 5´11˝/235 lbs; Syracuse; 2003: Sea, rnd 5; B11/8/1979 Tampa, FL   **2003** Sea 1 (0)

DAVIS, CLARENCE Clarence Eugene, RB, 5´10˝/195 lbs; USC; 1971: Oak, rnd 4; B6/28/1949 Birmingham, AL **[R]**

1971	Oak	14	54	321	5.9(39)	2	15	97	6.5(18)	0	—	—	—	—	—	—	—	—	—	k	—	12	719
1972	†Oak	11	71	363	5.1(45)	6	8	82	10.3(26)	0	—	—	—	—	—	—	—	—	—	kp	—	36	658
1973	†Oak	13	116	609	5.3(32)	4	7	76	10.9(19)	0	—	—	—	—	—	—	—	—	—	k	—	24	906
1974	†Oak	11(7, RB)	129	554	4.3(41)	2	11	145	13.2(45)	1	—	—	—	—	—	—	—	—	—	k	—	18	714
1975	†Oak	11(8, RB)	112	486	4.3(41)	4	11	126	11.5(31)	1	—	—	—	—	—	—	—	—	—	k	—	30	727
1976	†Oak	12(RB)	114	516	4.5(31)	3	27	191	7.1(37)	0	—	—	—	—	—	—	—	—	—	—	—	18	642
1977	†Oak	14(14, RB)	194	787	4.1(37)	5	16	124	7.8(38)	0	—	—	—	—	—	—	—	—	—	k	—	30	917
1978	Oak	2(2)	14	4	0.3(7)	0	4	24	6.0(13)	0	—	—	—	—	—	—	—	—	—	—	—	0	16
NFL	8	88(31)	804	3640	4.5(45)	26	99	865	8.7(45)	2	—	—	—	—	—	—	—	—	—	kp	—	168	5298

DAVIS, CORBY Richard Corbett, BB-FB-K, 5´11˝/212 lbs; Indiana; 1938: Cle, rnd 1; B12/18/1914 Lowell, IN, D5/28/1968, **[K]**

1938	Cle	11(5)	71	202	2.8	3	1	2	2.0(2)	0	1 0	0.0	0	0	0	0	—	—	—	K	—	19	233
1939	Cle	11(0)	13	15	1.2	1	3	49	16.3	0	—	—	—	—	—	—	—	—	—	KP	—	13	50
1941	Cle	8(5, BB)	31	110	3.5(18)	0	13	64	4.9(12)	0	—	—	—	—	—	—	—	—	—	Pp	—	0	143
1942	Cle	9(2)	28	55	2.0(12)	0	2	18	9.0(14)	0	2 1	50.0	22	11.0(22)	0	1	—	—	—	Pi	—	0	33
NFL	4	39(12)	143	382	2.7(18)	4	19	133	7.0(14)	0	3 1	33.3	22	7.3(22)	0	1	—	—	—	KPpi	—	32	459

DAVIS, DARRELL Darrell Odell, DE, 6´2˝/258 lbs; TCU; 1990: NYJ, rnd 12; B3/10/1966 Houston, TX   **1990** NYJ 15 (0)   **1991** NYJ 13 (0)   **NFL** 28 (0) [2 yrs]

DAVIS, DAVE David Glenn, WR, 6´0˝/175 lbs; Tennessee State; 1971: GB, rnd 7; B7/5/1948 Alcoa, TN

1971	GB	14	—	—	—	—	6	59	9.8(20)	0	—	—	—	—	—	—	—	—	—	kp	—	0	43
1972	GB	10	2	0	0.0(7)	0	4	119	29.8(68)	1	—	—	—	—	—	—	—	—	—	kp	—	6	65
1973	Pit	2	—	—	—	—	1	14	14.0(14)	0	—	—	—	—	—	—	—	—	—	—	—	0	7
1974	NO	7	—	—	—	—	—	—	—	—	—	—	—	—	—	—	—	—	—	k	—	0	-1
NFL	4	33	2	0	0.0(7)	0	11	192	17.5(68)	1	—	—	—	—	—	—	—	—	—	kp	—	6	113

DAVIS, DEXTER Dexter Wendell Jackson, DB, 5´10˝/190 lbs; Clemson; 1991: Phx, rnd 4; B3/20/1970 Brooklyn, NY   **1991** Phx 11 (0)   **1992** Phx 16 (2)   **1993** Phx 6 (1)   **1993** LARm 6 (3)   **1994** LARm 4 (0)   **1995** SL 16 (0)   **NFL** 59 (6) [5 yrs]

DAVIS, DICK Richard Earl, DE, 6´2˝/230 lbs; Vanderbilt; Kansas; B2/6/1938 Jackson, TN   **1962**†DalT-A 12

DAVIS, DICK Richard C., RB, 5´11˝/215 lbs; Nebraska; 1969: Cle, rnd 12; B11/28/1946 Omaha, NE   **1970** Den 2

| 1970 | NO | 4 | 27 | 94 | 3.5(25) | 0 | 4 | 29 | 7.3(13) | 0 | — | — | — | — | — | — | — | — | — | — | — | 0 | 109 |
| NFL | 1 | 6 | 27 | 94 | 3.5(25) | 0 | 4 | 29 | 7.3(13) | 0 | — | — | — | — | — | — | — | — | — | — | — | 0 | 109 |

DAVIS, DOC Edward C., T-G, 5´9˝/200 lbs; Indiana; B2/13/1889, D7/1963   **1920** Mun 1 (1, RT)   **1920** Day 7 (3)   **1922** Col 1 (1)   **NFL** 9 (5) [2 yrs]

YEAR	TEAM	G(GS, POS)	RUSH	YD	AVG(LG)	TD	REC	YD	AVG(LG)	TD	PASS	COMP	PCT	YD	AVG(LG)	TD	INT	SK	YD	QBR	KPR	OTD	PTS	TAY

DAVIS, DOMANICK Domanick, RB, 5′9″/216 lbs; LSU; 2003: Hou, rnd 4; B10/1/1980 Lafayette, LA

2003	Hou	14(10, RB)	238	1031	4.3(51)	8	47	351	7.5(17)	0	—	—	—	—	—	—	—	—	—	—	k	—	48	1303
2004	Hou	15(15, RB)	302	1188	3.9(44)	13	68	588	8.6(38)	1	—	—	—	—	—	—	—	—	—	—	—	—	84	1617
2005	Hou	11(11, RB)	230	976	4.2(44)	2	39	337	8.6(33)	4	1	0	0.0	0	0.0	0	0	—	—	—	kp	—	36	1208
NFL	3	40(36)	770	3195	4.1(51)	23	154	1276	8.3(38)	5	1	0	0.0	0	0.0	0	0	—	—	—	kp	—	168	4127

DAVIS, DON Donald Earl, DT, 6′6″/285 lbs; Los Angeles State; 1966: NYG, rnd 2/SD, rnd 1; B12/16/1943 Santa Ana, CA **1966** NYG 14 (RDT)

DAVIS, DON Donald Earl, LB, 6′1″/235 lbs; Kansas; B12/17/1972 Olathe, KS **1996** NO 11 (0) **1997** NO 11 (0) **1998** NO 4 (0) **1998** TB 5 (0) **1999**†TB 14 (0) **2000**†TB 16 (0) **2001**†SL 12 (8, llb) **2002** SL 16 (7, llb) **2003**†NE 15 (0) **2004**†NE 16 (2) **2005**†NE 16 (0) **NFL** 136 (17) [10 yrs]

DAVIS, DONNIE Donnie Ray, WR-TE, 6′3″/225 lbs; Southern (LA); 1962: Dal, rnd 6; B9/18/1940 Opelousas, LA, D1/19/2004 Houston, TX **1970** Hou 14

| 1962 | Dal | 11 | — | — | — | — | 2 | 31 | 15.5(24) | 0 | — | — | — | — | — | — | — | — | — | — | k | — | 0 | 22 |
| NFL | 2 | 25 | — | — | — | — | 2 | 31 | 15.5(24) | 0 | — | — | — | — | — | — | — | — | — | — | k | — | 0 | -9 |

DAVIS, DORSETT Dorsett Terrell, DE-DT, 6′5″/305 lbs; Mississippi State; 2002: Den, rnd 3; B1/24/1979 Shelby, MA **2003** Den 14 (0)

DAVIS, DOUG Douglas Sherone, T, 6′4″/255 lbs; Kentucky; 1966: Min, rnd 5; B7/22/1944 Elkton, MD **1966** Min 13 (12, RT) **1967** Min 11 (7, RT) **1968**†Min 14 (7, RT) **1969**†Min 10 (8, RT) **1970** Min 12 **1971**†Min 14 **1972** Min 5 **NFL** 79 (34) [7 yrs]

DAVIS, EDWARD Edward, G, /185 lbs; Chicago; deceased **1920** Ham 6 (2, RG)

DAVIS, ELGIN Elgin, RB, 5′10″/192 lbs; Central Florida; 1987: NE, rnd 12; B10/23/1965 Jacksonville, FL **1988** NE 5 (0)

| 1987 | NE | 4(0) | 9 | 43 | 4.8(27) | 0 | — | — | — | — | — | — | — | — | — | — | — | — | — | — | k | — | 0 | 102 |
| NFL | 2 | 9(0) | 9 | 43 | 4.8(27) | 0 | — | — | — | — | — | — | — | — | — | — | — | — | — | — | k | — | 0 | 118 |

DAVIS, ERIC Eric Wayne, DB, 5′11″/185 lbs; Jacksonville State; 1990: SF, rnd 2; B1/26/1968 Anniston, AL [I] **1990**†SF 16 (0) **1991** SF 2 (2) **1992**†SF 16 (16, LCB) **1993**†SF 16 (16, LCB) **1994** SF 16 (16, LCB) **1995**†SF★15 (15, LCB) **1996**†Car☆16 (16, LCB) **1997** Car 14 (14, LCB) **1998** Car 16 (16, LCB) **1999** Car 16 (16, LCB) **2000** Car 16 (16, LCB) **2001** Den 13 (8, fs) **NFL** 188 (151) [13 yrs]

DAVIS, FRED Frederick Lee, T-DT, 6′3″/244 lbs; Alabama; 1941: Was, rnd 3; B2/15/1918 Louisville, KY, D3/10/1995 Selma, AL **1941** Was 11 (1) **1942**†Was◇11 (4) **1945**†Was 4 (1) **1946**†ChiB◇11 (7, LT) **1947** ChiB☆12 (8, LT) **1948** ChiB☆12 (7, LT) **1949** ChiB 12 (6, lt) **1950**†ChiB◇12 (LDT) **1951** ChiB 12 (LDT) **NFL** 97 (34) [9 yrs]

DAVIS, FRED Frederick, DB, 5′10″/182 lbs; Western Carolina; B7/18/1964 **1987** Sea 1 (1)

DAVIS, GAINES Trenton Gaines, G, 5′11″/230 lbs; Texas Tech; B10/20/1913, D12/1983 Waco, TX **1936** NYG 6 (0)

DAVIS, GARY Gary Curtis, RB, 5′10″/202 lbs; Cal Poly-San Luis Obispo; 1976: Mia, rnd 6; B9/7/1954 Los Angeles, CA [R]

1976	Mia	14(1)	31	160	5.2(57)	1	2	8	4.0(6)	0	—	—	—	—	—	—	—	—	—	—	k	—	6	401
1977	Mia	14(6, rb)	126	533	4.2(60)	2	14	151	10.8(32)	1	—	—	—	—	—	—	—	—	—	—	kp	—	18	844
1978	Mia	14(1)	62	313	5.0(65)	3	24	218	9.1(34)	0	—	—	—	—	—	—	—	—	—	—	kp	—	18	534
1979	†Mia	15(3)	98	383	3.9(42)	1	34	215	6.3(18)	0	—	—	—	—	—	—	—	—	—	—	k	—	6	498
1980	TB	15(2)	7	21	3.0(12)	0	9	79	8.8(15)	0	—	—	—	—	—	—	—	—	—	—	k	—	0	352
1981	TB	7(0)	—	—	—	—	—	—	—	—	—	—	—	—	—	—	—	—	—	—	k	—	0	6
NFL	6	79(13)	324	1410	4.4(65)	7	83	671	8.1(34)	1	—	—	—	—	—	—	—	—	—	—	k	—	48	2634

DAVIS, GLENN Glenn Woodward 'Mr. Outside', HB, 5′9″/172 lbs; Cal Poly-Pomona; Army; 1947: Det, rnd 1/SF-A, rnd S; B12/26/1924 Burbank, CA, D3/9/2005 La Quinta, CA

1950	†LARm◇	12(LH)	88	416	4.7(51)	3	42	592	14.1(50)	4	5	3	60.0	97	19.4(58)	2	0	—	—	—	kp	—	42	877
1951	†LARm	11(LH)	64	200	3.1(23)	1	8	90	11.3(21)	1	2	1	50.0	5	2.5(5)	0	0	—	—	—	kp	—	12	317
NFL	2	23	152	616	4.1(51)	4	50	682	13.6(50)	5	7	4	57.1	102	14.6(58)	2	0	—	—	—	kp	—	54	1193

DAVIS, GLENN Glenn Ashby, WR, 6′0″/180 lbs; Ohio State; B9/12/1934 Wellsburg, WV

1960	Det	4	—	—	—	—	1	17	17.0(17)	0	—	—	—	—	—	—	—	—	—	—	—	—	0	9
1961	Det	8	—	—	—	—	9	115	12.8(19)	0	—	—	—	—	—	—	—	—	—	—	—	—	0	58
NFL	2	12	—	—	—	—	10	132	13.2(19)	0	—	—	—	—	—	—	—	—	—	—	—	—	0	66

DAVIS, GREG Gregory Brian, K, 6′0″/202 lbs; The Citadel; 1987: TB, rnd 9; B10/29/1965 Atlanta, GA [K] **1987** Atl 3 (0) **1988** Atl 16 (0) **1989** NE 9 (0) **1989** Atl 6 (0) **1990** Atl 16 (0) **1991** Phx 16 (0) **1992** Phx 16 (0) **1993** Phx 16 (0) **1994** Arz 14 (0) **1995** Arz 9 (0) **1996** Arz 16 (0) **1997** Min 4 (0) **1997** SD 12 (0) **1998** Oak 16 (0) **NFL** 169 (0) [12 yrs]

DAVIS, HARPER Julius Harper, DB, 5′11″/173 lbs; Mississippi State; 1948: LAD-A, rnd 12/1949: Pit, rnd 2; B12/11/1925 Clarksdale, MS

1949	LAD-A	11(0)	13	32	2.5	1	2	13	6.5	0	—	—	—	—	—	—	—	—	—	—	kpi	—	6	99
1950	†ChiB	12(DB)	10	57	5.7(36)	1	2	15	7.5(8)	0	—	—	—	—	—	—	—	—	—	—	pi	—	6	123
1951	GB	12(DB)	—	—	—	—	1	15	15.0(15)	0	—	—	—	—	—	—	—	—	—	—	pi	—	0	36
NFL	2	24	—	57	5.7(36)	1	3	30	10.1(15)	0	—	—	—	—	—	—	—	—	—	—	pi	—	6	158

DAVIS, HARRISON Harrison Paul, WR, 6′4″/219 lbs; Virginia; 1974: SD, rnd 4; B2/20/1952 Salisbury, NC

| 1974 | SD | 12(7, WR) | 2 | -7 | -3.5(2) | 0 | 18 | 432 | 24.0(70) | 2 | — | — | — | — | — | — | — | — | — | — | p | — | 12 | 233 |

DAVIS, HENRY Henry Louis, LB, 6′3″/235 lbs; Grambling State; 1968: NYG, rnd 11; B11/8/1942 Slaughter, LA, D6/11/2000 Baton Rouge, LA **1968** NYG 14 (MLB) **1969** NYG 13 (LLB) **1970** Pit 14 (llb) **1971** Pit 14 **1972**†Pit 14 (MLB) **1973**†Pit 14 (MLB) **NFL** 83 [6 yrs]

DAVIS, HERB Herbert A., WB-E-BB, 5′11″/173 lbs; Xavier (OH); B4/2/1899, NJ, D1/1/1986 San Lorenzo, CA **1925** Col 4 (0) **1926** Col 6 (0) **NFL** 10 (0) [2 yrs]

DAVIS, HERMIT Hermit, E, 5′11″/205 lbs; Birmingham-Southern; B3/31/1911 Double Springs, AL

| 1936 | ChiC | 2(1) | — | — | — | — | 1 | 36 | 36.0(36) | 0 | — | — | — | — | — | — | — | — | — | — | — | — | 0 | 18 |

DAVIS, ISAAC John Isaac Earl Lamont, G, 6′3″/320 lbs; Arkansas; 1994: SD, rnd 2; B4/8/1972 Malvern, AR **1994**†SD 13 (2) **1995**†SD 16 (10, RG) **1996** SD 14 (5, rg) **1997** SD 12 (12, RG) **1997** NO 3 (2) **NFL** 58 (31) [4 yrs]

DAVIS, JACK John James, G, 6′0″/225 lbs; Maryland; 1958: Was, rnd 15; B3/12/1932 Braddock, PA **1960** Den-A 2

DAVIS, JACK Jack Owen, G, 6′2″/235 lbs; Arizona; B2/19/1933 Heavener, OK **1960** Bos-A☆14 (RG)

DAVIS, JAMES James Steven, DB, 6′0″/193 lbs; Southern (LA); 1981: Oak, rnd 5; B6/12/1957 Los Angeles, CA **1982**†LARd 9 (0) **1983**†LARd 16 (0) **1984**†LARd 15 (0) **1985**†LARd 15 (1) **1986** LARd 16 (0) **1987** LARd 12 (1) **NFL** 83 (2) [6 yrs]

DAVIS, JAMES James, LB, 6′1″/221 lbs; West Virginia; 2003: Det, rnd 5; B4/26/1979 Stuart, FL **2003** Det 8 (1) **2004** Det 16 (15, LLB) **2005** Det 16 (14, RLB) **NFL** 40 (30) [3 yrs]

DAVIS, JEFF Jeffrey Eugene, LB, 6′0″/230 lbs; Clemson; 1982: TB, rnd 5; B1/26/1960 Greensboro, NC **1982**†TB 9 (0) **1983** TB 15 (14, LILB) **1984** TB 16 (16, LILB) **1985** TB 16 (16, LILB) **1986** TB 16 (16, LILB) **1987** TB 11 (10, LILB) **NFL** 83 (72) [6 yrs]

DAVIS, JEROME Jerome, NT, 6′1″/260 lbs; Ball State; B2/27/1962 Cincinnati, OH **1987** Det 3 (3)

DAVIS, JEROME Jerome Devon, T, 6′5″/290 lbs; Minnesota; B2/4/1974 Detroit, MI **2002**†SF 2 (0) **2003** SF 2 (0) **2004** SF 2 (0) **NFL** 6 (0) [3 yrs]

DAVIS, JERRY Jerome W., DB-HB, 5′10″/178 lbs; Southeastern Louisiana; 1948: ChiC, rnd 19; B1/5/1924 Savannah, GA [I] **1949** ChiC 9 (0) **1950** ChiC 11 (DB) **1952** DalT 7 (DB)

1948	†ChiC	11(3)	12	77	6.4(35)	0	—	—	—	—	—	—	—	—	—	—	—	—	—	—	kpi	2	12	590
1951	ChiC	8(DB)	1	-7	-7.0(-7)	0	4	24	6.0(15)	0	—	—	—	—	—	—	—	—	—	—	pi	—	0	21
NFL	5	46(3)	13	70	5.4(35)	0	4	24	6.0(15)	0	—	—	—	—	—	—	—	—	—	—	kpi	4	24	804

DAVIS, JERRY Jerry Wayne, DB, 5′11″/182 lbs; Morris Brown; B2/5/1951 Macon, GA **1975** NYJ 6

DAVIS, JIM Jim, DE, 6′3″/276 lbs; Virginia Tech; B10/4/1981 Richmond, VA **2005** Jax 1 (0)

DAVIS, JOE Joseph Austin, E-DE, 6′2″/195 lbs; USC; B11/20/1919 St. Anthony, ID, D5/26/1992 Bakersfield, CA [K]

| 1946 | Bkn-A | 14(12, RE) | — | — | — | — | 22 | 337 | 15.3 | 1 | — | — | — | — | — | — | — | — | — | — | Kk | — | 7 | 176 |

DAVIS, JOHN John, FB-WB-TB-BB, /155 lbs; none; B1896, deceased **1920** Col 8 (2)

DAVIS, JOHN John Leonard, TE, 6′4″/257 lbs; Emporia State; 1994: Dal, rnd S5; B5/14/1973 Jasper, TX

1997	TB	8(2)	—	—	—	—	3	35	11.7(16)	0	—	—	—	—	—	—	—	—	—	—	—	—	0	18
1998	TB	16(0)	—	—	—	—	2	12	6.0(11)	1	—	—	—	—	—	—	—	—	—	—	—	—	6	11
1999	TB	16(0)	—	—	—	—	2	7	3.5(6)	1	—	—	—	—	—	—	—	—	—	—	—	—	6	9

YEAR	TEAM	G (GS, POS)	RUSH	YD	AVG (LG)	TD	REC	YD	AVG (LG)	TD	PASS	COMP	PCT	YD	AVG (LG)	TD	INT	SK	YD	QBR	KPR	OTD	PTS	TAY
2000	Min	15(9, TE)	—	—	—	—	17	202	11.9(37)	1	—	—	—	—	—	—	—	—	—	—	—	—	6	106
2001	ChiB	16(7, te)	—	—	—	—	11	68	6.2(14)	0	—	—	—	—	—	—	—	—	—	—	—	—	0	34
2002	ChiB	10(8, TE)	—	—	—	—	20	193	9.6(37)	3	—	—	—	—	—	—	—	—	—	—	—	—	18	112
NFL	6	81(26)	—	—	—	—	55	517	9.4(37)	6	—	—	—	—	—	—	—	—	—	—	—	—	36	289

DAVIS, JOHN John Henry, G-T-C, 6´4˝/310 lbs; Georgia Tech; 1987: Hou, rnd 11; B8/22/1965 Ellijay, GA **1987** Hou 6 (0) **1988**†Hou 13 (0) **1989**†Buf 16 (0) **1990**†Buf 16 (15, RG) **1991** Buf 12 (12, RG) **1992**†Buf 9 (0) **1993**†Buf 16 (16, RG) **1994** Buf 16 (16, RG) **NFL** 104 (59) [8 yrs]

DAVIS, JOHNNY Johnny Lee, RB, 6´1˝/235 lbs; Alabama; 1978: TB, rnd 2; B7/17/1956 Montgomery, AL

YEAR	TEAM	G (GS, POS)	RUSH	YD	AVG (LG)	TD	REC	YD	AVG (LG)	TD	PASS	COMP	PCT	YD	AVG (LG)	TD	INT	SK	YD	QBR	KPR	OTD	PTS	TAY
1978	TB	16(10, FB)	97	370	3.8(18)	3	5	13	2.6(7)	0	—	—	—	—	—	—	—	—	—	—	—	—	18	407
1979	†TB	16(4)	59	221	3.7(18)	2	5	57	11.4(24)	0	—	—	—	—	—	—	—	—	—	—	—	—	12	270
1980	TB	14(6, rb)	39	130	3.3(8)	1	4	17	4.3(9)	0	—	—	—	—	—	—	—	—	—	—	—	—	6	149
1981	†SF	16(5, rb)	94	297	3.2(14)	7	3	-1	-0.3(3)	0	—	—	—	—	—	—	—	—	—	—	k	—	42	352
1982	Cle	2(0)	4	3	0.8(2)	1	—	—	—	—	—	—	—	—	—	—	—	—	—	—	—	—	6	13
1983	Cle	16(3)	13	42	3.2(16)	0	5	20	4.0(10)	0	—	—	—	—	—	—	—	—	—	—	k	—	0	45
1984	Cle	16(4)	3	15	5.0(8)	1	—	—	—	—	—	—	—	—	—	—	—	—	—	—	—	—	6	25
1985	†Cle	16(0)	4	9	2.3(5)	0	—	—	—	—	—	—	—	—	—	—	—	—	—	—	—	—	0	9
1986	Cle	6(0)	—	—	—	—	—	—	—	—	—	—	—	—	—	—	—	—	—	—	—	—	—	—
1987	Cle	1(0)	1	7	7.0(7)	0	—	—	—	—	—	—	—	—	—	—	—	—	—	—	—	—	0	7
NFL	10	119(32)	314	1094	3.5(18)	15	22	106	4.8(24)	0	—	—	—	—	—	—	—	—	—	—	k	—	90	1275

DAVIS, KEITH Keith, DB, 5´10˝/193 lbs; Sam Houston State; B12/30/1978 Dallas, TX **2002** Dal 8 (0) **2004** Dal 15 (0) **2005** Dal 16 (15, FS) **NFL** 39 (15) [3 yrs]

DAVIS, KELVIN Kelvin, G, 6´2˝/260 lbs; Johnson C. Smith; B2/7/1963 **1987** NYG 1 (1)

DAVIS, KENNETH Kenneth Earl, RB, 5´10˝/208 lbs; TCU; 1986: GB, rnd 2; B4/16/1962 Williamson County, TX

YEAR	TEAM	G (GS, POS)	RUSH	YD	AVG (LG)	TD	REC	YD	AVG (LG)	TD	PASS	COMP	PCT	YD	AVG (LG)	TD	INT	SK	YD	QBR	KPR	OTD	PTS	TAY
1986	GB	16(6, RB)	114	519	4.6(50)	0	21	142	6.8(18)	1	—	—	—	—	—	—	—	—	—	—	k	—	6	646
1987	GB	10(8, RB)	109	413	3.8(39)	3	14	110	7.9(35)	0	—	—	—	—	—	—	—	—	—	—	—	—	18	498
1988	GB	9(7, rb)	39	121	3.1(27)	1	11	81	7.4(11)	0	—	—	—	—	—	—	—	—	—	—	—	—	6	172
1989	†Buf	16(0)	29	149	5.1(21)	1	6	92	15.3(29)	2	—	—	—	—	—	—	—	—	—	—	k	—	18	222
1990	†Buf	16(0)	64	302	4.7(47)	4	9	78	8.7(16)	1	—	—	—	—	—	—	—	—	—	—	—	—	30	386
1991	†Buf	16(1)	129	624	4.8(78)	4	20	118	5.9(14)	1	—	—	—	—	—	—	—	—	—	—	k	—	30	741
1992	†Buf	16(0)	139	613	4.4(64)	6	15	80	5.3(22)	0	—	—	—	—	—	—	—	—	—	—	k	—	36	754
1993	†Buf	16(0)	109	391	3.6(19)	6	21	95	4.5(28)	0	—	—	—	—	—	—	—	—	—	—	k	—	36	479
1994	Buf	16(1)	91	381	4.2(60)	2	18	82	4.6(12)	0	—	—	—	—	—	—	—	—	—	—	k	—	12	427
NFL	9	131(23)	823	3513	4.3(78)	27	135	878	6.5(35)	5	—	—	—	—	—	—	—	—	—	—	k	—	192	4324

DAVIS, KYLE Kyle Wayne, C, 6´3˝/240 lbs; Oklahoma; 1975: Dal, rnd 5; B10/1/1952 Cordell, OK **1975**†Dal 14 **1978** SF 7 **NFL** 21 [2 yrs]

DAVIS, LAMAR Raymond Lamar, E-DE, 6´1˝/185 lbs; Georgia; 1943: Phi, rnd 2; B6/15/1921 Brunswick, GA

YEAR	TEAM	G (GS, POS)	RUSH	YD	AVG (LG)	TD	REC	YD	AVG (LG)	TD	PASS	COMP	PCT	YD	AVG (LG)	TD	INT	SK	YD	QBR	KPR	OTD	PTS	TAY
1946	Mia-A	14(8, le)	14	64	4.6	0	22	275	12.5	2	—	—	—	—	—	—	—	—	—	—	kp	—	12	406
1947	Bal-A	13(2)	3	14	4.7	0	46	515	11.2	2	1	0	0.0	0	0.0	0	0	—	—	—	kpi	—	12	331
1948	†Bal-A	14(9, LE)	—	—	—	—	41	765	18.7	7	—	—	—	—	—	—	—	—	—	—	pi	—	42	508
1949	Bal-A	12(9, LE)	—	—	—	—	38	548	14.4	1	—	—	—	—	—	—	—	—	—	—	ki	—	6	307
AAFC	4	53(28)	17	78	4.6	0	147	2103	14.3	12	1	0	0.0	0	0.0	0	0	—	—	—	kpi	—	72	1551

DAVIS, LEE Lee Andrew, DB, 5´11˝/198 lbs; Mississippi; 1985: Cin, rnd 5; B12/18/1962 Okolona, MS **1985** Cin 7 (0) **1987** Ind 3 (0) **NFL** 10 (0) [2 yrs]

DAVIS, LEONARD Leonard Barrett, T-G, 6´6˝/375 lbs; Texas; 2001: Arz, rnd 1; B9/5/1978 Wortham, TX **2001** Arz 16 (16, RG) **2002** Arz 15 (15, RT) **2003** Arz 14 (14, RG) **2004** Arz 15 (15, LT) **2005** Arz 15 (15, LT) **NFL** 75 (75) [5 yrs]

DAVIS, LORENZO Lorenzo Edward, WR, 5´11˝/185 lbs; Youngstown State; B2/12/1968 Fort Lauderdale, FL **1990** Pit 4 (0)

DAVIS, MARVIN Marvin Daniel, DE, 6´4˝/252 lbs; Wichita State; 1965: Den, rnd R3/LA, rnd 15; B6/6/1943 Jacksonville, FL **1966** Den-A 1

DAVIS, MARVIN Marvin Eugene, LB, 6´4˝/235 lbs; Southern (LA); B5/25/1952 Shreveport, LA **1974** Hou 13

DAVIS, MIKE Michael Leonar, DB, 6´3˝/203 lbs; Colorado; 1977: Oak, rnd 2; B4/15/1956 Los Angeles, CA **1978** Oak 16 (1) **1979** Oak 16 (13, SS) **1980**†Oak 16 (16, SS) **1981** Oak 7 (2) **1982**†LARd 9 (9, SS) **1983**†LARd 16 (16, SS) **1984**†LARd 16 (16, SS) **1985**†LARd 11 (10, SS) **1987** SD 8 (0) **NFL** 115 (83) [9 yrs]

DAVIS, MIKE Michael Allen, DB, 6´1˝/192 lbs; Cincinnati; 1994: Hou, rnd 4; B1/14/1972 Springfield, OH **1994** Hou 16 (0) **1995** Cle 3 (0) **NFL** 19 (0) [2 yrs]

DAVIS, MILT Milton Eugene, DB, 6´1˝/188 lbs; UCLA; 1954: Det, rnd 8; B5/31/1929 Muskogee, OK **[I]** **1957** Bal☆12 (DB) **1958**†Bal 10 (DB) **1959**†Bal☆11 (DB) **1960** Bal 12 (RCB) **NFL** 45 [4 yrs]

DAVIS, NATHAN Nathan Michael, DE, 6´5˝/312 lbs; Indiana; 1997: Atl, rnd 2; B2/6/1974 Hartford, CT **1997** Atl 2 (0) **1999** Dal 4 (0) **NFL** 6 (0) [2 yrs]

DAVIS, NICK Nick, WR, 6´0˝/180 lbs; Wisconsin; B10/6/1979 Manchester, MI **2003** Min 1 (0)

YEAR	TEAM	G (GS, POS)	RUSH	YD	AVG (LG)	TD	REC	YD	AVG (LG)	TD	PASS	COMP	PCT	YD	AVG (LG)	TD	INT	SK	YD	QBR	KPR	OTD	PTS	TAY
2002	Min	15(0)	1	11	11.0(11)	0	—	—	—	—	—	—	—	—	—	—	—	—	—	—	kp	—	0	179
NFL	2	16(0)	1	11	11.0(11)	0	—	—	—	—	—	—	—	—	—	—	—	—	—	—	—	—	0	11

DAVIS, NORMAN Norman, G, 6´2˝/245 lbs; Grambling State; 1967: Bal, rnd 3; B8/8/1945 Cocoa, FL **1967** Bal 14 **1969** NO 12 **1970** Phi 14 **NFL** 40 [3 yrs]

DAVIS, OLIVER Oliver James, DB, 6´1˝/203 lbs; Tennessee State; 1977: Cle, rnd 4; B8/29/1954 Columbus, GA **1977** Cle 14 (14, RCB) **1978** Cle 13 (13, RCB) **1979** Cle 16 (RCB) **1980**†Cle 15 (1) **1981**†Cin 10 (0) **1982**†Cin 9 (0) **NFL** 77 (28) [6 yrs]

DAVIS, PAHL Pahl George, G-E-FB, 5´10˝/185 lbs; Wisconsin-Oshkosh; Marquette; B3/26/1897 Oconto, WI, D10/15/1971 Hemet, CA **1922** GB 7 (2)

DAVIS, PASCHALL Paschall Tederall, LB, 6´2˝/225 lbs; Texas A&M-Kingsville; B6/5/1969 Bryan, TX **1995** SL 3 (0) **1996** SL 11 (0) **NFL** 14 (0) [2 yrs]

DAVIS, PAUL Paul James, FB-DB, 6´1˝/188 lbs; Otterbein; 1947: Pit, rnd 24; B3/21/1925 Ashland, KY, D2/21/1989 Loxahatchee, FL

YEAR	TEAM	G (GS, POS)	RUSH	YD	AVG (LG)	TD	REC	YD	AVG (LG)	TD	PASS	COMP	PCT	YD	AVG (LG)	TD	INT	SK	YD	QBR	KPR	OTD	PTS	TAY
1947	†Pit	5(0)	4	5	1.3(6)	0	—	—	—	—	—	—	—	—	—	—	—	—	—	—	—	—	0	5
1948	Pit	6(3)	2	-1	-0.5(1)	0	—	—	—	—	—	—	—	—	—	—	—	—	—	—	kpi	—	0	13
NFL	2	11(3)	6	4	0.7(6)	0	—	—	—	—	—	—	—	—	—	—	—	—	—	—	kpi	—	0	18

DAVIS, PAUL Paul Calvin, LB, 6´2˝/221 lbs; North Carolina; B7/10/1958 Appalachia, VA **1981** Atl 13 (0) **1982**†Atl 9 (1) **1983** NYG 3 (0) **1983** SL 6 (0) **NFL** 31 (1) [3 yrs]

DAVIS, PERNELL Pernell, DT, 6´2˝/320 lbs; Alabama-Birmingham; 1999: Phi, rnd 7; B5/19/1976 Birmingham, AL **1999** Phi 2 (0)

DAVIS, PRESTON Preston, DB, 5´11˝/180 lbs; Baylor; B3/10/1962 Lubbock, TX **1984** Ind 12 (8, LCB) **1985** Ind 16 (16, LCB) **1986** Ind 8 (0) **NFL** 36 (24) [3 yrs]

DAVIS, RALPH Ralph Gordon, G, 5´11˝/205 lbs; Wisconsin; B5/30/1922 Seymour, WI, D9/26/1992 Northbrook, IL **1947** GB 11 (4) **1948** GB 11 (2) **NFL** 22 (6) [2 yrs]

DAVIS, RASHIED Rashied, DB, 5´10˝/180 lbs; San Jose State; B7/24/1979 Los Angeles, CA **2005**†ChiB 12 (0)

DAVIS, RAY Raymond Elswood, C-G-T-E, 6´1˝/198 lbs; Samford; B9/14/1907 Birmingham, AL, D8/26/1972 Fort Walton Beach, FL **1932** Por 11 (8, C) **1933** Por 4 (0) **NFL** 15 (8) [2 yrs]

DAVIS, RED Sylvester Edward, TB, 5´11˝/195 lbs; Geneva; B11/14/1907 Franks, OH, D8/5/1988 Garden Grove, CA **[K]** **1933** Por 1 (0)

YEAR	TEAM	G (GS, POS)	RUSH	YD	AVG (LG)	TD	REC	YD	AVG (LG)	TD	PASS	COMP	PCT	YD	AVG (LG)	TD	INT	SK	YD	QBR	KPR	OTD	PTS	TAY
1933	Phi	7(7, TB)	15	57	3.8	1	4	50	12.5	0	6	2	33.3	62	10.3	1	3	—	—	—	K	—	9	8
NFL	1	8(7)	15	57	3.8	1	4	50	12.5	0	6	2	33.3	62	10.3	1	3	—	—	—	K	—	9	8

DAVIS, REGGIE Reginald DeSean, TE, 6´3˝/233 lbs; Washington; B9/3/1976 Long Beach, CA

YEAR	TEAM	G (GS, POS)	RUSH	YD	AVG (LG)	TD	REC	YD	AVG (LG)	TD	PASS	COMP	PCT	YD	AVG (LG)	TD	INT	SK	YD	QBR	KPR	OTD	PTS	TAY
1999	SD	16(3)	—	—	—	—	12	137	11.4(46)	1	—	—	—	—	—	—	—	—	—	—	—	—	6	74
2000	SD	10(0)	—	—	—	—	1	8	8.0(8)	0	—	—	—	—	—	—	—	—	—	—	—	—	0	4
NFL	2	26(3)	—	—	—	—	13	145	11.2(46)	1	—	—	—	—	—	—	—	—	—	—	—	—	6	78

DAVIS, REUBEN Reuben Cordell, DE-DT, 6´5˝/302 lbs; North Carolina; 1988: TB, rnd 9; B5/7/1965 Greensboro, NC **1988** TB 16 (13, LDE) **1989** TB 16 (15, LDE) **1990** TB 16 (16, LDE) **1991** TB 12 (11, RDT) **1992** TB 5 (0) **1992** Phx 11 (5, rde) **1993** Phx 16 (15, RDE/ldt) **1994**†SD 16 (16, RDT) **1995**†SD 16 (16, RDT) **1996** SD 15 (15, RDT) **NFL** 139 (122) [9 yrs]

DAVIS, RICKY Richard Terrell, DB, 6´1˝/179 lbs; Alabama; 1975: Cin, rnd 8; B5/18/1953 Birmingham, AL **1975**†Cin 14 **1977** KC 13 (5, ss)

YEAR	TEAM	G (GS, POS)	RUSH	YD	AVG (LG)	TD	REC	YD	AVG (LG)	TD	PASS	COMP	PCT	YD	AVG (LG)	TD	INT	SK	YD	QBR	KPR	OTD	PTS	TAY
1976	TB	11	—	—	—	—	—	—	—	—	1	1	100.0	7	-7.0(-7)	0	0	—	—	—	—	—	0	-4
NFL	3	38(5)	—	—	—	—	—	—	—	—	1	1	100.0	7	-7.0(-7)	0	0	—	—	—	i	—	0	18

YEAR	TEAM	G (GS, POS)	RUSH	YD	AVG(LG)	TD	REC	YD	AVG(LG)	TD	PASS	COMP	PCT	YD	AVG(LG)	TD	INT	SK	YD	QBR	KPR	OTD	PTS	TAY

DAVIS, ROB   Robert Emmett, C, 6'3"/284 lbs; Shippensburg (PA); B12/10/1968 Washington, DC   **1996** ChiB 16 (0)   **1997**†GB 7 (0)   **1998**†GB 16 (0)   **1999** GB 16 (0)   **2000** GB 16 (0)   **2001**†GB 16 (0)   **2002**†GB 16 (0)   **2003**†GB 16 (0)   **2004**†GB 16 (0)   **2005** GB 16 (0)   **NFL** 151 (0) [10 yrs]

DAVIS, ROD   Rod, LB, 6'3"/246 lbs; Southern Mississippi; 2004: Min, rnd 5; B4/21/1981 Gulfport, MS   **2004**†Min 14 (0)   **2005** Min 16 (1)   **NFL** 30 (1) [2 yrs]

DAVIS, ROGER   Roger Wilfred, G-T, 6'3"/240 lbs; Syracuse; 1960: Chi, rnd 1/Den, rnd 1; B6/23/1938 Cleveland, OH   **1960** ChiB 12   **1961** ChiB 14 (RG)   **1962** ChiB 9 (RG)   **1963**†ChiB 13 (13, RG)   **1964** LARm 11   **1965** NYG 3   **1966** NYG 10   **NFL** 72 (13) [7 yrs]

DAVIS, RON   Ronald Willard, G, 6'2"/235 lbs; Virginia State; 1972: SF, rnd 16; B9/16/1950 Camden, NJ   **1973** SL 2

DAVIS, RON   Ronald Rozelle, DB, 5'10"/190 lbs; Tennessee; 1995: Atl, rnd 2; B2/24/1972 Bartlett, TN   **1995**†Atl 12 (5, lcb)

DAVIS, ROSEY   Roosevelt, DE, 6'5"/260 lbs; Tennessee State; 1965: Bal, rnd 8; B11/29/1941 Jackson, MS   **1965** NYG 14   **1966** NYG 7 (RDE)   **1967** NYG 1   **NFL** 22 [3 yrs]

DAVIS, RUSSELL   Russell W., RB, 6'0"/227 lbs; Michigan; 1979: Pit, rnd 4; B9/15/1956 Millen, GA

1980	Pit	14(2)	33	132	4.0(12)	1	—	—	—	—	—	—	—	—	—	—	—	—	—	—	k	—	6	167
1981	Pit	16(0)	47	270	5.7(28)	1	4	34	8.5(19)	0	—	—	—	—	—	—	—	—	—	—	k	—	6	290
1982	†Pit	7(0)	24	72	3.0(9)	0	1	11	11.0(11)	0	—	—	—	—	—	—	—	—	—	—	—	—	0	78
1983	Pit	5(0)	—	—	—	—	—	—	—	—	—	—	—	—	—	—	—	—	—	—	—	—	—	—
NFL	4	42(2)	104	474	4.6(28)	2	5	45	9.0(19)	0	—	—	—	—	—	—	—	—	—	—	k	—	12	535

DAVIS, RUSSELL   Russell Morgan, DT-DE, 6'4"/314 lbs; North Carolina; 1999: Chi, rnd 2; B3/28/1975 Hampton, VA   **1999** ChiB 11 (8, rde)   **2000** Arz 14 (9, LDT)   **2001** Arz 16 (16, LDT)   **2002** Arz 15 (15, LDT)   **2003** Arz 16 (16, LDT)   **2004** Arz 3 (3)   **NFL** 91 (83) [7 yrs]

DAVIS, SAM   Samuel Ruel, G, 6'1"/255 lbs; Allen; B7/5/1944 Jacksonville, FL   **1967** Pit 14   **1968** Pit 14   **1969** Pit 12 (2)   **1970** Pit 14 (14, LG)   **1971** Pit 12 (12, LG)   **1972**†Pit 11 (11, LG)   **1973**†Pit 12 (12, LG)   **1974**†Pit 11 (11, LG)   **1975**†Pit 14 (1, rg/lg)   **1976**†Pit 14 (12, LG)   **1977**†Pit 11 (9, LG)   **1978**†Pit 16 (16, LG)   **1979**†Pit 13 (12, LG)   **NFL** 168 (112) [13 yrs]

DAVIS, SAMMY   Samuel J., DB, 6'0"/190 lbs; Texas A&M; 2003: SD, rnd 1; B4/8/1980 Humble, TX   **2003** SD 16 (16, RCB)   **2004** SD 12 (10, LCB)   **2005** SD 16 (4)   **NFL** 44 (30) [3 yrs]

DAVIS, SCOTT   Scott Michael, DT-DE-LB, 6'7"/280 lbs; Illinois; 1988: LARd, rnd 1; B7/8/1965 Joliet, IL   **1988** LARd 15 (2)   **1989** LARd 14 (13, RDE)   **1990**†LARd 16 (16, RDT)   **1991**†LARd 16 (16, RDT)   **1994** LARd 14 (1)   **NFL** 75 (48) [5 yrs]

DAVIS, SCOTT   Scott L., G, 6'3"/292 lbs; Iowa; 1993: NYG, rnd 6; B1/29/1970 Glenwood, IA   **1993**†NYG 4 (0)   **1994** NYG 15 (4)   **1997** Atl 2 (2)   **NFL** 21 (6) [3 yrs]

DAVIS, SHOCKMAIN   Shockmain Natase, WR, 6'0"/205 lbs; Angelo State (TX); B8/20/1977 Port Arthur, TX

| 2000 | NE | 12(1) | — | — | — | — | 2 | 12 | 6.0(9) | 0 | — | — | — | — | — | — | — | — | — | — | k | — | 0 | 21 |

DAVIS, SONNY   Arnold Allen, LB, 6'2"/219 lbs; Baylor; 1961: Dal, rnd 4; B9/25/1938 Corpus Christi, TX   **1961** Dal 2

DAVIS, SONNY   Albert Lee, RB, 5'11"/215 lbs; Tennessee State; 1971: Phi, rnd 11; B1/16/1948 Alcoa, TN

| 1971 | Phi | 14(fb) | 47 | 163 | 3.5(21) | 1 | 11 | 46 | 4.2(12) | 0 | 1 | 0 | 0.0 | 0 | 0.0 | 0 | 0 | — | — | — | k | — | 6 | 210 |

DAVIS, STAN   Stanley Wayne, WR, 5'10"/180 lbs; Memphis; 1973: Phi, rnd 13; B7/13/1950 Memphis, TN

| 1973 | Phi | 8 | — | — | — | — | 1 | 6 | 6.0(6) | 0 | — | — | — | — | — | — | — | — | — | — | kp | — | 0 | 79 |

DAVIS, STEPHEN   Stephen Lamont, RB, 6'0"/230 lbs; Auburn; 1996: Was, rnd 4; B3/1/1974 Spartanburg, SC

1996	Was	12(0)	23	139	6.0(39)	2	—	—	—	—	—	—	—	—	—	—	—	—	—	—	—	—	12	159
1997	Was	14(6, rb)	141	567	4.0(18)	3	18	134	7.4(19)	0	—	—	—	—	—	—	—	—	—	—	k	—	18	681
1998	Was	16(12, FB)	34	109	3.2(12)	0	21	263	12.5(30)	2	—	—	—	—	—	—	—	—	—	—	—	—	12	251
1999	†Was★	14(14, RB)	290	**1405**	4.8(76)	17	23	111	4.8(21)	0	—	—	—	—	—	—	—	—	—	—	—	—	104	1631
2000	Was◇	15(15, RB)	332	1318	4.0(50)	11	33	313	9.5(39)	0	—	—	—	—	—	—	—	—	—	—	—	—	66	1585
2001	Was	16(16, RB)	**356**	**1432**	4.0(32)	5	28	205	7.3(29)	0	—	—	—	—	—	—	—	—	—	—	—	—	32	1585
2002	Was	12(12, RB)	207	820	4.0(33)	7	23	142	6.2(14)	1	—	—	—	—	—	—	—	—	—	—	—	—	48	966
2003	†Car◇	14(14, RB)	318	1444	4.5(40)	8	14	159	11.4(25)	0	—	—	—	—	—	—	—	—	—	—	—	—	48	1604
2004	Car	2(2)	24	92	3.8(12)	0	2	32	16.0(21)	0	—	—	—	—	—	—	—	—	—	—	—	—	0	108
2005	Car	13(11, rb)	180	549	3.1(39)	12	5	45	9.0(21)	0	—	—	—	—	—	—	—	—	—	—	—	—	72	692
NFL	10	128(102)	1905	7875	4.1(76)	65	167	1404	8.4(39)	3	—	—	—	—	—	—	—	—	—	—	k	—	412	9259

DAVIS, STEVE   Steven Timothy, RB, 6'1"/218 lbs; Delaware State; 1971: Pit, rnd 3; B11/10/1948 Lexington, VA

1972	†Pit	11	20	85	4.3(28)	1	1	5	5.0(5)	0	—	—	—	—	—	—	—	—	—	—	k	—	6	200
1973	†Pit	14	67	266	4.0(27)	2	7	31	4.4(9)	1	—	—	—	—	—	—	—	—	—	—	k	—	18	486
1974	†Pit	14	71	246	3.5(22)	2	11	152	13.8(61)	1	—	—	—	—	—	—	—	—	—	—	k	—	18	436
1975	NYJ	14(1)	70	290	4.1(24)	1	6	56	9.3(18)	0	—	—	—	—	—	—	—	—	—	—	k	—	6	511
1976	NYJ	12(RB)	94	418	4.4(26)	3	8	57	7.1(21)	0	—	—	—	—	—	—	—	—	—	—	—	—	18	477
NFL	5	65(1)	322	1305	4.1(28)	9	33	301	9.1(61)	2	—	—	—	—	—	—	—	—	—	—	k	—	66	2109

DAVIS, TED   Richard Kenneth, LB, 6'1"/232 lbs; Georgia Tech; 1964: Bal, rnd 4/SD, rnd 1; B7/27/1942 Memphis, TN   **1964**†Bal 14   **1965** Bal 14   **1966** Bal 10   **1967** NO 10 (mlb)   **1968** NO 14 (LLB)   **1969** NO 14   **1970**†Mia 14 (6, llb)   **NFL** 90 (6) [7 yrs]

DAVIS, TERRELL   Terrell Lamar, RB, 5'11"/206 lbs; Long Beach State; Georgia; 1995: Den, rnd 6; B10/28/1972 San Diego, CA

1995	Den☆	14(14, RB)	237	1117	**4.7(60)**	7	49	367	7.5(31)	1	—	—	—	—	—	—	—	—	—	—	—	—	48	1376
1996	†Den★	16(16, RB)	**345**	**1538**	4.5(71)	13	36	310	8.6(23)	2	—	—	—	—	—	—	—	—	—	—	—	—	90	1833
1997	†Den★	15(15, RB)	369	**1750**	4.7(50)	15	42	287	6.8(25)	0	—	—	—	—	—	—	—	—	—	—	—	—	96	**2044**
1998	†Den★	16(16, RB)	**392**	**2008**	**5.1(70)**	21	25	217	8.7(35)	2	—	—	—	—	—	—	—	—	—	—	—	—	138	**2337**
1999	Den	4(4)	67	211	3.1(26)	2	3	26	8.7(10)	0	—	—	—	—	—	—	—	—	—	—	—	—	12	244
2000	Den	5(4)	78	282	3.6(24)	2	2	4	2.0(5)	0	—	—	—	—	—	—	—	—	—	—	—	—	12	304
2001	Den	8(8, RB)	167	701	4.2(57)	0	12	69	5.8(16)	0	—	—	—	—	—	—	—	—	—	—	—	—	0	736
NFL	7	78(77)	1655	7607	4.6(71)	60	169	1280	7.6(35)	5	—	—	—	—	—	—	—	—	—	—	—	—	396	8872

DAVIS, THABITI   Thabiti Naeem, WR, 6'2"/205 lbs; Wake Forest; B3/24/1975 Charlotte, NC

2000	†NYG	13(0)	—	—	—	—	2	40	20.0(27)	0	—	—	—	—	—	—	—	—	—	—	—	—	0	20
2001	NYG	16(0)	—	—	—	—	3	34	11.3(20)	0	—	—	—	—	—	—	—	—	—	—	—	—	0	17
NFL	2	29(0)	—	—	—	—	5	74	14.8(27)	0	—	—	—	—	—	—	—	—	—	—	—	—	0	37

DAVIS, THOMAS   Thomas Antonio, LB, 6'1"/231 lbs; Georgia; 2005: Car, rnd 1; B3/22/1983 Shellman, GA   **2005**†Car 16 (2)

DAVIS, TOMMY   Tommy Ray, K-P, 6'0"/215 lbs; LSU; 1957: SF, rnd 11; B10/13/1934 Shreveport, LA, D4/2/1987 Millbrae, CA [KP]   **1959** SF 12   **1960** SF 12   **1961** SF 14   **1962** SF◇14   **1964** SF 14   **1967** SF 14   **1968** SF 9

1963	SF◇	14	—	—	—	—	—	—	—	—	1	0	0.0	0	0.0	0	0	0	—	—	KP	—	54	0
1965	SF☆	14	1	21	21.0(21)	0	—	—	—	—	—	—	—	—	—	—	—	—	—	—	KP	—	103	21
1966	SF	14	3	43	14.3(22)	0	—	—	—	—	—	—	—	—	—	—	—	—	—	—	KP	—	86	43
1969	SF	7	2	21	10.5(16)	0	—	—	—	—	—	—	—	—	—	—	—	—	—	—	KP	—	22	21
NFL	11	138	6	85	14.2(22)	0	—	—	—	—	1	0	0.0	0	0.0	0	0	0	—	—	KP	—	738	85

DAVIS, TONY   Michael Edward, RB, 5'11"/212 lbs; Nebraska; 1976: Cin, rnd 4; B1/21/1953 Tecumseh, NE

1976	Cin	14	36	178	4.9(16)	1	4	29	7.3(11)	0	—	—	—	—	—	—	—	—	—	—	kp	—	6	164
1977	Cin	14	27	81	3.0(13)	2	9	83	9.2(28)	0	—	—	—	—	—	—	—	—	—	—	kp	—	12	265
1978	Cin	14	21	57	2.7(15)	2	2	23	11.5(14)	0	—	—	—	—	—	—	—	—	—	—	kp	—	12	115
1979	†TB	16	—	—	—	—	—	—	—	—	—	—	—	—	—	—	—	—	—	—	kp	—	0	-25
1980	TB	15(2)	5	24	4.8(8)	0	12	115	9.6(18)	1	—	—	—	—	—	—	—	—	—	—	kp	—	6	85
1981	†TB	16(0)	2	5	2.5(3)	0	—	—	—	—	—	—	—	—	—	—	—	—	—	—	k	—	0	11
NFL	6	89(2)	91	345	3.8(16)	5	27	250	9.3(28)	1	—	—	—	—	—	—	—	—	—	—	kp	—	36	613

DAVIS, TRAVIS   Travis Horace, DB, 6'0"/203 lbs; Notre Dame; 1995: NO, rnd 7; B1/10/1973 Wilmington, CA   **1995** Jax 9 (5, ss)   **1996**†Jax 16 (7, ss)   **1997**†Jax 16 (16, SS)   **1998**†Jax 16 (5, fs)   **1999** Pit 16 (16, FS)   **NFL** 73 (49) [5 yrs]

DAVIS, TRAVIS   Travis Neil, NT, 6'2"/279 lbs; Michigan State; 1990: Phx, rnd 4; B5/10/1966 Warren, OH   **1990**†NO 2 (0)   **1991** Ind 16 (8, NT)   **NFL** 18 (8) [2 yrs]

YEAR	TEAM	G (GS, POS)	RUSH	YD	AVG(LG)	TD	REC	YD	AVG(LG)	TD	PASS	COMP	PCT	YD	AVG(LG)	TD	INT	SK	YD°	QBR	KPR	OTD	PTS	TAY

DAVIS, TROY   Troy, RB, 5´7˝/191 lbs; Iowa State; 1997: NO, rnd 3; B9/14/1975 Miami, FL

1997	NO	16(7, rb)	75	271	3.6(20)	0	13	85	6.5(18)	0	—	—	—	—	—	—	—	—	—	—	k	—	0	352
1998	NO	14(2)	55	143	2.6(14)	1	16	99	6.2(19)	0	—	—	—	—	—	—	—	—	—	—	k	—	6	194
1999	NO	16(3)	20	32	1.6(7)	0	7	53	7.6(20)	0	—	—	—	—	—	—	—	—	—	—	k	—	0	183
NFL	3	46(12)	150	446	3.0(20)	1	36	237	6.6(20)	0	—	—	—	—	—	—	—	—	—	—	k	—	6	728

DAVIS, TYREE   Tyree Bernard, WR, 5´9˝/175 lbs; Central Arkansas; 1993: TB, rnd 7; B9/23/1970 Altheimer, AR   **1995** TB 1 (0)

| 1997 | Sea | 13(1) | — | — | — | — | 2 | 48 | 24.0(37) | 0 | — | — | — | — | — | — | — | — | — | — | kp | — | 0 | 43 |
| NFL | 2 | 14(1) | — | — | — | — | 2 | 48 | 24.0(37) | 0 | — | — | — | — | — | — | — | — | — | — | — | — | 0 | 24 |

DAVIS, TYRONE   Joseph Tyrone, DB, 6´1˝/190 lbs; Clemson; 1985: NYG, rnd 3; B11/17/1961 Athens, GA   **1985** NYG 7 (0)

DAVIS, TYRONE   Tyrone, TE-WR, 6´4˝/240 lbs; Virginia; 1995: NYJ, rnd 4; B6/30/1972 Halifax, VA

1995	NYJ	4(0)	—	—	—	—	1	9	9.0(9)	0	—	—	—	—	—	—	—	—	—	—	—	—	0	5
1996	NYJ	2(0)	—	—	—	—	1	6	6.0(6)	0	—	—	—	—	—	—	—	—	—	—	—	—	0	3
1997	†GB	13(0)	—	—	—	—	2	28	14.0(26)	1	—	—	—	—	—	—	—	—	—	—	—	1	12	19
1998	†GB	13(1)	—	—	—	—	18	250	13.9(60)	7	—	—	—	—	—	—	—	—	—	—	—	—	42	160
1999	GB	16(13, TE)	—	—	—	—	20	204	10.2(33)	2	—	—	—	—	—	—	—	—	—	—	—	—	12	112
2000	GB	14(9, TE)	—	—	—	—	19	177	9.3(41)	2	—	—	—	—	—	—	—	—	—	—	—	—	14	99
2001	†GB	4(2)	—	—	—	—	3	14	4.7(7)	0	—	—	—	—	—	—	—	—	—	—	—	—	0	7
2002	†GB	9(5)	—	—	—	—	9	107	11.9(24)	1	—	—	—	—	—	—	—	—	—	—	—	—	6	59
NFL	8	75(27)	—	—	—	—	73	795	10.9(60)	13	—	—	—	—	—	—	—	—	—	—	—	1	86	463

DAVIS, VAN   Van Andrew, DE-E, 6´2˝/215 lbs; Georgia; 1943: GB, rnd 12; B10/5/1921 Philomath, GA, D7/11/1987 Carrollton, GA

1947	†NYY-A	13(0)	—	—	—	—	8	179	22.4	0	—	—	—	—	—	—	—	—	—	—	k	—	0	84
1948	NYY-A	13(4)	—	—	—	—	4	49	12.3	1	—	—	—	—	—	—	—	—	—	—	i	—	6	30
1949	†NYY-A	11(1)	—	—	—	—	2	26	13.0	0	—	—	—	—	—	—	—	—	—	—	—	—	0	13
AAFC	3	37(5)	—	—	—	—	14	254	18.1	1	—	—	—	—	—	—	—	—	—	—	ki	—	6	126

DAVIS, VERN   Vernon Charles, DB, 6´4˝/208 lbs; Western Michigan; B11/2/1949 Dowagiac, MI   **1971** Phi 3

DAVIS, WAYNE   Wayne Elliott, DB, 5´11˝/175 lbs; Indiana State; 1985: SD, rnd 2; B6/17/1963 Cincinnati, OH   **1985** SD 16 (6, lcb)   **1986** SD 16 (5, lcb)   **1987** Buf 10 (0)
1988†Buf 16 (3)   **1989** Buf 6 (0)   **1989** Was 1 (0)   **NFL** 73 (14) [6 yrs]

DAVIS, WAYNE   Chris Wayne, LB, 6´1˝/213 lbs; Alabama; 1987: SL, rnd 9; B3/10/1964 Tuscaloosa, AL   **1987** SL 12 (1)   **1988** Phx 16 (0)   **NFL** 28 (1) [2 yrs]

DAVIS, WENDELL   Wendell Tyrone, WR, 5´11˝/188 lbs; LSU; 1988: Chi, rnd 1; B1/3/1966 Shreveport, LA

1988	†ChiB	16(0)	1	3	3.0(3)	0	15	220	14.7(36)	0	—	—	—	—	—	—	—	—	—	—	p	—	0	115
1989	ChiB	14(7, wr)	—	—	—	—	26	397	15.3(52)	3	—	—	—	—	—	—	—	—	—	—	—	—	18	214
1990	†ChiB	14(12, WR)	—	—	—	—	39	572	14.7(51)	3	—	—	—	—	—	—	—	—	—	—	—	—	18	301
1991	†ChiB	16(16, WR)	—	—	—	—	61	945	15.5(75)	6	—	—	—	—	—	—	—	—	—	—	—	—	36	503
1992	ChiB	16(15, WR)	4	42	10.5(21)	0	54	734	13.6(40)	2	—	—	—	—	—	—	—	—	—	—	—	—	12	419
1993	ChiB	5(4)	—	—	—	—	12	132	11.0(17)	0	—	—	—	—	—	—	—	—	—	—	—	—	0	66
NFL	6	81(54)	5	45	9.0(21)	0	207	3000	14.5(75)	14	—	—	—	—	—	—	—	—	—	—	p	—	84	1617

DAVIS, WENDELL   Wendell, DB, 5´10˝/201 lbs; Oklahoma; 1996: Dal, rnd 6; B6/27/1973 Wichita, KS   **1996** Dal 13 (0)   **1997** Dal 15 (0)   **1999** Dal 6 (0)   **NFL** 34 (0) [3 yrs]

DAVIS, WENDELL   Wendell, TE, 6´2˝/246 lbs; Temple; B10/24/1975 Escatawapa, MS

| 1998 | SD | 11(7, TE) | — | — | — | — | 4 | 23 | 5.8(8) | 0 | — | — | — | — | — | — | — | — | — | — | — | — | 0 | 12 |

DAVIS, WILLIE   William Delford, DE-DT, 6´3˝/243 lbs; Grambling State; 1956: Cle, rnd 15; B7/24/1934 Lisbon, LA; HOF 1981   **1958**†Cle 12 (lde/rde)   **1959** Cle 12 (ldt)
1960†GB 12 (LDE)   **1961**†GB 14 (LDE)   **1962**†GB☆14 (LDE)   **1963** GB★(LDE)   **1964** GB★14 (LDE)   **1965**†GB★14 (LDE)   **1966**†GB★14 (LDE)   **1967**†GB★14 (LDE)
1968 GB 14 (LDE)   **1969** GB 14 (LDE)   **NFL** 162 [12 yrs]

DAVIS, WILLIE   Willie Clark, WR, 6´0˝/180 lbs; Central Arkansas; B10/10/1967 Little Rock, AR

1991	KC	1(0)	—	—	—	—	—	—	—	—	—	—	—	—	—	—	—	—	—	—	—	—	—	—
1992	†KC	16(14, WR)	1	-11	-11.0(-11)	0	36	756	**21.0(74)**	3	—	—	—	—	—	—	—	—	—	—	—	—	18	382
1993	†KC	16(15, WR)	—	—	—	—	52	909	17.5(66)	7	—	—	—	—	—	—	—	—	—	—	—	—	42	490
1994	†KC	14(13, WR)	—	—	—	—	51	822	16.1(62)	5	—	—	—	—	—	—	—	—	—	—	—	—	32	436
1995	†KC	16(16, WR)	—	—	—	—	33	527	16.0(60)	5	—	—	—	—	—	—	—	—	—	—	—	—	30	289
1996	Hou	16(14, WR)	1	15	15.0(15)	0	39	464	11.9(49)	6	—	—	—	—	—	—	—	—	—	—	—	—	36	277
1997	Ten	15(14, WR)	—	—	—	—	43	564	13.1(46)	4	1	1	100.0	22	22.0(22)	1	0	—	—	—	—	—	24	318
1998	Ten	13(10, WR)	—	—	—	—	32	461	14.4(38)	3	—	—	—	—	—	—	—	—	—	—	—	—	18	246
NFL	8	108(97)	2	4	2.0(15)	0	286	4503	15.7(74)	33	1	1	100.0	22	22.0(22)	1	0	—	—	—	—	—	200	2437

DAVIS, ZOLA   Zola Nakia, WR, 6´0˝/185 lbs; South Carolina; B1/16/1975 Charleston, SC

| 1999 | Cle | 6(1) | — | — | — | — | 3 | 38 | 19.0(25) | 1 | — | — | — | — | — | — | — | — | — | — | — | — | 0 | 19 |

DAVISON, ANDREW   Andrew, DB, 5´11˝/185 lbs; Kansas; B12/9/1979 Detroit, MI   **2002** NYJ 6 (0)   **2003** Dal 4 (0)   **NFL** 10 (0) [2 yrs]

DAVISON, JERONE   Jerone Lamar, RB, 6´1˝/235 lbs; Arizona State; B9/16/1970 Picayune, MS

1996	Oak	2(0)	—	—	—	—	4	21	5.3(8)	0	—	—	—	—	—	—	—	—	—	—	—	—	0	11
1997	Oak	8(1)	2	4	2.0(5)	0	2	34	17.0(25)	0	—	—	—	—	—	—	—	—	—	—	—	—	0	21
NFL	2	10(1)	2	4	2.0(5)	0	6	55	9.2(25)	0	—	—	—	—	—	—	—	—	—	—	—	—	0	32

DAVLIN, MIKE   Michael Francis, T, 6´1˝/230 lbs; Notre Dame; San Francisco; B11/2/1927 Omaha, NE, D3/28/1996 Petaluma, CA   **1955** Was 9

DAWKINS, BRIAN   Brian Patrick, DB, 5´11˝/205 lbs; Clemson; 1996: Phi, rnd 2; B10/13/1973 Jacksonville, FL [I]   **1996**†Phi 14 (13, FS)   **1997** Phi 15 (15, FS)   **1998** Phi 14 (14, FS)
1999 Phi★16 (16, FS)   **2000**†Phi 13 (13, FS)   **2001**†Phi★15 (15, FS)   **2003**†Phi 7 (7, fs)   **2004**†Phi★15 (15, FS)   **2005** Phi◇16 (16, FS)

| 2002 | †Phi★ | 16(16, FS) | — | — | — | — | 1 | 57 | 57.0(57) | 1 | — | — | — | — | — | — | — | — | — | — | iS | — | 6 | 51 |
| NFL | 10 | 141(140) | — | — | — | — | 1 | 57 | 57.0(57) | 1 | — | — | — | — | — | — | — | — | — | — | iS | 3 | 24 | 365 |

DAWKINS, DALE   Dale V., WR, 6´1˝/190 lbs; Miami (FL); 1990: NYJ, rnd 9; B10/30/1966 Vero Beach, FL   **1992** NYJ 6 (0)   **1993** NYJ 4 (0)

1990	NYJ	11(0)	—	—	—	—	5	68	13.6(31)	0	—	—	—	—	—	—	—	—	—	—	—	—	0	34
1991	NYJ	15(0)	—	—	—	—	3	38	12.7(24)	0	—	—	—	—	—	—	—	—	—	—	k	—	0	11
NFL	4	36(0)	—	—	—	—	8	106	13.3(31)	0	—	—	—	—	—	—	—	—	—	—	k	—	0	40

DAWKINS, JOE   Joseph, RB, 6´0˝/223 lbs; Wisconsin; 1970: Hou, rnd 10; B1/27/1948 Los Angeles, CA

1970	Hou	14(FB)	124	517	4.2(49)	2	15	94	6.3(17)	0	—	—	—	—	—	—	—	—	—	—	p	—	12	579
1971	Hou	6	42	135	3.2(21)	2	9	53	5.9(13)	0	—	—	—	—	—	—	—	—	—	—	—	—	12	182
1971	Den	8	—	—	—	—	—	—	—	—	—	—	—	—	—	—	—	—	—	—	k	—	0	4
1972	Den	14(5, fb)	56	243	4.3(19)	2	18	242	13.4(60)	0	—	—	—	—	—	—	—	—	—	—	k	—	12	516
1973	Den	14(14, FB)	160	706	4.4(32)	2	30	329	11.0(42)	0	—	—	—	—	—	—	—	—	—	—	k	—	12	963
1974	NYG	14(FB)	156	561	3.6(16)	2	46	332	7.2(51)	0	—	—	—	—	—	—	—	—	—	—	k	—	30	856
1975	NYG	14(FB)	129	438	3.4(15)	2	24	245	10.2(39)	0	—	—	—	—	—	—	—	—	—	—	k	—	12	598
1976	Hou	14	31	61	2.0(7)	1	3	21	7.0(14)	0	—	—	—	—	—	—	—	—	—	—	—	—	6	82
NFL	7	98(19)	698	2661	3.8(72)	13	145	1316	9.1(60)	0	—	—	—	—	—	—	—	—	—	—	kp	—	96	3778

DAWKINS, JULIUS   Julius, WR, 6´1˝/196 lbs; Pittsburgh; 1983: Buf, rnd 12; B1/4/1961 Monessen, PA

1983	Buf	11(2)	—	—	—	—	11	123	11.2(28)	1	—	—	—	—	—	—	—	—	—	—	—	—	6	67
1984	Buf	16(3)	—	—	—	—	21	295	14.0(37)	2	—	—	—	—	—	—	—	—	—	—	—	—	12	158
NFL	2	27(5)	—	—	—	—	32	418	13.1(37)	3	—	—	—	—	—	—	—	—	—	—	—	—	18	224

DAWKINS, SEAN   Sean Russell, WR, 6´4˝/215 lbs; California; 1993: Ind, rnd 1; B2/3/1971 Red Bank, NJ

1993	Ind	16(7, wr)	—	—	—	—	26	430	16.5(68)	1	—	—	—	—	—	—	—	—	—	—	—	—	6	220
1994	Ind	16(16, WR)	—	—	—	—	51	742	14.5(49)	5	—	—	—	—	—	—	—	—	—	—	—	—	30	396
1995	†Ind	16(13, WR)	—	—	—	—	52	784	15.1(52)	3	—	—	—	—	—	—	—	—	—	—	—	—	18	407
1996	†Ind	15(14, WR)	—	—	—	—	54	751	13.9(42)	1	—	—	—	—	—	—	—	—	—	—	—	—	6	381

YEAR	TEAM	G(GS, POS)	RUSH	YD	AVG(LG)	TD	REC	YD	AVG(LG)	TD	PASS	COMP	PCT	YD	AVG(LG)	TD	INT	SK	YD	QBR	KPR	OTD	PTS	TAY
1997	Ind	14(12, WR)	—	—	—	—	68	804	11.8(51)	2	—	—	—	—	—	—	—	—	—	—	—	—	12	412
1998	NO	15(15, WR)	—	—	—	—	53	823	15.5(64)	1	—	—	—	—	—	—	—	—	—	—	—	—	6	417
1999	†Sea	16(13, WR)	—	—	—	—	58	992	17.1(45)	7	—	—	—	—	—	—	—	—	—	—	—	—	42	531
2000	Sea	16(16, WR)	—	—	—	—	63	731	11.6(40)	5	—	—	—	—	—	—	—	—	—	—	—	—	30	391
2001	Jax	16(3)	—	—	—	—	20	234	11.7(28)	0	—	—	—	—	—	—	—	—	—	—	—	—	0	117
NFL	9	140(109)	—	—	—	—	445	6291	14.1(68)	25	—	—	—	—	—	—	—	—	—	—	—	—	150	3271
DAWKINS, TOMMY Tommy Earl, DE, 6´3˝/260 lbs; Appalachian State; B5/8/1965 Lexington, NC **1987** Pit 2 (2)																								
DAWLEY, FRED Frederick Martin, FB, 5´9˝/190 lbs; Michigan; B3/11/1921 Bay City, MI, D4/13/1994 Palm City, FL																								
1944	Det	2(0)	2	16	8.0(13)	0	—	—	—	—	—	—	—	—	—	—	—	—	—	—	—	—	0	16
DAWSEY, LAWRENCE Lawrence Leneir, WR, 6´0˝/192 lbs; Florida State; 1991: TB, rnd 3; B11/16/1967 Dothan, AL																								
1991	TB	16(10, WR)	1	9	9.0(9)	1	55	818	14.9(65)	3	—	—	—	—	—	—	—	—	—	—	—	—	24	443
1992	TB	15(12, WR)	—	—	—	—	60	776	12.9(41)	1	—	—	—	—	—	—	—	—	—	—	—	—	6	393
1993	TB	4(4)	—	—	—	—	15	203	13.5(24)	0	—	—	—	—	—	—	—	—	—	—	—	—	0	102
1994	TB	10(5, wr)	—	—	—	—	46	673	14.6(46)	1	—	—	—	—	—	—	—	—	—	—	—	—	6	342
1995	TB	12(10, WR)	—	—	—	—	30	372	12.4(26)	0	—	—	—	—	—	—	—	—	—	—	—	—	0	186
1996	NYG	16(4)	—	—	—	—	18	233	12.9(28)	0	—	—	—	—	—	—	—	—	—	—	—	—	0	117
1999	NO	10(0)	—	—	—	—	16	196	12.3(57)	1	—	—	—	—	—	—	—	—	—	—	k	—	6	108
NFL	7	83(45)	1	9	9.0(9)	1	240	3271	13.6(65)	6	—	—	—	—	—	—	—	—	—	—	k	—	42	1690
DAWSEY, STACEY Stacey L., WR, 5´9˝/154 lbs; Indiana; B10/24/1965 Bradenton, FL																								
1987	NO	3(3)	—	—	—	—	13	142	10.9(29)	0	—	—	—	—	—	—	—	—	—	—	—	—	0	71
DAWSON, BILL William, TE-DE, 6´3˝/240 lbs; Florida State; 1964: Bos, rnd 19/LA, rnd 12; B12/4/1942 **1965** Bos-A 9																								
DAWSON, DALE Dale, K, 6´0˝/213 lbs; Eastern Kentucky; B11/2/1964 West Palm Beach, FL **[K]** **1987** Min 3 (0) **1988** Phi 1 (0) **1988** GB 4 (0) **NFL** 8 (0) [2 yrs]																								
DAWSON, DERMONTTI Dermontti Fara, C-G, 6´2˝/288 lbs; Kentucky; 1988: Pit, rnd 2; B6/17/1965 Lexington, KY **1988** Pit 8 (5, rg) **1989†**Pit 16 (16, C) **1990** Pit 16 (16, C) **1991** Pit 16 (16, C) **1992†**Pit✧16 (16, C) **1993†**Pit★16 (16, C) **1994†**Pit★16 (16, C) **1995†**Pit★16 (16, C) **1996†**Pit★16 (16, C) **1997†**Pit★16 (16, C) **1998** Pit★16 (16, C) **1999** Pit 7 (7, c) **2000** Pit 9 (9, C) **NFL** 184 (181) [13 yrs]																								
DAWSON, DOUG Douglas Arlin, G, 6´3˝/238 lbs; Texas; 1984: SL, rnd 2; B12/27/1961 Houston, TX **1984** SL 15 (1) **1985** SL 16 (16, LG) **1986** SL 1 (1) **1990†**Hou 16 (1) **1991†**Hou 14 (10, RG) **1992†**Hou 16 (16, RG) **1993†**Hou 16 (16, RG) **1994†**Cle 12 (9, LG) **NFL** 106 (70) [8 yrs]																								
DAWSON, GIB Gilbert Henry, HB, 5´11˝/190 lbs; Texas; 1953: GB, rnd 4; B8/27/1930 Bisbee, AZ, D7/30/2005 Phoenix, AZ																								
1953	GB	7	5	18	3.6(18)	0	—	—	—	—	—	—	—	—	—	—	—	—	—	—	kp	1	6	107
DAWSON, JAJUAN JaJuan LaTroy, WR, 6´1˝/197 lbs; Tulane; 2000: Cle, rnd 3; B11/5/1977 Houston, TX																								
2000	Cle	2(2)	—	—	—	—	9	97	10.8(26)	1	—	—	—	—	—	—	—	—	—	—	—	—	6	54
2001	Cle	14(0)	—	—	—	—	22	281	12.8(44)	1	—	—	—	—	—	—	—	—	—	—	—	—	6	146
2002	Hou	14(2)	—	—	—	—	21	286	13.6(28)	0	—	—	—	—	—	—	—	—	—	—	—	—	0	143
NFL	3	30(4)	—	—	—	—	52	664	12.8(44)	2	—	—	—	—	—	—	—	—	—	—	—	—	12	342
DAWSON, LAKE Lake, WR, 6´1˝/204 lbs; Notre Dame; 1994: KC, rnd 3; B1/2/1972 Boston, MA																								
1994	†KC	12(6, wr)	3	24	8.0(13)	0	37	537	14.5(50)	2	—	—	—	—	—	—	—	—	—	—	—	—	12	303
1995	†KC	16(9, WR)	1	-9	-9.0(-9)	0	40	513	12.8(45)	5	—	—	—	—	—	—	—	—	—	—	—	—	30	273
1996	KC	4(0)	—	—	—	—	5	83	16.6(25)	1	—	—	—	—	—	—	—	—	—	—	—	—	6	47
1997	†KC	11(11, WR)	—	—	—	—	21	273	13.0(27)	2	—	—	—	—	—	—	—	—	—	—	—	—	12	147
NFL	4	43(26)	4	15	3.8(13)	0	103	1406	13.7(50)	10	—	—	—	—	—	—	—	—	—	—	—	—	60	768
DAWSON, LEN Leonard Ray, QB, 6´0˝/190 lbs; Purdue; 1957: Pit, rnd 1; B6/20/1935 Alliance, OH; HOF 1987 **[K]**																								
1957	Pit	3	3	31	10.3(27)	0	—	—	—	—	4	2	50.0	25	6.3(15)	0	0	—	—	—	K	—	0	44
1958	Pit	4	2	-1	-0.5(1)	0	—	—	—	—	6	1	16.7	11	1.8(11)	0	2	—	—	—	—	—	0	-76
1959	Pit	12	4	20	5.0(10)	0	—	—	—	—	7	3	42.9	60	8.6(32)	1	0	—	—	—	—	—	0	55
1960	Cle	2	1	0	0.0(0)	0	—	—	—	—	13	8	61.5	23	1.8(23)	0	0	—	—	—	—	—	0	12
1961	Cle	7	1	-10	-10.0(-10)	0	—	—	—	—	15	7	46.7	85	5.7(17)	1	3	—	—	—	—	—	0	-83
1962	†DalT-A★	14(14, QB)	38	252	6.6(22)	3	—	—	—	—	310	189	**61.0**	2759	**8.9(92)**	**29**	17	—	—	**98.3**	—	—	18	1127
1963	KC-A	14(13, QB)	37	272	7.4(43)	2	—	—	—	—	352	190	54.0	2389	6.8(82)	**26**	19	—	—	77.5	—	—	12	857
1964	KC-A★	14(14, QB)	40	89	2.2(18)	2	—	—	—	—	354	199	**56.2**	2879	8.1(72)	30	18	—	—	**89.9**	—	—	12	979
1965	KC-A	14(12, QB)	43	142	3.3(40)	2	—	—	—	—	305	163	**53.4**	2262	7.4(67)	**21**	14	—	—	**81.3**	—	—	12	838
1966	†KC-A★	14(14, QB)	24	167	7.0(18)	0	—	—	—	—	284	159	**56.0**	2527	**8.9(89)**	**26**	10	—	—	**101.7**	—	—	0	1161
1967	KC-A✧	14(14, QB)	20	68	3.4(24)	0	—	—	—	—	357	206	**57.7**	2651	7.4(71)	24	17	—	—	**83.7**	—	—	0	834
1968	†KC-A★	14(14, QB)	20	40	2.0(22)	0	—	—	—	—	224	131	**58.5**	2109	**9.4(92)**	17	9	—	—	**98.6**	—	—	0	820
1969	†KC-A✧	9(7, QB)	1	3	3.0(3)	0	—	—	—	—	166	98	**59.0**	1323	8.0(55)	9	13	13	89	69.9	—	—	0	190
1970	KC	14(12, QB)	11	46	4.2(21)	0	—	—	—	—	262	141	53.8	1876	7.2(61)	13	14	34	277	71.0	—	—	0	489
1971	†KC★	14(13, QB)	12	24	2.0(8)	0	—	—	—	—	301	167	55.5	2504	**8.3(82)**	15	13	30	303	81.6	—	—	0	831
1972	KC	14(12, QB)	15	75	5.0(20)	0	—	—	—	—	305	175	**57.4**	1835	6.0(44)	13	12	28	255	72.8	—	—	0	578
1973	KC	8(6, qb)	6	40	6.7(13)	0	—	—	—	—	101	66	65.3	725	7.2(48)	2	5	14	104	—	—	—	0	213
1974	KC	14(8, QB)	11	28	2.5(10)	0	—	—	—	—	235	138	58.7	1573	6.7(84)	7	13	25	199	65.8	—	—	0	330
1975	KC	12(5, qb)	5	7	1.4(9)	0	—	—	—	—	140	93	**66.4**	1095	7.8(51)	5	4	23	196	—	—	—	0	420
NFL	19	211(158)	294	1293	4.4(43)	9	—	—	—	—	3741	2136	57.1	28711	7.7(92)	239	183	167	1423	82.6	K	—	54	9614
DAWSON, LIN James Linwood, TE, 6´3˝/240 lbs; North Carolina State; 1981: NE, rnd 8; B6/24/1959 Norfolk, VA																								
1981	NE	15(3)	—	—	—	—	7	126	18.0(42)	0	—	—	—	—	—	—	—	—	—	—	—	—	0	63
1982	†NE	8(4)	—	—	—	—	13	160	12.3(26)	1	—	—	—	—	—	—	—	—	—	—	—	—	6	85
1983	NE	13(10, TE)	—	—	—	—	9	84	9.3(14)	1	—	—	—	—	—	—	—	—	—	—	—	—	6	47
1984	NE	16(15, TE)	—	—	—	—	39	427	10.9(27)	4	—	—	—	—	—	—	—	—	—	—	—	—	24	234
1985	†NE	16(13, TE)	—	—	—	—	17	148	8.7(26)	0	—	—	—	—	—	—	—	—	—	—	—	—	0	74
1987	NE	12(11, TE)	—	—	—	—	12	81	6.8(14)	0	—	—	—	—	—	—	—	—	—	—	—	—	0	41
1988	NE	6(6, te)	—	—	—	—	8	106	13.3(38)	2	—	—	—	—	—	—	—	—	—	—	—	—	12	63
1989	NE	16(13, TE)	—	—	—	—	12	101	8.4(17)	0	—	—	—	—	—	—	—	—	—	—	—	—	0	51
1990	NE	3(0)	—	—	—	—	—	—	—	—	—	—	—	—	—	—	—	—	—	—	—	—	—	—
NFL	9	105(75)	—	—	—	—	117	1233	10.5(42)	8	—	—	—	—	—	—	—	—	—	—	—	—	48	657
DAWSON, MIKE Michael Daniel, DT-NT-DE, 6´4˝/270 lbs; Arizona; 1976: SL, rnd 1; B10/16/1953 Dorking, England **1976** SL 13 (10, RDT) **1977** SL 14 (14, RDT) **1978** SL 16 (16, NT) **1979** SL 16 (15, RDE) **1980** SL 4 (4) **1981** SL 16 (16, LDT/nt) **1982†**SL 9 (9, LDT) **1983†**Det 16 (7, LDT) **1984** KC 9 (0) **NFL** 113 (91) [9 yrs]																								
DAWSON, PHIL Phil, K, 5´11˝/195 lbs; Texas; B1/23/1975 West Palm Beach, FL **[K]** **2000** Cle 16 (0) **2001** Cle 16 (0) **2002†**Cle 16 (0) **2004** Cle 16 (0) **2005** Cle 16 (0)																								
1999	Cle	15(0)	1	4	4.0(4)	1	—	—	—	—	—	—	—	—	—	—	—	—	—	—	K	—	53	14
2003	Cle	13(0)	1	14	14.0(14)	0	—	—	—	—	—	—	—	—	—	—	—	—	—	—	KP	—	74	14
NFL	7	108(0)	2	18	9.0(14)	1	—	—	—	—	—	—	—	—	—	—	—	—	—	—	KP	—	581	28
DAWSON, RHETT Rhett Motte, WR, 6´1˝/185 lbs; Florida State; 1972: Hou, rnd 10; B12/22/1948 Valdosta, GA																								
1972	Hou	14	—	—	—	—	6	78	13.0(20)	1	—	—	—	—	—	—	—	—	—	—	—	—	6	44
1973	Min	2	—	—	—	—	2	24	12.0(19)	0	—	—	—	—	—	—	—	—	—	—	—	—	0	12
NFL	2	16	—	—	—	—	8	102	12.8(20)	1	—	—	—	—	—	—	—	—	—	—	—	—	6	56
DAY, AL Albert Edward, LB, 6´2˝/216 lbs; Eastern Michigan; B3/18/1938 **1960** Den-A 14 (RLB)																								
DAY, EAGLE Herman Sidney, QB, 6´0˝/183 lbs; Mississippi; 1956: Was, rnd 17; B10/2/1932 Columbia, MS																								
1959	Was	4(1)	3	27	9.0(18)	0	—	—	—	—	13	6	46.2	79	6.1(20)	0	1	—	—	—	—	—	0	27
1960	Was	12	3	1	0.3(5)	0	—	—	—	—	19	9	47.4	115	6.1(27)	0	1	—	—	—	P	—	0	19
NFL	2	16(1)	6	28	4.7(18)	0	—	—	—	—	32	15	46.9	194	6.1(27)	0	2	—	—	—	P	—	0	45
DAY, FRED Frederic Samuel, T, 6´2˝/195 lbs; Ohio Wesleyan; B7/4/1896 Pandora, OH, D5/18/1963 Fort Lauderdale, FL **1921** Cin 1 (0)																								

YEAR	TEAM	G(GS, POS)	RUSH	YD	AVG(LG)	TD	REC	YD	AVG(LG)	TD	PASS	COMP	PCT	YD	AVG(LG)	TD	INT	SK	YD	QBR	KPR	OTD	PTS	TAY

DAY, TERRY Terry Lee, DE, 6´4˝/290 lbs; Mississippi State; 1997: NYJ, rnd 4; B9/18/1974 Pickens, MS **1997** NYJ 1 (0)

DAY, TOM Thomas Frederick, DE-G-DT-T, 6´2˝/252 lbs; North Carolina A&T; 1960: SL, rnd 20/Buf, rnd 2; B8/20/1935 Washington, DC, D8/21/2000 Getzville, NY **1960** SL 10 (rg) **1961** Buf-A 12 **1962** Buf-A 14 (RG) **1963**†Buf-A 14 (RG) **1964**†Buf-A☆14 (RDE) **1965**†Buf-A★14 (RDE) **1966**†Buf-A☆14 (RDE) **1967** SD-A 11 (rde) **1968** Buf-A 14 (14, RDE) **NFL** 117 (14) [9 yrs]

DAYHOFF, HARRY Harry Oscar, B, 5´9˝/180 lbs; Bucknell; B5/25/1896 Gettysburg, PA, D2/17/1963 Harrisburg, PA **1924** Fra 11 (3), 12 **1925** Pot 1 (1) **NFL** 12 (4) [2 yrs]

DAYKIN, TONY Anthony Albert, LB, 6´1˝/215 lbs; Georgia Tech; 1977: Det, rnd 11; B5/13/1955 Taipei, Taiwan **1977** Det 14 **1979** Atl 11 **1980**†Atl 16 (0)

YEAR	TEAM	G(GS, POS)	RUSH	YD	AVG(LG)	TD	REC	YD	AVG(LG)	TD	PASS	COMP	PCT	YD	AVG(LG)	TD	INT	SK	YD	QBR	KPR	OTD	PTS	TAY
1978	Det	16	1	8	8.0(8)	0	—	—	—	—	—	—	—	—	—	—	—	—	—	—	—	—	0	8
1981	Atl	16(0)	1	2	2.0(2)	0	—	—	—	—	—	—	—	—	—	—	—	—	—	—	—	—	0	2
NFL	5	73	2	10	5.0(8)	0	—	—	—	—	—	—	—	—	—	—	—	—	—	—	k	—	0	-2

DAYNE, RON Ron, RB, 5´10˝/250 lbs; Wisconsin; 2000: NYG, rnd 1; B3/14/1978 Berlin, NJ

YEAR	TEAM	G(GS, POS)	RUSH	YD	AVG(LG)	TD	REC	YD	AVG(LG)	TD	PASS	COMP	PCT	YD	AVG(LG)	TD	INT	SK	YD	QBR	KPR	OTD	PTS	TAY
2000	†NYG	16(4, rb)	228	770	3.4(50)	5	3	11	3.7(12)	0	—	—	—	—	—	—	—	—	—	—	—	—	30	826
2001	NYG	16(7, rb)	180	690	3.8(61)	7	8	67	8.4(21)	0	—	—	—	—	—	—	—	—	—	—	—	—	44	794
2002	†NYG	16(1)	125	428	3.4(30)	3	11	49	4.5(8)	0	—	—	—	—	—	—	—	—	—	—	—	—	18	483
2004	NYG	14(2)	52	179	3.4(15)	1	1	7	7.0(7)	0	—	—	—	—	—	—	—	—	—	—	k	—	6	189
2005	†Den	10(0)	53	270	5.1(55)	1	3	17	5.7(7)	0	—	—	—	—	—	—	—	—	—	—	—	—	6	289
NFL	5	72(14)	638	2337	3.7(61)	17	26	151	5.8(21)	0	—	—	—	—	—	—	—	—	—	—	k	—	104	2579

DEAL, RUFUS Rufus Copeland, B, 6´0˝/220 lbs; Auburn; 1942: Was, rnd 3; B12/7/1917 Moundsville, AL, D3/14/2005 Tuscaloosa, AL

YEAR	TEAM	G(GS, POS)	RUSH	YD	AVG(LG)	TD	REC	YD	AVG(LG)	TD	PASS	COMP	PCT	YD	AVG(LG)	TD	INT	SK	YD	QBR	KPR	OTD	PTS	TAY
1942	Was✧	6(0)	5	12	2.4(6)	0	—	—	—	—	—	—	—	—	—	—	—	—	—	—	—	—	0	12

DEAN, FLOYD Thomas Floyd, LB, 6´4˝/236 lbs; Florida; 1962: SF, rnd 4/Oak, rnd 15; B8/19/1940 **1964** SF 6 **1965** SF 9 **NFL** 15 [2 yrs]

DEAN, FRED Frederic Rudolph, DE, 6´3˝/230 lbs; Louisiana Tech; 1975: SD, rnd 2; B2/24/1952 Arcadia, LA **1975** SD 14 (13, LDE) **1976** SD 14 (14, RDE) **1977** SD 11 (11, RDE) **1978** SD 15 (14, RDE) **1979**†SD★13 (12, RDE) **1980**†SD★14 (11, RDE) **1981** SD 3 (2) **1981**†SF★11 (2) **1982** SF 9 (1) **1983**†SF★16 (2) **1984**†SF 5 (0) **1985**†SF 16 (0) **NFL** 141 (82) [11 yrs]

DEAN, FRED Frederick Gregory, T-G, 6´3˝/253 lbs; Texas Southern; B3/30/1955 Gainesville, FL **1977**†ChiB 0 **1978** Was 8 **1979** Was 15 (1) **1980** Was 12 (8, lt) **1982**†Was 5 (0) **NFL** 40 (9) [5 yrs]

DEAN, HAL Hal Stone, G-LB, 6´0˝/205 lbs; Ohio State; 1947: LA, rnd 30; B10/30/1922 Wooster, OH **1947** LARm 12 (3) **1948** LARm 11 (9, LG) **1949**†LARm 12 (12, LG) **NFL** 35 (24) [3 yrs]

DEAN, JIMMY James, DE, 6´4˝/252 lbs; Texas A&M; 1977: Buf, rnd 4; B1/8/1955 Bryan, TX **1978** Hou 3

DEAN, KEVIN Kevin James, LB, 6´1˝/235 lbs; TCU; B2/5/1965 Newton, TX **1987** SF 4 (1)

DEAN, RANDY Randolph Hume, QB, 6´3˝/195 lbs; Northwestern; 1977: NYG, rnd 5; B6/10/1955 Milwaukee, WI

YEAR	TEAM	G(GS, POS)	RUSH	YD	AVG(LG)	TD	REC	YD	AVG(LG)	TD	PASS	COMP	PCT	YD	AVG(LG)	TD	INT	SK	YD	QBR	KPR	OTD	PTS	TAY
1977	NYG	1	—	—	—	—	—	—	—	—	—	—	—	—	—	—	—	—	—	—	—	—	—	—
1978	NYG	6(2)	14	94	6.7(19)	0	—	—	—	—	39	19	48.7	188	4.8(48)	1	3	2	16	—	—	—	0	73
1979	NYG	16	8	56	7.0(19)	1	—	—	—	—	26	11	42.3	91	3.5(20)	0	2	3	23	—	—	—	6	32
NFL	3	23(2)	22	150	6.8(19)	1	—	—	—	—	65	30	46.2	279	4.3(48)	1	5	5	39	—	—	—	6	105

DEAN, TED Theodore Curtis, FB-HB, 6´2˝/213 lbs; Wichita State; 1960: Phi, rnd 4/Buf, rnd 1; B3/24/1938 Radnor, PA

YEAR	TEAM	G(GS, POS)	RUSH	YD	AVG(LG)	TD	REC	YD	AVG(LG)	TD	PASS	COMP	PCT	YD	AVG(LG)	TD	INT	SK	YD	QBR	KPR	OTD	PTS	TAY
1960	†Phi	12(FB)	113	304	2.7(32)	0	15	218	14.5(49)	3	—	—	—	—	—	—	—	—	—	—	kp	—	18	556
1961	Phi✧	14(hb)	66	321	4.9(44)	2	21	335	16.0(60)	1	—	—	—	—	—	—	—	—	—	—	kp	—	18	711
1962	Phi	2	—	—	—	—	—	—	—	—	—	—	—	—	—	—	—	—	—	—	k	—	0	23
1963	Phi	14(FB)	79	268	3.4(26)	0	14	108	7.7(20)	0	—	—	—	—	—	—	—	—	—	—	kp	—	0	531
1964	Min	2	5	30	6.0(9)	0	1	23	23.0(23)	0	—	—	—	—	—	—	—	—	—	—	kp	—	0	37
NFL	5	44	263	923	3.5(44)	2	51	684	13.4(60)	4	—	—	—	—	—	—	—	—	—	—	kp	—	36	1857

DEAN, TOM Thomas Edward, T, 6´2˝/247 lbs; Arkansas State; SMU; 1945: Bos, rnd 2; B5/27/1923 Fostoria, TX, D7/23/2003 Dallas, TX **1946** Bos 9 (8, LT) **1947** Bos 12 (7, LT) **NFL** 21 (15) [2 yrs]

DEAN, VERNON Vernon, DB, 5´11˝/178 lbs; U.S. International; San Diego State; 1982: Was, rnd 2; B5/5/1959 Los Angeles, CA **[I]** **1982**†Was☆9 (8, RCB) **1983**†Was 16 (13, RCB) **1984**†Was 16 (14, RCB) **1985** Was 16 (16, RCB) **1986**†Was 16 (8, RCB) **1987**†Was 12 (0) **1988**†Sea 16 (0) **NFL** 101 (59) [7 yrs]

DEAN, WALTER Walter Kevin, RB, 5´10˝/216 lbs; Grambling State; 1991: GB, rnd 6; B6/1/1968 Ruston, LA **1991** GB 9 (0)

DEARTH, JAMES James, TE, 6´4˝/270 lbs; Tulsa; Tarleton State; 1999: Cle, rnd 6; B1/22/1976 Fort Ord, CA **1999** Cle 2 (0) **2002**†NYJ 16 (0) **2003** NYJ 16 (0) **2004**†NYJ 16 (0) **2005** NYJ 16 (0)

YEAR	TEAM	G(GS, POS)	RUSH	YD	AVG(LG)	TD	REC	YD	AVG(LG)	TD	PASS	COMP	PCT	YD	AVG(LG)	TD	INT	SK	YD	QBR	KPR	OTD	PTS	TAY
2001	†NYJ	16(0)	—	—	—	—	3	10	3.3(9)	1	—	—	—	—	—	—	—	—	—	—	k	—	6	2
NFL	6	82(0)	—	—	—	—	3	10	3.3(9)	1	—	—	—	—	—	—	—	—	—	—	k	—	6	-4

DEAYALA, KIKI Julian Lewis, LB, 6´1˝/225 lbs; Texas; 1983: Cin, rnd 6; B10/23/1961 Miami, FL **1986** Cin 16 (0) **1987** Cin 12 (2) **NFL** 28 (2) [2 yrs]

DEBERG, STEVE Steven Leroy, QB, 6´3˝/210 lbs; San Jose State; 1977: Dal, rnd 10; B1/19/1954 Oakland, CA

YEAR	TEAM	G(GS, POS)	RUSH	YD	AVG(LG)	TD	REC	YD	AVG(LG)	TD	PASS	COMP	PCT	YD	AVG(LG)	TD	INT	SK	YD	QBR	KPR	OTD	PTS	TAY
1978	SF	12(11, QB)	15	20	1.3(7)	1	—	—	—	—	302	137	45.4	1570	5.2(58)	8	22	17	156	40.0	—	—	6	-25
1979	SF	16(15, QB)	17	10	0.6(8)	0	—	—	—	—	**578**	**347**	**60.0**	**3652**	6.3(50)	17	21	17	119	73.1	—	—	0	1081
1980	SF	11(9, QB)	6	4	0.7(7)	0	—	—	—	—	321	186	57.9	1998	6.2(**93**)	12	17	14	114	66.7	—	—	0	383
1981	Den	14(1)	9	40	4.4(11)	0	—	—	—	—	108	64	59.3	797	7.4(44)	6	6	7	67	—	—	—	0	229
1982	Den	9(5, QB)	8	27	3.4(6)	1	—	—	—	—	223	131	58.7	1405	6.3(51)	7	11	16	130	67.2	—	—	6	335
1983	†Den	10(5, qb)	13	28	2.2(11)	1	—	—	—	—	215	119	55.3	1617	7.5(54)	9	7	25	201	—	—	—	6	612
1984	TB	16(13, QB)	28	59	2.1(14)	2	—	—	—	—	509	308	60.5	3554	7.0(55)	19	18	35	308	79.3	—	—	12	1231
1985	TB	11(11, QB)	9	28	3.1(13)	0	—	—	—	—	370	197	53.2	2488	6.7(57)	19	18	19	143	71.3	—	—	0	647
1986	TB	16(2)	2	1	0.5(1)	1	—	—	—	—	96	50	52.1	610	6.4(45)	5	12	9	68	—	—	—	6	-139
1987	TB	12(8, QB)	8	-8	-1.0(0)	0	—	—	—	—	275	159	57.8	1891	6.9(64)	14	7	20	185	85.3	—	—	0	728
1988	KC	13(11, QB)	18	30	1.7(13)	1	—	—	—	—	414	224	54.1	2935	7.1(80)	16	16	30	246	73.5	—	—	6	948
1989	KC	12(10, QB)	14	-8	-0.6(15)	0	—	—	—	—	324	196	**60.5**	2529	7.8(50)	11	16	14	111	75.8	—	—	0	672
1990	†KC	16(16, QB)	21	-5	-0.2(6)	0	—	—	—	—	444	258	58.1	3444	7.8(**90**)	23	4	22	191	96.3	—	—	0	1672
1991	†KC	16(15, QB)	21	-15	-0.7(0)	0	—	—	—	—	434	256	59.0	2965	6.8(63)	17	14	19	161	79.3	—	—	0	993
1992	TB	6(2)	3	3	1.0(4)	0	—	—	—	—	125	76	60.8	710	5.7(28)	3	4	8	66	—	—	—	0	213
1993	TB	3(1)	—	—	—	—	—	—	—	—	39	23	59.0	186	**4.8(24)**	1	3	3	27	—	—	—	0	-22
1993	Mia	5(4, qb)	4	-4	-1.0(-1)	0	—	—	—	—	188	113	60.1	1521	**8.1(47)**	6	7	15	116	—	—	—	0	507
1998	Atl	8(1)	8	-10	-1.3(2)	0	—	—	—	—	59	30	50.8	369	6.3(35)	3	1	6	60	—	—	—	0	150
NFL	17	206(140)	204	200	1.0(15)	7	—	—	—	—	5024	2874	57.2	34241	6.8(93)	196	204	296	2469	74.2	—	—	42	10211

DEBERNARDI, FRED Frank Frederick, DE, 6´5˝/250 lbs; Texas-El Paso; 1972: Bal, rnd 11; B3/2/1949 Santa Clarita, CA **1974** KC 7

DEBRUIJN, CASE Case, P, 6´0˝/176 lbs; Idaho State; 1982: KC, rnd 8; B4/11/1960 Denhaague, Netherlands **1982** KC 1 (0)

DECARBO, NICK Nicholas Fred, G, 5´9˝/185 lbs; Duquesne; B3/21/1910 New Castle, PA, D8/21/1991 Mayfield Heights, OH **1933** Pit 11 (0)

DECARLO, ART Arthur Anthony, DB-E, 6´2˝/196 lbs; Georgia; 1953: ChiB, rnd 6; B3/23/1931 Youngstown, OH **1953** Pit 12 (SS) **1956** Was 12 (DB) **1957** Was 2 **1957** Bal 6 (DB) **1959** Bal 8

YEAR	TEAM	G(GS, POS)	RUSH	YD	AVG(LG)	TD	REC	YD	AVG(LG)	TD	PASS	COMP	PCT	YD	AVG(LG)	TD	INT	SK	YD	QBR	KPR	OTD	PTS	TAY
1958	†Bal	12	—	—	—	—	1	10	10.0(10)	0	—	—	—	—	—	—	—	—	—	—	k	—	0	-10
1960	Bal	9	—	—	—	—	8	116	14.5(22)	0	—	—	—	—	—	—	—	—	—	—	—	—	0	58
NFL	6	61	—	—	—	—	9	126	14.0(22)	0	—	—	—	—	—	—	—	—	—	—	kpi	—	0	117

DECLERK, FRANK Francis P., C, 5´9˝/191 lbs; St. Ambrose; B1899, NE, deceased **1923** RI 6 (4) **1924** RI 8 (2) **1925** RI 6 (1) **NFL** 20 (7) [3 yrs]

DECORREVONT, BILLY William John, B, 6´0˝/186 lbs; Northwestern; 1942: Was, rnd 14; B11/26/1918 Chicago, IL, D9/6/1995 St. Petersburg, FL

YEAR	TEAM	G(GS, POS)	RUSH	YD	AVG(LG)	TD	REC	YD	AVG(LG)	TD	PASS	COMP	PCT	YD	AVG(LG)	TD	INT	SK	YD	QBR	KPR	OTD	PTS	TAY
1945	†Was	10(6, RH)	22	91	4.1(18)	0	4	36	9.0(27)	0	—	—	—	—	—	—	—	—	—	—	kp	—	0	184
1946	Det	9(5, wb)	8	-32	-4.0(-5)	0	10	278	27.8(72)	2	19	8	42.1	155	8.2(70)	2	2	—	—	—	Pkp	—	12	209
1947	†ChiC	12(2)	29	149	5.1(27)	1	4	52	13.0(19)	0	—	—	—	—	—	—	—	—	—	—	kpi	—	6	198
1948	ChiB	10(2)	16	25	1.6(7)	0	2	7	3.5(6)	0	—	—	—	—	—	—	—	—	—	—	kpi	—	0	152

YEAR	TEAM	G (GS, POS)	RUSH	YD	AVG (LG)	TD	REC	YD	AVG (LG)	TD	PASS	COMP	PCT	YD	AVG (LG)	TD	INT	SK	YD	QBR	KPR	OTD	PTS	TAY
1949	ChiB	8(0)	—	—	—	—	1	44	44.0(44)	0	—	—	—	—	—	—	—	—	—	—	i	—	0	55
NFL	5	49(15)	75	233	3.1(27)	1	21	417	19.9(72)	2	19	8	42.1	155	8.2(70)	2	2	—	—	—	Pkpi	—	18	797

DEE, BOB Robert Henry, DE-DT, 6´3˝/248 lbs; Holy Cross; 1955: Was, rnd 19; B5/18/1933 Quincy, MA, D4/18/1979 Portsmouth, NH **1957** Was 11 **1958** Was 11 **1960** Bos-A☆14 (14, LDE) **1961** Bos-A★14 (14, LDE) **1962** Bos-A☆14 (14, LDE) **1963**†Bos-A✧14 (14, LDE) **1964** Bos-A★14 (14, LDE) **1965** Bos-A✧14 (14, LDE) **1966** Bos-A 14 (14, LDE) **1967** Bos-A 14 (14, LDE) **NFL** 134 (112) [10 yrs]

DEE, DONNIE Donald Francis, TE, 6´4˝/247 lbs; Tulsa; 1988: Ind, rnd 11; B3/17/1965 Kansas City, MO **1988** Ind 13 (0) **1989** Ind 1 (0) **1989** Sea 3 (3) **NFL** 17 (3) [2 yrs]

DEEKS, DON Donald Phillips, T-G, 6´4˝/238 lbs; Washington; 1945: Bos, rnd 4; B2/10/1923 Portland, OR, D9/4/1995 Bend, OR **1945** Bos 7 (0) **1946** Bos 8 (7, lt) **1947** Bos 3 (1) **1947** Was 3 (0) **1948** GB 8 (1) **NFL** 29 (9) [4 yrs]

DEER SLAYER, DICK Dick, E, /190 lbs; none; deceased **1922** Oor 2 (1)

DEES, BOB Robert Leslie, DT-T, 6´4˝/245 lbs; Southwest Missouri State; 1952: LA, rnd 18; B9/26/1929 St. Louis, MO **1952** GB 9 (RDT)

DEESE, DERRICK Derrick, T-G, 6´3˝/289 lbs; USC; B5/17/1970 Culver City, CA **1994**†SF 16 (15, RG) **1995** SF 2 (2) **1996**†SF 16 (0) **1997**†SF 16 (13, LT) **1998**†SF 16 (16, LT/rt) **1999** SF 16 (16, RT) **2000** SF 13 (13, LT) **2001**†SF 16 (16, LT) **2002**†SF 14 (14, LT) **2003** SF 11 (11, LT) **2004** TB 16 (16, LT) **NFL** 152 (132) [11 yrs]

DEFELICE, NICK Nicholas Francis, T, 6´3˝/250 lbs; Southern Connecticut State; B2/4/1940 Derby, CT **1965** NYJ-A 14

DEFILIPPO, LOU Louis Phillip, T-C, 6´2˝/230 lbs; Fordham; 1941: NYG, rnd 6; B8/28/1916 East Haven, CT, D3/5/2000 Hartford, CT **1941** NYG 11 (0) **1945** NYG 10 (5, rt) **1946**†NYG 11 (0) **1947** NYG 4 (0) **NFL** 36 (5) [4 yrs]

DEFOREST, JOE Joseph John, LB, 6´1˝/240 lbs; Louisiana-Lafayette; B4/17/1965 Teaneck, NJ **1987** NO 3 (3)

DEFRANCE, CHRIS Christopher Anthony, WR, 6´1˝/205 lbs; Arizona State; 1979: Dal, rnd 6; B9/13/1956 Waldo, AR **1979** Was 4 (1)

DEFRUITER, BOB Robert Albert, HB, 6´0˝/190 lbs; Nebraska; B6/3/1918 Springfield, NE, D1/12/2000 Corpus Christi, TX

YEAR	TEAM	G (GS, POS)	RUSH	YD	AVG (LG)	TD	REC	YD	AVG (LG)	TD	PASS	COMP	PCT	YD	AVG (LG)	TD	INT	SK	YD	QBR	KPR	OTD	PTS	TAY
1945	†Was	3(0)	7	36	5.1(17)	0	1	19	19.0(19)	0	—	—	—	—	—	—	—	—	—	—	—	—	0	46
1946	Was	7(1)	2	-2	-1.0(0)	0	1	9	9.0(9)	0	—	—	—	—	—	—	—	—	—	—	—	—	0	3
1947	Was	1(0)	—	—	—	—	—	—	—	—	—	—	—	—	—	—	—	—	—	—	—	—	—	—
1947	Det	8(2)	1	-2	-2.0(-2)	0	—	—	—	—	—	—	—	—	—	—	—	—	—	—	i	—	0	-9
1948	LARm	3(0)	3	4	1.3(4)	0	—	—	—	—	—	—	—	—	—	—	—	—	—	—	—	—	0	4
NFL	4	22(3)	13	36	2.8(17)	0	2	28	14.0(19)	0	—	—	—	—	—	—	—	—	—	—	i	—	0	43

DEGEN, DICK Richard G., LB, 6´1˝/220 lbs; Long Beach State; B3/4/1942 Jamestown, ND **1965**†SD-A 12 (llb) **1966** SD-A 10 (LLB) **NFL** 22 [2 yrs]

DEGRAFFENREID, ALLEN Allen, T, 6´4˝/293 lbs; Vanderbilt; B6/3/1974 Kansas City, MO **1998** Arz 5 (0)

DEGRAFFENREID, ALLEN Allen Justice, WR, 6´3˝/200 lbs; Ohio State; B5/1/1970 Cincinnati, OH **1993** Cin 2 (0)

DEGRATE, TONY Tony, NT, 6´4˝/280 lbs; Texas; 1985: Cin, rnd 5; B4/25/1962 Snyder, TX **1985** GB 1 (0)

DEGREE, CY Walter George, T-G, 6´1˝/210 lbs; Notre Dame; B7/7/1898 St. Cloud, MN, D11/1961 Detroit, MI **[K]** **1921** Det 7 (7, LT), 3

DEGRENIER, JACK Jack Thomas, RB, 6´1˝/225 lbs; Northern Arizona; Texas-Arlington; B2/25/1951 Chicago, IL

YEAR	TEAM	G (GS, POS)	RUSH	YD	AVG (LG)	TD	REC	YD	AVG (LG)	TD	PASS	COMP	PCT	YD	AVG (LG)	TD	INT	SK	YD	QBR	KPR	OTD	PTS	TAY
1974	NO	12	33	110	3.3(10)	0	4	13	3.3(8)	0	—	—	—	—	—	—	—	—	—	—	—	—	0	117

DEIBEL, ART Arthur Francis, T-G, 6´3˝/220 lbs; Lafayette; B4/3/1896 Clinton, OH, D4/1984 **1926** Can 7 (6, lt)

DEJURNETT, CHARLES Charles Ray, NT-DT, 6´4˝/263 lbs; San Jose State; 1974: SD, rnd 17; B6/17/1952 Picayune, MS **1976** SD 13 **1977** SD 11 (3) **1978** SD 15 (3) **1979**†SD 12 (4) **1980**†SD 15 (4) **1982** LARm 4 (0) **1983**†LARm 10 (6, nt) **1984**†LARm 16 (0) **1985**†LARm 15 (14, NT) **1986** LARm 7 (6, nt) **NFL** 118 (40) [10 yrs]

DEKDEBRUN, AL Allen Edward, B, 5´11˝/185 lbs; Cornell; 1946: Bos, rnd 9; B5/11/1921 Buffalo, NY, D3/29/2005 Cape Coral, FL

YEAR	TEAM	G (GS, POS)	RUSH	YD	AVG (LG)	TD	REC	YD	AVG (LG)	TD	PASS	COMP	PCT	YD	AVG (LG)	TD	INT	SK	YD	QBR	KPR	OTD	PTS	TAY
1946	Buf-A	14(8, QB)	25	-55	-2.2	0	—	—	—	—	66	28	42.4	517	7.8	8	8	—	—	—	ki	—	0	-47
1947	ChiR-A	12(5, qb)	20	71	3.6	0	—	—	—	—	75	45	60.0	556	7.4	5	7	—	—	—	—	—	0	94
1948	NYY-A	4(0)	7	24	3.4	0	—	—	—	—	20	10	50.0	149	7.4	0	2	—	—	—	kpi	—	0	37
AAFC	3	30(13)	52	40	0.8	0	—	—	—	—	161	83	51.6	1222	7.6	13	17	—	—	—	kpi	—	0	84
1948	Bos	2(0)	2	14	7.0(13)	0	—	—	—	—	3	1	33.3	2	0.7(2)	0	1	—	—	—	—	—	0	-25

DEKKER, PAUL Paul Nelson, E, 6´5˝/220 lbs; Michigan State; 1953: Was, rnd 3; B2/24/1931 Muskegon, MI, D5/8/2001 Burlington, Canada

YEAR	TEAM	G (GS, POS)	RUSH	YD	AVG (LG)	TD	REC	YD	AVG (LG)	TD	PASS	COMP	PCT	YD	AVG (LG)	TD	INT	SK	YD	QBR	KPR	OTD	PTS	TAY
1953	Was	11(RE)	—	—	—	—	14	182	13.0(34)	1	—	—	—	—	—	—	—	—	—	—	—	—	6	96

DEL BELLO, JACK Ameleto Vincent, QB, 6´1˝/190 lbs; Miami (FL); B12/9/1927 Philadelphia, PA

YEAR	TEAM	G (GS, POS)	RUSH	YD	AVG (LG)	TD	REC	YD	AVG (LG)	TD	PASS	COMP	PCT	YD	AVG (LG)	TD	INT	SK	YD	QBR	KPR	OTD	PTS	TAY
1953	Bal	5	14	14	1.0(9)	0	—	—	—	—	61	27	44.3	229	3.8(66)	1	5	—	—	—	—	—	0	-67

DEL GAIZO, JIM James Robert, QB, 6´1˝/198 lbs; Tampa; Syracuse; B5/31/1947 Everett, MA

YEAR	TEAM	G (GS, POS)	RUSH	YD	AVG (LG)	TD	REC	YD	AVG (LG)	TD	PASS	COMP	PCT	YD	AVG (LG)	TD	INT	SK	YD	QBR	KPR	OTD	PTS	TAY
1972	Mia	4	1	0	0.0(0)	0	—	—	—	—	9	5	55.6	165	18.3(51)	2	1	—	—	—	—	—	0	53
1973	GB	8	4	1	0.3(3)	0	—	—	—	—	62	27	43.5	318	5.1(28)	2	6	8	77	—	—	—	0	-70
1974	NYG	4	3	15	5.0(6)	0	—	—	—	—	32	12	37.5	165	5.2(44)	0	3	1	11	—	—	—	0	-23
NFL	3	16	8	16	2.0(6)	0	—	—	—	—	103	44	42.7	648	6.3(51)	4	10	9	88	—	—	—	0	-40

DEL GRECO, AL Albert Louis, K, 5´10˝/196 lbs; Auburn; B3/2/1962 Providence, RI **[K]** **1984** GB 9 (0) **1985** GB 16 (0) **1986** GB 16 (0) **1987** GB 5 (0) **1987** SL 3 (0) **1989** Phx 16 (0) **1990** Phx 16 (0) **1991**†Hou 7 (0) **1992**†Hou 16 (0) **1993**†Hou 16 (0) **1994** Hou 16 (0) **1995** Hou 16 (0) **1996** Hou☆16 (0) **1997** Ten 16 (0) **1998** Ten 16 (0) **1999**†Ten 16 (0) **2000**†Ten 16 (0)

YEAR	TEAM	G (GS, POS)	RUSH	YD	AVG (LG)	TD	REC	YD	AVG (LG)	TD	PASS	COMP	PCT	YD	AVG (LG)	TD	INT	SK	YD	QBR	KPR	OTD	PTS	TAY
1988	Phx	16(0)	1	8	8.0(8)	0	—	—	—	—	—	—	—	—	—	—	—	—	—	—	K	—	78	8
NFL	17	248(0)	1	8	8.0(8)	0	—	—	—	—	—	—	—	—	—	—	—	—	—	—	KP	—	1584	8

DEL RIO, JACK Jack L., LB, 6´4˝/246 lbs; USC; 1985: NO, rnd 3; B4/4/1963 Castro Valley, CA **[C]** **1985** NO 16 (9, RILB) **1987** KC 10 (7, ROLB) **1988** KC 15 (10, LOLB) **1989** Dal 14 (12, LLB) **1990** Dal 16 (16, LLB) **1991**†Dal 16 (16, MLB) **1992**†Min 16 (16, MLB) **1993**†Min 16 (16, MLB) **1994**†Min★16 (16, MLB) **1995** Min 9 (9, MLB)

YEAR	TEAM	G (GS, POS)	RUSH	YD	AVG (LG)	TD	REC	YD	AVG (LG)	TD	PASS	COMP	PCT	YD	AVG (LG)	TD	INT	SK	YD	QBR	KPR	OTD	PTS	TAY
1986	NO	16(1)	1	16	16.0(16)	0	—	—	—	—	—	—	—	—	—	—	—	—	—	—	—	—	0	16
NFL	11	160(128)	1	16	16.0(16)	0	—	—	—	—	—	—	—	—	—	—	—	—	—	—	kiS	3	18	78

DELAMIELLEURE, JOE Joseph Michael, G, 6´3˝/254 lbs; Michigan State; 1973: Buf, rnd 1; B3/16/1951 Detroit, MI; HOF 2003 **1973** Buf 14 (14, RG) **1974**†Buf☆14 (14, RG) **1975** Buf★14 (14, RG) **1976** Buf★14 (14, RG) **1977** Buf★14 (14, RG) **1978** Buf★16 (16, RG) **1979** Buf★16 (16, RG) **1980**†Cle★16 (13, RG) **1981** Cle☆16 (16, RG) **1982**†Cle 9 (9, RG) **1983** Cle☆16 (16, RG) **1984** Cle 16 (16, RG) **1985** Buf 10 (3) **NFL** 185 (175) [13 yrs]

DELANEY, JEFF Jeffrey John, DB, 6´0˝/195 lbs; Pittsburgh; 1979: LA, rnd 7; B10/25/1956 Pittsburgh, PA **1980**†LARm 16 (0) **1981** Det 5 (0) **1981**†TB 2 (0) **1982** Bal 8 (1) **1983** Bal 11 (5, ss) **NFL** 42 (6) [4 yrs]

DELANEY, JOE Joe Alton, RB, 5´10˝/184 lbs; Northwestern State (LA); 1981: KC, rnd 2; B10/30/1958 Henderson, TX, D6/29/1983 Monroe, LA

YEAR	TEAM	G (GS, POS)	RUSH	YD	AVG (LG)	TD	REC	YD	AVG (LG)	TD	PASS	COMP	PCT	YD	AVG (LG)	TD	INT	SK	YD	QBR	KPR	OTD	PTS	TAY
1981	KC★	15(10, RB)	234	1121	4.8(82)	3	22	246	11.2(61)	0	—	—	—	—	—	—	—	—	—	—	k	—	18	1270
1982	KC	8(7, RB)	95	380	4.0(36)	0	11	53	4.8(13)	0	—	—	—	—	—	—	—	—	—	—	—	—	0	407
NFL	2	23(17)	329	1501	4.6(82)	3	33	299	9.1(61)	0	—	—	—	—	—	—	—	—	—	—	k	—	18	1677

DELAPORTE, DAROLL Darroll Austin, BB, none; B10/30/1903 Brown County, WI, D12/25/1980 Bartow, FL **1925** Mil 1 (1)

DELAUER, BOB Robert, C, 6´1˝/218 lbs; USC; 1942: Cle, rnd 10; B8/30/1920 San Francisco, CA, D11/27/2002 Los Angeles, CA **[K]** **1945**†Cle 2 (0) **1946** LARm 11 (6, C) **NFL** 13 (6) [2 yrs]

DELEONE, TOM Thomas Denning, C, 6´2˝/248 lbs; Ohio State; 1972: Cin, rnd 5; B8/13/1950 Ravenna, OH **1972** Cin 13 **1973**†Cin 14 **1974** Cle 12 **1975** Cle 14 (9, C) **1976** Cle 14 (14, C) **1977** Cle 14 (14, C) **1978** Cle 15 (15, C) **1979** Cle✧16 (16, C) **1980**†Cle★16 (16, C) **1981** Cle 8 (8, C) **1982**†Cle 9 (9, C) **1983** Cle 16 (1) **1984** Cle 15 (0) **NFL** 176 (102) [13 yrs]

DELEVAN, BURT Darrel Burton, T, 6´2˝/236 lbs; Pacific; 1952: LA, rnd 7; B12/2/1929 Westwood, CA **1955** ChiC 12 **1956** ChiC 2 **NFL** 14 [2 yrs]

DELHOMME, JAKE Jake Christopher, QB, 6´2˝/205 lbs; Louisiana-Lafayette; B1/10/1975 Breaux Bridge, LA

YEAR	TEAM	G (GS, POS)	RUSH	YD	AVG (LG)	TD	REC	YD	AVG (LG)	TD	PASS	COMP	PCT	YD	AVG (LG)	TD	INT	SK	YD	QBR	KPR	OTD	PTS	TAY
1999	NO	2(2)	11	72	6.5(27)	2	—	—	—	—	76	42	55.3	521	6.9(51)	3	5	6	42	—	—	—	12	168
2002	NO	4(0)	4	-2	-0.5(6)	0	—	—	—	—	10	8	80.0	113	11.3(54)	0	0	—	—	—	—	—	0	55
2003	†Car	16(15, QB)	42	39	0.9(9)	1	—	—	—	—	449	266	59.2	3219	7.2(67)	19	16	23	168	80.6	—	—	6	1114
2004	Car	16(16, QB)	25	71	2.8(13)	1	—	—	—	—	533	310	58.2	3886	7.3(63)	29	15	33	246	87.3	—	—	6	1569
2005	†Car✧	16(16, QB)	24	31	1.3(12)	1	—	—	—	—	435	262	60.2	3421	7.9(80)	**24**	16	28	214	88.1	—	—	6	1232
NFL	5	54(49)	106	211	2.0(27)	5	—	—	—	—	1503	888	59.1	11160	7.4(80)	75	52	90	670	84.5	—	—	30	4136

YEAR	TEAM	G (GS, POS)	RUSH	YD	AVG(LG)	TD	REC	YD	AVG(LG)	TD	PASS	COMP	PCT	YD	AVG(LG)	TD	INT	SK	YD	QBR	KPR	OTD	PTS	TAY

DeLine, Steve   Steven Braun, K, 5´11˝/185 lbs; Colorado State; 1987: SF, rnd 7; B8/19/1961 Denver, CO **[K]**   **1988** SD 5 (0)   **1989** Phi 3 (0)   **NFL** 8 (0) [2 yrs]

DeLisle, Jim   James Roger, DT, 6´4˝/255 lbs; Wisconsin; B1/20/1949 Wausau, WI   **1971** GB 9

Dell Isola, Johnny   John Joseph, G-C, 5´11˝/201 lbs; Fordham; B2/12/1912 Everett, MA, D10/21/1986 Arlington, MA   **1934** NYG 6 (0)   **1935**†NYG 9 (2)   **1936** NYG 10 (8, LG)   **1937** NYG☆9 (8, LG)   **1938**†NYG☆11 (5, lg)   **1939**†NYG☆11 (11, LG)   **1940** NYG 10 (7, RG)   **NFL** 66 (41) [7 yrs]

Dellenbach, Jeff   Jeffrey Alan, C-T-G, 6´6˝/290 lbs; Wisconsin; 1985: Mia, rnd 4; B2/14/1963 Wausau, WI   **1985**†Mia 11 (1)   **1986** Mia 13 (6, lt)   **1987** Mia 11 (6, c)   **1988** Mia 16 (16, C)   **1989** Mia 16 (16, LT)   **1990** Mia 15 (0)   **1991** Mia 15 (2)   **1992**†Mia 16 (16, C/rg)   **1993** Mia 16 (16, RT)   **1994**†Mia 16 (16, C)   **1995** NE 15 (5, c)   **1996** NE 2 (0)   **1996**†GB 3 (0)   **1997** GB 14 (5, c)   **1998**†GB 16 (3)   **1999** Phi 16 (15, RG)   **NFL** 211 (115) [15 yrs]

Dellerba, Spiro   Spiro, LB-FB, 5´11˝/200 lbs; Ohio State; B1/25/1923 Ashtabula, OH, D8/1968   **1949** Bal-A 9 (2)

1947	Cle-A	8 (0)	29	176	6.1	0	1	14	14.0 (14)	0	—	—	—	—	—	—	—	—	—	—	k	1	6	202
1948	†Bal-A	14 (2)	2	0	0.0	0	—	—	—	—	—	—	—	—	—	—	—	—	—	—	ki		0	5
AAFC	3	31 (4)	31	176	5.7	0	1	14	14.0 (14)	0	—	—	—	—	—	—	—	—	—	—	ki	1	6	207

Dellinger, Larry   Lawrence, G-T, 5´11˝/204 lbs; none; B1893, deceased   **1920** Day 6 (5, LG)   **1921** Day 7 (3)   **1922** Day 3 (2)   **1923** Day 7 (4)   **NFL** 23 (14) [4 yrs]

DeLoach, Jerry   Jerry, DE, 6´2˝/315 lbs; California; B7/17/1977 Sacramento, CA   **2001** Was 15 (4)   **2002** Hou 16 (16, RDE)   **2003** Hou 16 (16, RDE)   **2004** Hou 15 (3)   **2005** Hou 11 (1)   **NFL** 73 (40) [5 yrs]

DeLoach, Ralph   Ralph Alan, DE, 6´5˝/255 lbs; California; 1979: Dal, rnd 4; B1/13/1957 Sacramento, CA   **1981** NYJ 1 (0)

DeLoatch, Curtis   Curtis, DB, 6´2˝/217 lbs; North Carolina A&T; B10/4/1981 Murfreesboro, NC   **2004** NYG 16 (0)   **2005**†NYG 16 (13, RCB)   **NFL** 32 (13) [2 yrs]

DeLong, Greg   Gregory Andrew, TE, 6´4˝/250 lbs; North Carolina; B4/3/1973 Orefield, PA

1995	Min	2 (2)	—	—	—	—	6	38	6.3 (9)	0	—	—	—	—	—	—	—	—	—	—	—	0	19
1996	†Min	16 (8, TE)	—	—	—	—	8	34	4.3 (9)	0	—	—	—	—	—	—	—	—	—	k		0	5
1997	†Min	16 (3)	—	—	—	—	8	75	9.4 (23)	0	—	—	—	—	—	—	—	—	—	—		0	38
1998	†Min	15 (5, te)	—	—	—	—	8	58	7.3 (17)	0	—	—	—	—	—	—	—	—	—	—		0	29
1999	Bal	16 (7, te)	—	—	—	—	13	52	4.0 (9)	1	—	—	—	—	—	—	—	—	—	—		6	27
2000	Jax	4 (1)	—	—	—	—	—	—	—	—	—	—	—	—	—	—	—	—	—	—			
NFL	6	69 (26)	—	—	—	—	43	257	6.0 (23)	1	—	—	—	—	—	—	—	—	—	k		6	118

DeLong, Keith   Keith Allen, LB, 6´2˝/245 lbs; Tennessee; 1989: SF, rnd 1; B8/14/1967 San Diego, CA   **1989**†SF 15 (0)   **1990**†SF 16 (13, RILB)   **1991** SF 15 (14, LILB)   **1992**†SF 14 (9, LILB)   **1993** SF 4 (3)   **NFL** 64 (39) [5 yrs]

DeLong, Steve   Steven Cyril, DE-DT, 6´2˝/252 lbs; Tennessee; 1965: SD, rnd 1/Chi, rnd 1; B7/3/1943 Norfolk, VA   **1965** SD-A 12   **1966** SD-A 14 (RDT)   **1967** SD-A 7   **1968** SD-A 14 (14, RDE)   **1969** SD-A★14 (RDE)   **1970** SD 14 (RDE)   **1971** SD 14 (RDE)   **1972** ChiB 14 (RDE)   **NFL** 103 (14) [8 yrs]

Deloplaine, Jack   Jack A., RB, 5´10˝/205 lbs; Salem; 1976: Pit, rnd 6; B4/21/1954 Pottstown, PA

1976	Pit	14	17	91	5.4 (19)	1	3	3.0 (3)		—	—	—	—	—	—	—	—	—	—	kp	—	12	308
1977	Pit	8	2	7	3.5 (5)	0	—	—	—	—	—	—	—	—	—	—	—	—	—	kp	—	0	12
1978	Was	2	—	—	—	—	—	—	—	—	—	—	—	—	—	—	—	—	—	—	—		
1978	†Pit	10	11	49	4.5 (19)	0	—	—	—	—	—	—	—	—	—	—	—	—	—	k	—	0	53
1979	ChiB	5	7	18	2.6 (6)	0	2	13	6.5 (15)	0	—	—	—	—	—	—	—	—	—	—	—	0	25
1979	Pit	1	—	—	—	—	—	—	—	—	—	—	—	—	—	—	—	—	—	—	—		
NFL	4	40	37	165	4.5 (19)	2	3	16	5.3 (15)	0	—	—	—	—	—	—	—	—	—	kp	—	12	397

Delpino, Robert   Robert Lewis, RB, 6´0˝/205 lbs; Missouri; 1988: LARm, rnd 5; B11/2/1965 Dodge City, KS

1988	†LARm☆	15 (3)	34	147	4.3 (13)	0	30	312	10.4 (38)	2	—	—	—	—	—	—	—	—	—	k	—	12	436
1989	†LARm	16 (1)	78	368	4.7 (32)	1	34	334	9.8 (25)	1	—	—	—	—	—	—	—	—	—	k	—	12	629
1990	LARm	15 (3)	13	52	4.0 (13)	0	15	172	11.5 (42)	4	—	—	—	—	—	—	—	—	—	k	—	24	247
1991	LARm	16 (15, RB)	214	688	3.2 (36)	9	55	617	11.2 (78)	1	—	—	—	—	—	—	—	—	—	k	—	60	1086
1992	LARm	10 (4)	32	115	3.6 (31)	0	18	139	7.7 (12)	1	—	—	—	—	—	—	—	—	—	k	—	6	183
1993	†Den	16 (4)	131	445	3.4 (18)	8	26	195	7.5 (25)	0	—	—	—	—	—	—	—	—	—	k	—	48	664
NFL	6	88 (30)	502	1815	3.6 (36)	18	178	1769	9.9 (78)	9	—	—	—	—	—	—	—	—	—	k	—	162	3244

DeLuca, Sam   Samuel Frank, G-T, 6´2˝/250 lbs; South Carolina; 1957: NYG, rnd 2; B5/2/1936 Brooklyn, NY   **1960**†LAC-A 14   **1961** SD-A 14 (RG)   **1963**†SD-A 14 (lg)   **1964** NYJ-A 11 (RG)   **1965** NYJ-A 14 (LG)   **1966** NYJ-A☆14 (LG)   **NFL** 81 [6 yrs]

DeLuca, Tony   Anthony Lawrence, NT, 6´4˝/250 lbs; Rhode Island; B11/16/1960 Greenwich, CT, D4/16/1999 Stamford, CT   **1984** GB 1 (0)

DeLucca, Jerry   Gerald Joseph, T-DT, 6´2˝/247 lbs; Tennessee; Middle Tennessee State; 1957: ChiB, rnd 7; B7/17/1936 Peabody, MA   **1959** Phi 12 (LT)   **1960** Bos-A 12 (RT)   **1961** Bos-A☆14 (RT)   **1962** Buf-A 14   **1963** Buf-A 2   **1963** Bos-A 3   **1964** Bos-A 2   **NFL** 59 [6 yrs]

DeMao, Al   Albert Marcellus, C-LB, 6´2˝/214 lbs; Duquesne; 1942: Was, rnd 11; B2/29/1920 New Kensington, PA   **1945**†Was 5 (0)   **1946** Was 11 (1)   **1947** Was 12 (5, c)   **1948** Was 9 (8, C)   **1949** Was 12 (10, C)   **1951** Was 12 (C)   **1952** Was 12 (C)   **1953** Was 12 (c)

| 1950 | Was | 12 (C) | — | — | — | — | 1 | 4 | 4.0 (4) | 0 | — | — | — | — | — | — | — | — | — | — | — | 0 | 2 |
| NFL | 9 | 97 (24) | — | — | — | — | 1 | 4 | 4.0 (4) | 0 | — | — | — | — | — | — | — | — | — | i | — | 0 | 84 |

DeMar, Enoch   Enoch, G-T, 6´4˝/317 lbs; Indiana; B9/7/1980 Indianapolis, IN   **2003** Cle 5 (2)   **2004** Cle 15 (11, LG)   **NFL** 20 (13) [2 yrs]

DeMarco, Bob   Robert Albert, C-G, 6´2˝/248 lbs; Indiana; Dayton; 1960: SL, rnd 14/LAC, rnd 2; B9/16/1938 Jersey City, NJ   **1961** SL 4   **1962** SL (C)   **1963** SL★14 (C)   **1964** SL☆12 (C)   **1965** SL☆9 (C)   **1967** SL★14 (C)   **1968** SL☆14 (C)   **1969** SL☆12 (C)   **1970** Mia 11 (11, C)   **1971**†Mia☆14 (14, C)   **1972**†Cle 12 (C)   **1973** Cle 13 (C)   **1974** Cle 14 (C)   **1975**†LARm 14   **NFL** 185 (25) [15 yrs]

DeMarco, Brian   Brian Thomas, G-T, 6´7˝/323 lbs; Michigan State; 1995: Jax, rnd 2; B4/9/1972 Berea, OH   **1995** Jax 16 (16, RT)   **1996**†Jax 10 (9, RG)   **1997** Jax 14 (5, rg)   **1998**†Jax 16 (9, RG)   **1999** Cin 7 (7, rg)   **NFL** 63 (46) [5 yrs]

DeMarco, Mario   Mario, G-LB, 5´11˝/200 lbs; Miami (FL); B7/24/1924 Boonton, NJ, D9/1967   **1949** Det 12 (11, LG)

Demaree, Chris   Christopher John, DT, 6´2˝/315 lbs; Kentucky; B3/12/1980 Louisville, KY   **2002** SD 2 (0)

Demarie, John   John E., G-T-C, 6´3˝/246 lbs; LSU; 1967: Cle, rnd 6; B8/28/1945 Lake Charles, LA   **1967**†Cle 14 (rt)   **1968**†Cle 14 (LG)   **1969**†Cle 14 (LG)   **1970** Cle 14 (LG)   **1971**†Cle 14 (LG)   **1972**†Cle 14 (RG/rt)   **1973** Cle 14 (RG)   **1975** Cle 14 (c)   **1976** Sea 9 (7, RG)   **NFL** 132 (7) [10 yrs]

Demas, George   George James, G, 6´0˝/194 lbs; Washington & Jefferson; B1/7/1907 Johnstown, PA, D11/1977 Miami, FL   **1932** SI 4 (2)   **1934** Bkn 1 (0)   **NFL** 5 (2) [2 yrs]

Demery, Calvin   Calvin Louis, WR, 6´1˝/190 lbs; Arizona State; 1972: Min, rnd 8; B8/17/1950 Phoenix, AZ   **1972** Min 5

Demko, George   George, DE, 6´3˝/240 lbs; Appalachian State; B8/10/1935   **1961** Pit 1

Demmy, John   John, aka John Demyanovich, T, /190 lbs; none; B3/5/1904 Bayonne, NJ, D3/1970 Bay Head, NJ   **1930** SI 6 (3)   **1931** SI 3 (5)   **NFL** 9 (3) [2 yrs]

Demory, Bill   John William, QB, 6´2˝/195 lbs; Arizona; B12/1/1950 Indianola, IA   **1974** NYJ 1

| 1973 | NYJ | 6 | 4 | -1 | -0.3 (0) | 0 | — | — | — | — | 39 | 12 | 30.8 | 159 | 4.1 (31) | 2 | 8 | 8 | 73 | — | — | — | 0 | -232 |
| NFL | 7 | 4 | -1 | -0.3 | 0 | — | — | — | — | 39 | 12 | 30.8 | 159 | 4.1 (31) | 2 | 8 | 8 | 73 | — | — | — | 0 | -232 |

DeMoss, Bob   Robert Alonzo, QB, 6´2˝/175 lbs; Purdue; 1949: NYB, rnd 2/Bal-A, rnd 28; B1/27/1927 Dayton, KY

| 1949 | NYB | 3 (0) | 5 | 1 | 0.2 (4) | 0 | — | — | — | — | 18 | 6 | 33.3 | 60 | 3.3 (20) | 0 | 2 | — | — | — | — | — | 0 | -49 |

Demps, Will   Will Henry, DB, 6´0˝/205 lbs; San Diego State; B11/7/1979 Charleston, SC   **2002** Bal 14 (10, FS)   **2003**†Bal 16 (9, fs)   **2004** Bal 16 (16, FS)   **2005** Bal 11 (11, FS)   **NFL** 57 (46) [4 yrs]

Dempsey, Frank   James Franklin, LB-MG-G-T, 6´3˝/235 lbs; Florida; 1950: ChiB, rnd 13; B5/27/1925 Dothan, AL   **1950**†ChiB 6   **1951** ChiB 12   **1952** ChiB 10 (LLB)   **1953** ChiB 11 (MG)   **NFL** 39 [4 yrs]

Dempsey, Jack   John Bernard, T, 6´2˝/225 lbs; Bucknell; B3/12/1912 Scranton, PA, D8/26/1988 Saratoga, CA   **1934** Phi 1 (0)   **1934** Pit 1 (1)   **1937** Phi 2 (1)   **NFL** 4 (2) [2 yrs]

Dempsey, Tom   Thomas John, K, 6´2˝/255 lbs; Palomar College; B1/12/1947 Milwaukee, WI **[K]**   **1969** NO★14   **1970** NO 14   **1971** Phi 5   **1972** Phi 14   **1973** Phi 14   **1974** Phi 14   **1975**†LARm 14   **1976**†LARm 14   **1977** Hou 5   **1978** Buf 16   **1979** Buf 3   **NFL** 127 [11 yrs]

DeMulling, Rick   Rick Elwood, G, 6´4˝/304 lbs; Idaho; 2001: Ind, rnd 7; B7/21/1977 Cheney, WA   **2001** Ind 7 (0)   **2002**†Ind 14 (14, LG)   **2003**†Ind 16 (16, LG)   **2004**†Ind 11 (11, LG)   **2005** Det 13 (5, lg)   **NFL** 61 (46) [5 yrs]

YEAR	TEAM	G(GS, POS)	RUSH	YD	AVG(LG)	TD	REC	YD	AVG(LG)	TD	PASS	COMP	PCT	YD	AVG(LG)	TD	INT	SK	YD	QBR	KPR	OTD	PTS	TAY

DEN HERDER, VERN Vern Wayne, DE-NT, 6´6˝/250 lbs; Iowa Central; 1971: Mia, rnd 9; B11/28/1948 Le Mars, IA　**1971**†Mia 14　**1972**†Mia☆14 (14, LDE)　**1973**†Mia 14 (14, LDE) **1974**†Mia 14 (14, LDE)　**1975** Mia 14 (14, LDE)　**1976** Mia 14 (14, LDE)　**1977** Mia 11 (11, LDE)　**1979**†Mia 16 (16, LDE)　**1980** Mia 16 (16, LDE)　**1981**†Mia 16 (14, RDE) **1982**†Mia 7 (1)

| **1978** | †Mia | 16 (16, LDE) | — | — | — | — | 1 | 7 | 7.0(7) | 1 | — | — | — | — | — | — | — | — | — | — | — | — | 6 | 9 |
| **NFL** | 12 | 166 (144) | — | — | — | — | 1 | 7 | 7.0(7) | 1 | — | — | — | — | — | — | — | — | — | — | i | — | 6 | 28 |

DENDY, PATRICK Patrick, DB, 6´0˝/190 lbs; Rice; B3/10/1982 Austin, TX　**2005** GB 4 (0)

DENFELD, FRED Frederick, G-T, 6´0˝/198 lbs; Navy; B10/26/1898 Duluth, MN, D1/18/1990 St. Paul, MN　**1920** RI☆5 (2)　**1925** Dul 3 (2, RG)　**NFL** 8 (4) [2 yrs]

DENMAN, ANTHONY Anthony Ray, LB, 5´11˝/235 lbs; Notre Dame; 2001: Jax, rnd 7; B10/30/1979 Lufkin, TX　**2001** Cle 11 (0)　**2002** Buf 16 (0)　**NFL** 27 (0) [2 yrs]

DENNARD, MARK Mark Wesley, C, 6´1˝/253 lbs; Texas A&M; 1978: Mia, rnd 10; B11/2/1955 Bay City, TX　**1979**†Mia 16 (7, c)　**1980** Mia 16 (16, C)　**1981**†Mia 11 (11, C) **1982**†Mia 8 (0)　**1983** Mia 8 (0)　**1984** Phi 16 (16, C)　**1985** Phi 16 (16, C)　**NFL** 91 (66) [7 yrs]

DENNARD, PRESTON Preston Jackson, WR, 6´1˝/185 lbs; New Mexico; B11/28/1955 Cordele, GA

1978	†LARm	11	—	—	—	—	3	35	11.7(15)	0	—	—	—	—	—	—	—	—	—	—	—	—	0	18
1979	†LARm	15 (11, WR)	4	32	8.0(15)	0	43	766	17.8(50)	4	—	—	—	—	—	—	—	—	—	—	—	—	24	435
1980	†LARm	16 (16, WR)	2	20	10.0(21)	0	36	596	16.6(44)	6	—	—	—	—	—	—	—	—	—	—	—	—	36	348
1981	LARm	15 (15, WR)	6	29	4.8(21)	0	49	821	16.8(64)	4	—	—	—	—	—	—	—	—	—	—	—	—	24	460
1982		9 (9, WR)	—	—	—	—	25	383	15.3(39)	2	—	—	—	—	—	—	—	—	—	—	—	—	12	202
1983	†LARm	14 (13, WR)	—	—	—	—	33	465	14.1(61)	5	—	—	—	—	—	—	—	—	—	—	—	—	30	258
1984	Buf	16 (13, WR)	—	—	—	—	30	417	13.9(68)	7	—	—	—	—	—	—	—	—	—	—	—	—	42	244
1985	GB	16 (0)	—	—	—	—	13	182	14.0(34)	2	—	—	—	—	—	—	—	—	—	—	—	—	12	101
NFL	8	112 (77)	12	81	6.8(21)	0	232	3665	15.8(68)	30	—	—	—	—	—	—	—	—	—	—	—	—	180	2064

DENNERLEIN, JERRY Gerald E., T, 6´2˝/235 lbs; St. Mary's (CA); 1937: NYG, rnd 3; B12/1/1915 Ambridge, PA, D7/29/1966 Los Angeles County, CA　**1937** NYG 11 (6, LT) **1940** NYG 11 (3)　**NFL** 22 (9) [2 yrs]

DENNERY, MIKE Michael Kevin, LB, 6´0˝/222 lbs; Southern Mississippi; 1974: Oak, rnd 13; B6/26/1950 Philadelphia, PA　**1974**†Oak 14　**1975**†Oak 14　**1976** Mia 3　**NFL** 31 [3 yrs]

DENNERY, VINCE Vincent Paul, E, 5´11˝/190 lbs; Fordham; B11/17/1916 Jersey City, NJ, D8/9/1989 Philadelphia, PA

| **1941** | NYG | 9 (0) | — | — | — | — | 1 | 65 | 65.0(65) | 1 | — | — | — | — | — | — | — | — | — | — | — | — | 6 | 38 |

DENNEY, AUSTIN Austin Cheek, TE, 6´2˝/230 lbs; Tennessee; 1966: Dal, rnd 11/NYJ, rnd R2; B1/2/1944 Nashville, TN

1967	ChiB	7 (TE)	—	—	—	—	12	113	9.4(19)	0	—	—	—	—	—	—	—	—	—	—	—	—	0	57
1968	ChiB	14 (TE)	1	-1	-1.0(-1)	0	23	247	10.7(46)	2	—	—	—	—	—	—	—	—	—	—	—	—	12	133
1969	ChiB	14 (TE)	1	4	4.0(4)	0	22	203	9.2(29)	1	—	—	—	—	—	—	—	—	—	—	—	—	6	111
1970	Buf	14 (TE)	—	—	—	—	14	201	14.4(31)	0	—	—	—	—	—	—	—	—	—	—	—	—	0	101
1971	Buf	1	—	—	—	—	—	—	—	—	—	—	—	—	—	—	—	—	—	—	—	—	—	—
NFL	5	50	2	3	1.5(4)	0	71	764	10.8(46)	3	—	—	—	—	—	—	—	—	—	—	—	—	18	400

DENNEY, JOHN John, DE, 6´5˝/275 lbs; Brigham Young; B12/13/1978 Denver, CO　**2005** Mia 16 (0)

DENNEY, RYAN Ryan Craig, DE, 6´7˝/275 lbs; Brigham Young; 2002: Buf, rnd 2; B6/15/1977 Denver, CO　**2002** Buf 8 (0)　**2003** Buf 16 (13, LDE)　**2004** Buf 16 (5, lde) **2005** Buf 16 (0)　**NFL** 56 (18) [4 yrs]

DENNIS, AL Albert Rudolph, G, 6´4˝/250 lbs; Grambling State; B6/24/1951 Independence, LA　**1973** SD 7　**1976** Cle 10　**1977** Cle 14　**NFL** 31 [3 yrs]

DENNIS, GUY Guy Dorell, G-C, 6´2˝/255 lbs; Florida; 1969: Cin, rnd 5; B2/28/1947 Walnut Hill, FL　**1969** Cin-A 14 (rg)　**1970**†Cin 14　**1971** Cin 14　**1972** Cin 13 **1973** Det 10 (8, LG)　**1974** Det 12 (5, lg)　**1975** Det 12　**NFL** 89 (13) [7 yrs]

DENNIS, MARK Mark Francis, T, 6´6˝/300 lbs; Illinois; 1987: Mia, rnd 8; B4/15/1965 Junction City, KS　**1987** Mia 5 (2)　**1988** Mia 13 (7, lt)　**1989** Mia 8 (1)　**1990**†Mia 16 (16, RT) **1991** Mia 16 (16, RT)　**1992**†Mia 16 (8, rt)　**1993** Mia 16 (0)　**1994** Cin 7 (1)　**1996** Car 16 (8, rt/lt)

| **1995** | Car | 12 (9, RT) | — | — | — | — | 1 | 3 | 3.0(3) | 0 | — | — | — | — | — | — | — | — | — | — | — | — | 0 | 2 |
| **NFL** | 10 | 125 (68) | — | — | — | — | 1 | 3 | 3.0(3) | 0 | — | — | — | — | — | — | — | — | — | — | — | — | 0 | 2 |

DENNIS, MIKE Walter Michael, RB, 6´1˝/207 lbs; Mississippi; 1966: Atl, rnd 3/Buf, rnd 1; B7/22/1944 Philadelphia, MS　**1969** LARm 1

| **1968** | LARm | 14 | 29 | 136 | 4.7(16) | 0 | 8 | 53 | 6.6(17) | 0 | 2 | 0 | 0.0 | 0 | 0.0 | 0 | 0 | — | — | k | — | 0 | 135 |
| **NFL** | 2 | 15 | 29 | 136 | 4.7(16) | 0 | 8 | 53 | 6.6(17) | 0 | 2 | 0 | 0.0 | 0 | 0.0 | 0 | 0 | — | — | k | — | 0 | 163 |

DENNIS, MIKE Michael Dwayne, DB, 5´10˝/190 lbs; Wyoming; B6/6/1958 Los Angeles, CA　**1980** NYG 13 (10, RCB)　**1981**†NYG 16 (0)　**1982** NYG 9 (1)　**1983** NYG 16 (5, rcb) **1984** SD 2 (0)　**1984** NYJ 4 (2)　**NFL** 60 (18) [5 yrs]

DENNIS, PAT Patrick, DB, 6´0˝/207 lbs; Louisiana-Monroe; 2000: KC, rnd 5; B6/3/1978 Shreveport, LA　**2000** KC 16 (13, LCB)　**2001** Dal 11 (0)　**2002** Hou 3 (0)　**2004** Was 11 (0) **NFL** 41 (13) [4 yrs]

DENNISON, DOUG William Douglas, RB, 6´1˝/202 lbs; Kutztown; B12/18/1951 Lancaster, PA

1974	Dal	12	16	52	3.3(14)	4	2	23	11.5(13)	0	—	—	—	—	—	—	—	—	—	k	—	24	113
1975	†Dal	13 (3)	111	383	3.5(27)	7	2	5	2.5(4)	0	—	—	—	—	—	—	—	—	—	k	—	42	523
1976	†Dal	14 (10, RB)	153	542	3.5(14)	6	8	67	8.4(33)	0	—	—	—	—	—	—	—	—	—	k	—	36	636
1977	†Dal	8	12	60	5.0(17)	1	1	9	9.0(9)	0	—	—	—	—	—	—	—	—	—	k	—	6	90
1978	Dal	5	14	75	5.4(23)	1	1	6	6.0(6)	0	—	—	—	—	—	—	—	—	—	k	—	6	106
NFL	5	52 (13)	306	1112	3.6(27)	19	14	110	7.9(33)	0	—	—	—	—	—	—	—	—	—	k	—	114	1466

DENNISON, GLENN Glenn, TE, 6´3˝/225 lbs; Miami (FL); 1984: NYJ, rnd 2; B11/17/1961 Beaver Falls, PA

1984	NYJ	16 (9, te)	1	4	4.0(4)	0	16	141	8.8(20)	1	—	—	—	—	—	—	—	—	—	—	—	6	80
1987	Was	2 (1)	—	—	—	—	2	8	4.0(5)	0	—	—	—	—	—	—	—	—	—	—	—	0	4
NFL	2	18 (10)	1	4	4.0(4)	0	18	149	8.3(20)	1	—	—	—	—	—	—	—	—	—	—	—	6	84

DENNISON, RICK Rick Steven, LB, 6´3˝/220 lbs; Colorado State; B6/22/1958 Kalispell, MT　**1982** Den 9 (0)　**1983**†Den 16 (1)　**1984**†Den 16 (15, LILB)　**1985** Den 15 (7, lilb) **1986**†Den 16 (2)　**1987**†Den 12 (0)　**1988** Den 16 (16, RILB)　**1989**†Den 15 (11, RILB)　**1990** Den 13 (0)　**NFL** 128 (52) [9 yrs]

DENNY, EARL Earl Livingston, RB, 6´1˝/205 lbs; Missouri; 1967: Min, rnd 3; B7/21/1945 El Paso, TX　**1967** Min 13

| **1968** | †Min | 14 | 2 | 9 | 4.5(9) | 0 | — | — | — | — | — | — | — | — | — | — | — | — | — | k | — | 0 | -17 |
| **NFL** | 2 | 27 | 2 | 9 | 4.5(9) | 0 | — | — | — | — | — | — | — | — | — | — | — | — | — | k | — | 0 | -14 |

DENSON, AL Alfred Freddie, FL-TE-SE-WR, 6´2˝/208 lbs; Florida A&M; 1964: Den, rnd 6/Phi, rnd 6; B1/2/1942 Jacksonville, FL

1964	Den-A	14 (fl)	—	—	—	—	25	383	15.3(82)	1	—	—	—	—	—	—	—	—	—	—	—	8	197
1965	Den-A	14 (te)	1	-4	-4.0(-4)	0	9	102	11.3(19)	0	—	—	—	—	—	—	—	—	—	—	—	0	47
1966	Den-A☆	14 (TE)	—	—	—	—	36	725	20.1(65)	3	—	—	—	—	—	—	—	—	—	—	—	18	378
1967	Den-A★	14 (FL)	1	-2	-2.0(-2)	0	46	899	19.5(68)	11	—	—	—	—	—	—	—	—	—	—	—	66	503
1968	Den-A	8 (SE)	—	—	—	—	34	586	17.2(44)	5	—	—	—	—	—	—	—	—	—	—	—	30	318
1969	Den-A★	13 (13, SE)	1	9	9.0(9)	0	53	809	15.3(62)	10	—	—	—	—	—	—	—	—	—	—	—	60	464
1970	Den	14 (14, WR)	—	—	—	—	47	646	13.7(42)	2	—	—	—	—	—	—	—	—	—	—	—	12	333
1971	Min	7	1	0	0.0(0)	0	10	125	12.5(17)	0	—	—	—	—	—	—	—	—	—	—	—	0	63
NFL	8	98 (27)	4	3	0.8(9)	0	260	4275	16.4(82)	32	—	—	—	—	—	—	—	—	—	—	—	194	2301

DENSON, AUTRY Autry Lamont, RB, 5´10˝/193 lbs; Notre Dame; 1999: TB, rnd 7; B12/8/1976 Davie, FL

1999	†Mia	6 (1)	28	98	3.5(20)	0	4	28	7.0(10)	0	—	—	—	—	—	—	—	—	—	—	—	0	112
2000	†Mia	11 (0)	31	108	3.5(12)	0	14	105	7.5(28)	0	—	—	—	—	—	—	—	—	—	k	—	0	356
2001	†ChiB	16 (0)	1	4	4.0(4)	0	—	—	—	—	—	—	—	—	—	—	—	—	—	kp	—	0	193
2002	Ind	1 (0)	2	2	1.0(3)	0	—	—	—	—	—	—	—	—	—	—	—	—	—	k	—	0	10
NFL	4	34 (1)	62	212	3.4(20)	0	18	133	7.4(28)	0	—	—	—	—	—	—	—	—	—	kp	—	0	671

DENSON, DAMON Damon Michael, G, 6´4˝/305 lbs; Michigan; 1997: NE, rnd 4; B2/8/1975 Pittsburgh, PA　**1997** NE 1 (0)　**1998**†NE 11 (4)　**1999** NE 2 (0)　**NFL** 14 (4) [3 yrs]

DENSON, KEITH Keith Armando, WR, 5´8˝/165 lbs; San Diego State; B8/30/1952 Camp Lejeune, NC　**1976** NYJ 2

YEAR	TEAM	G (GS, POS)	RUSH	YD	AVG(LG)	TD	REC	YD	AVG(LG)	TD	PASS	COMP	PCT	YD	AVG(LG)	TD	INT	SK	YD	QBR	KPR	OTD	PTS	TAY

DENSON, MOSES   Moses, RB, 6´1˝/215 lbs; Maryland-Eastern Shore; 1972: Was, rnd 8; B7/6/1944 Vredenburgh, AL

1974	†Was	13(8, FB)	103	391	3.8(23)	0	26	174	6.7(27)	2	—	—	—	—	—	—	—	—	—	—	k	—	12	507
1975	Was	13(9, FB)	56	195	3.5(14)	0	13	81	6.2(14)	0	—	—	—	—	—	—	—	—	—	—		—	0	236
NFL	2	26(17)	159	586	3.7(23)	0	39	255	6.5(27)	2	—	—	—	—	—	—	—	—	—	—	k	—	12	743

DENT, BURNELL   Burnell Joseph, LB, 6´1˝/236 lbs; Tulane; 1986: GB, rnd 6; B3/16/1963 New Orleans, LA   **1986** GB 16 (1)   **1987** GB 9 (0)   **1988** GB 10 (3)   **1989** GB 16 (1)
1990 GB 15 (2)   **1991** GB 14 (1)   **1992** GB 15 (3)   **NFL** 95 (11) [7 yrs]

DENT, RICHARD   Richard Lamar, DE, 6´5˝/265 lbs; Tennessee State; 1983: Chi, rnd 8; B12/13/1960 Atlanta, GA [S]   **1983** ChiB 16 (3)   **1984**†ChiB★16 (10, RDE)
1985†ChiB★16 (16, RDE)   **1986**†ChiB 16 (14, RDE)   **1987**ChiB 12 (12, RDE)   **1988** ChiB☆13 (12, RDE)   **1989** ChiB 15 (15, RDE)   **1990**†ChiB★16 (16, RDE)
1991†ChiB 16 (16, RDE)   **1992** ChiB 16 (16, RDE)   **1993** ChiB★16 (16, RDE)   **1994**†SF 2 (2)   **1995** ChiB 3 (1)   **1996**†Ind 16 (1)   **1997** Phi 15 (0)   **NFL** 203 (150) [15 yrs]

DENTON, BOB   Robert George, DE-T, 6´3˝/244 lbs; Pacific; 1959: Cle, rnd 6; B7/24/1934 Fresno, CA   **1960** Cle 12   **1961** Min 14   **1962** Min 14   **1963** Min 14   **1964** Min 14
NFL 68 [5 yrs]

DENTON, TIM   Tim, DB, 5´11˝/182 lbs; Oklahoma; Sam Houston State; B2/2/1973 Galveston, TX   **1998** Was 16 (0)   **1999**†Was 16 (0)   **2000** SD 5 (0)   **NFL** 37 (0) [3 yrs]

DENTON, WINNIE   Winfield Kirkpatrick, G, 6´1˝/200 lbs; DePauw; B10/28/1896 Evansville, IN, D11/2/1971 Evansville, IN   **1922** Evv 1 (1)

DENVIR, JOHN   John William, G, 6´4˝/245 lbs; West Virginia; Colorado; 1962: SD, rnd 30/1961: GB, rnd 12; B4/30/1938 Connellsville, PA   **1962** Den-A 11 (LG)

DeOSSIE, STEVE   Steven Leonard, LB, 6´2˝/248 lbs; Boston College; 1984: Dal, rnd 4; B11/22/1962 Tacoma, WA   **1984** Dal 16 (0)   **1985**†Dal 16 (0)   **1986** Dal 16 (0)
1987 Dal 11 (2)   **1988** Dal 16 (1)   **1989**†NYG 9 (3)   **1990**†NYG 16 (13, LILB)   **1991** NYG 16 (2)   **1992** NYG 12 (11, RILB)   **1993** NYG 8 (0)   **1993** NYJ 7 (0)   **1994**†NE 16 (0)
1995 NE 16 (0)   **NFL** 175 (32) [12 yrs]

DePASCAL, CARMINE   Carmine Ralph, E, 6´0˝/188 lbs; Wichita State; B4/13/1918 Aliquippa, PA, D3/26/2002 Tucson, AZ   **1945** Pit 1 (0)

DePASO, TOM   Thomas James, LB, 6´2˝/222 lbs; Penn State; 1978: Cin, rnd 10; B2/22/1956 White Plains, NY   **1978** Cin 12

DePAUL, HENRY   Henry J., G, 5´11˝/225 lbs; Duquesne; B4/12/1917 Beaver Falls, PA, D10/28/1985 Beaver Falls, PA   **1945** Pit 4 (0)

DEPLER, JACK   John Charles, C-T, 5´10˝/220 lbs; Illinois; B1/6/1899 Lewistown, IL, D12/5/1970 Lewistown, IL [C]   **1921** Ham 5 (4, C)   **1929** Ora 2 (0)   **NFL** 7 (4) [2 yrs]

DEPNER, JOHN   John, E, 5´9˝/180 lbs; none; B5/2/1907, PA, D1/23/1978 Covington, KY   **1929** Day 1 (1)

DePOYSTER, JERRY   Jerry Dean, K, 6´1˝/200 lbs; Wyoming; 1968: Det, rnd 2; B7/6/1946 Omaha, NE [K]

1968	Det	14	1	20	20.0(20)	0	—	—	—	—	—	—	—	—	—	—	—	—	—	—	KP	—	27	20
1971	Oak	12	1	-14	-14.0(-14)	0	—	—	—	—	—	—	—	—	—	—	—	—	—	—	P	—	0	-14
1972	†Oak	14					—	—	—	—	—	—	—	—	—	—	—	—	—	—	P	—	0	0
NFL	3	40	2	6	3.0(20)	0	—	—	—	—	—	—	—	—	—	—	—	—	—	—	KP	—	27	6

DeRAMUS, LEE   Lee Collins, WR, 6´0˝/205 lbs; Wisconsin; 1995: NO, rnd 6; B8/24/1972 Stratford, NJ

1995	NO	8(0)	—	—	—	—	6	76	12.7(27)	0	—	—	—	—	—	—	—	—	—	—		—	0	38
1996	NO	15(4)	1	2	2.0(2)	0	15	182	12.1(28)	1	—	—	—	—	—	—	—	—	—	—		—	6	98
NFL	2	23(4)	1	2	2.0(2)	0	21	258	12.3(28)	1	—	—	—	—	—	—	—	—	—	—		—	6	136

DeRATT, JIMMY   James Harold, DB, 6´0˝/203 lbs; North Carolina; B1/19/1953 Wilson, NC   **1975** NO 6

DERBY, DEAN   Clarence Dean, DB, 6´0˝/185 lbs; Washington; 1957: LA, rnd 5; B6/11/1935 Leavenworth, WA [KI]   **1958** Pit 12 (DB)   **1959** Pit★12 (DB)   **1960** Pit☆12 (LS)
1961 Pit 5   **1961** Min 8   **1962** Min 11 (11, LCB)

| 1957 | Pit | 8 | 18 | 49 | 2.7(7) | 1 | 4 | 79 | 19.8(36) | 0 | — | — | — | — | — | — | — | — | — | — | Kkp | — | 15 | 133 |
| NFL | 6 | 68(11) | 18 | 49 | 2.7(7) | 1 | 4 | 79 | 19.8(36) | 0 | — | — | — | — | — | — | — | — | — | — | Kkpi | — | 15 | 241 |

DERBY, GLENN   Glenn Evans, T-G, 6´6˝/290 lbs; Wisconsin; 1988: NO, rnd 8; B6/27/1964 Oconomowoc, WI   **1989** NO 3 (0)   **1990** NO 4 (0)   **NFL** 7 (0) [2 yrs]

DERBY, JOHN   John Leslie, LB, 6´0˝/232 lbs; Iowa; B3/24/1968 Oconomowoc, WI   **1992** Det 1 (0)

DERCHER, DAN   Daniel Lawrence, T, 6´5˝/293 lbs; Kansas; B6/2/1976 Kansas City, KS   **1999** SF 9 (0)   **2000** SF 2 (0)   **NFL** 11 (0) [2 yrs]

DEREMER, ART   Arthur Martin, C, 6´3˝/208 lbs; Niagara; 1942: Bkn, rnd 13; B12/16/1917 Pittsburgh, PA, D3/14/2001 Pittsburgh, PA   **1942** Bkn 5 (0)

DeRIGGI, FRED   Fred John, NT, 6´2˝/265 lbs; Syracuse; 1990: Buf, rnd 7; B1/15/1967 Scranton, PA   **1990** NE 2 (0)

DERLETH, ROBERT   Robert J., T, 6´3˝/230 lbs; Michigan; 1944: Det, rnd 29/1947: ChiR-A, rnd 3; B1922 Marquette, MI   **1947** Det 1 (0)

DeROGATIS, AL   Albert John, DT-T, 6´4˝/238 lbs; Duke; 1949: NYG, rnd 2/1947: SF-A, rnd 16; B5/5/1927 Newark, NJ, D12/26/1995 Neptune, NJ   **1949** NYG 11 (7, RT)
1950†NYG◇12 (RDT)   **1951** NYG★11 (RDT)   **1952** NYG☆12   **NFL** 46 (7) [4 yrs]

DeROO, BRIAN   Brian Charles, WR, 6´3˝/193 lbs; Redlands; 1978: NYG, rnd 5; B4/25/1956 Redlands, CA

1979	Bal	16(1)	—	—	—	—	4	82	20.5(67)	1	—	—	—	—	—	—	—	—	—	—		—	6	46
1980	Bal	16(0)	—	—	—	—	2	34	17.0(18)	0	—	—	—	—	—	—	—	—	—	—		—	0	17
1981	Bal	16(0)	—	—	—	—	1	38	38.0(38)	0	—	—	—	—	—	—	—	—	—	—		—	0	19
NFL	3	48(1)	—	—	—	—	7	154	22.0(67)	1	—	—	—	—	—	—	—	—	—	—		—	6	82

DeROSE, DAN   Daniel Eugene, LB, 6´0˝/230 lbs; Colorado; Southern Colorado; B1/25/1962   **1987** NYG 3 (2)

DERR, BEN   Benjamin Harrison, B, 5´10˝/180 lbs; Pennsylvania; B6/25/1892 Turton, SD, D7/3/1977 Mesa, AZ   **1920** ChiT 3 (2)   **1921** Ham 4 (4, WB)   **NFL** 7 (6) [2 yrs]

DES JARDIEN, PAUL   Paul Raymond, C-E, 6´4˝/210 lbs; Chicago; B8/24/1893 Coffeyville, KS, D3/7/1956 Monrovia, CA   **1920** ChiT☆8 (7, C)   **1922** Min 1 (0)   **NFL** 9 (7) [2 yrs]

DeSANTIS, DAN   Daniel Joseph, HB, 6´0˝/180 lbs; Niagara; B9/20/1918 Niagara Falls, NY [K]

| 1941 | Phi | 11(4) | 45 | 125 | 2.8(26) | 0 | 4 | 53 | 13.3(19) | 0 | 7 | 3 | 42.9 | 78 | 11.1(40) | 1 | 1 | — | — | — | KPkpi | — | 1 | 272 |

DESCHAINE, DICK   Richard, K, 6´0˝/206 lbs; none; B4/28/1932 Menomonie, MI   **1955** GB 12   **1956** GB 12   **1957** GB 12   **1958**†Cle 12   **NFL** 48 [4 yrs]

DeSHANE, CHUCK   Charles Frederick, B-G, 6´1˝/212 lbs; Alabama; B12/10/1918 Waukesha, WI [K]   **1947** Det 11 (10, RG)   **1948** Det 10 (0)   **1949** Det☆8 (1)

1945	Det	9(5, wb)	—	—	—	—	2	29	14.5(17)	0	—	—	—	—	—	—	—	—	—	—	Kpi	2	12	177
1946	Det	10(6, BB)	2	3	1.5(2)	0	2	13	6.5(13)	0	1	0	0.0	0	0.0	0	0	—	—	—	Ki	—	10	8
NFL	5	48(22)	2	3	1.5(2)	0	4	42	10.5(17)	0	1	0	0.0	0	0.0	0	0	—	—	—	Kpi	2	22	179

DESKIN, VERSIL   Virgil Eugene, E, 6´0˝/200 lbs; Drake; B2/14/1913 Avery, IA, D3/7/1992 Ankeny, IA

1935	ChiC	1(0)	—	—	—	—	—	—	—	—	—	—	—	—	—	—	—	—	—	—		—	0	
1936	ChiC	9(0)	—	—	—	—	3	60	20.0	1	—	—	—	—	—	—	—	—	—	—		—	6	35
1937	ChiC	11(8, RE)	—	—	—	—	3	48	16.0	1	—	—	—	—	—	—	—	—	—	—		—	6	29
1938	ChiC	11(1)	—	—	—	—	6	57	9.5	0	—	—	—	—	—	—	—	—	—	—		—	0	29
1939	ChiC	10(3)	—	—	—	—	4	84	21.0	0	—	—	—	—	—	—	—	—	—	—		—	0	42
NFL	5	42(12)	—	—	—	—	16	249	15.6	2	—	—	—	—	—	—	—	—	—	—		—	12	135

ᵒDESKINS, DON   Donald Richard, DT-G, 6´3˝/240 lbs; Michigan; 1960: Oak, rnd 1; B5/10/1932 Brooklyn, NY   **1960** Oak-A 14 (RDT)

DESS, DARRELL   Darrell Charles, G-T, 6´0˝/243 lbs; North Carolina State; 1958: Was, rnd 11; B7/11/1935 New Castle, PA   **1958** Pit 12 (rg)   **1959**†NYG 12 (LG)   **1961**†NYG 14 (LG)
1962†NYG◇14 (LG)   **1963**†NYG★14 (LG)   **1964** NYG 14 (LG)   **1965** Was 13   **1966** Was 1   **1966** NYG 10   **1968** NYG 13 (RG)   **1969** NYG 6

1960	NYG	9(LG)	—	—	—	—	1	3	3.0(3)	0	—	—	—	—	—	—	—	—	—	—		—	0	2
1967	NYG	14(RG)	0	1	(1)	1	—	—	—	—	—	—	—	—	—	—	—	—	—	—		—	6	11
NFL	12	146	0	1	(1)	1	1	3	3.0(3)	0	—	—	—	—	—	—	—	—	—	—		—	6	13

DeSTEFANO, FRED   Frederick Walter, B, /195 lbs; Princeton; Columbia; Northwestern; B4/4/1900 Coal City, IL, D6/27/1974 Houston, TX   **1924** ChiC 4 (1), 6   **1925** ChiC 2 (1)
NFL 6 (2) [2 yrs]

DeSUTTER, WAYNE   Wayne Edward, T, 6´4˝/255 lbs; Illinois; Western Illinois; 1966: Buf, rnd 12/Det, rnd 6; B5/17/1944 Geneseo, IL   **1966**†Buf-A 14

DETERS, HAROLD   Harold Lee, K, 6´0˝/200 lbs; North Carolina State; 1967: Dal, rnd 12; B1/16/1944 Du Bois, PA [K]   **1967** Dal 3

DETMER, KOY   Koy Dennis, QB, 6´1˝/195 lbs; Colorado; 1997: Phi, rnd 7; B7/5/1973 San Antonio, TX

1998	Phi	8(5, qb)	7	20	2.9(8)	0	—	—	—	—	181	97	53.6	1011	5.6(61)	5	5	5	29	—	—	—	0	351
1999	Phi	1(1)	2	-2	-1.0(-1)	0	—	—	—	—	29	10	34.5	181	6.2(50)	3	2	—	—	—	—	—	0	24
2000	†Phi	16(0)	1	8	8.0(8)	0	—	—	—	—	1	0	0.0	0	0.0	0	1	—	—	—	—	—	0	-32

YEAR	TEAM	G (GS, POS)	RUSH	YD	AVG (LG)	TD	REC	YD	AVG (LG)	TD	PASS	COMP	PCT	YD	AVG (LG)	TD	INT	SK	YD	QBR	KPR	OTD	PTS	TAY
2001	†Phi	16(0)	8	6	0.8(14)	0	—	—	—	—	14	5	35.7	51	3.6(16)	0	1	1	9	—	—	—	0	-9
2002	†Phi	14(1)	2	4	2.0(3)	1	—	—	—	—	28	19	67.9	224	8.0(37)	2	0	1	8	—	—	—	6	136
2003	†Phi	16(0)	—	—	—	—	—	—	—	—	5	3	60.0	32	6.4(15)	0	0	—	—	—	—	—	0	16
2004	†Phi	16(1)	10	-7	-0.7(2)	0	—	—	—	—	40	18	45.0	207	5.2(31)	0	2	2	16	—	—	—	0	17
2005	Phi	16(0)	1	1	1.0(1)	0	—	—	—	—	56	32	57.1	238	4.3(24)	0	3	3	15	—	—	—	0	0
NFL	8	103(8)	31	30	1.0(14)	1	—	—	—	—	354	184	52.0	1944	5.5(61)	10	14	12	77	—	—	—	6	502
DETMER, TY Ty Hubert, QB, 6´0˝/189 lbs; Brigham Young; 1992: GB, rnd 9; B10/30/1967 San Marcos, TX																								
1993	†GB	3(0)	1	-2	-2.0(-2)	0	—	—	—	—	5	3	60.0	26	5.2(25)	0	0	—	—	—	—	—	0	11
1995	GB	4(0)	3	3	1.0(5)	0	—	—	—	—	16	8	50.0	81	5.1(25)	1	1	—	—	—	—	—	0	9
1996	†Phi	13(11, QB)	31	59	1.9(9)	1	—	—	—	—	401	238	59.4	2911	7.3(42)	15	13	27	171	—	—	—	6	1080
1997	Phi	8(7, QB)	14	46	3.3(14)	1	—	—	—	—	244	134	54.9	1567	6.4(57)	7	6	19	94	—	—	—	6	635
1998	†SF	16(1)	8	7	0.9(10)	0	—	—	—	—	38	24	63.2	312	8.2(36)	4	3	5	20	—	—	—	0	63
1999	Cle	5(2)	6	38	6.3(11)	1	—	—	—	—	91	47	51.6	548	6.0(35)	4	2	4	26	—	—	—	6	262
2001	Det	4(4, qb)	9	26	2.9(9)	0	—	—	—	—	151	92	60.9	906	6.0(27)	3	10	12	75	—	—	—	0	94
2003	Det	1(0)	—	—	—	—	—	—	—	—	—	—	—	—	—	—	—	—	—	—	—	—	—	—
NFL	8	54(25)	72	177	2.5(14)	3	—	—	—	—	946	546	57.7	6351	6.7(57)	34	35	67	386	74.7	—	—	18	2153
DETWILER, CHUCK Charles Michael, DB, 6´0˝/185 lbs; Utah State; B3/6/1947 Rome, NY **1970** SD 11 **1971** SD 1 **1972** SD 13 (FS) **1973** SL 10 (fs) **NFL** 35 [4 yrs]																								
DETWILER, JOHN John Ely, FB-BB, 5´8˝/190 lbs; Kansas; B3/14/1892 Smith Center, KS, D2/6/1988 Smith Center, KS **1923** Ham 3 (1) **1924** Ham 1 (0) **NFL** 4 (1) [2 yrs]																								
DEVAUGHN, DENNIS Dennis Wayne, DB, 5´10˝/175 lbs; Bishop; 1982: Phi, rnd 5; B10/28/1960 Los Angeles, CA **1982** Phi 4 (0) **1983** Phi 9 (0) **NFL** 13 (0) [2 yrs]																								
DEVINE, KEVIN Kevin L., DB, 5´9˝/179 lbs; California; B12/11/1974 Jackson, MS **1997**†Jax 12 (0) **1998**†Jax 5 (0) **1999** Min 2 (0) **NFL** 19 (0) [3 yrs]																								
DEVITA, ROB Robert Gerard, LB, 6´2˝/222 lbs; Illinois Benedictine; Eastern Illinois; B11/29/1965 **1987** Sea 1 (0)																								
DEVLEIGHER, CHUCK Charles, DT, 6´4˝/265 lbs; Memphis; 1968: Buf, rnd 14; B1/2/1947 Paterson, NJ **1969** Buf-A 4																								
DEVLIN, CHRIS Christopher James, LB, 6´2˝/226 lbs; Penn State; 1975: Cin, rnd 7; B11/22/1953 Wexford, PA **1975** Cin 14 **1976** Cin 9 **1978** Cin 1 (1) **1978** ChiB 6 (1) **NFL** 30 (2) [3 yrs]																								
DEVLIN, JOE Joseph Gregory, T-G, 6´5˝/261 lbs; Iowa; 1976: Buf, rnd 2; B2/23/1954 Phoenixville, PA **1976** Buf 14 (2) **1977** Buf 14 (14, RT) **1978** Buf 14 (14, RT) **1979** Buf 16 (16, RT) **1980**†Buf 16 (16, RT) **1981**†Buf 16 (16, RT) **1982** Buf 9 (9, RT) **1984** Buf 16 (16, RT) **1985** Buf 16 (16, RT) **1986** Buf 16 (16, RT) **1987** Buf 12 (12, RT) **1988**†Buf 16 (16, RT) **1989**†Buf 16 (16, RG) **NFL** 191 (179) [13 yrs]																								
DEVLIN, MARK Mark H., BB, 5´10˝/180 lbs; Holy Cross; B12/5/1894 Lawrence, MA, D12/11/1973 Lawrence, MA **1920** Cle 4 (2) **1920** RI 1 (0) **1921** NYG 1 (1, BB) **NFL** 6 (3) [2 yrs]																								
DEVLIN, MIKE Michael Richard, C-G, 6´2˝/305 lbs; Iowa; 1993: Buf, rnd 5; B11/16/1969 Blacksburg, VA **1993**†Buf 12 (0) **1994** Buf 16 (0) **1995**†Buf 16 (0) **1996** Arz 11 (11, C) **1997** Arz 15 (13, C) **1998**†Arz 15 (3) **1999** Arz 16 (0) **NFL** 101 (27) [7 yrs]																								
DEVOE, TODD Todd, WR, 6´2˝/198 lbs; Central Missouri State; B4/5/1980 Fort Lauderdale, FL																								
2005	†Den	14(0)	—	—	—	—	9	87	9.7(44)	1	—	—	—	—	—	—	—	—	—	—	—	—	6	49
DEVRIES, JARED Jared, DE, 6´4˝/272 lbs; Iowa; 1999: Det, rnd 3; B6/11/1976 Aplington, IA **1999** Det 2 (0) **2000** Det 15 (1) **2001** Det 11 (0) **2002** Det 10 (0) **2003** Det 13 (2) **2004** Det 15 (0) **2005** Det 16 (0) **NFL** 82 (3) [7 yrs]																								
DEVRIES, JED Jed, T, 6´6˝/300 lbs; Utah State; B1/6/1971 Ogden, UT **1995** Cle 2 (0)																								
DEWAR, JIM James Alexander, B, 6´1˝/190 lbs; Indiana; 1947: Cle-A, rnd 10/LARm, rnd 19; B6/17/1922 Oak Park, IL, D6/30/1989 **1948** Bkn-A 1 (0)																								
1947	Cle-A	10(0)	14	64	4.6	1	—	—	—	—	—	—	—	—	—	—	—	—	—	—	kpi	—	6	126
AAFC	2	11(0)	14	64	4.6	1	—	—	—	—	—	—	—	—	—	—	—	—	—	—	—	—	6	74
DEWEESE, EBBY Everett, G-BB, 6´0˝/188 lbs; none; B1906 Miamisburg, OH, deceased **1927** Day 6 (4, RG) **1928** Day 1 (0) **1930** Por 11 (4) **NFL** 18 (8) [3 yrs]																								
DEWELL, BILLY William Austin, E, 6´4˝/208 lbs; SMU; 1939: Phi, rnd 4; B1/2/1917 Concordia, KS, D1/19/2000 Dallas, TX																								
1940	ChiC	4(3)	—	—	—	—	2	29	14.5	0	—	—	—	—	—	—	—	—	—	—	—	—	0	15
1941	ChiC★	11(8, LE)	1	-1	-1.0(-1)	0	27	362	13.4(30)	1	—	—	—	—	—	—	—	—	—	—	—	—	6	185
1945	ChiC	9(5, LE)	—	—	—	—	26	370	14.2(70)	1	—	—	—	—	—	—	—	—	—	—	—	—	6	190
1946	ChiC☆	11(6, LE)	—	—	—	—	27	643	**23.8**(**82**)	**7**	—	—	—	—	—	—	—	—	—	—	—	—	42	357
1947	†ChiC	11(9, LE)	—	—	—	—	42	576	13.7(46)	4	—	—	—	—	—	—	—	—	—	—	—	—	24	308
1948	†ChiC	11(11, LE)	—	—	—	—	33	442	13.4(48)	2	—	—	—	—	—	—	—	—	—	—	—	—	12	231
1949	ChiC	12(9, LE)	—	—	—	—	20	235	11.8(25)	2	—	—	—	—	—	—	—	—	—	—	—	—	12	128
NFL	7	69(51)	1	-1	-1.0(-1)	0	177	2657	15.0(82)	17	—	—	—	—	—	—	—	—	—	—	—	—	102	1413
DEWITZ, HERB Herbert Arnold, HB, 5´9˝/175 lbs; Nebraska; B8/14/1902 Stanton, NE, D8/17/2001 Boise, ID **1927** Cle 13 (0), 12																								
DEWITZ, RUFE Rufus Elbeno, B, 5´9˝/175 lbs; Nebraska; B6/9/1900 Stanton, NE, D3/1984 Roselle, IL **[K]** **1924** KC 8 (7, WB), 4 **1926** KC 8 (5, WB), 6 **NFL** 16 (12), 10 [2 yrs]																								
DEWVEALL, WILLARD Willard Charles, E, 6´4˝/224 lbs; SMU; 1958: ChiB, rnd 2; B4/29/1936 Springtown, TX																								
1959	ChiB	11	—	—	—	—	20	420	21.0(76)	3	—	—	—	—	—	—	—	—	—	—	—	—	18	225
1960	ChiB☆	12	—	—	—	—	43	804	18.7(**91**)	5	—	—	—	—	—	—	—	—	—	—	—	—	30	427
1961	†Hou-A	7	—	—	—	—	12	200	16.7(66)	3	—	—	—	—	—	—	—	—	—	—	—	—	18	115
1962	†Hou-A✧	14(WR)	—	—	—	—	33	576	17.5(**98**)	5	—	—	—	—	—	—	—	—	—	—	—	—	30	313
1963	Hou-A	14(WR)	—	—	—	—	58	752	13.0(35)	7	—	—	—	—	—	—	—	—	—	—	—	—	42	411
1964	Hou-A	14(TE)	—	—	—	—	38	552	14.5(60)	4	—	—	—	—	—	—	—	—	—	—	—	—	24	296
NFL	6	72	—	—	—	—	204	3304	16.2(98)	27	—	—	—	—	—	—	—	—	—	—	—	—	162	1787
DEXTER, JAMES James Roland, T-G, 6´7˝/319 lbs; South Carolina; 1996: Arz, rnd 5; B3/3/1973 Fort Ord, CA **1996** Arz 6 (1) **1997** Arz 10 (9, RT) **1998**†Arz 16 (16, RT) **1999** Arz 8 (5, lg) **2000** Car 9 (2) **NFL** 49 (33) [5 yrs]																								
DIAL, ALAN Alan Roy, DB, 6´1˝/188 lbs; UCLA; B2/2/1965 Anniston, AL **1989** Phi 1 (0)																								
DIAL, BENJY Benjamin Franklin, QB, 6´1˝/185 lbs; Eastern New Mexico; 1966: Pit, rnd 13; B5/21/1943 Memphis, TN, D4/5/2001 Duncanville, TX																								
1967	Phi	1	—	—	—	—	—	—	—	—	3	1	33.3	5	1.7(5)	0	0	1	18	—	—	—	0	3
DIAL, BUDDY Gilbert Leroy, SE-FL, 6´1˝/194 lbs; Rice; 1959: NYG, rnd 2; B1/17/1937 Ponca City, OK																								
1959	Pit	12(fl)	—	—	—	—	16	428	26.8(68)	6	—	—	—	—	—	—	—	—	—	—	—	—	36	244
1960	Pit	12(SE)	1	8	8.0(8)	0	40	972	**24.3**(**70**)	9	—	—	—	—	—	—	—	—	—	—	—	—	54	539
1961	Pit★	14(SE)	3	6	2.0(15)	0	53	1047	19.8(88)	12	—	—	—	—	—	—	—	—	—	—	—	—	72	590
1962	Pit	14(SE)	—	—	—	—	50	981	19.6(62)	6	—	—	—	—	—	—	—	—	—	—	—	—	36	521
1963	Pit★	14(SE)	—	—	—	—	60	1295	**21.6**(**83**)	9	—	—	—	—	—	—	—	—	—	—	—	—	54	693
1964	Dal	10	—	—	—	—	11	178	16.2(41)	0	—	—	—	—	—	—	—	—	—	—	—	—	0	89
1965	Dal	12(7, FL)	—	—	—	—	17	283	16.6(46)	1	—	—	—	—	—	—	—	—	—	—	—	—	6	147
1966	†Dal	10(3)	—	—	—	—	14	252	18.0(39)	1	—	—	—	—	—	—	—	—	—	—	—	—	6	131
NFL	8	98(10)	4	14	3.5(15)	0	261	5436	20.8(88)	44	—	—	—	—	—	—	—	—	—	—	—	—	264	2952
DIAMOND, BILL William Michael, G, 6´0˝/240 lbs; Miami (FL); 1962: SL, rnd 13; B8/14/1939 Miami, FL **1963** KC-A 5																								
DIAMOND, CHARLEY Charles John, T, 6´2˝/262 lbs; Miami (FL); B7/19/1936 Miami, FL **1960** DalT-A 14 (LT) **1961** DalT-A 14 (LT) **1962**†DalT-A 14 (RT) **1963** KC-A 9 (rt) **NFL** 51 [4 yrs]																								
DIAMOND, LORENZO Lorenzo, TE, 6´3˝/260 lbs; Auburn; B12/15/1978 Biloxi, MS																								
2004	Arz	5(4)	—	—	—	—	3	19	6.3(8)	0	—	—	—	—	—	—	—	—	—	—	—	—	0	10
2005	Mia	16(7, TE)	—	—	—	—	8	54	6.8(18)	0	—	—	—	—	—	—	—	—	—	—	—	—	0	27
NFL	2	21(11)	—	—	—	—	11	73	6.6(18)	0	—	—	—	—	—	—	—	—	—	—	—	—	0	37
DIANA, RICH Richard, RB, 5´9˝/220 lbs; Yale; 1982: Mia, rnd 5; B9/6/1960 Hamden, CT																								
1982	†Mia	9(0)	8	31	3.9(7)	0	2	21	10.5(13)	0	—	—	—	—	—	—	—	—	—	—	k	—	0	42

YEAR	TEAM	G(GS, POS)	RUSH	YD	AVG(LG)	TD	REC	YD	AVG(LG)	TD	PASS COMP	PCT	YD	AVG(LG)	TD	INT	SK	YD	QBR	KPR	OTD	PTS	TAY

DIAZ, JORGE Jorge Armando, G, 6´4˝/308 lbs; Texas A&M-Kingsville; B11/15/1973 New York, NY **1996** TB 11 (6, lg) **1997**†TB 16 (16, RG) **1998** TB 12 (12, LG) **1999**†TB 13 (11, LG) **2000** Dal 9 (0) **NFL** 61 (45) [5 yrs]

DIAZ-INFANTE, DAVID Gustavo David Miguel, G-C, 6´3˝/291 lbs; San Jose State; B3/31/1964 San Jose, CA **1987** SD 3 (0) **1996** Den 9 (2) **1997**†Den 16 (7, lg) **1998**†Den 10 (0) **1999** Phi 15 (0) **2001** Den 16 (0) **NFL** 69 (9) [6 yrs]

DIBB, JOHN John, T, 6´0˝/200 lbs; Army; B12/24/1903 England, D6/30/1993 Pinehurst, NC **1930** Nwk 3 (0)

DIBBLE, DORNE Dorne Allen, E-DB, 6´2˝/195 lbs; Michigan State; 1951: Det, rnd 3; B4/26/1929 Adrian, MI

1951	Det	12(LE)	—	—	—	—	30	613	20.4(47)	6	—	—	—	—	—	—	—	—	—	i	—	36	358
1953	†Det	12(le)	—	—	—	—	16	274	17.1(47)	3	—	—	—	—	—	—	—	—	—	—	—	18	152
1954	†Det☆	12(LE)	—	—	—	—	46	768	16.7(45)	6	—	—	—	—	—	—	—	—	—	—	—	36	414
1955	Det	8(le)	—	—	—	—	14	179	12.8(44)	2	—	—	—	—	—	—	—	—	—	—	—	12	100
1956	Det	12(LE)	1	8	8.0(8)	0	32	597	18.7(56)	2	—	—	—	—	—	—	—	—	—	—	—	12	317
1957	†Det	12	1	5	5.0(5)	0	8	121	15.1(23)	0	—	—	—	—	—	—	—	—	—	—	—	0	66
NFL	6	68	2	13	6.5(8)	0	146	2552	17.5(56)	19	—	—	—	—	—	—	—	—	—	i	—	114	1405

DIBERNARDO, RICK Richard Anthony, LB, 6´3˝/230 lbs; Notre Dame; B6/12/1964 Redondo Beach, CA **1986** SL 16 (0) **1987** LARm 3 (3) **NFL** 19 (3) [2 yrs]

DICK, JIM James Brian, LB, 6´1˝/230 lbs; North Dakota State; B6/18/1964, IL **1987** Min 3 (2)

DICKEL, DAN Daniel Lee, LB, 6´3˝/225 lbs; Iowa; 1974: Bal, rnd 7; B8/24/1952 Fort Riley, KS **1974** Bal 14 **1975** Bal 14 **1976** Bal 14 **1977** Bal 14 **1978** Det 4 **NFL** 60 [5 yrs]

DICKERSON, ANDY Andrew Charles, G, 6´5˝/260 lbs; Miami (FL); California Lutheran; B3/10/1963 Philadelphia, PA **1987** LARd 1 (0)

DICKERSON, ANTHONY Anthony Charles, LB, 6´2˝/220 lbs; SMU; B6/9/1957 Texas City, TX **1980**†Dal 16 (0) **1981**†Dal 16 (0) **1982**†Dal 9 (1) **1983**†Dal 16 (15, RLB) **1984** Dal 16 (15, RLB) **1985** Buf 16 (0) **NFL** 89 (31) [6 yrs]

DICKERSON, ERIC Eric Demetric, RB, 6´3˝/220 lbs; SMU; 1983: LARm, rnd 1; B9/2/1960 Sealy, TX; HOF 1999

1983	†LARm★	16(16, RB)	**390**	**1808**	4.6(85)	18	51	404	7.9(37)	2	—	—	—	—	—	—	—	—	—	—	—	120	**2200**
1984	†LARm★	16(16, RB)	379	**2105**	5.6(66)	**14**	21	139	6.6(19)	0	1	0	0.0	0	0.0	0	1	—	—	—	—	84	**2275**
1985	†LARm	14(14, RB)	292	1234	4.2(43)	12	20	126	6.3(33)	0	—	—	—	—	—	—	—	—	—	—	—	72	1417
1986	†LARm★	16(16, RB)	**404**	1821	4.5(42)	11	26	205	7.9(28)	0	1	1	100.0	15	15.0(15)	1	0	—	—	—	—	66	**2046**
1987	LARm	3(2)	60	277	4.6(57)	1	5	38	7.6(13)	0	—	—	—	—	—	—	—	—	—	—	—	6	306
1987	†Ind★	9(8, RB)	223	1011	4.5(53)	5	13	133	10.2(20)	0	—	—	—	—	—	—	—	—	—	—	—	30	1128
1988	Ind★	16(16, RB)	**388**	1659	4.3(41)	14	36	377	10.5(50)	1	—	—	—	—	—	—	—	—	—	—	—	90	**1993**
1989	Ind◇	15(14, RB)	314	1311	4.2(21)	7	30	211	7.0(22)	1	0	0	0.0	0	0.0	0	0	1	6	—	—	48	1492
1990	Ind	11(8, RB)	166	677	4.1(43)	4	18	92	5.1(19)	0	—	—	—	—	—	—	—	—	—	—	—	24	763
1991	Ind	10(9, RB)	167	536	3.2(28)	2	41	269	6.6(26)	1	—	—	—	—	—	—	—	—	—	—	—	18	696
1992	LARd	16(15, RB)	187	729	3.9(40)	2	14	85	6.1(15)	0	—	—	—	—	—	—	—	—	—	—	—	18	797
1993	Atl	4(2)	26	91	3.5(10)	0	6	58	9.7(30)	0	—	—	—	—	—	—	—	—	—	—	—	0	120
NFL	11	146(136)	2996	13259	4.4(85)	90	281	2137	7.6(50)	6	2	1	50.0	15	7.5(15)	1	1	1	6	—	—	576	15230

DICKERSON, KORI Kori, TE, 6´4˝/235 lbs; USC; B12/6/1978 Los Angeles, CA **2003**†Phi 2 (0)

DICKERSON, RON Ronald Lee, RB-WR, 6´0˝/211 lbs; Arkansas; B8/31/1971 Denver, CO **1993** KC 6 (0)

| 1994 | KC | 9(0) | 1 | 0 | 0.0(0) | 0 | 2 | 11 | 5.5(6) | 0 | — | — | — | — | — | — | — | — | — | k | — | 0 | 163 |
| NFL | 2 | 15(0) | 1 | 0 | 0.0(0) | 0 | 2 | 11 | 5.5(6) | 0 | — | — | — | — | — | — | — | — | — | k | — | 0 | 235 |

DICKEY, CHARLIE Charles Joseph, G, 6´3˝/270 lbs; Arizona; B12/31/1962 Ottumwa, IA **1987** Pit 1 (0)

DICKEY, CURTIS Curtis Raymond, RB, 6´1˝/213 lbs; Texas A&M; 1980: Bal, rnd 1; B11/27/1956 Madisonville, TX

1980	Bal	15(5, rb)	176	800	4.5(51)	11	25	204	8.2(32)	2	—	—	—	—	—	—	—	—	—	k	—	78	1048
1981	Bal	15(15, RB)	164	779	4.8(67)	7	37	419	11.3(50)	3	—	—	—	—	—	—	—	—	—	—	—	60	1074
1982	Bal	8(6, RB)	66	232	3.5(25)	1	21	228	10.9(34)	0	—	—	—	—	—	—	—	—	—	—	—	6	356
1983	Bal	16(16, RB)	254	1122	4.4(56)	4	24	483	20.1(72)	3	—	—	—	—	—	—	—	—	—	—	—	42	1419
1984	Ind	10(9, RB)	131	523	4.0(30)	3	14	135	9.6(33)	0	1	1	100.0	63	63.0(63)	1	0	—	—	—	—	18	657
1985	Ind	6(0)	9	34	3.8(11)	0	3	30	10.0(11)	0	—	—	—	—	—	—	—	—	—	—	—	0	49
1985	†Cle	1(0)	2	6	3.0(5)	0	—	—	—	—	—	—	—	—	—	—	—	—	—	—	—	0	6
1986	†Cle	14(10, RB)	135	523	3.9(47)	6	10	78	7.8(12)	0	—	—	—	—	—	—	—	—	—	—	—	36	622
NFL	7	85(61)	937	4019	4.3(67)	32	134	1577	11.8(72)	8	1	1	100.0	63	63.0(63)	1	0	—	—	—	k	—	240	5230

DICKEY, ELDRIGE Eldridge Reno, WR, 6´2˝/198 lbs; Tennessee State; 1968: Oak, rnd 1; B12/24/1945 Houston, TX

1968	†Oak-A	11	—	—	—	—	1	34	34.0(34)	0	—	—	—	—	—	—	—	—	—	kp	—	0	37
1971	Oak	7(2)	—	—	—	—	4	78	19.5(31)	1	—	—	—	—	—	—	—	—	—	—	—	6	44
NFL	2	18(2)	—	—	—	—	5	112	22.4(34)	1	—	—	—	—	—	—	—	—	—	kp	—	6	81

DICKEY, LYNN Clifford Lynn, QB, 6´3˝/214 lbs; Kansas State; 1971: Hou, rnd 3; B10/19/1949 Paola, KS **[K]**

1971	Hou	7	1	4	4.0(4)	0	—	—	—	—	57	19	33.3	315	5.5(42)	0	9	3	21	—	—	—	0	-199
1973	Hou	12(4)	6	9	1.5(6)	0	—	—	—	—	120	71	59.2	888	7.4(66)	6	10	13	138	—	K	—	1	83
1974	Hou	14(4)	3	7	2.3(7)	0	—	—	—	—	113	63	55.8	704	6.2(59)	2	8	10	73	—	—	—	0	49
1975	Hou	14	1	3	3.0(3)	0	—	—	—	—	4	2	50.0	46	11.5(28)	0	1	3	20	—	—	—	0	-14
1976	GB	10(10, QB)	11	19	1.7(12)	1	—	—	—	—	243	115	47.3	1465	6.0(69)	7	14	28	279	52.2	—	—	6	237
1977	GB	9(9, QB)	5	24	4.8(10)	0	—	—	—	—	220	113	51.4	1346	6.1(54)	5	14	21	181	51.4	—	—	0	162
1979	GB	5(3)	5	13	2.6(8)	0	—	—	—	—	119	60	50.4	787	6.6(52)	2	4	15	120	—	—	—	0	272
1980	GB	16(16, QB)	19	11	0.6(7)	1	—	—	—	—	478	278	58.2	3529	7.4(69)	15	**25**	37	314	70.0	—	—	6	861
1981	GB	13(13, QB)	19	6	0.3(13)	0	—	—	—	—	354	204	57.6	2593	7.3(75)	17	15	40	290	79.0	—	—	0	788
1982	†GB	9(9, QB)	13	19	1.5(11)	0	—	—	—	—	218	124	56.9	1790	8.2(80)	12	**14**	25	196	75.3	—	—	0	414
1983	GB☆	16(16, QB)	21	12	0.6(13)	3	—	—	—	—	484	289	59.7	**4458**	9.2(75)	**32**	**29**	40	307	87.3	—	—	18	1271
1984	GB	15(15, QB)	18	6	0.3(9)	3	—	—	—	—	401	237	59.1	3195	8.0(79)	25	**19**	32	243	85.6	—	—	18	999
1985	GB	12(10, QB)	18	-12	-0.7(3)	1	—	—	—	—	314	172	54.8	2206	7.0(63)	15	17	30	226	70.4	—	—	6	496
NFL	13	152(109)	140	121	0.9(13)	9	—	—	—	—	3125	1747	55.9	23322	7.5(95)	141	179	297	2423	70.9	K	—	55	5417

DICKEY, WALLACE Wallace, T, 6´3˝/260 lbs; Southwest Texas State; 1965: Det, rnd 15; B2/15/1941 San Antonio, TX **1968** Den-A 10 **1969** Den-A 12 **NFL** 22 [2 yrs]

DICKINSON, BO Richard Lee, FB, 6´2˝/220 lbs; Southern Mississippi; 1957: ChiB, rnd 6; B7/18/1935 Hattiesburg, MS

1960	DalT-A	14	35	143	4.1(31)	1	3	38	12.7(21)	0	—	—	—	—	—	—	—	—	—	k	—	6	171
1961	DalT-A	14	71	263	3.7(65)	3	14	209	14.9(48)	2	—	—	—	—	—	—	—	—	—	—	—	34	408
1962	Den-A	14(FB)	73	247	3.4(42)	0	60	554	9.2(33)	4	—	—	—	—	—	—	—	—	—	k	—	24	540
1963	Den-A	6	5	31	6.2(13)	0	1	9	9.0(9)	0	—	—	—	—	—	—	—	—	—	—	—	0	36
1963	Hou-A	5	1	1	1.0(1)	1	5	48	9.6(18)	0	—	—	—	—	—	—	—	—	—	—	—	6	35
1964	Oak-A	7	4	8	2.0(6)	0	3	28	9.3(18)	0	—	—	—	—	—	—	—	—	—	—	—	0	6
NFL	5	60	189	693	3.7(65)	5	86	886	10.3(48)	6	—	—	—	—	—	—	—	—	—	k	—	70	1196

DICKINSON, PARNELL Parnell, QB, 6´2˝/185 lbs; Mississippi Valley State; 1976: TB, rnd 7; B3/14/1953 Brighton, AL

| 1976 | TB | 8(1) | 13 | 103 | 7.9(46) | 0 | — | — | — | — | 39 | 15 | 38.5 | 210 | 5.4(49) | 1 | 5 | 14 | 124 | — | — | — | 0 | 13 |

DICKINSON, TOM Thomas Passmore, E, 5´8˝/175 lbs; Syracuse; B7/20/1897 Detroit, MI, deceased **1920** Det 3 (1)

DICKSON, PAUL Paul Serafin, DT-T, 6´5˝/252 lbs; Baylor; 1959: LA, rnd 1; B2/26/1937 Waco, TX **1959** LARm 10 **1960** Dal 8 (8, RT) **1961** Min 7 **1962** Min 14 (14, RDT) **1963** Min 14 (14, RDT) **1964** Min 14 (14, RDT) **1965** Min 14 (14, RDT) **1966** Min 12 (12, RDT) **1967** Min 14 (13, RDT) **1968**†Min 13 **1969**†Min 13 **1970**†Min 14 **1971** SL 5 **NFL** 152 (89) [13 yrs]

DICUS, CHUCK Charles Wayne, WR, 6´0˝/183 lbs; Arkansas; 1971: SD, rnd 7; B10/2/1948 Odessa, TX

1971	SD	14	1	-2	-2.0(-2)	0	6	89	14.8(29)	1	—	—	—	—	—	—	—	—	—	—	—	6	48
1972	SD	10(WR)	1	-11	-11.0(-11)	0	18	227	12.6(46)	2	—	—	—	—	—	—	—	—	—	—	—	12	113
NFL	2	24	2	-13	-6.5(-2)	0	24	316	13.2(46)	3	—	—	—	—	—	—	—	—	—	—	—	18	160

DIDIER, CLINT Clint Bradley, TE, 6´5˝/240 lbs; Portland State; 1981: Was, rnd 12; B4/4/1959 Connell, WA

YEAR	TEAM	G (GS, POS)	RUSH	YD	AVG (LG)	TD	REC	YD	AVG (LG)	TD	PASS	COMP	PCT	YD	AVG (LG)	TD	INT	SK	YD	QBR	KPR	OTD	PTS	TAY
1982	†Was	8(0)	—	—	—	—	2	10	5.0(8)	1	—	—	—	—	—	—	—	—	—	—	—	—	6	10
1983	†Was	16(3)	—	—	—	—	9	153	17.0(40)	4	—	—	—	—	—	—	—	—	—	—	—	1	30	97
1984	†Was	11(2)	—	—	—	—	30	350	11.7(44)	5	—	—	—	—	—	—	—	—	—	—	—	—	30	200
1985	Was	16(14, TE)	—	—	—	—	41	433	10.6(29)	4	—	—	—	—	—	—	—	—	—	—	—	—	24	237
1986	†Was	14(11, TE)	—	—	—	—	34	691	20.3(71)	4	—	—	—	—	—	—	—	—	—	—	—	—	24	366
1987	†Was	9(6, TE)	—	—	—	—	13	178	13.7(25)	1	—	—	—	—	—	—	—	—	—	—	—	—	6	94
1988	GB	15(0)	—	—	—	—	5	37	7.4(15)	1	—	—	—	—	—	—	—	—	—	—	—	—	6	24
1989	GB	16(4)	—	—	—	—	7	71	10.1(24)	1	—	—	—	—	—	—	—	—	—	—	k	—	6	26
NFL	8	105(40)	—	—	—	—	141	1923	13.6(71)	21	—	—	—	—	—	—	—	—	—	—	k	1	132	1052

DIDIO, MARK Mark Vincent, WR, 5´11˝/181 lbs; Connecticut; B2/17/1969 Syracuse, NY

YEAR	TEAM	G (GS, POS)	RUSH	YD	AVG (LG)	TD	REC	YD	AVG (LG)	TD	PASS	COMP	PCT	YD	AVG (LG)	TD	INT	SK	YD	QBR	KPR	OTD	PTS	TAY
1992	Pit	2(0)	—	—	—	—	3	39	13.0(18)	0	—	—	—	—	—	—	—	—	—	—	—	—	0	20

DIDION, JOHN John Lawrence, C-LB, 6´4˝/245 lbs; Oregon State; 1969: Was, rnd 7; B10/24/1947 Woodland, CA **1969** Was 14 **1970** Was 10 **1971** NO 14 (C) **1972** NO 14 (C) **1973** NO 14 (C) **1974** NO 14 (C) **NFL** 80 [6 yrs]

DIEDRICK, DAHRRAN Dahrran, RB, 6´0˝/225 lbs; Nebraska; B1/11/1979 Montego Bay, Jamaica **2004** Was 1 (0)

DIEHL, CHARLIE Charles Christian, G-T, 6´0˝/208 lbs; Idaho; B1/13/1905, D5/26/1981 Auburn Lake Trails, CA **1930** ChiC 6 (4) **1931** ChiC 8 (7, RG) **1934** SL 1 (1) **NFL** 15 (12) [3 yrs]

DIEHL, DAVE David Douglas, E, 6´0˝/195 lbs; Michigan State; B9/30/1918 Dansville, MI, D9/15/1994 Dansville, MI

YEAR	TEAM	G (GS, POS)	RUSH	YD	AVG (LG)	TD	REC	YD	AVG (LG)	TD	PASS	COMP	PCT	YD	AVG (LG)	TD	INT	SK	YD	QBR	KPR	OTD	PTS	TAY
1939	Det	3(1)	—	—	—	—	1	12	12.0(12)	0	—	—	—	—	—	—	—	—	—	—	—	—	0	6
1940	Det	10(2)	—	—	—	—	12	131	10.9	0	—	—	—	—	—	—	—	—	—	—	—	1	6	66
1944	Det	10(10, LE)	—	—	—	—	18	426	23.7(57)	4	—	—	—	—	—	—	—	—	—	—	—	—	24	233
1945	Det	3(0)	—	—	—	—	1	9	9.0(9)	0	—	—	—	—	—	—	—	—	—	—	—	—	0	5
NFL	4	26(13)	—	—	—	—	32	578	18.1(57)	4	—	—	—	—	—	—	—	—	—	—	—	1	30	309

DIEHL, DAVID David Michael, G-T, 6´5˝/315 lbs; Illinois; 2003: NYG, rnd 5; B9/15/1980 Chicago, IL **2003** NYG 16 (16, RG) **2004** NYG 16 (16, RT) **2005**†NYG 16 (16, LG) **NFL** 48 (48) [3 yrs]

DIEHL, JOHN John Albright, DT, 6´7˝/265 lbs; Virginia; 1958: Bal, rnd 7; B1/27/1936 Philadelphia, PA **1961** Bal 3 **1962** Bal 14 **1963** Bal 14 **1964**†Bal 14 **1965** Oak-A 8 **NFL** 53 [5 yrs]

DIEHL, WALLY Glenn Walter, FB, 6´0˝/204 lbs; Pennsylvania; Bucknell; B1905 Mount Carmel, PA, D5/29/1954 Philadelphia, PA **1928** Fra☆14 (11, FB), 30 **1929** Fra☆18 (16, FB), 36 **1930** Fra 6 (3) **NFL** 38 (30), 66 [3 yrs]

DIEKEN, DOUG Douglas Heye, T, 6´5˝/254 lbs; Illinois; 1971: Cle, rnd 6; B2/12/1949 Streator, IL **1971**†Cle 14 (5, lt) **1972**†Cle 14 (14, LT) **1973** Cle 14 (14, LT) **1974** Cle 14 (14, LT) **1975** Cle 14 (14, LT) **1976** Cle 14 (14, LT) **1977** Cle 14 (14, LT) **1978** Cle 16 (16, LT) **1979** Cle 16 (16, LT) **1980**†Cle★16 (16, LT) **1981** Cle 16 (16, LT) **1982**†Cle 9 (9, LT) **1984** Cle 16 (16, LT)

YEAR	TEAM	G (GS, POS)	RUSH	YD	AVG (LG)	TD	REC	YD	AVG (LG)	TD	PASS	COMP	PCT	YD	AVG (LG)	TD	INT	SK	YD	QBR	KPR	OTD	PTS	TAY
1983	Cle	16(16, LT)	—	—	—	—	1	14	14.0(14)	1	—	—	—	—	—	—	—	—	—	—	—	—	6	12
NFL	14	203(194)	—	—	—	—	1	14	14.0(14)	1	—	—	—	—	—	—	—	—	—	—	k	—	8	-3

DIELMAN, KRIS Kris, G, 6´4˝/310 lbs; Indiana; B2/3/1981 Goshen, IN **2003** SD 6 (0) **2004**†SD 15 (0) **2005** SD 16 (14, LG) **NFL** 37 (14) [3 yrs]

DIEM, RYAN Ryan, T-G, 6´6˝/331 lbs; Northern Illinois; 2001: Ind, rnd 4; B7/1/1979 Carol Stream, IL **2001** Ind 15 (8, rg) **2002**†Ind 16 (16, RG) **2003**†Ind 13 (13, RT) **2004**†Ind 16 (16, RT) **2005**†Ind 14 (14, RT) **NFL** 74 (67) [5 yrs]

DIERDORF, DAN Daniel Lee, T-G-C, 6´3˝/275 lbs; Michigan; 1971: SL, rnd 2; B6/29/1949 Canton, OH; HOF 1996 **1971** SL 12 (rg) **1972** SL 14 (LT) **1973** SL 14 (LT) **1974**†SL★14 (14, RT) **1975**†SL★14 (14, RT) **1976** SL★14 (RT) **1977** SL★12 (RT) **1978** SL★16 (RT) **1979** SL 2 **1980** SL★16 (16, RT) **1981** SL 16 (16, RT) **1982**†SL 9 (9, C) **1983** SL 7 (4) **NFL** 160 (73) [13 yrs]

DIERKING, SCOTT Scott Edward, RB, 5´10˝/218 lbs; Purdue; 1977: NYJ, rnd 4; B5/24/1955 Great Lakes Naval Base, IL

YEAR	TEAM	G (GS, POS)	RUSH	YD	AVG (LG)	TD	REC	YD	AVG (LG)	TD	PASS	COMP	PCT	YD	AVG (LG)	TD	INT	SK	YD	QBR	KPR	OTD	PTS	TAY
1977	NYJ	14(5, RB)	79	315	4.0(21)	0	4	29	7.3(15)	1	—	—	—	—	—	—	—	—	—	—	k	—	6	336
1978	NYJ	15(13, RB)	170	681	4.0(26)	4	19	152	8.0(17)	0	1	0	0.0	0	0.0	0	0	—	—	—	—	—	24	797
1979	NYJ	16(14, RB)	186	767	4.1(40)	3	10	121	12.1(27)	0	—	—	—	—	—	—	—	—	—	—	—	—	18	858
1980	NYJ	16(13, RB)	156	567	3.6(15)	6	19	138	7.3(22)	1	—	—	—	—	—	—	—	—	—	—	—	—	42	701
1981	†NYJ	16(4)	74	328	4.4(15)	1	26	228	8.8(23)	1	—	—	—	—	—	—	—	—	—	—	—	—	12	457
1982	†NYJ	9(0)	38	130	3.4(11)	1	12	80	6.7(13)	1	—	—	—	—	—	—	—	—	—	—	—	—	12	185
1983	NYJ	16(1)	28	113	4.0(31)	3	33	275	8.3(19)	0	—	—	—	—	—	—	—	—	—	—	—	—	18	281
1984	TB	8(2)	3	14	4.7(9)	0	1	5	5.0(5)	1	—	—	—	—	—	—	—	—	—	—	—	—	6	22
NFL	8	110(52)	734	2915	4.0(40)	18	124	1028	8.3(27)	5	1	0	0.0	0	0.0	0	0	—	—	—	k	—	138	3635

DIETER, HERB Herbert Erwin, G-T-E, 6´1˝/195 lbs; Pennsylvania; B3/3/1896 Springfield, OH, D12/3/1953 New York, NY **1922** Buf 9 (4)

DIETERICH, CHRIS Christian Jeffrey, T-G, 6´3˝/262 lbs; North Carolina State; 1980: Det, rnd 6; B7/27/1958 Freeport, NY **1980** Det 16 (3) **1981** Det 16 (0) **1982**†Det 9 (4) **1983**†Det 16 (16, LT) **1984** Det 16 (16, LG/lt) **1985** Det 16 (7, LG) **1986** Det 16 (3) **NFL** 105 (49) [7 yrs]

DIETTRICH, JOHN John Michael, K, 6´2˝/190 lbs; Ball State; B5/9/1963 Fort Wayne, IN **[K]** **1987** Hou 2 (0)

DIFILIPPO, DAVE David Edward, G, 5´10˝/210 lbs; Villanova; B10/9/1916 Philadelphia, PA, D8/29/1983 Ocean City, NJ **1941** Phi 5 (2)

DIGGS, NA'IL Na'il Ronald, LB, 6´4˝/238 lbs; Ohio State; 2000: GB, rnd 4; B7/8/1978 Phoenix, AZ **2000** GB 13 (12, LLB) **2001**†GB 16 (16, LLB) **2002**†GB 16 (16, LLB) **2003**†GB 16 (16, RLB) **2004**†GB 14 (14, RLB) **2005** GB 9 (6, llb) **NFL** 84 (80) [6 yrs]

DIGGS, SHELTON Shelton, WR, 6´1˝/190 lbs; USC; 1977: Atl, rnd 5; B4/22/1955 San Bernardino, CA

YEAR	TEAM	G (GS, POS)	RUSH	YD	AVG (LG)	TD	REC	YD	AVG (LG)	TD	PASS	COMP	PCT	YD	AVG (LG)	TD	INT	SK	YD	QBR	KPR	OTD	PTS	TAY
1977	NYJ	7	1	16	16.0(16)	0	—	—	—	—	—	—	—	—	—	—	—	—	—	—	—	—	0	16

DIGIACOMO, CURT Curt Joseph, G-C, 6´4˝/270 lbs; Arizona; B10/24/1963 San Diego, CA **1986** SD 3 (0) **1988** KC 12 (0) **NFL** 15 (0) [2 yrs]

DIGRIS, BERNIE Bernard John, T-G, 6´0˝/212 lbs; Holy Cross; B6/9/1919 Union City, CT, D11/1/1978 Roanoke, VA **1943** ChiB 2 (0)

DILFER, TRENT Trent Farris, QB, 6´4˝/225 lbs; Fresno State; 1994: TB, rnd 1; B3/13/1972 Santa Cruz, CA

YEAR	TEAM	G (GS, POS)	RUSH	YD	AVG (LG)	TD	REC	YD	AVG (LG)	TD	PASS	COMP	PCT	YD	AVG (LG)	TD	INT	SK	YD	QBR	KPR	OTD	PTS	TAY
1994	TB	5(2)	2	27	13.5(15)	0	—	—	—	—	82	38	46.3	433	5.3(42)	1	6	8	42	—	—	—	0	9
1995	TB	16(16, QB)	23	115	5.0(21)	2	—	—	—	—	415	224	54.0	2774	6.7(64)	4	18	47	331	60.1	—	—	12	822
1996	TB	16(16, QB)	32	124	3.9(19)	0	—	—	—	—	482	267	55.4	2859	5.9(45)	12	19	28	207	64.8	—	—	0	854
1997	†TB✧	16(16, QB)	33	99	3.0(17)	1	—	—	—	—	386	217	56.2	2555	6.6(59)	21	11	32	196	82.8	—	—	6	1052
1998	TB	16(16, QB)	40	141	3.5(17)	2	—	—	—	—	429	225	52.4	2729	6.4(79)	21	15	27	172	74.0	—	—	12	1031
1999	TB	10(10, QB)	35	144	4.1(28)	0	—	—	—	—	244	146	59.8	1619	6.6(62)	11	11	26	189	—	—	—	0	569
2000	†Bal	11(8, QB)	20	75	3.8(19)	0	1	-1	-1.0(-1)	0	226	134	59.3	1502	6.6(59)	12	11	23	135	—	—	—	0	446
2001	Sea	6(4)	11	17	1.5(11)	0	1	-5	-5.0(-5)	0	122	73	59.8	1014	8.3(54)	7	4	10	72	—	—	—	0	397
2002	Sea	6(6, qb)	10	27	2.7(13)	0	—	—	—	—	168	94	56.0	1182	7.0(83)	4	6	7	36	—	—	—	0	398
2003	Sea	5(0)	2	-1	-0.5(0)	0	—	—	—	—	8	4	50.0	31	3.9(14)	1	1	1	8	—	—	—	0	-21
2004	Sea	5(2)	10	14	1.4(11)	0	—	—	—	—	58	25	43.1	333	5.7(56)	1	3	4	21	—	—	—	0	66
2005	Cle	11(11, QB)	20	46	2.3(12)	0	—	—	—	—	333	199	59.8	2321	7.0(80)	11	12	23	139	76.9	—	—	0	782
NFL	12	123(107)	238	828	3.5(28)	5	2	-6	-3.0(-1)	0	2953	1646	55.7	19352	6.6(83)	106	117	236	1548	71.3	—	—	30	6401

DILGER, KEN Kenneth Ray, TE, 6´5˝/250 lbs; Illinois; 1995: Ind, rnd 2; B2/2/1971 Mariah Hill, IN

YEAR	TEAM	G (GS, POS)	RUSH	YD	AVG (LG)	TD	REC	YD	AVG (LG)	TD	PASS	COMP	PCT	YD	AVG (LG)	TD	INT	SK	YD	QBR	KPR	OTD	PTS	TAY
1995	†Ind	16(13, TE)	—	—	—	—	42	635	15.1(42)	4	—	—	—	—	—	—	—	—	—	—	—	—	24	338
1996	†Ind	16(16, TE)	—	—	—	—	42	503	12.0(51)	4	—	—	—	—	—	—	—	—	—	—	—	—	24	272
1997	Ind	14(14, TE)	—	—	—	—	27	380	14.1(43)	3	—	—	—	—	—	—	—	—	—	—	—	—	18	205
1998	Ind	16(16, TE)	—	—	—	—	31	303	9.8(27)	1	—	—	—	—	—	—	—	—	—	—	—	—	18	205
1999	†Ind	15(15, TE)	—	—	—	—	40	479	12.0(30)	2	—	—	—	—	—	—	—	—	—	—	k	—	8	156
2000	†Ind	16(16, TE)	—	—	—	—	47	538	11.4(32)	3	—	—	—	—	—	—	—	—	—	—	k	—	18	269
2001	Ind✧	16(16, TE)	—	—	—	—	32	343	10.7(44)	1	1	1	100.0	39	39.0(39)	1	0	—	—	—	—	—	8	201
2002	†TB	16(15, TE)	—	—	—	—	34	329	9.7(40)	2	—	—	—	—	—	—	—	—	—	—	—	—	12	175
2003	TB	15(15, TE)	—	—	—	—	22	244	11.1(48)	1	—	—	—	—	—	—	—	—	—	—	—	—	6	127

YEAR	TEAM	G (GS, POS)	RUSH	YD	AVG (LG)	TD	REC	YD	AVG (LG)	TD	PASS	COMP	PCT	YD	AVG (LG)	TD	INT	SK	YD	QBR	KPR	OTD	PTS	TAY
2004	TB	16(14, TE)	—	—	—	—	39	345	8.8(45)	3	—	—	—	—	—	—	—	—	—	—	—	—	20	188
NFL	10	156(150)	—	—	—	—	356	4099	11.5(51)	24	1	1	100.0	39	39.0(39)	1	0	—	—	—	k	—	150	2178

DILL, SCOTT Gerald Scott, T-G-C, 6´5˝/294 lbs; Memphis; 1988: Phx, rnd 9; B4/5/1966 Birmingham, AL **1988** Phx 13 (0) **1989** Phx 16 (0) **1990** TB 3 (2) **1991** TB 8 (0) **1992** TB 4 (3) **1993** TB 16 (16, RT/lt) **1994** TB 16 (16, RT) **1995** TB 12 (12, RT) **1996**†Min 9 (1) **1997** Min 13 (5, rg) **NFL** 110 (55) [10 yrs]

DILLAHUNT, ELLIS Ellis Arto, DB, 5´11˝/198 lbs; East Carolina; 1988: Cin, rnd 10; B11/25/1964 New Bern, NC **1988** Cin 8 (0)

DILLARD, STACEY Stacey Bertrand, NT-DT, 6´5˝/290 lbs; Oklahoma; 1992: NYG, rnd 6; B9/17/1968 Clarksville, TN **1992** NYG 12 (0) **1993**†NYG 16 (16, NT) **1994** NYG 16 (0) **1995** NYG 15 (3) **NFL** 59 (19) [4 yrs]

DILLON, BOBBY Bobby Dan, DB, 6´1˝/180 lbs; Texas; 1952: GB, rnd 3; B2/23/1930 Temple, TX [I] **1952** GB 12 (DB) **1953** GB☆10 (DB) **1954** GB☆12 (DB) **1955** GB★12 (DB) **1956** GB★12 (DB) **1957** GB★12 (DB) **1958** GB★12 (DB) **1959** GB☆12 **NFL** 94 [8 yrs]

DILLON, COREY Corey James, RB, 6´1˝/225 lbs; Washington; 1997: Cin, rnd 2; B10/24/1974 Seattle, WA

YEAR	TEAM	G (GS, POS)	RUSH	YD	AVG (LG)	TD	REC	YD	AVG (LG)	TD	PASS	COMP	PCT	YD	AVG (LG)	TD	INT	SK	YD	QBR	KPR	OTD	PTS	TAY
1997	Cin	16(6, RB)	233	1129	4.8(66)	10	27	259	9.6(28)	0	—	—	—	—	—	—	—	—	—	—	k	—	60	1451
1998	Cin	15(15, RB)	262	1130	4.3(66)	4	28	178	6.4(41)	1	—	—	—	—	—	—	—	—	—	—	—	—	30	1264
1999	Cin✧	15(15, RB)	263	1200	4.6(50)	5	31	290	9.4(23)	1	—	—	—	—	—	—	—	—	—	—	k	—	36	1389
2000	Cin✧	16(16, RB)	315	1435	4.6(80)	7	18	158	8.8(31)	0	—	—	—	—	—	—	—	—	—	—	—	—	42	1584
2001	Cin✧	16(16, RB)	**340**	1315	3.9(96)	10	34	228	6.7(17)	3	1	0	0.0	0	0.0	0	1	—	—	—	—	—	78	1504
2002	Cin	16(16, RB)	314	1311	4.2(67)	7	43	298	6.9(19)	0	—	—	—	—	—	—	—	—	—	—	—	—	42	1530
2003	Cin	13(11, rb)	138	541	3.9(39)	2	11	71	6.5(14)	0	—	—	—	—	—	—	—	—	—	—	—	—	12	597
2004	†NE✧	15(14, RB)	345	1635	4.7(44)	12	15	103	6.9(20)	1	—	—	—	—	—	—	—	—	—	—	—	—	80	1812
2005	†NE	12(10, RB)	209	733	3.5(29)	12	22	181	8.2(25)	1	—	—	—	—	—	—	—	—	—	—	—	—	78	949
NFL	9	134(119)	2419	10429	4.3(96)	69	229	1766	7.7(41)	7	1	0	0.0	0	0.0	0	1	—	—	—	k	—	458	12078

DILLON, TERRY Terry Gilbert, DB, 6´0˝/193 lbs; Montana; 1963: Oak, rnd 18; B8/18/1941 Waukesha, WI, D5/28/1964 Tarkio, MT **1963** Min 7

DILS, STEVE Stephen Whitfield, QB, 6´1˝/190 lbs; Stanford; 1979: Min, rnd 4; B12/8/1955 Seattle, WA

YEAR	TEAM	G (GS, POS)	RUSH	YD	AVG (LG)	TD	REC	YD	AVG (LG)	TD	PASS	COMP	PCT	YD	AVG (LG)	TD	INT	SK	YD	QBR	KPR	OTD	PTS	TAY
1979	Min	1	—	—	—	—	—	—	—	—	—	—	—	—	—	—	—	—	—	—	—	—	—	—
1980	†Min	16(1)	3	26	8.7(19)	0	—	—	—	—	51	32	62.7	352	6.9(58)	3	0	4	32	—	—	—	0	217
1981	Min	2(2)	4	14	3.5(7)	0	—	—	—	—	102	54	52.9	607	6.0(44)	1	2	8	66	—	—	—	0	243
1982	†Min	9(0)	1	5	5.0(5)	0	—	—	—	—	26	11	42.3	68	2.6(12)	0	0	1	8	—	—	—	0	39
1983	Min	16(12, QB)	16	28	1.8(8)	0	—	—	—	—	444	239	53.8	2840	6.4(68)	11	16	37	254	66.8	—	—	0	863
1984	Min	3(0)	—	—	—	—	—	—	—	—	—	—	—	—	—	—	—	—	—	—	—	—	—	—
1984	†LARm	7(0)	—	—	—	—	—	—	—	—	7	4	57.1	44	6.3(14)	1	1	1	8	—	—	—	0	-13
1985	†LARm	15(0)	2	-4	-2.0(-2)	0	—	—	—	—	—	—	—	—	—	—	—	—	—	—	—	—	0	-4
1986	†LARm	15(5, qb)	10	5	0.5(5)	0	—	—	—	—	129	59	45.7	693	5.4(65)	4	4	7	44	—	—	—	0	212
1987	LARm	15(4)	7	-4	-0.6(5)	0	—	—	—	—	114	56	49.1	646	5.7(51)	5	4	7	51	—	—	—	0	184
1988	Atl	7(3)	2	1	0.5(1)	1	—	—	—	—	99	49	49.5	566	5.7(50)	2	5	15	112	—	—	—	6	104
NFL	10	106(27)	45	71	1.6(19)	1	—	—	—	—	972	504	51.9	5816	6.0(68)	27	32	80	575	65.8	—	—	6	1844

DILTS, BUCKY Douglas Riggs, P, 5´9˝/185 lbs; Georgia; B12/6/1953 Corpus Christi, TX [P]

YEAR	TEAM	G (GS, POS)	RUSH	YD	AVG (LG)	TD	REC	YD	AVG (LG)	TD	PASS	COMP	PCT	YD	AVG (LG)	TD	INT	SK	YD	QBR	KPR	OTD	PTS	TAY
1977	†Den	14	1	0	0.0(0)	0	—	—	—	—	—	—	—	—	—	—	—	—	—	—	P	—	0	0
1978	†Den	16	—	—	—	—	—	—	—	—	—	—	—	—	—	—	—	—	—	—	P	—	0	0
1979	Bal	16	1	-14	-14.0(-14)	0	—	—	—	—	—	—	—	—	—	—	—	—	—	—	P	—	0	-14
NFL	3	46	2	-14	-7.0	0	—	—	—	—	—	—	—	—	—	—	—	—	—	—	P	—	0	-14

DILWEG, ANTHONY Anthony Hume, QB, 6´3˝/215 lbs; Duke; 1989: GB, rnd 3; B3/28/1965 Washington, DC

YEAR	TEAM	G (GS, POS)	RUSH	YD	AVG (LG)	TD	REC	YD	AVG (LG)	TD	PASS	COMP	PCT	YD	AVG (LG)	TD	INT	SK	YD	QBR	KPR	OTD	PTS	TAY
1989	GB	1(0)	—	—	—	—	—	—	—	—	1	1	100.0	7	7.0(7)	0	0	—	—	—	—	—	0	4
1990	GB	9(7, qb)	21	114	5.4(22)	0	—	—	—	—	192	101	52.6	1267	6.6(59)	8	7	22	150	—	—	—	0	508
NFL	2	10(7)	21	114	5.4(22)	0	—	—	—	—	193	102	52.8	1274	6.6(59)	8	7	22	150	—	—	—	0	511

DILWEG, LAVVIE LaVern Ralph, E, 6´3˝/200 lbs; Marquette; B1/11/1903 Milwaukee, WI, D1/2/1968 St. Petersburg, FL [K] **1926** Mil☆9 (9, LE) **1927** GB☆10 (10, LE), 12 **1928** GB☆12 (12, LE) **1929** GB☆13 (9, LE), 18 **1930** GB☆12 (10, LE), 18 **1931** GB☆14 (10, LE), 25

YEAR	TEAM	G (GS, POS)	RUSH	YD	AVG (LG)	TD	REC	YD	AVG (LG)	TD	PASS	COMP	PCT	YD	AVG (LG)	TD	INT	SK	YD	QBR	KPR	OTD	PTS	TAY
1932	GB☆	14(4)	—	—	—	—	5	83	16.6	0	—	—	—	—	—	—	—	—	—	—	K	—	1	42
1933	GB☆	11(6, le)	—	—	—	—	13	225	17.3	0	—	—	—	—	—	—	—	—	—	—	—	—	0	113
1934	GB	12(2)	—	—	—	—	5	135	27.0(39)	2	—	—	—	—	—	—	—	—	—	—	—	—	12	78
NFL	9	107(72)	—	—	—	—	23	443	19.3(39)	12	—	—	—	—	—	—	—	—	—	—	K	2	86	302

DIMANCHEFF, BABE Boris Stephan, HB, 5´11˝/178 lbs; Butler; Purdue; 1944: Bos, rnd 2; B9/6/1922 Indianapolis, IN

YEAR	TEAM	G (GS, POS)	RUSH	YD	AVG (LG)	TD	REC	YD	AVG (LG)	TD	PASS	COMP	PCT	YD	AVG (LG)	TD	INT	SK	YD	QBR	KPR	OTD	PTS	TAY
1945	Bos	5(2)	30	69	2.3(15)	0	1	15	15.0(15)	0	—	—	—	—	—	—	—	—	—	—	kpi	—	0	194
1946	Bos	8(6, LH)	57	238	4.2(24)	0	5	121	24.2(45)	1	—	—	—	—	—	—	—	—	—	—	kpi	—	6	380
1947	†ChiC	12(2)	30	116	3.9(14)	0	22	438	19.9(80)	4	—	—	—	—	—	—	—	—	—	—	k	—	24	385
1948	†ChiC	12(0)	27	117	4.3(26)	1	13	260	20.0(52)	3	—	—	—	—	—	—	—	—	—	—	k	—	24	300
1949	ChiC	10(1)	38	151	4.0(22)	3	10	130	13.0(50)	1	—	—	—	—	—	—	—	—	—	—	k	—	24	264
1950	ChiC	7	8	5	0.6(5)	0	5	53	10.6(17)	0	—	—	—	—	—	—	—	—	—	—	—	—	0	32
1952	ChiB	9	17	106	6.2(77)	1	5	69	13.8(41)	1	—	—	—	—	—	—	—	—	—	—	kp	—	12	201
NFL	7	63(11)	207	802	3.9(77)	5	61	1086	17.8(80)	10	—	—	—	—	—	—	—	—	—	—	kpi	—	90	1754

DIMIDIO, TONY Antonio James, T-C, 6´3˝/250 lbs; West Chester; 1964: KC, rnd 9/NYG, rnd 5; B8/20/1942 Bryn Mawr, PA **1966**†KC-A 14 **1967** KC-A 12 (2) **NFL** 26 (2) [2 yrs]

DIMITROFF, TOM Thomas George, QB, 5´11˝/200 lbs; Miami (OH); 1957: Cle, rnd 25; B6/6/1935, D1/20/1996 Strongsville, OH

YEAR	TEAM	G (GS, POS)	RUSH	YD	AVG (LG)	TD	REC	YD	AVG (LG)	TD	PASS	COMP	PCT	YD	AVG (LG)	TD	INT	SK	YD	QBR	KPR	OTD	PTS	TAY
1960	Bos-A	3	—	—	—	—	—	—	—	—	2	0	0.0	0	0.0	0	0	—	—	—	—	—	0	0

DIMLER, RICH Richard Alan, DT, 6´6˝/260 lbs; USC; 1979: Cle, rnd 5; B7/18/1956 Bayonne, NJ, D9/30/2000 Torrance, CA **1979** Cle 12 (2) **1980** GB 3 (0) **NFL** 15 (2) [2 yrs]

DIMMICK, DON Donald L., HB, 5´8˝/160 lbs; Hobart; B1/26/1902, NY, D1/9/1990 **1926** Buf 1 (0)

DIMMICK, TOM Thomas Evans, C-T-LB, 6´6˝/253 lbs; Houston; 1956: Phi, rnd 10; B5/1/1931 Opelousas, LA **1956** Phi 12 **1960** DalT-A 13 **NFL** 25 [2 yrs]

DIMRY, CHARLES Charles Louis, DB, 6´0˝/176 lbs; UNLV; 1988: Atl, rnd 5; B1/31/1966 San Diego, CA [I] **1988** Atl 16 (1) **1989** Atl 16 (5, rcb) **1990** Atl 16 (12, LCB) **1991**†Den 16 (1) **1992** Den 16 (6, rcb) **1993** Den 12 (11, RCB) **1994** TB 16 (16, RCB) **1995** TB 16 (16, RCB) **1996** TB 16 (7, rcb) **1997** Phi 15 (9, RCB) **1998** SD 16 (15, LCB) **1999** SD 12 (7, lcb) **NFL** 183 (106) [12 yrs]

DINAPOLI, GENNARO Gennaro L., C-G, 6´3˝/287 lbs; Virginia Tech; 1998: Oak, rnd 4; B5/25/1975 Manhasset, NY **1999** Oak 11 (9, RG) **2001** Ten 5 (2) **2002**†Ten 16 (16, C) **2003** Dal 7 (0) **NFL** 39 (27) [4 yrs]

DINGLE, ADRIAN Adrian Kennell, DE, 6´3˝/272 lbs; Clemson; 1999: SD, rnd 5; B6/25/1977 Holly Hill, SC **2000** SD 14 (1) **2001** SD 14 (0) **2002** SD 16 (3) **2003** SD 16 (15, RDE) **2004**†SD 10 (2) **NFL** 70 (21) [5 yrs]

DINGLE, ANTONIO Antonio Demetric, DT, 6´2˝/315 lbs; Virginia; 1999: Pit, rnd 7; B10/7/1976 Fayetteville, NC **1999** GB 6 (0) **1999** Car 3 (0) **NFL** 9 (0) [1 yr]

DINGLE, MIKE Miguel Bryce, RB, 6´2˝/240 lbs; South Carolina; 1991: Cin, rnd 8; B1/30/1969 Moncks Corner, SC

YEAR	TEAM	G (GS, POS)	RUSH	YD	AVG (LG)	TD	REC	YD	AVG (LG)	TD	PASS	COMP	PCT	YD	AVG (LG)	TD	INT	SK	YD	QBR	KPR	OTD	PTS	TAY
1991	Cin	8(0)	21	91	4.3(21)	0	5	23	4.6(12)	1	—	—	—	—	—	—	—	—	—	—	k	—	6	179

DINGLE, NATE Nathan Hunter, LB, 6´2˝/252 lbs; Cincinnati; B7/23/1971 East Machias, ME **1995** Phi 6 (0) **1996** Jax 2 (0) **1997** SL 9 (0) **NFL** 17 (0) [3 yrs]

DINKEL, TOM Thomas, LB, 6´3˝/240 lbs; Kansas; 1978: Cin, rnd 5; B7/25/1956 Topeka, KS **1980** Cin 16 (12, LOLB) **1981**†Cin 16 (0) **1982**†Cin 9 (0) **1983** Cin 16 (11, LOLB) **1985** Cin 3 (0)

YEAR	TEAM	G (GS, POS)	RUSH	YD	AVG (LG)	TD	REC	YD	AVG (LG)	TD	PASS	COMP	PCT	YD	AVG (LG)	TD	INT	SK	YD	QBR	KPR	OTD	PTS	TAY
1978	Cin	16	1	20	20.0(20)	0	—	—	—	—	—	—	—	—	—	—	—	—	—	—	i	—	0	16
1979	Cin	16	2	14	7.0(9)	0	—	—	—	—	—	—	—	—	—	—	—	—	—	—	—	—	0	14
NFL	7	92(23)	3	34	11.3(20)	0	—	—	—	—	—	—	—	—	—	—	—	—	—	—	kiS	—	0	1

DINKINS, DARNELL Darrell Joseph, TE, 6´3˝/255 lbs; Pittsburgh; B1/20/1977 Pittsburgh, PA

YEAR	TEAM	G (GS, POS)	RUSH	YD	AVG (LG)	TD	REC	YD	AVG (LG)	TD	PASS	COMP	PCT	YD	AVG (LG)	TD	INT	SK	YD	QBR	KPR	OTD	PTS	TAY
2002	NYG	2(0)	—	—	—	—	—	—	—	—	—	—	—	—	—	—	—	—	—	—	—	—	—	—
2003	NYG	7(0)	—	—	—	—	2	16	8.0(10)	0	—	—	—	—	—	—	—	—	—	—	—	—	0	8
2004	Bal	10(4)	—	—	—	—	9	94	10.4(18)	1	—	—	—	—	—	—	—	—	—	—	k	—	6	44
2005	Bal	16(4)	—	—	—	—	6	55	9.2(15)	0	—	—	—	—	—	—	—	—	—	—	k	—	0	23
NFL	4	35(8)	—	—	—	—	17	165	9.7(18)	1	—	—	—	—	—	—	—	—	—	—	k	—	6	75

YEAR	TEAM	G (GS, POS)	RUSH	YD	AVG (LG)	TD	REC	YD	AVG (LG)	TD	PASS	COMP	PCT	YD	AVG (LG)	TD	INT	SK	YD	QBR	KPR	OTD	PTS	TAY

DINKINS, HOWARD Howard James, LB, 6´1˝/230 lbs; Florida State; 1992: Atl, rnd 3; B4/26/1969 Jacksonville, FL **1993** Atl 3 (0)

DION, TERRY Terry Mark, DE, 6´6˝/254 lbs; Oregon; 1980: Sea, rnd 4; B11/22/1957 Shelton, WA **1980** Sea 9 (2)

DIORIO, JERRY Gerald J., TE, 6´3˝/245 lbs; Michigan; B1/11/1962 Youngstown, OH **1987** Det 2 (0)

DIPIERRO, RAY Ramon Frank, G, 5´11˝/210 lbs; Ohio State; B8/22/1926 Toledo, OH **1950** GB 12 (RG) **1951** GB 6 **NFL** 18 [2 yrs]

DIRDEN, JOHNNIE Johnnie, WR, 6´0˝/188 lbs; Sam Houston State; 1978: Hou, rnd S10; B3/14/1952 Houston, TX **1978**†Hou 16 **1979** KC 4 **1981** Pit 6 (0) **NFL** 26 [3 yrs]

DIRENZO, FRED Frederick E., FB, 5´11˝/234 lbs; New Haven; B1/28/1961 Dover, NJ

| 1987 | NYG | 1(0) | 1 | 5 | 5.0(5) | 0 | — | — | — | — | — | — | — | — | — | — | — | — | — | — | — | — | 0 | 5 |

DIRICO, ROBERT Robert J., RB, 5´10˝/202 lbs; West Chester; Kutztown; B11/22/1963 Norristown, PA

| 1987 | NYG | 3(1) | 25 | 90 | 3.6(14) | 0 | 2 | 22 | 11.0(15) | 0 | — | — | — | — | — | — | — | — | — | — | k | — | 0 | 102 |

DIRKS, MIKE Marion Gearhart, DT-G, 6´2˝/246 lbs; Wyoming; 1968: Phi, rnd 5; B8/28/1946 Monticello, GA **1968** Phi 14 **1969** Phi 12 **1970** Phi 12 **1971** Phi 5 **NFL** 43 [4 yrs]

DISCENZO, TONY Anthony N., T, 6´5˝/240 lbs; Michigan State; B1936 **1960** Bos-A 3 **1960** Buf-A 5 **NFL** 8 [1 yr]

DISEND, LEO Leo, T, 6´2˝/224 lbs; Albright; B11/7/1915 New York, NY, D5/13/1985 Baldwin, NY **1938** Bkn 11 (8, RT) **1939** Bkn 11 (8, LT) **1940** GB 5 (2) **NFL** 27 (18) [3 yrs]

DISHMAN, CHRIS Chris, G-C, 6´3˝/339 lbs; Nebraska; 1997: Arz, rnd 4; B2/27/1974 Cozad, NE **1997** Arz 8 (0) **1998**†Arz 12 (11, LG) **1999** Arz 13 (10, LG) **2000** Arz 14 (12, C/lg) **2001** Arz 16 (5, lg) **2002** Arz 14 (14, RG) **2003** Arz 14 (2) **2004** SL 7 (5, lg) **NFL** 98 (59) [8 yrs]

DISHMAN, CRIS Cris Edward, DB, 6´0˝/187 lbs; Purdue; 1988: Hou, rnd 5; B8/13/1965 Louisville, KY [I] **1988**†Hou 15 (2) **1989**†Hou 16 (0) **1990**†Hou 16 (14, LCB) **1991**†Hou★15 (15, LCB) **1992**†Hou 15 (15, LCB) **1993**†Hou 16 (16, LCB) **1994** Hou 16 (16, LCB) **1995** Hou 15 (15, LCB) **1996** Hou 16 (16, LCB) **1997** Was★16 (15, LCB) **1998** Was 16 (16, LCB) **1999** KC 16 (16, LCB) **2000** Min 11 (9, LCB) **NFL** 199 (165) [13 yrs]

DITKA, MIKE Michael Keller 'Iron Mike', TE, 6´3˝/228 lbs; Pittsburgh; 1961: Chi, rnd 1/Hou, rnd 1; B10/18/1939 Carnegie, PA; HOF 1988 [C]

1961	· ChiB★	14(TE)	—	—	—	—	56	1076	19.2(76)	12	—	—	—	—	—	—	—	—	—	—	—	—	72	598
1962	ChiB★	14(14, TE)	—	—	—	—	58	904	15.6(69)	5	—	—	—	—	—	—	—	—	—	—	—	1	36	477
1963	†ChiB★	14(14, TE)	—	—	—	—	59	794	13.5(63)	8	—	—	—	—	—	—	—	—	—	—	—	—	48	437
1964	ChiB★	14(14, TE)	—	—	—	—	75	897	12.0(34)	5	—	—	—	—	—	—	—	—	—	—	—	1	36	474
1965	ChiB★	14(14, TE)	—	—	—	—	36	454	12.6(44)	2	—	—	—	—	—	—	—	—	—	—	—	—	12	237
1966	ChiB☆	14(14, TE)	—	—	—	—	32	378	11.8(30)	2	—	—	—	—	—	—	—	—	—	—	—	—	12	199
1967	Phi	9(TE)	—	—	—	—	26	274	10.5(25)	2	—	—	—	—	—	—	—	—	—	—	—	—	12	147
1968	Phi	11(te)	—	—	—	—	13	111	8.5(18)	2	—	—	—	—	—	—	—	—	—	—	—	—	12	66
1969	†Dal	12(4)	—	—	—	—	17	268	15.8(51)	3	—	—	—	—	—	—	—	—	—	—	—	—	18	149
1970	†Dal	14	—	—	—	—	8	98	12.3(26)	0	—	—	—	—	—	—	—	—	—	—	—	—	0	49
1971	†Dal	14(4)	2	2	1.0(11)	0	30	360	12.0(29)	1	—	—	—	—	—	—	—	—	—	—	—	—	6	172
1972	†Dal	14(TE)	—	—	—	—	17	198	11.6(26)	1	—	—	—	—	—	—	—	—	—	k	—	—	6	104
NFL	12	158(78)	2	2	1.0(11)	0	427	5812	13.6(76)	43	—	—	—	—	—	—	—	—	—	k	—	2	270	3108

DITTRICH, JOHN John Francis, G, 6´1˝/236 lbs; Wisconsin; 1956: ChiC, rnd 6; B5/7/1933 Sheboygan, WI **1956** ChiC 12 (RG) **1959** GB 12 **1960** Oak-A 11 (rg) **1961** Buf-A 12 **NFL** 47 [4 yrs]

DIVITO, JOE Joseph Charles, QB-P, 6´2˝/205 lbs; Boston College; B9/2/1945

| 1968 | Den-A | 3 | 1 | -1 | -1.0(-1) | 0 | — | — | — | — | 6 | 1 | 16.7 | 16 | 2.7(16) | 0 | 0 | — | — | P | — | — | 0 | 7 |

DIXON, AL Albert D., TE, 6´5˝/230 lbs; Iowa State; 1977: NYG, rnd 7; B4/5/1954 Drew, MS

1977	NYG	8	—	—	—	—	6	78	13.0(21)	0	—	—	—	—	—	—	—	—	—	—	—	—	0	39
1978	NYG	15(10, TE)	—	—	—	—	18	376	20.9(47)	3	—	—	—	—	—	—	—	—	—	—	—	—	18	203
1979	NYG	5(1)	—	—	—	—	2	18	9.0(11)	0	—	—	—	—	—	—	—	—	—	—	—	—	0	9
1979	KC	3(1)	—	—	—	—	—	—	—	—	—	—	—	—	—	—	—	—	—	—	—	—	—	—
1980	KC	12(0)	—	—	—	—	7	115	16.4(32)	1	—	—	—	—	—	—	—	—	—	—	—	—	6	48
1981	KC	16(13, TE)	1	-5	-5.0(-5)	0	29	356	12.3(48)	2	—	—	—	—	—	—	—	—	—	k	—	—	12	183
1982	KC	8(6, te)	—	—	—	—	18	251	13.9(37)	2	—	—	—	—	—	—	—	—	—	—	—	—	12	136
1983	Phi	10(1)	—	—	—	—	4	54	13.5(22)	0	—	—	—	—	—	—	—	—	—	—	—	—	0	27
1984	SF	2(0)	—	—	—	—	—	—	—	—	—	—	—	—	—	—	—	—	—	—	—	—	—	—
NFL	8	79(32)	1	-5	-5.0(-5)	0	84	1248	14.9(48)	8	—	—	—	—	—	—	—	—	—	k	—	—	48	644

DIXON, ANDRE Andre Lee, DB, 6´1˝/200 lbs; Northeastern; B12/4/1975 Philadelphia, PA **1999** Det 4 (0)

DIXON, CAL Calvert Roy, C, 6´4˝/302 lbs; Florida; 1992: NYJ, rnd 5; B10/11/1969 Fort Lauderdale, FL **1992** NYJ 11 (0) **1993** NYJ 16 (0) **1994** NYJ 15 (0) **1995** NYJ 13 (12, C) **1996** Mia 11 (0) **NFL** 66 (12) [5 yrs]

DIXON, DAVID David Tukatahi, G, 6´5˝/343 lbs; Arizona State; 1992: NE, rnd 9; B1/5/1969 Papakura, New Zealand **1994** Min 1 (0) **1995** Min 15 (6, rg) **1996**†Min 13 (6, rg) **1997**†Min 13 (13, RG) **1998**†Min 16 (16, RG) **1999**†Min 16 (16, RG) **2000**†Min 16 (16, RG) **2001** Min 15 (14, RG) **2002** Min 15 (15, RG) **2003** Min 16 (16, RG) **2004**†Min 16 (16, RG) **NFL** 152 (134) [11 yrs]

DIXON, DWAYNE Dwayne Keith, WR, 6´1˝/205 lbs; Florida; B8/2/1962 Gainesville, FL

1984	TB	10(0)	—	—	—	—	5	69	13.8(21)	0	—	—	—	—	—	—	—	—	—	—	—	—	0	35
1987	TB	2(0)	—	—	—	—	1	18	18.0(18)	0	—	—	—	—	—	—	—	—	—	—	—	—	0	9
NFL	2	12(0)	—	—	—	—	6	87	14.5(21)	0	—	—	—	—	—	—	—	—	—	—	—	—	0	44

DIXON, ERNEST Ernest James, LB, 6´1˝/243 lbs; South Carolina; B10/17/1971 York, SC **1994** NO 15 (1) **1995** NO 16 (5, mlb) **1996** NO 16 (0) **1997** NO 15 (0) **1998** Oak 3 (0) **1998** KC 1 (0) **NFL** 66 (6) [5 yrs]

DIXON, FLOYD Floyd Eugene, WR, 5´9˝/170 lbs; Stephen F. Austin State; 1986: Atl, rnd 6; B4/9/1964 Beaumont, TX

1986	Atl	16(12, WR)	11	67	6.1(23)	0	42	617	14.7(65)	2	—	—	—	—	—	—	—	—	—	kp	—	—	12	405
1987	Atl	12(12, WR)	3	-3	-1.0(7)	0	36	600	16.7(51)	5	—	—	—	—	—	—	—	—	—	—	—	—	30	322
1988	Atl	14(14, WR)	7	69	9.9(24)	0	28	368	13.1(36)	2	—	—	—	—	—	—	—	—	—	—	—	—	12	263
1989	Atl	16(5, wr)	2	-23	-11.5(0)	0	25	357	14.3(53)	2	—	—	—	—	—	—	—	—	—	—	—	—	12	166
1990	Atl	16(2)	—	—	—	—	38	399	10.5(34)	4	—	—	—	—	—	—	—	—	—	k	—	—	24	205
1991	†Atl	10(3)	—	—	—	—	12	146	12.2(23)	1	—	—	—	—	—	—	—	—	—	—	—	—	6	78
1992	Phi	7(0)	—	—	—	—	3	36	12.0(19)	0	—	—	—	—	—	—	—	—	—	—	—	—	0	18
NFL	7	91(48)	23	110	4.8(24)	0	184	2523	13.7(65)	16	—	—	—	—	—	—	—	—	—	—	—	—	96	1456

DIXON, GERALD Gerald Scott, LB, 6´3˝/250 lbs; South Carolina; 1992: Cle, rnd 3; B6/20/1969 Charlotte, NC **1993** Cle 11 (0) **1994**†Cle 16 (0) **1995** Cle 16 (9, RLB) **1996** Cin 16 (1) **1997** Cin 15 (12, ROLB) **1998** SD 16 (6, llb) **1999** SD 14 (1) **2000** SD 16 (16, LLB) **2001** SD 16 (15, LLB) **NFL** 136 (60) [9 yrs]

DIXON, HANFORD Hanford Lee, DB, 5´11˝/186 lbs; Southern Mississippi; 1981: Cle, rnd 1; B12/25/1958 Mobile, AL [I] **1981** Cle 16 (14, RCB) **1982**†Cle 9 (9, RCB) **1983** Cle 16 (15, RCB) **1984** Cle 16 (16, RCB) **1985**†Cle 16 (16, RCB) **1986**†Cle★16 (16, RCB) **1987**†Cle★12 (12, RCB) **1988**†Cle★15 (15, RCB) **1989**†Cle 15 (15, RCB) **NFL** 131 (128) [9 yrs]

DIXON, HEWRITT Hewritt Frederick, RB-TE, 6´1˝/230 lbs; Florida A&M; 1963: Den, rnd 8/Pit, rnd 11; B1/8/1940 Alachua, FL, D11/24/1992 Los Angeles, CA

1963	Den-A	5(hb)	23	105	4.6(18)	2	10	130	13.0(30)	0	—	—	—	—	—	—	—	—	—	kp	—	—	12	293
1964	Den-A	14(TE)	18	25	1.4(17)	0	38	585	15.4(62)	1	—	—	—	—	—	—	—	—	—	k	—	—	6	322
1965	Den-A	14(TE)	—	—	—	—	25	354	14.2(59)	2	—	—	—	—	—	—	—	—	—	k	—	—	12	180
1966	Oak-A◇	14(fb)	68	277	4.1(23)	5	29	345	11.9(76)	4	—	—	—	—	—	—	—	—	—	—	—	—	54	520
1967	†Oak-A★	13(FB)	153	559	3.7(40)	5	59	563	9.5(48)	2	—	—	—	—	—	—	—	—	—	—	—	—	42	901
1968	†Oak-A★	14(13, FB)	206	865	4.2(28)	2	38	360	9.5(41)	2	—	—	—	—	—	—	—	—	—	—	—	—	26	1075
1969	†Oak-A	11(10, FB)	107	398	3.7(19)	0	33	275	8.3(37)	1	—	—	—	—	—	—	—	—	—	—	—	—	6	541
1970	†Oak★	14(14, FB)	197	861	4.4(30)	1	31	207	6.7(46)	1	—	—	—	—	—	—	—	—	—	—	—	—	12	980
NFL	8	99(37)	772	3090	4.0(40)	15	263	2819	10.7(76)	13	—	—	—	—	—	—	—	—	—	kp	—	—	170	4810

DIXON, JAMES James Anthony, WR-RB, 5´9˝/181 lbs; Houston; B2/2/1967 Vernon, TX [R]

| 1989 | Dal | 16(7, wr) | 3 | 30 | 10.0(13) | 0 | 24 | 477 | 19.9(75) | 2 | — | — | — | — | — | — | — | — | — | k | 1 | 18 | 765 |
| 1990 | Dal | 15(1) | 11 | 43 | 3.9(18) | 0 | 2 | 26 | 13.0(21) | 0 | — | — | — | — | — | — | — | — | — | k | — | 0 | 252 |

YEAR	TEAM	G (GS, POS)	RUSH	YD	AVG(LG)	TD	REC	YD	AVG(LG)	TD PASS	COMP	PCT	YD	AVG(LG)	TD	INT	SK	YD	QBR	KPR	OTD	PTS	TAY
1991	Dal	7(0)	—	—	—	—	—	—	—	—	—	—	—	—	—	—	—	—	—	k		0	128
NFL	3	38(8)	14	73	5.2(18)	0	26	503	19.3(75)	2	—	—	—	—	—	—	—	—	—	k		1	18	1145

DIXON, JOE   Willie Joe, NT, 6′3″/275 lbs; Tulsa; B1/8/1964 Fort Smith, AR   **1987** Hou 2 (0)

DIXON, MARK   Mark Keller, G-T, 6′4″/295 lbs; Virginia; B11/26/1970 Charlottesville, NC   **1998** Mia 11 (10, LG)   **1999**†Mia 13 (13, LG)   **2000**†Mia 15 (15, LG)   **2001** Mia 10 (10, LG)   **2002** Mia 13 (12, LT)   **NFL** 62 (60) [5 yrs]

DIXON, RANDY   Randall Charles, G, 6′3″/305 lbs; Pittsburgh; 1987: Ind, rnd 4; B3/12/1965 Clewiston, FL   **1987** Ind 3 (0)   **1988** Ind 16 (16, LG)   **1989** Ind 16 (16, LG)   **1990** Ind 15 (14, LG)   **1991** Ind 12 (11, LG)   **1992** Ind 15 (15, LG)   **1993** Ind 15 (15, LG)   **1994** Ind 14 (14, LG)   **1995**†Ind 12 (9, LG)   **NFL** 118 (110) [9 yrs]

DIXON, RICH   Richard Marvin, LB, 6′2″/235 lbs; California; B8/6/1959 Roswell, NM   **1983** Atl 14 (0)

DIXON, RICKEY   Rickey, DB, 5′11″/183 lbs; Oklahoma; 1988: Cin, rnd 1; B12/26/1966 Dallas, TX   **1988**†Cin 15 (0)   **1989** Cin 16 (16, FS)   **1990** Cin 13 (5, fs)   **1991** Cin 15 (9, FS)   **1992** Cin 14 (2)   **1993**†LARd 9 (0)   **NFL** 82 (32) [6 yrs]

DIXON, RON   Ronald, WR, 6′0″/190 lbs; West Georgia; Lambuth; 2000: NYG, rnd 3; B5/28/1976 Wildwood, FL

2000	†NYG	12(0)	2	13	6.5(12)	0	6	92	15.3(34)	1	—	—	—	—	—	—	—	—	—	k		6	257
2001	NYG	15(0)	1	0	0.0(0)	0	8	227	28.4(62)	1	—	—	—	—	—	—	—	—	—	kp		6	246
2002	†NYG	10(3)	—	—	—	—	22	377	17.1(33)	2	—	—	—	—	—	—	—	—	—	k		12	230
NFL	3	37(3)	3	13	4.3(12)	0	36	696	19.3(62)	4	—	—	—	—	—	—	—	—	—	kp		24	732

DIXON, RONNIE   Ronnie Christopher, DT-NT, 6′3″/301 lbs; Cincinnati; 1993: NO, rnd 6; B5/10/1971 Clinton, NC   **1993** NO 2 (0)   **1995** Phi 16 (10, RDT)   **1996**†Phi 16 (4)   **1997** NYJ 5 (3)   **1998** KC 4 (0)   **NFL** 43 (17) [5 yrs]

DIXON, TITUS   Titus L., WR, 5′6″/152 lbs; Troy State; 1989: NYJ, rnd 6; B6/15/1966 Clewiston, FL   **1989** NYJ 3 (0)   **1989** Ind 1 (0)   **NFL** 4 (0) [1 yr]

DIXON, TONY   Tony, DB, 6′1″/213 lbs; Alabama; 2001: Dal, rnd 2; B6/18/1979 Tuscaloosa, AL   **2001** Dal 8 (0)   **2002** Dal 16 (7, ss)   **2003**†Dal 16 (0)   **2004** Dal 16 (7, ss)   **NFL** 56 (14) [4 yrs]

DIXON, ZACHARY   Zachary C., RB, 6′0″/203 lbs; Temple; 1979: Den, rnd 11; B3/5/1956 Boston, MA **[R]**

1979	Den	5	3	9	3.0(7)	0	—	—	—	—	—	—	—	—	—	—	—	—	—	k		0	17
1979	NYG	3	—	—	—	—	—	—	—	—	—	—	—	—	—	—	—	—	—				
1980	Phi	5(0)	2	8	4.0(5)	0	1	5	5.0(5)	0	—	—	—	—	—	—	—	—	—	k		0	11
1980	Bal	1(0)	—	—	—	—	—	—	—	—	—	—	—	—	—	—	—	—	—				
1981	Bal	16(1)	73	285	3.9(41)	0	17	169	9.9(41)	1	—	—	—	—	—	—	—	—	—	k		6	572
1982	Bal	9(3)	58	249	4.3(32)	1	20	185	9.3(24)	0	—	—	—	—	—	—	—	—	—	k		6	384
1983	Bal	2(0)	5	14	2.8(7)	0	1	2	2.0(2)	0	—	—	—	—	—	—	—	—	—	k		0	8
1983	†Sea	13(0)	4	18	4.5(6)	0	—	—	—	—	—	—	—	—	—	—	—	—	—	k		6	441
1984	Sea	13(2)	52	149	2.9(17)	2	2	6	3.0(6)	0	—	—	—	—	—	—	—	—	—	kp		12	243
NFL	6	67(6)	197	732	3.7(41)	3	41	367	9.0(41)	1	—	—	—	—	—	—	—	—	—	kp		30	1675

DOANE, DINGER   Erling Eugene, FB, 5′10″/190 lbs; Tufts; B10/14/1893 Natick, MA, D6/5/1949   **1920** Cle 4 (3)   **1921** NYG 1 (1, FB)   **1922** Mil 9 (8, FB), 6   **1923** Mil☆9 (9, FB), 12   **1924** Mil 11 (11, FB), 24   **1925** Det 11 (3), 30   **1926** Det 12 (2), 18   **1927** Pot 2 (0)   **1927** Pro 5 (2)   **NFL** 64 (39), 90 [8 yrs]

DOBBINS, HERB   Herbert, T, 6′4″/260 lbs; San Diego State; B6/22/1951 Statesville, NC   **1974** Phi 3

DOBBINS, OLIVER   Oliver Wendel, DB, 6′0″/182 lbs; Morgan State; 1964: Pit, rnd 18; B11/30/1941 Philadelphia, PA   **1964**†Buf-A 14

DOBBS, GLENN   Glenn, TB-QB, 6′4″/210 lbs; Tulsa; 1943: ChiC, rnd 1; B7/12/1920 McKinney, TX, D11/12/2002 Tulsa, OK

1946	Bkn-A☆	12(11, TB)	95	208	2.2(58)	4	1	-5	-5.0(-5)	0	269	135	50.2	1886	7.0	13	15	—	—	Pkpi	2	36	843
1947	Bkn-A	2(0)	14	41	2.9	—	—	—	—	34	12	35.3	112	3.3	1	1	—	—	P	1	12	72
1947	LAD-A	9(3, qb)	28	90	3.2	0	2	21	10.5	0	109	49	45.0	650	6.0	6	7	—	—	Pkpi		0	359
1948	LAD-A☆	14(10, TB)	91	539	5.9(50)	4	2	11	5.5	0	369	185	50.1	2403	6.5	21	20	—	—	Pki		24	1126
1949	LAD-A	12(6, TB)	34	161	4.7	3	—	—	—	—	153	65	42.5	825	5.4	4	9	—	—	P		18	264
AAFC	4	49(30)	262	1039	4.0(58)	12	5	27	5.4	0	934	446	47.8	5876	6.3	45	52	—	61.0	Pkpi	3	90	2663

DOBELEIT, DICK   Richard Frank, B, 5′4″/155 lbs; Ohio State; B7/4/1903 Germany, D3/2/1978 Lake Wales, FL   **1925** Day 6 (3)   **1926** Day 6 (6, WB)   **NFL** 12 (9) [2 yrs]

DOBELSTEIN, BOB   Robert Edward, G, 5′11″/214 lbs; Tennessee; 1945: ChiC, rnd 4; B10/27/1922 Bridgeport, CT   **1946**†NYG 10 (9, LG)   **1947** NYG 12 (11, LG)   **1948** NYG 11 (9, LG)   **NFL** 33 (29) [3 yrs]

1949 LAD-A 8 (5, rg)

DOBLER, CONRAD   Conrad Francis, G, 6′3″/254 lbs; Wyoming; 1972: SL, rnd 5; B10/1/1950 Chicago, IL   **1972** SL 12 (LG)   **1973** SL 12 (RG)   **1974**†SL 14 (14, RG)   **1975**†SL★14 (14, RG)   **1976** SL★14 (14, RG)   **1977** SL★14 (RG)   **1978** NO 3 (3)   **1979** NO☆16 (16, RG)   **1980**†Buf 16 (16, RG)   **1981**†Buf 14 (13, RG)   **NFL** 129 (90) [10 yrs]

DOBRY, EMIL   Emil A., E, 5′11″/175 lbs; none; B8/10/1895, D7/1972 Decatur, IL   **1928** Fra 1 (0)

DOCKERY, DERRICK   Derrick, G, 6′6″/345 lbs; Texas; 2003: Was, rnd 3; B9/7/1980 Garland, TX   **2003** Was 16 (13, LG)   **2004** Was 16 (16, LG)   **2005**†Was 16 (16, LG)   **NFL** 48 (45) [3 yrs]

DOCKERY, JOHN   John Patrick, DB, 6′0″/185 lbs; Harvard; B9/6/1944 Brooklyn, NY   **1968**†NYJ-A 3   **1970** NYJ 14   **1971** NYJ 14 (LCB)   **1972**†Pit 6   **1973** Pit 10

| 1969 | NYJ-A | 14(LCB) | — | — | — | — | 1 | 6 | 6.0(6) | 0 | — | — | — | — | — | — | — | — | — | i | | 0 | 76 |
| NFL | 6 | 61 | — | — | — | — | 1 | 6 | 6.0(6) | 0 | — | — | — | — | — | — | — | — | — | i | | 0 | 74 |

DOCKETT, DARNELL   Darnell, DT, 6′4″/280 lbs; Florida State; 2004: Arz, rnd 3; B5/27/1981 Burtonsville, MD   **2004** Arz 16 (15, RDT)   **2005** Arz 16 (16, RDT)   **NFL** 32 (31) [2 yrs]

DODD, AL   Alvin Roy, WR-SE-DB, 6′0″/185 lbs; Northwestern State (LA); 1967: Chi, rnd 4; B8/21/1945 New Orleans, LA, D4/9/1987 Opelika, AL **[R]**

1967	ChiB	6	—	—	—	—	—	—	—	—	—	—	—	—	—	—	—	—	—	kp		0	-18
1969	NO	14(SE)	3	12	4.0(9)	0	37	600	16.2(52)	1	—	—	—	—	—	—	—	—	—	kp		6	399
1970	NO	14(WR)	5	31	6.2(16)	0	28	484	17.3(45)	1	1	0	0.0	0	0.0	0	0	—	—	kp	1	12	431
1971	NO	10(WR)	1	7	7.0(7)	0	15	298	19.9(49)	0	—	—	—	—	—	—	—	—	—	kp		0	251
1973	Atl	13(WR)	—	—	—	—	19	291	15.3(25)	1	—	—	—	—	—	—	—	—	—	p		6	279
1974	Atl	14(WR)	—	—	—	—	12	130	10.8(17)	1	—	—	—	—	—	—	—	—	—	p		6	175
NFL	6	71	9	50	5.6(16)	0	111	1803	16.2(52)	3	1	0	0.0	0	0.0	0	0	—	—	kp	1	24	1517

DODGE, DEDRICK   Dedrick Allen, DB, 6′2″/184 lbs; Florida State; B6/14/1967 Neptune, NJ   **1991** Sea 11 (0)   **1992** Sea 14 (0)   **1994**†SF 15 (0)   **1995**†SF 16 (0)   **1996**†SF 16 (3)   **1997**†Den 16 (1)   **1998** SD 8 (0)   **NFL** 96 (4) [7 yrs]

DODGE, KIRK   Kirk James, LB, 6′1″/231 lbs; UNLV; 1984: Atl, rnd 7; B6/4/1962 Whittier, CA   **1984** Det 11 (0)   **1986** Hou 9 (0)   **1987** Den 3 (1)   **NFL** 23 (1) [3 yrs]

DODRILL, DALE   Dale Fike, MG-LB, 6′1″/215 lbs; Colorado State; 1951: Pit, rnd 6; B2/27/1926 Stockton, KS   **1951** Pit 7   **1952** Pit☆12 (MG)   **1953** Pit★12 (MG)   **1954** Pit★12 (MG)   **1955** Pit★12 (MG)   **1956** Pit☆12 (MG)   **1957** Pit☆12 (MLB)   **1958** Pit☆12 (MLB)   **1959** Pit 12 (MLB)   **NFL** 103 [9 yrs]

DODSON, LES   James Leslie, B, 6′1″/180 lbs; Mississippi; 1941: Phi, rnd 14; B4/18/1916 Birmingham, AL, D7/25/1998 Lakeland, FL

| 1941 | Pit | 2(0) | 2 | -4 | -2.0(6) | 0 | — | — | — | — | 8 | 1 | 12.5 | 7 | 0.9(7) | 0 | 3 | — | — | P | | 0 | -121 |

DOEHRING, JOHN   John H., B, 6′0″/216 lbs; none; B11/6/1909 Milwaukee, WI, D11/18/1972 Milwaukee, WI

1932	ChiB	7(0)	36	28	0.8	1	—	—	—	—	26	10	38.5	203	7.8	2	1	—	—	—		6	110
1933	ChiB	8(0)	13	58	4.5	0	1	9	9.0(9)	0	5	1	19.2	123	4.7	1	8	—	—	—		0	-191
1934	ChiB	2(0)	8	6	0.8	0	1	14	14.0(14)	0	11	3	27.3	48	4.4	1	0	—	—	—		0	42
1935	Pit	2(1)	3	-6	-2.0	0	—	—	—	—	8	4	50.0	.83	10.4	2	1	—	—	—		0	6
1936	ChiB	6(0)	18	101	5.6	0	1	19	19.0(19)	0	12	5	41.7	145	12.1	1	0	—	—	—		0	188
1937	ChiB	3(0)	9	33	3.7	0	—	—	—	—	3	2	66.7	25	8.3	0	0	—	—	—		0	46
NFL	6	28(1)	87	220	2.5	1	3	42	14.0(19)	0	86	29	33.7	627	7.3	7	10	—	—	—		6	200

DOELL, SONNY   Walter A., T, 6′0″/200 lbs; Texas; B12/8/1906 Mason, TX   **1933** Cin 1 (0)

DOELLING, FRED   Fred Frank, DB, 5′10″/190 lbs; Pennsylvania; B9/27/1938 Valparaiso, IN   **1960** Dal 2 (2)

DOERGER, JERRY   Jerome William, C-T, 6′5″/270 lbs; Wisconsin; 1982: Chi, rnd 8; B7/18/1960 Cincinnati, OH   **1982** ChiB 2 (0)   **1985** SD 8 (0)   **NFL** 10 (0) [2 yrs]

YEAR	TEAM	G(GS, POS)	RUSH	YD	AVG(LG)	TD	REC	YD	AVG(LG)	TD	PASS COMP	PCT	YD	AVG(LG)	TD	INT	SK	YD	QBR	KPR	OTD	PTS	TAY

DOERING, CHRIS Christopher Paul, WR, 6´4˝/202 lbs; Florida; 1996: Jax, rnd 6; B5/19/1973 Gainesville, FL

1996	Ind	1(0)	—	—	—	—	1	10	10.0(10)	0	—	—	—	—	—	—	—	—	—	—	—	0	5
1997	Ind	2(0)	—	—	—	—	2	12	6.0(8)	0	—	—	—	—	—	—	—	—	—	—	—	0	6
1999	Den	3(0)	—	—	—	—	3	22	7.3(9)	0	—	—	—	—	—	—	—	—	—	—	—	0	11
2002	Was	15(3)	—	—	—	—	18	192	10.7(33)	2	1	0	0.0	0	0.0	0	0	—	—	—	—	14	106
2003	Pit	16(0)	—	—	—	—	18	240	13.3(53)	1	—	—	—	—	—	—	—	—	—	—	—	6	134
2004	Pit	3(0)	—	—	—	—	—	—	—	—	—	—	—	—	—	—	—	—	—	—	—	—	—
NFL	6	40(3)	—	—	—	—	42	476	11.3(53)	3	1	0	0.0	0	0.0	0	0	—	—	—	—	20	262

DOERING, JASON Jason James, DB, 6´0˝/201 lbs; Wisconsin; 2001: Ind, rnd 6; B4/22/1978 Rhinelander, WI **2001** Ind 16 (1) **2002**†Ind 15 (6, ss) **2003**†Ind 16 (0) **2004** Was 6 (0) NFL 53 (7) [4 yrs]

DOGINS, KEVIN Kevin Ray, G-C, 6´1˝/295 lbs; Texas A&M-Kingsville; B12/7/1972 Eagle Lake, TX **1996** TB 1 (0) **1997**†TB 0 (0) **1998** TB 6 (4) **1999**†TB 11 (5, lg) 2001†ChiB 16 (0) **2002** ChiB 15 (8, LG) NFL 49 (17) [6 yrs]

DOHERTY, GEORGE George Edward, T-G, 6´1˝/218 lbs; Louisiana Tech; 1944: Bkn, rnd 20; B9/5/1920 Camden, MS, D12/31/1987 Natchitoches, LA **1944** Bkn 10 (7, RT) 1945 Bos 9 (7, RT) NFL 19 (14) [2 yrs]

1946 NYY-A 1 (0) **1946** Buf-A 12 (7, RT) **1947** Buf-A 11 (8, RT) AAFC 24 (15) [2 yrs]

DOHERTY, MEL Melvin, C, 5´11˝/190 lbs; Marietta; B1883, deceased **1921** Cin 4 (4, C)

DOHRING, TOM Tom Edward, T, 6´6˝/290 lbs; Michigan; 1991: KC, rnd 8; B5/24/1968 Detroit, MI **1992** KC 3 (1)

DOIG, STEVE Stephen Gugel, LB, 6´2˝/240 lbs; New Hampshire; 1982: Det, rnd 3; B3/28/1960 Melrose, MA **1982**†Det 9 (0) **1983** Det 9 (0) **1984** Det 16 (4) **1986**†NE 5 (0) 1987 NE 1 (0) NFL 40 (4) [5 yrs]

DOKES, PHIL Philip Dennis, DT-DE, 6´4˝/258 lbs; Oklahoma State; 1977: Buf, rnd 1; B9/7/1955 North Little Rock, AR, D12/7/1990 Jacksonville, FL **1977** Buf 12 1978 Buf 10 (10, RDT) NFL 22 (10) [2 yrs]

DOLAWAY, CLIFF Clifford Theodore, E, 6´0˝/215 lbs; Carnegie Mellon; B12/11/1913, D12/18/1968

| 1935 | Pit | 4(0) | — | — | — | — | 2 | 42 | 21.0 | 0 | — | — | — | — | — | — | — | — | — | — | — | 0 | 21 |

DOLBIN, JACK John Tice, WR, 5´10˝/180 lbs; Wake Forest; B10/12/1948 Pottsville, PA

1975	Den	14(1)	5	72	14.4(25)	0	22	421	19.1(41)	3	—	—	—	—	—	—	—	—	—	—	1	24	298
1976	Den	14(5, wr)	2	5	2.5(8)	0	19	354	18.6(40)	1	—	—	—	—	—	—	—	—	—	—	—	6	187
1977	†Den	14(13, WR)	2	12	6.0(14)	0	26	443	17.0(81)	3	—	—	—	—	—	—	—	—	—	—	—	18	263
1978	†Den	16(14, WR)	—	—	—	—	24	284	11.8(21)	0	—	—	—	—	—	—	—	—	—	—	—	0	142
1979	Den	4	—	—	—	—	3	74	24.7(45)	0	—	—	—	—	—	—	—	—	—	—	—	0	37
NFL	5	62(33)	9	89	9.9(25)	0	94	1576	16.8(81)	7	—	—	—	—	—	—	—	—	—	—	1	48	926

DOLEMAN, CHRIS Christopher John, DE-LB, 6´5˝/270 lbs; Pittsburgh; 1985: Min, rnd 1; B10/16/1961 Indianapolis, IN [S] **1985** Min 16 (13, LOLB) **1986** Min 16 (9, llb) 1987†Min★12 (12, RDE) **1988**†Min★16 (16, RDE) **1989**†Min★16 (16, RDE) **1990** Min★16 (16, RDE) **1991** Min 16 (16, RDE) **1992**†Min★16 (16, RDE) **1993**†Min★16 (16, RDE) 1994 Atl 14 (7, rde) **1995**†Atl◇16 (16, RDE) **1996**†SF 16 (16, RDE) **1997**†SF◇16 (16, RDE) **1998**†SF 16 (16, RDE) **1999** Min 14 (12, RDE) NFL 232 (213) [15 yrs]

DOLL, DON Donald LeRoy, DB, 5´10˝/185 lbs; USC; 1948: Det, rnd 9/ChiR-A, rnd 20; B8/29/1926 Los Angeles, CA [I] **1950** Det★11 (DB) **1951** Det★12 (DB) **1952**†Det◇12 (db) 1953 Was◇12 (DB) **1954** LARm 12 (DB)

| 1949 | Det☆ | 12(1) | 8 | 25 | 3.1(10) | 1 | 1 | -5 | -5.0(-5) | 0 | — | — | — | — | — | — | — | — | kpi | — | 1 | 12 | 537 |
| NFL | 6 | 71(1) | 8 | 25 | 3.1(10) | 1 | 1 | -5 | -5.0(-5) | 0 | — | — | — | — | — | — | — | — | kpi | — | 2 | 18 | 872 |

DOLLINGER, TONY Anthony Dennis, RB, 5´11˝/205 lbs; Evangel (MO); B10/18/1962 Winter Park, FL

| 1987 | Det | 2(1) | 8 | 22 | 2.8(8) | 0 | 2 | 25 | 8.3(15) | 0 | — | — | — | — | — | — | — | — | — | — | — | 0 | 35 |

DOLLY, DICK John Rrichard, E, 6´3˝/211 lbs; West Virginia; B12/12/1917 Onego, WV, D5/30/1959 North Augusta, SC

1941	Pit	9(4)	1	2	2.0(2)	0	—	—	—	—	—	—	—	—	—	—	—	—	—	—	—	0	2
1945	Pit	10(9, LE)	—	—	—	—	8	122	15.3(47)	0	—	—	—	—	—	—	—	—	—	—	—	0	61
NFL	2	19(13)	1	2	2.0(2)	0	8	122	15.3(47)	0	—	—	—	—	—	—	—	—	—	—	—	0	63

DOMBROSKI, PAUL Paul Matthew, DB, 6´0˝/185 lbs; Hawaii; Linfield; B8/8/1956 Sumter, SC **1980** KC 16 (1) **1981** KC 5 (0) **1981** NE 6 (0) **1982**†NE 9 (0) **1983** NE 7 (0) 1984 NE 14 (0) **1985** TB 6 (0) NFL 63 (1) [6 yrs]

DOMBROWSKI, JIM James Matthew, G-T, 6´5˝/300 lbs; Virginia; 1986: NO, rnd 1; B10/19/1963 Williamsville, NY **1986** NO 3 (3) **1987**†NO 10 (10, LT) **1988** NO 16 (16, LT) 1989 NO 16 (16, LT/lg) **1990**†NO 16 (16, LG) **1991**†NO 16 (16, LG) **1992**†NO 16 (16, LG) **1993** NO 16 (2) **1994** NO 16 (16, LG) **1995** NO 16 (16, LG) **1996** NO 10 (10, LG) NFL 151 (137) [11 yrs]

DOMBROWSKI, LEON Leon Raymond, LB, 6´0˝/215 lbs; Delaware; 1960: Oak, rnd 1; B4/9/1938 Wilmington, DE **1960** NYT-A 1

DOMINGUEZ, MATT Matt, TE, 6´2˝/219 lbs; Sam Houston State; B6/27/1978 Georgetown, TX

| 2001 | Den | 12(0) | — | — | — | — | 3 | 26 | 8.7(12) | 0 | — | — | — | — | — | — | — | — | — | — | — | 0 | 13 |

DOMNANOVICH, JOE Joseph John, C-LB, 6´1˝/213 lbs; Alabama; 1943: Bkn, rnd 4; B3/18/1919 South Bend, IN **1946** Bos 11 (11, C) **1947** Bos 8 (6, C) **1948** Bos 12 (10, C) 1949 NYB 12 (12, C) **1950** NYY 12 (MLB) **1951** NYY 12 (c) NFL 67 (39) [6 yrs]

DOMRES, MARTY Martin Francis, QB, 6´4˝/220 lbs; Columbia; 1969: SD, rnd 1; B4/17/1947 Ithaca, NY

1969	SD-A	10(4)	19	145	7.6(22)	4	—	—	—	—	112	47	42.0	631	5.6(55)	2	10	14	101	—	—	24	111
1970	SD	8(2)	14	39	2.8(7)	0	—	—	—	—	55	28	50.9	491	8.9(80)	2	4	13	93	—	—	0	135
1971	SD	4	1	0	0.0(0)	0	—	—	—	—	12	7	58.3	97	8.1(25)	1	3	3	26	—	—	0	-67
1972	Bal	12(QB)	30	137	4.6(15)	1	—	—	—	—	222	115	51.8	1392	6.3(62)	11	6	11	96	—	—	6	658
1973	Bal	11(QB)	32	126	3.9(14)	2	—	—	—	—	191	93	48.7	1153	6.0(66)	9	13	18	145	—	—	12	248
1974	Bal	14(qb)	22	145	6.6(21)	2	—	—	—	—	153	77	50.3	803	5.2(44)	0	12	13	71	—	—	12	87
1975	†Bal	14	4	46	11.5(20)	1	—	—	—	—	10	8	80.0	123	12.3(32)	1	0	—	—	—	—	6	123
1976	SF	5	4	18	4.5(8)	0	—	—	—	—	14	7	50.0	101	7.2(41)	0	1	3	32	—	—	0	29
1977	NYJ	12	4	23	5.8(11)	0	—	—	—	—	40	17	42.5	113	2.8(17)	1	4	4	24	—	—	0	45
NFL	9	90(6)	130	679	5.2(22)	10	—	—	—	—	809	399	49.3	4904	6.1(80)	27	50	79	588	53.8	—	—	60	1366

DOMRES, TOM Thomas Bruce, DT, 6´3˝/260 lbs; Wisconsin; 1968: Hou, rnd 10; B10/19/1946 Marshfield, WI, D11/8/1999 Rosemont, WA **1968** Hou-A 14 **1969**†Hou-A 14 (RDT) 1970 Hou 14 (RDT) **1971** Hou 5 **1971** Den 5 (2) **1972** Den 11 (3) NFL 63 (5) [5 yrs]

DONAHUE, JACK John, G-T, 6´2˝/230 lbs; Boston College; B1905, deceased **1926** Pro 13 (9, LG)

DONAHUE, MARK Mark Joseph, G, 6´3˝/256 lbs; Michigan; 1978: Cin, rnd 11; B1/29/1956 Evergreen Park, IL **1978** Cin 15 **1979** Cin 16 NFL 31 [2 yrs]

DONAHUE, MITCH Mitchell Todd, LB, 6´2˝/254 lbs; Wyoming; 1991: SF, rnd 4; B2/4/1968 Los Angeles, CA **1991** SF 13 (0) **1992** SF 2 (0) **1993**†Den 13 (0) **1994** Den 3 (0) NFL 31 (0) [4 yrs]

DONAHUE, OSCAR Oscar, WR, 6´3˝/195 lbs; San Jose State; 1962: GB, rnd 6/Oak, rnd 12; B6/7/1937

| 1962 | Min | 13 | — | — | — | — | 16 | 285 | 17.8(53) | 1 | — | — | — | — | — | — | — | — | — | — | — | 6 | 148 |

DONALDSON, GENE Eugene, G, 5´9˝/215 lbs; Kentucky; 1953: Cle, rnd 3; B9/29/1930 **1953**†Cle 11

DONALDSON, GENE Eugene Harold, RB, 6´2˝/230 lbs; Purdue; 1964: Was, rnd 11; B11/4/1942 Birmingham, AL

| 1967 | Buf-A | 2 | 3 | -1 | -0.3(2) | 0 | 1 | 20 | 20.0(20) | 0 | — | — | — | — | — | — | — | — | — | — | — | 0 | 9 |

DONALDSON, JEFF Jeffrey Michael, DB, 6´0˝/192 lbs; Colorado; 1984: Hou, rnd 9; B4/19/1962 Fort Collins, CO **1984** Hou 16 (2) **1985** Hou 16 (0) **1986** Hou 16 (7, fs) 1987†Hou 12 (12, FS) **1988**†Hou 16 (16, FS) **1989** Hou 14 (14, FS) **1990**†KC 16 (9, FS) **1991** Atl 16 (0) **1992** Atl 16 (16, SS) **1993** Atl 13 (2) NFL 151 (78) [10 yrs]

DONALDSON, JOHN John Colvin, DB-TB, 5´10˝/180 lbs; Georgia; B8/22/1925 Jessup, GA **1949** LAD-A 1 (0)

| 1949 | ChiH-A | 7(0) | 1 | -2 | -2.0(-2) | 0 | — | — | — | — | 1 | 0 | 0.0 | 0 | 0.0 | 0 | 0 | — | — | k | — | 0 | 10 |
| AAFC | 1 | 8(0) | 1 | -2 | -2.0(-2) | 0 | — | — | — | — | 1 | 0 | 0.0 | 0 | 0.0 | 0 | 0 | — | — | kp | — | 0 | 46 |

DONALDSON, RAY Raymond Canute, C, 6´3˝/311 lbs; Georgia; 1980: Bal, rnd 2; B5/18/1958 Rome, GA **1980** Bal 16 (0) **1981** Bal 16 (16, C) **1982** Bal 9 (9, C) **1983** Bal 16 (16, C) **1984** Ind 16 (16, C) **1985** Ind 16 (16, C) **1986** Ind★16 (16, C) **1987**†Ind★12 (12, C) **1989** Ind★16 (16, C) **1990** Ind 16 (16, C) **1991** Ind 3 (3) **1992** Ind 16 (16, C) **1993** Sea 16 (16, C) **1994** Sea 16 (16, C) **1995** Dal✧12 (12, C) **1996**†Dal★16 (16, C)

YEAR	TEAM	G (GS, POS)	RUSH	YD	AVG (LG)	TD	REC	YD	AVG (LG)	TD	PASS	COMP	PCT	YD	AVG (LG)	TD	INT	SK	YD	QBR	KPR	OTD	PTS	TAY
1988	Ind★	16 (16, C)	—	—	—	—	1	-3	-3.0 (-3)	0	—	—	—	—	—	—	—	—	—	—	—	—	0	-2
NFL	17	244 (228)	—	—	—	—	1	-3	-3.0 (-3)	0	—	—	—	—	—	—	—	—	—	—	—	—	0	-2

DON CARLOS, WALDO Waldo Emerson, C, 6´2˝/190 lbs; Drake; B10/16/1909 Greenfield, IA, D6/18/1997 **1931** GB 12 (6, C)

DONCHEZ, TOM Thomas Frederick, RB, 6´2˝/216 lbs; Penn State; 1975: Buf, rnd 4; B3/10/1952 Bethlehem, PA **1975** ChiB 14

DONCKERS, BILL William Lewis, QB, 6´1˝/205 lbs; San Diego State; B1/8/1951 Renton, WA

YEAR	TEAM	G (GS, POS)	RUSH	YD	AVG (LG)	TD	REC	YD	AVG (LG)	TD	PASS	COMP	PCT	YD	AVG (LG)	TD	INT	SK	YD	QBR	KPR	OTD	PTS	TAY
1976	SL	1	—	—	—	—	—	—	—	—	1	1	100.0	16	16.0 (16)	0	0	—	—	—	—	—	0	8
1977	SL	5	—	—	—	—	—	—	—	—	5	5	100.0	38	7.6 (16)	0	0	1	11	—	—	—	0	19
NFL	2	6	—	—	—	—	—	—	—	—	6	6	100.0	54	9.0 (16)	0	0	1	11	—	—	—	0	27

DONELLI, AL Allen A., HB, 5´7˝/165 lbs; Duquesne; B12/22/1917 Morgan, PA, D8/8/2002 Blacksburg, VA

YEAR	TEAM	G (GS, POS)	RUSH	YD	AVG (LG)	TD	REC	YD	AVG (LG)	TD	PASS	COMP	PCT	YD	AVG (LG)	TD	INT	SK	YD	QBR	KPR	OTD	PTS	TAY
1941	Pit	7 (0)	15	20	1.3 (7)	0	2	25	12.5 (14)	0	8	2	25.0	13	1.6 (10)	1	3	—	—	—	Pkpi	—	0	-34
1942	Pit	4 (1)	2	-4	-2.0 (0)	0	—	—	—	—	—	—	—	—	—	—	—	—	—	—		—	0	-4
NFL	2	11 (1)	17	16	0.9 (7)	0	2	25	12.5 (14)	0	8	2	25.0	13	1.6 (10)	1	3	—	—	—	Pkpi	—	0	-38

DONLEY, DOUG Douglas Max, WR, 6´0˝/175 lbs; Ohio State; 1981: Dal, rnd 2; B2/6/1959 Cambridge, OH

YEAR	TEAM	G (GS, POS)	RUSH	YD	AVG (LG)	TD	REC	YD	AVG (LG)	TD	PASS	COMP	PCT	YD	AVG (LG)	TD	INT	SK	YD	QBR	KPR	OTD	PTS	TAY
1981	†Dal	11 (0)	—	—	—	—	3	32	10.7 (17)	0	—	—	—	—	—	—	—	—	—	—	p	—	0	14
1982	†Dal	6 (0)	—	—	—	—	2	23	11.5 (12)	0	—	—	—	—	—	—	—	—	—	—	kp	—	0	52
1983	†Dal	11 (1)	—	—	—	—	18	370	20.6 (47)	2	—	—	—	—	—	—	—	—	—	—	p	—	12	191
1984	Dal	15 (9, wr)	2	5	2.5 (6)	0	32	473	14.8 (49)	2	—	—	—	—	—	—	—	—	—	—	—	—	12	252
NFL	4	43 (10)	2	5	2.5 (6)	0	55	898	16.3 (49)	4	—	—	—	—	—	—	—	—	—	—	kp	—	24	508

DONLIN, JIM James Mikeal, G, /210 lbs; none; B9/25/1900 Hartford, CT, D11/26/1957 Manchester, CT **1926** Har 2 (0)

DONNAHOO, ROGER Roger J., DB, 6´0˝/185 lbs; Michigan State; B8/5/1937 Greenville, SC **1960** NYT-A 14 (LCB)

DONNALLEY, KEVIN Kevin Dale, DB, 5´11˝/177 lbs; North Dakota State; 1981: SL, rnd 7; B1/17/1958 Warren, OH **1981** NE 1 (0)

DONNALLEY, KEVIN Kevin Thomas, G-T, 6´5˝/310 lbs; Davidson; North Carolina; 1991: Hou, rnd 3; B6/10/1968 St. Louis, MO **1991**†Hou 16 (0) **1992**†Hou 16 (2) **1993**†Hou 16 (6, lt) **1994** Hou 13 (11, RG) **1995** Hou 16 (16, RG) **1996** Hou 16 (16, RG) **1997** Ten 16 (16, RG) **1998**†Mia 14 (14, RG) **1999**†Mia 16 (9, RG) **2000**†Mia 16 (16, RG) **2001** Car 6 (6, RG) **2002** Car 16 (16, RG) **2003**†Car 16 (16, RG) **NFL** 193 (144) [13 yrs]

DONNALLEY, RICK William Frederick, C-G, 6´2˝/261 lbs; North Carolina; 1981: Pit, rnd 3; B12/11/1958 Wilmington, DE **1982**†Pit 5 (0) **1983**†Pit 16 (7, rg) **1984**†Was 15 (8, c) **1985** Was 13 (12, C) **1986**†KC 16 (16, C) **1987** KC 6 (6, c) **NFL** 71 (49) [6 yrs]

DONNELL, BEN Ben Clay, DE, 6´5˝/248 lbs; Vanderbilt; 1959: Det, rnd 7; B7/17/1936 Old Hickory, TN **1960** LAC-A 3

DONNELLY, GEORGE George, DB, 6´3˝/210 lbs; Illinois; 1965: SF, rnd 1/Den, rnd 4; B9/4/1942 Chicago, IL **1965** SF 14 (5, rs) **1966** SF 7 (7, RS) **1967** SF 12 (6, rs) **NFL** 33 (18) [3 yrs]

DONNELLY, RICK Richard Patrick, P, 6´0˝/195 lbs; Wyoming; B5/17/1962 Miller Place, NY **[KP]** **1986** Atl 16 (0) **1988** Atl☆16 (0) **1990** Sea 16 (0) **1991** Sea 3 (0)

YEAR	TEAM	G (GS, POS)	RUSH	YD	AVG (LG)	TD	REC	YD	AVG (LG)	TD	PASS	COMP	PCT	YD	AVG (LG)	TD	INT	SK	YD	QBR	KPR	OTD	PTS	TAY
1985	Atl	11 (0)	2	-5	-2.5 (0)	0	—	—	—	—	—	—	—	—	—	—	—	—	—	—	P	—	0	-5
1987	Atl☆	12 (0)	3	-6	-2.0 (0)	0	—	—	—	—	—	—	—	—	—	—	—	—	—	—	P	—	0	-6
NFL	6	74 (0)	5	-11	-2.2	0	—	—	—	—	—	—	—	—	—	—	—	—	—	—	KP	—	1	-11

D'ONOFRIO, MARK Mark Emil, LB, 6´2˝/235 lbs; Penn State; 1992: GB, rnd 2; B3/17/1969 Hoboken, NJ **1992** GB 2 (2)

DONOHOE, BILL William Wilson, B, 5´9˝/165 lbs; Carnegie Mellon; B1904 **1927** Fra 8 (3), 12

DONOHOE, MIKE Michael Pierce, TE, 6´3˝/225 lbs; San Francisco; 1968: Min, rnd 9; B5/6/1945 San Francisco, CA

YEAR	TEAM	G (GS, POS)	RUSH	YD	AVG (LG)	TD	REC	YD	AVG (LG)	TD	PASS	COMP	PCT	YD	AVG (LG)	TD	INT	SK	YD	QBR	KPR	OTD	PTS	TAY
1968	Atl	14	—	—	—	—	6	52	8.7 (14)	1	—	—	—	—	—	—	—	—	—	—	k	—	6	38
1970	Atl	14	—	—	—	—	2	36	18.0 (22)	1	—	—	—	—	—	—	—	—	—	—	—	—	6	23
1971	Atl	9	—	—	—	—	—	—	—	—	—	—	—	—	—	—	—	—	—	—	—	—	—	—
1973	GB	13	—	—	—	—	1	10	10.0 (10)	0	—	—	—	—	—	—	—	—	—	—	—	—	0	5
1974	GB	14	—	—	—	—	1	8	8.0 (8)	0	—	—	—	—	—	—	—	—	—	—	—	—	0	4
NFL	5	64	—	—	—	—	10	106	10.6 (22)	2	—	—	—	—	—	—	—	—	—	—	k	—	12	70

DONOHUE, LEON Leon, G-T, 6´4˝/245 lbs; San Jose State; 1961: SF, rnd 9/1962: Oak, rnd 29; B3/25/1939 Star City, AR **1962** SF 14 **1963** SF 14 (14, RG) **1964** SF 14 (13, RG) **1965** Dal 14 (14, RG) **1966**†Dal 14 (RG) **1967**†Dal 14 (RG) **NFL** 84 (41) [6 yrs]

DONOVAN, ART Arthur James 'Fatso', DT-T, 6´2˝/263 lbs; Boston College; 1947: NYG, rnd 22/1949: Buf-A, rnd 17; B6/5/1925 Bronx, NY; HOF 1968 **1950** Bal 12 (RDT) **1951** NYY 12 (LDT) **1952** DalT 6 (1, LDT) **1953** Bal✧12 (LDT) **1954** Bal★11 (LDT) **1955** Bal★12 (LDT) **1956** Bal★11 (LDT) **1957** Bal★12 (LDT) **1958**†Bal☆12 (LDT) **1959**†Bal 12 (LDT) **1960** Bal☆12 (12, LDT) **1961** Bal 14 (LDT) **NFL** 138 (13) [12 yrs]

DONOVAN, PAT Patrick Emery, T, 6´5˝/253 lbs; Stanford; 1975: Dal, rnd 4; B7/1/1953 Helena, MT **1975**†Dal 13 (1) **1976**†Dal 14 **1977**†Dal 14 (RT) **1978**†Dal☆16 (LT) **1979**†Dal★16 (LT) **1980**†Dal★16 (16, LT) **1981**†Dal★16 (16, LT) **1982**†Dal★9 (9, LT) **1983**†Dal☆15 (15, LT) **NFL** 129 (57) [9 yrs]

DONOVAN, TOM Thomas Edward, WR, 5´11˝/179 lbs; Penn State; 1980: KC, rnd 9; B1/13/1957 Queens, NY **1980** NO 5 (0)

DOOLAN, JOHN John James, HB-E, 6´1˝/190 lbs; Georgetown (DC); B5/16/1919 Brooklyn, NY, D3/23/2002 Sarasota, FL

YEAR	TEAM	G (GS, POS)	RUSH	YD	AVG (LG)	TD	REC	YD	AVG (LG)	TD	PASS	COMP	PCT	YD	AVG (LG)	TD	INT	SK	YD	QBR	KPR	OTD	PTS	TAY
1945	Was	1 (0)	—	—	—	—	—	—	—	—	—	—	—	—	—	—	—	—	—	—	—	—	—	—
1945	NYG	5 (0)	10	26	2.6 (10)	0	6	50	8.3 (23)	0	—	—	—	—	—	—	—	—	—	—	k	—	0	93
1946	†NYG	5 (3)	12	33	2.8 (24)	0	3	28	9.3 (13)	0	—	—	—	—	—	—	—	—	—	—	p	—	0	81
1947	†ChiC	12 (3)	—	—	—	—	1	17	17.0 (17)	0	—	—	—	—	—	—	—	—	—	—	—	—	0	9
1948	ChiC	12 (2)	—	—	—	—	—	—	—	—	—	—	—	—	—	—	—	—	—	—	—	—	0	0
NFL	4	35 (8)	22	59	2.7 (24)	0	10	95	9.5 (23)	0	—	—	—	—	—	—	—	—	—	—	kp	—	0	183

DOOLEY, JIM James William, B-E-FL-TE, 6´4˝/198 lbs; Miami (FL); 1952: ChiB, rnd 1; B2/8/1930 Stoutsville, MO **[C]**

YEAR	TEAM	G (GS, POS)	RUSH	YD	AVG (LG)	TD	REC	YD	AVG (LG)	TD	PASS	COMP	PCT	YD	AVG (LG)	TD	INT	SK	YD	QBR	KPR	OTD	PTS	TAY
1952	ChiB	12 (DB)	1	0	0.0 (0)	0	—	—	—	—	—	—	—	—	—	—	—	—	—	—	i	—	0	5
1953	ChiB	12 (LE)	—	—	—	—	53	841	15.9 (72)	4	—	—	—	—	—	—	—	—	—	—	—	—	24	441
1954	ChiB	12 (FL)	—	—	—	—	34	658	19.4 (69)	7	—	—	—	—	—	—	—	—	—	—	—	—	42	364
1956	†ChiB	3	—	—	—	—	4	47	11.8 (15)	0	—	—	—	—	—	—	—	—	—	—	—	—	0	24
1957	ChiB	12 (RE)	—	—	—	—	37	530	14.3 (32)	1	—	—	—	—	—	—	—	—	—	—	—	—	6	270
1959	ChiB	12 (RH)	—	—	—	—	41	580	14.1 (41)	3	—	—	—	—	—	—	—	—	—	—	—	—	18	305
1960	ChiB	12 (TE)	—	—	—	—	36	426	11.8 (28)	1	—	—	—	—	—	—	—	—	—	—	—	—	6	218
1961	ChiB	6	—	—	—	—	6	90	15.0 (25)	0	—	—	—	—	—	—	—	—	—	—	—	—	0	45
NFL	8	81	1	0	0.0	0	211	3172	15.0 (72)	16	—	—	—	—	—	—	—	—	—	—	i	—	96	1671

DOOLEY, JOHN John M., T-G, 6´1˝/224 lbs; Syracuse; Bucknell; B9/29/1897 Fairmount, NY, D10/31/1991 Syracuse, NY **1922** Roc 5 (5, LG) **1923** Mil 1 (1) **1924** Roc 5 (5, RT) **1925** Roc 6 (6, LT) **NFL** 17 (17) [4 yrs]

DOORNINK, DAN Daniel Glenn, RB, 6´3˝/210 lbs; Washington State; 1978: NYG, rnd 7; B2/1/1956 Yakima, WA

YEAR	TEAM	G (GS, POS)	RUSH	YD	AVG (LG)	TD	REC	YD	AVG (LG)	TD	PASS	COMP	PCT	YD	AVG (LG)	TD	INT	SK	YD	QBR	KPR	OTD	PTS	TAY
1978	NYG	12 (3)	60	306	5.1 (24)	1	12	66	5.5 (24)	0	—	—	—	—	—	—	—	—	—	—	—	—	6	349
1979	Sea	16 (12, FB)	152	500	3.3 (26)	8	54	432	8.0 (41)	1	—	—	—	—	—	—	—	—	—	—	k	—	54	799
1980	Sea	15 (14, RB)	100	344	3.4 (22)	3	31	237	7.6 (16)	2	—	—	—	—	—	—	—	—	—	—	—	—	30	503
1981	Sea	15 (8, FB)	65	194	3.0 (11)	1	27	350	13.0 (80)	4	—	—	—	—	—	—	—	—	—	—	—	—	30	399
1982	Sea	8 (6, FB)	45	178	4.0 (46)	0	22	176	8.0 (44)	0	—	—	—	—	—	—	—	—	—	—	P	—	0	266
1983	†Sea	16 (0)	40	99	2.5 (9)	2	24	328	13.7 (47)	2	—	—	—	—	—	—	—	—	—	—	—	—	24	293
1984	†Sea	16 (3)	57	215	3.8 (25)	0	31	365	11.8 (32)	2	—	—	—	—	—	—	—	—	—	—	—	—	12	408
1985	Sea	6 (1)	4	0	0.0 (3)	0	8	52	6.5 (19)	0	—	—	—	—	—	—	—	—	—	—	—	—	0	26
NFL	8	104 (47)	523	1836	3.5 (46)	15	209	2006	9.6 (80)	11	—	—	—	—	—	—	—	—	—	—	Pk	—	156	3042

DORAN, JIM James Robert, E-DE, 6´2˝/201 lbs; Buena Vista; Iowa State; 1951: Det, rnd 5; B8/11/1927 Beaver, IA, D6/30/1994 Lake City, IA

YEAR	TEAM	G (GS, POS)	RUSH	YD	AVG (LG)	TD	REC	YD	AVG (LG)	TD	PASS	COMP	PCT	YD	AVG (LG)	TD	INT	SK	YD	QBR	KPR	OTD	PTS	TAY
1951	Det	12 (LDE)	2	23	11.5 (25)	0	10	225	22.5 (48)	2	—	—	—	—	—	—	—	—	—	—	i	—	12	179
1952	†Det	11 (LDE)	1	36	36.0 (36)	0	10	147	14.7 (31)	1	—	—	—	—	—	—	—	—	—	—	—	—	6	115

YEAR	TEAM	G(GS, POS)	RUSH	YD	AVG(LG)	TD	REC	YD	AVG(LG)	TD	PASS	COMP	PCT	YD	AVG(LG)	TD	INT	SK	YD	QBR	KPR	OTD	PTS	TAY
1953	†Det	7	—	—	—	—	6	75	12.5(30)	0	—	—	—	—	—	—	—	—	—	—	—	—	0	38
1954	†Det	7(LDE)	—	—	—	—	10	203	20.3(49)	4	—	—	—	—	—	—	—	—	—	—	—	—	24	122
1955	Det	10(LE)	—	—	—	—	38	552	14.5(38)	2	—	—	—	—	—	—	—	—	—	—	—	—	12	286
1956	Det	11(re)	—	—	—	—	25	448	17.9(31)	0	—	—	—	—	—	—	—	—	—	—	—	—	0	224
1957	†Det	12(RE)	—	—	—	—	33	624	18.9(65)	5	—	—	—	—	—	—	—	—	—	—	—	—	30	337
1958	Det	9(LE)	—	—	—	—	22	495	22.5(65)	4	—	—	—	—	—	—	—	—	—	—	—	—	24	268
1959	Det	10	—	—	—	—	14	191	13.6(25)	1	—	—	—	—	—	—	—	—	—	—	—	—	24	268
1960	Dal✧	12(9, TE)	—	—	—	—	31	554	17.9(75)	3	—	—	—	—	—	—	—	—	—	—	—	1	12	101
1961	Dal	14	—	—	—	—	13	153	11.8(29)	2	—	—	—	—	—	—	—	—	—	—	k	—	18	292
NFL	11	115(9)	3	59	19.7(36)	0	212	3667	17.3(75)	24	—	—	—	—	—	—	—	—	—	—	ki	1	150	2031

D'ORAZIO, JOE Joseph, T, 5´11˝/220 lbs; Ithaca; B10/5/1914, D9/1972 **1944** Det 5 (1)

DORENBOS, JON Jon, C, 6´0˝/250 lbs; Texas-El Paso; B7/21/1980 Humble, TX **2003** Buf 16 (0) **2004** Buf 13 (0) **2005** Ten 9 (0) **NFL** 38 (0) [3 yrs]

DORFMAN, ART Arthur, C, 5´10˝/210 lbs; Boston University; B5/9/1908 Odessa, Ukraine, D9/23/1997 Boston, MA **1929** Buf 9 (8, C)

DORN, TORIN Torin Damon, DB, 6´0˝/200 lbs; North Carolina; 1990: LARd, rnd 4; B2/29/1968 Greenwood, SC **1990** LARd 16 (0) **1991** LARd 16 (1) **1992** LARd 15 (0) **1993** LARd 15 (0) **1995** SL 12 (3) **1996** SL 10 (0) **NFL** 84 (4) [6 yrs]

DORNBROOK, THOM Thomas John, G-C, 6´2˝/240 lbs; Kentucky; B12/1/1956 Pittsburgh, PA **1979**†Pit 16 (1) **1980** Mia 4 (0) **NFL** 20 (1) [2 yrs]

DORNEY, KEITH Keith Robert, T-G, 6´5˝/268 lbs; Penn State; 1979: Det, rnd 1; B12/3/1957 Allentown, PA **1979** Det 16 (16, RT) **1980** Det 9 (8, RT) **1981** Det☆16 (16, RT) **1982**†Det✧9 (9, RT) **1983**†Det 13 (12, RT) **1984** Det 16 (16, RT) **1985** Det☆16 (16, RT/rg) **1986** Det 12 (12, RG) **1987** Det 5 (5, rg) **NFL** 112 (110) [9 yrs]

DORNING, DALE Dale Scott, DE, 6´5˝/260 lbs; Oregon; B2/7/1962 Burien, WA **1987** Sea 3 (3)

DOROW, AL Albert Richard, QB, 6´0˝/193 lbs; Michigan State; 1952: Was, rnd 3; B11/15/1929 Imlay City, MI

YEAR	TEAM	G(GS, POS)	RUSH	YD	AVG(LG)	TD	REC	YD	AVG(LG)	TD	PASS	COMP	PCT	YD	AVG(LG)	TD	INT	SK	YD	QBR	KPR	OTD	PTS	TAY
1954	Was	11(QB)	34	117	3.4(14)	3	—	—	—	—	138	70	50.7	997	7.2(80)	8	17	—	—	54.2	—	—	18	6
1955	Was	8	8	49	6.1(19)	0	—	—	—	—	12	2	16.7	37	3.1(19)	0	1	—	—	—	—	—	0	28
1956	Was✧	12(QB)	30	105	3.5(30)	0	—	—	—	—	112	55	49.1	730	6.5(51)	8	8	—	—	64.2	—	—	0	190
1957	Phi	6	17	52	3.1(14)	2	—	—	—	—	36	17	47.2	212	5.9(49)	1	4	—	—	—	—	—	12	23
1960	NYT-A☆	14(QB)	90	453	5.0(15)	7	—	—	—	—	396	201	50.8	2748	6.9(56)	**26**	26	—	—	67.8	P	—	42	987
1961	NYT-A✧	14(QB)	54	317	5.9(40)	4	—	—	—	—	**438**	**197**	45.0	2651	6.1(68)	19	**30**	—	—	50.7	—	—	24	578
1962	Buf-A	4	15	57	3.8(15)	0	—	—	—	—	75	30	40.0	333	4.4(34)	2	7	—	—	—	—	—	0	-47
NFL	7	69	248	1150	4.6(40)	16	—	—	—	—	1207	572	47.4	7708	6.4(80)	64	93	—	—	53.8	P	—	96	1764

DORRIS, ANDY Andrew Michael, DE, 6´4˝/238 lbs; New Mexico State; 1973: Cle, rnd 4; B8/11/1951 Bellaire, OH **1973** SL 4 **1973** NO 1 **1974** NO 14 **1975** NO 13 (LDE) **1976** NO 14 (6, lde) **1977** Sea 4 (1) **1977** Hou 5 **1978**†Hou 16 **1979**†Hou 16 (16, LDE) **1980**†Hou 16 (16, LDE) **1981** Hou 15 (15, LDE) **NFL** 118 (54) [9 yrs]

DORRIS, DEREK Derek Russell, WR, 6´2˝/206 lbs; Texas Tech; B12/1/1978 Arlington, TX **2002**†NYG 6 (0)

DORSCH, TRAVIS Travis Edward, P, 6´6˝/227 lbs; Purdue; 2002: Cin, rnd 4; B9/4/1979 Bozeman, MT **2002** Cin 1 (0)

DORSETT, ANTHONY Anthony Drew, DB, 5´11˝/205 lbs; Pittsburgh; 1996: Hou, rnd 6; B9/14/1973 Aliquippa, PA **1996** Hou 8 (0) **1997** Ten 16 (0) **1998** Ten 16 (0) **1999**†Ten 16 (1) **2000**†Oak 16 (16, FS) **2001**†Oak 16 (16, FS) **2002**†Oak 16 (7, ss) **2003** Oak 14 (6, fs) **NFL** 118 (46) [8 yrs]

DORSETT, MATTHEW Matthew Herbert, DB, 5´11˝/187 lbs; Southern (LA); B8/23/1973 New Orleans, LA **1995**†GB 10 (0)

DORSETT, TONY Anthony Drew, RB, 5´11˝/192 lbs; Pittsburgh; 1977: Dal, rnd 1; B4/7/1954 Rochester, PA; HOF 1994

YEAR	TEAM	G(GS, POS)	RUSH	YD	AVG(LG)	TD	REC	YD	AVG(LG)	TD	PASS	COMP	PCT	YD	AVG(LG)	TD	INT	SK	YD	QBR	KPR	OTD	PTS	TAY
1977	†Dal☆	14(4, RB)	208	1007	4.8(84)	12	29	273	9.4(23)	1	1	1	100.0	34	34.0(34)	0	0	—	—	—	—	—	78	1286
1978	†Dal★	16(15, RB)	290	1325	4.6(63)	7	37	378	10.2(**91**)	2	1	0	0.0	0	0.0	0	0	—	—	—	—	1	60	1594
1979	†Dal	14(14, RB)	250	1107	4.4(41)	6	45	375	8.3(32)	1	—	—	—	—	—	—	—	—	—	—	—	—	42	1360
1980	†Dal	15(15, RB)	278	1185	4.3(56)	11	34	263	7.7(27)	0	1	0	0.0	0	0.0	0	0	—	—	—	—	—	66	1427
1981	†Dal★	16(16, RB)	342	1646	4.8(75)	4	32	325	10.2(73)	2	—	—	—	—	—	—	—	—	—	—	—	—	36	1859
1982	†Dal★	9(9, RB)	**177**	**745**	4.2(99)	5	24	179	7.5(18)	0	1	0	0.0	0	0.0	0	0	—	—	—	—	—	30	885
1983	†Dal★	16(16, RB)	289	1321	4.6(77)	8	40	287	7.2(24)	1	1	0	0.0	0	0.0	0	0	—	—	—	—	—	54	1550
1984	Dal	16(16, RB)	302	1189	3.9(31)	6	51	459	9.0(68)	1	1	0	0.0	0	0.0	0	1	—	—	—	—	—	42	1444
1985	†Dal	16(16, RB)	305	1307	4.3(60)	7	46	449	9.8(56)	3	—	—	—	—	—	—	—	—	—	—	—	—	60	1617
1986	Dal	13(12, RB)	184	748	4.1(33)	5	25	267	10.7(36)	1	—	—	—	—	—	—	—	—	—	—	—	—	36	937
1987	Dal	12(6, rb)	130	456	3.5(24)	1	19	177	9.3(33)	1	—	—	—	—	—	—	—	—	—	—	—	—	12	560
1988	Den	16(13, RB)	181	703	3.9(26)	5	16	122	7.6(16)	0	2	1	50.0	7	3.5(7)	1	0	—	—	—	—	—	30	823
NFL	12	173(152)	2936	12739	4.3(99)	77	398	3554	8.9(91)	13	8	2	25.0	41	5.1(34)	1	1	—	—	—	—	1	546	15337

DORSEY, CHAR-RON Char-ron, T, 6´6˝/367 lbs; Florida State; 2001: Dal, rnd 7; B11/5/1978 Jacksonville, FL **2001** Dal 8 (2) **2002** Dal 1 (0) **2002** Hou 2 (1) **NFL** 11 (3) [2 yrs]

DORSEY, DEAN Dean, K, 5´11˝/190 lbs; Toronto; B3/13/1957 Toronto, Canada **[K]** **1988** Phi 3 (0) **1988** GB 3 (0) **NFL** 6 (0) [1 yr]

DORSEY, DICK Richard LeRoy, SE-WR, 6´3˝/200 lbs; USC; Oklahoma; 1958: LA, rnd 19; B3/11/1936 Malvern, IA

YEAR	TEAM	G(GS, POS)	RUSH	YD	AVG(LG)	TD	REC	YD	AVG(LG)	TD	PASS	COMP	PCT	YD	AVG(LG)	TD	INT	SK	YD	QBR	KPR	OTD	PTS	TAY
1962	Oak-A	11(SE)	—	—	—	—	21	344	16.4(90)	2	—	—	—	—	—	—	—	—	—	—	—	—	12	182

DORSEY, ERIC Eric Hall, DE, 6´5˝/280 lbs; Notre Dame; 1986: NYG, rnd 1; B8/5/1964 Washington, DC **1986**†NYG 16 (0) **1987** NYG 12 (3) **1988** NYG 16 (16, LDE) **1989**†NYG 2 (2) **1990**†NYG 16 (11, LDE) **1991** NYG 11 (10, LDE) **1992** NYG 16 (16, LDE) **NFL** 89 (58) [7 yrs]

DORSEY, JOHN John Michael, LB, 6´2˝/240 lbs; Connecticut; 1984: GB, rnd 4; B8/31/1960 Leonardtown, MD **1984** GB 16 (0) **1985** GB 16 (0) **1986** GB 16 (9, RILB) **1987** GB 12 (0) **1988** GB 16 (6, rilb) **NFL** 76 (15) [5 yrs]

DORSEY, KEN Kenneth Simon, QB, 6´5˝/208 lbs; Miami (FL); 2003: SF, rnd 7; B4/22/1981 Orinda, CA

YEAR	TEAM	G(GS, POS)	RUSH	YD	AVG(LG)	TD	REC	YD	AVG(LG)	TD	PASS	COMP	PCT	YD	AVG(LG)	TD	INT	SK	YD	QBR	KPR	OTD	PTS	TAY
2004	SF	9(7, qb)	5	7	1.4(3)	0	—	—	—	—	226	123	54.4	1231	5.4(59)	6	9	13	94	62.4	—	—	0	293
2005	SF	3(3)	4	11	2.8(6)	0	—	—	—	—	90	48	53.3	481	5.3(44)	2	2	6	28	—	—	—	0	182
NFL	2	12(10)	9	18	2.0(6)	0	—	—	—	—	316	171	54.1	1712	5.4(59)	8	11	19	122	63.7	—	—	0	474

DORSEY, LARRY Larry Darnnell, WR, 6´1˝/195 lbs; Tennessee State; 1976: SD, rnd 3; B8/15/1953 Corinth, MS

YEAR	TEAM	G(GS, POS)	RUSH	YD	AVG(LG)	TD	REC	YD	AVG(LG)	TD	PASS	COMP	PCT	YD	AVG(LG)	TD	INT	SK	YD	QBR	KPR	OTD	PTS	TAY
1976	SD	13(2)	1	-12	-12.0(-12)	0	8	108	13.5(19)	0	—	—	—	—	—	—	—	—	—	—	—	—	0	42
1977	SD	13	—	—	—	—	10	198	19.8(67)	2	—	—	—	—	—	—	—	—	—	—	—	—	12	109
1978	KC	16	—	—	—	—	9	169	18.8(33)	2	—	—	—	—	—	—	—	—	—	—	p	—	12	93
NFL	3	42(2)	1	-12	-12.0(-12)	0	27	475	17.6(67)	4	—	—	—	—	—	—	—	—	—	—	p	—	24	244

DORSEY, NAT Nathaniel Willie, T, 6´6˝/324 lbs; Georgia Tech; 2004: Min, rnd 4; B9/9/1983 New Orleans, LA **2004**†Min 13 (7, RT) **2005** Cle 9 (0) **NFL** 22 (7) [2 yrs]

DORSEY, NATE Nathaniel Eugene, WR, 6´4˝/240 lbs; Mississippi Valley State; 1973: Pit, rnd 7; B12/6/1950 Tampa, FL **1973** NE 2

DOSS, MIKE Michael Allen, DB, 5´10˝/207 lbs; Ohio State; 2003: Ind, rnd 2; B3/24/1981 Canton, OH **2003**†Ind 15 (15, SS) **2004**†Ind 10 (9, SS) **2005**†Ind 15 (14, SS) **NFL** 40 (38) [3 yrs]

DOSS, NOBLE Noble Webster, HB, 6´0˝/186 lbs; Texas; 1942: Phi, rnd 11; B5/22/1920 Temple, TX

YEAR	TEAM	G(GS, POS)	RUSH	YD	AVG(LG)	TD	REC	YD	AVG(LG)	TD	PASS	COMP	PCT	YD	AVG(LG)	TD	INT	SK	YD	QBR	KPR	OTD	PTS	TAY
1947	Phi	9(0)	11	45	4.1(20)	0	2	17	8.5(19)	0	—	—	—	—	—	—	—	—	—	—	i	—	0	75
1948	Phi	11(0)	62	193	3.1(18)	0	8	96	12.0(30)	0	—	—	—	—	—	—	—	—	—	—	kp	—	0	247
NFL	2	20(0)	73	238	3.3(20)	0	10	113	11.3(30)	0	—	—	—	—	—	—	—	—	—	—	kpi	—	0	322
1949	NYY-A	4(0)	5	15	3.0	0	—	—	—	—	—	—	—	—	—	—	—	—	—	—	k	—	0	22

DOSS, REGGIE Reginald Lee, DE-DT, 6´4˝/265 lbs; Hampton; 1978: LA, rnd 7; B12/7/1956 Mobile, AL **1978**†LARm 16 **1979**†LARm 16 **1980**†LARm 16 (0) **1981** LARm 16 (8, rdt) **1982** LARm 9 (9, RDE) **1983**†LARm 16 (16, RDE) **1984**†LARm 16 (16, RDE) **1985**†LARm 16 (15, RDE) **1986**†LARm 16 (16, RDE) **1987** LARm 12 (9, RDE) **NFL** 149 (89) [10 yrs]

DOTSON, AL Alphonse Alan, DT, 6´4˝/260 lbs; Grambling State; 1965: KC, rnd R1/GB, rnd 2; B2/25/1943 Houston, TX **1965** KC-A 1 **1966** Mia-A 9 **1968**†Oak-A 13 (1) **1969**†Oak-A 13 (1) **1970**†Oak 11 (2) **NFL** 47 (4) [5 yrs]

DOTSON, DEWAYNE Jack DeWayne, LB, 6´1˝/254 lbs; Tennessee; Mississippi; 1994: Dal, rnd 4; B6/10/1971 Nashville, TN **1994**†Mia 0 (0) **1995** Mia 15 (0)

YEAR	TEAM	G(GS, POS)	RUSH	YD	AVG(LG)	TD	REC	YD	AVG(LG)	TD	PASS	COMP	PCT	YD	AVG(LG)	TD	INT	SK	YD	QBR	KPR	OTD	PTS	TAY
1997	Mia	10(2)	—	—	—	—	1	4	4.0(4)	0	—	—	—	—	—	—	—	—	—	—	—	—	0	2
NFL	3	25(2)	—	—	—	—	1	4	4.0(4)	0	—	—	—	—	—	—	—	—	—	—	—	—	0	2

DOTSON, EARL Earl Christopher, T, 6´4˝/315 lbs; Texas A&M-Kingsville; 1993: GB, rnd 3; B12/17/1970 Beaumont, TX **1993**†GB 13 (0) **1994** GB 4 (0) **1995**†GB 16 (16, RT) **1996**†GB 15 (15, RT) **1997**†GB 13 (13, RT) **1998**†GB 16 (16, RT) **1999** GB 15 (15, RT) **2000** GB 2 (2) **2001**†GB 12 (0) **2002**†GB 14 (11, RT) **NFL** 120 (88) [10 yrs]

DOTSON, SANTANA Santana N., DT-DE, 6´5˝/278 lbs; Baylor; 1992: TB, rnd 5; B12/19/1969 New Orleans, LA **1992** TB 16 (16, RDT) **1993** TB 16 (13, RDT) **1994** TB 16 (9, RDT) **1995** TB 16 (8, rdt) **1996**†GB 16 (15, RDT) **1997**†GB 16 (16, RDT) **1998**†GB 16 (16, RDT) **1999** GB 12 (12, RDT) **2000** GB 12 (11, RDT) **2001**†GB 16 (13, RDT) **NFL** 152 (129) [10 yrs]

DOTTLEY, JOHN John Albert, FB, 6´1˝/200 lbs; Mississippi; 1950: ChiB, rnd 2; B8/25/1928 Birmingham, AL

YEAR	TEAM	G (GS, POS)	RUSH	YD	AVG (LG)	TD	REC	YD	AVG (LG)	TD	PASS	COMP	PCT	YD	AVG (LG)	TD	INT	SK	YD	QBR	KPR	OTD	PTS	TAY
1951	ChiB★	12 (FB)	127	670	5.3 (38)	3	14	225	16.1 (77)	1	—	—	—	—	—	—	—	—	—	—	—	—	24	818
1952	ChiB	5	65	302	4.6 (44)	3	9	113	12.6 (25)	1	—	—	—	—	—	—	—	—	—	—	—	—	24	394
1953	ChiB	10 (fb)	58	150	2.6 (12)	1	5	21	4.2 (8)	0	—	—	—	—	—	—	—	—	—	—	—	—	6	171
NFL	3	27	250	1122	4.5 (44)	7	28	359	12.8 (77)	2	—	—	—	—	—	—	—	—	—	—	—	—	54	1382

DOUBIAGO, DAN Daniel Clarke, T, 6´5˝/283 lbs; Utah; B9/25/1960 Escondido, CA **1987** KC 3 (0)

DOUDS, JAP Forrest McCreery, T-G-C, 5´10˝/216 lbs; Washington & Jefferson; B4/21/1905 Rochester, PA, D8/16/1979 Sewickley, PA **[C]** **1930** Pro 9 (7, LT) **1930** Por☆3 (3) **1931** Por☆13 (13, LT) **1932** ChiC 10 (4) **1934** Pit 11 (8, LG)

YEAR	TEAM	G (GS, POS)	RUSH	YD	AVG (LG)	TD	REC	YD	AVG (LG)	TD	PASS	COMP	PCT	YD	AVG (LG)	TD	INT	SK	YD	QBR	KPR	OTD	PTS	TAY
1933	Pit	7 (5, rt)	1	2	2.0 (2)	0	—	—	—	—	—	—	—	—	—	—	—	—	—	—	—	—	0	2
NFL	5	53 (40)	1	2	2.0 (2)	0	—	—	—	—	—	—	—	—	—	—	—	—	—	—	—	—	0	2

DOUGHERTY, BOB Robert William, LB, 6´1˝/240 lbs; Cincinnati; Kentucky; 1954: LA, rnd 20; B4/20/1932 Bellevue, KY, deceased **1957** LARm 10 (LLB) **1958** Pit 12 (LLB) **1960** Oak-A☆14 (LLB) **1961** Oak-A 14 (LLB) **1962** Oak-A 14 (LLB) **1963** Oak-A 5 (llb) **NFL** 69 [6 yrs]

DOUGHERTY, PHIL Philip Frances, C, 5´11˝/185 lbs; Santa Clara; 1938: ChiC, rnd 9; B9/20/1912 San Francisco, CA, D9/28/2000 Granite Bay, CA **1938** ChiC✧8 (4, C)

DOUGHTY, GLENN Glenn Martin, WR, 6´2˝/204 lbs; Michigan; 1972: Bal, rnd 2; B1/30/1947 Detroit, MI

YEAR	TEAM	G (GS, POS)	RUSH	YD	AVG (LG)	TD	REC	YD	AVG (LG)	TD	PASS	COMP	PCT	YD	AVG (LG)	TD	INT	SK	YD	QBR	KPR	OTD	PTS	TAY
1972	Bal	5	2	33	16.5 (17)	0	3	31	10.3 (19)	0	—	—	—	—	—	—	—	—	—	—	—	—	0	49
1973	Bal	14 (14, WR)	10	96	9.6 (30)	0	25	587	23.5 (66)	4	—	—	—	—	—	—	—	—	—	—	—	—	24	410
1974	Bal	13 (12, WR)	7	51	7.3 (17)	0	24	300	12.5 (27)	2	—	—	—	—	—	—	—	—	—	—	—	—	12	211
1975	†Bal	14 (14, WR)	1	5	5.0 (5)	0	39	666	17.1 (63)	4	—	—	—	—	—	—	—	—	—	—	—	—	24	358
1976	†Bal	14 (14, WR)	3	7	2.3 (3)	0	40	628	15.7 (41)	5	—	—	—	—	—	—	—	—	—	—	—	—	30	346
1977	†Bal	13 (13, WR)	2	11	5.5 (16)	0	28	435	15.5 (57)	4	—	—	—	—	—	—	—	—	—	—	k	—	24	234
1978	Bal	15 (15, WR)	1	-1	-1.0 (-1)	0	25	390	15.6 (46)	3	—	—	—	—	—	—	—	—	—	—	—	—	18	209
1979	Bal	15 (15, WR)	—	—	—	—	35	510	14.6 (54)	2	—	—	—	—	—	—	—	—	—	—	—	—	12	265
NFL	8	103 (97)	26	202	7.8 (30)	0	219	3547	16.2 (66)	24	—	—	—	—	—	—	—	—	—	—	k	—	144	2081

DOUGLAS, BEN Frank Benjamin, HB, 6´0˝/185 lbs; Grinnell; B3/12/1909 Denver, CO, D12/4/1985 Brandon, FL

YEAR	TEAM	G (GS, POS)	RUSH	YD	AVG (LG)	TD	REC	YD	AVG (LG)	TD	PASS	COMP	PCT	YD	AVG (LG)	TD	INT	SK	YD	QBR	KPR	OTD	PTS	TAY
1933	Bkn	6 (0)	4	6	1.5	0	5	86	17.2	1	—	—	—	—	—	—	—	—	—	—	—	—	6	54

DOUGLAS, BOB Robert, FB, 6´0˝/195 lbs; Kansas State; B1915

YEAR	TEAM	G (GS, POS)	RUSH	YD	AVG (LG)	TD	REC	YD	AVG (LG)	TD	PASS	COMP	PCT	YD	AVG (LG)	TD	INT	SK	YD	QBR	KPR	OTD	PTS	TAY
1938	Pit	2 (0)	4	10	2.5	0	—	—	—	—	—	—	—	—	—	—	—	—	—	—	—	—	0	10

DOUGLAS, DAMEANE Dameane, WR, 6´0˝/195 lbs; California; 1999: Oak, rnd 4; B3/15/1976 Hanford, CA

YEAR	TEAM	G (GS, POS)	RUSH	YD	AVG (LG)	TD	REC	YD	AVG (LG)	TD	PASS	COMP	PCT	YD	AVG (LG)	TD	INT	SK	YD	QBR	KPR	OTD	PTS	TAY
1999	Phi	14 (0)	—	—	—	—	8	79	9.9 (29)	1	—	—	—	—	—	—	—	—	—	—	—	—	6	45
2000	†Phi	6 (0)	—	—	—	—	1	9	9.0 (9)	0	—	—	—	—	—	—	—	—	—	—	k	—	0	25
2001	†Phi	16 (0)	—	—	—	—	5	77	15.4 (27)	2	—	—	—	—	—	—	—	—	—	—	k	—	12	51
2002	†Phi	16 (0)	—	—	—	—	—	—	—	—	—	—	—	—	—	—	—	—	—	—	k	—	0	17
NFL	4	52 (0)	—	—	—	—	14	165	11.8 (29)	3	—	—	—	—	—	—	—	—	—	—	k	—	18	137

DOUGLAS, DAVID David Glenn, C-T-G, 6´4˝/280 lbs; Tennessee; 1986: Cin, rnd 8; B3/20/1963 Spring City, TN **1986** Cin 14 (0) **1987** Cin 12 (4) **1988**†Cin 14 (0) **1989** NE 5 (1) **1990** NE 11 (5, C) **NFL** 56 (10) [5 yrs]

DOUGLAS, DERRICK Derrick DeWayne, RB, 5´10˝/222 lbs; Louisiana Tech; 1990: TB, rnd 6; B8/10/1968 Shreveport, LA **1991** Cle 2 (0)

DOUGLAS, EVERETT Everett Dewayne, T, 6´3˝/240 lbs; Florida; 1953: NYG, rnd 4; B12/22/1931, D4/11/2000 Gainesville, FL **1953** NYG 10

DOUGLAS, FREDDIE Freddie Joe, WR, 5´9˝/185 lbs; Arkansas; B3/28/1954 McGehee, AR

YEAR	TEAM	G (GS, POS)	RUSH	YD	AVG (LG)	TD	REC	YD	AVG (LG)	TD	PASS	COMP	PCT	YD	AVG (LG)	TD	INT	SK	YD	QBR	KPR	OTD	PTS	TAY
1976	TB	7 (1)	—	—	—	—	3	58	19.3 (35)	0	—	—	—	—	—	—	—	—	—	—	kp	—	0	149

DOUGLAS, HUGH Hugh Lamont, DE, 6´2˝/281 lbs; Central State (OH); 1995: NYJ, rnd 1; B8/23/1971 Mansfield, OH **[S]** **1995** NYJ 15 (3) **1996** NYJ 10 (10, RDE) **1997** NYJ 15 (15, RDE) **1998** Phi 15 (13, RDE) **1999** Phi 4 (2) **2000**†Phi★16 (15, RDE) **2001**†Phi✧15 (15, RDE) **2002**†Phi★16 (16, RDE) **2003** Jax 16 (16, RDE) **2004**†Phi 16 (3) **NFL** 138 (108) [10 yrs]

DOUGLAS, JAY Jay Rufus, C, 6´6˝/250 lbs; Arkansas; Memphis; 1973: SD, rnd 11; B9/1/1950 Palco, KS **1973** SD 14 **1974** SD 14 **NFL** 28 [2 yrs]

DOUGLAS, JOHN John Louis, LB, 6´2˝/228 lbs; Missouri; 1968: Dal, rnd 4; B9/6/1945 Columbia, MD **1970** NYG 14 **1971** NYG 14 (RLB) **1972** NYG 14 **1973** NYG 14 (LLB) **NFL** 56 [4 yrs]

DOUGLAS, JOHN John Henry, DB, 6´1˝/195 lbs; Texas Southern; 1967: NO, rnd 5; B1/12/1945 Fort Worth, TX, D4/5/2005 Hurst, TX **1967** NO 14 (RCB) **1968** NO 14 (RCB) **1969**†Hou-A 8 **NFL** 36 [3 yrs]

DOUGLAS, LELAND Leland Cleveland, WR, 6´0˝/179 lbs; Baylor; B9/23/1963 Beaumont, TX

YEAR	TEAM	G (GS, POS)	RUSH	YD	AVG (LG)	TD	REC	YD	AVG (LG)	TD	PASS	COMP	PCT	YD	AVG (LG)	TD	INT	SK	YD	QBR	KPR	OTD	PTS	TAY
1987	Mia	3 (2)	—	—	—	—	9	92	10.2 (17)	1	—	—	—	—	—	—	—	—	—	—	—	—	6	51

DOUGLAS, MARQUES Marques Lamont, DE, 6´2˝/280 lbs; Howard; B3/5/1977 Greensboro, NC **2000** NO 1 (0) **2001** Bal 2 (0) **2002** Bal 5 (1) **2003**†Bal 16 (16, RDE) **2004** Bal 16 (15, RDE) **2005** SF 16 (15, RDE) **NFL** 56 (47) [6 yrs]

DOUGLAS, MERRILL Merrill George, FB-HB, 6´0˝/204 lbs; Utah; 1958: ChiB, rnd 6; B3/15/1936 Salt Lake City, UT

YEAR	TEAM	G (GS, POS)	RUSH	YD	AVG (LG)	TD	REC	YD	AVG (LG)	TD	PASS	COMP	PCT	YD	AVG (LG)	TD	INT	SK	YD	QBR	KPR	OTD	PTS	TAY
1958	ChiB	12	10	53	5.3 (18)	0	—	—	—	—	—	—	—	—	—	—	—	—	—	—	—	—	0	53
1959	ChiB	12	24	47	2.0 (9)	2	1	17	17.0 (17)	0	—	—	—	—	—	—	—	—	—	—	—	—	12	76
1960	ChiB	12	11	82	7.5 (29)	0	2	11	5.5 (9)	0	—	—	—	—	—	—	—	—	—	—	—	—	0	88
1961	Dal	6	5	24	4.8 (6)	0	1	-2	-2.0 (-2)	0	—	—	—	—	—	—	—	—	—	—	k	—	0	20
1962	Phi	13	4	7	1.8 (6)	0	—	—	—	—	—	—	—	—	—	—	—	—	—	—	k	—	0	53
NFL	5	55	54	213	3.9 (29)	2	4	26	6.5 (17)	0	—	—	—	—	—	—	—	—	—	—	k	—	12	289

DOUGLAS, OMAR Omar Kareem, WR, 5´10˝/182 lbs; Minnesota; B6/3/1972 New Orleans, LA

YEAR	TEAM	G (GS, POS)	RUSH	YD	AVG (LG)	TD	REC	YD	AVG (LG)	TD	PASS	COMP	PCT	YD	AVG (LG)	TD	INT	SK	YD	QBR	KPR	OTD	PTS	TAY
1994	NYG	6 (0)	—	—	—	—	—	—	—	—	—	—	—	—	—	—	—	—	—	—	—	—	—	—
1995	NYG	8 (1)	—	—	—	—	2	15	7.5 (11)	0	—	—	—	—	—	—	—	—	—	—	k	1	6	6
1996	NYG	4 (0)	—	—	—	—	1	8	8.0 (8)	0	—	—	—	—	—	—	—	—	—	—	k	—	0	0
NFL	3	18 (1)	—	—	—	—	3	23	7.7 (11)	0	—	—	—	—	—	—	—	—	—	—	k	1	6	6

DOUGLAS, OTIS Otis Whitfield, T, 6´1˝/224 lbs; William & Mary; B7/25/1911 Reedville, VA, D3/21/1989 Kilmarnock, VA **1946** Phi 11 (0) **1947**†Phi 12 (3) **1948**†Phi 5 (0) **1949** Phi 2 (0) **NFL** 30 (3) [4 yrs]

DOUGLAS, STEVE Stephen, G-T, /200 lbs; none **1926** Mil 2 (0)

DOUGLASS, BOBBY Robert Gilchrist, QB, 6´4˝/225 lbs; Kansas; 1969: Chi, rnd 2; B6/22/1947 Manhattan, KS **[K]**

YEAR	TEAM	G (GS, POS)	RUSH	YD	AVG (LG)	TD	REC	YD	AVG (LG)	TD	PASS	COMP	PCT	YD	AVG (LG)	TD	INT	SK	YD	QBR	KPR	OTD	PTS	TAY
1969	ChiB	11 (QB)	51	408	8.0 (39)	2	—	—	—	—	148	68	45.9	773	5.2 (48)	5	8	37	312	—	—	—	12	520
1970	ChiB	3	7	22	3.1 (7)	0	—	—	—	—	30	12	40.0	218	7.3 (53)	4	3	7	46	—	—	—	0	31
1971	ChiB	12 (QB)	39	284	7.3 (30)	3	—	—	—	—	225	91	40.4	1164	5.2 (64)	5	15	30	235	37.0	K	—	19	321
1972	ChiB	14 (QB)	141	968	**6.9** (**57**)	8	—	—	—	—	198	75	37.9	1246	6.3 (85)	9	12	32	175	—	—	—	48	1236
1973	ChiB	13 (QB)	94	525	**5.6** (**42**)	5	—	—	—	—	174	81	46.6	1057	6.1 (63)	5	7	27	215	—	—	—	30	849
1974	ChiB	7 (1)	36	229	6.4 (17)	1	—	—	—	—	100	41	41.0	387	3.9 (40)	2	4	9	69	—	—	—	6	283
1975	ChiB	1 (1)	5	34	6.8 (18)	1	—	—	—	—	20	8	40.0	87	4.3 (34)	0	2	2	13	—	—	—	6	8
1975	SD	3	10	42	4.2 (9)	0	—	—	—	—	27	7	25.9	53	2.0 (22)	0	1	4	43	—	—	—	0	29
1976	NO	11 (6, qb)	21	92	4.4 (19)	2	1	-2	-2.0 (-2)	0	213	103	48.4	1288	6.0 (74)	4	8	26	189	—	—	—	12	455
1977	NO	4	2	23	11.5 (20)	0	—	—	—	—	31	16	51.6	130	4.2 (31)	1	3	5	29	—	—	—	0	-27
1978	GB	12	4	27	6.8 (17)	0	—	—	—	—	12	5	41.7	90	7.5 (30)	1	1	1	9	—	—	—	0	37
NFL	10	91 (8)	410	2654	6.5 (57)	22	1	-2	-2.0 (-2)	0	1178	507	43.0	6493	5.5 (85)	36	64	180	1335	48.5	K	—	133	3740

DOUGLASS, LEO Leo Frederick, FB-TB, 5´11˝/190 lbs; Lehigh; Vermont; B2/13/1901 Wakefield, MA, D4/3/1985 Wakefield, MA **1926** Bkn 4 (0) **1926** Fra 2 (0) **NFL** 6 (0) [1 yr]

DOUGLASS,[P] MAURICE Maurice Gerrard, DB, 5´11˝/210 lbs; Kentucky; 1986: Chi, rnd 8; B2/12/1964 Muncie, IN **1986**†ChiB 4 (0) **1987**†ChiB 12 (1) **1988**†ChiB 15 (9, FS) **1989** ChiB 10 (1) **1990**†ChiB 11 (0) **1991**†ChiB 16 (0) **1992** ChiB 16 (0) **1993** ChiB 16 (1) **1994**†ChiB☆16 (3) **1995** NYG 8 (0) **1996** NYG 15 (0) **NFL** 139 (15) [11 yrs]

DOUGLASS, MIKE Michael Reese, LB, 6´0˝/220 lbs; Arizona State; San Diego State; 1978: GB, rnd 5; B3/15/1955 St. Louis, MO **1978** GB 16 (3) **1979** GB 16 (16, RLB) **1980** GB 16 (16, ROLB) **1981** GB☆16 (16, ROLB) **1982**†GB☆9 (9, ROLB) **1983** GB 15 (15, ROLB) **1984** GB 16 (16, ROLB) **1985** GB 15 (15, ROLB) **1986** SD 7 (0) **NFL** 126 (106) [9 yrs]

DOUTHARD, TY Talib Yakee, RB, 6´1˝/215 lbs; Illinois; B5/27/1973 Cincinnati, OH **1997** Cin 1 (0)

DOUTHITT, EARL Earl, DB, 6´2˝/188 lbs; Iowa; 1975: Chi, rnd 7; B9/8/1952 Cleveland, OH **1975** ChiB 9

DOVE, BOB Robert Leo Patrick, DE-E, 6´2˝/222 lbs; Notre Dame; 1943: Was, rnd 5; B2/21/1921 Youngstown, OH, D4/19/2006 Austintown, OH **[C]**

YEAR	TEAM	G (GS, POS)	RUSH	YD	AVG (LG)	TD	REC	YD	AVG (LG)	TD	PASS	COMP	PCT	YD	AVG (LG)	TD	INT	SK	YD	QBR	KPR	OTD	PTS	TAY
1946	ChiR-A	14 (5, le)	—	—	—	—	7	67	9.6	1	—	—	—	—	—	—	—	—	—	—	—	—	6	39
1947	ChiR-A	13 (3)	—	—	—	—	6	61	10.2	1	—	—	—	—	—	—	—	—	—	—	k	—	6	37
AAFC	2	27 (8)	—	—	—	—	13	128	9.8	2	—	—	—	—	—	—	—	—	—	—	k	—	12	75

1949 ChiC 12 (0) **1950** ChiC✧12 (LDE) **1951** ChiC 12 **1952** ChiC 11 (LDE) **1953** ChiC 4 **1953** Det 4 **1954**†Det 12

YEAR	TEAM	G (GS, POS)	RUSH	YD	AVG (LG)	TD	REC	YD	AVG (LG)	TD	PASS	COMP	PCT	YD	AVG (LG)	TD	INT	SK	YD	QBR	KPR	OTD	PTS	TAY
1948	ChiC	12 (0)	1	-2	-2.0 (-2)	0	—	—	—	—	—	—	—	—	—	—	—	—	—	—	—	—	0	-2
NFL	7	79	1	-2	-2.0 (-2)	0	—	—	—	—	—	—	—	—	—	—	—	—	—	—	i	—	0	-7

DOVE, EDDIE Edward Everett, DB, 6´2˝/181 lbs; Colorado; 1959: SF, rnd 3; B4/4/1937 Hygiene, CO **1959** SF 12 (DB) **1960** SF 12 (12, RS) **1961** SF★14 (14, RS) **1962** SF 14 (10, RS) **1963** SF 2 **1963**†NYG 12 **NFL** 66 (36) [5 yrs]

DOVE, JEROME Jerome, DB, 6´0˝/190 lbs; Colorado State; 1976: Oak, rnd 8; B10/3/1953 Newport News, VA **1977** SD 14 (4) **1978** SD 14 (7, lcb) **1979**†SD 16 **1980**†SD 16 (2) **NFL** 60 (13) [4 yrs]

DOVE, WES Wesley Walker, DE, 6´7˝/270 lbs; Syracuse; 1987: Sea, rnd 12; B2/9/1964 Buffalo, NY, D3/24/1989 Gaithersburg, MD **1987** Sea 2 (0)

DOW, HARLEY Harley Duane, G-T, 6´2˝/220 lbs; San Jose State; 1950: SF, rnd 11; B10/19/1925 Mt. Hope, KS **1950** SF 12

DOW, KEN Kenneth William, FB, 5´10˝/198 lbs; Oregon State; 1941: Was, rnd 16; B11/18/1917 Ephrata, WA, D11/17/1988 Helena, MT **1941** Was 2 (0)

DOW, WOODY Jess Elwood, BB-FB, 6´0˝/195 lbs; West Texas A&M; B12/16/1916 Littlefield, TX, D12/24/2003 Orange, CT

YEAR	TEAM	G (GS, POS)	RUSH	YD	AVG (LG)	TD	REC	YD	AVG (LG)	TD	PASS	COMP	PCT	YD	AVG (LG)	TD	INT	SK	YD	QBR	KPR	OTD	PTS	TAY
1938	Phi	10 (10, BB)	4	20	5.0	0	5	88	17.6	1	—	—	—	—	—	—	—	—	—	—	—	—	6	69
1939	Phi	9 (2)	1	-7	-7.0 (-7)	0	5	58	11.6	0	—	—	—	—	—	—	—	—	—	—	—	—	0	22
1940	Phi	11 (0)	—	—	—	—	—	—	—	—	—	—	—	—	—	—	—	—	—	—	—	—	—	—
NFL	3	30 (12)	5	13	2.6	0	10	146	14.6	1	—	—	—	—	—	—	—	—	—	—	—	—	6	91

DOWD, JERRY Jerry, C, 6´0˝/210 lbs; St. Mary's (CA); 1939: Cle, rnd 7; B11/29/1916, CA, D8/24/1995 **1939** Cle 9 (0)

DOWDA, HARRY Harry Clinton, DB-HB, 6´2˝/195 lbs; Wake Forest; 1947: Was, rnd 19; B12/29/1922 Atlanta, GA, D6/24/1996 Wintergreen, VA

YEAR	TEAM	G (GS, POS)	RUSH	YD	AVG (LG)	TD	REC	YD	AVG (LG)	TD	PASS	COMP	PCT	YD	AVG (LG)	TD	INT	SK	YD	QBR	KPR	OTD	PTS	TAY
1949	Was	12 (6, rh)	65	239	3.7 (21)	2	11	187	17.0 (67)	1	—	—	—	—	—	—	—	—	—	—	i	—	18	379
1950	Was	12 (DB)	23	47	2.0 (11)	0	2	16	8.0 (10)	0	—	—	—	—	—	—	—	—	—	—	i	1	6	73
1951	Was	12 (DB)	29	111	3.8 (32)	0	2	54	27.0 (48)	0	—	—	—	—	—	—	—	—	—	—	k	—	0	284
1952	Was	12 (DB)	6	5	0.8 (5)	0	3	20	6.7 (12)	1	—	—	—	—	—	—	—	—	—	—	i	—	6	44
1953	Was	12 (DB)	1	3	3.0 (3)	0	—	—	—	—	—	—	—	—	—	—	—	—	—	—	i	1	6	55
1954	Phi	12 (DB)	—	—	—	—	—	—	—	—	—	—	—	—	—	—	—	—	—	—	i	—	0	24
1955	Phi	12 (DB)	—	—	—	—	—	—	—	—	—	—	—	—	—	—	—	—	—	—	—	—	0	0
NFL	7	84 (6)	124	405	3.3 (32)	2	18	277	15.4 (67)	2	—	—	—	—	—	—	—	—	—	—	ki	2	36	859

DOWDELL, MARCUS Marcus Llewellyn, WR, 5´10˝/179 lbs; Tennessee State; 1992: NO, rnd 10; B5/22/1970 Birmingham, AL

YEAR	TEAM	G (GS, POS)	RUSH	YD	AVG (LG)	TD	REC	YD	AVG (LG)	TD	PASS	COMP	PCT	YD	AVG (LG)	TD	INT	SK	YD	QBR	KPR	OTD	PTS	TAY
1992	NO	4 (0)	—	—	—	—	1	6	6.0 (6)	0	—	—	—	—	—	—	—	—	—	—	p	—	0	-20
1993	NO	9 (1)	—	—	—	—	6	46	7.7 (11)	1	—	—	—	—	—	—	—	—	—	—	—	—	6	80
1995	Arz	13 (0)	—	—	—	—	10	96	9.6 (23)	0	—	—	—	—	—	—	—	—	—	—	kp	—	0	117
1996	Arz	15 (0)	—	—	—	—	20	318	15.9 (64)	2	—	—	—	—	—	—	—	—	—	—	kp	—	12	343
NFL	4	41 (1)	—	—	—	—	37	466	12.6 (64)	3	—	—	—	—	—	—	—	—	—	—	kp	—	18	520

DOWDEN, COREY Corey, DB, 5´11˝/190 lbs; Tulane; B10/18/1968 New Orleans, LA **1996** GB 9 (0) **1996** Bal 3 (0) **1997** ChiB 2 (0) **NFL** 14 (0) [2 yrs]

DOWDEN, STEVE Stephen Henry, T, 6´2˝/235 lbs; Baylor; 1952: Det, rnd 10; B2/24/1929 Natchitoches, LA, D1/24/2001 Spring, TX **1952** GB 12 (RT)

DOWDLE, MIKE Donald Michael, LB-FB, 6´3˝/235 lbs; Texas; 1960: SF, rnd 15/Den, rnd 1; B12/6/1937 Eliasville, TX, D12/5/1993 Houston, TX **1960** Dal 2 **1961** Dal 14 (6, llb) **1962** Dal 14 (LLB) **1963** SF 13 (13, MLB) **1964** SF 14 (14, MLB) **1965** SF 10 (10, MLB) **1966** SF 14 **NFL** 81 (43) [7 yrs]

DOWELL, MULE Gwyn Clark, B, 6´2˝/206 lbs; Texas Tech; B6/27/1913 Ben Franklin, TX, D8/12/1992 Richardson, TX

YEAR	TEAM	G (GS, POS)	RUSH	YD	AVG (LG)	TD	REC	YD	AVG (LG)	TD	PASS	COMP	PCT	YD	AVG (LG)	TD	INT	SK	YD	QBR	KPR	OTD	PTS	TAY
1935	ChiC	5 (1)	6	4	0.7	0	—	—	—	—	—	—	—	—	—	—	—	—	—	—	—	—	0	4
1936	ChiC	10 (7, FB)	54	151	2.8	0	—	—	—	—	2	1	50.0	6	3.0 (6)	0	0	—	—	—	—	—	0	154
NFL	2	15 (8)	60	155	2.6	0	—	—	—	—	2	1	50.0	6	3.0 (6)	0	0	—	—	—	—	—	0	158

DOWLER, BOYD Boyd Hamilton, FL-SE-WR, 6´5˝/224 lbs; Colorado; 1959: GB, rnd 3; B10/18/1937 Rock Springs, WY

YEAR	TEAM	G (GS, POS)	RUSH	YD	AVG (LG)	TD	REC	YD	AVG (LG)	TD	PASS	COMP	PCT	YD	AVG (LG)	TD	INT	SK	YD	QBR	KPR	OTD	PTS	TAY
1959	GB	12 (FL)	1	20	20.0 (20)	0	32	549	17.2 (35)	4	—	—	—	—	—	—	—	—	—	—	—	—	24	315
1960	†GB	12 (FL)	1	8	8.0 (8)	0	30	505	16.8 (**91**)	2	—	—	—	—	—	—	—	—	—	—	P	—	12	271
1961	†GB	14 (FL)	—	—	—	—	36	633	17.6 (78)	3	—	—	—	—	—	—	—	—	—	—	P	—	18	332
1962	†GB☆	14 (FL)	—	—	—	—	49	724	14.8 (41)	2	—	—	—	—	—	—	—	—	—	—	P	—	12	372
1963	GB	14 (FL)	—	—	—	—	53	901	17.0 (53)	6	—	—	—	—	—	—	—	—	—	—	—	—	36	481
1964	GB	14 (FL)	—	—	—	—	45	623	13.8 (50)	5	—	—	—	—	—	—	—	—	—	—	—	—	30	337
1965	†GB✧	14 (SE)	—	—	—	—	44	610	13.9 (47)	4	—	—	—	—	—	—	—	—	—	—	—	—	24	325
1966	†GB	14 (FL)	—	—	—	—	29	392	13.5 (40)	0	—	—	—	—	—	—	—	—	—	—	—	—	0	196
1967	†GB★	14 (SE)	—	—	—	—	54	836	15.5 (57)	4	—	—	—	—	—	—	—	—	—	—	—	—	24	438
1968	GB	14 (SE)	—	—	—	—	45	668	14.8 (72)	6	—	—	—	—	—	—	—	—	—	—	—	—	36	364
1969	GB	14 (WR)	—	—	—	—	31	477	15.4 (45)	4	—	—	—	—	—	—	—	—	—	—	P	—	24	259
1971	†Was	12 (7, WR)	—	—	—	—	26	352	13.5 (30)	0	—	—	—	—	—	—	—	—	—	—	—	—	0	176
NFL	12	162 (7)	2	28	14.0 (20)	0	474	7270	15.3 (91)	40	—	—	—	—	—	—	—	—	—	—	P	—	240	3863

DOWLER, TOMMY Thomas Moran, WB, 5´8˝/160 lbs; Colgate; B7/3/1908 Erie, PA, D12/6/1986 Atlanta, GA **1931** Bkn 2 (0)

DOWLING, BRIAN Brian John, QB, 6´2˝/210 lbs; Yale; 1969: Min, rnd 11; B4/1/1947 Cleveland, OH

YEAR	TEAM	G (GS, POS)	RUSH	YD	AVG (LG)	TD	REC	YD	AVG (LG)	TD	PASS	COMP	PCT	YD	AVG (LG)	TD	INT	SK	YD	QBR	KPR	OTD	PTS	TAY
1972	NE	14	7	35	5.0 (11)	3	—	—	—	—	54	29	53.7	383	7.1 (42)	2	1	4	63	—	—	—	18	227
1973	NE	11	—	—	—	—	—	—	—	—	—	—	—	—	—	—	—	—	—	—	—	—	—	—
1977	GB	2	—	—	—	—	—	—	—	—	1	0	0.0	0	0.0	0	0	—	—	—	—	—	0	0
NFL	3	27	7	35	5.0 (11)	3	—	—	—	—	55	29	52.7	383	7.0 (42)	2	1	4	63	—	—	—	18	227

DOWLING, PAT Patrick Arthur, E, 5´11˝/185 lbs; DePaul; B4/14/1901 Chicago, IL, D7/1984 Chicago, IL **1929** ChiC 13 (10, LE)

DOWLING, SEAN Sean, G-T, 6´4˝/280 lbs; C.W. Post; B2/19/1963 New York, NY **1987** Buf 3 (3)

DOWNING, ERIC Eric Lamont, DT, 6´3˝/315 lbs; Syracuse; 2001: KC, rnd 3; B9/16/1978 Ahoskie, NC **2001** KC 15 (9, LDT) **2002** KC 13 (4) **2003** KC 14 (0) **2004** SD 3 (0) **NFL** 45 (13) [4 yrs]

DOWNING, WALT Walter Tyson, G-C, 6´3˝/259 lbs; Michigan; 1978: SF, rnd 2; B6/11/1956 Coatesville, PA **1978** SF 16 (15, RG) **1979** SF 16 **1980** SF 14 (0) **1981**†SF 16 (0) **1982** SF 9 (2) **1983**†SF 12 (1) **NFL** 83 (18) [6 yrs]

DOWNS, BOB Robert LeRoy, G, 5´10˝/210 lbs; USC; B1927 Los Angeles, CA **1951** SF 1

DOWNS, GARY Gary McLinton, RB, 6´1˝/212 lbs; North Carolina State; 1994: NYG, rnd 3; B6/6/1972 Columbus, GA **1995** Den 1 (0) **1997** Atl 16 (0) **2000** Atl 16 (0)

YEAR	TEAM	G (GS, POS)	RUSH	YD	AVG (LG)	TD	REC	YD	AVG (LG)	TD	PASS	COMP	PCT	YD	AVG (LG)	TD	INT	SK	YD	QBR	KPR	OTD	PTS	TAY
1994	NYG	14 (0)	15	51	3.4 (8)	0	2	15	7.5 (10)	0	—	—	—	—	—	—	—	—	—	—	—	—	0	59
1996	NYG	6 (1)	29	94	3.2 (27)	0	3	20	6.7 (13)	0	—	—	—	—	—	—	—	—	—	—	—	—	0	104
1998	†Atl	16 (1)	1	4	4.0 (4)	0	4	31	7.8 (11)	0	—	—	—	—	—	—	—	—	—	—	—	—	0	20
NFL	6	69 (2)	45	149	3.3 (27)	0	9	66	7.3 (13)	0	—	—	—	—	—	—	—	—	—	—	—	—	0	182

DOWNS, MICHAEL Michael Lynn, DB, 6´3˝/205 lbs; Rice; B6/9/1959 Dallas, TX **[I]** **1981**†Dal 15 (15, FS) **1982**†Dal 9 (9, FS) **1983**†Dal 16 (16, FS) **1984** Dal☆16 (16, FS) **1985**†Dal☆16 (16, FS) **1986** Dal 16 (16, FS) **1987** Dal 12 (12, FS) **1988** Dal 16 (16, FS) **1989** Phx 5 (0) **NFL** 121 (116) [9 yrs]

YEAR	TEAM	G (GS, POS)	RUSH	YD	AVG(LG)	TD	REC	YD	AVG(LG)	TD	PASS COMP	PCT	YD	AVG(LG)	TD	INT	SK	YD	QBR	KPR	OTD	PTS	TAY

DOWNWIND, XAVIER   Xavier, aka Red Fang, T-E, 6´0˝/200 lbs; Carlisle Indian; B12/24/1893 Red Lake Indian Reservation, MN, D7/24/1968 Bemidji, MN   **1922** Oor 5 (3)
1923 Oor 2 (1)   **NFL** 7 (4) [2 yrs]

DOWRICK, PERRY   Pirre, FB, /172 lbs; none; B7/1894 Washington, DC   **1921** Was 2 (0)

DOXZON, TODD   Todd Matthew, WR, 6´1˝/186 lbs; Iowa State; B3/28/1975 Sioux City, IA
| 1998 | Mia | 9(0) | — | 2 | 6 | 3.0(3) | 0 | — | — | — | — | — | — | — | — | — | — | — | — | — | — | — | 0 | 6 |

DOYLE, DICK   Richard Albert, DB, 6´0˝/193 lbs; Ohio State; 1952: Pit, rnd 27; B3/25/1930   **1955** Pit 12 (DB)   **1960** Den-A 6   **NFL** 18 [2 yrs]

DOYLE, ED   Edward Joseph, G, 5´10˝/190 lbs; Canisius; B7/5/1905 Buffalo, NY, D3/15/1997 Niagara-on-the-Lake, Canada   **1927** Buf 5 (0)

DOYLE, EDDIE   Edward James, E, 5´9˝/173 lbs; Army; B8/17/1898 New York, NY, D11/8/1942 Morocco   **1924** Fra 10 (6, re), 12   **1925** Pot 9 (6, le), 6   **NFL** 19 (12), 18 [2 yrs]

DOYLE, TED   Theodore Dennison, T-G, 6´2˝/224 lbs; Nebraska; 1938: NYG, rnd 8; B1/12/1914 Maywood, NE   **1938** Pit 9 (0)   **1939** Pit 9 (3)   **1940** Pit 6 (0)   **1941** Pit 9 (2)
1942 Pit 11 (0)   **1943** P-P 10 (5, RT)   **1944** C-P 10 (3)   **1945** Pit 10 (10, RT)   **NFL** 74 (23) [8 yrs]

DOZIER, CORNELIUS   Cornelius Leslie, DB, 6´2˝/190 lbs; SMU; B2/5/1964 Ennis, TX   **1987** KC 2 (0)

DOZIER, D.J.   William Henry, RB, 6´0˝/200 lbs; Penn State; 1987: Min, rnd 1; B9/21/1965 Norfolk, VA
1987	†Min	9(3)	69	257	3.7(19)	5	12	89	7.4(20)	2	—	—	—	—	—	—	—	—	—	k	—	42	355
1988	Min	8(1)	42	167	4.0(19)	2	5	49	9.8(20)	0	—	—	—	—	—	—	—	—	—	k	—	12	242
1989	†Min	14(6, rb)	46	207	4.5(38)	0	14	148	10.6(30)	0	1	1	100.0	19	19.0(19)	1	0	—	—	k	—	0	374
1990	Min	6(1)	6	12	2.0(4)	0	1	12	12.0(12)	0	—	—	—	—	—	—	—	—	—	—	—	0	18
1991	†Det	6(0)	9	48	5.3(29)	0	1	3	3.0(3)	0	—	—	—	—	—	—	—	—	—	k	—	0	50
NFL	5	43(11)	172	691	4.0(38)	7	33	301	9.1(30)	2	1	1	100.0	19	19.0(19)	1	0	—	—	k	—	54	1037

DRAFT, CHRIS   Chris, LB, 5´11˝/232 lbs; Stanford; 1998: Chi, rnd 6; B2/26/1976 Anaheim, CA   **1998** ChiB 1 (0)   **1999** SF 7 (0)   **2000** Atl 13 (8, LLB)   **2001** Atl 13 (10, LLB)
2002†Atl 15 (5, rilb)   **2003** Atl 16 (16, RILB)   **2004** Atl 14 (13, MLB)   **2005**†Car 16 (3)   **NFL** 95 (55) [8 yrs]

DRAGON, OSCAR   Oscar Lee, RB, 6´0˝/214 lbs; Arizona State; 1972: SD, rnd 17; B3/2/1950 Madera, CA
| 1972 | SD | 13 | 9 | 30 | 3.3(7) | 0 | — | — | — | — | — | — | — | — | — | — | — | — | — | — | — | 0 | 30 |

DRAGOS, SCOTT   Scott, FB-TE, 6´2˝/245 lbs; Boston College; B10/28/1975 Old Rochester, MA   **2001** ChiB 6 (0)
| 2000 | ChiB | 9(2) | — | — | — | — | 4 | 28 | 7.0(10) | 0 | — | — | — | — | — | — | — | — | — | — | — | 0 | 14 |
| NFL | 2 | 15(2) | — | — | — | — | 4 | 28 | 7.0(10) | 0 | — | — | — | — | — | — | — | — | — | — | — | 0 | 14 |

DRAKE, BILL   William Donald, DB-WR, 6´1˝/195 lbs; Oregon; B5/22/1950 Portland, OR   **1973** LARm 4   **1974** LARm 9   **NFL** 13 [2 yrs]

DRAKE, JERRY   Jerry, DT-DE, 6´5˝/298 lbs; Hastings; B7/9/1969 Kingston, NY   **1995** Arz 2 (0)   **1996** Arz 11 (0)   **1998** Arz 1 (1)   **1999** Arz 16 (16, RDT)   **NFL** 30 (17) [4 yrs]

DRAKE, JOE   Joe Lynn, NT, 6´2˝/290 lbs; Arizona; 1985: Phi, rnd 9; B5/28/1963 San Francisco, CA, D   **1985** Phi 16 (0)   **1987** SF 3 (1)   **NFL** 19 (1) [2 yrs]

DRAKE, JOHNNY   John William, B, 6´1˝/213 lbs; Purdue; 1937: Cle, rnd 1; B3/27/1916 Chicago, IL, D3/25/1973 Detroit, MI **[K]**
1937	Cle☆	11(9, FB)	98	333	3.4	3	10	172	17.2	2	1	0	0.0	0	0.0	0	0	—	—	—	—	30	459
1938	Cle★	11(8, FB)	74	188	2.5	1	2	13	6.5	0	3	1	33.3	8	2.7(8)	0	0	—	—	—	—	6	209
1939	Cle★	11(11, FB)	118	453	3.8	9	5	53	10.6	0	—	—	—	—	—	—	—	—	—	—	—	54	570
1940	Cle★	11(8, FB)	134	480	3.6	9	8	81	10.1	0	4	2	50.0	16	4.0(9)	2	0	—	—	Ki	—	56	626
1941	Cle☆	11(8, FB)	101	246	2.4(15)	2	16	211	13.2(48)	1	2	0	0.0	0	0.0	0	0	—	—	ki	—	18	437
NFL	5	55(44)	525	1700	3.2(15)	24	41	530	12.9(48)	3	10	3	30.0	24	2.4(9)	2	0	—	—	Kki	—	164	2299

DRAKE, TROY   Troy Adam, T, 6´6˝/294 lbs; Indiana; B5/15/1972 Rockford, IL   **1995** Phi 1 (0)   **1996** Phi 11 (0)   **1997** Phi 9 (2)   **1998** Was 11 (2)   **NFL** 32 (4) [4 yrs]

DRAKEFORD, TYRONNE   Tyronne James, DB, 5´11˝/185 lbs; Virginia Tech; 1994: SF, rnd 2; B6/21/1971 Camden, SC   **1994**†SF 13 (0)   **1995**†SF 16 (2)   **1996**†SF 16 (16, LCB)
1997†SF 16 (2)   **1998** NO 16 (15, RCB)   **1999** NO 10 (5, rcb)   **2000** Was 9 (1)   **2001**†SF 1 (0)   **NFL** 97 (41) [8 yrs]

DRANE, DWIGHT   Dwight, DB, 6´1˝/200 lbs; Oklahoma; 1984: Buf, rnd S1; B5/6/1962 Miami, FL   **1986** Buf 13 (1)   **1987** Buf 11 (6, SS)   **1988**†Buf 16 (4)   **1989**†Buf 16 (1)
1990†Buf 12 (0)   **1991** Buf 14 (0)   **NFL** 82 (12) [6 yrs]

DRAVELING, LEO   Leo Frank, T, 6´2˝/210 lbs; Michigan; B6/23/1907 Port Huron, MI, D7/2/1955 Port Huron, MI   **1933** Cin 9 (2)

DRAYER, CLARENCE   Clarence Tilghman, T, 6´4˝/225 lbs; Illinois; B8/29/1901 Columbus, OH, D10/8/1977 Indianapolis, IN   **1925** Day 4 (4, LT)

DRAYTON, TROY   Troy Anthony, TE, 6´3˝/260 lbs; Penn State; 1993: LARm, rnd 2; B6/29/1970 Harrisburg, PA
1993	LARm	16(2)	1	7	7.0(7)	0	27	319	11.8(27)	4	—	—	—	—	—	—	—	—	—	k	—	24	157
1994	LARm	16(16, TE)	1	4	4.0(4)	0	32	276	8.6(22)	6	—	—	—	—	—	—	—	—	—	—	—	36	172
1995	SL	16(16, TE)	—	—	—	47	458	9.7(31)	4	—	—	—	—	—	—	—	—	—	—	—	24	249
1996	SL	3(3)	—	—	—	2	11	5.5(6)	0	—	—	—	—	—	—	—	—	—	—	—	0	6
1996	Mia	10(10, TE)	—	—	—	26	320	12.3(51)	0	—	—	—	—	—	—	—	—	—	—	—	2	160
1997	†Mia	16(15, TE)	—	—	—	39	558	14.3(34)	4	—	—	—	—	—	—	—	—	—	—	—	24	299
1998	†Mia	15(15, TE)	—	—	—	30	334	11.1(35)	3	—	—	—	—	—	—	—	—	—	—	—	18	182
1999	†Mia	14(13, TE)	—	—	—	32	299	9.3(26)	1	—	—	—	—	—	—	—	—	—	—	—	6	155
2000	KC	16(1)	—	—	—	8	70	8.8(21)	2	—	—	—	—	—	—	—	—	—	—	—	12	45
NFL	8	122(91)	2	11	5.5(7)	0	243	2645	10.9(51)	24	—	—	—	—	—	—	—	—	—	k	—	146	1424

DRAZENOVICH, CHUCK   Charles Mark, LB-FB, 6´1˝/225 lbs; Penn State; 1949: Det, rnd 9/LAD-A, rnd 11; B8/7/1927 Jere, WV, D2/27/1992 Annandale, VA
1950	Was	12(LLB)	35	155	4.4(28)	1	3	38	12.7(23)	0	—	—	—	—	—	—	—	—	—	ki	—	6	210
1951	Was	9(LLB)	34	76	2.2(7)	3	1	27	27.0(27)	0	—	—	—	—	—	—	—	—	—	i	—	18	137
1952	Was	12(LLB)	29	66	2.3(15)	3	4	62	15.5(20)	0	—	—	—	—	—	—	—	—	—	i	—	18	170
1953	Was	8(LLB)	11	27	2.5(9)	1	—	—	—	—	—	—	—	—	—	—	—	—	—	—	—	6	37
1954	Was	12(12, LLB)	8	6	0.8(3)	0	1	15	15.0(15)	0	—	—	—	—	—	—	—	—	—	ki	—	0	16
1955	Was◇	12(12, MLB)	—	—	—	1	-3	-3.0(-3)	0	—	—	—	—	—	—	—	—	—	i	—	0	-2
1956	Was★	12(12, MLB)	—	—	—	—	—	—	—	—	—	—	—	—	—	—	—	—	i	—	0	0
1957	Was★	12(12, MLB)	—	—	—	—	—	—	—	—	—	—	—	—	—	—	—	—	i	—	0	-4
1958	Was★	12(12, MLB)	—	—	—	—	—	—	—	—	—	—	—	—	—	—	—	—	i	—	0	6
1959	Was	12(MLB)	—	—	—	—	—	—	—	—	—	—	—	—	—	—	—	—	i	—	0	-5
NFL	10	113(60)	117	330	2.8(28)	8	10	139	13.9(27)	0	—	—	—	—	—	—	—	—	—	ki	—	48	565

DRECHSLER, DAVE   David Edwin, G, 6´3˝/264 lbs; North Carolina; 1983: GB, rnd 2; B7/18/1960 Bethesda, MO   **1983** GB 16 (12, LG)   **1984** GB 16 (3)   **NFL** 32 (15) [2 yrs]

DREESSEN, JOEL   Joel Clifford, TE, 6´4˝/260 lbs; Colorado State; 2005: NYJ, rnd 6; B7/26/1982 Ida Grove, IA
| 2005 | NYJ | 14(0) | — | — | — | 5 | 41 | 8.2(17) | 0 | — | — | — | — | — | — | — | — | — | — | — | 0 | 21 |

DREHER, FRED   Ferdinand Adolphus, E, 6´3˝/205 lbs; Denver; 1938: ChiB, rnd 12; B2/23/1913 Jonesboro, AR, D12/28/1996 Jonesboro, AR
| 1938 | ChiB | 3(0) | — | — | — | 3 | 69 | 23.0(32) | 0 | — | — | — | — | — | — | — | — | — | — | — | 6 | 40 |

DRESSEL, CHRIS   Christopher John, TE, 6´4˝/238 lbs; Stanford; 1983: Hou, rnd 3; B2/7/1961 Palcentia, CA
1983	Hou	16(14, TE)	1	3	3.0(3)	0	32	316	9.9(35)	4	—	—	—	—	—	—	—	—	—	k	—	24	161
1984	Hou	16(16, TE)	—	—	—	40	378	9.4(42)	2	—	—	—	—	—	—	—	—	—	—	—	12	199
1985	Hou	16(0)	—	—	—	3	17	5.7(12)	1	—	—	—	—	—	—	—	—	—	—	—	6	14
1986	Hou	16(0)	—	—	—	—	—	—	—	—	—	—	—	—	—	—	—	—	—	—	0	0
1987	SF	1(0)	—	—	—	1	8	8.0(8)	0	—	—	—	—	—	—	—	—	—	—	—	0	4
1989	KC	7(0)	—	—	—	9	136	15.1(49)	1	—	—	—	—	—	—	—	—	—	—	—	6	73
1989	NYJ	8(1)	—	—	—	3	55	18.3(43)	0	—	—	—	—	—	—	—	—	—	—	—	0	28
1990	NYJ	15(4)	—	—	—	6	66	11.0(21)	0	—	—	—	—	—	—	—	—	—	k	—	0	25
1991	†NYJ	15(5, te)	—	—	—	17	122	7.2(22)	0	—	—	—	—	—	—	—	—	—	k	—	0	46
1992	SF	1(0)	—	—	—	—	—	—	—	—	—	—	—	—	—	—	—	—	—	—	0	0
NFL	9	111(40)	1	3	3.0(3)	0	111	1098	9.9(49)	8	—	—	—	—	—	—	—	—	—	k	—	48	549

DRESSEN, CHUCK   Charles Walter, B, 5´6˝/147 lbs; none; B9/20/1898 Decatur, IL, D8/10/1966 Detroit, MI   **1920** Dec 4 (3), 12   **1922** Rac 7 (7, BB), 12   **1923** Rac 1 (0)
NFL 12 (7) [3 yrs]

DRESSLER, DOUG Douglas J., RB, 6´3˝/228 lbs; Cal State-Chico; B8/19/1948 Beaver Falls, PA

YEAR	TEAM	G(GS, POS)	RUSH	YD	AVG(LG)	TD	REC	YD	AVG(LG)	TD	PASS	COMP	PCT	YD	AVG(LG)	TD	INT	SK	YD	QBR	KPR	OTD	PTS	TAY
1970	†Cin	14	18	77	4.3(17)	0	—	—	—	—	—	—	—	—	—	—	—	—	—	—	k	—	0	65
1971	Cin	14	54	204	3.8(13)	1	19	145	7.6(26)	0	—	—	—	—	—	—	—	—	—	—	Pk	—	6	292
1972	Cin	14(FB)	128	565	4.4(43)	6	39	348	8.9(33)	1	—	—	—	—	—	—	—	—	—	—	—	—	42	804
1974	Cin	13	72	255	3.5(17)	2	29	196	6.8(23)	0	—	—	—	—	—	—	—	—	—	—	k	—	12	360
1975	NE	5	3	8	2.7(6)	0	1	-1	-1.0(-1)	0	—	—	—	—	—	—	—	—	—	—	—	—	0	8
1975	KC	8	3	16	5.3(11)	0	2	7	3.5(4)	1	—	—	—	—	—	—	—	—	—	—	Pk	—	6	28
NFL	5	68	278	1125	4.0(43)	9	90	695	7.7(33)	2	—	—	—	—	—	—	—	—	—	—	Pk	—	66	1556

DREWREY, WILLIE Willie James, WR, 5´7˝/184 lbs; West Virginia; 1985: Hou, rnd 11; B4/28/1963 Columbus, NJ **[R]**

YEAR	TEAM	G(GS, POS)	RUSH	YD	AVG(LG)	TD	REC	YD	AVG(LG)	TD	PASS	COMP	PCT	YD	AVG(LG)	TD	INT	SK	YD	QBR	KPR	OTD	PTS	TAY
1985	Hou	14(0)	2	-4	-2.0(5)	0	2	28	14.0(19)	0	—	—	—	—	—	—	—	—	—	—	kp	—	0	357
1986	Hou	15(0)	—	—	—	—	18	299	16.6(31)	0	—	—	—	—	—	—	—	—	—	—	kp	—	0	367
1987	†Hou	12(0)	—	—	—	—	11	148	13.5(35)	0	—	—	—	—	—	—	—	—	—	—	kp	—	0	86
1988	Hou	14(0)	—	—	—	—	11	172	15.6(55)	1	—	—	—	—	—	—	—	—	—	—	kp	—	6	84
1989	TB	16(0)	—	—	—	—	14	157	11.2(18)	1	—	—	—	—	—	—	—	—	—	—	kp	—	6	215
1990	TB	16(1)	—	—	—	—	7	182	26.0(89)	1	—	—	—	—	—	—	—	—	—	—	kp	—	6	199
1991	TB	16(0)	—	—	—	—	26	375	14.4(87)	2	—	—	—	—	—	—	—	—	—	—	kp	—	12	434
1992	TB	9(2)	—	—	—	—	16	237	14.8(32)	2	—	—	—	—	—	—	—	—	—	—	p	—	12	156
1993	†Hou	16(0)	—	—	—	—	1	3	3.0(3)	0	—	—	—	—	—	—	—	—	—	—	kp	—	0	140
NFL	9	128(3)	2	-4	-2.0(5)	0	106	1601	15.1(89)	7	—	—	—	—	—	—	—	—	—	—	kp	—	42	2036

DREWS, TED Theodore Williams, E, 6´0˝/185 lbs; Princeton; B12/15/1902 Chicago, IL, D4/15/1982 Daytona Beach, FL **[K]** **1926** Bkn 3 (3) **1928** ChiB 7 (7, RE), 1 **NFL** 10 (10) [2 yrs]

DREYER, WALLY Walter Otto, DB-HB, 5´10˝/170 lbs; Wisconsin; Michigan; 1947: ChiB, rnd 17; B2/25/1923 Milwaukee, WI, D9/27/2002 Brookfield, WI

YEAR	TEAM	G(GS, POS)	RUSH	YD	AVG(LG)	TD	REC	YD	AVG(LG)	TD	PASS	COMP	PCT	YD	AVG(LG)	TD	INT	SK	YD	QBR	KPR	OTD	PTS	TAY
1949	ChiB	12(1)	45	172	3.8(38)	0	7	94	13.4(24)	0	—	—	—	—	—	—	—	—	—	—	kp	—	0	427
1950	GB	12(DB)	1	0	0.0(0)	0	—	—	—	—	—	—	—	—	—	—	—	—	—	—	pi	1	6	80
NFL	2	24(1)	46	172	3.7(38)	0	7	94	13.4(24)	0	—	—	—	—	—	—	—	—	—	—	kpi	1	6	507

DRISCOLL, PADDY John Leo, HB-QB-TB-BB, 5´11˝/160 lbs; Northwestern; B1/11/1895 Evanston, IL, D6/29/1968 Chicago, IL; HOF 1965 **[KC]** **1920** ChiC 9 (6, QB) **1920** Dec☆1 (0) **1921** ChiC 8 (8, QB), 25 **1922** ChiC☆11 (11, LH), 40 **1923** ChiC☆10 (9, LH), 78 **1924** ChiC☆10 (10, LH), 34 **1925** ChiC☆13 (12, TB), 67 **1926** ChiB☆16 (16, LH), 86 **1927** ChiB☆14 (10, LH), 43 **1928** ChiB☆12 (12, LH), 20 **1929** ChiB 14 (9, lh), 9 **NFL** 118 (103), 402 [10 yrs]

DRISKILL, JOE Joseph Guyon, DB, 6´1˝/195 lbs; Louisiana-Monroe; B8/10/1937 Arcadia, LA **1960** SL 6 (LCB) **1961** SL 14 (rs) **NFL** 20 [2 yrs]

DRIVER, DONALD Donald Jerome, WR, 6´0˝/188 lbs; Alcorn State; 1999: GB, rnd 7; B2/2/1975 Houston, TX

YEAR	TEAM	G(GS, POS)	RUSH	YD	AVG(LG)	TD	REC	YD	AVG(LG)	TD	PASS	COMP	PCT	YD	AVG(LG)	TD	INT	SK	YD	QBR	KPR	OTD	PTS	TAY
1999	GB	6(0)	—	—	—	—	3	31	10.3(12)	1	—	—	—	—	—	—	—	—	—	—	—	—	6	21
2000	GB	16(2)	1	4	4.0(4)	0	21	322	15.3(49)	1	—	—	—	—	—	—	—	—	—	—	—	—	8	170
2001	†GB	13(2)	3	38	12.7(31)	1	13	167	12.8(37)	1	—	—	—	—	—	—	—	—	—	—	—	—	12	137
2002	†GB✧	16(16, WR)	8	70	8.8(17)	0	70	1064	15.2(**85**)	9	—	—	—	—	—	—	—	—	—	—	—	—	54	647
2003	†GB	15(15, WR)	5	51	10.2(45)	0	52	621	11.9(41)	2	—	—	—	—	—	—	—	—	—	—	—	—	12	372
2004	†GB	16(11, WR)	3	4	1.3(14)	0	84	1208	14.4(50)	9	—	—	—	—	—	—	—	—	—	—	—	—	56	653
2005	GB	16(16, WR)	2	13	6.5(9)	0	86	1221	14.2(59)	5	—	—	—	—	—	—	—	—	—	—	—	—	30	649
NFL	7	98(62)	22	180	8.2(45)	1	329	4634	14.1(85)	28	—	—	—	—	—	—	—	—	—	—	—	—	178	2647

DRIVER, STACEY Stacey Staphon, RB, 5´7˝/190 lbs; Clemson; B3/4/1964 Griffin, GA

YEAR	TEAM	G(GS, POS)	RUSH	YD	AVG(LG)	TD	REC	YD	AVG(LG)	TD	PASS	COMP	PCT	YD	AVG(LG)	TD	INT	SK	YD	QBR	KPR	OTD	PTS	TAY
1987	Cle	2(0)	9	31	3.4(16)	0	—	—	—	—	—	—	—	—	—	—	—	—	—	—	k	—	0	32

DRIVER, TONY Tony D., DB, 6´1˝/207 lbs; Notre Dame; 2001: Buf, rnd 6; B8/4/1977 Louisville, KY **2001** Buf 5 (0) **2002** Buf 6 (0) **NFL** 11 (0) [2 yrs]

DRONETT, SHANE Carlton Shane, DT-DE, 6´6˝/281 lbs; Texas; 1992: Den, rnd 2; B1/12/1971 Orange, TX **1992** Den 16 (2) **1993**†Den 16 (16, RDE) **1994** Den 16 (15, LDE) **1995** Den 13 (2) **1996** Atl 5 (0) **1996** Det 7 (0) **1997** Atl 16 (1) **1998**†Atl 16 (16, RDT) **1999** Atl 16 (16, RDT) **2000** Atl 3 (3) **2001** Atl 15 (15, RDT) **NFL** 139 (86) [10 yrs]

DROST, JEFF Jeffrey Wayne, DT, 6´5˝/286 lbs; Iowa; 1987: GB, rnd 8; B1/27/1964 San Angelo, TX **1987** GB 2 (0)

DROUGAS, TOM Thomas Christopher, T-G, 6´4˝/257 lbs; Oregon; 1972: Bal, rnd 1; B12/25/1949 Portland, OR **1972** Bal 14 **1973** Bal 13 (LT) **1974** Den 3 **1974** KC 7 **1975** Mia 14 **1976** Mia 14 **NFL** 65 [5 yrs]

DROUGHNS, REUBEN Reuben, RB, 5´11˝/207 lbs; Oregon; 2000: Det, rnd 3; B8/21/1978 Chicago, IL

YEAR	TEAM	G(GS, POS)	RUSH	YD	AVG(LG)	TD	REC	YD	AVG(LG)	TD	PASS	COMP	PCT	YD	AVG(LG)	TD	INT	SK	YD	QBR	KPR	OTD	PTS	TAY
2001	Det	9(3)	30	72	2.4(15)	0	4	21	5.3(8)	1	—	—	—	—	—	—	—	—	—	—	—	—	6	88
2002	Den	16(0)	4	11	2.8(9)	1	5	53	10.6(22)	1	—	—	—	—	—	—	—	—	—	—	k	—	12	269
2003	†Den	15(4)	6	14	2.3(12)	0	9	87	9.7(15)	2	—	—	—	—	—	—	—	—	—	—	k	—	12	181
2004	†Den	16(15, RB)	275	1240	4.5(51)	6	32	241	7.5(23)	2	—	—	—	—	—	—	—	—	—	—	k	—	48	1565
2005	Cle	16(16, RB)	309	1232	4.0(75)	2	39	369	9.5(51)	0	—	—	—	—	—	—	—	—	—	—	k	—	12	1481
NFL	5	72(38)	624	2569	4.1(75)	9	89	771	8.7(51)	6	—	—	—	—	—	—	—	—	—	—	k	—	90	3582

DROZDOV, DARREN Darren, NT, 6´3˝/280 lbs; Maryland; B4/7/1969 Mays Landing, NJ, D10/5/1999 Kansas City, MO **1993**†Den 6 (2)

DRUCKENMILLER, JIM James David, QB, 6´4˝/241 lbs; Virginia Tech; 1997: SF, rnd 1; B9/19/1972 Allentown, PA

YEAR	TEAM	G(GS, POS)	RUSH	YD	AVG(LG)	TD	REC	YD	AVG(LG)	TD	PASS	COMP	PCT	YD	AVG(LG)	TD	INT	SK	YD	QBR	KPR	OTD	PTS	TAY
1997	SF	4(1)	10	-6	-0.6(2)	0	—	—	—	—	52	21	40.4	239	4.6(33)	1	4	4	32	—	—	—	0	-42
1998	SF	2(0)	3	-4	-1.3(-1)	0	—	—	—	—	—	—	—	—	—	—	—	—	—	—	—	—	0	-4
NFL	2	6(1)	13	-10	-0.8(2)	0	—	—	—	—	52	21	40.4	239	4.6(33)	1	4	4	32	—	—	—	0	-46

DRULIS, AL Albert Anthony, B, 5´10˝/193 lbs; Temple; 1943: ChiC, rnd 27; B8/30/1921 Girardville, PA

YEAR	TEAM	G(GS, POS)	RUSH	YD	AVG(LG)	TD	REC	YD	AVG(LG)	TD	PASS	COMP	PCT	YD	AVG(LG)	TD	INT	SK	YD	QBR	KPR	OTD	PTS	TAY
1945	ChiC	9(7, FB)	12	49	4.1(13)	0	6	49	8.2(17)	0	—	—	—	—	—	—	—	—	—	—	k	—	0	58
1946	ChiC	5(1)	1	0	0.0(0)	0	—	—	—	—	—	—	—	—	—	—	—	—	—	—	—	—	0	0
1947	†Pit	10(2)	—	—	—	—	—	—	—	—	—	—	—	—	—	—	—	—	—	—	—	—	0	0
NFL	3	24(10)	13	49	3.8(13)	0	6	49	8.2(17)	0	—	—	—	—	—	—	—	—	—	—	k	—	0	58

DRULIS, CHUCK Charles John, G-LB, 5´10˝/216 lbs; Temple; B3/8/1918 Girardville, PA, D8/23/1972 Little Rock, AR **[C]** **1942**†ChiB✧11 (0) **1945** ChiB 3 (0) **1946**†ChiB 11 (8, LG) **1947** ChiB 12 (8, LG) **1948** ChiB☆12 (10, LG) **1949** ChiB 12 (6, LG) **1950** GB 11 **NFL** 72 (32) [7 yrs]

DRUMMOND, EDDIE Eddie, WR, 5´9˝/185 lbs; Penn State; B4/12/1980 Pittsburgh, PA **[R]**

YEAR	TEAM	G(GS, POS)	RUSH	YD	AVG(LG)	TD	REC	YD	AVG(LG)	TD	PASS	COMP	PCT	YD	AVG(LG)	TD	INT	SK	YD	QBR	KPR	OTD	PTS	TAY
2002	Det	9(0)	4	38	9.5(23)	0	2	-3	-1.5(-1)	0	—	—	—	—	—	—	—	—	—	—	kp	1	6	534
2003	Det	6(0)	1	1	1.0(1)	0	—	—	—	—	—	—	—	—	—	—	—	—	—	—	kp	1	6	256
2004	Det★	11(1)	1	9	9.0(9)	0	—	—	—	—	—	—	—	—	—	—	—	—	—	—	kp	4	24	722
2005	Det	12(0)	1	-3	-3.0(-3)	0	—	—	—	—	—	—	—	—	—	—	—	—	—	—	kp	—	0	366
NFL	4	38(1)	7	45	6.4(23)	0	2	-3	-1.5(-1)	0	—	—	—	—	—	—	—	—	—	—	kp	6	36	1878

DRUMMOND, ROBERT Robert C., RB, 6´1˝/205 lbs; Syracuse; 1989: Phi, rnd 3; B6/21/1967 Apopka, FL

YEAR	TEAM	G(GS, POS)	RUSH	YD	AVG(LG)	TD	REC	YD	AVG(LG)	TD	PASS	COMP	PCT	YD	AVG(LG)	TD	INT	SK	YD	QBR	KPR	OTD	PTS	TAY
1989	†Phi	16(1)	32	127	4.0(16)	0	17	180	10.6(21)	1	—	—	—	—	—	—	—	—	—	—	—	—	6	222
1990	Phi	4(0)	8	33	4.1(9)	1	5	39	7.8(29)	0	—	—	—	—	—	—	—	—	—	—	—	—	6	63
1991	Phi	16(0)	12	27	2.3(7)	2	—	—	—	—	—	—	—	—	—	—	—	—	—	—	—	—	12	47
NFL	3	36(1)	52	187	3.6(16)	3	22	219	10.0(29)	1	—	—	—	—	—	—	—	—	—	—	—	—	24	332

DRUMSTEAD, WOP Walter, aka Walter Dremstadt, G, /185 lbs; none; B9/1898 Hammond, IN, deceased **1925** Ham 1 (1)

DRUNGO, ELBERT Elbert J., T-G, 6´5˝/265 lbs; Tennessee State; 1969: Hou, rnd 3; B4/30/1943 Columbus, MS **1969**†Hou-A 14 **1970** Hou 14 (RG) **1971** Hou 11 (RG) **1973** Hou 14 (RT) **1974** Hou 13 (RT) **1975** Hou 13 (RT) **1976** Hou 14 (RT) **1977** Hou 14 (14, RG) **1978** Buf 13 (4) **NFL** 120 (18) [9 yrs]

DRURY, HOOT Lyle Thomas, E, 6´4˝/189 lbs; St. Louis; B2/18/1906, D8/26/1989 Itasca, IL **1930** ChiB 14 (8, re) **1931** ChiB 10 (6, RE), 6 **NFL** 24 (14) [2 yrs]

DRUSCHEL, RICH Richard Dennis, T-G, 6´2˝/248 lbs; North Carolina State; 1974: Pit, rnd 6; B1/15/1952 Ellwood City, PA **1974**†Pit 11

DRUZE, JOHNNY John Francis, E, 6´0˝/195 lbs; Fordham; 1938: Bkn, rnd 11; B7/3/1914 Newark, NJ, D12/27/2005 Scottsdale, AZ

YEAR	TEAM	G(GS, POS)	RUSH	YD	AVG(LG)	TD	REC	YD	AVG(LG)	TD	PASS	COMP	PCT	YD	AVG(LG)	TD	INT	SK	YD	QBR	KPR	OTD	PTS	TAY
1938	Bkn	10(5, RE)	—	—	—	—	4	29	7.3	0	—	—	—	—	—	—	—	—	—	—	—	—	0	15

YEAR	TEAM	G (GS, POS)	RUSH	YD	AVG (LG)	TD	REC	YD	AVG (LG)	TD	PASS	COMP	PCT	YD	AVG (LG)	TD	INT	SK	YD	QBR	KPR	OTD	PTS	TAY
DRYER, FRED John Frederick, DE, 6´6˝/240 lbs; San Diego State; 1969: NYG, rnd 1; B7/6/1946 Hawthorne, CA **1969** NYG 14 (14, RDE) **1970** NYG 14 (14, RDE) **1971** NYG 14 (14, RDE) **1972** LARm 14 (3) **1973**†LARm 14 (14, RDE) **1974**†LARm☆14 (14, RDE) **1975**†LARm★14 (14, RDE) **1976**†LARm 14 (14, RDE) **1977**†LARm 14 (14, RDE) **1978**†LARm 16 (16, RDE) **1979**†LARm 16 (16, RDE) **1980**†LARm 16 (16, RDE) **1981** LARm 2 (0) **NFL** 176 (163) [13 yrs]																								
DRZEWIECKI, RON Ronald John, HB-DB, 5´11˝/185 lbs; Marquette; 1955: ChiB, rnd 1; B1/25/1933 Milwaukee, WI																								
1955	ChiB	12	10	54	5.4(19)	1	1	1	1.0(1)	0	—	—	—	—	—	—	—	—	—	—	kp	—	6	281
1957	ChiB	8	5	11	2.2(6)	0	1	7	7.0(7)	0	—	—	—	—	—	—	—	—	—	—	kp	—	0	89
NFL	2	20	15	65	4.3(19)	1	2	8	4.0(7)	0	—	—	—	—	—	—	—	—	—	—	kp	—	6	369
DUARTE, GEORGE George Luis, DB, 5´9˝/178 lbs; Arizona State; Northern Arizona; B2/9/1964 Tucson, AZ **1987** ChiB 3 (0)																								
DUBENION, ELBERT Elbert, FL-WR-HB, 5´11˝/187 lbs; Bluffton; 1959: Cle, rnd 14; B2/16/1933 Griffin, GA																								
1960	Buf-A☆	14(FL)	16	94	5.9(66)	1	42	752	17.9(64)	7	—	—	—	—	—	—	—	—	—	—	kp	—	48	519
1961	Buf-A	14(FL)	17	173	10.2(72)	2	31	461	14.9(61)	6	—	—	—	—	—	—	—	—	—	—	kp	—	48	541
1962	Buf-A	14(FL)	7	40	5.7(43)	0	33	571	17.3(75)	5	—	—	—	—	—	—	—	—	—	—	k	1	36	487
1963	†Buf-A☆	14(FL)	—	—	—	—	53	959	18.1(89)	4	—	—	—	—	—	—	—	—	—	—	k	—	24	638
1964	†Buf-A★	14(FL)	1	20	20.0(20)	0	42	1139	**27.1**(**72**)	10	—	—	—	—	—	—	—	—	—	—	—	—	60	640
1965	Buf-A	3	—	—	—	—	18	281	15.6(46)	1	—	—	—	—	—	—	—	—	—	—	—	—	6	146
1966	†Buf-A	14(FL)	3	16	5.3(17)	0	50	747	14.9(44)	2	—	—	—	—	—	—	—	—	—	—	—	—	12	400
1967	Buf-A	12(FL)	2	-17	-8.5(-1)	0	25	384	15.4(42)	0	—	—	—	—	—	—	—	—	—	—	—	—	0	175
1968	Buf-A	4	—	—	—	—	—	—	—	—	—	—	—	—	—	—	—	—	—	—	—	—	—	—
NFL	9	103	46	326	7.1(72)	3	294	5294	18.0(89)	35	—	—	—	—	—	—	—	—	—	—	kp	1	234	3543
DUBINETZ, GREG Gregory George, G, 6´4˝/260 lbs; Yale; 1975: Cin, rnd 9; B4/15/1954 Chicago, IL **1979** Was 15																								
DUBLINSKI, TOM Thomas Eugene, QB, 6´2˝/212 lbs; Utah; 1952: Det, rnd 8; B8/8/1930 Chicago, IL																								
1952	†Det	6	1	3	3.0(3)	0	—	—	—	—	6	1	16.7	39	6.5(39)	0	1	—	—	—	—	—	0	-18
1953	Det	7	6	39	6.5(17)	0	—	—	—	—	30	14	46.7	174	5.8(26)	0	5	—	—	—	—	—	0	-74
1954	†Det	12	21	76	3.6(15)	1	—	—	—	—	138	77	55.8	1073	7.8(66)	8	7	—	—	—	—	—	6	383
1958	NYG	1	—	—	—	—	—	—	—	—	3	1	33.3	14	4.7(14)	0	0	—	—	—	—	—	0	7
1960	Den-A	3	—	—	—	—	—	—	—	—	—	—	—	—	—	—	—	—	—	—	—	—	—	—
NFL	5	29	28	118	4.2(17)	1	—	—	—	—	177	93	52.5	1300	7.3(66)	8	13	—	—	—	—	—	6	298
DUBOFSKY, MAURY Maurice, G, 5´10˝/210 lbs; Georgetown (DC); B1909 Hartford, CT, D1/25/1970 Bethesda, MD **1932** NYG 5 (2)																								
DUBOIS, PHIL Phillip Donn, TE, 6´2˝/220 lbs; San Diego State; B11/16/1956 Rochester, MN **1979** Was 15																								
1980	Was	2(1)	—	—	—	—	1	16	16.0(16)	0	—	—	—	—	—	—	—	—	—	—	—	—	0	8
NFL	2	17(1)	—	—	—	—	1	16	16.0(16)	0	—	—	—	—	—	—	—	—	—	—	—	—	0	8
DUBOSE, DEMETRIOUS Adolphus Demetrius, LB, 6´1˝/235 lbs; Notre Dame; 1993: TB, rnd 2; B3/23/1971 Seattle, WA, D7/24/1999 La Jolla, CA **1993** TB 15 (4) **1994** TB 16 (1) **1995** TB 15 (0) **1996** TB 14 (0) **NFL** 60 (5) [4 yrs]																								
DUBOSE, DOUG Donald Douglas, RB, 5´11˝/190 lbs; Nebraska; B3/14/1964 New London, CT																								
1987	SF	2(0)	10	33	3.3(11)	0	4	37	9.3(14)	0	—	—	—	—	—	—	—	—	—	—	—	—	0	52
1988	SF	14(0)	24	116	4.8(37)	2	6	57	9.5(13)	0	—	—	—	—	—	—	—	—	—	—	k	—	12	293
NFL	2	16(0)	34	149	4.4(37)	2	10	94	9.4(14)	0	—	—	—	—	—	—	—	—	—	—	k	—	12	344
DUBOSE, JIMMY Jimmy DuWayne, RB, 5´11˝/217 lbs; Florida; 1976: TB, rnd 2; B10/25/1954 Enterprise, AL																								
1976	TB	14(4)	20	62	3.1(24)	0	5	26	5.2(18)	0	—	—	—	—	—	—	—	—	—	—	k	—	0	94
1977	TB	13(6, FB)	71	284	4.0(13)	0	11	89	8.1(17)	0	—	—	—	—	—	—	—	—	—	—	—	—	0	329
1978	TB	6(5, fb)	93	358	3.8(12)	4	1	3	3.0(3)	0	—	—	—	—	—	—	—	—	—	—	—	—	24	400
NFL	3	33(15)	184	704	3.8(24)	4	17	118	6.9(18)	0	—	—	—	—	—	—	—	—	—	—	k	—	24	822
DUBZINSKI, WALT Walter John, C-G, 5´10˝/205 lbs; Boston College; B10/26/1919 Gardner, MA **1943** NYG 5 (0) **1944** Bos 3 (2) **NFL** 8 (2) [2 yrs]																								
DUCKENS, MARK Mark Anthony, DE-DT, 6´4˝/270 lbs; Wichita State; Arizona State; B3/4/1965 Wichita, KS **1989**†NYG 15 (0) **1990** Det 15 (0) **1992** TB 5 (3) **NFL** 35 (3) [3 yrs]																								
DUCKETT, DAMANE Damane Jerrel, DT, 6´6˝/300 lbs; East Carolina; B1/21/1981 Waterbury, CT **2004** Car 2 (0) **2004** NYG 4 (1) **2005**†NYG 8 (0) **NFL** 14 (1) [2 yrs]																								
DUCKETT, FOREY William Forey, DB, 6´3˝/195 lbs; Nevada-Reno; 1993: Cin, rnd 5; B2/5/1970 Oakland, CA **1994** Cin 2 (0) **1994** GB 3 (0) **1994** Sea 2 (0) **NFL** 7 (0) [1 yr]																								
DUCKETT, KENNY Kenneth Wayne, WR, 6´0˝/184 lbs; Wake Forest; 1982: NO, rnd 3; B10/1/1959 Winston-Salem, NC, D3/15/1998 Winston-Salem, NC																								
1982	NO	7(0)	—	—	—	—	12	196	16.3(31)	2	—	—	—	—	—	—	—	—	—	—	k	—	12	117
1983	NO	14(1)	2	-16	-8.0(2)	0	19	283	14.9(48)	2	—	—	—	—	—	—	—	—	—	—	k	—	12	360
1984	NO	11(0)	1	-3	-3.0(-3)	0	3	24	8.0(11)	0	—	—	—	—	—	—	—	—	—	—	k	—	0	154
1985	NO	1(0)	—	—	—	—	—	—	—	—	—	—	—	—	—	—	—	—	—	—	—	—	—	—
1985	†Dal	3(0)	—	—	—	—	—	—	—	—	—	—	—	—	—	—	—	—	—	—	k	—	0	38
NFL	4	36(1)	3	-19	-6.3(2)	0	34	503	14.8(48)	4	—	—	—	—	—	—	—	—	—	—	k	—	24	669
DUCKETT, T.J. Todd Jeffrey, RB, 6´0˝/254 lbs; Michigan State; 2002: Atl, rnd 1; B2/17/1981 Kalamazoo, MI																								
2002	†Atl	11(4)	130	507	3.9(33)	4	9	61	6.8(20)	0	—	—	—	—	—	—	—	—	—	—	k	—	24	567
2003	Atl	16(10, RB)	197	779	4.0(55)	11	11	94	8.5(21)	0	1	0	0.0	0	0.0	0	0	—	—	—	—	—	66	936
2004	†Atl	13(0)	104	509	4.9(35)	8	3	15	5.0(11)	0	—	—	—	—	—	—	—	—	—	—	—	—	48	597
2005	Atl	14(0)	121	380	3.1(25)	8	6	63	10.5(19)	0	—	—	—	—	—	—	—	—	—	—	k	—	48	498
NFL	4	54(14)	552	2175	3.9(55)	31	29	233	8.0(21)	0	1	0	0.0	0	0.0	0	0	—	—	—	k	—	186	2597
DUCKSWORTH, ROBERT Robert Charles, DB, 5´11˝/200 lbs; Southern Mississippi; 1986: NYJ, rnd 8; B1/5/1963 Biloxi, MS **1986** NYJ 2 (0)																								
DUCKWORTH, BOBBY Bobby Ray, WR, 6´3˝/198 lbs; Arkansas; 1981: SD, rnd 6; B11/27/1958 Crossett, AR																								
1982	SD	5(0)	—	—	—	—	2	77	38.5(55)	0	—	—	—	—	—	—	—	—	—	—	—	—	0	39
1983	SD	16(2)	—	—	—	—	20	422	21.1(59)	5	—	—	—	—	—	—	—	—	—	—	—	—	30	236
1984	SD	16(1)	—	—	—	—	25	715	28.6(88)	4	—	—	—	—	—	—	—	—	—	—	—	—	24	378
1985	†LARm	14(6, wr)	—	—	—	—	25	422	16.9(42)	3	—	—	—	—	—	—	—	—	—	—	—	—	18	226
1986	LARm	7(6, wr)	—	—	—	—	9	141	15.7(32)	1	—	—	—	—	—	—	—	—	—	—	—	—	6	76
1986	Phi	4(0)	—	—	—	—	1	7	7.0(7)	0	—	—	—	—	—	—	—	—	—	—	—	—	0	4
NFL	5	62(15)	—	—	—	—	82	1784	21.8(88)	13	—	—	—	—	—	—	—	—	—	—	—	—	78	957
DUCKWORTH, JOE Joseph Walter, E, 6´2˝/220 lbs; Colgate; B7/3/1921 Orange, NJ																								
1947	Was	12(1)	—	—	—	—	14	250	17.9(55)	3	—	—	—	—	—	—	—	—	—	—	—	—	18	140
DUCOTE, MOON Richard Joseph, WB-TB, 5´11˝/190 lbs; Auburn; B8/28/1897, D9/1985 Plaucheville, LA **1920** Cle 1 (1)																								
DUDA, MARK Mark David, DT, 6´3˝/273 lbs; Maryland; 1983: SL, rnd 4; B2/4/1961 Wilkes-Barre, PA **1983** SL 14 (6, ldt) **1984** SL 8 (6, RDT) **1985** SL 16 (16, RDT) **1986** SL 14 (3) **1987** SL 3 (3) **NFL** 55 (34) [5 yrs]																								
DUDEK, JOE Joseph Anthony, RB, 6´0˝/200 lbs; Plymouth State; B1/22/1964 Boston, MA																								
1987	Den	2(2)	35	154	4.4(16)	2	7	41	5.9(19)	0	—	—	—	—	—	—	—	—	—	—	—	—	12	195
DUDEK, MITCH Mitchell Richard, T, 6´4˝/245 lbs; Xavier (OH); 1965: NYJ, rnd 19; B11/9/1943 Evanston, IL **1966** NYJ-A 14																								
DUDEN, DICK Henry Richard, DE-E, 6´3˝/212 lbs; Navy; B11/29/1924 Pottstown, PA																								
1949	NYG	12(2)	—	—	—	—	2	15	7.5(10)	0	—	—	—	—	—	—	—	—	—	—	—	—	0	8
DUDISH, ANDY Andrew Charles, HB, 5´11˝/182 lbs; Georgia; B10/13/1921 Wilkes-Barre, PA, D1/19/2001 Snellville, GA																								
1946	Buf-A	11(2)	30	106	3.5	0	2	33	16.5	0	—	—	—	—	—	—	—	—	—	—	kp	—	0	262
1947	Bal-A	14(4)	28	30	1.1	1	7	130	18.6	1	—	—	—	—	—	—	—	—	—	—	kp	—	12	270
AAFC	2	25(6)	58	136	2.3	1	9	163	18.1	1	—	—	—	—	—	—	—	—	—	—	kp	—	12	532
1948	Det	4(0)	1	5	5.0(5)	0	—	—	—	—	—	—	—	—	—	—	—	—	—	—	kp	—	0	13

YEAR	TEAM	G (GS, POS)	RUSH	YD	AVG(LG)	TD	REC	YD	AVG(LG)	TD	PASS	COMP	PCT	YD	AVG(LG)	TD	INT	SK	YD	QBR	KPR	OTD	PTS	TAY

DUDLEY, BILL William McGarvey, HB-TB-QB, 5´10˝/182 lbs; Virginia; 1942: Pit, rnd 1; B12/24/1919 Bluefield, VA; HOF 1966 [KRI]

1942	Pit★	11(11, TB)	**162**	**696**	4.3(66)	5	1	24	24.0(24)	0	94	35	37.2	438	4.7(38)	2	5	—	—	—	Pkpi	1	36	**1146**
1945	Pit	4(4, TB)	57	204	3.6(32)	3	—	—	—	—	32	10	31.3	58	1.8(32)	0	2	—	—	—	KPkpi	—	20	235
1946	Pit☆	11(11, TB)	146	604	4.1(41)	2	4	109	27.3(80)	1	90	32	35.6	452	5.0(37)	2	9	—	—	—	KPkpi	2	48	**1082**
1947	Det☆	9(8, LH)	80	302	3.8(28)	2	27	375	13.9(64)	7	4	3	75.0	24	6.0(11)	2	0	—	—	—	Pkpi	2	66	927
1948	Det☆	7(4, LH)	33	97	2.9(11)	0	20	210	10.5(22)	6	1	0	0.0	0	0.0	0	1	—	—	—	Pkpi	1	42	271
1949	Det	12(11, LH)	125	402	3.2(26)	3	27	190	7.0(18)	2	—	—	—	—	—	—	—	—	—	—	KPkp	1	81	742
1950	Was★	12(RH)	66	339	5.1(27)	1	22	172	7.8(17)	1	—	—	—	—	—	—	—	—	—	—	KPkp	1	64	596
1951	Was★	12(LH)	91	398	4.4(40)	2	22	303	13.8(40)	1	1	1	100.0	13	13.0(13)	0	0	—	—	—	KPkp	—	69	726
1953	Was	12	5	15	3.0(7)	0	—	—	—	—	—	—	—	—	—	—	—	—	—	—	Kp	—	58	9
NFL	9	90(49)	765	3057	4.0(66)	18	123	1383	11.2(80)	18	222	81	36.5	985	4.4(38)	6	17	—	—	—	KPkpi	8	484	5733

DUDLEY, BRIAN Brian Christopher, DB, 6´1˝/180 lbs; Bethune-Cookman; B8/30/1960 Los Angeles, CA **1987** Cle 3 (3)

DUDLEY, KEVIN Kevin, RB, 6´0˝/238 lbs; Michigan; B1/2/1982 Brookville, IL **2005** Atl 1 (0)

DUDLEY, PAUL Paul Eugene, HB, 6´0˝/185 lbs; Arkansas; 1961: GB, rnd 4/1962: SD, rnd 29; B1/16/1939 Fort Smith, AR

1962	NYG	11	27	100	3.7(38)	0	9	112	12.4(38)	1	1	0	0.0	0	0.0	0	1	—	—	—	k	—	6	230
1963	Phi	10	11	21	1.9(6)	0	1	8	8.0(8)	0	0	0	0.0	0	0.0	0	0	1	10	—	k	—	0	25
NFL	2	21	38	121	3.2(38)	0	10	120	12.0(38)	1	1	0	0.0	0	0.0	0	1	1	10	—	k	—	6	255

DUDLEY, RICKEY Rickey DeShun, TE, 6´6˝/255 lbs; Ohio State; 1996: Oak, rnd 1; B7/15/1972 Henderson, TX

1996	Oak	16(15, TE)	—	—	—	—	34	386	11.4(62)	4	—	—	—	—	—	—	—	—	—	—	—	—	24	213
1997	Oak	16(16, TE)	—	—	—	—	48	787	16.4(76)	7	—	—	—	—	—	—	—	—	—	—	—	—	42	429
1998	Oak	16(15, TE)	1	-2	-2.0(-2)	0	36	549	15.3(32)	5	—	—	—	—	—	—	—	—	—	—	—	—	32	298
1999	Oak	16(16, TE)	—	—	—	—	39	555	14.2(35)	9	—	—	—	—	—	—	—	—	—	—	—	—	54	323
2000	†Oak	16(16, TE)	1	-7	-7.0(-7)	0	29	350	12.1(30)	4	—	—	—	—	—	—	—	—	—	—	—	—	24	188
2001	Cle	4(4)	—	—	—	—	9	115	12.8(27)	0	—	—	—	—	—	—	—	—	—	—	—	—	0	58
2002	†TB	14(3)	—	—	—	—	16	192	12.0(35)	3	—	—	—	—	—	—	—	—	—	—	—	—	18	111
2003	TB	7(2)	—	—	—	—	7	42	6.0(9)	1	—	—	—	—	—	—	—	—	—	—	—	—	6	26
2004	TB	3(0)	—	—	—	—	3	48	16.0(24)	0	—	—	—	—	—	—	—	—	—	—	—	—	0	24
NFL	9	108(87)	2	-9	-4.5(-2)	0	221	3024	13.7(76)	33	—	—	—	—	—	—	—	—	—	—	—	—	200	1668

DUERSON, DAVE David Russell, DB, 6´1˝/207 lbs; Notre Dame; 1983: Chi, rnd 3; B11/28/1960 Muncie, IN [I] **1983** ChiB 16 (6, fs) **1984**†ChiB 16 (0) **1985**†ChiB☆15 (15, SS) **1986**†ChiB★16 (16, SS) **1987**†ChiB★12 (12, FS) **1988**†ChiB★15 (15, SS) **1989** ChiB 12 (12, SS) **1990**†NYG 16 (2) **1991** Phx 11 (4) **1992** Phx 15 (0) **1993** Phx 16 (4) **NFL** 160 (86) [11 yrs]

DUFAULT, PAUL Paul Henry, C, 6´4˝/255 lbs; New Hampshire; B2/15/1964 Bridgeport, CT **1987** LARd 1 (0)

DUFEK, DON Donald Patrick, DB, 6´0˝/195 lbs; Michigan; 1976: Sea, rnd 5; B4/28/1954 Ann Arbor, MI **1976** Sea 14 **1977** Sea 13 (5, ss) **1979** Sea 13 **1980** Sea 8 (0) **1981** Sea 15 (0) **1982** Sea 9 (1) **1983**†Sea 14 (0) **1984**†Sea 9 (0) **NFL** 95 (6) [8 yrs]

DUFEK, JOE Joseph Edward, QB, 6´4˝/215 lbs; Yale; B8/23/1961 Ann Arbor, MI **1983** Buf 5 (0)

| 1984 | Buf | 5(5, qb) | 9 | 22 | 2.4(13) | 1 | — | — | — | — | 150 | 74 | 49.3 | 829 | 5.5(64) | 4 | 8 | 10 | 86 | — | — | — | 6 | 147 |
| NFL | 2 | 10(5) | 9 | 22 | 2.4(13) | 1 | — | — | — | — | 150 | 74 | 49.3 | 829 | 5.5(64) | 4 | 8 | 10 | 86 | — | — | — | 6 | 147 |

DUFF, BILL William Brian, DT, 6´3˝/284 lbs; Tennessee; B2/24/1974 Delran, NJ **1999** Cle 5 (0)

DUFF, JAMAL Jamal Edwin, DE-DT, 6´7˝/276 lbs; San Diego State; 1995: NYG, rnd 6; B3/11/1972 Columbus, OH **1995** NYG 15 (2) **1997** Was 13 (5, lde) **1998** Was 13 (3) **NFL** 41 (10) [3 yrs]

DUFF, JOHN John Edward, TE, 6´7˝/250 lbs; New Mexico; B7/31/1967 Columbus, OH **1993**†LARd 1 (0) **1994** LARd 4 (0) **NFL** 5 (0) [2 yrs]

DUFFT, JIM James Henry, G-T, 6´6˝/250 lbs; Rutgers; Fordham; B6/25/1896, deceased **1921** Roc 1 (1) **1921** NYG 1 (0) **1922** Mil 8 (7, RG) **NFL** 10 (8) [2 yrs]

DUFFY, PAT Joseph Patrick, B, 5´10˝/185 lbs; Dayton; B12/6/1906 Dayton, OH; D10/14/1965 Dayton, OH [K] **1929** Day 5 (1), 1

DUFFY, ROGER Roger Thomas, G-C, 6´3˝/300 lbs; Penn State; 1990: NYJ, rnd 8; B7/16/1967 Pittsburgh, PA **1990** NYJ 16 (2) **1991**†NYJ 12 (0) **1992** NYJ 16 (6, lg) **1993** NYJ 16 (1) **1994** NYJ 16 (14, LG) **1995** NYJ 16 (16, LG) **1996** NYJ 16 (16, C/lg) **1997** NYJ 15 (15, C) **1998** Pit 15 (4) **1999** Pit 16 (11, C) **2000** Pit 13 (7, c) **2001**†Pit 8 (0) **NFL** 175 (92) [12 yrs]

DUFORD, DUKES Wilfred Joseph, E-B, 5´10˝/180 lbs; Marquette; B6/11/1898 Menomonie, WI, D5/8/1981 Davenport, IA **1924** GB 3 (0)

DUFOUR, DAN Daniel Arthur, G, 6´5˝/280 lbs; UCLA; B10/18/1960 Lynn, MA **1983** Atl 16 (0) **1984** Atl 6 (3) **NFL** 22 (3) [2 yrs]

DUGAN, BILL William H., G-T, 6´4˝/275 lbs; Penn State; 1981: Sea, rnd 3; B6/5/1959 Hornell, NY **1981** Sea 16 (2) **1982** Sea 9 (2) **1983**†Sea 15 (1) **1984** Min 1 (0) **1987** NYG 3 (3) **NFL** 44 (8) [5 yrs]

DUGAN, FRED John Frederick, E, 6´3˝/205 lbs; Dayton; 1957: SF, rnd 7; B5/12/1933 Stamford, CT

1958	SF	12	—	—	—	—	9	122	13.6(23)	0	—	—	—	—	—	—	—	—	—	—	—	—	0	61
1959	SF	12	—	—	—	—	6	72	12.0(13)	0	—	—	—	—	—	—	—	—	—	—	—	—	0	36
1960	Dal	12(SE)	—	—	—	—	29	461	15.9(49)	1	—	—	—	—	—	—	—	—	—	—	—	—	6	236
1961	Was	13(TE)	—	—	—	—	53	817	15.4(80)	4	—	—	—	—	—	—	—	—	—	—	—	—	24	429
1962	Was	12(TE)	1	-9	-9.0(-9)	0	36	466	12.9(27)	5	—	—	—	—	—	—	—	—	—	—	—	—	30	249
1963	Was	14(TE)	—	—	—	—	20	288	14.4(41)	3	—	—	—	—	—	—	—	—	—	—	—	—	18	159
NFL	6	75—	1	-9	-9.0(-9)	0	153	2226	14.5(80)	13	—	—	—	—	—	—	—	—	—	—	—	—	78	1169

DUGAN, JEFF Jeffery Steven, TE, 6´4˝/261 lbs; Maryland; 2004: Min, rnd 7; B4/8/1981 Allison Park, PA **2004**†Min 14 (2) **2005** Min 1 (0) **NFL** 15 (2) [2 yrs]

DUGAN, LEN Leonard Mark, C-LB, 6´0˝/218 lbs; Wichita State; B2/19/1910, D6/22/1967 **1936** NYG 3 (1) **1937** ChiC 11 (5, c) **1938** ChiC 8 (3) **1939** ChiC 4 (0) **1939** Pit 1 (0) **NFL** 27 (9) [4 yrs]

DUGANS, RON Ron, WR, 6´2˝/205 lbs; Florida State; 2000: Cin, rnd 3; B4/27/1977 Tallahassee, FL

2000	Cin	14(5, wr)	—	—	—	—	14	125	8.9(17)	1	—	—	—	—	—	—	—	—	—	—	—	—	6	68
2001	Cin	16(3)	—	—	—	—	28	251	9.0(31)	2	—	—	—	—	—	—	—	—	—	—	—	—	14	136
2002	Cin	16(5, wr)	—	—	—	—	47	421	9.0(31)	0	—	—	—	—	—	—	—	—	—	—	k	—	0	202
NFL	3	46(13)	—	—	—	—	89	797	9.0(31)	3	—	—	—	—	—	—	—	—	—	—	k	—	20	405

DUGGAN, EDDIE Edward Dean, FB, 6´0˝/200 lbs; Notre Dame; B5/19/1891 Franklin, IN, D10/16/1950 Houston, TX **1921** RI 3 (1)

DUGGAN, GIL Gilford Earl, T, 6´3˝/229 lbs; Oklahoma; 1939: NYG, rnd 15; B12/26/1914 Benton, AR, D10/18/1974 Harrah, OK **1940** NYG 10 (0) **1942** ChiC 11 (11, LT) **1943** ChiC 10 (10, LT) **1944** C-P 10 (8, LT) **1945** ChiC 8 (5, lt) **NFL** 49 (34) [5 yrs]

1946 LAD-A 11 (0) **1947** Buf-A 12 (2) **AAFC** 23 (2) [2 yrs]

DUGGER, JACK John Richard, T-DE, 6´3˝/230 lbs; Ohio State; 1945: Pit, rnd 2; B1/13/1923 Pittsburgh, PA, D2/23/1988 Charlotte, NC

| 1946 | Buf-A | 7(0) | — | — | — | — | 1 | 15 | 15.0(15) | 0 | — | — | — | — | — | — | — | — | — | — | — | 1 | 6 | 8 |

1947 Det 12 (3) **1948** Det 12 (7, RT)

| 1949 | ChiB | 6(2) | — | — | — | — | 1 | 11 | 11.0(11) | 0 | — | — | — | — | — | — | — | — | — | — | k | — | 0 | -2 |
| NFL | 3 | 30(12) | — | — | — | — | 1 | 11 | 11.0(15) | 0 | — | — | — | — | — | — | — | — | — | — | ki | — | 0 | -1 |

DUGGINS, HERB George Herbert, E, 6´3˝/200 lbs; Purdue; B3/25/1912 New Albany, IN, D7/20/1988 Yelm, WA

| 1934 | ChiC | 11(11, RE) | — | — | — | — | 5 | 52 | 10.4 | 0 | — | — | — | — | — | — | — | — | — | — | — | — | 0 | 26 |

DUHART, PAUL Paul Albert, B, 6´0˝/180 lbs; Florida; 1945: Pit, rnd 1; B12/30/1920 Montreal, Canada

1944	†GB	8(2)	51	183	3.6(16)	2	9	176	19.6(32)	2	13	4	30.8	42	3.2(12)	0	0	—	—	—	kpi	—	24	345
1945	Pit	2(2)	11	7	0.6(0)	1	—	—	—	—	3	1	33.3	1	0.3(1)	0	0	—	—	—	k	—	6	37
1945	Bos	3(3)	6	10	1.7(9)	0	—	—	—	—	6	2	33.3	26	4.3(21)	0	2	—	—	—	k	—	0	-55
NFL	2	13(7)	68	200	2.9(16)	3	9	176	19.6(32)	2	22	7	31.8	69	3.1(21)	0	2	—	—	—	kpi	—	30	327

YEAR	TEAM	G (GS, POS)	RUSH	YD	AVG (LG)	TD	REC	YD	AVG (LG)	TD	PASS	COMP	PCT	YD	AVG (LG)	TD	INT	SK	YD	QBR	KPR	OTD	PTS	TAY

DUHE, A.J. Adam Joseph, LB-DE, 6´4˝/247 lbs; LSU; 1977: Mia, rnd 1; B11/27/1955 New Orleans, LA **1977** Mia 14 (14, RDE) **1978**†Mia 13 (10, RDE) **1979**†Mia 13 (2) **1980** Mia 16 (15, RILB) **1981**†Mia☆16 (16, LILB) **1982**†Mia 9 (9, LILB) **1983**†Mia☆15 (15, LILB) **1984**†Mia✧12 (8, LILB) **NFL** 108 (89) [8 yrs]

DUHON, BOBBY Robert Joseph, RB, 6´0˝/195 lbs; Tulane; 1968: NYG, rnd 3; B9/24/1946 Abbeville, LA

YEAR	TEAM	G (GS, POS)	RUSH	YD	AVG (LG)	TD	REC	YD	AVG (LG)	TD	PASS	COMP	PCT	YD	AVG (LG)	TD	INT	SK	YD	QBR	KPR	OTD	PTS	TAY
1968	NYG	13 (FB)	101	362	3.6 (13)	3	37	373	10.1 (51)	1	2	2	100.0	24	12.0 (19)	0	0	—	—	—	kp	—	24	614
1970	NYG	14	18	111	6.2 (38)	0	4	58	14.5 (22)	0	2	2	100.0	28	14.0 (15)	0	0	—	—	—	kp	1	6	271
1971	NYG	13 (RB)	93	344	3.7 (27)	1	25	266	10.6 (26)	0	1	0	0.0	0	0.0	0	1	—	—	—	kp	—	6	499
1972	NYG	4	9	23	2.6 (7)	0	2	20	10.0 (12)	0	—	—	—	—	—	—	—	—	—	—	kp	—	0	60
NFL	4	44	221	840	3.8 (38)	4	68	717	10.5 (51)	1	5	4	80.0	52	10.4 (19)	0	1	—	—	—	kp	1	36	1444

DUICH, STEVE Steven John, G, 6´3˝/248 lbs; San Diego State; 1968: GB, rnd 5; B2/28/1946 Long Beach, CA **1968** Atl 12 (4) **1969** Was 11 **NFL** 23 (4) [2 yrs]

DUKE, PAUL Paul Anderson, C-LB, 6´1˝/210 lbs; Georgia Tech; 1947: SF-A, rnd 3/1946: NYG, rnd 4; B9/24/1924 DeKalb County, GA **1947**†NYY-A 10 (0)

DUKE, WESLEY Wesley, TE, 6´5˝/225 lbs; Mercer; B6/21/1981 Grand Prairie, TX

YEAR	TEAM	G (GS, POS)	RUSH	YD	AVG (LG)	TD	REC	YD	AVG (LG)	TD	PASS	COMP	PCT	YD	AVG (LG)	TD	INT	SK	YD	QBR	KPR	OTD	PTS	TAY
2005	†Den	2 (0)	—	—	—	—	2	22	11.0 (21)	1	—	—	—	—	—	—	—	—	—	—	—	—	6	16

DUKES, CHAD Chad Everett, RB, 6´0˝/230 lbs; Pittsburgh; B12/29/1971 Albany, NY **2000** Was 1 (0)

YEAR	TEAM	G (GS, POS)	RUSH	YD	AVG (LG)	TD	REC	YD	AVG (LG)	TD	PASS	COMP	PCT	YD	AVG (LG)	TD	INT	SK	YD	QBR	KPR	OTD	PTS	TAY
2000	Jax	1 (0)	2	2	1.0 (2)	0	—	—	—	—	—	—	—	—	—	—	—	—	—	—	—	—	0	2
NFL	1	2 (0)	2	2	1.0 (2)	0	—	—	—	—	—	—	—	—	—	—	—	—	—	—	—	—	0	2

DUKES, JAMIE Jamie Donnell, C-G, 6´1˝/285 lbs; Florida State; B6/14/1964 Schenectady, NY **1986** Atl 14 (4) **1987** Atl 4 (0) **1988** Atl 12 (5, lg) **1989** Atl 16 (16, C) **1990** Atl 16 (16, C) **1991**†Atl 16 (16, C) **1992** Atl 16 (16, C) **1993** Atl 16 (16, C) **1994** GB 6 (6, c) **1995** Arz 8 (8, c) **NFL** 124 (103) [10 yrs]

DUKES, MIKE Michael Francis, LB, 6´3˝/235 lbs; Clemson; 1959: SF, rnd 14; B3/16/1936 Louisville, KY **1960**†Hou-A☆11 (RLB) **1961**†Hou-A 14 (RLB) **1962**†Hou-A 14 (RLB) **1963** Hou-A 14 (RLB) **1964** Bos-A 14 **1965** Bos-A 11 **1965** NYJ-A 3 **NFL** 81 [6 yrs]

DULAC, BILL William Frank, G, 6´4˝/250 lbs; Eastern Michigan; 1973: LA, rnd 7; B1/15/1951 Detroit, MI **1974** NE 13 (1) **1975** NE 13 (1) **NFL** 26 (2) [2 yrs]

DULANEY, MIKE see Mike Faulkerson

DULIBAN, CHRIS Christopher E., LB, 6´2˝/216 lbs; Texas; 1986: Dal, rnd 12; B1/9/1963 Champaign, IL **1987** Dal 3 (3)

DULIN, GARY Gary Wayne, DE-DT, 6´4˝/275 lbs; Ohio State; B1/20/1957 Madisonville, KY **1986** SL 3 (3) **1987** SL 3 (3) **NFL** 6 (6) [2 yrs]

DUMAS, MIKE Michael Dion, DB, 6´0˝/190 lbs; Indiana; 1991: Hou, rnd 2; B3/18/1969 Grand Rapids, MI **1991**†Hou 13 (0) **1992**†Hou 16 (1) **1994** Buf 14 (0) **1995** Jax 14 (8, FS) **1997** SD 16 (15, FS) **1998** SD 3 (3) **1999** SD 14 (14, FS) **2000** SD 12 (12, FS) **NFL** 102 (53) [8 yrs]

DUMAS, TROY Troy, LB, 6´3˝/242 lbs; Nebraska; 1995: KC, rnd 3; B9/30/1972 Riverside, CA **1996** KC 5 (0) **1997** KC 8 (0) **1997** SL 2 (0) **NFL** 15 (0) [2 yrs]

DUMBAULD, JON Jonathan Jordan, DE, 6´4˝/259 lbs; Kentucky; 1986: NO, rnd 10; B2/14/1963 Anaheim, CA **1986** NO 9 (0) **1987** Phi 6 (0) **1988** Phi 1 (0) **1988** NO 1 (0) **NFL** 17 (0) [3 yrs]

DUMLER, DOUG Douglas Marvin, C, 6´3˝/243 lbs; Nebraska; 1973: NE, rnd 5; B12/15/1950 Hoisington, KS **1973** NE 14 **1974** NE 14 **1975** NE 14 (3) **1976**†Min 14 **1977**†Min 14 **NFL** 70 (3) [5 yrs]

DUMOE, BILLY William George, E, 5´10˝/175 lbs; none; B3/14/1898 Duluth, MN, D5/6/1983 Minneapolis, MN **1921** GB 6 (6, LE), 12

DUMOE, JOE Joseph Thomas, E, 5´9˝/178 lbs; Syracuse; Fordham; Lafayette; B9/11/1894 Duluth, MN, D2/23/1959 Los Angeles County, CA **1920** Roc 2 (0) **1921** Roc 2 (2) **NFL** 4 (2) [2 yrs]

DUMONT, JIM James, LB, 6´1˝/224 lbs; Rutgers; 1984: Cle, rnd 7; B7/16/1961 Bristol, PA **1984** Cle 12 (0)

DUNAWAY, CRAIG Craig Carter, TE, 6´2˝/233 lbs; Michigan; 1983: Pit, rnd 8; B3/27/1961 Lake Charles, LA **1983**†Pit 11 (0)

DUNAWAY, DAVE David Harry, WR, 6´2˝/205 lbs; Duke; 1967: GB, rnd 2; B1/19/1945 Philadelphia, PA, D3/12/2001 Cary, NC **1968** GB 2 **1968** Atl 8

YEAR	TEAM	G (GS, POS)	RUSH	YD	AVG (LG)	TD	REC	YD	AVG (LG)	TD	PASS	COMP	PCT	YD	AVG (LG)	TD	INT	SK	YD	QBR	KPR	OTD	PTS	TAY
1969	NYG	3	1	4	4.0 (4)	0	2	37	18.5 (25)	0	—	—	—	—	—	—	—	—	—	—	P	—	0	23
NFL	2	13	1	4	4.0 (4)	0	2	37	18.5 (25)	0	—	—	—	—	—	—	—	—	—	—	—	—	0	23

DUNAWAY, JIM James Kenneth, DT, 6´4˝/277 lbs; Mississippi; 1963: Buf, rnd 2/Min, rnd 1; B9/3/1941 Columbia, MS **1963**†Buf-A 14 (10, LDT) **1964**†Buf-A 14 (LDT) **1965**†Buf-A★14 (LDT) **1966**†Buf-A★14 (LDT) **1967** Buf-A✧14 (LDT) **1968** Buf-A✧14 (LDT) **1969** Buf-A☆14 (LDT) **1970** Buf 14 (LDT) **1971** Buf 14 (LDT) **1972** Mia 6 (6, rdt) **NFL** 132 (16) [10 yrs]

DUNBAR, JUBILEE Allen, WR, 6´0˝/196 lbs; Southern (LA); 1972: SF, rnd 3; B5/17/1949 New Orleans, LA

YEAR	TEAM	G (GS, POS)	RUSH	YD	AVG (LG)	TD	REC	YD	AVG (LG)	TD	PASS	COMP	PCT	YD	AVG (LG)	TD	INT	SK	YD	QBR	KPR	OTD	PTS	TAY
1973	NO	14 (WR)	3	3	1.0 (13)	0	23	447	19.4 (65)	4	—	—	—	—	—	—	—	—	—	—	—	—	24	247
1974	Cle	5 (wr)	—	—	—	—	6	74	12.3 (25)	0	—	—	—	—	—	—	—	—	—	—	—	—	0	37
NFL	2	19	3	3	1.0 (13)	0	29	521	18.0 (65)	4	—	—	—	—	—	—	—	—	—	—	—	—	24	284

DUNBAR, KARL Karmichael MacKenzie, DE, 6´4˝/275 lbs; LSU; 1990: Pit, rnd 8; B5/18/1967 Opelousas, LA **1993** NO 13 (1) **1994** Arz 4 (0) **1995** Arz 4 (0) **NFL** 21 (1) [3 yrs]

DUNBAR, LATARENCE LaTarence Eugene, WR, 5´11˝/196 lbs; TCU; 2003: Atl, rnd 6; B8/15/1980 Dallas, TX **2003** Atl 5 (0)

DUNBAR, VAUGHN Vaughn Allen, RB, 5´10˝/204 lbs; Northeastern State (OK); Indiana; 1992: NO, rnd 1; B9/4/1968 Fort Wayne, IN

YEAR	TEAM	G (GS, POS)	RUSH	YD	AVG (LG)	TD	REC	YD	AVG (LG)	TD	PASS	COMP	PCT	YD	AVG (LG)	TD	INT	SK	YD	QBR	KPR	OTD	PTS	TAY
1992	†NO	16 (8, RB)	154	565	3.7 (25)	3	9	62	6.9 (13)	0	—	—	—	—	—	—	—	—	—	—	k	—	18	663
1994	NO	8 (0)	3	9	3.0 (3)	0	—	—	—	—	—	—	—	—	—	—	—	—	—	—	k	—	0	22
1995	NO	1 (0)	—	—	—	—	—	—	—	—	—	—	—	—	—	—	—	—	—	—	—	—	—	—
1995	Jax	14 (7, rb)	110	361	3.3 (26)	2	2	11	5.5 (8)	0	—	—	—	—	—	—	—	—	—	—	k	—	12	389
NFL	3	39 (15)	267	935	3.5 (26)	5	11	73	6.6 (13)	0	—	—	—	—	—	—	—	—	—	—	k	—	30	1074

DUNCAN, BRIAN James Brian, RB, 6´0˝/201 lbs; SMU; B3/31/1952 Olney, TX

YEAR	TEAM	G (GS, POS)	RUSH	YD	AVG (LG)	TD	REC	YD	AVG (LG)	TD	PASS	COMP	PCT	YD	AVG (LG)	TD	INT	SK	YD	QBR	KPR	OTD	PTS	TAY
1976	Cle	14	11	44	4.0 (11)	0	6	49	8.2 (17)	1	—	—	—	—	—	—	—	—	—	—	k	—	6	129
1977	Cle	14	5	16	3.2 (10)	0	1	5	5.0 (5)	1	—	—	—	—	—	—	—	—	—	—	k	—	6	97
1978	†Hou	5	1	0	0.0 (0)	0	2	0	0.0 (0)	0	—	—	—	—	—	—	—	—	—	—	k	—	0	8
NFL	3	33	17	60	3.5 (11)	0	9	54	6.0 (17)	2	—	—	—	—	—	—	—	—	—	—	k	—	12	233

DUNCAN, CLYDE Clyde Lewis, WR, 6´1˝/202 lbs; Tennessee; 1984: SL, rnd 1; B2/5/1961 Oxon Hill, MD **1984** SL 8 (0)

YEAR	TEAM	G (GS, POS)	RUSH	YD	AVG (LG)	TD	REC	YD	AVG (LG)	TD	PASS	COMP	PCT	YD	AVG (LG)	TD	INT	SK	YD	QBR	KPR	OTD	PTS	TAY
1985	SL	11 (0)	—	—	—	—	4	39	9.8 (14)	1	—	—	—	—	—	—	—	—	—	—	k	—	6	155
NFL	2	19 (0)	—	—	—	—	4	39	9.8 (14)	1	—	—	—	—	—	—	—	—	—	—	—	—	6	25

DUNCAN, CURTIS Curtis Everett, WR, 5´11˝/184 lbs; Northwestern; 1987: Hou, rnd 10; B1/26/1965 Detroit, MI

YEAR	TEAM	G (GS, POS)	RUSH	YD	AVG (LG)	TD	REC	YD	AVG (LG)	TD	PASS	COMP	PCT	YD	AVG (LG)	TD	INT	SK	YD	QBR	KPR	OTD	PTS	TAY
1987	†Hou	10 (0)	—	—	—	—	13	237	18.2 (48)	5	—	—	—	—	—	—	—	—	—	—	kp	—	30	253
1988	†Hou	16 (0)	—	—	—	—	22	302	13.7 (36)	1	—	—	—	—	—	—	—	—	—	—	kp	—	6	202
1989	†Hou	16 (1)	1	0	0.0 (0)	0	43	613	14.3 (55)	5	—	—	—	—	—	—	—	—	—	—	—	—	30	332
1990	†Hou	16 (16, WR)	—	—	—	—	66	785	11.9 (37)	1	—	—	—	—	—	—	—	—	—	—	p	—	6	398
1991	†Hou	16 (16, WR)	—	—	—	—	55	588	10.7 (42)	4	—	—	—	—	—	—	—	—	—	—	p	—	24	308
1992	†Hou✧	16 (16, WR)	—	—	—	—	82	954	11.6 (72)	1	—	—	—	—	—	—	—	—	—	—	—	—	6	482
1993	†Hou	12 (12, WR)	—	—	—	—	41	456	11.1 (47)	3	—	—	—	—	—	—	—	—	—	—	—	—	18	243
NFL	7	102 (61)	1	0	0.0	0	322	3935	12.2 (72)	20	—	—	—	—	—	—	—	—	—	—	kp	—	120	2217

DUNCAN, FRANK Frank Milton, DB, 6´1˝/190 lbs; San Francisco State; 1979: SD, rnd 12; B11/16/1956 San Francisco, CA **1979** SD 4 **1980**†SD 15 (1) **1981** SD 7 (4) **NFL** 26 (5) [3 yrs]

DUNCAN, HOWARD Howard D., C, 6´3˝/225 lbs; Ohio State; 1948: Phi, rnd 6; B11/8/1924, D7/1986 Tucson, AZ **1948** Det 1 (1)

DUNCAN, JAMIE Jamie Robert, LB, 6´1˝/238 lbs; Vanderbilt; 1998: TB, rnd 3; B7/20/1975 Wilmington, DE **1998** TB 14 (6, mlb) **1999**†TB 16 (0) **2000**†TB 15 (15, MLB) **2001**†TB 15 (15, MLB) **2002** SL 16 (12, MLB) **2003**†SL 16 (6, mlb) **2004** Atl 4 (2) **NFL** 96 (56) [7 yrs]

DUNCAN, JIM James Howard, DE, 6´2˝/205 lbs; Duke; Wake Forest; 1950: Cle, rnd 9; B5/2/1925 Reidsville, NC, D5/2/1985 Alameda County, CA **1950**†NYG 8 (LDE) **1951** NYG 12 (LDE) **1952** NYG 12 (LDE) **1953** NYG 11 (LDE) **NFL** 43 [4 yrs]

DUNCAN, JIM James, DB, 6´2˝/200 lbs; Maryland-Eastern Shore; 1968: Bal, rnd 4; B8/3/1946 Lancaster, SC, D10/20/1972 Lancaster, SC **1969** Bal 13 **1970**†Bal 14 **1971** Bal 11 (RCB) **NFL** 38 [3 yrs]

DUNCAN, KEN Kenneth W., P, 6´2˝/210 lbs; Tulsa; 1971: Min, rnd 17; B2/28/1946 Rock Island, IL **1971** GB 2

YEAR	TEAM	G (GS, POS)	RUSH	YD	AVG(LG)	TD	REC	YD	AVG(LG)	TD	PASS COMP	PCT	YD	AVG(LG)	TD	INT	SK	YD	QBR	KPR	OTD	PTS	TAY

DUNCAN, MAURY   Maurice Perry, QB, 6´1˝/185 lbs; San Francisco State; B7/18/1931 Oakland, CA

1954	SF	6						14	4	28.6	82	5.9(29)	0	2	—	—	—	—	—		0	-39
1955	SF	11	1	-5	-5.0(-5)	0	—	—	—	—	12	4	33.3	40	3.3(27)	0	0	—	—	—	—	0	15
NFL	2	17	1	-5	-5.0(-5)	0	—	—	—	—	26	8	30.8	122	4.7(29)	0	2	—	—	—	—	0	-24

DUNCAN, RANDY   Hearst Randolph, QB, 6´0˝/185 lbs; Iowa; 1959: GB, rnd 1; B3/15/1937 Osage, IA

| 1961 | DalT-A | 14(2) | 5 | 42 | 8.4(19) | 0 | — | — | — | — | 67 | 25 | 37.3 | 361 | 5.4(47) | 1 | 3 | — | — | — | — | 0 | 108 |

DUNCAN, RICK   Richard Joe, P-K, 6´0˝/208 lbs; Eastern Montana; B8/14/1941 Mattoon, IL **[K]**   **1967** Den-A 2   **1968** Phi 1   **1969** Det 1   **NFL** 4 [3 yrs]

DUNCAN, RON   Ronald Neely, TE, 6´6˝/255 lbs; Wittenberg; B9/8/1943 Lakeland, FL   **1967** Cle 3

DUNCAN, SPEEDY   Leslie Herbert, DB, 5´10˝/180 lbs; Jackson State; B8/10/1942 Tuscaloosa, AL **[RI]**   **1964**†SD-A 5   **1965**†SD-A★14 (RCB)   **1966** SD-A★14 (RCB)   **1967** SD-A★14 (RCB)   **1968** SD-A 10 (RCB)   **1969** SD 6   **1970** SD 6   **1971**†Was◊14   **1972** Was 8   **1973**†Was 14   **1974** Was 2   **NFL** 115 [11 yrs]

DUNCAN, TIM   Tim, K, 6´2˝/210 lbs; Oklahoma; B6/12/1979 Tulsa, OK **[K]**   **2003** Arz 5 (0)

DUNCUM, BOB   Robert Eldon, T, 6´3˝/255 lbs; West Texas A&M; 1967; SL, rnd 13; B8/14/1944 Austin, TX   **1968** SL 4

DUNEK, KEN   Kenneth Robert, TE, 6´6˝/235 lbs; Memphis; B6/20/1957 Chicago, IL   **1980** Phi 2 (0)

DUNGY, TONY   Anthony Kevin, DB-QB, 6´0˝/188 lbs; Minnesota; B10/6/1955 Jackson, MI **[C]**   **1978**†Pit 16 (2)   **1979** SF 15 (7, FS)

| 1977 | †Pit | 14 | 3 | 8 | 2.7(6) | 0 | — | — | — | — | 8 | 3 | 37.5 | 43 | 5.4(18) | 0 | 2 | — | — | i | — | 0 | -29 |
| NFL | 3 | 45(9) | 3 | 8 | 2.7(6) | 0 | — | — | — | — | 8 | 3 | 37.5 | 43 | 5.4(18) | 0 | 2 | — | — | pi | — | 0 | 49 |

DUNIVEN, TOM   James Thomas, QB, 6´3˝/210 lbs; Texas Tech; 1977: Cin, rnd 6; B5/20/1954 Pampa, TX   **1977** Hou 1

DUNLAP, BOB   Robert Louis, DB-QB, 6´1˝/191 lbs; Oklahoma; B10/29/1912 Haskell, OK, D7/30/1966 Wilmette, OH

1935	ChiB	12(1)	7	-16	-2.3	0	1	9	9.0(9)	0	37	11	29.7	121	3.3	1	2	—	—	—	—	0	-26
1936	NYG	5(0)	8	20	2.5	0	—	—	—	—	1	0	0.0	0	0.0	0	0	—	—	—	—	0	20
NFL	2	17(1)	15	4	0.3	0	1	9	9.0(9)	0	38	11	28.9	121	3.2	1	2	—	—	—	—	0	-6

DUNLAP, LENNY   Leonard, DB, 6´1˝/196 lbs; North Texas; 1971: Bal, rnd 1; B6/25/1949 Monroe, LA   **1971** Bal 4   **1972** SD 14 (RCB)   **1973** SD 14 (14, RCB)   **1974** SD 8 (2)   **1975** Det 6 (1)   **NFL** 46 (17) [5 yrs]

DUNN, ANTHONY   Anthony, DE, 6´2˝/255 lbs; Northern Colorado; B7/1/1980 Denver, CO   **2003** Ten 2 (0)

DUNN, BOB   Robert E., C-T, 6´1˝/200 lbs; NYU; B7/1/1905, D1/1984 Springfield, MA   **1929** SI 6 (6, C)

DUNN, COYE   Coye Elvis, B, 6´0˝/198 lbs; USC; B3/7/1916 Vilas, CO, D2/8/2000   **1943** Was 3 (0)

DUNN, DAMON   Damon Jerrel, WR, 5´9˝/182 lbs; Stanford; B3/15/1976 Fort Worth, TX   **1999** Cle 1 (0)   **2000** NYJ 1 (0)

| 2000 | Cle | 3(0) | — | — | — | — | 1 | 6 | 6.0(6) | 0 | — | — | — | — | — | — | — | — | — | — | — | 0 | 3 |
| NFL | 2 | 5(0) | — | — | — | — | 1 | 6 | 6.0(6) | 0 | — | — | — | — | — | — | — | — | — | kp | — | 0 | 3 |

DUNN, DAVID   David Leon, WR, 6´3˝/215 lbs; Fresno State; 1995: Cin, rnd 5; B6/10/1972 San Diego, CA **[R]**

1995	Cin	16(0)	1	-13	-13.0(-13)	0	17	209	12.3(37)	1	1	0	0.0	.0	0.0	0	0	—	—	k	—	6	439
1996	Cin	16(0)	—	—	—	—	32	509	15.9(40)	1	—	—	—	—	—	—	—	—	—	kp	1	12	546
1997	Cin	14(5, wr)	—	—	—	—	27	414	15.3(39)	1	—	—	—	—	—	—	—	—	—	k	—	12	419
1998	Cin	1(0)	—	—	—	—	—	—	—	—	—	—	—	—	—	—	—	—	—	—	—	0	—
1998	Pit	10(0)	—	—	—	—	9	87	9.7(24)	0	—	—	—	—	—	—	—	—	—	k	—	0	254
1999	Cle	6(0)	—	—	—	—	1	4	4.0(4)	0	—	—	—	—	—	—	—	—	—	kp	—	0	52
2000	†Oak	16(0)	—	—	—	—	4	33	8.3(14)	0	—	—	—	—	—	—	—	—	—	kp	1	6	499
2001	Oak	10(0)	—	—	—	—	1	8	8.0(8)	0	—	—	—	—	—	—	—	—	—	kp	—	0	236
NFL	7	89(5)	1	-13	-13.0(-13)	0	91	1264	13.9(40)	4	1	0	0.0	0	0.0	0	0	—	—	kp	2	36	2443

DUNN, GARY   Gary Edward, NT-DT-DE, 6´3˝/258 lbs; Miami (FL); 1976: Pit, rnd 6; B8/24/1953 Coral Gables, FL   **1976** Pit 5   **1978**†Pit 16   **1979**†Pit 16 (15, RDT)   **1980** Pit 16 (1)   **1981** Pit 16 (15, RDT)   **1982**†Pit 9 (9, NT)   **1983**†Pit 13 (12, NT)   **1984**†Pit◊16 (16, NT)   **1985** Pit 10 (7, NT)   **1986** Pit 16 (16, NT)   **1987** Pit 13 (13, NT)   **NFL** 146 (104) [11 yrs]

DUNN, JASON   Jason Adam, TE, 6´6˝/276 lbs; Eastern Kentucky; 1996: Phi, rnd 2; B11/15/1973 Harrodsburg, KY

1996	†Phi	16(12, TE)	—	—	—	—	15	332	22.1(58)	2	—	—	—	—	—	—	—	—	—	—	—	12	176
1997	Phi	15(4)	—	—	—	—	7	93	13.3(31)	2	—	—	—	—	—	—	—	—	—	k	—	12	59
1998	Phi	10(10, TE)	1	-5	-5.0(-5)	0	18	132	7.3(21)	0	—	—	—	—	—	—	—	—	—	—	—	0	61
2000	KC	14(2)	—	—	—	—	2	26	13.0(20)	0	—	—	—	—	—	—	—	—	—	—	—	0	13
2001	KC	15(5, te)	—	—	—	—	4	54	13.5(28)	1	—	—	—	—	—	—	—	—	—	k	—	6	36
2002	KC	11(4)	—	—	—	—	2	16	8.0(11)	0	—	—	—	—	—	—	—	—	—	—	—	0	8
2003	†KC	16(4)	—	—	—	—	5	35	7.0(15)	3	—	—	—	—	—	—	—	—	—	—	—	18	33
2004	KC	16(0)	—	—	—	—	17	120	7.1(17)	3	—	—	—	—	—	—	—	—	—	—	—	18	75
2005	KC	16(2)	—	—	—	—	5	53	10.6(24)	0	—	—	—	—	—	—	—	—	—	—	—	0	27
NFL	9	129(43)	1	-5	-5.0(-5)	0	75	861	11.5(58)	11	—	—	—	—	—	—	—	—	—	k	—	66	487

DUNN, K.D.   Keldrick Arthur, TE, 6´3˝/235 lbs; Clemson; 1985: SL, rnd 5; B4/28/1963 Fort Hood, TX

1985	TB	7(0)	—	—	—	—	—	—	—	—	—	—	—	—	—	—	—	—	—	—	—	0	—
1986	TB	7(0)	—	—	—	—	3	83	27.7(38)	0	—	—	—	—	—	—	—	—	—	k	—	0	27
1987	Was	3(0)	—	—	—	—	—	—	—	—	—	—	—	—	—	—	—	—	—	—	—	0	—
1988	NYJ	15(2)	—	—	—	—	6	67	11.2(26)	0	—	—	—	—	—	—	—	—	—	—	—	0	34
1989	NYJ	1(1)	—	—	—	—	2	13	6.5(8)	0	—	—	—	—	—	—	—	—	—	—	—	0	7
NFL	5	33(3)	—	—	—	—	11	163	14.8(38)	0	—	—	—	—	—	—	—	—	—	k	—	0	67

DUNN, PAUL   Paul, RB, 6´0˝/210 lbs; San Francisco State; U.S. International; 1970: Cin, rnd 13; B7/14/1948 Little Rock, AR   **1970** Cin 5

DUNN, PERRY LEE   Perry Lee, RB, 6´2˝/210 lbs; Mississippi; 1964: Dal, rnd 4/SD, rnd 3; B1/20/1941 Natchez, MS

1964	Dal	14	26	103	4.0(14)	1	2	30	15.0(18)	0	2	0	0.0	0	0.0	0	0	—	—	k	—	6	131
1965	Dal	13(7, HB)	54	171	3.2(12)	2	8	74	9.3(22)	1	—	—	—	—	—	—	—	—	—	—	—	18	233
1966	Atl	14	22	52	2.4(10)	0	5	45	9.0(16)	0	2	0	0.0	0	0.0	0	2	—	—	k	—	0	1
1967	Atl	14	27	63	2.3(11)	0	13	111	8.5(21)	0	2	1	50.0	32	16.0(32)	1	0	—	—	k	—	0	163
1968	Atl	14(HB)	72	219	3.0(15)	3	9	118	13.1(43)	0	—	—	—	—	—	—	—	—	—	—	—	18	308
1969	Bal	5	13	45	3.5(11)	0	5	30	6.0(10)	0	—	—	—	—	—	—	—	—	—	—	—	0	60
NFL	6	74(7)	214	653	3.1(15)	6	42	408	9.7(43)	1	6	1	16.7	32	5.3(32)	1	2	—	—	k	—	42	895

DUNN, RED   Joseph Aloysius, BB-TB, 5´11˝/177 lbs; Marquette; B6/21/1901 Milwaukee, WI, D1/15/1957 Milwaukee, WI **[K]**   **1924** Mil☆13 (13, BB), 47   **1925** ChiC 10 (9, BB), 28   **1926** ChiC 11 (9, BB), 15   **1927** GB 10 (6, BB), 13   **1928** GB 12 (12, BB), 1   **1929** GB 11 (8, BB), 17   **1930** GB☆13 (10, BB), 14   **1931** GB☆12 (4), 15   **NFL** 92 (71), 150 [8 yrs]

DUNN, RODDY   Roderick, T, 5´10˝/200 lbs; Syracuse; B8/8/1895 Duluth, MN, D12/20/1961 Los Angeles, CA   **1923** Dul 2 (0)

DUNN, WARRICK   Warrick De'Mon, RB, 5´9˝/180 lbs; Florida State; 1997: TB, rnd 1; B1/5/1975 Baton Rouge, LA

1997	†TB◊	16(10, RB)	224	978	4.4(76)	4	39	462	11.8(59)	3	—	—	—	—	—	—	—	—	—	kp	—	42	1326
1998	TB	16(14, RB)	245	1026	4.2(50)	2	44	344	7.8(31)	0	—	—	—	—	—	—	—	—	—	k	—	12	1228
1999	†TB	15(15, RB)	195	616	3.2(33)	0	64	589	9.2(68)	2	—	—	—	—	—	—	—	—	—	k	—	12	957
2000	†TB◊	16(14, RB)	248	1133	4.6(70)	8	44	422	9.6(45)	1	—	—	—	—	—	—	—	—	—	—	—	54	1429
2001	†TB	13(12, RB)	158	447	2.8(21)	3	68	557	8.2(31)	3	—	—	—	—	—	—	—	—	—	—	—	36	771
2002	†Atl	15(14, RB)	230	927	4.0(59)	7	50	377	7.5(31)	2	—	—	—	—	—	—	—	—	—	—	—	54	1196
2003	Atl	11(6, rb)	125	672	5.4(69)	3	37	336	9.1(86)	2	0	0	0.0	0	0.0	0	0	1	3	—	—	30	880
2004	†Atl	16(16, RB)	265	1106	4.2(60)	9	29	294	10.1(59)	0	—	—	—	—	—	—	—	—	—	—	—	54	1343
2005	Atl◊	16(16, RB)	280	1416	5.1(65)	3	29	220	7.6(24)	1	—	—	—	—	—	—	—	—	—	—	—	24	1561
NFL	9	134(117)	1970	8321	4.2(76)	39	404	3601	8.9(86)	14	0	0	0.0	0	0.0	0	0	1	3	kp	—	318	10690

DUNNE, PAT   Patrick, FB, /182 lbs; none; B1888, deceased   **1920** Det 8 (2, FB)   **1921** Det 2 (0)   **NFL** 10 (2) [2 yrs]

DUNNIGAN, PAT   Merton Arthur, T-G-E, 5´10˝/206 lbs; Minnesota; B1/24/1894 Bay City, MI, D3/30/1937 Hennepin County, MN   **1922** GB 2 (2)   **1924** Min 5 (5, LT)   **1925** Mil 6 (5, RT)   **1926** Mil 8 (8, RG)   **NFL** 21 (20) [4 yrs]

DUNSMORE, PAT Patrick Neil, TE, 6´3˝/237 lbs; Drake; 1983: Chi, rnd 4; B10/2/1957 Duluth, MN

YEAR	TEAM	G(GS, POS)	RUSH	YD	AVG(LG)	TD	REC	YD	AVG(LG)	TD	PASS	COMP	PCT	YD	AVG(LG)	TD	INT	SK	YD	QBR	KPR	OTD	PTS	TAY
1983	ChiB	16(1)	—	—	—	—	8	102	12.8(24)	0	—	—	—	—	—	—	—	—	—	—	—	—	0	51
1984	†ChiB	11(0)	—	—	—	—	9	106	11.8(25)	1	—	—	—	—	—	—	—	—	—	—	—	—	6	58
NFL	2	27(1)	—	—	—	—	17	208	12.2(25)	1	—	—	—	—	—	—	—	—	—	—	—	—	6	109

DUNSTAN, BILL William Elwyn, DT, 6´4˝/250 lbs; Utah State; 1971: SF, rnd 14; B1/3/1949 Oakland, CA **1973** Phi 14 **1974** Phi 14 (LDT) **1975** Phi 14 (14, RDT) **1976** Phi 14 **1977** Buf 14 (RDT) **1979** LARm 10 **NFL** 80 (14) [6 yrs]

DUNSTAN, ELWYN William Elwyn, T, 6´3˝/238 lbs; Portland; B2/4/1915 San Francisco, CA, D3/12/1999 **1938** ChiC 4 (0) **1939** Cle 7 (6, RT) **1941** Cle 11 (11, RT)

YEAR	TEAM	G(GS, POS)	RUSH	YD	AVG(LG)	TD	REC	YD	AVG(LG)	TD	PASS	COMP	PCT	YD	AVG(LG)	TD	INT	SK	YD	QBR	KPR	OTD	PTS	TAY
1939	ChiC	1(0)	3	2	0.7	0	—	—	—	—	—	—	—	—	—	—	—	—	—	—	—	—	0	2
1940	Cle	10(6, RT)	1	4	4.0(4)	0	—	—	—	—	—	—	—	—	—	—	—	—	—	—	—	—	0	4
NFL	4	33(23)	4	6	1.5(4)	0	—	—	—	—	—	—	—	—	—	—	—	—	—	—	p	1	6	46

DUPARD, REGGIE Jon Reginald, RB, 5´11˝/206 lbs; SMU; 1986: NE, rnd 1; B10/30/1963 New Orleans, LA

YEAR	TEAM	G(GS, POS)	RUSH	YD	AVG(LG)	TD	REC	YD	AVG(LG)	TD	PASS	COMP	PCT	YD	AVG(LG)	TD	INT	SK	YD	QBR	KPR	OTD	PTS	TAY
1986	†NE	6(0)	15	39	2.6(11)	0	—	—	—	—	—	—	—	—	—	—	—	—	—	—	k	—	0	44
1987	NE	8(3)	94	318	3.4(49)	3	3	1	0.3(2)	0	—	—	—	—	—	—	—	—	—	—	k	—	18	350
1988	NE	16(2)	52	151	2.9(15)	2	34	232	6.8(15)	0	—	—	—	—	—	—	—	—	—	—	—	—	12	287
1989	NE	7(2)	25	63	2.5(10)	1	6	70	11.7(45)	0	—	—	—	—	—	—	—	—	—	—	—	—	6	108
1989	Was	7(0)	12	48	4.0(19)	0	—	—	—	—	—	—	—	—	—	—	—	—	—	—	—	—	0	48
1990	†Was	7(0)	19	85	4.5(11)	0	—	—	—	—	—	—	—	—	—	—	—	—	—	—	k	—	0	55
NFL	5	51(7)	217	704	3.2(49)	6	43	303	7.0(45)	0	—	—	—	—	—	—	—	—	—	—	k	—	36	892

DUPER, MARK Mark Super, aka Mark Kirby Dupas, WR, 5´9˝/185 lbs; Northwestern State (LA); 1982: Mia, rnd 2; B1/25/1959 Pineville, LA

YEAR	TEAM	G(GS, POS)	RUSH	YD	AVG(LG)	TD	REC	YD	AVG(LG)	TD	PASS	COMP	PCT	YD	AVG(LG)	TD	INT	SK	YD	QBR	KPR	OTD	PTS	TAY
1982	Mia	2(0)	—	—	—	—	—	—	—	—	—	—	—	—	—	—	—	—	—	—	—	—	—	—
1983	†Mia★	16(11, WR)	—	—	—	—	51	1003	**19.7**(**85**)	10	—	—	—	—	—	—	—	—	—	—	—	—	60	552
1984	†Mia★	16(16, WR)	—	—	—	—	71	1306	18.4(80)	8	—	—	—	—	—	—	—	—	—	—	—	—	48	693
1985	†Mia	9(8, WR)	—	—	—	—	35	650	18.6(67)	3	—	—	—	—	—	—	—	—	—	—	—	—	18	340
1986	Mia✧	16(16, WR)	1	-10	-10.0(-10)	0	67	1313	19.6(**85**)	11	—	—	—	—	—	—	—	—	—	—	—	—	66	702
1987	Mia	11(11, WR)	—	—	—	—	33	597	18.1(59)	**8**	—	—	—	—	—	—	—	—	—	—	—	—	48	339
1988	Mia	13(13, WR)	—	—	—	—	39	626	16.1(56)	1	—	—	—	—	—	—	—	—	—	—	—	—	6	318
1989	Mia	15(14, WR)	—	—	—	—	49	717	14.6(41)	1	—	—	—	—	—	—	—	—	—	—	—	—	6	364
1990	†Mia	16(15, WR)	—	—	—	—	52	810	15.6(69)	5	—	—	—	—	—	—	—	—	—	—	—	—	30	430
1991	Mia	16(16, WR)	—	—	—	—	70	1085	15.5(43)	5	—	—	—	—	—	—	—	—	—	—	—	—	30	568
1992	†Mia	16(16, WR)	—	—	—	—	44	762	17.3(62)	7	—	—	—	—	—	—	—	—	—	—	—	—	42	416
NFL	11	146(136)	1	-10	-10.0(-10)	0	511	8869	17.4(85)	59	—	—	—	—	—	—	—	—	—	—	—	—	354	4720

DUPRE, CHARLIE Charles Leroy, DB, 6´1˝/195 lbs; Baylor; 1956: ChiC, rnd 6; B11/11/1933 Texas City, TX **1960** NYT-A 14

DUPRE, L.G. Louis George 'Long Gone', HB, 5´11˝/190 lbs; Baylor; 1955: Bal, rnd 3; B9/10/1932 New Orleans, LA, D8/9/2001 Texas City, TX

YEAR	TEAM	G(GS, POS)	RUSH	YD	AVG(LG)	TD	REC	YD	AVG(LG)	TD	PASS	COMP	PCT	YD	AVG(LG)	TD	INT	SK	YD	QBR	KPR	OTD	PTS	TAY
1955	Bal	11(LH)	88	338	3.8(60)	1	10	153	15.3(30)	0	—	—	—	—	—	—	—	—	—	—	—	—	6	425
1956	Bal	11(LH)	49	182	3.7(21)	2	16	216	13.5(49)	2	—	—	—	—	—	—	—	—	—	—	Pk	—	24	363
1957	Bal	12(LH)	101	375	3.7(22)	2	32	339	10.6(43)	2	—	—	—	—	—	—	—	—	—	—	P	—	24	575
1958	†Bal	10(LH)	95	390	4.1(39)	3	13	111	8.5(22)	0	—	—	—	—	—	—	—	—	—	—	P	—	18	476
1959	Bal	4	23	54	2.3(21)	0	6	47	7.8(18)	1	1	0	0.0	0	0.0	0	0	—	—	—	—	—	6	83
1960	Dal	11(5, hb)	104	362	3.5(18)	3	21	216	10.3(36)	2	—	—	—	—	—	—	—	—	—	—	k	—	30	524
1961	Dal	10	16	60	3.8(12)	0	6	49	8.2(17)	0	—	—	—	—	—	—	—	—	—	—	kp	—	0	99
NFL	7	69(5)	476	1761	3.7(60)	11	104	1131	10.9(49)	7	1	0	0.0	0	0.0	0	0	—	—	—	Pkp	—	108	2543

DUPREE, BILLY JOE Billy Joe, TE, 6´4˝/225 lbs; Michigan State; 1973: Dal, rnd 1; B3/7/1950 Monroe, LA

YEAR	TEAM	G(GS, POS)	RUSH	YD	AVG(LG)	TD	REC	YD	AVG(LG)	TD	PASS	COMP	PCT	YD	AVG(LG)	TD	INT	SK	YD	QBR	KPR	OTD	PTS	TAY
1973	†Dal	14(TE)	2	2	1.0(6)	0	29	392	13.5(40)	5	—	—	—	—	—	—	—	—	—	—	—	—	30	223
1974	Dal	14(TE)	4	43	10.8(20)	0	29	466	16.1(42)	4	—	—	—	—	—	—	—	—	—	—	—	—	24	296
1975	†Dal	14(5, te)	1	3	3.0(3)	0	9	138	15.3(28)	1	—	—	—	—	—	—	—	—	—	—	—	—	6	77
1976	†Dal★	14(14, TE)	7	50	7.1(13)	0	42	680	16.2(38)	2	—	—	—	—	—	—	—	—	—	—	—	—	12	400
1977	†Dal★	14(14, TE)	3	9	3.0(7)	0	28	347	12.4(23)	3	—	—	—	—	—	—	—	—	—	—	—	—	18	222
1978	†Dal★	16(16, TE)	1	15	15.0(15)	0	34	509	15.0(38)	**9**	—	—	—	—	—	—	—	—	—	—	—	—	54	315
1979	†Dal	16(16, TE)	2	19	9.5(20)	0	29	324	11.2(33)	5	—	—	—	—	—	—	—	—	—	—	—	—	30	206
1980	†Dal	16(16, TE)	4	19	4.8(11)	0	29	312	10.8(39)	7	—	—	—	—	—	—	—	—	—	—	—	—	42	210
1981	†Dal	16(15, TE)	1	12	12.0(12)	0	19	214	11.3(33)	2	—	—	—	—	—	—	—	—	—	—	—	—	12	129
1982	†Dal	9(1)	1	6	6.0(6)	1	7	41	5.9(12)	2	—	—	—	—	—	—	—	—	—	—	—	—	18	47
1983	†Dal	16(5, te)	—	—	—	—	12	142	11.8(28)	1	—	—	—	—	—	—	—	—	—	—	—	—	6	76
NFL	11	159(102)	26	178	6.8(20)	1	267	3565	13.4(42)	41	—	—	—	—	—	—	—	—	—	—	—	—	252	2200

DUPREE, MARCUS Marcus L., RB, 6´2˝/225 lbs; Oklahoma; Southern Mississippi; 1986: LARm, rnd 12; B5/22/1964 Philadelphia, PA

YEAR	TEAM	G(GS, POS)	RUSH	YD	AVG(LG)	TD	REC	YD	AVG(LG)	TD	PASS	COMP	PCT	YD	AVG(LG)	TD	INT	SK	YD	QBR	KPR	OTD	PTS	TAY
1990	LARm	7(1)	19	72	3.8(13)	0	—	—	—	—	—	—	—	—	—	—	—	—	—	—	—	—	0	72
1991	LARm	8(1)	49	179	3.7(24)	1	6	46	7.7(21)	0	—	—	—	—	—	—	—	—	—	—	—	—	6	212
NFL	2	15(2)	68	251	3.7(24)	1	6	46	7.7(21)	0	—	—	—	—	—	—	—	—	—	—	—	—	6	284

DUPREE, MYRON Myron Ray, DB, 5´11˝/180 lbs; North Carolina Central; 1983: Den, rnd 7; B10/15/1961 New York, NY **1983**†Den 16 (0)

DURANKO, PETE Peter Nicholas, DE-DT, 6´2˝/250 lbs; Notre Dame; 1966: Den, rnd R2/Cle, rnd 4; B12/15/1943 Johnstown, PA **1967** Den-A 14 (lde) **1968** Den-A 14 (LDE) **1969** Den-A 14 (14, RDE) **1970** Den 14 (14, RDE) **1972** Den 14 (13, LDT/lde) **1973** Den 14 (14, LDE) **1974** Den 14 (9, RDT) **NFL** 98 (64) [7 yrs]

DURDAN, DON Donald Edgar, HB-DB, 5´9˝/175 lbs; Oregon State; B9/21/1920 Arcata, CA, D6/28/1971 Corvallis, OR

YEAR	TEAM	G(GS, POS)	RUSH	YD	AVG(LG)	TD	REC	YD	AVG(LG)	TD	PASS	COMP	PCT	YD	AVG(LG)	TD	INT	SK	YD	QBR	KPR	OTD	PTS	TAY
1946	SF-A	12(1)	32	132	4.1	0	2	27	13.5	1	—	—	—	—	—	—	—	—	—	—	Ppi	—	6	201
1947	SF-A	1(0)	1	2	2.0(2)	0	—	—	—	—	—	—	—	—	—	—	—	—	—	—	—	—	0	2
AAFC	2	13(1)	33	134	4.1(2)	0	2	27	13.5	1	—	—	—	—	—	—	—	—	—	—	Ppi	—	6	203

DUREN, CLARENCE Clarence Edward, DB, 6´1˝/190 lbs; California; B12/9/1950 Compton, CA **1973** SL 11 (9, FS) **1974**†SL 14 (14, FS) **1975**†SL 13 (11, FS) **1976** SL 13 **1977** SD 14 (14, FS) **NFL** 65 (48) [5 yrs]

DURHAM, STEVE Steven Allen, DE, 6´5˝/256 lbs; Clemson; 1981: Sea, rnd 6; B10/11/1958 Greer, SC **1982** Bal 8 (0)

DURISHAN, JACK John Donald, T-G, 6´2˝/230 lbs; Pittsburgh; 1947: NYY-A, rnd 5/1943: Pit, rnd 29; B7/7/1922, D5/13/1977 **1947** NYY-A 6 (1)

DURKEE, CHARLIE Charles Michael, K, 5´11˝/165 lbs; Oklahoma State; B6/25/1944 Tulsa, OK **[K]** **1967** NO 14 **1968** NO 14 **1971** NO 12 **1972** NO 6 **NFL** 46 [4 yrs]

DURKO, JOHN John Joseph, E, 6´4˝/235 lbs; Albright; B7/23/1914 Mahanoy City, PA, D1/1/1963 **1945** ChiC 1 (0)

YEAR	TEAM	G(GS, POS)	RUSH	YD	AVG(LG)	TD	REC	YD	AVG(LG)	TD	PASS	COMP	PCT	YD	AVG(LG)	TD	INT	SK	YD	QBR	KPR	OTD	PTS	TAY
1944	Phi	6(0)	—	—	—	—	2	31	15.5(23)	1	—	—	—	—	—	—	—	—	—	—	—	—	6	21
NFL	2	7(0)	—	—	—	—	2	31	15.5(23)	1	—	—	—	—	—	—	—	—	—	—	—	—	6	21

DURKO, SANDY Sandy Vincent, DB, 6´1˝/185 lbs; USC; 1970: Cin, rnd 6; B8/29/1948 Los Angeles, CA **1970** Cin 1 **1973** NE 14 (14, SS) **1974** NE 11 (4)

YEAR	TEAM	G(GS, POS)	RUSH	YD	AVG(LG)	TD	REC	YD	AVG(LG)	TD	PASS	COMP	PCT	YD	AVG(LG)	TD	INT	SK	YD	QBR	KPR	OTD	PTS	TAY
1971	Cin	14(FS)	1	7	7.0(7)	0	—	—	—	—	—	—	—	—	—	—	—	—	—	—	pi	—	0	17
NFL	4	40(18)	1	7	7.0(7)	0	—	—	—	—	—	—	—	—	—	—	—	—	—	—	kpi	—	0	15

DURKOTA, JEFF Jeffrey George, FB-LB, 6´0˝/205 lbs; Penn State; 1948: Cle-A, rnd 1/1947: Phi, rnd 16; B12/20/1923 Pittsburgh, PA

YEAR	TEAM	G(GS, POS)	RUSH	YD	AVG(LG)	TD	REC	YD	AVG(LG)	TD	PASS	COMP	PCT	YD	AVG(LG)	TD	INT	SK	YD	QBR	KPR	OTD	PTS	TAY
1948	LAD-A	12(4)	14	66	4.7	0	2	12	6.0	0	—	—	—	—	—	—	—	—	—	—	ki	—	0	148

DURRETTE, MICHAEL Michael Ray, G, 6´4˝/280 lbs; Ferrum; West Virginia; B8/11/1957 Charlottesville, VA **1986** SF 9 (0) **1987** SF 3 (3) **NFL** 12 (3) [2 yrs]

DUSBABEK, MARK Mark Edward, LB, 6´3˝/232 lbs; Minnesota; 1987: Hou, rnd 4; B6/23/1964 Fairbault, MN **1989**†Min 16 (1) **1990** Min 14 (11, LLB) **1991** Min 1 (1) **NFL** 31 (13) [3 yrs]

DUSEK, BRAD John Bradley, LB, 6´2˝/220 lbs; Texas A&M; 1973: NE, rnd 3; B12/13/1950 Temple, TX **1974**†Was 14 **1975** Was 14 (14, LLB) **1976**†Was 14 (14, LLB) **1977** Was 14 (14, LLB) **1978** Was 16 (16, LLB) **1979** Was☆16 (16, LLB) **1980** Was 16 (14, LLB) **1981** Was 10 (9, LLB) **NFL** 114 (97) [8 yrs]

DUSENBERY, BILL William, RB, 6´2˝/198 lbs; Johnson C. Smith; 1970: Hou, rnd 2; B9/15/1948 Washington, DC

YEAR	TEAM	G(GS, POS)	RUSH	YD	AVG(LG)	TD	REC	YD	AVG(LG)	TD	PASS	COMP	PCT	YD	AVG(LG)	TD	INT	SK	YD	QBR	KPR	OTD	PTS	TAY
1970	NO	8	4	6	1.5(3)	0	—	—	—	—	—	—	—	—	—	—	—	—	—	—	k	—	0	39

DUSOSSOIT, JOE Florimond Joseph, aka Florimund DuSossoit Duke, E, 5´11˝/185 lbs; Dartmouth; B10/2/1895 Rochester, NY, D4/4/1969 Phoenix, AZ **1921** NYG 1 (1, RE)

YEAR	TEAM	G(GS,POS)	RUSH	YD	AVG(LG)	TD	REC	YD	AVG(LG)	TD	PASS	COMP	PCT	YD	AVG(LG)	TD	INT	SK	YD	QBR	KPR	OTD	PTS	TAY

DUTTON, BILL   William Earl, HB, 5´10˝/180 lbs; Pittsburgh; 1943: Was, rnd 3; B12/9/1918 Morgantown, WV, D8/2/1951 Pittsburgh, PA

| 1946 | Pit | 11(3) | 53 | 169 | 3.2(38) | 2 | 2 | 68 | 34.0(52) | 0 | 6 | 4 | 66.7 | 31 | 5.2(11) | 0 | 0 | — | — | — | kp | — | 12 | 267 |

DUTTON, JOHN   John Owen, DT-DE, 6´6˝/266 lbs; Nebraska; 1974: Bal, rnd 1; B2/6/1951 Rapid City, SD   **1974** Bal 14 (RDE)   **1975**†Bal★14 (14, RDE)   **1976**†Bal★14 (RDE)
1977†Bal◇12 (RDE)   **1978** Bal 14 (14, RDE)   **1979**†Dal 8 (5, lde)   **1980**†Dal 16 (0)   **1981**Dal 16 (16, LDT)   **1982**†Dal 9 (9, LDT)   **1983**†Dal 16 (16, LDT)   **1984** Dal 16 (16, LDT)
1985†Dal 16 (15, LDT)   **1986** Dal 16 (16, LDT)   **1987** Dal 4 (1)   **NFL** 185 (122) [14 yrs]

DUVALL, EARL   Earl S., G-T-E, 6´0˝/220 lbs; Ohio University; B6/20/1899 Duvall, OH, D8/6/1966 Marble Cliff, OH   **1924** Col 8 (7, LG)   **1925** Col 8 (5, LG)   **1926** Col 5 (2)
NFL 21 (14) [3 yrs]

DVORAK, BEN   Benjamin Anton, TB, 5´10˝/170 lbs; Minnesota; B1/20/1895, D5/7/1974 Minneapolis, MN   **1921** Min 4 (4, TB), 12

DVORAK, RICK   Richard Joseph, DT-DE, 6´4˝/240 lbs; Wichita State; 1974: NYG, rnd 3; B4/21/1952 Spearville, KS   **1974** NYG 13   **1975** NYG 14 (LDT)   **1976** NYG 14
1977 NYG 5   **1977** Mia 1   **NFL** 47 [4 yrs]

DWIGHT, TIM   Timothy John, WR, 5´9˝/180 lbs; Iowa; 1998: Atl, rnd 4; B7/13/1975 Iowa City, IA [R]

1998	†Atl	12(0)	8	19	2.4(7)	0	4	94	23.5(44)	1	2	1	50.0	22	11.0(22)	0	0	—	—	—	kp	1	12	633
1999	Atl	12(8, WR)	5	28	5.6(9)	1	32	669	20.9(60)	7	—	—	—	—	—	—	—	—	—	—	kp	1	54	822
2000	Atl	14(1)	8	13	1.6(5)	0	26	406	15.6(52)	3	—	—	—	—	—	—	—	—	—	—	kp	1	24	580
2001	SD	10(2)	2	24	12.0(16)	1	25	406	16.2(78)	0	—	—	—	—	—	—	—	—	—	—	p	1	12	398
2002	SD	16(14, WR)	12	108	9.0(20)	1	50	623	12.5(42)	2	—	—	—	—	—	—	—	—	—	—	kp	—	18	622
2003	SD	9(3)	9	88	9.8(20)	0	14	193	13.8(32)	0	—	—	—	—	—	—	—	—	—	—	kp	0	0	333
2004	†SD	12(0)	4	54	13.5(48)	0	2	31	15.5(23)	1	—	—	—	—	—	—	—	—	—	—	kp	1	12	558
2005	†NE	16(1)	4	11	2.8(12)	0	19	332	17.5(59)	3	—	—	—	—	—	—	—	—	—	—	kp	—	18	405
NFL	8	101(29)	49	340	6.9(48)	3	172	2764	16.0(78)	17	2	1	50.0	22	11.0(22)	0	0	—	—	—	kp	5	150	4349

DWORSKY, DAN   Daniel Leonard, LB, 6´0˝/211 lbs; Michigan; 1948: Cle-A, rnd 15/1949: GB, rnd 2; B10/4/1927 Minneapolis, MN   **1949** LAD-A 11 (0)

DWYER, BOB   Robert E., WB, 5´9˝/160 lbs; Georgetown (DC); B8/30/1905 Orange, NJ, D3/27/1974 Washington, DC   **1929** Ora 1 (0)

DWYER, JACK   John Joseph, DB, 5´11˝/175 lbs; Loyola Marymount; 1951: Phi, rnd 5; B1/15/1927 Los Angeles, CA   **1951** Was 12 (DB)   **1952** LARm 9   **1953** LARm 12
1954 LARm 11 (DB)   **1955** LARm 2   **NFL** 46 [5 yrs]

DWYER, MIKE   Francis Michael, DT, 6´3˝/280 lbs; Rhode Island; Massachusetts; B6/13/1963 Boston, MA   **1987** Dal 3 (3)

DYAL, MIKE   Michael Eben, TE, 6´2˝/240 lbs; Texas A&M-Kingsville; B5/20/1966 San Antonio, TX

1989	LARd	16(16, TE)	—	—	—	—	27	499	18.5(67)	2	—	—	—	—	—	—	—	—	—	—	—	—	12	260
1990	†LARd	3(2)	—	—	—	—	3	51	17.0(29)	0	—	—	—	—	—	—	—	—	—	—	—	—	0	26
1992	KC	3(0)	—	—	—	—	1	7	7.0(7)	0	—	—	—	—	—	—	—	—	—	—	—	—	0	4
1993	KC	6(0)	—	—	—	—	7	83	11.9(34)	0	—	—	—	—	—	—	—	—	—	—	—	—	0	42
1993	SD	4(0)	—	—	—	—	—	—	—	—	—	—	—	—	—	—	—	—	—	—	—	—	—	—
NFL	4	32(18)	—	—	—	—	38	640	16.8(67)	2	—	—	—	—	—	—	—	—	—	—	—	—	12	330

DYE, ERNEST   Ernest Thaddius, T-G, 6´6˝/330 lbs; South Carolina; 1993: Phx, rnd 1; B7/15/1971 Greenwood, SC   **1993** Phx 7 (1)   **1994** Arz 16 (16, LG)   **1995** Arz 6 (6, LT)
1996 Arz 8 (1)   **1997** SL 13 (0)   **NFL** 50 (24) [5 yrs]

DYE, LES   Lester Henry, E, 6´1˝/181 lbs; Syracuse; B7/15/1916 Forestville, NY, D8/11/2000 Roanoke, VA

1944	Was	9(2)	—	—	—	—	24	281	11.7(61)	2	—	—	—	—	—	—	—	—	—	—	—	—	12	151
1945	†Was	10(1)	—	—	—	—	8	84	10.5(25)	2	—	—	—	—	—	—	—	—	—	—	—	—	12	52
NFL	2	19(3)	—	—	—	—	32	365	11.4(61)	4	—	—	—	—	—	—	—	—	—	—	—	—	24	203

DYER, DEON   Deon Joseph, FB, 6´0˝/255 lbs; North Carolina; 2000: Mia, rnd 4; B10/2/1977 Chesapeake, VA   **2001**†Mia 16 (0)   **2002** Mia 13 (0)

| 2000 | †Mia | 16(0) | — | — | — | — | 2 | 14 | 7.0(13) | 0 | — | — | — | — | — | — | — | — | — | — | — | — | 0 | 7 |
| NFL | 3 | 45(0) | — | — | — | — | 2 | 14 | 7.0(13) | 0 | — | — | — | — | — | — | — | — | — | — | k | — | 0 | 1 |

DYER, HENRY   Henry Louis, RB, 6´2˝/230 lbs; Grambling State; 1966: LA, rnd 4; B1/28/1945 Baton Rouge, LA

1966	LARm	8	—	—	—	—	—	—	—	—	—	—	—	—	—	—	—	—	—	—	k	—	0	-14
1968	LARm	8	55	136	2.5(15)	1	8	37	4.6(15)	0	—	—	—	—	—	—	—	—	—	—	—	—	6	165
1969	Was	13	6	18	3.0(9)	0	2	86	43.0(69)	1	—	—	—	—	—	—	—	—	—	—	k	—	6	108
1970	Was	12(2)	21	102	4.9(12)	0	4	37	9.3(20)	0	—	—	—	—	—	—	—	—	—	—	k	—	0	124
NFL	4	41(2)	82	256	3.1(15)	1	14	160	11.4(69)	1	—	—	—	—	—	—	—	—	—	—	k	—	12	382

DYER, KEN   Kenneth James, DB-WR, 6´3˝/190 lbs; Arizona State; 1968: SD, rnd 4; B3/16/1946 Ann Arbor, MI   **1970**†Cin 12 (FS)   **1971** Cin 1

| 1968 | SD-A | 14 | — | — | — | — | 1 | 22 | 22.0(22) | 0 | — | — | — | — | — | — | — | — | — | — | i | 1 | 6 | 11 |
| NFL | 3 | 27 | — | — | — | — | 1 | 22 | 22.0(22) | 0 | — | — | — | — | — | — | — | — | — | — | i | 1 | 6 | 41 |

DYKES, DONALD   Donald Ray, DB, 5´11˝/182 lbs; Southeastern Louisiana; 1979: NYJ, rnd 3; B8/24/1955 Independence, MO   **1979** NYJ 16 (2)   **1980** NYJ 16 (16, RCB)
1981†NYJ 14 (9, rcb)   **1982** SD 1 (0)   **NFL** 47 (27) [4 yrs]

DYKES, HART LEE   Hart Lee, WR, 6´4˝/218 lbs; Oklahoma State; 1989: NE, rnd 1; B9/2/1966 Bay City, TX

1989	NE	16(8, wr)	—	—	—	—	49	795	16.2(42)	5	—	—	—	—	—	—	—	—	—	—	—	—	30	423
1990	NE	10(10, WR)	—	—	—	—	34	549	16.1(35)	2	—	—	—	—	—	—	—	—	—	—	—	—	12	285
NFL	2	26(18)	—	—	—	—	83	1344	16.2(42)	7	—	—	—	—	—	—	—	—	—	—	—	—	42	707

DYKES, SEAN   Sean Rene, DB, 5´10˝/170 lbs; Bowling Green State; B8/8/1964 New Orleans, LA   **1987** NYJ 6 (2)

DYKO, CHRIS   Christopher Edward, T, 6´6˝/305 lbs; Washington State; 1989: Chi, rnd 8; B3/16/1966 Champaign, IL   **1989** ChiB 8 (1)

DYSON, ANDRE   Andre, DB, 5´10˝/183 lbs; Utah; 2001: Ten, rnd 2; B5/25/1979 Logan, UT   **2001** Ten 14 (12, LCB)   **2002**†Ten 16 (16, LCB)   **2003**†Ten 16 (16, LCB)
2004 Ten 16 (16, LCB)   **2005**†Sea 10 (6, lcb)   **NFL** 72 (66) [5 yrs]

DYSON, KEVIN   Kevin Tyree, WR, 6´1˝/208 lbs; Utah; 1998: Ten, rnd 1; B6/23/1975 Logan, UT

1998	Ten	13(9, wr)	1	4	4.0(4)	0	21	263	12.5(45)	2	—	—	—	—	—	—	—	—	—	—	—	—	12	146
1999	†Ten	16(16, WR)	1	3	3.0(3)	0	54	658	12.2(47)	4	—	—	—	—	—	—	—	—	—	—	—	—	24	352
2000	Ten	2(2)	—	—	—	—	6	104	17.3(30)	1	—	—	—	—	—	—	—	—	—	—	—	—	6	57
2001	Ten	16(16, WR)	—	—	—	—	54	825	15.3(68)	7	—	—	—	—	—	—	—	—	—	—	—	—	44	448
2002	Ten	11(11, WR)	2	-4	-2.0(5)	0	41	460	11.2(40)	4	—	—	—	—	—	—	—	—	—	—	—	—	24	246
2003	†Car	1(0)	—	—	—	—	2	15	7.5(9)	0	—	—	—	—	—	—	—	—	—	—	p	—	0	17
NFL	6	59(54)	4	3	0.8(5)	0	178	2325	13.1(68)	18	—	—	—	—	—	—	—	—	—	—	p	—	110	1265

DYSON, MATT   Matthew A., LB, 6´4˝/275 lbs; Michigan; 1995: Oak, rnd 5; B8/1/1972 La Plata, MD   **1995** Oak 4 (0)

EADDY, JAMES   James, NT, 6´2˝/280 lbs; C.W. Post; New York Tech; B5/31/1963 Queens, NY   **1987** Cin 2 (0)

EAGLE FEATHER   FB-HB, 6´0˝/220 lbs; none   **1922** Oor 7 (7, FB), 6   **1923** Oor 11 (7, FB)   **NFL** 18 (14) [2 yrs]

EAGLE, ALEX   Alexander Franklin, T, 6´2˝/220 lbs; Oregon; B3/19/1913 San Francisco, CA, D3/5/1999   **1935** Bkn 10 (1)

EAGLIN, LARRY   Lawrence, DB, 6´3˝/195 lbs; Stephen F. Austin State; 1973: Hou, rnd 11; B8/27/1948 Raywood, TX   **1973** Hou 11

EAKIN, KAY   Oliver Kay, HB, 6´0˝/180 lbs; Arkansas; 1940: Pit, rnd 1; B8/3/1917 Atkins, AR, D2/15/1993 Fort Smith, AR [K]

1940	NYG	7(1)	14	20	1.4	0	—	—	—	—	17	39.5	199	4.6	0	3	—	—	—	P	—	0	-1
1941	†NYG	11(1)	27	-5	-0.2(17)	0	5	81	16.2(38)	1	19	26.3	71	3.7(41)	1	4	—	—	—	KPi	—	6	-56
NFL	2	18(2)	41	15	0.4(17)	0	5	81	16.2(38)	1	62	22	35.5	270	4.4(41)	1	7	—	—	—	KPi	—	6	-57
1946	Mia-A	13(1)	15	-41	-2.7	0	6	67	11.2	0	45	19	42.2	331	7.4	2	5	—	—	—	Pkpi	—	0	-5

EARHART, RALPH   Ralph Gloyd, HB, 5´10˝/165 lbs; Pittsburg State; Texas Tech; 1948: GB, rnd 32; B3/29/1923 Milburn, OK

1948	GB	12(2)	30	140	4.7(72)	1	17	194	11.4(64)	0	—	—	—	—	—	—	—	—	—	—	kp	—	18	360
1949	GB	12(0)	20	54	2.7(14)	0	5	109	21.8(50)	1	—	—	—	—	—	—	—	—	—	—	kp	1	6	232
NFL	2	24(2)	50	194	3.9(72)	1	22	303	13.8(64)	1	—	—	—	—	—	—	—	—	—	—	kp	1	24	592

EARL, GLENN   Glenn, DB, 6´1˝/205 lbs; Notre Dame; 2004: Hou, rnd 4; B6/10/1981 Lisle, IL   **2004** Hou 12 (9, SS)   **2005** Hou 10 (7, ss)   **NFL** 22 (16) [2 yrs]

YEAR	TEAM	G (GS, POS)	RUSH	YD	AVG (LG)	TD	REC	YD	AVG (LG)	TD	PASS	COMP	PCT	YD	AVG (LG)	TD	INT	SK	YD	QBR	KPR	OTD	PTS	TAY

EARL, ROBIN   Robin Daniel, TE-RB, 6´5˝/242 lbs; Washington; 1977: Chi, rnd 3; B3/18/1955 Boise, ID

1977	†ChiB	14(3)	56	233	4.2(34)	1	6	32	5.3(20)	0	—	—	—	—	—	—	—	—	—	—	k	—	6	267
1978	ChiB	16	3	17	5.7(9)	0	1	1	1.0(1)	0	—	—	—	—	—	—	—	—	—	—	k	—	0	21
1979	†ChiB	13(2)	35	132	3.8(12)	0	8	56	7.0(19)	0	—	—	—	—	—	—	—	—	—	—	—	—	0	160
1980	ChiB	16(13, TE)	—	—	—	—	18	223	12.4(28)	3	—	—	—	—	—	—	—	—	—	—	k	—	18	123
1981	ChiB	16(15, TE)	—	—	—	—	10	118	11.8(24)	1	—	—	—	—	—	—	—	—	—	—	—	—	6	64
1982	ChiB	9(1)	—	—	—	—	4	56	14.0(18)	0	—	—	—	—	—	—	—	—	—	—	—	—	0	28
NFL	6	84(34)	94	382	4.1(34)	1	47	486	10.3(28)	4	—	—	—	—	—	—	—	—	—	—	k	—	30	662

EARLEY, JIM   James H., RB, 6´1˝/230 lbs; Michigan State; 1978: NYJ, rnd 7; B1/23/1956 Dayton, OH   **1978** NYJ 2

EARLY, GUY   Guy Burdette, G-FB, 6´3˝/210 lbs; Miami (OH); B10/1892   **1920** Day 4 (1)   **1921** Cin 1 (1)   **NFL** 5 (2) [2 yrs]

EARLY, QUINN   Quinn Remar, WR, 6´0˝/190 lbs; Iowa; 1988: SD, rnd 3; B4/13/1965 West Hempstead, NY

1988	SD	16(11, WR)	7	63	9.0(37)	0	29	375	12.9(38)	4	—	—	—	—	—	—	—	—	—	—	—	—	24	271
1989	SD	6(3)	1	19	19.0(19)	0	11	126	11.5(21)	0	—	—	—	—	—	—	—	—	—	—	—	—	0	82
1990	SD	14(3)	—	—	—	—	15	238	15.9(45)	1	—	—	—	—	—	—	—	—	—	—	—	—	6	124
1991	†NO	15(12, WR)	3	13	4.3(6)	0	32	541	16.9(52)	2	—	—	—	—	—	—	—	—	—	—	k	—	12	327
1992	†NO	16(16, WR)	3	-1	-0.3(7)	0	30	566	18.9(59)	5	—	—	—	—	—	—	—	—	—	—	—	—	30	307
1993	NO	16(15, WR)	2	32	16.0(26)	0	45	670	14.9(63)	6	—	—	—	—	—	—	—	—	—	—	—	—	36	397
1994	NO	16(13, WR)	2	10	5.0(8)	0	82	894	10.9(33)	4	—	—	—	—	—	—	—	—	—	—	—	—	24	477
1995	NO	16(15, WR)	2	-3	-1.5(9)	0	81	1087	13.4(70)	8	—	—	—	—	—	—	—	—	—	—	—	—	48	581
1996	†Buf	16(13, WR)	3	39	13.0(29)	0	50	798	16.0(95)	4	—	—	—	—	—	—	—	—	—	—	—	—	26	458
1997	Buf	16(16, WR)	—	—	—	—	60	853	14.2(45)	5	—	—	—	—	—	—	—	—	—	—	—	—	30	452
1998	Buf	16(2)	—	—	—	—	19	217	11.4(37)	1	—	—	—	—	—	—	—	—	—	—	—	—	6	114
1999	NYJ	16(3)	—	—	—	—	6	83	13.8(24)	0	—	—	—	—	—	—	—	—	—	—	—	—	0	42
NFL	12	179(122)	23	172	7.5(37)	0	460	6448	14.0(95)	40	—	—	—	—	—	—	—	—	—	—	k	—	242	3629

EARON, BLAINE   Blaine Allen, DE, 6´1˝/195 lbs; Duke; 1952: Det, rnd 19; B1/15/1927 Altoona, PA   **1952**†Det 12 (RDE)   **1953** Det 6 (RDE)   **NFL** 18 [2 yrs]

EARP, JUG   Francis Lewis, C-T-G, 6´0˝/236 lbs; Monmouth (NJ); B7/22/1897 Monmouth, IL, D1/8/1969 Green Bay, WI   **1921** RI 6 (6, C)   **1922** RI 2 (2)   **1922** GB 7 (7, RT)   **1923** GB 8 (8, RT)   **1924** GB 11 (11, C)   **1925** Fra 1 (0)   **1925** GB 13 (13, RT)   **1926** GB 12 (12, C)   **1927** GB 10 (10, RT)   **1927** NYY 3 (3)   **1928** GB 13 (9, C)   **1929** GB☆11 (6, c)   **1930** GB 13 (7, c)   **1931** GB 12 (2)   **1932** GB 10 (3)   **NFL** 132 (99) [12 yrs]

EASLEY, KENNY   Kenneth Mason, DB, 6´3˝/206 lbs; UCLA; 1981: Sea, rnd 1; B1/15/1959 Chesapeake, VA [I]   **1981** Sea 14 (14, SS)   **1982** Sea☆8 (8, SS)   **1983**†Sea★16 (15, SS)   **1984**†Sea★16 (16, SS)   **1985** Sea★13 (13, SS)   **1986** Sea☆10 (10, SS)   **1987**†Sea★12 (11, SS)   **NFL** 89 (87) [7 yrs]

EASLEY, WALT   Walter Edward, RB, 6´2˝/226 lbs; West Virginia; B9/8/1957 Charleston, WV

1981	†SF	12(1)	76	224	2.9(9)	1	9	62	6.9(21)	0	1	1	100.0	5	5.0(5)	0	0	0	—	—	—	—	6	268
1982	SF	1(0)	5	11	2.2(5)	0	—	—	—	—	—	—	—	—	—	—	—	—	—	—	—	—	0	11
NFL	2	13(1)	81	235	2.9(9)	1	9	62	6.9(21)	0	1	1	100.0	5	5.0(5)	0	0	0	—	—	—	—	6	279

EASLICK, DOUG   Arthur Doug, RB, 5´11˝/243 lbs; Virginia Tech; B12/4/1980 Mount Holly, NJ

| 2004 | Mia | 3(1) | — | — | — | — | 1 | 4 | 4.0(4) | 0 | — | — | — | — | — | — | — | — | — | — | — | — | 0 | 2 |

EASMON, RICKY   Charles Richard, DB, 5´10˝/158 lbs; Florida; B7/3/1963 Inverness, FL   **1985** Dal 8 (1)   **1985** TB 6 (0)   **1986** TB 9 (2)   **NFL** 23 (3) [2 yrs]

EASON, BO   James Lawrence, DB, 6´2˝/200 lbs; California-Davis; 1984: Hou, rnd 2; B3/10/1961 Walnut Grove, CA   **1984** Hou 10 (1)   **1985** Hou☆16 (16, FS)   **1986** Hou 9 (9, FS)   **1987**†Hou 3 (0)   **NFL** 38 (26) [4 yrs]

EASON, JOHN   Areenouis John, WR, 6´2˝/220 lbs; Florida A&M; 1968: Oak, rnd 9; B7/30/1945 Ocala, FL   **1968** Oak-A 3

EASON, NICK   Nicholas, DT, 6´3˝/301 lbs; Clemson; 2003: Den, rnd 4; B5/29/1980 Lyons, GA   **2004** Cle 1 (0)   **2005** Cle 16 (0)   **NFL** 17 (0) [2 yrs]

EASON, NIJRELL   Nijrell, DB, 6´1˝/205 lbs; Arizona State; B5/20/1979 Long Beach, CA   **2002** Arz 1 (0)

EASON, ROGER   Charles Roger, G, 6´1˝/227 lbs; Oklahoma; 1942: Cle, rnd 3; B7/31/1918 Pauls Valley, OK, D4/28/1998 Houston, TX   **1945**†Cle 2 (0)   **1946** LARm 9 (8, LG)   **1947** LARm 11 (10, RG)   **1948** LARm 10 (6, rg)   **1949** GB 12 (2)   **NFL** 44 (26) [5 yrs]

EASON, TONY   Charles Carroll, QB, 6´4˝/212 lbs; Illinois; 1983: NE, rnd 1; B10/8/1959 Blythe, CA

1983	NE	16(4)	19	39	2.1(12)	0	—	—	—	—	95	46	48.4	557	5.9(35)	1	5	16	139	—	—	—	0	123
1984	NE	16(13, QB)	40	154	3.8(25)	5	—	—	—	—	431	259	60.1	3228	7.5(76)	23	8	59	409	93.4	—	—	30	1613
1985	†NE	16(10, QB)	22	70	3.2(23)	1	—	—	—	—	299	168	56.2	2156	7.2(90)	11	17	28	229	67.5	—	—	6	533
1986	†NE	15(14, QB)	35	170	4.9(26)	0	—	—	—	—	448	276	61.6	3328	7.4(49)	19	10	43	336	89.2	—	—	0	1529
1987	NE	4(3)	3	25	8.3(13)	0	—	—	—	—	79	42	53.2	453	5.7(45)	3	2	8	70	—	—	—	0	187
1988	NE	2(2)	5	18	3.6(10)	0	—	—	—	—	43	28	65.1	249	5.8(26)	0	2	2	12	—	—	—	0	63
1989	NE	3(3)	2	-2	-1.0(0)	0	—	—	—	—	105	57	54.3	761	7.2(45)	3	4	10	78	—	—	—	0	234
1989	NYJ	2(2)	1	0	0.0(0)	0	—	—	—	—	36	22	61.1	255	7.1(63)	1	2	7	42	—	—	—	0	53
1990	NYJ	16(0)	7	29	4.1(24)	0	—	—	—	—	28	13	46.4	155	5.5(31)	1	4	35	—	—	—	—	0	67
NFL	8	90(51)	134	503	3.8(26)	6	—	—	—	—	1564	911	58.2	11142	7.1(90)	61	51	177	1350	79.7	—	—	36	4399

EAST, RON   Ronald Allan, DT-DE, 6´4˝/250 lbs; Montana State; Oregon State; B8/26/1943 Portland, OR   **1967**†Dal 14   **1968**†Dal 14   **1969**†Dal 14 (3)   **1970**†Dal 14   **1971** SD 14 (LDT)   **1972** SD 12 (LDT)   **1973** SD 13 (LDT)   **1975** Cle 14 (14, LDE)   **1976** Atl 14   **1977** Sea 14 (14, LDT)   **NFL** 137 (31) [10 yrs]

EASTERLING, RAY   Charles Ray, DB, 6´0˝/195 lbs; Richmond; 1972: Atl, rnd 9; B9/3/1949 Richmond, VA   **1972** Atl 8   **1973** Atl 1   **1974** Atl 14   **1975** Atl 14 (SS)   **1976** Atl 14 (14, FS)   **1977** Atl 14 (FS)   **1978** Atl 2   **1979** Atl 16 (FS/ss)   **NFL** 83 (14) [8 yrs]

EASY, OMAR   Omar Xavier, FB, 6´1˝/245 lbs; Penn State; 2002: KC, rnd 4; B10/29/1977 Spanish Town, Jamaica

2002	KC	7(0)	—	—	—	—	3	23	7.7(13)	1	—	—	—	—	—	—	—	—	—	—	—	—	6	17
2003	†KC	15(0)	—	—	—	—	3	19	6.3(8)	0	—	—	—	—	—	—	—	—	—	—	—	—	0	10
2004	KC	15(0)	4	1	0.3(4)	0	—	—	—	—	—	—	—	—	—	—	—	—	—	—	—	—	0	1
2005	Oak	16(0)	—	—	—	—	—	—	—	—	—	—	—	—	—	—	—	—	—	—	—	—	—	—
NFL	4	53(0)	4	1	0.3(4)	0	6	42	7.0(13)	1	—	—	—	—	—	—	—	—	—	—	—	—	6	27

EATMAN, IRV   Irving Humphrey, T, 6´7˝/293 lbs; UCLA; 1983: KC, rnd 8; B1/1/1961 Birmingham, AL   **1986**†KC 16 (16, LT)   **1987** KC 12 (8, RT)   **1988** KC 16 (14, RT)   **1989** KC 13 (13, RT)   **1990**†KC 12 (0)   **1991**†NYJ 16 (16, RT)   **1992** NYJ 12 (12, RT)   **1993** LARm 16 (16, LT)   **1994** Atl 4 (0)   **1995** Hou 16 (7, rt)   **1996** Hou 16 (16, RT)   **NFL** 149 (118) [11 yrs]

EATON, CHAD   Chad Everett, DT-NT, 6´5˝/303 lbs; Washington State; 1995: Arz, rnd 7; B4/6/1972 Exeter, NH   **1996**†NE 4 (0)   **1997**†NE 16 (1)   **1998**†NE 15 (14, LDT)   **1999** NE 16 (16, LDT)   **2000** NE 14 (13, NT)   **2001** Sea 16 (16, LDT)   **2002** Sea 16 (16, LDT)   **2004** Dal 6 (1)   **NFL** 103 (77) [8 yrs]

EATON, LOU   Louis Standish, T, 6´2˝/215 lbs; California; B1915   **1945** NYG 2 (0)

EATON, SCOTT   Thomas Scott, DB, 6´3˝/205 lbs; Oregon State; 1967: NYG, rnd 8; B8/20/1944 Salem, OR   **1968** NYG 14 (LCB)   **1969** NYG 14 (LCB)   **1970** NYG 8 (LCB)   **1971** NYG 12 (SS)

| 1967 | NYG | 12(LCB) | — | — | — | — | 1 | 18 | 18.0(18) | 0 | — | — | — | — | — | — | — | — | — | — | i | — | 0 | 6 |
| NFL | 5 | 60 | — | — | — | — | 1 | 18 | 18.0(18) | 0 | — | — | — | — | — | — | — | — | — | — | ki | 1 | 6 | 9 |

EATON, TRACEY   Tracey Bruce, DB, 6´1˝/195 lbs; Portland State; 1988: Hou, rnd 7; B7/19/1965 Medford, OR   **1988**†Hou 1 (0)   **1989**†Hou 16 (2)   **1990** Phx 11 (0)   **1991**†Atl 16 (0)   **1993** Atl 16 (1)   **NFL** 60 (3) [5 yrs]

EATON, VIC   Victor Roe, QB-DB, 6´2˝/200 lbs; Missouri; 1955: Pit, rnd 11; B1/3/1933 Savannah, GA

| 1955 | Pit | 12 | — | — | — | — | — | — | — | — | 2 | 0 | 0.0 | 0 | 0.0 | 0 | 2 | — | — | — | Pp | — | 0 | -42 |

EBDING, HARRY   Harry Joseph, E, 5´11˝/199 lbs; St. Mary's (CA); B9/12/1906 Walla Walla, WA, D9/11/1980 Mecca, CA

1931	Por	14(13, RE)	—	—	—	—	—	—	—	—	—	—	—	—	—	—	—	—	—	—	—	—	—	—
1932	Por	12(12, RE)	—	—	—	—	14	171	12.2	1	—	—	—	—	—	—	—	—	—	—	—	—	6	91
1933	Por☆	11(8, RE)	—	—	—	—	8	125	15.6	0	—	—	—	—	—	—	—	—	—	—	—	—	0	63
1934	Det☆	12(7, RE)	—	—	—	—	10	**264**	26.4	2	—	—	—	—	—	—	—	—	—	—	—	—	12	142
1935	Det	11(4)	—	—	—	—	8	128	16.0	1	—	—	—	—	—	—	—	—	—	—	—	—	6	69

YEAR	TEAM	G (GS, POS)	RUSH	YD	AVG(LG)	TD	REC	YD	AVG(LG)	TD	PASS COMP	PCT	YD	AVG(LG)	TD	INT	SK	YD	QBR	KPR	OTD	PTS	TAY
1936	Det	11(4)	—	—	—	—	10	194	19.4	3	—	—	—	—	—	—	—	—	—	—	1	24	112
1937	Det	10(5, re)	—	—	—	—	5	89	17.8	1	—	—	—	—	—	—	—	—	—	—	2	18	50
NFL	7	81(53)	—	—	—	—	55	971	17.7	8	—	—	—	—	—	—	—	—	—	—	3	66	526

EBER, RICK   Richard Lee, WR, 6'0"/185 lbs; Tulsa; 1968: Atl, rnd 6; B4/17/1945 Torrance, CA

1968	Atl	1	—	—	—	—	—	—	—	—	—	—	—	—	—	—	—	—	—	—	—	—	—
1969	SD-A	5	—	—	—	—	9	141	15.7(43)	1	—	—	—	—	—	—	—	—	—	—	—	6	76
1970	SD	6	—	—	—	—	2	43	21.5(31)	0	—	—	—	—	—	—	—	—	—	—	0	22
NFL	3	12	—	—	—	—	11	184	16.7(43)	1	—	—	—	—	—	—	—	—	—	—	—	6	97

EBERDT, JESS   Jess Samuel, C, 6'2"/215 lbs; Alabama; B4/17/1908 Blytheville, AR, D1/29/1995 Williamsburg, VA   **1932** Bkn 4 (0)

EBERSOLE, HAL   Harold Leon, G, 6'3"/190 lbs; Cornell; B9/24/1899 St. Louis, MO, D9/25/1984 Atlanta, GA   **1923** Cle 2 (1)

EBERSOLE, JOHN   John Joel, LB, 6'3"/234 lbs; Penn State; 1970: NYJ, rnd 4; B11/5/1948 Altoona, PA   **1970** NYJ 14   **1971** NYJ 14   **1972** NYJ 14   **1973** NYJ 13 (MLB)
1974 NYJ 14 (RLB)   **1975** NYJ 13 (7, MLB)   **1976** NYJ 13 (MLB)   **1977** NYJ 13 (12, MLB)   **NFL** 108 (19) [8 yrs]

EBERTS, BEANIE   Bernard L., G-T-BB, 5'11"/198 lbs; Catholic; B5/21/1901 Columbus, OH, D4/20/1983 Chevy Chase, MD   **1924** Min 3 (1)

EBLI, RAY   Raymond Henry, E, 6'3"/210 lbs; Notre Dame; B10/6/1919 Bessemer, MI, D1/19/2005 Green Bay, WI

1942	ChiC	6(0)	—	—	—	—	6	83	13.8(31)	0	—	—	—	—	—	—	—	—	—	—	—	0	42
1946	Buf-A	9(7, LE)	—	—	—	—	2	15	7.5	1	—	—	—	—	—	—	—	—	—	—	—	6	13
1947	ChiR-A	5(2)	—	—	—	—	4	38	9.5	1	—	—	—	—	—	—	—	—	—	—	—	6	24
AAFC	2	14(9)	—	—	—	—	6	53	8.8(31)	2	—	—	—	—	—	—	—	—	—	—	—	12	37

EBY, BYRON   Byron, B, 6'0"/185 lbs; Ohio State; B12/11/1904, D9/11/1990   **1930** Por 3 (1), 6

ECCLES, SCOTT   Scott Michael, TE, 6'5"/240 lbs; Eastern New Mexico; 1987: LARd, rnd 9; B6/28/1963 New Orleans, LA   **1987** Hou 1 (0)

ECHEMANDU, ADIMCHINOBE   Adimchinobe, aka Joe Ecehma, RB, 5'10"/225 lbs; California; 2004: Cle, rnd 7; B11/21/1980 Lagos, Nigeria   **2005** Min 2 (0)

| 2004 | Cle | 4(0) | 8 | 25 | 3.1(6) | 0 | 3 | 25 | 8.3(19) | 0 | 1 | 0 | 0.0 | 0 | 0.0 | 0 | 0 | — | — | — | — | 0 | 38 |
| NFL | 2 | 6(0) | 8 | 25 | 3.1(6) | 0 | 3 | 25 | 8.3(19) | 0 | 1 | 0 | 0.0 | 0 | 0.0 | 0 | 0 | — | — | — | — | 0 | 38 |

ECHOLS, DONNIE   Donald Wayne, TE, 6'4"/240 lbs; Oklahoma State; B12/16/1957 Dallas, TX   **1987** Cle 3 (0)

ECHOLS, FATE   Fate Leonard, T-DT, 6'1"/258 lbs; Northwestern; 1962: SL, rnd 1/NYT, rnd 3; B6/29/1939 Union Springs, AL, D10/10/2002 Springfield, IL   **1962** SL 5   **1963** SL 3
NFL 8 [2 yrs]

ECHOLS, MIKE   Michael Kitome, DB, 5'10"/190 lbs; Wisconsin; 2002: Ten, rnd 4; B10/13/1978 Youngstown, OH   **2002** Ten 4 (0)   **2003** Ten 5 (0)   **NFL** 9 (0) [2 yrs]

ECHOLS, TERRY   Terry Lee, LB, 6'0"/220 lbs; Marshall; B1/10/1962 Mullens, WV   **1984** Pit 4 (0)

ECK, KEITH   Keith Curren, C-G, 6'5"/255 lbs; UCLA; B11/28/1955 Newport Beach, CA   **1979** NYG 13

ECKBERG, GUS   Gustavus Anthony, FB, 5'9"/180 lbs; Minnesota; West Virginia; B8/25/1898 Minneapolis, MN, deceased   **1925** Cle 1 (0)

ECKER, ED   Enrique Edward, DT-T, 6'7"/276 lbs; John Carroll; B1/21/1923 Cleveland, OH, D1/4/1990 Los Angeles, CA   **1948** ChiR-A 8 (2)
1947 ChiB 12 (0)   **1950** GB 12   **1951** GB 7   **1952** Was 9 (LDT)   **NFL** 40 [4 yrs]

ECKHARDT, OX   Oscar George, FB, 6'1"/190 lbs; Texas; B12/23/1901 Yorktown, TX, D4/22/1951 Yorktown, TX [K]   **1928** NYG 11 (6, fb), 13

ECKL, BOB   Robert Joseph, T, 6'1"/233 lbs; Wisconsin; B11/20/1917 Milwaukee, WI, D9/1961   **1945** ChiC 6 (0)

ECKLUND, BRAD   Bradford Sterling, C-LB, 6'3"/215 lbs; Oregon; 1947: GB, rnd 20; B5/9/1922 Los Angeles, CA   **1949†**NYY-A 12 (9, C)
1950 NYY◊12 (C)   **1951** NYY◊12 (C)   **1952** DalT 12 (12, C)   **1953** Bal☆12 (C)   **NFL** 48 (12) [4 yrs]

ECKSTEIN, DOLPH   Adolph William, C, 5'10"/185 lbs; Brown; B5/7/1902 Elizabeth, NJ, D6/28/1963 Providence, RI   **1925** Pro☆12 (12, C)   **1926** Pro 13 (12, C)   **NFL** 25 (24) [2 yrs]

ECKWOOD, JERRY   Jerry Louis, RB, 6'0"/198 lbs; Arkansas; 1979: TB, rnd 3; B12/26/1954 Brinkley, AR

1979	†TB	16(10, RB)	194	690	3.6(61)	2	22	268	12.2(31)	0	1	0	0.0	0	0.0	0	0	—	—	—	—	12	844
1980	TB	15(8, RB)	149	504	3.4(35)	1	47	475	10.1(40)	0	4	0	0.0	0	0.0	0	0	—	—	—	—	18	767
1981	†TB	16(12, RB)	172	651	3.8(59)	2	24	213	8.9(33)	0	0	0	0.0	0	0.0	0	0	1	1	—	—	12	778
NFL	3	47(30)	515	1845	3.6(61)	5	93	956	10.3(40)	0	5	0	0.0	0	0.0	0	0	1	1	—	—	42	2388

EDDINGS, FLOYD   Floyd, WR, 5'11"/177 lbs; California; B12/15/1958 Birmingham, AL

1982	NYG	4(1)	2	12	6.0(16)	0	14	275	19.6(47)	0	—	—	—	—	—	—	—	—	—	—	—	0	150
1983	NYG	9(6, wr)	1	3	3.0(3)	0	14	231	16.5(33)	0	—	—	—	—	—	—	—	—	—	—	—	0	119
NFL	2	13(7)	3	15	5.0(16)	0	28	506	18.1(47)	0	—	—	—	—	—	—	—	—	—	—	—	0	268

EDDY, NICK   Nicholas Matthew, RB, 6'1"/210 lbs; Notre Dame; 1966: Det, rnd 2/Den, rnd R1; B8/23/1944 Dunsmuir, CA

1968	Det	5	48	176	3.7(20)	0	8	91	11.4(28)	0	—	—	—	—	—	—	—	—	p	—	—	0	212
1969	Det	11(HB)	78	272	3.5(26)	2	10	78	7.8(14)	1	—	—	—	—	—	—	—	—	p	—	—	18	336
1970	Det	11	18	47	2.6(9)	1	4	22	5.5(9)	0	—	—	—	—	—	—	—	—	kp	—	—	6	136
1972	Det	2	8	28	3.5(10)	0	2	46	23.0(36)	1	—	—	—	—	—	—	—	—	—	—	—	6	56
NFL	4	29	152	523	3.4(26)	3	24	237	9.9(36)	2	—	—	—	—	—	—	—	—	kp	—	—	30	740

EDELMAN, BRAD   Bradley Martin, G, 6'6"/265 lbs; Missouri; 1982: NO, rnd 2; B9/3/1960 Jacksonville, FL   **1982** NO 9 (9, LG)   **1983** NO 16 (16, LG)   **1984** NO 11 (11, LG)
1985 NO 8 (8, LG)   **1986** NO 13 (13, LG)   **1987†**NO★11 (9, LG)   **1988** NO 14 (13, LG)   **1989** NO 8 (8, LG)   **NFL** 90 (87) [8 yrs]

EDGAR, BILL   Alexander Willis, G-B, 6'2"/185 lbs; Washington & Jefferson; Pittsburgh; Bucknell; B9/17/1898 Morning Sun, IA, D12/18/1970 Butler, PA   **1923** Buf 2 (2)
1923 Akr 3 (3)   **NFL** 5 (5) [1 yr]

EDGE, SHAYNE   Randall Shayne, P, 5'11"/174 lbs; Florida; B8/21/1971 Lake City, FL

| 1996 | Pit | 4(0) | 1 | -16 | -16.0(-16) | 0 | — | — | — | — | — | — | — | — | — | — | — | — | P | — | — | 0 | -16 |

EDGERSON, BOOKER   Booker Tyrone, DB, 5'10"/183 lbs; Western Illinois; B7/5/1939 Baxter, AR [I]   **1962** Buf-A 14 (RCB)   **1963†**Buf-A 14 (RCB)   **1964** Buf-A 10 (LCB)
1965†Buf-A◊14 (LCB)   **1966†**Buf-A 7   **1967** Buf-A 14 (LCB)   **1968** Buf-A 13 (LCB)   **1969** Buf-A☆14 (LCB)   **1970** Den 6   **NFL** 106 [9 yrs]

EDINGER, PAUL   Paul E., K, 5'8"/175 lbs; Michigan State; 2000: Chi, rnd 6; B1/17/1978 Frankfort, MI [K]   **2000** ChiB 16 (0)   **2001†**ChiB 16 (0)   **2002** ChiB 16 (0)   **2003** ChiB 16 (0)
2005 Min 16 (0)

| 2004 | ChiB | 16(0) | — | — | — | — | — | — | — | — | 1 | 0 | 0.0 | 0 | 0.0 | 0 | 1 | — | — | KP | — | 67 | -40 |
| NFL | 6 | 96(0) | — | — | — | — | — | — | — | — | 1 | 0 | 0.0 | 0 | 0.0 | 0 | 1 | — | — | KP | — | 569 | -40 |

EDLER, DEKE   Robert Karl, WB, 5'9"/170 lbs; Ohio Wesleyan; B8/29/1898, D6/1/1953 Peoria, IL   **1923** Cle 5 (1), 6

EDMONDS, BOBBY JOE   Bobby Joe, RB, 5'11"/186 lbs; Arkansas; 1986: Sea, rnd 5; B9/26/1964 Nashville, TN [R]   **1987†**Sea 11 (0)   **1988†**Sea 16 (0)   **1989** LARd 7 (0)

1986	Sea★	15(0)	1	-11	-11.0(-11)	0	—	—	—	—	—	—	—	—	—	—	—	—	kp	—	1	6	502
1995	TB	16(0)	5	28	5.6(9)	0	1	8	8.0(8)	0	—	—	—	—	—	—	—	—	kp	—	—	0	457
NFL	5	65(0)	6	17	2.8(9)	0	1	8	8.0(8)	0	—	—	—	—	—	—	—	—	kp	—	1	6	1883

EDMONDS, CHRIS   Chris, FB, 6'3"/250 lbs; West Virginia; B1/1/1978 Newark, NJ   **2002** Cin 8 (0)   **2003** Cin 4 (0)   **NFL** 12 (0) [2 yrs]

EDMONDSON, VAN   August Van, C, 5'10"/210 lbs; Oklahoma; B6/8/1899 Delaware County, OK, D3/4/1998 San Antonio, TX   **1926** Buf 5 (3)

EDMUNDS, FERRELL   Ferrell, TE, 6'6"/254 lbs; Maryland; 1988: Mia, rnd 3; B4/16/1965 South Boston, VA

1988	Mia	16(14, TE)	1	-8	-8.0(-8)	0	33	575	17.4(80)	3	—	—	—	—	—	—	—	—	k	—	—	18	300
1989	Mia★	16(16, TE)	—	—	—	—	32	382	11.9(30)	3	—	—	—	—	—	—	—	—	—	—	—	18	206
1990	†Mia◊	16(16, TE)	1	-7	-7.0(-7)	0	31	446	14.4(35)	1	—	—	—	—	—	—	—	—	—	—	—	6	221
1991	Mia	8(6, te)	—	—	—	—	11	118	10.7(22)	1	—	—	—	—	—	—	—	—	—	—	—	6	69
1992	†Mia	10(6, te)	—	—	—	—	10	91	9.1(15)	1	—	—	—	—	—	—	—	—	—	—	—	6	51
1993	Sea	16(16, TE)	—	—	—	—	24	239	10.0(32)	2	—	—	—	—	—	—	—	—	—	—	—	12	130
1994	Sea	7(7, te)	—	—	—	—	7	43	6.1(8)	0	—	—	—	—	—	—	—	—	—	—	—	0	22
NFL	7	89(83)	2	-15	-7.5(-7)	0	148	1894	12.8(80)	12	—	—	—	—	—	—	—	—	k	—	—	72	997

YEAR	TEAM	G (GS, POS)	RUSH	YD	AVG(LG)	TD	REC	YD	AVG(LG)	TD	PASS COMP	PCT	YD	AVG(LG)	TD	INT	SK	YD	QBR	KPR	OTD	PTS	TAY

EDMUNDS, RANDY George Randall, LB, 6´2˝/220 lbs; Georgia Tech; 1968: Mia, rnd 8; B6/24/1946 Washington, GA **1968** Mia-A 14 (14, LLB) **1969** Mia-A 14 (14, LLB)
1971 NE 14 **1972** Bal 3 **NFL** 45 (28) [4 yrs]

EDWARDS, AL Albert, WR, 5´8˝/171 lbs; Northwestern State (LA); 1990: Buf, rnd 11; B5/18/1967 New Orleans, LA

1990	†Buf	14 (2)	—	—	—	—	2	11	5.5 (6)	0	—	—	—	—	—	—	—	—	—	kp	—	0	119
1991	†Buf	16 (5, wr)	1	17	17.0 (17)	0	22	228	10.4 (33)	1	—	—	—	—	—	—	—	—	—	kp	1	12	308
1992	Buf	7 (0)	1	8	8.0 (8)	0	2	25	12.5 (20)	0	—	—	—	—	—	—	—	—	—	k	—	0	115
NFL	3	37 (7)	2	25	12.5 (17)	0	26	264	10.2 (33)	1	—	—	—	—	—	—	—	—	—	kp	1	12	541

EDWARDS, ANTHONY Anthony Quinn, WR, 5´10˝/195 lbs; New Mexico Highlands; B5/26/1966 Casa Grande, AZ

1989	†Phi	9 (0)	—	—	—	—	2	74	37.0 (66)	0	—	—	—	—	—	—	—	—	—	kp	—	0	44
1990	Phi	5 (0)	—	—	—	—	—	—	—	—	—	—	—	—	—	—	—	—	—	kp	—	0	11
1991	Phx	13 (0)	—	—	—	—	—	—	—	—	—	—	—	—	—	—	—	—	—	kp	—	0	68
1992	Phx	16 (0)	—	—	—	—	14	147	10.5 (25)	1	—	—	—	—	—	—	—	—	—	k	—	6	102
1993	Phx	16 (0)	—	—	—	—	13	326	25.1 (65)	1	—	—	—	—	—	—	—	—	—	kp	—	6	171
1995	Arz	15 (0)	—	—	—	—	29	417	14.4 (28)	2	—	—	—	—	—	—	—	—	—	kp	—	12	265
1996	Arz	16 (1)	1	-8	-8.0 (-8)	0	29	311	10.7 (31)	1	—	—	—	—	—	—	—	—	—	p	—	6	174
1997	Arz	16 (1)	—	—	—	—	20	203	10.1 (33)	0	—	—	—	—	—	—	—	—	—	p	—	0	96
NFL	8	106 (2)	1	-8	-8.0 (-8)	0	107	1478	13.8 (66)	5	—	—	—	—	—	—	—	—	—	kp	—	30	929

EDWARDS, ANTONIO Antonio, DE, 6´3˝/271 lbs; Valdosta State; 1993: Sea, rnd 8; B3/10/1970 Moultrie, GA **1993** Sea 9 (0) **1994** Sea 15 (14, LDE/rde) **1995** Sea 13 (7, rde)
1996 Sea 12 (3) **1997** Sea 1 (0) **1997**†NYG 3 (0) **1998**†Atl 15 (0) **1999** Car 14 (7, lde) **NFL** 82 (31) [7 yrs]

EDWARDS, ANTUAN Antuan Minye´, DB, 6´1˝/212 lbs; Clemson; 1999: GB, rnd 1; B5/26/1977 Starkville, MA **1999** GB 16 (1) **2000** GB 12 (3) **2001** GB 3 (0) **2002**†GB 12 (4)
2003 GB 10 (10, SS) **2004** Mia 8 (8, fs) **2004**†SL 6 (5, fs) **2005** Atl 4 (1) **NFL** 71 (32) [7 yrs]

EDWARDS, BRAD Bradford Wayne, DB, 6´2˝/208 lbs; South Carolina; 1988: Min, rnd 2; B3/22/1966 Lumberton, NC **1988**†Min 16 (6, fs) **1989**†Min 9 (1) **1990**†Was 16 (1)
1991†Was 16 (16, FS) **1992**†Was☆16 (16, FS) **1993** Was 16 (16, FS) **1994** Atl 4 (0) **1996** Atl 16 (7, fs) **NFL** 122 (63) [9 yrs]

EDWARDS, BRAYLON Braylon Jamel, WR, 6´3˝/211 lbs; Michigan; 2005: Cle, rnd 1; B2/21/1983 Detroit, MI

| 2005 | Cle | 10 (7, wr) | — | — | — | — | 32 | 512 | 16.0 (80) | 3 | — | — | — | — | — | — | — | — | — | — | — | 18 | 271 |

EDWARDS, BUD Charles Halleck, B, 5´11˝/190 lbs; Brown; B3/21/1908 Chicago, IL, D8/11/1986 Scottsdale, AZ **1930** Pro 9 (3), 6 **1931** ChiB 1 (0) **1931** Pro 9 (4)
NFL 19 (7) [2 yrs]

EDWARDS, CAP Howard Eugene, G, 6´0˝/207 lbs; Notre Dame; B5/1888 South Bend, IN, D11/23/1944 South Bend, IN [C] **1920** Can 7 (5, LG) **1921** Can 2 (2) **1922** Tol 9 (8, LG)
1923 Cle 2 (0) **1924** Cle 7 (2) **NFL** 27 (17) [5 yrs]

EDWARDS, CID Cleophus J., RB, 6´3˝/230 lbs; Tennessee State; B10/10/1943 Selma, AL

1968	SL	14	31	214	6.9 (42)	1	1	2	2.0 (2)	0	—	—	—	—	—	—	—	—	—	—	—	6	225
1969	SL	14 (FB)	107	504	4.7 (48)	3	23	309	13.4 (37)	0	—	—	—	—	—	—	—	—	—	—	—	18	689
1970	SL	11 (FB)	70	350	5.0 (22)	1	19	150	7.9 (39)	1	—	—	—	—	—	—	—	—	—	—	—	12	440
1971	SL	12 (fb)	108	316	2.9 (14)	4	12	122	10.2 (38)	0	—	—	—	—	—	—	—	—	—	k	—	24	428
1972	SD	12 (FB)	157	679	4.3 (31)	5	40	557	13.9 (61)	2	—	—	—	—	—	—	—	—	—	—	—	42	1018
1973	SD	13 (FB)	133	609	4.6 (50)	1	25	164	6.6 (28)	0	—	—	—	—	—	—	—	—	—	—	—	6	701
1974	SD	10	65	261	4.0 (30)	0	13	102	7.8 (16)	0	—	—	—	—	—	—	—	—	—	—	—	0	312
1975	ChiB	8	27	73	2.7 (16)	0	11	86	7.8 (14)	1	—	—	—	—	—	—	—	—	—	—	—	6	121
NFL	8	94	698	3006	4.3 (50)	15	144	1492	10.4 (61)	4	—	—	—	—	—	—	—	—	—	k	—	114	3933

EDWARDS, DAN Daniel Moody, E, 6´1˝/197 lbs; Georgia; 1948: Bkn-A, rnd 3/Pit, rnd 1; B7/18/1926 Osage, TX, D8/7/2001 Gatesville, TX

1948	Bkn-A	11 (7, RE)	—	—	—	—	23	176	7.7		—	—	—	—	—	—	—	—	—	k	—	0	94
1949	ChiH-A	12 (12, RE)	—	—	—	—	42	573	13.6 (66)	3	—	—	—	—	—	—	—	—	—	k	1	24	311
AAFC	2	23 (19)	—	—	—	—	65	749	11.5 (66)	3	—	—	—	—	—	—	—	—	—	k	1	24	405
1950	NYY★	12 (RE)	—	—	—	—	52	775	14.9 (82)	6	—	—	—	—	—	—	—	—	—	—	—	36	418
1951	NYY	10 (RE)	—	—	—	—	39	509	13.1 (53)	3	—	—	—	—	—	—	—	—	—	—	—	18	270
1952	DalT	1 (1)	—	—	—	—	3	22	7.3 (13)	0	—	—	—	—	—	—	—	—	—	—	—	0	11
1953	Bal	12 (RE)	—	—	—	—	35	312	8.9 (32)	3	—	—	—	—	—	—	—	—	—	—	—	18	171
1954	Bal	12 (RE)	—	—	—	—	40	531	13.3 (42)	1	—	—	—	—	—	—	—	—	—	—	—	6	271
NFL	5	47 (1)	—	—	—	—	169	2149	12.7 (82)	13	—	—	—	—	—	—	—	—	—	—	—	78	1140

EDWARDS, DAVE David Monroe, LB, 6´1˝/225 lbs; Auburn; 1962: Den, rnd 25; B12/14/1939 Columbia, AL **1963** Dal 14 (6, rlb) **1964** Dal 14 (4) **1965** Dal 14 (RLB)
1966†Dal 14 (RLB) **1967**†Dal 14 (RLB) **1968**†Dal 14 (RLB) **1969**†Dal 14 (LLB) **1970**†Dal 13 (LLB) **1971**†Dal 14 (LLB) **1972**†Dal 14 (LLB) **1973**†Dal 14 (LLB)
1974 Dal 14 (LLB) **1975**†Dal 14 (LLB) **NFL** 181 (10) [13 yrs]

EDWARDS, DAVE David Lee, DB, 6´0˝/195 lbs; Illinois; B3/31/1962 Senoia, GA **1985** Pit 14 (0) **1986** Pit 16 (1) **1987** Pit 3 (3) **NFL** 33 (4) [3 yrs]

EDWARDS, DENNIS Dennis Ray, DE, 6´4˝/253 lbs; USC; 1982: Buf, rnd 9; B10/6/1959 Stockton, CA **1987** LARm 3 (0)

EDWARDS, DEVONTE Devonte, DB, 6´0˝/182 lbs; North Carolina State; B10/17/1982 Chapel Hill, NC **2005** Min 12 (0)

EDWARDS, DIXON Dixon Voledean, LB, 6´1˝/230 lbs; Michigan State; 1991: Dal, rnd 2; B3/25/1968 Cincinnati, OH **1991**†Dal 12 (1) **1992**†Dal 16 (9) **1993**†Dal 16 (15, LLB)
1994†Dal 16 (15, LLB) **1995**†Dal 15 (15, LLB) **1996**†Min 14 (13, RLB) **1997**†Min 16 (16, RLB) **1998**†Min 15 (14, LLB) **NFL** 120 (90) [8 yrs]

EDWARDS, DONNIE Donnie Lewis, LB, 6´2˝/227 lbs; UCLA; 1996: KC, rnd 4; B4/6/1973 San Diego, CA [I] **1996** KC 15 (1) **1997**†KC 16 (16, RILB) **1998** KC 15 (15, RILB)
1999 KC 16 (16, RLB) **2000** KC 16 (16, RLB) **2001** KC 16 (16, RLB) **2002** SD★16 (16, MLB) **2003** SD 16 (16, RLB) **2004**†SD☆16 (16, LILB) **2005** SD 16 (16, LILB)
NFL 158 (144) [10 yrs]

EDWARDS, DWAN Dwan Sedaine, DT, 6´3˝/305 lbs; Oregon State; 2004: Bal, rnd 2; B5/16/1981 Billings, MT **2004** Bal 4 (0) **2005** Bal 12 (1) **NFL** 16 (1) [2 yrs]

EDWARDS, EARL Earl, DT-DE, 6´7˝/260 lbs; Wichita State; 1969: SF, rnd 5; B3/17/1946 Statesboro, GA **1970**†SF 14 **1971**†SF 14 (14, RDT) **1972**†SF 13 (12, RDT)
1973 Buf 14 (14, RDE) **1974**†Buf 14 (14, RDE) **1975** Buf 14 (14, RDE) **1976** Cle 14 **1977** Cle 14 (14, LDT) **1978** Cle 16 (16, LDT) **1979** GB 9 (LDT)

| 1969 | SF | 14 | — | — | — | — | 1 | 1 | 1.0 (1) | — | — | — | — | — | — | — | — | — | — | k | — | 0 | -42 |
| NFL | 11 | 150 (98) | — | — | — | — | 1 | 1 | 1.0 (1) | — | — | — | — | — | — | — | — | — | — | k | — | 0 | -42 |

EDWARDS, EDDIE Eddie Lee, DE-DT, 6´5˝/256 lbs; Miami (FL); 1977: Cin, rnd 1; B4/25/1954 Sumter, SC **1977** Cin 12 (LDT) **1978** Cin 16 (RDT) **1979** Cin 14 (LDT)
1980 Cin 16 (16, LDE) **1981**†Cin☆14 (13, LDE) **1982**†Cin 9 (9, LDE) **1983** Cin 16 (16, LDE) **1984** Cin 16 (16, LDE) **1985** Cin 16 (16, LDE) **1986** Cin 16 (16, LDE)
1987 Cin 14 (14, LDE) **1988**†Cin 11 (0) **NFL** 170 (116) [12 yrs]

EDWARDS, EMMETT Emmett Lee, WR, 6´1˝/187 lbs; Kansas; 1975: Hou, rnd 2; B6/6/1952 Tulsa, OK

1975	Hou	11	1	-4	-4.0 (-4)	0	2	22	11.0 (18)	0	—	—	—	—	—	—	—	—	—	—	—	0	7
1976	Hou	3	—	—	—	—	—	—	—	—	—	—	—	—	—	—	—	—	—	—	—	0	
1976	Buf	6 (1)	1	0	0.0 (0)	0	2	53	26.5 (46)	0	—	—	—	—	—	—	—	—	—	—	—	0	27
NFL	2	20 (1)	2	-4	-2.0	0	4	75	18.8 (46)	0	—	—	—	—	—	—	—	—	—	—	—	0	34

EDWARDS, ERIC Timothy Eric, TE, 6´5˝/256 lbs; LSU; B8/4/1980 Monroe, LA

2004	Arz	16 (1)	—	—	—	—	5	51	10.2 (19)	0	—	—	—	—	—	—	—	—	—	k	—	0	21
2005	Arz	16 (9, TE)	—	—	—	—	12	133	11.1 (63)	1	—	—	—	—	—	—	—	—	—	—	—	6	72
NFL	2	32 (10)	—	—	—	—	17	184	10.8 (63)	1	—	—	—	—	—	—	—	—	—	k	—	6	92

EDWARDS, GLEN Glen, DB, 6´0˝/185 lbs; Florida A&M; B7/31/1947 St. Petersburg, FL [RI] **1971** Pit 8 (6, FS) **1972**†Pit 12 **1973**†Pit☆14 (14, FS) **1974**†Pit 14 (14, FS)
1975†Pit☆14 (14, FS) **1976**†Pit☆14 (14, FS) **1977**†Pit 13 (8, FS) **1978** SD 14 (2) **1979**†SD 15 (13, FS) **1980**†SD 16 (14, FS) **1981** SD 8 (8, FS) **NFL** 142 (107) [11 yrs]

EDWARDS, HERMAN Herman Lee, DB, 6´0˝/194 lbs; California; San Diego State; B4/27/1954 Fort Monmouth, NJ [IC] **1977** Phi 14 (14, RCB) **1978**†Phi 16 (16, RCB)
1979†Phi 16 (16, RCB) **1980**†Phi 16 (16, RCB) **1981** Phi 16 (16, RCB) **1982** Phi☆9 (9, RCB) **1983** Phi 16 (16, RCB) **1984** Phi 16 (16, RCB) **1985** Phi 16 (16, RCB)
1986 LARm 4 (0) **1986** Atl 3 (0) **NFL** 142 (135) [10 yrs]

EDWARDS, JIMMY James Leroy, RB, 5´9˝/185 lbs; Oklahoma; Louisiana-Monroe; B9/19/1952 Oklahoma City, OK

| 1979 | Min | 14 | — | — | — | — | 1 | 2 | 2.0 (2) | 0 | — | — | — | — | — | — | — | — | — | kp | — | 0 | 465 |

YEAR	TEAM	G (GS, POS)	RUSH	YD	AVG(LG)	TD	REC	YD	AVG(LG)	TD	PASS COMP	PCT	YD	AVG(LG)	TD	INT	SK	YD	QBR	KPR	OTD	PTS	TAY

EDWARDS, KALIMBA Kalimba, DE, 6´5˝/264 lbs; South Carolina; 2002: Det, rnd 2; B12/26/1979 East Point, GA **2002** Det 16 (4) **2003** Det 15 (4) **2004** Det 16 (0) **2005** Det 16 (2) **NFL** 63 (6) [4 yrs]

EDWARDS, KELVIN Kelvin Mack, WR, 6´2˝/202 lbs; Liberty; 1986: NO, rnd 4; B7/19/1964 Birmingham, AL

1986	NO	14(3)	1	6	6.0(6)	0	10	132	13.2(24)	0	—	—	—	—	—	—	—	—	p	—	0	59
1987	Dal	13(9, WR)	2	61	30.5(62)	1	34	521	15.3(38)	3	—	—	—	—	—	—	—	—	kp	—	24	432
1988	Dal	8(2)	—	—	—	—	5	93	18.6(27)	0	—	—	—	—	—	—	—	—	—	—	0	47
NFL	3	35(14)	3	67	22.3(62)	1	49	746	15.2(38)	3	—	—	—	—	—	—	—	—	kp	—	24	537

EDWARDS, LLOYD Lloyd B., TE, 6´3˝/248 lbs; San Diego State; 1969: Oak, rnd 3; B11/26/1946 Long Beach, CA **1969**†Oak-A 14

EDWARDS, MARC Marc Alexander, FB, 6´0˝/249 lbs; Notre Dame; 1997: SF, rnd 2; B11/17/1974 Cincinnati, OH

1997	†SF	15(1)	5	17	3.4(6)	0	6	48	8.0(19)	0	—	—	—	—	—	—	—	—	k	—	0	56
1998	†SF	16(10, FB)	22	94	4.3(32)	1	22	218	9.9(47)	2	—	—	—	—	—	—	—	—	—	—	18	223
1999	Cle	16(14, FB)	6	35	5.8(28)	0	27	212	7.9(27)	2	—	—	—	—	—	—	—	—	—	—	12	151
2000	Cle	16(8, FB)	2	9	4.5(6)	0	16	128	8.0(21)	2	—	—	—	—	—	—	—	—	—	—	12	92
2001	†NE	16(13, FB)	51	141	2.8(14)	1	25	166	6.6(17)	2	—	—	—	—	—	—	—	—	k	—	18	252
2002	NE	16(10, FB)	31	96	3.1(17)	0	23	196	8.5(27)	0	—	—	—	—	—	—	—	—	k	—	0	176
2003	Jax	16(16, FB)	7	13	1.9(3)	1	31	226	7.3(32)	0	—	—	—	—	—	—	—	—	k	—	6	150
2004	Jax	13(5, FB)	—	—	—	—	7	41	5.9(15)	0	—	—	—	—	—	—	—	—	k	—	0	14
2005	ChiB	8(5, fb)	—	—	—	—	10	66	6.6(13)	2	—	—	—	—	—	—	—	—	k	—	12	43
NFL	9	132(82)	124	405	3.3(32)	3	167	1301	7.8(47)	10	—	—	—	—	—	—	—	—	k	—	78	1157

EDWARDS, MARIO Mario L., DB, 6´0˝/199 lbs; Florida State; 2000: Dal, rnd 6; B12/1/1975 Gautier, MS **2000** Dal 11 (1) **2001** Dal 16 (15, RCB) **2002** Dal 15 (15, RCB) **2003**†Dal 16 (16, RCB) **2004** TB 15 (3) **NFL** 73 (50) [5 yrs]

EDWARDS, MARSHALL Marshall, FB, 6´1˝/190 lbs; Wake Forest; B4/1/1916

| 1943 | Bkn | 1(0) | 1 | 5 | 5.0(5) | 0 | 1 | -4 | -4.0(-4) | 0 | — | — | — | — | — | — | — | — | — | — | 0 | 3 |

EDWARDS, MONK William Bennett, G-C-T, 6´3˝/213 lbs; Baylor; 1940: NYG, rnd 18; B7/19/1920 Ireland, TX **1940** NYG 9 (0) **1941**†NYG☆11 (10, LG) **1942** NYG☆11 (10, LG) **1946**†NYG☆10 (1) **NFL** 41 (21) [4 yrs]

EDWARDS, RANDY Richard Randolph, DE-NT, 6´4˝/264 lbs; Alabama; B3/9/1961 Marietta, GA **1984**†Sea 13 (0) **1985** Sea 16 (0) **1986** Sea 16 (4) **1987** Sea 7 (0) **NFL** 52 (4) [4 yrs]

EDWARDS, ROBERT Robert Lee, RB, 5´11˝/218 lbs; Georgia; 1998: NE, rnd 1; B10/2/1974 Tennille, GA

1998	†NE	16(15, RB)	291	1115	3.8(53)	9	35	331	9.5(46)	3	—	—	—	—	—	—	—	—	—	—	72	1386
2002	Mia	12(0)	20	107	5.3(19)	1	18	126	7.0(14)	1	—	—	—	—	—	—	—	—	—	—	12	185
NFL	2	28(15)	311	1222	3.9(53)	10	53	457	8.6(46)	4	—	—	—	—	—	—	—	—	—	—	84	1571

EDWARDS, RON Ronald H., DT, 6´3˝/320 lbs; Texas A&M; 2001: Buf, rnd 3; B7/12/1979 Columbus, OH **2001** Buf 7 (3) **2002** Buf 16 (16, LDT) **2003** Buf 5 (0) **2004** Buf 16 (2) **2005** Buf 4 (4) **NFL** 48 (25) [5 yrs]

EDWARDS, STAN Stanley J., RB, 6´0˝/208 lbs; Michigan; 1982: Hou, rnd 3; B5/20/1960 Detroit, MI

1982	Hou	7(4, FB)	15	58	3.9(8)	0	9	53	5.9(21)	0	—	—	—	—	—	—	—	—	—	—	0	85
1983	Hou	14(1)	16	40	2.5(9)	0	9	79	8.8(20)	1	—	—	—	—	—	—	—	—	—	—	6	85
1984	Hou	14(1)	60	267	4.4(20)	1	20	151	7.6(20)	0	—	—	—	—	—	—	—	—	—	—	6	353
1985	Hou	15(0)	25	96	3.8(19)	1	7	71	10.1(31)	0	—	—	—	—	—	—	—	—	—	—	6	142
1986	Hou	3(0)	1	3	3.0(3)	0	—	—	—	—	—	—	—	—	—	—	—	—	—	—	0	3
1987	Det	3(3)	32	69	2.2(13)	0	7	82	11.7(21)	0	—	—	—	—	—	—	—	—	—	—	0	110
NFL	6	56(9)	149	533	3.6(20)	2	52	436	8.4(31)	1	—	—	—	—	—	—	—	—	—	—	18	776

EDWARDS, STEVE Steve, G-T, 6´5˝/340 lbs; Tennessee State; Central Florida; B2/20/1979 Chicago, IL **2002** ChiB 1 (0) **2003** ChiB 16 (16, LG) **2004** ChiB 15 (8, RG) **2005**†ChiB 7 (0) **NFL** 39 (24) [4 yrs]

EDWARDS, TERRENCE Terrence, WR, 6´0˝/176 lbs; Georgia; B4/29/1979 Tennille, GA

| 2003 | Atl | 6(0) | — | — | — | — | 1 | 10 | 10.0(10) | 0 | — | — | — | — | — | — | — | — | p | — | 0 | 2 |

EDWARDS, TIM Timothy, DT, 6´1˝/270 lbs; Delta State; 1991: NE, rnd 12; B8/29/1968 Philadelphia, MS **1992** NE 14 (1)

EDWARDS, TOM Thomas Leighton, T, 5´11˝/185 lbs; Central Michigan; Michigan; B12/12/1899 Traverse City, MI; D1/28/1980 Central Lake, MI **1926** Det 12 (11, RT)

EDWARDS, TROY Troy, WR, 5´10˝/191 lbs; Louisiana Tech; 1999: Pit, rnd 1; B4/7/1977 Shreveport, LA

1999	Pit	16(6, wr)	—	—	—	—	61	714	11.7(41)	5	—	—	—	—	—	—	—	—	kp	—	30	530
2000	Pit	14(1)	3	4	1.3(15)	0	18	215	11.9(27)	0	—	—	—	—	—	—	—	—	kp	—	0	185
2001	†Pit	16(0)	5	28	5.6(12)	1	19	283	14.9(57)	0	—	—	—	—	—	—	—	—	kp	1	12	375
2002	SL	14(0)	3	21	7.0(27)	0	18	157	8.7(48)	2	—	—	—	—	—	—	—	—	k	—	12	171
2003	Jax	13(11, WR)	3	-9	-3.0(4)	0	35	487	13.9(**84**)	3	—	—	—	—	—	—	—	—	k	—	18	255
2004	Jax	16(4)	2	2	1.0(2)	0	50	533	10.7(36)	1	—	—	—	—	—	—	—	—	kp	—	6	395
2005	Det	3(0)	—	—	—	—	2	15	7.5(8)	0	—	—	—	—	—	—	—	—	—	—	0	8
NFL	7	92(22)	16	46	2.9(27)	1	203	2404	11.8(84)	11	—	—	—	—	—	—	—	—	k	1	78	1916

EDWARDS, TURK Albert Glen, T, 6´2˝/255 lbs; Washington State; B9/28/1907 Mold, VA; D1/2/1973 Seattle, WA; HOF 1969 [KC] **1932** Bos☆6 (5, lt) **1933** Bos☆12 (12, LT) **1934** Bos☆12 (11, LT) **1935** Bos☆11 (11, LT) **1936**†Bos☆12 (11, LT) **1937** Was☆11 (11, LT) **1938** Was☆9 (8, LT) **1939** Was★11 (7, LT) **1940** Was 2 (1) **NFL** 86 (77) [9 yrs]

EDWARDS, VERNON Vernon Lajvin, DE, 6´4˝/255 lbs; SMU; B6/23/1972 Houston, TX **1996** SD 5 (1)

EDWARDS, WELDON Weldon Bertrand, T, 6´0˝/225 lbs; Texas-Arlington; TCU; 1947: Was, rnd 14/1948: LAD-A, rnd 7; B4/15/1924 Comanche, TX, D5/6/1988 Tulsa, OK **1948** Was 5 (0)

EGAN, DICK Dick, E-B, /175 lbs; DePaul; deceased **1920** ChiC 7 (2) **1921** ChiC 1 (0) **1922** ChiC 9 (9, LE) **1923** ChiC 4 (1) **1924** Ken 2 (2) **NFL** 23 (14) [5 yrs]

EGAN, DICK Richard Francis, G, /165 lbs; Wilmington; B2/2/1904 Wilmington, OH, D5/15/1984 Wilmington, OH **1924** Day 3 (3)

EGGERS, DOUG Douglas Boyd, LB, 6´0˝/213 lbs; South Dakota State; B9/21/1930 Wagner, SD **1954** Bal 11 (RLB) **1955** Bal 12 (RLB) **1956** Bal 12 (RLB) **1957** Bal 11 (RLB) **1958** ChiC 8 **NFL** 54 [5 yrs]

EGLOFF, RON Ronald Barry, TE, 6´5˝/230 lbs; Wisconsin; B10/3/1955 Garden City, MI

1977	†Den	13	—	—	—	—	2	27	13.5(20)	0	—	—	—	—	—	—	—	—	—	—	0	14
1978	Den	8	—	—	—	—	4	33	8.3(15)	1	—	—	—	—	—	—	—	—	—	—	6	22
1979	†Den	15(4)	—	—	—	—	5	70	14.0(22)	0	—	—	—	—	—	—	—	—	k	—	0	20
1980	Den	16(4)	—	—	—	—	6	85	14.2(24)	0	—	—	—	—	—	—	—	—	—	—	0	43
1981	Den	16(6, te)	—	—	—	—	17	231	13.6(40)	1	—	—	—	—	—	—	—	—	k	—	6	113
1982	Den	9(1)	—	—	—	—	10	96	9.6(17)	0	—	—	—	—	—	—	—	—	—	—	0	48
1983	†Den	16(10, TE)	—	—	—	—	20	205	10.3(32)	2	—	—	—	—	—	—	—	—	k	—	12	113
1984	SD	12(4)	—	—	—	—	11	92	8.4(10)	0	—	—	—	—	—	—	—	—	—	—	0	36
NFL	8	105(29)	—	—	—	—	75	839	11.2(40)	4	—	—	—	—	—	—	—	—	k	—	24	407

EGU, PATRICK Okechukwu Patrick, RB, 5´11˝/205 lbs; Nevada-Reno; 1989: TB, rnd 9; B2/20/1967 Owerri, Nigeria

| 1989 | NE | 7(0) | 3 | 20 | 6.7(15) | 1 | — | — | — | — | — | — | — | — | — | — | — | — | k | — | 6 | 26 |

EHIN, CHUCK Charles Kalev, NT-DE-LB, 6´4˝/261 lbs; Brigham Young; 1983: SD, rnd 12; B7/1/1961 Marysville, CA **1983** SD 9 (0) **1984** SD 16 (15, LDE) **1985** SD 16 (15, NT) **1986** SD 12 (9, NT) **1987** SD 12 (4) **NFL** 65 (43) [5 yrs]

EHLERS, TOM Thomas Slick, LB, 6´2˝/218 lbs; Kentucky; 1975: Phi, rnd 13; B7/14/1952 South Bend, IN **1975** Phi 14 **1976** Phi 14 **1977** Phi 14 (3) **1978** Buf 8 **NFL** 50 (3) [4 yrs]

EHRHARDT, CLYDE Clyde Walter, C, 6´1˝/232 lbs; Georgia; 1944: Was, rnd 19; B7/4/1921 Bardwell, KY, D2/4/1963 **1946** Was 10 (1) **1948** Was 12 (5, c) **1949** Was 12 (2) **NFL** 34 (8) [3 yrs]

EHRMANN, JOE Joseph Charles, DT, 6´5˝/260 lbs; Syracuse; 1973: Bal, rnd 1; B3/29/1949 Buffalo, NY **1973** Bal 12 (9, RDT) **1974** Bal 14 (12, RDT) **1975**†Bal 14 (14, RDT) **1976**†Bal☆14 (14, RDT) **1977**†Bal 9 (8, RDT) **1978** Bal 14 (10, RDT) **1979** Bal 15 (4) **1980** Bal 16 (1) **1981** Det 4 (2) **1982**†Det 9 (1) **NFL** 121 (75) [10 yrs]

YEAR	TEAM	G (GS, POS)	RUSH	YD	AVG(LG)	TD	REC	YD	AVG(LG)	TD	PASS COMP	PCT	YD	AVG(LG)	TD	INT	SK	YD	QBR	KPR	OTD	PTS	TAY

EIBNER, JOHN John R., T, 6´2˝/228 lbs; Kentucky; 1941: Pit, rnd 15; B3/13/1914 Elyria, OH, D11/1973   **1941** Phi 11 (9, LT)   **1942** Phi 10 (7, RT)   **1946** Phi 9 (0)   **NFL** 30 (16) [3 yrs]

EICHENLAUB, RAY Raymond Joseph, FB, 6´0˝/225 lbs; Notre Dame; B7/15/1892 Columbus, OH, D11/9/1949 Chicago, IL   **1925** Col 4 (2)

EIDEN, ED Edmund Joseph, C, 6´0˝/205 lbs; Scranton; 1944: Phi, rnd 26; B11/16/1921 Scranton, PA   **1944** Det 1 (0)

EIDEN, JIM Harold Charles, T, 5´8˝/185 lbs; none; B10/16/1901 Evanston, IL, D4/17/1990 Stuart, FL   **1926** Lou 1 (1)

EIDSON, JIM James Milton, G-C, 6´3˝/264 lbs; Mississippi State; 1976: Dal, rnd 2; B5/10/1954 Anderson, SC   **1976** Dal 9

EIFRID, JIM James John, LB, 6´1˝/240 lbs; Colorado State; 1960: NYT, rnd 1/Was, rnd 11; B10/22/1938 Fort Wayne, IN   **1961** Den-A 1

EIKENBERG, CHARLEY Charles Virgil, QB, 6´2˝/205 lbs; Louisiana-Lafayette; Rice; 1945: Bkn, rnd 18/1947: ChiR-A, rnd 9; B2/22/1924 Old Gulf, TX, D1/30/1987 Houston, TX

| 1948 | ChiC | 9(1) | 2 | 9 | 4.5(18) | 0 | — | — | — | — | 19 | 6 | 31.6 | 116 | 6.1(52) | 3 | 2 | — | — | — | P | — | 0 | 2 |

EILERS, PAT Patrick Christopher, DB, 5´11˝/197 lbs; Notre Dame; B9/3/1966 St. Paul, MN   **1990** Min 8 (0)   **1991** Min 16 (0)   **1992** Was 1 (0)   **1993** Was 11 (0)   **1994** Was 16 (0)   **1995** ChiB 9 (0)   **NFL** 61 (0) [6 yrs]

EISCHEID, MIKE Michael Duncan, K, 6´0˝/190 lbs; Upper Iowa; B9/29/1940 Orange City, IA **[KP]**   **1966** Oak-A 12   **1967**†Oak-A 14   **1970**†Oak 14   **1971** Oak 2   **1973**†Min 14

1968	†Oak-A	14	2	41	20.5(24)	0	—	—	—	—	—	—	—	—	—	—	—	—	—	P	—	0	41
1969	†Oak-A	14	1	10	10.0(10)	0	—	—	—	—	—	—	—	—	—	—	—	—	—	P	—	0	10
1972	Min	14	1	-13	-13.0(-13)	0	—	—	—	—	—	—	—	—	—	—	—	—	—	P	—	0	-13
1974	†Min	14	—	—	—	—	—	—	—	—	1	1	100.0	6	6.0(6)	0	0	—	—	P	—	0	3
NFL		9	112	4	38	9.5(24)	0	—	—	—	—	1	1	100.0	6	6.0(6)	0	0	—	—	KP	—	70	41

EISENHAUER, LARRY Lawrence Conway, DE, 6´5˝/250 lbs; Boston College; 1961: Bos, rnd 6; B2/22/1940 Hicksville, NY   **1961** Bos-A☆14 (RDE)   **1962** Bos-A★14 (RDE)   **1963**†Bos-A★14 (RDE)   **1964** Bos-A★14 (RDE)   **1965** Bos-A 14 (RDE)   **1966** Bos-A★14 (RDE)   **1967** Bos-A 9 (RDE)   **1968** Bos-A 8 (8, RDE)   **1969** Bos-A 14 (13, RDE)   **NFL** 115 (21) [9 yrs]

EISENHOOTH, JOHN John Levere, NT, 6´2˝/265 lbs; Lock Haven; B3/3/1962 Harrisburg, PA   **1987** Sea 1 (0)

EISENHOOTH, STAN Stanley Emerson, C-T, 6´5˝/287 lbs; Towson State; B7/8/1963 Harrisburg, PA   **1988** Sea 13 (0)   **1989** Ind 16 (0)   **NFL** 29 (0) [2 yrs]

EISSLER, ALFRED Alfred F., HB, none; B11/1896 Cicero, IL, D11/19/1954 Albion, MI   **1920** ChiT 2 (0)

EITZMANN, CHRIS Chris John, TE, 6´5˝/255 lbs; Harvard; B4/1/1977 Belleville, KS   **2000** NE 5 (1)

EKEJIUBA, ISAIAH Isaiah, LB, 6´4˝/219 lbs; Virginia; B10/5/1981 Chestnut Ridge, NY   **2005** Oak 10 (0)

EKERN, ANDY Anderson Erik, TE, 6´6˝/265 lbs; Missouri; 1983: NE, rnd 12; B7/26/1961 Columbia, MO   **1984** Ind 2 (0)

EKERN, CARL Carl Frederick, LB, 6´3˝/223 lbs; San Jose State; 1976: LA, rnd 5; B5/27/1954 Richland, WA, D8/1/1990 Ridgecrest, CA   **1976**†LARm 14   **1977**†LARm 14   **1978**†LARm 16   **1980**†LARm 15 (0)   **1981** LARm 16 (16, MLB)   **1982** LARm 3 (3, LLB)   **1983**†LARm 16 (16, LILB)   **1984**†LARm 16 (16, LILB)   **1985**†LARm 16 (16, LILB)   **1986**†LARm★13 (13, LILB)   **1987** LARm 11 (11, LILB)   **1988**†LARm 16 (16, LILB)   **NFL** 166 (107) [12 yrs]

EKUBAN, EBENEZER Ebenexer, DE, 6´3˝/265 lbs; North Carolina; 1999: Dal, rnd 1; B5/29/1976, Ghana   **1999**†Dal 16 (2)   **2000** Dal 12 (2)   **2001** Dal 1 (1)   **2002** Dal 16 (15, RDE)   **2003**†Dal 15 (14, RDE)   **2004** Cle 16 (11, LDE)   **2005**†Den 16 (4)   **NFL** 92 (49) [7 yrs]

ELAM, CLEVELAND Cleveland, DT-DE, 6´4˝/252 lbs; Tennessee State; 1975: SF, rnd 4; B4/5/1952 Memphis, TN   **1975** SF 14   **1976** SF★14 (14, RDT)   **1977** SF★14 (14, RDT)   **1978** SF 12 (4)   **1979** Det 8   **NFL** 62 (32) [5 yrs]

ELAM, JASON Jason Douglas, K, 5´11˝/200 lbs; Hawaii; 1993: Den, rnd 3; B3/8/1970 Fort Walton Beach, FL **[K]**   **1993**†Den 16 (0)   **1994** Den 16 (0)   **1995** Den★16 (0)   **1996**†Den 16 (0)   **1997**†Den 15 (0)   **1998**†Den★16 (0)   **1999** Den 16 (0)   **2000**†Den 13 (0)   **2001** Den★16 (0)   **2002** Den 16 (0)   **2003**†Den 16 (0)   **2004**†Den 16 (0)   **2005**†Den 16 (0)   **NFL** 204 (0) [13 yrs]

ELAM, ONZY Onzy Warren, LB, 6´2˝/225 lbs; Tennessee State; 1987: NYJ, rnd 3; B12/1/1964 Miami, FL   **1987** NYJ 5 (0)   **1988** NYJ 4 (0)   **1989** Dal 1 (0)   **NFL** 10 (0) [3 yrs]

ELAM, SHANE Shane Farrar, LB, 6´1˝/240 lbs; Mississippi; B11/6/1977 Covington, TN   **2001** SF 4 (0)

ELDER, DONNIE Donald Eugene, DB, 5´9˝/175 lbs; Memphis; 1985: NYJ, rnd 3; B12/13/1962 Chattanooga, TN **[R]**   **1985** NYJ 10 (0)   **1986** Pit 9 (0)   **1986** Det 3 (0)   **1988** TB 16 (0)   **1989** TB 16 (0)   **1990** SD 12 (0)   **1991** SD 16 (1)   **NFL** 82 (1) [6 yrs]

ELEWONIBI, MOHAMMED Mohammed Thomas David, T, 6´4˝/286 lbs; Brigham Young; 1990: Was, rnd 3; B12/16/1965 Lagos, Nigeria   **1992** Was 5 (4)   **1993** Was 15 (15, LT)   **1995**†Phi 6 (0)   **NFL** 26 (19) [3 yrs]

ELEY, CLIFTON Clifton, TE, 6´5˝/230 lbs; Mississippi State; B6/21/1961 Clarksdale, MS   **1987** Min 2 (0)

ELEY, MONROE Monroe, RB, 6´2˝/210 lbs; Arizona State; 1974: Atl, rnd 5; B4/17/1949 Rocky Mount, NC

1975	Atl	6	1	3	3.0(3)	0	—	—	—	—	—	—	—	—	—	—	—	—	—	kp	—	0	40
1977	Atl	7	97	273	2.8(16)	1	9	60	6.7(14)	0	—	—	—	—	—	—	—	—	—	k	—	6	314
NFL		2	13	98	276	2.8(16)	1	9	60	6.7(14)	0	—	—	—	—	—	—	—	—	kp	—	6	354

ELIA, BRUCE Bruce Louis, LB, 6´1˝/222 lbs; Ohio State; 1975: Mia, rnd 4; B1/10/1953 Hoboken, NJ   **1975** Mia 14   **1976** SF 12 (2)   **1977** SF 13 (7, MLB)

| 1978 | SF | 16 | 1 | 0 | 0.0(0) | 0 | — | — | — | — | — | — | — | — | — | — | — | — | — | — | — | 0 | 0 |
| NFL | | 4 | 55(9) | 1 | 0 | 0.0 | — | — | — | — | — | — | — | — | — | — | — | — | — | p | — | 0 | -4 |

ELIAS, HOMER Homer Cary, G-T, 6´3˝/255 lbs; Tennessee State; 1978: Det, rnd 4; B5/1/1955 Fort Benning, GA   **1978** Det 16 (16, LG)   **1979** Det 15 (14, LG)   **1980** Det 14 (13, LG/rt)   **1981** Det 16 (16, LG)   **1982**†Det 9 (9, LG)   **1983**†Det 14 (14, LG)   **1984** Det 12 (4)   **NFL** 96 (86) [7 yrs]

ELIAS, KEITH Keith Hector, RB, 5´9˝/198 lbs; Princeton; B2/3/1972 Lacey Township, NJ

1994	NYG	2(0)	2	4	2.0(5)	0	—	—	—	—	—	—	—	—	—	—	—	—	—	—	—	0	4
1995	NYG	15(0)	10	44	4.4(8)	0	9	69	7.7(18)	0	—	—	—	—	—	—	—	—	—	—	—	0	79
1996	NYG	9(0)	9	24	2.7(8)	0	8	51	6.4(11)	0	—	—	—	—	—	—	—	—	—	—	—	0	50
1998	Ind	13(0)	8	24	3.0(8)	0	1	11	11.0(11)	0	—	—	—	—	—	—	—	—	—	k	—	0	137
1999	†Ind	14(0)	13	28	2.2(8)	0	4	16	4.0(7)	0	—	—	—	—	—	—	—	—	—	k	—	0	43
NFL		5	53(0)	42	124	3.0(8)	0	22	147	6.7(18)	0	—	—	—	—	—	—	—	—	k	—	0	312

ELIASON, DON Donald Carlton, E, 6´2˝/215 lbs; Hamline; B7/24/1918 Owatonna, MN, D8/18/2003, **[K]**

1942	Bkn	4(0)	—	—	—	—	1	36	36.0(36)	0	—	—	—	—	—	—	—	—	—	—	—	0	18
1946	Bos	3(0)	—	—	—	—	1	9	9.0(9)	0	—	—	—	—	—	—	—	—	—	K	—	0	5
NFL		2	7(0)	—	—	—	—	2	45	22.5(36)	0	—	—	—	—	—	—	—	—	—	K	—	0	23

ELIOPULOS, JIM James A., LB, 6´2˝/230 lbs; Westminster (MO); Wyoming; 1982: Dal, rnd 3; B4/18/1959 Dearborn, MI   **1983** SL 4 (0)   **1983** NYJ 8 (0)   **1984** NYJ 11 (0)   **1985** NYJ 8 (0)   **NFL** 31 (0) [3 yrs]

ELKINS, CHIEF Fait Vernon, B, 5´11˝/190 lbs; Haskell Indian; Southwestern Oklahoma State; Nebraska; B8/16/1899 Utica, NY, D8/1966 Philadelphia, PA **[K]**   **1928** Fra 10 (3), 13   **1929** Fra 7 (4)   **1929** ChiC 2 (2), 3   **1933** Cin 1 (1)   **NFL** 20 (10), 16 [3 yrs]

ELKINS, EV Everett Lee, B, 5´11˝/190 lbs; Marshall; 1939: ChiC, rnd 17; B11/17/1917 Hamlin, WV, D6/8/1977 Hamlin, WV   **1940** ChiC 1 (0)

ELKINS, LARRY Lawrence Clayton, WR, 6´1˝/192 lbs; Baylor; 1965: Hou, rnd 1/GB, rnd 1; B7/28/1943 Brownwood, TX

1966	Hou-A	14	—	—	—	—	21	283	13.5(62)	3	—	—	—	—	—	—	—	—	—	—	—	18	157
1967	Hou-A	4	2	19	9.5(14)	0	3	32	10.7(16)	0	—	—	—	—	—	—	—	—	—	—	—	0	35
NFL		2	18	2	19	9.5(14)	0	24	315	13.1(62)	3	—	—	—	—	—	—	—	—	—	—	—	18	192

ELKINS, MIKE Michael David, QB, 6´3˝/221 lbs; Wake Forest; 1989: KC, rnd 2; B7/20/1966 Greensboro, NC

| 1989 | KC | 1(0) | — | — | — | — | — | — | — | — | 2 | 1 | 50.0 | 5 | 2.5(5) | 0 | 1 | — | — | — | — | 0 | -38 |

ELKO, BILL William, NT-G, 6´5˝/278 lbs; Arizona State; LSU; 1983: SD, rnd 7; B12/28/1959 New York, NY   **1983** SD 11 (3)   **1984** SD 15 (12, NT)   **1987** Ind 3 (1)   **NFL** 29 (16) [3 yrs]

ELLARD, HENRY Henry Austin, WR, 5´11˝/180 lbs; Fresno State; 1983: LARm, rnd 2; B7/21/1961 Fresno, CA **[R]**

1983	†LARm	12(0)	3	7	2.3(12)	0	16	268	16.8(44)	0	—	—	—	—	—	—	—	—	—	kp	1	6	377
1984	LARm★	16(16, WR)	3	-5	-1.7(5)	0	34	622	18.3(63)	6	—	—	—	—	—	—	—	—	—	kp	2	48	603
1985	†LARm☆	16(16, WR)	3	8	2.7(16)	0	54	811	15.0(64)	5	—	—	—	—	—	—	—	—	—	p	1	36	765
1986	†LARm	9(8, WR)	1	-15	-15.0(-15)	0	34	447	13.1(34)	0	—	—	—	—	—	—	—	—	—	kp	—	24	289

YEAR	TEAM	G (GS, POS)	RUSH	YD	AVG(LG)	TD	REC	YD	AVG(LG)	TD	PASS	COMP	PCT	YD	AVG(LG)	TD	INT	SK	YD	QBR	KPR	OTD	PTS	TAY
1987	LARm	12(12, WR)	1	4	4.0(4)	0	51	799	15.7(81)	3	—	—	—	—	—	—	—	—	—	—	kp	—	18	444
1988	†LARm★	16(15, WR)	1	7	7.0(7)	0	86	1414	16.4(68)	10	—	—	—	—	—	—	—	—	—	—	p	—	60	798
1989	†LARm★	14(12, WR)	2	10	5.0(6)	0	70	1382	19.7(53)	8	—	—	—	—	—	—	—	—	—	—	p	—	48	751
1990	LARm	15(15, WR)	2	21	10.5(13)	0	76	1294	17.0(50)	4	—	—	—	—	—	—	—	—	—	—	p	—	24	693
1991	LARm	16(16, WR)	—	—	—	—	64	1052	16.4(38)	3	—	—	—	—	—	—	—	—	—	—		—	18	541
1992	LARm	16(15, WR)	—	—	—	—	47	727	15.5(33)	3	—	—	—	—	—	—	—	—	—	—		—	18	379
1993	LARm	16(16, WR)	2	18	9.0(15)	0	61	945	15.5(54)	2	—	—	—	—	—	—	—	—	—	—	p	—	12	509
1994	Was	16(16, WR)	1	-5	-5.0(-5)	0	74	1397	18.9(73)	6	—	—	—	—	—	—	—	—	—	—		—	36	724
1995	Was	15(15, WR)	—	—	—	—	56	1005	17.9(59)	5	—	—	—	—	—	—	—	—	—	—		—	30	528
1996	Was	16(16, WR)	—	—	—	—	52	1014	19.5(51)	5	—	—	—	—	—	—	—	—	—	—		—	12	517
1997	Was	16(11, WR)	—	—	—	—	32	485	15.2(27)	4	—	—	—	—	—	—	—	—	—	—		—	24	263
1998	NE	5(0)	—	—	—	—	5	86	17.2(19)	0	—	—	—	—	—	—	—	—	—	—		—	0	43
1998	Was	2(0)	—	—	—	—	2	29	14.5(19)	0	—	—	—	—	—	—	—	—	—	—		—	0	15
NFL	16	228(199)	19	50	2.6(16)	0	814	13777	16.9(81)	65	—	—	—	—	—	—	—	—	—	—	kp	4	414	8235

ELLENA, JACK Jack Duane, G-LB, 6′1″/225 lbs; UCLA; 1953: LA, rnd 19; B10/27/1931 Susanville, CA **1955**†LARm 12 **1956** LARm 9 **NFL** 21 [2 yrs]

ELLENBOGEN, BILL William A., G-T, 6′5″/258 lbs; Buffalo; Virginia Tech; B12/8/1950 Glen Cove, NY **1976** NYG 11 (2) **1977** NYG 12 **NFL** 23 (2) [2 yrs]

ELLENDER, RICH Richard, RB, 5′11″/171 lbs; McNeese State; 1979: Hou, rnd 9; B6/9/1957 Sulphur, LA

1979	†Hou	13	—	—	—	—	1	15	15.0(15)	0	—	—	—	—	—	—	—	—	—	—	kp	—	0	210

ELLENSON, GENE Eugene, T, 6′1″/210 lbs; Georgia; B3/24/1921 Chippewa Falls, WI, D3/17/1995 Gainesville, FL **1946** Mia-A 13 (11, RT)

ELLER, CARL Carl Lee, DE, 6′6″/247 lbs; Minnesota; 1964: Min, rnd 1/Buf, rnd 1; B2/25/1942 Winston-Salem, NC; HOF 2004 **1964** Min 14 (14, LDE) **1965** Min 14 (14, LDE) **1966** Min 14 (14, LDE) **1967** Min☆14 (13, LDE) **1968**†Min★14 (14, LDE) **1969**†Min★14 (14, LDE) **1970**†Min★14 (14, LDE) **1971**†Min★14 (14, LDE) **1972** Min☆14 (14, LDE) **1973**†Min★14 (14, LDE) **1974**†Min★14 (14, LDE) **1975**†Min☆14 (14, LDE) **1976**†Min 13 (13, LDE) **1977**†Min 14 (14, LDE) **1978**†Min 14 (7, lde) **1979** Sea 16 (8, LDE) **NFL** 225 (209) [16 yrs]

ELLERSICK, DON Donald K., DB, 6′1″/193 lbs; Washington State; 1960: LA, rnd 6/NYT, rnd 1; B5/7/1938 Ione, WA **1960** LARm 12

ELLERSON, GARY Gary Tobius, RB, 5′11″/220 lbs; Wisconsin; 1985: GB, rnd 7; B7/17/1963 Albany, GA

1985	GB	15(0)	32	205	6.4(37)	2	2	15	7.5(11)	0	—	—	—	—	—	—	—	—	—	—	k	—	12	319
1986	GB	16(6, rb)	90	287	3.2(18)	3	12	130	10.8(32)	0	—	—	—	—	—	—	—	—	—	—	k	—	18	431
1987	Det	8(2)	47	196	4.2(33)	3	5	48	9.6(23)	1	—	—	—	—	—	—	—	—	—	—		—	24	255
NFL	3	39(8)	169	688	4.1(37)	8	19	193	10.2(32)	1	—	—	—	—	—	—	—	—	—	—	k	—	54	1005

ELLING, AARON Aaron, K, 6′2″/201 lbs; Wyoming; B5/31/1978 Waconia, MN **[K]** **2003** Min 16 (0) **2004** Ten 1 (0) **2004** Min 7 (0) **2005** Bal 9 (0) **NFL** 33 (0) [3 yrs]

ELLINGTON, DANTE Dante, T, 6′6″/330 lbs; Alabama; B2/29/1980 Leighton, AL **2005** Arz 2 (0)

ELLIOTT, AL Alvah Charles, B, 5′9″/175 lbs; Wisconsin; B10/13/1894 Muscoda, WI, D12/18/1975 Naperville, IL **[K]** **1922** Rac 11 (9, TB), 12 **1923** Rac 10 (8, TB), 12 **1924** Rac 7 (6, TB), 9 **NFL** 28 (23), 33 [3 yrs]

ELLIOTT, CARL Carlton Batt, DE-E, 6′4″/230 lbs; Virginia; 1950: GB, rnd 13; B11/12/1927 Laurel, DE, D7/18/2005 Garland, TX

1951	GB	12(le)	—	—	—	—	35	317	9.1(33)	5	—	—	—	—	—	—	—	—	—	—	k	—	30	183
1952	GB	12(RDE)	—	—	—	—	12	114	9.5(15)	1	—	—	—	—	—	—	—	—	—	—		—	6	62
1953	GB	12(RDE)	—	—	—	—	13	150	11.5(19)	0	—	—	—	—	—	—	—	—	—	—		1	6	75
1954	GB	12(RDE)	—	—	—	—	—	—	—	—	—	—	—	—	—	—	—	—	—	—		—	0	0
NFL	4	48	—	—	—	—	60	581	9.7(33)	6	—	—	—	—	—	—	—	—	—	—	k	1	42	320

ELLIOTT, CHARLIE Charles Junior, T, 6′2″/240 lbs; Oregon; 1947: NYY-A, rnd 14/LARm, rnd 22; B12/30/1921 Corvallis, OR, D9/15/1980 Oregon City, OR **1947** NYY-A 10 (0) **1948** ChiR-A 1 (0) **1948** SF-A.3 (1) **AAFC** 14 (0) [2 yrs]

ELLIOTT, DOC Wallace John, B, 5′10″/209 lbs; Lafayette; B4/6/1900 Youngstown, OH, D1/11/1976 Fort Myers, FL **[K]** **1922** Can☆7 (7, FB), 12 **1923** Can☆9 (8, FB), 36 **1924** Cle☆7 (5, fb), 40 **1925** Cle 14 (12, FB), 27 **1931** Cle 2 (1), 6 **NFL** 39 (33), 121 [5 yrs]

ELLIOTT, JAMIN Jamin, WR, 6′0″/187 lbs; Delaware; 2002: Chi, rnd 6; B10/5/1979 Portsmouth, VA **2002** ChiB 1 (0)

ELLIOTT, JIM James Lawrence, P, 5′11″/184 lbs; Presbyterian; B8/18/1944 Montgomery, AL **1967** Pit 14

ELLIOTT, JOHN Darrell John, DT-DE, 6′4″/244 lbs; Texas; 1967: NYJ, rnd 7; B10/26/1944 Beaumont, TX **1967** NYJ-A 13 **1968** NYJ-A★14 (RDT) **1969** NYJ-A★14 (RDT) **1970** NYJ-A★14 (RDT) **1971** NYJ 4 **1972** NYJ 13 (RDT) **1973** NYJ 13 (RDT) **NFL** 85 [7 yrs]

ELLIOTT, JUMBO John Stuart, T, 6′7″/308 lbs; Michigan; 1988: NYG, rnd 2; B4/1/1965 Lake Ronkonkoma, NY **1988** NYG 16 (5, lt) **1989**†NYG 13 (11, LT) **1990**†NYG 8 (8, lt) **1991** NYG 16 (16, LT) **1992** NYG 16 (16, LT) **1993** NYG◇11 (11, LT) **1994** NYG 16 (15, LT) **1995** NYG 16 (16, LT) **1996** NYJ 14 (14, LT) **1997** NYJ 13 (13, LT) **1998**†NYJ 16 (16, LT) **1999** NYJ 16 (15, LT) **2002**†NYJ 16 (0)

2000	NYJ	9(0)	—	—	—	—	1	3	3.0(3)	1	—	—	—	—	—	—	—	—	—	—		—	6	7
NFL	14	196(156)	—	—	—	—	1	3	3.0(3)	1	—	—	—	—	—	—	—	—	—	—		—	6	7

ELLIOTT, LENVIL Lenvil Olon, RB, 6′0″/205 lbs; Truman State; 1973: Cin, rnd 10; B9/2/1951 Lexington, MO

1973	†Cin	6	22	122	5.5(15)	1	1	12	12.0(12)	1	—	—	—	—	—	—	—	—	—	—		—	12	143
1974	Cin	10	68	345	5.1(26)	1	18	187	10.4(28)	1	1	1	100.0	17	17.0(17)	0	0	—	—	—	k	—	12	449
1975	†Cin	14(rb)	71	308	4.3(27)	1	20	196	9.8(31)	1	—	—	—	—	—	—	—	—	—	—	k	—	24	508
1976	Cin	12	69	276	4.0(24)	0	22	188	8.5(29)	3	—	—	—	—	—	—	—	—	—	—	k	—	18	408
1977	Cin	14	65	269	4.1(32)	0	29	238	8.2(33)	1	—	—	—	—	—	—	—	—	—	—	k	—	6	401
1978	Cin	10	29	75	2.6(12)	0	12	100	8.3(18)	0	—	—	—	—	—	—	—	—	—	—		—	0	125
1979	SF	16	33	135	4.1(12)	3	23	197	8.6(30)	0	—	—	—	—	—	—	—	—	—	—	k	—	18	299
1980	SF	15(3)	76	341	4.5(20)	2	27	285	10.6(45)	1	—	—	—	—	—	—	—	—	—	—	k	—	18	560
1981	†SF	4(0)	7	29	4.1(9)	0	7	81	11.6(19)	0	—	—	—	—	—	—	—	—	—	—		—	0	70
NFL	9	101(3)	440	1900	4.3(32)	8	159	1484	9.3(45)	10	1	1	100.0	17	17.0(17)	0	0	—	—	—	k	—	108	2962

ELLIOTT, LIN Lindley Franklin, K, 6′0″/182 lbs; Texas Tech; B11/11/1968 Euless, TX **[K]** **1992**†Dal 16 (0) **1993** Dal 2 (0) **1994**†KC 16 (0) **1995**†KC 16 (0) **NFL** 50 (0) [4 yrs]

ELLIOTT, MATT Eric Matthew, G-C, 6′3″/288 lbs; Michigan; 1992: Was, rnd 12; B10/1/1968 Carmel, IN **1992**†Was 16 (2) **1995** Car 15 (14, RG) **1996**†Car 16 (12, LG/c) **1997** Car 16 (6, lg) **NFL** 63 (34) [4 yrs]

ELLIOTT, TED Theodore, NT, 6′6″/275 lbs; Mankato State; B11/16/1964 Inver Grove Heights, MN **1987** NO 3 (0)

ELLIOTT, TONY Anthony Robert, NT, 6′2″/282 lbs; Wisconsin; North Texas; 1982: NO, rnd 5; B4/23/1959 New York, NY **1982** NO 9 (0) **1983** NO 12 (0) **1984** NO 4 (3) **1985** NO 16 (16, NT) **1986** NO 15 (15, NT) **1987**†NO 14 (14, NT) **1988** NO 14 (12, NT) **NFL** 84 (60) [7 yrs]

ELLIOTT, TONY Anthony Fitzgerald, DB, 5′10″/195 lbs; Central Michigan; B1/10/1964 Detroit, MI **1987** GB 1 (0)

ELLIS, ALLAN Allan Delon, DB, 5′11″/185 lbs; UCLA; 1973: Chi, rnd 5; B8/19/1951 Los Angeles, CA **[I]** **1973** ChiB 14 **1974** ChiB 14 (14, LCB) **1975** ChiB 14 (14, LCB) **1976** ChiB 14 (14, LCB) **1977**†ChiB★14 (14, LCB) **1979**†ChiB 8 (4) **1980** ChiB 16 (16, RCB) **1981**†SD 11 (6, rcb) **NFL** 105 (82) [8 yrs]

ELLIS, CLARENCE Clarence Joseph, DB, 5′11″/193 lbs; Notre Dame; 1972: Atl, rnd 1; B2/11/1950 Grand Rapids, MI **1972** Atl 13 (FS) **1973** Atl 14 (FS) **1974** Atl 14 (FS) **NFL** 41 [3 yrs]

ELLIS, CRAIG Craig, RB, 5′11″/185 lbs; San Diego State; B1/26/1961 Los Angeles, CA

1986	Mia	9(0)	3	6	2.0(2)	0	—	—	—	—	—	—	—	—	—	—	—	—	—	—	kp	—	0	201
1987	LARd	3(1)	33	138	4.2(14)	2	5	39	7.8(15)	0	—	—	—	—	—	—	—	—	—	—		—	12	178
NFL	2	12(1)	36	144	4.0(14)	2	5	39	7.8(15)	0	—	—	—	—	—	—	—	—	—	—	kp	—	12	379

ELLIS, DREW Benjamin Drew, T, 6′1″/215 lbs; TCU; 1937: Phi, rnd 3; B12/27/1914 Ochtree County, TX, D5/18/1988 Perryton, TX **1938** Phi 11 (10, LT)

1939	Phi	11(9, LT)	1	6	6.0(6)	0	—	—	—	—	—	—	—	—	—	—	—	—	—	—		—	0	6
NFL	2	22(19)	1	6	6.0(6)	0	—	—	—	—	—	—	—	—	—	—	—	—	—	—		—	0	6

ELLIS, ED Edward Key, T, 6′5″/325 lbs; Buffalo; 1997: NE, rnd 4; B10/13/1975 New Haven, CT **1997** NE 1 (0) **1998** NE 7 (0) **1999** NE 1 (1) **2000** Was 12 (0) **2001** SD 16 (2) **2002** SD 15 (3) **2003** SD 2 (1) **NFL** 54 (7) [7 yrs]

YEAR	TEAM	G (GS, POS)	RUSH	YD	AVG(LG)	TD	REC	YD	AVG(LG)	TD	PASS	COMP	PCT	YD	AVG(LG)	TD	INT	SK	YD	QBR	KPR	OTD	PTS	TAY

ELLIS, GERRY   Garry Lemont, RB, 6´11˝/221 lbs; Missouri; 1980: LA, rnd 7; B11/12/1957 Columbia, MO

1980	GB	15(13, FB)	126	545	4.3(22)	5	48	496	10.3(69)	3	—	—	—	—	—	—	—	—	—	—	—	—	48	858
1981	GB	16(16, FB)	196	860	4.4(29)	4	65	499	7.7(46)	3	2	1	50.0	23	11.5(23)	0	0	—	—	—	—	—	42	1176
1982	†GB	9(8, FB)	62	228	3.7(29)	1	18	140	7.8(20)	0	—	—	—	—	—	—	—	—	—	—	—	—	6	308
1983	GB	15(14, FB/rb)	141	696	4.9(71)	4	52	603	11.6(56)	2	5	2	40.0	31	6.2(20)	1	1	—	—	—	—	—	36	1028
1984	GB	16(16, RB/fb)	123	581	4.7(50)	4	36	312	8.7(22)	2	4	1	25.0	17	4.3(17)	0	0	1	3	—	—	—	36	796
1985	GB	16(8, rb)	104	571	5.5(59)	5	24	206	8.6(35)	1	1	0	0.0	0	0.0	0	0	—	—	k	—	—	30	776
1986	GB	16(6, rb)	84	345	4.1(24)	2	24	258	10.8(29)	0	—	—	—	—	—	—	—	—	—	k	—	—	12	494
NFL	7	103(81)	836	3826	4.6(71)	25	267	2514	9.4(69)	10	12	4	33.3	71	5.9(23)	1	1	3	—	k	—	—	210	5436

ELLIS, GREG   Gregory Lemont, DE, 6´6˝/277 lbs; North Carolina; 1998: Dal, rnd 1; B8/14/1975 Wendell, NC **[S]**   **1998**†Dal 16 (16, RDE)   **1999** Dal 13 (13, RDE)   **2000** Dal 16 (16, LDE)   **2001** Dal 16 (16, LDE)   **2002** Dal 15 (15, LDE)   **2003**†Dal 16 (16, LDE)   **2004** Dal 16 (16, LDE)   **2005** Dal 16 (13, RDE)   **NFL** 124 (120) [8 yrs]

ELLIS, HERB   Herbert Wayne, C-LB, 6´2˝/205 lbs; Texas A&M; B12/18/1925 Vernon, TX, deceased   **1949** NYB 12 (0)

ELLIS, JIM   James Kevin, LB, 6´3˝/240 lbs; Boise State; 1987: LARd, rnd 10; B3/25/1964 Pomona, CA   **1987** LARd 3 (2)

ELLIS, JOHN   John Wharton, G, 5´10˝/212 lbs; Vanderbilt; B12/21/1919 Sherman, TX   **1944** Bkn 6 (1)

ELLIS, KEN   Kenneth Alfonzo, DB, 5´10˝/190 lbs; Southern (LA); 1970: GB, rnd 4; B9/27/1947 Woodbine, GA **[I]**   **1970** GB 13 (13, LCB)   **1971** GB 14 (14, LCB)   **1972**†GB☆14 (14, RCB)   **1973** GB★14 (14, RCB)   **1974** GB★14 (14, RCB)   **1975** GB 14 (14, RCB)   **1976** Mia 12   **1976** Hou 1   **1977** Cle 9   **1979** Det 7   **1979**†LARm 3   **NFL** 115 (83) [9 yrs]

ELLIS, KWAME   Kwame Delaney, DB, 5´10˝/188 lbs; Stanford; B2/27/1974 Berkeley, CA   **1996** NYJ 8 (0)

ELLIS, LARRY   Lawrence Richard, LB, 6´1˝/204 lbs; Syracuse; B5/27/1922 York, ME   **1948** Det 4 (1)

ELLIS, RAY   Kerwin Ray, DB, 6´1˝/192 lbs; Ohio State; 1981: Phi, rnd 12; B4/27/1959 Canton, OH   **1981**†Phi 16 (0)   **1982** Phi 9 (0)   **1983** Phi 16 (4)   **1984** Phi 16 (16, SS)   **1985** Phi 16 (16, SS)   **1986** Cle 15 (15, SS)   **1987** Cle 12 (10, SS)   **NFL** 100 (61) [7 yrs]

ELLIS, ROGER   Roger Calvin, LB-C, 6´3˝/233 lbs; Maine; 1959: NYG, rnd 14; B2/1/1938 Boston, ME   **1960** NYT-A 14 (MLB)   **1961** NYT-A 14   **1962** NYT-A 14   **1963** NYJ-A 1   **NFL** 43 [4 yrs]

ELLIS, SHAUN   MeShaunda Pizarrur, DE, 6´5˝/294 lbs; Tennessee; 2000: NYJ, rnd 1; B6/24/1977 Anderson, SC   **2000** NYJ 16 (2)   **2001**†NYJ 16 (16, LDE)   **2002**†NYJ 16 (16, LDE)   **2003** NYJ✧16 (16, LDE)   **2004**†NYJ 15 (15, LDE)   **2005** NYJ 13 (13, LDE)   **NFL** 92 (78) [6 yrs]

ELLIS, WALT   Walter Joseph, T, 5´11˝/224 lbs; Detroit Mercy; B11/1898 Groton, CT, deceased   **1924** Col 8 (8, LT)   **1925** Col 9 (9, LT)   **1925** Det 1 (1)   **1926** ChiC☆10 (9, RT)   **1927** ChiC 8 (4)   **NFL** 36 (31) [4 yrs]

ELLISON, GLENN   Glenn F., RB, 6´1˝/215 lbs; Arkansas; B3/9/1947 Jacksonville, FL   **1971** Oak 1

ELLISON, JERRY   Jerry Ernest, RB, 5´10˝/204 lbs; Tennessee-Chattanooga; B12/20/1971 Augusta, GA

1995	TB	16(3)	26	218	8.4(75)	5	7	44	6.3(14)	0	—	—	—	—	—	—	—	—	k	—	30	326
1996	TB	16(2)	35	106	3.0(13)	0	18	208	11.6(42)	0	—	—	—	—	—	—	—	—	k	—	0	210
1997	†TB	16(0)	2	10	5.0(5)	0	1	8	8.0(8)	0	—	—	—	—	—	—	—	—	k	—	0	45
1998	TB	16(0)	9	24	2.7(10)	0	—	—	—	—	—	—	—	—	—	—	—	—	k	—	0	28
1999	NE	12(0)	2	10	5.0(8)	0	4	50	12.5(23)	0	—	—	—	—	—	—	—	—	k	—	0	33
NFL	5	76(5)	74	368	5.0(75)	5	30	310	10.3(42)	0	—	—	—	—	—	—	—	—	k	—	30	642

ELLISON, MARK   Marshall Mark, G, 6´2˝/250 lbs; Dayton; 1971: NYG, rnd 11; B4/15/1948 Pittsburgh, PA   **1972** NYG 14   **1973** NYG 14   **NFL** 28 [2 yrs]

ELLISON, 'OMAR   Omar Ryan, WR, 6´1˝/200 lbs; Florida State; 1995: SD, rnd 5; B10/8/1971 Griffin, GA

1995	SD	2(0)	—	—	—	—	1	6	6.0(6)	0	—	—	—	—	—	—	—	—	—	—	0	3
1996	SD	10(1)	—	—	—	—	3	15	5.0(6)	0	—	—	—	—	—	—	—	—	—	—	0	8
NFL	2	12(1)	—	—	—	—	4	21	5.3(6)	0	—	—	—	—	—	—	—	—	—	—	0	11

ELLISON, RIKI   Riki Morgan, LB, 6´2˝/225 lbs; USC; 1983: SF, rnd 5; B8/15/1960 Christchurch, New Zealand   **1983**†SF 16 (15, LILB)   **1984**†SF 16 (16, LILB)   **1985**†SF 16 (16, LILB)   **1986**†SF 16 (16, LILB)   **1987**†SF 3 (1)   **1988**†SF 13 (13, LILB)   **1990**†LARd 16 (15, MLB)   **1991**†LARd 16 (15, MLB)   **1992** LARd 12 (12, MLB)   **NFL** 124 (119) [9 yrs]

ELLISON, WILLIE   William Henry, RB, 6´2˝/210 lbs; Texas Southern; 1967: LA, rnd 2; B11/1/1945 Lockhart, TX

1967	†LARm	14	14	84	6.0(42)	0	1	18	18.0(18)	0	—	—	—	—	—	—	—	—	k	—	0	238
1968	LARm	14(8, HB)	151	616	4.1(52)	5	20	248	12.4(36)	2	1	0	0.0	0	0.0	0	0	—	—	k	—	42	888
1969	†LARm	14	20	56	2.8(15)	1	4	31	7.8(14)	1	2	0	0.0	0	0.0	0	0	—	—	k	—	12	95
1970	LARm	14	90	381	4.2(24)	5	10	84	8.4(20)	2	—	—	—	—	—	—	—	—	k	—	42	488
1971	LARm★	14(13, RB)	211	1000	4.7(80)	4	32	238	7.4(49)	0	—	—	—	—	—	—	—	—	—	—	24	1159
1972	LARm	13(12, FB)	170	764	4.5(37)	5	23	141	6.1(39)	1	—	—	—	—	—	—	—	—	k	—	36	1025
1973	KC	10(fb)	108	411	3.8(19)	2	9	64	7.1(17)	0	—	—	—	—	—	—	—	—	—	—	12	463
1974	KC	5	37	114	3.1(11)	2	5	64	12.8(26)	0	—	—	—	—	—	—	—	—	—	—	12	166
NFL	8	98(33)	801	3426	4.3(80)	24	104	888	8.5(49)	6	3	0	0.0	0	0.0	0	0	—	—	k	—	180	4521

ELLISS, LUTHER   Luther John, DT-DE, 6´5˝/318 lbs; Utah; 1995: Det, rnd 1; B3/22/1973 Mancos, CO   **1995**†Det 16 (16, LDE)   **1996** Det 14 (14, RDT)   **1997**†Det 16 (16, RDT)   **1998** Det 16 (16, RDT)   **1999**†Det★15 (14, RDT)   **2000** Det✧16 (16, RDT)   **2001** Det 14 (13, RDT)   **2002** Det 14 (14, RDT)   **2003** Det 5 (0)   **2004** Den 8 (0)   **NFL** 134 (119) [10 yrs]

ELLOR, BUD   Albert Wesley, G-E, 6´1˝/205 lbs; Bucknell; B1905 Bloomfield, NJ, D2/11/1932 Jersey City, NJ   **1930** Nwk 12 (6, LG), 6

ELLSTROM, SWEDE   Marvin Lawrence, WB-HB, 6´1˝/203 lbs; Oklahoma; B5/15/1906 Moline, IL, D4/25/1994 Tonkawa, OK

1934	Bos	3(1)	10	32	3.2	0	—	—	—	—	2	0	0.0	0	0.0	0	0	—	—	—	0	32
1934	Phi	8(7, WB)	72	287	4.0	1	1	18	18.0(18)	0	14	3	21.4	40	2.9	1	5	—	—	—	6	131
1935	Pit	3(1)	10	14	1.4	0	1	12	12.0(12)	0	7	6	85.7	68	9.7	0	0	—	—	—	0	54
1936	ChiC	1(0)	4	12	3.0	0	—	—	—	—	—	—	—	—	—	—	—	—	—	—	0	12
NFL	3	15(9)	96	345	3.6	1	2	30	15.0(18)	0	23	9	39.1	108	4.7	1	5	—	—	—	6	229

ELLSWORTH, PERCY   Percy Daniel, DB, 6´2˝/213 lbs; Virginia; B10/19/1974 Drewryville, VA **[I]**   **1996** NYG 14 (4)   **1997**†NYG 16 (1)   **1998** NYG 16 (9, ss)   **1999** NYG 14 (14, FS)   **2000** Cle 16 (16, FS)   **2001** Cle 11 (9, FS)   **NFL** 87 (53) [6 yrs]

ELLZEY, CHARLEY   Charles Melvin, C-LB, 6´3˝/240 lbs; Southern Mississippi; 1960: SL, rnd 3/DalT, rnd 2; B2/17/1938 Meridian, MS   **1960** SL 9   **1961** SL 5   **NFL** 14 [2 yrs]

EL-MASHTOUB, HICHAM   Hicham, C, 6´2˝/288 lbs; Arizona; 1995: Hou, rnd 6; B5/11/1972 Lebanon   **1995** Hou 2 (0)   **1996** Hou 1 (0)   **NFL** 3 (0) [2 yrs]

ELMENDORF, DAVE   David Cole, DB, 6´1˝/195 lbs; Texas A&M; 1971: LA, rnd 3; B6/20/1949 San Antonio, TX **[I]**   **1971** LARm 14 (14, FS)   **1972** LARm☆14 (14, SS)   **1973**†LARm 14 (14, SS)   **1974**†LARm☆14 (14, SS)   **1975**†LARm☆14 (14, SS)   **1976** LARm 14 (14, SS)   **1977**†LARm 14 (14, SS)   **1978**†LARm 16 (16, SS)   **1979**†LARm 16 (16, SS)   **NFL** 130 (130) [9 yrs]

ELMORE, DOUG   James Douglas, P, 6´0˝/188 lbs; Mississippi; 1961: Was, rnd 13/1962: SD, rnd 31; B12/15/1939 Reform, AL, D9/28/2002 Jackson, MS

| 1962 | Was | 14 | 1 | -14 | -14.0(-14) | 0 | — | — | — | — | 1 | 0 | 0.0 | 0 | 0.0 | 0 | 0 | — | — | Pi | — | 0 | 4 |

ELNESS, SHORTY   Leland, HB-QB, 5´8˝/166 lbs; Bradley; B5/10/1906, D11/3/1965   **1929** ChiB 4 (0)

ELOMS, JOEY   Joey, DB, 5´10˝/181 lbs; Indiana; B4/4/1976 Fort Wayne, IN   **1998** Sea 1 (0)   **1999**†Sea 4 (0)   **NFL** 5 (0) [2 yrs]

ELROD, JIMBO   James Whittington, LB, 6´0˝/220 lbs; Oklahoma; 1976: KC, rnd 5; B5/25/1954 Memphis, TN   **1976** KC 6 (3)   **1977** KC 14   **1978** KC 16   **1979** Hou 4   **NFL** 40 (3) [4 yrs]

ELSER, EARL   Earl Howard, T, 6´1˝/229 lbs; Butler; B3/21/1908, D8/1974 Gary, IN   **1933** Por 4 (0)   **1934** Cin 8 (7, RT)   **1934** SL 1 (0)   **NFL** 13 (7) [2 yrs]

ELSEY, EARL   Earl D., HB, 5´8˝/175 lbs; Loyola Marymount; B6/23/1920, D1/8/1998

| 1946 | LAD-A | 13(3) | 47 | 165 | 3.5 | 0 | 14 | 179 | 12.8 | 0 | — | — | — | — | — | — | — | — | kpi | — | 0 | 459 |

ELSHIRE, NEIL   Neil James, DE, 6´6˝/260 lbs; Oregon; B3/8/1958 Salem, OR   **1981** Min 4 (0)   **1982** Min 5 (0)   **1983** Min 16 (10, RDE)   **1984** Min 12 (10, LDE)   **1985** Min 16 (3)   **1986** Min 10 (4)   **NFL** 63 (27) [6 yrs]

Elston, Dutch Arthur Warren, C-BB, 5´11˝/190 lbs; South Carolina; B11/19/1918 Texhoma, TX, D9/10/1989 Daly City, CA **1946** SF-A 13 (11, C) **1947** SF-A 9 (3) **1948** SF-A 12 (0) **AAFC** 34 (14) [3 yrs]

YEAR	TEAM	G(GS, POS)	RUSH	YD	AVG(LG)	TD	REC	YD	AVG(LG)	TD	PASS	COMP	PCT	YD	AVG(LG)	TD	INT	SK	YD	QBR	KPR	OTD	PTS	TAY
1942	Cle	11(8, BB)	1	15	15.0(15)	0	4	58	14.5(18)	0	—	—	—	—	—	—	—	—	—	—	k	—	0	60

Elter, Leo Leo William, FB-HB, 5´10˝/201 lbs; Duquesne; Villanova; B10/21/1929 Pittsburgh, PA

YEAR	TEAM	G(GS, POS)	RUSH	YD	AVG(LG)	TD	REC	YD	AVG(LG)	TD	PASS	COMP	PCT	YD	AVG(LG)	TD	INT	SK	YD	QBR	KPR	OTD	PTS	TAY
1953	Pit	12	26	81	3.1(10)	0	3	29	9.7(15)	0	—	—	—	—	—	—	—	—	—	—	k	—	0	104
1954	Pit	11	13	54	4.2(12)	0	4	16	4.0(26)	0	—	—	—	—	—	—	—	—	—	—	k	—	0	64
1955	Was	11(fb)	97	361	3.7(33)	3	13	219	16.8(70)	1	—	—	—	—	—	—	—	—	—	—	—	—	24	506
1956	Was✧	12(FB)	145	544	3.8(48)	2	11	99	9.0(17)	0	—	—	—	—	—	—	—	—	—	—	k	—	12	641
1957	Was	12	45	211	4.7(22)	2	6	94	15.7(49)	1	—	—	—	—	—	—	—	—	—	—	—	—	18	283
1958	Pit	7	37	104	2.8(18)	2	6	68	11.3(22)	0	—	—	—	—	—	—	—	—	—	—	—	—	12	158
1959	Pit	8	8	25	3.1(9)	0	3	31	10.3(28)	0	—	—	—	—	—	—	—	—	—	—	—	—	0	41
NFL	7	73	371	1380	3.7(48)	9	46	556	12.1(70)	2	—	—	—	—	—	—	—	—	—	—	k	—	66	1795

Elway, John John Albert, QB, 6´3˝/215 lbs; Stanford; 1983: Bal, rnd 1; B6/28/1960 Port Angeles, WA; HOF 2004

YEAR	TEAM	G(GS, POS)	RUSH	YD	AVG(LG)	TD	REC	YD	AVG(LG)	TD	PASS	COMP	PCT	YD	AVG(LG)	TD	INT	SK	YD	QBR	KPR	OTD	PTS	TAY
1983	†Den	11(10, QB)	28	146	5.2(23)	1	—	—	—	—	259	123	47.5	1663	6.4(49)	7	14	28	218	54.9	—	—	6	463
1984	†Den	15(14, QB)	56	237	4.2(21)	1	—	—	—	—	380	214	56.3	2598	6.8(73)	18	15	24	158	76.8	—	—	6	1036
1985	Den	16(16, QB)	51	253	5.0(22)	0	—	—	—	—	**605**	327	54.0	3891	6.4(65)	22	**23**	38	307	70.2	—	—	0	1389
1986	†Den★	16(16, QB)	52	257	4.9(24)	1	1	23	23.0(23)	1	504	280	55.6	3485	6.9(53)	19	13	32	233	79.0	—	—	12	1601
1987	†Den★	12(12, QB)	66	304	4.6(29)	4	—	—	—	—	410	224	54.6	3198	**7.8**(**72**)	19	12	20	138	83.4	P	—	24	**1558**
1988	Den	15(15, QB)	54	234	4.3(26)	1	—	—	—	—	496	274	55.2	3309	6.7(86)	17	19	30	237	71.4	P	—	6	1224
1989	†Den✧	15(15, QB)	48	244	5.1(31)	3	—	—	—	—	416	223	53.6	3051	7.3(69)	18	18	35	298	73.7	P	—	18	1170
1990	Den	16(16, QB)	50	258	5.2(21)	3	—	—	—	—	502	294	58.6	3526	7.0(66)	15	14	43	311	78.5	P	—	18	1566
1991	†Den✧	16(16, QB)	55	255	4.6(17)	6	1	24	24.0(24)	0	451	242	53.7	3253	7.2(71)	13	12	45	305	75.4	P	—	36	1539
1992	Den	12(12, QB)	34	94	2.8(9)	2	—	—	—	—	316	174	55.1	2242	7.1(80)	10	17	36	272	65.7	—	—	12	605
1993	†Den★	16(16, QB)	44	153	3.5(18)	0	—	—	—	—	**551**	**348**	**63.2**	**4030**	7.3(63)	**25**	10	39	293	**92.8**	—	—	0	**1893**
1994	Den✧	14(14, QB)	58	235	4.1(22)	4	—	—	—	—	494	307	62.1	3490	7.1(63)	16	10	46	303	85.7	—	—	24	1700
1995	Den	16(16, QB)	41	176	4.3(25)	1	—	—	—	—	542	316	58.3	**3970**	7.3(62)	26	14	22	180	86.4	—	—	8	1741
1996	†Den★	15(15, QB)	50	249	5.0(22)	4	—	—	—	—	466	287	61.6	3328	7.1(51)	26	14	26	194	**89.2**	—	—	24	1523
1997	†Den★	16(16, QB)	50	218	4.4(23)	1	—	—	—	—	502	280	55.8	3635	7.2(78)	27	11	34	203	87.5	—	—	6	1741
1998	†Den✧	13(12, QB)	37	94	2.5(16)	1	1	14	14.0(14)	0	356	210	59.0	2806	**7.9**(**58**)	22	10	18	135	93.0	—	—	6	1224
NFL	16	234(231)	774	3407	4.4(31)	33	3	61	20.3(24)	1	7250	4123	56.9	51475	7.1(86)	300	226	516	3785	79.9	P	—	206	21970

Elwell, Jack John Matthew, WR, 6´3˝/200 lbs; Purdue; 1962: SL, rnd 6/Buf, rnd 3; B8/1/1940 Cleveland, OH

YEAR	TEAM	G(GS, POS)	RUSH	YD	AVG(LG)	TD	REC	YD	AVG(LG)	TD	PASS	COMP	PCT	YD	AVG(LG)	TD	INT	SK	YD	QBR	KPR	OTD	PTS	TAY
1962	SL	13	—	—	—	—	1	11	11.0(11)	0	—	—	—	—	—	—	—	—	—	—	—	—	0	6

Ely, Harold Harold E., T, 6´2˝/268 lbs; Iowa; B12/26/1909 Des Moines, IA, D7/12/1983 Jasper, AL **1932** ChiB 6 (1) **1932** Bkn 3 (2) **1933** Bkn 10 (8, RT) **1934** Bkn 11 (10, RT) **NFL** 30 (21) [3 yrs]

Ely, Larry Lawrence Orlo, LB, 6´1˝/230 lbs; Iowa; 1970: Cin, rnd 16; B12/19/1947 Iowa City, IA **1970** Cin 11 **1971** Cin 6 **1975** ChiB 12 (MLB) **NFL** 29 [3 yrs]

Elzey, Paul Paul Vincent, LB, 6´3˝/235 lbs; Toledo; 1968: Bal, rnd 5; B5/13/1946 Toledo, OH **1968** Cin-A 5

Emanuel, Ben Ben, DB, 6´3˝/213 lbs; UCLA; 2005: Car, rnd 5; B6/18/1982 Texas City, TX **2005** SF 11 (8, ss)

Emanuel, Bert Bert Tyrone, WR, 5´10˝/180 lbs; UCLA; Rice; 1994: Atl, rnd 2; B10/26/1970 Kansas City, MO

YEAR	TEAM	G(GS, POS)	RUSH	YD	AVG(LG)	TD	REC	YD	AVG(LG)	TD	PASS	COMP	PCT	YD	AVG(LG)	TD	INT	SK	YD	QBR	KPR	OTD	PTS	TAY
1994	Atl	16(16, WR)	2	4	2.0(2)	0	46	649	14.1(85)	4	1	0	0.0	0	0.0	0	1	—	—	—	—	—	24	309
1995	†Atl	16(16, WR)	1	0	0.0(0)	0	74	1039	14.0(52)	5	—	—	—	—	—	—	—	—	—	—	—	—	30	545
1996	Atl	14(13, WR)	—	—	—	—	75	921	12.3(53)	6	—	—	—	—	—	—	—	—	—	—	—	—	36	491
1997	Atl	16(16, WR)	—	—	—	—	65	991	15.2(56)	9	—	—	—	—	—	—	—	—	—	—	—	—	54	541
1998	TB	11(11, WR)	1	11	11.0(11)	0	41	636	15.5(62)	2	—	—	—	—	—	—	—	—	—	—	—	—	12	339
1999	†TB	11(10, WR)	—	—	—	—	22	238	10.8(39)	1	—	—	—	—	—	—	—	—	—	—	—	—	6	124
2000	Mia	11(0)	3	-2	-0.7(0)	0	7	132	18.9(53)	1	—	—	—	—	—	—	—	—	—	—	—	—	6	69
2001	NE	2(1)	—	—	—	—	4	25	6.3(16)	0	—	—	—	—	—	—	—	—	—	—	—	—	0	13
2001	Det	6(4)	—	—	—	—	17	221	13.0(29)	0	—	—	—	—	—	—	—	—	—	—	—	—	0	111
NFL	8	103(87)	7	13	1.9(11)	0	351	4852	13.8(85)	28	1	0	0.0	0	0.0	0	1	—	—	—	—	—	168	2539

Emanuel, Charles Charles Edward, DB, 6´0˝/196 lbs; West Virginia; B6/3/1973 Stuart, FL **1997** Phi 5 (1)

Emanuel, Frank Thomas Frank, LB, 6´3˝/225 lbs; Tennessee; 1966: Mia, rnd 2/Phi, rnd 4; B12/4/1942 Clio, SC **1966** Mia-A 14 (11, MLB) **1967** Mia-A 14 (8, MLB) **1968** Mia-A 14 (12, MLB) **1969** Mia-A 14 **1970** NO 3 **NFL** 59 (31) [5 yrs]

Embray, Keith Keith, DE, 6´4˝/265 lbs; Utah; B11/29/1974 San Diego, CA **2000**†Ten 14 (0)

Embree, John John William, FL-WR, 6´4˝/194 lbs; Compton CC (CA); B7/13/1944 St. Louis, MO

YEAR	TEAM	G(GS, POS)	RUSH	YD	AVG(LG)	TD	REC	YD	AVG(LG)	TD	PASS	COMP	PCT	YD	AVG(LG)	TD	INT	SK	YD	QBR	KPR	OTD	PTS	TAY
1969	Den-A	13(5, fl)	—	—	—	—	29	469	16.2(79)	5	—	—	—	—	—	—	—	—	—	—	—	—	30	260
1970	Den	7(1)	—	—	—	—	4	50	12.5(20)	0	—	—	—	—	—	—	—	—	—	—	—	—	0	25
NFL	2	20(6)	—	—	—	—	33	519	15.7(79)	5	—	—	—	—	—	—	—	—	—	—	—	—	30	285

Embree, Jon Jon William, TE, 6´2˝/234 lbs; Colorado; 1987: LARm, rnd 6; B10/15/1965 Los Angeles, CA **1987** LARm 1 (0) **1988** LARm 12 (0) **NFL** 13 (0) [2 yrs]

Embree, Mel Melvin Belton, E, 6´3˝/190 lbs; Pepperdine; B1/26/1927 Los Angeles, CA, D8/30/1996 Los Angeles, CA

YEAR	TEAM	G(GS, POS)	RUSH	YD	AVG(LG)	TD	REC	YD	AVG(LG)	TD	PASS	COMP	PCT	YD	AVG(LG)	TD	INT	SK	YD	QBR	KPR	OTD	PTS	TAY
1953	Bal	12(LE)	—	—	—	—	23	272	11.8(24)	1	—	—	—	—	—	—	—	—	—	—	—	—	6	141
1954	ChiC	5	—	—	—	—	2	20	10.0(15)	0	—	—	—	—	—	—	—	—	—	—	—	—	0	10
NFL	2	17	—	—	—	—	25	292	11.7(24)	1	—	—	—	—	—	—	—	—	—	—	—	—	6	151

Emerick, Bob Robert William, T-G, 6´2˝/225 lbs; Miami (OH); B2/21/1913 Stockton, CA, D8/28/2003 Charlotte, NC **1934** Det 9 (1) **1937** Cle 11 (5, lt) **NFL** 20 (6) [2 yrs]

Emerson, Ox Grover Conner, G-C, 5´11˝/203 lbs; Texas; B12/18/1907 Douglas, TX, D11/26/1998 Austin, TX **1931** Por 12 (9, RG) **1932** Por☆12 (12, RG) **1933** Por☆11 (10, RG) **1934** Det☆13 (13, RG) **1935**†Det☆7 (7, RG) **1936** Det☆10 (3) **1937** Det☆10 (6, LG) **1938** Bkn 11 (7, RG) **NFL** 86 (67) [8 yrs]

Emerson, Vern Vernon Merlin, T, 6´5˝/260 lbs; Minnesota-Duluth; 1968: SL, rnd 12; B9/2/1945 Anoka, MN **1969** SL 5 **1970** SL 14 **1971** SL 4 **NFL** 23 [3 yrs]

Emery, Larry Larry George, RB, 5´9˝/195 lbs; Wisconsin; 1987: Atl, rnd 12; B7/13/1964 Macon, GA

YEAR	TEAM	G(GS, POS)	RUSH	YD	AVG(LG)	TD	REC	YD	AVG(LG)	TD	PASS	COMP	PCT	YD	AVG(LG)	TD	INT	SK	YD	QBR	KPR	OTD	PTS	TAY
1987	Atl	5(0)	1	5	5.0(5)	0	5	31	6.2(13)	0	—	—	—	—	—	—	—	—	—	—	k	—	0	146

Emmons, Carlos Carlos Antoine, LB, 6´5˝/250 lbs; Arkansas State; 1996: Pit, rnd 7; B9/3/1973 Greenwood, MS **1996**†Pit 15 (0) **1997**†Pit 5 (0) **1998** Pit 15 (14, ROLB) **1999** Pit 16 (16, ROLB) **2000**†Phi 16 (13, RLB) **2001**†Phi 16 (15, RLB) **2002**†Phi 13 (13, RLB) **2003** Phi 15 (15, RLB) **2004** NYG 15 (15, LLB) **2005** NYG 9 (8, llb) **NFL** 135 (109) [10 yrs]

Emmons, Frank Frank Boone, B, 6´1˝/213 lbs; Oregon; 1940: Phi, rnd 5; B9/17/1918 Portland, OR, D11/5/2005 Edmonds, WA

YEAR	TEAM	G(GS, POS)	RUSH	YD	AVG(LG)	TD	REC	YD	AVG(LG)	TD	PASS	COMP	PCT	YD	AVG(LG)	TD	INT	SK	YD	QBR	KPR	OTD	PTS	TAY
1940	Phi	11(5, fb)	29	77	2.7	1	3	19	6.3(19)	1	—	—	—	—	—	—	—	—	—	—	—	—	12	102

Emslie, Red Percy Gordon, G, none; B4/29/1895 Buffalo, NY, D8/3/1964 Buffalo, NY **1923** Roc 1 (1)

Emtman, Steve Steven Charles, DE-DT, 6´4˝/290 lbs; Washington; 1992: Ind, rnd 1; B4/16/1970 Spokane, WA **1992** Ind 9 (9, LDE) **1993** Ind 5 (5, lde) **1994** Ind 4 (0) **1995**†Mia 16 (1) **1996** Mia 13 (4) **1997** Was 3 (0) **NFL** 50 (19) [6 yrs]

Ena, Justin Justin, LB, 6´3˝/247 lbs; Brigham Young; B11/20/1977 Shelton, WA **2002**†Phi 9 (0) **2003**†Phi 16 (0) **2004** Ten 16 (5, llb) **2005** Phi 6 (0) **NFL** 47 (5) [4 yrs]

Enderle, Dick Richard Allyn, G, 6´2˝/250 lbs; Minnesota; 1969: Atl, rnd 7; B11/6/1947 Breckenridge, MN **1969** Atl 14 (LG) **1970** Atl 12 (RG) **1971** Atl 14 **1972** NYG 14 (LG) **1973** NYG 14 (LG) **1974** NYG 14 **1975** NYG 9 **1976** SF 2 **1976** GB 3 **NFL** 96 [8 yrs]

Endress, Al Albert James, DE-E, 6´2˝/200 lbs; St. Mary's (CA); San Francisco State; B2/18/1929 Oakland, CA **1952** SF 2

Endress, Vic Victor F., BB, none; B5/25/1903 Evansville, IN, D8/29/1970 Moline, IL **1922** Evv 1 (1, BB)

Engebretsen, Tiny Paul J., T-G, 6´1˝/238 lbs; Northwestern; B7/27/1910 Chariton, IA, D3/31/1979 Chariton, IA **[K]** **1932** ChiB 14 (12, LT) **1933** Pit 9 (5, lt) **1933** ChiC 2 (2) **1934** Bkn 5 (0) **1934** GB 5 (0) **1935** GB 9 (3) **1936**†GB 11 (8, LG) **1937** GB 9 (4) **1938**†GB 10 (4) **1939**†GB✧11 (4) **1940** GB 8 (2) **1941** GB 1 (0) **NFL** 94 (44) [10 yrs]

Engel, Greg Gregory Allen, C, 6´3˝/285 lbs; Illinois; B1/18/1971 Davenport, IA **1995**†SD 10 (0) **1996** SD 12 (9, C) **1997** SD 9 (0) **1999** Det 1 (0) **NFL** 32 (9) [4 yrs]

YEAR	TEAM	G(GS, POS)	RUSH	YD	AVG(LG)	TD	°REC	YD	AVG(LG)	TD	PASS COMP	PCT	♂ YD	AVG(LG)	TD	INT	SK	YD	QBR	KPR	OTD	PTS	TAY

ENGEL, STEVE   William Stephen, RB, 6´1˝/218 lbs; Colorado; 1970: Cle, rnd 5; B10/13/1947 Englewood, CO **1970** Cle 3

ENGELBERGER, JOHN   John Albert, DE, 6´4˝/268 lbs; Virginia Tech; 2000: SF, rnd 2; B10/18/1976 Heidelberg, Germany **2000** SF 16 (13, RDE) **2001** SF 15 (14, RDE)
2002†SF 15 (0) **2003** SF 16 (16, LDE) **2004** SF 16 (15, LDE) **2005** Den 14 (0) **NFL** 92 (58) [6 yrs]

ENGELHARD, JOE   Joseph Adolphus, B, 5´11˝/185 lbs; Rose Hulman Tech; B10/15/1898 Owensboro, KY, D7/4/1981 Louisville, KY **1921** Lou 1 (1, BB) **1922** Lou 1 (0)
NFL 2 (1) [2 yrs]

ENGELMANN, WUERT   Wuert, B, 6´3˝/191 lbs; South Dakota State; B2/11/1908 Miller, SD, D1/8/1979 Green Bay, WI **1930** GB 9 (9, WB), 18 **1931** GB 14 (7, tb), 24

1932	GB	12(7, wb)	35	184	5.3	0	1	33	33.0(33)	0	—	—	—	—	—	—	—	—	—	—	1	6	211
1933	GB	9(5, hb)	23	79	3.4	0	4	54	13.5(23)	0	—	—	—	—	—	—	—	—	—	—	2	12	116
NFL		44(28)	58	263	4.5	2	5	87	17.4(33)	0	—	—	—	—	—	—	—	—	—	—	4	60	377

ENGLAND, ERIC   Eric Jevon, DE, 6´2˝/283 lbs; Texas A&M; 1994: Arz, rnd 3; B3/25/1971 Fort Wayne, IN **1994** Arz 11 (1) **1995** Arz 15 (0) **1996** Arz 11 (1) **NFL** 37 (3) [3 yrs]

ENGLER, DEREK   Derek Michael, C, 6´5˝/300 lbs; Wisconsin; B7/11/1974 St. Paul, MN **1997** NYG 5 (5, c) **1998** NYG 11 (0) **1999** NYG 10 (4) **2000**†NYG 8 (0) **NFL** 34 (9) [4 yrs]

ENGLES, RICK   Richard B., P, 5´11˝/177 lbs; Tulsa; 1976: Sea, rnd 3; B8/18/1954 Tulsa, OK **1977** Sea 1 **1977**†Pit 1

1976	Sea	14	3	37	12.3(15)	0	—	—	—	—	1	1	100.0	8	8.0(8)	0	0	—	—	—	P	—	0	41
1978	Phi	6	1	16	16.0(16)	0	—	—	—	—	1	1	100.0	-2	-2.0(-2)	0	0	—	—	—	P	—	0	15
NFL		22	4	53	13.3(16)	0	—	—	—	—	2	2	100.0	6	3.0(8)	0	0	—	—	—	P	—	0	56

ENGLISH, DOUG   Lowell Douglas, DT-NT, 6´5˝/255 lbs; Texas; 1975: Det, rnd 2; B8/25/1953 Dallas, TX **1975** Det 14 **1976** Det 7 (5, ldt) **1977** Det 14 (14, RDT)
1978 Det★14 (13, RDT) **1979** Det 16 (RDT) **1981** Det★16 (16, RDT) **1982**†Det★9 (9, RDT) **1983**†Det★15 (15, RDT) **1984** Det☆16 (16, RDT) **1985** Det 10 (10, NT)
NFL 131 (98) [10 yrs]

ENGLISH, KEITH   Kéith Alan, P, 6´3˝/220 lbs; Colorado; B3/10/1966 Denver, CO

| 1990 | LARm | 16(0) | 2 | -19 | -9.5(-8) | 0 | — | — | — | — | — | — | — | — | — | — | — | — | — | — | P | — | 0 | -19 |

ENGLUND, HARRY   Harry C., E-HB, 6´0˝/185 lbs; none; B8/13/1900 Rockford, IL, D3/16/1989 Rockford, IL **1921** ChiS 5 (0) **1922** ChiB 11 (3) **NFL** 16 (3) [2 yrs]

ENGRAM, BOBBY   Simon, WR, 5´10˝/188 lbs; Penn State; 1996: Chi, rnd 2; B1/7/1973 Camden, SC [R]

1996	ChiB	16(2)	—	—	—	—	33	389	11.8(24)	6	—	—	—	—	—	—	—	—	—	kp	—	36	557
1997	ChiB	11(11, WR)	—	—	—	—	45	399	8.9(23)	2	—	—	—	—	—	—	—	—	—	kp	—	14	206
1998	ChiB	16(16, WR)	1	3	3.0(3)	0	64	987	15.4(79)	5	—	—	—	—	—	—	—	—	—	—	—	30	522
1999	ChiB	16(14, WR)	2	11	5.5(9)	0	88	947	10.8(56)	4	—	—	—	—	—	—	—	—	—	—	—	24	505
2000	ChiB	3(3)	1	1	1.0(1)	0	16	109	6.8(25)	0	—	—	—	—	—	—	—	—	—	—	—	0	56
2001	Sea	16(4)	—	—	—	—	29	400	13.8(31)	0	—	—	—	—	—	—	—	—	—	kp	—	0	257
2002	Sea	15(6, wr)	—	—	—	—	50	619	12.4(38)	1	—	—	—	—	—	—	—	—	—	p	1	6	439
2003	†Sea	16(7, wr)	—	—	—	—	52	637	12.3(34)	6	—	—	—	—	—	—	—	—	—	p	1	42	527
2004	†Sea	13(7, WR)	—	—	—	—	36	499	13.9(60)	2	—	—	—	—	—	—	—	—	—	p	—	12	328
2005	†Sea	13(13, WR)	—	—	—	—	67	778	11.6(56)	3	—	—	—	—	—	—	—	—	—	p	—	18	408
NFL	10	135(83)	4	15	3.8(9)	0	480	5764	12.0(79)	28	—	—	—	—	—	—	—	—	—	kp	2	182	3801

ENGSTROM, ART   Arthur Edward, G, 5´9˝/185 lbs; Chicago; B8/23/1901 Knox, IN, D11/1970 Watertown, MN **1924** Dul 1 (1)

ENICH, STEVE   Steve, G, 5´10˝/210 lbs; Marquette; 1945: Bkn, rnd 4; B4/21/1923 Hibbing, MN, D11/10/2004 Elm Grove, WI **1945** ChiC 5 (1)

ENIS, CURTIS   Curtis D., RB, 6´0˝/242 lbs; Penn State; 1998: Chi, rnd 1; B6/15/1976 Union City, OH

1998	ChiB	9(1)	133	497	3.7(29)	0	6	20	3.3(7)	0	—	—	—	—	—	—	—	—	—	—	—	0	507
1999	ChiB	15(12, RB)	287	916	3.2(19)	3	45	340	7.6(28)	2	—	—	—	—	—	—	—	—	—	—	—	30	1126
2000	ChiB	12(5, FB)	36	84	2.3(11)	1	8	68	8.5(18)	0	—	—	—	—	—	—	—	—	—	k	—	6	128
NFL	3	36(18)	456	1497	3.3(29)	4	59	428	7.3(28)	2	—	—	—	—	—	—	—	—	—	k	—	36	1761

ENIS, HUNTER   George Hunter, QB, 6´2˝/195 lbs; TCU; B12/10/1936 Fort Worth, TX

1960	DalT-A	14	9	23	2.6(11)	3	—	—	—	—	54	30	55.6	357	6.6(39)	1	2	—	—	—	—	—	18	157
1961	†SD-A	13	16	13	0.8(9)	2	—	—	—	—	55	23	41.8	365	6.6(45)	2	3	—	—	—	—	—	12	106
1962	Den-A	4	—	—	—	—	—	—	—	—	2	1	50.0	8	4.0(8)	0	0	—	—	—	—	—	0	4
1962	Oak-A	7	2	24	12.0(13)	0	—	—	—	—	49	26	53.1	217	4.4(17)	1	1	—	—	—	—	—	0	98
NFL	3	38	27	60	2.2(13)	5	—	—	—	—	160	80	50.0	947	5.9(45)	4	6	—	—	—	—	—	30	364

ENKE, FRED   Frederick William, QB, 6´1˝/208 lbs; Arizona; 1948: Det, rnd 7/NYY-A, rnd 22; B12/15/1924 Louisville, KY

1948	Det	12(10, QB)	74	365	4.9(41)	0	1	6	6.0(6)	0	221	100	45.2	1328	6.0(51)	11	17	—	—	49.4	k	—	0	408
1949	Det	12(7, QB)	36	134	3.7(33)	1	1	14	14.0(14)	0	142	63	44.4	793	5.6(58)	6	5	—	—	61.7	—	—	6	378
1950	Det	12	9	16	1.8(16)	0	—	—	—	—	53	22	41.5	424	8.0(46)	5	7	—	—	—	kp	—	0	-33
1951	Det	12	4	6	1.5(4)	0	—	—	—	—	9	2	22.2	22	2.4(12)	0	1	—	—	—	—	—	0	-23
1952	Phi	9	14	25	1.8(12)	0	2	19	9.5(18)	0	67	22	32.8	377	5.6(65)	1	5	—	—	—	—	—	0	28
1953	Bal	8(QB)	28	91	3.3(25)	0	—	—	—	—	169	71	42.0	1054	6.2(55)	8	15	—	—	41.9	—	—	0	58
1954	Bal	3	5	3	0.6(5)	0	—	—	—	—	28	17	60.7	171	6.1(42)	0	3	—	—	—	—	—	0	-32
NFL	7	68(17)	170	640	3.8(41)	1	4	39	9.8(18)	0	689	297	43.1	4169	6.1(65)	31	53	—	—	46.2	kp	—	6	784

ENRIGHT, REX   Rex Edward, FB, 5´10˝/198 lbs; Notre Dame; B3/19/1901 Rockford, IL, D4/6/1960 Columbia, SC **1926** GB 10 (4), 6 **1927** GB 9 (6, FB), 24 **NFL** 19 (10), 30 [2 yrs]

ENYART, BILL   William Donald, RB-LB, 6´4˝/235 lbs; Oregon State; 1969: Buf, rnd 2; B4/28/1947 Pawhuska, OK

1969	Buf-A	14	47	191	4.1(29)	1	19	186	9.8(32)	2	—	—	—	—	—	—	—	—	—	k	—	18	301
1970	Buf	14	58	196	3.4(17)	0	35	235	6.7(37)	1	—	—	—	—	—	—	—	—	—	k	—	6	334
1971	Oak	1	—	—	—	—	—	—	—	—	—	—	—	—	—	—	—	—	—	—	—	0	—
NFL	3	29	105	387	3.7(26)	1	54	421	7.8(37)	3	—	—	—	—	—	—	—	—	—	k	—	24	635

ENZOR, JAMAR   Jamar, LB, 6´1˝/237 lbs; Cincinnati; B12/28/1981 Tallahassee, FL **2005** NYJ 1 (0)

EPHRAIM, ALONZO   Alonzo Brandon, C, 6´4˝/312 lbs; Alabama; B11/9/1981 Birmingham, AL **2003**†Phi 16 (0) **2004**†Phi 14 (2) **2005** Mia 13 (3) **NFL** 43 (5) [3 yrs]

EPPERSON, PAT   John Patrick, E, 6´3˝/225 lbs; Adams State; B11/3/1935 Los Angeles, CA

| 1960 | Den-A | 9(te) | — | — | — | — | 11 | 99 | 9.0(16) | 0 | — | — | — | — | — | — | — | — | — | — | — | 0 | 50 |

EPPS, BOBBY   Robert Hezekiah, FB, 5´9˝/198 lbs; Pittsburgh; 1954: NYG, rnd 14; B3/25/1932 Swissvale, PA

1954	NYG	10	30	110	3.7(11)	0	5	20	4.0(10)	0	—	—	—	—	—	—	—	—	—	—	—	0	120
1955	NYG	9(FB)	95	375	3.9(24)	2	5	8	1.6(5)	0	—	—	—	—	—	—	—	—	—	—	—	12	399
1957	NYG	12(fb)	63	286	4.5(55)	0	8	81	10.1(34)	0	1	0	0.0	0	0.0	0	0	—	—	—	—	—	0	327
NFL	3	31	188	771	4.1(55)	2	18	109	6.1(34)	0	1	0	0.0	0	0.0	0	0	—	—	—	—	—	12	846

EPPS, JACK   John Michael, DB, 6´0˝/197 lbs; Kansas State; B3/20/1963 Tulsa, OK **1987** KC 3 (2)

EPPS, PHIL   Phillip Earl, WR, 5´10˝/165 lbs; TCU; 1982: GB, rnd 12; B11/11/1958 Atlanta, GA [R]

1982	†GB	9(1)	—	—	—	—	10	226	22.6(50)	2	—	—	—	—	—	—	—	—	—	p	—	12	173
1983	GB	16(0)	—	—	—	—	18	313	17.4(45)	0	—	—	—	—	—	—	—	—	—	p	1	6	311
1984	GB	16(4)	—	—	—	—	26	435	16.7(56)	3	—	—	—	—	—	—	—	—	—	kp	—	18	339
1985	GB	16(16, WR)	5	103	20.6(34)	1	44	683	15.5(63)	3	—	—	—	—	—	—	—	—	—	kp	—	24	640
1986	GB	12(12, WR)	4	18	4.5(20)	0	49	612	12.5(53)	4	—	—	—	—	—	—	—	—	—	k	—	24	350
1987	GB	10(9, WR)	1	0	0.0(0)	0	34	516	15.2(40)	2	—	—	—	—	—	—	—	—	—	p	—	12	268
1988	GB	6(3)	—	—	—	—	11	99	9.0(25)	0	—	—	—	—	—	—	—	—	—	—	—	0	50
1989	NYJ	10(0)	1	14	14.0(14)	0	8	108	13.5(21)	0	—	—	—	—	—	—	—	—	—	k	—	0	87
NFL	8	95(45)	11	135	12.3(34)	1	200	2992	15.0(63)	14	—	—	—	—	—	—	—	—	—	kp	1	96	2216

EPPS, TORY   Torrean Douglas, NT-DT, 6´1˝/280 lbs; Memphis; 1990: Atl, rnd 8; B5/28/1967 Uniontown, PA, D6/1/2005 Uniontown, PA **1990** Atl 16 (15, NT) **1991**†Atl 16 (2)
1992 Atl 16 (5, nt) **1993** Atl 2 (0) **1993** ChiB 3 (0) **1994** ChiB 5 (0) **1995** NO 12 (0) **NFL** 70 (22) [6 yrs]

EPSTEIN, HAYDEN   Hayden Scott, K, 6´2˝/214 lbs; Michigan; 2002: Jax, rnd 7; B11/16/1980 San Diego, CA [K] **2002** Jax 6 (0) **2002** Min 9 (0) **NFL** 15 (0) [1 yr]

YEAR	TEAM	G (GS, POS)	RUSH	YD	AVG (LG)	TD	REC	YD	AVG (LG)	TD	PASS	COMP	PCT	YD	AVG (LG)	TD	INT	SK	YD	QBR	KPR	OTD	PTS	TAY
ERDLITZ, DICK Richard Alfred, HB, 5´10˝/181 lbs; Northwestern; B2/16/1920 Menomonie, MI **[K]**																								
1942	Phi	10(1)	21	69	3.3(17)	1	5	78	15.6(42)	0	—	—	—	—	—	—	—	—	—	—	Kki	—	14	123
1945	Phi	7(0)	6	24	4.0(16)	0	—	—	—	—	—	—	—	—	—	—	—	—	—	—	i	—	0	22
NFL	2	17(1)	27	93	3.4(17)	1	5	78	15.6(42)	0	—	—	—	—	—	—	—	—	—	—	Kki	—	14	145
1946	Mia-A	14(7, RH)	26	38	1.5	1	7	31	4.4	0	1	1	100.0	10	10.0(10)	0	0	—	—	—	Kki	—	34	90
EREHART, ARCH Archibald Dean, WB, 5´8˝/165 lbs; Indiana; B3/27/1894, deceased **1920** Mun 1 (1, WB)																								
ERENBERG, RICH Richard Mark, RB, 5´10˝/200 lbs; Colgate; 1984: Pit, rnd 9; B4/17/1962 Chappaqua, NY																								
1984	†Pit	16(9, RB)	115	405	3.5(31)	2	38	358	9.4(25)	1	—	—	—	—	—	—	—	—	—	—	k	—	18	764
1985	Pit	14(0)	17	67	3.9(12)	0	33	326	9.9(35)	3	—	—	—	—	—	—	—	—	—	—	k	—	18	371
1986	Pit	16(1)	42	170	4.0(17)	1	27	217	8.0(19)	3	—	—	—	—	—	—	—	—	—	—	—	—	24	304
NFL	3	46(10)	174	642	3.7(31)	3	98	901	9.2(35)	7	—	—	—	—	—	—	—	—	—	—	k	—	60	1439
ERICKSON, BERNIE John Bernard, LB, 6´2˝/240 lbs; Abilene Christian; 1967: SD, rnd 5; B10/16/1944 Clifton, TX **1967** SD-A 13 **1968** SD-A 8 **1968** Cin-A 5 **NFL** 26 [2 yrs]																								
ERICKSON, BILL William Clarence, G, 6´2˝/210 lbs; North Carolina; Mississippi; 1948: NYG, rnd 6/LAD-A, rnd 15; B12/4/1921, deceased **1948** NYG 9 (3) **1949** NYY-A 6 (1)																								
ERICKSON, BUD Carlton Lyons, C, 6´1˝/198 lbs; Washington; B4/10/1916 Seattle, WA, D10/1969 **1938** Was 2 (1) **1939** Was 1 (0) **NFL** 3 (1) [2 yrs]																								
ERICKSON, CRAIG Craig Neil, QB, 6´2˝/209 lbs; Miami (FL); 1992: TB, rnd 4; B5/17/1969 Boynton Beach, FL																								
1992	TB	6(0)	1	-1	-1.0(-1)	0	—	—	—	—	26	15	57.7	121	4.7(24)	0	0	2	9	—	—	—	0	60
1993	TB	16(15, QB)	26	96	3.7(15)	0	—	—	—	—	457	233	51.0	3054	6.7(67)	18	21	35	236	66.4	—	—	0	873
1994	TB	15(14, QB)	26	68	2.6(17)	1	—	—	—	—	399	225	56.4	2919	7.3(71)	16	10	22	129	82.5	—	—	6	1218
1995	Ind	6(3)	9	14	1.6(15)	0	—	—	—	—	83	50	60.2	586	7.1(39)	3	4	10	68	—	—	—	0	162
1996	Mia	7(3)	11	16	1.5(12)	0	—	—	—	—	99	55	55.6	780	7.9(61)	4	2	11	72	—	—	—	0	346
1997	Mia	2(0)	4	8	2.0(4)	0	—	—	—	—	28	13	46.4	165	5.9(27)	0	1	2	21	—	—	—	0	51
NFL	6	52(35)	77	201	2.6(17)	1	—	—	—	—	1092	591	54.1	7625	7.0(71)	41	38	82	535	74.3	—	—	6	2709
ERICKSON, HAL Harold A., B, 5´9˝/193 lbs; St. Olaf; Washington & Jefferson; B3/10/1899 Maynard, MN, D1/28/1963, **[KC]** **1923** Mil☆10 (10, WB), 6 **1924** Mil 4 (4), 18 **1925** Chi C 14 (12, WB), 42 **1926** ChiC 11 (7, TB), 6 **1927** ChiC 8 (4) **1928** ChiC 6 (4, TB), 6 **1929** Min 10 (9, TB), 4 **1930** Min 4 (1) **NFL** 67 (51), 82 [8 yrs]																								
ERICKSON, HAROLD Harold, T, /195 lbs; none; B8/2/1894, D1/28/1963 **1921** Min 4 (4, RT) **1922** Min 4 (4, RT) **NFL** 8 (8) [2 yrs]																								
ERICKSON, MICKEY Milton Leroy, C, 6´2˝/208 lbs; Northwestern; B5/16/1905 Cambridge, MN, D1/26/1984 Phoenix, AZ **1930** ChiC 12 (10, C) **1931** ChiC 8 (4) **1932** ChiC 1 (0) **1932** Bos 9 (5, C) **NFL** 30 (19) [3 yrs]																								
ERICKSON, SWEDE Swede, E, /215 lbs; deceased **1924** Ken 1 (0)																								
ERICKSON, WALDEN Walden D., T, 6´1˝/205 lbs; Washington; B9/3/1902, D12/1968 Chicago, IL **1927** Pot 12 (11, LT)																								
ERLANDSON, TOM Thomas Dean, LB, 6´3˝/235 lbs; Washington State; B3/24/1940 Seattle, WA **1962** Den-A 4 **1963** Den-A 11 (llb) **1964** Den-A 5 (llb) **1965** Den-A 14 (LLB) **1966** Mia-A✧14 (14, LLB) **1967** Mia-A 10 (6, LLB) **1968** SD-A 10 (RLB) **NFL** 68 (20) [7 yrs]																								
ERLANDSON, TOM Thomas Dean, LB, 6´1˝/220 lbs; Washington; 1988: Buf, rnd 12; B6/19/1966 Denver, CO **1988** Buf 4 (0)																								
ERNST, JACK John Oliver, B, 5´11˝/180 lbs; Lafayette; B12/4/1899 Llewellyn, PA, D3/9/1968 South Williamsport, PA **[K]** **1925** Pot 12 (11, BB), 19 **1926** Pot 14 (14, BB), 6 **1927** Pot 12 (10, BB) **1928** Pot 10 (10, BB), 12 **1928** NYY 1 (1) **1929** Bos 7 (7, BB), 1 **1930** Fra 8 (4), 6 **NFL** 64 (57), 44 [6 yrs]																								
ERNST, MIKE Michael Paul, QB, 6´1˝/190 lbs; Cal State-Fullerton; B10/12/1950 Lynwood, CA **1973**†Cin 1																								
1972	Den	1	1	4	4.0(4)	0	—	—	—	—	4	1	25.0	10	2.5(10)	0	0	—	—	—	—	—	0	9
NFL	2	2	1	4	4.0(4)	0	—	—	—	—	4	1	25.0	10	2.5(10)	0	0	—	—	—	—	—	0	9
ERNSTER, PAUL Paul, K, 6´1˝/217 lbs; Northern Arizona; 2005: Den, rnd 7; B1/26/1982 Phoenix, AZ **2005** Den 1 (0)																								
ERVINS, RICKY Ricky, RB, 5´7˝/195 lbs; USC; 1991: Was, rnd 3; B12/7/1968 Fort Wayne, IN																								
1991	†Was	15(0)	145	680	4.7(65)	3	16	181	11.3(28)	1	—	—	—	—	—	—	—	—	—	—	k	—	24	873
1992	Was	16(0, rb)	151	495	3.3(25)	2	32	252	7.9(19)	0	—	—	—	—	—	—	—	—	—	—	—	—	12	641
1993	Was	15(1)	50	201	4.0(18)	0	16	123	7.7(20)	0	—	—	—	—	—	—	—	—	—	—	k	—	0	262
1994	Was	16(10, RB)	185	650	3.5(49)	3	51	293	5.7(21)	1	—	—	—	—	—	—	—	—	—	—	k	—	24	834
1995	†SF	14(0)	23	88	3.8(13)	0	2	21	10.5(11)	0	—	—	—	—	—	—	—	—	—	—	k	—	0	56
NFL	5	76(11)	554	2114	3.8(65)	8	117	870	7.4(28)	2	—	—	—	—	—	—	—	—	—	—	k	—	60	2664
ERWIN, TERRY Terrence Lester, RB, 6´0˝/190 lbs; Boston College; B8/30/1946 Weymouth, MA																								
1968	Den-A	9	24	76	3.2(9)	0	2	21	10.5(17)	0	—	—	—	—	—	—	—	—	—	—	k	—	0	97
ERXLEBEN, RUSSELL Russell Allen, P, 6´4˝/223 lbs; Texas; 1979: NO, rnd 1; B1/13/1956 Seguin, TX **[KP]**																								
1979	NO	1	—	—	—	—	—	—	—	—	1	0	0.0	0	0.0	0	1	—	—	—	KP	—	10	-40
1980	NO	16(0)	—	—	—	—	—	—	—	—	1	0	0.0	0	0.0	0	0	—	—	—	KP	—	8	0
1981	NO	16(0)	2	10	5.0(26)	0	—	—	—	—	—	—	—	—	—	—	—	—	—	—	P	—	0	10
1982	NO	9(0)	—	—	—	—	—	—	—	—	2	1	50.0	39	19.5(39)	1	0	—	—	—	KP	—	1	25
1983	NO	16(0)	2	-9	-4.5(1)	0	—	—	—	—	1	1	100.0	24	24.0(24)	0	0	—	—	—	P	—	0	3
1987	Det	1(0)	—	—	—	—	—	—	—	—	—	—	—	—	—	—	—	—	—	—	P	—	0	0
NFL	6	59	4	1	0.3(26)	0	—	—	—	—	5	2	40.0	63	12.6(39)	1	1	—	—	—	KP	—	19	-3
ESCHBACH, HERB Harold Heins, C, 6´0˝/190 lbs; Penn State; B4/26/1907 Lancaster, PA, deceased **1930** Pro 7 (4) **1931** Pro 4 (1) **NFL** 11 (5) [2 yrs]																								
ESHMONT, LEN Leonard Charles, HB-FB, 5´11˝/179 lbs; Fordham; 1941: NYG, rnd 5; B8/26/1917 Mount Carmel, PA, D5/12/1957 Charlottesville, VA																								
1941	†NYG	9(5, FB)	50	164	3.3(25)	0	1	4	4.0(4)	0	3	2	66.7	32	10.7(16)	1	0	—	—	—	Pkp	—	0	312
1946	SF-A	10(9, LH)	73	340	4.7	**6**	16	287	16.9	2	2	1	50.0	42	21.0(42)	1	0	—	—	—	kp	1	54	709
1947	SF-A	13(13, LH)	84	381	4.5	0	19	303	15.9	2	—	—	—	—	—	—	—	—	—	—	kpi	—	12	625
1948	SF-A	13(8, LH)	50	296	5.9	1	14	214	15.3	0	—	—	—	—	—	—	—	—	—	—	ki	1	12	425
1949	†SF-A	12(6, LH)	25	164	6.6	0	3	107	35.7	2	—	—	—	—	—	—	—	—	—	—	ki	—	12	267
AAFC	4	48(36)	232	1181	5.1(25)	7	53	911	17.2(4)	6	2	1	50.0	42	21.0(42)	1	0	—	—	—	kpi	2	90	2025
ESIASON, BOOMER Norman Julius, QB, 6´5˝/224 lbs; Maryland; 1984: Cin, rnd 2; B4/17/1961 West Islip, NY																								
1984	Cin	10(4)	19	63	3.3(9)	2	—	—	—	—	102	51	50.0	530	5.2(36)	3	3	5	52	—	—	—	12	243
1985	Cin	15(14, QB)	33	79	2.4(20)	1	—	—	—	—	431	251	58.2	3443	8.0(68)	27	12	32	289	93.2	—	—	6	1466
1986	Cin✧	16(16, QB)	44	146	3.3(23)	1	—	—	—	—	469	273	58.2	3959	**8.4(57)**	24	17	26	194	87.7	P	—	6	1576
1987	Cin	12(12, QB)	52	241	4.6(19)	0	—	—	—	—	440	240	54.5	**3321**	7.5(61)	16	**19**	26	209	73.1	P	—	0	1222
1988	†Cin★	16(16, QB)	43	248	5.8(24)	1	—	—	—	—	388	223	57.5	3572	**9.2(86)**	**28**	14	30	245	**97.4**	P	—	6	1624
1989	Cin★	16(15, QB)	47	278	5.9(24)	0	—	—	—	—	455	258	56.7	3525	7.7(74)	**28**	11	36	288	**92.1**	—	—	0	**1741**
1990	†Cin	16(16, QB)	49	157	3.2(21)	0	—	—	—	—	402	224	55.7	3031	7.5(53)	24	**22**	31	198	77.0	—	—	0	913
1991	Cin	14(14, QB)	24	66	2.8(16)	0	—	—	—	—	413	233	56.4	2883	7.0(53)	13	16	25	190	72.5	—	—	0	933
1992	Cin	12(11, QB)	21	66	3.1(15)	0	—	—	—	—	278	144	51.8	1407	5.1(38)	11	15	19	150	57.0	—	—	0	225
1993	NYJ✧	16(16, QB)	45	118	2.6(17)	1	1	-8	-8.0(-8)	0	473	288	60.9	3421	7.2(77)	16	11	18	139	84.5	—	—	6	1475
1994	NYJ	15(14, QB)	28	59	2.1(15)	0	—	—	—	—	440	255	58.0	2782	6.3(69)	17	13	19	134	77.3	—	—	0	1015
1995	NYJ	12(12, QB)	19	14	0.7(19)	0	—	—	—	—	389	221	56.8	2275	5.8(43)	16	15	27	198	71.4	—	—	0	632
1996	Arz	10(8, QB)	15	52	3.5(13)	1	—	—	—	—	339	190	56.0	2293	6.8(64)	11	14	17	109	70.6	—	—	8	704
1997	Cin	7(5, qb)	8	11	1.4(8)	0	—	—	—	—	186	118	**63.4**	1478	**7.9(77)**	13	2	7	43	—	—	—	0	735
NFL	14	187(173)	447	1598	3.6(24)	7	1	-8	-8.0(-8)	0	5205	2969	57.0	37920	7.3(86)	247	184	318	2438	81.1	P	—	44	14499
ESPIE, AL David Allen, T, none; B1900 Kuttawa, KY, D3/25/1961 Louisville, KY **1923** Lou 1 (1, RT)																								
ESPINOZA, ALEX Alex A., QB, 6´1˝/193 lbs; Cal State-Fullerton; Iowa State; B5/31/1964 Los Angeles, CA																								
1987	KC	1(0)	1	5	5.0(5)	0	—	—	—	—	14	9	64.3	69	4.9(16)	0	2	2	17	—	—	—	0	-41

YEAR	TEAM	G(GS, POS)	RUSH	YD	AVG(LG)	TD	REC	YD	AVG(LG)	TD	PASS	COMP	PCT	YD	AVG(LG)	TD	INT	SK	YD	QBR	KPR	OTD	PTS	TAY

ESPOSITO, MIKE   Michael John, RB, 6′0″/183 lbs; Boston College; 1975: Atl, rnd 7; B4/24/1953 Everett, MA

1976	Atl	10(FB)	60	317	5.3(36)	2	17	88	5.2(13)	0	1	0	0.0	0	0.0	0	0	—	—	—	kp	—	12	379
1977	Atl	14	34	101	3.0(23)	0	1	-1	-1.0(-1)	0	1	0	0.0	0	0.0	0	0	—	—	—	i	—	0	151
1978	†Atl	16	7	21	3.0(7)	0	3	10	3.3(4)	0	—	—										—	0	26
NFL	3	40	101	439	4.3(36)	2	21	97	4.6(13)	0	2	0	0.0	0	0.0	0	0	—	—	—	kpi	—	12	556

ESSER, CLARENCE   Clarence Joseph, E, 6′0″/190 lbs; Wisconsin; 1947: ChiC, rnd 20; B3/27/1921 Madison, WI   **1947** ChiC 7 (0)

ESSEX, TRAI   Trai J., T, 6′4″/324 lbs; Northwestern; 2005: Pit, rnd 3; B12/5/1982 Fort Wayne, IN   **2005** Pit 6 (4)

ESSINK, RON   Ronald Arden, T-TE, 6′6″/260 lbs; Grand Valley State; 1980: Sea, rnd 10; B7/30/1958 Zeeland, MI   **1981** Sea 16 (16, LT)   **1982** Sea 7 (7, LT)   **1983**†Sea 16 (16, LT)   **1984**†Sea 16 (16, LT)   **1985** Sea 12 (12, LT)

| 1980 | Sea | 16(3) | — | — | — | | 1 | 2 | 2.0(2) | 1 | | | | | | | | | | | | | 6 | 6 |
| NFL | 6 | 83(70) | — | — | — | | 1 | 2 | 2.0(2) | 1 | | | | | | | | | | | | | 6 | 6 |

ESSMAN, CHARLIE   Charles Peter, G, 6′0″/220 lbs; Christian Brothers (MO); B1/31/1881 Jackson, OH, D10/12/1965 Columbus, OH   **1920** Col 1 (0)

ESTELL, RICHARD   Richard Wayne, WR, 6′2″/210 lbs; Kansas; B10/12/1963 Kansas City, KS

| 1987 | KC | 2(0) | — | — | — | | 3 | 24 | 8.0(11) | 0 | | | | | | | | | | | | | 0 | 12 |

ESTEP, MIKE   Michael Lawrence, G-T, 6′4″/270 lbs; Bowling Green State; B12/29/1963 Northampton, England   **1987** GB 1 (0)   **1987** Buf 2 (0)   **NFL** 3 (0) [1 yr]

ESTES, DON   Donald Olarey, G, 6′3″/250 lbs; LSU; 1963: Hou, rnd 2/SL, rnd 4; B10/14/1938 Tomball, TX   **1966** SD-A 5

ESTES, LARRY   Lawrence G., DE, 6′6″/255 lbs; Alcorn State; 1970: NO, rnd 8; B12/9/1946 Louisville, MS   **1970** NO 14   **1971** NO 8   **1972** Phi 7   **1975** KC 4   **1976** KC 14 (3)   **NFL** 47 (3) [5 yrs]

ESTES, PATRICK   Patrick Brion, TE, 6′6″/268 lbs; Virginia; 2005: SF, rnd 7; B2/4/1983 Richmond, VA   **2005** SF 7 (0)

ETCHEVERRY, SAM   Samuel, QB, 5′11″/190 lbs; Denver; B5/20/1930 Carlsbad, NM

1961	SL	14(QB)	33	73	2.2(44)	0	—	—	—		196	96	49.0	1275	6.5(78)	14	11	—	—	70.4	—	—	0	341
1962	SL	14(qb)	8	5	0.6(13)	0	—	—	—		106	58	54.7	707	6.7(68)	2	10	—	—		P	—	0	-32
NFL	2	28	41	78	1.9(44)	0	—	—	—		302	154	51.0	1982	6.6(78)	16	21	—	—	60.6	P	—	0	309

ETELMAN, CARL   Carl Edward, B, 5′8″/160 lbs; Boston University; Harvard; Tufts; B4/2/1900 Fairhaven, MA, deceased   **1926** Pro 1 (1)

ETHEREDGE, CARLOS   Carlos Sebastian, TE, 6′5″/236 lbs; Miami (FL); 1993: Ind, rnd 6; B8/10/1970 Albuquerque, NM

| 1994 | Ind | 9(0) | — | — | — | | 1 | 6 | 6.0(6) | 0 | | | | | | | | | | | k | — | 0 | -4 |

ETHERLY, DAVE   David, DB, 6′1″/190 lbs; Oregon State; Portland State; B12/22/1962 Alburgu, Mexico   **1987** Was 3 (0)

ETHRIDGE, JOE   Joe Paul, TE, 6′0″/230 lbs; SMU; 1949: GB, rnd 6/LAD-A, rnd 29; B4/15/1928 Conway, TX [K]   **1949** GB 12 (2)

ETHRIDGE, RAY   Raymond Arthur, WR, 5′10″/180 lbs; Pasadena City College (JC); 1992: SD, rnd 3; B12/12/1968 San Diego, CA   **1997** Bal 2 (0)

| 1996 | Bal | 14(1) | — | — | — | | 2 | 24 | 12.0(15) | 0 | | | | | | | | | | | kp | — | 0 | 61 |
| NFL | 2 | 16(1) | — | — | — | | 2 | 24 | 12.0(15) | 0 | | | | | | | | | | | kp | — | 0 | 64 |

ETIENNE, LARRY   LeRoy Joseph, LB, 6′2″/245 lbs; Nebraska; B7/21/1966 Lafayette, LA   **1990**†SF 10 (0)

ETTENHAUS, EARL   Earl, G, none; B1902 Perry, NY, deceased   **1921** Roc 1 (0)

ETTER, BOB   Robert Glenn, K, 5′11″/157 lbs; Georgia; B8/8/1945 Chattanooga, TN [K]   **1968** Atl 14   **1969** Atl✧14   **NFL** 28 [2 yrs]

ETTINGER, DON   Donald Nesbitt, LB-G, 6′2″/213 lbs; Kansas; 1948: NYG, rnd 19/Bal-A, rnd 11; B11/20/1922 Independence, MO, D2/13/1992 Cookeville, KS   **1948** NYG✩10 (2)   **1949** NYG 11 (4)   **1950**†NYG 12   **NFL** 33 (6) [3 yrs]

EUHUS, TIM   Tim, TE, 6′5″/247 lbs; Oregon State; 2004: Buf, rnd 4; B10/2/1980 Eugene, OR

2004	Buf	12(5, te)	—	—	—		11	98	8.9(17)	2	—											—	12	59
2005	Buf	11(3)	—	—	—		3	17	5.7(9)	0	—										k	—	0	-7
NFL	2	23(8)	—	—	—		14	115	8.2(17)	2	—										k	—	12	53

EVANS, BOB   Robert Delbert, DE, 6′3″/250 lbs; Texas A&M; 1965: SD, rnd 18; B2/9/1942 Houston, TX   **1965** Hou-A 4

EVANS, BYRON   Byron Nelson, LB, 6′2″/235 lbs; Arizona; 1987: Phi, rnd 4; B2/23/1964 Phoenix, AZ   **1987** Phi 12 (3)   **1988**†Phi 16 (5, mlb)   **1989**†Phi 16 (16, MLB)   **1990**†Phi✧16 (16, MLB)   **1991** Phi 16 (15, MLB)   **1992**†Phi✧16 (16, MLB)   **1993** Phi 11 (10, MLB)   **1994** Phi 10 (10, MLB)   **NFL** 113 (91) [8 yrs]

EVANS, CHARLES   Charles, RB, 6′1″/240 lbs; Clark Atlanta; 1992: Min, rnd 11; B4/16/1967 Augusta, GA

1993	Min	3(0)	14	32	2.3(5)	0	4	39	9.8(21)	0	—										k	—	0	48
1994	Min	14(0)	6	20	3.3(8)	0	1	2	2.0(2)	0	—										k	—	0	10
1995	Min	16(7, FB)	19	59	3.1(12)	1	18	119	6.6(24)	1	—											—	12	134
1996	†Min	16(6, fb)	13	29	2.2(9)	0	22	135	6.1(10)	0	—											—	0	97
1997	†Min	16(13, FB)	43	157	3.7(13)	2	21	152	7.2(17)	0	—											—	14	253
1998	†Min	16(8, fb)	23	67	2.9(12)	1	12	84	7.0(14)	0	—											—	6	119
1999	Bal	16(10, FB)	38	134	3.5(12)	0	32	235	7.3(27)	1	—											—	8	257
2000	†Bal	1(0)	—				—				—												—	0	
NFL	8	98(44)	156	498	3.2(13)	4	110	766	7.0(27)	2	—										k	—	40	916

EVANS, CHARLIE   Jack Charles, RB, 6′1″/220 lbs; Utah; USC; 1971: NYG, rnd 14; B1/10/1948 Gardena, CA

1971	NYG	6	48	171	3.6(17)	4	13	144	11.1(25)	0	—											—	30	293
1972	NYG	8(FB)	91	317	3.5(24)	4	26	182	7.0(18)	1	—											—	30	453
1973	NYG	5	34	77	2.3(15)	1	13	100	7.7(20)	0	—											—	6	137
1974	†Was	6	32	79	2.5(9)	2	2	44	22.0(44)	0	—										k	—	12	121
NFL	4	25	205	644	3.1(24)	12	54	470	8.7(44)	1	—										k	—	78	1004

EVANS, CHUCK   Charles Allen, LB, 6′3″/235 lbs; Stanford; 1980: NO, rnd 8; B12/19/1956 West Covina, CA   **1980** NO 10 (2)   **1981** NO 16 (1)   **NFL** 26 (3) [2 yrs]

EVANS, DALE   Jay Dale, HB, 6′3″/210 lbs; Kansas State; 1961: Den, rnd 6/SL, rnd 6; B9/10/1939 St. Francis, KS   **1961** Den-A 5

EVANS, DAVID   David Wayne, DB, 6′0″/178 lbs; Central Arkansas; B5/1/1959 Naples, TX   **1986** Min 16 (1)   **1987** Min 3 (3)   **NFL** 19 (4) [2 yrs]

EVANS, DEMETRIC   Demetric Untrell, DE, 6′3″/289 lbs; Georgia; B9/3/1979 Haynesville, LA   **2001** Dal 16 (0)   **2002** Dal 4 (0)   **2004** Was 12 (8, RDE)   **2005**†Was 16 (3)   **NFL** 48 (11) [4 yrs]

EVANS, DICK   Richard Jacob, E, 6′3″/205 lbs; Iowa; B5/31/1918 Chicago, IL

1940	GB	7(0)	—	—	—		2	40	20.0(30)	0	—											—	0	20
1941	ChiC	7(0)	—	—	—		3	34	11.3(22)	0	—											—	0	17
1942	ChiC	3(1)	—	—	—		—				—												—		
1943	GB	10(1)	—	—	—		8	71	8.9(13)	0	—											—	0	36
NFL	4	27(2)	—	—	—		13	145	11.2(30)	0	—											—	0	73

EVANS, DONALD   Donald Lee, DE-DT, 6′2″/282 lbs; Winston-Salem State; 1987: LARm, rnd 2; B3/14/1964 Raleigh, NC   **1988** Phi 5 (0)   **1990** Pit 16 (16, RDE)   **1991** Pit 16 (14, RDE)   **1992**†Pit 16 (16, RDE)   **1993**†Pit 16 (16, RDE)   **1994** NYJ 16 (16, LDT)   **1995** NYJ 4 (4)

| 1987 | LARm | 1(0) | 3 | 10 | 3.3(5) | 0 | — | | | | — | | | | | | | | | | | | — | 0 | 10 |
| NFL | 8 | 90(82) | 3 | 10 | 3.3(5) | 0 | — | | | | — | | | | | | | | | S | | | — | 0 | 10 |

EVANS, DOUG   Douglas Edwards, DB, 6′1″/188 lbs; Louisiana Tech; 1993: GB, rnd 6; B5/13/1970 Shreveport, LA [I]   **1993**†GB 16 (0)   **1994**†GB 16 (15, RCB)   **1995**†GB 16 (16, RCB)   **1996**†GB 16 (16, RCB)   **1997**†GB✧15 (15, RCB)   **1998** Car 9 (7, RCB)   **1999** Car 16 (16, RCB)   **2000** Car 16 (16, RCB)   **2001** Car 16 (16, RCB)   **2002** Sea 15 (0)   **2003** Sea 2 (0)   **2003** Det 9 (3)   **NFL** 162 (120) [11 yrs]

EVANS, EARL   Earl, T-G, 5′11″/204 lbs; Marquette; Harvard; B4/14/1900 Lucas, IA, D3/18/1992 San Francisco, CA   **1925** ChiC 14 (11, LT), 6   **1926** ChiB 14 (2)   **1927** ChiB 11 (6, lt)   **1928** ChiB 10 (4)   **1929** ChiB 6 (5, rg)   **NFL** 55 (28) [5 yrs]

EVANS, FRED   Frederick Owen, HB, 5′11″/185 lbs; Notre Dame; 1943: ChiB, rnd 3; B5/23/1921 Grand Rapids, MI

| 1946 | Cle-A | 6(0) | 8 | 27 | 3.4 | 0 | 1 | 7 | 7.0(7) | 0 | — | | | | | | | | | | Ppi | — | 0 | 42 |
| 1947 | Buf-A | 4(0) | 11 | 14 | 1.3 | 0 | 1 | 31 | 31.0(31) | 1 | — | | | | | | | | | | kp | — | 6 | 15 |

YEAR	TEAM	G (GS, POS)	RUSH	YD	AVG (LG)	TD	REC	YD	AVG (LG)	TD	PASS	COMP	PCT	YD	AVG (LG)	TD	INT	SK	YD	QBR	KPR	OTD	PTS	TAY
1947	ChiR-A	9 (6, LH)	20	110	5.5	1	4	53	13.3	0	2	0	0.0	0	0.0	0	0	—	—	—	Pkp	—	6	196
AAFC	2	19 (6)	39	151	3.9	1	6	91	15.2 (31)	1	2	0	0.0	0	0.0	0	0	—	—	—	Pkpi	—	12	252
1948	ChiB	3 (0)	10	15	1.5 (7)	0	1	-2	-2.0 (-2)	0	—	—	—	—	—	—	—	—	—	—	p	2	12	24

EVANS, GREG Gregory G., DB, 6´1˝/217 lbs; TCU; B6/28/1971 Daingerfield, TX **1995**†Buf 16 (4) **1998** Was 13 (0) **NFL** 29 (4) [2 yrs]

EVANS, HEATH Bryan Heath, FB, 6´0˝/245 lbs; Auburn; 2001: Sea, rnd 3; B12/30/1978 West Palm Beach, FL

YEAR	TEAM	G (GS, POS)	RUSH	YD	AVG (LG)	TD	REC	YD	AVG (LG)	TD	PASS	COMP	PCT	YD	AVG (LG)	TD	INT	SK	YD	QBR	KPR	OTD	PTS	TAY
2001	Sea	16 (0)	2	11	5.5 (7)	0	—	—	—	—	—	—	—	—	—	—	—	—	—	—	k	—	0	6
2002	Sea	16 (1)	17	53	3.1 (8)	0	8	41	5.1 (13)	0	—	—	—	—	—	—	—	—	—	—	k	—	0	68
2003	†Sea	14 (0)	7	24	3.4 (8)	0	2	34	17.0 (20)	0	—	—	—	—	—	—	—	—	—	—	k	—	0	40
2004	†Sea	15 (0)	7	20	2.9 (7)	0	2	12	6.0 (9)	0	—	—	—	—	—	—	—	—	—	—	k	—	0	32
2005	Mia	6 (3)	1	0	0.0 (0)	0	4	17	4.3 (5)	0	—	—	—	—	—	—	—	—	—	—	—	—	0	9
2005	†NE	6 (1)	51	192	3.8 (21)	0	10	88	8.8 (19)	0	—	—	—	—	—	—	—	—	—	—	—	—	2	236
NFL	5	73 (5)	85	300	3.5 (21)	0	26	192	7.4 (20)	0	—	—	—	—	—	—	—	—	—	—	k	—	2	390

EVANS, JACK John Alexander, BB, 5´9˝/175 lbs; California; B8/17/1906 Colorado Springs, CO, D9/5/1988 Claremont, CA **1929** GB 2 (2)

EVANS, JAMES James Marcus, RB, 6´0˝/220 lbs; Southern (LA); 1987: KC, rnd 10; B8/17/1963 Prichard, AL **1987** KC 2 (0)

EVANS, JERRY Gerald Kristin, TE, 6´4˝/250 lbs; Toledo; 1991: Phx, rnd 8; B9/28/1968 Lorain, OH

YEAR	TEAM	G (GS, POS)	RUSH	YD	AVG (LG)	TD	REC	YD	AVG (LG)	TD	PASS	COMP	PCT	YD	AVG (LG)	TD	INT	SK	YD	QBR	KPR	OTD	PTS	TAY
1993	†Den	14 (2)	—	—	—	—	—	—	—	—	—	—	—	—	—	—	—	—	—	—	—	—	—	—
1994	Den	16 (12, TE)	—	—	—	—	13	127	9.8 (20)	2	—	—	—	—	—	—	—	—	—	—	k	—	12	65
1995	Den	13 (4)	—	—	—	—	12	124	10.3 (22)	1	—	—	—	—	—	—	—	—	—	—	—	—	6	67
NFL	3	43 (18)	—	—	—	—	25	251	10.0 (22)	3	—	—	—	—	—	—	—	—	—	—	k	—	18	132

EVANS, JIM James, WR, 6´1˝/190 lbs; Texas-El Paso; 1964: NYJ, rnd 4/Dal, rnd 6; B10/24/1939

YEAR	TEAM	G (GS, POS)	RUSH	YD	AVG (LG)	TD	REC	YD	AVG (LG)	TD	PASS	COMP	PCT	YD	AVG (LG)	TD	INT	SK	YD	QBR	KPR	OTD	PTS	TAY
1964	NYJ-A	12 (1)	—	—	—	—	7	56	8.0 (17)	0	—	—	—	—	—	—	—	—	—	—	k	—	0	92
1965	NYJ-A	9	—	—	—	—	2	24	12.0 (17)	0	—	—	—	—	—	—	—	—	—	—	—	—	0	12
NFL	2	21 (1)	—	—	—	—	9	80	8.9 (17)	0	—	—	—	—	—	—	—	—	—	—	k	—	0	104

EVANS, JOHN John Stuart, TE, 6´2˝/243 lbs; Stephen F. Austin State; B6/13/1964 Houston, TX

YEAR	TEAM	G (GS, POS)	RUSH	YD	AVG (LG)	TD	REC	YD	AVG (LG)	TD	PASS	COMP	PCT	YD	AVG (LG)	TD	INT	SK	YD	QBR	KPR	OTD	PTS	TAY
1987	Atl	1 (1)	—	—	—	—	1	8	8.0 (8)	0	—	—	—	—	—	—	—	—	—	—	—	—	0	4

EVANS, JOHNNY John Albert, P-QB, 6´1˝/197 lbs; North Carolina State; 1978: Cle, rnd 2; B2/18/1956 High Point, NC

YEAR	TEAM	G (GS, POS)	RUSH	YD	AVG (LG)	TD	REC	YD	AVG (LG)	TD	PASS	COMP	PCT	YD	AVG (LG)	TD	INT	SK	YD	QBR	KPR	OTD	PTS	TAY
1978	Cle	16	2	12	6.0 (12)	0	—	—	—	—	1	1	100.0	19	19.0 (19)	0	0	—	—	—	P	—	0	22
1979	Cle	16	—	—	—	—	—	—	—	—	2	1	50.0	14	7.0 (14)	0	0	—	—	—	P	—	0	7
1980	†Cle	16 (0)	3	-6	-2.0 (0)	0	—	—	—	—	—	—	—	—	—	—	—	—	—	—	P	—	0	-6
NFL	3	48	5	6	1.2 (12)	0	—	—	—	—	3	2	66.7	33	11.0 (19)	0	0	—	—	—	P	—	0	23

EVANS, JON Jon Albert, E, 6´4˝/205 lbs; Oklahoma State; 1958: Pit, rnd 26; B1/31/1936 Tyler, TX, D8/19/1979 Raleigh, NC **1958** Pit 1

EVANS, JOSH Mijoshki Antwon, DT, 6´3˝/280 lbs; Alabama-Birmingham; B9/6/1972 Langdale, AL **1995** Hou 7 (0) **1996** Hou 8 (0) **1997** Ten 15 (0) **1998** Ten 14 (11, RDT) **1999**†Ten 11 (10, LDT) **2001** Ten 16 (16, LDT) **2002**†NYJ 16 (16, RDT) **2003** NYJ 6 (0) **2004** NYJ 1 (0) **NFL** 94 (53) [9 yrs]

EVANS, LARRY Lawrence Eugene, LB, 6´2˝/216 lbs; Mississippi College; 1976: Den, rnd 14; B7/11/1953 Biloxi, MS **1976** Den 14 **1977**†Den 14 **1978**†Den 16 **1979**†Den 16 (4) **1980** Den 16 (12, LILB) **1981** Den 16 (16, LILB) **1982** Den 9 (9, LILB) **1983** SD 3 (0) **NFL** 104 (41) [8 yrs]

EVANS, LEE Lee, WR, 5´11˝/202 lbs; Wisconsin; 2004: Buf, rnd 1; B3/11/1981 Bedford, OH

YEAR	TEAM	G (GS, POS)	RUSH	YD	AVG (LG)	TD	REC	YD	AVG (LG)	TD	PASS	COMP	PCT	YD	AVG (LG)	TD	INT	SK	YD	QBR	KPR	OTD	PTS	TAY
2004	Buf	16 (11, WR)	5	85	17.0 (48)	0	48	843	17.6 (69)	9	—	—	—	—	—	—	—	—	—	—	—	—	54	552
2005	Buf	16 (15, WR)	4	38	9.5 (39)	0	48	743	15.5 (65)	7	—	—	—	—	—	—	—	—	—	—	—	—	42	445
NFL	2	32 (26)	9	123	13.7 (48)	0	96	1586	16.5 (69)	16	—	—	—	—	—	—	—	—	—	—	—	—	96	996

EVANS, LEOMONT Leomont Dozier, DB, 6´1˝/202 lbs; Clemson; 1996: Was, rnd 5; B7/12/1974 Abbeville, SC **1996** Was 12 (0) **1997** Was 16 (0) **1998** Was 16 (13, SS) **1999**†Was 15 (15, FS) **NFL** 59 (28) [4 yrs]

EVANS, LEON Leon, DE, 6´5˝/282 lbs; Miami (FL); B10/12/1961 Silver Spring, MD **1985** Det 8 (0) **1986** Det 16 (0) **NFL** 24 (0) [2 yrs]

EVANS, LON Lon Worth, G-T, 6´2˝/223 lbs; TCU; B12/25/1911 Fort Worth, TX, D12/11/1992 Fort Worth, TX **1933** GB 12 (5, lg) **1934** GB 11 (6, LT) **1935** GB☆11 (9, RG) **1936**†GB☆12 (7, RG) **1937** GB☆11 (8, RG) **NFL** 57 (35) [5 yrs]

EVANS, MIKE William Michael, C, 6´5˝/250 lbs; Boston College; 1968: Phi, rnd 9; B8/6/1946 Philadelphia, PA **1968** Phi 6 **1969** Phi 13 (C) **1970** Phi 14 (C) **1971** Phi 14 (C) **1972** Phi 12 (C) **1973** Phi 14 (5, c) **NFL** 73 (5) [6 yrs]

EVANS, MIKE Michael James, DT-DE, 6´3˝/289 lbs; Michigan; 1992: KC, rnd 4; B6/2/1967 St. Croix, Virgin Islands **1992** KC 12 (1)

EVANS, MURRAY Murray Charles, BB-QB, 6´1˝/203 lbs; Hardin-Simmons; 1942: Det, rnd 6; B6/23/1919 Goodlettsville, TN, D3/10/2004 Abilene, TX

YEAR	TEAM	G (GS, POS)	RUSH	YD	AVG (LG)	TD	REC	YD	AVG (LG)	TD	PASS	COMP	PCT	YD	AVG (LG)	TD	INT	SK	YD	QBR	KPR	OTD	PTS	TAY
1942	Det	10 (1)	1	-1	-1.0 (-1)	0	2	32	16.0 (19)	0	17	7	41.2	64	3.8 (15)	0	1	—	—	—	—	—	0	7
1943	Det	9 (5, BB)	2	3	1.5 (2)	0	3	31	10.3 (16)	0	5	1	20.0	8	1.6 (8)	0	2	—	—	—	—	—	0	-58
NFL	2	19 (6)	3	2	0.7 (2)	0	5	63	12.6 (19)	0	22	8	36.4	72	3.3 (15)	0	3	—	—	—	—	—	0	-51

EVANS, NORM Norman Earl, T, 6´5˝/250 lbs; TCU; 1965: Hou, rnd 14; B9/28/1942 Santa Fe, NM **1965** Hou-A 14 (RT) **1966** Mia-A 14 (14, RT) **1967** Mia-A 14 (14, RT) **1968** Mia-A 13 (12, RT) **1969** Mia-A 13 (12, RT) **1970**†Mia 14 (14, RT) **1971**†Mia 14 (14, RT) **1972**†Mia✧14 (14, RT) **1973**†Mia☆14 (14, RT) **1974**†Mia★14 (14, RT) **1975** Mia 14 (13, RT) **1976** Sea 10 (10, RT) **1977** Sea 13 (13, RT) **1978** Sea 13 (2) **NFL** 188 (160) [14 yrs]

EVANS, RAY Raymond Richard, TB-HB, 6´1˝/195 lbs; Kansas; 1944: ChiB, rnd 1; B9/22/1922 Kansas City, KS, D4/24/1999 Priairie Village, KS

YEAR	TEAM	G (GS, POS)	RUSH	YD	AVG (LG)	TD	REC	YD	AVG (LG)	TD	PASS	COMP	PCT	YD	AVG (LG)	TD	INT	SK	YD	QBR	KPR	OTD	PTS	TAY
1948	Pit	9 (8, TB)	99	343	3.5 (24)	2	7	93	13.3 (36)	0	137	64	46.7	924	6.7 (66)	5	17	—	—	41.7	Pkp	—	12	317

EVANS, RAY Raymond L., G-T, 6´1˝/225 lbs; Texas-El Paso; 1947: Bkn-A, rnd 25/1946: ChiC, rnd 16; B1/10/1924 Electra, TX **1949**†SF-A 10 (0)

1950 SF 12

EVANS, REGGIE Reginald Leon, RB, 5´11˝/201 lbs; Richmond; B1/5/1959 Newport News, VA

YEAR	TEAM	G (GS, POS)	RUSH	YD	AVG (LG)	TD	REC	YD	AVG (LG)	TD	PASS	COMP	PCT	YD	AVG (LG)	TD	INT	SK	YD	QBR	KPR	OTD	PTS	TAY
1983	†Was	15 (0)	16	11	0.7 (5)	4	—	—	—	—	—	—	—	—	—	—	—	—	—	—	k	—	24	42

EVANS, RUSSELL Russell, WR, 5´8˝/165 lbs; Truman State; B2/3/1965 **1987** Sea 1 (0)

EVANS, SCOTT Scott Allen, DE, 6´3˝/261 lbs; Oklahoma; 1991: Phx, rnd 8; B3/29/1968 Cincinnati, OH **1991** Phx 1 (0)

EVANS, TROY Troy Lyn, LB, 6´3˝/243 lbs; Cincinnati; B12/3/1977 Bay City, MI **2002** Hou 12 (0) **2003** Hou 15 (0) **2004** Hou 13 (0) **2005** Hou 16 (0) **NFL** 56 (0) [4 yrs]

EVANS, VINCE Vincent Tobias, QB, 6´2˝/215 lbs; USC; 1977: Chi, rnd 6; B6/14/1955 Greensboro, NC

YEAR	TEAM	G (GS, POS)	RUSH	YD	AVG (LG)	TD	REC	YD	AVG (LG)	TD	PASS	COMP	PCT	YD	AVG (LG)	TD	INT	SK	YD	QBR	KPR	OTD	PTS	TAY
1977	ChiB	7	1	0	0.0 (0)	0	—	—	—	—	—	—	—	—	—	—	—	—	—	—	k	—	0	58
1978	ChiB	3	6	23	3.8 (13)	0	—	—	—	—	3	1	33.3	38	12.7 (38)	0	1	2	25	—	—	—	0	2
1979	ChiB	4 (3)	12	72	6.0 (17)	1	—	—	—	—	63	32	50.8	508	8.1 (65)	4	5	8	75	—	—	—	6	156
1980	ChiB	13 (10, QB)	60	306	5.1 (58)	8	—	—	—	—	278	148	53.2	2039	7.3 (89)	11	16	26	205	66.2	—	—	48	821
1981	ChiB	16 (16, QB)	43	218	5.1 (25)	3	—	—	—	—	436	195	44.7	2354	5.4 (85)	11	20	23	173	51.1	—	—	18	680
1982	ChiB	4 (0)	2	0	0.0 (6)	0	—	—	—	—	28	12	42.9	125	4.5 (19)	0	4	2	17	—	—	—	0	-98
1983	ChiB	9 (3)	22	142	6.5 (27)	1	—	—	—	—	145	76	52.4	1108	7.6 (72)	5	7	11	92	69.0	—	—	6	451
1987	LARd	3 (3)	11	144	13.1 (24)	1	—	—	—	—	83	39	47.0	630	7.6 (47)	5	4	7	38	—	—	—	6	334
1989	LARd	1 (0)	1	16	16.0 (16)	0	—	—	—	—	2	2	100.0	50	25.0 (40)	0	0	2	19	—	—	—	0	41
1990	†LARd	5 (0)	1	-2	-2.0 (-2)	0	—	—	—	—	1	1	100.0	36	36.0 (36)	0	0	—	—	—	—	—	0	16
1991	LARd	4 (0)	8	20	2.5 (11)	0	—	—	—	—	14	6	42.9	127	9.1 (80)	1	2	2	20	—	—	—	0	9
1992	LARd	5 (0)	11	79	7.2 (16)	0	—	—	—	—	53	29	54.7	372	7.0 (50)	4	3	3	26	—	—	—	0	165
1993	LARd	8 (1)	14	51	3.6 (17)	0	—	—	—	—	76	45	59.2	640	8.4 (68)	3	4	12	87	—	—	—	0	226
1994	LARd	9 (0)	6	24	4.0 (23)	0	—	—	—	—	33	18	54.5	222	6.7 (65)	2	0	9	57	—	—	—	0	145
1995	Oak	9 (3, qb)	14	36	2.6 (11)	0	—	—	—	—	175	100	57.1	1236	7.1 (73)	6	8	11	70	71.5	—	—	0	364
NFL	15	100 (39)	212	1129	5.3 (58)	14	—	—	—	—	1390	704	50.6	9485	6.8 (89)	52	74	118	904	63.0	k	—	84	3370

EVANSEN, PAUL Paul Arnold, G, 6´3˝/240 lbs; Oregon State; B5/10/1922 San Francisco, CA **1948** SF-A 1 (0)

EVERETT, ERIC Eric Eugene, DB, 5´10˝/165 lbs; Texas Tech; 1988: Phi, rnd 5; B7/13/1966 Daingerfield, TX **1988**†Phi 16 (1) **1989**†Phi 16 (1) **1990** TB 16 (0) **1991**†KC 11 (0) **1992**†Min 16 (0) **NFL** 75 (2) [5 yrs]

YEAR	TEAM	G (GS, POS)	RUSH	YD	AVG (LG)	TD	REC	YD	AVG (LG)	TD	PASS	COMP	PCT	YD	AVG (LG)	TD	INT	SK	YD	QBR	KPR	OTD	PTS	TAY

EVERETT, JIM James Samuel, QB, 6´5˝/212 lbs; Purdue; 1986: Hou, rnd 1; B1/3/1963 Emporia, KS

1986	†LARm	6(5, qb)	16	46	2.9(14)	1	—	—	—	—	147	73	49.7	1018	6.9(60)	8	8	8	50	—	—	—	6	285
1987	LARm	11(11, QB)	18	83	4.6(16)	1	—	—	—	—	302	162	53.6	2064	6.8(81)	10	13	17	139	68.4	—	—	6	655
1988	†LARm☆	16(16, QB)	34	104	3.1(19)	0	—	—	—	—	517	308	59.6	3964	7.7(69)	31	18	28	197	89.2	—	—	0	1521
1989	†LARm☆	16(16, QB)	25	31	1.2(13)	1	—	—	—	—	518	304	58.7	4310	8.3(78)	29	17	29	214	90.6	—	—	6	1661
1990	LARm◇	16(16, QB)	20	31	1.5(15)	1	—	—	—	—	554	307	55.4	3989	7.2(55)	23	17	30	198	79.3	—	—	6	1471
1991	LARm	16(16, QB)	27	44	1.6(10)	0	—	—	—	—	490	277	56.5	3438	7.0(78)	11	20	30	200	68.9	—	—	0	1018
1992	LARm	16(16, QB)	32	133	4.2(22)	0	—	—	—	—	475	281	59.2	3323	7.0(67)	22	18	26	204	80.2	—	—	0	1185
1993	LARm	10(9, QB)	19	38	2.0(14)	0	—	—	—	—	274	135	49.3	1652	6.0(60)	8	12	18	125	59.7	—	—	0	424
1994	NO	16(16, QB)	15	35	2.3(14)	0	—	—	—	—	540	346	64.1	3855	7.1(78)	22	18	21	164	84.9	—	—	0	1353
1995	NO	16(16, QB)	24	42	1.8(9)	0	—	—	—	—	567	345	60.8	3970	7.0(70)	26	14	27	210	87.0	—	—	0	1597
1996	NO	15(15, QB)	22	3	0.1(3)	0	—	—	—	—	464	267	57.5	2797	6.0(51)	12	16	19	154	69.4	—	—	0	822
1997	SD	4(1)	5	6	1.2(6)	0	—	—	—	—	75	36	48.0	457	6.1(62)	1	4	4	30	—	—	—	0	80
NFL	12	158(153)	257	596	2.3(22)	4	—	—	—	—	4923	2841	57.7	34837	7.1(81)	203	175	257	1885	78.6	—	—	24	12070

EVERETT, MAJOR Major Daniel, RB, 5´10˝/215 lbs; Mississippi College; B1/4/1960 New Hebron, MS

1983	Phi	16(0)	5	7	1.4(7)	0	2	18	9.0(11)	0	—	—	—	—	—	—	—	—	—	—	k	—	0	81
1984	Phi	16(0)	—	—	—	—	—	—	—	—	—	—	—	—	—	—	—	—	—	—	k	—	0	-5
1985	Phi	15(0)	4	13	3.3(8)	0	4	25	6.3(11)	0	—	—	—	—	—	—	—	—	—	—	k	—	0	26
1986	†Cle	9(0)	12	43	3.6(8)	0	—	—	—	—	—	—	—	—	—	—	—	—	—	—	k	—	0	43
1987	Cle	4(3)	34	95	2.8(16)	0	8	41	5.1(10)	0	—	—	—	—	—	—	—	—	—	—	k	—	0	116
1987	Atl	7(0)	—	—	—	—	—	—	—	—	—	—	—	—	—	—	—	—	—	—	k	—	0	3
NFL	5	67(3)	55	158	2.9(16)	0	14	84	6.0(11)	0	—	—	—	—	—	—	—	—	—	—	k	—	0	263

EVERETT, THOMAS Thomas Gregory, DB, 5´9˝/190 lbs; Baylor; 1987: Pit, rnd 4; B11/21/1964 Daingerfield, TX **[I]** **1987** Pit 12 (9, FS) **1988** Pit 14 (12, FS) **1989**†Pit 16 (16, FS) **1990** Pit 15 (14, FS) **1991** Pit 16 (16, FS) **1992**†Dal 11 (9, SS) **1993**†Dal◇16 (16, FS) **1994** TB 15 (15, FS) **1995** TB 13 (10, FS) **NFL** 128 (117) [9 yrs]

EVERITT, STEVE Steven Michael, C-G, 6´5˝/295 lbs; Michigan; 1993: Cle, rnd 1; B8/21/1970 Miami, FL **1993** Cle 16 (16, C) **1994**†Cle 15 (15, C) **1995** Cle 15 (14, C) **1996** Bal 8 (7, c) **1997** Phi 16 (16, C) **1998** Phi 13 (13, C) **1999** Phi 16 (16, C) **2000** SL 4 (1) **NFL** 103 (98) [8 yrs]

EVERS, WILLIAM William, DB, 5´10˝/175 lbs; Florida A&M; B9/24/1968 Cairo, GA **1990** Atl 2 (0) **1991** Atl 2 (0) **NFL** 4 (0) [2 yrs]

EVEY, DICK Richard Theodore, DT-DE-G, 6´4˝/245 lbs; Tennessee; 1964: Chi, rnd 1/Buf, rnd 2; B2/12/1941 State College, PA **1964** ChiB 14 (LDE) **1965** ChiB 14 (14, LDE) **1966** ChiB 14 (RDT) **1967** ChiB 12 (RDT) **1968** ChiB 14 (RDT) **1969** ChiB 14 (LDE) **1970** LARm 9 (RDT) **1971** Det 11 (LDT) **NFL** 102 (14) [8 yrs]

EYRE, NICK Nicholas G., T, 6´5˝/276 lbs; Brigham Young; 1981: Hou, rnd 4; B6/16/1959 Las Vegas, NV **1981** Hou 6 (0)

EZEKIEL, LIAM Liam, LB, 6´0˝/249 lbs; Northeastern; B10/30/1982 Arlington, MA **2005** Buf 2 (0)

EZERINS, VILNIS Vilnis Raymond, RB, 6´2˝/217 lbs; Wisconsin-Whitewater; 1966: LA, rnd 8; B4/22/1944 Latvia

| 1968 | LARm | 14 | 2 | 2 | 1.0(1) | 0 | — | — | — | — | — | — | — | — | — | — | — | — | — | — | k | — | 0 | -13 |

EZOR, BLAKE Blake, RB, 5´9˝/181 lbs; Michigan State; B10/11/1966 Las Vegas, NV

| 1990 | Den | 9(0) | 23 | 81 | 3.5(15) | 0 | — | — | — | — | — | — | — | — | — | — | — | — | — | — | k | — | 0 | 100 |

FAAOLA, NUU Sinatausilinuu, RB, 5´11˝/215 lbs; Hawaii; 1986: NYJ, rnd 9; B1/15/1964 Honolulu, HI

1986	†NYJ	12(0)	3	5	1.7(2)	0	—	—	—	—	—	—	—	—	—	—	—	—	—	—	k	—	0	5
1987	NYJ	12(0)	14	43	3.1(18)	2	1	16	16.0(16)	0	—	—	—	—	—	—	—	—	—	—	k	—	12	60
1988	NYJ	16(0)	1	13	13.0(13)	0	—	—	—	—	—	—	—	—	—	—	—	—	—	—	k	—	0	-8
1989	NYJ	2(0)	—	—	—	—	—	—	—	—	—	—	—	—	—	—	—	—	—	—	k	—	0	
1989	Mia	10(1)	2	10	5.0(5)	0	1	8	8.0(8)	0	—	—	—	—	—	—	—	—	—	—	k	—	0	14
NFL	4	52(1)	20	71	3.6(18)	2	2	24	12.0(16)	0	—	—	—	—	—	—	—	—	—	—	k	—	12	71

FABINI, JASON Jason T., T, 6´7˝/304 lbs; Cincinnati; 1998: NYJ, rnd 4; B8/25/1974 Fort Wayne, IN **1998**†NYJ 16 (16, RT) **1999** NYJ 9 (9, RT) **2000** NYJ 16 (16, RT) **2001**†NYJ 16 (16, LT) **2002**†NYJ 16 (16, LT) **2003** NYJ 16 (16, LT) **2004**†NYJ 16 (16, LT) **2005** NYJ 9 (9, RT) **NFL** 114 (114) [8 yrs]

FADA, ROB Robert Alan, G, 6´2˝/265 lbs; Pittsburgh; 1983: Chi, rnd 9; B5/7/1961 Fairborn, OH **1983** ChiB 5 (3) **1984**†ChiB 14 (1) **1985** KC 5 (0) **NFL** 24 (4) [3 yrs]

FAGAN, JULIAN Julian Walter, P, 6´3˝/205 lbs; Mississippi; 1970: Hou, rnd 17; B2/21/1948 Laurel, MS **[P]**

1970	NO☆	14	1	-6	-6.0(-6)	0	—	—	—	—	—	—	—	—	—	—	—	—	—	P	—	0	-6
1971	NO	14	1	-17	-17.0(-17)	0	—	—	—	—	—	—	—	—	—	—	—	—	—	P	—	0	-17
1972	NO	14	—	—	—	—	—	—	—	—	—	—	—	—	—	—	—	—	—	P	—	0	0
1973	NYJ	14	2	47	23.5(26)	0	—	—	—	—	—	—	—	—	—	—	—	—	—	P	—	0	47
NFL	4	56	4	24	6.0(26)	0	—	—	—	—	—	—	—	—	—	—	—	—	—	P	—	0	24

FAGAN, KEVIN Kevin Scott, DE, 6´3˝/260 lbs; Miami (FL); 1986: SF, rnd 4; B4/25/1963 Lake Worth, FL **1987**†SF 7 (2) **1988**†SF 14 (14, RDE) **1989**†SF 16 (15, RDE) **1990**†SF☆16 (16, RDE) **1991** SF 8 (7, rde) **1992**†SF 15 (13, RDE) **1993** SF 7 (7, RDE) **NFL** 83 (74) [7 yrs]

FAGGINS, DEMARCUS Demarcus, DB, 5´10˝/178 lbs; Kansas State; 2002: Hou, rnd 6; B6/13/1979 Irving, TX **2002** Hou 2 (0) **2003** Hou 8 (1) **2004** Hou 16 (2) **2005** Hou 13 (10, LCB) **NFL** 39 (13) [4 yrs]

FAGIOLO, CARL Carl, G, 6´0˝/200 lbs; none; B4/26/1917 **1944** Phi 2 (0)

FAHAY, JOHN John Lloyd, E-B-G, 6´0˝/189 lbs; St. Thomas; Marquette; B6/16/1902 Mason City, IL, D1/18/1980 Fort Lauderdale, FL **1925** Mil 1 (0) **1926** Rac 2 (2) **1929** Min 5 (1) **NFL** 8 (3) [3 yrs]

FAHNHORST, JIM James John, LB, 6´4˝/230 lbs; Minnesota; 1982: Min, rnd 4; B11/8/1958 St. Cloud, MN **1984** SF 14 (2) **1985**†SF 15 (2) **1986**†SF 16 (14, RILB) **1987**†SF 11 (10, LILB) **1988**†SF 16 (3) **1989** SF 7 (7, mlb) **1990** SF 3 (0) **NFL** 82 (38) [7 yrs]

FAHNHORST, KEITH Keith Victor, T, 6´6˝/273 lbs; Minnesota; 1974: SF, rnd 2; B2/6/1952 St. Cloud, MN **1974** SF 14 **1976** SF 13 (6, rt) **1977** SF 14 (14, RT) **1978** SF 15 (15, RT) **1979** SF 16 (16, RT) **1980** SF 16 (16, RT) **1981**†SF 16 (16, RT) **1982** SF 9 (9, RT) **1983**†SF☆16 (16, RT) **1984**†SF★15 (15, RT) **1985**†SF☆16 (16, RT) **1986**†SF 16 (16, RT) **1987** SF 3 (3)

| 1975 | SF | 14(3) | — | — | — | 1 | 1 | 1.0(1) | 0 | — | — | — | — | — | — | — | — | — | — | — | k | — | 0 | -2 |
| NFL | 14 | 193(161) | — | — | — | 1 | 1 | 1.0(1) | 0 | — | — | — | — | — | — | — | — | — | — | — | k | — | 0 | -2 |

FAILING, FRED Fred C., G, 5´11˝/200 lbs; Central Michigan; B6/7/1904 Caro, MI, D9/7/1972 Green Bay, WI **1930** ChiC 1 (0)

FAIN, RICHARD Richard Alexander, DB, 5´10˝/183 lbs; Florida; 1991: Cin, rnd 6; B2/29/1968 North Fort Myers, FL **1991** Cin 6 (2) **1991** Phx 2 (0) **1992** ChiB 16 (6, rcb) **NFL** 24 (8) [2 yrs]

FAINE, JEFF Jeffrey Kalei, C, 6´3˝/303 lbs; Notre Dame; 2003: Cle, rnd 1; B4/6/1981 Milwaukie, OR

2003	Cle	9(9, c)	1	0	0.0(0)	0	—	—	—	—	—	—	—	—	—	—	—	—	—	—	—	—	0	0
2004	Cle	13(13, C)	—	—	—	—	—	—	—	—	—	—	—	—	—	—	—	—	—	—	—	—	0	0
2005	Cle	14(14, C)	—	—	—	1	-1	-1.0(-1)	0	—	—	—	—	—	—	—	—	—	—	—	—	—	0	-1
NFL	3	36(36)	1	0	0.0	0	1	-1	-1.0(-1)	0	—	—	—	—	—	—	—	—	—	—	—	—	0	-1

FAIR, CARL Carl, RB, 6´1˝/219 lbs; Alabama-Birmingham; B6/8/1979 Starkville, MS **2001** Cle 3 (0)

FAIR, TERRY Terrance Delon, DB, 5´9˝/185 lbs; Tennessee; 1998: Det, rnd 1; B7/20/1976 Phoenix, AZ **[R]** **1998** Det☆14 (10, RCB) **1999** Det 11 (11, RCB) **2000** Det 15 (15, RCB) **2001** Det 12 (12, RCB) **2002** Car 3 (0) **2005** SL 5 (0) **NFL** 60 (48) [6 yrs]

FAIRBAND, BILL William Robert, LB, 6´3˝/228 lbs; Colorado; 1967: Oak, rnd 3; B6/11/1941 Los Gatos, CA **1967** Oak-A 7 **1968** Oak-A 2 **NFL** 9 [2 yrs]

FAIRBANKS, DON Donald Lee, DE, 6´3˝/253 lbs; Colorado; 1986: Sea, rnd 10; B2/13/1964 Lakewood, CO **1987** Sea 3 (3)

FAIRCHILD, GREG Gregory Thompson, G-T-C, 6´4˝/258 lbs; Tulsa; 1976: Cin, rnd 4; B3/10/1954 St. Louis, MO **1976** Cin 12 **1977** Cin 13 **1978** Cle 2 **NFL** 27 [3 yrs]

FAIRCHILD, PAUL Paul Jay, G-C, 6´4˝/270 lbs; Kansas; 1984: NE, rnd 5; B9/14/1961 Carroll, IA **1984** NE 7 (0) **1985**†NE 16 (2) **1986**†NE 15 (15, LG) **1987** NE 11 (2) **1988** NE 16 (3) **1989** NE 14 (14, RG) **1990** NE 4 (2) **NFL** 83 (38) [7 yrs]

FAIRCLOTH, ART Arthur Terman, B, 6´0˝/190 lbs; North Carolina State; Guilford; 1944: Bos, rnd 19; B7/8/1921 Richmond, VA

YEAR	TEAM	G (GS, POS)	RUSH	YD	AVG (LG)	TD	REC	YD	AVG (LG)	TD	PASS	COMP	PCT	YD	AVG (LG)	TD	INT	SK	YD	QBR	KPR	OTD	PTS	TAY
1947	NYG	3(0)	10	9	0.9(7)	0	—	—	—	—	5	3	60.0	30	6.0(14)	1	0	—	—	—	Pk	—	0	61
1948	NYG	2(0)	1	-1	-1.0(-1)	0	—	—	—	—	—	—	—	—	—	—	—	—	—	—	i	—	0	-11
NFL	2	5(0)	11	8	0.7(7)	0	—	—	—	—	5	3	60.0	30	6.0(14)	1	0	—	—	—	Pki	—	0	50

FAIRLEY, LEONARD Leonard, DB, 5´11˝/200 lbs; Alcorn State; 1974: Hou, rnd 7; B1/2/1951 Biloxi, MS **1974** Hou 2

FAIRS, ERIC Eric Jerome, LB, 6´3˝/240 lbs; Memphis; B2/17/1964 Memphis, TN **1986** Hou 12 (0) **1987**†Hou 12 (0) **1988**†Hou 16 (0) **1989**†Hou 16 (3) **1990**†Hou 16 (1) **1991** Hou 16 (0) **1992** Atl 2 (0) **NFL** 90 (4) [7 yrs]

FAISON, DERRICK Derrick, WR, 6´4˝/200 lbs; Howard; B8/24/1967 Lake City, SC

YEAR	TEAM	G (GS, POS)	RUSH	YD	AVG (LG)	TD	REC	YD	AVG (LG)	TD	PASS	COMP	PCT	YD	AVG (LG)	TD	INT	SK	YD	QBR	KPR	OTD	PTS	TAY
1990	LARm	15(0)	—	—	—	—	3	27	9.0(12)	1	—	—	—	—	—	—	—	—	—	—	—	—	6	19

FAISON, EARL William Earl, DE, 6´5˝/270 lbs; Indiana; 1961: SD, rnd 1/Det, rnd 5; B1/31/1939 Newport News, VA **1961**†SD-A★14 (LDE) **1962** SD-A★8 (LDE) **1963**†SD-A★14 (LDE) **1964**†SD-A★14 (LDE) **1965**†SD-A★14 (LDE) **1966** SD-A 3 **1966** Mia-A 6 **NFL** 73 [6 yrs]

FALASCHI, NELLO Nello Donald, BB, 6´0˝/195 lbs; Santa Clara; 1937: Was, rnd 2; B3/19/1913 Dos Palos, CA, D7/29/1986 Oakland, CA

YEAR	TEAM	G (GS, POS)	RUSH	YD	AVG (LG)	TD	REC	YD	AVG (LG)	TD	PASS	COMP	PCT	YD	AVG (LG)	TD	INT	SK	YD	QBR	KPR	OTD	PTS	TAY
1938	†NYG✧	9(4)	1	6	6.0(6)	0	—	—	—	—	1	0	0.0	0	0.0	0	0	—	—	—	—	—	0	6
1939	†NYG✧	11(9, BB)	1	4	4.0(4)	0	4	27	6.8(25)	0	—	—	—	—	—	—	—	—	—	—	—	—	0	18
1940	NYG	11(9, BB)	—	—	—	—	2	9	4.5(8)	0	—	—	—	—	—	—	—	—	—	—	i	—	0	23
1941	†NYG✧	11(11, BB)	—	—	—	—	1	3	3.0(3)	0	—	—	—	—	—	—	—	—	—	—	ki	—	0	9
NFL	4	42(33)	2	10	5.0(6)	0	7	39	5.6(25)	0	1	0	0.0	0	0.0	0	0	—	—	—	ki	—	0	55

FALCON, DICK Raymond Chester, G, 5´9˝/175 lbs; none; B4/26/1896 Evanston, IL, D9/15/1949 Evanston, IL **1920** ChiT 2 (0)

FALCON, GUIL Guilford W., FB, 5´10˝/220 lbs; none; B12/15/1892 Evanston, IL, D7/28/1982 Hollywood, FL **[C]** **1920** Ham 8 (1) **1920** ChiT☆7 (7, FB) **1921** Ham 1 (0) **1921** Can 7 (7, FB), 12 **1922** Tol 9 (6, FB), 6 **1923** Tol 2 (0) **1924** Ham 5 (4, FB), 12 **1925** Ham 1 (0) **1925** Akr 8 (7, FB) **1925** Roc 1 (0) **NFL** 49 (32), 30 [6 yrs]

FALCON, TERRY Theodore Lee, G-T, 6´3˝/260 lbs; Minot State; Montana; 1978: NE, rnd 8; B8/30/1955 Culbertson, MT **1978**†NE 8 **1979** NE 10 **1980** NYG 13 (2) **NFL** 31 (2) [3 yrs]

FALKENSTEIN, TONY Anthony Joseph, FB-BB, 5´10˝/205 lbs; St. Mary's (CA); 1938: GB, rnd 12; B2/16/1915 Pueblo, CO, D10/9/1994 Ceres, CA

YEAR	TEAM	G (GS, POS)	RUSH	YD	AVG (LG)	TD	REC	YD	AVG (LG)	TD	PASS	COMP	PCT	YD	AVG (LG)	TD	INT	SK	YD	QBR	KPR	OTD	PTS	TAY
1943	GB	10(4)	58	198	3.4(59)	1	3	39	13.0(18)	0	—	—	—	—	—	—	—	—	—	—	k	—	6	245
1944	Bkn	6(1)	3	1	0.3(2)	0	—	—	—	—	—	—	—	—	—	—	—	—	—	—	—	—	0	1
1944	Bos	2(0)	1	1	1.0(1)	0	1	21	21.0(21)	0	—	—	—	—	—	—	—	—	—	—	—	—	0	12
NFL	2	18(5)	62	200	3.2(59)	1	4	60	15.0(21)	0	—	—	—	—	—	—	—	—	—	—	k	—	6	257

FALLON, MICKEY Michael William, G-E, 5´9˝/175 lbs; Muhlenberg; Syracuse; B4/15/1898 Hartford, CT, D3/21/1972 New York, NY **1922** Mil 8 (4)

FALLS, MIKE Michael Lee, G, 6´2˝/240 lbs; Minnesota; 1956: NYG, rnd 20; B3/3/1934 Bemidji, MN **1960** Dal 11 (5, rg) **1961** Dal 14 (RG) **NFL** 25 (5) [2 yrs]

FAMIGLIETTI, GARY Gary J., FB-HB, 6´0˝/225 lbs; Boston University; 1938: ChiB, rnd 3; B11/28/1913 Boston, MA, D7/13/1986 Chicago, IL **[K]**

YEAR	TEAM	G (GS, POS)	RUSH	YD	AVG (LG)	TD	REC	YD	AVG (LG)	TD	PASS	COMP	PCT	YD	AVG (LG)	TD	INT	SK	YD	QBR	KPR	OTD	PTS	TAY
1938	ChiB	9(3)	33	129	3.9	0	—	—	—	—	—	—	—	—	—	—	—	—	—	—	—	—	0	129
1939	ChiB	10(2)	33	128	3.9	0	3	72	24.0	0	—	—	—	—	—	—	—	—	—	—	K	—	1	164
1940	†ChiB★	11(2, fb)	93	320	3.4	4	1	11	11.0(11)	0	—	—	—	—	—	—	—	—	—	—	i	—	24	364
1941	†ChiB✧	7(2)	36	101	2.8(10)	1	—	—	—	—	—	—	—	—	—	—	—	—	—	—	—	—	6	111
1942	†ChiB★	10(8, FB)	118	503	4.3(21)	**8**	1	12	12.0(12)	0	—	—	—	—	—	—	—	—	—	—	Kki	—	48	588
1943	†ChiB	10(4, FB)	64	229	3.6(31)	2	1	10	10.0(10)	0	—	—	—	—	—	—	—	—	—	—	—	—	12	254
1944	ChiB	10(1)	63	282	4.5(16)	2	1	23	23.0(23)	1	—	—	—	—	—	—	—	—	—	—	—	—	18	319
1945	ChiB	10(0)	65	235	3.6(14)	3	4	42	10.5(13)	0	—	—	—	—	—	—	—	—	—	—	k	—	18	290
1946	Bos	11(0)	23	54	2.3(13)	4	1	17	17.0(17)	0	1	1	100.0	6	6.0(6)	0	0	—	—	—	K	—	24	106
NFL	9	88(22)	528	1981	3.8(31)	24	12	187	15.6(23)	1	1	1	100.0	6	6.0(6)	0	0	—	—	—	Kki	—	151	2324

FANECA, ALAN Alan Joseph, G-T, 6´5˝/312 lbs; LSU; 1998: Pit, rnd 1; B12/7/1976 New Orleans, LA **1998** Pit 16 (12, LG) **1999** Pit 15 (14, LG) **2000** Pit 16 (16, LG) **2001**†Pit★15 (15, LG) **2002**†Pit★16 (16, LG) **2003** Pit★16 (16, LT/lg) **2004**†Pit★16 (16, LG) **2005**†Pit★16 (16, LG) **NFL** 126 (121) [8 yrs]

FANENE, JONATHAN Jonathan David, DE, 6´3˝/290 lbs; Utah; 2005: Cin, rnd 7; B3/19/1982 Pago Pago, American Samoa **2005** Cin 3 (1)

FANN, CHAD Chad Fitzgerald, TE, 6´3˝/252 lbs; Mississippi; Florida A&M; B6/7/1970 Jacksonville, FL

YEAR	TEAM	G (GS, POS)	RUSH	YD	AVG (LG)	TD	REC	YD	AVG (LG)	TD	PASS	COMP	PCT	YD	AVG (LG)	TD	INT	SK	YD	QBR	KPR	OTD	PTS	TAY
1993	Phx	1(0)	—	—	—	—	—	—	—	—	—	—	—	—	—	—	—	—	—	—	—	—	—	—
1994	Arz	16(9, TE)	—	—	—	—	12	96	8.0(16)	0	—	—	—	—	—	—	—	—	—	—	—	—	0	48
1995	Arz	16(3)	—	—	—	—	5	41	8.2(13)	0	—	—	—	—	—	—	—	—	—	—	—	—	0	21
1997	†SF	11(0)	—	—	—	—	5	78	15.6(21)	0	—	—	—	—	—	—	—	—	—	—	k	—	0	24
1998	†SF	12(0)	—	—	—	—	—	—	—	—	—	—	—	—	—	—	—	—	—	—	—	—	—	—
1999	SF	16(3)	—	—	—	—	2	8	4.0(6)	0	—	—	—	—	—	—	—	—	—	—	—	—	0	4
NFL	6	72(15)	—	—	—	—	24	223	9.3(21)	0	—	—	—	—	—	—	—	—	—	—	k	—	0	97

FANNING, MIKE Michael LaVern, DT-DE-NT, 6´6˝/255 lbs; Notre Dame; 1975: LA, rnd 1; B2/2/1953 Mount Clemens, MI **1975**†LARm 8 **1976**†LARm 14 **1977**†LARm 14 **1978**†LARm 16 (2) **1979**†LARm 16 (16, RDT) **1980**†LARm 15 (3) **1981** LARm 16 (16, LDT) **1982** LARm 8 (8, LDT) **1983** Det 14 (5, ldt) **1984**†Sea 16 (0) **NFL** 137 (50) [10 yrs]

FANNING, STAN Stanley Lynn, T-DE-DT, 6´7˝/270 lbs; Idaho; 1960: Chi, rnd 11/Hou, rnd 2; B11/22/1937 Peoria, IL **1960** ChiB 12 (RT) **1961** ChiB 14 **1962** ChiB 4 **1963** LARm 10 **1964** Hou-A 5 **1964** Den-A 7 **NFL** 52 [5 yrs]

FANTETTI, KEN Kenneth Mark, LB, 6´2˝/230 lbs; Wyoming; 1979: Det, rnd 2; B4/7/1957 Toledo, OR **1979** Det 16 (8, mlb) **1980** Det 16 (16, MLB) **1981** Det 16 (16, MLB) **1982**†Det 9 (9, MLB) **1983**†Det 16 (16, MLB) **1984** Det 14 (13, MLB) **1985** Det 8 (4) **NFL** 95 (82) [7 yrs]

FANUCCHI, LEDIO Ledio, T-DT, 6´2˝/225 lbs; Fresno State; 1954: ChiC, rnd 22; B3/27/1931 Fresno, CA **1954** ChiC 12

FANUCCI, MIKE Michael Joseph, DE, 6´4˝/235 lbs; Arizona State; 1971: Was, rnd 9; B9/25/1949 Scranton, PA **1972**†Was 14 **1973** Hou 13 **1974** GB 13 **NFL** 40 [3 yrs]

FARASOPOULOS, CHRIS Chris Vitos, DB, 6´0˝/210 lbs; Brigham Young; 1971: NYJ, rnd 3; B7/20/1949 Athens, Greece **1971** NYJ 14 **1972** NYJ 13 (FS) **1973** NYJ 9 (FS) **1974** NO 6 **NFL** 42 [4 yrs]

FARBER, HAP Louis Allen, LB, 6´1˝/220 lbs; Mississippi; 1970: Min, rnd 7; B7/1/1948 Norfolk, VA **1970** Min 3 **1970** NO 5 **NFL** 8 [1 yr]

FARGAS, JUSTIN Justin, FB, 6´1˝/220 lbs; Michigan; USC; 2003: Oak, rnd 3; B1/25/1980 Encino, CA

YEAR	TEAM	G (GS, POS)	RUSH	YD	AVG (LG)	TD	REC	YD	AVG (LG)	TD	PASS	COMP	PCT	YD	AVG (LG)	TD	INT	SK	YD	QBR	KPR	OTD	PTS	TAY
2003	Oak	10(1)	40	203	5.1(53)	0	2	2	1.0(6)	0	—	—	—	—	—	—	—	—	—	—	k	—	0	279
2004	Oak	12(0)	35	126	3.6(15)	1	11	68	6.2(21)	0	—	—	—	—	—	—	—	—	—	—	—	—	6	170
2005	Oak	14(0)	5	28	5.6(15)	0	1	9	9.0(9)	0	—	—	—	—	—	—	—	—	—	—	—	—	0	33
NFL	3	36(1)	80	357	4.5(53)	1	14	79	5.6(21)	0	—	—	—	—	—	—	—	—	—	—	k	—	6	482

FARINA, NICK Ralph Robert, C, 5´8˝/180 lbs; Villanova; B2/21/1905 Steelton, PA, D9/22/1984 Harrisburg, PA **1927** Pot 1 (0)

FARKAS, ANDY Andrew Geza, FB-HB-WB, 5´10˝/189 lbs; Detroit Mercy; 1938: Was, rnd 1; B5/2/1916 Clay Center, OH, D4/10/2001 Traverse City, MI **[K]**

YEAR	TEAM	G (GS, POS)	RUSH	YD	AVG (LG)	TD	REC	YD	AVG (LG)	TD	PASS	COMP	PCT	YD	AVG (LG)	TD	INT	SK	YD	QBR	KPR	OTD	PTS	TAY
1938	Was	9(4, FB)	75	315	4.2(53)	**6**	9	66	7.3(21)	0	—	—	—	—	—	—	—	—	—	—	K	—	37	408
1939	Was★	11(7, FB)	**139**	547	3.9	5	16	437	27.3(**99**)	5	—	—	—	—	—	—	—	—	—	—	K	1	**68**	**851**
1940	†Was	1(0)	1	0	0.0	0	—	—	—	—	—	—	—	—	—	—	—	—	—	—	i	—	0	-5
1941	Was	11(2, fb)	85	224	2.6(10)	2	12	77	6.4(44)	0	—	—	—	—	—	—	—	—	—	—	kpi	1	18	397
1942	†Was★	10(8, FB)	125	468	3.7(22)	3	11	143	13.0(35)	2	—	—	—	—	—	—	—	—	—	—	Kkpi	1	39	886
1943	†Was☆	10(8, FB)	110	327	3.0(36)	5	19	202	10.6(55)	4	—	—	—	—	—	—	—	—	—	—	kp	—	54	735
1944	Was	10(6, LH)	21	85	4.0(20)	0	4	29	7.3(12)	0	—	—	—	—	—	—	—	—	—	—	kpi	—	0	236
1945	Det	8(3, WB)	31	137	4.4(27)	0	9	132	14.7(29)	2	—	—	—	—	—	—	—	—	—	—	kp	—	12	324
NFL	8	70(38)	587	2103	3.6(53)	21	80	1086	13.6(99)	13	—	—	—	—	—	—	—	—	—	—	Kkpi	3	228	3830

FARLEY, DALE Dale Rice, LB, 6´3˝/225 lbs; West Virginia; 1971: Mia, rnd 3; B9/27/1949 Sparta, TN **1971**†Mia 4 **1972** Buf 7 **1973** Buf 2 **NFL** 13 [3 yrs]

FARLEY, DICK Richard Joseph, DB, 5´11˝/185 lbs; Boston University; 1968: SD, rnd 16; B5/30/1946 Danvers, MA **1968** SD-A 10 **1969** SD-A 14 **NFL** 24 [2 yrs]

FARLEY, JOHN John Howard, RB, 5´10˝/202 lbs; Sacramento State; 1984: Cin, rnd 4; B8/11/1961 Stockton, CA

YEAR	TEAM	G (GS, POS)	RUSH	YD	AVG (LG)	TD	REC	YD	AVG (LG)	TD	PASS	COMP	PCT	YD	AVG (LG)	TD	INT	SK	YD	QBR	KPR	OTD	PTS	TAY
1984	Cin	13(0)	7	11	1.6(5)	0	2	11	5.5(10)	0	—	—	—	—	—	—	—	—	—	—	k	—	0	20

YEAR	TEAM	G(GS, POS)	RUSH	YD	AVG(LG)	TD	REC	YD	AVG(LG)	TD	PASS	COMP	PCT	YD	AVG(LG)	TD	INT	○SK	YD	QBR	KPR	OTD	PTS	TAY
Farman, Dick Richard George, G, 6´0˝/219 lbs; Washington State; 1939: Was, rnd 16; B7/26/1916 Belmond, IA, D5/5/2002 Seattle, WA **1939** Was 10 (2) **1940**†Was☆11 (11, LG) **1941** Was 11 (1) **1942**†Was★11 (8, LG) **1943** Was☆6 (6, LG) **NFL** 49 (28) [5 yrs]																								
Farmer, Danny Daniel Steven, WR, 6´3˝/217 lbs; UCLA; 2000: Pit, rnd 4; B5/21/1977 Los Angeles, CA																								
2000	Cin	13(2)	—	—	—	—	19	268	14.1(38)	0	—	—	—	—	—	—	—	—	—	—	—	—	0	134
2001	Cin	12(1)	—	—	—	—	15	228	15.2(27)	1	—	—	—	—	—	—	—	—	—	—	p	—	6	125
2002	Cin	8(1)	—	—	—	—	9	115	12.8(51)	0	—	—	—	—	—	—	—	—	—	—	p	—	0	58
NFL	3	33(4)	—	—	—	—	43	611	14.2(51)	1	—	—	—	—	—	—	—	—	—	—	p	—	6	317
Farmer, Dave David W., RB, 6´0˝/205 lbs; USC; 1977: Atl, rnd 11; B5/20/1954 Phoenix, AZ **1978** TB 3																								
Farmer, George George Thaxton, WR, 6´4˝/214 lbs; UCLA; 1970: Chi, rnd 3; B4/19/1948 Chattanooga, TN																								
1970	ChiB	11(WR)	—	—	—	—	31	496	16.0(60)	2	—	—	—	—	—	—	—	—	—	—	—	—	12	258
1971	ChiB	14(WR)	1	11	11.0(11)	0	46	737	16.0(64)	5	—	—	—	—	—	—	—	—	—	—	—	—	30	405
1972	ChiB	14(WR)	2	-13	-6.5(-2)	0	14	380	27.1(85)	2	—	—	—	—	—	—	—	—	—	—	—	—	12	187
1973	ChiB	14(WR)	1	8	8.0(8)	0	15	219	14.6(25)	1	—	—	—	—	—	—	—	—	—	—	—	—	6	123
1974	ChiB	9	—	—	—	—	5	45	9.0(17)	0	—	—	—	—	—	—	—	—	—	—	—	—	0	23
1975	ChiB	2	—	—	—	—	2	32	16.0(17)	0	—	—	—	—	—	—	—	—	—	—	—	—	0	16
1975	Det	6(1)	—	—	—	—	6	86	14.3(22)	0	—	—	—	—	—	—	—	—	—	—	—	—	0	43
NFL	6	70(1)	4	6	1.5(11)	0	119	1995	16.8(85)	10	—	—	—	—	—	—	—	—	—	—	—	—	60	1054
Farmer, George George, WR, 5´10˝/175 lbs; Southern (LA); 1980: LA, rnd 9; B12/5/1958 Los Angeles, CA																								
1982	LARm	8(0)	—	—	—	—	17	344	20.2(42)	2	—	—	—	—	—	—	—	—	—	—	—	—	12	182
1983	†LARm	16(16, WR)	1	-9	-9.0(-9)	0	40	556	13.9(46)	5	—	—	—	—	—	—	—	—	—	—	—	—	30	294
1984	†LARm	14(0)	—	—	—	—	7	75	10.7(23)	0	—	—	—	—	—	—	—	—	—	—	—	—	0	38
1987	Mia	1(0)	—	—	—	—	1	5	5.0(5)	0	—	—	—	—	—	—	—	—	—	—	k	—	0	14
NFL	4	39(16)	1	-9	-9.0(-9)	0	65	980	15.1(46)	7	—	—	—	—	—	—	—	—	—	—	k	—	42	527
Farmer, Karl Karl Anthony, WR, 5´11˝/165 lbs; Pittsburgh; 1976: Atl, rnd 7; B8/28/1954 Oklahoma City, OK **1976** Atl 1 **1978** TB 2																								
1977	Atl	14	1	4	4.0(4)	0	2	39	19.5(23)	0	—	—	—	—	—	—	—	—	—	—	k	—	0	128
NFL	3	17	1	4	4.0(4)	0	2	39	19.5(23)	0	—	—	—	—	—	—	—	—	—	—	kp	—	0	123
Farmer, Lonnie Lonnie Wayne, LB, 6´0˝/220 lbs; Northwestern; Tennessee-Chattanooga; 1964: Bos, rnd 20; B3/28/1940 Steubenville, OH **1964** Bos-A 14 **1965** Bos-A 3 **1966** Bos-A 14 (RLB) **NFL** 31 [3 yrs]																								
Farmer, Ray Harvey Ray, LB, 6´3˝/225 lbs; Duke; 1996: Phi, rnd 4; B7/1/1974 White Plains, NY **1996** Phi 16 (11, LLB) **1997** Phi 14 (5, llb) **1998** Phi 2 (0) **NFL** 32 (16) [3 yrs]																								
Farmer, Robert Robert, RB, 5´11˝/217 lbs; Notre Dame; B3/4/1974 Lincoln, NE **1999** NYJ 13 (0)																								
Farmer, Roger Roger Anderson, WR, 6´3˝/195 lbs; Baker; B11/10/1955 Barbados **1979** NYJ 4																								
Farmer, Ted Clanton Carter, RB, 5´11˝/175 lbs; Oregon; B9/8/1953 St. Louis, MO																								
1978	SL	2	1	4	4.0(4)	0	—	—	—	—	—	—	—	—	—	—	—	—	—	—	—	—	0	4
Farmer, Tom Thomas Manduis, HB, 5´11˝/190 lbs; Iowa; 1943: Cle, rnd 2; B4/17/1921 Cedar Rapids, IA, D7/1/1980 Iowa City, IA																								
1946	LARm	8(1)	28	90	3.2(17)	1	6	17	2.8(13)	0	2	0	0.0	0	0.0	0	0	—	—	—	kp	—	6	198
1947	Was	10(6, RH)	15	29	1.9(9)	1	8	137	17.1(31)	0	—	—	—	—	—	—	—	—	—	—	ki	—	6	163
1948	Was	9(5, LH)	52	188	3.6(17)	1	12	148	12.3(48)	2	—	—	—	—	—	—	—	—	—	—	kp	—	18	368
NFL	3	27(12)	95	307	3.2(17)	3	26	302	11.6(48)	2	2	0	0.0	0	0.0	0	0	—	—	—	kpi	—	30	728
Farquhar, John John Christian Mowat, TE, 6´6˝/278 lbs; Duke; B3/22/1972 Stanford, CA **1996** TB 1 (0) **1996**†Pit 4 (0)																								
1997	NO	11(8, te)	—	—	—	—	17	253	14.9(42)	1	—	—	—	—	—	—	—	—	—	—	—	—	6	132
1998	NO	5(0)	—	—	—	—	1	13	13.0(13)	0	—	—	—	—	—	—	—	—	—	—	—	—	0	7
NFL	3	21(8)	—	—	—	—	18	266	14.8(42)	1	—	—	—	—	—	—	—	—	—	—	—	—	6	138
Farr, D'Marco D'Marco Marcellus, DT, 6´1˝/276 lbs; Washington; B6/9/1971 San Pablo, CA **1994** LARm 10 (3) **1995** SL 16 (16, RDT) **1996** SL 16 (16, RDT) **1997** SL 16 (16, RDT) **1998** SL 16 (16, RDT) **1999**†SL 16 (16, RDT) **2000**†SL 10 (5, rdt) **NFL** 100 (88) [7 yrs]																								
Farr, Mel Melvin, RB, 6´2˝/210 lbs; UCLA; 1967: Det, rnd 1; B11/3/1944 Beaumont, TX																								
1967	Det✧	13(FB)	206	860	4.2(57)	3	39	317	8.1(31)	3	2	0	0.0	0	0.0	0	0	—	—	—	—	—	36	1064
1968	Det	9(HB)	128	597	4.7(46)	3	24	375	15.6(86)	4	—	—	—	—	—	—	—	—	—	—	—	—	42	835
1969	Det	5(hb)	58	245	4.2(52)	4	13	94	7.2(24)	0	1	0	0.0	0	0.0	0	0	—	—	—	—	—	24	332
1970	†Det★	12(FB)	166	717	4.3(36)	9	29	213	7.3(58)	2	—	—	—	—	—	—	—	—	—	—	—	—	66	924
1971	Det	9	22	64	2.9(14)	0	5	60	12.0(39)	1	—	—	—	—	—	—	—	—	—	—	—	—	6	99
1972	Det	10	62	216	3.5(22)	3	10	132	13.2(42)	0	—	—	—	—	—	—	—	—	—	—	—	—	18	312
1973	Det	11	97	373	3.8(32)	4	26	183	7.0(27)	0	—	—	—	—	—	—	—	—	—	—	—	—	24	505
NFL	7	69	739	3072	4.2(57)	26	146	1374	9.4(86)	10	3	0	0.0	0	0.0	0	0	—	—	—	—	—	216	4069
Farr, Mel Melvin, RB, 6´0˝/222 lbs; UCLA; 1988: Den, rnd 9; B8/12/1966 Santa Monica, CA **1989**†LARm 1 (0)																								
Farr, Mike Michael Anthony, WR, 5´10˝/192 lbs; UCLA; B8/8/1967 Santa Monica, CA																								
1990	Det	12(8, wr)	—	—	—	—	12	170	14.2(44)	0	—	—	—	—	—	—	—	—	—	—	—	—	0	85
1991	†Det	16(13, WR)	—	—	—	—	42	431	10.3(34)	1	—	—	—	—	—	—	—	—	—	—	—	—	6	221
1992	Det	14(9, WR)	—	—	—	—	15	115	7.7(14)	0	—	—	—	—	—	—	—	—	—	—	—	—	0	58
NFL	3	42(30)	—	—	—	—	69	716	10.4(44)	1	—	—	—	—	—	—	—	—	—	—	—	—	6	363
Farr, Miller Miller, DB, 6´1˝/190 lbs; Wichita State; 1965: Den, rnd R1; B4/8/1943 Beaumont, TX [I] **1965** Den-A 7 (LS) **1965**†SD-A 3 **1966** SD-A 14 (LCB) **1967**†Hou-A★14 (LCB) **1968** Hou-A★14 (LCB) **1969**†Hou-A★14 (LCB) **1970** SL 14 (LCB) **1971** SL 14 (LCB) **1972** SL 13 (RCB) **1973** Det 6 **NFL** 113 [9 yrs]																								
Farragut, Ken Kenneth David, C-LB, 6´4˝/240 lbs; Mississippi; 1951: Phi, rnd 6; B12/23/1928 Ponchatoula, LA **1951** Phi 11 (LLB) **1952** Phi 12 (C) **1953** Phi✧12 (C) **1954** Phi 8 **NFL** 43 [4 yrs]																								
Farrar, Venice Venice, G-BB, 5´10˝/200 lbs; North Carolina State; B12/22/1910 Youngstown, OH, D1/1/1973 Youngstown, OH **1938** Pit 1 (0) **1939** Pit 6 (0) **NFL** 7 (0) [2 yrs]																								
Farrell, Scrapper Edward Francis, FB, 5´9˝/204 lbs; Muhlenberg; B7/12/1915 Catasauqua, PA, D4/16/1986 Lebanon, PA																								
1938	Pit	5(2)	46	176	3.8	0	—	—	—	—	—	—	—	—	—	—	—	—	—	—	—	—	0	176
1938	Bkn	7(5, FB)	63	249	4.0	3	—	—	—	—	2	0	0.0	0	0.0	0	1	—	—	—	—	—	18	239
1939	Bkn	2(0)	—	—	—	—	—	—	—	—	—	—	—	—	—	—	—	—	—	—	—	—	—	—
NFL	2	14(7)	109	425	3.9	3	—	—	—	—	2	0	0.0	0	0.0	0	1	—	—	—	—	—	18	415
Farrell, Sean Sean Ward, G-T, 6´3˝/260 lbs; Penn State; 1982: TB, rnd 1; B5/25/1960 Southampton, NY **1982**†TB 9 (7, RT/rg) **1983** TB 10 (9, RG) **1984** TB☆15 (14, RG) **1985** TB 14 (14, RG) **1986** TB 16 (15, RG) **1987** NE 14 (14, LG) **1989** NE 14 (14, LG) **1990** Den 5 (0) **1991**†Den 5 (4) **1992** Sea 6 (0)																								
1988	NE	15(15, LG)	—	—	—	—	1	4	4.0(4)	0	—	—	—	—	—	—	—	—	—	—	—	—	0	2
NFL	11	123(106)	—	—	—	—	1	4	4.0(4)	0	—	—	—	—	—	—	—	—	—	—	—	—	0	2
Farren, Paul Paul Vincent, T-G, 6´5˝/272 lbs; Boston University; 1983: Cle, rnd 12; B12/24/1960 Weymouth, MA **1983** Cle 16 (0) **1984** Cle 15 (6, rt) **1985** Cle 13 (13, LT) **1986** Cle 16 (16, LT/lg) **1987** Cle 12 (12, LT) **1988** Cle 15 (15, LT) **1989** Cle 16 (13, LT) **1990** Cle 16 (16, LT) **1991** Cle 13 (0) **NFL** 132 (91) [9 yrs]																								
Farrier, Curt Curtis James, DT, 6´6˝/264 lbs; Montana State; 1963: KC, rnd 10/LA, rnd 10; B6/25/1941 Yakima, WA **1963** KC-A 5 **1964** KC-A 14 **1965** KC-A 8 **NFL** 27 [3 yrs]																								
Farrington, Bo John R., SE-WR, 6´3˝/217 lbs; Prairie View A&M; 1960: Chi, rnd 16/Bos, rnd 2; B1/18/1936 DeWalt, TX, D7/26/1964 Rensselaer, IN																								
1960	ChiB	6	1	-2	-2.0(-2)	0	—	—	—	—	—	—	—	—	—	—	—	—	—	—	—	—	0	-2
1961	ChiB	11(SE)	—	—	—	—	21	349	16.6(**98**)	4	—	—	—	—	—	—	—	—	—	—	—	—	24	195
1962	ChiB	14(SE)	—	—	—	—	13	197	15.2(51)	1	—	—	—	—	—	—	—	—	—	—	—	—	6	104
1963	†ChiB	14(SE)	—	—	—	—	21	335	16.0(58)	2	—	—	—	—	—	—	—	—	—	—	—	—	12	178
NFL	4	45	1	-2	-2.0(-2)	0	55	881	16.0(98)	7	—	—	—	—	—	—	—	—	—	—	—	—	42	474
Farrior, James James Alfred, LB, 6´2˝/242 lbs; Virginia; 1997: NYJ, rnd 1; B1/6/1975 Richmond, VA **1997** NYJ 16 (15, ROLB) **1998**†NYJ 12 (2) **1999** NYJ 16 (4) **2000** NYJ 16 (6, rolb) **2001**†NYJ 16 (16, RLB) **2002**†Pit 14 (14, RILB) **2003** Pit 16 (16, LILB) **2004**†Pit★16 (16, LILB) **2005**†Pit 14 (14, LILB) **NFL** 136 (103) [9 yrs]																								

YEAR	TEAM	G (GS, POS)	RUSH	YD	AVG(LG)	TD	REC	YD	AVG(LG)	TD	PASS COMP	PCT	YD	AVG(LG)	TD	INT	SK	YD	QBR	KPR	OTD	PTS	TAY

FARRIS, JIMMY James Robert, WR, 6'0"/200 lbs; Montana; B4/13/1978 Lewiston, ID

2003	Atl	16(0)	—	—	—	—	6	100	16.7(42)	2	—	—	—	—	—	—	—	—	—	—	—	12	60
2004	Atl	14(0)	—	—	—	—	—	—	—	—	—	—	—	—	—	—	—	—	—	—	—		
2005	†Was	4(0)	—	—	—	—	1	18	18.0(18)	0	—	—	—	—	—	—	—	—	—	—	—	0	9
NFL	3	34(0)	—	—	—	—	7	118	16.9(42)	2	—	—	—	—	—	—	—	—	—	—	—	12	69

FARRIS, JOHN John Speed, G, 6'4"/245 lbs; San Diego State; 1964: SD, rnd 17/LA, rnd 11; B11/2/1943 Kansas City, MO   **1965**†SD-A 14 **1966** SD-A 14 **NFL** 28 [2 yrs]

FARRIS, KRIS Kristofer Martin, T, 6'8"/318 lbs; UCLA; 1999: Pit, rnd 3; B3/26/1977 St. Paul, MN   **2001** Buf 3 (1)

FARRIS, TOM Thomas George, QB, 6'1"/185 lbs; Wisconsin; 1942: GB, rnd 11; B9/16/1920 Casper, WY, D11/16/2002 Citrus Heights, CA

1946	†ChiB	11(3)	12	-11	-0.9(6)	0	1	16	16.0(16)	0	21	8	38.1	108	5.1(20)	1	2	—	—	—	kpi	—	0	5
1947	ChiB	9(0)	1	-3	-3.0(-3)	0	—	—	—	—	—	—	—	0	0.0	0	—	—	—	—	i	—	0	-6
NFL	2	20(3)	13	-14	-1.1(6)	0	1	16	16.0(16)	0	23	8	34.8	108	4.7(20)	1	2	—	—	—	kpi	—	0	-1
1948	ChiR-A	13(0)	4	5	1.3	0	—	—	—	—	9	3	33.3	24	2.7	0	3	—	—	—	—	—	0	-103

FARYNIARZ, BRETT Brett Allen, LB, 6'3"/230 lbs; San Diego State; B7/23/1965 Carmichael, CA   **1988**†LARm 15 (0)   **1989**†LARm 16 (0)   **1990** LARm 16 (3) **1991** LARm 12 (8, LLB) **1993** SF 2 (0) **1994** Hou 16 (0) **1995** Car 15 (1) **NFL** 92 (12) [7 yrs]

FARWELL, HEATH Heath, LB, 6'0"/235 lbs; San Diego State; B12/31/1981 Corona, CA   **2005** Min 7 (0)

FASANI, RANDY Randy Mark, QB, 6'3"/234 lbs; Stanford; 2002: Car, rnd 5; B9/18/1978 Granite City, CA

| 2002 | Car | 4(1) | 18 | 95 | 5.3(19) | 0 | — | — | — | — | 44 | 15 | 34.1 | 171 | 3.9(27) | 0 | 4 | 7 | 60 | — | — | — | 0 | 21 |

FASON, CIATRICK Ciatrick Antione, RB, 6'1"/207 lbs; Florida; 2005: Min, rnd 4; B10/29/1982 Atlanta, GA

| 2005 | Min | 13(0) | 32 | 62 | 1.9(15) | 4 | — | — | — | — | — | — | — | — | — | — | — | — | — | — | k | — | 24 | 76 |

FATAFEHI, MARIO Mario, DT, 6'2"/300 lbs; Kansas State; 2001: Arz, rnd 5; B1/27/1979 Chicago, IL   **2001** Arz 7 (1) **2002** Car 6 (0) **2003**†Den 16 (9, LDT) **2004**†Den 16 (16, LDT) **NFL** 45 (26) [4 yrs]

FAUCETTE, CHUCK Charles, LB, 6'3"/242 lbs; Maryland; 1987: NYG, rnd 10; B10/7/1963 Levittown, PA   **1987** SD 2 (1) **1988** SD 8 (8, LILB) **NFL** 10 (9) [2 yrs]

FAULK, KEVIN Kevin Tony, RB, 5'8"/202 lbs; LSU; 1999: NE, rnd 2; B6/5/1976 Lafayette, LA **[R]**

1999	NE	11(2)	67	227	3.4(43)	1	12	98	8.2(19)	1	—	—	—	—	—	—	—	—	—	—	kp	—	12	689
2000	NE	16(9, RB)	164	570	3.5(18)	4	51	465	9.1(52)	1	—	—	—	—	—	—	—	—	—	—	kp	—	32	1122
2001	†NE	15(1)	41	169	4.1(24)	1	30	189	6.3(28)	2	1	1	100.0	23	23.0(23)	0	0	—	—	—	kp	—	18	469
2002	NE	15(0)	52	271	5.2(45)	2	37	379	10.2(36)	3	1	0	0.0	0	0.0	0	0	—	—	—	kp	2	42	876
2003	†NE	15(8, RB)	178	638	3.6(23)	0	48	440	9.2(27)	0	1	0	0.0	0	0.0	0	0	—	—	—	kp	—	0	956
2004	†NE	11(1)	54	255	4.7(20)	2	26	248	9.5(31)	1	—	—	—	—	—	—	—	—	—	—	kp	—	18	450
2005	†NE	8(2)	51	145	2.8(13)	0	29	260	9.0(23)	0	—	—	—	—	—	—	—	—	—	—	k	—	0	296
NFL	7	91(23)	607	2275	3.7(45)	10	233	2079	8.9(52)	8	3	1	33.3	23	7.7(23)	0	0	—	—	—	kp	2	122	4857

FAULK, LARRY see Abdul Salaam

FAULK, MARSHALL Marshall William, RB, 5'10"/211 lbs; San Diego State; 1994: Ind, rnd 1; B2/26/1973 New Orleans, LA

1994	Ind★	16(16, RB)	314	1282	4.1(52)	11	52	522	10.0(85)	1	—	—	—	—	—	—	—	—	—	—	—	—	72	1658
1995	†Ind★	16(16, RB)	289	1078	3.7(40)	11	56	475	8.5(34)	3	—	—	—	—	—	—	—	—	—	—	—	—	84	1441
1996	†Ind	13(13, RB)	198	587	3.0(43)	7	56	428	7.6(30)	0	—	—	—	—	—	—	—	—	—	—	—	—	42	871
1997	Ind	16(16, RB)	264	1054	4.0(45)	7	47	471	10.0(58)	1	—	—	—	—	—	—	—	—	—	—	—	—	48	1365
1998	Ind★	16(15, RB)	324	1319	4.1(68)	6	86	908	10.6(78)	4	—	—	—	—	—	—	—	—	—	—	—	—	60	1853
1999	†SL★	16(16, RB)	253	1381	**5.5(58)**	7	87	1048	12.0(57)	5	1	0	0.0	0	0.0	0	0	—	—	—	—	—	74	**2000**
2000	†SL★	14(14, RB)	253	1359	5.4(36)	**18**	81	830	10.2(72)	8	—	—	—	—	—	—	—	—	—	—	k	—	**160**	1997
2001	†SL★	14(14, RB)	260	1382	5.3(71)	**12**	83	765	9.2(45)	9	1	0	0.0	0	0.0	0	0	—	—	—	—	—	**128**	1930
2002	SL◇	14(10, RB)	212	953	4.5(44)	8	80	537	6.7(40)	2	—	—	—	—	—	—	—	—	—	—	—	—	60	1312
2003	†SL	11(11, RB)	209	818	3.9(52)	10	45	290	6.4(30)	1	—	—	—	—	—	—	—	—	—	—	—	—	66	1068
2004	†SL	14(14, RB)	195	774	4.0(40)	3	50	310	6.2(25)	1	—	—	—	—	—	—	—	—	—	—	k	—	28	949
2005	SL	16(1)	65	292	4.5(20)	0	44	291	6.6(18)	1	—	—	—	—	—	—	—	—	—	—	—	—	8	443
NFL	12	176(156)	2836	12279	4.3(71)	100	767	6875	9.0(85)	36	2	0	0.0	0	0.0	0	0	—	—	—	k	—	830	16885

FAULK, TREV Treverance Donta, LB, 6'3"/254 lbs; LSU; B8/6/1981 Lafayette, LA   **2004**†SL 13 (2) **2005** SL 16 (5, mlb) **NFL** 29 (7) [2 yrs]

FAULKERSON, MIKE Michael Wayne, aka Mike Dulaney, RB, 6'0"/245 lbs; North Carolina; B9/9/1970 Kingsport, TN   **1997** ChiB 7 (0) **1998** Car 8 (0)

1995	ChiB	5(1)	—	—	—	—	2	22	11.0(12)	0	—	—	—	—	—	—	—	—	—	—	—	—	0	11
1996	ChiB	16(0)	—	—	—	—	1	1	1.0(1)	1	—	—	—	—	—	—	—	—	—	—	k	—	6	9
NFL	4	36(1)	—	—	—	—	3	23	7.7(12)	1	—	—	—	—	—	—	—	—	—	—	kp	—	6	15

FAULKNER, CHRIS Christopher Alan, TE, 6'4"/255 lbs; Florida; 1983: Dal, rnd 4; B4/13/1960 Tipton, IN

1984	LARm	8(0)	—	—	—	—	1	6	6.0(6)	0	—	—	—	—	—	—	—	—	—	—	—	—	0	3
1985	SD	9(0)	—	—	—	—	1	12	12.0(12)	0	—	—	—	—	—	—	—	—	—	—	—	—	0	6
NFL	2	17(0)	—	—	—	—	2	18	9.0(12)	0	—	—	—	—	—	—	—	—	—	—	—	—	0	9

FAULKNER, JEFF Jeffrey E., DE-DT, 6'4"/305 lbs; Southern (LA); B4/4/1964 St. Thomas, Virgin Islands   **1987** KC 3 (1) **1990** Ind 7 (0) **1991** Phx 16 (14, LDE) **1992** Phx 16 (14) **1993** Was 5 (3) **1996** NYJ 4 (0) **NFL** 52 (23) [6 yrs]

FAULKNER, STALEY Staley, T, 6'3"/245 lbs; Texas; 1963: Hou, rnd 21/Cle, rnd 14; B4/2/1941 Pampa, TX   **1964** Hou-A 1

FAUMUI, TA'ASE Ta'ase, DE, 6'3"/278 lbs; Hawaii; 1994: Pit, rnd 4; B3/19/1971 Western Samoa   **1994** Pit 5 (0) **1995** Pit 3 (0) **NFL** 8 (0) [2 yrs]

FAUMUINA, WILSON Wilson, DT-DE-NT, 6'5"/275 lbs; San Jose State; 1977: Atl, rnd 1; B8/11/1954 American Samoa   **1977** Atl 14 **1978**†Atl 16 **1979** Atl 14 (14, LDT) **1980**†Atl 14 (4) **1981** Atl 16 (6, rde) **NFL** 74 (24) [5 yrs]

FAURIA, CHRISTIAN Christian Ashley, TE, 6'4"/250 lbs; Colorado; 1995: Sea, rnd 2; B9/22/1971 Northridge, CA

1995	Sea	14(9, TE)	—	—	—	—	17	181	10.6(20)	1	—	—	—	—	—	—	—	—	—	—	—	—	6	96
1996	Sea	10(9, TE)	—	—	—	—	18	214	11.9(23)	1	—	—	—	—	—	—	—	—	—	—	k	—	6	105
1997	Sea	16(3)	—	—	—	—	10	110	11.0(25)	0	—	—	—	—	—	—	—	—	—	—	—	—	0	55
1998	Sea	16(15, TE)	—	—	—	—	37	377	10.2(25)	2	—	—	—	—	—	—	—	—	—	—	k	—	12	184
1999	†Sea	16(16, TE)	—	—	—	—	35	376	10.7(25)	0	—	—	—	—	—	—	—	—	—	—	k	—	0	173
2000	Sea	15(10, TE)	—	—	—	—	28	237	8.5(16)	2	—	—	—	—	—	—	—	—	—	—	k	—	12	123
2001	Sea	16(11, TE)	—	—	—	—	21	188	9.0(30)	1	—	—	—	—	—	—	—	—	—	—	k	—	8	84
2002	NE	16(13, TE)	—	—	—	—	27	253	9.4(33)	7	—	—	—	—	—	—	—	—	—	—	—	—	44	162
2003	†NE	16(12, TE)	—	—	—	—	28	285	10.2(28)	2	—	—	—	—	—	—	—	—	—	—	—	—	12	153
2004	NE	16(10, te)	—	—	—	—	16	195	12.2(25)	2	—	—	—	—	—	—	—	—	—	—	—	—	12	108
2005	†NE	16(10, TE)	—	—	—	—	8	57	7.1(18)	2	—	—	—	—	—	—	—	—	—	—	—	—	12	39
NFL	11	167(118)	—	—	—	—	245	2473	10.1(33)	20	—	—	—	—	—	—	—	—	—	—	k	—	124	1279

FAUROT, RON Ronald Edward, DE-DT, 6'7"/262 lbs; Arkansas; 1984: NYJ, rnd 1; B1/27/1962 Wichita, KS   **1984** NYJ 15 (9, RDE) **1985** NYJ 5 (4) **NFL** 20 (13) [2 yrs]

FAUSCH, FRANK Franklin Leo, FB-T, 6'3"/250 lbs; Kalamazoo; B6/13/1895 Goshen, IN, deceased **[C]**   **1921** Evv 4 (4, FB), 18 **1922** Evv 3 (3, RT) **NFL** 7 (7) [2 yrs]

FAUST, DICK Richard A., T-G-E, 6'1"/208 lbs; Otterbein; B1903; D4/15/1955   **1924** Day 1 (0) **1928** Day 7 (5, rt) **1929** Day 6 (5, RT) **NFL** 14 (10) [3 yrs]

FAUST, GEORGE George John, BB, 6'1"/205 lbs; Minnesota; 1939: ChiC, rnd 6; B9/28/1917 Parkston, SD, D5/28/1993 Edina, MN **[K]**

| 1939 | ChiC | 9(6, bb) | 22 | 71 | 3.2 | 0 | 4 | 85 | 21.3 | 0 | 0 | 0 | — | 0 | — | 0 | 1 | — | — | — | KP | — | 1 | 74 |

FAUST, PAUL Paul Timothy, LB, 6'1"/225 lbs; Minnesota; B7/23/1943 Minneapolis, MN   **1967** Min 1

FAVERTY, HAL Harold Edward, LB-DE-C, 6'2"/220 lbs; Wisconsin; 1949: ChiB, rnd 15; B9/26/1927 Hammond, IN   **1952** GB 11

FAVORS, GREG Gregory Bernard, LB-DE, 6'1"/242 lbs; Mississippi State; 1998: KC, rnd 4; B9/30/1974 Atlanta, GA   **1998** KC 16 (4) **1999**†Ten 15 (0) **2000**†Ten 16 (15, LLB) **2001** Ten 16 (12, LLB) **2002** Buf 6 (0) **2003**†Car 16 (12, LLB) **2004** Jax 15 (10, RDE) **2005**†Jax 1 (0) **NFL** 101 (53) [8 yrs]

FAVRE, BRETT Brett Lorenzo, QB, 6´2˝/225 lbs; Southern Mississippi; 1991: Atl, rnd 2; B10/10/1969 Gulfport, MS

YEAR	TEAM	G (GS, POS)	RUSH	YD	AVG (LG)	TD	REC	YD	AVG (LG)	TD	PASS	COMP	PCT	YD	AVG (LG)	TD	INT	SK	YD	QBR	KPR	OTD	PTS	TAY
1991	Atl	2(0)	—	—	—	—	—	—	—	—	5	0	0.0	0	0.0	0	2	1	11	—	—	—	0	-80
1992	GB✧	15(13, QB)	47	198	4.2(19)	1	1	-7	-7.0(-7)	0	471	**302**	64.1	3227	6.9(76)	18	13	34	208	85.3	—	—	6	1388
1993	†GB✧	16(16, QB)	58	216	3.7(27)	1	—	—	—	—	**522**	**318**	60.9	3303	6.3(66)	19	**24**	30	199	72.2	—	—	6	1013
1994	†GB	16(16, QB)	42	202	4.8(36)	2	—	—	—	—	582	363	62.4	3882	6.7(49)	33	14	31	188	90.7	—	—	12	1768
1995	†GB★	16(16, QB)	39	181	4.6(40)	3	—	—	—	—	570	359	63.0	**4413**	7.7(**99**)	**38**	13	33	217	**99.5**	—	—	18	2088
1996	†GB★	16(16, QB)	49	136	2.8(23)	2	—	—	—	—	**543**	**325**	59.9	**3899**	7.2(80)	**39**	13	40	241	95.8	—	—	12	**1781**
1997	†GB★	16(16, QB)	58	187	3.2(16)	1	—	—	—	—	513	**304**	59.3	**3867**	7.5(74)	**35**	16	25	176	92.6	—	—	6	1666
1998	†GB	16(16, QB)	40	133	3.3(35)	1	—	—	—	—	**551**	**347**	**63.0**	**4212**	7.6(84)	31	**23**	38	223	87.8	—	—	6	1484
1999	GB	16(16, QB)	28	142	5.1(20)	0	—	—	—	—	**595**	341	57.3	4091	6.9(74)	22	23	35	223	74.7	—	—	0	1378
2000	GB	16(16, QB)	27	108	4.0(18)	0	—	—	—	—	**580**	338	58.3	3812	6.6(67)	20	16	33	236	78.0	—	—	0	1474
2001	†GB★	16(16, QB)	38	56	1.5(14)	1	—	—	—	—	510	314	61.6	3921	7.7(67)	32	15	22	151	94.1	—	—	6	1587
2002	†GB★	16(16, QB)	25	73	2.9(17)	0	—	—	—	—	**551**	**341**	61.9	3658	6.6(**85**)	**27**	16	26	188	85.6	—	—	0	1397
2003	†GB★	16(16, QB)	18	15	0.8(7)	0	—	—	—	—	471	308	**65.4**	3361	7.1(66)	**32**	21	19	137	90.4	—	—	0	1016
2004	†GB	16(16, QB)	16	36	2.3(17)	0	—	—	—	—	540	346	64.1	4088	7.6(79)	30	17	12	93	92.4	—	—	0	1550
2005	GB	16(16, QB)	18	62	3.4(20)	0	—	—	—	—	**607**	**372**	61.3	**3881**	6.4(59)	20	**29**	24	170	70.9	—	—	0	943
NFL	15	225(221)	503	1745	3.5(40)	12	1	-7	-7.0(-7)	0	7611	4678	61.5	53615	7.0(99)	396	255	403	2661	86.0	—	—	72	20449

FAVRON, CALVIN Calvin Joseph, LB, 6´1˝/225 lbs; Southeastern Louisiana; 1979: SL, rnd 2; B7/3/1957 New Orleans, LA, D4/19/1999 Baton Rouge, LA **1979** SL 16 (7, rolb) **1980** SL 16 (7, lilb) **1981** SL 14 (7, lolb) **1982** SL 4 (0) **NFL** 50 (21) [4 yrs]

FAWCETT, JAKE Jacob Robert, T-G, 5´11˝/223 lbs; SMU; B5/29/1919 Hillsboro, TX, D6/1979 San Antonio, TX **1942** Cle 10 (0) **1943** Bkn 10 (10, LG) **1946** LARm 4 (0)

YEAR	TEAM	G (GS, POS)	RUSH	YD	AVG (LG)	TD	REC	YD	AVG (LG)	TD	PASS	COMP	PCT	YD	AVG (LG)	TD	INT	SK	YD	QBR	KPR	OTD	PTS	TAY
1944	Cle	10(10, RT)	—	—	—	—	1	9	9.0(9)	0	—	—	—	—	—	—	—	—	—	—	k	—	0	-24
NFL	4	34(20)	—	—	—	—	1	9	9.0(9)	0	—	—	—	—	—	—	—	—	—	—	ki	—	0	-24

FAY, DOC Allen, E, /175 lbs; Marquette **1922** GB 1 (0)

FAYLOR, JOHN John Joseph, DB, 6´1˝/197 lbs; Santa Clara; B2/10/1963 South Bend, IN **1987** SF 3 (0)

FAZANDE, JERMAINE Jermaine Keith, RB, 6´2˝/255 lbs; Oklahoma; 1999: SD, rnd 2; B1/14/1975 Marrero, LA

YEAR	TEAM	G (GS, POS)	RUSH	YD	AVG (LG)	TD	REC	YD	AVG (LG)	TD	PASS	COMP	PCT	YD	AVG (LG)	TD	INT	SK	YD	QBR	KPR	OTD	PTS	TAY
1999	SD	7(3)	91	365	4.0(54)	2	—	—	—	—	—	—	—	—	—	—	—	—	—	—	—	—	12	385
2000	SD	13(7, RB)	119	368	3.1(26)	2	16	104	6.5(17)	0	—	—	—	—	—	—	—	—	—	—	—	—	12	440
NFL	2	20(10)	210	733	3.5(54)	4	16	104	6.5(17)	0	—	—	—	—	—	—	—	—	—	—	—	—	24	825

FAZIO, RON Ronald Anthony, TE, 6´4˝/242 lbs; Maryland; B6/5/1962 Meadowbrook, PA **1987** Phi 1 (0)

FEACHER, RICKY Ivory Ricky, WR, 5´10˝/174 lbs; Mississippi Valley State; 1976: NE, rnd 10; B2/11/1954 Crystal River, FL

YEAR	TEAM	G (GS, POS)	RUSH	YD	AVG (LG)	TD	REC	YD	AVG (LG)	TD	PASS	COMP	PCT	YD	AVG (LG)	TD	INT	SK	YD	QBR	KPR	OTD	PTS	TAY
1976	NE	3	—	—	—	—	2	38	19.0(21)	0	—	—	—	—	—	—	—	—	—	—	k	—	0	109
1976	Cle	10	—	—	—	—	—	—	—	—	—	—	—	—	—	—	—	—	—	—	kp	—	0	178
1977	Cle	14	—	—	—	—	—	—	—	—	—	—	—	—	—	—	—	—	—	—	kp	—	0	59
1978	Cle	16(1)	—	—	—	—	4	76	19.0(42)	0	—	—	—	—	—	—	—	—	—	—	—	—	0	38
1979	Cle	16	1	-1	-1.0(-1)	0	7	103	14.7(25)	1	—	—	—	—	—	—	—	—	—	—	k	—	6	77
1980	†Cle	16(0)	—	—	—	—	10	244	24.4(55)	4	—	—	—	—	—	—	—	—	—	—	—	—	24	142
1981	Cle	16(7, wr)	1	-1	-1.0(-1)	0	29	654	22.6(48)	3	—	—	—	—	—	—	—	—	—	—	—	—	18	341
1982	†Cle	9(9, WR)	—	—	—	—	28	408	14.6(46)	3	—	—	—	—	—	—	—	—	—	—	—	—	18	219
1983	Cle	9(5, wr)	—	—	—	—	13	217	16.7(42)	3	—	—	—	—	—	—	—	—	—	—	—	—	18	124
1984	Cle	16(3)	—	—	—	—	22	382	17.4(64)	1	—	—	—	—	—	—	—	—	—	—	—	—	6	196
NFL	9	125(25)	2	-2	-1.0(-1)	0	115	2122	18.5(64)	15	—	—	—	—	—	—	—	—	—	—	kp	—	90	1482

FEAGIN, WILEY Thomas Wiley, G, 6´2˝/235 lbs; Texas; Houston; B8/28/1937 Conroe, TX **1961** Bal 14 **1962** Bal 14 **1963** Was 2 **NFL** 30 [3 yrs]

FEAGLES, JEFF Jeffrey Allan, P, 6´1˝/215 lbs; Miami (FL); B3/7/1966 Anaheim, CA **[KP]**

YEAR	TEAM	G (GS, POS)	RUSH	YD	AVG (LG)	TD	REC	YD	AVG (LG)	TD	PASS	COMP	PCT	YD	AVG (LG)	TD	INT	SK	YD	QBR	KPR	OTD	PTS	TAY
1988	NE	16(0)	1	0	0.0(0)	0	—	—	—	—	—	—	—	—	—	—	—	—	—	—	P	—	0	0
1989	NE	16(0)	—	—	—	—	—	—	—	—	2	0	0.0	0	0.0	0	0	—	—	—	P	—	0	0
1990	†Phi	16(0)	2	3	1.5(3)	0	—	—	—	—	1	0	0.0	0	0.0	0	0	—	—	—	P	—	0	3
1991	Phi	16(0)	3	-1	-0.3(11)	0	—	—	—	—	—	—	—	—	—	—	—	—	—	—	P	—	0	-1
1992	†Phi	16(0)	—	—	—	—	—	—	—	—	—	—	—	—	—	—	—	—	—	—	P	—	0	0
1993	Phi	16(0)	2	6	3.0(6)	0	—	—	—	—	—	—	—	—	—	—	—	—	—	—	P	—	0	6
1994	Arz	16(0)	2	8	4.0(12)	0	—	—	—	—	—	—	—	—	—	—	—	—	—	—	P	—	0	8
1995	Arz★	16(0)	2	4	2.0(4)	0	—	—	—	—	—	—	—	—	—	—	—	—	—	—	P	—	0	4
1996	Arz	16(0)	1	0	0.0(0)	0	—	—	—	—	—	—	—	—	—	—	—	—	—	—	P	—	0	0
1997	Arz	16(0)	—	—	—	—	—	—	—	—	—	—	—	—	—	—	—	—	—	—	P	—	0	0
1998	Sea	16(0)	—	—	—	—	—	—	—	—	—	—	—	—	—	—	—	—	—	—	P	—	0	0
1999	†Sea	16(0)	2	0	0.0(0)	0	—	—	—	—	—	—	—	—	—	—	—	—	—	—	P	—	0	0
2000	Sea	16(0)	—	—	—	—	—	—	—	—	1	0	0.0	0	0.0	0	0	—	—	—	P	—	0	0
2001	Sea	16(0)	—	—	—	—	—	—	—	—	2	0	0.0	0	0.0	0	0	—	—	—	P	—	0	0
2002	Sea	16(0)	2	-23	-11.5(-8)	0	—	—	—	—	—	—	—	—	—	—	—	—	—	—	P	—	0	-23
2003	NYG	16(0)	1	0	0.0(0)	0	—	—	—	—	—	—	—	—	—	—	—	—	—	—	KP	—	0	0
2004	NYG	16(0)	—	—	—	—	—	—	—	—	1	0	0.0	0	0.0	0	0	—	—	—	P	—	0	0
2005	†NYG	16(0)	—	—	—	—	—	—	—	—	—	—	—	—	—	—	—	—	—	—	P	—	0	0
NFL	18	288(0)	18	-3	-0.2(12)	0	—	—	—	—	7	0	0.0	0	0.0	0	0	—	—	—	KP	—	0	-3

FEAMSTER, TOM Thomas Ofey, T-DE, 6´7˝/260 lbs; William & Mary; Florida State; 1955: LA, rnd 4; B10/23/1930 Warwick, VA **[K]** **1956** Bal 12

FEARS, TOM Thomas Jesse, E, 6´2˝/216 lbs; Santa Clara; UCLA; 1945: Cle, rnd 11; B12/3/1923 Los Angeles, CA, D1/4/2000 Palm Desert, CA; HOF 1970 **[KC]**

YEAR	TEAM	G (GS, POS)	RUSH	YD	AVG (LG)	TD	REC	YD	AVG (LG)	TD	PASS	COMP	PCT	YD	AVG (LG)	TD	INT	SK	YD	QBR	KPR	OTD	PTS	TAY
1948	LARm☆	12(1, le)	2	8	4.0(8)	0	**51**	698	13.7(80)	4	—	—	—	—	—	—	—	—	—	—	i	1	30	414
1949	†LARm☆	12(10, LE)	1	-3	-3.0(-3)	0	**77**	1013	13.2(51)	**9**	—	—	—	—	—	—	—	—	—	—	—	—	54	549
1950	†LARm★	12(LE)	—	—	—	—	**84**	**1116**	13.3(53)	7	—	—	—	—	—	—	—	—	—	—	—	—	42	593
1951	†LARm☆	7(LE)	—	—	—	—	32	528	16.5(54)	3	—	—	—	—	—	—	—	—	—	—	K	—	24	279
1952	†LARm	12(RE)	1	0	0.0(0)	0	48	600	12.5(36)	6	—	—	—	—	—	—	—	—	—	—	—	—	36	330
1953	LARm	8(FL)	—	—	—	—	23	278	12.1(31)	4	—	—	—	—	—	—	—	—	—	—	K	—	32	159
1954	LARm	10(FL)	1	10	10.0(10)	0	36	546	15.2(43)	3	—	—	—	—	—	—	—	—	—	—	K	—	19	298
1955	†LARm☆	12(LE)	—	—	—	—	44	569	12.9(31)	2	—	—	—	—	—	—	—	—	—	—	K	—	12	295
1956	LARm	2	—	—	—	—	5	49	9.8(18)	0	—	—	—	—	—	—	—	—	—	—	—	—	0	25
NFL	9	87(11)	5	15	3.0(10)	0	400	5397	13.5(80)	38	—	—	—	—	—	—	—	—	—	—	Ki	1	249	2941

FEARS, WILLIE Willie Bert, DE, 6´3˝/278 lbs; Northwestern State (LA); B6/4/1964 Chicago, IL **1987** Cin 3 (1) **1990** Min 2 (0) **NFL** 5 (1) [2 yrs]

FEASEL, GRANT Grant Earl, C, 6´7˝/278 lbs; Abilene Christian; 1983: Bal, rnd 6; B6/28/1960 Barstow, GA **1983** Bal 11 (0) **1984** Ind 6 (0) **1984** Min 9 (3) **1987**†Sea 12 (2) **1988**†Sea 16 (2) **1990** Sea 16 (16, C) **1991** Sea 15 (15, C) **1992** Sea 16 (0)

YEAR	TEAM	G (GS, POS)	RUSH	YD	AVG (LG)	TD	REC	YD	AVG (LG)	TD	PASS	COMP	PCT	YD	AVG (LG)	TD	INT	SK	YD	QBR	KPR	OTD	PTS	TAY
1989	Sea	16(16, C)	—	—	—	—	1	5	5.0(5)	0	—	—	—	—	—	—	—	—	—	—	—	—	0	3
NFL	8	117(54)	—	—	—	—	1	5	5.0(5)	0	—	—	—	—	—	—	—	—	—	—	—	—	0	3

FEASEL, GREG Gregory Duane, T, 6´7˝/300 lbs; Abilene Christian; B11/7/1958 Barstow, GA **1986** GB 15 (0) **1987** SD 3 (3) **NFL** 18 (3) [2 yrs]

FEASTER, BILL William George, T-C, 6´0˝/205 lbs; Fordham; B1904, D12/11/1950 Plainfield, NJ **1929** Ora 12 (12, LT) **1930** Nwk 10 (8, LT) **NFL** 22 (20) [2 yrs]

FEATHER, TINY Elwin Elton, B, 6´0˝/197 lbs; Kansas State; B2/23/1902 **1927** Cle 11 (11, BB) **1928** Det 10 (10, FB), 42 **1929** NYG 15 (15, BB), 18 **1930** NYG 15 (14, BB), 6 **1931** SI 10 (5, HB) **1931** NYG 2 (2)

YEAR	TEAM	G (GS, POS)	RUSH	YD	AVG (LG)	TD	REC	YD	AVG (LG)	TD	PASS	COMP	PCT	YD	AVG (LG)	TD	INT	SK	YD	QBR	KPR	OTD	PTS	TAY
1932	NYG	9(7, wb)	28	47	1.7	0	2	15	7.5	0	5	1	20.0	15	3.0(15)	0	1	—	—	—	—	—	0	22
1933	NYG	9(2)	2	4	2.0(3)	0	2	38	19.0(22)	0	—	—	—	—	—	—	—	—	—	—	—	—	0	23
1934	Cin	5(3)	—	—	—	—	3	26	8.7	0	—	—	—	—	—	—	—	—	—	—	—	—	0	13
NFL	8	86(69)	30	51	1.7(3)	8	7	79	11.3(22)	2	5	1	20.0	15	3.0(15)	1	1	—	—	—	—	1	66	163

YEAR	TEAM	G (GS, POS)	RUSH	YD	AVG(LG)	TD	REC	YD	AVG(LG)	TD	PASS	COMP	PCT	YD	AVG(LG)	TD	INT	SK	YD	QBR	KPR	OTD	PTS	TAY

FEATHERS, BEATTIE William Beattie, HB-WB, 5´10˝/185 lbs; Tennessee; B8/4/1908 Bristol, VA, D3/10/1979 Winston-Salem, NC **[K]**

1934	ChiB☆	11(10, LH)	119	**1004**	8.4(82)	8	6	174	29.0	1	12	4	33.3	41	3.4	2	2	—	—	—	K	—	55	**1127**
1935	ChiB	8(5, LH)	56	281	5.0	3	3	18	6.0	0	14	5	35.7	53	3.8	1	2	—	—	—		—	18	272
1936	ChiB☆	12(12, LH)	97	350	3.6	2	2	5	2.5	0	11	1	9.1	10	0.9(10)	1	2	—	—	—		—	12	303
1937	†ChiB	11(7, LH)	66	211	3.2	1	—	—	—	—	6	2	33.3	12	2.0	0	0	—	—	—		—	6	227
1938	Bkn	7(5, wb)	28	94	3.4	2	3	34	11.3	0	—	—	—	—	—	—	—	—	—	—		—	12	131
1939	Bkn	4(0)	8	21	2.6	0	1	12	12.0(12)	0	—	—	—	—	—	—	—	—	—	—		—	0	27
1940	GB	1(0)	4	19	4.8	0	—	—	—	—	—	—	—	—	—	—	—	—	—	—		—	0	19
NFL	7	54(39)	378	1980	5.2(82)	16	15	243	16.2(12)	1	43	12	27.9	116	2.7(10)	4	6	—	—	—	K	—	103	2105

FEDERICO, CREIG Creig Ronald, DB, 6´2˝/205 lbs; Iowa Central; Illinois State; B5/7/1963 Chicago, IL   **1987** Det 3 (2)

FEDEROVITCH, JOHN John Lawrence, T, 6´5˝/263 lbs; Davis & Elkins; 1941: ChiB, rnd 7; B6/26/1917 Wyano, PA, D1/20/2003 Youngstown, OH   **1941**†ChiB◇11 (0)   **1946** ChiB 3 (0)
NFL 14 (0) [2 yrs]

FEDERSPIEL, JOE Joseph Michael, LB, 6´1˝/230 lbs; Kentucky; 1972: NO, rnd 4; B5/6/1950 Louisville, KY   **1972** NO 14 (MLB)   **1973** NO 13 (MLB)   **1974** NO 14 (MLB)
1975 NO 14 (14, MLB)   **1976** NO 14 (14, MLB)   **1977** NO 14 (14, MLB)   **1978** NO 16 (16, MLB)   **1979** NO 16 (16, MLB)   **1980** NO 15 (14, MLB)   **1981** Bal 11 (10, MLB)
NFL 141 (98) [10 yrs]

FEDORA, WALT Walter Jack, FB, 6´1˝/190 lbs; George Washington; 1942: Bkn, rnd 22; B9/15/1918 Decatur, IL, D9/1968

| 1942 | Bkn | 8(0) | 16 | 34 | 2.1(12) | 0 | — | — | — | — | — | — | — | — | — | — | — | — | — | — | k | — | 0 | 49 |

FEEHERY, GERRY Gerald, C-G, 6´2˝/268 lbs; Syracuse; B3/9/1960 Philadelphia, PA   **1983** Phi 2 (0)   **1984** Phi 6 (0)   **1985** Phi 15 (0)   **1986** Phi 6 (6, c)   **1987** Phi 12 (12, C)
1988 KC 6 (6, c)   **NFL** 47 (24) [6 yrs]

FEELEY, A.J. Adam Joshua, QB, 6´3˝/217 lbs; Oregon; 2001: Phi, rnd 5; B5/16/1977 Caldwell, ID

2001	Phi	1(0)	—	—	—	—	—	—	—	—	14	10	71.4	143	10.2(27)	2	1	—	—	—		—	0	42
2002	Phi	6(5, qb)	12	6	0.5(6)	0	—	—	—	—	154	86	55.8	1011	6.6(53)	6	5	7	48	—		—	0	342
2004	Mia	11(8, QB)	14	13	0.9(7)	1	—	—	—	—	356	191	53.7	1893	5.3(38)	11	15	23	136	61.7		—	6	425
NFL	3	18(13)	26	19	0.7(7)	1	—	—	—	—	524	287	54.8	3047	5.8(53)	19	21	30	184	67.3		—	6	808

FEELY, JAY Thomas, K, 5´10˝/206 lbs; Michigan; B5/23/1976 Odessa, FL **[K]**   **2002**†Atl 16 (0)   **2003** Atl 16 (0)   **2005**†NYG 16 (0)

2001	Atl	16(0)	—	—	—	—	1	-2	-2.0(-2)	0	—	—	—	—	—	—	—	—	—	—	K	—	115	-1
2004	†Atl	16(0)	—	—	—	—	1	-2	-2.0(-2)	0	—	—	—	—	—	—	—	—	—	—	K	—	94	-1
NFL	5	80(0)	—	—	—	—	2	-4	-2.0(-2)	0	—	—	—	—	—	—	—	—	—	—	K	—	584	-2

FEENEY, AL Albert George, C, 6´0˝/210 lbs; Notre Dame; B11/12/1891 Indianapolis, IN, D11/2/1950 Indianapolis, IN **[K]**   **1920** Can 11 (8, C)   **1921** Can 8 (8, C), 6
NFL 19 (16) [2 yrs]

FEGGINS, HOWARD Howard Anthony, DB, 5´10˝/190 lbs; North Carolina; B5/6/1965 South Hill, VA   **1989** NE 11 (0)

FEHER, NICK Nicholas John, G, 6´0˝/224 lbs; Georgia; 1951: SF, rnd 10; B7/13/1926 Youngstown, OH, D1/28/1992 Kingman, AZ   **1951** SF 12 (LG)   **1952** SF 6   **1953** SF 10
1954 SF 12 (LG)   **1955** Pit 2   **NFL** 42 [5 yrs]

FEIBISH, BERNIE Bernard, C, 6´2˝/223 lbs; NYU; B1918, deceased   **1941** Phi 3 (0)

FEICHTINGER, ANDY Andrew Joseph, E, 5´10˝/170 lbs; none; B11/16/1897 Salem, OR, D12/1962, OR   **1920** Dec 4 (0)

FEIST, LOU Louis, E-T-FB, 6´1˝/200 lbs; Columbia; Canisius; B1903, D11/12/1926 Buffalo, NY   **1924** Buf 10 (9, LT)   **1925** Buf 7 (5, RE)   **1926** Buf 5 (4)   **NFL** 22 (18) [3 yrs]

FEKETE, GENE Eugene H., FB-LB, 6´0˝/195 lbs; Ohio State; 1945: Det, rnd 6; B8/31/1922 Sugar Creek, OH

| 1946 | †Cle-A | 6(2) | 26 | 106 | 4.1 | 1 | 2 | 2.0(12) | 0 | — | — | — | — | — | — | — | — | — | — | — | k | — | 6 | 123 |

FEKETE, JOHN John Michael, HB-DB, 5´11˝/200 lbs; Ohio University; 1943: Bkn, rnd 14; B10/28/1919 Morgantown, WV, D7/26/1988 Cleveland, OH

| 1946 | Buf-A | 3(0) | 1 | -1 | -1.0 | 0 | — | — | — | — | — | — | — | — | — | — | — | — | — | — | | — | 0 | -1 |

FELBER, NIP Frederick Emmett, E, 6´2˝/190 lbs; North Dakota; B3/25/1909 Le Seuer, MN, D5/1978 Minot, ND   **1932** Bos 10 (0)

| 1933 | Phi | 1(0) | — | — | — | — | 1 | 8 | 8.0(8) | 0 | — | — | — | — | — | — | — | — | — | — | | — | 0 | 4 |
| NFL | 2 | 11(0) | — | — | — | — | 1 | 8 | 8.0(8) | 0 | — | — | — | — | — | — | — | — | — | — | | — | 0 | 4 |

FELDHAUS, BILL William Bernard, G-T, 6´0˝/226 lbs; Cincinnati; B12/8/1912 Cincinnati, OH, D6/2/1974 Cincinnati, OH   **1937** Det 11 (5, rg)   **1938** Det 11 (6, RG)
1939 Det 10 (10, RG)   **1940** Det 11 (11, RG)   **NFL** 43 (32) [4 yrs]

FELDHAUSEN, PAUL Paul Elvie, T, 6´6˝/260 lbs; Northland (WI); 1968: Bos, rnd 11; B6/14/1946 Madison, WI   **1968** Bos-A 2

FELDMAN, TODD Todd Mitchell, WR, 5´10˝/184 lbs; Kent State; B8/7/1962 Philadelphia, PA   **1987** Mia 1 (0)

FELKER, GENE Eugene Marvin, E, 6´1˝/198 lbs; Wisconsin; 1952: DalT, rnd 19; B3/4/1929 Milwaukee, WI

| 1952 | DalT | 6(3) | — | — | — | — | 6 | 63 | 10.5(17) | 1 | — | — | — | — | — | — | — | — | — | — | | — | 6 | 37 |

FELLER, HAPPY James Patrick, K, 5´11˝/185 lbs; Texas; 1971: Phi, rnd 4; B6/13/1949 Fredericksburg, TX **[K]**   **1971** Phi 9   **1972** NO 6   **1973** NO 6   **NFL** 21 [3 yrs]

FELLOWS, MARK Charles Mark, LB, 6´1˝/233 lbs; Montana State; 1985: SD, rnd 7; B2/26/1963 Billings, MT   **1985** SD 2 (0)   **1986** SD 1 (0)   **NFL** 3 (0) [2 yrs]

FELLOWS, RON Ronald Lee, DB, 6´0˝/178 lbs; Missouri; 1981: Dal, rnd 7; B11/7/1958 South Bend, IN   **1981**†Dal 16 (0)   **1982**†Dal 9 (0)   **1983**†Dal 16 (0)   **1984** Dal 16 (16, RCB)
1985†Dal 13 (11, RCB)   **1986** Dal 16 (16, RCB)   **1987** LARd 12 (2)   **1988** LARd 14 (10, LCB)   **NFL** 112 (55) [8 yrs]

FELT, DICK Richard George, DB, 6´1˝/185 lbs; Brigham Young; B3/4/1933 Lehi, UT   **1960** NYT-A 14 (RCB)   **1961** NYT-A★14 (LS)   **1962** Bos-A★14 (RCB)   **1963**†Bos-A 14 (RCB)
1964 Bos-A 9 (RCB)   **1965** Bos-A 1   **1966** Bos-A 14   **NFL** 80 [7 yrs]

FELTON, ERIC Eric Norman, DB, 6´0˝/200 lbs; Texas Tech; 1978: NO, rnd 5; B10/8/1955 Austin, TX   **1978** NO 16 (2)   **1979** NO 13 (10, RCB)   **1980** NYG 6 (3)   **NFL** 35 (15) [3 yrs]

FELTON, JOE Joseph James, G, 6´2˝/266 lbs; Albion; B10/16/1964 Saginaw, MI   **1987** Det 2 (2)

FELTON, RALPH Ralph Dwaine, LB-DB-FB, 5´11˝/210 lbs; Maryland; 1954: Was, rnd 4; B5/21/1932 Midway, PA **[K]**   **1955** Was 12 (RLB)   **1956** Was 7 (rlb)   **1957** Was 12 (RLB)
1958 Was 8 (7, LLB)   **1959** Was 12 (LLB)   **1960** Was 12 (MLB)   **1961** Buf-A☆14 (LLB)   **1962** Buf-A 4

| 1954 | Was | 12(DB) | 3 | 8 | 2.7(5) | 0 | — | — | — | — | — | — | — | — | — | — | — | — | — | — | Kkpi | — | 19 | -12 |
| NFL | 9 | 93(7) | 3 | 8 | 2.7(5) | 0 | — | — | — | — | — | — | — | — | — | — | — | — | — | — | Kkpi | — | 19 | -12 |

FELTS, BOBBY Bobby, HB, 6´2˝/202 lbs; Florida A&M; 1965: Bal, rnd 6/Hou, rnd 13; B6/26/1942 Miami, FL

1965	Bal	7	2	0	0.0(2)	0	—	—	—	—	—	—	—	—	—	—	—	—	—	—	k	—	0	43
1965	Det	7	20	58	2.9(6)	0	3	28	9.3(17)	0	1	0	0.0	0	0.0	0	—	—	—	—	kp	—	0	193
1966	Det	10	34	83	2.4(14)	2	2	1	0.5(1)	0	—	—	—	—	—	—	—	—	—	—	kp	—	12	206
1967	Det	14	10	66	6.6(22)	0	—	—	—	—	—	—	—	—	—	—	—	—	—	—	p	—	0	60
NFL	3	38	66	207	3.1(22)	2	5	29	5.8(17)	0	1	0	0.0	0	0.0	0	—	—	—	—	kp	—	12	502

FENA, TOM Thomas Mitchell, G, 5´11˝/200 lbs; Denver; B12/27/1909 Cleveland, OH, D9/7/1985 Burlingame, CA   **1937** Det 2 (0)

FENCIK, GARY John Gary, DB, 6´1˝/194 lbs; Yale; 1976: Mia, rnd 10; B6/11/1954 Chicago, IL **[I]**   **1976** ChiB 13   **1977**†ChiB 14 (14, SS)   **1978** ChiB 16 (16, SS)
1979†ChiB☆14 (14, SS)   **1980** ChiB★15 (15, SS)   **1981** ChiB★16 (16, SS)   **1982** ChiB☆9 (9, SS)   **1983** ChiB 7 (7, FS)   **1984**†ChiB 16 (16, FS)   **1985**†ChiB☆16 (16, FS)
1986†ChiB 16 (16, FS)   **1987**†ChiB 12 (1)   **NFL** 164 (140) [12 yrs]

FENCL, DICK Richard John, E, 5´11˝/160 lbs; Northwestern; B2/24/1909 Chicago, IL, D6/25/1972 Chicago, IL

| 1933 | Phi | 5(1) | — | — | — | — | 1 | 20 | 20.0(20) | 0 | — | — | — | — | — | — | — | — | — | — | | — | 0 | 10 |

FENDERSON, JAMES James E., RB, 5´9˝/200 lbs; Hawaii; B10/24/1976 Mililani, HI

2001	NO	4(0)	—	—	—	—	—	—	—	—	—	—	—	—	—	—	—	—	—	—		—	—	—
2002	NO	16(1)	13	65	5.0(17)	1	6	38	6.3(13)	0	—	—	—	—	—	—	—	—	—	—	k	—	6	107
2003	NO	9(0)	4	14	3.5(6)	0	1	5	5.0(5)	0	—	—	—	—	—	—	—	—	—	—		—	2	17
NFL	3	29(1)	17	79	4.6(17)	1	7	43	6.1(13)	0	—	—	—	—	—	—	—	—	—	—	k	—	8	124

FENENBOCK, CHUCK Charles Bernard, HB-TB, 5´9˝/174 lbs; UCLA; B8/28/1917 Oakland, CA

1943	Det	10(6, tb)	46	180	3.9(25)	0	5	45	9.0(33)	1	58	20	34.5	338	5.8(72)	3	9	—	—	—	Pkpi	—	6	138
1945	Det	10(4, TB)	72	143	2.0(37)	1	1	24	24.0(24)	0	110	45	40.9	754	6.9(56)	7	11	—	—	46.4	Pkpi	1	12	273
NFL	2	20(8)	118	323	2.7(37)	1	6	69	11.5(33)	1	168	65	38.7	1092	6.5(72)	10	20	—	—	41.7	Pkpi	1	18	411

YEAR	TEAM	G (GS, POS)	RUSH	YD	AVG (LG)	TD	REC	YD	AVG (LG)	TD	PASS	COMP	PCT	YD	AVG (LG)	TD	INT	SK	YD	QBR	KPR	OTD	PTS	TAY
1946	LAD-A	13 (7, lh)	50	420	8.4	3	11	67	6.1	0	1	0	0.0	0	0.0	0	0	—	—	—	kp	1	24	937
1947	LAD-A	14 (12, LH)	58	185	3.2	3	20	276	13.8	2	7	1	14.3	7	1.0 (7)	0	2	—	—	—	kp	1	36	594
1948	LAD-A	1 (0)	—	—	—	—	—	—	—	—	—	—	—	—	—	—	—	—	—	—	—	—	—	—
1948	ChiR-A	13 (5, lh)	43	174	4.0	0	8	111	13.9	1	15	4	26.7	136	9.1 (60)	2	1	—	—	—	kp	—	6	458
AAFC	3	41 (24)	151	779	5.2 (37)	6	39	454	11.6 (33)	3	23	5	21.7	143	6.2 (72)	2	3	—	—	42.4	kp	2	66	1988

FENERTY, GILL Lawrence Gill, RB, 6´0˝/205 lbs; Holy Cross; 1986: NO, rnd 7; B8/24/1963 New Orleans, LA

YEAR	TEAM	G (GS, POS)	RUSH	YD	AVG (LG)	TD	REC	YD	AVG (LG)	TD	PASS	COMP	PCT	YD	AVG (LG)	TD	INT	SK	YD	QBR	KPR	OTD	PTS	TAY
1990	†NO	15 (0)	73	355	4.9 (60)	2	18	209	11.6 (28)	0	—	—	—	—	—	—	—	—	—	—	k	—	12	632
1991	†NO	16 (12, RB)	139	477	3.4 (54)	3	26	235	9.0 (50)	2	—	—	—	—	—	—	—	—	—	—	kp	—	30	628
NFL	2	31 (12)	212	832	3.9 (60)	5	44	444	10.1 (50)	2	—	—	—	—	—	—	—	—	—	—	kp	—	42	1259

FENIMORE, BOB Robert Dale, HB, 6´1˝/190 lbs; Oklahoma State; 1947: ChiB, rnd B1/Buf-A, rnd S; B10/6/1925 Woodward, OK

YEAR	TEAM	G (GS, POS)	RUSH	YD	AVG (LG)	TD	REC	YD	AVG (LG)	TD	PASS	COMP	PCT	YD	AVG (LG)	TD	INT	SK	YD	QBR	KPR	OTD	PTS	TAY
1947	ChiB	10 (0)	53	189	3.6 (13)	1	15	219	14.6 (29)	2	3	2	66.7	27	9.0 (15)	0	0	—	—	—	pi	—	18	411

FENNEMA, CARL Carl H., C-LB, 6´2˝/210 lbs; Washington; B10/17/1926 San Francisco, CA **1948** NYG 8 (0) **1949** NYG 3 (0) **NFL** 11 (0) [2 yrs]

FENNER, DERRICK Derrick Steven, RB, 5´11˝/240 lbs; Gardner-Webb; North Carolina; 1989: Sea, rnd 10; B4/6/1967 Washington, DC

YEAR	TEAM	G (GS, POS)	RUSH	YD	AVG (LG)	TD	REC	YD	AVG (LG)	TD	PASS	COMP	PCT	YD	AVG (LG)	TD	INT	SK	YD	QBR	KPR	OTD	PTS	TAY
1989	Sea	5 (1)	11	41	3.7 (9)	1	3	23	7.7 (9)	0	—	—	—	—	—	—	—	—	—	—	—	—	6	63
1990	Sea	16 (15, RB)	215	859	4.0 (36)	**14**	17	143	8.4 (50)	1	—	—	—	—	—	—	—	—	—	—	—	—	90	1076
1991	Sea	11 (7, RB)	91	267	2.9 (15)	4	11	72	6.5 (15)	0	—	—	—	—	—	—	—	—	—	—	—	—	24	343
1992	Cin	16 (1)	112	500	4.5 (35)	7	7	41	5.9 (15)	1	—	—	—	—	—	—	—	—	—	—	k	—	48	604
1993	Cin	15 (14, FB)	121	482	4.0 (26)	1	48	427	8.9 (40)	0	—	—	—	—	—	—	—	—	—	—	—	—	6	706
1994	Cin	16 (12, FB)	141	468	3.3 (21)	1	36	276	7.7 (29)	1	—	—	—	—	—	—	—	—	—	—	—	—	12	621
1995	Oak	16 (13, FB)	39	110	2.8 (10)	0	35	252	7.2 (23)	3	—	—	—	—	—	—	—	—	—	—	—	—	18	251
1996	Oak	16 (11, FB)	67	245	3.7 (17)	4	31	252	8.1 (23)	4	—	—	—	—	—	—	—	—	—	—	—	—	48	431
1997	Oak	9 (7, FB)	7	24	3.4 (7)	0	14	92	6.6 (13)	0	—	—	—	—	—	—	—	—	—	—	—	—	0	70
NFL	9	120 (81)	804	2996	3.7 (36)	32	202	1578	7.8 (50)	10	—	—	—	—	—	—	—	—	—	—	k	—	252	4163

FENNER, HAROLD Leonard Harold, E, 5´10˝/171 lbs; none; B11/10/1895 Hillsboro, MI, D4/1/1963 Cincinnati, OH **[K]** **1920** Day 8 (1) **1921** Day 8 (4) **1922** Day 6 (1), 3 **1923** Day 5 (0) **1924** Day 7 (6, LE), 6 **1925** Day 8 (8, LE) **1926** Day 6 (6, LE) **1927** Day 6 (5, LE) **1929** Day 6 (5, RE) **1930** Por 1 (0) **NFL** 61 (36), 9 [10 yrs]

FENNER, LANE Lane Bryce, WR, 6´5˝/210 lbs; Florida State; 1968: SD, rnd 7; B12/7/1945 Evansville, IN **1968** SD-A 11

FENNEY, RICK Ricky Dale, RB, 6´1˝/235 lbs; Washington; 1987: Min, rnd 8; B12/7/1964 Everett, WA

YEAR	TEAM	G (GS, POS)	RUSH	YD	AVG (LG)	TD	REC	YD	AVG (LG)	TD	PASS	COMP	PCT	YD	AVG (LG)	TD	INT	SK	YD	QBR	KPR	OTD	PTS	TAY
1987	†Min	11 (0)	42	174	4.1 (12)	2	7	27	3.9 (18)	0	—	—	—	—	—	—	—	—	—	—	—	—	12	208
1988	†Min	13 (3)	55	271	4.9 (28)	3	15	224	14.9 (42)	0	—	—	—	—	—	—	—	—	—	—	—	—	18	413
1989	†Min	16 (8, fb)	151	588	3.9 (25)	4	30	254	8.5 (26)	2	—	—	—	—	—	—	—	—	—	—	k	—	36	762
1990	Min	12 (5, fb)	87	376	4.3 (27)	2	17	112	6.6 (17)	0	—	—	—	—	—	—	—	—	—	—	—	—	12	452
1991	Min	11 (0)	23	99	4.3 (17)	0	2	11	5.5 (8)	0	—	—	—	—	—	—	—	—	—	—	—	—	0	105
NFL	5	63 (16)	358	1508	4.2 (28)	11	71	628	8.8 (42)	2	—	—	—	—	—	—	—	—	—	—	k	—	78	1939

FERGERSON, DUKE Duke, WR, 6´1˝/189 lbs; Washington State; San Diego State; 1976: Dal, rnd 3; B4/21/1954 Boise, ID

YEAR	TEAM	G (GS, POS)	RUSH	YD	AVG (LG)	TD	REC	YD	AVG (LG)	TD	PASS	COMP	PCT	YD	AVG (LG)	TD	INT	SK	YD	QBR	KPR	OTD	PTS	TAY
1977	Sea	13 (8, WR)	—	—	—	—	19	374	19.7 (45)	2	—	—	—	—	—	—	—	—	—	—	kp	—	12	286
1978	Sea	16	—	—	—	—	11	116	10.5 (17)	0	—	—	—	—	—	—	—	—	—	—	k	—	0	144
1979	Sea	4	—	—	—	—	2	12	6.0 (10)	0	—	—	—	—	—	—	—	—	—	—	—	—	0	6
1980	†Buf	9 (0)	—	—	—	—	3	41	13.7 (19)	0	—	—	—	—	—	—	—	—	—	—	—	—	0	21
NFL	4	42 (8)	—	—	—	—	35	543	15.5 (45)	2	—	—	—	—	—	—	—	—	—	—	kp	—	12	457

FERGUSON, BILL William Michael, LB, 6´3˝/225 lbs; Washington; San Diego State; 1973: NYJ, rnd 4; B7/7/1951 San Diego, CA **1973** NYJ 11 (RLB) **1974** NYJ 13 **NFL** 24 [2 yrs]

FERGUSON, BOB Robert Eugene, FB, 5´11˝/220 lbs; Ohio State; 1962: Pit, rnd 1/SD, rnd 1; B8/29/1939 Columbus, OH, D12/30/2004 Columbus, OH

YEAR	TEAM	G (GS, POS)	RUSH	YD	AVG (LG)	TD	REC	YD	AVG (LG)	TD	PASS	COMP	PCT	YD	AVG (LG)	TD	INT	SK	YD	QBR	KPR	OTD	PTS	TAY
1962	Pit	13	20	37	1.9 (13)	0	1	6	6.0 (6)	0	—	—	—	—	—	—	—	—	—	—	k	—	0	40
1963	Pit	5	43	171	4.0 (19)	1	3	7	2.3 (9)	0	—	—	—	—	—	—	—	—	—	—	—	—	6	185
1963	Min	2	3	1	0.3 (1)	0	—	—	—	—	—	—	—	—	—	—	—	—	—	—	—	—	0	1
NFL	2	20	66	209	3.2 (19)	1	4	13	3.3 (9)	0	—	—	—	—	—	—	—	—	—	—	k	—	6	226

FERGUSON, CHARLEY Charles Edward, WR-TE, 6´5˝/217 lbs; Tennessee State; B11/13/1939 Dallas, TX

YEAR	TEAM	G (GS, POS)	RUSH	YD	AVG (LG)	TD	REC	YD	AVG (LG)	TD	PASS	COMP	PCT	YD	AVG (LG)	TD	INT	SK	YD	QBR	KPR	OTD	PTS	TAY
1961	Cle	12	—	—	—	—	2	68	34.0 (60)	1	—	—	—	—	—	—	—	—	—	—	—	—	6	39
1962	Min	10 (9, WR)	—	—	—	—	14	364	26.0 (**89**)	6	—	—	—	—	—	—	—	—	—	—	—	—	36	212
1963	†Buf-A	12	—	—	—	—	9	181	20.1 (72)	3	—	—	—	—	—	—	—	—	—	—	—	—	18	106
1965	†Buf-A✧	12 (te)	—	—	—	—	21	262	12.5 (30)	2	—	—	—	—	—	—	—	—	—	—	—	—	12	141
1966	†Buf-A	14	—	—	—	—	16	293	18.3 (32)	1	—	—	—	—	—	—	—	—	—	—	k	—	6	122
1969	Buf-A	4	—	—	—	—	—	—	—	—	—	—	—	—	—	—	—	—	—	—	—	—	—	—
NFL	6	64 (9)	—	—	—	—	62	1168	18.8 (89)	13	—	—	—	—	—	—	—	—	—	—	k	—	78	619

FERGUSON, GENE Eugene Bransford, T-DT, 6´8˝/300 lbs; Norfolk State; 1969: SD, rnd 3; B6/5/1947 Lynchburg, VA **1969** SD-A 12 (RT) **1970** SD 14 **1971** Hou 14 (LT) **1972** Hou 1 **NFL** 41 [4 yrs]

FERGUSON, HOWIE Howard, FB-HB, 6´2˝/218 lbs; none; B8/5/1930 New Iberia, LA, D12/18/2005 New Iberia, LA

YEAR	TEAM	G (GS, POS)	RUSH	YD	AVG (LG)	TD	REC	YD	AVG (LG)	TD	PASS	COMP	PCT	YD	AVG (LG)	TD	INT	SK	YD	QBR	KPR	OTD	PTS	TAY
1953	GB	11 (rh)	52	134	2.6 (12)	0	15	86	5.7 (23)	0	—	—	—	—	—	—	—	—	—	—	k	—	0	195
1954	GB	12 (FB)	83	276	3.3 (25)	0	41	398	9.7 (49)	0	—	—	—	—	—	—	—	—	—	—	k	—	0	476
1955	GB★	12 (FB)	192	859	4.5 (57)	4	22	153	7.0 (16)	0	—	—	—	—	—	—	—	—	—	—	k	—	24	981
1956	GB	11 (FB)	99	367	3.7 (24)	0	22	214	9.7 (25)	0	—	—	—	—	—	—	—	—	—	—	k	—	0	482
1957	GB	12 (RH)	59	216	3.7 (40)	1	15	107	7.1 (17)	1	1	0	0.0	0	0.0	0	0	—	—	—	—	—	12	285
1958	GB	7	59	268	4.5 (29)	1	12	121	10.1 (27)	0	1	0	0.0	0	0.0	0	0	—	—	—	—	—	6	339
1960	†LAC-A	14 (FB)	126	438	3.5 (30)	4	21	168	8.0 (26)	2	—	—	—	—	—	—	—	—	—	—	—	—	36	572
NFL	7	79	670	2558	3.8 (57)	10	148	1247	8.4 (49)	3	2	0	0.0	0	0.0	0	0	—	—	—	k	—	78	3329

FERGUSON, JAMES James Thomas, C-LB, 6´4˝/240 lbs; USC; 1968: NO, rnd 17; B10/15/1942 Oakland, CA **1968** NO 4 **1969** Atl 2 **1969** ChiB 4 **NFL** 10 [2 yrs]

FERGUSON, JASON Jason O., DT-NT, 6´3˝/305 lbs; Georgia; 1997: NYJ, rnd 7; B11/28/1974 Nettleton, MS **1997** NYJ 13 (1) **1998** NYJ 16 (16, LDT) **1999** NYJ 9 (9, NT) **2000** NYJ 15 (11, NT) **2002** NYJ 16 (16, LDT) **2003** NYJ 16 (16, RDT) **2004** NYJ 16 (14, RDT) **2005** Dal 16 (5, nt) **NFL** 117 (88) [8 yrs]

FERGUSON, JOE Joe Carlton, QB, 6´1˝/195 lbs; Arkansas; 1973: Buf, rnd 3; B4/23/1950 Alvin, TX

YEAR	TEAM	G (GS, POS)	RUSH	YD	AVG (LG)	TD	REC	YD	AVG (LG)	TD	PASS	COMP	PCT	YD	AVG (LG)	TD	INT	SK	YD	QBR	KPR	OTD	PTS	TAY
1973	Buf	14 (14, QB)	48	147	3.1 (24)	2	1	-3	-3.0 (-3)	0	164	73	44.5	939	5.7 (42)	4	10	20	164	—	—	—	12	255
1974	†Buf	14 (14, QB)	54	111	2.1 (15)	2	—	—	—	—	232	119	51.3	1588	6.8 (55)	12	12	32	235	69.0	—	—	12	505
1975	Buf	14 (14, QB)	23	82	3.6 (17)	1	—	—	—	—	321	169	52.6	2426	7.6 (77)	**25**	17	20	153	81.3	—	—	6	750
1976	Buf	7 (7, qb)	18	81	4.5 (19)	0	—	—	—	—	151	74	49.0	1086	7.2 (58)	9	1	11	80	—	—	—	0	629
1977	Buf	14 (14, QB)	41	279	6.8 (41)	2	—	—	—	—	**457**	221	48.4	**2803**	6.1 (42)	12	**24**	36	273	54.8	—	—	12	801
1978	Buf	16 (16, QB)	27	76	2.8 (12)	0	1	-6	-6.0 (-6)	0	330	175	53.0	2136	6.5 (**92**)	16	15	29	243	70.5	—	—	0	621
1979	Buf	16 (16, QB)	22	68	3.1 (15)	1	—	—	—	—	458	238	52.0	3572	7.8 (**84**)	14	15	43	387	74.4	—	—	6	1334
1980	†Buf	16 (16, QB)	31	65	2.1 (15)	0	—	—	—	—	439	251	57.2	2805	6.4 (69)	20	18	13	129	74.5	—	—	0	848
1981	†Buf	16 (16, QB)	20	29	1.5 (16)	1	—	—	—	—	498	252	50.6	3652	7.3 (67)	24	20	15	137	74.1	—	—	6	1185
1982	Buf	9 (9, QB)	16	46	2.9 (13)	1	—	—	—	—	264	144	54.5	1597	6.0 (47)	7	**16**	11	105	56.3	—	1	12	250
1983	Buf	16 (16, QB)	20	88	4.4 (19)	0	—	—	—	—	508	281	55.3	2995	5.9 (43)	**26**	25	27	266	69.3	—	—	0	716
1984	Buf	12 (11, QB)	19	102	5.4 (20)	0	—	—	—	—	344	191	55.5	1991	5.8 (68)	12	17	35	357	63.5	—	—	0	478
1985	Det	8 (1)	4	12	3.0 (15)	1	—	—	—	—	54	31	57.4	364	6.7 (38)	2	3	4	35	—	—	—	6	94
1986	Det	6 (4, qb)	5	25	5.0 (14)	0	—	—	—	—	155	73	47.1	941	6.1 (73)	7	7	10	101	—	—	—	0	251
1988	TB	2 (1)	1	0	0.0 (0)	0	—	—	—	—	46	31	67.4	368	8.0 (34)	3	1	1	8	—	—	—	0	159
1989	TB	5 (2)	4	6	1.5 (7)	0	—	—	—	—	90	44	48.9	533	5.9 (69)	3	6	5	37	—	—	—	0	48
1990	Ind	1 (0)	—	—	—	—	—	—	—	—	8	2	25.0	21	2.6 (13)	0	2	—	—	—	—	—	0	-70
NFL	17	186 (171)	353	1217	3.4 (41)	11	2	-9	-4.5 (-3)	0	4519	2369	52.4	29817	6.6 (92)	196	209	312	2710	68.4	—	1	72	8851

FERGUSON, KEITH Keith Tyrone, DE, 6´5˝/252 lbs; Ohio State; 1981: SD, rnd 5; B4/3/1959 Miami, FL **1981**†SD 16 (1) **1982**†SD 9 (8, RDE) **1983** SD 16 (16, LDE) **1984** SD 16 (16, RDE) **1985** SD 10 (7, rde) **1985** Det 5 (4) **1986** Det 16 (15, LDE) **1987** Det 12 (9, RDE) **1988** Det 14 (14, RDE) **1989** Det 4 (1) **1990** Det 16 (14, RDE) **NFL** 134 (105) [10 yrs]

YEAR	TEAM	G (GS, POS)	RUSH	YD	AVG (LG)	TD	REC	YD	AVG (LG)	TD	PASS	COMP	PCT	°YD	AVG (LG)	TD	INT	SK	YD	QBR	KPR	OTD	PTS	TAY

FERGUSON, KEVIN Kevin Howard, TE, 6´2˝/223 lbs; Virginia; B12/4/1965 Lynchburg, VA **1987** SD 3 (0)

FERGUSON, LARRY Lawrence Pearly, HB, 5´10˝/195 lbs; Iowa; 1962: Det, rnd 4/Oak, rnd 17; B3/19/1940 Madison, IL

| 1963 | Det | 7 | 13 | 23 | 1.8(5) | 0 | 2 | 8 | 4.0(7) | 0 | — | — | — | — | — | — | — | — | — | — | kp | — | 0 | 176 |

FERGUSON, NICK Nick, DB, 5´11˝/201 lbs; Morris Brown; Georgia Tech; B11/27/1974 Miami, FL **2000** NYJ 7 (0) **2001**†NYJ 16 (1) **2002**†NYJ 16 (0) **2003** Den 15 (10, FS/ss) **2004**†Den 16 (1) **2005**†Den 16 (16, SS) **NFL** 86 (28) [6 yrs]

FERGUSON, ROBERT Robert Charles, WR, 6´1˝/209 lbs; Texas A&M; 2001: GB, rnd 2; B12/17/1979 Houston, TX

2001	GB	1(0)	—	—	—	—	—	—	—	—	—	—	—	—	—	—	—	—	—	—	kp	—	0	1
2002	†GB	16(1)	—	—	—	—	22	293	13.3(40)	3	—	—	—	—	—	—	—	—	—	—	k	—	18	185
2003	†GB	15(12, WR)	1	-8	-8.0(-8)	0	38	520	13.7(47)	4	—	—	—	—	—	—	—	—	—	—	k	—	24	315
2004	GB	13(5, wr)	—	—	—	—	24	367	15.3(48)	1	—	—	—	—	—	—	—	—	—	—	k	—	8	400
2005	GB	11(7, WR)	—	—	—	—	27	366	13.6(51)	3	—	—	—	—	—	—	—	—	—	—	k	—	20	212
NFL	5	56(25)	1	-8	-8.0(-8)	0	111	1546	13.9(51)	11	—	—	—	—	—	—	—	—	—	—	kp	—	70	1112

FERGUSON, TOM Thomas B., T, none; B9/24/1893, IN, D12/8/1979 Plantation, FL **1921** Lou 2 (2, LT)

FERGUSON, VAGAS Vasquero Diaz, RB, 6´1˝/204 lbs; Notre Dame; 1980: NE, rnd 1; B3/6/1957 Richmond, IN

1980	NE	16(16, RB)	211	818	3.9(44)	2	22	173	7.9(18)	0	—	—	—	—	—	—	—	—	—	—	—	—	12	925
1981	NE	13(5, rb)	78	340	4.4(19)	3	4	39	9.8(20)	0	—	—	—	—	—	—	—	—	—	—	—	—	18	390
1982	NE	2(0)	1	5	5.0(5)	0	—	—	—	—	—	—	—	—	—	—	—	—	—	—	—	—	0	5
1983	Hou	1(0)	—	—	—	—	—	—	—	—	—	—	—	—	—	—	—	—	—	—	—	—	0	6
1983	Cle	1(0)	—	—	—	—	—	—	—	—	—	—	—	—	—	—	—	—	—	—	k	—	0	6
NFL	4	33(21)	290	1163	4.0(44)	5	26	212	8.2(20)	0	—	—	—	—	—	—	—	—	—	—	—	—	30	1325

FERKO, FRITZ John Frederick, T, 6´1˝/242 lbs; West Chester; Mount St. Mary's; B7/6/1912, D3/1984 Perth Amboy, NJ **1937** Phi 10 (5, RT) **1938** Phi 2 (0) **NFL** 12 (5) [2 yrs]

FERNANDES, RON Ronald Michael, DE-DT, 6´4˝/251 lbs; Eastern Michigan; 1973: Mia, rnd 10; B9/11/1951 Ypsilanti, MI **1976**†Bal 13 **1977**†Bal 14 (7, rdt) **1979** Bal 13 (8, RDE) **NFL** 40 (15) [3 yrs]

FERNANDEZ, MANNY Manuel Jose, DT-DE, 6´2˝/250 lbs; Utah; B7/3/1946 Oakland, CA **1968** Mia-A 13 (11, RDE) **1969** Mia-A 14 (13, LDT) **1970**†Mia☆14 (12, LDT) **1971**†Mia☆14 (14, LDT) **1972**†Mia☆14 (14, LDT) **1973**†Mia☆13 (13, LDT) **1974**†Mia 12 (12, LDT) **1975** Mia 10 **NFL** 103 (89) [8 yrs]

FERNANDEZ, MERVYN Mervyn, WR, 6´3˝/205 lbs; San Jose State; 1983: LARd, rnd 10; B12/29/1959 Merced, CA

1987	LARd	7(7, WR)	—	—	—	—	14	236	16.9(47)	0	—	—	—	—	—	—	—	—	—	—	—	—	0	118
1988	LARd	16(1)	1	9	9.0(9)	0	31	805	26.0(45)	4	—	—	—	—	—	—	—	—	—	—	—	—	24	432
1989	LARd	16(13, WR)	2	16	8.0(12)	0	57	1069	18.8(75)	9	—	—	—	—	—	—	—	—	—	—	—	—	54	596
1990	†LARd	16(15, WR)	3	10	3.3(9)	0	52	839	16.1(66)	5	—	—	—	—	—	—	—	—	—	—	—	—	30	455
1991	†LARd	16(13, WR)	—	—	—	—	46	694	15.1(59)	1	—	—	—	—	—	—	—	—	—	—	—	—	6	352
1992	LARd	15(1)	—	—	—	—	9	121	13.4(21)	0	—	—	—	—	—	—	—	—	—	—	p	—	0	61
NFL	6	86(50)	6	35	5.8(12)	0	209	3764	18.0(85)	19	—	—	—	—	—	—	—	—	—	—	p	—	114	2012

FERRAGAMO, VINCE Vincent Anthony, QB, 6´3˝/212 lbs; California; Nebraska; 1977: LA, rnd 4; B4/24/1954 Torrance, CA

1977	†LARm	3	1	0	0.0(0)	0	—	—	—	—	15	9	60.0	83	5.5(17)	2	0	1	10	—	—	—	0	52
1978	†LARm	9	2	10	5.0(12)	0	—	—	—	—	20	7	35.0	114	5.7(28)	0	2	2	19	—	—	—	0	-13
1979	†LARm	8(5, qb)	3	-2	-0.7(2)	0	—	—	—	—	110	53	48.2	778	7.1(71)	5	10	11	115	—	—	—	0	12
1980	†LARm	16(15, QB)	15	34	2.3(15)	1	—	—	—	—	404	240	59.4	3199	**7.9(74)**	30	19	23	191	89.7	—	—	6	1034
1982	LARm	7(5, QB)	4	3	0.8(2)	1	—	—	—	—	209	118	56.5	1609	7.7(85)	9	8	9	77.6	—	—	—	6	503
1983	†LARm	16(16, QB)	22	17	0.8(8)	0	—	—	—	—	464	274	59.1	3276	7.1(61)	22	23	21	178	75.9	—	—	0	845
1984	LARm	3(3)	4	0	0.0(2)	0	—	—	—	—	66	29	43.9	317	4.8(68)	2	8	7	42	—	—	—	0	-152
1985	Buf	10(9, QB)	8	15	1.9(5)	1	—	—	—	—	287	149	51.9	1677	5.8(48)	5	17	19	135	50.8	—	—	6	209
1986	GB	3(0)	1	0	0.0(0)	0	—	—	—	—	40	23	57.5	283	7.1(50)	1	3	3	15	—	—	—	0	27
NFL	9	75(53)	60	77	1.3(15)	3	—	—	—	—	1615	902	55.9	11336	7.0(85)	76	91	94	770	70.1	—	—	18	2515

FERRANTE, JACK Jack Anthony, E-DE, 6´1˝/197 lbs; none; B3/9/1916 Camden, NJ

1941	Phi	3(0)	—	—	—	—	2	22	11.0(14)	0	—	—	—	—	—	—	—	—	—	—	—	—	0	11
1944	Phi	10(4, LE)	—	—	—	—	3	66	22.0(45)	1	—	—	—	—	—	—	—	—	—	—	—	—	6	38
1945	Phi☆	10(8, LE)	—	—	—	—	21	464	22.1(74)	7	—	—	—	—	—	—	—	—	—	—	i	—	42	277
1946	Phi	11(9, LE)	—	—	—	—	28	451	16.1(48)	4	—	—	—	—	—	—	—	—	—	—	—	—	24	246
1947	†Phi	11(10, LE)	—	—	—	—	18	341	18.9(54)	4	—	—	—	—	—	—	—	—	—	—	k	—	24	185
1948	†Phi	12(0)	—	—	—	—	28	444	15.9(66)	7	—	—	—	—	—	—	—	—	—	—	—	—	42	257
1949	†Phi☆	12(7, LE)	—	—	—	—	34	508	14.9(64)	5	—	—	—	—	—	—	—	—	—	—	—	—	30	279
1950	Phi	12(LE)	—	—	—	—	35	588	16.8(58)	3	—	—	—	—	—	—	—	—	—	—	—	—	18	309
NFL	8	81(38)	—	—	—	—	169	2884	17.1(74)	31	—	—	—	—	—	—	—	—	—	—	ki	—	186	1601

FERRANTE, ORLANDO Orlando C., G, 6´0˝/230 lbs; USC; B9/24/1932 Los Angeles, CA **1960**†LAC-A 14 (LG) **1961**†SD-A 14 (LG) **NFL** 28 [2 yrs]

FERRARA, FRANK Frank, DE, 6´3˝/280 lbs; Rhode Island; B12/7/1975 Brooklyn, NY **2001** NYG 9 (0) **2002**†NYG 16 (1) **2003** NYG 2 (0) **NFL** 27 (1) [3 yrs]

FERRARI, RON Ronald Lee, LB, 6´0˝/212 lbs; Lakeland; Illinois; 1982: SF, rnd 7; B7/30/1959 Springfield, IL **1982** SF 9 (0) **1983**†SF 16 (0) **1984** SF 11 (0) **1985**†SF 16 (0) **1986**†SF 16 (0) **NFL** 68 (0) [5 yrs]

FERRARIO, BILL William James, G, 6´2˝/315 lbs; Wisconsin; 2001: GB, rnd 4; B9/22/1978 Scranton, PA **2002**†GB 16 (0)

FERRELL, BOB Robert Steven, RB, 6´0˝/216 lbs; UCLA; B11/13/1952 Los Angeles, CA

1976	SF	10	9	28	3.1(11)	1	1	9	9.0(9)	0	—	—	—	—	—	—	—	—	—	—	k	—	6	40
1977	SF	14	41	160	3.9(12)	1	2	12	6.0(7)	0	—	—	—	—	—	—	—	—	—	—	k	—	6	166
1978	SF	16(8, fb)	125	471	3.8(20)	1	16	123	7.7(14)	0	—	—	—	—	—	—	—	—	—	—	k	—	6	552
1979	SF	16	8	33	4.1(8)	0	2	4	2.0(3)	0	—	—	—	—	—	—	—	—	—	—	k	—	0	23
1980	SF	12(0)	—	—	—	—	—	—	—	—	—	—	—	—	—	—	—	—	—	—	p	—	0	-4
NFL	5	68(8)	183	692	3.8(20)	3	21	148	7.0(14)	0	—	—	—	—	—	—	—	—	—	—	kp	—	18	776

FERRELL, EARL Earl Thomas, RB, 6´0˝/225 lbs; East Tennessee State; 1982: SL, rnd 5; B3/27/1958 Halifax, VA

1982	†SL	9(0)	—	—	—	—	—	—	—	—	—	—	—	—	—	—	—	—	—	—	kp	—	0	29
1983	SL	16(0)	7	53	7.6(21)	1	—	—	—	—	—	—	—	—	—	—	—	—	—	—	kp	—	6	137
1984	SL	16(9, FB)	44	203	4.6(25)	1	26	218	8.4(21)	1	—	—	—	—	—	—	—	—	—	—	k	—	12	312
1985	SL	11(9, FB)	46	208	4.5(30)	2	25	277	11.1(30)	2	—	—	—	—	—	—	—	—	—	—	—	—	24	377
1986	SL	16(15, FB)	124	548	4.4(25)	0	56	434	7.8(30)	3	—	—	—	—	—	—	—	—	—	—	k	—	18	776
1987	SL	11(11, FB)	113	512	4.5(35)	7	23	262	11.4(36)	0	—	—	—	—	—	—	—	—	—	—	k	—	42	708
1988	Phx	16(16, FB)	202	924	4.6(47)	7	38	315	8.3(30)	1	—	—	—	—	—	—	—	—	—	—	k	—	54	1157
1989	Phx	15(15, FB)	149	502	3.4(44)	6	18	122	6.8(25)	0	—	—	—	—	—	—	—	—	—	—	—	—	36	623
NFL	8	110(75)	685	2950	4.3(47)	24	186	1628	8.8(36)	8	—	—	—	—	—	—	—	—	—	—	kp	—	192	4118

FERRIS, NEIL Neil George, DB-HB, 5´11˝/181 lbs; Loyola Marymount; B10/31/1927 Bell, CA, D1/30/1996 Lake Havasu City, AZ **1951** Was 12 (DB) **1952** Phi 8 (DB) **1953** LARm 5

| 1952 | Was | 4 | 11 | 22 | 2.0(11) | 1 | 1 | 8 | 8.0(8) | 0 | — | — | — | — | — | — | — | — | — | — | kp | — | 6 | 68 |
| **NFL** | 3 | 29 | 11 | 22 | 2.0(11) | 1 | 1 | 8 | 8.0(8) | 0 | — | — | — | — | — | — | — | — | — | — | kp | — | 6 | 62 |

FERRY, LOU Louis Anthony, DT-T, 6´2˝/244 lbs; Villanova; 1949: GB, rnd 3/Bkn-A, rnd 2; B12/1/1927 Chester, PA, D1/25/2004 Bryn Mawr, PA **1949** GB 12 (3) **1951** ChiC 12 (LDT) **1952** Pit 12 (LDT) **1953** Pit 12 (LDT) **1954** Pit 11 (LDT) **1955** Pit 12 **NFL** 71 (3) [6 yrs]

FERSEN, PAUL Paul Clinton, T, 6´5˝/260 lbs; Georgia; 1973: NO, rnd 14; B2/16/1950 Columbus, GA **1973** NO 3 **1974** NO 1 **NFL** 4 [2 yrs]

FEST, HOWARD Howard Arthur, G-T, 6´6˝/262 lbs; Texas; 1968: Cin, rnd 6; B4/11/1946 San Antonio, TX **1968** Cin-A 14 (RT) **1969** Cin-A 14 (RT) **1970**†Cin 14 (LG) **1971** Cin 14 (LG) **1972** Cin 14 (LG) **1973**†Cin 14 (LG) **1974** Cin 14 (LG) **1975**†Cin 14 (LG) **1976** TB 14 (14, LG) **1977** TB 1 **NFL** 127 (14) [10 yrs]

FETHERSTON, JIM James Steven, LB, 6´2˝/225 lbs; California; B6/1/1945 Merced, CA **1968** SD-A 13 (7, mlb) **1969** SD-A 14 **NFL** 27 (7) [2 yrs]

FETZ, GUS Gustave, HB, /158 lbs; none; B1900, deceased **1923** ChiB 9 (1), 6

YEAR	TEAM	G (GS, POS)	RUSH	YD	AVG (LG)	TD	REC	YD	AVG (LG)	TD	PASS COMP	PCT	YD	AVG (LG)	TD	INT	SK	YD	QBR	KPR	OTD	PTS	TAY

FIALA, JOHN John Charles, LB, 6´2˝/232 lbs; Washington; 1997: Mia, rnd 6; B11/25/1973 Fullerton, CA **1998** Pit 16 (0) **1999** Pit 16 (0) **2000** Pit 16 (0) **2001**†Pit 16 (0)
2002 Pit 11 (1) **NFL** 75 (1) [5 yrs]

FICCA, DAN Daniel Robert, G, 6´1˝/245 lbs; USC; 1961: SD, rnd 29/Phi, rnd 4; B2/7/1939 Atlas, PA **1962** Oak-A 14 **1963** NYJ-A 14 (LG) **1964** NYJ-A 14 (LG) **1965** NYJ-A☆14
1966 NYJ-A 14 **NFL** 70 [5 yrs]

FICHMAN, LEON Leon, T, 6´1˝/215 lbs; Alabama; B2/23/1921 Los Angeles, CA **1946** Det 11 (5, rt) **1947** Det 1 (0) **NFL** 12 (5) [2 yrs]

FICHTEL, BRAD Brad Alan, C, 6´2˝/285 lbs; Eastern Illinois; 1993: LARm, rnd 7; B3/10/1970 Aurora, IL **1994** LARm 1 (0)

FICHTNER, ROSS Ross William, DB, 6´0˝/185 lbs; Purdue; 1960: Cle, rnd 3/Buf, rnd 1; B10/26/1938 McKeesport, PA **[I]** **1960** Cle 12 **1961** Cle 13 **1962** Cle 14 (LS)
1963 Cle 13 (RS) **1964**†Cle 8 (rs) **1965**†Cle 14 (LS) **1966** Cle☆14 (LS/rs) **1967**†Cle 14 (RS/ls) **1968** NO 4 **NFL** 106 [9 yrs]

FIEDLER, BILL William Ferdinand, G, 5´9˝/200 lbs; Pennsylvania; B11/9/1914, D2/1976 **1938** Phi 1 (0)

FIEDLER, JAY Jay Brian, QB, 6´2˝/225 lbs; Dartmouth; B12/29/1971 Oceanside, NY

YEAR	TEAM	G (GS, POS)	RUSH	YD	AVG (LG)	TD	REC	YD	AVG (LG)	TD	PASS COMP	PCT	YD	AVG (LG)	TD	INT	SK	YD	QBR	KPR	OTD	PTS	TAY
1995	†Phi	0 (0)	—	—	—	—	—	—	—	—	—	—	—	—	—	—	—	—	—	—	—	0	0
1998	Min	5 (0)	4	-6	-1.5 (-1)	0	—	—	—	—	7	3	42.9	41	5.9 (19)	0	1	—	—	—	—	0	-26
1999	†Jax	8 (1)	13	26	2.0 (15)	0	—	—	—	—	94	61	64.9	656	7.0 (25)	2	2	7	47	—	—	0	284
2000	†Mia	15 (15, QB)	54	267	4.9 (30)	1	—	—	—	—	357	204	57.1	2402	6.7 (61)	14	14	23	129	74.5	—	6	988
2001	†Mia	16 (16, QB)	73	321	4.4 (26)	4	—	—	—	—	450	273	60.7	3290	7.3 (74)	20	19	27	178	80.3	—	24	1346
2002	Mia	11 (10, QB)	28	99	3.5 (12)	3	—	—	—	—	292	179	61.3	2024	6.9 (59)	14	9	13	89	85.2	—	18	851
2003	Mia	12 (11, QB)	34	88	2.6 (14)	3	—	—	—	—	314	179	57.0	2138	6.8 (59)	11	13	19	126	72.4	—	18	722
2004	Mia	8 (7, qb)	12	59	4.9 (26)	0	—	—	—	—	190	101	53.2	1186	6.2 (71)	7	8	25	165	67.1	—	0	367
2005	NYJ	2 (0)	1	0	0.0 (0)	0	—	—	—	—	13	8	61.5	107	8.2 (23)	1	0	—	—	—	—	0	59
NFL	9	77 (60)	219	854	3.9 (30)	11	—	—	—	—	1717	1008	58.7	11844	6.9 (74)	69	66	114	734	77.1	—	66	4591

FIELD, AMOD Arnold Lloyd, WR, 5´11˝/186 lbs; Montclair State; B10/11/1967 **1991** Phx 2 (0)

FIELD, DOAK Richard Doak, LB, 6´2˝/228 lbs; Baylor; 1981: Phi, rnd 7; B10/8/1958 Burnet, TX **1981** SL 7 (0)

FIELD, HARRY Harry Nuuanu, T, 6´1˝/226 lbs; Hawaii; Oregon State; B8/18/1911 Iao Valley, HI, D5/23/1964 Honolulu, HI **1934** ChiC☆11 (11, LT) **1935** ChiC 10 (4)
1936 ChiC 12 (12, RT) **NFL** 33 (27) [3 yrs]

FIELDER, DON Donald Sinclair, DE, 6´3˝/260 lbs; Kentucky; B10/20/1959 Las Cruces, NM **1985** TB 11 (0)

FIELDINGS, ANTHONY Anthony, LB, 6´1˝/237 lbs; Morningside; B7/7/1971 Eustis, FL **1995** Dal 4 (3)

FIELDS, AARON Aaron, DE, 6´4˝/243 lbs; Troy State; B1/9/1976 Notasulga, AL **2000** Dal 3 (0)

FIELDS, ANGELO Angelo Bertell, T, 6´6˝/321 lbs; Michigan State; 1980: Hou, rnd 2; B9/15/1957 Washington, DC **1980**†Hou 16 (3) **1981** Hou 14 (0) **1982**†GB 0 (0)
NFL 30 (3) [3 yrs]

FIELDS, ANTHONY Anthony Bernard, DB, 6´1˝/192 lbs; Eastern Michigan; B1/17/1964 Mobile, AL **1987** Det 3 (0)

FIELDS, EDGAR Edgar Eugene, DT-DE, 6´2˝/255 lbs; Texas A&M; 1977: Atl, rnd 3; B3/10/1954 Austin, TX **1977** Atl 14 **1978**†Atl 16 (2) **1979** Atl 16 (15, RDT) **1980**†Atl 14 (1)
1981 Det 2 (0) **NFL** 62 (18) [5 yrs]

FIELDS, FLOYD Floyd Cornelius, DB, 6´0˝/208 lbs; Arizona State; 1991: SD, rnd 5; B1/7/1969 South Holland, IL **1991** SD 1 (0) **1992**†SD 16 (14, SS) **1993** SD 13 (2)
NFL 30 (16) [3 yrs]

FIELDS, GEORGE George, DT-DE, 6´3˝/245 lbs; Bakersfield College (CA); B1936 **1960** Oak-A 14 (LDT) **1961** Oak-A 1 **NFL** 15 [2 yrs]

FIELDS, GREG Gregory Keith, DE, 6´7˝/260 lbs; Grambling State; B1/23/1955 San Francisco, CA **1979** Bal 16 (4) **1980** Bal 16 (6, rde) **NFL** 32 (10) [2 yrs]

FIELDS, JAIME Jaime, LB, 5´11˝/230 lbs; Washington; 1993: KC, rnd 4; B8/28/1970 Compton, CA, D8/29/1999 Downey, CA **1993**†KC 6 (0) **1994** KC 11 (2) **NFL** 17 (2) [2 yrs]

FIELDS, JEFF Jeff, DT, 6´3˝/320 lbs; Arkansas State; 1991: LARm, rnd 9; B7/3/1967 Jackson, MS **1995** Car 2 (0)

FIELDS, JERRY Jerry Eugene, LB, 6´1˝/222 lbs; Ohio State; 1961: NYG, rnd 13; B5/24/1938 Ironton, OH **1961** NYT-A 5 **1962** NYT-A 14 **NFL** 19 [2 yrs]

FIELDS, JITTER Alfred Gene, DB, 5´8˝/185 lbs; Texas; 1984: NO, rnd 5; B8/16/1962 Dallas, TX **1984** NO 13 (0) **1987** Ind 1 (0) **1987** KC 5 (0) **NFL** 19 (0) [2 yrs]

FIELDS, JOE Joseph Charles, C-G, 6´2˝/250 lbs; Rutgers-Camden; Widener; 1975: NYJ, rnd 14; B11/14/1953 Woodbury, NJ **1975** NYJ 14 **1976** NYJ 14 (10, C)
1977 NYJ 14 (14, C) **1978** NYJ 16 (16, C) **1979** NYJ 15 (15, C) **1980** NYJ 13 (13, C) **1981**†NYJ☆16 (16, C) **1982**†NYJ☆9 (9, C) **1983** NYJ 12 (12, C) **1984** NYJ 16 (16, C)
1985†NYJ☆15 (14, C) **1986**†NYJ 9 (9, C) **1987** NYJ 10 (10, RG) **1988** NYG 13 (0) **NFL** 186 (154) [14 yrs]

FIELDS, MARK Mark Lee, LB, 6´2˝/244 lbs; Washington State; 1995: NO, rnd 1; B11/9/1972 Los Angeles, CA **1995** NO 16 (3) **1996** NO 16 (15, RLB) **1997** NO 16 (15, RLB)
1998 NO 15 (15, RLB) **1999** NO 14 (14, RLB) **2000**†NO◇16 (14, RLB) **2001**†SL 14 (12, RLB) **2002** Car 15 (15, LLB) **2004** Car◇14 (10, LLB) **NFL** 136 (113) [9 yrs]

FIELDS, RONALD Ronald J., DT, 6´2˝/322 lbs; Mississippi State; 2005: SF, rnd 5; B9/13/1981 Bogalusa, LA **2005** SF 4 (0)

FIELDS, SCOTT Scott, LB, 6´2˝/220 lbs; USC; B4/22/1973 Ontario, CA **1996** Atl 6 (0) **1999** Sea 2 (0) **NFL** 8 (0) [2 yrs]

FIFE, RALPH Ralph David, G, 5´11˝/207 lbs; Pittsburgh; B1/26/1920 Canton, OH, D1/21/2000 Mount Lebanon, PA **1942** ChiC 4 (3) **1945** ChiC 1 (1) **1946** Pit 10 (9, LG)
NFL 15 (13) [3 yrs]

FIFER, BILL William Charles, T, 6´4˝/250 lbs; West Texas A&M; 1978: Det, rnd 4; B10/26/1955 Kerrville, TX **1978** Det 8 **1978** NO 4 **NFL** 12 [1 yr]

FIGARO, CEDRIC Cedric Noah, LB, 6´2˝/255 lbs; Notre Dame; 1988: SD, rnd 6; B8/17/1966 Lafayette, LA **1988** SD 6 (5, lilb) **1989** SD 16 (14, RILB) **1990** SD 16 (1)
1991 Ind 1 (0) **1991** Cle 12 (0) **1992** Cle 16 (0) **1995** SL 16 (1) **1996** SL 15 (0) **NFL** 98 (21) [7 yrs]

FIGNER, GEORGE George Kendall, DB, 6´0˝/185 lbs; Colorado; B4/30/1931 Dayton, OH **1953** ChiB 5

FIGURES, DEON Deon Juniel, DB, 6´0˝/200 lbs; Colorado; 1993: Pit, rnd 1; B1/20/1970 Bellflower, CA **1993**†Pit 15 (4) **1994**†Pit 16 (15, RCB) **1995**†Pit 14 (1) **1996**†Pit 16 (3)
1997†Jax 16 (12, RCB) **1998**†Jax 16 (5, rcb) **NFL** 93 (40) [6 yrs]

FIKE, DAN Dan Clement, G-T, 6´7˝/280 lbs; Florida; 1983: NYJ, rnd 10; B6/16/1961 Mobile, AL **1985**†Cle 13 (13, RG) **1986**†Cle☆16 (16, RG) **1987**†Cle☆12 (12, RG)
1988†Cle 16 (16, RG) **1989** Cle 13 (13, RG) **1990** Cle 10 (0) **1991** Cle 16 (16, RT) **1992** Cle 16 (16, RT) **1993** Pit 3 (0) **NFL** 115 (102) [9 yrs]

FILAK, JOHN John, T-G, 6´0˝/190 lbs; Penn State; B10/13/1903, deceased **1927** Fra 11 (5, rt) **1928** Fra 14 (2) **1929** Fra 14 (11, rt) **NFL** 39 (18) [3 yrs]

FILCHOCK, FRANK Frank Joseph, TB-QB-HB, 5´10˝/193 lbs; Indiana; 1938: Pit, rnd 2; B10/18/1916 Crucible, PA, D1/20/1994 Washington County, OR **[C]**

YEAR	TEAM	G (GS, POS)	RUSH	YD	AVG (LG)	TD	REC	YD	AVG (LG)	TD	PASS COMP	PCT	YD	AVG (LG)	TD	INT	SK	YD	QBR	KPR	OTD	PTS	TAY
1938	Pit	6 (3)	17	20	1.2	0	—	—	—	—	74	30	40.5	392	5.3	3	7	—	—	—	—	0	-49
1938	Was	6 (2)	52	178	3.4	1	2	4	2.0	0	27	11	40.7	77	2.9	0	4	—	—	—	—	6	69
1939	Was★	11 (9, TB)	103	413	4.0	1	—	—	—	—	89	55	61.8	1094	12.3 (99)	11	7	—	—	—	—	6	745
1940	†Was	10	50	126	2.5	2	—	—	—	—	54	28	51.9	460	8.5	6	9	—	—	i	—	12	27
1941	Was◇	11 (10, tb)	115	383	3.3 (51)	1	—	—	—	—	68	28	41.2	327	4.8 (35)	1	11	—	—	Pkp	—	1	12	305
1944	Was☆	10 (6, QB)	33	-34	-1.0 (9)	0	3	51	17.0 (28)	0	147	84	57.1	1139	7.7 (61)	13	9	—	—	86.0	kp	—	0	253
1945	†Was	10	9	21	2.3 (29)	0	3	33	11.0 (17)	0	46	18	39.1	169	3.7 (27)	1	7	—	—	pi	—	0	-146
1946	†NYG☆	11 (4, TB)	98	371	3.8 (70)	2	1	-6	-6.0 (-6)	0	169	87	51.5	1262	7.5 (57)	12	25	—	—	60.2	kpi	—	12	162
1950	Bal	1	—	—	—	—	—	—	—	—	3	1	33.3	1	0.3 (1)	0	0	—	—	—	—	0	1
NFL	8	76 (34)	477	1478	3.1 (70)	7	9	82	9.1 (28)	0	677	342	50.5	4921	7.3 (99)	47	79	—	—	58.0	Pkpi	1	48	1366

FILES, JIM James Dale, LB, 6´4˝/240 lbs; Oklahoma; 1970: NYG, rnd 1; B1/16/1948 Paris, AR **1970** NYG 14 (MLB) **1971** NYG 14 (MLB) **1972** NYG 14 (LLB)
1973 NYG 14 (MLB) **NFL** 56 [4 yrs]

FILIPOVIC, FILIP Filip, P, 6´2˝/216 lbs; South Dakota; B11/5/1977 Belgrade, Yugoslavia **2002** Dal 9 (0)

FILIPOWICZ, STEVE Stephen Charles, FB-BB, 5´8˝/200 lbs; Fordham; 1943: NYG, rnd 1; B6/28/1921 Donora, PA, D2/21/1975 Wilkes-Barre, PA

YEAR	TEAM	G (GS, POS)	RUSH	YD	AVG (LG)	TD	REC	YD	AVG (LG)	TD	PASS COMP	PCT	YD	AVG (LG)	TD	INT	SK	YD	QBR	KPR	OTD	PTS	TAY
1945	NYG	10 (5, FB)	53	142	2.7 (13)	1	4	49	12.3 (26)	1	2	0	0.0	0	0.0	0	0	—	—	—	kp	—	12	212
1946	†NYG	11 (7, BB)	2	3	1.5 (2)	1	7	84	12.0 (29)	1	—	—	—	—	—	—	—	—	—	—	ki	—	18	103
NFL	2	21 (12)	55	145	2.6 (13)	2	11	133	12.1 (29)	2	2	0	0.0	0	0.0	0	0	—	—	—	kpi	—	30	315

YEAR	TEAM	G (GS, POS)	RUSH	YD	AVG(LG)	TD	REC	YD	AVG(LG)	TD	PASS	COMP	PCT	YD	AVG(LG)	TD	INT	SK	YD	QBR	KPR	OTD	PTS	TAY
FILIPSKI, GENE	Eugene C., HB, 5´11˝/185 lbs; Army; Villanova; 1953: Cle, rnd 7; B6/14/1931 Webster, MA, D8/23/1994 Calgary, Canada																							
1956	†NYG	12	13	85	6.5(35)	1	3	37	12.3(21)	0	—	—	—	—	—	—	—	—	—	—	kp	—	6	239
1957	NYG	12	22	89	4.0(11)	0	1	7	7.0(7)	0	—	—	—	—	—	—	—	—	—	—	kp	—	0	307
NFL	2	24	35	174	5.0(35)	1	4	44	11.0(21)	0	—	—	—	—	—	—	—	—	—	—		—	6	545
FINA, JOHN	John Joseph, T, 6´4˝/287 lbs; Arizona; 1992: Buf, rnd 1; B3/11/1969 Rochester, MN **1994** Buf 12 (12, LT) **1995**†Buf 16 (16, LT) **1996**†Buf 15 (15, LT) **1997** Buf 16 (16, LT) **1998**†Buf 14 (14, LT) **1999**†Buf 16 (16, LT) **2000** Buf 14 (14, LT) **2001** Buf 13 (12, LT) **2002** Arz 7 (0)																							
1992	†Buf	16(0)	—	—	—	—	1	1	1.0(1)	1	—	—	—	—	—	—	—	—	—	—	—	—	6	6
1993	†Buf	16(16, LT)	1	-2	-2.0(-2)	0	—	—	—	—	—	—	—	—	—	—	—	—	—	—	—	—	0	-2
NFL	11	155(131)	1	-2	-2.0(-2)	0	1	1	1.0(1)	1	—	—	—	—	—	—	—	—	—	—	—	—	6	4
FINCH, BULL	Olin, BB-FB, 5´8˝/180 lbs; Whittier; B1893, D1956 **1926** LA 7 (5, BB)																							
FINCH, KARL	Karl Lee, WR, 6´3˝/195 lbs; Iowa; Cal Poly-San Luis Obispo; B7/7/1939 Modesto, CA **1962** LARm 7																							
FINCH, STEVE	Stephen, WR, 6´0˝/200 lbs; Elmhurst; B1/2/1961 Great Lakes, IL																							
1987	Min	1(1)	—	—	—	—	3	54	18.0(20)	0	—	—	—	—	—	—	—	—	—	—	—	—	0	27
FINCHER, ALFRED	Alfred William, LB, 6´1˝/241 lbs; Connecticut; 2005: NO, rnd 3; B8/15/1983 Key West, FL **2005** NO 11 (0)																							
FINK, MIKE	Paul Michael, DB, 5´11˝/181 lbs; Missouri; 1973: NO, rnd 9; B12/24/1950 Kansas City, MO **1973** NO 13																							
FINKES, MIKE	Matthew Scott, DE, 6´3˝/272 lbs; Ohio State; 1997: Car, rnd 6; B2/12/1975 Piqua, OH **1997** NYJ 8 (0)																							
FINKS, JIM	James Edward, QB-DB-TB, 5´11˝/180 lbs; Tulsa; 1949: Pit, rnd 12/ChiH-A, rnd 4; B8/31/1927 St. Louis, MO, D5/8/1994 New Orleans, LA; HOF 1995																							
1949	Pit	11(0)	35	135	3.9(38)	1	1	17	17.0(17)	1	71	24	33.8	322	4.5(35)	2	8	—	—	i	—	—	12	19
1950	Pit	9(DB)	1	2	2.0(2)	0	—	—	—	—	9	5	55.6	35	3.9(19)	0	1	—	—	i	—	—	0	-12
1951	Pit	12(DB)	3	27	9.0(22)	0	—	—	—	—	24	14	58.3	201	8.4(40)	1	1	—	—	pi	—	1	6	149
1952	Pit◇	12(QB)	23	37	1.6(20)	5	—	—	—	—	336	158	47.0	2307	6.9(60)	20	19	—	—	66.2	P	—	30	581
1953	Pit	11(QB)	12	0	0.0(4)	2	—	—	—	—	292	131	44.9	1484	5.1(77)	8	14	—	—	49.8	—	—	12	242
1954	Pit	12(QB)	9	17	1.9(6)	0	—	—	—	—	306	164	53.6	2003	6.5(78)	14	19	—	—	63.4	—	—	0	329
1955	Pit	12(QB)	35	76	2.2(9)	4	—	—	—	—	344	165	48.0	2270	6.6(62)	10	26	—	—	47.7	—	—	24	261
NFL	7	79	118	294	2.5(38)	12	1	17	17.0(17)	1	1382	661	47.8	8622	6.2(78)	55	88	—	—	54.7	Ppi	1	84	1568
FINLAY, JACK	Jack Alexander, G-LB, 6´1˝/217 lbs; UCLA; B9/8/1921 Los Angeles, CA **1947** LARm 12 (0) **1948** LARm 12 (2) **1949**†LARm 12 (0) **1950**†LARm 10 (LG) **1951**†LARm 9 **NFL** 55 (2) [5 yrs]																							
FINLEY, CLINT	Clint Cade, DB, 6´0˝/210 lbs; Nebraska; B3/27/1977 Andrews, TX **2002** KC 1 (0) **2003**†KC 3 (0) **NFL** 4 (0) [2 yrs]																							
FINN, BERNIE	Bernard Francis, B, 5´10˝/180 lbs; Holy Cross; B6/4/1907, D9/26/1993 Toms River, NJ **1930** Nwk 10 (8, BB) **1930** SI 4 (4)																							
1932	SI	1(1)	3	9	3.0	0	—	—	—	—	1	1	100.0	9	9.0(9)	0	0	—	—	—	—	—	0	14
1932	ChiC	2(1)	—	—	—	—	3	37	12.3	0	—	—	—	—	—	—	—	—	—	—	—	—	0	19
NFL	2	17(14)	3	9	3.0	0	3	37	12.3	0	1	1	100.0	9	9.0(9)	0	0	—	—	—	—	—	0	32
FINN, JACK	John Thomas, B, 5´7˝/172 lbs; Villanova; Moravian; B8/27/1895 Bethlehem, PA, D12/25/1970 Hellertown, PA **[K]** **1924** Fra 9 (1), 20																							
FINN, JIM	James, FB, 6´0˝/245 lbs; Pennsylvania; 1999: Chi, rnd 7; B12/9/1976 Teaneck, NJ																							
2000	†Ind	16(1)	1	1	1.0(1)	0	4	13	3.3(6)	0	—	—	—	—	—	—	—	—	—	—	—	—	6	13
2001	Ind	15(0)	—	—	—	—	—	—	—	—	—	—	—	—	—	—	—	—	—	—	k	—	0	-16
2002	Ind	12(2)	5	8	1.6(5)	0	6	31	5.2(12)	0	—	—	—	—	—	—	—	—	—	—	k	—	0	24
2003	NYG	15(9, FB)	—	—	—	—	14	115	8.2(27)	0	—	—	—	—	—	—	—	—	—	—	k	—	0	62
2004	NYG	16(9, FB)	3	7	2.3(5)	0	15	112	7.5(15)	0	—	—	—	—	—	—	—	—	—	—	k	—	0	64
2005	†NYG	16(13, FB)	—	—	—	—	13	98	7.5(15)	0	—	—	—	—	—	—	—	—	—	—	k	—	0	49
NFL	6	90(34)	9	16	1.8(5)	0	52	369	7.1(27)	1	—	—	—	—	—	—	—	—	—	—	k	—	6	195
FINNEGAN, JAMES	James Patrick, E-QB, 5´8˝/160 lbs; St. Louis; B1/20/1901 St. Louis, MO, D9/6/1967 Crestwood, MO **1923** SL 2 (0)																							
FINNERAN, BRIAN	Brian, WR, 6´5˝/210 lbs; Villanova; B1/31/1976 Mission Viejo, CA																							
1999	Phi	3(0)	—	—	—	—	2	21	10.5(11)	0	—	—	—	—	—	—	—	—	—	—	—	—	0	11
2000	Atl	11(0)	—	—	—	—	7	60	8.6(14)	0	—	—	—	—	—	—	—	—	—	—	k	—	0	17
2001	Atl	16(1)	—	—	—	—	23	491	21.3(52)	3	—	—	—	—	—	—	—	—	—	—	—	—	18	261
2002	†Atl	16(16, WR)	—	—	—	—	56	838	15.0(47)	6	—	—	—	—	—	—	—	—	—	—	p	—	36	439
2003	Atl	12(10, WR)	—	—	—	—	26	368	14.2(38)	2	—	—	—	—	—	—	—	—	—	—	—	—	12	194
2004	†Atl	12(1)	—	—	—	—	23	258	11.2(26)	2	—	—	—	—	—	—	—	—	—	—	p	—	12	139
2005	Atl	16(6, wr)	—	—	—	—	50	611	12.2(53)	2	—	—	—	—	—	—	—	—	—	—	p	—	18	313
NFL	7	86(34)	—	—	—	—	187	2647	14.2(53)	15	—	—	—	—	—	—	—	—	—	—	kp	—	96	1373
FINNERAN, GARY	Gary, DE-DT, 6´3˝/240 lbs; USC; B2/23/1934 **1960**†LAC-A 13 **1961** Oak-A 13 (LDE) **NFL** 26 [2 yrs]																							
FINNIE, ROGER	Roger Lewis, T-G-DT, 6´3˝/245 lbs; Florida A&M; 1969: NYJ, rnd 14; B11/6/1945 Miami, FL **1969**†NYJ-A 14 (RT) **1970** NYJ 3 **1971** NYJ 7 (ldt) **1972** NYJ 14 **1973** SL 12 (1, rt) **1974**†SL 14 (7, lg) **1975**†SL 14 (14, LT) **1976** SL 14 (LT) **1977** SL 14 (LT) **1978** SL 7 **1979** NO 8 **NFL** 121 (22) [11 yrs]																							
FINNIN, TOM	Thomas R., DT, 6´2˝/262 lbs; Detroit Mercy; 1950: NYG, rnd 24; B9/28/1927 Chicago, IL, D6/22/2003 Chicago, IL **1953** Bal 11 (RDT) **1954** Bal 12 (RDT) **1955** Bal 11 (RDT) **1956** Bal 10 (RDT) **1957** ChiC 8 **1957** GB 3 **NFL** 55 [5 yrs]																							
FINSTERWALD, RUSS	Russell Walter, WB, 5´9˝/165 lbs; Ohio University; Syracuse; B8/1896 Athens, OH, D6/13/1962 Athens, OH **1920** Det 2 (1)																							
FINZER, DAVE	David Mangan, P, 6´1˝/195 lbs; Illinois; DePauw; B2/3/1959 Chicago, IL																							
1984	†ChiB	16(0)	2	0	0.0(5)	0	—	—	—	—	—	—	—	—	—	—	—	—	—	P	—	—	0	0
1985	Sea	12(0)	1	-2	-2.0(-2)	0	—	—	—	—	1	0	0.0	0	0.0	0	1	—	—	P	—	—	0	-42
NFL	2	28(0)	3	-2	-0.7(5)	0	—	—	—	—	1	0	0.0	0	0.0	0	1	—	—	P	—	—	0	-42
FIORE, DAVE	David Allan, G-T, 6´4˝/293 lbs; Hofstra; B8/10/1974 Hackensack, NJ **1998**†SF 9 (3) **1999** SF 16 (16, LT) **2000** SF 15 (15, RG) **2001**†SF 16 (16, RG) **2002** SF 3 (3) **2003** Was 3 (3) **NFL** 62 (56) [6 yrs]																							
FIORENTINO, AL	Albert M., G, 5´7˝/200 lbs; Boston College; B2/28/1917 Watertown, NY, D2/28/2001 Butler, PA **1943**†Was 10 (0) **1944** Was 10 (10, LG) **1945** Bos 8 (1) **NFL** 28 (11) [3 yrs]																							
FIORENTINO, ED	Edward Angelo, DE, 6´1˝/210 lbs; Boston College; Brown; 1944: Bos, rnd 12; B9/21/1923 Everett, MA, D8/2/1989 Boston, MA **1947** Bos 4 (0)																							
FISCHER, BILL	William Anton, T-G-DT, 6´2˝/248 lbs; Notre Dame; 1949: ChiC, rnd 1/ChiR-A, rnd S2; B3/10/1927 Chicago, IL **1949** ChiC 12 (7, LT) **1950** ChiC◇12 (12, LT) **1951** ChiC★12 (LT) **1952** ChiC★12 (RG) **1953** ChiC 11 **NFL** 59 (19) [5 yrs]																							
FISCHER, CLARKE	Clarke John, HB, 5´8˝/165 lbs; Marquette; Campion; Catholic; B3/30/1900 Hermansville, MI, D10/21/1979 Pana, IL **1926** Mil 2 (0)																							
FISCHER, CLETE	Cletus Paul, HB, 5´9˝/170 lbs; Nebraska; 1949: NYG, rnd 23; B6/11/1925 St. Edward, NE, D12/3/2000 Lincoln, NE																							
1949	NYG	11(1)	26	72	2.8(10)	0	3	45	15.0(36)	1	—	—	—	—	—	—	—	—	—	—	kpi	—	6	197
FISCHER, MARK	Mark Raymond, C, 6´3˝/293 lbs; Purdue; 1998: Was, rnd 5; B7/29/1974 Cincinnati, OH **1998** Was 6 (0) **1999**†Was 0 (0) **2000** Was 16 (16, C) **NFL** 22 (16) [3 yrs]																							
FISCHER, PAT	Patrick, DB, 5´9˝/170 lbs; Nebraska; 1961: SL, rnd 17; B1/2/1940 St. Edward, NE **[I]** **1962** SL 12 **1963** SL 14 (LCB) **1964** SL★14 (LCB) **1965** SL★14 (LCB) **1966** SL 7 (lcb) **1967** SL 14 (LCB) **1968** Was☆14 (LCB) **1969** Was★14 (LCB) **1970** Was 14 (14, LCB) **1971**†Was 14 (14, LCB) **1972**†Was☆14 (14, LCB) **1973**†Was 14 (14, LCB) **1974**†Was 14 (14, LCB) **1975** Was☆11 (11, LCB) **1976**†Was 14 (14, LCB) **1977** Was 3 (3)																							
1961	SL	12	—	—	—	—	1	22	22.0(22)	0	—	—	—	—	—	—	—	—	—	—	kp	—	0	180
NFL	17	213(98)	—	—	—	—	1	22	22.0(22)	0	—	—	—	—	—	—	—	—	—	—	kpi	5	30	945
FISHBACK, JOE	Joe Edward, DB, 6´0˝/205 lbs; Carson-Newman; B11/29/1967 Knoxville, TN **1991**†Atl 14 (0) **1992** NYJ 5 (0) **1992** Atl 8 (0) **1993**†Dal 6 (0) **1994**†Dal 12 (0) **NFL** 45 (0) [4 yrs]																							
FISHEL, DICK	Richard Edward, B, 5´9˝/190 lbs; Syracuse; B9/19/1909 Brooklyn, NY, D8/12/1972																							
1933	Bkn	8(2)	22	61	2.8	1	—	—	—	—	7	3	42.9	50	7.1	0	1	—	—	—	—	—	6	56

YEAR	TEAM	G (GS, POS)	RUSH	YD	AVG (LG)	TD	REC	YD	AVG (LG)	TD	PASS	COMP	PCT	YD	AVG (LG)	TD	INT	SK	YD	QBR	KPR	OTD	PTS	TAY

Fisher, Bob Robert Arthur, T, 6´2˝/220 lbs; USC; B8/27/1916 Los Angeles, CA, D5/29/1983 Laguna Beach, CA **1940**†Was 7 (1)

Fisher, Bob Robert Lee, TE, 6´3˝/240 lbs; SMU; 1980: Chi, rnd 12; B3/17/1958 Pasadena, CA **1981** ChiB 6 (1)

YEAR	TEAM	G (GS, POS)	RUSH	YD	AVG (LG)	TD	REC	YD	AVG (LG)	TD	PASS	COMP	PCT	YD	AVG (LG)	TD	INT	SK	YD	QBR	KPR	OTD	PTS	TAY
1980	ChiB	16(2)	—	—	—	—	12	203	16.9(56)	2	—	—	—	—	—	—	—	—	—	—	k	—	12	99
NFL	2	22(3)	—	—	—	—	12	203	16.9(56)	2	—	—	—	—	—	—	—	—	—	—	k	—	12	93

Fisher, Bryce Bryce Alexander, DE, 6´3˝/272 lbs; Air Force; 1999: Buf, rnd 7; B5/12/1977 Renton, WA **2001** Buf 13 (2) **2002** SL 4 (0) **2003**†SL 16 (1) **2004**†SL 16 (14, RDE) **2005**†Sea 16 (15, LDE) **NFL** 65 (32) [5 yrs]

Fisher, Charles Charles, DB, 6´0˝/185 lbs; West Virginia; 1999: Cin, rnd 2; B2/2/1976 Aliquippa, PA **1999** Cin 1 (1)

Fisher, Darrell Darrell Charles, TB-FB, 5´11˝/190 lbs; Iowa; B5/10/1903, IL, deceased **1925** Buf 5 (2)

Fisher, Doug Douglas Gene, LB, 6´1˝/225 lbs; San Diego State; 1969: Pit, rnd 12; B3/8/1947 Fresno, CA **1969** Pit 6 **1970** Pit 4 **NFL** 10 [2 yrs]

Fisher, Ed Edwin Louis, G-C-DE, 6´3˝/249 lbs; Arizona State; B5/31/1949 Stockton, CA **1974** Hou 11 **1975** Hou 14 (14, RG) **1976** Hou 14 (14, RG) **1977** Hou 14 **1978**†Hou 16 (16, RG) **1979**†Hou 16 (16, RG) **1980**†Hou 16 (16, RG) **1981** Hou 16 (16, RG) **1982** Hou 9 (9, RG) **NFL** 126 (101) [9 yrs]

Fisher, Eddie Edward, G, 5´11˝/210 lbs; Columbia; B7/18/1901 Tonawanda, NY, D2/1984 Buffalo, NY **1925** Buf 2 (1)

Fisher, Ev Everett Earl, BB-E, 5´11˝/205 lbs; Santa Clara; B3/1/1914, deceased

YEAR	TEAM	G (GS, POS)	RUSH	YD	AVG (LG)	TD	REC	YD	AVG (LG)	TD	PASS	COMP	PCT	YD	AVG (LG)	TD	INT	SK	YD	QBR	KPR	OTD	PTS	TAY
1938	ChiC	11(0)	—	—	—	—	3	48	16.0	0	—	—	—	—	—	—	—	—	—	—	—	—	0	24
1939	ChiC	11(7, BB)	18	63	3.5	0	6	62	10.3	0	—	—	—	—	—	—	—	—	—	—	—	—	0	94
1940	Pit	4(0)	—	—	—	—	2	12	6.0	0	—	—	—	—	—	—	—	—	—	—	—	—	0	6
NFL	3	26(7)	18	63	3.5	0	11	122	11.1	0	—	—	—	—	—	—	—	—	—	—	—	—	0	124

Fisher, George George Louis, T, 6´0˝/210 lbs; Indiana; B8/17/1901 Jackson County, IN, D10/30/1968 Lewisburg, IN **1926** Ham 2 (1)

Fisher, Jeff Jeffrey Michael, DB, 5´10˝/188 lbs; USC; 1981: Chi, rnd 7; B2/25/1958 Culver City, CA **[RC]** **1981** ChiB 16 (0) **1982** ChiB 9 (0) **1983** ChiB 8 (3) **1984**†ChiB 16 (0) **NFL** 49 (3) [4 yrs]

Fisher, Levar Levar, LB, 6´1˝/239 lbs; North Carolina State; 2002: Arz, rnd 2; B7/2/1979 Beaufort, NC **2002** Arz 7 (0) **2003** Arz 16 (15, RLB) **NFL** 23 (15) [2 yrs]

Fisher, Mike James Michael, WR, 5´11˝/172 lbs; Baylor; 1981: SL, rnd 8; B4/22/1958 Gatesville, TX **1981** SL 2 (0)

Fisher, Ray Raymond Edward, DT-T-G, 6´0˝/230 lbs; Eastern Illinois; B2/12/1934 Charleston, IL **1959** Pit 12 (RDT)

Fisher, Tony Antoine Maurice, RB, 6´1˝/222 lbs; Notre Dame; B10/12/1979 Euclid, OH

YEAR	TEAM	G (GS, POS)	RUSH	YD	AVG (LG)	TD	REC	YD	AVG (LG)	TD	PASS	COMP	PCT	YD	AVG (LG)	TD	INT	SK	YD	QBR	KPR	OTD	PTS	TAY
2002	†GB	15(1)	70	283	4.0(28)	2	18	70	3.9(11)	0	—	—	—	—	—	—	—	—	—	—	k	—	12	350
2003	†GB	15(0)	40	200	5.0(19)	1	21	206	9.8(32)	2	—	—	—	—	—	—	—	—	—	—	—	—	18	323
2004	†GB	16(0)	65	224	3.4(24)	0	38	277	7.3(25)	2	1	1	100.0	8	8.0(8)	1	0	—	—	—	—	—	12	382
2005	GB	14(4)	60	173	2.9(17)	1	48	347	7.2(15)	1	1	1	100.0	14	14.0(14)	0	0	—	—	—	—	—	12	369
NFL	4	60(5)	235	880	3.7(28)	4	125	900	7.2(32)	5	2	2	100.0	22	11.0(14)	1	0	—	—	—	k	—	54	1423

Fisher, Travis Travis Lamon, DB, 5´10˝/189 lbs; Central Florida; 2002: SL, rnd 2; B9/12/1979 Tallahassee, FL **2002** SL 14 (11, LCB) **2003**†SL 15 (15, RCB) **2004**†SL 10 (10, RCB) **2005** SL 8 (8, RCB) **NFL** 47 (44) [4 yrs]

Fishman, Alec Alexander, G-FB, 5´11˝/218 lbs; none; B1898, IL, deceased **1921** Evv 5 (5, LG), 6

Fisk, Bill William G., E-DE, 6´0˝/200 lbs; USC; 1940: Det, rnd 3; B11/5/1916 Los Angeles, CA

YEAR	TEAM	G (GS, POS)	RUSH	YD	AVG (LG)	TD	REC	YD	AVG (LG)	TD	PASS	COMP	PCT	YD	AVG (LG)	TD	INT	SK	YD	QBR	KPR	OTD	PTS	TAY
1940	Det	10(3)	2	0	0.0	0	1	10	10.0(10)	0	—	—	—	—	—	—	—	—	—	—	—	—	0	5
1941	Det	11(8, LE)	—	—	—	—	9	140	15.6(32)	2	—	—	—	—	—	—	—	—	—	—	—	—	12	80
1942	Det	11(11, LE)	—	—	—	—	15	177	11.8(27)	0	—	—	—	—	—	—	—	—	—	—	k	—	0	84
1943	Det☆	10(9, LE)	—	—	—	—	11	137	12.5(28)	0	—	—	—	—	—	—	—	—	—	—	k	—	0	59
NFL	4	42(31)	2	0	0.0	0	36	464	12.9(32)	2	—	—	—	—	—	—	—	—	—	—	k	—	12	227
1946	SF-A	14(12, LE)	—	—	—	—	19	186	9.8	1	—	—	—	—	—	—	—	—	—	—	—	—	6	98
1947	SF-A	14(1)	—	—	—	—	5	39	7.8	0	—	—	—	—	—	—	—	—	—	—	—	—	0	20
1948	LAD-A	13(2)	—	—	—	—	9	102	11.3	0	—	—	—	—	—	—	—	—	—	—	—	—	0	51
AAFC	3	41(15)	—	—	—	—	33	327	9.9(32)	1	—	—	—	—	—	—	—	—	—	—	—	—	6	169

Fisk, Jason Jason Michael, DT-NT, 6´3˝/295 lbs; Stanford; 1995: Min, rnd 7; B9/4/1972 Davis, CA **1995** Min 8 (0) **1996**†Min 16 (6, ldt) **1997**†Min 16 (10, LDT) **1998**†Min 16 (0) **1999**†Ten 16 (16, RDT) **2000**†Ten 15 (15, RDT) **2001** Ten 16 (16, RDT) **2002** SD 16 (14, RDT) **2003** SD 16 (16, RDT) **2004**†SD 15 (1) **2005** Cle 16 (14, NT) **NFL** 166 (108) [11 yrs]

Fiske, Max Max Joseph, B-E, 6´0˝/199 lbs; DePaul; B9/27/1913 Chicago, IL, D3/15/1973 Chicago, IL

YEAR	TEAM	G (GS, POS)	RUSH	YD	AVG (LG)	TD	REC	YD	AVG (LG)	TD	PASS	COMP	PCT	YD	AVG (LG)	TD	INT	SK	YD	QBR	KPR	OTD	PTS	TAY
1936	Pit	11(0)	58	92	1.6	0	7	96	13.7	0	15	6	40.0	64	4.3	0	3	—	—	—	—	—	0	52
1937	Pit	7(1)	28	44	1.6	0	1	0	0.0	0	43	17	39.5	318	7.4	4	4	—	—	—	—	—	0	63
1938	Pit	10(2)	29	83	2.9	0	—	—	—	—	37	11	29.7	121	3.3	0	4	—	—	—	—	—	0	-17
1939	Pit	1(0)	—	—	—	—	—	—	—	—	—	—	—	—	—	—	—	—	—	—	—	—	—	—
NFL	4	29(3)	115	219	1.9	0	8	96	12.0	0	95	34	35.8	503	5.3	4	11	—	—	—	—	—	0	99

Fiss, Galen Galen Toyce, LB, 6´0˝/227 lbs; Kansas; 1953: Cle, rnd 13; B7/10/1931 Johnson, KS **1956** Cle 12 (RLB) **1957**†Cle 12 (LLB) **1958**†Cle 12 (LLB) **1959** Cle 12 (LLB) **1960** Cle 12 (LLB) **1961** Cle 13 (llb) **1962** Cle★14 (LLB) **1963** Cle✧13 (RLB) **1964**†Cle 13 (RLB) **1965**†Cle 12 (llb/rlb) **1966** Cle 14 **NFL** 139 [11 yrs]

Fitzgerald, France Francis J., BB-HB, 5´10˝/185 lbs; Detroit Mercy; B5/20/1896 County Kerry, Ireland, D3/6/1976 Springfield, MA **1923** Tol 7 (6, BB)

Fitzgerald, Freeman Freeman Charles, C-G, 6´0˝/195 lbs; Notre Dame; B8/21/1891 Jervis, OR, D5/6/1942 Milwaukee, WI **1920** RI 9 (6, C) **1921** RI 2 (1) **NFL** 11 (7) [2 yrs]

Fitzgerald, Greg Gregory M., DE, 6´4˝/265 lbs; Iowa; B7/3/1963 Chicago, IL **1987** ChiB 3 (0)

Fitzgerald, Jamie Edgar James, DB, 6´0˝/180 lbs; Idaho State; B4/30/1965 Spokane, WA **1987** Min 2 (0)

Fitzgerald, Jim James Peter, C, 5´11˝/215 lbs; Holy Cross; B3/7/1907 Waltham, MA, D9/23/1978 Boston, MA **1930** SI 11 (9, C) **1931** SI 10 (5, c) **NFL** 21 (14) [2 yrs]

Fitzgerald, Joe Joseph, E, /150 lbs; none; deceased **1920** Det 8 (2, LE)

Fitzgerald, John John Robert, C-G, 6´5˝/255 lbs; Boston College; 1970: Dal, rnd 4; B4/16/1948 Southbridge, MA **1971**†Dal 14 **1972**†Dal 14 **1973**†Dal 14 (C) **1974** Dal 12 (C) **1975**†Dal 14 (C) **1976**†Dal 14 (14, C) **1977**†Dal 12 (C) **1978**†Dal 14 (14, C) **1979**†Dal 15 (C) **1980**†Dal 14 (14, C) **NFL** 137 (42) [10 yrs]

Fitzgerald, Kevin Kevin Lee, TE, 6´3˝/235 lbs; Wisconsin-Eau Claire; B6/30/1964 **1987** GB 1 (0)

Fitzgerald, Larry Larry Darnell, WR, 6´3˝/225 lbs; Pittsburgh; 2004: Arz, rnd 1; B8/31/1983 Minneapolis, MN

YEAR	TEAM	G (GS, POS)	RUSH	YD	AVG (LG)	TD	REC	YD	AVG (LG)	TD	PASS	COMP	PCT	YD	AVG (LG)	TD	INT	SK	YD	QBR	KPR	OTD	PTS	TAY
2004	Arz	16(16, WR)	8	14	1.8(10)	0	58	780	13.4(48)	8	0	0	0.0	0	0.0	0	0	1	7	—	—	—	48	444
2005	Arz✧	16(16, WR)	8	41	5.1(15)	0	**103**	1409	13.7(47)	10	—	—	—	—	—	—	—	—	—	—	—	—	60	796
NFL	2	32(32)	16	55	3.4(15)	0	161	2189	13.6(48)	18	0	0	0.0	0	0.0	0	0	1	7	—	—	—	108	1240

Fitzgeral9, Mickey Marion Maxwell, RB, 6´2˝/235 lbs; Virginia Tech; B4/10/1958 Lynchburg, VA **1981** Atl 1 (0) **1981** Phi 1 (0) **NFL** 2 (0) [1 yr]

Fitzgerald, Mike Michael, DB, 5´10˝/180 lbs; Iowa State; B5/4/1941 Detroit, MI **1966** Min 9 **1967** Min 6 **1967** NYG 2 **1967** Atl 2 **NFL** 19 [2 yrs]

Fitzgibbon, Paul Paul Joseph, B, 5´8˝/176 lbs; Creighton; B3/21/1903, deceased **[K]** **1926** Dul 14 (7, tb), 6 **1927** Fra 11 (5, BB) **1928** ChiC 6 (1) **1930** GB 9 (0), 18 **1931** GB 11 (7, BB), 1

YEAR	TEAM	G (GS, POS)	RUSH	YD	AVG (LG)	TD	REC	YD	AVG (LG)	TD	PASS	COMP	PCT	YD	AVG (LG)	TD	INT	SK	YD	QBR	KPR	OTD	PTS	TAY
1932	GB	4(2)	2	-1	-0.5	0	1	25	25.0(25)	0	5	1	20.0	9	1.8(9)	0	0	—	—	—	—	—	0	16
NFL	6	55(22)	2	-1	-0.5	2	1	25	25.0(25)	2	5	1	20.0	9	1.8(9)	3	0	—	—	—	K	—	25	61

Fitzhugh, Steve Stephen Allen, DB, 5´11˝/188 lbs; Miami (OH); B1/28/1963 Akron, OH **1987** Den 3 (1)

Fitzke, Bob Paul Frederick Herman, WB, 5´10˝/195 lbs; Wyoming; Idaho; B7/30/1900 La Crosse, WI, D6/30/1950 Sacramento, CA **1925** Fra 16 (13, wb), 6

Fitzkee, Scott Scott Austin, WR, 6´0˝/187 lbs; Penn State; 1979: Phi, rnd 5; B4/8/1957 York, PA

YEAR	TEAM	G (GS, POS)	RUSH	YD	AVG (LG)	TD	REC	YD	AVG (LG)	TD	PASS	COMP	PCT	YD	AVG (LG)	TD	INT	SK	YD	QBR	KPR	OTD	PTS	TAY
1979	†Phi	15(1)	—	—	—	—	8	105	13.1(19)	1	—	—	—	—	—	—	—	—	—	—	—	—	6	58
1980	†Phi	7(0)	1	15	15.0(15)	0	6	169	28.2(49)	2	—	—	—	—	—	—	—	—	—	—	—	—	12	110
1981	SD	5(0)	—	—	—	—	—	—	—	—	—	—	—	—	—	—	—	—	—	—	—	—	—	—
1982	†SD	9(0)	—	—	—	—	3	47	15.7(18)	1	—	—	—	—	—	—	—	—	—	—	—	—	6	29
NFL	4	36(1)	1	15	15.0(15)	0	17	321	18.9(49)	4	—	—	—	—	—	—	—	—	—	—	—	—	24	196

YEAR	TEAM	G(GS, POS)	RUSH	YD	AVG(LG)	TD	REC	YD	AVG(LG)	TD	PASS COMP	PCT	YD	AVG(LG)	TD	INT	SK	YD	QBR	KPR	OTD	PTS	TAY

FitzPatrick, James James Joseph, T-G, 6´8˝/305 lbs; USC; 1986: SD, rnd 1; B2/1/1964 Heidelberg, Germany **1986** SD 4 (0) **1987** SD 10 (9, LG) **1988** SD 11 (0)
1989 SD 13 (5, rt) **1990** LARd 11 (1) **1991**†LARd 16 (4) **NFL** 65 (19) [6 yrs]

Fitzpatrick, Ryan Ryan Joseph, QB, 6´2˝/221 lbs; Harvard; 2005: SL, rnd 7; B11/24/1982 Gilbert, AZ

| 2005 | | 4(3) | 14 | 64 | 4.6(14) | 2 | — | — | — | — | 135 | 76 | 56.3 | 777 | 5.8(56) | 4 | 8 | 9 | 49 | 58.2 | — | — | 12 | 173 |

Fitzsimmons, Casey Casey, TE, 6´3˝/250 lbs; Carroll (MT); B10/10/1980 Wolf Point, MT

2003	Det	16(11, TE)	—	—	—	—	23	160	7.0(22)	2	—	—	—	—	—	—	—	—	—	—	—	12	90
2004	Det	16(2)	—	—	—	—	10	103	10.3(27)	0	—	—	—	—	—	—	—	—	—	—	—	0	52
2005	Det	14(2)	—	—	—	—	10	45	4.5(11)	1	—	—	—	—	—	—	—	—	—	—	—	6	28
NFL	3	46(15)	—	—	—	—	43	308	7.2(27)	3	—	—	—	—	—	—	—	—	—	—	—	18	169

Flagerman, Jack Jack Michael, C-LB, 6´0˝/218 lbs; St. Mary's (CA); B3/27/1922 San Francisco, CA, D6/12/2005 Rohnert Park, CA

| 1948 | LAD-A | 14(0) | — | — | — | — | 0 | 6 | (6) | 0 | — | — | — | — | — | — | — | — | — | — | — | 0 | 3 |

Flagler, Terrence Robert Terrence, RB, 6´0˝/200 lbs; Clemson; 1987: SF, rnd 1; B9/24/1964 New York, NY

1987	SF	3(1)	6	11	1.8(5)	0	2	28	14.0(24)	0	—	—	—	—	—	—	—	—	—	k	—	0	11
1988	†SF	3(0)	3	5	1.7(4)	0	4	72	18.0(57)	0	—	—	—	—	—	—	—	—	—	k	—	0	41
1989	†SF	15(0)	33	129	3.9(29)	1	6	51	8.5(30)	0	—	—	—	—	—	—	—	—	—	k	—	6	328
1990	Phx	13(0)	13	85	6.5(29)	1	13	130	10.0(21)	1	—	—	—	—	—	—	—	—	—	k	—	12	182
1991	Phx	7(0)	1	7	7.0(7)	0	8	85	10.6(17)	0	—	—	—	—	—	—	—	—	—	k	—	0	78
NFL	5	41(1)	56	237	4.2(29)	2	33	366	11.1(57)	1	—	—	—	—	—	—	—	—	—	k	—	18	639

Flaherty, Dick Richard Thomas, E, 5´10˝/200 lbs; Gonzaga; Marquette; B8/8/1900 Seattle, WA, D2/4/1984 Spokane, WA **1926** GB 12 (10, RE), 12

Flaherty, Harry Harry Edward, LB, 6´1˝/232 lbs; Holy Cross; B12/25/1961 **1987** Dal 2 (0)

Flaherty, Jim James Wilson, E-HB, /198 lbs; Georgetown (DC); B12/26/1895 Washington, DC, D1/30/1978 Winter Haven, FL **1923** ChiB 12 (0)

Flaherty, Ray Raymond Paul, E-DE, 6´0˝/190 lbs; Washington State; Gonzaga; B9/1/1903 Spokane, WA, D7/19/1994 Coeur d'Alene, ID; HOF 1976 [KC] **1927** NYY 13 (11, LE),
24 **1928** NYG 1 (0) **1928** NYY☆15 (9, RE), 6 **1929** NYG☆15 (13, LE), 49 **1931** NYG 14 (11, RE), 12

1932	NYG☆	12(11, RE)	—	—	—	—	21	350	16.7	5	4	3	75.0	33	8.3	0	0	—	—	—	—	30	217
1933	†NYG☆	11(10, RE)	—	—	—	—	11	177	16.1	0	—	—	—	—	—	—	—	—	—	—	—	0	89
1934	†NYG☆	9(7, RE)	—	—	—	—	8	76	9.5	1	—	—	—	—	—	—	—	—	—	—	—	6	43
1935	NYG	2(0)	—	—	—	—	1	23	23.0(23)	0	—	—	—	—	—	—	—	—	—	—	—	0	12
NFL	8	88(72)	—	—	—	—	41	626	15.3(23)	20	4	3	75.0	33	8.3	0	0	—	—	K	1	127	430

Flaherty, Tom Thomas Francis, LB, 6´3˝/223 lbs; Northwestern; 1986: Cin, rnd 11; B9/24/1964 Chicago, IL **1987** Cin 3 (3)

Flanagan, Dick Richard Eugene, LB-G-C, 6´0˝/216 lbs; Ohio State; 1948: ChiR-A, rnd 17/ChiB, rnd 10; B10/31/1926 Sidney, OH, deceased **1949** ChiB 12 (2) **1950** ChiB 1
1950 Det 7 **1951** Det 12 (LLB) **1952**†Det 12 (LLB) **1953** Pit 12 (LLB) **1954** Pit 5 (llb) **1955** Pit 12 (LLB)

| 1948 | ChiB | 11(1) | 5 | 14 | 2.8(6) | 0 | — | — | — | — | — | — | — | — | — | — | — | — | — | — | — | 0 | 14 |
| NFL | 8 | 84(3) | 5 | 14 | 2.8(6) | 0 | — | — | — | — | — | — | — | — | — | — | — | ki | — | 0 | 24 |

Flanagan, Ed Edward Joseph, C, 6´3˝/245 lbs; Purdue; 1965: Det, rnd 5; B2/23/1944 San Bernardino, CA **1965** Det 14 (14, C) **1966** Det 14 (14, C) **1968** Det 14 (14, C)
1969 Det★14 (C) **1970**†Det★14 (C) **1971** Det★14 (C) **1972** Det 14 (C) **1973** Det✧14 (C) **1974** Det 13 (13, C) **1975** SD 14 (14, C) **1976** SD 12 (C)

| 1967 | Det | 14(14, C) | 0 | 5 | (5) | 0 | — | — | — | — | — | — | — | — | — | — | — | — | — | — | — | 0 | 5 |
| NFL | 12 | 165(83) | 0 | 5 | (5) | 0 | — | — | — | — | — | — | — | — | — | — | — | — | — | — | — | 0 | 5 |

Flanagan, Hoot William Harold, TB-WB, 6´0˝/169 lbs; West Virginia Wesleyan; Pittsburgh; B4/28/1901 Buckhannon, WV, D2/3/1975 Martinsburg, WV **1925** Pot 10 (9, TB), 42
1926 Pot 8 (6, WB) **NFL** 18 (15) [2 yrs]

Flanagan, Latham Latham, E, 6´2˝/185 lbs; Carnegie Mellon; B1/17/1907 Buckhannon, WV, D5/18/1981 Eugene, OR **1931** ChiB 2 (2) **1931** ChiC 2 (1) **NFL** 4 (3) [1 yr]

Flanagan, Mike Michael Christopher, C-T, 6´5˝/297 lbs; UCLA; 1996: GB, rnd 3; B11/10/1973 Washington, DC **1998** GB 2 (0) **1999** GB 15 (0) **2000** GB 16 (2)
2001†GB 16 (16, C) **2002**†GB 16 (13, LT/c) **2003**†GB✧16 (16, C) **2004** GB 3 (3) **2005** GB 14 (14, C) **NFL** 98 (64) [8 yrs]

Flanigan, Jim James Michael, LB, 6´3˝/240 lbs; Pittsburgh; 1967: GB, rnd 2; B4/15/1945 Pittsburgh, PA **1967**†GB 12 **1968** GB 13 **1969** GB 4 **1970** GB 11 **1971** NO 14 (MLB)
NFL 54 [5 yrs]

Flanigan, Jim James Michael, DT, 6´2˝/290 lbs; Notre Dame; 1994: Chi, rnd 3; B8/27/1971 Green Bay, WI **1994**†ChiB 14 (0) **1997** ChiB 16 (16, LDT) **1998** ChiB 16 (16, LDT)
1999 ChiB 16 (16, LDT) **2000** ChiB 16 (14, LDT) **2001**†GB 16 (8, ldt) **2002**†SF 15 (1) **2003** Phi 6 (0)

1995	ChiB	16(12, LDT)	1	0	0.0(0)	0	2	6	3.0(4)	2	—	—	—	—	—	—	—	—	—	S	—	12	13
1996	ChiB	14(14, LDT)	—	—	—	—	1	1	1.0(1)	1	—	—	—	—	—	—	—	—	—	S	—	6	6
NFL	10	145(97)	1	0	0.0	0	3	7	2.3(4)	3	—	—	—	—	—	—	—	—	—	kiS	—	20	10

Flannery, John John Joseph, G-C, 6´4˝/303 lbs; Syracuse; 1991: Hou, rnd 2; B1/13/1969 Pottsville, PA **1991**†Hou 16 (9, rg) **1992**†Hou 15 (2) **1994** Hou 16 (16, LG)
1996 Dal 1 (0) **1997** Dal 16 (4)

| 1998 | SL | 16(15, C) | — | — | — | — | 1 | 2 | 2.0(2) | 0 | — | — | — | — | — | — | — | — | — | — | — | 0 | 1 |
| NFL | 6 | 80(46) | — | — | — | — | 1 | 2 | 2.0(2) | 0 | — | — | — | — | — | — | — | — | — | k | — | 0 | -17 |

Flannigan, Bill William, T, /210 lbs; none; B1902, deceased **1926** Lou 2 (2)

Flatley, Paul Paul Richard, WR-FL, 6´1˝/187 lbs; Northwestern; 1963: Min, rnd 4/Den, rnd 7; B1/30/1941 Richmond, IN

1963	Min	14(14, WR)	—	—	—	—	51	867	17.0(62)	4	—	—	—	—	—	—	—	—	—	—	—	24	454
1964	Min	10(9, WR)	—	—	—	—	28	450	16.1(48)	3	—	—	—	—	—	—	—	—	—	—	—	18	240
1965	Min✧	14(14, WR)	—	—	—	—	50	896	17.9(58)	7	—	—	—	—	—	—	—	—	—	—	—	42	483
1966	Min✧	13(12, WR)	—	—	—	—	50	777	15.5(41)	3	—	—	—	—	—	—	—	—	—	—	—	18	404
1967	Min	13(13, WR)	—	—	—	—	23	232	10.1(27)	0	—	—	—	—	—	—	—	—	—	—	—	0	116
1968	Atl	14(5, FL)	—	—	—	—	20	305	15.3(66)	0	—	—	—	—	—	—	—	—	—	—	—	0	153
1969	Atl	14(FL)	—	—	—	—	45	834	18.5(71)	6	—	—	—	—	—	—	—	—	—	—	—	36	447
1970	Atl	14(WR)	—	—	—	—	39	544	13.9(35)	1	—	—	—	—	—	—	—	—	—	—	—	6	277
NFL	8	106(67)	—	—	—	—	306	4905	16.0(71)	24	—	—	—	—	—	—	—	—	—	—	—	144	2573

Flattery, Willie Wilson Immel, G-E, 5´11˝/220 lbs; Wooster; B2/4/1904 Wooster, OH, D4/4/1957 Wooster, OH **1925** Can 6 (5, LG) **1926** Can 10 (9, RG) **NFL** 16 (14) [2 yrs]

Flavin, Jack John Henry, FB, 5´11˝/187 lbs; Georgetown (DC); B1/1900 Portland, ME, D7/8/1965 New York, NY **1923** Buf 1 (1), 12 **1924** Buf 2 (2) **NFL** 3 (3) [2 yrs]

Fleck, P.J. P.J. John, WR, 5´10˝/191 lbs; Northern Illinois; B11/29/1980 Sugar Grove, IL **2004** SF 1 (0)

Fleckenstein, Bill William P., G-E-T-C, 6´5˝/208 lbs; Carleton; Iowa; B11/4/1903 Fairbault, MN, D1/25/1967 Los Angeles, CA **1925** ChiB 16 (12, LG) **1926** ChiB 10 (3)
1927 ChiB 11 (6, lg) **1928** ChiB 12 (9, lg), 6 **1929** ChiB 15 (10, lg) **1930** ChiB 2 (0) **1930** Por 10 (7, RE) **1931** Fra 6 (3) **1931** Bkn 2 (0) **NFL** 84 (50) [7 yrs]

Fleischmann, Jack Godfrey Jacob, G, 5´6˝/184 lbs; Purdue; B8/15/1901 Monroe, MI, D4/27/1988 Monroe, LA **1925** Det 9 (3) **1926** Det 11 (10, LG) **1927** Pro 14 (12, LG)
1928 Pro 11 (6, RG) **1929** Pro 12 (12, RG) **NFL** 57 (43) [5 yrs]

Fleming, Cory Cory Lamont, WR, 6´1˝/216 lbs; Tennessee; 1994: SF, rnd 3; B3/19/1971 Nashville, TN **1994** Dal 2 (0)

| 1995 | †Dal | 16(0) | — | — | — | — | 6 | 83 | 13.8(16) | 0 | — | — | — | — | — | — | — | — | — | — | — | 0 | 42 |
| NFL | 2 | 18(0) | — | — | — | — | 6 | 83 | 13.8(16) | 0 | — | — | — | — | — | — | — | — | — | — | — | 0 | 42 |

Fleming, Don Donald Denver, DB, 6´0˝/188 lbs; Florida; 1959: ChiC, rnd 28; B6/11/1937 Bellaire, OH, D6/4/1963 Winter Park, FL **1960** Cle 12 (LS) **1961** Cle 14 (LS)
1962 Cle☆12 (rs) **NFL** 38 [3 yrs]

Fleming, George George, HB-K, 5´11˝/188 lbs; Washington; 1961: Oak, rnd 2/Chi, rnd 6; B6/29/1938, TX [K]

| 1961 | Oak-A | 14 | 21 | 112 | 3.6(23) | 1 | 10 | 49 | 4.9(22) | 0 | — | — | 0.0 | 0 | 0.0 | 0 | 0 | — | — | — | Kkp | — | 63 | 269 |

Fleming, Marv Marvin Xavier, TE-SE, 6´4˝/232 lbs; Utah; 1963: GB, rnd 11/Den, rnd 9; B1/2/1942 Longview, TX

1963	GB	14	—	—	—	—	7	132	18.9(33)	2	—	—	—	—	—	—	—	—	—	k	—	12	61
1964	GB	14	—	—	—	—	4	36	9.0(10)	0	—	—	—	—	—	—	—	—	—	—	—	0	18
1965	†GB	13(TE)	—	—	—	—	14	141	10.1(31)	2	—	—	—	—	—	—	—	—	—	—	—	12	81
1966	†GB	14(SE)	—	—	—	—	31	361	11.6(53)	2	—	—	—	—	—	—	—	—	—	—	—	12	191
1967	†GB	14(TE)	—	—	—	—	10	126	12.6(19)	1	—	—	—	—	—	—	—	—	—	—	—	6	68

YEAR	TEAM	G (GS, POS)	RUSH	YD	AVG(LG)	TD	REC	YD	AVG(LG)	TD	PASS	COMP	PCT	YD	AVG(LG)	TD	INT	SK	YD	QBR	KPR	OTD	PTS	TAY
1968	GB	14(TE)	—	—	—	—	25	278	11.1(32)	3	—	—	—	—	—	—	—	—	—	—	—	—	18	154
1969	GB	12(TE)	—	—	—	—	18	226	12.6(23)	2	—	—	—	—	—	—	—	—	—	—	—	—	12	123
1970	†Mia	14(14, TE)	—	—	—	—	18	205	11.4(36)	0	—	—	—	—	—	—	—	—	—	—	—	—	0	103
1971	†Mia	14(13, TE)	—	—	—	—	13	137	10.5(23)	2	—	—	—	—	—	—	—	—	—	—	—	—	12	79
1972	†Mia	14(14, TE)	—	—	—	—	13	156	12.0(31)	1	—	—	—	—	—	—	—	—	—	—	—	—	6	83
1973	†Mia	11(11, TE)	—	—	—	—	3	22	7.3(15)	0	—	—	—	—	—	—	—	—	—	—	—	—	0	11
1974	†Mia	14	—	—	—	—	1	3	3.0(3)	1	—	—	—	—	—	—	—	—	—	—	—	—	6	7
NFL	12	162(52)	—	—	—	—	157	1823	11.6(53)	16	—	—	—	—	—	—	—	—	—	k	—	—	96	977

FLEMING, TROY Troy Majors, RB, 6´2˝/230 lbs; Tennessee; 2004: Ten, rnd 6; B10/1/1980 Franklin, TN

2004	Ten	16(0)	7	40	5.7(13)	0	19	164	8.6(37)	2	—	—	—	—	—	—	—	—	—	k	—	—	12	178
2005	Ten	13(2)	—	—	—	—	10	69	6.9(18)	1	—	—	—	—	—	—	—	—	—	k	—	—	6	34
NFL	2	29(2)	7	40	5.7(13)	0	29	233	8.0(37)	3	—	—	—	—	—	—	—	—	—	k	—	—	18	212

FLEMING, WILMER Clarence Wilmer, HB, 5´11˝/165 lbs; Mount Union; B9/30/1901 Cambridge, OH, D3/13/1969 Toledo, OH   **1925** Can 1 (0)

FLEMISTER, ZERON Zeron, TE, 6´4˝/250 lbs; Iowa; B9/8/1976 Chicago, IL

2000	Was	5(0)	—	—	—	—	1	8	8.0(8)	0	—	—	—	—	—	—	—	—	—	—	—	—	0	4
2001	Was	16(1)	—	—	—	—	18	196	10.9(30)	2	—	—	—	—	—	—	—	—	—	—	—	—	12	108
2002	Was	15(7, te)	—	—	—	—	10	146	14.6(25)	2	—	—	—	—	—	—	—	—	—	k	—	—	12	83
2003	Was	12(9, TE)	—	—	—	—	9	89	9.9(18)	0	—	—	—	—	—	—	—	—	—	k	—	—	0	37
2005	Oak	12(4)	—	—	—	—	1	3	3.0(3)	0	—	—	—	—	—	—	—	—	—	k	—	—	0	-14
NFL	5	60(21)	—	—	—	—	38	439	11.6(33)	4	—	—	—	—	—	—	—	—	—	k	—	—	24	218

FLEMONS, RONALD Ronald, DE, 6´5˝/265 lbs; Texas A&M; 2001: Atl, rnd 7; B10/20/1979 San Antonio, TX   **2001** Atl 1 (0) **2002** Atl 4 (0) **2004** Mia 1 (0) **NFL** 6 (0) [3 yrs]

FLENNIKEN, MACK Mack, B, 6´1˝/200 lbs; Centenary; Geneva; B1905, D5/26/1956 Geneva, PA   **1930** ChiC 10 (3), 18 **1931** NYG 4 (1), 6 **NFL** 14 (4), 24 [2 yrs]

FLETCHER, ANDREW Andrew, FB, 5´6˝/165 lbs; Maryland; deceased   **1920** Buf 2 (1)

FLETCHER, ARTHUR Arthur A., E, 6´3˝/215 lbs; Washburn; B12/22/1924 Fort Huachuca, AZ, D7/12/2005 Washington, DC

| 1950 | Bal | 1 | — | — | — | — | 2 | 18 | 9.0(10) | 0 | — | — | — | — | — | — | — | — | — | — | — | — | 0 | 9 |

FLETCHER, BILLY Billy Ray, DB, 5´10˝/190 lbs; Memphis; B5/2/1943 Memphis, TN   **1966** Den-A 1

FLETCHER, BRYAN Bryan, TE, 6´5˝/238 lbs; UCLA; 2002: Chi, rnd 6; B3/23/1979 St. Louis, MQ

| 2005 | †Ind | 16(12, TE) | — | — | — | — | 18 | 202 | 11.2(23) | 3 | — | — | — | — | — | — | — | — | — | — | — | — | 18 | 116 |

FLETCHER, CHRIS Christopher C., DB, 5´11˝/185 lbs; Temple; 1970: SD, rnd 9; B12/25/1948 Morristown, NJ   **1970** SD 13 **1971** SD 14 (14, FS) **1972** SD 1 (1) **1973** SD 9 (4) **1974** SD 12 (12, SS) **1975** SD 14 (14, FS) **1976** SD 13 (12, FS) **NFL** 76 (57) [7 yrs]

FLETCHER, DERRICK Derrick W., T-G, 6´6˝/348 lbs; Baylor; 1999: NE, rnd 5; B9/9/1975 Houston, TX   **2000** NE 2 (2) **2000** Was 1 (0) **2002** Car 5 (0) **2005**†Jax 12 (1) **NFL** 20 (3) [3 yrs]

FLETCHER, JAMAR Jamar Mondell, DB, 5´9˝/186 lbs; Wisconsin; 2001: Mia, rnd 1; B8/28/1979 St. Louis, MO   **2001** Mia 14 (2) **2002** Mia 16 (4) **2003** Mia 11 (0) **2004**†SD 16 (0) **2005** SD 14 (0) **NFL** 71 (6) [5 yrs]

FLETCHER, JOHN John Williams, G, 6´3˝/293 lbs; Texas A&M-Kingsville; B8/22/1965 Uvalde, TX   **1987** Cin 3 (0)

FLETCHER, LONDON London Levi, LB, 5´10˝/245 lbs; John Carroll; B5/19/1975 Cleveland, OH   **1998** SL 16 (1) **1999**†SL 16 (16, MLB) **2000**†SL 16 (15, MLB) **2001**†SL 16 (16, MLB) **2002** Buf 16 (16, MLB) **2003** Buf 16 (16, MLB) **2004** Buf 16 (16, MLB) **2005** Buf 16 (16, MLB) **NFL** 128 (112) [8 yrs]

FLETCHER, OLIVER Oliver, G, 6´3˝/210 lbs; USC; 1949: Was, rnd 20; B2/5/1923, D5/10/1994 Bullhead City, AZ   **1949** LAD-A 3 (0)

FLETCHER, SIMON Simon Raynard, LB-DE, 6´5˝/240 lbs; Houston; 1985: Den, rnd 2; B2/18/1962 Bay City, TX [S]   **1985** Den 16 (1) **1986**†Den 16 (2) **1987**†Den 12 (12, LOLB) **1988** Den 16 (16, LOLB) **1989**†Den 16 (16, LOLB) **1990** Den 16 (16, LOLB) **1991**†Den 16 (16, LOLB) **1992** Den 16 (16, ROLB) **1993**†Den 16 (16, ROLB) **1994** Den 16 (16, RDE) **1995** Den 16 (16, RDE) **NFL** 172 (143) [11 yrs]

FLETCHER, TERRELL Terrell Antoine, RB, 5´8˝/196 lbs; Wisconsin; 1995: SD, rnd 2; B9/14/1973 St. Louis, MO

1995	†SD	16(0)	26	140	5.4(46)	1	3	26	8.7(15)	0	—	—	—	—	—	—	—	—	—	kp	—	—	6	165
1996	SD	16(0)	77	282	3.7(19)	0	61	476	7.8(41)	2	—	—	—	—	—	—	—	—	—	—	—	—	12	530
1997	SD	13(1)	51	161	3.2(13)	0	39	292	7.5(25)	0	—	—	—	—	—	—	—	—	—	—	—	—	0	307
1998	SD	12(5, rb)	153	543	3.5(21)	5	30	188	6.3(22)	0	1	1	100.0	23	23.0(23)	1	0	—	—	—	k	—	—	30	730
1999	SD	15(2)	48	126	2.6(16)	0	45	360	8.0(25)	0	—	—	—	—	—	—	—	—	—	k	—	—	0	313
2000	SD	16(6, rb)	116	384	3.3(21)	3	48	355	7.4(26)	1	—	—	—	—	—	—	—	—	—	k	—	—	24	597
2001	SD	13(0)	29	107	3.7(16)	0	23	184	8.0(27)	0	—	—	—	—	—	—	—	—	—	k	—	—	0	195
2002	SD	10(0)	26	128	4.9(15)	1	10	62	6.2(13)	0	—	—	—	—	—	—	—	—	—	k	—	—	6	176
NFL	8	111(14)	526	1871	3.6(46)	10	259	1943	7.5(41)	3	1	1	100.0	23	23.0(23)	1	0	—	—	—	kp	—	—	78	3012

FLICK, TOM Thomas Lyle, QB, 6´2˝/190 lbs; Washington; 1981: Was, rnd 4; B8/30/1958 Patuxent River, MD

1981	Was	6(0)	—	—	—	—	—	—	—	—	27	13	48.1	143	5.3(33)	0	2	2	18	—	—	—	0	-9
1982	NE	3(0)	—	—	—	—	—	—	—	—	5	0	0.0	0	0.0	0	0	—	—	—	—	—	0	0
1984	Cle	1(0)	—	—	—	—	—	—	—	—	1	1	100.0	2	2.0(2)	0	0	—	—	—	—	—	0	1
1986	SD	11(0)	6	5	0.8(7)	1	—	—	—	—	73	33	45.2	361	4.9(26)	2	8	6	49	—	—	—	6	-115
NFL	4	21(0)	6	5	0.8(7)	1	—	—	—	—	106	47	44.3	506	4.8(33)	2	10	10	80	—	—	—	6	-122

FLINN, PAUL Paul Augustine, E, 6´0˝/180 lbs; Minnesota; B9/11/1895 St. Paul, MN, D12/1980 St. Paul, MN   **1922** Min 3 (3) **1923** Min 8 (8, RE) **NFL** 11 (11) [2 yrs]

FLINN, RYAN Ryan, P, 6´5˝/205 lbs; Central Florida; B2/14/1980 Fort Myers, FL   **2005** GB 2 (0)

FLINT, GEORGE George Howard, G, 6´4˝/240 lbs; Arizona State; B2/26/1939 Erie, PA   **1962** Buf-A 14 **1963** Buf-A 9 (rg) **1964**†Buf-A 14 **1965**†Buf-A◊14 **1968** Buf-A 14 **NFL** 65 [5 yrs]

FLINT, JUDSON Judson Rochelle, DB, 6´0˝/201 lbs; Memphis; California (PA); 1979: NE, rnd 7; B1/26/1957 Farrell, PA   **1980**†Cle 13 (0) **1981** Cle 16 (0) **1982**†Cle 9 (0) **1983** Buf 1 (0) **NFL** 39 (0) [4 yrs]

FLONES, BRIAN Brian Lee, LB, 6´1˝/228 lbs; Washington State; B9/1/1959 Mount Vernon, WA   **1981** Sea 4 (0) **1982** Sea 9 (0) **NFL** 13 (0) [2 yrs]

FLORENCE, ANTHONY Anthony Wesly, DB, 6´0˝/185 lbs; Bethune-Cookman; 1989: TB, rnd 4; B12/11/1966 Delray Beach, FL   **1991** Cle 6 (0)

FLORENCE, DRAYTON Drayton, DB, 6´0˝/195 lbs; Tennessee-Chattanooga; Tuskegee; 2003: SD, rnd 2; B12/19/1980 Waycross, GA   **2003** SD 16 (0) **2004**†SD 13 (5, rcb) **2005** SD 13 (12, RCB) **NFL** 42 (17) [3 yrs]

FLORENCE, PAUL Paul Robert, E, 6´1˝/180 lbs; Loyola (IL); Georgetown (DC); B4/22/1900 Chicago, IL, D5/28/1986 Gainesville, FL   **1920** ChiC 9 (5, RE)

FLORES, MIKE Michael Andre, DE, 6´3˝/256 lbs; Louisville; 1991: Phi, rnd 11; B12/1/1966 Youngstown, OH   **1991** Phi 4 (0) **1992** Phi 15 (0) **1993** Phi 16 (11, LDE) **1994** Phi 15 (2) **1995** Was 11 (0) **1995**†SF 0 (0) **NFL** 61 (13) [5 yrs]

FLORES, TOM Thomas Raymond, QB, 6´1˝/202 lbs; Pacific; B3/21/1937 Fresno, CA [C]

1960	Oak-A	14(QB)	19	123	6.5(31)	3	—	—	—	—	252	136	**54.0**	1738	6.9(61)	12	12	—	—	**71.8**	—	—	18	602
1961	Oak-A	14(QB)	23	36	1.6(13)	1	—	—	—	—	366	190	51.9	2176	5.9(85)	15	19	—	—	62.1	—	—	6	449
1963	Oak-A	14(QB)	12	2	0.2(7)	0	—	—	—	—	247	113	45.7	2101	8.5(93)	20	13	—	—	80.7	—	—	0	633
1964	Oak-A	14(QB)	11	64	5.8(27)	0	—	—	—	—	200	98	49.0	1389	6.9(77)	7	14	—	—	54.4	—	—	0	234
1965	Oak-A	14(11, QB)	11	32	2.9(15)	0	—	—	—	—	269	122	45.4	1593	5.9(69)	14	11	—	—	64.9	—	—	0	459
1966	Oak-A◊	14(QB)	5	50	10.0(27)	0	—	—	—	—	306	151	49.3	2638	8.6(78)	24	14	—	—	86.2	—	—	6	939
1967	Buf-A	14	—	—	—	—	—	—	—	—	64	22	34.4	260	4.1(59)	0	8	—	—	—	—	—	0	-190
1968	Buf-A	4	—	—	—	—	—	—	—	—	5	3	60.0	15	3.0(12)	0	1	—	—	—	—	—	0	-33
1969	Buf-A	2	—	—	—	—	—	—	—	—	5	2	40.0	16	3.2(14)	0	0	1	11	—	—	—	0	8
1969	KC-A	5	1	0	0.0(0)	0	—	—	—	—	1	1	100.0	33	33.0(33)	1	0	—	—	—	—	—	0	22
NFL	9	106(11)	82	307	3.7(31)	5	—	—	—	—	1715	838	48.9	11959	7.0(93)	93	92	1	11	67.6	—	—	30	3122

YEAR	TEAM	G (GS, POS)	RUSH	YD	AVG(LG)	TD	REC	YD	AVG(LG)	TD	PASS COMP	PCT	YD	AVG(LG)	TD	INT	SK	YD	QBR	KPR	OTD	PTS	TAY

FLOWER, JIM James Tod, aka Jim Reeves, T-E-C-G, 6'1"/193 lbs; Ohio State; B10/17/1895 Akron, OH, D5/6/1965 Fremont, OH   **1920** Col 4 (4, RE)   **1921** Akr 9 (6, LE) **1922** Akr☆10 (9, C) **1923** Akr 7 (7, RT) **1924** Akr 8 (8, LT) **1925** Akr 1 (0) **NFL** 39 (34) [6 yrs]

FLOWERS, BERNIE Benjamin Bernard, E, 6'2"/190 lbs; Purdue; 1953: Bal, rnd 2; B2/14/1930 Erie, PA   **1956** Bal 1

FLOWERS, BOB Robert O.C., C-LB, 6'1"/210 lbs; Texas; Texas Tech; B8/6/1917 Big Spring, TX, D12/8/1962 Big Spring, TX   **1942** GB 3 (1) **1943** GB 8 (3) **1944** GB 8 (4) **1945** GB 10 (4) **1946** GB 10 (0) **1947** GB 12 (0) **1948** GB 11 (5, c) **1949** GB 1 (0) **NFL** 63 (17) [8 yrs]

FLOWERS, CHARLIE Charles, FB, 6'1"/220 lbs; Mississippi; 1960: LAC, rnd 1; B6/28/1937 Marianna, AR

1960	†LAC-A	10	39	161	4.1(25)	1	12	153	12.8(55)	0	—		—								—	12	253
1961	†SD-A	14(FB)	51	177	3.5(11)	3	16	175	10.9(31)	0	—		—								—	18	295
1962	NYT-A	4	21	78	3.7(14)	0	7	55	7.9(14)	0	—		—								—	0	106
NFL	3	28	111	416	3.7(25)	4	35	383	10.9(55)	0	—		—								—	30	653

FLOWERS, DICK Richard R., QB, 6'0"/190 lbs; Northwestern; B8/13/1927 South Bend, IN

| 1953 | Bal | 1 | — | — | | | — | — | | | 4 | 2 | 50.0 | 18 | 4.5(12) | 0 | 0 | — | — | | | — | 0 | 9 |

FLOWERS, ERIK Eril Mathews, DE-LB, 6'4"/273 lbs; Arizona State; 2000: Buf, rnd 1; B3/1/1978 San Antonio, TX   **2000** Buf 16 (0) **2001** Buf 15 (5, rde) **2002** Hou 14 (0) **2003**†SL 4 (0) **2004**†SL 9 (0) **NFL** 58 (5) [5 yrs]

FLOWERS, KEITH Keith Duane, C-LB, 6'0"/211 lbs; TCU; 1952: Det, rnd 11; B4/24/1930 Perryton, TX, D11/12/1993 Richardson, TX [K]   **1952** Det 3 **1952** DalT 6 **NFL** 9 [1 yr]

FLOWERS, KENNY Kenneth Charles, RB, 6'0"/210 lbs; Clemson; 1987: Atl, rnd 2; B3/14/1964 Daytona Beach, FL

1987	Atl	8(1)	14	61	4.4(14)	0	7	50	7.1(24)	0	—		—							k	—	0	98
1989	Atl	8(1)	13	24	1.8(4)	1	—	—			—		—								—	6	34
NFL	2	16(2)	27	85	3.1(14)	1	7	50	7.1(24)	0	—		—							k	—	6	132

FLOWERS, LARRY Larry Darnell, DB, 6'1"/190 lbs; Texas Tech; 1980: TB, rnd 4; B4/19/1958 Temple, TX   **1981**†NYG 16 (2) **1982** NYG 6 (0) **1983** NYG 14 (0) **1984**†NYG 16 (0) **1985** NYG 9 (0) **1985**†NYJ 6 (0) **NFL** 67 (2) [5 yrs]

FLOWERS, LEE Lethon, DB, 6'0"/213 lbs; Georgia Tech; 1995: Pit, rnd 5; B1/14/1973 Columbia, SC   **1995**†Pit 10 (0) **1996**†Pit 16 (0) **1997**†Pit 10 (0) **1998** Pit 16 (16, SS) **1999** Pit 15 (15, SS) **2000** Pit 14 (14, SS) **2001**†Pit 15 (15, SS) **2002**†Pit 16 (15, SS) **NFL** 112 (75) [8 yrs]

FLOWERS, RICHMOND Richmond McDavid, DB-WR, 6'0"/180 lbs; Tennessee; 1969: Dal, rnd 2; B6/13/1947 Montgomery, AL   **1969**†Dal 6 **1970**†Dal 14 (3) **1971** Dal 5 **1971** NYG 8 **1972** NYG 14 (SS) **1973** NYG 8 (SS) **NFL** 55 (3) [5 yrs]

FLOYD, ANTHONY Anthony, DB, 5'10"/202 lbs; Louisville; B2/1/1981 Youngstown, OH   **2003**†Ind 6 (0) **2004** Ind 11 (2) **NFL** 17 (2) [2 yrs]

FLOYD, BOBBY JACK Bobby Jack, FB, 6'0"/210 lbs; TCU; 1952: GB, rnd 15; B12/8/1929 Paris, TX

1952	GB	12(fb)	61	236	3.9(17)	1	11	129	11.7(44)	0	—		—							k	—	6	311
1953	ChiB	8	16	70	4.4(16)	0	9	63	7.0(16)	0	—		—								—	0	102
NFL	2	20	77	306	4.0(17)	1	20	192	9.6(44)	0	—		—							k	—	6	412

FLOYD, CHRIS Christopher Michael, RB, 6'0"/231 lbs; Michigan; 1998: NE, rnd 3; B6/23/1975 Detroit, MI

1998	†NE	16(2)	6	22	3.7(10)	0	1	6	6.0(6)	0	—		—								—	0	25
1999	NE	13(0)	6	12	2.0(6)	0	2	16	8.0(11)	0	—		—								—	0	20
2000	NE	11(0)	2	-1	-0.5(0)	0	1	21	21.0(21)	0	—		—								—	0	10
2000	Cle	2(0)	—	—			—	—			—		—								—		
NFL	3	42(2)	14	33	2.4(10)	0	4	43	10.8(21)	0	—		—								—	0	55

FLOYD, DON Donald Wayne, DE, 6'3"/245 lbs; TCU; 1960: NYT, rnd 1/Bal, rnd 2; B7/10/1938 Abilene, TX, D3/9/1980 Arlington, TX   **1960**†Hou-A 14 (RDE) **1961**†Hou-A★14 (RDE) **1962**†Hou-A★14 (RDE) **1963** Hou-A☆9 (RDE) **1964** Hou-A☆14 (RDE) **1965** Hou-A 14 (RDE) **1966** Hou-A 6 (RDE) **1967**†Hou-A 12 (RDE) **NFL** 97 [8 yrs]

FLOYD, ERIC Eric Cunningham, G-T, 6'5"/310 lbs; Auburn; B10/28/1965 Rome, GA   **1990** SD 16 (6, lt) **1991** SD 2 (0) **1992**†Phi 16 (16, RG) **1993** Phi 3 (3) **1995** Arz 1 (0) **NFL** 38 (25) [5 yrs]

FLOYD, GEORGE George, DB, 5'11"/190 lbs; Eastern Kentucky; 1982: NYJ, rnd 4; B12/21/1960 Tampa, FL   **1982**†NYJ 7 (0) **1984** NYJ 8 (2) **NFL** 15 (2) [2 yrs]

FLOYD, JOHN John Manuel, WR, 6'1"/195 lbs; Louisiana-Monroe; 1979: SD, rnd 4; B9/10/1956 Big Sandy, TX

1979	†SD	8(2)	—	—			10	152	15.2(40)	1	—		—								—	6	81
1980	†SD	15(0)	—	—			1	31	31.0(31)	1	—		—							p	—	6	16
1981	SL	4(1)	—	—			3	32	10.7(16)	0	—		—								—	0	16
NFL	3	27(3)	—	—			14	215	15.4(40)	2	—		—							p	—	12	113

FLOYD, MALCOLM Malcolm Gregory Ali, aka Malcolm Seabron, WR, 6'0"/194 lbs; Fresno State; 1994: Hou, rnd 3; B12/19/1972 San Francisco, CA

1994	Hou	13(0)	—	—			—	—			—		—								—		
1995	Hou	15(1)	—	—			12	167	13.9(34)	1	—		—								—	6	89
1996	Hou	16(0)	—	—			10	145	14.5(63)	1	—		—							p	—	6	117
1997	Ten	1(0)	—	—			—	—			—		—								—		
1997	SL	4(0)	—	—			4	39	9.8(14)	0	—		—							p	—	0	15
NFL	4	49(1)	—	—			26	351	13.5(63)	2	—		—							p	—	12	220

FLOYD, MALCOM Malcom, WR, 6'5"/201 lbs; Wyoming; B9/8/1981 Sacramento, CA

| 2004 | †SD | 4(2) | — | — | | | 3 | 49 | 16.3(27) | 1 | — | | — | | | | | | | | — | 6 | 30 |

FLOYD, MARCUS Marcus D., DB, 5'9"/180 lbs; Indiana; B10/12/1978 Bartow, FL   **2002** NYJ 2 (0) **2002** Buf 2 (0) **NFL** 4 (0) [1 yr]

FLOYD, OWEN Owen Glen, C, 6'0"/195 lbs; Rose Hulman Tech; B12/7/1896 Marshall, IN, D9/26/1960 Beaumont, TX   **1920** Mun 1 (1, C) **1921** Mun 2 (2, C) **NFL** 3 (3) [2 yrs]

FLOYD, VICTOR Victor Leonard, RB, 6'1"/201 lbs; Florida State; 1989: SD, rnd 11; B1/24/1966 Pensacola, FL

| 1989 | SD | 6(0) | 8 | 15 | 1.9(5) | 0 | 1 | 6 | 6.0(6) | 0 | — | | — | | | | | | | k | — | 0 | -15 |

FLOYD, WILLIAM William Ali, FB, 6'1"/242 lbs; Florida State; 1994: SF, rnd 1; B2/17/1972 St. Petersburg, FL

1994	†SF	16(11, FB)	87	305	3.5(26)	6	19	145	7.6(15)	1	—		—								—	36	438
1995	SF	8(8, FB)	64	237	3.7(23)	2	47	348	7.4(23)	1	—		—								—	18	436
1996	†SF	9(8, FB)	47	186	4.0(12)	2	26	197	7.6(24)	1	—		—								—	18	310
1997	†SF	15(15, FB)	78	231	3.0(22)	3	37	321	8.7(44)	1	—		—								—	24	427
1998	Car	16(13, FB)	28	71	2.5(7)	3	24	123	5.1(20)	1	1	0	0.0	0	0.0	0	1			k	—	24	135
1999	Car	16(16, FB)	35	78	2.2(16)	3	21	179	8.5(25)	0	—		—								—	18	198
2000	Car	10(8, FB)	16	33	2.1(8)	1	17	114	6.7(15)	1	—		—								—	12	105
NFL	7	90(79)	355	1141	3.2(26)	20	191	1427	7.5(44)	5	1	0	0.0	0	0.0	0	1			k	—	150	2047

FLUTIE, DARREN Darren Paul, WR, 5'10"/184 lbs; Boston College; B11/18/1966 Baltimore, MD

| 1988 | SD | 16(0) | — | — | | | 18 | 208 | 11.6(28) | 0 | — | | — | | | | | | | kp | — | 12 | 110 |

FLUTIE, DOUG Douglas Richard, QB, 5'10"/180 lbs; Boston College; 1985: LARm, rnd 11; B10/23/1962 Manchester, MD [K]

1986	†ChiB	4(1)	9	36	4.0(19)	1	—	—			46	23	50.0	361	7.8(58)	3	2	6	30	—	—	—	6	162
1987	ChiB	1(0)	—	—			—	—			—		—								—		
1987	NE	1(1)	6	43	7.2(13)	0	—	—			25	15	60.0	199	8.0(30)	1	0	1	3	—	—	—	0	148
1988	NE	11(9, QB)	38	179	4.7(16)	1	—	—			179	92	51.4	1150	6.4(80)	8	10	11	65	63.3	—	—	6	404
1989	NE	5(3)	16	87	5.4(22)	0	—	—			91	36	39.6	493	5.4(36)	2	4	6	52	—	—	—	0	184
1998	†Buf◇	13(10, QB)	48	248	5.2(23)	1	—	—			354	202	57.1	2711	7.7(84)	20	11	12	78	87.4	—	—	6	1519
1999	Buf	15(15, QB)	88	476	5.4(24)	1	—	—			478	264	55.2	3171	6.6(54)	19	16	26	176	75.1	—	—	6	1527
2000	Buf	11(5, qb)	36	161	4.5(32)	1	—	—			231	132	57.1	1700	7.4(52)	8	3	10	68	86.5	—	—	6	941
2001	SD	16(16, QB)	53	192	3.6(16)	1	—	—			521	294	56.4	3464	6.6(78)	15	18	25	168	72.0	—	—	6	1289
2002	SD	1(0)	1	6	6.0(6)	0	—	—			11	3	27.3	64	5.8(47)	0	0	—	—	—	—	—	0	38
2003	SD	7(5, qb)	33	168	5.1(17)	2	—	—			167	91	54.5	1097	6.6(73)	9	4	8	27	82.8	—	—	12	622
2004	SD	2(1)	5	39	7.8(20)	0	—	—			38	20	52.6	276	7.3(29)	1	0	1	7	—	—	—	12	202
2005	NE	5(0)	5	-1	-0.2(2)	0	—	—			10	5	50.0	29	2.9(13)	0	1	0	1	—	K	—	1	14
NFL	12	92(66)	338	1634	4.8(32)	10	—	—			2151	1177	54.7	14715	6.8(84)	86	68	107	687	76.3	K	—	61	6802

YEAR	TEAM	G (GS, POS)	RUSH	YD	AVG(LG)	TD	REC	YD	AVG(LG)	TD	PASS COMP	PCT	YD	AVG(LG)	TD	INT	SK	YD	QBR	KPR	OTD	PTS	TAY

FLYNN, DON   Don Max, DB-K, 6′0″/205 lbs; Houston; B9/14/1934   **1960** DalT-A 14 (LS)   **1961** DalT-A 6   **1961** NYT-A 7   **NFL** 27 [2 yrs]

FLYNN, FURLONG   Furlonge Harold, G-T, 6′0″/210 lbs; Cornell; B12/27/1901 Waterford, NY, D11/1/1977 Vernon, CT   **1926** Har 9 (6, LG)

FLYNN, MIKE   Michael Patrick, C-G, 6′3″/305 lbs; Maine; B6/15/1974 Doylestown, PA   **1998** Bal 2 (0)   **1999** Bal 12 (0)   **2000**†Bal 16 (16, RG)   **2001**†Bal 16 (16, C)
2002 Bal 15 (15, C)   **2003**†Bal 16 (16, C)   **2004** Bal 9 (5, rg)   **2005** Bal 16 (16, C)   **NFL** 102 (84) [8 yrs]

FLYNN, TOM   Thomas Jeffrey, DB, 6′0″/195 lbs; Pittsburgh; 1984: GB, rnd 5; B3/24/1962 Verona, PA   **1984** GB 15 (15, FS)   **1985** GB 16 (15, FS)   **1986** GB 7 (6, fs)
1986†NYG 2 (0)   **1987** NYG 12 (0)   **1988** NYG 16 (0)   **NFL** 68 (36) [5 yrs]

FLYTHE, MARK   Mark Lloyd, DE, 6′7″/270 lbs; Penn State; B10/4/1968 Philadelphia, PA   **1993** NYG 2 (0)

FOGGIE, FRED   Fred Jerome, DB, 6′0″/200 lbs; Minnesota; B6/10/1969 Waterloo, SC   **1992** Cle 2 (0)   **1994**†Pit 3 (0)   **NFL** 5 (0) [2 yrs]

FOGLE, DESHAWN   DeShawn Casey, LB, 6′1″/220 lbs; Kansas State; B4/1/1975 Brooklyn, NY   **1997** Phi 5 (0)

FOLAU, SPENCER   Spencer Sione, T, 6′5″/315 lbs; Idaho; B4/5/1973 Nuku'Alofa, Tonga   **1997** Bal 10 (0)   **1998** Bal 3 (3)   **1999** Bal 7 (1)   **2000**†Bal 11 (4)   **2001**†Mia 16 (15, LT)
2002 NO 16 (16, RT)   **2003** NO 14 (1)   **2004** NO 16 (3)   **NFL** 93 (43) [8 yrs]

FOLDBERG, HANK   Henry Christian, E, 6′2″/205 lbs; Texas A&M; Army; 1947: Bkn-A, rnd 20/Was, rnd 5; B3/12/1923 Dallas, TX, D3/6/2001 Bella Vista, AR

1948	Bkn-A	13(6, LE)	—	—	—	—	16	129	8.1	0	—	—	—	—	—	—	—	—	—	—	1	6	65
1949	ChiH-A	12(9, LE)	—	—	—	—	15	202	13.5	0	—	—	—	—	—	—	—	—	—	—	—	0	101
AAFC	2	25(15)	—	—	—	—	31	331	10.7	0	—	—	—	—	—	—	—	—	—	—	1	6	166

FOLEY, DAVE   David Edward, T-C, 6′5″/255 lbs; Ohio State; 1969: NYJ, rnd 1; B10/28/1947 Cincinnati, OH   **1969** NYJ-A 1   **1970** NYJ 14 (RT)   **1971** NYJ 14   **1972** Buf 12 (12, LT)
1973 Buf◇14 (14, LT)   **1974**†Buf 14 (14, LT)   **1975** Buf 14 (14, LT)   **1976** Buf 14 (14, LT)   **1977** Buf 13 (LT)   **NFL** 110 (68) [9 yrs]

FOLEY, GLENN   Glenn Edward, QB, 6′2″/210 lbs; Boston College; 1994: NYJ, rnd 7; B10/10/1970 Cherry Hill, NJ

1994	NYJ	1(0)	—	—	—	—	—	—	—	—	8	5	62.5	45	5.6(16)	0	1	—	—	—	—	0	-18
1995	NYJ	1(0)	1	9	9.0(9)	0	1	-9	-9.0(-9)	0	29	16	55.2	128	4.4(32)	0	1	4	21	—	—	0	29
1996	NYJ	5(3)	7	40	5.7(12)	0	—	—	—	—	110	54	49.1	559	5.1(46)	3	7	9	65	—	—	0	55
1997	NYJ	6(2)	3	-5	-1.7(-1)	0	—	—	—	—	97	56	57.7	705	7.3(35)	3	1	3	24	—	—	0	323
1998	NYJ	5(3)	5	-11	-2.2(-1)	0	—	—	—	—	108	58	53.7	749	6.9(48)	4	6	5	49	—	—	0	144
1999	Sea	3(1)	3	-1	-0.3(0)	0	—	—	—	—	30	18	60.0	283	9.4(49)	2	0	6	34	—	—	0	151
NFL	6	21(9)	19	32	1.7(12)	0	1	-9	-9.0(-9)	0	382	207	54.2	2469	6.5(49)	12	16	27	193	—	—	0	682

FOLEY, JIM   James Edward, B, 5′8″/165 lbs; Syracuse; B1903, deceased   **1926** Har 9 (5, WB)

FOLEY, STEVE   Stephen James, DB, 6′2″/189 lbs; Tulane; 1975: Den, rnd 8; B11/11/1953 New Orleans, LA [I]   **1976** Den 14 (6, rcb)   **1977**†Den 13 (13, RCB)
1979†Den 16 (16, RCB)   **1980** Den 16 (16, FS/rcb)   **1981** Den 16 (13, FS)   **1982** Den 1 (1)   **1983**†Den 14 (13, FS)   **1984**†Den 16 (16, FS)   **1985** Den 12 (11, FS)
1986†Den 16 (15, FS)

| 1978 | †Den☆ | 16(16, RCB) | 1 | 14 | 14.0(14) | 0 | — | — | — | — | — | — | — | — | — | — | — | — | — | i | — | 0 | 68 |
| NFL | 11 | 150(136) | 1 | 14 | 14.0(14) | 0 | — | — | — | — | — | — | — | — | — | — | — | — | — | pi | 2 | 12 | 443 |

FOLEY, STEVE   Steve, LB, 6′3″/260 lbs; Louisiana-Monroe; 1998: Cin, rnd 3; B9/11/1975 Little Rock, AR   **1998** Cin 10 (1)   **1999** Cin 16 (16, LOLB/llb)   **2000** Cin 16 (16, LLB)
2001 Cin 12 (12, LLB)   **2003** Hou 13 (3)   **2004**†SD 16 (16, ROLB)   **2005** SD 13 (13, ROLB)   **NFL** 96 (77) [7 yrs]

FOLEY, TIM   Thomas David, DB, 6′0″/194 lbs; Purdue; 1970: Mia, rnd 3; B1/22/1948 Evanston, IL [I]   **1970** Mia 14   **1971**†Mia 14 (14, LCB)   **1972** Mia 14 (13, LCB)
1973†Mia 11 (10, LCB)   **1974**†Mia 13 (10, LCB)   **1975** Mia 14 (9, LCB)   **1976** Mia 2   **1977** Mia☆14 (10, SS)   **1978**†Mia 16 (16, SS)   **1979**†Mia★15 (15, SS)   **1980** Mia 7 (4)
NFL 134 (101) [11 yrs]

FOLEY, TIM   Timothy John, T, 6′6″/275 lbs; Notre Dame; 1980: Bal, rnd 2; B5/30/1958 Cincinnati, OH   **1981** Bal 6 (0)

FOLK, DICK   Richard Armand, FB, 6′0″/200 lbs; Arkansas State; Illinois Wesleyan; B5/21/1915 Polo, IL, D6/1970 Bishopville, SC   **1939** Bkn 3 (0)

FOLKINS, LEE   Lloyd Leroy, TE-DE, 6′5″/215 lbs; Washington; 1961: GB, rnd 6; B7/4/1939 Wallace, ID

1961	†GB	14	—	—	—	—	—	—	—	—	—	—	—	—	—	—	—	—	—	—	—	—	—
1962	Dal	14(11, TE)	—	—	—	—	39	536	13.7(52)	6	—	—	—	—	—	—	—	—	—	—	—	36	298
1963	Dal◇	13(TE)	—	—	—	—	31	407	13.1(35)	4	—	—	—	—	—	—	—	—	—	—	—	24	224
1964	Dal	14	1	9	9.0(9)	0	5	41	8.2(11)	0	—	—	—	—	—	—	—	—	—	Pk	—	0	15
1965	Pit	8	—	—	—	—	5	58	11.6(16)	0	—	—	—	—	—	—	—	—	—	—	1	6	29
NFL	5	63(11)	1	9	9.0(9)	0	80	1042	13.0(52)	10	—	—	—	—	—	—	—	—	—	Pk	1	66	565

FOLLET, BERYL   Beryl Millard, TB-HB, 5′9″/165 lbs; NYU; B4/26/1908 Manlius, NY, D5/1/1982 Stony Brook, NY   **1930** SI 10 (9, TB)   **1931** SI 2 (0)   **NFL** 12 (9) [2 yrs]

FOLMAR, BRENDAN   Brendan Arthur, QB, 6′1″/200 lbs; California (PA); B4/2/1964 Birmingham, AL   **1987** Det 1 (0)

FOLSOM, STEVE   Steven Mark, TE, 6′5″/235 lbs; Long Beach State; Utah; 1981: Mia, rnd 10; B3/21/1958 Los Angeles, CA   **1981** Phi 3 (0)   **1987** Dal 9 (0)   **1990** Dal 1 (0)

1988	Dal	16(4)	—	—	—	—	9	84	9.3(20)	2	—	—	—	—	—	—	—	—	—	—	—	12	52
1989	Dal	16(16, TE)	—	—	—	—	28	265	9.5(20)	2	—	—	—	—	—	—	—	—	—	—	—	12	143
NFL	5	45(20)	—	—	—	—	37	349	9.4(20)	4	—	—	—	—	—	—	—	—	—	—	—	24	195

FOLSTON, JAMES   James Edward, LB, 6′3″/236 lbs; Louisiana-Monroe; 1994: LARd, rnd 2; B8/14/1971 Cocoa, FL   **1994** LARd 7 (0)   **1995** Oak 15 (0)   **1996** Oak 12 (0)
1997 Oak 16 (7, rlb)   **1999** Arz 6 (0)   **2000** Arz 13 (3)

| 1998 | Oak | 16(5, llb) | — | — | — | — | 1 | -1 | -1.0(-1) | 0 | — | — | — | — | — | — | — | — | — | S | — | 0 | -1 |
| NFL | 7 | 85(15) | — | — | — | — | 1 | -1 | -1.0(-1) | 0 | — | — | — | — | — | — | — | — | — | S | — | 0 | -1 |

FOLTZ, VERN   Vernon Jay, C-LB, 6′1″/205 lbs; St. Vincent; B8/27/1918 Clearfield, PA   **1944** Was 10 (6, C)   **1945** Pit 4 (0)   **NFL** 14 (6) [2 yrs]

FOLZ, ART   Arthur, B, 5′7″/157 lbs; Chicago; B1903, deceased [K]   **1923** ChiC 4 (2), 7   **1924** ChiC 9 (5, lh), 6   **1925** ChiC 5 (1), 24   **NFL** 18 (8), 37 [3 yrs]

FONOTI, TONIU   Toniuoleviavea Satele, G, 6′4″/349 lbs; Nebraska; 2002: SD, rnd 2; B11/26/1981 American Samoa   **2002** SD 15 (14, RG)   **2004**†SD 16 (16, LG)   **2005** SD 2 (2)
2005 Min 1 (1)   **NFL** 34 (33) [3 yrs]

FONTENOT, ALBERT   Albert Paul, DE-DT, 6′4″/275 lbs; Baylor; 1993: Chi, rnd 4; B9/17/1970 Houston, TX   **1993** ChiB 16 (0)   **1994**†ChiB 16 (8, LDT)   **1995** ChiB 13 (5, rde)
1996 ChiB 16 (15, LDE)   **1997** Ind 16 (16, LDE)   **1998** Ind 7 (5, lde)   **1999** SD 15 (15, LDE)   **2000** SD 15 (15, LDE)   **2001** SD 16 (2)   **NFL** 130 (81) [9 yrs]

FONTENOT, CHRIS   Christopher Dwight, TE, 6′3″/250 lbs; McNeese State; B7/11/1974 Lafayette, LA

| 1998 | Phi | 5(3) | — | — | — | — | 8 | 90 | 11.3(19) | 0 | — | — | — | — | — | — | — | — | — | — | — | 0 | 45 |

FONTENOT, HERMAN   Herman Joseph, RB, 6′0″/206 lbs; LSU; B9/12/1963 St. Elizabeth, TX

1985	†Cle	9(0)	—	—	—	—	2	19	9.5(17)	0	1	0	0.0	0	0.0	0	—	—	—	k	—	0	105
1986	†Cle	16(3)	25	105	4.2(16)	1	47	559	11.9(72)	1	1	1	100.0	46	46.0(46)	1	0	—	—	k	—	12	422
1987	†Cle	12(0)	15	33	2.2(14)	0	4	40	10.0(25)	0	1	1	100.0	14	14.0(14)	0	—	—	—	k	—	0	55
1988	†Cle	16(1)	28	87	3.1(17)	0	19	170	8.9(15)	1	1	0	0.0	0	0.0	0	—	—	—	k	1	12	297
1989	GB	16(0)	17	69	4.1(19)	1	40	372	9.3(38)	3	0	0	0.0	0	0.0	0	1	9	—	k	—	24	280
1990	GB	14(0)	17	76	4.5(18)	0	31	293	9.5(59)	1	—	—	—	—	—	—	—	—	—	k	—	6	271
NFL	6	83(4)	102	370	3.6(19)	2	143	1453	10.2(72)	6	4	2	50.0	60	15.0(46)	1	0	1	9	k	1	54	1429

FONTENOT, JERRY   Jerry Paul, C-G, 6′3″/300 lbs; Texas A&M; 1989: Chi, rnd 3; B11/21/1966 Lafayette, LA   **1989** ChiB 16 (0)   **1990**†ChiB 16 (2)   **1991**†ChiB 16 (7, lg)
1992 ChiB 16 (16, C)   **1993** ChiB 16 (16, C)   **1994**†ChiB 16 (16, C)   **1995** ChiB 16 (16, C)   **1996** ChiB 16 (16, C)   **1997** NO 16 (16, C)   **1998** NO 4 (4)   **1999** NO 16 (16, C)
2000†NO 16 (16, C)   **2001** NO 16 (16, C)   **2002** NO 16 (16, C)   **2003** NO 16 (16, C)   **2004** Cin 11 (16, c)   **NFL** 239 (195) [16 yrs]

FONTENOT, THERRIAN   Therrian, DB, 5′10″/187 lbs; Fresno State; B6/28/1981 Lawndale, CA   **2005** GB 1 (0)

FONTES, WAYNE   Wayne Howard Joseph, DB, 6′0″/190 lbs; Michigan State; 1961: NYT, rnd 22/Phi, rnd 9; B2/2/1940 New Bedford, MA [C]   **1962** NYT-A 9

FOOTE, CHRIS   Christopher D., C-G, 6′3″/256 lbs; USC; 1980: Bal, rnd 6; B12/2/1956 Louisville, KY   **1980** Bal 16 (0)   **1981** Bal 16 (0)   **1982** NYG 7 (0)   **1983** NYG 11 (0)
1987†Min 6 (0)   **1988**†Min 16 (5, c)   **1989**†Min 16 (0)   **1990** Min 16 (3)   **NFL** 104 (8) [8 yrs]

FOOTE, LARRY   Lawrence Edward, LB, 6′0″/234 lbs; Michigan; 2002: Pit, rnd 4; B6/12/1980 Detroit, MI   **2002**†Pit 14 (3)   **2003** Pit 16 (0)   **2004**†Pit 16 (16, RILB)
2005†Pit 16 (16, RILB)   **NFL** 62 (35) [4 yrs]

FOOTMAN, DAN   Daniel Ellis, DE-DT-NT, 6′5″/290 lbs; Florida State; 1993: Cle, rnd 2; B1/13/1969 Tampa, FL   **1993** Cle 8 (0)   **1994**†Cle 16 (2)   **1995** Cle 16 (16, RDT)
1996 Bal 10 (8, nt)   **1997** Ind 16 (10, RDE)   **1998** Ind 3 (3)   **NFL** 69 (39) [6 yrs]

YEAR	TEAM	G (GS, POS)	RUSH	YD	AVG(LG)	TD	REC	YD	AVG(LG)	TD	PASS	COMP	PCT	YD	AVG(LG)	TD	INT	SK	YD	QBR	KPR	OTD	PTS	TAY

FORBES, MARLON — Marlon Darryl, DB, 6'1"/215 lbs; Penn State; B12/25/1971 Brooklyn, NY   **1996** ChiB 15 (0)   **1997** ChiB 16 (1)   **1998** ChiB 16 (2)   **1999** Cle 16 (1)   **NFL** 63 (4) [4 yrs]

FORD, ADRIAN — Adrian Grainger, B, 5'10"/190 lbs; Lafayette; B1/1/1904 Youngstown, OH, D7/7/1977 Youngstown, OH   **1927** Pot 2 (0)   **1927** Fra 9 (6, tb), 12   **NFL** 11 (6) [1 yr]

FORD, BERNARD — K. Bernard, WR, 5'9"/168 lbs; Central Florida; 1988: Buf, rnd 3; B2/27/1966 Cordele, GA

1989	Dal	10(1)	—	—	—	—	7	78	11.1(21)	1													6	44
1990	†Hou	14(0)	—	—	—	—	10	98	9.8(24)	1											k		6	63
NFL	2	24(1)	—	—	—	—	17	176	10.4(24)	2											k		12	107

FORD, BRAD — Brad Jamar, DB, 5'10"/170 lbs; Alabama; 1996: Det, rnd 4; B1/11/1974 Alexander City, AL   **1996** Det 14 (0)

FORD, CARL — Carl, WR, 6'0"/183 lbs; Toledo; 2004: GB, rnd 4; B10/8/1980 Monroe, MI   **2005** ChiB 10 (0)

FORD, CHARLIE — Charles Glenn, DB, 6'3"/185 lbs; Houston; 1971: Chi, rnd 2; B12/10/1948 Beaumont, TX   **1971** ChiB 14 (LCB)   **1972** ChiB 14 (LCB)   **1973** ChiB 13 (LCB)   **1974** Phi 6   **1975** Buf 5 (4)   **1975** NYG 8   **NFL** 60 (4) [5 yrs]

FORD, CHRIS — Christopher David, WR, 6'1"/185 lbs; Lamar; B5/20/1967 Houston, TX   **1990** TB 1 (0)

FORD, COLE — Cole, K, 6'2"/210 lbs; USC; 1995: Pit, rnd 7; B12/31/1972 Tucson, AZ [K]   **1995** Oak 5 (0)   **1996** Oak 16 (0)   **1997** Oak 16 (0)   **1998** Buf 1 (0)   **NFL** 38 (0) [4 yrs]

FORD, DARRYL — Darryl Dewayne, LB, 6'1"/225 lbs; New Mexico State; B6/22/1966 Dallas, TX   **1992** Pit 8 (0)   **1992** Det 1 (0)   **1993** Det 11 (0)   **1994** Atl 15 (0)   **NFL** 35 (0) [3 yrs]

FORD, FRED — Frederick, HB, 5'8"/180 lbs; Cal Poly-Pomona; B3/30/1938

1960	Buf-A	3	18	40	2.2(7)	0	1	5	5.0(5)	0	—	—		—	—		—	—			k		0	74
1960	†LAC-A	6	20	154	7.7(53)	2	—	—	—		1	0	0.0	0	0.0	0	0				kp		12	269
NFL	1	9	38	194	5.1(53)	2	1	5	5.0(5)	0	1	0	0.0	0	0.0	0	0				kp		12	343

FORD, GARRETT — Garrett William, RB, 6'2"/230 lbs; West Virginia; 1968: Den, rnd 3; B5/4/1945 Washington, DC

| 1968 | Den-A | 14(FB) | 41 | 186 | 4.5(23) | 1 | 6 | 40 | 6.7(12) | 0 | | | | | | | | | | | — | | 6 | 216 |

FORD, HENRY — Henry, HB-DB, 6'0"/180 lbs; Pittsburgh; 1955: Cle, rnd 9; B11/1/1931 Homestead, PA

1955	Cle	2	2	1	0.5(1)	0	—	—	—												p		0	-4
1956	Pit	12	12	26	2.2(16)	2	3	7	2.3(8)	0											kpi		12	127
NFL	2	14	14	27	1.9(16)	2	3	7	2.3(8)	0											kpi		12	123

FORD, HENRY — Henry, DT-DE, 6'3"/295 lbs; Arkansas; 1994: Hou, rnd 1; B10/30/1971 Fort Worth, TX   **1994** Hou 11 (0)   **1995** Hou 16 (16, RDE)   **1996** Hou 15 (14, RDT)   **1997** Ten 16 (16, RDT)   **1998** Ten 13 (5, rdt)   **1999**†Ten 12 (9, RDE)   **2000**†Ten 14 (3)   **2001** Ten 16 (0)   **2002**†Ten 16 (13, RDT)   **2003** NO 4 (0)   **NFL** 133 (76) [10 yrs]

FORD, JAMES — James Leon, RB, 6'0"/200 lbs; Texas Southern; 1971: Dal, rnd 18; B9/11/1949 Jacksonville, FL

1971	NO	9(fb)	93	379	4.1(35)	2	7	54	7.7(10)	1													12	426
1972	NO	5	11	28	2.5(9)	0	1	9	9.0(9)	1													0	33
NFL	2	14	104	407	3.9(35)	2	8	63	7.9(10)	0													12	459

FORD, JOHN — John Allen, WR, 6'2"/204 lbs; Virginia; 1989: Det, rnd 2; B7/31/1966 Belle Glade, FL

| 1989 | Det | 7(1) | — | — | — | — | 5 | 56 | 11.2(37) | 0 | | | | | | | | | | | — | | 0 | 28 |

FORD, LEN — Leonard Guy, DE-E, 6'4"/245 lbs; Morgan State; Michigan; B2/18/1926 Washington, DC, D3/13/1972 Detroit, MI; HOF 1976   **1950**†Cle 5 (RDE)   **1951**†Cle★12 (RDE)   **1952**†Cle★12 (RDE)   **1953**†Cle★12 (RDE)   **1954**†Cle★12 (RDE)   **1955**†Cle☆12 (RDE)   **1956** Cle☆12 (RDE)   **1957**†Cle★11 (RDE)   **1958** GB 11   **NFL** 99 [9 yrs]

1948	LAD-A	14(10, RE)	—	—	—	—	31	598	19.3	7											ki		42	338
1949	LAD-A	12(8, RE)	—	—	—	—	36	577	16.0	1											i		6	334
AAFC	2	26(18)	—	—	—	—	67	1175	17.5	8											ki		48	672

FORD, MOSES — Moses, WR, 6'2"/220 lbs; Fayetteville State; B2/19/1964 Dillon, SC   **1987** Pit 1 (0)

FORDE, SALEM — Salem Holland, B, 5'7"/150 lbs; Louisville; B2/14/1896 Louisville, KY, D6/16/1976 Louisville, KY   **1922** Lou 3 (1)   **1923** Lou 1 (0)   **NFL** 4 (1) [2 yrs]

FORDE, BRIAN — Brian Michael, LB, 6'2"/230 lbs; Washington State; 1988: NO, rnd 7; B11/1/1963 Montreal, Canada   **1988** NO 16 (0)   **1989** NO 16 (1)   **1990**†NO 16 (0)   **1991**†NO 16 (0)   **NFL** 64 (1) [4 yrs]

FORDHAM, JIM — James Abner, FB, 5'11"/215 lbs; Georgia; 1940: ChiB, rnd 8; B12/6/1916 Graymont, GA, D4/1969

1944	ChiB	10(8, FB)	73	381	5.2(40)	4	1	13	13.0(13)	0											k		24	440
1945	ChiB	9(5, FB)	45	153	3.4(11)	1	4	34	8.5(19)	0													6	180
NFL	2	19(13)	118	534	4.5(40)	5	5	47	9.4(19)	0											k		30	620

FORDHAM, TODD — Lindsay Todd, T, 6'5"/320 lbs; Florida State; B10/9/1973 Atlanta, GA   **1997** Jax 1 (0)   **1998** Jax 11 (1)   **2000** Jax 16 (8, rt)   **2001** Jax 12 (12, LT)   **2002** Jax 16 (9, RT)   **2003** Pit 11 (6, rt)   **2004** Car 15 (7, rt)   **2005**†Car 16 (0)   **NFL** 98 (43) [8 yrs]

FOREMAN, CHUCK — Walter Eugene, RB, 6'2"/210 lbs; Miami (FL); 1973: Min, rnd 1; B10/26/1950 Frederick, MD

1973	†Min◇	12(11, FB)	182	801	4.4(50)	4	37	362	9.8(35)	2													36	1032
1974	†Min★	13(13, FB)	199	777	3.9(32)	9	53	586	11.1(66)	6											k		90	1205
1975	†Min★	14(12, RB)	280	1070	3.8(31)	13	73	691	9.5(33)	9											k		132	1580
1976	†Min★	14(14, RB)	278	1155	4.2(46)	13	55	567	10.3(41)	1													84	1574
1977	†Min★	14(14, RB)	270	1112	4.1(51)	6	38	308	8.1(31)	3													54	1341
1978	†Min	14(14, FB)	237	749	3.2(21)	5	61	396	6.5(20)	2													42	1007
1979	Min	12	87	223	2.6(16)	2	19	147	7.7(22)	0													12	317
1980	NE	16(0)	23	63	2.7(7)	1	14	99	7.1(18)	0													6	123
NFL	8	109(78)	1556	5950	3.8(51)	53	350	3156	9.0(66)	23											k		456	8177

FOREMAN, JAY — Jamal A., LB, 6'1"/240 lbs; Nebraska; 1999: Buf, rnd 5; B2/18/1976 Eden Prairie, MN   **1999** Buf 7 (0)   **2000** Buf 15 (3)   **2001** Buf 16 (16, RLB)   **2002** Hou 16 (16, LILB)   **2003** Hou 16 (16, LILB)   **2004** Hou 11 (11, LILB)   **2005**†NYG 1 (0)   **NFL** 82 (62) [7 yrs]

FORESTER, BILL — George William, LB-MG-DT, 6'3"/237 lbs; SMU; 1953: GB, rnd 3; B8/9/1932 Dallas, TX [I]   **1953** GB 12 (MG)   **1954** GB 12 (MG)   **1955** GB 12 (MG)   **1956** GB 12 (MG)   **1957** GB 12 (RLB)   **1958** GB 12 (RLB)   **1959** GB★12 (RLB)   **1960**†GB★12 (RLB)   **1961**†GB★14 (RLB)   **1962**†GB★14 (RLB)   **1963** GB☆14 (RLB)   **NFL** 138 [11 yrs]

FORESTER, HERSCHEL — Herschel Vincent, G, 6'0"/230 lbs; SMU; 1952: Cle, rnd 8; B4/14/1931 Dallas, TX   **1954**†Cle 12   **1955**†Cle 12 (rg)   **1956** Cle 12 (RG)   **1957**†Cle 12 (lg)   **NFL** 48 [4 yrs]

FORKOVITCH, NICK — Nicholas John, FB, 5'11"/195 lbs; William & Mary; 1945: ChiB, rnd 29; B3/1/1920 McKeesport, PA

| 1948 | Bkn-A | 9(0) | 1 | 4 | 4.0(4) | 0 | — | — | — | | | | | | | | | | | | | | 0 | 4 |

FORNEY, KYNAN — Kynan, G, 6'3"/307 lbs; Hawaii; 2001: Atl, rnd 7; B9/8/1978 Nacogdoches, TX   **2001** Atl 12 (8, rg)   **2002**†Atl 14 (12, RG)   **2003** Atl 16 (16, RG)   **2004**†Atl 16 (16, RG)   **2005** Atl 16 (16, RG)   **NFL** 74 (68) [5 yrs]

FORNEY, PHIL — Philip L., LB, 6'2"/230 lbs; East Tennessee State; B9/18/1963 Rutherfordton, NC   **1987** SL 3 (0)

FORREST, EDDIE — Edwin George, G, 5'11"/210 lbs; Santa Clara; 1943: GB, rnd 20; B6/12/1921 San Francisco, CA, D5/30/2001 Palo Alto, CA   **1946** SF-A 11 (0)   **1947** SF-A 14 (5, rg)   **AAFC** 25 (5) [2 yrs]

FORREST, TOM — Thomas Wesley, G, 6'2"/255 lbs; Cincinnati; 1974: SD, rnd 8; B4/11/1952 Washington, DC   **1974** ChiB 8

FORSBERG, FRED — Frederick Carl, LB, 6'1"/235 lbs; Washington; 1966: Den, rnd 14; B7/4/1944 Tacoma, WA   **1968** Den-A 13 (RLB)   **1970** Den 14 (13, MLB)   **1971** Den 14 (14, MLB)   **1972** Den 9 (6, LLB)   **1973** Den 3   **1973** Buf 10   **1974** SD 6 (1)   **NFL** 69 (34) [6 yrs]

FORSEY, BROCK — Brock, RB, 5'11"/203 lbs; Boise State; 2003: Chi, rnd 6; B2/11/1980 Meridian, ID

2003	ChiB	9(2)	50	191	3.8(17)	2	3	37	12.3(22)	0													12	230
2004	Mia	7(0)	19	53	2.8(15)	0	—	—	—														0	53
NFL	2	16(2)	69	244	3.5(17)	2	3	37	12.3(22)	0													12	283

FORST, DUTCH — Arthur Henry, FB, 5'8"/195 lbs; Villanova; B2/17/1891 Derby, CT, D10/5/1963 Seymour, CT   **1926** Pro 2 (2)

FORSYTH, BEN — Charles Benjamin, C, /190 lbs; Rochester; Syracuse; B6/4/1890 Rochester, NY, D11/11/1968 Rochester, NY   **1920** Roc 2 (0)

FORTE, ALDO Aldo John, G-T, 6´0˝/213 lbs; Montana; 1939: ChiB, rnd 21; B1/20/1918 Chicago, IL **1939** ChiB 10 (1) **1940**†ChiB✧10 (4) **1941**†ChiB★10 (4) **1946**†ChiB 6 (1) **1947** GB 10 (1) **1946** Det 3 (1) **NFL** 49 (12) [6 yrs]

FORTE, BOB Robert Dominic, HB-LB-DB, 6´0˝/199 lbs; Arkansas; 1943: GB, rnd 11; B7/15/1922 Lake Village, AR, D3/12/1996 Dallas, TX **[I]**

YEAR	TEAM	G (GS, POS)	RUSH	YD	AVG (LG)	TD	REC	YD	AVG (LG)	TD	PASS	COMP	PCT	YD	AVG (LG)	TD	INT	SK	YD	QBR	KPR	OTD	PTS	TAY
1946	GB	9(4)	17	73	4.3(20)	0	2	5	2.5(4)	0	7	3	42.9	28	4.0(15)	1	1	—	—	—	i	—	0	68
1947	GB	12(10, RH)	29	80	2.8(12)	0	7	80	11.4(22)	2	2	1	50.0	8	4.0(8)	0	0	—	—	—	kpi	1	18	247
1948	GB	12(9, RH)	12	30	2.5(9)	0	6	63	10.5(19)	1	—	—	—	—	—	—	—	—	—	—	ki	—	6	98
1949	GB	12(11, RH)	40	135	3.4(25)	0	7	85	12.1(28)	0	1	0	0.0	0	0.0	0	0	—	—	—	kpi	—	0	247
1950	GB	12(DB)	9	13	1.4(11)	0	2	9	4.5(10)	0	2	2	100.0	24	12.0(14)	0	0	—	—	—	Pki	—	0	58
1952	GB	12(RLB)	—	—	—	—	—	—	—	—	2	2	100.0	4	2.0(5)	0	0	—	—	—	i	—	0	32
1953	GB	11(RLB)	—	—	—	—	—	—	—	—	—	—	—	—	—	—	—	—	—	—	—	—	0	0
NFL	7	80(34)	107	331	3.1(25)	0	24	242	10.1(28)	3	14	8	57.1	64	4.6(15)	1	1	—	—	—	Pkpi	1	24	748

FORTE, IKE Donald Ray, RB, 6´0˝/203 lbs; Arkansas; 1976: NE, rnd 2; B3/8/1954 Texarkana, AR

YEAR	TEAM	G (GS, POS)	RUSH	YD	AVG (LG)	TD	REC	YD	AVG (LG)	TD	PASS	COMP	PCT	YD	AVG (LG)	TD	INT	SK	YD	QBR	KPR	OTD	PTS	TAY
1976	NE	10(1)	25	100	4.0(26)	1	3	9	3.0(6)	1	—	—	—	—	—	—	—	—	—	—	k	—	12	137
1977	NE	13	62	157	2.5(16)	2	8	88	11.0(22)	0	—	—	—	—	—	—	—	—	—	—	p	—	12	220
1978	Was	13	4	4	1.0(2)	0	—	—	—	—	—	—	—	—	—	—	—	—	—	—	kp	—	0	72
1979	Was	11	25	125	5.0(20)	1	10	105	10.5(22)	0	—	—	—	—	—	—	—	—	—	—	k	—	6	279
1980	Was	12(0)	30	51	1.7(6)	1	15	174	11.6(28)	1	—	—	—	—	—	—	—	—	—	—	k	—	12	207
1981	†NYG	5(3)	19	74	3.9(15)	0	3	11	3.7(6)	0	—	—	—	—	—	—	—	—	—	—	—	—	0	80
NFL	6	64(4)	165	511	3.1(26)	5	39	387	9.9(28)	2	—	—	—	—	—	—	—	—	—	—	kp	—	42	994

FORTIN, ROMAN Roman Brian, C-T-G, 6´5˝/297 lbs; Oregon State; San Diego State; 1990: Det, rnd 8; B2/26/1967 Columbus, OH **1992** Atl 16 (1) **1993** Atl 16 (1) **1994** Atl 16 (16, C) **1995**†Atl 16 (15, C) **1996** Atl 16 (16, C) **1997** Atl 3 (3) **1998** SD 16 (16, C) **1999** SD 16 (16, C) **2000** SD 16 (16, C)

YEAR	TEAM	G (GS, POS)	RUSH	YD	AVG (LG)	TD	REC	YD	AVG (LG)	TD	PASS	COMP	PCT	YD	AVG (LG)	TD	INT	SK	YD	QBR	KPR	OTD	PTS	TAY
1991	†Det	16(2)	—	—	—	—	1	4	4.0(4)	0	—	—	—	—	—	—	—	—	—	—	—	—	0	2
NFL	10	147(102)	—	—	—	—	1	4	4.0(4)	0	—	—	—	—	—	—	—	—	—	—	k	—	0	-8

FORTMANN, DANNY Daniel John, G-LB, 6´0˝/210 lbs; Colgate; 1936: ChiB, rnd 9; B4/11/1916 Pearl River, NY, D5/24/1995 Los Angeles County, CA; HOF 1965 **1936** ChiB☆12 (9, RG) **1937**†ChiB☆10 (9, LG) **1938** ChiB☆11 (10, LG) **1939** ChiB☆11 (10, LG) **1940**†ChiB★10 (10, LG) **1941**†ChiB★11 (11, LG) **1942**†ChiB★11 (11, LG) **1943**†ChiB☆10 (9, LG) **NFL** 86 (79) [8 yrs]

FORTUNATO, JOE Joseph Francis, LB, 6´1˝/225 lbs; VMI; Mississippi State; 1952: ChiB, rnd 7; B3/28/1930 Mingo Junction, OH **1955** ChiB 12 (RLB) **1956**†ChiB 12 (RLB) **1958** ChiB★12 (RLB) **1959** ChiB 12 (RLB) **1960** ChiB 12 (LLB) **1961** ChiB 14 (LLB) **1962** ChiB★14 (LLB) **1963**†ChiB★14 (LLB) **1964** ChiB★13 (LLB) **1965** ChiB★14 (LLB) **1966** ChiB☆14 (LLB)

YEAR	TEAM	G (GS, POS)	RUSH	YD	AVG (LG)	TD	REC	YD	AVG (LG)	TD	PASS	COMP	PCT	YD	AVG (LG)	TD	INT	SK	YD	QBR	KPR	OTD	PTS	TAY
1957	ChiB	12(RLB)	2	-9	-4.5(1)	1	—	—	—	—	—	—	—	—	—	—	—	—	—	—	—	—	6	1
NFL	12	155	2	-9	-4.5(1)	1	—	—	—	—	—	—	—	—	—	—	—	—	—	—	i	2	18	87

FORTUNE, BILL William Peter, G, 5´11˝/218 lbs; Michigan; B10/14/1897 Joliet, IL, D3/12/1947 Chicago, IL **1920** ChiC 1 (0) **1924** Ham 4 (4, RG) **1925** Ham 5 (4, RG) **NFL** 10 (8) [3 yrs]

FORTUNE, ELLIOTT Elliott David, DE, 6´4˝/275 lbs; Georgia Tech; B5/28/1974 Roosevelt, NY **1996** Bal 14 (0)

FORTUNE, HOSEA Hosea Gerard, WR, 6´0˝/174 lbs; Rice; B3/4/1959 New Orleans, LA **1983** SD 4 (0)

FORURIA, JOHN John George, DB, 6´2˝/205 lbs; Idaho; 1967: Pit, rnd 8; B11/26/1944 Emmett, ID **1967** Pit 3 **1968** Pit 6 **NFL** 9 [2 yrs]

FOSCHI, JOHN PAUL John Paul, FB-TE, 6´4˝/270 lbs; Georgia Tech; B5/19/1982 Queens, NY

YEAR	TEAM	G (GS, POS)	RUSH	YD	AVG (LG)	TD	REC	YD	AVG (LG)	TD	PASS	COMP	PCT	YD	AVG (LG)	TD	INT	SK	YD	QBR	KPR	OTD	PTS	TAY
2005	Oak	10(5, fb)	—	—	—	—	6	37	6.2(11)	0	—	—	—	—	—	—	—	—	—	—	—	—	0	19

FOSDICK, BOB Robert Everett, G-T, 5´10˝/225 lbs; Iowa; B11/11/1894 Knoxville, IA, D1/30/1990 Tucson, AZ **1923** Min 5 (5, RG)

FOSTER, BARRY Barry, RB, 5´10˝/223 lbs; Arkansas; 1990: Pit, rnd 5; B12/8/1968 Hurst, TX

YEAR	TEAM	G (GS, POS)	RUSH	YD	AVG (LG)	TD	REC	YD	AVG (LG)	TD	PASS	COMP	PCT	YD	AVG (LG)	TD	INT	SK	YD	QBR	KPR	OTD	PTS	TAY
1990	Pit	16(1)	36	203	5.6(38)	1	1	2	2.0(2)	0	—	—	—	—	—	—	—	—	—	—	k	—	6	198
1991	Pit	10(9, RB)	96	488	5.1(56)	1	9	117	13.0(31)	1	—	—	—	—	—	—	—	—	—	—	—	—	12	562
1992	†Pit★	16(15, RB)	**390**	**1690**	4.3(69)	**11**	36	344	9.6(42)	0	1	0	0.0	0	0.0	0	0	—	—	—	—	—	66	**1972**
1993	Pit	9(9, RB)	177	711	4.0(38)	8	27	217	8.0(21)	1	—	—	—	—	—	—	—	—	—	—	—	—	54	905
1994	†Pit	11(10, RB)	216	851	3.9(29)	5	20	124	6.2(27)	0	—	—	—	—	—	—	—	—	—	—	—	—	30	963
NFL	5	62(44)	915	3943	4.3(69)	26	93	804	8.6(42)	2	1	0	0.0	0	0.0	0	0	—	—	—	k	—	168	4599

FOSTER, BOB Robins J., B-G-T, 5´10˝/192 lbs; none; B10/1886, deceased **1922** Rac 10 (2), 18 **1923** Rac 8 (1) **1924** Mil 2 (2) **NFL** 20 (5) [3 yrs]

FOSTER, DERRICK Derrick, RB, 5´11˝/205 lbs; William Paterson; B10/12/1963

YEAR	TEAM	G (GS, POS)	RUSH	YD	AVG (LG)	TD	REC	YD	AVG (LG)	TD	PASS	COMP	PCT	YD	AVG (LG)	TD	INT	SK	YD	QBR	KPR	OTD	PTS	TAY
1987	NYJ	3(0)	1	9	9.0(9)	0	1	9	9.0(9)	0	—	—	—	—	—	—	—	—	—	—	p	—	0	12

FOSTER, DESHAUN DeShaun Xavier, RB, 6´0˝/222 lbs; UCLA; 2002: Car, rnd 2; B1/10/1980 Charlotte, NC

YEAR	TEAM	G (GS, POS)	RUSH	YD	AVG (LG)	TD	REC	YD	AVG (LG)	TD	PASS	COMP	PCT	YD	AVG (LG)	TD	INT	SK	YD	QBR	KPR	OTD	PTS	TAY
2003	†Car	14(2)	113	429	3.8(21)	0	26	207	8.0(47)	2	—	—	—	—	—	—	—	—	—	—	—	—	12	543
2004	Car	4(3)	59	255	4.3(71)	2	9	76	8.4(42)	0	—	—	—	—	—	—	—	—	—	—	k	—	12	299
2005	†Car	15(5, RB)	205	879	4.3(70)	2	34	372	10.9(47)	1	1	0	0.0	0	0.0	0	0	—	—	—	—	—	18	1090
NFL	3	33(10)	377	1563	4.1(71)	4	69	655	9.5(47)	3	1	0	0.0	0	0.0	0	0	—	—	—	k	—	42	1932

FOSTER, EDDIE Edward Ervin, WR, 5´10˝/185 lbs; Houston; 1977: Hou, rnd 8; B6/5/1954 Houston, TX **1979** Hou 1

YEAR	TEAM	G (GS, POS)	RUSH	YD	AVG (LG)	TD	REC	YD	AVG (LG)	TD	PASS	COMP	PCT	YD	AVG (LG)	TD	INT	SK	YD	QBR	KPR	OTD	PTS	TAY
1977	Hou	14(14, WR)	—	—	—	—	15	208	13.9(56)	0	—	—	—	—	—	—	—	—	—	—	k	—	0	120
NFL	2	15(14)	—	—	—	—	15	208	13.9(56)	0	—	—	—	—	—	—	—	—	—	—	—	—	0	104

FOSTER, FRED Frederick Frank, FB-BB, 5´11˝/185 lbs; Syracuse; B4/25/1898 Niagara Falls, NY, D12/19/1968 Tallahassee, FL **1923** Buf 1 (1) **1923** Roc 1 (1) **1924** Roc 5 (2) **NFL** 7 (4) [2 yrs]

FOSTER, GENE Irving Eugene, RB, 6´0˝/220 lbs; Arizona State; 1965: SD, rnd 10/Dal, rnd 15; B3/20/1942 Salem, NJ

YEAR	TEAM	G (GS, POS)	RUSH	YD	AVG (LG)	TD	REC	YD	AVG (LG)	TD	PASS	COMP	PCT	YD	AVG (LG)	TD	INT	SK	YD	QBR	KPR	OTD	PTS	TAY
1965	†SD-A	14(FB)	121	469	3.9(22)	2	17	199	11.7(23)	0	3	2	66.7	31	10.3(21)	0	0	—	—	—	k	—	12	637
1966	SD-A	14(FB)	81	352	4.3(37)	1	26	260	10.0(63)	2	—	—	—	—	—	—	—	—	—	—	—	—	18	502
1967	SD-A	10	38	78	2.1(13)	0	9	46	5.1(11)	0	1	0	0.0	0	0.0	0	0	—	—	—	—	—	0	101
1968	SD-A	10(FB)	109	394	3.6(22)	1	23	224	9.7(48)	0	7	6	85.7	169	24.1(50)	0	0	—	—	—	—	—	6	601
1969	SD-A	13	64	236	3.7(24)	0	14	83	5.9(28)	1	5	2	40.0	39	7.8(30)	1	0	—	—	—	k	—	6	293
1970	SD	7	32	84	2.6(15)	0	10	92	9.2(48)	0	3	1	33.3	9	3.0(9)	0	0	1	8	—	—	—	0	135
NFL	6	68	445	1613	3.6(37)	4	99	904	9.1(63)	3	19	11	57.9	248	13.1(50)	1	0	1	8	—	k	—	42	2268

FOSTER, GEORGE George, T, 6´5˝/338 lbs; Georgia; 2003: Den, rnd 1; B6/9/1980 Macon, GA **2003** Den 1 (0) **2004**†Den 16 (16, RT) **2005**†Den 16 (16, RT) **NFL** 33 (32) [3 yrs]

FOSTER, JEROME Jerome, DE-DT, 6´2˝/268 lbs; Ohio State; 1983: Hou, rnd 5; B7/25/1960 Detroit, MI **1983** Hou 16 (1) **1984** Hou 9 (3) **1986** Mia 14 (0) **1986**†NYJ 1 (0) **1987** NYJ 4 (0) **NFL** 44 (4) [4 yrs]

FOSTER, LARRY Larry, WR, 5´10˝/195 lbs; LSU; B11/7/1976 Harvey, LA

YEAR	TEAM	G (GS, POS)	RUSH	YD	AVG (LG)	TD	REC	YD	AVG (LG)	TD	PASS	COMP	PCT	YD	AVG (LG)	TD	INT	SK	YD	QBR	KPR	OTD	PTS	TAY
2000	Det	10(0)	2	31	15.5(16)	0	17	175	10.3(40)	1	—	—	—	—	—	—	—	—	—	—	—	—	6	124
2001	Det	13(5, WR)	2	6	3.0(3)	0	22	283	12.9(36)	0	—	—	—	—	—	—	—	—	—	—	kp	—	0	197
2002	Det	13(0)	—	—	—	—	14	152	10.9(22)	0	—	—	—	—	—	—	—	—	—	—	kp	—	0	191
2003	Arz	1(1)	—	—	—	—	1	7	7.0(7)	0	—	—	—	—	—	—	—	—	—	—	—	—	0	4
NFL	4	37(6)	4	37	9.3(16)	0	54	617	11.4(40)	1	—	—	—	—	—	—	—	—	—	—	kp	—	6	515

FOSTER, RALPH Ralph Ellsworth, T, 6´0˝/230 lbs; Idaho; Oklahoma State; 1940: ChiC, rnd 17; B6/12/1917 Perry, OK, D6/3/1999 **1945** ChiC 9 (5, LT) **1946** ChiC 10 (4, LT) **NFL** 19 (9) [2 yrs]

FOSTER, RON Ronald Calvin, DB, 6´0˝/200 lbs; Cal State-Northridge; B11/25/1963 Los Angeles, CA **1987** LARd 3 (2)

FOSTER, ROY Roy Allen, G-T, 6´4˝/282 lbs; USC; 1982: Mia, rnd 1; B5/24/1960 Los Angeles, CA **1982**†Mia 9 (0) **1983**†Mia 16 (1) **1984**†Mia☆16 (16, LG) **1985**†Mia★16 (16, LG) **1986** Mia★16 (16, LG) **1987** Mia 12 (12, LG) **1988** Mia 15 (15, LG) **1989** Mia☆16 (16, LG) **1990**†Mia 16 (3) **1991** SF 16 (16, RG) **1992**†SF 16 (16, RG) **1993** SF 1 (0) **NFL** 165 (127) [12 yrs]

FOSTER, WALLY James Wallace, BB, 5´10˝/165 lbs; Bucknell; B10/29/1902 Pittsburgh, PA, D8/31/1978 Oakmont, PA **[K]** **1925** Buf 9 (9, BB), 1

FOSTER, WILL William Henry, LB, 6´2˝/230 lbs; Eastern Michigan; 1972: Phi, rnd 7; B10/2/1948 Grady, AL **1973** NE 9 (1) **1974** NE 12 **NFL** 21 (1) [2 yrs]

YEAR	TEAM	G(GS, POS)	RUSH	YD	AVG(LG)	TD	REC	YD	AVG(LG)	TD	PASS	COMP	PCT	YD	AVG(LG)	TD	INT	SK	YD	QBR	KPR	OTD	PTS	TAY

FOULES, ELBERT   Elbert, DB, 5′11″/185 lbs; Alcorn State; B7/4/1961 Greenville, MS   **1983** Phi 16 (0)   **1984** Phi 16 (12, LCB)   **1985** Phi 16 (3)   **1986** Phi 16 (3)   **1987** Phi 9 (8, RCB)   **NFL** 73 (26) [5 yrs]

FOUNTAINE, JAMAL   Jamal David, DE, 6′3″/240 lbs; Washington; B1/29/1971 San Francisco, CA   **1995** SF 7 (0)   **1997** Atl 3 (0)   **NFL** 10 (0) [2 yrs]

FOURCADE, JOHN   John Charles, QB, 6′1″/208 lbs; Mississippi; B10/11/1960 Gretna, LA

1987	NO	3(3)	19	134	7.1(18)	0	—	—	—	—	89	48	53.9	597	6.7(82)	4	3	6	67	—	—	—	0	333
1988	NO	1(0)	—	—	—	—	—	—	—	—	1	0	0.0	0	0.0	0	0	—	—	—	—	—	0	0
1989	NO	13(3)	14	91	6.5(14)	1	—	—	—	—	107	61	57.0	930	8.7(54)	7	4	13	96	—	—	—	6	441
1990	†NO	7(5, qb)	15	77	5.1(12)	1	—	—	—	—	116	50	43.1	785	6.8(68)	3	8	8	44	—	—	—	6	175
NFL		4	24(11)	48	302	6.3(18)	2	—	—	—	—	313	159	50.8	2312	7.4(82)	14	15	27	207	—	—	—	12	948

FOURCADE, KEITH   Keith Joseph, LB, 5′11″/225 lbs; Mississippi; B10/20/1961 Marrero, LA   **1987** NO 3 (0)

FOURNET, SID   Sidney Fredrick, G-LB-DB, 6′0″/235 lbs; LSU; 1955: LA, rnd 2; B8/27/1932 Bogalusa, LA   **1955**†LARm 12   **1956** LARm 12   **1957** Pit 2   **1960** DalT-A 14 (LG)   **1961** DalT-A 14 (LG)   **1962** NYT-A 14 (RG)   **1963** NYJ-A 14 (RG)   **NFL** 82 [7 yrs]

FOUTS, DAN   Daniel Francis, QB, 6′3″/204 lbs; Oregon; 1973: SD, rnd 3; B6/10/1951 San Francisco, CA; HOF 1993

1973	SD	10(6, QB)	7	32	4.6(16)	0	—	—	—	—	194	87	44.8	1126	5.8(69)	6	13	14	129	46.0	—	—	0	105
1974	SD	11(11, QB)	19	63	3.3(16)	1	—	—	—	—	237	115	48.5	1732	7.3(75)	8	13	12	99	61.4	—	—	6	459
1975	SD	10(9, QB)	23	170	7.4(32)	2	—	—	—	—	195	106	54.4	1396	7.2(57)	2	10	25	197	59.3	—	—	12	498
1976	SD	14(13, QB)	18	65	3.6(13)	0	—	—	—	—	359	208	57.9	2535	7.1(81)	14	15	39	220	75.4	—	—	0	803
1977	SD	4(4)	6	13	2.2(11)	0	—	—	—	—	109	69	63.3	869	8.0(67)	4	6	10	77	—	—	—	0	228
1978	SD	15(14, QB)	20	43	2.2(22)	2	—	—	—	—	381	224	58.8	2999	7.9(55)	24	20	12	130	83.0	—	—	12	883
1979	†SD★	16(16, QB)	26	49	1.9(26)	2	—	—	—	—	530	332	62.6	4082	7.7(65)	24	24	28	195	82.6	—	—	12	1270
1980	†SD★	16(16, QB)	23	15	0.7(9)	1	—	—	—	—	589	348	59.1	4715	8.0(65)	30	24	32	210	84.7	—	—	12	1583
1981	†SD★	16(16, QB)	22	56	2.5(13)	0	—	—	—	—	609	360	59.1	4802	7.9(67)	33	17	19	134	90.6	—	—	0	1942
1982	†SD★	9(9, QB)	9	8	0.9(9)	1	—	—	—	—	330	204	61.8	2883	8.7(44)	17	11	12	94	93.3	—	—	6	1105
1983	†SD★	10(10, QB)	12	-5	-0.4(3)	1	—	—	—	—	340	215	63.2	2975	8.8(59)	20	15	14	107	92.5	—	—	6	993
1984	SD	13(13, QB)	12	-29	-2.4(3)	0	1	0	0.0(0)	0	507	317	62.5	3740	7.4(61)	19	17	29	228	83.4	—	—	0	1256
1985	SD★	14(12, QB)	11	-1	-0.1(7)	0	—	—	—	—	430	254	59.1	3638	8.5(75)	27	20	18	135	88.1	—	—	0	1153
1986	SD	12(12, QB)	4	-3	-0.8(0)	0	—	—	—	—	430	252	58.6	3031	7.0(45)	16	22	21	173	71.4	—	—	0	713
1987	SD	11(10, QB)	12	0	0.0(2)	0	—	—	—	—	364	206	56.6	2517	6.9(46)	10	15	24	176	70.0	—	—	12	729
NFL		15	181(171)	224	476	2.1(32)	13	1	0	0.0	0	5604	3297	58.8	43040	7.7(81)	254	242	319	2304	80.2	—	—	78	13716

FOWLER, AMOS   Amos Emanuel, C-G, 6′3″/250 lbs; Southern Mississippi; 1978: Det, rnd 5; B2/11/1956 Pensacola, FL   **1978** Det 16   **1979** Det 12 (1)   **1980** Det 13 (12, C)   **1981** Det 16 (16, C)   **1982**†Det 9 (9, C)   **1983**†Det 16 (4)   **1984** Det 15 (7, C)   **NFL** 97 (49) [7 yrs]

FOWLER, AUBREY   Robert Aubey, HB, 5′10″/160 lbs; Arkansas Tech; Arkansas; 1948: Bal-A, rnd 9/Phi, rnd 18; B6/12/1920 Hamburg, AR, D2/29/1996 Dumas, AR

| 1948 | †Bal-A | 13(0) | 6 | 30 | 5.0 | 0 | — | — | — | — | — | — | — | — | — | — | — | — | — | | kpi | — | 0 | 22 |

FOWLER, BOBBY   Robert, FB, 5′11″/212 lbs; Tennessee-Martin; B1936

| 1962 | NYT-A | 7 | 25 | 5.4(15) | 0 | — | — | — | — | — | — | — | — | — | — | — | — | — | — | — | — | — | 0 | 27 |

FOWLER, BOBBY   Bobby Lane, FB, 6′2″/230 lbs; Texas-El Paso; Louisiana Tech; B9/11/1960 Temple, TX

| 1985 | NO | 10(0) | 2 | 4 | 2.0(3) | 0 | 5 | 43 | 8.6(11) | 0 | — | — | — | — | — | — | — | — | — | | k | — | 0 | 44 |

FOWLER, CHARLIE   Charles Clark, G, 6′2″/265 lbs; Auburn; Houston; 1967: Cle, rnd 12; B11/10/1944 Nashville, TN   **1967** Mia-A 6 (2)   **1968** Mia-A 14 (7, LG)   **NFL** 20 (9) [2 yrs]

FOWLER, DAN   Daniel Gabriel, G, 6′4″/260 lbs; Kentucky; 1979: NYG, rnd 10; B4/12/1956 Euclid, OH   **1979** NYG 1

FOWLER, JERRY   Jerry Marston, T, 6′3″/255 lbs; Northwestern State (LA); B4/26/1940 Shreveport, LA   **1964** Hou-A 4

FOWLER, MELVIN   Melvin Thaddeus, C-G, 6′3″/310 lbs; Maryland; 2002: Cle, rnd 3; B3/31/1979 Brooklyn, NY   **2002** Cle 1 (1)   **2003** Cle 14 (10, C/lg)   **2004** Cle 15 (3)   **2005** Min 11 (9, C)   **NFL** 41 (23) [4 yrs]

FOWLER, RYAN   Ryan, LB, 6′3″/243 lbs; Duke; B5/20/1982   **2004** Dal 2 (0)   **2005** Dal 14 (3)   **NFL** 16 (3) [2 yrs]

FOWLER, TODD   Steven Todd, TE, 6′3″/221 lbs; Stephen F. Austin State; 1984: Dal, rnd S1; B6/9/1962 Van, TX

1985	†Dal	8(1)	7	25	3.6(6)	0	5	24	4.8(10)	0	—	—	—	—	—	—	—	—	—		k	—	0	40
1986	Dal	16(0)	6	5	0.8(2)	0	1	19	19.0(19)	0	—	—	—	—	—	—	—	—	—			—	0	15
1987	Dal	12(1)	—	—	—	—	1	6	6.0(6)	0	—	—	—	—	—	—	—	—	—			—	0	3
1988	Dal	16(6, te)	3	6	2.0(4)	0	10	64	6.4(13)	0	—	—	—	—	—	—	—	—	—			—	0	38
NFL		4	52(8)	16	36	2.3(6)	0	17	113	6.6(19)	0	—	—	—	—	—	—	—	—		k	—	0	96

FOWLER, WAYNE   Byron Wayne, C, 6′3″/260 lbs; Richmond; 1970: Buf, rnd 7; B1/23/1948 Baltimore, MD   **1970** Buf 10

FOWLER, WILLMER   Willmer, HB, 5′10″/185 lbs; Northwestern; 1959: Phi, rnd 8; B6/3/1937 Andalusia, AL

1960	Buf-A	11(HB)	93	370	4.0(76)	1	10	99	9.9(28)	0	—	—	—	—	—	—	—	—	—		k	—	6	451
1961	Buf-A	2	1	2	2.0(2)	0	—	—	—	—	—	—	—	—	—	—	—	—	—			—	0	2
NFL		2	13	94	372	4.0(76)	1	10	99	9.9(28)	0	—	—	—	—	—	—	—	—		k	—	6	453

FOWLKES, DENNIS   Dennis James, LB, 6′2″/238 lbs; West Virginia; B3/11/1961 Columbus, OH   **1983** Min 11 (0)   **1984** Min 14 (0)   **1985** Min 15 (8, RILB)   **1987** Mia 3 (3)   **NFL** 43 (11) [4 yrs]

FOX, CHAS   Charles Eldon, WR, 5′11″/180 lbs; Furman; 1986: KC, rnd 4; B10/3/1963 Lafayette, IN

| 1986 | SL | 4(3) | — | — | — | — | 5 | 59 | 11.8(38) | 1 | — | — | — | — | — | — | — | — | — | | k | — | 6 | 106 |

FOX, KEYARON   Keyaron James, LB, 6′3″/220 lbs; Georgia Tech; 2004: KC, rnd 3; B1/24/1982 Atlanta, GA   **2004** KC 12 (0)   **2005** KC 2 (0)   **NFL** 14 (0) [2 yrs]

FOX, MIKE   Michael James, DE-DT-NT, 6′8″/285 lbs; West Virginia; 1990: NYG, rnd 2; B8/5/1967 Akron, OH   **1990**†NYG 16 (0)   **1991** NYG 15 (5, lde)   **1992** NYG 16 (4)   **1993**†NYG 16 (16, RDE)   **1994** NYG 16 (16, LDT)   **1995** Car 16 (16, LDE)   **1996** Car 11 (11, LDE)   **1997** Car 11 (9, lde)   **1998** Car 16 (7, nt)   **NFL** 133 (84) [9 yrs]

FOX, SAM   Samuel S., E, 6′2″/215 lbs; Ohio State; B5/4/1918 Washington, DC, D4/11/2004 Kendall, FL

| 1945 | NYG | 8(6, LE) | — | — | — | — | 10 | 120 | 12.0(28) | 1 | — | — | — | — | — | — | — | — | — | | k | — | 12 | 69 |

FOX, SCOTT   Scott, LB, 6′2″/222 lbs; Austin Peay State; B12/28/1963   **1987** Hou 2 (0)

FOX, TERRY   Terrence Patrick, FB-LB, 6′1″/208 lbs; Miami (FL); 1941: Pit, rnd 17; B7/6/1918 Newark, NJ, D4/1/1981 Miami, FL

1941	Phi	11(2)	21	97	4.6(13)	0	6	71	11.8(21)	0	—	—	—	—	—	—	—	—	—		k	—	0	134
1945	Phi	2(0)	—	—	—	—	—	—	—	—	—	—	—	—	—	—	—	—	—			—	0	—
NFL		2	13(2)	21	97	4.6(13)	0	6	71	11.8(21)	0	—	—	—	—	—	—	—	—	—			—	0	133
1946	Mia-A	8(2)	12	26	2.2	0	3	27	9.0	0	—	—	—	—	—	—	—	—	—		Pk	—	0	49

FOX, TIM   Timothy Richard, DB, 5′11″/186 lbs; Ohio State; 1976: NE, rnd 1; B11/1/1953 Canton, OH [I]   **1976**†NE 13 (13, FS)   **1977** NE 14 (14, FS)   **1978**†NE 16 (16, FS)   **1979** NE 16 (16, FS)   **1980** NE✧16 (16, FS)   **1981** NE 16 (16, FS)   **1982**†SD☆7 (7, FS)   **1983** SD 12 (8, fs)   **1984** SD 11 (10, FS)   **1985**†LARm 6 (0)   **1986**†LARm 14 (0)   **NFL** 141 (116) [11 yrs]

FOX, VERNON   Vernon Lee, DB, 5′9″/200 lbs; Fresno State; B10/9/1979 Las Vegas, NV   **2002** SD 16 (3)   **2003** SD 12 (2)   **2004** Det 14 (0)   **2005** Det 14 (0)   **NFL** 56 (5) [4 yrs]

FOXWORTH, DOMONIQUE   Domonique, DB, 5′11″/178 lbs; Maryland; 2005: Den, rnd 3; B3/27/1983 Oxford, England   **2005**†Den 16 (7, rcb)

FOXX, DION   Dion Lamont, LB, 6′3″/250 lbs; James Madison; B6/11/1971 Richmond, VA   **1994**†Mia 16 (0)   **1995** Mia 1 (0)   **1995** Was 2 (0)   **NFL** 19 (0) [2 yrs]

FRAHM, DICK   Herald Samuel, WB-T, 5′10″/195 lbs; Nebraska; B4/11/1906 Liberty, NE, D10/19/1977 St. Louis, MO [K]

1932	SI	9(7, WB)	1	8	8.0(8)	0	2	10	5.0	0	—	—	—	—	—	—	—	—	—		K	—	2	13
1935	Phi	1(0)	—	—	—	—	—	—	—	—	—	—	—	—	—	—	—	—	—			—	0	—
1935	Bos	1(0)	—	—	—	—	1	1	100.0	12	12.0(12)	0	0	—	—	—	—	—	—		K	—	1	6
NFL		3	11(7)	1	8	8.0(8)	0	2	1	100.0	12	12.0(12)	0	0	—	—	—	—	—		K	—	3	19

FRAIN, TODD   Todd Leslie, TE, 6′2″/240 lbs; Nebraska; B1/31/1962 Council Bluffs, IA   **1986** Was 1 (0)

| 1987 | NE | 3(2) | — | — | — | — | 2 | 22 | 11.0(11) | 0 | — | — | — | — | — | — | — | — | — | | | — | 0 | 11 |
| **NFL** | | 2 | 4(2) | — | — | — | — | 2 | 22 | 11.0(11) | 0 | — | — | — | — | — | — | — | — | | | — | 0 | 11 |

YEAR	TEAM	G(GS, POS)	RUSH	YD	AVG(LG)	TD	REC	YD	AVG(LG)	TD	PASS COMP	PCT	YD	AVG(LG)	TD	INT	SK	YD	QBR	KPR	OTD	PTS	TAY

FRALEY, HANK   Henry F., C-G, 6´2˝/300 lbs; Robert Morris; B9/21/1977 Gaithersburg, MD   **2001**†Phi 16 (15, C)   **2002**†Phi 16 (16, C)   **2003**†Phi 16 (16, C)   **2004**†Phi 16 (16, C)   **2005** Phi 8 (8, C)   **NFL** 72 (71) [5 yrs]

FRALIC, BILL   William P., G-T, 6´5˝/280 lbs; Pittsburgh; 1985: Atl, rnd 1; B10/31/1962 Penn Hills, PA   **1985** Atl 15 (14, RG)   **1986** Atl★16 (16, RG)   **1987** Atl★12 (12, RG)

| 1988 | Atl★14 (14, RG) | | | | | | | | | | | | | | | | | | | | | | |

1989 Atl★15 (15, RG)   **1990** Atl 16 (16, RG)   **1991**†Atl 12 (12, RG)   **1992** Atl 16 (16, RG)

| 1993 | †Det | 16(16, RG) | — | — | — | — | 1 | -4 | -4.0(-4) | 0 | — | — | — | — | — | — | — | — | — | — | — | 0 | -2 |
| NFL | 9 | 132(131) | — | — | — | — | 1 | -4 | -4.0(-4) | 0 | — | — | — | — | — | — | — | — | — | — | — | 0 | -2 |

FRANCE, DOUG   Frederick Douglas, T, 6´5˝/270 lbs; Ohio State; 1975: LA, rnd 1; B4/26/1953 Dayton, OH   **1975**†LARm 14 (1)   **1976**†LARm 14 (14, LT)   **1977**†LARm♢13 (13, LT)   **1978**†LARm★16 (16, LT)   **1979**†LARm☆16 (13, LT)   **1980**†LARm☆16 (16, LT)   **1981** LARm 8 (1)   **1983** Hou 13 (13, LT)   **NFL** 110 (87) [8 yrs]

FRANCE, TODD   Todd, K, 6´3˝/200 lbs; Toledo; B2/13/1980 Toledo, OH **[K]**   **2005** Phi 3 (0)   **2005** TB 1 (0)   **NFL** 4 (0) [1 yr]

FRANCESCHI, PETE   Peter Louis, HB-DB, 5´9˝/170 lbs; San Francisco; B9/28/1919 San Francisco, CA, D7/22/1989 San Francisco, CA

| 1946 | SF-A | .9(1) | 8 | -5 | -0.6 | 1 | 3 | 35 | 11.7 | — | — | — | — | — | — | — | — | — | — | p | — | 12 | 29 |

FRANCI, JASON   Jason Arthur, WR, 6´1˝/210 lbs; California-Santa Barbara; B10/17/1943 Fort Bragg, CA

| 1966 | Den-A | 10 | — | — | — | — | 1 | 8 | 8.0(8) | 0 | — | — | — | — | — | — | — | — | — | — | — | 0 | 4 |

FRANCIS, CARLOS   Carlos Miguel, WR, 5´10˝/197 lbs; Texas Tech; 2004: Oak, rnd 4; B1/3/1981 Fort Worth, TX   **2004** Oak 5 (0)

FRANCIS, DAVE   David Lee, FB, 6´1˝/210 lbs; Ohio State; 1963: Was, rnd 7; B4/15/1941 Columbus, OH   **1963** Was 8

FRANCIS, GENE   Eugene Arthur, FB, 5´10˝/190 lbs; Chicago; B7/1/1903 Chicago, IL, D11/1968 Wickenberg, AZ   **1926** ChiC 11 (5, fb), 6

FRANCIS, JAMES   James Henry, LB, 6´5˝/253 lbs; Baylor; 1990: Cin, rnd 1; B8/4/1968 Houston, TX   **1990**†Cin 16 (16, ROLB)   **1991** Cin 16 (16, LOLB)   **1992** Cin 14 (13, LOLB)   **1993** Cin 14 (12, LOLB)   **1994** Cin 16 (16, LLB)   **1995** Cin 11 (11, LLB)   **1996** Cin 16 (16, LLB)   **1997** Cin 16 (16, LOLB)   **1998** Cin 14 (14, LOLB)   **1999**†Was 10 (1)   **NFL** 143 (131) [10 yrs]

FRANCIS, JEFF   Jeffrey Lee, QB, 6´4˝/225 lbs; Tennessee; 1989: LARd, rnd 6; B7/7/1966 Park Ridge, IL

| 1990 | Cle | 1(0) | — | — | — | — | — | — | — | — | 2 | 2 | 100.0 | 26 | 13.0(17) | 0 | 0 | — | — | — | — | 0 | 13 |

FRANCIS, JOE   Joseph Charles, QB-HB, 6´1˝/195 lbs; Oregon State; 1958: GB, rnd 5; B4/21/1936 Honolulu, HI

1958	GB	12	24	153	6.4(20)	1	—	—	—	—	31	15	48.4	175	5.6(50)	2	5	—	—	—	—	6	181
1959	GB	12	2	5	2.5(8)	0	—	—	—	—	18	5	27.8	91	5.1(24)	0	1	—	—	k	—	0	33
NFL	2	24	26	158	6.1(20)	1	—	—	—	—	49	20	40.8	266	5.4(50)	2	3	—	—	k	—	6	213

FRANCIS, JON   Jon Charles Naekauna, RB, 5´11˝/207 lbs; Colorado State; Boise State; 1986: NYG, rnd 7; B6/21/1964 Corvallis, OR

| 1987 | LARm | 9(0) | 35 | 138 | 3.9(23) | 0 | 8 | 38 | 4.8(7) | 1 | — | — | — | — | — | — | — | — | — | — | — | 12 | 167 |

FRANCIS, PHIL   Phillip Kevin, RB, 6´1˝/205 lbs; Stanford; 1979: SF, rnd 7; B1/10/1957 Kewanee, IL

1979	SF	16	31	118	3.8(16)	1	32	198	6.2(19)	0	—	—	—	—	—	—	—	—	—	k	—	6	225
1980	SF	5(1)	7	36	5.1(14)	0	3	23	7.7(15)	0	—	—	—	—	—	—	—	—	—	k	—	0	33
NFL	2	21(1)	38	154	4.1(16)	1	35	221	6.3(19)	0	—	—	—	—	—	—	—	—	—	k	—	6	258

FRANCIS, RON   Ronald Bernard, DB, 5´9˝/201 lbs; Baylor; 1987: Dal, rnd 2; B4/7/1964 La Marque, TX   **1987** Dal 11 (11, RCB)   **1988** Dal 13 (2)   **1989** Dal 15 (4)   **1990** Dal 15 (0)   **NFL** 54 (17) [4 yrs]

FRANCIS, RUSS   Russell Ross, TE, 6´6˝/240 lbs; Oregon; 1975: NE, rnd 1; B4/3/1953 Seattle, WA

1975	NE	14(11, TE)	—	—	—	—	35	636	18.2(48)	4	—	—	—	—	—	—	—	—	—	—	—	24	338
1976	†NE☆	13(12, TE)	2	12	6.0(8)	0	26	367	14.1(48)	3	—	—	—	—	—	—	—	—	—	—	—	18	211
1977	NE☆	10(10, TE)	—	—	—	—	16	229	14.3(31)	4	—	—	—	—	—	—	—	—	—	—	—	24	135
1978	†NE☆	15(15, TE)	—	—	—	—	39	543	13.9(53)	4	—	—	—	—	—	—	—	—	—	—	—	24	292
1979	NE	12(12, TE)	—	—	—	—	39	557	14.3(44)	5	—	—	—	—	—	—	—	—	—	—	—	30	304
1980	NE★	15(15, TE)	—	—	—	—	41	664	16.2(39)	8	—	—	—	—	—	—	—	—	—	—	—	48	372
1982	SF	9(3)	—	—	—	—	23	278	12.1(26)	2	1	1	100.0	45	45.0(45)	0	0	—	—	—	—	12	172
1983	†SF	16(16, TE)	—	—	—	—	33	357	10.8(25)	4	—	—	—	—	—	—	—	—	—	—	—	24	199
1984	†SF	10(8, te)	—	—	—	—	23	285	12.4(32)	2	—	—	—	—	—	—	—	—	—	—	—	12	153
1985	†SF	16(16, TE)	—	—	—	—	44	478	10.9(25)	3	—	—	—	—	—	—	—	—	—	—	—	18	254
1986	†SF	14(14, TE)	—	—	—	—	41	505	12.3(52)	1	—	—	—	—	—	—	—	—	—	—	—	6	258
1987	SF	8(7, TE)	—	—	—	—	22	202	9.2(19)	0	—	—	—	—	—	—	—	—	—	—	—	0	101
1987	NE	1(0)	—	—	—	—	—	—	—	—	—	—	—	—	—	—	—	—	—	—	—	—	—
1988	NE	12(8, TE)	—	—	—	—	11	161	14.6(51)	0	—	—	—	—	—	—	—	—	—	—	—	0	81
NFL	13	167(147)	2	12	6.0(8)	0	393	5262	13.4(53)	40	1	1	100.0	45	45.0(45)	0	0	—	—	—	—	240	2866

FRANCIS, SAM   Harrison Samuel, FB-HB, 6´0˝/207 lbs; Nebraska; 1937: Phi, rnd 1; B10/26/1913 Dunbar, NE, D4/23/2002 Springfield, MO **[K]**

1937	†ChiB	8(3)	48	129	2.7	0	1	-9	-9.0(-9)	0	6	3	50.0	34	5.7	1	2	—	—	K	1	7	77
1938	ChiB	11(1)	85	297	3.5	3	1	8	8.0(8)	0	3	1	33.3	0	0.0	0	0	—	—	K	—	18	331
1939	Pit	5(3)	55	171	3.1	1	1	5	5.0(5)	0	—	—	—	—	—	—	—	—	—	P	—	6	184
1939	Bkn	5(3)	21	59	2.8	0	1	0	0.0	0	—	—	—	—	—	—	—	—	—	P	—	0	59
1940	Bkn	11(0)	44	217	4.9	1	—	—	—	—	—	—	—	—	—	—	—	—	—	KPi	—	6	229
NFL	4	40(10)	253	873	3.5	5	4	4	1.0(8)	0	9	4	44.4	34	3.8	1	2	—	—	KPi	1	37	879

FRANCIS, WALLACE   Wallace Diron, WR, 5´11˝/190 lbs; Arkansas-Pine Bluff; 1973: Buf, rnd 5; B11/7/1951 Franklin, LA **[R]**

1973	Buf	12	—	—	—	—	—	—	—	—	—	—	—	—	—	—	—	—	—	k	2	12	362
1974	†Buf	14	—	—	—	—	—	—	—	—	—	—	—	—	—	—	—	—	—	k	—	0	392
1975	Atl	14	2	12	6.0(9)	0	13	270	20.8(67)	4	—	—	—	—	—	—	—	—	—	k	—	24	222
1976	Atl	14	—	—	—	—	2	24	12.0(12)	0	—	—	—	—	—	—	—	—	—	k	—	0	33
1977	Atl	14(14, WR)	4	6	1.5(11)	0	26	390	15.0(32)	1	—	—	—	—	—	—	—	—	—	k	—	6	213
1978	†Atl	16(16, WR)	2	-11	-5.5(-5)	0	45	695	15.4(54)	3	—	—	—	—	—	—	—	—	—	—	—	18	352
1979	Atl	16(16, WR)	—	—	—	—	74	1013	13.7(42)	8	—	—	—	—	—	—	—	—	—	—	—	48	547
1980	†Atl	16(16, WR)	1	2	2.0(1)	0	54	862	16.0(45)	7	—	—	—	—	—	—	—	—	—	—	—	42	468
1981	Atl	16(16, WR)	1	8	8.0(8)	1	30	441	14.7(36)	4	—	—	—	—	—	—	—	—	—	—	—	30	259
NFL	9	132(78)	10	17	1.7(11)	1	244	3695	15.1(81)	27	—	—	—	—	—	—	—	—	—	k	2	180	2847

FRANCISCO, AARON   Aaron, DB, 6´2˝/212 lbs; Brigham Young; B7/5/1983 Honolulu, HI   **2005** Arz 11 (0)

FRANCK, GEORGE   George Henning, HB, 6´0˝/185 lbs; Minnesota; 1941: NYG, rnd 1; B9/23/1918 Davenport, IA

1941	†NYG	11(3)	48	101	2.1(17)	3	8	95	11.9(44)	1	0	0	0.0	0	0.0	0	0	—	—	Pkpi	—	24	447
1945	NYG	5(0)	29	42	1.4(9)	0	3	39	13.0(18)	0	1	1	100.0	4	4.0(4)	0	0	—	—	Pkp	—	0	90
1946	NYG	10(1)	43	270	6.3(46)	0	6	137	22.8(50)	1	—	—	—	—	—	—	—	—	—	Pkp	—	6	454
1947	NYG	7(0)	24	93	3.9(25)	0	10	265	26.5(88)	3	—	—	—	—	—	—	—	—	—	Pkpi	—	18	282
NFL	4	33(4)	144	506	3.5(46)	3	27	536	19.9(88)	5	2	1	50.0	4	2.0(4)	0	0	—	—	Pkpi	—	48	1271

FRANCKHAUSER, TOM   Thomas Anthony, DB, 6´0˝/195 lbs; Purdue; 1959: LA, rnd 3; B5/26/1937 Steubenville, OH, D4/17/1997 Houston, TX   **1959** LARm 12 (DB)   **1960** Dal 12 (LCB)   **1961** Dal 6 (4)   **1962** Min 14   **1963** Min 14   **NFL** 58 (4) [5 yrs]

FRANCKOWIAK, MIKE   Michael Jerome, RB, 6´3˝/220 lbs; Central Michigan; 1975: Den, rnd 3; B3/25/1953 Grand Rapids, MI

1975	Den	14	1	1	1.0(1)	0	—	—	—	—	—	—	—	—	—	—	—	—	—	—	—	0	1
1976	Den	14(1)	12	25	2.1(7)	0	4	42	10.5(11)	0	—	—	—	—	—	—	—	—	—	k	—	0	38
1977	Buf	13	1	0	0.0(0)	0	—	—	—	—	—	—	—	—	—	—	—	—	—	k	—	0	-6
1978	Buf	16	—	—	—	—	—	—	—	—	—	—	—	—	—	—	—	—	—	k	—	0	-15
NFL	4	57(1)	14	26	1.9(7)	0	4	42	10.5(11)	0	—	—	—	—	—	—	—	—	—	k	—	0	18

FRANCO, BRIAN   Brian David, K, 5´8˝/165 lbs; Penn State; B12/3/1959 Annapolis, MD **[K]**   **1987** Cle 2 (0)

FRANCO, ED   Edmund Joseph, T, 5´8˝/205 lbs; Fordham; 1938: Cle, rnd 5; B4/24/1915 New York, NY, D11/18/1992 Bayonne, NJ   **1944** Bos 10 (9, LT)

FRANK, BILL   William B., T, 6´5˝/255 lbs; Colorado; 1963: Dal, rnd 18/SD, rnd 24; B4/13/1938 Denver, CO   **1964** Dal 4

Frank, Donald Donald Lee, DB, 6´0˝/192 lbs; Winston-Salem State; B10/24/1965 Edgecombe County, NC **1990** SD 16 (2) **1991** SD 16 (1) **1992**†SD 16 (0) **1993** SD 16 (16, LCB) **1994** LARd 16 (0) **1995** Min 12 (5, lcb) **NFL** 92 (24) [6 yrs]

Frank, Joe Joseph C., T, 6´1˝/217 lbs; Georgetown (DC); B7/14/1915 Bronx, NY, D8/11/1981 Queens, NY **1941** Phi 11 (0) **1942** Phi 1 (0) **1943** P-P 2 (0) **NFL** 14 (0) [3 yrs]

Frank, John John E., TE, 6´3˝/225 lbs; Ohio State; 1984: SF, rnd 2; B4/17/1962 Pittsburgh, PA

YEAR	TEAM	G(GS, POS)	RUSH	YD	AVG(LG)	TD	REC	YD	AVG(LG)	TD	PASS	COMP	PCT	YD	AVG(LG)	TD	INT	SK	YD	QBR	KPR	OTD	PTS	TAY
1984	†SF	15(2)	—	—	—	—	7	60	8.6(21)	1	—	—	—	—	—	—	—	—	—	—		—	6	35
1985	†SF	16(3)	—	—	—	—	7	50	7.1(14)	1	—	—	—	—	—	—	—	—	—	—	k	—	6	16
1986	†SF	16(6, te)	1	-3	-3.0(-3)	0	9	61	6.8(17)	2	—	—	—	—	—	—	—	—	—	—	k	—	12	32
1987	†SF	12(6, te)	1	2	2.0(2)	0	26	296	11.4(27)	3	—	—	—	—	—	—	—	—	—	—		—	18	165
1988	†SF	7(6, te)	—	—	—	—	16	195	12.2(38)	3	—	—	—	—	—	—	—	—	—	—		—	18	113
NFL	5	66(23)	2	-1	-0.5(2)	0	65	662	10.2(38)	10	—	—	—	—	—	—	—	—	—	—	k	—	60	360

Frank, Malcolm Baldwin Malcolm, DB, 5´8˝/178 lbs; Baylor; B12/5/1968 Mamou, LA **1992** Sea 15 (0)

Frank, Paul Paul, B, /200 lbs; Waynesburg; B5/8/1907, D11/1970 **1930** Nwk 3 (1)

Frankian, Ike Malcolm John, E, 5´11˝/208 lbs; St. Mary's (CA); B4/3/1907 Worcester, MA, D4/14/1963 Merced County, CA

YEAR	TEAM	G(GS, POS)	RUSH	YD	AVG(LG)	TD	REC	YD	AVG(LG)	TD	PASS	COMP	PCT	YD	AVG(LG)	TD	INT	SK	YD	QBR	KPR	OTD	PTS	TAY
1933	Bos	12(10, LE)	—	—	—	—	6	75	12.5	1	—	—	—	—	—	—	—	—	—	—		—	6	43
1934	†NYG	13(6, re)	—	—	—	—	1	5	5.0(5)	0	—	—	—	—	—	—	—	—	—	—		—	0	3
1935	†NYG	12(5, le)	—	—	—	—	7	39	5.6	1	—	—	—	—	—	—	—	—	—	—		—	6	25
NFL	3	37(21)	—	—	—	—	14	119	8.5(5)	2	—	—	—	—	—	—	—	—	—	—		—	12	70

Franklin, Andra Andra Bernard, RB, 5´10˝/225 lbs; Nebraska; 1981: Mia, rnd 2; B8/22/1959 Anniston, AL

YEAR	TEAM	G(GS, POS)	RUSH	YD	AVG(LG)	TD	REC	YD	AVG(LG)	TD	PASS	COMP	PCT	YD	AVG(LG)	TD	INT	SK	YD	QBR	KPR	OTD	PTS	TAY
1981	†Mia	16(11, FB)	201	711	3.5(29)	7	3	6	2.0(3)	1	—	—	—	—	—	—	—	—	—	—		—	48	789
1982	†Mia★	9(9, FB)	**177**	701	4.0(25)	7	3	9	3.0(6)	0	—	—	—	—	—	—	—	—	—	—		—	42	776
1983	†Mia	15(12, FB)	224	746	3.3(18)	8	—	—	—	—	—	—	—	—	—	—	—	—	—	—		—	48	826
1984	Mia	2(2)	20	74	3.7(12)	0	—	—	—	—	—	—	—	—	—	—	—	—	—	—		—	0	74
NFL	4	42(34)	622	2232	3.6(29)	22	6	15	2.5(6)	1	—	—	—	—	—	—	—	—	—	—		—	138	2465

Franklin, Arnold Arnold Lee, TE, 6´3˝/246 lbs; North Carolina; 1986: Mia, rnd 11; B12/16/1963 Cincinnati, OH **1987** NE 3 (0)

Franklin, Aubrayo Aubrayo Razyo, DT, 6´1˝/320 lbs; Tennessee; 2003: Bal, rnd 5; B8/27/1980 Johnson City, TN **2003** Bal 1 (0) **2004** Bal 6 (0) **2005** Bal 15 (1) **NFL** 22 (1) [3 yrs]

Franklin, Bobby Bobby Ray, DB, 5´11˝/182 lbs; Mississippi; 1960: Cle, rnd 11/LAC, rnd 1; B10/5/1936 Clarksdale, MS **1960** Cle 12 (rs) **1962** Cle 9 (RS) **1964**†Cle 14 (RS) **1966** Cle 9

YEAR	TEAM	G(GS, POS)	RUSH	YD	AVG(LG)	TD	REC	YD	AVG(LG)	TD	PASS	COMP	PCT	YD	AVG(LG)	TD	INT	SK	YD	QBR	KPR	OTD	PTS	TAY
1961	Cle	14(RS)	1	12	12.0(12)	1	—	—	—	—	—	—	—	—	—	—	—	—	—	—	i	—	6	32
1963	Cle	14	1	-10	-10.0(-10)	0	—	—	—	—	—	—	—	—	—	—	—	—	—	—	ki	—	0	9
1965	†Cle	14	1	-11	-11.0(-11)	1	—	—	—	—	—	—	—	—	—	—	—	—	—	—	Pk	—	0	-26
NFL	7	86	3	-9	-3.0(12)	1	—	—	—	—	—	—	—	—	—	—	—	—	—	—	Pkpi	2	18	122

Franklin, Brad Michael Bradford, DB, 6´1˝/184 lbs; Louisiana-Lafayette; 2002: Car, rnd 7; B12/22/1979 Baton Rouge, LA **2003** Jax 4 (0)

Franklin, Byron Byron Paul, WR, 6´1˝/179 lbs; Auburn; 1981: Buf, rnd 2; B9/4/1958 Florence, AL

YEAR	TEAM	G(GS, POS)	RUSH	YD	AVG(LG)	TD	REC	YD	AVG(LG)	TD	PASS	COMP	PCT	YD	AVG(LG)	TD	INT	SK	YD	QBR	KPR	OTD	PTS	TAY
1981	†Buf	13(0)	1	-11	-11.0(-11)	0	2	29	14.5(16)	0	—	—	—	—	—	—	—	—	—	—	kp	—	0	145
1983	Buf	15(5, wr)	1	3	3.0(3)	0	30	452	15.1(43)	4	—	—	—	—	—	—	—	—	—	—		—	24	249
1984	Buf	16(16, WR)	1	-7	-7.0(-7)	0	69	862	12.5(64)	4	—	—	—	—	—	—	—	—	—	—		—	24	444
1985	Sea	13(0)	1	5	5.0(5)	0	10	119	11.9(28)	0	—	—	—	—	—	—	—	—	—	—		—	0	65
1986	Sea	14(1)	1	2	2.0(2)	0	33	547	16.6(49)	2	—	—	—	—	—	—	—	—	—	—		—	12	286
1987	Sea	6(0)	—	—	—	—	1	7	7.0(7)	0	—	—	—	—	—	—	—	—	—	—		—	0	4
NFL	6	77(22)	5	-8	-1.6(5)	0	145	2016	13.9(64)	10	—	—	—	—	—	—	—	—	—	—	kp	—	60	1191

Franklin, Cleveland Cleveland, RB, 6´2˝/216 lbs; Baylor; 1977: Phi, rnd 8; B4/24/1955 Brenham, TX

YEAR	TEAM	G(GS, POS)	RUSH	YD	AVG(LG)	TD	REC	YD	AVG(LG)	TD	PASS	COMP	PCT	YD	AVG(LG)	TD	INT	SK	YD	QBR	KPR	OTD	PTS	TAY
1977	Phi	14	1	0	0.0(0)	0	—	—	—	—	—	—	—	—	—	—	—	—	—	—		—	0	0
1978	†Phi	16(4)	60	167	2.8(9)	0	7	46	6.6(15)	0	—	—	—	—	—	—	—	—	—	—		—	0	190
1980	Bal	13(13, FB)	83	264	3.2(21)	2	14	112	8.0(16)	0	—	—	—	—	—	—	—	—	—	—		—	12	340
1981	Bal	9(0)	21	52	2.5(8)	1	6	39	6.5(10)	0	—	—	—	—	—	—	—	—	—	—		—	6	82
1982	Bal	9(0)	43	152	3.5(19)	0	9	61	6.8(15)	0	—	—	—	—	—	—	—	—	—	—	k	—	0	176
NFL	5	61(17)	208	635	3.1(21)	3	36	258	7.2(16)	0	—	—	—	—	—	—	—	—	—	—	k	—	18	787

Franklin, Dennis Dennis E., WR, 6´1˝/185 lbs; Michigan; 1975: Det, rnd 6; B8/24/1953 Massillon, OH

YEAR	TEAM	G(GS, POS)	RUSH	YD	AVG(LG)	TD	REC	YD	AVG(LG)	TD	PASS	COMP	PCT	YD	AVG(LG)	TD	INT	SK	YD	QBR	KPR	OTD	PTS	TAY
1975	Det	4(2)	—	—	—	—	5	109	21.8(36)	0	—	—	—	—	—	—	—	—	—	—		—	0	55
1976	Det	5	—	—	—	—	1	16	16.0(16)	0	—	—	—	—	—	—	—	—	—	—		—	0	8
NFL	2	9(2)	—	—	—	—	6	125	20.8(36)	0	—	—	—	—	—	—	—	—	—	—		—	0	63

Franklin, George George Eugene, RB, 6´3˝/225 lbs; Texas A&M-Kingsville; 1977: SL, rnd 2; B7/5/1954 Seguin, TX

YEAR	TEAM	G(GS, POS)	RUSH	YD	AVG(LG)	TD	REC	YD	AVG(LG)	TD	PASS	COMP	PCT	YD	AVG(LG)	TD	INT	SK	YD	QBR	KPR	OTD	PTS	TAY
1978	†Atl	15	1	-8	-8.0(-8)	0	1	19	19.0(19)	0	—	—	—	—	—	—	—	—	—	—	k	—	0	95

Franklin, Jerrell Jerrell Lynn, G, 6´3˝/287 lbs; Kansas State; Southern (LA); B5/4/1959 Houston, TX **1987** Hou 3 (3)

Franklin, Jethro Jethro Fitzgerald, DE, 6´1˝/258 lbs; Fresno State; 1988: Hou, rnd 11; B10/25/1965 St. Laziare, France **1989** Sea 7 (1)

Franklin, Keith Keith Lamont, LB, 6´2˝/230 lbs; South Carolina; B3/4/1970 Los Angeles, CA **1995** Oak 2 (0)

Franklin, Larry Lawrence Darnell, WR, 6´1˝/185 lbs; Jackson State; B8/2/1955 Memphis, TN **1978** TB 2

Franklin, P.J. David L., WR, 5´10˝/180 lbs; Tulane; B9/28/1977 Independence, LA

YEAR	TEAM	G(GS, POS)	RUSH	YD	AVG(LG)	TD	REC	YD	AVG(LG)	TD	PASS	COMP	PCT	YD	AVG(LG)	TD	INT	SK	YD	QBR	KPR	OTD	PTS	TAY
1999	NO	3(0)	1	0	0.0(0)	0	2	13	6.5(8)	0	—	—	—	—	—	—	—	—	—	—		—	0	7

Franklin, Pat Patrick Dijon, RB, 6´1˝/232 lbs; Southwest Texas State; Houston; 1986: Cin, rnd 7; B8/16/1963 Bay City, TX **1987** Cin 2 (0)

YEAR	TEAM	G(GS, POS)	RUSH	YD	AVG(LG)	TD	REC	YD	AVG(LG)	TD	PASS	COMP	PCT	YD	AVG(LG)	TD	INT	SK	YD	QBR	KPR	OTD	PTS	TAY
1986	TB	8(1)	7	7	1.0(4)	0	7	29	4.1(9)	1	—	—	—	—	—	—	—	—	—	—	k	1	12	5
NFL	2	10(1)	7	7	1.0(4)	0	7	29	4.1(9)	1	—	—	—	—	—	—	—	—	—	—		1	12	27

Franklin, Paul Paul R., B-E, 6´2˝/198 lbs; Franklin (IN); B2/10/1906 Plainfield, IN, D8/26/1959 Mount Prospect, IL

YEAR	TEAM	G(GS, POS)	RUSH	YD	AVG(LG)	TD	REC	YD	AVG(LG)	TD	PASS	COMP	PCT	YD	AVG(LG)	TD	INT	SK	YD	QBR	KPR	OTD	PTS	TAY
1931	ChiB	12(3)	—	—	—	—	—	—	—	—	—	—	—	—	—	—	—	—	—	—		—	—	—
1932	ChiB	8(2)	26	14	0.5	0	—	—	—	—	—	—	—	—	—	—	—	—	—	—		—	0	14
1933	ChiB	3(0)	2	5	2.5	0	—	—	—	—	—	—	—	—	—	—	—	—	—	—		—	0	5
NFL	3	23(5)	28	19	0.7	1	—	—	—	—	—	—	—	—	—	—	—	—	—	—		—	6	29

Franklin, Red Norman Clifford, TB-HB, 5´10˝/163 lbs; Oregon State; B12/13/1911 Hope, RI, D12/1984 Santa Ana, CA

YEAR	TEAM	G(GS, POS)	RUSH	YD	AVG(LG)	TD	REC	YD	AVG(LG)	TD	PASS	COMP	PCT	YD	AVG(LG)	TD	INT	SK	YD	QBR	KPR	OTD	PTS	TAY
1935	Bkn	12(9, TB)	100	284	2.8	3	1	12	12.0(12)	0	57	12	21.1	175	3.1(44)	2	7	—	—	—	—	—	18	138
1936	Bkn	2(1)	15	70	4.7	1	—	—	—	—	7	1	14.3	17	2.4(17)	0	0	—	—	—	—	—	6	89
1937	Bkn	1(0)	4	12	3.0	0	—	—	—	—	4	0	0.0	0	0.0	0	0	—	—	—	—	—	0	12
NFL	3	15(10)	119	366	3.1	4	1	12	12.0(12)	0	68	13	19.1	192	2.8(44)	2	7	—	—	—	—	—	24	238

Franklin, Tony Anthony Ray, K, 5´8˝/182 lbs; Texas A&M; 1979: Phi, rnd 3; B11/18/1956 Big Spring, TX **[K]** **1979**†Phi☆16 **1980**†Phi 16 (0) **1981**†Phi 16 (0) **1982** Phi 9 (0) **1983** Phi 16 (0) **1984** NE 16 (0) **1986**†NE★16 (0) **1987** NE 14 (0) **1988** Mia 5 (0)

YEAR	TEAM	G(GS, POS)	RUSH	YD	AVG(LG)	TD	REC	YD	AVG(LG)	TD	PASS	COMP	PCT	YD	AVG(LG)	TD	INT	SK	YD	QBR	KPR	OTD	PTS	TAY
1985	†NE	16(0)	1	-5	-5.0(-5)	0	—	—	—	—	—	—	—	—	—	—	—	—	—	—	K	—	112	-5
NFL	10	140	1	-5	-5.0(-5)	0	—	—	—	—	—	—	—	—	—	—	—	—	—	—	KP	—	872	-5

Franklin, Willie Willie, WR, 6´2˝/195 lbs; Oklahoma; B10/9/1949 San Diego, CA **1972** Bal 4

Frankowski, Ray Raymond William, G, 5´11˝/223 lbs; Washington; 1942: GB, rnd 3; B9/14/1919 Chicago, IL, D11/27/2001 Laguna Niguel, CA **1945** GB 2 (0) **1946** LAD-A 12 (2) **1947** LAD-A 14 (8, RG) **1948** LAD-A 14 (3) **AAFC** 40 (13) [3 yrs]

Franks, Bubba Daniel Lamont, TE, 6´6˝/263 lbs; Miami (FL); 2000: GB, rnd 1; B1/6/1978 Riverside, CA

YEAR	TEAM	G(GS, POS)	RUSH	YD	AVG(LG)	TD	REC	YD	AVG(LG)	TD	PASS	COMP	PCT	YD	AVG(LG)	TD	INT	SK	YD	QBR	KPR	OTD	PTS	TAY
2000	GB	16(13, TE)	—	—	—	—	34	363	10.7(27)	1	—	—	—	—	—	—	—	—	—	—		—	6	187
2001	†GB✧	16(14, TE)	—	—	—	—	36	322	8.9(31)	9	—	—	—	—	—	—	—	—	—	—		—	54	206
2002	†GB✧	16(15, TE)	—	—	—	—	54	442	8.2(20)	7	1	1	100.0	31	31.0(31)	1	0	—	—	—		—	42	277

YEAR	TEAM	G (GS, POS)	RUSH	YD	AVG(LG)	TD	REC	YD	AVG(LG)	TD	PASS	COMP	PCT	YD	AVG(LG)	TD	INT	SK	YD	QBR	KPR	OTD	PTS	TAY
2003	†GB◇	16(15, TE)	—	—	—	—	30	241	8.0(24)	4	—	—	—	—	—	—	—	—	—	—	—	—	28	141
2004	†GB	16(14, TE)	—	—	—	—	34	361	10.6(29)	7	—	—	—	—	—	—	—	—	—	—	—	—	42	216
2005	GB	10(8, te)	—	—	—	—	25	207	8.3(24)	1	—	—	—	—	—	—	—	—	—	—	—	—	6	109
NFL	6	90(79)	—	—	—	—	213	1936	9.1(31)	29	1	1	100.0	31	31.0(31)	1	0	—	—	—	—	—	178	1134

FRANKS, DENNIS   Dennis John, C, 6´1˝/241 lbs; Michigan; B5/29/1953 McKeesport, PA   **1976** Phi 14   **1977** Phi 14 (1)   **1978**†Phi 14   **1979** Det 13   **NFL** 57 (1) [4 yrs]

FRANKS, ELVIS   Elvis Andrea, DE, 6´4˝/252 lbs; Morgan State; 1980: Cle, rnd 5; B7/9/1957 Doucette, TX   **1980**†Cle 16 (0)   **1981** Cle 16 (1)   **1982**†Cle 9 (0)   **1983** Cle 16 (7, rde)   **1984** Cle 16 (0)   **1985**†LARd 3 (1)   **1986** LARd 4 (0)   **1986** NYJ 3 (0)   **NFL** 83 (9) [7 yrs]

FRANTA, CHIEF   Herbert J., T-G, 6´1˝/220 lbs; St. Thomas; B3/10/1905 New Ulm, MN, deceased   **1929** Min 10 (10, RT)   **1930** Min 6 (3, RT)   **1930** GB 2 (1)   **NFL** 18 (14) [2 yrs]

FRANTZ, JOHN   John Edward, C, 6´3˝/230 lbs; California; 1968: Buf, rnd 16; B7/1/1945 Kokomo, IN   **1968** Buf-A 2

FRANZ, NOLAN   Nolan Clarence, WR, 6´2˝/185 lbs; Tulane; B9/11/1959 New Orleans, LA

YEAR	TEAM	G (GS, POS)	RUSH	YD	AVG(LG)	TD	REC	YD	AVG(LG)	TD	PTS	TAY
1986	GB	1(0)	—	—	—	—	1	7	7.0(7)	0	0	4

FRANZ, TODD   Stephen Todd, DB, 6´0˝/202 lbs; Tulsa; 2000: Det, rnd 5; B4/12/1976 Enid, OK   **2000** NO 5 (0)   **2000** Cle 2 (0)   **2002** GB 2 (0)   **2003** Was 16 (1)   **2004** Was 16 (0)   **2005** GB 5 (0)   **NFL** 46 (1) [5 yrs]

FRANZ, TRACY   Tracy Mark, G, 6´5˝/270 lbs; San Jose State; B3/26/1960 Sacramento, CA   **1987** SF 3 (3)

FRASE, PAUL   Paul Miles, DE-DT-NT, 6´5˝/272 lbs; Syracuse; 1988: NYJ, rnd 6; B5/6/1965 Elmira, NY   **1988** NYJ 16 (7, lde)   **1989** NYJ 16 (14, LDE)   **1991**†NYJ 16 (2)   **1992** NYJ 16 (12, RDT)   **1993** NYJ 16 (4)   **1994** NYJ 16 (5, rdt)   **1995** Jax 9 (5, rde)   **1996**†Jax 14 (0)   **1997**†GB 9 (0)   **1998** Bal 11 (0)   **NFL** 139 (49) [10 yrs]

FRASER, JIM   James Gallagher, LB-P, 6´3˝/236 lbs; Wisconsin; 1959: Cle, rnd 21; B5/29/1936 Philadelphia, PA **[KP]**   **1962** Den-A◇14 (LLB)   **1963** Den-A◇14 (RLB)   **1964** Den-A◇14 (RLB)   **1965** KC-A 14   **1966** Bos-A 14   **1968** NO 2   **NFL** 72 [6 yrs]

FRASER, SIMON   Simon, DE-DT, 6´6˝/288 lbs; Ohio State; B3/27/1983 Upper Arlington, OH   **2005** Cle 16 (0)

FRAZIER, AL   Adolphus Cornelius, FL-HB, 5´11˝/180 lbs; Florida A&M; 1957: ChiB, rnd 20; B5/28/1935 Jacksonville, FL

YEAR	TEAM	G (GS, POS)	RUSH	YD	AVG(LG)	TD	REC	YD	AVG(LG)	TD	PASS	COMP	PCT	YD	AVG(LG)	TD	INT	SK	YD	QBR	KPR	OTD	PTS	TAY
1961	Den-A	14(FL)	23	110	4.8(43)	0	47	799	17.0(87)	6	1	0	0.0	0	0.0	0	1	—	—	—	kp	2	50	895
1962	Den-A	14(fl)	39	168	4.3(35)	2	11	211	19.2(96)	1	—	—	—	—	—	—	—	—	—	—	kp	—	18	409
1963	Den-A	3	—	—	—	—	—	—	—	—	—	—	—	—	—	—	—	—	—	—	kp	—	0	107
NFL	3	31	62	278	4.5(43)	2	58	1010	17.4(96)	7	1	0	0.0	0	0.0	0	1	—	—	—	kp	2	68	1410

FRAZIER, ANDRE   Andre, LB, 6´5˝/234 lbs; Cincinnati; B6/29/1982 Cincinnati, OH   **2005**†Pit 11 (0)

FRAZIER, CHARLEY   Charles Douglas, WR, 6´0˝/190 lbs; Texas Southern; B8/12/1939 Houston, TX

YEAR	TEAM	G (GS, POS)	RUSH	YD	AVG(LG)	TD	REC	YD	AVG(LG)	TD	PTS	TAY
1962	†Hou-A	14	—	—	—	—	7	155	22.1(73)	1	6	83
1963	Hou-A	10	—	—	—	—	16	279	17.4(80)	1	6	145
1964	Hou-A	11(WR)	1	-4	-4.0(-4)	0	29	404	13.9(46)	1	6	203
1965	Hou-A	12(WR)	1	10	10.0(8)	0	38	717	18.9(64)	6	36	399
1966	Hou-A◇	14(WR)	—	—	—	—	57	1129	19.8(79)	12	72	625
1967	†Hou-A	13(WR)	—	—	—	—	23	253	11.0(53)	1	6	132
1968	Hou-A	13	—	—	—	—	9	123	13.7(19)	0	0	62
1969	Bos-A	14(12, WR)	2	-1	-0.5(9)	0	19	306	16.1(50)	7	42	187
1970	Bos	9(1)	—	—	—	—	9	86	9.6(16)	0	0	43
NFL	9	110(13)	4	5	1.3(9)	0	207	3452	16.7(80)	29	174	1876

FRAZIER, CLIFF   Clifford Henry, DT, 6´4˝/265 lbs; UCLA; 1976: KC, rnd 2; B11/23/1952 St. Louis, MO   **1977** KC 14

FRAZIER, CURT   Curtis, DB, 5´11˝/193 lbs; Fresno State; B3/11/1945 Berkeley, CA   **1968** Cin-A 14

FRAZIER, DERRICK   Derrick Lothair, DB, 5´11˝/178 lbs; Texas A&M; 1993: Phi, rnd 3; B4/29/1970 Sugar Land, TX   **1994** Phi 12 (0)   **1995**†Phi 7 (4)   **1996** Ind 6 (4)   **NFL** 25 (8) [3 yrs]

FRAZIER, FRANK   Frank Lee, G, 6´5˝/290 lbs; Miami (FL); B6/15/1960 Tampa, FL, D11/23/2000 Miami, FL   **1987** Was 3 (0)

FRAZIER, GUY   Guy Shelton, LB, 6´2˝/215 lbs; Wyoming; 1981: Cin, rnd 4; B7/20/1959 Detroit, MI   **1981**†Cin 16 (0)   **1982**†Cin 9 (0)   **1983** Cin 10 (5, lolb)   **1984** Cin 16 (5, lolb)   **1985** Buf 16 (16, LOLB/rolb)   **1986** Buf 7 (7, lolb)   **NFL** 74 (33) [6 yrs]

FRAZIER, LANCE   Elance Antonio, DB, 5´10˝/183 lbs; West Virginia; B5/23/1981 Boynton Beach, FL   **2004** Dal 12 (8, RCB)

FRAZIER, LESLIE   Leslie Antonio, DB, 6´0˝/189 lbs; Alcorn State; B4/3/1959 Columbus, MS **[I]**   **1981** ChiB 13 (0)   **1982** ChiB 9 (6, RCB)   **1983** ChiB 16 (16, RCB)   **1984**†ChiB 11 (11, RCB)   **1985**†ChiB 16 (16, RCB)   **NFL** 65 (49) [5 yrs]

FRAZIER, PAUL   Daniel Paul, RB, 5´8˝/188 lbs; Northwestern State (LA); B11/12/1967 Beaumont, TX

YEAR	TEAM	G (GS, POS)	RUSH	YD	AVG(LG)	TD	REC	YD	AVG(LG)	TD	KPR	OTD	PTS	TAY
1989	NO	15(0)	25	112	4.5(21)	1	3	25	8.3(22)	0	k	—	6	172

FRAZIER, RANDY   Phillip Randy, LB, 6´3˝/235 lbs; Morehead State; B6/18/1964 Letcher County, KY   **1987** KC 3 (0)

FRAZIER, WAYNE   William Wayne, C-LB, 6´3˝/245 lbs; Auburn; 1962: SD, rnd 32/1961: Chi, rnd 16; B3/5/1939 Evergreen, AL   **1962** SD-A 7 (C)   **1965** Hou-A 14 (c)   **1966**†KC-A 14 (C)   **1967** KC-A 7 (c)   **1967** Buf-A 6   **NFL** 48 [4 yrs]

FRAZIER, WILLIE   Willie C., TE, 6´4˝/245 lbs; Arkansas-Pine Bluff; B6/19/1942

YEAR	TEAM	G (GS, POS)	RUSH	YD	AVG(LG)	TD	REC	YD	AVG(LG)	TD	KPR	OTD	PTS	TAY
1964	Hou-A	14(te)	—	—	—	—	11	227	20.6(80)	2	k	—	12	109
1965	Hou-A★	12(TE)	—	—	—	—	37	521	14.1(57)	8	—	—	48	301
1966	SD-A	14	—	—	—	—	9	144	16.0(30)	2	—	—	12	82
1967	SD-A★	14(TE)	—	—	—	—	57	922	16.2(72)	10	—	—	60	511
1968	SD-A	9(te)	—	—	—	—	16	237	14.8(48)	3	—	—	18	134
1969	SD-A◇	11(TE)	—	—	—	—	17	205	12.1(50)	0	—	—	0	103
1970	SD	14(TE)	5	120	24.0(70)	1	38	497	13.1(51)	6	—	1	48	409
1971	Hou	6(te)	—	—	—	—	8	113	14.1(33)	0	—	—	0	57
1971	†KC	8	1	-2	-2.0(-2)	0	2	41	20.5(23)	0	—	—	0	19
1972	KC	14(te)	—	—	—	—	13	172	13.2(35)	5	—	—	30	111
1975	Hou	5	—	—	—	—	1	9	9.0(9)	0	—	—	0	5
NFL	10	121	6	118	19.7(70)	1	209	3088	14.8(80)	36	k	1	228	1837

FREDERICK, ANDY   Andrew Brian, T, 6´6˝/257 lbs; New Mexico; 1977: Dal, rnd 5; B7/25/1954 Oak Park, IL   **1977**†Dal 13   **1978**†Dal 16 (5, rt)   **1979**†Dal 16   **1980**†Dal 16 (1)   **1981**†Dal 16 (0)   **1982** Cle 7 (0)   **1983** ChiB 16 (6, rt)   **1984**†ChiB 16 (2)   **1985**†ChiB 16 (1)   **NFL** 132 (15) [9 yrs]

FREDERICK, MIKE   Thomas Michael, DE, 6´5˝/280 lbs; Virginia; 1995: Cle, rnd 3; B8/6/1972 Abington, PA   **1995** Cle 16 (0)   **1996** Bal 16 (11, LDE)   **1997** Bal 16 (1)   **1998** Bal 10 (0)   **1999** Ten 13 (0)   **NFL** 71 (12) [5 yrs]

FREDERICKSON, TUCKER   Ivan Charles, RB, 6´2˝/220 lbs; Auburn; 1965: NYG, rnd 1; B1/12/1943 Fort Lauderdale, FL

YEAR	TEAM	G (GS, POS)	RUSH	YD	AVG(LG)	TD	REC	YD	AVG(LG)	TD	PASS	COMP	PCT	YD	AVG(LG)	TD	INT	SK	YD	QBR	KPR	OTD	PTS	TAY
1965	NYG◇	13(FB)	195	659	3.4(41)	5	24	177	7.4(31)	1	1	0	0.0	0	0.0	0	—	—	—	—	—	—	36	763
1967	NYG	10(FB)	97	311	3.2(17)	2	19	153	8.1(29)	0	—	—	—	—	—	—	—	—	—	—	k	—	12	412
1968	NYG	14	142	486	3.4(19)	1	10	64	6.4(14)	2	—	—	—	—	—	—	—	—	—	—	k	—	18	521
1969	NYG	5	33	136	4.1(19)	0	14	95	6.8(16)	1	—	—	—	—	—	—	—	—	—	—	—	—	6	189
1970	NYG	14(FB)	120	375	3.1(15)	1	40	408	10.2(57)	3	—	—	—	—	—	—	—	—	—	—	—	—	24	604
1971	NYG	10(FB)	64	242	3.8(37)	0	21	114	5.4(20)	1	—	—	—	—	—	—	—	—	—	—	—	—	6	304
NFL	6	66	651	2209	3.4(41)	9	128	1011	7.9(57)	8	1	0	0.0	0	0.0	0	1	—	—	—	k	—	102	2792

FREDRICKSON, ROB   Robert J., LB, 6´4˝/240 lbs; Michigan State; 1994: LARd, rnd 1; B5/13/1971 St. Joseph, MO   **1994** LARd 16 (12, LLB)   **1995** Oak 16 (15, LLB)   **1996** Oak 10 (10, LLB)   **1997** Oak 16 (14, LLB)   **1998** Det 16 (16, LLB)   **1999** Arz 16 (16, LLB)   **2000** Arz 13 (12, RLB)   **2001** Arz 15 (15, RLB)   **2002** Arz 10 (10, RLB)   **NFL** 128 (120) [9 yrs]

FREELON, SOLOMON   Solomon, G, 6´2˝/250 lbs; Grambling State; 1972: Hou, rnd 3; B2/19/1951 Monroe, LA   **1972** Hou 14   **1973** Hou 11 (LG)   **1974** Hou 14   **NFL** 39 [3 yrs]

FREEMAN, ANTONIO   Antonio Michael, WR, 6´1˝/198 lbs; Virginia Tech; 1995: GB, rnd 3; B5/27/1972 Baltimore, MD

YEAR	TEAM	G (GS, POS)	RUSH	YD	AVG(LG)	TD	REC	YD	AVG(LG)	TD	KPR	OTD	PTS	TAY
1995	†GB	11(0)	—	—	—	—	8	106	13.3(28)	0	kp	—	6	361
1996	†GB	12(12, WR)	—	—	—	—	56	933	16.7(51)	9	k	—	54	513

YEAR	TEAM	G (GS, POS)	RUSH	YD	AVG (LG)	TD	REC	YD	AVG (LG)	TD	PASS	COMP	PCT	YD	AVG (LG)	TD	INT	SK	YD	QBR	KPR	OTD	PTS	TAY
1997	†GB	16(16, WR)	1	14	14.0(14)	0	81	1243	15.3(58)	12	—	—	—	—	—	—	—	—	—	—	—	—	72	696
1998	†GB★	15(15, WR)	3	5	1.7(10)	0	84	**1424**	17.0(84)	14	—	—	—	—	—	—	—	—	—	—	—	—	86	787
1999	GB	16(16, WR)	1	-2	-2.0(-2)	0	74	1074	14.5(51)	6	—	—	—	—	—	—	—	—	—	—	—	—	36	565
2000	GB	15(15, WR)	2	5	2.5(3)	0	62	912	14.7(67)	9	—	—	—	—	—	—	—	—	—	—	—	—	54	506
2001	†GB	16(16, WR)	1	-5	-5.0(-5)	0	52	818	15.7(63)	6	—	—	—	—	—	—	—	—	—	—	kp	—	38	461
2002	†Phi	16(1)	—	—	—	—	46	600	13.0(59)	4	—	—	—	—	—	—	—	—	—	—	—	—	24	320
2003	†GB	15(0)	—	—	—	—	14	141	10.1(15)	0	—	—	—	—	—	—	—	—	—	—	—	—	0	71
NFL	9	132(91)	8	17	2.1(14)	0	477	7251	15.2(84)	61	—	—	—	—	—	—	—	—	—	—	kp	—	370	4279

Freeman, Arturo Arturo C., DB, 6´0˝/198 lbs; South Carolina; 2000: Mia, rnd 5; B10/27/1976 Orangeburg, SC **2000**†Mia 8 (0) **2001**†Mia 16 (4) **2002** Mia 16 (16, SS) **2003** Mia 16 (0) **2004** Mia 16 (9, FS) **2005** NE 2 (1) **NFL** 74 (30) [6 yrs]

Freeman, Bobby Robert Clayton, DB, 6´1˝/202 lbs; Auburn; 1955: Cle, rnd 3; B10/19/1932 Birmingham, AL, D12/30/2003 Auburn, AL **1957**†Cle 9 (db) **1959** GB 12 (DB) **1960**†Phi 12 (RS) **1961** Phi 14 (RS) **1962** Was 14

YEAR	TEAM	G (GS, POS)	RUSH	YD	AVG (LG)	TD	REC	YD	AVG (LG)	TD	PASS	COMP	PCT	YD	AVG (LG)	TD	INT	SK	YD	QBR	KPR	OTD	PTS	TAY
1958	†Cle	12(db)	2	1	0.5(9)	0	—	—	—	—	—	—	—	—	—	—	—	—	—	—	i	—	0	7
NFL	6	73	2	1	0.5(9)	0	—	—	—	—	—	—	—	—	—	—	—	—	—	—	ki	—	0	130

Freeman, Eddie Eddie V., DE, 6´5˝/307 lbs; Alabama-Birmingham; 2002: KC, rnd 2; B1/4/1978 Mobile, AL **2002** KC 15 (0) **2003** KC 5 (0) **NFL** 20 (0) [2 yrs]

Freeman, Jack Jack Lenard, G, 6´0˝/198 lbs; Texas; 1943: Pit, rnd 27; B1/20/1922 Mexia, TX **1946** Bkn-A 12 (3)

Freeman, Lorenzo Lorenzo Z., NT-DT, 6´5˝/300 lbs; Pittsburgh; 1987: GB, rnd 4; B5/23/1964 Camden, NJ **1987** Pit 6 (0) **1988** Pit 13 (2) **1989**†Pit 16 (0) **1990** Pit 11 (1) **1991** NYG 16 (4) **NFL** 62 (7) [5 yrs]

Freeman, Mike Michael, DB, 5´11˝/179 lbs; Fresno State; 1968: Min, rnd 4; B7/13/1944 Los Angeles, CA **1968** Atl 9 **1969** Atl 14 **1970** Atl 14 **NFL** 37 [3 yrs]

Freeman, Mike Michael Joseph, C-G, 6´3˝/256 lbs; Arizona; B10/13/1961 Mount Holly, NJ **1984**†Den 9 (0) **1986**†Den 4 (0) **1987**†Den 13 (9, C) **1988** LARd 2 (0) **NFL** 28 (9) [4 yrs]

Freeman, Phil Phillip Emery, WR, 5´11˝/185 lbs; Arizona; 1985: TB, rnd 8; B12/9/1962 St. Paul, MN **[R]**

YEAR	TEAM	G (GS, POS)	RUSH	YD	AVG (LG)	TD	REC	YD	AVG (LG)	TD	PASS	COMP	PCT	YD	AVG (LG)	TD	INT	SK	YD	QBR	KPR	OTD	PTS	TAY
1985	TB	14(0)	—	—	—	—	—	—	—	—	—	—	—	—	—	—	—	—	—	—	k	—	0	365
1986	TB	15(6, wr)	—	—	—	—	14	229	16.4(33)	2	—	—	—	—	—	—	—	—	—	—	k	—	12	242
1987	TB	8(4)	1	1	1.0(1)	0	8	141	17.6(64)	2	—	—	—	—	—	—	—	—	—	—	—	—	12	82
NFL	3	37(10)	1	1	1.0(1)	0	22	370	16.8(64)	4	—	—	—	—	—	—	—	—	—	—	k	—	24	688

Freeman, Reggie Reginald Prince, LB, 6´1˝/233 lbs; Florida State; 1993: NO, rnd 2; B5/8/1970 Clewiston, FL **1993** NO 10 (0)

Freeman, Russ Russell Williams, T, 6´7˝/290 lbs; Georgia Tech; B9/2/1969 Homestead, PA **1992** Den 16 (16, LT) **1993**†Den 14 (14, RT) **1994** Den 13 (7, rt) **1995** Oak 15 (1) **NFL** 58 (38) [4 yrs]

Freeman, Steve Steven Jay, DB, 5´11˝/185 lbs; Mississippi State; 1975: NE, rnd 5; B5/8/1953 Lamesa, TX **[I]** **1975** Buf 14 (FS) **1976** Buf 14 **1977** Buf 14 **1978** Buf 16 (7, ss) **1979** Buf 16 (16, SS) **1980**†Buf 16 (16, SS) **1981**†Buf 16 (16, SS) **1982** Buf 9 (9, SS) **1983** Buf☆16 (16, FS/ss) **1984** Buf 15 (15, SS) **1985** Buf 16 (16, SS) **1986** Buf 16 (16, FS) **1987**†Min 12 (0) **NFL** 190 (127) [13 yrs]

Freeney, Dwight Dwight Jason, DE, 6´1˝/268 lbs; Syracuse; 2002: Ind, rnd 1; B2/19/1980 Hartford, CT **[S]** **2002**†Ind 16 (8, RDE) **2003**†Ind★15 (13, RDE) **2004**†Ind★16 (16, RDE) **2005**†Ind★16 (13, RDE) **NFL** 63 (50) [4 yrs]

Freitas, Jesse Jesse, QB, 5´10˝/170 lbs; Santa Clara; 1944: Pit, rnd 7; B2/7/1921 Red Bluff, CA

YEAR	TEAM	G (GS, POS)	RUSH	YD	AVG (LG)	TD	REC	YD	AVG (LG)	TD	PASS	COMP	PCT	YD	AVG (LG)	TD	INT	SK	YD	QBR	KPR	OTD	PTS	TAY
1946	SF-A	10(0)	6	-21	-3.5	0	—	—	—	—	44	22	50.0	234	5.3	3	7	—	—	—	pi	—	0	-134
1947	SF-A	10(0)	6	-9	-1.5	0	—	—	—	—	33	13	39.4	215	6.5	4	2	—	—	—	Pi	—	0	45
1948	ChiR-A	10(9, QB)	24	25	1.0	0	—	—	—	—	167	84	50.3	1425	8.5	14	16	—	—	—	—	—	0	168
1949	Buf-A	1(0)	3	13	4.3	0	—	—	—	—	9	4	44.4	10	1.1	0	2	—	—	—	—	—	0	-62
AAFC	4	31(9)	39	8	0.2	0	—	—	—	—	253	123	48.6	1884	7.4	21	27	—	—	—	Ppi	—	0	16

Freitas, Jesse Jesse Lee, QB, 6´1˝/203 lbs; Stanford; San Diego State; 1974: SD, rnd 6; B9/10/1951 San Mateo, CA

YEAR	TEAM	G (GS, POS)	RUSH	YD	AVG (LG)	TD	REC	YD	AVG (LG)	TD	PASS	COMP	PCT	YD	AVG (LG)	TD	INT	SK	YD	QBR	KPR	OTD	PTS	TAY
1974	SD	5(3)	6	16	2.7(9)	0	—	—	—	—	109	49	45.0	719	6.6(71)	3	8	11	76	—	—	—	0	71
1975	SD	8(4)	11	56	5.1(17)	0	—	—	—	—	110	49	44.5	525	4.8(42)	5	5	20	138	—	—	—	0	144
NFL	2	13(7)	17	72	4.2(17)	0	—	—	—	—	219	98	44.7	1244	5.7(71)	8	13	31	214	—	—	—	0	214

Freitas, Makoa Rockne Makoa, T-G, 6´4˝/307 lbs; Arizona; 2003: Ind, rnd 6; B11/23/1979 Honolulu, HI **2003**†Ind 12 (6, lt) **2004**†Ind 16 (0) **NFL** 28 (6) [2 yrs]

Freitas, Rocky Rockne Crowningburg, T, 6´6˝/270 lbs; Oregon State; 1967: Pit, rnd 3; B9/7/1945 Kailua, HI **1968** Det 6 **1969** Det 14 (14, RT) **1971** Det 14 (14, RT) **1972** Det★14 (14, RT) **1973** Det 14 (14, RT) **1974** Det 14 (14, RT) **1975** Det 14 (14, RT) **1976** Det 14 (14, RT) **1977** Det 3 **1978** TB 13 (2)

YEAR	TEAM	G (GS, POS)	RUSH	YD	AVG (LG)	TD	REC	YD	AVG (LG)	TD	PASS	COMP	PCT	YD	AVG (LG)	TD	INT	SK	YD	QBR	KPR	OTD	PTS	TAY
1970	†Det☆	14(14, RT)	—	—	—	—	1	-8	-8.0(-8)	0	—	—	—	—	—	—	—	—	—	—	—	—	0	-4
NFL	11	134(114)	—	—	—	—	1	-8	-8.0(-8)	0	—	—	—	—	—	—	—	—	—	—	—	—	0	-4

French, Barry Barry Alden, G-T, 6´0˝/225 lbs; Purdue; 1944: ChiB, rnd 19; B2/12/1922 Chamberlain, SD, D3/16/1990 Vero Beach, FL **1947** Bal-A 14 (14, LG) **1949** Bal-A 11 (4) **AAFC** 25 (18) [2 yrs] **1950** Bal 12 (11, RT) **1951** Det 12 **NFL** 24 (11) [2 yrs]

French, Ernest Ernest Clauzell, DB, 5´11˝/195 lbs; Alabama A&M; B9/5/1959 Tensaw, AL **1982** Pit 3 (0)

French, Walter Walter Edward, B, 5´7˝/155 lbs; Rutgers; Army; B7/12/1899 Moorestown, NJ, D5/13/1984 Mountain Home, AR **1922** Roc 1 (0) **1925** Pot☆9 (2), 30 **NFL** 10 (2) [2 yrs]

Frerotte, Gus Gustave Joseph, QB, 6´3˝/237 lbs; Tulsa; 1994: Was, rnd 7; B7/31/1971 Kittanning, PA

YEAR	TEAM	G (GS, POS)	RUSH	YD	AVG (LG)	TD	REC	YD	AVG (LG)	TD	PASS	COMP	PCT	YD	AVG (LG)	TD	INT	SK	YD	QBR	KPR	OTD	PTS	TAY
1994	Was	4(4)	4	1	0.3(2)	0	—	—	—	—	100	46	46.0	600	6.0(51)	5	5	3	18	—	—	—	0	126
1995	Was	16(11, QB)	22	16	0.7(10)	1	—	—	—	—	396	199	50.3	2751	6.9(73)	13	13	23	192	70.2	—	—	6	947
1996	Was✧	16(16, QB)	28	16	0.6(17)	0	—	—	—	—	470	270	57.4	3453	7.3(52)	12	11	22	134	79.3	—	—	0	1363
1997	Was	13(13, QB)	24	65	2.7(14)	2	—	—	—	—	402	204	50.7	2682	6.7(52)	17	12	23	146	73.8	—	—	12	1031
1998	Was	3(2)	3	20	6.7(20)	0	—	—	—	—	54	25	46.3	283	5.2(22)	1	3	12	61	—	—	—	0	47
1999	†Det	9(6, qb)	15	33	2.2(8)	0	—	—	—	—	288	175	60.8	2117	7.4(77)	9	7	28	202	83.6	—	—	0	857
2000	†Den	10(6, qb)	22	64	2.9(13)	1	—	—	—	—	232	138	59.5	1776	7.7(44)	9	8	12	77	82.1	—	—	6	687
2001	Den	4(1)	10	9	0.9(4)	1	—	—	—	—	48	30	62.5	308	6.4(26)	3	0	3	21	—	—	—	6	188
2002	Cin	4(3)	4	22	5.5(9)	0	—	—	—	—	85	44	51.8	437	5.1(51)	1	5	10	74	—	—	—	0	46
2003	Min	16(2)	12	-2	-0.2(4)	0	—	—	—	—	65	38	58.5	690	10.6(72)	7	2	5	22	—	—	—	0	298
2004	†Min	16(0)	—	—	—	—	—	—	—	—	1	0	0.0	0	0.0	0	0	—	—	—	—	—	0	0
2005	Mia	16(15, QB)	27	61	2.3(14)	0	—	—	—	—	494	257	52.0	2996	6.1(60)	18	13	26	158	71.9	—	—	0	1129
NFL	12	127(79)	171	305	1.8(20)	5	—	—	—	—	2635	1426	54.1	18093	6.9(77)	95	79	167	1105	75.3	—	—	30	6717

Frerotte, Mitch Paul Mitchell, G, 6´3˝/281 lbs; Penn State; B3/30/1965 Kittanning, PA **1987** Buf 12 (0) **1990**†Buf 16 (0) **1991**†Buf 16 (0)

YEAR	TEAM	G (GS, POS)	RUSH	YD	AVG (LG)	TD	REC	YD	AVG (LG)	TD	PASS	COMP	PCT	YD	AVG (LG)	TD	INT	SK	YD	QBR	KPR	OTD	PTS	TAY
1992	†Buf	14(3)	—	—	—	—	2	4	2.0(2)	2	—	—	—	—	—	—	—	—	—	—	k	—	12	-3
NFL	4	58(3)	—	—	—	—	2	4	2.0(2)	2	—	—	—	—	—	—	—	—	—	—	—	—	12	12

Frey, Dick Richard H., DE, 6´2˝/235 lbs; Texas A&M; B12/17/1929 **1960** DalT-A 14 **1961**†Hou-A 7 **NFL** 21 [2 yrs]

Frey, Glenn Glenn Joseph, B, 5´10˝/193 lbs; Temple; B3/6/1912 Tunkhannock, PA, D1/5/1980 New Port Richey, FL

YEAR	TEAM	G (GS, POS)	RUSH	YD	AVG (LG)	TD	REC	YD	AVG (LG)	TD	PASS	COMP	PCT	YD	AVG (LG)	TD	INT	SK	YD	QBR	KPR	OTD	PTS	TAY
1936	Phi	12(8, bb)	7	8	1.1	0	3	65	21.7	0	—	—	—	—	—	—	—	—	—	—	—	—	0	41
1937	Phi	6(5, BB)	5	11	2.2	0	4	19	4.8	0	1	0	0.0	0	0.0	0	0	—	—	—	—	—	0	21
NFL	2	18(13)	12	19	1.6	0	7	84	12.0	0	1	0	0.0	0	0.0	0	0	—	—	—	—	—	0	61

Frick, Ray Raymond Augustus, C, 6´1˝/205 lbs; Pennsylvania; 1941: Bkn, rnd 5; B1/16/1919 Bloomfield, NJ, D3/2/2005 Flemington, NJ **1941** Bkn 3 (0)

Fricke, Ben Ben, C-G, 6´0˝/295 lbs; Houston; 1998: NYG, rnd 7; B11/3/1975 Austin, TX **1999** Dal 3 (0) **2000** Dal 8 (5, c) **2001** Dal 5 (0) **NFL** 16 (5) [3 yrs]

Frickey, Walt Walter Henry, E, 5´11˝/220 lbs; none; B8/8/1895 Rochester, NY, D3/12/1972 Rochester, NY **1920** Roc 1 (0)

Friday, Larry Lawrence, DB, 6´4˝/215 lbs; Alcorn State; Mississippi State; 1981: Cle, rnd 11; B1/23/1958 Jackson, MS **1987** Buf 1 (0)

YEAR	TEAM	G (GS, POS)	RUSH	YD	AVG(LG)	TD	REC	YD	AVG(LG)	TD	PASS COMP	PCT	YD	AVG(LG)	TD	INT	SK	YD	QBR	KPR	OTD	PTS	TAY

FRIEDE, MIKE Michael Gordon, WR, 6´3˝/205 lbs; Indiana; 1980: Det, rnd 3; B9/22/1957 Havre, MT

1980	Det	4(0)	—	—	—	—	1	21	21.0(21)	0	—	—	—	—	—	—	—	—	—	—	—	0	11
1980	NYG	7(4)	—	—	—	—	21	350	16.7(48)	0	—	—	—	—	—	—	—	—	—	—	—	0	175
1981	†NYG	16(15, WR)	—	—	—	—	18	250	13.9(43)	1	—	—	—	—	—	—	—	—	—	—	—	6	130
NFL	2	27(19)	—	—	—	—	40	621	15.5(48)	1	—	—	—	—	—	—	—	—	—	—	—	6	316

FRIEDLUND, BOB Robert Memler, E, 6´3˝/210 lbs; Michigan State; B1/6/1920 Galesburg, IL, D8/24/1991 Indian River County, FL **1946** Phi 2 (0)

FRIEDMAN, BENNY Benjamin, TB-DB, 5´10˝/183 lbs; Michigan; B3/18/1905 Cleveland, OH, D11/23/1982 New York, NY; HOF 2005 **[KC]** **1927** Cle☆13 (13, TB), 23
1928 Det☆10 (10, TB), 55 **1929** NYG☆15 (14, TB), 32 **1930** NYG☆15 (13, TB), 49 **1931** NYG 9 (5, TB), 12

1932	Bkn	11(10, TB)	88	250	2.8	0	5	67	13.4	0	74	23	31.1	319	4.3	5	10	—	—	12.2	K	—	8	68
1933	Bkn☆	7(5, TB)	-55	177	3.2	0	—	—	—	—	80	42	52.5	594	7.4	5	7	—	—	61.1	K	—	6	219
1934	Bkn	1(1)	9	31	3.4	0	—	—	—	—	13	5	38.5	16	1.2	0	2	—	—	—	—	—	0	-41
NFL	8	152(71)	152	458	3.0	0	18	5	67	13.4	0	167	70	41.9	929	5.6	66	19	—	—	60.2	K	—	185	706

FRIEDMAN, BOB Robert Allen, T, 6´2˝/215 lbs; Washington; 1943: Phi, rnd 18; B9/11/1921 Allentown, PA, D12/9/1989 Fort Lauderdale, FL **1944** Phi 10 (8, LT)

FRIEDMAN, JAKE Jacob, E, none; B3/23/1896 Bridgeport, CT, D11/9/1988 Port Salerno, FL **1926** Har 3 (0)

FRIEDMAN, LENNIE Leonard Lebrecht, G, 6´3˝/283 lbs; Duke; 1999: Den, rnd 2; B10/13/1976 Livingston, NJ **2000**†Den 16 (8, lg) **2001** Den 15 (14, LG) **2002** Den 2 (0)
2003 Was 16 (8, lg) **2004** Was 5 (2) **2005** Was 10 (0) **2005** ChiB 1 (0) **NFL** 65 (32) [6 yrs]

FRIEND, BEN Benjamin W., T, 6´5˝/248 lbs; LSU; 1939: Cle, rnd 15; B1/30/1912 **1939** Cle 10 (4)

FRIER, MIKE Michael, DE, 6´5˝/300 lbs; Appalachian State; 1992: Sea, rnd 7; B3/20/1969 Jacksonville, NC **1992** Cin 15 (3) **1993** Cin 16 (6, rde) **1994** Cin 1 (0) **1994** Sea 3 (0)
NFL 35 (9) [3 yrs]

FRIES, SHERWOOD Sherwood Marshall, G, 6´1˝/235 lbs; Colorado State; B11/24/1920 Los Angeles, CA, D12/9/1986 San Juan Capistrano, CA **1943** GB 5 (0)

FRIESZ, JOHN John Melvin, QB, 6´4˝/214 lbs; Idaho; 1990: SD, rnd 6; B5/19/1967 Missoula, MT

1990	SD	1(1)	1	3	3.0(3)	0	—	—	—	—	22	11	50.0	98	4.5(17)	1	1	1	7	—	—	—	0	17
1991	SD	16(16, QB)	10	18	1.8(11)	0	—	—	—	—	487	262	53.8	2896	5.9(58)	12	15	32	214	67.1	—	—	0	926
1993	SD	12(6, qb)	10	3	0.3(2)	0	—	—	—	—	238	128	53.8	1402	5.9(66)	6	4	14	98	72.8	—	—	0	574
1994	Was	16(4, qb)	1	1	1.0(1)	0	—	—	—	—	180	105	58.3	1266	7.0(73)	10	9	46	45	—	—	—	0	324
1995	Sea	6(3)	11	0	0.0(2)	0	—	—	—	—	120	64	53.3	795	6.6(43)	6	3	3	12	—	—	—	0	308
1996	Sea	8(6, qb)	12	1	0.1(3)	0	—	—	—	—	211	120	56.9	1629	7.7(80)	8	4	12	77	—	—	—	0	696
1997	Sea	2(1)	1	0	0.0(0)	0	—	—	—	—	36	15	41.7	138	3.8(22)	0	3	2	11	—	—	—	0	-51
1998	Sea	6(1)	5	5	1.0(8)	0	—	—	—	—	49	29	59.2	409	8.3(81)	2	2	1	7	—	—	—	0	140
1999	NE	1(0)	2	-2	-1.0(-1)	0	—	—	—	—	—	—	—	—	—	—	—	—	—	—	—	—	0	-2
2000	NE	1(0)	—	—	—	—	—	—	—	—	21	11	52.4	66	3.1(17)	0	1	3	16	—	—	—	0	-7
NFL	10	69(38)	53	29	0.5(11)	0	—	—	—	—	1364	745	54.6	8699	6.4(81)	45	42	74	487	72.3	—	—	0	2924

FRISCH, BYRON Byron Arthur, DE, 6´5˝/267 lbs; Brigham Young; 2000: Ten, rnd 3; B12/17/1976 Roseville, CA **2001** Dal 13 (0) **2002**†NYG 10 (0) **NFL** 23 (0) [2 yrs]

FRISCH, DAVID David Joseph, TE, 6´7˝/260 lbs; Iowa Central; Missouri; Colorado State; B6/22/1970 Kirkwood, MO **1994** Cin 16 (0) **1995** NE 2 (0) **1997** Was 2 (0)

1993	Cin	11(2)	—	—	—	—	6	43	7.2(12)	0	—	—	—	—	—	—	—	—	—	—	—	0	22
1996	Min	10(1)	—	—	—	—	3	27	9.0(2)	1	—	—	—	—	—	—	—	—	—	—	—	6	19
NFL	5	41(3)	—	—	—	—	9	70	7.8(21)	1	—	—	—	—	—	—	—	—	—	k	—	6	33

FRITSCH, ERNIE Ernest A., LB, 6´0˝/230 lbs; Detroit Mercy; B1/14/1937 Massillon, OH **1960** SL 1

FRITSCH, LOUIE Louis E., G, /240 lbs; Georgetown (KY); B10/9/1879 Evansville, IN, D1/20/1958 Indianapolis, IN **1921** Evv 1 (0)

FRITSCH, TED Theodore Edward, FB, 5´10˝/210 lbs; Wisconsin-Stevens Point; B10/31/1920 Spencer, WI, D10/5/1979 Green Bay, WI **[K]**

1942	GB	11(8, FB)	74	323	4.4(55)	1	9	60	6.7(31)	0	—	—	—	—	—	—	—	—	—	KPkp	—	13	392
1943	GB	10(6, FB)	54	169	3.1(14)	4	2	55	27.5(32)	0	—	—	—	—	—	—	—	—	—	KPk	—	24	276
1944	†GB	9(7, FB)	94	322	3.4(18)	4	3	5	1.7(5)	0	—	—	—	—	—	—	—	—	—	Pki	1	30	583
1945	GB☆	10(9, FB)	89	282	3.2(31)	7	3	13	4.3(9)	0	—	—	—	—	—	—	—	—	—	Kki	1	57	592
1946	GB☆	11(8, FB)	128	444	3.5(32)	9	2	13	6.5(12)	1	—	—	—	—	—	—	—	—	—	KPki	—	100	579
1947	GB	12(12, FB)	68	247	3.6(48)	6	—	—	—	—	—	—	—	—	—	—	—	—	—	Kki	—	56	339
1948	GB	12(11, FB)	37	173	4.7(30)	0	—	—	—	—	—	—	—	—	—	—	—	—	—	Kki	1	29	222
1949	GB	12(8, FB)	69	227	3.3(27)	1	6	81	13.5(35)	0	1	0	0.0	0	0.0	0	0	—	—	—	Kk	—	32	286
1950	GB	12	7	13	1.9(5)	0	—	—	—	—	—	—	—	—	—	—	—	—	—	Kk	—	39	17
NFL	9	99(69)	620	2200	3.5(55)	31	25	227	9.1(35)	1	1	0	0.0	0	0.0	0	0	—	—	—	KPkpi	3	380	3284

FRITSCH, TED Theodroe Edward, C, 6´2˝/242 lbs; St. Norbert; B8/26/1950 Green Bay, WI **1972** Atl 14 **1973** Atl 14 **1974** Atl 14 **1976**†Was 14 **1977** Was 14 **1978** Was 16
1979 Was 16 **NFL** 102 [7 yrs]

FRITSCH, TONI Anton, K, 5´7˝/190 lbs; none; B7/10/1945 Petronell, Austria, D9/13/2005 Vienna, Austria **[K]** **1971** Dal 2 **1972**†Dal 14 **1973**†Dal 13 **1975**†Dal☆14 **1976** SD 5
1977 Hou 9 **1978**†Hou 16 **1979**†Hou★16 **1980**†Hou 15 (0) **1982** Hou 16 (0) **1982** NO 5 (0) **NFL** 115 [11 yrs]

FRITTS, GEORGE George Henry, T, 5´11˝/205 lbs; Clemson; B12/30/1919 Lenor City, TN, D2/7/1987 Savannah, GA **1945** Phi 10 (1)

FRITTS, STAN Stanley Allen, RB, 6´1˝/215 lbs; Murray State; North Carolina State; 1975: Cin, rnd 4; B12/18/1952 Oak Ridge, TN

1975	†Cin	13(RB)	94	375	4.0(22)	8	6	63	10.5(17)	2	4	2	50.0	31	7.8(16)	0	0	—	—	—	—	60	512
1976	Cin	13	47	200	4.3(13)	3	9	75	8.3(19)	2	—	—	—	—	—	—	—	—	—	k	—	18	263
NFL	2	26	141	575	4.1(22)	11	15	138	9.2(19)	2	4	2	50.0	31	7.8(16)	0	0	—	—	—	k	—	78	775

FRITZ, RALPH Ralph C., G, 5´9˝/202 lbs; Michigan; 1941: Pit, rnd 10; B11/23/1917 New Kensington, PA, D2/4/2002 Miami, FL **1941** Phi 10 (1)

FRITZSCHE, JIM James Brian, T-G, 6´8˝/265 lbs; Purdue; 1982: Phi, rnd 8; B10/11/1960 Parma, OH **1983** Phi 15 (0)

FRIZZELL, WILLIAM William Jasper, DB, 6´3˝/203 lbs; North Carolina Central; 1984: Det, rnd 10; B9/8/1962 Greenville, NC **1984** Det 16 (0) **1985** Det 8 (0) **1986** Phi 8 (0)
1987 Phi 12 (5, rcb) **1988**†Phi 16 (0) **1989**†Phi 16 (0) **1990**†Phi 16 (1) **1991** TB 16 (4) **1992**†Phi 10 (1) **1993** Phi 16 (2) **NFL** 134 (13) [10 yrs]

FRKETICH, LEN Leonard Lawrence, T, 6´1˝/290 lbs; Penn State; B11/18/1917 Monessen, PA, D12/18/1999 **1945** Pit 2 (0)

FROHBOSE, BILL William Joseph, DB, 6´0˝/185 lbs; Miami (FL); B5/20/1952 Washington, DC **1974** Det 2

FRONCZEK, ANDY Andrew Anthony, T, 6´0˝/200 lbs; Richmond; B9/21/1916 Harvey, IL **1941** Bkn 11 (0)

FRONGILLO, JOHN John Richard, C-G, 6´3˝/255 lbs; Baylor; 1961: Hou, rnd 28/Cle, rnd 8; B10/12/1939 Mansfield, MA **1962**†Hou-A 14 **1963** Hou-A 3 **1964** Hou-A 14
1965 Hou-A 9 (C) **1966** Hou-A 14 **NFL** 54 [5 yrs]

FROST, DERRICK Derrick, P, 6´4˝/200 lbs; Northern Iowa; B11/25/1980 St. Louis, MO **2005**†Was 14 (0)

| 2004 | Cle | 16(0) | 1 | 1 | 1.0(1) | 0 | — | — | — | — | — | — | — | — | — | — | — | — | P | — | 0 | 1 |
| NFL | 2 | 30(0) | 1 | 1 | 1.0(1) | 0 | — | — | — | — | — | — | — | — | — | — | — | — | P | — | 0 | 1 |

FROST, KEN Carroll Kenneth, DT, 6´4˝/242 lbs; Tennessee; B11/17/1938 Brentwood, TN **1961** Dal 14 **1962** Dal 3 (3) **NFL** 17 (3) [2 yrs]

FROST, SCOTT Scott Andrew, DB, 6´3˝/218 lbs; Stanford; Nebraska; 1998: NYJ, rnd 3; B1/4/1975 Wood River, NE **1998**†NYJ 13 (0) **1999** NYJ 14 (0) **2000** NYJ 16 (1)
2003 TB 4 (0)

| 2001 | Cle | 12(0) | 1 | 1 | 1.0(1) | 0 | — | — | — | — | — | — | — | — | — | — | — | — | p | — | 0 | 1 |
| NFL | 5 | 59(1) | 1 | 1 | 1.0(1) | 0 | — | — | — | — | — | — | — | — | — | — | — | — | piS | — | 0 | -8 |

FRUGONE, JIM James Gregory, TB, 5´10˝/165 lbs; Syracuse; B10/23/1897 Brooklyn, NY, D6/7/1972 Brooklyn, NY **1925** NYG 3 (0)

FRUMP, BABE Maurice Elwood, G, 6´0˝/225 lbs; Ohio Wesleyan; B7/15/1901 OH, D8/14/1979 Boynton Beach, FL **1930** ChiB 9 (8, RG)

FRUTIG, ED Edward C., E, 6´1˝/190 lbs; Michigan; 1941: GB, rnd 5; B8/19/1920 River Rouge, MI

1941	GB	8(2)	1	11	11.0(11)	0	2	40	20.0(34)	0	—	—	—	—	—	—	—	—	—	—	—	0	31
1945	GB	1(0)	—	—	—	—	—	—	—	—	—	—	—	—	—	—	—	—	—	—	—	0	—
1945	Det	8(0)	—	—	—	—	2	5	2.5(3)	1	—	—	—	—	—	—	—	—	—	—	—	6	5

YEAR	TEAM	G (GS, POS)	RUSH	YD	AVG (LG)	TD	REC	YD	AVG (LG)	TD	PASS	COMP	PCT	YD	AVG (LG)	TD	INT	SK	YD	QBR	KPR	OTD	PTS	TAY
1946	Det	7(0)	—	—	—	—	8	72	9.0(17)	2	—	—	—	—	—	—	—	—	—	—	k	—	12	48
NFL	3	24(2)	1	11	11.0(11)	0	12	117	9.8(34)	3	—	—	—	—	—	—	—	—	—	—	k	—	18	84

FRY, BOB Robert Moellerig, T-G, 6´4˝/235 lbs; Kentucky; 1953: LA, rnd 3; B11/11/1930 Cincinnati, OH **1953** LARm 12 (LT) **1956** LARm 12 (LT) **1957** LARm 12 (LT) **1958** LARm 12 (LT) **1959** LARm 12 (LT) **1960** Dal 12 (LT) **1961** Dal 14 (LT) **1962** Dal 14 (LT) **1963** Dal 14 (14, LT/rt) **1964** Dal 12 (5, rt) **NFL** 126 (19) [10 yrs]

FRY, HARRY Harry Glen, E, 6´3˝/210 lbs; Bucknell; B10/4/1909 Hughesville, PA, D12/1983 Matamoras, PA **1932** SI 5 (2)

FRY, WES Wesley Leonard, B, 5´10˝/190 lbs; Iowa; B12/10/1902 Hartley, IA, D11/11/1970 La Mesa, CA **[K]** **1927** NYY 15 (8, fb), 25

FRYAR, IRVING Irving Dale, WR, 6´0˝/200 lbs; Nebraska; 1984: NE, rnd 1; B9/28/1962 Mount Holly, NJ **[R]**

YEAR	TEAM	G (GS, POS)	RUSH	YD	AVG (LG)	TD	REC	YD	AVG (LG)	TD	PASS	COMP	PCT	YD	AVG (LG)	TD	INT	SK	YD	QBR	KPR	OTD	PTS	TAY
1984	NE	14(2)	2	-11	-5.5(0)	0	11	164	14.9(26)	1	—	—	—	—	—	—	—	—	—	—	kp	—	6	263
1985	†NE★	16(14, WR)	7	27	3.9(13)	1	39	670	17.2(56)	7	—	—	—	—	—	—	—	—	—	—	kp	2	60	756
1986	†NE	14(13, WR)	4	80	20.0(31)	0	43	737	17.1(69)	6	—	—	—	—	—	—	—	—	—	—	kp	1	42	722
1987	NE	12(12, WR)	9	52	5.8(16)	0	31	467	15.1(40)	5	—	—	—	—	—	—	—	—	—	—	kp	—	30	424
1988	NE	15(14, WR)	6	12	2.0(6)	0	33	490	14.8(80)	5	—	—	—	—	—	—	—	—	—	—	kp	—	30	478
1989	NE	11(5, wr)	2	15	7.5(11)	0	29	537	18.5(52)	3	—	—	—	—	—	—	—	—	—	—	kp	—	18	378
1990	NE	16(15, WR)	2	-4	-2.0(-1)	0	54	856	15.9(56)	4	—	—	—	—	—	—	—	—	—	—	p	—	24	437
1991	NE	16(15, WR)	2	11	5.5(9)	0	68	1014	14.9(56)	3	1	0	0.0	0	0.0	0	0	—	—	—	p	—	18	533
1992	NE	15(14, WR)	1	6	6.0(6)	0	55	791	14.4(54)	4	—	—	—	—	—	—	—	—	—	—	p	—	24	422
1993	Mia✧	16(16, WR)	3	-4	-1.3(2)	0	64	1010	15.8(65)	5	—	—	—	—	—	—	—	—	—	—	k	—	30	521
1994	†Mia★	16(16, WR)	—	—	—	—	73	1270	17.4(54)	7	—	—	—	—	—	—	—	—	—	—	—	—	46	670
1995	†Mia	16(16, WR)	—	—	—	—	62	910	14.7(67)	8	—	—	—	—	—	—	—	—	—	—	—	—	48	495
1996	†Phi✧	16(16, WR)	1	-4	-4.0(-4)	0	88	1195	13.6(42)	**11**	—	—	—	—	—	—	—	—	—	—	—	—	66	649
1997	Phi✧	16(16, WR)	—	—	—	—	86	1316	15.3(72)	6	—	—	—	—	—	—	—	—	—	—	—	—	36	688
1998	Phi	16(16, WR)	3	46	15.3(32)	0	48	556	11.6(61)	2	—	—	—	—	—	—	—	—	—	—	—	—	12	334
1999	†Was	16(1)	—	—	—	—	26	254	9.8(30)	2	—	—	—	—	—	—	—	—	—	—	—	—	12	137
2000	Was	14(5, wr)	2	16	8.0(15)	0	41	548	13.4(34)	5	—	—	—	—	—	—	—	—	—	—	—	—	30	315
NFL	17	255(206)	44	242	5.5(32)	1	851	12785	15.0(80)	84	1	0	0.0	0	0.0	0	0	—	—	—	kp	3	532	8220

FRYE, CHARLIE Charlie, QB, 6´4˝/217 lbs; Akron; 2005: Cle, rnd 3; B8/28/1981 Willard, OH

YEAR	TEAM	G (GS, POS)	RUSH	YD	AVG (LG)	TD	REC	YD	AVG (LG)	TD	PASS	COMP	PCT	YD	AVG (LG)	TD	INT	SK	YD	QBR	KPR	OTD	PTS	TAY
2005	Cle	7(5, qb)	18	60	3.3(16)	1	—	—	—	—	164	98	59.8	1002	6.1(45)	4	5	22	135	72.8	—	—	6	391

FRYE, DAVID David William, LB, 6´2˝/223 lbs; Purdue; B6/21/1961 Cincinnati, OH **1983** Atl 16 (2) **1984** Atl 16 (11, LLB) **1985** Atl 14 (5, rlb) **1986** Mia 9 (2) **1987** Mia 12 (1) **1988** Mia 8 (0) **1989** Mia 11 (0) **NFL** 86 (21) [7 yrs]

FRYE, PHIL Philip Todd, RB, 5´11˝/180 lbs; Utah State; B12/20/1958 Washington, DC

YEAR	TEAM	G (GS, POS)	RUSH	YD	AVG (LG)	TD	REC	YD	AVG (LG)	TD	PASS	COMP	PCT	YD	AVG (LG)	TD	INT	SK	YD	QBR	KPR	OTD	PTS	TAY
1987	Min	1(1)	4	4	1.0(2)	0	3	25	8.3(12)	0	—	—	—	—	—	—	—	—	—	—	—	—	0	17

FRYER, BRIAN Brian, WR, 6´1˝/185 lbs; Edmonton (Canada); 1976: Was, rnd 8; B7/16/1953 Edmonton, Canada **1976** Was 4

FRYER, KENNY Kenneth Wesley, TB, 6´0˝/200 lbs; West Virginia; B11/17/1918 Wellsburg, WV

YEAR	TEAM	G (GS, POS)	RUSH	YD	AVG (LG)	TD	REC	YD	AVG (LG)	TD	PASS	COMP	PCT	YD	AVG (LG)	TD	INT	SK	YD	QBR	KPR	OTD	PTS	TAY
1944	Bkn	3(2)	15	15	1.0(9)	0	—	—	—	—	24	9	37.5	91	3.8(25)	0	2	—	—	—	P	—	0	-20

FUAMATU-MA'AFALA, CHRIS Chris, RB, 5´11˝/254 lbs; Utah; 1998: Pit, rnd 6; B3/4/1977 Honolulu, HI

YEAR	TEAM	G (GS, POS)	RUSH	YD	AVG (LG)	TD	REC	YD	AVG (LG)	TD	PASS	COMP	PCT	YD	AVG (LG)	TD	INT	SK	YD	QBR	KPR	OTD	PTS	TAY
1998	Pit	12(0)	7	30	4.3(10)	2	9	84	9.3(26)	1	—	—	—	—	—	—	—	—	—	—	—	—	18	97
1999	Pit	10(0)	1	4	4.0(4)	0	—	—	—	—	—	—	—	—	—	—	—	—	—	—	k	—	0	-2
2000	Pit	7(1)	21	149	7.1(23)	1	11	107	9.7(25)	0	—	—	—	—	—	—	—	—	—	—	—	—	6	213
2001	†Pit	16(5, rb)	120	453	3.8(46)	3	16	127	7.9(54)	1	—	—	—	—	—	—	—	—	—	—	—	—	24	552
2002	†Pit	8(0)	23	115	5.0(17)	0	2	12	6.0(6)	0	—	—	—	—	—	—	—	—	—	—	—	—	0	121
2003	Jax	13(0)	35	144	4.1(18)	1	1	2	2.0(2)	0	—	—	—	—	—	—	—	—	—	—	—	—	6	155
2004	Jax	7(1)	20	69	3.5(10)	1	4	19	4.8(8)	0	—	—	—	—	—	—	—	—	—	—	—	—	6	89
NFL	7	73(7)	227	964	4.2(46)	8	43	351	8.2(54)	2	—	—	—	—	—	—	—	—	—	—	k	—	60	1224

FUCCI, DOM Dominic A., DB, 5´11˝/190 lbs; Kentucky; 1951: Was, rnd 18; B9/14/1928 New Village, NJ, D6/22/1987 Lexington, KY **1955** Det 12

FUGETT, JEAN Jean Schloss, TE, 6´3˝/225 lbs; Amherst; 1972: Dal, rnd 13; B12/16/1951 Baltimore, MD

YEAR	TEAM	G (GS, POS)	RUSH	YD	AVG (LG)	TD	REC	YD	AVG (LG)	TD	PASS	COMP	PCT	YD	AVG (LG)	TD	INT	SK	YD	QBR	KPR	OTD	PTS	TAY
1972	†Dal	14	3	2	0.7(9)	0	7	94	13.4(29)	0	—	—	—	—	—	—	—	—	—	—	k	—	0	34
1973	†Dal	12	1	34	34.0(34)	0	9	168	18.7(48)	3	—	—	—	—	—	—	—	—	—	—	—	—	18	133
1974	Dal	12	—	—	—	—	4	60	15.0(24)	1	—	—	—	—	—	—	—	—	—	—	—	—	6	35
1975	†Dal	14(9, TE)	1	2	2.0(2)	0	38	488	12.8(54)	3	—	—	—	—	—	—	—	—	—	—	—	—	18	261
1976	†Was	12(12, TE)	2	0	0.0(10)	0	27	334	12.4(33)	6	—	—	—	—	—	—	—	—	—	—	—	—	36	197
1977	Was★	14(14, TE)	—	—	—	—	36	631	17.5(52)	5	—	—	—	—	—	—	—	—	—	—	—	—	30	341
1978	Was	14(12, TE)	—	—	—	—	25	367	14.7(49)	7	—	—	—	—	—	—	—	—	—	—	—	—	42	219
1979	Was	11(6, te)	—	—	—	—	10	128	12.8(30)	3	—	—	—	—	—	—	—	—	—	—	—	—	18	79
NFL	8	103(53)	7	38	5.4(34)	0	156	2270	14.6(54)	28	—	—	—	—	—	—	—	—	—	—	k	—	168	1298

FUGLER, DICK Richard Guy, T-DT, 6´2˝/238 lbs; Tulane; 1952: ChiC, rnd 5; B7/19/1931 Dallas, TX **1954** ChiC 12 **1952** Pit 12 (LT) **NFL** 24 [2 yrs]

FUJITA, SCOTT Scott Anthony, LB, 6´5˝/247 lbs; California; 2002: KC, rnd 5; B4/28/1979 Ventura, CA **2002** KC 16 (9, LLB) **2003**†KC 16 (16, LLB) **2004** KC 16 (16, LLB) **2005** Dal 16 (8, LOLB) **NFL** 64 (49) [4 yrs]

FULCHER, BILL William Marcus, LB-G, 6´0˝/193 lbs; Georgia Tech; B2/9/1934 Augusta, GA **1956** Was 9 (RLB) **1957** Was 2 **1958** Was 12 (7, llb) **NFL** 23 (7) [3 yrs]

FULCHER, DAVID David Dwayne, DB, 6´3˝/236 lbs; Arizona State; 1986: Cin, rnd 3; B9/28/1964 Los Angeles, CA **[I]** **1986** Cin 16 (16, SS) **1987** Cin 11 (11, SS) **1988**†Cin★16 (16, SS) **1989** Cin★16 (16, SS) **1990**†Cin★13 (12, SS) **1991** Cin 16 (16, SS) **1992** Cin 12 (11, SS) **1993**†LARd 3 (0) **NFL** 103 (98) [8 yrs]

FULCHER, MONDRIEL Mondriel DeCarlos A., TE, 6´3˝/250 lbs; Miami (FL); 2000: Oak, rnd 7; B10/15/1976 Coffeyville, KS **2000** Oak 10 (0) **2001**†Oak 13 (1) **2002** Oak 2 (0) **NFL** 25 (1) [3 yrs]

FULHAGE, SCOTT Scott Alan, P, 5´11˝/191 lbs; Kansas State; B1/17/1961 Beloit, KS **[P]** **1987** Cin 11 (0) **1988** Cin 13 (0) **1990** Atl 16 (0) **1991**†Atl 16 (0)

YEAR	TEAM	G (GS, POS)	RUSH	YD	AVG (LG)	TD	REC	YD	AVG (LG)	TD	PASS	COMP	PCT	YD	AVG (LG)	TD	INT	SK	YD	QBR	KPR	OTD	PTS	TAY
1989	Atl	16(0)	1	0	0.0(0)	0	—	—	—	—	1	1	100.0	12	12.0(12)	0	0	—	—	—	P	—	0	6
1992	Atl	16(0)	1	0	0.0(0)	0	—	—	—	—	—	—	—	—	—	—	—	—	—	—	P	—	0	0
NFL	6	88(0)	2	0	0.0	0	—	—	—	—	1	1	100.0	12	12.0(12)	0	0	—	—	—	P	—	0	6

FULLER, CHARLEY Charles Earl, HB, 5´11˝/175 lbs; San Francisco State; 1961: Oak, rnd 19/SF, rnd 16; B1/22/1939 Vicksburg, MS, D8/8/2001 Oakland, CA

YEAR	TEAM	G (GS, POS)	RUSH	YD	AVG (LG)	TD	REC	YD	AVG (LG)	TD	PASS	COMP	PCT	YD	AVG (LG)	TD	INT	SK	YD	QBR	KPR	OTD	PTS	TAY
1961	Oak-A	14	38	134	3.5(19)	0	12	277	23.1(85)	2	1	0	0.0	0	0.0	0	0	—	—	—	kp	—	12	350
1962	Oak-A	3	—	—	—	—	5	67	13.4(25)	0	—	—	—	—	—	—	—	—	—	—	—	—	0	34
NFL	2	17	38	134	3.5(19)	0	17	344	20.2(85)	2	1	0	0.0	0	0.0	0	0	—	—	—	kp	—	12	383

FULLER, COREY Corey Bushe, DB, 5´10˝/220 lbs; Florida State; 1995: Min, rnd 2; B5/1/1971 Tallahassee, FL **1995** Min 16 (10, LCB) **1996**†Min 16 (14, LCB) **1997**†Min 16 (16, LCB) **1998**†Min 16 (16, LCB) **1999** Cle 16 (16, FS) **2000** Cle 15 (15, LCB) **2001** Cle 16 (16, LCB) **2002**†Cle 13 (12, LCB) **2003**†Bal 14 (10, RCB) **2004** Bal 14 (2) **NFL** 152 (127) [10 yrs]

FULLER, CURTIS Curtis, DB, 5´11˝/191 lbs; TCU; 2001: Sea, rnd 4; B7/25/1978 Fort Worth, TX **2001** Sea 10 (1) **2002** Sea 16 (1) **2003**†GB 9 (0) **2004** GB 1 (0) **2004** Car 6 (0) **NFL** 42 (2) [4 yrs]

FULLER, EDDIE Eddie Jerome, RB, 5´9˝/201 lbs; LSU; 1990: Buf, rnd 4; B6/22/1968 Leesville, LA **1991** Buf 5 (0) **1993**†Buf 7 (0)

YEAR	TEAM	G (GS, POS)	RUSH	YD	AVG (LG)	TD	REC	YD	AVG (LG)	TD	PASS	COMP	PCT	YD	AVG (LG)	TD	INT	SK	YD	QBR	KPR	OTD	PTS	TAY
1992	Buf	8(0)	6	39	6.5(15)	0	2	17	8.5(17)	0	—	—	—	—	—	—	—	—	—	—	k	—	0	62
NFL	3	20(0)	6	39	6.5(15)	0	2	17	8.5(17)	0	—	—	—	—	—	—	—	—	—	—	k	—	0	67

FULLER, FRANK Frank Andrew, DT-T-G-C-DE, 6´4˝/244 lbs; Kentucky; 1952: LA, rnd 26; B8/8/1929 Du Bois, PA, D12/10/1993 Los Angeles, CA **1953** LARm 9 **1955**†LARm 12 **1957** LARm 10 (RDT) **1958** LARm 12 (RDT) **1959** ChiC★10 (RDT) **1960** SL☆9 (RDT) **1961** SL 14 (RDT) **1962** SL 14 (RDT) **1963** Phi 5 **NFL** 95 [9 yrs]

FULLER, JAMES James Ray, DB, 5´11˝/208 lbs; Portland State; 1992: SD, rnd 8; B8/5/1969 Tacoma, WA **1992**†SD 0 (0) **1993** SD 10 (0) **1996**†Phi 13 (2) **NFL** 23 (2) [3 yrs]

FULLER, JEFF Jeffery Avery, DB-LB, 6´2˝/216 lbs; Texas A&M; 1984: SF, rnd 5; B8/8/1962 Dallas, TX **1984**†SF 13 (1) **1985**†SF 16 (0) **1986**†SF 6 (0) **1987**†SF 14 (13, SS) **1988**†SF 16 (16, SS) **1989** SF 6 (4) **NFL** 71 (34) [6 yrs]

FULLER, JOE Joe Robert, DB, 5´11˝/180 lbs; Northern Iowa; B9/25/1964 Milligan, FL **1990** SD 4 (1) **1991** GB 16 (0) **NFL** 20 (1) [2 yrs]

YEAR	TEAM	G (GS, POS)	RUSH	YD	AVG (LG)	TD	REC	YD	AVG (LG)	TD	PASS COMP	PCT	YD	AVG (LG)	TD	INT	SK	YD	QBR	KPR	OTD	PTS	TAY

FULLER, JOHNNY   John Charles, DB, 6´0˝/186 lbs; Lamar; 1968: SF, rnd 4; B3/3/1946 Beaumont, TX   **1968** SF 14 (10, RS)   **1969** SF 7   **1970**†SF 14   **1971**†SF 14
1972†SF 14 (5, fs)   **1973** NO 13 (SS)   **1974** NO 12 (SS)   **1975** NO 11 (11, FS)   **NFL** 99 (26) [8 yrs]

FULLER, LARRY   Lawrence, B, 5´10˝/192 lbs; none; B1/28/1923 Faust, NY, D2/18/1992 Tupper Lake, NY   **1945** Was 1 (0)   **1945** ChiC 1 (0)

| 1944 | Was | 5(0) | 4 | 10 | 2.5(6) | 0 | 5 | 82 | 16.4(47) | 1 | — | — | — | — | — | — | — | — | — | — | — | 6 | 56 |
| NFL | | 2 | 7(0) | 4 | 10 | 2.5(6) | 0 | 5 | 82 | 16.4(47) | 1 | — | — | — | — | — | — | — | — | — | 6 | 56 |

FULLER, MIKE   Michael Darwin, DB, 5´10˝/188 lbs; Auburn; 1975: SD, rnd 3; B4/7/1953 Jackson, MS **[KR]**   **1975** SD 14 (6, ss)   **1976** SD 14 (14, SS)   **1978** SD 16 (16, SS)
1981†Cin 15 (6, ss)   **1982**†Cin 9 (2)

1977	SD	14(14, SS)	1	7	7.0(7)	1	—	—	—	—	—	—	—	—	—	—	—	—	pi	1	12	283
1979	†SD	16(SS)	1	0	0.0(0)	0	—	—	—	1	0	0.0	0	0.0	0	0	—	—	kpi	—	0	262
1980	†SD	16(4)	2	0	0.0(0)	0	—	—	—	1	0	0.0	0	0.0	0	0	—	—	kp	—	0	212
NFL		8	114(62)	4	7	1.8(7)	1	—	—	—	1	0	0.0	0	0.0	0	0	—	Kkpi	3	25	2054

FULLER, RANDY   Randy Lamar, DB, 5´10˝/180 lbs; Tennessee State; 1994: Den, rnd 4; B6/2/1970 Griffin, GA   **1994** Den 10 (1)   **1995**†Pit 13 (0)   **1996**†Pit 14 (1)   **1997**†Pit 12 (3)
1998†Atl 13 (0)   **1999** Sea 2 (0)   **NFL** 64 (5) [6 yrs]

FULLER, STEVE   Stephen Ray, QB, 6´4˝/198 lbs; Clemson; 1979: KC, rnd 1; B1/5/1957 Enid, OK

1979	KC	16(12, QB)	50	264	5.3(49)	1	—	—	—	—	270	146	54.1	1484	5.5(40)	6	14	37	244	55.8	—	—	6	486
1980	KC	14(13, QB)	60	274	4.6(38)	4	—	—	—	—	320	193	60.3	2250	7.0(77)	10	12	49	348	76.4	—	—	24	1009
1981	KC	13(3)	19	118	6.2(27)	0	—	—	—	—	134	77	57.5	934	7.0(53)	3	4	17	117	—	—	—	0	440
1982	KC	9(3)	10	56	5.6(12)	0	—	—	—	—	93	49	52.7	665	7.2(51)	3	2	17	143	—	—	—	0	324
1984	†ChiB	6(4)	15	89	5.9(26)	1	—	—	—	—	78	53	67.9	595	7.6(31)	3	0	7	41	—	—	—	6	412
1985	†ChiB	16(5, qb)	24	77	3.2(13)	5	—	—	—	—	107	53	49.5	777	7.3(69)	1	5	17	102	—	—	—	30	321
1986	†ChiB	16(2)	8	30	3.8(10)	0	—	—	—	—	64	34	53.1	451	7.0(50)	2	4	8	53	—	—	—	0	106
NFL		7	90(42)	186	908	4.9(49)	11	—	—	—	—	1066	605	56.8	7156	6.7(77)	28	41	152	1048	70.1	—	—	66	3096

FULLER, VINCENT   Vincent, DB, 6´1˝/189 lbs; Virginia Tech; 2005: Ten, rnd 4; B8/3/1982 Baltimore, MD   **2005** Ten 2 (0)

FULLER, WILLIAM   William Henry, DE, 6´3˝/271 lbs; North Carolina; 1984: LARm, rnd S1; B3/8/1962 Norfolk, VA **[S]**   **1986** Hou 13 (0)   **1987**†Hou 12 (1)   **1988**†Hou 16 (15, RDE)
1989†Hou 15 (8, rde)   **1990**†Hou 16 (16, LDE)   **1991**†Hou★16 (16, LDE)   **1992** Hou 15 (14, LDE)   **1993**†Hou 16 (16, LDE)   **1994** Phi★16 (16, LDE)   **1995**†Phi★14 (13, LDE)
1996†Phi★16 (16, LDE)   **1997** SD 16 (16, LDE)   **1998** SD 13 (13, LDE)   **NFL** 194 (160) [13 yrs]

FULLERTON, ED   Edward Reno, DB, 5´10˝/190 lbs; Maryland; 1953: SF, rnd 4; B4/7/1931 Pittsburgh, PA   **1953** Pit 1

FULLINGTON, DARRELL   Darrell, DB, 6´1˝/197 lbs; Miami (FL); 1988: Min, rnd 5; B4/17/1964 New Smyrna Beach, FL   **1988**†Min 15 (0)   **1989**†Min 16 (2)   **1990** Min 16 (11, FS)
1991 NE 5 (0)   **1991** TB 11 (0)

| 1992 | TB | 16(13, FS) | — | — | — | — | 1 | 12 | 12.0(12) | 0 | — | — | — | — | — | — | — | i | — | 0 | 16 |
| NFL | | 5 | 79(26) | — | — | — | — | 1 | 12 | 12.0(12) | 0 | — | — | — | — | — | — | iS | — | 0 | 61 |

FULLWOOD, BRENT   Brent Leanrd, RB, 5´11˝/209 lbs; Auburn; 1987: GB, rnd 1; B10/10/1963 Kissimmee, FL

1987	GB	11(1)	84	274	3.3(18)	5	2	11	5.5(12)	0	—	—	—	—	—	—	—	k	—	30	480
1988	GB	14(10, FB)	101	483	4.8(33)	7	20	128	6.4(30)	1	—	—	—	—	—	—	—	k	—	48	728
1989	GB◇	15(15, FB)	204	821	4.0(38)	5	19	214	11.3(67)	0	—	—	—	—	—	—	—	k	—	30	1056
1990	GB	5(4)	44	124	2.8(16)	1	3	17	5.7(10)	0	—	—	—	—	—	—	—		—	6	143
1990	Cle	1(0)	—	—	—	—	—	—	—	—	—	—	—	—	—	—	—	k	—	0	29
NFL		4	46(30)	433	1702	3.9(38)	18	44	370	8.4(67)	1	—	—	—	—	—	—	—	k	—	114	2435

FULTON, DANNY   Daniel B., WR, 6´2˝/184 lbs; Nebraska; Nebarska-Omaha; 1978: Buf, rnd 3; B9/2/1956 Memphis, TN

1979	Buf	6	—	—	—	—	2	34	17.0(18)	0	—	—	—	—	—	—	—	—	0	17
1981	Cle	5(0)	—	—	—	—	2	38	19.0(27)	0	—	—	—	—	—	—	—	—	0	19
1982	†Cle	9(0)	—	—	—	—	1	9	9.0(9)	0	—	—	—	—	—	—	—	—	0	5
NFL		3	20	—	—	—	—	5	81	16.2(27)	0	—	—	—	—	—	—	—	—	0	41

FULTON, ED   Edward Ulmer, G, 6´3˝/250 lbs; Maryland; 1977: LA, rnd 3; B1/27/1955 Abington, PA   **1978** LARm 4   **1979** Buf 5   **NFL** 9 [2 yrs]

FULTON, KEN   Kenneth L., G, none; B6/5/1899 Muncie, IN, D3/12/1948 Muncie, IN   **1921** Mun 1 (1, RG)

FULTON, TED   Theodore Walton, G, 6´0˝/203 lbs; Oglethorpe; B11/5/1905 Memphis, TN, D3/2/1991 Atlanta, GA   **1931** Bkn 12 (6, lg)   **1932** Bkn 1 (0)   **NFL** 13 (6) [2 yrs]

FULTZ, MIKE   Michael Dwayne, DT, 6´5˝/278 lbs; Nebraska; 1977: NO, rnd 2; B1/28/1954 Lincoln, NE   **1977** NO 12 (5, ldt)   **1978** NO 12   **1979** NO 13 (1)   **1980** NO 12 (8, LDT)
1981 Mia 4 (0)   **1981** Bal 5 (5, rdt)   **NFL** 58 (19) [5 yrs]

FUNCHESS, TOM   Thomas, T, 6´5˝/265 lbs; Jackson State; 1968: Bos, rnd 2; B9/12/1944 Crystal Springs, MS   **1968** Bos-A 14 (13, LT)   **1969** Bos-A 14 (14, LT)   **1970** Bos 11 (11, LT)
1971 Hou 12   **1972** Hou 14 (LT)   **1973** Hou 14 (LT)   **1974**†Mia 8 (3, LT)   **NFL** 87 (41) [7 yrs]

FUQUA, JOHN   John William 'Frenchy', RB, 5´11˝/205 lbs; Morgan State; 1969: NYG, rnd 11; B9/12/1946 Detroit, MI

1969	NYG	13	20	89	4.4(35)	0	3	11	3.7(6)	0	—	—	—	—	—	—	—	k	—	0	194
1970	Pit	14(FB)	138	691	**5.0(85)**	7	23	289	12.6(57)	2	—	—	—	—	—	—	—		—	54	916
1971	Pit	12(FB)	155	625	4.0(30)	4	49	427	8.7(40)	1	—	—	—	—	—	—	—	p	—	30	879
1972	†Pit	13(FB)	150	665	4.4(47)	4	18	152	8.4(28)	0	—	—	—	—	—	—	—		—	24	781
1973	†Pit	11	117	457	3.9(25)	2	17	150	8.8(22)	0	—	—	—	—	—	—	—	k	—	12	559
1974	†Pit	9	50	156	3.1(14)	2	6	68	11.3(18)	0	—	—	—	—	—	—	—		—	12	210
1975	†Pit	14(3)	74	285	3.9(18)	1	18	146	8.1(21)	0	—	—	—	—	—	—	—	k	—	6	353
1976	Pit	15	63	4.2(12)	1	4	16	4.0(4)	0	—	—	—	—	—	—	—	—	kp	—	6	112
NFL		8	100(3)	719	3031	4.2(85)	21	135	1247	9.2(57)	3	—	—	—	—	—	—	—	kp	—	144	4003

FUQUA, RAY   Raymond Earl, E, 6´0˝/190 lbs; SMU; B3/21/1912 Shreveport, LA, D10/26/1983 Houston, TX

1935	Bkn	10(7, RE)	—	—	—	—	8	82	10.3	1	—	—	—	—	—	—	—	—	6	46
1936	Bkn	12(9, RE)	—	—	—	—	1	2	2.0(2)	0	—	—	—	—	—	—	—	—	0	1
NFL		2	22(16)	—	—	—	—	9	84	9.3(2)	1	—	—	—	—	—	—	—	—	6	47

FUREY, JIM   James Andrew, LB, 6´0˝/228 lbs; Kansas State; 1956: Cle, rnd 13; B9/12/1932 Newark, NJ   **1961** NYT-A 9

FURJANIC, TONY   Anthony Joseph, LB, 6´1˝/228 lbs; Notre Dame; 1986: Buf, rnd 8; B2/26/1964 Chicago, IL   **1986** Buf 14 (1)   **1987** Buf 8 (0)   **1988** Mia 6 (0)   **NFL** 28 (1) [3 yrs]

FURNESS, STEVE   Stephen Robert, DT-DE, 6´4˝/255 lbs; Rhode Island; 1972: Pit, rnd 5; B12/5/1950 Providence, RI, D2/10/2000 Bethel Park, PA   **1972**†Pit 2   **1973** Pit 6
1974†Pit 14 (1)   **1975**†Pit 14 (6, ldt)   **1976**†Pit 9 (4)   **1977**†Pit 14 (14, RDT/lde)   **1978**†Pit 10 (6, rdt)   **1979**†Pit 12 (2)   **1980** Pit 16 (16, RDT)   **1981** Det 9 (2)   **NFL** 106 (51) [10 yrs]

FURRER, WILL   William Mason, QB, 6´3˝/210 lbs; Virginia Tech; 1992: Chi, rnd 4; B2/5/1968 Danville, PA

1992	ChiB	2(1)	—	—	—	—	—	—	—	—	25	9	36.0	89	3.6(16)	0	3	4	39	—	—	—	0	-76
1995	Hou	7(1)	8	20	2.5(11)	0	—	—	—	—	99	48	48.5	483	4.9(48)	2	7	5	35	—	—	—	0	-9
NFL		2	9(2)	8	20	2.5(11)	0	—	—	—	—	124	57	46.0	572	4.6(48)	2	10	9	74	—	—	—	0	-84

FURREY, MIKE   Michael Thomas, DB-WR, 6´0˝/185 lbs; Northern Iowa; B5/12/1977 Grove City, OH

2003	†SL	13(0)	3	5	1.7(2)	0	20	189	9.4(24)	0	—	—	—	—	—	—	—	kp	—	0	199
2004	†SL	8(0)	—	—	—	—	1	8	8.0(8)	0	—	—	—	—	—	—	—	k	—	0	41
2005	SL	16(11, FS)	—	—	—	—	—	—	—	—	—	—	—	—	—	—	—	pi	1	6	141
NFL		3	37(11)	3	5	1.7(2)	0	21	197	9.4(24)	0	—	—	—	—	—	—	—	kpi	1	6	381

FURST, TONY   Anthony Raymond, T, 6´1˝/217 lbs; Dayton; B4/26/1918 Dayton, OH   **1940** Det 9 (4)   **1941** Det 10 (6, RT)   **1944** Det 2 (0)   **NFL** 21 (10) [3 yrs]

FUSINA, CHUCK   Charles Anthony, QB, 6´1˝/197 lbs; Penn State; 1979: TB, rnd 5; B5/31/1957 Pittsburgh, PA

1979	TB	1	—	—	—	—	—	—	—	—	—	—	—	—	—	—	—	—	—	—	0	
1980	TB	2(0)	1	14	14.0(14)	0	—	—	—	—	4	2	50.0	18	4.5(13)	0	1	1	0	—	—	—	0	-17
1981	TB	4(0)	3	1	0.1(7)	0	—	—	—	—	1	1	100.0	2	2.0(2)	1	0	0	0	—	—	—	9	9
1986	GB	7(0)	7	11	1.6(6)	0	—	—	—	—	32	19	59.4*	178	5.6(42)	0	1	1	3	—	—	—	0	60
NFL		4	14	11	28	2.5(14)	0	—	—	—	—	37	22	59.5	198	5.4(42)	1	2	2	3	—	—	—	0	52

FUSSELL, THOMAS   Thomas Paul, DE, 6´3˝/250 lbs; LSU; 1967: Bos, rnd 8; B5/25/1945 Cleveland, OH   **1967** Bos-A 12 (2)

YEAR	TEAM	G(GS, POS)	RUSH	YD	AVG(LG)	TD	REC	YD	AVG(LG)	TD	PASS	COMP	PCT	YD	AVG(LG)	TD	INT	SK	YD	QBR	KPR	OTD	PTS	TAY
FUTRELL, BOBBY Bobby Lee, DB, 5´11˝/190 lbs; Elizabeth City State; B8/4/1963 Ahoskie, NC, D5/31/1992 Tampa, FL **[R]** **1986** TB 16 (0) **1987** TB 12 (1) **1988** TB 16 (15, RCB) **1989** TB 16 (1) **1990** TB 1 (0) **NFL** 61 (17) [5 yrs]																								
GABBARD, STEVE Stephen Edward, DT, 6´4˝/297 lbs; Florida State; B7/19/1966 Lexington, KY **1991** GB 4 (0)																								
GABLER, JOHN John H., G, none; B4/16/1906 Dayton, OH, D3/25/1975 Dayton, OH **1925** Day 1 (0)																								
GABRIEL, DOUG Douglas, WR, 6´2˝/215 lbs; Central Florida; 2003: Oak, rnd 5; B8/27/1980 Miami, FL **[R]**																								
2003	Oak	12(0)	—	—	—	—	1	17	17.0(17)	0	—	—	—	—	—	—	—	—	—	—	k	1	6	230
2004	Oak	16(5, WR)	2	7	3.5(4)	0	33	551	16.7(58)	2	—	—	—	—	—	—	—	—	—	—	kp	—	12	635
2005	Oak	14(2)	1	5	5.0(5)	0	37	554	15.0(38)	3	—	—	—	—	—	—	—	—	—	—	k	—	18	301
NFL	3	42(7)	3	12	4.0(5)	0	71	1122	15.8(58)	5	—	—	—	—	—	—	—	—	—	—	kp	1	36	1165
GABRIEL, ROMAN Roman Ildonzo, QB, 6´5˝/220 lbs; North Carolina State; 1962: LA, rnd 1/Oak, rnd 1; B8/5/1940 Wilmington, NC																								
1962	LARm	6(4)	18	93	5.2(15)	0	—	—	—	—	101	57	56.4	670	6.6(65)	3	2	—	—	—	—	—	0	363
1963	LARm	12(9, QB)	39	132	3.4(16)	3	—	—	—	—	281	130	46.3	1947	6.9(77)	8	11	—	—	62.7	—	—	18	736
1964	LARm	7(qb)	11	5	0.5(6)	1	—	—	—	—	143	65	45.5	1236	8.6(70)	9	5	—	—	—	—	—	6	478
1965	LARm	7(QB)	23	79	3.4(17)	2	—	—	—	—	173	83	48.0	1321	7.6(60)	11	5	—	—	—	—	—	12	615
1966	LARm	14(QB)	52	176	3.4(14)	3	—	—	—	—	397	217	54.7	2540	6.4(84)	10	16	—	—	65.9	—	—	18	886
1967	†LARm✧	14(QB)	43	198	4.6(23)	6	—	—	—	—	371	196	52.8	2779	7.5(80)	25	13	—	—	85.2	—	—	36	1253
1968	LARm★	14(14, QB)	34	139	4.1(19)	4	1	-5	-5.0(-5)	0	366	184	50.3	2364	6.5(60)	19	16	—	—	70.0	—	—	24	814
1969	†LARm★	14(14, QB)	35	156	4.5(22)	5	—	—	—	—	399	217	54.4	2549	6.4(**93**)	**24**	7	14	112	86.8	—	—	30	1321
1970	LARm	14(14, QB)	28	104	3.7(15)	1	—	—	—	—	**407**	211	51.8	2552	6.3(71)	16	12	20	134	72.2	—	—	6	990
1971	LARm	14(14, QB)	18	48	2.7(10)	2	—	—	—	—	352	180	51.1	2238	6.4(68)	17	10	25	200	75.4	—	—	12	872
1972	LARm	14(13, QB)	14	16	1.1(11)	1	—	—	—	—	323	165	51.1	2027	6.3(57)	12	15	12	102	63.8	—	—	6	500
1973	Phi✧	14(QB)	12	10	0.8(5)	1	—	—	—	—	**460**	**270**	58.7	**3219**	7.0(80)	**23**	12	31	219	86.0	—	—	6	1265
1974	Phi	11(QB)	14	76	5.4(11)	0	—	—	—	—	338	193	57.1	1867	5.5(64)	9	12	35	259	66.8	—	—	0	575
1975	Phi	11(9, QB)	13	70	5.4(39)	1	—	—	—	—	292	151	51.7	1644	5.6(62)	13	11	18	131	67.8	—	—	6	527
1976	Phi	4	4	2	0.5(1)	0	—	—	—	—	92	46	50.0	476	5.2(34)	2	2	13	111	—	—	—	0	170
1977	Phi	13	—	—	—	—	—	—	—	—	3	1	33.3	15	5.0(15)	0	0	—	—	—	—	—	0	8
NFL	16	183(91)	358	1304	3.6(39)	30	1	-5	-5.0(-5)	0	4498	2366	52.6	29444	6.5(93)	201	149	168	1268	74.3	—	—	180	11369
GADBOIS, DENNIS Dennis Richard, WR, 6´1˝/183 lbs; Boston University; B9/18/1963 Biddeford, ME **1988** NE 2 (0)																								
1987	NE	3(1)	—	—	—	—	3	51	17.0(20)	0	—	—	—	—	—	—	—	—	—	—	—	—	0	26
NFL	2	5(1)	—	—	—	—	3	51	17.0(20)	0	—	—	—	—	—	—	—	—	—	—	—	—	0	26
GADDIS, BOB Robert, WR, 5´11˝/178 lbs; Mississippi Valley State; 1975: Pit, rnd 13; B1/20/1952 Jackson, MS **1976** Buf 2																								
GADO, SAMKON Samkon, RB, 5´11˝/210 lbs; Liberty; B11/13/1982 Columbia, SC																								
2005	GB	8(5, RB)	143	582	4.1(64)	6	10	77	7.7(30)	1	1	0	0.0	0	0.0	0	0	—	—	—	—	—	42	686
GADSDEN, ORONDE Oronde Benjamin, WR, 6´2˝/215 lbs; Winston-Salem State; B8/20/1971 Charleston, SC																								
1998	†Mia	16(12, WR)	—	—	—	—	48	713	14.9(50)	7	—	—	—	—	—	—	—	—	—	—	—	—	42	392
1999	†Mia	16(7, wr)	—	—	—	—	48	803	16.7(62)	6	—	—	—	—	—	—	—	—	—	—	—	—	36	432
2000	†Mia	16(16, WR)	—	—	—	—	56	786	14.0(61)	6	—	—	—	—	—	—	—	—	—	—	—	—	36	423
2001	†Mia	14(14, WR)	—	—	—	—	55	674	12.3(61)	3	—	—	—	—	—	—	—	—	—	—	—	—	18	352
2002	Mia	6(6, wr)	—	—	—	—	16	228	14.3(29)	0	—	—	—	—	—	—	—	—	—	—	—	—	0	114
2003	Mia	6(0)	—	—	—	—	4	48	12.0(23)	0	—	—	—	—	—	—	—	—	—	—	—	—	0	24
NFL	6	74(55)	—	—	—	—	227	3252	14.3(62)	22	—	—	—	—	—	—	—	—	—	—	—	—	132	1736
GAECHTER, MIKE Michael Theodore, DB, 6´0˝/190 lbs; Oregon; B1/9/1940 Santa Monica, CA **[I]** **1962** Dal 14 (9, LCB) **1963** Dal 14 (10, LS) **1964** Dal 11 (4) **1965** Dal 14 (5, ls) **1966**†Dal 14 (LS) **1967**†Dal 14 (LS) **1968**†Dal 14 (LS) **1969**†Dal 13 (LS) **NFL** 108 (28) [8 yrs]																								
GAFFNEY, DERRICK Derrick Tyrone, WR, 6´1˝/181 lbs; Florida; 1978: NYJ, rnd 8; B5/24/1955 Jacksonville, FL																								
1978	NYJ	16(16, WR)	2	-2	-1.0(1)	0	38	691	18.2(50)	3	—	—	—	—	—	—	—	—	—	—	—	—	18	359
1979	NYJ	16(16, WR)	—	—	—	—	32	534	16.7(43)	1	—	—	—	—	—	—	—	—	—	—	—	—	6	272
1980	NYJ	13(5, wr)	—	—	—	—	24	397	16.5(36)	2	—	—	—	—	—	—	—	—	—	—	—	—	12	209
1981	†NYJ	16(13, WR)	—	—	—	—	14	246	17.6(39)	0	—	—	—	—	—	—	—	—	—	—	—	—	0	123
1982	†NYJ	9(2)	—	—	—	—	11	207	18.8(45)	1	—	—	—	—	—	—	—	—	—	—	—	—	6	109
1983	NYJ	16(9, WR)	—	—	—	—	17	243	14.3(35)	0	—	—	—	—	—	—	—	—	—	—	—	—	0	122
1984	NYJ	12(7, wr)	—	—	—	—	19	285	15.0(29)	0	—	—	—	—	—	—	—	—	—	—	k	—	0	134
1987	NYJ	2(0)	—	—	—	—	1	10	10.0(10)	0	—	—	—	—	—	—	—	—	—	—	—	—	0	5
NFL	8	100(68)	2	-2	-1.0(1)	0	156	2613	16.8(50)	7	—	—	—	—	—	—	—	—	—	—	k	—	42	1331
GAFFNEY, JABAR Derrick Jabar, WR, 6´1˝/193 lbs; Florida; 2002: Hou, rnd 2; B12/1/1980 San Antonio, TX																								
2002	Hou	16(14, WR)	—	—	—	—	41	483	11.8(27)	1	1	1	100.0	39	39.0(39)	1	0	—	—	—	p	—	8	253
2003	Hou	16(11, WR)	1	13	13.0(13)	0	34	402	11.8(33)	2	1	0	0.0	0	0.0	0	0	—	—	—	p	—	12	226
2004	Hou	16(12, WR)	4	30	7.5(10)	0	41	632	15.4(69)	2	3	0	0.0	0	0.0	0	0	—	—	—	k	—	12	357
2005	Hou	16(13, WR)	4	13	3.3(10)	0	55	492	8.9(29)	2	—	—	—	—	—	—	—	—	—	—	—	—	12	269
NFL	4	64(50)	9	56	6.2(13)	0	171	2009	11.7(69)	7	5	1	20.0	39	7.8(39)	1	0	—	—	—	kp	—	44	1105
GAFFNEY, JEFF John Francis, K, 6´2˝/195 lbs; Virginia; B10/22/1964 Washington, DC **[K]** **1987** SD 3 (0)																								
GAFFNEY, JIM James Thomas, QB-HB, 6´1˝/204 lbs; Tennessee; 1944: Was, rnd 15; B4/21/1921 Cumberland, MD																								
1945	Was	2(0)	1	-6	-6.0(-6)	0	—	—	—	—	—	—	—	—	—	—	—	—	—	—	—	—	0	-6
1946	Was	10(5, qb)	25	96	3.8(12)	0	7	85	12.1(41)	1	—	—	—	—	—	—	—	—	—	—	k	—	6	153
NFL	2	12(5)	26	90	3.5(12)	0	7	85	12.1(41)	1	—	—	—	—	—	—	—	—	—	—	k	—	6	147
GAFFORD, MONK Roy Haynes, B, 5´11˝/195 lbs; Auburn; 1943: Phi, rnd 3; B10/1/1920 Fort Deposit, AL, D2/19/1987 Montgomery, AL																								
1946	Mia-A	11(8, LH)	22	60	2.7	1	14	270	19.3	4	5	1	20.0	3	-0.6(-3)	0	2	—	—	—	Pkpi	—	30	393
1946	Bkn-A	2(0)	2	6	3.0	0	—	—	—	—	—	—	—	—	—	—	—	—	—	—	Pki	—	0	77
1947	Bkn-A	14(13, HB)	46	232	5.0	1	8	113	14.1	0	—	—	—	—	—	—	—	—	—	—	kpi	—	6	681
1948	Bkn-A	12(6, WB)	30	51	1.7	1	15	274	18.3	4	39	17	43.6	268	6.9	4	2	—	—	—	kp	—	30	566
AAFC	3	39(27)	100	349	3.5	3	37	657	17.8	8	44	18	40.9	265	6.0	4	4	—	—	—	Pkpi	—	66	1716
GAGE, BOB Robert, DB-TB, 5´11˝/175 lbs; Clemson; 1949: Pit, rnd 1/Bal-A, rnd 2; B1/15/1928 Chester, SC, D4/19/2005 Greenville, SC																								
1949	Pit	12(4)	46	228	5.0(97)	3	1	8	8.0(8)	0	36	17	47.2	329	9.1(52)	2	4	—	—	—	Pkpi	—	18	494
1950	Pit	10(DB)	39	106	2.7(18)	3	6	127	21.2(48)	2	58	21	36.2	294	5.1(42)	1	5	—	—	—	Pkpi	—	30	389
NFL	2	22(4)	85	334	3.9(97)	6	7	135	19.3(48)	2	94	38	40.4	623	6.6(52)	3	9	—	—	—	Pkpi	—	48	882
GAGE, JUSTIN Justin, WR, 6´4˝/208 lbs; Missouri; 2003: Chi, rnd 5; B1/25/1981 Indianapolis, IN																								
2003	ChiB	10(3)	—	—	—	—	17	338	19.9(57)	2	—	—	—	—	—	—	—	—	—	—	—	—	12	179
2004	ChiB	16(2)	—	—	—	—	12	156	13.0(32)	0	—	—	—	—	—	—	—	—	—	—	—	—	0	134
2005	†ChiB	15(11, WR)	—	—	—	—	31	346	11.2(25)	2	—	—	—	—	—	—	—	—	—	—	—	—	12	183
NFL	3	41(16)	—	—	—	—	60	840	14.0(57)	4	—	—	—	—	—	—	—	—	—	—	—	—	24	496
GAGE, STEVE Steven Glen, DB, 6´3˝/210 lbs; Tulsa; 1987: Was, rnd 6; B5/10/1964 Claremore, OK **1987** Was 4 (1) **1988** Was 16 (1) **NFL** 20 (2) [2 yrs]																								
GAGLIANO, BOB Robert Frank, QB, 6´3˝/200 lbs; U.S. International; Utah State; 1981: KC, rnd 12; B9/5/1958 Los Angeles, CA																								
1982	KC	1(0)	—	—	—	—	—	—	—	—	1	1	100.0	7	7.0(7)	0	0	—	—	—	—	—	0	4
1983	KC	1(0)	—	—	—	—	—	—	—	—	—	—	—	—	—	—	—	—	—	—	—	—	—	—
1987	SF	3(1)	—	—	—	—	—	—	—	—	29	16	55.2	229	7.9(50)	1	1	4	22	—	—	—	0	80
1989	Det	11(7, qb)	41	192	4.7(19)	4	—	—	—	—	232	117	50.4	1671	7.2(75)	6	12	25	153	61.2	—	—	24	618
1990	Det	9(4, qb)	46	145	3.2(22)	0	—	—	—	—	159	87	54.7	1190	7.5(47)	10	10	13	83	—	—	—	0	390
1991	SD	2(0)	3	19	6.3(16)	0	—	—	—	—	23	9	39.1	76	3.3(17)	0	1	3	22	—	—	—	0	17

YEAR	TEAM	G(GS,POS)	RUSH	YD	AVG(LG)	TD	REC	YD	AVG(LG)	TD	PASS	COMP	PCT	YD	AVG(LG)	TD	INT	SK	YD	QBR	KPR	OTD	PTS	TAY
1992	†SD	5(1)	3	-4	-1.3(0)	0	—	—	—	—	42	19	45.2	258	6.1(55)	0	3	5	50	—	—	—	0	5
NFL	7	32(13)	93	352	3.8(22)	4	—	—	—	—	486	249	51.2	3431	7.1(75)	17	27	50	330	62.7	—	—	24	1113

GAGNER, LARRY Lawrence Joseph, G, 6´3˝/240 lbs; Florida; 1966: Pit, rnd 2/Mia, rnd 3; B12/30/1943 Cleveland, OH **1966** Pit 14 (14, LG) **1967** Pit 14 (LG) **1968** Pit 12 (LG)
1969 Pit 12 (LG) **1972** KC 7 **NFL** 59 (14) [5 yrs]

GAGNON, DAVE David John, RB, 5´10˝/210 lbs; Ferris State; B1/17/1951 Garden City, MI

| 1974 | ChiB | 13 | 1 | 15 | 15.0(15) | 0 | 4 | 20 | 5.0(16) | 0 | — | — | — | — | — | — | — | — | — | — | k | — | 0 | 27 |

GAGNON, ROY Roy Joseph Maurice, G, 5´11˝/205 lbs; Oregon; B1/6/1913 Minneapolis, MN, D6/29/2000 Anoka, MS **1935** Det 4 (0)

GAIN, BOB Robert, DT-DE-MG-T, 6´3˝/256 lbs; Kentucky; 1951: GB, rnd 1; B6/21/1929 Akron, OH **[K]** **1952**†Cle 6 (LDT) **1954** Cle 2 **1955**†Cle☆11 (MG) **1956** Cle☆12 (RDT/ lde) **1957**†Cle★12 (LDT) **1958**†Cle★12 (LDT) **1959** Cle★12 (LDE) **1960** Cle☆12 (LDT) **1961** Cle★14 (LDT) **1962** Cle★14 (LDT) **1963** Cle★14 (LDT) **1964** Cle 4
NFL 125 [12 yrs]

GAINER, DERRICK Derrick Luther, RB, 5´11˝/235 lbs; Florida A&M; 1989: LARd, rnd 8; B8/15/1966 Plant City, FL

1990	Cle	16(1)	30	81	2.7(9)	1	7	85	12.1(20)	0	—	—	—	—	—	—	—	—	—	—	k	—	6	119
1992	LARd	2(0)	2	10	5.0(6)	0	—	—	—	—	—	—	—	—	—	—	—	—	—	—	—	—	0	10
1992	†Dal	5(0)	—	—	—	—	—	—	—	—	—	—	—	—	—	—	—	—	—	—	—	—	—	—
1993	†Dal	11(0)	9	29	3.2(8)	0	6	37	6.2(8)	0	—	—	—	—	—	—	—	—	—	—	—	—	0	48
NFL	3	34(1)	41	120	2.9(9)	1	13	122	9.4(20)	0	—	—	—	—	—	—	—	—	—	—	k	—	6	176

GAINES, CHRIS Christopher Randall, LB, 6´0˝/238 lbs; Vanderbilt; 1988: Phx, rnd 5; B2/3/1965 Nashville, TN **1988** Mia 4 (0)

GAINES, CLARK Clark Daniel, RB, 6´1˝/206 lbs; Wake Forest; B2/1/1954 Elberton, GA

1976	NYJ	14(8, FB)	157	724	4.6(33)	3	41	400	9.8(27)	2	—	—	—	—	—	—	—	—	—	—	k	—	30	954
1977	NYJ	14(13, FB)	158	595	3.8(19)	3	55	469	8.5(31)	1	—	—	—	—	—	—	—	—	—	—	—	—	24	865
1978	NYJ	16(1)	44	154	3.5(33)	2	3	23	7.7(13)	0	—	—	—	—	—	—	—	—	—	—	k	—	12	174
1979	NYJ	16(9, FB)	186	905	4.9(52)	0	29	219	7.6(15)	0	—	—	—	—	—	—	—	—	—	—	k	—	0	1014
1980	NYJ	5(4)	36	174	4.8(15)	0	36	310	8.6(16)	3	—	—	—	—	—	—	—	—	—	—	—	—	18	344
1981	KC	1(0)	—	—	—	—	—	—	—	—	—	—	—	—	—	—	—	—	—	—	—	—	—	—
1982	KC	9(0)	1	0	0.0(0)	0	2	17	8.5(10)	0	—	—	—	—	—	—	—	—	—	—	—	—	0	9
NFL	7	75(35)	582	2552	4.4(52)	8	166	1438	8.7(31)	6	—	—	—	—	—	—	—	—	—	—	k	—	84	3358

GAINES, GREG Gregory Scott, LB, 6´3˝/220 lbs; Tennessee; B10/16/1958 Martinsville, VA **1981** Sea 8 (1) **1983**†Sea 16 (6, rolb) **1984**†Sea 16 (11, ROLB) **1985** Sea 16 (0)
1986 Sea 16 (15, ROLB) **1987**†Sea 11 (10, ROLB) **1988**†Sea 6 (0) **NFL** 89 (43) [7 yrs]

GAINES, LAWRENCE Lawrence Edward, RB, 6´1˝/237 lbs; Wyoming; 1976: Det, rnd 1; B12/15/1953 Vernon, TX

1976	Det	14(7, fb)	155	659	4.3(26)	4	23	130	5.7(24)	1	—	—	—	—	—	—	—	—	—	—	—	—	30	769
1978	Det	13(1)	54	178	3.3(12)	1	2	16	8.0(9)	0	—	—	—	—	—	—	—	—	—	—	—	—	6	196
1979	Det	16	23	55	2.4(9)	0	—	—	—	—	—	—	—	—	—	—	—	—	—	—	—	—	0	55
NFL	3	43(8)	232	892	3.8(26)	5	25	146	5.8(24)	1	—	—	—	—	—	—	—	—	—	—	—	—	36	1020

GAINES, MICHAEL Michael, TE, 6´3˝/280 lbs; Central Florida; 2004: Car, rnd 7; B3/30/1980 Tallahassee, FL

2004	Car	15(6, te)	—	—	—	—	4	34	8.5(14)	0	—	—	—	—	—	—	—	—	—	—	—	—	0	17
2005	†Car	11(6, te)	—	—	—	—	12	155	12.9(38)	2	—	—	—	—	—	—	—	—	—	—	k	—	12	82
NFL	2	26(12)	—	—	—	—	16	189	11.8(38)	2	—	—	—	—	—	—	—	—	—	—	k	—	12	99

GAINES, SHELDON Sheldon, WR, 5´9˝/155 lbs; Long Beach State; B4/22/1964 Los Angeles, CA

| 1987 | Buf | 3(3) | — | — | — | — | 9 | 115 | 12.8(37) | 0 | — | — | — | — | — | — | — | — | — | — | — | — | 0 | 58 |

GAINES, WENDALL Wendall Lewis, TE-DE, 6´4˝/293 lbs; Oklahoma State; B1/17/1972 Vernon, TX

| 1995 | Arz | 16(11, TE) | — | — | — | — | 14 | 117 | 8.4(22) | 2 | — | — | — | — | — | — | — | — | — | — | — | — | 12 | 69 |

GAINES, WENTFORD Wentford Elijah, DB, 6´0˝/185 lbs; Ferrum; Tennessee Tech; Cincinnati; 1976: Pit, rnd 9; B2/4/1953 Anderson, SC **1978** Pit 1 **1978** ChiB 11 **1979**†ChiB 16
1980 ChiB 8 (0) **NFL** 36 [3 yrs]

GAINES, WILLIAM William Albert, DT, 6´5˝/310 lbs; Florida; 1994: Mia, rnd 5; B6/20/1971 Jackson, MS **1994** Mia 8 (0) **1995** Was 15 (11, RDT) **1996** Was 16 (6, ldt)
1997 Was 13 (7, ldt) **NFL** 52 (24) [4 yrs]

GAINOR, CHARLIE Charles Edward, DE, 6´3˝/190 lbs; North Dakota; 1939: Phi, rnd 18; B11/22/1916 Sargeant, ND, D9/10/1966 Fort Dodge, IA **1939** ChiC 1 (0)

GAISER, GEORGE George Nolan, T-G, 6´4˝/255 lbs; SMU; 1967: Buf, rnd 7; B5/9/1945 San Antonio, TX **1968** Den-A 10

GAISON, BLANE Blane Keith, DB, 6´0˝/185 lbs; Hawaii; B5/13/1958 Kaneohe, HI **1981** Atl 14 (0) **1982**†Atl 9 (0) **1983** Atl 16 (0) **1984** Atl 15 (0) **NFL** 54 (0) [4 yrs]

GAITER, TONY Tony Bernard, WR, 5´8˝/169 lbs; Miami (FL); 1997: NE, rnd 6; B7/15/1974 Miami, FL **1997** NE 1 (0) **1998** SD 5 (0) **NFL** 6 (0) [2 yrs]

GAITERS, BOB Robert James, HB, 5´11˝/210 lbs; New Mexico State; 1961: NYG, rnd 2/Den, rnd 1; B2/26/1938 Zanesville, OH

1961	†NYG	14	116	460	4.0(29)	6	11	54	4.9(14)	1	3	3	100.0	42	14.0(27)	2	0	—	—	—	k	—	42	706
1962	NYG	2	7	35	5.0(13)	0	3	34	11.3(15)	0	2	0	0.0	—	—	0	0	—	—	—	—	—	0	52
1962	SF	9	36	158	4.4(53)	0	2	13	6.5(13)	0	—	—	—	—	—	—	—	—	—	—	k	—	0	273
1963	Den-A	6	9	20	2.2(8)	0	1	74	74.0(74)	1	—	—	—	—	—	—	—	—	—	—	k	—	6	122
NFL	3	31	168	673	4.0(53)	6	17	175	10.3(74)	2	5	3	60.0	42	8.4(27)	2	0	—	—	—	k	—	48	1153

GAJAN, HOKIE Howard Lee, RB, 5´11˝/220 lbs; LSU; 1981: NO, rnd 10; B9/6/1959 Baton Rouge, LA

1982	NO	9(4)	19	77	4.1(12)	0	10	33	3.3(9)	0	—	—	—	—	—	—	—	—	—	—	k	—	0	85
1983	NO	16(12, FB)	81	415	5.1(58)	4	17	130	7.6(26)	0	1	0	0.0	—	—	0	0	—	—	—	—	—	24	520
1984	NO	14(14, FB)	102	615	6.0(62)	5	35	288	8.2(51)	2	1	1	100.0	34	34.0(34)	1	0	—	—	—	—	—	42	841
1985	NO	6(6, fb)	50	251	5.0(26)	2	8	87	10.9(22)	0	—	—	—	—	—	—	—	—	—	—	k	—	12	315
NFL	4	45(36)	252	1358	5.4(62)	11	63	515	8.2(51)	2	2	1	50.0	34	17.0(34)	1	0	—	—	—	k	—	78	1761

GALAZIN, STAN Stanley Bernard, C, 6´3˝/211 lbs; Villanova; B8/8/1915; D1/3/1989 Queens, NY **1937** NYG 1 (0) **1938**†NYG◇5 (0) **1939** NYG 3 (0) **NFL** 9 (0) [3 yrs]

GALBRAITH, SCOTT Alan Scott, TE, 6´2˝/258 lbs; USC; 1990: Cle, rnd 7; B1/7/1967 Sacramento, CA

1990	Cle	16(1)	—	—	—	—	4	62	15.5(28)	0	—	—	—	—	—	—	—	—	—	—	k	—	0	2
1991	Cle	16(13, TE)	—	—	—	—	27	328	12.1(42)	0	—	—	—	—	—	—	—	—	—	—	k	—	0	147
1992	Cle	14(2)	—	—	—	—	4	63	15.8(28)	1	—	—	—	—	—	—	—	—	—	—	—	—	6	37
1993	†Dal	7(0)	—	—	—	—	1	1	1.0(1)	1	—	—	—	—	—	—	—	—	—	—	—	—	6	6
1994	†Dal	15(2)	—	—	—	—	4	31	7.8(15)	0	—	—	—	—	—	—	—	—	—	—	—	—	0	16
1995	Was	16(16, TE)	—	—	—	—	10	80	8.0(25)	2	—	—	—	—	—	—	—	—	—	—	—	—	12	50
1996	Was	16(6, te)	—	—	—	—	8	89	11.1(30)	2	—	—	—	—	—	—	—	—	—	—	—	—	12	55
1997	Dal	16(0)	—	—	—	—	2	16	8.0(11)	0	—	—	—	—	—	—	—	—	—	—	k	—	0	2
1998	GB	1(0)	—	—	—	—	—	—	—	—	—	—	—	—	—	—	—	—	—	—	—	—	—	—
NFL	9	117(40)	—	—	—	—	60	670	11.2(42)	6	—	—	—	—	—	—	—	—	—	—	k	—	36	313

GALBREATH, HARRY Harry Curtis, G, 6´1˝/280 lbs; Tennessee; 1988: Mia, rnd 8; B1/1/1965 Clarksville, TN **1988** Mia 16 (13, RG) **1989** Mia 14 (14, RG) **1990**†Mia 16 (16, RG)
1991 Mia 16 (16, RG) **1992**†Mia 16 (16, RG) **1993**†GB 16 (16, RG) **1994**†GB 16 (16, RG) **1995**†GB 16 (16, RG) **1996** NYJ 15 (8, LG) **NFL** 141 (131) [9 yrs]

GALBREATH, TONY Anthony Dale, RB, 6´0˝/228 lbs; Missouri; 1976: NO, rnd 2; B1/29/1954 Fulton, MO **[K]**

1976	NO	14(13, RB)	136	570	4.2(74)	7	54	420	7.8(35)	1	—	—	—	—	—	—	—	—	—	—	kp	—	48	952
1977	NO	14(14, FB)	168	644	3.8(26)	3	41	265	6.5(30)	0	—	—	—	—	—	—	—	—	—	—	k	—	18	807
1978	NO	16(16, FB)	186	635	3.4(20)	5	74	582	7.9(35)	2	—	—	—	—	—	—	—	—	—	—	K	—	42	986
1979	NO	15(FB)	189	708	3.7(27)	9	58	484	8.3(38)	1	3	2	66.7	70	23.3(48)	0	1	—	—	—	K	—	67	1040
1980	NO	16(4)	81	308	3.8(26)	3	57	470	8.2(21)	2	—	—	—	—	—	—	—	—	—	—	k	—	30	579
1981	Min	14(1)	42	198	4.7(21)	2	18	144	8.0(23)	0	—	—	—	—	—	—	—	—	—	—	k	—	12	291
1982	†Min	8(3)	39	116	3.0(12)	1	17	153	9.0(32)	0	—	—	—	—	—	—	—	—	—	—	—	—	6	203
1983	Min	13(7, fb)	113	474	4.2(52)	4	45	348	7.7(31)	1	—	—	—	—	—	—	—	—	—	—	—	—	36	698
1984	†NYG	16(0)	22	97	4.4(11)	0	37	357	9.6(37)	0	1	1	100.0	13	13.0(13)	0	—	—	—	—	—	—	0	282
1985	†NYG	16(0)	29	187	6.4(18)	0	30	327	10.9(49)	1	—	—	—	—	—	—	—	—	—	—	—	—	6	371

YEAR	TEAM	G(GS, POS)	RUSH	YD	AVG(LG)	TD	REC	YD	AVG(LG)	TD	PASS	COMP	PCT	YD	AVG(LG)	TD	INT	SK	YD	QBR	KPR	OTD	PTS	TAY
1986	†NYG	16(0)	16	61	3.8(10)	0	33	268	8.1(19)	0	1	0	0.0	0	0.0	0	0	1	8	—	p	—	0	181
1987	NYG	12(0)	10	74	7.4(17)	0	26	248	9.5(21)	0	—	—	—	—	—	—	—	—	—	—	—	—	0	198
NFL	12	170(58)	1031	4072	3.9(74)	34	490	4066	8.3(49)	9	7	3	42.9	83	11.9(48)	0	1	1	8	—	Kkp	—	265	6587

GALIFFA, ARNIE Arnold Anthony, QB, 6´2˝/193 lbs; Army; 1950: GB, rnd 18; B1/29/1927 Donora, PA, D9/5/1978 Glenview, IL

YEAR	TEAM	G(GS, POS)	RUSH	YD	AVG(LG)	TD	REC	YD	AVG(LG)	TD	PASS	COMP	PCT	YD	AVG(LG)	TD	INT	SK	YD	QBR	KPR	OTD	PTS	TAY
1953	NYG	3	5	1	0.2(7)	0	—	—	—	—	13	4	30.8	129	9.9(75)	1	5	—	—	—	—	—	0	-130
1954	SF	4	1	2	2.0(2)	0	—	—	—	—	12	3	25.0	54	4.5(25)	0	0	—	—	—	—	—	0	29
NFL	2	7	6	3	0.5(7)	0	—	—	—	—	25	7	28.0	183	7.3(75)	1	5	—	—	—	—	—	0	-101

GALIGHER, ED Edward Albert, DT-DE, 6´4˝/255 lbs; UCLA; 1972: NYJ, rnd 4; B10/15/1950 Hayward, CA **1972** NYJ 13 **1973** NYJ 7 (LDE) **1974** NYJ 13 (LDE) **1975** NYJ 13 (11, RDT) **1976** NYJ 14 (RDT) **1977** SF 12 **1978** SF 15 (15, RDT) **NFL** 87 (26) [7 yrs]

GALIMORE, WILLIE Willie Lee, HB, 6´1˝/187 lbs; Florida A&M; 1956: ChiB, rnd 5; B3/30/1935 St. Augustine, FL, D7/26/1964 Rensselaer, IN

YEAR	TEAM	G(GS, POS)	RUSH	YD	AVG(LG)	TD	REC	YD	AVG(LG)	TD	PASS	COMP	PCT	YD	AVG(LG)	TD	INT	SK	YD	QBR	KPR	OTD	PTS	TAY
1957	ChiB☆	12(LH)	127	538	4.2(67)	5	15	201	13.4(56)	2	—	—	—	—	—	—	—	—	—	—	k	—	42	764
1958	ChiB★	12(LH)	130	619	4.8(36)	8	8	151	18.9(79)	3	1	0	0.0	0	0.0	0	1	—	—	—	k	1	72	963
1959	ChiB	12(lh)	58	199	3.4(36)	1	10	125	12.5(34)	2	—	—	—	—	—	—	—	—	—	—	k	—	18	346
1960	ChiB	12(LH)	74	368	5.0(54)	1	3	35	11.7(33)	0	—	—	—	—	—	—	—	—	—	—	k	—	6	508
1961	ChiB	14(HB)	153	707	4.6(60)	4	33	502	15.2(84)	3	—	—	—	—	—	—	—	—	—	—	k	—	42	1020
1962	ChiB	7	43	233	5.4(77)	2	5	56	11.2(29)	0	—	—	—	—	—	—	—	—	—	—	—	—	12	281
1963	†ChiB	13(HB)	85	321	3.8(51)	5	13	131	10.1(44)	0	—	—	—	—	—	—	—	—	—	—	k	—	30	441
NFL	7	82	670	2985	4.5(77)	26	87	1201	13.8(84)	10	1	0	0.0	0	0.0	0	1	—	—	—	k	1	222	4321

GALLAGHER, BERNIE Bernard John, G, 6´0˝/234 lbs; Princeton; Pennsylvania; 1947: ChiR-A, rnd S/Det, rnd 6; B11/8/1921 Philadelphia, PA, D11/17/1988 East Landsdowne, PA **1947** LAD-A 8 (0)

GALLAGHER, DAVE David Dillon, DE-DT, 6´4˝/256 lbs; Michigan; 1974: Chi, rnd 1; B1/2/1952 Piqua, OH **1974** ChiB 14 (11, LDE) **1975** NYG 12 (10, LDE) **1976** NYG 14 (LDT) **1978** Det 1 **1979** Det 10 (LDT) **NFL** 51 (21) [5 yrs]

GALLAGHER, ED Edward Barto, T, 6´1˝/205 lbs; Washington & Jefferson; B2/3/1903 Philadelphia, PA, D10/1963 **1928** NYY 11 (11, LT)

GALLAGHER, FRANK Francis Joseph, G, 6´2˝/245 lbs; North Carolina; B3/2/1943 Chester, PA **1967** Det 13 **1968** Det 14 (RG) **1969** Det 14 (RG) **1970**†Det 14 (RG) **1971** Det 14 **1972** Det 14 **1973** Atl 3 **1973**†Min 4 **NFL** 90 [7 yrs]

GALLAHER, ALLEN Allen Ross, T, 6´3˝/250 lbs; USC; 1973: NE, rnd 4; B11/13/1950 San Fernando, CA **1974** NE 14

GALLARNEAU, HUGH Hugh Harold, HB, 6´0˝/190 lbs; Stanford; 1941: ChiB, rnd 3; B4/2/1917 Detroit, MI, D7/14/1999 Northbrook, IL

YEAR	TEAM	G(GS, POS)	RUSH	YD	AVG(LG)	TD	REC	YD	AVG(LG)	TD	PASS	COMP	PCT	YD	AVG(LG)	TD	INT	SK	YD	QBR	KPR	OTD	PTS	TAY
1941	†ChiB✧	11(8, RH)	49	304	6.2(40)	**8**	11	204	18.5(46)	2	—	—	—	—	—	—	—	—	—	—	kpi	1	66	578
1942	†ChiB	10(9, RH)	68	292	4.3(20)	4	14	291	20.8(60)	3	—	—	—	—	—	—	—	—	—	—	kp	—	42	625
1945	ChiB	8(7, RH)	75	260	3.5(31)	2	7	58	8.3(36)	1	—	—	—	—	—	—	—	—	—	—	kpi	—	18	302
1946	†ChiB☆	11(5, RH)	112	476	4.3(52)	6	12	185	15.4(36)	1	—	—	—	—	—	—	—	—	—	—	kp	1	48	723
1947	ChiB	12(4)	39	89	2.3(8)	6	7	56	8.0(28)	0	—	—	—	—	—	—	—	—	—	—	ki	—	36	194
NFL	5	52(33)	343	1421	4.1(52)	26	51	794	15.6(60)	7	—	—	—	—	—	—	—	—	—	—	kpi	2	210	2421

GALLEGOS, CHON Chon Fernando, QB, 5´9˝/175 lbs; San Jose State; B9/28/1939 Gallup, NM

YEAR	TEAM	G(GS, POS)	RUSH	YD	AVG(LG)	TD	REC	YD	AVG(LG)	TD	PASS	COMP	PCT	YD	AVG(LG)	TD	INT	SK	YD	QBR	KPR	OTD	PTS	TAY
1962	Oak-A	6	3	25	8.3(16)	0	—	—	—	—	35	18	51.4	298	8.5(35)	2	3	—	—	—	—	—	0	64

GALLERY, JIM James Patrick, K, 6´1˝/190 lbs; Minnesota; 1984: TB, rnd 10; B9/15/1961 Redwood Falls, MN **[K]** **1987** SL 13 (0) **1989** Cin 4 (0) **1990** Min 2 (0) **NFL** 19 (0) [3 yrs]

GALLERY, NICK Nick Patrick, P, 6´4˝/245 lbs; Iowa; B2/15/1975 Manchester, IA **1998** NYJ 1 (0)

GALLERY, ROBERT Robert, T, 6´7˝/307 lbs; Iowa; 2004: Oak, rnd 1; B7/26/1980 Manchester, IA **2004** Oak 16 (15, RT) **2005** Oak 16 (16, RT) **NFL** 32 (31) [2 yrs]

GALLISHAW, LARONI Laroni, DB, 6´0˝/190 lbs; Murray State; B4/4/1981 Lakeland, FL **2005** Min 5 (0)

GALLOVICH, TONY Anthony Richard, WB, 5´9˝/170 lbs; Wake Forest; 1941: Cle, rnd 8; B9/10/1917 Vandergrift, PA, D4/18/1999 Richmond, VA

YEAR	TEAM	G(GS, POS)	RUSH	YD	AVG(LG)	TD	REC	YD	AVG(LG)	TD	PASS	COMP	PCT	YD	AVG(LG)	TD	INT	SK	YD	QBR	KPR	OTD	PTS	TAY
1941	Cle	3(0)	1	1	1.0(1)	0	—	—	—	—	—	—	—	—	—	—	—	—	—	—	—	—	0	1

GALLOWAY, DAVID David Lawrence, DT-DE-NT, 6´3˝/277 lbs; Florida; 1982: SL, rnd 2; B2/16/1959 Tampa, FL **1982**†SL 5 (0) **1983** SL 16 (13, RDT) **1984** SL 14 (14, LDT) **1985** SL 16 (16, LDT) **1986** SL 14 (13, NT) **1987** SL 4 (3) **1988** Phx 8 (6, lde) **1989** Phx 12 (11, RDE) **1990** Den 10 (0) **NFL** 99 (76) [9 yrs]

GALLOWAY, DUANE Duane Keith, DB, 5´8˝/181 lbs; Arizona State; B11/7/1961 Los Angeles, CA **1985** Det 2 (0) **1986** Det 16 (12, LCB) **1987** Det 10 (7, LCB) **NFL** 28 (19) [3 yrs]

GALLOWAY, JOEY Joseph Scott, WR, 5´11˝/197 lbs; Ohio State; 1995: Sea, rnd 1; B11/20/1971 Bellaire, OH **[R]**

YEAR	TEAM	G(GS, POS)	RUSH	YD	AVG(LG)	TD	REC	YD	AVG(LG)	TD	PASS	COMP	PCT	YD	AVG(LG)	TD	INT	SK	YD	QBR	KPR	OTD	PTS	TAY
1995	Sea	16(16, WR)	11	154	14.0(86)	1	67	1039	15.5(59)	7	—	—	—	—	—	—	—	—	—	—	kp	1	54	909
1996	Sea	16(16, WR)	15	127	8.5(51)	0	57	987	17.3(65)	7	—	—	—	—	—	—	—	—	—	—	p	1	48	749
1997	Sea	15(15, WR)	9	72	8.0(44)	0	72	1049	14.6(53)	**12**	0	0	0.0	0	0.0	0	0	1	15	—	—	—	72	657
1998	Sea	16(16, WR)	9	26	2.9(14)	0	65	1047	16.1(81)	**10**	—	—	—	—	—	—	—	—	—	—	p	2	72	746
1999	†Sea	8(4)	1	-1	-1.0(-1)	0	22	335	15.2(48)	1	—	—	—	—	—	—	—	—	—	—	p	—	6	211
2000	Dal	1(1)	—	—	—	—	4	62	15.5(22)	1	—	—	—	—	—	—	—	—	—	—	p	—	6	33
2001	Dal	16(16, WR)	3	32	10.7(16)	0	52	699	13.4(47)	3	1	1	100.0	1	-1.0(-1)	0	0	—	—	—	p	—	18	397
2002	Dal	16(16, WR)	4	31	7.8(21)	0	61	908	14.9(80)	6	—	—	—	—	—	—	—	—	—	—	p	—	36	621
2003	†Dal	15(13, WR)	4	22	5.5(10)	0	34	672	**19.8(64)**	2	—	—	—	—	—	—	—	—	—	—	kp	—	12	454
2004	TB	10(7, WR)	2	19	9.5(14)	0	33	416	12.6(36)	5	—	—	—	—	—	—	—	—	—	—	p	1	36	304
2005	†TB	16(16, WR)	2	4	2.0(4)	0	83	1287	15.5(80)	10	—	—	—	—	—	—	—	—	—	—	—	—	60	698
NFL	11	145(136)	60	486	8.1(86)	1	550	8501	15.5(81)	64	1	1	100.0	1	-1.0	0	0	1	15	—	kp	5	420	5776

GALLOWAY, MITCHELL Mitchell, WR, 5´8˝/178 lbs; East Carolina; B10/8/1974 Chesterfield County, SC **1997** Buf 3 (0)

GALVIN, JOHN John E., QB, 5´10˝/170 lbs; Purdue; B12/7/1920 Chicago, IL, D12/23/1998 Oak Lawn, IL

YEAR	TEAM	G(GS, POS)	RUSH	YD	AVG(LG)	TD	REC	YD	AVG(LG)	TD	PASS	COMP	PCT	YD	AVG(LG)	TD	INT	SK	YD	QBR	KPR	OTD	PTS	TAY
1947	Bal-A	13(1)	1	-4	-4.0(-4)	0	—	—	—	—	6	3	50.0	34	5.7	0	0	—	—	—	Pk	—	0	21

GALVIN, JOHN John Blake, LB, 6´3˝/226 lbs; Boston College; 1988: NYJ, rnd 11; B7/9/1965 Lowell, MA **1988** NYJ 16 (0) **1989**†Min 11 (0) **1990** NYJ 16 (0) **1991** NYJ 9 (0) **NFL** 52 (0) [4 yrs]

GALYON, SCOTT Gregory Scott, LB, 6´2˝/245 lbs; Tennessee; 1996: NYG, rnd 6; B3/23/1974 Seymour, TN **1996** NYG 16 (0) **1997**†NYG 16 (0) **1998** NYG 10 (1) **1999** NYG 16 (0) **2000** Mia 6 (1) **2001**†Mia 16 (2) **2002** Mia 15 (0) **NFL** 95 (4) [7 yrs]

GAMACHE, VINCENT Vincent Lucky, P, 5´11˝/174 lbs; Cal State-Fullerton; B11/18/1961 Los Angeles, CA **1986** Sea 16 (0) **1987** LARd 3 (0) **NFL** 19 (0) [2 yrs]

GAMBINO, LU Lucien Anthony, FB, 6´1˝/205 lbs; Indiana; Maryland; 1948: Cle-A, rnd 22/1945: ChiB, rnd 26; B9/21/1923 Berwyn, IL, D7/16/2003 Chicago, IL

YEAR	TEAM	G(GS, POS)	RUSH	YD	AVG(LG)	TD	REC	YD	AVG(LG)	TD	PASS	COMP	PCT	YD	AVG(LG)	TD	INT	SK	YD	QBR	KPR	OTD	PTS	TAY
1948	†Bal-A	9(1)	54	194	3.6	1	6	28	4.7	0	—	—	—	—	—	—	—	—	—	—	k	—	6	230
1949	Bal-A	10(6, FB)	56	208	3.7	0	10	67	6.7	1	—	—	—	—	—	—	—	—	—	—	—	—	6	247
AAFC	2	19(7)	110	402	3.7	1	16	95	5.9	1	—	—	—	—	—	—	—	—	—	—	k	—	12	477

GAMBLE, CHRIS Chris, DB, 6´2˝/195 lbs; Ohio State; 2004: Car, rnd 1; B3/11/1983 Boston, MA **2004** Car 16 (16, RCB) **2005**†Car 15 (15, RCB) **NFL** 31 (31) [2 yrs]

GAMBLE, DAVID David Anthony, WR, 6´1˝/190 lbs; New Hampshire; B6/14/1971 Albany, NY **1997** Den 2 (0)

GAMBLE, KENNY Kenneth Patrick, RB-DB, 5´10˝/197 lbs; Colgate; 1988: KC, rnd 10; B3/8/1965 Holyoke, MA

YEAR	TEAM	G(GS, POS)	RUSH	YD	AVG(LG)	TD	REC	YD	AVG(LG)	TD	PASS	COMP	PCT	YD	AVG(LG)	TD	INT	SK	YD	QBR	KPR	OTD	PTS	TAY
1988	KC	16(0)	—	—	—	—	1	-7	-7.0(-7)	0	—	—	—	—	—	—	—	—	—	—	ki	—	0	60
1989	KC	2(0)	6	24	4.0(20)	1	2	2	1.0(6)	0	—	—	—	—	—	—	—	—	—	—	k	—	6	45
1990	KC	1(0)	—	—	—	—	—	—	—	—	—	—	—	—	—	—	—	—	—	—	—	—	—	—
NFL	3	19(0)	6	24	4.0(20)	1	3	-5	-1.7(6)	0	—	—	—	—	—	—	—	—	—	—	ki	—	6	105

GAMBLE, R.C. R.C., RB, 6´3˝/220 lbs; South Carolina State; 1968: Bos, rnd 4; B9/27/1946 Greenville, SC

YEAR	TEAM	G(GS, POS)	RUSH	YD	AVG(LG)	TD	REC	YD	AVG(LG)	TD	PASS	COMP	PCT	YD	AVG(LG)	TD	INT	SK	YD	QBR	KPR	OTD	PTS	TAY
1968	Bos-A	14(8, HB)	78	311	4.0(45)	1	11	55	5.0(16)	1	—	—	—	—	—	—	—	—	—	—	k	—	12	339
1969	Bos-A	13(5, hb)	16	35	2.2(9)	0	7	74	10.6(20)	0	—	—	—	—	—	—	—	—	—	—	kp	—	0	80
NFL	2	27(13)	94	346	3.7(45)	1	18	129	7.2(20)	1	—	—	—	—	—	—	—	—	—	—	kp	—	12	419

GAMBLE, TRENT Trent Ashford, DB, 5´9˝/185 lbs; Wyoming; B7/24/1977 Denver, CO **2000**†Mia 16 (0) **2001** Mia 1 (0) **2002** Mia 13 (0) **2003** Mia 9 (1) **NFL** 39 (1) [4 yrs]

GAMBOL, CHRIS Christopher Hughes, G-T, 6´6˝/303 lbs; Iowa; 1987: Ind, rnd 3; B9/14/1964 Pittsburgh, PA **1988** Ind 1 (0) **1988** SD 11 (0) **1989** Det 6 (0) **1990** NE 16 (15, LG) **NFL** 34 (15) [3 yrs]

YEAR	TEAM	G(GS, POS)	RUSH	YD	AVG(LG)	TD	REC	YD	AVG(LG)	TD	PASS	COMP	PCT	YD	AVG(LG)	TD	INT	SK	YD	QBR	KPR	OTD	PTS	TAY

GAMBOLD, BOB   Robert Lee, QB, 6´4˝/215 lbs; Washington State; 1950: ChiC, rnd 24; B2/5/1929 Longview, WA

| 1953 | Phi | 3 | 2 | -2 | -1.0(0) | 0 | — | — | — | — | 14 | 6 | 42.9 | 107 | 7.6(41) | 0 | 2 | — | — | — | — | — | 0 | -29 |

GAMBRELL, BILLY   William Edward, SE-FL-WR, 5´10˝/175 lbs; South Carolina; 1963: Bos, rnd 12; B9/18/1941 Athens, GA

1963	SL	14	—	—	—	—	3	63	21.0(33)	0	—	—	—	—	—	—	—	—	—	—	p	—	0	88
1964	SL	14(se)	—	—	—	—	24	398	16.6(47)	2	—	—	—	—	—	—	—	—	—	—	kp	—	12	307
1965	SL	10	4	15	3.8(11)	0	9	171	19.0(59)	2	—	—	—	—	—	—	—	—	—	—	kp	—	12	186
1966	SL	14	3	26	8.7(24)	0	24	409	17.0(49)	5	—	—	—	—	—	—	—	—	—	—	kp	—	30	283
1967	SL	12(SE)	—	—	—	—	28	398	14.2(48)	2	—	—	—	—	—	—	—	—	—	—	—	—	12	209
1968	Det	14(FL)	—	—	—	—	28	492	17.6(50)	7	—	—	—	—	—	—	—	—	—	—	kp	—	42	278
NFL	6	78	7	41	5.9(24)	0	116	1931	16.6(59)	18	—	—	—	—	—	—	—	—	—	—	kp	—	108	1350

GAMMON, KENDALL   Kendall Robert, C-TE, 6´4˝/255 lbs; Pittsburg State; 1992: Pit, rnd 11; B10/23/1968 Wichita, KS   **1992**†Pit 16 (0)   **1993**†Pit 16 (0)   **1994**†Pit 16 (0)   **1995**†Pit 16 (0)   **1996** NO 16 (0)   **1997** NO 16 (0)   **1998** NO 16 (0)   **1999** NO 16 (0)   **2000** KC 16 (0)   **2001** KC 16 (0)   **2002** KC 16 (0)   **2003**†KC 16 (0)   **2004** KC◇16 (0)   **2005** KC 10 (0)   **NFL** 218 (0) [14 yrs]

GANAS, RUSTY   Russell Lindberg, DT, 6´4˝/257 lbs; South Carolina; B8/12/1949 Waycross, GA   **1971** Bal 1

GANDEE, SONNY   Sherman Kenneth, LB-DE, 6´1˝/216 lbs; Ohio State; 1952: Det, rnd 9; B2/27/1929 Akron, OH, D10/8/1985 Akron, OH   **1952** DalT 2   **1952** Det 8   **1953**†Det 8   **1954**†Det 11   **1955** Det 12 (RLB)   **1956** Det 12 (LLB)   **NFL** 53 [5 yrs]

GANDY, DYLAN   Dylan, G, 6´3˝/300 lbs; Texas Tech; 2005: Ind, rnd 4; B3/8/1982 Harlingen, TX   **2005**†Ind 16 (2)

GANDY, MIKE   Michael Joseph, T-G, 6´4˝/325 lbs; Notre Dame; 2001: Chi, rnd 3; B1/3/1979 Rockford, IL   **2002** ChiB 13 (11, LT/lg)   **2003** ChiB 14 (14, LT)   **2004** ChiB 5 (5, rg)   **2005** Buf 16 (16, LT)   **NFL** 48 (46) [4 yrs]

GANDY, WAYNE   Wayne Lamar, T, 6´4˝/308 lbs; Auburn; 1994: LARm, rnd 1; B2/10/1971 Haines City, FL   **1994** LARm 16 (9, RT)   **1995** SL 16 (16, LT)   **1996** SL 16 (16, LT)   **1997** SL 16 (16, RT)   **1998** SL 16 (16, RT)   **1999** Pit 16 (16, LT)   **2000** Pit 16 (16, LT)   **2001**†Pit 15 (15, LT)   **2002**†Pit 16 (16, LT)   **2003** NO 16 (16, LT)   **2004** NO 16 (16, LT)   **2005** NO 16 (16, LT)   **NFL** 191 (184) [12 yrs]

GANN, MIKE   Michael Alan, DE, 6´5˝/271 lbs; Notre Dame; 1985: Atl, rnd 2; B10/19/1963 Stillwater, OK   **1985** Atl 16 (16, RDE)   **1986** Atl 16 (16, LDE)   **1987** Atl 12 (12, LDE)   **1988** Atl 16 (16, LDE)   **1989** Atl 16 (16, LDE)   **1990** Atl 16 (15, LDE)   **1991** Atl 5 (5, lde)   **1992** Atl 13 (13, LDE)   **1993** Atl 8 (8, LDE)   **NFL** 118 (117) [9 yrs]

GANNON, CHRIS   Christopher Stephen, DE-TE, 6´6˝/265 lbs; Louisiana-Lafayette; 1989: NE, rnd 3; B1/20/1966 Brandon, FL   **1989** SD 10 (1)   **1991** NE 8 (0)   **1992** NE 12 (0)   **1993** NE 4 (1)

| 1990 | NE | 6(2) | 1 | 0 | 0.0(0) | 0 | — | — | — | — | — | — | — | — | — | — | — | — | — | — | S | — | 0 | 0 |
| NFL | 5 | 40(4) | 1 | 0 | 0.0 | 0 | — | — | — | — | — | — | — | — | — | — | — | — | — | — | S | — | 0 | 0 |

GANNON, RICH   Richard Joseph, QB, 6´3˝/210 lbs; Delaware; 1987: NE, rnd 4; B12/20/1965 Philadelphia, PA

1987	†Min	4(0)	—	—	—	—	—	—	—	—	6	2	33.3	18	3.0(12)	0	1	—	—	—	—	—	0	-31
1988	†Min	3(0)	4	29	7.3(15)	0	—	—	—	—	15	7	46.7	90	6.0(19)	0	0	3	22	—	—	—	0	74
1989	†Min	0(0)	—	—	—	—	—	—	—	—	—	—	—	—	—	—	—	—	—	—	—	—	0	0
1990	Min	14(12, QB)	52	268	5.2(27)	1	—	—	—	—	349	182	52.1	2278	6.5(78)	16	16	34	188	68.9	—	—	6	857
1991	Min	15(11, QB)	43	236	5.5(42)	2	1	0	0.0(0)	0	354	211	59.6	2166	6.1(50)	12	6	19	91	81.5	—	—	12	1159
1992	Min	12(12, QB)	45	187	4.2(14)	0	—	—	—	—	279	159	57.0	1905	6.8(60)	12	13	25	177	72.9	—	—	0	680
1993	Was	8(4)	21	88	4.2(12)	1	—	—	—	—	125	74	59.2	704	5.6(54)	3	7	16	87	—	—	—	6	185
1995	†KC	2(0)	8	25	3.1(12)	1	—	—	—	—	11	7	63.6	57	5.2(18)	0	0	—	—	—	—	—	6	64
1996	KC	4(3)	12	81	6.8(19)	0	—	—	—	—	90	54	60.0	491	5.5(25)	6	1	5	42	—	—	—	0	317
1997	KC	9(6, qb)	33	109	3.3(13)	2	—	—	—	—	175	98	56.0	1144	6.5(47)	7	4	13	86	—	—	—	12	576
1998	KC	12(10, QB)	44	168	3.8(21)	3	—	—	—	—	354	206	58.2	2305	6.5(55)	10	6	25	155	80.1	—	—	18	1161
1999	Oak◇	16(16, QB)	46	298	6.5(39)	2	1	-3	-3.0(-3)	0	515	304	59.0	3840	7.5(50)	24	14	49	241	86.5	—	—	12	1797
2000	†Oak★	16(16, QB)	89	529	5.9(23)	4	—	—	—	—	473	284	60.0	3430	7.3(84)	28	11	28	124	92.4	—	—	26	1984
2001	†Oak★	16(16, QB)	63	231	3.7(17)	2	—	—	—	—	549	361	65.8	3828	7.0(49)	27	9	27	155	95.5	—	—	14	1940
2002	†Oak★	16(16, QB)	50	156	3.1(14)	3	—	—	—	—	618	418	67.6	4689	7.6(75)	26	10	36	214	97.3	—	—	18	2261
2003	Oak	7(7, qb)	6	18	3.0(6)	0	—	—	—	—	225	125	55.6	1274	5.7(46)	6	4	17	90	73.5	—	—	0	525
2004	Oak	3(3)	5	26	5.2(20)	0	—	—	—	—	68	41	60.3	524	7.7(58)	3	2	5	17	—	—	—	0	223
NFL	17	157(132)	521	2449	4.7(42)	21	2	-3	-1.5	0	4206	2533	60.2	28743	6.8(84)	180	104	302	1689	84.7	—	—	130	13769

GANSBERG, AL   Alfred Henry, E-T, 5´11˝/187 lbs; Miami (OH); B10/16/1901 Lake Forest, IL, D8/24/1976 Evanston, IL   **1926** Lou 3 (0)

GANT, BRIAN   Brian Keith, LB, 6´0˝/235 lbs; Illinois State; B9/6/1965 Gary, IN   **1987** TB 11 (3)

GANT, EARL   Earl Leon, RB, 6´0˝/207 lbs; Missouri; 1979: KC, rnd 5; B7/6/1957 Chicago, IL

1979	KC	16	56	196	3.5(16)	1	15	101	6.7(26)	0	—	—	—	—	—	—	—	—	—	—	k	—	6	272
1980	KC	4(0)	9	32	3.6(11)	0	9	68	7.6(33)	0	—	—	—	—	—	—	—	—	—	—	k	—	0	65
NFL	2	20	65	228	3.5(16)	1	24	169	7.0(33)	0	—	—	—	—	—	—	—	—	—	—	k	—	6	337

GANT, KENNETH   Kenneth Dwayne, DB, 5´11˝/195 lbs; Albany State (GA); 1990: Dal, rnd 9; B4/18/1967 Bartow, FL   **1990** Dal 12 (0)   **1991**†Dal 16 (1)   **1992**†Dal 16 (4)   **1993**†Dal 12 (1)   **1994**†Dal 16 (0)   **1995** TB 16 (3)   **1996** TB 16 (0)   **1997**†TB 9 (0)   **NFL** 113 (9) [8 yrs]

GANT, REUBEN   Reuben Charles, TE-WR, 6´4˝/230 lbs; Oklahoma State; 1974: Buf, rnd 1; B4/12/1952 Tulsa, OK

1974	Buf	13	—	—	—	—	—	—	—	—	—	—	—	—	—	—	—	—	—	—	—	—	—	—
1975	Buf	14	—	—	—	—	9	107	11.9(19)	2	—	—	—	—	—	—	—	—	—	—	—	—	12	64
1976	Buf	14(7, wr)	—	—	—	—	12	263	21.9(39)	3	—	—	—	—	—	—	—	—	—	—	—	—	18	147
1977	Buf	14(1)	—	—	—	—	41	646	15.8(39)	2	—	—	—	—	—	—	—	—	—	—	—	—	12	333
1978	Buf	16(16, TE)	1	14	14.0(14)	0	34	408	12.0(25)	5	—	—	—	—	—	—	—	—	—	—	—	—	30	243
1979	Buf	14(14, TE)	—	—	—	—	19	245	12.9(22)	2	—	—	—	—	—	—	—	—	—	—	—	—	12	133
1980	†Buf	16(11, TE)	—	—	—	—	12	181	15.1(48)	1	—	—	—	—	—	—	—	—	—	—	—	—	6	96
NFL	7	101(49)	1	14	14.0(14)	0	127	1850	14.6(48)	15	—	—	—	—	—	—	—	—	—	—	—	—	90	1014

GANTENBEIN, MILT   Milton Edward, E-DE, 6´0˝/193 lbs; Wisconsin; B5/31/1910 New Albin, IA, D12/18/1988 Carmichael, CA

1931	GB	14(6, re)	—	—	—	—	—	—	—	—	—	—	—	—	—	—	—	—	—	—	—	—	—	—
1932	GB	9(8, RE)	—	—	—	—	2	71	35.5	0	—	—	—	—	—	—	—	—	—	—	—	—	0	36
1933	GB	12(10, RE)	—	—	—	—	6	144	24.0	1	—	—	—	—	—	—	—	—	—	—	—	—	6	77
1934	GB	10(7, LE)	—	—	—	—	10	155	15.5	0	—	—	—	—	—	—	—	—	—	—	—	—	0	78
1935	GB	11(9, RE)	—	—	—	—	12	168	14.0	1	—	—	—	—	—	—	—	—	—	—	—	—	6	89
1936	†GB☆	9(9, RE)	—	—	—	—	15	221	14.7	1	—	—	—	—	—	—	—	—	—	—	—	—	6	116
1937	†GB☆	11(9, RE)	—	—	—	—	12	237	19.8(77)	2	—	—	—	—	—	—	—	—	—	—	—	—	12	129
1938	†GB☆	11(7, RE)	—	—	—	—	12	164	13.7(29)	1	—	—	—	—	—	—	—	—	—	—	—	—	6	87
1939	†GB◇	11(5, re)	—	—	—	—	7	127	18.1(32)	1	—	—	—	—	—	—	—	—	—	—	—	—	6	69
1940	GB	5(1)	—	—	—	—	1	12	12.0(12)	0	—	—	—	—	—	—	—	—	—	—	—	—	0	6
NFL	10	103(71)	—	—	—	—	77	1299	16.9(77)	8	—	—	—	—	—	—	—	—	—	—	—	—	48	690

GANTT, GREG   Lewis Gregory, P, 5´11˝/188 lbs; Alabama; 1974: NYJ, rnd 8; B10/30/1951 Birmingham, AL [K]   **1974** NYJ 14

| 1975 | NYJ | 14 | — | — | — | — | — | — | — | — | 1 | 1 | 100.0 | 1 | 1.0(1) | 0 | 0 | — | — | — | P | — | 0 | 1 |
| NFL | 2 | 28 | — | — | — | — | — | — | — | — | 1 | 1 | 100.0 | 1 | 1.0(1) | 0 | 0 | — | — | — | KP | — | 1 | 1 |

GANTT, JERRY   Jerome Floyd, T, 6´4˝/266 lbs; North Carolina Central; 1970: Buf, rnd 4; B8/20/1948 Greensboro, NC   **1970** Buf 6

GAONA, BOB   Robert John, T, 6´3˝/243 lbs; Wake Forest; 1953: Pit, rnd 5; B1/3/1931 Ambridge, PA, D5/23/2001 Durham, NC   **1953** Pit 12 (LT)   **1955** Pit 12 (LT)   **1956** Pit 12 (LT)

1954	Pit	12(LT)	—	—	—	—	0	25	(25)	0	—	—	—	—	—	—	—	—	—	—	—	—	0	13
1957	Phi	12(RT)	—	—	—	—	1	-9	-9.0(-9)	0	—	—	—	—	—	—	—	—	—	—	—	—	0	-5
NFL	5	60	—	—	—	—	1	16	16.0(16)	0	—	—	—	—	—	—	—	—	—	—	k	—	0	-33

GARALCZYK, MARK   Mark Patrick, DT-DE, 6´5˝/272 lbs; Western Michigan; 1987: SL, rnd 5; B8/12/1964 Roseville, MI   **1987** SL 11 (3)   **1988** Phx 6 (0)   **1988** NYJ 7 (0)   **NFL** 24 (3) [2 yrs]

GARAY, ANTONIO   Antonio, DE, 6´4˝/300 lbs; Boston College; 2003: Cle, rnd 6; B11/30/1979 Rahway, NJ   **2003** Cle 4 (0)

YEAR	TEAM	G(GS, POS)	RUSH	YD	AVG(LG)	TD	REC	YD	AVG(LG)	TD	PASS	COMP	PCT	YD	AVG(LG)	TD	INT	SK	YD	QBR	KPR	OTD	PTS	TAY

GARBARCZYK, TONY Anthony Stephen, DE, 6´4˝/275 lbs; Wake Forest; 1986: Buf, rnd 11; B1/20/1964 Queens, NY **1987** NYJ 2 (0)

GARCIA, BUBBA Jesse Clarence, WR, 5´11˝/185 lbs; Texas-El Paso; 1980: KC, rnd 6; B10/18/1957 New Braunfels, TX **1981** KC 1 (0)

| 1980 | KC | 5 (0) | — | — | — | — | 3 | 27 | 9.0(10) | 1 | — | — | — | — | — | — | — | — | — | — | — | — | 6 | 19 |
| NFL | 2 | 6 (0) | — | — | — | — | 3 | 27 | 9.0(10) | 1 | — | — | — | — | — | — | — | — | — | — | — | — | 6 | 19 |

GARCIA, EDDIE Edgar Ivan, K, 5´8˝/178 lbs; SMU; 1982: GB, rnd 10; B4/15/1959 New Orleans, LA [K] **1983** GB 12 (0) **1984** GB 7 (0) **NFL** 19 (0) [2 yrs]

GARCIA, FRANK Frank Benitez, P, 6´0˝/205 lbs; Arizona State; UNLV; Arizona; B6/5/1957 Tucson, AZ [P] **1981** Sea 1 (0) **1983** TB☆16 (0) **1985** TB 16 (0) **1987** TB 12 (0)

1984	TB	16 (0)	—	—	—	—	—	—	—	—	1	0	0.0	0	0.0	0	0	—	—	P	—	—	0	0
1986	TB	16 (0)	1	-11	-11.0(-11)	0	—	—	—	—	0	0	—	—	—	—	—	—	—	P	—	—	0	-11
NFL	6	77 (0)	1	-11	-11.0(-11)	0	—	—	—	—	1	0	0.0	0	0.0	0	0	—	—	P	—	—	0	-11

GARCIA, FRANK Frank Christopher, C-G, 6´2˝/302 lbs; Washington; 1995: Car, rnd 4; B1/28/1972 Phoenix, AZ **1995** Car 15 (14, LG) **1996**†Car 14 (8, c/lg) **1997** Car 16 (16, C) **1998** Car 14 (14, LG/c) **1999** Car 16 (16, C) **2000** Car 16 (16, C) **2001**†SL 13 (2) **2002** SL 14 (3) **2003** Arz 7 (3) **NFL** 125 (92) [9 yrs]

GARCIA, JEFF Jeff, QB, 6´1˝/195 lbs; San Jose State; B2/24/1970 Gilroy, CA

1999	SF	13 (10, QB)	45	231	5.1(25)	2	—	—	—	—	375	225	60.0	2544	6.8(62)	11	11	15	104	77.9	—	—	12	1138
2000	SF◇	72	414	5.8(33)	4	—	—	—	—	561	355	63.3	4278	7.6(69)	31	10	24	155	97.6	—	—	24	2348		16 (16, QB)
2001	†SF◇	16 (16, QB)	72	254	3.5(25)	5	—	—	—	—	504	316	62.7	3538	7.0(61)	32	12	26	114	94.8	—	—	30	1753
2002	†SF◇	16 (16, QB)	73	353	4.8(21)	3	—	—	—	—	528	328	62.1	3344	6.3(76)	21	10	17	93	85.6	—	—	20	1760
2003	SF	13 (13, QB)	56	319	5.7(21)	7	1	6	6.0(6)	0	392	225	57.4	2704	6.9(75)	18	13	21	104	80.1	—	—	42	1314
2004	Cle	11 (10, QB)	35	169	4.8(21)	0	—	—	—	—	252	144	57.1	1731	6.9(99)	10	9	24	99	76.7	—	—	12	745
2005	Det	6 (5, qb)	17	51	3.0(14)	1	—	—	—	—	173	102	59.0	937	5.4(49)	3	6	6	34	65.1	—	—	6	305
NFL	7	91 (86)	370	1791	4.8(33)	24	1	6	6.0(6)	0	2785	1695	60.9	19076	6.8(99)	126	71	133	703	85.8	—	—	146	9362

GARCIA, JIM James Ronald, DE-DT, 6´4˝/250 lbs; Purdue; 1965: Cle, rnd 2/Den, rnd 7; B3/7/1944 Chicago, IL **1965**†Cle 12 **1966** NYG 10 **1967** NO 12 **1968** Atl 1 **NFL** 35 [4 yrs]

GARCIA, TEDDY Alfonso Teddy, K, 5´10˝/187 lbs; Louisiana-Monroe; 1988: NE, rnd 4; B6/4/1964 Caddo Parish, LA [K] **1988** NE 16 (0) **1989** Min 3 (0) **1990**†Hou 9 (0) **NFL** 28 (0) [3 yrs]

GARDELLA, GUS Augustus Michael, FB, /190 lbs; none; B7/22/1895 New York, NY, D6/4/1985 Bridgeport, CT **1922** GB 7 (3)

GARDEN, FRANK Frank, E, 5´11˝/188 lbs; none; B6/3/1898, D6/26/1966 Santa Monica, CA **1920** RI 2 (0) **1923** Cle 2 (0) **1925** Cle 1 (0) **NFL** 5 (0) [3 yrs]

GARDENER, DARYL Daryl Ronald, DT, 6´6˝/295 lbs; Baylor; 1996: Mia, rnd 1; B2/25/1973 Baltimore, MD **1996** Mia 16 (12, LDT) **1997**†Mia 16 (16, RDT) **1998**†Mia 16 (16, RDT) **1999**†Mia 16 (15, RDT) **2000**†Mia 10 (10, RDT) **2001** Mia 8 (8, RDT) **2002** Was 15 (15, RDT) **2003** Den 5 (2) **NFL** 102 (94) [8 yrs]

GARDIN, RON Ronald Lee, DB-WR, 5´11˝/180 lbs; Cameron; Arizona; 1970: Bal, rnd 6; B9/25/1944 New Haven, CT **1970**†Bal 13 **1971** Bal 1 **1971** NE 8 **NFL** 22 [2 yrs]

GARDNER, BARRY Barry Allan, LB, 6´1˝/245 lbs; Northwestern; 1999: Phi, rnd 2; B12/13/1976 Harvey, IL **1999** Phi 16 (5, llb) **2000**†Phi 16 (13, LLB) **2001**†Phi 16 (0) **2002**†Phi 16 (0) **2003** Cle 16 (0) **2004** Cle 14 (5, mlb) **2005** NYJ 16 (1) **NFL** 110 (24) [7 yrs]

GARDNER, BIRDIE William, T, 6´3˝/260 lbs; Carlisle Indian; B1883, deceased **1920** Can 1 (0)

GARDNER, CARWELL Carwell Ernest, FB, 6´2˝/240 lbs; Kentucky; Louisville; 1990: Buf, rnd 2; B11/27/1966 Baltimore, MD

1990	†Buf	7 (0)	15	41	2.7(14)	0	—	—	—	—	—	—	—	—	—	—	—	—	—	—	—	—	0	41
1991	†Buf	16 (5, fb)	42	146	3.5(18)	4	3	20	6.7(11)	0	—	—	—	—	—	—	—	—	—	—	k	—	24	191
1992	†Buf	16 (7, fb)	40	166	4.2(19)	2	7	67	9.6(17)	0	—	—	—	—	—	—	—	—	—	—	—	—	12	220
1993	†Buf	13 (0)	20	56	2.8(8)	0	4	50	12.5(22)	1	—	—	—	—	—	—	—	—	—	—	—	—	6	86
1994	Buf	16 (7, fb)	41	135	3.3(13)	4	11	89	8.1(21)	0	—	—	—	—	—	—	—	—	—	—	k	—	24	211
1995	†Buf	15 (4)	20	77	3.8(17)	0	2	17	8.5(13)	0	—	—	—	—	—	—	—	—	—	—	—	1	8	86
1996	Bal	13 (3)	26	108	4.2(19)	0	7	28	4.0(7)	0	—	—	—	—	—	—	—	—	—	—	—	—	2	122
1997	SD	5 (2)	7	20	2.9(5)	0	2	10	5.0(8)	0	—	—	—	—	—	—	—	—	—	—	—	—	0	25
NFL	8	101 (30)	211	749	3.5(19)	10	36	281	7.8(22)	1	—	—	—	—	—	—	—	—	—	—	k	1	76	981

GARDNER, DERRICK Derrick, DB, 6´0˝/185 lbs; California; B3/10/1977 Oakland, CA **1999** Atl 7 (0)

GARDNER, DONNIE Redondo Lee, DE, 6´3˝/260 lbs; Kentucky; 1990: TB, rnd 7; B2/17/1968 Louisville, KY **1991** Mia 10 (0)

GARDNER, ELLIS Ellis Peniston, T-G, 6´5˝/257 lbs; Georgia Tech; 1983: KC, rnd 6; B9/16/1961 Chattanooga, TN **1983** KC 8 (0) **1984** Ind 9 (0) **NFL** 17 (0) [2 yrs]

GARDNER, GILBERT Gilbert Ravelle, LB, 6´2˝/234 lbs; Purdue; 2004: Ind, rnd 3; B5/9/1982 Angleton, TX **2004**†Ind 11 (0) **2005**†Ind 11 (3) **NFL** 22 (3) [2 yrs]

GARDNER, MOE Morris, DT-NT, 6´2˝/265 lbs; Illinois; 1991: Atl, rnd 4; B8/10/1968 Indianapolis, IN **1991**†Atl 16 (13, NT) **1992** Atl 16 (14, NT) **1993** Atl 16 (16, RDT) **1994** Atl 16 (16, RDT) **1995**†Atl 16 (15, RDT) **1996** Atl 10 (10, RDT) **NFL** 90 (84) [6 yrs]

GARDNER, MOOSE Milton LeRoy, G, 6´1˝/220 lbs; Wisconsin; B7/2/1894 Ashland, WI, D12/23/1954 Rocky River, OH **1920** Det 2 (2) **1921** Det 7 (7, RG) **1921** Buf 1 (0) **1922** GB 9 (7, RG) **1923** GB 9 (7, RG) **1924** GB 11 (11, RG) **1925** GB 13 (10, RG), 6 **1926** GB 13 (13, RG) **NFL** 65 (57) [7 yrs]

GARDNER, RICH Richard James, DB, 5´11˝/185 lbs; Penn State; 2004: Ten, rnd 3; B2/1/1981 Carbondale, IL **2004** Ten 15 (1) **2005** Ten 13 (0) **NFL** 28 (1) [2 yrs]

GARDNER, ROD Roderick F., WR, 6´2˝/213 lbs; Clemson; 2001: Was, rnd 1; B10/26/1977 Jacksonville, FL

2001	Was	16 (16, WR)	1	16	16.0(16)	0	46	741	16.1(85)	4	—	—	—	—	—	—	—	—	—	—	—	—	24	407
2002	Was	16 (15, WR)	1	1	1.0(1)	0	71	1006	14.2(43)	8	1	0	0.0	0	0.0	0	0	—	—	—	—	—	48	544
2003	Was	16 (16, WR)	—	—	—	—	59	600	10.2(35)	5	3	2	66.7	46	15.3(36)	2	0	—	—	—	—	—	30	358
2004	Was	16 (14, WR)	3	7	2.3(11)	0	51	650	12.7(51)	5	3	0	0.0	0	0.0	0	0	—	—	—	—	—	30	357
2005	Car	10 (0)	—	—	—	—	9	84	9.3(15)	1	—	—	—	—	—	—	—	—	—	—	—	—	6	47
2005	GB	2 (1)	—	—	—	—	4	67	16.8(33)	0	—	—	—	—	—	—	—	—	—	—	—	—	0	34
NFL	5	76 (62)	5	24	4.8(16)	0	240	3148	13.1(85)	23	7	2	28.6	46	6.6(36)	2	0	—	—	—	—	—	138	1746

GARDNER, TALMAN Talman, WR, 6´1˝/205 lbs; Florida State; 2003: NO, rnd 7; B3/10/1980 New Orleans, LA

2003	NO	10 (1)	—	—	—	—	3	29	9.7(11)	0	—	—	—	—	—	—	—	—	—	—	—	—	0	15
2004	NO	11 (1)	—	—	—	—	1	23	23.0(23)	0	—	—	—	—	—	—	—	—	—	—	—	—	0	12
NFL	2	21 (2)	—	—	—	—	4	52	13.0(23)	0	—	—	—	—	—	—	—	—	—	—	—	—	0	26

GARDOCKI, CHRIS Christopher Alan, P, 6´1˝/200 lbs; Clemson; 1991: Chi, rnd 3; B2/7/1970 Stone Mountain, GA [P] **1991**†ChiB 4 (0) **1994**†ChiB 16 (0) **1996**†Ind★16 (0) **1997** Ind 16 (0) **1998** Ind 16 (0) **1999** Cle 16 (0) **2000** Cle☆16 (0) **2001** Cle 16 (0) **2002**†Cle 16 (0) **2003** Cle 16 (0) **2004**†Pit 16 (0)

1992	ChiB	16 (0)	—	—	—	—	—	—	—	—	3	1	33.3	43	14.3(43)	0	0	—	—	P	—	—	0	22
1993	ChiB	16 (0)	—	—	—	—	—	—	—	—	2	0	0.0	0	0.0	0	0	—	—	P	—	—	0	0
1995	†Ind	16 (0)	—	—	—	—	—	—	—	—	1	0	0.0	0	0.0	0	0	—	—	P	—	—	0	0
2005	†Pit	16 (0)	—	—	—	—	—	—	—	—	1	0	0.0	0	0.0	0	0	—	—	P	—	—	0	0
NFL	15	228 (0)	—	—	—	—	—	—	—	—	7	1	14.3	43	6.1(43)	0	0	—	—	P	—	—	0	22

GARLICH, CHRIS Christopher James, LB, 6´1˝/220 lbs; Missouri; B7/17/1957 St. Louis, MO **1979** SL 9

GARLIN, DON Donald Arthur, HB-DB, 5´11˝/188 lbs; USC; B11/10/1926 Porterville, CA, D7/29/1999 Bodega Bay, CA

| 1949 | †SF-A | 11 (0) | 21 | 113 | 5.4(60) | 1 | 6 | 64 | 10.7 | 0 | — | — | — | — | — | — | — | — | — | — | ki | — | 6 | 156 |
| 1950 | SF | 8 | 3 | 3 | 1.0(2) | 0 | — | — | — | — | — | — | — | — | — | — | — | — | — | — | — | — | 0 | 12 |

GARLINGTON, JOHN John M., LB, 6´1˝/218 lbs; LSU; 1968: Cle, rnd 2; B6/5/1946 Jonesboro, LA, D2/10/2000 Mill Creek, LA **1968**†Cle 13 (rlb) **1969**†Cle 14 (RLB) **1970** Cle 11 (rlb) **1971**†Cle 14 (llb) **1972** Cle 14 (rlb) **1973** Cle 14 (RLB) **1974** Cle 14 (RLB) **1975** Cle 7 (6, rlb) **1976** Cle 14 (RLB) **1977** Cle 13 (RLB) **NFL** 128 (6) [10 yrs]

GARMON, KELVIN Kelvin, G, 6´2˝/350 lbs; Baylor; 1999: Dal, rnd 7; B10/26/1976 Fort Worth, TX **2001** Dal 16 (16, RG) **2002** Dal 5 (5, rg) **2002** SD 7 (5, lg) **2003** SD 16 (16, LG) **2004** Cle 8 (8, RG) **NFL** 52 (50) [4 yrs]

GARNAAS, BILL Wilford Benjamin, QB, 5´11˝/187 lbs; Minnesota; 1944: ChiC, rnd 6; B10/8/1921 Oberon, ND, D5/9/2002 St. Paul, MN

1946	Pit	10 (3)	—	—	—	—	3	56	18.7(30)	1	—	—	—	—	—	—	—	—	—	k	—	—	6	32
1947	†Pit	10 (0)	—	—	—	—	5	144	28.8(68)	2	—	—	—	—	—	—	—	—	—	k	—	—	12	84
1948	Pit	6 (0)	—	—	—	—	—	—	—	—	—	—	—	—	—	—	—	—	—	k	—	—	0	3
NFL	3	26 (3)	—	—	—	—	8	200	25.0(68)	3	—	—	—	—	—	—	—	—	—	k	—	—	18	119

YEAR	TEAM	G (GS, POS)	RUSH	YD	AVG(LG)	TD	REC	YD	AVG(LG)	TD	PASS COMP	PCT	YD	AVG(LG)	TD	INT	SK	YD	QBR	KPR	OTD	PTS	TAY

GARNER, BOB   Robert Edward, T, 6'0"/238 lbs; none; B8/16/1923 North Adams, MA, D12/1972 **1945** NYG 1 (0)

GARNER, BOB   Robert, DB, 5'10"/189 lbs; Fresno State; B1935 **1960**†LAC-A 13 **1961** Oak-A 13 (RCB) **1962** Oak-A 14 (RCB) **NFL** 40 [3 yrs]

GARNER, CHARLIE   Charles, RB, 5'10"/190 lbs; Tennessee; 1994: Phi, rnd 2; B2/13/1972 Fairfax, VA

1994	Phi	10 (8, fb)	109	399	3.7(28)	3	8	74	9.3(28)	0	—	—	—	—	—	—	—	—	—	—	—	18	466
1995	†Phi	15 (3)	108	588	5.4(55)	6	10	61	6.1(29)	0	—	—	—	—	—	—	—	—	—	k	—	36	834
1996	†Phi	15 (1)	66	346	5.2(46)	1	14	92	6.6(13)	0	—	—	—	—	—	—	—	—	—	k	—	6	429
1997	Phi	16 (2)	116	547	4.7(26)	3	24	225	9.4(27)	0	—	—	—	—	—	—	—	—	—	—	—	18	690
1998	Phi	10 (3)	96	381	4.0(40)	4	19	110	5.8(21)	0	—	—	—	—	—	—	—	—	—	—	—	24	476
1999	SF	16 (15, RB)	241	1229	5.1(53)	4	56	535	9.6(53)	2	0	0	0.0	0	0.0	0	0	1	8	—	—	36	1547
2000	SF◇	16 (15, RB)	258	1142	4.4(42)	7	68	647	9.5(62)	3	—	—	—	—	—	—	—	—	—	—	—	60	1551
2001	†Oak	16 (16, RB)	211	839	4.0(38)	1	72	578	8.0(27)	2	—	—	—	—	—	—	—	—	—	—	—	18	1148
2002	†Oak	16 (15, RB)	182	962	5.3(36)	7	91	941	10.3(69)	4	—	—	—	—	—	—	—	—	—	—	—	66	1523
2003	Oak	14 (9, RB)	120	553	4.6(33)	3	48	386	8.0(46)	1	—	—	—	—	—	—	—	—	—	—	—	24	781
2004	TB	3 (3)	30	111	3.7(25)	0	9	62	6.9(31)	0	—	—	—	—	—	—	—	—	—	—	—	0	142
NFL	11	147 (90)	1537	7097	4.6(55)	39	419	3711	8.9(69)	12	0	0	0.0	0	0.0	0	0	1	8	—	—	306	9585

GARNER, DWIGHT   Dwight Eugene, RB, 5'8"/183 lbs; California; B10/25/1964 San Francisco, CA **1986**†Was 2 (0)

GARNER, HAL   Hal E., LB, 6'4"/228 lbs; Utah State; 1985: Buf, rnd 3; B1/18/1962 New Iberia, LA **1985** Buf 13 (0) **1986** Buf 16 (1) **1988**†Buf 12 (1) **1990**†Buf 10 (0) **1991**†Buf 16 (0) **NFL** 67 (2) [5 yrs]

GARNES, SAM   Sam Aaron, DB, 6'3"/225 lbs; Cincinnati; 1997: NYG, rnd 5; B7/12/1974 Bronx, NY **1997**†NYG 16 (15, SS) **1998** NYG 11 (11, SS) **1999** NYG 16 (16, SS) **2000**†NYG 15 (15, SS) **2001** NYG 16 (16, SS) **2002**†NYJ 16 (16, SS) **2003** NYJ 16 (16, SS) **NFL** 106 (105) [7 yrs]

GARNETT, DAVE   David Eugene, LB, 6'2"/219 lbs; Stanford; B12/6/1970 Pittsburgh, PA **1993**†Min 16 (0) **1994**†Min 9 (0) **1995** Den 3 (0) **1996**†Min 12 (4) **NFL** 40 (4) [4 yrs]

GARNETT, SCOTT   Scott Aaron, NT-DE, 6'2"/271 lbs; Washington; 1984: Den, rnd 8; B12/3/1962 Harrisburg, PA **1984**†Den 16 (1) **1985** SF 3 (0) **1985** SD 5 (0) **1987** Buf 3 (2) **NFL** 27 (3) [3 yrs]

GARNETT, WINFIELD   Winfield, DT, 6'6"/320 lbs; Ohio State; B7/24/1976 Chicago, IL **2001** Min 12 (2)

GARNJOST, BILL   William Tecumseh Sherman, G, 5'10"/190 lbs; Columbia; B12/1892, D1958 **1921** Evv 5 (4, RG)

GARRARD, DAVID   David Douglas, QB, 6'1"/244 lbs; East Carolina; 2002: Jax, rnd 4; B2/14/1978 East Orange, NJ

2002	Jax	4 (1)	25	139	5.6(41)	2	—	—	—	—	46	23	50.0	231	5.0(22)	1	2	7	40	—	—	—	12	200
2003	Jax	2 (0)	—	—	—	—	—	—	—	—	12	9	75.0	86	7.2(28)	1	0	—	—	—	—	—	0	48
2004	Jax	4 (2)	12	76	6.3(12)	1	—	—	—	—	72	38	52.8	374	5.2(36)	2	1	6	35	—	—	—	6	243
2005	†Jax	7 (5, qb)	31	172	5.5(28)	3	—	—	—	—	168	98	58.3	1117	6.6(37)	4	1	8	45	83.9	—	—	20	741
NFL	4	17 (8)	68	387	5.7(41)	6	—	—	—	—	298	168	56.4	1808	6.1(37)	8	4	21	120	77.7	—	—	38	1231

GARRETT, ALVIN   Alvin Lynn, WR-RB, 5'7"/178 lbs; Angelo State (TX); 1979: SD, rnd 9; B10/1/1956 Mineral Wells, TX

1980	NYG	15 (0)	9	31	3.4(10)	1	5	69	13.8(32)	1	—	—	—	—	—	—	—	—	—	kp	—	6	290
1981	NYG	9 (0)	1	2	2.0(2)	0	—	—	—	—	—	—	—	—	—	—	—	—	—	kp	—	0	140
1981	Was	4 (0)	—	—	—	—	—	—	—	—	—	—	—	—	—	—	—	—	—	k	—	0	10
1982	†Was	9 (0)	—	—	—	—	1	6	6.0(6)	0	—	—	—	—	—	—	—	—	—	k	—	0	8
1983	†Was	15 (6, wr)	2	0	0.0(4)	0	25	332	13.3(84)	1	—	—	—	—	—	—	—	—	—	k	—	6	191
1984	Was	3 (0)	—	—	—	—	1	5	5.0(5)	0	—	—	—	—	—	—	—	—	—	—	—	0	3
NFL	5	55 (6)	12	33	2.8(10)	0	32	412	12.9(84)	2	—	—	—	—	—	—	—	—	—	kp	—	12	641

GARRETT, BOBBY   Robert Driscoll, QB, 6'1"/198 lbs; Stanford; 1954: Cle, rnd B1; B8/16/1932 Los Angeles, CA, D12/5/1987 Westminster, CA

| 1954 | GB | 9 | 1 | -3 | -3.0(-3) | 0 | — | — | — | — | 30 | 15 | 50.0 | 143 | 4.8(16) | 0 | 1 | — | — | — | — | — | 0 | 29 |

GARRETT, BUDGE   Alfred Tennyson, E-G-FB, 5'9"/200 lbs; Rutgers; B4/17/1893 Muskogee, OK, D6/11/1950 Verona, NJ [C] **1920** Akr 7 (0) **1922** Mil 6 (6, LE) **NFL** 13 (6) [2 yrs]

GARRETT, CARL   Carl L., RB, 5'11"/210 lbs; New Mexico Highlands; 1969: Bos, rnd 3; B8/31/1947 Denton, TX [R]

1969	Bos-A★	14 (6, HB)	137	691	5.0(80)	5	29	267	9.2(34)	2	1	0	0.0	0	0.0	0	—	—	—	kp	—	42	1356
1970	Bos	13 (12, RB)	88	272	3.1(26)	4	26	216	8.3(29)	0	—	—	—	—	—	—	—	—	—	kp	—	24	654
1971	NE	14 (14, RB)	181	784	4.3(38)	1	22	265	12.0(80)	1	—	—	—	—	—	—	—	—	—	kp	—	12	1194
1972	NE	10 (7, RB)	131	488	3.7(41)	5	30	410	13.7(43)	0	1	0	0.0	0	0.0	0	0	1	4	—	kp	—	30	879
1973	ChiB	13 (RB)	175	655	3.7(35)	5	23	292	12.7(39)	0	1	0	0.0	0	0.0	0	—	—	—	k	—	30	1097
1974	ChiB	7	96	346	3.6(19)	1	16	132	8.3(20)	1	—	—	—	—	—	—	—	—	—	—	—	12	427
1975	NYJ	13 (RB)	122	566	4.6(40)	5	19	180	9.5(20)	1	—	—	—	—	—	—	—	—	—	k	—	36	765
1976	†Oak	12	48	220	4.6(17)	1	9	108	12.0(26)	0	—	—	—	—	—	—	—	—	—	k	—	6	402
1977	†Oak	14	53	175	3.3(13)	1	8	61	7.6(13)	2	—	—	—	—	—	—	—	—	—	k	—	18	331
NFL	9	110 (39)	1031	4197	4.1(80)	28	182	1931	10.6(80)	7	3	0	0.0	0	0.0	0	0	1	4	—	kp	—	210	7104

GARRETT, CURTIS   Curtis L., DE, 6'5"/302 lbs; Illinois; Illinois State; B6/9/1962 Chicago Heights, IL **1987** NYG 3 (3)

GARRETT, DRAKE   Drake F., DB, 5'9"/183 lbs; Michigan State; 1968: Den, rnd 4; B3/19/1946 Dayton, OH **1968** Den-A 14 (RCB) **1970** Den 1 **NFL** 15 [2 yrs]

GARRETT, DUB   William Davis, G-DT, 6'1"/235 lbs; Mississippi State; 1948: Bal-A, rnd 2/ChiB, rnd 3; B1/29/1925 Dundee, MS, D7/1976 **1948**†Bal-A 14 (14, RG) **1949** Bal-A 11 (7, RG) **AAFC** 25 (21) [2 yrs]

1950 ChiB 3

GARRETT, J.D.   John D., HB, 5'11"/195 lbs; Grambling State; 1964: Bos, rnd 8/NYG, rnd 18; B11/28/1941 Natchitoches, LA

1964	Bos-A	14	56	259	4.6(58)	2	8	101	12.6(57)	0	—	—	—	—	—	—	—	—	—	kp	—	12	617
1965	Bos-A	12	42	147	3.5(26)	1	7	49	7.0(15)	2	—	—	—	—	—	—	—	—	—	kp	—	18	258
1966	Bos-A	14	13	21	1.6(5)	0	1	7	7.0(7)	0	—	—	—	—	—	—	—	—	—	k	—	0	25
1967	Bos-A	10	5	7	1.4(8)	0	1	12	12.0(12)	0	—	—	—	—	—	—	—	—	—	k	1	6	26
NFL	4	50	116	434	3.7(58)	3	17	169	9.9(57)	2	—	—	—	—	—	—	—	—	—	kp	1	36	925

GARRETT, JASON   Jason Calvin, QB, 6'2"/200 lbs; Princeton; B3/28/1966 Abington, PA

1993	Dal	5 (1)	8	-8	-1.0(0)	0	—	—	—	—	19	9	47.4	61	3.2(16)	0	0	1	6	—	—	—	0	23
1994	Dal	2 (1)	3	-2	-0.7(0)	0	—	—	—	—	31	16	51.6	315	10.2(68)	2	1	2	13	—	—	—	0	126
1995	Dal	1 (0)	1	-1	-1.0(-1)	0	—	—	—	—	5	4	80.0	46	9.2(24)	1	0	—	—	—	—	—	0	27
1996	†Dal	1 (0)	—	—	—	—	—	—	—	—	3	3	100.0	44	14.7(32)	0	0	—	—	—	—	—	0	22
1997	Dal	1 (0)	—	—	—	—	—	—	—	—	14	10	71.4	56	4.0(12)	0	0	2	18	—	—	—	0	28
1998	Dal	8 (5, qb)	11	14	1.3(5)	0	—	—	—	—	158	91	57.6	1206	7.6(80)	5	3	10	52	—	—	—	0	522
1999	Dal	5 (2)	6	12	2.0(9)	0	—	—	—	—	64	32	50.0	314	4.9(37)	3	1	5	21	—	—	—	0	144
2000	†NYG	2 (0)	4	-4	-1.0(-1)	0	—	—	—	—	—	—	—	—	—	—	—	—	—	—	—	0	-4
NFL	8	25 (9)	33	11	0.3(9)	0	—	—	—	—	294	165	56.1	2042	6.9(80)	11	5	20	110	—	—	—	0	887

GARRETT, JOHN   John Morgan, WR, 5'11"/180 lbs; Columbia; Princeton; B3/2/1965 Danville, PA

| 1989 | Cin | 1 (0) | — | — | — | — | 2 | 29 | 14.5(18) | 0 | — | — | — | — | — | — | — | — | — | — | — | 0 | 15 |

GARRETT, KEVIN   Kevin Rashard, DB, 5'10"/194 lbs; SMU; 2003: SL, rnd 5; B7/29/1980 San Benito, TX **2003**†SL 9 (0) **2004**†SL 14 (1) **NFL** 23 (1) [2 yrs]

GARRETT, LEN   Leonard Neal, TE, 6'3"/230 lbs; New Mexico Highlands; 1971: GB, rnd 15; B12/18/1947 Silsbee, TX **1971** GB 14 **1973** GB 2 **1974** NO 10 **1975** NO 1 **1975** SF 2

1972	†GB	14 (TE)	—	—	—	—	4	66	16.5(21)	0	—	—	—	—	—	—	—	—	—	k	—	0	18
1973	NO	12	—	—	—	—	2	30	15.0(22)	0	—	—	—	—	—	—	—	—	—	k	—	0	15
NFL	5	55	—	—	—	—	6	96	16.0(22)	0	—	—	—	—	—	—	—	—	—	k	—	0	33

GARRETT, MIKE   Michael Lockett, RB, 5'9"/191 lbs; USC; 1966: KC, rnd 20/LA, rnd 2; B4/12/1944 Los Angeles, CA

| 1966 | †KC-A★ | 14 (HB) | 147 | 801 | 5.4(77) | 6 | 15 | 175 | 11.7(36) | 1 | 1 | 0 | 0.0 | 0 | 0.0 | 0 | 0 | — | — | — | kp | 1 | 48 | 1131 |
| 1967 | KC-A★ | 14 (HB) | 236 | 1087 | 4.6(58) | 9 | 46 | 261 | 5.7(34) | 1 | 1 | 1 | 25.0 | 17 | 4.3(17) | 1 | 0 | — | — | — | p | — | 60 | 1328 |

YEAR	TEAM	G (GS, POS)	RUSH	YD	AVG (LG)	TD	REC	YD	AVG (LG)	TD	PASS	COMP	PCT	YD	AVG (LG)	TD	INT	SK	YD	QBR	KPR	OTD	PTS	TAY
1968	†KC-A	13 (HB)	164	564	3.4 (37)	3	33	359	10.9 (43)	3	1	0	0.0	0	0.0	0	1	—	—	—	p	—	36	743
1969	†KC-A☆	14 (HB)	168	732	4.4 (34)	6	43	432	10.0 (41)	2	—	—	—	—	—	—	—	—	—	—	p	—	48	1006
1970	KC	3	21	62	3.0 (18)	0	4	4	1.0 (5)	0	—	—	—	—	—	—	—	—	—	—	p	—	0	79
1970	SD	9	46	146	3.2 (22)	1	10	127	12.7 (44)	1	0	0	0.0	0	0.0	0	0	1	5	—	—	—	12	225
1971	SD	13 (RB)	140	591	4.2 (36)	4	41	283	6.9 (40)	3	1	1	100.0	53	53.0 (53)	0	0	—	—	—	p	—	42	801
1972	SD	14 (RB)	272	1031	3.8 (41)	6	31	245	7.9 (27)	1	1	0	0.0	0	0.0	0	0	2	16	—	p	—	42	1219
1973	SD	10 (RB)	114	467	4.1 (68)	0	15	124	8.3 (30)	1	1	0	0.0	0	0.0	0	0	—	—	—	—	—	6	534
NFL	8	104	1308	5481	4.2 (77)	35	238	2010	8.4 (44)	13	9	2	22.2	70	7.8 (53)	1	1	3	21	—	kp	1	294	7064

GARRETT, MIKE Michael Steven, P, 6´1˝/184 lbs; Georgia; B6/13/1957 Atlanta, GA

YEAR	TEAM	G (GS, POS)	RUSH	YD	AVG (LG)	TD	REC	YD	AVG (LG)	TD	PASS	COMP	PCT	YD	AVG (LG)	TD	INT	SK	YD	QBR	KPR	OTD	PTS	TAY
1981	Bal	16 (0)	2	4	2.0 (3)	0	—	—	—	—	—	—	—	—	—	—	—	—	—	—	P	—	0	4

GARRETT, REGGIE Reginald Weldon, WR, 6´1˝/172 lbs; New Mexico Highlands; B11/22/1951 Silsbee, TX **1974**†Pit 14

YEAR	TEAM	G (GS, POS)	RUSH	YD	AVG (LG)	TD	REC	YD	AVG (LG)	TD	PASS	COMP	PCT	YD	AVG (LG)	TD	INT	SK	YD	QBR	KPR	OTD	PTS	TAY
1975	†Pit	14 (3)	—	—	—	—	13	178	13.7 (45)	1	—	—	—	—	—	—	—	—	—	—	—	—	6	94
NFL	2	28 (3)	—	—	—	—	13	178	13.7 (45)	1	—	—	—	—	—	—	—	—	—	—	—	—	6	94

GARRETT, SHANE Marcus Shane, WR, 5´11˝/185 lbs; Texas A&M; 1991: Cin, rnd 9; B11/16/1967 Lafayette, LA

YEAR	TEAM	G (GS, POS)	RUSH	YD	AVG (LG)	TD	REC	YD	AVG (LG)	TD	PASS	COMP	PCT	YD	AVG (LG)	TD	INT	SK	YD	QBR	KPR	OTD	PTS	TAY
1991	Cin	4 (0)	—	—	—	—	3	32	10.7 (13)	0	—	—	—	—	—	—	—	—	—	—	kp	—	0	37

GARRETT, THURMAN Thurman Edward, C, 6´3˝/268 lbs; Oklahoma State; B2/17/1923 Blackwell, OK, D6/11/2002 Sand Springs, OK **1947** ChiB 10 (1) **1948** ChiB 10 (0) **NFL** 20 (1) [2 yrs]

GARRISON, GARY Gary Lynn, WR-SE, 6´2˝/193 lbs; San Diego State; 1965: SD, rnd R1/Phi, rnd 6; B1/21/1944 Amarillo, TX

YEAR	TEAM	G (GS, POS)	RUSH	YD	AVG (LG)	TD	REC	YD	AVG (LG)	TD	PASS	COMP	PCT	YD	AVG (LG)	TD	INT	SK	YD	QBR	KPR	OTD	PTS	TAY
1966	SD-A	14 (12, SE)	1	-3	-3.0 (-3)	0	46	642	14.0 (36)	4	—	—	—	—	—	—	—	—	—	—	—	—	24	338
1967	SD-A	14 (14, SE)	1	1	1.0 (1)	0	44	772	17.5 (62)	2	—	—	—	—	—	—	—	—	—	—	—	—	12	397
1968	SD-A★	14 (14, SE)	—	—	—	—	52	1103	21.2 (84)	10	—	—	—	—	—	—	—	—	—	—	—	—	60	602
1969	SD-A	10 (10, SE)	—	—	—	—	40	804	20.1 (50)	7	—	—	—	—	—	—	—	—	—	—	—	—	42	437
1970	SD★	14 (14, WR)	4	7	1.8 (10)	0	44	1006	22.9 (67)	**12**	—	—	—	—	—	—	—	—	—	—	—	—	72	570
1971	SD★	14 (14, WR)	1	0	0.0 (0)	0	42	889	21.2 (77)	6	—	—	—	—	—	—	—	—	—	—	—	—	36	475
1972	SD★	14 (13, WR)	2	-6	-3.0 (0)	0	52	744	14.3 (52)	7	—	—	—	—	—	—	—	—	—	—	—	—	42	401
1973	SD	7 (5, wr)	—	—	—	—	14	292	20.9 (51)	2	—	—	—	—	—	—	—	—	—	—	—	—	12	156
1974	SD	14 (14, WR)	—	—	—	—	41	785	19.1 (71)	5	—	—	—	—	—	—	—	—	—	—	—	—	30	418
1975	SD	14 (14, WR)	3	30	10.0 (20)	0	27	438	16.2 (40)	2	—	—	—	—	—	—	—	—	—	—	—	—	12	259
1976	SD	2 (2)	—	—	—	—	2	58	29.0 (36)	1	—	—	—	—	—	—	—	—	—	—	—	—	6	34
1977	Hou	3	—	—	—	—	1	5	5.0 (5)	0	—	—	—	—	—	—	—	—	—	—	—	—	0	3
NFL	12	134 (126)	12	29	2.4 (20)	0	405	7538	18.6 (84)	58	—	—	—	—	—	—	—	—	—	—	—	—	348	4088

GARRISON, WALT Walter Benton, RB, 6´0˝/205 lbs; Oklahoma State; 1966: Dal, rnd 5/KC, rnd 17; B7/23/1944 Denton, TX

YEAR	TEAM	G (GS, POS)	RUSH	YD	AVG (LG)	TD	REC	YD	AVG (LG)	TD	PASS	COMP	PCT	YD	AVG (LG)	TD	INT	SK	YD	QBR	KPR	OTD	PTS	TAY
1966	†Dal	14	16	62	3.9 (13)	1	2	18	9.0 (17)	0	—	—	—	—	—	—	—	—	—	—	k	—	6	226
1967	†Dal	13	24	146	6.1 (26)	0	2	17	8.5 (14)	0	—	—	—	—	—	—	—	—	—	—	k	—	0	221
1968	†Dal	14	45	271	6.0 (22)	5	7	111	15.9 (53)	0	—	—	—	—	—	—	—	—	—	—	—	—	30	377
1969	†Dal	13 (FB)	176	818	4.6 (21)	2	13	131	10.1 (25)	0	—	—	—	—	—	—	—	—	—	—	k	—	12	891
1970	†Dal	11 (10, FB)	126	507	4.0 (18)	3	21	205	9.8 (36)	2	—	—	—	—	—	—	—	—	—	—	—	—	30	650
1971	†Dal	13 (FB)	127	429	3.4 (34)	1	40	396	9.9 (36)	1	—	—	—	—	—	—	—	—	—	—	—	—	12	642
1972	†Dal✧	14 (FB)	167	784	4.7 (41)	7	37	390	10.5 (26)	3	—	—	—	—	—	—	—	—	—	—	—	—	60	1064
1973	†Dal	13 (8, FB)	105	440	4.2 (33)	6	26	273	10.5 (53)	2	1	0	0.0	0	0.0	0	0	—	—	—	—	—	48	647
1974	Dal	14 (FB)	113	429	3.8 (18)	5	34	253	7.4 (30)	1	—	—	—	—	—	—	—	—	—	—	—	—	36	611
NFL	9	119 (18)	899	3886	4.3 (41)	30	182	1794	9.9 (53)	9	1	0	0.0	0	0.0	0	0	—	—	—	k	—	234	5326

GARRITY, GREGG Gregg David, WR, 5´10˝/171 lbs; Penn State; 1983: Pit, rnd 5; B11/24/1960 Pittsburgh, PA

YEAR	TEAM	G (GS, POS)	RUSH	YD	AVG (LG)	TD	REC	YD	AVG (LG)	TD	PASS	COMP	PCT	YD	AVG (LG)	TD	INT	SK	YD	QBR	KPR	OTD	PTS	TAY
1983	†Pit	15 (3)	—	—	—	—	19	279	14.7 (38)	1	—	—	—	—	—	—	—	—	—	—	—	—	6	145
1984	Pit	6 (0)	—	—	—	—	2	22	11.0 (12)	0	—	—	—	—	—	—	—	—	—	—	—	—	0	11
1984	Phi	4 (0)	—	—	—	—	—	—	—	—	—	—	—	—	—	—	—	—	—	—	—	—	—	—
1985	Phi	12 (1)	—	—	—	—	7	142	20.3 (34)	0	—	—	—	—	—	—	—	—	—	—	—	—	0	71
1986	Phi	12 (0)	—	—	—	—	12	227	18.9 (34)	0	—	—	—	—	—	—	—	—	—	—	p	1	6	226
1987	Phi	12 (0)	—	—	—	—	12	242	20.2 (41)	2	—	—	—	—	—	—	—	—	—	—	p	—	12	127
1988	†Phi	9 (4)	—	—	—	—	17	208	12.2 (20)	1	—	—	—	—	—	—	—	—	—	—	—	—	6	109
1989	†Phi	9 (0)	—	—	—	—	13	209	16.1 (31)	2	—	—	—	—	—	—	—	—	—	—	—	—	12	115
NFL	7	79 (8)	—	—	—	—	82	1329	16.2 (41)	6	—	—	—	—	—	—	—	—	—	—	p	1	42	803

GARRON, LARRY Lawrence, HB-FB, 6´0˝/195 lbs; Western Illinois; B5/23/1937 Marks, MS **[R]**

YEAR	TEAM	G (GS, POS)	RUSH	YD	AVG (LG)	TD	REC	YD	AVG (LG)	TD	PASS	COMP	PCT	YD	AVG (LG)	TD	INT	SK	YD	QBR	KPR	OTD	PTS	TAY
1960	Bos-A	4	8	27	3.4 (9)	0	1	8	8.0 (8)	0	—	—	—	—	—	—	—	—	—	—	k	—	0	37
1961	Bos-A★	14 (hb)	69	389	5.6 (85)	2	24	341	14.2 (51)	3	—	—	—	—	—	—	—	—	—	—	k	1	36	803
1962	Bos-A	11 (FB)	67	392	5.9 (41)	2	18	236	13.1 (63)	3	3	1	33.3	39	13.0 (39)	0	0	—	—	—	k	1	36	901
1963	†Bos-A✧	14 (FB)	175	750	4.3 (47)	2	26	418	16.1 (76)	2	1	0	0.0	0	0.0	0	0	—	—	—	kp	—	24	1280
1964	Bos-A✧	14 (FB)	183	585	3.2 (16)	2	40	350	8.8 (52)	7	2	0	0.0	0	0.0	0	0	—	—	—	k	—	54	863
1965	Bos-A	10 (HB)	74	259	3.5 (59)	1	15	222	14.8 (52)	1	—	—	—	—	—	—	—	—	—	—	k	—	12	451
1966	Bos-A	14 (HB)	101	319	3.2 (54)	4	30	416	13.9 (61)	5	—	—	—	—	—	—	—	—	—	—	k	—	54	611
1967	Bos-A✧	14 (HB)	46	163	3.5 (20)	0	30	507	16.9 (66)	5	—	—	—	—	—	—	—	—	—	—	k	—	30	470
1968	Bos-A	4 (2)	36	97	2.7 (18)	1	1	4	4.0 (4)	0	—	—	—	—	—	—	—	—	—	—	—	—	6	109
NFL	9	99 (2)	759	2981	3.9 (85)	14	185	2502	13.5 (76)	26	6	1	16.7	39	6.5 (39)	0	0	—	—	—	kp	2	252	5524

GARROR, LEON Leon, DB, 6´0˝/180 lbs; Alcorn State; 1972: Buf, rnd 5; B5/2/1948 Mobile, AL **1972** Buf 12 **1973** Buf 4 **NFL** 16 [2 yrs]

GARRY, BEN Benjamin Earl, RB, 6´0˝/215 lbs; Southern Mississippi; 1978: Bal, rnd 6; B2/11/1956 Hazelhurst, MS

YEAR	TEAM	G (GS, POS)	RUSH	YD	AVG (LG)	TD	REC	YD	AVG (LG)	TD	PASS	COMP	PCT	YD	AVG (LG)	TD	INT	SK	YD	QBR	KPR	OTD	PTS	TAY
1979	Bal	11	13	41	3.2 (14)	0	3	9	3.0 (12)	0	—	—	—	—	—	—	—	—	—	—	k	—	0	61
1980	Bal	3 (0)	—	—	—	—	1	9	9.0 (9)	0	—	—	—	—	—	—	—	—	—	—	k	—	0	15
NFL	2	14	13	41	3.2 (14)	0	4	18	4.5 (12)	0	—	—	—	—	—	—	—	—	—	—	k	—	0	75

GARTNER, CHRIS Sven Chris, K, 6´0˝/170 lbs; Indiana; B7/12/1950 Gothenburg, Sweden **1974** Cle 11

GARVEY, FRANNY Francis Daniel, E, 6´1˝/175 lbs; Holy Cross; B5/18/1901 Worcester, MA, D11/18/1972 Chelsea, MA **[K]** **1925** Pro 9 (8, LE), 12 **1926** Pro 10 (7, LE), 1 **NFL** 19 (15), 13 [2 yrs]

GARVEY, HEC Arthur Aloysius, G-E-T-C, 6´1˝/235 lbs; Notre Dame; B2/20/1900 Holyoke, MA, D9/22/1973 Chicago, IL **1922** ChiB 12 (12, LE) **1923** ChiB☆12 (12, RG) **1926** Har 4 (3) **1926** Bkn 1 (1) **1927** NYG 8 (8, LG) **1928** NYG 11 (9, RG) **1929** Pro 9 (7, LG) **1930** Bkn 12 (12, LG) **1931** SI 11 (7, LG) **NFL** 80 (71) [8 yrs]

GARY, CLEVELAND Cleveland Everett, RB, 6´0˝/226 lbs; Georgia; Miami (FL); 1989: LARm, rnd 1; B5/4/1966 Stuart, FL

YEAR	TEAM	G (GS, POS)	RUSH	YD	AVG (LG)	TD	REC	YD	AVG (LG)	TD	PASS	COMP	PCT	YD	AVG (LG)	TD	INT	SK	YD	QBR	KPR	OTD	PTS	TAY
1989	†LARm	10 (0)	37	163	4.4 (18)	1	2	13	6.5 (8)	0	—	—	—	—	—	—	—	—	—	—	k	—	6	169
1990	LARm	15 (7, RB)	204	808	4.0 (48)	**14**	30	150	5.0 (22)	1	—	—	—	—	—	—	—	—	—	—	—	—	90	1028
1991	LARm	10 (2)	68	245	3.6 (14)	1	13	110	8.5 (22)	0	—	—	—	—	—	—	—	—	—	—	—	—	6	310
1992	LARm	16 (16, RB)	279	1125	4.0 (63)	7	52	293	5.6 (22)	3	—	—	—	—	—	—	—	—	—	—	—	—	60	1357
1993	LARm	15 (4)	79	293	3.7 (15)	1	36	289	8.0 (60)	1	1	1	100.0	8	8.0 (8)	0	0	—	—	—	—	—	12	457
1994	Mia	2 (0)	7	11	1.6 (4)	0	2	19	9.5 (11)	0	—	—	—	—	—	—	—	—	—	—	—	—	0	21
NFL	6	68 (29)	674	2645	3.9 (63)	24	135	874	6.5 (60)	5	1	1	100.0	8	8.0 (8)	0	0	—	—	—	k	—	174	3340

GARY, KEITH Keith Jerrold, DE, 6´3˝/263 lbs; Ferrum; Oklahoma; 1981: Pit, rnd 1; B9/14/1959 Bethesda, MD **1983**†Pit 16 (2) **1984**†Pit 16 (11, RDE) **1985** Pit 12 (7, RDE) **1986** Pit 16 (0) **1987** Pit 11 (6, rde) **1988** Pit 15 (9, RDE) **NFL** 86 (35) [6 yrs]

GARY, OLANDIS Olandic C., RB, 5´11˝/218 lbs; Marshall; Georgia; 1999: Den, rnd 4; B5/18/1975 Washington, DC

YEAR	TEAM	G (GS, POS)	RUSH	YD	AVG (LG)	TD	REC	YD	AVG (LG)	TD	PASS	COMP	PCT	YD	AVG (LG)	TD	INT	SK	YD	QBR	KPR	OTD	PTS	TAY
1999	Den	12 (12, RB)	276	1159	4.2 (71)	7	21	159	7.6 (21)	0	—	—	—	—	—	—	—	—	—	—	—	—	44	1309
2000	Den	1 (0)	13	80	6.2 (25)	0	3	10	3.3 (7)	0	—	—	—	—	—	—	—	—	—	—	—	—	0	85
2001	Den	9 (1)	57	228	4.0 (29)	1	4	29	7.3 (11)	0	—	—	—	—	—	—	—	—	—	—	k	—	6	256
2002	Den	13 (2)	37	147	4.0 (26)	1	18	148	8.2 (19)	0	—	—	—	—	—	—	—	—	—	—	k	—	6	229

YEAR	TEAM	G (GS, POS)	RUSH	YD	AVG(LG)	TD	REC	YD	AVG(LG)	°TD	PASS	COMP	PCT	YD	AVG(LG)	TD	INT	SK	YD	QBR	KPR	OTD	PTS	TAY
2003	Det	13(1)	113	384	3.4(27)	2	13	69	5.3(13)	0	—	—	—	—	—	—	—	—	—	—	—	—	12	439
NFL	5	48(16)	496	1998	4.0(71)	11	59	415	7.0(21)	0	—	—	—	—	—	—	—	—	—	—	k	—	68	2317

GARY, RUSSELL Russell Craig, DB, 5´11˝/195 lbs; Nebraska; 1981: NO, rnd 2; B7/31/1959 Minneapolis, MN **1981** NO 14 (14, SS) **1982** NO 9 (9, SS) **1983** NO☆14 (14, SS)
1984 NO 16 (16, SS) **1985** NO 2 (2) **1986** NO 7 (3) **1986** Phi 6 (0) **1987** Phi 12 (0) **NFL** 80 (58) [7 yrs]

GARY, WILLIE Willie Frank, DB, 5´10˝/195 lbs; Kentucky; B11/1/1978 Valdosta, GA **2001**†SL 7 (0)

GARZA, DAN Daniel Robert, E, 6´3˝/203 lbs; North Texas; Central Missouri State; Oregon; 1949: NYY-A, rnd 7/1948: NYG, rnd 15; B2/21/1924 Anderson, SC, D3/6/2002 Tucson, AZ

| 1949 | †NYY-A | 12(0) | — | — | — | — | 9 | 193 | 21.4 | — | — | — | — | — | — | — | — | — | — | — | k | — | 0 | 103 |
| 1951 | NYY | 11(LE) | — | — | — | — | 31 | 470 | 15.2(69) | 4 | — | — | — | — | — | — | — | — | — | — | — | — | 24 | 255 |

GARZA, ROBERTO Roberto, G-C, 6´2˝/296 lbs; Texas A&M-Kingsville; 2001: Atl, rnd 4; B3/26/1979 Rio Hondo, TX **2001** Atl 16 (4) **2002** Atl 6 (4) **2003** Atl 14 (8, LG)
2004†Atl 16 (15, LG) **2005**†ChiB 16 (7, lg) **NFL** 68 (38) [5 yrs]

GARZA, SAMMY Samuel Mayorga, QB, 6´1˝/184 lbs; Texas-El Paso; 1987: Sea, rnd 8; B7/10/1965 Corpus Christi, TX

| 1987 | SL | 2(1) | 8 | 31 | 3.9(10) | 1 | — | — | — | — | 20 | 11 | 55.0 | 183 | 9.1(38) | 1 | 2 | 1 | 13 | — | — | — | 6 | 58 |

GARZONI, MIKE Michael John, G, 5´11˝/218 lbs; Santa Clara; Fresno State; USC; 1947: Was, rnd 6; B8/19/1923 Los Angeles, CA **1947** Was 10 (0) **1948** NYG 5 (0)
NFL 15 (0) [2 yrs]

1948 NYY-A 2 (0)

GASH, SAM Samuel Lee, FB, 6´0˝/242 lbs; Penn State; 1992: NE, rnd 8; B3/7/1969 Hendersonville, NC

1992	NE	15(0)	5	7	1.4(4)	1	—	—	—	—	—	—	—	—	—	—	—	—	—	—	—	—	6	17
1993	NE	15(4)	48	149	3.1(14)	1	14	93	6.6(15)	0	—	—	—	—	—	—	—	—	—	—	—	—	6	206
1994	†NE	13(6, fb)	30	86	2.9(10)	0	9	61	6.8(19)	0	—	—	—	—	—	—	—	—	—	—	k	—	0	111
1995	NE	15(12, FB)	8	24	3.0(9)	0	26	242	9.3(30)	1	—	—	—	—	—	—	—	—	—	—	—	—	6	150
1996	NE	14(9, FB)	8	15	1.9(3)	0	33	276	8.4(28)	2	—	—	—	—	—	—	—	—	—	—	—	—	14	163
1997	†NE	16(5, fb)	6	10	1.7(4)	0	22	154	7.0(19)	3	—	—	—	—	—	—	—	—	—	—	—	—	18	102
1998	†Buf★	16(12, FB)	11	32	2.9(11)	0	19	165	8.7(20)	3	—	—	—	—	—	—	—	—	—	—	k	—	18	126
1999	†Buf★	15(12, FB)	—	—	—	—	20	163	8.1(31)	0	—	—	—	—	—	—	—	—	—	—	k	—	12	90
2000	†Bal	15(4)	2	2	1.0(1)	0	6	30	5.0(9)	1	—	—	—	—	—	—	—	—	—	—	—	—	6	22
2001	†Bal	16(4)	2	-1	-0.5(0)	0	9	80	8.9(16)	1	—	—	—	—	—	—	—	—	—	—	—	—	6	44
2002	Bal	11(0)	—	—	—	—	—	—	—	—	—	—	—	—	—	—	—	—	—	—	k	—	0	-1
2003	Buf	16(10, FB)	1	3	3.0(3)	0	11	83	7.5(18)	0	—	—	—	—	—	—	—	—	—	—	—	—	0	45
NFL	12	177(78)	121	327	2.7(14)	2	169	1347	8.0(31)	13	—	—	—	—	—	—	—	—	—	—	k	—	92	1073

GASH, THANE Thane Alvin, DB, 6´0˝/200 lbs; East Tennessee State; 1988: Cle, rnd 7; B9/1/1965 Hendersonville, NC **1988**†Cle 16 (1) **1989**†Cle 16 (15, FS) **1990** Cle 16 (16, FS)
1992†SF 16 (3) **NFL** 64 (35) [4 yrs]

GASKINS, PERCELL Percell McGahee, LB, 6´0˝/230 lbs; Northwestern Oklahoma State; Kansas State; 1996: SL, rnd 4; B4/25/1972 Daytona Beach, FL **1996** SL 15 (1)
1997 Car 12 (0) **NFL** 27 (1) [2 yrs]

GASPARELLA, JOE Joseph Richard, BB-QB, 6´4˝/222 lbs; Notre Dame; 1948: Pit, rnd 6; B2/5/1927 Apollo, PA, D11/21/2000 Pittsburgh, PA

1948	Pit	9(3)	1	5	5.0(5)	0	—	—	—	—	57	23	40.4	294	5.2(43)	0	4	—	—	—	—	—	0	-8
1950	Pit	11(bb)	—	—	—	—	1	3	3.0(3)	—	54	23	42.6	383	7.1(51)	3	5	—	—	—	—	—	0	8
1951	Pit	4	—	—	—	—	—	—	—	—	2	0	0.0	0	0.0	0	1	—	—	—	—	—	0	-40
1951	ChiC	2	—	—	—	—	—	—	—	—	—	—	—	—	—	—	—	—	—	—	—	—		
NFL	3	26(3)	1	5	5.0(5)	0	1	3	3.0(3)	0	113	46	40.7	677	6.0(51)	3	10	—	—	—	—	—	0	-40

GASSERT, RON Ronald Earl, DT, 6´3˝/260 lbs; Virginia; 1962: GB, rnd 4/Buf, rnd 13; B7/22/1940 Campbelltown, PA **1962** GB 10

GASTINEAU, MARK Marcus Dell, DE, 6´5˝/266 lbs; Arizona State; East Central (OK); 1979: NYJ, rnd 2; B11/20/1956 Ardmore, OK **[S]** **1979** NYJ 16 (1) **1980** NYJ 16 (16, LDE)
1981†NYJ★16 (16, LDE) **1982**†NYJ★9 (9, LDE) **1983** NYJ★16 (16, LDE) **1984** NYJ★16 (16, LDE) **1985**†NYJ★16 (12, LDE) **1986**†NYJ 10 (7, rde) **1987** NYJ 15 (7, lde)
1988 NYJ 7 (7, LDE) **NFL** 137 (107) [10 yrs]

GATES G, none; deceased **1920** Det 1 (0)

GATES, ANTONIO Antonio, TE, 6´4˝/260 lbs; Kent State; B6/18/1980 Detroit, MI

2003	SD	15(11, TE)	—	—	—	—	24	389	16.2(48)	2	—	—	—	—	—	—	—	—	—	—	—	—	12	205
2004	†SD★	15(15, TE)	—	—	—	—	81	964	11.9(72)	13	—	—	—	—	—	—	—	—	—	—	—	—	78	547
2005	SD★	15(15, TE)	—	—	—	—	89	1101	12.4(38)	10	—	—	—	—	—	—	—	—	—	—	—	—	60	601
NFL	3	45(41)	—	—	—	—	194	2454	12.6(72)	25	—	—	—	—	—	—	—	—	—	—	—	—	150	1352

GATEWOOD, LES Lester Buddy, C, 6´2˝/198 lbs; Baylor; Tulane; 1943: GB, rnd 8; B5/30/1921 Dallas, TX **1946** GB 11 (0) **1947** GB 12 (6, c) **NFL** 23 (6) [2 yrs]

GATEWOOD, TOM Thomas, TE-WR, 6´3˝/215 lbs; Notre Dame; 1972: NYG, rnd 5; B3/7/1950 Baltimore, MD **1972** NYG 10 **1973** NYG 7 **NFL** 17 [2 yrs]

GATSKI, FRANK Frank 'Gunner', C-LB, 6´3˝/233 lbs; Marshall; Auburn; B3/18/1922 Farmington, WV, D11/23/2005 Morgantown, WV; HOF 1985 **1946**†Cle-A 10 (1)
1947†Cle-A 12 (3) **1948**†Cle-A 14 (14, C) **1949**†Cle-A 12 (11, C) **AAFC** 48 (29) [4 yrs]
1950†Cle 12 (C) **1951**†Cle☆12 (C) **1952**†Cle☆12 (C) **1953**†Cle☆12 (C) **1954**†Cle☆12 (C) **1955**†Cle★12 (C) **1956**†Cle 12 (C) **1957**†Det 12 (C) **NFL** 96 [8 yrs]

GAUBATZ, DENNIS Dennis Earl, LB, 6´2˝/232 lbs; LSU; 1963: Det, rnd 8/Bos, rnd 25; B2/11/1940 Needville, TX **1963** Det 14 (MLB) **1964** Det 14 (MLB) **1965**†Bal 14 (MLB)
1966 Bal 13 (MLB) **1967** Bal 14 (MLB) **1968**†Bal 14 (MLB) **1969** Bal 12 **NFL** 95 [7 yrs]

GAUDIO, BOB Angelo Robert, G, 5´10˝/219 lbs; Ohio State; B7/13/1925 Ashtabula, OH, D5/10/2003 Miami, FL **1947**†Cle-A 14 (1)

1948	†Cle-A	13(12, RG)	1	2	2.0(2)	0	—	—	—	—	—	—	—	—	—	—	—	—	—	—	—	—	0	2
1949	†Cle-A	12(0)	1	-2	-2.0(-2)	0	—	—	—	—	—	—	—	—	—	—	—	—	—	—	—	—	0	-2
AAFC	3	39(13)	2	0	0	0	—	—	—	—	—	—	—	—	—	—	—	—	—	—	—	—	0	0

1951†Cle 12 (RG)

GAUER, CHARLIE Charles Edward, FB-E, 6´2˝/213 lbs; Colgate; B9/24/1921 Chicago, IL, D10/22/1973 Philadelphia, PA

1943	P-P	9(1)	12	69	5.8(25)	0	2	18	9.0(14)	0	—	—	—	—	—	—	—	—	—	—	i	—	0	73
1944	Phi	7(4)	—	—	—	—	2	35	17.5(18)	0	—	—	—	—	—	—	—	—	—	—	i	—	0	15
1945	Phi	7(0)	—	—	—	—	—	—	—	—	—	—	—	—	—	—	—	—	—	—	—	—		
NFL	3	23(5)	12	69	5.8(25)	0	4	53	13.3(18)	0	—	—	—	—	—	—	—	—	—	—	i	—	0	88

GAUL, FRANK Francis Edward, T, 6´0˝/200 lbs; Notre Dame; 1949: NYB, rnd 20/Buf-A, rnd 5; B8/8/1926 Cleveland, OH **1949** NYB 12 (0)

GAULKE, HAL Harold M., B, 5´7˝/175 lbs; none; B8/1894 Columbus, OH, D4/30/1971 Columbus, OH **1920** Col 10 (4, BB) **1921** Col 4 (4) **1922** Col 7 (7, BB) **NFL** 21 (15) [3 yrs]

GAULT, BILLY William, HB, 6´1˝/185 lbs; TCU; 1961: Min, rnd 11; B12/19/1936 Monroe, LA **1961** Min 4

GAULT, DON Donald J., QB, 6´2˝/190 lbs; Hofstra; B8/30/1946 Lynbrook, NY

| 1970 | Cle | 2 | — | — | — | — | — | — | — | — | 19 | 2 | 10.5 | 67 | 3.5(44) | 0 | 3 | 1 | 5 | — | — | — | 0 | -87 |

GAULT, WILLIE Willie James, WR, 6´0˝/181 lbs; Tennessee; 1983: Chi, rnd 1; B9/5/1960 Griffin, GA

1983	ChiB	16(13, WR)	4	31	7.8(22)	0	40	836	20.9(87)	8	—	—	—	—	—	—	—	—	—	—	kp	—	48	585
1984	†ChiB	16(16, WR)	—	—	—	—	34	587	17.3(61)	6	—	—	—	—	—	—	—	—	—	—	k	—	36	321
1985	†ChiB	16(16, WR)	5	18	3.6(11)	0	33	704	21.3(70)	1	—	—	—	—	—	—	—	—	—	—	k	1	12	632
1986	†ChiB	16(16, WR)	8	79	9.9(33)	0	42	818	19.5(53)	5	—	—	—	—	—	—	—	—	—	—	k	—	30	518
1987	†ChiB	12(12, WR)	2	16	8.0(9)	0	35	705	20.1(56)	7	—	—	—	—	—	—	—	—	—	—	k	—	42	404
1988	LARd	15(6, wr)	1	4	4.0(4)	0	16	392	24.5(57)	2	—	—	—	—	—	—	—	—	—	—	—	—	12	210
1989	LARd	16(16, WR)	—	—	—	—	28	690	24.6(84)	4	—	—	—	—	—	—	—	—	—	—	k	—	24	366
1990	†LARd	16(16, WR)	—	—	—	—	50	985	19.7(68)	3	—	—	—	—	—	—	—	—	—	—	—	—	18	508
1991	†LARd	16(15, WR)	—	—	—	—	20	346	17.3(59)	4	—	—	—	—	—	—	—	—	—	—	—	—	24	193
1992	LARd	16(16, WR)	1	6	6.0(6)	0	27	508	18.8(53)	4	—	—	—	—	—	—	—	—	—	—	—	—	24	280
1993	†LARd	15(0)	—	—	—	—	14	64	8.0(12)	0	—	—	—	—	—	—	—	—	—	—	—	—	0	114
NFL	11	170(141)	21	154	7.3(33)	0	333	6635	19.9(87)	44	—	—	—	—	—	—	—	—	—	—	kp	1	270	4130

YEAR	TEAM	G (GS, POS)	RUSH	YD	AVG(LG)	TD	REC	YD	AVG(LG)	TD	PASS	COMP	PCT	YD	AVG(LG)	TD	INT	SK	YD	QBR	KPR	OTD	PTS	TAY

GAUNTY, STEVE Steven, WR, 5´10˝/175 lbs; Northern Colorado; B5/3/1957 Chicago, IL

| 1979 | KC | 9 | — | — | — | — | 5 | 87 | 17.4(23) | 1 | — | — | — | — | — | — | — | — | — | — | k | — | 6 | 140 |

GAUSE, FRANK Frank O., C-G, /190 lbs; none; B2/11/1905, D8/15/1972 Minneapolis, MN   **1929** Min 3 (2)

GAUSTAD, DUTCH Arthur Millert, G, /212 lbs; none; B6/1889, MN, D3/23/1945 Hennepin County, MN   **1921** Min 4 (4, LG)   **1922** Min 4 (3, RG)   **1923** Min 6 (4)   **NFL** 14 (11) [3 yrs]

GAUTT, PRENTICE Prentice, HB-FB, 6´1˝/210 lbs; Oklahoma; 1960: Cle, rnd 2/NYT, rnd 1; B2/8/1938 Oklahoma City, OK, D3/17/2005 Lawrence, KS

1960	Cle	12	28	159	5.7(23)	1	1	10	10.0(10)	0	—	—	—	—	—	—	—	—	—	—	k	—	6	176
1961	SL	14(HB)	129	523	4.1(54)	3	12	132	11.0(45)	3	11	6	54.5	100	9.1(22)	1	1	—	—	—	—	—	36	649
1962	SL	13	114	470	4.1(34)	2	16	240	15.0(39)	0	—	—	—	—	—	—	—	—	—	—	k	—	12	644
1963	SL	1	3	5	1.7(2)	0	1	3	3.0(3)	0	1	0	0.0	0	0.0	0	0	—	—	—	—	—	0	7
1964	SL	13(fb)	59	191	3.2(30)	1	9	72	8.0(15)	1	—	—	—	—	—	—	—	—	—	—	k	—	12	271
1965	SL	7	44	175	4.0(20)	2	9	128	14.2(54)	1	1	0	0.0	0	0.0	0	0	—	—	—	—	—	12	259
1966	SL	14(fb)	110	370	3.4(23)	1	16	114	7.1(22)	1	—	—	—	—	—	—	—	—	—	—	—	—	12	442
1967	SL	14(HB)	142	573	4.0(30)	1	15	202	13.5(32)	1	—	—	—	—	—	—	—	—	—	—	—	—	12	689
NFL	8	88	629	2466	3.9(54)	11	79	901	11.4(54)	6	13	6	46.2	100	7.7(22)	1	1	—	—	—	k	—	102	3137

GAVAGAN, MIKE Maurice Thomas, FB-BB, 5´10˝/176 lbs; St. Bonaventure; B4/10/1899 Warsaw, TX, deceased   **1923** Roc 2 (2, FB)

GAVIN, BUCK Patrick Marvin, B, 5´10˝/179 lbs; none; B6/22/1895 Amenia, NY, D4/12/1981 Daytona Beach, FL   **1920** Buf 5 (1)   **1921** Det 3 (2)   **1921** RI 3 (2)   **1922** RI 7 (6, FB), 30   **1922** Buf 3 (3), 6   **1923** GB 9 (9, FB)   **1924** RI 9 (8, FB), 42   **1925** RI 5 (5, fb)   **1926** Ham 3 (3, FB)   **NFL** 47 (39), 78 [7 yrs]

GAVIN, CHUCK Charles E., DE, 6´1˝/250 lbs; Tennessee State; B12/26/1933 Lake, MS   **1960** Den-A 11 (RDE)   **1961** Den-A 8 (RDE)   **1962** Den-A 14 (LDE)   **1963** Den-A 14 (RDE)   **NFL** 47 [4 yrs]

GAVRIC, MOMCILO Momcilo, K, 5´10˝/167 lbs; Belgrade; B8/4/1938 Senj, Croatia **[K]**   **1969** SF 7

GAY, BEN Benjamin Stevenson, RB, 6´1˝/227 lbs; Baylor; B2/28/1980 Houston, TX

| 2001 | Cle | 16(0) | 51 | 172 | 3.4(40) | 1 | 4 | 11 | 2.8(7) | 0 | — | — | — | — | — | — | — | — | — | — | k | — | 6 | 356 |

GAY, BILLY William Thodore, DB, 5´11˝/180 lbs; Notre Dame; 1950: ChiC, rnd 7; B11/12/1927 Chicago, IL   **1951** ChiC 3

GAY, BLENDA Blenda Glen, DE, 6´5˝/254 lbs; Fayetteville State; 1973: Oak, rnd S1; B11/22/1950 Greenville, NC, D12/19/1976 Freeport, NY   **1974** SD 2   **1975** Phi 14 (8, RDE)   **1976** Phi 14 (LDE)   **NFL** 30 (8) [3 yrs]

GAY, CHET Chester Joseph, G-T-C, 6´0˝/215 lbs; Minnesota; B1/8/1900 Moose Lake, WI, D3/12/1978 Moose Lake, MN   **1925** Buf 8 (6, LG)   **1926** Mil 6 (3)   **NFL** 14 (9) [2 yrs]

GAY, EVERETT Everett Carlton, WR, 6´2˝/209 lbs; Texas; 1987: Dal, rnd 5; B10/23/1964 Houston, TX

| 1988 | Dal | 16(0) | — | — | — | — | 15 | 205 | 13.7(25) | 1 | — | — | — | — | — | — | — | — | — | — | — | — | 6 | 108 |

GAY, MATT Matthew Gilbert, DB, 5´11˝/197 lbs; Kansas; B4/3/1970 Chicago, IL   **1994** KC 2 (0)

GAY, RANDALL Randall Jerome, DB, 5´11˝/186 lbs; LSU; B5/5/1982 Baton Rouge, LA   **2004**†NE 15 (9, RCB)   **2005** NE 5 (2)   **NFL** 20 (11) [2 yrs]

GAY, WILLIAM William Howard, DE-DT-TE, 6´5˝/250 lbs; USC; 1978: Den, rnd 2; B5/28/1955 San Francisco, CA   **1978** Det 16   **1979** Det 15 (2)   **1980** Det 16 (9, LDT)   **1981** Det 16 (14, LDT)   **1982**†Det 9 (8, LDT)   **1983**†Det☆15 (15, RDE/ldt)   **1984** Det 16 (16, RDE)   **1985** Det 16 (16, RDE)   **1986** Det 16 (16, RDE)   **1987** Det 11 (5, rde)   **1988** Min 5 (1)   **NFL** 151 (102) [11 yrs]

GAYDOS, KENT Kent Bryan, WR, 6´6˝/225 lbs; Florida State; 1972: Oak, rnd 12; B9/8/1949 South Bend, IN   **1975** GB 4

GAYER, CHUCK Walter Edward, T, 5´11˝/205 lbs; St. Mary's (MN); Creighton; B7/29/1901 Janesville, MN, D1/1961   **1926** Dul 9 (6, rt)

GAYLE, RASHID Rashid Ali, DB, 5´8˝/174 lbs; Boise State; B4/16/1974 Harlem, NY   **1996** Jax 2 (0)

GAYLE, SHAUN Shaun Lenard, DB, 5´11˝/202 lbs; Ohio State; 1984: Chi, rnd 10; B3/8/1962 Newport News, VA   **1984** ChiB 15 (6, rcb)   **1985**†ChiB 16 (16)   **1986**†ChiB 16 (0)   **1987**†ChiB 8 (0)   **1988** ChiB 4 (4)   **1989** ChiB 14 (14, FS)   **1990**†ChiB 16 (16, SS)   **1991**†ChiB◇12 (9, SS)   **1992** ChiB 11 (11, SS)   **1993** ChiB 16 (16, SS)   **1994**†ChiB 16 (16, SS)   **1995**†SD 16 (16, SS)   **NFL** 160 (108) [12 yrs]

GAYLOR, TREVOR Trevor Alexander, WR, 6´3˝/195 lbs; Miami (OH); 2000: SD, rnd 4; B11/3/1977 St. Louis, MO

2000	SD	14(2)	—	—	—	—	13	182	14.0(62)	1	—	—	—	—	—	—	—	—	—	—	—	—	6	96
2001	SD	7(3)	—	—	—	—	14	217	15.5(31)	0	—	—	—	—	—	—	—	—	—	—	—	—	0	109
2002	†Atl	13(2)	—	—	—	—	25	385	15.4(74)	3	—	—	—	—	—	—	—	—	—	—	—	—	18	208
NFL	3	34(7)	—	—	—	—	52	784	15.1(74)	4	—	—	—	—	—	—	—	—	—	—	—	—	24	412

GAYNOR, DOUG Douglas, QB, 6´2˝/205 lbs; Long Beach State; 1986: Cin, rnd 4; B7/5/1963 Fresno, CA

| 1986 | Cin | 1(0) | 1 | 4 | 4.0(4) | 0 | — | — | — | — | 3 | 3 | 100.0 | 30 | 10.0(16) | 0 | 0 | 1 | 5 | — | — | — | 0 | 19 |

GAZIANO, FRANK Francis Joseph, G, 5´8˝/218 lbs; Holy Cross; B5/2/1916 Realemonte, Italy   **1944** Bos 9 (1)

GBAJA-BIAMILA, AKBAR Akbar, DE, 6´5˝/270 lbs; San Diego State; B5/6/1979 Los Angeles, CA   **2003** Oak 13 (0)   **2004** Oak 14 (0)   **NFL** 27 (0) [2 yrs]

GBAJA-BIAMILA, KABEER Muhammad Kabeer Olarewaja, DE, 6´4˝/255 lbs; San Diego State; 2000: GB, rnd 5; B9/24/1977 Los Angeles, CA **[S]**   **2000** GB 7 (0)   **2001**†GB 16 (0)   **2002**†GB 15 (11, RDE)   **2003**†GB◇16 (16, RDE)   **2004**†GB 16 (15, RDE)   **2005** GB 16 (16, RDE)   **NFL** 86 (58) [6 yrs]

GEASON, CORY Cory, TE, 6´3˝/255 lbs; Tulane; B8/12/1975 St. James, LA   **2001**†Pit 7 (0)   **2002** Buf 10 (0)

| 2000 | Pit | 9(3) | — | — | — | — | 3 | 66 | 22.0(36) | 0 | — | — | — | — | — | — | — | — | — | — | — | — | 0 | 33 |
| NFL | 3 | 26(3) | — | — | — | — | 3 | 66 | 22.0(36) | 0 | — | — | — | — | — | — | — | — | — | — | — | — | 0 | 33 |

GEATER, RON Ronald Ray, DE, 6´6˝/272 lbs; Iowa; 1992: Den, rnd 7; B4/23/1969 Marion, IA   **1992** Den 3 (0)

GEATHERS, JUMPY James Allen, DE-DT, 6´7˝/290 lbs; Wichita State; 1984: NO, rnd 2; B6/26/1960 Georgetown, SC **[S]**   **1984** NO 16 (0)   **1985** NO 16 (0)   **1986** NO 16 (2)   **1987**†NO 1 (0)   **1988** NO 16 (6, lde)   **1989** NO 15 (15, RDE)   **1990**†Was 9 (1)   **1991**†Was 16 (0)   **1992**†Was 16 (0)   **1993** Atl 14 (0)   **1994** Atl 16 (1)   **1995**†Atl 16 (2)   **1996**†Den 16 (0)   **NFL** 183 (27) [13 yrs]

GEATHERS, ROBERT Robert L., DE, 6´3˝/270 lbs; Georgia; 2004: Cin, rnd 4; B8/11/1983 Georgetown, SC   **2004** Cin 14 (1)   **2005**†Cin 16 (16, RDE)   **NFL** 30 (17) [2 yrs]

GEDDES, BOB Robert Eric, LB, 6´2˝/240 lbs; UCLA; 1970: LA, rnd 14; B4/22/1946 Seattle, WA   **1972** Den 14 (3)   **1973** NE 2   **1974** NE 9 (5, lilb)   **1975** NE 13 (1)   **NFL** 38 (9) [4 yrs]

GEDDES, KEN Kenneth Lewis, LB, 6´3˝/235 lbs; Nebraska; 1970: Det, rnd 7; B9/27/1946 Jacksonville, FL   **1971** LARm 14   **1972** LARm 2   **1973**†LARm 14 (14, LLB)   **1974**†LARm 14 (14, LLB)   **1975**†LARm 14 (14, LLB)   **1976** Sea 11 (9, LLB)   **1977** Sea 14 (14, RLB)   **1978** Sea 12 (2)   **NFL** 95 (67) [8 yrs]

GEDMAN, GENE Eugene William, HB, 5´11˝/195 lbs; Indiana; 1953: Det, rnd 2; B1/9/1932 Duquesne, PA, D8/19/1974 Chicago, IL

1953	†Det	12(rh)	83	255	3.1(27)	3	14	121	8.6(25)	0	—	—	—	—	—	—	—	—	—	—	kp	—	18	353
1956	Det	12(RH)	135	479	3.5(33)	7	15	142	9.5(43)	1	—	—	—	—	—	—	—	—	—	—	—	—	48	625
1957	†Det	10(LH)	67	278	4.1(59)	3	10	135	13.5(47)	0	2	0	0.0	0	0.0	0	0	—	—	—	—	k	—	18	444
1958	Det	11(LH)	92	209	2.3(17)	4	14	106	7.6(24)	3	3	2	66.7	111	37.0(81)	1	0	—	—	—	—	k	—	42	404
NFL	4	45	377	1221	3.2(59)	17	53	504	9.5(47)	4	5	2	40.0	111	22.2(81)	1	0	—	—	—	—	kp	—	126	1825

GEDNEY, CHRIS Christopher Joseph, TE, 6´5˝/258 lbs; Syracuse; 1993: Chi, rnd 3; B8/9/1970 Liverpool, NY

1993	ChiB	7(4)	—	—	—	—	10	98	9.8(24)	0	—	—	—	—	—	—	—	—	—	—	—	—	0	49
1994	ChiB	7(7, te)	—	—	—	—	13	157	12.1(37)	3	—	—	—	—	—	—	—	—	—	—	—	—	18	94
1995	ChiB	14(1)	—	—	—	—	5	52	10.4(15)	0	—	—	—	—	—	—	—	—	—	—	—	—	0	26
1997	Arz	16(3)	1	15	15.0(15)	0	23	261	11.3(37)	4	—	—	—	—	—	—	—	—	—	—	k	—	24	162
1998	†Arz	16(3)	—	—	—	—	22	271	12.3(32)	1	—	—	—	—	—	—	—	—	—	—	k	—	6	123
2000	Arz	13(3)	—	—	—	—	10	75	7.5(24)	0	—	—	—	—	—	—	—	—	—	—	—	—	0	38
NFL	6	73(21)	1	15	15.0(15)	0	83	914	11.0(37)	8	—	—	—	—	—	—	—	—	—	—	k	—	48	490

GEHRING, MARK Mark, TE, 6´4˝/235 lbs; Eastern Washington; B4/16/1964 Burien, WA

| 1987 | Hou | 6(3) | — | — | — | — | 5 | 64 | 12.8(31) | 1 | — | — | — | — | — | — | — | — | — | — | — | — | 6 | 37 |

GEHRKE, BRUCE Bruce R., E, 6´2˝/190 lbs; Columbia; 1948: NYG, rnd 4/Bkn-A, rnd 8; B9/12/1924 Long Island, NY, D4/6/1976 Mineola, NY

| 1948 | NYG | 8(0) | — | — | — | — | 9 | 109 | 12.1(27) | 0 | — | — | — | — | — | — | — | — | — | — | — | — | 6 | 60 |

YEAR	TEAM	G (GS, POS)	RUSH	YD	AVG (LG)	TD	REC	YD	AVG (LG)	TD	PASS	COMP	PCT	YD	AVG (LG)	TD	INT	SK	YD	QBR	KPR	OTD	PTS	TAY

GEHRKE, FRED Clarence Fred, HB, 5´11˝/189 lbs; Utah; B4/24/1918 Salt Lake City, UT, D2/9/2002 Palm Springs, CA **[K]**

1940	Cle	3(0)	—	—	—	—	1	-2	-2.0(-2)	0	1	0	0.0	0	0.0	0	0	—	—	—		—	0	-1
1945	†Cle☆	10(7, LH)	74	467	**6.3(72)**	7	8	90	11.3(23)	1	—	—	—	—	—						kpi	—	48	701
1946	LARm	10(10, LH)	71	371	**5.2(53)**	3	11	83	7.5(21)	2	1	1	100.0	29	29.0(29)	0	0	—	—	—	kpi	—	30	600
1947	LARm	11(8, LH)	59	304	5.2(29)	0	6	19	3.2(11)	0	—	—	—	—	—						Kkpi	1	13	410
1948	LARm	12(8, LH)	56	246	4.4(24)	1	16	173	10.8(34)	1	1	0	0.0	0	0.0	0	0	—	—	—	Kkpi	1	19	708
1949	†LARm	12(7, LH)	58	203	3.5(53)	2	9	140	15.6(42)	2	—	—	—	—	—						K	1	32	303
1950	ChiC	7(1)	3	4	1.3(9)	0	2	-3	-1.5(13)	0	—	—	—	—	—						i	—	0	11
1950	SF	4	22	69	3.1(12)	1	3	29	9.7(13)	1	—	—	—	—	—						kp	—	12	145
NFL	7	69(41)	343	1664	4.9(72)	14	56	529	9.4(42)	7	1	33.3		29	9.7(29)	0	0	—	—	—	Kkpi	3	154	2875

GEHRKE, JACK John Fred, WR, 6´0˝/178 lbs; Utah; 1968: KC, rnd 10; B1/14/1946 Salt Lake City, UT

1968	KC-A	2	—	—	—	—	—	—	—	—	—	—	—	—	—							—		
1969	Cin-A	10	—	—	—	—	—	—	—	—	1	1	100.0	13	13.0(13)	0	0	—	—	—	p	—	0	7
1971	Den	14(10, WR)	1	2	2.0(2)	0	14	254	18.1(48)	0	2	1	50.0	19	9.5(19)	0	0	—	—	—		—	0	139
NFL	3	26(10)	1	2	2.0(2)	0	14	254	18.1(48)	0	3	2	66.7	32	10.7(19)	0	0	—	—	—	p	—	0	145

GEILE, CHRIS Christopher L., G, 6´4˝/305 lbs; Eastern Illinois; B4/14/1964 Anaheim, CA **1987** Det 3 (1)

GELATKA, CHUCK Charles T., E, 6´1˝/185 lbs; Mississippi State; 1937: NYG, rnd 10; B1/28/1914 Chicago, IL, D5/23/2001 Red Bank, NJ **[K]**

1937	NYG	4(0)	—	—	—	—	1	17	17.0(17)	0	—	—	—	—	—							—	0	9
1938	†NYG✧	10(3)	—	—	—	—	7	106	15.1	1	—	—	—	—	—						K	1	12	68
1939	†NYG	10(0)	—	—	—	—	6	71	11.8	0	—	—	—	—	—							—	0	36
1940	NYG	10(0)	—	—	—	—	6	56	9.3	0	—	—	—	—	—							—	0	28
NFL	4	34(3)	—	—	—	—	20	250	12.5(17)	1	—	—	—	—	—						K	1	12	140

GELBAUGH, STAN Stanley Morris, QB, 6´3˝/207 lbs; Maryland; 1986: Dal, rnd 6; B12/4/1962 Carlisle, PA

1989	Buf	1(0)	1	-3	-3.0(-3)	0	—	—	—	—	—	—	—	—	—							—	0	-3
1991	Phx	6(3)	9	23	2.6(13)	0	—	—	—	—	118	61	51.7	674	5.7(34)	2	6	11	94			—	0	-25
1992	Sea	10(8, QB)	16	79	4.9(22)	0	—	—	—	—	255	121	47.5	1307	5.1(57)	6	11	34	265	—		—	0	323
1993	Sea	1(0)	1	-1	-1.0(-1)	0	—	—	—	—	5	3	60.0	39	7.8(22)	0	1	1	7	—		—	0	-22
1994	Sea	2(0)	1	10	10.0(10)	0	—	—	—	—	11	7	63.6	80	7.3(25)	1	0	—	—	—		—	0	55
1996	Sea	1(1)	—	—	—	—	—	—	—	—	2	0	0.0	0	0.0	0	3	1	11	—		—	0	0
NFL	6	21(12)	28	108	3.9(22)	0	—	—	—	—	391	192	49.1	2100	5.4(57)	10	22	46	377	—		—	0	328

GENT, PETE George Davis, FL-WR, 6´4˝/205 lbs; Michigan State; B8/23/1942 Bangor, MI

1964	Dal	7	—	—	—	—	—	—	—	—	—	—	—	—	—							—		
1965	Dal	10(7, fl)	—	—	—	—	16	233	14.6(20)	2	—	—	—	—	—							—	12	127
1966	†Dal	14(10, FL)	—	—	—	—	27	474	17.6(84)	1	—	—	—	—	—							—	6	242
1967	Dal	7	—	—	—	—	9	88	9.8(16)	1	—	—	—	—	—							—	6	49
1968	†Dal	10	2	-5	-2.5(0)	0	16	194	12.1(22)	0	—	—	—	—	—							—	0	92
NFL	5	48(17)	2	-5	-2.5	0	68	989	14.5(84)	4	—	—	—	—	—							—	24	510

GENTRY, BYRON Byron Burk, G, 5´11˝/227 lbs; USC; B10/20/1913, WA, D2/10/1992 Paso Robles, CA **1937** Pit 3 (2) **1938** Pit★11 (11, LG) **1939** Pit★11 (11, LG)
NFL 25 (24) [3 yrs]

GENTRY, CURT Curtis William, DB, 6´0˝/185 lbs; Maryland-Eastern Shore; 1966: Chi, rnd 17; B8/8/1941 Waco, TX **1966** ChiB 13 **1967** ChiB 14 (RCB) **1968** ChiB 11
NFL 38 [3 yrs]

GENTRY, DALE Dale LuAuverene, E, 6´3˝/223 lbs; St. Mary's (CA); Washington State; B7/2/1917 Umapine, OR, D1/30/1966

1946	LAD-A	14(9, RE)	5	29	5.8		24	341	14.2	3	—	—	—	—	—						p	1	30	234
1947	LAD-A	14(13, RE)	—	—	—		22	352	16.0	2	—	—	—	—	—							—	12	186
1948	LAD-A	14(5, re)	—	—	—		28	308	11.0	0	—	—	—	—	—							—	0	154
AAFC	3	42(27)	5	29	5.8	1	74	1001	13.5	5	—	—	—	—	—						p	1	42	574

GENTRY, DENNIS Dennis Louis, WR-RB, 5´8˝/181 lbs; Baylor; 1982: Chi, rnd 4; B2/10/1959 Lubbock, TX **[R]**

1982	ChiB	9(0)	4	21	5.3(9)	0	1	9	9.0(9)	0	—	—	—	—	—						kp	—	0	56
1983	ChiB	15(0)	16	65	4.1(17)	0	2	8	4.0(6)	0	—	—	—	—	—						k	—	0	94
1984	†ChiB	16(0)	21	79	3.8(28)	1	4	29	7.3(13)	0	—	—	—	—	—						k	—	6	148
1985	†ChiB	16(0)	30	160	5.3(21)	2	5	77	15.4(30)	0	—	—	—	—	—						k	1	18	472
1986	†ChiB☆	15(2)	11	103	9.4(29)	1	19	238	12.5(41)	0	—	—	—	—	—						k	2	18	518
1987	†ChiB☆	12(0)	6	41	6.8(12)	0	17	183	10.8(38)	1	—	—	—	—	—						k	1	12	394
1988	†ChiB☆	16(16, WR)	7	86	12.3(58)	1	33	486	14.7(45)	2	—	—	—	—	—						k	—	24	527
1989	ChiB	16(6, wr)	17	106	6.2(29)	0	39	463	11.9(79)	1	—	—	—	—	—						k	—	6	590
1990	†ChiB	14(5, wr)	11	43	3.9(11)	0	23	320	13.9(80)	2	—	—	—	—	—						k	—	12	331
1991	ChiB	15(0)	9	58	6.4(17)	0	16	149	9.3(18)	0	—	—	—	—	—						k	—	0	165
1992	ChiB	15(1)	5	2	0.4(3)	0	12	114	9.5(18)	0	—	—	—	—	—						k	—	0	149
NFL	11	159(30)	137	764	5.6(58)	5	171	2076	12.1(80)	7	—	—	—	—	—						kp	4	96	3441

GENTRY, LEE Elmer Lee, HB, 6´0˝/198 lbs; Tulsa; 1941: Was, rnd 22; B12/1/1918 Shawnee, OK, D12/1992

| 1941 | Was | 5(0) | 5 | 13 | 2.6(7) | 0 | — | — | — | — | — | — | — | — | — | | | | | | i | — | 0 | 17 |

GENTRY, WELDON Weldon Christopher, G, 5´10˝/195 lbs; Arkansas; Oklahoma; B9/9/1906 Lawton, OK, D3/19/1990 Oklahoma City, OK **1930** Pro 4 (0) **1931** Pro 7 (4)
NFL 11 (4) [2 yrs]

GEORGE, BILL William J., LB-G-MG-DT, 6´2˝/237 lbs; Wake Forest; 1951: ChiB, rnd 2; B10/27/1929 Waynesburg, PA, D9/30/1982 Davis Junction, IL; HOF 1974 **[K]**
1952 ChiB 12 (RG) **1953** ChiB 12 (RG) **1954** ChiB✧12 (MG) **1955** ChiB★12 (MLB) **1956**†ChiB★12 (MLB) **1957** ChiB★12 (MLB) **1958** ChiB★12 (MLB) **1959** ChiB 12 (MLB)
1960 ChiB★12 (MLB) **1961** ChiB★14 (MLB) **1962** ChiB 13 (MLB) **1963**†ChiB★14 (MLB) **1964** ChiB 8 (MLB) **1965** ChiB 12 (MLB) **1966** LARm 14 (MLB) **NFL** 173 [15 yrs]

GEORGE, CARL Carl W., G, 5´11˝/175 lbs; Carroll (WI); Loras; B3/13/1892, NY, D10/8/1965 Union County, OH **1922** Rac 3 (1)

GEORGE, ED Edward Gary, T, 6´4˝/270 lbs; Ferrum; Wake Forest; 1970: Pit, rnd 4; B8/10/1946 Norfolk, VA **1975**†Bal 12 (2) **1976** Phi 14 (14, RT) **1977** Phi 14 (RT) **1978**†Phi 16
NFL 56 (16) [4 yrs]

GEORGE, EDDIE Edward Nathan, RB, 6´3˝/235 lbs; Ohio State; 1996: Hou, rnd 1; B9/24/1973 Philadelphia, PA

1996	Hou☆	16(16, RB)	335	1368	4.1(76)	8	23	182	7.9(17)	0	—	—	—	—	—							—	48	1539
1997	Ten✧	16(16, RB)	357	1399	3.9(30)	6	7	44	6.3(15)	1	—	—	—	—	—							—	44	1486
1998	Ten✧	16(16, RB)	348	1294	3.7(37)	5	37	310	8.4(29)	1	—	—	—	—	—							—	38	1504
1999	†Ten★	16(16, RB)	320	1304	4.1(40)	9	47	458	9.7(54)	4	—	—	—	—	—							—	78	1643
2000	†Ten★	16(16, RB)	**403**	1509	3.7(35)	14	50	453	9.1(24)	2	—	—	—	—	—							—	96	1886
2001	Ten	16(16, RB)	315	939	3.0(27)	5	37	279	7.5(25)	0	—	—	—	—	—							—	30	1129
2002	Ten	16(16, RB)	343	1165	3.4(35)	12	36	255	7.1(14)	2	—	—	—	—	—							—	86	1423
2003	†Ten	16(16, RB)	312	1031	3.3(27)	5	22	163	7.4(22)	0	—	—	—	—	—							—	30	1163
2004	Dal	13(8, rb)	132	432	3.3(24)	4	9	83	9.2(28)	0	—	—	—	—	—							—	24	514
NFL	9	141(136)	2865	10441	3.6(76)	68	268	2227	8.3(54)	10	—	—	—	—	—							—	474	12285

GEORGE, JEFF Jeffrey Scott, QB, 6´4˝/218 lbs; Purdue; Illinois; 1990: Ind, rnd 1; B12/8/1967 Indianapolis, IN

1990	Ind	13(12, QB)	11	2	0.2(6)	0	—	—	—	—	334	181	54.2	2152	6.4(75)	16	13	37	320	73.8	—		6	648
1991	Ind	16(16, QB)	16	36	2.3(13)	0	—	—	—	—	485	292	60.2	2910	6.0(49)	10	12	56	481	73.8	—		0	1061
1992	Ind	10(10, QB)	14	26	1.9(13)	1	—	—	—	—	306	167	54.6	1963	6.4(62)	7	15	27	188	61.5	—		6	453
1993	Ind	13(11, QB)	13	39	3.0(14)	0	—	—	—	—	407	234	57.5	2526	6.2(72)	8	6	26	190	76.3	—		0	1102
1994	Atl	16(16, QB)	30	66	2.2(10)	0	—	—	—	—	524	322	61.5	3734	7.1(85)	23	18	32	206	83.3	—		0	1328
1995	†Atl	16(16, QB)	27	17	0.6(6)	0	—	—	—	—	557	336	60.3	4143	7.4(62)	24	11	43	270	89.5	—		0	1769
1996	Atl	3(3)	5	10	2.0(5)	0	—	—	—	—	99	56	56.6	698	7.1(67)	3	3	11	84	—		—	0	254
1997	Oak	16(16, QB)	17	44	2.6(12)	0	—	—	—	—	521	290	55.7	**3917**	7.5(76)	**29**	9	58	430	91.2	—		0	1788

YEAR	TEAM	G (GS, POS)	RUSH	YD	AVG(LG)	TD	REC	YD	AVG(LG)	TD	PASS	COMP	PCT	YD	AVG(LG)	TD	INT	SK	YD	QBR	KPR	OTD	PTS	TAY
1998	Oak	8(7, QB)	8	2	0.3(8)	0	—	—	—	—	169	93	55.0	1186	7.0(75)	4	5	22	162	—	—	—	0	415
1999	†Min	12(10, QB)	16	41	2.6(17)	0	—	—	—	—	329	191	58.1	2816	8.6(80)	23	12	28	228	94.2	—	—	0	1084
2000	Was	6(5, qb)	7	24	3.4(14)	0	—	—	—	—	194	113	58.2	1389	7.2(50)	7	6	12	94	—	—	—	0	514
2001	Was	2(2)	4	0	0.0(2)	0	—	—	—	—	42	23	54.8	168	4.0(17)	0	3	6	38	—	—	—	0	-36
NFL	12	131(124)	168	307	1.8(17)	2	—	—	—	—	3967	2298	57.9	27602	7.0(85)	154	113	358	2691	80.4	—	—	12	10378

GEORGE, JEFF   Jeffrey L., DB, 6´1˝/185 lbs; Illinois State; B12/24/1957 Atchison, KS   **1987** TB 2 (1)

GEORGE, MATT   Matthew Michael, P-K, 5´11˝/190 lbs; Chapman; B1/13/1975 Santa Clara, CA [K]   **1998** Pit 1 (0)

GEORGE, RAY   Raymond Edward, T, 6´0˝/229 lbs; USC; 1939: Det, rnd 10; B1/7/1918 St. Louis, MO, D1/12/1995 Costa Mesa, CA   **1939** Det◇11 (11, RT)   **1940** Phi 2 (2)   **NFL** 13 (13) [2 yrs]

GEORGE, RON   Ronald Lawrence, LB, 6´2˝/233 lbs; Air Force; Stanford; 1993: Atl, rnd 5; B3/20/1970 Heidelberg, Germany   **1993** Atl 12 (4)   **1994** Atl 16 (9, RLB)   **1995** Atl 16 (0)   **1996** Atl 16 (15, RLB)   **1997** Min 16 (0)   **1998** KC 16 (0)   **1999** KC 16 (0)   **2000** KC 16 (0)   **NFL** 124 (28) [8 yrs]

GEORGE, SPENCER   Spencer James, RB, 5´9˝/202 lbs; Rice; B10/28/1973 Beaumont, TX   **1997** Ten 5 (0)   **1998** Ten 5 (0)   **1999** Ten 8 (0)   **NFL** 18 (0) [3 yrs]

GEORGE, STEVE   Stephen Elwood, DT, 6´5˝/265 lbs; Houston; 1974: SL, rnd 3; B4/11/1951 Sulphur Springs, TX   **1974**†SL 13   **1976** Atl 1   **NFL** 14 [2 yrs]

GEORGE, TIM   Timothy Anderson, WR, 6´5˝/225 lbs; Carson-Newman; 1973: Cin, rnd 3; B10/4/1951 Alcoa, TN   **1974** Cle 8

| 1973 | Cin | 12(WR) | — | — | — | — | 2 | 28 | 14.0(19) | 0 | — | — | — | — | — | — | — | — | — | — | — | — | 0 | 14 |
| NFL | 2 | 20 | — | — | — | — | 2 | 28 | 14.0(19) | 0 | — | — | — | — | — | — | — | — | — | — | — | — | 0 | 14 |

GEORGE, TONY   Houston Antonio, DB, 5´11˝/205 lbs; Florida; 1999: NE, rnd 3; B8/10/1975 Cincinnati, OH   **1999** NE 16 (1)   **2000** NE 15 (0)   **NFL** 31 (1) [2 yrs]

GEPFORD, SID   Sidney, HB, 5´6˝/152 lbs; Millikin; Bethany (WV); B12/1896 Decatur, IL, deceased   **1920** Dec 2 (0)

GERAK, JOHN   John Matthew, G-C, 6´3˝/290 lbs; Penn State; 1993: Min, rnd 3; B1/6/1970 Youngstown, OH   **1993**†Min 4 (0)   **1994**†Min 13 (3)   **1996**†Min 14 (10, RG)   **1997** SL 16 (16, LG)

| 1995 | Min | 15(6, RG) | — | — | — | — | 1 | 3 | 3.0(3) | 0 | — | — | — | — | — | — | — | — | — | k | — | — | 0 | 6 |
| NFL | 5 | 62(35) | — | — | — | — | 1 | 3 | 3.0(3) | 0 | — | — | — | — | — | — | — | — | — | k | — | — | 0 | 4 |

GERARDI, PATSY   Pasqual, E, /165 lbs; none; B2/27/1892 Washington, DC, D6/13/1973 Kensington, MD   **1921** Was 1 (0)

GERBER, WOODY   Elwood George, G, 6´0˝/223 lbs; Alabama; B8/7/1920 Kankakee, IL, D10/19/2001 Lakeland, FL   **1941** Phi 5 (1)   **1942** Phi 11 (9, LG)   **NFL** 16 (10) [2 yrs]

GEREDINE, TOM   Thomas Allen, WR, 6´2˝/195 lbs; Truman State; 1973: Atl, rnd 4; B6/17/1950 St. Louis, MO

1973	Atl	12(WR)	1	-3	-3.0(-3)	0	12	231	19.3(46)	1	—	—	—	—	—	—	—	—	—	k	—	6	194
1974	Atl	12	—	—	—	—	4	69	17.3(24)	0	—	—	—	—	—	—	—	—	—	k	—	0	119
1976	†LARm	10	1	8	8.0(8)	0	1	23	23.0(23)	1	—	—	—	—	—	—	—	—	—	k	—	6	71
NFL	3	34	2	5	2.5(8)	0	17	323	19.0(46)	2	—	—	—	—	—	—	—	—	—	k	—	12	383

GERELA, ROY   Carl Roy, K, 5´10˝/185 lbs; New Mexico State; 1969: Hou, rnd 4; B4/2/1948 Sarrail, Canada [K]   **1969** Hou-A 14   **1970** Hou 14   **1971** Pit 14   **1972** Pit★14   **1973** Pit☆14   **1974** Pit★14   **1975** Pit☆14   **1976** Pit 14   **1977** Pit 16   **1978** Pit 16   **1979** SD 3   **NFL** 145 [11 yrs]

GERHARD, CHRIS   Chris, DB, 5´10˝/185 lbs; East Stroudsburg; B7/6/1964 Allentown, PA   **1987** Phi 3 (0)

GERHART, TOM   Thomas Edward, DB, 6´1˝/195 lbs; Salem (NC); Ohio University; B6/4/1965 Lebanon, PA   **1992** Phi 1 (0)

GERI, JOE   Joseph Steven, TB-HB, 5´10˝/185 lbs; Georgia; 1949: Pit, rnd 4/LAD-A, rnd 6; B10/20/1924 Phoenixville, PA, D4/20/2002 Milledgeville, GA [K]

1949	Pit	12(1, TB)	133	543	4.1(25)	5	—	—	—	—	77	31	40.3	554	7.2(63)	5	5	—	—	—	KPp	—	45	713
1950	Pit★	12(TB)	188	705	3.8(42)	2	1	33	33.0(33)	1	113	41	36.3	866	7.7(78)	6	15	—	—	42.4	KP	—	64	610
1951	Pit★	12(tb)	90	252	2.8(17)	3	3	59	19.7(49)	1	90	29	32.2	506	5.6(77)	2	7	—	—	—	KPk	—	67	378
1952	ChiC	12	20	50	2.5(21)	0	—	—	—	—	—	—	—	—	—	—	—	—	—	—	KP	—	28	50
NFL	4	48(1)	431	1550	3.6(47)	10	4	92	23.0(49)	2	280	101	36.1	1926	6.9(78)	13	27	—	—	36.7	KPkp	—	204	1750

GERMAINE, JOE   Joe Berton, QB, 6´0˝/220 lbs; Ohio State; 1999: SL, rnd 4; B8/11/1975 Denver, CO

| 1999 | SL | 3(0) | 3 | 0 | 0.0(2) | 0 | — | — | — | — | 9 | 9 | 56.3 | 136 | 8.5(63) | 1 | 2 | 3 | 23 | — | — | — | 0 | -7 |

GERMAN, JAMMI   Jammi Darnell, WR, 6´0˝/187 lbs; Miami (FL); 1998: Atl, rnd 3; B7/4/1974 Fort Myers, FL

1998	Atl	6(0)	—	—	—	—	—	—	—	—	—	—	—	—	—	—	—	—	—	—	—	—	—	—
1999	Atl	14(0)	—	—	—	—	12	219	18.3(62)	3	—	—	—	—	—	—	—	—	—	k	—	18	111
2000	Atl	9(0)	—	—	—	—	1	10	10.0(10)	0	—	—	—	—	—	—	—	—	—	—	—	0	5
2001	Cle	6(0)	—	—	—	—	7	65	9.3(18)	0	—	—	—	—	—	—	—	—	—	—	—	0	33
NFL	4	35(0)	—	—	—	—	20	294	14.7(62)	3	—	—	—	—	—	—	—	—	—	k	—	18	148

GERMAN, JIMMY   James, TB, 6´0˝/180 lbs; Centre; 1939: Was, rnd 11; B11/6/1917 Louisville, KY, D8/8/1945 Burma   **1940** ChiC 1 (0)

| 1939 | Was | 8(1) | 17 | 58 | 3.4(15) | 2 | — | — | — | — | 12 | 6 | 50.0 | 97 | 8.1(63) | 1 | 2 | — | — | — | — | — | 12 | 52 |
| NFL | 2 | 9(1) | 17 | 58 | 3.4(15) | 2 | — | — | — | — | 12 | 6 | 50.0 | 97 | 8.1(63) | 1 | 2 | — | — | — | — | — | 12 | 52 |

GERMANY, REGGIE   Reggie, WR, 6´1˝/180 lbs; Ohio State; 2001: Buf, rnd 7; B3/19/1978 Hazelwood, MO

| 2001 | Buf | 16(1) | — | — | — | — | 12 | 203 | 16.9(39) | 0 | — | — | — | — | — | — | — | — | — | — | — | 0 | 102 |

GERMANY, WILLIE   Willie James, DB, 6´0˝/192 lbs; Morgan State; 1971: Was, rnd 7; B5/9/1948 Columbus, GA   **1972** Atl 12   **1973** Det 6   **1975** Hou 14 (SS)   **1976**†NE 10   **NFL** 42 [4 yrs]

GERSBACH, CARL   Carl Robert, LB, 6´1˝/230 lbs; Duke; West Chester; B1/8/1947 Syracuse, NY   **1970** Phi 6   **1971**†Min 13 (10, MLB)   **1972** Min 14   **1973** SD 14 (8, MLB)   **1974** SD 12 (7, llb)   **1975** ChiB 10   **1976** SL 7   **NFL** 76 (25) [7 yrs]

GERVAIS, RICK   Richard Paul, DB, 5´11˝/190 lbs; Stanford; B11/4/1959 Bend, OR   **1981**†SF 8 (0)   **1982** SF 8 (1)   **1983** SF 5 (5, ss)   **NFL** 21 (6) [3 yrs]

GESEK, JOHN   John Christian, G-C, 6´5˝/282 lbs; Sacramento State; 1987: LARd, rnd 10; B2/18/1963 San Francisco, CA   **1987** LARd 3 (1)   **1988** LARd 12 (6, lg)   **1989** LARd 16 (16, LG)   **1990** Dal 15 (12, RG)   **1991**†Dal 16 (15, RG)   **1993**†Dal 14 (0)   **1994** Was 15 (12, C)   **1995** Was 16 (16, C)

| 1992 | †Dal | 16(16, RG) | — | — | — | — | 1 | 4 | 4.0(4) | 0 | — | — | — | — | — | — | — | — | — | — | — | 0 | 2 |
| NFL | 9 | 123(94) | — | — | — | — | 1 | 4 | 4.0(4) | 0 | — | — | — | — | — | — | — | — | — | — | — | 0 | 2 |

GETCHELL, GORHAM   Charles Gorham, E-DE, 6´4˝/225 lbs; Temple; B8/14/1920 Abington, PA, D7/7/1980 Manhattan Beach, CA

| 1947 | Bal-A | 8(1) | — | — | — | — | 2 | 17 | 8.5 | 0 | — | — | — | — | — | — | — | — | — | — | — | 0 | 9 |

GETTY, CHARLIE   Charles Matthew, T-G, 6´4˝/265 lbs; Penn State; 1974: KC, rnd 2; B7/24/1952 Pompton Lakes, NJ   **1974** KC 14 (LT)   **1975** KC 14 (14, LT)   **1977** KC 14 (5, lg)   **1978** KC 16 (10, RT)   **1979** KC 16 (LT)   **1980** KC 6 (6, rt)   **1981** KC 16 (16, RT)   **1982** KC 9 (8, RT)   **1983** GB 15 (4)

| 1976 | KC | 14(14, LG) | — | — | — | — | 1 | -5 | -5.0(-5) | 0 | — | — | — | — | — | — | — | — | — | — | — | 0 | -3 |
| NFL | 10 | 134(77) | — | — | — | — | 1 | -5 | -5.0(-5) | 0 | — | — | — | — | — | — | — | — | — | k | — | 0 | -3 |

GETZ, FRED   Frederick, E, 6´1˝/192 lbs; Tennessee-Chattanooga; B3/16/1909 Memphis, TN, D10/1971 Norfolk, VA   **1930** Bkn 1 (0)

GETZ, LEE   E. Lee, G, 6´3˝/250 lbs; Rutgers; B4/2/1964 Hunterton County, NJ   **1987** KC 3 (0)

GEYER, BILL   William Herbert, HB, 5´10˝/173 lbs; Colgate; 1942: ChiB, rnd 11; B10/3/1919 Bloomfield, NJ, D6/4/2004 Glen Ridge, NJ

1942	ChiB	5(0)	9	18	2.0(6)	0	1	22	22.0(22)	0	—	—	—	—	—	—	—	—	—	p	—	0	47
1943	ChiB	3(3)	16	36	2.3(15)	1	5	123	24.6(64)	2	—	—	—	—	—	—	—	—	—	kpi	1	24	152
1946	ChiB	1(0)	—	—	—	—	—	—	—	—	—	—	—	—	—	—	—	—	—	k	—	0	-1
NFL	3	9(3)	25	54	2.2(15)	1	6	145	24.2(64)	2	—	—	—	—	—	—	—	—	—	kpi	1	24	198

GHECAS, LOU   Louis James, HB, 5´9˝/175 lbs; Georgetown (DC); B7/14/1918 Danbury, CT, D5/13/1997 Wilmington, DE

| 1941 | Phi | 8(0) | — | — | — | — | — | — | — | — | — | — | — | — | — | — | — | — | — | kp | — | 0 | 8 |

GHEE, MILT   Milton Pomeroy, B, 5´7˝/167 lbs; Dartmouth; B11/17/1891 Wilmette, IL, D3/16/1975 Costa Madera, CA   **1920** ChiT 8 (7, BB)   **1921** Cle 5 (4, BB), 12   **NFL** 13 (11) [2 yrs]

GHERSANICH, VERN   Vernon George, G, 5´11˝/219 lbs; Auburn; B12/22/1919 New Orleans, LA, deceased   **1943** ChiC 4 (0)

GHIACIUC, ERIC   Eric, C, 6´4˝/302 lbs; Central Michigan; 2005: Cin, rnd 4; B5/28/1981 Detroit, MI   **2005** Cin 5 (1)

GIACOMARRO, RALPH Ralph J., P, 6´1˝/190 lbs; Penn State; 1983: Atl, rnd 10; B1/17/1961 Passaic, NJ **1985** Atl 5 (0) **1987** Den 3 (0)

YEAR	TEAM	G(GS, POS)	RUSH	YD	AVG(LG)	TD	REC	YD	AVG(LG)	TD	PASS	COMP	PCT	YD	AVG(LG)	TD	INT	SK	YD	QBR	KPR	OTD	PTS	TAY
1983	Atl	16(0)	2	13	6.5(13)	0	—	—	—	—	1	1	100.0	23	23.0(23)	0	0	—	—	—	P	—	0	25
1984	Atl	16(0)	1	0	0.0(0)	0	—	—	—	—	—	—	—	—	—	—	—	—	—	—	P	—	0	0
NFL	4	40(0)	3	13	4.3(13)	0	—	—	—	—	1	1	100.0	23	23.0(23)	0	0	—	—	—	P	—	0	25

GIAMMONA, LOUIE Louis Jean, RB, 5´9˝/180 lbs; Utah State; 1976: NYJ, rnd 8; B3/3/1953 St. Helena, CA

YEAR	TEAM	G(GS, POS)	RUSH	YD	AVG(LG)	TD	REC	YD	AVG(LG)	TD	PASS	COMP	PCT	YD	AVG(LG)	TD	INT	SK	YD	QBR	KPR	OTD	PTS	TAY
1976	NYJ	14(3)	39	150	3.8(35)	1	15	145	9.7(28)	0	—	—	—	—	—	—	—	—	—	—	kp	—	6	472
1978	†Phi	7	4	6	1.5(3)	0	—	—	—	—	—	—	—	—	—	—	—	—	—	—	kp	—	0	71
1979	†Phi	15	15	38	2.5(9)	0	—	—	—	—	—	—	—	—	—	—	—	—	—	—	kp	—	0	124
1980	†Phi	16(4)	97	361	3.7(44)	4	17	178	10.5(30)	1	3	3	100.0	55	18.3(27)	1	0	—	—	—	kp	—	30	508
1981	Phi	8(1)	35	98	2.8(9)	1	6	54	9.0(19)	1	—	—	—	—	—	—	—	—	—	—	k	—	12	144
1982	Phi	9(0)	11	29	2.6(8)	1	8	67	8.4(16)	0	1	0	0.0	0	0.0	0	1	—	—	—	p	—	6	33
NFL	6	69(8)	201	682	3.4(44)	7	46	444	9.7(30)	2	4	3	75.0	55	13.8(27)	1	1	—	—	—	kp	—	54	1351

GIANCANELLI, HAL Harold Arthur, HB, 5´10˝/182 lbs; Loyola Marymount; B5/21/1929 Farr, CO

YEAR	TEAM	G(GS, POS)	RUSH	YD	AVG(LG)	TD	REC	YD	AVG(LG)	TD	PASS	COMP	PCT	YD	AVG(LG)	TD	INT	SK	YD	QBR	KPR	OTD	PTS	TAY
1953	Phi	12	44	131	3.0(30)	1	20	346	17.3(47)	5	—	—	—	—	—	—	—	—	—	—	kp	—	36	345
1954	Phi	10	33	47	1.4(11)	0	14	195	13.9(49)	4	—	—	—	—	—	—	—	—	—	—	k	—	24	297
1955	Phi	12(LH)	97	385	4.0(20)	2	25	379	15.2(59)	1	—	—	—	—	—	—	—	—	—	—	kp	—	18	707
1956	Phi	7(RH)	42	148	3.5(21)	1	10	104	10.4(18)	0	—	—	—	—	—	—	—	—	—	—	kp	—	6	279
NFL	4	41	216	711	3.3(30)	4	69	1024	14.8(59)	10	—	—	—	—	—	—	—	—	—	—	kp	—	84	1627

GIANELLI, MARIO Mario, MG-G, 6´0˝/265 lbs; Boston College; 1945: Bos, rnd 20/1947: Cle-A, rnd 12; B12/24/1920 Everett, MA, D6/29/2003 Chelsea, MA **1948**†Phi 12 (1) **1949**†Phi 10 (1) **1950** Phi 12 (MG) **1951** Phi 10 (MG) **NFL** 44 (2) [4 yrs]

GIANNETTI, FRANK Frank John, NT, 6´2˝/267 lbs; Penn State; 1991: Ind, rnd 10; B3/14/1968 Toms River, NJ **1991** Ind 3 (1)

GIANNONI, JOHN John Michael, E, 6´1˝/210 lbs; St. Mary's (CA); B8/27/1914 Sacramento, CA, D5/24/2000 Sacramento, CA **1938** Cle 3 (0)

GIAQUINTO, NICK Nicholas Albert, RB, 5´11˝/205 lbs; Bridgeport; Connecticut; B4/4/1955 Bridgeport, CT

YEAR	TEAM	G(GS, POS)	RUSH	YD	AVG(LG)	TD	REC	YD	AVG(LG)	TD	PASS	COMP	PCT	YD	AVG(LG)	TD	INT	SK	YD	QBR	KPR	OTD	PTS	TAY
1980	Mia	16(0)	5	16	3.2(5)	0	24	192	8.0(25)	1	—	—	—	—	—	—	—	—	—	—	kp	1	12	128
1981	Mia	8(0)	3	31	10.3(20)	0	7	38	5.4(16)	1	—	—	—	—	—	—	—	—	—	—	k	—	6	62
1981	Was	6(0)	17	73	4.3(5)	0	5	55	11.0(25)	1	—	—	—	—	—	—	—	—	—	—	—	—	6	106
1982	†Was	7(0)	1	5	5.0(5)	0	2	65	32.5(36)	0	—	—	—	—	—	—	—	—	—	—	kp	—	0	53
1983	†Was	16(0)	14	53	3.8(11)	1	27	372	13.8(35)	0	—	—	—	—	—	—	—	—	—	—	kp	—	6	236
NFL	4	53(0)	40	178	4.4(20)	1	65	722	11.1(36)	3	—	—	—	—	—	—	—	—	—	—	kp	1	30	584

GIAVER, BILL Einar William, B, 5´9˝/190 lbs; Georgia Tech; B5/29/1898 Chicago, IL, deceased **1922** Ham 5 (4, WB) **1923** RI 7 (5, TB), 24 **1924** Rac 10 (6, WB) **1925** Ham 4 (4, FB) **1926** Lou 2 (1) **NFL** 28 (20) [5 yrs]

GIBBONS, JIM James Edwin, E-TE, 6´2˝/220 lbs; Iowa; 1958: Cle, rnd 5; B9/26/1936 Chicago, IL

YEAR	TEAM	G(GS, POS)	RUSH	YD	AVG(LG)	TD	REC	YD	AVG(LG)	TD	PASS	COMP	PCT	YD	AVG(LG)	TD	INT	SK	YD	QBR	KPR	OTD	PTS	TAY
1958	Det	12(le)	—	—	—	—	25	367	14.7(35)	2	—	—	—	—	—	—	—	—	—	—	k	—	12	183
1959	Det	12(LE)	—	—	—	—	31	431	13.9(38)	1	—	—	—	—	—	—	—	—	—	—	—	—	6	221
1960	Det✧	12(TE)	—	—	—	—	51	604	11.8(65)	2	—	—	—	—	—	—	—	—	—	—	—	—	12	312
1961	Det✧	14(TE)	—	—	—	—	45	566	12.6(36)	1	—	—	—	—	—	—	—	—	—	—	p	—	6	297
1962	Det	14(TE)	—	—	—	—	33	318	9.6(22)	2	—	—	—	—	—	—	—	—	—	—	—	—	12	169
1963	Det	14(TE)	—	—	—	—	32	412	12.9(32)	1	—	—	—	—	—	—	—	—	—	—	—	—	6	211
1964	Det✧	14(TE)	—	—	—	—	45	605	13.4(82)	8	—	—	—	—	—	—	—	—	—	—	—	—	48	343
1965	Det	13(TE)	—	—	—	—	12	111	9.3(24)	2	—	—	—	—	—	—	—	—	—	—	—	—	12	66
1966	Det	7	—	—	—	—	1	2	2.0(2)	1	—	—	—	—	—	—	—	—	—	—	—	—	6	6
1967	Det	14(te)	—	—	—	—	10	107	10.7(21)	0	—	—	—	—	—	—	—	—	—	—	—	—	0	54
1968	Det	14	—	—	—	—	2	38	19.0(20)	0	—	—	—	—	—	—	—	—	—	—	—	—	0	19
NFL	11	140	—	—	—	—	287	3561	12.4(82)	20	—	—	—	—	—	—	—	—	—	—	kp	—	120	1879

GIBBONS, MIKE Michael Leslie, T, 6´4˝/262 lbs; Southwestern Oklahoma State; B1/23/1951 Duncan, OK **1976** NYG 11 (2) **1977** NYG 5 (4) **NFL** 16 (6) [2 yrs]

GIBBS, DONNIE Donald R., DB, 6´2˝/205 lbs; TCU; B12/31/1945 Tyler, TX, D2/21/2006, PA **1974** NO 1

GIBBS, PAT Patrick Henry, DB, 5´10˝/188 lbs; Lamar; 1972: Phi, rnd 9; B4/5/1950 Marshall, TX **1972** Phi 2

GIBBS, SONNY Guy Gilbert, QB, 6´7˝/230 lbs; TCU; 1962: Dal, rnd 2/Den, rnd 14; B10/25/1939 Graham, TX

YEAR	TEAM	G(GS, POS)	RUSH	YD	AVG(LG)	TD	REC	YD	AVG(LG)	TD	PASS	COMP	PCT	YD	AVG(LG)	TD	INT	SK	YD	QBR	KPR	OTD	PTS	TAY
1964	Det	2	—	—	—	—	—	—	—	—	3	1	33.3	3	1.0(3)	0	1	—	—	—	—	—	0	-39

GIBLER, ANDY James Andrew, TE, 6´4˝/235 lbs; Missouri; B4/30/1961 Independence, MO **1983** Cin 2 (0)

GIBLIN, ROBERT Robert James, DB, 6´2˝/205 lbs; Houston; 1975: NYG, rnd 4; B11/18/1952 Omaha, NE **1975** NYG 12 **1977** SL 11 **NFL** 23 [2 yrs]

GIBRON, ABE Abraham, G, 5´11˝/243 lbs; Valparaiso; Purdue; 1949: Buf-A, rnd S1/NYG, rnd 6; B9/22/1925 Michigan City, IN, D9/23/1997 Belleair, FL **[C]**

YEAR	TEAM	G(GS, POS)	RUSH	YD	AVG(LG)	TD	REC	YD	AVG(LG)	TD	PASS	COMP	PCT	YD	AVG(LG)	TD	INT	SK	YD	QBR	KPR	OTD	PTS	TAY
1949	†Buf-A	10(9, LG)	—	—	—	—	0	3	(3)	0	—	—	—	—	—	—	—	—	—	—	—	—	0	2

1950†Cle 12 (LG) **1951**†Cle☆12 (LG) **1952**†Cle✧12 (LG) **1954**†Cle★12 (LG) **1955**†Cle★12 (LG) **1956** Cle 7 (LG) **1956** Phi 2 **1957** Phi 12 (LG) **1958** ChiB 12 (LG) **1959** ChiB 12 (LG)

YEAR	TEAM	G(GS, POS)	RUSH	YD	AVG(LG)	TD	REC	YD	AVG(LG)	TD	PASS	COMP	PCT	YD	AVG(LG)	TD	INT	SK	YD	QBR	KPR	OTD	PTS	TAY
1953	†Cle★	10(LG)	0	-7	(-7)	0	—	—	—	—	—	—	—	—	—	—	—	—	—	—	—	—	0	-7
NFL	10	115	0	-7	(-7)	0	—	—	—	—	—	—	—	—	—	—	—	—	—	—	k	—	0	-40

GIBSON, AARON Aaron, T-G, 6´6˝/375 lbs; Wisconsin; 1999: Det, rnd 1; B9/27/1977 Indianapolis, IN **2000** Det 10 (10, RT) **2001** Det 6 (5, rt) **2001** Dal 1 (0) **2002** Dal 1 (0) **2003** ChiB 16 (16, RT) **2004** ChiB 4 (3) **NFL** 38 (34) [5 yrs]

GIBSON, ALEC Alexander Raymond, DE, 6´4˝/270 lbs; Illinois; B12/9/1963 Columbus, OH **1987** Was 3 (3)

GIBSON, ANTONIO Antonio Maurice, DB, 6´3˝/206 lbs; Cincinnati; B7/5/1962 Jackson, MS **1986** NO 16 (13, SS) **1987**†NO 10 (10, SS) **1988** NO 10 (10, SS) **1989** NO 16 (3) **1992**†NO 6 (0) **NFL** 58 (36) [5 yrs]

GIBSON, BUTCH Denver E., G-T, 5´9˝/204 lbs; Grove City; B1904 Middlebranch, OH, D5/1960 **1930** NYG 14 (2) **1931** NYG☆14 (14, LG) **1932** NYG☆12 (8, LG) **1933**†NYG☆14 (12, LG) **1934**†NYG☆13 (9, RG) **NFL** 67 (45) [5 yrs]

GIBSON, CLAUDE Claude Andrew, DB, 6´1˝/190 lbs; North Carolina State; 1961: SD, rnd 7/Chi, rnd 3; B5/26/1939 Spruce Pine, NC **[RI]** **1961**†SD-A☆14 (LCB) **1962** SD-A 14 (LCB) **1963** Oak-A 14 (RCB) **1964** Oak-A 14 (rs) **1965** Oak-A 14 **NFL** 70 [5 yrs]

GIBSON, DAMON Damon O'Keith, WR, 5´8˝/185 lbs; Iowa; B2/25/1975 Houston, TX **1999** Cle 2 (0) **2002** Jax 1 (0) **2002** Atl 1 (0)

YEAR	TEAM	G(GS, POS)	RUSH	YD	AVG(LG)	TD	REC	YD	AVG(LG)	TD	PASS	COMP	PCT	YD	AVG(LG)	TD	INT	SK	YD	QBR	KPR	OTD	PTS	TAY
1998	Cin	16(0)	1	9	9.0(9)	0	19	258	13.6(76)	3	—	—	—	—	—	—	—	—	—	—	kp	1	24	363
2001	Jax	16(0)	2	19	9.5(18)	0	2	13	6.5(9)	0	—	—	—	—	—	—	—	—	—	—	kp	—	0	290
NFL	4	36(0)	3	28	9.3(18)	0	21	271	12.9(76)	3	—	—	—	—	—	—	—	—	—	—	kp	1	24	662

GIBSON, DAVID David, DB, 6´1˝/210 lbs; USC; 2000: TB, rnd 6; B11/5/1977 Santa Ana, CA **2000**†TB 9 (0) **2001**†TB 13 (0) **2002** TB 3 (0) **2002**†Ind 13 (9, SS) **2003** TB 9 (0) **NFL** 47 (9) [4 yrs]

GIBSON, DENNIS Dennis Michael, LB, 6´2˝/240 lbs; Iowa State; 1987: Det, rnd 8; B2/8/1964 Des Moines, IA **1987** Det 12 (12, RILB) **1988** Det 16 (16, RILB) **1989** Det 6 (6, rilb) **1990** Det 11 (11, RILB) **1991**†Det 16 (16, RILB) **1992** Det 16 (16, RILB) **1993**†Det 15 (15, RILB) **1994**†SD 16 (15, MLB) **1995**†SD 13 (13, MLB) **NFL** 121 (120) [9 yrs]

GIBSON, DERRICK Derrick, DB, 6´2˝/215 lbs; Florida State; 2001: Oak, rnd 1; B3/22/1979 Miami, FL **2001**†Oak 16 (0) **2002**†Oak 16 (11, SS) **2003** Oak 15 (14, SS) **2005** Oak 6 (6, ss) **NFL** 53 (31) [4 yrs]

GIBSON, DICK Richard M., T-G, 6´0˝/188 lbs; Centre; B12/5/1900, D11/23/1968 Greenville, IN **1922** Lou 2 (2, RT) **1923** Lou 3 (3, LT) **NFL** 5 (5) [2 yrs]

GIBSON, ERNEST Ernest Gerard, DB, 5´10˝/189 lbs; Furman; 1984: NE, rnd 6; B10/3/1961 Jacksonville, FL **1984** NE 15 (8, LCB) **1985**†NE 9 (0) **1986**†NE 15 (1) **1987** NE 12 (5, rcb) **1988** NE 16 (0) **1989** Mia 5 (0) **NFL** 72 (14) [6 yrs]

GIBSON, GEORGE George Randall, G, 6´0˝/208 lbs; Minnesota; B10/2/1905 Kendaia, NY, D8/19/2004 Midland, TX **[C]** **1930** Fra 5 (4) **1930** Min☆9 (8, RG) **NFL** 14 (12) [1 yr]

GIBSON, JOE Billy Joe, C-E, 6´3˝/213 lbs; Cameron; Tulsa; B6/28/1919 Nacona, TX, D10/19/2002 Sacramento, CA **1943**†Was 5 (0) **1944** Cle 10 (1)

YEAR	TEAM	G(GS, POS)	RUSH	YD	AVG(LG)	TD	REC	YD	AVG(LG)	TD	PASS	COMP	PCT	YD	AVG(LG)	TD	INT	SK	YD	QBR	KPR	OTD	PTS	TAY
1942	Cle	11(8, RE)	—	—	—	—	6	79	13.2(19)	0	—	—	—	—	—	—	—	—	—	—	—	—	0	40
NFL	3	26(9)	—	—	—	—	6	79	13.2(19)	0	—	—	—	—	—	—	—	—	—	—	—	—	0	40

YEAR	TEAM	G(GS, POS)	RUSH	YD	AVG(LG)	TD	REC	YD	AVG(LG)	TD	PASS	COMP	PCT	YD	AVG(LG)	TD	INT	SK	YD	QBR	KPR	OTD	PTS	TAY

1946 Bkn-A 14 (5, c) **1947** Bkn-A 14 (4) **AAFC** 26 (9) [3 yrs]

GIBSON, OLIVER Oliver Donnovan, DT-NT, 6´2˝/304 lbs; Notre Dame; 1995: Pit, rnd 4; B3/15/1972 Chicago, IL **1995** Pit 12 (0) **1996**†Pit 16 (0) **1997**†Pit 16 (0) **1998** Pit 16 (0) **1999** Cin 16 (16, NT/rdt) **2000** Cin 16 (16, LDT) **2001** Cin 16 (16, LDT) **2002** Cin 9 (9, LDT) **2003** Cin 16 (0) **NFL** 133 (57) [9 yrs]

GIBSON, PAUL Paul Edward, E-QB-DB-DE; 6´2˝/195 lbs; North Carolina State; 1947: Buf-A, rnd 9/Pit, rnd 10; B10/28/1921 Winston-Salem, NC, D1975

YEAR	TEAM	G(GS, POS)	RUSH	YD	AVG(LG)	TD	REC	YD	AVG(LG)	TD	PASS	COMP	PCT	YD	AVG(LG)	TD	INT	SK	YD	QBR	KPR	OTD	PTS	TAY
1947	Buf-A	14(8, LE)	—	—	—	—	8	154	19.3	0	—	—	—	—	—	—	—	—	—	—	—	—	0	77
1948	†Buf-A	7(5, RE)	—	—	—	—	11	216	19.6	0	—	—	—	—	—	—	—	—	—	—	—	—	0	108
1949	†Buf-A	9(2)	—	—	—	—	3	32	10.7	0	—	—	—	—	—	—	—	—	—	—	i	—	0	20
AAFC	3	30(15)	—	—	—	—	22	402	18.3	0	—	—	—	—	—	—	—	—	—	—	i	—	0	205

GIBSON, PAUL Paul Dean, WR, 6´2˝/195 lbs; Texas-El Paso; 1972: Buf, rnd 8; B6/20/1948 Paris, AR, D5/23/1975 El Paso, TX **1972** GB 1

GIBSON, TOM Thomas Anthony, DE-DT, 6´7˝/257 lbs; Northern Arizona; 1987: NE, rnd 5; B12/20/1963 San Fernando, CA **1989**†Cle 16 (1) **1990** Cle 12 (3) **1991** LARm 5 (1) **NFL** 33 (5) [3 yrs]

GIDDENS, FRANK Frank David, T, 6´7˝/300 lbs; New Mexico; B1/20/1959 Lubbock, TX **1981**†Phi 16 (0) **1982** Phi 9 (3) **NFL** 25 (3) [2 yrs]

GIDDENS, WIMPY Herschel Orine, T, 6´2˝/220 lbs; Louisiana Tech; B11/25/1914 Ringgold, LA **1938** Phi 9 (0) **1944** Bos 7 (0) **NFL** 16 (0) [2 yrs]

GIESLER, JON Jon William, T, 6´5˝/262 lbs; Michigan; 1979: Mia, rnd 1; B12/23/1956 Toledo, OH **1979**†Mia 16 **1980** Mia 10 (10, LT) **1981**†Mia 16 (16, LT) **1982**†Mia 9 (9, LT) **1983**†Mia 16 (16, LT) **1984**†Mia☆16 (16, LT) **1985**†Mia 13 (13, LT) **1986** Mia☆7 (7, LT) **1987** Mia 10 (9, LT) **1988** Mia 13 (9, LT) **NFL** 126 (105) [10 yrs]

GIFFORD, BOB Robert F., BB, 6´0˝/200 lbs; Denver; 1942: Bkn, rnd 9; B11/12/1918 Chicago, IL, D8/31/1994 Westminster, CO **1942** Bkn 5 (0)

GIFFORD, FRANK Frank Newton, HB-FL-DB-WR, 6´1˝/197 lbs; USC; 1952: NYG, rnd 1; B8/16/1930 Santa Monica, CA; HOF 1977 **[K]**

YEAR	TEAM	G(GS, POS)	RUSH	YD	AVG(LG)	TD	REC	YD	AVG(LG)	TD	PASS	COMP	PCT	YD	AVG(LG)	TD	INT	SK	YD	QBR	KPR	OTD	PTS	TAY
1952	NYG	10(lh)	38	116	3.1(15)	0	5	36	7.2(11)	0	2	1	50.0	18	9.0(18)	1	0	—	—	—	kpi	—	0	251
1953	NYG★	12(lh/db)	50	157	3.1(15)	2	18	292	16.2(49)	4	6	3	50.0	47	7.8(21)	1	0	—	—	—	Kkpi	1	47	601
1954	NYG✧	9(LH)	66	368	5.6(30)	2	14	154	11.0(35)	1	8	4	50.0	155	19.4(83)	3	1	—	—	—	kp	—	18	509
1955	NYG★	11(LH)	86	351	4.1(49)	3	33	437	13.2(54)	4	6	2	33.3	96	16.0(71)	2	0	—	—	—	k	—	42	717
1956	†NYG★	12(LH)	159	819	5.2(69)	5	51	603	11.8(48)	4	5	2	40.0	35	7.0(29)	2	1	—	—	—	K	—	65	1178
1957	NYG☆	12(LH)	136	528	3.9(41)	5	41	588	14.3(63)	4	6	4	66.7	143	23.8(66)	2	0	—	—	—	—	—	54	974
1958	†NYG★	10(LH)	115	468	4.1(33)	8	29	330	11.4(41)	2	10	3	30.0	109	10.9(63)	1	1	—	—	—	—	—	60	743
1959	†NYG★	11(LH)	106	540	5.1(79)	3	42	768	18.3(77)	4	11	5	45.5	151	13.7(43)	2	2	—	—	—	—	—	42	980
1960	NYG	8(LH)	77	232	3.0(15)	4	24	344	14.3(44)	3	6	3	50.0	24	4.0(13)	0	1	—	—	—	—	—	42	431
1962	†NYG	14(FL)	2	18	9.0(12)	1	39	796	20.4(63)	7	2	1	50.0	12	6.0(12)	0	0	—	—	—	—	—	48	467
1963	†NYG✧	14(FL)	4	10	2.5(12)	0	42	657	15.6(64)	7	—	—	—	—	—	—	—	—	—	—	—	—	42	374
1964	NYG	13(FL)	1	2	2.0(2)	1	29	429	14.8(40)	3	1	1	100.0	33	33.0(33)	0	0	—	—	—	—	—	24	258
NFL	12	136	840	3609	4.3(79)	34	367	5434	14.8(77)	43	63	29	46.0	823	13.1(83)	14	6	—	—	—	Kkpi	1	484	7480

GIFT, WAYNE Leland Wayne, QB, 5´8˝/175 lbs; Purdue; B10/21/1915 Medina, OH, D2/13/1998 Louisville, KY

YEAR	TEAM	G(GS, POS)	RUSH	YD	AVG(LG)	TD	REC	YD	AVG(LG)	TD	PASS	COMP	PCT	YD	AVG(LG)	TD	INT	SK	YD	QBR	KPR	OTD	PTS	TAY
1937	Cle	10(1)	3	7	2.3	0	3	20	6.7	0	3	0	0.0	0	0.0	0	0	—	—	—	—	—	0	17

GILBERT, DAREN Daren K., T, 6´6˝/285 lbs; Cal State-Fullerton; 1985: NO, rnd 2; B10/3/1963 San Diego, CA **1985** NO 16 (0) **1986** NO 9 (0) **1987** NO 6 (5, lt) **1988** NO 11 (6, rt) **NFL** 42 (11) [4 yrs]

GILBERT, FREDDIE Freddie Gene, DE, 6´4˝/275 lbs; Georgia; 1984: Den, rnd S1; B4/8/1962 Griffin, GA **1986**†Den 15 (0) **1987** Den 7 (3) **1988** Den 13 (5, lde) **1989** Phx 2 (0) **NFL** 37 (8) [4 yrs]

GILBERT, GALE Gale Reed, QB, 6´3˝/209 lbs; California; B12/20/1961 Red Bluff, CA

YEAR	TEAM	G(GS, POS)	RUSH	YD	AVG(LG)	TD	REC	YD	AVG(LG)	TD	PASS	COMP	PCT	YD	AVG(LG)	TD	INT	SK	YD	QBR	KPR	OTD	PTS	TAY
1985	Sea	9(0)	7	4	0.6(8)	0	—	—	—	—	40	19	47.5	218	5.4(37)	1	2	1	9	—	—	—	0	38
1986	Sea	16(2)	3	8	2.7(12)	0	—	—	—	—	76	42	55.3	485	6.4(38)	3	3	4	34	—	—	—	0	146
1990	Buf	1(0)	—	—	—	—	—	—	—	—	15	8	53.3	106	7.1(23)	2	2	1	9	—	—	—	0	-17
1993	Buf	1(0)	—	—	—	—	—	—	—	—	—	—	—	—	—	—	—	—	—	—	—	—	—	—
1994	†SD	15(1)	8	-3	-0.4(5)	0	—	—	—	—	67	41	61.2	410	6.1(26)	3	1	4	28	—	—	—	0	177
1995	†SD	16(1)	6	11	1.8(8)	0	—	—	—	—	61	36	59.0	325	5.3(41)	0	4	9	43	—	—	—	0	14
NFL	6	58(4)	24	20	0.8(12)	0	—	—	—	—	259	146	56.4	1544	6.0(41)	9	12	19	123	—	—	—	0	357

GILBERT, KLINE Kline, T-G, 6´2˝/233 lbs; Mississippi; 1953: ChiB, rnd 6; B11/22/1930 Hollandale, MS, D6/14/1987 Jackson, MS **1953** ChiB 12 (RT) **1954** ChiB 12 (RG) **1955** ChiB 12 (RT) **1956**†ChiB 12 (RT) **1957** ChiB✧12 (RT) **NFL** 60 [5 yrs]

GILBERT, LEWIS Lewis Howe, TE, 6´4˝/225 lbs; Florida; B5/24/1956 Naples, FL **1978**†Atl 4 **1980** SF 6 (0) **1981** LARm 6 (0)

YEAR	TEAM	G(GS, POS)	RUSH	YD	AVG(LG)	TD	REC	YD	AVG(LG)	TD	PASS	COMP	PCT	YD	AVG(LG)	TD	INT	SK	YD	QBR	KPR	OTD	PTS	TAY
1980	Phi	3(0)	—	—	—	—	1	7	7.0(7)	0	—	—	—	—	—	—	—	—	—	—	—	—	0	4
NFL	3	19	—	—	—	—	1	7	7.0(7)	0	—	—	—	—	—	—	—	—	—	—	—	—	0	4

GILBERT, SEAN Sean, DT-DE, 6´5˝/318 lbs; Pittsburgh; 1992: LARm, rnd 1; B4/10/1970 Aliquippa, PA **1992** LARm 16 (16, RDT) **1993** LARm★16 (16, RDT) **1994** LARm 14 (14, RDT) **1995** SL 14 (14, RDE) **1996** Was 16 (16, RDT) **1998** Car 16 (16, RDE) **1999** Car 16 (16, RDT) **2000** Car 15 (15, RDT) **2001** Car 9 (9, ldt) **2002** Car 8 (0) **2003** Oak 6 (0) **NFL** 146 (132) [11 yrs]

GILBERT, TONY Antonio C., LB, 6´1˝/257 lbs; Georgia; 2003: Arz, rnd 6; B10/16/1979 Macon, GA **2003** Jax 8 (0) **2004** Jax 16 (0) **2005**†Jax 16 (0) **NFL** 40 (0) [3 yrs]

GILBERT, WALLY Walter John, TB-WB, 6´1˝/180 lbs; Valparaiso; B12/19/1900 Oscoda, MI, D9/7/1958 Duluth, MN **[K]** **1923** Dul 7 (3), 6 **1924** Dul 5 (4, TB), 18 **1925** Dul 2 (1) **1926** Dul 3 (1) **NFL** 17 (9), 24 [4 yrs]

GILBURG, TOM Thomas deMagnin, T-P, 6´5˝/245 lbs; Syracuse; 1961: Bal, rnd 2/Buf, rnd 3; B11/27/1938 Bronxville, NY **1961** Bal 14 **1962** Bal 14 (8, LT) **1963** Bal 13 **1964**†Bal 14 **1965**†Bal 14 **NFL** 69 (8) [5 yrs]

GILCHRIST, COOKIE Carlton Chester, FB, 6´3˝/251 lbs; none; B5/25/1935 Brackenridge, PA **[K]**

YEAR	TEAM	G(GS, POS)	RUSH	YD	AVG(LG)	TD	REC	YD	AVG(LG)	TD	PASS	COMP	PCT	YD	AVG(LG)	TD	INT	SK	YD	QBR	KPR	OTD	PTS	TAY
1962	Buf-A★	14(FB)	214	**1096**	5.1(44)	**13**	24	319	13,3(74)	2	—	—	—	—	—	—	—	—	—	—	Kk	—	128	1441
1963	†Buf-A★	14(FB)	**232**	979	4.2(32)	**12**	24	211	8.8(42)	2	1	1	100.0	35	35.0(35)	0	0	—	—	—	—	—	84	1232
1964	†Buf-A★	14(FB)	**230**	**981**	4.3(67)	**6**	30	345	11.5(37)	0	—	—	—	—	—	—	—	—	—	—	—	—	36	1214
1965	Den-A★	14(FB)	**252**	954	3.8(44)	**6**	18	154	8.6(29)	1	—	—	—	—	—	—	—	—	—	—	—	—	42	1096
1966	Mia-A	8(5, fb)	72	262	3.6(22)	0	13	110	8.5(22)	1	—	—	—	—	—	—	—	—	—	—	—	—	6	322
1967	Den-A	1	10	21	2.1(6)	0	1	-4	-4.0(-4)	0	—	—	—	—	—	—	—	—	—	—	—	—	0	19
NFL	6	65(5)	1010	4293	4.3(67)	37	110	1135	10.3(74)	6	1	1	100.0	35	35.0(35)	0	0	—	—	—	Kk	—	296	5323

GILCHRIST, GEORGE George Robert, DT, 6´0˝/260 lbs; Tennessee State; B1/19/1928 Memphis, TN, D7/16/1980 Chicago, IL **1953** ChiC 11

GILDEA, DENNIS Dennis Anthony, C-T-G, 5´9˝/190 lbs; Holy Cross; B10/9/1898 Boston, MA, D2/22/1976 Lynn, MA **1926** Har 7 (2)

GILDEA, JOHNNY John Thomas, B, 6´2˝/205 lbs; St. Bonaventure; B3/9/1910 Boston Run, PA, D11/20/1979 Tamaqua, PA **[K]**

YEAR	TEAM	G(GS, POS)	RUSH	YD	AVG(LG)	TD	REC	YD	AVG(LG)	TD	PASS	COMP	PCT	YD	AVG(LG)	TD	INT	SK	YD	QBR	KPR	OTD	PTS	TAY
1935	Pit	12(10, TB)	49	1	0.0	0	4	61	15.3	0	105	28	26.7	529	5.0	2	**20**	—	—	14.8	—	—	0	-494
1936	Pit	12(9, BB)	35	31	0.9	0	5	70	14.0	0	29	9	31.0	147	5.1	1	5	—	—	—	—	—	0	-56
1937	Pit☆	11(8, TB)	49	65	1.3	1	3	47	15.7	0	47	14	29.8	288	6.1	2	9	—	—	—	—	—	6	-108
1938	†NYG✧	9(2)	1	2	2.0(2)	0	1	3	3.0(3)	0	—	—	—	—	—	—	—	—	—	—	K	—	0	4
NFL	4	44(29)	134	99	0.7(2)	1	13	181	13.9(3)	0	181	51	28.2	964	5.3	5	34	—	—	18.9	K	—	6	-654

GILDON, JASON Jason Larue, LB, 6´4˝/255 lbs; Oklahoma State; 1994: Pit, rnd 3; B7/31/1972 Altus, OK **[S]** **1994**†Pit 16 (1) **1995**†Pit 16 (0) **1996**†Pit 14 (13, LOLB) **1997**†Pit 16 (16, LOLB) **1998** Pit 16 (16, LOLB) **1999** Pit 16 (16, LOLB) **2000** Pit✧16 (16, LOLB) **2001**†Pit★16 (16, LOLB) **2002**†Pit✧16 (16, LOLB) **2003** Pit 16 (16, LOLB) **2004** Jax 9 (0) **NFL** 167 (126) [11 yrs]

GILES, JIMMIE Jimmie, TE, 6´3˝/239 lbs; Alcorn State; 1977: Hou, rnd 3; B11/8/1954 Natchez, MS

YEAR	TEAM	G(GS, POS)	RUSH	YD	AVG(LG)	TD	REC	YD	AVG(LG)	TD	PASS	COMP	PCT	YD	AVG(LG)	TD	INT	SK	YD	QBR	KPR	OTD	PTS	TAY
1977	Hou	14(3)	1	-10	-10.0(-10)	0	17	147	8.6(17)	0	—	—	—	—	—	—	—	—	—	—	—	—	0	64
1978	TB	16(10, TE)	1	-1	-1.0(-1)	0	23	324	14.1(38)	2	—	—	—	—	—	—	—	—	—	—	k	—	12	156
1979	†TB	16(16, TE)	2	7	3.5(9)	0	40	579	14.5(66)	7	—	—	—	—	—	—	—	—	—	—	—	—	42	332
1980	TB★	16(15, TE)	—	—	—	—	33	602	18.2(51)	4	—	—	—	—	—	—	—	—	—	—	—	—	24	321
1981	†TB★	16(16, TE)	—	—	—	—	45	786	17.5(81)	6	—	—	—	—	—	—	—	—	—	—	—	—	36	423
1982	†TB★	9(9, TE)	1	1	1.0(1)	0	28	499	17.8(48)	3	—	—	—	—	—	—	—	—	—	—	—	—	18	266
1983	TB	11(9, TE)	—	—	—	—	25	349	14.0(80)	1	—	—	—	—	—	—	—	—	—	—	—	—	6	180
1984	TB	14(14, TE)	—	—	—	—	24	310	12.9(38)	2	—	—	—	—	—	—	—	—	—	—	—	—	12	165

YEAR	TEAM	G (GS, POS)	RUSH	YD	AVG (LG)	TD	REC	YD	AVG (LG)	TD	PASS	COMP	PCT	YD	AVG (LG)	TD	INT	SK	YD	QBR	KPR	OTD	PTS	TAY
1985	TB★	16(16, TE)	—	—	—	—	43	673	15.7(44)	8	—	—	—	—	—	—	—	—	—	—	—	—	48	377
1986	TB	7(7, te)	—	—	—	—	18	178	9.9(20)	1	—	—	—	—	—	—	—	—	—	—	—	—	6	94
1986	Det	9(8, TE)	—	—	—	—	19	198	10.4(30)	3	—	—	—	—	—	—	—	—	—	—	—	—	18	114
1987	Det	4(1)	—	—	—	—	6	62	10.3(25)	0	—	—	—	—	—	—	—	—	—	—	—	—	0	31
1987	Phi	8(0)	—	—	—	—	7	95	13.6(40)	1	—	—	—	—	—	—	—	—	—	—	—	—	6	53
1988	†Phi	16(1)	—	—	—	—	6	57	9.5(17)	1	—	—	—	—	—	—	—	—	—	—	—	—	6	34
1989	†Phi	16(5, te)	—	—	—	—	16	225	14.1(66)	2	—	—	—	—	—	—	—	—	—	—	—	—	12	123
NFL	13	188(130)	5	-3	-0.6(9)	0	350	5084	14.5(81)	41	—	—	—	—	—	—	—	—	—	—	k	—	246	2729
GILL, OWEN Owen, RB, 6´1˝/230 lbs; Iowa; 1985: Sea, rnd 2; B2/19/1962 London, England																								
1985	Ind	15(0)	45	262	5.8(67)	2	5	52	10.4(20)	0	—	—	—	—	—	—	—	—	—	—	k	—	12	299
1986	Ind	16(1)	53	228	4.3(18)	1	16	137	8.6(15)	0	—	—	—	—	—	—	—	—	—	—	k	—	6	305
1987	LARm	1(0)	—	—	—	—	—	—	—	—	—	—	—	—	—	—	—	—	—	—	—	—	—	—
NFL	3	32(1)	98	490	5.0(67)	3	21	189	9.0(20)	0	—	—	—	—	—	—	—	—	—	—	k	—	18	604
GILL, RANDY Randy, LB, 6´2˝/230 lbs; San Jose State; 1978: SL, rnd 10; B8/1/1956 Ventura, CA, D2/10/2002 Winnipeg, Canada **1978** SL 7 **1978** TB 1 **NFL** 8 [1 yr]																								
GILL, ROGER Roger Ewing, WR-HB, 6´1˝/200 lbs; Texas Tech; 1963: Phi, rnd 12/SD, rnd 22; B10/14/1940 League City, TX																								
1964	Phi	12	—	—	—	—	4	58	14.5(29)	0	—	—	—	—	—	—	—	—	—	—	kp	—	0	122
1965	Phi	13	—	—	—	—	1	27	27.0(27)	0	—	—	—	—	—	—	—	—	—	—	kp	—	0	17
NFL	2	25	—	—	—	—	5	85	17.0(29)	0	—	—	—	—	—	—	—	—	—	—	kp	—	0	139
GILL, SLOK Sloko, C-LB-G, 5´7˝/180 lbs; Youngstown State; B3/8/1918 Campbell, OH, D12/22/1995 Boardman, OH **1942** Det 11 (2)																								
GILLEN, JOHN John Francis, LB, 6´3˝/227 lbs; Illinois; 1981: SL, rnd 5; B11/5/1958 Arlington Heights, IL **1981** SL 16 (0) **1982**†SL 4 (0) **1983** NE 8 (0) **NFL** 28 (0) [3 yrs]																								
GILLESPIE, SCOOP Fernadars, RB, 5´10˝/185 lbs; William Jewell; 1984: Pit, rnd 12; B2/26/1962 St. Louis, MO																								
1984	†Pit	14(0)	7	18	2.6(9)	0	1	12	12.0(12)	0	—	—	—	—	—	—	—	—	—	—	k	—	0	21
GILLESPIE, WILLIE Willie E., WR, 5´9˝/170 lbs; Tennessee-Chattanooga; B10/24/1961 Starkville, MS																								
1986	TB	2(0)	—	—	—	—	1	18	18.0(18)	0	—	—	—	—	—	—	—	—	—	—	—	—	0	9
1987	Min	1(1)	—	—	—	—	2	28	14.0(14)	0	—	—	—	—	—	—	—	—	—	—	—	—	0	14
NFL	2	3(1)	—	—	—	—	3	46	15.3(18)	0	—	—	—	—	—	—	—	—	—	—	—	—	0	23
GILLETT, FRED Frederick L., C-LB-G, 6´3˝/225 lbs; Los Angeles State; 1962: Bal, rnd 19; B12/16/1936 **1964** Oak-A 3																								
1962	SD-A	6	2	8	4.0(5)	0	—	—	—	—	—	—	—	—	—	—	—	—	—	—	—	—	0	8
NFL	2	9	2	8	4.0(5)	0	—	—	—	—	—	—	—	—	—	—	—	—	—	—	—	—	0	8
GILLETTE, JIM James Thomas, HB, 6´1˝/185 lbs; Virginia; 1940: GB, rnd 18; B12/19/1917 Courtland, VA, D1/9/1990 Richmond, VA																								
1940	Cle	4(0)	1	1	1.0(1)	0	—	—	—	—	4	0	0.0	0	0.0	0	2	—	—	—	—	—	0	-79
1944	Cle	7(2)	26	131	5.0(58)	2	—	—	—	—	—	—	—	—	—	—	—	—	—	—	kpi	—	12	231
1945	†Cle☆	10(7, RH)	63	390	6.2(52)	1	6	48	8.0(15)	0	—	—	—	—	—	—	—	—	—	—	kpi	—	6	436
1946	Bos	11(4)	30	99	3.3(46)	1	5	96	19.2(60)	1	—	—	—	—	—	—	—	—	—	—	kpi	—	12	212
1947	GB	10(1)	50	207	4.1(26)	0	12	224	18.7(50)	1	—	—	—	—	—	—	—	—	—	—	kp	—	6	458
1948	Det	10(2)	2	3	1.5(2)	0	1	8	8.0(8)	0	—	—	—	—	—	—	—	—	—	—	pi	—	0	-6
NFL	6	52(16)	172	831	4.8(58)	4	24	376	15.7(60)	2	4	0	0.0	0	0.0	0	2	—	—	—	kpi	—	36	1252
GILLETTE, WALKER Walker Adams, WR, 6´5˝/200 lbs; Richmond; 1970: SD, rnd 1; B3/16/1947 Norfolk, VA																								
1970	SD	13	—	—	—	—	2	21	10.5(12)	0	—	—	—	—	—	—	—	—	—	—	—	—	0	11
1971	SD	12	—	—	—	—	10	147	14.7(25)	2	—	—	—	—	—	—	—	—	—	—	—	—	12	84
1972	SL	14(WR)	—	—	—	—	33	550	16.7(65)	2	—	—	—	—	—	—	—	—	—	—	—	—	12	285
1973	SL	14(wr)	—	—	—	—	20	244	12.2(48)	1	—	—	—	—	—	—	—	—	—	—	—	—	6	127
1974	NYG	11(WR)	—	—	—	—	29	466	16.1(72)	3	—	—	—	—	—	—	—	—	—	—	—	—	18	248
1975	NYG	14(WR)	—	—	—	—	43	600	14.0(50)	2	—	—	—	—	—	—	—	—	—	—	—	—	12	310
1976	NYG	13	1	-4	-4.0(-4)	0	16	263	16.4(62)	2	—	—	—	—	—	—	—	—	—	—	—	—	12	138
NFL	7	91	1	-4	-4.0(-4)	0	153	2291	15.0(72)	12	—	—	—	—	—	—	—	—	—	—	—	—	72	1202
GILLIAM, DONDRE Dondre, WR, 6´0˝/185 lbs; Cheyney; Millersville; B2/9/1977 Baltimore, MD **2002** SD 2 (0)																								
2003	SD	5(1)	—	—	—	—	6	95	15.8(37)	0	—	—	—	—	—	—	—	—	—	—	—	—	0	48
NFL	2	7(1)	—	—	—	—	6	95	15.8(37)	0	—	—	—	—	—	—	—	—	—	—	—	—	0	48
GILLIAM, JOE Joseph Wiley 'Jefferson Street Joe', QB, 6´2˝/187 lbs; Tennessee State; 1972: Pit, rnd 11; B12/29/1950 Charleston, WV, D12/25/2000 Nashville, TN																								
1972	Pit	2	2	0	0.0(0)	0	—	—	—	—	11	7	63.6	48	4.4(9)	0	0	2	8	—	—	—	0	24
1973	Pit	5(1)	6	23	3.8(14)	0	—	—	—	—	60	20	33.3	331	5.5(46)	2	6	3	17	—	—	—	0	-42
1974	†Pit	9(6, qb)	14	41	2.9(13)	1	—	—	—	—	212	96	45.3	1274	6.0(61)	4	8	7	79	55.4	—	—	6	388
1975	Pit	4	—	—	—	—	—	—	—	—	48	24	50.0	450	9.4(53)	3	3	—	—	—	—	—	0	120
NFL	4	20(7)	22	64	2.9(14)	1	—	—	—	—	331	147	44.4	2103	6.4(61)	9	17	12	104	53.2	—	—	6	491
GILLIAM, JOHN John Rally, WR-FL, 6´1˝/195 lbs; South Carolina State; 1967: NO, rnd 2; B8/7/1945 Greenwood, SC																								
1967	NO	13(fl)	7	41	5.9(19)	0	22	264	12.0(35)	1	—	—	—	—	—	—	—	—	—	—	kp	1	12	407
1968	NO	14	2	36	18.0(29)	0	24	284	11.8(39)	0	—	—	—	—	—	—	—	—	—	—	kp	—	0	266
1969	SL	14(FL)	1	-4	-4.0(-4)	0	52	997	19.2(84)	9	—	—	—	—	—	—	—	—	—	—	k	1	60	724
1970	SL	14(WR)	5	68	13.6(48)	1	45	952	21.2(79)	5	—	—	—	—	—	—	—	—	—	—	k	—	36	611
1971	SL	14(WR)	2	16	8.0(12)	0	42	837	19.9(54)	3	—	—	—	—	—	—	—	—	—	—	p	—	18	466
1972	Min★	14(14, WR)	8	14	1.8(14)	0	47	1035	**22.0**(**66**)	7	—	—	—	—	—	—	—	—	—	—	k	—	42	726
1973	†Min★	14(14, WR)	5	71	14.2(44)	1	42	907	21.6(54)	8	—	—	—	—	—	—	—	—	—	—	k	—	54	599
1974	†Min✧	14(14, WR)	2	16	8.0(9)	0	26	578	22.2(80)	5	—	—	—	—	—	—	—	—	—	—	k	—	30	371
1975	†Min★	14(14, WR)	3	35	11.7(22)	0	50	777	15.5(46)	7	—	—	—	—	—	—	—	—	—	—	—	—	42	459
1976	Atl	14(WR)	—	—	—	—	21	292	13.9(49)	2	—	—	—	—	—	—	—	—	—	—	—	—	12	156
1977	ChiB	2	—	—	—	—	—	—	—	—	—	—	—	—	—	—	—	—	—	—	—	—	—	—
1977	NO	10(WR)	—	—	—	—	11	133	12.1(23)	1	—	—	—	—	—	—	—	—	—	—	—	—	6	72
NFL	11	151(56)	35	293	8.4(48)	2	382	7056	18.5(84)	48	—	—	—	—	—	—	—	—	—	—	kp	2	312	4854
GILLIAM, JON Jon Ray, C, 6´2˝/240 lbs; Oklahoma State; Texas A&M-Commerce; 1960: Buf, rnd 1/GB, rnd 14; B10/22/1938 Oklahoma City, OK **1962**†DalT-A 14 (14, C) **1963** KC-A 14 (14, C) **1964** KC-A 14 (14, C) **1965** KC-A 14 (14, C) **1966**†KC-A 1 **1967** KC-A 5 (C)																								
1961	DalT-A✧	14(14, C)	1	-6	-6.0(-6)	0	—	—	—	—	—	—	—	—	—	—	—	—	—	—	k	—	0	2
NFL	7	76(70)	1	-6	-6.0(-6)	0	—	—	—	—	—	—	—	—	—	—	—	—	—	—	—	—	0	-6
GILLIARD, CORY Cory Rashad, DB, 6´0˝/210 lbs; Ball State; 1997: Den, rnd 4; B10/10/1974 Bronx, NY **1997** Cin 1 (0)																								
GILLIES, FRED Frederick Montague, T, 6´3˝/218 lbs; Cornell; B12/9/1895 Chicago, IL, D5/8/1974 Flossmoor, IL **[C]** **1920** ChiC 9 (6, LT) **1921** ChiC 8 (8, LT) **1922** ChiC☆11 (9, RT) **1923** ChiC 11 (6, rt) **1924** ChiC 10 (9, RT) **1925** ChiC 14 (10, RT) **1926** ChiC 7 (4) **1928** ChiC 1 (0) **NFL** 71 (52) [8 yrs]																								
GILLINGHAM, GALE Gale Herbert, G-DT, 6´3˝/255 lbs; Minnesota; 1966: GB, rnd 1; B2/3/1944 Madison, WI **1966**†GB 14 (2) **1967**†GB 14 (14, LG) **1968** GB☆14 (14, LG) **1969** GB★14 (RG) **1970** GB★14 (RG) **1971** GB★14 (RG) **1972** GB 2 **1973** GB★14 (RG) **1974** GB★14 (RG) **1976** GB 14 (RG) **NFL** 128 (30) [10 yrs]																								
GILLIS, DON Donald, C, 6´3˝/245 lbs; Rice; 1957: Cle, rnd 8; B3/31/1935 Corpus Christi, TX **1958** ChiC 12 (C) **1959** ChiC 12 (C) **1960** SL 12 (7, C) **1961** SL 9 (C) **NFL** 45 (7) [4 yrs]																								
GILLIS, JOE Joseph Augustus, G-T, 5´8˝/210 lbs; Tufts; Detroit Mercy; B4/24/1896 Medford, MA, D12/19/1967 Detroit, MI **1923** Tol 7 (2)																								
GILLO, HANK Henry Charles, B, 5´10˝/195 lbs; Colgate; B10/5/1894 Milwaukee, WI, D9/6/1948 Manchester Township, WI **[KC]** **1920** Ham 7 (3, FB) **1921** Ham 1 (1) **1922** Rac 11 (10, FB), 52 **1923** Rac☆10 (10, FB), 44 **1924** Rac 10 (9, FB), 48 **1925** Mil 2 (0) **1926** Rac 4 (0) **NFL** 45 (33), 144 [7 yrs]																								
GILLOM, HORACE Horace Albert, E-DE, 6´1˝/221 lbs; Ohio State; Nevada-Reno; B3/3/1921 Roanoke, AL **[P]**																								
1947	†Cle-A	14(4)	—	—	—	—	2	24	12.0	0	—	—	—	—	—	—	—	—	—	—	Pi	—	0	36
1948	†Cle-A	13(8, re)	—	—	—	—	20	295	14.8	1	—	—	—	—	—	—	—	—	—	—	Pk	—	6	118

YEAR	TEAM	G (GS, POS)	RUSH	YD	AVG (LG)	TD	REC	YD	AVG (LG)	TD	PASS	COMP	PCT	YD	AVG (LG)	TD	INT	SK	YD	QBR	KPR	OTD	PTS	TAY
1949	†Cle-A	12 (4)	2	8	4.0	0	23	359	15.6	0	—	—	—	—	—	—	—	—	—	—	P	—	0	188
AAFC	3	39 (16)	2	8	4.0	0	45	678	15.1	1	—	—	—	—	—	—	—	—	—	—	Pki	—	6	341
1950	†Cle	12 (rde)	—	—	—	—	2	54	27.0 (38)	1	1	1	100.0	3	3.0 (3)	0	0	—	—	—	Pk	—	6	40
1951	†Cle	12 (le)	—	—	—	—	11	164	14.9 (24)	0	—	—	—	—	—	—	—	—	—	—	Pk	1	6	77
1952	†Cle✧	12	—	—	—	—	4	45	11.3 (21)	1	—	—	—	—	—	—	—	—	—	—	Pk	—	6	15
1953	†Cle	12	—	—	—	—	7	80	11.4 (23)	0	—	—	—	—	—	—	—	—	—	—	P	—	0	40
1954	†Cle	12	—	—	—	—	5	62	12.4 (24)	0	—	—	—	—	—	—	—	—	—	—	P	—	0	31
1955	†Cle	12	1	-15	-15.0 (-15)	0	—	—	—	—	—	—	—	—	—	—	—	—	—	—	P	—	0	-15
1956	Cle	5	—	—	—	—	—	—	—	—	—	—	—	—	—	—	—	—	—	—	P	—	0	0
NFL	7	77	1	-15	-15.0	0	29	405	14.0 (38)	2	1	1	100.0	3	3.0 (3)	0	0	—	—	—	Pk	1	18	187

GILLSON, BOB Robert William, G, 6´0˝/208 lbs; Colgate; B5/4/1905 Binghamton, NY, D11/16/1992 **1930** Bkn 12 (11, RG/lg) **1931** Bkn 11 (8, RG) **NFL** 23 (19) [2 yrs]

GILLUS, WILLIE Willie Harden, QB, 6´4˝/215 lbs; Norfolk State; B9/1/1963 Emporia, VA

YEAR	TEAM	G (GS, POS)	RUSH	YD	AVG (LG)	TD	REC	YD	AVG (LG)	TD	PASS	COMP	PCT	YD	AVG (LG)	TD	INT	SK	YD	QBR	KPR	OTD	PTS	TAY
1987	GB	1 (0)	—	—	—	—	—	—	—	—	5	2	40.0	28	5.6 (15)	0	0	3	14	—	—	—	0	14

GILMER, HARRY Harry Vincent, QB-HB, 6´0˝/169 lbs; Alabama; 1948: Was, rnd B1/Bkn-A, rnd 1; B4/14/1926 Birmingham, AL **[C]**

YEAR	TEAM	G (GS, POS)	RUSH	YD	AVG (LG)	TD	REC	YD	AVG (LG)	TD	PASS	COMP	PCT	YD	AVG (LG)	TD	INT	SK	YD	QBR	KPR	OTD	PTS	TAY
1948	Was	1 (0)	—	—	—	—	—	—	—	—	5	2	40.0	69	13.8 (45)	0	0	—	—	—	—	—	0	35
1949	Was	12 (3, qb)	31	167	5.4 (25)	0	5	37	7.4 (13)	0	132	49	37.1	869	6.6 (61)	4	15	—	—	31.0	—	—	0	40
1950	Was✧	10 (qb)	22	145	6.6 (20)	1	—	—	—	—	141	63	44.7	948	6.7 (74)	8	12	—	—	50.8	—	—	6	189
1951	Was	10 (qb)	19	141	7.4 (37)	0	—	—	—	—	68	31	45.6	391	5.8 (47)	1	6	—	—	—	pi	—	0	258
1952	Was✧	12 (LH)	100	365	3.7 (30)	0	15	143	9.5 (37)	1	58	31	53.4	555	9.6 (61)	4	4	—	—	—	kp	—	6	644
1954	Was	12	6	19	3.2 (11)	0	—	—	—	—	7	2	28.6	18	2.6 (10)	0	1	—	—	—	—	—	0	-12
1955	Det	8 (qb)	15	67	4.5 (19)	0	—	—	—	—	122	58	47.5	633	5.2 (34)	2	4	—	—	55.1	—	—	0	234
1956	Det	11 (qb)	8	19	2.4 (6)	0	—	—	—	—	46	27	58.7	303	6.6 (41)	4	3	—	—	—	—	—	0	71
NFL	8	76 (3)	201	923	4.6 (37)	1	20	180	9.0 (37)	1	579	263	45.4	3786	6.5 (74)	23	45	—	—	48.0	kpi	—	12	1457

GILMORE, BRYAN Bryan, WR, 6´0˝/200 lbs; Midwestern State; B1/21/1978 Lufkin, TX

YEAR	TEAM	G (GS, POS)	RUSH	YD	AVG (LG)	TD	REC	YD	AVG (LG)	TD	PASS	COMP	PCT	YD	AVG (LG)	TD	INT	SK	YD	QBR	KPR	OTD	PTS	TAY
2000	Arz	1 (0)	—	—	—	—	—	—	—	—	—	—	—	—	—	—	—	—	—	—	—	—	—	—
2001	Arz	3 (0)	—	—	—	—	—	—	—	—	—	—	—	—	—	—	—	—	—	—	—	—	—	—
2002	Arz	7 (0)	—	—	—	—	1	14	14.0 (14)	0	—	—	—	—	—	—	—	—	—	—	—	—	0	7
2003	Arz	14 (10, WR)	1	0	0.0 (0)	0	17	208	12.2 (32)	2	—	—	—	—	—	—	—	—	—	—	—	—	12	114
2004	Mia	16 (2)	—	—	—	—	15	206	13.7 (37)	1	—	—	—	—	—	—	—	—	—	—	k	—	6	158
2005	Mia	15 (1)	—	—	—	—	5	105	21.0 (44)	1	—	—	—	—	—	—	—	—	—	—	k	—	6	97
NFL	6	56 (13)	1	0	0.0	0	38	533	14.0 (44)	4	—	—	—	—	—	—	—	—	—	—	k	—	24	376

GILMORE, JIM James Thomas, T-G, 6´5˝/269 lbs; Villanova; Ohio State; B12/19/1962 Philadelphia, PA **1986** Phi 2 (0) **1987** Mia 3 (2) **NFL** 5 (2) [2 yrs]

GILMORE, JOHN John Henry, TE, 6´4˝/260 lbs; Penn State; 2002: NO, rnd 6; B9/21/1979 Marquette, MI

YEAR	TEAM	G (GS, POS)	RUSH	YD	AVG (LG)	TD	REC	YD	AVG (LG)	TD	PASS	COMP	PCT	YD	AVG (LG)	TD	INT	SK	YD	QBR	KPR	OTD	PTS	TAY
2002	ChiB	8 (4)	—	—	—	—	10	130	13.0 (30)	0	—	—	—	—	—	—	—	—	—	—	—	—	0	65
2003	ChiB	15 (1)	—	—	—	—	—	—	—	—	—	—	—	—	—	—	—	—	—	—	k	—	0	-20
2004	ChiB	16 (1)	—	—	—	—	1	11	11.0 (11)	0	—	—	—	—	—	—	—	—	—	—	—	—	0	6
2005	†ChiB	16 (0)	—	—	—	—	1	1	1.0 (1)	1	—	—	—	—	—	—	—	—	—	—	k	—	6	-5
NFL	4	55 (6)	—	—	—	—	12	142	11.8 (30)	1	—	—	—	—	—	—	—	—	—	—	k	—	6	46

GILROY, JOHN Roland John, B, 5´11˝/178 lbs; Georgetown (DC); B10/24/1895 Hudson, MA, D6/1983 Smithtown, NY **1920** Can 6 (3) **1920** Cle 2 (1) **1921** Was 1 (1) **NFL** 9 (5) [2 yrs]

GINN, HUBERT Hubert A., RB, 5´10˝/185 lbs; Florida A&M; 1970: Mia, rnd 9; B1/4/1947 Savannah, GA

YEAR	TEAM	G (GS, POS)	RUSH	YD	AVG (LG)	TD	REC	YD	AVG (LG)	TD	PASS	COMP	PCT	YD	AVG (LG)	TD	INT	SK	YD	QBR	KPR	OTD	PTS	TAY
1970	†Mia	12	5	-1	-0.2 (8)	0	—	—	—	—	—	—	—	—	—	—	—	—	—	—	k	—	0	-17
1971	†Mia	14	22	97	4.4 (46)	0	—	—	—	—	—	—	—	—	—	—	—	—	—	—	k	—	0	199
1972	†Mia	14	27	142	5.3 (22)	1	1	23	23.0 (23)	0	—	—	—	—	—	—	—	—	—	—	k	—	6	174
1973	Mia	3	—	—	—	—	—	—	—	—	—	—	—	—	—	—	—	—	—	—	—	—	—	—
1973	Bal	9	16	47	2.9 (8)	0	3	2	0.7 (6)	0	—	—	—	—	—	—	—	—	—	—	k	—	0	111
1974	†Mia	9	26	99	3.8 (41)	2	2	3	1.5 (3)	0	—	—	—	—	—	—	—	—	—	—	k	—	12	176
1975	Mia	11	21	78	3.7 (14)	0	3	21	7.0 (8)	0	—	—	—	—	—	—	—	—	—	—	kp	—	0	188
1976	†Oak	7	10	53	5.3 (16)	0	—	—	—	—	—	—	—	—	—	—	—	—	—	—	k	—	0	65
1977	†Oak	10	5	6	1.2 (5)	0	—	—	—	—	—	—	—	—	—	—	—	—	—	—	k	—	0	35
1978	Oak	1	—	—	—	—	—	—	—	—	—	—	—	—	—	—	—	—	—	—	—	—	—	—
NFL	9	90	132	521	3.9 (46)	3	9	49	5.4 (23)	0	—	—	—	—	—	—	—	—	—	—	kp	—	18	930

GINN, TOMMIE Tommie Webster, C-G, 6´3˝/253 lbs; Arkansas; 1980: Det, rnd 5; B1/25/1958 Scotia, CA **1980** Det 14 (5, c) **1981** Det 13 (0) **NFL** 27 (5) [2 yrs]

GINNEY, JERRY Jerald Warren, G, 5´11˝/217 lbs; Santa Clara; 1939: NYG, rnd 6; B4/9/1916 Dayton, OH, D10/22/1984 San Jose, CA **1940** Phi 1 (0)

GIORDANO, MATT Matt, DB, 5´11˝/194 lbs; California; 2005: Ind, rnd 4; B10/16/1982 Fresno, CA **2005** Ind 15 (0)

GIPSON, PAUL Paul Theodis, RB, 6´0˝/210 lbs; Houston; 1969: Atl, rnd 2; B3/21/1946 Jacksonville, TX, D1/16/1985 Houston, TX

YEAR	TEAM	G (GS, POS)	RUSH	YD	AVG (LG)	TD	REC	YD	AVG (LG)	TD	PASS	COMP	PCT	YD	AVG (LG)	TD	INT	SK	YD	QBR	KPR	OTD	PTS	TAY
1969	Atl	10	62	303	4.9 (33)	1	4	33	8.3 (18)	0	1	0	0.0	0	0.0	0	1	—	—	—	k	—	6	300
1970	Atl	13	52	177	3.4 (16)	0	16	186	11.6 (51)	3	—	—	—	—	—	—	—	—	—	—	k	—	18	354
1971	Det	5	4	12	3.0 (5)	0	1	21	21.0 (21)	0	—	—	—	—	—	—	—	—	—	—	k	—	0	53
1973	NE	5	5	-1	-0.2 (4)	0	—	—	—	—	—	—	—	—	—	—	—	—	—	—	—	—	0	-1
NFL	4	33	123	491	4.0 (33)	1	21	240	11.4 (51)	3	1	0	0.0	0	0.0	0	1	—	—	—	k	—	24	705

GIPSON, THOMAS Thomas Allen, DT, 6´7˝/280 lbs; North Texas; 1971: Oak, rnd 14; B7/28/1948 Refugio, TX **1971** Oak 4

GIRARD, JUG Earl Francis, E-HB-QB-DB, 5´11˝/176 lbs; Wisconsin; 1948: GB, rnd 1/NYY-A, rnd 27; B1/25/1927 Marinette, WI, D1/17/1997 Rochester Hills, MI **[KP]**

YEAR	TEAM	G (GS, POS)	RUSH	YD	AVG (LG)	TD	REC	YD	AVG (LG)	TD	PASS	COMP	PCT	YD	AVG (LG)	TD	INT	SK	YD	QBR	KPR	OTD	PTS	TAY
1948	GB	10 (0)	13	26	2.0 (7)	0	1	2	2.0 (2)	0	14	4	28.6	117	8.4 (40)	1	1	—	—	—	Pki	—	0	85
1949	GB	12 (10, QB)	45	198	4.4 (35)	1	1	13	13.0 (13)	0	175	62	35.4	881	5.0 (50)	4	12	—	—	31.6	Pkpi	—	6	261
1950	GB	12	14	39	2.8 (11)	0	4	89	22.3 (55)	0	—	—	—	—	—	—	—	—	—	—	Pki	—	0	95
1951	GB	12 (DB)	4	20	5.0 (32)	0	10	220	22.0 (75)	2	—	—	—	—	—	—	—	—	—	—	Ppi	—	12	144
1952	Det	11 (LH)	61	222	3.6 (36)	2	17	316	18.6 (39)	2	4	0	0.0	0	0.0	0	0	—	—	—	k	—	24	411
1953	†Det	11	19	73	3.8 (17)	0	2	24	12.0 (15)	0	1	0	0.0	0	0.0	0	0	—	—	—	kp	—	0	243
1954	†Det	12 (re)	9	36	4.0 (16)	0	27	421	15.6 (41)	7	—	—	—	—	—	—	—	—	—	—	Pkp	—	42	327
1955	Det	12 (RE)	10	27	2.7 (10)	0	23	301	13.1 (34)	0	1	0	0.0	0	0.0	0	0	—	—	—	Pkp	—	0	170
1956	Det	10 (lh)	17	67	3.9 (11)	0	3	33	11.0 (16)	0	1	1	100.0	19	19.0 (19)	0	0	—	—	—	Pp	—	0	90
1957	Pit	12 (LE)	2	-5	-2.5 (0)	0	21	419	20.0 (46)	4	1	0	0.0	0	0.0	0	0	—	—	—	KP	—	29	225
NFL	10	114 (10)	194	703	3.6 (36)	3	109	1838	16.9 (75)	15	197	67	34.0	1017	5.2 (50)	5	13	—	—	32.9	KPkpi	—	113	2049

GISLER, MIKE Michael, C-G, 6´4˝/295 lbs; Houston; 1992: NO, rnd 11; B8/26/1969 Runge, TX **1993** NE 12 (0) **1994** NE 15 (5, c) **1995** NE 16 (0) **1996**†NE 14 (0) **1997**†NE 16 (2) **1998** NYJ 16 (0) **1999** NYJ 16 (0) **NFL** 105 (7) [7 yrs]

GISSINGER, ANDREW Andrew, T, 6´5˝/280 lbs; Syracuse; 1981: SD, rnd 6; B7/4/1959 Barberton, OH **1982**†SD 9 (0) **1983** SD 16 (16, RT)

YEAR	TEAM	G (GS, POS)	RUSH	YD	AVG (LG)	TD	REC	YD	AVG (LG)	TD	PASS	COMP	PCT	YD	AVG (LG)	TD	INT	SK	YD	QBR	KPR	OTD	PTS	TAY
1984	SD	16 (4)	—	—	—	—	1	3	3.0 (3)	0	—	—	—	—	—	—	—	—	—	—	—	—	0	2
NFL	3	41 (20)	—	—	—	—	1	3	3.0 (3)	0	—	—	—	—	—	—	—	—	—	—	k	—	0	-14

GIUGLIANO, PATSY Pasquale Raphael, BB, 5´4˝/140 lbs; none; B12/11/1900 Louisville, KY, D3/1976 Louisville, KY **1923** Lou 1 (0)

GIVENS, DAVID David Lamar, WR, 6´0˝/212 lbs; Notre Dame; 2002: NE, rnd 7; B8/16/1980 Youngstown, OH

YEAR	TEAM	G (GS, POS)	RUSH	YD	AVG (LG)	TD	REC	YD	AVG (LG)	TD	PASS	COMP	PCT	YD	AVG (LG)	TD	INT	SK	YD	QBR	KPR	OTD	PTS	TAY
2002	NE	12 (0)	—	—	—	—	9	92	10.2 (30)	1	—	—	—	—	—	—	—	—	—	—	—	—	6	51
2003	†NE	13 (5, wr)	—	—	—	—	34	510	15.0 (57)	6	1	0	0.0	0	0.0	0	1	—	—	—	k	—	36	246
2004	†NE	15 (12, WR)	—	—	—	—	56	874	15.6 (50)	3	—	—	—	—	—	—	—	—	—	—	—	—	18	452
2005	†NE	13 (10, WR)	2	13	6.5 (9)	0	59	738	12.5 (40)	2	—	—	—	—	—	—	—	—	—	—	—	—	12	392
NFL	4	53 (27)	2	13	6.5 (9)	0	158	2214	14.0 (57)	12	1	0	0.0	0	0.0	0	1	—	—	—	k	—	72	1141

GIVENS, REGGIE Reginald Alonzo, LB, 6´0˝/234 lbs; Penn State; 1993: Dal, rnd 8; B10/3/1971 Emporia, VA **1998**†SF 16 (0) **1999** SF 16 (0) **2000** Was 9 (0) **NFL** 41 (0) [3 yrs]

YEAR	TEAM	G (GS, POS)	RUSH	YD	AVG (LG)	TD	REC	YD	AVG (LG)	TD	PASS COMP	PCT	YD	AVG (LG)	TD	INT	SK	YD	QBR	KPR	OTD	PTS	TAY

GIVINS, ERNEST Ernest Pastell, WR-TE, 5´9˝/178 lbs; Northeastern Oklahoma A&M; Louisville; 1986: Hou, rnd 2; B9/3/1964 St. Petersburg, FL

1986	Hou	15(15, WR)	9	148	16.4(43)	1	61	1062	17.4(60)	3	2	0	0.0	0	0.0	0	0	—	—	p	—	24	744
1987	†Hou	12(12, WR)	1	-13	-13.0(-13)	0	53	933	17.6(**83**)	6	—	—	—	—	—	—	—	—	—	—	—	36	484
1988	†Hou	16(16, WR)	4	26	6.5(10)	0	60	976	16.3(46)	5	—	—	—	—	—	—	—	—	—	—	—	30	539
1989	†Hou	15(15, WR)	—	—	—	—	55	794	14.4(48)	3	—	—	—	—	—	—	—	—	—	—	—	18	412
1990	†Hou★	16(16, TE)	3	65	21.7(31)	0	72	979	13.6(80)	**9**	—	—	—	—	—	—	—	—	—	—	—	54	600
1991	†Hou	16(16, TE)	4	30	7.5(23)	0	70	996	14.2(49)	5	—	—	—	—	—	—	—	—	—	p	—	30	605
1992	†Hou✧	16(16, TE)	7	75	10.7(44)	0	67	787	11.7(41)	**10**	—	—	—	—	—	—	—	—	—	—	—	60	519
1993	†Hou	16(16, TE)	6	19	3.2(16)	0	68	887	13.0(**80**)	4	—	—	—	—	—	—	—	—	—	—	—	24	483
1994	Hou	16(16, WR)	1	-5	-5.0(-5)	0	36	521	14.5(76)	1	—	—	—	—	—	—	—	—	—	kp	1	12	308
1995	Jax	9(9, WR)	—	—	—	—	29	280	9.7(18)	3	—	—	—	—	—	—	—	—	—	p	—	18	138
NFL	10	147(147)	35	345	9.9(44)	1	571	8215	14.4(83)	49	2	0	0.0	0	0.0	0	0	—	—	kp	1	306	4830

GIZZI, CHRIS Christopher Aaron, LB, 6´0˝/235 lbs; Air Force; B3/8/1975 Brunswick, OH   **2000** GB 11 (0) **2001** GB 12 (1) **NFL** 23 (1) [2 yrs]

GLACKEN, SCOTTY Edward Scott, QB, 6´0˝/190 lbs; Duke; 1966: Den, rnd 7; B7/28/1944 Washington, DC

1966	Den-A	8(1)	2	-1	-0.5(5)	0	—	—	—	—	11	6	54.5	84	7.6(22)	1	0	—	—	—	—	0	46
1967	Den-A	2	1	10	10.0(10)	0	—	—	—	—	4	0	0.0	0	0.0	0	0	—	—	—	—	0	10
NFL	2	10(1)	3	9	3.0(10)	0	—	—	—	—	15	6	40.0	84	5.6(22)	1	0	—	—	—	—	0	56

GLADCHUK, CHET Chester Stephen, C-G-T, 6´4˝/248 lbs; Boston College; 1941: Pit, rnd 2; B4/4/1917 Bridgeport, CT, D9/4/1967 Northampton, MA   **1941**†NYG 7 (0)
1946†NYG 11 (11, C) **1947** NYG 10 (8, C) **NFL** 28 (19) [3 yrs]

GLADDEN, MACK James Mack, E, 6´2˝/195 lbs; Missouri; B5/22/1909 Turley, MO, D3/1985 Rolla, MO   **1934** SL 3 (3, RE)

GLADIEUX, BOB Robert Joseph, RB, 5´11˝/195 lbs; Notre Dame; 1969: Bos, rnd 8; B1/2/1947 Louisville, OH

1969	Bos-A	10	—	—	—	—	—	—	—	—	—	—	—	—	—	—	—	—	—	kp	—	0	1
1970	Bos	8	4	8	2.0(8)	0	—	—	—	—	—	—	—	—	—	—	—	—	—	p	—	0	8
1970	Buf	2	—	—	—	—	—	—	—	—	—	—	—	—	—	—	—	—	—	—	—	—	—
1971	NE	14	37	175	4.7(31)	0	6	60	10.0(25)	0	2	1	50.0	48	24.0(48)	0	0	—	—	kp	—	0	204
1972	NE	11(6, fb)	24	56	2.3(11)	0	19	192	10.1(31)	0	1	0	0.0	0	0.0	0	1	—	—	p	—	0	96
NFL	4	45(6)	65	239	3.7(31)	0	25	252	10.1(31)	0	3	1	33.3	48	16.0(48)	0	1	—	—	kp	—	0	309

GLADMAN, CHARLES Charles R., RB, 5´11˝/205 lbs; Pittsburgh; B9/2/1966 Akron, OH

| 1987 | TB | 2(0) | 12 | 29 | 2.4(6) | 0 | 2 | 8 | 4.0(5) | 0 | — | — | — | — | — | — | — | — | — | k | — | 0 | 34 |

GLADNEY, TOM Anthony Lamont, WR, 6´3˝/200 lbs; UNLV; B7/20/1964 San Mateo, CA

| 1987 | SF | 2(0) | — | — | — | — | 4 | 60 | 15.0(19) | 0 | — | — | — | — | — | — | — | — | — | — | — | 0 | 30 |

GLAMP, JOE Joseph J., HB, 5´11˝/180 lbs; LSU; B5/13/1921, D1/13/1989 Greensburg, PA **[K]**

1947	†Pit	12(5, HB)	1	2	2.0(2)	0	—	—	—	—	—	—	—	—	—	—	—	—	—	K	—	48	2
1948	Pit	12(2)	28	167	6.0(55)	1	9	138	15.3(39)	2	1	0	0.0	0	0.0	0	0	—	—	Kkp	—	56	319
1949	Pit	8(0)	3	-8	-2.7(2)	0	1	14	14.0(14)	0	—	—	—	—	—	—	—	—	—	K	—	21	-1
NFL	3	32(7)	32	161	5.0(55)	1	10	152	15.2(39)	2	1	0	0.0	0	0.0	0	0	—	—	Kkp	—	125	320

GLASGOW, BRIAN Brian Gene, TE, 6´2˝/230 lbs; Northern Illinois; B6/9/1961 Burlington, IA

| 1987 | ChiB | 3(1) | — | — | — | — | 1 | 8 | 8.0(11) | 0 | — | — | — | — | — | — | — | — | — | — | — | 0 | 8 |

GLASGOW, NESBY Nesby Lee, DB, 5´10˝/185 lbs; Washington; 1979: Bal, rnd 8; B4/15/1957 Los Angeles, CA **[R]**   **1979** Bal 16 (4) **1980** Bal 16 (16, FS) **1981** Bal 14 (13, FS)
1982 Bal 9 (9, FS) **1983** Bal 16 (15, FS/ss) **1984** Ind 16 (16, FS) **1985** Ind 14 (14, SS) **1986** Ind 14 (14, SS) **1987**†Ind 11 (11, SS) **1988**†Sea 16 (0) **1990** Sea 16 (13, SS)
1991 Sea 16 (1) **1992** Sea 13 (0)

| 1989 | Sea | 16(16, SS) | — | — | — | — | 1 | 4 | 4.0(4) | 0 | — | — | — | — | — | — | — | — | — | kpiS | — | 1 | 6 | 2 |
| NFL | 14 | 203(142) | — | — | — | — | 1 | 4 | 4.0(4) | 0 | — | — | — | — | — | — | — | — | — | kpiS | 2 | 12 | 1008 |

GLASS, BILL William Sheppeard, DE-C-T, 6´5˝/252 lbs; Baylor; 1957: Det, rnd 1; B8/16/1935 Texarkana, TX   **1958** Det 12 (C) **1959** Det 12 (RDE) **1960** Det 12 (RDE)
1961 Det 14 (RDE) **1962** Cle★14 (RDE) **1963** Cle★14 (RDE) **1964**†Cle★14 (RDE) **1965**†Cle☆14 (RDE) **1966** Cle 14 (14, RDE) **1967**†Cle★14 (RDE/lde) **1968**†Cle 10 (RDE)
NFL 144 (14) [11 yrs]

GLASS, CHIP Charles Ferdinand, TE, 6´4˝/235 lbs; Florida State; 1969: Cle, rnd 3; B6/25/1947 Homestead, FL

1969	†Cle	14(te)	—	—	—	—	4	91	22.8(40)	2	—	—	—	—	—	—	—	—	—	—	—	12	56
1970	Cle	14(te)	—	—	—	—	19	403	21.2(78)	2	—	—	—	—	—	—	—	—	—	k	—	12	197
1971	†Cle	14	—	—	—	—	1	4	4.0(4)	1	—	—	—	—	—	—	—	—	—	k	—	6	-7
1972	†Cle	14	—	—	—	—	5	61	12.2(24)	0	—	—	—	—	—	—	—	—	—	—	—	0	31
1973	Cle	12(te)	—	—	—	—	2	60	30.0(47)	0	—	—	—	—	—	—	—	—	—	—	—	0	30
1974	NYG	13	—	—	—	—	3	23	7.7(11)	0	—	—	—	—	—	—	—	—	—	—	—	0	12
NFL	6	81	—	—	—	—	34	642	18.9(78)	5	—	—	—	—	—	—	—	—	—	k	—	30	317

GLASS, GLENN Glenn Murray, DB-WR, 6´1˝/205 lbs; Tennessee; 1962: Chi, rnd 17/Buf, rnd 2; B2/16/1940 Holopaw, FL   **1962** Pit 7 **1963** Pit 14 (14, RS) **1964** Phi 13 (ls)
1966 Atl 3 **1966** Den-A 6

| 1965 | Phi | 12 | — | — | — | — | 15 | 201 | 13.4(41) | 0 | — | — | — | — | — | — | — | — | — | — | — | 0 | 101 |
| NFL | 5 | 55(14) | — | — | — | — | 15 | 201 | 13.4(41) | 0 | — | — | — | — | — | — | — | — | — | kpi | — | 0 | 298 |

GLASS, LELAND Leland Strother, WR, 6´0˝/185 lbs; Oregon; 1972: GB, rnd 8; B11/5/1950 Sacramento, CA

1972	†GB	14(WR)	2	13	6.5(13)	0	15	261	17.4(31)	1	—	—	—	—	—	—	—	—	—	p	—	6	145
1973	GB	12(wr)	—	—	—	—	11	119	10.8(23)	0	—	—	—	—	—	—	—	—	—	—	—	0	60
NFL	2	26	2	13	6.5(13)	0	26	380	14.6(31)	1	—	—	—	—	—	—	—	—	—	p	—	6	204

GLASS, WILLIAM William Parker, G, 6´4˝/261 lbs; Baylor; 1980: Cin, rnd 4; B12/21/1957 Harlingen, TX   **1980** Cin 15 (0)

GLASSGOW, BILL Willis Allen, WB-HB, 5´10˝/187 lbs; Nebraska; Iowa; B4/21/1907 Wheeling, MO, D11/1/1959 Cedar Rapids, IA **[K]**   **1930** Por☆12 (9, WB), 28
1931 ChiC 9 (7, WB) **NFL** 21 (16) [2 yrs]

GLASSIC, TOM Thomas Joseph, G, 6´3˝/254 lbs; Virginia; 1976: Den, rnd 1; B4/17/1954 Elizabeth, NJ   **1976** Den 14 (14, LG) **1977**†Den 14 (14, LG) **1978**†Den 11 (10, LG)
1979†Den 16 (16, LG) **1980** Den 13 (13, LG) **1981** Den 16 (16, LG) **1982** Den 9 (9, LG) **1983**†Den 12 (0) **NFL** 105 (92) [8 yrs]

GLASSMAN, FRANK Frank, G-T, 6´0˝/210 lbs; Wilmington; Bliss; B5/14/1908 Columbus, OH, D8/1/1996 Columbus, OH   **1929** Buf 9 (5, rg)

GLASSMAN, MORRIS Morris, E, 5´10˝/166 lbs; none; B2/19/1900 Russia, D2/18/1980 Columbus, OH   **1921** Col 9 (6, LE) **1922** Col 6 (6, RE) **NFL** 15 (12) [2 yrs]

GLATZ, FRED Fred Joseph, E, 6´1˝/200 lbs; Pittsburgh; 1956: Pit, rnd 20; B7/31/1933 Pittsburgh, PA   **1956** Pit 4

GLAZE, CHARLES Charles Otis, DB, 5´11˝/200 lbs; South Carolina State; B9/12/1965 Lincolnton, GA   **1987** Sea 3 (2)

GLAZEBROOK, BOB Robert, DB, 6´1˝/200 lbs; Fresno State; 1978: Oak, rnd 11; B3/7/1956 Fresno, CA   **1978**†Atl 8 **1980**†Atl 16 (9, SS) **1981** Atl 16 (16, SS) **1982**†Atl 9 (9, SS)
1983 Atl 16 (8, fs)

| 1979 | Atl | 13 | — | — | — | — | 1 | 20 | 20.0(20) | 0 | — | — | — | — | — | — | — | — | — | p | — | 0 | 4 |
| NFL | 6 | 78(42) | — | — | — | — | 1 | 20 | 20.0(20) | 0 | — | — | — | — | — | — | — | — | — | kpi | 1 | 6 | 1 |

GLEASON, STEVE Stephen, DB, 5´11˝/215 lbs; Washington State; B3/19/1977 Spokane, WA   **2000**†NO 3 (0) **2001** NO 7 (0) **2002** NO 14 (0) **2003** NO 16 (0) **2004** NO 15 (0)
2005 NO 13 (1) **NFL** 68 (1) [6 yrs]

GLENN, AARON Aaron DeVon, DB, 5´9˝/185 lbs; Texas A&M; 1994: NYJ, rnd 1; B7/16/1972 Humble, TX **[RI]**   **1994** NYJ 15 (15, LCB) **1995** NYJ 16 (16, LCB)
1996 NYJ 16 (16, LCB) **1997** NYJ★16 (16, LCB) **1998**†NYJ★13 (13, LCB) **1999** NYJ 16 (16, LCB) **2000** NYJ 16 (16, LCB) **2001**†NYJ 13 (12, LCB) **2002** Hou★16 (16, LCB)
2003 Hou 11 (11, LCB) **2004** Hou 16 (16, LCB) **2005** Dal 16 (7, rcb) **NFL** 180 (170) [12 yrs]

GLENN, BILL William Joseph, QB, 6´0˝/157 lbs; Eastern Illinois; 1941: ChiB, rnd 17; B3/15/1918 St. Louis, MO, D12/11/2000 Boise, ID

| 1944 | ChiB | 2(0) | 1 | 1 | 1.0(1) | 0 | — | — | — | — | 4 | 1 | 25.0 | 22 | 5.5(22) | 0 | 0 | — | — | — | — | 0 | 12 |

GLENN, HOWARD Howard Earl, G, 6´0˝/235 lbs; Linfield; B9/26/1934 Vancouver, Canada, D10/9/1960 Houston, TX   **1960** NYT-A 4

YEAR	TEAM	G(GS, POS)	RUSH	YD	AVG(LG)	TD	REC	YD	AVG(LG)	TD	PASS	COMP	PCT	YD	AVG(LG)	TD	INT	SK	YD	QBR	KPR	OTD	PTS	TAY

GLENN, JASON Jason, LB, 6´0˝/231 lbs; Texas A&M; 2001: Det, rnd 6; B8/20/1979 Aldine, TX **2001**†NYJ 15 (0) **2002**†NYJ 16 (0) **2003** NYJ 14 (1) **2004**†NYJ 10 (0) **2005** Mia 16 (0) **NFL** 71 (1) [5 yrs]

GLENN, KERRY Kerry Raymond, DB, 5´9˝/175 lbs; Minnesota; 1985: NYJ, rnd 10; B1/3/1962 East St. Louis, IL **1985**†NYJ 16 (6, rcb) **1986** NYJ 1 (1) **1987** NYJ 8 (2) **1989** NYJ 14 (0) **1990**†Mia 16 (0) **1991** Mia 3 (0) **1992**†Mia 16 (1) **NFL** 74 (10) [7 yrs]

GLENN, TARIK Tarik, T-G, 6´5˝/332 lbs; California; 1997: Ind, rnd 1; B5/25/1976 Cleveland, OH **1998** Ind 16 (16, LT) **1999**†Ind 16 (16, LT) **2000**†Ind 16 (16, LT) **2001** Ind 16 (16, LT) **2002**†Ind 16 (16, LT) **2003**†Ind 10 (10, LT) **2004**†Ind✧16 (16, LT) **2005**†Ind✧16 (16, LT)

YEAR	TEAM	G(GS, POS)	RUSH	YD	AVG(LG)	TD	REC	YD	AVG(LG)	TD	PASS	COMP	PCT	YD	AVG(LG)	TD	INT	SK	YD	QBR	KPR	OTD	PTS	TAY
1997	Ind	16(16, RG)	—	—	—	—	1	3	3.0(3)	0	—	—	—	—	—	—	—	—	—	—	—	—	0	2
NFL	9	138(138)	—	—	—	—	1	3	3.0(3)	0	—	—	—	—	—	—	—	—	—	—	—	—	0	2

GLENN, TERRY Terry Tyree, WR, 5´11˝/195 lbs; Ohio State; 1996: NE, rnd 1; B7/23/1974 Columbus, OH

YEAR	TEAM	G(GS, POS)	RUSH	YD	AVG(LG)	TD	REC	YD	AVG(LG)	TD	PASS	COMP	PCT	YD	AVG(LG)	TD	INT	SK	YD	QBR	KPR	OTD	PTS	TAY
1996	†NE☆	15(15, WR)	5	42	8.4(26)	0	90	1132	12.6(37)	6	—	—	—	—	—	—	—	—	—	—	—	—	36	638
1997	†NE	9(9, WR)	—	—	—	—	27	431	16.0(50)	2	—	—	—	—	—	—	—	—	—	—	—	—	12	226
1998	NE	10(9, WR)	2	-1	-0.5(7)	0	50	792	15.8(**86**)	3	—	—	—	—	—	—	—	—	—	—	—	—	18	410
1999	NE	14(13, WR)	—	—	—	—	69	1147	16.6(67)	4	—	—	—	—	—	—	—	—	—	—	—	—	24	594
2000	NE	16(15, WR)	4	39	9.8(35)	0	79	963	12.2(39)	6	—	—	—	—	—	—	—	—	—	—	—	—	36	551
2001	NE	4(1)	—	—	—	—	14	204	14.6(23)	1	—	—	—	—	—	—	—	—	—	—	—	—	6	107
2002	†GB	15(14, WR)	—	—	—	—	56	817	14.6(49)	2	—	—	—	—	—	—	—	—	—	—	—	—	12	419
2003	†Dal	16(14, WR)	3	55	18.3(47)	0	52	754	14.5(51)	5	1	0	0.0	0	0.0	0	0	—	—	—	—	—	30	457
2004	Dal	6(6, wr)	1	-3	-3.0(-3)	0	24	400	16.7(48)	2	1	0	0.0	0	0.0	0	0	—	—	—	—	—	12	207
2005	Dal	16(16, WR)	2	-4	-2.0(6)	1	62	1136	**18.3**(**71**)	7	—	—	—	—	—	—	—	—	—	—	—	—	48	609
NFL	10	121(112)	17	128	7.5(47)	1	523	7776	14.9(86)	38	2	0	0.0	0	0.0	0	0	—	—	—	—	—	234	4216

GLENN, VENCIE Vencie Leonard, DB, 6´0˝/205 lbs; Indiana State; 1986: NE, rnd 2; B10/26/1964 Grambling, LA **[I]** **1986** NE 4 (0) **1986** SD 12 (7, fs) **1987** SD 12 (12, FS) **1988** SD 16 (16, FS) **1989** SD 16 (16, FS) **1990** SD 14 (14, FS) **1991**†NO 16 (1) **1992**†Min 16 (3) **1993**†Min 16 (16, FS) **1994**†Min 16 (16, FS) **1995** NYG 15 (15, FS) **NFL** 153 (116) [10 yrs]

GLENNIE, GEORGE George William, G-E-T, 6´2˝/185 lbs; Ripon; B3/30/1902 North Andover, MA, D6/8/1980 Andover, MA **1926** Rac 5 (1)

GLICK, ED Edward Isadore, B, 5´8˝/165 lbs; Lawrence; Marquette; B4/23/1900 Marinette, WI, D8/13/1976 DePere, WI **1922** GB 6 (1)

GLICK, FRED Frederick Couture, DB, 6´1˝/195 lbs; Colorado State; 1959: ChiC, rnd 23; B2/25/1937 Aurora, CO **[I]** **1959** ChiC 1 **1960** SL 4 **1961**†Hou-A 12 (RS) **1962**†Hou-A✧14 (RS) **1963** Hou-A★14 (RS) **1964** Hou-A★14 (RS) **1965** Hou-A 14 (RS) **1966** Hou-A 10 (LS) **NFL** 83 [8 yrs]

GLICK, GARY Gary Gaylen, DB-HB, 6´2˝/195 lbs; Colorado State; 1956: Pit, rnd B1; B5/14/1930 Grant, NE **[K]** **1956** Pit 8 (DB) **1957** Pit 12 (DB) **1958** Pit 12 (DB) **1959** Pit 2 **1959** Was 9 (9, DB) **1961** Bal 11 (RCB) **1963**†SD-A 6 (RS)

YEAR	TEAM	G(GS, POS)	RUSH	YD	AVG(LG)	TD	REC	YD	AVG(LG)	TD	PASS	COMP	PCT	YD	AVG(LG)	TD	INT	SK	YD	QBR	KPR	OTD	PTS	TAY
1960	Was	11(LS)	1	15	15.0(15)	0	—	—	—	—	—	—	—	—	—	—	—	—	—	—	i	1	6	4
NFL	7	71(9)	1	15	15.0(15)	0	—	—	—	—	—	—	—	—	—	—	—	—	—	—	Kpi	2	65	64

GLOCKSON, NORM Norman Stanley, G, 6´2˝/230 lbs; none; B6/15/1894 Blue Island, FL, D8/5/1955 Maywood, IL **1922** Rac 1 (1)

GLODEN, FRED Frederick Jean, HB, 5´10˝/187 lbs; Tulane; B12/21/1918 Dubuque, IA

YEAR	TEAM	G(GS, POS)	RUSH	YD	AVG(LG)	TD	REC	YD	AVG(LG)	TD	PASS	COMP	PCT	YD	AVG(LG)	TD	INT	SK	YD	QBR	KPR	OTD	PTS	TAY
1941	Phi	6(0)	22	55	2.5(10)	0	2	13	6.5(11)	0	—	—	—	—	—	—	—	—	—	—	—	—	0	62
1946	Mia-A	7(0)	13	24	1.8	1	—	—	—	—	—	—	—	—	—	—	—	—	—	—	k	—	6	39

GLOSSON, CLYDE Clyde P., WR, 5´11˝/175 lbs; Texas-El Paso; 1970: KC, rnd 7; B1/22/1947 San Antonio, TX

YEAR	TEAM	G(GS, POS)	RUSH	YD	AVG(LG)	TD	REC	YD	AVG(LG)	TD	PASS	COMP	PCT	YD	AVG(LG)	TD	INT	SK	YD	QBR	KPR	OTD	PTS	TAY
1970	Buf	11	—	—	—	—	2	16	8.0(14)	0	—	—	—	—	—	—	—	—	—	—	k	—	0	9

GLOVER, ANDREW Andrew Lee, TE, 6´6˝/250 lbs; Grambling State; 1991: LARd, rnd 10; B8/12/1967 New Orleans, LA

YEAR	TEAM	G(GS, POS)	RUSH	YD	AVG(LG)	TD	REC	YD	AVG(LG)	TD	PASS	COMP	PCT	YD	AVG(LG)	TD	INT	SK	YD	QBR	KPR	OTD	PTS	TAY
1991	†LARd	16(1)	—	—	—	—	5	45	9.0(18)	3	—	—	—	—	—	—	—	—	—	—	—	—	18	38
1992	LARd	16(2)	—	—	—	—	15	178	11.9(30)	1	—	—	—	—	—	—	—	—	—	—	—	—	6	94
1993	LARd	15(0)	—	—	—	—	4	55	13.8(26)	1	—	—	—	—	—	—	—	—	—	—	—	—	6	33
1994	LARd	16(16, TE)	—	—	—	—	33	371	11.2(27)	2	—	—	—	—	—	—	—	—	—	—	—	—	12	196
1995	Oak	16(7, te)	—	—	—	—	26	220	8.5(25)	3	—	—	—	—	—	—	—	—	—	—	—	—	18	125
1996	Oak	14(4)	—	—	—	—	9	101	11.2(25)	1	—	—	—	—	—	—	—	—	—	—	—	—	6	56
1997	†Min	13(11, TE)	—	—	—	—	32	378	11.8(43)	3	—	—	—	—	—	—	—	—	—	—	—	—	18	204
1998	†Min	16(12, TE)	—	—	—	—	35	522	14.9(36)	5	—	—	—	—	—	—	—	—	—	—	—	—	30	286
1999	†Min	16(13, TE)	—	—	—	—	28	327	11.7(31)	1	—	—	—	—	—	—	—	—	—	—	—	—	6	169
2000	†NO	16(15, TE)	—	—	—	—	21	281	13.4(39)	4	—	—	—	—	—	—	—	—	—	—	—	—	24	161
NFL	10	154(81)	—	—	—	—	208	2478	11.9(43)	24	—	—	—	—	—	—	—	—	—	—	—	—	144	1359

GLOVER, CLYDE Clyde M., DT, 6´6˝/280 lbs; Fresno State; B7/16/1960 New Orleans, LA **1987**†SF 13 (1)

GLOVER, KEVIN Kevin Bernard, C-G, 6´2˝/278 lbs; Maryland; 1985: Det, rnd 2; B6/17/1963 Washington, DC **1985** Det 10 (0) **1986** Det 4 (1) **1987** Det 12 (9, RG) **1988** Det 16 (16, LG) **1989** Det 16 (16, C) **1990** Det 16 (16, C) **1991**†Det 16 (16, C) **1992** Det 7 (7, C) **1993**†Det 16 (16, C) **1994**†Det☆16 (16, C) **1995**†Det★16 (16, C) **1996** Det★16 (16, C) **1997**†Det★16 (16, C) **1998** Sea 8 (8, C) **1999** Sea 6 (6, c) **NFL** 191 (175) [15 yrs]

GLOVER, LA'ROI La'Roi Damon, DT-NT, 6´2˝/285 lbs; San Diego State; 1996: Oak, rnd 5; B7/4/1974 San Diego, CA **[S]** **1996** Oak 2 (0) **1997** NO 15 (2) **1998** NO☆16 (15, RDT) **1999** NO 16 (16, RDT) **2000**†NO★16 (16, RDT) **2001** NO✧16 (16, RDT) **2002** Dal★16 (16, RDT) **2003**†Dal★16 (16, RDT) **2004** Dal✧16 (16, RDT) **2005** Dal 16 (13, NT) **NFL** 145 (126) [10 yrs]

GLOVER, LAVAR Lavar, DB, 5´9˝/177 lbs; Cincinnati; 2002: Pit, rnd 7; B12/17/1978 Dayton, OH **2002** Cin 2 (0)

GLOVER, PHIL Phil Dwyain, LB, 5´11˝/241 lbs; Washington State; Utah; 1999: Ten, rnd 7; B12/17/1975 San Fernando, CA **1999** Ten 1 (0) **2000**†Ind 9 (0) **NFL** 10 (0) [2 yrs]

GLOVER, RICH Richard Edward, DT, 6´1˝/240 lbs; Nebraska; 1973: NYG, rnd 3; B2/6/1950 Bayonne, NJ **1973** NYG 13 **1975** Phi 14 (14, LDT) **NFL** 27 (14) [2 yrs]

GLUECK, LARRY Lawrence David, DB, 6´0˝/190 lbs; Villanova; 1963: Chi, rnd 3/SD, rnd 5; B10/5/1941 Norristown, PA **1963**†ChiB 14 **1964** ChiB 11 **1965** ChiB 12 **NFL** 37 [3 yrs]

GLYMPH, JUNIOR Clarence, DE, 6´5˝/270 lbs; Carson-Newman; B9/2/1980 Hackensack, NJ **2004** Atl 3 (0) **2005** Atl 3 (0) **NFL** 6 (0) [2 yrs]

GOAD, PAUL Paul Ellis, FB, 6´0˝/195 lbs; Vanderbilt; Abilene Christian; 1956: SF, rnd 25; B9/7/1934 Cincinnati, OH, D11/29/1978 Little Rock, AR **1956** SF 4

GOAD, TIM Timothy Ray, NT-DT, 6´3˝/280 lbs; North Carolina; 1988: NE, rnd 4; B2/28/1966 Claudville, VA **1988** NE 16 (14, NT) **1989** NE 16 (16, NT) **1990** NE 16 (16, NT) **1991** NE 16 (15, NT) **1992** NE 16 (16, NT) **1993** NE 16 (15, NT) **1994** NE 13 (13, NT) **1995** Cle 16 (13, LDT) **1996** Bal 16 (5, nt) **NFL** 141 (123) [9 yrs]

GOB, ART Arthur Jerome, DE, 6´4˝/230 lbs; Pittsburgh; 1959: Was, rnd 22; B1/7/1937 Pittsburgh, PA **1959** Was 11 (6, RDE) **1960** Was 1 **1960** LAC-A 3 **NFL** 15 (6) [2 yrs]

GOBLE, LES Lester Bois, HB-DB, 5´11˝/158 lbs; Alfred; 1954: ChiC, rnd 13; B7/23/1932 Waverly, NY

YEAR	TEAM	G(GS, POS)	RUSH	YD	AVG(LG)	TD	REC	YD	AVG(LG)	TD	PASS	COMP	PCT	YD	AVG(LG)	TD	INT	SK	YD	QBR	KPR	OTD	PTS	TAY
1954	ChiC	12	30	42	1.4(8)	1	1	-1	-1.0(-1)	0	—	—	—	—	—	—	—	—	—	—	kpi	2	18	355
1955	ChiC	9	7	11	1.6(5)	0	—	—	—	—	—	—	—	—	—	—	—	—	—	—	k	—	0	51
NFL	2	21	37	53	1.4(8)	1	1	-1	-1.0(-1)	0	—	—	—	—	—	—	—	—	—	—	kpi	2	18	406

GODDARD, ED Edwin Vinson, B, 5´10˝/183 lbs; Washington State; 1937: Bkn, rnd 1; B10/28/1914 San Diego, CA, D7/20/1992 Lake San Marcos, CA **[K]**

YEAR	TEAM	G(GS, POS)	RUSH	YD	AVG(LG)	TD	REC	YD	AVG(LG)	TD	PASS	COMP	PCT	YD	AVG(LG)	TD	INT	SK	YD	QBR	KPR	OTD	PTS	TAY
1937	Bkn	4(3)	19	65	3.4	1	3	18	6.0	0	23	4	17.4	46	2.0	1	5	—	—	—	—	—	6	-88
1937	Cle	4(3)	38	97	2.6	1	3	43	14.3	0	18	9	50.0	134	7.4	0	3	—	—	—	K	—	7	76
1938	Cle✧	10(1)	40	-16	-0.4	0	6	128	21.3(53)	1	43	19	44.2	238	5.5	0	6	—	—	—	K	—	7	-68
NFL	2	18(7)	97	146	1.5	2	12	189	15.8(53)	1	84	32	38.1	418	5.0	1	14	—	—	—	K	—	20	-81

GODDARD, JONATHAN Jonathan Bruce, DE, 6´1˝/242 lbs; Marshall; 2005: Det, rnd 6; B5/11/1981 San Diego, CA **2005** Ind 1 (0)

GODFREY, CHRIS Christopher James, G-T-DE-DT, 6´3˝/263 lbs; Michigan; B5/17/1958 Detroit, MI **1980** NYJ 6 (0) **1984**†NYG 10 (8, rg) **1985**†NYG 16 (16, RG) **1986**†NYG☆16 (16, RG) **1987** NYG 8 (5, rg) **1988**†Sea 9 (2) **NFL** 65 (47) [6 yrs]

GODFREY, HERB Herbert L., E, 6´1˝/187 lbs; Washington State; B8/23/1919 Port Angeles, WA, D9/16/2002 Juneau, AK **1942** Cle 3 (0)

GODFREY, RANDALL Randall Euralentris, LB, 6´2˝/245 lbs; Georgia; 1996: Dal, rnd 2; B4/6/1973 Valdosta, GA **1996**†Dal 16 (6, llb) **1997** Dal 16 (16, LLB) **1998**†Dal 16 (16, LLB) **1999**†Dal 16 (16, MLB) **2000**†Ten☆16 (16, MLB) **2001** Ten 14 (14, MLB) **2002**†Ten 8 (5, mlb) **2003** Sea 15 (14, MLB) **2004**†SD 15 (15, RILB) **2005** SD 14 (14, RILB) **NFL** 146 (132) [10 yrs]

GODWIN, BILL William Domont, C-LB, 6´3˝/241 lbs; Georgia; 1943: ChiC, rnd 8; B5/8/1919 Blytheville, AR, D3/26/1998 Columbus, GA **1947** Bos 12 (5, c) **1948** Bos 12 (3) **NFL** 24 (8) [2 yrs]

YEAR	TEAM	G (GS, POS)	RUSH	YD	AVG (LG)	TD	REC	YD	AVG (LG)	TD	PASS	COMP	PCT	YD	AVG (LG)	TD	INT	SK	YD	QBR	KPR	OTD	PTS	TAY

GODWIN, WALT   Walter Hampton, G, 5´7˝/205 lbs; Georgia Tech; B9/29/1899, D10/1954   **1929** SI 9 (5, RG)

GOEAS, LEO   Leo Douglas, G-T, 6´4˝/300 lbs; Hawaii; 1990: SD, rnd 3; B8/15/1966 Honolulu, HI   **1990** SD 15 (10, LT)   **1991** SD 9 (4)   **1992**†SD 16 (4)   **1993** LARm 16 (16, RG) **1994** LARm 13 (13, RG)   **1995** SL 15 (14, LG)   **1996** SL 16 (13, LG)   **1997** Bal 11 (7, lg)   **NFL** 111 (81) [8 yrs]

GOEBEL, BRAD   Bradley Arlen, QB, 6´3˝/202 lbs; Baylor; B10/13/1967 Cuero, TX

1991	Phi	5(2)	1	2	2.0(2)	0	—				56	30	53.6	267	4.8(26)	0	6	6	37	—	—	—	0	-105
1992	Cle	1(0)	—				—				3	2	66.7	32	10.7(22)	0	0	—	—	—	—	—	0	16
1994	Cle	1(0)	—				—				—													
NFL	3	7(2)	1	2	2.0(2)	0	—				59	32	54.2	299	5.1(26)	0	6	6	37	—	—	—	0	-89

GOEBEL, HANK   Henry Walter, T, 6´7˝/270 lbs; Cal State-Fullerton; 1986: LARm, rnd 8; B11/1/1964 Evergreen Park, IL   **1987** LARm 3 (3)

GOEBEL, JOE   Joseph Robert, C, 6´5˝/264 lbs; UCLA; 1987: SD, rnd 11; B12/12/1963 Tulsa, OK   **1987** SD 2 (0)

GOEBEL, PAUL   Paul Gordon, E, 6´3˝/200 lbs; Michigan; B5/28/1901 Grand Rapids, MI, D1/26/1988 Grand Rapids, MI **[K]**   **1923** Col☆10 (10, RE), 8   **1924** Col☆8 (8, RE), 18 **1925** Col 8 (8, RE)   **NFL** 26 (26), 26 [3 yrs]

GOEDDEKE, GEORGE   George Aloysius, G-C-T, 6´3˝/253 lbs; Notre Dame; 1967: Den, rnd 3; B7/29/1945 Detroit, MI   **1967** Den-A 10 (LG)   **1968** Den-A 14 (LG) **1969** Den-A◇14 (14, LG)   **1970** Den 14 (14, LG)   **1971** Den 12 (12, C)   **1972** Den 2 (1)   **NFL** 66 (41) [6 yrs]

GOERKE, ART   Arthur C., E, 5´6˝/165 lbs; none; B9/14/1896, NY, D2/5/1970 Rochester, NY   **1921** Ton 1 (1, LE)

GOETZ, GUS   Angus Gerald, E-T, 6´3˝/198 lbs; Michigan; B7/6/1897 DeTour, MI, D7/24/1977 Grosse Pointe, MI   **1922** Buf 7 (7, LE)   **1923** Col 2 (2)   **NFL** 9 (9) [2 yrs]

GOFF, CLARK   Clark William, T, 6´3˝/215 lbs; Florida; 1940: Pit, rnd 5; B12/6/1917, D3/1998 Pittsburgh, PA   **1940** Pit 11 (5, lt)

GOFF, MIKE   Michael J., G, 6´5˝/306 lbs; Iowa; 1998: Cin, rnd 3; B1/6/1976 Spring Valley, IL   **1998** Cin 10 (5, rg)   **1999** Cin 14 (1)   **2000** Cin 16 (16, RG)   **2001** Cin 16 (16, RG) **2002** Cin 13 (13, RG)   **2003** Cin 16 (16, RG)   **2004†**SD 16 (16, RG)   **2005** SD 16 (16, RG)   **NFL** 117 (99) [8 yrs]

GOFF, ROBERT   Robert Lamar, DE-DT-NT, 6´3˝/280 lbs; Auburn; 1988: TB, rnd 4; B10/2/1965 Rochester, NY   **1988** TB 16 (6, rde)   **1989** TB 12 (12, RDE)   **1990†**NO 15 (10, NT) **1991†**NO 15 (0)   **1992†**NO 16 (0)   **1993** NO 16 (9, RDE)   **1994** NO 16 (0)   **1995** NO 11 (6, ldt)   **1996** Min 4 (0)   **NFL** 121 (43) [9 yrs]

GOFF, WILLARD   Willard E., DT, 6´3˝/268 lbs; West Texas A&M; Illinois; B10/17/1961 Lamar, CO   **1985** Atl 7 (0)   **1987** SD 1 (0)   **NFL** 8 (0) [2 yrs]

GOFOURTH, DERREL   Darrel Glen, G-C, 6´3˝/260 lbs; Oklahoma State; 1977: GB, rnd 7; B3/20/1955 Parsons, KS   **1977** GB 13   **1978** GB 16 (16, LG)   **1979** GB 16 (16, LG) **1980** GB 16 (16, LG)   **1981** GB 15 (15, LG)   **1982** GB 9 (7, LG)   **1983** SD 15 (0)   **1984** SD 16 (2)   **NFL** 116 (72) [8 yrs]

GOGAN, KEVIN   Kevin Patrick, G-T, 6´7˝/317 lbs; Washington; 1987: Dal, rnd 8; B11/2/1964 Pacifica, CA   **1987** Dal 11 (10, RT)   **1988** Dal 15 (15, RT)   **1989** Dal 13 (13, RT) **1990** Dal 16 (4)   **1991†**Dal 16 (16, LG)   **1992†**Dal 16 (1)   **1993†**Dal 16 (16, RG)   **1994** LARd◇16 (16, RG)   **1995** Oak 16 (16, RG)   **1996** Oak 16 (16, RG)   **1997†**SF◇16 (16, RG) **1998†**SF★16 (16, RG)   **1999†**Mia 16 (10, rg)   **2000** SD 14 (14, RG)   **NFL** 213 (179) [14 yrs]

GOGANIOUS, KEITH   Keith Lorenzo, LB, 6´2˝/239 lbs; Penn State; 1992: Buf, rnd 3; B12/7/1968 Virginia Beach, VA   **1992†**Buf 13 (0)   **1993†**Buf 16 (7, rilb)   **1994** Buf 16 (1) **1995** Jax 16 (15, LLB)   **1996** Bal 13 (8, ROLB)   **NFL** 74 (31) [5 yrs]

GOGOLAK, CHARLIE   Charles Paul, K, 5´10˝/165 lbs; Princeton; 1966: Was, rnd 1/KC, rnd 7; B12/29/1944 Rapahidveg, Hungary **[K]**   **1966** Was☆14   **1967** Was 11   **1968** Was 14 **1970** Bos 6   **1971** NE 14   **1972** NE 6   **NFL** 55 [6 yrs]

GOGOLAK, PETE   Peter Kornel, K, 6´1˝/190 lbs; Cornell; 1964: Buf, rnd 12; B4/18/1942 Budapest, Hungary **[K]**   **1964†**Buf-A 14   **1965†**Buf-A★14   **1966** NYG 14   **1967** NYG 9 **1968** NYG 14   **1969** NYG 14   **1970** NYG 14   **1971** NYG 14   **1972** NYG 14   **1973** NYG 14   **1974** NYG 14   **NFL** 149 [11 yrs]

GOICH, DAN   Dandennis John, DT, 6´4˝/240 lbs; California; 1966: SL, rnd 8/Hou, rnd R10; B4/30/1944 Chicago, IL   **1969** Det 14   **1970†**Det 14   **1971** NO 10   **1972** NYG 4 **1973** NYG 14 (LDT)   **NFL** 56 [5 yrs]

GOINGS, NICK   Nick Aaron, RB, 6´0˝/225 lbs; Pittsburgh; B1/26/1978 Columbus, OH

2001	Car	13(2)	66	197	3.0(16)	0	8	39	4.9(11)	0	—			—			—		—	—	—	—	0	217
2002	Car	14(2)	50	188	3.8(20)	0	18	91	5.1(14)	0	—			—			—		—	—	—	—	2	234
2003	†Car	15(0)	10	69	6.9(17)	0	12	97	8.1(14)	1	—			—			—		—	—	—	—	6	123
2004	Car	16(8, RB)	217	821	3.8(57)	6	45	394	8.8(37)	1	—			—			—		—	—	—	—	42	1083
2005	†Car	16(1)	37	133	3.6(17)	0	14	151	10.8(30)	0	—			—			—		—	—	k	—	0	215
NFL	5	74(13)	380	1408	3.7(57)	6	97	772	8.0(37)	2	—			—			—		—	—	k	—	50	1870

GOLD, IAN   Ian Maurice, LB, 6´0˝/223 lbs; Michigan; 2000: Den, rnd 2; B8/23/1978 Ann Arbor, MI   **2000†**Den 16 (0)   **2001** Den★16 (0)   **2002** Den 16 (16, RLB)   **2003** Den 6 (6, rlb) **2004** TB 16 (13, LLB)   **2005†**Den 16 (16, RLB)   **NFL** 86 (51) [6 yrs]

GOLDBERG, ADAM   Adam, G-T, 6´7˝/310 lbs; Wyoming; B8/12/1980 Edina, MN   **2004†**Min 13 (6, rt)   **2005** Min 16 (12, RG)   **NFL** 29 (18) [2 yrs]

GOLDBERG, BILL   William Scott, NT-DT, 6´2˝/272 lbs; Georgia; 1990: LARm, rnd 11; B12/27/1966 Tulsa, OK   **1992** Atl 4 (1)   **1993** Atl 5 (0)   **1994** Atl 5 (0)   **NFL** 14 (1) [3 yrs]

GOLDBERG, MARSHALL   Marshall 'Biggie', B, 5´11˝/190 lbs; Pittsburgh; 1939: ChiC, rnd 2; B10/25/1917 Elkins, WV, D4/3/2006 Chicago, IL

1939	ChiC	10(8, FB)	56	152	2.7	2	5	90	18.0	1	14.3	1	14.3	4	0.6(4)	0	1	—		—	—	—	—	18	184
1940	ChiC	11(7, FB)	87	325	3.7	2	2	29	14.5	1	2	0	0.0	0	0.0	0	0	—		—	Pi	—	—	18	370
1941	ChiC★	11(10, FB)	117	427	3.6(25)	3	16	313	19.6(76)	1	19	7	36.8	110	5.8(44)	1	2	—		—	kpi	—	—	24	820
1942	ChiC	11(7, FB)	116	369	3.2(29)	1	9	108	12.0(27)	0	—			—			—		—	kpi	—	1	12	665
1943	ChiC	1(1)	6	6	1.0(5)	0	4	31	7.8(11)	0	—			—			—		—	kpi	—	—	6	55
1946	ChiC	10(8, LH)	43	210	4.9(32)	3	17	152	8.9(22)	1	—			—			—		—	kpi	—	—	24	386
1947	†ChiC☆	12(10, RH)	51	155	3.0(10)	0	7	52	7.4(19)	0	—			—			—		—	p	—	—	0	197
1948	†ChiC	11(0)	—				—				—			—			—		—	i	—	—	0	-1
NFL	8	77(51)	476	1644	3.5(32)	11	75	775	12.9(76)	5	28	8	28.6	114	4.1(44)	1	3	—		—	Pkpi	—	1	102	2675

GOLDEN, JACK   Jack Danta', LB, 6´1˝/240 lbs; Oklahoma State; B1/28/1977 Harvey, IL   **2000†**NYG 16 (0)   **2001** NYG 16 (0)   **2002†**TB 13 (0)   **2003** TB 4 (0)   **NFL** 49 (0) [4 yrs]

GOLDEN, TIM   Timothy George, LB, 6´1˝/220 lbs; Florida; B11/15/1959 Pahokee, FL   **1982†**NE 9 (0)   **1983** NE 16 (1)   **1984** NE 15 (0)   **1985** Phi 2 (0)   **NFL** 42 (1) [4 yrs]

GOLDENBERG, BUCKETS   Charles Robert, G-BB, 5´10˝/215 lbs; Wisconsin; B3/10/1911 Odessa, Ukraine, D4/16/1986 Glendale, WI   **1938†**GB 11 (11, RG)   **1939†**GB★9 (9, RG) **1940** GB 11 (8, RG)   **1941†**GB 8 (3)   **1942** GB☆11 (10, RG)   **1943** GB 10 (6, RG)   **1944†**GB 9 (9, RG)   **1945** GB 4 (0)

1933	GB	11(4)	52	213	4.1	4	4	43	10.8(18)	1	—			—			—		—	—	—	—	2	42	290
1934	GB	10(5, bb)	30	73	2.4	2	4	26	6.5(9)	0	—			—			—		—	—	—	—	12	106
1935	GB	11(6, BB)	16	52	3.3	0	3	42	14.0(21)	0	—			—			—		—	—	—	—	0	73
1936	†GB	7(2)	6	9	1.5	0	—				—			—			—		—	—	—	—	0	9
1937	GB	8(3)	4	18	4.5	0	—				—			—			—		—	—	—	1	6	28
NFL	13	120(69)	108	365	3.4	6	11	111	10.1(21)	1	—			—			—		—	—	i	—	3	60	539

GOLDING, JOE   Joseph Griffith, HB-DB, 6´0˝/184 lbs; Oklahoma; 1946: ChiC, rnd 5; B2/26/1921 Eufaula, OK, D12/26/1971 Muskogee, OK

1947	Bos	12(7, LH)	26	71	2.7(15)	1	6	52	8.7(24)	2	—			—			—		—	kpi	—	—	18	245
1948	Bos	12(8, RH)	24	36	1.5(9)	0	9	159	17.7(34)	4	—			—			—		—	kpi	—	2	36	507
1949	NYB	11(11, RH)	63	240	3.8(39)	0	12	78	6.5(16)	2	—			—			—		—	kpi	—	1	18	455
1950	NYY	12(DB)	1	2	2.0(2)	0	—				—			—			—		—	i	—	2	12	122
1951	NYY	11(DB)	—				—				—			—			—		—	i	—	—	0	-1
NFL	5	58(26)	114	349	3.1(39)	1	27	289	10.7(34)	8	—			—			—		—	kpi	—	5	84	1328

GOLDMAN, SAM   Samuel, E, 6´3˝/228 lbs; Ohio State; Samford; B11/10/1916 Cleveland, OH, D11/8/1978 Pensacola, FL

1944	Bos	4(0)	—				2	21	10.5(11)	0	—			—			—		—	k	—	—	0	-5
1946	Bos	11(11, LE)	2	-3	-1.5(-1)	0	15	154	10.3(27)	0	—			—			—		—	k	—	—	0	85
1947	Bos	12(6, LE)	—				1	9	9.0(9)	0	—			—			—		—	k	—	—	0	-10
1948	†ChiC	11(0)	—				—				—			—			—		—	k	—	—	0	0
1949	Det	8(1)	—				—				—			—			—		—	k	—	—	0	1
NFL	5	46(18)	2	-3	-1.5(-1)	0	18	184	10.2(27)	0	—			—			—		—	k	—	—	0	71

GOLDSBERRY, JOHN   John Gerard, DT-T, 6´2˝/245 lbs; Indiana; 1949: ChiC, rnd 4/NYY-A, rnd 10; B11/22/1926 Indianapolis, IN, D1/23/1972   **1949** ChiC 10 (0)   **1950** ChiC 10 (RDT) **NFL** 20 [2 yrs]

GOLDSMITH, EARL   Arthur Earl, E-WB, /182 lbs; Indiana; B4/14/1894 Evansville, IN, D1/9/1971 Richmond, IN   **1921** Evv 5 (5, LE), 6   **1922** Evv 2 (1)   **NFL** 7 (6) [2 yrs]

YEAR	TEAM	G (GS, POS)	RUSH	YD	AVG(LG)	TD	REC	YD	AVG(LG)	TD	PASS COMP	PCT	YD	AVG(LG)	TD	INT	SK	YD	QBR	KPR	OTD	PTS	TAY

GOLDSMITH, WENDELL   Wendell Eugene, C, 6´0˝/202 lbs; Emporia State; B12/15/1917 Malvern, KS, D11/6/1998 Wakeeney, KS   **1940** NYG 1 (0)

GOLDSTEIN, ALAN   Alan, E, 6´0˝/204 lbs; North Carolina; 1960: Buf, rnd 1; B1/8/1936 Brooklyn, NY, D10/14/1991 West Bloomfield, MI

| 1960 | Oak-A | 14 (FL) | 3 | -2 | -0.7(16) | 1 | 27 | 354 | 13.1(44) | 1 | — | — | — | — | — | — | — | — | — | — | — | 12 | 190 |

GOLDSTON, RALPH   Ralph Peter, HB-DB, 5´11˝/195 lbs; Indiana; Youngstown State; 1952: Phi, rnd 11; B2/25/1929 Campbell, OH

1952	Phi	9 (LH)	65	210	3.2(20)	3	2	12	6.0(8)	0	—	—	—	—	—	—	—	—	—	—	—	18	246
1954	Phi	8									—	—	—	—	—	—	—	—	—	—	—		
1955	Phi	10	14	-7	-0.5(7)	0	2	8	4.0(9)	0	—	—	—	—	—	—	—	—	—	—	—	0	-3
NFL	3	27	79	203	2.6(20)	3	4	20	5.0(9)	0	—	—	—	—	—	—	—	—	—	—	—	18	243

GOLEMBESKI, ARCHIE   Anthony Edward, E-G-C, 5´10˝/185 lbs; Holy Cross; B5/25/1900 Lyon Mountain, KY, D3/9/1976 Worcester, MA **[KC]**   **1925** Pro 11 (11, RG), 12
1926 Pro 9 (7, RE), 7   **1929** Pro 8 (5, c)   **NFL** 28 (23), 19 [3 yrs]

GOLEMGESKE, JOHN   John William, T-G, 6´2˝/225 lbs; Wisconsin; 1937: Bkn, rnd 6; B11/14/1915 Waukesha, WI   **1937** Bkn 10 (9, RT)   **1938** Bkn☆11 (8, LG)   **1939** Bkn 11 (4)
1940 Bkn 10 (5, rt)   **NFL** 42 (26) [4 yrs]

GOLIC, BOB   Robert Perry, NT-DT-LB-DE, 6´2˝/264 lbs; Notre Dame; 1979: NE, rnd 2; B10/26/1957 Cleveland, OH   **1979** NE 1   **1980** NE 16 (3)   **1981** NE 16 (9, rilb)
1982†Cle 6 (4)   **1983** Cle 16 (16, NT)   **1984** Cle 15 (15, NT)   **1985**†Cle★16 (16, NT)   **1986**†Cle★16 (16, NT)   **1987** Cle 12 (12, NT)   **1988**†Cle 16 (16, NT)   **1989** LARd 16 (16, NT)
1990†LARd 16 (16, LDT)   **1991**†LARd 16 (14, LDT)   **1992** LARd 9 (7, ldt)   **NFL** 187 (160) [14 yrs]

GOLIC, MIKE   Michael Louis, DT-NT-DE, 6´5˝/274 lbs; Notre Dame; 1985: Hou, rnd 10; B12/12/1962 Willowick, OH   **1986** Hou 16 (9, NT)   **1987** Hou 2 (0)   **1987** Phi 6 (0)
1988†Phi 12 (1)   **1989**†Phi 16 (0)   **1990**†Phi 16 (13, LDT)   **1991** Phi 16 (6, ldt)   **1992**†Phi 16 (13, RDT) · **1993** Mia 15 (7, rdt)   **NFL** 115 (49) [8 yrs]

GOLLOMB, RUDY   Rudolph Peter, G, 5´11˝/205 lbs; Wisconsin; Carroll (WI); B11/6/1910 Oshkosh, WI, D9/11/1991 Oshkosh, WI   **1936** Phi 4 (0)

GOLSEN, GENE   Eugene William, FB-TB, 5´11˝/188 lbs; Georgetown (DC); B7/6/1902, D11/19/1935 Bound Brook, NJ   **1926** Lou 3 (3, FB)

GOLSEN, TOM   Thomas Joseph, G, 5´11˝/175 lbs; Georgetown (DC); B7/6/1902, D11/23/1986 Chicago, IL   **1926** Lou 1 (0)

GOLSTEYN, JERRY   Jerry Mark, QB, 6´4˝/207 lbs; Northern Illinois; 1976: NYG, rnd 12; B8/6/1954 West Allis, WI

1977	NYG	6 (3)	3	-4	-1.3(-1)	0	—	—	—	—	70	31	44.3	416	5.9(47)	2	8	14	113	—	—	—	0	-106
1978	NYG	7 (2)	1	-3	-3.0(-3)	0	—	—	—	—	40	12	30.0	110	2.8(20)	0	1	8	62	—	—	—	0	12
1979	Det	1	1	0	0.0(0)	0	—	—	—	—	9	2	22.2	16	1.8(15)	0	2	2	18	—	—	—	0	-72
1979	Bal	1																		—	—	—		
1982	TB	1 (0)					—	—	—	—	1	0	0.0	0	0.0	0	0	—	—	—	—	—	0	0
1983	TB	5 (3)	5	3	0.6(2)	0	—	—	—	—	97	47	48.5	535	5.5(52)	0	2	7	52	—	—	—	0	191
NFL	5	21 (8)	10	-4	-0.4(2)	0	—	—	—	—	217	92	42.4	1077	5.0(52)	2	13	31	245	—	—	—	0	25

GOLTZ, RICK   Ricardo Eugene, DE, 6´4˝/255 lbs; Simon Fraser; British Columbia; B3/19/1955 Vancouver, Canada   **1987** LARd 1 (1)

GOLUB, CHRIS   Christopher David, DB, 6´2˝/196 lbs; Kansas; 1977: KC, rnd 7; B12/2/1954 Kansas City, MO   **1977** KC 1

GOMPERS, BILL   William George, HB, 6´1˝/185 lbs; Notre Dame; B3/20/1928 Wheeling, WV

| 1948 | †Buf-A | 14 (3) | 48 | 219 | 4.6 | | | | | | — | — | — | — | — | — | — | — | — | — | kpi | — | 6 | 300 |

GONDA, GEORGE   George John, HB, 5´10˝/175 lbs; Duquesne; B2/23/1919 Alverton, PA, D9/19/1994 Woodville, PA

| 1942 | Pit | 5 (1) | 17 | 147 | 8.6(68) | 2 | 1 | 7 | 7.0(7) | 0 | — | — | — | — | — | — | — | — | — | — | pi | — | 12 | 210 |

GONSOULIN, GOOSE   Austin William, DB, 6´3˝/210 lbs; Baylor; 1960: DalT, rnd 2/SF, rnd 17; B6/7/1938 Port Arthur, TX **[I]**   **1960** Den-A★14 (RS)   **1961** Den-A★14 (RS)
1962 Den-A★14 (RS)   **1963** Den-A★14 (RS)   **1964** Den-A★14 (RS)   **1965** Den-A 14 (RS)   **1966** Den-A☆10 (RS)   **1967** SF 14 (7, RS)   **NFL** 108 (7) [8 yrs]

GONYA, BOB   Robert James, T, 6´2˝/208 lbs; Northwestern; B6/15/1910 Chicago, IL, D1/15/1999 Tempe, AZ   **1933** Phi 2 (1)

| 1934 | Phi | 9 (4) | — | — | — | | 1 | 4 | 4.0(4) | 1 | — | — | — | — | — | — | — | — | — | — | — | — | 6 | 7 |
| NFL | 2 | 11 (2) | — | — | — | | 1 | 4 | 4.0(4) | 1 | — | — | — | — | — | — | — | — | — | — | — | — | 6 | 7 |

GONZAGA, JOHN   John Louis, T-G-DE-DT, 6´3˝/247 lbs; none; B3/6/1933 Martinez, CA   **1956** SF 9   **1957**†SF 12 (LT)   **1958** SF 12 (LT)   **1959** SF 12   **1960** Dal 11 (RDE)
1961 Det 13 (LT)   **1962** Det 14 (LT)   **1963** Det 14 (LG)   **1964** Det 14 (LG)   **1965** Det 10   **1966** Den-A 11 (RG)   **NFL** 132 [11 yrs]

GONZALEZ, JOAQUIN   Joaquin Antonio, T, 6´5˝/310 lbs; Miami (FL); 2002: Cle, rnd 7; B9/7/1979 Miami, FL   **2002**†Cle 9 (0)   **2003** Cle 16 (3)   **2004** Cle 16 (11, RT)   **2005** Ind 5 (0)
NFL 46 (14) [4 yrs]

GONZALEZ, LEON   Leon Eugene, WR, 5´10˝/162 lbs; Bethune-Cookman; 1985: Dal, rnd 8; B9/21/1963 Jacksonville, FL

1985	Dal	11 (0)	—	—	—		3	28	9.3(13)	0	—	—	—	—	—	—	—	—	—	—	p	—	0	-3
1987	Atl	2 (0)	—	—	—		3	40	13.3(22)	0	—	—	—	—	—	—	—	—	—	—		—	0	20
NFL	2		—	—	—		6	68	11.3(22)	0	—	—	—	—	—	—	—	—	—	—	p	—	0	17

GONZALEZ, NOE   Noe Mio, RB, 6´1˝/210 lbs; Southwest Texas State; 1974: Oak, rnd 12; B2/5/1951 Alice, TX   **1974** NE 2

GONZALEZ, PETE   Pete, QB, 6´1˝/216 lbs; Pittsburgh; B7/4/1974 Miami, FL

| 1999 | Pit | 1 (0) | 2 | -3 | -1.5(-1) | 0 | — | — | — | — | 1 | 1 | 100.0 | 8 | 8.0(8) | 0 | 0 | — | — | — | — | — | 0 | 1 |

GONZALEZ, TONY   Anthony David, TE, 6´4˝/248 lbs; California; 1997: KC, rnd 1; B2/27/1976 Torrance, CA

1997	†KC	16 (0)	—	—	—		33	368	11.2(30)	2	—	—	—	—	—	—	—	—	—	—	—	—	14	194
1998	KC	16 (16, TE)	—	—	—		59	621	10.5(32)	2	—	—	—	—	—	—	—	—	—	—	—	—	12	321
1999	KC★	15 (15, TE)	—	—	—		76	849	11.2(73)	11	—	—	—	—	—	—	—	—	—	—	—	—	66	480
2000	KC★	16 (16, TE)	—	—	—		93	1203	12.9(39)	9	—	—	—	—	—	—	—	—	—	—	—	—	54	647
2001	KC★	16 (16, TE)	1	9	9.0(9)	0	73	917	12.6(36)	6	1	1	100.0	40	40.0(40)	0	0	—	—	—	—	—	38	518
2002	KC★	16 (16, TE)	—	—	—		63	773	12.3(42)	7	—	—	—	—	—	—	—	—	—	—	—	—	42	422
2003	†KC★	16 (16, TE)	—	—	—		71	916	12.9(67)	10	—	—	—	—	—	—	—	—	—	—	—	—	60	508
2004	KC★	16 (16, TE)	1	5	5.0(5)	0	102	1258	12.3(32)	7	—	—	—	—	—	—	—	—	—	—	—	—	42	669
2005	KC◇	16 (16, TE)	—	—	—		78	905	11.6(39)	2	—	—	—	—	—	—	—	—	—	—	—	—	12	463
NFL	9	143 (127)	2	14	7.0(9)	0	648	7810	12.1(73)	56	1	1	100.0	40	40.0(40)	0	0	—	—	—	—	—	340	4219

GOOCH, JEFF   Jeffrey Lance, LB, 5´11˝/226 lbs; Austin Peay State; B10/31/1974 Nashville, TN   **1996** TB 15 (0)   **1997**†TB 14 (5, llb)   **1998** TB 16 (16, LLB)   **1999**†TB 15 (0)
2000 TB 16 (0)   **2001**†TB 13 (0)   **2002** Det 16 (2)   **2003** Det 16 (0)   **2004** TB 16 (1)   **NFL** 137 (24) [9 yrs]

GOOD, TOM   Thomas Maynard, LB, 6´0˝/230 lbs; Marshall; 1965: SD, rnd R6/NYG, rnd 16; B12/23/1944 South Charleston, WV   **1966** SD-A 2

GOODBREAD, ROYCE   Royce Ethelbert, WB-HB, 5´11˝/207 lbs; Florida; B8/23/1907 Crystal River, FL, D5/19/1991 Dallas County, TX   **1930** Fra 13 (10, WB), 6   **1930** Min 1 (0)
1931 Pro 4 (2)   **NFL** 18 (12) [2 yrs]

GOODBURN, KELLY   Kelly Joe, P, 6´2˝/195 lbs; Emporia State; Iowa State; B4/14/1962 Cherokee, IA **[P]**   **1989** KC 16 (0)   **1990**†Was 4 (0)   **1991**†Was 16 (0)   **1993** Was 1 (0)

1987	KC	.13 (0)	1	16	16.0(16)	0	—	—	—	—	—	—	—	—	—	—	—	—	—	P	—	—	0	16
1988	KC	16 (0)	1	15	15.0(15)	0	—	—	—	—	—	—	—	—	—	—	—	—	—	P	—	—	0	15
1990	KC	3 (0)	1	5	5.0(5)	0	—	—	—	—	—	—	—	—	—	—	—	—	—	P	—	—	0	5
1992	†Was	16 (0)	2	1	0.5(5)	0	—	—	—	—	—	—	—	—	—	—	—	—	—	P	—	—	0	1
NFL	7	85 (0)	5	37	7.4(16)	0	—	—	—	—	—	—	—	—	—	—	—	—	—	P	—	—	0	37

GOODE, CHRIS   Christopher Kimberly, DB, 6´0˝/195 lbs; North Alabama; Alabama; 1987: Ind, rnd 10; B9/17/1963 Town Creek, AL   **1987**†Ind 8 (0)   **1988** Ind 13 (8, lcb)
1989 Ind 15 (8, LCB)   **1990** Ind 16 (10, LCB)   **1991** Ind 15 (15, LCB)   **1992** Ind 15 (15, LCB)   **1993** Ind 14 (10, LCB)   **NFL** 96 (66) [7 yrs]

GOODE, CONRAD   Conrad Lawrence, T-G-C, 6´6˝/285 lbs; Missouri; 1984: NYG, rnd 4; B1/19/1962 St. Louis, MO   **1984**†NYG 8 (0)   **1985**†NYG 16 (2)   **1987** TB 11 (2)
NFL 35 (4) [3 yrs]

GOODE, DON   Donald Ray, LB, 6´2˝/234 lbs; Kansas; 1974: SD, rnd 1; B6/21/1951 Houston, TX   **1974** SD 14 (7, LLB)   **1975** SD 13 (12, LLB)   **1976** SD 14 (14, LLB)
1977 SD 14 (14, LLB)   **1978** SD 14 (14, LLB)   **1979**†SD 12 (1)   **1980**†Cle 15 (2)   **1981** Cle 16 (16, LOLB)   **NFL** 112 (80) [8 yrs]

GOODE, IRV   Irvin Lee, G-T-C, 6´5˝/255 lbs; Kentucky; 1962: SL, rnd 1/DalT, rnd 4; B10/12/1940 Newport, KY   **1962** SL 14   **1963** SL 13 (LT)   **1964** SL◇14 (LG)   **1965** SL 12 (LG)
1966 SL 11 (LG/c)   **1967** SL◇14 (LG)   **1968** SL 14 (LG)   **1969** SL 14 (LG)   **1970** SL☆14 (LG)   **1971** SL 14 (LG)   **1973**†Mia 14   **1974**†Mia 14   **NFL** 162 [12 yrs]

GOODE, JOHN John Timothy, TE, 6´2˝/233 lbs; Youngstown State; 1984: SL, rnd 5; B11/5/1962 Cleveland Heights, OH **1985** Phi 14 (0)

YEAR	TEAM	G(GS, POS)	RUSH	YD	AVG(LG)	TD	REC	YD	AVG(LG)	TD	PASS	COMP	PCT	YD	AVG(LG)	TD	INT	SK	YD	QBR	KPR	OTD	PTS	TAY
1984	SL	16(1)	—	—	—		3	23	7.7(10)	0	—	—	—	—	—	—	—	—	—	—	—	—	0	12
NFL	2	30(1)	—	—	—		3	23	7.7(10)	0	—	—	—	—	—	—	—	—	—	—	—	—	0	12

GOODE, KERRY Kerry DeAnglo, RB, 5´11˝/200 lbs; Alabama; 1988: TB, rnd 7; B7/28/1965 Town Creek, AL **1989** Mia 1 (0)

YEAR	TEAM	G(GS, POS)	RUSH	YD	AVG(LG)	TD	REC	YD	AVG(LG)	TD	KPR	PTS	TAY
1988	TB	14(5, rb)	63	231	3.7(22)	0	7	68	9.7(22)	0		2	265
NFL	2	15(5)	63	231	3.7(22)	0	7	68	9.7(22)	0	k	2	258

GOODE, ROB Robert Leslie, B, 6´4˝/222 lbs; Texas A&M; 1949: Was, rnd 1/Buf-A, rnd 16; B6/5/1927 Roby, TX

YEAR	TEAM	G(GS, POS)	RUSH	YD	AVG(LG)	TD	REC	YD	AVG(LG)	TD	KPR	OTD	PTS	TAY
1949	Was	12(7, LH)	61	261	4.3(54)	2	16	279	17.4(54)	0	ki		12	441
1950	Was	12(FB)	136	560	4.1(80)	5	19	160	8.4(56)	1	i		36	714
1951	Was◇	12(FB)	208	951	4.6(33)	9	3	45	15.0(26)	0			54	**1064**
1954	Was◇	12(FB)	108	462	4.3(44)	0	4	4	1.0(10)	0	k	1	6	508
1955	Was	3	7	23	3.3(0)	0	1	15	15.0(15)	0			0	31
1955	Phi	8(FB)	76	274	3.6(36)	0	10	137	13.7(50)	0	k		0	349
NFL	5	59(7)	596	2531	4.2(80)	16	53	640	12.1(56)	1	ki	1	108	3105

GOODE, TOM Thomas Guinn, C-LB, 6´3˝/245 lbs; Mississippi State; 1961: Hou, rnd 2/Det, rnd 17; B12/1/1938 West Point, MS **1962**†Hou-A 14 **1963** Hou-A 14 **1964** Hou-A 14 (C) **1965** Hou-A 14 **1966** Mia-A 14 (13, C) **1967** Mia-A 14 (14, C) **1968** Mia-A 14 (14, C) **1969** Mia-A◇ 14 (14, C) **1970**†Bal 1 **NFL** 113 (55) [9 yrs]

GOODLOW, DARRYL Darryl, LB, 6´2˝/235 lbs; Oklahoma; 1984: Phi, rnd S2; B11/2/1960 St. Louis, MO **1987** LARd 2 (0)

GOODLOW, EUGENE Eugene, WR, 6´2˝/185 lbs; Kansas State; 1982: NO, rnd 3; B12/19/1958 St. Louis, MO

YEAR	TEAM	G(GS, POS)	RUSH	YD	AVG(LG)	TD	REC	YD	AVG(LG)	TD	PTS	TAY
1983	NO	16(7, WR)	1	3	3.0(3)	0	41	487	11.9(26)	2	12	257
1984	NO	10(6, wr)	1	5	5.0(5)	0	22	281	12.8(23)	3	18	161
1985	NO	12(11, WR)	1	3	3.0(3)	0	32	603	18.8(76)	3	18	320
1986	NO	16(6, wr)	—	—	—		20	306	15.3(29)	2	12	163
NFL	4	54(30)	3	11	3.7(5)	0	115	1677	14.6(76)	10	60	900

GOODMAN, ANDRE´ Andre´, DB, 5´10˝/185 lbs; South Carolina; 2002: Det, rnd 3; B8/11/1978 Greenville, SC **2002** Det 14 (6, rcb) **2003** Det 3 (3) **2004** Det 11 (4) **2005** Det 15 (8, LCB) **NFL** 43 (21) [4 yrs]

GOODMAN, AUBREY Aubrey Louis, T, 6´3˝/225 lbs; Baylor; Chicago; B2/18/1904 Lott, TX, D3/7/1972 Waco, TX **1927** ChiC 1 (0)

GOODMAN, BRIAN Brian Harbert, G, 6´2˝/250 lbs; UCLA; B12/7/1949 Los Angeles, CA **1973** Hou 3 **1974** Hou 14 (RG) **NFL** 17 [2 yrs]

GOODMAN, DON Weldon Charles, RB, 5´11˝/214 lbs; Cincinnati; B4/23/1959 Los Angeles, CA **1987** SL 3 (0)

GOODMAN, HARVEY Harvey Franklin, G, 6´4˝/260 lbs; Colorado; 1975: SL, rnd 5; B9/16/1952 Los Angeles, CA **1976** Den 14

GOODMAN, HANK Henry Joseph, T, 6´4˝/230 lbs; St. Bonaventure; George Washington; West Virginia; B4/18/1917 Bradford, PA **1942** Det 11 (1)

GOODMAN, HERBERT Herbert James, RB, 5´11˝/203 lbs; Graceland College (IA); B8/31/1977 Miami, FL

YEAR	TEAM	G(GS, POS)	RUSH	YD	AVG(LG)	TD	REC	YD	AVG(LG)	TD	KPR	PTS	TAY
2000	GB	5(0)	3	-2	-0.7(3)	0	1	0	0.0(0)	0	k	0	67
2001	†GB	7(0)	1	-1	-1.0(-1)	0	—	—	—		k	0	5
NFL	2	12(0)	4	-3	-0.8(3)	0	1	0	0.0(0)	0	k	0	72

GOODMAN, JOHN John Richard, DE-DT-NT, 6´6˝/253 lbs; Oklahoma; 1980: Pit, rnd 2; B11/21/1958 Oklahoma City, OK **1981** Pit 15 (10, LDE) **1982**†Pit 9 (9, LDE) **1983** Pit 14 (11, LDE) **1984**†Pit 14 (14, LDE) **1985** Pit 12 (6, rde) **NFL** 64 (50) [5 yrs]

GOODMAN, LES Leslie Edward, RB, 5´11˝/206 lbs; Yankton; 1972: Atl, rnd 3; B9/1/1950 Port Jefferson, NY

YEAR	TEAM	G(GS, POS)	RUSH	YD	AVG(LG)	TD	REC	YD	AVG(LG)	TD	KPR	PTS	TAY
1973	GB	6	18	88	4.9(19)	1	2	19	9.5(12)	0		6	108
1974	GB	13	20	101	5.1(47)	0	5	19	3.8(12)	0	k	0	100
NFL	2	19	38	189	5.0(47)	1	7	38	5.4(12)	0	k	6	207

GOODNIGHT, CLYDE Clyde Davis, E, 6´1˝/196 lbs; Tulsa; 1945: GB, rnd 3; B3/3/1924 Holland, TX, D12/28/2002 Little River, TX

YEAR	TEAM	G(GS, POS)	RUSH	YD	AVG(LG)	TD	REC	YD	AVG(LG)	TD	KPR	PTS	TAY
1945	GB	10(9, LE)	8	26	3.3(12)	0	7	283	40.4(75)	3	k	18	176
1946	GB	8(8, LE)	—	—	—		16	308	19.3(51)	1		6	159
1947	GB	11(8, LE)	1	-1	-1.0(-1)	0	38	593	15.6(69)	6	k	36	318
1948	GB	8(5, le)	—	—	—		28	448	16.0(57)	3	k	18	236
1949	GB	1(1)											
1949	Was	10(1)	—	—	—		11	150	13.6(30)	0		0	75
1950	Was	10	—	—	—		12	185	15.4(33)	2		12	100
NFL	6	58(32)	9	25	2.8(12)	0	112	1967	17.6(75)	15	k	90	1063

GOODNIGHT, OWEN Owen L., HB, 6´0˝/200 lbs; Hardin-Simmons; 1940: Cle, rnd 15; B8/27/1917 Holland, TX, D5/13/1967 Hays County, TX

YEAR	TEAM	G(GS, POS)	RUSH	YD	AVG(LG)	TD	PASS	COMP	PCT	YD	AVG(LG)	TD	INT	QBR	PTS	TAY
1941	Cle	9(1)	21	-54	-2.6(7)	0	36	12	33.3	182	5.1(61)	1	5	Pkpi	0	-110

GOODRICH, DWAYNE Dwayne Lewis, DB, 5´11˝/198 lbs; Tennessee; 2000: Dal, rnd 2; B5/29/1978 Oak Lawn, IL **2000** Dal 5 (0) **2002** Dal 11 (1) **NFL** 16 (1) [2 yrs]

GOODRIDGE, BOB Robert Wayne, WR, 6´2˝/190 lbs; Vanderbilt; 1968: Min, rnd 6; B5/11/1946 Boston, MA

YEAR	TEAM	G(GS, POS)	RUSH	YD	AVG(LG)	TD	REC	YD	AVG(LG)	TD	PTS	TAY
1968	Min	11	—	—	—		1	5	5.0(5)	0	0	3

GOODRUM, CHARLES Charles Leo, G-T, 6´3˝/256 lbs; Florida A&M; 1972: Min, rnd 2; B1/11/1950 Miami, FL **1973**†Min 10 **1974**†Min 12 (12, LT) **1975** Min 14 (7, LT) **1976**†Min 14 (14, LG) **1977**†Min 14 (14, LG) **1978**†Min 16 (16, LG) **1979** Min 15 (9, LG) **NFL** 95 (72) [7 yrs]

GOODSON, JOHN John Warren, P, 6´3˝/204 lbs; Texas; 1982: Pit, rnd 8; B3/18/1960 Houston, TX **1982**†Pit 9 (0)

GOODSPEED, JOEY Joey Allen, FB, 6´1˝/247 lbs; Notre Dame; B2/22/1978 Berwyn, IL **2002** SD 12 (0) **2003**†SL 8 (4)

YEAR	TEAM	G(GS, POS)	RUSH	YD	AVG(LG)	TD	REC	YD	AVG(LG)	TD	KPR	PTS	TAY
2004	†SL	16(5, fb)	3	6	2.0(2)	1	11	71	6.5(13)	0	k	6	46
NFL	3	36(9)	3	6	2.0(2)	1	11	71	6.5(13)	0	k	6	32

GOODSPEED, MARK Mark Judson, T, 6´5˝/270 lbs; Nebraska; 1980: Mia, rnd 9; B12/1/1956 Kansas City, KS, D1/10/1998 Kansas City, MO **1980** SL 3 (0)

GOODWIN, DOUG Douglas McArthur, RB, 6´2˝/228 lbs; Maryland-Eastern Shore; 1965: Buf, rnd 11/GB, rnd 5; B3/11/1942 Charleston, SC **1966** Buf-A 3 **1968** Atl 2 **NFL** 5 [2 yrs]

GOODWIN, EARL Earl, E, 6´1˝/195 lbs; West Texas A&M; Bucknell; B1/21/1901 Paducah, KY, D7/1/1976 Durango, CO **1928** Pot 8 (3)

GOODWIN, HUNTER Robert Hunter, TE, 6´5˝/268 lbs; Texas A&M-Kingsville; Texas A&M; 1996: Min, rnd 4; B10/10/1972 Bellville, TX

YEAR	TEAM	G(GS, POS)	RUSH	YD	AVG(LG)	TD	REC	YD	AVG(LG)	TD	KPR	PTS	TAY
1996	†Min	9(6, te)	—	—	—		1	24	24.0(24)	0		0	12
1997	†Min	16(5, te)	—	—	—		7	61	8.7(14)	0		0	31
1998	†Min	15(0)	—	—	—		3	16	5.3(9)	0		0	8
1999	†Mia	15(5, te)	—	—	—		8	55	6.9(14)	0		0	28
2000	†Mia	16(16, TE)	—	—	—		6	36	6.0(9)	1	k	6	-1
2001	†Mia	16(11, TE)	—	—	—		4	27	6.8(9)	0		0	14
2002	Min	16(6, te)	—	—	—		4	20	5.0(8)	1		6	15
2003	Min	16(5, te)	—	—	—		4	26	6.5(12)	0		2	13
NFL	8	119(54)	—	—	—		37	265	7.2(24)		k	14	119

GOODWIN, JONATHAN Jonathan Scott, G, 6´3˝/318 lbs; Ohio University; Michigan; 2002: NYJ, rnd 5; B12/2/1978 Columbia, SC **2002** NYJ 12 (0) **2003** NYJ 15 (0) **2004**†NYJ 15 (3) **2005** NYJ 16 (10, LG) **NFL** 58 (13) [4 yrs]

GOODWIN, MYRL Myrl, B-E, 6´1˝/195 lbs; West Texas A&M; Bucknell; B1/21/1901 Paducah, KY, D2/14/1979 Reno, NV **1928** Pot 4 (0)

GOODWIN, RON Ronald Ray, FL-SE-WR, 5´11˝/180 lbs; Baylor; 1963: Phi, rnd 16/Buf, rnd 11; B1/9/1941 Phillips, TX

YEAR	TEAM	G(GS, POS)	RUSH	YD	AVG(LG)	TD	REC	YD	AVG(LG)	TD	PTS	TAY
1963	Phi	10(SE)	—	—	—		15	215	14.3(35)	4	24	128
1964	Phi	14(FL)	1	-23	-23.0(-23)	0	23	335	14.6(44)	3	18	160
1965	Phi	11(FL)	—	—	—		18	252	14.0(35)	1	6	131
1966	Phi	12(FL)	—	—	—		16	212	13.3(30)	1	6	111
1967	Phi	7	1	1	1.0(1)	0	6	65	10.8(23)	0	0	34
1968	Phi	2										
NFL	6	56	2	-22	-11.0(1)	0	78	1079	13.8(44)	9	54	563

YEAR	TEAM	G(GS, POS)	RUSH	YD	AVG(LG)	TD	REC	YD	AVG(LG)	TD	PASS	COMP	PCT	YD	AVG(LG)	TD	INT	SK	YD	QBR	KPR	OTD	PTS	TAY

GORDON, TOD Charles Tod, E, 6'0"/184 lbs; West Virginia; B12/5/1911 Wheeling, WV, D1/7/1997

YEAR	TEAM	G(GS,POS)	RUSH	YD	AVG(LG)	TD	REC	YD	AVG(LG)	TD	KPR	OTD	PTS	TAY
1935	†NYG☆	12(8, RE)	—	—	—	—	26	432	16.6(65)	4	—	—	24	236
1936	NYG	8(6, RE)	3	-1	-0.3	0	7	79	11.3(23)	2	—	—	12	49
NFL	2	20(14)	3	-1	-0.3	0	33	511	15.5(65)	6	—	—	36	285

GOODYEAR, JOHN John Martin, B, 6'0"/190 lbs; Marquette; 1942: Was, rnd 10; B1/10/1920 La Grange, IL, D3/7/2002 Sacramento, CA

1942	Was	3(0)	2	1	0.5(1)	0	—					—	0	1

GOOLSBY, MIKE Mike, LB, 6'4"/242 lbs; Notre Dame; B9/10/1982 Joliet, IL **2005** SL 2 (0)

GOOLSBY, SHAG James Earl, C, 6'2"/198 lbs; Mississippi State; 1940: Cle, rnd 12; B7/24/1917 Columbus, MS, D5/7/1975 Columbus, MS **1940** Cle 8 (0)

GOOSBY, TOM Thomas Aaron, G-LB, 6'0"/235 lbs; Baldwin-Wallace; 1962: Cle, rnd 15; B5/24/1939 Alliance, OH **1963** Cle 1 **1966** Was 14 **NFL** 15 [2 yrs]

GOOVERT, RON Ronald Edward, LB, 5'11"/225 lbs; Michigan State; B2/15/1944 Detroit, MI **1967** Det 14

GORDON, ALEX Alex Groncier, LB, 6'5"/246 lbs; Cincinnati; 1987: NYJ, rnd 2; B9/14/1964 Jacksonville, FL **1987** NYJ 12 (12, LOLB) **1988** NYJ 13 (13, LOLB) **1989** NYJ 16 (15, LOLB) **1990**†LARd 10 (0) **1991** Cin 14 (1) **1992** Cin 15 (3) **1993** Cin 16 (3) **NFL** 96 (47) [7 yrs]

GORDON, AMON Amon, DT, 6'3"/275 lbs; Stanford; 2004: Cle, rnd 5; B10/13/1981 San Diego, CA **2004** Cle 6 (0)

GORDON, BOBBY Bobby Lee, DB, 6'0"/195 lbs; Tennessee; 1958: ChiC, rnd 6; B12/7/1935 Pulaski, TN, D8/16/1990 Strawberry Plains, TN **1960**†Hou-A 13 (LS)

1958	ChiC	12(DB)	2	10	5.0(12)	0	—				Ppi	—	0	34
NFL	2	25	2	10	5.0(12)	0	—				Ppi	—	0	64

GORDON, CORNELL Cornell Kermit, DB, 6'0"/187 lbs; North Carolina A&T; 1964: NYJ, rnd 23/SF, rnd 16; B1/6/1941 Norfolk, VA **1965** NYJ-A 14 **1966** NYJ-A 10 (1) **1967** NYJ-A 2 **1968**†NYJ-A 14 (4) **1969**†NYJ-A 14 (RCB) **1970** Den 14 (14, LCB) **1971** Den 14 **1972** Den 1 **NFL** 83 (19) [8 yrs]

GORDON, DARRIEN Darrien X. Jamal, DB, 5'11"/184 lbs; Stanford; 1993: SD, rnd 1; B11/14/1970 Shawnee, OK [R] **1993** SD 16 (7, rcb) **1994**†SD☆16 (16, LCB) **1996** SD☆16 (6, lcb) **1997**†Den☆16 (16, RCB) **1998**†Den 16 (16, RCB) **1999** Oak 16 (2) **2000**†Oak 13 (0) **2001** Atl☆16 (2) **2002** GB 13 (0) **NFL** 138 (65) [9 yrs]

GORDON, DICK Richard Frederick, WR-SE-FL, 5'11"/190 lbs; Michigan State; 1965: Chi, rnd 7; B1/1/1944 Cincinnati, OH [R]

1965	ChiB	14	2	10	5.0(6)	0	13	279	21.5(51)	3	kp	—	18	189
1966	ChiB	14(FL)	1	2	2.0(12)	0	15	210	14.0(40)	1	kp	—	6	323
1967	ChiB	14(SE)	3	-7	-2.3(9)	0	31	534	17.2(93)	5	kp	—	30	464
1968	ChiB	14(SE)	—	—	—	—	29	477	16.4(51)	4	kp	—	24	311
1969	ChiB	14(WR)	2	28	14.0(22)	0	36	414	11.5(41)	4	kp	—	24	276
1970	ChiB★	14(WR)	4	17	4.3(7)	0	71	1026	14.5(69)	13	—	—	78	595
1971	ChiB★	13(WR)	—	—	—	—	43	610	14.2(45)	5	—	—	30	330
1972	LARm	4	—	—	—	—	3	29	9.7(17)	1	—	—	6	101
1973	LARm	5	1	19	19.0(19)	0	—				k	—	0	42
1973	GB	1	1	-4	-4.0(-4)	0	—				—	—	0	-4
1974	SD	7	1	25	25.0(25)	0	2	15	7.5(17)	0	kp	—	0	176
NFL	10	115	15	90	6.0(25)	0	243	3594	14.8(93)	36	kp	—	216	2801

GORDON, DWAYNE Dwayne Kirk, LB, 6'1"/240 lbs; New Hampshire; 1993: Mia, rnd 9; B11/2/1969 White Plains, NY **1993** Atl 5 (0) **1994** Atl 16 (0) **1995**†SD 16 (3) **1996** SD 13 (0) **1997** NYJ 16 (8, LILB) **1998**†NYJ 16 (4) **1999** NYJ 16 (4) **2000** NYJ 15 (1) **NFL** 113 (20) [8 yrs]

GORDON, IRA Ira Lawrence, G-T, 6'3"/275 lbs; Kansas State; 1970: Phi, rnd 8; B5/5/1947 Kilbourne, LA **1970** SD 8 **1971** SD 14 **1972** SD 6 **1973** SD 6 **1974** SD 14 (14, RG) **1975** SD 14 (RG) **NFL** 62 (14) [6 yrs]

GORDON, JOHN John David, DT, 6'6"/260 lbs; New Mexico State; Hawaii; B8/29/1948 Detroit, MI **1972** Det 2

GORDON, LAMAR Lamar Deshawn, RB, 6'1"/228 lbs; North Dakota State; 2002: SL, rnd 3; B1/7/1980 Milwaukee, WI

2002	SL	13(5, rb)	65	228	3.5(29)	1	30	278	9.3(25)	2	k	—	18	401
2003	SL	10(4)	71	298	4.2(20)	1	8	59	7.4(21)	0	—	—	6	338
2004	Mia	3(2)	35	64	1.8(11)	0	13	74	5.7(20)	0	—	—	0	101
2005	Phi	14(4)	54	182	3.4(11)	1	11	79	7.2(18)	0	k	—	6	251
NFL	4	40(15)	225	772	3.4(29)	2	62	490	7.9(25)	2	k	—	30	1090

GORDON, LARRY Larry Wayne, LB, 6'4"/230 lbs; Arizona State; 1976: Mia, rnd 1; B7/8/1953 Monroe, LA, D6/25/1983 Phoenix, AZ **1976** Mia 14 (14, LLB) **1977** Mia 14 (14, ROLB) **1978**†Mia 16 (15, ROLB) **1979**†Mia 16 (16, ROLB) **1980** Mia 15 (14, ROLB) **1981**†Mia 16 (16, ROLB) **1982**†Mia 9 (9, ROLB) **NFL** 100 (98) [7 yrs]

GORDON, LENNOX Lennox Constantine, RB, 6'0"/201 lbs; New Mexico; B4/9/1978 Higley, AZ

1999	†Buf	8(0)	11	38	3.5(13)	0	—				k	—	0	34
2000	†Ind	9(0)	4	13	3.3(6)	0	—				k	—	0	13
NFL	2	17(0)	15	51	3.4(13)	0	—				k	—	0	47

GORDON, LOU Louis James, T-G-E, 6'5"/224 lbs; Illinois; B7/15/1908 Chicago, IL, D4/4/1976 Chicago, IL **1930** ChiC 10 (3) **1931** ChiC 1 (0) **1931** Bkn 6 (5, lt) **1932** ChiC☆8 (7, RT) **1934** ChiC 11 (11, RT) **1935** ChiC 12 (5, rt) **1936**†GB 12 (5, RT) **1937** GB☆10 (8, RT) **1938** ChiB 2 (1)

1933	ChiC☆	11(11, RT)	—				1	8	8.0(8)	0	—	0	4
NFL	9	83(56)	—				1	8	8.0(8)	0	—	0	4

GORDON, SONNY Denman Preston, DB, 5'11"/192 lbs; Ohio State; 1987: Cin, rnd 6; B7/30/1965 Lynn, MA **1987** TB 7 (0)

GORDON, STEVE Steve Duane, C, 6'3"/288 lbs; California; 1992: NE, rnd 10; B4/15/1969 Fort Ord, CA **1998** SF 13 (1)

GORDON, TIM Timothy Carvelle, DB, 6'0"/188 lbs; Tulsa; B5/7/1965 Ardmore, OK **1987** Atl 11 (8, FS) **1988** Atl 16 (5, fs) **1989** Atl 14 (13, FS) **1990** Atl 5 (0) **1991** NE 11 (7, fs) **1992** NE 10 (7, SS) **NFL** 67 (40) [6 yrs]

GORDY, JOHN John Thomas, G-T, 6'3"/248 lbs; Tennessee; 1957: Det, rnd 2; B6/17/1935 Nashville, TN **1957**†Det 12 (rt) **1959** Det 12 (RG) **1960** Det 12 (RG) **1961** Det 14 (RG) **1962** Det 14 (RG) **1963** Det☆14 (RG) **1964** Det★14 (RG) **1965** Det★14 (RG) **1966** Det☆14 (RG) **1967** Det☆14 (RG) **NFL** 134 [10 yrs]

GORE, FRANK Franklin, RB, 5'9"/217 lbs; Miami (FL); 2005: SF, rnd 3; B5/14/1983 Coral Gables, FL

2005	SF	14(1)	127	608	4.8(72)	3	15	131	8.7(47)	0	—	18	704

GORE, GORDON Wilfred Gordon, HB, 6'0"/215 lbs; Southwestern Oklahoma State; B6/28/1913 Clinton, OK

1939	Det	7(1)	8	7	0.9	0	1	20	20.0(20)	0	0	0	0.0	0	—	0	17

GORE, STACY Stacy Lynn, P, 6'0"/200 lbs; Arkansas State; B5/20/1963 Jonesboro, AR **1987** Mia 3 (0)

GORECKI, CHUCK Charles Michael, LB, 6'4"/237 lbs; Boston College; B4/7/1964 Bryn Mawr, PA **1987** Phi 3 (0)

GORGAL, ALEX Alex, FB-WB, 5'9"/180 lbs; none; B1/16/1900 Czechoslovakia, D6/1/1986 Peru, IN **1923** RI 5 (2)

GORGAL, KEN Kenneth Robert, DB, 6'2"/200 lbs; Purdue; 1950: Cle, rnd 6; B2/13/1929 La Salle, IL **1950**†Cle 12 **1953**†Cle☆12 (DB) **1954**†Cle 11 (DB) **1955** ChiB 12 (DB) **1956** ChiB 6 (db) **1956** GB 5 **NFL** 58 [5 yrs]

GORGONE, PETE Pietro Orris, HB, 6'0"/220 lbs; Muhlenberg; B5/8/1920 Bruca, Italy, D12/1/1992 Salisbury Township, PA **1946**†NYG 9 (3)

GORIN, BRANDON Brandon Michael, T, 6'6"/308 lbs; Purdue; 2001: SD, rnd 7; B7/17/1978 Muncie, IN **2003**†NE 6 (0) **2004**†NE 14 (10, RT) **2005**†NE 12 (8, rt) **NFL** 32 (18) [3 yrs]

GORINSKI, WALT Walter A., FB, 6'1"/207 lbs; LSU; 1943: Phi, rnd 17; B12/20/1919 Mutual, PA, D7/3/1977 Bossier City, LA

1946	Pit	6(1)	1	3	3.0(3)	0	—				—	0	3

GORMAN, DOC Otho Addison, E, St. Louis; B7/23/1893 Pawnee, IL, D9/22/1938 Evanston, IL **1921** Evv 1 (1) **1922** Evv 1 (1) **NFL** 2 (2) [2 yrs]

GORMAN, EARL Earl Patrick, G-T, /225 lbs; none; B6/27/1896 Halder, WI, D11/6/1962 Milwaukee, WI **1922** Rac 11 (9, LG) **1923** Rac 10 (6, LG) **1924** Ken 3 (1) **NFL** 24 (16) [3 yrs]

GORMLEY, TOM Thomas Francis, G-T, 5'11"/225 lbs; Villanova; Ursinus; Catholic; Georgetown (DC); B8/8/1891 Bridgeport, CT, D7/24/1951 Washington, DC **1920** Cle 8 (6, LG) **1920** Can 1 (0) **1921** NYG 1 (1, RT) **1921** Was 2 (2, RG) **NFL** 12 (9) [2 yrs]

GORRILL, FLOP Charles Virgil, E, 5'11"/178 lbs; Ohio State; B1903 Fostoria, OH, D12/19/1945 Fostoria, OH **1926** Col 7 (6, RE), 6

YEAR	TEAM	G(GS, POS)	RUSH	YD	AVG(LG)	TD	REC	YD	AVG(LG)	TD	PASS	COMP	PCT	YD	AVG(LG)	TD	INT	SK	YD	QBR	KPR	OTD	PTS	TAY

GOSS, ANTONIO Antonio Derrell, LB, 6´4˝/228 lbs; North Carolina; 1989: SF, rnd 12; B8/11/1966 Randleman, NC **1989**†SF 8 (0) **1991** SF 14 (0) **1992**†SF 16 (0) **1993**†SF 14 (1) **1994**†SF 16 (1) **1995**†SF 16 (0) **1996** SL 8 (3) **NFL** 92 (5) [7 yrs]

GOSS, DONALD Robert Donald, T-DT, 6´5˝/260 lbs; SMU; 1954: Cle, rnd 10; B5/19/1933 Dallas, TX, D9/15/1998 Duncanville, TX **1956** Cle 6

GOSS, JASON Jason Tamon, DB, 5´10˝/185 lbs; TCU; B10/4/1979 Fort Worth, TX **2003** Arz 4 (0)

GOSSAGE, GENE Ezra Gene, DE-DT-G, 6´3˝/240 lbs; Northwestern; 1960: DalT, rnd 1; B2/17/1935 Columbia, TN **1960**†Phi 12 **1961** Phi 14 **1962** Phi 14 (lde) **NFL** 40 [3 yrs]

GOSSETT, BRUCE Daniel Bruce, K, 6´1˝/204 lbs; Ferrum; Clarion; Duquesne; Richmond; B11/9/1941 Canonsburg, PA **[K]** **1964** LARm☆14 **1965** LARm 14 **1966** LARm★14 **1967**†LARm 14 **1968** LARm✧14 **1969**†LARm 14 **1970**†SF 14 **1971**†SF 14 **1972**†SF 14 **1973** SF☆14 **1974** SF 14 **NFL** 154 [11 yrs]

GOSSETT, JEFF Jeffrey Alan, P, 6´2˝/200 lbs; Eastern Illinois; B1/25/1957 Charleston, IL **[P]** **1981** KC 7 (0) **1982** KC 8 (0) **1983** Cle 16 (0) **1987**†Cle 5 (0) **1987** Hou 4 (0) **1988** LARd 16 (0) **1990**†LARd 16 (0) **1994** LARd 16 (0) **1995** Oak 16 (0)

YEAR	TEAM	G(GS, POS)	RUSH	YD	AVG(LG)	TD	REC	YD	AVG(LG)	TD	PASS	COMP	PCT	YD	AVG(LG)	TD	INT	SK	YD	QBR	KPR	OTD	PTS	TAY
1985	†Cle	16(0)	—	—	—	—	—	—	—	—	1	0	0.0	0	0.0	0	0	—	—	—	P	—	0	0
1986	†Cle	16(0)	—	—	—	—	—	—	—	—	2	1	50.0	30	15.0(30)	0	1	—	—	—	P	—	0	-25
1989	LARd	16(0)	—	—	—	—	—	—	—	—	1	0	0.0	0	0.0	0	0	—	—	—	P	—	0	0
1991	†LARd★	16(0)	—	—	—	—	—	—	—	—	1	1	100.0	34	34.0(34)	0	0	—	—	—	P	—	0	17
1992	LARd	16(0)	1	-12	-12.0(-12)	0	—	—	—	—	—	—	—	—	—	—	—	—	—	—	P	—	0	-12
1993	†LARd	16(0)	1	-10	-10.0(-10)	0	—	—	—	—	—	—	—	—	—	—	—	—	—	—	P	—	0	-10
1996	Oak	12(0)	3	28	9.3(18)	0	—	—	—	—	—	—	—	—	—	—	—	—	—	—	Pk	—	0	13
NFL	15	212(0)	5	6	1.2(18)	0	—	—	—	—	5	2	40.0	64	12.8(34)	0	1	—	—	—	Pk	—	0	-17

GOTHARD, PRESTON Sherrill Preston, TE, 6´4˝/239 lbs; Alabama; B2/23/1962 Montgomery, AL

YEAR	TEAM	G(GS, POS)	RUSH	YD	AVG(LG)	TD	REC	YD	AVG(LG)	TD	PASS	COMP	PCT	YD	AVG(LG)	TD	INT	SK	YD	QBR	KPR	OTD	PTS	TAY
1985	Pit	16(0)	—	—	—	—	6	83	13.8(24)	0	—	—	—	—	—	—	—	—	—	—	—	—	0	42
1986	Pit	16(16, TE)	—	—	—	—	21	246	11.7(34)	1	—	—	—	—	—	—	—	—	—	—	—	—	6	128
1987	Pit	2(2)	—	—	—	—	2	9	4.5(7)	1	—	—	—	—	—	—	—	—	—	—	—	—	6	10
1988	Pit	16(15, TE)	—	—	—	—	12	121	10.1(26)	1	—	—	—	—	—	—	—	—	—	—	—	—	6	66
NFL	4	50(33)	—	—	—	—	41	459	11.2(34)	3	—	—	—	—	—	—	—	—	—	—	—	—	18	245

GOTSHALK, LEN Leonard William, T-G, 6´4˝/259 lbs; Humboldt State; 1971: Phi, rnd 8; B10/21/1949 Lakeport, CA **1972** Atl 14 **1973** Atl 14 **1974** Atl 10 (LT) **1975** Atl 14 (RT) **1976** Atl 14 (RT) **NFL** 66 [5 yrs]

GOTTSCHALK, DARREN Darren K., TE, 6´4˝/225 lbs; California Lutheran; B12/1/1964 Merced, CA **1987** NO 1 (0)

GOULD, ROBBIE Robbie, K, 6´1˝/181 lbs; Penn State; B12/6/1982 Jersey Shore, PA **[K]** **2005**†ChiB 13 (0)

GOUVEIA, KURT Kurt Keola, LB, 6´1˝/233 lbs; Brigham Young; 1986: Was, rnd 8; B9/14/1964 Honolulu, HI **1987**†Was 11 (1) **1988** Was 16 (0) **1989** Was 15 (1) **1990**†Was 16 (7, mlb) **1991**†Was 14 (1) **1992**†Was 16 (14, MLB) **1993** Was 16 (16, MLB) **1994** Was 14 (1) **1995**†Phi 16 (16, MLB) **1996** SD 16 (16, MLB) **1997** SD 7 (6, mlb) **1998** SD 14 (12, MLB) **1999**†Was 12 (0) **NFL** 183 (91) [13 yrs]

GOVERNALI, PAUL Paul Vincent, QB-TB, 5´11˝/193 lbs; Columbia; 1943: Bkn, rnd 1; B1/5/1921 Bronx, NY, D2/14/1978 San Diego, CA

YEAR	TEAM	G(GS, POS)	RUSH	YD	AVG(LG)	TD	REC	YD	AVG(LG)	TD	PASS	COMP	PCT	YD	AVG(LG)	TD	INT	SK	YD	QBR	KPR	OTD	PTS	TAY
1946	Bos	11(1, QB)	33	-186	-5.6(4)	2	—	—	—	—	192	83	43.2	1293	6.7(62)	13	10	—	—	67.0	P	—	12	146
1947	Bos	4(0)	4	19	4.8(0)	0	—	—	—	—	55	23	41.8	314	5.7(78)	3	6	—	—	—	—	—	0	-49
1947	NYG	8(2, TB)	36	132	3.7(28)	2	—	—	—	—	197	85	43.1	1461	7.4(53)	14	16	—	—	58.8	P	—	12	313
1948	NYG	9(2)	6	-48	-8.0(10)	0	—	—	—	—	56	27	48.2	280	5.0(24)	1	1	—	—	—	—	—	0	57
NFL	3	32(5)	79	-83	-1.1(28)	4	—	—	—	—	500	218	43.6	3348	6.7(78)	31	33	—	—	59.5	P	—	24	466

GOWDY, CORNELL Cornell Anthony, DB, 6´1˝/196 lbs; Morgan State; B10/2/1963 Washington, DC **1986** Dal 3 (0) **1987** Pit 13 (3) **1988** Pit 16 (14, SS) **NFL** 32 (17) [3 yrs]

GOWIN, TOBY Toby Lee, P, 5´10˝/167 lbs; North Texas; B3/30/1975 Jacksonville, TX **[KP]** **1997** Dal 16 (0) **1999**†Dal 16 (0) **2001** NO 16 (0) **2002** NO 15 (0) **2003**†Dal 16 (0) **2004**†NYJ 16 (0)

YEAR	TEAM	G(GS, POS)	RUSH	YD	AVG(LG)	TD	REC	YD	AVG(LG)	TD	PASS	COMP	PCT	YD	AVG(LG)	TD	INT	SK	YD	QBR	KPR	OTD	PTS	TAY
1998	†Dal	16(0)	1	33	33.0(33)	0	—	—	—	—	—	—	—	—	—	—	—	—	—	—	P	—	0	33
2000	†NO	16(0)	1	5	5.0(5)	0	—	—	—	—	—	—	—	—	—	—	—	—	—	—	P	—	0	5
NFL	8	127(0)	2	38	19.0(33)	0	—	—	—	—	—	—	—	—	—	—	—	—	—	—	KP	—	0	38

GOWINS, BRIAN Brian, K, 5´9˝/174 lbs; Northwestern; B6/3/1976 Birmingham, AL **[K]** **1999** ChiB 2 (0)

GOZDOWSKI, HIPPO Casimir, FB-G-C, none; B3/4/1897, D7/1976 Spring Lake, NJ **1922** Tol 3 (0), 12

GRABINSKI, TED Thaddeus, C-LB-G, 6´2˝/207 lbs; Duquesne; B2/6/1916 **1939** Pit 10 (2) **1940** Pit 11 (9, C) **NFL** 21 (11) [2 yrs]

GRABOSKY, GENE Harry Eugene, DT, 6´5˝/275 lbs; Syracuse; 1959: Was, rnd 26; B9/1/1936 Syracuse, NY, D5/4/2001 Liverpool, NY **1960** Buf-A 3

GRABOWSKI, JIM James Steven, RB, 6´2˝/220 lbs; Illinois; 1966: GB, rnd 1/Mia, rnd 1; B9/9/1944 Chicago, IL

YEAR	TEAM	G(GS, POS)	RUSH	YD	AVG(LG)	TD	REC	YD	AVG(LG)	TD	PASS	COMP	PCT	YD	AVG(LG)	TD	INT	SK	YD	QBR	KPR	OTD	PTS	TAY
1966	†GB	14	29	127	4.4(36)	1	4	13	3.3(7)	0	—	—	—	—	—	—	—	—	—	—	—	—	6	144
1967	†GB	9(FB)	120	466	3.9(24)	2	12	171	14.3(53)	1	—	—	—	—	—	—	—	—	—	—	—	—	18	577
1968	GB	14(FB)	135	518	3.8(25)	3	18	210	11.7(67)	1	—	—	—	—	—	—	—	—	—	—	—	—	24	658
1969	GB	14(FB)	73	261	3.6(22)	1	12	98	8.2(25)	1	—	—	—	—	—	—	—	—	—	—	—	—	12	325
1970	GB	12(FB)	67	210	3.1(17)	1	19	83	4.4(19)	0	—	—	—	—	—	—	—	—	—	—	—	—	6	262
1971	ChiB	12(FB)	51	149	2.9(16)	0	17	100	5.9(25)	0	—	—	—	—	—	—	—	—	—	—	—	—	0	199
NFL	6	75	475	1731	3.6(36)	8	82	675	8.2(67)	3	—	—	—	—	—	—	—	—	—	—	—	—	66	2164

GRACE, LES Leslie, E, 5´11˝/200 lbs; Temple; B1905, D8/19/1968 **1930** Nwk 2 (0)

GRACE, STEVEN Steven Kanoeau, C, 6´3˝/296 lbs; Arizona; B2/13/1979 Honolulu, HI **2002** Arz 1 (0)

GRADDY, SAM Samuel Louis, WR, 5´10˝/165 lbs; Tennessee; B2/10/1964 Gaffney, SC

YEAR	TEAM	G(GS, POS)	RUSH	YD	AVG(LG)	TD	REC	YD	AVG(LG)	TD	PASS	COMP	PCT	YD	AVG(LG)	TD	INT	SK	YD	QBR	KPR	OTD	PTS	TAY
1987	Den	1(0)	—	—	—	—	—	—	—	—	—	—	—	—	—	—	—	—	—	—	—	—	—	—
1988	Den	7(0)	—	—	—	—	1	30	30.0(30)	0	—	—	—	—	—	—	—	—	—	—	—	—	0	15
1990	†LARd	16(0)	—	—	—	—	1	47	47.0(47)	1	—	—	—	—	—	—	—	—	—	—	—	—	6	29
1991	†LARd	12(0)	—	—	—	—	6	195	32.5(80)	1	—	—	—	—	—	—	—	—	—	—	k	—	6	146
1992	LARd	7(1)	—	—	—	—	10	205	20.5(48)	1	—	—	—	—	—	—	—	—	—	—	k	—	6	118
NFL	5	43(1)	—	—	—	—	18	477	26.5(80)	3	—	—	—	—	—	—	—	—	—	—	k	—	18	307

GRADISHAR, RANDY Randolph Charles, LB, 6´3˝/233 lbs; Ohio State; 1974: Den, rnd 1; B3/3/1952 Warren, OH **[I]** **1974** Den 14 (3) **1975** Den✧14 (14, MLB) **1976** Den☆14 (14, RILB/mlb) **1977**†Den★14 (14, RILB) **1978**†Den★16 (16, RILB) **1979**†Den★16 (15, RILB) **1980** Den☆16 (16, RILB) **1981** Den★16 (16, RILB) **1982** Den★9 (9, RILB) **1983**†Den★16 (16, LILB) **NFL** 145 (133) [10 yrs]

GRADY, GARRY Garry L., DB, 5´10˝/185 lbs; Eastern Michigan; B10/11/1946 Northville, MI **1969** Mia-A 2

GRAF, DAVE David Francis, LB, 6´2˝/215 lbs; Penn State; 1975: Cle, rnd 17; B8/5/1953 Dunkirk, NY **1975** Cle 14 **1976** Cle 14 **1977** Cle 14 **1978** Cle 7 **1979** Cle 16 **1981** Was 6 (0) **NFL** 71 [6 yrs]

GRAF, RICK Richard Glenn, LB, 6´5˝/244 lbs; Wisconsin; 1987: Mia, rnd 2; B8/29/1964 Iowa City, IA **1987** Mia 12 (5, lolb) **1988** Mia 16 (16, LOLB) **1989** Mia 4 (4) **1990** Mia 8 (0) **1991**†Hou 12 (0) **1992**†Hou 16 (5, llb) **1993** Was 5 (0) **NFL** 73 (30) [7 yrs]

GRAFF, NEIL Neil Howard, QB, 6´3˝/205 lbs; Wisconsin; 1972: Min, rnd 16; B1/12/1950 Sioux Falls, SD

YEAR	TEAM	G(GS, POS)	RUSH	YD	AVG(LG)	TD	REC	YD	AVG(LG)	TD	PASS	COMP	PCT	YD	AVG(LG)	TD	INT	SK	YD	QBR	KPR	OTD	PTS	TAY
1974	NE	14	—	—	—	—	—	—	—	—	1	1	100.0	20	20.0(20)	0	0	—	—	—	—	—	0	10
1975	NE	11(2)	2	2	1.0(2)	0	—	—	—	—	35	18	51.4	221	6.3(31)	2	3	4	34	—	—	—	0	3
1977	†Pit	4	5	3	0.6(4)	0	—	—	—	—	12	6	50.0	47	3.9(21)	0	0	1	10	—	—	—	0	27
NFL	3	29(2)	7	5	0.7(4)	0	—	—	—	—	48	25	52.1	288	6.0(31)	2	3	5	44	—	—	—	0	39

GRAGG, SCOTT Christopher Scott, T, 6´8˝/315 lbs; Montana; 1995: NYG, rnd 2; B2/28/1972 Silverton, OR **1995** NYG 13 (0) **1996** NYG 16 (16, RT) **1997**†NYG 16 (16, RT) **1998** NYG 16 (16, RT) **1999** NYG 16 (16, RT) **2000** SF 16 (16, RT) **2001**†SF 16 (16, RT) **2002**†SF 16 (16, RT) **2003** SF 15 (14, RT) **2004** SF 16 (16, RT) **2005** NYJ 15 (7, rt) **NFL** 171 (149) [11 yrs]

GRAHAM, AARON Aaron Geddes, C, 6´4˝/293 lbs; Nebraska; 1996: Arz, rnd 4; B5/22/1973 Las Vegas, NM **1996** Arz 16 (7, c) **1997** Arz 16 (4) **1998**†Arz 14 (13, C) **1999** Arz 16 (16, C) **2001**†Oak 14 (0) **2002**†Ten 16 (0) **NFL** 92 (40) [6 yrs]

GRAHAM, AL Alfred, G, 6´0˝/211 lbs; none; B9/27/1905, D10/18/1969 Knoxville, TN **1925** Day 8 (8, RG) **1926** Day 6 (6, LG) **1927** Day☆8 (8, LG), 6 **1928** Day☆7 (6, LG) **1929** Day 5 (5, LG), 6 **1930** Por 3 (3) **1930** Pro 9 (9, RG) **1931** Pro☆11 (10, LG) **1932** ChiC 8 (5, RG) **1933** ChiC 8 (1) **NFL** 73 (61), 12 [9 yrs]

YEAR	TEAM	G (GS, POS)	RUSH	YD	AVG(LG)	TD	REC	YD	AVG(LG)	TD	PASS	COMP	PCT	YD	AVG(LG)	TD	INT	SK	YD	QBR	KPR	OTD	PTS	TAY

GRAHAM, ART — Arthur William, SE-WR, 6'1"/205 lbs; Boston College; 1963: Bos, rnd 1/Cle, rnd 11; B7/31/1941 Somerville, MA

YEAR	TEAM	G (GS, POS)	RUSH	YD	AVG(LG)	TD	REC	YD	AVG(LG)	TD	KPR	OTD	PTS	TAY
1963	†Bos-A	14	—	—	—	—	21	550	26.2(77)	5		—	30	300
1964	Bos-A	14(SE)	—	—	—	—	45	720	16.0(80)	6		—	36	390
1965	Bos-A	10(se)	—	—	—	—	25	316	12.6(33)	0		—	0	158
1966	Bos-A	14(SE)	—	—	—	—	51	673	13.2(42)	4		—	24	357
1967	Bos-A	12(SE)	1	-5	-5.0(-5)	0	41	606	14.8(79)	4		—	24	318
1968	Bos-A	11(6, WR)	—	—	—	—	16	242	15.1(34)	1	kp	—	6	121
NFL	6	75(6)	1	-5	-5.0(-5)	0	199	3107	15.6(80)	20	kp	—	120	1644

GRAHAM, BEN — Ben, P, 6'5"/230 lbs; Deakin (Australia); B11/2/1973 Melbourne, Australia

YEAR	TEAM	G (GS, POS)	RUSH	YD	AVG(LG)	TD	QBR	KPR	OTD	PTS	TAY
2005	NYJ	16(0)	1	0	0	—		P	—	0	0

GRAHAM, CLARENCE — Clarence, B, none   1928 Day 2 (1)

GRAHAM, DANIEL — Daniel, TE, 6'3"/257 lbs; Colorado; 2002: NE, rnd 1; B11/16/1978 Torrance, CA

YEAR	TEAM	G (GS, POS)	RUSH	YD	AVG(LG)	TD	REC	YD	AVG(LG)	TD	OTD	PTS	TAY
2002	NE	12(6, te)	—	—	—	—	15	150	10.0(31)	1	—	6	80
2003	†NE	14(9, TE)	—	—	—	—	38	409	10.8(38)	4	—	24	225
2004	†NE	14(14, TE)	—	—	—	—	30	364	12.1(48)	7	—	42	217
2005	†NE	11(9, te)	—	—	—	—	16	235	14.7(45)	3	—	18	133
NFL	4	51(38)	—	—	—	—	99	1158	11.7(48)	15	—	90	654

GRAHAM, DAVE — David Elliott, T, 6'3"/250 lbs; Virginia; 1960: Phi, rnd 13/Hou, rnd 2; B2/1/1939 Bridgeport, CT   **1963** Phi 14 (14, LT)   **1964** Phi 13 (LT)   **1965** Phi 14   **1966** Phi 14   **1968** Phi 14   **1969** Phi 14   **NFL** 83 (14) [6 yrs]

GRAHAM, DAVID — David Jerome, DE-NT, 6'6"/250 lbs; Morehouse; B4/6/1959 Chicago, IL   **1982** Sea 3 (0)   **1987** Sea 3 (2)   **NFL** 6 (2) [2 yrs]

GRAHAM, DeMINGO — DeMingo, G, 6'3"/310 lbs; Hofstra; B9/10/1973 Newark, NJ   **1999** SD 16 (10, RG)   **2000** SD 14 (1)   **2001** SD 16 (16, RG)   **2002** Hou 14 (11, LG)   **NFL** 60 (38) [4 yrs]

GRAHAM, DERRICK — Dettrice Anthony, G-T, 6'4"/310 lbs; Appalachian State; 1990: KC, rnd 5; B3/18/1967 Groveland, FL   **1990** KC 6 (0)   **1991**†KC 16 (1)   **1992** KC 2 (2)   **1993**†KC 11 (2)   **1994**†KC 16 (11, RT)   **1995** Car 11 (7, rt)   **1996** Sea 16 (16, RG)   **1997** Sea 9 (9, RG)   **1998** Oak 12 (12, RG)   **NFL** 99 (60) [9 yrs]

GRAHAM, DON — Donald John, LB, 6'2"/244 lbs; Penn State; 1987: TB, rnd 4; B1/31/1964 Pittsburgh, PA   **1987** TB 2 (0)   **1988** Buf 10 (0)   **1989** Was 1 (0)   **NFL** 13 (0) [3 yrs]

GRAHAM, EARNEST — Earnest, RB, 5'9"/215 lbs; Florida; B1/15/1980 Naples, FL

YEAR	TEAM	G (GS, POS)	RUSH	YD	AVG(LG)	TD	KPR	OTD	PTS	TAY
2004	TB	9(0)	13	73	5.6(13)	0	k	—	0	80
2005	†TB	16(0)	28	83	3.0(16)	0	k	—	0	97
NFL	2	25(0)	41	156	3.8(16)	0	k	—	0	177

GRAHAM, FRED — Frederick Hartley, E, 6'0"/175 lbs; Indiana State; West Virginia; B12/11/1900 Masontown, WV, D8/29/1952 Fairmont, WV   **1926** Fra 1 (1)   **1926** Pro 1 (0)   **NFL** 2 (1) [1 yr]

GRAHAM, HASON — Hason Aaron, WR, 5'10"/176 lbs; Georgia; B3/21/1971 Decatur, GA

YEAR	TEAM	G (GS, POS)	RUSH	YD	AVG(LG)	TD	REC	YD	AVG(LG)	TD	OTD	PTS	TAY
1995	NE	10(1)	—	—	—	—	10	156	15.6(37)	2	—	12	88
1996	†NE	9(0)	—	—	—	—	5	64	12.8(23)	0	—	0	32
NFL	2	19(1)	—	—	—	—	15	220	14.7(37)	2	—	12	120

GRAHAM, JAY — Herman Jason, RB, 5'11"/220 lbs; Tennessee; 1997: Bal, rnd 3; B7/14/1975 Concord, NC

YEAR	TEAM	G (GS, POS)	RUSH	YD	AVG(LG)	TD	REC	YD	AVG(LG)	TD	KPR	OTD	PTS	TAY
1997	Bal	13(3)	81	299	3.7(19)	2	12	51	4.3(19)	0	k	—	12	370
1998	Bal	5(1)	35	109	3.1(12)	0	5	41	8.2(14)	0	k	—	0	137
1999	Bal	4(0)												
2001	Sea	11(0)	12	43	3.6(19)	0	1	6	6.0(6)	0	k	—	0	57
2002	GB	3(0)	1	3	3.0(3)	0	2	6	3.0(4)	0		—	0	6
NFL	5	36(4)	129	454	3.5(19)	2	20	104	5.2(19)	0	k	—	12	569

GRAHAM, JEFF — Jeffrey Todd, WR, 6'2"/200 lbs; Ohio State; 1991: Pit, rnd 2; B2/14/1969 Dayton, OH

YEAR	TEAM	G (GS, POS)	RUSH	YD	AVG(LG)	TD	REC	YD	AVG(LG)	TD	KPR	OTD	PTS	TAY
1991	Pit	13(1)	—	—	—	—	2	21	10.5(15)	0	kp	—	0	20
1992	Pit	14(10, WR)	—	—	—	—	49	711	14.5(51)	1	—	—	6	361
1993	†Pit	15(12, WR)	—	—	—	—	38	579	15.2(51)	0	—	—	0	290
1994	†ChiB	16(15, WR)	—	—	—	—	68	944	13.9(76)	4	p	1	32	567
1995	ChiB	16(16, WR)	—	—	—	—	82	1301	15.9(51)	4	kp	—	24	736
1996	NYJ	11(9, wr)	—	—	—	—	50	788	15.8(78)	6	—	—	36	424
1997	NYJ	16(15, WR)	—	—	—	—	42	542	12.9(47)	2	—	—	12	281
1998	Phi	15(15, WR)	—	—	—	—	47	600	12.8(45)	2	—	—	12	310
1999	SD	16(11, WR)	—	—	—	—	57	968	17.0(54)	2	—	—	12	494
2000	SD	14(13, WR)	—	—	—	—	55	907	16.5(83)	4	p	—	24	466
2001	SD	14(12, WR)	—	—	—	—	52	811	15.6(61)	5	—	—	30	431
NFL	11	160(129)	—	—	—	—	542	8172	15.1(83)	30	kp	1	188	4377

GRAHAM, KENNY — James Kenneth, DB, 6'0"/210 lbs; Washington State; 1964: SD, rnd 13/Bal, rnd 12; B11/25/1941 Texarkana, TX [I]   **1964**†SD-A 14 (LS)   **1965**†SD-A★14 (LS)   **1966** SD-A☆13 (LS)   **1967** SD-A★13 (LS)   **1968** SD-A★14 (LS)   **1969** SD-A★14 (LS)   **1970** Cin 5   **1970** Pit 3   **NFL** 90 [7 yrs]

GRAHAM, KENT — Kent Douglas, QB, 6'5"/231 lbs; Notre Dame; Ohio State; 1992: NYG, rnd 8; B11/1/1968 Wheaton, IL

YEAR	TEAM	G (GS, POS)	RUSH	YD	AVG(LG)	TD	REC	YD	AVG(LG)	TD	PASS	COMP	PCT	YD	AVG(LG)	TD	INT	SK	YD	QBR	OTD	PTS	TAY
1992	NYG	6(3)	6	36	6.0(15)	0	—	—	—	—	97	42	43.3	470	4.8(44)	1	4	7	49	—	—	0	116
1993	NYG	9(0)	2	-3	-1.5(-1)	0	—	—	—	—	22	8	36.4	79	3.6(18)	0	0	3	28	—	—	0	37
1994	NYG	13(1)	2	11	5.5(9)	0	—	—	—	—	53	24	45.3	295	5.6(55)	3	2	2	22	—	—	0	94
1996	Arz	10(8, qb)	21	87	4.1(19)	0	—	—	—	—	274	146	53.3	1624	5.9(69)	12	7	19	120	75.1	—	0	679
1997	Arz	8(6, qb)	13	23	1.8(10)	2	—	—	—	—	250	130	52.0	1408	5.6(47)	4	5	16	115	65.9	—	12	567
1998	NYG	11(6, qb)	27	138	5.1(23)	2	1	16	16.0(16)	0	205	105	51.2	1219	5.9(87)	7	5	12	75	—	—	12	611
1999	NYG	9(9, QB)	35	132	3.8(17)	1	1	-1	-1.0(-1)	0	271	160	59.0	1697	6.3(56)	9	9	26	184	74.6	—	6	675
2000	Pit	14(5, qb)	8	7	0.9(7)	0	—	—	—	—	148	66	44.6	878	5.9(77)	1	1	13	70	—	—	0	411
2001	Was	3(0)	7	-7	-1.0(0)	0	—	—	—	—	19	13	68.4	131	6.9(16)	2	0	2	16	—	—	0	69
NFL	9	83(38)	121	424	3.5(23)	5	2	15	7.5(16)	0	1339	694	51.8	7801	5.8(87)	39	33	100	679	69.0	—	30	3257

GRAHAM, LES — Lester James, G, 6'0"/215 lbs; Tulsa; B7/1/1916 Hominy, OK, deceased   **1938** Det 11 (2)

GRAHAM, LYLE — Samuel Lyle, C, 6'3"/210 lbs; Richmond; B10/28/1915 Kenbridge, VA   **1941** Phi 11 (7, C)

GRAHAM, MIKE — Michael N., B, 6'0"/198 lbs; Cincinnati; 1948: LAD-A, rnd 13/LARm, rnd 9; B4/3/1923 Warren, OH, D7/7/2003 Warren, OH

YEAR	TEAM	G (GS, POS)	RUSH	YD	AVG(LG)	TD	REC	YD	AVG(LG)	TD	KPR	OTD	PTS	TAY
1948	LAD-A	14(1)	19	69	3.6	1	0	2	(2)	0	ki	—	6	150

GRAHAM, MILT — Milton Russell, T-DT, 6'6"/235 lbs; Colgate; 1956: ChiB, rnd 14; B7/28/1934, MA   **1961** Bos-A 3   **1962** Bos-A 14 (RT)   **1963**†Bos-A 11 (RT)   **NFL** 28 [3 yrs]

GRAHAM, OTTO — Otto Everett 'Automatic Otto', QB-DB, 6'1"/196 lbs; Northwestern; 1944: Det, rnd 1; B12/6/1921 Waukegan, IL, D12/17/2003 Sarasota, FL; HOF 1965 [C]

YEAR	TEAM	G (GS, POS)	RUSH	YD	AVG(LG)	TD	PASS	COMP	PCT	YD	AVG(LG)	TD	INT	QBR	KPR	OTD	PTS	TAY
1946	†Cle-A☆	14(9, QB)	30	-125	-4.2	1	174	95	54.6	1834	10.5(79)	17	5	—	pi	1	12	843
1947	†Cle-A☆	14(9, QB)	19	72	3.8	1	269	163	60.6	2753	10.2(99)	25	11	—	pi	—	6	1210
1948	†Cle-A☆	14(14, QB)	23	146	6.3	6	333	173	52.0	2713	8.1(78)	25	15	—	pi	—	36	1090
1949	†Cle-A☆	12(11, QB)	27	107	4.0	3	285	161	56.5	2785	9.8(74)	19	10	—	pi	—	18	1225
AAFC	4	54(43)	99	200	2.0	11	1061	592	55.8	10085	9.5(99)	86	41	99.1	pi	1	72	4367
1950	†Cle★	12(QB)	55	145	2.6(20)	6	253	137	54.2	1943	7.7(80)	14	20	64.7	—	—	36	447
1951	†Cle★	12(QB)	35	29	0.8(12)	3	265	147	55.5	2205	8.3(81)	17	16	79.2	—	1	24	607
1952	†Cle★	12(QB)	42	130	3.1(21)	4	364	181	49.7	2816	7.7(68)	20	24	66.6	—	—	24	718
1953	†Cle★	12(QB)	43	143	3.3(21)	6	258	167	64.7	2722	10.6(70)	11	9	99.7	—	—	36	1259
1954	†Cle★	12(QB)	63	114	1.8(14)	8	240	142	59.2	2092	8.7(77)	11	17	73.5	—	—	48	615
1955	†Cle☆	12(QB)	68	121	1.8(36)	6	185	98	53.0	1721	9.3(61)	15	8	94.0	—	—	36	797
NFL	6	72	306	682	2.2(36)	33	1565	872	55.7	13499	8.6(99)	88	94	78.2	—	1	204	4442

GRAHAM, ROGER — Roger Alton, RB, 5'11"/217 lbs; New Haven; B11/8/1972 Bronx, NY   **1996** Jax 1 (0)

Graham, Scottie James Otis, RB, 5´9˝/217 lbs; Ohio State; 1992: Pit, rnd 7; B3/28/1969 Long Beach, NY

YEAR	TEAM	G(GS, POS)	RUSH	YD	AVG(LG)	TD	REC	YD	AVG(LG)	TD	PASS	COMP	PCT	YD	AVG(LG)	TD	INT	SK	YD	QBR	KPR	OTD	PTS	TAY
1992	NYJ	2(0)	14	29	2.1(6)	0	—	—	—	—	—	—	—	—	—	—	—	—	—	—	—	—	0	29
1993	†Min	7(3)	118	488	4.1(31)	3	7	46	6.6(11)	0	—	—	—	—	—	—	—	—	—	—	k	—	18	542
1994	†Min	16(0)	64	207	3.2(11)	2	1	1	1.0(1)	0	—	—	—	—	—	—	—	—	—	—	—	—	12	228
1995	Min	16(6, rb)	110	406	3.7(26)	2	4	30	7.5(11)	0	—	—	—	—	—	—	—	—	—	—	—	—	12	441
1996	†Min	11(0)	57	138	2.4(12)	0	7	48	6.9(18)	0	—	—	—	—	—	—	—	—	—	—	—	—	0	162
1997	Cin	5(0)	1	-1	-1.0(-1)	0	1	1	1.0(1)	0	—	—	—	—	—	—	—	—	—	—	—	—	0	-1
NFL	6	57(9)	364	1267	3.5(31)	7	20	126	6.3(18)	0	—	—	—	—	—	—	—	—	—	—	k	—	42	1401

Graham, Shayne Michael Shayne, K, 6´0˝/197 lbs; Virginia Tech; B12/9/1977 Radford, VA **[K]** **2001** Buf 6 (0) **2002** Car 11 (0) **2003** Cin 16 (0) **2004** Cin 16 (0) **2005**†Cin★16 (0) **NFL** 65 (0) [5 yrs]

Graham, Tom Thomas, G, 6´3˝/210 lbs; Temple; B8/14/1909, D8/1961 **1935** Phi 2 (0)

Graham, Tom Thomas Lawrence, LB, 6´2˝/235 lbs; Oregon; 1972: Den, rnd 4; B4/15/1950 Los Angeles, CA **1972** Den 14 (9, MLB) **1973** Den 14 (14, MLB) **1974** Den 5 **1974** KC 8 **1975** SD 14 (8, MLB) **1976** SD 10 (8, MLB) **1977** SD 12 (MLB) **1978** Buf 11 (mlb) **NFL** 88 (39) [7 yrs]

Graham, William William Roger, DB, 5´11˝/191 lbs; Texas; 1982: Det, rnd 5; B9/27/1959 Silsbee, TX **1982** Det 7 (1) **1983** Det 14 (14, FS) **1984** Det 14 (13, FS) **1985** Det 16 (16, FS) **1986** Det 16 (0) **1987** Det 2 (1) **NFL** 69 (45) [6 yrs]

Grain, Ed Edwin Elswin, G, 6´0˝/230 lbs; Pennsylvania; 1947: NYY-A, rnd 15/Det, rnd 7; B2/25/1922 Baltimore, MD, D10/6/1984 Evanston, IL **1947** NYY-A 2 (0) **1947** Bal-A 10 (2) **1948** Bal-A 11 (1) **AAFC** 23 (3) [2 yrs]

Gramatica, Bill Guillermo, K, 5´10˝/189 lbs; Florida State; South Florida; 2001: Arz, rnd 4; B7/10/1978 Buenos Aires, Argentina **[K]** **2001** Arz 13 (0) **2002** Arz 16 (0) **2003** Arz 4 (0) **2004** Mia 1 (0) **NFL** 34 (0) [4 yrs]

Gramatica, Martin Martin, K, 5´8˝/170 lbs; Kansas State; 1999: TB, rnd 3; B11/27/1975 Buenos Aires, Argentina **[K]** **1999**†TB 16 (0) **2000**†TB★16 (0) **2002**†TB 16 (0) **2003** TB 16 (0) **2004**†Ind 4 (0) **2004** TB 11 (0)

YEAR	TEAM	G(GS, POS)	RUSH	YD	AVG(LG)	TD	REC	YD	AVG(LG)	TD	PASS	COMP	PCT	YD	AVG(LG)	TD	INT	SK	YD	QBR	KPR	OTD	PTS	TAY
2001	†TB	14(0)	—	—	—	—	—	—	—	—	1	0	0.0	0	0.0	0	0	—	—	—	K	—	97	0
NFL	6	93(0)	—	—	—	—	—	—	—	—	1	0	0.0	0	0.0	0	0	—	—	—	KP	—	592	0

Granby, John John Edward, WR, 6´1˝/200 lbs; Virginia Tech; 1992: Den, rnd 12; B11/11/1968 Virginia Beach, VA **1992** Den 4 (1)

Grandberry, Ken Kenneth James, RB, 6´0˝/195 lbs; Washington State; 1974: Chi, rnd 8; B1/25/1952 Waco, TX

YEAR	TEAM	G(GS, POS)	RUSH	YD	AVG(LG)	TD	REC	YD	AVG(LG)	TD	PASS	COMP	PCT	YD	AVG(LG)	TD	INT	SK	YD	QBR	KPR	OTD	PTS	TAY
1974	ChiB	14(RB)	144	475	3.3(31)	2	30	212	7.1(40)	0	—	—	—	—	—	—	—	—	—	—	k	—	12	839

Grandelius, Sonny Everett John, HB, 6´0˝/195 lbs; Michigan State; 1951: NYG, rnd 3; B4/16/1929 Muskegon, MI

YEAR	TEAM	G(GS, POS)	RUSH	YD	AVG(LG)	TD	REC	YD	AVG(LG)	TD	PASS	COMP	PCT	YD	AVG(LG)	TD	INT	SK	YD	QBR	KPR	OTD	PTS	TAY
1953	NYG	12(LH)	108	278	2.6(31)	1	15	80	5.3(26)	0	—	—	—	—	—	—	—	—	—	—	—	—	6	328

Granderson, Rufus Rufus Will, DT, 6´5˝/277 lbs; Prairie View A&M; 1959: Det, rnd 19; B8/13/1936 Waco, TX **1960** DalT-A 6

Grandinette, George George J., G, 5´9˝/215 lbs; Fordham; B4/13/1917 New Haven, CT, D4/16/1984 Lauderdale Lake, FL **1943** Bkn 10 (0)

Grange, Gardie Garland Arthur, HB-E, 6´0˝/173 lbs; Illinois; B12/2/1906 Forksville, PA, D5/28/1981 Miami, FL **[K]** **1929** ChiB 14 (3, LH), 12 **1930** ChiB 12 (8, RE), 1 **1931** ChiB 12 (3, LH), 7 **NFL** 38 (14), 20 [3 yrs]

Grange, Red Harold Edward 'The Galloping Ghost', HB-BB-DB-TB, 6´0˝/180 lbs; Illinois; B6/13/1903 Forksville, PA, D1/28/1991 Lake Wales, FL; HOF 1963 **[K]** **1925** ChiB 5 (5, lh), 18 **1927** NYY 13 (9, bb), 6 **1929** ChiB 14 (10), 13 **1930** ChiB☆14 (14, LH), 49 **1931** ChiB☆13 (11), 42

YEAR	TEAM	G(GS, POS)	RUSH	YD	AVG(LG)	TD	REC	YD	AVG(LG)	TD	PASS	COMP	PCT	YD	AVG(LG)	TD	INT	SK	YD	QBR	KPR	OTD	PTS	TAY
1932	ChiB☆	12(12, LH)	57	136	2.4	3	11	168	15.3	4	13	5	38.5	96	7.4	0	0	—	—	—	—	—	42	318
1933	ChiB	13(2)	81	277	3.4	1	3	74	24.7	0	33	13	39.4	169	5.1	2	3	—	—	—	—	—	6	299
1934	ChiB	12(0)	32	156	4.9	1	2	46	23.0(36)	2	25	6	24.0	81	3.2	1	7	—	—	—	—	—	18	-36
NFL	8	96(63)	170	569	3.3	21	16	288	18.0(36)	10	71	24	33.8	346	4.9	10	10	—	—	—	K	1	194	806

Granger, Charley Charles, T, 6´2˝/240 lbs; Southern (LA); 1961: Bos, rnd 26; B8/9/1938 Lake Charles, LA **1961** Dal 8 (7, RT) **1961** SL 6 **NFL** 14 (7) [1 yr]

Granger, Hoyle Hoyle John, RB, 6´1˝/225 lbs; Mississippi State; 1966: Hou, rnd 5/Bal, rnd 4; B3/7/1944 Oberlin, LA

YEAR	TEAM	G(GS, POS)	RUSH	YD	AVG(LG)	TD	REC	YD	AVG(LG)	TD	PASS	COMP	PCT	YD	AVG(LG)	TD	INT	SK	YD	QBR	KPR	OTD	PTS	TAY
1966	Hou-A	11	56	388	6.9(69)	1	12	104	8.7(26)	1	—	—	—	—	—	—	—	—	—	—	—	—	12	455
1967	†Hou-A★	14(FB)	236	1194	5.1(67)	6	31	300	9.7(43)	3	—	—	—	—	—	—	—	—	—	—	—	—	54	**1419**
1968	Hou-A✧	13(FB)	202	848	4.2(47)	7	26	361	13.9(55)	0	—	—	—	—	—	—	—	—	—	—	—	—	42	1099
1969	†Hou-A	13(FB)	186	740	4.0(23)	3	27	330	12.2(53)	1	—	—	—	—	—	—	—	—	—	—	—	—	24	940
1970	Hou	5(fb)	51	169	3.3(15)	1	11	118	10.7(22)	0	—	—	—	—	—	—	—	—	—	—	k	—	6	223
1971	NO	14	32	139	4.3(16)	1	12	52	4.3(11)	0	—	—	—	—	—	—	—	—	—	—	—	—	6	175
1972	Hou	13(fb)	42	175	4.2(14)	0	15	74	4.9(20)	0	—	—	—	—	—	—	—	—	—	—	k	—	0	202
NFL	7	83	805	3653	4.5(69)	19	134	1339	10.0(55)	5	—	—	—	—	—	—	—	—	—	—	k	—	144	4513

Granger, Norm Norman Lance, RB, 5´9˝/225 lbs; Iowa; 1984: Dal, rnd 5; B9/14/1961 Newark, NJ **1984** Dal 15 (0)

YEAR	TEAM	G(GS, POS)	RUSH	YD	AVG(LG)	TD	REC	YD	AVG(LG)	TD	PASS	COMP	PCT	YD	AVG(LG)	TD	INT	SK	YD	QBR	KPR	OTD	PTS	TAY
1987	Atl	3(1)	6	12	2.0(6)	0	2	34	17.0(26)	0	—	—	—	—	—	—	—	—	—	—	—	—	0	29
NFL	2	18(1)	6	12	2.0(6)	0	2	34	17.0(26)	0	—	—	—	—	—	—	—	—	—	—	k	—	0	5

Grannell, Dave David Matthew, TE, 6´4˝/230 lbs; Arizona State; 1974: SD, rnd 11; B10/4/1952 Denver, CO

YEAR	TEAM	G(GS, POS)	RUSH	YD	AVG(LG)	TD	REC	YD	AVG(LG)	TD	PASS	COMP	PCT	YD	AVG(LG)	TD	INT	SK	YD	QBR	KPR	OTD	PTS	TAY
1974	SD	9	—	—	—	—	3	51	17.0(22)	0	—	—	—	—	—	—	—	—	—	—	—	—	0	26

Grant, Aaron Aaron T., C, 6´2˝/285 lbs; Tennessee Wesleyan; Tennessee-Chattanooga; B7/3/1908 Roane County, TN, D9/1966 **1930** Por 1 (0)

Grant, African African Nigeria, DB, 6´0˝/200 lbs; Illinois; B8/2/1965 New York, NY **1990** Mia 4 (0)

Grant, Alan Alan Hays, DB, 5´10˝/187 lbs; Stanford; 1990: Ind, rnd 4; B10/1/1966 Pasadena, CA **1990** Ind 16 (7, lcb) **1991** Ind 16 (1) **1992**†SF 15 (0) **1993** SF 3 (0) **1993** Cin 9 (1) **1994** Was 13 (0) **NFL** 72 (9) [5 yrs]

Grant, Bob Robert Bernard, LB, 6´2˝/225 lbs; Wake Forest; 1968: Bal, rnd 2; B10/14/1946 Jacksonville, FL **1968** Bal 7 **1969** Bal 14 (LLB) **1970**†Bal 14 (LLB) **1971** Was 6 **NFL** 41 [4 yrs]

Grant, Bud Harold Peter, E-DE, 6´3˝/199 lbs; Minnesota; 1950: Phi, rnd 1; B5/20/1927 Superior, WI; HOF 1994 **[C]** **1951** Phi 12

YEAR	TEAM	G(GS, POS)	RUSH	YD	AVG(LG)	TD	REC	YD	AVG(LG)	TD	PASS	COMP	PCT	YD	AVG(LG)	TD	INT	SK	YD	QBR	KPR	OTD	PTS	TAY
1952	Phi	12(RE)	—	—	—	—	56	997	17.8(84)	7	—	—	—	—	—	—	—	—	—	—	—	—	42	534
NFL	2	24	—	—	—	—	56	997	17.8(84)	7	—	—	—	—	—	—	—	—	—	—	p	—	42	538

Grant, Charles Charles Gabriel, DE, 6´3˝/282 lbs; Georgia; 2002: NO, rnd 1; B9/3/1978 Colquitt, GA **2002** NO 16 (6, lde) **2003** NO 16 (16, LDE/rde) **2004** NO 16 (16, LDE) **2005** NO 16 (14, RDE) **NFL** 64 (52) [4 yrs]

Grant, Cie Willie, LB, 6´0˝/228 lbs; Ohio State; 2003: NO, rnd 3; B11/27/1979 New Philadelphia, OH **2003** NO 7 (0)

Grant, Darryl Darryl Baris, DT-G-C-T, 6´1˝/269 lbs; Rice; 1981: Was, rnd 9; B11/22/1959 San Antonio, TX **1981** Was 15 (0) **1982**†Was 9 (4) **1983**†Was 16 (16, RDT) **1984**†Was 15 (15, RDT) **1985** Was 8 (8, RDT) **1986**†Was 16 (8, RDT) **1987**†Was 12 (11, RDT) **1988** Was 16 (16, RDT) **1989** Was 16 (16, RDT) **1990**†Was 16 (15, RDT) **1991** TB 2 (0) **NFL** 141 (109) [11 yrs]

Grant, David David John, DE-NT, 6´4˝/277 lbs; West Virginia; 1988: Cin, rnd 4; B9/17/1965 Belleville, NJ **1988**†Cin 16 (0) **1989** Cin 16 (0) **1990**†Cin 16 (9, RDE) **1991** Cin 13 (13, RDE) **1992** TB 2 (0) **1993** GB 7 (0) **NFL** 70 (22) [6 yrs]

Grant, DeLawrence DeLawrence, DE-LB, 6´3˝/280 lbs; Oregon State; 2001: Oak, rnd 3; B11/18/1979 Compton, CA **2001** Oak 2 (0) **2002**†Oak 16 (14, LDE) **2003** Oak 13 (4) **2004** Oak 9 (9, LLB) **2005** Oak 9 (0) **NFL** 49 (27) [5 yrs]

Grant, Deon Deon D'Marquis, DB, 6´2˝/207 lbs; Tennessee; 2000: Car, rnd 2; B3/14/1979 Augusta, GA **2001** Car 16 (16, FS) **2002** Car 16 (16, FS) **2003**†Car 16 (16, FS) **2004** Jax 16 (16, FS) **2005**†Jax 16 (16, FS) **NFL** 80 (80) [5 yrs]

Grant, Ducky Hugh E., BB, 5´11˝/175 lbs; St. Mary's (CA); B12/24/1902, D9/1985 Fountain Valley, CA **[K]** **1928** ChiC 6 (6, BB), 1

Grant, Ernest Ernest Jovoa, DT, 6´5˝/310 lbs; Arkansas-Pine Bluff; 2000: Mia, rnd 6; B5/17/1976 Atlanta, GA **2000** Mia 2 (0) **2001**†Mia 11 (3) **2002** ChiB 11 (0) **NFL** 24 (3) [3 yrs]

Grant, Frank Frank, WR, 5´11˝/181 lbs; Southern Colorado; 1972: Was, rnd 13; B2/15/1950 Brooklyn, NY

YEAR	TEAM	G(GS, POS)	RUSH	YD	AVG(LG)	TD	REC	YD	AVG(LG)	TD	PASS	COMP	PCT	YD	AVG(LG)	TD	INT	SK	YD	QBR	KPR	OTD	PTS	TAY
1973	†Was	13	—	—	—	—	1	12	12.0(12)	1	—	—	—	—	—	—	—	—	—	—	—	—	6	11
1974	†Was	14(1)	1	-10	-10.0(-10)	0	9	196	21.8(69)	1	—	—	—	—	—	—	—	—	—	—	—	—	6	93
1975	Was	14(9, WR)	3	46	15.3(25)	0	41	776	18.9(**96**)	8	—	—	—	—	—	—	—	—	—	—	—	—	48	490
1976	†Was☆	14(14, WR)	1	-9	-9.0(-9)	0	50	818	16.4(53)	5	—	—	—	—	—	—	—	—	—	—	—	—	30	425

YEAR	TEAM	G (GS, POS)	RUSH	YD	AVG(LG)	TD	REC	YD	AVG(LG)	TD	PASS	COMP	PCT	YD	AVG(LG)	TD	INT	SK	YD	QBR	KPR	OTD	PTS	TAY
1977	Was	14(14, WR)	—	—	—	—	34	480	14.1(59)	3	—	—	—	—	—	—	—	—	—	—	—	—	18	255
1978	Was	6(4)	—	—	—	—	6	92	15.3(23)	0	—	—	—	—	—	—	—	—	—	—	—	—	0	46
1978	TB	10(6, wr)	—	—	—	—	8	112	14.0(20)	0	—	—	—	—	—	—	—	—	—	—	—	—	0	56
NFL	6	85(48)	5	27	5.4(25)	0	149	2486	16.7(96)	18	—	—	—	—	—	—	—	—	—	—	—	—	108	1376

GRANT, JOHN   John David, DT-DE-NT, 6′3″/241 lbs; USC; 1973: Den, rnd 7; B6/28/1950 Boise, ID   **1973** Den 13 **1974** Den 13 (13, LDT) **1975** Den 14 (13, LDT) **1976** Den 13 (3) **1977**†Den 14 **1978**†Den 16 **1979**†Den 16 **NFL** 99 (29) [7 yrs]

GRANT, LEN   Leonard W., T, 6′3″/235 lbs; NYU; B1/17/1906 Boston, MA, D8/6/1938 Dedham, MA   **1930** NYG 12 (8, lt) **1931** NYG☆11 (9, LT) **1932** NYG☆12 (9, LT) **1933**†NYG☆14 (9, LT) **1934**†NYG 12 (7, LT) **1935**†NYG 12 (11, RT) **1936** NYG 10 (8, rt) **1937** NYG 9 (7, RT) **NFL** 92 (68) [8 yrs]

GRANT, ORANTES   Orantes Laquay, LB, 6′0″/228 lbs; Georgia; 2000: Dal, rnd 7; B3/18/1979 Atlanta, GA   **2000** Dal 13 (0) **2001** Dal 10 (1) **2002** Was 1 (0) **2003** Was 1 (0) **2003** Cle 1 (0) **NFL** 26 (1) [4 yrs]

GRANT, OTIS   Otis, WR, 6′3″/197 lbs; Michigan State; 1983: LARm, rnd 5; B8/13/1961 Atlanta, GA

YEAR	TEAM	G (GS, POS)	RUSH	YD	AVG(LG)	TD	REC	YD	AVG(LG)	TD	PASS	COMP	PCT	YD	AVG(LG)	TD	INT	SK	YD	QBR	KPR	OTD	PTS	TAY
1983	†LARm	16(3)	2	-10	-5.0(1)	0	12	221	18.4(57)	1	—	—	—	—	—	—	—	—	—	—	—	—	6	106
1984	LARm	14(0)	—	—	—	—	9	64	7.1(15)	0	—	—	—	—	—	—	—	—	—	—	—	—	0	32
1987	Phi	3(3)	1	20	20.0(20)	0	16	280	17.5(41)	0	1	0	0.0	0	0.0	0	—	—	—	—	—	—	0	160
NFL	3	33(6)	3	10	3.3(20)	0	37	565	15.3(57)	1	1	0	0.0	0	0.0	0	—	—	—	—	—	—	6	298

GRANT, REGGIE   Reginald Leon, DB, 5′9″/185 lbs; Oregon; 1978: NYJ, rnd 9; B9/2/1955 Atlanta, GA   **1978** NYJ 14

GRANT, ROSIE   Ross Stewart, G, 5′10″/198 lbs; NYU; B4/16/1908 Chicago, IL, D4/26/1974 Cedar Lake, IN   **1932** SI 12 (11, RG) **1933** Cin 8 (3) **1934** Cin 2 (0) **NFL** 22 (14) [3 yrs]

GRANT, RUPERT   Rupert, RB, 6′1″/233 lbs; Howard; B11/5/1973 Washington, DC

YEAR	TEAM	G (GS, POS)	RUSH	YD	AVG(LG)	TD	REC	YD	AVG(LG)	TD	PASS	COMP	PCT	YD	AVG(LG)	TD	INT	SK	YD	QBR	KPR	OTD	PTS	TAY
1995	NE	7(1)	—	—	—	—	1	4	4.0(4)	0	—	—	—	—	—	—	—	—	—	—	—	k	—	0	-6

GRANT, STEVE   Stephen Mitchell, LB, 6′0″/240 lbs; West Virginia; 1992: Ind, rnd 10; B12/23/1969 Miami, FL   **1992** Ind 16 (0) **1993** Ind 16 (0) **1994** Ind 16 (12, LLB) **1995**†Ind 15 (15, LLB) **1996** Ind 16 (11, LLB) **1997** Ind 9 (9, MLB) **NFL** 83 (47) [6 yrs]

GRANT, WES   Wesley Louis, DE-DT, 6′3″/245 lbs; UCLA; 1970: NYG, rnd 4; B9/24/1946 Los Angeles, CA   **1971** Buf 3 **1971** SD 2 **1972** Cle 3 **1973** Hou 3 **NFL** 11 [3 yrs]

GRANT, WILL   Wilfred L., C, 6′3″/254 lbs; Idaho State; Kentucky; 1978: Buf, rnd 10; B3/7/1954 Milton, MA   **1978** Buf 16 **1979** Buf 16 **1980**†Buf 16 (16, C) **1981**†Buf 16 (16, C) **1982** Buf 9 (9, C) **1983** Buf 16 (16, C) **1984** Buf 16 (16, C) **1985** Buf 16 (15, C) **1986** Sea 7 (6, c) **1987** Buf 1 (1) **NFL** 129 (95) [10 yrs]

GRANTHAM, LARRY   James Larry, LB, 6′0″/210 lbs; Mississippi; 1960: NYT, rnd 1/Bal, rnd 15; B9/16/1938 Crystal Springs, MS [I]   **1960** NYT-A☆14 (LLB) **1961** NYT-A☆11 (RLB) **1962** NYT-A☆14 (RLB) **1963** NYJ-A☆14 (RLB) **1964** NYJ-A☆14 (RLB) **1965** NYJ-A☆14 (RLB) **1966** NYJ-A☆14 (RLB) **1967** NYJ-A☆14 (RLB) **1968**†NYJ-A☆13 (RLB) **1969**†NYJ-A★14 (RLB) **1970** NYJ 14 (RLB) **1971** NYJ☆14 (RLB) **1972** NYJ 11 (RLB) **NFL** 175 (14) [13 yrs]

GRANVILLE, BILLY   William Lamont, LB, 6′3″/252 lbs; Duke; B3/11/1974 Trenton, NJ   **1997** Cin 12 (4) **1998** Cin 16 (0) **1999** Cin 16 (0) **2000** Cin 14 (0) **NFL** 58 (4) [4 yrs]

GRASMANIS, PAUL   Paul Ryan, DT, 6′3″/298 lbs; Notre Dame; 1996: Chi, rnd 4; B8/2/1974 Grand Rapids, MI   **1996** ChiB 14 (3) **1997** ChiB 16 (1) **1998** ChiB 15 (0) **1999** Den 5 (0) **2000**†Phi 16 (0) **2001**†Phi 14 (2) **2002**†Phi 16 (3) **2003** Phi 2 (0) **2004** Phi 4 (0) **2005** Phi 2 (0) **NFL** 104 (9) [10 yrs]

GRATE, CARL   Carl F., G, 6′0″/215 lbs; Georgia; 1944: NYG, rnd 11; B1920   **1945** NYG 6 (2)

GRATE, WILLIE   Willie, TE, 6′4″/225 lbs; South Carolina State; 1969: Hou, rnd 6; B5/25/1946 Georgetown, SC

YEAR	TEAM	G (GS, POS)	RUSH	YD	AVG(LG)	TD	REC	YD	AVG(LG)	TD	PASS	COMP	PCT	YD	AVG(LG)	TD	INT	SK	YD	QBR	KPR	OTD	PTS	TAY
1969	Buf-A	11	—	—	—	—	1	19	19.0(19)	1	—	—	—	—	—	—	—	—	—	—	—	—	6	15
1970	Buf	14	—	—	—	—	7	147	21.0(32)	2	—	—	—	—	—	—	—	—	—	—	—	—	12	84
NFL	2	25	—	—	—	—	8	166	20.8(32)	3	—	—	—	—	—	—	—	—	—	—	—	—	18	98

GRAU, JEFF   Jeffrey Alan, C, 6′3″/257 lbs; UCLA; 2002: Was, rnd 7; B12/16/1979 Inglewood, CA   **2002** Dal 16 (0) **2003** Mia 11 (0) **NFL** 27 (0) [2 yrs]

GRAVELLE, GORDON   Gordon Carr, T, 6′5″/250 lbs; Brigham Young; 1972: Pit, rnd 2; B6/12/1949 Oakland, CA   **1972**†Pit 14 (3) **1973** Pit 6 **1974**†Pit 14 (13, RT) **1975**†Pit 14 (14, RT) **1976** Pit 6 (2) **1977** NYG 14 (14, LT) **1979**†LARm 8 (3) **NFL** 96 (68) [8 yrs]

GRAVES, MARSHARNE   Marsharne DeWayne, T, 6′3″/268 lbs; Arizona; B7/8/1962 Memphis, TN   **1984**†Den 1 (0) **1987** Ind 3 (3) **NFL** 4 (3) [2 yrs]

GRAVES, RAY   Samuel Ray, C, 6′1″/205 lbs; Tennessee Wesleyan; Tennessee; 1942: Phi, rnd 9; B12/31/1918 Rockwood, TN [K]   **1942** Phi 11 (6, C) **1943** P-P 10 (9, C) **1946** Phi 7 (0) **NFL** 28 (15) [3 yrs]

GRAVES, RORY   Rory Anthony, T, 6′6″/288 lbs; Ohio State; B7/21/1963 Atlanta, GA   **1988** LARd 16 (15, RT) **1989** LARd 15 (15, LT) **1990**†LARd 15 (15, LT) **1991** LARd 3 (0) **NFL** 49 (45) [4 yrs]

GRAVES, TOM   Thomas Edward, LB, 6′3″/228 lbs; Michigan State; 1979: Pit, rnd 8; B12/18/1955 Norfolk, VA   **1979**†Pit 11

GRAVES, WHITE   White Solomon, DB, 6′0″/190 lbs; LSU; 1965: Bos, rnd 17; B3/20/1942 Jackson, MS   **1965** Bos-A 14 **1966** Bos-A 14 **1967** Bos-A 12 **1968** Cin-A 2 **NFL** 42 [4 yrs]

GRAY, BILL   William Robertson, G-C-BB, 5′11″/210 lbs; USC; Oregon State; 1947: Was, rnd 7; B12/27/1922 Portland, OR, D7/1978 Manassas, VA   **1947** Was 12 (3) **1948** Was 12 (1) **NFL** 24 (4) [2 yrs]

GRAY, BOBBY   Bobby Wayne, DB, 6′0″/212 lbs; Louisiana Tech; 2002: Chi, rnd 5; B4/30/1978 Houston, TX   **2002** ChiB 3 (0) **2003** ChiB 16 (9, SS) **2004** ChiB 10 (4) **NFL** 29 (13) [3 yrs]

GRAY, CARLTON   Carlton Patrick, DB, 6′0″/195 lbs; UCLA; 1993: Sea, rnd 2; B6/26/1971 Cincinnati, OH   **1993** Sea 10 (2) **1994** Sea 11 (11, LCB) **1995** Sea 16 (16, LCB) **1996** Sea 16 (16, LCB) **1997** Ind 15 (13, LCB) **1998** NYG 14 (3) **1999** KC 16 (0) **2000** KC 4 (1) **NFL** 102 (62) [8 yrs]

GRAY, CECIL   Cecil Tarik, DE-T, 6′4″/305 lbs; North Carolina; 1990: Phi, rnd 9; B2/16/1968 Harlem, NY   **1990** Phi 12 (1) **1991** Phi 2 (2) **1992** GB 2 (0) **1993** Ind 6 (2) **1994** Ind 16 (5, lde) **1995** Arz 7 (4) **NFL** 45 (14) [6 yrs]

GRAY, CHRIS   Christopher William, G-C, 6′4″/308 lbs; Auburn; 1993: Mia, rnd 5; B6/19/1970 Birmingham, AL   **1993** Mia 5 (0) **1994**†Mia 16 (2) **1995** Mia 10 (10, RG) **1996** Mia 11 (11, RG) **1997** ChiB 8 (2) **1998** Sea 15 (8, c) **1999**†Sea 16 (10, C) **2000** Sea 16 (16, C) **2001** Sea 16 (16, RG) **2002** Sea 16 (16, LG) **2003** Sea 16 (16, RG) **2004**†Sea 16 (16, RG) **2005**†Sea 16 (16, RG) **NFL** 177 (139) [13 yrs]

GRAY, DAN   Daniel Thomas, DT, 6′6″/240 lbs; Rutgers; 1978: Det, rnd 5; B1/29/1956 Phillipsburg, NJ   **1978** Det 14

GRAY, DAVID   David Allen, DB, 6′0″/187 lbs; Oregon State; San Diego State; B3/28/1955 San Diego, CA   **1979** NO 16 (6, rcb)

GRAY, DERWIN   Derwin Lamont, DB, 5′11″/198 lbs; Brigham Young; 1993: Ind, rnd 4; B4/9/1971 San Antonio, TX   **1993** Ind 11 (0) **1994** Ind 16 (2) **1995**†Ind 16 (0) **1996**†Ind 10 (1) **1997** Ind 11 (0) **1998** Car 3 (0) **NFL** 67 (3) [6 yrs]

GRAY, EARNEST   Ernest L., WR, 6′3″/195 lbs; Memphis; 1979: NYG, rnd 2; B3/2/1957 Greenwood, MS

YEAR	TEAM	G (GS, POS)	RUSH	YD	AVG(LG)	TD	REC	YD	AVG(LG)	TD	PASS	COMP	PCT	YD	AVG(LG)	TD	INT	SK	YD	QBR	KPR	OTD	PTS	TAY
1979	NYG	16(WR)	2	2	1.0(9)	0	28	537	19.2(53)	4	—	—	—	—	—	—	—	—	—	—	k	—	24	276
1980	NYG	16(16, WR)	—	—	—	—	52	777	14.9(50)	10	—	—	—	—	—	—	—	—	—	—	—	—	60	439
1981	†NYG	16(3)	—	—	—	—	22	360	16.4(45)	2	—	—	—	—	—	—	—	—	—	—	—	—	12	190
1982	NYG	9(9, WR)	—	—	—	—	25	426	17.0(47)	4	—	—	—	—	—	—	—	—	—	—	—	—	24	233
1983	NYG	16(16, WR)	—	—	—	—	78	1139	14.6(62)	5	—	—	—	—	—	—	—	—	—	—	—	—	30	595
1984	†NYG	12(11, WR)	—	—	—	—	38	529	13.9(31)	2	—	—	—	—	—	—	—	—	—	—	—	—	12	275
1985	SL	5(0)	—	—	—	—	3	22	7.3(12)	0	—	—	—	—	—	—	—	—	—	—	—	—	0	11
NFL	7	90(55)	2	2	1.0(9)	0	246	3790	15.4(62)	27	—	—	—	—	—	—	—	—	—	—	k	—	162	2017

GRAY, HECTOR   Hector Bernard, DB, 6′1″/192 lbs; Florida State; B1/2/1957 Miami, FL   **1981** Det 16 (4) **1982**†Det 8 (2) **1983** Det 1 (0) **NFL** 25 (6) [3 yrs]

GRAY, JACK   Jack, E, 5′11″/175 lbs; Princeton; deceased   **1923** SL 4 (2) **1923** GB 1 (1) **NFL** 5 (3) [1 yr]

GRAY, JERRY   Jerry Don, DB, 6′0″/183 lbs; Texas; 1985: LARm, rnd 1; B12/16/1962 Lubbock, TX [I]   **1985** LARm 16 (1) **1986**†LARm★16 (16, LCB) **1987** LARm★12 (12, LCB) **1988**†LARm★16 (16, LCB) **1989**†LARm★16 (16, LCB) **1990** LARm 12 (12, LCB) **1991** LARm 16 (9, LCB) **1992**†Hou 16 (16, RCB) **1993** TB 14 (5, fs) **NFL** 134 (103) [9 yrs]

GRAY, JIM   James H., DB, 6′0″/180 lbs; Toledo; 1965: NYJ, rnd 11/Phi, rnd 16; B8/23/1941   **1966** NYJ-A 6 **1967** Phi 3 **NFL** 9 [2 yrs]

GRAY, JOHNNIE   Johnnie Lee, DB, 5′11″/185 lbs; Cal State-Fullerton; B12/18/1953 Lake Charles, LA [RI]   **1975** GB 14 (14, FS) **1976** GB 14 (14, FS) **1977** GB 14 (14, FS) **1978** GB 16 (16, FS) **1979** GB 16 (16, FS) **1980** GB 16 (16, FS) **1981** GB 9 (9, SS) **1982**†GB 9 (9, SS) **1983** GB 16 (16, SS) **NFL** 124 (124) [9 yrs]

YEAR	TEAM	G (GS, POS)	RUSH	YD	AVG (LG)	TD	REC	YD	AVG (LG)	TD	PASS	COMP	PCT	YD	AVG (LG)	TD	INT	SK	YD	QBR	KPR	OTD	PTS	TAY

GRAY, KEN Kenneth Don, G-LB, 6´2˝/245 lbs; Howard Payne; 1958: GB, rnd 6; B3/10/1936 San Saba, TX **1958** ChiC 10 **1959** ChiC 12 (RG) **1960** SL 10 (RG) **1961** SL✧13 (RG) **1962** SL 14 (RG) **1963** SL★14 (RG) **1964** SL★14 (RG) **1965** SL☆14 (RG) **1966** SL★11 (RG) **1967** SL★13 (RG) **1968** SL★14 (RG) **1969** SL☆12 (RG) **1970** Hou 11 (LG) **NFL** 162 [13 yrs]

GRAY, KEVIN Kevin, DB, 5´11˝/179 lbs; Eastern Illinois; B9/11/1957 Chicago, IL **1982** NO 8 (0)

GRAY, LEON Leon, T-G, 6´3˝/256 lbs; Jackson State; 1973: Mia, rnd 3; B11/15/1951 Olive Branch, MS, D11/11/2001 Boston, MA **1973** NE 9 (8, lg) **1974** NE 14 (14, LT) **1975** NE 14 (14, LT) **1976**†NE★14 (14, LT) **1977** NE☆11 (11, LT) **1978**†NE★16 (16, LT) **1979**†Hou★16 (16, LT) **1980** Hou☆14 (14, LT) **1981** Hou★16 (16, LT) **1982** NO 7 (0) **1983** NO 11 (0) **NFL** 142 (123) [11 yrs]

GRAY, MEL Melvin Dean, WR, 5´9˝/175 lbs; Missouri; 1971: SL, rnd 6; B9/28/1948 Fresno, CA

YEAR	TEAM	G (GS, POS)	RUSH	YD	AVG (LG)	TD	REC	YD	AVG (LG)	TD	PASS	COMP	PCT	YD	AVG (LG)	TD	INT	SK	YD	QBR	KPR	OTD	PTS	TAY
1971	SL	14 (wr)	2	56	28.0 (38)	0	18	534	29.7 (80)	4	—	—	—	—	—	—	—	—	—	—	k	—	24	633
1972	SL	7	—	—	—	—	3	62	20.7 (33)	0	—	—	—	—	—	—	—	—	—	—	kp	—	0	140
1973	SL	12 (WR)	—	—	—	—	29	513	17.7 (80)	7	—	—	—	—	—	—	—	—	—	—	k	—	42	305
1974	†SL★	14 (14, WR)	—	—	—	—	39	770	19.7 (80)	6	—	—	—	—	—	—	—	—	—	—	—	—	36	415
1975	†SL★	14 (WR)	1	6	6.0 (6)	0	48	**926**	19.3 (74)	**11**	—	—	—	—	—	—	—	—	—	—	p	—	66	542
1976	SL★	11 (WR)	—	—	—	—	36	686	19.1 (77)	5	—	—	—	—	—	—	—	—	—	—	—	—	30	368
1977	SL✧	14 (WR)	1	-1	-1.0 (-1)	0	38	782	**20.6** (**69**)	5	—	—	—	—	—	—	—	—	—	—	—	—	30	415
1978	SL	13 (WR)	5	51	10.2 (27)	1	44	871	19.8 (74)	1	—	—	—	—	—	—	—	—	—	—	—	—	12	502
1979	SL	13 (13, WR)	4	41	10.3 (38)	0	25	447	17.9 (78)	1	—	—	—	—	—	—	—	—	—	—	—	—	6	270
1980	SL	16 (16, WR)	1	-3	-3.0 (-3)	0	40	709	17.7 (69)	3	—	—	—	—	—	—	—	—	—	—	—	—	18	367
1981	SL	12 (12, WR)	1	4	4.0 (4)	0	27	310	11.5 (41)	2	—	—	—	—	—	—	—	—	—	—	—	—	12	169
1982	SL	5 (0)	—	—	—	—	4	34	8.5 (13)	0	—	—	—	—	—	—	—	—	—	—	—	—	0	17
NFL	12	145 (55)	15	154	10.3 (38)	1	351	6644	18.9 (80)	45	—	—	—	—	—	—	—	—	—	—	kp	—	276	4141

GRAY, MEL Melvin James, RB-WR, 5´9˝/167 lbs; Purdue; 1984: NO, rnd S2; B3/16/1961 Williamsburg, VA **[R]** **1988** NO 14 (0) **1990** Det★16 (0) **1992** Det★15 (0) **1993**†Det☆11 (0) **1994**†Det★16 (0) **1995** Hou 15 (0) **1996** Hou 14 (0) **1997** Ten 11 (0) **1997** Phi 3 (0)

YEAR	TEAM	G (GS, POS)	RUSH	YD	AVG (LG)	TD	REC	YD	AVG (LG)	TD	PASS	COMP	PCT	YD	AVG (LG)	TD	INT	SK	YD	QBR	KPR	OTD	PTS	TAY
1986	NO☆	16 (0)	6	29	4.8 (11)	0	2	45	22.5 (38)	0	—	—	—	—	—	—	—	—	—	—	k	1	6	463
1987	†NO☆	12 (1)	8	37	4.6 (12)	1	6	30	5.0 (12)	0	—	—	—	—	—	—	—	—	—	—	kp	—	6	480
1989	Det☆	10 (1)	3	22	7.3 (14)	0	2	47	23.5 (30)	0	—	—	—	—	—	—	—	—	—	—	kp	—	0	347
1991	†Det★	16 (0)	2	11	5.5 (6)	0	3	42	14.0 (31)	0	—	—	—	—	—	—	—	—	—	—	kp	1	6	691
NFL	12	169 (2)	19	99	5.2 (14)	1	13	164	12.6 (38)	0	—	—	—	—	—	—	—	—	—	—	kp	9	60	5709

GRAY, MOSES Moses William, T-DT, 6´3˝/260 lbs; Indiana; 1961: NYT, rnd 27/NYG, rnd 9; B4/12/1937 Conemaugh, PA **1961** NYT-A 3 **1962** NYT-A 2 **NFL** 5 [2 yrs]

GRAY, OSCAR Oscar Ray, RB, 6´1˝/255 lbs; Arkansas; B9/25/1972 Houston, TX

YEAR	TEAM	G (GS, POS)	RUSH	YD	AVG (LG)	TD	REC	YD	AVG (LG)	TD	PASS	COMP	PCT	YD	AVG (LG)	TD	INT	SK	YD	QBR	KPR	OTD	PTS	TAY
1996	Sea	9 (0)	2	4	2.0 (2)	0	1	5	5.0 (5)	0	—	—	—	—	—	—	—	—	—	—	—	—	0	7

GRAY, PAUL Paul David, LB, 6´2˝/231 lbs; Western Kentucky; 1984: NO, rnd 10; B6/20/1962 Tulsa, OK **1987** Atl 2 (0)

GRAY, QUINN Quinn, QB, 6´3˝/246 lbs; Florida A&M; B5/21/1979 Fort Lauderdale, FL

YEAR	TEAM	G (GS, POS)	RUSH	YD	AVG (LG)	TD	REC	YD	AVG (LG)	TD	PASS	COMP	PCT	YD	AVG (LG)	TD	INT	SK	YD	QBR	KPR	OTD	PTS	TAY
2005	Jax	1 (0)	3	1	0.3 (3)	0	—	—	—	—	14	8	57.1	100	7.1 (26)	2	0	1	7	—	—	—	0	61

GRAY, SAM Samuel Wilbur, E, 6´0˝/195 lbs; Tulsa; 1944: Pit, rnd 12; B1/1/1919 Independence, KS, D6/12/1979 Houston, TX **1947** Pit 10 (0)

YEAR	TEAM	G (GS, POS)	RUSH	YD	AVG (LG)	TD	REC	YD	AVG (LG)	TD	PASS	COMP	PCT	YD	AVG (LG)	TD	INT	SK	YD	QBR	KPR	OTD	PTS	TAY
1946	Pit	6 (0)	—	—	—	—	1	20	20.0 (20)	0	—	—	—	—	—	—	—	—	—	—	—	—	0	10
NFL	2	16 (0)	—	—	—	—	1	20	20.0 (20)	0	—	—	—	—	—	—	—	—	—	—	—	—	0	10

GRAY, TIM Timothy, DB, 6´1˝/200 lbs; Texas A&M; 1975: SL, rnd 1; B11/11/1952 Houston, TX **1975**†SL 14 **1976** KC 12 (11, SS) **1977** KC 10 (9, SS) **1978** KC 14 (SS) **1979** SF 16 (15, SS) **NFL** 66 (35) [5 yrs]

GRAY, TORRIAN Torrian Deshon, DB, 6´0˝/200 lbs; Virginia Tech; 1997: Min, rnd 2; B3/18/1974 Bartow, FL **1997**†Min 16 (3) **1998** Min 9 (1) **NFL** 25 (4) [2 yrs]

GRAYBILL, MIKE Michael Alton, T, 6´7˝/275 lbs; Boston University; 1989: Cle, rnd 7; B10/14/1966 Washington, DC **1989** Cle 6 (0)

GRAY HORSE HB, 5´8˝/190 lbs; none; deceased **1923** Oor 2 (1)

GRAYSON, DAVE David Lee, DB, 5´10˝/187 lbs; Oregon; B6/6/1939 San Diego, CA **[RI]** **1961** DalT-A 13 (RCB) **1962**†DalT-A✧14 (RCB) **1963** KC-A★14 (RCB) **1964** KC-A★14 (RCB) **1965** Oak-A★14 (RCB) **1966** Oak-A★14 (RCB) **1967**†Oak-A 14 **1968**†Oak-A☆14 (14, RS) **1969**†Oak-A★14 (14, RS) **1970**†Oak☆14 (14, FS) **NFL** 139 (42) [10 yrs]

GRAYSON, DAVID David Lee, LB, 6´2˝/230 lbs; Cal Poly-Pomona; Fresno State; 1987: SF, rnd 8; B2/27/1964 San Diego, CA **1987**†Cle 11 (5, rolb) **1988**†Cle 16 (14, LOLB) **1989**†Cle 10 (10, RLB) **1990** Cle 16 (8, RLB) **1991** SD 1 (0) **NFL** 54 (37) [5 yrs]

GRAZIANI, TONY Anthony Robert, QB, 6´2˝/210 lbs; Oregon; 1997: Atl, rnd 7; B12/23/1973 Las Vegas, NV

YEAR	TEAM	G (GS, POS)	RUSH	YD	AVG (LG)	TD	REC	YD	AVG (LG)	TD	PASS	COMP	PCT	YD	AVG (LG)	TD	INT	SK	YD	QBR	KPR	OTD	PTS	TAY
1997	Atl	3 (1)	3	19	6.3 (10)	0	—	—	—	—	23	7	30.4	41	1.8 (13)	0	2	1	7	—	—	—	0	-41
1998	Atl	4 (1)	4	21	5.3 (12)	0	—	—	—	—	33	16	48.5	199	6.0 (32)	0	2	2	15	—	—	—	0	41
1999	Atl	11 (3)	9	11	1.2 (10)	0	—	—	—	—	118	62	52.5	759	6.4 (62)	2	4	12	78	—	—	—	0	241
NFL	3	18 (5)	16	51	3.2 (12)	0	—	—	—	—	174	85	48.9	999	5.7 (62)	2	8	15	100	—	—	—	0	241

GRBAC, ELVIS Elvis, QB, 6´5˝/232 lbs; Michigan; 1993: SF, rnd 8; B8/13/1970 Cleveland, OH

YEAR	TEAM	G (GS, POS)	RUSH	YD	AVG (LG)	TD	REC	YD	AVG (LG)	TD	PASS	COMP	PCT	YD	AVG (LG)	TD	INT	SK	YD	QBR	KPR	OTD	PTS	TAY
1994	†SF	12 (0)	13	1	0.1 (6)	0	—	—	—	—	50	35	70.0	393	7.9 (42)	2	1	4	36	—	—	—	0	168
1995	†SF	16 (5, qb)	20	33	1.6 (11)	2	—	—	—	—	183	127	**69.4**	1469	**8.0** (**81**)	8	5	6	36	—	—	—	12	628
1996	†SF	15 (4, qb)	23	21	0.9 (12)	2	—	—	—	—	197	122	61.9	1236	6.3 (40)	8	10	6	30	—	—	—	12	299
1997	†KC	10 (10, QB)	30	168	5.6 (20)	1	—	—	—	—	314	179	57.0	1943	6.2 (55)	11	6	19	150	79.1	—	—	6	965
1998	KC	8 (6, qb)	7	27	3.9 (10)	0	—	—	—	—	188	98	52.1	1142	6.1 (65)	5	12	11	57	—	—	—	0	143
1999	KC	16 (16, QB)	19	10	0.5 (8)	0	—	—	—	—	499	294	58.9	3389	6.8 (86)	22	15	26	170	81.7	—	—	0	1215
2000	KC✧	15 (15, QB)	30	110	3.7 (22)	1	—	—	—	—	547	326	59.6	4169	7.6 (81)	28	14	29	213	89.9	—	—	6	1785
2001	†Bal	14 (14, QB)	21	18	0.9 (6)	1	—	—	—	—	467	265	56.7	3033	6.5 (77)	15	18	28	215	71.1	—	—	6	900
NFL	8	106 (70)	163	388	2.4 (22)	7	—	—	—	—	2445	1446	59.1	16774	6.9 (86)	99	81	129	907	79.6	—	—	42	6100

GREAVES, GARY Gary, T, 6´3˝/235 lbs; Miami (FL); B10/28/1935 **1960**†Hou-A 7

GRECNI, DICK Richard, LB, 6´1˝/230 lbs; Ohio University; 1960: Cle, rnd 13/Bos, rnd 2; B3/27/1938 Akron, OH **1961** Min 12

GRECO, DON Donald, G, 6´3˝/260 lbs; Western Illinois; 1981: Det, rnd 3; B4/1/1959 St. Louis, MO **1982**†Det 9 (4) **1983**†Det 12 (12, RG) **1984** Det 16 (16, RG) **1985** Det 8 (6, rg) **NFL** 45 (38) [4 yrs]

GREELEY, BUCKY Paul Domero, C, 6´2˝/285 lbs; Penn State; B7/30/1972 Wilkes-Barre, PA **1997** Car 6 (0)

GREEN, AHMAN Ahman Rashad, RB, 6´0˝/217 lbs; Nebraska; 1998: Sea, rnd 3; B2/16/1977 Omaha, NE

YEAR	TEAM	G (GS, POS)	RUSH	YD	AVG (LG)	TD	REC	YD	AVG (LG)	TD	PASS	COMP	PCT	YD	AVG (LG)	TD	INT	SK	YD	QBR	KPR	OTD	PTS	TAY
1998	Sea	16 (0)	35	209	6.0 (64)	1	3	2	0.7 (3)	0	—	—	—	—	—	—	—	—	—	—	k	—	6	435
1999	†Sea	14 (0)	26	120	4.6 (21)	0	—	—	—	—	—	—	—	—	—	—	—	—	—	—	k	—	0	398
2000	GB	16 (11, RB)	263	1175	4.5 (39)	10	73	559	7.7 (31)	3	1	0	0.0	0	0.0	0	0	—	—	—	—	—	78	1570
2001	†GB★	16 (16, RB)	304	1387	4.6 (83)	9	62	594	9.6 (42)	2	—	—	—	—	—	—	—	—	—	—	—	—	66	1784
2002	†GB✧	14 (14, RB)	286	1240	4.3 (43)	7	57	393	6.9 (23)	2	—	—	—	—	—	—	—	—	—	—	—	—	54	1517
2003	†GB★	16 (16, RB)	**355**	**1883**	5.3 (98)	**15**	50	367	7.3 (27)	5	—	—	—	—	—	—	—	—	—	—	—	—	120	**2242**
2004	†GB✧	15 (15, RB)	259	1163	4.5 (90)	7	40	275	6.9 (48)	1	1	1	100.0	20	20.0 (20)	1	0	—	—	—	—	—	48	1391
2005	GB	5 (5, rb)	77	255	3.3 (13)	0	19	147	7.7 (20)	0	—	—	—	—	—	—	—	—	—	—	—	—	0	329
NFL	8	112 (77)	1605	7432	4.6 (98)	49	304	2337	7.7 (48)	13	2	1	50.0	20	10.0 (20)	1	0	—	—	—	k	—	372	9664

GREEN, ALEX William Alexander, DB, 6´1˝/194 lbs; Indiana; B11/3/1965 **1987** Dal 3 (3)

GREEN, ALLEN Allen Leiden, K, 6´2˝/216 lbs; Mississippi; 1961: NYG, rnd 8; B2/15/1938 Hanceville, AL **[K]** **1961** Dal 14

GREEN, ARTHUR Arthur, RB, 5´11˝/198 lbs; Albany State (GA); B9/18/1947 Atlanta, GA

YEAR	TEAM	G (GS, POS)	RUSH	YD	AVG (LG)	TD	REC	YD	AVG (LG)	TD	PASS	COMP	PCT	YD	AVG (LG)	TD	INT	SK	YD	QBR	KPR	OTD	PTS	TAY
1972	NO	7	14	51	3.6 (14)	0	7	49	7.0 (15)	0	—	—	—	—	—	—	—	—	—	—	k	—	0	143

GREEN, BARRETT Barrett, LB, 6´0˝/226 lbs; West Virginia; 2000: Det, rnd 2; B10/29/1977 West Palm Beach, FL **2000** Det 9 (0) **2001** Det 14 (10, RLB) **2002** Det 15 (14, LLB) **2003** Det 16 (16, LLB) **2004** NYG 10 (9, RLB) **2005** NYG 1 (0) **NFL** 65 (49) [6 yrs]

YEAR	TEAM	G(GS, POS)	RUSH	YD	AVG(LG)	TD	REC	YD	AVG(LG)	TD	PASS	COMP	PCT	YD	AVG(LG)	TD	INT	SK	YD	QBR	KPR	OTD	PTS	TAY

GREEN, BOBBY JOE Bobby Joe, P, 5'11"/175 lbs; Florida; 1960: Den, rnd 2; B5/7/1936 Vernon, TX, D5/28/1993 Gainesville, FL [KP]

YEAR	TEAM	G(GS, POS)	RUSH	YD	AVG(LG)	TD	REC	YD	AVG(LG)	TD	PASS	COMP	PCT	YD	AVG(LG)	TD	INT	KPR	OTD	PTS	TAY
1960	Pit	12																P	—	0	0
1961	Pit	14	2	37	18.5(33)	0					1	0	0.0	0	0.0	0	0	KP	—	0	37
1962	ChiB	14																P	—	0	0
1963	†ChiB	14	2	-10	-5.0(-6)	0					1	0	0.0	0	0.0	0	0	P	—	0	-10
1964	ChiB	14	2	-2	-1.0(7)	0												P	—	0	-2
1965	ChiB	14																P	—	0	0
1966	ChiB	14																P	—	0	0
1967	ChiB	14																P	—	0	0
1968	ChiB	7	1	4	4.0(4)	0												P	—	0	4
1969	ChiB	14	1	17	17.0(17)	0					2	2	100.0	30	15.0(19)	0	0	P	—	0	32
1970	ChiB◇	14	1	7	7.0(7)	0					2	2	100.0	37	18.5(34)	0	0	P	—	0	26
1971	ChiB	14									2	1	50.0	13	6.5(13)	0	0	P	—	0	7
1972	ChiB	14									2	1	50.0	23	11.5(23)	0	1	P	—	0	-29
1973	ChiB	14																P	—	0	0
NFL	14	187	9	53	5.9(33)	0					10	6	60.0	103	10.3(34)	0	1	KP	—	0	65

GREEN, BOYCE Boyce Keith, RB, 5'11"/215 lbs; Carson-Newman; 1983: Cle, rnd 11; B6/24/1960 Beaufort, SC

YEAR	TEAM	G(GS, POS)	RUSH	YD	AVG(LG)	TD	REC	YD	AVG(LG)	TD	PASS	COMP	PCT	YD	AVG(LG)	TD	INT	KPR	OTD	PTS	TAY
1983	Cle	13(2)	104	497	4.8(29)	3	25	167	6.7(33)	1								k	—	24	711
1984	Cle	16(10, RB)	202	673	3.3(29)	0	12	124	10.3(44)	0								k	—	6	740
1985	†Cle	13(0)																k	—	0	-10
1986	†KC	16(7, rb)	90	314	3.5(27)	3	19	137	7.2(17)	0	1	0	0.0	0	0.0	0	1	k	1	24	487
1987	Sea	2(2)	21	77	3.7(17)	0												k	—	0	82
NFL	5	60(21)	417	1561	3.7(29)	6	56	428	7.6(44)	2	1	0	0.0	0	0.0	0	1	k	1	54	2009

GREEN, BRANDON James Brandon, DE, 6'2"/264 lbs; Rice; 2003: Jax, rnd 6; B9/5/1980 Victoria, TX **2004** Jax 3 (0) **2005** SL 16 (1) **NFL** 19 (1) [2 yrs]

GREEN, BUBBA Anthony Wayne, DT, 6'4"/278 lbs; North Carolina State; 1981: Bal, rnd 6; B9/30/1957 Cape May, NJ **1981** Bal 15 (10, RDT)

GREEN, CHARLIE Charles Harold, QB, 6'0"/190 lbs; Wittenberg; 1965: Bos, rnd 13; B3/14/1943 Dayton, OH

YEAR	TEAM	G(GS, POS)	PASS	COMP	PCT	YD	AVG(LG)	TD	INT	OTD	PTS	TAY
1966	Oak-A	14	2	2	100.0	17	8.5(11)	0	0	—	0	9

GREEN, CHRIS Christopher Allen, DB, 5'11"/192 lbs; Illinois; 1991: Mia, rnd 7; B2/26/1968 Lawrenceburg, IN **1991** Mia 16 (0) **1992** Mia 4 (2) **1993** Mia 14 (0) **1994**†Mia 16 (1) **1995**†Buf 16 (1) **NFL** 66 (4) [5 yrs]

GREEN, CLEVELAND Cleveland Carl, T, 6'3"/265 lbs; Southern (LA); B9/11/1957 Bolton, MS **1979**†Mia 16 **1980** Mia 12 (3) **1981** Mia 6 (0) **1982**†Mia 3 (0) **1983**†Mia 16 (1) **1984**†Mia 16 (12, RT) **1985**†Mia 12 (11, RT) **1986** Mia 11 (5, lt) **NFL** 92 (32) [8 yrs]

GREEN, CORNELL Cornell, DB, 6'3"/208 lbs; Utah State; B2/10/1940 Oklahoma City, OK [I] **1962** Dal 14 **1963** Dal 14 (LCB) **1964** Dal 14 (LCB) **1965** Dal◇14 (LCB) **1966**†Dal★14 (LCB) **1967**†Dal★14 (LCB) **1968**†Dal☆14 (LCB) **1969**†Dal☆14 (LCB) **1970**†Dal 14 (SS) **1971**†Dal★14 (SS) **1972**†Dal★14 (SS) **1973**†Dal 14 (SS) **1974** Dal 14 (SS) **NFL** 182 [13 yrs]

GREEN, CORNELL Cornell Duane, T-G, 6'6"/315 lbs; Central Florida; B8/25/1976 St. Petersburg, FL **2002**†TB 16 (3) **2005**†Den 14 (0)

YEAR	TEAM	G(GS, POS)	RUSH	YD	AVG(LG)	TD	OTD	PTS	TAY
2003	TB	7(5, rt)	0	-3	(-3)	0	—	0	-2
NFL	3	37(8)	0	-3	(-3)	0	—	0	-2

GREEN, CURTIS Curtis, DE-DT-NT, 6'3"/256 lbs; Alabama State; 1981: Det, rnd 2; B6/3/1957 Quincy, FL **1981** Det 14 (4) **1982**†Det 7 (1) **1983**†Det 16 (16, LDE) **1984** Det 16 (15, LDT) **1985** Det 15 (8, lde) **1986** Det 16 (1) **1987** Det 12 (0) **1988** Det 11 (0) **1989** Det 16 (0) **NFL** 123 (45) [9 yrs]

GREEN, DARRELL Darrell Ray, DB, 5'8"/176 lbs; Texas A&M-Kingsville; 1983: Was, rnd 1; B2/15/1960 Houston, TX [I] **1983**†Was 16 (16, LCB) **1984**†Was★16 (16, LCB) **1986**†Was★16 (15, LCB) **1987**†Was★12 (12, LCB) **1988** Was 15 (15, RCB) **1989** Was 7 (7, rcb) **1990**†Was★16 (16, RCB) **1991**†Was★16 (16, RCB) **1992**†Was 8 (7, rcb) **1993** Was (16, RCB) **1994** Was 16 (16, RCB) **1995** Was 16 (16, RCB) **1996** Was◇16 (16, RCB) **1997** Was◇16 (16, RCB) **1998** Was 16 (16, RCB) **1999**†Was 16 (16, RCB) **2000** Was 13 (2) **2001** Was 16 (4) **2002** Was 16 (4)

YEAR	TEAM	G(GS, POS)	RUSH	YD	AVG(LG)	TD	KPR	OTD	PTS	TAY
1985	Was	16(16, LCB)	1	6	6.0(6)	0	pi	—	0	130
NFL	20	295(258)	1	6	6.0(6)	0	kpiS	8	48	767

GREEN, DAVE David Elliott, P, 5'11"/206 lbs; Ohio University; 1972: Cin, rnd 17; B9/21/1949 Mason City, IA [KP]

YEAR	TEAM	G(GS, POS)	RUSH	YD	AVG(LG)	TD	REC	YD	AVG(LG)	TD	PASS	COMP	PCT	YD	AVG(LG)	TD	INT	KPR	OTD	PTS	TAY
1973	Hou	4																P	—	0	0
1974	Cin	14									2	1	50.0	22	11.0(22)	0	0	P	—	0	11
1975	†Cin	14									1	0	0.0	0	0.0	0	0	KP	—	70	0
1976	TB	14	1	0	0.0(0)	0	1	9	9.0(9)	0								KP	—	35	5
1977	TB	14	1	0	0.0(0)	0					2	2	100.0	59	29.5(45)	0	0	KP	—	17	30
1978	TB	16	1	0	0.0(0)	0					3	2	66.7	25	8.3(25)	0	0	KP	—	3	13
NFL	6	76	3	0	0.0	0	1	9	9.0(9)	0	8	5	62.5	106	13.3(45)	0	0	KP	—	125	58

GREEN, DAVID David Fendell, RB, 5'10"/200 lbs; Chowan Coll (NC); Edinboro; B9/7/1953 Jacksonville, NC **1982**†Cle 9 (0)

GREEN, DAVID David G., RB, 5'11"/193 lbs; Boston College; B4/18/1972 Mount Kisco, NY **1995** NE 2 (0)

GREEN, DONNIE Donald Gerald, T, 6'7"/272 lbs; Purdue; 1971: Buf, rnd 5; B7/12/1948 Washington, DC **1971** Buf 10 (RT) **1972** Buf 14 (RT) **1973** Buf 14 (RT) **1975** Buf 14 (14, RT) **1976** Buf 13 (11, RT) **1977** Phi 10 **1978** Det 7

YEAR	TEAM	G(GS, POS)	RUSH	YD	AVG(LG)	TD	REC	YD	AVG(LG)	TD	OTD	PTS	TAY
1974	†Buf	10(10, RT)					1	0	0.0(0)	0	—	0	0
NFL	8	92(35)					1	0	0.0	0	—	0	0

GREEN, DONNY Donny Jamal, LB, 6'2"/238 lbs; Virginia; B9/18/1977 Jessup, GA **2001** Jax 1 (0) **2001** Was 1 (0) **NFL** 2 (0) [1 yr]

GREEN, E.G. Ernest G., WR, 5'11"/188 lbs; Florida State; 1998: Ind, rnd 3; B6/28/1975 Fort Walton Beach, FL

YEAR	TEAM	G(GS, POS)	REC	YD	AVG(LG)	TD	OTD	PTS	TAY
1998	Ind	11(0)	15	177	11.8(25)	1	—	6	94
1999	†Ind	11(4)	21	287	13.7(50)	0	—	0	144
2000	†Ind	7(0)	18	201	11.2(34)	1	—	6	106
NFL	3	29(4)	54	665	12.3(50)	2	—	12	343

GREEN, ERIC Bernard Eric, TE, 6'5"/280 lbs; Liberty; 1990: Pit, rnd 1; B6/22/1967 Savannah, GA

YEAR	TEAM	G(GS, POS)	REC	YD	AVG(LG)	TD	KPR	OTD	PTS	TAY
1990	Pit☆	13(7, te)	34	387	11.4(46)	7	k	—	42	230
1991	Pit	11(11, TE)	41	582	14.2(49)	6		—	36	321
1992	†Pit	7(5, te)	14	152	10.9(24)	2		—	12	86
1993	†Pit◇	16(16, TE)	63	942	15.0(71)	5		—	30	496
1994	†Pit◇	15(14, TE)	46	618	13.4(46)	4		—	24	329
1995	†Mia	14(14, TE)	43	499	11.6(31)	3		—	20	265
1996	Bal	6(3)	15	150	10.0(23)	1		—	6	80
1997	Bal	16(15, TE)	65	601	9.2(37)	5		—	30	326
1998	Bal	12(12, TE)	34	422	12.4(56)	1		—	6	216
1999	NYJ	10(7, te)	7	37	5.3(10)	2		—	12	29
NFL	10	120(104)	362	4390	12.1(71)	36	k	—	218	2376

GREEN, ERIC Eric Denaud, DB, 5'11"/197 lbs; Virginia Tech; 2005: Arz, rnd 3; B3/16/1982 Pahokee, FL **2005** Arz 12 (5, lcb)

GREEN, ERNIE Ernest E., HB-FB, 6'2"/205 lbs; Louisville; 1962: GB, rnd 14; B10/15/1938 Columbus, GA

YEAR	TEAM	G(GS, POS)	RUSH	YD	AVG(LG)	TD	REC	YD	AVG(LG)	TD	KPR	OTD	PTS	TAY
1962	Cle	13	31	139	4.5(45)	0	17	194	11.4(65)	1	kp	—	6	302
1963	Cle	14(HB)	87	526	6.0(72)	0	28	305	10.9(35)	3	kp	—	18	867
1964	†Cle	14(HB)	109	491	4.5(37)	6	25	283	11.3(32)	4		—	60	713
1965	†Cle	14(HB)	111	436	3.9(41)	2	25	298	11.9(69)	0	k	—	24	604
1966	Cle◇	14(FB)	144	750	5.2(35)	3	45	445	9.9(31)	6	p	—	54	1033
1967	†Cle◇	13(FB)	145	710	4.9(59)	4	39	369	9.5(41)	2		—	36	945
1968	†Cle	8(FB)	41	152	3.7(14)	0	16	142	8.9(62)	2		—	12	233
NFL	7	89	668	3204	4.8(72)	15	195	2036	10.4(69)	20	kp	—	210	4695

Green, Gary Gary Francis, DB, 5´11˝/187 lbs; Baylor; 1977: KC, rnd 1; B10/22/1955 San Antonio, TX [I] **1977** KC 11 (10, LCB) **1978** KC 16 (16, LCB) **1979** KC 16 (16, LCB) **1980** KC 16 (16, LCB) **1981** KC★16 (16, LCB) **1982** KC★9 (9, LCB) **1983** KC★16 (16, LCB) **1984**†LARm☆16 (16, LCB) **1985**†LARm★16 (16, LCB) **NFL** 132 (131) [9 yrs]

Green, Gaston Gaston Alfred, RB, 5´10˝/189 lbs; UCLA; 1988: LARm, rnd 1; B8/1/1966 Los Angeles, CA

YEAR	TEAM	G (GS, POS)	RUSH	YD	AVG (LG)	TD	REC	YD	AVG (LG)	TD	PASS	COMP	PCT	YD	AVG (LG)	TD	INT	SK	YD	QBR	KPR	OTD	PTS	TAY
1988	LARm	10(0)	35	117	3.3(13)	0	6	57	9.5(19)	0	—	—	—	—	—	—	—	—	—	—	k	—	0	236
1989	LARm	6(1)	26	73	2.8(9)	0	1	-5	-5.0(-5)	0	—	—	—	—	—	—	—	—	—	—	—	—	0	71
1990	LARm	15(2)	68	261	3.8(31)	0	2	23	11.5(16)	1	—	—	—	—	—	—	—	—	—	—	k	1	12	473
1991	†Den★	13(12, RB)	261	1037	4.0(63)	4	13	78	6.0(13)	0	—	—	—	—	—	—	—	—	—	—	—	—	24	1116
1992	Den	14(13, RB)	161	648	4.0(67)	2	10	79	7.9(33)	0	—	—	—	—	—	—	—	—	—	—	k	—	12	709
NFL	5	58(28)	551	2136	3.9(67)	6	32	232	7.3(33)	1	—	—	—	—	—	—	—	—	—	—	k	1	48	2603

Green, Harold Harold, RB, 6´2˝/222 lbs; South Carolina; 1990: Cin, rnd 2; B1/29/1968 Ladson, SC

YEAR	TEAM	G (GS, POS)	RUSH	YD	AVG (LG)	TD	REC	YD	AVG (LG)	TD	PASS	COMP	PCT	YD	AVG (LG)	TD	INT	SK	YD	QBR	KPR	OTD	PTS	TAY
1990	†Cin	12(9, FB)	83	353	4.3(39)	1	12	90	7.5(22)	1	—	—	—	—	—	—	—	—	—	—	—	—	12	413
1991	Cin	14(10, FB)	158	731	4.6(75)	2	16	136	8.5(18)	0	—	—	—	—	—	—	—	—	—	—	k	—	12	825
1992	Cin✧	16(15, RB)	265	1170	4.4(53)	2	41	214	5.2(19)	0	—	—	—	—	—	—	—	—	—	—	—	—	12	1297
1993	Cin	15(15, RB)	215	589	2.7(25)	0	22	115	5.2(16)	0	—	—	—	—	—	—	—	—	—	—	—	—	0	647
1994	Cin	14(11, RB)	76	223	2.9(22)	1	27	267	9.9(34)	1	—	—	—	—	—	—	—	—	—	—	k	—	12	410
1995	Cin	15(15, RB)	171	661	3.9(23)	2	27	182	6.7(24)	1	—	—	—	—	—	—	—	—	—	—	—	—	18	777
1996	SL	16(5, rb)	127	523	4.1(35)	4	37	246	6.6(19)	1	—	—	—	—	—	—	—	—	—	—	—	—	32	691
1997	Atl	16(1)	36	78	2.2(22)	1	29	360	12.4(47)	0	—	—	—	—	—	—	—	—	—	—	k	—	6	276
1998	†Atl	6(0)	20	37	1.9(6)	0	2	34	17.0(28)	0	—	—	—	—	—	—	—	—	—	—	k	—	0	63
NFL	9	124(81)	1151	4365	3.8(75)	13	213	1644	7.7(47)	4	—	—	—	—	—	—	—	—	—	—	k	—	104	5398

Green, Howard Howard, DT, 6´2˝/320 lbs; LSU; 2002: Hou, rnd 6; B1/12/1979 Donaldsonville, LA **2002** Bal 1 (0) **2003** NO 4 (0) **2004** NO 14 (12, LDT) **NFL** 19 (12) [3 yrs]

Green, Hugh Hugh Donell, LB, 6´2˝/225 lbs; Pittsburgh; 1981: TB, rnd 1; B7/27/1959 Natchez, MS **1981**†TB 16 (16, ROLB) **1982**†TB★9 (9, ROLB) **1983** TB★16 (15, ROLB) **1984** TB 8 (8, ROLB) **1985** TB 5 (5, rolb) **1985**†Mia 11 (11, ROLB) **1986** Mia 3 (3) **1987** Mia 9 (1) **1988** Mia 16 (16, ROLB) **1989** Mia 16 (16, ROLB) **1990**†Mia 16 (16, ROLB) **1991** Mia 11 (3) **NFL** 136 (119) [11 yrs]

Green, Jacob Jacob Carl, DE, 6´3˝/255 lbs; Texas A&M; 1980: Sea, rnd 1; B1/21/1957 Pasadena, TX [S] **1980** Sea 14 (13, LDE) **1981** Sea 16 (16, LDE) **1982** Sea 9 (9, LDE) **1983**†Sea☆16 (16, LDE) **1984**†Sea☆16 (16, LDE) **1985** Sea☆16 (16, LDE) **1986** Sea✧16 (16, LDE) **1987**†Sea★12 (12, LDE) **1988**†Sea 16 (16, LDE) **1989** Sea 15 (14, LDE) **1990** Sea 16 (16, LDE) **1991** Sea 16 (16, LDE) **1992** SF 2 (0) **NFL** 180 (176) [13 yrs]

Green, Jacquez D'Tanyian Jacquez, WR, 5´9˝/172 lbs; Florida; 1998: TB, rnd 2; B1/15/1976 Fort Valley, GA

YEAR	TEAM	G (GS, POS)	RUSH	YD	AVG (LG)	TD	REC	YD	AVG (LG)	TD	PASS	COMP	PCT	YD	AVG (LG)	TD	INT	SK	YD	QBR	KPR	OTD	PTS	TAY
1998	TB	12(1)	3	12	4.0(18)	0	14	251	17.9(64)	2	—	—	—	—	—	—	—	—	—	—	kp	1	18	540
1999	†TB	16(10, WR)	3	8	2.7(15)	0	56	791	14.1(62)	3	—	—	—	—	—	—	—	—	—	—	kp	—	18	543
2000	†TB	16(16, WR)	5	13	2.6(6)	0	51	773	15.2(75)	1	—	—	—	—	—	—	—	—	—	—	kp	—	6	392
2001	†TB	12(10, WR)	—	—	—	—	36	402	11.2(35)	1	—	—	—	—	—	—	—	—	—	—	—	—	6	206
2002	Was	9(0)	2	9	4.5(8)	0	5	94	18.8(44)	0	—	—	—	—	—	—	—	—	—	—	kp	1	6	168
2002	Det	1(0)	—	—	—	—	—	—	—	—	—	—	—	—	—	—	—	—	—	—	—	—	—	—
NFL	5	66(37)	13	42	3.2(18)	0	162	2311	14.3(75)	7	—	—	—	—	—	—	—	—	—	—	kp	2	54	1848

Green, Jamaal Jamaal Hakeem, DE, 6´2˝/272 lbs; Miami (FL); 2003: Phi, rnd 4; B6/5/1980 Camden, NJ **2004** Phi 8 (0) **2005**†ChiB 0 (0) **NFL** 8 (0) [2 yrs]

Green, Jarvis Jarvis Pernell, DE, 6´3˝/290 lbs; LSU; 2002: NE, rnd 4; B1/12/1979 Thibodeaux, LA **2002** NE 15 (4) **2003**†NE 16 (7, rde) **2004**†NE 16 (1) **2005**†NE 15 (5, rde) **NFL** 62 (17) [4 yrs]

Green, Jerry Jerome Albert, E, 6´0˝/190 lbs; Georgia Tech; B4/16/1936 Atlanta, GA

YEAR	TEAM	G (GS, POS)	RUSH	YD	AVG (LG)	TD	REC	YD	AVG (LG)	TD	PASS	COMP	PCT	YD	AVG (LG)	TD	INT	SK	YD	QBR	KPR	OTD	PTS	TAY
1960	Bos-A	2	—	—	—	—	3	52	17.3(31)	0	—	—	—	—	—	—	—	—	—	—	—	—	0	26

Green, Jessie Jessie Ray, WR, 6´3˝/191 lbs; Tulsa; 1976: GB, rnd 10; B2/21/1954 Malakoff, TX

YEAR	TEAM	G (GS, POS)	RUSH	YD	AVG (LG)	TD	REC	YD	AVG (LG)	TD	PASS	COMP	PCT	YD	AVG (LG)	TD	INT	SK	YD	QBR	KPR	OTD	PTS	TAY
1976	GB	1	—	—	—	—	—	—	—	—	—	—	—	—	—	—	—	—	—	—	—	—	—	—
1979	Sea	12	—	—	—	—	1	9	9.0(9)	0	—	—	—	—	—	—	—	—	—	—	—	—	0	5
1980	Sea	11(0)	—	—	—	—	4	47	11.8(19)	0	—	—	—	—	—	—	—	—	—	—	k	1	6	73
NFL	3	24	—	—	—	—	5	56	11.2(19)	0	—	—	—	—	—	—	—	—	—	—	k	1	6	77

Green, Joe Joseph David, DB, 5´11˝/195 lbs; Bowling Green State; B11/20/1948 Aberdeen, MS **1970** NYG 14 **1971** NYG 14 **NFL** 28 [2 yrs]

Green, John John Lincoln, DE-E, 6´1˝/192 lbs; Tulsa; 1944: Phi, rnd 16; B10/14/1921 Hastings, OK, D3/6/1989 Bergland, MI **1947** Phi 12 (1) **1948** Phi 12 (9, LE) **1949** Phi 7 (2) **1950** Phi✧12 (LDE) **1951** Phi 1 **NFL** 44 (12) [5 yrs]

Green, Johnny John Edward, QB, 6´3˝/198 lbs; Tennessee-Chattanooga; 1959: Pit, rnd 21; B10/12/1937 West Point, MS

YEAR	TEAM	G (GS, POS)	RUSH	YD	AVG (LG)	TD	REC	YD	AVG (LG)	TD	PASS	COMP	PCT	YD	AVG (LG)	TD	INT	SK	YD	QBR	KPR	OTD	PTS	TAY
1960	Buf-A	10(QB)	21	29	1.4(11)	2	1	0	0.0(0)	0	228	89	39.0	1267	5.6(70)	10	10	—	—	54.1	—	—	12	333
1961	Buf-A	8(qb)	14	15	1.1(14)	1	—	—	—	—	126	56	44.4	903	7.2(61)	6	5	—	—	—	—	—	6	307
1962	NYT-A	11(QB)	17	35	2.1(8)	3	—	—	—	—	258	128	49.6	1741	6.7(63)	10	18	—	—	55.4	P	—	18	266
1963	NYJ-A	1	—	—	—	—	—	—	—	—	6	2	33.3	10	1.7(6)	0	1	—	—	—	—	—	0	-35
NFL	4	30	52	79	1.5(14)	6	1	0	0.0	0	618	275	44.5	3921	6.3(70)	26	34	—	—	56.7	P	—	36	870

Green, Justin Justin, FB, 5´11˝/250 lbs; Montana; 2005: Bal, rnd 5; B4/30/1982 San Diego, CA

YEAR	TEAM	G (GS, POS)	RUSH	YD	AVG (LG)	TD	REC	YD	AVG (LG)	TD	PASS	COMP	PCT	YD	AVG (LG)	TD	INT	SK	YD	QBR	KPR	OTD	PTS	TAY
2005	Bal	12(4)	5	4	0.8(4)	0	7	32	4.6(8)	0	—	—	—	—	—	—	—	—	—	—	k	—	2	15

Green, Lamont Lamont, LB, 6´3˝/230 lbs; Florida State; B7/10/1976 Miami, FL **1999** Atl 1 (0)

Green, Larry Lawrence Edward, E, 6´0˝/180 lbs; Georgetown (DC); B6/3/1894 Yorkshire, England, D11/29/1976 St. Petersburg, FL **1920** Can 4 (1)

Green, Louis Louis Edward, LB, 6´3˝/228 lbs; Alcorn State; B9/23/1979 Vicksburg, MS **2004**†Den 6 (0) **2005**†Den 14 (0) **NFL** 20 (0) [2 yrs]

Green, Mark Mark Anthony, RB, 5´11˝/184 lbs; Notre Dame; 1989: Chi, rnd 5; B3/22/1967 Riverside, CA

YEAR	TEAM	G (GS, POS)	RUSH	YD	AVG (LG)	TD	REC	YD	AVG (LG)	TD	PASS	COMP	PCT	YD	AVG (LG)	TD	INT	SK	YD	QBR	KPR	OTD	PTS	TAY
1989	ChiB	10(0)	5	46	9.2(37)	1	5	48	9.6(21)	0	—	—	—	—	—	—	—	—	—	—	kp	—	6	215
1990	†ChiB	12(1)	27	126	4.7(14)	0	4	26	6.5(10)	1	—	—	—	—	—	—	—	—	—	—	k	—	6	151
1991	†ChiB	16(4)	61	217	3.6(18)	3	6	54	9.0(15)	0	—	—	—	—	—	—	—	—	—	—	kp	—	18	277
1992	ChiB	15(0)	23	107	4.7(18)	2	7	85	12.1(43)	0	—	—	—	—	—	—	—	—	—	—	k	—	12	229
NFL	4	53(5)	116	496	4.3(37)	6	22	213	9.7(43)	1	—	—	—	—	—	—	—	—	—	—	kp	—	42	872

Green, Michael Michael Wayne, DB, 6´0˝/195 lbs; Northwestern State (LA); 2000: Chi, rnd 7; B12/6/1976 Ruston, LA **2000** ChiB 7 (0) **2001**†ChiB 16 (2) **2002** ChiB 16 (16, SS) **2003** ChiB 10 (8, ss) **2004** ChiB 16 (16, SS) **2005**†ChiB 16 (3) **NFL** 81 (45) [6 yrs]

Green, Mike Michael James, LB, 6´0˝/235 lbs; Oklahoma State; 1983: SD, rnd 9; B6/29/1961 Port Arthur, TX **1983** SD 16 (16, LILB) **1984** SD 16 (16, LILB) **1985** SD 15 (15, LILB) **NFL** 47 (47) [3 yrs]

Green, Mike Mike Lewayne, RB, 6´0˝/249 lbs; Houston; 2000: Ten, rnd 7; B9/2/1976 Ruston, LA

YEAR	TEAM	G (GS, POS)	RUSH	YD	AVG (LG)	TD	REC	YD	AVG (LG)	TD	PASS	COMP	PCT	YD	AVG (LG)	TD	INT	SK	YD	QBR	KPR	OTD	PTS	TAY
2000	†Ten	1(0)	—	—	—	—	—	—	—	—	—	—	—	—	—	—	—	—	—	—	—	—	—	—
2001	Ten	16(1)	15	71	4.7(21)	1	12	64	5.3(10)	1	2	0	0.0	0	0.0	0	2	—	—	—	k	—	12	28
2002	†Ten	15(2)	21	71	3.4(12)	0	7	57	8.1(21)	1	—	—	—	—	—	—	—	—	—	—	k	—	6	100
NFL	3	32(3)	36	142	3.9(21)	1	19	121	6.4(21)	2	2	0	0.0	0	0.0	0	2	—	—	—	k	—	18	128

Green, Paul Paul Earl, TE, 6´3˝/236 lbs; USC; 1989: Den, rnd 8; B10/8/1966 Coalinga, CA

YEAR	TEAM	G (GS, POS)	RUSH	YD	AVG (LG)	TD	REC	YD	AVG (LG)	TD	PASS	COMP	PCT	YD	AVG (LG)	TD	INT	SK	YD	QBR	KPR	OTD	PTS	TAY
1989	†Den	0(0)	—	—	—	—	—	—	—	—	—	—	—	—	—	—	—	—	—	—	—	—	0	0
1992	Sea	4(4)	—	—	—	—	9	67	7.4(15)	1	—	—	—	—	—	—	—	—	—	—	—	—	6	39
1993	Sea	15(8, te)	—	—	—	—	23	178	7.7(20)	1	—	—	—	—	—	—	—	—	—	—	—	—	6	94
1994	Sea	16(10, TE)	—	—	—	—	30	208	6.9(20)	1	—	—	—	—	—	—	—	—	—	—	—	—	6	109
1996	NO	14(5, te)	—	—	—	—	7	91	13.0(23)	0	—	—	—	—	—	—	—	—	—	—	—	—	0	46
NFL	5	49(27)	—	—	—	—	69	544	7.9(23)	3	—	—	—	—	—	—	—	—	—	—	—	—	18	287

Green, Ray Raymond, DB, 6´3˝/195 lbs; South Carolina; B3/22/1977 Queens, NY **2000** Car 16 (0) **2001**†Mia 4 (0) **2002** Mia 8 (0) **2003** NYJ 8 (0) **2003** NYG 2 (0) **NFL** 38 (0) [4 yrs]

YEAR	TEAM	G (GS, POS)	RUSH	YD	AVG (LG)	TD	REC	YD	AVG (LG)	TD	PASS	COMP	PCT	YD	AVG (LG)	TD	INT	SK	YD	QBR	KPR	OTD	PTS	TAY
Green, Robert Robert David, RB, 5´8˝/212 lbs; William & Mary; B9/10/1970 Washington, DC																								
1992	†Was	15(0)	8	46	5.8(23)	0	1	5	5.0(5)	0	—	—	—	—	—	—	—	—	—	—	k	—	0	43
1993	ChiB	16(0)	15	29	1.9(10)	0	13	63	4.8(9)	0	—	—	—	—	—	—	—	—	—	—	k	—	0	67
1994	†ChiB	15(0)	25	122	4.9(14)	0	24	199	8.3(39)	2	—	—	—	—	—	—	—	—	—	—	k	—	12	219
1995	ChiB	12(3)	107	570	5.3(38)	3	28	246	8.8(28)	0	—	—	—	—	—	—	—	—	—	—	k	—	18	707
1996	ChiB	10(3)	60	249	4.2(19)	0	13	78	6.0(18)	0	—	—	—	—	—	—	—	—	—	—	—	—	0	288
1997	Min	3(1)	6	22	3.7(8)	0	1	5	5.0(5)	0	—	—	—	—	—	—	—	—	—	—	—	—	0	25
NFL	6	71(7)	221	1038	4.7(38)	3	80	596	7.4(39)	2	—	—	—	—	—	—	—	—	—	—	k	—	30	1347
Green, Roderick Roderick, LB, 6´2˝/243 lbs; Central Missouri State; 2004: Bal, rnd 5; B4/26/1982 Brenham, TX **2004** Bal 9 (0) **2005** Bal 16 (0) **NFL** 25 (0) [2 yrs]																								
Green, Rogerick Rogerick, DB, 6´0˝/182 lbs; Kansas State; 1992: TB, rnd 5; B12/15/1969 San Antonio, TX **1992** TB 1 (1) **1994** TB 11 (0) **1995** Jax 14 (0) **NFL** 26 (1) [3 yrs]																								
Green, Ron Ronald Morris, WR, 6´1˝/200 lbs; North Dakota; 1966: Min, rnd 9; B11/27/1943 Fargo, ND **1967** Cle 4 **1968**†Cle 1 **NFL** 5 [2 yrs]																								
Green, Roy Roy Calvin, WR-DB, 6´0˝/195 lbs; Henderson State; 1979: SL, rnd 4; B6/30/1957 Magnolia, AR **[R]**																								
1979	SL☆	16	—	—	—	—	1	15	15.0(15)	0	—	—	—	—	—	—	—	—	—	—	kp	1	6	410
1980	SL	15(6, fs)	—	—	—	—	—	—	—	—	—	—	—	—	—	—	—	—	—	—	kpi	1	6	368
1981	SL	16(2)	3	60	20.0(44)	1	33	708	**21.5**(**60**)	4	—	—	—	—	—	—	—	—	—	—	ki	—	30	488
1982	†SL	9(9, WR)	6	8	1.3(13)	0	32	453	14.2(42)	3	1	0	0.0	0	0.0	0	0	1	9	—	p	—	18	255
1983	SL★	16(15, WR)	4	49	12.3(25)	0	**78**	1227	15.7(71)	**14**	—	—	—	—	—	—	—	—	—	—	k	—	84	732
1984	SL★	16(16, WR)	1	-10	-10.0(-10)	0	78	**1555**	19.9(83)	**12**	—	—	—	—	—	—	—	—	—	—	kp	—	72	831
1985	SL	13(13, WR)	1	2	2.0(2)	0	50	693	13.9(47)	5	—	—	—	—	—	—	—	—	—	—	—	—	30	374
1986	SL	11(10, WR)	2	-4	-2.0(1)	0	42	517	12.3(48)	6	—	—	—	—	—	—	—	—	—	—	—	—	36	285
1987	SL	12(12, WR)	2	34	17.0(26)	0	43	731	17.0(57)	4	—	—	—	—	—	—	—	—	—	—	—	—	24	420
1988	Phx	16(16, WR)	4	1	0.3(18)	0	68	1097	16.1(52)	7	—	—	—	—	—	—	—	—	—	—	—	—	42	585
1989	Phx	12(12, WR)	—	—	—	—	44	703	16.0(59)	7	—	—	—	—	—	—	—	—	—	—	—	—	42	387
1990	Phx	16(16, WR)	—	—	—	—	53	797	15.0(54)	4	1	1	100.0	20	20.0(20)	0	0	—	—	—	k	—	24	429
1991	Phi	13(3)	—	—	—	—	29	364	12.6(42)	0	—	—	—	—	—	—	—	—	—	—	k	—	0	177
1992	†Phi	9(0)	—	—	—	—	8	105	13.1(21)	0	—	—	—	—	—	—	—	—	—	—	—	—	0	53
NFL	14	190(130)	23	140	6.1(44)	1	559	8965	16.0(83)	66	2	1	50.0	20	10.0(20)	0	0	1	9	—	kpi	2	414	5789
Green, Sammy Samuel Lee, LB, 6´2˝/228 lbs; Florida; 1976: Sea, rnd 2; B10/12/1954 Bradenton, FL **1976** Sea 14 (5, llb) **1977** Sea 14 (14, LLB) **1978** Sea 16 (16, LLB) **1979** Sea 16 (9, LLB) **1980** Hou 2 (0) **NFL** 62 (44) [5 yrs]																								
Green, Tim Timothy John, LB-DE, 6´2˝/249 lbs; Syracuse; 1986: Atl, rnd 1; B12/16/1963 Liverpool, NY **1986** Atl 11 (1) **1987** Atl 9 (5, LOLB) **1988** Atl 10 (5, rolb) **1989** Atl 16 (14, ROLB) **1990** Atl 16 (16, RDE) **1991**†Atl 16 (16, RDE) **1992** Atl 12 (11, RDE) **1993** Atl 9 (3) **NFL** 99 (71) [8 yrs]																								
Green, Tony Anthony Edward, RB, 5´9˝/185 lbs; Florida; 1978: Was, rnd 6; B9/26/1956 Rochester, NY **1979** NYG 4 **1979** Sea 11																								
1978	Was★	16	22	82	3.7(13)	1	4	89	22.3(34)	0	—	—	—	—	—	—	—	—	—	—	kp	2	18	750
NFL	2	31	22	82	3.7(13)	1	4	89	22.3(34)	0	—	—	—	—	—	—	—	—	—	—	kp	2	18	964
Green, Trent Trent Jason, QB, 6´3˝/217 lbs; Indiana; 1993: SD, rnd 8; B7/9/1970 St. Louis, MO																								
1997	Was	1(0)	—	—	—	—	—	—	—	—	1	0	0.0	0	0.0	0	0	—	—	—	—	—	0	0
1998	Was	15(14, QB)	42	117	2.8(13)	2	2	-8	-4.0(0)	0	509	278	54.6	3441	6.8(75)	23	11	49	338	81.8	—	—	12	1529
2000	SL	8(5, qb)	20	69	3.5(18)	1	—	—	—	—	240	145	60.4	2063	8.6(64)	16	5	24	145	—	—	—	6	991
2001	KC	16(16, QB)	35	158	4.5(16)	0	1	1	1.0(1)	0	523	296	56.6	3783	7.2(67)	17	**24**	39	198	71.1	—	—	2	1175
2002	KC	16(16, QB)	31	225	7.3(24)	1	—	—	—	—	470	287	61.1	3690	**7.9**(**99**)	26	13	26	141	92.6	—	—	8	1690
2003	†KC✧	16(16, QB)	26	83	3.2(14)	2	—	—	—	—	523	330	63.1	4039	7.7(67)	24	12	20	130	92.6	—	—	12	1763
2004	KC	16(16, QB)	25	85	3.4(13)	0	—	—	—	—	**556**	**369**	66.4	**4591**	8.3(70)	27	17	32	227	95.2	—	—	0	1836
2005	KC✧	16(16, QB)	35	82	2.3(13)	0	—	—	—	—	507	317	62.5	4014	7.9(60)	17	10	32	204	90.1	—	—	0	1774
NFL	8	104(99)	214	819	3.8(24)	6	3	-7	-2.3(1)	0	3329	2022	60.7	25621	7.7(99)	150	92	222	1383	88.3	—	—	40	10756
Green, Van Van Harold, DB, 6´1˝/192 lbs; Shaw; 1973: Cle, rnd 6; B4/21/1951 Auburndale, FL **1973** Cle 14 (ss/fs) **1976** Cle 1 **1976** Buf 5																								
1974	Cle	14(RCB/ss)	—	—	—	—	1	27	27.0(27)	0	—	—	—	—	—	—	—	—	—	—	i	1	6	70
1975	Cle	14(SS/fs)	—	—	—	—	1	-1	-1.0(-1)	0	—	—	—	—	—	—	—	—	—	—	pi	—	0	-11
NFL	4	48	—	—	—	—	2	26	13.0(27)	0	—	—	—	—	—	—	—	—	—	—	pi	2	12	59
Green, Vee Vivian Julius, T, 6´0˝/195 lbs; Illinois; B10/9/1900 Oakwood, IL, D5/13/1967 Urbana, IL **1926** Lou 2 (2, LT)																								
Green, Victor Victor Bernard, DB, 5´11˝/210 lbs; Akron; B12/8/1969 Americus, GA **[I]** **1993** NYJ 11 (0) **1994** NYJ 16 (0) **1995** NYJ 16 (12, SS) **1996** NYJ 16 (16, SS) **1997** NYJ 16 (16, SS) **1998**†NYJ 16 (16, SS) **1999** NYJ 16 (16, SS) **2000** NYJ 16 (16, SS) **2001**†NYJ 16 (16, SS) **2002** NE 16 (6, fs) **2003** NO 13 (1) **NFL** 168 (115) [11 yrs]																								
Green, William William, RB, 6´0˝/215 lbs; Boston College; 2002: Cle, rnd 1; B12/17/1979 Atlantic City, NJ																								
2002	†Cle	16(10, RB)	243	887	3.7(64)	6	16	113	7.1(18)	0	—	—	—	—	—	—	—	—	—	—	—	—	36	1004
2003	Cle	7(7, RB)	142	559	3.9(26)	1	10	50	5.0(12)	0	—	—	—	—	—	—	—	—	—	—	—	—	6	594
2004	Cle	15(12, RB)	163	585	3.6(46)	2	14	84	6.0(17)	0	—	—	—	—	—	—	—	—	—	—	—	—	12	647
2005	Cle	8(0)	20	78	3.9(17)	0	5	30	6.0(14)	0	—	—	—	—	—	—	—	—	—	—	k	—	0	97
NFL	4	46(29)	568	2109	3.7(64)	9	45	277	6.2(18)	0	—	—	—	—	—	—	—	—	—	—	k	—	54	2342
Green, Willie Willie Aaron, WR, 6´4˝/185 lbs; Mississippi; 1990: Det, rnd 8; B4/2/1966 Athens, GA																								
1991	†Det	16(15, WR)	—	—	—	—	39	592	15.2(73)	7	—	—	—	—	—	—	—	—	—	—	—	—	42	331
1992	Det	15(13, WR)	—	—	—	—	33	586	17.8(73)	5	—	—	—	—	—	—	—	—	—	—	—	—	30	318
1993	†Det	16(6, WR)	—	—	—	—	28	462	16.5(47)	2	—	—	—	—	—	—	—	—	—	—	—	—	12	241
1994	TB	5(0)	—	—	—	—	9	150	16.7(28)	0	—	—	—	—	—	—	—	—	—	—	—	—	0	75
1995	Car	16(7, wr)	—	—	—	—	47	882	**18.8**(**89**)	6	—	—	—	—	—	—	—	—	—	—	—	—	36	471
1996	†Car	15(10, WR)	1	1	1.0(1)	0	46	614	13.3(50)	3	—	—	—	—	—	—	—	—	—	—	—	—	18	323
1997	†Den	16(1)	—	—	—	—	19	240	12.6(31)	2	—	—	—	—	—	—	—	—	—	—	—	—	12	130
1998	†Den	15(0)	—	—	—	—	16	194	12.1(50)	1	—	—	—	—	—	—	—	—	—	—	—	—	6	102
NFL	8	114(52)	1	1	1.0(1)	0	237	3720	15.7(89)	26	—	—	—	—	—	—	—	—	—	—	—	—	156	1991
Green, Woody Woodrow, RB, 6´0˝/205 lbs; Arizona State; 1974: KC, rnd 1; B6/20/1951 Warren, OR																								
1974	KC	10(FB)	135	509	3.8(43)	3	26	247	9.5(69)	1	—	—	—	—	—	—	—	—	—	—	kp	—	24	665
1975	KC	12(FB)	167	611	3.7(42)	5	23	215	9.3(28)	1	—	—	—	—	—	—	—	—	—	—	k	—	36	877
1976	KC	6(6, RB)	73	322	4.4(27)	1	9	100	11.1(31)	0	—	—	—	—	—	—	—	—	—	—	k	—	6	419
NFL	3	28(6)	375	1442	3.8(43)	9	58	562	9.7(69)	2	—	—	—	—	—	—	—	—	—	—	kp	—	66	1960
Green, Yatil Yatil Devon, WR, 6´2˝/205 lbs; Miami (FL); 1997: Mia, rnd 1; B11/25/1973 Gainesville, FL																								
1999	Mia	8(1)	—	—	—	—	18	234	13.0(27)	0	—	—	—	—	—	—	—	—	—	—	—	—	0	117
Greenberg, Ben Benjamin Norman, FB-TB, 5´9˝/170 lbs; Rutgers; B1907, D2/76 **1930** Bkn 2 (0)																								
Greene, A.J. Anthony Jerome, DB, 5´8˝/167 lbs; Wake Forest; 1989: NYG, rnd 9; B6/24/1966 Hendersonville, NC **1991** NYG 2 (0)																								
Greene, Al Albert, aka Al Greenstein, HB, 5´8˝/160 lbs; none; B3/1/1901, Russia, D1/19/1977 North Miami, FL **1922** Mil 2 (1)																								
Greene, Andrew Andrew Kirkpatrick, G, 6´3˝/304 lbs; Indiana; 1995: Mia, rnd 2; B9/24/1969 Kingston, Jamaica **1995**†Mia 6 (1) **1998** Sea 4 (0) **NFL** 10 (1) [2 yrs]																								
Greene, Danny Theodore Daniel, WR, 5´11˝/190 lbs; Washington; 1985: Sea, rnd 3; B12/26/1961 Compton, CA																								
1985	Sea	4(0)	—	—	—	—	2	10	5.0(7)	1	—	—	—	—	—	—	—	—	—	—	kp	—	6	84
Greene, Doug Douglas Parks, DB, 6´2˝/205 lbs; Texas A&M-Kingsville; 1978: SL, rnd 3; B2/10/1956 Los Angeles, CA **1978** SL 15 (4) **1979** Buf 15 **1980** Buf 8 (0) **NFL** 38 (4) [3 yrs]																								
Greene, Ed Edward, G-E, 5´11˝/185 lbs; Loyola (IL); B9/28/1900, D9/1960 **1926** ChiC 9 (3)																								
Greene, Frank Frank Stokes, BB, 5´11˝/190 lbs; Tulsa; B3/29/1910 San Diego, CA, deceased																								
1934	ChiC	11(6, BB)	31	82	2.6	0	4	32	8.0	0	41	7	17.1	71	1.7	0	2	—	—	—	—	—	0	54

YEAR	TEAM	G (GS, POS)	RUSH	YD	AVG (LG)	TD	REC	YD	AVG (LG)	TD	PASS	COMP	PCT	YD	AVG (LG)	TD	INT	SK	YD	QBR	KPR	OTD	PTS	TAY

GREENE, JOE Charles Edward 'Mean Joe', DT, 6´4˝/275 lbs; North Texas; 1969: Pit, rnd 1; B9/24/1946 Temple, TX; HOF 1987 **1969** Pit★14 (14, LDT) **1970** Pit★14 (14, LDT) **1971** Pit★14 (14, LDT) **1972**†Pit★14 (14, LDT) **1973**†Pit★14 (13, LDT) **1974**†Pit★14 (14, LDT) **1975**†Pit★10 (9, LDT) **1976**†Pit★14 (14, LDT) **1977**†Pit☆13 (13, LDT) **1978**†Pit★16 (16, LDT) **1979**†Pit★15 (15, LDT) **1980** Pit 15 (15, LDT) **1981** Pit 14 (7, ldt) **NFL** 181 (172) [13 yrs]

GREENE, JOHN John Joseph, E-G-B, 6´0˝/210 lbs; Michigan; 1944: Det, rnd 5; B4/21/1920 Pittsburgh, PA

YEAR	TEAM	G (GS, POS)	RUSH	YD	AVG (LG)	TD	REC	YD	AVG (LG)	TD	PASS	COMP	PCT	YD	AVG (LG)	TD	INT	SK	YD	QBR	KPR	OTD	PTS	TAY
1944	Det	9 (5, LG)	—	—	—	—	—	—	—	—	—	—	—	—	—	—	—	—	—	—	i	—	0	12
1945	Det	10 (10, LE)	—	—	—	—	26	550	21.2 (63)	5	—	—	—	—	—	—	—	—	—	—	i	—	30	350
1946	Det	11 (2)	—	—	—	—	22	289	13.1 (**88**)	2	—	—	—	—	—	—	—	—	—	—	k	—	14	154
1947	Det	12 (6, LE)	—	—	—	—	38	621	16.3 (47)	5	—	—	—	—	—	—	—	—	—	—	k	—	30	325
1948	Det	12 (5, re)	—	—	—	—	25	595	**23.8** (**83**)	5	—	—	—	—	—	—	—	—	—	—	k	—	30	319
1949	Det	12 (11, RE)	—	—	—	—	42	542	12.9 (28)	7	—	—	—	—	—	—	—	—	—	—	—	—	42	306
1950	Det	12 (re)	—	—	—	—	22	368	16.7 (46)	2	—	—	—	—	—	—	—	—	—	—	—	1	18	194
NFL	7	78 (39)	—	—	—	—	175	2965	16.9 (88)	26	—	—	—	—	—	—	—	—	—	—	ki	1	164	1659

GREENE, KEN Kenneth Edward, DB, 6´3˝/203 lbs; Washington State; 1978: SL, rnd 1; B5/8/1956 Lewiston, ID **1978** SL 16 (12, SS) **1979** SL 16 (16, SS) **1980** SL 12 (8, ss) **1981** SL 15 (15, FS) **1982**†SL 8 (0) **1983** SD 16 (9, FS) **1984** SD 15 (13, SS) **NFL** 98 (73) [7 yrs]

GREENE, KEVIN Kevin Darwin, LB-DE, 6´3˝/247 lbs; Auburn; 1985: LARm, rnd 5; B7/31/1962 New York, NY **[S]** **1985**†LARm 15 (0) **1986**†LARm 16 (0) **1987** LARm 9 (0) **1988**†LARm 16 (14, LOLB) **1989**†LARm★16 (16, LOLB) **1990** LARm 15 (15, LOLB) **1991** LARm 16 (16, RDE/lde) **1992** LARm 16 (16, LLB) **1993**†Pit 16 (16, LOLB) **1994**†Pit★16 (16, LOLB) **1995**†Pit✧16 (16, LOLB) **1996**†Car★16 (16, LOLB) **1997**†SF 14 (4) **1998** Car✧15 (15, LOLB) **1999** Car 16 (16, LLB) **NFL** 228 (176) [15 yrs]

GREENE, MARCELLUS Marcellus Lamont, DB, 6´0˝/185 lbs; Arizona; 1981: LA, rnd 11; B12/12/1957 Indianapolis, IN **1984** Min 14 (0)

GREENE, NELSON Nelson R., T, 6´2˝/235 lbs; Tulsa; 1947: NYG, rnd 5; B3/21/1924 Houston, TX, D5/3/1983 Houston, TX **1948** NYY-A 14 (10, RT)

GREENE, SCOTT Scott Clayton, RB, 5´11˝/240 lbs; Michigan State; 1996: Car, rnd 6; B6/1/1972 Honeoye, NY

YEAR	TEAM	G (GS, POS)	RUSH	YD	AVG (LG)	TD	REC	YD	AVG (LG)	TD	PASS	COMP	PCT	YD	AVG (LG)	TD	INT	SK	YD	QBR	KPR	OTD	PTS	TAY
1996	†Car	8 (0)	—	—	—	—	2	7	3.5 (6)	1	—	—	—	—	—	—	—	—	—	—	k	—	6	-12
1997	Car	16 (14, FB)	45	157	3.5 (10)	1	40	277	6.9 (25)	1	—	—	—	—	—	—	—	—	—	—	k	—	12	284
1998	Ind	5 (0)	—	—	—	—	1	2	2.0 (2)	0	—	—	—	—	—	—	—	—	—	—	—	—	0	1
1999	†Ind	5 (0)	—	—	—	—	1	4	4.0 (4)	0	—	—	—	—	—	—	—	—	—	—	k	—	0	1
NFL	4	34 (14)	45	157	3.5 (10)	1	44	290	6.6 (25)	2	—	—	—	—	—	—	—	—	—	—	k	—	18	274

GREENE, TED Theodore William, LB, 6´1˝/230 lbs; Tampa; B1/25/1932 **1960** DalT-A 14 **1961** DalT-A 14 **1962**†DalT-A 4 **NFL** 32 [3 yrs]

GREENE, TIGER George Everett, DB, 6´0˝/194 lbs; Western Carolina; B2/15/1962 Hendersonville, NC **1985** Atl 10 (7, FS) **1986** GB 13 (10, SS) **1987** GB 11 (1) **1988** GB 16 (4) **1989** GB 16 (0) **1990** GB 16 (8, fs) **NFL** 82 (30) [6 yrs]

GREENE, TOM Thomas W., QB-P, 6´1˝/190 lbs; Holy Cross; B1938 **1961** DalT-A 1

YEAR	TEAM	G (GS, POS)	RUSH	YD	AVG (LG)	TD	REC	YD	AVG (LG)	TD	PASS	COMP	PCT	YD	AVG (LG)	TD	INT	SK	YD	QBR	KPR	OTD	PTS	TAY
1960	Bos-A	10	7	44	6.3 (21)	0	—	—	—	—	63	27	42.9	251	4.0 (31)	1	6	—	—	—	Pk	—	0	-78
NFL	2	11	7	44	6.3 (21)	0	—	—	—	—	63	27	42.9	251	4.0 (31)	1	6	—	—	—	—	—	0	-66

GREENE, TONY Anthony, DB, 5´10˝/170 lbs; Maryland; B8/29/1949 Clocksburg, MD **[I]** **1971** Buf 14 **1972** Buf 14 (RCB) **1973** Buf 14 (FS) **1974** Buf☆12 (12, FS) **1975** Buf 14 (12, LCB/fs) **1976** Buf 14 (14, FS) **1977** Buf★14 (FS) **1978** Buf 16 (FS) **1979** Buf 16 (12, FS) **NFL** 128 (50) [9 yrs]

GREENE, TRACY Tracy Lamar, TE, 6´5˝/270 lbs; Grambling State; 1994: KC, rnd 7; B11/5/1972 Monroe, LA **1995**†Pit 16 (0)

YEAR	TEAM	G (GS, POS)	RUSH	YD	AVG (LG)	TD	REC	YD	AVG (LG)	TD	PASS	COMP	PCT	YD	AVG (LG)	TD	INT	SK	YD	QBR	KPR	OTD	PTS	TAY
1994	KC	7 (1)	—	—	—	—	6	69	11.5 (20)	1	—	—	—	—	—	—	—	—	—	—	—	—	6	40
NFL	2	23 (1)	—	—	—	—	6	69	11.5 (20)	1	—	—	—	—	—	—	—	—	—	—	k	—	6	32

GREENEY, NORM Norman Junior, G, 5´11˝/212 lbs; Notre Dame; B5/7/1910 Cleveland, OH, D10/20/1985 Kelley's Island, OH **1933** GB 7 (4) **1934** Pit 11 (3) **1935** Pit 1 (0) **NFL** 19 (7) [3 yrs]

GREENFIELD, TOM Thomas Guy, C-LB, 6´4˝/213 lbs; Arizona; 1939: GB, rnd 15; B11/10/1917 Glendale, AZ **1939**†GB✧8 (0) **1940** GB 9 (3) **1941**†GB 5 (0) **NFL** 22 (3) [3 yrs]

GREENHALGH, BOB Robert Clyde, FB, 6´1˝/200 lbs; Notre Dame; San Francisco; 1948: NYG, rnd 29; B5/23/1924

YEAR	TEAM	G (GS, POS)	RUSH	YD	AVG (LG)	TD	REC	YD	AVG (LG)	TD	PASS	COMP	PCT	YD	AVG (LG)	TD	INT	SK	YD	QBR	KPR	OTD	PTS	TAY
1949	NYG	10 (6, FB)	62	188	3.0 (14)	0	3	23	7.7 (14)	0	—	—	—	—	—	—	—	—	—	—	—	—	0	200

GREENICH, DUKE Harley Max, B, 5´11˝/185 lbs; Mississippi; B10/16/1921 Coldwater, MI, D3/4/1989 Lindenhurst, NY **1944** ChiB 1 (0)

GREENLEE, FRITZ William Frederick, LB, 6´2˝/230 lbs; Northern Arizona; 1966: Chi, rnd 9/Mia, rnd R5; B11/5/1943 Des Moines, IA **1969** SF 4

GREENSHIELDS, DONN Donn, T, 6´1˝/190 lbs; Penn State; B5/1/1904, deceased **1932** Bkn 11 (8, RT) **1933** Bkn 2 (0) **NFL** 13 (8) [2 yrs]

GREENWOOD, CARL Carlanditt Keith, DB, 5´11˝/186 lbs; UCLA; 1995: NYJ, rnd 5; B3/11/1972 Fort Ord, CA **1995** NYJ 10 (0) **1996** NYJ 14 (1) **NFL** 24 (1) [2 yrs]

GREENWOOD, DAVID David Mark, DB, 6´3˝/210 lbs; Wisconsin; 1983: NO, rnd 8; B3/25/1960 Park Falls, WI **1985** TB 16 (9, SS) **1986** GB 9 (0) **1988** LARd 2 (0) **NFL** 27 (9) [3 yrs]

GREENWOOD, DON Donald Adams, B, 6´0˝/190 lbs; Missouri; Illinois; B2/18/1921 Detroit, MI, D3/21/1983 Princeville, IL

YEAR	TEAM	G (GS, POS)	RUSH	YD	AVG (LG)	TD	REC	YD	AVG (LG)	TD	PASS	COMP	PCT	YD	AVG (LG)	TD	INT	SK	YD	QBR	KPR	OTD	PTS	TAY
1945	†Cle☆	9 (6, FB)	101	376	3.7 (35)	4	3	72	24.0 (42)	0	—	—	—	—	—	—	—	—	—	—	k	—	24	483
1946	†Cle-A	13 (10, RH)	77	274	3.6	**6**	4	0	0.0	0	1	1	100.0	27	27.0 (27)	0	0	—	—	—	ki	—	36	424
1947	Cle-A	11 (6, RH)	18	94	5.2	0	5	49	9.8	0	—	—	—	—	—	—	—	—	—	—	i	—	0	118
AAFC	2	24 (16)	95	368	3.9 (35)	6	9	49	5.4 (42)	0	1	1	100.0	27	27.0 (27)	0	0	—	—	—	ki	—	36	541

GREENWOOD, GLENN Glenn Jackson, FB, 5´10˝/185 lbs; Iowa; B2/5/1896, IA, D7/1/1970 Los Angeles, CA **1926** Lou 1 (0)

GREENWOOD, L.C. L.C. Henderson, DE, 6´6˝/245 lbs; Arkansas-Pine Bluff; 1969: Pit, rnd 10; B9/8/1946 Canton, MS **1969** Pit 12 **1970** Pit 12 **1971** Pit 14 (14, LDE) **1972**†Pit 13 (13, LDE) **1973**†Pit★14 (14, LDE) **1974**†Pit★14 (14, LDE) **1975**†Pit★14 (14, LDE) **1976**†Pit★13 (12, LDE) **1977**†Pit 9 (8, LDE) **1978**†Pit★14 (14, LDE) **1979**†Pit★12 (11, LDE) **1980** Pit 15 (15, LDE) **1981** Pit 14 (5, lde) **NFL** 170 (134) [13 yrs]

GREENWOOD, MORLON Morlon O'Neil, LB, 6´0˝/238 lbs; Syracuse; 2001: Mia, rnd 3; B7/17/1978 Jamaica, West Indies **2001**†Mia 14 (12, RLB) **2002** Mia 16 (13, RLB) **2003** Mia 16 (11, RLB) **2004** Mia 16 (15, RLB) **2005** Hou 16 (16, RILB) **NFL** 78 (67) [5 yrs]

GREER, AL Albert, E, 6´4˝/190 lbs; Jackson State; 1963: Det, rnd 18; B4/15/1940 Anniston, AL **1963** Det 1

GREER, CHARLIE Charles Anthony, DB, 6´0˝/205 lbs; Colorado; 1968: Den, rnd 13; B4/4/1946 Atlanta, GA, D12/7/1999 Atlanta, GA **1968** Den-A 14 (LCB) **1969** Den-A 12 (9, LS) **1970** Den 14 (14, SS) **1971** Den 13 (13, SS) **1972** Den 14 (14, SS) **1973** Den 10 (10, FS) **1974** Den 11 (10, FS) **NFL** 88 (70) [7 yrs]

GREER, CURTIS Curtis William, DE, 6´4˝/255 lbs; Michigan; 1980: SL, rnd 1; B11/10/1957 Detroit, MI **[S]** **1980** SL 11 (2) **1981** SL 16 (12, RDE) **1982**†SL 9 (9, RDE) **1983** SL 16 (16, RDE) **1984** SL☆16 (16, RDE) **1985** SL 16 (15, RDE) **1987** SL 10 (9, RDE) **NFL** 94 (79) [7 yrs]

GREER, DONOVAN Donovan Orlando, DB, 5´9˝/178 lbs; Texas A&M; B9/11/1974 Houston, TX **1997** Atl 1 (0) **1997** NO 6 (1) **1998**†Buf 11 (2) **1999**†Buf 16 (0) **2000** Buf 13 (1) **2001** Was 2 (0) **2002** Det 1 (0) **NFL** 50 (4) [6 yrs]

GREER, JABARI Jabari Amin, DB, 5´11˝/169 lbs; Tennessee; B2/2/1982 Jackson, TN **2005** Buf 16 (2)

YEAR	TEAM	G (GS, POS)	RUSH	YD	AVG (LG)	TD	REC	YD	AVG (LG)	TD	PASS	COMP	PCT	YD	AVG (LG)	TD	INT	SK	YD	QBR	KPR	OTD	PTS	TAY
2004	Buf	12 (1)	1	-6	-6.0 (-6)	0	—	—	—	—	—	—	—	—	—	—	—	—	—	—	S	—	0	-6
NFL	2	28 (3)	1	-6	-6.0 (-6)	0	—	—	—	—	—	—	—	—	—	—	—	—	—	—	S	—	0	-6

GREER, JIM James Daniel, E, 6´3˝/215 lbs; Elizabeth City State; 1955: Cle, rnd 23; B7/7/1931 Huntington, WV

YEAR	TEAM	G (GS, POS)	RUSH	YD	AVG (LG)	TD	REC	YD	AVG (LG)	TD	PASS	COMP	PCT	YD	AVG (LG)	TD	INT	SK	YD	QBR	KPR	OTD	PTS	TAY
1960	Den-A	14 (se)	—	—	—	—	22	284	12.9 (33)	1	—	—	—	—	—	—	—	—	—	—	k		6	143

GREER, TERRY Terry Lee, WR, 6´1˝/192 lbs; Alabama State; 1980: LA, rnd 11; B9/27/1957 Memphis, TN

YEAR	TEAM	G (GS, POS)	RUSH	YD	AVG (LG)	TD	REC	YD	AVG (LG)	TD	PASS	COMP	PCT	YD	AVG (LG)	TD	INT	SK	YD	QBR	KPR	OTD	PTS	TAY
1986	Cle	11 (1)	—	—	—	—	3	51	17.0 (22)	0	—	—	—	—	—	—	—	—	—	—	—	—	0	26
1987	SF	3 (1)	—	—	—	—	6	111	18.5 (50)	1	—	—	—	—	—	—	—	—	—	—	—	—	6	61
1988	†SF	10 (0)	—	—	—	—	8	120	15.0 (31)	0	—	—	—	—	—	—	—	—	—	—	—	—	0	60
1989	SF	11 (0)	—	—	—	—	1	26	26.0 (26)	0	—	—	—	—	—	—	—	—	—	—	kp	—	0	13
1990	Det	15 (9, WR)	—	—	—	—	20	332	16.6 (68)	3	—	—	—	—	—	—	—	—	—	—	—	—	18	181
NFL	5	50 (11)	—	—	—	—	38	640	16.8 (68)	4	—	—	—	—	—	—	—	—	—	—	kp	—	24	340

GREFE, TED Theodore Fred, E, 6´0˝/205 lbs; Northwestern; B10/26/1917 Des Moines, IA, D10/27/1989 Fairfax, VA **1945** Det 2 (0)

GREGG, EDD Edd R., E, 5´6˝/135 lbs; Kentucky; B8/4/1897 Louisville, KY, D11/9/1961 Louisville, KY **1922** Lou 2 (2, RE)

YEAR	TEAM	G(GS, POS)	RUSH	YD	AVG(LG)	TD	REC	YD	AVG(LG)	TD	PASS	COMP	PCT	YD	AVG(LG)	TD	INT	SK	YD	QBR	KPR	OTD	PTS	TAY

GREGG, FORREST Alvis Forrest, T-G-DT, 6´4˝/249 lbs; SMU; 1956: GB, rnd 2; B10/18/1933 Birthright, TX; HOF 1977 [C] **1956** GB 11 **1958** GB 12 **1959** GB★12 (RT)
1960†GB★12 (RT) **1961**†GB★14 (RT/rg) **1962**†GB★14 (RT) **1963**†GB★14 (RT) **1964** GB★14 (RT) **1965**†GB★14 (LG) **1966**†GB★14 (RT) **1967**†GB★14 (RT)
1968 GB◇14 (RT) **1969** GB 14 (RT) **1970** GB 14 **1971** Dal 6 **NFL** 193 [15 yrs]

GREGG, KELLY Kelly, NT-DT, 6´0˝/310 lbs; Oklahoma; 1999: Cin, rnd 6; B11/1/1976 Wichita, KS **1999** Phi 3 (0) **2001**†Bal 8 (1) **2002** Bal 16 (16, NT) **2003**†Bal 16 (15, NT)
2004 Bal 14 (14, NT) **2005** Bal 16 (16, RDT) **NFL** 73 (62) [6 yrs]

GREGOR, BOB Robert Lee, DB, 6´2˝/192 lbs; Washington State; 1980: SD, rnd 4; B2/10/1957 Riverside, CA **1981**†SD 14 (6, fs) **1982**†SD 4 (3) **1983** SD 5 (5, ss) **1984** SD 7 (2)
NFL 30 (16) [4 yrs]

GREGORY, BEN Bennett Maurice, RB, 6´3˝/220 lbs; Nebraska; 1968: Buf, rnd 5; B10/31/1946 Uniontown, PA, D4/10/1997 Boulder, CO

| 1968 | Buf-A | 6(FB) | 52 | 283 | 5.4(67) | 1 | 5 | 21 | 4.2(8) | 0 | — | — | — | — | — | — | — | — | — | — | — | — | 6 | 304 |

GREGORY, BILL William Penn, DE-DT, 6´5˝/255 lbs; Wisconsin; 1971: Dal, rnd 3; B12/14/1949 Galveston, TX **1971**†Dal 14 **1972**†Dal 13 **1973**†Dal 14 **1974** Dal 14
1975†Dal 14 (6, rdt) **1976**†Dal 14 (6, rdt) **1977**†Dal 13 **1978** Sea 16 (14, RDE) **1979** Sea 16 (14, RDE) **1980** Sea 14 (13, RDE) **NFL** 142 (55) [10 yrs]

GREGORY, BRUCE Bruce Robert, TB-WB, 5´10˝/170 lbs; Michigan; B5/13/1903 Battle Creek, MI, D12/26/1960 Frederick, MD **1926** Det 12 (11, TB), 12

GREGORY, DAMIAN Damian K., DT, 6´2˝/305 lbs; Indiana; Illinois State; B1/21/1977 Ann Arbor, MI **2001** Mia 2 (0) **2002** Cle 1 (0) **2004** TB 6 (0) **NFL** 9 (0) [3 yrs]

GREGORY, GARLAND Garland D., G-LB, 5´11˝/185 lbs; Louisiana Tech; B3/8/1919 Columbia, LA **1946** SF-A☆13 (6, lg) **1947** SF-A 14 (14, LG) **AAFC** 27 (20) [2 yrs]

GREGORY, GIL Frank Gilbert, FB-WB, 5´11˝/165 lbs; Williams; B1/18/1898 Newark, NJ, D11/11/1980 Hamburg, NY **1923** Buf 1 (0) **1924** Buf 3 (0) **NFL** 4 (0) [2 yrs]

GREGORY, GLYNN Glynn Stephens, E-DB, 6´2˝/195 lbs; SMU; 1961: Dal, rnd 9/DalT, rnd 13; B7/6/1939 Paris, TX

1961	Dal	14	—	—	—	—	3	30	10.0(13)	0	—	—	—	—	—	—	—	—	—	i	—	0	31
1962	Dal	6	—	—	—	—	3	70	23.3(44)	0	—	—	—	—	—	—	—	—	—	—	—	0	35
NFL	2	20	—	—	—	—	6	100	16.7(44)	0	—	—	—	—	—	—	—	—	i	—	0	66

GREGORY, JACK Earl Jackson, G, 6´2˝/215 lbs; Alabama; Tennessee-Chattanooga; 1940: Cle, rnd 13; B2/14/1916 Okolona, MS, D11/5/2003 Okolona, MS **1941** Cle 7 (0)

GREGORY, JACK Earl Jackson, DE, 6´5˝/250 lbs; Tennessee-Chattanooga; Delta State; 1966: Cle, rnd 9/Buf, rnd R1; B10/3/1944 Okolona, MS **1967**†Cle 14 **1968**†Cle 14 (6, lde/
rde) **1969**†Cle★14 (RDE) **1970** Cle◇14 (RDE) **1971**†Cle 14 (RDE) **1972** NYG★14 (RDE) **1973** NYG 13 (RDE) **1974** NYG 14 (RDE) **1975** NYG 14 (RDE) **1976** NYG 11 (RDE)
1977 NYG 14 (RDE) **1978** NYG 16 (16, RDE) **1979** Cle 16 (16, RDE) **NFL** 182 (22) [13 yrs]

GREGORY, KEN Kenneth, E, 6´1˝/190 lbs; Whittier; 1961: Bal, rnd 4/Hou, rnd 24; B2/1/1937 **1961** Bal 14 **1962** Phi 2

| 1963 | NYJ-A | 14 | — | — | — | — | 9 | 90 | 10.0(16) | 0 | — | — | — | — | — | — | — | — | — | — | — | 0 | 45 |
| NFL | 3 | 30 | — | — | — | — | 9 | 90 | 10.0(16) | 0 | — | — | — | — | — | — | — | — | k | — | 0 | 33 |

GREGORY, MIKE Mitchell Oscar, C, 5´11˝/215 lbs; Denison; B7/30/1905 Pittsburgh, PA, D7/30/1957 Granville, OH **1931** Cle 7 (3)

GREGORY, TED Theodore Anthony, NT, 6´1˝/260 lbs; Syracuse; 1988: Den, rnd 1; B2/11/1965 Queens, NY **1988** NO 3 (0)

GREISEN, CHRIS Chris, QB, 6´3˝/227 lbs; Northwest Missouri State; 1999: Arz, rnd 7; B7/2/1976 Sturgeon Bay, WI

1999	Arz	2(0)	—	—	—	—	—	—	—	—	6	1	16.7	4	0.7(4)	0	0	—	—	—	—	0	2
2000	Arz	3(0)	1	1	1.0(1)	0	—	—	—	—	10	6	60.0	65	6.5(26)	1	0	3	24	—	—	0	39
NFL	2	5(0)	1	1	1.0(1)	0	—	—	—	—	16	7	43.8	69	4.3(26)	1	0	3	24	—	—	0	41

GREISEN, NICK Nick, LB, 6´1˝/245 lbs; Wisconsin; 2002: NYG, rnd 5; B8/10/1979 Sturgeon Bay, WI **2002**†NYG 8 (1) **2003** NYG 15 (0) **2004** NYG 15 (7, rlb)
2005†NYG 16 (12, RLB) **NFL** 54 (20) [4 yrs]

GREMMINGER, HANK Charles Henry, DB, 6´1˝/201 lbs; Baylor; 1956: GB, rnd 7; B9/1/1933 Windthorst, TX, D11/2/2001 Weatherford, TX [I] **1956** GB 12 (DB) **1957** GB 12 (DB)
1958 GB 12 (DB) **1959** GB 12 (DB) **1960**†GB 12 (RS) **1961**†GB 14 (LS) **1962**†GB 14 (LS) **1963** GB 14 (LS) **1964** GB 13 **1965**†GB 8 **1966** LARm 8 **NFL** 131 [11 yrs]

GRESHAM, BOB Robert Clark, RB, 5´11˝/195 lbs; West Virginia; 1971: NO, rnd 8; B7/9/1948 Porter, AL

1971	NO	13(RB)	127	383	3.0(18)	6	17	203	11.9(37)	0	—	—	—	—	—	—	—	—	—	k	—	36	560
1972	NO	14(RB)	121	381	3.1(23)	4	29	192	6.6(54)	0	1	0	0.0	0	0	0	0	—	—	k	—	18	507
1973	Hou	13(RB)	104	400	3.8(52)	2	28	244	8.7(62)	1	—	—	—	—	—	—	—	—	—	k	1	24	875
1974	Hou	14	3	6	2.0(3)	0	3	19	6.3(9)	0	—	—	—	—	—	—	—	—	—	—	—	6	61
1975	NYJ	10	25	98	3.9(16)	1	2	4	2.0(6)	0	—	—	—	—	—	—	—	—	—	k	—	6	158
1976	NYJ	11	30	92	3.1(24)	0	11	66	6.0(13)	0	1	1	100.0	29	29.0(29)	0	0	—	—	—	—	0	140
NFL	6	75	410	1360	3.3(52)	12	90	728	8.1(62)	1	2	1	50.0	29	14.5(29)	0	0	—	—	k	1	84	2300

GRGICH, VISCO Visco Gerald, G-MG-T-LB, 5´11˝/217 lbs; Santa Clara; 1946: ChiB, rnd 24; B1/19/1923 Zlarin, Yugoslavia, D12/26/2005 Modesto, CA **1946** SF-A 12 (0)
1947 SF-A 14 (0) **1948** SF-A 14 (14, RG) **1949**†SF-A☆12 (10, RG) **AAFC** 52 (24) [4 yrs]

1950 SF◇12 (MG) **1951** SF 12 (MG) **1952** SF 2 **NFL** 26 [3 yrs]

GRICE, SHANE Shane, G, 6´1˝/307 lbs; Mississippi; B12/20/1976 Tupelo, MS **2001** TB 1 (0)

GRIER, MARRIO Marrio Darnell, RB, 5´10˝/229 lbs; Clemson; Tennessee-Chattanooga; 1996: NE, rnd 6; B12/5/1971 Charlotte, NC

1996	†NE	16(0)	27	105	3.9(26)	1	1	8	8.0(8)	0	1	0	0.0	0	0	0	0	—	—	—	—	6	119
1997	†NE	16(0)	33	75	2.3(12)	1	—	—	—	—	—	—	—	—	—	—	—	—	—	—	—	6	85
NFL	2	32(0)	60	180	3.0(26)	2	1	8	8.0(8)	0	1	0	0.0	0	0	0	0	—	—	—	—	12	204

GRIER, ROSEY Roosevelt, DT-DE, 6´5˝/284 lbs; Penn State; 1955: NYG, rnd 3; B7/14/1932 Cuthbert, GA **1955** NYG 12 (RDE) **1956**†NYG★12 (RDT) **1958**†NYG☆10 (RDT)
1959†NYG☆12 (RDT) **1960** NYG★12 (RDT) **1961**†NYG☆14 (RDT) **1962**†NYG★13 (RDT) **1963** LARm☆14 (RDT) **1964** LARm 14 (14, RDT) **1965** LARm 14 (RDT)
1966 LARm 14 (RDT) **NFL** 141 (41) [11 yrs]

GRIESE, BOB Robert Allen, QB, 6´1˝/190 lbs; Purdue; 1967: Mia, rnd 1; B2/3/1945 Evansville, IN; HOF 1990

1967	Mia-A◇	12(11, QB)	37	157	4.2(22)	1	—	—	—	—	331	166	50.2	2005	6.1(68)	15	18	25	240	61.6	—	—	6	525
1968	Mia-A★	13(13, QB)	42	230	5.5(35)	1	—	—	—	—	355	186	52.4	2473	7.0(50)	21	16	43	372	75.7	—	—	6	942
1969	Mia-A	9(9, QB)	21	102	4.9(22)	0	—	—	—	—	252	121	48.0	1695	6.7(53)	10	16	33	289	56.9	—	—	0	360
1970	†Mia★	14(14, QB)	26	89	3.4(16)	2	—	—	—	—	245	142	58.0	2019	8.2(54)	12	17	31	282	72.1	—	—	12	499
1971	†Mia★	14(13, QB)	26	82	3.2(21)	0	—	—	—	—	263	145	55.1	2089	7.9(86)	19	9	23	248	90.9	—	—	0	862
1972	†Mia	6(5, qb)	3	11	3.7(5)	1	—	—	—	—	97	53	54.6	638	6.6(39)	4	4	7	45	—	—	—	6	200
1973	†Mia★	13(13, QB)	13	20	1.5(21)	0	—	—	—	—	218	116	53.2	1422	6.5(46)	17	8	11	75	84.3	—	—	0	496
1974	†Mia◇	13(13, QB)	16	66	4.1(22)	1	—	—	—	—	253	152	60.1	1968	7.8(52)	16	15	27	202	80.9	—	—	6	540
1975	Mia	10(10, QB)	17	59	3.5(17)	1	—	—	—	—	191	118	61.8	1693	8.9(79)	14	13	16	131	86.6	—	—	6	466
1976	Mia	13(13, QB)	23	108	4.7(26)	0	—	—	—	—	272	162	59.6	2097	7.7(47)	11	12	30	266	78.9	—	—	0	732
1977	†Mia★	14(14, QB)	16	30	1.9(13)	0	—	—	—	—	307	180	58.6	2252	7.3(73)	22	13	36	303	87.8	—	—	0	746
1978	†Mia◇	11(9, QB)	9	10	1.1(9)	0	—	—	—	—	235	148	63.0	1791	7.6(63)	11	11	18	165	82.4	—	—	0	521
1979	†Mia	14(12, QB)	11	30	2.7(18)	0	—	—	—	—	310	176	56.8	2160	7.0(51)	14	16	26	223	72.0	—	—	0	540
1980	Mia	5(3)	1	0	0.0(0)	0	—	—	—	—	100	61	61.0	790	7.9(54)	6	4	9	89	—	—	—	0	265
NFL	14	161(152)	261	994	3.8(35)	7	—	—	—	—	3429	1926	56.2	25092	7.3(86)	192	172	335	2930	77.1	—	—	42	7690

GRIESE, BRIAN Brian David, QB, 6´3˝/215 lbs; Michigan; 1998: Den, rnd 3; B3/18/1975 Miami, FL

1998	Den	1(0)	4	-4	-1.0(0)	0	—	—	—	—	3	1	33.3	2	0.7(2)	0	1	—	—	—	—	0	-43
1999	Den	14(13, QB)	46	138	3.0(23)	2	—	—	—	—	452	261	57.7	3032	6.7(88)	14	14	27	176	75.6	—	—	12	1184
2000	Den◇	10(10, QB)	29	102	3.5(18)	1	—	—	—	—	336	216	64.3	2688	8.0(61)	19	4	17	139	102.9	—	—	6	1391
2001	Den	15(15, QB)	50	173	3.5(24)	1	1	-6	-6.0(-6)	0	451	275	61.0	2827	6.3(65)	23	19	38	241	78.5	—	—	6	949
2002	Den	13(13, QB)	37	107	2.9(13)	1	—	—	—	—	436	291	66.7	3214	7.4(82)	15	15	34	237	85.6	—	—	6	1199
2003	Mia	5(5, qb)	5	15	3.0(9)	0	—	—	—	—	130	74	56.9	813	6.3(80)	5	6	12	83	69.2	—	—	0	207
2004	TB	11(10, QB)	30	17	0.6(7)	0	1	-4	-4.0(-4)	0	336	233	69.3	2632	7.8(68)	20	12	26	169	97.5	—	—	0	951
2005	TB	6(6, qb)	13	12	0.9(7)	0	—	—	—	—	174	112	64.4	1136	6.5(82)	7	7	19	122	81.6	—	—	0	335
NFL	8	75(72)	214	560	2.6(24)	5	2	-10	-5.0(-4)	0	2318	1463	63.1	16344	7.1(88)	103	78	166	1121	84.8	—	—	30	6172

GRIFFEN, HAL Harold Winslow, C-T, 6´1˝/247 lbs; Iowa; B3/1/1902 Sioux City, IA, deceased [C] **1928** GB 5 (4) **1930** Por 2 (0) **1932** Por 2 (0) **NFL** 9 (4) [3 yrs]

GRIFFIN, ARCHIE Archie Mason, RB, 5´9˝/189 lbs; Ohio State; 1976: Cin, rnd 1; B8/21/1954 Columbus, OH

YEAR	TEAM	G (GS, POS)	RUSH	YD	AVG (LG)	TD	REC	YD	AVG (LG)	TD	PASS	COMP	PCT	YD	AVG (LG)	TD	INT	SK	YD	QBR	KPR	OTD	PTS	TAY
1976	Cin	14(RB)	138	625	4.5(77)	3	16	138	8.6(23)	0	—	—	—	—	—	—	—	—	—	—	k	—	18	735
1977	Cin	12(RB)	137	549	4.0(31)	0	28	240	8.6(24)	0	1	1	100.0	18	18.0(18)	1	0	1	3	—	k	—	0	740
1978	Cin	16(RB)	132	484	3.7(30)	0	35	284	8.1(27)	3	3	2	66.7	21	7.0(18)	1	0	—	—	—	k	—	18	691
1979	Cin	16(RB)	140	688	4.9(63)	0	43	417	9.7(52)	2	—	—	—	—	—	—	—	—	—	—	—	—	12	907
1980	Cin	15(7, rb)	85	260	3.1(14)	0	28	196	7.0(19)	0	—	—	—	—	—	—	—	—	—	—	—	—	0	358
1981	†Cin	16(2)	47	163	3.5(23)	3	20	160	8.0(17)	1	—	—	—	—	—	—	—	—	—	—	k	—	24	307
1982	†Cin	9(0)	12	39	3.3(10)	1	22	172	7.8(22)	0	—	—	—	—	—	—	—	—	—	—	—	—	6	135
NFL	7	98(9)	691	2808	4.1(77)	7	192	1607	8.4(52)	6	4	3	75.0	39	9.8(18)	2	0	1	3	—	k	—	78	3872

GRIFFIN, BOB Robert Lloyd, LB-C, 6´3˝/235 lbs; Arkansas; 1952: LA, rnd 2; B2/12/1929 Fort Worth, TX **1953** LARm 2 **1954** LARm 12 (LLB) **1955**†LARm 12 (RLB) **1956** LARm 6 **1957** LARm 12 (C) **1961** SL 5 **NFL** 49 [6 yrs]

GRIFFIN, BOBBIE Bobbie Joel, DB, 6´0˝/180 lbs; Baylor; 1950: NYY, rnd 19; B5/27/1928 Fort Worth, TX **1951** NYY 12 (DB)

GRIFFIN, CORNELIUS Cornelius, DT, 6´3˝/300 lbs; Alabama; 2000: NYG, rnd 2; B12/3/1976 Brundidge, AL **2000**†NYG 15 (0) **2001** NYG 16 (16, LDT) **2002**†NYG 14 (14, LDT) **2003** NYG 15 (15, LDT) **2004** Was 15 (15, RDT) **2005**†Was 13 (12, LDT) **NFL** 88 (72) [6 yrs]

GRIFFIN, COURTNEY Courtney, DB, 5´10˝/180 lbs; Fresno State; B12/19/1966 Madera, CA **1993** LARm 7 (1)

GRIFFIN, DAMON Damon Gilbert, WR, 5´9˝/186 lbs; Oregon; B6/14/1976 Los Angeles, CA

YEAR	TEAM	G (GS, POS)	RUSH	YD	AVG (LG)	TD	REC	YD	AVG (LG)	TD	PASS	COMP	PCT	YD	AVG (LG)	TD	INT	SK	YD	QBR	KPR	OTD	PTS	TAY
1999	Cin	13(0)	—	—	—	—	12	112	9.3(20)	0	—	—	—	—	—	—	—	—	—	—	kp	—	0	207
2000	Cin	8(0)	—	—	—	—	2	25	12.5(16)	0	—	—	—	—	—	—	—	—	—	—	kp	—	0	26
NFL	2	21(0)	—	—	—	—	14	137	9.8(20)	0	—	—	—	—	—	—	—	—	—	—	kp	—	0	233

GRIFFIN, DON Donald Dean, HB-DB, 5´11˝/190 lbs; Illinois; 1944: GB, rnd 14; B10/15/1922 Benton Harbor, MI, D1/17/2005 Aurora, IL

YEAR	TEAM	G (GS, POS)	RUSH	YD	AVG (LG)	TD	REC	YD	AVG (LG)	TD	PASS	COMP	PCT	YD	AVG (LG)	TD	INT	SK	YD	QBR	KPR	OTD	PTS	TAY
1946	ChiR-A	13(4)	28	13	0.5	0	5	28	5.6	0	1	0	0.0	0	0.0	0	1	—	—	—	ki	—	0	2

GRIFFIN, DON Donald Frederick, DB, 6´0˝/176 lbs; Middle Tennessee State; 1986: SF, rnd 6; B3/17/1964 Pelham, GA **[I]** **1986**†SF 16 (15, RCB) **1987**†SF☆12 (10, RCB) **1988**†SF 10 (6, rcb) **1989**†SF☆16 (16, RCB) **1990**†SF☆16 (16, RCB) **1991** SF 16 (16, RCB) **1992**†SF 16 (16, RCB) **1993**†SF 12 (12, RCB) **1994**†Cle 15 (15, RCB) **1995** Cle 16 (16, RCB) **1996**†Phi 16 (1) **NFL** 161 (139) [11 yrs]

GRIFFIN, JAMES James Victor, DB, 6´2˝/197 lbs; Middle Tennessee State; 1983: Cin, rnd 7; B9/7/1961 Camilla, GA **1983** Cin 16 (0) **1984** Cin 16 (0) **1985** Cin 16 (11, FS) **1986** Det 16 (0). **1987** Det 12 (12, SS) **1988** Det 16 (6, fs) **1989** Det 16 (1) **NFL** 108 (30) [7 yrs]

GRIFFIN, JEFF Jeffrey Earl, DB, 6´0˝/185 lbs; Utah; 1981: SL, rnd 3; B7/19/1958 Carson, CA **1981** SL 16 (9, LCB) **1982**†SL 9 (8, LCB) **1983** SL 3 (3) **1984** SL 8 (1) **1985** SL 12 (0) **1987** Phi 2 (2) **NFL** 50 (23) [6 yrs]

GRIFFIN, JIM James Bauman, DE, 6´3˝/265 lbs; Grambling State; 1964: SF, rnd 15; B2/8/1942 Lake Charles, LA **1966** SD-A 14 **1967** SD-A 14 **1968** Cin-A 14 (LDE) **NFL** 42 [3 yrs]

GRIFFIN, JOHN John Watson, DB, 6´1˝/190 lbs; Memphis; 1963: LA, rnd 4/Den, rnd 8; B11/2/1939 Nashville, TN **1963** LARm 10 **1964** Den-A 7 (rcb) **1965** Den-A 14 (ls) **1966** Den-A 5 **NFL** 36 [4 yrs]

GRIFFIN, KEITH Keith B., RB, 5´8˝/185 lbs; Miami (FL); 1984: Was, rnd 10; B10/26/1961 Columbus, OH

YEAR	TEAM	G (GS, POS)	RUSH	YD	AVG (LG)	TD	REC	YD	AVG (LG)	TD	PASS	COMP	PCT	YD	AVG (LG)	TD	INT	SK	YD	QBR	KPR	OTD	PTS	TAY
1984	†Was	16(2)	97	408	4.2(31)	0	8	43	5.4(8)	0	—	—	—	—	—	—	—	—	—	—	k	—	0	459
1985	Was	16(0)	102	473	4.6(66)	3	37	285	7.7(28)	0	—	—	—	—	—	—	—	—	—	—	k	—	18	683
1986	†Was	16(1)	62	197	3.2(12)	0	11	110	10.0(28)	0	—	—	—	—	—	—	—	—	—	—	k	—	0	288
1987	†Was	9(2)	62	242	3.9(13)	0	3	13	4.3(6)	1	—	—	—	—	—	—	—	—	—	—	k	—	6	357
1988	Was	8(0)	6	23	3.8(9)	0	2	9	4.5(5)	1	—	—	—	—	—	—	—	—	—	—	k	—	6	33
NFL	5	65(5)	329	1343	4.1(66)	3	61	460	7.5(28)	2	—	—	—	—	—	—	—	—	—	—	k	—	30	1818

GRIFFIN, KRIS Kris, LB, 6´3˝/232 lbs; Indiana (PA); B5/27/1981 Rochester, PA **2005** KC 8 (0)

GRIFFIN, LARRY Larry Anthony, DB, 6´0˝/197 lbs; North Carolina; 1986: Hou, rnd 8; B1/11/1963 Chesapeake, VA **1986** Hou 3 (0) **1987** Pit 7 (3) **1988** Pit 15 (3) **1989**†Pit 16 (1) **1990** Pit 16 (3) **1991** Pit 6 (0) **1992**†Pit 14 (2) **1993**†Pit 12 (0) **NFL** 89 (12) [8 yrs]

GRIFFIN, LEONARD Leonard James, DE-NT, 6´4˝/268 lbs; Grambling State; 1986: KC, rnd 3; B9/22/1962 Lake Providence, LA **1986**†KC 9 (0) **1987** KC 12 (2) **1988** KC 15 (9, LDE) **1989** KC 16 (11, RDE) **1990**†KC 16 (2) **1991**†KC 16 (2) **1992**†KC 15 (10, RDE) **1993** KC 4 (1) **NFL** 103 (37) [8 yrs]

GRIFFIN, QUENTIN Quentin LaVell, RB, 5´7˝/195 lbs; Oklahoma; 2003: Den, rnd 4; B1/12/1981 Houston, TX

YEAR	TEAM	G (GS, POS)	RUSH	YD	AVG (LG)	TD	REC	YD	AVG (LG)	TD	PASS	COMP	PCT	YD	AVG (LG)	TD	INT	SK	YD	QBR	KPR	OTD	PTS	TAY
2003	†Den	10(1)	94	345	3.7(23)	0	8	61	7.6(24)	0	—	—	—	—	—	—	—	—	—	—	—	—	0	376
2004	Den	6(4)	85	311	3.7(47)	2	10	68	6.8(22)	1	—	—	—	—	—	—	—	—	—	—	k	—	18	362
NFL	2	16(5)	179	656	3.7(47)	2	18	129	7.2(24)	1	—	—	—	—	—	—	—	—	—	—	k	—	18	738

GRIFFIN, RAY Raymond Eric, DB, 5´10˝/186 lbs; Ohio State; 1978: Cin, rnd 2; B6/29/1956 Columbus, OH **1978** Cin 15 **1979** Cin 12 **1980** Cin 16 (11, LCB) **1981**†Cin 8 (2) **1982**†Cin 9 (3) **1983** Cin 16 (0) **1984** Cin 12 (2) **NFL** 88 (18) [7 yrs]

GRIFFIN, STEPHEN Stephen Giovanni, RB, 5´10˝/205 lbs; Tennessee State; B8/14/1964 **1987** KC 1 (0)

GRIFFIN, STEVE Steve Broadus, RB, 5´10˝/185 lbs; Clemson; B12/17/1963 Charlotte, NC

YEAR	TEAM	G (GS, POS)	RUSH	YD	AVG (LG)	TD	REC	YD	AVG (LG)	TD	PASS	COMP	PCT	YD	AVG (LG)	TD	INT	SK	YD	QBR	KPR	OTD	PTS	TAY
1987	Atl	4(0)	1	-2	-2.0(-2)	0	—	—	—	—	—	—	—	—	—	—	—	—	—	—	k	—	0	4

GRIFFIN, STEVE Steven Leroy, WR, 5´11˝/198 lbs; Purdue; 1986: Atl, rnd 12; B12/24/1964 Miami, FL **1987** Atl 2 (0)

GRIFFIN, WADE Wade Hampton, T, 6´5˝/260 lbs; Mississippi; B8/7/1954 Winona, MS **1977**†Bal 14 **1978** Bal 16 (16, LT) **1979** Bal 16 (16, LT) **1980** Bal 16 (16, LT) **1981** Bal 15 (15, LT) **NFL** 77 (63) [5 yrs]

GRIFFING, GLYNN Wilbur Glynn, QB, 6´1˝/200 lbs; Mississippi; 1962: NYG, rnd 4/Hou, rnd 14; B12/1/1940 Bentonia, MA

YEAR	TEAM	G (GS, POS)	RUSH	YD	AVG (LG)	TD	REC	YD	AVG (LG)	TD	PASS	COMP	PCT	YD	AVG (LG)	TD	INT	SK	YD	QBR	KPR	OTD	PTS	TAY
1963	†NYG	13	5	20	4.0(10)	0	—	—	—	—	40	16	40.0	306	7.7(64)	3	4	4	39	—	—	—	0	28

GRIFFITH, FORREST Forrest Martin, HB, 5´11˝/190 lbs; Kansas; 1950: NYG, rnd 5; B2/15/1928 Lee's Summit, MO

YEAR	TEAM	G (GS, POS)	RUSH	YD	AVG (LG)	TD	REC	YD	AVG (LG)	TD	PASS	COMP	PCT	YD	AVG (LG)	TD	INT	SK	YD	QBR	KPR	OTD	PTS	TAY
1950	NYG	6	45	162	3.6(39)	2	1	26	26.0(26)	0	—	—	—	—	—	—	—	—	—	—	—	—	12	195
1951	NYG	10(LH)	54	115	2.1(27)	0	2	19	9.5(22)	0	—	—	—	—	—	—	—	—	—	—	k	—	0	123
NFL	2	16	99	277	2.8(39)	2	3	45	15.0(26)	0	—	—	—	—	—	—	—	—	—	—	k	—	12	318

GRIFFITH, HOMER Homer Oliver, TB, 5´11˝/165 lbs; USC; B7/24/1912 Los Angeles, CA, D1/31/1990 Tarzana, CA

YEAR	TEAM	G (GS, POS)	RUSH	YD	AVG (LG)	TD	REC	YD	AVG (LG)	TD	PASS	COMP	PCT	YD	AVG (LG)	TD	INT	SK	YD	QBR	KPR	OTD	PTS	TAY
1934	ChiC	9(6, TB)	57	66	1.2	0	—	—	—	—	29	8	27.6	51	1.8	0	3	—	—	—	—	2	12	-19

GRIFFITH, HOWARD Howard Thomas, RB, 6´0˝/230 lbs; Illinois; 1991: Ind, rnd 9; B11/17/1967 Chicago, IL

YEAR	TEAM	G (GS, POS)	RUSH	YD	AVG (LG)	TD	REC	YD	AVG (LG)	TD	PASS	COMP	PCT	YD	AVG (LG)	TD	INT	SK	YD	QBR	KPR	OTD	PTS	TAY
1993	LARm	15(0)	—	—	—	—	—	—	—	—	—	—	—	—	—	—	—	—	—	—	k	—	0	49
1994	LARm	16(10, FB)	9	30	3.3(7)	0	16	113	7.1(13)	1	—	—	—	—	—	—	—	—	—	—	k	—	6	97
1995	Car	15(7, fb)	65	197	3.0(15)	1	11	63	5.7(15)	1	—	—	—	—	—	—	—	—	—	—	—	—	12	244
1996	†Car	16(14, FB)	12	7	0.6(3)	1	27	223	8.3(21)	1	—	—	—	—	—	—	—	—	—	—	—	—	12	134
1997	†Den	15(13, FB)	9	34	3.8(9)	0	11	55	5.0(20)	0	—	—	—	—	—	—	—	—	—	—	—	—	0	62
1998	†Den	14(13, FB)	4	13	3.3(16)	0	15	97	6.5(15)	3	—	—	—	—	—	—	—	—	—	—	—	—	18	77
1999	Den	16(16, FB)	17	66	3.9(13)	1	26	192	7.4(20)	1	—	—	—	—	—	—	—	—	—	—	—	—	12	177
2000	†Den	14(14, FB)	5	4	0.8(3)	0	16	101	6.3(16)	2	—	—	—	—	—	—	—	—	—	—	—	—	12	65
NFL	8	121(87)	121	351	2.9(16)	3	122	844	6.9(21)	9	—	—	—	—	—	—	—	—	—	—	k	—	72	902

GRIFFITH, JUSTIN Justin Montrel, FB, 5´11˝/232 lbs; Mississippi State; 2003: Atl, rnd 4; B4/13/1981 Magee, MS

YEAR	TEAM	G (GS, POS)	RUSH	YD	AVG (LG)	TD	REC	YD	AVG (LG)	TD	PASS	COMP	PCT	YD	AVG (LG)	TD	INT	SK	YD	QBR	KPR	OTD	PTS	TAY
2003	Atl	16(11, FB)	38	168	4.4(15)	0	21	122	5.8(24)	2	—	—	—	—	—	—	—	—	—	—	—	—	12	239
2004	Atl	12(11, FB)	9	39	4.3(10)	0	22	220	10.0(62)	1	—	—	—	—	—	—	—	—	—	—	k	—	6	170
2005	Atl	16(15, FB)	15	65	4.3(19)	0	21	111	5.3(17)	3	—	—	—	—	—	—	—	—	—	—	k	—	18	165
NFL	3	44(37)	62	272	4.4(19)	0	64	453	7.1(62)	6	—	—	—	—	—	—	—	—	—	—	k	—	36	574

GRIFFITH, RICH Richard Pope, TE, 6´5˝/262 lbs; Arizona; 1993: NE, rnd 5; B7/31/1969 Batesville, AR **1993** NE 3 (0) **1997**†Jax 16 (1) **1998** Jax 7 (0) **1999**†Jax 16 (0) **2000** Jax 16 (1)

YEAR	TEAM	G (GS, POS)	RUSH	YD	AVG (LG)	TD	REC	YD	AVG (LG)	TD	PASS	COMP	PCT	YD	AVG (LG)	TD	INT	SK	YD	QBR	KPR	OTD	PTS	TAY
1995	Jax	16(15, TE)	—	—	—	—	16	243	15.2(39)	0	—	—	—	—	—	—	—	—	—	—	k	—	0	116
1996	†Jax	16(2)	—	—	—	—	5	53	10.6(18)	0	—	—	—	—	—	—	—	—	—	—	k	—	0	21
NFL	7	90(19)	—	—	—	—	21	296	14.1(39)	0	—	—	—	—	—	—	—	—	—	—	k	—	0	136

YEAR	TEAM	G (GS, POS)	RUSH	YD	AVG(LG)	TD	REC	YD	AVG(LG)	TD	PASS	COMP	PCT	YD	AVG(LG)	TD	INT	SK	YD	QBR	KPR	OTD	PTS	TAY

GRIFFITH, ROBERT   Robert Otis, DB, 5´11˝/197 lbs; San Diego State; B11/30/1970 Lanham, MD [I]   **1994**†Min 15 (0)   **1995** Min 16 (1)   **1996**†Min 14 (14, SS)
1997†Min 16 (16, SS)   **1998**†Min☆16 (16, SS)   **1999**†Min☆16 (16, SS)   **2000**†Min◇16 (16, SS)   **2001** Min 10 (9, SS)   **2002**†Cle 12 (12, SS)   **2003** Cle 16 (16, SS)
2004 Cle 16 (16, SS)   **2005** Arz 16 (16, FS)   **NFL** 179 (148) [12 yrs]

GRIFFITH, RUSSELL   Russell M., P, 5´11˝/175 lbs; Utah State; Weber State; B2/5/1964

| 1987 | Sea | 2(0) | 1 | 0 | 0.0(0) | 0 | — | — | — | — | — | — | — | — | — | — | — | — | — | P | — | 0 | 0 |

GRIFFITHS, RED   Percy Wilfred, G, 5´8˝/190 lbs; Bloomsburg; Penn State; B3/30/1893 Taylor, PA, D6/12/1983 Clearwater, FL   **1921** Can 1 (1)

GRIGAS, JOHN   John Joseph, FB-HB, 6´0˝/204 lbs; Holy Cross; 1943: ChiC, rnd 2; B8/19/1920 Chelsea, MA, D5/19/2000 Shrewsbury, MA

1943	ChiC	10(7, FB)	105	333	3.2(28)	3	19	225	11.8(39)	0	19	4	21.1	98	5.2(50)	0	4	—	—	—	kpi	—	18	397
1944	C-P☆	9(9, FB)	185	610	3.3(29)	3	2	33	16.5(36)	0	131	50	38.2	690	5.3(72)	6	21	—	—	31.5	Pkpi	—	18	330
1945	Bos	10(8, LH)	64	160	2.5(45)	2	5	59	11.8(29)	0	14	5	35.7	85	6.1(30)	0	1	—	—	—	ki	—	12	215
1946	Bos	11(9, FB)	84	426	5.1(59)	2	3	61	20.3(44)	1	2	1	50.0	16	8.0(16)	0	1	—	—	—	Pki	—	18	438
1947	Bos	9(2)	27	52	1.9(13)	0	1	1	1.0(1)	0	—	—	—	—	—	—	—	—	—	—	k	—	0	57
NFL	5	49(35)	465	1581	3.4(59)	10	30	379	12.6(44)	1	166	60	36.1	889	5.4(72)	6	27	—	—	27.0	Pkpi	—	66	1435

GRIGG, TEX   Cecil Burkett, B, 5´11˝/191 lbs; Austin; Texas; B2/15/1891 Nashville, TN, D9/5/1968 Houston, TX [KC]   **1920** Can 12 (5, BB)   **1921** Can 7 (7, TB), 6   **1922** Can 4 (2)
1923 Can☆12 (10, WB), 24   **1924** Roc 1 (1)   **1925** Roc 7 (7, BB), 2   **1926** NYG 12 (10, BB)   **1927** Fra 1 (1)   **NFL** 56 (43), 32 [8 yrs]

GRIGG, CHUBBY   Forrest Porter, DT-T, 6´2˝/294 lbs; Tulsa; B1/10/1926 El Dorado, AR, D10/10/1983 Ore City, TX [K]   **1946** Buf-A 8 (0)   **1947** ChiR-A 13 (7, lt)   **1948**†Cle-A 14 (0)

| 1949 | †Cle-A | 12(0) | — | — | — | — | 0 | 2 | (2) | 0 | — | — | — | — | — | — | — | — | — | — | — | — | 0 | 1 |
| AAFC | 4 | 47(7) | — | — | — | — | 0 | 2 | (2) | 0 | — | — | — | — | — | — | — | — | — | — | — | — | 0 | 1 |

1950†Cle 11 (LDT)   **1951**†Cle 11 (LDT)   **1952** DalT 10 (ldt)   **NFL** 47 (7) [4 yrs]

GRIGGS, ANTHONY   Anthony G., LB, 6´3˝/227 lbs; Villanova; Ohio State; 1982: Phi, rnd 4; B2/12/1960 Lawton, OK   **1982** Phi 9 (0)   **1983** Phi 16 (16, RILB)   **1984** Phi 16 (16, RILB)
1985 Phi 16 (16, RILB)   **1986**†Cle 16 (15, RILB)   **1987**†Cle 12 (2)   **1988** Cle 5 (0)   **NFL** 90 (65) [7 yrs]

GRIGGS, BILLY   William Edward, TE, 6´3˝/230 lbs; Virginia; 1984: NYJ, rnd 8; B8/4/1962 Camden, NJ

1985	†NYJ	16(3)	—	—	—	—	—	—	—	—	—	—	—	—	—	—	—	—	—	—	—	0	—
1986	†NYJ	16(1)	—	—	—	—	—	—	—	—	—	—	—	—	—	—	—	—	—	—	—	0	—
1987	NYJ	12(1)	—	—	—	—	2	17	8.5(13)	1	—	—	—	—	—	—	—	—	—	k	—	6	12
1988	NYJ	15(8, te)	—	—	—	—	14	133	9.5(21)	0	—	—	—	—	—	—	—	—	—	—	—	0	67
1989	NYJ	5(3)	—	—	—	—	9	112	12.4(23)	0	—	—	—	—	—	—	—	—	—	—	—	0	56
NFL	5	64(16)	—	—	—	—	25	262	10.5(23)	1	—	—	—	—	—	—	—	—	—	k	—	6	134

GRIGGS, DAVID   David Wesley, LB-DE, 6´3˝/245 lbs; Virginia; 1989: NO, rnd 7; B2/5/1967 Camden, NJ, D6/19/1995 Davie, FL   **1989** Mia 5 (0)   **1990**†Mia 16 (16, LOLB)
1991 Mia 16 (16, LOLB)   **1992**†Mia 16 (13, LDE/lolb)   **1993** Mia 9 (0)   **1994**†SD 16 (15, LLB)   **NFL** 78 (60) [6 yrs]

GRIGGS, HAL   Haldane Alfred, WB-HB, 5´10˝/170 lbs; Butler; B11/27/1900 Toronto, Canada, D12/29/1987 Orange County, CA   **1926** Akr 5 (5, WB), 12

GRIGGS, PERRY   Perry, WR, 5´10˝/183 lbs; Troy State; 1977: NYJ, rnd 5; B9/17/1954 Lafayette, AL   **1977** Bal 1

GRIGONIS, FRANK   Frank John, FB, 5´10˝/190 lbs; Tennessee-Chattanooga; B10/10/1916 Calumet City, IL, D9/2/2003

| 1942 | Det | 10(2) | 37 | 131 | 3.5(12) | 1 | 1 | 17 | 17.0(17) | 0 | — | — | — | — | — | — | — | — | — | i | — | 6 | 171 |

GRIGSBY, BOOMER   James, LB, 6´1˝/242 lbs; Illinois State; 2005: KC, rnd 5; B11/15/1981 Canton, IL   **2005** KC 16 (0)

GRIM, BOB   Robert Lee, WR, 6´0˝/200 lbs; Oregon State; 1967: Min, rnd 2; B5/8/1945 Oakland, CA

1967	Min	13	1	20	20.0(20)	0	6	108	18.0(26)	1	—	—	—	—	—	—	—	—	—	kp	—	6	218
1968	†Min	2	—	—	—	—	—	—	—	—	—	—	—	—	—	—	—	—	—	—	—	0	—
1969	†Min	14	—	—	—	—	10	155	15.5(44)	1	—	—	—	—	—	—	—	—	—	p	—	6	75
1970	†Min	14(9, WR)	—	—	—	—	23	287	12.5(35)	0	—	—	—	—	—	—	—	—	—	p	—	0	165
1971	†Min★	14(14, WR)	6	127	21.2(54)	0	45	691	15.4(55)	7	1	0	0.0	0	0	0	0	—	—	kp	—	42	524
1972	NYG	13	—	—	—	—	5	67	13.4(17)	1	—	—	—	—	—	—	—	—	—	p	—	6	14
1973	NYG	14(WR)	1	-10	-10.0(-10)	0	37	593	16.0(48)	2	—	—	—	—	—	—	—	—	—	—	—	12	297
1974	NYG	14(WR)	—	—	—	—	28	466	16.6(53)	2	—	—	—	—	—	—	—	—	—	—	—	12	243
1975	ChiB	14(12, WR)	—	—	—	—	28	374	13.4(57)	2	1	0	0.0	0	0	0	0	—	—	—	—	12	197
1976	†Min	8	—	—	—	—	9	108	12.0(27)	0	—	—	—	—	—	—	—	—	—	—	—	0	54
1977	†Min	14	—	—	—	—	3	65	21.7(23)	0	—	—	—	—	—	—	—	—	—	kp	—	0	36
NFL	11	134(35)	8	137	17.1(54)	0	194	2914	15.0(57)	16	2	0	0.0	0	0	0	0	—	—	kp	—	96	1820

GRIMES, BILLY   William Joseph, HB, 6´1˝/195 lbs; Oklahoma State; 1949: LAD-A, rnd 5/ChiB, rnd 2; B7/27/1927 County Line, OK, D3/26/2005 Oklahoma City, OK [R]

1949	LAD-A	12(7, RH)	83	429	5.2(51)	4	13	189	14.5	2	3	3	100.0	105	35.0	1	0	—	—	—	kp	—	36	844
1950	GB★	12(RH)	84	480	5.7(73)	5	17	261	15.4(96)	1	—	—	—	—	—	—	—	—	—	kp	2	48	**1306**
1951	GB◇	12(RH)	44	123	2.8(18)	1	15	170	11.3(38)	1	—	—	—	—	—	—	—	—	—	kp	—	12	480
1952	GB	12	17	59	3.5(31)	0	—	—	—	—	—	—	—	—	—	—	—	—	—	kp	—	0	300
NFL	3	36	145	662	4.6(73)	6	32	431	13.5(96)	2	—	—	—	—	—	—	—	—	—	kp	2	60	2086

GRIMES, GEORGE   George Stanley, DB-WB, 5´11˝/190 lbs; North Carolina; Virginia; 1948: LARm, rnd 6/Buf-A, rnd 13; B7/3/1922 Jewell Ridge, VA, D4/1971, [K]

| 1948 | Det | 9(2) | 1 | 8 | 8.0(8) | 0 | 1 | 17 | 17.0(17) | 0 | — | — | — | — | — | — | — | — | — | KPpi | — | 6 | 42 |

GRIMES, PHIL   Philip, DE, 6´4˝/230 lbs; Central Missouri State; B2/26/1965 Montgomery, AL   **1987** LARd 2 (0)

GRIMES, RANDY   Randall Collins, C-G, 6´4˝/270 lbs; Baylor; 1983: TB, rnd 2; B7/20/1960 Tyler, TX   **1983** TB 15 (10, LG/c)   **1984** TB 10 (3)   **1985** TB 16 (16, C)   **1986** TB 16 (16, C)
1987 TB 12 (12, C)   **1988** TB 16 (16, C)   **1989** TB 16 (16, C)   **1990** TB 16 (15, C)   **1992** TB 2 (0)   **NFL** 118 (104) [9 yrs]

GRIMES, REGGIE   Reginald Dewayne, DE, 6´4˝/290 lbs; Alabama; B11/7/1976 Nashville, TN   **2000** NE 8 (0)

GRIMM, DAN   Daniel Jay, G, 6´3˝/245 lbs; Colorado; 1963: GB, rnd 5/Den, rnd 20; B2/7/1941 Perry, IA   **1963** GB 14   **1964** GB 14 (RG)   **1965**†GB 14   **1966** Atl 14 (RG)   **1967** Atl 2
1968 Atl 14 (RG)   **1969** Bal 2   **1969** Was 6   **NFL** 80 [7 yrs]

GRIMM, RUSS   Russell Scott, G-C, 6´3˝/273 lbs; Pittsburgh; 1981: Was, rnd 3; B5/2/1959 Scottsdale, PA   **1981** Was 14 (13, LG)   **1982**†Was☆9 (9, LG)   **1983**†Was★16 (16, LG)
1984†Was★16 (16, LG)   **1985** Was★16 (16, LG)   **1986**†Was★15 (14, LG)   **1987**†Was 6 (5, C)   **1988** Was 5 (4)   **1989** Was 12 (9, LG)   **1990**†Was 15 (11, LG)   **1991**†Was 16 (1)
NFL 140 (114) [11 yrs]

GRIMSLEY, ED   Edward Paul, LB, 6´0˝/235 lbs; Akron; B3/22/1963 Canton, OH   **1987** Ind 5 (3)

GRIMSLEY, JOHN   John Glenn, LB, 6´2˝/235 lbs; Kentucky; 1984: Hou, rnd 6; B2/25/1962 Canton, OH   **1984** Hou 16 (0)   **1985** Hou 15 (1)   **1986** Hou 16 (10, LILB)
1987 Hou 12 (12, LILB)   **1988**†Hou☆16 (16, LILB)   **1989**†Hou☆16 (16, LILB)   **1990** Hou 15 (13, LLB)   **1992** Mia 14 (11, LILB)   **1993** Mia 13 (9, LLB)   **NFL** 133 (88) [9 yrs]

GROCE, CLIF   Clifton Allen, RB, 5´11˝/245 lbs; Texas A&M; B7/30/1972 College Station, TX

1995	†Ind	1(0)	—	—	—	—	—	—	—	—	—	—	—	—	—	—	—	—	—	—	—	0	—
1996	†Ind	15(8, FB)	46	184	4.0(24)	0	13	106	8.2(24)	0	—	—	—	—	—	—	—	—	—	k	—	0	240
1997	Ind	7(0)	10	66	6.6(29)	0	—	—	—	—	—	—	—	—	—	—	—	—	—	k	—	0	66
1999	Cin	16(15, FB)	8	22	2.8(8)	1	25	154	6.2(14)	0	—	—	—	—	—	—	—	—	—	—	—	6	109
2000	Cin	8(6, fb)	3	4	1.3(5)	0	11	45	4.1(14)	0	—	—	—	—	—	—	—	—	—	—	—	0	27
NFL	5	47(29)	67	276	4.1(29)	1	49	305	6.2(24)	0	—	—	—	—	—	—	—	—	—	k	—	6	442

GROCE, DeJUAN   DeJuan Anthony, DB, 5´10˝/192 lbs; Nebraska; 2003: SL, rnd 4; B2/17/1980 Garfield Heights, OH   **2003** SL 16 (1)   **2004**†SL 11 (4)   **2005** SL 15 (15, LCB)
NFL 42 (20) [3 yrs]

GROCE, RON   Ronald, RB, 6´2˝/211 lbs; Macalester; 1976: Min, rnd 15; B7/1/1954 Minneapolis, MN

| 1976 | †Min | 4 | 3 | 18 | 6.0(13) | 0 | — | — | — | — | — | — | — | — | — | — | — | — | — | — | — | 0 | 18 |

GROGAN, STEVE   Steven James, QB, 6´4˝/210 lbs; Kansas State; 1975: NE, rnd 5; B7/24/1953 San Antonio, TX

1975	NE	13(7, QB)	30	110	3.7(14)	3	—	—	—	—	274	139	50.7	1976	7.2(62)	11	18	22	207	60.4	—	—	18	463
1976	†NE	14(14, QB)	60	397	6.6(41)	12	—	—	—	—	302	145	48.0	1903	6.3(58)	18	20	18	155	60.2	—	1	78	759
1977	NE	14(14, QB)	61	324	5.3(41)	1	—	—	—	—	305	160	52.5	2162	7.1(68)	17	21	14	155	65.2	—	—	6	660
1978	†NE	16(16, QB)	81	539	**6.7(31)**	5	—	—	—	—	362	181	50.0	2824	7.8(75)	15	23	21	184	63.6	—	—	30	1156

YEAR	TEAM	G (GS, POS)	RUSH	YD	AVG (LG)	TD	REC	YD	AVG (LG)	TD	PASS	COMP	PCT	YD	AVG (LG)	TD	INT	SK	YD	QBR	KPR	OTD	PTS	TAY
1979	NE	16 (16, QB)	64	368	5.8 (26)	2	—	—	—	—	423	206	48.7	3286	7.8 (63)	**28**	20	45	341	77.4	—	—	12	1371
1980	NE	12 (12, QB)	30	112	3.7 (19)	1	—	—	—	—	306	175	57.2	2475	**8.1 (71)**	18	22	17	138	73.1	—	—	6	570
1981	NE	8 (7, qb)	12	49	4.1 (24)	2	2	27	13.5 (16)	0	216	117	54.2	1859	**8.6 (76)**	7	16	24	165	—	—	—	12	407
1982	†NE	6 (6, QB)	9	42	4.7 (19)	1	—	—	—	—	122	66	54.1	930	7.6 (62)	7	4	8	48	—	—	—	6	392
1983	NE	12 (12, QB)	23	108	4.7 (17)	2	1	-8	-8.0 (-8)	0	303	168	55.4	2411	8.0 (76)	15	12	29	195	81.4	—	—	12	925
1984	NE	3 (3)	7	12	1.7 (1)	0	—	—	—	—	68	32	47.1	444	6.5 (65)	3	6	7	45	—	—	—	0	9
1985	†NE	7 (6, qb)	20	29	1.5 (12)	2	—	—	—	—	156	85	54.5	1311	8.4 (56)	7	5	11	86	—	—	—	12	540
1986	NE	4 (2)	9	23	2.6 (10)	1	—	—	—	—	102	62	60.8	976	9.6 (69)	9	2	4	31	—	—	—	6	486
1987	NE	7 (6, QB)	20	37	1.9 (8)	2	—	—	—	—	161	93	57.8	1183	7.3 (40)	10	9	7	55	—	—	—	12	339
1988	NE	6 (4)	6	12	2.0 (6)	1	—	—	—	—	140	67	47.9	834	6.0 (41)	4	13	8	77	—	—	—	6	-61
1989	NE	7 (6, QB)	9	19	2.1 (7)	0	—	—	—	—	261	133	51.0	1697	6.5 (55)	9	14	8	64	60.8	—	—	0	353
1990	NE	4 (4)	4	-5	-1.3 (0)	0	—	—	—	—	92	50	54.3	615	6.7 (48)	4	3	9	68	—	—	—	0	203
NFL	16	149 (135)	445	2176	4.9 (41)	35	3	19	6.3 (16)	0	3593	1879	52.3	26886	7.5 (76)	182	208	252	2014	69.6	—	1	216	8569

GROMAN, BILL William Frederick, WR-FL, 6´0˝/194 lbs; Heidelberg; B7/17/1936 Tiffin, OH

YEAR	TEAM	G (GS, POS)	RUSH	YD	AVG (LG)	TD	REC	YD	AVG (LG)	TD	PASS	COMP	PCT	YD	AVG (LG)	TD	INT	SK	YD	QBR	KPR	OTD	PTS	TAY
1960	†Hou-A☆	14 (WR)	—	—	—	—	72	**1473**	**20.5 (92)**	12	1	1	100.0	3	3.0 (3)	1	0	—	—	—	—	—	72	803
1961	†Hou-A☆	14 (WR)	1	2	2.0 (2)	1	50	1175	**23.5 (80)**	**17**	1	0	0.0	0	0.0	0	0	—	—	—	—	—	108	685
1962	†Hou-A	14	—	—	—	—	21	328	15.6 (54)	3	—	—	—	—	—	—	—	—	—	—	—	—	18	179
1963	Den-A	14 (fl)	—	—	—	—	27	437	16.2 (74)	3	—	—	—	—	—	—	—	—	—	—	—	—	18	243
1964	Buf-A	5	—	—	—	—	4	68	17.0 (22)	1	—	—	—	—	—	—	—	—	—	—	—	—	6	39
1965	†Buf-A	5	—	—	—	—	—	—	—	—	—	—	—	—	—	—	—	—	—	—	—	—	—	—
NFL	6	66	1	2	2.0 (2)	1	174	3481	20.0 (92)	36	2	1	50.0	3	1.5 (3)	1	0	—	—	—	—	—	222	1948

GROOM, ANDY Andy, P, 6´0˝/196 lbs; Ohio State; B9/10/1979 **2005** Was 2 (0)

GROOM, JERRY Jerome Paul, MG-DT-C-LB, 6´3˝/236 lbs; Notre Dame; 1951: ChiC, rnd 1; B8/15/1929 Des Moines, IA **1951** ChiC 12 (MG) **1952** ChiC 12 (MG) **1953** ChiC 12 (MG) **1954** ChiC✧11 (RDT) **1955** ChiC 11 (RDT) **NFL** 58 [5 yrs]

GROOMES, MEL Melvin Harold, HB, 6´0˝/178 lbs; Indiana; B3/6/1927 Trenton, NJ

YEAR	TEAM	G (GS, POS)	RUSH	YD	AVG (LG)	TD	REC	YD	AVG (LG)	TD	PASS	COMP	PCT	YD	AVG (LG)	TD	INT	SK	YD	QBR	KPR	OTD	PTS	TAY
1948	Det	6 (1)	2	1	0.5 (7)	0	2	18	9.0 (10)	0	—	—	—	—	—	—	—	—	—	—	—	—	0	10
1949	Det	3 (0)	1	1	1.0 (1)	0	3	33	11.0 (20)	1	—	—	—	—	—	—	—	—	—	—	i	—	6	43
NFL	2	9 (1)	3	2	0.7 (7)	0	5	51	10.2 (20)	1	—	—	—	—	—	—	—	—	—	—	i	—	6	53

GROOMS, ELOIS Elois, DE-DT, 6´4˝/249 lbs; Tennessee Tech; 1975: NO, rnd 3; B5/20/1953 Tompkinsville, KY **1975** NO 10 **1976** NO 11 (1) **1978** NO 16 (16, LDE) **1979** NO 16 (16, LDE) **1980** NO 16 (16, LDE) **1981** NO 16 (16, RDE) **1982**†SL 9 (9, LDE) **1983** SL 11 (11, LDT) **1984** SL 11 (6, rdt) **1985** SL 5 (0) **1987** Phi 3 (3)

YEAR	TEAM	G (GS, POS)	RUSH	YD	AVG (LG)	TD	REC	YD	AVG (LG)	TD	PASS	COMP	PCT	YD	AVG (LG)	TD	INT	SK	YD	QBR	KPR	OTD	PTS	TAY
1977	NO	14 (14, LDE)	—	—	—	—	1	3	3.0 (3)	1	—	—	—	—	—	—	—	—	—	—	—	—	6	7
NFL	12	138 (108)	—	—	—	—	1	3	3.0 (3)	1	—	—	—	—	—	—	—	—	—	—	iS	1	14	37

GROOTEGOED, MATT Matt, LB, 5´11˝/215 lbs; USC; B5/6/1982 Huntington Beach, CA **2005** Det 3 (0)

GROS, EARL Earl Roy, FB, 6´3˝/220 lbs; LSU; 1962: GB, rnd 1/Hou, rnd 2; B8/29/1940 Lafourche Parish, LA

YEAR	TEAM	G (GS, POS)	RUSH	YD	AVG (LG)	TD	REC	YD	AVG (LG)	TD	PASS	COMP	PCT	YD	AVG (LG)	TD	INT	SK	YD	QBR	KPR	OTD	PTS	TAY
1962	†GB	14	29	155	5.3 (56)	2	—	—	—	—	—	—	—	—	—	—	—	—	—	—	k	—	12	167
1963	GB	14	48	203	4.2 (19)	2	1	19	19.0 (19)	0	—	—	—	—	—	—	—	—	—	—	k	—	12	408
1964	Phi	13 (FB)	154	748	4.9 (59)	2	29	234	8.1 (29)	0	1	0	0.0	0	0.0	0	0	—	—	—	k	—	12	893
1965	Phi	14 (FB)	145	479	3.3 (33)	7	29	271	9.3 (37)	2	2	1	50.0	63	31.5 (63)	1	0	—	—	—	—	—	54	731
1966	Phi	14 (FB)	102	396	3.9 (26)	7	18	214	11.9 (48)	2	1	0	0.0	0	0.0	0	0	1	5	—	—	—	54	583
1967	Pit	12 (fb)	72	252	3.5 (23)	1	19	175	9.2 (22)	0	—	—	—	—	—	—	—	—	—	—	—	—	6	350
1968	Pit	13 (FB)	151	579	3.8 (44)	3	27	211	7.8 (21)	3	—	—	—	—	—	—	—	—	—	—	—	—	36	730
1969	Pit	13 (FB)	116	343	3.0 (16)	4	17	131	7.7 (20)	3	—	—	—	—	—	—	—	—	—	—	—	—	42	464
1970	NO	1	4	2	0.5 (4)	0	2	0	0.0 (1)	0	—	—	—	—	—	—	—	—	—	—	—	—	0	2
NFL	9	108	821	3157	3.8 (59)	28	142	1255	8.8 (48)	10	4	1	25.0	63	15.8 (63)	1	0	1	5	—	k	—	228	4326

GROSS, AL Alfred Ellis, DB, 6´3˝/191 lbs; Arizona; 1983: Dal, rnd 9; B1/4/1961 Stockton, CA **1983** Cle 16 (0) **1984** Cle 16 (16, SS) **1985**†Cle 16 (16, SS) **1986**†Cle 4 (1) **1987** Cle 6 (5, fs) **NFL** 58 (38) [5 yrs]

GROSS, ANDY Andrew, G, 6´0˝/230 lbs; Auburn; B10/13/1945 Burkam, Austria **1967** NYG 14 **1968** NYG 14 **NFL** 28 [2 yrs]

GROSS, GEORGE George, DT, 6´3˝/270 lbs; Auburn; 1962: SD, rnd 16/SL, rnd 8; B1/26/1941 Wellau, Romania **1963**†SD-A 14 (RDT) **1964**†SD-A 14 (RDT) **1965**†SD-A 14 (LDT) **1966** SD-A 14 (LDT) **1967** SD-A 14 **NFL** 70 [5 yrs]

GROSS, JORDAN Jordan Alan, T, 6´4˝/300 lbs; Utah; 2003: Car, rnd 1; B7/20/1980 Fruitland, ID **2003**†Car 16 (16, RT) **2004** Car 16 (16, LT) **2005**†Car 16 (16, RT) **NFL** 48 (48) [3 yrs]

GROSS, LEE Lee Monroe, C, 6´3˝/237 lbs; Auburn; 1975: NO, rnd 2; B7/29/1953 Montgomery, AL **1975** NO 9 **1976** NO 14 **1977** NO 9 **1979** Bal 16 **NFL** 48 [4 yrs]

GROSSCUP, LEE Clyde Lee Edward, QB, 6´1˝/187 lbs; Washington; Utah; 1959: NYG, rnd 1; B12/27/1936 Santa Monica, CA

YEAR	TEAM	G (GS, POS)	RUSH	YD	AVG (LG)	TD	REC	YD	AVG (LG)	TD	PASS	COMP	PCT	YD	AVG (LG)	TD	INT	SK	YD	QBR	KPR	OTD	PTS	TAY
1960	NYG	4	3	1	0.3 (5)	0	—	—	—	—	25	11	44.0	144	5.8 (26)	1	1	—	—	—	—	—	0	38
1961	NYG	4	2	10	5.0 (10)	0	—	—	—	—	22	5	22.7	87	4.0 (32)	1	3	—	—	—	—	—	0	-62
1962	NYT-A	8	8	62	7.8 (18)	0	—	—	—	—	126	57	45.2	855	6.8 (86)	8	8	—	—	—	—	—	0	210
NFL	3	16	13	73	5.6 (18)	0	—	—	—	—	173	73	42.2	1086	6.3 (86)	10	12	—	—	—	—	—	0	186

GROSSMAN, BURT Burton L., DE, 6´4˝/270 lbs; Pittsburgh; 1989: SD, rnd 1; B4/10/1967 Philadelphia, PA **1989** SD 16 (16, RDE) **1990** SD 15 (15, RDE) **1991** SD 16 (16, RDE) **1992**†SD 15 (14, LDE) **1993** SD 10 (10, LDE) **1994** Phi 14 (2) **NFL** 86 (73) [6 yrs]

GROSSMAN, JACK Jack, B, 6´1˝/193 lbs; Rutgers; B11/1/1910, Poland, D2/6/1983 Hollywood, FL **[K]**

YEAR	TEAM	G (GS, POS)	RUSH	YD	AVG (LG)	TD	REC	YD	AVG (LG)	TD	PASS	COMP	PCT	YD	AVG (LG)	TD	INT	SK	YD	QBR	KPR	OTD	PTS	TAY
1932	Bkn☆	12 (9, FB)	129	323	2.5	2	8	129	16.1	3	32	11	34.4	178	5.6	0	3	—	—	—	—	—	30	392
1934	Bkn	11 (3)	35	115	3.3	0	11	161	14.6	1	8	1	12.5	47	5.9 (47)	1	3	—	—	—	—	1	12	119
1935	Bkn	11 (3)	67	208	3.1	2	4	66	16.5	0	35	9	25.7	149	4.3	0	7	—	—	—	K	—	13	56
NFL	3	34 (15)	231	646	2.8	4	23	356	15.5	4	75	21	28.0	374	5.0 (47)	1	13	—	—	—	K	1	55	566

GROSSMAN, RANDY Curt Randy, TE, 6´1˝/218 lbs; Temple; B9/20/1952 Philadelphia, PA

YEAR	TEAM	G (GS, POS)	RUSH	YD	AVG (LG)	TD	REC	YD	AVG (LG)	TD	PASS	COMP	PCT	YD	AVG (LG)	TD	INT	SK	YD	QBR	KPR	OTD	PTS	TAY
1974	†Pit	14	—	—	—	—	13	164	12.6 (32)	0	—	—	—	—	—	—	—	—	—	—	—	—	0	82
1975	†Pit	14 (1)	—	—	—	—	11	135	12.3 (21)	1	—	—	—	—	—	—	—	—	—	—	—	—	6	73
1976	†Pit	14 (5, te)	—	—	—	—	15	181	12.1 (35)	1	—	—	—	—	—	—	—	—	—	—	—	—	6	96
1977	†Pit	13 (4)	—	—	—	—	5	57	11.4 (20)	0	—	—	—	—	—	—	—	—	—	—	—	—	0	29
1978	†Pit	16 (10, TE)	—	—	—	—	37	448	12.1 (26)	1	—	—	—	—	—	—	—	—	—	—	—	—	6	229
1979	†Pit	16 (8, te)	—	—	—	—	12	217	18.1 (54)	1	—	—	—	—	—	—	—	—	—	—	—	—	6	114
1980	Pit	15 (14, TE)	—	—	—	—	23	293	12.7 (35)	0	—	—	—	—	—	—	—	—	—	—	—	—	0	147
1981	Pit	16 (1)	—	—	—	—	3	19	6.3 (14)	1	—	—	—	—	—	—	—	—	—	—	—	—	6	15
NFL	8	118 (43)	—	—	—	—	119	1514	12.7 (54)	5	—	—	—	—	—	—	—	—	—	—	—	—	30	782

GROSSMAN, REX Rex Daniel, LB-FB, 6´1˝/215 lbs; Indiana; 1948: Bal-A, rnd 29/Phi, rnd 29; B2/5/1924 Huntington, IN, D6/13/1980 Bloomington, IN **[K]**

YEAR	TEAM	G (GS, POS)	RUSH	YD	AVG (LG)	TD	REC	YD	AVG (LG)	TD	PASS	COMP	PCT	YD	AVG (LG)	TD	INT	SK	YD	QBR	KPR	OTD	PTS	TAY
1948	Bal-A	14 (1)	8	-3	-0.4	0	—	—	—	—	—	—	—	—	—	—	—	—	—	—	Ki	—	73	0
1949	Bal-A	11 (0)	—	—	—	—	—	—	—	—	1	0	0.0	0	0.0	0	1	—	—	—	KP	—	37	-40
AAFC	2	25 (1)	8	-3	-0.4	0	—	—	—	—	1	0	0.0	0	0.0	0	1	—	—	—	KPi	—	110	-40
1950	Bal	8	—	—	—	—	1	4	4.0 (4)	0	—	—	—	—	—	—	—	—	—	—	K	—	16	2
1950	Det	4	—	—	—	—	—	—	—	—	—	—	—	—	—	—	—	—	—	—	k	—	0	0
NFL	1	12	—	—	—	—	1	4	4.0 (4)	0	—	—	—	—	—	—	—	—	—	—	Kk	—	16	2

GROSSMAN, REX Rex, QB, 6´1˝/222 lbs; Florida; 2003: Chi, rnd 1; B8/23/1980 Bloomington, IN

YEAR	TEAM	G (GS, POS)	RUSH	YD	AVG (LG)	TD	REC	YD	AVG (LG)	TD	PASS	COMP	PCT	YD	AVG (LG)	TD	INT	SK	YD	QBR	KPR	OTD	PTS	TAY
2003	ChiB	3 (3)	3	-1	-0.3 (0)	0	—	—	—	—	72	38	52.8	437	6.1 (59)	2	1	4	41	—	—	—	0	188
2004	ChiB	3 (3)	11	48	4.4 (8)	1	—	—	—	—	84	47	56.0	607	7.2 (40)	1	3	5	22	—	—	—	6	247
2005	†ChiB	2 (1)	—	—	—	—	—	—	—	—	39	20	51.3	259	6.6 (54)	1	2	1	9	—	—	—	0	55
NFL	3	8 (7)	14	47	3.4 (8)	1	—	—	—	—	195	105	53.8	1303	6.7 (59)	4	6	10	72	—	—	—	6	489

YEAR	TEAM	G (GS, POS)	RUSH	YD	AVG(LG)	TD	REC	YD	AVG(LG)	TD	PASS COMP	PCT	YD	AVG(LG)	TD	INT	SK	YD	QBR	KPR	OTD	PTS	TAY

GROSVENOR, GEORGE George A., TB-HB, 6´0˝/175 lbs; Colorado; B8/4/1910 Jefferson, OK, D9/20/2001 Pueblo, CO

1935	ChiB	11 (3)	55	234	4.3	0	—	—	—	—	15	6	40.0	69	4.6	0	1	—	—	—	—	0	229
1936	ChiB	1 (0)	1	3	3.0(3)	0	—	—	—	—	—	—	—	—	—	—	—	—	—	—	—	0	3
1936	ChiC☆	9 (8, TB)	169	609	3.6	4	1	6	6.0(6)	0	34	12	35.3	173	5.1	0	6	—	—	—	1	30	509
1937	ChiC	11 (7, TB)	143	461	3.2	2	—	—	—	—	50	21	42.0	325	6.5	3	7	—	—	—	—	12	379
NFL	3	32 (18)	368	1307	3.6(3)	6	1	6	6.0(6)	0	99	39	39.4	567	5.7	3	14	—	—	—	1	42	1119

GROTH, JEFF Jeffrey Eugene, WR, 5´10˝/176 lbs; Bowling Green State; 1979: Mia, rnd 8; B7/2/1957 Mankato, MN [R]

1979	Mia	4	—	—	—	—	—	—	—	—	—	—	—	—	—	—	—	—	—	—	—	—	—
1979	†Hou	6	—	—	—	—	1	6	6.0(6)	0	—	—	—	—	—	—	—	—	—	—	k	—	0	9
1980	Hou	16 (0)	—	—	—	—	4	47	11.8(18)	0	—	—	—	—	—	—	—	—	—	—	kp	—	0	55
1981	NO	15 (13, WR)	2	27	13.5(28)	0	20	380	19.0(54)	1	—	—	—	—	—	—	—	—	—	—	kp	—	6	478
1982	NO	9 (9, WR)	1	1	1.0(1)	0	30	383	12.8(39)	1	—	—	—	—	—	—	—	—	—	—	p	—	6	237
1983	NO	16 (14, WR)	1	15	15.0(15)	0	49	585	11.9(42)	1	—	—	—	—	—	—	—	—	—	—	p	—	6	393
1984	NO	16 (13, WR)	—	—	—	—	33	487	14.8(31)	0	—	—	—	—	—	—	—	—	—	—	p	—	0	246
1985	NO	12 (2)	—	—	—	—	15	238	15.9(56)	2	—	—	—	—	—	—	—	—	—	—	p	—	12	124
NFL	7	94 (51)	4	43	10.8(28)	0	152	2126	14.0(56)	5	—	—	—	—	—	—	—	—	—	—	—	—	30	1540

GROTTKAU, BOB Robert Fred, G, 6´4˝/228 lbs; Oregon; 1959: Det, rnd 4; B3/22/1937 San Rafael, CA **1959** Det 12 **1960** Det 5 **1961** Dal 13 **NFL** 30 [3 yrs]

GROVE, JAKE Charles Jacob, C-G, 6´3˝/286 lbs; Virginia Tech; 2004: Oak, rnd 2; B1/22/1980 Johnson City, TN **2004** Oak 9 (8, RG) **2005** Oak 10 (8, c) **NFL** 19 (16) [2 yrs]

GROVE, ROGER Roger Robert, BB-HB-QB, 6´0˝/182 lbs; Michigan State; B6/19/1908 Greenville, OH, D12/19/1986 Torrance, CA [K]

1931	GB	14 (3)	—	—	—	—	—	—	—	—	—	—	—	—	—	—	—	—	—	—	—	—	—	—
1932	GB	11 (5, bb)	12	21	1.8	0	9	149	16.6(34)	3	—	—	—	—	—	—	—	—	—	—	K	—	23	111
1933	GB	13 (11, BB)	1	4	4.0	0	17	215	12.6	0	3	1	33.3	44	14.7(44)	0	0	—	—	—	K	—	8	134
1934	GB	10 (6, hb)	62	262	4.2	1	6	125	20.8(37)	3	10	5	50.0	34	3.4(34)	0	0	—	—	—	K	—	25	367
1935	GB	3 (1)	7	21	3.0	0	—	—	—	—	—	—	—	—	—	—	—	—	—	—	K	—	0	21
NFL	5	51 (26)	82	308	3.8	1	32	489	15.3(37)	6	13	6	46.2	78	6.0(44)	2	0	—	—	—	K	—	58	642

GROVES, GEORGE George Noah, G-LB, 5´11˝/195 lbs; Marquette; 1945: ChiB, rnd 32; B6/10/1921 Hammond, IN **1947** Buf-A 7 (0) **1948** Bal-A 2 (0) **AAFC** 9 (0) [2 yrs]

GROW, MONTY Monty Roy, DB, 6´4˝/214 lbs; Florida; B9/4/1971 Inverness, FL **1994** †KC 15 (0) **1995** Jax 4 (1) **NFL** 19 (1) [2 yrs]

GROZA, LOU Louis Roy 'The Toe', T-C-DT-K, 6´3˝/240 lbs; Ohio State; B1/25/1924 Martins Ferry, OH, D11/29/2000 Middleburg Heights, OH; HOF 1974 [K] **1946**†Cle-A☆14 (5, c) **1947**†Cle-A 12 (5, rt) **1948**†Cle-A 14 (14, LT) **1949**†Cle-A 12 (12, LT) **AAFC** 52 (36) [4 yrs]

1951†Cle★12 (LT) **1952**†Cle★12 (LT) **1953**†Cle★12 (LT) **1954**†Cle★12 (LT) **1955**†Cle★12 (LT) **1956** Cle☆12 (LT) **1957**†Cle★12 (LT) **1958**†Cle◇12 (LT) **1959** Cle◇12 (LT) **1961** Cle 14 **1962** Cle 14 **1964**†Cle★14 **1967** Cle 14

1950	†Cle◇	10 (LT)	—	—	—	—	1	23	23.0(23)	1	1	0	0	0	0.0	0	0	—	—	—	K	—	74	17
1963	Cle	14	—	—	—	—	—	—	—	—	1	0	0.0	0	0.0	0	1	—	—	—	K	—	85	-40
1965	†Cle☆	14	—	—	—	—	—	—	—	—	1	0	0.0	0	0.0	0	0	—	—	—	K	—	93	0
1966	Cle	14	—	—	—	—	—	—	—	—	1	1	100.0	7	-7.0(-7)	0	0	—	—	—	K	—	78	-4
NFL	1 7	216	—	—	—	—	1	23	23.0(23)	1	4	1	25.0	7	-1.8	0	1	—	—	—	K	—	1349	-27

GRUBE, CHARLIE Charles William, E, 5´10˝/175 lbs; Michigan; B6/11/1904 Saginaw, MI, D1/21/1976 Hollywood, FL **1926** Det 2 (1)

GRUBE, FRANK Franklin Thomas, E, 5´9˝/180 lbs; Lafayette; B1/7/1905 Easton, PA, D7/2/1945 New York, NY [K] **1928** NYY 11 (10, LE), 1

GRUBER, BOB Robert Leon, T, 6´5˝/275 lbs; Pittsburgh; 1980: LA, rnd 10; B6/7/1958 Del Rio, TX **1987** GB 1 (0)

GRUBER, HERB Herbert C., E, 5´9˝/155 lbs; Kentucky; B12/22/1901 Shelbyville, KY, D2/1/1979 St. Matthews, KY **1921** Lou 2 (2, LE) **1922** Lou 3 (3, LE) **1923** Lou 3 (2) **NFL** 8 (7) [3 yrs]

GRUBER, PAUL Paul Blake, T, 6´5˝/292 lbs; Wisconsin; 1988: TB, rnd 1; B2/24/1965 Madison, WI **1988** TB 16 (16, LT) **1989** TB☆16 (16, LT) **1990** TB 16 (16, LT) **1991** TB☆16 (16, LT) **1992** TB☆16 (16, LT) **1993** TB 10 (10, LT) **1994** TB 16 (16, LT) **1995** TB 16 (16, LT) **1996** TB 13 (13, LT) **1997**†TB 16 (16, LT) **1998** TB 16 (16, LT) **1999** TB 16 (16, LT) **NFL** 183 (183) [12 yrs]

GRUNEISEN, SAM Samuel Kenneth, C-G-LB, 6´1˝/242 lbs; Villanova; 1962: SD, rnd 25; B1/16/1941 Louisville, KY **1962** SD-A 9 **1963** SD-A 7 (LG) **1964**†SD-A 11 **1965**†SD-A 14 (14, C) **1966** SD-A 14 (14, C) **1967** SD-A 14 (14, C) **1968** SD-A 14 (14, C) **1969** SD-A 14 (C) **1970** SD 14 (C) **1971** SD 2 **1972** SD 7 **1973** Hou 10 (C) **NFL** 130 (56) [12 yrs]

GRUNHARD, TIM Timothy Gerard, C, 6´2˝/304 lbs; Notre Dame; 1990: KC, rnd 2; B5/17/1968 Chicago, IL **1990**†KC 14 (9, C) **1991**†KC 16 (16, C) **1992**†KC 12 (12, C) **1993**†KC 16 (16, C) **1994**†KC 16 (16, C) **1995**†KC 16 (16, C) **1996** KC 16 (16, C) **1997**†KC 16 (16, C) **1998** KC 16 (16, C) **1999** KC 16 (16, C) **2000** KC 15 (15, C) **NFL** 169 (164) [11 yrs]

GRUPP, BOB Robert William, P, 5´11˝/193 lbs; Duke; 1977: NYJ, rnd 7; B5/8/1955 Philadelphia, PA

1979	KC★	16	—	—	—	—	—	—	—	—	1	0	0.0	0	0.0	0	0	—	—	—	P	—	0	0
1980	KC	16 (0)	3	-14	-4.7(0)	0	—	—	—	—	—	—	—	—	—	—	—	—	—	—	P	—	0	-14
1981	KC	9 (0)	1	-19	-19.0(-19)	0	—	—	—	—	—	—	—	—	—	—	—	—	—	—	P	—	0	-19
NFL	3	41	4	-33	-8.3	0	—	—	—	—	1	0	0.0	0	0.0	0	0	—	—	—	P	—	0	-33

GRUTTADAURIA, MIKE Michael Jason, C, 6´3˝/297 lbs; Central Florida; B12/6/1972 Fort Lauderdale, FL **1996** SL 9 (3) **1998** SL 11 (3) **1999**†SL 16 (16, C) **2000** Arz 8 (8, c) **2002** Arz 8 (8, c)

1997	SL	14 (14, C)	—	—	—	—	1	0	0.0(0)	0	—	—	—	—	—	—	—	—	—	—	—	—	0	0
2001	Arz	15 (15, C)	1	1	1.0(1)	0	—	—	—	—	—	—	—	—	—	—	—	—	—	—	—	—	0	1
NFL	7	81 (67)	1	1	1.0(1)	0	1	0	0.0(0)	0	—	—	—	—	—	—	—	—	—	—	—	—	0	1

GRYGO, AL Aloysius Joseph, HB, 5´10˝/173 lbs; South Carolina; B8/14/1918 Erie, PA, D9/27/1971 Columbia, SC

1944	ChiB	9 (8, RH)	53	322	6.1(66)	2	5	42	8.4(15)	0	—	—	—	—	—	—	—	—	—	—	Pkpi	—	12	524
1945	ChiB	10 (2)	23	98	4.3(16)	0	5	68	13.6(33)	1	1	1	100.0	11	11.0(11)	0	0	—	—	—	Pkpi	—	6	171
NFL	2	19 (10)	76	420	5.5(66)	2	10	110	11.0(33)	1	1	1	100.0	11	11.0(11)	0	0	—	—	—	Pkpi	—	18	695

GRYMES, DARRELL Darrell Anthony, WR, 6´2˝/182 lbs; Central State (OH); B12/4/1961 Washington, DC

| 1987 | Det | 2 (2) | — | — | — | — | 9 | 140 | 15.6(36) | 2 | — | — | — | — | — | — | — | — | — | — | — | — | 12 | 80 |

GUARNIERI, AL George Albert, E, 5´10˝/175 lbs; Niagara; Canisius; B7/1/1899 Ashtabula, OH, D4/28/1980 Ashtabula, OH **1924** Buf 11 (10, RE), 12 **1925** Can 1 (0) **NFL** 12 (10) [2 yrs]

GUCCIARDO, PAT Pasquale John, DB, 5´11˝/185 lbs; Kent State; B4/21/1944 **1966** NYJ-A 1

GUDAUSKAS, PETE Peter, G, 6´2˝/222 lbs; Murray State; B10/19/1916 Georgetown, IL, D10/27/2003, [K] **1940** Cle 1 (0) **1943** ChiB 6 (0) **1944** ChiB☆10 (7, LG) **1945** ChiB 8 (6, LG) **NFL** 25 (13) [4 yrs]

GUDD, LEN Leonard William, E, 6´3˝/212 lbs; Temple; B9/25/1910 Taylor Springs, IL, D6/5/1992 **1934** Phi 1 (0)

GUDE, HENRY Henry Paul, C-G, 6´1˝/225 lbs; Vanderbilt; 1942: ChiB, rnd 14; B2/25/1919 Memphis, TN, D10/6/1998 Heber Springs, AR **1946** Phi 2 (0)

GUDMUNDSON, SCOTT Wayne Scott, QB, 5´10˝/178 lbs; George Washington; B4/3/1921 Ogden, UT

1944	Bos	7 (4)	14	-21	-1.5(6)	0	—	—	—	—	38	16	42.1	226	5.9(38)	1	4	—	—	—	Pkp	—	0	-31
1945	Bos	10 (0)	23	4	0.2(20)	0	1	-8	-8.0(-8)	0	43	17	39.5	299	7.0(43)	1	5	—	—	—	Ppi	—	0	-17
NFL	2	17 (4)	37	-17	-0.5(20)	0	1	-8	-8.0(-8)	0	81	33	40.7	525	6.5(43)	2	9	—	—	—	Pkpi	—	0	-48

GUENDLING, MIKE Michael Anthony, LB, 6´3˝/238 lbs; Northwestern; 1984: SD, rnd 2; B6/18/1962 Chicago, IL **1985** SD 9 (0)

GUENO, JIM James Andre, LB, 6´2˝/220 lbs; Tulane; 1976: GB, rnd 9; B1/15/1954 Crowley, LA **1976** GB 14 **1977** GB 14 **1978** GB 15 (1) **1980** GB 16 (7, lolb)

| 1979 | GB | 16 | — | — | — | — | 1 | 23 | 23.0(23) | 0 | — | — | — | — | — | — | — | — | — | — | — | — | 0 | 12 |
| NFL | 5 | 75 (8) | — | — | — | — | 1 | 23 | 23.0(23) | 0 | — | — | — | — | — | — | — | — | — | — | k | — | 0 | -10 |

GUENTHER, GREGG Gregg, TE, 6´8˝/255 lbs; USC; B1/29/1982 Calabasas, CA

| 2005 | Ten | 5 (0) | — | — | — | — | 2 | 13 | 6.5(8) | 0 | — | — | — | — | — | — | — | — | — | — | — | — | 0 | 7 |

YEAR	TEAM	G(GS, POS)	RUSH	YD	AVG(LG)	TD	REC	YD	AVG(LG)	TD	PASS COMP	PCT	YD	AVG(LG)	TD	INT	SK	YD	QBR	KPR	OTD	PTS	TAY

GUESMAN, DICK   Richard Eugene, DT-K, 6´4˝/255 lbs; West Virginia; 1959: Det, rnd 6; B1/22/1938 Brownsville, PA **[K]**   **1960** NYT-A 10 (RDT)   **1961** NYT-A 14 (RDT)
1962 NYT-A 7 (RDT)   **1963** NYJ-A☆14 (RDT)   **1964** Den-A 14 (LDT)   **NFL** 59 [5 yrs]

GUESS, TERRY   Terry, WR, 6´0˝/200 lbs; Gardner-Webb; 1996: NO, rnd 5; B9/22/1974 Orangeburg, SC
| 1996 | NO | 3(2) | 2 | -4 | -2.0(-1) | 0 | 2 | 69 | 34.5(57) | 1 | — | — | — | — | — | — | — | — | — | p | — | 6 | 38 |

GUFFEY, ROY   Roy Cornelius, E, 6´0˝/194 lbs; Oklahoma; B9/18/1902 Columbus Grove, OH, D3/25/1994 Dallas, TX   **1926** Buf 9 (9, RE), 6

GUGGEMOS, NEAL   Neal Evan, DB, 6´0˝/187 lbs; St. Thomas; B6/14/1964 Winsted, MN   **1986** Min 4 (0)   **1987**†Min 12 (1)   **1988** NYG 11 (0)   **NFL** 27 (1) [3 yrs]

GUGLIELMI, RALPH   Ralph Vincent, QB, 6´1˝/196 lbs; Notre Dame; 1955: Was, rnd 1; B6/26/1933 Columbus, OH
1955	Was	9(4)	18	51	2.8(17)	1	—	—	—	—	62	20	32.3	242	3.9(43)	2	4	—	—	—	—	6	32
1958	Was	8(qb)	17	74	4.4(17)	0	—	—	—	—	81	34	42.0	458	5.7(64)	2	6	—	—	—	—	0	73
1959	Was	9(qb)	26	97	3.7(19)	0	—	—	—	—	89	36	40.4	617	6.9(70)	4	11	—	—	—	—	0	-15
1960	Was	11(QB)	79	247	3.1(16)	0	—	—	—	—	223	125	56.1	1547	6.9(50)	9	19	—	55.7	—	—	0	306
1961	SL	9(qb)	22	101	4.6(23)	1	—	—	—	—	116	56	48.3	927	8.0(80)	5	8	—	—	—	—	6	280
1962	†NYG	14	11	40	3.6(18)	0	—	—	—	—	31	14	45.2	210	6.8(41)	2	1	—	—	—	—	0	115
1963	NYG	2	3	3	1.0(2)	0	—	—	—	—	17	5	29.4	89	5.2(32)	0	3	7	67	—	—	0	-73
1963	Phi	4	1	20	20.0(20)	0	—	—	—	—	7	2	28.6	29	4.1(19)	0	4	27	—	—	—	0	35
NFL	7	66(4)	177	633	3.6(23)	2	—	—	—	—	626	292	46.6	4119	6.6(80)	24	52	11	94	46.5	—	—	12	753

GUIDRY, KEVIN   Kevin Dale, DB, 6´0˝/176 lbs; LSU; 1988: Den, rnd 3; B5/16/1964 Lake Charles, LA   **1988** Den 14 (0)   **1989** Phx 3 (0)   **NFL** 17 (0) [2 yrs]

GUIDRY, PAUL   Paul Michael, LB, 6´3˝/227 lbs; LSU; McNeese State; 1966: Buf, rnd 8; B1/14/1944 Breaux Bridge, LA   **1966**†Buf-A 14   **1967** Buf-A 14 (4)   **1968** Buf-A 14 (14, LLB)
1969 Buf-A 8 (LLB)   **1970** Buf☆14 (LLB)   **1971** Buf 14 (LLB)   **1972** Buf 14 (LLB)   **1973** Hou 14   **NFL** 106 (18) [8 yrs]

GUILBEAU, RUSTY   David Ruston, LB-DE, 6´4˝/242 lbs; McNeese State; 1982: SL, rnd 3; B11/20/1958 Opelousas, LA   **1982**†NYJ 4 (0)   **1983** NYJ 16 (0)   **1984** NYJ 16 (2)
1985 NYJ 14 (7, ROLB)   **1986**†NYJ 6 (4)   **1987** Cle 1 (0)   **NFL** 57 (13) [6 yrs]

GUILLORY, JOHN   John Lee, DB, 5´10˝/190 lbs; Stanford; B7/28/1945 Berkeley, CA   **1969** Cin-A 11   **1970**†Cin 7   **NFL** 18 [2 yrs]

GUILLORY, TONY   Anthony R., LB, 6´4˝/236 lbs; Nebraska; Lamar; 1965: LA, rnd 4/Hou, rnd 15; B11/10/1942 Opelousas, LA   **1965** LARm 14 (14, LLB)   **1967**†LARm 14
1968 LARm 13   **1969** Phi 12 (LLB)   **NFL** 53 (14) [4 yrs]

GULIAN, MIKE   Milanese J., T, 6´0˝/205 lbs; Brown; B7/29/1900 Marash, Armenia, D1/10/1970 Boston, MA   **1923** Buf 11 (11, RT)   **1924** Fra 14 (10, RT)   **1925** Pro 8 (8, RT)
1926 Pro 13 (12, RT)   **1927** Pro 2 (1)   **NFL** 48 (42) [5 yrs]

GULIFORD, ERIC   Eric Andre, WR, 5´8˝/170 lbs; Arizona State; B10/25/1969 Kansas City, KS **[R]**
1993	Min	10(0)	—	—	—	—	1	45	45.0(45)	0	—	—	—	—	—	—	—	—	—	kp	—	0	116
1994	Min	7(1)	—	—	—	—	—	—	—	—	—	—	—	—	—	—	—	—	—	p	—	0	-11
1995	Car	14(9, WR)	2	2	1.0(1)	0	29	444	15.3(49)	1	2	1	50.0	46	23.0(46)	0	1	—	—	—	p	1	12	482
1997	NO	16(2)	1	-2	-2.0(-2)	0	27	362	13.4(47)	1	—	—	—	—	—	—	—	—	—	kp	1	12	940
1998	NO	5(1)	—	—	—	—	10	124	12.4(24)	0	—	—	—	—	—	—	—	—	—	kp	—	0	274
NFL	5	52(13)	3	0	0.0(1)	0	67	975	14.6(49)	2	2	1	50.0	46	23.0(46)	0	1	—	—	—	kp	2	24	1801

GULLEDGE, DAVID   David, DB, 6´1˝/203 lbs; Jacksonville State; 1991: Was, rnd 11; B10/26/1967 Pell City, AL   **1992** Was 4 (0)

GULSETH, DON   Donald Maurice, LB, 6´1˝/240 lbs; North Dakota; B9/11/1942 Tracy, MN   **1966** Den-A 5

GULYANICS, GEORGE   George, HB, 6´0˝/198 lbs; Alabama; B6/11/1921 Mishakawa, IN, D1/19/1990 Mishawaka, IN
1947	ChiB	12(4)	35	212	6.1(46)	4	3	22	7.3(16)	0	2	1	50.0	55	27.5(55)	0	1	—	—	—	Pkpi	—	24	328
1948	ChiB	12(8, LH)	119	439	3.7(24)	4	8	130	16.3(36)	1	—	—	—	—	—	—	—	—	—	P	—	30	549
1949	ChiB	11(11, LH)	102	452	4.4(31)	5	16	165	10.3(34)	1	1	0	0.0	0	0.0	0	0	—	—	—	P	—	36	590
1950	†ChiB	12(LH)	146	571	3.9(31)	2	12	137	11.4(42)	0	1	1	100.0	16	16.0(16)	0	0	—	—	—	P	—	12	668
1951	ChiB	12(LH)	105	403	3.8(30)	4	13	146	11.2(32)	0	—	—	—	—	—	—	—	—	—	—	—	24	516
1952	ChiB	2	2	4	2.0(3)	0	—	—	—	—	—	—	—	—	—	—	—	—	—	—	—	0	4
NFL	6	61(23)	509	2081	4.1(46)	19	52	600	11.5(42)	2	4	2	50.0	71	17.8(55)	0	1	—	—	—	Pkpi	—	126	2654

GUMAN, MIKE   Michael Donald, RB, 6´2˝/216 lbs; Penn State; 1980: LA, rnd 6; B4/21/1958 Allentown, PA
1980	†LARm	16(0)	100	410	4.1(17)	4	18	131	9.4(41)	0	1	1	100.0	31	31.0(31)	1	0	1	5	—	kp	—	24	527
1981	LARm	16(4)	115	433	3.8(18)	4	18	130	7.2(14)	0	1	1	100.0	7	7.0(7)	1	0	—	—	—	k	—	24	542
1982	LARm	9(9, FB)	69	266	3.9(15)	2	31	310	10.0(46)	0	1	0	0.0	0	0.0	0	1	—	—	—	k	—	12	383
1983	†LARm	16(14, FB)	7	42	6.0(11)	0	34	347	10.2(60)	4	—	—	—	—	—	—	—	—	—	k	—	24	236
1984	†LARm	16(13, FB)	1	2	2.0(2)	0	19	161	8.5(29)	0	—	—	—	—	—	—	—	—	—	k	1	6	121
1985	†LARm	8(1)	11	32	2.9(6)	0	3	23	7.7(11)	0	—	—	—	—	—	—	—	—	—	k	—	0	44
1986	LARm	12(3)	2	2	1.0(3)	0	9	68	7.6(13)	0	—	—	—	—	—	—	—	—	—	k	—	0	34
1987	LARm	12(8, FB)	36	98	2.7(7)	1	22	263	12.0(33)	0	—	—	—	—	—	—	—	—	—	k	—	6	228
1988	LARm	1(0)	1	1	1.0(1)	0	—	—	—	—	—	—	—	—	—	—	—	—	—	—	—	0	1
NFL	9	106(52)	342	1286	3.8(18)	11	150	1433	9.6(60)	4	3	2	66.7	38	12.7(31)	2	1	1	5	—	kp	—	96	2114

GUMP, ANDY   Andy, G-T, /210 lbs; none; deceased   **1922** Col 3 (0)

GUNDERMAN, BOB   Robert Edward, E, 6´3˝/220 lbs; Virginia; 1957: Det, rnd 19; B10/8/1934 Sparta, NJ   **1957** Pit 1

GUNDERSON, HARRY   Arthur Henry, C-G, 6´2˝/203 lbs; Iowa; B11/9/1887 Rolfe, IA, D11/24/1975 Everett, WA   **1920** RI 4 (2)   **1921** Min 4 (4, C)   **1922** Min 2 (0)   **NFL** 10 (6) [3 yrs]

GUNDLACH, HERMAN   Herman, G, 6´0˝/205 lbs; Harvard; B7/16/1913 Houghton, MI, D5/5/2005 Rochester, MN   **1935** Bos 2 (0)

GUNN, JIMMY   James, LB, 6´1˝/220 lbs; USC; 1970: Chi, rnd 13; B11/27/1948 Augusta, AR   **1970** ChiB 14   **1971** ChiB 14   **1972** ChiB 14   **1973** ChiB 3   **1974** ChiB 14 (RLB)
1975 ChiB 4   **1975** NYG 10   **1976** TB 13 (13, LLB)   **NFL** 86 (13) [7 yrs]

GUNN, LANCE   Lance Cameron, DB, 6´3˝/222 lbs; Texas; 1993: Cin, rnd 7; B1/9/1970 Whiteman AFB, MO   **1993** Cin 8 (8, SS)

GUNN, MARK   Mark Pierre, DT-DE, 6´5˝/288 lbs; Pittsburgh; 1991: NYJ, rnd 4; B7/24/1968 Cleveland, OH   **1991** NYJ 15 (1)   **1992** NYJ 16 (12, LDE)   **1993** NYJ 12 (0)
1994 NYJ 3 (0)   **1995**†Phi 12 (6, rdt)   **1996** NYJ 8 (0)   **NFL** 69 (19) [6 yrs]

GUNNELS, RILEY   John Riley, DT-DE, 6´3˝/253 lbs; Georgia; 1959: Pit, rnd 10; B9/24/1937 Atlanta, GA   **1960**†Phi 12   **1961** Phi 14 (2)   **1962** Phi 14 (LDT)   **1963** Phi 9 (LDT)
1964 Phi 14   **1965** Pit 14   **1966** Pit 14   **NFL** 91 (2) [7 yrs]

GUNNER, HARRY   Harry James, DE, 6´6˝/250 lbs; Oregon State; 1968: Cin, rnd 8; B11/25/1944 Port Arthur, TX   **1968** Cin-A 14 (RDE)   **1969** Cin-A 14   **1970** ChiB 14
NFL 42 [3 yrs]

GUNTER, MICHAEL   Michael Wayne, RB, 5´11˝/205 lbs; Tulsa; 1984: TB, rnd 4; B2/18/1961 Gladewater, TX
| 1984 | KC | 4(0) | 15 | 12 | 0.8(4) | 0 | — | — | — | — | — | — | — | — | — | — | — | — | — | — | — | 0 | 12 |

GURLEY, BUCK   Sheddrick Tobias, DT, 6´2˝/295 lbs; Florida; B4/7/1978 Quincy, FL   **2002** TB 7 (0)

GURODE, ANDRE   Andre, G-C, 6´4˝/326 lbs; Colorado; 2002: Dal, rnd 2; B3/6/1978 Houston, TX   **2002** Dal 14 (14, RG/c)   **2003**†Dal 16 (15, RG)   **2004** Dal 14 (13, RG)
2005 Dal 16 (2)   **NFL** 60 (44) [4 yrs]

GURSKY, ALBERT   Albert Lenart, LB, 6´1˝/215 lbs; Penn State; 1962: NYG, rnd 12/Bos, rnd 27; B11/23/1940 West Reading, PA   **1963**†NYG 2

GUSSIE, MIKE   Michael, G, 6´0˝/204 lbs; West Virginia; 1940: Bkn, rnd 13; B9/16/1917 Everettstown, PA, D2/24/1977 Alexandria, VA
| 1940 | Bkn | 8(0) | — | — | — | — | 1 | 9 | 9.0(9) | 1 | — | — | — | — | — | — | — | — | — | — | — | 6 | 10 |

GUSTAFSON, ED   Edsel Warren, C-LB, 6´3˝/205 lbs; Dartmouth; George Washington; B4/4/1922 Moline, IL   **1947** Bkn-A 13 (9, C)
| 1948 | Bkn-A | 14(8, C) | 1 | 7 | 7.0(7) | 0 | — | — | — | — | — | — | — | — | — | — | — | — | — | — | — | 0 | 7 |
| AAFC | 2 | 27(17) | 1 | 7 | 7.0(7) | 0 | — | — | — | — | — | — | — | — | — | — | — | — | — | — | — | 0 | 7 |

GUSTAFSON, JIM   James Joel, WR, 6´1˝/177 lbs; St. Thomas; B3/16/1961 Minneapolis, MN
1986	Min	14(0)	—	—	—	—	5	61	12.2(18)	2	—	—	—	—	—	—	—	—	—	—	—	12	41
1987	†Min	12(0)	1	-2	-2.0(-2)	0	4	55	13.8(23)	0	—	—	—	—	—	—	—	—	—	—	—	0	26
1988	†Min	16(0)	—	—	—	—	15	231	15.4(47)	1	—	—	—	—	—	—	—	—	—	—	—	6	121

YEAR	TEAM	G(GS, POS)	RUSH	YD	AVG(LG)	TD	REC	YD	AVG(LG)	TD	PASS	COMP	PCT	YD	AVG(LG)	TD	INT	SK	YD	QBR	KPR	OTD	PTS	TAY
1989	†Min	16(0)	—	—	—	—	14	144	10.3(22)	2	—	—	—	—	—	—	—	—	—	—	—	—	12	82
NFL	4	58(0)	1	-2	-2.0(-2)	0	38	491	12.9(47)	5	—	—	—	—	—	—	—	—	—	—	—	—	30	269

Guthrie, Grant Grant Morrow, K, 6´0˝/210 lbs; Florida State; 1970: Buf, rnd 6; B2/9/1948 Waynesboro, PA **[K]** **1970** Buf 14 **1971** Buf 6 **NFL** 20 [2 yrs]

Guthrie, Keith Keith Edwin, NT, 6´4˝/264 lbs; Texas A&M; 1984: SD, rnd 6; B8/17/1961 Tyler, TX **1984** SD 11 (2)

Gutierrez, Brock James Brock, C, 6´3˝/304 lbs; Central Michigan; B9/25/1973 Charlotte, MI **1997** Cin 5 (0) **1998** Cin 1 (0) **1999** Cin 16 (0) **2000** Cin 16 (7, c) **2001** Cin 15 (0) **2002** Cin 16 (1) **2003** SF 12 (0) **2004** SF 16 (15, C) **2005** Det 14 (0) **NFL** 111 (23) [9 yrs]

Gutknecht, Al Albert Rudolph, G-LB, 6´0˝/205 lbs; Niagara; B6/11/1917 Arnold, PA, D3/25/1996 Springfield, PA **1943** Bkn 2 (0) **1944** Cle 1 (0) **NFL** 3 (0) [2 yrs]

Gutowsky, Ace LeRoy Erwin, FB-TB, 5´11˝/201 lbs; Oklahoma City; B8/2/1909 Komolty, Russia, D12/4/1976 Oklahoma City, OK

YEAR	TEAM	G(GS, POS)	RUSH	YD	AVG(LG)	TD	REC	YD	AVG(LG)	TD	PASS	COMP	PCT	YD	AVG(LG)	TD	INT	SK	YD	QBR	KPR	OTD	PTS	TAY
1932	Por☆	8(4, fb)	63	247	3.9	3	—	—	—	—	3	1	33.3	26	8.7(26)	0	0	—	—	—	—	—	18	290
1933	Por	10(6, FB)	103	385	3.7	1	—	—	—	—	11	4	36.4	24	2.2	1	1	—	—	—	—	—	6	372
1934	Det☆	13(6, fb)	**146**	517	3.5	5	—	—	—	—	12	2	16.7	12	1.0	0	3	—	—	—	—	—	30	453
1935	†Det	12(7, FB)	102	296	2.9	2	1	9	9.0(9)	0	9	5	55.6	95	10.6	2	1	—	—	—	—	—	12	338
1936	Det☆	12(6, FB)	191	827	4.3	6	1	30	30.0(30)	0	13	2	15.4	21	1.6	0	4	—	—	—	—	—	36	753
1937	Det☆	11(11, FB)	128	361	2.8	1	—	—	—	—	8	1	12.5	30	3.8(30)	0	2	—	—	—	—	—	6	306
1938	Det☆	11(9, FB)	131	444	3.4	2	1	25	25.0(25)	0	7	3	42.9	41	5.9	0	0	—	—	—	—	—	12	**497**
1939	Bkn	9(4)	58	202	3.5	0	—	—	—	—	1	1	100.0	5	5.0(5)	0	0	—	—	—	—	—	0	205
NFL	8	86(53)	922	3279	3.6	20	3	64	21.3(30)	0	64	19	29.7	254	4.0(30)	3	11	—	—	—	—	—	120	3213

Gutteron, Bill William Alexander, BB, 5´5˝/155 lbs; Nevada-Reno; B11/26/1899 Belize, D5/30/1987 Middleton, WI **1926** LA 2 (1)

Guy, Buzz Melwood Norman, G-T-DT, 6´3˝/248 lbs; Duke; 1958: Cle, rnd 3; B3/20/1936 New Castle, PA **1958**†NYG 10 **1959** NYG 12 **1960** Dal 12 (7, RG) **1961** Hou-A 1 **1961** Den-A 9 **NFL** 44 (7) [4 yrs]

Guy, Charlie Charles Howgate, C-G-BB, 6´0˝/170 lbs; Dartmouth; Washington & Jefferson; B12/5/1896 Schenectady, NY, D4/9/1974 Tampa, FL **1920** Det 7 (4, RG) **1921** Det 7 (7, C) **1921** Buf 5 (5, c) **1922** Buf 10 (10, C) **1923** Cle☆7 (7, C) **1925** Day 5 (1) **NFL** 41 (34) [5 yrs]

Guy, Louis Louis Burton, DB, 6´0˝/190 lbs; Mississippi; 1963: Phi, rnd 3/NYJ, rnd 7; B5/26/1941 McComb, MS **1963**†NYG 5 **1964** Oak-A 6 (rcb) **NFL** 11 [2 yrs]

Guy, Ray William Ray, P, 6´3˝/195 lbs; Southern Mississippi; 1973: Oak, rnd 1; B12/22/1949 Swainsboro, GA **[KP]**

YEAR	TEAM	G(GS, POS)	RUSH	YD	AVG(LG)	TD	REC	YD	AVG(LG)	TD	PASS	COMP	PCT	YD	AVG(LG)	TD	INT	SK	YD	QBR	KPR	OTD	PTS	TAY
1973	†Oak★	14	1	21	21.0(21)	0	—	—	—	—	—	—	—	—	—	—	—	—	—	—	P	—	0	21
1974	†Oak★	14	—	—	—	—	—	—	—	—	1	0	0.0	0	0.0	0	1	—	—	—	P	—	0	-40
1975	†Oak★	14	—	—	—	—	—	—	—	—	1	1	100.0	22	22.0(22)	0	0	—	—	—	P	—	0	11
1976	†Oak★	14	1	0	0.0(0)	0	—	—	—	—	—	—	—	—	—	—	—	—	—	—	KP	—	0	0
1977	†Oak★	14	—	—	—	—	—	—	—	—	—	—	—	—	—	—	—	—	—	—	P	—	0	0
1978	Oak★	16	—	—	—	—	—	—	—	—	—	—	—	—	—	—	—	—	—	—	P	—	0	0
1979	Oak☆	16	—	—	—	—	—	—	—	—	—	—	—	—	—	—	—	—	—	—	P	—	0	0
1980	†Oak★	16(0)	3	38	12.7(24)	0	—	—	—	—	1	1	100.0	32	32.0(32)	0	0	—	—	—	P	—	0	54
1981	Oak☆	16(0)	—	—	—	—	—	—	—	—	0	0	0.0	0	0.0	0	0	1	12	—	P	—	0	0
1982	†LARd	9(0)	2	-3	-1.5(7)	0	—	—	—	—	—	—	—	—	—	—	—	—	—	—	P	—	0	-3
1983	†LARd	16(0)	2	-13	-6.5(-3)	0	—	—	—	—	—	—	—	—	—	—	—	—	—	—	P	—	0	-13
1984	†LARd	16(0)	—	—	—	—	—	—	—	—	—	—	—	—	—	—	—	—	—	—	P	—	0	0
1985	†LARd	16(0)	1	0	0.0(0)	0	—	—	—	—	—	—	—	—	—	—	—	—	—	—	P	—	0	0
1986	LARd	16(0)	1	0	0.0(0)	0	—	—	—	—	—	—	—	—	—	—	—	—	—	—	P	—	0	0
NFL	14	207	11	43	3.9(24)	0	—	—	—	—	3	2	66.7	54	18.0(32)	0	1	1	12	—	KP	—	0	30

Guynes, Thomas Thomas, T, 6´5˝/300 lbs; Michigan; B9/9/1974 Marion, IN **1997** Arz 4 (0)

Guyon, Joe Joseph Napleoen, WB-TB-BB-FB, 5´10˝/195 lbs; Carlisle Indian; Georgia Tech; B11/26/1892 White Earth, MN, D11/27/1971 Louisville, KY; HOF 1966 **[K]** **1920** Can☆13 (7, WB) **1921** Was 1 (1) **1921** Cle 8 (8, WB), 28 **1922** Oor 9 (9, TB), 33 **1923** Oor 4 (4), 12 **1924** RI 3 (1) **1925** KC 1 (1) **1927** NYG 7 (2) **NFL** 46 (33), 73 [7 yrs]

Guyton, Myron Myron Mynard, DB, 6´1˝/205 lbs; Eastern Kentucky; 1989: NYG, rnd 8; B8/26/1967 Metcalf, GA **1989**†NYG 16 (15, SS) **1990**†NYG 16 (16, FS) **1991** NYG 16 (16, FS) **1992** NYG 4 (4) **1993**†NYG 16 (16, SS) **1994**†NE 16 (16, FS) **1995** NE 14 (14, FS) **NFL** 98 (97) [7 yrs]

Guzik, John John Paul, LB, 6´3˝/231 lbs; Pittsburgh; 1958: LA, rnd 4; B7/12/1936 Lawrence, PA **1959** LARm 12 **1960** LARm 12 **1961** Hou-A 3 **NFL** 27 [3 yrs]

Guzik, John John Joseph, NT-DE, 6´4˝/270 lbs; Ohio University; B9/25/1962 Cleveland, OH **1987** NE 3 (2)

Gwinn, Ross Charles Ross, G, 6´3˝/273 lbs; Northwestern State (LA); B7/25/1944 Deport, TX **1968** NO 2

Gwosden, Milo Milo, E, 6´0˝/185 lbs; Indiana (PA); Pittsburgh; B10/20/1898 Angram, Austria, D10/25/1989 Pittsburgh, PA **1925** Buf 6 (3)

Haak, Bob Robert Ally, G-T, 6´1˝/245 lbs; Indiana; 1939: Bkn, rnd 2; B3/26/1915 Hammond, IN, D11/1/1992 Bloomington, IN **1939** Bkn 10 (6, LG)

Haas, Bob Robert K., B, Worcester State; B5/25/1906 Springfield, OH, D9/1979 Huntsville, OH **1929** Day 5 (3)

Haas, Bruno Bruno Phillip, B, 5´10˝/180 lbs; none; B5/5/1891 Worcester, MA, D6/5/1952 Sarasota, FL **1921** Akr 1 (1) **1921** Cle 9 (5, TB), 6 **1922** Day 1 (0) **NFL** 11 (6) [2 yrs]

Haase, Andy Andrew Scott, TE, 6´4˝/260 lbs; Northern Colorado; B7/10/1974 Odessa, WA

YEAR	TEAM	G(GS, POS)	RUSH	YD	AVG(LG)	TD	REC	YD	AVG(LG)	TD	PASS	COMP	PCT	YD	AVG(LG)	TD	INT	SK	YD	QBR	KPR	OTD	PTS	TAY
1998	NYG	7(1)	—	—	—	—	2	33	16.5(27)	0	—	—	—	—	—	—	—	—	—	—	—	—	0	17

Haaven, Ira Ira Laeon, E, 6´2˝/192 lbs; Minnesota-Crookston; Hamlin; B6/6/1894 McIntosh, MN, D6/28/1971 Minneapolis, MN **1923** Dul 3 (2)

Haayer, Adam Adam, T, 6´6˝/298 lbs; Minnesota; 2001: Ten, rnd 6; B2/22/1977 Wyoming, MN **2002** Min 4 (0) **2004**†Min 4 (1) **2005** Arz 12 (4) **NFL** 20 (5) [3 yrs]

Habib, Brian Brian Richard, G-T, 6´7˝/299 lbs; Washington; 1988: Min, rnd 10; B12/2/1964 Ellensburg, WA **1989**†Min 16 (0) **1990** Min 16 (0) **1991** Min 16 (8, rg) **1992**†Min 16 (15, RG) **1993**†Den 16 (16, RG) **1994** Den 16 (16, RG) **1995** Den 16 (16, RG) **1996**†Den 16 (16, RG) **1997**†Den 14 (14, RG) **1998** Sea 16 (16, RG) **1999**†Sea 16 (16, RG) **NFL** 174 (133) [11 yrs]

Hachten, Bill William Andrews, G, 6´0˝/210 lbs; California; Stanford; 1947: NYG, rnd 13; B11/30/1924 Wichita, KS **1947** NYG 8 (1)

Hackbart, Dale Dale Leonard, DB, 6´3˝/210 lbs; Wisconsin; 1960: GB, rnd 5/Oak, rnd 1; B7/21/1938 Madison, WI **1960**†GB 12 **1961** GB 2 **1961** Was 12 (11, RS) **1962** Was 14 (RS) **1963** Was 14 (RS) **1966** Min 14 (13, RS) **1967** Min 13 (12, RS) **1968**†Min 14 **1969**†Min 12 **1970**†Min 14 **1971** SL 14 **1972** SL 14 **1973** Den 3 (2) **NFL** 152 (38) [12 yrs]

Hackenbruck, Johnny John Anthony, T, 6´2˝/215 lbs; Oregon State; 1940: Det, rnd 17; B10/20/1915 The Dalles, OR, D10/26/1988 Corvallis, OR **1940** Det 7 (2)

Hackett, D.J. D.J., WR, 6´2˝/199 lbs; Colorado; 2004: Sea, rnd 5; B7/31/1981 Fontana, CA

YEAR	TEAM	G(GS, POS)	RUSH	YD	AVG(LG)	TD	REC	YD	AVG(LG)	TD	PASS	COMP	PCT	YD	AVG(LG)	TD	INT	SK	YD	QBR	KPR	OTD	PTS	TAY
2005	†Sea	13(3)	—	—	—	—	28	400	14.3(47)	2	—	—	—	—	—	—	—	—	—	—	—	—	12	210

Hackett, Dino Barry Dean, LB, 6´3˝/228 lbs; Appalachian State; 1986: KC, rnd 2; B6/28/1964 Greensboro, NC **1986**†KC 16 (16, LILB) **1987** KC 11 (11, RILB) **1988** KC★13 (13, RILB) **1989** KC 13 (13, RILB) **1990**†KC 16 (15, RILB) **1991**†KC 16 (14, RILB) **1993** Sea 3 (0) **NFL** 88 (82) [7 yrs]

Hackett, Joey Joseph Glenn, TE, 6´5˝/267 lbs; Elon; B9/29/1958 Greensboro, NC

YEAR	TEAM	G(GS, POS)	RUSH	YD	AVG(LG)	TD	REC	YD	AVG(LG)	TD	PASS	COMP	PCT	YD	AVG(LG)	TD	INT	SK	YD	QBR	KPR	OTD	PTS	TAY
1986	†Den	16(4)	—	—	—	—	3	48	16.0(19)	0	—	—	—	—	—	—	—	—	—	—	—	—	0	24
1987	GB	11(0)	—	—	—	—	—	—	—	—	—	—	—	—	—	—	—	—	—	—	—	—	—	—
1988	GB	9(0)	—	—	—	—	1	2	2.0(2)	1	—	—	—	—	—	—	—	—	—	—	k	—	6	0
NFL	3	36(4)	—	—	—	—	4	50	12.5(19)	1	—	—	—	—	—	—	—	—	—	—	k	—	6	24

Hackney, Elmer Elmer Loyd, FB, 6´2˝/205 lbs; Kansas State; 1940: Phi, rnd 11; B7/8/1916 Oberlin, KS, D5/30/1969 Manhattan, KS

YEAR	TEAM	G(GS, POS)	RUSH	YD	AVG(LG)	TD	REC	YD	AVG(LG)	TD	PASS	COMP	PCT	YD	AVG(LG)	TD	INT	SK	YD	QBR	KPR	OTD	PTS	TAY
1940	Phi	8(1)	32	101	3.2	1	2	4	2.0	0	—	—	—	—	—	—	—	—	—	—	—	—	6	113
1941	Pit	11(4)	63	253	4.0(31)	1	1	10	10.0(10)	0	1	0	0.0	0	0.0	0	0	—	—	—	p	—	6	266
1942	Det	8(2)	34	208	6.1(78)	2	3	22	7.3(12)	0	—	—	—	—	—	—	—	—	—	—	k	—	12	228
1943	Det	10(2)	27	87	3.2(16)	2	5	51	10.2(16)	0	3	1	33.3	1	-0.3(-1)	0	0	—	—	—	kpi	1	18	267
1944	Det	10(1)	58	184	3.2(16)	4	8	48	6.0(10)	1	1	1	100.0	19	19.0(19)	0	0	—	—	—	i	—	30	289
1945	Det	8(3)	6	13	2.2(6)	0	—	—	—	—	—	—	—	—	—	—	—	—	—	—	—	—	0	13
1946	Det	6(1)	—	—	—	—	—	—	—	—	—	—	—	—	—	—	—	—	—	—	—	—	—	—
NFL	7	61(14)	220	846	3.8(78)	10	19	135	7.1(16)	1	5	2	40.0	18	3.6(19)	0	0	—	—	—	kpi	1	72	1176

Hadd, Gary Gary Alan, DT-NT, 6´4˝/274 lbs; Minnesota; 1988: Det, rnd 8; B10/19/1965 St. Paul, MN **1988** Det 5 (0) **1989** Phx 10 (4) **NFL** 15 (4) [2 yrs]

YEAR	TEAM	G (GS, POS)	RUSH	YD	AVG (LG)	TD	REC	YD	AVG (LG)	TD	PASS	COMP	PCT	YD	AVG (LG)	TD	INT	SK	YD	QBR	KPR	OTD	PTS	TAY
HADDAD, DREW Andrew George, WR, 5´11˝/187 lbs; Buffalo; 2000: Buf, rnd 7; B8/15/1978 Cleveland, OH **2004** Buf 1 (0)																								
2002	†Ind	1(0)	—	—	—	—	1	11	11.0(11)	0	—	—	—	—	—	—	—	—	—	—	kp	—	0	-6
NFL	2	2(0)	—	—	—	—	1	11	11.0(11)	0	—	—	—	—	—	—	—	—	—	—	—	—	0	6
HADDEN, AL Aldous Bernard, B-E, 5´9˝/186 lbs; Washington & Jefferson; B11/8/1899 Toledo, OH, D2/26/1969 Toledo, OH **1925** Det 12 (12, WB), 24 **1926** Det 12 (8, WB), 6 **1927** Pro 10 (7, WB) **1928** ChiB 1 (0) **1928** Pro 9 (7, FB) **1929** Pro 9 (7, LE) **1930** Pro 9 (4) **NFL** 62 (45), 30 [6 yrs]																								
HADDIX, MICHAEL Michael Mcglamery, RB, 6´2˝/225 lbs; Mississippi State; 1983: Phi, rnd 1; B12/27/1961 Tippah County, MS																								
1983	Phi	14(6, rb)	91	220	2.4(11)	2	23	254	11.0(34)	0	—	—	—	—	—	—	—	—	—	—	k	—	12	373
1984	Phi	14(0)	48	130	2.7(21)	1	33	231	7.0(22)	0	—	—	—	—	—	—	—	—	—	—	—	—	6	256
1985	Phi	16(15, FB)	67	213	3.2(12)	0	43	330	7.7(17)	0	—	—	—	—	—	—	—	—	—	—	—	—	0	378
1986	Phi	16(9, FB)	79	276	3.5(18)	0	26	150	5.8(29)	0	—	—	—	—	—	—	—	—	—	—	—	—	0	351
1987	Phi	12(4)	59	165	2.8(11)	0	7	58	8.3(23)	0	—	—	—	—	—	—	—	—	—	—	k	—	0	180
1988	†Phi	16(3)	57	185	3.2(15)	0	12	82	6.8(14)	0	—	—	—	—	—	—	—	—	—	—	—	—	0	226
1989	GB	16(1)	44	135	3.1(10)	0	15	111	7.4(23)	1	—	—	—	—	—	—	—	—	—	—	—	—	6	196
1990	GB	16(12, FB)	98	311	3.2(13)	0	13	94	7.2(28)	2	—	—	—	—	—	—	—	—	—	—	—	—	12	368
NFL	8	120(50)	543	1635	3.0(21)	3	172	1310	7.6(34)	3	—	—	—	—	—	—	—	—	—	—	k	—	36	2327
HADDIX, WAYNE Samuel LaWayne, DB, 6´1˝/203 lbs; Liberty; B7/23/1965 Bolivar, TN **1987** NYG 5 (0) **1988** NYG 7 (0) **1990** TB★16 (16, RCB) **1991** TB 6 (4) **1991** Cin 7 (7, LCB) **NFL** 41 (27) [4 yrs]																								
HADEN, JACK Jack Crandon, T, 6´4˝/233 lbs; Arkansas; B10/2/1914 Fort Worth, TX, D1/25/1996 Odessa, TX **1936** NYG 9 (1) **1937** NYG 10 (2) **1938** NYG✧11 (4) **NFL** 30 (7) [3 yrs]																								
HADEN, NICK Nicholas Scott, G-C, 6´2˝/270 lbs; Penn State; 1985: LARd, rnd 7; B11/7/1962 Pittsburgh, PA **1986** Phi 8 (6, lg)																								
HADEN, PAT Patrick Capper, QB, 5´11˝/182 lbs; USC; 1975: LA, rnd 7; B1/23/1953 Westbury, NY																								
1976	†LARm	10(7, qb)	25	84	3.4(16)	4	—	—	—	—	105	60	57.1	896	8.5(65)	8	4	13	86	—	—	—	24	452
1977	†LARm★	12(10, QB)	29	106	3.7(23)	2	—	—	—	—	216	122	56.5	1551	7.2(58)	11	6	17	151	84.5	—	—	12	717
1978	†LARm	16(16, QB)	33	206	6.2(24)	0	—	—	—	—	444	229	51.6	2995	6.7(68)	13	19	32	216	65.1	—	—	0	1009
1979	LARm	10(10, QB)	16	97	6.1(17)	0	—	—	—	—	290	163	56.2	1854	6.4(50)	11	14	21	178	68.1	—	—	0	519
1980	†LARm	4(1)	3	12	4.0(6)	0	—	—	—	—	41	19	46.3	185	4.5(24)	0	4	4	30	—	—	—	0	-56
1981	LARm	13(11, QB)	18	104	5.8(16)	0	—	—	—	—	267	138	51.7	1815	6.8(67)	9	13	28	227	64.4	—	—	0	537
NFL	6	65(55)	124	609	4.9(24)	6	—	—	—	—	1363	731	53.6	9296	6.8(68)	52	60	115	888	69.6	—	—	36	3177
HADL, JOHN John Willard, QB, 6´1˝/214 lbs; Kansas; 1962: SD, rnd 3/Det, rnd 1; B2/15/1940 Lawrence, KS																								
1962	SD-A	14(10, QB)	40	139	3.5(18)	1	—	—	—	—	260	107	41.2	1632	6.3(72)	15	24	—	—	43.3	—	—	6	80
1963	†SD-A	14	8	26	3.3(33)	0	—	—	—	—	64	28	43.8	502	7.8(69)	6	6	—	—	—	P	—	0	67
1964	†SD-A✧	14(9, QB)	20	70	3.5(20)	1	—	—	—	—	274	147	53.6	2157	7.9(76)	18	15	11	124	78.7	P	—	6	649
1965	†SD-A★	14(14, QB)	28	91	3.3(23)	1	—	—	—	—	348	174	50.0	**2798**	**8.0(85)**	20	21	—	—	71.3	P	—	6	760
1966	SD-A☆	14(14, QB)	38	95	2.5(21)	2	2	-13	-6.5(4)	0	375	200	53.3	2846	7.6(78)	23	14	—	—	83.0	—	—	12	1087
1967	SD-A	14(14, QB)	37	107	2.9(26)	3	—	—	—	—	427	217	50.8	3365	7.9(72)	24	22	9	91	74.5	P	—	18	1060
1968	SD-A★	14(14, QB)	23	14	0.6(9)	2	—	—	—	—	**440**	**208**	47.3	**3473**	7.9(84)	**27**	**32**	10	110	64.5	—	—	12	626
1969	SD-A✧	14(10, QB)	26	109	4.2(17)	2	—	—	—	—	324	158	48.8	2253	7.0(76)	10	11	18	190	67.8	—	—	12	866
1970	SD	14(12, QB)	28	188	6.7(34)	1	—	—	—	—	327	162	49.5	2388	7.3(67)	**22**	15	42	327	**77.1**	P	—	6	902
1971	SD	14(14, QB)	18	75	4.2(37)	1	—	—	—	—	**431**	**233**	54.1	**3075**	7.1(77)	**21**	25	16	145	68.9	—	—	6	728
1972	SD✧	14(14, QB)	22	99	4.5(17)	1	1	4	4.0(4)	0	**370**	**190**	51.4	2449	6.6(61)	15	**26**	19	187	56.7	—	—	6	371
1973	†LARm★	14(14, QB)	14	5	0.4(6)	0	—	—	—	—	258	135	52.3	2008	7.8(69)	22	11	17	126	88.8	—	—	0	679
1974	LARm	6(5, qb)	11	28	2.5(9)	0	—	—	—	—	115	53	46.1	680	5.9(38)	5	6	6	36	57.9	—	—	0	153
1974	GB	8(qb)	8	-3	-0.4(6)	0	—	—	—	—	184	89	48.4	1072	5.8(68)	3	8	9	70	54.0	—	—	0	228
1975	GB	14(QB)	20	47	2.3(9)	0	—	—	—	—	353	191	54.1	2095	5.9(54)	6	**21**	35	284	52.8	—	—	0	285
1976	Hou	14(4)	7	11	1.6(8)	0	—	—	—	—	113	60	53.1	634	5.6(69)	7	8	15	123	—	—	—	0	43
1977	Hou	14	3	11	3.7(6)	1	—	—	—	—	24	11	45.8	76	3.2(18)	0	3	2	26	—	—	—	6	-61
NFL	16	224(148)	351	1112	3.2(37)	16	3	-9	-3.0(4)	0	4687	2363	50.4	33503	7.1(85)	244	268	209	1839	67.4	P	—	96	8519
HADLEY, DAVID David, DB, 5´9˝/186 lbs; Alcorn State; 1970: KC, rnd 3; B10/8/1948 Amory, MS **1970** KC 14 **1971**†KC 14 **NFL** 28 [2 yrs]																								
HADLEY, RON Ronald Arthur, LB, 6´2˝/240 lbs; Washington; 1986: NYJ, rnd 5; B11/9/1963 Caldwell, ID **1987** SF 3 (2) **1988**†SF 3 (0) **NFL** 6 (2) [2 yrs]																								
HADNOT, JAMES James Weldon, RB, 6´2˝/244 lbs; Texas Tech; 1980: KC, rnd 3; B7/11/1957 Jasper, TX																								
1980	KC	13(5, rb)	76	244	3.2(11)	2	15	97	6.5(18)	0	—	—	—	—	—	—	—	—	—	—	—	—	12	313
1981	KC	16(16, FB)	140	603	4.3(30)	3	23	215	9.3(20)	0	1	0	0.0	0	0.0	0	1	—	—	—	—	—	18	701
1982	KC	9(2)	46	172	3.7(25)	0	14	96	6.9(28)	0	—	—	—	—	—	—	—	—	—	—	—	—	0	220
1983	KC	5(0)	4	10	2.5(7)	0	2	18	9.0(16)	0	—	—	—	—	—	—	—	—	—	—	—	—	0	19
NFL	4	43(23)	266	1029	3.9(30)	5	54	426	7.9(28)	0	1	0	0.0	0	0.0	0	1	—	—	—	—	—	30	1252
HADNOT, REX Rex, G-C, 6´2˝/310 lbs; Houston; 2004: Mia, rnd 6; B1/28/1982 Lufkin, TX **2004** Mia 14 (7, rg) **2005** Mia 16 (16, RG) **NFL** 30 (23) [2 yrs]																								
HAFEN, BARNEY Banard Ervin, DE-E, 6´2˝/195 lbs; Utah; 1948: Det, rnd 19/1949: NYY-A, rnd 18; B11/20/1921 Santa Clara, UT **1950** Det 12 (LDE)																								
1949	Det	12(0)	—	—	—	—	1	10	10.0(10)	0	—	—	—	—	—	—	—	—	—	—	—	—	0	5
NFL	2	24	—	—	—	—	1	10	10.0(10)	0	—	—	—	—	—	—	—	—	—	—	—	—	0	5
HAFFNER, MIKE Michael Arthur, WR-FL, 6´2˝/200 lbs; UCLA; B7/7/1942 Waterloo, IA																								
1968	Den-A	14	2	2	1.0(1)	0	12	232	19.3(52)	1	1	1	100.0	18	18.0(18)	0	0	—	—	—	—	—	6	132
1969	Den-A	9(9, FL)	—	—	—	—	35	563	16.1(46)	5	—	—	—	—	—	—	—	—	—	—	—	—	30	307
1970	Den	11(6, WR)	1	1	1.0(1)	0	12	196	16.3(28)	1	—	—	—	—	—	—	—	—	—	—	—	—	6	104
1971	Cin	3	—	—	—	—	—	—	—	—	—	—	—	—	—	—	—	—	—	—	—	—	—	—
NFL	4	37(15)	3	3	1.0(1)	0	59	991	16.8(52)	7	1	1	100.0	18	18.0(18)	0	0	—	—	—	—	—	42	543
HAGBERG, ROGER Roger Wheeler, FB-FL, 6´2˝/216 lbs; Minnesota; 1961: GB, rnd 10; B2/28/1939 Winnebago, MN, D4/15/1970 Lafayette, CA																								
1965	Oak-A	14(fl)	48	171	3.6(19)	1	12	121	10.1(18)	0	—	—	—	—	—	—	—	—	—	—	kp	—	6	245
1966	Oak-A	14(FB)	62	282	4.5(30)	0	21	248	11.8(37)	1	—	—	—	—	—	—	—	—	—	—	k	—	6	409
1967	†Oak-A	12	44	146	3.3(11)	2	11	114	10.4(25)	1	—	—	—	—	—	—	—	—	—	—	k	—	18	210
1968	†Oak-A	14(1)	39	164	4.2(16)	1	8	78	9.8(22)	1	—	—	—	—	—	—	—	—	—	—	k	—	12	224
1969	†Oak-A	14(3)	1	3	3.0(3)	0	6	84	14.0(20)	1	—	—	—	—	—	—	—	—	—	—	—	—	6	50
NFL	5	68(4)	194	766	3.9(30)	4	58	645	11.1(37)	4	—	—	—	—	—	—	—	—	—	—	kp	—	48	1138
HAGBERG, SWEDE Rudolph E., C-B-T, 6´4˝/219 lbs; West Virginia; B6/18/1907 Charleroi, PA, D11/25/1960 Steubenville, OH **1929** Buf 9 (9, WB), 18 **1930** Bkn☆12 (12, C), 6 **NFL** 21 (21), 24 [2 yrs]																								
HAGEMAN, FRED Fred John, C-LB, 6´5˝/242 lbs; Arkansas; Kansas; 1960: NYG, rnd 8/Oak, rnd 2; B6/30/1937 Bunkie, LA **1961** Was 13 (13, MLB) **1962** Was 14 (14, C) **1963** Was 14 (C) **1964** Was 14 (c) **NFL** 55 (27) [4 yrs]																								
HAGEN, HALVOR Halvor Reini, G-DE-T-C, 6´5˝/245 lbs; Weber State; 1969: Dal, rnd 3; B2/4/1947 Oslo, Norway **1969**†Dal 12 **1970** Dal 6 **1971** NE 14 (14, LG) **1972** NE 12 **1973** Buf 5 **1974**†Buf 8 **1975** Buf 13 **NFL** 70 (14) [7 yrs]																								
HAGEN, MIKE Michael Christopher, RB, 6´0˝/240 lbs; Montana; B6/30/1959 Auburn, WA																								
1987	Sea	2(1)	2	3	1.5(4)	0	—	—	—	—	—	—	—	—	—	—	—	—	—	—	—	—	0	3
HAGENBUCKLE, VERN Vernon Bertram, E, 5´8˝/185 lbs; Dartmouth; B12/6/1901 Mount Vernon, NY, D11/17/1997 Brattleboro, VT **1926** Pro 2 (2)																								
HAGER, BRITT Britt Harley, LB, 6´1˝/231 lbs; Texas; 1989: Phi, rnd 3; B2/20/1966 Odessa, TX **1989**†Phi 16 (0) **1990**†Phi 16 (1) **1991** Phi 16 (0) **1992** Phi 10 (0) **1993** Phi 16 (7, mlb) **1994** Phi 16 (5, mlb) **1995** Den 16 (5, rlb) **1996** Den 2 (0) **1997** SL 13 (0) **NFL** 121 (18) [9 yrs]																								
HAGERTY, JACK John Leo, B, 5´9˝/164 lbs; Georgetown (DC); B7/3/1903 Boston, MA, D3/23/1982 Washington, DC [K] **1926** NYG 10 (7, WB), 12 **1927** NYG 12 (3), 18 **1928** NYG 11 (8, BB) **1929** NYG 14 (1), 18 **1930** NYG 12 (4), 30																								
1932	NYG	4(4)	10	22	2.2	0	—	—	—	—	32	17	53.1	158	4.9	2	2	—	—	—	K	—	2	31
NFL	6	63(27)	10	22	2.2	4	—	—	—	—	32	17	53.1	158	4.9	3	2	—	—	—	K	2	80	131

YEAR	TEAM	G (GS, POS)	RUSH	YD	AVG(LG)	TD	REC	YD	AVG(LG)	TD	PASS	COMP	PCT	YD	AVG(LG)	TD	INT	SK	YD	QBR	KPR	OTD	PTS	TAY

HAGERTY, HORSE   Loris James, FB-TB, 5´10˝/185 lbs; Iowa; B4/16/1905 Blanchard, IA, D3/26/1991   **1930** Bkn 9 (2)

HAGGAN, MARIO   Mario Marcel, LB, 6´3˝/248 lbs; Mississippi State; 2003: Buf, rnd 7; B3/3/1980 Clarksdale, MS   **2003** Buf 1 (0)   **2004** Buf 16 (0)   **2005** Buf 16 (0)
NFL 33 (0) [3 yrs]

HAGGANS, CLARK   Clark Cromwell, LB, 6´3˝/251 lbs; Colorado State; 2000: Pit, rnd 5; B1/10/1977 Torrance, CA   **2000** Pit 2 (0)   **2001**†Pit 16 (1)   **2002**†Pit 16 (1)   **2003** Pit 16 (2)
2004†Pit 13 (13, LOLB)   **2005**†Pit 13 (13, LOLB)   NFL 76 (30) [6 yrs]

HAGGERTY, DOC   John F., G, 6´0˝/205 lbs; Tufts; B5/9/1895, OH, D7/ 1964, NY   **1920** Cle 5 (4, RG)   **1920** Can 1 (0)   **1921** NYG 1 (1, RG)   NFL 7 (5) [2 yrs]

HAGGERTY, MIKE   Michael K., T, 6´4˝/245 lbs; Miami (FL); 1967: Pit, rnd 6; B10/14/1945 Royal Oak, MI   **1967** Pit 14 (LT)   **1968** Pit 1   **1969** Pit 14 (lt)   **1970** Pit 14 (LT)   **1971** NE 13
1973 Det 4   NFL 60 [6 yrs]

HAGGERTY, STEVE   Steven Thomas, WR, 5´10˝/175 lbs; Colorado; UNLV; 1975: Den, rnd 10; B5/17/1953 Denver, CO   **1975** Den 1

HAGGINS, ODELL   Odell, NT, 6´2˝/278 lbs; Florida State; 1990: SF, rnd 9; B2/27/1967 Lakeland, FL   **1991** Buf 5 (0)

HAGINS, ISAAC   Isaac Ben, WR, 5´9˝/179 lbs; Southern (LA); 1976: Min, rnd 9; B3/2/1954 Shreveport, LA

1976	TB	1	—	—	—	—	—	—	—	—	—	—	—	—	—	—	—	—	—	—	kp	—	0	2
1977	TB	13(3)	1	2	2.0(2)	0	15	196	13.1(56)	0	—	—	—	—	—	—	—	—	—	—	kp	—	0	278
1978	TB	4(1)	—	—	—	—	6	65	10.8(21)	0	—	—	—	—	—	—	—	—	—	—	kp	—	0	45
1979	†TB	16(14, WR)	—	—	—	—	39	692	17.7(57)	3	—	—	—	—	—	—	—	—	—	—	k	—	18	422
1980	TB	16(14, WR)	3	24	8.0(26)	0	23	364	15.8(48)	2	—	—	—	—	—	—	—	—	—	—	k	—	12	238
NFL		50(32)	4	26	6.5(26)	0	83	1317	15.9(57)	5	—	—	—	—	—	—	—	—	—	—	kp	—	30	985

HAGLER, SCOTT   William Scott, K, 5´8˝/160 lbs; South Carolina; B7/19/1964, [K]   **1987** Sea 2 (0)

HAGOOD, JAY   Jay Dwight, T, 6´4˝/306 lbs; Virginia Tech; B8/9/1973 Easley, SC   **1997** NYJ 2 (0)

HAGOOD, RICKEY   Rickey Gabriel, NT, 6´2˝/286 lbs; South Carolina; 1984: Sea, rnd 4; B4/24/1961 Easley, SC   **1984** SD 2 (0)

HAGY, JOHN   John Kevin, DB, 5´11˝/190 lbs; Texas; 1988: Buf, rnd 8; B12/9/1965 Okinawa, Japan   **1988**†Buf 3 (0)   **1989** Buf 9 (0)   **1990**†Buf 16 (11, FS)   NFL 28 (11) [3 yrs]

HAHN, RAY   Raymond Dryer, E, 5´10˝/190 lbs; Kansas State; B11/19/1897 Clay Center, KS, D11/8/1989 McPherson, KS   **1926** Ham 3 (3, RE)

HAIGHT, MIKE   Michael James, G-T, 6´4˝/281 lbs; Iowa; 1986: NYJ, rnd 1; B10/6/1962 Manchester, IA   **1986** NYJ 2 (0)   **1987** NYJ 6 (1)   **1988** NYJ 14 (9, LG)
1989 NYJ 13 (13, LG)   **1990** NYJ 14 (14, LG)   **1991** NYJ 7 (6, lg)   **1992** Was 7 (0)   NFL 63 (43) [7 yrs]

HAIK, MAC   Joseph Michael, WR, 6´1˝/195 lbs; Mississippi; 1968: Hou, rnd 2; B1/19/1946 Meridian, MS

1968	Hou-A	14(WR)	2	7	3.5(5)	0	32	584	18.3(59)	8	—	—	—	—	—	—	—	—	—	—	—	48	339
1969	Hou-A	13(WR)	2	21	10.5(11)	0	27	375	13.9(42)	1	—	—	—	—	—	—	—	—	—	—	—	6	214
1970	Hou	13	—	—	—	—	17	190	11.2(35)	0	—	—	—	—	—	—	—	—	—	—	—	0	95
1971	Hou	4	—	—	—	—	—	—	—	—	—	—	—	—	—	—	—	—	—	—	—	—	—
NFL		44	4	28	7.0(11)	0	76	1149	15.1(59)	9	—	—	—	—	—	—	—	—	—	—	—	54	648

HAINES, BY   Byron Dalton, HB, 5´11˝/185 lbs; Washington; 1937: Pit, rnd 7; B11/30/1914 Bend, OR

| **1937** | Pit | 5(1) | 24 | 29 | 1.2 | 0 | 2 | 17 | 8.5 | 0 | 6 | 1 | 16.7 | 14 | 2.3(14) | 0 | 1 | — | — | — | — | 0 | 5 |

HAINES, HINKEY   Henry Luther, B, 5´10˝/170 lbs; Lebanon Valley; Penn State; B12/23/1898 Red Lion, PA, D1/9/1979 Sharon Hill, PA [C]   **1925** NYG 11 (9, TB), 18
1926 NYG☆12 (11, TB), 36   **1927** NYG☆13 (11, TB), 36   **1928** NYG 9 (6, tb), 30   **1929** SI 4 (4), 12   **1931** SI 4 (1)   NFL 53 (42), 132 [6 yrs]

HAINES, HOOT   Harry Jepson, T-G-E, 6´0˝/205 lbs; Colgate; B2/25/1907 Philadelphia, PA, D8/17/1965 Brighton, NY   **1930** Bkn 8 (7, RT)   **1931** Bkn 7 (3)   **1931** SI 2 (0)
NFL 17 (10) [2 yrs]

HAINES, JOHN   John Yancy, NT-DE-DT, 6´6˝/266 lbs; Texas; 1984: Min, rnd 7; B12/16/1961 Fort Worth, TX   **1984** Min 8 (0)   **1986** Ind 11 (0)   NFL 19 (0) [2 yrs]

HAINES, KRIS   David Kris, WR, 5´11˝/183 lbs; Notre Dame; 1979: Was, rnd 9; B7/23/1957 Akron, OH   **1979** Was 1   **1979**†ChiB 2   **1981** ChiB 1 (0)   **1987** Buf 1 (0)

| **1980** | ChiB | 16(1) | — | — | — | — | 4 | 83 | 20.8(35) | 0 | — | — | — | — | — | — | — | — | — | — | k | — | 0 | 27 |
| NFL | | 21(1) | — | — | — | — | 4 | 83 | 20.8(35) | 0 | — | — | — | — | — | — | — | — | — | — | — | — | 0 | 42 |

HAIRSTON, CARL   Carl Blake, DE-DT-LB, 6´3˝/260 lbs; Maryland-Eastern Shore; 1976: Phi, rnd 7; B12/15/1952 Martinsville, VA   **1976** Phi 14 (9, RDT)   **1977** Phi 14 (14, RDE)
1978†Phi 16 (16, RDE)   **1979**†Phi☆15 (15, RDE)   **1980**†Phi☆16 (16, RDE)   **1981**†Phi☆16 (16, RDE)   **1982** Phi 9 (9, RDE)   **1983** Phi 16 (11, RDE)   **1984** Cle 16 (0)
1985†Cle 16 (16, RDE)   **1986**†Cle 16 (16, RDE)   **1987**†Cle☆14 (14, RDE)   **1988**†Cle 14 (13, RDE)   **1989**†Cle 16 (16, LDT)   **1990** Phx 16 (3)   NFL 224 (184) [15 yrs]

HAIRSTON, RUSSELL   Russell Jonathan, DB, 6´3˝/208 lbs; Kentucky; B2/10/1964

| **1987** | Pit | 3(2) | — | — | — | — | 2 | 16 | 8.0(11) | 1 | — | — | — | — | — | — | — | — | — | — | — | — | 6 | 13 |

HAIRSTON, STACEY   Stacey, DB, 5´9˝/185 lbs; Ohio Northern; B8/16/1967 Columbus, OH   **1993** Cle 16 (0)   **1994**†Cle 15 (0)   NFL 31 (0) [2 yrs]

HAJEK, CHUCK   Charles Joseph, C-LB, 6´1˝/210 lbs; South Carolina; Northwestern; B11/11/1910 Chicago, IL, D2/21/1979 Centerport, NY   **1934** Phi 11 (2)

HAJI-SHEIKH, ALI   Ali, K, 6´0˝/172 lbs; Michigan; 1983: NYG, rnd 9; B1/11/1961 Ann Arbor, MI [K]   **1983** NYG★16 (0)   **1984**†NYG 16 (0)   **1985** NYG 2 (0)   **1986** Atl 6 (0)
1987†Was 11 (0)   NFL 51 (0) [5 yrs]

HAKIM, AZ-ZAHIR   Az-Zahir Ali, WR, 5´10˝/189 lbs; San Diego State; 1998: SL, rnd 4; B6/3/1977 Los Angeles, CA [R]

1998	SL	9(4)	2	30	15.0(34)	1	20	247	12.4(22)	1	—	—	—	—	—	—	—	—	—	—	—	12	169
1999	†SL	15(0)	4	44	11.0(31)	0	36	677	18.8(75)	8	—	—	—	—	—	—	—	—	—	—	kp	1	54	679
2000	†SL☆	16(4)	5	19	3.8(5)	0	53	734	13.8(80)	4	—	—	—	—	—	—	—	—	—	—	kp	1	30	732
2001	†SL	16(2)	11	50	4.5(12)	0	39	374	9.6(33)	3	1	1	100.0	51	51.0(51)	1	0	—	—	—	p	—	18	433
2002	Det	10(10, WR)	4	3	0.8(10)	0	37	541	14.6(64)	3	—	—	—	—	—	—	—	—	—	—	p	—	24	397
2003	Det	14(12, WR)	3	51	17.0(35)	0	49	449	9.2(28)	4	1	1	100.0	21	21.0(21)	0	0	—	—	—	p	—	26	346
2004	Det	12(5, wr)	1	0	0.0(0)	0	31	533	17.2(39)	3	—	—	—	—	—	—	—	—	—	—	—	—	18	282
2005	NO	12(2)	—	—	—	—	34	489	14.4(42)	2	—	—	—	—	—	—	—	—	—	—	kp	—	12	381
NFL		104(39)	30	197	6.6(35)	1	299	4044	13.5(80)	28	2	2	100.0	72	36.0(51)	1	0	—	—	—	kp	3	194	3416

HALAPIN, MIKE   Richard Michael, DT, 6´4˝/294 lbs; Pittsburgh; B7/1/1973 New Kensington, PA   **1996** Hou 9 (0)   **1997** Ten 3 (1)   **1999** NO 9 (3)   NFL 21 (4) [3 yrs]

HALAS, GEORGE   George Stanley 'Papa Bear', E, 6´0˝/182 lbs; Illinois; B2/2/1895 Chicago, IL, D10/31/1983 Chicago, IL; HOF 1963 [KC]   **1920** Dec☆12 (8, RE)
1921 ChiS 11 (11, RE), 18   **1922** ChiB 12 (11, RE), 14   **1923** ChiB 12 (12, RE), 6   **1924** ChiB 11 (10, RE)   **1925** ChiB 17 (17, RE)   **1926** ChiB 15 (15, RE)   **1927** ChiB 10 (1), 18
1928 ChiB 4 (0), 6   NFL 104 (85), 62 [9 yrs]

HALE, CHRIS   Christopher, DB, 5´7˝/164 lbs; Nebraska; USC; 1989: Buf, rnd 7; B1/4/1966 Monrovia, CA   **1989**†Buf 16 (0)   **1990**†Buf 8 (0)   **1991**†Buf 5 (0)   **1992** Buf 14 (0)
NFL 43 (0) [4 yrs]

HALE, DAVE   David Robert, DT-DE, 6´8˝/225 lbs; Ottawa (KS); 1969: Chi, rnd 12; B6/21/1947 McCook, NE   **1969** ChiB 3   **1970** ChiB 14   **1971** ChiB 12   **1973** ChiB 1
NFL 30 [4 yrs]

HALE, RYAN   Ryan, DT, 6´4˝/300 lbs; Arkansas; 1999: NYG, rnd 7; B7/10/1975 Rogers, AR   **1999** NYG 9 (0)   **2000**†NYG 16 (0)   NFL 25 (0) [2 yrs]

HALEY, ART   Arthur Reed, HB, 5´8˝/165 lbs; Akron; B10/7/1895 Beaver Falls, PA, D2/14/1946 Zanesville, OH   **1920** Can 1 (0)   **1921** Day 2 (0)   **1923** Akr 3 (0)   NFL 6 (0) [3 yrs]

HALEY, CHARLES   Charles Lewis, DE-LB, 6´5˝/242 lbs; James Madison; 1986: SF, rnd 4; B1/6/1964 Gladys, VA [S]   **1986**†SF 16 (1)   **1987**†SF 12 (2)   **1988**†SF★16 (14, LOLB)
1989†SF 16 (16, LOLB)   **1990**†SF★16 (16, LOLB)   **1991** SF☆14 (14, LOLB)   **1992**†Dal 15 (13, RDE)   **1993**†Dal 14 (11, RDE)   **1994**†Dal☆16 (16, RDE)   **1995**†Dal★13 (11, RDE)
1996 Dal 5 (5, rde)   **1998**†SF 16 (0)   NFL 169 (119) [13 yrs]

HALEY, DARRYL   Darryl, T-G, 6´4˝/269 lbs; Utah; 1982: NE, rnd 2; B2/16/1961 Los Angeles, CA   **1982** NE 9 (0)   **1983** NE 16 (2)   **1984** NE 16 (16, RT)   **1986**†NE 16 (6, rt)
1987†Cle 9 (1)   **1988** GB 13 (0)   NFL 79 (25) [6 yrs]

HALEY, DENNIS   Dennis, LB, 6´1˝/247 lbs; Virginia; B2/18/1982 Roanoke, VA   **2005** Bal 4 (0)

HALEY, DICK   George Richard, DB-HB-E, 5´10˝/183 lbs; Pittsburgh; 1959: Was, rnd 9; B10/2/1937 Midway, PA   **1961** Pit 8   **1962** Pit 14 (LCB)   **1963** Pit 14 (LCB)
1964 Pit 13 (LCB)

1959	Was	12(8, DB)	14	51	3.6(15)	1	2	14	7.0(8)	0	—	—	—	—	—	—	—	—	—	—	kpi	—	6	149
1960	Was	10	—	—	—	—	3	21	7.0(11)	0	—	—	—	—	—	—	—	—	—	—	—	—	0	11
1961	Min	4	—	—	—	—	3	43	14.3(22)	0	—	—	—	—	—	—	—	—	—	—	—	—	0	22
NFL		75(8)	14	51	3.6(15)	1	8	78	9.8(22)	0	—	—	—	—	—	—	—	—	—	—	kpi	1	12	318

YEAR	TEAM	G (GS, POS)	RUSH	YD	AVG(LG)	TD	REC	YD	AVG(LG)	TD	PASS	COMP	PCT	YD	AVG(LG)	TD	INT	SK	YD	QBR	KPR	OTD	PTS	TAY

HALEY, JERMAINE Jermaine, DT, 6´4˝/325 lbs; Butte J.C. (CA); 1999: Mia, rnd 7; B2/23/1973 Fresno, CA   **2000**†Mia 15 (4)   **2001**†Mia 12 (5, rdt)   **2002** Mia 16 (0)   **2003** Was 6 (5, ldt)   **2004** Was 13 (1)   **NFL** 62 (15) [5 yrs]

HALIBURTON, RONNIE Ronnie Maurice, TE, 6´4˝/230 lbs; LSU; 1990: Den, rnd 6; B4/14/1968 New Orleans, LA   **1990** Den 9 (0)   **1991** Den 8 (0)   **NFL** 17 (0) [2 yrs]

HALICKI, ED Edward Henry, B, 5´9˝/185 lbs; Bucknell; B12/23/1905 Kingston, PA, D4/27/1986 Ashley, PA **[K]**   **1929** Fra 17 (8, TB), 45   **1930** Fra 13 (10, TB), 29   **1930** Min 1 (1)   **NFL** 31 (19), 74 [2 yrs]

HALL, ALVIN Alvin, DB, 6´0˝/198 lbs; none; B8/12/1934 Fayette, MS   **1961** LARm 9 (9, RCB)   **1962** LARm 14   **1963** LARm 3   **NFL** 26 (9) [3 yrs]

HALL, ALVIN Alvin Eugene, DB, 5´10˝/193 lbs; Miami (OH); B8/12/1958 Dayton, OH **[R]**   **1981** Det 16 (1)   **1982**†Det 9 (9, FS)   **1983**†Det 16 (16, SS)   **1984** Det 16 (16, SS)   **1985** Det 16 (0)   **1987** Det 3 (3)   **NFL** 76 (45) [6 yrs]

HALL, ANDY Andy, QB, 6´3˝/218 lbs; Delaware; 2004: Phi, rnd 6; B11/26/1980 Cheraw, SC   **2005** Phi 1 (0)

HALL, CARLOS Carlos DeShaun, DE, 6´4˝/261 lbs; Arkansas; 2002: Ten, rnd 7; B1/16/1979 Marianna, AR   **2002**†Ten 15 (13, RDE)   **2003**†Ten 16 (4)   **2004** Ten 14 (14, RDE)   **2005** KC 14 (2)   **NFL** 59 (33) [4 yrs]

HALL, CHARLIE Charles Leslie, LB, 6´3˝/220 lbs; Houston; 1971: Cle, rnd 3; B12/2/1948 Yoakum, TX   **1971**†Cle 14   **1972**†Cle 14 (LLB)   **1973** Cle 14 (LLB)   **1974** Cle 14 (14, LLB)   **1975** Cle 14 (14, LLB)   **1976** Cle 14 (14, LLB)   **1977** Cle 14 (14, LLB)   **1978** Cle 16 (16, LLB)   **1979** Cle 16 (16, LLB/lolb)   **1980**†Cle 16 (16, LOLB)   **NFL** 146 (104) [10 yrs]

HALL, CHARLIE Charles Val, DB, 6´1˝/193 lbs; Pittsburgh; 1971: GB, rnd 3; B3/31/1948 Philadelphia, PA, D5/15/1998 Orangeburg County, SC   **1971** GB 14   **1972**†GB 14   **1973** GB 13   **1974** GB 14 (3)   **1975** GB 14

| 1976 | GB | 14 (1) | — | — | — | — | 1 | 18 | 18.0 (18) | 0 | — | — | — | — | — | — | — | — | — | — | — | — | 0 | 9 |
| NFL | 6 | 83 (4) | — | — | — | — | 1 | 18 | 18.0 (18) | 0 | — | — | — | — | — | — | — | — | — | pi | — | — | 0 | 16 |

HALL, CHRIS Charles Christopher, DB, 6´2˝/184 lbs; East Carolina; 1992: Dal, rnd 9; B4/25/1970 Fort Dix, NJ   **1993** Dal 1 (0)

HALL, COREY Corey, DB, 6´4˝/203 lbs; Appalachian State; 2001: Atl, rnd 7; B1/17/1979 Athens, GA   **2001** Atl 3 (0)

HALL, CORY Cory, DB, 6´0˝/213 lbs; Fresno State; 1999: Cin, rnd 3; B12/5/1976 Bakersfield, CA   **1999** Cin 16 (12, FS)   **2000** Cin 16 (6, ss)   **2001** Cin 16 (15, FS/ss)   **2002** Cin 14 (14, FS)   **2003** Atl 11 (10, FS)   **2004**†Atl 14 (13, FS)   **NFL** 87 (70) [6 yrs]

HALL, COURTNEY Courtney Caeser, C-G, 6´2˝/281 lbs; Rice; 1989: SD, rnd 2; B8/26/1968 Los Angeles, CA   **1989** SD 16 (16, C)   **1990** SD 16 (16, LG)   **1991** SD 16 (16, C)   **1992**†SD 16 (16, C)   **1993** SD 16 (16, C)   **1994**†SD☆15 (15, C)   **1995**†SD 16 (16, C)   **1996** SD 7 (7, c)   **NFL** 118 (118) [8 yrs]

HALL, DANA Dana Eric, DB, 6´3˝/208 lbs; Washington; 1992: SF, rnd 1; B7/8/1969 Bellflower, CA   **1992**†SF 15 (15, FS)   **1993**†SF 13 (7, fs)   **1994**†SF 16 (4)   **1995** Cle 15 (2)   **1996**†Jax 16 (10, SS)

| 1997 | †Jax | 16 (0) | — | — | — | — | 1 | 22 | 22.0 (22) | 0 | — | — | — | — | — | — | — | — | — | — | — | — | 0 | 11 |
| NFL | 6 | 91 (38) | — | — | — | — | 1 | 22 | 22.0 (22) | 0 | — | — | — | — | — | — | — | — | — | iS | — | — | 0 | 71 |

HALL, DANTE Damieon Dante, WR, 5´8˝/187 lbs; Texas A&M; 2000: KC, rnd 5; B9/20/1978 Lufkin, TX **[R]**

2000	KC	5 (0)	—	—	—	—	—	—	—	—	—	—	—	—	—	—	—	—	—	kp	—	0	110
2001	KC	13 (0)	2	10	5.0 (6)	0	—	—	—	—	—	—	—	—	—	—	—	—	—	kp	—	0	409
2002	KC★	16 (0)	11	54	4.9 (21)	0	20	322	16.1 (75)	3	—	—	—	—	—	—	—	—	—	kp	3	36	1004
2003	†KC★	16 (2)	16	73	4.6 (16)	0	40	423	10.6 (67)	1	0	0	0.0	0	0.0	0	0	1	2	kp	4	30	1280
2004	KC	16 (6, wr)	8	56	7.0 (17)	0	25	230	9.2 (22)	0	—	—	—	—	—	—	—	—	—	kp	2	12	1006
2005	KC	16 (3)	7	11	1.6 (7)	0	34	436	12.8 (52)	3	—	—	—	—	—	—	—	—	—	kp	1	24	905
NFL	6	82 (11)	44	204	4.6 (21)	0	119	1411	11.9 (75)	7	0	0	0.0	0	0.0	0	0	1	2	kp	10	102	4714

HALL, DARRYL Darryl Cavada, DB, 5´10˝/185 lbs; San Diego State; B10/23/1959 Greensboro, NC   **1987** LARm 1 (0)

HALL, DARRYL Darryl Cavada, DB, 6´2˝/210 lbs; Washington; B8/1/1966 Oscoda, MI   **1993**†Den 16 (2)   **1994** Den 16 (3)   **1995**†SF 12 (0)   **NFL** 44 (5) [3 yrs]

HALL, DeANGELO DeAngelo Eugene, DB, 5´11˝/200 lbs; Virginia Tech; 2004: Atl, rnd 1; B11/19/1983 Chesapeake, VA   **2004**†Atl 10 (9, LCB)   **2005** Atl◇15 (15, LCB)   **NFL** 25 (24) [2 yrs]

HALL, DELTON Delton Dwayne, DB, 6´1˝/205 lbs; Clemson; 1987: Pit, rnd 2; B1/16/1965 Greensboro, NC   **1987** Pit 12 (12, RCB)   **1988** Pit 14 (4)   **1989**†Pit 16 (2)   **1990** Pit 12 (1)   **1991** Pit 6 (0)   **1992** SD 16 (1)   **NFL** 76 (20) [6 yrs]

HALL, DICK Richard Lewis, T, 6´2˝/220 lbs; Butler; Illinois; B6/6/1903 Logansport, IN, D9/6/1971 Homewood, IL   **1927** NYY 15 (13, RT)

HALL, DINO Donald Richard, RB, 5´7˝/165 lbs; Rowan; B12/6/1955 Atlantic City, NJ **[R]**

1979	Cle	11	22	152	6.9 (52)	1	2	14	7.0 (8)	0	—	—	—	—	—	—	—	—	—	kp	—	6	583
1980	†Cle	16 (0)	2	26	13.0 (19)	0	—	—	—	—	—	—	—	—	—	—	—	—	—	kp	—	0	248
1981	Cle	12 (0)	—	—	—	—	—	—	—	—	—	—	—	—	—	—	—	—	—	kp	—	0	356
1982	†Cle	9 (0)	2	14	7.0 (13)	0	5	78	15.6 (31)	1	—	—	—	—	—	—	—	—	—	kp	—	6	171
1983	Cle	16 (0)	1	2	2.0 (2)	0	4	33	8.3 (18)	0	—	—	—	—	—	—	—	—	—	kp	—	0	180
NFL	5	64	27	194	7.2 (52)	1	11	125	11.4 (31)	1	—	—	—	—	—	—	—	—	—	kp	—	12	1538

HALL, FORREST Forrest J., B, 5´8˝/155 lbs; Duquesne; San Francisco; 1945: Phi, rnd 9; B10/29/1921 Oil City, PA, D2/14/2001 Scottsdale, AZ

| 1948 | SF-A | 14 (5, lh) | 66 | 413 | 6.3 (65) | 2 | 4 | 87 | 21.8 | 0 | — | — | — | — | — | — | — | — | — | kp | — | 12 | 733 |

HALL, GALEN Galen Samuel, QB, 5´10˝/216 lbs; Penn State; B8/14/1940 Altoona, PA

1962	Was	3	2	2	1.0 (1)	1	—	—	—	—	32	19	59.4	274	8.6 (48)	2	1	—	—	—	—	6	119
1963	NYJ-A	13	9	24	2.7 (11)	1	—	—	—	—	118	45	38.1	611	5.2 (73)	3	9	—	—	—	—	6	-6
NFL	2	16	11	26	2.4 (11)	2	—	—	—	—	150	64	42.7	885	5.9 (73)	5	10	—	—	—	—	12	114

HALL, HAROLD Harold Benjamin, C, 6´2˝/210 lbs; Springfield; B4/29/1914 Brooklyn, NY, D8/4/1992 Longwood, FL   **1942** NYG 1 (0)

HALL, HARRY Harry Archibald, B, 5´11˝/165 lbs; Chicago; Illinois; B10/5/1902 Waukegan, IL, D2/25/1951 Minneapolis, MN   **1925** RI 1 (1)

HALL, IRV Irving Alger, FB, 6´0˝/210 lbs; Brown; 1939: Phi, rnd 16; B11/23/1913 Raynham, MA, D1/24/1964 Orlando, FL

| 1942 | Phi | 8 (3) | 8 | 14 | 1.8 (11) | 0 | 2 | 18 | 9.0 (14) | 0 | — | — | — | — | — | — | — | — | — | Pk | — | 0 | 30 |

HALL, JAMES James, LB, 6´1˝/252 lbs; Northwestern State (LA); B1/27/1963 Natchez, MS   **1987** Atl 3 (0)

HALL, JAMES James, DE, 6´2˝/270 lbs; Michigan; B2/4/1977 New Orleans, LA   **2000** Det 5 (0)   **2001** Det 15 (0)   **2002** Det 16 (14, RDE)   **2003** Det 16 (16, RDE)   **2004** Det 16 (16, RDE)   **2005** Det 14 (14, RDE)   **NFL** 82 (60) [6 yrs]

HALL, JEFF Paul Jeffery, K, 5´11˝/190 lbs; Tennessee; 1999: Was, rnd 6; B7/30/1976 Winchester, TN **[K]**   **2000** SL 3 (0)

HALL, JOHN John Wesley, DE, 6´1˝/220 lbs; Iowa; 1955: Cle, rnd 3; B6/30/1933 Chicago, IL   **1955** NYG 2

HALL, JOHN John, K, 6´3˝/240 lbs; Wisconsin; B3/17/1974 Port Charlotte, FL **[K]**   **1997** NYJ 16 (0)   **1998**†NYJ 16 (0)   **1999** NYJ 15 (0)   **2000** NYJ 16 (0)   **2001**†NYJ 16 (0)   **2002**†NYJ 16 (0)   **2003** Was 16 (0)   **2004** Was 8 (0)   **2005**†Was 10 (0)   **NFL** 129 (0) [9 yrs]

HALL, JOHNNY John Robert, WB-HB, 6´0˝/195 lbs; TCU; 1939: GB, rnd 9; B12/14/1916 Kaufman, TX, D12/7/1996 Collin County, TX

1940	ChiC	11 (7, WB)	41	88	2.1	4	4	111	27.8	2	3	0	0.0	0	0.0	0	2	—	—	i	2	30	139
1941	ChiC	11 (7, WB)	53	165	3.1 (24)	2	16	302	18.9 (80)	2	1	0	0.0	0	0.0	0	2	—	—	k	—	24	396
1942	Det	7 (3)	2	-8	-4.0 (0)	0	1	42	42.0 (42)	0	1	0	0.0	0	0.0	0	0	—	—	kpi	—	0	61
1943	ChiC	8 (4)	22	51	2.3 (14)	0	7	82	11.7 (67)	1	4	2	50.0	2	6.0 (15)	0	0	—	—	kpi	—	6	85
NFL	4	37 (21)	118	296	2.5 (24)	3	28	537	19.2 (80)	5	9	2	22.2	24	2.7 (15)	0	4	—	—	kpi	2	60	681

HALL, KEN Charles Kenneth, HB-P, 6´1˝/205 lbs; Texas A&M; 1958: Bal, rnd 14; B12/13/1935 Sugar Land, TX

1959	ChiC	12	14	81	5.8 (20)	0	4	60	15.0 (31)	1	—	—	—	—	—	—	—	—	—	kp	1	12	211
1960	†Hou-A	11	30	118	3.9 (16)	0	—	—	—	—	—	—	—	—	—	—	—	—	—	Pkp	1	6	479
1961	Hou-A	3	7	13	1.9 (9)	0	1	20	20.0 (20)	0	—	—	—	—	—	—	—	—	—	Pkp	—	6	69
1961	SL	8	—	—	—	—	3	38	12.7 (18)	0	—	—	—	—	—	—	—	—	—	—	—	0	19
NFL	3	34	51	212	4.2 (20)	0	8	118	14.8 (31)	1	—	—	—	—	—	—	—	—	—	Pkp	2	24	778

HALL, LAMONT James Lamont, TE, 6´4˝/260 lbs; Clemson; B11/16/1974 York, SC

1999	GB	14 (0)	—	—	—	—	3	33	11.0 (13)	0	—	—	—	—	—	—	—	—	—	—	—	0	17
2000	†NO	16 (5, te)	—	—	—	—	5	33	6.6 (13)	0	—	—	—	—	—	—	—	—	—	—	—	6	22
2001	NO	16 (6, te)	—	—	—	—	2	15	7.5 (9)	0	—	—	—	—	—	—	—	—	—	—	—	0	8

YEAR	TEAM	G (GS, POS)	RUSH	YD	AVG (LG)	TD	REC	YD	AVG (LG)	TD	PASS	COMP	PCT	YD	AVG (LG)	TD	INT	SK	YD	QBR	KPR	OTD	PTS	TAY
2002	NO	16(1)	—	—	—	—	2	6	3.0(4)	0	—	—	—	—	—	—	—	—	—	—	—	—	0	3
2004	NO	16(2)	—	—	—	—	1	4	4.0(4)	1	—	—	—	—	—	—	—	—	—	—	k	—	6	-18
2005	NO	16(4)	—	—	—	—	6	36	6.0(8)	0	—	—	—	—	—	—	—	—	—	—	k	—	0	-3
NFL	6	94(18)	—	—	—	—	19	127	6.7(13)	2	—	—	—	—	—	—	—	—	—	—	k	—	12	28

HALL, LEMANSKI Lemanski S., LB, 6´0˝/231 lbs; Alabama; 1994: Hou, rnd 7; B11/24/1970 Valley, AL **1995** Hou 12 (0) **1996** Hou 3 (0) **1997** Ten 16 (2) **1998** ChiB 15 (0) **1999**†Dal 10 (0) **2000**†Min 15 (1) **2001** Min 16 (13, LLB) **2002** Min 14 (4) **NFL** 101 (20) [8 yrs]

HALL, MARK Mark James, DE, 6´4˝/285 lbs; Louisiana-Lafayette; 1989: GB, rnd 7; B8/21/1965 Morgan City, IA **1989** GB 7 (0) **1990** GB 3 (0) **NFL** 10 (0) [2 yrs]

HALL, PARKER Linus Parker, TB-HB, 6´0˝/198 lbs; Mississippi; 1939: Cle, rnd 1; B12/10/1916 Tunica, MS, D2/8/2005 Vicksburg, MS

YEAR	TEAM	G (GS, POS)	RUSH	YD	AVG (LG)	TD	REC	YD	AVG (LG)	TD	PASS	COMP	PCT	YD	AVG (LG)	TD	INT	SK	YD	QBR	KPR	OTD	PTS	TAY
1939	Cle★	11(11, TB)	120	458	3.8	2	1	-16	-16.0(-16)	0	**208**	**106**	**51.0**	1227	5.9	9	13	—	—	57.5	P	—	12	609
1940	Cle☆	11(7, TB)	94	365	3.9	1	—	—	—	—	183	77	42.1	1108	6.1	7	16	—	—	38.7	Pi	—	6	314
1941	Cle	10(8, TB)	57	232	4.1(60)	2	—	—	—	—	190	84	44.2	863	4.5(39)	7	**19**	—	—	30.5	Pkpi	—	12	35
1942	Cle	10(8, TB)	41	-3	-0.1(13)	1	—	—	—	—	140	62	44.3	815	5.8(59)	7	19	—	—	40.3	Pkpi	—	6	-173
NFL	4	42(34)	312	1052	3.4(60)	6	1	-16	-16.0(-16)	0	721	329	45.6	4013	5.6(59)	30	67	—	—	38.5	Pkpi	—	36	785
1946	SF-A	11(0)	17	31	1.8	0	2	25	12.5	0	8	2	25.0	15	1.9	0	0	—	—	—	k	—	0	58

HALL, PETE Peter William, E, 6´2˝/200 lbs; Marquette; 1960: NYG, rnd 12/Buf, rnd 2; B2/28/1939 Sharon, PA

YEAR	TEAM	G (GS, POS)	RUSH	YD	AVG (LG)	TD	REC	YD	AVG (LG)	TD	PASS	COMP	PCT	YD	AVG (LG)	TD	INT	SK	YD	QBR	KPR	OTD	PTS	TAY
1961	NYG	12	—	—	—	—	2	22	11.0(20)	0	—	—	—	—	—	—	—	—	—	—	—	—	0	11

HALL, RANDY Randy Lee, DB, 6´3˝/190 lbs; Idaho; 1974: Bal, rnd 13; B2/8/1952 East Wenatchee, WA **1974** Bal 14 **1976**†Bal 13 **NFL** 27 [2 yrs]

HALL, RAY Hayward Ray, DT, 6´4˝/294 lbs; Washington State; B3/2/1971 Seattle, WA **1995** Jax 12 (0)

HALL, RHETT Rhett Floyd, DT, 6´2˝/270 lbs; California; 1991: TB, rnd 6; B12/5/1968 San Jose, CA **1991** TB 16 (0) **1992** TB 4 (0) **1993** TB 1 (0) **1994**†SF 12 (2) **1995** Phi 2 (1) **1996**†Phi 16 (16, RDT) **1997** Phi 15 (15, RDT) **1998** Phi 2 (0) **NFL** 68 (34) [8 yrs]

HALL, RON Ronald Gene, DB, 6´0˝/190 lbs; Missouri Valley; 1959: Pit, rnd 28; B4/30/1937 Goreville, IL **[I]** **1959** Pit 2 **1961** Bos-A 9 (LS) **1962** Bos-A 14 (RS) **1963**†Bos-A★14 (RS) **1964** Bos-A☆14 (RS) **1965** Bos-A 14 (RS) **1966** Bos-A 14 (RS) **1967** Bos-A 9 (3) **NFL** 90 (3) [8 yrs]

HALL, RON Ronald Edwin, TE, 6´4˝/245 lbs; Cal Poly-Pomona; Hawaii; 1987: TB, rnd 4; B3/15/1964 Fort Huachuca, AZ

YEAR	TEAM	G (GS, POS)	RUSH	YD	AVG (LG)	TD	REC	YD	AVG (LG)	TD	PASS	COMP	PCT	YD	AVG (LG)	TD	INT	SK	YD	QBR	KPR	OTD	PTS	TAY
1987	TB	10(3)	—	—	—	—	16	169	10.6(29)	1	—	—	—	—	—	—	—	—	—	—	—	—	6	90
1988	TB	15(14, TE)	—	—	—	—	39	555	14.2(37)	0	—	—	—	—	—	—	—	—	—	—	—	—	0	278
1989	TB	16(15, TE)	—	—	—	—	30	331	11.0(32)	2	—	—	—	—	—	—	—	—	—	—	—	—	12	176
1990	TB	16(16, TE)	—	—	—	—	31	464	15.0(54)	2	—	—	—	—	—	—	—	—	—	—	k	—	12	227
1991	TB	15(15, TE)	—	—	—	—	31	284	9.2(24)	0	—	—	—	—	—	—	—	—	—	—	k	—	0	128
1992	TB	12(11, TE)	—	—	—	—	39	351	9.0(32)	4	—	—	—	—	—	—	—	—	—	—	—	—	24	196
1993	TB	16(16, TE)	—	—	—	—	23	268	11.7(37)	1	—	—	—	—	—	—	—	—	—	—	—	—	6	139
1994	Det	13(10, TE)	—	—	—	—	10	106	10.6(18)	0	—	—	—	—	—	—	—	—	—	—	—	—	0	53
1995	Det	6(6, te)	—	—	—	—	11	81	7.4(15)	0	—	—	—	—	—	—	—	—	—	—	—	—	0	41
NFL	9	119(106)	—	—	—	—	230	2609	11.3(54)	10	—	—	—	—	—	—	—	—	—	—	k	—	60	1326

HALL, STEVE Steven Lamont, DB, 6´0˝/209 lbs; Kentucky; B4/15/1973 Fort Wayne, IN **1996** Min 1 (0) **1996** Ind 2 (0) **NFL** 3 (0) [1 yr]

HALL, TIM Timothy, RB, 5´11˝/218 lbs; Robert Morris; 1996: Oak, rnd 6; B2/17/1974 Kansas City, MO, D9/30/1998 Kansas City, MO

YEAR	TEAM	G (GS, POS)	RUSH	YD	AVG (LG)	TD	REC	YD	AVG (LG)	TD	PASS	COMP	PCT	YD	AVG (LG)	TD	INT	SK	YD	QBR	KPR	OTD	PTS	TAY
1996	Oak	2(0)	3	7	2.3(4)	0	—	—	—	—	—	—	—	—	—	—	—	—	—	—	—	—	0	7
1997	Oak	16(0)	23	120	5.2(15)	0	1	9	9.0(9)	0	—	—	—	—	—	—	—	—	—	—	k	—	0	172
NFL	2	18(0)	26	127	4.9(15)	0	1	9	9.0(9)	0	—	—	—	—	—	—	—	—	—	—	k	—	0	179

HALL, TOM Thomas Francis, WR-DB, 6´1˝/195 lbs; Minnesota; 1962: Det, rnd 7/Buf, rnd 22; B4/3/1940 Wilmington, DE

YEAR	TEAM	G (GS, POS)	RUSH	YD	AVG (LG)	TD	REC	YD	AVG (LG)	TD	PASS	COMP	PCT	YD	AVG (LG)	TD	INT	SK	YD	QBR	KPR	OTD	PTS	TAY
1962	Det	13	—	—	—	—	—	—	—	—	—	—	—	—	—	—	—	—	—	—	k	—	0	1
1963	Det	14	—	—	—	—	3	29	9.7(23)	1	—	—	—	—	—	—	—	—	—	—	kpi	—	6	160
1964	Min	14	4	-4	-1.0(5)	0	23	325	14.1(32)	2	—	—	—	—	—	—	—	—	—	—	—	—	12	169
1965	Min	14	—	—	—	—	15	287	19.1(69)	2	—	—	—	—	—	—	—	—	—	—	kp	—	12	193
1966	Min	14	—	—	—	—	23	271	11.8(30)	2	—	—	—	—	—	—	—	—	—	—	k	—	12	182
1967	NO	11	—	—	—	—	19	249	13.1(21)	0	—	—	—	—	—	—	—	—	—	—	—	—	0	125
1968	†Min	13(13, WR)	—	—	—	—	19	268	14.1(37)	1	—	—	—	—	—	—	—	—	—	—	—	—	6	139
1969	Min	3	—	—	—	—	1	12	12.0(12)	0	—	—	—	—	—	—	—	—	—	—	—	—	0	6
NFL	8	96(13)	4	-4	-1.0(5)	0	103	1441	14.0(69)	8	—	—	—	—	—	—	—	—	—	—	kpi	—	48	973

HALL, TRAVIS Travis Todd, DT-DE, 6´5˝/295 lbs; Brigham Young; 1995: Atl, rnd 6; B8/3/1972 Kenai, AK **1995** Atl 1 (0) **1996** Atl 14 (13, LDT) **1997** Atl 16 (16, LDT) **1998**†Atl 14 (13, LDT) **1999** Atl 16 (15, LDT) **2000** Atl 16 (16, LDT) **2001** Atl 16 (16, LDT) **2002**†Atl 11 (1) **2003** Atl 15 (2) **2004**†Atl 15 (0) **2005** SF 16 (1) **NFL** 150 (93) [11 yrs]

HALL, WILLIE William Charles, LB, 6´2˝/223 lbs; USC; 1972: NO, rnd 2; B9/30/1949 Montrose, GA **1972** NO 14 **1973** NO 7 (LLB) **1975**†Oak 7 **1976**†Oak 14 (LILB) **1977**†Oak 14 (14, RILB) **1978** Oak 11 (11, RILB) **NFL** 67 (25) [6 yrs]

HALL, WINDLAN Windlan Edsel, DB, 5´11˝/178 lbs; Arizona State; 1972: SF, rnd 4; B3/11/1950 Los Angeles, CA **1972**†SF 14 **1973** SF 14 (fs) **1974** SF 13 (12, FS/ss) **1975** SF 13 (13, fs/ss) **1976**†Min 14 (1) **1977** Min 5 **1977** Was 8 **NFL** 81 (26) [6 yrs]

HALLADAY, DICK Robert Thayer, E-WB, 6´0˝/175 lbs; Chicago; B10/29/1900 Chicago, IL, D11/12/1988 Hinsdale, IL **1923** Rac 7 (6, RE), 6 **1924** Rac 10 (10, RE), 6 **NFL** 17 (16), 12 [2 yrs]

HALLECK, NEIL Neil, BB-WB, /190 lbs; none; B1902, deceased **1924** Col 6 (2)

HALLECK, PAUL Paul Charles, E, 6´0˝/195 lbs; Ohio University; B7/11/1912 Youngstown, OH, D3/1974

YEAR	TEAM	G (GS, POS)	RUSH	YD	AVG (LG)	TD	REC	YD	AVG (LG)	TD	PASS	COMP	PCT	YD	AVG (LG)	TD	INT	SK	YD	QBR	KPR	OTD	PTS	TAY
1937	Cle	11(2)	—	—	—	—	3	57	19.0	0	—	—	—	—	—	—	—	—	—	—	—	—	0	29

HALLEN, BOB Robert Joseph, G-C, 6´3˝/295 lbs; Kent State; 1998: Atl, rnd 2; B3/9/1975 Mentor, OH **1998**†Atl 12 (0) **1999** Atl 16 (14, LG) **2000** Atl 16 (5, lg) **2001** Atl 15 (12, LG) **2002** SD 13 (11, LG) **2003** SD 3 (2) **2004**†SD 2 (0) **2005** SD 9 (3) **NFL** 86 (47) [8 yrs]

HALLER, ALAN Alan Glenn, DB, 5´11˝/186 lbs; Michigan State; 1992: Pit, rnd 5; B8/9/1970 Lansing, MI **1992** Pit 3 (0) **1992** Cle 3 (0) **1993**†Pit 4 (0) **1995** Car 2 (0) **NFL** 12 (0) [3 yrs]

HALLIDAY, JACK Jack P., T, 6´3˝/238 lbs; SMU; 1950: Bal, rnd 5; B6/5/1928, D5/28/2000 Gulfport, MS **1951**†LARm 11

HALLOCK, TY Ty Edward, RB-TE-LB, 6´2˝/252 lbs; Michigan State; 1993: Det, rnd 7; B4/30/1971 Grand Rapids, MI

YEAR	TEAM	G (GS, POS)	RUSH	YD	AVG (LG)	TD	REC	YD	AVG (LG)	TD	PASS	COMP	PCT	YD	AVG (LG)	TD	INT	SK	YD	QBR	KPR	OTD	PTS	TAY
1993	†Det	16(4)	—	—	—	—	8	88	11.0(24)	2	—	—	—	—	—	—	—	—	—	—	k	—	12	50
1994	†Det	15(10, TE)	—	—	—	—	7	75	10.7(21)	0	—	—	—	—	—	—	—	—	—	—	—	—	0	38
1996	†Jax	7(0)	—	—	—	—	1	5	5.0(5)	0	—	—	—	—	—	—	—	—	—	—	—	—	0	3
1997	†Jax	15(8, FB)	4	21	5.3(11)	0	18	131	7.3(23)	1	—	—	—	—	—	—	—	—	—	—	k	—	6	83
1998	ChiB	16(12, FB)	13	41	3.2(14)	1	25	166	6.6(16)	0	—	—	—	—	—	—	—	—	—	—	—	—	6	134
1999	ChiB	15(4)	—	—	—	—	6	22	3.7(7)	0	—	—	—	—	—	—	—	—	—	—	k	—	0	-9
2000	ChiB	2(0)	—	—	—	—	—	—	—	—	—	—	—	—	—	—	—	—	—	—	—	—	—	—
NFL	7	86(38)	17	62	3.6(14)	1	65	487	7.5(24)	3	—	—	—	—	—	—	—	—	—	—	k	—	24	298

HALLORAN, DIMP Clarence R., TB, 5´8˝/175 lbs; Boston College; Fordham; B5/27/1896 Framington, MA, D11/17/1970 Framington, MA **1926** Har 3 (0)

HALLORAN, SHAWN Shawn Michael, QB, 6´4˝/217 lbs; Boston College; B4/23/1964 Gardner, MA

YEAR	TEAM	G (GS, POS)	RUSH	YD	AVG (LG)	TD	REC	YD	AVG (LG)	TD	PASS	COMP	PCT	YD	AVG (LG)	TD	INT	SK	YD	QBR	KPR	OTD	PTS	TAY
1987	SL	3(2)	3	-9	-3.0(2)	0	—	—	—	—	42	18	42.9	263	6.3(49)	0	1	5	34	—	—	—	0	83

HALLQUIST, STONE Stone Conrad, BB-HB-TB, 5´9˝/168 lbs; Middlebury; B4/8/1902 Soderholm, Sweden, D6/1/1981 Sun City, AZ **1926** Mil 9 (4, BB)

HALLSTROM, RON Ronald David, G-T, 6´6˝/300 lbs; Iowa Central; Iowa; 1982: GB, rnd 1; B6/11/1959 Holden, MA **1982**†GB 6 (0) **1983** GB 16 (0) **1984** GB 16 (13, RG) **1985** GB 16 (15, RG) **1986** GB 16 (16, RG) **1987** GB 12 (12, RG) **1988** GB 16 (16, RG) **1989** GB☆16 (16, RG) **1990** GB 16 (4) **1991** GB 16 (16, RG) **1992** GB 16 (16, RG) **1993** Phi 12 (8, RG) **NFL** 174 (132) [12 yrs]

HALPERIN, BUCK Robert Sherman, HB, 5´11˝/200 lbs; none; B1/26/1908 Chicago, IL, D3/8/1985 Palm Springs, CA

YEAR	TEAM	G (GS, POS)	RUSH	YD	AVG (LG)	TD	REC	YD	AVG (LG)	TD	PASS	COMP	PCT	YD	AVG (LG)	TD	INT	SK	YD	QBR	KPR	OTD	PTS	TAY
1932	Bkn	2(0)	9	-4	-0.4	0	—	—	—	—	2	1	50.0	23	11.5(23)	0	0	—	—	—	—	—	0	8

HALPERN, WILLIE Robert William, T, 5´11˝/220 lbs; CCNY; B7/10/1908 Brooklyn, NY, D11/24/1990 Hollywood, FL **1930** SI 3 (2)

YEAR	TEAM	G (GS, POS)	RUSH	YD	AVG (LG)	TD	REC	YD	AVG (LG)	TD	PASS COMP	PCT	YD	AVG (LG)	TD	INT	SK	YD	QBR	KPR	OTD	PTS	°TAY

HALSTROM, BERNIE Bernard Christian, HB, 5´9˝/160 lbs; Illinois; B4/18/1895 Chicago, IL, D1951 Dade County, FL **1920** ChiC 8 (5, LH) **1921** ChiC 5 (4, LH) **NFL** 13 (9) [2 yrs]

HALUSKA, JIM James David, QB, 6´0˝/190 lbs; Wisconsin; 1954: ChiB, rnd 30; B10/9/1932 Racine, WI

| 1956 | ChiB | 5 | — | — | — | — | — | — | — | — | 4 | 25.0 | 8 | 2.0(8) | 0 | 0 | — | — | — | — | 0 | 4 |

HALVERSON, BILL William Meral, T, 6´3˝/242 lbs; Oregon State; 1942: Phi, rnd 8; B5/4/1919 Davenport, IA **1942** Phi 8 (0)

HALVERSON, DEAN Robert Dean, LB, 6´2˝/230 lbs; Washington; 1968: LA, rnd 13; B8/24/1946 Olympia, WA **1968** LARm 1 **1970** Atl 7 **1971** LARm 12 **1972** LARm 14 **1973** Phi 5 **1974** Phi 13 **1975** Phi 14 **NFL** 66 [7 yrs]

HAM, DERRICK Derrick Jerome, DE, 6´4˝/257 lbs; Miami (FL); B3/23/1975 Merritt Island, FL **2000** Was 1 (0) **2001** Cle 1 (0) **NFL** 2 (0) [2 yrs]

HAM, JACK Jack Raphael, LB, 6´1˝/225 lbs; Penn State; 1971: Pit, rnd 2; B12/23/1948 Johnstown, PA; HOF 1988 [I] **1971** Pit 14 (14, LLB) **1972**†Pit☆14 (14, LLB) **1973**†Pit★13 (13, LLB) **1974**†Pit★14 (14, LLB) **1975**†Pit★14 (14, LLB) **1976**†Pit★14 (14, LLB) **1977**†Pit★14 (14, LLB) **1978**†Pit★14 (14, LLB) **1979** Pit★15 (15, LLB) **1980** Pit★16 (16, LLB) **1981** Pit 12 (11, LLB) **1982**†Pit 8 (8, LOLB) **NFL** 162 (161) [12 yrs]

HAMAN, JACK John Adam, C, 6´2˝/215 lbs; Northwestern; 1940: Cle, rnd 3; B8/18/1918 Naperville, IL, D9/1972 **1941** Cle 10 (3)

| 1940 | Cle | 11(9, C) | — | — | — | — | 1 | 5 | 5.0(5) | 0 | — | — | — | — | — | — | — | — | i | — | 1 | 6 | 68 |
| NFL | 2 | 21(12) | — | — | — | — | 1 | 5 | 5.0(5) | 0 | — | — | — | — | — | — | — | — | i | — | 1 | 6 | 69 |

HAMAS, STEVEN Steven V., FB-WB, 6´0˝/195 lbs; Penn State; B1/9/1907 Passaic, NJ, D10/11/1974 Northport, NY **1929** Ora 12 (5, fb)

HAMBACHER, ERNIE Ernest Adam, FB-TB, 5´8˝/170 lbs; Bucknell; B12/12/1906 Bloomfield, NJ, D9/3/1990 **1929** Ora 3 (1)

HAMBRICK, DARREN Darren, LB, 6´1˝/227 lbs; Florida; South Carolina; 1998: Dal, rnd 5; B8/30/1975 Lacoochee, FL **1998**†Dal 14 (0) **1999**†Dal 16 (12, LLB) **2000** Dal 16 (16, LLB) **2001** Dal 5 (5, llb) **2001** Car 9 (8, RLB) **2002**†Cle 16 (15, LLB) **NFL** 76 (56) [5 yrs]

HAMBRICK, TROY Troy, RB, 6´1˝/233 lbs; South Carolina; Savannah State; B11/6/1976 Lacoochee, FL

2000	Dal	3(0)	6	28	4.7(13)	0	—	—	—	—	—	—	—	—	—	—	—	—	—	—	0	28
2001	Dal	16(11, FB)	113	579	5.1(80)	2	4	62	15.5(27)	0	—	—	—	—	—	—	—	—	—	—	12	630
2002	Dal	16(0)	79	317	4.0(18)	1	21	99	4.7(14)	0	—	—	—	—	—	—	—	—	—	—	6	377
2003	†Dal	16(16, RB)	275	972	3.5(42)	5	17	99	5.8(13)	0	—	—	—	—	—	—	—	—	—	—	30	1072
2004	Arz	10(0)	63	283	4.5(62)	1	4	16	4.0(9)	1	—	—	—	—	—	—	—	—	—	—	12	306
NFL	5	61(27)	536	2179	4.1(80)	9	46	276	6.0(27)	1	—	—	—	—	—	—	—	—	—	—	60	2412

HAMBY, MIKE Michael Bradley, DE, 6´4˝/270 lbs; Utah State; 1985: Buf, rnd 6; B11/12/1962 Salt Lake City, UT **1986** Buf 16 (1)

HAMDAN, GIBRAN Gibran, QB, 6´6˝/240 lbs; Indiana; 2003: Was, rnd 7; B2/8/1981 San Diego, CA

| 2003 | Was | 1(0) | — | — | — | — | — | — | — | — | 2 | 50.0 | 7 | 3.5(7) | 0 | 0 | 1 | 2 | — | — | 0 | 4 |

HAMEL, DEAN Dean Edward, DT, 6´3˝/279 lbs; Tulsa; 1985: Was, rnd 12; B7/7/1961 Detroit, MI **1985** Was 16 (8, rdt) **1986**†Was 16 (8, rdt) **1987**†Was 12 (1) **1988** Was 16 (0) **1989** Dal 16 (13, LDT/rdt) **1990** Dal 12 (11, LDT) **NFL** 88 (41) [6 yrs]

HAMER, TEX Ernest Alexander, B, 6´1˝/191 lbs; Pennsylvania; B10/4/1901 Junction, TX, D5/9/1981 Dallas, TX [K] **1924** Fra☆14 (14, FB), 72 **1925** Fra☆19 (15, WB), 45 **1926** Fra ☆17 (12, WB), 15 **1927** Fra 5 (3) **NFL** 55 (44), 132 [4 yrs]

HAMILTON, ANDY Andrew Ladelle, WR, 6´3˝/190 lbs; LSU; 1972: KC, rnd 4; B11/8/1950 Ruston, LA

1973	KC	5	—	—	—	—	2	35	17.5(20)	0	—	—	—	—	—	—	—	—	—	—	0	18
1974	KC	10	—	—	—	—	2	25	12.5(19)	0	—	—	—	—	—	—	—	—	—	—	0	13
1975	NO	9	—	—	—	—	12	210	17.5(44)	0	—	—	—	—	—	—	—	—	—	—	0	105
NFL	3	24	—	—	—	—	16	270	16.9(44)	0	—	—	—	—	—	—	—	—	—	—	0	135

HAMILTON, BEN Benjamin Thomas, G-C, 6´4˝/283 lbs; Minnesota; 2001: Den, rnd 4; B8/18/1977 Minneapolis, MN **2002** Den 16 (16, C/lg) **2003**†Den 16 (16, LG) **2004**†Den 16 (16, LG) **2005**†Den 16 (16, LG) **NFL** 64 (64) [4 yrs]

HAMILTON, BOBBY Bobby Jerome, DE-DT, 6´5˝/280 lbs; Southern Mississippi; B1/7/1971 Denver, CO **1996** NYJ 15 (11, LDE) **1997** NYJ 16 (0) **1998**†NYJ 16 (1) **1999** NYJ 7 (0) **2000** NE 16 (16, RDE) **2001**†NE 16 (15, LDE) **2002** NE 16 (15, LDT/lde) **2003**†NE 16 (16, LDE) **2004** Oak 16 (15, RDE) **2005** Oak 14 (13, LDE) **NFL** 148 (102) [10 yrs]

HAMILTON, CONRAD Conrad, DB, 5´10˝/195 lbs; Eastern New Mexico; 1996: NYG, rnd 7; B11/5/1974 Alamagordo, NM **1996** NYG 15 (1) **1997**†NYG 14 (0) **1998** NYG 16 (16, RCB) **1999** NYG 3 (2) **2001** Atl 6 (0) **NFL** 54 (18) [5 yrs]

HAMILTON, DARRELL Darrell Franklin, T, 6´6˝/298 lbs; North Carolina; 1989: Den, rnd 3; B5/11/1965 Washington, DC **1990** Den 15 (8, lt) **1991** Den 6 (0) **NFL** 21 (8) [2 yrs]

HAMILTON, DERRICK Derrick T., WR, 6´4˝/200 lbs; Clemson; 2004: SF, rnd 3; B11/30/1981 Dillon, SC **2004** SF 2 (0)

HAMILTON, HARRY Harry Edwin, DB, 6´0˝/194 lbs; Penn State; 1984: NYJ, rnd 7; B11/29/1962 Queens, NY [I] **1984** NYJ 8 (0) **1985**†NYJ 11 (11, FS) **1986**†NYJ 15 (11, FS) **1987** NYJ 12 (12, FS) **1988** TB 16 (16, FS) **1989** TB☆13 (13, FS) **1990** TB 16 (16, FS) **1991** TB 7 (5, fs) **NFL** 98 (84) [8 yrs]

HAMILTON, JAMES James Samuel, LB, 6´5˝/243 lbs; North Carolina; 1997: Jax, rnd 4; B4/17/1974 Hartford, CT **1997**†Jax 9 (0) **1998** Jax 7 (0) **NFL** 16 (0) [2 yrs]

HAMILTON, JOE Joseph Fitzgerald, QB, 5´10˝/190 lbs; Georgia Tech; 2000: TB, rnd 7; B3/13/1977 Alvin, SC

| 2000 | TB | 1(0) | 1 | -2 | -2.0(-2) | 0 | — | — | — | — | 0 | 0.0 | 0 | — | 0 | 0 | 1 | 1 | — | — | 0 | -2 |

HAMILTON, KEITH Keith Lamarr, DT-DE, 6´6˝/295 lbs; Pittsburgh; 1992: NYG, rnd 4; B5/25/1971 Paterson, NJ [S] **1992** NYG 16 (0) **1993**†NYG 16 (16, LDE) **1994** NYG 15 (15, LDE) **1995** NYG 14 (14, LDT) **1996** NYG 14 (14, RDT) **1997**†NYG 16 (16, RDT) **1998** NYG 16 (16, RDT) **1999** NYG 16 (16, RDT) **2000**†NYG☆16 (16, RDT) **2001** NYG 13 (13, RDT) **2002** NYG 6 (6, rdt) **2003** NYG 15 (15, RDT) **NFL** 173 (157) [12 yrs]

HAMILTON, LAWRENCE Lawrence, WR, 6´3˝/204 lbs; Stephen F. Austin State; B8/31/1980 Marshall, TX **2003** Cin 5 (1) **2004** Arz 1 (0) **NFL** 6 (1) [2 yrs]

HAMILTON, MALCOLM Malcolm Xavier, LB, 6´1˝/238 lbs; Baylor; B12/31/1972 Dallas, TX **1998** Was 2 (0) **1999** Was 4 (0) **NFL** 6 (0) [2 yrs]

HAMILTON, MICHAEL Michael Antonio, LB, 6´2˝/245 lbs; North Carolina A&T; 1997: SD, rnd 3; B2/3/1973 Greenville, SC **1997** SD 6 (0) **1998** SD 13 (0) **1999** SD 14 (2) **2000** Mia 3 (0) **2000** Cle 1 (0) **NFL** 37 (2) [4 yrs]

HAMILTON, RAY Raymond, E, 6´4˝/212 lbs; Arkansas; 1938: Cle, rnd 6; B1/21/1916 Sheridan, AR

1938	Cle	9(6, RE)	—	—	—	—	10	187	18.7	0	—	—	—	—	—	—	—	—	—	—	0	94
1939	Det	8(0)	—	—	—	—	3	53	17.7	0	—	—	—	—	—	—	—	—	—	—	0	27
1944	Cle	9(0)	—	—	—	—	3	113	37.7(70)	1	—	—	—	—	—	—	—	—	—	—	6	62
1945	†Cle	9(0)	—	—	—	—	4	50	12.5(14)	0	—	—	—	—	—	—	—	—	—	—	0	25
1946	LARm	11(7, RE)	—	—	—	—	8	92	11.5(16)	0	—	—	—	—	—	—	—	—	—	—	0	46
1947	LARm	12(5, RE)	—	—	—	—	12	193	16.1(39)	1	—	—	—	—	—	—	—	—	k	—	6	97
NFL	6	58(18)	—	—	—	—	40	688	17.2(70)	2	—	—	—	—	—	—	—	—	k	—	12	349

HAMILTON, RAY Raymond Lee 'Sugar Bear', NT-DE, 6´1˝/244 lbs; Oklahoma; 1973: NE, rnd 14; B1/20/1951 Omaha, NE **1973** NE 14 (14, LDE) **1974** NE 14 (14, NT) **1975** NE 14 (14, NT) **1976**†NE 14 (14, NT) **1977** NE 14 (14, NT) **1978**†NE 16 (16, NT) **1979** NE 16 (16, NT) **1980** NE 15 (15, NT) **1981** NE 15 (0) **NFL** 132 (117) [9 yrs]

HAMILTON, REMY Remy, K, 5´11˝/189 lbs; Michigan; B8/30/1974 Wildwood, NJ [K] **2005** Det 1 (0)

HAMILTON, RICK Richard, LB, 6´2˝/241 lbs; Central Florida; 1993: Was, rnd 3; B4/19/1970 Inverness, FL **1993** Was 16 (0) **1994** Was 1 (0) **1994**†KC 2 (0) **1996** NYJ 15 (4) **NFL** 34 (4) [3 yrs]

HAMILTON, RUFFIN Ruffin, LB, 6´1˝/235 lbs; Tulane; 1994: GB, rnd 6; B3/2/1971 Detroit, MI **1994**†GB 5 (0) **1997** Atl 12 (0) **1998**†Atl 16 (0) **1999** Atl 11 (1) **NFL** 44 (1) [4 yrs]

HAMILTON, SKIP Lenwood, DT, 6´2˝/265 lbs; North Carolina State; Southern (LA); B5/14/1959 Philadelphia, PA **1987** Phi 1 (0)

HAMILTON, STEVE Steven, DE-DT, 6´4˝/263 lbs; East Carolina; 1984: Was, rnd 2; B9/28/1961 Niagara Falls, NY **1985** Was 7 (0) **1986**†Was 12 (2) **1987**†Was 12 (0) **1988** Was 15 (0) **NFL** 46 (2) [4 yrs]

HAMILTON, WES Wesley Dean, G, 6´3˝/261 lbs; Tulsa; 1976: Min, rnd 3; B4/24/1953 Texas City, TX **1976**†Min 13 (1) **1977**†Min 14 (6, rg) **1978**†Min 16 (15, RG) **1979** Min 16 (16, RG) **1980**†Min 13 (13, RG) **1981** Min☆16 (16, RG) **1982**†Min 9 (9, RG) **1983** Min 15 (15, RG) **1984** Min 4 (1) **NFL** 116 (92) [9 yrs]

HAMITER, UHURU Uhuru, DE, 6´4˝/280 lbs; Delaware State; B3/14/1973 Kingstree, SC **1999** NO 5 (0) **2000**†Phi 7 (0) **2001** Phi 1 (0) **NFL** 13 (0) [3 yrs]

HAMLIN, GENE Eugene Robert, C, 6´3˝/245 lbs; Western Michigan; B7/26/1946 Detroit, MI **1970** Was 4 **1971** ChiB 7 **1972** Det 5 **NFL** 16 [3 yrs]

HAMLIN, KEN Ken, DB, 6´2˝/209 lbs; Arkansas; 2003: Sea, rnd 2; B1/20/1981 Memphis, TN **2003**†Sea 16 (14, FS) **2004** Sea 16 (16, FS) **2005** Sea 6 (6, fs) **NFL** 38 (36) [3 yrs]

HAMM, BOB Robert, DE, 6´4˝/260 lbs; Nevada-Reno; B4/24/1959 Kansas City, MO **1983** Hou 16 (12, LDE) **1984** Hou 12 (12, LDE) **1985** KC 14 (5, rde) **1987** Ind 3 (0) **NFL** 45 (29) [4 yrs]

HAMMACK, MAL Malcolm Eugene, FB-LB, 6´2˝/205 lbs; Florida; 1955: ChiC, rnd 3; B6/19/1933 Roscoe, TX, D7/19/2004 Valley Park, MO

YEAR	TEAM	G (GS, POS)	RUSH	YD	AVG (LG)	TD	REC	YD	AVG (LG)	TD	PASS	COMP	PCT	YD	AVG (LG)	TD	INT	SK	YD	QBR	KPR	OTD	PTS	TAY
1955	ChiC	9	51	160	3.1(17)	2	5	13	2.6(10)	0	—	—	—	—	—	—	—	—	—	—	k	—	12	189
1957	ChiC	12	30	158	5.3(17)	0	1	14	14.0(14)	0	—	—	—	—	—	—	—	—	—	—	k	—	0	168
1958	ChiC	10(FB)	35	121	3.5(15)	1	3	11	3.7(13)	0	—	—	—	—	—	—	—	—	—	—	—	—	6	137
1959	ChiC	12(FB)	49	237	4.8(19)	0	4	69	17.3(20)	0	—	—	—	—	—	—	—	—	—	—	k	1	6	284
1960	SL	9(FB)	96	347	3.6(24)	2	4	36	9.0(26)	0	—	—	—	—	—	—	—	—	—	—	k	—	12	378
1961	SL	7	18	79	4.4(28)	1	5	70	14.0(26)	0	—	—	—	—	—	—	—	—	—	—	k	—	6	117
1962	SL	14(FB)	38	160	4.2(23)	1	4	27	6.8(15)	0	—	—	—	—	—	—	—	—	—	—	k	—	6	190
1963	SL	13	3	16	5.3(9)	0	1	15	15.0(15)	0	—	—	—	—	—	—	—	—	—	—	k	—	0	24
1964	SL	14(llb)	—	—	—	—	—	—	—	—	—	—	—	—	—	—	—	—	—	—	k	—	0	31
1965	SL	14	—	—	—	—	—	—	—	—	—	—	—	—	—	—	—	—	—	—	k	—	0	-11
1966	SL	14	—	—	—	—	—	—	—	—	—	—	—	—	—	—	—	—	—	—	—	—	—	—
NFL	11	128	320	1278	4.0(28)	7	27	255	9.4(26)	0	—	—	—	—	—	—	—	—	—	—	k	1	48	1505

HAMMERSTEIN, MIKE Michael Scott, DE-NT, 6´4˝/270 lbs; Michigan; 1986: Cin, rnd 3; B3/29/1963 Kokomo, IN **1986** Cin 15 (0) **1987** Cin 11 (0) **1989** Cin 15 (0) **1990**†Cin 15 (2) **NFL** 56 (2) [4 yrs]

HAMMILL, CHING James E., BB, 5´7˝/158 lbs; Connecticut; Villanova; Georgetown (DC); B1902, D11/25/1926 Bridgeport, CT **1925** Pro 1 (1)

HAMMOND, BOBBY Robert Lee, RB, 5´10˝/171 lbs; Morgan State; B2/20/1952 Orangeburg, SC

YEAR	TEAM	G (GS, POS)	RUSH	YD	AVG (LG)	TD	REC	YD	AVG (LG)	TD	PASS	COMP	PCT	YD	AVG (LG)	TD	INT	SK	YD	QBR	KPR	OTD	PTS	TAY
1976	NYG	2	—	—	—	—	—	—	—	—	—	—	—	—	—	—	—	—	—	—	k	—	0	14
1977	NYG☆	14(rb)	154	577	3.7(30)	3	19	136	7.2(28)	0	—	—	—	—	—	—	—	—	—	—	kp	1	24	993
1978	NYG	14(10, rb)	131	554	4.2(39)	1	20	173	8.6(26)	2	—	—	—	—	—	—	—	—	—	—	kp	—	18	773
1979	NYG	4	—	—	—	—	—	—	—	—	—	—	—	—	—	—	—	—	—	—	kp	—	0	56
1979	Was	5	2	5	2.5(3)	0	2	16	8.0(12)	0	—	—	—	—	—	—	—	—	—	—	kp	—	0	136
1980	Was	15(2)	45	265	5.9(36)	0	24	203	8.5(38)	1	—	—	—	—	—	—	—	—	—	—	—	—	6	372
NFL	5	54(12)	332	1401	4.2(39)	4	65	528	8.1(38)	3	—	—	—	—	—	—	—	—	—	—	kp	1	48	2343

HAMMOND, GARY Gary Allen, WR-RB, 5´11˝/184 lbs; SMU; 1972: NYJ, rnd 3; B7/31/1949 Port Arthur, TX

YEAR	TEAM	G (GS, POS)	RUSH	YD	AVG (LG)	TD	REC	YD	AVG (LG)	TD	PASS	COMP	PCT	YD	AVG (LG)	TD	INT	SK	YD	QBR	KPR	OTD	PTS	TAY
1973	SL	9	4	11	2.8(7)	0	4	39	9.8(23)	0	1	0	0.0	0	0.0	0	0	—	—	—	kp	—	0	190
1974	†SL	12	—	—	—	—	2	14	7.0(9)	0	1	1	100.0	81	81.0(**81**)	0	0	—	—	—	kp	—	0	191
1975	†SL	14	3	13	4.3(6)	0	2	6	3.0(10)	0	—	—	—	—	—	—	—	—	—	—	kp	—	0	100
1976	SL	14	—	—	—	—	1	5	5.0(5)	0	—	—	—	—	—	—	—	—	—	—	kp	—	0	10
NFL	4	49	7	24	3.4(7)	0	9	64	7.1(23)	0	2	1	50.0	81	40.5(81)	0	0	—	—	—	kp	—	0	490

HAMMOND, HENRY Henry Thomas, E, 5´11˝/190 lbs; Rhodes; 1937: ChiB, rnd 4; B2/23/1913 Memphis, TN, D8/19/2004 Memphis, TN **1937** ChiB 6 (3)

HAMMOND, KIM Kim Crane, QB, 6´1˝/190 lbs; Florida State; 1968: Mia, rnd 6; B10/12/1944 Miami, FL

YEAR	TEAM	G (GS, POS)	RUSH	YD	AVG (LG)	TD	REC	YD	AVG (LG)	TD	PASS	COMP	PCT	YD	AVG (LG)	TD	INT	SK	YD	QBR	KPR	OTD	PTS	TAY
1968	Mia-A	3	1	0	0.0(0)	0	—	—	—	—	26	13	50.0	116	4.5(25)	0	2	2	11	—	—	—	0	-22
1969	Bos-A	3	—	—	—	—	—	—	—	—	6	2	33.3	31	5.2(18)	0	0	—	—	—	—	—	2	16
NFL	2	6	1	0	0.0	0	—	—	—	—	32	15	46.9	147	4.6(25)	0	2	2	11	—	—	—	2	-7

HAMMOND, STEVE Steven Reed, LB, 6´4˝/225 lbs; Wake Forest; B2/25/1960 Hartford, CT **1988** NYJ 2 (0)

HAMMOND, WAYNE Wayne Roger, DT, 6´5˝/257 lbs; Montana State; 1975: LA, rnd 5; B1/30/1953 Minneapolis, MN **1976** Den 5

HAMMONDS, SHELLY Shelton Cornelius, DB, 5´10˝/189 lbs; Penn State; 1994: Min, rnd 5; B2/13/1971 Barnwell, SC **1995** Min 1 (0)

HAMPTON, ALONZO Alonzo, DB, 5´10˝/191 lbs; Pittsburgh; 1990: Min, rnd 4; B1/19/1967 Butler, AL **1990** Min 10 (0) **1991** TB 15 (3) **NFL** 25 (3) [2 yrs]

HAMPTON, CASEY Casey, NT-DT, 6´1˝/320 lbs; Texas; 2001: Pit, rnd 1; B9/3/1977 Galveston, TX **2001**†Pit 16 (11, NT) **2002**†Pit 16 (15, NT) **2003** Pit✧16 (16, NT) **2004** Pit 6 (6, nt) **2005**†Pit✧16 (15, NT) **NFL** 70 (63) [5 yrs]

HAMPTON, DAN Daniel Oliver, DE-DT, 6´5˝/264 lbs; Arkansas; 1979: Chi, rnd 1; B9/19/1957 Oklahoma City, OK; HOF 2002 **[S]** **1979**†ChiB 16 (16, LDE) **1980** ChiB★16 (16, LDE) **1981** ChiB 16 (16, LDE) **1982** ChiB★9 (9, RDT) **1983** ChiB 11 (11, RDE) **1984**†ChiB★15 (15, RDT) **1985**†ChiB★16 (15, LDE/rdt) **1986**†ChiB☆16 (16, LDE) **1987**†ChiB 8 (8, LDE) **1988**†ChiB☆16 (16, RDT) **1989** ChiB 4 (4) **1990**†ChiB 14 (9, RDT) **NFL** 157 (151) [12 yrs]

HAMPTON, DAVE David, RB, 6´0˝/210 lbs; Wyoming; 1969: GB, rnd 9; B5/7/1947 Akron, OH **[R]**

YEAR	TEAM	G (GS, POS)	RUSH	YD	AVG (LG)	TD	REC	YD	AVG (LG)	TD	PASS	COMP	PCT	YD	AVG (LG)	TD	INT	SK	YD	QBR	KPR	OTD	PTS	TAY
1969	GB	14	80	365	4.6(53)	4	15	216	14.4(50)	2	—	—	—	—	—	—	—	—	—	—	k	1	42	785
1970	GB	6	48	115	2.4(14)	0	7	23	3.3(12)	0	—	—	—	—	—	—	—	—	—	—	k	1	6	235
1971	GB	13	67	307	4.6(41)	3	3	37	12.3(19)	1	—	—	—	—	—	—	—	—	—	—	k	1	30	995
1972	Atl☆	13(FB)	230	995	4.3(56)	6	23	244	10.6(43)	1	—	—	—	—	—	—	—	—	—	—	k		42	1342
1973	Atl☆	14(FB)	263	997	3.8(25)	4	25	273	10.9(22)	1	—	—	—	—	—	—	—	—	—	—	k	—	30	1272
1974	Atl	9(FB)	127	464	3.7(34)	2	13	111	8.5(21)	0	—	—	—	—	—	—	—	—	—	—	—	—	12	540
1975	Atl☆	14(FB)	250	1002	4.0(22)	5	21	195	9.3(24)	1	—	—	—	—	—	—	—	—	—	—	—	—	36	1155
1976	Atl	2	12	24	2.0(10)	0	—	—	—	—	—	—	—	—	—	—	—	—	—	—	—	—	0	24
1976	Phi	8	71	267	3.8(59)	1	12	57	4.8(19)	0	—	—	—	—	—	—	—	—	—	—	k	—	6	307
NFL	8	93	1148	4536	4.0(59)	25	119	1156	9.7(50)	6	—	—	—	—	—	—	—	—	—	—	k	3	204	6652

HAMPTON, JERMAINE Jermaine, DB, 6´0˝/205 lbs; Northern Illinois; B6/12/1979 Riverdale, IL **2001** Ind 10 (0)

HAMPTON, KWANTE Kwante Lavon, WR, 6´1˝/182 lbs; Oregon; Long Beach State; B12/11/1963 Los Angeles, CA **1987** Atl 1 (0)

HAMPTON, LORENZO Lorenzo Timothy, RB, 5´11˝/205 lbs; Florida; 1985: Mia, rnd 1; B3/12/1962 Lake Wales, FL **[R]**

YEAR	TEAM	G (GS, POS)	RUSH	YD	AVG (LG)	TD	REC	YD	AVG (LG)	TD	PASS	COMP	PCT	YD	AVG (LG)	TD	INT	SK	YD	QBR	KPR	OTD	PTS	TAY
1985	†Mia	16(1)	105	369	3.5(15)	3	8	56	7.0(15)	0	—	—	—	—	—	—	—	—	—	—	k	—	18	772
1986	Mia	16(16, RB)	186	830	4.5(54)	9	61	446	7.3(19)	3	—	—	—	—	—	—	—	—	—	—	k	—	72	1205
1987	Mia	12(6, RB)	75	289	3.9(34)	1	23	223	9.7(24)	0	—	—	—	—	—	—	—	—	—	—	k	—	6	475
1988	Mia	16(10, RB)	117	414	3.5(33)	9	23	204	8.9(39)	3	—	—	—	—	—	—	—	—	—	—	k	—	72	702
1989	Mia	10(0)	17	47	2.8(9)	0	8	25	3.1(12)	0	—	—	—	—	—	—	—	—	—	—	k	—	0	108
NFL	5	70(33)	500	1949	3.9(54)	22	123	954	7.8(39)	6	—	—	—	—	—	—	—	—	—	—	k	—	168	3261

HAMPTON, RODNEY Rodney Craig, RB, 5´11˝/221 lbs; Georgia; 1990: NYG, rnd 1; B4/3/1969 Houston, TX

YEAR	TEAM	G (GS, POS)	RUSH	YD	AVG (LG)	TD	REC	YD	AVG (LG)	TD	PASS	COMP	PCT	YD	AVG (LG)	TD	INT	SK	YD	QBR	KPR	OTD	PTS	TAY
1990	†NYG	15(2)	109	455	4.2(41)	2	32	274	8.6(27)	2	—	—	—	—	—	—	—	—	—	—	k	—	24	662
1991	NYG	14(14, RB)	256	1059	4.1(44)	10	43	283	6.6(19)	0	—	—	—	—	—	—	—	—	—	—	k	—	60	1355
1992	NYG✧	16(16, RB)	257	1141	4.4(63)	14	28	215	7.7(31)	0	—	—	—	—	—	—	—	—	—	—	—	—	84	1389
1993	†NYG✧	12(10, RB)	292	1077	3.7(20)	5	18	210	11.7(62)	0	—	—	—	—	—	—	—	—	—	—	—	—	30	1232
1994	NYG	14(13, RB)	327	1075	3.3(27)	6	14	103	7.4(17)	0	—	—	—	—	—	—	—	—	—	—	—	—	38	1187
1995	NYG	16(15, RB)	306	1182	3.9(32)	10	24	142	5.9(18)	0	—	—	—	—	—	—	—	—	—	—	—	—	62	1353
1996	NYG	15(14, RB)	254	827	3.3(25)	1	15	82	5.5(16)	0	—	—	—	—	—	—	—	—	—	—	—	—	6	878
1997	†NYG	2(0)	23	81	3.5(22)	1	—	—	—	—	—	—	—	—	—	—	—	—	—	—	—	—	6	91
NFL	8	104(84)	1824	6897	3.8(63)	49	174	1309	7.5(62)	2	—	—	—	—	—	—	—	—	—	—	k	—	310	8146

HAMPTON, WILLIAM William Louis, DB, 5´10˝/190 lbs; Murray State; B3/7/1975 Little Rock, AR **2001**†Phi 13 (0) **2003** Car 5 (0) **2004** Car 4 (0) **NFL** 22 (0) [3 yrs]

HAMRICK, JAMES James McNeil, K, 5´11˝/177 lbs; Rice; B8/31/1963 Jacksonville, FL **[K]** **1987** KC 3 (0)

HANBURGER, CHRIS Christian, LB, 6´2˝/218 lbs; North Carolina; 1965: Was, rnd 18; B8/13/1941 Fort Bragg, NC **1965** Was 14 (5, rlb) **1966** Was✧13 (13, RLB) **1968** Was☆14 (RLB) **1969** Was★14 (RLB) **1970** Was☆14 (14, RLB) **1971**†Was 14 (14, RLB) **1972**†Was☆14 (14, RLB) **1973**†Was★14 (14, RLB) **1974**†Was★14 (14, RLB) **1975** Was★14 (14, RLB) **1976**†Was★14 (14, RLB) **1977** Was 5 (4) **1978** Was 16 (16, RLB)

YEAR	TEAM	G (GS, POS)	RUSH	YD	AVG (LG)	TD	REC	YD	AVG (LG)	TD	PASS	COMP	PCT	YD	AVG (LG)	TD	INT	SK	YD	QBR	KPR	OTD	PTS	TAY
1967	Was✧	13(13, RLB)	—	—	—	—	1	1	1.0(1)	0	—	—	—	—	—	—	—	—	—	—	—	—	0	1
NFL	14	187(149)	—	—	—	—	1	1	1.0(1)	0	—	—	—	—	—	—	—	—	—	—	ki	5	30	261

HANCOCK, ANTHONY Anthony Duane, WR, 6´0˝/200 lbs; Tennessee; 1982: KC, rnd 1; B6/10/1960 Cleveland, OH

YEAR	TEAM	G (GS, POS)	RUSH	YD	AVG (LG)	TD	REC	YD	AVG (LG)	TD	PASS	COMP	PCT	YD	AVG (LG)	TD	INT	SK	YD	QBR	KPR	OTD	PTS	TAY
1982	KC	9(0)	—	—	—	—	7	116	16.6(41)	1	—	—	—	—	—	—	—	—	—	—	kp	—	6	310
1983	KC	16(7, wr)	—	—	—	—	37	584	15.8(50)	1	—	—	—	—	—	—	—	—	—	—	kp	—	6	388

YEAR	TEAM	G (GS, POS)	RUSH	YD	AVG (LG)	TD	REC	YD	AVG (LG)	TD	PASS	COMP	PCT	YD	AVG (LG)	TD	INT	SK	YD	QBR	KPR	OTD	PTS	TAY
1984	KC	14 (0)	—	—	—	—	10	217	21.7 (46)	1	—	—	—	—	—	—	—	—	—	—	kp	—	6	115
1985	KC	16 (1)	—	—	—	—	15	286	19.1 (48)	2	—	—	—	—	—	—	—	—	—	—	k	—	12	188
1986	KC	4 (0)	—	—	—	—	4	63	15.8 (25)	0	—	—	—	—	—	—	—	—	—	—	—	—	0	32
NFL	5	59 (8)	—	—	—	—	73	1266	17.3 (50)	5	—	—	—	—	—	—	—	—	—	—	kp	—	30	1032

HANCOCK, KEVIN Kevin Drew, LB, 6´2˝/224 lbs; Baylor; 1985: Det, rnd 4; B1/6/1962 Longview, TX **1987**†Ind 1 (0)

HANCOCK, MIKE Carl Michael, TE, 6´4˝/220 lbs; Idaho State; 1973: Was, rnd 8; B2/25/1950 Woodlake, CA **1974** Was 11

YEAR	TEAM	G (GS, POS)	RUSH	YD	AVG (LG)	TD	REC	YD	AVG (LG)	TD	PASS	COMP	PCT	YD	AVG (LG)	TD	INT	SK	YD	QBR	KPR	OTD	PTS	TAY
1973	†Was	10	—	—	—	—	2	3	1.5 (2)	2	—	—	—	—	—	—	—	—	—	—	—	—	12	12
NFL	2	21	—	—	—	—	2	3	1.5 (2)	2	—	—	—	—	—	—	—	—	—	—	—	—	12	12

HAND, JON Jon Thomas, DE, 6´7˝/300 lbs; Alabama; 1986: Ind, rnd 1; B11/13/1963 Sylacauga, AL **1986** Ind 15 (15, RDE) **1987**†Ind 12 (11, RDE) **1988** Ind 15 (15, RDE) **1989** Ind 16 (15, RDE) **1990** Ind 12 (12, RDE) **1991** Ind 16 (16, RDE) **1992** Ind 15 (9, RDE) **1993** Ind 15 (14, RDE) **1994** Ind 5 (3) **NFL** 121 (110) [9 yrs]

HAND, LARRY Lawrence Thomas, DE-DT, 6´4˝/250 lbs; Appalachian State; 1964: Det, rnd 10/NYJ, rnd 21; B7/10/1940 Paterson, NJ **1965** Det 14 **1966** Det 14 (RDE) **1967** Det 14 (RDE) **1968** Det 1 **1969** Det 14 (RDE) **1970**†Det☆14 (RDE) **1971** Det 14 (RDE) **1972** Det☆14 (RDE) **1973** Det 14 (RDE) **1974** Det 13 (8, RDE) **1975** Det 14 (RDT) **1976** Det 10 (10, RDT) **1977** Det 14 **NFL** 164 (18) [13 yrs]

HAND, NORMAN Norman L., DT, 6´3˝/310 lbs; Mississippi; 1995: Mia, rnd 5; B9/4/1972 Queens, NY **1996** Mia 9 (0) **1997** SD 15 (1) **1998** SD 16 (16, LDT) **1999** SD 14 (14, LDT) **2000**†NO 15 (15, LDT) **2001** NO 13 (13, LDT) **2002** NO 16 (13, RDT) **2003** Sea 6 (4) **2004** NYG 11 (11, LDT) **NFL** 115 (87) [9 yrs]

HAND, OMARI Omari Sean, DE, 6´4˝/265 lbs; Tennessee; B7/3/1980 Philadelphia, PA **2003** SD 1 (0)

HANDLER, PHIL Philip Jacob, G, 6´0˝/212 lbs; TCU; B7/21/1908 Fort Worth, TX, D12/8/1968 Skokie, IL **[C]** **1930** ChiC 9 (3) **1931** ChiC 7 (2) **1932** ChiC 9 (4) **1933** ChiC 8 (5, RG) **1934** ChiC 8 (6, RG) **1935** ChiC☆10 (8, RG) **1936** ChiC 2 (0) **NFL** 53 (28) [7 yrs]

HANDLEY, DICK Richard H., C-LB, 6´1˝/215 lbs; Fresno State; B5/22/1922 Tulare, CA **1947** Bal-A 14 (3)

HANGARTNER, GEOFF Geoffrey Thomas, C, 6´5˝/301 lbs; Texas A&M; 2005: Car, rnd 5; B4/22/1982 New Braunfels, TX **2005**†Car 4 (0)

HANKE, CARL Carl Christopher, E, 6´0˝/190 lbs; Minnesota; B12/31/1897, D5/1964 Chicago, IL **1921** Ham 5 (4, RE), 6 **1922** ChiB 2 (0) **1922** Ham 1 (1) **1923** Ham 7 (7, RE) **1924** ChiC 8 (5, le), 12 **NFL** 23 (17), 18 [4 yrs]

HANKEN, RAY Raymond George, E, 5´11˝/190 lbs; George Washington; B12/3/1911, D11/1980 Vienna, WA

YEAR	TEAM	G (GS, POS)	RUSH	YD	AVG (LG)	TD	REC	YD	AVG (LG)	TD	PASS	COMP	PCT	YD	AVG (LG)	TD	INT	SK	YD	QBR	KPR	OTD	PTS	TAY
1937	NYG	11 (2)	—	—	—	—	4	51	12.8	0	—	—	—	—	—	—	—	—	—	—	—	—	0	26
1938	NYG✧	10 (1)	—	—	—	—	5	73	14.6	2	—	—	—	—	—	—	—	—	—	—	—	—	12	47
NFL	2	21 (3)	—	—	—	—	9	124	13.8	2	—	—	—	—	—	—	—	—	—	—	—	—	12	72

HANKS, BEN Benjamin Ujean, LB, 6´2˝/223 lbs; Florida; B7/31/1971 Miami, FL **1996** Min 12 (0) **1997**†Det 2 (0) **NFL** 14 (0) [2 yrs]

HANKS, MERTON Merton Edward, DB, 6´2˝/185 lbs; Iowa; 1991: SF, rnd 5; B3/12/1968 Dallas, TX **[I]** **1991** SF 13 (8, LCB) **1992**†SF 16 (5, ss) **1993**†SF 16 (14, FS) **1994**†SF★16 (16, FS) **1995**†SF★16 (16, FS) **1996**†SF★16 (16, FS) **1997**†SF★16 (16, FS) **1998**†SF 16 (16, FS) **1999** Sea 12 (1) **NFL** 137 (108) [9 yrs]

HANKTON, CORTEZ Cortez, WR, 6´0˝/200 lbs; Texas Southern; B1/20/1981 New Orleans, LA

YEAR	TEAM	G (GS, POS)	RUSH	YD	AVG (LG)	TD	REC	YD	AVG (LG)	TD	PASS	COMP	PCT	YD	AVG (LG)	TD	INT	SK	YD	QBR	KPR	OTD	PTS	TAY
2003	Jax	16 (0)	—	—	—	—	17	166	9.8 (22)	0	—	—	—	—	—	—	—	—	—	—	—	—	0	83
2004	Jax	12 (0)	—	—	—	—	9	81	9.0 (14)	2	—	—	—	—	—	—	—	—	—	—	—	—	12	51
2005	Jax	5 (0)	—	—	—	—	3	15	5.0 (8)	0	—	—	—	—	—	—	—	—	—	—	—	—	0	8
NFL	3	33 (0)	—	—	—	—	29	262	9.0 (22)	2	—	—	—	—	—	—	—	—	—	—	—	—	12	141

HANKTON, KARL Karl Christopher, WR, 6´2˝/202 lbs; LSU; Trinity (IL); B7/24/1970 New Orleans, LA

YEAR	TEAM	G (GS, POS)	RUSH	YD	AVG (LG)	TD	REC	YD	AVG (LG)	TD	PASS	COMP	PCT	YD	AVG (LG)	TD	INT	SK	YD	QBR	KPR	OTD	PTS	TAY
1998	Phi	10 (0)	1	-4	-4.0 (-4)	0	—	—	—	—	—	—	—	—	—	—	—	—	—	—	k	—	0	-1
2000	Car	16 (0)	—	—	—	—	4	38	9.5 (14)	0	—	—	—	—	—	—	—	—	—	—	—	—	0	19
2001	Car	11 (0)	—	—	—	—	—	—	—	—	—	—	—	—	—	—	—	—	—	—	—	—	—	—
2002	Car	16 (1)	2	-4	-2.0 (2)	0	9	146	16.2 (31)	0	—	—	—	—	—	—	—	—	—	—	—	—	0	69
2003	†Car	14 (0)	—	—	—	—	2	27	13.5 (15)	0	—	—	—	—	—	—	—	—	—	—	—	—	0	14
2004	Car	15 (0)	—	—	—	—	2	25	12.5 (20)	0	—	—	—	—	—	—	—	—	—	—	—	—	0	13
2005	†Car	16 (0)	—	—	—	—	—	—	—	—	—	—	—	—	—	—	—	—	—	—	—	—	0	0
NFL	7	98 (1)	3	-8	-2.7 (2)	0	17	236	13.9 (31)	0	—	—	—	—	—	—	—	—	—	—	k	—	0	113

HANLEY, BO Edward Louis, WB, 5´7˝/150 lbs; Marquette; B12/14/1887 Milwaukee, WI, D9/21/1980 Milwaukee, WI **[C]** **1920** Det 3 (3, WB)

HANLEY, DICK Richard Edgar, WB, 5´10˝/175 lbs; Washington; Washington State; B11/19/1894 Cloquet, MN, D12/16/1970 Palo Alto, CA **[C]** **1924** Rac 1 (0)

HANLON, BOB Robert Seldon, HB-DB, 6´1˝/195 lbs; Notre Dame; Loras; 1948: ChiC, rnd 14; B8/24/1924 Springfield, OH, D7/20/1995 Chicago, IL

YEAR	TEAM	G (GS, POS)	RUSH	YD	AVG (LG)	TD	REC	YD	AVG (LG)	TD	PASS	COMP	PCT	YD	AVG (LG)	TD	INT	SK	YD	QBR	KPR	OTD	PTS	TAY
1948	ChiC	10 (1)	6	11	1.8 (5)	0	—	—	—	—	—	—	—	—	—	—	—	—	—	—	i	—	0	31
1949	Pit	12 (7, hb)	6	13	2.2 (7)	0	1	4	4.0 (4)	0	—	—	—	—	—	—	—	—	—	—	ki	—	0	77
NFL	2	22 (8)	12	24	2.0 (7)	0	1	4	4.0 (4)	0	—	—	—	—	—	—	—	—	—	—	ki	—	0	108

HANNA, JIM Jimmy Glenn, NT, 6´4˝/255 lbs; Louisville; B8/10/1971 West Palm Beach, FL **1994** NO 7 (0)

HANNA, ZIP Elzaphan McConnell, G, 5´10˝/218 lbs; South Carolina; B12/1/1916 Chester, SC, D1/18/2001 Asheville, NC **1945**†Was 9 (7, RG)

HANNAH, CHARLEY Charles Alvin, G-T-DE, 6´5˝/260 lbs; Alabama; 1977: TB, rnd 3; B7/26/1955 Albertville, AL **1977** TB 9 **1978** TB 16 (14, LDE) **1979**†TB 14 (14, RT) **1981**†TB 15 (12, RT) **1982**†TB 7 (5, rt) **1983**†LARd 16 (16, LG) **1984**†LARd 15 (9, LG) **1985**†LARd 15 (15, LG) **1986** LARd 12 (12, LG) **1987** LARd 5 (5, lg) **1988** LARd 8 (8, LG)

YEAR	TEAM	G (GS, POS)	RUSH	YD	AVG (LG)	TD	REC	YD	AVG (LG)	TD	PASS	COMP	PCT	YD	AVG (LG)	TD	INT	SK	YD	QBR	KPR	OTD	PTS	TAY
1980	TB	16 (16, RT)	—	—	—	—	—	—	—	—	1	0	0.0	0	0.0	0	0	—	—	—	—	—	0	0
NFL	12	148 (126)	—	—	—	—	—	—	—	—	1	0	0.0	0	0.0	0	0	—	—	—	—	—	0	0

HANNAH, HERB Herbert, T, 6´3˝/220 lbs; Alabama; 1951: NYG, rnd 6; B7/21/1921 Laoma, TN

YEAR	TEAM	G (GS, POS)	RUSH	YD	AVG (LG)	TD	REC	YD	AVG (LG)	TD	PASS	COMP	PCT	YD	AVG (LG)	TD	INT	SK	YD	QBR	KPR	OTD	PTS	TAY
1951	NYG	12 (RT)	—	—	—	—	0	8	(8)	0	—	—	—	—	—	—	—	—	—	—	—	—	0	4

HANNAH, JOHN John Allen, G, 6´2˝/265 lbs; Alabama; 1973: NE, rnd 1; B4/4/1951 Canton, GA; HOF 1991 **1973** NE 13 (13, LG) **1974** NE☆14 (14, LG) **1975** NE 14 (14, LG) **1976**†NE★14 (14, LG) **1977** NE☆11 (11, LG) **1978**†NE★16 (16, LG) **1979** NE★16 (16, LG) **1980** NE★16 (16, LG) **1981** NE★16 (16, LG) **1982**†NE★8 (8, LG) **1983** NE★16 (16, LG) **1984** NE★15 (15, LG) **1985**†NE★14 (14, LG) **NFL** 183 (183) [13 yrs]

HANNAH, TRAVIS Travis Lamont, WR, 5´7˝/161 lbs; USC; 1993: Hou, rnd 4; B1/31/1970 Los Angeles, CA

YEAR	TEAM	G (GS, POS)	RUSH	YD	AVG (LG)	TD	REC	YD	AVG (LG)	TD	PASS	COMP	PCT	YD	AVG (LG)	TD	INT	SK	YD	QBR	KPR	OTD	PTS	TAY
1993	†Hou	12 (0)	—	—	—	—	—	—	—	—	—	—	—	—	—	—	—	—	—	—	—	—	—	—
1994	Hou	9 (0)	—	—	—	—	3	24	8.0 (11)	0	—	—	—	—	—	—	—	—	—	—	kp	—	0	66
1995	Hou	16 (1)	1	5	5.0 (5)	0	10	142	14.2 (42)	0	—	—	—	—	—	—	—	—	—	—	p	—	0	87
NFL	3	37 (1)	1	5	5.0 (5)	0	13	166	12.8 (42)	0	—	—	—	—	—	—	—	—	—	—	kp	—	0	153

HANNAM, RYAN Ryan, TE, 6´2˝/248 lbs; Northern Iowa; 2002: Sea, rnd 5; B2/24/1980 St. Ansgar, IA

YEAR	TEAM	G (GS, POS)	RUSH	YD	AVG (LG)	TD	REC	YD	AVG (LG)	TD	PASS	COMP	PCT	YD	AVG (LG)	TD	INT	SK	YD	QBR	KPR	OTD	PTS	TAY
2002	Sea	15 (0)	—	—	—	—	1	16	16.0 (16)	1	—	—	—	—	—	—	—	—	—	—	—	—	6	13
2003	Sea	5 (0)	—	—	—	—	—	—	—	—	—	—	—	—	—	—	—	—	—	—	k	—	0	2
2004	†Sea	16 (0)	—	—	—	—	8	110	13.8 (36)	0	—	—	—	—	—	—	—	—	—	—	p	—	0	56
2005	†Sea	16 (5, te)	—	—	—	—	13	89	6.8 (20)	1	—	—	—	—	—	—	—	—	—	—	—	—	6	50
NFL	4	52 (5)	—	—	—	—	22	215	9.8 (36)	2	—	—	—	—	—	—	—	—	—	—	kp	—	12	121

HANNEMAN, CHUCK Charles Bennett, E, 6´0˝/220 lbs; Eastern Michigan; B9/26/1914 Flint, MI, D3/31/1999 Cadillac, MI **[K]**

YEAR	TEAM	G (GS, POS)	RUSH	YD	AVG (LG)	TD	REC	YD	AVG (LG)	TD	PASS	COMP	PCT	YD	AVG (LG)	TD	INT	SK	YD	QBR	KPR	OTD	PTS	TAY
1937	Det	10 (0)	2	53	26.5 (50)	1	1	9	9.0 (9)	0	—	—	—	—	—	—	—	—	—	—	—	—	6	68
1938	Det	10 (2)	1	6	6.0 (6)	0	4	80	20.0	1	—	—	—	—	—	—	—	—	—	—	—	—	6	51
1939	Det	10 (10, RE)	—	—	—	—	12	257	21.4	2	—	—	—	—	—	—	—	—	—	—	KP	—	29	139
1940	Det☆	9 (6, RE)	—	—	—	—	14	224	16.0	0	—	—	—	—	—	—	—	—	—	—	Ki	—	16	136
1941	Det	6 (4)	—	—	—	—	4	48	12.0 (46)	1	—	—	—	—	—	—	—	—	—	—	K	—	13	29
1941	Cle	1 (0)	—	—	—	—	—	—	—	—	—	—	—	—	—	—	—	—	—	—	—	—	—	—
NFL	5	46 (22)	3	59	19.7 (50)	1	35	618	17.7 (46)	4	—	—	—	—	—	—	—	—	—	—	KPi	—	70	422

HANNEMAN, CLIFF Clifford Paul, LB, 6´2˝/235 lbs; Fresno State; B10/21/1964 Duarte, CA **1987** Cle 3 (3)

HANNEMAN, CRAIG Craig Lewis, DE-DT, 6´3˝/240 lbs; Oregon State; 1971: Pit, rnd 6; B7/1/1949 Salem, OR **1972**†Pit 13 **1973**†Pit 14 **1974** NE 9 **1975** NE 11 (3) **NFL** 47 (3) [4 yrs]

YEAR	TEAM	G (GS, POS)	RUSH	YD	AVG (LG)	TD	REC	YD	AVG (LG)	TD	PASS COMP	PCT	YD	AVG (LG)	TD	INT	SK	YD	QBR	KPR	OTD	PTS	TAY

HANNER, DAVE   Joel David 'Hawg', DT, 6´2˝/257 lbs; Arkansas; 1952: GB, rnd 5; B5/22/1930 Parkin, AR   **1952** GB 12 (LDT)   **1953** GB✧12 (RDT)   **1954** GB✧12 (RDT)
1955 GB 12 (RDT)   **1956** GB 12 (RDT)   **1957** GB✩12 (RDT)   **1958** GB 12 (LDT)   **1959** GB✩12 (LDT)   **1960**†GB 12 (LDT)   **1961**†GB 13 (LDT)   **1962**†GB 14 (LDT)   **1963** GB 14 (ldt)
1964 GB 11   **NFL** 160 [13 yrs]

HANNON, TOM   Thomas Edward, DB, 5´11˝/193 lbs; Michigan State; 1977: Min, rnd 3; B3/5/1955 Massillon, OH   **1977**†Min 12   **1978**†Min 16 (14, FS)   **1979** Min 16 (16, SS)
1980†Min 16 (16, SS)   **1981** Min 16 (16, SS)   **1982**†Min 9 (9, SS)   **1983** Min 16 (16, SS)   **1984** Min 16 (16, SS)   **NFL** 117 (103) [8 yrs]

HANNULA, JIM   James Frank, T, 6´6˝/264 lbs; Northern Illinois; 1981: Cin, rnd 9; B7/12/1959 Elgin, IL   **1983** Cin 15 (0)

HANNY, DUKE   Frank Matthew, E-T-G-FB, 6´0˝/199 lbs; Indiana; B12/10/1897 Aurora, IL, D9/3/1946 Aurora, IL [K]   **1923** ChiB✩11 (11, LE), 6   **1924** ChiB✩11 (11, LE), 6
1925 ChiB✩17 (17, LE), 6   **1926** ChiB✩16 (14, LE), 24   **1927** ChiB 14 (14, RE)   **1928** Pro 11 (10, LE), 6   **1929** Pro 11 (7, LT), 1   **1930** GB 2 (1)   **1930** Por 4 (1)   **NFL** 97 (86), 49 [8 yrs]

HANOUSEK, MATT   Matthew Joseph, G-T, 6´4˝/265 lbs; Drake; Utah State; B8/16/1963 St. Paul, MN   **1987** Sea 3 (3)

HANRATTY, TERRY   Terrence Hugh, QB, 6´1˝/210 lbs; Notre Dame; 1969: Pit, rnd 2; B1/19/1948 Butler, PA
1969	Pit	8 (5, qb)	10	106	10.6 (31)	0	—	—	—	—	126	52	41.3	716	5.7 (41)	8	13	20	168	41.7	—	—	0	-16
1970	Pit	13 (6, qb)	4	-5	-1.3 (0)	0	—	—	—	—	163	64	39.3	842	5.2 (72)	5	8	3	33	46.1	—	—	0	121
1971	Pit	6 (1)	1	3	3.0 (3)	1	—	—	—	—	29	7	24.1	159	5.5 (40)	2	3	3	32	—	—	—	6	-18
1972	†Pit	7	—	—	—	—	—	—	—	—	4	2	50.0	23	5.8 (14)	0	0	1	2	—	—	—	0	12
1973	Pit	9 (4)	3	0	0.0 (0)	0	—	—	—	—	69	31	44.9	643	9.3 (53)	8	5	3	27	—	—	—	0	162
1974	Pit	3 (1)	1	-6	-6.0 (-6)	0	—	—	—	—	26	3	11.5	95	3.7 (35)	1	5	1	13	—	—	—	0	-154
1975	†Pit	1	1	0	0.0 (0)	0	—	—	—	—	—	—	—	—	—	—	—	—	—	—	—	—	0	0
1976	TB	3 (1)	1	1	1.0 (1)	0	—	—	—	—	14	6	42.9	32	2.3 (12)	0	1	3	24	—	—	—	0	-23
NFL	8	50 (18)	21	99	4.7 (31)	1	—	—	—	—	431	165	38.3	2510	5.8 (72)	24	35	34	299	43.0	—	—	6	84

HANSEN, BRIAN   Brian Dean, P, 6´4˝/215 lbs; Sioux Falls; 1984: NO, rnd 9; B10/26/1960 Hawarden, IA [P]
1984	NO★	16 (0)	2	-27	-13.5 (-12)	0	—	—	—	—	—	—	—	—	—	—	—	—	—	—	P	—	0	-27
1985	NO	16 (0)	—	—	—	—	—	—	—	—	1	1	100.0	8	8.0 (8)	0	0	—	—	—	P	—	0	4
1986	NO	16 (0)	1	0	0.0 (0)	0	—	—	—	—	—	—	—	—	—	—	—	—	—	—	P	—	0	0
1987	†NO	12 (0)	2	-6	-3.0 (-3)	0	—	—	—	—	—	—	—	—	—	—	—	—	—	—	P	—	0	-6
1988	NO	16 (0)	1	10	10.0 (10)	0	—	—	—	—	—	—	—	—	—	—	—	—	—	—	P	—	0	10
1990	NE	16 (0)	1	0	0.0 (0)	0	—	—	—	—	—	—	—	—	—	—	—	—	—	—	P	—	0	0
1991	Cle	16 (0)	2	-3	-1.5 (0)	0	—	—	—	—	1	1	100.0	11	11.0 (11)	1	0	—	—	—	P	—	0	8
1992	Cle	16 (0)	—	—	—	—	—	—	—	—	—	—	—	—	—	—	—	—	—	—	P	—	0	0
1993	Cle	16 (0)	—	—	—	—	—	—	—	—	—	—	—	—	—	—	—	—	—	—	P	—	0	0
1994	NYJ	16 (0)	—	—	—	—	—	—	—	—	—	—	—	—	—	—	—	—	—	—	P	—	0	0
1995	NYJ	16 (0)	—	—	—	—	—	—	—	—	—	—	—	—	—	—	—	—	—	—	P	—	0	0
1996	NYJ	16 (0)	1	1	1.0 (1)	0	—	—	—	—	—	—	—	—	—	—	—	—	—	—	P	—	0	1
1997	NYJ	15 (0)	—	—	—	—	—	—	—	—	1	1	100.0	26	26.0 (26)	0	0	—	—	—	P	—	0	13
1998	NYJ	7 (0)	—	—	—	—	—	—	—	—	—	—	—	—	—	—	—	—	—	—	P	—	0	0
1999	Was	2 (0)	—	—	—	—	—	—	—	—	—	—	—	—	—	—	—	—	—	—	P	—	0	0
NFL	15	212 (0)	10	-25	-2.5 (10)	0	—	—	—	—	3	3	100.0	45	15.0 (26)	1	0	—	—	—	P	—	0	3

HANSEN, BRUCE   Bruce B., RB, 6´1˝/225 lbs; Brigham Young; B9/18/1961 American Fork, UT
| 1987 | NE | 6 (2) | 16 | 44 | 2.8 (7) | 0 | 1 | 22 | 22.0 (22) | 0 | — | — | — | — | — | — | — | — | — | — | k | — | 0 | 54 |

HANSEN, CARL   David Carl, DE, 6´5˝/282 lbs; Stanford; 1998: Sea, rnd 6; B1/25/1976 Houston, TX   **1998** NYJ 5 (0)

HANSEN, CLIFF   Clifford Harold, HB, 6´1˝/190 lbs; Luther; B6/29/1910 Thief River Falls, MN, D11/11/2001 Minneapolis, MN
| 1933 | ChiC | 5 (0) | 9 | 55 | 6.1 | 0 | — | — | — | — | 10 | 1 | 10.0 | 8 | 0.8 (8) | 0 | 3 | — | — | — | — | — | 0 | -61 |

HANSEN, DALE   Warren Dale, T, 6´3˝/2223 lbs; Michigan State; B1/27/1921 Detroit, MI, D5/6/1978 Birmingham, MI   **1944** Det 2 (0)   **1948** Det 12 (2)   **NFL** 14 (2) [2 yrs]

HANSEN, DON   Donald Ray, LB, 6´2˝/235 lbs; Illinois; 1966: Min, rnd 3/Mia, rnd 7; B8/20/1944 Warrick County, IN   **1966** Min 13 (8, rlb)   **1967** Min 12   **1969** Atl 11 (MLB)
1970 Atl 14 (RLB)   **1971** Atl 14 (MLB)   **1972** Atl 14 (LLB)   **1973** Atl 14 (LLB)   **1974** Atl 14 (LLB)   **1975** Atl 14 (LLB)   **1976** Sea 2   **1976** GB 12 (10, MLB)   **1977** GB 8
NFL 142 (18) [11 yrs]

HANSEN, HAL   Harlan C., FB-E, 5´10˝/200 lbs; Minnesota; B9/3/1892 Anita, IA, D9/8/1977 Des Moines, IA   **1923** GB 1 (0)

HANSEN, PHIL   Phillip Allen, DE, 6´5˝/278 lbs; North Dakota State; 1991: Buf, rnd 2; B5/20/1968 Ellendale, ND [S]   **1991**†Buf 14 (10, RDE)   **1992**†Buf 16 (16, LDE)
1993†Buf 11 (9, LDE)   **1994** Buf 16 (16, LDE)   **1995**†Buf 16 (16, LDE)   **1996**†Buf 16 (16, LDE)   **1997** Buf 16 (16, LDE)   **1998** Buf 15 (15, LDE)   **1999**†Buf 14 (14, LDE)
2000 Buf 10 (8, LDE)   **2001** Buf 12 (12, LDE)   **NFL** 156 (148) [11 yrs]

HANSEN, RON   Ronald Melrich, G-LB, 6´0˝/220 lbs; Minnesota; 1954: Was, rnd 28; B2/10/1932 Northfield, MN   **1954** Was 12

HANSEN, ROSCOE   Roscoe Harold, T-DT, 6´3˝/215 lbs; North Carolina; 1951: Phi, rnd 29; B9/24/1929 New York, NY   **1951** Phi 9

HANSEN, WAYNE   George Wayne, LB-C-G-T, 6´2˝/231 lbs; Texas-El Paso; 1950: ChiB, rnd 6; B10/6/1928 McCarney, TX, D8/24/1987 El Paso, TX   **1950**†ChiB 12   **1951** ChiB 12
1952 ChiB 10 (C)   **1953** ChiB 12 (C)   **1954** ChiB 12   **1955** ChiB 12 (LLB)   **1956**†ChiB 12 (LLB)   **1957** ChiB 12 (LLB)   **1958** ChiB 5   **1960** Dal 12 (LLB)   **NFL** 111 [10 yrs]

HANSHAW, TIM   Timothy Eugene, G, 6´5˝/300 lbs; Brigham Young; 1995: SF, rnd 4; B4/27/1970 Spokane, WA   **1996** SF 1 (0)   **1997**†SF 13 (3)   **1998**†SF 16 (0)   **NFL** 30 (3) [3 yrs]

HANSON, CHRIS   Christopher David, P, 6´3˝/223 lbs; Marshall; B10/25/1976 Riverdale, GA [P]   **1999** GB 1 (0)   **2002** Jax★16 (0)   **2003** Jax 5 (0)   **2004** Jax 16 (0)   **2005**†Jax 16 (0)
| 2001 | Jax | 16 (0) | 2 | 0 | 0.0 (0) | 0 | — | — | — | — | — | — | — | — | — | — | — | — | — | — | P | — | 0 | 0 |
| NFL | 6 | 70 (0) | 2 | 0 | 0.0 (0) | 0 | — | — | — | — | — | — | — | — | — | — | — | — | — | — | P | — | 0 | 0 |

HANSON, DICK   Richard Alan, T, 6´6˝/280 lbs; North Dakota State; B12/25/1949 Hillsboro, ND   **1971** NYG 3

HANSON, HAL   Harold William, C-G-T, 6´1˝/190 lbs; South Dakota; B11/18/1895 La Crosse, WI, D10/10/1973 Sarasota, FL [C]   **1921** RI 6 (0)   **1923** Min 1 (0)   **NFL** 7 (0) [2 yrs]

HANSON, HAL   Harold Walter, G, Minnesota; B8/10/1905 Stewart, MN, D9/29/1977 Mora, MN   **1928** Fra 16 (16, LG)   **1929** Fra✩18 (15, LG)   **1930** Fra 16 (12, LG)   **1930** Min✩1 (1)
NFL 51 (44) [3 yrs]

HANSON, HOMER   Homer Peter, C-G-LB, 6´0˝/217 lbs; Kansas State; B7/25/1910 Riley, KS, D10/5/1989 Marysville, KS   **1934** Cin 2 (0)   **1935** ChiC 1 (0)   **1935** Phi 1 (0)
1936 ChiC 1 (0)   **NFL** 5 (0) [3 yrs]

HANSON, JASON   Jason Douglas, K, 5´11˝/182 lbs; Washington State; 1992: Det, rnd 2; B6/17/1970 Spokane, WA [K]   **1992** Det 16 (0)   **1993**†Det✩16 (0)   **1994**†Det 16 (0)
1995†Det 16 (0)   **1996** Det 16 (0)   **1997**†Det★16 (0)   **1998** Det 16 (0)   **1999**†Det★16 (0)   **2000** Det 16 (0)   **2001** Det 16 (0)   **2002** Det 16 (0)   **2003** Det 16 (0)   **2004** Det 16 (0)
2005 Det 15 (0)   **NFL** 223 (0) [14 yrs]

HANSON, JOSELIO   Joselio Basilio, DB, 5´9˝/175 lbs; Texas Tech; B8/13/1981 Inglewood, CA   **2004** SF 13 (3)

HANSON, MARK   Mark, G, 6´2˝/260 lbs; Mankato State; B2/3/1965 Fairbault, MN   **1987** Min 1 (0)

HANSON, RAY   Raymond W., G-C-T, 5´11˝/190 lbs; Ohio State; Ohio Wesleyan; B7/16/1893 London, OH, D9/1968 Minerva, OH   **1923** Col 2 (1)

HANSON, STEVE   Steven Harold, E, 6´2˝/192 lbs; Carthage; B4/27/1902 Racine, WI, D8/1/1981 Racine, WI   **1926** Lou 1 (1)

HANSON, SWEDE   Thomas Tucker, B, 6´1˝/192 lbs; Temple; B11/10/1907 Navesink, NJ, D8/5/1970 Philadelphia, PA [K]
1931	Bkn	11 (3)	—	—	—	—	—	—	—	—	—	—	—	—	—	—	—	—	—	—	—	—	—	71
1932	SI	3 (2)	46	165	3.6	1	—	—	—	—	10	2	20.0	31	3.1	0	3	—	—	—	—	—	6	71
1933	Phi✩	9 (7, FB)	133	475	3.6	3	10	186	18.6 (35)	1	28	7	25.0	50	1.8	0	4	—	—	—	—	—	24	468
1934	Phi✩	11 (8, FB)	**146**	805	5.5	7	5	22	4.4	0	12	4	33.3	28	2.3	0	2	—	—	—	K	1	50	830
1935	Phi	11 (8, HB)	77	209	2.7	0	4	82	20.5	0	1	1	100.0	23	23.0 (23)	0	0	—	—	—	—	—	0	262
1936	Phi	12 (10, TB)	119	359	3.0	1	3	33	11.0	0	15	0	0.0	0	0.0	0	0	—	—	—	—	—	6	226
1937	Phi	2 (0)	18	59	3.3	1	—	—	—	—	2	0	0.0	0	0.0	0	0	—	—	—	—	—	6	69
1938	Pit	5 (1)	15	50	3.3	0	1	2	2.0 (2)	0	—	—	—	—	—	—	—	—	—	—	—	—	0	51
NFL	8	64 (39)	554	2122	3.8	13	23	325	14.1 (35)	1	68	14	20.6	132	1.9 (23)	0	13	—	—	—	K	1	92	1976

YEAR	TEAM	G (GS, POS)	RUSH	YD	AVG (LG)	TD	REC	YD	AVG (LG)	TD	PASS	COMP	PCT	YD	AVG (LG)	TD	INT	SK	YD	QBR	KPR	OTD	PTS	TAY
HANSPARD, BYRON Byron Courtenay, RB, 5´10˝/198 lbs; Texas Tech; 1997: Atl, rnd 2; B1/23/1976 Dallas, TX																								
1997	Atl	16(0)	53	335	6.3(77)	0	6	53	8.8(21)	1	—	—	—	—	—	—	—	—	—	—	k	2	18	774
1999	Atl	12(4)	136	383	2.8(15)	1	10	93	9.3(34)	0	—	—	—	—	—	—	—	—	—	—	—	—	6	440
NFL	2	28(4)	189	718	3.8(77)	1	16	146	9.1(34)	1	—	—	—	—	—	—	—	—	—	—	k	2	24	1213
HANTLA, BOB Robert Dean, G-LB-DE, 6´1˝/230 lbs; Kansas; 1954: SF, rnd 5; B10/3/1931 St. John, KS **1954** SF 12 **1955** SF 12 **NFL** 24 [2 yrs]																								
HANULAK, CHET Chester Edward, HB, 5´10˝/185 lbs; Maryland; 1954: Cle, rnd 2; B3/28/1933 Hackensack, NJ																								
1954	†Cle	12(lh)	59	296	5.0(24)	4	6	80	13.3(22)	0	—	—	—	—	—	—	—	—	—	—	kp	—	24	411
1957	†Cle	12(LH)	125	375	3.0(64)	3	3	38	12.7(19)	0	2	1	50.0	32	16.0(32)	1	0	—	—	—	p	—	18	419
NFL	2	24	184	671	3.6(64)	7	9	118	13.1(22)	0	2	1	50.0	32	16.0(32)	1	0	—	—	—	kp	—	42	830
HAPE, PATRICK Patrick Stephen, TE-FB, 6´4˝/262 lbs; Alabama; 1997: TB, rnd 5; B6/6/1974 Killen, AL																								
1997	†TB	14(3)	1	1	1.0(1)	0	4	22	5.5(13)	1	—	—	—	—	—	—	—	—	—	—	—	—	6	17
1998	TB	16(2)	—	—	—	—	4	27	6.8(11)	0	—	—	—	—	—	—	—	—	—	—	—	—	2	14
1999	†TB	15(1)	—	—	—	—	5	12	2.4(4)	1	—	—	—	—	—	—	—	—	—	—	—	—	6	11
2000	†TB	16(2)	—	—	—	—	6	39	6.5(13)	0	—	—	—	—	—	—	—	—	—	—	—	—	0	20
2001	Den	15(8, FB)	2	0	0.0(0)	0	15	96	6.4(25)	3	—	—	—	—	—	—	—	—	—	—	—	—	18	63
2002	Den	16(0)	—	—	—	—	6	26	4.3(7)	2	—	—	—	—	—	—	—	—	—	—	k	—	12	24
2003	†Den	16(0)	—	—	—	—	3	30	10.0(12)	0	—	—	—	—	—	—	—	—	—	—	—	—	0	15
2004	†Den	16(5, te)	—	—	—	—	8	35	4.4(11)	4	—	—	—	—	—	—	—	—	—	—	—	—	24	38
NFL	8	124(21)	3	1	0.3(1)	0	51	287	5.6(25)	11	—	—	—	—	—	—	—	—	—	—	k	—	68	201
HAPES, MERLE Merle Alison, FB, 5´10˝/190 lbs; Mississippi; 1942: NYG, rnd 1; B5/9/1919 Garden Grove, CA, D7/18/1994 Biloxi, MS																								
1942	NYG	11(10, FB)	95	363	3.8(52)	3	10	79	7.9(16)	2	2	2	100.0	12	-6.0(-2)	0	0	—	—	—	Pkpi	—	30	666
1946	NYG	10(1)	56	161	2.9(26)	5	3	40	13.3(33)	0	—	—	—	—	—	—	—	—	—	—	Pkp	—	30	239
NFL	2	21(11)	151	524	3.5(52)	8	13	119	9.2(33)	2	2	2	100.0	12	-6.0(-2)	0	0	—	—	—	Pkpi	—	60	905
HARBAUGH, JIM James Joseph, QB, 6´3˝/215 lbs; Michigan; 1987: Chi, rnd 1; B12/23/1963 Toledo, OH																								
1987	ChiB	6(0)	4	15	3.8(9)	0	—	—	—	—	11	8	72.7	62	5.6(21)	0	0	4	45	—	—	—	0	46
1988	ChiB	10(2)	19	110	5.8(19)	1	—	—	—	—	97	47	48.5	514	5.3(56)	0	2	6	49	—	—	—	6	297
1989	ChiB	12(5, qb)	45	276	6.1(26)	3	—	—	—	—	178	111	62.4	1204	6.8(49)	5	9	18	106	—	—	—	18	573
1990	ChiB	14(14, QB)	51	321	6.3(17)	4	—	—	—	—	312	180	57.7	2178	7.0(80)	10	6	31	206	81.9	—	—	24	1260
1991	†ChiB	16(16, QB)	70	338	4.8(20)	2	—	—	—	—	478	275	57.5	3121	6.5(84)	15	16	24	163	73.7	—	—	12	1354
1992	ChiB	16(13, QB)	47	272	5.8(17)	1	—	—	—	—	358	202	56.4	2486	6.9(83)	13	12	31	167	76.2	—	—	6	1110
1993	ChiB	15(15, QB)	60	277	4.6(25)	4	1	1	1.0(1)	0	325	200	61.5	2002	6.2(48)	7	11	43	210	72.1	—	—	24	914
1994	Ind	12(9, QB)	39	223	5.7(41)	0	—	—	—	—	202	125	61.9	1440	7.1(85)	9	6	17	72	—	—	—	0	748
1995	†Ind★	15(12, QB)	52	235	4.5(21)	2	1	-9	-9.0(-9)	0	314	200	63.7	2575	**8.2(52)**	17	5	36	219	**100.7**	—	—	12	1423
1996	†Ind	14(14, QB)	48	192	4.0(21)	1	—	—	—	—	405	232	57.3	2630	6.5(51)	13	11	36	190	76.3	—	—	6	1142
1997	Ind	12(11, QB)	36	206	5.7(18)	0	—	—	—	—	309	189	61.2	2060	6.7(58)	10	4	41	256	86.2	—	—	0	1126
1998	Bal	14(12, QB)	40	172	4.3(15)	0	—	—	—	—	293	164	56.0	1839	6.3(66)	12	11	23	145	72.9	—	—	0	712
1999	SD	14(12, QB)	34	126	3.7(16)	0	—	—	—	—	434	249	57.4	2761	6.4(80)	10	14	37	208	70.6	—	—	0	997
2000	SD	7(5, qb)	16	24	1.5(7)	0	—	—	—	—	202	123	60.9	1416	7.0(62)	8	10	14	96	—	—	—	0	372
NFL	14	177(140)	561	2787	5.0(41)	18	2	-8	-4.0(1)	0	3918	2305	58.8	26288	6.7(85)	129	117	361	2132	77.6	—	—	108	12072
HARBOUR, DAVE David Lynn, C, 6´4˝/265 lbs; Illinois; B10/23/1965 Boston, MA **1988** Was 15 (0) **1989** Was 16 (0) **NFL** 31 (0) [2 yrs]																								
HARBOUR, JAMES James Edward, WR, 6´1˝/192 lbs; Mississippi; 1985: Ind, rnd 7; B11/10/1962 Meridian, MS																								
1986	Ind	9(0)	—	—	—	—	4	46	11.5(28)	0	—	—	—	—	—	—	—	—	—	—	—	—	0	23
HARDAWAY, BUDDY Milton Buddy, T, 6´9˝/309 lbs; Oklahoma State; 1978: SD, rnd 2; B12/12/1954 Seguin, TX **1978** SD 12																								
HARDEE, BILLY William Abraham, DB, 6´0˝/184 lbs; Virginia Tech; B8/12/1954 Lakeland, FL **1976** Den 2 **1977** NYJ 14 (9, LCB) **NFL** 16 (9) [2 yrs]																								
HARDEMAN, BUDDY Willie Riley, RB, 6´0˝/196 lbs; Iowa State; B10/21/1954 Auburn, NY																								
1979	Was	10	31	124	4.0(22)	0	21	197	9.4(41)	1	2	1	50.0	30	15.0(30)	0	1	—	—	—	kp	—	6	409
1980	Was	15(2)	40	132	3.3(13)	0	16	178	11.1(46)	0	1	0	0.0	0	0.0	0	0	—	—	—	—	—	0	221
NFL	2	25(2)	71	256	3.6(22)	0	37	375	10.1(46)	1	3	1	33.3	30	10.0(30)	0	1	—	—	—	kp	—	6	630
HARDEMAN, DON Donald Ray, RB, 6´2˝/235 lbs; Texas A&M-Kingsville; 1975: Hou, rnd 1; B8/13/1952 Killeen, TX																								
1975	Hou	13(FB)	166	648	3.9(39)	5	5	10	2.0(9)	0	—	—	—	—	—	—	—	—	—	—	—	—	30	703
1976	Hou	13	32	114	3.6(21)	1	7	25	3.6(11)	0	—	—	—	—	—	—	—	—	—	—	k	—	6	203
1977	Hou	12	42	162	3.9(18)	2	11	47	4.3(9)	1	—	—	—	—	—	—	—	—	—	—	—	—	18	211
1978	Bal	13	48	244	5.1(46)	0	10	88	8.8(19)	0	—	—	—	—	—	—	—	—	—	—	k	—	0	279
1979	Bal	13(FB)	109	292	2.7(16)	3	25	115	4.6(14)	1	—	—	—	—	—	—	—	—	—	—	—	—	24	385
NFL	5	64	397	1460	3.7(46)	11	58	285	4.9(19)	2	—	—	—	—	—	—	—	—	—	—	k	—	78	1780
HARDEN, BOBBY Bobby Lee, DB, 6´0˝/192 lbs; Miami (FL); 1990: Mia, rnd 12; B2/8/1967 Pahokee, FL **1990** Mia 1 (0) **1991** Mia 16 (5, ss) **1992** Mia 4 (0) **1993** Mia 8 (0) **NFL** 29 (5) [4 yrs]																								
HARDEN, CEDRIC Cedric Bernard, DE, 6´6˝/260 lbs; Florida A&M; 1998: SD, rnd 5; B10/19/1974 Atlanta, GA **1999** SD 5 (0)																								
HARDEN, DERRICK Derrick, WR, 6´1˝/175 lbs; Eastern New Mexico; B4/21/1964 Milwaukee, WI																								
1987	GB	3(0)	—	—	—	—	2	29	14.5(15)	0	—	—	—	—	—	—	—	—	—	—	k	—	0	27
HARDEN, LEE Leon Maurice, DB, 5´11˝/195 lbs; Texas-El Paso; 1969: GB, rnd 11; B8/17/1947 Kansas City, MO **1970** GB 8																								
HARDEN, MICHAEL Michael, DB, 5´11˝/190 lbs; Missouri; B10/21/1981 **2005** Sea 4 (0)																								
HARDEN, MIKE Michael, DB, 6´1˝/192 lbs; Michigan; 1980: Den, rnd 5; B2/16/1958 Memphis, TN **[I]** **1980** Den 16 (0) **1981** Den 16 (3) **1982** Den 5 (4, FS) **1983**†Den 15 (15, RCB) **1984**†Den 16 (16, RCB) **1985** Den 16 (16, RCB) **1986**†Den 16 (16, RCB) **1987**†Den 12 (12, RCB) **1988** Den 16 (16, FS) **1989** LARd 15 (12, SS) **1990**†LARd 15 (15, SS) **NFL** 158 (125) [11 yrs]																								
HARDER, PAT Marlin Martin, FB-LB, 5´11˝/203 lbs; Wisconsin; 1944: ChiC, rnd 1; B5/6/1922 Milwaukee, WI, D9/6/1992 Waukesha, WI **[K]**																								
1946	ChiC☆	11(6, FB)	106	545	5.1(55)	4	11	128	11.6(24)	1	—	—	—	—	—	—	—	—	—	—	Kkp	—	35	676
1947	ChiC☆	12(7, FB)	113	371	3.3(45)	7	9	78	8.7(21)	0	—	—	—	—	—	—	—	—	—	—	K	—	**102**	480
1948	ChiC☆	12(7, FB)	126	554	4.4(71)	6	13	93	7.2(26)	0	—	—	—	—	—	—	—	—	—	—	K	—	**110**	661
1949	ChiC☆	11(9, FB)	106	447	4.2(42)	7	12	100	8.3(44)	1	—	—	—	—	—	—	—	—	—	—	K	—	**102**	572
1950	ChiC★	12(12, FB)	99	454	4.6(22)	1	15	111	7.4(35)	0	—	—	—	—	—	—	—	—	—	—	Kk	—	40	542
1951	Det	12(FB)	101	380	3.8(28)	6	17	193	11.4(26)	2	1	0	0.0	0	0.0	0	0	—	—	—	Kk	—	57	546
1952	Det★	11(FB)	81	244	3.0(22)	2	14	142	10.1(22)	1	—	—	—	—	—	—	—	—	—	—	K	—	85	340
1953	Det	5	8	21	2.6(10)	0	1	19	19.0(19)	0	—	—	—	—	—	—	—	—	—	—	—	—	0	31
NFL	8	86(41)	740	3016	4.1(71)	33	92	864	9.4(44)	5	1	0	0.0	0	0.0	0	0	—	—	—	Kkp	—	531	3846
HARDIN, STEVE Steven John, G, 6´7˝/334 lbs; Oregon; B12/30/1971 Bellevue, WA **1996** Ind 1 (0)																								
HARDING, GREG Gregory, DB, 6´2˝/197 lbs; Nicholls State; B7/31/1960 New Orleans, LA **1984** NO 3 (0) **1987** Phi 1 (0) **NFL** 4 (0) [2 yrs]																								
HARDING, ROGER Roger Paul, C-LB, 6´2˝/217 lbs; California; 1945: Cle, rnd 5; B6/11/1923 Oakland, CA **1945**†Cle 6 (0) **1946** LARm 10 (1) **1947**†Phi 6 (0) **1948** Det 11 (4) **1949** NYB 3 (0) **1949** GB 6 (0) **NFL** 42 (5) [5 yrs]																								
HARDISON, DEE William David, DE-DT-NT-DE, 6´4˝/274 lbs; North Carolina; 1978: Buf, rnd 2; B5/2/1956 Jacksonville, NC **1978** Buf 16 (15, LDT) **1979** Buf 16 (3) **1980**†Buf 16 (0) **1981**†NYG 0 (0) **1982** NYG 5 (1) **1983** NYG 16 (13, RDE) **1984**†NYG 15 (5, rde) **1985**†NYG 13 (0) **1986** SD 15 (0) **1987** SD 3 (0) **1988** KC 7 (1) **NFL** 122 (38) [11 yrs]																								
HARDMAN, CEDRICK Cedrick Ward, DE, 6´3˝/255 lbs; North Texas; 1970: SF, rnd 1; B10/4/1948 Houston, TX **1970**†SF 14 **1971**†SF★14 (RDE) **1972**†SF 14 (12, RDE) **1973** SF 14 (11, RDE) **1974** SF 14 (14, RDE) **1975** SF★14 (14, RDE) **1976** SF 11 (11, RDE) **1977** SF 14 (14, RDE) **1978** SF 16 (16, RDE) **1979** SF 14 (11, RDE) **1980**†Oak 16 (0) **1981** Oak 16 (0) **NFL** 171 (103) [12 yrs]																								
HARDWICK, NICK Nicholas Adam, C, 6´4˝/282 lbs; Purdue; 2004: SD, rnd 3; B9/12/1981 Franklin, IN **2004**†SD 14 (14, C) **2005** SD 13 (13, C) **NFL** 27 (27) [2 yrs]																								

HARDY, ADRIAN Adrian Paul, DB, 5´11˝/194 lbs; Northwestern State (LA); 1993: SF, rnd 2; B8/16/1970 New Orleans, LA **1993** SF 10 (0) **1994** SF 2 (0) **1994** Cin 14 (0) **1995** Cin 10 (0) **NFL** 36 (0) [3 yrs]

HARDY, ANDRE Andre Elton, RB, 6´1˝/233 lbs; Weber State; St. Mary's (CA); 1984: Phi, rnd 5; B11/28/1961 San Diego, CA

YEAR	TEAM	G (GS, POS)	RUSH	YD	AVG (LG)	TD	REC	YD	AVG (LG)	TD	PASS	COMP	PCT	YD	AVG (LG)	TD	INT	SK	YD	QBR	KPR	OTD	PTS	TAY
1984	Phi	6(0)	14	41	2.9(10)	0	2	22	11.0(13)	0	—	—	—	—	—	—	—	—	—	—	k	—	0	57
1985	Sea	3(1)	5	5	1.0(4)	0	3	7	2.3(3)	0	—	—	—	—	—	—	—	—	—	—	—	—	0	9
1987	SF	1(0)	7	48	6.9(14)	0	1	7	7.0(7)	0	—	—	—	—	—	—	—	—	—	—	—	—	0	52
NFL	3	10(1)	26	94	3.6(14)	0	6	36	6.0(13)	0	—	—	—	—	—	—	—	—	—	—	k	—	0	117

HARDY, BRUCE Bruce Alan, TE-WR-QB, 6´5˝/235 lbs; Arizona State; 1978: Mia, rnd 9; B6/1/1956 Murray, UT

YEAR	TEAM	G (GS, POS)	RUSH	YD	AVG (LG)	TD	REC	YD	AVG (LG)	TD	PASS	COMP	PCT	YD	AVG (LG)	TD	INT	SK	YD	QBR	KPR	OTD	PTS	TAY
1978	†Mia	16	—	—	—	—	4	32	8.0(15)	2	—	—	—	—	—	—	—	—	—	—	k	—	12	23
1979	†Mia	16(14, TE)	—	—	—	—	30	386	12.9(28)	3	1	0	0.0	0	0.0	0	0	—	—	—	—	—	18	208
1980	Mia	16(12, WR)	—	—	—	—	19	159	8.4(19)	2	—	—	—	—	—	—	—	—	—	—	—	—	12	90
1981	†Mia	16(4)	—	—	—	—	15	174	11.6(21)	0	—	—	—	—	—	—	—	—	—	—	—	—	0	87
1982	†Mia	9(6, TE)	—	—	—	—	12	66	5.5(19)	2	—	—	—	—	—	—	—	—	—	—	—	—	12	43
1983	†Mia	15(8, te)	1	2	2.0(2)	0	22	202	9.2(25)	0	—	—	—	—	—	—	—	—	—	—	—	—	0	103
1984	†Mia	16(5, te)	—	—	—	—	28	257	9.2(19)	5	—	—	—	—	—	—	—	—	—	—	—	—	30	154
1985	†Mia	16(16, TE)	—	—	—	—	39	409	10.5(31)	4	—	—	—	—	—	—	—	—	—	—	k	—	24	221
1986	Mia	16(16, TE)	—	—	—	—	54	430	8.0(18)	5	—	—	—	—	—	—	—	—	—	—	k	—	30	234
1987	Mia	12(12, TE)	—	—	—	—	28	292	10.4(31)	2	—	—	—	—	—	—	—	—	—	—	k	—	12	143
1988	Mia	2(2)	—	—	—	—	4	46	11.5(19)	0	—	—	—	—	—	—	—	—	—	—	k	—	0	25
1989	Mia	1(0)	—	—	—	—	1	2	2.0(2)	0	—	—	—	—	—	—	—	—	—	—	—	—	0	1
NFL	12	151(95)	1	2	2.0(2)	0	256	2455	9.6(31)	25	1	0	0.0	0	0.0	0	0	—	—	—	k	—	150	1331

HARDY, CARROLL Carroll William, HB, 6´0˝/185 lbs; Colorado; 1955: SF, rnd 3; B5/18/1933 Sturgis, SD

YEAR	TEAM	G (GS, POS)	RUSH	YD	AVG (LG)	TD	REC	YD	AVG (LG)	TD	PASS	COMP	PCT	YD	AVG (LG)	TD	INT	SK	YD	QBR	KPR	OTD	PTS	TAY
1955	SF	10	15	37	2.5(14)	0	12	338	28.2(78)	4	—	—	—	—	—	—	—	—	—	—	k	—	24	246

HARDY, CHARLIE Charles, SE-WR, 6´0˝/183 lbs; San Jose State; B11/7/1933 Monroe, LA

YEAR	TEAM	G (GS, POS)	RUSH	YD	AVG (LG)	TD	REC	YD	AVG (LG)	TD	PASS	COMP	PCT	YD	AVG (LG)	TD	INT	SK	YD	QBR	KPR	OTD	PTS	TAY
1960	Oak-A	14(SE)	—	—	—	—	24	423	17.6(52)	3	—	—	—	—	—	—	—	—	—	—	—	—	18	227
1961	Oak-A	14(SE)	—	—	—	—	24	337	14.0(55)	4	—	—	—	—	—	—	—	—	—	—	—	—	24	189
1962	Oak-A	5(se)	—	—	—	—	6	80	13.3(16)	0	—	—	—	—	—	—	—	—	—	—	—	—	0	40
NFL	3	33	—	—	—	—	54	840	15.6(55)	7	—	—	—	—	—	—	—	—	—	—	—	—	42	455

HARDY, CLIFF Clifton, DB, 6´0˝/188 lbs; Michigan State; 1971: Chi, rnd 11; B1/28/1947 Fairfield, AL **1971** ChiB 1

HARDY, DARRYL Daryl Gerrod, LB, 6´2˝/230 lbs; Tennessee; 1992: Atl, rnd 10; B11/22/1968 Cincinnati, OH **1995** Arz 4 (0) **1995** Dal 5 (0) **1997** Dal 12 (0) **1997** Sea 2 (0) **NFL** 23 (0) [2 yrs]

HARDY, DAVID David Robert, K, 5´7˝/180 lbs; Texas A&M; B7/7/1959 Fort Worth, TX **[K]** **1987** LARd 2 (0)

HARDY, ED Edgar Charles, G, 6´4˝/242 lbs; Jackson State; 1972: SF, rnd 7; B3/11/1951 Magee, MS **1973** SF 3

HARDY, ISHAM Isham Trotter, G, 5´9˝/185 lbs; William & Mary; B3/28/1899 Blackstone, VA, D1/23/1983 Richmond, VA **1923** Akr 1 (0) **1926** Akr 2 (0) **NFL** 3 (0) [2 yrs]

HARDY, JERMAINE Jermaine, DB, 5´10˝/213 lbs; Virginia; B3/20/1982 Roanoke, VA **2005** Car 3 (0)

HARDY, JIM James Fred, QB-DB, 6´0˝/180 lbs; USC; 1945: Was, rnd 1; B4/24/1923 San Pedro, CA **[K]**

YEAR	TEAM	G (GS, POS)	RUSH	YD	AVG (LG)	TD	REC	YD	AVG (LG)	TD	PASS	COMP	PCT	YD	AVG (LG)	TD	INT	SK	YD	QBR	KPR	OTD	PTS	TAY
1946	LARm	9(0)	10	-10	-1.0(6)	0	—	—	—	—	64	24	37.5	285	4.5(60)	2	7	—	—	—	Pi	—	0	-135
1947	LARm	9(0)	3	-6	-2.0(7)	0	—	—	—	—	57	23	40.4	388	6.8(64)	5	7	—	—	—	P	—	0	-67
1948	LARm	12(3, qb)	5	14	2.8(9)	0	—	—	—	—	211	112	53.1	1390	6.6(69)	14	7	—	—	82.1	P	—	0	499
1949	ChiC	12(5, qb)	7	6	0.9(4)	1	—	—	—	—	150	63	42.0	748	5.0(48)	10	13	—	—	44.0	P	—	6	-80
1950	ChiC✧	11(11, QB)	10	14	1.4(19)	1	—	—	—	—	257	117	45.5	1636	6.4(58)	17	**24**	—	—	49.7	P	—	6	-33
1951	ChiC	7(qb)	12	38	3.2(16)	0	—	—	—	—	114	56	49.1	809	7.1(80)	3	10	—	—	44.8	—	—	0	58
1952	Det	9	5	16	3.2(9)	0	—	—	—	—	59	28	47.5	434	7.4(49)	3	5	—	—	—	K	—	1	48
NFL	7	69(19)	52	72	1.4(19)	2	—	—	—	—	912	423	46.4	5690	6.2(80)	54	73	—	—	53.1	KPi	—	13	290

HARDY, JOHN John Louis, DB, 5´10˝/166 lbs; California; B6/11/1968 Pasadena, CA **1991** ChiB 4 (0)

HARDY, KEVIN Kevin Thomas, DT, 6´5˝/276 lbs; Notre Dame; 1968: NO, rnd 1; B7/28/1945 Oakland, CA **1968** SF 12 **1970** GB 14 **1971** SD 13 (RDT) **1972** SD 6 **NFL** 45 [4 yrs]

HARDY, KEVIN Kevin Lamont, LB, 6´4˝/259 lbs; Illinois; 1996: Jax, rnd 1; B7/24/1973 Evansville, IN **1996**†Jax 16 (15, RLB) **1997**†Jax 13 (11, LLB) **1998**†Jax 16 (16, RLB) **1999**†Jax★16 (16, RLB) **2000** Jax 16 (16, LLB/rlb) **2001** Jax 9 (9, LLB) **2002** Dal 16 (15, LLB) **2003** Cin 16 (16, MLB) **2004** Cin 16 (14, LLB) **NFL** 134 (128) [9 yrs]

HARDY, LARRY Lawrence, TE, 6´3˝/234 lbs; Jackson State; 1978: NO, rnd 12; B7/9/1956 Mendenhall, MS

YEAR	TEAM	G (GS, POS)	RUSH	YD	AVG (LG)	TD	REC	YD	AVG (LG)	TD	PASS	COMP	PCT	YD	AVG (LG)	TD	INT	SK	YD	QBR	KPR	OTD	PTS	TAY
1978	NO	16(1)	—	—	—	—	5	131	26.2(71)	1	—	—	—	—	—	—	—	—	—	—	k	—	6	44
1979	NO	16	—	—	—	—	1	3	3.0(3)	1	—	—	—	—	—	—	—	—	—	—	—	—	6	7
1980	NO	16(3)	—	—	—	—	13	197	15.2(44)	0	—	—	—	—	—	—	—	—	—	—	—	—	0	99
1981	NO	16(16, TE)	—	—	—	—	23	275	12.0(27)	1	—	—	—	—	—	—	—	—	—	—	—	—	6	143
1982	NO	9(2)	—	—	—	—	8	67	8.4(31)	1	—	—	—	—	—	—	—	—	—	—	—	—	6	39
1983	NO	6(1)	—	—	—	—	2	29	14.5(22)	0	—	—	—	—	—	—	—	—	—	—	—	—	0	15
1984	NO	6(0)	—	—	—	—	4	50	12.5(28)	1	—	—	—	—	—	—	—	—	—	—	—	—	6	30
1985	NO	16(0)	—	—	—	—	15	208	13.9(31)	2	—	—	—	—	—	—	—	—	—	—	—	—	12	114
NFL	8	101(23)	—	—	—	—	71	960	13.5(71)	7	—	—	—	—	—	—	—	—	—	—	k	—	42	488

HARDY, RICHARD Richard Earle, T, 5´10˝/210 lbs; Boston College; B9/1/1904, MA, D2/27/1970 Togus, ME **1926** Rac 5 (5, LT)

HARDY, ROBERT Robert Emmitt, DT, 6´2˝/250 lbs; Jackson State; 1979: Sea, rnd 10; B7/3/1956 Tulsa, OK **1979** Sea 16 (16, LDT) **1980** Sea 16 (16, LDT) **1981** Sea 14 (13, LDT) **1982** Sea 8 (8, LDT) **NFL** 54 (53) [4 yrs]

HARDY, ROBERT Robert Kenneth, RB, 5´10˝/210 lbs; Carson-Newman; B9/1/1967 Gaffney, SC **1991** TB 16 (0)

HARDY, TERRY Terry, TE, 6´4˝/266 lbs; Southern Mississippi; 1998: Arz, rnd 5; B5/31/1976 Montgomery, AL

YEAR	TEAM	G (GS, POS)	RUSH	YD	AVG (LG)	TD	REC	YD	AVG (LG)	TD	PASS	COMP	PCT	YD	AVG (LG)	TD	INT	SK	YD	QBR	KPR	OTD	PTS	TAY
1998	Arz	9(0)	—	—	—	—	—	—	—	—	—	—	—	—	—	—	—	—	—	—	—	—	—	—
1999	Arz	16(16, TE)	—	—	—	—	30	222	7.4(23)	0	—	—	—	—	—	—	—	—	—	—	—	—	0	111
2000	Arz	16(15, TE)	—	—	—	—	27	160	5.9(13)	1	—	—	—	—	—	—	—	—	—	—	—	—	6	85
2001	Arz	8(6, te)	—	—	—	—	11	79	7.2(13)	2	—	—	—	—	—	—	—	—	—	—	—	—	12	50
NFL	4	49(37)	—	—	—	—	68	461	6.8(23)	3	—	—	—	—	—	—	—	—	—	—	—	—	18	246

HARE, CECE Cecil J., B, 5´11˝/195 lbs; Gonzaga; B3/2/1919 Glenbush, Canada, D4/14/1963 Spokane, WA

YEAR	TEAM	G (GS, POS)	RUSH	YD	AVG (LG)	TD	REC	YD	AVG (LG)	TD	PASS	COMP	PCT	YD	AVG (LG)	TD	INT	SK	YD	QBR	KPR	OTD	PTS	TAY
1941	Was✧	11(9, BB)	5	19	3.8(6)	0	1	25	25.0(25)	0	—	—	—	—	—	—	—	—	—	—	i	—	0	31
1942	†Was✧	11(4, BB)	14	57	4.1(11)	1	3	35	11.7(33)	1	—	—	—	—	—	—	—	—	—	—	kp	1	12	85
1945	†Was	9(3)	3	0	0.0(0)	0	3	83	27.7(66)	0	—	—	—	—	—	—	—	—	—	—	k	—	0	42
1946	NYG	8(0)	—	—	—	—	2	30	15.0(20)	0	—	—	—	—	—	—	—	—	—	—	k	—	0	19
NFL	4	39(16)	22	76	3.5(11)	1	9	173	19.2(66)	1	—	—	—	—	—	—	—	—	—	—	kpi	1	12	176

HARE, EDDIE Edward Everett, P, 6´4˝/209 lbs; Tulsa; 1979: NE, rnd 4; B5/30/1957 Ulysses, KS

YEAR	TEAM	G (GS, POS)	RUSH	YD	AVG (LG)	TD	REC	YD	AVG (LG)	TD	PASS	COMP	PCT	YD	AVG (LG)	TD	INT	SK	YD	QBR	KPR	OTD	PTS	TAY
1979	NE	16	1	0	0.0(0)	0	—	—	—	—	1	1	100.0	4	4.0(4)	0	0	—	—	—	P	—	0	2

HARE, RAY Raymond Lewis, B, 6´1˝/204 lbs; Gonzaga; B11/21/1917 North Battleford, Canada, D6/2/1975 Chewelah, WA

YEAR	TEAM	G (GS, POS)	RUSH	YD	AVG (LG)	TD	REC	YD	AVG (LG)	TD	PASS	COMP	PCT	YD	AVG (LG)	TD	INT	SK	YD	QBR	KPR	OTD	PTS	TAY
1940	†Was	5(1)	1	2	2.0(2)	0	—	—	—	—	—	—	—	—	—	—	—	—	—	—	—	—	0	2
1941	Was	11(0)	12	51	4.3(12)	1	12	87	7.3(18)	0	—	—	—	—	—	—	—	—	—	—	k	—	6	117
1942	†Was✧	11(7)	27	197	7.3(47)	1	5	57	11.4(27)	0	—	—	—	—	—	—	—	—	—	—	kpi	1	12	316
1943	†Was	10(10, BB)	21	96	4.6(16)	0	2	9	4.5(8)	0	—	—	—	—	—	—	—	—	—	—	kpi	—	0	105
1944	Bkn	10(9, HB)	72	196	2.7(36)	0	9	206	22.9(65)	1	1	0	0.0	0	0.0	0	0	—	—	—	kpi	—	6	366
NFL	5	47(27)	133	542	4.1(47)	2	28	359	12.8(65)	1	1	0	0.0	0	0.0	0	0	—	—	—	kpi	1	24	905
1946	NYY-A	4(1)	—	—	—	—	—	—	—	—	—	—	—	—	—	—	—	—	—	—	—	—	—	—

HARGAIN, TONY Anthony Michael, WR, 6´0˝/194 lbs; Oregon; 1991: SF, rnd 8; B12/26/1967 Palo Alto, CA

YEAR	TEAM	G (GS, POS)	RUSH	YD	AVG (LG)	TD	REC	YD	AVG (LG)	TD	PASS	COMP	PCT	YD	AVG (LG)	TD	INT	SK	YD	QBR	KPR	OTD	PTS	TAY
1992	†KC	12(0)	—	—	—	—	17	205	12.1(25)	0	—	—	—	—	—	—	—	—	—	—	—	—	0	103

Hargett, Ed Edward Eugene, QB, 5´11˝/185 lbs; Texas A&M; 1969: NO, rnd 16; B6/26/1947 Marietta, TX

YEAR	TEAM	G (GS, POS)	RUSH	YD	AVG (LG)	TD	REC	YD	AVG (LG)	TD	PASS	COMP	PCT	YD	AVG (LG)	TD	INT	SK	YD	QBR	KPR	OTD	PTS	TAY
1969	NO	6	5	15	3.0(11)	0	—	—	—	—	52	31	59.6	403	7.8(32)	0	0	3	18	—	—	—	0	217
1970	NO	10(qb)	4	7	1.8(7)	0	—	—	—	—	175	78	44.6	1133	6.5(49)	5	5	9	77	63.8	—	—	0	399
1971	NO	14(qb)	9	24	2.7(11)	1	—	—	—	—	210	96	45.7	1191	5.7(49)	6	5	10	68	63.4	—	—	6	460
1972	NO	14	—	—	—	—	—	—	—	—	—	—	—	—	—	—	—	—	—	—	—	—	—	—
1973	Hou	5	—	—	—	—	—	—	—	—	—	—	—	—	—	—	—	—	—	—	—	—	—	—
NFL	5	49	18	46	2.6(11)	1	—	—	—	—	437	205	46.9	2727	6.2(49)	11	10	22	163	66.0	—	—	6	1075

Hargrove, Anthony Anthony La'Ron, DE, 6´4˝/255 lbs; Georgia Tech; 2004: SL, rnd 3; B7/20/1983 Brooklyn, NY **2004** SL 15 (2) **2005** SL 16 (15, RDE) **NFL** 31 (17) [2 yrs]

Hargrove, Jim James Lawrence, LB, 6´2˝/233 lbs; Howard Payne; 1967: Min, rnd 14; B2/21/1945 Temple, TX **1967** Min 14 **1969**†Min 6 **1970** Min 12 **1971** SL 14 **1972** SL 10 **NFL** 56 [5 yrs]

Hargrove, Jimmy Jimmy Rogers, RB, 6´2˝/228 lbs; Wake Forest; B11/13/1957 Newton Grove, NC

YEAR	TEAM	G (GS, POS)	RUSH	YD	AVG (LG)	TD	REC	YD	AVG (LG)	TD	PASS	COMP	PCT	YD	AVG (LG)	TD	INT	SK	YD	QBR	KPR	OTD	PTS	TAY
1981	†Cin	15(0)	16	66	4.1(27)	1	1	0	0.0(0)	0	—	—	—	—	—	—	—	—	—	—	—	—	6	76
1987	GB	2(2)	11	38	3.5(7)	1	1	6	6.0(6)	0	—	—	—	—	—	—	—	—	—	—	—	—	6	51
NFL	2	17(2)	27	104	3.9(27)	2	2	6	3.0(6)	0	—	—	—	—	—	—	—	—	—	—	—	—	12	127

Hargrove, Marvin Marvin Andre, WR, 5´10˝/178 lbs; Richmond; B4/23/1968 Philadelphia, PA

YEAR	TEAM	G (GS, POS)	RUSH	YD	AVG (LG)	TD	REC	YD	AVG (LG)	TD	PASS	COMP	PCT	YD	AVG (LG)	TD	INT	SK	YD	QBR	KPR	OTD	PTS	TAY
1990	Phi	7(0)	—	—	—	—	1	34	34.0(34)	1	—	—	—	—	—	—	—	—	—	—	kp	—	6	101

Harkey, Lance Lance Marcel, DB, 5´10˝/180 lbs; Illinois; B10/30/1965 Selma, AL **1987** LARd 2 (0)

Harkey, Lem Lemuel, FB, 6´1˝/205 lbs; College of Emporia; 1955: Pit, rnd 6; B1/7/1934 Oklahoma City, OK, D7/3/2004 San Antonio, TX

YEAR	TEAM	G (GS, POS)	RUSH	YD	AVG (LG)	TD	REC	YD	AVG (LG)	TD	PASS	COMP	PCT	YD	AVG (LG)	TD	INT	SK	YD	QBR	KPR	OTD	PTS	TAY
1955	SF	4	6	27	4.5(15)	0	—	—	—	—	—	—	—	—	—	—	—	—	—	—	—	—	0	27

Harkey, Steve Stephen Douglas, RB, 6´0˝/215 lbs; Georgia Tech; 1971: NYJ, rnd 16; B8/3/1949 Atlanta, GA

YEAR	TEAM	G (GS, POS)	RUSH	YD	AVG (LG)	TD	REC	YD	AVG (LG)	TD	PASS	COMP	PCT	YD	AVG (LG)	TD	INT	SK	YD	QBR	KPR	OTD	PTS	TAY
1971	NYJ	14	20	62	3.1(10)	0	5	28	5.6(10)	0	—	—	—	—	—	—	—	—	—	—	k	—	0	63
1972	NYJ	11	45	129	2.9(10)	0	9	114	12.7(24)	0	—	—	—	—	—	—	—	—	—	—	—	—	0	186
NFL	2	25	65	191	2.9(10)	0	14	142	10.1(24)	0	—	—	—	—	—	—	—	—	—	—	k	—	0	249

Harlan, Jim James Thomas, T, 6´4˝/250 lbs; Howard Payne; 1977: SF, rnd 6; B6/14/1954 Shreveport, LA **1978** Was 14 (2)

Harley, Chic Charles Wesley, WB-HB, 5´8˝/165 lbs; Ohio State; B9/15/1895 Columbus, OH, D4/21/1974 Danville, IL **1921** ChiS 9 (5, wb)

Harlow, Pat Patrick Christopher, T, 6´6˝/295 lbs; USC; 1991: NE, rnd 1; B3/16/1969 Norco, CA **1991** NE 16 (16, RT) **1992** NE 16 (16, RT/lt) **1993** NE 16 (16, RT) **1994**†NE 16 (16, RT) **1995** NE 10 (0) **1996** Oak 10 (9, LT) **1997** Oak 16 (16, LT) **1998** Oak 5 (5, lt) **NFL** 105 (94) [8 yrs]

Harmon, Andy Andrew Phillip, DT-DE, 6´4˝/272 lbs; Kent State; 1991: Phi, rnd 6; B4/6/1969 Dayton, OH **1991** Phi 16 (0) **1992**†Phi 16 (13, LDT) **1993** Phi 16 (15, LDT) **1994** Phi 16 (16, LDT) **1995**†Phi☆15 (15, LDT) **1996** Phi 2 (2) **1997** Phi 5 (0) **NFL** 86 (61) [7 yrs]

Harmon, Clarence Clarence, RB, 5´11˝/204 lbs; Mississippi State; B11/30/1955 Kosciusko, MS

YEAR	TEAM	G (GS, POS)	RUSH	YD	AVG (LG)	TD	REC	YD	AVG (LG)	TD	PASS	COMP	PCT	YD	AVG (LG)	TD	INT	SK	YD	QBR	KPR	OTD	PTS	TAY
1977	Was	12(9, FB)	94	310	3.3(21)	0	14	119	8.5(22)	1	—	—	—	—	—	—	—	—	—	—	k	—	6	378
1978	Was	16(3)	34	141	4.1(47)	0	11	112	10.2(22)	1	—	—	—	—	—	—	—	—	—	—	kp	—	6	209
1979	Was	16(1)	65	267	4.1(18)	0	32	434	13.6(40)	5	—	—	—	—	—	—	—	—	—	—	kp	—	30	502
1980	Was	16(14, FB)	128	484	3.8(23)	4	54	534	9.9(45)	4	—	—	—	—	—	—	—	—	—	—	—	—	48	811
1981	Was	5(0)	1	4	4.0(4)	0	11	98	8.9(23)	0	—	—	—	—	—	—	—	—	—	—	—	—	0	53
1982	†Was	9(0)	38	168	4.4(20)	1	11	86	7.8(28)	0	—	—	—	—	—	—	—	—	—	—	k	—	6	219
NFL	6	74(27)	360	1374	3.8(47)	5	133	1383	10.4(45)	11	—	—	—	—	—	—	—	—	—	—	kp	—	96	2172

Harmon, Derrick Derrick Todd, RB, 5´10˝/202 lbs; Cornell; 1984: SF, rnd 9; B4/26/1963 New York, NY

YEAR	TEAM	G (GS, POS)	RUSH	YD	AVG (LG)	TD	REC	YD	AVG (LG)	TD	PASS	COMP	PCT	YD	AVG (LG)	TD	INT	SK	YD	QBR	KPR	OTD	PTS	TAY
1984	†SF	16(0)	39	192	4.9(19)	1	1	2	2.0(2)	0	2	0	0.0	0	0.0	0	0	—	—	—	k	—	6	365
1985	†SF	15(3)	28	92	3.3(17)	0	14	123	8.8(42)	0	1	0	0.0	0	0.0	0	0	—	—	—	k	—	0	276
1986	SF	8(2)	27	77	2.9(15)	1	8	78	9.8(15)	0	—	—	—	—	—	—	—	—	—	—	k	—	6	148
NFL	3	39(5)	94	361	3.8(19)	2	23	203	8.8(42)	0	3	0	0.0	0	0.0	0	0	—	—	—	k	—	12	789

Harmon, Ed Edward Charles, LB, 6´4˝/235 lbs; Louisville; 1968: Dal, rnd 3; B12/16/1946 North Tonawanda, NY **1969** Cin-A 11

Harmon, Ham Hamilton S., C, 6´0˝/220 lbs; Tulsa; 1937: ChiC, rnd 5; B4/2/1913 **1937** ChiC 6 (6, C)

Harmon, Kevin Kevin Anthony, RB, 6´0˝/190 lbs; Iowa; 1988: Sea, rnd 4; B10/26/1965 Queens, NY

YEAR	TEAM	G (GS, POS)	RUSH	YD	AVG (LG)	TD	REC	YD	AVG (LG)	TD	PASS	COMP	PCT	YD	AVG (LG)	TD	INT	SK	YD	QBR	KPR	OTD	PTS	TAY
1988	†Sea	5(0)	2	13	6.5(8)	0	—	—	—	—	—	—	—	—	—	—	—	—	—	—	k	—	0	30
1989	Sea	4(0)	1	24	24.0(24)	0	—	—	—	—	—	—	—	—	—	—	—	—	—	—	k	—	0	18
NFL	2	9(0)	3	37	12.3(24)	0	—	—	—	—	—	—	—	—	—	—	—	—	—	—	k	—	0	48

Harmon, Mike Michael, WR, 6´0˝/185 lbs; Mississippi; 1983: NYJ, rnd 11; B7/24/1961 Kosciusko, MS

YEAR	TEAM	G (GS, POS)	RUSH	YD	AVG (LG)	TD	REC	YD	AVG (LG)	TD	PASS	COMP	PCT	YD	AVG (LG)	TD	INT	SK	YD	QBR	KPR	OTD	PTS	TAY
1983	NYJ	9(0)	—	—	—	—	1	4	4.0(4)	0	—	—	—	—	—	—	—	—	—	—	p	—	0	51

Harmon, Ronnie Ronnie Keith, RB-WR, 5´11˝/200 lbs; Iowa; 1986: Buf, rnd 1; B5/7/1964 Queens, NY **[R]**

YEAR	TEAM	G (GS, POS)	RUSH	YD	AVG (LG)	TD	REC	YD	AVG (LG)	TD	PASS	COMP	PCT	YD	AVG (LG)	TD	INT	SK	YD	QBR	KPR	OTD	PTS	TAY
1986	Buf	14(2)	54	172	3.2(38)	0	22	185	8.4(27)	1	—	—	—	—	—	—	—	—	—	—	k	—	6	321
1987	Buf	12(10, RB)	116	485	4.2(21)	2	56	477	8.5(42)	2	—	—	—	—	—	—	—	—	—	—	k	—	24	769
1988	†Buf	16(1)	57	212	3.7(32)	1	37	427	11.5(36)	3	—	—	—	—	—	—	—	—	—	—	k	—	24	535
1989	†Buf	15(2)	17	99	5.8(24)	0	29	363	12.5(42)	4	—	—	—	—	—	—	—	—	—	—	k	—	24	440
1990	SD	16(2)	66	363	5.5(41)	0	46	511	11.1(36)	2	—	—	—	—	—	—	—	—	—	—	—	—	12	629
1991	SD	16(0)	89	544	**6.1(33)**	1	59	555	9.4(36)	1	—	—	—	—	—	—	—	—	—	—	k	—	12	832
1992	†SD✧	16(2, rb)	55	235	4.3(33)	3	79	914	11.6(55)	1	—	—	—	—	—	—	—	—	—	—	k	—	24	718
1993	SD	16(1)	46	216	4.7(19)	0	73	671	9.2(37)	2	—	—	—	—	—	—	—	—	—	—	k	—	12	565
1994	†SD	16(0)	25	94	3.8(15)	1	58	615	10.6(35)	1	—	—	—	—	—	—	—	—	—	—	k	—	18	439
1995	†SD	16(1)	51	187	3.7(48)	1	63	673	10.7(44)	5	—	—	—	—	—	—	—	—	—	—	k	—	36	524
1996	Hou	16(6, wr)	29	131	4.5(25)	1	42	488	11.6(43)	2	—	—	—	—	—	—	—	—	—	—	k	—	18	404
1997	Ten	11(0)	8	30	3.8(14)	0	16	189	11.8(27)	0	—	—	—	—	—	—	—	—	—	—	k	—	0	126
1997	ChiB	1(0)	2	6	3.0(4)	0	2	8	4.0(6)	0	—	—	—	—	—	—	—	—	—	—	—	—	0	10
NFL	12	181(27)	615	2774	4.5(48)	10	582	6076	10.4(55)	24	—	—	—	—	—	—	—	—	—	—	k	—	210	6307

Harmon, Tom Thomas Dudley 'Old 98', HB, 6´1˝/197 lbs; Michigan; 1941: ChiB, rnd 1; B9/28/1919 Gary, IN, D3/15/1990 Los Angeles, CA

YEAR	TEAM	G (GS, POS)	RUSH	YD	AVG (LG)	TD	REC	YD	AVG (LG)	TD	PASS	COMP	PCT	YD	AVG (LG)	TD	INT	SK	YD	QBR	KPR	OTD	PTS	TAY
1946	LARm	10(3)	47	236	5.0(84)	2	10	199	19.9(45)	2	—	—	—	—	—	—	—	—	—	—	kpi	1	30	534
1947	LARm	12(1)	60	306	5.1(32)	1	5	89	17.8(33)	1	3	1	33.3	31	10.3(31)	0	0	—	—	—	kpi	2	24	827
NFL	2	22(4)	107	542	5.1(84)	3	15	288	19.2(45)	3	3	1	33.3	31	10.3(31)	0	0	—	—	—	kpi	3	54	1361

Harmon, Tom Thomas Rockwell, G, 6´4˝/238 lbs; Gustavus Adolphus; B7/1/1945 Omaha, NE **1967** Atl 10

Harms, Art Arthur Gustav, T, 6´1˝/200 lbs; Vermont; B7/25/1902 New York, NY, D7/24/1986 New Providence, NJ **1925** Fra 9 (9, RT) **1926** NYG 5 (1) **NFL** 14 (10) [2 yrs]

Harness, Jim James, DB, 5´11˝/180 lbs; Mississippi State; 1956: Bal, rnd 21; B4/6/1934 Dyersburg, TN **1956** Bal 1

Harold, George George Alton, DB, 6´3˝/194 lbs; Allen; 1965: Bal, rnd 10; B4/13/1942 Augusta, GA **1966** Bal 12 **1967** Bal 2 **1968** Was 8 **NFL** 22 [3 yrs]

Harper, Alan Alan, DT, 6´1˝/285 lbs; Fresno State; 2002: NYJ, rnd 4; B9/6/1979 Fontana, CA **2004**†NYJ 11 (0)

Harper, Alvin Alvin Craig, WR, 6´3˝/210 lbs; Tennessee; 1991: Dal, rnd 1; B7/6/1968 Lake Wales, FL

YEAR	TEAM	G (GS, POS)	RUSH	YD	AVG (LG)	TD	REC	YD	AVG (LG)	TD	PASS	COMP	PCT	YD	AVG (LG)	TD	INT	SK	YD	QBR	KPR	OTD	PTS	TAY
1991	†Dal	15(5, wr)	—	—	—	—	20	326	16.3(39)	1	—	—	—	—	—	—	—	—	—	—	—	—	6	168
1992	†Dal	16(13, WR)	1	15	15.0(15)	0	35	562	16.1(52)	4	—	—	—	—	—	—	—	—	—	—	i	—	24	312
1993	†Dal	16(15, WR)	—	—	—	—	36	777	**21.6(80)**	5	1	1	100.0	46	46.0(46)	0	0	—	—	—	—	—	30	437
1994	†Dal	16(14, WR)	—	—	—	—	33	821	**24.9(90)**	8	—	—	—	—	—	—	—	—	—	—	—	—	48	451
1995	TB	13(13, WR)	—	—	—	—	46	633	13.8(49)	2	—	—	—	—	—	—	—	—	—	—	—	—	12	327
1996	TB	12(7, wr)	—	—	—	—	19	289	15.2(40)	1	—	—	—	—	—	—	—	—	—	—	—	—	6	150
1997	Was	12(0)	—	—	—	—	2	65	32.5(52)	0	—	—	—	—	—	—	—	—	—	—	—	—	0	33
1999	Dal	2(0)	—	—	—	—	—	—	—	—	—	—	—	—	—	—	—	—	—	—	—	—	—	—
NFL	8	102(67)	1	15	15.0(15)	0	191	3473	18.2(90)	21	1	1	100.0	46	46.0(46)	0	0	—	—	—	i	—	126	1876

HARPER, BRUCE Bruce S., RB-WR, 5´8˝/174 lbs; Kutztown; B6/20/1955 Englewood, NJ [R]

YEAR	TEAM	G (GS, POS)	RUSH	YD	AVG (LG)	TD	REC	YD	AVG (LG)	TD	PASS	COMP	PCT	YD	AVG (LG)	TD	INT	SK	YD	QBR	KPR	OTD	PTS	TAY
1977	NYJ	14(2)	44	198	4.5(18)	0	21	209	10.0(55)	1	1	0	0.0	0	0.0	0	0	—	—	—	kp	—	6	968
1978	NYJ	16	58	303	5.2(32)	2	13	196	15.1(44)	2	—	—	—	—	—	—	—	—	—	—	kp	1	30	1124
1979	NYJ	16	65	282	4.3(31)	0	17	250	14.7(72)	2	—	—	—	—	—	—	—	—	—	—	kp	—	12	875
1980	NYJ	15(1)	45	126	2.8(22)	0	50	634	12.7(52)	3	—	—	—	—	—	—	—	—	—	—	kp	—	18	895
1981	†NYJ	16(7, rb)	81	393	4.9(29)	4	52	459	8.8(24)	1	—	—	—	—	—	—	—	—	—	—	kp	—	30	893
1982	†NYJ	9(0)	20	125	6.3(40)	0	14	177	12.6(39)	1	—	—	—	—	—	—	—	—	—	—	kp	—	6	386
1983	NYJ	9(2)	51	354	6.9(78)	1	48	413	8.6(33)	2	—	—	—	—	—	—	—	—	—	—	k	—	18	582
1984	NYJ	4(0)	10	48	4.8(16)	1	5	71	14.2(28)	0	—	—	—	—	—	—	—	—	—	—	—	—	6	94
NFL	8	99(12)	374	1829	4.9(78)	8	220	2409	10.9(72)	12	1	0	0.0	0	0.0	0	0	—	—	—	kp	1	126	5815

HARPER, CHARLIE Charles Lynwood, T-G-DT, 6´0˝/250 lbs; Oklahoma State; 1966: NYG, rnd 8; B8/14/1944 Haskell, OK **1966** NYG 14 **1967** NYG 14 (RT) **1968** NYG 14 **1969** NYG 14 **1970** NYG 14 (LG) **1971** NYG 14 (RT) **1972** NYG 1 **NFL** 85 [7 yrs]

HARPER, DARRELL Darrell L., HB-K, 6´1˝/195 lbs; Michigan; 1960: Buf, rnd 2/Det, rnd 15; B6/18/1938, [K]

YEAR	TEAM	G (GS, POS)	RUSH	YD	AVG (LG)	TD	REC	YD	AVG (LG)	TD	PASS	COMP	PCT	YD	AVG (LG)	TD	INT	SK	YD	QBR	KPR	OTD	PTS	TAY
1960	Buf-A	4	1	3	3.0(3)	0	—	—	—	—	—	—	—	—	—	—	—	—	—	—	K	—	7	3

HARPER, DAVE David Douglas, LB, 6´1˝/220 lbs; Humboldt State; 1990: Dal, rnd 11; B5/5/1966 Eureka, CA **1990** Dal 6 (0)

HARPER, DEVERON Deveron Alfredo, DB, 5´11˝/187 lbs; Notre Dame; B11/15/1977 Orangeburg, SC **2000** Car 16 (0) **2001** Car 8 (1) **2003** NO 14 (0) **2004** NO 5 (0) **NFL** 43 (1) [4 yrs]

HARPER, DWAYNE Dwayne Anthony, DB, 5´11˝/175 lbs; South Carolina State; 1988: Sea, rnd 11; B3/29/1966 Orangeburg, SC [I] **1988**†Sea 16 (1) **1989** Sea 16 (13, LCB) **1990** Sea 16 (16, LCB) **1991** Sea 16 (16, LCB) **1992** Sea 16 (16, LCB) **1993** Sea 14 (14, LCB) **1994**†SD 16 (16, RCB) **1995**†SD 16 (16, LCB) **1996** SD 6 (6, LCB) **1997** SD 12 (12, LCB) **1998** SD 1 (1) **1999** Det 3 (1) **NFL** 148 (128) [12 yrs]

HARPER, JACK Jack Ridley, RB, 5´11˝/190 lbs; Florida; B10/8/1944 Lakeland, FL **1968** Mia-A 5

YEAR	TEAM	G (GS, POS)	RUSH	YD	AVG (LG)	TD	REC	YD	AVG (LG)	TD	PASS	COMP	PCT	YD	AVG (LG)	TD	INT	SK	YD	QBR	KPR	OTD	PTS	TAY
1967	Mia-A	9(6, HB)	41	197	4.8(37)	1	11	212	19.3(40)	3	—	—	—	—	—	—	—	—	—	—	p	—	24	323
NFL	2	14(6)	41	197	4.8(37)	1	11	212	19.3(40)	3	—	—	—	—	—	—	—	—	—	—	kp	—	24	328

HARPER, JOHN John, LB, 6´3˝/230 lbs; Southern Illinois; 1983: Atl, rnd 4; B6/12/1960 Memphis, TN **1983** Atl 13 (0)

HARPER, LASALLE LaSalle, LB, 6´1˝/235 lbs; Arkansas; 1989: Chi, rnd 9; B5/16/1967 Galveston, TX **1989** NYG 1 (0) **1989** ChiB 3 (0) **NFL** 4 (0) [1 yr]

HARPER, MARK Mark, DB, 5´9˝/174 lbs; Alcorn State; B11/5/1961 Memphis, TN **1986**†Cle 16 (1) **1987**†Cle 12 (0) **1988**†Cle 13 (1) **1989**†Cle 16 (2) **1990** Cle 5 (2) **NFL** 62 (6) [5 yrs]

HARPER, MAURICE Maurice Sydney, C, 6´4˝/227 lbs; Austin; B5/14/1910 Bandera, TX, D12/23/1991 Los Angeles, CA **1937** Phi 9 (3) **1938** Phi 11 (9, C) **1939** Phi 11 (8, C) **1940** Phi 9 (6, C) **NFL** 40 (26) [4 yrs]

HARPER, MICHAEL Michael, WR, 5´10˝/180 lbs; USC; 1984: LARm, rnd 11; B5/11/1961 Kansas City, MO **1986**†NYJ 16 (0) **1988** NYJ 10 (0)

YEAR	TEAM	G (GS, POS)	RUSH	YD	AVG (LG)	TD	REC	YD	AVG (LG)	TD	PASS	COMP	PCT	YD	AVG (LG)	TD	INT	SK	YD	QBR	KPR	OTD	PTS	TAY
1987	NYJ	3(2)	—	—	—	—	18	225	12.5(35)	1	—	—	—	—	—	—	—	—	—	—	kp	1	12	216
1989	NYJ	6(4)	1	3	3.0(3)	0	7	127	18.1(48)	0	—	—	—	—	—	—	—	—	—	—	—	—	0	67
NFL	4	35(6)	1	3	3.0(3)	0	25	352	14.1(48)	1	—	—	—	—	—	—	—	—	—	—	kp	1	12	257

HARPER, NICK Nicholas Necosi, DB, 5´10˝/182 lbs; Fort Valley State (GA); B9/10/1974 Baldwin, GA **2001** Ind 13 (2) **2002**†Ind 16 (1) **2003**†Ind 16 (13, RCB) **2004**†Ind 14 (14, LCB) **2005**†Ind 15 (15, LCB) **NFL** 74 (45) [5 yrs]

HARPER, ROGER Roger Michael, DB, 6´2˝/225 lbs; Ohio State; 1993: Atl, rnd 2; B10/26/1970 Columbus, OH **1993** Atl 16 (12, SS) **1994** Atl 10 (10, FS) **1995**†Atl 16 (12, FS) **1996**†Dal 14 (0) **NFL** 56 (34) [4 yrs]

HARPER, ROLAND Roland, RB, 5´11˝/208 lbs; Louisiana Tech; 1975: Chi, rnd 17; B2/28/1953 Seguin, TX

YEAR	TEAM	G (GS, POS)	RUSH	YD	AVG (LG)	TD	REC	YD	AVG (LG)	TD	PASS	COMP	PCT	YD	AVG (LG)	TD	INT	SK	YD	QBR	KPR	OTD	PTS	TAY
1975	ChiB	13(10, FB)	100	453	4.5(32)	1	27	191	7.1(27)	0	—	—	—	—	—	—	—	—	—	—	k	—	6	566
1976	ChiB	14(14, FB)	147	625	4.3(28)	2	29	291	10.0(39)	1	—	—	—	—	—	—	—	—	—	—	k	—	18	825
1977	†ChiB	11(10, FB)	120	457	3.8(19)	0	19	142	7.5(34)	0	2	0	0.0	0	0.0	0	0	—	—	—	k	—	0	527
1978	ChiB	16(16, FB)	240	992	4.1(31)	6	43	340	7.9(33)	2	1	0	0.0	0	0.0	0	1	—	—	—	—	—	48	1192
1980	ChiB	12(12, FB)	113	404	3.6(13)	5	7	31	4.4(16)	0	—	—	—	—	—	—	—	—	—	—	—	—	30	470
1981	ChiB	15(2)	34	106	3.1(11)	1	2	10	5.0(8)	0	—	—	—	—	—	—	—	—	—	—	—	—	6	121
1982	ChiB	8(0)	3	7	2.3(8)	0	1	8	8.0(8)	0	—	—	—	—	—	—	—	—	—	—	k	—	0	-9
NFL	7	89(64)	757	3044	4.0(32)	15	128	1013	7.9(39)	3	3	0	0.0	0	0.0	0	1	—	—	—	k	—	108	3691

HARPER, SHAWN Aaron Shawn, T, 6´3˝/290 lbs; Indiana; 1992: LARm, rnd 4; B7/9/1968 Columbus, OH **1995** Ind 9 (0)

HARPER, WILLIE Willie Miles, LB, 6´2˝/215 lbs; Nebraska; 1973: SF, rnd 2; B7/30/1950 Toledo, OH **1973** SF 14 (12, RLB) **1974** SF 14 (14, RLB) **1975** SF 13 **1976** SF 14 **1977** SF 12 (10, llb) **1979** SF 16 (16, RLB) **1980** SF 14 (12, LLB/lolb) **1981**†SF 16 (16, LOLB) **1982** SF 5 (5, LOLB) **1983**†SF 16 (16, LOLB) **NFL** 134 (101) [10 yrs]

HARRAH, DENNIS Dennis Wayne, G-C, 6´5˝/260 lbs; Miami (FL); 1975: LA, rnd 1; B3/9/1953 Charleston, WV **1975**†LARm 14 **1977** LARm 8 (8, RG) **1978**†LARm★13 (12, RG) **1979**†LARm★13 (12, RG) **1980**†LARm★15 (8, rg) **1981** LARm 15 (13, RG) **1982** LARm 9 (9, RG) **1983**†LARm 15 (15, RG) **1984**†LARm☆16 (16, RG) **1985**†LARm★10 (10, RG) **1986**†LARm★16 (16, RG) **1987** LARm★8 (8, RG)

YEAR	TEAM	G (GS, POS)	RUSH	YD	AVG (LG)	TD	REC	YD	AVG (LG)	TD	PASS	COMP	PCT	YD	AVG (LG)	TD	INT	SK	YD	QBR	KPR	OTD	PTS	TAY
1976	†LARm	14(14, RG)	—	—	—	—	0	3	(3)	0	—	—	—	—	—	—	—	—	—	—	—	—	0	2
NFL	13	168(144)	—	—	—	—	0	3	(3)	0	—	—	—	—	—	—	—	—	—	—	—	—	0	2

HARRAWAY, CHARLIE Charles Edward, RB, 6´2˝/215 lbs; San Jose State; 1966: Cle, rnd 18/KC, rnd 14; B9/21/1944 Oklahoma City, OK

YEAR	TEAM	G (GS, POS)	RUSH	YD	AVG (LG)	TD	REC	YD	AVG (LG)	TD	PASS	COMP	PCT	YD	AVG (LG)	TD	INT	SK	YD	QBR	KPR	OTD	PTS	TAY
1966	Cle	14	7	40	5.7(18)	0	—	—	—	—	—	—	—	—	—	—	—	—	—	—	k	—	0	98
1967	†Cle	14	5	-14	-2.8(2)	0	—	—	—	—	—	—	—	—	—	—	—	—	—	—	p	—	0	-12
1968	†Cle	13(fb)	91	334	3.7(23)	0	12	162	13.5(63)	1	—	—	—	—	—	—	—	—	—	—	—	—	6	420
1969	Was	14(FB)	141	428	3.0(17)	6	55	489	8.9(64)	3	—	—	—	—	—	—	—	—	—	—	—	—	54	748
1970	Was	13(13, FB)	146	577	4.0(57)	5	24	136	5.7(29)	0	—	—	—	—	—	—	—	—	—	—	—	—	30	695
1971	†Was	14(14, FB)	156	635	4.1(57)	2	20	121	6.1(20)	0	—	—	—	—	—	—	—	—	—	—	—	—	12	716
1972	†Was	14(14, FB)	148	567	3.8(24)	6	15	105	7.0(24)	0	—	—	—	—	—	—	—	—	—	—	—	—	36	680
1973	†Was	14(14, FB)	128	452	3.5(16)	1	32	291	9.1(31)	3	—	—	—	—	—	—	—	—	—	—	—	—	24	623
NFL	8	110(55)	822	3019	3.7(57)	20	158	1304	8.3(64)	7	—	—	—	—	—	—	—	—	—	—	kp	—	162	3966

HARRELL, GARY Gary Lamar, WR, 5´7˝/170 lbs; Howard; B1/23/1972 Miami, FL **1995** NYG 4 (0)

HARRELL, JAMES James Clarence, LB, 6´1˝/224 lbs; Florida; B7/19/1957 Tampa, FL **1979** Det 9 (8, RLB) **1980** Det 5 (0) **1981** Det 16 (0) **1982**†Det 9 (3) **1983**†Det 16 (0) **1985** Det 7 (2) **1986** Det 16 (15, LILB) **1987** KC 11 (4) **NFL** 89 (32) [8 yrs]

HARRELL, RICK Richard Lee, C, 6´3˝/238 lbs; Clemson; 1973: NYJ, rnd 6; B8/8/1951 Morristown, NJ **1973** NYJ 4

HARRELL, SAM Samuel Delmar, RB, 6´2˝/217 lbs; East Carolina; 1980: Min, rnd 11; B2/7/1957 Ahoskie, NC

YEAR	TEAM	G (GS, POS)	RUSH	YD	AVG (LG)	TD	REC	YD	AVG (LG)	TD	PASS	COMP	PCT	YD	AVG (LG)	TD	INT	SK	YD	QBR	KPR	OTD	PTS	TAY
1981	Min	4(0)	1	7	7.0(7)	0	2	23	11.5(17)	0	—	—	—	—	—	—	—	—	—	—	—	—	0	19
1982	Min	1(0)	—	—	—	—	—	—	—	—	—	—	—	—	—	—	—	—	—	—	k	—	0	-9
1987	Min	1(1)	5	8	1.6(4)	0	3	20	6.7(8)	0	—	—	—	—	—	—	—	—	—	—	k	—	0	7
NFL	3	6(1)	6	15	2.5(7)	0	5	43	8.6(17)	0	—	—	—	—	—	—	—	—	—	—	k	—	0	17

HARRELL, WILLARD Willard Race, RB, 5´8˝/162 lbs; Pacific; 1975: GB, rnd 3; B9/16/1952 Stockton, CA [R]

YEAR	TEAM	G (GS, POS)	RUSH	YD	AVG (LG)	TD	REC	YD	AVG (LG)	TD	PASS	COMP	PCT	YD	AVG (LG)	TD	INT	SK	YD	QBR	KPR	OTD	PTS	TAY
1975	GB	14(14, RB)	121	359	3.0(26)	1	34	261	7.7(36)	2	5	3	60.0	61	12.2(24)	3	0	—	—	—	kp	—	18	619
1976	GB	13(8, RB)	130	435	3.3(56)	3	17	201	11.8(69)	1	4	1	25.0	40	10.0(40)	1	1	1	7	—	p	—	24	534
1977	GB	13(3)	60	140	2.3(9)	1	19	194	10.2(48)	0	1	1	100.0	33	33.0(33)	0	0	1	10	—	kp	1	12	390
1978	SL	13(2)	35	134	3.8(15)	0	3	5	1.7(2)	0	—	—	—	—	—	—	—	—	—	—	kp	1	6	342
1979	SL	14	19	100	5.3(19)	0	3	33	11.0(15)	0	1	0	0.0	0	0.0	0	0	—	—	—	kp	—	0	329
1980	SL	16(0)	42	170	4.0(26)	3	9	52	5.8(14)	0	—	—	—	—	—	—	—	—	—	—	kp	—	18	265
1981	SL	16(0)	5	6	1.2(4)	1	14	131	9.4(62)	1	—	—	—	—	—	—	—	—	—	—	kp	—	12	103
1982	†SL	7(0)	4	14	3.5(8)	0	11	127	11.5(36)	0	1	1	100.0	10	10.0(10)	0	0	—	—	—	kp	—	0	109
1983	SL	14(0)	4	13	3.3(8)	0	3	25	8.3(13)	0	—	—	—	—	—	—	—	—	—	—	kp	—	0	49
1984	SL	16(0)	6	7	1.2(4)	1	14	106	7.6(15)	0	—	—	—	—	—	—	—	—	—	—	k	—	6	106
NFL	10	136(27)	426	1378	3.2(56)	10	127	1135	8.9(69)	4	12	6	50.0	144	12.0(40)	4	1	2	17	—	kp	2	96	2843

YEAR	TEAM	G (GS, POS)	RUSH	YD	AVG(LG)	TD	REC	YD	AVG(LG)	TD	PASS	COMP	PCT	YD	AVG(LG)	TD	INT	SK	YD	QBR	KPR	OTD	PTS	TAY

HARRINGTON, JOEY John Joseph, QB, 6'4"/220 lbs; Oregon; 2002: Det, rnd 1; B10/21/1978 Portland, OR

YEAR	TEAM	G (GS, POS)	RUSH	YD	AVG(LG)	TD	REC	YD	AVG(LG)	TD	PASS	COMP	PCT	YD	AVG(LG)	TD	INT	SK	YD	QBR	KPR	OTD	PTS	TAY
2002	Det	14(12, QB)	7	4	0.6(6)	0	—	—	—	—	429	215	50.1	2294	5.3(64)	12	16	8	75	59.9	—	—	0	571
2003	Det	16(16, QB)	30	86	2.9(26)	0	1	8	8.0(8)	0	554	309	55.8	2880	5.2(72)	17	22	9	55	63.9	—	—	0	735
2004	Det	16(16, QB)	48	175	3.6(17)	0	—	—	—	—	489	274	56.0	3047	6.2(62)	19	12	36	196	77.5	—	—	0	1314
2005	Det	13(11, QB)	24	80	3.3(15)	0	1	-4	-4.0(-4)	0	330	188	57.0	2021	6.1(86)	12	12	24	136	72.0	—	—	0	669
NFL 4		59(55)	109	345	3.2(26)	0	2	4	2.0(8)	0	1802	986	54.7	10242	5.7(86)	60	62	77	462	68.1	—	—	0	3288

HARRINGTON, JOHN John Patrick, E-DE, 6'3"/198 lbs; Marquette; 1945: ChiC, rnd 8; B4/15/1921 Reedsburg, WI; D1/8/1992 Green Bay, WI

YEAR	TEAM	G (GS, POS)	RUSH	YD	AVG(LG)	TD	REC	YD	AVG(LG)	TD	KPR	OTD	PTS	TAY
1946	†Cle-A	12(2)	—	—	—	—	8	136	17.0	0	k	—	0	54
1947	ChiR-A	13(3)	—	—	—	—	17	233	13.7	3	k	—	18	132
AAFC 2		25(5)	—	—	—	—	25	369	14.8	3	k	—	18	186

HARRINGTON, LaRUE LaRue Henry, RB, 6'0"/210 lbs; Norfolk State; 1980: SD, rnd 6; B6/28/1957 Norfolk, VA

YEAR	TEAM	G (GS, POS)	RUSH	YD	AVG(LG)	TD	OTD	PTS	TAY
1980	SD	4(0)	4	-7	-1.8(-1)	0	—	0	-7

HARRINGTON, PERRY Perry Donell, RB, 5'11"/210 lbs; Jackson State; 1980: Phi, rnd 2; B3/13/1958 Bentonia, MS

YEAR	TEAM	G (GS, POS)	RUSH	YD	AVG(LG)	TD	REC	YD	AVG(LG)	TD	KPR	OTD	PTS	TAY
1980	†Phi	14(1)	32	166	5.2(19)	1	3	24	8.0(17)	0	k	—	6	202
1981	Phi	4(4)	34	140	4.1(16)	2	9	27	3.0(12)	0		—	12	174
1982	Phi	9(8, FB)	56	231	4.1(37)	1	13	74	5.7(17)	0		—	6	278
1983	Phi	15(1)	23	98	4.3(35)	1	1	19	19.0(19)	0	k	—	6	137
1984	SL	6(0)	3	6	2.0(5)	0	—	—	—	—		—	0	6
1985	SL	11(0)	7	42	6.0(22)	1	—	—	—	—	k	—	6	69
NFL 6		59(14)	155	683	4.4(37)	6	26	144	5.5(19)	0	k	—	36	865

HARRIS, AL Alfred Carl, DE-LB, 6'5"/250 lbs; Arizona State; 1979: Chi, rnd 1; B12/31/1956 Bangor, ME **1979**†ChiB 4 **1980** ChiB 16 (0) **1982** ChiB 8 (7, RDE) **1983** ChiB 13 (11, RLB) **1984**†ChiB 16 (16, RLB) **1986**†ChiB 16 (3) **1987**†ChiB 12 (5, lde) **1988**†ChiB 16 (14, LDE) **1989**†Phi 16 (16, RLB) **1990**†Phi 16 (4)

YEAR	TEAM	G (GS, POS)	RUSH	YD	AVG(LG)	TD	REC	YD	AVG(LG)	TD	KPR	OTD	PTS	TAY
1981	ChiB	16(11, RDE)	—	—	—	—	1	18	18.0(18)	0	i	1	6	58
NFL 11		149(87)	—	—	—	—	1	18	18.0(18)	0	iS	1	8	95

HARRIS, AL Alshinard, DB, 6'1"/185 lbs; Texas A&M-Kingsville; 1997: TB, rnd 6; B12/7/1974 Pompano Beach, FL **1998** Phi 16 (7, rcb) **1999** Phi 16 (6, rcb) **2000**†Phi 16 (4) **2001**†Phi 16 (2) **2002**†Phi 16 (2) **2003**†GB 16 (16, RCB) **2004**†GB 16 (16, RCB) **2005** GB 16 (16, RCB) **NFL** 128 (69) [8 yrs]

HARRIS, AMOS Edwin Amos, G, 5'11"/175 lbs; Mississippi State; B1921 **1947** Bkn-A 14 (2) **1948** Bkn-A 14 (2) **AAFC** 28 (4) [2 yrs]

HARRIS, ANTHONY Anthony Jerrod, LB, 6'1"/231 lbs; Auburn; B1/25/1973 Fort Pierce, FL **1996** Mia 7 (3) **1997**†Mia 16 (16, LLB) **1998**†Mia 5 (0) **1999**†Mia 4 (0) **NFL** 32 (19) [4 yrs]

HARRIS, ANTWAN Melvin Antwan, DB, 5'9"/194 lbs; Virginia; 2000: NE, rnd 6; B5/29/1977 Raleigh, NC **2000** NE 14 (0) **2001**†NE 11 (1) **2002** NE 14 (0) **2003** NE 13 (1) **NFL** 52 (2) [4 yrs]

HARRIS, ARCHIE Archie Lee, T, 6'6"/270 lbs; William & Mary; 1987: Chi, rnd 7; B11/17/1964 Richmond, VA **1987** Den 3 (0)

HARRIS, ARLEN Arlen Quincy, RB, 5'10"/212 lbs; Virginia; Hofstra; B4/22/1980 Chester, PA [R]

YEAR	TEAM	G (GS, POS)	RUSH	YD	AVG(LG)	TD	REC	YD	AVG(LG)	TD	KPR	OTD	PTS	TAY
2003	†SL	16(2)	85	255	3.0(18)	4	15	102	6.8(26)	0	kp	—	24	757
2004	SL	14(1)	20	63	3.2(14)	0	4	44	11.0(21)	0	k	—	0	331
2005	SL	16(0)	13	21	1.6(10)	1	4	34	8.5(17)	0	k	—	8	54
NFL 3		46(3)	118	339	2.9(18)	5	23	180	7.8(26)	0	kp	—	32	1142

HARRIS, ATNAF Atnaf DeShawn, WR, 6'1"/182 lbs; Fresno State; Cal State-Northridge; B2/27/1979 Fresno, CA

YEAR	TEAM	G (GS, POS)	RUSH	YD	AVG(LG)	TD	REC	YD	AVG(LG)	TD	OTD	PTS	TAY
2002	Hou	1(1)	—	—	—	—	1	8	8.0(8)	0	—	0	4

HARRIS, BERNARDO Bernardo Jamaine, LB, 6'2"/247 lbs; North Carolina; B10/15/1971 Chapel Hill, NC **1995**†GB 11 (0) **1996**†GB 16 (0) **1997**†GB 16 (16, MLB) **1998**†GB 16 (16, MLB) **1999** GB 16 (15, MLB) **2000** GB 16 (16, MLB) **2001**†GB 16 (16, MLB) **2002** Bal 13 (11, RILB) **NFL** 120 (90) [8 yrs]

HARRIS, BILLY William Walter, E-DE, 6'2"/196 lbs; Hardin-Simmons; B9/1/1914 Waco, TX; D6/7/1979 San Benito, TX **1937** Pit 1 (0)

HARRIS, BILLY William Andrews, RB, 6'2"/204 lbs; Colorado; 1968: Atl, rnd 13; B1/17/1946 Galveston, TX

YEAR	TEAM	G (GS, POS)	RUSH	YD	AVG(LG)	TD	REC	YD	AVG(LG)	TD	KPR	OTD	PTS	TAY
1968	Atl	6	53	144	2.7(11)	0	3	118	39.3(55)	1	k	—	6	209
1969	†Min	13	6	13	2.2(5)	0	2	13	6.5(10)	0	k	—	0	28
1971	NO	1	1	1	1.0(1)	0	—	—	—	—			0	1
NFL 3		20	60	158	2.6(11)	0	5	131	26.2(55)	1	k	—	6	238

HARRIS, BO Clinton Lee, LB, 6'3"/225 lbs; LSU; 1975: Cin, rnd 3; B1/16/1953 Leesville, LA **1975** Cin 12 **1976** Cin 14 (LLB) **1977** Cin 14 (LLB) **1978** Cin 8 **1979** Cin 15 (LLB) **1980** Cin 15 (7, lolb) **1981**†Cin 16 (16, LOLB) **1982**†Cin 9 (9, LOLB) **NFL** 103 (32) [8 yrs]

HARRIS, BOB Robert Huel, LB-DB, 6'2"/219 lbs; Auburn; 1983: SL, rnd 8; B11/11/1960 Everett, WA **1983** SL 8 (8, LLB) **1984** SL 16 (3) **1985** SL 10 (0) **1987** KC 3 (3) **NFL** 37 (14) [4 yrs]

HARRIS, CHRIS Chris, DB, 6'1"/206 lbs; Louisiana-Monroe; 2005: Chi, rnd 6; B8/6/1982 Little Rock, AR **2005**†ChiB 14 (13, FS)

HARRIS, CHUCK Charles William, T, 6'3"/225 lbs; West Virginia; B10/7/1961 Columbus, OH **1987** ChiB 3 (2)

HARRIS, CLIFF Clifford Allen, DB, 6'0"/188 lbs; Ouachita Baptist; B11/12/1948 Fayetteville, AR [I] **1970**†Dal 11 (5, fs) **1971**†Dal 14 (11, FS) **1972**†Dal 14 (FS) **1973**†Dal 14 (FS) **1974** Dal★14 (FS) **1975**†Dal★14 (FS) **1976**†Dal☆14 (12, FS) **1977**†Dal★14 (FS) **1978**†Dal★16 (FS) **1979**†Dal★16 (FS) **NFL** 141 (28) [10 yrs]

HARRIS, COREY Corey Lamont, DB, 5'11"/213 lbs; Vanderbilt; 1992: Hou, rnd 3; B10/25/1969 Indianapolis, IN [R] **1992** Hou 5 (0) **1994**†GB 16 (2) **1995** Sea 16 (16, RCB) **1996** Sea 16 (16, RCB) **1997**†Mia 16 (7, FS) **1998** Bal 16 (6, fs) **1999** Bal 16 (0) **2000**†Bal 16 (0) **2001** Bal 16 (16, SS) **2002** Det 16 (16, SS) **2003** Det 13 (13, SS)

YEAR	TEAM	G (GS, POS)	RUSH	YD	AVG(LG)	TD	REC	YD	AVG(LG)	TD	KPR	OTD	PTS	TAY
1992	GB	10(0)	2	10	5.0(7)	0	—	—	—	—		—	0	150
1993	†GB	11(0)	—	—	—	—	2	11	5.5(6)	0	k	—	0	248
NFL 12		183(92)	2	10	5.0(7)	0	2	11	5.5(6)	0	kpiS	4	24	2063

HARRIS, COREY Corey Alan, DB, 5'10"/187 lbs; The Citadel; North Alabama; B11/28/1976 Jacksonville, FL **1999** NO 3 (0) **2000** NO 3 (1) **2001** KC 4 (0) **2002** KC 14 (0) **2003** KC 3 (0) **NFL** 27 (1) [5 yrs]

HARRIS, DARRYL Darryl Lynn, RB, 5'10"/178 lbs; Arizona State; B2/20/1966 Jackson, MS

YEAR	TEAM	G (GS, POS)	RUSH	YD	AVG(LG)	TD	REC	YD	AVG(LG)	TD	KPR	OTD	PTS	TAY
1988	†Min	14(0)	34	151	4.4(34)	1	6	30	5.0(7)	0	k	—	6	424

HARRIS, DERRICK Sidney Derrick, RB, 6'0"/253 lbs; Miami (FL); 1996: SL, rnd 6; B9/18/1972 Angleton, TX

YEAR	TEAM	G (GS, POS)	RUSH	YD	AVG(LG)	TD	REC	YD	AVG(LG)	TD	KPR	OTD	PTS	TAY
1996	SL	11(6, FB)	3	5	1.7(3)	0	4	17	4.3(8)	0		—	0	14
1998	SL	16(14, FB)	14	38	2.7(15)	0	12	57	4.8(8)	2		—	12	77
1999	SL	1(0)	—	—	—	—	—	—	—	—				
2001	SD	16(0)	—	—	—	—	1	7	7.0(7)	0	k	1	6	8
NFL 4		44(20)	17	43	2.5(15)	0	17	81	4.8(8)	2	k	1	18	98

HARRIS, DICK Richard May, DB, 5'11"/187 lbs; McNeese State; B7/24/1937 Denver, CO [I] **1960**†LAC-A☆14 (RCB) **1961**†SD-A★14 (RCB) **1962** SD-A☆14 (RCB) **1963**†SD-A☆14 (RCB) **1964**†SD-A 6 **1965**†SD-A 14 **NFL** 76 [6 yrs]

HARRIS, DON Donald Lesley, DB, 6'2"/185 lbs; Rutgers; 1977: Was, rnd 11; B2/8/1954 Elizabeth, NJ **1978** Was 16 **1979** Was 16 **1980** NYG 11 (4) **NFL** 43 (4) [3 yrs]

HARRIS, DUD Edmund Dudley, T, 6'2"/240 lbs; Ohio State; B10/24/1903 Quitsna, NC; D2/13/1989 Palm Springs, CA **1930** Por 13 (9, RT)

HARRIS, DURIEL Duriel LaDon, WR, 5'11"/179 lbs; New Mexico State; 1976: Mia, rnd 5; B11/27/1954 Port Arthur, TX

YEAR	TEAM	G (GS, POS)	RUSH	YD	AVG(LG)	TD	REC	YD	AVG(LG)	TD	KPR	OTD	PTS	TAY
1976	Mia☆	12(2)	—	—	—	—	22	372	16.9(44)	1	kp	—	6	529
1977	Mia	14(4)	—	—	—	—	34	601	17.7(47)	5	k	—	30	357
1978	†Mia	16(15, WR)	—	—	—	—	45	654	14.5(63)	3	k	—	18	564
1979	†Mia	15(14, WR)	1	20	20.0(20)	0	42	798	19.0(51)	3	k	—	18	434
1980	Mia	12(3)	—	—	—	—	33	583	17.7(54)	2		—	12	316
1981	†Mia	15(12, WR)	—	—	—	—	53	911	17.2(55)	2	k	—	12	471
1982	†Mia	9(8, WR)	1	13	13.0(13)	0	22	331	15.0(45)	1		—	6	184
1983	†Mia	12(3)	1	0	0.0(0)	0	15	260	17.3(64)	1		—	6	135
1984	Cle	11(11, WR)	—	—	—	—	32	512	16.0(43)	2	p	—	12	294

YEAR	TEAM	G (GS, POS)	RUSH	YD	AVG(LG)	TD	REC	YD	AVG(LG)	TD	PASS	COMP	PCT	YD	AVG(LG)	TD	INT	SK	YD	QBR	KPR	OTD	PTS	TAY
1984	Dal	5(0)	—	—	—	—	1	9	9.0(9)	0	—												—	0	5
1985	Mia	6(0)	—	—	—	—	3	24	8.0(11)	0	—												—	0	12
NFL	10	127(72)	3	33	11.0(20)	0	302	5055	16.7(64)	20	—											kp	—	120	3299

HARRIS, ELMORE   Elmore Thomas, HB, 5´11˝/175 lbs; Morgan State; B6/3/1922 Huntsville, AL, D12/8/1968 Queens, NY

YEAR	TEAM	G (GS, POS)	RUSH	YD	AVG(LG)	TD	REC	YD	AVG(LG)	TD											KPR	OTD	PTS	TAY
1947	Bkn-A	10(2)	3	-2	-0.7	0	—														k	—	0	117

HARRIS, ELROY   Elroy, RB, 5´9˝/218 lbs; Eastern Kentucky; 1989: Sea, rnd 3; B8/18/1966 Orlando, FL

| 1989 | Sea | 14(0) | 8 | 23 | 2.9(8) | 0 | 3 | 26 | 8.7(11) | 0 | — | | | | | | | | | | k | — | 0 | 100 |

HARRIS, ERIC   Eric Wayne, DB, 6´3˝/198 lbs; Memphis; 1977: KC, rnd 4; B8/11/1955 Memphis, TN [I]   **1980** KC 15 (13, RCB)   **1981** KC☆16 (16, RCB)   **1982** KC 8 (8, RCB)   **1983**†LARm 16 (11, LCB)   **1984**†LARm 7 (7, fs)   **1985** LARm 9 (0)   **NFL** 71 (55) [6 yrs]

HARRIS, FATTY   George Arthur, T, none; B3/8/1884 Flemingsburg, KY, D10/2/1963 Ashland, KY   **1921** Lou 1 (0)

HARRIS, FRANCO   Franco, RB, 6´2˝/230 lbs; Penn State; 1972: Pit, rnd 1; B3/7/1950 Fort Dix, NJ; HOF 1990

YEAR	TEAM	G (GS, POS)	RUSH	YD	AVG(LG)	TD	REC	YD	AVG(LG)	TD	PASS	COMP	PCT	YD	AVG(LG)	TD	INT	SK	YD	QBR	KPR	OTD	PTS	TAY
1972	†Pit★	14(9, RB)	188	1055	**5.6(75)**	10	21	180	8.6(29)	1											k	—	66	1313
1973	†Pit◇	12(12, RB)	188	698	3.7(35)	3	10	69	6.9(19)	0											k	—	18	771
1974	†Pit★	12(12, FB)	208	1006	4.8(54)	5	23	200	8.7(31)	1												—	36	1161
1975	†Pit★	14(14, FB)	262	1246	4.8(36)	10	28	214	7.6(44)	1											k	—	66	1470
1976	†Pit★	14(14, FB)	289	1128	3.9(30)	14	23	151	6.6(39)	0												—	84	1344
1977	†Pit★	14(14, FB)	300	1162	3.9(61)	11	11	62	5.6(15)	0												—	66	1303
1978	†Pit★	16(16, FB)	**310**	1082	3.5(37)	8	22	144	6.5(15)	0	1	0	0.0	0	0.0	0	0	0			k	—	48	1234
1979	†Pit★	15(15, FB)	267	1186	4.4(71)	11	36	291	8.1(21)	1												—	72	1447
1980	Pit◇	13(13, FB)	208	789	3.8(26)	4	30	196	6.5(31)	2												—	36	937
1981	Pit	16(16, FB)	242	987	4.1(50)	8	37	250	6.8(26)	1												—	54	1197
1982	Pit	9(9, FB)	140	604	4.3(21)	2	31	249	8.0(20)	0												—	12	749
1983	†Pit	16(16, FB)	279	1007	3.6(19)	5	34	278	8.2(29)	2												—	42	1206
1984	Sea	8(6, fb)	68	170	2.5(16)	0	1	3	3.0(3)	0												—	0	172
NFL	13	173(166)	2949	12120	4.1(75)	91	307	2287	7.4(44)	9	1	0	0.0	0	0.0	0	0	0			k	—	600	14302

HARRIS, FRANK   Frank Harmon, RB, 6´1˝/196 lbs; North Carolina State; B7/1/1964 Waukesha, WI

| 1987 | ChiB | 3(0) | 6 | 23 | 3.8(18) | 0 | — | | | | | | | | | | | | | | | | — | 0 | 23 |

HARRIS, HANK   Henry Franklin, G-T, 6´0˝/265 lbs; Texas; 1947: Was, rnd 8; B2/26/1923 Camden, AL   **1947** Was 10 (2)   **1948** Was 2 (0)   **NFL** 12 (2) [2 yrs]

HARRIS, HARRY   Harry Frank, BB, 5´9˝/175 lbs; West Virginia Wesleyan; West Virginia; B9/10/1895, D3/1969 Martins Ferry, OH   **1920** Akr 11 (9, BB)

HARRIS, HERBERT   Herbert H., WR, 6´1˝/206 lbs; Lamar; B5/4/1961 Houston, TX   **1987** NO 2 (0)

YEAR	TEAM	G (GS, POS)	RUSH	YD	AVG(LG)	TD	REC	YD	AVG(LG)	TD											KPR	OTD	PTS	TAY
1986	NO	7(1)	—	—	—	—	11	148	13.5(27)	0											k	—	0	91
NFL	2	9(1)	—	—	—	—	11	148	13.5(27)	0												—	0	74

HARRIS, IKE   Isiah, WR, 6´3˝/210 lbs; Iowa State; 1974: SL, rnd 4; B11/27/1952 West Memphis, AR

YEAR	TEAM	G (GS, POS)	RUSH	YD	AVG(LG)	TD	REC	YD	AVG(LG)	TD	PASS	COMP	PCT	YD	AVG(LG)	TD	INT	SK	YD	QBR	KPR	OTD	PTS	TAY
1975	†SL	14(4)	—	—	—	—	15	266	17.7(36)	0												—	0	133
1976	SL	12(12, WR)	—	—	—	—	52	782	15.0(40)	1												—	6	396
1977	SL	14(14, WR)	—	—	—	—	40	547	13.7(38)	3												—	18	289
1978	NO	15(15, WR)	2	22	11.0(22)	0	40	590	14.8(45)	4	1	0	0.0	0	0.0	0	0	0				—	24	337
1979	NO	14(14, WR)	2	9	4.5(16)	0	25	395	15.8(42)	2												—	12	217
1980	NO	16(16, WR)	—	—	—	—	37	692	18.7(44)	6												—	36	376
1981	NO	3(3)	—	—	—	—	2	33	16.5(20)	0												—	0	17
NFL	7	88(78)	4	31	7.8(22)	0	211	3305	15.7(45)	16	1	0	0.0	0	0.0	0	0	0				—	96	1764

HARRIS, JACK   Welton John, FB-E-HB, 5´11˝/190 lbs; Wisconsin; B9/29/1902 Jackson, MI, D12/28/1973 Indianapolis, IN   **1925** GB 11 (7, fb), 6   **1926** GB 10 (5, re), 12   **NFL** 21 (12), 18 [2 yrs]

HARRIS, JACKIE   Jackie Bernard, TE, 6´4˝/244 lbs; Louisiana-Monroe; 1990: GB, rnd 4; B1/4/1968 Pine Bluff, AR

YEAR	TEAM	G (GS, POS)	RUSH	YD	AVG(LG)	TD	REC	YD	AVG(LG)	TD											KPR	OTD	PTS	TAY
1990	GB	16(3)	—	—	—	—	12	157	13.1(26)	0												—	0	79
1991	GB	16(6, te)	1	1	1.0(1)	0	24	264	11.0(35)	3												—	18	148
1992	GB☆	16(11, TE)	—	—	—	—	55	595	10.8(40)	2												—	12	308
1993	GB	12(12, TE)	—	—	—	—	42	604	14.4(66)	4												—	24	322
1994	TB	9(9, TE)	—	—	—	—	26	337	13.0(48)	3												—	20	184
1995	TB	16(16, TE)	—	—	—	—	62	751	12.1(33)	1												—	6	381
1996	TB	13(12, TE)	—	—	—	—	30	349	11.6(36)	1												—	8	180
1997	†TB	12(11, TE)	—	—	—	—	19	197	10.4(39)	1												—	6	104
1998	Ten	16(16, TE)	—	—	—	—	43	412	9.6(32)	2											k	—	12	204
1999	†Ten	12(2)	—	—	—	—	26	297	11.4(62)	1												—	8	154
2000	Dal	16(7, te)	—	—	—	—	39	306	7.8(21)	5												—	32	178
2001	Dal	13(12, TE)	—	—	—	—	15	141	9.4(28)	2												—	12	81
NFL	12	167(117)	1	1	1.0(1)	0	393	4410	11.2(66)	25											k	—	158	2319

HARRIS, JAMES   James Larnell, QB, 6´4˝/210 lbs; Grambling State; 1969: Buf, rnd 8; B7/20/1947 Monroe, LA

YEAR	TEAM	G (GS, POS)	RUSH	YD	AVG(LG)	TD	REC	YD	AVG(LG)	TD	PASS	COMP	PCT	YD	AVG(LG)	TD	INT	SK	YD	QBR	KPR	OTD	PTS	TAY
1969	Buf-A	4(1)	10	25	2.5(9)	0	—	—	—	—	36	15	41.7	270	7.5(55)	1	9	70			—	—	0	125
1970	Buf	7	3	-8	-2.7(1)	0	—	—	—	—	50	24	48.0	338	6.8(32)	3	4	7	63		—	—	0	16
1971	Buf	7(2)	6	42	7.0(13)	0	—	—	—	—	103	51	49.5	512	5.0(62)	1	6	16	145		—	—	0	63
1973	†LARm	8	4	29	7.3(19)	0	—	—	—	—	11	7	63.6	68	6.2(27)	0	0				—	—	0	63
1974	†LARm◇	11(8, QB)	42	112	2.7(15)	5	—	—	—	—	198	106	53.5	1544	**7.8(50)**	11	6	12	101	85.1	—	—	30	749
1975	†LARm	13(13, QB)	18	45	2.5(15)	1	—	—	—	—	285	157	55.1	2148	7.5(54)	14	15	21	180	73.8	—	—	6	599
1976	LARm	7(5, QB)	12	76	6.3(20)	2	—	—	—	—	158	91	57.6	1460	**9.2(80)**	8	6	14	151	—	—	—	12	626
1977	SD	9(9, QB)	10	13	1.3(12)	0	—	—	—	—	211	109	51.7	1240	5.9(78)	5	11	12	106	55.8	—	—	12	238
1978	SD	9(2)	10	7	0.7(9)	0	—	—	—	—	88	42	47.7	518	5.9(34)	2	9	8	43	—	—	—	0	-84
1979	SD	8	6	26	4.3(18)	0	—	—	—	—	9	5	55.6	38	4.2(10)	0	1	2	15	—	—	—	0	5
NFL	10	83(40)	121	367	3.0(20)	10	—	—	—	—	1149	607	52.8	8136	7.1(80)	45	59	101	874	67.3	—	—	60	2400

HARRIS, JAMES   James Edward, DE, 6´6˝/266 lbs; Temple; B5/13/1968 East St. Louis, IL   **1993** Min 6 (0)   **1994**†Min 16 (16, RDE)   **1995** Min 12 (3)   **1996** SL 16 (0)   **1998** Oak 16 (16, LDE)   **1999** Oak 16 (16, LDE)   **NFL** 82 (51) [6 yrs]

HARRIS, JIM   James C., DB, 6´0˝/173 lbs; Houston; Howard Payne; 1970: Was, rnd 7; B9/18/1946 Brownwood, TX   **1970** Was 3   **1971** Cin 2   **NFL** 5 [2 yrs]

HARRIS, JIM   James, DT, 6´4˝/280 lbs; Utah State; 1965: NYJ, rnd 7/Min, rnd 4; B2/24/1943 Lake Charles, LA   **1965** NYJ-A 14 (14, RDT)   **1966** NYJ-A 14 (RDT)   **1967** NYJ-A 14 (RDT)   **NFL** 42 [3 yrs]

HARRIS, JIMMY   James Bedford, DB, 6´1˝/178 lbs; Oklahoma; 1957: Phi, rnd 5; B11/12/1934 Terrell, TX   **1957** Phi 12 (DB)   **1958** LARm 12 (DB)   **1960** DalT-A 14 (RS)   **1961** Dal 11 (4)   **NFL** 49 (4) [4 yrs]

HARRIS, JOE   Joseph Alexander, LB, 6´1˝/225 lbs; Georgia Tech; 1975: Chi, rnd 8; B12/6/1952 Fayetteville, NC   **1977** Was 11   **1978** SF 16 (16, LLB)   **1979** Min 2   **1979**†LARm 13   **1980**†LARm 16 (2)   **1981** LARm 16 (1)   **1982** Bal 9 (0)   **NFL** 83 (19) [6 yrs]

HARRIS, JOEY   Joseph Andreas, RB, 5´10˝/205 lbs; Purdue; B12/18/1980 Houston, TX

| 2004 | Car | 4(0) | 15 | 53 | 3.5(19) | 0 | — | | | | | | | | | | | | | | | | — | 0 | 53 |

HARRIS, JOHN   John T., HB, /196 lbs; none; B1898, CT, deceased   **1926** Har 2 (2)

HARRIS, JOHN   John Hiram, DB-HB, 6´1˝/195 lbs; Santa Monica Coll (CA); B5/7/1933 San Antonio, TX   **1960** Oak-A 14   **1961** Oak-A 14   **NFL** 28 [2 yrs]

HARRIS, JOHN   John Edward, DB, 6´2˝/200 lbs; Arizona State; 1978: Sea, rnd 7; B6/13/1956 Fort Benning, GA [I]   **1978** Sea 16 (16, FS)   **1979** Sea 14 (6, fs)   **1980** Sea 16 (16, FS)   **1981** Sea 16 (16, FS)   **1982** Sea 9 (9, FS)   **1983**†Sea 16 (16, FS)   **1984**†Sea 16 (16, FS)   **1985** Sea 16 (16, FS)   **1986** Min 16 (15, FS)   **1987**†Min 12 (12, FS)   **1988**†Min 13 (10, FS)   **NFL** 160 (148) [11 yrs]

YEAR	TEAM	G (GS, POS)	RUSH	YD	AVG(LG)	TD	REC	YD	AVG(LG)	TD	PASS	COMP	PCT	YD	AVG(LG)	TD	INT	SK	YD	QBR	KPR	OTD	PTS	TAY

HARRIS, JOHNNIE Johnnie, DB, 6´0˝/215 lbs; Mississippi State; B8/21/1972 Chicago, IL **1999** Oak 4 (0) **2000**†Oak 15 (2) **2001**†Oak 16 (5, ss) **2002**†NYG 9 (0) **2003** NYG 14 (5, ss) **NFL** 58 (12) [5 yrs]

HARRIS, JON Jonathan Cecil, DE, 6´7˝/300 lbs; Virginia; 1997: Phi, rnd 1; B6/9/1974 Inwood, NY **1997** Phi 8 (4) **1998** Phi 16 (4) **NFL** 24 (8) [2 yrs]

HARRIS, KEN Kenneth M., FB, 6´0˝/190 lbs; Syracuse; Columbia; B6/1894 Duluth, MN, deceased **1923** Dul 6 (6, FB)

HARRIS, KENNY Kenneth Lamont, DB, 6´1˝/198 lbs; North Carolina State; B4/25/1975 Durham, NC **1997** Arz 11 (0)

HARRIS, KWAME Kwame, T, 6´7˝/310 lbs; Stanford; 2003: SF, rnd 1; B3/15/1982, Jamaica **2003** SF 14 (5, lt) **2004** SF 14 (7, lt) **2005** SF 16 (16, RT) **NFL** 44 (28) [3 yrs]

HARRIS, LEONARD Leonard Milton, WR, 5´8˝/162 lbs; Austin; Texas Tech; B11/27/1960 McKinney, TX

YEAR	TEAM	G (GS, POS)	RUSH	YD	AVG(LG)	TD	REC	YD	AVG(LG)	TD	KPR	OTD	PTS	TAY
1986	TB	6(1)	—	—	—	—	3	52	17.3(23)	0	kp	—	0	30
1987	Hou	3(3)	1	17	17.0(17)	0	10	164	16.4(39)	0	k	—	0	141
1988	†Hou	16(0)	—	—	—	—	10	136	13.6(42)	0	k	—	0	236
1989	†Hou	11(0)	—	—	—	—	13	202	15.5(36)	2	k	—	12	232
1990	†Hou	14(0)	—	—	—	—	13	172	13.2(42)	3	—	—	18	101
1991	†Hou	9(0)	—	—	—	—	8	101	12.6(29)	0	k	—	0	55
1992	†Hou	14(7, wr)	1	8	8.0(8)	0	35	435	12.4(47)	2	—	—	12	236
1993	Hou	4(2)	—	—	—	—	4	53	13.3(17)	1	—	—	6	32
1994	Atl	8(2)	—	—	—	—	9	113	12.6(26)	0	k	—	0	74
NFL	9	85(15)	2	25	12.5(17)	0	105	1428	13.6(47)	8	kp	—	48	1135

HARRIS, LEOTIS Leotis, G, 6´1˝/267 lbs; Arkansas; 1978: GB, rnd 6; B6/28/1955 Little Rock, AR **1978** GB 13 **1979** GB 15 (12, RG) **1980** GB 16 (16, RG) **1981** GB 16 (16, RG) **1982**†GB 9 (8, RG) **1983** GB 5 (3) **NFL** 74 (55) [6 yrs]

HARRIS, LEROY Leroy, RB, 5´9˝/226 lbs; Arkansas State; 1977: Mia, rnd 5; B7/3/1954 Savannah, GA

YEAR	TEAM	G (GS, POS)	RUSH	YD	AVG(LG)	TD	REC	YD	AVG(LG)	TD	OTD	PTS	TAY
1977	Mia	11(5, fb)	91	417	4.6(77)	4	7	29	4.1(11)	0	—	24	472
1978	†Mia	15(11, FB)	123	512	4.2(51)	2	25	211	8.4(57)	0	—	12	638
1979	†Phi	15(13, FB)	107	504	4.7(80)	2	22	107	4.9(15)	0	—	12	578
1980	†Phi	15(15, FB)	104	341	3.3(22)	3	15	207	13.8(51)	1	—	24	480
1982	Phi	7(1)	17	39	2.3(14)	2	3	17	5.7(9)	0	—	12	68
NFL	5	63(45)	442	1813	4.1(80)	13	72	571	7.9(57)	1	—	84	2234

HARRIS, LOU Louis Richard, DB, 6´0˝/180 lbs; Kent State; 1968: Pit, rnd 14; B3/25/1946 Washington, DC **1968** Pit 14

HARRIS, M.L. Michael Lee, TE, 6´5˝/238 lbs; Tampa; Kansas State; B1/16/1954 Columbus, OH

YEAR	TEAM	G (GS, POS)	RUSH	YD	AVG(LG)	TD	REC	YD	AVG(LG)	TD	KPR	OTD	PTS	TAY
1980	Cin	12(0)	1	0	0.0(0)	0	10	137	13.7(26)	0	—	—	0	69
1981	†Cin	15(0)	—	—	—	—	13	181	13.9(42)	2	—	—	12	101
1982	†Cin	9(0)	2	-3	-1.5(5)	0	10	103	10.3(17)	3	—	—	18	64
1983	Cin	12(1)	—	—	—	—	8	66	8.3(14)	2	—	—	12	43
1984	Cin	16(16, TE)	1	-2	-2.0(-2)	0	48	759	15.8(80)	2	k	—	12	385
1985	Cin	10(0)	—	—	—	—	10	123	12.3(22)	1	—	—	6	67
NFL	6	74(17)	4	-5	-1.3(5)	0	99	1369	13.8(80)	10	k	—	60	727

HARRIS, MARK Mark Edward, WR, 6´4˝/201 lbs; Southern Utah; Stanford; B4/28/1970 Clovis, NM

YEAR	TEAM	G (GS, POS)	RUSH	YD	AVG(LG)	TD	REC	YD	AVG(LG)	TD	KPR	OTD	PTS	TAY
1996	SF	1(0)	—	—	—	—	—	—	—	—	—	—	—	—
1997	†SF	10(0)	—	—	—	—	5	53	10.6(16)	0	—	—	0	27
1998	SF	10(0)	—	—	—	—	2	67	33.5(42)	0	—	—	0	34
1999	SF	16(2)	—	—	—	—	6	66	11.0(33)	0	kp	—	0	17
NFL	4	37(2)	—	—	—	—	13	186	14.3(42)	0	kp	—	0	77

HARRIS, MARQUES Marques, LB, 6´1˝/231 lbs; Southern Utah State; B9/20/1981 Salt Lake City, UT **2005** SD 11 (0)

HARRIS, MARSHALL Marshall Kurt, DE-NT, 6´6˝/261 lbs; TCU; 1979: NYJ, rnd 8; B12/6/1955 San Antonio, TX **1980**†Cle 16 (15, LDE) **1981** Cle 15 (12, LDE) **1982**†Cle 9 (9, LDE) **1983** NE 6 (2) **NFL** 46 (38) [4 yrs]

HARRIS, MARV Marvin Keith, LB, 6´1˝/237 lbs; Stanford; 1964: LA, rnd 13; B7/8/1942 Coos Bay, OR **1964** LARm 14

HARRIS, MICHAEL Anthony Michael, C-G, 6´4˝/306 lbs; Grambling State; B8/30/1966 Shreveport, LA **1989** KC 3 (0)

HARRIS, NAPOLEON Napoleon Bill, LB, 6´2˝/255 lbs; Northwestern; 2002: Oak, rnd 1; B2/25/1979 Chicago, IL **2002**†Oak 15 (13, MLB) **2003** Oak 16 (16, MLB) **2004** Oak 14 (9, RLB) **2005** Min 15 (3) **NFL** 60 (41) [4 yrs]

HARRIS, NICK Nicholas John, P, 6´2˝/218 lbs; California; 2001: Den, rnd 4; B7/23/1978 Phoenix, AZ [P] **2001** Cin 16 (0) **2002** Cin 15 (0) **2003** Cin 5 (0) **2005** Det 16 (0)

YEAR	TEAM	G (GS, POS)	RUSH	YD	AVG(LG)	TD	REC	PASS	COMP	PCT	YD	AVG(LG)	TD	INT	KPR	OTD	PTS	TAY
2003	Det	11(0)	—	—	—	—	—	1	0	0.0	0	0.0	0	—	P	—	0	0
2004	Det	16(0)	1	-7	-7.0(-7)	0	—	—	—	—	—	—	—	—	P	—	0	-7
NFL	5	79(0)	1	-7	-7.0(-7)	0	—	1	0	0.0	0	0.0	0	—	P	—	0	-7

HARRIS, ODIE Odie Lazar, DB, 6´0˝/190 lbs; Sam Houston State; B4/1/1966 Bryan, TX **1988** TB 16 (7, ss) **1989** TB 16 (2) **1990** TB 16 (0) **1991** Cle 16 (0) **1992** Cle 4 (0) **1992** Phx 8 (0) **1993** Phx 16 (0) **1994** Arz 13 (0) **1995** Hou 16 (2) **NFL** 121 (11) [8 yrs]

HARRIS, PAUL Paul Christopher, LB, 6´3˝/220 lbs; Alabama; 1977: Pit, rnd 6; B2/19/1954 Mobile, AL **1977** TB 14 (3) **1978** Min 1 **1978** TB 5 **NFL** 20 (3) [2 yrs]

HARRIS, PHIL Phillip Leon, DB, 6´0˝/195 lbs; Texas; 1966: NYG, rnd 7; B9/13/1944 Jackson Hole, WY **1966** NYG 14

HARRIS, QUENTIN Quentin Hugh, DB, 6´1˝/214 lbs; Syracuse; B1/26/1977 Wilkes-Barre, PA **2002** Arz 6 (0) **2003** Arz 16 (1) **2004** Arz 16 (4) **2005** Arz 16 (1) **NFL** 54 (6) [4 yrs]

HARRIS, RAYMONT Raymont LeShawn, RB, 6´0˝/226 lbs; Ohio State; 1994: Chi, rnd 4; B12/23/1970 Lorain, OH

YEAR	TEAM	G (GS, POS)	RUSH	YD	AVG(LG)	TD	REC	YD	AVG(LG)	TD	KPR	OTD	PTS	TAY
1994	ChiB	16(11, FB)	123	464	3.8(13)	1	39	236	6.1(18)	0	k	—	6	595
1995	ChiB	1(1)	—	—	—	—	1	4	4.0(4)	0	—	—	0	2
1996	ChiB	12(10, RB)	194	748	3.9(23)	4	32	296	9.3(47)	1	—	—	30	941
1997	ChiB	13(13, RB)	275	1033	3.8(68)	10	28	115	4.1(16)	0	—	—	60	1191
1998	GB	8(3)	79	228	2.9(14)	1	10	68	6.8(12)	0	—	—	6	272
2000	Den	3(0)	10	22	2.2(6)	0	2	19	9.5(16)	0	—	—	0	32
2000	NE	1(0)	3	14	4.7(7)	0	2	1	0.5(2)	0	—	—	0	15
NFL	6	54(38)	684	2509	3.7(68)	16	114	739	6.5(47)	1	k	—	102	3047

HARRIS, RICHARD Richard Drew, DE-DT, 6´5˝/260 lbs; Grambling State; 1971: Phi, rnd 1; B1/21/1948 Shreveport, LA **1971** Phi 14 (LDE) **1972** Phi 14 (LDE) **1973** Phi 11 (RDT) **1974** ChiB 14 (3) **1975** ChiB 12 (8, RDE) **1976** Sea 14 (8, RDT) **1977** Sea 14 (8, LDE) **NFL** 93 (33) [7 yrs]

HARRIS, RICKIE Rickie Calvin, DB, 5´11˝/182 lbs; Arizona; B5/15/1943 St. Louis, MO [R] **1965** Was 14 (2) **1966** Was 13 (LCB) **1967** Was 14 (LCB) **1968** Was 14 (RCB) **1969** Was 14 (RS) **1970** Was 14 (12, FS) **1971** NE 14 (10, SS) **1972** NE 14 (11, FS) **NFL** 111 (35) [8 yrs]

HARRIS, ROBERT Robert Lee, DT-DE, 6´4˝/295 lbs; Southern (LA); 1992: Min, rnd 2; B6/13/1969 Riviera Beach, FL **1992**†Min 7 (0) **1993**†Min 16 (0) **1994**†Min 11 (1) **1995** NYG 15 (15, RDE) **1996** NYG 16 (15, LDT) **1997**†NYG 16 (16, LDT) **1998** NYG 10 (10, LDT) **1999** NYG 6 (6, ldt) **NFL** 97 (63) [8 yrs]

HARRIS, ROD Roderick World, WR, 5´10˝/183 lbs; Texas A&M; 1989: Hou, rnd 4; B11/14/1966 Dallas, TX [R] **1989** NO 11 (0) **1990** Dal 7 (0) **1990**†Phi 4 (0)

YEAR	TEAM	G (GS, POS)	RUSH	YD	AVG(LG)	TD	REC	YD	AVG(LG)	TD	KPR	OTD	PTS	TAY
1991	Phi	16(0)	—	—	—	—	2	28	14.0(22)	0	kp	—	0	218
NFL	3	38(0)	—	—	—	—	2	28	14.0(22)	0	kp	—	0	460

HARRIS, RONNIE Ronnie James, WR, 5´11˝/179 lbs; Oregon; B6/4/1970 Granada Hills, CA

YEAR	TEAM	G (GS, POS)	RUSH	YD	AVG(LG)	TD	REC	YD	AVG(LG)	TD	KPR	OTD	PTS	TAY
1993	NE	5(0)	—	—	—	—	—	—	—	—	kp	—	0	86
1994	NE	1(0)	—	—	—	—	1	11	11.0(11)	0	p	—	0	17
1994	Sea	1(0)	—	—	—	—	—	—	—	—	—	—	—	—
1995	Sea	13(0)	—	—	—	—	—	—	—	—	kp	—	0	22
1996	Sea	15(0)	—	—	—	—	2	26	13.0(21)	0	kp	—	0	172
1997	Sea	13(0)	—	—	—	—	4	81	20.3(34)	0	kp	—	0	188
1998	Sea	2(0)	—	—	—	—	—	—	—	—	kp	—	0	-10
1998	†Atl	6(0)	—	—	—	—	1	14	14.0(14)	0	kp	—	0	2

YEAR	TEAM	G(GS, POS)	RUSH	YD	AVG(LG)	TD	REC	YD	AVG(LG)	TD	PASS	COMP	PCT	YD	AVG(LG)	TD	INT	SK	YD	QBR	KPR	OTD	PTS	TAY
1999	Atl	13(0)	—	—	—	—	10	164	16.4(24)	0	—	—	—	—	—	—	—	—	—	—	k	—	0	72
NFL	7	69(0)	—	—	—	—	18	296	16.4(34)	0	—	—	—	—	—	—	—	—	—	—	kp	—	0	548

HARRIS, ROY Roy Elliott, DE-DT, 6´2˝/264 lbs; Florida; B3/26/1961 Winter Garden, FL **1984** Atl 15 (0) **1985** Atl 5 (0) **1987** TB 3 (2) **NFL** 23 (2) [3 yrs]

HARRIS, RUDY Onzell Andre, RB, 6´1˝/255 lbs; Clemson; 1993: TB, rnd 4; B9/18/1971 Brockton, MA

YEAR	TEAM	G(GS, POS)	RUSH	YD	AVG(LG)	TD	REC	YD	AVG(LG)	TD	PASS	COMP	PCT	YD	AVG(LG)	TD	INT	SK	YD	QBR	KPR	OTD	PTS	TAY
1993	TB	10(2)	7	29	4.1(12)	0	4	48	12.0(25)	0	—	—	—	—	—	—	—	—	—	—	—	—	0	53
1994	TB	8(0)	2	0	0.0(3)	0	2	11	5.5(8)	0	—	—	—	—	—	—	—	—	—	—	k	—	0	3
NFL	2	18(2)	9	29	3.2(12)	0	6	59	9.8(25)	0	—	—	—	—	—	—	—	—	—	—	k	—	0	56

HARRIS, SEAN Sean Eugene, LB, 6´3˝/245 lbs; Arizona; 1995: Chi, rnd 3; B2/25/1972 Tucson, AZ **1995** ChiB 11 (0) **1996** ChiB 15 (0) **1997** ChiB 11 (1) **1998** ChiB 16 (14, RLB) **1999** ChiB 14 (10, MLB) **2000** ChiB 15 (13, LLB/rlb) **2001** Ind 1 (0) **NFL** 83 (38) [7 yrs]

HARRIS, STEVE Steven, RB, 5´11˝/194 lbs; Northern Iowa; B12/12/1962 Chicago, IL

YEAR	TEAM	G(GS, POS)	RUSH	YD	AVG(LG)	TD	REC	YD	AVG(LG)	TD	PASS	COMP	PCT	YD	AVG(LG)	TD	INT	SK	YD	QBR	KPR	OTD	PTS	TAY
1987	Min	2(0)	4	3	0.8(2)	0	2	17	8.5(16)	0	—	—	—	—	—	—	—	—	—	—	—	—	0	12

HARRIS, TIM Timothy David, LB-DE, 6´6˝/260 lbs; Memphis; 1986: GB, rnd 4; B9/10/1964 Birmingham, AL **[S]** **1986** GB 16 (10, LOLB) **1987** GB 12 (12, ROLB) **1988** GB☆16 (16, ROLB) **1989** GB★16 (16, ROLB) **1990** GB 16 (16, ROLB) **1991** SF 11 (4) **1992**†SF 16 (15, LOLB) **1993** Phi 4 (3) **1994**†SF 5 (1) **1995**†SF 10 (0) **NFL** 122 (93) [10 yrs]

HARRIS, TIM Timothy Allen, RB, 5´9˝/206 lbs; Washington State; B6/15/1961 Compton, CA

YEAR	TEAM	G(GS, POS)	RUSH	YD	AVG(LG)	TD	REC	YD	AVG(LG)	TD	PASS	COMP	PCT	YD	AVG(LG)	TD	INT	SK	YD	QBR	KPR	OTD	PTS	TAY
1983	†Pit	14(0)	2	15	7.5(10)	0	—	—	—	—	—	—	—	—	—	—	—	—	—	—	kp	—	0	31

HARRIS, TOMMIE Tommie, DT, 6´3˝/289 lbs; Oklahoma; 2004: Chi, rnd 1; B4/29/1983 Killeen, TX **2004** ChiB 16 (16, LDT) **2005**†ChiB★16 (16, RDT) **NFL** 32 (32) [2 yrs]

HARRIS, TONY Anthony, DB, 6´2˝/190 lbs; Toledo; 1971: SF, rnd 4; B4/20/1949 Cleveland, OH **1971** SF 4

HARRIS, WALT Walter Lee, DB, 6´1˝/195 lbs; Stanford; B4/1/1964 Stockton, CA **1987** SD 3 (0)

HARRIS, WALT Walter Lee, DB, 5´11˝/192 lbs; Mississippi State; 1996: Chi, rnd 1; B8/10/1974 La Grange, GA **[I]** **1996** ChiB 15 (13, RCB) **1997** ChiB 16 (16, RCB) **1998** ChiB 14 (14, RCB) **1999** ChiB 15 (15, LCB) **2000** ChiB 12 (12, LCB) **2001** ChiB 15 (13, LCB) **2002** Ind 15 (15, LCB) **2003** Ind 16 (15, LCB) **2004** Was 16 (2) **2005**†Was 13 (12, LCB) **NFL** 147 (127) [10 yrs]

HARRIS, WENDELL Wendell Preston, DB-K, 5´11˝/185 lbs; LSU; 1962: Bal, rnd 1/SD, rnd 7; B10/2/1940 Baton Rouge, LA **[K]** **1962** Bal 14 (9, RCB) **1963** Bal 14 **1964**†Bal 14 (4) **1965**†Bal 14 (RS) **1966** NYG 13 (LS) **1967** NYG 14 (LS) **NFL** 83 (13) [6 yrs]

HARRIS, WILLIAM William Milton, TE, 6´4˝/239 lbs; Texas; Bishop; 1987: SL, rnd 7; B2/10/1965 Houston, TX

YEAR	TEAM	G(GS, POS)	RUSH	YD	AVG(LG)	TD	REC	YD	AVG(LG)	TD	PASS	COMP	PCT	YD	AVG(LG)	TD	INT	SK	YD	QBR	KPR	OTD	PTS	TAY
1987	SL	10(3)	—	—	—	—	1	8	8.0(8)	0	—	—	—	—	—	—	—	—	—	—	—	—	0	4
1989	TB	16(2)	—	—	—	—	11	102	9.3(21)	1	—	—	—	—	—	—	—	—	—	—	—	—	6	56
1990	GB	4(0)	—	—	—	—	—	—	—	—	—	—	—	—	—	—	—	—	—	—	—	—	—	—
NFL	3	30(5)	—	—	—	—	12	110	9.2(21)	1	—	—	—	—	—	—	—	—	—	—	—	—	6	60

HARRISON, ANTHONY Willie Anthony, DB, 6´1˝/195 lbs; Georgia Tech; B9/26/1965 Toccoa, GA **1987** GB 3 (3)

HARRISON, BOB Robert, DB, 5´11˝/185 lbs; Ohio University; B11/15/1938 St. Louis, MO **1961** Bal 13 (RS)

HARRISON, BOB Robert Lucius, LB, 6´2˝/225 lbs; Oklahoma; 1959: SF, rnd 2; B8/8/1937 Stamford, TX **1959** SF 12 **1960** SF 12 (6, MLB) **1961** SF 14 (10, MLB) **1962** Phi 13 (LLB) **1963** Phi 9 **1964** Pit 11 (RLB) **1965** SF 7 **1966** SF 14 **1967** SF 14 **NFL** 106 (16) [9 yrs]

HARRISON, CHRIS Christopher Allen, G, 6´3˝/290 lbs; Virginia; B2/25/1972 Washington, DC **1996** Det 2 (0)

HARRISON, DENNIS Dennis, DE, 6´8˝/275 lbs; Vanderbilt; 1978: Phi, rnd 4; B7/31/1956 Cleveland, OH **1978**†Phi 16 (6, lde) **1979**†Phi 12 (1) **1980**†Phi 15 (15, LDE) **1981**†Phi 13 (12, LDE) **1982** Phi★9 (9, LDE) **1983** Phi 16 (16, LDE) **1984** Phi 16 (16, LDE) **1985**†LARm 12 (0) **1986** SF 5 (0) **1986** Atl 11 (0) **1987** Atl 11 (5, rde) **NFL** 136 (80) [10 yrs]

HARRISON, DICK Richard Proctor, E-DB, 6´0˝/195 lbs; Boston College; B4/13/1916 Buffalo, NY, D5/30/1981 Boston, MA

YEAR	TEAM	G(GS, POS)	RUSH	YD	AVG(LG)	TD	REC	YD	AVG(LG)	TD	PASS	COMP	PCT	YD	AVG(LG)	TD	INT	SK	YD	QBR	KPR	OTD	PTS	TAY
1944	Bos	4(0)	—	—	—	—	1	9	9.0(9)	0	—	—	—	—	—	—	—	—	—	—	—	—	0	5

HARRISON, DWIGHT Dwight Webster, DB-WR, 6´1˝/187 lbs; Texas A&M-Kingsville; 1971: Den, rnd 2; B10/12/1948 Beaumont, TX **1973** Buf 14 (RCB) **1974**†Buf 13 (RCB) **1975** Buf 13 (13, RCB) **1976** Buf 12 (12, RCB) **1977** Buf 12 (RCB) **1978** Bal 15 (6, ss) **1979** Bal 7 **1980** Oak 3 (0)

YEAR	TEAM	G(GS, POS)	RUSH	YD	AVG(LG)	TD	REC	YD	AVG(LG)	TD	PASS	COMP	PCT	YD	AVG(LG)	TD	INT	SK	YD	QBR	KPR	OTD	PTS	TAY
1971	Den	10(5, wr)	5	36	7.2(16)	0	19	265	13.9(43)	2	—	—	—	—	—	—	—	—	—	—	—	—	12	179
1972	Den	2(1)	1	9	9.0(9)	0	—	—	—	—	—	—	—	—	—	—	—	—	—	—	—	—	0	9
1972	Buf	7	—	—	—	—	1	16	16.0(16)	0	—	—	—	—	—	—	—	—	—	—	p	—	0	5
NFL	10	108(37)	6	45	7.5(16)	0	20	281	14.1(43)	2	—	—	—	—	—	—	—	—	—	—	pi	1	18	372

HARRISON, ED Edward A., E, 6´0˝/178 lbs; Boston College; B12/3/1902 New York, NY, D5/1981 Bronxville, NY **1926** Bkn 3 (1)

HARRISON, GLYNN Glynn Alan, RB, 5´11˝/191 lbs; Georgia; 1976: SD, rnd 9; B5/25/1954 Atlanta, GA

YEAR	TEAM	G(GS, POS)	RUSH	YD	AVG(LG)	TD	REC	YD	AVG(LG)	TD	PASS	COMP	PCT	YD	AVG(LG)	TD	INT	SK	YD	QBR	KPR	OTD	PTS	TAY
1976	KC	8	16	41	2.6(7)	0	1	12	12.0(12)	0	—	—	—	—	—	—	—	—	—	—	k	—	0	130

HARRISON, GRAN Granville Pearl, E, 6´3˝/211 lbs; Mississippi State; B7/1/1917 Ashland, MS, D12/13/1997 **1941** Phi 1 (0)

YEAR	TEAM	G(GS, POS)	RUSH	YD	AVG(LG)	TD	REC	YD	AVG(LG)	TD	PASS	COMP	PCT	YD	AVG(LG)	TD	INT	SK	YD	QBR	KPR	OTD	PTS	TAY
1942	Det	4(1)	—	—	—	—	3	21	7.0(9)	0	—	—	—	—	—	—	—	—	—	—	—	—	0	11
NFL	2	5(1)	—	—	—	—	3	21	7.0(9)	0	—	—	—	—	—	—	—	—	—	—	—	—	0	11

HARRISON, JAMES James, LB, 6´0˝/242 lbs; Kent State; B5/4/1978 Akron, OH **2002** Pit 1 (0) **2004**†Pit 16 (4) **2005**†Pit 16 (3) **NFL** 33 (7) [3 yrs]

HARRISON, JIM Hulet James, RB, 6´4˝/235 lbs; Missouri; 1971: Chi, rnd 2; B9/10/1948 San Antonio, TX

YEAR	TEAM	G(GS, POS)	RUSH	YD	AVG(LG)	TD	REC	YD	AVG(LG)	TD	PASS	COMP	PCT	YD	AVG(LG)	TD	INT	SK	YD	QBR	KPR	OTD	PTS	TAY
1971	ChiB	2	5	13	2.6(12)	0	2	18	9.0(12)	0	—	—	—	—	—	—	—	—	—	—	—	—	0	22
1972	ChiB	14(FB)	167	622	3.7(19)	2	8	30	3.8(20)	1	—	—	—	—	—	—	—	—	—	—	—	—	18	662
1973	ChiB	13(FB)	100	370	3.7(17)	1	21	200	9.5(44)	2	—	—	—	—	—	—	—	—	—	—	—	—	18	490
1974	ChiB	9	36	94	2.6(16)	1	5	38	7.6(14)	0	—	—	—	—	—	—	—	—	—	—	—	—	6	123
NFL	4	38	308	1099	3.6(19)	4	36	286	7.9(44)	3	—	—	—	—	—	—	—	—	—	—	—	—	42	1297

HARRISON, KENNY Kenneth Wayne, WR, 6´0˝/176 lbs; SMU; 1976: SF, rnd 9; B12/12/1953 Beaumont, TX

YEAR	TEAM	G(GS, POS)	RUSH	YD	AVG(LG)	TD	REC	YD	AVG(LG)	TD	PASS	COMP	PCT	YD	AVG(LG)	TD	INT	SK	YD	QBR	KPR	OTD	PTS	TAY
1976	SF	11	—	—	—	—	3	65	21.7(41)	0	—	—	—	—	—	—	—	—	—	—	—	—	0	33
1977	SF	14(10, WR)	6	15	2.5(15)	0	15	217	14.5(46)	1	1	0	0.0	0	0.0	0	0	—	—	—	—	—	6	129
1978	SF	8(6, WR)	—	—	—	—	16	320	20.0(50)	0	—	—	—	—	—	—	—	—	—	—	—	—	0	160
1980	Was	9(0)	2	-11	-5.5(-3)	0	8	66	8.3(12)	0	—	—	—	—	—	—	—	—	—	—	—	—	0	22
NFL	4	42(16)	8	4	0.5(15)	0	42	668	15.9(50)	1	1	0	0.0	0	0.0	0	0	—	—	—	—	—	6	343

HARRISON, LLOYD Lloyd, DB, 5´10˝/190 lbs; North Carolina State; 2000: Was, rnd 3; B6/21/1977 Kingston, Jamaica **2000** Was 2 (0) **2001** SD 12 (1) **2002** Mia 2 (0) **NFL** 16 (1) [3 yrs]

HARRISON, MARTIN Martin Allen, DE-LB, 6´5˝/252 lbs; Washington; 1990: SF, rnd 10; B9/20/1967 Livermore, CA **1990** SF 2 (0) **1992**†SF 16 (1) **1993** SF 11 (1) **1994**†Min 13 (0) **1995** Min 11 (0) **1996**†Min 16 (8, rde) **1997** Sea 8 (0) **1999** Min 4 (0) **NFL** 81 (10) [8 yrs]

HARRISON, MARVIN Marvin Daniel, WR, 6´0˝/175 lbs; Syracuse; 1996: Ind, rnd 1; B8/25/1972 Philadelphia, PA

YEAR	TEAM	G(GS, POS)	RUSH	YD	AVG(LG)	TD	REC	YD	AVG(LG)	TD	PASS	COMP	PCT	YD	AVG(LG)	TD	INT	SK	YD	QBR	KPR	OTD	PTS	TAY
1996	†Ind	16(15, WR)	3	15	5.0(15)	0	64	836	13.1(41)	8	—	—	—	—	—	—	—	—	—	—	p	—	48	560
1997	Ind	16(15, WR)	2	-7	-3.5(0)	0	73	866	11.9(44)	6	—	—	—	—	—	—	—	—	—	—	p	—	40	456
1998	Ind	12(12, WR)	—	—	—	—	59	776	13.2(61)	7	—	—	—	—	—	—	—	—	—	—	—	—	44	423
1999	†Ind★	16(16, WR)	1	4	4.0(4)	0	115	**1663**	14.5(57)	**12**	—	—	—	—	—	—	—	—	—	—	—	—	74	896
2000	†Ind★	16(16, WR)	—	—	—	—	**102**	1413	13.9(78)	**14**	—	—	—	—	—	—	—	—	—	—	—	—	84	777
2001	Ind★	16(16, WR)	1	3	3.0(3)	0	109	**1524**	14.0(68)	**15**	—	—	—	—	—	—	—	—	—	—	—	—	90	840
2002	†Ind★	16(16, WR)	2	10	5.0(8)	0	**143**	**1722**	12.0(69)	11	—	—	—	—	—	—	—	—	—	—	—	—	68	926
2003	†Ind★	15(15, WR)	1	3	3.0(3)	0	94	1272	13.5(79)	10	—	—	—	—	—	—	—	—	—	—	p	—	60	689
2004	†Ind★	16(16, WR)	—	—	—	—	86	1113	12.9(59)	**15**	—	—	—	—	—	—	—	—	—	—	—	—	90	632
2005	†Ind★	15(15, WR)	—	—	—	—	82	1146	14.0(80)	**12**	—	—	—	—	—	—	—	—	—	—	p	—	72	638
NFL	10	154(152)	10	28	2.8(15)	0	927	12331	13.3(80)	110	—	—	—	—	—	—	—	—	—	—	p	—	670	6836

HARRISON, MAX Maxwell Lamar, E, 6´1˝/208 lbs; Auburn; B1/29/1921 Cottonwood, AL

YEAR	TEAM	G(GS, POS)	RUSH	YD	AVG(LG)	TD	REC	YD	AVG(LG)	TD	PASS	COMP	PCT	YD	AVG(LG)	TD	INT	SK	YD	QBR	KPR	OTD	PTS	TAY
1940	NYG	8(2)	—	—	—	—	4	96	24.0	0	—	—	—	—	—	—	—	—	—	—	—	—	0	48

Harrison, Nolan Nolan, DE-DT, 6´5˝/280 lbs; Indiana; 1991: LARd, rnd 6; B1/25/1969 Chicago, IL **1991**†LARd 14 (3) **1992** LARd 14 (14, RDT) **1993**†LARd 16 (14, RDT/rde) **1994** LARd 16 (16, LDE) **1995** Oak 7 (6, lde) **1996** Oak 15 (2) **1997**†Pit 16 (16, LDE) **1998** Pit 9 (7, lde) **1999** Pit 5 (3) **2000** Was 16 (2) **NFL** 128 (83) [10 yrs]

Harrison, Pat F.M., T, 6´2˝/215 lbs; Samford; B11/21/1911 Tallat Springs, AL **1937** Bkn 3 (0)

Harrison, Reggie Reginald, RB, 5´11˝/218 lbs; Cincinnati; 1974: SL, rnd 9; B1/9/1951 Somerville, NJ

YEAR	TEAM	G(GS, POS)	RUSH	YD	AVG(LG)	TD	REC	YD	AVG(LG)	TD	PASS	COMP	PCT	YD	AVG(LG)	TD	INT	SK	YD	QBR	KPR	OTD	PTS	TAY
1974	SL	1	—	—	—	—	—	—	—	—	—	—	—	—	—	—	—	—	—	—	—	—	—	—
1974	†Pit	4	6	30	5.0(15)	1	1	2	2.0(2)	0	—	—	—	—	—	—	—	—	—	—	k	—	6	53
1975	†Pit	14	43	191	4.4(17)	3	1	4	4.0(4)	0	—	—	—	—	—	—	—	—	—	—	—	—	18	223
1976	†Pit	12	54	235	4.4(27)	4	2	19	9.5(10)	0	—	—	—	—	—	—	—	—	—	—	k	—	24	296
1977	†Pit	14(1)	36	175	4.9(33)	0	3	11	3.7(7)	0	—	—	—	—	—	—	—	—	—	—	—	—	0	181
NFL	4	45(1)	139	631	4.5(33)	8	7	36	5.1(10)	0	—	—	—	—	—	—	—	—	—	—	k	—	48	752

Harrison, Rob Robert, DB, 6´2˝/220 lbs; San Diego State; Sacramento State; 1987: LARd, rnd 10; B8/31/1963 Fortuna, CA

YEAR	TEAM	G(GS, POS)	RUSH	YD	AVG(LG)	TD	REC	YD	AVG(LG)	TD	PASS	COMP	PCT	YD	AVG(LG)	TD	INT	SK	YD	QBR	KPR	OTD	PTS	TAY
1987	LARd	2(1)	9	49	5.4(13)	0	2	18	9.0(15)	0	—	—	—	—	—	—	—	—	—	—	—	—	0	58

Harrison, Rodney Rodney Scott, DB, 6´1˝/220 lbs; Western Illinois; 1994: SD, rnd 5; B12/15/1972 Markham, IL [I] **1994**†SD 15 (0) **1995**†SD 11 (0) **1996** SD 16 (16, SS) **1997** SD 16 (16, SS) **1998** SD★16 (16, SS) **1999** SD 6 (6, ss) **2000** SD 16 (16, SS) **2001** SD★14 (14, SS) **2002** SD 13 (13, SS) **2003**†NE☆16 (16, SS) **2004**†NE☆16 (16, SS) **2005** NE 3 (3) **NFL** 158 (132) [12 yrs]

Harrison, Todd Todd Lewis, TE, 6´4˝/260 lbs; North Carolina State; 1992: Chi, rnd 5; B3/20/1969 Gainesville, FL **1992** TB 1 (0)

Harrison, Tyreo Tyreo Tremayne, LB, 6´2˝/238 lbs; Notre Dame; 2002: Phi, rnd 6; B5/15/1980 Sulphur Springs, TX **2002** Phi 2 (0) **2003**†Phi 12 (0) **NFL** 14 (0) [2 yrs]

Harrison, Vic Victor Mack, WR, 5´9˝/184 lbs; North Carolina; B2/9/1961 Vance County, NC **1987** NO 3 (0)

Harry, Carl Carl David, WR, 5´9˝/168 lbs; Utah; B10/26/1967 Fountain Valley, CA **1989** Was 1 (0) **1992**†Was 1 (0) **NFL** 2 (0) [2 yrs]

Harry, Emile Emile Michael, WR, 5´11˝/175 lbs; Stanford; 1985: Atl, rnd 4; B4/5/1963 Los Angeles, CA

YEAR	TEAM	G(GS, POS)	RUSH	YD	AVG(LG)	TD	REC	YD	AVG(LG)	TD	PASS	COMP	PCT	YD	AVG(LG)	TD	INT	SK	YD	QBR	KPR	OTD	PTS	TAY
1986	†KC	12(0)	—	—	—	—	9	211	23.4(53)	1	—	—	—	—	—	—	—	—	—	—	kp	—	6	126
1988	KC	16(2)	—	—	—	—	26	362	13.9(38)	1	—	—	—	—	—	—	—	—	—	—	—	—	6	186
1989	KC	16(6, wr)	1	9	9.0(9)	0	33	430	13.0(25)	2	—	—	—	—	—	—	—	—	—	—	p	—	12	230
1990	†KC	16(1)	—	—	—	—	41	519	12.7(60)	2	—	—	—	—	—	—	—	—	—	—	p	—	12	267
1991	†KC	12(7, wr)	—	—	—	—	35	431	12.3(36)	3	—	—	—	—	—	—	—	—	—	—	—	—	18	231
1992	KC	7(0)	1	27	27.0(27)	0	5	46	9.2(13)	0	—	—	—	—	—	—	—	—	—	—	—	—	0	50
1992	LARm	4(0)	—	—	—	—	1	12	12.0(12)	0	—	—	—	—	—	—	—	—	—	—	p	—	0	10
NFL	6	83(16)	2	36	18.0(27)	0	150	2011	13.4(60)	9	—	—	—	—	—	—	—	—	—	—	kp	—	54	1099

Hart, Ben Benjamin Franklin, E, 6´2˝/205 lbs; Oklahoma; 1967: NO, rnd 3; B8/19/1945 Oklahoma City, OK, D8/27/2004 Garden City, KS **1967** NO 1

Hart, Clinton Clinton Glenn, DB, 6´0˝/205 lbs; Central Florida; B7/20/1977 Dade City, FL **2003**†Phi 16 (9, FS) **2004**†SD 14 (0) **2005** SD 16 (6, ss) **NFL** 46 (15) [3 yrs]

Hart, Dick Richard Kay, G, 6´2˝/253 lbs; none; B3/4/1943 Morrisville, PA **1967** Phi 14 (14, LG) **1968** Phi 14 (LG) **1969** Phi 14 (LG) **1970** Phi 14 (LG) **1972** Buf 5 (rg) **NFL** 61 (14) [5 yrs]

Hart, Doug Douglas Wayne, DB, 6´0˝/190 lbs; Texas-Arlington; B6/3/1939 Fort Worth, TX **1964** GB 14 (RCB) **1965**†GB 14 **1966**†GB 14 **1967**†GB 14 **1968** GB 14 (3) **1969** GB 14 (LS) **1970** GB 14 (SS) **1971** GB 14 (SS) **NFL** 112 (3) [8 yrs]

Hart, Harold Harold Jerome, RB, 6´0˝/206 lbs; Texas Southern; 1974: Oak, rnd 11; B7/13/1952 Lake City, FL

YEAR	TEAM	G(GS, POS)	RUSH	YD	AVG(LG)	TD	REC	YD	AVG(LG)	TD	PASS	COMP	PCT	YD	AVG(LG)	TD	INT	SK	YD	QBR	KPR	OTD	PTS	TAY
1974	†Oak	13	51	268	5.3(25)	2	1	4	4.0(4)	0	—	—	—	—	—	—	—	—	—	—	k	1	18	486
1975	†Oak	9(4)	56	173	3.1(19)	3	6	27	4.5(15)	0	—	—	—	—	—	—	—	—	—	—	k	1	24	490
1977	NYG	1	—	—	—	—	—	—	—	—	—	—	—	—	—	—	—	—	—	—	—	—	—	—
1978	Oak	7	7	44	6.3(16)	0	1	1	1.0(1)	0	—	—	—	—	—	—	—	—	—	—	k	—	0	132
NFL	4	30(4)	114	485	4.3(25)	5	8	32	4.0(15)	0	—	—	—	—	—	—	—	—	—	—	k	2	42	1107

Hart, Jeff Jeffrey Alan, T, 6´5˝/266 lbs; Oregon State; 1975: SF, rnd 3; B9/10/1953 Portland, OR **1975** SF 14 **1976** NO 14 **1979** Bal 16 (14, RT) **1980** Bal 16 (10, RT) **1981** Bal 16 (16, RT) **1982** Bal 9 (9, RT) **1983** Bal 14 (8, RT) **NFL** 99 (57) [7 yrs]

Hart, Jim James Warren, QB, 6´1˝/215 lbs; Southern Illinois; B4/29/1944 Evanston, IL

YEAR	TEAM	G(GS, POS)	RUSH	YD	AVG(LG)	TD	REC	YD	AVG(LG)	TD	PASS	COMP	PCT	YD	AVG(LG)	TD	INT	SK	YD	QBR	KPR	OTD	PTS	TAY
1966	SL	1	—	—	—	—	—	—	—	—	11	4	36.4	29	2.6(15)	0	0	—	—	—	—	—	0	15
1967	SL	14(14, QB)	13	36	2.8(23)	3	—	—	—	—	397	192	48.4	3008	7.6(76)	19	**30**	—	—	58.4	—	—	18	465
1968	SL	13(12, QB)	19	20	1.1(3)	6	—	—	—	—	316	140	44.3	2059	6.5(80)	15	18	—	—	58.2	—	—	36	465
1969	SL	9(3, qb)	7	16	2.3(10)	2	—	—	—	—	169	84	49.7	1086	6.4(60)	6	12	10	100	52.5	—	—	12	129
1970	SL	14(14, QB)	18	18	1.0(4)	0	—	—	—	—	373	171	45.8	2575	6.9(79)	14	18	26	216	61.5	—	—	0	656
1971	SL	11(9, QB)	13	9	0.7(3)	0	—	—	—	—	243	110	45.3	1626	6.7(57)	8	14	13	139	54.7	—	—	0	302
1972	SL	6(3, qb)	9	17	1.9(8)	0	—	—	—	—	119	60	50.4	857	7.2(**98**)	5	5	7	56	—	—	—	0	271
1973	SL	12(12, QB)	3	-3	-1.0(0)	0	—	—	—	—	320	178	55.6	2223	6.9(69)	15	10	22	168	80.0	—	—	0	784
1974	†SL★	14(14, QB)	10	21	2.1(16)	2	—	—	—	—	**388**	**200**	51.5	2411	6.2(80)	**20**	8	16	134	79.5	—	—	12	1027
1975	†SL✧	14(14, QB)	11	7	0.6(6)	1	—	—	—	—	345	182	52.8	2507	7.3(80)	19	19	6	43	71.7	—	—	6	606
1976	SL✧	14(14, QB)	8	7	0.9(10)	0	—	—	—	—	388	218	56.2	2946	7.6(77)	**18**	13	17	132	82.0	—	—	0	1050
1977	SL✧	14(14, QB)	11	18	1.6(13)	0	—	—	—	—	355	186	52.4	2542	7.2(69)	13	20	13	89	64.3	—	—	0	554
1978	SL	15(15, QB)	11	11	1.0(9)	2	—	—	—	—	477	240	50.3	3121	6.5(74)	16	18	20	166	66.7	—	—	12	952
1979	SL	14(11, QB)	6	11	1.8(12)	0	1	-4	-4.0(-4)	0	378	194	51.3	2218	5.9(51)	9	20	25	183	55.2	—	—	0	363
1980	SL	15(15, QB)	9	11	1.2(12)	0	—	—	—	—	425	228	53.6	2946	6.9(69)	16	20	39	292	68.6	—	—	0	764
1981	SL	10(9, QB)	3	2	0.7(4)	0	—	—	—	—	241	134	55.6	1694	7.0(58)	11	14	16	119	68.7	—	—	0	344
1982	†SL	4(0)	—	—	—	—	—	—	—	—	33	19	57.6	199	6.0(22)	1	0	—	—	—	—	—	0	105
1983	SL	5(3)	5	12	2.4(13)	0	—	—	—	—	91	50	54.9	592	6.5(39)	4	8	13	99	—	—	—	0	8
1984	Was	2(0)	3	-6	-2.0(-2)	0	—	—	—	—	7	3	42.9	26	3.7(13)	0	0	—	—	—	—	—	0	7
NFL	19	201(176)	159	207	1.3(23)	16	1	-4	-4.0(-4)	0	5076	2593	51.1	34665	6.8(98)	209	247	243	1936	66.6	—	—	96	8863

Hart, Lawrence Lawrence Edward, TE, 6´4˝/271 lbs; Southern (LA); 1998: NYJ, rnd 7; B9/19/1976 New Orleans, LA **2001** Arz 1 (0)

Hart, Leo Marion Leo, QB, 6´3˝/203 lbs; Duke; 1971: Atl, rnd 3; B3/3/1949 Kinston, NC

YEAR	TEAM	G(GS, POS)	RUSH	YD	AVG(LG)	TD	REC	YD	AVG(LG)	TD	PASS	COMP	PCT	YD	AVG(LG)	TD	INT	SK	YD	QBR	KPR	OTD	PTS	TAY
1971	Atl	1	—	—	—	—	—	—	—	—	1	0	0.0	0	0.0	0	0	—	—	—	—	—	0	0
1972	Buf	2	5	19	3.8(16)	0	—	—	—	—	15	6	40.0	53	3.5(13)	0	3	4	32	—	—	—	0	-75
NFL	2	3	5	19	3.8(16)	0	—	—	—	—	16	6	37.5	53	3.3(13)	0	3	4	32	—	—	—	0	-75

Hart, Leon Leon Joseph, E-FB-DE, 6´5˝/257 lbs; Notre Dame; 1950: Det, rnd B1; B11/2/1928 Pittsburgh, PA, D9/24/2002 South Bend, IN

YEAR	TEAM	G(GS, POS)	RUSH	YD	AVG(LG)	TD	REC	YD	AVG(LG)	TD	PASS	COMP	PCT	YD	AVG(LG)	TD	INT	SK	YD	QBR	KPR	OTD	PTS	TAY
1950	Det	12(RE)	—	—	—	—	31	505	16.3(66)	1	—	—	—	—	—	—	—	—	—	—	—	—	6	258
1951	Det★	12(RE/RDE)	4	-6	-1.5(3)	0	35	544	15.5(33)	12	—	—	—	—	—	—	—	—	—	—	i	—	72	338
1952	†Det	11(RE)	3	10	3.3(11)	0	32	376	11.8(24)	4	—	—	—	—	—	—	—	—	—	—	—	—	24	218
1953	†Det	12(RE)	1	2	2.0(2)	0	25	472	18.9(49)	7	—	—	—	—	—	—	—	—	—	—	—	—	42	273
1954	†Det☆	12(RE/rde)	—	—	—	—	24	377	15.7(40)	0	—	—	—	—	—	—	—	—	—	—	—	1	6	189
1955	Det	11(FB)	35	159	4.5(21)	0	9	54	6.0(14)	1	—	—	—	—	—	—	—	—	—	—	k	—	6	217
1956	Det☆	11(FB)	76	348	4.6(46)	5	14	116	8.3(29)	1	—	—	—	—	—	—	—	—	—	—	—	—	36	461
1957	†Det	11(fb)	24	99	4.1(15)	0	4	55	13.8(22)	0	—	—	—	—	—	—	—	—	—	—	—	—	0	127
NFL	8	92	143	612	4.3(46)	5	174	2499	14.4(66)	26	—	—	—	—	—	—	—	—	—	—	ki	1	192	2080

Hart, Les Joseph Leslie, BB, 5´11˝/180 lbs; Colgate; B3/7/1908 Yonkers, NY **1931** SI 5 (2)

Hart, Pete Dee Whitfield, FB, 5´9˝/190 lbs; Hardin-Simmons; 1959: ChiC, rnd 17; B4/19/1933 Aspermont, TX

YEAR	TEAM	G(GS, POS)	RUSH	YD	AVG(LG)	TD	REC	YD	AVG(LG)	TD	PASS	COMP	PCT	YD	AVG(LG)	TD	INT	SK	YD	QBR	KPR	OTD	PTS	TAY
1960	NYT-A	14	25	113	4.5(16)	0	3	19	6.3(12)	0	—	—	—	—	—	—	—	—	—	—	—	—	0	123

Hart, Roy Roy, NT-DT, 6´1˝/280 lbs; South Carolina; 1988: Sea, rnd 6; B7/10/1965 Tifton, GA **1989** Sea 16 (1) **1991**†LARd 1 (0) **NFL** 17 (1) [2 yrs]

Hart, Tommy Tommy Lee, DE-LB, 6´4˝/245 lbs; Morris Brown; 1968: SF, rnd 10; B11/7/1944 Macon, GA **1968** SF 5 **1969** SF 14 **1970**†SF 14 (14, LDE) **1971**†SF 14 (14, LDE) **1972**†SF 14 (14, LDE) **1973** SF 14 (14, LDE) **1974** SF 14 (14, LDE) **1975** SF 14 (14, LDE) **1976** SF★14 (14, LDE) **1977** SF 14 (14, LDE) **1978** ChiB 16 (16, LDE) **1979**†ChiB 15 **1980** NO 15 (12, RDE) **NFL** 177 (140) [13 yrs]

YEAR	TEAM	G(GS, POS)	RUSH	YD	AVG(LG)	TD	REC	YD	AVG(LG)	TD	PASS COMP	PCT	YD	AVG(LG)	TD	INT	SK	YD	QBR	KPR	OTD	PTS	TAY

HARTENSTINE, MIKE   Michael Albert, DE, 6´3˝/251 lbs; Penn State; 1975: Chi, rnd 2; B7/27/1953 Bethlehem, PA   **1975** ChiB 14 (14, LDE)   **1976** ChiB 14 (14, LDE)
1977†ChiB 14 (11, LDE)   **1978** ChiB 16 (RDE)   **1979**†ChiB 16 (16, RDE)   **1980** ChiB 16 (16, RDE)   **1981** ChiB 16 (5, rde)   **1982** ChiB 9 (9, LDE)   **1983** ChiB 16 (16, LDE)
1984†ChiB 16 (14, LDE)   **1985**†ChiB 16 (8, lde)   **1986**†ChiB 16 (2)   **1987** Min 5 (0)   **NFL** 184 (125) [13 yrs]

HARTINGS, JEFF   Jeffrey Allen, C-G, 6´3˝/301 lbs; Penn State; 1996: Det, rnd 1; B9/7/1972 St. Henry, OH   **1996** Det 11 (10, RG)   **1997**†Det 16 (16, RG)   **1998** Det 13 (13, RG)
1999†Det 16 (16, RG)   **2000** Det 16 (16, RG)   **2001**†Pit☆16 (16, C)   **2002**†Pit 13 (11, C)   **2003** Pit 16 (16, C)   **2004**†Pit☆16 (16, C)   **2005**†Pit◇16 (16, C)   **NFL** 149 (146) [10 yrs]

HARTLE, GREG   Gregory Alan, LB, 6´2˝/225 lbs; Newberry; 1974: SL, rnd 10; B2/14/1951 Savannah, GA   **1974**†SL 14 (3)   **1975**†SL 13 (3)   **1976** SL 1   **NFL** 28 (6) [3 yrs]

HARTLEY, FRANK   Frank, TE, 6´2˝/268 lbs; Illinois; B12/15/1967 Chicago, IL

1994	Cle	10(5, te)	—	—	—	—	3	13	4.3(8)	1	—	—	—	—	—	—	—	—	—	—	—	6	12
1995	Cle	15(13, TE)	—	—	—	—	11	137	12.5(23)	1	—	—	—	—	—	—	—	—	—	—	—	6	74
1996	Bal	8(0)																					
1997	SD	16(16, TE)	—	—	—	—	19	246	12.9(35)	1	—	—	—	—	—	—	—	—	—	—	—	6	128
1998	SD	16(3)	—	—	—	—	2	28	14.0(17)	0	—	—	—	—	—	—	—	—	—	k	—	0	10
NFL	5	65(37)	—	—	—	—	35	424	12.1(35)	3	—	—	—	—	—	—	—	—	—	k	—	18	223

HARTLEY, HOWARD   Howard Paul, B, 6´0˝/185 lbs; Duke; B9/26/1924 Ravenswood, WV [I]   **1949** Pit 12 (0)   **1951** Pit 12 (DB)   **1952** Pit 9 (DB)

1948	Was	12(2)	5	40	8.0(26)	1	1	10	10.0(10)	0	—	—	—	—	—	—	—	—	—	—	kpi	—	6	151
1950	Pit	12(DB)	—	—	—	—	2	27	13.5(24)	0	—	—	—	—	—	—	—	—	—	—	kpi	—	0	100
NFL	5	57(2)	5	40	8.0(26)	1	3	37	12.3(24)	0	—	—	—	—	—	—	—	—	—	—	kpi	—	6	470

HARTLEY, KEN   Kenneth P., P, 6´2˝/200 lbs; Catawba; B4/28/1957 Bermuda, CO   **1981** NE 2 (0)

HARTMAN, BILL   William Coleman, B, 6´0˝/188 lbs; Georgia; 1938: Was, rnd 8; B3/17/1915 Thomaston, GA, D3/16/2006

| 1938 | Was | 10(4, tb) | 71 | 195 | 2.7 | 0 | 1 | 6 | 6.0(6) | 0 | 77 | 38 | 49.4 | 558 | 7.2(62) | 4 | 10 | — | — | — | — | — | 0 | 97 |

HARTMAN, FRED   Frederick Lilburn, T, 6´1˝/229 lbs; Schreiner College; Rice; 1941: ChiB, rnd 8; B5/21/1917 Dallas, TX, D4/30/1984 Houston, TX   **1947** ChiB 11 (0)   **1948** Phi 12 (0)
NFL 23 (0) [2 yrs]

HARTMAN, JIM   James, E, 6´2˝/205 lbs; Colorado State; B1913   **1936** Bkn 3 (0)

HARTNETT, PERRY   Perry Edmond, G, 6´5˝/278 lbs; SMU; 1982: Chi, rnd 5; B4/28/1960 Galveston, TX   **1982** ChiB 9 (4)   **1983** ChiB 2 (0)   **1987** GB 1 (1)   **NFL** 12 (5) [3 yrs]

HARTONG, GEORGE   George Howard, G-T-C, 6´0˝/210 lbs; Chicago; B7/18/1896 Joliet, IL, D8/1973 Hinsdale, IL   **1921** Ham 3 (3, LG)   **1923** Rac 8 (7, RG)   **1924** ChiC 10 (8, LG)
NFL 21 (18) [3 yrs]

HARTS, SHAUNARD   Shaunard Trudell, DB, 6´0˝/207 lbs; Boise State; 2001: KC, rnd 7; B8/4/1978 Pittsburg, CA   **2001** KC 3 (0)   **2002** KC 16 (11, FS)   **2003**†KC 16 (0)
2004 KC 16 (6, fs)   **NFL** 51 (17) [4 yrs]

HARTSELL, MARK   Mark, QB, 6´4˝/225 lbs; Boston College; B12/7/1973 Brockton, MA

| 2000 | ChiB | 1(0) | | | | | | | | | 1 | 0 | 0.0 | 0 | 0.0 | 0 | 0 | — | — | — | — | — | 0 | 0 |

HARTSHORN, LARRY   Lawrence L., G, 6´0˝/225 lbs; Kansas State; B5/19/1933   **1955** ChiC 2

HARTSOCK, BEN   Ben, TE, 6´4˝/264 lbs; Ohio State; 2004: Ind, rnd 3; B7/5/1980 Chillicothe, OH

2004	Ind	16(3)	—	—	—	—	4	33	8.3(17)	0	—	—	—	—	—	—	—	—	—	—	—	0	17
2005	Ind	7(0)	—	—	—	—	2	8	4.0(7)	0	—	—	—	—	—	—	—	—	—	—	—	0	4
NFL	2	23(3)	—	—	—	—	6	41	6.8(17)	0	—	—	—	—	—	—	—	—	—	—	—	0	21

HARTWELL, ED   Edgerton, LB, 6´1˝/250 lbs; Western Illinois; 2001: Bal, rnd 4; B5/27/1978 Las Vegas, NV   **2001** Bal 16 (0)   **2002** Bal 16 (16, LILB)   **2003**†Bal 16 (15, LILB)
2004 Bal 16 (16, LILB)   **2005** Atl 5 (5, mlb)   **NFL** 69 (52) [5 yrs]

HARTWIG, CARTER   Carter, DB, 6´0˝/205 lbs; USC; 1979: Hou, rnd 8; B2/27/1956 Culver City, CA   **1979**†Hou 16   **1980**†Hou 15 (0)   **1981** Hou 16 (1)   **1982** Hou 9 (3)
1983 Hou 16 (16, FS)   **1984** Hou 14 (14, FS)   **NFL** 86 (34) [6 yrs]

HARTWIG, JUSTIN   Justin James, C-G, 6´4˝/305 lbs; Kansas; 2002: Ten, rnd 6; B11/21/1978 Mankato, MN   **2002** Ten 3 (0)   **2003**†Ten 16 (16, C)   **2004** Ten 15 (15, C)
2005 Ten 16 (16, C)   **NFL** 50 (47) [4 yrs]

HARTWIG, KEITH   Malcolm Keith, WR, 6´0˝/186 lbs; Arizona; 1977: Min, rnd 11; B12/10/1953 Corona Del Mar, CA   **1977** GB 4

HARTY, JOHN   John Daniel, NT-DE, 6´4˝/260 lbs; Iowa; 1981: SF, rnd 2; B12/17/1958 Sioux City, IA   **1981**†SF 14 (0)   **1982** SF 9 (7, NT)   **1983** SF 5 (2)   **1985**†SF 7 (3)
1986 SF 7 (5, lde)   **NFL** 42 (17) [5 yrs]

HARTZOG, BUG   Howard Gallamore, G, 5´11˝/195 lbs; Baylor; B4/11/1901 Terrell, TX, D5/18/1968 Port Lavaca, TX   **1928** NYG 13 (3)

HARVEY, CLAUDE   Claude E., LB, 6´4˝/225 lbs; Prairie View A&M; B3/27/1948 Willis, TX   **1970** Hou 5

HARVEY, FRANK   Willie Frank, RB, 6´0˝/245 lbs; Georgia; 1994: Arz, rnd 7; B1/19/1971 Dawson, GA   **1994** Arz 2 (0)

HARVEY, GEORGE   George Everett, T, 6´4˝/245 lbs; Kansas; 1967: NO, rnd 6; B8/18/1945 Topeka, KS   **1967** NO 6

HARVEY, JAMES   James M., G-T, 6´3˝/265 lbs; Jackson State; B11/27/1965 New Orleans, LA   **1987** KC 3 (3)   **1988** KC 1 (0)   **NFL** 4 (3) [2 yrs]

HARVEY, JIM   James Britton, G-T, 6´5˝/255 lbs; Mississippi; 1965: Oak, rnd R2/GB, rnd 5; B8/20/1943 Jackson, MS   **1966** Oak-A 14 (RG)   **1967**†Oak-A 10
1968†Oak-A 14 (11, RG)   **1969**†Oak-A 14 (14, RG)   **1970**†Oak 14 (14, RG)   **1971** Oak 12   **NFL** 78 (39) [6 yrs]

HARVEY, JOHN   John Lewis, RB, 5´11˝/185 lbs; Texas-El Paso; B12/28/1966 New York, NY

| 1990 | TB | 20 | 27 | 113 | 4.2(14) | 0 | 11 | 86 | 7.8(18) | 1 | — | — | — | — | — | — | — | — | — | k | — | 6 | 188 |

HARVEY, KEN   Kenneth Ray, LB, 6´2˝/237 lbs; California; 1988: Phx, rnd 1; B5/6/1965 Austin, TX [S]   **1988** Phx 16 (0)   **1989** Phx 16 (16, RLB)   **1990** Phx 16 (16, ROLB)
1991 Phx 16 (16, ROLB)   **1992** Phx 10 (10, ROLB)   **1993** Phx 16 (6, rlb)   **1994** Was★16 (16, LLB)   **1995** Was★16 (16, LLB)   **1996** Was★16 (16, LLB)   **1997** Was◇15 (14, LLB)
1998 Was 11 (9, LLB)   **NFL** 164 (135) [11 yrs]

HARVEY, MARVIN   Marvin Dwight, TE-WR, 6´3˝/220 lbs; Southern Mississippi; 1981: KC, rnd 3; B10/17/1959 Donalsonville, GA   **1981** KC 7 (0)

HARVEY, MAURICE   Maurice, DB, 5´10˝/190 lbs; Ball State; 1978: Oak, rnd 4; B1/14/1956 Cincinnati, OH   **1978**†Den 16   **1980** Den 15 (3)   **1981** GB 16 (16, FS)
1982†GB 9 (9, FS)   **1983** GB 4 (4)   **1984** TB 15 (0)   **1987** Det 2 (2)   **NFL** 86 (34) [7 yrs]

HARVEY, NORM   Norman C., T-E-C-G, 6´0˝/196 lbs; Detroit Mercy; B8/27/1896 Calumet, MI, D2/16/1983 Clearwater, FL   **1925** Buf 5 (5, LT)   **1926** Det 8 (1)   **1927** Buf 5 (5, LT)
1927 NYY 9 (7, LT)   **1928** Pro 9 (4)   **1929** Pro 8 (2)   **NFL** 44 (24) [5 yrs]

HARVEY, RICHARD   Richard Clermont, DB, 6´2˝/190 lbs; Jackson State; 1969: LA, rnd 8; B10/22/1945 Gulfport, MS   **1970** Phi 4   **1971** NO 3   **NFL** 7 [2 yrs]

HARVEY, RICHARD   Richard Clemont, LB, 6´1˝/235 lbs; Tulane; 1989: Buf, rnd 11; B9/11/1966 Pascagoula, MS   **1990** NE 16 (9, LILB)   **1991** NE 1 (0)   **1992**†Buf 12 (0)
1993†Buf 15 (0)   **1994** Den 16 (1)   **1995** NO 16 (14, RLB)   **1996** NO 14 (7, llb)   **1997** NO 14 (13, LLB)   **1998** Oak 16 (16, RLB)   **1999** Oak 15 (15, RLB)   **2000** SD 7 (0)
NFL 142 (75) [11 yrs]

HARVEY, STACY   Stacy Lamonte, LB, 6´4˝/245 lbs; Arizona State; B3/8/1965 Pasadena, CA   **1989** KC 9 (0)

HARVEY, WADDEY   James Wallace, DT, 6´4˝/282 lbs; Virginia Tech; 1969: Buf, rnd 8; B3/26/1947 Richmond, VA   **1969** Buf-A 14   **1970** Buf 14 (RDT)   **NFL** 28 [2 yrs]

HARVIN, ALLEN   Allen Nathaniel, RB, 5´9˝/200 lbs; Cincinnati; B3/18/1959 Philadelphia, PA   **1987** Was 1 (0)

HASBROUCK, JOHN   John Hutton, B-E, 6´0˝/190 lbs; Rutgers; B1/20/1895 Port Ewen, NY, D10/19/1944 Port Ewen, NY   **1921** Roc 2 (0)   **1921** RI 3 (1)   **NFL** 5 (1) [1 yr]

HASELRIG, CARLTON   Carlton Lee, G, 6´1˝/295 lbs; Pittsburgh-Johnstown; 1989: Pit, rnd 12; B1/22/1966 Johnstown, PA   **1990** Pit 16 (0)   **1991** Pit 16 (16, RG)
1992†Pit★16 (16, RG)   **1993**†Pit 9 (4)   **1995** NYJ 11 (11, RG)   **NFL** 68 (47) [5 yrs]

HASENOHRL, GEORGE   George Joseph, DT, 6´1˝/260 lbs; Ohio State; 1973: NYG, rnd 8; B3/10/1951 Cleveland, OH, D10/31/2002 Maple Heights, OH   **1974** NYG 5

HASKINS, JON   Jon Radcliffe, LB, 6´2˝/240 lbs; Stanford; 1998: SD, rnd 7; B10/6/1975 Des Moines, IA   **1998** SD 2 (0)

HASLERIG, CLINT   Clinton Edward, WR-HB, 6´0˝/189 lbs; Michigan; 1974: SF, rnd 4; B4/9/1952 Cincinnati, OH   **1974** ChiB 3   **1974** Buf 8   **1976** NYJ 5

1975	Buf	3	2	9	4.5(6)	0	—	—	—	—	—	—	—	—	—	—	—	—	—	—	—	0	9
1975	Min	7	—	—	—	—	2	28	14.0(17)	0	—	—	—	—	—	—	—	—	—	—	—	0	14
NFL	3	26	2	9	4.5(6)	0	2	28	14.0(17)	0	—	—	—	—	—	—	—	—	—	—	—	0	23

HASLETT, JIM James Donald, LB, 6´3˝/232 lbs; Indiana (PA); 1979: Buf, rnd 2; B12/9/1955 Pittsburgh, PA **[C]** **1979** Buf 16 (16, LILB) **1980**†Buf☆16 (16, LILB) **1981**†Buf 16 (16, LILB) **1983** Buf 5 (0) **1984** Buf 15 (15, LILB) **1985** Buf 16 (16, RILB) **1987** NYJ 3 (2)

YEAR	TEAM	G (GS, POS)	RUSH	YD	AVG (LG)	TD	REC	YD	AVG (LG)	TD	PASS	COMP	PCT	YD	AVG (LG)	TD	INT	SK	YD	QBR	KPR	OTD	PTS	TAY
1982	Buf	7(5, RILB)	—	—	—	—	1	4	4.0(4)	0	—	—	—	—	—	—	—	—	—	—	—	—	0	2
NFL	8	94(86)	—	—	—	—	1	4	4.0(4)	0	—	—	—	—	—	—	—	—	—	—	iS	—	0	66

HASLIP, WILBERT Wilbert, RB, 5´11˝/212 lbs; Hawaii; 1979: SD, rnd 8; B12/8/1956 El Centro, CA

YEAR	TEAM	G (GS, POS)	RUSH	YD	AVG (LG)	TD	REC	YD	AVG (LG)	TD	PASS	COMP	PCT	YD	AVG (LG)	TD	INT	SK	YD	QBR	KPR	OTD	PTS	TAY
1979	KC	5	2	1	0.5(1)	0	—	—	—	—	—	—	—	—	—	—	—	—	—	—	k	—	0	-7

HASSELBACH, HARALD Harald, DE-DT, 6´6˝/281 lbs; Washington; B9/22/1967 Amsterdam, Netherlands **1994** Den 16 (9, RDT) **1995** Den 16 (10, LDE) **1996**†Den 16 (1) **1997**†Den 16 (3) **1998**†Den 16 (3) **1999** Den 16 (2) **2000**†Den 16 (1) **NFL** 112 (29) [7 yrs]

HASSELBECK, DON Donald William, TE, 6´7˝/245 lbs; Colorado; 1977: NE, rnd 2; B4/1/1955 Cincinnati, OH

YEAR	TEAM	G (GS, POS)	RUSH	YD	AVG (LG)	TD	REC	YD	AVG (LG)	TD	PASS	COMP	PCT	YD	AVG (LG)	TD	INT	SK	YD	QBR	KPR	OTD	PTS	TAY
1977	NE	14(1)	—	—	—	—	9	76	8.4(21)	4	—	—	—	—	—	—	—	—	—	—	—	—	24	58
1978	†NE	16(4)	—	—	—	—	7	107	15.3(24)	0	—	—	—	—	—	—	—	—	—	—	—	—	0	54
1979	NE	16(3)	—	—	—	—	13	158	12.2(41)	0	—	—	—	—	—	—	—	—	—	—	—	—	0	79
1980	NE	16(2)	—	—	—	—	8	130	16.3(35)	4	—	—	—	—	—	—	—	—	—	—	—	—	24	85
1981	NE	14(14, TE)	—	—	—	—	46	808	17.6(51)	6	—	—	—	—	—	—	—	—	—	—	k	—	36	426
1982	†NE	9(5, TE)	—	—	—	—	15	158	10.5(41)	1	—	—	—	—	—	—	—	—	—	—	—	—	6	84
1983	NE	1(0)	—	—	—	—	1	7	7.0(7)	0	—	—	—	—	—	—	—	—	—	—	—	—	0	4
1983	†LARd	14(0)	—	—	—	—	2	17	8.5(13)	2	—	—	—	—	—	—	—	—	—	—	—	—	12	19
1984	Min	16(0)	—	—	—	—	1	10	10.0(10)	0	—	—	—	—	—	—	—	—	—	—	—	—	0	5
1985	†NYG	7(0)	—	—	—	—	5	71	14.2(30)	1	—	—	—	—	—	—	—	—	—	—	k	—	6	47
NFL	9	123(29)	—	—	—	—	107	1542	14.4(51)	18	—	—	—	—	—	—	—	—	—	—	k	—	108	859

HASSELBECK, MATT Matthew Michael, QB, 6´4˝/223 lbs; Boston College; 1998: GB, rnd 6; B9/25/1975 Westwood, MA

YEAR	TEAM	G (GS, POS)	RUSH	YD	AVG (LG)	TD	REC	YD	AVG (LG)	TD	PASS	COMP	PCT	YD	AVG (LG)	TD	INT	SK	YD	QBR	KPR	OTD	PTS	TAY
1999	GB	16(0)	6	15	2.5(13)	0	—	—	—	—	10	3	30.0	41	4.1(19)	1	0	1	9	—	—	—	0	41
2000	GB	16(0)	4	-5	-1.3(-1)	0	—	—	—	—	19	10	52.6	104	5.5(27)	1	0	1	2	—	—	—	0	52
2001	Sea	13(12, QB)	40	141	3.5(17)	0	—	—	—	—	321	176	54.8	2023	6.3(64)	7	8	38	251	70.9	—	—	0	868
2002	Sea	16(10, QB)	40	202	5.1(21)	1	—	—	—	—	419	267	63.7	3075	7.3(49)	15	10	26	143	87.8	—	—	8	1425
2003	†Sea✧	16(16, QB)	36	125	3.5(18)	2	—	—	—	—	513	313	61.0	3841	7.5(80)	26	15	42	246	88.8	—	—	12	1596
2004	†Sea	14(14, QB)	27	90	3.3(19)	1	—	—	—	—	474	279	58.9	3382	7.1(60)	22	15	30	155	83.1	—	—	6	1301
2005	†Sea★	16(16, QB)	36	124	3.4(23)	1	—	—	—	—	449	294	65.5	3459	7.7(56)	**24**	9	24	154	**98.2**	—	—	6	1624
NFL	7	107(68)	189	692	3.7(23)	5	—	—	—	—	2205	1342	60.9	15925	7.2(80)	96	57	162	960	86.6	—	—	32	6905

HASSELBECK, TIM Timothy Thomas, QB, 6´1˝/211 lbs; Boston College; B4/6/1978 Norfolk, MA

YEAR	TEAM	G (GS, POS)	RUSH	YD	AVG (LG)	TD	REC	YD	AVG (LG)	TD	PASS	COMP	PCT	YD	AVG (LG)	TD	INT	SK	YD	QBR	KPR	OTD	PTS	TAY
2002	Phi	2(0)	—	—	—	—	—	—	—	—	—	—	—	—	—	—	—	—	—	—	—	—	—	—
2003	Was	7(5, qb)	15	41	2.7(11)	0	—	—	—	—	177	95	53.7	1012	5.7(40)	5	7	9	44	63.6	—	—	0	292
2005	NYG	5(0)	2	-3	-1.5(-1)	0	—	—	—	—	—	—	—	—	—	—	—	—	—	—	—	—	0	-3
NFL	3	14(5)	17	38	2.2(11)	0	—	—	—	—	177	95	53.7	1012	5.7(40)	5	7	9	44	63.6	—	—	0	289

HASTINGS, ANDRE Andre Orlando, WR, 6´1˝/190 lbs; Georgia; 1993: Pit, rnd 3; B11/7/1971 Macon, GA **[R]**

YEAR	TEAM	G (GS, POS)	RUSH	YD	AVG (LG)	TD	REC	YD	AVG (LG)	TD	PASS	COMP	PCT	YD	AVG (LG)	TD	INT	SK	YD	QBR	KPR	OTD	PTS	TAY
1993	†Pit	6(0)	—	—	—	—	3	44	14.7(18)	0	—	—	—	—	—	—	—	—	—	—	k	—	0	19
1994	†Pit	16(8, WR)	—	—	—	—	20	281	14.1(46)	2	—	—	—	—	—	—	—	—	—	—	p	—	12	156
1995	†Pit	16(0)	1	14	14.0(14)	0	48	502	10.5(36)	1	—	—	—	—	—	—	—	—	—	—	p	1	12	514
1996	†Pit	16(10, WR)	4	71	17.8(37)	0	72	739	10.3(38)	6	—	—	—	—	—	—	—	—	—	—	kp	—	36	555
1997	NO	16(16, WR)	4	35	8.8(27)	0	48	722	15.0(39)	5	—	—	—	—	—	—	—	—	—	—	p	—	32	414
1998	NO	16(12, WR)	3	32	10.7(4)	0	35	455	13.0(89)	3	—	—	—	—	—	—	—	—	—	—	kp	—	18	473
1999	NO	15(5, wr)	1	4	4.0(4)	0	40	564	14.1(42)	1	—	—	—	—	—	—	—	—	—	—	—	—	6	291
2000	TB	3(0)	—	—	—	—	—	—	—	—	—	—	—	—	—	—	—	—	—	—	p	—	0	25
NFL	8	104(51)	13	156	12.0(37)	0	266	3307	12.4(89)	18	—	—	—	—	—	—	—	—	—	—	kp	1	116	2446

HASTINGS, GEORGE George William, T, 6´2˝/190 lbs; Ohio University; B9/21/1905 Malden, MA, D8/9/1981 Boston, MA **1930** Por 1 (0) **1931** Por 1 (0) **NFL** 2 (0) [2 yrs]

HASTINGS, SANDY Charles Elliott, B, 5´8˝/178 lbs; Pittsburgh; B1/24/1893 Brookville, PA, deceased **1920** Cle 3 (2)

HASTY, JAMES James Edward, DB, 6´0˝/203 lbs; Central Washington; Washington State; 1988: NYJ, rnd 3; B5/23/1965 Seattle, WA **[I]** **1988** NYJ 15 (15, RCB) **1989** NYJ 16 (16, RCB) **1990** NYJ 16 (16, RCB) **1991**†NYJ 16 (16, RCB) **1992** NYJ 16 (16, RCB) **1993** NYJ 16 (16, RCB) **1994** NYJ 16 (16, RCB) **1995**†KC 16 (16, RCB) **1996** KC 15 (14, RCB) **1997**†KC★16 (15, RCB) **1998** KC 16 (14, RCB) **1999** KC✧15 (15, RCB) **2000** KC 16 (15, RCB) **2001** Oak 1 (0) **NFL** 206 (200) [14 yrs]

HATCH, JEFF Jeff, T, 6´6˝/305 lbs; Pennsylvania; 2002: NYG, rnd 3; B9/28/1979 Annapolis, MD **2003** NYG 4 (4)

HATCHER, ARMON Armon Merrell, DB, 6´0˝/212 lbs; Oregon State; 1999: Buf, rnd 6; B7/15/1976 Diamond Bar, CA **2000** SD 4 (0)

HATCHER, DALE Roger Dale, P, 6´2˝/209 lbs; Clemson; 1985: LARm, rnd 3; B4/5/1963 Cheraw, SC **[P]** **1985**†LARm★16 (0) **1986**†LARm 16 (0) **1987** LARm 15 (0) **1988**†LARm 7 (0) **1991** LARm 13 (0) **1993** Mia 16 (0)

YEAR	TEAM	G (GS, POS)	RUSH	YD	AVG (LG)	TD	REC	YD	AVG (LG)	TD	PASS	COMP	PCT	YD	AVG (LG)	TD	INT	SK	YD	QBR	KPR	OTD	PTS	TAY
1989	†LARm	16(0)	1	0	0.0(0)	0	—	—	—	—	—	—	—	—	—	—	—	—	—	—	P	—	0	0
NFL	7	99(0)	1	0	0.0	0	—	—	—	—	—	—	—	—	—	—	—	—	—	—	P	—	0	0

HATCHER, RON Ronald Allan, FB, 5´11˝/215 lbs; Michigan State; 1962: Was, rnd 8/NYT, rnd 21; B7/3/1939 Pittsburgh, PA **1962** Was 3

HATCHETT, DERRICK Derrick Kingston, DB, 5´11˝/182 lbs; Texas; 1980: Bal, rnd 1; B8/14/1958 Bryan, TX **1980** Bal 16 (16, LCB) **1981** Bal 16 (13, LCB) **1982** Bal 9 (9, RCB) **1983** Bal 7 (6, RCB) **1983** Hou 1 (0) **NFL** 49 (44) [4 yrs]

HATCHETTE, MATTHEW Matthew Isaac, WR, 6´3˝/200 lbs; Mercyhurst; Langston; 1997: Min, rnd 7; B5/1/1974 Cleveland, OH

YEAR	TEAM	G (GS, POS)	RUSH	YD	AVG (LG)	TD	REC	YD	AVG (LG)	TD	PASS	COMP	PCT	YD	AVG (LG)	TD	INT	SK	YD	QBR	KPR	OTD	PTS	TAY
1997	†Min	16(0)	—	—	—	—	3	54	18.0(38)	0	—	—	—	—	—	—	—	—	—	—	—	—	0	27
1998	†Min	5(0)	—	—	—	—	15	216	14.4(25)	0	—	—	—	—	—	—	—	—	—	—	—	—	0	108
1999	†Min	13(0)	—	—	—	—	9	180	20.0(80)	2	—	—	—	—	—	—	—	—	—	—	—	—	12	100
2000	†Min	14(4)	—	—	—	—	16	190	11.9(39)	2	—	—	—	—	—	—	—	—	—	—	—	—	12	105
2001	NYJ	11(0)	—	—	—	—	2	44	22.0(29)	0	—	—	—	—	—	—	—	—	—	—	—	—	0	22
2003	Jax	6(4)	—	—	—	—	15	203	13.5(45)	2	—	—	—	—	—	—	—	—	—	—	—	—	12	112
NFL	6	65(8)	—	—	—	—	60	887	14.8(80)	6	—	—	—	—	—	—	—	—	—	—	—	—	36	474

HATHAWAY, RUSS Russell Grant, T-G, 5´11˝/238 lbs; Indiana; B1/14/1896 Terre Haute, IN, D8/19/1988 Clay City, IN **[K]** **1920** Mun 1 (1, RG) **1920** Day 2 (1) **1921** Day 9 (7, LT), 24 **1922** Can 2 (0) **1922** Day☆8 (8, LT), 15 **1923** Day☆8 (8, LT), 10 **1924** Day 8 (8, LT), 6 **1925** Pot 12 (12, LT) **1926** Pot 10 (7, RT), 3 **1927** Buf 4 (0) **NFL** 64 (52), 58 [8 yrs]

HATHAWAY, STEVE Steven Francis, LB, 6´4˝/238 lbs; West Virginia; 1984: Ind, rnd 12; B4/26/1962 Beaver, PA **1984** Ind 6 (1)

HATHCOCK, DAVE David Gary, DB, 6´0˝/195 lbs; Memphis; 1966: GB, rnd 17; B7/20/1943 Memphis, TN **1966**†GB 14 **1967** NYG 6 **NFL** 20 [2 yrs]

HATLEY, JOHNNY Johnny Ray, G-DT, 6´3˝/249 lbs; Baylor; Sul Ross State; 1953: ChiB, rnd 16; B3/16/1930 Lometa, TX, D2/10/2001 Albuquerque, NM **1953** ChiB 10 **1954** ChiC 12 (LG) **1955** ChiC 12 **1960** Den-A 14 (RDT) **NFL** 48 [4 yrs]

HAUCK, TIM Timothy Christian, DB, 5´10˝/187 lbs; Pacific (OR); Montana; B12/20/1966 Butte, MT **1990** GB 10 (0) **1991** GB 16 (0) **1992** GB 16 (0) **1993**†GB 13 (0) **1994**†GB 13 (3) **1995** Den 16 (0) **1996**†Den 16 (0) **1997** Sea 16 (0) **1998** Ind 16 (7, fs) **1999** Phi 16 (15, SS) **2000**†Phi 16 (3) **2001**†Phi 16 (0) **2002** SF 3 (0) **NFL** 183 (28) [13 yrs]

HAUSER, ART Arthur A., DT-T-G, 6´0˝/237 lbs; Xavier (OH); 1954: LA, rnd 5; B6/19/1929 Rubican, WI **1954** LARm 12 (LDT) **1955**†LARm 12 (RDT) **1956** LARm 12 (RDT) **1957** LARm 12 (LDT) **1959** ChiC 2 **1959**†NYG 4 **1960** Bos-A 8 **1961** Den-A 14 **NFL** 76 [7 yrs]

HAUSER, EARL William Earl, E-T, 6´1˝/190 lbs; Miami (OH); B2/22/1897, D11/1974 Akron, OH **1920** Day 6 (2) **1921** Cin 4 (4, LE), 6 **NFL** 10 (6) [2 yrs]

HAUSER, KEN Kenneth, FB-BB, 6´1˝/224 lbs; none; B1899, deceased **1927** Buf 2 (2, FB) **1930** Nwk 5 (2) **NFL** 7 (4) [2 yrs]

HAUSS, LEN Leonard Moore, C, 6´2˝/235 lbs; Georgia; 1964: Was, rnd 9; B7/11/1942 Jessup, GA **1964** Was 14 (C) **1965** Was 14 (14, C) **1966** Was✧14 (14, C) **1967** Was 14 (14, C) **1968** Was✧14 (C) **1969** Was✧14 (C) **1970** Was✧14 (14, C) **1971**†Was☆14 (14, C) **1972**†Was★14 (14, C) **1973**†Was☆14 (14, C) **1974**†Was☆14 (14, C) **1975** Was☆14 (14, C) **1976**†Was☆14 (14, C) **1977** Was☆14 (14, C) **NFL** 196 (154) [14 yrs]

HAVENS, CHARLIE Charles William, C-T, 5´10˝/205 lbs; Colgate; Western Maryland; B7/12/1903 Rome, NY, D5/12/1996 Gaithersburg, MD **1930** Fra 13 (11, C)

HAVERDICK, DAVE David George, DT, 6´4˝/245 lbs; Morehead State; 1970: Det, rnd 13; B1/19/1948 Canton, OH **1970** Det 8

Haverdink, Kevin Kevin Dean, T, 6´5˝/285 lbs; Western Michigan; 1989: NO, rnd 5; B10/20/1965 Holland, MI **1989** NO 16 (7, lt) **1990**†NO 15 (15, LT) **1991** NO 10 (5, lt) **NFL** 41 (27) [3 yrs]

Havig, Dennis Dennis Eugene, G, 6´2˝/253 lbs; Colorado; 1971: Atl, rnd 8; B5/6/1949 Powell, WY **1972** Atl 14 (RG) **1973** Atl 14 (RG) **1974** Atl 14 (RG) **1975** Atl 13 (13, RG) **1976** Hou 14 **1977** GB 7 (lg) **NFL** 76 (13) [6 yrs]

Havrilak, Sam Samuel Charles, WR-RB, 6´2˝/195 lbs; Bucknell; 1969: Bal, rnd 8; B12/13/1947 Charleroi, PA

YEAR	TEAM	G (GS, POS)	RUSH	YD	AVG (LG)	TD	REC	YD	AVG (LG)	TD	PASS	COMP	PCT	YD	AVG (LG)	TD	INT	SK	YD	QBR	KPR	OTD	PTS	TAY
1969	Bal	14	5	49	9.8(29)	1	1	5	5.0(5)	0	—	—	—	—	—	—	—	—	—	—	p	—	6	53
1970	†Bal	13	54	159	2.9(26)	0	14	141	10.1(33)	0	2	2	100.0	82	41.0(54)	0	0	—	—	—	kp	—	0	277
1971	†Bal	14	—	—	—	—	1	12	12.0(12)	0	—	—	—	—	—	—	—	—	—	—	—	—	0	6
1972	Bal	14(WR)	12	72	6.0(32)	2	33	571	17.3(62)	4	1	0	0.0	0	0.0	0	0	—	—	—	—	—	36	398
1973	Bal	14	2	9	4.5(8)	0	1	9	9.0(9)	0	—	—	—	—	—	—	—	—	—	—	—	—	0	14
1974	NO	6	—	—	—	—	1	23	23.0(23)	0	—	—	—	—	—	—	—	—	—	—	—	—	0	12
NFL	6	75	73	289	4.0(32)	3	51	761	14.9(62)	4	3	2	66.7	82	27.3(54)	0	0	—	—	—	kp	—	42	758

Hawkes, Michael Michael Tranzo, LB, 6´0˝/242 lbs; Virginia Tech; B4/11/1977 Richmond, VA **2000** Car 1 (0) **2001** Car 2 (0) **NFL** 3 (0) [2 yrs]

Hawkins, Alex Clifton Alexander, HB-FL-WR, 6´0˝/190 lbs; South Carolina; 1959: GB, rnd 2; B7/2/1937 Welch, WV

YEAR	TEAM	G (GS, POS)	RUSH	YD	AVG (LG)	TD	REC	YD	AVG (LG)	TD	PASS	COMP	PCT	YD	AVG (LG)	TD	INT	SK	YD	QBR	KPR	OTD	PTS	TAY
1959	†Bal	11	12	44	3.7(11)	0	—	—	—	—	—	—	—	—	—	—	—	—	—	—	k	—	0	50
1960	Bal	12(HB)	76	267	3.5(17)	2	25	280	11.2(49)	3	—	—	—	—	—	—	—	—	—	—	—	—	30	442
1961	Bal	11(HB)	86	379	4.4(39)	4	20	158	7.9(22)	1	—	—	—	—	—	—	—	—	—	—	p	—	30	503
1962	Bal	13	29	87	3.0(13)	4	4	37	9.3(14)	0	1	0	0.0	0	0.0	0	0	—	—	—	kp	—	24	138
1963	Bal	14	3	-2	-0.7(-1)	0	3	41	13.7(19)	0	—	—	—	—	—	—	—	—	—	—	p	—	0	90
1964	†Bal	14	—	—	—	—	2	42	21.0(27)	1	—	—	—	—	—	—	—	—	—	—	p	—	6	68
1965	†Bal	14	—	—	—	—	2	32	16.0(27)	1	—	—	—	—	—	—	—	—	—	—	kp	—	6	-11
1966	Atl	12(FL)	—	—	—	—	44	661	15.0(42)	2	—	—	—	—	—	—	—	—	—	—	k	—	12	356
1967	Atl	3	—	—	—	—	—	—	—	—	—	—	—	—	—	—	—	—	—	—	—	—	—	—
1967	Bal	11	2	12	6.0(7)	0	27	469	17.4(54)	4	—	—	—	—	—	—	—	—	—	—	—	—	24	267
1968	†Bal	10	—	—	—	—	2	31	15.5(18)	0	—	—	—	—	—	—	—	—	—	—	—	—	0	16
NFL	10	125	208	787	3.8(39)	10	129	1751	13.6(54)	12	1	0	0.0	0	0.0	0	0	—	—	—	kp	—	132	1917

Hawkins, Andy Anthony James, LB, 6´2˝/225 lbs; Texas A&M-Kingsville; 1980: TB, rnd 10; B3/31/1958 Bay City, TX **1980** TB 16 (1) **1981**†TB 16 (12, LOLB) **1982**†TB 9 (9, LOLB) **1983** TB 6 (5, lolb) **1986** SD 10 (0) **1987** SD 2 (1) **1988** KC 7 (3) **NFL** 66 (31) [7 yrs]

Hawkins, Artrell Artrell, DB, 5´10˝/190 lbs; Cincinnati; 1998: Cin, rnd 2; B11/24/1976 Johnstown, PA **1998** Cin 16 (16, RCB) **1999** Cin 14 (13, RCB) **2000** Cin 16 (6, rcb) **2001** Cin 14 (13, RCB) **2002** Cin 15 (15, RCB) **2003** Cin 14 (9, LCB) **2004** Car 14 (4) **2005**†NE 5 (4, SS) **NFL** 108 (80) [8 yrs]

Hawkins, Ben Benjamin Charles, WR-SE-FL, 6´1˝/180 lbs; Arizona State; 1966: Phi, rnd 3/NYJ, rnd 5; B3/22/1944 Newark, NJ

YEAR	TEAM	G (GS, POS)	RUSH	YD	AVG (LG)	TD	REC	YD	AVG (LG)	TD	PASS	COMP	PCT	YD	AVG (LG)	TD	INT	SK	YD	QBR	KPR	OTD	PTS	TAY
1966	Phi	14	—	—	—	—	14	143	10.2(23)	0	—	—	—	—	—	—	—	—	—	—	kp	—	0	59
1967	Phi	14(SE)	—	—	—	—	59	**1265**	21.4(87)	10	—	—	—	—	—	—	—	—	—	—	k	—	60	783
1968	Phi	14(FL)	—	—	—	—	42	707	16.8(92)	5	—	—	—	—	—	—	—	—	—	—	kp	—	30	453
1969	Phi	14(SE)	1	-3	-3.0(-3)	0	43	761	17.7(58)	8	—	—	—	—	—	—	—	—	—	—	p	—	48	419
1970	Phi	14(WR)	2	3	1.5(4)	0	30	612	20.4(78)	4	—	—	—	—	—	—	—	—	—	—	kp	—	24	280
1971	Phi	14(WR)	4	8	2.0(10)	0	37	650	17.6(65)	4	—	—	—	—	—	—	—	—	—	—	p	1	30	354
1972	Phi	14(WR)	3	0	0.0(12)	0	30	512	17.1(67)	1	—	—	—	—	—	—	—	—	—	—	—	—	6	261
1973	Phi	4	—	—	—	—	6	114	19.0(37)	0	—	—	—	—	—	—	—	—	—	—	—	—	0	57
1974	Cle	2	—	—	—	—	—	—	—	—	—	—	—	—	—	—	—	—	—	—	—	—	—	—
NFL	9	104	10	8	0.8(12)	0	261	4764	18.3(92)	32	—	—	—	—	—	—	—	—	—	—	kp	1	198	2664

Hawkins, Bill William E., DE-DT, 6´6˝/269 lbs; Miami (FL); 1989: LARm, rnd 1; B5/9/1966 Miami, FL **1989** LARm 13 (1) **1990** LARm 15 (0) **1991** LARm 6 (0) **1992** LARm 8 (7, RDE) **NFL** 42 (8) [4 yrs]

Hawkins, Clarence Clarence L., RB, 6´0˝/205 lbs; Florida A&M; B7/15/1956 Tallahassee, FL

YEAR	TEAM	G (GS, POS)	RUSH	YD	AVG (LG)	TD	REC	YD	AVG (LG)	TD	PASS	COMP	PCT	YD	AVG (LG)	TD	INT	SK	YD	QBR	KPR	OTD	PTS	TAY
1979	Oak	7	21	72	3.4(34)	0	2	24	12.0(20)	1	—	—	—	—	—	—	—	—	—	—	k	—	6	99

Hawkins, Courtney Courtney Tyrone, WR, 5´9˝/183 lbs; Michigan State; 1992: TB, rnd 2; B12/12/1969 Flint, MI

YEAR	TEAM	G (GS, POS)	RUSH	YD	AVG (LG)	TD	REC	YD	AVG (LG)	TD	PASS	COMP	PCT	YD	AVG (LG)	TD	INT	SK	YD	QBR	KPR	OTD	PTS	TAY
1992	TB	16(5, wr)	—	—	—	—	20	336	16.8(49)	2	—	—	—	—	—	—	—	—	—	—	kp	—	12	149
1993	TB	16(12, WR)	—	—	—	—	62	933	15.0(67)	5	—	—	—	—	—	—	—	—	—	—	p	—	30	583
1994	TB	13(12, WR)	—	—	—	—	37	438	11.8(32)	5	—	—	—	—	—	—	—	—	—	—	p	—	30	247
1995	TB	16(3)	4	5	1.3(11)	0	41	493	12.0(47)	0	—	—	—	—	—	—	—	—	—	—	—	—	0	252
1996	TB	16(16, WR)	1	-13	-13.0(-13)	0	46	544	11.8(45)	1	—	—	—	—	—	—	—	—	—	—	p	—	6	258
1997	†Pit	15(3)	5	17	3.4(11)	0	45	555	12.3(44)	3	—	—	—	—	—	—	—	—	—	—	p	—	18	358
1998	Pit	15(14, WR)	10	41	4.1(14)	0	66	751	11.4(53)	1	—	—	—	—	—	—	—	—	—	—	p	—	6	522
1999	Pit	11(11, WR)	—	—	—	—	30	285	9.5(23)	0	—	—	—	—	—	—	—	—	—	—	p	—	0	137
2000	Pit	13(5, wr)	—	—	—	—	19	238	12.5(33)	1	—	—	—	—	—	—	—	—	—	—	p	—	6	119
NFL	9	131(81)	20	50	2.5(14)	0	366	4573	12.5(67)	18	—	—	—	—	—	—	—	—	—	—	kp	—	108	2623

Hawkins, Frank Frank, RB, 5´9˝/210 lbs; Nevada-Reno; 1981: Oak, rnd 10; B7/3/1959 Las Vegas, NV

YEAR	TEAM	G (GS, POS)	RUSH	YD	AVG (LG)	TD	REC	YD	AVG (LG)	TD	PASS	COMP	PCT	YD	AVG (LG)	TD	INT	SK	YD	QBR	KPR	OTD	PTS	TAY
1981	Oak	13(0)	40	165	4.1(19)	0	10	109	10.9(35)	0	—	—	—	—	—	—	—	—	—	—	k	—	0	212
1982	†LARd	9(0)	27	54	2.0(11)	2	7	35	5.0(9)	1	—	—	—	—	—	—	—	—	—	—	—	—	18	97
1983	†LARd	16(2)	110	526	4.8(32)	6	20	150	7.5(28)	2	—	—	—	—	—	—	—	—	—	—	—	—	48	671
1984	†LARd	16(0)	108	376	3.5(17)	3	7	51	7.3(15)	0	—	—	—	—	—	—	—	—	—	—	—	—	18	432
1985	†LARd	16(16, FB)	84	269	3.2(21)	4	27	174	6.4(20)	0	—	—	—	—	—	—	—	—	—	—	k	—	24	395
1986	LARd	16(15, FB)	58	245	4.2(15)	0	25	166	6.6(16)	0	—	—	—	—	—	—	—	—	—	—	k	—	0	328
1987	LARd	2(1)	4	24	6.0(7)	0	1	6	6.0(6)	0	—	—	—	—	—	—	—	—	—	—	—	—	0	27
NFL	7	88(34)	431	1659	3.8(32)	15	97	691	7.1(35)	3	—	—	—	—	—	—	—	—	—	—	k	—	108	2161

Hawkins, Garland Garland Anthony, DE, 6´3˝/253 lbs; Syracuse; B2/19/1970 Washington, DC **1995** ChiB 1 (0)

Hawkins, Michael Michael, DB, 6´1˝/175 lbs; Oklahoma; 2005: GB, rnd 5; B7/15/1983 Dallas, TX **2005** GB 11 (1)

Hawkins, Mike Michael Douglas, LB, 6´2˝/235 lbs; Texas A&M-Kingsville; 1978: NE, rnd 7; B10/29/1955 Bay City, TX **1978**†NE 12 **1979** NE 16 (14, LOLB) **1980** NE 16 (16, LOLB) **1981** NE 15 (15, LOLB) **1982** LARd 3 (0) **NFL** 62 (45) [5 yrs]

Hawkins, Nate Nathaniel Alfred, WR, 6´1˝/190 lbs; UNLV; 1972: Pit, rnd 16; B2/8/1950 Houston, TX

YEAR	TEAM	G (GS, POS)	RUSH	YD	AVG (LG)	TD	REC	YD	AVG (LG)	TD	PASS	COMP	PCT	YD	AVG (LG)	TD	INT	SK	YD	QBR	KPR	OTD	PTS	TAY
1975	Hou	11	—	—	—	—	1	32	32.0(32)	0	—	—	—	—	—	—	—	—	—	—	—	—	0	16

Hawkins, Rip Ross Cooper, LB, 6´3˝/235 lbs; North Carolina; 1961: Min, rnd 2/Bos, rnd 2; B4/21/1939 Winchester, TN **1961** Min 14 (13, MLB) **1962** Min 14 (11, MLB) **1963** Min★14 (14, MLB) **1964** Min 14 (14, MLB) **1965** Min 14 (14, MLB) **NFL** 70 (66) [5 yrs]

Hawkins, Steve Steven, WR, 6´5˝/210 lbs; Tennessee State; Western Michigan; 1994: NE, rnd 6; B3/16/1971 Detroit, MI

YEAR	TEAM	G (GS, POS)	RUSH	YD	AVG (LG)	TD	REC	YD	AVG (LG)	TD	PASS	COMP	PCT	YD	AVG (LG)	TD	INT	SK	YD	QBR	KPR	OTD	PTS	TAY
1994	NE	7(0)	—	—	—	—	2	22	11.0(14)	0	—	—	—	—	—	—	—	—	—	—	—	—	0	11

Hawkins, Wayne Wayne Allen, G, 6´0˝/240 lbs; Pacific; 1960: Den, rnd 1; B6/17/1938 Fort Peck, MT **1960** Oak-A 14 (RG) **1961** Oak-A☆14 (RG) **1962** Oak-A 14 (RG) **1963** Oak-A★14 (LG) **1964** Oak-A★14 (RG) **1965** Oak-A★14 (RG) **1966** Oak-A★14 (LG) **1967**†Oak-A★14 (RG) **1968**†Oak-A 10 (3) **1969**†Oak-A 14 **NFL** 136 (3) [10 yrs]

Haworth, Steve Steven, DB, 5´11˝/189 lbs; Oklahoma; 1983: Hou, rnd 6; B9/16/1961 Manilla, Philippines **1983** Atl 11 (0) **1984** Atl 5 (0) **NFL** 16 (0) [2 yrs]

Haws, Kurt Kurt Leroy, TE, 6´5˝/248 lbs; Utah; 1994: Was, rnd 4; B9/25/1969 Mesa, AZ **1994** Was 6 (0)

Haws, Les Harvey Lester, B, 5´8˝/165 lbs; Dartmouth; B11/28/1899 Ardmore, PA, D1/20/1966 Norristown, PA **1924** Fra 13 (13, BB), 24 **1925** Fra 13 (8, bb), 6 **NFL** 26 (21), 30 [2 yrs]

Hawthorne, Anttaj Anttaj, DT, 6´2˝/310 lbs; Wisconsin; 2005: Oak, rnd 6; B11/15/1981 New Haven, CT **2005** Oak 2 (0)

Hawthorne, Duane Duane, DB, 5´10˝/175 lbs; Northern Illinois; B8/26/1976 St. Louis, MO **1999**†Dal 13 (0) **2000** Dal 14 (0) **2001** Dal 16 (11, LCB) **2002** Dal 10 (5, lcb) **2002**†SF 3 (0) **NFL** 56 (16) [4 yrs]

Hawthorne, Ed Edward William, NT, 6´1˝/305 lbs; Minnesota; B7/30/1970 St. Louis, MO **1995** Mia 1 (0)

YEAR	TEAM	G (GS, POS)	RUSH	YD	AVG(LG)	TD	REC	YD	AVG(LG)	TD	PASS	COMP	PCT	YD	AVG(LG)	TD	INT	SK	YD	QBR	KPR	OTD	PTS	TAY

HAWTHORNE, GREG Gregory Dale, RB-TE-WR, 6´2˝/228 lbs; Baylor; 1979: Pit, rnd 1; B9/5/1956 Fort Worth, TX

1979	†Pit	15	28	123	4.4(19)	1	8	47	5.9(17)	0	—	—	—	—	—	—	—	—	—	—	k	—	6	173
1980	Pit	15(6, rb)	63	226	3.6(15)	4	12	158	13.2(33)	0	—	—	—	—	—	—	—	—	—	—	k	—	24	379
1981	Pit	10(0)	25	58	2.3(16)	2	4	23	5.8(12)	0	—	—	—	—	—	—	—	—	—	—	k	—	12	123
1982	†Pit	9(1)	15	68	4.5(11)	0	12	182	15.2(46)	3	—	—	—	—	—	—	—	—	—	—	—	—	18	174
1983	Pit	10(4)	5	47	9.4(20)	0	19	300	15.8(52)	0	—	—	—	—	—	—	—	—	—	—	—	—	0	197
1984	NE	14(1)	—	—	—	—	7	127	18.1(26)	0	—	—	—	—	—	—	—	—	—	—	k	—	0	63
1985	†NE	15(0)	—	—	—	—	3	42	14.0(28)	1	—	—	—	—	—	—	—	—	—	—	k	—	6	24
1986	†NE	14(10, TE)	1	5	5.0(5)	0	24	192	8.0(17)	0	—	—	—	—	—	—	—	—	—	—	k	—	0	84
1987	Ind	3(3)	—	—	—	—	3	41	13.7(21)	0	—	—	—	—	—	—	—	—	—	—	—	—	0	21
NFL	9	105(25)	137	527	3.8(20)	7	92	1112	12.1(52)	4	—	—	—	—	—	—	—	—	—	—	k	—	66	1236

HAWTHORNE, MICHAEL Michael Seneca, DB, 6´3˝/200 lbs; Purdue; 2000: NO, rnd 6; B1/26/1977 Sarasota, FL   **2000**†NO 11 (1) **2001** NO 11 (2) **2002** NO 6 (4) **2003**†GB 14 (2) **2004**†GB 16 (5, lcb) **2005** SL 5 (5, fs) **NFL** 63 (19) [6 yrs]

HAYCRAFT, KEN Kenneth C., E, 6´0˝/178 lbs; Minnesota; B2/16/1907 Bemidji, MN, D6/29/1995 Kaneohe, HI   **1929** Min 10 (9, LE), 12 **1930** Min 5 (5, LE) **1930** GB 1 (1) **NFL** 16 (15) [2 yrs]

HAYDEN, AARON Aaron Chautezz, RB, 6´0˝/216 lbs; Tennessee; 1995: SD, rnd 4; B4/13/1973 Detroit, MI

1995	†SD	7(4)	128	470	3.7(20)	3	5	53	10.6(16)	0	—	—	—	—	—	—	—	—	—	—	—	—	18	527
1996	SD	11(0)	55	166	3.0(13)	0	1	10	10.0(10)	0	—	—	—	—	—	—	—	—	—	—	—	—	0	171
1997	†GB	14(0)	32	148	4.6(21)	1	2	11	5.5(7)	0	—	—	—	—	—	—	—	—	—	—	k	—	6	215
1998	Phi	1(0)	—	—	—	—	—	—	—	—	—	—	—	—	—	—	—	—	—	—	k	—	0	7
NFL	4	33(4)	215	784	3.6(21)	4	8	74	9.3(16)	0	—	—	—	—	—	—	—	—	—	—	k	—	24	919

HAYDEN, KEN Kenneth Mack, C, 6´0˝/205 lbs; Arkansas; B10/21/1917 Hamburg, AR, D8/1968 Smackover, AR   **1942** Phi 9 (5, c) **1943**†Was 8 (2) **NFL** 17 (7) [2 yrs]

HAYDEN, KELVIN Kelvin, DB, 5´10˝/198 lbs; Illinois; 2005: Ind, rnd 2; B7/23/1983 Chicago, IL   **2005**†Ind 16 (0)

HAYDEN, LEO Leophus, RB, 6´0˝/210 lbs; Ohio State; 1971: Min, rnd 1; B6/2/1948 Louisville, KY   **1971** Min 7 **1973** SL 2

| 1972 | SL | 4 | 8 | 11 | 1.4(5) | 1 | 1 | 17 | 17.0(17) | 0 | — | — | — | — | — | — | — | — | — | — | — | — | 6 | 30 |
| NFL | 3 | 13 | 8 | 11 | 1.4(5) | 1 | 1 | 17 | 17.0(17) | 0 | — | — | — | — | — | — | — | — | — | — | k | — | 6 | 53 |

HAYDUK, HENRY Henry Harold, G, 6´0˝/200 lbs; Washington State; B9/26/1913, NY, D8/27/1969 Seattle, WA   **1935** Bkn 1 (0)

| 1935 | Pit | 8(0) | 1 | 3 | 3.0(3) | 0 | — | — | — | — | — | — | — | — | — | — | — | — | — | — | — | — | 0 | 3 |
| NFL | 1 | 9(0) | 1 | 3 | 3.0(3) | 0 | — | — | — | — | — | — | — | — | — | — | — | — | — | — | — | — | 0 | 3 |

HAYE, JOVAN Jovan, DE, 6´2˝/284 lbs; Vanderbilt; 2005: Car, rnd 6; B6/21/1982 Jamaica   **2005** Car 2 (0)

HAYES, BILLIE William, DB, 6´1˝/175 lbs; San Diego State; 1970: Cin, rnd 4; B6/22/1947 Riverside, CA   **1972** NO 14 (lcb)

HAYES, BOB Robert Lee 'Bullet Bob', SE-WR, 6´0˝/187 lbs; Florida A&M; 1964: Dal, rnd 7/Den, rnd 14; B12/20/1942 Jacksonville, FL, D9/18/2002 Jacksonville, FL [R]

1965	Dal★	13(SE)	4	-8	-2.0(11)	1	46	1003	21.8(82)	12	—	—	—	—	—	—	—	—	—	—	kp	—	78	852
1966	†Dal★	14(SE)	1	-1	-1.0(-1)	0	64	1232	19.3(95)	13	—	—	—	—	—	—	—	—	—	—	p	—	78	701
1967	†Dal★	13(SE)	—	—	—	—	49	998	20.4(64)	10	—	—	—	—	—	—	—	—	—	—	kp	1	66	717
1968	†Dal☆	14(SE)	4	2	0.5(6)	0	53	909	17.2(54)	10	—	—	—	—	—	—	—	—	—	—	kp	2	72	769
1969	†Dal	10(10, SE)	4	17	4.3(8)	0	40	746	18.6(67)	4	—	—	—	—	—	—	—	—	—	—	kp	—	24	534
1970	†Dal	13(9, WR)	4	34	8.5(13)	1	34	889	26.1(89)	10	—	—	—	—	—	—	—	—	—	—	p	—	66	580
1971	†Dal	14(WR)	3	18	6.0(11)	0	35	840	24.0(85)	8	—	—	—	—	—	—	—	—	—	—	kp	—	48	477
1972	†Dal	12(6, wr)	2	8	4.0(7)	0	15	200	13.3(29)	0	—	—	—	—	—	—	—	—	—	—	—	—	0	108
1973	†Dal	13(WR)	—	—	—	—	22	360	16.4(47)	3	—	—	—	—	—	—	—	—	—	—	—	—	18	195
1974	Dal	12	—	—	—	—	7	118	16.9(35)	1	—	—	—	—	—	—	—	—	—	—	p	—	6	65
1975	SF	4	2	-2	-1.0(-1)	0	6	119	19.8(36)	1	—	—	—	—	—	—	—	—	—	—	—	—	0	58
NFL	11	132(25)	24	68	2.8(13)	2	371	7414	20.0(95)	71	—	—	—	—	—	—	—	—	—	—	kp	3	456	5054

HAYES, BRANDON William Brandon, G, 6´4˝/308 lbs; Central State (OH); B3/11/1973 Muncie, IN   **1996** Car 6 (0)

HAYES, CHRIS Christopher Kareem, DB, 6´0˝/206 lbs; Washington State; 1996: NYJ, rnd 7; B5/7/1972 San Bernardino, CA   **1996**†GB 2 (0) **1997** NYJ 16 (0) **1998**†NYJ 15 (0) **1999** NYJ 15 (0) **2000** NYJ 16 (8, FS) **2001**†NYJ 16 (1) **2002** NE 4 (0) **NFL** 84 (9) [7 yrs]

HAYES, DAVE David Vincent, E, 5´8˝/165 lbs; Notre Dame; B3/1894 Hartford, CT, deceased   **1921** RI 3 (2), 6 **1921** GB 6 (6, RE) **1922** GB 7 (6, LE) **NFL** 16 (14) [2 yrs]

HAYES, DONALD Donald Ross, WR, 6´4˝/220 lbs; Wisconsin; 1998: Car, rnd 4; B7/13/1975 Madison, WI

1998	Car	7(0)	—	—	—	—	3	62	20.7(35)	0	—	—	—	—	—	—	—	—	—	—	—	—	0	31
1999	Car	13(1)	—	—	—	—	11	270	24.5(56)	2	—	—	—	—	—	—	—	—	—	—	—	—	12	145
2000	Car	15(15, WR)	—	—	—	—	66	926	14.0(43)	3	—	—	—	—	—	—	—	—	—	—	—	—	18	478
2001	Car	16(15, WR)	—	—	—	—	52	597	11.5(48)	2	—	—	—	—	—	—	—	—	—	—	—	—	12	309
2002	NE	12(1)	—	—	—	—	12	133	11.1(40)	2	—	—	—	—	—	—	—	—	—	—	—	—	12	77
NFL	5	63(32)	—	—	—	—	144	1988	13.8(56)	9	—	—	—	—	—	—	—	—	—	—	—	—	54	1039

HAYES, ED Edward Rogers, DB, 6´1˝/185 lbs; Morgan State; 1969: Den, rnd 4; B8/14/1946 Jacksonville, FL   **1970** Phi 4

HAYES, ERIC Eric Gerard, DT-DE-NT, 6´3˝/292 lbs; Florida State; 1990: Sea, rnd 5; B11/12/1967 Tampa, FL   **1990** Sea 16 (0) **1991** Sea 5 (3) **1992** LARm 1 (0) **1993** TB 2 (0) **NFL** 24 (3) [4 yrs]

HAYES, GARY Gary L., DB, 5´10˝/180 lbs; Fresno State; B8/19/1957 Tucson, AZ   **1984** GB 16 (0) **1985** GB 16 (0) **1986** GB 10 (0) **NFL** 42 (0) [3 yrs]

HAYES, GERALD Gerald, LB, 6´1˝/237 lbs; Pittsburgh; 2003: Arz, rnd 3; B10/10/1980 Paterson, NJ   **2003** Arz 12 (2) **2004** Arz 16 (1) **NFL** 28 (3) [2 yrs]

HAYES, JARIUS Jarius, TE, 6´3˝/266 lbs; North Alabama; 1996: Arz, rnd 7; B3/27/1973 Sheffield, AL   **1996** Arz 4 (0) **1998**†Arz 16 (0) **NFL** 20 (0) [2 yrs]

HAYES, JEFF Jeffrey Clyde, P, 5´11˝/175 lbs; North Carolina; B8/19/1959 Elkin, NC [P]   **1982**†Was 9 (0) **1985** Was 4 (0) **1987** Mia 2 (0)

1983	†Was	16(0)	2	63	31.5(48)	0	—	—	—	—	—	—	—	—	—	—	—	—	—	—	P	—	0	63
1984	†Was	16(0)	2	13	6.5(24)	0	—	—	—	—	—	—	—	—	—	—	—	—	—	—	P	—	0	13
1986	Cin	16(0)	3	92	30.7(61)	1	—	—	—	—	—	—	—	—	—	—	—	—	—	—	P	—	6	102
NFL	6	63(0)	7	168	24.0(61)	1	—	—	—	—	—	—	—	—	—	—	—	—	—	—	P	—	6	178

HAYES, JIM James William, DT-DE, 6´4˝/263 lbs; Jackson State; B11/26/1940 Meridian, MS, D4/19/2001 Meridian, MS   **1965** Hou-A 14 **1966** Hou-A 14 **NFL** 28 [2 yrs]

HAYES, JOE Joseph Herman, RB-WR, 5´9˝/185 lbs; Texas A&M-Kingsville; Central Oklahoma; 1984: Phi, rnd 7; B9/15/1960 Dallas, TX   **1984** Phi 12 (0)

HAYES, JONATHAN Jonathan Michael, TE, 6´5˝/248 lbs; Iowa; 1985: KC, rnd 2; B8/11/1962 South Fayette, PA

1985	KC	16(0)	—	—	—	—	5	39	7.8(12)	1	—	—	—	—	—	—	—	—	—	—	k	—	6	10
1986	†KC	16(4)	—	—	—	—	8	69	8.6(16)	0	—	—	—	—	—	—	—	—	—	—	—	—	0	35
1987	KC	12(8, TE)	—	—	—	—	21	272	13.0(33)	2	—	—	—	—	—	—	—	—	—	—	—	—	12	146
1988	KC	16(9, TE)	—	—	—	—	22	233	10.6(25)	1	—	—	—	—	—	—	—	—	—	—	—	—	6	122
1989	KC	16(16, TE)	—	—	—	—	18	229	12.7(23)	2	—	—	—	—	—	—	—	—	—	—	—	—	12	125
1990	†KC	12(11, te)	—	—	—	—	9	83	9.2(21)	1	—	—	—	—	—	—	—	—	—	—	—	—	6	47
1991	†KC	16(16, TE)	—	—	—	—	19	208	10.9(23)	2	—	—	—	—	—	—	—	—	—	—	—	—	12	114
1992	†KC	16(16, TE)	—	—	—	—	9	77	8.6(21)	2	—	—	—	—	—	—	—	—	—	—	—	—	12	49
1993	†KC	16(16, TE)	—	—	—	—	24	331	13.8(49)	1	—	—	—	—	—	—	—	—	—	—	—	—	6	171
1994	†Pit	16(6, te)	—	—	—	—	5	50	10.0(17)	1	—	—	—	—	—	—	—	—	—	—	—	—	6	30
1995	†Pit	16(6, te)	—	—	—	—	11	113	10.3(32)	0	—	—	—	—	—	—	—	—	—	—	—	—	0	57
1996	†Pit	16(6, te)	—	—	—	—	2	14	7.0(7)	0	—	—	—	—	—	—	—	—	—	—	—	—	0	7
NFL	12	184(114)	—	—	—	—	153	1718	11.2(49)	13	—	—	—	—	—	—	—	—	—	—	k	—	78	909

HAYES, LARRY Larry Gene, C-LB, 6´3˝/220 lbs; Vanderbilt; B7/21/1935 Nashville, TN   **1961**†NYG 14 **1962** LARm 9 (C) **1963** LARm 9 **NFL** 32 [3 yrs]

YEAR	TEAM	G (GS, POS)	RUSH	YD	AVG(LG)	TD	REC	YD	AVG(LG)	TD	PASS	COMP	PCT	YD	AVG(LG)	TD	INT	SK	YD	QBR	KPR	OTD	PTS	TAY

HAYES, LESTER Lester 'The Molester', DB, 6´0˝/200 lbs; Texas A&M; 1977: Oak, rnd 5; B1/22/1955 Houston, TX **[I]** **1977**†Oak 14 (2) **1978** Oak 16 (16, LCB)
1979 Oak☆16 (16, LCB) **1980**†Oak★16 (16, LCB) **1981** Oak☆16 (16, LCB) **1982**†LARd★9 (9, LCB) **1983**†LARd★16 (16, LCB) **1984**†LARd★16 (16, LCB)
1985†LARd 16 (13, LCB) **1986** LARd 14 (14, LCB) **NFL** 149 (134) [10 yrs]

HAYES, LUTHER Luther E., E, 6´4˝/202 lbs; USC; 1961: SD, rnd 27/Phi, rnd 10; B1/1/1939 San Diego, CA

| 1961 | †SD-A | 14 | — | — | — | — | 14 | 280 | 20.0(39) | 3 | | | | | | | | | | | — | — | 18 | 155 |

HAYES, MELVIN Melvin Anthony, T, 6´6˝/328 lbs; Mississippi State; 1995: NYJ, rnd 4; B4/28/1973 New Orleans, LA **1995** NYJ 3 (0) **1996** NYJ 1 (0) **NFL** 4 (0) [2 yrs]

HAYES, MERCURY Mercury Wayne, WR, 5´11˝/195 lbs; Michigan; 1996: NO, rnd 5; B1/1/1973 Houston, TX **1997** NO 4 (0) **1997** Atl 2 (0)

| 1996 | NO | 7(0) | 2 | 7 | 3.5(5) | 0 | 4 | 101 | 25.3(50) | 0 | — | — | — | — | — | — | — | — | — | — | k | — | 0 | 58 |
| NFL | 2 | 13(0) | 2 | 7 | 3.5(5) | 0 | 4 | 101 | 25.3(50) | 0 | — | — | — | — | — | — | — | — | — | — | — | — | 0 | 58 |

HAYES, NORBERT Norbert P., E–FB, 5´11˝/175 lbs; Marquette; B11/21/1896 Kaukauna, WI, D7/1945 **1922** Rac 11 (7, LE) **1923** GB 6 (5, le) **NFL** 17 (12) [2 yrs]

HAYES, RAY Raymond, FB, 6´3˝/235 lbs; Maryland-Eastern Shore; Central Oklahoma; 1961: Min, rnd 13; B5/25/1935 Pawhuska, OK

| 1961 | Min | 13 | 73 | 319 | 4.4(22) | 2 | 16 | 121 | 7.6(22) | 0 | — | — | — | — | — | — | — | — | — | — | k | — | 12 | 385 |

HAYES, RAYMOND Raymond Roy, DT, 6´5˝/248 lbs; Toledo; 1968: NYJ, rnd 12; B9/5/1946 Hazel Park, MI **1968** NYJ-A 6

HAYES, RUDY Richard Rudolph, LB, 6´0˝/217 lbs; Clemson; 1959: Pit, rnd 20; B1/12/1935 Pickens, SC **1959** Pit 12 **1960** Pit 12 (LLB) **1962** Pit 4 **NFL** 28 [3 yrs]

HAYES, TOM Thomas J., DB, 6´1˝/199 lbs; San Diego State; 1971: Atl, rnd 6; B4/18/1946 Riverside, CA **1971** Atl 14 (14, RCB) **1972** Atl 14 (14, RCB) **1973** Atl 14 (14, RCB)
1974 Atl 13 (13, RCB) **1975** Atl 14 (14, RCB) **1976** SD 9 (8, lcb) **NFL** 78 (77) [6 yrs]

HAYES, WENDELL Wendell, RB, 6´1˝/220 lbs; Humboldt State; B8/5/1940 Dallas, TX

1963	Dal	1	—	—	—	—	—	—	—	—	—	—	—	—	—	—	—	—	—	—	k	—	0	18
1965	Den-A	14(14, HB)	130	526	4.0(43)	5	24	294	12.3(66)	2	1	0	0.0	0	0.0	0	0	1	—	—	k	—	44	726
1966	Den-A	11(FB)	105	417	4.0(56)	1	8	49	6.1(29)	0	—	—	—	—	—	—	—	—	—	—	—	—	6	452
1967	Den-A	14(fb)	85	255	3.0(18)	4	13	125	9.6(24)	0	—	—	—	—	—	—	—	—	—	—	k	—	26	417
1968	†KC-A	11	85	340	4.0(25)	4	12	108	9.0(22)	1	—	—	—	—	—	—	—	—	—	—	—	—	30	439
1969	†KC-A	14	62	208	3.4(11)	4	9	64	7.1(17)	0	—	—	—	—	—	—	—	—	—	—	k	—	24	331
1970	KC	14(FB)	109	381	3.5(22)	5	26	219	8.4(28)	0	—	—	—	—	—	—	—	—	—	—	—	—	30	541
1971	†KC	14(FB)	132	537	4.1(27)	1	16	150	9.4(29)	1	—	—	—	—	—	—	—	—	—	—	k	—	12	642
1972	KC	13(FB)	128	536	4.2(28)	0	31	295	9.5(29)	3	—	—	—	—	—	—	—	—	—	—	—	—	18	699
1973	KC	13(FB)	95	352	3.7(27)	2	18	134	7.4(27)	0	—	—	—	—	—	—	—	—	—	—	—	—	12	439
1974	KC	14(fb)	57	206	3.6(19)	2	4	23	5.8(9)	0	—	—	—	—	—	—	—	—	—	—	—	—	12	238
NFL	11	133(14)	988	3758	3.8(56)	28	161	1461	9.1(66)	7	1	0	0.0	0	0.0	0	0	1	—	—	k	—	214	4940

HAYES, WINDRELL Windrell Mansa, WR, 5´11˝/198 lbs; San Jose State; USC; 2000: NYJ, rnd 5; B12/14/1976 Stockton, CA **2001** NYJ 1 (0)

| 2000 | NYJ | 8(0) | 1 | 2 | 2.0(2) | 0 | 6 | 126 | 21.0(32) | 0 | — | — | — | — | — | — | — | — | — | — | — | — | 0 | 65 |
| NFL | 2 | 9(0) | 1 | 2 | 2.0(2) | 0 | 6 | 126 | 21.0(32) | 0 | — | — | — | — | — | — | — | — | — | — | — | — | 0 | 65 |

HAYGOOD, HERB Herbert Donta, WR, 5´11˝/193 lbs; Michigan State; 2002: Den, rnd 5; B12/30/1977 Sarasota, FL **2002** Den 4 (0)

HAYHOE, BILL William J., T, 6´8˝/258 lbs; USC; 1969: GB, rnd 5; B9/6/1946 Los Angeles, CA **1969** GB 14 **1970** GB 13 **1971** GB 14 **1972**†GB 14 (LT) **1973** GB 6 (lt)
NFL 61 [5 yrs]

HAYMAN, CONWAY Conway, G–T, 6´3˝/264 lbs; Delaware; 1971: Was, rnd 6; B1/9/1949 Wilmington, DE **1975** Hou 14 **1976** Hou 14 (14, LG) **1977** Hou 12 (2)
1978†Hou 16 (16, RT/lg) **1979**†Hou 16 (16, LG) **1980**†Hou 5 (3) **NFL** 77 (51) [6 yrs]

HAYMAN, GARY Gary Wesley, RB, 6´1˝/198 lbs; Penn State; 1974: Buf, rnd 5; B9/8/1951 Newark, DE

1974	Buf	1	7	31	4.4(8)	0	—	—	—	—	—	—	—	—	—	—	—	—	—	—	p	—	0	34
1975	Buf	14	10	30	3.0(7)	0	—	—	—	—	—	—	—	—	—	—	—	—	—	—	kp	—	0	180
NFL	2	15	17	61	3.6(8)	0	—	—	—	—	—	—	—	—	—	—	—	—	—	—	kp	—	0	214

HAYMOND, ALVIN Alvin Henry, DB, 6´0˝/194 lbs; Southern (LA); 1964: Bal, rnd 18; B8/31/1942 New Orleans, LA **[R]** **1964** Bal 9 **1965**†Bal 14 **1966** Bal 14 (RS) **1967** Bal 8
1968 Phi 11 (RCB) **1969**†LARm 14 **1970** LARm 14 **1971** LARm 10 **1972**†Was 4 **1973** Hou 6 **NFL** 104 [10 yrs]

HAYNES, ABNER Abner, HB, 6´0˝/190 lbs; North Texas; 1960: Oak, rnd 1/Pit, rnd 5; B9/19/1937 Denton, TX **[R]**

1960	DalT-A☆	14(HB)	156	875	5.6(67)	9	55	576	10.5(34)	3	1	0	0.0	0	0.0	0	0	0	—	—	kp	—	72	**1562**
1961	DalT-A★	14(HB)	179	841	4.7(59)	9	34	558	16.4(69)	3	—	—	—	—	—	—	—	—	—	—	kp	1	78	1486
1962	†DalT-A★	14(HB)	221	1049	4.7(71)	13	39	573	14.7(78)	6	1	0	0.0	0	0.0	0	0	0	—	—	kp	—	114	**1552**
1963	KC-A	14(HB)	99	352	3.6(46)	4	33	470	14.2(73)	2	1	1	100.0	24	24.0(24)	0	0	0	—	—	kp	—	36	813
1964	KC-A★	14(HB)	139	697	5.0(80)	4	38	562	14.8(68)	3	1	0	0.0	0	0.0	0	0	0	—	—	kp	1	48	1137
1965	Den-A	14	41	166	4.0(47)	3	26	216	8.3(71)	2	1	0	0.0	0	0.0	0	0	0	—	—	kp	1	36	766
1966	Den-A	14(HB)	129	304	2.4(20)	2	46	480	10.4(52)	1	2	0	0.0	0	0.0	0	0	0	—	—	kp	—	18	652
1967	Mia-A	11	56	274	4.9(65)	1	16	100	6.3(22)	0	—	—	—	—	—	—	—	—	—	—	kp	—	12	465
1967	NYJ-A	3	16	72	4.5(14)	0	—	—	—	—	—	—	—	—	—	—	—	—	—	—	k	—	0	137
NFL	8	112	1036	4630	4.5(80)	46	287	3535	12.3(78)	20	7	1	14.3	24	3.4(24)	0	0	0	—	—	kp	3	414	8570

HAYNES, HALL Hall Gibson, DB, 6´0˝/187 lbs; Santa Clara; 1950: Was, rnd 2; B10/3/1928 Duncan, OK, D6/13/1988 Santa Clara County, CA **1954** LARm 11 (DB) **1955** LARm 9

1950	Was	12(DB)	2	20	10.0(17)	0	—	—	—	—	—	—	—	—	—	—	—	—	—	—	Pkpi	1	6	233
1953	Was	8	2	0	0.0(4)	0	—	—	—	—	—	—	—	—	—	—	—	—	—	—	kp	—	0	85
NFL	4	40	4	20	5.0(17)	0	—	—	—	—	—	—	—	—	—	—	—	—	—	—	Pkpi	1	6	313

HAYNES, JAMES James, LB, 6´2˝/230 lbs; Mississippi Valley State; B8/9/1960 Tallulah, LA **1984** NO 10 (0) **1986** NO 16 (16, ROLB) **1987**†NO 12 (0) **1988** NO 4 (0)
1989 NO 3 (2)

| 1985 | NO | 16(5, rolb) | — | — | — | — | 1 | 8 | 8.0(8) | 0 | — | — | — | — | — | — | — | — | — | — | S | — | 0 | 4 |
| NFL | 6 | 61(23) | — | — | — | — | 1 | 8 | 8.0(8) | 0 | — | — | — | — | — | — | — | — | — | — | iS | 1 | 6 | 26 |

HAYNES, JOE Joseph H., C–G, 6´3˝/225 lbs; Oklahoma; Tulsa; 1947: Phi, rnd 23; B3/26/1921 Barnsdall, OK, D3/9/1994 Tupelo, MS **1947** Buf-A 9 (0)

HAYNES, LOUIS Louis Jules, LB, 6´0˝/227 lbs; Bishop; North Texas; 1982: KC, rnd 4; B1/17/1960 New Orleans, LA, D12/2/2002 New Orleans, LA **1982** KC 6 (0) **1983** KC 5 (0)
NFL 11 (0) [2 yrs]

HAYNES, MARK Mark, DB, 5´11˝/194 lbs; Colorado; 1980: NYG, rnd 1; B11/6/1958 Kansas City, KS **1980** NYG 15 (11, LCB/rcb) **1981**†NYG☆16 (16, LCB)
1982 NYG★9 (9, LCB) **1983** NYG★15 (15, LCB) **1984** NYG★15 (15, LCB) **1985** NYG 5 (1) **1986**†Den 11 (0) **1987**†Den 12 (12, LCB) **1988** Den 15 (15, LCB) **1989**†Den 14 (0)
NFL 127 (94) [10 yrs]

HAYNES, MICHAEL Michael David, WR, 6´0˝/184 lbs; Northern Arizona; 1988: Atl, rnd 7; B12/24/1965 New Orleans, LA

1988	Atl	15(5, wr)	—	—	—	—	13	232	17.8(49)	4	—	—	—	—	—	—	—	—	—	—	k	—	24	159
1989	Atl	13(11, WR)	4	35	8.8(21)	0	40	681	17.0(72)	4	—	—	—	—	—	—	—	—	—	—	—	—	24	396
1990	Atl	13(10, WR)	—	—	—	—	31	445	14.4(60)	0	—	—	—	—	—	—	—	—	—	—	—	—	0	223
1991	†Atl	16(16, WR)	—	—	—	—	50	1122	**22.4(80)**	11	—	—	—	—	—	—	—	—	—	—	—	—	66	616
1992	Atl	14(14, WR)	—	—	—	—	48	808	16.8(89)	10	—	—	—	—	—	—	—	—	—	—	—	—	60	454
1993	Atl	16(16, WR)	—	—	—	—	72	778	10.8(98)	4	—	—	—	—	—	—	—	—	—	—	—	—	24	409
1994	NO	16(16, WR)	4	43	10.8(15)	0	77	985	12.8(78)	5	—	—	—	—	—	—	—	—	—	—	—	—	30	561
1995	NO	16(15, WR)	—	—	—	—	41	597	14.6(48)	4	—	—	—	—	—	—	—	—	—	—	—	—	24	319
1996	NO	16(11, WR)	—	—	—	—	44	786	17.9(51)	4	—	—	—	—	—	—	—	—	—	—	—	—	26	413
1997	Atl	12(0)	—	—	—	—	12	154	12.8(34)	1	—	—	—	—	—	—	—	—	—	—	—	—	6	82
NFL	10	147(114)	8	78	9.8(21)	0	428	6588	15.4(98)	47	—	—	—	—	—	—	—	—	—	—	k	—	284	3630

HAYNES, MICHAEL Michael Washington Augustis, DE, 6´3˝/281 lbs; Penn State; 2003: Chi, rnd 1; B9/13/1980 Brooklyn, NY **2003** ChiB 16 (0) **2004** ChiB 16 (4) **2005** ChiB 10 (0)
NFL 42 (4) [3 yrs]

HAYNES, MIKE Michael James, DB, 6´2˝/192 lbs; Arizona State; 1976: NE, rnd 1; B7/1/1953 Denison, TX; HOF 1997 **[RI]** **1976**†NE★14 (14, RCB) **1977** NE★14 (14, RCB)
1978†NE★16 (16, RCB) **1979** NE★16 (15, RCB) **1980** NE★13 (12, RCB) **1981** NE 8 (6, RCB) **1982**†NE★9 (9, LCB) **1983** LARd 5 (3) **1984**†LARd★16 (16, RCB)
1985†LARd★16 (16, RCB) **1986** LARd☆13 (13, RCB) **1987** LARd 8 (7, RCB) **1988** LARd 16 (16, RCB) **1989** LARd 13 (1) **NFL** 177 (158) [14 yrs]

YEAR	TEAM	G(GS, POS)	RUSH	YD	AVG(LG)	TD	REC	YD	AVG(LG)	TD	PASS COMP	PCT	YD	AVG(LG)	TD	INT	SK	YD	QBR	KPR	OTD	PTS	TAY

HAYNES, REGGIE Reginald Eugene, TE, 6´2˝/229 lbs; UNLV; 1977: Was, rnd 7; B9/15/1954 Denison, TX

| 1978 | Was | 14(4) | | 1 | 13 | 13.0(13) | 0 | 2 | 32 | 16.0(21) | 0 | — | | | | | | | | | | — | 0 | 29 |

HAYNES, TOMMY Thomas Walton, DB, 6´0˝/190 lbs; USC; B2/6/1963 Chicago, IL **1987** Dal 3 (3)

HAYNES, VERRON Verron Ulric, RB, 5´10˝/223 lbs; Georgia; 2002: Pit, rnd 5; B2/17/1979 Woodstock, GA

2002	Pit	14(0)	10	51	5.1(20)	0	3	10	3.3(7)	0	—										—	0	56
2003	Pit	12(0)	20	63	3.2(15)	0	7	57	8.1(13)	0	—										—	0	92
2004	†Pit	13(0)	55	272	4.9(18)	0	18	142	7.9(26)	2	—									p	—	12	353
2005	†Pit	14(0)	74	274	3.7(20)	3	11	113	10.3(18)	0	—										—	18	361
NFL	4	53(0)	159	660	4.2(20)	3	39	322	8.3(26)	2	—									p	—	30	861

HAYNESWORTH, ALBERT Albert, DT, 6´6˝/320 lbs; Tennessee; 2002: Ten, rnd 1; B6/17/1981 Hartsville, SC **2002** Ten 16 (3) **2003** †Ten 12 (11, RDT) **2004** Ten 10 (10, RDT) **2005** Ten 14 (14, RDT) **NFL** 52 (30) [4 yrs]

HAYS, GEORGE George William, DE-E, 6´2˝/211 lbs; St. Bonaventure; B8/29/1924 Glassport, PA, D1988 **1950** Pit 12 **1951** Pit 12 (LDE) **1952** Pit 11 **1953** GB 9 **NFL** 44 [4 yrs]

HAYS, HAROLD Leo Harold, LB, 6´2˝/225 lbs; Southern Mississippi; 1962: Dal, rnd 14/Hou, rnd 26; B9/24/1939 Gulfport, MS **1963** Dal 14 **1964** Dal 14 **1965** Dal 14 **1966** †Dal 14 **1967** †Dal 14 **1968** SF 14 **1969** SF 12 **NFL** 96 [7 yrs]

HAYWARD, REGGIE Reginald Joseph, DE, 6´5˝/270 lbs; Iowa State; 2001: Den, rnd 3; B3/14/1979 Chicago, IL **2001** Den 6 (2) **2002** Den 9 (0) **2003** †Den 16 (2) **2004** †Den 16 (15, RDE) **2005** †Jax 15 (15, LDE) **NFL** 62 (34) [5 yrs]

HAYWOOD, AL Alfred, RB, 5´11˝/215 lbs; Bethune-Cookman; B8/6/1948 Jacksonville, FL **1975** Den 2

HAYWORTH, TRACY Tracy Keith, LB, 6´3˝/260 lbs; Tennessee; 1990: Det, rnd 7; B12/18/1967 Winchester, TN **1990** Det 16 (0) **1991** †Det 16 (14, ROLB) **1992** Det 4 (0) **1993** †Det 11 (2) **1994** †Det 9 (1) **1995** †Det 16 (14, LLB) **NFL** 72 (31) [6 yrs]

HAZELHURST, ROBERT Robert Gerald, HB, 6´0˝/188 lbs; Denver; 1947: Bos, rnd 10/Cle-A, rnd 8; B7/21/1924 Denver, CO, D11/11/1988 Denver, CO

| 1948 | Bos | 12(3) | 11 | 15 | 1.4(7) | 0 | — | | | | | — | | | | | | | | | Pk | — | 0 | 16 |

HAZELTINE, MATT Matthew Emery, LB, 6´1˝/220 lbs; California; 1955: SF, rnd 4; B8/2/1933 Ross, CA, D1/13/1987 San Francisco, CA **1955** SF 12 (LLB) **1956** SF 12 (RLB) **1957** †SF 12 (LLB) **1958** SF 12 (RLB) **1959** †SF☆12 (RLB) **1960** SF 12 (RLB) **1961** SF☆14 (14, RLB) **1962** SF★14 (14, RLB) **1963** SF 13 (13, RLB) **1964** SF★14 (14, RLB) **1965** SF 8 (8, RLB) **1966** SF 14 (12, RLB) **1967** SF 13 (12, RLB) **1968** SF 14 (14, RLB) **1970** NYG 14 (RLB) **NFL** 190 (113) [15 yrs]

HAZELTON, MAJOR Major F., DB, 6´1˝/185 lbs; Florida A&M; 1968: Chi, rnd 3; B9/9/1944 Bartow, FL **1968** ChiB 14 **1969** ChiB 9 **1970** NO 3 **NFL** 26 [3 yrs]

HAZELWOOD, TED Theodore Eugene, T-DT, 6´1˝/235 lbs; Purdue; North Carolina; 1946: ChiB, rnd 16; B4/24/1924 Silverwood, IN **1949** ChiH-A 9 (2)

1953 Was 6

HAZUGA, JEFF Jeff, DE, 6´5˝/277 lbs; St. Cloud State; Wisconsin-Stout; B4/29/1978 Thorp, WI **2001** Min 3 (0)

HEADEN, ANDY Andrew Roosevelt, LB, 6´5˝/240 lbs; Clemson; 1983: NYG, rnd 8; B7/8/1960 Asheboro, NC **1983** NYG 16 (0) **1984** †NYG 11 (6, lolb) **1985** †NYG 16 (1) **1986** NYG 15 (0) **1987** NYG 12 (2) **1988** NYG 4 (3) **NFL** 74 (12) [6 yrs]

HEADRICK, SHERRILL Sherrill Dalton, LB, 6´2˝/240 lbs; TCU; B3/13/1937 Waco, TX **1960** DalT-A☆12 (MLB) **1961** DalT-A✩14 (MLB) **1962** DalT-A✩14 (MLB) **1963** KC-A 14 (MLB) **1964** KC-A☆14 (MLB) **1965** KC-A◇14 (MLB) **1966** †KC-A✩14 (MLB) **1967** KC-A 12 (MLB) **1968** Cin-A 8 (MLB) **NFL** 116 [9 yrs]

HEALEY, ED Edward Francis, T-G-E, 6´1˝/207 lbs; Dartmouth; B12/28/1894 Indian Orchard, MA, D12/10/1978 South Bend, IN; HOF 1964 **1920** RI 7 (3) **1921** RI 7 (4, LT), 6 **1922** RI 7 (7, LT) **1922** ChiB☆3 (2) **1923** ChiB✩11 (11, LT) **1924** ChiB✩11 (10, LT) **1925** ChiB☆17 (16, LT) **1926** ChiB☆14 (11, LT) **1927** ChiB 11 (8, LT) **NFL** 88 (72) [8 yrs]

HEALY, CHIP William Raymond, LB, 6´2˝/235 lbs; Vanderbilt; 1969: SL, rnd 3; B8/16/1947 Atlanta, GA **1969** SL 14 (mlb) **1970** SL 14 **NFL** 28 [2 yrs]

HEALY, DON Michael Donald, DT-G, 6´3˝/259 lbs; Maryland; 1958: ChiB, rnd 3; B8/28/1936 Rome, NY **1958** ChiB 12 **1959** ChiB 12 **1960** Dal 12 (LDT) **1961** Dal 14 (LDT) **1962** Buf-A 1 **NFL** 51 [5 yrs]

HEAP, JOE Joseph Lawrence, HB, 5´11˝/185 lbs; Notre Dame; 1955: NYG, rnd 1; B10/26/1931 Abita Springs, LA

| 1955 | NYG | 12 | 8 | 29 | 3.6(16) | 0 | — | | | | | — | | | | | | | | | kp | — | 0 | 102 |

HEAP, TODD Todd Benjamin, TE, 6´5˝/252 lbs; Arizona State; 2001: Bal, rnd 1; B3/16/1980 Mesa, AZ

2001	†Bal	12(7, TE)	—				16	206	12.9(24)	1	—										—	6	108
2002	Bal◇	16(16, TE)	4	38	9.5(15)	0	68	836	12.3(43)	6	1	0	0.0		0	0.0		0	—			—	38	486
2003	†Bal★	16(16, TE)	3	21	7.0(9)	0	57	693	12.2(33)	3	—										—	26	383
2004	Bal	6(6, te)	—				27	303	11.2(37)	3	—										—	18	167
2005	Bal	16(16, TE)	—				75	855	11.4(48)	7	—										—	42	463
NFL	5	66(61)	7	59	8.4(15)	0	243	2893	11.9(48)	20	1	0	0.0		0	0.0		0	—			—	130	1606

HEAP, WALT Walter Richmond, B, 6´1˝/210 lbs; Texas; 1947: LAD-A, rnd 10/Bos, rnd 2; B9/18/1921 Taylor, TX, D5/20/1989 Dallas, TX

1947	LAD-A	13(2)	5	3	0.6	0	2	0	0.0	1	—								i			1	12	100
1948	LAD-A	14(7, BB)	3	12	4.0	0	2	9	4.5	0	—								i			1	6	96
AAFC	2	27(9)	8	15	1.9	0	4	9	2.3	1	—								i			2	18	196

HEARD, HERMAN Herman Willie, RB, 5´10˝/184 lbs; Fort Lewis; Southern Colorado; 1984: KC, rnd 3; B11/24/1961 Denver, CO

1984	KC	16(9, RB)	165	684	4.1(69)	4	25	223	8.9(17)	0	—										—	24	836
1985	KC	16(12, RB)	164	595	3.6(33)	4	31	257	8.3(27)	0	—										—	36	774
1986	†KC	15(7, RB)	71	295	4.2(40)	2	17	83	4.9(13)	0	—										—	12	357
1987	KC	12(6, RB)	82	466	5.7(64)	3	14	118	8.4(15)	0	—										—	18	555
1988	KC	12(5, rb)	106	438	4.1(20)	0	20	198	9.9(32)	0	—										—	0	537
1989	KC	16(10, RB)	63	216	3.4(28)	0	25	246	9.8(27)	1	—										—	6	344
NFL	6	87(49)	651	2694	4.1(69)	13	132	1125	8.5(32)	3	—										—	96	3402

HEARD, RONNIE Ronnie E., DB, 6´3˝/215 lbs; Mississippi; B10/5/1976 Bay City, TX **2000** SF 13 (3) **2001** †SF 16 (0) **2002** †SF 12 (6, FS) **2003** SF 12 (1) **2004** SF 16 (14, FS) **2005** Atl 16 (5, fs) **NFL** 85 (29) [6 yrs]

HEARDEN, LES Lester Christopher, HB, 5´8˝/175 lbs; Marquette; St. Ambrose; B4/24/1902 Lawrence, WI, D12/25/1978 Green Bay, WI **1924** GB 2 (0), 6

HEARDEN, TOM Thomas Francis, HB, 5´9˝/178 lbs; Notre Dame; B9/8/1904 Appleton, WI, D12/27/1964 Green Bay, WI **1927** GB 4 (2) **1928** GB 1 (1) **1929** ChiB 1 (0) **NFL** 6 (3) [3 yrs]

HEARST, GARRISON Gerald Garrison, RB, 5´11˝/215 lbs; Georgia; 1993: Phx, rnd 1; B1/4/1971 Lincolnton, GA

1993	Phx	6(5, rb)	76	264	3.5(57)	1	6	18	3.0(9)	0	1	0	0.0		0	1		—	—			—	6	243
1994	Arz	8(0)	37	169	4.6(36)	1	6	49	8.2(29)	0	1	1	100.0	10	10.0(10)	1	0	—				—	6	214
1995	Arz	16(15, RB)	284	1070	3.8(38)	1	29	243	8.4(39)	1	2	1	50.0	16	8.0(16)	0	0	—				—	12	1215
1996	Cin	16(12, RB)	225	847	3.8(24)	0	12	131	10.9(40)	1	—										—	8	918
1997	†SF	13(13, RB)	234	1019	4.4(51)	4	21	194	9.2(69)	0	—										—	36	1166
1998	†SF★	16(16, RB)	310	1570	5.1(96)	7	39	535	13.7(81)	2	—										—	56	1918
2001	†SF◇	16(16, RB)	252	1206	4.8(43)	4	41	347	8.5(60)	1	—										—	30	1425
2002	†SF	16(16, RB)	215	972	4.5(40)	8	48	317	6.6(16)	1	—										—	56	1216
2003	SF	12(12, RB)	178	768	4.3(36)	2	25	211	8.4(26)	1	—										—	24	909
2004	Den	7(0)	20	81	4.1(11)	1	2	20	10.0(15)	0	—										—	6	101
NFL	10	126(105)	1831	7966	4.4(96)	30	229	2065	9.0(81)	9	4	2	50.0	26	6.5(16)	1	1	—				—	240	9322

HEATER, DON Donald Perry, RB, 6´2˝/205 lbs; Montana Tech; 1972: SL, rnd 6; B6/22/1950 Helena, MT **1972** SL 2

HEATER, LARRY Larry, RB, 5´11˝/205 lbs; Arizona; 1980: KC, rnd 6; B1/9/1958 Cincinnati, OH

1980	NYG	14(4)	111	360	3.2(11)	3	10	139	13.9(43)	0	—									k	—	18	488
1982	NYG	9(0)	3	13	4.3(8)	0	2	15	7.5(12)	0	—									k	—	0	30
1983	NYG	6(0)	—				—					—									k	—	0	-4
NFL	3	29(4)	114	373	3.3(11)	3	12	154	12.8(43)	0	—									k	—	18	513

HEATER, RED William Alfred, T, 6´2˝/220 lbs; Syracuse; B9/22/1918 Reading, PA, D10/24/2003 Syracuse, NY **1940** Bkn 8 (0)

YEAR	TEAM	G (GS, POS)	RUSH	YD	AVG(LG)	TD	REC	YD	AVG(LG)	TD	PASS	COMP	PCT	YD	AVG(LG)	TD	INT	SK	YD	QBR	KPR	OTD	PTS	TAY

HEATH, CLAYTON Clayton Donnie, RB, 5´11˝/195 lbs; Wake Forest; 1974: Mia, rnd 13; B2/15/1951 Chester County, SC   **1976** Buf 2

| 1976 | Mia | 6 | 1 | 0 | 0.0(0) | 0 | — | — | — | — | — | — | — | — | — | — | — | — | — | — | — | — | 0 | 0 |
| NFL | 1 | 8 | 1 | 0 | 0.0 | 0 | — | — | — | — | — | — | — | — | — | — | — | — | — | — | — | — | 0 | 0 |

HEATH, JO JO Joseph Leroy, DB, 5´10˝/182 lbs; Pittsburgh; 1980: Cin, rnd 6; B3/9/1957 Monessen, PA, D12/30/2002 Charleroi, PA   **1980** Cin 10 (0)   **1981** Phi 15 (0)
1987 NYJ 2 (0)   **NFL** 27 (0) [3 yrs]

HEATH, LEON Herman Leon, FB-HB, 6´1˝/203 lbs; Oklahoma; 1951: Was, rnd 1; B10/27/1928 Hollis, OK

1951	Was	11(RH)	64	159	2.5(16)	0	1	3	3.0(3)	0	—	—	—	—	—	—	—	—	—	—	—	—	0	161
1952	Was	11(FB)	90	388	4.3(74)	2	23	146	6.3(27)	1	—	—	—	—	—	—	—	—	—	—	—	—	18	486
1953	Was	9(fb)	76	266	3.5(43)	4	5	45	9.0(17)	0	—	—	—	—	—	—	—	—	—	—	—	—	24	329
NFL	3	31	230	813	3.5(74)	6	29	194	6.7(27)	1	—	—	—	—	—	—	—	—	—	—	—	—	42	975

HEATH, RODNEY Rodney Larece, DB, 5´10˝/175 lbs; Minnesota; B10/29/1974 Cincinnati, OH   **1999** Cin 16 (9, LCB)   **2000** Cin 13 (9, RCB)   **2001** Cin 5 (5, lcb)   **2002** Atl 1 (0)
NFL 35 (23) [4 yrs]

HEATH, STAN Stanley R., QB, 6´1˝/190 lbs; Wisconsin; Nevada-Reno; 1949: GB, rnd 1/ChiH-A, rnd 1; B3/5/1927 Toledo, OH

| 1949 | GB | 12(1, qb) | 10 | 25 | 2.5(18) | 1 | — | — | — | — | 106 | 26 | 24.5 | 355 | 3.3(42) | 1 | 14 | — | — | — | — | — | 6 | -343 |

HEBERT, BOBBY Bobby Joseph, QB, 6´4˝/215 lbs; Northwestern State (LA); B8/19/1960 Baton Rouge, LA

1985	NO	6(6, qb)	12	26	2.2(8)	0	1	7	7.0(7)	0	181	97	53.6	1208	6.7(76)	5	4	17	150	—	—	—	6	504
1986	NO	5(3)	5	14	2.8(7)	0	1	1	1.0(1)	0	79	41	51.9	498	6.3(84)	2	8	5	34	—	—	—	0	-47
1987	†NO	12(12, QB)	13	95	7.3(19)	0	—	—	—	—	294	164	55.8	2119	7.2(67)	15	9	20	119	82.9	—	—	0	870
1988	NO	16(16, QB)	37	79	2.1(16)	0	2	0	0.0(0)	0	478	280	58.6	3156	6.6(40)	20	15	24	171	79.3	—	—	0	1157
1989	NO	14(13, QB)	25	87	3.5(11)	0	—	—	—	—	353	222	62.9	2686	7.6(54)	15	15	22	171	82.7	—	—	0	905
1991	NO	9(9, QB)	18	56	3.1(16)	0	—	—	—	—	248	149	60.1	1676	6.8(65)	9	8	3	26	79.0	—	—	0	619
1992	†NO	16(16, QB)	32	95	3.0(18)	0	—	—	—	—	422	249	59.0	3287	7.8(72)	19	16	15	119	82.9	—	—	0	1194
1993	Atl◊	14(12, QB)	24	49	2.0(14)	0	—	—	—	—	430	263	61.2	2978	6.9(98)	24	17	29	190	84.0	—	—	0	978
1994	Atl	10(0)	9	43	4.8(20)	0	—	—	—	—	103	52	50.5	614	5.9(40)	2	6	3	17	—	—	—	0	118
1995	Atl	4(0)	5	-1	-0.2(2)	0	—	—	—	—	45	28	62.2	313	7.0(37)	2	1	—	—	—	—	—	0	126
1996	Atl	14(13, QB)	15	59	3.9(25)	1	—	—	—	—	488	294	60.2	3152	6.5(57)	22	25	27	150	72.9	—	—	6	755
NFL	11	120(100)	195	602	3.1(25)	1	4	8	2.0(7)	0	3121	1839	58.9	21683	6.9(98)	135	124	165	1147	78.0	—	—	12	7178

HEBERT, BUD Darryl Ray, DB, 6´0˝/190 lbs; Oklahoma; 1980: NYG, rnd 7; B10/12/1956 Beaumont, TX   **1980** NYG 10 (6, fs)

HEBERT, KEN Kenneth Daniel, WR, 6´0˝/200 lbs; Houston; 1968: Pit, rnd 3; B9/9/1944 San Bernardino, CA   **1968** Pit 3

HEBRON, VAUGHN Vaughn Harlen, RB, 5´8˝/195 lbs; Virginia Tech; B10/7/1970 Baltimore, MD [R]

1993	Phi	16(4)	84	297	3.5(33)	3	11	82	7.5(12)	0	—	—	—	—	—	—	—	—	—	—	k	—	18	358
1994	Phi	16(1)	82	325	4.0(19)	2	18	137	7.6(29)	0	—	—	—	—	—	—	—	—	—	—	k	—	12	542
1996	†Den	16(0)	49	262	5.3(47)	0	7	43	6.1(11)	0	—	—	—	—	—	—	—	—	—	—	k	—	0	708
1997	†Den	16(1)	49	222	4.5(46)	1	3	36	12.0(21)	0	—	—	—	—	—	—	—	—	—	—	k	—	6	614
1998	†Den☆	15(0)	9	31	3.4(8)	1	2	5	2.5(3)	0	—	—	—	—	—	—	—	—	—	—	k	1	12	580
NFL	5	79(6)	273	1143	4.2(47)	7	41	303	7.4(29)	0	—	—	—	—	—	—	—	—	—	—	k	1	48	2801

HECHT, GEORGE Alfred George, G, 6´0˝/235 lbs; Alabama; 1943: ChiC, rnd 5; B9/17/1920 Chicago Heights, IL, D10/24/1994 Collinsville, AL   **1947** ChiR-A 10 (2)

HECK, ANDY Andrew Robert, T-G, 6´6˝/298 lbs; Notre Dame; 1989: Sea, rnd 1; B1/1/1967 Fargo, ND   **1989** Sea 16 (9, LT)   **1990** Sea 16 (16, LT)   **1991** Sea 16 (16, LT)
1992 Sea 13 (13, LG)   **1993** Sea 16 (16, RT)   **1994**†ChiB 14 (14, LT)   **1995** ChiB☆16 (16, LT)   **1996** ChiB 16 (16, LT)   **1997** ChiB 16 (16, LT)   **1998** ChiB 14 (14, LT)
1999†Was 16 (16, LT)   **2000** Was 16 (2)   **NFL** 185 (164) [12 yrs]

HECK, BOB Robert Elgin, DE-E, 6´4˝/210 lbs; Purdue; 1948: SF-A, rnd 22/LARm, rnd 13; B6/17/1925 South Bend, IN   **1949** ChiH-A 4 (0)

HECK, RALPH Ralph Adam, LB, 6´1˝/230 lbs; Colorado; 1963: Phi, rnd 1; B11/6/1941 Pittsburgh, PA   **1963** Phi 14   **1964** Phi 14   **1965** Phi 12   **1966** Atl 14   **1967** Atl 14 (RLB)
1968 Atl 13 (RLB)   **1969** NYG 14 (MLB)   **1970** NYG 14 (LLB)   **1971** NYG 11 (LLB)   **NFL** 120 [9 yrs]

HECKARD, STEVE Robert Stephen, WR, 6´1˝/195 lbs; USC; Davidson; B4/12/1943 Winston-Salem, NC

1965	LARm	13	—	—	—	—	1	4	4.0(4)	0	—	—	—	—	—	—	—	—	—	—	—	—	0	2
1966	LARm	12	—	—	—	—	5	102	20.4(50)	0	—	—	—	—	—	—	—	—	—	—	—	—	0	51
NFL	2	25	—	—	—	—	6	106	17.7(50)	0	—	—	—	—	—	—	—	—	—	—	—	—	0	53

HECKER, NORB Norbert Earl, DB, 6´2˝/193 lbs; Baldwin-Wallace; 1951: LA, rnd 6; B5/26/1927 Berea, OH, D3/13/2004 Los Altos, CA [KIC]   **1952**†LARm 10   **1956** Was 12 (DB)
1957 Was 8 (DB)

1951	†LARm	10(DB)	—	—	—	—	4	35	8.8(20)	1	—	—	—	—	—	—	—	—	—	Ki	—	—	6	82
1953	LARm	12(DB)	—	—	—	—	2	25	12.5(16)	0	—	—	—	—	—	—	—	—	—	i	—	—	0	69
1955	Was	12(DB)	—	—	—	—	3	31	10.3(13)	1	—	—	—	—	—	—	—	—	—	Ki	—	—	8	43
NFL	6	64	—	—	—	—	9	91	10.1(20)	2	—	—	—	—	—	—	—	—	—	Ki	1	20	248

HECKER, ROBERT Robert, DB, 6´1˝/185 lbs; Baldwin-Wallace; B7/29/1925   **1952** LARm 2   **1952** ChiC 1   **NFL** 3 [1 yr]

HECTOR, JOHNNY Johnny Lyndell, RB, 5´11˝/204 lbs; Texas A&M; 1983: NYJ, rnd 2; B11/26/1960 Lafayette, LA

1983	NYJ	10(1)	16	85	5.3(42)	0	5	61	12.2(22)	1	—	—	—	—	—	—	—	—	—	—	k	—	6	185
1984	NYJ	13(2)	124	531	4.3(64)	1	20	182	9.1(26)	0	—	—	—	—	—	—	—	—	—	—	—	—	6	632
1985	†NYJ	14(5, rb)	145	572	3.9(22)	6	17	164	9.6(28)	0	—	—	—	—	—	—	—	—	—	—	k	—	36	823
1986	NYJ	13(6, rb)	164	605	3.7(41)	8	33	302	9.2(23)	0	—	—	—	—	—	—	—	—	—	—	—	—	48	836
1987	NYJ	11(6, rb)	111	435	3.9(20)	11	32	249	7.8(27)	0	—	—	—	—	—	—	—	—	—	—	—	—	66	670
1988	NYJ	16(16)	137	561	4.1(19)	10	26	237	9.1(30)	0	1	0	0.0	0	0.0	0	—	—	—	—	—	—	60	780
1989	NYJ	15(9, RB)	177	702	4.0(24)	3	38	330	8.7(32)	2	—	—	—	—	—	—	—	—	—	—	—	—	30	907
1990	NYJ	15(4)	91	377	4.1(22)	2	8	72	9.0(25)	0	—	—	—	—	—	—	—	—	—	—	—	—	12	433
1991	†NYJ	14(1)	62	345	5.6(47)	0	7	51	7.3(16)	0	—	—	—	—	—	—	—	—	—	—	k	—	0	423
1992	NYJ	5(1)	24	67	2.8(14)	0	2	13	6.5(9)	0	—	—	—	—	—	—	—	—	—	—	k	—	0	74
NFL	10	126(36)	1051	4280	4.1(64)	41	188	1661	8.8(32)	3	1	0	0.0	0	0.0	0	0	0	0	—	k	—	264	5761

HECTOR, WILLIE Willie, T, 6´2˝/220 lbs; Pacific; 1961: LA, rnd 5; B12/23/1939 New Iberia, LA   **1961** LARm 12

HEDBERG, RANDY Randolph R., QB, 6´3˝/200 lbs; Minot State; 1977: TB, rnd 8; B12/27/1954 Parshall, ND

| 1977 | TB | 7(4) | 9 | 35 | 3.9(12) | 0 | — | — | — | — | 90 | 25 | 27.8 | 244 | 2.7(19) | 0 | 10 | 15 | 131 | — | — | — | 0 | -243 |

HEDGECOCK, MADISON Madison Smith, FB, 6´3˝/266 lbs; North Carolina; 2005: SL, rnd 7; B8/27/1981 Winston-Salem, NC

| 2005 | SL | 16(7, fb) | 1 | 0 | 0.0(0) | 0 | 9 | 69 | 7.7(15) | 0 | — | — | — | — | — | — | — | — | — | — | — | — | 0 | 35 |

HEENAN, PAT Patrick Dennis, DB-E, 6´2˝/191 lbs; Notre Dame; B3/1/1938 Detroit, MI   **1960** Was 11 (RCB)   **1961** Was 1   **NFL** 12 [2 yrs]

HEETER, GENE Eugene Elwood, TE, 6´4˝/230 lbs; West Virginia; 1963: SD, rnd 8; B4/19/1941 Windber, PA

1963	NYJ-A	9(TE)	—	—	—	—	8	160	20.0(40)	1	—	—	—	—	—	—	—	—	—	—	—	—	6	85
1964	NYJ-A	14(TE)	—	—	—	—	13	153	11.8(21)	1	—	—	—	—	—	—	—	—	—	k	—	—	6	67
1965	NYJ-A	2	—	—	—	—	1	14	14.0(14)	0	—	—	—	—	—	—	—	—	—	—	—	—	0	7
NFL	3	25	—	—	—	—	22	327	14.9(40)	2	—	—	—	—	—	—	—	—	—	k	—	12	159

HEFFERN, SHAWN Shawn Patrick, T, 6´5˝/270 lbs; Notre Dame; B3/15/1964 Toledo, OH   **1987** Ind 1 (0)

HEFFERNAN, DAVE David Roy, G, 6´4˝/255 lbs; Miami (FL); 1985: KC, rnd 7; B10/28/1962 Boston, MA   **1987** TB 2 (0)

HEFLIN, VICTOR Victor, DB, 6´0˝/184 lbs; Delaware State; 1983: Den, rnd 6; B7/7/1960 Springfield, MA   **1983** SL 8 (0)   **1984** SL 16 (0)   **NFL** 24 (0) [2 yrs]

HEFLIN, VINCE Vincent George, WR, 6´0˝/185 lbs; Central State (OH); B7/7/1959 Dayton, OH   **1982**†Mia 6 (0)   **1983**†Mia 14 (0)   **1984**†Mia 16 (0)

1985	Mia	5(0)	—	—	—	—	6	98	16.3(46)	1	—	—	—	—	—	—	—	—	—	—	—	—	6	54
1986	TB	6(3)	—	—	—	—	3	42	14.0(15)	0	—	—	—	—	—	—	—	—	—	k	1	6	21
NFL	5	47(3)	—	—	—	—	9	140	15.6(46)	1	—	—	—	—	—	—	—	—	—	kp	1	12	161

HEFNER, LARRY Larry Douglas, LB, 6´2˝/230 lbs; Clemson; 1972: GB, rnd 14; B8/2/1949 Charlotte, NC   **1972**†GB 2   **1973** GB 14   **1974** GB 14   **1975** GB 4 (1)   **NFL** 34 (1) [4 yrs]

YEAR	TEAM	G(GS, POS)	RUSH	YD	AVG(LG)	TD	REC	YD	AVG(LG)	TD	PASS COMP	PCT	YD	AVG(LG)	TD	INT	SK	YD	QBR	KPR	OTD	PTS	TAY

HEGAMIN, GEORGE George Russell, T-G, 6'7"/331 lbs; North Carolina State; 1994: Dal, rnd 3; B2/14/1973 Camden, NJ   **1994** Dal 2 (0)   **1995**†Dal 0 (0)   **1996**†Dal 16 (1)
1997 Dal 13 (9, LT)   **1998** Phi 16 (6, lg)   **1999**†TB 1 (0)   **2000**†TB 16 (1)   **NFL** 64 (17) [7 yrs]

HEGARTY, BILL William Michael, DE-T, 6'4"/240 lbs; Georgia; Villanova; 1952: LA, rnd 15; B6/30/1931 Medford, MA   **1953** Pit 1   **1953** Was 2   **NFL** 3 [1 yr]

HEGMAN, MIKE Michael William, LB, 6'1"/227 lbs; Alabama A&M; Tennessee State; 1975: Dal, rnd 7; B1/17/1953 Memphis, TN   **1976**†Dal 14   **1977**†Dal 14   **1978**†Dal 16 (6, llb)
1979†Dal 16 (5, mlb)   **1980**†Dal 16 (16, LLB)   **1981**†Dal 11 (10, LLB)   **1982**†Dal 9 (9, LLB)   **1983**†Dal 16 (15, LLB)   **1984** Dal 16 (16, LLB)   **1985**†Dal 16 (15, LLB)
1986 Dal 16 (16, LLB)   **1987** Dal 10 (10, LLB)   **NFL** 170 (118) [12 yrs]

HEIDEL, JIMMY James Byrnes, DB, 6'1"/185 lbs; Mississippi; 1965: SL, rnd 9/NYJ, rnd R3; B12/1/1943 Yazoo City, MS   **1966** SL 14   **1967** NO 14 (LS)   **NFL** 28 [2 yrs]

HEIDEN, STEVE Steven Allen, TE, 6'5"/265 lbs; South Dakota State; 1999: SD, rnd 3; B9/21/1976 Rushford, MN

1999	SD	11(0)	—	—	—	—	—	—	—	—	—	—	—	—	—	—	—	—	—	—	—	0	
2000	SD	15(3)	—	—	—	—	6	32	5.3(10)	1	—	—	—	—	—	—	—	—	—	—	—	6	21
2001	SD	16(10, TE)	—	—	—	—	8	55	6.9(16)	1	—	—	—	—	—	—	—	—	—	—	—	6	33
2002	†Cle	16(6, TE)	—	—	—	—	17	105	6.2(16)	1	—	—	—	—	—	—	—	—	—	—	—	6	58
2003	Cle	9(9, TE)	—	—	—	—	18	134	7.4(17)	0	—	—	—	—	—	—	—	—	—	—	—	0	67
2004	Cle	13(13, TE)	—	—	—	—	28	287	10.3(30)	5	—	—	—	—	—	—	—	—	—	—	—	32	169
2005	Cle	15(13, TE)	—	—	—	—	43	401	9.3(62)	3	—	—	—	—	—	—	—	—	—	—	—	18	216
NFL	7	95(54)	—	—	—	—	120	1014	8.4(62)	11	—	—	—	—	—	—	—	—	—	—	—	68	562

HEIKKINEN, RALPH Ralph I., G, 5'10"/180 lbs; Michigan; 1939: Bkn, rnd 12; B5/14/1917 Hancock, MI, D1/11/1990 Pontiac, MI   **1939** Bkn 3 (0)

HEILEMAN, CHARLES Charles Donald, E, 6'2"/197 lbs; Iowa State; 1939: ChiB, rnd 7; B1/25/1915 Fort Dodge, IA, D2/23/1966 Clinton, IA   **1939** ChiB 2 (0)

HEIMBURGER, CRAIG Craig Andre, G, 6'2"/314 lbs; Missouri; 1999: GB, rnd 5; B2/3/1977 Belleville, IL   **1999** GB 2 (0)   **2001** Buf 11 (0)   **NFL** 13 (0) [2 yrs]

HEIMKREITER, STEVE Steven, LB, 6'2"/228 lbs; Notre Dame; 1979: Bal, rnd 8; B6/9/1957 Cincinnati, OH   **1980** Bal 15 (0)

HEIMSCH, JOHNNY John Cyrus, B, 5'10"/175 lbs; Marquette; B9/18/1902 Rosebush, MI, D5/27/1991 Boulder Junction, WI   **1926** Mil 9 (9, WB), 18

HEIMULI, LAKEI Lakei, RB, 5'11"/219 lbs; Brigham Young; 1987: Chi, rnd 9; B6/24/1965 Vavau, Tonga

| 1987 | ChiB | 3(3) | 34 | 128 | 3.8(12) | 0 | 5 | 51 | 10.2(17) | 1 | — | — | — | — | — | — | — | — | — | — | — | 6 | 159 |

HEIN, BOB Robert William, E, 6'3"/220 lbs; Kent State; B2/6/1921 Cleveland, OH, D3/17/1999 Louisville, KY

| 1947 | Bkn-A | 5(0) | — | — | — | — | 1 | 7 | 7.0(7) | 0 | — | — | — | — | — | — | — | — | — | — | — | 0 | 4 |

HEIN, MEL Melvin Jack 'Old Indestructible', C-LB, 6'2"/225 lbs; Washington State; B8/22/1909 Redding, CA, D1/31/1992 San Clemente, CA; HOF 1963 [C]   **1931** NYG☆14 (10, C)
1932†NYG☆12 (10, C)   **1933**†NYG☆12 (10, C)   **1935**†NYG☆12 (10, C)   **1936** NYG★11 (10, C)   **1938**†NYG★11 (11, C)   **1939**†NYG★11 (10, C)   **1940** NYG★11 (11, C)
1941†NYG★11 (11, C)   **1942** NYG 11 (11, C)   **1944**†NYG★10 (8, C)   **1945** NYG☆10 (10, C)

1934	†NYG☆	13(13, C)	1	1	1.0(1)	0	1	13	13.0(13)	0	—	—	—	—	—	—	—	—	—	—	—	0	8
1937	NYG☆	11(11, C)	—	—	—	—	1	7	7.0(7)	0	—	—	—	—	—	—	—	—	—	—	—	0	4
1943	†NYG	10(7, C)	—	—	—	—	—	—	—	—	1	0	0.0	0	0.0	0	0	—	—	i	—	0	26
NFL	15	170(153)	1	1	1.0(1)	0	2	20	10.0(13)	0	1	0	0.0	0	0.0	0	0	—	—	i	1	6	49

HEINEMAN, KEN Kenneth Roy, TB, 5'9"/168 lbs; Texas-El Paso; 1940: Cle, rnd 6; B1/13/1918 Yorktown, TX [K]

1940	Cle	3(0)	6	-5	-0.8	0	—	—	—	—	8	3	37.5	74	9.3	1	1	—	—	KPi	—	1	-3
1943	Bkn	8(6, TB)	49	126	2.6(43)	0	—	—	—	—	57	18	31.6	285	5.0(65)	3	8	—	—	Pkpi	—	0	189
NFL	2	11(6)	55	121	2.2(43)	0	—	—	—	—	65	21	32.3	359	5.5(65)	4	9	—	—	KPkpi	—	1	186

HEINISCH, FRITZ Godfred F., E-B, 5'10"/173 lbs; none; B6/22/1900 Racine, WI, D12/22/1983 Mount Pleasant, WI   **1922** Rac 5 (1)   **1923** Rac 6 (1)   **1924** Ken 3 (2, RE)
1926 Rac 3 (0)   **1926** Dul 1 (0)   **NFL** 18 (4) [4 yrs]

HEINLEIN, PETE George L., G-T, 5'10"/230 lbs; none; B5/2/1893, deceased   **1920** Roc 3 (0)

HEINRICH, DON Donald Alan, QB, 6'0"/182 lbs; Washington; 1952: NYG, rnd 3; B9/19/1930 Chicago, IL, D2/29/1992 Saratoga, CA

1954	NYG	2	1	0	0.0(0)	0	—	—	—	—	9	4	44.4	56	6.2(31)	0	2	—	—	—	—	0	-52
1955	NYG	10	7	4	0.6(5)	2	—	—	—	—	67	31	46.3	413	6.2(37)	2	2	—	—	—	—	12	161
1956	†NYG	12(qb)	5	-4	-0.8(2)	0	—	—	—	—	88	37	42.0	369	4.2(43)	5	5	—	—	—	—	0	6
1957	NYG	4	4	10	2.5(7)	2	—	—	—	—	26	11	42.3	224	8.6(63)	1	1	—	—	—	—	12	107
1958	†NYG	7(qb)	5	4	0.8(6)	1	—	—	—	—	68	26	38.2	369	5.4(41)	4	2	—	—	—	—	6	139
1959	NYG	8	2	3	1.5(9)	0	—	—	—	—	58	22	37.9	329	5.7(49)	1	6	—	—	—	—	0	-68
1960	Dal	12	2	3	1.5(3)	0	—	—	—	—	61	23	37.7	371	6.1(64)	3	3	4	39	—	—	0	84
1962	Oak-A	1	1	4	4.0(4)	0	—	—	—	—	29	10	34.5	156	5.4(25)	1	2	—	—	—	—	0	7
NFL	8	56	27	24	0.9(9)	5	—	—	—	—	406	164	40.4	2287	5.6(64)	17	23	4	39	—	—	30	383

HEINRICH, KEITH Keith Charles, TE, 6'5"/255 lbs; Sam Houston State; 2002: Car, rnd 6; B3/19/1979 Houston, TX

2002	Car	4(0)	—	—	—	—	—	—	—	—	—	—	—	—	—	—	—	—	—	k	—	0	-12
2003	Cle	7(3)	—	—	—	—	8	64	8.0(17)	2	—	—	—	—	—	—	—	—	—	—	—	12	42
2004	Cle	7(0)	—	—	—	—	1	1	1.0(1)	0	—	—	—	—	—	—	—	—	—	—	—	0	1
NFL	3	18(3)	—	—	—	—	9	65	7.2(17)	2	—	—	—	—	—	—	—	—	—	k	—	12	31

HEINZ, BOB Robert Kenneth, DT-DE, 6'6"/265 lbs; Pacific; 1969: Mia, rnd 2; B7/25/1947 Milwaukee, WI   **1969** Mia-A 14   **1970**†Mia 14   **1971**†Mia 14 (7, RDT)
1972†Mia 11 (8, RDT)   **1973**†Mia 14 (13, RDT)   **1974**†Mia 14 (13, RDT)   **1976** Mia 14 (4)   **1977** Mia 14   **1978** Was 2   **NFL** 111 (45) [9 yrs]

HEITMANN, ERIC Eric Wade, C, 6'3"/305 lbs; Stanford; 2002: SF, rnd 7; B2/24/1980 Brookshire, TX   **2002**†SF 16 (12, LG)   **2003** SF 9 (8, lg)   **2004** SF 16 (16, LG)
2005 SF 16 (16, RG/c)   **NFL** 57 (52) [4 yrs]

HEKKERS, GEORGE George James, T, 6'4"/241 lbs; Wisconsin; B2/18/1923 Milwaukee, WI   **1946** Mia-A 8 (4, rt)   **1947** Bal-A 3 (0)   **AAFC** 11 (4) [2 yrs]
1947 Det 6 (0)   **1948** Det 12 (4)   **1949** Det 12 (6, LT)   **NFL** 30 (10) [2 yrs]

HELD, PAUL Paul E., QB, 6'2"/195 lbs; San Jose State; 1953: Det, rnd 19; B10/20/1928 El Segundo, CA [K]

1954	Pit	8	3	3	1.0(3)	0	—	—	—	—	73	24	32.9	305	4.2(37)	1	6	—	—	—	K	—	23	-80
1955	GB	2	1	8	8.0(8)	0	—	—	—	—	4	2	50.0	27	6.8(18)	0	0	—	—	—	—	—	0	22
NFL	2	10	4	11	2.8(8)	0	—	—	—	—	77	26	33.8	332	4.3(37)	1	6	—	—	—	K	—	23	-58

HELDT, CARL Carl Diederich, T, 6'2"/205 lbs; Purdue; B3/20/1913 Evansville, IN, D7/20/1983 Kerrville, TX   **1935** Bkn 6 (6, LT)

| 1936 | Bkn | 12(9, LT) | — | — | — | — | 2 | 39 | 19.5 | 0 | — | — | — | — | — | — | — | — | — | — | — | 0 | 20 |
| NFL | 2 | 18(15) | — | — | — | — | 2 | 39 | 19.5 | 0 | — | — | — | — | — | — | — | — | — | — | — | 0 | 20 |

HELDT, JACK John Claussen, G-C, 5'9"/210 lbs; Iowa; B12/2/1899 Calumet, MI, D10/25/1975 Emmetsburg, IA [C]   **1923** Col 1 (1)   **1926** Col 6 (6, LG)   **NFL** 7 (7) [2 yrs]

HELLER, RON Ronald Jeffrey, TE, 6'3"/236 lbs; Oregon State; B9/18/1963 Grass Valley, CA

1987	SF	13(6, te)	—	—	—	—	12	165	13.8(39)	1	—	—	—	—	—	—	—	—	—	—	—	18	98
1988	†SF	16(8, TE)	—	—	—	—	14	140	10.0(22)	0	—	—	—	—	—	—	—	—	—	—	—	0	70
1989	Atl	15(13, TE)	—	—	—	—	33	324	9.8(30)	1	—	—	—	—	—	—	—	—	—	—	—	6	167
1990	Sea	16(5, te)	—	—	—	—	13	157	12.1(23)	1	—	—	—	—	—	—	—	—	—	—	—	6	84
1992	Sea	16(11, TE)	—	—	—	—	12	85	7.1(17)	0	—	—	—	—	—	—	—	—	—	—	—	0	43
NFL	5	76(43)	—	—	—	—	84	871	10.4(39)	3	—	—	—	—	—	—	—	—	—	—	—	30	461

HELLER, RON Ronald Ramon, T, 6'5"/298 lbs; Penn State; 1984: TB, rnd 4; B8/25/1962 East Meadow, NY   **1984** TB 14 (14, RT)   **1985** TB 16 (16, RT)   **1987** TB 12 (10, RT)
1988†Phi 15 (15, RT)   **1989**†Phi 16 (16, RT)   **1990** Phi 16 (14, LT)   **1991** Phi 16 (14, LT)   **1992** Phi 12 (12, LT)   **1993** Mia 16 (16, RT)   **1994**†Mia 16 (16, RT)   **1995** Mia 7 (7, rt)

| 1986 | TB | 16(16, RT) | — | — | — | — | 1 | 1 | 1.0(1) | 1 | — | — | — | — | — | — | — | — | — | — | — | 6 | 6 |
| NFL | 12 | 172(166) | — | — | — | — | 1 | 1 | 1.0(1) | 1 | — | — | — | — | — | — | — | — | — | — | — | 6 | 6 |

HELLER, WARREN Warren Willis, HB-TB, 5'11"/195 lbs; Pittsburgh; B11/24/1910 Pittsburgh, PA, D10/29/1982 Oakmont, PA

1934	Pit	12(12, TB)	132	528	4.0	1	6	96	16.0	0	112	31	27.7	511	4.6	2	15	—	—	12.5	—	—	6	252
1935	Pit	12(1)	37	112	3.0	0	2	16	8.0	0	41	9	22.0	88	2.1	0	8	—	—	—	—	—	0	-156
1936	Pit	12(4, HB)	106	332	3.1	0	12	160	13.3	3	5	0	0.0	0	0.0	0	1	—	—	—	—	—	18	387
NFL	3	36(17)	275	972	3.5	1	20	272	13.6	3	158	40	25.3	599	3.8	2	24	—	—	7.5	—	—	24	483

YEAR	TEAM	G (GS, POS)	RUSH	YD	AVG(LG)	TD	REC	YD	AVG(LG)	TD	PASS	COMP	PCT	YD	AVG(LG)	TD	INT	SK	YD	QBR	KPR	OTD	PTS	TAY

HELLER, WILL   Will Sanders, TE, 6'6"/250 lbs; Georgia Tech; B2/28/1981 Dunwoody, GA

YEAR	TEAM	G(GS,POS)	RUSH	YD	AVG(LG)	TD	REC	YD	AVG(LG)	TD	...	KPR	OTD	PTS	TAY
2003	TB	9(1)	—	—	—	—	2	15	7.5(11)	1		—	—	6	13
2004	TB	10(2)	—	—	—	—	12	98	8.2(22)	1		—	—	6	54
2005	Mia	7(0)	—	—	—	—	1	1	1.0(1)	1		k	—	6	2
NFL	3	26(3)	—	—	—	—	15	114	7.6(22)	3		k	—	18	68

HELLESTRAE, DALE   Dale Robert, T-G-C, 6'5"/282 lbs; SMU; 1985: Buf, rnd 4; B7/11/1962 Phoenix, AZ   **1985** Buf 4 (0)   **1986** Buf 8 (0)   **1988**†Buf 16 (2)   **1990** Dal 16 (0)   **1991**†Dal 16 (0)   **1992**†Dal 16 (0)   **1993**†Dal 16 (0)   **1994**†Dal 16 (0)   **1995**†Dal 16 (0)   **1996**†Dal 16 (0)   **1997** Dal 16 (0)   **1998**†Dal 16 (0)   **1999**†Dal 16 (0)   **2000** Dal 16 (0)   **2001**†Bal 1 (0)   **NFL** 205 (2) [15 yrs]

HELLUIN, JERRY   Francis Jerome, DT, 6'2"/272 lbs; Tulane; 1951: Cle, rnd 3; B8/8/1929 Houma, LA   **1952**†Cle 12   **1953**†Cle 6   **1954** GB 12 (LDT)   **1955** GB 12 (LDT)   **1956** GB 12 (LDT)   **1957** GB 12 (LDT)   **1960**†Hou-A 14 (RDT)   **NFL** 80 [7 yrs]

HELMS, JACK   John Ancel, DE, 6'4"/215 lbs; Georgia Tech; 1944: Det, rnd 17; B1921, [K]   **1946** Det 7 (0)

HELTON, BARRY   Barry Bret, P, 6'3"/205 lbs; Colorado; 1988: SF, rnd 4; B1/2/1965 Colorado Springs, CO

YEAR	TEAM	G(GS,POS)	RUSH	YD	AVG(LG)	TD	REC	...	PASS	COMP	PCT	YD	AVG(LG)	TD	INT	SK	...	KPR	OTD	PTS	TAY
1988	†SF	15(0)	1	0	0.0(0)	0	—		—	—	—	—	—	—	—	—		P	—	0	0
1989	†SF	16(0)	1	0	0.0(0)	0	—		—	—	—	—	—	—	—	—		P	—	0	0
1990	†SF	16(0)	—	—	—	—	—		1	1	100.0	0	0.0(0)	0	0	—		P	—	0	0
1991	LARm	3(0)	—	—	—	—	—		1	1	100.0	22	22.0(22)	0	0	—		P	—	0	11
NFL	4	50(0)	2	0	0.0(0)	0	—		2	2	100.0	22	11.0(22)	0	0	—		P	—	0	11

HELTON, DARIUS   Darius, G, 6'2"/260 lbs; North Carolina Central; 1977: KC, rnd 4; B10/2/1954 Charlotte, NC   **1977** KC 6

HELVIE, CHUCK   Charles L., E, 5'8"/180 lbs; none; B10/8/1891, IN, D5/17/1964 Columbus, OH   **1920** Mun 1 (0, RE)   **1920** Day 4 (1)   **1921** Mun 2 (2, RE)   **NFL** 7 (3) [2 yrs]

HELWIG, JOHN   John Francis, LB-DB-DE, 6'2"/208 lbs; Notre Dame; 1950: ChiB, rnd 11; B12/5/1927 Los Angeles, CA, D12/2/1994 Pontiac, MI   **1953** ChiB 12 (LLB)   **1954** ChiB 12 (DB)   **1955** ChiB 12   **1956**†ChiB 6   **NFL** 42 [4 yrs]

HEMPEL, BILL   William, T, 6'0"/238 lbs; Carroll (WI); B2/10/1920 Lincoln, NE, D1/19/2001 Fresno, CA   **1942** ChiB 8 (0)

HEMPHILL, DARRYL   Darryl Anthony, DB, 6'0"/195 lbs; West Texas A&M; 1982: NYJ, rnd 10; B3/29/1960 San Antonio, TX   **1982** Bal 3 (0)

HEMPSTEAD, HESSLEY   Hessley James, G, 6'1"/295 lbs; Kansas; 1995: Det, rnd 7; B1/29/1972 Upland, CA   **1995**†Det 3 (0)   **1996** Det 13 (0)   **1997**†Det 16 (1)   **NFL** 32 (1) [3 yrs]

HEMSLEY, NATE   Nathaniel Richard, LB, 6'0"/228 lbs; Syracuse; B5/15/1974 Willingboro, NJ   **1997** Dal 2 (0)   **1998** Dal 3 (0)   **1999** Dal 6 (0)   **2001** Car 9 (3)   **NFL** 20 (3) [4 yrs]

HENDEL, ANDY   Andrew Carey, LB, 6'1"/230 lbs; North Carolina State; B3/4/1961 Rochester, NY   **1986** Mia 16 (1)

HENDERSHOT, LARRY   Lawrence Leland, LB, 6'3"/240 lbs; Arizona State; 1967: Was, rnd 8; B1/15/1944 Indianapolis, IN   **1967** Was 4

HENDERSON, DEVERY   Devery Vaughn, WR, 5'11"/190 lbs; LSU; 2004: NO, rnd 2; B3/26/1982 Lafayette, LA   **2004** NO 1 (0)

YEAR	TEAM	G(GS,POS)	RUSH	YD	AVG(LG)	TD	REC	YD	AVG(LG)	TD	...	KPR	OTD	PTS	TAY
2005	NO	14(3)	1	9	9.0(9)	0	22	343	15.6(66)	3		—	—	18	196
NFL	2	15(3)	1	9	9.0(9)	0	22	343	15.6(66)	3		—	—	18	196

HENDERSON, E.J.   Eric N., LB, 6'1"/245 lbs; Maryland; 2003: Min, rnd 2; B8/3/1980 Aberdeen, MD   **2003** Min 16 (0)   **2004**†Min 14 (14, MLB)   **2005** Min 15 (14, RLB)   **NFL** 45 (28) [3 yrs]

HENDERSON, HERB   Herbert Raymond, WB-HB, 5'11"/170 lbs; Oberlin; Ohio State; B6/21/1899 Oberlin, OH, D1/14/1991 Odon, IN [K]   **1921** Evv 4 (4, WB), 29

HENDERSON, JAMIE   Jamie Concepcion, DB, 6'2"/202 lbs; Georgia; 2001: NYJ, rnd 4; B1/1/1979 Carrollton, GA   **2001**†NYJ 16 (0)   **2002** NYJ 2 (0)   **2003** NYJ 14 (0)   **NFL** 32 (0) [3 yrs]

HENDERSON, JEROME   Jerome Virgil, DB, 5'10"/193 lbs; Clemson; 1991: NE, rnd 2; B8/8/1969 Statesville, NC   **1991** NE 16 (1)   **1992** NE 16 (9, fs)   **1993** NE 1 (0)   **1993**†Buf 2 (0)   **1994** Buf 12 (0)   **1995** Phi 15 (0)   **1996**†NE 7 (0)   **1997** NYJ 16 (14, FS)   **1998**†NYJ 13 (9, FS)   **NFL** 98 (33) [8 yrs]

HENDERSON, JOHN   John William, WR-FL, 6'3"/195 lbs; Michigan; 1965: Phi, rnd 5/Buf, rnd 17; B3/21/1943 Dayton, OH

YEAR	TEAM	G(GS,POS)	RUSH	YD	AVG(LG)	TD	REC	YD	AVG(LG)	TD	...	KPR	OTD	PTS	TAY
1965	Det	12	—	—	—	—	8	140	17.5(31)	1		—	—	6	75
1966	Det	13	—	—	—	—	6	121	20.2(53)	0		—	—	0	61
1967	Det	14(fl)	—	—	—	—	13	144	11.1(41)	0		—	—	0	72
1968	†Min	7	—	—	—	—	4	42	10.5(12)	0		—	—	0	21
1969	†Min	14(14, WR)	—	—	—	—	34	553	16.3(47)	5		—	—	30	302
1970	†Min	14	—	—	—	—	31	527	17.0(52)	2		—	—	12	274
1971	†Min	7	—	—	—	—	2	18	9.0(12)	0		—	—	0	9
1972	Min	12	—	—	—	—	10	190	19.0(70)	2		—	—	12	105
NFL	8	93(14)	—	—	—	—	108	1735	16.1(70)	10		—	—	60	918

HENDERSON, JOHN   John Nathan, DT, 6'7"/328 lbs; Tennessee; 2002: Jax, rnd 1; B1/9/1979 Nashville, TN   **2002** Jax 16 (13, RDT)   **2003** Jax 16 (16, RDT)   **2004** Jax◇16 (16, RDT)   **2005**†Jax 16 (15, RDT)   **NFL** 64 (60) [4 yrs]

HENDERSON, JON   Jon Elliott, WR-DB, 6'0"/200 lbs; Colorado State; 1968: Pit, rnd 3; B12/17/1944 Pittsburgh, PA

YEAR	TEAM	G(GS,POS)	RUSH	YD	AVG(LG)	TD	REC	YD	AVG(LG)	TD	...	KPR	OTD	PTS	TAY
1968	Pit	14	—	—	—	—	3	26	8.7(13)	0		k	—	0	167
1969	Pit	9	—	—	—	—	12	188	15.7(45)	3		k	—	18	109
1970	Was	14	—	—	—	—	13	176	13.5(56)	3		k	—	18	88
NFL	3	37	—	—	—	—	28	390	13.9(56)	6		k	—	36	364

HENDERSON, KEITH   Keith Pernell, RB, 6'1"/220 lbs; Georgia; 1989: SF, rnd 3; B8/4/1966 Cartersville, GA

YEAR	TEAM	G(GS,POS)	RUSH	YD	AVG(LG)	TD	REC	YD	AVG(LG)	TD	PASS	COMP	PCT	YD	AVG(LG)	TD	INT	SK	YD	QBR	KPR	OTD	PTS	TAY
1989	†SF	6(0)	7	30	4.3(11)	1	3	130	43.3(78)	0	—	—	—	—	—	—	—	—			k	—	6	96
1990	†SF	2(0)	6	14	2.3(9)	0	4	35	8.8(9)	0	—	—	—	—	—	—	—	—			—	—	0	32
1991	SF	14(1)	137	561	4.1(25)	2	30	303	10.1(23)	0	—	—	—	—	—	—	—	—			k	—	12	733
1992	SF	2(0)	10	37	3.7(9)	0	1	4	4.0(4)	0	—	—	—	—	—	—	—	—			—	—	0	39
1992	Min	13(0)	34	113	3.3(12)	1	4	60	15.0(23)	0	1	1	100.0	36	36.0(36)	1	0	—			k	—	6	212
NFL	4	37(1)	194	755	3.9(25)	4	42	532	12.7(78)	0	1	1	100.0	36	36.0(36)	1	0	—			k	—	24	1111

HENDERSON, OTHELLO   Othello M., DB, 6'0"/204 lbs; UCLA; 1993: NO, rnd 7; B8/23/1972 Oakland, CA   **1993** NO 5 (1)   **1994** NO 16 (0)   **NFL** 21 (1) [2 yrs]

HENDERSON, REUBEN   Reuben Stanley, DB, 6'1"/196 lbs; Oklahoma State; San Diego State; 1981: Chi, rnd 6; B10/3/1958 Santa Monica, CA   **1981** ChiB 16 (16, RCB)   **1982** ChiB 4 (3)   **1983** SD 14 (4)   **1984** SD 12 (0)   **NFL** 46 (23) [4 yrs]

HENDERSON, THOMAS   Thomas Edward 'Hollywood', LB, 6'2"/221 lbs; Langston; 1975: Dal, rnd 1; B3/1/1953 Austin, TX   **1975**†Dal 13   **1976**†Dal 14   **1977**†Dal☆14 (14, LLB)   **1978**†Dal◇15 (13, LLB)   **1979** Dal 11 (10, LLB)   **1980** SF 1 (0)   **1980**†Hou 7 (0)   **NFL** 75 (37) [6 yrs]

HENDERSON, WILBUR   Wilbur W., FB, /195 lbs; none; B1898, IL, deceased   **1920** Ham 1 (0)

HENDERSON, WILLIAM   William Terrelle, FB, 6'1"/249 lbs; North Carolina; 1995: GB, rnd 3; B2/19/1971 Richmond, VA

YEAR	TEAM	G(GS,POS)	RUSH	YD	AVG(LG)	TD	REC	YD	AVG(LG)	TD	...	KPR	OTD	PTS	TAY
1995	†GB	15(1)	7	35	5.0(17)	0	3	21	7.0(9)	0		—	—	0	46
1996	†GB	16(11, FB)	39	130	3.3(14)	0	27	203	7.5(27)	1		k	—	6	245
1997	†GB	16(14, FB)	31	113	3.6(15)	0	41	367	9.0(25)	1		—	—	6	302
1998	†GB	16(10, FB)	23	70	3.0(9)	2	37	241	6.5(15)	1		—	—	18	216
1999	GB	16(13, FB)	7	29	4.1(10)	2	30	203	6.8(22)	1		k	—	18	149
2000	GB	16(6, fb)	2	16	8.0(12)	0	35	234	6.7(25)	1		k	—	6	143
2001	†GB	16(8, FB)	6	11	1.8(4)	0	21	193	9.2(26)	0		k	—	0	80
2002	†GB	15(12, FB)	7	27	3.9(10)	1	26	168	6.5(17)	3		k	—	24	136
2003	†GB	16(12, FB)	—	—	—	—	24	214	8.9(22)	3		—	—	18	110
2004	†GB★	16(8, FB)	—	—	—	—	34	239	7.0(38)	3		k	—	18	121
2005	GB	16(8, FB)	1	-5	-5.0(-5)	0	30	264	8.8(32)	0		k	—	0	117
NFL	11	174(103)	123	426	3.5(17)	5	308	2347	7.6(38)	14		k	—	114	1662

HENDERSON, WYATT   Wyatt Monroe, DB, 5'10"/180 lbs; Fresno State; B11/10/1956 Bakersfield, CA   **1981** SD 15 (0)

HENDERSON, WYMON   Wymon, DB, 5'10"/190 lbs; UNLV; B12/15/1961 North Miami Beach, FL   **1987**†Min 12 (8, LCB)   **1988**†Min 16 (0)   **1989**†Den 16 (15, RCB)   **1990** Den 15 (15, RCB)   **1991**†Den 16 (16, RCB)   **1992** Den 15 (11, RCB)   **1993** LARm 9 (4)   **1994** LARm 15 (1)   **NFL** 114 (70) [8 yrs]

YEAR	TEAM	G (GS, POS)	RUSH	YD	AVG (LG)	TD	REC	YD	AVG (LG)	TD	PASS	COMP	PCT	YD	AVG (LG)	TD	INT	SK	YD	QBR	KPR	OTD	PTS	TAY

HENDERSON, ZAC Zachary Ryall, DB, 6´1˝/190 lbs; Oklahoma; B10/14/1955 Jena, LA **1980**†Phi 12 (0)

HENDLEY, DAVID David, DB, 6´0˝/188 lbs; Southern Connecticut State; B6/29/1964 **1987** NE 2 (0)

HENDLEY, DICK Dickson Lafayette, BB, 6´0˝/198 lbs; Clemson; 1951: Pit, rnd 22; B8/6/1926 **1951** Pit 7

HENDLEY, JIM James Willis, C, 6´3˝/257 lbs; Florida State; B10/25/1964 Valdosta, GA **1987** Atl 3 (3)

HENDREN, BOB Robert Gerald, T-DT-DE, 6´8˝/244 lbs; Culver-Stockton; USC; 1946: Was, rnd 7/1948: NYY-A, rnd 12; B8/10/1923 Burlington Junction, MO **1949** Was 12 (1) **1950** Was 12 (RT) **1951** Was 12 (RDT) **NFL** 36 (1) [3 yrs]

HENDREN, JERRY Jerry Wayne, WR, 6´2˝/187 lbs; Idaho; 1970: Den, rnd 4; B11/4/1947 Spokane, WA **1970** Den 10

HENDREN, JOHNNY John Crowther, HB, 5´10˝/185 lbs; Bucknell; B4/25/1897 Philadelphia, PA, D6/3/1964 Media, PA **1920** Can 3 (1) **1921** Cle 5 (0), 6 **NFL** 8 (1) [2 yrs]

HENDRIAN, DUTCH Oscar George, B, 5´9˝/182 lbs; DePauw; Detroit Mercy; Pittsburgh; Princeton; B1/19/1896 Detroit, MI, D12/13/1953 Los Angeles, CA **[KC]** **1923** Akr 5 (5, BB), 1 **1923** Can 4 (0), 6 **1924** GB 11 (11, FB), 21 **1925** RI 1 (1) **1925** NYG 11 (8, BB), 22 **NFL** 32 (25), 50 [3 yrs]

HENDRICKS, TED Theodore Paul 'The Mad Stork', LB, 6´7˝/220 lbs; Miami (FL); 1969: Bal, rnd 2; B11/1/1947 Guatemala City, Guatemala; HOF 1990 **[I]** **1969** Bal 14 (RLB) **1970**†Bal 14 (RLB) **1971**†Bal★14 (RLB) **1972** Bal★14 (LLB) **1973** Bal★14 (LLB) **1974** GB★14 (LLB) **1975**†Oak 14 (5, rlb) **1976**†Oak☆14 (ROLB) **1977**†Oak☆14 (14, ROLB) **1978** Oak☆16 (16, LOLB) **1979** Oak 16 (16, LOLB) **1980**†Oak★16 (16, LOLB) **1981** Oak★16 (16, LOLB) **1982**†LARd★9 (9, LOLB) **1983**†LARd★16 (16, LOLB) **NFL** 215 (108) [15 yrs]

HENDRICKS, TOMMY Thomas Emmett, LB, 6´2˝/235 lbs; Michigan; B10/23/1978 Houston, TX **2000**†Mia 8 (0) **2001**†Mia 16 (1) **2002** Mia 16 (0) **2003** Mia 16 (2) **2004** Jax 15 (1) **NFL** 71 (4) [5 yrs]

HENDRICKSON, STEVE Steven Daniel, LB-RB-TE, 6´0˝/250 lbs; California; 1989: SF, rnd 6; B8/30/1966 Richmond, CA **1989** Dal 4 (0) **1989**†SF 11 (0) **1992**†SD 16 (2) **1995** Phi 3 (0) **1995** Hou 5 (1)

YEAR	TEAM	G (GS, POS)	RUSH	YD	AVG (LG)	TD	REC	YD	AVG (LG)	TD	PASS	COMP	PCT	YD	AVG (LG)	TD	INT	SK	YD	QBR	KPR	OTD	PTS	TAY
1990	SD	14(0)	—	—	—	—	1	12	12.0(12)	0	—	—	—	—	—	—	—	—	—	—	—	—	0	6
1991	SD	15(4)	1	3	3.0(3)	1	4	36	9.0(20)	1	—	—	—	—	—	—	—	—	—	—	—	—	12	36
1993	SD	16(10, LLB)	1	0	0.0(0)	0	—	—	—	—	—	—	—	—	—	—	—	—	—	—	ki	—	0	6
1994	†SD	16(0)	1	3	3.0(3)	0	—	—	—	—	—	—	—	—	—	—	—	—	—	—	—	—	0	3
NFL	7	100(17)	3	6	2.0(3)	1	5	48	9.6(20)	1	—	—	—	—	—	—	—	—	—	—	ki	—	12	35

HENDRIX, DAVE David Tyrone, DB, 6´1˝/213 lbs; Georgia Tech; B5/29/1972 Jessup, GA **1995**†SD 5 (0) **1996** SD 14 (0) **1997** SD 4 (0) **NFL** 23 (0) [3 yrs]

HENDRIX, MANNY Manuel, DB, 5´10˝/180 lbs; Utah; B10/20/1964 Phoenix, AZ **1986** Dal 13 (0) **1987** Dal 12 (1) **1988** Dal 16 (0) **1989** Dal 16 (3) **1990** Dal 16 (11, RCB) **1991**†Dal 16 (3) **NFL** 89 (18) [6 yrs]

HENDRIX, TIM Timothy John, TE, 6´5˝/241 lbs; Tennessee; B2/24/1965 De Soto, TX **1987** Dal 3 (0)

HENDY, JOHN John Herald, DB, 5´11˝/196 lbs; Long Beach State; 1985: SD, rnd 3; B10/9/1962 Guatemala City, Guatemala **1985** SD 16 (10, LCB)

HENESEY, BRIAN Brian P., RB, 5´10˝/215 lbs; Bucknell; B12/10/1969 Villanova, PA **1994** Arz 3 (0)

HENKE, BRAD Brad William, DE-NT, 6´3˝/275 lbs; Iowa State; Arizona; 1989: NYG, rnd 4; B4/10/1966 Columbus, NE **1989**†Den 2 (0)

HENKE, ED Edgar Edwin, DE-LB-G, 6´3˝/227 lbs; USC; 1949: Was, rnd 13; B12/13/1927 Ontario, CA

YEAR	TEAM	G (GS, POS)	RUSH	YD	AVG (LG)	TD	REC	YD	AVG (LG)	TD	PASS	COMP	PCT	YD	AVG (LG)	TD	INT	SK	YD	QBR	KPR	OTD	PTS	TAY
1949	LAD-A	11(0)	—	—	—	—	1	15	15.0(15)	0	—	—	—	—	—	—	—	—	—	—	—	—	0	8

1951 SF 12 (LDE) **1956** SF 12 (RG) **1957**†SF☆12 (LDE) **1958** SF 12 (LDE) **1959** SF 12 (LDE) **1960** SF 8 (6, mlb/rlb) **1961** SL 14 (RDE/lde) **1962** SL 8 **1963** SL 10

YEAR	TEAM	G (GS, POS)	RUSH	YD	AVG (LG)	TD	REC	YD	AVG (LG)	TD	PASS	COMP	PCT	YD	AVG (LG)	TD	INT	SK	YD	QBR	KPR	OTD	PTS	TAY
1952	SF★	12(LDE)	—	—	—	—	1	13	13.0(13)	0	—	—	—	—	—	—	—	—	—	—	—	—	0	7
NFL	1 0	112(6)	—	—	—	—	1	13	13.0(15)	0	—	—	—	—	—	—	—	—	—	—	—	—	0	7

HENKE, KARL Karl Alfred, DE-DT, 6´4˝/245 lbs; Tulsa; 1968: NYJ, rnd 8; B3/8/1945 Ventura, CA **1968** NYJ-A 6 **1969** Bos-A 10 (7, LDE) **NFL** 16 (7) [2 yrs]

HENLEY, CAREY Carey Ernest, HB, 5´10˝/201 lbs; Tennessee-Chattanooga; 1962: Buf, rnd 21; B9/24/1936 West Point, MS

YEAR	TEAM	G (GS, POS)	RUSH	YD	AVG (LG)	TD	REC	YD	AVG (LG)	TD	PASS	COMP	PCT	YD	AVG (LG)	TD	INT	SK	YD	QBR	KPR	OTD	PTS	TAY
1962	Buf-A	1	3	2	0.7(4)	0	—	—	—	—	—	—	—	—	—	—	—	—	—	—	k	—	0	17

HENLEY, DARRYL Darryl Keith, DB, 5´9˝/172 lbs; UCLA; 1989: LARm, rnd 2; B10/30/1966 Los Angeles, CA **1989**†LARm 15 (0) **1990** LARm 9 (6, rcb) **1991** LARm 16 (15, RCB) **1992** LARm 16 (15, RCB) **1993** LARm 5 (4) **1994** LARm 15 (14, LCB) **NFL** 76 (54) [6 yrs]

HENLEY, JUNE Charles Lee, RB, 5´10˝/226 lbs; Kansas; 1997: KC, rnd 5; B9/4/1975 Columbus, OH

YEAR	TEAM	G (GS, POS)	RUSH	YD	AVG (LG)	TD	REC	YD	AVG (LG)	TD	PASS	COMP	PCT	YD	AVG (LG)	TD	INT	SK	YD	QBR	KPR	OTD	PTS	TAY
1998	SL	11(3)	88	313	3.6(22)	3	35	252	7.2(43)	0	—	—	—	—	—	—	—	—	—	—	k	—	18	467

HENLEY, THOMAS Thomas Henry, WR, 5´11˝/185 lbs; Stanford; 1987: NO, rnd 6; B7/28/1965 Hillsboro, TX **1987** SF 1 (1)

HENNESSEY, TOM Thomas Edward, DB, 6´0˝/180 lbs; Holy Cross; B2/15/1942 Boston, MA **1965** Bos-A 14 (RCB) **1966** Bos-A 14 (RCB) **NFL** 28 [2 yrs]

HENNESSY, JERRY Jerome Joseph, DE, 6´2˝/219 lbs; Santa Clara; 1950: ChiC, rnd 13; B2/22/1926 Los Angeles, CA **1950** ChiC 7 **1951** ChiC 12 (RDE) **1952** Was 12 (lde) **1953** Was 8 (rde) **NFL** 39 [4 yrs]

HENNESSY, JOHN John William, LB-DE, 6´3˝/243 lbs; Michigan; 1977: NYJ, rnd 10; B3/12/1955 Chicago, IL **1977** NYJ 14 (2) **1978** NYJ 16 (16, LILB) **1979** NYJ 16 **NFL** 46 (18) [3 yrs]

HENNIGAN, CHARLEY Charles Taylor, WR, 6´1˝/187 lbs; LSU; Northwestern State (LA); B3/19/1935 Bienville, LA

YEAR	TEAM	G (GS, POS)	RUSH	YD	AVG (LG)	TD	REC	YD	AVG (LG)	TD	PASS	COMP	PCT	YD	AVG (LG)	TD	INT	SK	YD	QBR	KPR	OTD	PTS	TAY
1960	†Hou-A	11(WR)	—	—	—	—	44	722	16.4(73)	6	—	—	—	—	—	—	—	—	—	—	—	—	36	391
1961	†Hou-A★	14(WR)	—	—	—	—	82	**1746**	21.3(80)	12	—	—	—	—	—	—	—	—	—	—	—	—	72	933
1962	†Hou-A★	14(WR)	—	—	—	—	54	867	16.1(78)	8	—	—	—	—	—	—	—	—	—	—	—	—	48	474
1963	Hou-A★	14(WR)	—	—	—	—	61	1051	17.2(83)	10	—	—	—	—	—	—	—	—	—	—	—	—	60	576
1964	Hou-A★	14(WR)	—	—	—	—	**101**	**1546**	15.3(53)	8	—	—	—	—	—	—	—	—	—	—	—	—	48	813
1965	Hou-A✧	14(WR)	—	—	—	—	41	578	14.1(53)	4	—	—	—	—	—	—	—	—	—	—	—	—	24	309
1966	Hou-A	14(WR)	—	—	—	—	27	313	11.6(23)	3	—	—	—	—	—	—	—	—	—	—	—	—	18	172
NFL	7	95	—	—	—	—	410	6823	16.6(83)	51	—	—	—	—	—	—	—	—	—	—	—	—	306	3667

HENNIGAN, MIKE Thomas Michael, LB, 6´2˝/217 lbs; Parsons; Tennessee Tech; 1973: Det, rnd 4; B10/24/1951 Washington, IA **1973** Det 8 **1974** Det 14 **1975** Det 4 **1976** NYJ 12 **1977** NYJ 14 (2) **1978** NYJ 12 (12, RILB) **NFL** 64 (14) [6 yrs]

HENNING, DAN Daniel Ernest, QB, 6´0˝/195 lbs; William & Mary; B6/21/1942 Bronx, NY **[C]** **1966** SD-A 1

HENNINGS, CHAD Chad William, DT-DE, 6´6˝/287 lbs; Air Force; 1988: Dal, rnd 11; B10/20/1965 Elberon, IA **1992**†Dal 8 (0) **1993**†Dal 13 (0) **1994**†Dal 16 (0) **1995**†Dal 16 (7, rdt) **1996**†Dal 15 (15, LDT) **1997** Dal 11 (10, RDT) **1998**†Dal 16 (16, RDT) **1999**†Dal 16 (16, RDT) **2000** Dal 8 (8, ldt) **NFL** 119 (72) [9 yrs]

HENRICUS, RALPH Ralph Charles, HB, 6´0˝/175 lbs; none; B6/2/1896 Rochester, NY, D8/27/1949 Alameda County, CA **1922** Roc 2 (1)

HENRY, ANTHONY Anthony Daniel, DB, 6´1˝/205 lbs; South Florida; 2001: Cle, rnd 4; B11/3/1976 Fort Myers, FL **[I]** **2001** Cle 16 (2) **2002**†Cle 16 (10, rcb) **2003** Cle 14 (13, LCB) **2004** Cle 15 (14, LCB) **2005** Dal 12 (10, RCB) **NFL** 73 (49) [5 yrs]

HENRY, BERNARD Bernard, WR, 6´1˝/180 lbs; Arizona State; B4/9/1960 Los Angeles, CA

YEAR	TEAM	G (GS, POS)	RUSH	YD	AVG (LG)	TD	REC	YD	AVG (LG)	TD	PASS	COMP	PCT	YD	AVG (LG)	TD	INT	SK	YD	QBR	KPR	OTD	PTS	TAY
1982	Bal	6(0)	—	—	—	—	7	110	15.7(23)	0	—	—	—	—	—	—	—	—	—	—	—	—	0	55
1983	Bal	15(7, wr)	—	—	—	—	30	416	13.9(40)	4	—	—	—	—	—	—	—	—	—	—	—	—	24	228
1984	Ind	14(0)	—	—	—	—	11	139	12.6(19)	2	—	—	—	—	—	—	—	—	—	—	—	—	12	80
1985	Ind	1(1)	—	—	—	—	2	31	15.5(16)	0	—	—	—	—	—	—	—	—	—	—	—	—	0	16
1987	LARm	3(2)	—	—	—	—	1	13	13.0(13)	0	—	—	—	—	—	—	—	—	—	—	—	—	0	7
NFL	5	39(10)	—	—	—	—	51	709	13.9(40)	6	—	—	—	—	—	—	—	—	—	—	—	—	36	385

HENRY, CHARLES Charles W., TE, 6´4˝/230 lbs; Miami (FL); B4/18/1964 St. Petersburg, FL

YEAR	TEAM	G (GS, POS)	RUSH	YD	AVG (LG)	TD	REC	YD	AVG (LG)	TD	PASS	COMP	PCT	YD	AVG (LG)	TD	INT	SK	YD	QBR	KPR	OTD	PTS	TAY
1991	Mia	6(2)	—	—	—	—	2	17	8.5(9)	0	—	—	—	—	—	—	—	—	—	—	k	—	0	7

HENRY, CHRIS Chris, WR, 6´4˝/197 lbs; West Virginia; 2005: Cin, rnd 3; B3/17/1983 Belle Chasse, LA

YEAR	TEAM	G (GS, POS)	RUSH	YD	AVG (LG)	TD	REC	YD	AVG (LG)	TD	PASS	COMP	PCT	YD	AVG (LG)	TD	INT	SK	YD	QBR	KPR	OTD	PTS	TAY
2005	†Cin	14(5, wr)	—	—	—	—	31	422	13.6(47)	6	—	—	—	—	—	—	—	—	—	—	—	—	36	241

HENRY, FRITZ Fritz Earl, G, /190 lbs; none; B11/30/1895 Columbus, OH, D1/23/1974 Columbus, OH **1925** Akr 1 (1)

HENRY, KEVIN Kevin Lerell, DE, 6´4˝/282 lbs; Mississippi State; 1993: Pit, rnd 4; B10/23/1968 Mound Bayou, MS **1993** Pit 12 (1) **1994**†Pit 16 (5, rde) **1995**†Pit 13 (5, lde) **1996**†Pit 12 (10, RDE) **1997**†Pit 16 (16, RDE) **1998** Pit 16 (16, RDE) **1999** Pit 16 (13, RDE) **2000** Pit 15 (15, RDE) **NFL** 116 (81) [8 yrs]

YEAR	TEAM	G(GS, POS)	RUSH	YD	AVG(LG)	TD	REC	YD	AVG(LG)	TD	PASS COMP	PCT	YD	AVG(LG)	TD	INT	SK	YD	QBR	KPR	OTD	PTS	TAY

HENRY, LEONARD Leonard Charles, RB, 6′1″/210 lbs; East Carolina; 2002: Mia, rnd 7; B1/5/1978 Clinton, NC

| 2004 | Mia | 6(2) | 46 | 141 | 3.1(53) | 0 | 3 | 12 | 4.0(7) | 0 | — | — | — | — | — | — | — | — | — | — | — | 0 | 147 |

HENRY, MAURICE Maurice Eugene, LB, 5′11″/220 lbs; Kansas State; 1990: Det, rnd 6; B3/12/1967 Starkville, MS **1990** Phi 7 (0)

HENRY, MIKE Michael Dennis, LB, 6′2″/220 lbs; USC; 1958: Pit, rnd 9; B8/15/1936 Los Angeles, CA **1959** Pit 12 **1960** Pit 12 **1961** Pit 10 **1962** LARm 14 (MLB)
1963 LARm 14 (MLB) **1964** LARm 14 (MLB) **NFL** 76 [6 yrs]

HENRY, PETE Wilbur Francis 'Fats', T, 5′11″/245 lbs; Washington & Jefferson; B10/31/1897 Mansfield, OH, D2/7/1952 Washington, PA; HOF 1963 **[KC]** **1920** Can☆13 (8, RT)
1921 Can☆10 (10, RT) **1922** Can☆12 (11, RT), 10 **1923** Can☆12 (12, RT), 58 **1925** Can 6 (6, RT), 8 **1926** Can 13 (11, RT), 3 **1927** NYG 4 (4) **1927** Pot 9 (9, RT), 7
1928 Pot 7 (3), 2 **NFL** 86 (74), 88 [8 yrs]

HENRY, STEVE Steven Arlen, DB, 6′2″/190 lbs; Emporia State; 1979: SL, rnd 5; B3/5/1957 Kansas City, KS **1979** SL 8 **1980** NYG 5 (0) **1981** Bal 2 (0) **NFL** 15 [3 yrs]

HENRY, TOM Thomas E., WB, 5′10″/185 lbs; LSU; B4/1895 Alton, IL, deceased **1920** RI 1 (0)

HENRY, TRAVIS Travis Deion, RB, 5′9″/215 lbs; Tennessee; 2001: Buf, rnd 2; B10/29/1978 Frostproof, FL

2001	Buf	13(12, RB)	213	729	3.4(25)	4	22	179	8.1(40)	0	—	—	—	—	—	—	—	—	—	—	—	24	859
2002	Buf◇	16(16, RB)	325	1438	4.4(34)	13	43	309	7.2(26)	1	—	—	—	—	—	—	—	—	—	—	—	84	1728
2003	Buf	15(15, RB)	331	1356	4.1(64)	10	28	158	5.6(18)	1	1	0	0.0	0	0.0	0	0	1	—	—	—	66	1500
2004	Buf	10(5, rb)	94	326	3.5(19)	0	10	45	4.5(10)	0	—	—	—	—	—	—	—	—	—	—	—	0	349
2005	Ten	9(1)	88	335	3.8(29)	0	13	117	9.0(42)	0	—	—	—	—	—	—	—	—	—	—	—	0	394
NFL	5	63(49)	1051	4184	4.0(64)	27	116	808	7.0(42)	2	1	0	0.0	0	0.0	0	0	1	—	—	—	174	4828

HENRY, URBAN Urban A., DT, 6′4″/265 lbs; Georgia Tech; 1958: LA, rnd 4; B6/7/1935 Berwick, LA, D2/1979 **1961** LARm 14 (LDT) **1963** GB 14 **1964** Pit 10 **NFL** 38 [3 yrs]

HENRY, WALLY Wallace, WR, 5′8″/175 lbs; UCLA; B10/30/1954 San Diego, CA **[R]** **1978** Phi 3 **1979**†Phi★12 **1982** Phi 8 (0)

1977	Phi	10	1	-2	-2.0(-2)	0	2	16	8.0(14)	0	—	—	—	—	—	—	—	—	p	—	—	0	21
1980	†Phi	7(0)	—	—	—	—	4	68	17.0(22)	0	—	—	—	—	—	—	—	—	kp	—	—	0	175
1981	†Phi	16(0)	1	-2	-2.0(-2)	0	9	145	16.1(44)	2	—	—	—	—	—	—	—	—	kp	—	—	12	365
NFL	6	56	2	-4	-2.0(-2)	0	15	229	15.3(44)	2	—	—	—	—	—	—	—	—	kp	1	—	18	1267

HENRY, WILBUR Wilbur Amos, G, 5′10″/185 lbs; Stanford; B12/4/1891 Los Angeles, CA, D11/9/1947 Los Angeles, CA **1930** SI 2 (0)

HENSLEY, DICK Richard Earl, E-DE, 6′4″/213 lbs; Kentucky; 1949: NYG, rnd 11; B9/8/1927 Williamson, WV

1949	NYG	11(0)	—	—	—	—	3	24	8.0(10)	0	—	—	—	—	—	—	—	—	—	—	—	0	12
1952	Pit	11(LE)	—	—	—	—	12	217	18.1(60)	2	—	—	—	—	—	—	—	—	—	—	—	12	119
1953	ChiB	11	—	—	—	—	4	117	29.3(50)	0	—	—	—	—	—	—	—	—	—	—	—	2	59
NFL	3	33	—	—	—	—	19	358	18.8(60)	2	—	—	—	—	—	—	—	—	—	—	—	14	189

HENSON, CHAMP Harold R., RB, 6′3″/240 lbs; Ohio State; 1975: Min, rnd 4; B6/1/1953 Columbus, OH

| 1975 | Cin | 6 | 11 | 38 | 3.5(8) | 0 | 1 | -2 | -2.0(-2) | 0 | — | — | — | — | — | — | — | — | — | — | — | 0 | 37 |

HENSON, DREW Drew Daniel, QB, 6′4″/233 lbs; Michigan; 2003: Hou, rnd 6; B2/13/1980 San Diego, CA

| 2004 | Dal | 7(1) | 1 | 7 | 7.0(7) | 0 | — | — | — | — | 18 | 10 | 55.6 | 78 | 4.3(16) | 1 | 1 | 2 | 26 | — | — | 0 | 11 |

HENSON, GARY Gary Owen, E, 6′3″/200 lbs; Colorado; 1962: LA, rnd 14/Hou, rnd 28; B9/8/1940 Oklahoma City, OK **1963** Phi 11 **1964** Den-A 1 **NFL** 12 [2 yrs]

HENSON, KEN Kenneth Wayne, C, 6′6″/260 lbs; TCU; 1964: LA, rnd 5/Hou, rnd 14; B4/11/1943 San Angelo, TX, D11/24/2004 Richland Hills, TX **1965** Pit 4

HENSON, LUTHER Luther Martin, NT, 6′0″/275 lbs; Ohio State; B3/25/1959 Sandusky, OH **1982**†NE 8 (0) **1983** NE 4 (2) **1984** NE 9 (0) **NFL** 21 (2) [3 yrs]

HENTON, ANTHONY Oscar Anthony, LB, 6′1″/218 lbs; Troy State; 1986: Pit, rnd 9; B7/27/1963 Bessemer, AL **1986** Pit 16 (0) **1988** Pit 16 (4) **NFL** 32 (4) [2 yrs]

HENTRICH, CRAIG Craig Anthony, P, 6′3″/213 lbs; Notre Dame; 1993: NYJ, rnd 8; B5/18/1971 Alton, IL **[KP]**

1994	†GB	16(0)	—	—	—	—	—	—	—	—	—	—	—	—	—	—	—	—	P	—	—	0	0
1995	†GB	16(0)	—	—	—	—	—	—	—	—	—	—	—	—	—	—	—	—	KP	—	—	14	0
1996	†GB	16(0)	—	—	—	—	—	—	—	—	1	0	0.0	0	0.0	0	0	0	P	—	—	0	0
1997	†GB	16(0)	—	—	—	—	—	—	—	—	—	—	—	—	—	—	—	—	P	—	—	0	0
1998	Ten★	16(0)	1	-1	-1.0(-1)	0	—	—	—	—	1	1	100.0	13	13.0(13)	0	0	—	KP	—	—	0	6
1999	†Ten	16(0)	2	1	0.5(1)	0	—	—	—	—	—	—	—	—	—	—	—	—	P	—	—	0	1
2000	†Ten	16(0)	—	—	—	—	—	—	—	—	—	—	—	—	—	—	—	—	KP	—	—	0	0
2001	Ten	16(0)	—	—	—	—	—	—	—	—	2	0	0.0	0	0.0	0	1	—	P	—	—	0	-40
2002	†Ten	16(0)	1	5	5.0(5)	0	—	—	—	—	1	1	100.0	17	17.0(17)	0	0	—	P	—	—	0	14
2003	†Ten★	16(0)	—	—	—	—	—	—	—	—	5	2	40.0	25	5.0(15)	0	0	—	KP	—	—	13	13
2004	Ten	16(0)	1	8	8.0(8)	0	—	—	—	—	4	2	50.0	10	2.5(6)	0	0	—	KP	—	—	3	13
2005	Ten	16(0)	1	0	0.0(0)	0	—	—	—	—	2	1	50.0	26	13.0(26)	0	0	—	KP	—	—	0	13
NFL	12	192(0)	6	13	2.2(8)	0	—	—	—	—	16	7	43.8	91	5.7(26)	0	1	—	KP	—	—	30	19

HEPBURN, LONNIE Lionel Lorenzo, DB, 5′11″/180 lbs; Texas Southern; 1971: Mia, rnd 13; B5/12/1949 Miami, FL **1971**†Bal 3 **1972** Bal 14 (RCB) **1974** Den 14 (4)
NFL 31 (4) [3 yrs]

HEPPNER, KRIS Kris, K, 5′9″/180 lbs; Montana; B1/18/1977 Great Falls, MT **[K]** **2000** Sea 4 (0) **2000** Was 4 (0) **NFL** 8 (0) [1 yr]

HERBER, ARNIE Arnold Charles, TB-HB-DB-QB-BB, 5′11″/203 lbs; Wisconsin; Regis; B4/2/1910 Green Bay, WI, D10/14/1969 Green Bay, WI; HOF 1966 **[K]**

1930	GB	10(4)	—	—	—	—	—	—	—	—	—	—	—	—	—	—	—	—	—	—	—	—	—
1931	GB	3(0)	—	—	—	—	—	—	—	—	—	—	—	—	—	—	—	—	—	—	—	—	—
1932	GB☆	14(8, tb)	64	149	2.3	1	—	—	—	—	101	37	36.6	639	6.3	9	9	—	51.5	—	1	12	174
1933	GB	11(6, HB)	62	77	1.2	0	3	27	9.0(25)	0	124	50	40.3	656	5.3	3	12	—	26.2 K	—	1	-47
1934	GB	11(7, TB)	37	33	0.9	0	—	—	—	—	115	42	36.5	799	6.9(69)	8	12	—	45.1	—	0	-8
1935	GB☆	11(8, TB)	19	0	0.0	0	2	26	13.0(17)	0	109	40	36.7	729	6.7(83)	8	14	—	45.4 K	—	1	-143
1936	†GB☆	12(5, TB)	20	-32	-1.6	0	—	—	—	—	173	77	44.5	1239	7.2(58)	11	13	—	58.9	—	0	123
1937	GB	9(0, tb)	5	9	1.8	0	—	—	—	—	104	47	45.2	684	6.6(78)	7	10	—	50.0	—	0	-14
1938	†GB	8(4)	6	-1	-0.2	0	5	84	16.8(20)	2	55	22	40.0	336	6.1	3	4	—	K	—	12	74
1939	†GB◇	10(7, TB)	18	-11	-0.6	1	1	18	18.0(18)	0	139	57	41.0	1107	8.0(92)	8	9	—	61.6 P	—	6	242
1940	GB	10(4, tb)	6	-23	-3.8	0	—	—	—	—	89	38	42.7	560	6.3(55)	6	7	—	Pi	—	0	-3
1944	†NYG	10(3, TB)	7	-58	-8.3(-14)	0	—	—	—	—	86	36	41.9	651	7.6(58)	6	8	—	P	—	0	-23
1945	NYG	10(0, TB)	6	-27	-4.5(1)	0	—	—	—	—	80	35	43.8	641	8.0(54)	9	8	—	P	—	0	19
NFL	13	129(56)	250	116	0.5(1)	3	11	155	14.1(25)	3	1175	481	40.9	8041	6.8(92)	81	106	—	50.1 KPi	1	44	424

HERCHMAN, BILL William, DT, 6′2″/246 lbs; Texas Tech; 1956: SF, rnd 3; B3/10/1933 Vernon, TX **1956** SF 12 (RDT) **1957**†SF 12 (RDT) **1958** SF 12 (RDT) **1959** SF 12
1960 Dal 11 **1961** Dal 14 (RDT) **1962**†Hou-A 12 **NFL** 85 [7 yrs]

HERGERT, JOE Joseph Martin, LB-K, 6′1″/216 lbs; Florida; 1959: GB, rnd 24; B6/7/1936 Wilkes-Barre, PA **[K]** **1960** Buf-A 10 **1961** Buf-A 9 **NFL** 19 [2 yrs]

HERKENHOFF, MATT Matthew Bernard, T, 6′4″/267 lbs; Minnesota; 1974: KC, rnd 4; B4/2/1951 Melrose, MN **1976** KC 14 (12, LT) **1977** KC 14 (14, LT) **1978** KC 16 (16, LT)
1979 KC 5 **1980** KC 14 (14, LT) **1981** KC 16 (16, LT) **1982** KC 9 (9, LT) **1983** KC 12 (11, LT) **1984** KC 15 (15, LT) **1985** KC 10 (10, LT) **NFL** 125 (117) [10 yrs]

HERLINE, AL Alan Joseph, K-P, 6′0″/168 lbs; Vanderbilt; B9/16/1964 Monroe, LA **1987** NE 3 (0)

HERMAN, CHUCK Charles Martin, G, 6′3″/250 lbs; Arkansas; B10/7/1958 North Little Rock, AR **1980** Atl 2 (0)

HERMAN, DAVE David Jon, G-T, 6′1″/255 lbs; Michigan State; 1963: NYJ, rnd 27/NYG, rnd 8; B9/3/1941 Bryan, OH **1964** NYJ-A 5 **1965** NYJ-A 14 (14, RG)
1966 NYJ-A 14 (14, RG) **1967** NYJ-A☆14 (14, RG) **1968**†NYJ-A★14 (14, RG) **1969**†NYJ-A★12 (RG) **1970** NYJ 14 (RG) **1971** NYJ 14 (RG) **1972** NYJ 13 (RG)
1973 NYJ 14 (RG) **NFL** 128 (56) [10 yrs]

HERMAN, ED Edward Martin, E, 5′10″/175 lbs; Northwestern; B1/22/1902 Philadelphia, PA, D5/31/1979 Evanston, IL **1925** RI 1 (1)

HERMANN, DICK Richard, LB, 6′2″/215 lbs; Florida State; B7/11/1942 Marianna, FL **1965** Oak-A 14

HERMANN, JOHNNY John William, DB, 6′1″/180 lbs; UCLA; 1956: NYG, rnd 10; B10/17/1933 San Fernando, CA **1956** NYG 2 **1956** Bal 8 **NFL** 10 [1 yr]

YEAR	TEAM	G(GS, POS)	RUSH	YD	AVG(LG)	TD	REC	YD	AVG(LG)	TD	PASS	COMP	PCT	YD	AVG(LG)	TD	INT	SK	YD	QBR	KPR	OTD	PTS	TAY

HERMELING, TERRY Terry Allen, T-G-DE, 6´5˝/255 lbs; Nevada-Reno; B4/25/1946 Santa Maria, CA **1970** Was 5 **1971** Was 8 **1972**†Was 14 (14, LT) **1973**†Was 13 (13, LT) **1975** Was 9 (9, LT) **1976**†Was 12 (12, RG) **1977** Was 13 (12, RG) **1978** Was 16 (16, LT) **1979** Was 16 (16, LT) **1980** Was 14 (11, LT) **NFL** 120 (103) [10 yrs]

HERNANDEZ, JOE Jose M., WR, 6´2˝/180 lbs; Arizona; 1962: Was, rnd 2/Oak, rnd 5; B2/9/1940 Bakersfield, CA

YEAR	TEAM	G(GS, POS)	RUSH	YD	AVG(LG)	TD	REC	YD	AVG(LG)	TD	PASS	COMP	PCT	YD	AVG(LG)	TD	INT	SK	YD	QBR	KPR	OTD	PTS	TAY
1964	Was	14	—	—	—	—	1	18	18.0(18)	0	—	—	—	—	—	—	—	—	—	—	kp	—	0	37

HERNANDEZ, MATT Matthew J., T, 6´6˝/260 lbs; Purdue; 1983: Sea, rnd 8; B10/16/1961 Detroit, MI **1983**†Sea 8 (1) **1984** Min 13 (0) **NFL** 21 (1) [2 yrs]

HERNANDEZ, SCOTT Scott M., NT, 6´0˝/250 lbs; Kent State; B10/17/1959 Kenmore, NY **1987** Buf 2 (2)

HERNDON, DON Donald Eugene, HB, 6´0˝/195 lbs; Tampa; 1958: NYG, rnd 13; B6/4/1936

YEAR	TEAM	G(GS, POS)	RUSH	YD	AVG(LG)	TD	REC	YD	AVG(LG)	TD	PASS	COMP	PCT	YD	AVG(LG)	TD	INT	SK	YD	QBR	KPR	OTD	PTS	TAY
1960	NYT-A	8	—	—	—	—	5	57	11.4(16)	1	—	—	—	—	—	—	—	—	—	—	k	—	6	73

HERNDON, JIMMY James Scott, T, 6´8˝/318 lbs; Houston; 1996: Jax, rnd 5; B8/30/1973 Baytown, TX **1997** ChiB 7 (0) **1998** ChiB 9 (2) **2000** ChiB 10 (2) **2001**†ChiB 16 (0) **2002** Hou 12 (7, rt) **NFL** 54 (11) [5 yrs]

HERNDON, KELLY Kelly Errin, DB, 5´10˝/180 lbs; Toledo; B11/3/1976 Bedford, OH **2002** Den 14 (0) **2003**†Den 15 (11, RCB) **2004**†Den 16 (16, RCB) **2005**†Sea 12 (6, LCB) **NFL** 57 (33) [4 yrs]

HERNDON, STEVE Steven Marshall, G, 6´4˝/292 lbs; Georgia; B5/25/1977 La Grange, GA **2001** Den 5 (3) **2002** Den 15 (9, LG) **2003** Den 2 (0) **2004**†Atl 15 (1) **NFL** 37 (13) [4 yrs]

HEROCK, KEN Kenneth Barry, TE-LB, 6´2˝/230 lbs; West Virginia; B7/16/1941 Munhall, PA

YEAR	TEAM	G(GS, POS)	RUSH	YD	AVG(LG)	TD	REC	YD	AVG(LG)	TD	PASS	COMP	PCT	YD	AVG(LG)	TD	INT	SK	YD	QBR	KPR	OTD	PTS	TAY
1963	Oak-A	14(TE)	—	—	—	—	16	269	16.8(38)	2	—	—	—	—	—	—	—	—	—	—	k	1	18	133
1964	Oak-A	14(TE)	—	—	—	—	23	360	15.7(50)	2	—	—	—	—	—	—	—	—	—	—	—	—	12	190
1965	Oak-A	14(te)	—	—	—	—	18	221	12.3(22)	0	—	—	—	—	—	—	—	—	—	—	—	—	0	111
1967	†Oak-A	12	—	—	—	—	1	-1	-1.0(-1)	0	—	—	—	—	—	—	—	—	—	—	—	—	0	-1
1968	Cin-A	13	—	—	—	—	6	75	12.5(22)	0	—	—	—	—	—	—	—	—	—	—	—	—	0	38
1969	Bos-A	6	—	—	—	—	—	—	—	—	—	—	—	—	—	—	—	—	—	—	—	—	—	—
NFL	6	73	—	—	—	—	64	924	14.4(50)	4	—	—	—	—	—	—	—	—	—	—	k	1	30	470

HERON, FRED Frederick Roger, DT-DE, 6´4˝/260 lbs; San Jose State; 1966: GB, rnd 3; B10/6/1944 Stockton, CA **1966** SL 11 **1967** SL 12 **1968** SL 14 (LDT) **1969** SL 13 (LDT) **1970** SL 14 (LDT) **1971** SL 9 (ldt) **1972** SL 6 (ldt) **NFL** 79 [7 yrs]

HEROSIAN, BRIAN Brian Berge, DB, 6´3˝/200 lbs; Connecticut; B9/14/1950 Worcester, MA **1973** Bal 12

HERREMANS, TODD Todd, T, 6´6˝/321 lbs; Saginaw Valley State; 2005: Phi, rnd 4; B10/13/1982 Grand Rapids, MI **2005** Phi 4 (4)

HERRERA, ANTHONY Anthony, G, 6´2˝/315 lbs; Tennessee; B6/14/1980 Trinidad **2005** Min 10 (6, lg)

HERRERA, EFREN Efren, K, 5´9˝/185 lbs; UCLA; 1974: Det, rnd 7; B7/30/1951 Guadalajara, Mexico **[K]** **1974** Dal 11 **1976**†Dal☆14 **1977**†Dal★14 **1978** Sea 16 **1981** Sea 12 (0) **1982** Buf 7 (0)

YEAR	TEAM	G(GS, POS)	RUSH	YD	AVG(LG)	TD	REC	YD	AVG(LG)	TD	PASS	COMP	PCT	YD	AVG(LG)	TD	INT	SK	YD	QBR	KPR	OTD	PTS	TAY
1979	Sea☆	16	—	—	—	—	1	20	20.0(20)	0	—	—	—	—	—	—	—	—	—	—	KP	—	100	10
1980	Sea	16(0)	—	—	—	—	1	9	9.0(9)	0	—	—	—	—	—	—	—	—	—	—	KP	—	93	5
NFL	8	106	—	—	—	—	2	29	14.5(20)	0	—	—	—	—	—	—	—	—	—	—	KP	—	604	15

HERRIN, HOOT Houston Randolph, C-G, 5´10˝/190 lbs; St. Mary's (CA); B11/24/1904, OK, D4/6/1984 Visalia, CA **1931** Cle 1 (1)

HERRING, GEORGE George W., QB-P, 6´2˝/200 lbs; Southern Mississippi; 1960: Hou, rnd 1; B6/18/1934 Gadsden, AL

YEAR	TEAM	G(GS, POS)	RUSH	YD	AVG(LG)	TD	REC	YD	AVG(LG)	TD	PASS	COMP	PCT	YD	AVG(LG)	TD	INT	SK	YD	QBR	KPR	OTD	PTS	TAY
1960	Den-A	14	—	—	—	—	—	—	—	—	22	9	40.9	137	6.2(21)	0	1	—	—	—	P	—	0	29
1961	Den-A	14(qb)	15	74	4.9(20)	2	—	—	—	—	211	93	44.1	1160	5.5(54)	5	22	—	—	30.0	P	—	12	-181
NFL	2	28	15	74	4.9(20)	2	—	—	—	—	233	102	43.8	1297	5.6(54)	5	23	—	—	29.3	P	—	12	-153

HERRING, HAL Harold Moreland, LB-C, 6´1˝/211 lbs; Auburn; 1949: ChiC, rnd 9; B2/24/1924 Lanett, AL **1949** Buf-A 12 (0) **1950**†Cle 12 (RLB) **1951**†Cle 10 (RLB) **1952**†Cle 12 (RLB) **NFL** 34 [3 yrs]

HERRING, KIM Kimani Masai, DB, 6´0˝/200 lbs; Penn State; 1997: Bal, rnd 2; B9/10/1975 Detroit, MI **1997** Bal 15 (4) **1998** Bal 7 (7, FS) **1999** Bal 16 (16, SS) **2000**†Bal 16 (16, SS) **2001**†SL 16 (15, FS) **2002** SL 16 (16, FS) **2004** Cin 12 (10, SS) **NFL** 98 (84) [7 yrs]

HERRMANN, DON Donald Bruce, WR-FL, 6´2˝/205 lbs; Waynesburg; 1969: NYG, rnd 15; B6/5/1947 Newark, NJ

YEAR	TEAM	G(GS, POS)	RUSH	YD	AVG(LG)	TD	REC	YD	AVG(LG)	TD	PASS	COMP	PCT	YD	AVG(LG)	TD	INT	SK	YD	QBR	KPR	OTD	PTS	TAY
1969	NYG	12(FL)	—	—	—	—	33	423	12.8(62)	5	—	—	—	—	—	—	—	—	—	—	—	—	30	237
1970	NYG	13(WR)	—	—	—	—	24	290	12.1(2)	2	—	—	—	—	—	—	—	—	—	—	—	—	12	155
1971	NYG	9(WR)	—	—	—	—	27	297	11.0(22)	1	—	—	—	—	—	—	—	—	—	—	—	—	6	154
1972	NYG	14(WR)	3	9	3.0(11)	0	28	422	15.1(63)	5	—	—	—	—	—	—	—	—	—	—	—	—	30	245
1973	NYG	14(WR)	—	—	—	—	43	520	12.1(46)	2	—	—	—	—	—	—	—	—	—	—	—	—	12	270
1974	NYG	8	—	—	—	—	10	97	9.7(16)	0	—	—	—	—	—	—	—	—	—	—	—	—	0	49
1975	NO	3	—	—	—	—	3	47	15.7(28)	1	—	—	—	—	—	—	—	—	—	—	—	—	6	29
1976	NO	14(14, WR)	—	—	—	—	34	535	15.7(57)	0	—	—	—	—	—	—	—	—	—	—	—	—	0	268
1977	NO	13(13, WR)	1	-17	-17.0(-17)	0	32	408	12.8(39)	0	—	—	—	—	—	—	—	—	—	—	—	—	0	187
NFL	9	100(27)	4	-8	-2.0(11)	0	234	3039	13.0(63)	16	—	—	—	—	—	—	—	—	—	—	—	—	96	1592

HERRMANN, MARK Mark Donald, QB, 6´4˝/200 lbs; Purdue; 1981: Den, rnd 4; B1/8/1959 Cincinnati, OH

YEAR	TEAM	G(GS, POS)	RUSH	YD	AVG(LG)	TD	REC	YD	AVG(LG)	TD	PASS	COMP	PCT	YD	AVG(LG)	TD	INT	SK	YD	QBR	KPR	OTD	PTS	TAY
1982	Den	2(1)	3	7	2.3(6)	1	—	—	—	—	60	32	53.3	421	7.0(39)	1	4	4	48	—	—	—	6	73
1983	Bal	2(1)	1	0	0.0(0)	0	—	—	—	—	36	18	50.0	256	7.1(35)	0	3	7	62	—	—	—	0	8
1984	Ind	3(2)	—	—	—	—	—	—	—	—	56	29	51.8	352	6.3(74)	1	6	7	65	—	—	—	0	-59
1985	SD	9(4, qb)	18	-8	-0.4(11)	0	—	—	—	—	201	132	**65.7**	1537	7.6(59)	10	10	19	157	—	—	—	0	411
1986	SD	6(1)	2	6	3.0(6)	0	—	—	—	—	97	51	52.6	627	6.5(28)	2	3	5	43	—	—	—	0	210
1987	SD	3(2)	4	-1	-0.3(0)	0	—	—	—	—	57	37	64.9	405	7.1(34)	1	5	3	37	—	—	—	0	7
1988	LARm	6(0)	1	-1	-1.0(-1)	0	—	—	—	—	5	4	80.0	38	7.6(15)	0	0	—	—	—	—	—	0	18
1989	LARm	3(0)	2	-1	-0.5(0)	0	—	—	—	—	5	4	80.0	59	11.8(23)	0	1	3	22	—	—	—	0	-12
1990	Ind	3(0)	—	—	—	—	—	—	—	—	1	1	100.0	6	6.0(6)	0	0	—	—	—	—	—	0	3
1991	Ind	2(0)	1	-1	-1.0(-1)	0	—	—	—	—	19	11	57.9	137	7.2(26)	0	3	—	—	—	—	—	0	-53
1992	Ind	1(1)	3	-2	-0.7(0)	0	—	—	—	—	24	15	62.5	177	7.4(27)	1	1	1	5	—	—	—	0	52
NFL	11	40(12)	35	-1	-0.0(11)	1	—	—	—	—	561	334	59.5	4015	7.2(74)	16	36	49	439	64.3	—	—	6	657

HERROD, JEFF Jeff Sylvester, LB, 6´0˝/249 lbs; Mississippi; 1988: Ind, rnd 9; B7/29/1966 Birmingham, AL **1988** Ind 16 (0) **1989** Ind 15 (14, LILB) **1990** Ind 13 (13, LILB) **1991** Ind 14 (14, RILB) **1992** Ind 16 (16, RILB) **1993** Ind 14 (14, RLB) **1994** Ind 15 (15, MLB) **1995**†Ind 16 (16, MLB) **1996**†Ind 14 (14, MLB) **1997** Phi 10 (2) **1998** Ind 10 (7, mlb) **NFL** 153 (125) [11 yrs]

HERRON, ANTHONY Anthony, DE, 6´3˝/280 lbs; Iowa; B9/24/1979 Bollingbrook, IL **2001** Det 1 (0)

HERRON, BRUCE Bruce Wayne, LB, 6´2˝/220 lbs; New Mexico; 1977: Mia, rnd 7; B4/14/1954 Victoria, TX **1978** ChiB 15 (1) **1979**†ChiB 16 **1980** ChiB 15 (0) **1981** ChiB 16 (0) **1982** ChiB 9 (0) **NFL** 71 (1) [5 yrs]

HERRON, MACK Mack Willie, RB, 5´5˝/170 lbs; Kansas State; 1970: Atl, rnd 6; B7/24/1948 Biloxi, MS **[R]**

YEAR	TEAM	G(GS, POS)	RUSH	YD	AVG(LG)	TD	REC	YD	AVG(LG)	TD	PASS	COMP	PCT	YD	AVG(LG)	TD	INT	SK	YD	QBR	KPR	OTD	PTS	TAY
1973	NE	14(1)	61	200	3.3(17)	2	18	265	14.7(29)	1	—	—	—	—	—	—	—	—	—	—	kp	1	24	992
1974	NE	14(14, RB)	231	824	3.6(28)	7	38	474	12.5(48)	5	—	—	—	—	—	—	—	—	—	—	kp	—	72	1707
1975	NE	7(5, rb)	61	274	4.5(53)	0	5	50	10.0(19)	0	—	—	—	—	—	—	—	—	—	—	kp	—	0	373
1975	Atl	4	1	0	0.0(0)	0	—	—	—	—	—	—	—	—	—	—	—	—	—	—	kp	—	0	68
NFL	3	39(20)	354	1298	3.7(53)	9	61	789	12.9(48)	6	—	—	—	—	—	—	—	—	—	—	kp	1	96	3140

HERRON, NOAH Noah Scott, RB, 5´11˝/224 lbs; Northwestern; 2005: Pit, rnd 7; B4/3/1982 Mattawan, MI

YEAR	TEAM	G(GS, POS)	RUSH	YD	AVG(LG)	TD	REC	YD	AVG(LG)	TD	PASS	COMP	PCT	YD	AVG(LG)	TD	INT	SK	YD	QBR	KPR	OTD	PTS	TAY
2005	Pit	2(0)	3	2	0.7(1)	0	—	—	—	—	—	—	—	—	—	—	—	—	—	—	—	—	0	2
2005	GB	5(0)	45	121	2.7(17)	2	—	—	—	—	—	—	—	—	—	—	—	—	—	—	—	—	12	141
NFL	1	7(0)	48	123	2.6(17)	2	—	—	—	—	—	—	—	—	—	—	—	—	—	—	—	—	12	143

HERRON, PAT James Patrick, E, 5´7˝/170 lbs; Pittsburgh; B8/12/1894 New Kensington, PA, D12/21/1967 Monongahela, PA **1920** Cle 1 (1)

YEAR	TEAM	G (GS, POS)	RUSH	YD	AVG(LG)	TD	REC	YD	AVG(LG)	TD	PASS	COMP	PCT	YD	AVG(LG)	TD	INT	SK	YD	QBR	KPR	OTD	PTS	TAY

HERSHEY, KIRK   Kirk, E, 6'2"/215 lbs; Carroll (WI); Cornell; 1941: Cle, rnd 17; B7/7/1918 Philadelphia, PA, D1/23/1979 North Palm Beach, FL   **1941** Cle 2 (0)

| 1941 | Phi | 6(0) | — | — | — | — | 1 | 11 | 11.0(11) | 0 | — | — | — | — | — | — | — | — | — | — | — | — | 0 | 6 |
| NFL | 1 | 8(0) | — | — | — | — | 1 | 11 | 11.0(11) | 0 | — | — | — | — | — | — | — | — | — | — | — | — | 0 | 6 |

HERTEL, ROB   Robert Alden, QB, 6'2"/195 lbs; USC; 1978: Cin, rnd 5; B2/21/1955 Montebello, CA

| 1978 | Cin | 3 | 1 | 0 | 0.0(0) | 0 | — | — | — | — | 4 | 1 | 25.0 | 9 | 2.3(9) | 0 | 0 | — | — | — | — | — | 0 | 5 |

HERTWIG, CRAIG   John Craig, T, 6'8"/270 lbs; Georgia; 1975: Det, rnd 4; B1/15/1952 Columbus, GA   **1975** Det 9 (1)   **1976** Det 14 (9, LT)   **1977** Det 14 (14, RT)   **NFL** 37 (24) [3 yrs]

HERTZ, FRANK   Frank W., E, 5'10"/185 lbs; Carroll (WI); B11/6/1902, D7/20/1963   **1926** Mil 8 (1)

HESS, WALLY   Walter Bernard, B, 5'9"/177 lbs; Indiana; B10/28/1894 Hammond, IN, D8/1963 Hammond, IN **[C]**   **1920** Ham 2 (1)   **1921** Ham 4 (4, TB)   **1922** Ham 6 (4, BB)   **1923** Ham 7 (7, TB)   **1924** Ham 4 (4, BB)   **1925** Ham 5 (3, BB), 6   **NFL** 28 (23) [6 yrs]

HESSE, JON   Jonathan Andrew, LB, 6'4"/250 lbs; Nebraska; 1997: Jax, rnd 7; B6/6/1973 Lincoln, NE   **1998** SL 5 (0)

HESTER, JESSIE   Jessie Lee, WR, 5'11"/175 lbs; Florida State; 1985: LARd, rnd 1; B1/21/1963 Belle Glade, FL

1985	†LARd	16(16, WR)	1	13	13.0(13)	1	32	665	20.8(59)	4	—	—	—	—	—	—	—	—	—	—	—	—	30	376
1986	LARd	13(1)	—	—	—	—	23	632	27.5(81)	6	—	—	—	—	—	—	—	—	—	—	—	—	36	346
1987	LARd	10(0)	—	—	—	—	1	30	30.0(30)	0	—	—	—	—	—	—	—	—	—	—	—	—	0	15
1988	Atl	16(3)	1	3	3.0(3)	0	12	176	14.7(41)	0	—	—	—	—	—	—	—	—	—	—	—	—	0	91
1990	Ind	16(14, WR)	4	9	2.3(10)	0	54	924	17.1(64)	6	—	—	—	—	—	—	—	—	—	—	—	—	36	501
1991	Ind	16(16, WR)	—	—	—	—	60	753	12.6(49)	5	—	—	—	—	—	—	—	—	—	—	—	—	30	402
1992	Ind	16(16, WR)	—	—	—	—	52	792	15.2(81)	1	—	—	—	—	—	—	—	—	—	—	—	—	6	401
1993	Ind	16(16, WR)	—	—	—	—	64	835	13.0(58)	1	—	—	—	—	—	—	—	—	—	—	—	—	6	423
1994	LARm	16(15, WR)	2	28	14.0(24)	0	45	644	14.3(41)	3	—	—	—	—	—	—	—	—	—	—	—	—	18	365
1995	SL	12(7, WR)	—	—	—	—	30	399	13.3(38)	1	—	—	—	—	—	—	—	—	—	—	—	—	18	215
NFL	10	147(104)	8	53	6.6(24)	1	373	5850	15.7(81)	29	—	—	—	—	—	—	—	—	—	—	—	—	180	3133

HESTER, JIMMY   James Conway, TE, 6'4"/238 lbs; North Dakota; 1967: NO, rnd 14; B12/13/1944 Rock Island, IL, D11/14/2002 Davenport, IA

1967	NO	5	—	—	—	—	2	10	5.0(7)	0	—	—	—	—	—	—	—	—	—	—	—	—	0	5
1968	NO	14(te)	—	—	—	—	17	300	17.6(51)	2	—	—	—	—	—	—	—	—	—	—	—	—	12	160
1969	NO	10	—	—	—	—	3	44	14.7(22)	1	—	—	—	—	—	—	—	—	—	—	k	—	6	16
1970	ChiB	5	—	—	—	—	7	54	7.7(16)	0	—	—	—	—	—	—	—	—	—	—	—	—	0	27
NFL	4	34	—	—	—	—	29	408	14.1(51)	3	—	—	—	—	—	—	—	—	—	—	k	—	18	208

HESTER, RAY   Raymond William, LB, 6'2"/215 lbs; Tulane; B3/31/1949 New Orleans, LA, D3/15/1977 Metairie, LA   **1971** NO 14 (llb)   **1972** NO 7   **1973** NO 6   **NFL** 27 [3 yrs]

HESTER, RON   Ronald, LB, 6'2"/222 lbs; Florida State; 1982: Mia, rnd 6; B5/26/1959 Atlanta, GA   **1982**†Mia 9 (0)

HETHERINGTON, CHRIS   Christopher Raymond, FB, 6'3"/245 lbs; Yale; B11/27/1972 North Branford, CT

1996	†Ind	6(0)	—	—	—	—	—	—	—	—	—	—	—	—	—	—	—	—	—	—	k	—	0	1
1997	Ind	16(0)	—	—	—	—	—	—	—	—	—	—	—	—	—	—	—	—	—	—	k	—	0	-7
1998	Ind	14(1)	—	—	—	—	—	—	—	—	—	—	—	—	—	—	—	—	—	—	k	—	0	-4
1999	Car	14(0)	2	7	3.5(5)	0	—	—	—	—	—	—	—	—	—	—	—	—	—	—	k	—	0	8
2000	Car	16(5, fb)	23	65	2.8(14)	2	14	116	8.3(19)	1	—	—	—	—	—	—	—	—	—	—	k	—	18	139
2001	Car	16(1)	5	12	2.4(8)	0	23	124	5.4(15)	0	—	—	—	—	—	—	—	—	—	—	k	—	0	45
2002	SL	6(4)	1	0	0.0(0)	0	1	2	2.0(2)	0	—	—	—	—	—	—	—	—	—	—	—	—	0	1
2003	Oak	14(1)	—	—	—	—	2	23	11.5(17)	0	—	—	—	—	—	—	—	—	—	—	—	—	0	12
2004	Oak	5(2)	1	4	4.0(4)	0	3	28	9.3(14)	0	—	—	—	—	—	—	—	—	—	—	k	—	0	26
2005	SF	16(6, fb)	1	3	3.0(3)	0	5	26	5.2(11)	0	—	—	—	—	—	—	—	—	—	—	k	—	0	16
NFL	10	123(20)	33	91	2.8(14)	2	48	319	6.6(19)	1	—	—	—	—	—	—	—	—	—	—	k	—	18	237

HETTEMA, DAVE   David Gary, T, 6'5"/250 lbs; New Mexico; 1965: SF, rnd 16/Bos, rnd R10; B11/7/1942 Pasadena, CA   **1967** SF 7   **1970** Atl 6   **NFL** 13 [2 yrs]

HEWITT, BILL   William Ernest 'The Off-Side Kid', E-DE, 5'9"/190 lbs; Michigan; B10/8/1909 Bay City, MI, D1/14/1947 Sellersville, PA; HOF 1971

1932	ChiB	13(12, RE)	1	29	29.0(29)	1	7	77	11.0	0	—	—	—	—	—	—	—	—	—	—	—	—	6	78
1933	†ChiB☆	13(13, LE)	2	1	0.5(1)	0	14	273	19.5(29)	2	7	4	57.1	59	8.4(34)	3	0	—	—	—	—	1	18	192
1934	†ChiB☆	13(12, LE)	1	14	14.0(14)	0	11	151	13.7	5	2	1	50.0	4	2.0(4)	0	0	—	—	—	—	—	30	117
1935	ChiB	12(12, LE)	1	0	0.0	0	5	80	16.0	1	0	0	0.0	0	0.0	0	0	—	—	—	—	—	0	40
1936	ChiB☆	12(12, LE)	2	-9	-4.5	0	15	358	23.9(45)	6	—	—	—	—	—	—	—	—	—	—	—	1	42	200
1937	Phi☆	11(11, LE)	—	—	—	—	16	197	12.3	5	—	—	—	—	—	—	—	—	—	—	—	—	30	124
1938	Phi☆	11(11, LE)	—	—	—	—	18	237	13.2	4	—	—	—	—	—	—	—	—	—	—	—	—	24	139
1939	Phi	10(2)	1	1	1.0(1)	0	15	243	16.2	1	—	—	—	—	—	—	—	—	—	—	—	—	6	128
1943	P-P	6(4)	—	—	—	—	2	22	11.0(11)	0	—	—	—	—	—	—	—	—	—	—	—	—	0	11
NFL	9	101(89)	8	36	4.5(29)	1	103	1638	15.9(45)	23	10	5	50.0	63	6.3(34)	3	0	—	—	—	—	2	156	1027

HEWITT, CHRIS   Christopher Horace, DB, 6'0"/210 lbs; Cincinnati; B7/22/1974 Kingston, Jamaica   **1997** NO 11 (2)   **1998** NO 16 (2)   **1999** NO 12 (0)   **NFL** 39 (4) [3 yrs]

HEWKO, BOB   Robert Todd, QB, 6'3"/195 lbs; Florida; B6/8/1960 Abington, PA   **1983** TB 2 (0)

HEWS, BOB   Robert Ellsworth, T-DE, 6'5"/240 lbs; Princeton; 1970: KC, rnd 6; B12/30/1947 Portland, ME   **1971** Buf 2

HEYWARD, CRAIG   Craig William 'Ironhead', RB, 5'11"/260 lbs; Pittsburgh; 1988: NO, rnd 1; B9/26/1966 Passaic, NJ

1988	NO	11(8, fb)	74	355	4.8(73)	1	13	105	8.1(18)	0	—	—	—	—	—	—	—	—	—	—	—	—	6	418
1989	NO	16(6, fb)	49	183	3.7(15)	1	13	69	5.3(12)	0	—	—	—	—	—	—	—	—	—	—	—	—	6	228
1990	†NO	16(15, FB)	129	599	4.6(47)	4	18	121	6.7(12)	0	1	0	0.0	0	0.0	0	1	—	—	—	k	—	24	657
1991	NO	7(4)	76	260	3.4(15)	4	4	34	8.5(22)	1	1	1	100.0	44	44.0(44)	0	0	—	—	—	—	—	30	344
1992	†NO	16(13, FB)	104	416	4.0(23)	3	19	159	8.4(21)	0	—	—	—	—	—	—	—	—	—	—	k	—	18	525
1993	ChiB	16(14, FB)	68	206	3.0(11)	0	16	132	8.3(20)	0	—	—	—	—	—	—	—	—	—	—	k	—	0	269
1994	Atl	16(11, RB)	183	779	4.3(17)	7	32	335	10.5(34)	1	—	—	—	—	—	—	—	—	—	—	k	—	48	1014
1995	†Atl◇	16(16, RB)	236	1083	4.6(31)	6	37	350	9.5(25)	2	—	—	—	—	—	—	—	—	—	—	—	—	48	1328
1996	Atl	15(5, rb)	72	321	4.5(34)	3	16	168	10.5(25)	0	—	—	—	—	—	—	—	—	—	—	kp	—	18	433
1997	SL	16(12, FB)	34	84	2.5(8)	1	8	77	9.6(25)	0	—	—	—	—	—	—	—	—	—	—	—	—	6	133
1998	Ind	4(3)	6	15	2.5(8)	0	1	9	9.0(9)	0	—	—	—	—	—	—	—	—	—	—	—	—	0	20
NFL	11	149(107)	1031	4301	4.2(73)	30	177	1559	8.8(34)	4	2	1	50.0	44	22.0(44)	0	1	—	—	—	kp	—	204	5366

HEYWOOD, RALPH   Ralph Alvin, E-DE, 6'2"/203 lbs; USC; 1944: Det, rnd 3; B9/11/1921 Los Angeles, CA

1946	ChiR-A	14(8, LE)	—	—	—	—	20	287	14.4	4	—	—	—	—	—	—	—	—	—	—	P	—	24	164
1947	Det	12(1)	—	—	—	—	13	198	15.2(39)	2	—	—	—	—	—	—	—	—	—	—	—	—	12	109
1948	Det	2(0)	—	—	—	—	3	31	10.3(0)	0	—	—	—	—	—	—	—	—	—	—	P	—	0	16
1948	Bos	8(6, RE)	1	11	11.0(11)	0	11	177	16.1(42)	1	—	—	—	—	—	—	—	—	—	—	Pk	2	18	98
1949	NYB	12(2)	3	-6	-2.0(2)	0	37	499	13.5(61)	3	—	—	—	—	—	—	—	—	—	—	P	1	24	259
NFL	3	34(9)	4	5	1.3(11)	0	64	905	14.1(61)	6	—	—	—	—	—	—	—	—	—	—	Pk	3	54	481

HIBBS, JESSE   Jesse John, T, 6'0"/195 lbs; USC; B1/11/1906 Normal, IL, D2/4/1985 Ojai, CA   **1931** ChiB 9 (4)

HIBLER, MIKE   Michael Keith, LB, 6'1"/235 lbs; Stanford; 1967: Oak, rnd 5; B1/29/1946 Mountain View, CA   **1968** Cin-A 11

HICKERSON, GENE   Robert Eugene, G, 6'3"/248 lbs; Mississippi; 1957: Cle, rnd 7; B2/15/1935 Trenton, NJ   **1958**†Cle 12 (rg)   **1959** Cle 12 (RG)   **1960** Cle 12 (RG)   **1962** Cle 12 (rg)   **1963** Cle 14 (RG)   **1964**†Cle☆14 (RG)   **1965** Cle★14 (RG)   **1966** Cle★14 (RG)   **1967**†Cle★14 (RG)   **1968**†Cle★14 (RG)   **1969**†Cle★14 (RG)   **1970** Cle★14 (RG)   **1971**†Cle 14 (RG)   **1972** Cle 14 (LG)   **1973** Cle 14 (LG)   **NFL** 202 [15 yrs]

HICKEY, BO   Thomas Henry, RB, 5'11"/230 lbs; Maryland; 1967: SL, rnd 14; B10/7/1945 Stamford, CT

| 1967 | Den-A | 12(FB) | 73 | 263 | 3.6(20) | 4 | 7 | 36 | 5.1(22) | 1 | — | — | — | — | — | — | — | — | — | — | — | — | 30 | 326 |

YEAR	TEAM	G(GS, POS)	RUSH	YD	AVG(LG)	TD	REC	YD	AVG(LG)	TD	PASS COMP	PCT	YD	AVG(LG)	TD	INT	SK	YD	QBR	KPR	OTD	PTS	TAY

HICKEY, RED Howard Wayne, E, 6´2˝/204 lbs; Arkansas; 1941: Phi, rnd 6; B2/14/1917 Clarksville, AR, D3/30/2006 Santa Cruz, CA [C]

1941	Pit	1(0)	—	—	—	—	—	—	—	—	—	—	—	—	—	—	—	—	—	—	—	—	—
1941	Cle	9(3)	7	7	1.0(7)	0	21	294	14.0(39)	4	—	—	—	—	—	—	—	—	—	—	—	24	174
1945	†Cle	8(2)	—	—	—	—	4	76	19.0(33)	0	—	—	—	—	—	—	—	—	—	—	—	0	38
1946	LARm	8(0)	—	—	—	—	8	213	26.6(60)	3	—	—	—	—	—	—	—	—	—	—	—	18	121
1947	LARm	11(4)	—	—	—	—	12	196	16.3(42)	2	—	—	—	—	—	—	—	—	—	k	—	12	108
1948	LARm	12(0)	—	—	—	—	30	509	17.0(69)	7	—	—	—	—	—	—	—	—	—	—	—	42	290
NFL	5	49(9)	7	7	1.0(7)	0	75	1288	17.2(69)	16	—	—	—	—	—	—	—	—	—	k	—	96	730

HICKL, RAY Raymond William, LB, 6´2˝/220 lbs; Texas A&M-Kingsville; 1969: NYG, rnd 9; B12/24/1946 El Maton, TX **1969** NYG 9 **1970** NYG 1 **NFL** 10 [2 yrs]

HICKMAN, DALLAS Dallas Mark, DE-LB, 6´6˝/238 lbs; California; 1975: Was, rnd 9; B2/16/1952 Martinez, CA **1976**†Was 14 **1977** Was 14 **1978** Was 16 **1979** Was 16
1980 Was 16 (0) **1981** Bal 5 (0) **NFL** 91 [6 yrs]

HICKMAN, DONNIE Donald J., G, 6´2˝/261 lbs; USC; 1977: LA, rnd 5; B6/11/1955 Flagstaff, AZ **1978** Was 3 **1978** Det 7 **NFL** 10 [1 yr]

HICKMAN, HERMAN Herman Michael, G, 5´10˝/246 lbs; Tennessee; B10/1/1911 Johnson City, TN, D4/25/1958 Washington, DC [K] **1932** Bkn 3 (2) **1933** Bkn☆10 (9, RG)
1934 Bkn☆11 (10, RG) **NFL** 24 (21) [3 yrs]

HICKMAN, KEVIN Kevin Joseph, TE, 6´4˝/258 lbs; Navy; 1995: Det, rnd 6; B8/20/1971 Cherry Hill, NJ **1995** Det 6 (0) **1997** Det 4 (0) **1998** Det 3 (0) **NFL** 13 (0) [3 yrs]

HICKMAN, LARRY Lawrence Dean, FB, 6´2˝/227 lbs; Baylor; 1959: LA, rnd 3; B10/9/1935 Spring Hill, TX

1959	ChiC	12	5	18	3.6(5)	0	1	11	11.0(11)	0	—	—	—	—	—	—	—	—	—	—	—	0	24
1960	GB	12	7	22	3.1(4)	0	—	—	—	—	—	—	—	—	—	—	—	—	—	k	—	0	31
NFL	2	24	12	40	3.3(5)	0	1	11	11.0(11)	0	—	—	—	—	—	—	—	—	—	k	—	0	55

HICKS, ARTIS Artis, G-T, 6´4˝/303 lbs; Memphis; B11/28/1978 Jackson, TN **2003**†Phi 10 (4) **2004**†Phi 14 (13, LG) **2005** Phi 14 (14, LG) **NFL** 38 (31) [3 yrs]

HICKS, BRANDON Brandon Elliott George, DT, 6´0˝/282 lbs; Bowling Green State; B11/17/1977 Shields, IL **2003** Ind 4 (0)

HICKS, BRYAN Mark Bryan, DB, 6´0˝/192 lbs; McNeese State; 1980: Cin, rnd 5; B1/24/1957 Lake Charles, LA **1980** Cin 16 (6, fs) **1981**†Cin 16 (12, FS) **1982**†Cin 7 (7, FS)
NFL 39 (25) [3 yrs]

HICKS, CLIFF Clifford Wendell, DB, 5´9˝/190 lbs; Oregon; 1987: LARm, rnd 3; B8/18/1964 San Diego, CA [R] **1987** LARm 11 (0) **1988**†LARm 7 (0) **1989** LARm 15 (6, rcb)
1990 LARm 1 (0) **1990**†Buf 4 (0) **1991**†Buf 16 (0) **1992**†Buf 12 (2) **1993** NYJ 10 (0) **1994** NYJ 16 (0) **1995** Den 6 (0) **NFL** 98 (8) [9 yrs]

HICKS, DWIGHT Dwight, DB, 6´1˝/190 lbs; Michigan; 1978: Det, rnd 6; B4/5/1956 Mount Holly, NJ [I] **1979** SF 8 (4) **1980** SF 16 (16, FS) **1981**†SF★16 (16, FS)
1982 SF◇9 (9, FS) **1983**†SF★15 (15, FS) **1984**†SF★16 (16, FS) **1985**†SF 16 (16, FS/lcb) **1986** Ind 9 (6, FS) **NFL** 105 (98) [8 yrs]

HICKS, DWONE Kenneth Dwone, RB, 5´10˝/222 lbs; Middle Tennessee State; B4/25/1981 Huntsville, AL **2003** Ten 3 (0)

HICKS, EDDIE Edward James, RB, 6´2˝/210 lbs; East Carolina; 1979: NYG, rnd 6; B7/26/1955 Henderson, NC **1979** NYG 14

| 1980 | NYG | 3(1) | 19 | 50 | 2.6(9) | 0 | 4 | 4 | 4.0(4) | 0 | — | — | — | — | — | — | — | — | — | — | — | 0 | 52 |
| NFL | 2 | 17(1) | 19 | 50 | 2.6(9) | 0 | 4 | 4 | 4.0(4) | 0 | — | — | — | — | — | — | — | — | — | k | — | 0 | 58 |

HICKS, ERIC Eric David, DE, 6´6˝/280 lbs; Maryland; B6/17/1976 Erie, PA **1998** KC 3 (0) **1999** KC 16 (16, LDE) **2000** KC 13 (11, LDE) **2001** KC 16 (16, LDE)
2002 KC 16 (15, LDE) **2003**†KC 16 (16, LDE) **2004** KC 16 (16, LDE) **2005** KC 16 (14, LDE) **NFL** 112 (104) [8 yrs]

HICKS, IVAN Ivan Lemuel, DB, 6´2˝/185 lbs; Michigan; B6/30/1963 Camden, NJ **1987** Det 1 (0)

HICKS, JOHN John Charles, G, 6´2˝/258 lbs; Ohio State; 1974: NYG, rnd 1; B3/21/1951 Cleveland, OH **1974** NYG 14 (14, RG) **1976** NYG 14 (14, RG) **1977** NYG 10 (RG)

| 1975 | NYG | 14(14, RG) | — | — | — | — | 1 | 5 | 5.0(5) | 0 | — | — | — | — | — | — | — | — | — | — | — | 0 | 3 |
| NFL | 4 | 52(42) | — | — | — | — | 1 | 5 | 5.0(5) | 0 | — | — | — | — | — | — | — | — | — | — | — | 0 | 3 |

HICKS, KERRY Kerry Dale, DE, 6´6˝/283 lbs; Colorado; 1996: Car, rnd 7; B12/29/1972 Bountiful, UT **1997** KC 2 (0)

HICKS, MARK Mark Anthony, LB, 6´2˝/225 lbs; Arizona State; B11/7/1960 Los Angeles, CA **1983**†Sea 10 (1) **1987** Det 1 (0) **NFL** 11 (1) [2 yrs]

HICKS, MAURICE Maurice, RB, 5´11˝/200 lbs; North Carolina A&T; B7/22/1978 Emporia, VA

2004	SF	9(2)	96	362	3.8(35)	2	16	154	9.6(19)	0	—	—	—	—	—	—	—	—	—	k	—	12	617
2005	SF	14(3)	59	308	5.2(73)	3	12	47	3.9(11)	0	—	—	—	—	—	—	—	—	—	k	—	18	541
NFL	2	23(5)	155	670	4.3(73)	5	28	201	7.2(19)	0	—	—	—	—	—	—	—	—	—	k	—	30	1158

HICKS, MAX Max, E, /175 lbs; Geneva; B7/1/1894, deceased [C] **1920** Ham 1 (0) **1921** Ham 1 (0) **NFL** 2 (0) [2 yrs]

HICKS, MICHAEL Michael, RB, 6´0˝/194 lbs; South Carolina State; 1996: Chi, rnd 7; B2/1/1973 Barnesville, GA

1996	ChiB	4(0)	27	92	3.4(23)	0	1	-1	-1.0(-5)	0	—	—	—	—	—	—	—	—	—	—	—	0	92
1997	ChiB	3(0)	4	14	3.5(8)	0	—	—	—	—	—	—	—	—	—	—	—	—	—	—	—	0	14
NFL	2	7(0)	31	106	3.4(23)	0	1	-1	-1.0(-5)	0	—	—	—	—	—	—	—	—	—	—	—	0	106

HICKS, R.W. Richard Winslow, C, 6´4˝/250 lbs; Southwestern (TX); Humboldt State; B1/4/1951 Cleveland, OH **1975** Det 14

HICKS, ROBERT Robert Otis, T, 6´7˝/338 lbs; Mississippi State; 1998: Buf, rnd 3; B11/17/1974 Atlanta, GA **1998**†Buf 9 (2) **2000** Buf 14 (7, rt)

| 1999 | †Buf | 14(14, RT) | 1 | -2 | -2.0(-2) | 0 | 1 | -6 | -6.0(-6) | 0 | — | — | — | — | — | — | — | — | — | — | — | 0 | -5 |
| NFL | 3 | 37(23) | 1 | -2 | -2.0(-2) | 0 | 1 | -6 | -6.0(-6) | 0 | — | — | — | — | — | — | — | — | — | — | — | 0 | -5 |

HICKS, SKIP Brian LaVell, RB, 6´0˝/230 lbs; UCLA; 1998: Was, rnd 3; B10/13/1974 Corsicana, TX

1998	Was	9(5, rb)	122	433	3.5(28)	8	4	23	5.8(9)	0	—	—	—	—	—	—	—	—	—	—	—	48	525
1999	†Was	10(2)	78	257	3.3(24)	3	8	72	9.0(25)	0	—	—	—	—	—	—	—	—	—	—	—	18	323
2000	Was	10(1)	29	78	2.7(12)	1	5	43	8.6(25)	0	—	—	—	—	—	—	—	—	—	k	—	6	112
2001	Ten	9(0)	56	341	6.1(51)	1	5	22	4.4(9)	0	—	—	—	—	—	—	—	—	—	—	—	6	362
NFL	4	38(8)	285	1109	3.9(51)	13	22	160	7.3(25)	0	—	—	—	—	—	—	—	—	—	k	—	78	1321

HICKS, SYLVESTER Sylvester, DE, 6´4˝/251 lbs; Tennessee State; 1978: KC, rnd 2; B4/2/1955 Jackson, TN **1978** KC 16 (RDE) **1979** KC 16 (13, RDE) **1980** KC 10 (0)
1981 KC 1 (0) **NFL** 43 (13) [4 yrs]

HICKS, TOM Thomas Logan, LB, 6´4˝/235 lbs; Illinois; 1975: Chi, rnd 6; B12/18/1952 Chicago, IL **1976** ChiB 14 **1977**†ChiB 12 (5, MLB) **1978** ChiB 9 (9, MLB)
1979†ChiB 15 (MLB) **1980** ChiB 14 (14, MLB) **NFL** 64 (28) [5 yrs]

HICKS, VICTOR Victor Lonell, TE, 6´3˝/250 lbs; Oklahoma; 1979: LA, rnd 5; B1/19/1957 Lubbock, TX

| 1980 | †LARm | 16(14, TE) | 1 | 19 | 19.0(19) | 0 | 23 | 318 | 13.8(32) | 3 | — | — | — | — | — | — | — | — | — | — | — | 18 | 193 |

HICKS, W.K. William Kenzie, DB, 6´1˝/195 lbs; Texas Southern; B7/14/1942 Texarkana, AR [I] **1964** Hou-A 14 (LS) **1965** Hou-A☆14 (RCB) **1966** Hou-A◇14 (RCB)
1967†Hou-A 14 (RCB) **1968** Hou-A 14 (RS) **1969**†Hou-A 14 (RS) **1970** NYJ 14 (FS) **1971** NYJ 13 (FS) **1972** NYJ 14 **NFL** 125 [9 yrs]

HIEMSTRA, ED Edward Paul, G, 6´0˝/200 lbs; Sterling; B3/8/1919 Columbus, MT **1942** NYG 11 (0)

HIGDON, ALEX Alexander, TE, 6´5˝/247 lbs; Ohio State; 1988: Atl, rnd 3; B9/9/1966 Cincinnati, OH

| 1988 | Atl | 3(0) | — | — | — | — | 3 | 60 | 20.0(34) | 2 | — | — | — | — | — | — | — | — | — | — | — | 12 | 40 |

HIGGINS, AUSTIN Austin George, C-E, 5´9˝/168 lbs; none; B11/29/1897 Louisville, KY, D3/3/1976 Kingsley, KY [C] **1921** Lou 2 (2, C) **1922** Lou 4 (4, C) **1923** Lou 1 (1)
NFL 7 (7) [3 yrs]

HIGGINS, BOB Robert Arlington, E, 5´10˝/195 lbs; Penn State; B12/24/1893 Corning, NY, D6/6/1969 State College, PA [K] **1920** Can 3 (3, LE) **1921** Can 9 (9, RE), 14
NFL 12 (12) [2 yrs]

HIGGINS, JIM James Benton, T-G, 6´1˝/250 lbs; Xavier (OH); 1964: Cle, rnd 19; B1/20/1942 Cincinnati, OH, deceased **1966** Mia-A 7

HIGGINS, JIM James Benton, G-LB, 6´1˝/210 lbs; Trinity (TX); B1/10/1920 Maypearl, TX, D6/6/1991 Beaumont, TX **1941** ChiC 4 (1)

HIGGINS, LUKE Luke Martin, G, 6´0˝/210 lbs; Notre Dame; 1945: Cle, rnd 23; B5/3/1921 Edgewater, NJ, D10/11/1991 **1947** Bal-A 11 (0)

HIGGINS, TOM Thomas Joseph John, T-G-DT, 6´2˝/230 lbs; North Carolina; 1953: ChiC, rnd 6; B2/26/1930 Newark, NJ **1953** ChiC 12 (LT) **1954** Phi 5 **1955** Phi 12
NFL 29 [3 yrs]

HIGGINS, TOM Thomas Joseph John, LB, 6´2˝/235 lbs; North Carolina State; B7/13/1954 Newark, NJ **1979** Buf 16

YEAR	TEAM	G (GS, POS)	RUSH	YD	AVG(LG)	TD	REC	YD	AVG(LG)	TD	PASS	COMP	PCT	YD	AVG(LG)	TD	INT	SK	YD	QBR	KPR	OTD	PTS	TAY

HIGGS, MARK Mark Deyon, RB, 5´7˝/199 lbs; Kentucky; 1988: Dal, rnd 8; B4/11/1966 Chicago, IL

1988	Dal	5(0)	—	—	—	—	—	—	—	—	—	—	—	—	—	—	—	—	—	—	k	—	0	1
1989	†Phi	15(1)	49	184	3.8(13)	0	3	9	3.0(8)	0	—	—	—	—	—	—	—	—	—	—	k	—	0	242
1990	Mia	12(0)	10	67	6.7(27)	0	—	—	—	—	—	—	—	—	—	—	—	—	—	—	k	1	6	127
1991	Mia	14(10, RB)	231	905	3.9(24)	4	11	80	7.3(13)	0	—	—	—	—	—	—	—	—	—	—	—	—	24	985
1992	Mia	16(15, RB)	256	915	3.6(23)	7	16	142	8.9(21)	0	—	—	—	—	—	—	—	—	—	—	—	—	42	1056
1993	Mia	16(8, RB)	186	693	3.7(31)	3	10	72	7.2(15)	0	—	—	—	—	—	—	—	—	—	—	—	—	18	759
1994	Mia	5(1)	19	68	3.6(21)	0	—	—	—	—	—	—	—	—	—	—	—	—	—	—	—	—	0	68
1994	Arz	6(0)	43	127	3.0(16)	0	—	—	—	—	—	—	—	—	—	—	—	—	—	—	k	—	0	122
1995	Arz	1(0)	—	—	—	—	—	—	—	—	—	—	—	—	—	—	—	—	—	—	k	—	0	-4
NFL	8	90(35)	794	2959	3.7(31)	14	40	303	7.6(21)	0	—	—	—	—	—	—	—	—	—	—	k	1	90	3356

HIGH, LENNY Leonard L., E, 5´11˝/195 lbs; Eastern Illinois; B2/17/1895, D11/16/1975 La Habra, CA **1920** Dec 1 (0)

HIGHSMITH, ALONZO Alonzo Walter, RB, 6´1˝/234 lbs; Miami (FL); 1987: Hou, rnd 1; B2/26/1965 Bartow, FL

1987	†Hou	8(3)	29	106	3.7(25)	1	4	55	13.8(33)	1	—	—	—	—	—	—	—	—	—	—	—	—	12	149
1988	†Hou	16(16, FB)	94	466	5.0(42)	2	12	131	10.9(28)	0	—	—	—	—	—	—	—	—	—	—	—	—	12	552
1989	†Hou	16(16, FB)	128	531	4.1(25)	4	18	201	11.2(32)	2	—	—	—	—	—	—	—	—	—	—	—	—	36	682
1990	Dal	7(5, fb)	19	48	2.5(7)	0	3	13	4.3(7)	0	—	—	—	—	—	—	—	—	—	—	—	—	0	55
1991	Dal	2(0)	—	—	—	—	—	—	—	—	—	—	—	—	—	—	—	—	—	—	—	—	—	—
1991	TB	11(0)	5	21	4.2(10)	0	—	—	—	—	—	—	—	—	—	—	—	—	—	—	—	—	0	21
1992	TB	5(2)	8	23	2.9(5)	0	5	28	5.6(11)	0	—	—	—	—	—	—	—	—	—	—	—	—	0	37
NFL	6	65(42)	283	1195	4.2(42)	7	42	428	10.2(33)	3	—	—	—	—	—	—	—	—	—	—	—	—	60	1494

HIGHSMITH, BUZZ Walter, G-T-C, 6´3˝/247 lbs; Florida A&M; B8/27/1943 Tampa, FL **1968** Den-A 14 **1969** Den-A 9 **1972** Hou 9 **NFL** 32 [3 yrs]

HIGHSMITH, DON Donald Cornelius, RB, 6´0˝/210 lbs; Michigan State; 1970: Oak, rnd 13; B3/12/1948 New Brunswick, NJ

1970	†Oak	8	2	2	1.0(4)	0	—	—	—	—	—	—	—	—	—	—	—	—	—	—	—	—	0	2
1971	Oak	14(3)	76	307	4.0(26)	1	10	109	10.9(47)	0	—	—	—	—	—	—	—	—	—	—	kp	—	6	506
1972	Oak	8(1)	9	11	1.2(12)	1	2	34	17.0(22)	0	—	—	—	—	—	—	—	—	—	—	—	—	6	38
1973	GB	7	7	7	1.0(4)	0	—	—	—	—	—	—	—	—	—	—	—	—	—	—	k	—	0	10
NFL	4	37(4)	94	327	3.5(26)	2	12	143	11.9(47)	0	—	—	—	—	—	—	—	—	—	—	kp	—	12	556

HIGHTOWER, BEN John Benjamin, E, 6´2˝/184 lbs; Sam Houston State; 1942: Cle, rnd 11; B12/5/1918 Beaumont, TX, D1/1/2003 Austin, TX

1942	Cle	10(2)	—	—	—	—	19	317	16.7(59)	3	—	—	—	—	—	—	—	—	—	—	—	—	18	174
1943	Det	8(7, RE)	1	-5	-5.0(-5)	0	10	172	17.2(46)	1	—	—	—	—	—	—	—	—	—	—	i	—	6	90
NFL	2	18(9)	1	-5	-5.0(-5)	0	29	489	16.9(59)	4	—	—	—	—	—	—	—	—	—	—	i	—	24	264

HILBERT, JON Jonathan Samuel, K, 6´2˝/228 lbs; Louisville; B7/15/1975 West Palm Beach, FL **[K]** **2001** Dal 8 (0) **2002** Car 1 (0) **NFL** 9 (0) [2 yrs]

HILES, VAN Lavanda Van, DB, 6´0˝/195 lbs; Kentucky; 1997: Chi, rnd 5; B11/1/1975 Baton Rouge, LA **1997** ChiB 16 (1)

HILGENBERG, JAY Jay Walter, C-G, 6´3˝/259 lbs; Iowa; B3/21/1959 Iowa City, IA **1981** ChiB 16 (0) **1982** ChiB 9 (0) **1983** ChiB 16 (8, c) **1984**†ChiB 16 (16, C) **1985**†ChiB★16 (16, C) **1986**†ChiB★16 (16, C) **1987**†ChiB 12 (12, C) **1988**†ChiB 16 (16, C) **1989** ChiB★16 (16, C) **1990**†ChiB★14 (14, C) **1991**†ChiB★16 (16, C) **1992** Cle 16 (16, C) **1993** NO 9 (6, C) **NFL** 188 (152) [13 yrs]

HILGENBERG, JOEL Joel C., C-G, 6´3˝/250 lbs; Iowa; 1984: NO, rnd 4; B7/10/1962 Iowa City, IA **1984** NO 10 (0) **1985** NO 15 (5, c) **1986** NO 16 (2) **1987**†NO 12 (12, C) **1988** NO 16 (10, RG) **1989** NO 16 (13, C) **1991**†NO 16 (14, C) **1992**†NO◇16 (16, C) **1993** NO 9 (9, C)

| 1990 | †NO | 16(16, C) | — | — | — | — | 1 | 9 | 9.0(9) | 0 | — | — | — | — | — | — | — | — | — | — | — | — | 0 | 5 |
| NFL | 10 | 142(97) | — | — | — | — | 1 | 9 | 9.0(9) | 0 | — | — | — | — | — | — | — | — | — | — | — | — | 0 | 5 |

HILGENBERG, WALLY Walter William, LB-G, 6´3˝/229 lbs; Iowa; 1964: Det, rnd 4/Den, rnd 8; B9/19/1942 Marshalltown, IA **1964** Det 14 **1965** Det 13 (llb) **1966** Det 14 (RLB) **1968**†Min 14 (7, rlb) **1969**†Min 14 (14, RLB) **1970**†Min 14 (14, RLB) **1971**†Min 14 (14, RLB) **1972** Min 14 (14, RLB) **1973**†Min☆13 (13, RLB) **1974**†Min 13 (13, RLB) **1975**†Min 14 (14, RLB) **1976**†Min 14 (14, RLB) **1977**†Min 11 **1978**†Min 15 (1) **1979** Min 8 **NFL** 199 (118) [15 yrs]

HILGER, RUSTY Russell Todd, QB, 6´4˝/205 lbs; Oklahoma State; 1985: LARd, rnd 6; B5/9/1962 Oklahoma City, OK

1985	LARd	4(0)	3	8	2.7(4)	0	—	—	—	—	13	4	30.8	54	4.2(29)	1	0	3	32	—	—	—	0	40
1986	LARd	2(0)	6	48	8.0(16)	0	—	—	—	—	38	19	50.0	266	7.0(54)	1	1	3	22	—	—	—	0	146
1987	LARd	5(5, qb)	8	8	1.0(6)	0	—	—	—	—	106	55	51.9	706	6.7(49)	2	6	12	80	—	—	—	0	131
1988	Det	11(9, QB)	18	27	1.5(11)	0	—	—	—	—	306	126	41.2	1558	5.1(56)	7	12	31	251	48.9	—	—	0	361
1991	Ind	1(0)	—	—	—	—	—	—	—	—	1	0	0.0	0	—	0	0	0	0	—	—	—	0	0
NFL	5	23(14)	35	91	2.6(16)	0	—	—	—	—	464	204	44.0	2584	5.6(56)	11	19	49	385	52.8	—	—	0	678

HILL, BARRY Barry Stephen, DB, 6´3˝/185 lbs; Iowa State; 1975: Mia, rnd 5; B1/26/1953 Eglin AFB, FL **1975** Mia 14 **1976** Mia 6 (6, FS) **NFL** 20 (6) [2 yrs]

HILL, BILL William, DB, 5´9˝/172 lbs; Rutgers; B4/21/1959 Neptune, NJ **1987** Dal 3 (1)

HILL, BOB Haskell, aka War Horse, G, 5´10˝/190 lbs; Carlisle Indian; B1890, deceased **1922** Oor 6 (6, LG)

HILL, BRUCE Bruce Edward, WR, 6´0˝/178 lbs; Arizona State; 1987: TB, rnd 4; B2/29/1964 Fort Dix, NJ

1987	TB	8(1)	3	3	1.0(9)	0	23	403	17.5(40)	2	—	—	—	—	—	—	—	—	—	—	k	—	12	208
1988	TB	14(14, WR)	2	-11	-5.5(3)	0	58	1040	17.9(42)	9	—	—	—	—	—	—	—	—	—	—	—	—	54	554
1989	TB	16(16, WR)	—	—	—	—	50	673	13.5(53)	5	—	—	—	—	—	—	—	—	—	—	—	—	30	362
1990	TB	13(13, WR)	1	0	0.0(0)	0	42	641	15.3(48)	5	—	—	—	—	—	—	—	—	—	—	—	—	30	346
1991	TB	6(6, wr)	—	—	—	—	17	185	10.9(18)	2	—	—	—	—	—	—	—	—	—	—	—	—	12	103
NFL	5	57(50)	6	-8	-1.3(9)	0	190	2942	15.5(53)	23	—	—	—	—	—	—	—	—	—	—	k	—	138	1571

HILL, CALVIN Calvin, RB, 6´4˝/227 lbs; Yale; 1969: Dal, rnd 1; B1/2/1947 Baltimore, MD

1969	†Dal★	13(HB)	204	942	4.6(55)	8	20	232	11.6(28)	0	3	3	100.0	137	45.7(59)	2	0	—	—	—	k	—	48	1282
1970	†Dal	12(9, RB)	153	577	3.8(20)	4	13	95	7.3(21)	0	4	1	25.0	12	3.0(12)	0	0	—	—	—	—	—	24	671
1971	†Dal	8(5, rb)	106	468	4.4(17)	8	19	244	12.8(27)	3	1	0	0.0	0	—	0	1	—	—	—	—	—	66	645
1972	†Dal◇	14(RB)	245	1036	4.2(26)	6	43	364	8.5(33)	3	3	1	33.3	55	18.3(55)	1	0	—	—	—	—	—	54	1326
1973	†Dal★	14(RB)	273	1142	4.2(21)	6	32	290	9.1(29)	0	1	0	0.0	0	—	0	0	—	—	—	—	—	36	**1347**
1974	Dal★	12(RB)	185	844	4.6(27)	7	12	134	11.2(39)	0	1	0	0.0	0	—	0	0	—	—	—	—	—	42	981
1976	†Was	14	79	301	3.8(15)	1	7	100	14.3(23)	0	1	0	0.0	0	—	0	0	—	—	—	—	—	6	361
1977	Was	14(1)	69	257	3.7(34)	0	18	154	8.6(23)	1	—	—	—	—	—	—	—	—	—	—	—	—	6	339
1978	Cle	12(1)	80	289	3.6(21)	1	25	334	13.4(53)	6	0	0	0.0	0	—	0	0	—	—	—	—	—	42	496
1979	Cle	14(RB)	53	193	3.6(33)	1	38	381	10.0(31)	2	0	0	0.0	0	—	0	0	—	—	—	—	—	18	404
1980	†Cle	15(0)	1	11	11.0(11)	0	27	383	14.2(50)	6	—	—	—	—	—	—	—	—	—	—	—	—	36	233
1981	Cle	14(0)	4	23	5.8(9)	0	17	150	8.8(23)	2	—	—	—	—	—	—	—	—	—	—	—	—	12	108
NFL	12	156(16)	1452	6083	4.2(55)	42	271	2861	10.6(53)	23	13	5	38.5	204	15.7(59)	3	1	1	2	—	k	—	390	8191

HILL, CHARLEY Charles Leland, TB-QB-FB-BB, 6´0˝/183 lbs; Baker; B1900 Paola, KS, deceased **[K]** **1924** KC 7 (4, TB), 6 **1925** KC 8 (3, TB), 25 **1926** KC 10 (7, tb), 6 **NFL** 25 (14), 37 [3 yrs]

HILL, CHARLES Charles LeDawnta, DT, 6´3˝/320 lbs; Maryland; 2002: Hou, rnd 3; B11/1/1980 Palmer Park, MD **2002** Hou 16 (0)

HILL, CHUCK Charles Kelley, FB-WB-E, 5´8˝/190 lbs; Iowa State; B5/26/1904, D1/19/1986 Saratoga, CA **1925** RI 1 (1)

HILL, COWBOY Harry Franklin, TB-WB-BB, 5´8˝/176 lbs; Oklahoma; B3/30/1899 Pittsburg, OK, D2/3/1966 Norman, OK **1923** Tol 8 (8, TB) **1924** KC 5 (4) **1925** KC 8 (5), 6 **1925** NYG 2 (0) **1926** NYG 10 (4), 12 **NFL** 33 (21), 36 [4 yrs]

HILL, DARRELL Darrell Frederick, WR, 6´3˝/200 lbs; Northern Illinois; 2002: Ten, rnd 7; B6/19/1979 Chicago, IL **2002**†Ten 7 (0) **2003**†Ten 12 (0) **2004** Ten 14 (0) **NFL** 33 (0) [3 yrs]

HILL, DAVE David Harris, T, 6´5˝/260 lbs; Auburn; 1963: KC, rnd 24/NYG, rnd 5; B2/1/1941 Lanett, AL **1963** KC-A 11 (RT) **1964** KC-A 14 (RT) **1965** KC-A 14 (RT) **1966**†KC-A 14 (RT) **1967** KC-A 14 (RT) **1968**†KC-A 14 (RT) **1969**†KC-A☆14 (RT) **1970** KC 14 (RT) **1971**†KC 14 (RT) **1972** KC 14 (RT) **1973** KC 8 (rt) **1974** KC 5 **NFL** 150 [12 yrs]

HILL, DAVID David Earl, TE, 6´2˝/229 lbs; Texas A&M-Kingsville; 1976: Det, rnd 2; B1/1/1954 San Antonio, TX

YEAR	TEAM	G(GS, POS)	RUSH	YD	AVG(LG)	TD	REC	YD	AVG(LG)	TD	PASS	COMP	PCT	YD	AVG(LG)	TD	INT	SK	YD	QBR	KPR	OTD	PTS	TAY
1976	Det	14(1)	—	—	—	—	19	249	13.1(24)	5	1	0	0.0	0	0.0	0	1	—	—	—	—	—	30	110
1977	Det	14(12, TE)	4	10	2.5(14)	0	32	465	14.5(61)	2	1	0	0.0	0	0.0	0	0	—	—	—	—	—	12	253
1978	Det✧	16(16, TE)	3	12	4.0(13)	0	53	633	11.9(32)	4	—	—	—	—	—	—	—	—	—	—	—	—	24	349
1979	Det✧	16(15, TE)	1	15	15.0(15)	0	47	569	12.1(40)	3	—	—	—	—	—	—	—	—	—	—	—	—	18	315
1980	Det	16(16, TE)	—	—	—	—	39	424	10.9(29)	1	—	—	—	—	—	—	—	—	—	—	—	—	6	217
1981	Det	15(15, TE)	—	—	—	—	33	462	14.0(34)	4	—	—	—	—	—	—	—	—	—	—	—	—	24	251
1982	†Det	9(8, TE)	—	—	—	—	22	252	11.5(27)	4	—	—	—	—	—	—	—	—	—	—	—	—	24	146
1983	†LARm	16(2)	—	—	—	—	28	280	10.0(34)	2	—	—	—	—	—	—	—	—	—	—	—	—	12	150
1984	†LARm	16(16, TE)	—	—	—	—	31	300	9.7(26)	1	—	—	—	—	—	—	—	—	—	—	—	—	6	155
1985	†LARm	16(16, TE)	—	—	—	—	29	271	9.3(37)	1	—	—	—	—	—	—	—	—	—	—	—	—	6	141
1986	†LARm	16(15, TE)	—	—	—	—	14	202	14.4(33)	1	—	—	—	—	—	—	—	—	—	—	—	—	6	106
1987	LARm	12(12, TE)	—	—	—	—	11	105	9.5(24)	0	—	—	—	—	—	—	—	—	—	—	—	—	0	53
NFL	12	176(144)	8	37	4.6(15)	0	358	4212	11.8(61)	28	2	0	0.0	0	0.0	0	1	—	—	—	—	—	168	2243

HILL, DEREK Derek Keith, WR, 6´1˝/193 lbs; Arizona; 1989: Pit, rnd 3; B11/4/1967 Detroit, MI

YEAR	TEAM	G(GS, POS)	RUSH	YD	AVG(LG)	TD	REC	YD	AVG(LG)	TD	PASS	COMP	PCT	YD	AVG(LG)	TD	INT	SK	YD	QBR	KPR	OTD	PTS	TAY
1989	†Pit	16(8, WR)	—	—	—	—	28	455	16.3(53)	1	—	—	—	—	—	—	—	—	—	—	p	—	6	230
1990	Pit	16(11, WR)	—	—	—	—	25	391	15.6(66)	0	—	—	—	—	—	—	—	—	—	—	p	—	0	191
NFL	2	32(19)	—	—	—	—	53	846	16.0(66)	1	—	—	—	—	—	—	—	—	—	—	p	—	6	420

HILL, DON Donald Kinman, TB-WB-HB-C, 5´10˝/175 lbs; Stanford; B9/18/1904 Hiawatha, KS, D2/9/1967 Glendale, CA **1929** GB 3 (1) **1929** ChiC 10 (7, TB), 6 **NFL** 13 (8) [1 yr]

HILL, DREW Andrew, WR, 5´9˝/170 lbs; Georgia Tech; 1979: LA, rnd 12; B10/5/1956 Newman, GA **[R]**

YEAR	TEAM	G(GS, POS)	RUSH	YD	AVG(LG)	TD	REC	YD	AVG(LG)	TD	PASS	COMP	PCT	YD	AVG(LG)	TD	INT	SK	YD	QBR	KPR	OTD	PTS	TAY
1979	†LARm	16(4)	—	—	—	—	4	94	23.5(43)	1	—	—	—	—	—	—	—	—	—	—	kp	—	6	250
1980	†LARm	16(0)	1	4	4.0(4)	0	19	416	21.9(74)	2	—	—	—	—	—	—	—	—	—	—	k	1	18	467
1981	LARm	16(2)	1	14	14.0(14)	0	16	355	22.2(45)	3	—	—	—	—	—	—	—	—	—	—	kp	—	18	489
1982	LARm	9(0)	—	—	—	—	7	92	13.1(23)	0	—	—	—	—	—	—	—	—	—	—	k	—	0	58
1984	†LARm	16(16, WR)	—	—	—	—	14	390	27.9(68)	4	—	—	—	—	—	—	—	—	—	—	k	—	24	368
1985	Hou	16(16, WR)	—	—	—	—	64	1169	18.3(57)	9	—	—	—	—	—	—	—	—	—	—	k	—	54	637
1986	Hou	16(16, WR)	—	—	—	—	65	1112	17.1(81)	5	—	—	—	—	—	—	—	—	—	—	—	—	30	581
1987	†Hou	12(12, WR)	—	—	—	—	49	989	20.2(52)	6	1	0	0.0	0	0.0	0	0	—	—	—	—	—	36	525
1988	†Hou★	16(16, WR)	—	—	—	—	72	1141	15.8(57)	10	—	—	—	—	—	—	—	—	—	—	—	—	60	621
1989	†Hou	14(12, WR)	—	—	—	—	66	938	14.2(50)	8	—	—	—	—	—	—	—	—	—	—	—	—	48	509
1990	†Hou★	16(16, WR)	—	—	—	—	**74**	1019	13.8(57)	5	—	—	—	—	—	—	—	—	—	—	—	—	30	535
1991	†Hou	16(16, WR)	1	1	1.0(1)	0	90	1109	12.3(61)	4	—	—	—	—	—	—	—	—	—	—	—	—	24	576
1992	Atl	16(14, WR)	—	—	—	—	60	623	10.4(43)	3	—	—	—	—	—	—	—	—	—	—	—	—	18	327
1993	Atl	16(7, wr)	—	—	—	—	34	384	11.3(30)	0	—	—	—	—	—	—	—	—	—	—	—	—	0	192
NFL	14	211(147)	3	19	6.3(14)	0	634	9831	15.5(81)	60	1	0	0.0	0	0.0	0	0	—	—	—	kp	1	366	6132

HILL, EDDIE Eddie Wayne, RB, 6´2˝/205 lbs; Memphis; 1979: LA, rnd 2; B5/13/1957 Nashville, TN

YEAR	TEAM	G(GS, POS)	RUSH	YD	AVG(LG)	TD	REC	YD	AVG(LG)	TD	PASS	COMP	PCT	YD	AVG(LG)	TD	INT	SK	YD	QBR	KPR	OTD	PTS	TAY
1979	†LARm	16	29	114	3.9(27)	1	4	36	9.0(21)	1	—	—	—	—	—	—	—	—	—	—	k	—	12	227
1980	LARm	7(1)	39	120	3.1(19)	0	4	29	7.3(11)	0	—	—	—	—	—	—	—	—	—	—	—	—	0	135
1981	†Mia	11(3)	37	146	3.9(24)	1	12	73	6.1(16)	1	1	1	100.0	14	14.0(14)	0	0	—	—	—	k	—	12	201
1982	†Mia	9(0)	13	51	3.9(13)	0	6	33	5.5(10)	0	1	0	0.0	0	0.0	0	0	—	—	—	—	—	0	68
1983	†Mia	16(0)	2	12	6.0(10)	0	—	—	—	—	—	—	—	—	—	—	—	—	—	—	—	—	0	12
1984	†Mia	16(0)	—	—	—	—	—	—	—	—	—	—	—	—	—	—	—	—	—	—	k	—	0	-1
NFL	6	75(4)	120	443	3.7(27)	2	26	171	6.6(21)	2	2	1	50.0	14	7.0(14)	0	0	—	—	—	k	—	24	641

HILL, ERIC Eric Dwayne, LB, 6´2˝/258 lbs; LSU; 1989: Phx, rnd 1; B11/14/1966 Blytheville, AR **1989** Phx 15 (14, MLB) **1990** Phx 16 (16, RILB) **1991** Phx 16 (15, RILB) **1992** Phx 16 (16, RILB/rlb) **1993** Phx 13 (12, LLB/rlb) **1994** Arz 16 (15, MLB) **1995** Arz 14 (14, MLB) **1996** Arz 16 (16, MLB) **1997** Arz 11 (10, MLB) **1998** SL 15 (15, MLB) **1999** SD 12 (10, MLB) **NFL** 160 (153) [11 yrs]

HILL, FRED Frederick Gordon, TE-SE-WR, 6´2˝/215 lbs; USC; 1965: Phi, rnd 4/Oak, rnd 16; B8/13/1943 Los Angeles, CA

YEAR	TEAM	G(GS, POS)	RUSH	YD	AVG(LG)	TD	REC	YD	AVG(LG)	TD	PASS	COMP	PCT	YD	AVG(LG)	TD	INT	SK	YD	QBR	KPR	OTD	PTS	TAY
1965	Phi	12	—	—	—	—	1	21	21.0(21)	0	—	—	—	—	—	—	—	—	—	—	—	—	0	11
1966	Phi	14(SE)	1	5	5.0(5)	0	29	304	10.5(36)	0	—	—	—	—	—	—	—	—	—	—	—	—	0	157
1967	Phi	14(1)	—	—	—	—	9	144	16.0(57)	0	—	—	—	—	—	—	—	—	—	—	—	—	0	72
1968	Phi	14(TE)	—	—	—	—	30	370	12.3(31)	3	—	—	—	—	—	—	—	—	—	—	—	—	18	200
1969	Phi	8	—	—	—	—	6	64	10.7(23)	1	—	—	—	—	—	—	—	—	—	—	—	—	6	37
1970	Phi	14	—	—	—	—	3	10	3.3(9)	1	—	—	—	—	—	—	—	—	—	—	—	—	6	10
1971	Phi	7	—	—	—	—	7	92	13.1(35)	0	—	—	—	—	—	—	—	—	—	—	—	—	0	46
NFL	7	83(1)	1	5	5.0(5)	0	85	1005	11.8(57)	5	—	—	—	—	—	—	—	—	—	—	—	—	30	533

HILL, GARY Gary H., DB, 6´0˝/200 lbs; USC; B6/29/1943 **1965** Min 8

HILL, GREG Gregory Michael, DB, 6´1˝/194 lbs; Oklahoma State; 1983: Hou, rnd 4; B2/12/1961 Orange, TX **1983** Hou 14 (0) **1984** KC 15 (1) **1985** KC 16 (1) **1986** KC 13 (1) **1987** LARd 2 (2) **1987** KC 4 (0) **1988** KC 15 (0) **NFL** 79 (5) [6 yrs]

HILL, GREG Gregory LaMonte, RB, 5´11˝/207 lbs; Texas A&M; 1994: KC, rnd 1; B2/23/1972 Dallas, TX

YEAR	TEAM	G(GS, POS)	RUSH	YD	AVG(LG)	TD	REC	YD	AVG(LG)	TD	PASS	COMP	PCT	YD	AVG(LG)	TD	INT	SK	YD	QBR	KPR	OTD	PTS	TAY
1994	†KC	16(2)	141	574	4.1(20)	1	16	92	5.8(21)	0	—	—	—	—	—	—	—	—	—	—	—	—	6	630
1995	KC	16(1, rb)	155	667	4.3(27)	1	7	45	6.4(13)	0	—	—	—	—	—	—	—	—	—	—	—	—	6	700
1996	KC	15(1)	135	645	4.8(28)	4	3	60	20.0(34)	1	—	—	—	—	—	—	—	—	—	—	—	—	30	720
1997	†KC	16(16, RB)	157	550	3.5(38)	0	12	126	10.5(39)	0	—	—	—	—	—	—	—	—	—	—	—	—	0	613
1998	SL	2(2)	40	240	6.0(46)	4	1	6	6.0(6)	0	—	—	—	—	—	—	—	—	—	—	—	—	24	283
1999	Det	14(8, RB)	144	542	3.8(45)	2	13	77	5.9(15)	0	—	—	—	—	—	—	—	—	—	—	—	—	12	601
NFL	6	79(30)	772	3218	4.2(46)	12	52	406	7.8(39)	1	—	—	—	—	—	—	—	—	—	—	—	—	78	3546

HILL, HARLON Harlon Junious, E-DB, 6´3˝/199 lbs; North Alabama; 1954: ChiB, rnd 15; B5/4/1932 Killen, AL

YEAR	TEAM	G(GS, POS)	RUSH	YD	AVG(LG)	TD	REC	YD	AVG(LG)	TD	PASS	COMP	PCT	YD	AVG(LG)	TD	INT	SK	YD	QBR	KPR	OTD	PTS	TAY
1954	ChiB★	12(LE)	—	—	—	—	45	1124	**25.0**(**76**)	**12**	—	—	—	—	—	—	—	—	—	—	—	—	72	622
1955	ChiB★	12(LE)	—	—	—	—	42	789	18.8(86)	**9**	—	—	—	—	—	—	—	—	—	—	—	—	54	440
1956	†ChiB★	12(LE)	2	24	12.0(12)	0	47	1128	**24.0**(**79**)	11	1	0	0.0	0	0.0	0	0	—	—	—	—	—	66	643
1957	ChiB	8(LE)	2	7	3.5(8)	0	21	483	23.0(53)	2	—	—	—	—	—	—	—	—	—	—	—	—	12	259
1958	ChiB	8(LE)	—	—	—	—	27	365	13.5(40)	3	—	—	—	—	—	—	—	—	—	—	—	—	18	198
1959	ChiB	11(LE)	1	0	0.0(0)	0	36	578	16.1(**88**)	3	—	—	—	—	—	—	—	—	—	—	—	—	18	304
1960	ChiB	12	—	—	—	—	5	98	19.6(45)	0	—	—	—	—	—	—	—	—	—	—	—	—	0	49
1961	ChiB	14	—	—	—	—	3	51	17.0(23)	0	—	—	—	—	—	—	—	—	—	—	i	—	0	63
1962	Pit	7	7	72	10.3(24)	0	7	101	14.4(25)	0	—	—	—	—	—	—	—	—	—	—	—	—	0	123
1962	Det	7	—	—	—	—	—	—	—	—	—	—	—	—	—	—	—	—	—	—	—	—	—	—
NFL	9	103	12	103	8.6(24)	0	233	4717	20.2(88)	40	1	0	0.0	0	0.0	0	0	—	—	—	i	—	240	2699

HILL, HAROLD James Harold, E, 6´0˝/200 lbs; Samford; B12/8/1914 Gadsden, AL, D3/26/2003 Bessemer, AL

YEAR	TEAM	G(GS, POS)	RUSH	YD	AVG(LG)	TD	REC	YD	AVG(LG)	TD	PASS	COMP	PCT	YD	AVG(LG)	TD	INT	SK	YD	QBR	KPR	OTD	PTS	TAY
1938	Bkn	8(2)	—	—	—	—	3	61	20.3	0	—	—	—	—	—	—	—	—	—	—	—	—	0	31
1939	Bkn	9(4)	—	—	—	—	7	150	21.4	0	—	—	—	—	—	—	—	—	—	—	—	—	0	75
1940	Bkn	9(0)	—	—	—	—	1	9	9.0(9)	0	—	—	—	—	—	—	—	—	—	—	—	—	0	5
NFL	3	26(6)	—	—	—	—	11	220	20.0(9)	0	—	—	—	—	—	—	—	—	—	—	—	—	0	110

HILL, IKE Talmaldga L., WB-DB, 5´10˝/180 lbs; Catawba; 1970: Oak, rnd 9; B4/15/1947 Winston-Salem, NC **[R]**

YEAR	TEAM	G(GS, POS)	RUSH	YD	AVG(LG)	TD	REC	YD	AVG(LG)	TD	PASS	COMP	PCT	YD	AVG(LG)	TD	INT	SK	YD	QBR	KPR	OTD	PTS	TAY
1970	Buf	6	—	—	—	—	—	—	—	—	—	—	—	—	—	—	—	—	—	—	kp	—	0	37
1971	Buf	14	—	—	—	—	5	55	11.0(26)	1	—	—	—	—	—	—	—	—	—	—	kp	1	12	206
1973	ChiB	14	3	-14	-4.7(5)	0	10	119	11.9(18)	0	1	1	100.0	35	35.0(35)	0	0	—	—	—	kp	2	12	339
1974	ChiB	13	—	—	—	—	7	109	15.6(28)	1	1	0	0.0	0	0.0	0	0	—	—	—	p	—	6	78
1976	Mia	2	—	—	—	—	—	—	—	—	—	—	—	—	—	—	—	—	—	—	—	—	—	—
NFL	5	49	3	-14	-4.7(5)	0	22	283	12.9(28)	2	2	1	50.0	35	17.5(35)	0	0	—	—	—	kp	3	30	659

YEAR	TEAM	G (GS, POS)	RUSH	YD	AVG(LG)	TD	REC	YD	AVG(LG)	TD	PASS COMP	PCT	YD	AVG(LG)	TD	INT	SK	YD	QBR	KPR	OTD	PTS	TAY
HILL, IRV Irvin Pate, BB-FB-LB-DB, 6´1˝/207 lbs; Trinity (TX); B12/8/1908 Fort Worth, TX, D11/7/1978 Dallas, TX **[K]**																						
1931	ChiC	9(7, BB)	—	—	—	—	—	—	—	—	—	—	—	—	—	—	—	—	—	—	—	0	—
1932	ChiC	7(2)	45	162	3.6	3	3	28	9.3	0	—	—	—	—	—	—	—	—	—	K	—	22	206
1933	Bos	1(0)	1	1	1.0	0	—	—	—	—	—	—	—	—	—	—	—	—	—	—	—	0	1
NFL	3	17(9)	46	163	3.5	3	3	28	9.3	0	—	—	—	—	—	—	—	—	—	K	—	22	207
HILL, J.D. James D., WR, 6´1˝/202 lbs; Arizona State; 1971: Buf, rnd 1; B10/30/1948 Stockton, CA																						
1971	Buf	5	1	2	2.0(2)	0	11	216	19.6(47)	2	—	—	—	—	—	—	—	—	—	—	—	12	120
1972	Buf◇	14(WR)	1	11	11.0(11)	0	52	754	14.5(58)	5	—	—	—	—	—	—	—	—	—	kp	—	30	419
1973	Buf	14(WR)	—	—	—	—	29	422	14.6(42)	—	—	—	—	—	—	—	—	—	—	p	—	0	197
1974	†Buf	14(WR)	—	—	—	—	32	572	17.9(55)	6	—	—	—	—	—	—	—	—	—	—	—	36	316
1975	Buf	14(WR)	1	1	1.0(1)	0	36	667	18.5(77)	7	—	—	—	—	—	—	—	—	—	—	—	42	370
1976	Det	1	—	—	—	—	2	2	1.0(2)	0	—	—	—	—	—	—	—	—	—	—	—	0	1
1977	Det	11(WR)	—	—	—	—	24	247	10.3(23)	1	—	—	—	—	—	—	—	—	—	—	—	6	129
NFL	7	73	3	14	4.7(11)	0	185	2880	15.6(77)	21	—	—	—	—	—	—	—	—	—	kp	—	126	1551
HILL, JACK Jack Flint, WR-K, 6´1˝/185 lbs; Utah State; 1956: Bal, rnd 13; B10/17/1932 Ogden, UT, D9/26/2005 Kaysville, UT **[K]**																						
1961	Den-A	14	—	—	—	—	4	33	8.3(15)	0	—	—	—	—	—	—	—	—	—	Kk	—	31	25
HILL, JAMES James, TE, 6´4˝/246 lbs; Abilene Christian; B10/25/1974 Dallas, TX **2000** Sea 10 (0)																						
HILL, JEFF Jeffrey Martin, WR, 5´11˝/178 lbs; Purdue; B9/24/1972 Mount Healthy, OH **1994** Cin 1 (0) **1996** Cin 9 (0)																						
1995	Cin	16(1)	1	-3	-3.0(-3)	0	4	44	11.0(18)	0	—	—	—	—	—	—	—	—	—	k	—	0	218
NFL	3	26(1)	1	-3	-3.0(-3)	0	4	44	11.0(18)	0	—	—	—	—	—	—	—	—	—	k	—	0	293
HILL, JERRY Gerald Allen, RB, 5´11˝/210 lbs; Wyoming; 1961: Bal, rnd 3/Den, rnd 2; B10/12/1939 Torrington, WY																						
1961	Bal	1	1	4	4.0(4)	0	—	—	—	—	—	—	—	—	—	—	—	—	—	—	—	0	4
1963	Bal	14	100	440	4.4(20)	5	22	304	13.8(55)	1	—	—	—	—	—	—	—	—	—	kp	—	36	644
1964	†Bal	13(FB)	88	384	4.4(50)	5	14	113	8.1(27)	0	—	—	—	—	—	—	—	—	—	k	—	36	521
1965	†Bal	14(FB)	147	516	3.5(20)	5	20	112	5.6(20)	0	—	—	—	—	—	—	—	—	—	k	—	30	610
1966	Bal	11(fb)	104	395	3.8(14)	0	5	18	3.6(7)	0	—	—	—	—	—	—	—	—	—	—	—	0	404
1967	Bal	14	90	311	3.5(18)	2	19	156	8.2(33)	0	—	—	—	—	—	—	—	—	—	—	—	12	409
1968	†Bal	9(FB)	91	360	4.0(21)	1	18	161	8.9(19)	1	—	—	—	—	—	—	—	—	—	—	—	12	456
1969	Bal	14(FB)	49	143	2.9(14)	2	11	44	4.0(12)	0	—	—	—	—	—	—	—	—	—	—	—	12	185
1970	†Bal	12(FB)	36	115	3.2(15)	2	8	62	7.8(13)	0	—	—	—	—	—	—	—	—	—	—	—	12	166
NFL	9	102	706	2668	3.8(50)	22	117	970	8.3(55)	3	—	—	—	—	—	—	—	—	—	kp	—	150	3398
HILL, JIM James Clifford, DB, 6´0˝/188 lbs; Tennessee; 1951: Det, rnd 15; B7/21/1929 Knoxville, TN, D5/5/2003 Maryville, TN **1951** Det 12 **1952**†Det 9 **1955** Pit 10 (DB) **NFL** 31 [3 yrs]																						
HILL, JIM James Webster, DB, 6´2˝/190 lbs; Texas A&M-Kingsville; 1968: SD, rnd 1; B10/21/1946 San Antonio, TX **1969** SD-A 14 (RS) **1970** SD 14 (SS) **1971** SD 14 **1972**†GB 14 (FS) **1973** GB 13 (FS) **1974** GB 14 (FS) **1975** Cle 11 **NFL** 94 [7 yrs]																						
HILL, JIMMY James, DB, 6´2˝/192 lbs; Sam Houston State; B6/27/1928 Dallas, TX **[I]** **1955** ChiC 9 **1956** ChiC 12 (DB) **1957** ChiC 10 (DB) **1959** ChiC 12 (DB) **1960** SL◇12 (RCB/rs) **1961** SL★13 (RCB) **1962** SL★14 (RCB) **1963** SL☆12 (RCB) **1964** SL 10 (rcb) **1965** Det 4 **1966** KC-A 3 **NFL** 111 [11 yrs]																						
HILL, JOHN John Stark, C-T, 6´2˝/249 lbs; Lehigh; 1972: NYG, rnd 6; B4/16/1950 East Orange, NJ **1972** NYG 14 **1973** NYG 12 **1974** NYG 12 **1975** NO 14 (13, C/lt) **1977** NO 14 (14, C) **1978** NO 16 (16, C) **1979** NO 16 (16, C) **1980** NO 15 (14, C) **1981** NO 13 (11, C) **1982** NO 9 (9, C) **1983** NO 16 (16, C) **1984** NO 11 (11, C) **1985**†SF 1 (0) **NFL** 177 (134) [14 yrs]																						
HILL, KAHLIL Kahlil, WR, 6´2˝/200 lbs; Iowa; 2002: Atl, rnd 6; B3/18/1979 Iowa City, IA **2002** Atl 1 (0)																						
HILL, KENNY Kenneth W., DB, 6´0˝/194 lbs; Yale; 1980: Oak, rnd 8; B7/25/1958 Oak Grove, LA **1981** Oak 9 (0) **1982**†LARd 9 (0) **1983**†LARd 16 (0) **1984**†NYG 12 (7, ss) **1985**†NYG 12 (11, SS) **1986** NYG 16 (16, SS) **1987** NYG 12 (12, SS) **1988** NYG 16 (16, SS) **1989** KC 8 (0) **NFL** 110 (62) [9 yrs]																						
HILL, KENT Kent Angelo, G-T, 6´5˝/260 lbs; Georgia Tech; 1979: LA, rnd 1; B3/7/1957 Americus, GA **1979**†LARm★16 (9, LG) **1980**†LARm★16 (16, LG) **1981** LARm 16 (11, LG) **1982** LARm★9 (9, LG) **1983**†LARm★16 (16, LG) **1984**†LARm★16 (16, LG) **1985**†LARm★16 (16, LG) **1986** LARm 2 (2) **1986** Hou 13 (13, RG) **1987**†Hou 12 (6, rg) **NFL** 132 (114) [9 yrs]																						
HILL, KID John Anthony, T, 5´11˝/185 lbs; Amherst; B5/6/1904 Washington, DC, D12/3/1973 Puerto Vallarta, Mexico **1926** NYG 2 (0)																						
HILL, KING Stuart King, QB, 6´3˝/212 lbs; Rice; 1958: ChiC, rnd B1; B11/8/1936 Hamilton, TX **[P]**																						
1958	ChiC	7	1	0	0.0(0)	0	—	—	—	9	1	11.1	18	2.0(18)	0	2	—	—	—	P	—	0	-71
1959	ChiC	11(QB)	39	167	4.3(29)	5	—	—	—	181	82	45.3	1015	5.6(31)	7	13	—	—	46.2	P	—	30	240
1960	SL	12	16	47	2.9(10)	1	—	—	—	55	20	36.4	205	3.7(25)	1	5	—	—	—	P	—	6	-36
1961	Phi	14	2	9	4.5(7)	0	—	—	—	12	6	50.0	101	8.4(23)	2	2	—	—	—	P	—	0	-11
1962	Phi	14	4	40	10.0(22)	0	—	—	—	61	31	50.8	361	5.9(37)	0	5	—	—	—	P	—	6	31
1963	Phi	14(qb)	3	-1	-0.3(6)	0	—	—	—	186	91	48.9	1213	6.5(80)	10	17	9	104	49.9	P	—	0	-25
1964	Phi	8(3)	8	27	3.4(14)	0	—	—	—	88	49	55.7	641	7.3(38)	3	4	8	61	—	P	—	0	203
1965	Phi	7	7	20	2.9(7)	0	—	—	—	113	60	53.1	857	7.6(50)	5	10	4	21	—	P	—	12	94
1966	Phi	10	7	-2	-0.3(2)	0	—	—	—	97	53	54.6	571	5.9(30)	5	7	6	42	—	P	—	0	29
1967	Phi	1	—	—	—	—	—	—	—	7	2	28.6	33	4.7(18)	1	0	—	—	—	—	—	0	22
1968	Phi	3	1	1	1.0(1)	0	—	—	—	71	33	46.5	531	7.5(92)	3	6	4	36	—	—	—	0	42
1968	†Min	8	—	—	—	—	—	—	—	—	—	—	—	—	—	—	—	—	—	P	—	0	0
1969	SL	14	—	—	—	—	—	—	—	1	1	100.0	7	7.0(7)	0	0	—	—	—	P	—	0	4
NFL	12	123(3)	88	308	3.5(29)	9	—	—	—	881	429	48.7	5553	6.3(92)	37	71	31	264	49.3	P	—	54	520
HILL, LEROY LeRoy, LB, 6´1˝/224 lbs; Clemson; 2005: Sea, rnd 3; B9/14/1982 Haddock, GA **2005**†Sea 15 (8, lolb)																						
HILL, LONZELL Lonzell Ramon, WR, 5´11˝/189 lbs; Washington; 1987: NO, rnd 2; B9/25/1965 Stockton, CA																						
1987	†NO	10(1)	1	-9	-9.0(-9)	0	19	322	16.9(36)	2	—	—	—	—	—	—	—	—	—	—	—	12	162
1988	NO	16(15, WR)	2	7	3.5(5)	0	66	703	10.7(35)	7	1	0	0.0	0	—	0	—	—	—	p	—	42	452
1989	NO	16(12, WR)	1	-7	-7.0(-7)	0	48	636	13.3(46)	4	0	0	0.0	0	—	0	1	4	—	kp	—	24	335
1990	†NO	13(0)	—	—	—	—	3	35	11.7(13)	0	—	—	—	—	—	—	—	—	—	—	—	0	18
NFL	4	55(28)	4	-9	-2.3(5)	0	136	1696	12.5(46)	13	1	0	0.0	0	—	0	1	4	—	kp	—	78	966
HILL, MACK LEE Mack Lee, FB-HB, 5´11˝/225 lbs; Southern (LA); B8/17/1940 Quincy, FL, D12/14/1965 Kansas City, MO																						
1964	KC-A◇	14(FB)	105	576	**5.5(71)**	4	19	144	7.6(34)	2	—	—	—	—	—	—	—	—	—	—	—	36	698
1965	KC-A☆	13(HB)	125	627	5.0(66)	2	21	264	12.6(46)	1	—	—	—	—	—	—	—	—	—	—	—	18	784
NFL	2	27	230	1203	5.2(71)	6	40	408	10.2(46)	3	—	—	—	—	—	—	—	—	—	—	—	54	1482
HILL, MADRE Madre, RB, 5´11˝/199 lbs; Arkansas; 1999: Cle, rnd 7; B1/2/1976 Malvern, AR **1999** Cle 5 (0) **2002** Oak 2 (0) **NFL** 7 (0) [2 yrs]																						
HILL, MARQUISE Marquise, DE, 6´6˝/297 lbs; LSU; 2004: NE, rnd 2; B8/7/1982 New Orleans, LA **2004** NE 1 (0) **2005**†NE 8 (0) **NFL** 9 (0) [2 yrs]																						
HILL, MATT Matt, T, 6´6˝/304 lbs; Boise State; 2002: Sea, rnd 5; B11/10/1978 Grangeville, ID **2002** Sea 13 (0) **2003**†Sea 13 (2) **NFL** 26 (2) [2 yrs]																						
HILL, NATE Nathaniel, DE, 6´4˝/273 lbs; Auburn; 1988: GB, rnd 6; B2/21/1966 La Grange, GA **1988** GB 3 (0) **1988** Mia 1 (0) **NFL** 4 (0) [1 yr]																						
HILL, RAION Raion Yance, DB, 6´0˝/200 lbs; LSU; B9/2/1976 Marrero, LA **2000** Buf 16 (0) **2001** Buf 15 (13, SS) **NFL** 31 (13) [2 yrs]																						
HILL, RALPH Ralph Edward, C, 6´1˝/245 lbs; Florida A&M; B11/10/1949 Chicago, IL **1976** NYG 14 **1977** NYG 12 **NFL** 26 [2 yrs]																						
HILL, RANDAL Randal Thrill, WR, 5´10˝/180 lbs; Miami (FL); 1991: Mia, rnd 1; B9/21/1969 Miami, FL																						
1991	Mia	1(0)	—	—	—	—	—	—	—	—	—	—	—	—	—	—	—	—	—	k	—	0	18
1991	Phx	15(4)	—	—	—	—	43	495	11.5(31)	1	—	—	—	—	—	—	—	—	—	k	—	6	246
1992	Phx	16(14, WR)	1	4	4.0(4)	0	58	861	14.8(49)	3	—	—	—	—	—	—	—	—	—	—	—	18	450
1993	Phx	16(9, wr)	—	—	—	—	35	519	14.8(58)	4	—	—	—	—	—	—	—	—	—	—	—	24	280
1994	Arz	14(14, WR)	—	—	—	—	38	544	14.3(51)	0	—	—	—	—	—	—	—	—	—	—	—	0	272

YEAR	TEAM	G (GS, POS)	RUSH	YD	AVG (LG)	TD	REC	YD	AVG (LG)	TD	PASS	COMP	PCT	YD	AVG (LG)	TD	INT	SK	YD	QBR	KPR	OTD	PTS	TAY
1995	†Mia	12 (0)	—	—	—	—	12	260	21.7 (58)	0	—	—	—	—	—	—	—	—	—	—	k	—	0	237
1996	Mia	14 (5, wr)	—	—	—	—	21	409	19.5 (61)	4	—	—	—	—	—	—	—	—	—	—	k	—	24	199
1997	NO	15 (15, WR)	1	11	11.0 (11)	0	55	761	13.8 (**89**)	2	0	0	0.0	0	0.0	0	0	1	8	—	—	—	12	402
NFL	7	103 (61)	2	15	7.5 (11)	0	262	3849	14.7 (89)	14	0	0	0.0	0	0.0	0	0	1	8	—	k	—	84	2102

Hill, Ray Raymond Millous, DB, 6´0˝/182 lbs; Michigan State; B8/7/1975 Detroit, MI **1998** Buf 4 (0) **1998**†Mia 2 (0) **1999**†Mia 16 (0) **2000** Mia 3 (0) **2000** Buf 5 (0) **NFL** 30 (0) [3 yrs]

Hill, Renaldo Renaldo, DB, 5´11˝/194 lbs; Michigan State; 2001: Arz, rnd 7; B11/12/1978 Detroit, MI **2001** Arz 14 (1) **2002** Arz 14 (7, lcb) **2003** Arz 14 (14, LCB) **2004** Arz 13 (10, LCB) **2005** Oak 16 (13, CB) **NFL** 71 (45) [5 yrs]

Hill, Reynaldo Reynaldo, DB, 5´11˝/187 lbs; Florida; 2005: Ten, rnd 7; B8/28/1982 Pahokee, FL **2005** Ten 15 (10, LCB)

Hill, Rod Rodrick, DB, 6´0˝/185 lbs; Kentucky State; 1982: Dal, rnd 1; B3/14/1959 Detroit, MI **1982**†Dal 9 (0) **1983** Dal 14 (0) **1984** Buf 2 (0) **1985** Buf 10 (5, lcb) **1986** Buf 6 (2) **1986** Det 3 (0) **1987** LARd 4 (3) **NFL** 48 (10) [6 yrs]

Hill, Sean Sean Terrell, DB, 5´10˝/179 lbs; Montana State; 1994: Mia, rnd 7; B8/14/1971 Dowagiac, MI **1994**†Mia 16 (1) **1995**†Mia 16 (0) **1996** Mia 12 (5, fs) **NFL** 44 (6) [3 yrs]

Hill, Shaun Shaun, QB, 6´5˝/210 lbs; Maryland; B1/9/1980 Parsons, KS

YEAR	TEAM	G (GS, POS)	RUSH	YD	AVG (LG)	TD	REC	YD	AVG (LG)	TD	PASS	COMP	PCT	YD	AVG (LG)	TD	INT	SK	YD	QBR	KPR	OTD	PTS	TAY
2005	Min	1 (0)	2	-2	-1.0 (-1)	0	—	—	—	—	—	—	—	—	—	—	—	—	—	—	—	—	0	-2

Hill, Tony Leroy Anthony, WR, 6´2˝/199 lbs; Stanford; 1977: Dal, rnd 3; B6/23/1956 San Diego, CA

YEAR	TEAM	G (GS, POS)	RUSH	YD	AVG (LG)	TD	REC	YD	AVG (LG)	TD	PASS	COMP	PCT	YD	AVG (LG)	TD	INT	SK	YD	QBR	KPR	OTD	PTS	TAY
1977	†Dal	14	—	—	—	—	2	21	10.5 (12)	0	—	—	—	—	—	—	—	—	—	—	kp	—	0	104
1978	†Dal★	16 (WR)	3	17	5.7 (14)	0	46	823	17.9 (54)	6	1	0	0.0	0	0.0	0	0	—	—	—	p	—	36	505
1979	†Dal★	16 (WR)	2	18	9.0 (12)	0	60	1062	17.7 (75)	10	—	—	—	—	—	—	—	—	—	—	kp	—	60	629
1980	†Dal	16 (13, WR)	4	27	6.8 (15)	0	60	1055	17.6 (58)	8	—	—	—	—	—	—	—	—	—	—	—	—	48	595
1981	†Dal	16 (9, WR)	1	-3	-3.0 (-3)	0	46	953	20.7 (63)	4	—	—	—	—	—	—	—	—	—	—	—	—	24	494
1982	†Dal	9 (8, WR)	1	22	22.0 (22)	0	35	526	15.0 (47)	1	—	—	—	—	—	—	—	—	—	—	—	—	6	290
1983	†Dal	12 (10, WR)	1	2	2.0 (3)	0	49	801	16.3 (75)	7	—	—	—	—	—	—	—	—	—	—	—	—	42	438
1984	Dal	11 (11, WR)	1	7	7.0 (7)	0	58	864	14.9 (66)	5	—	—	—	—	—	—	—	—	—	—	—	—	30	464
1985	†Dal★	15 (14, WR)	1	-6	-6.0 (-6)	0	74	1113	15.0 (53)	7	1	1	100.0	42	42.0 (42)	0	0	—	—	—	—	—	42	607
1986	Dal	16 (16, WR)	—	—	—	—	49	770	15.7 (63)	3	—	—	—	—	—	—	—	—	—	—	—	—	18	400
NFL	10	141 (81)	14	84	6.0 (22)	0	479	7988	16.7 (75)	51	2	1	50.0	42	21.0 (42)	0	0	—	—	—	kp	—	306	4523

Hill, Tony Antonio LaVosia, DE, 6´6˝/250 lbs; Tennessee-Chattanooga; 1991: Dal, rnd 4; B10/23/1968 Augusta, GA **1991**†Dal 8 (0) **1992** Dal 5 (0) **NFL** 13 (0) [2 yrs]

Hill, Travis Travis LaVell, LB, 6´2˝/240 lbs; Nebraska; 1993: Cle, rnd 7; B10/3/1969 Texas City, TX **1994**†Cle 14 (0) **1995** Car 3 (0) **1995** Cle 4 (0) **NFL** 21 (0) [2 yrs]

Hill, Will Willie Jay, DB, 6´0˝/200 lbs; Bishop; B3/5/1963 Vero Beach, FL **1988** Cle 16 (1)

Hill, Winston Winston Cordell, T, 6´4˝/270 lbs; Texas Southern; 1963: Bal, rnd 11; B10/23/1941 Seguin, TX **1963** NYJ-A 13 (LT) **1964** NYJ-A★14 (14, LT) **1965** NYJ-A 14 (LT) **1966** NYJ-A 14 (LT) **1967** NYJ-A✧14 (LT) **1968**†NYJ-A★14 (LT) **1969**†NYJ-A★14 (LT) **1970** NYJ★14 (LT) **1971** NYJ★14 (RT) **1972** NYJ★14 (RT) **1973** NYJ★14 (RT) **1974** NYJ☆14 (RT) **1975** NYJ 14 (14, RT) **1976** NYJ 14 (rt) **1977**†LARm 3 **NFL** 198 (28) [15 yrs]

Hillary, Ira Ira McDonald, WR, 5´10˝/190 lbs; South Carolina; 1985: KC, rnd 8; B11/13/1962 Edgefield, SC

YEAR	TEAM	G (GS, POS)	RUSH	YD	AVG (LG)	TD	REC	YD	AVG (LG)	TD	PASS	COMP	PCT	YD	AVG (LG)	TD	INT	SK	YD	QBR	KPR	OTD	PTS	TAY
1987	Cin	11 (0)	—	—	—	—	5	65	13.0 (23)	0	0	0	0.0	0	0.0	0	0	1	13	—	k	—	0	33
1988	†Cin	16 (0)	—	—	—	—	5	76	15.2 (31)	1	—	—	—	—	—	—	—	—	—	—	kp	—	6	139
1989	Cin	16 (1)	1	-2	-2.0 (-2)	0	17	162	9.5 (17)	1	—	—	—	—	—	—	—	—	—	—	kp	—	6	86
1990	Min	3 (0)	—	—	—	—	—	—	—	—	—	—	—	—	—	—	—	—	—	—	kp	—	0	-4
NFL	4	46 (1)	1	-2	-2.0 (-2)	0	27	303	11.2 (31)	2	0	0	0.0	0	0.0	0	0	1	13	—	kp	—	12	254

Hillebrand, Jerry Gerald John, LB, 6´3˝/240 lbs; Colorado; 1962: NYG, rnd 1/Den, rnd 2; B3/28/1940 Davenport, IA **[K]** **1963**†NYG 14 **1964** NYG 11 **1965** NYG 13 (MLB) **1966** NYG 11 (LLB) **1967** SL 14 **1969** Pit 10 (LLB) **1970** Pit 12 (LLB)

YEAR	TEAM	G (GS, POS)	RUSH	YD	AVG (LG)	TD	REC	YD	AVG (LG)	TD	PASS	COMP	PCT	YD	AVG (LG)	TD	INT	SK	YD	QBR	KPR	OTD	PTS	TAY
1968	Pit	14 (LLB)	—	—	—	—	1	27	27.0 (27)	0	—	—	—	—	—	—	—	—	—	—	i	—	0	36
NFL	8	99	—	—	—	—	1	27	27.0 (27)	0	—	—	—	—	—	—	—	—	—	—	Ki	3	18	153

Hillenbrand, Billy William Frank, HB-BB, 6´0˝/188 lbs; Indiana; 1944: NYG, rnd 1; B3/29/1922 Armstrong, IN, D7/14/1994 Indianapolis, IN

YEAR	TEAM	G (GS, POS)	RUSH	YD	AVG (LG)	TD	REC	YD	AVG (LG)	TD	PASS	COMP	PCT	YD	AVG (LG)	TD	INT	SK	YD	QBR	KPR	OTD	PTS	TAY
1946	ChiR-A	14 (9, BB)	50	175	3.5	2	21	315	15.0	4	3	0	0.0	0	0.0	0	2	—	—	—	kpi	2	48	550
1947	Bal-A	13 (13, LH)	66	204	3.1	2	39	702	18.0	7	1	0	0.0	0	0.0	0	1	—	—	—	kpi	1	60	955
1948	†Bal-A☆	14 (13, LH)	100	510	5.1	7	50	**970**	19.4	6	—	—	—	—	—	—	—	—	—	—	kp	—	78	1352
AAFC	3	41 (35)	216	889	4.1	11	110	1987	18.1	17	4	0	0.0	0	0.0	0	3	—	—	—	kpi	3	186	2857

Hillenmeyer, Hunter Hunter Taverner, LB, 6´4˝/238 lbs; Vanderbilt; 2003: GB, rnd 5; B10/28/1980 Nashville, TN **2003** ChiB 13 (0) **2004** ChiB 16 (11, LLB) **2005**†ChiB 13 (12, LLB) **NFL** 42 (23) [3 yrs]

Hillhouse, Andy Andrew Fitch, HB, 6´2˝/190 lbs; Brown; B9/15/1896 Willimantic, CT, D3/6/1979 Boynton Beach, FL **1921** Buf 1 (0)

Hilliard, Dalton Dalton Andrea, RB, 5´8˝/204 lbs; LSU; 1986: NO, rnd 2; B1/21/1964 Patterson, LA

YEAR	TEAM	G (GS, POS)	RUSH	YD	AVG (LG)	TD	REC	YD	AVG (LG)	TD	PASS	COMP	PCT	YD	AVG (LG)	TD	INT	SK	YD	QBR	KPR	OTD	PTS	TAY
1986	NO	16 (5, rb)	121	425	3.5 (36)	5	17	107	6.3 (17)	0	3	1	33.3	29	9.7 (29)	1	0	—	—	—	—	—	30	548
1987	†NO	12 (1)	123	508	4.1 (30)	7	23	264	11.5 (38)	1	1	1	100.0	23	23.0 (23)	1	0	—	—	—	k	—	48	830
1988	NO	16 (9, RB)	204	823	4.0 (36)	5	34	335	9.9 (26)	1	2	1	50.0	27	13.5 (27)	1	0	—	—	—	k	—	36	1085
1989	NO★	16 (16, RB)	**344**	1262	3.7 (40)	13	52	514	9.9 (54)	5	1	1	100.0	35	35.0 (35)	1	0	—	—	—	k	—	108	1702
1990	†NO	6 (6, rb)	90	284	3.2 (17)	0	14	125	8.9 (20)	1	—	—	—	—	—	—	—	—	—	—	—	—	6	352
1991	†NO	10 (3)	79	252	3.2 (65)	4	21	127	6.0 (14)	1	—	—	—	—	—	—	—	—	—	—	—	—	30	361
1992	†NO	16 (4)	115	445	3.9 (22)	3	48	465	9.7 (41)	4	—	—	—	—	—	—	—	—	—	—	k	—	42	753
1993	NO	16 (0)	50	165	3.3 (16)	2	40	296	7.4 (34)	1	—	—	—	—	—	—	—	—	—	—	k	—	18	340
NFL	8	108 (44)	1126	4164	3.7 (65)	39	249	2233	9.0 (54)	14	7	4	57.1	114	16.3 (35)	4	0	—	—	—	k	—	318	5969

Hilliard, Ike Isaac Jason, WR, 5´11˝/210 lbs; Florida; 1997: NYG, rnd 1; B4/5/1976 Patterson, LA

YEAR	TEAM	G (GS, POS)	RUSH	YD	AVG (LG)	TD	REC	YD	AVG (LG)	TD	PASS	COMP	PCT	YD	AVG (LG)	TD	INT	SK	YD	QBR	KPR	OTD	PTS	TAY
1997	NYG	2 (2)	—	—	—	—	2	42	21.0 (23)	0	—	—	—	—	—	—	—	—	—	—	—	—	0	21
1998	NYG	16 (16, WR)	1	4	4.0 (4)	0	51	715	14.0 (50)	2	—	—	—	—	—	—	—	—	—	—	—	—	12	372
1999	NYG	16 (16, WR)	3	16	5.3 (24)	0	72	996	13.8 (46)	3	—	—	—	—	—	—	—	—	—	—	—	—	18	529
2000	†NYG	14 (14, WR)	3	19	6.3 (17)	0	55	787	14.3 (59)	8	—	—	—	—	—	—	—	—	—	—	—	—	48	453
2001	NYG	14 (9, WR)	1	21	21.0 (21)	0	52	659	12.7 (38)	6	—	—	—	—	—	—	—	—	—	—	—	—	36	381
2002	NYG	7 (7, WR)	1	7	7.0 (7)	0	27	386	14.3 (38)	2	—	—	—	—	—	—	—	—	—	—	—	—	12	210
2003	NYG	13 (12, WR)	2	19	9.5 (13)	0	60	608	10.1 (38)	6	—	—	—	—	—	—	—	—	—	—	—	—	36	353
2004	NYG	16 (15, WR)	3	34	11.3 (17)	0	49	437	8.9 (43)	0	—	—	—	—	—	—	—	—	—	—	p	—	0	259
2005	†TB	16 (2)	—	—	—	—	35	282	8.1 (22)	1	—	—	—	—	—	—	—	—	—	—	—	—	6	146
NFL	9	114 (93)	14	120	8.6 (24)	0	403	4912	12.2 (59)	28	—	—	—	—	—	—	—	—	—	—	p	—	168	2722

Hilliard, Jason Jason Bradley, T, 6´6˝/328 lbs; Louisville; B6/29/1981 Jeffersonville, IN **2004** NYG 2 (0)

Hilliard, John JohnEdward, DE, 6´2˝/285 lbs; Mississippi State; 2000: Sea, rnd 6; B4/16/1976 Coushatta, LA **2000** Sea 5 (0) **2001** Sea 16 (8, rde) **2002** Sea 6 (3) **NFL** 27 (11) [3 yrs]

Hilliard, Randy Randy, DB, 5´11˝/165 lbs; Northwestern State (LA); 1990: Cle, rnd 6; B2/6/1967 New Orleans, LA **1990** Cle 15 (0) **1991** Cle 14 (10, RCB) **1992** Cle 16 (4) **1993** Cle 12 (5, lcb) **1994** Den 15 (4) **1995** Den 12 (0) **1996**†Den 13 (2) **1997**†Den 14 (0) **1998** ChiB 9 (2) **NFL** 120 (27) [9 yrs]

Hillman, Bill William Joseph, B, 5´11˝/200 lbs; Tennessee; 1947: Det, rnd 27; B11/11/1921 Erie, PA, D1952

YEAR	TEAM	G (GS, POS)	RUSH	YD	AVG (LG)	TD	REC	YD	AVG (LG)	TD	PASS	COMP	PCT	YD	AVG (LG)	TD	INT	SK	YD	QBR	KPR	OTD	PTS	TAY
1947	Det	2 (0)	2	0	0.0 (4)	0	1	25	25.0 (25)	0	—	—	—	—	—	—	—	—	—	—	k	—	0	13

Hills, Keno Keno J., G-T, 6´6˝/305 lbs; Kent State; Louisiana-Lafayette; 1996: NO, rnd 6; B6/13/1973 Tampa, FL **1996** NO 1 (0) **1997** NO 9 (6, rg) **1998** NO 12 (1) **NFL** 22 (7) [3 yrs]

Hilpert, Hal Harold, E-B, 5´9˝/188 lbs; Oklahoma City; B1908 **1930** NYG 10 (2) **1933** Cin 1 (1) **NFL** 11 (3) [2 yrs]

Hilton, Carl Carl Patrick, TE, 6´3˝/232 lbs; Houston; 1986: Min, rnd 7; B2/8/1964 Galveston, TX **1986** Min 16 (0) **1989** Min 1 (0)

YEAR	TEAM	G (GS, POS)	RUSH	YD	AVG (LG)	TD	REC	YD	AVG (LG)	TD	PASS	COMP	PCT	YD	AVG (LG)	TD	INT	SK	YD	QBR	KPR	OTD	PTS	TAY
1987	†Min	11 (1)	—	—	—	—	2	16	8.0 (8)	2	—	—	—	—	—	—	—	—	—	—	k	—	12	16
1988	†Min	8 (0)	—	—	—	—	1	1	1.0 (1)	1	—	—	—	—	—	—	—	—	—	—	—	—	6	6
NFL	4	36 (1)	—	—	—	—	3	17	5.7 (8)	3	—	—	—	—	—	—	—	—	—	—	k	—	18	22

YEAR	TEAM	G (GS, POS)	RUSH	YD	AVG(LG)	TD	REC	YD	AVG(LG)	TD	PASS COMP	PCT	YD	AVG(LG)	TD	INT	SK	YD	QBR	KPR	OTD	PTS	TAY

HILTON, JOHN John Justin, TE, 6´5˝/225 lbs; Richmond; 1964: Det, rnd 6/Buf, rnd 16; B3/12/1942 Albany, NY

1965	Pit	14 (TE)	—	—	—	—	4	32	8.0(12)	0	—	—	—	—	—	—	—	—	—	—	—	0	16
1966	Pit	14 (TE)	—	—	—	—	46	603	13.1(32)	4	—	—	—	—	—	—	—	—	—	k	—	24	307
1967	Pit	13 (TE)	1	15	15.0(15)	0	26	343	13.2(43)	5	—	—	—	—	—	—	—	—	—	k	—	30	197
1968	Pit	14 (TE)	—	—	—	—	20	285	14.3(37)	1	—	—	—	—	—	—	—	—	—	k	—	6	142
1969	Pit	11 (TE)	—	—	—	—	12	231	19.3(34)	0	—	—	—	—	—	—	—	—	—	—	—	0	116
1970	GB	14 (TE)	—	—	—	—	25	350	14.0(65)	1	—	—	—	—	—	—	—	—	—	k	—	24	195
1971	Min	7	—	—	—	—	—	—	—	—	—	—	—	—	—	—	—	—	—	—	—	—	—
1972	Det	5	—	—	—	—	5	133	26.6(66)	1	—	—	—	—	—	—	—	—	—	—	—	6	72
1973	Det	14	—	—	—	—	6	70	11.7(31)	1	—	—	—	—	—	—	—	—	—	—	—	6	40
NFL	9	106	1	15	15.0(15)	0	144	2047	14.2(66)	16	—	—	—	—	—	—	—	—	—	k	—	96	1083

HILTON, ROY Roy Lee, DE, 6´6˝/240 lbs; Jackson State; 1965: Bal, rnd 15/Hou, rnd 8; B3/23/1943 Georgetown, MS **1965**†Bal 14 **1966** Bal 14 **1967** Bal 14 (LDE) **1968**†Bal 14
1969 Bal 14 (RDE) **1970**†Bal 14 (RDE) **1971**†Bal 14 (RDE) **1972** Bal 14 (RDE) **1973** Bal 13 **1974** NYG 14 (LDE) **1975** Atl 12 **NFL** 151 [11 yrs]

HILTON, SCOTT Scott, LB, 6´4˝/230 lbs; Salem (NC); B5/28/1954 Harrisburg, PA **1979** SF 7 (LLB) **1980** SF 13 (8, mlb/rilb) **NFL** 20 (8) [2 yrs]

HILTON, ZACHARY Zachary Thomas, TE, 6´8˝/262 lbs; North Carolina; B7/2/1980 Washington, DC **2003** NO 3 (0)

| 2005 | NO | 15 (6, te) | — | — | — | — | 35 | 396 | 11.3(29) | 1 | — | — | — | — | — | — | — | — | — | — | — | 6 | 203 |
| NFL | 2 | 18 (6) | — | — | — | — | 35 | 396 | 11.3(29) | 1 | — | — | — | — | — | — | — | — | — | — | — | 6 | 203 |

HIMES, DICK Richard Dean, T, 6´4˝/244 lbs; Ohio State; 1968: GB, rnd 3; B5/25/1946 Canton, OH **1968** GB 14 **1969** GB 14 **1970** GB 11 (11, RT) **1971** GB 14 (14, RT)
1972†GB 14 (14, RT) **1973** GB 14 (13, RT) **1974** GB 13 (13, RT) **1975** GB 14 (14, RT) **1976** GB 14 (14, RT) **1977** GB 13 (RT) **NFL** 135 (93) [10 yrs]

HINCHMAN, CURLY Hubert Edward, B, 5´10˝/190 lbs; Butler; B11/12/1907, IL, D1/9/1968 Anderson, IN

1933	ChiC	10 (1, FB)	49	156	3.2	1	1	9	9.0(9)	0	4	2	50.0	33	8.3	0	0	—	—	—	—	—	0	177
1934	ChiC	9 (0)	10	15	1.5	0	—	—	—	—	—	—	—	—	—	—	—	—	—	—	—	0	15
1934	Det	3 (1)	—	—	—	—	1	18	18.0(18)	0	—	—	—	—	—	—	—	—	—	—	—	0	9
NFL	2	22 (6)	59	171	2.9	0	2	27	13.5(18)	0	4	2	50.0	33	8.3	0	0	—	—	—	—	0	201

HINDMAN, STAN Stanley Chatham, DE-DT, 6´3˝/235 lbs; Mississippi; 1966: SF, rnd 1/Hou, rnd 2; B3/1/1944 Houlton, ME **1966** SF 14 **1967** SF 13 (13, LDE)
1968 SF 14 (14, LDE) **1969** SF 10 (10, LDE) **1970**†SF 8 **1971**†SF 9 **1974** SF 8 **NFL** 76 (37) [7 yrs]

HINES, ANDRE Andre Pierre, T, 6´6˝/275 lbs; Stanford; 1980: Sea, rnd 2; B2/28/1958 Oakland, CA **1980** Sea 9 (0)

HINES, GLEN RAY Glen Ray, T, 6´5˝/265 lbs; Arkansas; 1965: Hou, rnd R2/StL, rnd 6; B10/26/1943 El Dorado, AR **1966** Hou-A 14 (9, RT) **1967**†Hou-A 14 (RT)
1968 Hou-A◇14 (RT) **1969**†Hou-A◇14 (RT) **1970** Hou 14 (RT) **1971** NO 14 (RT) **1972** NO 14 (RT) **1973**†Pit 14 (RT) **NFL** 112 (9) [8 yrs]

HINES, JIMMY James, WR, 6´0˝/175 lbs; Texas Southern; 1968: Mia, rnd 6; B9/10/1946 Dumas, AR **1970** KC 1

| 1969 | Mia-A | 9 | 1 | 7 | 7.0(7) | 0 | 2 | 23 | 11.5(22) | 0 | — | — | — | — | — | — | — | — | — | k | — | 0 | 26 |
| NFL | 2 | 10 | 1 | 7 | 7.0(7) | 0 | 2 | 23 | 11.5(22) | 0 | — | — | — | — | — | — | — | — | — | — | — | 0 | 19 |

HINKLE, BRYAN Bryan Eric, LB, 6´1˝/222 lbs; Oregon; 1981: Pit, rnd 6; B6/4/1959 Long Beach, CA **1982** Pit 9 (1) **1983**†Pit 16 (0) **1984**†Pit 15 (15, ROLB)
1985 Pit 14 (14, ROLB) **1986** Pit 12 (12, ROLB) **1987** Pit 12 (12, ROLB) **1988** Pit 13 (13, LOLB) **1989**†Pit 13 (13, LOLB) **1990** Pit 16 (16, LOLB) **1991** Pit 14 (14, LOLB)
1992†Pit 13 (1) **1993**†Pit 12 (1) **NFL** 163 (116) [12 yrs]

HINKLE, CLARKE William Clarke, FB-LB-HB-DB, 5´11˝/202 lbs; Bucknell; B4/10/1909 Toronto, OH, D11/9/1988 Steubenville, OH; HOF 1964 **[K]**

1932	GB☆	13 (9, FB)	95	331	3.5(27)	3	—	—	—	—	1	1	100.0	23	23.0(23)	0	0	—	—	—	K	—	19	373
1933	GB☆	13 (8, FB)	139	413	3.0(33)	4	6	38	6.3	—	27	12	44.4	147	5.4	0	3	—	—	—	K	—	30	426
1934	GB☆	12 (10, FB)	144	359	2.5(32)	1	11	113	10.3(69)	1	19	9	47.4	87	4.6	0	2	—	—	—	K	—	27	394
1935	GB☆	9 (6, FB)	77	273	3.5(17)	2	1	-4	-4.0(-4)	0	—	—	—	—	—	—	—	—	—	—	K	—	18	291
1936	†GB☆	12 (10, FB)	100	476	4.8(57)	5	—	—	—	—	2	1	50.0	10	5.0(10)	0	0	—	—	—	K	—	31	531
1937	GB☆	11 (10, FB)	129	552	4.3(41)	5	8	116	14.5(49)	2	3	2	66.7	43	14.3	0	0	—	—	—	K	—	57	692
1938	†GB★	11 (8, FB)	114	299	2.6(46)	3	7	98	14.0(32)	4	2	1	50.0	6	3.0(6)	0	0	—	—	—	K	—	**58**	401
1939	†GB★	11 (5, fb)	135	381	2.8(29)	5	4	70	17.5(25)	0	—	—	—	—	—	—	—	—	—	—	KP	—	35	466
1940	†GB★	10 (8, FB)	109	383	3.5(31)	2	4	28	7.0(12)	1	—	—	—	—	—	—	—	—	—	—	KPi	—	48	423
1941	†GB☆	11 (8, FB)	**129**	393	3.0(20)	5	8	78	9.8(28)	1	—	—	—	—	—	—	—	—	—	—	KPkpi	—	56	528
NFL	10	113 (82)	1171	3860	3.3(57)	35	49	537	11.0(69)	9	54	26	48.1	316	5.9(23)	0	5	—	—	—	KPkpi	—	379	4524

HINKLE, GEORGE George Allen, DE-NT-DT, 6´4˝/273 lbs; Arizona; 1988: SD, rnd 11; B3/17/1965 St. Louis, MO **1988** SD 3 (1) **1989** SD 14 (0) **1990** SD 16 (3)
1991 SD 13 (13, LDE) **1992** Min 9 (0) **1993** Cin 13 (9, RDE) **NFL** 68 (26) [6 yrs]

HINKLE, JACK John M., B, 6´0˝/195 lbs; Syracuse; B10/31/1917 Milton, PA

1940	NYG	3 (0)	—	—	—	—	3	23	7.7	0	—	—	—	—	—	—	—	—	—	—	—	0	12
1941	Phi	1 (0)	—	—	—	—	—	—	—	—	—	—	—	—	—	—	—	—	—	k	—	0	-10
1943	P-P☆	10 (9, RH)	116	571	4.9(56)	3	1	3	3.0(3)	0	—	—	—	—	—	—	—	—	—	Pkpi	1	24	758
1944	Phi	10 (7, RH)	92	421	4.6(26)	2	2	34	17.0(22)	0	—	—	—	—	—	—	—	—	—	kpi	1	18	576
1945	Phi	3 (2)	11	40	3.6(14)	0	1	8	8.0(8)	0	—	—	—	—	—	—	—	—	—	kpi	—	0	71
1946	Phi	10 (3)	18	33	1.8(8)	0	—	—	—	—	—	—	—	—	—	—	—	—	—	kpi	—	0	69
1947	Phi	3 (0)	1	2	2.0(2)	0	—	—	—	—	—	—	—	—	—	—	—	—	—	—	—	0	2
NFL	7	40 (21)	238	1067	4.5(56)	5	7	68	9.7(22)	0	—	—	—	—	—	—	—	—	—	Pkpi	2	42	1477

HINNANT, MIKE Michael Wesley, TE, 6´3˝/268 lbs; Temple; 1988: Pit, rnd 8; B9/8/1966 Washington, DC

1988	Pit	16 (1)	—	—	—	—	1	23	23.0(23)	0	—	—	—	—	—	—	—	—	—	—	—	0	12
1989	Pit	5 (0)	—	—	—	—	—	—	—	—	—	—	—	—	—	—	—	—	—	k	—	0	-2
1992	Det	15 (1)	—	—	—	—	3	28	9.3(13)	0	—	—	—	—	—	—	—	—	—	—	—	0	14
NFL	3	36 (2)	—	—	—	—	4	51	12.8(23)	0	—	—	—	—	—	—	—	—	—	k	—	0	24

HINTE, HAL Harold Hale, E, 6´1˝/195 lbs; Pittsburgh; B1/25/1920 Pittsburgh, PA, D2/3/1996 Jacksonville, FL **1942** GB 1 (0) **1942** Pit 3 (0) **NFL** 4 (0) [1 yr]

HINTON, CHRIS Christopher Jerrod, T-G, 6´4˝/300 lbs; Northwestern; 1983: Den, rnd 1; B7/31/1961 Chicago, IL **1983** Bal★16 (15, LG) **1984** Ind 6 (6, lt) **1985** Ind★16 (16, LT)
1986 Ind★16 (16, LT) **1987**†Ind★12 (12, LT) **1989** Ind★14 (14, LT) **1990** Atl 15 (15, RT) **1991**†Atl◇16 (16, RT) **1994**†Min 16 (16, RT) **1995** Min 4 (4)

1988	Ind★	14 (13, LT)	—	—	—	—	1	1.0(1)	—	0	—	—	—	—	—	—	—	—	—	—	—	0	1
1992	Atl	16 (16, RT)	—	—	—	—	1	-2	-2.0(-2)	0	—	—	—	—	—	—	—	—	—	—	—	0	-1
1993	Atl☆	16 (16, RG)	—	—	—	—	1	-8	-8.0(-8)	0	—	—	—	—	—	—	—	—	—	—	—	0	-4
NFL	13	177 (172)	—	—	—	—	3	-9	-3.0(1)	0	—	—	—	—	—	—	—	—	—	—	—	0	-5

HINTON, CHUCK Charles Dudley, DT, 6´5˝/257 lbs; North Carolina Central; 1962: Cle, rnd 2/DalT, rnd 4; B8/11/1939 Raleigh, NC, D1/30/1999 Raleigh, NC **1964** Pit 14 (RDT)
1965 Pit 14 (RDT) **1966** Pit 14 (RDT) **1967** Pit 14 (RDT) **1968** Pit 14 (RDT) **1969** Pit 14 (RDT) **1970** Pit 14 (RDT) **1971** NYJ 12 (RDT) **1972** Bal 13 **NFL** 123 [9 yrs]

HINTON, CHUCK Charles Richard, C, 6´2˝/235 lbs; Mississippi; 1964: NYG, rnd 15/SD, rnd 22; B12/6/1942 Wilkinson, MS **1967** NYG 10 **1968** NYG 14 **1969** NYG 8
NFL 32 [3 yrs]

HINTON, EDDIE Edward Gerald, WR, 6´0˝/200 lbs; Oklahoma; 1969: Bal, rnd 1; B6/26/1947 Lawton, OK

1969	Bal	12	1	-3	-3.0(-3)	0	13	269	20.7(46)	1	—	—	—	—	—	—	—	—	—	k	—	6	146
1970	†Bal	13 (WR)	5	58	11.6(21)	2	47	733	15.6(40)	5	—	—	—	—	—	—	—	—	—	—	—	42	470
1971	†Bal	14 (WR)	4	56	14.0(30)	0	25	436	17.4(33)	2	—	—	—	—	—	—	—	—	—	—	—	12	284
1972	Bal	8	—	—	—	—	11	146	13.3(63)	0	—	—	—	—	—	—	—	—	—	—	—	6	78
1973	Hou	11	1	-2	-2.0(-2)	0	13	202	15.5(34)	1	—	—	—	—	—	—	—	—	—	k	—	6	125
1974	NE	9 (1)	1	1	1.0(1)	0	2	36	18.0(20)	1	—	—	—	—	—	—	—	—	—	kp	—	0	52
NFL	6	67 (1)	12	110	9.2(30)	2	111	1822	16.4(63)	10	—	—	—	—	—	—	—	—	—	kp	—	72	1154

HINTON, GRASSY J.W., TB-QB, 6´0˝/185 lbs; TCU; B6/30/1907, D12/10/1944 East Indies

| 1932 | StL | 12 (6, tb) | 19 | 64 | 3.4 | 1 | 4 | 69 | 17.3 | 0 | 19 | 5 | 26.3 | 46 | 2.4 | 0 | 2 | — | — | — | — | — | 6 | 52 |

HINTON, MARCUS Marcus, TE, 6´4˝/260 lbs; Alcorn State; B12/27/1971 Wiggins, MS **1996** Oak 2 (0)

HINTZ, MIKE Michael Kerry, DB, 6´1˝/190 lbs; Wisconsin-Platteville; B8/8/1965 Eau Claire, WI **1987** ChiB 3 (0)

HIPA, SAM Samuel Vincent, E, 5´11˝/165 lbs; Dayton; B10/12/1900 Mapulhu, HI, D10/17/1961 **1927** Day 1 (1) **1928** Day 4 (4) **NFL** 5 (5) [2 yrs]

HIPP, I.M. Isiah Moses Walter, RB, 5´11˝/201 lbs; Nebraska; 1980: Atl, rnd 4; B2/15/1956 Chapin, SC **1980** Oak 1 (0)

HIPPLE, ERIC Eric Ellsworth, QB, 6´2˝/196 lbs; Utah State; 1980: Det, rnd 4; B9/16/1957 Lubbock, TX

YEAR	TEAM	G (GS, POS)	RUSH	YD	AVG (LG)	TD	REC	YD	AVG (LG)	TD	PASS	COMP	PCT	YD	AVG (LG)	TD	INT	SK	YD	QBR	KPR	OTD	PTS	TAY
1980	Det	15(0)	—	—	—	—	—	—	—	—	—	—	—	—	—	—	—	—	—	—	—	—	—	—
1981	Det	16(10, QB)	41	168	4.1(18)	7	—	—	—	—	279	140	50.2	2358	**8.5**(**94**)	14	15	27	208	73.4	—	—	42	887
1982	†Det	9(4)	10	57	5.7(20)	0	—	—	—	—	86	36	41.9	411	4.8(52)	2	4	11	97	—	—	—	0	113
1983	Det	16(16, QB)	41	171	4.2(27)	3	—	—	—	—	387	204	52.7	2577	6.7(80)	12	18	37	274	64.7	—	—	18	830
1984	Det	8(1)	2	3	1.5(2)	0	—	—	—	—	38	16	42.1	246	6.5(40)	1	1	7	62	—	—	—	0	91
1985	Det	16(15, QB)	32	89	2.8(26)	2	—	—	—	—	406	223	54.9	2952	7.3(56)	17	18	49	343	73.6	—	—	12	950
1986	Det	16(10, QB)	16	46	2.9(13)	0	—	—	—	—	305	192	**63.0**	1919	6.3(46)	9	11	21	153	75.6	—	—	0	611
1988	Det	5(0)	1	5	5.0(5)	0	—	—	—	—	27	12	44.4	158	5.9(31)	0	0	3	25	—	—	—	0	84
1989	Det	1(1)	2	11	5.5(10)	1	—	—	—	—	18	7	38.9	90	5.0(30)	0	3	5	26	—	—	—	6	-54
NFL	9	102(57)	145	550	3.8(27)	13	—	—	—	—	1546	830	53.7	10711	6.9(94)	55	70	160	1188	68.7	—	—	78	3511

HIPPS, CLAUDE Claude Marion, DB, 6´1˝/189 lbs; Georgia; 1952: Pit, rnd 7; B4/21/1927 Hazlehurst, GA **1952** Pit 12 (SS) **1953** Pit 5 **NFL** 17 [2 yrs]

HIRE, DOUG Douglas, C, 6´2˝/245 lbs; Linfield; B4/22/1965 **1987** Sea 3 (1)

HIRSCH, BUCKETS Edward Norman, QB-FB, 5´10˝/207 lbs; Northwestern; 1944: ChiB, rnd 16; B3/26/1921 Clarence, NY, D1/28/2000 Irving, NY **1948**†Buf-A 13 (0) **1949**†Buf-A 7 (0)

YEAR	TEAM	G (GS, POS)	RUSH	YD	AVG (LG)	TD	REC	YD	AVG (LG)	TD	PASS	COMP	PCT	YD	AVG (LG)	TD	INT	SK	YD	QBR	KPR	OTD	PTS	TAY
1947	Buf-A	14(2, qb)	4	7	1.8	0	—	—	—	—	—	—	—	—	—	—	—	—	—	—	i	1	6	75
AAFC	3	34(2)	4	7	1.8	0	—	—	—	—	—	—	—	—	—	—	—	—	—	—	—	1	6	7

HIRSCH, ELROY Elroy Leon 'Crazy Legs', E-HB-DE, 6´2˝/190 lbs; Wisconsin; Michigan; 1945: Cle, rnd 1; B6/17/1923 Wausau, WI, D1/28/2004 Madison, WI; HOF 1968 **[K]**

YEAR	TEAM	G (GS, POS)	RUSH	YD	AVG (LG)	TD	REC	YD	AVG (LG)	TD	PASS	COMP	PCT	YD	AVG (LG)	TD	INT	SK	YD	QBR	KPR	OTD	PTS	TAY
1946	ChiR-A	14(12, HB)	87	226	2.6	1	27	347	12.9(68)	3	20	12	60.0	156	7.8	1	2	—	—	—	Kkpi	2	36	839
1947	ChiR-A	5(4, lh)	23	51	2.2	1	10	282	28.2(76)	3	1	0	0.0	0	0.0	0	0	—	—	—	kp	—	24	313
1948	ChiR-A	5(3)	23	93	4.0	0	7	101	14.4	1	—	—	—	—	—	—	—	—	—	—	kpi	—	6	210
AAFC	3	24(19)	133	370	2.8	2	44	730	16.6(76)	7	21	12	57.1	156	7.4	1	2	—	—	—	Kkpi	2	66	1361
1949	†LARm	12(3)	68	287	4.2(51)	1	22	326	14.8(48)	4	—	—	—	—	—	—	—	—	—	—	i	1	36	525
1950	†LARm	12(RE)	2	19	9.5(15)	0	42	687	16.4(58)	7	1	0	0.0	0	0.0	0	0	—	—	—	Ki	—	47	406
1951	†LARm★	12(RE)	1	3	3.0(3)	0	**66**	**1495**	**22.7**(**91**)	**17**	—	—	—	—	—	—	—	—	—	—	K	—	**102**	836
1952	†LARm★	10(LE)	—	—	—	—	25	590	**23.6**(**84**)	4	—	—	—	—	—	—	—	—	—	—	—	—	24	315
1953	LARm★	12(LE)	1	-6	-6.0(-6)	0	61	941	15.4(70)	4	—	—	—	—	—	—	—	—	—	—	K	—	28	485
1954	LARm	12(LE)	1	6	6.0(6)	0	35	720	20.6(66)	3	—	—	—	—	—	—	—	—	—	—	i	—	18	388
1955	†LARm	9(RE)	—	—	—	—	25	460	18.4(72)	2	—	—	—	—	—	—	—	—	—	—	—	—	12	240
1956	LARm☆	12(LE)	—	—	—	—	35	603	17.2(76)	6	—	—	—	—	—	—	—	—	—	—	—	—	36	332
1957	LARm	12(LE)	1	8	8.0(8)	0	32	477	14.9(45)	6	—	—	—	—	—	—	—	—	—	—	—	—	36	277
NFL	9	103(3)	74	317	4.3(51)	1	343	6299	18.4(91)	53	1	0	0.0	0	0.0	0	0	—	—	—	Ki	1	339	3802

HIRSCH, STEVE Steven Wendell, DB, 6´0˝/195 lbs; Northern Illinois; B5/18/1962 Pontiac, MI **1987** Det 3 (1)

HITCHCOCK, BILL William Frederick, T-G, 6´6˝/296 lbs; Purdue; 1990: Sea, rnd 8; B8/26/1965 Kirkland, Canada **1991** Sea 16 (9, RT) **1992** Sea 16 (11, RT) **1993** Sea 14 (14, RG) **1994** Sea 5 (5, rg) **NFL** 51 (39) [4 yrs]

HITCHCOCK, JIMMY Jimmy Davis, DB, 5´10˝/190 lbs; North Carolina; 1995: NE, rnd 3; B11/9/1970 Concord, NC **1995** NE 8 (0) **1996** NE 13 (5, rcb) **1997**†NE 15 (15, RCB) **1998**†Min 16 (16, RCB) **1999**†Min 16 (16, RCB) **2000** Car 16 (2) **2001** Car 16 (7, lcb) **2002** NE 1 (0) **NFL** 101 (61) [8 yrs]

HITCHCOCK, RAY Raebern Brooks, C, 6´2˝/289 lbs; Minnesota; 1987: Was, rnd 12; B6/20/1965 St. Paul, MN **1987** Was 5 (0)

HITT, JOEL Joel Reuben, E, 6´1˝/180 lbs; Mississippi College; 1939: Cle, rnd 13; B12/30/1916 Clinton, MS, D6/2/2003 Mobile, AL

YEAR	TEAM	G (GS, POS)	RUSH	YD	AVG (LG)	TD	REC	YD	AVG (LG)	TD	PASS	COMP	PCT	YD	AVG (LG)	TD	INT	SK	YD	QBR	KPR	OTD	PTS	TAY
1939	Cle	3(0)	1	3	3.0(3)	0	4	51	12.8	0	—	—	—	—	—	—	—	—	—	—	—	—	0	29

HIX, BILLY William Stewart, E, 6´2˝/215 lbs; Arkansas; 1950: Phi, rnd 14; B1/18/1929 Batesville, AR

YEAR	TEAM	G (GS, POS)	RUSH	YD	AVG (LG)	TD	REC	YD	AVG (LG)	TD	PASS	COMP	PCT	YD	AVG (LG)	TD	INT	SK	YD	QBR	KPR	OTD	PTS	TAY
1950	Phi	11	—	—	—	—	2	25	12.5(20)	0	—	—	—	—	—	—	—	—	—	—	—	—	0	13

HOAGE, TERRY Terrell Lee, DB, 6´2˝/201 lbs; Georgia; 1984: NO, rnd 3; B4/11/1962 Ames, IA **[I]** **1984** NO 14 (0) **1985** NO 16 (13, SS) **1986** Phi 16 (12, FS) **1987** Phi 11 (11, FS) **1989**†Phi 6 (0) **1990**†Phi 16 (3) **1991**†Was 6 (0) **1993** SF 4 (0) **1993**†Hou 3 (0) **1994** Arz 16 (16, FS) **1995** Arz 13 (7, fs) **1996** Arz 5 (3)

YEAR	TEAM	G (GS, POS)	RUSH	YD	AVG (LG)	TD	REC	YD	AVG (LG)	TD	PASS	COMP	PCT	YD	AVG (LG)	TD	INT	SK	YD	QBR	KPR	OTD	PTS	TAY
1988	†Phi☆	16(0)	1	38	38.0(38)	1	—	—	—	—	—	—	—	—	—	—	—	—	—	—	iS	—	6	124
NFL	12	142(65)	1	38	38.0(38)	1	—	—	—	—	—	—	—	—	—	—	—	—	—	—	iS	1	12	233

HOAGLIN, FRED George Frederick, C, 6´4˝/250 lbs; Pittsburgh; 1966: Cle, rnd 6; B1/28/1944 Alliance, OH **1966** Cle 6 (6, c) **1967**†Cle 14 (14, C) **1968**†Cle 14 (14, C) **1969**†Cle✧14 (C) **1970** Cle 14 (C) **1971**†Cle 11 (C) **1972**†Cle 14 (c) **1973** Bal 14 **1974** Hou 14 (c) **1975** Hou 14 **1976** Sea 13 (7, C) **NFL** 142 (41) [11 yrs]

HOAGUE, JOE Joseph Daniell, FB-HB, 6´2˝/203 lbs; Colgate; 1941: Phi, rnd 13; B2/8/1918 Brookline, MA, D1/4/1991 Lakeville, MA

YEAR	TEAM	G (GS, POS)	RUSH	YD	AVG (LG)	TD	REC	YD	AVG (LG)	TD	PASS	COMP	PCT	YD	AVG (LG)	TD	INT	SK	YD	QBR	KPR	OTD	PTS	TAY
1941	Pit	10(1)	33	112	3.4(29)	1	2	21	10.5(14)	1	1	0	0.0	0	0.0	0	0	—	—	—	Pk	—	12	140
1942	Pit	11(0)	65	168	2.6(42)	1	—	—	—	—	1	0	0.0	0	0.0	0	0	—	—	—	Pi	—	6	188
1946	Bos	7(1)	1	2	2.0(2)	0	1	4	4.0(4)	0	—	—	—	—	—	—	—	—	—	—	i	—	0	7
NFL	3	28(2)	99	282	2.8(42)	2	3	25	8.3(14)	1	2	0	0.0	0	0.0	0	0	—	—	—	Pki	—	18	335

HOAK, DICK Richard John, RB-FL, 5´11˝/195 lbs; Penn State; 1961: Pit, rnd 7; B12/8/1939 Jeannette, PA

YEAR	TEAM	G (GS, POS)	RUSH	YD	AVG (LG)	TD	REC	YD	AVG (LG)	TD	PASS	COMP	PCT	YD	AVG (LG)	TD	INT	SK	YD	QBR	KPR	OTD	PTS	TAY
1961	Pit	14(FL)	85	302	3.6(22)	0	3	18	6.0(7)	0	3	1	33.3	13	4.3(13)	1	1	—	—	—	—	—	0	283
1962	Pit	14(FL)	117	442	3.8(39)	4	9	133	14.8(23)	0	1	0	0.0	0	0.0	0	0	—	—	—	k	—	24	559
1963	Pit	12(HB)	216	679	3.1(17)	6	11	118	10.7(23)	1	—	—	—	—	—	—	—	—	—	—	—	—	42	803
1964	Pit	14(HB)	84	258	3.1(17)	2	12	137	11.4(22)	3	1	0	0.0	0	0.0	0	0	—	—	—	—	—	30	362
1965	Pit	14(HB)	131	426	3.3(42)	5	19	228	12.0(48)	1	—	—	—	—	—	—	—	—	—	—	—	—	36	595
1966	Pit	13(HB)	81	212	2.6(16)	1	23	239	10.4(31)	0	6	4	66.7	87	14.5(42)	1	0	—	—	—	—	—	6	390
1967	Pit	14	52	142	2.7(11)	1	17	111	6.5(20)	1	8	4	50.0	69	8.6(21)	1	1	—	—	—	—	—	12	212
1968	Pit★	14(HB)	175	858	4.9(77)	3	28	253	9.0(30)	1	16	7	43.8	188	11.8(62)	0	1	—	—	—	—	—	24	1074
1969	Pit	14(HB)	151	531	3.5(13)	2	20	190	9.5(26)	1	3	2	66.7	30	10.0(16)	0	0	1	10	—	p	—	18	670
1970	Pit	12	40	115	2.9(13)	1	4	25	6.3(18)	0	2	2	100.0	40	20.0(27)	1	0	—	—	—	—	—	6	163
NFL	10	135	1132	3965	3.5(77)	25	146	1452	9.9(48)	8	40	20	50.0	427	10.7(62)	4	3	1	10	—	kp	—	198	5109

HOARD, LEROY Leroy, RB, 5´11˝/225 lbs; Michigan; 1990: Cle, rnd 2; B5/15/1968 New Orleans, LA

YEAR	TEAM	G (GS, POS)	RUSH	YD	AVG (LG)	TD	REC	YD	AVG (LG)	TD	PASS	COMP	PCT	YD	AVG (LG)	TD	INT	SK	YD	QBR	KPR	OTD	PTS	TAY
1990	Cle	14(5, rb)	58	149	2.6(42)	3	10	73	7.3(17)	0	—	—	—	—	—	—	—	—	—	—	k	—	18	204
1991	Cle	16(9, RB)	37	154	4.2(52)	2	48	567	11.8(71)	9	—	—	—	—	—	—	—	—	—	—	—	—	66	503
1992	Cle	16(9, RB)	54	236	4.4(37)	0	26	310	11.9(46)	1	—	—	—	—	—	—	—	—	—	—	k	—	6	400
1993	Cle	16(7, fb)	56	227	4.1(30)	0	35	351	10.0(41)	0	1	0	0.0	0	0.0	0	0	—	—	—	k	—	0	494
1994	†Cle✧	16(12, FB)	209	890	4.3(39)	5	45	445	9.9(65)	4	—	—	—	—	—	—	—	—	—	—	k	—	54	1183
1995	Cle	12(12, RB)	136	547	4.0(25)	0	13	103	7.9(24)	0	—	—	—	—	—	—	—	—	—	—	k	—	0	597
1996	Bal	2(1)	15	61	4.1(10)	0	1	4	4.0(4)	0	—	—	—	—	—	—	—	—	—	—	—	—	0	63
1996	Car	3(0)	5	11	2.2(5)	0	—	—	—	—	—	—	—	—	—	—	—	—	—	—	k	—	0	15
1996	†Min	6(6, rb)	105	420	4.0(25)	3	10	129	12.9(37)	0	—	—	—	—	—	—	—	—	—	—	—	—	18	515
1997	†Min	12(1)	80	235	2.9(20)	4	11	84	7.6(30)	0	—	—	—	—	—	—	—	—	—	—	—	—	24	317
1998	†Min	16(1)	115	479	4.2(50)	9	22	198	9.0(24)	1	—	—	—	—	—	—	—	—	—	—	—	—	60	673
1999	†Min	15(3)	138	555	4.0(53)	10	17	166	9.8(29)	0	—	—	—	—	—	—	—	—	—	—	—	—	60	738
NFL	10	144(66)	1008	3964	3.9(53)	36	238	2430	10.2(71)	15	1	0	0.0	0	0.0	0	0	—	—	—	k	—	306	5699

HOBAN, MIKE Michael Angel, G, 6´2˝/235 lbs; Michigan; B1/19/1952 Chicago, IL **1974** ChiB 1

HOBBINS, JIM James Patrick, G, 6´6˝/275 lbs; Minnesota; B6/4/1964 Green Bay, WI **1987** GB 3 (3)

HOBBS, BILL Billie Glenn, LB, 6´0˝/218 lbs; Texas A&M; 1969: Phi, rnd 8; B9/18/1946 Mount Pleasant, TX, D8/21/2004 San Antonio, TX **1969** Phi 14 **1970** Phi 12 **1971** Phi 11 **1972** NO 6 **NFL** 43 [4 yrs]

YEAR	TEAM	G(GS, POS)	RUSH	YD	AVG(LG)	TD	REC	YD	AVG(LG)	TD	PASS	COMP	PCT	YD	AVG(LG)	TD	INT	SK	YD	QBR	KPR	OTD	PTS	TAY

HOBBS, DARYL   Daryl Ray, WR, 6´2˝/175 lbs; Pacific; B5/23/1968 Victoria, TX

1993	†LARd	3(0)	—	—	—	—	—	—	—	—	—	—	—	—	—	—	—	—	—	—	—	—	—	—
1994	LARd	10(0)	—	—	—	—	5	52	10.4(14)	0	—	—	—	—	—	—	—	—	—	—	—	—	0	26
1995	Oak	16(1)	—	—	—	—	38	612	16.1(54)	3	1	0	0.0	0	0.0	0	0	—	—	—	kp	—	18	331
1996	Oak	16(1)	—	—	—	—	44	423	9.6(29)	3	1	1	100.0	7	7.0(7)	0	0	—	—	—	kp	—	18	263
1997	NO	4(0)	—	—	—	—	2	41	20.5(21)	1	—	—	—	—	—	—	—	—	—	—	—	—	6	26
1997	Sea	10(0)	—	—	—	—	5	44	8.8(21)	0	—	—	—	—	—	—	—	—	—	—	—	—	0	22
NFL	5	59(2)	—	—	—	—	94	1172	12.5(54)	7	2	1	50.0	7	3.5(7)	0	0	—	—	—	kp	—	42	668

HOBBS, ELLIS   Ellis, DB, 5´9˝/188 lbs; Iowa State; 2005: NE, rnd 3; B5/16/1983 Niagara Falls, NY   **2005**†NE 16 (8, RCB)

HOBBS, HOMER   Homer Brown, G, 5´11˝/210 lbs; Georgia; 1949: SF-A, rnd 16/Was, rnd 11; B2/13/1923 Lexington, SC, D1/2/1999 Powder Springs, GA   **1949**†SF-A 12 (2)

1950 SF 10 (LG)

HOBBS, STEPHEN   Stephen, WR, 5´11˝/200 lbs; North Alabama; B11/14/1965 Mendenhall, MS

1990	†Was	7(0)	—	—	—	—	1	18	18.0(18)	1	—	—	—	—	—	—	—	—	—	—	k	—	6	16
1991	†Was	16(0)	—	—	—	—	3	24	8.0(10)	0	—	—	—	—	—	—	—	—	—	—	kp	—	0	18
1992	†Was	2(0)	—	—	—	—	—	—	—	—	—	—	—	—	—	—	—	—	—	—	—	—	—	—
NFL	3	25(0)	—	—	—	—	4	42	10.5(18)	1	—	—	—	—	—	—	—	—	—	—	kp	—	6	34

HOBBY, MARION   Marion Eugene, DE, 6´4˝/277 lbs; Tennessee; 1990: Min, rnd 3; B11/7/1966 Birmingham, AL   **1990** NE 16 (5, rde)   **1991** NE 15 (1)   **1992** NE 11 (2)
NFL 42 (8) [3 yrs]

HOBERT, BILLY JOE   Billy Joe, QB, 6´3˝/230 lbs; Washington; 1993: LARd, rnd 3; B1/8/1971 Puyallup, WA

1995	Oak	4(2)	3	5	1.7(6)	0	—	—	—	—	80	44	55.0	540	6.8(80)	6	4	3	11	—	—	—	0	145
1996	Oak	8(3)	2	13	6.5(14)	0	—	—	—	—	104	57	54.8	667	6.4(51)	4	5	9	52	—	P	—	0	167
1997	Buf	2(0)	2	7	3.5(7)	0	—	—	—	—	30	17	56.7	133	4.4(20)	0	2	2	7	—	—	—	0	-7
1997	NO	5(4)	12	36	3.0(15)	0	—	—	—	—	131	61	46.6	891	6.8(49)	6	8	4	29	—	—	—	0	192
1998	NO	1(1)	2	13	6.5(14)	0	—	—	—	—	23	11	47.8	170	7.4(35)	1	2	2	17	—	—	—	0	103
1999	NO	9(7, qb)	12	47	3.9(10)	1	—	—	—	—	159	85	53.5	970	6.1(90)	6	6	11	79	—	—	—	6	332
NFL	5	29(17)	33	121	3.7(15)	1	—	—	—	—	527	275	52.2	3371	6.4(90)	23	25	31	195	67.0	P	—	6	932

HOBGOOD-CHITTICK, NATE   Nate Broe, DT, 6´3˝/290 lbs; North Carolina; B11/30/1974 New Haven, CT   **1999**†SL 10 (0)   **2000** SF 5 (0)   **2000** SL 5 (0)   **2001** KC 10 (1)
2002 KC 3 (0)   **NFL** 33 (1) [4 yrs]

HOBLEY, LIFFORT   Liffort Wayne, DB, 6´0˝/207 lbs; LSU; 1985: Pit, rnd 3; B5/12/1962 Shreveport, LA   **1985** SL 5 (0)   **1987** Mia 14 (6, ss)   **1988** Mia 16 (13, SS)   **1989** Mia 16 (3)
1990 Mia 14 (0)   **1992**†Mia 15 (5, ss)   **1993** Mia 4 (2)   **NFL** 84 (29) [7 yrs]

HOBSCHEID, FRED   Fred John, T-G, 5´11˝/202 lbs; Chicago; B4/20/1904 Chicago, IL, D4/1967   **1926** Rac 5 (5, RT)

HOBSON, BEN   Benjamin Archibald, B, 5´10˝/190 lbs; none; B7/25/1902 Kansas City, KS, D7/5/1975 Leawood, KS   **1926** Buf 9 (9, FB), 6   **1927** Buf 5 (5, BB)   **NFL** 14 (14) [2 yrs]

HOBSON, VICTOR   Victor, LB, 6´0˝/252 lbs; Michigan; 2003: NYJ, rnd 2; B2/3/1980 Mount Laurel, NJ   **2003** NYJ 16 (1)   **2004**†NYJ 12 (10, LLB)   **2005** NYJ 16 (16, LLB)
NFL 44 (27) [3 yrs]

HOCHSTEIN, RUSS   Russ, C-G, 6´4˝/305 lbs; Nebraska; 2001: TB, rnd 5; B10/7/1977 Hartington, NE   **2002** TB 1 (0)   **2002** NE 1 (0)   **2003**†NE 14 (1)   **2004**†NE 16 (2)
2005†NE 16 (7, c)   **NFL** 48 (10) [4 yrs]

HOCK, JOHN   John Joseph, G, 6´2˝/230 lbs; Santa Clara; 1950: ChiC, rnd 8; B3/7/1927 Pittsburgh, PA, D12/9/2000 Ridgewood, NJ   **1950** ChiC 12   **1953** LARm 9
1955†LARm 12 (RG)   **1956** LARm◊12 (RG)   **1957** LARm 12 (RG)   **NFL** 57 [5 yrs]

HODEL, MERWIN   Merwin Luther, FB, 6´2˝/205 lbs; Colorado; 1952: NYG, rnd 4; B5/27/1931 Rockford, IL

1953	NYG	2	5	11	2.2(6)	0	2	-15	-7.5(0)	0	—	—	—	—	—	—	—	—	—	—	—	—	0	4

HODEL, NATHAN   Nathan William, TE, 6´2˝/249 lbs; Illinois; B11/12/1977 Maryville, IL   **2002** Arz 16 (0)   **2003** Arz 16 (0)   **2004** Arz 16 (0)   **2005** Arz 16 (0)   **NFL** 64 (0) [4 yrs]

HODGDON, DREW   Lincoln Andrew, C, 6´3˝/309 lbs; Arizona State; 2005: Hou, rnd 5; B11/15/1981 Palo Alto, CA   **2005** Hou 4 (3)

HODGE, DAMON   Damon, WR, 6´1˝/192 lbs; Alabama State; B2/16/1977 Thomaston, AL

2000	Dal	8(0)	—	—	—	—	4	60	15.0(20)	0	—	—	—	—	—	—	—	—	—	—	—	—	0	30

HODGE, FLOYD   Floyd, WR, 6´0˝/195 lbs; Utah; B7/18/1959 Compton, CA

1982	†Atl	9(0)	2	11	5.5(11)	0	14	160	11.4(23)	0	—	—	—	—	—	—	—	—	—	—	k	—	0	99
1983	Atl	12(6, wr)	—	—	—	—	25	280	11.2(76)	4	2	1	50.0	28	14.0(28)	0	1	—	—	—	—	—	24	134
1984	Atl	12(1)	2	17	8.5(9)	0	24	234	9.8(26)	0	—	—	—	—	—	—	—	—	—	—	—	—	0	134
NFL	3	33(7)	4	28	7.0(11)	0	63	674	10.7(76)	4	2	1	50.0	28	14.0(28)	0	1	—	—	—	k	—	24	367

HODGE, MILFORD   Milford, DE-NT, 6´3˝/278 lbs; Washington State; 1985: NE, rnd 8; B3/11/1961 Los Angeles, CA   **1986** NO 1 (0)   **1986**†NE 6 (0)   **1987** NE 12 (0)
1988 NE 15 (7, rde)   **1989** NE 16 (1)   **NFL** 50 (8) [4 yrs]

HODGE, SEDRICK   Sedrick Jamaine, LB, 6´4˝/244 lbs; North Carolina; 2001: NO, rnd 3; B9/13/1978 Fayetteville, GA   **2001** NO 16 (0)   **2002** NO 16 (16, RLB)   **2003** NO 9 (9, LLB)
2004 NO 9 (6, llb)   **2005** NO 13 (12, LLB)   **NFL** 63 (43) [5 yrs]

HODGES, ERIC   Eric Neal, WR, 6´0˝/190 lbs; Florida; B6/3/1964 Philadelphia, PA   **1987** KC 1 (0)

HODGES, HERMAN   J. Herman, E, 6´1˝/198 lbs; Samford; B11/22/1914 Ozark, AL, D4/6/2000

1939	Bkn	10(2)	—	—	—	—	4	45	11.3	0	—	—	—	—	—	—	—	—	—	—	—	1	6	33
1940	Bkn	9(0)	—	—	—	—	3	38	12.7	0	—	—	—	—	—	—	—	—	—	—	—	—	0	19
1941	Bkn	11(3)	—	—	—	—	12	128	10.7(32)	0	—	—	—	—	—	—	—	—	—	—	—	—	0	64
1942	Bkn	10(3)	—	—	—	—	4	74	18.5(40)	0	—	—	—	—	—	—	—	—	—	—	—	—	0	37
NFL	4	40(8)	—	—	—	—	23	285	12.4(40)	0	—	—	—	—	—	—	—	—	—	—	—	1	6	153

HODGES, REGGIE   Reggie A., P, 6´1˝/226 lbs; Ball State; 2005: SL, rnd 6; B1/26/1987 Champaign, IL   **2005** SL 5 (0)   **2005** Phi 3 (0)   **NFL** 8 (0) [1 yr]

HODGINS, JAMES   James, FB, 6´1˝/274 lbs; San Jose State; B4/30/1977 San Jose, CA

1999	†SL	15(0)	7	10	1.4(3)	1	6	35	5.8(10)	0	—	—	—	—	—	—	—	—	—	—	k	—	6	12
2000	†SL	15(2)	1	3	3.0(3)	0	5	25	5.0(3)	0	—	—	—	—	—	—	—	—	—	—	—	—	0	6
2001	†SL	16(10, FB)	2	5	2.5(5)	0	4	24	6.0(11)	1	—	—	—	—	—	—	—	—	—	—	—	—	6	22
2002	SL	9(8, fb)	3	7	2.3(5)	0	9	47	5.2(11)	0	—	—	—	—	—	—	—	—	—	—	—	—	0	31
2003	Arz	16(8, FB)	2	6	3.0(3)	0	14	58	4.1(9)	2	—	—	—	—	—	—	—	—	—	—	k	—	12	43
2005	Arz	1(0)	—	—	—	—	—	—	—	—	—	—	—	—	—	—	—	—	—	—	—	—	—	—
NFL	6	72(28)	15	31	2.1(5)	1	35	169	4.8(11)	3	—	—	—	—	—	—	—	—	—	—	k	—	24	113

HODGINS, NORM   Norman Francis, DB, 6´1˝/190 lbs; LSU; 1974: Chi, rnd 11; B3/1/1952 New Orleans, LA

1974	ChiB	14	1	3	3.0(3)	0	—	—	—	—	1	0	0.0	0	0.0	0	0	—	—	—	p	—	0	1

HODGSON, PAT   Patrick Shannon, WR, 6´2˝/190 lbs; Georgia; B1/30/1944 Columbus, GA   **1966** Was 10

HODSON, TOM   Thomas Paul, QB, 6´3˝/195 lbs; LSU; 1990: NE, rnd 3; B1/28/1967 Mathews, LA

1990	NE	7(6, qb)	12	79	6.6(23)	0	—	—	—	—	156	85	54.5	968	6.2(56)	4	5	20	147	—	—	—	0	383
1991	NE	16(3)	4	0	0.0(1)	0	—	—	—	—	68	36	52.9	345	5.1(32)	1	4	9	57	—	—	—	0	18
1992	NE	9(3)	5	11	2.2(5)	0	1	-6	-6.0(-6)	0	91	50	54.9	496	5.5(54)	2	2	12	96	—	—	—	0	186
1995	NO	4(0)	—	—	—	—	—	—	—	—	5	3	60.0	14	2.8(9)	0	0	—	—	—	—	—	0	7
NFL	4	36(12)	21	90	4.3(23)	0	1	-6	-6.0(-6)	0	320	174	54.4	1823	5.7(56)	7	11	41	300	—	—	—	0	594

HOEL, BOB   Robert Malcolm, G-T, 6´0˝/208 lbs; Pittsburgh; B6/5/1913 Alden, MN, D12/14/2001 Glenview, IL   **1935** Pit 12 (9, RG)   **1937** ChiC 1 (0)   **1938** ChiC 4 (1)
NFL 17 (10) [3 yrs]

HOELSCHER, DAVID   David Henry, DE, 6´6˝/261 lbs; Eastern Kentucky; B11/27/1975 Coldwater, OH   **1998** Was 1 (0)

HOERNER, DICK
Lester Junior, FB, 6′4″/220 lbs; Iowa; 1945: Cle, rnd 17/1947: Cle-A, rnd S; B7/25/1922 Dubuque, IA

YEAR	TEAM	G(GS, POS)	RUSH	YD	AVG(LG)	TD	REC	YD	AVG(LG)	TD	PASS	COMP	PCT	YD	AVG(LG)	TD	INT	SK	YD	QBR	KPR	OTD	PTS	TAY
1947	LARm	4(0)	30	124	4.1(23)	2	1	20	20.0(20)	0	—	—	—	—	—	—	—	—	—	—	—	—	12	154
1948	LARm	12(5, FB)	76	354	4.7(23)	4	18	227	12.6(45)	2	—	—	—	—	—	—	—	—	—	—	kpi	—	36	525
1949	†LARm	12(12, FB)	155	582	3.8(37)	6	17	213	12.5(29)	0	—	—	—	—	—	—	—	—	—	—	P	—	36	749
1950	†LARm★	12(FB)	95	381	4.0(64)	10	26	446	17.2(48)	1	—	—	—	—	—	—	—	—	—	—	—	—	66	709
1951	†LARm	12(fb)	94	569	6.1(43)	6	8	102	12.8(21)	1	—	—	—	—	—	—	—	—	—	—	k	—	42	692
1952	DalT	11(5, fb)	56	162	2.9(14)	2	10	172	17.2(54)	0	—	—	—	—	—	—	—	—	—	—	—	—	12	286
NFL	6	63(22)	506	2172	4.3(64)	30	80	1180	14.8(54)	4	—	—	—	—	—	—	—	—	—	—	Pkpi	—	204	3114

HOERNSCHEMEYER, BOB
Robert James 'Hunchy', B, 5′11″/194 lbs; Indiana; Navy; 1947: NYG, rnd 11; B9/24/1925 Cincinnati, OH, D6/17/1980 Detroit, MI

YEAR	TEAM	G(GS, POS)	RUSH	YD	AVG(LG)	TD	REC	YD	AVG(LG)	TD	PASS	COMP	PCT	YD	AVG(LG)	TD	INT	SK	YD	QBR	KPR	OTD	PTS	TAY
1946	ChiR-A☆	14(10, TB)	111	375	3.4(57)	0	1	11	11.0(11)	0	193	95	49.2	1266	6.6	14	14	—	—	—	Pkpi	—	0	730
1947	ChiR-A	2(2)	5	2	0.4	0	1	4	4.0(4)	0	22	9	40.9	143	6.5	1	0	—	—	—	k	—	6	82
1947	Bkn-A	12(5, TB)	147	702	4.8(84)	5	—	—	—	—	151	64	42.4	783	5.2	3	11	—	—	—	Ppi	—	30	736
1948	Bkn-A	14(6, tb)	110	574	5.2(61)	3	11	173	15.7(42)	3	155	71	45.8	854	5.5	8	15	—	—	—	Pkp	1	42	619
1949	ChiH-A☆	12(12, TB)	133	456	3.4	2	—	—	—	—	167	69	41.3	1063	6.4	6	11	—	—	—	Pkp	—	12	760
AAFC	4	54(35)	506	2109	4.2(84)	10	13	188	14.5(42)	4	688	308	44.8	4109	6.0	32	51	—	—	48.9	Pkpi	1	90	2925
1950	Det	10(RH)	84	471	5.6(96)	1	8	78	9.8(41)	1	4	1	25.0	19	4.8(19)	1	1	—	—	—	P	—	12	500
1951	Det★	11(RH)	132	678	5.1(85)	2	23	263	11.4(48)	3	4	2	50.0	46	11.5(30)	2	0	—	—	—	kp	—	30	917
1952	†Det★	10(RH)	106	457	4.3(41)	0	17	139	8.2(28)	0	4	2	50.0	14	3.5(10)	2	1	—	—	—	—	—	24	552
1953	†Det☆	12(RH)	101	482	4.8(49)	7	23	282	12.3(35)	1	5	2	40.0	16	3.2(8)	1	1	—	—	—	k	—	54	671
1954	†Det	11(RH)	94	242	2.6(35)	2	20	153	7.7(26)	1	7	3	42.9	81	11.6(66)	3	1	—	—	—	k	—	18	372
1955	Det	5(rh)	36	109	3.0(10)	1	5	36	7.2(15)	0	2	1	50.0	17	8.5(17)	1	1	—	—	—	—	—	6	111
NFL	6	59	553	2439	4.4(96)	17	96	951	9.9(48)	7	26	11	42.3	193	7.4(66)	10	5	—	—	68.3	Pkp	—	144	3121

HOEY, GEORGE
George William, DB, 5′10″/174 lbs; Michigan; 1969: Det, rnd 14; B11/14/1946 Gaffney, SC **1971** SL 6 **1972** NE 12 (6, rcb) **1973** NE 13 (12, LCB) **1974** SD 13 (8, fs) **1975** Den 1 **1975** NYJ 5 (3) **NFL** 50 (29) [5 yrs]

HOFER, PAUL
Paul David, RB, 6′0″/195 lbs; Mississippi; 1976: SF, rnd 11; B5/13/1952 Memphis, TN

YEAR	TEAM	G(GS, POS)	RUSH	YD	AVG(LG)	TD	REC	YD	AVG(LG)	TD	KPR	OTD	PTS	TAY
1976	SF	14	18	74	4.1(17)	0	4	45	11.3(13)	1	k	—	6	118
1977	SF	14	34	106	3.1(10)	0	5	46	9.2(16)	0	k	—	0	460
1978	SF	16(6, rb)	121	465	3.8(40)	7	12	170	14.2(46)	0	k	—	42	736
1979	SF	15(7, rb)	123	615	5.0(47)	7	58	662	11.4(44)	2	k	—	54	1030
1980	SF	6(6, RB)	60	293	4.9(26)	1	41	467	11.4(28)	2	k	—	18	534
1981	SF	12(0)	60	193	3.2(12)	1	27	244	9.0(22)	0	k	—	6	325
NFL	6	77(19)	416	1746	4.2(47)	16	147	1634	11.1(46)	5	k	—	126	3202

HOFFMAN, BILL
J. William, G, 5′10″/227 lbs; Lehigh; B3/31/1902 Raubsville, PA, D6/12/1994 **1924** Fra 1 (0) **1925** Fra 19 (17, LG) **1926** Fra 16 (16, LG) **NFL** 36 (33) [3 yrs]

HOFFMAN, BOB
Wayne Robert, B, 6′1″/208 lbs; USC; 1940: Was, rnd 9; B12/13/1917 Star City, WV, D4/13/2005 Kern, CA

YEAR	TEAM	G(GS, POS)	RUSH	YD	AVG(LG)	TD	REC	YD	AVG(LG)	TD	KPR	OTD	PTS	TAY
1940	†Was	8(3)	3	7	2.3	0	—	—	—	—	i	—	0	8
1941	Was	2(3)	1	2	2.0(2)	0	—	—	—	—	—	—	0	2
1946	LARm	10(2)	43	162	3.8(19)	3	—	—	—	—	—	—	18	192
1947	LARm	10(4)	42	159	3.8(20)	3	2	22	11.0(12)	0	ki	—	18	206
1948	LARm	11(4)	22	68	3.1(8)	4	3	28	9.3(13)	1	k	—	30	116
NFL	5	42(15)	111	398	3.6(20)	10	5	50	10.0(13)	1	ki	—	66	524
1949	LAD-A	12(5, bb)	—	—	—	—	2	21	10.5	—	ki	—	0	12

HOFFMAN, DALTON
Johnnie Dalton, FB, 6′0″/207 lbs; Baylor; B12/23/1941 Ballinger, TX

YEAR	TEAM	G(GS, POS)	RUSH	YD	AVG(LG)	TD	REC	YD	AVG(LG)	TD	KPR	OTD	PTS	TAY
1964	Hou-A	5	2	3	1.5(1)	1	1	1	1.0(1)	0	k	—	6	36
1965	Hou-A	4	1	11	11.0(11)	0	—	—	—	—	—	—	0	11
NFL	2	9	3	14	4.7(11)	1	1	1	1.0(1)	0	k	—	6	47

HOFFMAN, GARY
Gary Edward, T, 6′7″/285 lbs; Santa Clara; 1984: GB, rnd 10; B9/28/1961 Sacramento, CA **1984** GB 1 (0) **1987** SF 3 (0) **NFL** 4 (0) [2 yrs]

HOFFMAN, JACK
Jack Howard, DE, 6′5″/234 lbs; Xavier (OH); 1952: ChiB, rnd 5; B3/11/1930 Cincinnati, OH, D12/13/2001 Cincinnati, OH **1952** ChiB 12 (lde) **1956**†ChiB 12 (LDE) **1957** ChiB 12 (LDE) **1958** ChiB 7 (LDE)

YEAR	TEAM	G(GS, POS)	REC	YD	AVG(LG)	TD	KPR	OTD	PTS	TAY
1955	ChiB	12(LDE)	6	86	14.3(32)	0	—	—	0	43
NFL	5	55	6	86	14.3(32)	0	i	—	0	44

HOFFMAN, JAKE
Jacob H., FB, 5′8″/170 lbs; none; B7/21/1895 Syracuse, NY, D2/11/1977 Jordan, NY **1925** Roc 4 (2)

HOFFMAN, JOHN
John Wilks, HB-FB-E-LB, 6′2″/215 lbs; Arkansas; 1949: ChiB, rnd 5; B12/8/1925 Little Rock, AR, D4/15/1987 Little Rock, AR

YEAR	TEAM	G(GS, POS)	RUSH	YD	AVG(LG)	TD	REC	YD	AVG(LG)	TD	KPR	OTD	PTS	TAY
1949	ChiB	12(6, fb)	53	216	4.1(27)	1	25	373	14.9(94)	2	k	—	18	522
1950	†ChiB	12	42	154	3.7(25)	0	8	161	20.1(44)	2	kpi	1	18	351
1951	ChiB	12(LE)	1	-3	-3.0(-3)	0	28	394	14.1(78)	2	—	—	12	204
1952	ChiB	4	—	—	—	—	1	9	9.0(9)	0	ki	—	0	53
1953	ChiB◇	12(RH)	32	95	3.0(34)	3	28	341	12.2(40)	1	ki	—	24	325
1954	ChiB	12	39	178	4.6(19)	1	28	354	12.6(54)	1	kp	—	12	378
1955	ChiB◇	12(LH)	94	454	4.8(47)	0	11	153	13.9(37)	1	—	—	8	536
1956	†ChiB	12(RH)	56	272	4.9(39)	2	7	85	12.1(35)	0	—	—	12	335
NFL	8	88(6)	317	1366	4.3(47)	7	136	1870	13.8(78)	9	kpi	1	104	2701

HOFFMAN, JOHN
John Frederick, DE, 6′7″/260 lbs; USC; Hawaii; B8/2/1943 Santa Monica, CA **1969** Was 13 (lde) **1970** Was 13 (9, LDE) **1971** ChiB 1 **1972** SL 2 **1972** Den 2 (1) **NFL** 31 (10) [4 yrs]

HOFFMANN, DAVE
David Paul, LB, 6′2″/233 lbs; Washington; 1993: Chi, rnd 6; B7/24/1970 San Luis Obispo, CA **1993** Pit 1 (0)

HOGAN, DARRELL
Darrell, LB-G, 5′10″/210 lbs; Baylor; Trinity (TX); B7/2/1926 San Antonio, TX **1949** Pit☆12 (2) **1950** Pit 12 (RLB) **1951** Pit 12 (RLB) **1952** Pit 12 (LLB) **1953** Pit 12 (RLB) **NFL** 60 (2) [5 yrs]

HOGAN, MARC
Marc Christian, DB, 6′0″/180 lbs; Tennessee; B4/21/1962 Pittsburgh, PA **1987** NYJ 3 (3)

HOGAN, MIKE
Michael L., RB, 6′2″/213 lbs; Tennessee-Chattanooga; 1976: Phi, rnd 9; B11/1/1954 Floyd County, GA

YEAR	TEAM	G(GS, POS)	RUSH	YD	AVG(LG)	TD	REC	YD	AVG(LG)	TD	KPR	OTD	PTS	TAY
1976	Phi	8(7, FB)	123	561	4.6(32)	0	15	89	5.9(18)	0	—	—	0	606
1977	Phi	12(12, FB)	155	546	3.5(19)	0	19	118	6.2(51)	1	—	—	6	610
1978	†Phi	14(12, FB)	145	607	4.2(33)	4	31	164	5.3(16)	1	—	—	30	734
1979	SF	2(2)	9	31	3.4(6)	0	9	65	7.2(27)	0	—	—	0	64
1980	NYG	7(4)	22	46	2.1(9)	1	5	46	9.2(12)	0	—	—	6	79
1980	Phi	6(0)	12	44	3.7(12)	1	—	—	—	—	—	—	6	54
NFL	5	49(37)	466	1835	3.9(33)	6	79	482	6.1(51)	2	—	—	48	2146

HOGAN, PAUL
Paul Timothy, B, 5′8″/170 lbs; Notre Dame; Niagara; Washington & Jefferson; Detroit Mercy; B9/5/1898 Ashtabula, OH, D8/13/1976 Las Vegas, NV [K] **1924** Akr 6 (3, WB), 5 **1925** Can 6 (4) **1926** NYG 10 (4), 3 **1926** Fra 3 (0), 2 **1927** ChiC 1 (0), 6 **NFL** 26 (11), 16 [4 yrs]

HOGAN, TOM
Thomas Francis, T-G-C-E, 6′2″/193 lbs; Detroit Mercy; Fordham; B4/26/1898 Boston, MA, D1/27/1975 Boston, MA **1924** Min 5 (0) **1925** Det 11 (8, RT) **1926** ChiC 1 (0) **NFL** 17 (8) [3 yrs]

HOGE, MERRIL
Merrill DuAine, RB, 6′2″/225 lbs; Idaho State; 1987: Pit, rnd 10; B1/26/1965 Pocatello, ID

YEAR	TEAM	G(GS, POS)	RUSH	YD	AVG(LG)	TD	REC	YD	AVG(LG)	TD	KPR	OTD	PTS	TAY
1987	Pit	13(0)	3	8	2.7(5)	0	7	97	13.9(27)	1	k	—	6	60
1988	Pit	16(8, FB)	170	705	4.1(20)	3	50	487	9.7(40)	3	—	—	36	994
1989	†Pit	16(16, FB)	186	621	3.3(31)	8	34	271	8.0(22)	0	k	—	48	837
1990	Pit	16(15, FB)	203	772	3.8(41)	7	40	342	8.6(27)	3	—	—	60	1028
1991	Pit	16(16, FB)	165	610	3.7(24)	2	49	379	7.7(25)	1	—	—	18	825
1992	†Pit	16(11, FB)	41	150	3.7(15)	0	28	231	8.3(20)	1	k	—	6	269
1993	†Pit	16(13, FB)	51	249	4.9(30)	1	33	247	7.5(18)	4	k	—	30	391

YEAR	TEAM	G (GS, POS)	RUSH	YD	AVG (LG)	TD	REC	YD	AVG (LG)	TD	PASS	COMP	PCT	YD	AVG (LG)	TD	INT	SK	YD	QBR	KPR	OTD	PTS	TAY
1994	ChiB	5(5, fb)	6	24	4.0(8)	0	13	79	6.1(11)	0	—	—	—	—	—	—	—	—	—	—	—	—	0	64
NFL	8	114(84)	825	3139	3.8(41)	21	254	2133	8.4(40)	13	—	—	—	—	—	—	—	—	—	—	k	—	204	4465

HOGEBOOM, GARY Gary Keith, QB, 6´4˝/205 lbs; Central Michigan; 1980: Dal, rnd 5; B8/21/1958 Grand Rapids, MI

YEAR	TEAM	G (GS, POS)	RUSH	YD	AVG (LG)	TD	REC	YD	AVG (LG)	TD	PASS	COMP	PCT	YD	AVG (LG)	TD	INT	SK	YD	QBR	KPR	OTD	PTS	TAY
1980	†Dal	2(0)	—	—	—	—	—	—	—	—	—	—	—	—	—	—	—	—	—	—	—	—	—	—
1981	Dal	1(0)	—	—	—	—	—	—	—	—	—	—	—	—	—	—	—	—	—	—	—	—	—	—
1982	†Dal	4(0)	3	0	0.0(0)	0	—	—	—	—	8	3	37.5	45	5.6(26)	0	1	—	—	—	—	—	0	-18
1983	Dal	6(0)	6	-10	-1.7(-1)	0	—	—	—	—	17	11	64.7	161	9.5(24)	1	1	—	—	—	—	—	0	36
1984	Dal	16(10, QB)	15	19	1.3(11)	0	—	—	—	—	367	195	53.1	2366	6.4(68)	7	14	22	178	63.7	—	—	0	677
1985	Dal	16(2)	8	48	6.0(15)	1	—	—	—	—	126	70	55.6	978	7.8(58)	5	7	14	118	—	—	—	6	292
1986	Ind	5(5, qb)	10	20	2.0(6)	1	—	—	—	—	144	85	59.0	1154	8.0(60)	6	6	18	144	—	—	—	6	397
1987	Ind	6(6, qb)	3	3	1.0(2)	0	—	—	—	—	168	99	58.9	1145	6.8(72)	9	5	8	63	—	—	—	0	421
1988	Ind	9(1)	11	-8	-0.7(6)	1	—	—	—	—	131	76	58.0	996	7.6(58)	7	7	12	88	—	—	—	6	255
1989	Phx	14(13, QB)	27	89	3.3(15)	1	—	—	—	—	364	204	56.0	2591	7.1(59)	14	19	40	266	69.5	—	—	6	705
NFL	10	79(37)	83	161	1.9(15)	4	—	—	—	—	1325	743	56.1	9436	7.1(72)	49	60	114	857	71.9	—	—	24	2764

HOGGARD, D.D. William Benjamin, DB, 6´0˝/188 lbs; North Carolina State; B5/20/1961 Ahoskie, NC **1985** Cle 2 (0) **1986**†Cle 16 (0) **1987**†Cle 1 (0) **NFL** 19 (0) [3 yrs]

HOGLAND, DOUG M. Douglas, G-T, 6´4˝/245 lbs; Oregon State; 1953: SF, rnd 8; B5/8/1931 Farmington, NM **1954** SF 12 (LT) **1955** SF 12 (LG) **1956** ChiC 12 (LG) **1957** ChiC 12 (LG) **1958** ChiC 2 **1958** Det 10

YEAR	TEAM	G (GS, POS)	RUSH	YD	AVG (LG)	TD	REC	YD	AVG (LG)	TD	PASS	COMP	PCT	YD	AVG (LG)	TD	INT	SK	YD	QBR	KPR	OTD	PTS	TAY
1953	SF	12(LT)	—	—	—	—	1	-2	-2.0(-2)	0	—	—	—	—	—	—	—	—	—	—	—	—	0	-1
NFL	6	72	—	—	—	—	1	-2	-2.0(-2)	0	—	—	—	—	—	—	—	—	—	—	k	—	0	-14

HOGUE, FRANK Francis E., B, none; B1/18/1899 Cleveland, OH, D1/10/1967 Holmes County, OH **1924** Akr 3 (0)

HOGUE, MURRELL Murrell E., G-T, 6´1˝/208 lbs; Centenary; B8/13/1904 Amarillo, TX, D11/27/1990 Shreveport, LA **1928** NYY 10 (9, RG) **1929** ChiC 11 (3) **1930** Min 1 (0) **NFL** 22 (12) [3 yrs]

HOHENSEE, MIKE Michael Louis, QB, 6´0˝/205 lbs; Minnesota; B2/22/1961 Rowland Heights, CA

YEAR	TEAM	G (GS, POS)	RUSH	YD	AVG (LG)	TD	REC	YD	AVG (LG)	TD	PASS	COMP	PCT	YD	AVG (LG)	TD	INT	SK	YD	QBR	KPR	OTD	PTS	TAY
1987	ChiB	2(2)	9	56	6.2(26)	0	—	—	—	—	52	28	53.8	343	6.6(28)	4	1	3	19	—	—	—	0	208

HOHMAN, JON Jon Carl, G, 6´1˝/245 lbs; Wisconsin; 1965: Den, rnd 8; B10/23/1942 Antigo, WI **1965** Den-A 10 **1966** Den-A 14 (rg) **NFL** 24 [2 yrs]

HOHN, BOB Robert Huber, DB, 6´0˝/185 lbs; Nebraska; 1964: LA, rnd 20/KC, rnd 20; B6/4/1941 Beatrice, NE **1965** Pit 10 **1966** Pit 4 **1967** Pit 13 (RCB) **1968** Pit 8 **1969** Pit 11 (LCB) **NFL** 46 [5 yrs]

HOISINGTON, AL Allan G., E, 6´3˝/200 lbs; Pasadena City College (JC); B11/18/1933 Chicago, IL

YEAR	TEAM	G (GS, POS)	RUSH	YD	AVG (LG)	TD	REC	YD	AVG (LG)	TD	PASS	COMP	PCT	YD	AVG (LG)	TD	INT	SK	YD	QBR	KPR	OTD	PTS	TAY
1960	Oak-A	9	—	—	—	—	4	96	24.0(61)	2	—	—	—	—	—	—	—	—	—	—	k	—	12	53
1960	Buf-A	5	—	—	—	—	4	45	11.3(20)	0	—	—	—	—	—	—	—	—	—	—	—	—	0	23
NFL	1	14	—	—	—	—	8	141	17.6(61)	2	—	—	—	—	—	—	—	—	—	—	k	—	12	76

HOKE, CHRIS Chris, NT-DT, 6´3˝/296 lbs; Brigham Young; B4/6/1976 Long Beach, CA **2004**†Pit 14 (10, NT) **2005**†Pit 15 (0) **NFL** 29 (10) [2 yrs]

HOKE, JONATHAN Jonathan David, DB, 5´11˝/175 lbs; Ball State; B1/24/1957 Hamilton, OH **1980** ChiB 11 (0)

HOKUF, STEVE Stephen Melvin, B-E, 6´0˝/199 lbs; Nebraska; B9/26/1910 Wilber, NE, D7/1/2000 Cockeysville, MD **[K]**

YEAR	TEAM	G (GS, POS)	RUSH	YD	AVG (LG)	TD	REC	YD	AVG (LG)	TD	PASS	COMP	PCT	YD	AVG (LG)	TD	INT	SK	YD	QBR	KPR	OTD	PTS	TAY
1933	Bos	12(5, le)	16	56	3.5	0	2	19	9.5	0	18	8	44.4	105	5.8	0	0	—	—	—	—	—	0	118
1934	Bos	10(9, BB)	25	98	3.9	0	6	34	5.7	0	51	13	25.5	203	4.0	3	10	—	—	—	K	—	4	-169
1935	Bos	7(4)	12	25	2.1	0	1	1	1.0(1)	0	1	0	0.0	0	0.0	0	0	—	—	—	—	—	0	26
NFL	3	29(18)	53	179	3.4	0	9	54	6.0(1)	0	70	21	30.0	308	4.4	3	10	—	—	—	K	—	4	-25

HOLCOMB, KELLY Bryan Kelly, QB, 6´2˝/212 lbs; Middle Tennessee State; B7/9/1973 Fayetteville, TN

YEAR	TEAM	G (GS, POS)	RUSH	YD	AVG (LG)	TD	REC	YD	AVG (LG)	TD	PASS	COMP	PCT	YD	AVG (LG)	TD	INT	SK	YD	QBR	KPR	OTD	PTS	TAY
1997	Ind	5(1)	5	5	1.0(3)	0	—	—	—	—	73	45	61.6	454	6.2(41)	1	8	11	76	—	—	—	0	-83
2001	Cle	1(0)	1	0	0.0(0)	0	—	—	—	—	12	7	58.3	114	9.5(25)	1	0	—	—	—	—	—	0	62
2002	†Cle	4(2)	8	9	1.1(7)	0	—	—	—	—	106	64	60.4	790	7.5(44)	8	4	5	40	—	—	—	0	284
2003	Cle	10(8, QB)	8	7	0.9(6)	0	—	—	—	—	302	193	63.9	1797	6.0(68)	10	12	21	166	74.6	—	—	0	476
2004	Cle	4(2)	3	-2	-0.7(0)	0	—	—	—	—	87	59	67.8	737	8.5(55)	7	5	5	31	—	—	—	0	202
2005	Buf	10(8, QB)	18	11	0.6(8)	1	—	—	—	—	230	155	67.4	1509	6.6(65)	10	8	17	140	85.6	—	—	6	506
NFL	6	34(21)	43	30	0.7(8)	1	—	—	—	—	810	523	64.6	5401	6.7(68)	37	37	59	453	79.9	—	—	6	1446

HOLCOMB, TEX William L., T, 6´2˝/235 lbs; Texas Tech; B6/21/1913 Amarillo, TX, D5/20/1974 Dallas, TX **1937** Pit 7 (3) **1937** Phi 1 (1) **NFL** 8 (4) [1 yr]

HOLCOMBE, ROBERT Robert Wayne, RB, 5´11˝/208 lbs; Illinois; 1998: SL, rnd 2; B12/11/1975 Houston, TX

YEAR	TEAM	G (GS, POS)	RUSH	YD	AVG (LG)	TD	REC	YD	AVG (LG)	TD	PASS	COMP	PCT	YD	AVG (LG)	TD	INT	SK	YD	QBR	KPR	OTD	PTS	TAY
1998	SL	13(6, RB)	98	230	2.3(12)	2	6	34	5.7(14)	0	—	—	—	—	—	—	—	—	—	—	—	—	12	267
1999	†SL	15(7, fb)	78	294	3.8(34)	4	14	163	11.6(30)	1	—	—	—	—	—	—	—	—	—	—	—	—	30	421
2000	†SL	14(9, FB)	21	70	3.3(11)	3	8	90	11.3(19)	1	—	—	—	—	—	—	—	—	—	—	—	—	24	150
2001	†SL	16(0)	13	42	3.2(11)	1	1	14	14.0(14)	0	—	—	—	—	—	—	—	—	—	—	—	—	6	59
2002	†Ten	8(0)	47	242	5.1(39)	0	10	91	9.1(18)	0	—	—	—	—	—	—	—	—	—	—	—	—	0	288
2003	†Ten	15(0)	63	201	3.2(21)	1	19	121	6.4(11)	1	—	—	—	—	—	—	—	—	—	—	k	—	14	255
2004	Ten	16(8, FB)	17	62	3.6(20)	0	11	60	5.5(9)	0	—	—	—	—	—	—	—	—	—	—	k	—	0	73
NFL	7	97(30)	337	1141	3.4(39)	11	69	573	8.3(30)	3	—	—	—	—	—	—	—	—	—	—	k	—	86	1512

HOLD, MIKE James Michel, QB, 6´0˝/190 lbs; South Carolina; B3/16/1963 Phoenix, AZ

YEAR	TEAM	G (GS, POS)	RUSH	YD	AVG (LG)	TD	REC	YD	AVG (LG)	TD	PASS	COMP	PCT	YD	AVG (LG)	TD	INT	SK	YD	QBR	KPR	OTD	PTS	TAY
1987	TB	2(0)	7	69	9.9(35)	0	—	—	—	—	24	8	33.3	123	5.1(61)	2	1	3	18	—	—	—	0	101

HOLDEN, CURTIS Curtis, LB, 6´2˝/232 lbs; Washington State; B3/17/1979 San Francisco, CA **2001** NO 12 (0)

HOLDEN, SAM Samuel Lee, T, 6´3˝/258 lbs; Southern Illinois; Grambling State; 1971: NO, rnd 2; B2/24/1947 Magnolia, MS **1971** NO 9

HOLDEN, STEVE Steven Anthony, WR, 6´0˝/195 lbs; Arizona State; 1973: Cle, rnd 1; B8/2/1951 Los Angeles, CA

YEAR	TEAM	G (GS, POS)	RUSH	YD	AVG (LG)	TD	REC	YD	AVG (LG)	TD	PASS	COMP	PCT	YD	AVG (LG)	TD	INT	SK	YD	QBR	KPR	OTD	PTS	TAY
1973	Cle	11	—	—	—	—	3	27	9.0(17)	0	—	—	—	—	—	—	—	—	—	—	kp	—	0	75
1974	Cle	10(WR)	1	6	6.0(6)	0	30	452	15.1(53)	3	—	—	—	—	—	—	—	—	—	—	—	—	18	247
1975	Cle	13(WR)	2	-4	-2.0(0)	0	21	320	15.2(28)	0	—	—	—	—	—	—	—	—	—	—	—	—	0	156
1976	Cle	14	—	—	—	—	8	128	16.0(26)	1	—	—	—	—	—	—	—	—	—	—	kp	—	6	295
1977	Cin	6	—	—	—	—	—	—	—	—	—	—	—	—	—	—	—	—	—	—	kp	—	0	11
NFL	5	54	3	2	0.7(6)	0	62	927	15.0(53)	4	—	—	—	—	—	—	—	—	—	—	kp	—	24	784

HOLDER, LEW Lewis C., E, 6´0˝/191 lbs; Texas; B10/10/1923 Dallas, TX

YEAR	TEAM	G (GS, POS)	RUSH	YD	AVG (LG)	TD	REC	YD	AVG (LG)	TD	PASS	COMP	PCT	YD	AVG (LG)	TD	INT	SK	YD	QBR	KPR	OTD	PTS	TAY
1949	LAD-A	12(1)	1	-1	-1.0(-1)	0	5	71	14.2	0	—	—	—	—	—	—	—	—	—	—	—	—	0	35

HOLDMAN, WARRICK Warrick Donte, LB, 6´1˝/234 lbs; Texas A&M; 1999: Chi, rnd 4; B11/22/1975 Alief, TX **1999** ChiB 16 (5, rlb) **2000** ChiB 10 (10, RLB) **2001**†ChiB 16 (15, RLB) **2002** ChiB 4 (4) **2003** ChiB 13 (13, RLB) **2004** Cle 16 (14, RLB) **2005**†Was 14 (7, rlb) **NFL** 89 (68) [7 yrs]

HOLE, ERNIE Ernest Bradford, G, none; B1901, deceased **1920** Mun 1 (1, LG) **1921** Mun 2 (2, LG) **NFL** 3 (3) [2 yrs]

HOLE, MICKEY Michael, B, 5´9˝/180 lbs; none; B2/1892, deceased **1920** Mun 1 (1, TB) **1921** Mun 2 (2, FB) **NFL** 3 (3) [2 yrs]

HOLECEK, JOHN John Francis, LB, 6´2˝/240 lbs; Illinois; 1995: Buf, rnd 5; B5/7/1972 Steger, IL **1995** Buf 1 (0) **1997** Buf 14 (8, rilb) **1998**†Buf 13 (13, LILB) **1999**†Buf 14 (14, LILB) **2000** Buf 16 (16, LILB) **2001** SD 11 (0) **2002** Atl 12 (11, RILB) **NFL** 81 (62) [7 yrs]

HOLIDAY, CARLYLE Carlyle, WR, 6´2˝/217 lbs; Notre Dame; B10/4/1981 San Antonio, TX **2005** Arz 1 (0)

HOLIFIELD, JIM James Lee, DB, 6´3˝/195 lbs; Jackson State; 1968: NYG, rnd 12; B1/18/1946 Bessemer, AL **1968** NYG 14 **1969** NYG 14 **NFL** 28 [2 yrs]

HOLIFIELD, JOHN Johnathan Mark, RB, 6´0˝/202 lbs; West Virginia; 1987: Cin, rnd 12; B7/14/1964 Wayne, MI

YEAR	TEAM	G (GS, POS)	RUSH	YD	AVG (LG)	TD	REC	YD	AVG (LG)	TD	PASS	COMP	PCT	YD	AVG (LG)	TD	INT	SK	YD	QBR	KPR	OTD	PTS	TAY
1989	Cin	3(0)	11	20	1.8(11)	0	2	18	9.0(14)	0	—	—	—	—	—	—	—	—	—	—	k	—	0	14

HOLLADAY, BOB Robert B., DB, 5´11˝/175 lbs; Tulsa; B3/13/1932 Shreveport, LA **1956** LARm 4 **1956** SF 7 **1957** SF 7 (DB) **NFL** 18 [2 yrs]

HOLLAND, DARIUS Darius Jerome, DT, 6´5˝/330 lbs; Colorado; 1995: GB, rnd 3; B11/10/1973 Petersburg, VA **1995**†GB 14 (4) **1996**†GB 16 (0) **1997**†GB 12 (1) **1998** KC 6 (0) **1998** Det 10 (4) **1999** Cle 15 (11, LDT) **2000** Cle 16 (1) **2002** Min 4 (0) **2003**†Den 16 (14, RDT) **2004** Den 2 (0) **NFL** 111 (35) [9 yrs]

YEAR	TEAM	G (GS, POS)	RUSH	YD	AVG(LG)	TD	REC	YD	AVG(LG)	TD	PASS COMP	PCT	YD	AVG(LG)	TD	INT	SK	YD	QBR	KPR	OTD	PTS	TAY

HOLLAND, JAMIE Jamie Lorenza, WR-RB, 6´1˝/192 lbs; Ohio State; 1987: SD, rnd 7; B2/1/1964 Raleigh, NC [R]

YEAR	TEAM	G (GS, POS)	RUSH	YD	AVG(LG)	TD	REC	YD	AVG(LG)	TD	KPR	OTD	PTS	TAY
1987	SD	12 (0)	1	17	17.0(17)	0	6	138	23.0(45)	0	k	—	0	211
1988	SD	16 (6, wr)	3	19	6.3(10)	0	39	536	13.7(45)	1	k	1	12	647
1989	SD	16 (6, WR)	6	46	7.7(24)	0	26	336	12.9(37)	0	k	—	0	289
1990	†LARd	16 (0)	—	—	—	—	—	—	—	—	k	—	0	175
1991	†LARd	16 (0)	—	—	—	—	—	—	—	—	k	—	0	91
1992	Cle	4 (3)	—	—	—	—	2	27	13.5(16)	0	—	—	0	14
NFL	6	80 (15)	10	82	8.2(24)	0	73	1037	14.2(45)	1	k	1	12	1427

HOLLAND, JOHN John Calvin, WR, 6´0˝/190 lbs; Tennessee State; 1974: Min, rnd 2; B2/28/1952 Beckley, WV

YEAR	TEAM	G (GS, POS)	REC	YD	AVG(LG)	TD	KPR	OTD	PTS	TAY
1974	Min	10	5	84	16.8(20)	0	—	—	0	42
1975	Buf	12	7	144	20.6(63)	1	kp	—	6	102
1976	Buf	13 (8, WR)	15	299	19.9(58)	2	kp	1	18	153
1977	Buf	3	8	107	13.4(27)	0	—	—	0	54
NFL	4	38 (8)	35	634	18.1(63)	3	kp	1	24	350

HOLLAND, JOHNNY Johnny Ray, LB, 6´2˝/231 lbs; Texas A&M; 1987: GB, rnd 2; B3/11/1965 Bellville, TX   **1987** GB 12 (12, RILB) **1988** GB 13 (13, RILB/lilb) **1989** GB 16 (15, RILB) **1990** GB 16 (16, RILB) **1991** GB 16 (14, RILB) **1992** GB 14 (14, RILB) **1993** GB 16 (16, RILB) **NFL** 103 (100) [7 yrs]

HOLLAND, MONTRAE Montrae Rondell, G, 6´2˝/333 lbs; Florida State; 2003: NO, rnd 4; B5/21/1980 Jefferson, TX   **2003** NO 16 (7, lg) **2004** NO 13 (13, RG) **2005** NO 15 (10, RG) **NFL** 44 (30) [3 yrs]

HOLLAND, VERN Vernon Edward, T, 6´5˝/268 lbs; Tennessee State; 1971: Cin, rnd 1; B6/27/1948 San Antonio, TX, D4/21/1998 Nashville, TN   **1971** Cin 14 (RT) **1972** Cin 14 (RT) **1973**†Cin 14 (RT) **1974** Cin 3 **1975**†Cin☆14 (RT) **1976** Cin 14 (RT) **1977** Cin 14 (RT) **1978** Cin 16 (RT) **1979** Cin 16 (RT) **1980** Det 2 (0) **1980** NYG 10 (5, rt) **NFL** 131 (5) [10 yrs]

HOLLAR, JOHN John Henry, FB, 6´0˝/223 lbs; Appalachian State; 1948: ChiC, rnd 13; B8/7/1922 Boone, NC

YEAR	TEAM	G (GS, POS)	RUSH	YD	AVG(LG)	TD	REC	YD	AVG(LG)	TD	OTD	PTS	TAY
1948	Was	9 (4)	4	7	1.8(6)	0	—	—	—	—	—	0	7
1949	Det	6 (5, fb)	8	21	2.6(12)	0	—	—	—	—	—	0	21
1949	Was	2 (0)	5	14	2.8(0)	1	4	38	9.5(15)	1	—	12	48
NFL	2	17 (9)	17	42	2.5(12)	1	4	38	9.5(15)	1	—	12	-76

HOLLAS, DONALD Donald Wayne, QB, 6´3˝/215 lbs; Rice; 1991: Cin, rnd 4; B11/22/1967 Kingsville, TX

YEAR	TEAM	G (GS, POS)	RUSH	YD	AVG(LG)	TD	PASS COMP	PCT	YD	AVG(LG)	TD	INT	SK	YD	QBR	OTD	PTS	TAY
1991	Cin	8 (1)	12	66	5.5(27)	0	— 55 32	58.2	310	5.6(23)	1	4	7	57	—	—	0	66
1992	Cin	10 (1)	20	109	5.4(24)	0	— 58 35	60.3	335	5.8(24)	2	0	8	45	—	—	0	287
1994	Cin	2 (0)	—	—	—	—	— 2 0	0.0	0	0.0	0	1	1	20	—	—	0	-40
1998	Oak	12 (6, qb)	29	120	4.1(14)	1	— 260 135	51.9	1754	6.7(47)	10	16	36	207	60.6	—	6	417
NFL	4	32 (8)	61	295	4.8(27)	1	— 375 202	53.9	2399	6.4(47)	13	21	52	329	61.8	—	6	730

HOLLAS, HUGO Hugo Andrew, DB, 6´1˝/190 lbs; Rice; B11/30/1945 High Hill, TX, D9/6/1995 Schulenburg, TX   **1970** NO 11 (SS) **1971** NO 14 (SS) **1972** NO 14 (SS) **1974** SF 7 **NFL** 46 [4 yrs]

HOLLE, ERIC Eric Warner, NT-DE, 6´5˝/260 lbs; Texas; 1984: KC, rnd 5; B9/5/1960 Houston, TX   **1984** KC 16 (1) **1985** KC 16 (16, nt) **1986**†KC 16 (0) **1987** KC 8 (1) **NFL** 56 (7) [4 yrs]

HOLLER, ED James Edward, LB, 6´2˝/235 lbs; South Carolina; 1963: GB, rnd 14; B1/23/1940 Bluefield, WV   **1963** GB 2

YEAR	TEAM	G (GS, POS)	RUSH	YD	AVG(LG)	TD	KPR	OTD	PTS	TAY
1964	Pit	13	1	8	8.0(8)	0	Pi	—	0	5
NFL	2	15	1	8	8.0(8)	0	—	—	0	8

HOLLERAN, TOM Thomas Vincent, B, 5´7˝/171 lbs; Pittsburgh; B12/18/1896 Pittsburgh, PA, D7/27/1972 Pittsburgh, PA   **1923** Buf 5 (5, TB), 12

HOLLERAN, TOMMY Thomas, BB, none; B3/6/1892, D1/1976 Reynoldsburg, OH   **1920** Akr 1 (0) **1922** Tol 1 (1) **NFL** 2 (1) [2 yrs]

HOLLEY, KEN Kenneth Joseph, QB, 5´10˝/185 lbs; Holy Cross; B10/9/1919 Hartford, CT, D3/1/1986 Livingston, NJ

YEAR	TEAM	G (GS, POS)	RUSH	YD	AVG(LG)	TD	PASS COMP	PCT	YD	AVG(LG)	TD	INT	OTD	PTS	TAY
1946	Mia-A	5 (0)	2	-22	-11.0	0	— 11 3	27.3	36	3.3	0	4	—	0	-164

HOLLIDAY, COREY Corey Lamont, WR, 6´2˝/208 lbs; North Carolina; B1/31/1971 Richmond, VA   **1995**†Pit 3 (0) **1997** Pit 2 (0)

YEAR	TEAM	G (GS, POS)	REC	YD	AVG(LG)	TD	OTD	PTS	TAY
1996	†Pit	12 (0)	1	7	7.0(7)	0	—	0	4
NFL	3	17 (0)	1	7	7.0(7)	0	—	0	4

HOLLIDAY, MARCUS Marcus Edward, RB, 5´11˝/222 lbs; Memphis; B7/16/1973 Memphis, TN   **1996** SL 1 (0)

HOLLIDAY, RON Ronald C., WR, 5´9˝/168 lbs; Pittsburgh; B2/12/1948 West Chester, PA [K]

YEAR	TEAM	G (GS, POS)	RUSH	YD	AVG(LG)	TD	REC	YD	AVG(LG)	TD	KPR	OTD	PTS	TAY
1973	SD	11 (6, WR)	6	70	11.7(22)	0	14	182	13.0(36)	0	K	1	119

HOLLIDAY, VONNIE Dimetry Giovonni, DE-DT, 6´5˝/290 lbs; North Carolina; 1998: GB, rnd 1; B12/11/1975 Camden, SC   **1998**†GB 12 (12, RDE) **1999** GB 16 (16, RDE) **2000** GB 12 (9, lde) **2001**†GB 16 (16, LDE) **2002**†GB 10 (10, LDE) **2003**†KC 16 (16, RDE) **2004** KC 9 (3) **2005** Mia 16 (16, RDT) **NFL** 107 (98) [8 yrs]

HOLLIE, DOUG James Douglas, DE, 6´4˝/265 lbs; SMU; 1984: Det, rnd S3; B12/15/1960 Detroit, MI   **1987** Sea 2 (0) **1988** Sea 3 (0) **NFL** 5 (0) [2 yrs]

HOLLIER, DWIGHT Dwight Leon, LB, 6´2˝/246 lbs; North Carolina; 1992: Mia, rnd 4; B4/21/1969 Hampton, VA   **1992**†Mia 16 (5, rilb) **1993** Mia 16 (10, mlb) **1994** Mia 11 (7, RLB) **1995**†Mia 16 (14, RLB) **1996** Mia 16 (15, LLB) **1997** Mia 16 (3) **1998**†Mia 16 (0) **1999** Mia 15 (0) **2000**†Ind 16 (15, MLB) **NFL** 138 (69) [9 yrs]

HOLLINGS, TONY Tony Terrell, RB, 5´10˝/216 lbs; Georgia Tech; 2003: Hou, rnd S2; B12/1/1981 Macon, GA

YEAR	TEAM	G (GS, POS)	RUSH	YD	AVG(LG)	TD	REC	YD	AVG(LG)	TD	KPR	OTD	PTS	TAY
2003	Hou	14 (1)	38	102	2.7(17)	0	25	12.5(19)	0	k	—	0	137
2004	Hou	7 (0)	11	47	4.3(13)	0	5	46	9.2(24)	0	k	—	0	78
2005	Hou	2 (0)	—	—	—	—	—	—	—	—	k	—	0	16
NFL	3	23 (1)	49	149	3.0(17)	0	7	71	10.1(27)	0	k	—	0	231

HOLLINGSWORTH, JOE Joseph DeWitt, FB, 6´0˝/198 lbs; Georgia; Eastern Kentucky; B6/20/1925 Durham, GA, D8/18/1975 Lynch, KY

YEAR	TEAM	G (GS, POS)	RUSH	YD	AVG(LG)	TD	REC	YD	AVG(LG)	TD	KPR	OTD	PTS	TAY
1949	Pit	11 (2)	6	13	2.2(7)	0	1	0	0.0	0	—	0	13
1950	Pit	10	1	2	2.0(2)	0	—	—	—	—	—	0	9
1951	Pit	10	7	11	1.6(6)	0	—	—	—	—	—	0	11
NFL	3	31 (2)	14	26	1.9(7)	0	1	0	0.0	0	k	—	0	33

HOLLINGSWORTH, SHAWN Shawn Lenor, T, 6´2˝/260 lbs; New Mexico; Angelo State; B12/4/1961 Brownwood, TX   **1983** Den 5 (0)

HOLLINQUEST, LAMONT Bertrell Lamont, LB, 6´3˝/250 lbs; USC; 1993: Was, rnd 8; B10/24/1970 Los Angeles, CA   **1993** Was 16 (0) **1994** Was 14 (0) **1996**†GB 16 (0) **1997**†GB 16 (0) **1998**†GB 14 (2) **NFL** 76 (2) [5 yrs]

HOLLIS, DAVID David Lanier, DB, 5´11˝/175 lbs; UNLV; B4/4/1965 Los Angeles, CA   **1987**†Sea 11 (0) **1988** KC 2 (0) **1988** Sea 6 (0) **1989** Sea 10 (0) **NFL** 29 (0) [3 yrs]

HOLLIS, MIKE Michael Shane, K, 5´7˝/179 lbs; Idaho; B5/22/1972 Kellogg, ID [K]   **1995** Jax 16 (0) **1996**†Jax 16 (0) **1997**†Jax✧16 (0) **1998**†Jax 16 (0) **1999**†Jax 16 (0) **2000** Jax 12 (0) **2001** Jax 16 (0) **2002** Buf 16 (0) **NFL** 124 (0) [8 yrs]

HOLLOMON, GUS Gus Martin, DB-P, 6´3˝/195 lbs; Houston; 1968: Den, rnd 4; B10/23/1945 Beaumont, TX   **1968** Den-A 13 (ls) **1969** Den-A 14 (5, ls) **1970** NYJ 14 (SS) **1971** NYJ 11 **1972** NYJ 14 (SS) **NFL** 66 (5) [5 yrs]

HOLLOWAY, BRIAN Brian Douglass, T-G, 6´7˝/284 lbs; Stanford; 1981: NE, rnd 1; B7/25/1959 Omaha, NE   **1981** NE 16 (16, lt) **1982**†NE 9 (9, LT) **1983** NE★16 (16, LT) **1984** NE★16 (16, LT) **1985**†NE★16 (16, LT) **1987** LARd 12 (8, LT) **1988** LARd 2 (0)

YEAR	TEAM	G (GS, POS)	REC	YD	AVG(LG)	TD	OTD	PTS	TAY
1986	†NE☆	15 (15, LT)	1	5	5.0(5)	0	—	0	3
NFL	8	102 (85)	1	5	5.0(5)	0	—	0	3

HOLLOWAY, CORNELL Cornell Duane, DB, 5´11˝/185 lbs; Pittsburgh; 1989: Cin, rnd 10; B1/30/1966 Alliance, OH   **1990** Ind 15 (0) **1991** Ind 10 (0) **1992** Ind 7 (0) **NFL** 32 (0) [3 yrs]

HOLLOWAY, DEREK Derek Lance, WR, 5´7˝/166 lbs; Arkansas; B1/17/1961 Riverside, NJ   **1987** TB 1 (0)

YEAR	TEAM	G (GS, POS)	REC	YD	AVG(LG)	TD	KPR	OTD	PTS	TAY
1986	Was	9 (1)	1	7	7.0(7)	0	k	—	0	3
NFL	2	10 (1)	1	7	7.0(7)	0	—	—	0	4

HOLLOWAY, GLEN Glen Leroy, G, 6´3˝/250 lbs; North Texas; 1970: Chi, rnd 10; B9/16/1948 Corpus Christi, TX   **1970** ChiB 14 (LG) **1971** ChiB 14 (LG) **1972** ChiB 14 (LG) **1973** ChiB 14 (LG) **1974** Cle 14 (rg) **NFL** 70 [5 yrs]

YEAR	TEAM	G (GS, POS)	RUSH	YD	AVG(LG)	TD	REC	YD	AVG(LG)	TD	PASS	COMP	PCT	YD	AVG(LG)	TD	INT	SK	YD	QBR	KPR	OTD	PTS	TAY

HOLLOWAY, JABARI   Jabari Jelani, TE, 6´2˝/260 lbs; Notre Dame; 2001: NE, rnd 4; B12/18/1978 Atlanta, GA

2002	Hou	11 (8, TE)	—	—	—	—	7	73	10.4(24)	0	—	—	—	—	—	—	—	—	—	—	—	—	0	37
2003	Hou	15 (9, TE)	—	—	—	—	8	84	10.5(33)	0	—	—	—	—	—	—	—	—	—	—	—	—	0	42
NFL	2	26 (17)	—	—	—	—	15	157	10.5(33)	0	—	—	—	—	—	—	—	—	—	—	—	—	0	79

HOLLOWAY, JOHNNY   Johnny Owen, DB, 5´11˝/181 lbs; Northwestern; Kansas; 1986: Dal, rnd 7; B11/8/1963 Galveston, TX   **1986** Dal 16 (0)   **1987** SL 3 (1)   **NFL** 19 (1) [2 yrs]

HOLLOWAY, RANDY   Randy, DE, 6´5˝/250 lbs; Pittsburgh; 1978: Min, rnd 1; B8/26/1955 Sharon, PA   **1978**†Min 16   **1979** Min 16   **1980**†Min 16 (16, RDE)   **1981** Min 16 (8, rde)   **1982**†Min 9 (0)   **1983** Min 16 (2)   **1984** Min 8 (5, rde)   **1984** SL 6 (1)   **NFL** 103 (32) [7 yrs]

HOLLOWAY, STAN   Stanley O'Neill, LB, 6´2˝/218 lbs; California; B9/28/1957 San Francisco, CA   **1980** NO 11 (2)

HOLLOWAY, STEVE   Steven Weymon, TE, 6´3˝/235 lbs; Tennessee State; B8/23/1964 Montgomery, AL

| 1987 | TB | 6 (4) | — | — | — | — | 10 | 127 | 12.7(26) | 0 | — | — | — | — | — | — | — | — | — | — | — | — | 0 | 64 |

HOLLOWAY, TONY   Anthony Lambert, DE-LB, 6´2˝/222 lbs; Nebraska; B4/21/1964 Puerto Rico   **1987** KC 1 (1)

HOLLOWELL, T.J.   Thomas Anthony, LB, 6´0˝/235 lbs; Nebraska; B4/8/1981 Copperas Cove, TX   **2004** NYG 4 (0)   **2005** NYJ 2 (0)   **NFL** 6 (0) [2 yrs]

HOLLY, BOB   Robert Charles, QB, 6´2˝/197 lbs; Princeton; 1982: Was, rnd 11; B6/1/1960 Clifton, NJ

1983	†Was	5 (0)	4	13	3.3(13)	0	—	—	—	—	1	1	100.0	5	5.0(5)	0	0	1	9	—	—	—	0	16
1985	Atl	4 (0)	3	36	12.0(20)	1	—	—	—	—	39	24	61.5	295	7.6(44)	1	2	8	61	—	—	—	6	119
NFL	9 (0)	7	49	7.0(20)	1	—	—	—	—	40	25	62.5	300	7.5(44)	1	2	9	70	—	—	—	6	134

HOLLY, DAVEN   Daven, DB, 5´10˝/186 lbs; Cincinnati; 2005: SF, rnd 7; B8/8/1982 McKeesport, PA   **2005** ChiB 3 (0)

HOLM, TONY   Bernard Patrick, B, 6´1˝/214 lbs; Alabama; B5/22/1908 Birmingham, AL, D7/15/1978 Waukegan, IL   **1930** Pro 3 (2)   **1931** Por 14 (5, fb), 12

1932	ChiC	8 (5, FB)	34	73	2.1	0	1	9	9.0(9)	0	—	—	—	—	—	—	—	—	—	—	—	—	0	78
1933	Pit	9 (9, FB)	58	160	2.8	0	2	13	6.5	0	52	17	32.7	406	7.8	2	13	—	—	—	—	—	0	-141
NFL	4	34 (21)	92	233	2.5	1	3	22	7.3(9)	1	52	17	32.7	406	7.8	2	13	—	—	—	—	—	12	-48

HOLMAN, JOHN   John, T, none; B1902 New Orleans, LA, deceased   **1928** NYG 1 (1)

HOLMAN, RASHAD   Rashad, DB, 5´11˝/191 lbs; Louisville; 2001: SF, rnd 6; B1/17/1978 Louisville, KY   **2001**†SF 16 (1)   **2002**†SF 16 (0)   **2003** SF 14 (0)   **NFL** 46 (1) [3 yrs]

HOLMAN, RODNEY   Rodney Alan, TE, 6´3˝/238 lbs; Tulane; 1982: Cin, rnd 3; B4/20/1960 Ypsilanti, MI

1982	†Cin	9 (0)	—	—	—	—	3	18	6.0(10)	1	—	—	—	—	—	—	—	—	—	—	—	—	6	14
1983	Cin	16 (0)	—	—	—	—	2	15	7.5(10)	0	—	—	—	—	—	—	—	—	—	—	—	—	0	8
1984	Cin	16 (2)	—	—	—	—	21	239	11.4(27)	1	—	—	—	—	—	—	—	—	—	—	—	—	6	125
1985	Cin	16 (16, TE)	—	—	—	—	38	479	12.6(64)	7	—	—	—	—	—	—	—	—	—	—	—	—	42	275
1986	Cin	16 (16, TE)	—	—	—	—	40	570	14.3(34)	2	—	—	—	—	—	—	—	—	—	—	k	—	12	298
1987	Cin	12 (12, TE)	—	—	—	—	28	438	15.6(61)	2	—	—	—	—	—	—	—	—	—	—	—	—	12	229
1988	†Cin★	16 (16, TE)	—	—	—	—	39	527	13.5(33)	3	—	—	—	—	—	—	—	—	—	—	—	—	18	279
1989	Cin★	16 (15, TE)	—	—	—	—	50	736	14.7(73)	9	—	—	—	—	—	—	—	—	—	—	—	—	54	413
1990	†Cin★	16 (15, TE)	—	—	—	—	40	596	14.9(53)	5	—	—	—	—	—	—	—	—	—	—	—	—	30	323
1991	Cin	16 (15, TE)	—	—	—	—	31	445	14.4(39)	2	—	—	—	—	—	—	—	—	—	—	k	—	12	233
1992	Cin	16 (13, TE)	—	—	—	—	26	266	10.2(26)	2	—	—	—	—	—	—	—	—	—	—	—	—	12	143
1993	†Det	16 (16, TE)	—	—	—	—	25	244	9.8(28)	2	—	—	—	—	—	—	—	—	—	—	—	—	12	132
1994	†Det	15 (7, te)	—	—	—	—	17	163	9.6(18)	0	—	—	—	—	—	—	—	—	—	—	—	—	0	82
1995	†Det	16 (3)	—	—	—	—	5	35	7.0(9)	0	—	—	—	—	—	—	—	—	—	—	—	—	0	18
NFL	14	212 (146)	—	—	—	—	365	4771	13.1(73)	36	—	—	—	—	—	—	—	—	—	—	k	—	216	2569

HOLMAN, SCOTT   Scott Huntington, WR, 6´2˝/195 lbs; Oregon; B9/27/1962 Portland, OR

1986	SL	3 (1)	—	—	—	—	3	41	13.7(18)	0	—	—	—	—	—	—	—	—	—	—	—	—	0	21
1987	NYJ	3 (2)	—	—	—	—	15	155	10.3(30)	0	—	—	—	—	—	—	—	—	—	—	—	—	0	78
NFL	2	6 (3)	—	—	—	—	18	196	10.9(30)	0	—	—	—	—	—	—	—	—	—	—	—	—	0	98

HOLMAN, WALTER   Walter Ree, RB, 5´10˝/208 lbs; West Virginia State; B4/6/1959 Vaiden, MS

| 1987 | Was | 3 (0) | 2 | 7 | 3.5(5) | 0 | — | — | — | — | — | — | — | — | — | — | — | — | — | — | — | — | 0 | 7 |

HOLMAN, WILLIE   Willie Joseph, DE-DT, 6´4˝/250 lbs; South Carolina State; 1968: Chi, rnd 7; B2/27/1945 St. Matthews, SC, D4/21/2002 Chicago, IL   **1968** ChiB 14   **1969** ChiB 14 (RDT)   **1970** ChiB 14 (LDE)   **1971** ChiB 14 (LDE)   **1972** ChiB 4   **1973** ChiB 6   **1973** Was 5   **NFL** 71 [6 yrs]

HOLMBERG, ROB   Robert Anthony, LB, 6´3˝/230 lbs; Navy; Penn State; 1994: LARd, rnd 7; B5/6/1971 McKeesport, PA   **1994** LARd 16 (0)   **1995** Oak 16 (0)   **1996** Oak 13 (1)   **1997** Oak 16 (0)   **1998** Ind 3 (0)   **1998**†NYJ 9 (0)   **1999**†Min 16 (0)   **2000** NE 16 (5, rilb)   **2001** NE 2 (0)   **2001** Car 1 (0)   **2001**†GB 4 (2)   **NFL** 112 (8) [8 yrs]

HOLMER, WALT   Walter R., B, 6´0˝/185 lbs; Northwestern; B12/5/1902 Moline, IL, D8/27/1976 Cashmere, WA [K]   **1929** ChiB☆15 (8, FB), 3   **1930** ChiB 12 (0), 18   **1931** ChiC 9 (5, TB)

1932	ChiC	10 (4)	65	230	3.5	1	—	—	—	—	78	25	32.1	449	5.8	2	1	—	—	—	K	—	8	435
1933	Bos	6 (0)	9	28	3.1	1	—	—	—	—	5	2	40.0	35	7.0	0	2	—	—	—	—	—	6	-25
1933	Pit	4 (4)	4	8	2.0	0	—	—	—	—	27	9	33.3	158	5.9	0	4	—	—	—	—	—	0	-73
NFL	5	56 (21)	78	266	3.4	4	—	—	—	—	110	36	32.7	642	5.8	7	7	—	—	—	K	1	35	392

HOLMES, ALEX   Alex, TE, 6´3˝/270 lbs; USC; B8/22/1982 Sherman Oaks, CA

| 2005 | Mia | 8 (0) | — | — | — | — | 1 | 2 | 2.0(2) | 0 | — | — | — | — | — | — | — | — | — | — | — | — | 0 | 1 |

HOLMES, BRUCE   Bruce Barton, LB, 6´2˝/235 lbs; Minnesota; 1987: KC, rnd 12; B10/24/1964 El Paso, TX   **1987** KC 3 (3)   **1993** Min 1 (0)   **NFL** 4 (3) [2 yrs]

HOLMES, CLAYTON   Clayton Antwan, DB, 5´10˝/181 lbs; Carson-Newman; 1992: Dal, rnd 3; B8/23/1969 Florence, SC   **1992**†Dal 15 (0)   **1994**†Dal 16 (1)   **1995** Dal 8 (6, lcb)   **NFL** 39 (7) [3 yrs]

HOLMES, DARICK   Darick Lamon, RB, 6´0˝/226 lbs; Portland State; 1995: Buf, rnd 7; B7/1/1971 Pasadena, CA

1995	Buf	16 (2, rb)	172	698	4.1(38)	4	24	214	8.9(47)	0	—	—	—	—	—	—	—	—	—	—	k	—	24	1059
1996	Buf	16 (1, rb)	189	571	3.0(37)	4	16	102	6.4(20)	1	—	—	—	—	—	—	—	—	—	—	k	—	32	667
1997	Buf	13 (0)	22	106	4.8(19)	2	13	106	8.2(22)	0	—	—	—	—	—	—	—	—	—	—	k	—	12	264
1998	Buf	3 (0)	2	8	4.0(5)	0	1	9	9.0(9)	0	—	—	—	—	—	—	—	—	—	—	k	—	0	18
1998	GB	11 (0)	93	386	4.2(13)	1	19	179	9.4(24)	0	—	—	—	—	—	—	—	—	—	—	—	—	6	486
1999	Ind	1 (0)	—	—	—	—	—	—	—	—	—	—	—	—	—	—	—	—	—	—	—	—	—	—
NFL	5	60 (7)	478	1769	3.7(38)	11	73	610	8.4(47)	0	—	—	—	—	—	—	—	—	—	—	k	—	74	2493

HOLMES, DARRYL   Darryl DeWayne, DB, 6´2˝/190 lbs; Fort Valley State; B9/6/1964 Birmingham, AL   **1987** NE 15 (3)   **1988** NE 16 (0)   **1989** NE 13 (0)   **NFL** 44 (3) [3 yrs]

HOLMES, DON   Donald Ira, WR, 5´10˝/180 lbs; Colorado; Mesa; 1984: Atl, rnd 12; B4/1/1961 Miami, FL

1986	SL	12 (0)	—	—	—	—	—	—	—	—	—	—	—	—	—	—	—	—	—	—	k	—	0	-13
1987	SL	11 (1)	—	—	—	—	11	132	12.0(23)	0	—	—	—	—	—	—	—	—	—	—	k	—	0	76
1988	Phx	16 (0)	—	—	—	—	1	10	10.0(10)	0	—	—	—	—	—	—	—	—	—	—	—	—	0	5
1989	Phx	15 (1)	—	—	—	—	13	271	20.8(77)	1	—	—	—	—	—	—	—	—	—	—	—	—	6	141
1990	Phx	6 (0)	—	—	—	—	—	—	—	—	—	—	—	—	—	—	—	—	—	—	—	—	0	—
NFL	5	60 (2)	—	—	—	—	25	413	16.5(77)	1	—	—	—	—	—	—	—	—	—	—	k	—	6	209

HOLMES, EARL   Earl L., LB, 6´2˝/242 lbs; Florida A&M; 1996: Pit, rnd 4; B4/28/1973 Tallahassee, FL   **1996** Pit 3 (1)   **1997**†Pit 16 (16, RILB)   **1998** Pit 14 (14, RILB)   **1999** Pit 16 (16, RILB)   **2000** Pit 16 (16, RILB)   **2001**†Pit 16 (16, LILB)   **2002**†Cle 16 (15, MLB)   **2003** Det 16 (13, MLB)   **2004** Det 16 (14, RLB)   **2005** Det 11 (10, MLB)   **NFL** 140 (131) [10 yrs]

HOLMES, ERNIE   Ernest Lee, DT-NT, 6´3˝/260 lbs; Texas Southern; 1971: Pit, rnd 8; B7/11/1948 Jamestown, TX   **1972**†Pit 14 (rdt)   **1973**†Pit 14 (RDT)   **1974**†Pit☆13 (RDT)   **1975**†Pit☆13 (RDT)   **1976**†Pit 14 (RDT)   **1977**†Pit 13 (rdt)   **1978**†NE 3   **NFL** 84 [7 yrs]

HOLMES, JACK   John, RB, 5´11˝/210 lbs; Texas Southern; 1975: Hou, rnd 15; B6/20/1953 Rolling Fork, MS

1978	NO	11	2	4	2.0(4)	0	—	—	—	—	—	—	—	—	—	—	—	—	—	—	k	—	0	7
1979	NO	16 (1)	17	68	4.0(14)	0	3	19	6.3(13)	0	—	—	—	—	—	—	—	—	—	—	k	—	0	78
1980	NO	16 (7, fb)	38	119	3.1(20)	2	29	226	7.8(16)	1	3	1	33.3	23	7.7(23)	1	0	—	—	—	—	—	18	274

YEAR	TEAM	G (GS, POS)	RUSH	YD	AVG (LG)	TD	REC	YD	AVG (LG)	TD	PASS	COMP	PCT	YD	AVG (LG)	TD	INT	SK	YD	QBR	KPR	OTD	PTS	TAY
1981	NO	16(15, FB)	58	194	3.3(11)	2	38	206	5.4(19)	0	—	—	—	—	—	—	—	—	—	—	—	—	12	317
1982	NO	5(0)	2	8	4.0(5)	0	1	2	2.0(2)	0	1	0	0.0	0	0.0	0	0	—	—	—	—	—	0	9
NFL	5	64(23)	117	393	3.4(20)	4	71	453	6.4(19)	1	4	1	25.0	23	5.8(23)	1	0	—	—	—	k	—	30	684

Holmes, Jaret Jaret D., K, 6´0˝/203 lbs; Auburn; B3/3/1976 Clinton, MS **[K]** **1999** ChiB 3 (0) **2000** NYG 4 (0) **2001** Jax 4 (0) **NFL** 11 (0) [3 yrs]

Holmes, Jerry Jerry Lee, DB, 6´2˝/175 lbs; Chowan Coll. (NC); West Virginia; B12/22/1957 Newport News, VA **[I]** **1980** NYJ 12 (0) **1981**†NYJ 16 (13, RCB) **1982**†NYJ 9 (9, RCB) **1983** NYJ 16 (16, RCB) **1986**†NYJ 15 (13, LCB) **1987** NYJ 8 (7, LCB) **1988** Det 16 (16, LCB) **1989** Det 16 (16, RCB) **1990** GB 16 (16, RCB) **1991** GB 13 (12, LCB) **NFL** 137 (118) [10 yrs]

Holmes, Johnny John L., DE, 6´2˝/248 lbs; Florida A&M; B11/3/1943 **1966** Mia-A 3

Holmes, Kenny Kenneth Jerome, DE, 6´4˝/265 lbs; Miami (FL); 1997: Ten, rnd 1; B10/24/1973 Vero Beach, FL **1997** Ten 16 (5, rde) **1998** Ten 14 (11, RDE) **1999**†Ten 14 (7, rde) **2000**†Ten 14 (13, RDE) **2001** NYG 16 (16, RDE) **2002**†NYG 15 (15, RDE) **2003** NYG 9 (9, RDE) **NFL** 98 (76) [7 yrs]

Holmes, Lester Lester, G, 6´4˝/304 lbs; Jackson State; 1993: Phi, rnd 1; B9/27/1969 Tylertown, MS **1993** Phi 12 (6, rg) **1994** Phi 16 (16, RG) **1995** Phi 2 (2) **1996** Phi 16 (14, RG) **1997** Oak 15 (15, RG) **1998**†Arz 16 (16, RG) **1999** Arz 13 (13, RG) **2000** Arz 12 (12, RG) **NFL** 102 (94) [8 yrs]

Holmes, Mel Melvin, G-T, 6´3˝/251 lbs; North Carolina A&T; 1971: Pit, rnd 5; B1/22/1950 Miami, FL **1971** Pit 14 **1972** Pit 14 **1973** Pit 1 **NFL** 29 [3 yrs]

Holmes, Mike Michael Raphael, DB-WR, 6´2˝/193 lbs; Texas Southern; 1973: SF, rnd 1; B11/18/1950 Galveston, TX **1974** SF 13 (6, fs) **1976** Buf 1

YEAR	TEAM	G (GS, POS)	RUSH	YD	AVG (LG)	TD	REC	YD	AVG (LG)	TD	PASS	COMP	PCT	YD	AVG (LG)	TD	INT	SK	YD	QBR	KPR	OTD	PTS	TAY
1975	SF	14(4)	1	-4	-4.0(-4)	0	16	220	13.8(25)	1	—	—	—	—	—	—	—	—	—	—	k	—	6	140
1976	Mia	3	—	—	—	—	1	11	11.0(11)	0	—	—	—	—	—	—	—	—	—	—	—	—	0	6
NFL	3	31(10)	1	-4	-4.0(-4)	0	17	231	13.6(25)	1	—	—	—	—	—	—	—	—	—	—	kpi	—	6	424

Holmes, Pat James Patrick, DE-DT, 6´5˝/255 lbs; Texas Tech; 1962: Phi, rnd 3; B8/3/1940 Durant, OK **1966** Hou-A 14 (14, LDT) **1967**†Hou-A★14 (LDE) **1968** Hou-A✧14 (LDE) **1969**†Hou-A 14 (LDE) **1970** Hou 14 (LDE) **1971** Hou 14 (LDE) **1972** Hou 14 (LDE) **1973** KC 10 **NFL** 108 (14) [8 yrs]

Holmes, Priest Priest Anthony, RB, 5´9˝/213 lbs; Texas; B10/7/1973 Fort Smith, AR

YEAR	TEAM	G (GS, POS)	RUSH	YD	AVG (LG)	TD	REC	YD	AVG (LG)	TD	PASS	COMP	PCT	YD	AVG (LG)	TD	INT	SK	YD	QBR	KPR	OTD	PTS	TAY
1997	Bal	7(0)	—	—	—	—	—	—	—	—	—	—	—	—	—	—	—	—	—	—	k	—	0	-1
1998	Bal	16(13, RB)	233	1008	4.3(56)	7	43	260	6.0(25)	0	1	0	0.0	0	0.0	0	1	—	—	—	k	—	42	1168
1999	Bal	9(4)	89	506	5.7(72)	1	13	104	8.0(34)	1	—	—	—	—	—	—	—	—	—	—	—	—	12	573
2000	†Bal	16(2)	137	588	4.3(21)	2	32	221	6.9(27)	0	—	—	—	—	—	—	—	—	—	—	k	—	12	711
2001	KC★	16(16, RB)	327	**1555**	4.8(41)	8	62	614	9.9(67)	2	—	—	—	—	—	—	—	—	—	—	—	—	60	**1952**
2002	KC★	14(14, RB)	313	1615	5.2(56)	**21**	70	672	9.6(64)	3	1	0	0.0	0	0.0	0	0	—	—	—	—	—	**144**	2176
2003	†KC★	16(16, RB)	320	1420	4.4(31)	**27**	74	690	9.3(36)	0	1	0	0.0	0	0.0	0	0	—	—	—	—	—	**162**	2035
2004	KC	8(8, RB)	196	892	4.6(33)	14	19	187	9.8(52)	1	—	—	—	—	—	—	—	—	—	—	—	—	90	1131
2005	KC	7(7, rb)	119	451	3.8(35)	6	21	197	9.4(60)	1	—	—	—	—	—	—	—	—	—	—	—	—	42	615
NFL	9	109(80)	1734	8035	4.6(72)	86	334	2945	8.8(67)	8	3	0	0.0	0	0.0	0	1	—	—	—	k	—	564	10359

Holmes, Robert Robert, RB, 5´9˝/221 lbs; Southern (LA); 1968: KC, rnd 14; B10/5/1945 Huntsville, TX

YEAR	TEAM	G (GS, POS)	RUSH	YD	AVG (LG)	TD	REC	YD	AVG (LG)	TD	PASS	COMP	PCT	YD	AVG (LG)	TD	INT	SK	YD	QBR	KPR	OTD	PTS	TAY
1968	†KC-A☆	14(FB)	174	866	5.0(76)	7	19	201	10.6(43)	0	—	—	—	—	—	—	—	—	—	—	—	—	42	1037
1969	†KC-A✧	14(FB)	150	612	4.1(25)	2	26	266	10.2(33)	3	—	—	—	—	—	—	—	—	—	—	k	—	30	804
1970	KC	14	63	206	3.3(22)	3	23	173	7.5(31)	1	—	—	—	—	—	—	—	—	—	—	k	—	24	578
1971	KC	6	21	35	1.7(6)	0	2	16	8.0(12)	0	—	—	—	—	—	—	—	—	—	—	k	—	0	109
1971	Hou	8(FB)	91	288	3.2(31)	4	17	138	8.1(22)	0	—	—	—	—	—	—	—	—	—	—	k	—	24	451
1972	Hou	6	43	172	4.0(18)	0	6	32	5.3(13)	0	—	—	—	—	—	—	—	—	—	—	k	—	0	197
1973	SD	13	78	289	3.7(24)	7	19	151	7.9(30)	0	—	—	—	—	—	—	—	—	—	—	—	—	42	435
1975	Hou	14	19	42	2.2(11)	0	1	5	5.0(5)	0	—	—	—	—	—	—	—	—	—	—	—	—	0	45
NFL	7	89	639	2510	3.9(76)	23	113	982	8.7(43)	4	—	—	—	—	—	—	—	—	—	—	k	—	162	3654

Holmes, Ron Ronald, DE, 6´4˝/261 lbs; Washington; 1985: TB, rnd 1; B8/26/1963 Fort Benning, GA **1985** TB 16 (14, RDE) **1986** TB 14 (12, RDE) **1987** TB 10 (8, RDE) **1988** TB 10 (10, RDE) **1989**†Den 15 (8, rde) **1990** Den 14 (10, RDE) **1991**†Den 15 (14, RDE) **1992** Den 8 (0) **NFL** 102 (76) [8 yrs]

Holmes, Rudy Rudell Leron, DB, 5´10˝/178 lbs; Drake; B7/19/1952 Oakland, CA **1974** Atl 8

Holmoe, Tom Thomas Allen, DB, 6´2˝/190 lbs; Brigham Young; 1983: SF, rnd 4; B3/7/1960 Los Angeles, CA **1983**†SF 16 (0) **1984**†SF 16 (1) **1986**†SF 16 (2) **1987**†SF 11 (0) **1988**†SF 16 (4) **1989** SF 7 (0) **NFL** 82 (7) [6 yrs]

Holohan, Pete Peter Joseph, TE, 6´4˝/237 lbs; Notre Dame; 1981: SD, rnd 7; B7/25/1959 Albany, NY

YEAR	TEAM	G (GS, POS)	RUSH	YD	AVG (LG)	TD	REC	YD	AVG (LG)	TD	PASS	COMP	PCT	YD	AVG (LG)	TD	INT	SK	YD	QBR	KPR	OTD	PTS	TAY
1981	SD	7(0)	—	—	—	—	1	14	14.0(14)	0	—	—	—	—	—	—	—	—	—	—	—	—	0	7
1982	†SD	9(0)	—	—	—	—	—	—	—	—	—	—	—	—	—	—	—	—	—	—	—	—	0	0
1983	SD	16(3)	—	—	—	—	23	272	11.8(35)	2	1	0	0.0	0	0.0	0	0	—	—	—	—	—	12	146
1984	SD	15(4)	—	—	—	—	56	734	13.1(51)	1	2	1	50.0	25	12.5(25)	1	0	—	—	—	—	—	6	390
1985	SD	15(3)	—	—	—	—	42	458	10.9(23)	3	1	0	0.0	0	0.0	0	0	1	8	—	k	—	18	229
1986	SD	16(6, te)	—	—	—	—	29	356	12.3(34)	1	2	1	50.0	21	10.5(21)	0	0	—	—	—	—	—	6	194
1987	SD	12(4)	—	—	—	—	20	239	11.9(18)	0	—	—	—	—	—	—	—	—	—	—	—	—	0	120
1988	†LARm	16(6, te)	—	—	—	—	59	640	10.8(29)	3	—	—	—	—	—	—	—	—	—	—	—	—	18	335
1989	†LARm	16(6, te)	1	3	3.0(3)	0	51	510	10.0(31)	2	—	—	—	—	—	—	—	—	—	—	—	—	12	268
1990	LARm	16(10, TE)	—	—	—	—	49	475	9.7(28)	2	—	—	—	—	—	—	—	—	—	—	—	—	12	248
1991	†KC	16(3)	—	—	—	—	13	113	8.7(26)	2	—	—	—	—	—	—	—	—	—	—	—	—	12	67
1992	Cle	9(3)	—	—	—	—	20	170	8.5(24)	0	—	—	—	—	—	—	—	—	—	—	—	—	0	85
NFL	12	163(48)	1	3	3.0(3)	0	363	3981	11.0(51)	16	6	2	33.3	46	7.7(25)	1	0	1	8	—	k	—	96	2087

Holovak, Mike Michael Joseph, FB-LB, 6´1˝/213 lbs; Boston College; 1943: Cle, rnd 1; B9/19/1919 Lansford, CA **[C]**

YEAR	TEAM	G (GS, POS)	RUSH	YD	AVG (LG)	TD	REC	YD	AVG (LG)	TD	PASS	COMP	PCT	YD	AVG (LG)	TD	INT	SK	YD	QBR	KPR	OTD	PTS	TAY
1946	LARm	11(2)	55	211	3.8(22)	3	2	6	3.0(8)	0	—	—	—	—	—	—	—	—	—	—	k	—	18	247
1947	ChiB	12(3)	51	281	5.5(52)	1	7	119	17.0(60)	0	—	—	—	—	—	—	—	—	—	—	k	—	6	368
1948	ChiB	11(5, fb)	30	228	7.6(47)	2	4	30	7.5(15)	0	—	—	—	—	—	—	—	—	—	—	i	—	12	276
NFL	3	34(10)	136	720	5.3(52)	6	13	155	11.9(60)	0	—	—	—	—	—	—	—	—	—	—	ki	—	36	891

Holsey, Bernard Leonard Bernard, DT-DE, 6´2˝/286 lbs; Duke; B12/10/1973 Rome, GA **1996** NYG 16 (0) **1997**†NYG 16 (4) **1998** NYG 16 (0) **1999** NYG 16 (0) **2000**†Ind 16 (13, LDE) **2002** NE 8 (0) **2003** Was 16 (16, LDT/rdt) **NFL** 104 (33) [7 yrs]

Holston, Mike Michael Anthony, WR, 6´3˝/189 lbs; Morgan State; 1981: Hou, rnd 3; B1/8/1958 Seat Pleasant, MD

YEAR	TEAM	G (GS, POS)	RUSH	YD	AVG (LG)	TD	REC	YD	AVG (LG)	TD	PASS	COMP	PCT	YD	AVG (LG)	TD	INT	SK	YD	QBR	KPR	OTD	PTS	TAY
1981	Hou	16(4)	—	—	—	—	27	427	15.8(50)	2	—	—	—	—	—	—	—	—	—	—	—	—	12	224
1982	Hou	9(5, WR)	—	—	—	—	5	116	23.2(38)	1	—	—	—	—	—	—	—	—	—	—	—	—	6	63
1983	Hou	16(0)	—	—	—	—	14	205	14.6(43)	0	—	—	—	—	—	—	—	—	—	—	—	—	0	103
1984	Hou	16(3)	—	—	—	—	22	287	13.0(28)	1	—	—	—	—	—	—	—	—	—	—	—	—	6	149
1985	Hou	3(0)	—	—	—	—	1	25	25.0(25)	0	—	—	—	—	—	—	—	—	—	—	—	—	0	13
1985	KC	4(0)	—	—	—	—	5	51	10.2(17)	0	—	—	—	—	—	—	—	—	—	—	—	—	0	26
NFL	5	64(12)	—	—	—	—	74	1111	15.0(50)	4	—	—	—	—	—	—	—	—	—	—	—	—	24	576

Holt, Harry Harry Thompson, TE, 6´4˝/236 lbs; Arizona; B12/29/1957 Harlingen, TX

YEAR	TEAM	G (GS, POS)	RUSH	YD	AVG (LG)	TD	REC	YD	AVG (LG)	TD	PASS	COMP	PCT	YD	AVG (LG)	TD	INT	SK	YD	QBR	KPR	OTD	PTS	TAY
1983	Cle	15(11, TE)	3	8	2.7(4)	0	29	420	14.5(48)	3	—	—	—	—	—	—	—	—	—	—	—	—	18	233
1984	Cle	12(8, TE)	1	12	12.0(12)	0	20	261	13.1(36)	0	—	—	—	—	—	—	—	—	—	—	k	—	0	129
1985	†Cle	11(2)	—	—	—	—	10	95	9.5(23)	1	—	—	—	—	—	—	—	—	—	—	—	—	6	53
1986	†Cle	14(0)	1	16	16.0(16)	1	4	61	15.3(34)	1	—	—	—	—	—	—	—	—	—	—	—	—	12	62
1987	SD	3(3)	—	—	—	—	7	56	8.0(17)	0	—	—	—	—	—	—	—	—	—	—	—	—	0	28
NFL	5	55(24)	5	36	7.2(16)	1	70	893	12.8(48)	5	—	—	—	—	—	—	—	—	—	—	k	—	36	504

Holt, Issiac Issiac, DB, 6´2˝/200 lbs; Alcorn State; 1985: Min, rnd 2; B10/4/1962 Birmingham, AL **[I]** **1985** Min 15 (1) **1986** Min 16 (15, LCB) **1987**†Min 9 (6, lcb) **1988**†Min 13 (9, LCB) **1989** Min 5 (1) **1989** Dal 9 (0) **1990** Dal☆15 (15, LCB) **1991**†Dal 15 (15, LCB) **1992**†Dal 16 (11, LCB) **NFL** 113 (73) [8 yrs]

Holt, John John Stephanie, DB, 5´11˝/180 lbs; West Texas A&M; 1981: TB, rnd 4; B5/14/1959 Lawton, OK **1981**†TB 16 (6, rcb) **1982**†TB 9 (0) **1983** TB 16 (16, LCB/rcb) **1984** TB 15 (15, RCB) **1985** TB 16 (16, RCB) **1986** Ind 16 (4) **1987**†Ind 12 (0) **1988** Ind 9 (1) **NFL** 109 (58) [8 yrs]

Holt, Pierce Leslie Pierce, DE-DT, 6´4˝/275 lbs; Angelo State (TX); 1988: SF, rnd 2; B1/1/1962 Marlin, TX **1988**†SF 9 (0) **1989**†SF 16 (11, LDE) **1990**†SF 16 (16, LDE) **1991** SF 13 (11, LDE) **1992**†SF★16 (16, LDE) **1993** Atl 16 (15, LDT) **1994** Atl 12 (12, LDT) **1995**†Atl 11 (10, LDT) **NFL** 109 (91) [8 yrs]

YEAR	TEAM	G (GS, POS)	RUSH	YD	AVG(LG)	TD	REC	YD	AVG(LG)	TD	PASS	COMP	PCT	YD	AVG(LG)	TD	INT	SK	YD	QBR	KPR	OTD	PTS	TAY

HOLT, ROBERT Robert James, WR, 6´1˝/182 lbs; Baylor; 1981: Buf, rnd 6; B10/4/1959 Denison, TX

| 1982 | Buf | 7(0) | 1 | 3 | 3.0(3) | 0 | 4 | 45 | 11.3(23) | 0 | — | — | — | — | — | — | — | — | — | — | kp | — | 0 | 72 |

HOLT, TERRENCE Terrence, DB, 6´2˝/208 lbs; North Carolina State; 2003: Det, rnd 5; B3/5/1980 Greensboro, NC   **2003** Det 11 (2) **2004** Det 16 (0) **2005** Det 10 (10, FS)
NFL 37 (12) [3 yrs]

HOLT, TORRY Torry Jabar, WR, 6´0˝/190 lbs; North Carolina State; 1999: SL, rnd 1; B6/5/1976 Greensboro, NC

1999	†SL	16(15, WR)	3	25	8.3(14)	0	52	788	15.2(63)	6	—	—	—	—	—	—	—	—	—	—	p	—	36	449
2000	†SL◇	16(15, WR)	2	7	3.5(7)	0	82	1635	19.9(85)	6	—	—	—	—	—	—	—	—	—	—	—	—	36	855
2001	†SL◇	16(14, WR)	2	0	0.0(2)	0	81	1363	16.8(51)	7	—	—	—	—	—	—	—	—	—	—	—	—	42	717
2002	SL	16(11, WR)	2	18	9.0(14)	0	91	1302	14.3(58)	4	—	—	—	—	—	—	—	—	—	—	—	—	24	689
2003	†SL★	16(15, WR)	1	5	5.0(5)	0	117	1696	14.5(48)	12	—	—	—	—	—	—	—	—	—	—	—	—	72	913
2004	†SL◇	16(16, WR)	—	—	—	—	94	1372	14.6(75)	10	—	—	—	—	—	—	—	—	—	—	—	—	60	736
2005	SL◇	14(14, WR)	1	2	2.0(2)	0	102	1331	13.0(44)	9	—	—	—	—	—	—	—	—	—	—	—	—	54	713
NFL	7	110(100)	11	57	5.2(14)	0	619	9487	15.3(85)	54	—	—	—	—	—	—	—	—	—	—	p	—	324	5071

HOLTZMAN, GLENN Glen, T-DE, 6´3˝/250 lbs; North Texas; 1954: LA, rnd 26; B10/9/1930 Shreveport, LA, D5/6/1980 Reno, NV   **1955**†LARm 12 **1956** LARm 12 (RT)
1957 LARm 12 **1958** LARm 12 (LDE) **NFL** 48 [4 yrs]

HOLUB, E.J. Emil Joseph, LB-C, 6´4˝/236 lbs; Texas Tech; 1961: DalT, rnd 1/Dal, rnd 2; B1/5/1938 Schulenburg, TX   **1961** DalT-A☆14 (LLB) **1962**†DalT-A★14 (LLB)
1963 KC-A☆14 (LLB) **1964** KC-A☆9 (LLB) **1965** KC-A☆14 (RLB) **1966**†KC-A★14 (RLB) **1967** KC-A 6 (rlb) **1968**†KC-A 14 (C) **1969**†KC-A☆14 (C) **1970** KC 14 (c)
NFL 127 [10 yrs]

HOLZ, GORDY Gordon Francis, DT-T, 6´4˝/260 lbs; Minnesota; 1955: Pit, rnd 23; B5/24/1933 St. Paul, MN   **1960** Den-A 14 (LT) **1961** Den-A 14 (RDT) **1962** Den-A 14 (RDT)
1963 Den-A 14 (RDT) **1964** NYJ-A 14 (RDT) **NFL** 70 [5 yrs]

HOLZER, TOM Thomas Robert, DE, 6´4˝/248 lbs; Louisville; 1967: SF, rnd 2; B8/2/1945 Indianapolis, IN   **1967** SF 14

HOMAN, DENNIS Dennis Frank, WR, 6´1˝/181 lbs; Alabama; 1968: Dal, rnd 1; B1/9/1946 Muscle Shoals, AL

1968	†Dal	10	—	—	—	—	4	92	23.0(36)	1	—	—	—	—	—	—	—	—	—	—	kp	—	6	37
1969	†Dal	11(4)	—	—	—	—	12	240	20.0(66)	0	—	—	—	—	—	—	—	—	—	—	—	—	0	120
1970	†Dal	10(5, wr)	2	-3	-1.5(0)	0	7	105	15.0(43)	0	—	—	—	—	—	—	—	—	—	—	—	—	0	50
1971	†KC	8	—	—	—	—	2	47	23.5(29)	0	—	—	—	—	—	—	—	—	—	—	p	—	0	35
1972	KC	7(WR)	—	—	—	—	12	135	11.3(38)	1	—	—	—	—	—	—	—	—	—	—	p	—	6	72
NFL	5	46(9)	2	-3	-1.5	0	37	619	16.7(66)	2	—	—	—	—	—	—	—	—	—	—	kp	—	12	313

HOMAN, TWO-BITS Ralph Henry, B, 5´5˝/145 lbs; Lebanon Valley; B6/7/1898 Reading, PA, D2/1966, NY   **1925** Fra 16 (14, BB), 12 **1926** Fra 7 (2), 18 **1927** Fra 16 (2), 12
1928 Fra 11 (6, bb), 6 **1929** Fra 17 (13, BB), 12 **1930** Fra 14 (6, bb) **NFL** 81 (43), 60 [6 yrs]

HOMCO, THOMAS Thomas Ross, LB, 6´1˝/245 lbs; Northwestern; B1/8/1970 Hammond, IN   **1993** LARm 16 (3) **1994** LARm 15 (0) **1995** SL 11 (0) **1996** SL 3 (0)
NFL 45 (3) [4 yrs]

HONAKER, CHARLIE Frank Charles, E, 5´11˝/185 lbs; Ohio State; B10/11/1899 Russell, KY, D4/21/1974 Huntington, WV   **1924** Cle 6 (2)

HONS, TODD Todd Hank, QB, 6´1˝/195 lbs; Arizona State; B9/5/1961 Torrance, CA

| 1987 | Det | 3(3) | 5 | 49 | 9.8(23) | 0 | — | — | — | — | 92 | 43 | 46.7 | 552 | 6.0(53) | 5 | 5 | 9 | 67 | — | — | — | 0 | 150 |

HOOD, ESTUS Estus, DB, 5´11˝/183 lbs; Illinois State; 1978: GB, rnd 3; B11/14/1955 Hattiesburg, MS   **1978** GB 16 **1979** GB 16 (16, LCB) **1980** GB 15 (15, LCB) **1981** GB 16 (0)
1982†GB 9 (1) **1983** GB 16 (0) **1984** GB 16 (0) **NFL** 104 (32) [7 yrs]

HOOD, FRANK Franklin, HB, 6´0˝/235 lbs; Pittsburgh; B10/5/1908, D9/1973

| 1933 | Pit | 3(1) | 1 | 1 | 1.0(1) | 0 | — | — | — | — | 18 | 6 | 33.3 | 45 | 2.5 | 0 | 4 | — | — | — | — | — | 0 | -137 |

HOOD, RODERICK Roderick, DB, 5´11˝/196 lbs; Auburn; B10/3/1981 Columbus, GA   **2003**†Phi 14 (0) **2004**†Phi 16 (2) **2005** Phi 16 (6, rcb) **NFL** 46 (8) [3 yrs]

HOOD, WINFORD Winford DeWayne, G-T, 6´3˝/262 lbs; Georgia; 1984: Den, rnd 8; B3/29/1962 Atlanta, GA   **1984**†Den 16 (2) **1985** Den 16 (3) **1986** Den 9 (2) **1987** Den 3 (2)
1988 Den 3 (0) **NFL** 47 (9) [5 yrs]

HOOKER, FAIR Fair, WR, 6´1˝/190 lbs; Arizona State; 1969: Cle, rnd 5; B5/22/1947 Los Angeles, CA

1969	†Cle	13	—	—	—	—	2	21	10.5(12)	0	—	—	—	—	—	—	—	—	—	—	—	—	0	11
1970	Cle	13(WR)	—	—	—	—	28	490	17.5(69)	2	—	—	—	—	—	—	—	—	—	—	—	—	12	255
1971	†Cle	14(WR)	—	—	—	—	45	649	14.4(48)	1	—	—	—	—	—	—	—	—	—	—	—	—	6	330
1972	†Cle	14(WR)	—	—	—	—	32	441	13.8(43)	2	—	—	—	—	—	—	—	—	—	—	—	—	12	231
1973	Cle	13(WR)	—	—	—	—	18	196	10.9(26)	2	—	—	—	—	—	—	—	—	—	—	—	—	12	108
1974	Cle	7(WR)	—	—	—	—	4	48	12.0(17)	1	—	—	—	—	—	—	—	—	—	—	—	—	6	29
NFL	6	74	—	—	—	—	129	1845	14.3(69)	8	—	—	—	—	—	—	—	—	—	—	—	—	48	963

HOOKS, ALVIN Alvin Lee, WR, 5´11˝/170 lbs; Cal State-Northridge; B5/7/1957 Los Angeles, CA   **1981** Phi 3 (0)

HOOKS, JIM James Earl, RB, 5´11˝/225 lbs; Central Oklahoma; 1973: Det, rnd 4; B10/23/1950 Oklahoma City, OK

1973	Det	11	19	110	5.8(24)	0	1	6	6.0(6)	0	—	—	—	—	—	—	—	—	—	—	k	—	0	135
1974	Det	8(6, fb)	44	143	3.3(17)	0	9	53	5.9(19)	0	—	—	—	—	—	—	—	—	—	—	k	—	0	170
1975	Det	12	4	-8	-2.0(3)	0	1	5	5.0(5)	0	—	—	—	—	—	—	—	—	—	—	k	—	0	-28
1976	Det	1	—	—	—	—	—	—	—	—	—	—	—	—	—	—	—	—	—	—	—	—	—	—
NFL	4	32(6)	67	245	3.7(24)	0	11	64	5.8(19)	0	—	—	—	—	—	—	—	—	—	—	k	—	0	277

HOOKS, ROLAND Roland, RB, 6´0˝/197 lbs; North Carolina State; 1975: Buf, rnd 10; B1/2/1953 Brooklyn, NY

1976	Buf	14(2)	25	116	4.6(24)	0	6	72	12.0(28)	0	—	—	—	—	—	—	—	—	—	—	kp	—	0	318
1977	Buf	14(7, rb)	128	497	3.9(66)	0	16	195	12.2(33)	0	—	—	—	—	—	—	—	—	—	—	—	—	0	595
1978	Buf	16	76	358	4.7(66)	2	15	110	7.3(21)	1	—	—	—	—	—	—	—	—	—	—	kp	—	18	454
1979	Buf	16	89	320	3.6(32)	6	26	254	9.8(42)	0	—	—	—	—	—	—	—	—	—	—	—	—	36	507
1980	†Buf	16(0)	25	118	4.7(25)	1	23	179	7.8(26)	0	—	—	—	—	—	—	—	—	—	—	kp	—	6	272
1981	†Buf	16(1)	51	250	4.9(19)	3	10	140	14.0(37)	2	—	—	—	—	—	—	—	—	—	—	kp	—	30	467
1982	Buf	6(0)	5	23	4.6(9)	0	—	—	—	—	—	—	—	—	—	—	—	—	—	—	p	—	0	16
NFL	7	98(10)	399	1682	4.2(66)	12	96	950	9.9(42)	3	—	—	—	—	—	—	—	—	—	—	kp	—	90	2628

HOOLIGAN, HARRY Harry, FB, 6´2˝/225 lbs; Bishop; B9/13/1938   **1965** Hou-A 1

HOOPER, TRELL John Lutrell, DB, 5´11˝/182 lbs; Memphis; 1986: Ind, rnd 8; B12/22/1961 Brownsville, TX   **1987** Mia 3 (3)

HOOPES, MITCH Mitchell Kent, P, 6´1˝/207 lbs; Arizona; 1975: Dal, rnd 8; B7/8/1953 Bisbee, AZ   **1976** Hou 1 **1977** Det 1

1975	†Dal	14	1	13	13.0(13)	0	—	—	—	—	3	1	33.3	21	7.0(21)	0	0	—	—	—	P	—	0	24
1976	SD	9	2	10	5.0(10)	0	—	—	—	—	—	—	—	—	—	—	—	—	—	—	P	—	0	10
NFL	3	25	3	23	7.7(13)	0	—	—	—	—	3	1	33.3	21	7.0(21)	0	0	—	—	—	P	—	0	34

HOOVER, BRAD Bradley R., FB, 6´0˝/242 lbs; Western Carolina; B11/11/1976 High Point, NC

2000	Car	16(4)	89	290	3.3(35)	1	15	112	7.5(16)	0	—	—	—	—	—	—	—	—	—	—	—	—	6	356
2001	Car	16(7, fb)	17	71	4.2(10)	0	26	185	7.1(19)	0	—	—	—	—	—	—	—	—	—	—	k	—	0	157
2002	Car	16(10, FB)	31	129	4.2(11)	0	17	187	11.0(33)	2	—	—	—	—	—	—	—	—	—	—	—	—	12	233
2003	†Car	16(9, fb)	6	21	3.5(5)	0	12	72	6.0(17)	1	—	—	—	—	—	—	—	—	—	—	k	—	6	47
2004	Car	14(9, FB)	68	246	3.6(16)	0	21	161	7.7(34)	2	—	—	—	—	—	—	—	—	—	—	k	—	12	337
2005	†Car	15(15, FB)	10	22	2.2(4)	0	14	87	6.2(12)	0	—	—	—	—	—	—	—	—	—	—	k	—	0	61
NFL	6	93(54)	221	779	3.5(35)	1	105	804	7.7(34)	5	—	—	—	—	—	—	—	—	—	—	k	—	36	1189

HOOVER, HOUSTON Houston Roosevelt, G-T, 6´2˝/295 lbs; Jackson State; 1988: Atl, rnd 6; B2/6/1965 Yazoo City, MS   **1988** Atl 15 (12, RT) **1989** Atl 16 (16, RT)
1990 Atl 16 (12, LG) **1991**†Atl 16 (16, LG) **1992** Atl 16 (16, LG) **1993** Cle 16 (16, LG) **1994** Mia 3 (0) **NFL** 98 (88) [7 yrs]

HOOVER, MELVIN Melvin Charles, WR, 6´0˝/185 lbs; Arizona State; 1981: NYG, rnd 6; B9/21/1959 Charlotte, NC

| 1982 | Phi | 7(0) | 1 | 5 | 5.0(5) | 0 | — | — | — | — | — | — | — | — | — | — | — | — | — | — | k | — | 0 | 13 |
| 1983 | Phi | 11(0) | — | — | — | — | 10 | 221 | 22.1(68) | 0 | — | — | — | — | — | — | — | — | — | — | p | — | 0 | 120 |

YEAR	TEAM	G(GS, POS)	RUSH	YD	AVG(LG)	TD	REC	YD	AVG(LG)	TD	PASS	COMP	PCT	YD	AVG(LG)	TD	INT	SK	YD	QBR	KPR	OTD	PTS	TAY
1984	Phi	12(1)	—	—	—	—	6	143	23.8(44)	2	—	—	—	—	—	—	—	—	—	—	—	—	12	82
1987	Det	2(0)	—	—	—	—	—	—	—	—	—	—	—	—	—	—	—	—	—	—	—	—	—	—
NFL	4	32(1)	1	5	5.0(5)	0	16	364	22.8(68)	2	—	—	—	—	—	—	—	—	—	—	kp	—	12	214

HOPE, CHARLES Charles Edward, G-C, 6´3˝/303 lbs; Central State (OH); B3/12/1970 Wilmington, DE **1994**†GB 6 (0)

HOPE, CHRIS Chris, DB, 6´0˝/214 lbs; Florida State; 2002: Pit, rnd 3; B9/29/1980 Rock Hill, SC **2002**†Pit 14 (0) **2004**†Pit 16 (16, FS) **2005**†Pit 16 (16, FS)

YEAR	TEAM	G(GS, POS)	RUSH	YD	AVG(LG)	TD	REC	YD	AVG(LG)	TD	PASS	COMP	PCT	YD	AVG(LG)	TD	INT	SK	YD	QBR	KPR	OTD	PTS	TAY
2003	Pit	16(0)	—	—	—	—	1	81	81.0(81)	1	—	—	—	—	—	—	—	—	—	—	—	—	6	46
NFL	4	62(32)	—	—	—	—	1	81	81.0(81)	1	—	—	—	—	—	—	—	—	—	—	i	—	6	127

HOPE, NEIL Neil Keith, LB, 6´2˝/235 lbs; USC; B3/22/1963 Memphis, TN **1987** LARm 3 (1)

HOPKINS, ANDY Andrew Pochae, RB, 5´10˝/186 lbs; Stephen F. Austin State; 1971: Hou, rnd 15; B10/19/1949 Crockett, TX

YEAR	TEAM	G(GS, POS)	RUSH	YD	AVG(LG)	TD	REC	YD	AVG(LG)	TD	PASS	COMP	PCT	YD	AVG(LG)	TD	INT	SK	YD	QBR	KPR	OTD	PTS	TAY
1971	Hou	2	2	2	1.0(2)	0	—	—	—	—	—	—	—	—	—	—	—	—	—	—	—	—	0	2

HOPKINS, BRAD Bradley Donnell, T, 6´3˝/305 lbs; Illinois; 1993: Hou, rnd 1; B9/5/1970 Columbia, SC **1993**†Hou 16 (11, LT) **1994** Hou 16 (15, LT) **1995** Hou 16 (16, LT) **1996** Hou 16 (16, LT) **1997** Ten 16 (16, LT) **1998** Ten 13 (13, LT) **1999**†Ten 16 (16, LT) **2000**†Ten★15 (15, LT) **2001** Ten 14 (14, LT) **2002**†Ten 14 (14, LT) **2003**†Ten 16 (16, LT) **2004** Ten 11 (11, LT) **2005** Ten 15 (15, LT) **NFL** 194 (188) [13 yrs]

HOPKINS, JERRY Jerry Wayne, LB, 6´2˝/235 lbs; Texas A&M; 1963: Hou, rnd 4; B1/24/1941 Chalk Bluff, TX **1963** Den-A 7 **1964** Den-A 14 (LLB) **1965** Den-A 14 (MLB) **1966** Den-A 14 (MLB) **1967** Mia-A 13 (6, llb) **1968**†Oak-A 5 **NFL** 67 (6) [6 yrs]

HOPKINS, ROY Roy Lee, RB, 6´1˝/235 lbs; Texas Southern; 1967: Hou, rnd 2; B2/18/1945 Gilmer, TX

YEAR	TEAM	G(GS, POS)	RUSH	YD	AVG(LG)	TD	REC	YD	AVG(LG)	TD	PASS	COMP	PCT	YD	AVG(LG)	TD	INT	SK	YD	QBR	KPR	OTD	PTS	TAY
1967	†Hou-A	14	13	42	3.2(19)	0	3	9	3.0(7)	0	—	—	—	—	—	—	—	—	—	—	k	—	0	58
1968	Hou-A	13	31	104	3.4(18)	0	4	40	10.0(26)	0	—	—	—	—	—	—	—	—	—	—	k	—	0	130
1969	Hou-A	14(HB)	131	473	3.6(43)	4	29	338	11.7(56)	1	—	—	—	—	—	—	—	—	—	—	—	—	30	687
1970	Hou	12	57	207	3.6(12)	3	14	142	10.1(43)	0	—	—	—	—	—	—	—	—	—	—	k	—	18	313
NFL	4	53	232	826	3.6(43)	7	50	529	10.6(56)	1	—	—	—	—	—	—	—	—	—	—	k	—	48	1188

HOPKINS, TAM Tam, G, 6´4˝/315 lbs; Ohio State; B3/22/1978 Winter Park, FL **2002**†NYG 16 (1)

HOPKINS, TED Edward J., E, 5´9˝/180 lbs; none; B12/5/1890 Canton, OH, D3/8/1973 Kettering, OH **1921** Col 3 (1) **1922** Col 5 (0) **NFL** 8 (1) [2 yrs]

HOPKINS, THOMAS Thomas, T, 6´6˝/260 lbs; Alabama A&M; 1983: Cle, rnd 10; B1/13/1960 Butler, AL **1983** Cle 2 (0)

HOPKINS, WES Wesley Carl, DB, 6´1˝/213 lbs; SMU; 1983: Phi, rnd 2; B9/26/1961 Birmingham, AL **[I]** **1983** Phi 14 (14, FS) **1984** Phi☆16 (15, FS) **1985** Phi★15 (15, FS) **1986** Phi 4 (4) **1988**†Phi 16 (16, FS) **1989**†Phi 16 (15, FS) **1990**†Phi 15 (12, FS) **1991** Phi 16 (16, FS) **1992** Phi 10 (10, FS) **1993** Phi 15 (8, ss) **NFL** 137 (125) [10 yrs]

HOPP, HARRY Harry, B, 6´0˝/209 lbs; Nebraska; 1941: Det, rnd 3; B12/13/1918 Hastings, NE, D12/22/1964 Hastings, NE

YEAR	TEAM	G(GS, POS)	RUSH	YD	AVG(LG)	TD	REC	YD	AVG(LG)	TD	PASS	COMP	PCT	YD	AVG(LG)	TD	INT	SK	YD	QBR	KPR	OTD	PTS	TAY
1941	Det	10(6, FB)	69	202	2.9(29)	1	2	7	3.5(5)	0	3	0	0.0	0	0.0	0	1	—	—	—	Pi	—	6	174
1942	Det✧	10(5, TB)	66	230	3.5(44)	0	—	—	—	—	68	20	29.4	258	3.8(50)	0	13	—	—	—	Pkpi	—	0	-92
1943	Det	10(9, FB)	56	99	1.8(16)	3	17	229	13.5(67)	3	8	5	62.5	60	7.5(36)	0	0	—	—	—	Pkpi	3	54	329
NFL	3	30(20)	191	531	2.8(44)	4	19	236	12.4(67)	3	79	25	31.6	318	4.0(50)	0	14	—	—	—	Pkpi	3	60	410
1946	Buf-A	9(2)	45	129	2.9	1	2	-1	-0.5	0	22	11	50.0	190	8.6	0	0	—	—	—	Pk	—	6	228
1946	Mia-A	3(2)	16	89	5.6(55)	2	—	—	—	—	—	—	—	—	—	—	—	—	—	—	k	—	12	138
1947	LAD-A	9(0)	10	52	5.2	0	3	59	19.7	0	—	—	—	—	—	—	—	—	—	—	ki	—	0	91
AAFC	2	21(4)	71	270	3.8(55)	3	5	58	11.6(67)	0	22	11	50.0	190	8.6(50)	0	0	—	—	—	Pki	—	18	456

HOPPER, DARREL Darrel, DB, 6´1˝/196 lbs; USC; B3/14/1963 Los Angeles, CA **1987** SD 4 (2)

HOPPOCK, DOUG Douglas Gene, T-G, 6´4˝/280 lbs; Kansas State; B1/30/1960 Wichita, KS **1987** KC 3 (3)

HOPSON, TYRONE Tyrone, G, 6´2˝/305 lbs; Eastern Kentucky; 1999: SF, rnd 5; B5/28/1976 Hopkinsville, KY **1999** SF 1 (0) **2000** SF 3 (1) **2002** Det 8 (0) **2004** Det 11 (0) **NFL** 23 (1) [4 yrs]

HOPTOWIT, AL Alphonse William, T, 6´1˝/217 lbs; Washington State; 1938: Cle, rnd 11; B9/7/1915 Yakima, WA, D4/6/1981 Yakima, WA **1942**†ChiB 11 (0) **1943**†ChiB 10 (10, RT) **1944** ChiB 10 (7, RT) **1945** ChiB 10 (2) **NFL** 41 (19) [4 yrs]

HORAN, MIKE Michael William, P, 5´11˝/192 lbs; Long Beach State; 1982: Atl, rnd 9; B2/1/1959 Orange, CA **[P]** **1984** Phi☆16 (0) **1987**†Den 12 (0) **1988** Den★16 (0) **1989**†Den 16 (0) **1990** Den☆15 (0) **1992** Den 7 (0) **1993**†NYG 8 (0) **1994** NYG 16 (0) **1996** NYG 16 (0) **1999**†SL 8 (0)

YEAR	TEAM	G(GS, POS)	RUSH	YD	AVG(LG)	TD	REC	YD	AVG(LG)	TD	PASS	COMP	PCT	YD	AVG(LG)	TD	INT	SK	YD	QBR	KPR	OTD	PTS	TAY
1985	Phi	16(0)	1	12	12.0(12)	0	—	—	—	—	—	—	—	—	—	—	—	—	—	—	P	—	0	12
1986	†Den	4(0)	1	0	0.0(0)	0	—	—	—	—	—	—	—	—	—	—	—	—	—	—	P	—	0	0
1991	†Den	16(0)	2	9	4.5(9)	0	—	—	—	—	—	—	—	—	—	—	—	—	—	—	P	—	0	9
1995	NYG	16(0)	1	0	0.0(0)	0	—	—	—	—	—	—	—	—	—	—	—	—	—	—	P	—	0	0
1997	SL	10(0)	1	-3	-3.0(-3)	0	—	—	—	—	—	—	—	—	—	—	—	—	—	—	P	—	0	-3
1998	ChiB	13(0)	—	—	—	—	—	—	—	—	2	1	50.0	18	9.0(18)	1	0	—	—	—	P	—	0	14
NFL	16	205(0)	6	18	3.0(12)	0	—	—	—	—	2	1	50.0	18	9.0(18)	1	0	—	—	—	P	—	0	32

HORD, ROY Ambrose Roy, G, 6´4˝/244 lbs; Duke; 1957: LA, rnd 8; B12/25/1934 Charlotte, NC, D10/24/2002 Riverside, CA **1960** LARm 12 (RG) **1961** LARm 14 (RG) **1962** LARm 3 **1962** Phi 11 (RG) **1963** NYJ-A 13 **NFL** 53 [4 yrs]

HORN, ALVIN Alvin Ramone, DB, 5´11˝/185 lbs; UNLV; B3/7/1965 Hanford, CA **1987** Cle 3 (3)

HORN, BOB Robert Allen, LB, 6´3˝/235 lbs; Oregon State; 1976: SD, rnd 4; B2/6/1954 Salem, OR **1976** SD 14 (6, mlb) **1977** SD 14 (3) **1978** SD 16 (16, MLB) **1979**†SD 16 (16, MLB) **1980**†SD 16 (16, MLB) **1981**†SD 16 (11, MLB) **1982** SF 9 (7, RILB) **1983** SF 8 (0) **NFL** 109 (75) [8 yrs]

HORN, CHRIS Christopher Michael, WR, 5´11˝/195 lbs; Rocky Mountain; B7/13/1977 Caldwell, ID

YEAR	TEAM	G(GS, POS)	RUSH	YD	AVG(LG)	TD	REC	YD	AVG(LG)	TD	PASS	COMP	PCT	YD	AVG(LG)	TD	INT	SK	YD	QBR	KPR	OTD	PTS	TAY
2004	KC	14(0)	1	12	12.0(12)	0	15	178	11.9(30)	1	—	—	—	—	—	—	—	—	—	—	k	—	6	90
2005	KC	14(2)	—	—	—	—	18	187	10.4(50)	0	—	—	—	—	—	—	—	—	—	—	k	—	0	80
NFL	2	28(2)	1	12	12.0(12)	0	33	365	11.1(50)	1	—	—	—	—	—	—	—	—	—	—	k	—	6	170

HORN, DICK Richard Henry, QB, 6´1˝/195 lbs; Stanford; 1952: DalT, rnd 17; B3/18/1930 Santa Monica, CA **1958** Bal 5

HORN, DON Donald Glenn, QB, 6´2˝/195 lbs; Washington State; San Diego State; 1967: GB, rnd 1; B3/9/1945 South Gate, CA

YEAR	TEAM	G(GS, POS)	RUSH	YD	AVG(LG)	TD	REC	YD	AVG(LG)	TD	PASS	COMP	PCT	YD	AVG(LG)	TD	INT	SK	YD	QBR	KPR	OTD	PTS	TAY
1967	†GB	3	1	-2	-2.0(-2)	0	—	—	—	—	24	12	50.0	171	7.1(29)	1	1	1	8	—	—	—	0	49
1968	GB	1	3	-7	-2.3(1)	0	—	—	—	—	16	10	62.5	187	11.7(67)	2	0	1	8	—	—	—	0	97
1969	GB	9(qb)	3	-7	-2.3(2)	1	—	—	—	—	168	89	53.0	1505	**9.0**(**60**)	11	11	10	85	—	—	—	6	371
1970	GB	7	5	4	0.8(4)	0	—	—	—	—	76	28	36.8	428	5.6(**89**)	2	10	6	59	—	—	—	0	-172
1971	Den	9(9, QB)	6	15	2.5(10)	0	—	—	—	—	173	89	51.4	1056	6.1(74)	3	14	8	67	—	—	—	0	-2
1972	Den	2	—	—	—	—	—	—	—	—	—	—	—	—	—	—	—	—	—	—	—	—	—	—
1973	Cle	14	—	—	—	—	—	—	—	—	8	4	50.0	22	2.8(12)	1	0	1	6	—	—	—	0	16
1974	SD	12	—	—	—	—	—	—	—	—	—	—	—	—	—	—	—	—	—	—	—	—	—	—
NFL	8	57(9)	18	3	0.2(10)	1	—	—	—	—	465	232	49.9	3369	7.2(89)	20	36	27	233	—	—	—	6	358

HORN, JOE Joseph, WR, 6´1˝/206 lbs; Itawamba J.C.; 1996: KC, rnd 5; B1/16/1972 New Haven, CT

YEAR	TEAM	G(GS, POS)	RUSH	YD	AVG(LG)	TD	REC	YD	AVG(LG)	TD	PASS	COMP	PCT	YD	AVG(LG)	TD	INT	SK	YD	QBR	KPR	OTD	PTS	TAY
1996	KC	9(0)	1	8	8.0(8)	0	2	30	15.0(21)	0	—	—	—	—	—	—	—	—	—	—	—	—	0	23
1997	†KC	8(0)	—	—	—	—	2	65	32.5(47)	0	—	—	—	—	—	—	—	—	—	—	—	—	0	33
1998	KC	16(1)	1	0	0.0(0)	0	14	198	14.1(57)	1	—	—	—	—	—	—	—	—	—	—	kp	—	6	173
1999	KC	16(1)	2	15	7.5(9)	0	35	586	16.7(76)	6	—	—	—	—	—	—	—	—	—	—	kp	—	36	381
2000	†NO✧	16(16, WR)	6	10	1.7(16)	0	94	1340	14.3(52)	8	—	—	—	—	—	—	—	—	—	—	—	—	48	720
2001	NO✧	16(16, WR)	1	4	4.0(4)	0	83	1265	15.2(56)	9	1	0	0.0	0	0.0	0	0	—	—	—	—	—	54	682
2002	NO✧	16(16, WR)	1	2	2.0(2)	0	88	1312	14.9(63)	7	—	—	—	—	—	—	—	—	—	—	—	—	44	693
2003	NO	15(14, WR)	2	15	7.5(13)	0	78	973	12.5(50)	10	1	1	100.0	14	14.0(14)	0	0	—	—	—	—	—	60	559
2004	NO✧	16(16, WR)	—	—	—	—	**94**	1399	14.9(57)	11	—	—	—	—	—	—	—	—	—	—	—	—	68	755
2005	NO	13(13, WR)	—	—	—	—	49	654	13.3(30)	1	—	—	—	—	—	—	—	—	—	—	—	—	6	332
NFL	10	141(93)	14	54	3.9(16)	0	539	7822	14.5(76)	53	2	1	50.0	14	7.0(14)	0	0	—	—	—	kp	—	322	4349

HORN, MARTY Martin Louis, QB, 6´2˝/205 lbs; Lehigh; B3/27/1963 Orange, NJ

YEAR	TEAM	G(GS, POS)	RUSH	YD	AVG(LG)	TD	REC	YD	AVG(LG)	TD	PASS	COMP	PCT	YD	AVG(LG)	TD	INT	SK	YD	QBR	KPR	OTD	PTS	TAY
1987	Phi	1(0)	1	0	0.0(0)	0	—	—	—	—	11	5	45.5	68	6.2(23)	0	0	1	7	—	—	—	0	34

HORN, ROD Rodney Lee, NT, 6´4˝/268 lbs; Nebraska; 1980: Cin, rnd 3; B11/23/1956 Fresno, CA **1980** Cin 7 (0) **1981**†Cin 16 (4) **NFL** 23 (4) [2 yrs]

YEAR	TEAM	G(GS,POS)	RUSH	YD	AVG(LG)	TD	REC	YD	AVG(LG)	TD	PASS COMP	PCT	YD	AVG(LG)	TD	INT	SK	YD	QBR	KPR	OTD	PTS	TAY

HORNBEAK, JAY Jay William, B, 5´11˝/185 lbs; Washington; B9/9/1911 Corsicana, TX, D7/15/1990 Palm Springs, CA

| 1935 | Bkn | 6(0) | 1 | 6 | 6.0(6) | 0 | 1 | 13 | 13.0(13) | 0 | — | — | — | — | — | — | — | — | — | — | — | 0 | 13 |

HORNE, DICK Richard Courtland, E, 6´2˝/214 lbs; Oregon; B9/4/1918 Denver, CO, D11/1964 **1941**†NYG 2 (0)

1946	Mia-A	10(3)	—	—	—	—	5	48	9.6	0	—	—	—	—	—	—	—	—	—	—	—	0	24
1947	SF-A	10(4)	—	—	—	—	3	69	23.0	0	—	—	—	—	—	—	—	—	—	—	—	0	35
AAFC	2	20(5)	—	—	—	—	8	117	14.6	0	—	—	—	—	—	—	—	—	—	—	—	0	59

HORNE, GREG Gregory Lee, P, 6´0˝/188 lbs; Arkansas; 1987: Cin, rnd 5; B11/22/1964 Russellville, AR **1987** Cin 4 (0) **1987** SL 5 (0)

| 1988 | Phx | 16(0) | 3 | 20 | 6.7(20) | 0 | — | — | — | — | — | — | — | — | — | — | — | — | P | — | — | 0 | 20 |
| NFL | 2 | 25(0) | 3 | 20 | 6.7(20) | 0 | — | — | — | — | — | — | — | — | — | — | — | — | P | — | — | 0 | 20 |

HORNE, TONY Antonio Tremaine, WR, 5´9˝/173 lbs; Clemson; B3/21/1976 Monthomery County, NC **[R]** **1998** SL 16 (0) **1999**†SL☆12 (0)

| 2000 | †SL | 11(0) | 2 | 6 | 3.0(9) | 0 | 4 | 32 | 8.0(18) | 2 | — | — | — | — | — | — | — | — | — | kp | 1 | 18 | 577 |
| NFL | 3 | 39(0) | 2 | 6 | 3.0(9) | 0 | 4 | 32 | 8.0(18) | 2 | — | — | — | — | — | — | — | — | — | kp | 4 | 36 | 1507 |

HORNER, SAM Samuel Watson, HB-DB-P, 6´0˝/198 lbs; VMI; 1960: Was, rnd 2/Den, rnd 2; B3/4/1938 Fort Sill, OK

1960	Was	10	22	80	3.6(16)	0	7	106	15.1(35)	0	—	—	—	—	—	—	—	—	—	Pkp	—	0	285
1961	Was	14(11, LH)	96	275	2.9(32)	0	10	113	11.3(20)	1	—	—	—	—	—	—	—	—	—	Pk	—	6	352
1962	†NYG	9	—	—	—	—	—	—	—	—	—	—	—	—	—	—	—	—	—	kp	—	0	65
NFL	3	33(11)	118	355	3.0(32)	0	17	219	12.9(35)	1	—	—	—	—	—	—	—	—	—	Pkp	—	6	702

HORNICK, BILL William Michael Thomas, T, 6´1˝/207 lbs; Tulane; B2/13/1919, D5/3/1995 Taylorsville, MS **1947** Pit 4 (0)

HORNING, STEAMER Clarence Edward, T, 6´0˝/198 lbs; Colgate; B11/15/1892 Phoenix, AZ, D1/24/1982 Southfield, MI **1920** Det 8 (4, RT) **1921** Det 7 (7, RT) **1921** Buf 4 (3), 6 **1922** Tol☆9 (8, RT), 6 **1923** Tol☆8 (8, RT) **NFL** 36 (30), 12 **[4 yrs]**

HORNSBY, RON Ronald Joseph, LB, 6´2˝/232 lbs; Southeastern Louisiana; 1971: NYG, rnd 3; B8/16/1949 Baton Rouge, LA **1971** NYG 14 **1972** NYG 13 (MLB) **1973** NYG 13 **1974** NYG 9 **NFL** 49 **[4 yrs]**

HORNUNG, PAUL Paul Vernon 'The Golden Boy', HB-FB-QB, 6´2˝/215 lbs; Notre Dame; 1957: GB, rnd B1; B12/23/1935 Louisville, KY; HOF 1986 **[K]**

1957	GB	12(FB)	60	319	5.3(72)	3	6	34	5.7(16)	0	6	1	16.7	1	-0.2(-1)	0	0	—	—	K	—	18	366
1958	GB	12(LH)	69	310	4.5(55)	2	15	137	9.1(39)	0	1	0	0.0	0	0.0	0	0	—	—	Kk	—	67	497
1959	GB★	12(LH)	152	681	4.5(63)	7	15	113	7.5(19)	0	8	5	62.5	95	11.9(30)	2	0	—	—	K	—	94	865
1960	†GB★	12(HB)	160	671	4.2(37)	13	28	257	9.2(33)	2	16	6	37.5	118	7.4(40)	2	0	—	—	K	—	176	1009
1961	†GB☆	12(HB)	127	597	4.7(54)	8	15	145	9.7(34)	2	5	3	60.0	42	8.4(20)	1	0	—	—	K	—	146	786
1962	†GB	9(HB)	57	219	3.8(37)	5	9	168	18.7(83)	2	6	4	66.7	80	13.3(41)	0	2	—	—	K	—	74	323
1964	GB	14(HB)	103	415	4.0(40)	5	9	98	10.9(40)	0	10	3	30.0	25	2.5(10)	0	1	—	—	K	—	107	487
1965	†GB	12(HB)	89	299	3.4(17)	5	19	336	17.7(65)	3	2	1	50.0	19	9.5(19)	0	1	13	—	—	—	48	502
1966	GB	9(HB)	76	200	2.6(9)	2	14	192	13.7(44)	3	1	1	100.0	5	5.0(5)	0	0	—	—	—	—	30	334
NFL	9	104	893	3711	4.2(72)	50	130	1480	11.4(83)	12	55	24	43.6	383	7.0(41)	5	4	1	13	—	Kk	—	760	5166

HORRELL, BILL William George, G, 5´11˝/222 lbs; Michigan State; B3/15/1930 New Kensington, PA **1952** Phi 4

HORSTMANN, ROY Roy Joseph, FB-HB, 6´0˝/188 lbs; Purdue; B12/6/1910 Aurora, IL, D1/23/1998 Hemet, CA

1933	Bos	8(1)	34	144	4.2	0	—	—	—	—	8	3	37.5	50	6.3	0	2	—	—	—	—	0	89
1934	ChiC	9(2)	18	36	2.0	1	—	—	—	—	3	1	33.3	12	4.0(12)	0	0	—	—	—	—	6	52
NFL	2	17(3)	52	180	3.5	1	—	—	—	—	11	4	36.4	62	5.6(12)	0	2	—	—	—	—	6	141

HORTON, BOB Robert, LB, 6´2˝/230 lbs; Boston University; 1964: SD, rnd 11/Chi, rnd 12; B9/15/1942 Chicago, IL **1964**†SD-A 10 **1965**†SD-A 12 **NFL** 22 **[2 yrs]**

HORTON, ETHAN Ethan Shane, TE-RB, 6´4˝/235 lbs; North Carolina; 1985: KC, rnd 1; B12/19/1962 Kannapolis, NC

1985	KC	16(0)	48	146	3.0(19)	3	28	185	6.6(22)	1	1	0	0.0	0	0.0	0	0	—	—	—	—	24	274
1987	LARd	4(2)	31	95	3.1(14)	0	3	44	14.7(32)	1	—	—	—	—	—	—	—	—	—	—	—	6	122
1989	LARd	16(1)	—	—	—	—	4	44	11.0(20)	1	—	—	—	—	—	—	—	—	—	—	—	6	27
1990	†LARd	16(14, TE)	—	—	—	—	33	404	12.2(36)	3	—	—	—	—	—	—	—	—	—	—	—	18	217
1991	†LARd◇	16(16, TE)	—	—	—	—	53	650	12.3(52)	5	—	—	—	—	—	—	—	—	—	—	—	30	350
1992	LARd	16(16, TE)	—	—	—	—	33	409	12.4(30)	2	—	—	—	—	—	—	—	—	—	—	—	12	215
1993	†LARd	16(16, TE)	—	—	—	—	43	467	10.9(32)	1	—	—	—	—	—	—	—	—	—	—	—	6	239
1994	Was	16(15, TE)	—	—	—	—	15	157	10.5(20)	3	—	—	—	—	—	—	—	—	—	—	—	18	94
NFL	8	116(80)	79	241	3.1(19)	3	212	2360	11.1(52)	17	1	0	0.0	0	0.0	0	0	—	—	—	—	120	1536

HORTON, GREG Gregory Keith, G-C, 6´4˝/245 lbs; Colorado; 1974: Chi, rnd 3; B1/7/1951 San Bernardino, CA **1976** LARm 14 **1977** LARm 14 (6, rg) **1978** LARm 2 **1978** TB 14 (12, LG) **1979** TB 16 (16, LG) **1980** LARm 3 (0) **NFL** 63 (34) **[5 yrs]**

HORTON, JASON Jason Dennard, DB, 6´0˝/193 lbs; North Carolina A&T; B2/16/1980 Ahoskie, NC **2004**†GB 14 (0) **2005** GB 9 (0) **NFL** 23 (0) **[2 yrs]**

HORTON, LARRY Lawrence, DE-DT, 6´4˝/248 lbs; Iowa; 1972: Chi, rnd 9; B4/29/1949 Gary, IN **1972** ChiB 10

HORTON, RAY Raymond Anthony, DB, 5´10˝/189 lbs; Washington; 1983: Cin, rnd 2; B4/12/1960 Tacoma, WA **1983** Cin 16 (5, lcb) **1984** Cin 15 (13, RCB) **1985** Cin 16 (16, RCB) **1986** Cin 16 (4) **1987** Cin 12 (8, LCB) **1988**†Cin 14 (0) **1989** Dal 16 (16, FS) **1990** Dal 14 (14, FS) **1991**†Dal 16 (16, FS) **1992** Dal 12 (7, fs) **NFL** 147 (99) **[10 yrs]**

HORVATH, LES Leslie, HB, 5´10˝/173 lbs; Ohio State; 1943: Cle, rnd 6; B10/12/1921 South Bend, IN, D11/14/1995 Glendale, CA

1947	LARm	10(1)	18	68	3.8(25)	0	3	29	9.7(14)	0	—	—	—	—	—	—	—	—	—	kp	—	0	105
1948	LARm	12(2)	30	118	3.9(19)	0	4	42	10.5(19)	0	—	—	—	—	—	—	—	—	—	kpi	1	6	282
NFL	2	22(3)	48	186	3.9(25)	0	7	71	10.1(19)	0	—	—	—	—	—	—	—	—	—	kpi	1	6	387
1949	Cle-A	12(0)	10	35	3.5	1	2	71	35.5	1	—	—	—	—	—	—	—	—	—	pi	1	18	84

HORWEEN, ARNIE Arnold, aka Arnold Horowitz, B, 5´11˝/206 lbs; Harvard; B7/7/1898 Chicago, IL, D8/5/1985 Chicago, IL **[KC]** **1921** ChiC 3 (3) **1922** ChiC 11 (11, QB), 27 **1923** ChiC 11 (7, QB), 9 **1924** ChiC 7 (3, QB) **NFL** 32 (24), 36 **[4 yrs]**

HORWEEN, RALPH Ralph, aka Ralph Horowitz, B, 5´10˝/200 lbs; Harvard; B8/3/1896 Chicago, IL, D5/26/1997 Charlottesville, VA **[K]** **1921** ChiC 2 (2), 3 **1922** ChiC 9 (2), 11 **1923** ChiC 11 (5, lh), 12 **NFL** 22 (9), 26 **[3 yrs]**

HOSKINS, BOB Robert Juan, DT-G, 6´2˝/246 lbs; Wichita State; 1969: SF, rnd 16; B9/16/1945 Highland, IL, D6/8/1980 Redwood City, CA **1970**†SF 14 **1971**†SF 7 **1972**†SF 14 **1973** SF 14 (13, RDT) **1974** SF 14 (14, RDT) **1975** SF 14 (14, RDT) **NFL** 77 (41) **[6 yrs]**

HOSKINS, DERRICK Derrick Tremayne, DB, 6´2˝/210 lbs; Southern Mississippi; 1992: LARd, rnd 5; B11/14/1970 Meridian, MS **1992** LARd 16 (0) **1993**†LARd 16 (16, SS) **1994** LARd 15 (9, SS) **1995** Oak 13 (13, SS) **1996** NO 1 (0) **NFL** 61 (38) **[5 yrs]**

HOSMER, CLARENCE Clarence Edward, G, 5´10˝/205 lbs; none; B7/28/1891 Tonawanda, NY, D11/1968 Buffalo, NY **1921** Ton 1 (0)

HOSS, CLARK Clark, TE, 6´8˝/235 lbs; Oregon State; 1972: NE, rnd 7; B2/19/1949 Portland, OR **1972** Phi 4

HOSTETLER, JEFF William Jeffrey, QB, 6´3˝/215 lbs; Penn State; West Virginia; 1984: NYG, rnd 3; B4/22/1961 Hollsopple, PA

1985	NYG	5(0)	—	—	—	—	—	—	—	—	—	—	—	—	—	—	—	—	—	—	—	—	—
1986	NYG	13(0)	1	1	1.0(1)	0	—	—	—	—	—	—	—	—	—	—	—	—	—	—	—	0	1
1988	NYG	16(1)	5	-3	-0.6(0)	0	1	10	10.0(10)	0	29	16	55.2	244	8.4(85)	1	2	5	31	—	—	—	0	49
1989	†NYG	16(1)	11	71	6.5(19)	2	—	—	—	—	39	20	51.3	294	7.5(35)	3	2	6	37	—	—	—	12	173
1990	†NYG	16(2)	39	190	4.9(30)	2	—	—	—	—	87	47	54.0	614	7.1(44)	3	1	9	38	—	—	—	12	492
1991	NYG	12(12, QB)	42	273	6.5(47)	2	—	—	—	—	285	179	62.8	2032	7.1(55)	5	4	20	100	84.1	—	—	12	1174
1992	NYG	13(9, QB)	35	172	4.9(27)	3	—	—	—	—	192	103	53.6	1225	6.4(46)	8	3	24	148	—	—	—	18	735
1993	†LARd	55	202	3.7(19)	5	—	—	—	—	419	236	56.3	3242	7.7(74)	14	10	38	206	82.5	—	—	30	1543
1994	LARd◇	16(16, QB)	46	159	3.5(14)	2	—	—	—	—	455	263	57.8	3334	7.3(77)	20	16	41	232	80.8	—	—	12	1306
1995	Oak	11(11, QB)	31	119	3.8(18)	0	—	—	—	—	286	172	60.1	1998	7.0(80)	12	9	22	133	82.2	—	—	0	818
1996	Oak	13(13, QB)	37	179	4.8(17)	1	—	—	—	—	402	242	60.2	2548	6.3(62)	23	14	32	181	83.2	—	—	6	1018
1997	Was	6(3)	14	28	2.0(11)	0	—	—	—	—	144	79	54.9	899	6.2(69)	5	10	10	52	—	—	—	0	103
NFL	12	152(83)	316	1391	4.4(47)	17	1	10	10.0(10)	0	2338	1357	58.0	16430	7.0(85)	94	71	207	1158	80.5	—	—	102	7411

HOUCK, BABE Orlan G., G, 6´0˝/275 lbs; Bliss; B8/20/1897 Gallipolis, OH, D7/6/1983 Athens, OH **1920** Col 4 (1) **1921** Col 7 (5, LG) **NFL** 11 (6) **[2 yrs]**

HOUGH, JIM James Husen, G-C, 6´2˝/267 lbs; Utah State; 1978: Min, rnd 4; B8/4/1956 Lynwood, CA **1978**†Min 15 (1) **1979** Min 16 (7, lg) **1980** Min 10 (10, LG) **1981** Min 16 (13, LG) **1982**†Min 9 (9, LG) **1983** Min 16 (16, LG) **1984** Min 9 (3) **1985** Min 4 (1) **1986** Min 16 (15, LG) **NFL** 111 (75) [9 yrs]

HOUGHTON, JERRY Gerald Haines, T-LB, 6´2˝/226 lbs; Washington State; 1950: Was, rnd 7; B4/18/1926 Yakima, WA, D6/1/2002 Bellevue, WA **1950** Was 12 **1951** ChiC 2 **NFL** 14 [2 yrs]

HOUGHTON, MIKE Michael Christopher, G-T, 6´3˝/315 lbs; San Diego State; 2002: GB, rnd 6; B12/1/1979 Northridge, CA **2002** Buf 1 (0)

HOULE, BILL Wilfred Theodore, BB-QB, 5´8˝/165 lbs; St. Thomas (MN); B7/14/1901, D12/26/1974 St. Paul, MN **1924** Min 6 (6, BB)

HOUSE, KEVIN Kevin Nathaniel, WR, 6´1˝/181 lbs; Southern Illinois; 1980: TB, rnd 2; B12/20/1957 St. Louis, MO

YEAR	TEAM	G (GS, POS)	RUSH	YD	AVG (LG)	TD	REC	YD	AVG (LG)	TD	PASS	COMP	PCT	YD	AVG (LG)	TD	INT	SK	YD	QBR	KPR	OTD	PTS	TAY
1980	TB	14(1)	1	32	32.0(32)	0	24	531	22.1(61)	5	—	—	—	—	—	—	—	—	—	—	—	—	30	323
1981	†TB	16(16, WR)	2	9	4.5(8)	0	56	1176	21.0(84)	9	1	0	0.0	0	0.0	0	0	—	—	—	—	—	54	642
1982	†TB	9(9, WR)	1	-1	-1.0(-1)	0	28	438	15.6(62)	2	—	—	—	—	—	—	—	—	—	—	—	—	12	228
1983	TB	16(16, WR)	1	-4	-4.0(-4)	0	47	769	16.4(74)	5	—	—	—	—	—	—	—	—	—	—	—	—	30	406
1984	TB☆	16(16, WR)	—	—	—	—	76	1005	13.2(55)	5	—	—	—	—	—	—	—	—	—	—	—	—	30	528
1985	TB	16(16, WR)	—	—	—	—	44	803	18.3(59)	5	—	—	—	—	—	—	—	—	—	—	—	—	30	427
1986	TB	7(7, WR)	2	5	2.5(4)	0	11	206	18.7(40)	0	—	—	—	—	—	—	—	—	—	—	—	—	0	108
1986	†LARm	8(3)	—	—	—	—	7	178	25.4(60)	2	0	0	0.0	0	0.0	0	0	1	6	—	—	—	12	99
1987	LARm	12(1)	—	—	—	—	6	63	10.5(15)	1	—	—	—	—	—	—	—	—	—	—	—	—	6	37
NFL	8	114(85)	7	41	5.9(32)	0	299	5169	17.3(84)	34	1	0	0.0	0	0.0	0	0	1	6	—	—	—	204	2796

HOUSE, KEVIN Kevin Nathaniel, DB, 6´0˝/185 lbs; South Carolina; B1/9/1979 St. Louis, MO **2002** SD 1 (0) **2003** SD 15 (0) **NFL** 16 (0) [2 yrs]

HOUSER, JOHN John Wesley, G-C-T, 6´3˝/238 lbs; Redlands; B6/21/1935 Oklahoma City, OK, D1/25/1999 Twin Falls, ID **1957** LARm 12 **1958** LARm 12 (rg) **1959** LARm 12 (RG) **1960** Dal 11 (C) **1961** Dal 14 (7, lg/rt) **1963** SL 7 **NFL** 68 (7) [6 yrs]

HOUSER, KEVIN Kevin J., C, 6´2˝/250 lbs; Ohio State; 2000: NO, rnd 7; B8/23/1977 Westlake, OH **2000**†NO 16 (0) **2001** NO 16 (0) **2002** NO 16 (0) **2003** NO 16 (0) **2004** NO 16 (0) **2005** NO 16 (0) **NFL** 96 (0) [6 yrs]

HOUSHMANDZADEH, T.J. Touraj, WR, 6´1˝/197 lbs; Oregon State; 2001: Cin, rnd 7; B9/26/1977 Victorville, CA

YEAR	TEAM	G (GS, POS)	RUSH	YD	AVG (LG)	TD	REC	YD	AVG (LG)	TD	PASS	COMP	PCT	YD	AVG (LG)	TD	INT	SK	YD	QBR	KPR	OTD	PTS	TAY
2001	Cin	12(1)	—	—	—	—	21	228	10.9(23)	0	—	—	—	—	—	—	—	—	—	—	kp	—	0	252
2002	Cin	16(5, wr)	—	—	—	—	41	492	12.0(31)	1	—	—	—	—	—	—	—	—	—	—	kp	—	6	341
2003	Cin	2(0)	—	—	—	—	—	—	—	—	—	—	—	—	—	—	—	—	—	—	—	—	—	—
2004	Cin	16(13, WR)	6	51	8.5(16)	0	73	978	13.4(62)	4	—	—	—	—	—	—	—	—	—	—	kp	—	24	670
2005	†Cin	14(12, WR)	8	62	7.8(17)	1	78	956	12.3(43)	7	—	—	—	—	—	—	—	—	—	—	—	—	48	585
NFL	5	60(31)	14	113	8.1(17)	1	213	2654	12.5(62)	12	—	—	—	—	—	—	—	—	—	—	kp	—	78	1848

HOUSMAN, WALT Walter Henry, T-G, 6´5˝/285 lbs; Iowa; Upsala; B10/13/1962 Marshall, MO **1987** NO 3 (0)

HOUSTON, BILL William Glenn, WR, 6´3˝/208 lbs; Jackson State; B8/22/1951 Oxford, MS

YEAR	TEAM	G (GS, POS)	RUSH	YD	AVG (LG)	TD	REC	YD	AVG (LG)	TD	PASS	COMP	PCT	YD	AVG (LG)	TD	INT	SK	YD	QBR	KPR	OTD	PTS	TAY
1974	Dal	13	—	—	—	—	6	72	12.0(19)	0	—	—	—	—	—	—	—	—	—	—	—	—	0	36

HOUSTON, BOBBY Bobby Darin, LB, 6´2˝/242 lbs; North Carolina State; 1990: GB, rnd 3; B10/26/1967 Washington, DC **1990** GB 1 (0) **1991**†NYJ 14 (0) **1992** NYJ 16 (15, LLB) **1993** NYJ 16 (15, LLB) **1994** NYJ 16 (16, LLB) **1995** NYJ 16 (15, LLB) **1996** NYJ 15 (15, LLB) **1997** KC 5 (0) **1997** SD 2 (0) **1998**†Min 8 (1) **NFL** 109 (77) [9 yrs]

HOUSTON, CEDRIC Cedric, RB, 5´11˝/225 lbs; Tennessee; 2005: NYJ, rnd 6; B6/28/1982 Little Rock, AR

YEAR	TEAM	G (GS, POS)	RUSH	YD	AVG (LG)	TD	REC	YD	AVG (LG)	TD	PASS	COMP	PCT	YD	AVG (LG)	TD	INT	SK	YD	QBR	KPR	OTD	PTS	TAY
2005	NYJ	12(4)	81	302	3.7(17)	2	8	66	8.3(16)	0	—	—	—	—	—	—	—	—	—	—	k	—	12	343

HOUSTON, JIM James Edward, LB-DE, 6´3˝/240 lbs; Ohio State; 1960: Cle, rnd 1/Buf, rnd 1; B11/3/1937 Massillon, OH **[K]** **1960** Cle 12 (lde) **1961** Cle 14 (LDE) **1962** Cle 14 **1963** Cle 14 (LLB) **1964**†Cle★14 (LLB) **1965**†Cle★12 (LLB) **1967**†Cle 13 (LLB/mlb) **1968**†Cle 14 (LLB) **1969**†Cle✧14 (LLB) **1970** Cle✧14 (LLB/mlb) **1971**†Cle 14 (LLB/mlb) **1972**†Cle 14 (mlb)

YEAR	TEAM	G (GS, POS)	RUSH	YD	AVG (LG)	TD	REC	YD	AVG (LG)	TD	PASS	COMP	PCT	YD	AVG (LG)	TD	INT	SK	YD	QBR	KPR	OTD	PTS	TAY
1966	Cle☆	14(LLB)	—	—	—	—	1	10	10.0(10)	1	—	—	—	—	—	—	—	—	—	—	Ki	—	7	27
NFL	13	177	—	—	—	—	1	10	10.0(10)	1	—	—	—	—	—	—	—	—	—	—	Kki	3	25	239

HOUSTON, KEN Kenneth Ray, DB, 6´3˝/197 lbs; Prairie View A&M; 1967: Hou, rnd 9; B11/12/1944 Lufkin, TX; HOF 1986 **[I]** **1967**†Hou-A 14 (LS) **1968** Hou-A★14 (9, LS) **1969**†Hou-A★14 (LS) **1970** Hou★14 (SS) **1971** Hou★14 (SS) **1972** Hou★14 (SS) **1973**†Was★14 (14, SS) **1974**†Was★14 (14, SS) **1975** Was★14 (14, SS) **1976**†Was★14 (14, SS) **1977** Was★14 (14, SS) **1978** Was★16 (16, SS) **1979** Was★13 (13, SS) **1980** Was 13 (5, ss) **NFL** 196 (113) [14 yrs]

HOUSTON, LIN Lindell Lee, G, 6´0˝/213 lbs; Ohio State; 1944: ChiB, rnd 11; B1/11/1921 Carbondale, IL, D9/8/1995 Canton, OH **1946**†Cle-A 12 (5, rg) **1947**†Cle-A 14 (1) **1948**†Cle-A 13 (2)

YEAR	TEAM	G (GS, POS)	RUSH	YD	AVG (LG)	TD	REC	YD	AVG (LG)	TD	PASS	COMP	PCT	YD	AVG (LG)	TD	INT	SK	YD	QBR	KPR	OTD	PTS	TAY
1949	†Cle-A	12(11, RG)	—	—	—	—	0	19	(19)	0	—	—	—	—	—	—	—	—	—	—	—	—	0	10
AAFC	4	51(19)	—	—	—	—	0	19	(19)	0	—	—	—	—	—	—	—	—	—	—	—	—	0	10

1950†Cle☆12 (RG) **1951**†Cle☆11 **1952**†Cle 12 (RG) **1953**†Cle 12 **NFL** 51 (19) [4 yrs]

HOUSTON, RICH Richard Charles, WR, 6´2˝/196 lbs; Texas A&M-Commerce; 1969: NYG, rnd 4; B11/16/1945 Texarkana, TX, D12/11/1982 Hackensack, NJ

YEAR	TEAM	G (GS, POS)	RUSH	YD	AVG (LG)	TD	REC	YD	AVG (LG)	TD	PASS	COMP	PCT	YD	AVG (LG)	TD	INT	SK	YD	QBR	KPR	OTD	PTS	TAY
1969	NYG	6	1	11	11.0(11)	0	2	69	34.5(46)	0	—	—	—	—	—	—	—	—	—	—	k	—	0	118
1970	NYG	13	—	—	—	—	4	68	17.0(35)	0	—	—	—	—	—	—	—	—	—	—	k	—	0	87
1971	NYG	13(WR)	2	2	1.0(2)	0	24	426	17.8(81)	4	—	—	—	—	—	—	—	—	—	—	—	—	24	235
1972	NYG	14(WR)	—	—	—	—	27	468	17.3(94)	3	—	—	—	—	—	—	—	—	—	—	—	—	18	249
1973	NYG	14	—	—	—	—	8	90	11.3(20)	0	—	—	—	—	—	—	—	—	—	—	k	—	0	195
NFL	5	60	3	13	4.3(11)	0	65	1121	17.2(94)	7	—	—	—	—	—	—	—	—	—	—	k	—	42	884

HOUSTON, WALT Loren Walter, G, 6´0˝/217 lbs; Miami (OH); Purdue; 1955: Was, rnd 26; B10/26/1932 Wolf Lake, IL **1955** Was 10 (LG)

HOVAN, CHRIS Christopher James, DT, 6´2˝/296 lbs; Boston College; 2000: Min, rnd 1; B5/12/1978 Rocky River, OH **2000**†Min 16 (13, LDT) **2001** Min 16 (16, RDT) **2002** Min☆16 (16, RDT) **2003** Min 16 (16, RDT) **2004** Min 13 (9, LDT) **2005**†TB 16 (16, LDT) **NFL** 93 (86) [6 yrs]

HOVER, DON Donald R., LB, 6´2˝/225 lbs; Washington State; 1978: Was, rnd 8; B12/13/1954 Seattle, WA **1978** Was 16 **1979** Was 16 (7, mlb) **NFL** 32 (7) [2 yrs]

HOVIOUS, JUNIE John A., HB, 5´8˝/180 lbs; Mississippi; 1942: NYG, rnd 18; B10/4/1919 Vicksburg, MS, D5/7/1998 Oxford, MS

YEAR	TEAM	G (GS, POS)	RUSH	YD	AVG (LG)	TD	REC	YD	AVG (LG)	TD	PASS	COMP	PCT	YD	AVG (LG)	TD	INT	SK	YD	QBR	KPR	OTD	PTS	TAY
1945	NYG	6(1)	22	-7	-0.3(7)	0	—	—	—	—	46	22	47.8	373	8.1(53)	4	5	—	—	—	k	—	0	5

HOWARD, ANTHONY Anthony Craig, NT, 6´3˝/267 lbs; Tennessee; B7/16/1960 Berkeley, CA **1987** NYG 3 (1)

HOWARD, BILLY William, DE-DT, 6´4˝/252 lbs; Alcorn State; 1974: Det, rnd 2; B7/17/1950 Clarksdale, MS **1974** Det 12 **1975** Det 13 (12, RDE) **1976** Det 13 (7, RDE) **NFL** 38 (19) [3 yrs]

HOWARD, BOB Robert Lee, DB, 6´2˝/174 lbs; Cal Poly-San Luis Obispo; San Diego State; 1967: SD, rnd 2; B11/24/1944 Tallulah, LA **[I]** **1967** SD-A 14 **1968** SD-A 14 (LCB) **1969** SD-A 14 (LCB) **1970** SD 14 (LCB) **1971** SD 14 (LCB) **1972** SD 5 (lcb) **1973** SD 13 (LCB) **1974** SD 14 (12, LCB) **1975** NE 14 (14, LCB) **1976**†NE 14 (14, LCB) **1977** NE 13 (12, LCB) **1978**†Phi 10 (6, lcb) **1979**†Phi 16 (LCB) **NFL** 169 (58) [13 yrs]

HOWARD, BOBBIE Bobbie Allen, LB, 5´10˝/232 lbs; Notre Dame; B6/14/1977 Rand, WV **2001**†ChiB 16 (0) **2002** ChiB 16 (9, RLB) **2003** ChiB 3 (0) **NFL** 35 (9) [3 yrs]

HOWARD, BOBBY Bobby Allen, RB, 6´0˝/213 lbs; Indiana; 1986: Phi, rnd 12; B6/1/1964 Pittsburgh, PA

YEAR	TEAM	G (GS, POS)	RUSH	YD	AVG (LG)	TD	REC	YD	AVG (LG)	TD	PASS	COMP	PCT	YD	AVG (LG)	TD	INT	SK	YD	QBR	KPR	OTD	PTS	TAY
1986	TB	7(2)	30	110	3.7(16)	1	5	60	12.0(29)	0	—	—	—	—	—	—	—	—	—	—	k	—	6	161
1987	TB	12(0)	30	100	3.3(31)	1	10	123	12.3(45)	0	—	—	—	—	—	—	—	—	—	—	k	—	6	162
1988	TB	1(0)	—	—	—	—	—	—	—	—	—	—	—	—	—	—	—	—	—	—	—	—	—	—
NFL	3	20(2)	60	210	3.5(31)	2	15	183	12.2(45)	0	—	—	—	—	—	—	—	—	—	—	k	—	12	323

HOWARD, BRIAN Brian Lewis, DT, 6´4˝/278 lbs; Idaho; B9/9/1981 Seattle, WA **2004** SL 15 (1) **2005** SL 5 (0) **NFL** 20 (1) [2 yrs]

HOWARD, BRYAN Bryan Edward, DB, 6´0˝/200 lbs; Tennessee State; 1982: Min, rnd 9; B3/6/1959 New Orleans, LA **1982** Min 2 (0)

HOWARD, CARL Carl Delano, DB, 6´2˝/188 lbs; Rutgers; B9/20/1961 Newark, NJ **1984** Dal 10 (0) **1985** TB 4 (0) **1985**†NYJ 3 (0) **1986**†NYJ 14 (3) **1987** NYJ 12 (7, RCB) **1988** NYJ 16 (1) **1989** NYJ 15 (0) **1990** NYJ 3 (0) **NFL** 77 (11) [7 yrs]

HOWARD, CHRIS Christopher L., RB, 5´10˝/223 lbs; Michigan; 1998: Den, rnd 5; B5/5/1975 Kenner, LA

YEAR	TEAM	G (GS, POS)	RUSH	YD	AVG (LG)	TD	REC	YD	AVG (LG)	TD	PASS	COMP	PCT	YD	AVG (LG)	TD	INT	SK	YD	QBR	KPR	OTD	PTS	TAY
1998	†Jax	8(0)	7	16	2.3(5)	0	1	3	3.0(3)	0	—	—	—	—	—	—	—	—	—	—	—	—	0	18
1999	†Jax	12(0)	13	55	4.2(22)	0	1	8	8.0(8)	0	—	—	—	—	—	—	—	—	—	—	—	—	0	59
2000	Jax	2(1)	21	52	2.5(19)	1	3	26	8.7(13)	0	—	—	—	—	—	—	—	—	—	—	—	—	6	75
NFL	3	22(1)	41	123	3.0(22)	1	5	37	7.4(13)	0	—	—	—	—	—	—	—	—	—	—	—	—	6	152

YEAR	TEAM	G (GS, POS)	RUSH	YD	AVG (LG)	TD	REC	YD	AVG (LG)	TD	PASS	COMP	PCT	YD	AVG (LG)	TD	INT	SK	YD	QBR	KPR	OTD	PTS	TAY

Howard, Dana Dana Cortez, LB, 6´0˝/238 lbs; Illinois; 1995: Dal, rnd 5; B2/25/1972 East St. Louis, IL **1995** SL 16 (0) **1996** ChiB 3 (0) **NFL** 19 (0) [2 yrs]

Howard, Darren Darren, DE, 6´3˝/281 lbs; Kansas State; 2000: NO, rnd 2; B11/19/1976 St. Petersburg, FL **2000**†NO 16 (16, LDE) **2001** NO 16 (16, LDE) **2002** NO 16 (16, RDE) **2003** NO 8 (8, rde) **2004** NO 13 (12, RDE) **2005** NO 12 (9, LDE) **NFL** 81 (77) [6 yrs]

Howard, David David, LB, 6´2˝/232 lbs; Oregon State; Long Beach State; 1984: Min, rnd S3; B12/8/1961 Enterprise, AL **1985** Min 16 (4) **1986** Min 14 (13, RLB) **1987**†Min 10 (7, RLB) **1988**†Min 16 (16, RLB) **1989** Min 5 (3) **1989** Dal 11 (0) **1990** Dal 16 (0) **1991** NE 16 (5, rolb) **1992** NE 16 (10, ROLB) **NFL** 120 (58) [8 yrs]

Howard, Desmond Desmond Kevin, WR, 5´10˝/185 lbs; Michigan; 1992: Was, rnd 1; B5/15/1970 Cleveland, OH **[R]**

YEAR	TEAM	G (GS, POS)	RUSH	YD	AVG (LG)	TD	REC	YD	AVG (LG)	TD	PASS	COMP	PCT	YD	AVG (LG)	TD	INT	SK	YD	QBR	KPR	OTD	PTS	TAY
1992	Was	16(1)	3	14	4.7(7)	0	3	20	6.7(8)	0	—	—	—	—	—	—	—	—	—	—	kp	1	6	220
1993	Was	16(5, wr)	2	17	8.5(9)	0	23	286	12.4(27)	0	—	—	—	—	—	—	—	—	—	—	kp	—	0	255
1994	Was	16(15, WR)	1	4	4.0(4)	0	40	727	18.2(81)	5	—	—	—	—	—	—	—	—	—	—	—	—	32	393
1995	Jax	13(7, wr)	1	8	8.0(8)	0	26	276	10.6(24)	1	—	—	—	—	—	—	—	—	—	—	kp	—	6	305
1996	†GB☆	16(0)	—	—	—	—	13	95	7.3(12)	0	—	—	—	—	—	—	—	—	—	—	kp	3	18	793
1997	Oak	15(0)	—	—	—	—	4	30	7.5(9)	0	—	—	—	—	—	—	—	—	—	—	kp	—	0	493
1998	Oak	15(1)	—	—	—	—	2	16	8.0(10)	0	—	—	—	—	—	—	—	—	—	—	kp	2	12	649
1999	GB	8(0)	—	—	—	—	—	—	—	—	—	—	—	—	—	—	—	—	—	—	kp	—	0	112
1999	Det	5(0)	—	—	—	—	—	—	—	—	—	—	—	—	—	—	—	—	—	—	kp	1	6	168
2000	Det★	15(0)	—	—	—	—	2	14	7.0(10)	0	—	—	—	—	—	—	—	—	—	—	kp	1	6	865
2001	Det	14(1)	5	25	5.0(7)	0	10	133	13.3(36)	1	—	—	—	—	—	—	—	—	—	—	kp	—	6	779
2002	Det	7(0)	—	—	—	—	—	—	—	—	—	—	—	—	—	—	—	—	—	—	kp	—	0	200
NFL	11	156(30)	12	68	5.7(9)	0	123	1597	13.0(81)	7	—	—	—	—	—	—	—	—	—	—	kp	8	92	5231

Howard, Dosey Robert Lee, G-T, 6´0˝/225 lbs; Marietta; B8/26/1902 Norman, OK, D5/15/1966 Alice, TX **1925** KC 8 (8, RG) **1926** KC 7 (6, rg) **1927** Cle 12 (11, RG) **1928** Det 9 (9, RG) **1929** NYG 12 (6, rg) **1930** NYG 16 (9, rg), 6 **NFL** 64 (49) [6 yrs]

Howard, Eddie Eddie, P, 6´1˝/203 lbs; Idaho; B10/16/1972 Covina, CA **1998** SF 2 (0)

Howard, Erik Erik Matthew, NT-DT-DE, 6´4˝/275 lbs; Washington State; 1986: NYG, rnd 2; B11/12/1964 Pittsfield, MA **1986**†NYG 8 (2) **1987** NYG 12 (4) **1988** NYG 16 (5, nt) **1989**†NYG 16 (16, NT) **1990**†NYG✧16 (16, NT) **1991** NYG 6 (4) **1992** NYG 16 (15, NT) **1993**†NYG 16 (0) **1994** NYG 16 (16, RDT) **1995** NYJ 16 (16, LDE) **1996** NYJ 1 (1) **NFL** 139 (95) [11 yrs]

Howard, Gene William Eugene, DB, 6´0˝/190 lbs; Langston; 1968: NO, rnd 7; B12/22/1946 Little Rock, AR **1968** NO 14 (LCB) **1969** NO 14 (LCB) **1970** NO 8 **1971** LARm 14 (14, RCB) **1972** LARm 13 (13, RCB) **NFL** 63 (27) [5 yrs]

Howard, Harry Harry J., DB, 6´1˝/189 lbs; Ohio State; 1972: LA, rnd 9; B10/7/1949 Cincinnati, OH **1976** NYJ 1

Howard, Joe see Joe Johnson

Howard, Joey Joseph Eissix, T, 6´5˝/305 lbs; Tennessee; 1988: SD, rnd 9; B9/14/1965 Springfield, OH **1989** SD 9 (2)

Howard, Leroy Leroy, DB, 5´11˝/175 lbs; Bishop; B6/16/1949 Port Arthur, TX **1971** Hou 7

Howard, Paul Paul Eugene, G, 6´3˝/260 lbs; Brigham Young; 1973: Den, rnd 3; B9/12/1950 Redding, CA **1973** Den 14 **1974** Den 14 (5, rg) **1975** Den 14 (14, RG) **1977**†Den 14 (14, RG) **1978**†Den 13 (13, RG) **1979**†Den 16 (16, RG) **1980** Den 14 (14, RG) **1981** Den 16 (15, RG) **1982** Den 9 (0) **1983**†Den 16 (14, RG) **1984**†Den 16 (14, RG) **1985** Den 16 (15, RG) **1986**†Den 15 (13, RG) **NFL** 187 (147) [13 yrs]

Howard, Percy Percy Lenard, WR, 6´4˝/210 lbs; Austin Peay State; B1/21/1952 Savannah, GA **1975**†Dal 8

Howard, Red Albert Franklin, G, 5´11˝/192 lbs; New Hampshire; Princeton; B11/23/1900 Haverhill, MA, D5/29/1973 Essex Falls, NJ **1926** Bkn 3 (3) **1927** NYG 1 (0) **NFL** 4 (3) [2 yrs]

Howard, Reggie Reginald Clement, DB, 6´0˝/190 lbs; Memphis; B5/17/1977 Memphis, TN **2000** NO 1 (0) **2000** Car 1 (0) **2001** Car 11 (0) **2002** Car 14 (14, RCB) **2003** Car 15 (15, RCB) **2004** Mia 15 (3) **2005** Mia 15 (7, cb) **NFL** 72 (39) [6 yrs]

Howard, Ron Ronald Ford, TE, 6´4˝/229 lbs; Seattle; B3/3/1951 Oakland, CA **1974** Dal 12 **1975**†Dal 10 **1979** Buf 1

YEAR	TEAM	G (GS, POS)	RUSH	YD	AVG (LG)	TD	REC	YD	AVG (LG)	TD	PASS	COMP	PCT	YD	AVG (LG)	TD	INT	SK	YD	QBR	KPR	OTD	PTS	TAY
1976	Sea	14(13, TE)	1	2	2.0(2)	0	37	422	11.4(30)	0	—	—	—	—	—	—	—	—	—	—	—	—	0	213
1977	Sea	12(12, TE)	—	—	—	—	17	177	10.4(24)	1	—	—	—	—	—	—	—	—	—	—	—	—	6	94
1978	Sea	16(11, TE)	—	—	—	—	18	251	13.9(42)	1	—	—	—	—	—	—	—	—	—	—	—	—	6	131
NFL	6	65(36)	1	2	2.0(2)	0	72	850	11.8(42)	2	—	—	—	—	—	—	—	—	—	—	—	—	12	437

Howard, Sherman Sherman John, HB-DB, 5´11˝/193 lbs; Iowa; Nevada-Reno; B11/28/1924 New Orleans, LA

YEAR	TEAM	G (GS, POS)	RUSH	YD	AVG (LG)	TD	REC	YD	AVG (LG)	TD	PASS	COMP	PCT	YD	AVG (LG)	TD	INT	SK	YD	QBR	KPR	OTD	PTS	TAY
1949	†NYY-A	12(6, RH)	117	459	3.9(79)	3	1	24	24.0(24)	0	—	—	—	—	—	—	—	—	—	—	ki	—	18	557
1950	NYY	12(rh)	71	362	5.1(60)	3	12	278	23.2(40)	5	—	—	—	—	—	—	—	—	—	—	kp	1	54	693
1951	NYY	12(RH)	94	343	3.6(31)	4	21	447	21.3(75)	3	—	—	—	—	—	—	—	—	—	—	—	—	42	622
1952	Cle	5	34	95	2.8(22)	0	11	219	19.9(57)	3	—	—	—	—	—	—	—	—	—	—	k	—	18	227
1953	†Cle	12	7	42	6.0(34)	0	—	—	—	—	—	—	—	—	—	—	—	—	—	—	ki	—	0	31
NFL	4	41	206	842	4.1(79)	7	44	944	21.5(75)	11	—	—	—	—	—	—	—	—	—	—	kpi	1	114	1572

Howard, Todd Walter Lee, LB, 6´2˝/235 lbs; Texas A&M; 1987: KC, rnd 3; B2/18/1965 Bryan, TX **1987** KC 12 (0) **1988** KC 7 (0) **NFL** 19 (0) [2 yrs]

Howard, Tom James Thomas, LB, 6´2˝/213 lbs; Texas Tech; 1977: KC, rnd 3; B8/18/1954 Lubbock, TX **1977** KC 13 (3) **1978** KC 16 (16, ROLB) **1979** KC 16 (16, ROLB) **1980** KC 16 (16, LOLB) **1981** KC 9 (7, lolb) **1982** KC 9 (9, LOLB) **1983** KC 16 (16, LOLB) **1984** SL 15 (13, LLB) **1985** SL 3 (2) **NFL** 113 (98) [9 yrs]

Howard, Tubby Lynn Wales, E-HB, 5´10˝/210 lbs; Ripon; Wisconsin; Indiana; B6/10/1894 Bloomington, IN, D5/1969 Prescott, AZ **1921** GB 4 (0), 6 **1922** GB 8 (7, RE) **NFL** 12 (7) [2 yrs]

Howard, Ty Ty L., DB, 5´9˝/185 lbs; Ohio State; 1997: Arz, rnd 3; B11/30/1973 Columbus, OH **1997** Arz 15 (2) **1998** Arz 9 (0) **1999** Cin 12 (3) **2000** Ten 1 (0) **NFL** 37 (5) [4 yrs]

Howard, William William Dotson, RB, 6´0˝/240 lbs; Tennessee; 1988: TB, rnd 5; B6/2/1964 Lima, OH

YEAR	TEAM	G (GS, POS)	RUSH	YD	AVG (LG)	TD	REC	YD	AVG (LG)	TD	PASS	COMP	PCT	YD	AVG (LG)	TD	INT	SK	YD	QBR	KPR	OTD	PTS	TAY
1988	TB	15(9, FB)	115	452	3.9(29)	1	11	97	8.8(16)	0	—	—	—	—	—	—	—	—	—	—	k	—	6	502
1989	TB	16(12, FB)	108	357	3.3(15)	1	30	188	6.3(18)	1	—	—	—	—	—	—	—	—	—	—	k	—	12	473
NFL	2	31(21)	223	809	3.6(29)	2	41	285	7.0(18)	1	—	—	—	—	—	—	—	—	—	—	k	—	18	975

Howard, Willie Willie, DE, 6´3˝/298 lbs; Stanford; 2001: Min, rnd 2; B12/26/1977 Mountain View, CA **2001** Min 8 (0)

Howe, Garry Gary William, NT, 6´1˝/298 lbs; Colorado; Drake; B6/20/1968 Spencer, IA **1992**†Pit 11 (2) **1993** Cin 1 (0) **1994** Ind 1 (0) **NFL** 13 (2) [3 yrs]

Howe, Glen Bobby Glen, T, 6´7˝/295 lbs; Southern Mississippi; 1984: Atl, rnd 9; B10/18/1961 New Albany, MS **1985** Pit 2 (0) **1985** Atl 5 (1) **1986** Atl 7 (3) **NFL** 14 (4) [2 yrs]

Howell, Bill Wilfred Daniel, E, 5´11˝/175 lbs; Catholic; B4/21/1904 Bath, Canada, D8/23/1981 Washington, DC **1929** Bos 4 (1)

Howell, Clarence John Clarence Maurice, E, 6´1˝/188 lbs; Texas A&M; B4/7/1927, D10/6/1981 Houston, TX

YEAR	TEAM	G (GS, POS)	RUSH	YD	AVG (LG)	TD	REC	YD	AVG (LG)	TD	PASS	COMP	PCT	YD	AVG (LG)	TD	INT	SK	YD	QBR	KPR	OTD	PTS	TAY
1948	SF-A	12(0)	—	—	—	—	1	9	9.0(9)	0	—	—	—	—	—	—	—	—	—	—	i	—	0	5

Howell, Delles Delles Ray, DB, 6´3˝/200 lbs; Grambling State; 1970: NO, rnd 4; B8/22/1948 Vallejo, CA **1970** NO 13 (RCB) **1971** NO 14 (RCB) **1972** NO 10 (RCB) **1973** NYJ 14 (LCB) **1974** NYJ 10 **1975** NYJ 10 (5, fs) **NFL** 71 (5) [6 yrs]

Howell, Dixie Millard Fillmore, HB, 5´11˝/175 lbs; Alabama; B11/24/1912 Hartford, AL, D3/2/1971 Los Angeles, CA

YEAR	TEAM	G (GS, POS)	RUSH	YD	AVG (LG)	TD	REC	YD	AVG (LG)	TD	PASS	COMP	PCT	YD	AVG (LG)	TD	INT	SK	YD	QBR	KPR	OTD	PTS	TAY
1937	Was	5(0)	5	9	1.8	0	—	—	—	—	6	1	16.7	14	2.3(14)	0	3	—	—	—	—	—	0	-104

Howell, Earl Earl Otto, HB, 5´10˝/180 lbs; Mississippi; 1949: LA, rnd 5; B9/28/1924 Talladega, AL

YEAR	TEAM	G (GS, POS)	RUSH	YD	AVG (LG)	TD	REC	YD	AVG (LG)	TD	PASS	COMP	PCT	YD	AVG (LG)	TD	INT	SK	YD	QBR	KPR	OTD	PTS	TAY
1949	LAD-A	12(3)	31	116	3.7	1	5	11	2.2	1	—	—	—	—	—	—	—	—	—	—	kp	—	12	153

Howell, Foster Foster C., T-G, 6´3˝/215 lbs; TCU; B2/12/1911 Lumpkin, GA, D8/7/1999 Fort Worth, TX **1934** Cin 6 (2)

Howell, Jim Lee James Lee, E, 6´5˝/210 lbs; Arkansas; B3/9/1915 Lonoke, AR, D1/4/1995 Lonoke, AR **[C]**

YEAR	TEAM	G (GS, POS)	RUSH	YD	AVG (LG)	TD	REC	YD	AVG (LG)	TD	PASS	COMP	PCT	YD	AVG (LG)	TD	INT	SK	YD	QBR	KPR	OTD	PTS	TAY
1937	NYG	8(7, RE)	—	—	—	—	4	32	8.0	0	—	—	—	—	—	—	—	—	—	—	—	—	0	16
1938	†NYG✧	10(7, RE)	—	—	—	—	12	163	13.6	2	—	—	—	—	—	—	—	—	—	—	—	—	12	92
1939	†NYG☆	7(5, re)	—	—	—	—	5	112	22.4	2	—	—	—	—	—	—	—	—	—	—	—	—	12	66
1940	NYG	11(9, RE)	—	—	—	—	14	255	18.2	2	—	—	—	—	—	—	—	—	—	—	i	—	12	133
1941	†NYG☆	11(11, RE)	—	—	—	—	4	62	15.5(42)	1	—	—	—	—	—	—	—	—	—	—	—	—	6	36
1942	NYG	10(0)	—	—	—	—	10	115	11.5(23)	0	—	—	—	—	—	—	—	—	—	—	—	—	0	58

YEAR	TEAM	G (GS, POS)	RUSH	YD	AVG(LG)	TD	REC	YD	AVG(LG)	TD	PASS	COMP	PCT	YD	AVG(LG)	TD	INT	SK	YD	QBR	KPR	OTD	PTS	TAY
1946	†NYG	11 (11, RE)	—	—	—	—	9	141	15.7 (33)	0	—	—	—	—	—	—	—	—	—	—	—	—	0	71
1947	NYG	6 (0)	—	—	—	—	3	41	13.7 (21)	0	—	—	—	—	—	—	—	—	—	—	—	—	0	21
NFL	8	74 (50)	—	—	—	—	61	921	15.1 (42)	7	—	—	—	—	—	—	—	—	—	—	i	—	42	491

HOWELL, JOHN John Searl, HB, 5´10˝/185 lbs; Nebraska; 1938: GB, rnd 9; B12/4/1915 Omaha, NE, deceased

| 1938 | GB | 6 (0) | 7 | 7 | 1.0 | 0 | — | — | — | — | — | — | — | — | — | — | — | — | — | — | — | — | 0 | 7 |

HOWELL, JOHN John Thomas, DB, 5´11˝/210 lbs; Colorado State; 2001: TB, rnd 4; B4/28/1978 North Platte, NE   **2001**†TB 14 (1) **2002**†TB 16 (1) **2003** TB 8 (0)
2004 TB 16 (6, fs) **2005** Sea 10 (0) **NFL** 64 (8) [5 yrs]

HOWELL, LANE Autrey Lane, T-DT, 6´5˝/257 lbs; Grambling State; 1963: NYG, rnd 15; B7/28/1941 Forndale, LA   **1963**†NYG 14 **1964** NYG 14 **1965** Phi 14 (LT)
1966 Phi 10 (10, LT) **1967** Phi 11 (11, LT) **1968** Phi 14 (LT) **1969** Phi 14 (LT) **NFL** 91 (21) [7 yrs]

HOWELL, MIKE Michael Lionel, DB, 6´1˝/195 lbs; Grambling State; 1965: Cle, rnd 8/SD, rnd 15; B7/5/1943 West Monroe, LA [I]   **1965**†Cle 14 **1966** Cle 14 (14, RCB)
1967†Cle 14 (RCB) **1968**†Cle 14 (RS/ls) **1969**†Cle☆14 (RS) **1970** Cle 14 (FS) **1971**†Cle 14 (FS) **1972** Cle 4 **1972** Mia 1 **NFL** 103 (14) [8 yrs]

HOWELL, PAT Patrick Gerrard, G, 6´5˝/257 lbs; USC; 1979: Atl, rnd 2; B3/12/1957 Fresno, CA   **1979** Atl 15 (5, rg) **1980**†Atl 5 (0) **1981** Atl 16 (2) **1982**†Atl 9 (9, LG)
1983 Atl 2 (0) **1983** Hou 7 (0) **1984** Hou 11 (5, rg) **1985** Hou 2 (0) **NFL** 67 (21) [7 yrs]

HOWELL, STEVE Stephen Glen, FB-TE, 6´2˝/227 lbs; Baylor; 1979: Mia, rnd 4; B12/20/1956 Corsicana, TX

1979	†Mia	16	3	8	2.7 (5)	0	3	23	7.7 (11)	0	—	—	—	—	—	—	—	—	—	—	—	—	0	20
1980	Mia	16 (8, FB)	60	206	3.4 (23)	1	5	38	7.6 (13)	0	—	—	—	—	—	—	—	—	—	—	—	—	6	235
1981	Mia	10 (2)	5	21	4.2 (9)	0	2	9	4.5 (5)	0	—	—	—	—	—	—	—	—	—	—	—	—	0	26
NFL	3	42 (10)	68	235	3.5 (23)	1	10	70	7.0 (13)	0	—	—	—	—	—	—	—	—	—	—	—	—	6	280

HOWER, KARL Karl, FB, none; B1902, deceased   **1921** Lou 1 (1, FB)

HOWFIELD, BOBBY Robert Michael, K, 5´9˝/180 lbs; none; B12/3/1936 Bushey, England [K]   **1968** Den-A 12 **1969** Den-A 14 **1970** Den 14 **1971** NYJ 14 **1972** NYJ 14
1973 NYJ 14 **1974** NYJ 7 **NFL** 89 [7 yrs]

HOWFIELD, IAN Ian Michael, K, 6´2˝/196 lbs; Tennessee; B6/4/1966 Watford, England [K]   **1991** Hou 9 (0)

HOWLEY, CHUCK Charles Louis, LB, 6´3˝/228 lbs; West Virginia; 1958: ChiB, rnd 1; B6/28/1936 Wheeling, WV [I]   **1958** ChiB 12 (LLB) **1959** ChiB 3
1961 Dal 13 (13, LLB/rlb) **1962** Dal☆14 (RLB) **1963** Dal☆14 (LLB) **1964** Dal 12 (9, LLB) **1965** Dal◇14 (LLB) **1966**†Dal★14 (LLB) **1967**†Dal★14 (LLB) **1968**†Dal★14 (LLB) **1969**†Dal★14 (RLB) **1970**†Dal☆14 (RLB) **1971**†Dal★14 (RLB) **1972** Dal 13 (RLB) **1973** Dal 1 **NFL** 180 (22) [15 yrs]

HOWRY, KEENAN Keenan Rashaun, WR, 5´10˝/172 lbs; Oregon; 2003: Min, rnd 7; B6/17/1981 Los Angeles, CA

2003	Min	16 (1)	—	—	—	—	2	15	7.5 (8)	0	—	—	—	—	—	—	—	—	—	—	kp	—	0	171
2004	Min	3 (0)	—	—	—	—	1	3	3.0 (3)	0	—	—	—	—	—	—	—	—	—	—	kp	—	0	40
2005	Min	4 (0)	—	—	—	—	—	—	—	—	—	—	—	—	—	—	—	—	—	—	p	—	0	18
NFL	3	23 (1)	—	—	—	—	3	18	6.0 (8)	0	—	—	—	—	—	—	—	—	—	—	kp	—	0	228

HOWSER, BILL William A., G-T, none; B1900, deceased   **1921** Lou 1 (1, RG)

HOWTON, BILLY William Harris, E, 6´2˝/191 lbs; Rice; 1952: GB, rnd 2; B7/5/1930 Littlefield, TX

1952	GB★	12 (RE)	—	—	—	—	53	1231	23.2 (90)	13	—	—	—	—	—	—	—	—	—	—	—	—	78	681
1953	GB	8 (RE)	—	—	—	—	25	463	18.5 (80)	4	—	—	—	—	—	—	—	—	—	—	—	—	24	252
1954	GB	12 (RE)	—	—	—	—	52	768	14.8 (59)	2	—	—	—	—	—	—	—	—	—	—	—	—	12	394
1955	GB★	12 (RE)	—	—	—	—	44	697	15.8 (60)	5	—	—	—	—	—	—	—	—	—	—	—	—	30	374
1956	GB★	12 (RE)	—	—	—	—	55	1188	21.6 (66)	12	—	—	—	—	—	—	—	—	—	—	—	—	72	654
1957	GB★	12 (RE)	4	20	5.0 (11)	0	38	727	19.1 (77)	5	—	—	—	—	—	—	—	—	—	—	—	—	30	409
1958	GB	12 (RE)	—	—	—	—	36	507	14.1 (50)	2	—	—	—	—	—	—	—	—	—	—	—	—	12	264
1959	Cle☆	12 (RE)	—	—	—	—	39	510	13.1 (36)	1	—	—	—	—	—	—	—	—	—	—	—	—	6	260
1960	Dal	11 (7, FL)	—	—	—	—	23	363	15.8 (41)	4	—	—	—	—	—	—	—	—	—	—	—	—	24	202
1961	Dal	14 (SE)	1	9	9.0 (9)	0	56	785	14.0 (53)	4	—	—	—	—	—	—	—	—	—	—	—	—	24	422
1962	Dal	14 (SE)	—	—	—	—	49	706	14.4 (69)	6	—	—	—	—	—	—	—	—	—	—	—	—	36	383
1963	Dal	11 (6, SE)	—	—	—	—	33	514	15.6 (44)	3	—	—	—	—	—	—	—	—	—	—	—	—	18	272
NFL	12	142 (13)	5	29	5.8 (11)	0	503	8459	16.8 (90)	61	—	—	—	—	—	—	—	—	—	—	—	—	366	4564

HOYEM, LYNN Lynn Douglas, G-T, 6´4˝/244 lbs; Long Beach State; 1961: Dal, rnd 19/1962: Den, rnd 29; B6/27/1939 Fargo, ND, D2/17/1973 Battle Ground, WA   **1962** Dal 14
1963 Dal 14 (6, lg) **1964** Phi 14 (8, RG) **1965** Phi 14 **1966** Phi 14 **1967** Phi 14 (6, rt) **NFL** 84 (20) [6 yrs]

HOYEM, STEVE Steven Randell, T, 6´7˝/287 lbs; Stanford; B11/12/1970 Boise, ID   **1994** Buf 6 (0)

HOYING, BOBBY Robert Carl, QB, 6´3˝/221 lbs; Ohio State; 1996: Phi, rnd 3; B9/20/1972 St. Henry, OH

1996	Phi	1 (0)	—	—	—	—	—	—	—	—	0	0	0.0	0	0.0	0	0	1	10	—	—	—	0	0
1997	Phi	7 (6, qb)	16	78	4.9 (30)	0	—	—	—	—	225	128	56.9	1573	7.0 (72)	11	6	28	183	—	—	—	0	680
1998	Phi	8 (7, QB)	22	84	3.8 (11)	0	—	—	—	—	224	114	50.9	961	4.3 (38)	0	9	35	185	—	—	—	0	205
1999	Oak	2 (0)	2	-3	-1.5 (-1)	0	—	—	—	—	5	2	40.0	10	2.0 (7)	0	0	0	0	—	—	—	0	2
2000	†Oak	4 (0)	2	-3	-1.5 (-1)	0	—	—	—	—	2	0	0.0	0	—	0	0	0	0	—	—	—	0	-3
NFL	5	22 (13)	42	156	3.7 (30)	0	—	—	—	—	456	244	53.5	2544	5.6 (72)	11	15	64	378	—	—	—	0	883

HRABETIN, FRANK Frank George, T, 6´4˝/233 lbs; Loyola Marymount; B12/1/1915 Cedar Rapids, IA, D3/27/2004 Tucson, AZ   **1942** Phi 7 (1)
1946 Mia-A 2 (0)

| 1946 | Bkn-A | 8 (2) | — | — | — | — | 1 | 17 | 17.0 (17) | 0 | — | — | — | — | — | — | — | — | — | — | — | — | 0 | 9 |
| AAFC | 1 | 10 (2) | — | — | — | — | 1 | 17 | 17.0 (17) | 0 | — | — | — | — | — | — | — | — | — | — | — | — | 0 | 9 |

HRIVNAK, GARY Gary Andrew, DE, 6´5˝/252 lbs; Purdue; 1973: Chi, rnd 2; B3/3/1951 Johnstown, PA   **1973** ChiB 13 **1974** ChiB 14 (7, RDE) **1975** ChiB 14 (4) **NFL** 41 (11) [3 yrs]

HUARD, BROCK Brock, QB, 6´4˝/232 lbs; Washington; 1999: Sea, rnd 3; B4/15/1976 Seattle, WA

2000	Sea	5 (4)	5	29	5.8 (10)	0	—	—	—	—	87	49	56.3	540	6.2 (45)	3	2	13	72	—	—	—	0	234
2001	Sea	1 (0)	1	11	11.0 (11)	0	—	—	—	—	17	9	52.9	127	7.5 (44)	1	0	1	5	—	—	—	0	80
2003	†Ind	2 (0)	3	8	2.7 (9)	0	—	—	—	—	3	2	66.7	22	7.3 (13)	0	0	1	3	—	—	—	0	19
NFL	3	8 (4)	9	48	5.3 (11)	0	—	—	—	—	107	60	56.1	689	6.4 (45)	4	2	15	80	—	—	—	0	333

HUARD, DAMON Damon Paul, QB, 6´3˝/215 lbs; Washington; B7/9/1973 Yakima, WA

1998	†Mia	2 (0)	—	—	—	—	—	—	—	—	9	6	66.7	85	9.4 (24)	0	1	1	9	—	—	—	0	3
1999	†Mia	16 (5, qb)	28	124	4.4 (25)	0	1	0	0.0 (0)	0	216	125	57.9	1288	6.0 (69)	8	4	28	185	—	—	—	0	648
2000	†Mia	16 (1)	—	—	—	—	—	—	—	—	63	39	61.9	318	5.0 (29)	1	3	4	22	—	—	—	0	44
2002	NE	2 (0)	1	4	4.0 (4)	0	—	—	—	—	0	0	0.0	0	—	0	0	0	0	—	—	—	0	4
2003	†NE	2 (0)	1	-1	-1.0 (-1)	0	—	—	—	—	1	0	0.0	0	—	0	0	0	0	—	—	—	0	-1
NFL	5	38 (6)	30	127	4.2 (25)	0	1	0	0.0	0	289	170	58.8	1691	5.9 (69)	9	8	33	216	—	—	—	0	698

HUARD, JOHN John Roland, LB, 6´0˝/228 lbs; Maine; 1967: Den, rnd 5; B3/9/1944 Waterville, ME   **1967** Den-A 14 (14, MLB) **1968** Den-A 14 (MLB) **1969** Den-A 14 (14, MLB)
1971 NO 1 **NFL** 43 (28) [4 yrs]

HUARTE, JOHN John Gregory, QB, 6´0˝/185 lbs; Notre Dame; 1965: NYJ, rnd 2/Phi, rnd 6; B4/6/1944 Anaheim, CA

1966	Bos-A	14	7	40	5.7 (13)	0	—	—	—	—	11	5	45.5	63	5.7 (17)	0	1	—	—	—	—	—	0	32
1967	Bos-A	4	2	5	2.5 (4)	0	—	—	—	—	9	3	33.3	25	2.8 (15)	0	1	5	36	—	—	—	0	-23
1968	Phi	2	2	9	4.5 (11)	0	—	—	—	—	15	7	46.7	110	7.3 (48)	1	2	2	17	—	—	—	0	-11
1970	KC	1	—	—	—	—	—	—	—	—	2	0	0.0	0	—	0	0	—	—	—	—	—	0	-40
1971	KC	1	—	—	—	—	—	—	—	—	6	2	33.3	18	3.0 (26)	0	1	1	5	—	—	—	0	9
1972	ChiB	2	1	-2	-2.0 (-2)	0	—	—	—	—	5	2	40.0	14	2.8 (8)	0	0	—	—	—	—	—	0	5
NFL	6	24	12	52	4.3 (13)	0	—	—	—	—	48	19	39.6	230	4.8 (48)	1	5	8	58	—	—	—	0	-28

HUBACH, MIKE Michael Andrew, P, 5´10˝/185 lbs; Kansas; 1980: NE, rnd 11; B1/26/1958 Cleveland, OH   **1981** NE 5 (0)

| 1980 | NE | 16 (0) | 1 | 0 | 0.0 (0) | 0 | — | — | — | — | — | — | — | — | — | — | — | — | — | — | P | — | 0 | 0 |
| NFL | 2 | 21 (0) | 1 | 0 | 0.0 | 0 | — | — | — | — | — | — | — | — | — | — | — | — | — | — | P | — | 0 | 0 |

Hubbard, Bud Wesley Lauren, E, 6´0˝/190 lbs; San Jose State; B1/8/1911 San Jose, CA, D6/8/1981 San Jose, CA

YEAR	TEAM	G(GS, POS)	RUSH	YD	AVG(LG)	TD	REC	YD	AVG(LG)	TD	PASS	COMP	PCT	YD	AVG(LG)	TD	INT	SK	YD	QBR	KPR	OTD	PTS	TAY
1935	Bkn	10(0)	1	1	1.0(1)	0	3	99	33.0	1	—	—	—	—	—	—	—	—	—	—	—	—	6	56

Hubbard, Cal Robert Calvin, T-E-DE-G, 6´2˝/253 lbs; Centenary; B10/11/1900 Keytesville, MO, D10/16/1977 St. Petersburg, FL; HOF 1963 **1927** NYG☆10 (10, RE) **1928** NYG☆13 (13, RE) **1929** GB☆12 (10, RT) **1930** GB 14 (13, LT), 6 **1931** GB☆12 (4) **1932** GB☆13 (11, LT) **1933** GB☆13 (8, LT) **1935** GB 11 (7, lt), 6 **1936** Pit 1 (0) **1936** NYG 6 (1) **NFL** 105 (77), 12 [9 yrs]

Hubbard, Dave David Allen, T, 6´7˝/270 lbs; Brigham Young; 1977: NO, rnd 5; B9/29/1955 Napa, CA **1977** NO 5

Hubbard, Marv Marvin Ronald, RB, 6´1˝/225 lbs; Colgate; 1968: Oak, rnd 11; B5/7/1946 Salamanca, NY

YEAR	TEAM	G(GS, POS)	RUSH	YD	AVG(LG)	TD	REC	YD	AVG(LG)	TD	PASS	COMP	PCT	YD	AVG(LG)	TD	INT	SK	YD	QBR	KPR	OTD	PTS	TAY
1969	†Oak-A	14	21	119	5.7(18)	0	2	30	15.0(20)	0	—	—	—	—	—	—	—	—	—	—	—	—	0	134
1970	†Oak	13	51	246	4.8(15)	1	—	—	—	—	—	—	—	—	—	—	—	—	—	—	k	—	6	267
1971	Oak✧	14(11, FB)	181	867	4.8(20)	5	22	167	7.6(31)	1	—	—	—	—	—	—	—	—	—	—	k	—	36	1007
1972	†Oak✧	14(14, FB)	219	1100	5.0(39)	4	22	103	4.7(21)	0	—	—	—	—	—	—	—	—	—	—	—	—	24	1192
1973	†Oak✧	14(14, FB)	193	903	4.7(50)	6	15	116	7.7(25)	0	—	—	—	—	—	—	—	—	—	—	—	—	36	1021
1974	†Oak	14(13, FB)	188	865	4.6(32)	4	11	95	8.6(15)	0	—	—	—	—	—	—	—	—	—	—	—	—	24	953
1975	†Oak	7(6, fb)	60	294	4.9(53)	2	7	81	11.6(16)	0	—	—	—	—	—	—	—	—	—	—	—	—	12	355
1977	Det	13	38	150	3.9(16)	1	6	36	6.0(9)	0	—	—	—	—	—	—	—	—	—	—	k	—	6	181
NFL	8	103(58)	951	4544	4.8(53)	23	85	628	7.4(31)	1	—	—	—	—	—	—	—	—	—	—	k	—	144	5108

Hubbell, Frank Franklin Sumner, E-DE, 6´2˝/222 lbs; Tennessee; 1944: Cle, rnd 15/1947: Mia-A, rnd 9; B1/19/1922 Bridgeport, CT, D4/9/2005 Knoxville, TN

YEAR	TEAM	G(GS, POS)	RUSH	YD	AVG(LG)	TD	REC	YD	AVG(LG)	TD	PASS	COMP	PCT	YD	AVG(LG)	TD	INT	SK	YD	QBR	KPR	OTD	PTS	TAY
1947	LARm	12(2)	—	—	—	—	2	60	30.0(45)	2	—	—	—	—	—	—	—	—	—	—	—	—	12	40
1948	LARm	12(11, LE)	—	—	—	—	10	134	13.4(48)	1	—	—	—	—	—	—	—	—	—	—	—	—	6	72
1949	†LARm	12(1)	—	—	—	—	3	32	10.7(12)	0	—	—	—	—	—	—	—	—	—	—	i	1	6	42
NFL	3	36(14)	—	—	—	—	15	226	15.1(48)	3	—	—	—	—	—	—	—	—	—	—	i	1	24	154

Hubbert, Brad Bradley, RB, 6´1˝/235 lbs; Arizona; 1966: SD, rnd R8; B6/5/1941 Boligee, AL

YEAR	TEAM	G(GS, POS)	RUSH	YD	AVG(LG)	TD	REC	YD	AVG(LG)	TD	PASS	COMP	PCT	YD	AVG(LG)	TD	INT	SK	YD	QBR	KPR	OTD	PTS	TAY
1967	SD-A✧	14(FB)	116	643	**5.5**(**80**)	2	19	214	11.3(49)	2	—	—	—	—	—	—	—	—	—	—	—	—	24	780
1968	SD-A	2	28	119	4.3(21)	2	5	11	2.2(10)	0	—	—	—	—	—	—	—	—	—	—	—	—	12	145
1969	SD-A	14(FB)	94	333	3.5(24)	4	11	43	3.9(18)	0	1	0	0.0	0	0.0	0	0	—	—	—	—	—	24	395
1970	SD	8	49	175	3.6(11)	1	7	44	6.3(11)	0	—	—	—	—	—	—	—	—	—	—	—	—	6	207
NFL	4	38	287	1270	4.4(80)	9	42	312	7.4(49)	2	1	0	0.0	0	0.0	0	0	—	—	—	—	—	66	1526

Hubka, Gene Eugene Lewis, TB, 5´11˝/175 lbs; Temple; Bucknell; B5/18/1924 Perth Amboy, NJ

YEAR	TEAM	G(GS, POS)	RUSH	YD	AVG(LG)	TD	REC	YD	AVG(LG)	TD	PASS	COMP	PCT	YD	AVG(LG)	TD	INT	SK	YD	QBR	KPR	OTD	PTS	TAY
1947	Pit	1(0)	2	4	2.0(3)	0	—	—	—	—	—	—	—	—	—	—	—	—	—	—	—	—	0	4

Huckleby, Harlan Harlan Charles, RB, 6´1˝/199 lbs; Michigan; 1979: NO, rnd 5; B12/30/1957 Detroit, MI

YEAR	TEAM	G(GS, POS)	RUSH	YD	AVG(LG)	TD	REC	YD	AVG(LG)	TD	PASS	COMP	PCT	YD	AVG(LG)	TD	INT	SK	YD	QBR	KPR	OTD	PTS	TAY
1980	GB	16(0)	6	11	1.8(9)	1	3	11	3.7(8)	0	—	—	—	—	—	—	—	—	—	—	k	—	6	41
1981	GB	16(12, RB)	139	381	2.7(22)	5	27	221	8.2(39)	3	—	—	—	—	—	—	—	—	—	—	k	—	48	586
1982	†GB	9(0)	4	19	4.8(7)	0	—	—	—	—	—	—	—	—	—	—	—	—	—	—	k	—	0	33
1983	GB	16(2)	50	182	3.6(20)	4	10	87	8.7(14)	0	—	—	—	—	—	—	—	—	—	—	k	—	24	408
1984	GB	16(0)	35	145	4.1(23)	0	8	65	8.1(13)	0	—	—	—	—	—	—	—	—	—	—	k	—	0	229
1985	GB	11(0)	8	41	5.1(15)	0	5	27	5.4(8)	0	—	—	—	—	—	—	—	—	—	—	—	—	0	55
NFL	6	84(14)	242	779	3.2(23)	10	53	411	7.8(39)	3	—	—	—	—	—	—	—	—	—	—	k	—	78	1350

Huddleston, Jim James Walden, G-T, 6´4˝/280 lbs; Virginia; 1986: Was, rnd 6; B9/22/1962 San Pedro, CA **1987** TB 1 (1)

Huddleston, John John Charles, LB, 6´3˝/231 lbs; Utah; 1976: Den, rnd 16; B4/10/1954 Los Angeles, CA **1978** Oak 11 **1979** Oak 16 **NFL** 27 [2 yrs]

Hudlow, Floyd Floyd Leroy, DB, 5´11˝/195 lbs; Arizona; 1965: Buf, rnd 10/Phi, rnd 9; B11/9/1943 Phoenix, AZ **1965** Buf-A 7 **1967** Atl 10 (10, LS) **1968** Atl 7 **NFL** 24 (10) [3 yrs]

Hudock, Mike Michael Edward, C, 6´2˝/245 lbs; Miami (FL); 1956: GB, rnd 11; B9/29/1934 Pittston, PA **1960** NYT-A 14 (C) **1961** NYT-A 11 (C) **1962** NYT-A 14 (C) **1963** NYJ-A 14 (C) **1964** NYJ-A☆11 (C) **1965** NYJ-A☆14 (C) **1966** Mia-A 14 **1967** KC-A 4 **NFL** 96 [8 yrs]

Hudson, Bill William Alex, DT, 6´4˝/270 lbs; Clemson; 1957: ChiC, rnd 3; B7/9/1935 Lamar, SC **1961**†SD-A★14 (LDT) **1962** SD-A 14 (LDT) **1963** Bos-A 4 **NFL** 32 [3 yrs]

Hudson, Bob Robert Willard, DB-LB-E, 6´4˝/225 lbs; Clemson; 1951: NYG, rnd 12; B4/5/1930 Lamar, SC **1953** Phi 12 (DB) **1954** Phi 12 (DB) **1955** Phi 12 (DB) **1957** Phi 12 (MLB) **1958** Phi 11 **1959** Was 3 **1960** DalT-A 5 **1960** Den-A 2 **1961** Den-A 14 (LLB)

YEAR	TEAM	G(GS, POS)	RUSH	YD	AVG(LG)	TD	REC	YD	AVG(LG)	TD	PASS	COMP	PCT	YD	AVG(LG)	TD	INT	SK	YD	QBR	KPR	OTD	PTS	TAY
1951	NYG	11	—	—	—	—	4	122	30.5(50)	0	—	—	—	—	—	—	—	—	—	—	—	—	0	61
1952	NYG	12	—	—	—	—	4	40	10.0(19)	0	—	—	—	—	—	—	—	—	—	—	—	—	0	20
NFL	10	106	—	—	—	—	8	162	20.3(50)	0	—	—	—	—	—	—	—	—	—	—	kpi	—	0	208

Hudson, Bob Robert Dale, RB, 5´11˝/210 lbs; Northeastern State (OK); 1972: GB, rnd 6; B3/21/1948 Hominy, OK

YEAR	TEAM	G(GS, POS)	RUSH	YD	AVG(LG)	TD	REC	YD	AVG(LG)	TD	PASS	COMP	PCT	YD	AVG(LG)	TD	INT	SK	YD	QBR	KPR	OTD	PTS	TAY
1972	†GB	12	15	62	4.1(17)	0	—	—	—	—	—	—	—	—	—	—	—	—	—	—	kp	—	0	139
1973	†Oak	14	4	3	0.8(5)	0	1	9	9.0(9)	0	—	—	—	—	—	—	—	—	—	—	kp	—	0	148
1974	†Oak	14	1	12	12.0(12)	0	—	—	—	—	—	—	—	—	—	—	—	—	—	—	—	—	0	12
NFL	3	40	20	77	3.8(17)	0	1	9	9.0(9)	0	—	—	—	—	—	—	—	—	—	—	kp	—	0	299

Hudson, Chris Christopher Resherd, DB, 5´10˝/199 lbs; Colorado; 1995: Jax, rnd 3; B10/6/1971 Houston, TX **1995** Jax 1 (0) **1996**†Jax 16 (16, FS) **1997**†Jax 16 (16, FS) **1998**†Jax 13 (13, FS) **1999** ChiB 16 (16, FS) **2001** Atl 15 (2) **NFL** 77 (63) [6 yrs]

Hudson, Dick Richard, B, /182 lbs; none; B10/7/1898, deceased **1923** Min 3 (3) **1925** Ham 3 (2) **1926** Ham 2 (2, BB) **NFL** 8 (7) [3 yrs]

Hudson, Dick Richard Smith, T-G, 6´3˝/272 lbs; Memphis; 1962: SD, rnd 2; B7/30/1940 Memphis, TN **1962** SD-A 14 **1963** Buf-A 2 **1965**†Buf-A✧14 (RT) **1966**†Buf-A☆14 (RT) **1967** Buf-A 8 (RT)

YEAR	TEAM	G(GS, POS)	RUSH	YD	AVG(LG)	TD	REC	YD	AVG(LG)	TD	PASS	COMP	PCT	YD	AVG(LG)	TD	INT	SK	YD	QBR	KPR	OTD	PTS	TAY
1964	†Buf-A	14(RT)	1	1	1.0(1)	0	—	—	—	—	—	—	—	—	—	—	—	—	—	—	—	—	0	1
NFL	6	66	1	1	1.0(1)	0	—	—	—	—	—	—	—	—	—	—	—	—	—	—	—	—	0	1

Hudson, Doug Benjamin Douglas, QB, 6´2˝/201 lbs; Nicholls State; 1987: KC, rnd 7; B9/11/1964 Memphis, TX

YEAR	TEAM	G(GS, POS)	RUSH	YD	AVG(LG)	TD	REC	YD	AVG(LG)	TD	PASS	COMP	PCT	YD	AVG(LG)	TD	INT	SK	YD	QBR	KPR	OTD	PTS	TAY
1987	KC	1(1)	1	0	0.0(0)	0	—	—	—	—	1	0	0.0	0	0.0	0	0	1	10	—	—	—	0	0

Hudson, Gordon Gordon Lynn, TE, 6´4˝/241 lbs; Brigham Young; 1984: Sea, rnd S1; B6/22/1962 Kennewick, WA

YEAR	TEAM	G(GS, POS)	RUSH	YD	AVG(LG)	TD	REC	YD	AVG(LG)	TD	PASS	COMP	PCT	YD	AVG(LG)	TD	INT	SK	YD	QBR	KPR	OTD	PTS	TAY
1986	Sea	16(4)	—	—	—	—	13	131	10.1(30)	1	—	—	—	—	—	—	—	—	—	—	—	—	6	71

Hudson, Jim James Clark, DB, 6´2˝/210 lbs; Texas; B3/31/1943 Steubenville, OH **1965** NYJ-A 2 **1967** NYJ-A 13 (LS) **1968**†NYJ-A☆14 (LS) **1969** NYJ-A 4 **1970** NYJ 7

YEAR	TEAM	G(GS, POS)	RUSH	YD	AVG(LG)	TD	REC	YD	AVG(LG)	TD	PASS	COMP	PCT	YD	AVG(LG)	TD	INT	SK	YD	QBR	KPR	OTD	PTS	TAY
1966	NYJ-A	14(RS)	—	—	—	—	—	—	—	—	1	0	0.0	0	0.0	0	0	—	—	—	pi	—	0	37
NFL	6	54	—	—	—	—	—	—	—	—	1	0	0.0	0	0.0	0	0	—	—	—	kpi	—	0	123

Hudson, John John Lewis, G-C, 6´2˝/270 lbs; Auburn; 1990: Phi, rnd 11; B1/29/1968 Memphis, TN **1991** Phi 16 (0) **1992** Phi 3 (0) **1993** Phi 16 (0) **1994** Phi 16 (0) **1995**†Phi 16 (0) **1996** NYJ 16 (0) **1997** NYJ 16 (0) **1998**†NYJ 16 (0) **1999** NYJ 16 (0) **2000**†Bal 8 (0) **NFL** 139 (0) [10 yrs]

Hudson, Johnnie John Randolph, HB-FB, 5´9˝/170 lbs; North Carolina State; B10/7/1898 Shelby, NC, deceased **1921** Was 3 (1), 6

Hudson, Mike Michael Todd, DB, 6´0˝/202 lbs; Oklahoma State; B12/25/1963 Pawhuska, OK **1987** SD 3 (0)

Hudson, Nat Nathaniel Lamar, G, 6´3˝/268 lbs; Georgia; 1981: NO, rnd 6; B10/11/1957 Rome, GA **1981** NO 16 (0) **1982** Bal 2 (2) **NFL** 18 (2) [2 yrs]

Hueller, Jack John C., G, 5´10˝/200 lbs; none; B9/29/1898 Milwaukee, WI, D8/29/1993 Milwaukee, WI **1922** Rac 9 (2) **1923** Rac 9 (3) **1924** Rac 4 (1) **NFL** 22 (6) [3 yrs]

Huerta, Carlos Carlos Antonio, K, 5´7˝/185 lbs; Miami (FL); 1992: SD, rnd 12; B6/29/1969 Coral Gables, FL **[K]** **1996** ChiB 3 (0) **1996** SL 1 (0) **NFL** 4 (0) [1 yr]

Huey, Gene Eugene Aaron, DB, 5´11˝/190 lbs; Wyoming; 1969: SL, rnd 5; B7/20/1947 Uniontown, PA **1969** SD-A 4

Huff, Alan Alan Edward, NT, 6´4˝/265 lbs; Marshall; B10/20/1963 East Liverpool, OH **1987** Pit 2 (1)

Huff, Charles Charles, DB, 5´11˝/195 lbs; Presbyterian; B2/24/1963 Statesboro, GA **1987** Atl 3 (2)

Huff, Gary Gary Earl, QB, 6´1˝/195 lbs; Florida State; 1973: Chi, rnd 2; B4/27/1951 Natchez, MS

YEAR	TEAM	G(GS, POS)	RUSH	YD	AVG(LG)	TD	REC	YD	AVG(LG)	TD	PASS	COMP	PCT	YD	AVG(LG)	TD	INT	SK	YD	QBR	KPR	OTD	PTS	TAY
1973	ChiB	8	11	22	2.0(8)	0	—	—	—	—	126	54	42.9	525	4.2(29)	3	8	22	180	—	—	—	0	-21
1974	ChiB	13(QB)	23	37	1.6(11)	2	—	—	—	—	283	142	50.2	1663	5.9(73)	6	**17**	24	260	50.4	—	—	12	239
1975	ChiB	14(9, QB)	5	7	1.4(10)	0	—	—	—	—	205	114	55.6	1083	5.3(49)	3	9	16	168	—	—	—	0	204
1976	ChiB	8	—	—	—	—	—	—	—	—	—	—	—	—	—	—	—	—	—	—	—	—	—	—

YEAR	TEAM	G(GS, POS)°	RUSH	YD	AVG(LG)	TD	REC	YD	AVG(LG)	TD	PASS	COMP	PCT	YD	AVG(LG)	TD	INT	SK	YD	QBR	KPR	OTD	PTS	TAY
1977	TB	8(6, QB)	8	10	1.3(2)	0	—	—	—	—	138	67	48.6	889	6.4(67)	3	13	15	150	—	—	—	0	-51
1978	TB	6	3	10	3.3(10)	0	—	—	—	—	36	15	41.7	169	4.7(31)	1	3	5	54	—	—	—	0	-21
NFL	6	57(15)	50	86	1.7(11)	2	—	—	—	—	788	392	49.7	4329	5.5(73)	16	50	82	812	46.8	—	—	12	351

HUFF, KEN   Kenneth Wayne, G, 6´4˝/260 lbs; North Carolina; 1975: Bal, rnd 1; B2/21/1953 Hutchinson, KS   **1975**†Bal 9   **1976** Bal 8   **1977**†Bal 14 (9, RG)   **1978** Bal 16 (16, RG)   **1979** Bal 14 (14, RG)   **1980** Bal 16 (16, RG)   **1982** Bal 9 (8, RG)   **1983**†Was 12 (1)   **1984**†Was 15 (9, RG)   **1985** Was 16 (15, RG)

| 1981 | Bal | 16(16, RG) | — | — | — | — | 1 | -1 | -1.0(-1) | 0 | — | — | — | — | — | — | — | — | — | — | — | — | 0 | -1 |
| NFL | 11 | 145(104) | — | — | — | — | 1 | -1 | -1.0(-1) | 0 | — | — | — | — | — | — | — | — | — | — | k | — | 0 | -16 |

HUFF, MARTY   Ralph Martin, LB, 6´2˝/234 lbs; Michigan; 1971: SF, rnd 5; B12/19/1948 Houston, TX   **1972**†SF 3

HUFF, ORLANDO   Orlando, LB, 6´2˝/250 lbs; Fresno State; 2001: Sea, rnd 4; B8/14/1978 Mobile, AL   **2001** Sea 12 (0)   **2002** Sea 16 (7, mlb)   **2003**†Sea 11 (2)   **2004**†Sea 16 (14, MLB)   **2005** Arz 16 (12, RLB)   **NFL** 71 (35) [5 yrs]

HUFF, SAM   Robert Lee, LB, 6´1˝/230 lbs; West Virginia; 1956: NYG, rnd 3; B10/4/1934 Edna Gas, WV; HOF 1982 [I]   **1956**†NYG 12 (MLB)   **1957** NYG☆12 (MLB)   **1958**†NYG★12 (MLB)   **1959**†NYG★12 (MLB)   **1960** NYG★12 (MLB)   **1961** NYG★14 (MLB)   **1962** NYG 14 (MLB)   **1963**†NYG☆14 (MLB)   **1964** Was★14 (MLB)   **1965** Was☆14 (MLB)   **1966** Was 14 (MLB)   **1967** Was 10 (MLB)   **NFL** 168 [13 yrs]

HUFFINE, KEN   Kenneth Wilbur, FB, 6´3˝/208 lbs; Purdue; B12/22/1897 Hammond, IN, D9/26/1977 Bradenton, FL [C]   **1920** Mun 1 (1, FB)   **1921** ChiS 10 (10, FB), 12   **1922** Day 8 (6, FB), 18   **1923** Day 8 (8, FB)   **1924** Day☆7 (5, FB)   **1925** Day 8 (6, FB)   **NFL** 42 (36), 30 [6 yrs]

HUFFMAN, DARVELL   Darvell Denario, WR, 5´8˝/158 lbs; Boston University; 1990: Ind, rnd 9; B5/5/1967 Boston, MA

| 1991 | Ind | 3(0) | 1 | -8 | -8.0(-8) | 0 | 3 | 14 | 4.7(7) | 0 | — | — | — | — | — | — | — | — | — | — | — | — | 0 | -1 |

HUFFMAN, DAVE   David Lambert, G-C, 6´6˝/280 lbs; Notre Dame; 1979: Min, rnd 2; B4/4/1957 Canton, OH, D11/21/1998 Lake Station, IN   **1979** Min 13   **1980**†Min 16 (2)   **1981** Min 13 (0)   **1982**†Min 9 (0)   **1983** Min 15 (0)   **1985** Min 15 (3)   **1986** Min 16 (1)   **1987**†Min 12 (12, LG)   **1988** Min 2 (1)   **1989**†Min 16 (3)   **1990** Min 1 (0)   **NFL** 128 (22) [11 yrs]

HUFFMAN, DICK   Richard Maxwell, T, 6´1˝/255 lbs; Tennessee; 1945: Cle, rnd 9; B3/27/1923 Charleston, WV, D9/13/1992 Charleston, WV   **1947** LARm☆11 (11, LT)   **1948** LARm☆11 (11, LT)   **1950**†LARm★12 (LT)

| 1949 | †LARm☆ | 12(12, LT) | — | — | — | — | 2 | 36 | 18.0(23) | 0 | — | — | — | — | — | — | — | — | — | — | — | — | 0 | 18 |
| NFL | 4 | 47(34) | — | — | — | — | 2 | 36 | 18.0(23) | 0 | — | — | — | — | — | — | — | — | — | — | — | 1 | 6 | 24 |

HUFFMAN, FRANK   Frank, T-E, 6´1˝/207 lbs; Marshall; 1939: ChiC, rnd 18; B5/22/1915 Pittsburgh, PA, D9/16/1980 Fayetteville, WV   **1939** ChiC 11 (1)   **1940** ChiC 9 (4)   **1941** ChiC 8 (3)   **NFL** 28 (8) [3 yrs]

HUFFMAN, IOLAS   Iolas Melitus, T-G, 5´11˝/228 lbs; Ohio State; B2/4/1898 Chandlersville, OH, D11/12/1989 Cleveland, OH   **1923** Cle 7 (6, RT)   **1924** Buf 6 (6, RT)   **NFL** 13 (12) [2 yrs]

HUFFMAN, TIM   Timothy Patrick, G-T, 6´5˝/277 lbs; Notre Dame; 1981: GB, rnd 9; B8/31/1959 Canton, OH   **1981** GB 5 (1)   **1982**†GB 9 (3)   **1983** GB 15 (6, rg)   **1984** GB 16 (15, LG)   **1985** GB 2 (0)   **NFL** 47 (25) [5 yrs]

HUFFMAN, VERN   Richard Vernon, BB-TB-HB-QB, 6´2˝/215 lbs; Indiana; 1937: Det, rnd 3; B12/18/1914 Moreland, IN, D3/18/1995 Bloomington, IN

1937	Det	11(7, BB)	35	187	5.3	0	8	104	13.0	0	23	5	21.7	102	4.4	1	6	—	—	—	—	1	6	65
1938	Det	11(8, TB)	69	181	2.6	1	1	17	17.0(17)	0	85	27	31.8	382	4.5	2	8	—	—	—	—	0	6	81
NFL	2	22(15)	104	368	3.5	1	9	121	13.4(17)	0	108	32	29.6	484	4.5	3	14	—	—	—	—	1	12	146

HUFFORD, DEL   Guy Darrell, E, 5´11˝/185 lbs; California; B1/18/1901, CA, D7/6/1984 Camarillo, CA   **1926** LA 10 (10, LE)

HUFNAGEL, JOHN   John Coleman, QB, 6´1˝/194 lbs; Penn State; 1973: Den, rnd 14; B9/13/1951 Pittsburgh, PA

1974	Den	4	2	22	11.0(18)	0	—	—	—	—	10	6	60.0	70	7.0(28)	0	1	1	7	—	—	—	0	17
1975	Den	5(1)	8	47	5.9(13)	0	—	—	—	—	51	16	31.4	287	5.6(80)	1	8	13	84	—	—	—	0	-125
NFL	2	9(1)	10	69	6.9(18)	0	—	—	—	—	61	22	36.1	357	5.9(80)	1	9	14	91	—	—	—	0	-108

HUGASIAN, HARRY   Harry, HB-DB, 6´1˝/192 lbs; Stanford; 1952: DalT, rnd 21; B8/29/1929 Pasadena, CA   **1955** ChiB 4

| 1955 | Bal | 2 | 12 | 34 | 2.8(15) | 0 | 3 | 32 | 10.7(13) | 0 | — | — | — | — | — | — | — | — | — | — | — | — | 0 | 50 |
| NFL | 1 | 6 | 12 | 34 | 2.8(15) | 0 | 3 | 32 | 10.7(13) | 0 | — | — | — | — | — | — | — | — | — | — | k | — | 0 | 35 |

HUGGINS, JOHNNY   Johnny, TE, 6´3˝/245 lbs; Alabama State; B3/29/1976 Zachary, LA

| 2001 | Dal | 10(2) | — | — | — | — | 8 | 36 | 4.5(10) | 0 | — | — | — | — | — | — | — | — | — | — | — | — | 0 | 18 |

HUGGINS, ROY   Roy, FB, 5´11˝/195 lbs; Vanderbilt; B10/6/1918 Nashville, TN, D4/1/1999

| 1944 | Cle | 5(0) | 12 | 41 | 3.4(15) | 0 | 1 | 0 | 0.0(0) | 0 | — | — | — | — | — | — | — | — | — | — | — | — | 0 | 41 |

HUGHES, BERNIE   Bernard B., C, 6´1˝/190 lbs; Oregon; B1/9/1910 Dorris, CA, D12/26/1967 Medford, OR   **1934** ChiC☆10 (6, C)   **1935** ChiC 10 (7, C)   **1936** ChiC 12 (12, C)   **NFL** 32 (25) [3 yrs]

HUGHES, BILL   William, G-C, 6´1˝/226 lbs; Texas; B4/11/1915 Van Alstyne, TX, D7/6/1978 Tampa, FL   **1937** Phi 11 (8, RG)   **1938** Phi 11 (6, rg)   **1939** Phi 11 (6, lg)   **1940** Phi 7 (6, RG)   **1941**†ChiB◊6 (0)   **NFL** 46 (26) [5 yrs]

HUGHES, BOB   Robert E., DE, 6´4˝/236 lbs; Jackson State; 1967: Phi, rnd 6; B11/17/1944 Columbus, MS   **1967** Atl 2   **1969** Atl 14   **NFL** 16 [2 yrs]

HUGHES, CHUCK   Charles Frederick, WR, 5´11˝/173 lbs; Texas-El Paso; 1967: Phi, rnd 4; B3/24/1943 Philadelphia, PA, D10/24/1971 Detroit, MI

1967	Phi	9	—	—	—	—	—	—	—	—	—	—	—	—	—	—	—	—	—	—	kp	—	0	17
1968	Phi	6	—	—	—	—	3	39	13.0(18)	0	—	—	—	—	—	—	—	—	—	—	—	—	0	20
1969	Phi	7	—	—	—	—	3	29	9.7(15)	0	—	—	—	—	—	—	—	—	—	—	p	—	0	10
1970	Det	13(wr)	—	—	—	—	8	162	20.3(42)	0	—	—	—	—	—	—	—	—	—	—	—	—	0	81
1971	Det	3	—	—	—	—	1	32	32.0(32)	0	—	—	—	—	—	—	—	—	—	—	p	—	0	16
NFL	5	38	—	—	—	—	15	262	17.5(42)	0	—	—	—	—	—	—	—	—	—	—	kp	—	0	143

HUGHES, DANAN   Robert Danan, WR, 6´2˝/205 lbs; Iowa; 1993: KC, rnd 7; B12/11/1970 Bayonne, NJ

1993	†KC	6(0)	—	—	—	—	—	—	—	—	—	—	—	—	—	—	—	—	—	—	kp	—	0	90
1994	†KC	16(0)	—	—	—	—	7	80	11.4(22)	0	—	—	—	—	—	—	—	—	—	—	kp	—	0	152
1995	†KC	16(0)	1	5	5.0(5)	0	14	103	7.4(15)	1	—	—	—	—	—	—	—	—	—	—	kp	—	6	59
1996	KC	15(2)	—	—	—	—	17	167	9.8(26)	1	1	1	100.0	30	30.0(30)	0	0	—	—	—	k	—	6	116
1997	†KC	16(1)	—	—	—	—	7	65	9.3(14)	2	—	—	—	—	—	—	—	—	—	—	k	1	18	49
1998	KC	16(0)	—	—	—	—	1	10	10.0(10)	0	1	1	100.0	25	25.0(25)	0	0	—	—	—	p	—	0	18
NFL	6	85(3)	1	5	5.0(5)	0	46	425	9.2(26)	4	2	2	100.0	55	27.5(30)	0	0	—	—	—	kp	1	30	482

HUGHES, DAVID   David Augustus, RB-FB, 6´0˝/220 lbs; Boise State; 1981: Sea, rnd 2; B6/1/1959 Honolulu, HI

1981	Sea	16(2)	47	135	2.9(15)	0	35	263	7.5(22)	0	—	—	—	—	—	—	—	—	—	—	—	—	12	277
1982	Sea	9(3)	30	106	3.5(13)	0	11	98	8.9(29)	1	—	—	—	—	—	—	—	—	—	—	k	—	6	162
1983	†Sea	16(6, fb)	83	313	3.8(26)	1	10	100	10.0(33)	1	—	—	—	—	—	—	—	—	—	—	k	—	12	480
1984	†Sea	16(6, fb)	94	327	3.5(14)	1	22	121	5.5(25)	1	—	—	—	—	—	—	—	—	—	—	k	—	12	496
1985	Sea	12(10, FB)	40	128	3.2(9)	0	19	184	9.7(26)	0	—	—	—	—	—	—	—	—	—	—	k	—	0	220
1986	Pit	5(0)	14	32	2.3(8)	0	10	98	9.8(22)	0	—	—	—	—	—	—	—	—	—	—	k	—	0	67
NFL	6	74(27)	308	1041	3.4(26)	2	107	864	8.1(33)	3	—	—	—	—	—	—	—	—	—	—	k	—	42	1701

HUGHES, DENNIS   Donald Dennis, TE, 6´1˝/225 lbs; Georgia; B2/22/1948 Seneca, SC   **1971** Pit 7

| 1970 | Pit | 11(TE) | 1 | -8 | -8.0(-8) | 0 | 24 | 332 | 13.8(72) | 3 | — | — | — | — | — | — | — | — | — | — | — | — | 18 | 173 |
| NFL | 2 | 18 | 1 | -8 | -8.0(-8) | 0 | 24 | 332 | 13.8(72) | 3 | — | — | — | — | — | — | — | — | — | — | — | — | 18 | 173 |

HUGHES, DENNY   Dennis, C, 5´11˝/185 lbs; George Washington; B1900, D1957, [K]   **1925** Pot 7 (6, c), 2

HUGHES, DICK   Richard, HB, 5´9˝/185 lbs; Tulsa; 1957: Pit, rnd 11; B9/26/1932 Buffalo, NY

| 1957 | Pit | 1 | 2 | 6 | 3.0(4) | 0 | — | — | — | — | — | — | — | — | — | — | — | — | — | — | p | — | 0 | 6 |

HUGHES, ED   Edward D., DB, 6´1˝/184 lbs; Cameron; North Carolina State; Tulsa; 1954: LA, rnd 10; B10/23/1927 Buffalo, NY, D6/23/2000 Libertyville, IL [C]   **1954** LARm 11   **1955**†LARm 12 (DB)   **1956**†NYG 12 (DB)   **1957** NYG 8 (DB)   **1958**†NYG 10 (DB)   **NFL** 53 [5 yrs]

HUGHES, ERNIE   Ernest Loyal, C-G, 6´3˝/259 lbs; Notre Dame; 1978: SF, rnd 3; B1/24/1955 Boise, ID   **1978** SF 15 (11, LG)   **1980** SF 3 (0)   **1981** NYG 10 (10, C)   **1982** NYG 5 (2)   **1983** NYG 12 (6, c)   **NFL** 45 (29) [5 yrs]

YEAR	TEAM	G (GS, POS)	RUSH	YD	AVG (LG)	TD	REC	YD	AVG (LG)	TD	PASS COMP	PCT	YD	AVG (LG)	TD	INT	SK	YD	QBR	KPR	OTD	PTS	TAY

HUGHES, GEORGE   George Samuel, T-G, 6´1˝/225 lbs; William & Mary; 1950: Pit, rnd 3; B8/19/1925 Norfolk, VA   **1950** Pit 12 (RG) **1951** Pit✧12 (RG) **1953** Pit✧12 (RT)
1954 Pit 12 (RT)

| 1952 | Pit | 12 (RT) | — | — | — | — | 0 | 2 | (2) | 0 | — | — | — | — | — | — | — | — | — | — | — | 0 | 1 |
| NFL | 5 | 60 | — | — | — | — | 0 | 2 | (2) | 0 | — | — | — | — | — | — | — | — | — | k | — | 0 | -14 |

HUGHES, HONOLULU   Henry Thomas, B, 5´10˝/195 lbs; Oregon State; B5/4/1907 Honolulu, HI, D12/27/1963 Honolulu, HI **[K]**

| 1932 | Bos | 10 (9, BB) | 14 | 28 | 2.0 | 0 | 2 | 35 | 17.5 | 0 | 57 | 11 | 19.3 | 134 | 2.4 | 1 | 9 | — | — | — | K | — | 5 | -243 |

HUGHES, PAT   William Patrick, LB-C, 6´2˝/240 lbs; Boston University; 1970: NYG, rnd 9; B6/2/1947 Everett, MA   **1970** NYG 14 **1971** NYG 14 **1972** NYG 14 (RLB)
1973 NYG 11 (RLB) **1974** NYG 14 (RLB) **1975** NYG 14 (LLB) **1976** NYG 14 (8, mlb) **1977** NO 14 (14, RLB) **1978** NO 16 (RLB) **1979** NO 16 (RLB) **NFL** 141 (22) [10 yrs]

HUGHES, RANDY   James Randall, DB; Oklahoma; 1975: Dal, rnd 4; B4/3/1953 Oklahoma City, OK   **1975**†Dal 14 **1976**†Dal 14 (2) **1977**†Dal 13 **1978**†Dal 16
1979†Dal 15 (SS) **1980**†Dal 5 (2) **NFL** 77 (2) [6 yrs]

HUGHES, TYRONE   Tyrone Christopher, DB, 5´9˝/175 lbs; Nebraska; 1993: NO, rnd 5; B1/14/1970 New Orleans, LA **[R]**   **1993** NO★16 (0) **1995** NO 16 (2) **1996** NO 16 (1)
1998†Dal 4 (0)

1994	NO	15 (5, rcb)	2	6	3.0 (7)	0	—	—	—	—	—	—	—	—	—	—	—	—	—	kpi	4	24	696
1997	ChiB	14 (0)	1	3	3.0 (3)	0	8	68	8.5 (16)	0	—	—	—	—	—	—	—	—	—	kp	—	0	478
NFL	6	81 (8)	3	9	3.0 (7)	0	8	68	8.5 (16)	0	—	—	—	—	—	—	—	—	—	kpi	7	42	3478

HUGHES, VAN   Curtis Van, DE, 6´3˝/280 lbs; Texas Tech; Southwest Texas State; 1984: Pit, rnd 5; B11/14/1960 Waco, TX   **1986** SL 7 (0) **1987** Sea 1 (1) **NFL** 8 (1) [2 yrs]

HUGHITT, TOMMY   Ernest Frederick, B, 5´8˝/159 lbs; Michigan; B12/27/1892 Genoa, Canada, D12/27/1961 Bartow, FL **[KC]**   **1920** Buf 11 (3, BB) **1921** Buf 12 (10, BB), 20
1922 Buf✩10 (9, BB), 12 **1923** Buf 12 (12, BB), 9 **1924** Buf 11 (7, WB) **NFL** 56 (41), 41 [5 yrs]

HUGHLEY, GEORGE   George Charles, FB, 6´2˝/223 lbs; Central Oklahoma; B6/26/1939 Los Angeles, CA, D2/27/1999 Glendale, CA

| 1965 | Was | 14 | 37 | 175 | 4.7 (19) | 0 | 9 | 93 | 10.3 (27) | 1 | — | — | — | — | — | — | — | — | — | kp | — | 6 | 329 |

HUGRET, JOE   Joseph Jon, E, 6´2˝/195 lbs; NYU; B4/11/1909 Torrington, CT, D9/1977 Minot, ND   **1934** Bkn 2 (0)

HULL, BILL   William Henry, DE, 6´6˝/245 lbs; Wake Forest; 1962: Bos, rnd 5/Chi, rnd 3; B8/4/1940   **1962**†DalT-A 14

HULL, KENT   James Kent, C, 6´5˝/284 lbs; Mississippi State; B1/13/1961 Pontotoc, MS   **1986** Buf 16 (16, C) **1987** Buf 12 (12, C) **1988**†Buf★16 (16, C) **1989**†Buf★16 (16, C)
1990†Buf★16 (16, C) **1991**†Buf 16 (16, C) **1992** Buf 16 (16, C) **1993**†Buf 14 (13, C) **1994** Buf 16 (16, C) **1995**†Buf✩16 (16, C) **1996**†Buf 16 (16, C) **NFL** 170 (169) [11 yrs]

HULL, MIKE   Michael Bruce, RB, 6´3˝/220 lbs; USC; 1968: Chi, rnd 1; B1/12/1945 Glendale, CA

1968	ChiB	14	12	22	1.8 (12)	0	4	20	5.0 (9)	0	—	—	—	—	—	—	—	—	—	—	—	0	32
1969	ChiB	10	29	81	2.8 (14)	1	12	63	5.3 (29)	0	—	—	—	—	—	—	—	—	—	—	—	6	123
1970	ChiB	13	32	99	3.1 (13)	0	13	44	3.4 (17)	0	—	—	—	—	—	—	—	—	—	—	—	0	121
1971	Was	11	2	8	4.0 (6)	0	—	—	—	—	—	—	—	—	—	—	—	—	—	—	—	0	8
1972	†Was	14	—	—	—	—	—	—	—	—	—	—	—	—	—	—	—	—	—	—	—	—	—
1973	†Was	13	2	-3	-1.5 (-1)	0	—	—	—	—	—	—	—	—	—	—	—	—	—	—	—	0	-3
1974	†Was	14	—	—	—	—	—	—	—	—	—	—	—	—	—	—	—	—	—	—	—	—	—
NFL	7	89	77	207	2.7 (14)	1	29	127	4.4 (29)	0	—	—	—	—	—	—	—	—	—	—	—	6	281

HULL, TOM   Thomas Michael, LB, 6´3˝/229 lbs; Penn State; 1974: SF, rnd 12; B6/30/1952 Cumberland, MD   **1974** SF 13 **1975** GB 12 **NFL** 25 [2 yrs]

HULSEY, COREY   Corey Spear, G-T, 6´4˝/325 lbs; Clemson; B7/26/1977 Lula, GA   **2001** Buf 16 (12, RG) **2003** Oak 4 (0) **2004** Oak 3 (0) **2005** Oak 11 (0) **NFL** 34 (12) [4 yrs]

HULTMAN, VIVIAN   Vivian Joseph, E, 5´8˝/178 lbs; Michigan State; B1/26/1903 Grand Rapids, MI, D12/27/1987 Largo, FL   **1925** Det 11 (11, LE), 6 **1926** Det 10 (5, le), 6
1927 Pot 9 (5, le), 6 **NFL** 30 (21), 18 [3 yrs]

HULTZ, DON   William Donald, DE-DT, 6´3˝/241 lbs; Southern Mississippi; B12/16/1940 Moss Point, MS   **1963** Min 14 (14, LDE) **1964** Phi 12 (3) **1965** Phi 14 (LDE)
1966 Phi 13 (LDE) **1967** Phi 13 (LDE) **1968** Phi 10 **1969** Phi 14 **1970** Phi 12 (LDT) **1971** Phi 14 (LDT) **1972** Phi 14 (LDT) **1973** Phi 3 **1974** ChiB 8 **NFL** 141 (17) [12 yrs]

HULTZ, GEORGE   George A., DT, 6´4˝/250 lbs; Southern Mississippi; 1961: SL, rnd 7/Bos, rnd 30; B3/7/1939 Moss Point, MS   **1962** SL 13

HUMBERT, DICK   Richard Elmer, E-DE, 6´1˝/179 lbs; Richmond; B12/31/1918 Reading, PA

1941	Phi★	11 (8, RE)	—	—	—	—	29	332	11.4 (33)	3	—	—	—	—	—	—	—	—	—	ki	↓	18	176
1945	Phi	4 (2)	—	—	—	—	6	53	8.8 (12)	0	—	—	—	—	—	—	—	—	—	—	—	0	27
1946	Phi	11 (4)	1	2	2.0 (2)	0	18	191	10.6 (22)	3	—	—	—	—	—	—	—	—	—	k	—	18	116
1947	†Phi	11 (1)	—	—	—	—	13	139	10.7 (19)	0	—	—	—	—	—	—	—	—	—	i	—	0	72
1948	†Phi	12 (0)	—	—	—	—	1	2	2.0 (2)	0	—	—	—	—	—	—	—	—	—	pi	—	0	13
1949	Phi	11 (0)	—	—	—	—	1	14	14.0 (14)	0	—	—	—	—	—	—	—	—	—	i	—	0	41
NFL	6	60 (15)	1	2	2.0 (2)	0	68	731	10.8 (33)	6	—	—	—	—	—	—	—	—	—	kpi	—	36	444

HUMBLE, WELDON   Weldon Gaston, G, 6´1˝/221 lbs; Rice; Louisiana-Lafayette; 1947: Mia-A, rnd 4/1943: ChiC, rnd 24; B4/24/1921 Nixon, TX, D4/14/1998 Nixon, TX
1948†Cle-A✩13 (0) **1949**†Cle-A 10 (2)

| 1947 | †Cle-A | 12 (9, LG) | 1 | 0 | 0.0 | 0 | — | — | — | — | — | — | — | — | — | — | — | — | — | i | — | 0 | 21 |
| AAFC | 3 | 35 (11) | 1 | 0 | 0.0 | 0 | — | — | — | — | — | — | — | — | — | — | — | — | — | i | — | 0 | 72 |

1952 DalT 11 (9, LG)

| 1950 | †Cle✧ | 12 (lg) | 1 | -10 | -10.0 (-10) | 0 | — | — | — | — | — | — | — | — | — | — | — | — | — | — | — | 0 | -10 |
| NFL | 2 | 23 (9) | 1 | -10 | -10.0 | 0 | — | — | — | — | — | — | — | — | — | — | — | — | — | k | — | 0 | -8 |

HUMISTON, MIKE   Michael David, LB, 6´3˝/238 lbs; Weber State; B1/8/1959 Oceanside, CA   **1981**†Buf 16 (0) **1982** Bal 7 (0) **1984** Ind 16 (1) **1987** SD 7 (5, rilb)
NFL 46 (6) [4 yrs]

HUMM, DAVID   David Henry, QB, 6´2˝/188 lbs; Nebraska; 1975: Oak, rnd 5; B4/2/1952 Las Vegas, NV

1975	Oak	7	7	21	3.0 (8)	0	—	—	—	—	38	18	47.4	246	6.5 (43)	3	2	2	9	—	—	—	0	79
1976	†Oak	14	—	—	—	—	—	—	—	—	5	3	60.0	41	8.2 (29)	0	0	1	16	—	—	—	0	21
1977	†Oak	14	—	—	—	—	—	—	—	—	—	—	—	—	—	—	—	—	—	—	—	—	—	—
1978	Oak	16	5	-4	-0.8 (4)	0	—	—	—	—	26	14	53.8	151	5.8 (23)	0	1	2	21	—	—	—	0	32
1979	Oak	16	—	—	—	—	—	—	—	—	—	—	—	—	—	—	—	—	—	—	—	—	—	—
1980	†Buf	16 (0)	1	5	5.0 (5)	0	—	—	—	—	14	4	28.6	39	2.8 (19)	0	1	2	9	—	—	—	0	-16
1981	Bal	1 (1)	—	—	—	—	—	—	—	—	24	7	29.2	90	3.8 (20)	0	2	1	8	—	—	—	0	-35
1982	Bal	2 (0)	—	—	—	—	—	—	—	—	23	13	56.5	130	5.7 (23)	0	1	1	10	—	—	—	0	25
1983	†LARd	6 (0)	1	-1	-1.0 (-1)	0	—	—	—	—	—	—	—	—	—	—	—	—	—	—	—	—	0	-1
1984	LARd	3 (0)	2	7	3.5 (9)	0	—	—	—	—	7	4	57.1	56	8.0 (21)	0	1	3	27	—	—	—	0	-5
NFL	10	95 (1)	16	28	1.8 (9)	0	—	—	—	—	137	63	46.0	753	5.5 (43)	3	8	12	100	—	—	—	0	100

HUMMELL, SWEDE   Arthur Joseph, FB-HB, /195 lbs; Lombard; B5/30/1902 Belleville, IL, D10/1964   **1926** KC 5 (5, fb) **1926** Pro 4 (3) **1927** ChiC 8 (4) **NFL** 17 (12) [2 yrs]

HUMMON, MACK   John Mack, E, 5´11˝/180 lbs; Wittenberg; B7/4/1901 Leipsic, OH, D2/27/1992 Oakwood, OH   **1926** Day 5 (2) **1928** Day 4 (4, RE) **NFL** 9 (6) [2 yrs]

HUMPHERY, BOBBY   Robert Charles, DB-WR, 5´10˝/178 lbs; New Mexico State; 1983: NYJ, rnd 9; B8/23/1961 Lubbock, TX **[R]**   **1986**†NYJ 16 (1) **1987** NYJ 12 (2)
1988 NYJ 16 (16, LCB) **1989** NYJ 16 (16, LCB) **1990** LARm 16 (0, RCB)

1984	NYJ☆	16 (4)	—	—	—	—	14	206	14.7 (44)	1	—	—	—	—	—	—	—	—	—	k	1	12	463
1985	†NYJ	12 (0)	1	10	10.0 (10)	0	—	—	—	—	—	—	—	—	—	—	—	—	—	kp	—	0	113
NFL	7	104 (49)	1	10	10.0 (10)	0	14	206	14.7 (44)	1	—	—	—	—	—	—	—	—	—	kpiS	4	32	1194

HUMPHREY, BOBBY   Bobby, RB, 6´1˝/201 lbs; Alabama; 1989: Den, rnd S1; B10/11/1966 Birmingham, AL

1989	†Den	16 (12, RB)	294	1151	3.9 (40)	7	22	156	7.1 (13)	1	2	1	50.0	17	8.5 (17)	1	0	—	—	—	k	—	48	1344
1990	Den✧	15 (14, RB)	288	1202	4.2 (37)	7	24	152	6.3 (26)	0	0	0	0.0	0	0.0	0	0	—	—	—	—	—	42	1348
1991	Den	4 (0)	11	33	3.0 (7)	0	—	—	—	—	—	—	—	—	—	—	—	—	—	—	—	0	33
1992	†Mia	16 (1)	102	471	4.6 (21)	1	54	507	9.4 (26)	1	—	—	—	—	—	—	—	—	—	k	—	12	743
NFL	4	51 (27)	695	2857	4.1 (40)	15	100	815	8.1 (26)	2	4	1	25.0	17	4.3 (17)	1	0	—	—	—	k	—	102	3467

HUMPHREY, BUDDY   Loyie Nawlin, QB, 6´1˝/198 lbs; Baylor; 1959: LA, rnd 2; B9/29/1935 Dallas, TX, D4/21/1988 Kilgore, TX

| 1959 | LARm | 2 | — | — | — | — | — | — | — | — | — | — | — | — | — | — | — | — | — | — | — | — | — |
| 1960 | LARm | 4 | 2 | 7 | 3.5 (6) | 0 | — | — | — | — | 24 | 9 | 37.5 | 78 | 3.3 (16) | 0 | 2 | — | — | — | — | — | 0 | -34 |

YEAR	TEAM	G (GS, POS)	RUSH	YD	AVG (LG)	TD	REC	YD	AVG (LG)	TD	PASS	COMP	PCT	YD	AVG (LG)	TD	INT	SK	YD	QBR	KPR	OTD	PTS	TAY
1961	Dal	2	—	—	—	—	—	—	—	—	2	1	50.0	16	8.0(16)	0	0	—	—	—	—	—	0	8
1963	SL	4	—	—	—	—	—	—	—	—	11	4	36.4	96	8.7(33)	1	0	—	—	—	—	—	0	53
1964	SL	1	—	—	—	—	—	—	—	—	1	0	0.0	0	0.0	0	0	—	—	—	—	—	0	0
1965	SL	7	2	4	2.0(2)	0	—	—	—	—	105	58	55.2	736	7.0(53)	1	9	—	—	—	—	—	0	17
1966	Hou-A	6	—	—	—	—	—	—	—	—	32	15	46.9	168	5.3(32)	2	1	—	—	—	—	—	0	54
NFL	7	26	4	11	2.8(6)	0	—	—	—	—	175	87	49.7	1094	6.3(53)	4	12	—	—	—	—	—	0	98

Humphrey, Claude Claude B., DE, 6´4˝/252 lbs; Tennessee State; 1968: Atl, rnd 1; B6/29/1944 Memphis, TN **1968** Atl 14 (LDE) **1969** Atl☆14 (LDE) **1970** Atl★12 (LDE) **1971** Atl★14 (LDE) **1972** Atl★14 (LDE) **1973** Atl★14 (LDE) **1974** Atl★14 (LDE) **1976** Atl☆13 (13, LDE) **1977** Atl★14 (14, LDE) **1978** Atl 4 **1979**†Phi 16 (16, LDE) **1980**†Phi 16 (1) **1981**†Phi 12 (4) **NFL** 171 (48) [13 yrs]

Humphrey, Deon Deon Morie, LB, 6´3˝/240 lbs; Florida State; B5/7/1976 Clewiston, FL **2000** Car 3 (0) **2000** SD 7 (0) **2001** SD 11 (0) **2003** Jax 8 (0) **NFL** 29 (0) [3 yrs]

Humphrey, Donnie Donnie Ray, NT-DE, 6´3˝/282 lbs; Auburn; 1984: GB, rnd 3; B4/20/1961 Huntsville, AL **1984** GB 16 (16, RDE) **1985** GB 16 (6, nt) **1986** GB 16 (5, nt) **NFL** 48 (27) [3 yrs]

Humphrey, Paul Paul Eugene, C, 6´0˝/210 lbs; Purdue; 1939: Phi, rnd 11; B7/18/1917 Terre Haute, IN **1939** Bkn 11 (1)

Humphrey, Ronald Ronald Lynn, RB, 5´10˝/211 lbs; Mississippi Valley State; 1992: Ind, rnd 8; B3/3/1969 Marland, TX

YEAR	TEAM	G (GS, POS)	RUSH	YD	AVG (LG)	TD	REC	YD	AVG (LG)	TD	PASS	COMP	PCT	YD	AVG (LG)	TD	INT	SK	YD	QBR	KPR	OTD	PTS	TAY
1994	Ind	15(0)	18	85	4.7(27)	0	3	19	6.3(12)	0	—	—	—	—	—	—	—	—	—	—	k	1	6	363
1995	†Ind	11(0)	2	6	3.0(5)	0	2	11	5.5(6)	0	—	—	—	—	—	—	—	—	—	—	k	—	0	150
NFL	2	26(0)	20	91	4.6(27)	0	5	30	6.0(12)	0	—	—	—	—	—	—	—	—	—	—	k	1	6	512

Humphrey, Tommy Thomas Gale, C, 6´6˝/260 lbs; Abilene Christian; 1973: Cle, rnd 10; B3/24/1950 Comanche, TX **1974** KC 5

Humphrey, Tommy Thomas Franklin, G-T, 6´3˝/280 lbs; Iowa; B12/16/1962 Huntington, WV **1987** NYJ 3 (3)

Humphrey, Tory Tory, TE, 6´2˝/257 lbs; Central Michigan; B1/20/1983 Saginaw, MI **2005** GB 1 (0)

Humphreys, Bob Robert Keith, K, 6´1˝/240 lbs; Wichita State; B3/30/1940 Los Angeles, CA **[K]** **1967** Den-A 8 **1968** Den-A 2 **NFL** 10 [2 yrs]

Humphries, Leonard Leonard Deshawn, DB, 5´9˝/180 lbs; Penn State; 1992: Buf, rnd 8; B6/19/1970 Akron, OH **1994** Ind 13 (0)

Humphries, Stan William Stanley, QB, 6´2˝/223 lbs; LSU; Louisiana-Monroe; 1988: Was, rnd 6; B4/14/1965 Shreveport, LA

YEAR	TEAM	G (GS, POS)	RUSH	YD	AVG (LG)	TD	REC	YD	AVG (LG)	TD	PASS	COMP	PCT	YD	AVG (LG)	TD	INT	SK	YD	QBR	KPR	OTD	PTS	TAY
1989	Was	2(0)	5	10	2.0(9)	0	—	—	—	—	10	5	50.0	91	9.1(39)	1	1	3	9	—	—	—	0	21
1990	Was	7(5, qb)	23	106	4.6(17)	2	—	—	—	—	156	91	58.3	1015	6.5(44)	3	10	9	62	—	—	—	12	249
1992	†SD	16(15, QB)	28	79	2.8(25)	4	—	—	—	—	454	263	57.9	3356	7.4(67)	16	18	28	218	76.4	—	—	24	1157
1993	SD	12(10, QB)	8	37	4.6(27)	0	—	—	—	—	324	173	53.4	1981	6.1(48)	12	10	18	142	71.5	—	—	0	688
1994	†SD	15(15, QB)	19	19	1.0(8)	0	—	—	—	—	453	264	58.3	3209	7.1(**99**)	17	12	25	223	81.6	—	—	0	1229
1995	†SD	15(15, QB)	33	53	1.6(18)	1	1	-4	-4.0(-4)	0	478	282	59.0	3381	7.1(51)	17	14	23	197	80.4	—	—	6	1277
1996	SD	13(13, QB)	21	28	1.3(7)	0	—	—	—	—	416	232	55.8	2670	6.4(63)	18	13	20	187	76.7	—	—	0	933
1997	SD	8(8, QB)	13	24	1.8(11)	0	—	—	—	—	225	121	53.8	1488	6.6(72)	5	6	18	144	—	—	—	0	553
NFL	8	88(81)	150	356	2.4(27)	7	1	-4	-4.0(-4)	0	2516	1431	56.9	17191	6.8(99)	89	84	144	1182	75.8	—	—	42	6105

Humphries, Stefan Stefan Govan, G, 6´3˝/265 lbs; Michigan; 1984: Chi, rnd 3; B1/20/1962 Fort Lauderdale, FL **1984** ChiB 10 (0) **1985**†ChiB 11 (0) **1986**†ChiB 4 (0) **1987**†Den 7 (7, RG) **1988** Den 1 (1) **NFL** 33 (8) [5 yrs]

Hundon, James James Henry, WR, 6´1˝/180 lbs; Portland State; B4/9/1971 San Francisco, CA

YEAR	TEAM	G (GS, POS)	RUSH	YD	AVG (LG)	TD	REC	YD	AVG (LG)	TD	PASS	COMP	PCT	YD	AVG (LG)	TD	INT	SK	YD	QBR	KPR	OTD	PTS	TAY
1996	Cin	5(0)	—	—	—	—	1	14	14.0(14)	1	—	—	—	—	—	—	—	—	—	—	kp	—	6	87
1997	Cin	16(0)	—	—	—	—	16	285	17.8(61)	2	—	—	—	—	—	—	—	—	—	—	k	—	12	172
1998	Cin	9(3)	—	—	—	—	10	112	11.2(17)	1	—	—	—	—	—	—	—	—	—	—	—	—	6	61
1999	Cin	6(0)	—	—	—	—	1	5	5.0(5)	0	—	—	—	—	—	—	—	—	—	—	—	—	0	3
NFL	4	36(3)	—	—	—	—	28	416	14.9(61)	4	—	—	—	—	—	—	—	—	—	—	kp	—	24	322

Huneke, Charlie Charles Franklin, T, 6´3˝/225 lbs; St. Mary's (TX); Benedictine; B1/1/1921 Lincoln, IL, D9/5/1990 **1946** ChiR-A 14 (11, RT) **1947** ChiR-A 1 (0) **1947** Bkn-A 12 (0) **1948** Bkn-A 2 (0) **AAFC** 29 (11) [3 yrs]

Hunley, LaMonte Kenneth LaMonte, LB, 6´2˝/240 lbs; Arizona; B1/31/1963 Richmond, VA **1985** Ind 16 (0) **1986** Ind 6 (2) **NFL** 22 (2) [2 yrs]

Hunley, Ricky Ricky Cardell, LB, 6´2˝/242 lbs; Arizona; 1984: Cin, rnd 1; B11/11/1961 Petersburg, VA **1984**†Den 8 (0) **1985** Den 16 (2) **1986**†Den 16 (15, RILB) **1987**†Den 12 (12, RILB) **1988** Phx 16 (0) **1989** LARd 12 (1) **1990** LARd 11 (0) **NFL** 91 (30) [7 yrs]

Hunnicutt, Jim James Edward, G, 6´0˝/175 lbs; South Carolina; 1947: LA, rnd 28; B6/10/1923 **1948** Det 1 (0)

Hunsinger, Chuck Charles Ray, HB, 6´0˝/188 lbs; Florida; 1950: ChiB, rnd 1; B7/25/1925 Harrisburg, IL, D3/23/1998 Carrier Mills, IL

YEAR	TEAM	G (GS, POS)	RUSH	YD	AVG (LG)	TD	REC	YD	AVG (LG)	TD	PASS	COMP	PCT	YD	AVG (LG)	TD	INT	SK	YD	QBR	KPR	OTD	PTS	TAY
1950	†ChiB	10	61	326	5.3(45)	2	1	20	20.0(20)	0	—	—	—	—	—	—	—	—	—	—	kp	—	12	518
1951	ChiB	12(lh)	73	369	5.1(39)	3	6	59	9.8(19)	1	—	—	—	—	—	—	—	—	—	—	kp	—	24	442
1952	ChiB	12(LH)	58	139	2.4(30)	0	16	170	10.6(30)	2	—	—	—	—	—	—	—	—	—	—	k	—	12	317
NFL	3	34	192	834	4.3(45)	5	23	249	10.8(30)	3	—	—	—	—	—	—	—	—	—	—	kp	—	48	1277

Hunt, Ben Ben, T, 5´9˝/185 lbs; Alabama; B9/16/1900 Scottsboro, AL, D6/1981 Scottsboro, AL **1923** Tol 3 (0)

Hunt, Bob Robert Steven, RB, 6´1˝/210 lbs; Heidelberg; 1974: Cle, rnd 14; B9/3/1951 Toledo, OH **1974** Cle 2

Hunt, Bobby Robert Kenneth, DB, 6´1˝/185 lbs; Auburn; 1962: DalT, rnd 11; B8/15/1940 Lanett, AL **[I]** **1962**†DalT-A☆14 (LS) **1963** KC-A 14 (LS) **1964** KC-A★14 (LS) **1965** KC-A 14 (LS) **1966**†KC-A☆14 (LS) **1967** KC-A 14 (LS) **1969** Cin-A 14 (RS)

YEAR	TEAM	G (GS, POS)	RUSH	YD	AVG (LG)	TD	REC	YD	AVG (LG)	TD	PASS	COMP	PCT	YD	AVG (LG)	TD	INT	SK	YD	QBR	KPR	OTD	PTS	TAY
1968	Cin-A	14(RS)	1	5	5.0(5)	1	—	—	—	—	—	—	—	—	—	—	—	—	—	—	i	—	6	25
NFL	8	112	1	5	5.0(5)	1	—	—	—	—	—	—	—	—	—	—	—	—	—	—	i	1	12	570

Hunt, Byron Byron Ray, LB, 6´5˝/238 lbs; SMU; 1981: NYG, rnd 9; B12/17/1958 Longview, TX **1981**†NYG 16 (3) **1982** NYG 9 (1) **1983** NYG 16 (5, rolb) **1984**†NYG 13 (6, LOLB) **1985**†NYG 16 (11, LOLB) **1986**†NYG 16 (0) **1987** NYG 12 (0) **1988** NYG 2 (0) **NFL** 100 (26) [8 yrs]

Hunt, Calvin Calvin Cornelius, C, 6´3˝/245 lbs; Baylor; 1970: Pit, rnd 11; B12/31/1947 Oceanside, CA **1970** Phi 7 **1972** Hou 10 (C) **1973** Hou 4 **NFL** 21 [3 yrs]

Hunt, Charlie Charles Edward, LB, 6´2˝/215 lbs; Florida State; 1973: SF, rnd 10; B2/1/1951 St. Augustine, FL **1973** SF 8 **1976** TB 5 **NFL** 13 [2 yrs]

Hunt, Cletidus Cletidus Marquell, DT-DE, 6´4˝/305 lbs; Kentucky State; 1999: GB, rnd 3; B1/2/1976 Memphis, TN **1999** GB 11 (1) **2000** GB 16 (11, LDE/rdt) **2001**†GB 12 (4) **2002**†GB 14 (14, RDT) **2003**†GB 16 (16, RDT) **2004**†GB 16 (14, RDT/ldt) **NFL** 85 (60) [6 yrs]

Hunt, Daryl Daryl Lynn, LB, 6´3˝/229 lbs; Oklahoma; 1979: Hou, rnd 6; B11/3/1956 Odessa, TX **1979**†Hou 16 **1980**†Hou 16 (6, lilb) **1981** Hou 16 (13, RILB) **1982** Hou 9 (9, RILB) **1983** Hou 16 (3) **1984** Hou 5 (0) **NFL** 78 (31) [6 yrs]

Hunt, Ervin Ervin J., DB, 6´2˝/ 190 lbs; Fresno State; 1970: GB, rnd 6; B7/1/1947 Fowler, CA **1970** GB 6

Hunt, Gary Gary Lynn, DB, 5´11˝/175 lbs; Memphis; 1986: Cin, rnd 6; B10/28/1963 Texarkana, TX **1987** Cin 3 (3)

Hunt, George George Arthur, K, 6´1˝/215 lbs; Tennessee; 1972: Cle, rnd 5; B8/3/1949 Marietta, GA **[K]** **1973** Bal 14 **1975** NYG 14 **NFL** 28 [2 yrs]

Hunt, Jackie John Seva, FB, 6´0˝/192 lbs; Marshall; 1942: ChiB, rnd 13; B2/17/1920 Huntington, WV, D6/21/1991 Huntington, WV

YEAR	TEAM	G (GS, POS)	RUSH	YD	AVG (LG)	TD	REC	YD	AVG (LG)	TD	PASS	COMP	PCT	YD	AVG (LG)	TD	INT	SK	YD	QBR	KPR	OTD	PTS	TAY
1945	ChiB	4(1)	1	1	1.0(1)	0	—	—	—	—	—	—	—	—	—	—	—	—	—	—	P	—	0	1

Hunt, Jim James Lee, DT-DE, 5´11˝/250 lbs; Prairie View A&M; 1960: SL, rnd 16; B10/5/1938 Atlanta, TX, D11/22/1975 Philadelphia, PA **1960** Bos-A 6 **1961** Bos-A★14 (RDT) **1962** Bos-A 14 (ldt) **1963**†Bos-A 14 (ldt) **1964** Bos-A 14 (LDT) **1965** Bos-A 14 (LDT) **1966** Bos-A★14 (LDT) **1967** Bos-A★14 (LDT) **1968** Bos-A☆14 (14, LDT) **1969** Bos-A✧14 (14, LDT) **1970** Bos 14 (13, LDT) **NFL** 146 (41) [11 yrs]

Hunt, John John Stephen, T-G, 6´4˝/254 lbs; Florida; 1984: Dal, rnd 9; B11/6/1962 Orlando, FL **1984** Dal 2 (1) **1987** TB 1 (0) **NFL** 3 (1) [2 yrs]

Hunt, Kevin Richard Kevin, T-G, 6´5˝/260 lbs; Doane; 1971: GB, rnd 10; B11/29/1948 Framington, MA **1972** GB 3 **1973** NE 1 **1973** Hou 4 **1974** Hou 13 **1975** Hou 13 **1976** Hou 13 (6, lt) **1977** Hou 13 (12, RT) **1978** NO 10 **NFL** 70 (18) [7 yrs]

Hunt, Mike Michael Anthony, LB, 6´2˝/240 lbs; Minnesota; 1978: GB, rnd 2; B10/6/1956 Madison, WI **1978** GB 16 (MLB) **1979** GB 3 **1980** GB 3 (3) **NFL** 22 (3) [3 yrs]

Hunt, Ron Ronald Michele, T, 6´6˝/261 lbs; Oregon; 1976: Cin, rnd 8; B1/27/1955 Los Angeles, CA **1976** Cin 12 **1977** Cin 13 (3) **1978** Cin 3 **NFL** 28 (3) [3 yrs]

Hunt, Sam Samuel Kay, LB, 6´1˝/248 lbs; Stephen F. Austin State; 1974: NE, rnd 15; B8/6/1951 Longview, TX **1974** NE 14 (14, RILB) **1975** NE 13 (13, RILB) **1976**†NE 14 (11, RILB) **1977** NE 13 (13, RILB) **1978**†NE 15 (15, RILB) **1979** NE 15 (15, RILB) **NFL** 84 (81) [6 yrs]

YEAR	TEAM	G (GS, POS)	RUSH	YD	AVG(LG)	TD	REC	YD	AVG(LG)	TD	PASS COMP	PCT	YD	AVG(LG)	TD	INT	SK	YD	QBR	KPR	OTD	PTS	TAY

HUNTER, AL Alfonse, RB, 5´11˝/195 lbs; Notre Dame; 1977: Sea, rnd S4; B2/21/1955 Greenville, NC [R]

1977	Sea	12	32	179	5.6(20)	1	5	42	8.4(20)	0	—	—	—	—	—	—	—	—	—	k	—	6	490
1978	Sea	16(5, rb)	105	348	3.3(55)	2	12	172	14.3(21)	0	—	—	—	—	—	—	—	—	—	k	—	12	599
1979	Sea	15	34	174	5.1(67)	1	7	77	11.0(18)	0	—	—	—	—	—	—	—	—	—	k	—	6	297
1980	Sea	9(0)	9	14	1.6(7)	0	3	40	13.3(18)	0	—	—	—	—	—	—	—	—	—	k	—	0	82
NFL	4	52(5)	180	715	4.0(67)	4	27	331	12.3(21)	0	—	—	—	—	—	—	—	—	—	k	—	24	1468

HUNTER, ART Arthur James, C-T, 6´4˝/245 lbs; Notre Dame; 1954: GB, rnd 1; B4/24/1933 Fairport Harbor, OH **1954** GB 12 (RT) **1956** Cle 8 **1957**†Cle 12 (C) **1958**†Cle 12 (C) **1959** Cle◊12 (C) **1960** LARm✧12 (C) **1961** LARm 14 (C) **1962** LARm 2 **1963** LARm 12 (C) **1964** LARm 14 (C) **1965** Pit 9 (C) **NFL** 119 [11 yrs]

HUNTER, BILLY George William, B, 6´1˝/185 lbs; Syracuse; B11/5/1942 Camden, NJ **1966** Mia-A 3

| 1965 | Was | 3 | — | — | — | — | 1 | 29 | 29.0(29) | 0 | — | — | — | — | — | — | — | — | — | k | — | 6 | 182 |
| NFL | 2 | 6 | — | — | — | — | 1 | 29 | 29.0(29) | 0 | — | — | — | — | — | — | — | — | — | k | — | 6 | 191 |

HUNTER, BRICE Brice H., WR, 6´2˝/206 lbs; Georgia; 1996: Mia, rnd 7; B4/21/1974 Coconut Creek, FL, D4/18/2004 Chicago, IL **1997** TB 3 (0)

| 1998 | TB | 10(0) | — | — | — | — | 4 | 73 | 18.3(45) | 0 | — | — | — | — | — | — | — | — | — | — | — | 8 | 42 |
| NFL | 2 | 13(0) | — | — | — | — | 4 | 73 | 18.3(45) | 0 | — | — | — | — | — | — | — | — | — | — | — | 8 | 42 |

HUNTER, DAMEON Dameon DeShawn, RB, 5´11˝/221 lbs; Utah; B2/18/1979 San Bernardino, CA **2002** Bal 1 (0)

HUNTER, DANIEL Daniel Lewis, DB, 5´11˝/178 lbs; Henderson State; B9/1/1962 Arkadelphia, AR **1985** Den 16 (0) **1986** Den 10 (0) **1986** SD 5 (2) **1987** SD 12 (0) **NFL** 43 (2) [3 yrs]

HUNTER, EARNEST Earnest, RB, 5´8˝/201 lbs; Southeastern Oklahoma State; B12/21/1970 Longview, TX

1995	Cle	10(0)	30	100	3.3(15)	0	5	42	8.4(17)	0	—	—	—	—	—	—	—	—	—	kp	—	0	309
1996	Bal	5(0)	1	0	0.0(0)	0	1	25	25.0(25)	0	—	—	—	—	—	—	—	—	—	kp	—	0	56
1996	NO	6(0)	14	44	3.1(9)	0	17	138	8.1(22)	0	1	0	0.0	0	0.0	0	0	—	—	—	k	—	0	118
NFL	2	21(0)	45	144	3.2(15)	0	23	205	8.9(25)	0	1	0	0.0	0	0.0	0	0	—	—	—	kp	—	0	483

HUNTER, EDDIE Edward Lee, RB, 5´10˝/205 lbs; Virginia Tech; 1987: NYJ, rnd 8; B1/20/1965 Reno, NV

1987	NYJ	3(3)	48	169	3.5(23)	0	5	24	4.8(8)	2	—	—	—	—	—	—	—	—	—	k	—	12	194
1987	TB	3(0)	8	41	5.1(11)	0	2	4	2.0(4)	0	—	—	—	—	—	—	—	—	—	—	—	0	43
NFL	1	6(3)	56	210	3.8(23)	0	7	28	4.0(8)	2	—	—	—	—	—	—	—	—	—	k	—	12	237

HUNTER, HERMAN Herman James, RB, 6´1˝/197 lbs; Tennessee State; 1985: Phi, rnd 11; B2/14/1961 Columbus, GA [R]

1985	Phi	16(5, rb)	27	121	4.5(74)	1	28	405	14.5(43)	1	2	1	50.0	38	19.0(38)	1	0	1	11	—	kp	—	12	691
1986	Det	16(0)	3	22	7.3(18)	0	25	218	8.7(18)	1	—	—	—	—	—	—	—	—	—	k	—	6	408
1987	Hou	3(0)	34	144	4.2(21)	0	3	17	5.7(11)	0	—	—	—	—	—	—	—	—	—	k	—	0	172
NFL	3	35(5)	64	287	4.5(74)	1	56	640	11.4(43)	2	2	1	50.0	38	19.0(38)	1	0	1	11	—	kp	—	18	1270

HUNTER, IVY JOE Ivy Joe, RB, 6´0˝/237 lbs; Kentucky; 1989: Ind, rnd 7; B11/16/1966 Gainesville, FL

1989	Ind	16(1)	13	47	3.6(11)	0	—	—	—	—	—	—	—	—	—	—	—	—	—	k	—	0	45
1990	Ind	16(1)	—	—	—	—	—	—	—	—	—	—	—	—	—	—	—	—	—	—	—	0	0
1991	NE	13(11, FB)	18	53	2.9(9)	0	11	97	8.8(25)	0	—	—	—	—	—	—	—	—	—	—	—	0	102
NFL	3	45(13)	31	100	3.2(11)	0	11	97	8.8(25)	0	—	—	—	—	—	—	—	—	—	—	—	0	147

HUNTER, JAMES James Edward, DB, 6´3˝/195 lbs; Grambling State; 1976: Det, rnd 1; B3/8/1954 Silsbee, TX [I] **1976** Det✩13 (8, FS) **1977** Det 14 (14, LCB) **1978** Det 9 (5, lcb) **1979** Det 15 (15, FS) **1980** Det 16 (16, RCB) **1981** Det 12 (12, RCB) **1982** Det 7 (7, RCB) **NFL** 86 (77) [7 yrs]

HUNTER, JAMES James Dale, NT-DE, 6´5˝/251 lbs; USC; 1981: Pit, rnd 9; B9/13/1957 Oklahoma City, OK **1982** Bal 9 (1)

HUNTER, JAVIN Javin Edward, WR, 5´11˝/190 lbs; Notre Dame; 2002: Bal, rnd 6; B5/9/1980 Detroit, MI

| 2002 | Bal | 12(3) | 1 | 9 | 9.0(9) | 0 | 5 | 35 | 7.0(8) | 0 | — | — | — | — | — | — | — | — | — | k | — | 0 | 72 |

HUNTER, JEFF Jeffrey Orlando, DE, 6´5˝/286 lbs; Albany State (GA); 1989: Phx, rnd 11; B4/12/1966 Hampton, VA **1990** Buf 3 (0) **1990** Det 7 (0) **1991**†Det 16 (0) **1992** Det 4 (0) **1992**†Mia 7 (0) **1993** Mia 5 (1) **1994** TB 1 (0) **NFL** 43 (1) [5 yrs]

HUNTER, JOHN John Rosel, T, 6´8˝/294 lbs; Brigham Young; 1989: Min, rnd 3; B8/16/1965 Roseburg, OR **1989** Atl 4 (0) **1990** Atl 15 (3) **1991** Atl 2 (0) **1992** Sea 5 (3) **NFL** 26 (6) [4 yrs]

HUNTER, MERLE Merle Lucas, T, /185 lbs; none; B4/28/1906 Ossian, IN, D7/15/1982 Ossian, IN **1925** Ham 3 (0) **1926** Ham 1 (0) **NFL** 4 (0) [2 yrs]

HUNTER, MONTY Orie Montgomery, DB, 6´0˝/202 lbs; Salem; 1982: Dal, rnd 4; B1/21/1959 Dover, OH **1982**†Dal 9 (0) **1983** SL 5 (0) **NFL** 14 (0) [2 yrs]

HUNTER, PATRICK Patrick Edward, DB, 5´11˝/186 lbs; Nevada-Reno; 1986: Sea, rnd 3; B10/24/1964 San Francisco, CA **1986** Sea 16 (0) **1987**†Sea 11 (11, RCB) **1988**†Sea 10 (7, rcb) **1989** Sea 16 (16, RCB) **1990** Sea 16 (16, RCB) **1991** Sea 15 (15, RCB) **1992** Sea 16 (16, RCB) **1993** Sea 15 (15, RCB) **1994** Sea 5 (5, rcb) **1995** Arz 5 (5, rcb) **NFL** 125 (104) [10 yrs]

HUNTER, PETE Ralph Everette, DB, 6´2˝/212 lbs; Virginia Union; 2002: Dal, rnd 5; B5/25/1980 Atlantic City, NJ **2002** Dal 11 (2) **2003**†Dal 16 (1) **2004** Dal 3 (3) **2005** Cle 4 (0) **NFL** 34 (6) [4 yrs]

HUNTER, RAMEY Raymond Q., E, 6´0˝/178 lbs; Marshall; B8/26/1910 Huntington, WV, D1/17/1992 Livingston, MT **1933** Por 2 (0)

HUNTER, SCOTT James Scott, QB, 6´2˝/205 lbs; Alabama; 1971: GB, rnd 6; B11/11/1947 Mobile, AL

1971	GB	13(QB)	21	50	2.4(16)	4	—	—	—	—	163	75	46.0	1210	7.4(77)	7	17	11	81	46.1	—	—	24	50
1972	†GB	14(QB)	22	37	1.7(15)	5	—	—	—	—	199	86	43.2	1252	6.3(49)	6	9	13	86	55.5	—	—	30	383
1973	GB	8(QB)	8	3	0.4(6)	1	—	—	—	—	84	35	41.7	442	5.3(30)	2	4	10	89	—	—	—	6	84
1974	Buf	1	—	—	—	—	—	—	—	—	—	—	—	—	—	—	—	—	—	—	—	—	—	—
1976	Atl	8(QB)	14	41	2.9(16)	1	—	—	—	—	110	51	46.4	633	5.8(34)	5	4	9	81	64.7	—	—	6	233
1977	Atl	7(qb)	28	70	2.5(18)	1	—	—	—	—	151	70	46.4	898	5.9(49)	2	3	11	88	61.6	—	—	6	419
1979	Det	13	2	3	1.5(2)	1	—	—	—	—	41	18	43.9	321	7.8(82)	1	1	4	33	—	—	—	6	139
NFL	7	64	95	204	2.1(18)	13	—	—	—	—	748	335	44.8	4756	6.4(82)	23	38	58	458	55.0	—	—	78	1307

HUNTER, STAN Stanford Keith, WR, 6´2˝/184 lbs; Bowling Green State; B11/29/1963 Dayton, OH

| 1987 | NYJ | 3(0) | — | — | — | — | 6 | 50 | 8.3(12) | 1 | — | — | — | — | — | — | — | — | — | — | — | 6 | 30 |

HUNTER, TONY Tony Wayne, TE, 6´4˝/237 lbs; Notre Dame; 1983: Buf, rnd 1; B5/22/1960 Cincinnati, OH

1983	Buf	13(3)	1	28	14.0(24)	0	36	402	11.2(40)	3	—	—	—	—	—	—	—	—	—	—	—	18	244
1984	Buf	11(9, TE)	1	6	6.0(6)	0	33	331	10.0(30)	2	—	—	—	—	—	—	—	—	—	—	—	12	182
1985	†LARm	16(9, TE)	—	—	—	—	50	562	11.2(47)	4	—	—	—	—	—	—	—	—	—	—	—	24	301
1986	LARm	7(1)	1	-6	-6.0(-6)	0	15	206	13.7(42)	0	—	—	—	—	—	—	—	—	—	—	—	0	97
NFL	4	47(22)	4	28	7.0(24)	0	134	1501	11.2(47)	9	—	—	—	—	—	—	—	—	—	—	—	54	824

HUNTER, TONY Anthony Fernando, RB, 5´9˝/215 lbs; Minnesota; B2/24/1963 Memphis, TN

| 1987 | GB | 1(0) | 1 | 0 | 0.0(0) | 0 | — | — | — | — | — | — | — | — | — | — | — | — | — | — | — | 0 | 0 |

HUNTER, TOREY Torey Hayward, DB, 5´9˝/176 lbs; Washington State; 1995: Hou, rnd 3; B2/10/1972 Tacoma, WA **1995** Hou 12 (0)

HUNTER, WAYNE Wayne, T, 6´5˝/303 lbs; Hawaii; 2003: Sea, rnd 3; B7/2/1981 Honolulu, HI **2004** Sea 1 (0) **2005** Sea 1 (0) **NFL** 2 (0) [2 yrs]

HUNTER, WILL Will, DB, 5´10˝/190 lbs; Syracuse; B3/24/1979 Crozer, PA **2005** Min 13 (0)

HUNTINGTON, GREG Gregory Gerard, C-G, 6´3˝/297 lbs; Penn State; 1993: Was, rnd 5; B9/22/1970 Morristown, NJ **1993** Was 9 (0) **1995** Jax 4 (0) **1996** Jax 2 (0) **1997** ChiB 1 (0) **1998** ChiB 2 (0) **NFL** 18 (0) [5 yrs]

HUNTLEY, RICHARD Richard Earl, RB, 5´11˝/224 lbs; Winston-Salem State; 1996: Atl, rnd 4; B9/18/1972 Monroe, NC

1996	Atl	1(0)	2	8	4.0(5)	0	1	14	14.0(14)	0	—	—	—	—	—	—	—	—	—	—	—	0	15
1998	Pit	16(1)	55	242	4.4(48)	3	18	6.0(7)		0	—	—	—	—	—	—	—	—	—	k	—	6	290
1999	Pit	16(2)	93	567	6.1(52)	5	27	253	9.4(25)	3	—	—	—	—	—	—	—	—	—	k	—	48	870
2000	Pit	13(0)	46	215	4.7(30)	3	10	91	9.1(19)	0	—	—	—	—	—	—	—	—	—	k	—	20	291
2001	Car	14(9, RB)	165	665	4.0(25)	2	21	101	4.8(23)	1	1	0	0.0	0	0.0	0	0	1	—	—	k	—	18	746

YEAR	TEAM	G (GS, POS)	RUSH	YD	AVG (LG)	TD	REC	YD	AVG (LG)	TD	PASS	COMP	PCT	YD	AVG (LG)	TD	INT	SK	YD	QBR	KPR	OTD	PTS	TAY
2002	Det	3(1)	3	4	1.3(3)	0	—	—	—	—	—	—	—	—	—	—	—	—	—	—	—	—	0	4
NFL	6	63(13)	364	1701	4.7(52)	11	62	477	7.7(25)	4	1	0	0.0	0	0.0	0	0	1	0	—	k	—	92	2215

Hupke, Tom Thomas George, G-T, 5´10˝/192 lbs; Alabama; B12/29/1910 East Chicago, IN, D9/7/1959 Detroit, MI **1934** Det 9 (1) **1935**†Det 10 (4) **1936** Det 7 (2) **1937** Det 11 (0) **1938** Cle 10 (7, RG) **1939** Cle 8 (1) **NFL** 55 (15) [6 yrs]

Hurd, Jeff Jeffrey Tonja, LB, 6´2˝/245 lbs; Kansas State; B5/25/1964 Monroe, LA **1987** Dal 5 (0)

Hurlburt, John John Blair, HB, 6´0˝/175 lbs; Chicago; B7/23/1898 Burlington, IA, D3/3/1968 Napa County, CA **1924** ChiC☆9 (7, RH), 18 **1925** ChiC 5 (1) **NFL** 14 (8) [2 yrs]

Hurley, Bill William John, DB, 5´11˝/195 lbs; Syracuse; 1980: Pit, rnd 4; B6/15/1957 Kenmore, NY **1983** NO 4 (0) **1983** Buf 10 (0)

YEAR	TEAM	G (GS, POS)	RUSH	YD	AVG (LG)	TD	REC	YD	AVG (LG)	TD	PASS	COMP	PCT	YD	AVG (LG)	TD	INT	SK	YD	QBR	KPR	OTD	PTS	TAY
1982	NO	9(0)	—	—	—	—	1	39	39.0(39)	1	—	—	—	—	—	—	—	—	—	—	i	—	6	46
NFL	2	23(0)	—	—	—	—	1	39	39.0(39)	1	—	—	—	—	—	—	—	—	—	—	pi	—	6	41

Hurley, George George Frank, G, 6´0˝/200 lbs; Washington State; B10/19/1909 San Francisco, CA, D12/17/1989 Twain Harte, CA **1932** Bos☆10 (10, RG) **1933** Bos☆10 (9, LG) **NFL** 20 (19) [2 yrs]

Hurley, John John J., E, 6´3˝/192 lbs; Washington State; B1/9/1907 San Francisco, CA, D1/1983 Santa Rosa, CA **1931** Cle 10 (8, LE)

Hurst, Bill William, T, 6´1˝/202 lbs; none; B6/23/1903 Rock Island, IL, D11/1966 **1924** Ken 5 (5, LT)

Hurst, Maurice Maurice Roy, DB, 5´10˝/185 lbs; Southern (LA); 1989: NE, rnd 4; B9/17/1967 New Orleans, LA **[I]** **1989** NE 16 (14, LCB) **1990** NE 16 (16, RCB) **1991** NE 15 (14, RCB) **1992** NE 16 (16, RCB) **1993** NE 16 (16, RCB) **1994**†NE 16 (16, RCB) **1995** NE 10 (10, RCB) **NFL** 105 (102) [7 yrs]

Hurston, Chuck Charles Frederick, DE-LB, 6´6˝/240 lbs; Auburn; 1965: Buf, rnd 12/GB, rnd 15; B11/9/1942 Columbus, GA **1965** KC-A 14 **1966**†KC-A 14 (RDE) **1967** KC-A 14 (RDE) **1968**†KC-A 14 **1969**†KC-A 14 **1970** KC 14 **1971** Buf 9 **NFL** 93 [7 yrs]

Hurt, Eric Eric, DB, 5´11˝/171 lbs; San Jose State; B6/11/1957 **1980** Dal 4 (0)

Husak, Todd Todd, QB, 6´3˝/216 lbs; Stanford; 2000: Was, rnd 6; B7/6/1978 Long Beach, CA

YEAR	TEAM	G (GS, POS)	RUSH	YD	AVG (LG)	TD	REC	YD	AVG (LG)	TD	PASS	COMP	PCT	YD	AVG (LG)	TD	INT	SK	YD	QBR	KPR	OTD	PTS	TAY
2000	Was	1(0)	1	-1	-1.0(-1)	0	—	—	—	—	2	2	100.0	2	-1.0(6)	0	0	—	—	—	—	—	0	-2

Husmann, Ed Edward Earl, DT-G-DE-LB, 6´2˝/245 lbs; Nebraska; 1953: ChiC, rnd 9; B8/6/1931 Schuyler, NE **1953** ChiC 12 (lg) **1956** ChiC 12 **1957** ChiC 12 **1958** ChiC 4 **1959** ChiC 12 **1960** Dal 12 (RDT) **1961**†Hou-A★14 (RDT) **1962**†Hou-A★14 (RDT) **1963** Hou-A★14 (RDT) **1964** Hou-A 14 (RDT) **1965** Hou-A 14 (RDT) **NFL** 134 [11 yrs]

Hust, Al Albert, E, 6´1˝/220 lbs; Tennessee; 1943: ChiC, rnd 4; B4/9/1921 Czechoslovakia, D4/16/1984 Knoxville, TN

YEAR	TEAM	G (GS, POS)	RUSH	YD	AVG (LG)	TD	REC	YD	AVG (LG)	TD	PASS	COMP	PCT	YD	AVG (LG)	TD	INT	SK	YD	QBR	KPR	OTD	PTS	TAY
1946	ChiC	10(4)	—	—	—	—	1	9	9.0(9)	0	—	—	—	—	—	—	—	—	—	—	—	—	0	5

Husted, Michael Michael James, K, 6´0˝/190 lbs; Virginia; B6/16/1970 El Paso, TX **[K]** **1993** TB 16 (0) **1994** TB 16 (0) **1995** TB 16 (0) **1996** TB 16 (0) **1997**†TB 16 (0) **1999** Oak 13 (0) **2000** Was 4 (0) **2002** KC 6 (0)

YEAR	TEAM	G (GS, POS)	RUSH	YD	AVG (LG)	TD	REC	YD	AVG (LG)	TD	PASS	COMP	PCT	YD	AVG (LG)	TD	INT	SK	YD	QBR	KPR	OTD	PTS	TAY
1998	TB	16(0)	1	20	20.0(20)	0	—	—	—	—	—	—	—	—	—	—	—	—	—	—	K	—	92	20
NFL	9	119(0)	1	20	20.0(20)	0	—	—	—	—	—	—	—	—	—	—	—	—	—	—	KP	—	618	20

Hutcherson, Ken Kenneth Lee, LB, 6´1˝/220 lbs; West Alabama; 1974: Dal, rnd 4; B7/14/1952 Anniston, AL **1974** Dal 14 **1975** SD 8 **NFL** 22 [2 yrs]

Hutchins, Paul Paul Andre, T, 6´5˝/335 lbs; Western Michigan; 1993: GB, rnd 6; B2/11/1970 Chicago, IL **1993** GB 1 (0) **1994**†GB 16 (1) **NFL** 17 (1) [2 yrs]

Hutchins, Von Tahaya De'Von, DB, 5´11˝/184 lbs; Mississippi; 2004: Ind, rnd 6; B2/14/1981 Natchez, MS **2004**†Ind 16 (1) **2005** Ind 3 (0) **NFL** 19 (1) [2 yrs]

Hutchinson, Bill Wiliam David, QB, 5´9˝/180 lbs; Dartmouth; B3/9/1916 Bronx, NY

YEAR	TEAM	G (GS, POS)	RUSH	YD	AVG (LG)	TD	REC	YD	AVG (LG)	TD	PASS	COMP	PCT	YD	AVG (LG)	TD	INT	SK	YD	QBR	KPR	OTD	PTS	TAY
1942	NYG	2(0)	7	27	3.9(15)	0	—	—	—	—	4	1	25.0	3	-0.8(-3)	0	2	—	—	—	Pp	—	0	-59

Hutchinson, Chad Chad Martin, QB, 6´5˝/237 lbs; Stanford; B2/21/1977 Boulder, CO

YEAR	TEAM	G (GS, POS)	RUSH	YD	AVG (LG)	TD	REC	YD	AVG (LG)	TD	PASS	COMP	PCT	YD	AVG (LG)	TD	INT	SK	YD	QBR	KPR	OTD	PTS	TAY
2002	Dal	9(9, QB)	18	74	4.1(18)	0	—	—	—	—	250	127	50.8	1555	6.2(58)	7	8	34	265	—	—	—	0	567
2003	Dal	1(0)	2	-3	-1.5(-1)	0	—	—	—	—	2	1	50.0	8	4.0(8)	0	0	—	—	—	—	—	0	1
2004	ChiB	5(5, QB)	6	14	2.3(11)	0	—	—	—	—	161	92	57.1	903	5.6(63)	4	3	23	160	73.6	—	—	0	366
NFL	3	15(14)	26	85	3.3(18)	0	—	—	—	—	413	220	53.3	2466	6.0(63)	11	11	57	425	69.1	—	—	0	933

Hutchinson, Ralph Ralph, T, 6´2˝/220 lbs; Tennessee-Chattanooga; 1948: NYG, rnd 8/1949: ChiH-A, rnd 7; B5/2/1924 Silas, AL, D1/10/1990 **1949** NYG 10 (1)

Hutchinson, Scott Scott Rawls, DE, 6´4˝/246 lbs; Florida; 1978: Buf, rnd 2; B5/27/1956 Winter Park, FL **1978** Buf 16 **1979** Buf 16 (5, rde) **1980**†Buf 16 (3) **1981**†TB 16 (0) **1983** Buf 5 (0) **NFL** 69 (8) [5 yrs]

Hutchinson, Steve Steven, G, 6´5˝/313 lbs; Michigan; 2001: Sea, rnd 1; B11/1/1977 Fort Lauderdale, FL **2001** Sea 16 (16, LG) **2002** Sea 4 (4) **2003**†Sea★16 (16, LG) **2004**†Sea★16 (16, LG) **2005**†Sea★16 (16, LG) **NFL** 68 (68) [5 yrs]

Hutchinson, Tom Thomas Edward, TE-WR, 6´1˝/190 lbs; Kentucky; 1963: Cle, rnd 1/Buf, rnd 2; B6/15/1941 Stanford, KY

YEAR	TEAM	G (GS, POS)	RUSH	YD	AVG (LG)	TD	REC	YD	AVG (LG)	TD	PASS	COMP	PCT	YD	AVG (LG)	TD	INT	SK	YD	QBR	KPR	OTD	PTS	TAY
1963	Cle	14	—	—	—	—	9	244	27.1(70)	0	—	—	—	—	—	—	—	—	—	—	—	—	0	122
1964	†Cle	14(te)	—	—	—	—	3	24	8.0(12)	0	—	—	—	—	—	—	—	—	—	—	—	—	0	12
1965	†Cle	14	—	—	—	—	6	113	18.8(24)	2	—	—	—	—	—	—	—	—	—	—	k	—	12	37
1966	Atl	5	—	—	—	—	1	28	28.0(28)	0	—	—	—	—	—	—	—	—	—	—	—	—	0	14
NFL	4	47	—	—	—	—	19	409	21.5(70)	2	—	—	—	—	—	—	—	—	—	—	k	—	12	185

Hutchison, Anthony Anthony LaRue, RB, 5´10˝/186 lbs; Texas Tech; 1983: Chi, rnd 10; B2/4/1961 Houston, TX

YEAR	TEAM	G (GS, POS)	RUSH	YD	AVG (LG)	TD	REC	YD	AVG (LG)	TD	PASS	COMP	PCT	YD	AVG (LG)	TD	INT	SK	YD	QBR	KPR	OTD	PTS	TAY
1983	ChiB	16(0)	6	13	2.2(5)	1	—	—	—	—	—	—	—	—	—	—	—	—	—	—	k	—	6	27
1984	†ChiB	12(0)	14	39	2.8(6)	1	1	7	7.0(7)	0	—	—	—	—	—	—	—	—	—	—	—	—	6	53
1985	Buf	5(0)	2	11	5.5(7)	0	—	—	—	—	—	—	—	—	—	—	—	—	—	—	k	—	0	70
NFL	3	33(0)	22	63	2.9(7)	2	1	7	7.0(7)	0	—	—	—	—	—	—	—	—	—	—	k	—	12	150

Hutchison, Chuck Charles Arthur, G, 6´3˝/250 lbs; Ohio State; 1970: SL, rnd 2; B11/17/1948 Canton, OH **1970** SL 7 **1971** SL 13 **1972** SL 4 **1973** Cle 2 **1974** Cle 7 **1975** Cle 14 (14, LG) **NFL** 47 (14) [6 yrs]

Hutchison, Elvin Elvin Clarence, HB, 6´0˝/195 lbs; Whittier; B10/14/1912 Guthrie Center, IA, D5/24/2001 Newport Beach, FL **1939** Det 2 (0)

Huth, Jerry Gerald Bernard, G, 6´0˝/226 lbs; Wake Forest; 1956: NYG, rnd 24; B7/23/1933 Floyds Knobs, IN **1956**†NYG 11 **1959** Phi 10 (LG) **1960**†Phi 12 (lg) **1961** Min 14 (14, LG) **1962** Min 14 (12, LG) **1963** Min 13 (12, LG) **NFL** 74 (38) [6 yrs]

Huther, Bruce Bruce Albert, LB, 6´1˝/221 lbs; New Hampshire; B7/23/1954 Paterson, NJ **1977**†Dal 14 **1978**†Dal 16 **1979**†Dal 16 **1980**†Dal 15 (0) **1981** Cle 16 (2) **1982** ChiB 4 (0) **1983**†Dal 11 (1) **NFL** 92 (3) [7 yrs]

Hutson, Brian Brian Sinclair, DB, 6´1˝/198 lbs; Mississippi State; B2/20/1965 Jackson, MS **1990** NE 2 (0)

Hutson, Don Donald Montgomery 'The Alabama Antelope', E-DB-DE, 6´1˝/183 lbs; Alabama; B1/31/1913 Pine Bluff, AR, D6/26/1997 Rancho Mirage, CA; HOF 1963 **[KI]**

YEAR	TEAM	G (GS, POS)	RUSH	YD	AVG (LG)	TD	REC	YD	AVG (LG)	TD	PASS	COMP	PCT	YD	AVG (LG)	TD	INT	SK	YD	QBR	KPR	OTD	PTS	TAY
1935	GB☆	9(5, LE)	6	22	3.7	0	18	420	**23.3(83)**	**6**	—	—	—	—	—	—	—	—	—	—	K	1	43	262
1936	†GB☆	12(5, LE)	1	-3	-3.0(-3)	0	**34**	**536**	15.8(58)	**8**	—	—	—	—	—	—	—	—	—	—	—	1	54	305
1937	GB☆	11(5, LE)	14	26	1.9	0	**41**	552	13.5(78)	**7**	4	0	0.0	0	0.0	0	1	—	—	—	—	—	42	297
1938	†GB☆	10(7, LE)	3	-1	-0.3	0	32	**548**	**17.1(54)**	**9**	—	—	—	—	—	—	—	—	—	—	K	—	57	318
1939	†GB★	11(8, LE)	5	26	5.2	0	**34**	**846**	**24.9(92)**	6	—	—	—	—	—	—	—	—	—	—	K	—	38	479
1940	GB★	11(6, LE)	—	—	—	—	45	664	14.8(36)	**7**	—	—	—	—	—	—	—	—	—	—	Ki	—	**57**	361
1941	†GB★	11(4, le)	4	22	5.5(18)	2	**58**	**738**	12.7(45)	**10**	—	—	—	—	—	—	—	—	—	—	Kki	—	**95**	481
1942	GB★	11(4)	3	4	1.3(9)	0	**74**	**1211**	**16.4(73)**	**17**	—	—	—	—	—	—	—	—	—	—	Ki	—	**138**	731
1943	GB☆	10(9, LE)	6	41	6.8(16)	0	**47**	**776**	16.5(79)	**11**	4	1	25.0	38	9.5(38)	1	1	—	—	—	Ki	1	**117**	635
1944	†GB☆	10(7, LE)	12	87	7.3(27)	0	**58**	**866**	14.9(55)	**9**	3	0	0.0	0	0.0	0	0	—	—	—	Ki	—	**85**	595
1945	GB☆	10(0)	8	60	7.5(18)	1	**47**	834	17.7(75)	9	—	—	—	—	—	—	—	—	—	—	Kki	—	97	504
NFL	11	116(60)	62	284	4.6(27)	3	488	7991	16.4(92)	99	11	1	9.1	38	3.5(38)	1	2	—	—	—	Kki	3	823	4968

Hutson, Merle Merle Albert, G-T, 6´0˝/210 lbs; Heidelberg; B8/27/1908 Wood, OH, D7/24/1999, OH **1931** Cle 10 (10, RG)

Hutson, Tony Tony, G, 6´3˝/306 lbs; Northeastern State (OK); B3/13/1974 Houston, TX **1997** Dal 5 (1) **1998** Dal 10 (1) **1999**†Dal 2 (2) **2000** Was 3 (0) **NFL** 20 (4) [4 yrs]

Hutton, Jack Leon John H., E-HB, 6´1˝/192 lbs; Purdue; B8/12/1906 Indianapolis, IN, D1/2/1969 Bristol, PA **1930** Fra 3 (2)

YEAR	TEAM	G(GS, POS)	RUSH	YD	AVG(LG)	TD	REC	YD	AVG(LG)	TD	PASS	COMP	PCT	YD	AVG(LG)	TD	INT	SK	YD	QBR	KPR	OTD	PTS	TAY

HUTTON, TOM   William Thomas, P-K, 6´1˝/193 lbs; Tennessee; B7/8/1972 Memphis, TN **[P]**   **1996**†Phi 16 (0)   **1998** Phi 16 (0)   **1999**†Mia 14 (0)

1995	†Phi	16(0)	1	0	0.0(0)	0	—	—	—	—	—	—	—	—	—	—	—	—	—	P	—	0	0
1997	Phi	16(0)	1	0	0.0(0)	0	—	—	—	—	—	—	—	—	—	—	—	—	—	P	—	0	0
NFL	5	78(0)	2	0	0.0(0)	0	—	—	—	—	—	—	—	—	—	—	—	—	—	P	—	0	0

HUTTON, TREVOR   Trevor, G, 6´2˝/308 lbs; Utah State; B2/28/1980 Hilo, HI   **2004** Ind 4 (0)

HUXHOLD, KEN   Kenneth Wayne, G, 6´1˝/226 lbs; Wisconsin; 1951: ChiC, rnd 27; B8/10/1929 Kenosha, WI   **1954** Phi 11 (6, LG)   **1955** Phi 12 (RG)   **1956** Phi 12 (LG)   **1957** Phi 12 (RG)   **1958** Phi 12 (RG)   **NFL** 59 (6) [5 yrs]

HUZVAR, JOHN   John Francis, FB, 6´4˝/247 lbs; North Carolina State; Pittsburgh; B8/6/1929 Carlisle, PA

1952	Phi	12(FB)	105	349	3.3(26)	2	13	37	2.8(12)	0	—	—	—	—	—	—	—	—	—	—	—	12	388
1953	Bal	12(FB)	119	515	4.3(36)	4	6	55	9.2(30)	1	—	—	—	—	—	—	—	—	—	—	—	30	588
1954	Bal	8	19	29	1.5(6)	0	—	—	—	—	—	—	—	—	—	—	—	—	k	—	*0	14
NFL	3	32	243	893	3.7(36)	6	19	92	4.8(30)	1	—	—	—	—	—	—	—	—	k	—	42	989

HYATT, FRED   Frederick Phillip, WR, 6´3˝/200 lbs; Auburn; 1968: SL, rnd 2; B6/28/1946 Roanoke, AL   **1968** SL 1   **1969** SL 6   **1970** SL 10   **1973** NO 1   **1973** Was 1

1971	SL	14	—	—	—	—	4	58	14.5(30)	0	—	—	—	—	—	—	—	—	—	—	0	29
1972	SL	12	—	—	—	—	2	32	16.0(25)	0	—	—	—	—	—	—	—	—	k	—	0	42
NFL	6	45	—	—	—	—	6	90	15.0(30)	0	—	—	—	—	—	—	—	—	k	—	0	71

HYCHE, STEVE   Steven Jay, LB, 6´3˝/241 lbs; West Alabama; B6/12/1963 Jasper, AL   **1989** ChiB 6 (0)   **1991** Phx 16 (0)   **1992** Phx 16 (1)   **1993** Phx 2 (0)   **NFL** 40 (1) [4 yrs]

HYDE, GLENN   Glenn Thatcher, T-G-C, 6´3˝/253 lbs; Pittsburgh; B3/14/1951 Boston, MA   **1976** Den 11   **1977**†Den 14   **1978**†Den 15 (5, rt)   **1979**†Den 16   **1980** Den 16 (5, lg)   **1981** Den 16 (2)   **1982** Bal 5 (0)   **1985** Den 11 (0)   **1986** Sea 3 (0)   **1987** KC 8 (1)   **NFL** 115 (13) [10 yrs]

HYDER, GAYLON   Gaylon, DT, 6´5˝/317 lbs; TCU; B10/18/1974 Longview, TX   **1999** SL 4 (0)   **2000** SL 5 (1)   **NFL** 9 (1) [2 yrs]

HYLAND, BOB   Robert Joseph, C-G, 6´5˝/255 lbs; Boston College; 1967: GB, rnd 1; B7/21/1945 White Plains, NY   **1967**†GB 14 (c)   **1968** GB 14   **1969** GB 14   **1970** ChiB 14 (C)   **1971** NYG 14 (LG)   **1972** NYG 10   **1974** NYG 11 (C)   **1975** NYG 14 (14, C)   **1976** GB 14   **1977** NE 3

| 1973 | NYG | 14 | — | — | — | — | 1 | 16 | 16.0(16) | 0 | — | — | — | — | — | — | — | — | — | — | 0 | 8 |
| NFL | 11 | 136(14) | — | — | — | — | 1 | 16 | 16.0(16) | 0 | — | — | — | — | — | — | — | — | k | — | 0 | -21 |

HYMES, RANDY   Randy, WR, 6´3˝/211 lbs; Grambling State; B8/7/1979 Galveston, TX

2002	Bal	7(2)	—	—	—	—	6	123	20.5(43)	0	—	—	—	—	—	—	—	—	—	—	0	62
2004	Bal	14(7, WR)	—	—	—	—	26	323	12.4(57)	2	1	0	0.0	0	0.0	0	—	—	—	—	12	172
2005	Bal	16(3)	—	—	—	—	11	132	12.0(21)	2	2	0	0.0	0	0.0	0	—	—	—	—	12	76
NFL	3	37(12)	—	—	—	—	43	578	13.4(57)	4	3	0	0.0	0	0.0	0	—	—	—	—	24	309

HYNES, PAUL   Paul Edward, DB, 6´1˝/210 lbs; Louisiana Tech; 1961: DalT, rnd 12/SF, rnd 10; B9/9/1939 Sulphur, LA   **1961** DalT-A 1   **1961** NYT-A 9   **1962** NYT-A 13 (RCB)   **NFL** 23 [2 yrs]

HYNOSKI, HENRY   Henry Philip, RB, 6´0˝/210 lbs; Temple; 1975: Cle, rnd 6; B5/30/1953 Mount Carmel, PA

| 1975 | Cle | 14 | 7 | 38 | 5.4(11) | 0 | 4 | 31 | 7.8(15) | 0 | 1 | 0 | 0.0 | 0 | 0.0 | 0 | — | — | — | kp | — | 0 | 134 |

IACAVAZZI, COSMO   Cosmo Joseph, HB, 5´11˝/209 lbs; Princeton; 1965: Min, rnd 20; B8/18/1943 Scranton, PA   **1965** NYJ-A 2

IAQUANIELLO, MIKE   Michael, DB, 6´3˝/208 lbs; Michigan State; B2/13/1968 Detroit, MI   **1991** Mia 15 (0)

IDONIJE, ISRAEL   Israel, DT, 6´7˝/290 lbs; Manitoba; B11/17/1980 Brandon, Canada   **2004** ChiB 15 (0)   **2005**†ChiB 11 (1)   **NFL** 26 (1) [2 yrs]

IEREMIA, MEKELI   Mekeli Tolufale, DT, 6´2˝/244 lbs; Brigham Young; 1978: Chi, rnd 6; B3/4/1954 Niosafutu, American Samoa   **1978** Buf 2

IFEANYI, ISRAEL   Israel, aka Israel Ifeanyichukwu, DE, 6´3˝/246 lbs; USC; 1996: SF, rnd 2; B11/21/1970 Lagos, Nigeria   **1996** SF 3 (0)

IGLEHART, FLOYD   Floyd Williams, HB, 6´4˝/197 lbs; Wiley; 1958: LA, rnd 6; B1/25/1934 Terrell, TX, D9/5/1987 Dallas, TX   **1958** LARm 1

IGWEBUIKE, DONALD   Donald Amechi, K, 5´9˝/181 lbs; Clemson; 1985: TB, rnd 10; B12/27/1960 Anamba, Nigeria **[K]**   **1985** TB 16 (0)   **1986** TB 16 (0)   **1987** TB 12 (0)   **1988** TB 12 (0)   **1989** TB 16 (0)   **1990** Min 8 (0)   **NFL** 80 (0) [6 yrs]

ILESIC, HANK   Henry, P, 6´1˝/210 lbs; none; B9/7/1959 Edmonton, Canada   **1989** SD 14 (0)

ILG, RAY   Raymond Arthur, LB, 6´1˝/220 lbs; Colgate; 1967: Bos, rnd 13; B11/25/1945 Wellesley, MA   **1967** Bos-A 14   **1968** Bos-A 14 (1)   **NFL** 28 (1) [2 yrs]

ILGENFRITZ, MARK   Mark Monteith, DE, 6´4˝/250 lbs; Vanderbilt; 1974: Cle, rnd 5; B9/9/1952 Honolulu, HI   **1974** Cle 14

ILKIN, TUNCH   Tunch Ali, T-G-C, 6´3˝/263 lbs; Indiana State; 1980: Pit, rnd 6; B9/23/1957 Istanbul, Turkey   **1980** Pit 10 (0)   **1981** Pit 16 (1)   **1982**†Pit 8 (1)   **1983**†Pit 11 (10, RT)   **1984**†Pit 16 (16, LT/rt)   **1985** Pit 16 (16, RT)   **1986** Pit 15 (15, RT)   **1987** Pit 11 (11, RT)   **1988** Pit★16 (16, RT)   **1989**†Pit✩16 (16, RT)   **1990** Pit 13 (13, RT)   **1991** Pit 16 (16, RT)   **1992**†Pit 12 (12, RT)   **1993**†GB 1 (0)   **NFL** 177 (143) [14 yrs]

ILLMAN, TED   Edward Walter, B, 6´0˝/190 lbs; Montana; B11/27/1902 Glasgow, MT, D3/29/1962 Glasgow, MT   **1928** ChiC 5 (2)

ILOWIT, ROY   Roy, T, 6´2˝/220 lbs; CCNY; B4/3/1917 New York, NY, D1/3/1990 Long Beach, NY   **1937** Bkn 4 (1)

IMAN, KEN   Kenneth Charles, C, 6´1˝/240 lbs; Southeast Missouri State; B2/8/1939 St. Louis, MO   **1960**†GB 12   **1961**†GB 14   **1962**†GB 14   **1963** GB 14   **1965** LARm 14 (14, C)   **1967**†LARm 14 (14, C)   **1968** LARm 14 (14, C)   **1969**†LARm✩14 (14, C)   **1970** LARm 14 (14, C)   **1971** LARm 14 (14, C)   **1972** LARm 14 (14, C)   **1973**†LARm 14 (14, C)   **1974**†LARm 14 (14, C)

| 1966 | LARm | 14(14, C) | 1 | 2 | 2.0(2) | 0 | — | — | — | — | — | — | — | — | — | — | — | — | — | — | 0 | 2 |
| NFL | 14 | 194(140) | 1 | 2 | 2.0(2) | 0 | — | — | — | — | — | — | — | — | — | — | — | — | — | — | 0 | 2 |

IMHOF, MARTIN   Martin Carl, DE-DT, 6´6˝/255 lbs; San Diego State; 1972: SL, rnd 4; B10/9/1949 Seattle, WA   **1972** SL 13 (rde)   **1974**†Was 13   **1975** NE 5 (3)   **1976** Den 1   **NFL** 32 (3) [4 yrs]

IMLAY, TUT   Talma W., B, 5´8˝/165 lbs; California; B3/20/1902 Panguitch, UT, D3/20/1976 Del Monte Forest, CA **[C]**   **1926** LA✩10 (10, TB), 24   **1927** NYG 7 (4)   **NFL** 17 (14) [2 yrs]

INGALLS, BOB   Donald Robert, C, 6´3˝/200 lbs; Michigan; 1942: GB, rnd 18; B1/17/1919 Marblehead, MA, D4/8/1970 Willimantic, CT   **1942** GB 10 (6, C)

INGLE, MARK   Mark B., G, none; B8/13/1891 Kingfisher County, OK, deceased   **1921** Evv 1 (0)

INGLIS, TIM   Timothy James, LB, 6´3˝/232 lbs; Toledo; B3/10/1964 Toledo, OH   **1987** Cin 8 (3)   **1988** Cin 4 (0)   **NFL** 12 (3) [2 yrs]

INGRAM, BRIAN   Brian DeWayne, LB, 6´4˝/236 lbs; Tennessee; 1982: NE, rnd 4; B10/31/1959 Memphis, TN   **1982**†NE 8 (0)   **1983** NE 4 (0)   **1984** NE 12 (0)   **1985**†NE 15 (0)   **1987** SD 1 (1)   **NFL** 40 (1) [5 yrs]

INGRAM, BYRON   Byron Kimble, G, 6´2˝/295 lbs; Eastern Kentucky; B11/17/1964 Lexington, KY   **1987** KC 1 (0)   **1988** KC 12 (5, rg)   **NFL** 13 (5) [2 yrs]

INGRAM, DARRYL   Darryl, TE, 6´3˝/240 lbs; California; 1989: Min, rnd 4; B5/2/1966 Lubbock, TX   **1991** Cle 2 (0)   **1992** GB 16 (0)   **1993**†GB 2 (0)

| 1989 | †Min | 16(2) | — | — | — | — | 5 | 47 | 9.4(21) | 1 | — | — | — | — | — | — | — | — | — | — | 6 | 29 |
| NFL | 4 | 36(2) | — | — | — | — | 5 | 47 | 9.4(21) | 1 | — | — | — | — | — | — | — | — | — | — | 6 | 29 |

INGRAM, JOHNATHAN   Johnathan, C, 6´2˝/300 lbs; San Diego State; B9/20/1980 LaQuinta, CA   **2005** KC 2 (0)

INGRAM, KEVIN   Kevin, QB, 6´0˝/178 lbs; East Carolina; B4/26/1962 Philadelphia, PA

| 1987 | NO | 2(0) | 2 | 14 | 7.0(9) | 0 | — | — | — | — | 2 | 1 | 50.0 | 5 | 2.5(5) | 1 | 0 | 1 | 6 | — | — | 0 | 22 |

INGRAM, MARK   Mark J., WR, 5´10˝/194 lbs; Michigan State; 1987: NYG, rnd 1; B8/23/1965 Rockford, IL

1987	NYG	9(0)	—	—	—	—	2	32	16.0(18)	0	—	—	—	—	—	—	—	—	—	k	—	0	40
1988	NYG	7(4)	—	—	—	—	13	158	12.2(32)	1	—	—	—	—	—	—	—	—	—	k	—	6	93
1989	†NYG	16(3)	1	1	1.0(1)	0	17	290	17.1(41)	1	—	—	—	—	—	—	—	—	—	k	—	6	153
1990	†NYG	16(14, WR)	1	4	4.0(4)	0	26	499	19.2(57)	5	—	—	—	—	—	—	—	—	—	k	—	30	276
1991	NYG	16(13, WR)	—	—	—	—	51	824	16.2(41)	3	1	0	0.0	0	0.0	0	0	1	2	—	kp	—	18	441
1992	NYG	12(12, WR)	—	—	—	—	27	408	15.1(34)	1	—	—	—	—	—	—	—	—	—	—	—	6	209
1993	Mia	16(16, WR)	—	—	—	—	44	707	16.1(77)	6	—	—	—	—	—	—	—	—	—	—	—	36	384
1994	Mia	15(9, WR)	—	—	—	—	44	506	11.5(64)	6	—	—	—	—	—	—	—	—	—	k	—	36	268
1995	†GB	16(9, WR)	1	-3	-3.0(-3)	0	39	469	12.0(29)	3	—	—	—	—	—	—	—	—	—	p	—	18	242

YEAR	TEAM	G (GS, POS)	RUSH	YD	AVG(LG)	TD	REC	YD	AVG(LG)	TD	PASS	COMP	PCT	YD	AVG(LG)	TD	INT	SK	YD	QBR	KPR	OTD	PTS	TAY
1996	Phi	5(0)	—	—	—	—	2	33	16.5(20)	0	—	—	—	—	—	—	—	—	—	—	—	—	0	17
NFL	10	128(84)	3	2	0.7(4)	0	265	3926	14.8(77)	26	1	0	0.0	0	0.0	0	0	1	2	—	kp	—	156	2121

INGRAM, STEVE   Stephen Anthony, T, 6´4˝/324 lbs; Maryland; 1995: TB, rnd 7; B5/8/1971 Cheverly, MD   **1995** TB 2 (0)   **1999**†Jax 6 (0)   **NFL** 8 (0) [2 yrs]

INGWERSEN, BURT   Burton Aherns, T, 5´11˝/180 lbs; Illinois; B8/29/1898 Fulton, IL, D7/17/1969 Champaign, IL   **1920** Dec 13 (7, LT)

INMAN, JERRY   Jerald Franklin, DT, 6´2˝/256 lbs; Boise State; Oregon; 1965: Den, rnd R6; B2/4/1940 Manhattan, KS   **1966** Den-A 14   **1967** Den-A 14 (LDT)   **1968** Den-A 7 (LDT)   **1969** Den-A 14 (12, LDT)   **1970** Den 11 (1)   **1971** Den 14 (3)   **1973** Den 8   **NFL** 82 (16) [7 yrs]

INMON, EARL   Earl, LB, 6´1˝/215 lbs; Bethune-Cookman; 1978: Oak, rnd 7; B3/21/1954 Umatilla, FL   **1978** TB 2

INNOCENT, DOU   Doudow, RB, 5´11˝/212 lbs; Mississippi; B7/9/1972 Pompano Beach, FL   **1996** Sea 4 (0)

INSLEY, TREVOR   Trevor, WR, 6´0˝/190 lbs; Nevada-Reno; B12/25/1977 San Clemente, CA

| 2001 | Ind | 11(0) | — | — | — | — | 14 | 165 | 11.8(26) | 1 | — | — | — | — | — | — | — | — | — | — | kp | — | 6 | 132 |

INTRIERI, MARNE   Marino Charles, C-G-T, 5´8˝/250 lbs; Loyola (MD); B9/13/1907 Steelton, PA, deceased   **1932** SI 11 (9, C)   **1933** Bos 3 (0)   **1934** Bos 6 (0)   **NFL** 20 (9) [3 yrs]

IOANE, JUNIOR   Junior Burton, DT, 6´4˝/320 lbs; Arizona State; 2000: Oak, rnd 4; B7/21/1977 American Samoa   **2001** Oak 3 (0)   **2002**†Oak 6 (0)   **2003** Hou 13 (4)   **2004** Hou 3 (0)   **2005** Hou 11 (1)   **NFL** 36 (5) [5 yrs]

IPPOLITO, TONY   Anthony Samuel, G, 5´10˝/220 lbs; Purdue; 1939: Phi, rnd 7; B9/19/1917 Chicago, IL, D11/12/1951 Evanston, IL   **1943**†ChiB 9 (0)

IRELAND, DARWIN   Darwin Dawan, LB, 5´11˝/240 lbs; Arkansas; B5/26/1971 Pine Bluff, AR   **1994** ChiB 2 (0)   **1995** ChiB 1 (0)   **NFL** 3 (0) [2 yrs]

IRGENS, BILL   Einer M., B-E, 5´8˝/175 lbs; none; B6/1883 Norway, D10/28/1947 Hennepin County, MN **[K]**   **1921** Min 2 (0)   **1922** Min 4 (3, BB), 1   **1923** Min 5 (4)   **NFL** 11 (7), 1 [3 yrs]

IRONS, GERALD   Gerald Dwayne, LB, 6´2˝/230 lbs; Maryland-Eastern Shore; 1970: Oak, rnd 3; B5/2/1947 Gary, IN   **1970**†Oak 14   **1971** Oak 7   **1972**†Oak 14 (14, RLB)   **1973**†Oak 14 (14, RLB)   **1974**†Oak 14 (14, RLB)   **1975**†Oak 14 (14, RLB)   **1976** Cle 14 (RLB)   **1977** Cle 14 (14, RLB)   **1978** Cle 14 (14, RLB)   **1979** Cle 16   **NFL** 135 (84) [10 yrs]

IRONS, GRANT   Grant Michael, DE, 6´5˝/265 lbs; Notre Dame; B7/7/1979 Middleburg Heights, OH   **2002** Buf 15 (0)   **2003** Oak 1 (0)   **2004** Oak 8 (2)   **2005** Oak 15 (1)   **NFL** 39 (3) [4 yrs]

IRONS, PAUL   Paul, TE, 6´2˝/242 lbs; Florida State; B12/23/1982 New Orleans, LA

| 2005 | Cle | 2(1) | — | — | — | — | 2 | 16 | 8.0(14) | 0 | — | — | — | — | — | — | — | — | — | — | — | — | 0 | 8 |

IRVIN, BARLOW   Barlow, G-T, 5´10˝/225 lbs; Texas A&M; B12/31/1903 Cotulla, TX, D11/26/1985 Bryan, TX   **1926** Buf 10 (10, RG)   **1927** Buf 5 (5, RT)   **NFL** 15 (15) [2 yrs]

IRVIN, DARRELL   Darrell Bruce, DE, 6´4˝/259 lbs; Oklahoma; B1/21/1957 Pawhuska, OK   **1980**†Buf 7 (0)   **1981**†Buf 13 (0)   **1982** Buf 9 (0)   **1983**†Sea 16 (0)   **NFL** 45 (0) [4 yrs]

IRVIN, KEN   Kenneth Pernell, DB, 5´11˝/182 lbs; Memphis; 1995: Buf, rnd 4; B7/11/1972 Rome, GA   **1995**†Buf 16 (3)   **1996**†Buf 16 (1)   **1997** Buf 16 (0)   **1998**†Buf 16 (16, LCB)   **1999** Buf 14 (14, LCB)   **2000** Buf 16 (16, RCB)   **2001** Buf 14 (4)   **2002** NO 16 (9, LCB)   **2003** Min 16 (8, RCB)   **2005** Min 7 (1)   **NFL** 147 (72) [10 yrs]

IRVIN, LEROY   LeRoy, DB, 5´11˝/184 lbs; Kansas; 1980: LA, rnd 3; B9/15/1957 Fort Dix, NJ **[RI]**   **1980**†LARm 16 (2)   **1981** LARm☆16 (7, lcb)   **1982** LARm☆9 (0)   **1983**†LARm 15 (13, RCB)   **1984**†LARm 16 (16, RCB)   **1985**†LARm★16 (16, RCB)   **1986**†LARm★16 (15, RCB)   **1987** LARm 10 (9, RCB)   **1988**†LARm 16 (16, RCB)   **1989**†LARm 13 (13, RCB)   **1990** Det 16 (16, RCB)   **NFL** 159 (123) [11 yrs]

IRVIN, MARK   Mark LaRue, DB, 5´10˝/190 lbs; Bethune-Cookman; B10/12/1964 Miami, FL   **1987** Mia 3 (0)

IRVIN, MICHAEL   Michael Jerome 'The Playmaker', WR, 6´2˝/207 lbs; Miami (FL); 1988: Dal, rnd 1; B3/5/1966 Fort Lauderdale, FL

1988	Dal	14(10, WR)	1	2	2.0(2)	0	32	654	20.4(61)	5	—	—	—	—	—	—	—	—	—	—	—	—	30	354
1989	Dal	6(6, wr)	1	6	6.0(6)	0	26	378	14.5(65)	2	—	—	—	—	—	—	—	—	—	—	—	—	12	205
1990	Dal	12(7, WR)	—	—	—	—	20	413	20.6(61)	5	—	—	—	—	—	—	—	—	—	—	—	—	30	232
1991	†Dal★	16(16, WR)	—	—	—	—	93	1523	16.4(66)	8	—	—	—	—	—	—	—	—	—	—	—	—	48	802
1992	†Dal★	16(14, WR)	1	-9	-9.0(-9)	0	78	1396	17.9(87)	7	—	—	—	—	—	—	—	—	—	—	—	—	42	724
1993	†Dal★	16(16, WR)	2	6	3.0(9)	0	88	1330	15.1(61)	7	—	—	—	—	—	—	—	—	—	—	—	—	42	706
1994	†Dal◇	16(16, WR)	—	—	—	—	79	1241	15.7(65)	6	—	—	—	—	—	—	—	—	—	—	—	—	36	651
1995	†Dal◇	16(16, WR)	—	—	—	—	111	1603	14.4(50)	10	—	—	—	—	—	—	—	—	—	—	—	—	60	852
1996	†Dal	11(11, WR)	—	—	—	—	64	962	15.0(61)	2	—	—	—	—	—	—	—	—	—	—	—	—	14	491
1997	Dal	16(16, WR)	—	—	—	—	75	1180	15.7(55)	9	—	—	—	—	—	—	—	—	—	—	—	—	54	635
1998	†Dal	16(15, WR)	1	1	1.0(1)	0	74	1057	14.3(51)	1	—	—	—	—	—	—	—	—	—	—	—	—	6	535
1999	Dal	4(4)	—	—	—	—	10	167	16.7(37)	3	—	—	—	—	—	—	—	—	—	—	—	—	18	99
NFL	12	159(147)	6	6	1.0(9)	0	750	11904	15.9(87)	65	—	—	—	—	—	—	—	—	—	—	—	—	392	6283

IRVIN, SEDRICK   Sedrick, RB, 5´11˝/226 lbs; Michigan State; 1999: Det, rnd 4; B3/30/1978 Miami, FL

1999	†Det	14(0)	36	133	3.7(51)	4	25	233	9.3(31)	0	—	—	—	—	—	—	—	—	—	—	kp	—	24	271
2000	Det	6(0)	9	49	5.4(32)	0	8	90	11.3(18)	0	—	—	—	—	—	—	—	—	—	—	—	—	0	94
NFL	2	20(0)	45	182	4.0(51)	4	33	323	9.8(31)	0	—	—	—	—	—	—	—	—	—	—	kp	—	24	365

IRVIN, TEX   Cecil Paul, T-FB-G, 6´0˝/225 lbs; Shreiner College; Davis & Elkins; B10/9/1906 DeLeon, TX, D2/11/1978 DeLeon, TX   **1931** Pro 10 (9, LT)   **1932** NYG 10 (6, rt)   **1934**†NYG 12 (6, rt)   **1935**†NYG 12 (2)

| 1933 | †NYG | 12(6, rt) | — | — | — | — | 1 | 15 | 15.0(15) | 1 | — | — | — | — | — | — | — | — | — | — | — | — | 6 | 13 |
| NFL | 5 | 56(29) | — | — | — | — | 1 | 15 | 15.0(15) | 1 | — | — | — | — | — | — | — | — | — | — | — | — | 6 | 13 |

IRVIN, WILLIE   Willie James, DE-E, 6´3˝/203 lbs; Florida A&M; 1953: Phi, rnd 15; B1/3/1930 St. Augustine, FL   **1953** Phi 3

IRVING, TERRY   Terry Duane, LB, 6´2˝/230 lbs; McNeese State; 1994: Arz, rnd 4; B7/3/1971 Galveston, TX   **1994** Arz 16 (0)   **1995** Arz 16 (8, llb/rlb)   **1996** Arz 16 (0)   **1997** Arz 16 (6, rlb)   **1998** Arz 6 (1)   **NFL** 70 (15) [5 yrs]

IRWIN, DON   Donald Emerson, FB-HB, 6´1˝/196 lbs; Colgate; 1936: Bos, rnd 7; B7/22/1913 New York, NY, D6/8/1983 Detroit, MI **[K]**

1936	†Bos	2(1)	17	78	4.6	2	2	31	15.5	0	5	0	0.0	—	—	—	0	1	—	—	—	—	12	74
1937	†Was	10(9, FB)	89	315	3.5	2	8	112	14.0	0	3	0	0.0	0	—	—	0	1	—	—	—	—	12	391
1938	Was	10(4)	56	130	2.3	1	16	138	8.6	0	6	0	0.0	0	—	—	0	0	—	—	K	—	6	129
1939	Was	7(1)	10	63	6.3	1	1	8	8.0(8)	0	0	0	0.0	0	—	—	0	2	—	—	K	—	6	77
NFL	4	29(15)	172	586	3.4	6	27	289	10.7(8)	0	14	0	0.0	0	—	—	0	3	—	—	K	—	36	671

IRWIN, DUTCH   Harry Stanton, HB, 5´7˝/170 lbs; Mercer; B8/11/1899 Rochester, NY, D6/6/1967 Fairport, NY   **1920** Roc 9 (0)

IRWIN, HEATH   Heath Spencer, G, 6´4˝/300 lbs; Colorado; 1996: NE, rnd 4; B6/27/1973 Boulder, CO   **1997**†NE 16 (1)   **1998**†NE 13 (3)   **1999** NE 15 (13, LG)   **2000**†Mia 13 (0)   **2001**†Mia 16 (7, lg)   **2002** SL 14 (5, lg)   **NFL** 87 (29) [6 yrs]

IRWIN, JIM   James C., FB, 5´7˝/165 lbs; none; B3/9/1897 Louisville, KY, D12/17/1965 Columbia, KY   **1921** Lou 1 (1)   **1922** Lou 3 (1)   **NFL** 4 (2) [2 yrs]

IRWIN, TIM   Timothy Edward, T, 6´7˝/300 lbs; Tennessee; 1981: Min, rnd 3; B12/13/1958 Knoxville, TN   **1981** Min 7 (0)   **1982**†Min 9 (9, RT)   **1983** Min 16 (16, RT)   **1984** Min 16 (16, RT)   **1985** Min 16 (16, RT)   **1986** Min 16 (16, RT)   **1987**†Min 12 (12, RT)   **1988**†Min 16 (16, RT)   **1989**†Min 16 (16, RT)   **1990** Min 16 (16, RT)   **1991** Min 16 (16, RT)   **1992**†Min 16 (16, RT)   **1993**†Min 16 (16, RT)   **1994** TB 16 (6, rt)   **1994**†Mia 5 (0)   **NFL** 201 (187) [14 yrs]

ISAACSON, TED   Theodore F., T-C, 6´4˝/272 lbs; Washington; B3/2/1912 Seattle, WA, deceased   **1934** ChiC 10 (0)   **1935** ChiC 12 (7, RT)   **NFL** 22 (7) [2 yrs]

ISABEL, WILMER   Wilmer Edward, TB-HB, 6´0˝/175 lbs; Ohio State; B10/1/1899 Columbus, OH, D9/7/1975 Bexley, OH   **1923** Col 10 (10, TB), 12   **1924** Col 7 (1)   **NFL** 17 (11) [2 yrs]

ISAIA, SALE   Sale, G, 6´5˝/320 lbs; UCLA; B6/13/1972 Honolulu, HI   **1996** Bal 9 (0)   **2000** NE 16 (14, RG)   **NFL** 25 (14) [2 yrs]

ISBELL, CECIL   Cecil Frank, TB-HB, 6´1˝/190 lbs; Purdue; 1938: GB, rnd 1; B7/11/1915 Houston, TX, D6/23/1985 Hammond, IN **[KC]**

1938	†GB★	11(4, tb)	85	445	5.2	2	5	104	20.8(49)	0	91	37	40.7	659	7.2(53)	8	10	—	—	—	—	—	12	487
1939	†GB★	11(5, tb)	132	407	3.1	2	9	71	7.9(20)	0	103	43	41.7	749	7.3(51)	6	5	—	—	66.4	KP	—	15	667
1940	GB☆	10(5, TB)	97	270	2.8	4	—	—	—	—	150	68	45.3	1037	6.9(47)	8	12	—	—	53.1	Pi	—	24	393
1941	†GB★	11(4, TB)	72	317	4.4(24)	1	1	-1	-1.0(-1)	0	206	117	56.8	1479	7.2(56)	15	11	—	—	81.4	kpi	—	6	702
1942	†GB★	11(6, TB)	36	83	2.3(32)	1	—	—	—	—	268	146	54.5	2021	7.5(73)	24	14	—	—	87.0	Pkpi	—	6	693
NFL	5	54(24)	422	1522	3.6(32)	10	15	174	11.6(49)	0	818	411	50.2	5945	7.3(73)	61	52	—	—	72.6	KPkpi	—	63	2941

ISBELL, JOE BOB   Joe Bob, G, 6´1˝/243 lbs; Houston; 1962: Hou, rnd 20; B7/7/1940 Gorman, TX   **1962** Dal 9 (1)   **1963** Dal 8 (1)   **1964** Dal 14 (10, RG/lg)   **1966** Cle 14   **NFL** 45 (10) [4 yrs]

YEAR	TEAM	G (GS, POS)	RUSH	YD	AVG (LG)	TD	REC	YD	AVG (LG)	TD	PASS COMP	PCT	YD	AVG (LG)	TD	INT	SK	YD	QBR	KPR	OTD	PTS	TAY

ISENBARGER, JOHN John Phillips, RB-WR, 6´3˝/203 lbs; Indiana; 1970: SF, rnd 2; B1/5/1947 Muncie, IN

1970	†SF	13	18	43	2.4(27)	0	8	158	19.8(61)	1	1	0	0.0	0	0	0.0	0	0	—	—	—	6	127
1971	†SF	14	5	34	6.8(22)	0	—	—	—		—				—					—		0	34
1972	†SF	14	3	9	3.0(7)	0	3	66	22.0(33)	1	0	0	0.0	0	0	0.0	0	0	—	—	—	6	47
1973	SF	14	1	-6	-6.0(-6)	0	10	67	6.7(18)	0	1	1	100.0	48	48.0(48)	0	0	0	0	—	—	—	0	52
NFL	4	55	27	80	3.0(27)	0	21	291	13.9(61)	2	3	1	33.3	48	16.0(48)	0	0	0	0	—	—	—	12	260

ISMAIL, QADRY Qadry Ramadan, WR, 6´0˝/196 lbs; Syracuse; 1993: Min, rnd 2; B11/8/1970 Newark, NJ [R]

1993	†Min	15(3)	3	14	4.7(6)	0	19	212	11.2(37)	1	—			—		—				k	—	6	397
1994	†Min	16(3)	—	—	—		45	696	15.5(65)	5	—			—		—				k	—	30	655
1995	Min	16(2)	1	7	7.0(7)	0	32	597	18.7(85)	3	—			—		—				k	—	18	728
1996	†Min	16(2)	—	—	—		22	351	16.0(54)	3	—			—		—				k	—	18	298
1997	Mia	3(0)					—	—	—		—			—		—				k	—	0	46
1998	NO	10(1)					—	—	—		—			—		—				k	—	0	170
1999	Bal	16(16, WR)	1	4	4.0(4)	0	68	1105	16.3(76)	6	—			—		—				k	—	36	582
2000	†Bal	15(13, WR)	—	—	—		49	655	13.4(53)	5	—			—		—				k	—	30	374
2001	†Bal	16(15, WR)	—	—	—		74	1059	14.3(77)	7	—			—		—					—	44	565
2002	Ind	14(14, WR)	—	—	—		44	462	10.5(42)	3	—			—		—					—	18	246
NFL	10	137(69)	5	25	5.0(7)	0	353	5137	14.6(85)	33	—			—		—				k	—	200	4059

ISMAIL, ROCKET Raghib Ramadian, WR, 5´11˝/180 lbs; Notre Dame; 1991: LARd, rnd 4; B11/18/1969 Elizabeth, NJ [R]

1993	†LARd	13(0)	4	-5	-1.3(10)	0	26	353	13.6(43)	1	—			—		—				k	—	6	407
1994	LARd	16(0)	4	31	7.8(13)	0	34	513	15.1(42)	5	—			—		—				k	—	30	591
1995	Oak	16(16, WR)	6	29	4.8(13)	0	28	491	17.5(73)	5	—			—		—				k	—	18	456
1996	†Car	13(5, wr)	8	80	10.0(35)	1	12	214	17.8(51)	0	—			—		—				k	—	6	222
1997	Car	13(2)	4	32	8.0(18)	0	36	419	11.6(59)	2	—			—		—					—	12	252
1998	Car	16(15, WR)	3	42	14.0(36)	0	69	1024	14.8(62)	8	—			—		—					—	48	594
1999	†Dal	16(14, WR)	13	110	8.5(27)	1	80	1097	13.7(76)	6	—			—		—					—	42	699
2000	Dal	9(9, WR)	8	73	9.1(37)	0	25	350	14.0(44)	1	—			—		—					—	8	253
2001	Dal	14(13, WR)	8	31	3.9(11)	0	53	834	15.7(80)	2	—			—		—				p	—	12	473
NFL	9	126(74)	58	423	7.3(37)	2	363	5295	14.6(80)	28	—			—		—				kp	—	182	3945

ISOM, JASEN Jasen J., FB, 6´1˝/243 lbs; Cincinnati; Western Illinois; B1/7/1977 Wheatley Heights, NY **2003** SF 2 (0)

| 2004 | SF | 5(1) | 1 | 0 | 0.0(0) | 0 | 1 | 1 | 1.0(1) | 0 | — | | | — | | — | | | | | — | 0 | 1 |
| NFL | 2 | 7(1) | 1 | 0 | 0.0 | 0 | 1 | 1 | 1.0(1) | 0 | — | | | — | | — | | | | | — | 0 | 1 |

ISOM, RAY Raymond Clinton, DB, 5´9˝/190 lbs; Penn State; B12/27/1965 Harrisburg, PA **1987** TB 6 (6, FS) **1988** TB 2 (1) **NFL** 8 (7) [2 yrs]

ISOM, RICKEY Rickey Lamarr, RB, 6´0˝/224 lbs; North Carolina State; 1986: Mia, rnd 12; B11/30/1963 Harrisburg, PA

| 1987 | Mia | 3(1) | 9 | 41 | 4.6(8) | 1 | 1 | 11 | 11.0(11) | 0 | — | | | — | | — | | | | k | — | 6 | 53 |

ISRAEL, RON Ron, DB, 6´0˝/212 lbs; Notre Dame; B1/5/1978 Voorhees, NJ **2003** Min 1 (0)

ISRAEL, STEVE Steven Douglas, DB, 5´11˝/194 lbs; Pittsburgh; 1992: LARm, rnd 2; B3/16/1969 Lawnside, NJ **1992** LARm 16 (1) **1993** LARm 16 (12, RCB) **1994** LARm 10 (2) **1995** SF 8 (0) **1996** †SF 14 (2) **1997** †NE 5 (0) **1998** †NE 11 (7, rcb) **1999** NE 13 (13, RCB) **2001** NO 9 (1) **NFL** 102 (38) [9 yrs]

ISSA, JABARI Jabari, DE-DT, 6´5˝/302 lbs; Washington; 2000: Arz, rnd 6; B4/18/1978 Foster City, CA **2000** Arz 11 (0) **2001** Arz 13 (5, lde) **NFL** 24 (5) [2 yrs]

ISSELHARDT, RALPH Ralph L., G, 6´1˝/205 lbs; Franklin (OH); B1/13/1910 Hillsboro, IL, D10/24/1972 East Grand Rapids, MI **1937** Det 1 (0) **1937** Cle 8 (0) **NFL** 9 (0) [1 yr]

ITZEL, JACK John F., FB, 6´0˝/190 lbs; Georgetown (DC); Pittsburgh; 1945: Pit, rnd 17; B11/12/1924, PA, D12/21/1966 Wilkinsburg, PA

| 1945 | Pit | 10(0) | 4 | 11 | 2.8(5) | 0 | 1 | 4 | 4.0(4) | 0 | — | | | — | | — | | | | i | — | 0 | 21 |

IVERSON, DUKE Christopher Arnold, B, 6´2˝/208 lbs; Oregon; 1947: NYG, rnd 7; B2/26/1920 Petaluma, CA **1950** NYY 7 (DB) **1951** NYY 9

1947	NYG	8(5, bb)	—	—	—		1	11	11.0(11)	0	—			—		—				k	—	0	7
NFL	3	24(5)	—	—	—		1	11	11.0(11)	0	—			—		—				ki	1	8	27
1948	NYY-A	10(1)	—	—	—		4	30	7.5	0	—			—		—				i	—	0	11
1949	†NYY-A	12(0)	6	50	8.3	0	—	—	—		—			—		—				ki	—	0	41
AAFC	2	22(1)	6	50	8.3	0	4	30	7.5	0	—			—		—				ki	—	0	52

IVERY, EDDIE LEE Eddie Lee, RB, 6´0˝/210 lbs; Georgia Tech; 1979: GB, rnd 1; B7/30/1957 McDuffie, GA

1979	GB	1	3	24	8.0(11)	0	—	—	—		—			—		—					—	0	24
1980	GB	16(16, RB)	202	831	4.1(38)	3	50	481	9.6(46)	1	—			—		—					—	24	1107
1981	GB	1(1)	14	72	5.1(28)	1	2	10	5.0(8)	0	—			—		—					—	6	87
1982	†GB	9(9, RB)	127	453	3.6(32)	9	16	186	11.6(62)	1	1	0	0.0	0	0.0	0	0	0	0	—	—	60	641
1983	GB	8(8, RB)	86	340	4.0(21)	2	16	139	8.7(17)	1	2	2	100.0	50	25.0(35)	0	0	0	0	k	—	18	462
1984	GB	10(5, rb)	99	552	5.6(49)	6	19	141	7.4(18)	1	—			—		—					—	42	688
1985	GB	15(10, RB)	132	636	4.8(34)	2	28	270	9.6(24)	2	1	0	0.0	0	0.0	0	0	1	7	—	—	24	801
1986	GB	12(1)	4	25	6.3(15)	0	31	385	12.4(42)	1	—			—		—					—	6	223
NFL	7	72(50)	667	2933	4.4(49)	23	162	1612	10.0(62)	7	4	2	50.0	50	12.5(35)	0	0	1	7	k	—	180	4031

IVLOW, JOHN John David, RB, 5´11˝/226 lbs; Northwestern; Colorado State; B1/26/1970 Joliet, IL **1993** ChiB 2 (0)

IVORY, BOB Robert James, G, 6´2˝/212 lbs; Detroit Mercy; 1945: Det, rnd 26; B1/29/1924 Detroit, MI, D2/25/1989 Detroit, MI **1947** Det 3 (0)

IVORY, HORACE Horace Orlando, RB, 6´0˝/197 lbs; Oklahoma; 1977: NE, rnd 2; B8/8/1954 Fort Worth, TX

1977	NE	5	3	10	3.3(9)	0	—	—	—		—			—		—					—	0	10
1978	†NE	15(3)	141	693	4.9(28)	11	14	122	8.7(18)	0	—			—		—				k	—	66	924
1979	NE	11(9, RB)	143	522	3.7(52)	2	23	216	9.4(24)	2	—			—		—				k	—	18	650
1980	NE☆	14(0)	42	111	2.6(20)	2	12	95	7.9(19)	0	—			—		—				k	1	18	641
1981	NE	1(0)	—	—	—		—	—	—		—			—		—				k	—	0	4
1981	Sea	6(0)	9	38	4.2(7)	0	—	—	—		—			—		—				k	—	0	94
1982	Sea	6(0)	13	51	3.9(27)	1	5	38	7.6(12)	0	—			—		—				k	—	6	154
NFL	6	58(12)	351	1425	4.1(52)	15	54	471	8.7(24)	2	—			—		—				k	1	108	2477

IVY, COREY Corey Terrell, DB, 5´8˝/183 lbs; Oklahoma; B3/29/1977 St. Louis, MO **2001** TB 1 (0) **2002** †TB 16 (0) **2003** TB 16 (2) **2004** TB 16 (0) **2005** SL 16 (5, cb) **NFL** 65 (7) [5 yrs]

IVY, POP Lee Frank, E, 6´3˝/208 lbs; Oklahoma; 1940: Pit, rnd 4; B1/25/1916 Skiatook, OK, D5/17/2003 Norman, OK [KC]

1940	Pit	4(0)	—	—	—		—	—	—		—			—		—					—	0	0
1940	ChiC	5(1)	—	—	—		2	32	16.0	0	—			—		—					—	0	16
1941	ChiC	11(9, RE)	—	—	—		20	183	9.1(16)	0	—			—		—				i	—	2	117
1942	ChiC◇	11(6, RE)	—	—	—		27	259	9.6(18)	0	—			—		—				K	—	2	130
1945	ChiC	3(0)	—	—	—		—	—	—		—			—		—					—	0	-5
1946	ChiC	11(4)	—	—	—		4	39	9.8(19)	1	—			—		—				i	—	6	42
1947	ChiC	12(1)	—	—	—		—	—	—		—			—		—				K	—	0	0
NFL	6	57(21)	—	—	—		53	513	9.7(19)	1	—			—		—				Ki	—	2	20	299

IWANOWSKI, MARK Mark David, TE, 6´4˝/230 lbs; Pennsylvania; B9/8/1955 Hazelton, PA **1978** NYJ 5

IWUOMA, CHIDI Chidi, DB, 5´8˝/184 lbs; California; B2/19/1978 Los Angeles, CA **2001** Det 13 (1) **2002** †Pit 13 (0) **2003** Pit 15 (0) **2004** †Pit 14 (0) **2005** †Pit 16 (0) **NFL** 71 (1) [5 yrs]

IZO, GEORGE George William, QB, 6´4˝/218 lbs; Notre Dame; 1960: SL, rnd 1/NYT, rnd 1; B9/20/1937 Barberton, OH

1960	SL	2(1)	—	—	—		—	—	—		24	10	41.7	115	4.8(24)	0	0	—	—	—	—	0	58
1961	Was	5	3	-1	-0.3(4)	0	—	—	—		40	16	40	214	5.3(33)	1	6	—	—	—	—	0	-129
1962	Was	1	1	-3	-3.0(-3)	0	—	—	—		37	17	45.9	284	7.7(49)	3	4	—	—	—	—	0	-6

YEAR	TEAM	G(GS, POS)	RUSH	YD	AVG(LG)	TD	REC	YD	AVG(LG)	TD	PASS	COMP	PCT	YD	AVG(LG)	TD	INT	SK	YD	QBR	KPR	OTD	PTS	TAY
1963	Was	5	3	4	1.3(2)	0	—	—	—	—	58	25	43.1	378	6.5(**99**)	3	6	—	—	—	—	—	0	-32
1964	Was	3	—	—	—	—	—	—	—	—	18	5	27.8	83	4.6(29)	1	2	—	—	—	—	—	0	-34
1965	Det	6	1	-5	-5.0(-5)	0	—	—	—	—	59	24	40.7	357	6.1(61)	2	6	—	—	—	—	—	0	-57
1966	Pit	4	2	-18	-9.0(-4)	0	—	—	—	—	81	35	43.2	360	4.4(37)	2	8	—	—	—	—	—	0	-148
NFL	7	26(1)	10	-23	-2.3(4)	0	—	—	—	—	317	132	41.6	1791	5.6(99)	12	32	—	—	—	—	—	0	-348

Izzo, Larry Lawrence Alexander, LB, 5´10˝/228 lbs; Rice; B9/26/1974 Fort Belvoir, VA **1998** Mia 13 (0) **1999**†Mia 16 (0) **2001**†NE 16 (0) **2002** NE★15 (0) **2003**†NE 16 (0) **2005**†NE 16 (0)

YEAR	TEAM	G(GS, POS)	RUSH	YD	AVG(LG)	TD	REC	YD	AVG(LG)	TD	PASS	COMP	PCT	YD	AVG(LG)	TD	INT	SK	YD	QBR	KPR	OTD	PTS	TAY
1996	Mia	16(0)	1	26	26.0(26)	0	—	—	—	—	—	—	—	—	—	—	—	—	—	—	—	—	0	26
2000	†Mia★	16(0)	1	39	39.0(39)	0	—	—	—	—	—	—	—	—	—	—	—	—	—	—	—	—	0	39
2004	†NE★	16(0)	1	0	0.0(0)	0	—	—	—	—	—	—	—	—	—	—	—	—	—	—	—	—	0	0
NFL	9	140(0)	3	65	21.7(39)	0	—	—	—	—	—	—	—	—	—	—	—	—	—	—	ki	—	0	45

Jack, Eric Eric Demond, DB, 5´10˝/177 lbs; New Mexico; B4/19/1972 Dallas, TX **1994** Atl 16 (0)

Jacke, Chris Christopher Lee, K, 6´0˝/205 lbs; Texas-El Paso; 1989: GB, rnd 6; B3/12/1966 Richmond, VA **[K]** **1989** GB 16 (0) **1990** GB☆16 (0) **1991** GB 16 (0) **1992** GB 16 (0) **1993**†GB☆16 (0) **1994**†GB 16 (0) **1995**†GB 14 (0) **1996**†GB 16 (0) **1997** Was 1 (0) **1998**†Arz 4 (0) **1999** Arz 16 (0) **NFL** 147 (0) [11 yrs]

Jackson, Al Alfonza, DB, 6´0˝/182 lbs; Georgia; B9/7/1971 Pensacola, FL **1994** Phi 11 (0)

Jackson, Al Alexander O'Neal, G, 6´3˝/306 lbs; LSU; B5/18/1977 Moss Point, MS **2000** Dal 3 (0) **2002** GB 2 (0) **NFL** 5 (0) [2 yrs]

Jackson, Alfred Alfred, WR, 5´11˝/176 lbs; Texas; 1978: Atl, rnd 7; B8/3/1955 Cameron, TX

YEAR	TEAM	G(GS, POS)	RUSH	YD	AVG(LG)	TD	REC	YD	AVG(LG)	TD	PASS	COMP	PCT	YD	AVG(LG)	TD	INT	SK	YD	QBR	KPR	OTD	PTS	TAY
1978	†Atl	15	—	—	—	—	26	526	20.2(71)	2	—	—	—	—	—	—	—	—	—	—	kp	—	12	367
1979	Atl	12	—	—	—	—	11	156	14.2(23)	0	—	—	—	—	—	—	—	—	—	—	k	—	0	83
1980	†Atl	16(0)	—	—	—	—	22	403	18.3(54)	7	—	—	—	—	—	—	—	—	—	—	k	—	42	262
1981	Atl	16(0)	2	5	2.5(5)	0	37	604	16.3(49)	6	—	—	—	—	—	—	—	—	—	—	—	1	42	337
1982	†Atl	9(9, WR)	1	4	4.0(4)	0	26	361	13.9(40)	1	—	—	—	—	—	—	—	—	—	—	—	—	6	190
1983	Atl	4(4)	—	—	—	—	13	220	16.9(54)	3	—	—	—	—	—	—	—	—	—	—	—	—	18	125
1984	Atl	16(15, WR)	—	—	—	—	52	731	14.1(50)	2	—	—	—	—	—	—	—	—	—	—	—	—	12	376
NFL	7	88(28)	3	9	3.0(5)	0	187	3001	16.0(71)	21	—	—	—	—	—	—	—	—	—	—	kp	1	132	1739

Jackson, Alfred Alfred Melvin, WR, 6´0˝/183 lbs; San Diego State; 1989: LARm, rnd 5; B7/10/1967 Tulare, CA **1989**†LARm 7 (0) **1990** LARm 5 (0) **1991** Cle 6 (1) **1992** Cle 5 (0) **1995** Min 8 (1) **1996**†Min 14 (2) **NFL** 45 (4) [6 yrs]

Jackson, Alonzo Alonzo, LB, 6´4˝/262 lbs; Florida State; 2003: Pit, rnd 2; B9/15/1980 Americus, GA **2003** Pit 2 (0) **2004** Pit 7 (0) **2005** Phi 1 (0) **2005**†NYG 8 (1) **NFL** 18 (1) [3 yrs]

Jackson, Andrew Andrew Leon, RB, 5´10˝/190 lbs; USC; Iowa State; B5/6/1964 Los Angeles, CA

YEAR	TEAM	G(GS, POS)	RUSH	YD	AVG(LG)	TD	REC	YD	AVG(LG)	TD	PASS	COMP	PCT	YD	AVG(LG)	TD	INT	SK	YD	QBR	KPR	OTD	PTS	TAY
1987	Hou	7(3)	60	232	3.9(16)	1	10	44	4.4(16)	0	—	—	—	—	—	—	—	—	—	—	—	—	6	264

Jackson, Arnold Arnold, WR, 5´8˝/168 lbs; Louisville; B4/9/1977 Jacksonville, FL

YEAR	TEAM	G(GS, POS)	RUSH	YD	AVG(LG)	TD	REC	YD	AVG(LG)	TD	PASS	COMP	PCT	YD	AVG(LG)	TD	INT	SK	YD	QBR	KPR	OTD	PTS	TAY
2001	Arz	16(1)	—	—	—	—	9	44	4.9(16)	0	—	—	—	—	—	—	—	—	—	—	kp	—	0	299
2002	Arz	16(0)	—	—	—	—	5	42	8.4(11)	1	—	—	—	—	—	—	—	—	—	—	p	—	6	53
NFL	2	32(1)	—	—	—	—	14	86	6.1(16)	1	—	—	—	—	—	—	—	—	—	—	kp	—	6	352

Jackson, Bernard Bernard Frank, DB, 6´0˝/178 lbs; Washington State; 1972: Cin, rnd 4; B8/24/1950 Washington, DC, D5/26/1997 Lompoc, CA **[R]** **1972** Cin 14 **1973**†Cin 14 **1975**†Cin 14 (FS) **1976** Cin 12 (fs) **1977**†Den 14 (13, FS) **1978**†Den 16 (16, FS) **1979**†Den 12 (9, FS) **1980** Den 4 (4) **1980** SD 4 (4)

YEAR	TEAM	G(GS, POS)	RUSH	YD	AVG(LG)	TD	REC	YD	AVG(LG)	TD	PASS	COMP	PCT	YD	AVG(LG)	TD	INT	SK	YD	QBR	KPR	OTD	PTS	TAY
1974	Cin	14(SS)	—	—	—	—	1	22	22.0(22)	0	—	—	—	—	—	—	—	—	—	—	ki	—	0	270
NFL	9	118(46)	—	—	—	—	1	22	22.0(22)	0	—	—	—	—	—	—	—	—	—	—	ki	—	0	1144

Jackson, Bernard Bernard, DE, 6´4˝/281 lbs; Tennessee; B5/10/1980 Louisville, KY **2002** Was 4 (0)

Jackson, Bill William Steven, DB, 6´1˝/202 lbs; North Carolina; 1982: Cle, rnd 8; B7/1/1960 Winston-Salem, NC **1982**†Cle 9 (0)

Jackson, Billy Billy Thurman, RB, 5´10˝/217 lbs; Alabama; 1981: KC, rnd 7; B9/13/1959 Phenix City, AL

YEAR	TEAM	G(GS, POS)	RUSH	YD	AVG(LG)	TD	REC	YD	AVG(LG)	TD	PASS	COMP	PCT	YD	AVG(LG)	TD	INT	SK	YD	QBR	KPR	OTD	PTS	TAY
1981	KC	16(1)	111	398	3.6(31)	10	6	31	5.2(10)	1	—	—	—	—	—	—	—	—	—	—	k	—	66	534
1982	KC	9(7, FB)	86	243	2.8(18)	3	5	41	8.2(13)	0	—	—	—	—	—	—	—	—	—	—	—	—	18	294
1983	KC	16(14, RB)	152	499	3.3(19)	2	32	243	7.6(29)	0	—	—	—	—	—	—	—	—	—	—	—	—	12	641
1984	KC	16(9, rb)	50	225	4.5(16)	1	15	101	6.7(11)	1	—	—	—	—	—	—	—	—	—	—	—	—	12	291
NFL	4	57(31)	399	1365	3.4(31)	16	58	416	7.2(29)	2	—	—	—	—	—	—	—	—	—	—	k	—	108	1758

Jackson, Bo Vincent Edward, RB, 6´1˝/227 lbs; Auburn; 1987: LARd, rnd 7; B11/30/1962 Bessemer, AL

YEAR	TEAM	G(GS, POS)	RUSH	YD	AVG(LG)	TD	REC	YD	AVG(LG)	TD	PASS	COMP	PCT	YD	AVG(LG)	TD	INT	SK	YD	QBR	KPR	OTD	PTS	TAY
1987	LARd	7(5, FB)	81	554	**6.8**(**91**)	4	16	136	8.5(23)	2	—	—	—	—	—	—	—	—	—	—	—	—	36	672
1988	LARd	10(9, FB)	136	580	4.3(25)	3	9	79	8.8(27)	0	—	—	—	—	—	—	—	—	—	—	—	—	18	650
1989	LARd☆	11(9, RB)	173	950	5.5(92)	4	9	69	7.7(20)	0	—	—	—	—	—	—	—	—	—	—	—	—	24	1025
1990	†LARd★	10(0)	125	698	**5.6**(**88**)	5	6	68	11.3(18)	0	—	—	—	—	—	—	—	—	—	—	—	—	30	782
NFL	4	38(23)	515	2782	5.4(92)	16	40	352	8.8(27)	2	—	—	—	—	—	—	—	—	—	—	—	—	108	3128

Jackson, Bob Robert Herman, FB, 5´11˝/210 lbs; North Carolina A&T; 1950: NYG, rnd 16; B10/26/1922 Mineral, VA

YEAR	TEAM	G(GS, POS)	RUSH	YD	AVG(LG)	TD	REC	YD	AVG(LG)	TD	PASS	COMP	PCT	YD	AVG(LG)	TD	INT	SK	YD	QBR	KPR	OTD	PTS	TAY
1950	†NYG	12	12	113	9.4(57)	2	—	—	—	—	—	—	—	—	—	—	—	—	—	—	—	—	12	133
1951	NYG	12	5	9	1.8(6)	0	—	—	—	—	—	—	—	—	—	—	—	—	—	—	k	—	0	21
NFL	2	24	17	122	7.2(57)	2	—	—	—	—	—	—	—	—	—	—	—	—	—	—	k	—	12	154

Jackson, Bobby Robert Dean, FB, 6´3˝/238 lbs; New Mexico State; 1962: SD, rnd 7/SL, rnd 2; B3/16/1940 Shreveport, LA

YEAR	TEAM	G(GS, POS)	RUSH	YD	AVG(LG)	TD	REC	YD	AVG(LG)	TD	PASS	COMP	PCT	YD	AVG(LG)	TD	INT	SK	YD	QBR	KPR	OTD	PTS	TAY
1962	SD-A	14(FB)	106	411	3.9(19)	5	13	136	10.5(33)	2	—	—	—	—	—	—	—	—	—	—	k	—	42	540
1963	SD-A	12	18	64	3.6(14)	4	8	85	10.6(26)	0	—	—	—	—	—	—	—	—	—	—	k	—	24	148
1964	Hou-A	6	8	11	1.4(5)	3	—	—	—	—	—	—	—	—	—	—	—	—	—	—	k	—	18	43
1964	Oak-A	8	15	53	3.5(14)	0	10	81	8.1(14)	0	—	—	—	—	—	—	—	—	—	—	p	—	0	89
1965	Hou-A	10	37	85	2.3(7)	2	1	31	31.0(31)	0	—	—	—	—	—	—	—	—	—	—	k	—	12	130
NFL	4	50	184	624	3.4(19)	14	32	333	10.4(33)	2	—	—	—	—	—	—	—	—	—	—	kp	—	96	949

Jackson, Bobby Robert Charles, DB, 5´9˝/178 lbs; Florida State; 1978: NYJ, rnd 6; B12/23/1956 Albany, GA **[I]** **1978** NYJ 16 (16, LCB) **1979** NYJ 16 (16, LCB) **1980** NYJ 15 (15, LCB) **1981**†NYJ 9 (6, LCB) **1982**†NYJ 9 (9, LCB) **1983** NYJ 15 (15, LCB) **1984** NYJ 3 (2) **1985** NYJ 12 (11, LCB) **NFL** 95 (90) [8 yrs]

Jackson, Bobby Bobby Gerald, DB, 6´1˝/190 lbs; Alabama; 1959: GB, rnd 7; B1/10/1936 Geneva, AL **1960**†Phi 12 **1961** ChiB 9 **NFL** 21 [2 yrs]

Jackson, Brad Bradley Michael, LB, 6´0˝/230 lbs; Cincinnati; 1998: Mia, rnd 3; B1/11/1975 Canton, OH **1999** Bal 13 (0) **2000**†Bal 10 (0) **2001**†Bal 16 (5, llb) **2002** Car 11 (0) **NFL** 50 (5) [4 yrs]

Jackson, Calvin Calvin Bernard, DB, 5´9˝/185 lbs; Auburn; B10/28/1972 Miami, FL **1994** Mia 2 (0) **1995**†Mia 9 (1) **1996** Mia 16 (15, RCB) **1997**†Mia 16 (16, RCB) **1998**†Mia 16 (15, SS) **1999**†Mia 16 (10, SS) **NFL** 75 (57) [6 yrs]

Jackson, Cedric Cedric Anthony, RB, 5´11˝/229 lbs; TCU; 1991: Det, rnd 8; B1/13/1968 Texarkana, TX

YEAR	TEAM	G(GS, POS)	RUSH	YD	AVG(LG)	TD	REC	YD	AVG(LG)	TD	PASS	COMP	PCT	YD	AVG(LG)	TD	INT	SK	YD	QBR	KPR	OTD	PTS	TAY
1991	Det	8(1)	17	55	3.2(10)	0	1	-2	-2.0(-2)	0	—	—	—	—	—	—	—	—	—	—	k	—	0	48

Jackson, Charles Charles Melvin, LB, 6´2˝/225 lbs; Washington; 1977: Den, rnd 9; B3/22/1955 Los Angeles, CA **1978** KC 16 **1979** KC 12 (4) **1980** KC 16 (0) **1981** KC 14 (10, ROLB) **1982** KC 9 (9, ROLB) **1983** KC 15 (15, ROLB) **1984** KC 4 (4) **1985**†NYJ 16 (14, LOLB) **1986**†NYJ 15 (14, LOLB) **NFL** 117 (70) [9 yrs]

Jackson, Charles Charles Edward, DB, 6´4˝/210 lbs; Texas Tech; B3/12/1962 Fort Gaines, GA **1987** Was 1 (1)

Jackson, Charlie Charles Robert, DB, 5´11˝/180 lbs; SMU; 1958: ChiC, rnd 13; B3/3/1936 Paris, TX **1958** ChiC 10 **1960** DalT-A 3 **NFL** 13 [2 yrs]

Jackson, Chris Chris, WR, 6´2˝/205 lbs; Washington State; B2/26/1975 Bristol, PA **2000** Ten 1 (0) **2002** GB 1 (0) **2003** GB 1 (0) **NFL** 3 (0) [3 yrs]

Jackson, Cleveland Cleveland Lee, TE, 6´4˝/230 lbs; Michigan State; UNLV; 1979: NYG, rnd 5; B10/1/1956 Crossett, AR

YEAR	TEAM	G(GS, POS)	RUSH	YD	AVG(LG)	TD	REC	YD	AVG(LG)	TD	PASS	COMP	PCT	YD	AVG(LG)	TD	INT	SK	YD	QBR	KPR	OTD	PTS	TAY
1979	NYG	2	—	—	—	—	1	7	7.0(7)	0	—	—	—	—	—	—	—	—	—	—	—	—	0	4

Jackson, Corey Corey, DE, 6´6˝/255 lbs; Nevada-Reno; B11/6/1978 Cassatt, SC **2004** Cle 1 (0)

JACKSON, CURTIS Curtis Ray, WR, 5´10˝/190 lbs; Texas; B9/22/1973 Fort Worth, TX

YEAR	TEAM	G(GS, POS)	RUSH	YD	AVG(LG)	TD	REC	YD	AVG(LG)	TD	PASS	COMP	PCT	YD	AVG(LG)	TD	INT	SK	YD	QBR	KPR	OTD	PTS	TAY
2000	NE	5(2)	—	—	—	—	5	44	8.8(13)	0	—	—	—	—	—	—	—	—	—	—	k	—	0	150
2001	NE	2(0)	—	—	—	—	2	16	8.0(12)	0	—	—	—	—	—	—	—	—	—	—	k	—	0	8
NFL	2	7(2)	—	—	—	—	7	60	8.6(13)	0	—	—	—	—	—	—	—	—	—	—	k	—	0	158

JACKSON, DARRELL Darrell Lamont, WR, 6´0˝/201 lbs; Florida; 2000: Sea, rnd 3; B12/6/1978 Dayton, OH

YEAR	TEAM	G(GS, POS)	RUSH	YD	AVG(LG)	TD	REC	YD	AVG(LG)	TD	PASS	COMP	PCT	YD	AVG(LG)	TD	INT	SK	YD	QBR	KPR	OTD	PTS	TAY
2000	Sea	16(10, WR)	1	-1	-1.0(-1)	0	53	713	13.5(71)	6	—	—	—	—	—	—	—	—	—	—	—	—	36	386
2001	Sea	16(16, WR)	1	9	9.0(9)	0	70	1081	15.4(64)	8	—	—	—	—	—	—	—	—	—	—	—	—	48	590
2002	Sea	13(13, WR)	3	3	1.0(4)	0	62	877	14.1(48)	4	—	—	—	—	—	—	—	—	—	—	p	—	24	474
2003	†Sea	16(16, WR)	—	—	—	—	68	1137	16.7(80)	9	—	—	—	—	—	—	—	—	—	—	—	—	54	614
2004	†Sea	16(16, WR)	—	—	—	—	87	1199	13.8(56)	7	—	—	—	—	—	—	—	—	—	—	—	—	44	635
2005	†Sea	6(6, wr)	1	7	7.0(7)	0	38	482	12.7(48)	3	—	—	—	—	—	—	—	—	—	—	—	—	18	263
NFL	6	83(77)	6	18	3.0(9)	0	378	5489	14.5(80)	37	—	—	—	—	—	—	—	—	—	—	p	—	224	2960

JACKSON, DAVID David Leonard, WR, 5´8˝/175 lbs; Southeast Missouri State; B1/2/1965 Baltimore, MD **1987** TB 1 (0)

JACKSON, DEXTER Dexter Lamar, DB, 6´0˝/205 lbs; Florida State; 1999: TB, rnd 4; B7/28/1977 Quincy, FL **1999**†TB 12 (0) **2000**†TB 13 (0) **2001**†TB 15 (15, FS) **2002**†TB 16 (16, FS) **2003** Arz 16 (16, FS) **2004** TB 6 (1) **2005**†TB 11 (10, FS) **NFL** 89 (58) [7 yrs]

JACKSON, DON Donald Fletcher, TB-DB, 5´11˝/184 lbs; North Carolina; B11/14/1913, D8/25/1946 Dallas, TX

YEAR	TEAM	G(GS, POS)	RUSH	YD	AVG(LG)	TD	REC	YD	AVG(LG)	TD	PASS	COMP	PCT	YD	AVG(LG)	TD	INT	SK	YD	QBR	KPR	OTD	PTS	TAY
1936	Phi	10(2)	46	76	1.7	0	—	—	—	—	35	7	20.0	80	2.3	0	11	—	—	—	—	—	0	-324

JACKSON, EARNEST Earnest, RB, 5´9˝/213 lbs; Texas A&M; 1983: SD, rnd 8; B12/18/1959 Needville, TX

YEAR	TEAM	G(GS, POS)	RUSH	YD	AVG(LG)	TD	REC	YD	AVG(LG)	TD	PASS	COMP	PCT	YD	AVG(LG)	TD	INT	SK	YD	QBR	KPR	OTD	PTS	TAY
1983	SD	12(0)	11	39	3.5(6)	0	5	42	8.4(10)	0	—	—	—	—	—	—	—	—	—	—	k	—	0	96
1984	SD★	16(14, RB)	**296**	**1179**	4.0(32)	8	39	222	5.7(21)	1	—	—	—	—	—	—	—	—	—	—	k	—	54	1370
1985	Phi	16(10, RB)	282	1028	3.6(59)	5	10	126	12.6(25)	1	—	—	—	—	—	—	—	—	—	—	—	—	36	1146
1986	Pit✧	13(12, FB)	216	910	4.2(31)	5	17	169	9.9(28)	0	—	—	—	—	—	—	—	—	—	—	—	—	30	1045
1987	Pit	12(9, FB)	180	696	3.9(39)	1	7	52	7.4(23)	0	—	—	—	—	—	—	—	—	—	—	—	—	6	732
1988	Pit	12(6, fb)	74	315	4.3(29)	3	9	84	9.3(24)	0	—	—	—	—	—	—	—	—	—	—	—	—	18	387
NFL	6	81(51)	1059	4167	3.9(59)	22	87	695	8.0(28)	2	—	—	—	—	—	—	—	—	—	—	k	—	144	4776

JACKSON, EDDIE Eddie Paul, DB, 6´0˝/190 lbs; Arkansas; B12/19/1980 Americus, GA **2004** Car 10 (0) **2005** Mia 15 (1) **NFL** 25 (1) [2 yrs]

JACKSON, ENIS Enis, DB, 5´9˝/180 lbs; Memphis; B5/16/1963 Helena, AR **1987** Cle 1 (0)

JACKSON, ERNIE Earnest, DB, 5´10˝/173 lbs; Duke; 1972: NO, rnd 7; B4/11/1950 Hopkins, SC **1972** NO 10 (LCB) **1973** NO 14 (LCB) **1974** NO 13 (LCB) **1975** NO 13 (13, LCB) **1976** NO 10 (9, LCB) **1977** NO 11 (LCB) **1978**†Atl 16 **1979** Det 2 **NFL** 89 (22) [8 yrs]

JACKSON, FRANK Frank Hardin, FL-FB-SE-WR-HB, 6´1˝/185 lbs; SMU; 1961: DalT, rnd 19; B4/14/1939 Levelland, TX

YEAR	TEAM	G(GS, POS)	RUSH	YD	AVG(LG)	TD	REC	YD	AVG(LG)	TD	PASS	COMP	PCT	YD	AVG(LG)	TD	INT	SK	YD	QBR	KPR	OTD	PTS	TAY
1961	DalT-A	14(FB)	65	386	5.9(49)	3	13	171	13.2(52)	2	2	1	50.0	9	4.5(9)	0	1	—	—	—	kp	—	30	758
1962	†DalT-A	14(FL)	47	251	5.3(35)	3	10	177	17.7(62)	1	—	—	—	—	—	—	—	—	—	—	kp	—	24	541
1963	KC-A	14(FL)	3	52	17.3(25)	1	50	785	15.7(82)	8	—	—	—	—	—	—	—	—	—	—	kp	—	54	540
1964	KC-A	14(FL)	2	5	2.5(12)	0	62	943	15.2(72)	9	—	—	—	—	—	—	—	—	—	—	p	—	54	570
1965	KC-A✧	14(FL)	1	26	26.0(26)	0	28	440	15.7(73)	1	—	—	—	—	—	—	—	—	—	—	kp	—	6	474
1966	Mia-A	10(7, SE)	2	22	11.0(24)	0	16	317	19.8(48)	2	—	—	—	—	—	—	—	—	—	—	kp	—	12	233
1967	Mia-A	10(6, FL)	1	48	48.0(48)	0	9	122	13.6(26)	1	—	—	—	—	—	—	—	—	—	—	—	—	6	114
NFL	7	90(13)	121	790	6.5(49)	7	188	2955	15.7(82)	24	2	1	50.0	9	4.5(9)	0	1	—	—	—	kp	—	186	3228

JACKSON, FRISMAN Frisman, WR, 6´3˝/215 lbs; Western Illinois; B6/12/1979 Chicago, IL

YEAR	TEAM	G(GS, POS)	RUSH	YD	AVG(LG)	TD	REC	YD	AVG(LG)	TD	PASS	COMP	PCT	YD	AVG(LG)	TD	INT	SK	YD	QBR	KPR	OTD	PTS	TAY
2002	Cle	7(0)	—	—	—	—	1	6	6.0(6)	0	1	0	0.0	0	0.0	0	0	—	—	—	k	—	0	16
2003	Cle	5(0)	—	—	—	—	2	29	14.5(19)	0	1	0	0.0	0	0.0	0	0	—	—	—	—	—	0	15
2004	Cle	10(0)	1	4	4.0(4)	0	13	168	12.9(24)	0	1	0	0.0	0	0.0	0	0	—	—	—	k	—	0	98
2005	Cle	12(0)	—	—	—	—	24	287	12.0(68)	1	0	0	0.0	0	0.0	0	0	1	2	—	k	—	6	149
NFL	4	34(0)	1	4	4.0(4)	0	40	490	12.3(68)	1	3	0	0.0	0	0.0	0	0	1	2	—	k	—	6	277

JACKSON, GERALD Gerald Eugene, DB, 6´1˝/195 lbs; Mississippi State; 1979: KC, rnd 10; B3/5/1956 Moss Point, MS **1979** KC 16

JACKSON, GRADY Grady O'Neal, DT, 6´2˝/330 lbs; Knoxville; 1997: Oak, rnd 6; B1/21/1973 Greensboro, AL **1997** Oak 5 (0) **1998** Oak 15 (1) **1999** Oak 15 (0) **2000**†Oak 16 (15, LDT) **2001**†Oak 16 (16, RDT) **2002** NO 15 (15, LDT) **2003** NO 7 (6, rdt) **2003**†GB 8 (1) **2004**†GB 10 (10, LDT) **2005** GB 16 (16, LDT) **NFL** 123 (80) [9 yrs]

JACKSON, GREG Greg Allen, DB, 6´1˝/205 lbs; LSU; 1989: NYG, rnd 3; B8/20/1966 Hialeah, FL **[I]** **1989**†NYG 16 (1) **1990**†NYG 14 (14, SS) **1991** NYG 13 (12, SS) **1992** NYG 16 (16, FS) **1993**†NYG 16 (16, FS) **1994** Phi 16 (16, FS) **1995**†Phi 16 (16, FS) **1996** NO 16 (15, FS) **1997** SD 13 (0) **1998** SD 16 (13, FS) **1999** SD 14 (9, SS) **2000** SD 2 (1) **NFL** 168 (129) [12 yrs]

JACKSON, HAROLD Harold, WR-FL, 5´10˝/175 lbs; Jackson State; 1968: LA, rnd 12; B1/6/1946 Hattiesburg, MS

YEAR	TEAM	G(GS, POS)	RUSH	YD	AVG(LG)	TD	REC	YD	AVG(LG)	TD	PASS	COMP	PCT	YD	AVG(LG)	TD	INT	SK	YD	QBR	KPR	OTD	PTS	TAY
1968	LARm	2	—	—	—	—	—	—	—	—	—	—	—	—	—	—	—	—	—	—	—	—	—	—
1969	Phi✧	14(14, FL)	2	10	5.0(6)	0	65	**1116**	17.2(65)	9	—	—	—	—	—	—	—	—	—	—	—	—	54	613
1970	Phi	14(14, WR)	1	-5	-5.0(-5)	0	41	613	15.0(79)	5	—	—	—	—	—	—	—	—	—	—	—	—	30	327
1971	Phi	14(14, WR)	5	41	8.2(18)	0	47	716	15.2(69)	3	—	—	—	—	—	—	—	—	—	—	k	—	18	432
1972	Phi★	14(14, WR)	9	76	8.4(34)	0	**62**	**1048**	16.9(77)	4	—	—	—	—	—	—	—	—	—	—	—	—	24	620
1973	†LARm★	14(14, WR)	2	-8	-4.0(-3)	0	40	874	**21.9(69)**	**13**	—	—	—	—	—	—	—	—	—	—	—	—	78	494
1974	†LARm	14(14, WR)	1	4	4.0(4)	0	30	514	17.1(44)	5	—	—	—	—	—	—	—	—	—	—	—	—	30	286
1975	†LARm✧	14(14, WR)	—	—	—	—	43	786	18.3(54)	7	—	—	—	—	—	—	—	—	—	—	—	—	42	428
1976	†LARm☆	14(14, WR)	1	15	15.0(15)	0	39	751	19.3(65)	5	—	—	—	—	—	—	—	—	—	—	—	—	30	416
1977	†LARm★	14(14, WR)	1	6	6.0(6)	0	48	666	13.9(58)	6	—	—	—	—	—	—	—	—	—	—	—	—	36	369
1978	†NE	16(13, WR)	1	7	7.0(7)	0	37	743	20.1(57)	6	—	—	—	—	—	—	—	—	—	—	—	—	36	409
1979	NE	16(16, WR)	3	12	4.0(12)	0	45	1013	22.5(59)	7	1	0	0.0	0	0.0	0	0	—	—	—	—	—	42	554
1980	NE	16(15, WR)	5	37	7.4(16)	0	35	737	21.1(40)	5	2	2	100.0	35	17.5(23)	0	0	—	—	—	—	—	30	448
1981	NE	16(15, WR)	2	-14	-7.0(-5)	0	39	669	17.2(45)	0	1	0	0.0	0	0.0	0	0	—	—	—	—	—	0	321
1982	†Min	1(0)	—	—	—	—	—	—	—	—	—	—	—	—	—	—	—	—	—	—	—	—	—	—
1983	†Sea	15(6, wr)	—	—	—	—	8	126	15.8(29)	1	—	—	—	—	—	—	—	—	—	—	—	—	6	68
NFL	16	208(191)	33	181	5.5(34)	0	579	10372	17.9(79)	76	4	2	50.0	35	8.8(23)	0	0	—	—	—	k	—	456	5783

JACKSON, HONOR Honor W., DB, 6´1˝/195 lbs; Pacific; 1971: Dal, rnd 9; B11/21/1948 New Orleans, LA **1972** NE 13 (10, SS) **1973** NE 4 (3) **1973** NYG 3 **1974** NYG 12 **NFL** 32 (13) [3 yrs]

JACKSON, JACK Elliott Cornelius, WR, 5´8˝/174 lbs; Florida; 1995: Chi, rnd 4; B11/11/1972 Moss Point, MS

YEAR	TEAM	G(GS, POS)	RUSH	YD	AVG(LG)	TD	REC	YD	AVG(LG)	TD	PASS	COMP	PCT	YD	AVG(LG)	TD	INT	SK	YD	QBR	KPR	OTD	PTS	TAY
1996	ChiB	12(0)	—	—	—	—	4	39	9.8(14)	0	—	—	—	—	—	—	—	—	—	—	k	—	0	234

JACKSON, JAMAAL Jamaal, C-G, 6´4˝/330 lbs; Delaware State; B5/8/1980 Miami, FL **2005** Phi 8 (8, c)

JACKSON, JAMES James Shurrate, RB, 5´10˝/215 lbs; Miami (FL); 2001: Cle, rnd 3; B8/4/1976 Belle Glade, FL

YEAR	TEAM	G(GS, POS)	RUSH	YD	AVG(LG)	TD	REC	YD	AVG(LG)	TD	PASS	COMP	PCT	YD	AVG(LG)	TD	INT	SK	YD	QBR	KPR	OTD	PTS	TAY
2001	Cle	11(10, RB)	195	554	2.8(22)	2	7	56	8.0(16)	0	—	—	—	—	—	—	—	—	—	—	—	—	12	602
2002	†Cle	16(0)	12	54	4.5(18)	0	3	9	3.0(5)	0	—	—	—	—	—	—	—	—	—	—	k	—	0	57
2003	Cle	12(6, rb)	102	382	3.7(18)	3	14	114	8.1(18)	0	—	—	—	—	—	—	—	—	—	—	k	—	18	522
2004	Cle	4(0)	12	81	6.8(38)	0	6	22	3.7(13)	0	—	—	—	—	—	—	—	—	—	—	k	—	0	101
2004	GB	1(0)	—	—	—	—	—	—	—	—	—	—	—	—	—	—	—	—	—	—	—	—	—	—
2005	Arz	8(0)	4	11	2.8(3)	0	2	31	15.5(19)	0	—	—	—	—	—	—	—	—	—	—	k	—	0	26
NFL	5	52(16)	325	1082	3.3(38)	5	32	232	7.3(19)	0	—	—	—	—	—	—	—	—	—	—	k	—	30	1307

JACKSON, JARIOUS Jarious K., QB, 6´0˝/228 lbs; Notre Dame; 2000: Den, rnd 7; B5/3/1977 Tupelo, MS

YEAR	TEAM	G(GS, POS)	RUSH	YD	AVG(LG)	TD	REC	YD	AVG(LG)	TD	PASS	COMP	PCT	YD	AVG(LG)	TD	INT	SK	YD	QBR	KPR	OTD	PTS	TAY
2000	†Den	2(0)	1	-1	-1.0(-1)	0	—	—	—	—	1	0	0.0	0	0.0	0	0	1	5	—	—	—	0	-1
2001	Den	1(0)	5	7	1.4(4)	0	—	—	—	—	12	7	58.3	73	6.1(19)	0	0	1	6	—	—	—	0	44
2002	Den	1(0)	—	—	—	—	—	—	—	—	—	—	—	—	—	—	—	—	—	—	—	—	—	—
2003	Den	1(1)	1	9	9.0(9)	0	—	—	—	—	9	4	44.4	41	4.6(16)	0	1	—	—	—	—	—	0	-11
NFL	4	5(1)	7	15	2.1(9)	0	—	—	—	—	22	11	50.0	114	5.2(19)	0	1	2	11	—	—	—	0	32

YEAR	TEAM	G (GS, POS)	RUSH	YD	AVG(LG)	TD	REC	YD	AVG(LG)	TD	PASS	COMP	PCT	YD	AVG(LG)	TD	INT	SK	YD	QBR	KPR	OTD	PTS	TAY

JACKSON, JAZZ   Clarence, RB, 5'8"/167 lbs; Western Kentucky; 1974: NYJ, rnd 16; B3/5/1952 Knoxville, TN

YEAR	TEAM	G (GS, POS)	RUSH	YD	AVG(LG)	TD	REC	YD	AVG(LG)	TD	KPR	OTD	PTS	TAY
1974	NYJ	13	20	74	3.7(16)	0	2	44	22.0(24)	1	kp	1	12	160
1975	NYJ	13	6	11	1.8(7)	0	5	54	10.8(14)	0	kp	—	0	55
1976	NYJ	7	1	6	6.0(6)	0	2	3	1.5(6)	0	kp	—	0	34
NFL	3	33	27	91	3.4(16)	0	9	101	11.2(24)	1	kp	1	12	249

JACKSON, JEFF   Jeffrey Paul, LB, 6'1"/235 lbs; Auburn; 1984: Atl, rnd 8; B10/9/1961 Shreveport, LA   **1984** Atl 16 (0)   **1985** Atl 11 (1)   **1987** SD 11 (6, lilb)   **1988** SD 14 (1)   **NFL** 52 (8) [4 yrs]

JACKSON, JIM   James George, DB-HB, 5'11"/193 lbs; Western Illinois; 1966: SF, rnd 13; B4/19/1944 Alton, IL   **1967** SF 3

YEAR	TEAM	G (GS, POS)	RUSH	YD	AVG(LG)	TD	REC	YD	AVG(LG)	TD	KPR	OTD	PTS	TAY
1966	SF	10	4	7	1.8(4)	0	1	63	63.0(63)	1	kp		6	76
NFL	2	13	4	7	1.8(4)	0	1	63	63.0(63)	1	kpi		6	93

JACKSON, JOE   Joseph Loyd, LB, 6'1"/225 lbs; San Francisco State; B10/15/1962   **1987** Sea 3 (0)

JACKSON, JOEY   William Joseph, DE-DT, 6'4"/270 lbs; New Mexico State; 1972: NYJ, rnd 6; B5/7/1949 Cincinnati, OH   **1972** NYJ 14   **1973** NYJ 3   **1977**†Min 3   **NFL** 20 [3 yrs]

JACKSON, JOHN   John, WR, 5'10"/175 lbs; USC; B1/2/1967 Brooklyn, NY   **1990** Phx 9 (0)   **1996** ChiB 5 (0)

YEAR	TEAM	G (GS, POS)	RUSH	YD	AVG(LG)	TD	REC	YD	AVG(LG)	TD	KPR	OTD	PTS	TAY
1991	Phx	16(3)	—	—	—	—	8	108	13.5(30)	0	kp		0	154
1992	Phx	6(0)	—	—	—	—	1	5	5.0(5)	0	k		6	10
NFL	4	36(3)	—	—	—	—	9	113	12.6(30)	1	kp		6	164

JACKSON, JOHN   John, T, 6'6"/297 lbs; Eastern Kentucky; 1988: Pit, rnd 10; B1/4/1965 Camp Kwe, Okinawa   **1988** Pit 16 (0)   **1989**†Pit 14 (12, LT)   **1990** Pit 16 (16, LT)   **1991** Pit 16 (16, LT)   **1992**†Pit 16 (16, LT)   **1993**†Pit☆16 (13, LT)   **1994**†Pit 16 (16, LT)   **1995**†Pit 11 (9, LT)   **1996**†Pit☆16 (16, LT)   **1997**†Pit 16 (16, LT)   **1998** SD 16 (16, LT)   **1999** SD 15 (15, LT)   **2000** Cin 8 (5, lt)   **2001** Cin 11 (0)   **NFL** 203 (166) [14 yrs]

JACKSON, JOHNNIE   Johnnie Bobby, DB, 6'1"/204 lbs; Houston; 1989: SF, rnd 5; B1/11/1967 Harlingen, TX   **1989**†SF 16 (2)   **1990**†SF 16 (4)   **1991** SF 16 (4)   **1992** SF 5 (1)   **1992** GB 2 (0)   **NFL** 55 (11) [4 yrs]

JACKSON, JOHNNY   John, NT, 6'3"/250 lbs; Tennessee State; Sourhern (LA); 1977: SL, rnd 9; B7/1/1953 Lima, OH   **1977** Phi 2

JACKSON, JONATHAN   Jonathan Alexander, LB, 6'2"/239 lbs; Oregon State; B9/2/1977 Dayton, OH   **2001** NO 1 (0)

JACKSON, KEITH   Keith Jerome, TE, 6'2"/250 lbs; Oklahoma; 1988: Phi, rnd 1; B4/19/1965 Little Rock, AR

YEAR	TEAM	G (GS, POS)	RUSH	YD	AVG(LG)	TD	REC	YD	AVG(LG)	TD	OTD	PTS	TAY
1988	†Phi★	16(15, TE)	—	—	—	—	81	869	10.7(41)	6		36	465
1989	†Phi★	14(12, TE)	—	—	—	—	63	648	10.3(33)	3		18	339
1990	†Phi★	14(14, TE)	—	—	—	—	50	670	13.4(37)	6		36	365
1991	Phi	16(16, TE)	—	—	—	—	48	569	11.9(73)	5		30	310
1992	†Mia★	13(11, TE)	—	—	—	—	48	594	12.4(42)	5		30	322
1993	Mia	15(15, TE)	—	—	—	—	39	613	15.7(57)	6		36	339
1994	†Mia	16(16, TE)	—	—	—	—	59	673	11.4(35)	7		44	372
1995	†GB	9(1)	—	—	—	—	13	142	10.9(22)	1		6	76
1996	†GB★	16(5, te)	—	—	—	—	40	505	12.6(51)	10		60	303
NFL	9	129(105)	—	—	—	—	441	5283	12.0(73)	49		296	2887

JACKSON, KEN   Kenneth Gene, T-G, 6'2"/236 lbs; Texas; 1951: NYY, rnd 2; B4/26/1929 Austin, TX, D1/28/1998 McGregor, TX   **1952** DalT 12 (10, RT)   **1953** Bal 12   **1954** Bal 12 (LT)   **1955** Bal 8   **1956** Bal 12 (LT)   **1957** Bal 12   **NFL** 68 (10) [6 yrs]

JACKSON, KENNY   Kenneth, WR, 6'0"/180 lbs; Penn State; 1984: Phi, rnd 1; B2/15/1962 Neptune, NJ

YEAR	TEAM	G (GS, POS)	RUSH	YD	AVG(LG)	TD	REC	YD	AVG(LG)	TD	KPR	OTD	PTS	TAY
1984	Phi	11(9, WR)	—	—	—	—	26	398	15.3(83)	1			6	204
1985	Phi	16(16, WR)	—	—	—	—	40	692	17.3(54)	1			6	351
1986	Phi	16(14, WR)	1	6	6.0(6)	0	30	506	16.9(49)	6			36	289
1987	Phi	12(12, WR)	6	27	4.5(10)	0	21	471	22.4(70)	1			18	278
1988	†Phi	7(0)												
1989	†Hou	10(0)	—	—	—	—	4	31	7.8(18)	0			0	16
1990	†Phi	14(0)	—	—	—	—	1	43	43.0(43)	0	k		0	57
1991	Phi	16(2)	1	18	18.0(18)	0	4	29	7.3(9)	0	k		0	33
NFL	8	102(53)	8	51	6.4(18)	0	126	2170	17.2(83)	11	k		66	1226

JACKSON, KIRBY   Kirby, DB, 5'10"/179 lbs; Mississippi State; 1987: NYJ, rnd 5; B2/2/1965 Sturgis, MS   **1987** LARm 5 (3)   **1988**†Buf 8 (0)   **1989**†Buf 14 (13, LCB)   **1990**†Buf 12 (11, LCB)   **1991**†Buf 16 (12, LCB)   **1992**†Buf 15 (10, LCB)   **NFL** 70 (49) [6 yrs]

JACKSON, LaDAIRIS   LaDairis, DE, 6'2"/261 lbs; Oregon State; B6/16/1979 Denver, CO   **2002** Was 15 (0)

JACKSON, LARRON   Larron Deonne, G-T, 6'3"/270 lbs; Missouri; 1971: Hou, rnd 4; B8/26/1949 St. Louis, MO   **1971** Den 14 (9, LG)   **1972** Den 14 (14, LG)   **1974** Den 14 (8, LG)   **1975** Atl 14 (LG)   **1976** Atl 14 (LG)

YEAR	TEAM	G (GS, POS)	RUSH	YD	AVG(LG)	TD	REC	YD	AVG(LG)	TD	OTD	PTS	TAY
1973	Den	13(12, LG)	—	—	—	—	1	-2	-2.0(-2)	0		0	-1
NFL	6	83(43)	—	—	—	—	1	-2	-2.0(-2)	0		0	-1

JACKSON, LARRY   Lawrence W., C-TB, /185 lbs; Loyola (IL); B11/4/1904, D3/1983 Princeton, IL   **1926** Lou 2 (0)

JACKSON, LAWRENCE   Lawrence Dennell, G, 6'1"/275 lbs; Presbyterian; B8/10/1964 Jacksonville, FL   **1987** Atl 3 (3)

JACKSON, LENZIE   Lenzie Maurice, WR, 6'0"/184 lbs; Arizona State; B6/17/1977 Santa Clara, CA   **1999** Jax 4 (0)   **2001**†Pit 11 (0)

YEAR	TEAM	G (GS, POS)	RUSH	YD	AVG(LG)	TD	REC	YD	AVG(LG)	TD	KPR	OTD	PTS	TAY
2000	Cle	5(0)	—	—	—	—	1	5	5.0(5)	0	k		0	36
NFL	3	20(0)	—	—	—	—	1	5	5.0(5)	0	k		0	84

JACKSON, LEONARD   Leonard Maurice, LB, 6'0"/240 lbs; Oklahoma State; B10/5/1964 Pine Bluff, AR   **1987** LARd 1 (1)   **1987** ChiB 1 (0)   **NFL** 2 (1) [1 yr]

JACKSON, LEROY   Leroy, HB, 6'0"/198 lbs; Western Illinois; 1962: Cle, rnd 1/Bos, rnd 2; B12/8/1939 Chicago Heights, IL

YEAR	TEAM	G (GS, POS)	RUSH	YD	AVG(LG)	TD	REC	YD	AVG(LG)	TD	KPR	OTD	PTS	TAY
1962	Was	10	49	112	2.3(14)	0	10	253	25.3(85)	1	k		6	366
1963	Was	5	3	30	10.0(17)	0					k		0	68
NFL	2	15	52	142	2.7(17)	0	10	253	25.3(85)	1	k		6	434

JACKSON, LOUIS   Louis Bernard, RB, 5'11"/195 lbs; Cal Poly-San Luis Obispo; 1981: NYG, rnd 7; B1/27/1958 Fresno, CA

YEAR	TEAM	G (GS, POS)	RUSH	YD	AVG(LG)	TD	REC	YD	AVG(LG)	TD	OTD	PTS	TAY
1981	†NYG	11(3)	27	68	2.5(9)	1	3	25	8.3(19)	0		6	91

JACKSON, MARCUS   Marcus Reginald, DE-NT, 6'5"/260 lbs; Purdue; 1980: Cle, rnd 12; B6/8/1957 Lima, OH   **1987** Ind 1 (0)

JACKSON, MARK   Mark Anthony, WR, 5'9"/180 lbs; Purdue; 1986: Den, rnd 6; B7/23/1963 Chicago, IL

YEAR	TEAM	G (GS, POS)	RUSH	YD	AVG(LG)	TD	REC	YD	AVG(LG)	TD	KPR	OTD	PTS	TAY
1986	†Den	16(1)	2	6	3.0(5)	0	38	738	19.4(59)	1	kp		6	378
1987	†Den	12(9, WR)	—	—	—	—	26	436	16.8(52)	2			12	228
1988	Den	12(4)	1	5	5.0(5)	0	46	852	18.5(63)	6			36	461
1989	†Den	16(16, WR)	5	13	2.6(8)	0	28	446	15.9(49)	2			12	246
1990	Den	16(15, WR)	5	28	5.6(16)	1	57	926	16.2(66)	4	k		30	524
1991	†Den	12(10, WR)	2	18	9.0(21)	0	33	603	18.3(71)	1			6	325
1992	Den	16(13, WR)	3	-1	-0.3(1)	0	48	745	15.5(51)	8			48	412
1993	†NYG	16(16, WR)	3	25	8.3(20)	0	58	708	12.2(40)	4			24	399
1994	NYG	2(0)												
1994	Ind	12(0)	—	—	—	—	8	97	12.1(22)	0	k		6	44
NFL	9	130(84)	21	94	4.5(21)	1	342	5551	16.2(71)	29	kp		180	3016

JACKSON, MARK   Mark Devalon, DB, 5'9"/180 lbs; Abilene Christian; B3/16/1962 Amarillo, TX   **1987** SL 11 (4)

JACKSON, MARLIN   Marlin Tyrell, DB, 6'0"/196 lbs; Michigan; 2005: Ind, rnd 1; B6/30/1983 Sharon, PA   **2005**†Ind 15 (1)

JACKSON, MELVIN   Melvin, G, 6'1"/267 lbs; USC; 1976: GB, rnd 12; B5/5/1954 Los Angeles, CA   **1977** GB 13 (RG)   **1978** GB 16 (RG)   **1979** GB 16   **1980** GB 6 (0)

YEAR	TEAM	G (GS, POS)	RUSH	YD	AVG(LG)	TD	REC	YD	AVG(LG)	TD	OTD	PTS	TAY
1976	GB	13	—	—	—	—	1	8	8.0(8)	0		0	4
NFL	5	64	—	—	—	—	1	8	8.0(8)	0		0	4

YEAR TEAM G (GS, POS) RUSH YD AVG (LG) TD REC YD AVG (LG) TD PASS COMP PCT YD AVG (LG) TD INT SK YD QBR KPR OTD PTS TAY

JACKSON, MICHAEL Michael Anthony, LB, 6´1˝/220 lbs; Washington; 1979: Sea, rnd 3; B7/15/1957 Pasco, WA **1979** Sea 15 (7, llb) **1980** Sea 15 (15, LLB) **1981** Sea 16 (16, LLB) **1982** Sea 8 (8, MLB) **1983**†Sea 11 (9, ROLB) **1984**†Sea 8 (5, rolb) **1985** Sea 16 (16, ROLB) **1986** Sea 16 (1) **NFL** 105 (77) [8 yrs]

JACKSON, MICHAEL Michael Dwayne, aka Michael Dyson, WR, 6´4˝/195 lbs; Southern Mississippi; 1991: Cle, rnd 6; B4/12/1969 Tangipahoa, LA

YEAR	TEAM	G (GS, POS)	RUSH	YD	AVG (LG)	TD	REC	YD	AVG (LG)	TD	PASS	COMP	PCT	YD	AVG (LG)	TD	INT	SK	YD	QBR	KPR	OTD	PTS	TAY
1991	Cle	16 (7, wr)	—	—	—	—	17	268	15.8 (65)	2	—	—	—	—	—	—	—	—	—	—	—	—	12	144
1992	Cle	16 (14, WR)	1	21	21.0 (21)	0	47	755	16.1 (69)	7	—	—	—	—	—	—	—	—	—	—	—	—	42	434
1993	Cle	15 (11, WR)	1	1	1.0 (1)	0	41	756	18.4 (62)	8	1	1	100.0	25	25.0 (25)	0	0	—	—	—	—	—	48	432
1994	†Cle	9 (7, WR)	—	—	—	—	21	304	14.5 (30)	2	2	0	0.0	0	0.0	0	0	—	—	—	—	—	12	162
1995	Cle	13 (10, WR)	—	—	—	—	44	714	16.2 (70)	9	1	0	0.0	0	0.0	0	1	—	—	—	—	—	54	362
1996	Bal	16 (16, WR)	—	—	—	—	76	1201	15.8 (86)	**14**	—	—	—	—	—	—	—	—	—	—	—	—	88	671
1997	Bal	16 (15, WR)	—	—	—	—	69	918	13.3 (54)	4	—	—	—	—	—	—	—	—	—	—	—	—	26	479
1998	Bal	13 (12, WR)	—	—	—	—	38	477	12.6 (53)	0	—	—	—	—	—	—	—	—	—	—	—	—	0	239
NFL	8	114 (92)	2	22	11.0 (21)	0	353	5393	15.3 (86)	46	4	1	25.0	25	6.3 (25)	0	1	—	—	—	—	—	282	2921

JACKSON, MONTE Monte Carl, DB, 5´11˝/193 lbs; San Diego State; 1975: LA, rnd 2; B7/14/1953 Sherman, TX **[I]** **1975**†LARm 14 (9, RCB) **1976**†LARm★14 (14, RCB) **1977**†LARm★14 (14, RCB) **1978** Oak 16 (14, RCB) **1979** Oak 8 (3) **1980**†Oak 16 (10, RCB) **1981** Oak 16 (10, RCB) **1982**†LARd 9 (0) **1983** LARm 5 (1) **NFL** 112 (75) [9 yrs]

JACKSON, NATE Nate, WR, 6´3˝/223 lbs; Menlo; B6/4/1979 San Jose, CA **2003** Den 1 (0) **2005** Den 2 (0)

YEAR	TEAM	G (GS, POS)	RUSH	YD	AVG (LG)	TD	REC	YD	AVG (LG)	TD	PASS	COMP	PCT	YD	AVG (LG)	TD	INT	SK	YD	QBR	KPR	OTD	PTS	TAY
2004	Den	12 (0)	—	—	—	—	8	73	9.1 (20)	0	—	—	—	—	—	—	—	—	—	—	—	—	0	37
NFL	3	15 (0)	—	—	—	—	8	73	9.1 (20)	0	—	—	—	—	—	—	—	—	—	—	—	—	0	37

JACKSON, NOAH Noah Dale, G, 6´2˝/267 lbs; Tampa; 1974: Bal, rnd 7; B4/14/1951 Jacksonville Beach, FL **1976** ChiB 12 (12, LG) **1977**†ChiB 14 (14, LG) **1978** ChiB 16 (16, LG) **1979**†ChiB 15 (15, LG) **1980** ChiB☆16 (16, LG) **1981** ChiB 16 (16, LG) **1982** ChiB 9 (9, LG) **1983** ChiB 13 (13, LG) **1984** TB 6 (3)

YEAR	TEAM	G (GS, POS)	RUSH	YD	AVG (LG)	TD	REC	YD	AVG (LG)	TD	PASS	COMP	PCT	YD	AVG (LG)	TD	INT	SK	YD	QBR	KPR	OTD	PTS	TAY
1975	ChiB	14 (14, LG)	—	—	—	—	1	17	17.0 (17)	0	—	—	—	—	—	—	—	—	—	—	—	—	0	9
NFL	10	131 (128)	—	—	—	—	1	17	17.0 (17)	0	—	—	—	—	—	—	—	—	—	—	—	—	0	9

JACKSON, PERRY Perry, aka Artha E. Shockley, T-E, 6´1˝/202 lbs; Southwestern Oklahoma State; B8/31/1903 McKinley Twp, MO, D4/27/1988 Mountain View, OK **1928** Pro 10 (7, RT) **1929** Pro 7 (5, rt) **1930** Pro 10 (5, rt) **NFL** 27 (17) [3 yrs]

JACKSON, PETE Harry R., FB-BB-WB, 5´10˝/200 lbs; Missouri; B8/13/1904, D3/1967 **1928** Det 5 (0), 12

JACKSON, RANDY Randy Joe, RB, 6´0˝/220 lbs; Wichita State; 1972: Buf, rnd 4; B11/13/1948 Atlanta, TX

YEAR	TEAM	G (GS, POS)	RUSH	YD	AVG (LG)	TD	REC	YD	AVG (LG)	TD	PASS	COMP	PCT	YD	AVG (LG)	TD	INT	SK	YD	QBR	KPR	OTD	PTS	TAY
1972	Buf	5	17	57	3.4 (15)	0	2	21	10.5 (13)	1	—	—	—	—	—	—	—	—	—	—	—	—	6	73
1973	SF	2	6	10	1.7 (5)	0	1	20	20.0 (20)	0	—	—	—	—	—	—	—	—	—	—	—	—	0	20
1974	Phi	14	7	3	0.4 (2)	0	2	17	8.5 (9)	0	—	—	—	—	—	—	—	—	—	—	k	—	0	141
NFL	3	21	30	70	2.3 (15)	0	5	58	11.6 (20)	1	—	—	—	—	—	—	—	—	—	—	k	—	6	233

JACKSON, RANDY Randall Belford, T, 6´5˝/250 lbs; Florida; 1966: Chi, rnd 4/Buf, rnd 3; B3/6/1944 Lake City, FL **1967** ChiB 14 (14, LT) **1968** ChiB 14 (14, LT) **1969** ChiB 14 (LT) **1970** ChiB 10 (LT) **1971** ChiB 14 (LT) **1972** ChiB 14 (LT) **1973** ChiB 14 (LT) **1974** ChiB 11 **NFL** 105 (28) [8 yrs]

JACKSON, RAY Raymond F., RB, 6´1˝/223 lbs; Michigan; Cincinnati; B8/1/1978 Indianapolis, IN **2003** Ten 1 (0)

JACKSON, RAYMOND Raymond DeWayne, DB, 5´10˝/189 lbs; Colorado State; 1996: Buf, rnd 5; B2/17/1973 East Chicago, IL **1996**†Buf 12 (0) **1997** Buf 9 (0) **1998**†Buf 14 (0) **1999** Cle 14 (0) **2000** Cle 9 (1) **2001** Cle 15 (0) **NFL** 73 (1) [6 yrs]

JACKSON, RED Colville Cameron, T, 6´0˝/200 lbs; Chicago; B4/15/1897 Chicago, IL, D11/1963, MS **1921** Evv 1 (0) **1921** Ham 1 (1) **NFL** 2 (1) [1 yr]

JACKSON, RICH Richard Samuel 'Tombstone', DE-LB, 6´3˝/255 lbs; Southern (LA); B7/22/1941 New Orleans, LA **1966** Oak-A 5 **1967** Den-A 14 (RDE) **1968** Den-A★14 (RDE) **1969** Den-A★14 (14, LDE) **1970** Den★14 (14, LDE) **1971** Den☆7 (7, LDE) **1972** Den 4 (3) **1972** Cle 10 (LDE) **NFL** 82 (38) [7 yrs]

JACKSON, RICKEY Rickey Anderson, LB-DE, 6´2˝/243 lbs; Pittsburgh; 1981: NO, rnd 2; B3/20/1958 Pahokee, FL **[S]** **1981** NO 16 (16, LOLB) **1982** NO 9 (9, LOLB) **1983** NO★16 (16, LOLB) **1984** NO★16 (16, LOLB) **1985** NO★16 (16, LOLB) **1986** NO★16 (16, LOLB) **1987**†NO☆12 (12, LOLB) **1988** NO 16 (16, LOLB) **1989** NO 14 (14, LOLB) **1990**†NO 16 (16, LOLB) **1991**†NO 16 (16, LOLB) **1992**†NO★16 (16, LOLB) **1993** NO★16 (16, LOLB) **1994**†SF 16 (14, RDE) **1995**†SF 16 (16, RDE) **NFL** 227 (225) [15 yrs]

JACKSON, ROBERT Robert Michael, DB, 5´10˝/184 lbs; Central Michigan; 1981: Cin, rnd 11; B10/10/1958 Grand Rapids, MI **1982** Cin 9 (0) **1983** Cin 16 (16, FS) **1984** Cin 16 (16, FS) **1985** Cin 16 (5, fs) **1986** Cin 7 (6, fs) **1987** Cin 12 (12, FS) **1989** Cin 14 (0) **NFL** 90 (55) [7 yrs]

JACKSON, ROBERT Robert Edward, G-T-C, 6´2˝/255 lbs; Duke; B4/1/1953 Charlotte, NC **1975** Cle 14 (7, rg) **1976** Cle 14 (14, RG) **1977** Cle 14 (14, RG) **1978** Cle 16 (16, RG) **1979** Cle 16 (16, RG) **1980**†Cle 14 (4) **1981** Cle 16 (13, LG) **1982**†Cle 9 (9, LG) **1983** Cle 16 (16, LG) **1984** Cle 16 (16, LG) **1985** Cle 15 (1) **NFL** 160 (126) [11 yrs]

JACKSON, ROBERT Robert Lee, LB, 6´1˝/230 lbs; Texas A&M; 1977: Cle, rnd 1; B8/7/1954 Houston, TX **1978** Cle 14 **1979** Cle 16 (5, rilb) **1980**†Cle 14 (14, LILB) **1981** Cle 14 (14, LILB) **1982**†Atl 4 (0) **NFL** 62 (33) [5 yrs]

JACKSON, ROGER Roger, DB, 6´0˝/186 lbs; Bethune-Cookman; B2/28/1959 Macon, AL **1982** Den 9 (0) **1983**†Den 16 (3) **1984**†Den 16 (0) **1985** Den 9 (0) **1987** Den 3 (2) **NFL** 53 (5) [5 yrs]

JACKSON, ROLAND Thomas Roland, FB-LB, 6´0˝/210 lbs; Rice; 1962: Hou, rnd 21; B1/5/1940 **1962** SL 5

JACKSON, RUSTY Dalton Sharman, P, 6´2˝/193 lbs; LSU; B11/17/1950 Tuscaloosa, AL, D4/14/1997 Chatom, WA **[P]** **1976**†LARm 14 **1979** Buf 16

YEAR	TEAM	G (GS, POS)	RUSH	YD	AVG (LG)	TD	REC	YD	AVG (LG)	TD	PASS	COMP	PCT	YD	AVG (LG)	TD	INT	SK	YD	QBR	KPR	OTD	PTS	TAY
1978	Buf	16	1	-13	-13.0 (-13)	0	—	—	—	—	—	—	—	—	—	—	—	—	—	—	P	—	0	-13
NFL	3	46	1	-13	-13.0 (-13)	0	—	—	—	—	—	—	—	—	—	—	—	—	—	—	P	—	0	-13

JACKSON, SHELDON Sheldon Blair, TE, 6´3˝/250 lbs; Nebraska; 1999: Buf, rnd 7; B7/24/1976 Diamond Bar, CA

YEAR	TEAM	G (GS, POS)	RUSH	YD	AVG (LG)	TD	REC	YD	AVG (LG)	TD	PASS	COMP	PCT	YD	AVG (LG)	TD	INT	SK	YD	QBR	KPR	OTD	PTS	TAY
1999	†Buf	13 (4)	—	—	—	—	4	34	8.5 (16)	0	—	—	—	—	—	—	—	—	—	—	—	—	0	17
2000	Buf	16 (8, TE)	—	—	—	—	5	36	7.2 (12)	1	—	—	—	—	—	—	—	—	—	—	—	—	6	23
2001	Buf	16 (1)	—	—	—	—	1	1	1.0 (1)	1	—	—	—	—	—	—	—	—	—	—	—	—	6	6
NFL	3	45 (13)	—	—	—	—	10	71	7.1 (16)	2	—	—	—	—	—	—	—	—	—	—	—	—	12	46

JACKSON, STEVE Stephen Franklin, LB, 6´1˝/225 lbs; Texas-Arlington; B12/8/1942 McKinney, TX **1966** Was 14 **1967** Was 11 **NFL** 25 [2 yrs]

JACKSON, STEVE Stephen Loran, DB, 6´1˝/192 lbs; LSU; B4/6/1955 Chatom, AL **1977**†Oak 6

JACKSON, STEVE Steven Wayne, DB, 5´8˝/188 lbs; Purdue; 1991: Hou, rnd 3; B4/8/1969 Houston, TX **1991**†Hou 15 (2) **1992**†Hou 16 (1) **1993**†Hou 16 (12, RCB) **1994** Hou 11 (0) **1995** Hou 10 (1) **1996** Hou 16 (1) **1997** Ten 12 (5, lcb) **1998** Ten 14 (4) **1999**†Ten 8 (0) **NFL** 118 (26) [9 yrs]

JACKSON, STEVEN Steven Rashad, RB, 6´3˝/229 lbs; Oregon State; 2004: SL, rnd 1; B7/22/1983 Las Vegas, NV

YEAR	TEAM	G (GS, POS)	RUSH	YD	AVG (LG)	TD	REC	YD	AVG (LG)	TD	PASS	COMP	PCT	YD	AVG (LG)	TD	INT	SK	YD	QBR	KPR	OTD	PTS	TAY
2004	†SL	14 (3)	134	673	5.0 (48)	4	19	189	9.9 (28)	0	—	—	—	—	—	—	—	—	—	—	k	—	26	827
2005	SL	15 (15, RB)	254	1046	4.1 (51)	8	43	320	7.4 (27)	2	—	—	—	—	—	—	—	—	—	—	—	—	60	1296
NFL	2	29 (18)	388	1719	4.4 (51)	12	62	509	8.2 (28)	2	—	—	—	—	—	—	—	—	—	—	k	—	86	2123

JACKSON, T.J. Trenton James, WR-DB, 6´0˝/180 lbs; Illinois; B2/28/1943 Cordele, GA **1966** Phi 3 **1967** Was 3 **NFL** 6 [2 yrs]

JACKSON, TERRY Terence Leon, DB, 5´10˝/197 lbs; San Diego State; 1978: NYG, rnd 5; B12/9/1955 Sherman, TX **[I]** **1978** NYG 15 (15, LCB) **1979** NYG 16 (16, LCB) **1980** NYG 8 (7, lcb) **1981**†NYG 16 (16, RCB) **1982** NYG 8 (8, RCB) **1983** NYG 12 (12, RCB) **1984**†Sea 16 (0) **1985** Sea 16 (0) **NFL** 107 (74) [8 yrs]

JACKSON, TERRY Terrance Bernard, FB, 6´0˝/232 lbs; Florida; 1999: SF, rnd 5; B1/10/1976 Gainesville, FL

YEAR	TEAM	G (GS, POS)	RUSH	YD	AVG (LG)	TD	REC	YD	AVG (LG)	TD	PASS	COMP	PCT	YD	AVG (LG)	TD	INT	SK	YD	QBR	KPR	OTD	PTS	TAY
1999	SF	16 (0)	15	75	5.0 (11)	0	3	6	2.0 (4)	0	—	—	—	—	—	—	—	—	—	—	—	—	0	78
2000	SF	15 (1)	5	6	1.2 (3)	1	5	48	9.6 (16)	1	—	—	—	—	—	—	—	—	—	—	k	—	14	39
2001	†SF	16 (1)	22	138	6.3 (15)	1	12	91	7.6 (14)	2	—	—	—	—	—	—	—	—	—	—	—	—	18	204
2002	SF	5 (0)	—	—	—	—	—	—	—	—	—	—	—	—	—	—	—	—	—	—	k	—	0	7
2003	SF	16 (0)	—	—	—	—	—	—	—	—	—	—	—	—	—	—	—	—	—	—	—	—	0	0
2004	SF	16 (0)	26	101	3.9 (13)	0	21	139	6.6 (22)	0	—	—	—	—	—	—	—	—	—	—	k	—	0	163
2005	SF	16 (0)	2	11	5.5 (11)	0	10	67	6.7 (12)	0	—	—	—	—	—	—	—	—	—	—	—	—	2	45
NFL	7	100 (2)	70	331	4.7 (15)	2	51	351	6.9 (22)	3	—	—	—	—	—	—	—	—	—	—	k	—	34	535

JACKSON, TIM Timothy Gerrard, DB, 5´11˝/192 lbs; Kansas State; Nebraska; 1989: Dal, rnd 9; B11/7/1965 Dallas, TX **1989** Dal 1 (0)

JACKSON, TOM Thomas Louie, LB, 5´11˝/220 lbs; Louisville; 1973: Den, rnd 4; B4/4/1951 Cleveland, OH **[I]** **1973** Den 8 (4) **1974** Den 13 (12, RLB/llb) **1975** Den 14 (14, LLB) **1976** Den 14 (14, ROLB/rlb) **1977**†Den★13 (13, ROLB) **1978**†Den★16 (16, ROLB) **1979**†Den★13 (13, ROLB) **1980** Den 16 (16, ROLB) **1981** Den 16 (16, ROLB) **1982** Den 9 (9, ROLB) **1983**†Den 15 (15, ROLB) **1984**†Den☆16 (16, ROLB) **1985** Den 12 (5, rolb) **1986**†Den 16 (14, ROLB) **NFL** 191 (177) [14 yrs]

JACKSON, TYOKA Tyoka, DE-DT, 6´2˝/280 lbs; Penn State; B11/22/1971 Washington, DC **1994**†Mia 1 (0) **1996** TB 13 (2) **1997**†TB 12 (0) **1998** TB 16 (12, LDE) **1999** TB 6 (1) **2000**†TB 16 (1) **2001**†SL 16 (0) **2002** SL 16 (0) **2003**†SL 16 (3) **2004** SL 14 (0) **2005** SL 16 (2) **NFL** 142 (21) [11 yrs]

YEAR	TEAM	G(GS, POS)	RUSH	YD	AVG(LG)	TD	REC	YD	AVG(LG)	TD	PASS COMP	PCT	YD	AVG(LG)	TD	INT	SK	YD	QBR	KPR	OTD	PTS	TAY

JACKSON, VESTEE   Vestee, DB-LB, 6´0˝/189 lbs; Washington; 1986: Chi, rnd 2; B8/14/1963 Fresno, CA   **1986**†ChiB 16 (8, RCB)   **1987**†ChiB 12 (12, RCB)
1988†ChiB 16 (16, RCB)   **1989** ChiB 16 (15, RCB)   **1990**†ChiB 16 (8, rcb)   **1991** Mia 16 (16, LCB/rcb)   **1992** Mia 11 (5, lilb)   **1993** Mia 16 (5, llb)   **NFL** 119 (85) [8 yrs]

JACKSON, VINCENT   Vincent, WR, 6´5˝/241 lbs; Northern Colorado; 2005: SD, rnd 2; B1/14/1983 Colorado Springs, CO

| 2005 | SD | 7(0) | — | — | — | — | 3 | 59 | 19.7(21) | 0 | — | — | — | — | — | — | — | — | — | — | — | 0 | 30 |

JACKSON, VICTOR   Victor Alan, DB, 6´0˝/205 lbs; Bowie State; B8/6/1959 Princess Anne, MD   **1986** Ind 2 (0)   **1987** Ind 2 (0)   **NFL** 4 (0) [2 yrs]

JACKSON, WAVERLY   Waverly Arthur, G-T, 6´2˝/310 lbs; Virginia Tech; B12/19/1972 South Hill, VA   **1998** Ind 6 (2)   **1999**†Ind 16 (16, RG)   **2000**†Ind 16 (0)   **2001** Ind 16 (0)
2002†Ind 14 (4)   **NFL** 68 (22) [5 yrs]

JACKSON, WILBUR   Wilbur, RB, 6´1˝/215 lbs; Alabama; 1974: SF, rnd 1; B11/19/1951 Ozark, AL

1974	SF	14(13, RB)	174	705	4.1(64)	0	23	190	8.3(31)	2	—	—	—	—	—	—	—	—	—	k	—	12	838
1975	SF	14(4)	78	303	3.9(44)	0	17	128	7.5(20)	0	—	—	—	—	—	—	—	—	—	—	—	0	367
1976	SF	14(14, FB)	200	792	4.0(24)	1	33	324	9.8(32)	1	—	—	—	—	—	—	—	—	—	—	—	12	969
1977	SF	14(14, FB)	179	780	4.4(80)	7	22	169	7.7(24)	0	—	—	—	—	—	—	—	—	—	—	—	42	935
1979	SF	16(14, FB)	114	375	3.3(16)	2	53	422	8.0(34)	0	—	—	—	—	—	—	—	—	—	—	—	12	606
1980	Was	16(12, RB)	176	708	4.0(55)	3	27	279	10.3(27)	1	—	—	—	—	—	—	—	—	—	k	—	24	967
1981	Was	5(2)	46	183	4.0(14)	0	7	51	7.3(16)	0	—	—	—	—	—	—	—	—	—	k	—	0	213
1982	†Was	1(0)	4	6	1.5(2)	0	1	9	9.0(9)	0	—	—	—	—	—	—	—	—	—	—	—	0	11
NFL	8	94(73)	971	3852	4.0(80)	13	183	1572	8.6(34)	4	—	—	—	—	—	—	—	—	—	k	—	102	4904

JACKSON, WILLIE   Willie Bernard, WR, 6´1˝/212 lbs; Florida; 1994: Dal, rnd 4; B8/16/1971 Gainesville, FL

1995	Jax	14(10, WR)	—	—	—	—	53	589	11.1(45)	0	—	—	—	—	—	—	—	—	—	kp	—	32	432
1996	†Jax	16(2)	1	2	2.0(2)	0	33	486	14.7(58)	3	—	—	—	—	—	—	—	—	—	k	—	20	304
1997	†Jax	16(1)	3	14	4.7(13)	0	17	206	12.1(45)	2	—	—	—	—	—	—	—	—	—	k	—	14	300
1998	Cin	8(0)	—	—	—	—	7	165	23.6(47)	0	—	—	—	—	—	—	—	—	—	—	—	0	83
1999	Cin	16(2)	—	—	—	—	31	369	11.9(29)	2	—	—	—	—	—	—	—	—	—	kp	—	14	280
2000	†NO	15(7, WR)	—	—	—	—	37	523	14.1(53)	6	—	—	—	—	—	—	—	—	—	—	—	36	292
2001	NO	16(16, WR)	—	—	—	—	81	1046	12.9(63)	6	—	—	—	—	—	—	—	—	—	—	—	32	548
2002	Atl	7(1)	—	—	—	—	18	199	11.1(29)	0	—	—	—	—	—	—	—	—	—	—	—	0	100
2002	Was	—	—	—	—	—	7	58	8.3(19)	1	—	—	—	—	—	—	—	—	—	k	—	6	36
NFL	8	113(39)	4	16	4.0(13)	0	284	3641	12.8(63)	24	—	—	—	—	—	—	—	—	—	kp	—	154	2373

JACKUNAS, FRANK   Frank Raymond, C, 6´3˝/225 lbs; Detroit Mercy; 1961: Buf, rnd 24/Pit, rnd 12; B10/5/1940 Detroit, MI   **1962** Buf-A 3

JACOBS, ALLEN   Allen Winnitt, FB-HB, 6´1˝/215 lbs; Utah; 1964: GB, rnd 10/Buf, rnd 26; B5/19/1941 Los Angeles, CA

1965	†GB	14	3	5	1.7(2)	0	—	—	—	—	—	—	—	—	—	—	—	—	—	—	—	0	5
1966	NYG	14	77	273	3.5(19)	1	10	69	6.9(29)	0	—	—	—	—	—	—	—	—	—	k	—	6	306
1967	NYG	6	11	23	2.1(5)	0	—	—	—	—	—	—	—	—	—	—	—	—	—	—	—	0	23
NFL	3	34	91	301	3.3(19)	1	10	69	6.9(29)	0	—	—	—	—	—	—	—	—	—	k	—	6	334

JACOBS, BRANDON   Brandon, RB, 6´4˝/256 lbs; Southern Illinois; 2005: NYG, rnd 4; B7/6/1982 Houma, LA

| 2005 | †NYG | 11 | 38 | 99 | 2.6(21) | 7 | — | — | — | — | — | — | — | — | — | — | — | — | — | k | — | 42 | 197 |

JACOBS, CAM   Thomas Cameron, LB, 6´2˝/230 lbs; Kentucky; 1985: Pit, rnd 5; B3/10/1962 Oklahoma City, OK   **1987** TB 3 (0)

JACOBS, DAVE   David Joseph, K, 5´7˝/151 lbs; Syracuse; 1979: Den, rnd 12; B7/1/1957 Scranton, PA **[K]**   **1979** NYJ 4   **1981** Cle 5 (0)   **1987** Phi 3 (0)   **NFL** 12 [3 yrs]

JACOBS, HARRY   Harry Edward, LB-DE, 6´1˝/226 lbs; Bradley; 1959: Det, rnd 11; B2/4/1937 Canton, IL   **1960** Bos-A 14   **1961** Bos-A 9 (MLB)   **1962** Bos-A 14
1963†Buf-A 14 (MLB)   **1964**†Buf-A 14 (MLB)   **1965**†Buf-A☆14 (14, MLB)   **1966**†Buf-A☆14 (14, MLB)   **1967** Buf-A 7 (7, MLB)   **1968** Buf-A 14 (14, MLB)   **1969** Buf-A◇14 (MLB)
1970 NO 6   **NFL** 134 (49) [11 yrs]

JACOBS, JACK   Jack, QB-TB-HB, 6´1˝/186 lbs; Oklahoma; 1942: Cle, rnd 2; B8/7/1919 Holdenville, OK, D1/12/1974 Greensboro, NC

1942	Cle	8(3, tb)	32	-31	-1.0(13)	0	—	—	—	—	93	43	46.2	640	6.9(67)	6	6	—	—	Pkpi	—	0	127
1945	Cle	2(1)	2	0	0.0(0)	0	—	—	—	—	5	3	60.0	12	2.4(11)	0	0	—	—	Pp	—	0	7
1946	Was	9(2)	18	34	1.9(9)	0	4	53	13.3(21)	0	12	5	41.7	98	8.2(35)	0	2	—	—	Ppi	—	0	89
1947	GB	12(8, QB)	18	64	3.6(15)	1	—	—	—	—	242	108	44.6	1615	6.7(69)	16	17	—	59.8	Ppi	—	6	325
1948	GB	12(8, QB)	24	73	3.0(23)	1	—	—	—	—	184	82	44.6	848	4.6(64)	5	21	—	27.9	Pp	—	6	-310
1949	GB	12(1)	—	—	—	—	—	—	—	—	16	3	18.8	55	3.4(39)	0	3	—	—	Ppi	—	0	-73
NFL	6	55(23)	94	140	1.5(23)	2	4	53	13.3(21)	0	552	244	44.2	3268	5.9(69)	27	49	—	42.9	Pkpi	—	12	165

JACOBS, MARV   Marvin Elzie, T, 6´2˝/235 lbs; none; B8/1/1925 Yakima, WA   **1948** ChiC 5 (0)

JACOBS, PROVERB   Proverb Gabriel, T-DT, 6´4˝/258 lbs; California; 1958: Phi, rnd 2; B5/25/1935 Marksville, LA   **1958** Phi 12 (LT)   **1960** NYG 8   **1961** NYT-A 10   **1962** NYT-A 4
1963 Oak-A 14 (LT)   **1964** Oak-A 6 (lt)   **NFL** 54 [6 yrs]

JACOBS, RAY   Herschel Ray, DT-DE, 6´3˝/285 lbs; Howard Payne; 1962: Hou, rnd 1/Dal, rnd 17; B11/21/1938 Corsicana, TX   **1963** Den-A 7 (LDE)   **1964** Den-A 14 (LDE)
1965 Den-A☆14 (LDT)   **1966** Den-A 14 (LDT)   **1967** Mia-A 14 (10, LDT)   **1968** Mia-A 11 (10, RDT)   **1969** Bos-A 8 (5, lde)   **NFL** 79 (25) [7 yrs]

JACOBS, RAY   Ray Anthony, LB, 6´2˝/244 lbs; North Carolina; B8/18/1972 Hamstead, NC   **1994** Den 16 (0)   **1995** Den 15 (0)   **NFL** 31 (0) [2 yrs]

JACOBS, STAN   Stanley, TB, none; B4/15/1897, D4/1966 Inkster, MI   **1920** Det 3 (1)

JACOBS, TAYLOR   Taylor Houser, WR, 6´0˝/198 lbs; Florida; 2003: Was, rnd 2; B5/30/1981 Tallahassee, FL

2003	Was	8(0)	—	—	—	—	3	37	12.3(19)	1	—	—	—	—	—	—	—	—	—	—	—	6	24
2004	Was	15(4)	1	-6	-6.0(-6)	0	16	178	11.1(45)	0	—	—	—	—	—	—	—	—	—	—	—	2	83
2005	†Was	15(3)	—	—	—	—	11	100	9.1(24)	0	—	—	—	—	—	—	—	—	—	—	—	0	50
NFL	3	38(7)	1	-6	-6.0(-6)	0	30	315	10.5(45)	1	—	—	—	—	—	—	—	—	—	—	—	8	157

JACOBS, TIM   Timothy, DB, 5´10˝/187 lbs; Delaware; B4/5/1970 Washington, DC   **1993** Cle 2 (0)   **1994**†Cle 10 (1)   **1995** Cle 14 (0)   **1996** Mia 12 (0)   **1997**†Mia 16 (1)
NFL 54 (2) [5 yrs]

JACOBSON, JACK   Jack Cliston, DB, 6´2˝/200 lbs; Oklahoma State; 1965: Det, rnd 13; B6/23/1941 Stillwater, OK   **1965** SD-A 3

JACOBSON, LARRY   Larry Paul, DT-DE, 6´6˝/260 lbs; Nebraska; 1972: NYG, rnd 1; B12/10/1949 Sioux Falls, SD   **1972** NYG 14 (LDT)   **1973** NYG 8   **1974** NYG 11   **NFL** 33 [3 yrs]

JACOBSON, STEVE   Stephen Dean, G, 6´3˝/255 lbs; Texas A&M; Abilene Christian; B11/18/1962 Corpus Christi, TX   **1987** Mia 3 (0)

JACOBY, JOE   Joseph Erwin, T-G, 6´7˝/305 lbs; Louisville; B7/6/1959 Louisville, KY   **1981** Was 14 (13, LT)   **1982**†Was 9 (9, LT)   **1983**†Was☆16 (16, LT)   **1984**†Was☆16 (16, LT)
1985 Was☆11 (11, LT)   **1986**†Was☆16 (16, LT)   **1987**†Was☆12 (12, LT)   **1988** Was 16 (13, LT)   **1989** Was 10 (10, RT)   **1990**†Was 16 (6, rt)   **1991**†Was 16 (16, RT)
1992†Was 13 (9, LG/rt)   **1993** Was 5 (1)   **NFL** 170 (148) [13 yrs]

JACOBY, MITCH   Mitchel Ray, TE, 6´4˝/260 lbs; Northern Illinois; B12/8/1973 Port Washington, WI

1997	SL	14(2)	—	—	—	—	2	10	5.0(10)	0	—	—	—	—	—	—	—	—	—	—	—	0	5
1998	SL	5(0)	—	—	—	—	—	—	—	—	—	—	—	—	—	—	—	—	—	—	—	0	—
1999	KC	5(0)	—	—	—	—	1	6	6.0(6)	0	—	—	—	—	—	—	—	—	—	—	—	0	3
NFL	3	24(2)	—	—	—	—	3	16	5.3(10)	0	—	—	—	—	—	—	—	—	—	—	—	0	8

JACOX, KENDYL   Kendyl LaMarc, G-C, 6´2˝/330 lbs; Kansas State; B6/10/1975 Dallas, TX   **1998** SD 16 (6, rg)   **1999** SD 10 (5, rg)   **2000** SD 16 (3)   **2001** SD 16 (16, C)
2002 NO 16 (16, LG)   **2003** NO 12 (11, LG)   **2004** NO 13 (13, LG)   **2005** NO 15 (15, LG)   **NFL** 114 (85) [8 yrs]

JACQUET, NATE   Nathaniel Martin, WR, 6´0˝/173 lbs; San Diego State; 1997: Ind, rnd 5; B9/2/1975 Duarte, CA **[R]**   **1997** Ind 5 (0)   **2000** Min 1 (0)   **2001** Min 10 (0)

1998	†Mia	15(0)	—	—	—	—	8	122	15.3(29)	0	—	—	—	—	—	—	—	—	—	k	—	0	104
1999	†Mia	13(0)	1	4	4.0(4)	0	1	18	18.0(18)	0	—	—	—	—	—	—	—	—	—	kp	—	0	235
2000	SD	11(0)	—	—	—	—	1	25	25.0(25)	0	—	—	—	—	—	—	—	—	—	p	—	0	74
NFL	5	55(0)	1	4	4.0(4)	0	10	165	16.5(29)	0	—	—	—	—	—	—	—	—	—	kp	—	0	876

JACQUITH, JIM   James M., BB, 5´9˝/175 lbs; College of Emporia; B4/1899 Council Grove, KS   **1926** KC 1 (0)

YEAR	TEAM	G (GS, POS)	RUSH	YD	AVG(LG)	TD	REC	YD	AVG(LG)	TD	PASS	COMP	PCT	YD	AVG(LG)	TD	INT	SK	YD	QBR	KPR	OTD	PTS	TAY

JACUNSKI, HARRY Harry Anthony, E, 6´2˝/200 lbs; Fordham; B10/20/1915 New Britain, CT, D2/20/2003 Branford, CT

YEAR	TEAM	G (GS, POS)	RUSH	YD	AVG(LG)	TD	REC	YD	AVG(LG)	TD	KPR	OTD	PTS	TAY
1939	†GB◇	11(2)	—	—	—	—	5	104	20.8(29)	2		—	12	62
1940	GB	10(5, le)	—	—	—	—	2	29	14.5(17)	0		—	0	15
1941	†GB	10(7, LE)	—	—	—	—	4	48	12.0(27)	0		—	0	24
1942	GB	5(1)	—	—	—	—	8	125	15.6(49)	1		—	6	68
1943	GB	10(9, RE)	—	—	—	—	24	528	22.0(86)	3	ki	—	18	299
1944	†GB	9(9, RE)	—	—	—	—	9	151	16.8(48)	0		—	0	76
NFL	6	55(33)	—	—	—	—	52	985	18.9(86)	6	ki	—	36	543

JAEGER, JEFF Jeff Todd, K, 5´11˝/190 lbs; Washington; 1987: Cle, rnd 3; B11/26/1964 Tacoma, WA [K] **1989** LARd 16 (0) **1990**†LARd 16 (0) **1991**†LARd★16 (0)
1992 LARd 16 (0) **1993**†LARd 16 (0) **1994** LARd 16 (0) **1995** Oak 11 (0) **1996** ChiB 13 (0) **1997** ChiB 16 (0) **1998** ChiB 16 (0) **1999** ChiB 3 (0)

YEAR	TEAM	G (GS, POS)	PASS	COMP	PCT	YD	AVG(LG)	TD	INT	SK	YD	QBR	KPR	OTD	PTS	TAY
1987	Cle	10(0)	1	0	0.0	0	0.0	0	0	—	—		K	—	75	0
NFL	12	165(0)	1	0	0.0	0	0.0	0	0	—	—		KP	—	1008	0

JAFFURS, JOHNNY John James, G, 5´10˝/200 lbs; Penn State; 1943: Was, rnd 29; B4/15/1923 Wilkinsburg, PA **1946** Was 8 (2)

JAGADE, CHICK Harry Charles, FB, 6´0˝/213 lbs; Indiana; 1948: Bal-A, rnd 27/Was, rnd 14; B12/9/1926 Chicago, IL, D11/24/1968 Washington Island, WA

YEAR	TEAM	G (GS, POS)	RUSH	YD	AVG(LG)	TD	REC	YD	AVG(LG)	TD	KPR	OTD	PTS	TAY
1949	Bal-A	10(3)	33	174	5.3	2	8	44	5.5		k	—	12	201
1951	†Cle	11(fb)	7	30	4.3(22)	0	—				k	—	0	36
1952	†Cle	12(fb)	57	373	6.5(30)	2	9	203	22.6(47)	1	k	—	18	513
1953	†Cle★	12(FB)	86	344	4.0(23)	4	20	193	9.6(37)	0		—	24	481
1954	ChiB	11(FB)	157	498	3.2(46)	3	24	172	7.2(26)	0	k	—	18	644
1955	ChiB	12	72	309	4.3(51)	2	7	16	2.3(15)	0	k	—	12	345
NFL	5	58	379	1554	4.1(51)	11	60	584	9.7(47)	1	k	—	72	2018

JAGIELSKI, HARRY Harry Anthony, DT-T, 6´0˝/257 lbs; Indiana; 1954: Was, rnd 7; B12/25/1931 Pittsburgh, PA, D10/9/1993 Chicago, IL **1956** ChiC 4 **1956** Was 5
1960 Bos-A 14 (LDT) **1961** Bos-A 5 **1961** Oak-A 8 (rdt) **NFL** 36 [3 yrs]

JAKES, VAN Van Keith, DB, 6´0˝/188 lbs; Kent State; B5/10/1961 Phenix City, AL **1983** KC 14 (1) **1984** KC 8 (0) **1986** NO 12 (0) **1987**†NO 12 (10, RCB)
1988 NO 16 (15, RCB) **1989** GB 16 (4) **NFL** 78 (30) [6 yrs]

JAKOWENKO, GEORGE George, K, 5´9˝/175 lbs; Syracuse; B6/26/1948 Charleroi, Belgium [K] **1974**†Oak 6 **1976** Buf 11 **NFL** 17 [2 yrs]

JAMERSON, LEFTY Charles Dewey, E, 6´1˝/195 lbs; Arkansas; B1/26/1900 Enfield, IL, D8/4/1980 Mocksville, NC **1926** Har 3 (0)

JAMES, ANGELO Michael Angelo, DB, 6´0˝/180 lbs; Sacramento State; B6/13/1962 Mobile, AL **1987** Phi 3 (3)

JAMES, ARRIKE Arrike, RB, 6´4˝/238 lbs; Delta State; B12/31/1964 Dumas, AR

YEAR	TEAM	G (GS, POS)	RUSH	YD	AVG(LG)	TD	REC	YD	AVG(LG)	TD	OTD	PTS	TAY
1987	Hou	3(0)	—	—	—		1	14	14.0(14)	0	—	0	7

JAMES, BRADIE Bradie Gene, LB, 6´2˝/243 lbs; LSU; 2003: Dal, rnd 4; B1/17/1981 Monroe, LA **2003**†Dal 14 (0) **2004** Dal 16 (2) **2005** Dal 16 (16, LILB) **NFL** 46 (18) [3 yrs]

JAMES, CEDRIC Cedric, WR, 6´1˝/199 lbs; TCU; 2001: Min, rnd 4; B3/19/1979 Fort Worth, TX

YEAR	TEAM	G (GS, POS)	RUSH	YD	AVG(LG)	TD	REC	YD	AVG(LG)	TD	KPR	OTD	PTS	TAY
2002	Min	5(0)	—	—	—		1	29	29.0(29)	0	k	—	0	93

JAMES, CLAUDIS Claudis Ray, WR-HB, 6´2˝/190 lbs; Jackson State; 1967: GB, rnd 14; B11/7/1943 Columbia, MS **1967** GB 1

YEAR	TEAM	G (GS, POS)	RUSH	YD	AVG(LG)	TD	REC	YD	AVG(LG)	TD	OTD	PTS	TAY
1968	GB	14	1	15	15.0(15)	0	8	148	18.5(24)	2	—	12	99
NFL	2	15	1	15	15.0(15)	0	8	148	18.5(24)	2	—	12	99

JAMES, CRAIG Jesse Craig, RB, 6´0˝/215 lbs; SMU; 1983: NE, rnd 7; B1/2/1961 Jacksonville, TX

YEAR	TEAM	G (GS, POS)	RUSH	YD	AVG(LG)	TD	REC	YD	AVG(LG)	TD	PASS	COMP	PCT	YD	AVG(LG)	TD	INT	KPR	OTD	PTS	TAY
1984	NE	15(7, RB)	160	790	4.9(73)	1	22	159	7.2(16)	0	—	—	—	—	—	—	—		—	6	880
1985	†NE◇	16(14, FB)	263	1227	4.7(65)	5	27	360	13.3(90)	2	2	2	100.0	16	8.0(11)	2	0	k	—	42	1470
1986	†NE	13(12, FB)	154	427	2.8(16)	4	18	129	7.2(17)	0	4	1	25.0	10	2.5(10)	1	1		—	24	502
1987	NE	2(0)	4	10	2.5(5)	0	—				—								—	0	10
1988	NE	6(0)	4	15	3.8(8)	1	14	171	12.2(32)	0	—								—	6	111
NFL	5	52(33)	585	2469	4.2(73)	11	81	819	10.1(90)	2	6	3	50.0	26	4.3(11)	3	1	k	—	78	2972

JAMES, DAN Daniel Anthony, T, 6´4˝/262 lbs; Ohio State; 1959: SF, rnd 1; B8/10/1937 Cincinnati, OH, D7/4/1987 Harrison, OH **1960** Pit 12 (LT) **1961** Pit 14 (RT) **1962** Pit 14 (RT)
1963 Pit 14 (RT) **1964** Pit 14 (RT) **1965** Pit 13 (RT) **1966** Pit 10 (RT) **1967** ChiB 2 **NFL** 93 [8 yrs]

JAMES, DICK Richard Alwin, HB-DB, 5´9˝/179 lbs; Oregon; 1956: Was, rnd 8; B5/22/1934 Grants Pass, OR, D6/28/2000 Medford, OR [R]

YEAR	TEAM	G (GS, POS)	RUSH	YD	AVG(LG)	TD	REC	YD	AVG(LG)	TD	PASS	COMP	PCT	YD	AVG(LG)	TD	INT	KPR	OTD	PTS	TAY
1956	Was	10(RH)	58	280	4.8(41)	1	7	127	18.1(34)	2	—	—	—	—	—	—	—	kpi	—	18	464
1957	Was	11(DB)	7	19	2.7(8)	0	—				—							kpi	—	0	119
1958	Was	12(12, DB)	24	88	3.7(14)	1	2	33	16.5(18)	0	—							kpi	—	6	222
1959	Was	12(RH)	100	384	3.8(39)	3	13	192	14.8(41)	1	—							kpi	—	24	695
1960	Was	12(RH)	73	199	2.7(27)	4	16	243	15.2(49)	2	1	0	0.0	0	0.0	0	0	kp	—	36	555
1961	Was◇	14(RH)	71	374	5.3(39)	3	20	298	14.9(44)	2	4	1	25.0	15	3.8(15)	0	0	Pkpi	—	30	926
1962	Was	14	9	13	1.4(7)	0	19	373	19.6(49)	5	—							kp	—	30	684
1963	Was	14(HB)	105	384	3.7(15)	4	15	302	20.1(77)	2	1	0	0.0	0	0.0	0	0	kpi	—	36	1110
1964	NYG	14(HB)	55	189	3.4(18)	3	12	101	8.4(34)	1	1	0	0.0	0	0.0	0	0	Pkp	—	24	453
1965	Min	4	—				—				—							kp	—	0	47
NFL	10	117(12)	502	1930	3.8(41)	19	104	1669	16.0(77)	15	7	1	14.3	15	2.1(15)	0	0	Pkpi	—	204	5272

JAMES, EDGERRIN Edgerrin Tyree, RB, 6´0˝/214 lbs; Miami (FL); 1999: Ind, rnd 1; B8/1/1978 Immokalee, FL

YEAR	TEAM	G (GS, POS)	RUSH	YD	AVG(LG)	TD	REC	YD	AVG(LG)	TD	OTD	PTS	TAY
1999	†Ind★	16(16, RB)	369	1553	4.2(72)	13	62	586	9.5(54)	4	—	102	1996
2000	†Ind★	16(16, RB)	387	1709	4.4(30)	13	63	594	9.4(60)	5	—	110	2161
2001	Ind	6(6, rb)	151	662	4.4(29)	3	24	193	8.0(27)	0	—	20	789
2002	†Ind	14(14, RB)	277	989	3.6(20)	2	61	354	5.8(23)	1	—	20	1191
2003	†Ind	13(13, RB)	310	1259	4.1(43)	11	51	292	5.7(17)	0	—	66	1515
2004	†Ind	16(16, RB)	334	1548	4.6(40)	9	51	483	9.5(56)	0	—	56	1880
2005	†Ind★	15(15, RB)	360	1506	4.2(33)	13	44	337	7.7(20)	1	—	84	1810
NFL	7	96(96)	2188	9226	4.2(72)	64	356	2839	8.0(60)	11	—	458	11341

JAMES, ERASMUS Erasmus, DE, 6´4˝/263 lbs; Wisconsin; 2005: Min, rnd 1; B11/4/1982 Saint Kitts **2005** Min 15 (9, RDE)

JAMES, GARRY Garry Malcolm, RB, 5´10˝/214 lbs; LSU; 1986: Det, rnd 2; B9/4/1963 Marrero, LA

YEAR	TEAM	G (GS, POS)	RUSH	YD	AVG(LG)	TD	REC	YD	AVG(LG)	TD	OTD	PTS	TAY
1986	Det	16(15, RB)	159	688	4.3(60)	3	34	219	6.4(26)	0	—	18	828
1987	Det	8(7, RB)	82	270	3.3(17)	4	16	215	13.4(46)	2	—	24	418
1988	Det	16(16, RB)	182	552	3.0(35)	2	39	382	9.8(39)	2	—	42	803
NFL	3	40(38)	423	1510	3.6(60)	12	89	816	9.2(46)	2	—	84	2048

JAMES, JENO Jenorris, G, 6´3˝/310 lbs; Auburn; 2000: Car, rnd 6; B1/12/1977 Montgomery, AL **2000** Car 16 (4) **2001** Car 14 (6, rg) **2002** Car 9 (2) **2003**†Car 16 (16, LG)
2004 Mia 14 (14, LG) **2005** Mia 16 (16, LG) **NFL** 85 (58) [6 yrs]

JAMES, JESSE Jesse, C, 6´4˝/311 lbs; Mississippi State; 1995: SL, rnd 2; B9/16/1971 Mobile, AL **1995** SL 2 (1) **1996** SL 1 (0) **NFL** 3 (0) [2 yrs]

JAMES, JOHN John Wilbur, P, 6´3˝/197 lbs; Florida; B1/21/1949 Panama City, FL [P] **1972** Atl 14 **1973** Atl 14 **1974** Atl 14 **1976** Atl★14 **1978**†Atl 16 **1982** Det 2 (0)
1982 Hou 5 (0) **1984** Hou 16 (0)

YEAR	TEAM	G (GS, POS)	RUSH	YD	AVG(LG)	TD	PASS	COMP	PCT	YD	AVG(LG)	TD	INT	KPR	OTD	PTS	TAY
1975	Atl★	14	—				1	1	100.0	25	25.0(25)	0	0	P	—	0	13
1977	Atl★	14	—				1	0	0.0	0	0.0	0	0	P	—	0	0
1979	Atl	16	1	1	0.0(0)	0	1	1	100.0	20	20.0(20)	0	0	P	—	0	10
1980	†Atl☆	16	1	13	13.0(13)	0	—							P	—	0	-27
1981	Atl	16(0)	1	-7	-7.0(-7)	0	—							P	—	0	-7
1983	Hou	16(0)	1	0	0.0(0)	0	1	1	100.0	7	7.0(7)	0	0	P	—	0	4
NFL	13	187	4	6	1.5(13)	0	6	3	50.0	52	8.7(25)	0	1	P	—	0	-8

JAMES, JUNE June, LB, 6´1˝/218 lbs; Texas; 1985: Det, rnd 9; B12/2/1962 Jennings, LA, D5/8/1990 Baton Rouge, LA **1985** Det 16 (0) **1987**†Ind 11 (0) **NFL** 27 (0) [2 yrs]

YEAR	TEAM	G (GS, POS)	RUSH	YD	AVG(LG)	TD	REC	YD	AVG(LG)	TD	PASS COMP	PCT	YD	AVG(LG)	TD	INT	SK	YD	QBR	KPR	OTD	PTS	TAY

JAMES, LIONEL　Lionel, RB-WR, 5´6˝/171 lbs; Auburn; 1984: SD, rnd 5; B5/25/1962 Albany, GA **[R]**

1984	SD	16(2)	25	115	4.6(20)	0	23	206	9.0(31)	0	2	0.0	0	0.0	—	0	1	—	—	kp	1	6	560
1985	SD☆	16(7, RB)	105	516	4.9(56)	2	86	1027	11.9(67)	6	—	—	—	—	—	—	—	—	—	kp	—	48	1407
1986	SD	7(1)	51	224	4.4(24)	0	23	173	7.5(18)	0	—	—	—	—	—	—	—	—	—	kp	—	0	405
1987	SD☆	12(11, WR)	27	102	3.8(15)	2	41	593	14.5(46)	3	—	—	—	—	—	—	—	—	—	kp	1	36	695
1988	SD	16(1)	23	105	4.6(23)	1	36	279	7.8(31)	1	0	0.0	0	0.0	0	0	1	8	—	p	—	6	388
NFL	**5**	67(22)	231	1062	4.6(56)	4	209	2278	10.9(67)	10	2	0.0	0	0.0	0	1	1	8	—	kp	2	96	3453

JAMES, LYNN　Lynn Fitzpatrick, WR, 6´0˝/191 lbs; SMU; Arizona State; 1990: Cin, rnd 5; B1/25/1965 Navasta, TX

1990	†Cin	11(0)	1	11	11.0(11)	0	3	36	12.0(16)	0	1	0.0	0	0.0	0	0	—	—	—	k	—	0	57
1991	Cin	10(1)	—	—	—	—	7	103	14.7(22)	1	—	—	—	—	—	—	—	—	—	kp	—	6	75
1991	Cle	4(0)	—	—	—	—	—	—	—	—	—	—	—	—	—	—	—	—	—	k	—	0	4
NFL	**2**	25(1)	1	11	11.0(11)	0	10	139	13.9(22)	1	1	0.0	0	0.0	0	0	—	—	—	kp	—	6	136

JAMES, NATE　Nathaniel, DB, 6´1˝/195 lbs; Florida A&M; 1968: Cle, rnd 6; B2/20/1945 Bartow, FL　**1968** Cle 12

JAMES, PHILLIP　Phillip Ray, G, 6´2˝/265 lbs; Southern (LA); B12/3/1964 Atlanta, GA　**1987** NO 3 (3)

JAMES, PO　Ronald, RB, 6´1˝/202 lbs; New Mexico State; 1972: Phi, rnd 4; B3/19/1949 New Brighton, PA

1972	Phi	14(RB)	182	565	3.1(22)	0	20	156	7.8(35)	1	—	—	—	—	—	—	—	—	—	—	—	6	648
1973	Phi	10	36	178	4.9(24)	1	17	94	5.5(13)	0	—	—	—	—	—	—	—	—	—	k	—	6	408
1974	Phi	11(5, rb)	67	276	4.1(15)	2	33	230	7.0(34)	0	—	—	—	—	—	—	—	—	—	k	—	12	469
1975	Phi	14	43	196	4.6(51)	1	32	267	8.3(47)	1	—	—	—	—	—	—	—	—	—	k	—	12	461
NFL	**4**	49(5)	328	1215	3.7(51)	4	102	747	7.3(47)	2	—	—	—	—	—	—	—	—	—	k	—	36	1986

JAMES, ROBERT　Robert Dematrice, DB, 6´1˝/184 lbs; Fisk; B7/7/1947 Murfreesboro, TN　**1970** Buf 14 (LCB)　**1971** Buf 14 (LCB)　**1972** Buf★14 (LCB)　**1973** Buf★13 (LCB)　**1974**†Buf★14 (LCB)

| 1969 | Buf-A | 14 | — | — | — | — | 1 | 19 | 19.0(19) | 0 | — | — | — | — | — | — | — | — | — | p | — | 0 | 7 |
| **NFL** | **6** | 83 | — | — | — | — | 1 | 19 | 19.0(19) | 0 | — | — | — | — | — | — | — | — | — | pi | — | 6 | -1 |

JAMES, ROLAND　Roland Orlando, DB, 6´2˝/191 lbs; Tennessee; 1980: NE, rnd 1; B2/18/1958 Xenia, OH **[I]**　**1980** NE 16 (10, SS)　**1981** NE 16 (6, rcb)　**1982** NE 7 (7, SS)　**1983** NE☆16 (16, SS)　**1984** NE 15 (15, SS)　**1985**†NE 16 (16, SS)　**1986**†NE 15 (15, SS)　**1987** NE 9 (4)　**1988** NE 15 (15, SS)　**1989** NE 14 (14, SS)　**1990** NE 6 (4)　**NFL** 145 (122) [11 yrs]

JAMES, TED　Theodore Lawrence, G-C, 6´2˝/190 lbs; Nebraska; B8/8/1906 Wymore, NE, D6/8/1999 Denver, CO　**1929** Fra 10 (6, lg)

JAMES, TOMMY　Thomas Laverne, DB-HB, 5´10˝/185 lbs; Ohio State; 1947: Det, rnd 17; B9/16/1923 Canton, OH **[I]**

1948	†Cle-A	14(0)	1	8	8.0(8)	0	1	44	44.0(44)	0	—	—	—	—	—	—	—	—	—	pi	—	0	69
1949	†Cle-A	12(1)	10	28	2.8	0	—	—	—	—	—	—	—	—	—	—	—	—	—	i	1	6	82
AAFC	**2**	26(1)	11	36	3.3(8)	0	1	44	44.0(44)	0	—	—	—	—	—	—	—	—	—	pi	1	6	151
1947	Det	2(0)	2	-1	-0.5(2)	0	—	—	—	—	—	—	—	—	—	—	—	—	—	p	—	0	-4
1950	†Cle☆	12(DB)	1	-1	-1.0(-1)	0	—	—	—	—	—	—	—	—	—	—	—	—	—	i	—	0	38
1951	†Cle	12(DB)	—	—	—	—	—	—	—	—	—	—	—	—	—	—	—	—	—	i	—	0	-9
1952	†Cle	12(DB)	—	—	—	—	—	—	—	—	—	—	—	—	—	—	—	—	—	i	—	0	20
1953	†Cle◇	12(DB)	—	—	—	—	—	—	—	—	—	—	—	—	—	—	—	—	—	i	1	6	-4
1954	†Cle☆	12(DB)	1	-6	-6.0(-6)	0	—	—	—	—	—	—	—	—	—	—	—	—	—	i	—	0	31
1955	†Cle	8(db)	1	2	2.0(2)	0	—	—	—	—	—	—	—	—	—	—	—	—	—	i	—	0	12
1956	Bal	2	—	—	—	—	—	—	—	—	—	—	—	—	—	—	—	—	—	—	—	—	—
NFL	**8**	72	5	-6	-1.2(8)	0	—	—	—	—	—	—	—	—	—	—	—	—	—	pi	1	6	84

JAMES, TORAN　Toran Clay, LB, 6´3˝/240 lbs; North Carolina A&T; 1997: SD, rnd 7; B3/8/1974 Richmond, VA　**1997** SD 14 (0)

JAMES, TORY　Tory Steven, DB, 6´2˝/186 lbs; LSU; 1996: Den, rnd 2; B5/18/1973 New Orleans, LA **[I]**　**1996** Den 16 (2)　**1998**†Den 16 (0)　**1999** Den 16 (4)　**2000**†Oak 16 (1)　**2001**†Oak 16 (2)　**2002**†Oak 14 (13, RCB)　**2003** Cin 16 (16, RCB)　**2004** Cin☆16 (16, RCB)　**2005**†Cin 16 (16, RCB)　**NFL** 142 (70) [9 yrs]

JAMESON, LARRY　George Larry, DT, 6´7˝/270 lbs; Indiana; 1975: SL, rnd 6; B2/1/1953 Washington, DC　**1976** TB 1

JAMESON, MICHAEL　Michael, DB, 5´11˝/205 lbs; Texas A&M; 2001: Cle, rnd 6; B7/14/1979 Killeen, TX　**2002**†Cle 11 (1)　**2003** Cle 15 (0)　**2004** Cle 16 (0)　**NFL** 42 (1) [3 yrs]

JAMIESON, DICK　Richard Alexander, QB, 6´1˝/191 lbs; Bradley; 1959: Phi, rnd 25; B11/13/1937 Streator, IL, D5/2/2001 St. Louis, MO　**1961** NYT-A 3

| 1960 | NYT-A | 11 | 2 | 10 | 5.0(6) | 0 | — | — | — | — | 70 | 35 | 50.0 | 586 | 8.4(65) | 6 | 2 | — | — | — | — | — | 0 | 253 |
| **NFL** | **2** | 14 | 2 | 10 | 5.0(6) | 0 | — | — | — | — | 70 | 35 | 50.0 | 586 | 8.4(65) | 6 | 2 | — | — | — | — | — | 0 | 253 |

JAMIESON, ROB　Robert John, C, 6´0˝/195 lbs; Franklin & Marshall; B2/3/1902, D6/1982 Palmerton, PA　**1924** Fra 3 (1)

JAMISON, AL　Alfred George, T, 6´5˝/250 lbs; Colgate; B5/11/1937　**1960**†Hou-A☆14 (LT)　**1961**†Hou-A★14 (LT)　**1962**†Hou-A★14 (LT)　**NFL** 42 [3 yrs]

JAMISON, GEORGE　George R., LB, 6´1˝/232 lbs; Cincinnati; 1984: Det, rnd S2; B9/30/1962 Bridgeton, NJ　**1987** Det 12 (0)　**1988** Det 16 (11, LOLB)　**1989** Det 10 (6, rolb)　**1990** Det 14 (7, lolb)　**1991**†Det 16 (16, LOLB)　**1992** Det 16 (16, LOLB)　**1993**†Det 16 (16, LOLB)　**1994**†KC 13 (12, LLB)　**1995** KC 14 (14, LOLB)　**1996** KC 5 (0)　**1997**†Det 16 (10, LLB)　**1998** Det 14 (0)　**NFL** 162 (108) [12 yrs]

JAMMER, QUENTIN　Quentin T., DB, 6´0˝/204 lbs; Texas; 2002: SD, rnd 1; B6/19/1979 Matagorda County, TX　**2002** SD 14 (4)　**2003** SD 16 (16, LCB)　**2004**†SD 16 (16, RCB)　**2005** SD 16 (16, LCB)　**NFL** 62 (52) [4 yrs]

JANATA, JOHN　John Michael, T, 6´7˝/274 lbs; Illinois; B4/10/1961 Chicago, IL　**1983** ChiB 15 (0)

JANCIK, BOBBY　Robert Lee, DB, 5´11˝/178 lbs; Lamar; 1962: Hou, rnd 19; B2/9/1940 Houston, TX **[R]**　**1962**†Hou-A 14 (rcb)　**1963** Hou-A☆14 (RCB)　**1965** Hou-A 14 (rs)　**1966** Hou-A 14　**1967**†Hou-A 11

| 1964 | Hou-A | 14(RCB) | — | — | — | — | 1 | 14 | 14.0(14) | 0 | — | — | — | — | — | — | — | — | — | kpi | 1 | 6 | 351 |
| **NFL** | **6** | 81 | — | — | — | — | 1 | 14 | 14.0(14) | 0 | — | — | — | — | — | — | — | — | — | kpi | 1 | 6 | 2279 |

JANECEK, CLARENCE　Clarence Robert, G, 6´0˝/200 lbs; Purdue; B4/1/1911 Chicago, IL, D1/16/1990　**1933** Pit 11 (11, RG)

JANERETTE, CHUCK　Charles Fletcher, DT-T-G, 6´3˝/253 lbs; Penn State; 1960: LA, rnd 5; B12/1/1938 Philadelphia, PA, D10/26/1984 Philadelphia, PA　**1960** LARm 12　**1961**†NYG 14　**1962**†NYG 12　**1963** NYJ-A 14 (LDT)　**1964** Den-A 14 (RDT)　**1965** Den-A 14 (RDT)　**NFL** 80 [6 yrs]

JANET, ERNIE　Ernest Jay, G, 6´4˝/250 lbs; Washington; 1971: SF, rnd 2; B7/22/1949 Renton, WA　**1972** ChiB 3　**1973** ChiB 12　**1974** ChiB 14 (LG)　**1975** GB 1　**1975** Phi 1　**NFL** 31 [4 yrs]

JANIAK, LEN　Leonard Joseph, B, 6´1˝/203 lbs; Ohio University; 1939: Bkn, rnd 6; B10/29/1915 Cleveland, OH, D5/22/1980 Cleveland, OH

1939	Bkn	10(1)	18	56	3.1	0	2	6	3.0	0	—	—	—	—	—	—	—	—	—	—	—	0	59
1940	Cle	11(3)	19	44	2.3	0	1	3	3.0(3)	0	—	—	—	—	—	—	—	—	—	P	—	0	46
1941	Cle	10(4)	14	20	1.4(12)	0	2	5	2.5(3)	0	—	—	—	—	—	—	—	—	—	ki	—	0	34
1942	Cle	9(3)	34	109	3.2(20)	0	6	51	8.5(19)	1	1	100.0	11	11.0(11)	0	0	—	—	—	—	—	6	145
NFL	**4**	40(11)	85	229	2.7(20)	0	11	65	5.9(19)	1	1	100.0	11	11.0(11)	0	0	—	—	—	Pki	—	6	283

JANIK, TOM　Thomas Alvin, DB, 6´3˝/190 lbs; Texas A&M; Texas A&M-Kingsville; 1963: Den, rnd 3/Det, rnd 12; B9/6/1940 Poth, TX **[PI]**　**1963** Den-A 14　**1964** Den-A 9　**1965**†Buf-A◇10　**1966**†Buf-A☆14 (LS)　**1967** Buf-A 14 (LS)　**1968** Buf-A 10, LS)　**1969** Bos-A 14　**1970** Bos 11　**1971** NE 14 (2)　**NFL** 114 (12) [9 yrs]

JANIKOWSKI, SEBASTIAN　Sebastian, K, 6´2˝/255 lbs; Florida State; 2000: Oak, rnd 1; B3/2/1978 Walbrzych, Poland **[K]**　**2000**†Oak 14 (0)　**2001**†Oak 15 (0)　**2002**†Oak 16 (0)　**2003** Oak 16 (0)　**2004** Oak 16 (0)　**2005** Oak 16 (0)　**NFL** 93 (0) [6 yrs]

JANKOVICH, KEEVER　Keever David, LB-DE, 6´0˝/215 lbs; Utah; Pacific; 1952: Cle, rnd 5; B1/6/1928 Wilmington, NC, D2/1979　**1952** DalT 10　**1953** ChiC 2　**NFL** 12 [2 yrs]

JANKOWSKI, BRUCE　Bruce David, WR, 5´11˝/185 lbs; Ohio State; 1971: KC, rnd 10; B8/12/1949 Paterson, NJ　**1971** KC 5

| 1972 | KC | 4 | — | — | — | — | 2 | 24 | 12.0(18) | 0 | — | — | — | — | — | — | — | — | — | — | — | 0 | 12 |
| **NFL** | **2** | 9 | — | — | — | — | 2 | 24 | 12.0(18) | 0 | — | — | — | — | — | — | — | — | — | — | — | 0 | 12 |

JANKOWSKI, ED　Edward Joe, FB, 5´9˝/201 lbs; Wisconsin; 1937: GB, rnd 1; B6/23/1913 Milwaukee, WI, D7/20/1996 Madison, WI **[K]**

1937	GB	11(1)	61	324	5.3	2	1	60	60.0(60)	1	—	—	—	—	—	—	—	—	—	K	1	25	389
1938	GB	11(3)	44	124	2.8	2	—	—	—	—	—	—	—	—	—	—	—	—	—	K	—	14	144
1939	GB◇	10(6, FB)	75	278	3.7	2	1	5	5.0(5)	0	—	—	—	—	—	—	—	—	—	—	—	12	301

YEAR	TEAM	G(GS, POS)	RUSH	YD	AVG(LG)	TD	REC	YD	AVG(LG)	TD	PASS	COMP	PCT	YD	AVG(LG)	TD	INT	SK	YD	QBR	KPR	OTD	PTS	TAY
1940	GB	7(1)	48	211	4.4	2	—	—	—	—	—	—	—	—	—	—	—	—	—	—	—	—	12	231
1941	GB	11(0)	47	65	1.4(13)	0	—	—	—	—	—	—	—	—	—	—	—	—	—	—	Ki	—	4	93
NFL	5	50(11)	275	1002	3.6(13)	8	2	65	32.5(60)	1	—	—	—	—	—	—	—	—	—	—	Ki	1	67	1158

Janowicz, Vic Victor Felix, HB, 5´9˝/187 lbs; Ohio State; 1952: Was, rnd 7; B2/26/1930 Elyria, OH, D2/27/1996 Columbus, OH **[K]**

YEAR	TEAM	G(GS, POS)	RUSH	YD	AVG(LG)	TD	REC	YD	AVG(LG)	TD	PASS	COMP	PCT	YD	AVG(LG)	TD	INT	SK	YD	QBR	KPR	OTD	PTS	TAY
1954	Was	10	6	13	2.2(3)	0	1	-1	-1.0(-1)	0	1	0	0.0	0	0.0	0	0	—	—	—	KPk	—	21	16
1955	Was	12(LH)	93	397	4.3(33)	4	11	149	13.5(48)	3	5	0	0.0	0	0.0	0	1	—	—	—	K	—	88	487
NFL	2	22	99	410	4.1(33)	4	12	148	12.3(48)	3	6	0	0.0	0	0.0	0	1	—	—	—	KPk	—	109	502

Jansante, Val Valerio Richard, E-DE, 6´1˝/190 lbs; Duquesne; Villanova; 1944: Pit, rnd 10; B9/27/1920 LaBelle, PA

YEAR	TEAM	G(GS, POS)	RUSH	YD	AVG(LG)	TD	REC	YD	AVG(LG)	TD	PASS	COMP	PCT	YD	AVG(LG)	TD	INT	SK	YD	QBR	KPR	OTD	PTS	TAY
1946	Pit	11(7, LE)	2	5	2.5(5)	0	10	136	13.6(34)	1	—	—	—	—	—	—	—	—	—	—	—	—	6	78
1947	†Pit☆	12(8, LE)	—	—	—	—	35	599	17.1(46)	5	—	—	—	—	—	—	—	—	—	—	k	—	32	337
1948	Pit	12(5, le)	1	-3	-3.0(-3)	0	39	623	16.0(66)	3	—	—	—	—	—	—	—	—	—	—	—	—	18	324
1949	Pit	12(10, LE)	—	—	—	—	29	445	15.3(47)	4	—	—	—	—	—	—	—	—	—	—	k	—	24	244
1950	Pit	12(LE)	—	—	—	—	26	353	13.6(40)	0	—	—	—	—	—	—	—	—	—	—	—	—	0	177
1951	Pit	6(le)	—	—	—	—	15	194	12.9(46)	1	—	—	—	—	—	—	—	—	—	—	—	—	6	102
1951	GB	3	—	—	—	—	1	6	6.0(6)	0	—	—	—	—	—	—	—	—	—	—	—	—	0	3
NFL	6	68(30)	3	2	0.7(5)	0	155	2356	15.2(66)	14	—	—	—	—	—	—	—	—	—	—	k	—	86	1263

Jansen, Jon Jonathan Ward, T, 6´6˝/305 lbs; Michigan; 1999: Was, rnd 2; B1/28/1976 Clawson, MI **1999**†Was 16 (16, RT) **2000** Was 16 (16, RT) **2001** Was 16 (16, RT) **2002** Was 16 (16, RT) **2003** Was 16 (16, RT) **2005**†Was☆16 (16, RT) **NFL** 96 (96) [6 yrs]

Jansing, Whitey Lee Irwin, FB, /175 lbs; none; B Louisville, KY, D7/21/1934 Louisville, KY **1922** Lou 3 (2)

January, Mike Michael Anthony, LB, 6´1˝/234 lbs; Texas; B6/30/1964 Lake Charles, LA **1987** ChiB 3 (3)

Janus, Paul Paul Scott, T, 6´4˝/294 lbs; Northwestern; B3/17/1975 Edgerton, WI **1998** Car 5 (1)

Jappe, Paul Paul Eugene, E-G-T, 6´1˝/195 lbs; Syracuse; B1/16/1898 Union Hill, NJ, D4/1/1989 Daytona Beach, FL **1925** NYG 12 (9, LE) **1926** Bkn 11 (11, LE/lt) **1927** NYG 13 (1) **1928** NYG 12 (7, LG) **NFL** 48 (28) [4 yrs]

Jaqua, Jon Jon V., DB, 6´0˝/190 lbs; Lewis & Clark; B9/10/1948 Eugene, OR **1970** Was 14 (2) **1971**†Was 14 (1) **1972**†Was 8 **NFL** 36 (3) [3 yrs]

Jaquess, Pete Lindel Glenn, DB, 6´0˝/185 lbs; Eastern New Mexico; 1964: Hou, rnd 20; B12/25/1940 Earth, TX **1964** Hou-A★14 (LCB) **1965** Hou-A 14 **1966** Mia-A 14 (9, LS) **1967** Mia-A 7 (4) **1967** Den-A 3 **1968** Den-A 13 (LS) **1969** Den-A 7 **1970** Den 13 (2) **NFL** 85 (15) [7 yrs]

Jarmoluk, Mike Michael, DT-T-MG, 6´5˝/232 lbs; Temple; 1945: Det, rnd 7; B10/22/1922 Philadelphia, PA, D11/23/2004 Ocala, FL **1946**†ChiB 11 (7, RT) **1948** Bos 12 (10, LT) **1949** NYB 2 (0) **1949**†Phi 9 (0) **1950** Phi 12 (RDT) **1951** Phi✧12 (RDT) **1952** Phi 12 (RDT) **1953** Phi 12 (RDT) **1954** Phi 12 (RDT) **1955** Phi 12 (RDT/mg)

YEAR	TEAM	G(GS, POS)	RUSH	YD	AVG(LG)	TD	REC	YD	AVG(LG)	TD	PASS	COMP	PCT	YD	AVG(LG)	TD	INT	SK	YD	QBR	KPR	OTD	PTS	TAY
1947	ChiB	12(1)	—	—	—	—	2	33	16.5(24)	1	—	—	—	—	—	—	—	—	—	—	k	—	6	7
NFL	10	118(18)	—	—	—	—	2	33	16.5(24)	1	—	—	—	—	—	—	—	—	—	—	ki	2	18	57

Jarostchuk, Ilia Ilia, LB, 6´3˝/231 lbs; New Hampshire; 1987: SL, rnd 5; B8/1/1964 Utica, NY **1987** SL 12 (0) **1988** Mia 6 (0) **1989** Phx 16 (1) **1990** NE 12 (1) **NFL** 46 (2) [4 yrs]

Jarrett, Craig Craig, P, 6´2˝/215 lbs; Michigan State; 2002: Sea, rnd 6; B7/17/1979 Martinsville, IN **2002** Was 4 (0)

Jarvi, Toimi Toimi, HB, 6´0˝/200 lbs; Northern Illinois; B2/28/1920 DeKalb, IL, D11/18/1977 Chicago, IL

YEAR	TEAM	G(GS, POS)	RUSH	YD	AVG(LG)	TD	REC	YD	AVG(LG)	TD	PASS	COMP	PCT	YD	AVG(LG)	TD	INT	SK	YD	QBR	KPR	OTD	PTS	TAY
1944	Phi	5(0)	5	16	3.2(4)	0	1	9	9.0(9)	0	—	—	—	—	—	—	—	—	—	—	pi	—	0	28
1945	Pit	1(0)	9	24	2.7(11)	0	—	—	—	—	10	4	40.0	50	5.0(21)	0	3	—	—	—	P	—	0	-71
NFL	2	6(0)	14	40	2.9(11)	0	1	9	9.0(9)	0	10	4	40.0	50	5.0(21)	0	3	—	—	—	Ppi	—	0	-44

Jarvis, Bruce J. Bruce, C, 6´7˝/250 lbs; Washington; 1971: Buf, rnd 3; B11/3/1948 Seattle, WA **1971** Buf 14 (C) **1972** Buf 1 **1973** Buf 8 (C) **1974** Buf 1 **NFL** 24 [4 yrs]

Jarvis, Curt Curtis Versil, NT-DE-DT, 6´2˝/266 lbs; Alabama; 1987: TB, rnd 7; B1/28/1965 Birmingham, AL **1987** TB 2 (0) **1988** TB 15 (15, NT) **1989** TB 14 (12, NT) **1990** TB 7 (7, NT) **NFL** 38 (34) [4 yrs]

Jarvis, Ralph Ralph A., DE, 6´4˝/255 lbs; Temple; 1988: Chi, rnd 3; B6/1/1965 Philadelphia, PA **1990** Ind 8 (0)

Jarvis, Ray Leon Raeminton, WR, 6´0˝/200 lbs; Norfolk State; 1971: Atl, rnd 5; B2/2/1949 Chesapeake, VA

YEAR	TEAM	G(GS, POS)	RUSH	YD	AVG(LG)	TD	REC	YD	AVG(LG)	TD	PASS	COMP	PCT	YD	AVG(LG)	TD	INT	SK	YD	QBR	KPR	OTD	PTS	TAY
1971	Atl	2	1	13	13.0(13)	0	—	—	—	—	—	—	—	—	—	—	—	—	—	—	—	—	0	13
1972	Atl	4	—	—	—	—	1	18	18.0(18)	0	—	—	—	—	—	—	—	—	—	—	—	—	0	9
1973	Buf	12	—	—	—	—	1	12	12.0(12)	0	—	—	—	—	—	—	—	—	—	—	k	—	0	15
1974	Det	13(2)	—	—	—	—	3	87	29.0(56)	0	—	—	—	—	—	—	—	—	—	—	kp	—	0	96
1975	Det	14(12, WR)	1	0	0.0(0)	0	29	501	17.3(62)	4	—	—	—	—	—	—	—	—	—	—	—	—	24	271
1976	Det	14(13, WR)	—	—	—	—	39	822	21.1(74)	5	—	—	—	—	—	—	—	—	—	—	—	—	30	436
1977	Det	14(WR)	—	—	—	—	28	353	12.6(28)	1	—	—	—	—	—	—	—	—	—	—	—	—	6	182
1978	Det	2(2)	—	—	—	—	1	9	9.0(9)	0	—	—	—	—	—	—	—	—	—	—	—	—	0	5
1979	NE	7	—	—	—	—	2	30	15.0(15)	1	—	—	—	—	—	—	—	—	—	—	—	—	6	20
NFL	9	82(29)	2	13	6.5(13)	0	104	1832	17.6(74)	11	—	—	—	—	—	—	—	—	—	—	kp	—	66	1045

Jasper, Ed Edward Vital, DT-NT, 6´2˝/293 lbs; Texas A&M; 1997: Phi, rnd 6; B1/18/1973 Tyler, TX **1997** Phi 10 (1) **1998** Phi 7 (0) **1999** Atl 13 (0) **2000** Atl 15 (15, RDT) **2001** Atl 16 (1) **2002**†Atl 16 (16, NT) **2003** Atl 14 (14, NT) **2004**†Atl 12 (12, RDT) **2005** Oak 15 (1) **NFL** 118 (60) [9 yrs]

Jasper, Vince Vincent Paul, G, 6´4˝/270 lbs; Iowa State; B11/30/1964 Hawarden, IA **1987** NYJ 3 (1)

Jaszewski, Floyd Floyd Roman, T, 6´4˝/230 lbs; Minnesota; 1950: Det, rnd 6; B6/5/1927 Minneapolis, MN **1950** Det 12 (LT) **1951** Det 12 (LT) **NFL** 24 [2 yrs]

Jauron, Dick Richard Manuel, DB, 6´0˝/190 lbs; Yale; 1973: Det, rnd 4; B10/7/1950 Swampscott, MA **[IC]** **1973** Det 14 (12, FS) **1974** Det✧14 (14, FS) **1975** Det 10 (10, FS) **1976** Det 6 (6, fs) **1977** Det 14 (9, FS) **1978** Cin 16 **1979** Cin 16 (FS) **1980** Cin 10 (10, FS) **NFL** 100 (61) [8 yrs]

Jawish, Heinie Henry King, T-G, 5´8˝/210 lbs; George Washington; Georgetown (DC); B2/15/1900 Syria, D3/14/1941 Washington, DC **1926** Pot 9 (4)

Jaworski, Matt Matthew Joseph, LB, 6´1˝/227 lbs; Colgate; B10/23/1967 Blasdell, NY **1991** Ind 8 (3)

Jaworski, Ron Ronald Vincent 'The Polish Rifle', QB, 6´2˝/196 lbs; Youngstown State; 1973: LA, rnd 2; B3/23/1951 Lackawanna, NY

YEAR	TEAM	G(GS, POS)	RUSH	YD	AVG(LG)	TD	REC	YD	AVG(LG)	TD	PASS	COMP	PCT	YD	AVG(LG)	TD	INT	SK	YD	QBR	KPR	OTD	PTS	TAY
1974	LARm	5	7	34	4.9(17)	1	—	—	—	—	24	10	41.7	144	6.0(22)	0	1	3	24	—	—	—	6	76
1975	†LARm	14(1)	12	33	2.8(21)	2	—	—	—	—	48	24	50.0	302	6.3(25)	0	2	9	75	—	—	—	12	124
1976	†LARm	5(2)	2	15	7.5(14)	1	—	—	—	—	52	20	38.5	273	5.3(42)	1	5	5	51	—	—	—	6	-34
1977	Phi	14(14, QB)	40	127	3.2(44)	5	—	—	—	—	346	166	48.0	2183	6.3(55)	**18**	**21**	47	342	60.4	—	—	30	519
1978	†Phi	16(16, QB)	30	79	2.6(15)	0	—	—	—	—	398	206	51.8	2487	6.2(56)	16	16	41	288	67.9	—	—	0	763
1979	†Phi	16(16, QB)	43	119	2.8(21)	2	—	—	—	—	374	190	50.8	2669	7.1(53)	18	12	34	272	76.8	—	—	12	1084
1980	†Phi★	16(16, QB)	27	95	3.5(19)	1	—	—	—	—	451	257	57.0	3529	7.8(56)	27	12	27	213	**91.0**	—	—	6	1525
1981	†Phi	16(16, QB)	22	128	5.8(26)	0	—	—	—	—	461	250	54.2	3095	6.7(85)	23	20	21	197	73.8	—	—	0	991
1982	Phi	9(9, QB)	10	9	0.9(6)	0	—	—	—	—	286	167	58.4	2076	7.3(57)	12	12	31	244	77.5	—	—	0	627
1983	Phi	16(16, QB)	25	129	5.2(29)	1	—	—	—	—	446	235	52.7	3315	7.4(83)	20	18	53	385	75.1	—	—	6	1177
1984	Phi	13(13, QB)	5	18	3.6(10)	1	—	—	—	—	427	234	54.8	2754	6.4(**90**)	16	14	34	270	73.5	—	—	6	925
1985	Phi	16(12, QB)	17	35	2.1(31)	2	—	—	—	—	484	255	52.7	3450	7.1(**99**)	17	20	34	289	70.2	—	—	12	1065
1986	Phi	10(9, QB)	13	33	2.5(10)	0	—	—	—	—	245	128	52.2	1405	5.7(56)	8	6	22	156	70.2	—	—	0	536
1988	Mia	16(0)	—	—	—	—	—	—	—	—	14	9	64.3	123	8.8(22)	1	0	1	10	—	—	—	0	67
1989	KC	6(3)	4	5	1.3(4)	0	—	—	—	—	61	36	59.0	385	6.3(32)	2	5	1	10	—	—	—	0	8
NFL	15	188(143)	257	859	3.3(44)	16	—	—	—	—	4117	2187	53.1	28190	6.8(99)	179	164	363	2826	72.8	—	—	96	9449

Jax, Garth James Garth, LB, 6´2˝/250 lbs; Florida State; 1986: Dal, rnd 11; B9/16/1963 Houston, TX **1986** Dal 16 (0) **1987** Dal 3 (0) **1988** Dal 16 (2) **1989** Phx 16 (0) **1990** Phx 16 (12, LILB) **1991** Phx 12 (9, LILB) **1992** Phx 16 (0) **1993** Phx 16 (0) **1994** Arz 16 (0) **1995** Arz 16 (5, rlb) **NFL** 143 (28) [10 yrs]

Jay, Craig Craig Adam, TE, 6´4˝/257 lbs; Mount Senario; B2/5/1963 Miami, FL **1987** GB 3 (2)

Jaynes, David David Duane, QB, 6´2˝/212 lbs; Kansas; 1974: KC, rnd 3; B12/12/1952 Kansas City, MO

YEAR	TEAM	G(GS, POS)	RUSH	YD	AVG(LG)	TD	REC	YD	AVG(LG)	TD	PASS	COMP	PCT	YD	AVG(LG)	TD	INT	SK	YD	QBR	KPR	OTD	PTS	TAY
1974	KC	2	1	0	0.0(0)	0	—	—	—	—	2	0	0.0	0	0.0	0	1	—	—	—	—	—	0	-40

Jean-Batiste, Garland Garland Anthony, RB, 6´0˝/208 lbs; LSU; B4/2/1965 Lafayette, LA

YEAR	TEAM	G(GS, POS)	RUSH	YD	AVG(LG)	TD	REC	YD	AVG(LG)	TD	PASS	COMP	PCT	YD	AVG(LG)	TD	INT	SK	YD	QBR	KPR	OTD	PTS	TAY
1987	NO	3(0)	8	18	2.3(7)	0	—	—	—	—	—	—	—	—	—	—	—	—	—	—	—	—	0	18

JECHA, RALPH Ralph LeRoy, G-LB, 6´2˝/235 lbs; Northwestern; 1953: ChiB, rnd 15; B12/1/1931 Chicago, IL **1955** ChiB 12 **1956** Pit 7 **NFL** 19 [2 yrs]

JEFFCOAT, JIM James Wilson, DE, 6´5˝/274 lbs; Arizona State; 1983: Dal, rnd 1; B4/1/1961 Long Branch, AL **[S]** **1983**†Dal 16 (0) **1984** Dal 16 (16, RDE) **1985**†Dal 16 (16, RDE) **1986** Dal 16 (16, RDE) **1987** Dal 12 (12, RDE) **1988** Dal 16 (15, RDE) **1989** Dal 16 (16, RDE) **1990** Dal 16 (13, RDE) **1991**†Dal 16 (16, RDE) **1992**†Dal 16 (3) **1993**†Dal 16 (3) **1994**†Dal 16 (1) **1995**†Buf 16 (2) **1996**†Buf 16 (0) **1997** Buf 7 (0) **NFL** 227 (129) [15 yrs]

JEFFERS, ED Edward Francis, G, 6´3˝/215 lbs; Oklahoma; Oklahoma State; 1945: GB, rnd 19; B11/6/1921 Hartshorne, OK **1947** Bkn-A 14 (0)

JEFFERS, PATRICK Patrick Christopher, WR, 6´3˝/217 lbs; Virginia; 1996: Den, rnd 5; B2/2/1973 Fort Campbell, KY

YEAR	TEAM	G (GS, POS)	RUSH	YD	AVG (LG)	TD	REC	YD	AVG (LG)	TD	PASS	COMP	PCT	YD	AVG (LG)	TD	INT	SK	YD	QBR	KPR	OTD	PTS	TAY
1996	†Den	4(0)	—	—	—	—	—	—	—	—	—	—	—	—	—	—	—	—	—	—	k	—	0	3
1997	†Den	10(0)	—	—	—	—	3	24	8.0(10)	0	—	—	—	—	—	—	—	—	—	—	—	—	0	12
1998	†Dal	8(1)	—	—	—	—	18	330	18.3(67)	2	—	—	—	—	—	—	—	—	—	—	—	—	12	175
1999	Car	15(10, WR)	2	16	8.0(23)	0	63	1082	17.2(88)	12	—	—	—	—	—	—	—	—	—	—	—	—	72	617
2001	Car	9(0)	—	—	—	—	14	127	9.1(21)	0	—	—	—	—	—	—	—	—	—	—	—	—	0	64
NFL	5	46(11)	2	16	8.0(23)	0	98	1563	15.9(88)	14	—	—	—	—	—	—	—	—	—	—	k	—	84	871

JEFFERSON, BEN William Benjamin, G, 6´9˝/330 lbs; Maryland; B1/15/1966 New Rochelle, NY **1990** Cle 4 (4)

JEFFERSON, BILLY William C., HB, 6´2˝/208 lbs; Mississippi State; 1941: Det, rnd 12; B3/17/1918 Pheba, MS, D3/10/1974 Memphis, TN

YEAR	TEAM	G (GS, POS)	RUSH	YD	AVG (LG)	TD	REC	YD	AVG (LG)	TD	PASS	COMP	PCT	YD	AVG (LG)	TD	INT	SK	YD	QBR	KPR	OTD	PTS	TAY
1941	Det	11(2)	56	164	2.9(20)	1	2	14	7.0(11)	0	72	18	25.0	181	2.5(32)	0	9	—	—	—	Pkpi	1	12	60
1942	Phi	5(0)	11	57	5.2(13)	0	—	—	—	—	1	0	0.0	0	0.0	0	0	—	—	—	Pk	—	0	86
1942	Bkn	3(0)	1	1	1.0(1)	0	—	—	—	—	3	1	33.3	11	3.7(11)	0	0	—	—	—	P	—	0	7
NFL	2	19(2)	68	222	3.3(20)	1	2	14	7.0(11)	0	76	19	25.0	192	2.5(32)	0	9	—	—	—	Pkpi	1	12	152

JEFFERSON, CHARLES Charles Ray, DB, 6´0˝/178 lbs; McNeese State; 1979: Den, rnd 4; B5/5/1957 New Orleans, LA **1979**†Hou 5

JEFFERSON, GREG Greg Benton, DE, 6´3˝/263 lbs; Central Florida; 1995: Phi, rnd 3; B8/31/1971 Orlando, FL **1995** Phi 3 (0) **1996** Phi 11 (0) **1997** Phi 12 (11, LDE) **1998** Phi 15 (14, LDE) **1999** Phi 16 (16, LDE) **NFL** 57 (41) [5 yrs]

JEFFERSON, JAMES James Andrew, DB, 6´1˝/199 lbs; Texas A&M-Kingsville; B11/18/1963 Portsmouth, VA **1989** Sea 16 (1) **1990** Sea 15 (2) **1991** Sea 16 (0) **1992** Sea 1 (0) **1993** Sea 10 (0) **NFL** 58 (3) [5 yrs]

JEFFERSON, JASON Jason, DT, 6´1˝/306 lbs; Wisconsin; 2005: NO, rnd 6; B12/20/1981 Chicago, IL **2005** Buf 5 (0)

JEFFERSON, JOE Joseph, DB, 6´1˝/202 lbs; Western Kentucky; 2002: Ind, rnd 3; B2/15/1980 Russellville, KY **2002**†Ind 14 (0) **2004**†Ind 9 (3) **2005** Ind 4 (2) **NFL** 27 (5) [3 yrs]

JEFFERSON, JOHN John Larry, WR, 6´1˝/198 lbs; Arizona State; 1978: SD, rnd 1; B2/3/1956 Dallas, TX

YEAR	TEAM	G (GS, POS)	RUSH	YD	AVG (LG)	TD	REC	YD	AVG (LG)	TD	PASS	COMP	PCT	YD	AVG (LG)	TD	INT	SK	YD	QBR	KPR	OTD	PTS	TAY
1978	SD★	14(14, WR)	1	7	7.0(7)	0	56	1001	17.9(46)	**13**	—	—	—	—	—	—	—	—	—	—	—	—	78	573
1979	†SD★	15(15, WR)	—	—	—	—	61	1090	17.9(65)	10	—	—	—	—	—	—	—	—	—	—	—	—	60	595
1980	†SD★	16(16, WR)	1	16	16.0(16)	0	82	**1340**	16.3(58)	**13**	—	—	—	—	—	—	—	—	—	—	k	—	78	736
1981	GB	13(13, WR)	2	22	11.0(15)	0	39	632	16.2(41)	4	—	—	—	—	—	—	—	—	—	—	k	—	24	346
1982	†GB✧	8(8, WR)	2	16	8.0(11)	0	27	452	16.7(50)	0	—	—	—	—	—	—	—	—	—	—	—	—	0	242
1983	GB	16(16, WR)	—	—	—	—	57	830	14.6(36)	7	—	—	—	—	—	—	—	—	—	—	—	—	42	450
1984	GB	13(12, WR)	—	—	—	—	26	339	13.0(33)	0	—	—	—	—	—	—	—	—	—	—	—	—	0	170
1985	Cle	7(2)	—	—	—	—	3	30	10.0(17)	0	—	—	—	—	—	—	—	—	—	—	—	—	0	15
NFL	8	102(96)	6	61	10.2(16)	0	351	5714	16.3(65)	47	—	—	—	—	—	—	—	—	—	—	k	—	282	3126

JEFFERSON, KEVIN Kevin Howard, LB, 6´2˝/232 lbs; Lehigh; B1/14/1974 Greensburg, PA **1994** Cin 6 (0) **1995** Cin 16 (0) **NFL** 22 (0) [2 yrs]

JEFFERSON, NORMAN Norman, DB, 5´10˝/183 lbs; LSU; 1987: GB, rnd 12; B8/7/1964 Marrero, LA **1987** GB 12 (0) **1988** GB 2 (0) **NFL** 14 (0) [2 yrs]

JEFFERSON, ROY Roy Lee, WR-SE, 6´2˝/195 lbs; Utah; 1965: Pit, rnd 2/SD, rnd 2; B11/9/1943 Texarkana, TX

YEAR	TEAM	G (GS, POS)	RUSH	YD	AVG (LG)	TD	REC	YD	AVG (LG)	TD	PASS	COMP	PCT	YD	AVG (LG)	TD	INT	SK	YD	QBR	KPR	OTD	PTS	TAY
1965	Pit	10	1	-1	-1.0(-1)	0	13	287	22.1(50)	1	—	—	—	—	—	—	—	—	—	—	p	—	6	183
1966	Pit	14(SE)	2	36	18.0(24)	0	32	772	**24.1**(**84**)	4	—	—	—	—	—	—	—	—	—	—	p	—	24	411
1967	Pit	13(se)	5	-11	-2.2(20)	0	29	459	15.8(58)	4	—	—	—	—	—	—	—	—	—	—	p	—	24	244
1968	Pit★	14(SE)	6	57	9.5(22)	0	58	**1074**	18.5(62)	11	—	—	—	—	—	—	—	—	—	—	p	1	72	793
1969	Pit★	14(SE)	4	46	11.5(22)	0	67	1079	16.1(63)	9	—	—	—	—	—	—	—	—	—	—	kp	—	54	654
1970	†Bal	14(WR)	4	47	11.8(19)	0	44	749	17.0(55)	7	—	—	—	—	—	—	—	—	—	—	k	—	42	453
1971	†Was★	14	2	13	6.5(13)	0	47	701	14.9(70)	4	—	—	—	—	—	—	—	—	—	—	—	—	24	384
1972	†Was	14(14, WR)	—	—	—	—	35	550	15.7(45)	3	—	—	—	—	—	—	—	—	—	—	—	—	18	290
1973	†Was	14(14, WR)	1	1	1.0(1)	0	41	595	14.5(36)	1	—	—	—	—	—	—	—	—	—	—	—	—	6	304
1974	†Was	14(WR)	—	—	—	—	43	654	15.2(43)	4	—	—	—	—	—	—	—	—	—	—	—	—	24	347
1975	Was	13(wr)	—	—	—	—	15	255	17.0(36)	2	—	—	—	—	—	—	—	—	—	—	—	—	12	138
1976	†Was	14(14, WR)	—	—	—	—	27	364	13.5(27)	2	—	—	—	—	—	—	—	—	—	—	—	—	12	192
NFL	12	162(42)	25	188	7.5(24)	0	451	7539	16.7(84)	52	—	—	—	—	—	—	—	—	—	—	kp	1	318	4390

JEFFERSON, SHAWN Vanchi LaShawn, WR, 5´11˝/185 lbs; Central Florida; 1991: Hou, rnd 9; B2/22/1969 Jacksonville, FL

YEAR	TEAM	G (GS, POS)	RUSH	YD	AVG (LG)	TD	REC	YD	AVG (LG)	TD	PASS	COMP	PCT	YD	AVG (LG)	TD	INT	SK	YD	QBR	KPR	OTD	PTS	TAY
1991	SD	16(3)	1	27	27.0(27)	0	12	125	10.4(29)	1	—	—	—	—	—	—	—	—	—	—	—	—	6	95
1992	†SD	16(1)	—	—	—	—	29	377	13.0(51)	2	—	—	—	—	—	—	—	—	—	—	—	—	12	199
1993	SD	16(4)	5	53	10.6(33)	0	30	391	13.0(39)	2	—	—	—	—	—	—	—	—	—	—	—	—	12	259
1994	†SD	16(16, WR)	3	40	13.3(22)	0	43	627	14.6(52)	3	—	—	—	—	—	—	—	—	—	—	—	—	18	369
1995	†SD	16(15, WR)	2	1	0.5(11)	0	48	621	12.9(45)	2	—	—	—	—	—	—	—	—	—	—	—	—	12	322
1996	†NE	15(15, WR)	1	6	6.0(6)	0	50	771	15.4(42)	4	—	—	—	—	—	—	—	—	—	—	—	—	24	412
1997	†NE	16(14, WR)	—	—	—	—	54	841	15.6(76)	2	—	—	—	—	—	—	—	—	—	—	—	—	12	431
1998	†NE	16(16, WR)	1	15	15.0(15)	0	34	771	**22.7**(**61**)	2	—	—	—	—	—	—	—	—	—	—	—	—	12	411
1999	NE	16(16, WR)	—	—	—	—	40	698	**17.5**(**68**)	6	—	—	—	—	—	—	—	—	—	—	—	—	36	379
2000	Atl	16(14, WR)	1	1	1.0(1)	0	60	822	13.7(49)	2	—	—	—	—	—	—	—	—	—	—	—	—	12	422
2001	Atl	16(6, wr)	—	—	—	—	37	539	14.6(48)	2	—	—	—	—	—	—	—	—	—	—	—	—	14	280
2002	†Atl	13(7, wr)	—	—	—	—	27	394	14.6(63)	1	—	—	—	—	—	—	—	—	—	—	—	—	6	202
2003	Det	7(3)	1	3	3.0(3)	0	6	46	7.7(13)	0	—	—	—	—	—	—	—	—	—	—	—	—	0	26
NFL	13	195(130)	15	146	9.7(33)	0	470	7023	14.9(76)	29	—	—	—	—	—	—	—	—	—	—	—	—	176	3803

JEFFERSON, THAD Thaddius Eugene, LB, 5´11˝/225 lbs; Hawaii; B3/11/1964 **1987** Hou 3 (3)

JEFFERY, TONY Tony Lorenzo, RB, 5´11˝/208 lbs; TCU; 1988: Phx, rnd 2; B7/8/1964 Gladewater, TX

YEAR	TEAM	G (GS, POS)	RUSH	YD	AVG (LG)	TD	REC	YD	AVG (LG)	TD	PASS	COMP	PCT	YD	AVG (LG)	TD	INT	SK	YD	QBR	KPR	OTD	PTS	TAY
1988	Phx	3(0)	3	8	2.7(9)	0	—	—	—	—	—	—	—	—	—	—	—	—	—	—	k	—	0	4

JEFFIRES, HAYWOOD Haywood Franklin, WR, 6´2˝/201 lbs; North Carolina State; 1987: Hou, rnd 1; B12/12/1964 Greensboro, NC

YEAR	TEAM	G (GS, POS)	RUSH	YD	AVG (LG)	TD	REC	YD	AVG (LG)	TD	PASS	COMP	PCT	YD	AVG (LG)	TD	INT	SK	YD	QBR	KPR	OTD	PTS	TAY
1987	†Hou	9(1)	—	—	—	—	7	89	12.7(23)	0	—	—	—	—	—	—	—	—	—	—	—	—	0	45
1988	†Hou	2(0)	—	—	—	—	2	49	24.5(42)	1	—	—	—	—	—	—	—	—	—	—	—	—	6	30
1989	†Hou	16(4)	—	—	—	—	47	619	13.2(45)	2	—	—	—	—	—	—	—	—	—	—	—	—	12	320
1990	†Hou	16(16, WR)	—	—	—	—	**74**	**1048**	14.2(87)	8	—	—	—	—	—	—	—	—	—	—	—	—	48	564
1991	†Hou★	16(16, WR)	—	—	—	—	**100**	**1181**	11.8(44)	7	—	—	—	—	—	—	—	—	—	—	—	—	42	626
1992	†Hou★	16(16, WR)	—	—	—	—	**90**	913	10.1(47)	9	—	—	—	—	—	—	—	—	—	—	—	—	54	502
1993	†Hou✧	16(16, WR)	—	—	—	—	66	753	11.4(66)	6	—	—	—	—	—	—	—	—	—	—	—	—	36	407
1994	Hou	16(16, WR)	—	—	—	—	68	783	11.5(50)	6	—	—	—	—	—	—	—	—	—	—	—	—	42	422
1995	Hou	16(16, WR)	—	—	—	—	61	684	11.2(35)	8	—	—	—	—	—	—	—	—	—	—	—	—	48	382
1996	NO	9(1)	—	—	—	—	20	215	10.8(27)	3	—	—	—	—	—	—	—	—	—	—	—	—	18	123
NFL	10	132(102)	—	—	—	—	535	6334	11.8(87)	50	—	—	—	—	—	—	—	—	—	—	—	—	306	3417

JEFFREY, NEAL James Neak, QB, 6´1˝/180 lbs; Baylor; 1975: SD, rnd 17; B7/23/1953 Fort Worth, TX

YEAR	TEAM	G (GS, POS)	RUSH	YD	AVG (LG)	TD	REC	YD	AVG (LG)	TD	PASS	COMP	PCT	YD	AVG (LG)	TD	INT	SK	YD	QBR	KPR	OTD	PTS	TAY
1976	SD	5	1	0	0.0(0)	0	—	—	—	—	2	2	100.0	11	5.5(7)	0	0	—	—	—	—	—	0	6

JEFFRIES, BOB Robert James, G, 6´2˝/206 lbs; Missouri; 1942: ChiB, rnd 7; B8/19/1919 Kansas City, MO **1942** Bkn 4 (0)

JEFFRIES, CURTIS Curtis Anthony, TE, 6´4˝/236 lbs; Louisville; B10/26/1964 Louisville, CA **1987** Cin 3 (0)

JEFFRIES, DAMEIAN Dameian, DE, 6´4˝/277 lbs; Alabama; 1995: NO, rnd 4; B5/7/1973 Sylacauga, AL **1995** NO 2 (0)

YEAR	TEAM	G(GS, POS)	RUSH	YD	AVG(LG)	TD	REC	YD	AVG(LG)	TD	PASS	COMP	PCT	YD	AVG(LG)	TD	INT	SK	YD	QBR	KPR	OTD	PTS	TAY

JEFFRIES, ERIC Eric Marcel, DB, 5´10˝/161 lbs; Texas; 1987: Chi, rnd 12; B7/25/1964 Springfield, MO **1987** ChiB 2 (0)

JEFFRIES, GREG Gregory Lamont, DB, 5´9˝/184 lbs; Virginia; 1993: Det, rnd 6; B10/16/1971 High Point, NC **1993** Det 7 (0) **1994**†Det 16 (1) **1995**†Det 14 (0) **1996** Det 16 (4) **1997**†Det 15 (2) **1998** Det 15 (3) **1999**†Mia 16 (0) **2000** Mia 11 (0) **NFL** 110 (10) [8 yrs]

JELACIC, JON Jon Francis, DE, 6´3˝/250 lbs; Minnesota; 1958: ChiC, rnd 7; B12/19/1936 Brainerd, MN, D9/17/1993 St. Paul, MN **1958** NYG 9 **1961** Oak-A 4 **1962** Oak-A 14 (LDE) **1963** Oak-A 14 (RDE) **1964** Oak-A 3 **NFL** 44 [5 yrs]

JELESKY, TOM Thomas John, T, 6´6˝/275 lbs; Purdue; B10/4/1960 Merrillville, IN **1985** Phi 16 (0) **1986** Phi 9 (7, LT) **NFL** 25 (7) [2 yrs]

JELLEY, TOM Thomas J., DE, 6´5˝/225 lbs; Miami (FL); 1951: ChiB, rnd 4; B11/18/1926 Pittsburgh, PA

| 1951 | Pit | 5 | — | — | — | — | 1 | 8 | 8.0(8) | 0 | — | — | — | — | — | — | — | — | — | — | — | — | 0 | 4 |

JELLS, DIETRICH Dietrich Davis, WR, 5´10˝/186 lbs; Pittsburgh; 1996: KC, rnd 6; B4/11/1972 Erie, PA

1996	NE	7(1)	—	—	—	—	1	5	5.0(5)	0	—	—	—	—	—	—	—	—	—	—	—	—	0	3
1997	NE	11(0)	—	—	—	—	1	9	9.0(9)	0	—	—	—	—	—	—	—	—	—	—	—	—	0	5
1998	Phi	9(0)	2	9	4.5(13)	0	2	53	26.5(37)	0	—	—	—	—	—	—	—	—	—	—	—	—	0	36
1999	Phi	14(3)	—	—	—	—	10	180	18.0(57)	2	—	—	—	—	—	—	—	—	—	—	—	—	12	100
NFL	4	41(4)	2	9	4.5(13)	0	14	247	17.6(57)	2	—	—	—	—	—	—	—	—	—	—	—	—	12	143

JEMAIL, JIMMY Manuel James, QB, 5´6˝/165 lbs; Brown; Navy; B9/12/1893 Biblos, Lebanon, D7/26/1978 New York, NY **1921** NYG 1 (1)

JENCKS, BOB Robert William, TE-K, 6´5˝/227 lbs; Miami (OH); 1963: Chi, rnd 2/Buf, rnd 5; B7/15/1941 Columbus, OH [K]

1963	†ChiB	14	—	—	—	—	1	6	6.0(6)	0	—	—	—	—	—	—	—	—	—	—	K	—	38	3
1964	ChiB	14	—	—	—	—	—	—	—	—	—	—	—	—	—	—	—	—	—	—	K	—	38	0
1965	Was	14	—	—	—	—	2	20	10.0(12)	0	—	—	—	—	—	—	—	—	—	—	K	—	59	10
NFL	3	42	—	—	—	—	3	26	8.7(12)	0	—	—	—	—	—	—	—	—	—	—	K	—	135	13

JENKE, NOEL Noel Charles, LB, 6´2˝/221 lbs; Minnesota; 1969: Min, rnd 12; B12/17/1946 Owatonna, MN **1971**†Min 14 **1972** Atl 1 **1973** GB 2 **1974** GB 8 **NFL** 25 [4 yrs]

JENKINS, A.J. A.J., LB-DE, 6´2˝/237 lbs; Cal State-Fullerton; 1989: Pit, rnd 9; B4/12/1966 Havelock, NC **1989**†Pit 16 (0) **1990** Pit 5 (0) **NFL** 21 (0) [2 yrs]

JENKINS, AL Alfred Joseph, G-T-DE-DT, 6´2˝/245 lbs; Southern Illinois; Tulsa; 1969: Cle, rnd 3; B7/15/1946 New Orleans, LA **1969** Cle 8 **1970** Cle 5 **1972** Mia 14 **1973** Hou 13 (RG) **NFL** 40 [4 yrs]

JENKINS, ALFRED Alfred Donell, WR, 5´10˝/170 lbs; Morris Brown; B1/25/1952 Hogansville, GA

1975	Atl	14(14, WR)	—	—	—	—	38	767	20.2(68)	6	—	—	—	—	—	—	—	—	—	—	kp	—	36	431
1976	Atl	14(14, WR)	—	—	—	—	41	710	17.3(34)	6	1	0	0.0	0	0.0	0	1	—	—	—	—	—	36	345
1977	Atl	14(14, WR)	2	7	3.5(9)	0	39	677	17.4(73)	4	—	—	—	—	—	—	—	—	—	—	—	—	24	366
1978	Atl	1(1)	—	—	—	—	2	28	14.0(22)	0	—	—	—	—	—	—	—	—	—	—	—	—	0	14
1979	Atl	16(16, WR)	—	—	—	—	50	858	17.2(57)	3	—	—	—	—	—	—	—	—	—	—	—	—	18	444
1980	†Atl◇	16(16, WR)	—	—	—	—	58	1035	17.8(57)	6	—	—	—	—	—	—	—	—	—	—	—	—	36	548
1981	Atl★	16(16, WR)	—	—	—	—	70	1358	19.4(67)	13	—	—	—	—	—	—	—	—	—	—	—	—	78	744
1982	†Atl	9(9, WR)	—	—	—	—	24	347	14.5(43)	1	—	—	—	—	—	—	—	—	—	—	—	—	6	179
1983	Atl	10(10, WR)	—	—	—	—	38	487	12.8(26)	1	—	—	—	—	—	—	—	—	—	—	—	—	6	249
NFL	9	110(110)	2	7	3.5(9)	0	360	6267	17.4(73)	40	1	0	0.0	0	0.0	0	1	—	—	—	kp	—	240	3318

JENKINS, BILLY Billy Leon, DB, 5´10˝/205 lbs; Howard; B7/8/1974 Albuquerque, NM **1997** SL 16 (2) **1998** SL 16 (13, SS) **1999**†SL 16 (16, SS) **2000** Den 16 (16, SS) **2001** Den 6 (0) **2001**†GB 6 (0) **2002** Buf 15 (1) **NFL** 91 (48) [6 yrs]

JENKINS, CARLOS Carlos Edward, LB, 6´3˝/217 lbs; Michigan State; 1991: Min, rnd 3; B7/12/1968 Palm Beach, FL **1991** Min 3 (0) **1992**†Min 16 (12, LLB) **1993**†Min 16 (16, LLB) **1994**†Min 16 (16, LLB) **1995** SL 16 (13, LLB) **1996** SL 13 (10, LLB) **NFL** 80 (67) [6 yrs]

JENKINS, COREY Corey LaVester, LB, 6´0˝/222 lbs; South Carolina; 2003: Mia, rnd 6; B8/25/1976 Columbia, SC **2003** Mia 16 (0) **2004** Mia 3 (0) **2004** ChiB 4 (0) **NFL** 23 (0) [2 yrs]

JENKINS, CULLEN Cullen Darome, DT, 6´3˝/292 lbs; Central Michigan; B1/20/1981 Detroit, MI **2004**†GB 16 (6, rdt) **2005** GB 16 (12, RDT) **NFL** 32 (18) [2 yrs]

JENKINS, DERON DeRon Charles, DB, 5´11˝/190 lbs; Tennessee; 1996: Bal, rnd 2; B11/14/1973 St. Louis, MO **1996** Bal 15 (2) **1997** Bal 16 (6, RCB) **1998** Bal 16 (7, rcb) **1999** Bal 16 (15, RCB) **2000** SD 15 (14, RCB) **2001** Ten 15 (6, lcb) **NFL** 93 (50) [6 yrs]

JENKINS, ED Eddie Jay, RB, 6´2˝/210 lbs; Holy Cross; 1972: Mia, rnd 11; B8/31/1950 Jacksonville, FL **1972**†Mia 3 **1974** NYG 4 **1974** NE 4

| 1974 | Buf | 3 | — | — | — | — | 1 | 12 | 12.0(12) | 0 | — | — | — | — | — | — | — | — | — | — | — | — | 0 | 6 |
| NFL | 2 | 14 | — | — | — | — | 1 | 12 | 12.0(12) | 0 | — | — | — | — | — | — | — | — | — | — | — | — | 0 | 6 |

JENKINS, FLETCHER Fletcher, DE-NT, 6´2˝/258 lbs; Washington; 1982: Bal, rnd 7; B11/4/1959 Tacoma, WA **1982** Bal 9 (9, RDE)

JENKINS, IZEL Izel, DB, 5´10˝/191 lbs; North Carolina State; 1988: Phi, rnd 11; B5/27/1964 Wilson, NC **1988**†Phi 16 (0) **1989**†Phi 16 (13, LCB) **1990**†Phi 15 (4) **1991** Phi 14 (5, lcb) **1992**†Phi 16 (6, lcb) **1993** Min 4 (0) **1993** NYG 5 (0) **NFL** 86 (28) [6 yrs]

JENKINS, J.R. John Robert, K, 6´1˝/195 lbs; Marshall; B1/31/1979 Springfield, IL [K] **2002** Bal 7 (0)

JENKINS, JACK Jacques Sumpter, FB, 6´1˝/206 lbs; Vanderbilt; 1943: Was, rnd 1; B5/6/1921 Texarkana, TX, D4/30/1982 Florence, AL [K]

1943	Was	2(0)	4	20	5.0(8)	0	—	—	—	—	—	—	—	—	—	—	—	—	—	—	K	—	1	20
1946	Was	8(6, FB)	64	200	3.1(15)	1	2	27	13.5(14)	0	—	—	—	—	—	—	—	—	—	—	pi	—	6	270
1947	Was	12(7, FB)	16	54	3.4(9)	0	5	96	19.2(37)	0	—	—	—	—	—	—	—	—	—	—	i	—	0	104
NFL	3	22(13)	84	274	3.3(15)	1	7	123	17.6(37)	0	—	—	—	—	—	—	—	—	—	—	Kpi	—	7	394

JENKINS, JAMES James, TE, 6´2˝/243 lbs; Rutgers; B8/17/1967 Staten Island, NY **1991**†Was 4 (0) **1992**†Was 5 (1) **1993** Was 15 (5, te) **1998** Was 16 (4) **2000** Was 13 (6, te)

1994	Was	16(3)	—	—	—	—	8	32	4.0(9)	4	—	—	—	—	—	—	—	—	—	—	k	—	24	25
1995	Was	16(5, te)	—	—	—	—	1	2	2.0(2)	0	—	—	—	—	—	—	—	—	—	—	k	—	0	-2
1996	Was	16(5, te)	—	—	—	—	1	7	7.0(7)	0	—	—	—	—	—	—	—	—	—	—	—	—	0	4
1997	Was	16(4)	—	—	—	—	4	43	10.8(20)	3	—	—	—	—	—	—	—	—	—	—	—	—	18	37
1999	†Was	16(4)	—	—	—	—	1	30	30.0(30)	0	—	—	—	—	—	—	—	—	—	—	k	—	0	10
NFL	10	133(37)	—	—	—	—	15	114	7.6(30)	7	—	—	—	—	—	—	—	—	—	—	k	—	42	58

JENKINS, JOHN John Eric, DB, 6´0˝/188 lbs; Pittsburgh; B5/11/1975 East McKeesport, PA **1998** Pit 1 (0)

JENKINS, JON Jonathan R., T, 6´2˝/225 lbs; Dartmouth; 1949: Bal-A, rnd 15/Phi, rnd 9; B6/17/1926 Frostburg, MD, D6/30/1999 Frostburg, MD **1949** Bal-A 11 (3) **1950** Bal 3 **1950** NYY 1 **NFL** 4 [1 yr]

JENKINS, KEN Kenneth Walton, RB, 5´8˝/183 lbs; Bucknell; B5/8/1959 Washington, DC [R] **1983**†Det 12 (0) **1986** Was 12 (0)

1984	Det	14(3)	78	358	4.6(25)	1	21	246	11.7(68)	0	1	0	0.0	0	0.0	0	0	—	—	—	kp	—	6	613
1985	Was	13(0)	2	39	19.5(37)	0	—	—	—	—	—	—	—	—	—	—	—	—	—	—	kp	—	0	584
NFL	4	51(3)	80	397	5.0(37)	1	21	246	11.7(68)	0	1	0	0.0	0	0.0	0	0	—	—	—	kp	—	6	1720

JENKINS, KERRY Kerry Cary, G, 6´5˝/305 lbs; LSU; Troy State; B9/6/1973 Tuscaloosa, AL **1997** NYJ 2 (2) **1998**†NYJ 16 (0) **1999** NYJ 16 (16, LG) **2000** NYJ 16 (16, LG) **2001**†NYJ 16 (16, LG) **2002** TB 15 (15, LG) **2003** TB 16 (11, LG) **NFL** 97 (76) [7 yrs]

JENKINS, KEYVAN Keyvan Lewis, RB, 5´10˝/190 lbs; UNLV; B1/6/1961 Stockton, CA **1988** KC 2 (0)

| 1987 | SD | 3(2) | 22 | 88 | 4.0(9) | 0 | 8 | 40 | 5.0(7) | 0 | — | — | — | — | — | — | — | — | — | — | k | — | 0 | 124 |
| NFL | 2 | 5(2) | 22 | 88 | 4.0(9) | 0 | 8 | 40 | 5.0(7) | 0 | — | — | — | — | — | — | — | — | — | — | k | — | 0 | 106 |

JENKINS, KRIS Kristopher Rudy-Charles, DT, 6´4˝/315 lbs; Maryland; 2001: Car, rnd 2; B8/3/1979 Ypsilanti, MI **2001** Car 16 (11, RDT) **2002** Car★16 (16, RDT) **2003**†Car★16 (16, RDT) **2004** Car 4 (4) **2005** Car 1 (1) **NFL** 53 (48) [5 yrs]

JENKINS, LEON Leon, DB, 5´11˝/165 lbs; West Virginia; 1972: Det, rnd 16; B8/26/1950 Columbus, OH **1972** Det 4

JENKINS, MARTAY MarTay, WR, 6´0˝/201 lbs; Nebraska-Omaha; 1999: Dal, rnd 6; B2/28/1975 Waterloo, IA [R]

1999	Arz	3(0)	—	—	—	—	—	—	—	—	—	—	—	—	—	—	—	—	—	—	—	—	—	—
2000	Arz	16(2)	1	-4	-4.0(-4)	0	17	219	12.9(34)	0	—	—	—	—	—	—	—	—	—	—	kp	1	6	1068
2001	Arz	13(3)	3	4	1.3(16)	0	32	518	16.2(53)	3	—	—	—	—	—	—	—	—	—	—	k	—	18	663

YEAR	TEAM	G (GS, POS)	RUSH	YD	AVG (LG)	TD	REC	YD	AVG (LG)	TD	PASS	COMP	PCT	YD	AVG (LG)	TD	INT	SK	YD	QBR	KPR	OTD	PTS	TAY
2002	Arz	8(1)	3	6	2.0(10)	0	21	250	11.9(65)	1	—	—	—	—	—	—	—	—	—	—	k	1	12	405
NFL	4	40(6)	7	6	0.9(16)	0	70	987	14.1(65)	4	—	—	—	—	—	—	—	—	—	—	kp	2	36	2136

JENKINS, MEL Melvin, DB, 5´10˝/172 lbs; Cincinnati; B3/16/1962 Jackson, MS **1987**†Sea 12 (1) **1988**†Sea 16 (16, RCB/lcb) **1989** Sea 16 (3) **1990** Sea 16 (0) **1991**†Det 16 (16, RCB) **1992** Det 16 (16, RCB) **1993** Atl 14 (3) **1993**†Det 1 (0) **NFL** 107 (55) [7 yrs]

JENKINS, MICHAEL Michael, WR, 6´5˝/215 lbs; Ohio State; 2004: Atl, rnd 1; B6/18/1982 Tampa, FL

YEAR	TEAM	G (GS, POS)	RUSH	YD	AVG (LG)	TD	REC	YD	AVG (LG)	TD	PASS	COMP	PCT	YD	AVG (LG)	TD	INT	SK	YD	QBR	KPR	OTD	PTS	TAY
2004	†Atl	16(0)	1	2	2.0(2)	0	7	119	17.0(46)	0	—	—	—	—	—	—	—	—	—	—	—	—	0	62
2005	Atl	14(13, WR)	—	—	—	—	36	508	14.1(58)	3	—	—	—	—	—	—	—	—	—	—	p	—	18	273
NFL	2	30(13)	1	2	2.0(2)	0	43	627	14.6(58)	3	—	—	—	—	—	—	—	—	—	—	p	—	18	335

JENKINS, MIKE Michael, WR, 6´4˝/200 lbs; Hampton; B8/25/1974 Portsmouth, VA **1997** Cin 4 (0)

JENKINS, ROBERT Robert Lloyd, aka Robert Cox, T, 6´5˝/258 lbs; UCLA; 1986: LARm, rnd 6; B12/30/1963 San Francisco, CA **1987** LARm 10 (0) **1988**†LARm 16 (0) **1989**†LARm 16 (2) **1990** LARm 11 (0) **1991** LARm 12 (8, lt) **1992** LARm 9 (0) **1993** LARm 8 (1) **1994** LARd 10 (4) **1995** Oak 15 (13, LT) **1996** Oak 10 (6, lt) **NFL** 117 (34) [10 yrs]

JENKINS, RONNEY Ronney Gene, RB, 5´11˝/185 lbs; Brigham Young; Northern Arizona; B5/25/1977 Los Angeles, CA **[R]** **2002** SD 13 (0) **2003** Oak 7 (0)

YEAR	TEAM	G (GS, POS)	RUSH	YD	AVG (LG)	TD	REC	YD	AVG (LG)	TD	PASS	COMP	PCT	YD	AVG (LG)	TD	INT	SK	YD	QBR	KPR	OTD	PTS	TAY
2000	SD	16(0)	8	6	0.8(4)	0	1	1	1.0(1)	0	—	—	—	—	—	—	—	—	—	—	k	1	6	543
2001	SD	16(0)	1	-1	-1.0(-1)	0	—	—	—	—	—	—	—	—	—	—	—	—	—	—	k	2	12	690
NFL	4	52(0)	9	5	0.6(4)	0	1	1	1.0(1)	0	—	—	—	—	—	—	—	—	—	—	k	3	18	1736

JENKINS, TREZELLE Trazelle Samuel, T, 6´7˝/317 lbs; Michigan; 1995: KC, rnd 1; B3/13/1973 Chicago, IL **1995** KC 1 (0) **1996** KC 6 (0) **1997** KC 2 (1) **NFL** 9 (1) [3 yrs]

JENKINS, WALT Walter B., DE-DT, 6´2˝/223 lbs; Wayne State (MI); 1955: Det, rnd 9; B12/9/1930 Detroit, MI **1955** Det 2

JENNINGS, BRANDON Brandon, DB, 6´0˝/195 lbs; Texas A&M; B7/15/1978 Houston, TX **2000** Oak 2 (0) **2001**†Oak 8 (0) **2002** Oak 10 (0) **NFL** 20 (0) [3 yrs]

JENNINGS, BRIAN Brian Lewis, TE, 6´5˝/245 lbs; Arizona State; 2000: SF, rnd 7; B10/14/1976 Mesa, AZ **2000** SF 16 (0) **2001** SF 16 (0) **2002** SF 16 (0) **2003** SF 16 (0) **2004** SF✧16 (0) **2005** SF 15 (0) **NFL** 95 (0) [6 yrs]

JENNINGS, DAVE David Tuthill, P, 6´4˝/203 lbs; St. Lawrence; B6/8/1952 New York, NY **[P]** **1974** NYG 14 **1975** NYG 14 **1976** NYG☆14 **1977** NYG 14 **1981**†NYG☆16 (0) **1982** NYG★9 (0) **1984**†NYG 16 (0) **1985**†NYJ 16 (0)

YEAR	TEAM	G (GS, POS)	RUSH	YD	AVG (LG)	TD	REC	YD	AVG (LG)	TD	PASS	COMP	PCT	YD	AVG (LG)	TD	INT	SK	YD	QBR	KPR	OTD	PTS	TAY
1978	NYG★	16	1	0	0.0(0)	0	—	—	—	—	1	1	100.0	1	-1.0(-1)	0	0	—	—	—	P	—	0	-1
1979	NYG★	16	2	11	5.5(9)	0	—	—	—	—	2	2	100.0	48	24.0(28)	0	0	—	—	—	P	—	0	35
1980	NYG★	16(0)	—	—	—	—	—	—	—	—	0	0	0.0	0	0.0	0	0	1	13	—	P	—	0	0
1983	NYG	16(0)	—	—	—	—	—	—	—	—	1	0	0.0	0	0.0	0	0	—	—	—	P	—	0	0
1986	†NYJ	16(0)	1	0	0.0(0)	0	—	—	—	—	—	—	—	—	—	—	—	—	—	—	P	—	0	0
1987	NYJ	12(0)	2	5	2.5(4)	0	—	—	—	—	1	1	100.0	16	16.0(16)	0	0	—	—	—	P	—	0	13
NFL	14	205	6	16	2.7(9)	0	—	—	—	—	5	4	80.0	63	12.6(28)	0	0	1	13	—	P	—	0	48

JENNINGS, JACK Jack Weldon, T, 6´4˝/245 lbs; Ohio State; 1950: ChiC, rnd 2; B2/23/1926 Columbus, OH, D6/11/1993 Rocky River, OH **1950** ChiC 12 (9, RT) **1951** ChiC 11 (RT) **1952** ChiC 7 (RT) **1953** ChiC 12 (RT) **1954** ChiC 12 (RT) **1955** ChiC☆12 (RT) **1956** ChiC 12 (RT) **1957** ChiC 12 (RT) **NFL** 90 (9) [8 yrs]

JENNINGS, JIM James Benton, DE-E, 6´3˝/195 lbs; Missouri; 1955: GB, rnd 26; B11/14/1933 Crystal City, MO **1955** GB 4

JENNINGS, JONAS Jonas D., T, 6´3˝/325 lbs; Georgia; 2001: Buf, rnd 3; B11/21/1977 College Park, GA **2001** Buf 12 (12, RT) **2002** Buf 15 (15, LT) **2003** Buf 11 (11, LT) **2004** Buf 14 (14, LT) **2005** SF 3 (3) **NFL** 55 (55) [5 yrs]

JENNINGS, KEITH Keith O'Neal, TE, 6´4˝/262 lbs; Clemson; 1989: Dal, rnd 5; B5/19/1966 Summerville, SC

YEAR	TEAM	G (GS, POS)	RUSH	YD	AVG (LG)	TD	REC	YD	AVG (LG)	TD	PASS	COMP	PCT	YD	AVG (LG)	TD	INT	SK	YD	QBR	KPR	OTD	PTS	TAY
1989	Dal	10(0)	—	—	—	—	6	47	7.8(14)	0	—	—	—	—	—	—	—	—	—	—	—	—	0	24
1991	†ChiB	10(3)	—	—	—	—	8	109	13.6(19)	0	—	—	—	—	—	—	—	—	—	—	—	—	0	55
1992	ChiB	16(14, TE)	—	—	—	—	23	264	11.5(23)	1	—	—	—	—	—	—	—	—	—	—	—	—	6	137
1993	ChiB	13(11, TE)	—	—	—	—	14	150	10.7(29)	0	—	—	—	—	—	—	—	—	—	—	—	—	0	75
1994	†ChiB	9(1)	—	—	—	—	11	75	6.8(23)	3	—	—	—	—	—	—	—	—	—	—	—	—	18	53
1995	ChiB	16(16, TE)	—	—	—	—	25	217	8.7(20)	6	—	—	—	—	—	—	—	—	—	—	—	—	36	139
1996	ChiB	6(5, TE)	—	—	—	—	6	56	9.3(20)	0	—	—	—	—	—	—	—	—	—	—	—	—	0	28
1997	ChiB	12(12, TE)	—	—	—	—	14	164	11.7(23)	0	—	—	—	—	—	—	—	—	—	—	—	—	0	82
NFL	8	92(62)	—	—	—	—	107	1082	10.1(29)	10	—	—	—	—	—	—	—	—	—	—	—	—	60	591

JENNINGS, LIGARIUS Ligarius Terez, DB, 5´8˝/202 lbs; Tennessee State; B11/3/1977 Birmingham, AL **2001** Cin 9 (0) **2002** Cin 9 (0) **NFL** 18 (0) [2 yrs]

JENNINGS, LOU Louis Walter, aka Hawk Feather, E-C, 6´3˝/230 lbs; Haskell Indian; Centenary; B3/5/1904, D11/1983 Dripping Springs, TX **[K]** **1929** Pro 2 (2), 4 **1930** Por 9 (9, LE) **NFL** 11 (11) [2 yrs]

JENNINGS, RICK Richard T., RB-WR, 5´9˝/180 lbs; Maryland; 1976: Oak, rnd 11; B4/17/1953 Houston, TX **1977** SF 3 **1977** Oak 2

YEAR	TEAM	G (GS, POS)	RUSH	YD	AVG (LG)	TD	REC	YD	AVG (LG)	TD	PASS	COMP	PCT	YD	AVG (LG)	TD	INT	SK	YD	QBR	KPR	OTD	PTS	TAY
1976	Oak	11	10	22	2.2(10)	0	1	10	10.0(10)	0	—	—	—	—	—	—	—	—	—	—	kp	—	0	219
NFL	2	16	10	22	2.2(10)	0	1	10	10.0(10)	0	—	—	—	—	—	—	—	—	—	—	kp	—	0	278

JENNINGS, STANFORD Stanford Jamison, RB, 6´1˝/205 lbs; Furman; 1984: Cin, rnd 3; B3/12/1962 Summerville, NC **[R]**

YEAR	TEAM	G (GS, POS)	RUSH	YD	AVG (LG)	TD	REC	YD	AVG (LG)	TD	PASS	COMP	PCT	YD	AVG (LG)	TD	INT	SK	YD	QBR	KPR	OTD	PTS	TAY
1984	Cin	15(4)	79	379	4.8(20)	2	35	346	9.9(43)	3	—	—	—	—	—	—	—	—	—	—	k	—	30	709
1985	Cin	16(0)	31	92	3.0(19)	1	12	101	8.4(24)	3	—	—	—	—	—	—	—	—	—	—	k	—	24	191
1986	Cin	16(0)	16	54	3.4(10)	1	6	86	14.3(34)	0	—	—	—	—	—	—	—	—	—	—	k	—	6	184
1987	Cin	12(5, rb)	70	314	4.5(18)	1	35	277	7.9(24)	2	—	—	—	—	—	—	—	—	—	—	k	—	18	475
1988	†Cin	16(1)	17	47	2.8(9)	1	5	75	15.0(31)	0	—	—	—	—	—	—	—	—	—	—	k	1	12	309
1989	Cin	16(6, fb)	83	293	3.5(17)	2	10	119	11.9(43)	1	—	—	—	—	—	—	—	—	—	—	k	—	18	513
1990	†Cin	16(0)	12	46	3.8(13)	1	4	23	5.8(13)	0	—	—	—	—	—	—	—	—	—	—	k	—	6	217
1991	NO	5(0)	—	—	—	—	—	—	—	—	—	—	—	—	—	—	—	—	—	—	k	—	0	33
1992	TB	11(0)	5	25	5.0(10)	0	9	69	7.7(20)	1	—	—	—	—	—	—	—	—	—	—	—	—	6	65
NFL	9	123(16)	313	1250	4.0(20)	9	116	1096	9.4(43)	10	—	—	—	—	—	—	—	—	—	—	k	1	120	2693

JENNISON, RAY Raymond Ellis, T, 6´3˝/198 lbs; South Dakota State; B1/19/1910 Oneida, SD, D5/3/1990, FL **1931** GB 2 (2)

JENSEN, BOB Robert Peter, DE-E, 6´2˝/220 lbs; Iowa State; 1948: Bkn-A, rnd 17/Bos, rnd 13; B12/29/1925 Chicago, IL, D12/1984 Sioux Falls, SD **1950** Bal 9 (RDE)

YEAR	TEAM	G (GS, POS)	RUSH	YD	AVG (LG)	TD	REC	YD	AVG (LG)	TD	PASS	COMP	PCT	YD	AVG (LG)	TD	INT	SK	YD	QBR	KPR	OTD	PTS	TAY
1948	ChiR-A	14(3)	—	—	—	—	20	276	13.8	1	—	—	—	—	—	—	—	—	—	—	k	—	6	138
1949	ChiH-A	11(0)	—	—	—	—	2	14	7.0	0	—	—	—	—	—	—	—	—	—	—	—	—	0	7
AAFC	2	25(3)	—	—	—	—	22	290	13.2	1	—	—	—	—	—	—	—	—	—	—	k	—	6	145

JENSEN, DERRICK Derrick, RB-TE, 6´1˝/221 lbs; Texas-Arlington; 1978: Oak, rnd 3; B4/27/1956 Waukegan, IL

YEAR	TEAM	G (GS, POS)	RUSH	YD	AVG (LG)	TD	REC	YD	AVG (LG)	TD	PASS	COMP	PCT	YD	AVG (LG)	TD	INT	SK	YD	QBR	KPR	OTD	PTS	TAY
1979	Oak	16(8, rb)	73	251	3.4(15)	0	7	23	3.3(7)	1	—	—	—	—	—	—	—	—	—	—	k	—	6	253
1980	†Oak	16(1)	14	30	2.1(4)	0	7	87	12.4(32)	0	—	—	—	—	—	—	—	—	—	—	k	1	6	102
1981	Oak	16(13, FB)	117	456	3.9(33)	4	28	271	9.7(21)	0	—	—	—	—	—	—	—	—	—	—	—	—	24	632
1982	†LARd	9(0)	—	—	—	—	—	—	—	—	—	—	—	—	—	—	—	—	—	—	k	—	0	12
1983	†LARd	16(0)	1	5	5.0(5)	0	1	2	2.0(2)	1	—	—	—	—	—	—	—	—	—	—	k	—	6	-4
1984	†LARd	16(0)	3	3	1.0(2)	1	1	1	1.0(1)	1	—	—	—	—	—	—	—	—	—	—	k	—	12	15
1985	†LARd	16(0)	16	35	2.2(8)	0	—	—	—	—	—	—	—	—	—	—	—	—	—	—	—	—	0	35
1986	LARd	1(0)	—	—	—	—	—	—	—	—	—	—	—	—	—	—	—	—	—	—	—	—	—	—
NFL	8	106(22)	224	780	3.5(33)	5	44	384	8.7(32)	3	—	—	—	—	—	—	—	—	—	—	k	1	54	1043

JENSEN, GREG Gregory George, C, 6´3˝/266 lbs; none; B1/23/1962 Saux City, WI **1987** GB 1 (0)

JENSEN, JERRY Jerry Joe, LB, 6´0˝/235 lbs; Washington; 1998: Car, rnd 5; B2/26/1975 Downey, CA **1998** Car 10 (0)

JENSEN, JIM James Christopher, WR-QB, 6´4˝/215 lbs; Boston University; 1981: Mia, rnd 11; B11/14/1958 Abington, PA

YEAR	TEAM	G (GS, POS)	RUSH	YD	AVG (LG)	TD	REC	YD	AVG (LG)	TD	PASS	COMP	PCT	YD	AVG (LG)	TD	INT	SK	YD	QBR	KPR	OTD	PTS	TAY
1981	†Mia	16(0)	—	—	—	—	—	—	—	—	—	—	—	—	—	—	—	—	—	—	—	—	—	—
1982	†Mia	6(0)	—	—	—	—	—	—	—	—	1	0	0.0	0	0.0	0	0	—	—	—	—	—	0	0
1983	†Mia	16(0)	—	—	—	—	—	—	—	—	—	—	—	—	—	—	—	—	—	—	—	—	—	—
1984	†Mia	16(2)	—	—	—	—	13	139	10.7(20)	2	1	1	100.0	35	35.0(35)	1	0	—	—	—	—	—	12	102
1985	†Mia	16(1)	—	—	—	—	1	4	4.0(4)	1	—	—	—	—	—	—	—	—	—	—	—	—	6	7

YEAR	TEAM	G (GS, POS)	RUSH	YD	AVG (LG)	TD	REC	YD	AVG (LG)	TD	PASS	COMP	PCT	YD	AVG (LG)	TD	INT	SK	YD	QBR	KPR	OTD	PTS	TAY
1986	Mia	16(0)	—	—	—	—	5	50	10.0(20)	1	2	0	0.0	0	0.0	0	0	—	—	—	—	—	6	30
1987	Mia	12(0)	4	18	4.5(9)	0	26	221	8.5(20)	1	—	—	—	—	—	—	—	—	—	—	—	—	6	134
1988	Mia	16(4)	10	68	6.8(23)	0	58	652	11.2(31)	5	—	—	—	—	—	—	—	—	—	—	—	—	30	419
1989	Mia	16(1)	8	50	6.3(14)	0	61	557	9.1(20)	6	1	1	100.0	19	19.0(19)	1	0	—	—	—	—	—	36	373
1990	†Mia	15(2)	4	6	1.5(2)	0	44	365	8.3(18)	1	1	1	100.0	31	31.0(31)	0	0	—	—	—	—	—	6	209
1991	Mia	16(0)	—	—	—	—	21	183	8.7(19)	2	1	1	100.0	17	17.0(17)	0	0	—	—	—	—	—	12	110
1992	Mia	3(0)	—	—	—	—	—	—	—	—	—	—	—	—	—	—	—	—	—	—	—	—	—	—
NFL	12	164(10)	26	142	5.5(23)	0	229	2171	9.5(31)	19	7	4	57.1	102	14.6(35)	2	0	—	—	—	—	—	114	1384

Jensen, Jim James Douglas, RB-TE, 6´3˝/230 lbs; Iowa; 1976: Dal, rnd 2; B11/28/1953 Waterloo, IA

YEAR	TEAM	G (GS, POS)	RUSH	YD	AVG (LG)	TD	REC	YD	AVG (LG)	TD	PASS	COMP	PCT	YD	AVG (LG)	TD	INT	SK	YD	QBR	KPR	OTD	PTS	TAY
1976	†Dal	14	—	—	—	—	—	—	—	—	—	—	—	—	—	—	—	—	—	—	k	—	0	118
1977	†Den	11	40	143	3.6(12)	1	4	63	15.8(34)	0	—	—	—	—	—	—	—	—	—	—	—	—	6	185
1979	†Den	16(7, fb)	106	400	3.8(30)	1	19	144	7.6(25)	1	—	—	—	—	—	—	—	—	—	—	—	—	12	487
1980	Den	14(13, FB)	101	476	4.7(32)	2	49	377	7.7(28)	1	—	—	—	—	—	—	—	—	—	—	k	—	18	680
1981	GB	15(1)	27	79	2.9(15)	0	5	49	9.8(16)	0	—	—	—	—	—	—	—	—	—	—	k	—	0	104
1982	†GB	8(0)	9	28	3.1(10)	0	3	18	6.0(11)	1	—	—	—	—	—	—	—	—	—	—	—	—	6	42
NFL	6	78(21)	283	1126	4.0(32)	4	80	651	8.1(34)	3	—	—	—	—	—	—	—	—	—	—	k	—	42	1615

Jensvold, Leo Leo Boyd, HB, 5´8˝/173 lbs; Iowa; B3/29/1908 Emmetsburg, IA, D5/30/1966 **1931** ChiB 1 (0) **1931** Cle 7 (4) **NFL** 8 (4) [1 yr]

Jeralds, Luther Luther Reginald, DE, 6´3˝/235 lbs; North Carolina Central; B8/20/1938 Roberson County, NC **1961** DalT-A 9

Jerman, Greg Gregory Stephen, T, 6´5˝/300 lbs; Baylor; B1/24/1979 Hyannis, MA **2002** Mia 2 (0) **2003** Mia 8 (1) **2004** Mia 1 (0) **2005** Buf 10 (3) **NFL** 21 (4) [4 yrs]

Jerue, Mark Mark Darrell, LB, 6´3˝/229 lbs; Washington; 1982: NYJ, rnd 5; B1/15/1960 Seattle, WA **1983**†LARm 16 (0) **1984**†LARm 16 (0) **1985**†LARm 16 (0) **1986**†LARm☆16 (16, RILB) **1987** LARm 4 (0) **1988** LARm 12 (11, RILB) **1989** LARm 6 (0) **NFL** 86 (27) [7 yrs]

Jervey, Travis Travis Richard, RB, 6´0˝/222 lbs; The Citadel; 1995: GB, rnd 5; B5/5/1972 Columbia, SC

YEAR	TEAM	G (GS, POS)	RUSH	YD	AVG (LG)	TD	REC	YD	AVG (LG)	TD	PASS	COMP	PCT	YD	AVG (LG)	TD	INT	SK	YD	QBR	KPR	OTD	PTS	TAY
1995	†GB	16(0)	—	—	—	—	—	—	—	—	—	—	—	—	—	—	—	—	—	—	k	—	0	45
1996	†GB	16(0)	26	106	4.1(12)	0	—	—	—	—	—	—	—	—	—	—	—	—	—	—	k	—	0	108
1997	†GB★	16(0)	—	—	—	—	—	—	—	—	—	—	—	—	—	—	—	—	—	—	—	—	—	—
1998	GB	8(5, RB)	83	325	3.9(16)	1	9	33	3.7(11)	0	—	—	—	—	—	—	—	—	—	—	—	—	6	352
1999	SF	8(0)	6	49	8.2(33)	1	1	2	2.0(2)	0	—	—	—	—	—	—	—	—	—	—	k	—	6	131
2000	SF	8(0)	1	0	0.0(0)	0	—	—	—	—	—	—	—	—	—	—	—	—	—	—	k	—	0	89
2001	Atl	16(0)	3	6	2.0(2)	0	—	—	—	—	—	—	—	—	—	—	—	—	—	—	—	—	0	6
2002	Atl	6(0)	10	17	1.7(9)	0	—	—	—	—	—	—	—	—	—	—	—	—	—	—	k	—	0	100
2003	Atl	15(0)	—	—	—	—	—	—	—	—	—	—	—	—	—	—	—	—	—	—	k	—	0	13
NFL	9	109(5)	129	503	3.9(33)	2	10	35	3.5(11)	0	—	—	—	—	—	—	—	—	—	—	k	—	12	844

Jessen, Ernie Ernest Robert, T, 6´1˝/225 lbs; Iowa; B5/1/1905 Dickinson, ND, D9/23/1987 Cedar Rapids, IA **1931** Cle 8 (6, RT)

Jessie, Ron Ronald Ray, WR, 6´0˝/185 lbs; Kansas; 1971: Dal, rnd 8; B2/4/1948 Yuma, AZ, D1/13/2006 Huntington Beach, CA

YEAR	TEAM	G (GS, POS)	RUSH	YD	AVG (LG)	TD	REC	YD	AVG (LG)	TD	PASS	COMP	PCT	YD	AVG (LG)	TD	INT	SK	YD	QBR	KPR	OTD	PTS	TAY
1971	Det	14	1	0	0.0(0)	0	4	87	21.8(51)	0	—	—	—	—	—	—	—	—	—	—	k	2	14	294
1972	Det	14(WR)	—	—	—	—	24	424	17.7(82)	4	1	0	0.0	0	0.0	0	0	—	—	—	k	—	24	445
1973	Det	14(WR)	5	31	6.2(17)	1	20	364	18.2(**84**)	3	—	—	—	—	—	—	—	—	—	—	k	—	24	302
1974	Det	12(11, WR)	6	17	2.8(18)	1	54	761	14.1(46)	3	—	—	—	—	—	—	—	—	—	—	k	—	24	448
1975	†LARm	14(14, WR)	2	15	7.5(9)	0	41	547	13.3(34)	3	—	—	—	—	—	—	—	—	—	—	—	—	18	304
1976	†LARm✧	14(14, WR)	4	37	9.3(22)	0	34	779	**22.9**(**58**)	6	—	—	—	—	—	—	—	—	—	—	—	—	36	457
1977	LARm	3(3)	—	—	—	—	9	139	15.4(21)	0	—	—	—	—	—	—	—	—	—	—	—	—	0	70
1978	†LARm	16(16, WR)	—	—	—	—	49	752	15.3(49)	4	—	—	—	—	—	—	—	—	—	—	—	—	24	396
1979	LARm	6(6, wr)	—	—	—	—	11	169	15.4(39)	2	—	—	—	—	—	—	—	—	—	—	—	—	12	95
1980	†Buf	16(2)	1	-9	-9.0(-9)	0	4	56	14.0(20)	1	—	—	—	—	—	—	—	—	—	—	—	—	6	24
1981	†Buf	15(0)	—	—	—	—	15	200	13.3(44)	0	—	—	—	—	—	—	—	—	—	—	—	—	0	100
NFL	11	138(66)	19	91	4.8(22)	2	265	4278	16.1(84)	26	1	0	0.0	0	0.0	0	0	—	—	—	k	2	182	2932

Jessie, Tim Timothy LaWayne, RB, 5´11˝/190 lbs; Auburn; 1987: Chi, rnd 11; B3/1/1963 Opp, AL

YEAR	TEAM	G (GS, POS)	RUSH	YD	AVG (LG)	TD	REC	YD	AVG (LG)	TD	PASS	COMP	PCT	YD	AVG (LG)	TD	INT	SK	YD	QBR	KPR	OTD	PTS	TAY
1987	Was	3(0)	10	37	3.7(14)	1	1	8	8.0(8)	0	—	—	—	—	—	—	—	—	—	—	k	—	6	64

Jessup, Bill William Dean, E-FL, 6´1˝/195 lbs; USC; 1951: SF, rnd 11; B3/17/1929 Wray, CO

YEAR	TEAM	G (GS, POS)	RUSH	YD	AVG (LG)	TD	REC	YD	AVG (LG)	TD	PASS	COMP	PCT	YD	AVG (LG)	TD	INT	SK	YD	QBR	KPR	OTD	PTS	TAY
1951	SF	10	—	—	—	—	7	99	14.1(31)	1	—	—	—	—	—	—	—	—	—	—	—	—	6	55
1952	SF	4	—	—	—	—	6	108	18.0(58)	1	—	—	—	—	—	—	—	—	—	—	—	—	6	59
1954	SF	12(le)	1	-5	-5.0(-5)	0	30	565	18.8(68)	3	—	—	—	—	—	—	—	—	—	—	—	—	18	293
1956	SF	3	—	—	—	—	2	7	3.5(10)	0	—	—	—	—	—	—	—	—	—	—	P	—	0	4
1957	†SF	12	—	—	—	—	2	29	14.5(22)	0	—	—	—	—	—	—	—	—	—	—	Pk	—	0	8
1958	SF	12	—	—	—	—	5	66	13.2(26)	1	1	0	0.0	0	0.0	0	1	—	—	—	Pp		6	-12
1960	Den-A	9(TE)	—	—	—	—	9	120	13.3(26)	1	—	—	—	—	—	—	—	—	—	—	—	—	6	65
NFL	7	62	1	-5	-5.0(-5)	0	61	994	16.3(68)	7	1	0	0.0	0	0.0	0	1	—	—	—	Pkp	—	42	470

Jeter, Bob Robert DeLafayette, DB-WR, 6´1˝/200 lbs; Iowa; 1960: GB, rnd 2/LAC, rnd 1; B5/9/1937 Union, SC **[I]** **1965**†GB 13 (RCB) **1966**†GB 14 (14, RCB) 1967†GB★14 (RCB) **1968** GB☆12 (RCB) **1969** GB✧14 (RCB) **1970** GB 14 (RCB) **1971** ChiB 9 **1972** ChiB 10 **1973** ChiB 13

YEAR	TEAM	G (GS, POS)	RUSH	YD	AVG (LG)	TD	REC	YD	AVG (LG)	TD	PASS	COMP	PCT	YD	AVG (LG)	TD	INT	SK	YD	QBR	KPR	OTD	PTS	TAY
1963	GB	13	—	—	—	—	1	2	2.0(2)	0	—	—	—	—	—	—	—	—	—	—	—	—	0	1
1964	GB	13	—	—	—	—	1	23	23.0(23)	0	—	—	—	—	—	—	—	—	—	—	—	—	0	12
NFL	11	139(14)	—	—	—	—	2	25	12.5(23)	0	—	—	—	—	—	—	—	—	—	—	i	2	12	236

Jeter, Gary Gary Michael, DE-DT, 6´4˝/259 lbs; USC; 1977: NYG, rnd 1; B1/24/1955 Weirton, WV **[S]** **1977** NYG 14 (6, lde) **1978** NYG 13 (8, rdt) **1979** NYG 16 (16, RDE) **1980** NYG 16 (16, RDE) **1981**†NYG 12 (11, RDE) **1982** NYG 4 (1) **1983**†LARm 16 (0) **1984**†LARm 5 (0) **1985**†LARm 16 (1) **1986**†LARm 15 (0) **1987** LARm 12 (0) **1988**†LARm 15 (1) **1989** NE 14 (0) **NFL** 168 (60) [13 yrs]

Jeter, Gene Eugene, LB, 6´3˝/235 lbs; Arkansas-Pine Bluff; Texas Southern; 1965: Den, rnd 10/GB, rnd 12; B2/9/1942 Montgomery, AL **1965** Den-A 14 **1966** Den-A 14 (LLB) **1967** Den-A 2 **NFL** 30 [3 yrs]

Jeter, Perry Perry, HB, 5´7˝/178 lbs; Cal Poly-San Luis Obispo; 1955: ChiB, rnd 26; B5/17/1931 Brevard, NC

YEAR	TEAM	G (GS, POS)	RUSH	YD	AVG (LG)	TD	REC	YD	AVG (LG)	TD	PASS	COMP	PCT	YD	AVG (LG)	TD	INT	SK	YD	QBR	KPR	OTD	PTS	TAY
1956	ChiB	7(rh)	60	316	5.3(51)	2	5	52	10.4(23)	0	1	0	0.0	0	0.0	0	0	—	—	—	kp	1	18	438
1957	ChiB	9	10	11	1.1(7)	0	2	9	4.5(11)	0	—	—	—	—	—	—	—	—	—	—	kp	—	0	26
NFL	2	16	70	327	4.7(51)	2	7	61	8.7(23)	0	1	0	0.0	0	0.0	0	0	—	—	—	kp	1	18	464

Jeter, Tommy Thomas Melvin, DT, 6´5˝/285 lbs; Texas; 1992: Phi, rnd 3; B9/20/1969 Nacogdoches, TX **1992**†Phi 15 (0) **1993** Phi 7 (0) **1994** Phi 14 (0) **1996** Car 1 (0) **NFL** 37 (0) [4 yrs]

Jeter, Tony Anthony John, TE, 6´3˝/223 lbs; Nebraska; 1966: GB, rnd 3/Oak, rnd 10; B9/8/1944 Steubenville, OH

YEAR	TEAM	G (GS, POS)	RUSH	YD	AVG (LG)	TD	REC	YD	AVG (LG)	TD	PASS	COMP	PCT	YD	AVG (LG)	TD	INT	SK	YD	QBR	KPR	OTD	PTS	TAY
1966	Pit	9	—	—	—	—	2	18	9.0(11)	0	—	—	—	—	—	—	—	—	—	—	—	—	0	9
1968	Pit	2	—	—	—	—	1	9	9.0(9)	0	—	—	—	—	—	—	—	—	—	—	—	—	0	5
NFL	2	11	—	—	—	—	3	27	9.0(11)	0	—	—	—	—	—	—	—	—	—	—	—	—	0	14

Jetmore, Cliff Clifford Norman, HB, none; B5/14/1895 New Dunkirk, IN, deceased **1923** Tol 1 (0)

Jett, James James Sherman, WR, 5´10˝/165 lbs; West Virginia; B12/28/1970 Charles Town, WV

YEAR	TEAM	G (GS, POS)	RUSH	YD	AVG (LG)	TD	REC	YD	AVG (LG)	TD	PASS	COMP	PCT	YD	AVG (LG)	TD	INT	SK	YD	QBR	KPR	OTD	PTS	TAY
1993	†LARd	16(1)	1	0	0.0(0)	0	33	771	**23.4**(**74**)	3	—	—	—	—	—	—	—	—	—	—	—	—	18	401
1994	LARd	16(1)	—	—	—	—	15	253	16.9(54)	0	—	—	—	—	—	—	—	—	—	—	—	—	0	127
1995	Oak	16(0)	—	—	—	—	13	179	13.8(26)	1	—	—	—	—	—	—	—	—	—	—	—	—	6	95
1996	Oak	16(16, WR)	—	—	—	—	43	601	14.0(58)	4	—	—	—	—	—	—	—	—	—	—	—	—	24	321
1997	Oak	16(16, WR)	—	—	—	—	46	804	17.5(56)	**12**	—	—	—	—	—	—	—	—	—	—	—	—	72	462
1998	Oak	16(16, WR)	1	3	3.0(3)	0	45	882	19.6(75)	6	—	—	—	—	—	—	—	—	—	—	—	—	36	474
1999	Oak	16(11, WR)	—	—	—	—	39	552	14.2(43)	2	—	—	—	—	—	—	—	—	—	—	—	—	14	286
2000	†Oak	16(11, WR)	—	—	—	—	20	356	17.8(**84**)	2	—	—	—	—	—	—	—	—	—	—	—	—	12	188
2001	†Oak	11(0)	—	—	—	—	2	19	9.5(10)	0	—	—	—	—	—	—	—	—	—	—	—	—	0	10

YEAR	TEAM	G (GS, POS)	RUSH	YD	AVG(LG)	TD	REC	YD	AVG(LG)	TD	PASS COMP	PCT	YD	AVG(LG)	TD	INT	SK	YD	QBR	KPR	OTD	PTS	TAY
2002	Oak	1(1)	—	—	—	—	—	—	—	—	—	—	—	—	—	—	—	—	—	—	—	—	—
NFL	10	140(73)	2	3	1.5(3)	0	256	4417	17.3(84)	30	—	—	—	—	—	—	—	—	—	—	—	182	2362

JETT, JOHN John, E, 6′7″/225 lbs; Wake Forest; 1941: Det, rnd 7; B2/9/1918 Canton, WV, D8/3/1975, NC

| 1941 | Det | 5(0) | — | — | — | — | 4 | 50 | 12.5(18) | 0 | — | — | — | — | — | — | — | — | — | k | — | 0 | 19 |

JETT, JOHN John, P, 6′0″/197 lbs; East Carolina; B11/11/1968 Richmond, VA [P]

1993	†Dal	16(0)	—	—	—	—	—	—	—	—	—	—	—	—	—	—	—	—	—	P	—	0	0
1994	†Dal	16(0)	—	—	—	—	—	—	—	—	—	—	—	—	—	—	—	—	—	P	—	0	0
1995	†Dal	16(0)	—	—	—	—	—	—	—	—	—	—	—	—	—	—	—	—	—	P	—	0	0
1996	†Dal	16(0)	1	-23	-23.0(-23)	0	—	—	—	—	—	—	—	—	—	—	—	—	—	P	—	0	-23
1997	†Det	16(0)	—	—	—	—	—	—	—	—	—	—	—	—	—	—	—	—	—	P	—	0	0
1998	Det	14(0)	—	—	—	—	—	—	—	—	1	0	0.0	0	0.0	0	0	—	—	P	—	0	0
1999	†Det	16(0)	2	-8	-4.0(0)	0	—	—	—	—	—	—	—	—	—	—	—	—	—	P	—	0	-8
2000	Det	16(0)	1	0	0.0(0)	0	—	—	—	—	—	—	—	—	—	—	—	—	—	P	—	0	0
2001	Det	13(0)	1	0	0.0(0)	0	—	—	—	—	—	—	—	—	—	—	—	—	—	P	—	0	0
2002	Det	16(0)	1	0	0.0(0)	0	—	—	—	—	—	—	—	—	—	—	—	—	—	P	—	0	0
2003	Det	4(0)	—	—	—	—	—	—	—	—	—	—	—	—	—	—	—	—	—	P	—	0	0
NFL	11	159(0)	6	-31	-5.2	0	—	—	—	—	1	0	0.0	0	0.0	0	0	—	—	P	—	0	-31

JETTON, PAUL Paul Ray, G-C, 6′4″/295 lbs; Texas; 1988: Cin, rnd 6; B10/6/1964 Houston, TX **1989** Cin 5 (2) **1990**†Cin 15 (0) **1991** Cin 8 (8, rg) **1992** NO 2 (0) **NFL** 30 (10) [4 yrs]

JEWETT, BOB Robert Gary, E, 6′2″/198 lbs; Michigan State; 1958: ChiB, rnd 5; B11/14/1934 Mason, MI

| 1958 | ChiB | 12 | — | — | — | — | 15 | 192 | 12.8(26) | 1 | — | — | — | — | — | — | — | — | — | — | — | 6 | 101 |

JIGGETTS, DAN Daniel Marcellus, T-G, 6′4″/274 lbs; Harvard; 1976: Chi, rnd 6; B3/10/1954 Brooklyn, NY **1976** ChiB 14 **1977** ChiB 12 **1978** ChiB 16 **1979**†ChiB 16 **1980** ChiB 15 (0) **1981** ChiB 16 (1) **1982** ChiB 9 (1) **NFL** 98 (2) [7 yrs]

JILEK, DAN Daniel Douglas, LB, 6′2″/220 lbs; Michigan; 1976: Buf, rnd 4; B12/3/1953 Cedar Rapids, IA, D3/6/2002 Ann Arbor, MI **1976** Buf 14 (14, RLB) **1977** Buf 14 (RLB) **1978** Buf 15 (1) **1979** Buf 15 **NFL** 58 (15) [4 yrs]

JILES, DWAYNE Dwayne Earl, LB, 6′4″/242 lbs; Texas Tech; 1985: Phi, rnd 5; B11/23/1961 Linden, TX **1985** Phi 10 (0) **1986** Phi 16 (3) **1987** Phi 9 (5, rlb) **1988**†Phi 16 (0) **1989**†Phi 1 (0) **1989** NYG 9 (0) **NFL** 61 (8) [5 yrs]

JIMERSON, A.J. Arthur, LB, 6′3″/233 lbs; Norfolk State; 1990: LARd, rnd 8; B5/12/1968 Erie, PA **1990** LARd 4 (0) **1991** LARd 13 (0) **NFL** 17 (0) [2 yrs]

JIMOH, ADE Ade, DB, 6′1″/190 lbs; Utah State; B4/18/1980 Los Angeles, CA **2003** Was 16 (0) **2004** Was 15 (0) **2005**†Was 16 (0) **NFL** 47 (0) [3 yrs]

JOACHIM, STEVE William Steven, QB, 6′3″/215 lbs; Penn State; Temple; 1975: Bal, rnd 7; B3/17/1952 Philadelphia, PA **1976** NYJ 1

JOBKO, BILL William Kermit, LB, 6′2″/224 lbs; Ohio State; 1958: LA, rnd 7; B10/7/1935 Bridgeport, OH, D12/18/2004 Snellville, GA **1958** LARm 9 (llb) **1959** LARm 12 (RLB) **1960** LARm 12 (RLB) **1961** LARm 11 (RLB) **1962** LARm 13 **1963** Min 13 **1964** Min 9 (9, RLB) **1965** Min 14 (13, RLB) **1966** Atl 14 (RLB) **NFL** 107 (22) [9 yrs]

JOCHER, ART Arthur Hamble, G, 6′1″/207 lbs; Manhattan; 1940: Bkn, rnd 9; B10/19/1915 Philadelphia, PA, D11/4/1997 **1942** Bkn 11 (4)

| 1940 | Bkn | 10(5, lg) | — | — | — | — | 1 | 2 | 2.0(2) | 1 | — | — | — | — | — | — | — | — | — | — | — | 6 | 6 |
| NFL | 2 | 21(9) | — | — | — | — | 1 | 2 | 2.0(2) | 1 | — | — | — | — | — | — | — | — | — | — | — | 6 | 6 |

JODAT, JIM James Steven, RB, 5′11″/210 lbs; Carthage; 1976: LA, rnd 12; B3/3/1954 Milwaukee, WI

1977	†LARm	14	5	15	3.0(5)	1	1	2	2.0(2)	1	—	—	—	—	—	—	—	—	—	k	—	12	85
1978	†LARm	16	26	100	3.8(18)	0	3	21	7.0(10)	0	—	—	—	—	—	—	—	—	—	k	—	0	228
1979	†LARm	7	6	6	1.0(4)	0	—	—	—	—	—	—	—	—	—	—	—	—	—	k	1	6	-5
1980	Sea	16(13, FB)	155	632	4.1(26)	5	26	190	7.3(14)	1	—	—	—	—	—	—	—	—	—	—	—	36	782
1981	Sea	12(6, fb)	31	106	3.4(15)	1	4	52	13.0(26)	0	—	—	—	—	—	—	—	—	—	—	—	6	142
1982	†SD	7(0)	3	7	2.3(3)	0	1	0	0.0(0)	0	—	—	—	—	—	—	—	—	—	k	—	0	7
1983	SD	15(0)	—	—	—	—	—	—	—	—	—	—	—	—	—	—	—	—	—	k	—	0	0
NFL	7	87(19)	226	866	3.8(26)	7	35	265	7.6(26)	2	—	—	—	—	—	—	—	—	—	k	1	60	1239

JOE, BILLY William, RB, 6′2″/235 lbs; Villanova; 1963: Den, rnd 11/Was, rnd 9; B10/14/1940 Aynor, SC

1963	Den-A☆	14(FB)	154	646	4.2(68)	4	19	90	6.0(34)	1	—	—	—	—	—	—	—	—	—	—	—	30	736
1964	Den-A	14(FB)	112	415	3.7(51)	2	12	16	1.3(15)	0	—	—	—	—	—	—	—	—	—	—	—	14	443
1965	†Buf-A◊	14(FB)	123	377	3.1(30)	4	27	271	10.0(78)	2	—	—	—	—	—	—	—	—	—	—	—	36	563
1966	Mia-A	14(7, FB)	71	232	3.3(14)	0	13	116	8.9(67)	1	—	—	—	—	—	—	—	—	—	—	—	8	295
1967	NYJ-A	11	37	154	4.2(26)	2	8	85	10.6(17)	0	—	—	—	—	—	—	—	—	—	—	—	12	217
1968	NYJ-A	10	42	186	4.4(32)	3	2	11	5.5(11)	0	—	—	—	—	—	—	—	—	—	—	—	18	222
1969	NYJ-A	1	—	—	—	—	—	—	—	—	—	—	—	—	—	—	—	—	—	—	—		
NFL	7	78(7)	539	2010	3.7(68)	15	77	589	7.6(78)	4	—	—	—	—	—	—	—	—	—	—	—	118	2475

JOE, LARRY Lawrence Edward, aka Lorenzo Giuseppe, B, 5′9″/190 lbs; Penn State; 1948: Buf-A, rnd 14/1947: ChiC, rnd 26; B7/6/1923 New Derry, PA, D4/1985

| 1949 | Buf-A | 1(0) | 2 | 18 | 9.0 | 0 | 2 | 52 | 26.0 | 0 | — | — | — | — | — | — | — | — | — | k | — | 0 | 41 |

JOE, LEON Leon, LB, 6′1″/223 lbs; Maryland; 2004: Chi, rnd 4; B10/26/1981 Fort Washington, MD **2004** Arz 4 (0) **2004** ChiB 1 (0) **2005**†ChiB 14 (0) **NFL** 19 (1) [2 yrs]

JOELSON, GREG Gregory Gordon, DE, 6′3″/270 lbs; Willamette; Arizona State; B8/22/1966 Roseburg, OR **1991** SF 4 (0)

JOESTING, HERB Herbert Walter, FB, 6′2″/194 lbs; Minnesota; B4/17/1905 Little Falls, MN, D10/1/1963 St. Paul, MN [C] **1929** Min 10 (10, FB), 12 **1930** Min 9 (9, FB), 6 **1930** Fra 5 (5, FB), 12 **1931** Fra 8 (7, FB), 6 **1931** ChiB 6 (2), 6

| 1932 | ChiB | 4(0) | 10 | 36 | 3.6 | 0 | — | — | — | — | 2 | 1 | 50.0 | 22 | 11.0(22) | 0 | 0 | — | — | — | — | 0 | 47 |
| NFL | 4 | 42(33) | 10 | 36 | 3.6 | 0 | — | — | — | — | 2 | 1 | 50.0 | 22 | 11.0(22) | 0 | 0 | — | — | — | — | 42 | 127 |

JOHANSSON, OVE Ove, K, 5′10″/175 lbs; Davis & Elkins; Abilene Christian; 1977: Hou, rnd 12; B3/31/1948 Gothenburg, Sweden [K] **1977** Phi 2

JOHNS, ED James Edward, G, 6′0″/175 lbs; Michigan State; Michigan; B2/22/1900, D12/1984 Marble Cliff, OH **1923** Cle 4 (4, LG) **1924** Min 2 (2) **NFL** 6 (6) [2 yrs]

JOHNS, FREEMAN Freeman, WR, 6′1″/175 lbs; SMU; 1976: LA, rnd 10; B12/20/1953 Waco, TX **1976** LARm 2 **1977**†LARm 5 **NFL** 7 [2 yrs]

JOHNS, PAUL Paul V., WR, 5′11″/173 lbs; Tulsa; B11/14/1958 Waco, TX

1981	Sea	16(0)	—	—	—	—	8	131	16.4(34)	1	—	—	—	—	—	—	—	—	—	kp	—	6	174
1982	Sea	9(9, WR)	1	-1	-1.0(-1)	0	15	234	15.6(35)	1	—	—	—	—	—	—	—	—	—	kp	—	6	248
1983	†Sea	11(9, WR)	2	12	6.0(26)	0	34	486	14.3(30)	4	—	—	—	—	—	—	—	—	—	p	1	30	461
1984	Sea	4(2)	—	—	—	—	17	207	12.2(32)	1	—	—	—	—	—	—	—	—	—	p	1	12	204
NFL	4	40(20)	3	11	3.7(26)	0	74	1058	14.3(35)	7	—	—	—	—	—	—	—	—	—	kp	2	54	1086

JOHNS, PETE Peter Murray, DB, 6′2″/190 lbs; Tulane; 1967: Hou, rnd 5; B8/14/1945 Cleveland, OH **1967**†Hou-A 13 **1968** Hou-A 9 **NFL** 22 [2 yrs]

JOHNSON, A.J. Anthony Sean, DB, 5′8″/175 lbs; Southwest Texas State; 1989: Was, rnd 6; B6/22/1967 Lompoc, CA **1989** Was 16 (8, RCB) **1990**†Was 5 (0) **1991**†Was 11 (0) **1992**†Was 14 (11, RCB) **1993** Was 13 (3) **1994** Was 11 (0) **1995** SD 1 (0) **NFL** 71 (22) [7 yrs]

JOHNSON, AL Stephen Alvin, QB-P, 6′0″/ lbs; Hardin-Simmons; 1947: Phi, rnd 14; B8/15/1922 Munday, TX **1948** Phi 5 (0)

JOHNSON, AL Albert Alphonso, DB-RB, 6′0″/200 lbs; Cincinnati; B6/17/1950 Baltimore, MD **1974** Hou 14 (SS) **1976** Hou 14 **1977** Hou 14 **1978**†Hou 7

1972	Hou	14	11	13	1.2(7)	0	6	24	4.0(16)	0	—	—	—	—	—	—	—	—	—	kp	—	0	64
1973	Hou	5	1	-3	-3.0(-3)	0	—	—	—	—	—	—	—	—	—	—	—	—	—	—	—	0	-3
NFL	6	68	12	10	0.8(7)	0	6	24	4.0(16)	0	—	—	—	—	—	—	—	—	—	kp	—	0	90

JOHNSON, AL Al, C, 6′3″/305 lbs; Wisconsin; 2003: Dal, rnd 2; B1/27/1979 Brussels, WI **2004** Dal 16 (15, C) **2005** Dal 16 (16, C) **NFL** 32 (31) [2 yrs]

JOHNSON, ALBERT Albert, WR, 5′9″/190 lbs; SMU; B11/11/1977 Houston, TX **2002** Mia 4 (0) **2003** NYJ 1 (0) **NFL** 5 (0) [2 yrs]

JOHNSON, ALEX Alex Dexter, WR, 5′9″/167 lbs; Miami (FL); 1991: Hou, rnd 12; B8/18/1968 Miami, FL **1991**†Hou 5 (0)

JOHNSON, ALONZO Alonzo Al, LB, 6′3″/222 lbs; Florida; 1986: Phi, rnd 2; B4/4/1963 Panama City, FL **1986** Phi 15 (9, RLB) **1987** Phi 3 (0) **NFL** 18 (9) [2 yrs]

JOHNSON, ALONZO Alonzo, WR, 5′11″/183 lbs; Central State (OH); B4/18/1973 Tuscaloosa, AL **1998** NO 1 (0)

YEAR	TEAM	G(GS, POS)	RUSH	YD	AVG(LG)	TD	REC	YD	AVG(LG)	TD	PASS	COMP	PCT	YD	AVG(LG)	TD	INT	SK	YD	QBR	KPR	OTD	PTS	TAY

JOHNSON, ANDRE Andre Lamont, WR, 6´2˝/221 lbs; Miami (FL); 2003: Hou, rnd 1; B7/11/1981 Miami, FL

2003	Hou	16(16, WR)	5	-10	-2.0(11)	0	66	976	14.8(46)	4	—			—								—	24	498
2004	Hou✧	16(16, WR)	4	12	3.0(14)	0	79	1142	14.5(54)	6	—			—								—	36	613
2005	Hou	13(13, WR)	6	10	1.7(5)	0	63	688	10.9(53)	2	—			—								—	12	364
NFL	3	45(45)	15	12	0.8(14)	0	208	2806	13.5(54)	12	—			—								—	72	1475

JOHNSON, ANDRE Andre T., T, 6´5˝/314 lbs; Penn State; 1996: Was, rnd 1; B8/25/1973 Southampton, NY **1997**†Det 0 (0) **1998** Det 3 (0) **NFL** 3 (0) [2 yrs]

JOHNSON, ANDY Anderson Sidney, RB, 6´0˝/204 lbs; Georgia; 1974: NE, rnd 5; B10/18/1952 Athens, GA

1974	NE	14(3)	2	-4	-2.0(-2)	0	8	147	18.4(34)	0	—			—							kp	—	0	148
1975	NE	14(9, RB)	117	488	4.2(66)	3	26	294	11.3(29)	1	—			—							kp	—	24	738
1976	†NE	14(13, RB)	169	699	4.1(69)	6	29	343	11.8(53)	4	2	0	0.0	0	0.0	0	0				—	—	60	951
1978	†NE	15(13, RB)	147	675	4.6(52)	3	26	267	10.3(31)	0	2	0	0.0	0	0.0	0	0				—	—	18	839
1979	NE	5(5, rb)	43	132	3.1(15)	1	9	68	7.6(11)	0	—			—							—	—	6	176
1980	NE	16(0)	11	26	2.4(11)	0	24	259	10.8(22)	3	—			—							—	—	18	171
1981	NE	16(0)	2	1	0.5(5)	0	39	429	11.0(36)	1	9	7	77.8	194	21.6(66)	4	1				k	—	6	306
1982	†NE	0(0)	—		—		—		—			—			—							—	—	0	0
NFL	8	94(43)	491	2017	4.1(69)	13	161	1807	11.2(53)	9	13	7	53.8	194	14.9(66)	4	1				kp	—	132	3327

JOHNSON, ANTHONY Anthony Scott, RB, 6´0˝/225 lbs; Notre Dame; 1990: Ind, rnd 2; B10/25/1967 Indianapolis, IN

1990	Ind	16(0)	—		—		5	32	6.4(15)	2	—			—							—	—	12	26
1991	Ind	9(6, fb)	22	94	4.3(15)	0	42	344	8.2(24)	0	—			—							—	—	0	266
1992	Ind	15(13, RB)	178	592	3.3(19)	0	49	517	10.6(57)	3	1	0	0.0	0	0.0	0	0				—	—	18	866
1993	Ind	15(8, FB)	95	331	3.5(14)	1	55	443	8.1(36)	0	1	0	0.0	0	0.0	0	1				—	—	6	523
1994	NYJ	15(0)	5	12	2.4(5)	0	5	31	6.2(9)	0	—			—							p	—	0	26
1995	ChiB	8(0)	6	30	5.0(11)	0	13	86	6.6(17)	0	—			—							—	—	0	73
1995	Car	7(0)	24	110	4.6(23)	1	16	121	7.6(37)	0	—			—							—	—	6	181
1996	†Car	16(11, RB)	300	1120	3.7(29)	6	26	192	7.4(55)	0	—			—							—	—	36	1276
1997	Car	16(7, rb)	97	358	3.7(20)	1	21	158	7.5(25)	1	—			—							—	—	8	442
1998	Car	16(2)	36	135	3.8(21)	0	27	242	9.0(38)	1	—			—							k	—	6	243
1999	Car	16(0)	25	72	2.9(23)	0	13	103	7.9(22)	0	—			—							kp	—	0	116
2000	Jax	12(3)	28	112	4.0(19)	1	12	153	12.8(48)	0	—			—							—	—	6	199
NFL	11	159(50)	816	2966	3.6(29)	9	284	2422	8.5(57)	7	2	0	0.0	0	0.0	0	2				kp	—	98	4234

JOHNSON, ART Arthur H., T-G, 5´11˝/189 lbs; Fordham; B1/14/1896 Duluth, MN, D4/25/1972 Duluth, MN **1923** Dul 7 (7, LT) **1924** Dul 6 (5, LG) **1925** Dul 3 (2, LT) **1926** Dul 12 (8, LT) **NFL** 28 (22) [4 yrs]

JOHNSON, BARRY Barry Wayne, WR, 6´2˝/197 lbs; Maryland; B2/1/1968 Baltimore, MD

| 1991 | †Den | 4(0) | — | | — | | 1 | 13 | 13.0(13) | 0 | — | | | — | | | | | | | — | — | 0 | 7 |

JOHNSON, BENNY Benny L., DB, 5´11˝/178 lbs; Johnson C. Smith; 1970: Hou, rnd 6; B6/29/1948 Fort Valley, GA **1970** Hou 14 **1971** Hou 10 (rcb) **1972** Hou 14 (RCB) **1973** Hou 13 **1976** NO 9 **NFL** 60 [5 yrs]

JOHNSON, BERT Albert Edward, FB-BB-HB, 6´0˝/212 lbs; Kentucky; 1937: Bkn, rnd 5; B2/18/1912 Ashland, KY, D8/10/1993 Lexington, KY

1937	Bkn	10(5, fb)	41	59	1.4	0	1	3	3.0(3)	0	11	0	0.0	0			0				—	—	0	21
1938	ChiB	9(7, FB)	37	138	3.7	2	—		—		2	1	50.0	4	2.0(4)	0	0				—	—	12	160
1939	ChiB	1(0)	3	4	1.3	0	—		—		—			—							—	—	0	4
1939	ChiC	9(4)	35	91	2.6	0	1	2	2.0(2)	0	40	14	35.0	208	5.2	0	5				P	—	0	-4
1940	ChiC	10(7, BB)	6	15	2.5	0	2	52	26.0	0	1	1	100.0	25	25.0(25)	0	0				Pi	—	0	93
1941	ChiC	10(3)	3	7	2.3(6)	0	4	90	22.5(29)	1	—			—							ki	—	6	82
1942	Phi	7(3)	27	54	2.0(13)	0	9	123	13.7(65)	2	—			—							k	—	12	136
NFL	6	56(29)	152	368	2.4(13)	2	17	270	15.9(65)	3	54	16	29.6	237	4.4(25)	0	6				Pki	—	30	491

JOHNSON, BETHEL Bethel, WR, 5´11˝/200 lbs; Texas A&M; 2003: NE, rnd 2; B2/11/1979 Corsicana, TX [R]

2003	†NE	15(5, wr)	1	-12	-12.0(-12)	0	16	209	13.1(45)	2	—			—							kp	1	18	507
2004	†NE	13(1)	2	8	4.0(11)	0	10	174	17.4(48)	1	—			—							kp	1	12	499
2005	NE	11(1)	—		—		4	67	16.8(55)	1	—			—							kp	—	6	274
NFL	3	39(7)	3	-4	-1.3(11)	0	30	450	15.0(55)	4	—			—							kp	2	36	1279

JOHNSON, BILL William Erick, DE, 6´1˝/196 lbs; Minnesota; B10/4/1916 Larrabee, IA, D3/8/2002 Bentonville, AR **1941**†GB 6 (0)

JOHNSON, BILL William Levi, C-LB, 6´3˝/228 lbs; Texas A&M; B7/14/1926 Tyler, TX [C] **1948** SF-A 5 (0) **1949**†SF-A 12 (10, C) **AAFC** 17 (10) [2 yrs]

1950 SF 12 (C) **1952** SF★11 (C) **1953** SF☆12 (C) **1954** SF☆12 (C) **1955** SF☆12 (C) **1956** SF 7 (C)

| 1951 | SF | 12(C) | — | | — | | 0 | 3 | (3) | 0 | — | | | — | | | | | | | — | — | 0 | 2 |
| NFL | 7 | 78 | — | | — | | 0 | 3 | (3) | 0 | — | | | — | | | | | | | — | — | 0 | 2 |

JOHNSON, BILL William Henry, P, 6´2˝/208 lbs; West Alabama; B7/9/1944 Tuscaloosa, AL **1970** NYG 11

JOHNSON, BILL William Thomas, RB, 6´2˝/230 lbs; Arkansas State; 1984: Cin, rnd S2; B10/31/1960 Poughkeepsie, NY

1985	Cin	13(0)	8	44	5.5(15)	0	—		—		—			—							—	—	0	44
1986	Cin	14(4)	39	226	5.8(34)	0	13	103	7.9(17)	0	—			—							—	—	0	278
1987	Cin	11(4)	39	205	5.3(20)	1	3	19	6.3(9)	0	—			—							—	—	6	225
NFL	3	38(8)	86	475	5.5(34)	1	16	122	7.6(17)	0	—			—							—	—	6	546

JOHNSON, BILL William Edward, DT-DE, 6´4˝/305 lbs; Michigan State; 1992: Cle, rnd 3; B12/9/1968 Chicago, IL **1992** Cle 15 (3) **1993** Cle 10 (0) **1994**†Cle 14 (13, LDT) **1995**†Pit 9 (0) **1996**†Pit 15 (8, lde) **1997** SL 16 (16, LDT) **1998** Phi 13 (13, RDT) **1999** Phi 6 (0) **NFL** 98 (53) [8 yrs]

JOHNSON, BILL William Orville, G-LB, 6´0˝/210 lbs; North Carolina; SMU; 1943: ChiB, rnd 22; B2/1/1921 Bryan, TX, D4/8/1978 Dallas, TX **1947** ChiB 6 (1)

JOHNSON, BILLY William Walter, DB, 5´10˝/180 lbs; Nebraska; B2/19/1943 Stanton, NE **1966** Bos-A 12 **1967** Bos-A 6 **1968** Bos-A 14 (5, ls) **NFL** 32 (5) [3 yrs]

JOHNSON, BILLY William Arthur 'White Shoes', WR, 5´9˝/170 lbs; Widener; 1974: Hou, rnd 15; B1/21/1952 Boothwyn, PA [R]

1974	Hou	14	5	82	16.4(47)	1	29	388	13.4(44)	0	—			—							kp	—	18	905
1975	Hou★	14(WR)	5	17	3.4(19)	0	37	393	10.6(30)	1	—			—							kp	4	30	974
1976	Hou	14(WR)	6	6	1.0(10)	0	47	495	10.5(40)	4	—			—							kp	—	24	676
1977	Hou★	14	6	102	17.0(61)	1	20	412	20.6(71)	3	0	0	0.0	0	0.0	0	0	1	8		kp	3	42	982
1978	Hou	5	—		—		1	10	10.0(10)	0	—			—							kp	—	0	38
1979	Hou	2	—		—		6	108	18.0(29)	1	—			—							kp	—	6	33
1980	†Hou	16(6, WR)	2	1	0.5(4)	0	31	343	11.1(57)	0	—			—							kp	—	12	183
1982	†Atl	9(0)	—		—		2	11	5.5(6)	0	—			—							p	—	0	159
1983	Atl★	16(1)	15	83	5.5(36)	0	64	709	11.1(47)	4	1	0	0.0	0	0.0	0	0				p	1	30	727
1984	Atl	6(0)	3	8	2.7(11)	0	24	371	15.5(45)	2	—			—							kp	—	18	295
1985	Atl	16(8, wr)	8	-8	-1.0(6)	0	62	830	13.4(62)	5	—			—							p	—	30	464
1986	Atl	4(0)	6	25	4.2(10)	0	6	57	9.5(27)	0	—			—							p	—	0	101
1987	Atl	12(1)	—		—		8	84	10.5(19)	0	—			—							p	—	0	105
1988	Was	1(0)	—		—		—		—		—			—							p	—	0	11
NFL	14	143(16)	56	316	5.6(61)	2	337	4211	12.5(71)	25	1	0	0.0	0	0.0	0	0	1	8		p	8	210	5650

JOHNSON, BOB Robert Douglas, C, 6´5˝/262 lbs; Tennessee; 1968: Cin, rnd 1; B8/19/1946 Gary, IN **1968** Cin-A★14 (C) **1969** Cin-A 14 (C) **1970**†Cin☆ 14 (C) **1971** Cin 14 (C) **1972** Cin☆14 (C) **1973**†Cin☆14 (C) **1975**†Cin☆14 (C) **1976** Cin☆14 (C) **1977** Cin 14 (C) **1978** Cin 13 **1979** Cin 5

| 1974 | Cin☆ | 10(C) | — | | — | | 1 | 3 | 3.0(3) | 0 | — | | | — | | | | | | | — | — | 0 | 2 |
| NFL | 12 | 154 | — | | — | | 1 | 3 | 3.0(3) | 0 | — | | | — | | | | | | | — | — | 0 | 2 |

JOHNSON, BOBBY Bobby Charles, DB, 6´0˝/191 lbs; Texas; B9/1/1960 La Grange, TX **1983** NO 16 (0) **1984** NO 16 (0) **1985** SL 11 (0) **1986** SL 3 (0) **1986** NO 8 (0) **NFL** 54 (0) [4 yrs]

YEAR	TEAM	G (GS, POS)	RUSH	YD	AVG (LG)	TD	REC	YD	AVG (LG)	TD	PASS	COMP	PCT	YD	AVG (LG)	TD	INT	SK	YD	QBR	KPR	OTD	PTS	TAY
JOHNSON, BOBBY Bobby Lee, WR, 5´11˝/170 lbs; Kansas; B12/14/1961 East St. Louis, IL																								
1984	†NYG	16 (16, WR)	—	—	—	—	48	795	16.6 (45)	7	—	—	—	—	—	—	—	—	—	—	—	—	42	433
1985	†NYG	16 (15, WR)	—	—	—	—	33	533	16.2 (42)	8	—	—	—	—	—	—	—	—	—	—	—	—	48	307
1986	†NYG	16 (12, WR)	2	28	14.0 (22)	0	31	534	17.2 (44)	5	—	—	—	—	—	—	—	—	—	—	—	—	30	320
NFL	3	48 (43)	2	28	14.0 (22)	0	112	1862	16.6 (45)	20	—	—	—	—	—	—	—	—	—	—	—	—	120	1059
JOHNSON, BRAD James Bradley, QB, 6´5˝/226 lbs; Florida State; 1992: Min, rnd 9; B9/13/1968 Marietta, GA																								
1994	Min	4 (0)	2	-2	-1.0 (-1)	0	—	—	—	—	37	22	59.5	150	4.1 (15)	0	0	1	5	—	—	—	0	73
1995	Min	5 (0)	9	-9	-1.0 (3)	0	—	—	—	—	36	25	69.4	272	7.6 (39)	0	2	2	18	—	—	—	0	47
1996	†Min	12 (8, qb)	34	90	2.6 (13)	1	—	—	—	—	311	195	62.7	2258	7.3 (**82**)	17	10	15	119	89.4	—	—	6	914
1997	Min	13 (13, QB)	35	139	4.0 (28)	0	1	3	3.0 (3)	1	452	275	60.8	3036	6.7 (56)	20	12	26	164	84.5	—	—	10	1284
1998	Min	4 (2)	12	15	1.3 (6)	0	—	—	—	—	101	65	64.4	747	7.4 (48)	7	5	4	30	—	—	—	0	224
1999	†Was✧	16 (16, QB)	26	31	1.2 (12)	2	—	—	—	—	519	316	60.9	4005	7.7 (65)	24	13	29	177	90.0	—	—	12	1654
2000	Was	12 (11, QB)	22	58	2.6 (21)	1	—	—	—	—	365	228	62.5	2505	6.9 (77)	11	15	20	150	75.7	—	—	6	776
2001	†TB	16 (16, QB)	39	120	3.1 (21)	3	—	—	—	—	559	340	60.8	3406	6.1 (47)	13	11	44	269	77.7	—	—	18	1478
2002	†TB✧	13 (13, QB)	13	30	2.3 (6)	0	—	—	—	—	451	281	62.3	3049	6.8 (76)	22	6	21	121	92.9	—	—	0	1425
2003	TB	16 (16, QB)	25	33	1.3 (13)	0	0	-2	(-2)	0	**570**	**354**	62.1	3811	6.7 (76)	26	21	20	111	81.5	—	—	0	1228
2004	TB	4 (4)	5	23	4.6 (7)	0	—	—	—	—	103	65	63.1	674	6.5 (54)	3	3	8	55	79.5	—	—	0	255
2005	Min	15 (9, QB)	18	53	2.9 (16)	0	—	—	—	—	294	184	62.6	1885	6.4 (80)	12	4	23	134	88.9	—	—	0	896
NFL	12	130 (108)	240	581	2.4 (28)	7	1	1	1.0 (3)	1	3798	2350	61.9	25798	6.8 (82)	155	102	213	1353	84.4	—	—	52	10251
JOHNSON, BRENT Brenton Howell, C, 6´2˝/255 lbs; Tennessee-Chattanooga; B5/16/1963 **1987** ChiB 3 (0)																								
JOHNSON, BRYAN Bryan, FB, 6´1˝/245 lbs; Boise State; B1/18/1978 Los Angeles, CA																								
2000	Was	1 (0)	—	—	—	—	—	—	—	—	—	—	—	—	—	—	—	—	—	—	—	—	—	—
2001	Was	16 (1)	—	—	—	—	9	129	14.3 (32)	0	—	—	—	—	—	—	—	—	—	—	k	—	0	56
2002	Was	16 (12, FB)	1	0	0.0 (0)	0	15	114	7.6 (23)	0	—	—	—	—	—	—	—	—	—	—	—	—	0	57
2003	Was	16 (11, FB)	2	5	2.5 (4)	0	9	71	7.9 (19)	0	—	—	—	—	—	—	—	—	—	—	k	—	0	41
2004	ChiB	12 (6, fb)	—	—	—	—	14	55	3.9 (14)	2	—	—	—	—	—	—	—	—	—	—	k	—	12	41
2005	ChiB	7 (6, FB)	1	5	5.0 (5)	0	5	15	3.0 (7)	0	—	—	—	—	—	—	—	—	—	—	—	—	0	13
NFL	6	68 (36)	4	10	2.5 (5)	0	52	384	7.4 (32)	2	—	—	—	—	—	—	—	—	—	—	k	—	12	206
JOHNSON, BRYANT Bryant Andrew, WR, 6´2˝/214 lbs; Penn State; 2003: Arz, rnd 1; B3/7/1981 Baltimore, MD																								
2003	Arz	15 (8, wr)	—	—	—	—	35	438	12.5 (54)	1	—	—	—	—	—	—	—	—	—	—	p	—	6	222
2004	Arz	16 (11, WR)	2	-6	-3.0 (1)	0	49	537	11.0 (40)	1	—	—	—	—	—	—	—	—	—	—	k	—	6	313
2005	Arz	14 (4)	1	0	0.0 (0)	0	40	432	10.8 (41)	1	—	—	—	—	—	—	—	—	—	—	kp	—	6	240
NFL	3	45 (23)	3	-6	-2.0 (1)	0	124	1407	11.3 (54)	3	—	—	—	—	—	—	—	—	—	—	kp	—	18	775
JOHNSON, BUTCH Michael McColly, WR, 6´1˝/187 lbs; California-Riverside; 1976: Dal, rnd 3; B5/28/1954 Los Angeles, CA **[R]**																								
1976	†Dal	14 (2)	—	—	—	—	5	84	16.8 (43)	2	—	—	—	—	—	—	—	—	—	—	kp	—	12	589
1977	†Dal	14	1	-3	-3.0 (-3)	0	12	135	11.3 (22)	1	—	—	—	—	—	—	—	—	—	—	kp	—	6	449
1978	†Dal	16	—	—	—	—	12	155	12.9 (23)	0	—	—	—	—	—	—	—	—	—	—	kp	—	0	392
1979	†Dal	11 (1)	1	13	13.0 (13)	0	6	105	17.5 (28)	1	—	—	—	—	—	—	—	—	—	—	—	—	6	71
1980	†Dal	16 (1)	—	—	—	—	19	263	13.8 (29)	4	—	—	—	—	—	—	—	—	—	—	—	—	24	152
1981	†Dal	16 (7, wr)	—	—	—	—	25	552	22.1 (55)	5	—	—	—	—	—	—	—	—	—	—	—	—	30	301
1982	†Dal	9 (1)	1	9	9.0 (9)	0	12	269	22.4 (49)	3	—	—	—	—	—	—	—	—	—	—	—	—	18	159
1983	†Dal	16 (5, wr)	1	0	0.0 (0)	0	41	561	13.7 (46)	3	—	—	—	—	—	—	—	—	—	—	—	—	18	296
1984	Den	16 (9, WR)	1	3	3.0 (3)	0	42	587	14.0 (49)	6	—	—	—	—	—	—	—	—	—	—	—	—	36	327
1985	Den	16 (8, WR)	—	—	—	—	19	380	20.0 (65)	3	—	—	—	—	—	—	—	—	—	—	—	—	18	205
NFL	10	144 (34)	5	22	4.4 (13)	0	193	3091	16.0 (65)	28	—	—	—	—	—	—	—	—	—	—	kp	—	168	2938
JOHNSON, BYRON Byron Eugene, DB, 6´1˝/220 lbs; Baylor; B10/21/1962 Bryan, TX **1987** Hou 3 (3)																								
JOHNSON, CARL Carl Knud, T-G, 6´3˝/248 lbs; Nebraska; 1972: NO, rnd 5; B12/26/1949 Phoenix, AZ **1972** NO 14 (LG) **1973** NO 14 (LT) **NFL** 28 [2 yrs]																								
JOHNSON, CARROLL Carroll William, E, 5´9˝/165 lbs; Northwestern; B2/10/1894, D4/6/1974 Oak Brook, IL **1920** Ham 7 (3, LE)																								
JOHNSON, CECIL Cecil Oran, TB-DB-HB, 5´11˝/197 lbs; Texas A&M-Commerce; B9/3/1921 Franklin, TX, D3/6/1961 Dallas, TX																								
1943	Bkn	9 (2)	26	38	1.5 (19)	0	9	136	15.1 (57)	2	8	4	50.0	16	2.0 (10)	0	1	—	—	—	Pki	—	12	116
1944	Bkn	7 (3)	30	41	1.4 (19)	0	—	—	—	—	25	10	40.0	193	7.7 (58)	2	4	—	—	—	Pp	—	0	55
NFL	2	16 (5)	56	79	1.4 (19)	0	9	136	15.1 (57)	2	33	14	42.4	209	6.3 (58)	2	5	—	—	—	Pkpi	—	12	171
JOHNSON, CECIL Cecil Ellord, LB, 6´2˝/230 lbs; Pittsburgh; B8/19/1955 Miami, FL **1977** TB 13 (12, ROLB) **1978** TB 13 (13, ROLB) **1979**†TB 15 (14, ROLB) **1980** TB 16 (16, ROLB) **1981**†TB 16 (16, LILB) **1982**†TB 9 (9, LILB) **1983** TB 5 (1) **1984** TB 8 (6, lolb) **1985** TB 16 (2) **NFL** 111 (89) [9 yrs]																								
JOHNSON, CHAD Chad, WR, 6´1˝/192 lbs; Oregon State; 2001: Cin, rnd 2; B1/9/1978 Miami, FL																								
2001	Cin	12 (3)	—	—	—	—	28	329	11.8 (28)	1	—	—	—	—	—	—	—	—	—	—	—	—	6	170
2002	Cin	16 (14, WR)	—	—	—	—	69	1166	16.9 (72)	5	—	—	—	—	—	—	—	—	—	—	—	—	30	608
2003	Cin★	16 (14, WR)	—	—	—	—	90	**1355**	15.1 (82)	10	—	—	—	—	—	—	—	—	—	—	—	—	60	728
2004	Cin★	16 (16, WR)	4	39	9.8 (18)	0	95	**1274**	13.4 (53)	9	—	—	—	—	—	—	—	—	—	—	—	—	54	721
2005	†Cin★	16 (16, WR)	5	33	6.6 (11)	0	**97**	**1432**	14.8 (70)	9	—	—	—	—	—	—	—	—	—	—	—	—	54	794
NFL	5	76 (63)	9	72	8.0 (18)	0	379	5556	14.7 (82)	34	—	—	—	—	—	—	—	—	—	—	—	—	204	3020
JOHNSON, CHARLES Charles Adrian, DB, 5´10˝/182 lbs; Grambling State; 1979: Atl, rnd 4; B5/8/1956 Mansfield, LA **1979** SF 4 **1980** SF 16 (14, RCB) **1981** SL 5 (0) **NFL** 25 (14) [3 yrs]																								
JOHNSON, CHARLES Charles Everett, WR, 6´0˝/195 lbs; Colorado; 1994: Pit, rnd 1; B1/3/1972 San Bernardino, CA																								
1994	†Pit	16 (9, WR)	4	-1	-0.3 (7)	0	38	577	15.2 (84)	3	—	—	—	—	—	—	—	—	—	—	kp	—	18	423
1995	Pit	15 (10, WR)	1	-10	-10.0 (-10)	0	38	432	11.4 (33)	0	—	—	—	—	—	—	—	—	—	—	k	—	0	223
1996	†Pit	16 (12, WR)	—	—	—	—	60	1008	16.8 (70)	3	—	—	—	—	—	—	—	—	—	—	k	—	20	540
1997	†Pit	13 (11, WR)	—	—	—	—	46	568	12.3 (49)	2	—	—	—	—	—	—	—	—	—	—	—	—	12	294
1998	Pit	16 (16, WR)	1	4	4.0 (4)	0	65	815	12.5 (55)	7	—	—	—	—	—	—	—	—	—	—	—	—	46	447
1999	Phi	11 (11, WR)	—	—	—	—	34	414	12.2 (36)	1	—	—	—	—	—	—	—	—	—	—	p	—	8	207
2000	†Phi	16 (15, WR)	5	18	3.6 (15)	0	56	642	11.5 (59)	7	—	—	—	—	—	—	—	—	—	—	—	—	42	374
2001	†NE	14 (3)	—	—	—	—	14	111	7.9 (24)	1	—	—	—	—	—	—	—	—	—	—	—	—	6	61
2002	Buf	16 (0)	—	—	—	—	3	39	13.0 (22)	0	—	—	—	—	—	—	—	—	—	—	—	—	0	20
NFL	9	133 (87)	11	11	1.0 (15)	0	354	4606	13.0 (84)	24	—	—	—	—	—	—	—	—	—	—	kp	—	152	2587
JOHNSON, CHARLES Charles Adrian, NT-DT, 6´1˝/262 lbs; Maryland; 1979; GB, rnd 3; B6/29/1957 Baltimore, MD **1979** GB 16 (12, RDT) **1980** GB 15 (15, NT) **1983** GB 14 (7, NT) **NFL** 45 (34) [3 yrs]																								
JOHNSON, CHARLEY Charles Lane, QB, 6´1˝/200 lbs; Schreiner College; New Mexico State; 1960: SL, rnd 10/1961: SD, rnd 8; B11/22/1938 Big Spring, TX																								
1961	SL	4 (qb)	1	-3	-3.0 (-3)	0	—	—	—	—	13	5	38.5	51	3.9 (16)	0	2	—	—	—	—	—	0	-58
1962	SL	11 (QB)	25	138	5.5 (19)	3	—	—	—	—	308	150	48.7	2440	7.9 (86)	16	20	—	—	65.9	—	—	18	668
1963	SL✧	14 (QB)	41	143	3.5 (16)	1	—	—	—	—	**423**	222	52.5	3280	7.8 (78)	28	21	—	—	79.5	—	—	6	1093
1964	SL	14 (QB)	31	93	3.0 (19)	2	—	—	—	—	**420**	**223**	53.1	**3045**	7.3 (78)	21	**24**	—	—	69.4	—	—	12	781
1965	SL	11 (QB)	25	60	2.4 (15)	1	—	—	—	—	322	155	48.1	2439	7.6 (78)	18	15	—	—	73.0	—	—	6	780
1966	SL	9 (QB)	20	39	2.0 (9)	2	—	—	—	—	205	103	50.2	1334	6.5 (69)	10	11	—	—	65.0	—	—	12	336
1967	SL	5	—	—	—	—	—	—	—	—	29	12	41.4	162	5.6 (36)	1	3	—	—	—	—	—	0	-34
1968	SL	7	5	-1	-0.2 (3)	0	—	—	—	—	67	29	43.3	330	4.9 (30)	1	1	—	—	—	—	—	0	129
1969	SL	12 (QB)	17	51	3.0 (15)	1	—	—	—	—	260	131	50.4	1847	7.1 (84)	13	13	11	101	69.5	—	—	6	530
1970	Hou	10 (10, QB)	5	3	0.6 (9)	0	—	—	—	—	281	144	51.2	1652	5.9 (63)	7	12	15	124	59.8	—	—	0	384
1971	Hou	14 (qb)	2	0	0.0 (0)	0	—	—	—	—	94	46	48.9	592	6.3 (70)	3	7	8	61	—	—	—	0	31
1972	Den	12 (9, QB)	3	0	0.0 (0)	0	—	—	—	—	238	132	55.5	1783	7.5 (60)	14	14	12	82	74.6	—	—	0	402

YEAR	TEAM	G (GS, POS)	RUSH	YD	AVG (LG)	TD	REC	YD	AVG (LG)	TD	PASS	COMP	PCT	YD	AVG (LG)	TD	INT	SK	YD	QBR	KPR	OTD	PTS	TAY
1973	Den☆	14 (14, QB)	7	-2	-0.3 (0)	0	—	—	—	—	346	184	53.2	2465	7.1 (62)	**20**	17	26	177	74.9	—	—	0	651
1974	Den	14 (12, QB)	4	-3	-0.8 (0)	0	—	—	—	—	244	136	55.7	1969	8.1 (73)	13	9	36	270	84.5	—	—	0	687
1975	Den	14 (6, qb)	10	21	2.1 (13)	0	—	—	—	—	142	65	45.8	1021	7.2 (90)	5	12	10	79	—	—	—	0	77
NFL	15	165 (51)	196	539	2.8 (19)	10	—	—	—	—	3392	1737	51.2	24410	7.2 (90)	170	181	118	894	69.2	—	—	60	6454

JOHNSON, CHARLIE Charles Wilbur, DT, 6´1˝/265 lbs; Louisville; 1966: SF, rnd 6; B9/29/1944 Columbus, GA **1966** SF 13 **1967** SF 14 **1968** SF 2 **NFL** 29 [3 yrs]

JOHNSON, CHARLIE Charles, NT, 6´3˝/266 lbs; Colorado; 1977: Phi, rnd 7; B2/17/1952 West Columbia, TX **1977** Phi 12 (9, NT) **1978**†Phi 16 (16, NT) **1979**†Phi★16 (16, NT) **1980**†Phi★16 (16, NT) **1981**†Phi★16 (16, NT) **1982**†Min 9 (6, NT) **1983** Min 16 (16, NT) **1984** Min 16 (15, NT) **NFL** 117 (110) [8 yrs]

JOHNSON, CHRIS Christopher T., DB, 6´4˝/225 lbs; Millersville; B12/3/1960 Miami, FL **1987** Phi 2 (0)

JOHNSON, CHRIS Christopher T'Maul, DB, 6´0˝/205 lbs; San Diego State; B8/7/1971 San Diego, CA **1996**†Min 5 (0)

JOHNSON, CHRIS Chris, DB, 5´11˝/198 lbs; Louisville; 2003: GB, rnd 7; B9/25/1979 Gladewater, TX **2005** SL 14 (1)

JOHNSON, CHUCK Charles Lewis, DT, 6´4˝/310 lbs; Auburn; B3/5/1969 Fayetteville, NC **1993** Phx 5 (0)

JOHNSON, CHUCK Charles Ray, T, 6´5˝/275 lbs; Texas; 1992: Den, rnd 4; B5/22/1969 Freeport, TX **1992** Den 16 (0)

JOHNSON, CLYDE Clyde Elmer, T, 6´6˝/269 lbs; Kentucky; 1943: Cle, rnd 5; B8/22/1917 Ashland, KY, D9/14/1997 **1946** LARm 11 (0) **1947** LARm 12 (1) **NFL** 23 (1) [2 yrs] **1948** LAD-A 9 (0)

JOHNSON, CLYDE Clyde A., DB, 5´10˝/191 lbs; Kansas State; B5/22/1970 Austin, TX **1997** KC 15 (0)

JOHNSON, CORNELIUS Cornelius Otis, G, 6´2˝/245 lbs; Virginia Union; 1967: Bal, rnd 8; B7/12/1943 Richmond, VA **1968**†Bal 14 **1969** Bal 14 **1970**†Bal 14 **1971**†Bal 7 **1972** Bal 13 **1973** Bal 12 **NFL** 74 [6 yrs]

JOHNSON, CURLEY John Curley, RB-P-TE, 6´0˝/215 lbs; Houston; 1957: Pit, rnd 7; B7/2/1935 Anna, TX **[P]**

YEAR	TEAM	G (GS, POS)	RUSH	YD	AVG (LG)	TD	REC	YD	AVG (LG)	TD	PASS	COMP	PCT	YD	AVG (LG)	TD	INT	SK	YD	QBR	KPR	OTD	PTS	TAY
1960	DalT-A	14	23	43	1.9 (8)	1	10	174	17.4 (36)	1	—	—	—	—	—	—	—	—	—	—	Pk	—	14	143
1961	NYT-A	12	1	3	3.0 (3)	0	1	32	32.0 (32)	0	—	—	—	—	—	—	—	—	—	—	Pk	—	0	28
1962	NYT-A	14	26	114	4.4 (25)	0	14	62	4.4 (12)	0	—	—	—	—	—	—	—	—	—	—	Pk	—	0	144
1963	NYJ-A	14	2	6	3.0 (5)	0	—	—	—	—	—	—	—	—	—	—	—	—	—	—	Pk	—	0	-7
1964	NYJ-A	14	6	22	3.7 (8)	0	—	—	—	—	1	0	0.0	0	0.0	0	0	—	—	—	Pk	—	0	24
1965	NYJ-A★	14	2	3	1.5 (2)	0	1	6	6.0 (6)	1	—	—	—	—	—	—	—	—	—	—	P	—	6	11
1966	NYJ-A	14	2	24	12.0 (20)	0	1	18	18.0 (18)	1	—	—	—	—	—	—	—	—	—	—	Pk	—	6	27
1967	NYJ-A	14	—	—	—	—	—	—	—	—	—	—	—	—	—	—	—	—	—	—	P	—	0	0
1968	†NYJ-A☆	14	2	-6	-3.0 (0)	0	5	78	15.6 (18)	0	—	—	—	—	—	—	—	—	—	—	P	—	0	33
1969	NYG	5	—	—	—	—	—	—	—	—	—	—	—	—	—	—	—	—	—	—	P	—	0	0
NFL	10	129	64	209	3.3 (25)	1	32	370	11.6 (36)	3	1	0	0.0	0	0.0	0	0	—	—	—	Pk	—	26	403

JOHNSON, CURTIS Curtis Wise, DB, 6´1˝/196 lbs; Toledo; 1970: Mia, rnd 4; B6/22/1948 Toledo, OH **[I]** **1970**†Mia 14 (14, LCB) **1971**†Mia 14 (10, RCB) **1972**†Mia 14 (13, RCB) **1973**†Mia 14 (13, RCB) **1974**†Mia 13 (12, RCB) **1975** Mia 14 (14, RCB) **1976** Mia 13 (9, RCB) **1977** Mia 14 (14, RCB) **1978**†Mia 15 (12, RCB) **NFL** 125 (111) [9 yrs]

JOHNSON, D.J. David Allen, DB, 6´0˝/187 lbs; Kentucky; 1989: Pit, rnd 7; B7/14/1966 Louisville, KY **1989**†Pit 16 (0) **1990** Pit 16 (15, LCB) **1991** Pit 16 (16, LCB) **1992**†Pit 15 (15, RCB) **1993**†Pit 16 (15, RCB) **1994** Atl 16 (16, RCB) **1995**†Atl 13 (12, RCB) **1996** Atl 2 (0) **1996** Arz 8 (0) **NFL** 118 (89) [8 yrs]

JOHNSON, DAMIAN Damian Curtis, G-T, 6´5˝/290 lbs; Kansas State; B12/18/1962 Great Bend, KS **1986**†NYG 16 (0) **1987** NYG 12 (7, RG) **1988** NYG 6 (6, rg) **1989**†NYG 4 (4) **1990** NE 16 (16, RG) **NFL** 54 (33) [5 yrs]

JOHNSON, DAMONE Damone, TE, 6´4˝/230 lbs; Cal Poly-San Luis Obispo; 1985: LARm, rnd 6; B3/2/1962 Los Angeles, CA

YEAR	TEAM	G (GS, POS)	RUSH	YD	AVG (LG)	TD	REC	YD	AVG (LG)	TD	PASS	COMP	PCT	YD	AVG (LG)	TD	INT	SK	YD	QBR	KPR	OTD	PTS	TAY
1986	†LARm	5 (0)	—	—	—	—	—	—	—	—	—	—	—	—	—	—	—	—	—	—	—	—	—	—
1987	LARm	12 (0)	—	—	—	—	21	198	9.4 (20)	2	—	—	—	—	—	—	—	—	—	—	—	—	12	109
1988	†LARm	16 (15, TE)	—	—	—	—	42	350	8.3 (23)	6	—	—	—	—	—	—	—	—	—	—	—	—	36	205
1989	†LARm	16 (16, TE)	—	—	—	—	25	148	5.9 (22)	5	—	—	—	—	—	—	—	—	—	—	—	—	30	99
1990	LARm	13 (9, te)	—	—	—	—	12	66	5.5 (11)	3	—	—	—	—	—	—	—	—	—	—	—	—	18	48
1991	LARm	16 (16, TE)	—	—	—	—	32	253	7.9 (27)	2	—	—	—	—	—	—	—	—	—	—	—	—	12	137
1992	LARm	4 (0)	—	—	—	—	—	—	—	—	—	—	—	—	—	—	—	—	—	—	—	—	—	—
NFL	7	82 (56)	—	—	—	—	132	1015	7.7 (27)	18	—	—	—	—	—	—	—	—	—	—	—	—	108	598

JOHNSON, DAN Daniel Jerome, TE, 6´3˝/240 lbs; Iowa State; 1982: Mia, rnd 7; B5/17/1960 Minneapolis, MN

YEAR	TEAM	G (GS, POS)	RUSH	YD	AVG (LG)	TD	REC	YD	AVG (LG)	TD	PASS	COMP	PCT	YD	AVG (LG)	TD	INT	SK	YD	QBR	KPR	OTD	PTS	TAY
1983	†Mia	16 (16, TE)	—	—	—	—	24	189	7.9 (33)	4	—	—	—	—	—	—	—	—	—	—	—	—	24	115
1984	†Mia	16 (16, TE)	—	—	—	—	34	426	12.5 (42)	3	—	—	—	—	—	—	—	—	—	—	—	—	18	228
1985	†Mia	12 (1)	—	—	—	—	13	192	14.8 (61)	3	—	—	—	—	—	—	—	—	—	—	—	—	18	111
1986	Mia	15 (1)	—	—	—	—	19	170	8.9 (20)	4	—	—	—	—	—	—	—	—	—	—	k	—	24	90
1987	Mia	7 (0)	—	—	—	—	4	35	8.8 (22)	2	—	—	—	—	—	—	—	—	—	—	k	—	12	11
NFL	5	66 (34)	—	—	—	—	94	1012	10.8 (61)	16	—	—	—	—	—	—	—	—	—	—	k	—	96	554

JOHNSON, DANNY Daniel, LB, 6´1˝/215 lbs; Tennessee State; 1978: KC, rnd 4; B5/7/1955 Normandy, TN **1978** GB 3

JOHNSON, DARRIEN Darrien, DB, 5´11˝/215 lbs; Iowa; B5/3/1980 **2005** NYJ 8 (0)

JOHNSON, DARRIUS Darrius Dashome, DB, 5´9˝/185 lbs; Oklahoma; 1996: Den, rnd 4; B5/18/1973 Terrell, TX **1996**†Den 13 (0) **1997**†Den 16 (0) **1998**†Den 16 (2) **1999** Den 16 (2) **2003** KC 2 (0) **NFL** 63 (4) [5 yrs]

JOHNSON, DARYL Daryl Evans, DB, 5´11˝/190 lbs; Morgan State; 1968: Bos, rnd 8; B8/11/1946 Richmond, VA **1968** Bos-A 14 (14, RCB) **1969** Bos-A 14 (14, RCB) **1970** Bos 14 (14, RCB) **NFL** 42 (42) [3 yrs]

JOHNSON, DEMETRIOUS Demetrious, DB, 5´11˝/190 lbs; Missouri; 1983: Det, rnd 5; B7/21/1961 St. Louis, MO **1983**†Det 14 (2) **1984** Det 16 (3) **1985** Det 16 (16, SS) **1986** Det 16 (16, SS) **1987** Mia 3 (2) **NFL** 65 (39) [5 yrs]

JOHNSON, DENNIS Dennis Craig, LB-DE, 6´3˝/234 lbs; USC; 1980: Min, rnd 4; B6/19/1958 Flint, MI **1980**†Min 12 (2) **1981** Min 16 (1) **1982**†Min 9 (9, LILB) **1983** Min 16 (16, RILB) **1984** Min 16 (15, RILB) **1985** Min 8 (6, rde) **1985** TB 8 (0) **NFL** 85 (49) [6 yrs]

JOHNSON, DENNIS Dennis Alan, DE, 6´5˝/269 lbs; Kentucky; 2002: Arz, rnd 3; B12/4/1979 Danville, KY **2002** Arz 13 (0) **2003** Arz 15 (10, LDE) **2004** SF 1 (0) **NFL** 29 (10) [3 yrs]

JOHNSON, DENNIS Dennis D., RB-TE, 6´3˝/220 lbs; Mississippi State; 1978: Buf, rnd 3; B2/26/1956 Weir, MS

YEAR	TEAM	G (GS, POS)	RUSH	YD	AVG (LG)	TD	REC	YD	AVG (LG)	TD	PASS	COMP	PCT	YD	AVG (LG)	TD	INT	SK	YD	QBR	KPR	OTD	PTS	TAY
1978	Buf	16	55	222	4.0 (30)	2	10	83	8.3 (28)	0	—	—	—	—	—	—	—	—	—	—	k	—	12	338
1979	Buf	3	3	5	1.7 (2)	0	—	—	—	—	—	—	—	—	—	—	—	—	—	—	—	—	0	5
1980	NYG	2 (0)	—	—	—	—	—	—	—	—	—	—	—	—	—	—	—	—	—	—	—	—	—	—
NFL	3	21	58	227	3.9 (30)	2	10	83	8.3 (28)	0	—	—	—	—	—	—	—	—	—	—	k	—	12	343

JOHNSON, DENNIS Dennis Leroy, DE-DT, 6´4˝/260 lbs; Delaware; 1973: Was, rnd 13; B10/22/1951 Passaic, NJ, D4/15/1996 **1974**†Was 13 **1975** Was 14 (14, RDE) **1976**†Was 13 (12, RDE) **1977** Was 11 (11, RDE) **1978** Buf 14 **NFL** 65 (37) [5 yrs]

JOHNSON, DERRICK Derrick, DB, 5´11˝/188 lbs; Washington; 2005: SF, rnd 6; B2/9/1982 Riverside, CA **2005** SF 14 (5, rcb)

JOHNSON, DERRICK Derrick O'Hara, LB, 6´3˝/234 lbs; Texas; 2005: KC, rnd 1; B11/11/1982 Waco, TX **2005** KC 16 (16, LOLB)

JOHNSON, DICK Richard John, WR, 6´4˝/220 lbs; Minnesota; B1939

YEAR	TEAM	G (GS, POS)	RUSH	YD	AVG (LG)	TD	REC	YD	AVG (LG)	TD	PASS	COMP	PCT	YD	AVG (LG)	TD	INT	SK	YD	QBR	KPR	OTD	PTS	TAY
1963	KC-A	5	—	—	—	—	2	17	8.5 (11)	1	—	—	—	—	—	—	—	—	—	—	—	—	6	14

JOHNSON, DIRK Dirk R., P, 6´0˝/205 lbs; Northern Colorado; B6/1/1975 Hoxie, KS **2002** NO 1 (0) **2003**†Phi 16 (0) **2004**†Phi 16 (0) **2005** Phi 7 (0) **NFL** 40 (0) [4 yrs]

JOHNSON, DON Donald Clifford, C-LB, 6´0˝/205 lbs; Northwestern; B9/14/1920 Chicago, IL **1942** Cle 1 (0)

JOHNSON, DON Donald Lee, HB, 6´0˝/187 lbs; California; 1953: Phi, rnd 3; B10/31/1931 Bakersfield, CA

YEAR	TEAM	G (GS, POS)	RUSH	YD	AVG (LG)	TD	REC	YD	AVG (LG)	TD	PASS	COMP	PCT	YD	AVG (LG)	TD	INT	SK	YD	QBR	KPR	OTD	PTS	TAY
1953	Phi	12 (lh)	83	439	5.3 (66)	5	12	227	18.9 (41)	2	—	—	—	—	—	—	—	—	—	—	kp	—	42	611
1954	Phi	6	7	16	2.3 (11)	0	1	20	20.0 (20)	0	—	—	—	—	—	—	—	—	—	—	k	—	0	88
1955	Phi	2	3	1	0.3 (4)	0	—	—	—	—	—	—	—	—	—	—	—	—	—	—	—	—	0	1
NFL	3	20	93	456	4.9 (66)	5	13	247	19.0 (41)	2	—	—	—	—	—	—	—	—	—	—	kp	—	42	700

JOHNSON, DONNELL Donnell, DE, 6´7˝/310 lbs; Johnson C. Smith; B12/24/1969 Miami, FL **1993** Cin 7 (0)

YEAR	TEAM	G(GS, POS)	RUSH	YD	AVG(LG)	TD	REC	YD	AVG(LG)	TD	PASS	COMP	PCT	YD	AVG(LG)	TD	INT	SK	YD	QBR	KPR	OTD	PTS	TAY

JOHNSON, DOUG Doug, QB, 6′2″/225 lbs; Florida; B10/27/1977 Gainesville, FL

2000	Atl	4(2)	3	11	3.7(8)	0	—	—	—	—	67	36	53.7	406	6.1(26)	2	3	13	75	—	—	—	0	104
2001	Atl	3(0)	5	12	2.4(8)	0	—	—	—	—	5	3	60.0	23	4.6(14)	1	0	2	13	—	—	—	0	29
2002	†Atl	6(1)	8	16	2.0(15)	1	—	—	—	—	57	37	64.9	448	7.9(63)	2	3	3	11	—	—	—	6	140
2003	Atl	10(8, QB)	14	21	1.5(13)	1	—	—	—	—	243	136	56.0	1655	6.8(86)	8	12	19	121	67.5	—	—	6	419
2004	Ten	2(0)	2	-2	-1.0(-1)	0	—	—	—	—	12	6	50.0	68	5.7(33)	0	0	1	6	—	—	—	0	32
NFL	5	25(11)	32	58	1.8(15)	2	—	—	—	—	384	218	56.8	2600	6.8(86)	13	18	38	226	69.4	—	—	12	723

JOHNSON, DUSTIN Dustin, FB, 6′2″/236 lbs; Brigham Young; 1998: NYJ, rnd 6; B8/5/1973 Eagar, AZ **1999** Sea 1 (0)

JOHNSON, DWIGHT Dwight O'Neal, DE, 6′4″/285 lbs; Baylor; B1/30/1977 Waco, TX **2000** Phi 4 (0) **2002**†NYG 10 (2) **NFL** 14 (2) [2 yrs]

JOHNSON, EARL Earl, DB, 6′0″/195 lbs; South Carolina; 1985: NO, rnd 9; B10/20/1963 Daytona Beach, FL **1985** NO 2 (0) **1987** Den 3 (3) **NFL** 5 (3) [2 yrs]

JOHNSON, EDDIE Eddie L., LB, 6′1″/220 lbs; Louisville; 1981: Cle, rnd 7; B2/3/1959 Albany, GA, D1/21/2003 Cleveland, OH **1981** Cle 16 (0) **1982**†Cle 9 (1) **1983** Cle 16 (2) **1984** Cle 16 (16, LILB) **1985**†Cle 16 (16, LILB) **1986**†Cle 16 (16, LILB) **1987**†Cle 12 (11, LILB) **1988**†Cle 15 (8, RILB) **1989**†Cle 16 (0) **1990** Cle 16 (0) **NFL** 148 (70) [10 yrs]

JOHNSON, EDDIE Eddie, P, 6′3″/236 lbs; Idaho State; 2003: Min, rnd 6; B3/2/1981 Newport Beach, CA

| 2003 | Min | 14(0) | — | — | — | — | — | — | — | — | 2 | 15 | 7.5(15) | 0 | — | — | — | — | — | P | — | — | 0 | 15 |

JOHNSON, ELLIS Ellis Edward, HB-WR, 6′0″/195 lbs; Southeastern Louisiana; 1965: Bos, rnd 4/Min, rnd 19; B7/9/1943 Baton Rouge, LA **1966** Bos-A 14

| 1965 | Bos-A | 14 | 19 | 29 | 1.5(9) | 0 | 4 | 29 | 7.3(23) | 0 | — | — | — | — | — | — | — | — | — | — | k | — | 0 | 43 |
| NFL | 2 | 28 | 19 | 29 | 1.5(9) | 0 | 4 | 29 | 7.3(23) | 0 | — | — | — | — | — | — | — | — | — | — | k | — | 0 | 58 |

JOHNSON, ELLIS Ellis Bernard, DT-DE, 6′2″/288 lbs; Florida; 1995: Ind, rnd 1; B10/30/1973 Wildwood, FL [S] **1995**†Ind 16 (2) **1996**†Ind 12 (6, Ide) **1997** Ind 15 (15, RDT) **1998** Ind 16 (16, RDT) **1999**†Ind 16 (16, RDT) **2000**†Ind 13 (13, RDT) **2001** Ind 16 (16, RDT) **2002**†Atl 16 (2) **2003** Atl 16 (3) **2004**†Den 13 (0) **NFL** 149 (89) [10 yrs]

JOHNSON, ERIC Eric, DB, 6′1″/192 lbs; Washington State; B7/23/1952 Ephrata, WA **1977** Phi 14 (2) **1978**†Phi 16 **1979** SF 8 **NFL** 38 (2) [3 yrs]

JOHNSON, ERIC Eric Maxwell, TE, 6′3″/256 lbs; Yale; 2001: SF, rnd 7; B9/15/1979 Needham, MA

2001	†SF	16(14, TE)	—	—	—	—	40	362	9.1(24)	3	—	—	—	—	—	—	—	—	—	—	—	—	20	196
2002	†SF	12(10, TE)	—	—	—	—	36	321	8.9(38)	0	—	—	—	—	—	—	—	—	—	—	—	—	0	161
2004	SF	16(14, TE)	—	—	—	—	82	825	10.1(25)	2	—	—	—	—	—	—	—	—	—	—	—	—	12	423
NFL	3	44(38)	—	—	—	—	158	1508	9.5(38)	5	—	—	—	—	—	—	—	—	—	—	—	—	32	779

JOHNSON, ERIC Eric, DB-LB, 6′0″/220 lbs; Nebraska; B4/30/1976 Carson, CA **2000**†Oak 16 (0) **2001** Oak 7 (0) **2002**†Oak 16 (0) **2003** Oak 16 (0) **2004**†Atl 16 (0) **2005** Arz 3 (0) **NFL** 74 (2) [6 yrs]

JOHNSON, ESSEX Essex L., RB, 5′9″/201 lbs; Grambling State; 1968: Cin, rnd 6; B10/15/1946 Shreveport, LA

1968	Cin-A	14	26	178	6.8(41)	3	1	33	33.0(33)	0	—	—	—	—	—	—	—	—	—	—	kp	—	18	282
1969	Cin-A	12	15	54	3.6(13)	0	1	3	3.0(3)	0	—	—	—	—	—	—	—	—	—	—	kp	—	0	178
1970	†Cin	13	65	273	4.2(26)	2	15	190	12.7(51)	2	—	—	—	—	—	—	—	—	—	—	kp	—	24	458
1971	Cin	14(rb)	85	522	6.1(86)	4	14	258	18.4(67)	2	—	—	—	—	—	—	—	—	—	—	kp	—	36	724
1972	Cin	14(RB)	212	825	3.9(19)	4	29	420	14.5(65)	2	—	—	—	—	—	—	—	—	—	—	kp	—	36	1080
1973	†Cin	14(RB)	195	997	5.1(46)	4	28	356	12.7(78)	3	—	—	—	—	—	—	—	—	—	—	—	—	42	1230
1974	Cin	5	19	44	2.3(11)	0	8	85	10.6(27)	1	—	—	—	—	—	—	—	—	—	—	—	—	6	92
1975	†Cin	12	58	177	3.1(15)	1	25	196	7.8(30)	1	—	—	—	—	—	—	—	—	—	—	—	—	12	290
1976	TB	14(1)	47	166	3.5(27)	1	25	201	8.0(38)	1	—	—	—	—	—	—	—	—	—	—	k	—	12	374
NFL	9	112(1)	722	3236	4.5(86)	19	146	1742	11.9(78)	12	—	—	—	—	—	—	—	—	—	—	kp	—	186	4706

JOHNSON, EZRA Ezra Ray, DE, 6′4″/250 lbs; Morris Brown; 1977: GB, rnd 1; B10/2/1955 Shreveport, LA [S] **1977** GB 14 **1978** GB◊16 (16, RDE) **1979** GB 11 (11, RDE) **1980** GB 15 (15, RDE) **1981** GB 16 (3) **1982**†GB 9 (9, RDE) **1983** GB 16 (16, RDE) **1984** GB 13 (0) **1985** GB 16 (16, RDE) **1986** GB 16 (0) **1987** GB 6 (0) **1988** Ind 10 (1) **1989** Ind 16 (1) **1990** Hou 16 (3) **1991**†Hou 2 (0) **NFL** 192 (91) [15 yrs]

JOHNSON, FARNHAM Farnham James, T-DE, 6′0″/215 lbs; Michigan; Wisconsin; B6/23/1924 St. Paul, MN, D12/12/2001 Winfield, AL [K] **1948** ChiR-A 8 (0, RT)

JOHNSON, FILMEL Filmel C., DB, 5′10″/187 lbs; Illinois; 1994: Buf, rnd 7; B12/24/1970 Orchard Lake, MI **1995**†Buf 2 (0)

JOHNSON, FLIP Fulton Frederick, WR, 5′10″/185 lbs; McNeese State; B7/13/1963 Cheek, TX

1988	†Buf	11(0)	—	—	—	—	9	170	18.9(66)	1	—	—	—	—	—	—	—	—	—	—	kp	—	6	122
1989	†Buf	16(5, wr)	—	—	—	—	25	303	12.1(36)	1	0	0	0.0	0	0.0	0	0	1	2	—	p	—	6	159
NFL	2	27(5)	—	—	—	—	34	473	13.9(66)	2	0	0	0.0	0	0.0	0	0	1	2	—	kp	—	12	281

JOHNSON, GARRETT Garrett, NT, 6′3″/295 lbs; Illinois; B12/31/1975 Delleville, IL **2000** NE 8 (2)

JOHNSON, GARY Gary Lynn 'Big Hands', DT-DE-NT, 6′2″/257 lbs; Grambling State; 1975: SD, rnd 1; B8/31/1952 Shreveport, LA **1975** SD 14 (8, RDT) **1976** SD 14 (14, RDT) **1977** SD 14 (14, RDT) **1978** SD 15 (14, RDT) **1979**†SD★16 (15, RDT) **1980**†SD★16 (16, RDT) **1981**†SD★16 (16, RDT) **1982**†SD★9 (9, RDT) **1983** SD 16 (16, RDE) **1984** SD 4 (1) **1984**†SF 12 (0) **1985** SF 11 (0) **NFL** 157 (123) [11 yrs]

JOHNSON, GENE Gene Paul, DB, 6′0″/187 lbs; Cincinnati; 1959: Phi, rnd 9; B9/18/1935 Clay, WV, D8/4/1997 Union Township, OH **1959** Phi 12 **1960**†Phi 11 **1961** Min 4 **1961** NYG 3 **NFL** 30 [3 yrs]

JOHNSON, GIL Gilbert, QB, 5′11″/195 lbs; SMU; 1949: NYY-A, rnd 17/1948: Phi, rnd 11; B12/4/1923 Tyler, TX, D7/10/1999 Dallas, TX

| 1949 | NYY-A | 9(0) | 3 | 21 | 7.0 | 0 | — | — | — | — | 36 | 12 | 33.3 | 179 | 5.0 | 0 | 5 | — | — | — | — | — | 0 | -90 |

JOHNSON, GILVANNI Giovanni Martinni, WR, 6′1″/195 lbs; Michigan; B9/12/1963 Birmingham, AL **1987** Det 3 (0)

JOHNSON, GLENN Glenn Murray, T, 6′4″/263 lbs; Arizona State; 1948: LA, rnd 10; B6/28/1922 Mesa, AZ **1948** NYY-A 9 (0)

1949 GB 8 (0)

JOHNSON, GREG Gregory Devon, DT-NT-DE, 6′4″/240 lbs; Florida State; 1976: Phi, rnd 5; B12/3/1953 Leesburg, FL **1977** Bal 2 **1977** TB 5 **NFL** 7 [1 yr]

JOHNSON, GREG Gregory Kent, T, 6′4″/295 lbs; Oklahoma; 1988: Mia, rnd 4; B12/19/1964 Oklahoma City, OK **1988** Mia 1 (0)

JOHNSON, GREGG Greggory Da-marr, DB, 6′1″/191 lbs; Oklahoma State; B10/20/1958 Houston, TX **1981** Sea 16 (3) **1982** Sea 9 (0) **1983**†Sea 16 (0) **1986** Sea 15 (0) **1987** SL 8 (3) **NFL** 64 (3) [5 yrs]

JOHNSON, HARVEY Harvey Paul, T-LB-BB-FB-G, 5′11″/212 lbs; William & Mary; 1943: Bkn, rnd 6; B6/22/1919 Bridgeton, NJ, D8/8/1983 Orchard Park, NY [KC] **1947**†NYY-A 14 (4, RT) **1949**†NYY-A 12 (0)

1946	†NYY-A	13(2, RT)	16	63	3.9	0	2	19	9.5	0	—	—	—	—	—	—	—	—	—	—	K	—	54	73
1948	NYY-A	14(0)	—	—	—	—	1	6	6.0(6)	0	—	—	—	—	—	—	—	—	—	—	K	—	43	3
AAFC	4	53(2)	16	63	3.9	0	3	25	8.3(6)	0	—	—	—	—	—	—	—	—	—	—	Ki	—	213	72

1951 NYY 12 (MLB)

JOHNSON, HENRY Henry William, LB, 6′1″/235 lbs; Georgia Tech; 1980: Min, rnd 7; B3/20/1958 Wrens, GA **1980**†Min 16 (0) **1981** Min 16 (0) **1982**†Min 9 (0) **1983** Min 5 (0) **NFL** 46 (0) [4 yrs]

JOHNSON, HERB Herbert Lorch, HB, 5′10″/172 lbs; Army; Washington; B7/10/1928

| 1954 | NYG | 11 | 42 | 168 | 4.0(26) | 1 | 10 | 89 | 8.9(24) | 0 | — | — | — | — | — | — | — | — | — | — | kp | 1 | 12 | 418 |

JOHNSON, HERBERT Herbert Lewis, WR, 5′11″/182 lbs; Missouri; B10/13/1963 Fulton, MO **1987** ChiB 3 (0)

JOHNSON, HOLBERT Holbert Dwayne, DB, 5′9″/180 lbs; New Mexico State; B7/14/1960 Los Angeles, CA **1987** LARm 3 (0)

JOHNSON, HOSS David G., T, 6′4″/295 lbs; Alabama; B6/8/1963 Huntsville, AL **1987** TB 1 (0)

JOHNSON, J.J. James E., RB, 6′1″/230 lbs; Mississippi State; 1999: Mia, rnd 2; B4/20/1974 Mobile, AL

1999	†Mia	13(4, rb)	164	558	3.4(34)	4	15	100	6.7(17)	0	—	—	—	—	—	—	—	—	—	—	k	—	24	644
2000	†Mia	13(1)	50	168	3.4(16)	1	10	61	6.1(11)	0	—	—	—	—	—	—	—	—	—	—	k	—	6	205
2001	†Mia	10(0)	5	22	4.4(9)	0	4	21	5.3(7)	0	—	—	—	—	—	—	—	—	—	—	k	—	0	34
NFL	3	36(5)	219	748	3.4(34)	5	29	182	6.3(17)	0	—	—	—	—	—	—	—	—	—	—	k	—	30	882

JOHNSON, J.R. Charles A., LB, 6′0″/240 lbs; Toledo; Syracuse; B6/20/1979 Los Angeles, CA **2002** Bal 4 (0) **2002** NO 1 (0) **NFL** 5 (0) [1 yr]

YEAR	TEAM	G(GS, POS)	RUSH	YD	AVG(LG)	TD	REC	YD	AVG(LG)	TD	PASS	COMP	PCT	YD	AVG(LG)	TD	INT	SK	YD	QBR	KPR	OTD	PTS	TAY

JOHNSON, JACK   John Denvil, T, 6´4˝/216 lbs; Utah; B11/28/1909 Grantsville, UT, D10/27/1978 Tooele, UT   **1934** Det 13 (12, LT)   **1935**†Det 10 (10, LT)   **1936** Det☆11 (8, LT)
1937 Det 11 (11, LT)   **1938** Det☆10 (7, LT)   **1939** Det★10 (9, LT)

| 1940 | Det | 11(6, LT) | — | — | — | — | 1 | 48 | 48.0(48) | 1 | — | — | — | — | — | — | — | — | — | — | — | — | 6 | 29 |
| NFL | 7 | 76(63) | — | — | — | — | 1 | 48 | 48.0(48) | 1 | — | — | — | — | — | — | — | — | — | — | — | 1 | 12 | 29 |

JOHNSON, JACK   Jack Connell, DB, 6´3˝/198 lbs; Miami (FL); 1957: ChiB, rnd 4; B12/11/1933 Pittsburgh, PA, deceased   **1957** ChiB 11   **1958** ChiB 12 (DB)   **1959** ChiB 6
1960 Buf-A 12   **1961** Buf-A 3   **1961** DalT-A 1   **NFL** 45 [5 yrs]

JOHNSON, JAMES   James Lenord, LB, 6´2˝/236 lbs; San Diego State; 1985: Det, rnd 3; B6/21/1962 Los Angeles, CA   **1986** Det 11 (0)   **1987** SF 1 (0)   **1987** SD 1 (0)
NFL 13 (0) [2 yrs]

JOHNSON, JARRET   Jarret Webster, DE, 6´3˝/285 lbs; Alabama; 2003: Bal, rnd 4; B8/14/1981 Homestead, FL   **2003**†Bal 15 (1)   **2004** Bal 16 (0)   **2005** Bal 16 (12, LDE)
NFL 47 (13) [3 yrs]

JOHNSON, JASON   Jason Mansfield, WR, 5´10˝/178 lbs; Illinois State; B11/8/1965 Gary, IN   **1989** Pit 14 (0)

| 1988 | Den | 8(0) | 1 | 3 | 3.0(3) | 0 | 1 | 6 | 6.0(6) | 0 | — | — | — | — | — | — | — | — | — | kp | — | 0 | 88 |
| NFL | 2 | 22(0) | 1 | 3 | 3.0(3) | 0 | 1 | 6 | 6.0(6) | 0 | — | — | — | — | — | — | — | — | — | kp | — | 0 | 98 |

JOHNSON, JASON   Jason Joseph, C, 6´3˝/290 lbs; Kansas State; B2/6/1974 Gladstone, MO   **1998** Ind 14 (0)   **1999**†Ind 16 (0)   **NFL** 30 (0) [2 yrs]

JOHNSON, JAY   Oliver Jay, LB, 6´3˝/230 lbs; Texas A&M-Commerce; B10/8/1945 East Orange, NJ   **1969** Phi 3   **1970** Phi 5   **NFL** 8 [2 yrs]

JOHNSON, JEREMI   Jeremi, FB, 5´11˝/265 lbs; Indiana; Western Kentucky; 2003: Cin, rnd 4; B9/4/1980 Louisville, KY

2003	Cin	16(13, FB)	15	41	2.7(12)	1	15	82	5.5(16)	1	—	—	—	—	—	—	—	—	—	k	—	12	98
2004	Cin	16(6, fb)	3	5	1.7(4)	0	16	53	3.3(9)	1	—	—	—	—	—	—	—	—	—	—	—	6	37
2005	†Cin	16(11, FB)	8	14	1.8(5)	0	12	65	5.4(27)	3	—	—	—	—	—	—	—	—	—	—	—	18	62
NFL	3	48(30)	26	60	2.3(12)	1	43	200	4.7(27)	5	—	—	—	—	—	—	—	—	—	k	—	36	196

JOHNSON, JERRY   Jerry, TB-WB-FB-BB, 5´11˝/195 lbs; Morningside; B1895, deceased [K]   **1921** RI 2 (1)   **1922** RI 5 (4, TB), 15   **1922** Rac 3 (2)   **NFL** 10 (7) [2 yrs]

JOHNSON, JERRY   Jerry M., DT, 6´0˝/290 lbs; Florida State; 2000: Den, rnd 4; B7/11/1977 Fort Pierce, FL   **2001** Den 9 (0)

JOHNSON, JESSE   Jesse, B, 6´3˝/185 lbs; Colorado; 1980: NYJ, rnd 4; B1/10/1958 Fort Collins, CO   **1980** NYJ 16 (1)   **1981** NYJ 16 (4)   **1982**†NYJ 9 (0)   **1983** NYJ 4 (0)
NFL 45 (5) [4 yrs]

JOHNSON, JIM   James Earl, DB, 6´1˝/195 lbs; South Carolina State; 1968: Cin, rnd 6; B11/30/1945 Charleston, SC   **1969** Cin-A 11

JOHNSON, JIMMIE   Jimmie Olden, TE, 6´2˝/252 lbs; Howard; 1989: Was, rnd 12; B10/6/1966 Augusta, GA

1989	Was	16(0)	—	—	—	—	4	84	21.0(39)	0	—	—	—	—	—	—	—	—	—	—	—	0	42
1990	†Was	16(5, te)	—	—	—	—	15	218	14.5(35)	2	—	—	—	—	—	—	—	—	—	—	—	12	119
1991	Was	6(0)	—	—	—	—	3	7	2.3(4)	2	—	—	—	—	—	—	—	—	—	—	—	12	14
1992	Det	16(5, te)	—	—	—	—	6	34	5.7(9)	0	—	—	—	—	—	—	—	—	—	k	—	0	2
1993	Det	6(5, te)	—	—	—	—	2	18	9.0(9)	0	—	—	—	—	—	—	—	—	—	—	—	0	9
1994	KC	7(1)	—	—	—	—	2	7	3.5(5)	0	—	—	—	—	—	—	—	—	—	—	—	0	4
1995	†Phi	16(1)	—	—	—	—	6	37	6.2(9)	0	—	—	—	—	—	—	—	—	—	—	—	0	19
1996	†Phi	16(3)	—	—	—	—	7	127	18.1(31)	0	—	—	—	—	—	—	—	—	—	—	—	0	64
1997	Phi	16(11, TE)	—	—	—	—	14	177	12.6(28)	1	—	—	—	—	—	—	—	—	—	k	—	6	71
1998	Phi	3(3)	—	—	—	—	2	14	7.0(9)	0	—	—	—	—	—	—	—	—	—	—	—	0	7
NFL	10	118(34)	—	—	—	—	61	723	11.9(39)	5	—	—	—	—	—	—	—	—	—	k	—	30	349

JOHNSON, JIMMY   James Earl, DB-HB, 6´2˝/187 lbs; UCLA; 1961: SF, rnd 1/SD, rnd 4; B3/31/1938 Dallas, TX; HOF 1994 [I]   **1961** SF 12 (7, rcb)   **1964** SF☆14 (14, LCB)
1965 SF☆14 (14, LCB)   **1966** SF☆14 (14, LCB)   **1967** SF 11 (11, LCB)   **1968** SF☆13 (13, LCB)   **1969** SF★14 (14, LCB)   **1970**†SF★14 (14, LCB)   **1971**†SF★14 (14, LCB)
1972†SF★14 (14, LCB)   **1973** SF 13 (13, LCB)   **1974** SF★13 (12, LCB)   **1975** SF 14 (14, LCB)   **1976** SF 13 (13, LCB)

1962	SF	12(8, rh)	—	—	—	—	34	627	18.4(80)	4	—	—	—	—	—	—	—	—	—	—	24	334
1963	SF	13(10, RS)	—	—	—	—	6	63	10.5(15)	0	—	—	—	—	—	—	i	—	—	—	0	58
NFL	16	213(199)	—	—	—	—	40	690	17.3(80)	4	—	—	—	—	—	—	i	—	—	—	2	38	765

JOHNSON, JOE   Joseph Cooper, E, 6´2˝/195 lbs; Mississippi; B9/15/1926

| 1948 | NYG | 11(0) | — | — | — | — | 19 | 217 | 11.4(23) | 2 | — | — | — | — | — | — | — | — | — | — | — | 12 | 119 |

JOHNSON, JOE   Joseph F., HB-E, 6´0˝/185 lbs; Boston College; 1953: GB, rnd 11; B11/3/1929 New Haven, CT, D11/1/2003 Las Vegas, NV

1954	GB	12	7	31	4.4(10)	0	10	72	7.2(17)	1	—	—	—	—	—	—	—	—	—	kp	—	6	116
1955	GB	12(RH)	49	210	4.3(21)	0	9	71	7.9(30)	1	—	—	—	—	—	—	—	—	—	kp	—	6	267
1956	GB	11(LH)	35	129	3.7(14)	0	28	258	9.2(20)	0	—	—	—	—	—	—	—	—	—	—	—	0	258
1957	GB	12	2	6	3.0(3)	0	7	75	10.7(14)	1	—	—	—	—	—	—	—	—	—	p	—	6	68
1958	GB	6	—	—	—	—	10	176	17.6(61)	1	—	—	—	—	—	—	—	—	—	—	—	6	93
1960	Bos-A	7(se)	—	—	—	—	11	186	16.9(51)	3	—	—	—	—	—	—	—	—	—	—	—	18	108
1961	Bos-A	6	—	—	—	—	9	82	9.1(21)	1	—	—	—	—	—	—	—	—	—	—	—	6	46
NFL	7	66	93	376	4.0(21)	0	84	920	11.0(61)	8	—	—	—	—	—	—	—	—	—	kp	—	48	955

JOHNSON, JOE   Joseph T., DE, 6´4˝/275 lbs; Louisville; 1994: NO, rnd 1; B7/11/1972 Cleveland, OH [S]   **1994** NO 15 (14, RDE)   **1995** NO 14 (14, LDE)   **1996** NO 13 (13, RDE)
1997 NO 16 (16, RDE)   **1998** NO✧16 (16, RDE)   **2000**†NO★16 (15, RDE)   **2001** NO 16 (16, RDE)   **2002** GB 5 (5, rde)   **2003** GB 6 (6, lde)   **NFL** 117 (115) [9 yrs]

JOHNSON, JOE   Joseph Pernell, aka Joe Howard, WR, 5´8˝/170 lbs; Notre Dame; B12/21/1962 Washington, DC   **1989** Was 15 (0)   **1991** Was 2 (0)

1990	†Was	15(0)	—	—	—	—	3	36	12.0(17)	0	—	—	—	—	—	—	—	—	—	kp	—	0	164
1992	†Min	15(6, wr)	4	26	6.5(9)	0	21	211	10.0(37)	1	—	—	—	—	—	—	—	—	—	kp	—	6	141
NFL	4	47(6)	4	26	6.5(9)	0	24	247	10.3(37)	1	—	—	—	—	—	—	—	—	—	kp	1	12	625

JOHNSON, JOHN   John Howard, DT, 6´5˝/260 lbs; Indiana; 1963: Chi, rnd 6/NYJ, rnd 20; B7/5/1941 Gary, IN   **1963**†ChiB 12   **1964** ChiB 14   **1965** ChiB 13 (LDT)
1966 ChiB 14 (LDT)   **1967** ChiB 14   **1968** ChiB 14 (3, LDT)   **1969** NYG 4   **NFL** 85 (3) [7 yrs]

JOHNSON, JOHN   John Vernard, LB, 6´3˝/240 lbs; Clemson; 1991: SF, rnd 2; B5/8/1968 La Grange, GA   **1991** SF 9 (0)   **1992**†SF 16 (2)   **1993**†SF 15 (12, LLB)   **1994** Cin 5 (0)
1995 NO 1 (0)   **NFL** 46 (14) [5 yrs]

JOHNSON, JOHN HENRY   John Henry, FB-HB, 6´2˝/210 lbs; St. Mary's (CA); Arizona State; 1953: Pit, rnd 2; B11/24/1929 Waterproof, LA; HOF 1987

1954	SF★	12(LH)	129	681	5.3(38)	9	28	183	6.5(34)	0	2	1	50.0	10	5.0(10)	1	0	—	—	k	—	54	868
1955	SF	7	19	69	3.6(12)	1	2	6	3.0(11)	0	—	—	—	—	—	—	—	—	—	pi	—	6	107
1956	SF	12(fb)	80	301	3.8(54)	2	8	90	11.3(28)	0	—	—	—	—	—	—	—	—	—	k	—	12	374
1957	†Det	12(FB)	129	621	4.8(62)	5	20	141	7.1(16)	0	—	—	—	—	—	—	—	—	—	—	—	30	742
1958	Det	9(FB)	56	254	4.5(19)	0	7	60	8.6(18)	0	—	—	—	—	—	—	—	—	—	—	—	0	284
1959	Det	10(fb)	82	270	3.3(39)	2	7	34	4.9(16)	1	—	—	—	—	—	—	—	—	—	—	—	18	312
1960	Pit	12(FB)	118	621	5.3(87)	2	12	112	9.3(26)	1	1	1	100.0	15	15.0(15)	0	0	—	—	—	—	18	715
1961	Pit	14(FB)	213	787	3.7(44)	6	24	262	10.9(51)	2	2	0	0.0	0	—	0	1	—	—	k	—	42	939
1962	Pit★	14(FB)	251	1141	4.5(40)	7	32	226	7.1(26)	2	—	—	—	—	—	—	—	—	—	—	—	54	1334
1963	Pit✧	12(FB)	186	773	4.2(48)	4	21	145	6.9(26)	1	—	—	—	—	—	—	—	—	—	—	—	30	891
1964	Pit✧	14(FB)	235	1048	4.5(45)	7	17	69	4.1(21)	1	—	—	—	—	—	—	—	—	—	—	—	48	1158
1965	Pit	1	3	11	3.7(7)	0	—	—	—	—	—	—	—	—	—	—	—	—	—	—	—	0	11
1966	Hou-A	14	70	226	3.2(28)	3	8	150	18.8(53)	0	—	—	—	—	—	—	—	—	—	—	—	18	331
NFL	13	143	1571	6803	4.3(87)	48	186	1478	7.9(53)	7	5	2	40.0	25	5.0(15)	2	1	—	—	kpi	—	330	8064

JOHNSON, JOHNNIE   Johnnie Junior, DB, 6´1˝/185 lbs; Texas; 1980: LA, rnd 1; B10/8/1956 La Grange, TX [I]   **1980** LARm 16 (16, SS)   **1981** LARm 16 (16, SS)
1982 LARm 9 (9, SS)   **1983**†LARm☆16 (16, FS)   **1984**†LARm 9 (7, FS)   **1985**†LARm 16 (15, FS)   **1986**†LARm 16 (5, fs)   **1987** LARm 7 (7, fs)   **1988** LARm 16 (16, FS)
1989 Sea 3 (1)   **1989**†LARm 0 (0)   **NFL** 124 (108) [10 yrs]

JOHNSON, JOHNNY   Johnny, RB, 6´3˝/220 lbs; San Jose State; 1990: Phx, rnd 7; B6/11/1968 Santa Clara, CA

1990	Phx✧	14(14, RB)	234	926	4.0(41)	5	25	241	9.6(35)	0	1	0	0.0	0	—	0	1	—	—	—	—	30	1057
1991	Phx	15(14, RB)	196	666	3.4(21)	4	29	225	7.8(51)	2	—	—	—	—	—	—	—	—	—	—	—	36	829
1992	Phx	12(8, RB)	178	734	4.1(42)	6	14	103	7.4(26)	0	—	—	—	—	—	—	—	—	—	—	—	36	846

YEAR	TEAM	G (GS, POS)	RUSH	YD	AVG (LG)	TD	REC	YD	AVG (LG)	TD	PASS	COMP	PCT	YD	AVG (LG)	TD	INT	SK	YD	QBR	KPR	OTD	PTS	TAY
1993	NYJ	15 (9, RB)	198	821	4.1 (57)	3	67	641	9.6 (48)	1	—	—	—	—	—	—	—	—	—	—	—	—	24	1177
1994	NYJ	16 (14, RB)	240	931	3.9 (90)	3	42	303	7.2 (24)	2	—	—	—	—	—	—	—	—	—	—	—	—	30	1123
NFL	5	72 (59)	1046	4078	3.9 (90)	21	177	1513	8.5 (51)	5	1	0	0.0	0	0.0	0	1	—	—	—	—	—	156	5030
Johnson, Kelley Kelley Antonio, WR, 5´8˝/168 lbs; Colorado; B6/3/1962 Carlsbad, NM																								
1987	Ind	3 (0)	—	—	—	—	1	15	15.0 (15)	0	—	—	—	—	—	—	—	—	—	—	kp	—	0	13
Johnson, Ken Kenneth, RB, 6´2˝/220 lbs; Miami (FL); 1979: NYG, rnd 11; B11/27/1956 Miami, FL																								
1979	NYG	9	62	168	2.7 (12)	0	16	108	6.8 (15)	1	—	—	—	—	—	—	—	—	—	—	—	—	6	227
Johnson, Ken Kenneth Eugene, DE, 6´5˝/253 lbs; Knoxville; 1979: Buf, rnd 4; B3/25/1955 Nashville, TN **1979** Buf 3 **1980**†Buf 16 (0) **1981**†Buf 16 (0) **1982** Buf 7 (0) **1983** Buf 16 (8, rde) **1984** Buf 16 (16, RDE) **1987** KC 2 (1) **NFL** 76 (25) [7 yrs]																								
Johnson, Ken Kenneth Lee, DB, 6´2˝/203 lbs; Florida A&M; B9/14/1966 Thomaston, GA **1989** Min 1 (0) **1990** Min 4 (0) **1990** NYJ 4 (0) **NFL** 9 (0) [2 yrs]																								
Johnson, Ken Ralph Kenneth, DE-DT, 6´6˝/265 lbs; Indiana; B3/12/1947 Anderson, IN **1971** Cin 9 **1972** Cin 11 **1973**†Cin 9 **1974** Cin 13 (LDE) **1975**†Cin 14 (LDE) **1976** Cin 13 **1977** Cin 10 **NFL** 79 [7 yrs]																								
Johnson, Kenneth Kenneth, DB, 6´0˝/185 lbs; Mississippi State; B12/28/1963 Weir, MS **1987** GB 12 (0)																								
Johnson, Kenny Kenneth Ray, DB, 5´10˝/176 lbs; Mississippi State; 1980: Atl, rnd 5; B1/7/1958 Columbia, MS **[R]** **1980**†Atl 16 (16, RCB) **1981** Atl 16 (16, RCB) **1982**†Atl 9 (9, RCB) **1983** Atl 16 (16, RCB) **1984** Atl 16 (16, SS) **1985** Atl 5 (3) **1986** Atl 7 (2) **1986** Hou 1 (0) **1987**†Hou 12 (3) **1988** Hou 13 (0) **1989**†Hou 16 (0) **NFL** 127 (81) [10 yrs]																								
Johnson, Kermit Kermit DeKoven, RB, 6´1˝/201 lbs; UCLA; 1974: SF, rnd 7; B2/22/1952 Los Angeles, CA																								
1975	SF	11	4	25	6.3 (19)	0	—	—	—	—	—	—	—	—	—	—	—	—	—	—	k	—	0	70
1976	SF	11 (1)	32	99	3.1 (16)	1	1	11	11.0 (11)	0	—	—	—	—	—	—	—	—	—	—	k	—	6	169
NFL	2	22 (1)	36	124	3.4 (19)	1	1	11	11.0 (11)	0	—	—	—	—	—	—	—	—	—	—	k	—	6	239
Johnson, Keshon Keshon Lorenzo, DB, 5´10˝/180 lbs; Arizona; 1993: Chi, rnd 7; B7/17/1970 Fresno, CA **1993** ChiB 15 (0) **1994** ChiB 6 (0) **1994**†GB 7 (0) **1995** ChiB 12 (0) **NFL** 40 (0) [3 yrs]																								
Johnson, Kevin Kevin L., WR, 5´11˝/185 lbs; Syracuse; 1999: Cle, rnd 2; B7/15/1976 Trenton, NJ																								
1999	Cle	16 (16, WR)	1	-6	-6.0 (-6)	0	66	986	14.9 (64)	8	1	0	0.0	0	0.0	0	0	—	—	—	kp	—	48	570
2000	Cle	16 (16, WR)	—	—	—	—	57	669	11.7 (79)	0	3	1	33.3	23	7.7 (23)	0	1	—	—	—	—	—	0	306
2001	Cle	16 (16, WR)	—	—	—	—	84	1097	13.1 (55)	9	—	—	—	—	—	—	—	—	—	—	p	—	54	641
2002	†Cle	16 (15, WR)	—	—	—	—	67	703	10.5 (30)	4	2	1	50.0	33	16.5 (33)	1	0	—	—	—	—	—	24	393
2003	Cle	9 (8, wr)	—	—	—	—	41	381	9.3 (41)	2	1	0	0.0	0	0.0	0	0	—	—	—	—	—	12	201
2003	Jax	6 (1)	—	—	—	—	17	253	14.9 (28)	1	—	—	—	—	—	—	—	—	—	—	—	—	6	132
2004	Bal	16 (5, wr)	1	0	0.0 (0)	0	35	373	10.7 (35)	1	—	—	—	—	—	—	—	—	—	—	—	—	6	192
2005	Det	6 (2)	—	—	—	—	17	133	7.8 (25)	0	—	—	—	—	—	—	—	—	—	—	k	—	0	66
NFL	7	101 (79)	2	-6	-3.0	0	384	4595	12.0 (79)	25	7	2	28.6	56	8.0 (33)	1	1	—	—	—	kp	—	150	2499
Johnson, Kevin Kevin Lamar, DT, 6´1˝/305 lbs; Texas Southern; 1993: NE, rnd 4; B10/30/1970 Los Angeles, CA **1995**†Phi 11 (1) **1996** Phi 12 (5, LDT) **1997** Oak 15 (0) **NFL** 38 (6) [3 yrs]																								
Johnson, Keyshawn Keyshawn Joseph, WR, 6´4˝/212 lbs; USC; 1996: NYJ, rnd 1; B7/22/1972 Los Angeles, CA																								
1996	NYJ	14 (11, WR)	—	—	—	—	63	844	13.4 (50)	8	—	—	—	—	—	—	—	—	—	—	—	—	50	462
1997	NYJ	16 (16, WR)	—	—	—	—	70	963	13.8 (39)	5	—	—	—	—	—	—	—	—	—	—	—	—	30	507
1998	†NYJ★	16 (16, WR)	2	60	30.0 (35)	1	83	1131	13.6 (41)	**10**	—	—	—	—	—	—	—	—	—	—	—	—	66	686
1999	NYJ✧	16 (16, WR)	5	6	1.2 (12)	0	89	1170	13.1 (65)	8	1	0	0.0	0	0.0	0	0	1	9	—	—	—	48	631
2000	†TB	16 (16, WR)	2	5	2.5 (3)	0	71	874	12.3 (38)	8	—	—	—	—	—	—	—	—	—	—	—	—	48	482
2001	†TB✧	15 (15, WR)	—	—	—	—	**106**	1266	11.9 (47)	1	—	—	—	—	—	—	—	—	—	—	—	—	6	638
2002	†TB	16 (16, WR)	—	—	—	—	76	1088	14.3 (76)	5	—	—	—	—	—	—	—	—	—	—	—	—	34	569
2003	TB	10 (10, WR)	—	—	—	—	45	600	13.3 (39)	3	—	—	—	—	—	—	—	—	—	—	—	—	18	315
2004	Dal	16 (16, WR)	2	13	6.5 (13)	0	70	981	14.0 (39)	6	2	0	0.0	0	0.0	0	1	—	—	—	—	—	36	494
2005	Dal	16 (14, WR)	1	3	3.0 (3)	0	71	839	11.8 (34)	6	1	0	0.0	0	0.0	0	0	—	—	—	—	—	38	453
NFL	10	151 (146)	12	87	7.3 (35)	1	744	9756	13.1 (76)	60	4	0	0.0	0	0.0	0	1	1	9	—	—	—	374	5235
Johnson, Kyle Albert Kyle, RB, 6´0˝/242 lbs; Syracuse; 2002: Car, rnd 5; B12/15/1978 Woodbridge, NJ																								
2004	Den	14 (3)	—	—	—	—	9	126	14.0 (31)	2	—	—	—	—	—	—	—	—	—	—	—	—	12	73
2005	†Den	16 (14, FB)	4	9	2.3 (4)	1	17	160	9.4 (33)	5	—	—	—	—	—	—	—	—	—	—	k	—	36	117
NFL	2	30 (17)	4	9	2.3 (4)	1	26	286	11.0 (33)	7	—	—	—	—	—	—	—	—	—	—	k	—	48	190
Johnson, Landon Landon Tremone, LB, 6´2˝/211 lbs; Purdue; 2004: Cin, rnd 3; B3/13/1981 Lubbock, TX **2004** Cin 16 (11, MLB) **2005**†Cin 16 (10, LLB) **NFL** 32 (21) [2 yrs]																								
Johnson, Larry Lawrence, LB-C-E, 6´3˝/223 lbs; Haskell Indian; B3/28/1909 Odanah, WI **1933** Bos 10 (3) **1935** Bos 2 (0) **1936** NYG 5 (0) **1937** NYG 8 (0) **1938**†NYG✧10 (0) **1939** NYG 4 (1) **1944** Was 5 (1)																								
1934	Bos	12 (3)	—	—	—	—	2	25	12.5	0	—	—	—	—	—	—	—	—	—	—	—	—	0	13
NFL	8	56 (8)	—	—	—	—	2	25	12.5	0	—	—	—	—	—	—	—	—	—	—	—	—	0	13
Johnson, Larry Larry Alphonso, RB, 6´1˝/228 lbs; Penn State; 2003: KC, rnd 1; B11/19/1979 State College, PA																								
2003	KC	6 (0)	20	85	4.3 (15)	1	1	2	2.0 (2)	0	—	—	—	—	—	—	—	—	—	—	—	—	6	96
2004	KC	10 (3)	120	581	4.8 (46)	9	22	278	12.6 (40)	2	—	—	—	—	—	—	—	—	—	—	—	—	66	820
2005	KC★	16 (9, RB)	336	**1750**	5.2 (49)	**20**	33	343	10.4 (36)	1	—	—	—	—	—	—	—	—	—	—	—	—	126	**2127**
NFL	3	32 (12)	476	2416	5.1 (49)	30	56	623	11.1 (40)	3	—	—	—	—	—	—	—	—	—	—	—	—	198	3043
Johnson, Lawrence Lawrence Wendell, DB, 5´11˝/204 lbs; Wisconsin; 1979: Cle, rnd 2; B9/11/1957 Gary, IN **1979** Cle 16 **1980** Cle 2 (2) **1981** Cle 16 (2) **1982** Cle 8 (7, LCB) **1983** Cle 16 (6, lcb) **1984** Cle 6 (3) **1984** Buf 10 (0) **1985** Buf 16 (3) **1987** Buf 6 (3) **NFL** 96 (26) [8 yrs]																								
Johnson, Lee Leo Daniel, WR, 6´1˝/200 lbs; Tennessee State; 1968: SF, rnd 6; B10/1/1944 Houston, TX **1970** SF 7																								
1969	SF	14	—	—	—	—	4	42	10.5 (14)	0	—	—	—	—	—	—	—	—	—	—	—	—	0	21
NFL	2	21	—	—	—	—	4	42	10.5 (14)	0	—	—	—	—	—	—	—	—	—	—	—	—	0	21
Johnson, Lee Leland Eric, P, 6´2˝/200 lbs; Brigham Young; 1985: Hou, rnd 5; B11/27/1961 Dallas, TX **[KP]**																								
1985	Hou	16 (0)	1	0	0.0 (0)	0	—	—	—	—	—	—	—	—	—	—	—	—	—	—	P	—	0	0
1986	Hou	16 (0)	—	—	—	—	—	—	—	—	—	—	—	—	—	—	—	—	—	—	P	—	0	0
1987	Hou	9 (0)	—	—	—	—	—	—	—	—	—	—	—	—	—	—	—	—	—	—	P	—	0	0
1987	†Cle	3 (0)	—	—	—	—	—	—	—	—	—	—	—	—	—	—	—	—	—	—	P	—	0	0
1988	Cle	3 (0)	—	—	—	—	—	—	—	—	—	—	—	—	—	—	—	—	—	—	P	—	0	0
1988	†Cin	12 (0)	—	—	—	—	—	—	—	—	—	—	—	—	—	—	—	—	—	—	KP	—	3	0
1989	Cin	16 (0)	1	-7	-7.0 (-7)	0	—	—	—	—	—	—	—	—	—	—	—	—	—	—	KP	—	0	-7
1990	†Cin	16 (0)	—	—	—	—	—	—	—	—	1	1	100.0	4	4.0 (4)	1	0	—	—	—	KP	—	0	7
1991	Cin	16 (0)	1	-2	-2.0 (-2)	0	—	—	—	—	1	1	100.0	3	3.0 (3)	0	0	—	—	—	KP	—	3	-1
1992	Cin	16 (0)	—	—	—	—	—	—	—	—	—	—	—	—	—	—	—	—	—	—	KP	—	0	0
1993	Cin	16 (0)	—	—	—	—	—	—	—	—	1	0	0.0	0	0.0	0	0	—	—	—	P	—	0	0
1994	Cin	16 (0)	—	—	—	—	—	—	—	—	1	1	100.0	7	7.0 (7)	1	0	—	—	—	P	—	0	9
1995	Cin	16 (0)	1	-16	-16.0 (-16)	0	—	—	—	—	1	1	100.0	5	5.0 (5)	0	0	—	—	—	P	—	0	-14
1996	Cin	16 (0)	—	—	—	—	—	—	—	—	—	—	—	—	—	—	—	—	—	—	P	—	0	0
1997	Cin	16 (0)	1	0	0.0 (0)	0	—	—	—	—	—	—	—	—	—	—	—	—	—	—	P	—	0	0
1998	Cin	13 (0)	—	—	—	—	—	—	—	—	—	—	—	—	—	—	—	—	—	—	P	—	0	0
1999	NE	16 (0)	2	13	6.5 (13)	0	—	—	—	—	—	—	—	—	—	—	—	—	—	—	P	—	0	13
2000	NE	16 (0)	2	-1	-0.5 (0)	0	—	—	—	—	1	1	100.0	18	18.0 (18)	0	0	—	—	—	P	—	0	8
2001	NE	5 (0)	1	-19	-19.0 (-19)	0	—	—	—	—	—	—	—	—	—	—	—	—	—	—	P	—	0	-19
2001	Min	4 (0)	—	—	—	—	—	—	—	—	—	—	—	—	—	—	—	—	—	—	P	—	0	0
2002	†Phi	2 (0)	—	—	—	—	—	—	—	—	—	—	—	—	—	—	—	—	—	—	P	—	0	0
NFL	18	259 (0)	10	-32	-3.2 (13)	0	—	—	—	—	6	5	83.3	37	6.2 (18)	2	0	—	—	—	KP	—	6	-4

JOHNSON, LEN Leonard C., BB, Syracuse; B11/15/1902, D4/1975 New York, NY **1926** Col 1 (1)

JOHNSON, LEN Leonard L., G-C, 6´2˝/250 lbs; St. Cloud State; B1/26/1946 Worthington, MN **1970** NYG 3

JOHNSON, LEON Leon, E, 5´11˝/185 lbs; Columbia; B9/30/1906, D9/1978 Florence, NJ **1929** Ora 5 (1)

JOHNSON, LEON William Leon, RB, 6´0˝/222 lbs; North Carolina; 1997: NYJ, rnd 4; B7/13/1974 Morganton, NC **[R]**

YEAR	TEAM	G(GS, POS)	RUSH	YD	AVG(LG)	TD	REC	YD	AVG(LG)	TD	PASS	COMP	PCT	YD	AVG(LG)	TD	INT	SK	YD	QBR	KPR	OTD	PTS	TAY
1997	NYJ	16(1)	48	158	3.3(20)	2	16	142	8.9(20)	0	2	0	0.0	0	0.0	0	1	—	—	—	kp	2	24	732
1998	NYJ	12(2)	41	185	4.5(40)	2	13	222	17.1(82)	2	0	0	0.0	0	0.0	0	0	1	7	—	kp	—	24	510
1999	NYJ	1(0)	1	2	2.0(2)	0	—	—	—	—	—	—	—	—	—	—	—	—	—	—	kp	—	0	4
2000	NYJ	3(0)	—	—	—	—	—	—	—	—	—	—	—	—	—	—	—	—	—	—	kp	—	0	39
2001	†ChiB	12(0)	20	99	4.9(34)	4	1	0	0.0(0)	0	1	1	100.0	18	18.0(18)	0	0	—	—	—	kp	—	24	339
2002	ChiB	16(4)	103	329	3.2(23)	1	16	125	7.8(31)	0	1	1	100.0	27	27.0(27)	0	0	1	0	—	kp	—	6	666
2003	SD	14(0)	4	26	6.5(18)	0	—	—	—	—	—	—	—	—	—	—	—	—	—	—	kp	—	0	491
NFL	7	74(7)	217	799	3.7(40)	9	46	489	10.6(82)	2	4	2	50.0	45	11.3(27)	0	1	2	7	—	kp	2	78	2781

JOHNSON, LESHON LeShon Eugene, RB, 6´0˝/205 lbs; Northern Illinois; 1994: GB, rnd 3; B1/15/1971 Tulsa, OK

YEAR	TEAM	G(GS, POS)	RUSH	YD	AVG(LG)	TD	REC	YD	AVG(LG)	TD	PASS	COMP	PCT	YD	AVG(LG)	TD	INT	SK	YD	QBR	KPR	OTD	PTS	TAY
1994	GB	12(0)	26	99	3.8(43)	0	13	168	12.9(33)	0	—	—	—	—	—	—	—	—	—	—	—	—	0	183
1995	GB	2(0)	2	-2	-1.0(0)	0	—	—	—	—	—	—	—	—	—	—	—	—	—	—	—	—	0	-2
1995	Arz	3(0)	—	—	—	—	—	—	—	—	—	—	—	—	—	—	—	—	—	—	k	—	0	94
1996	Arz	15(8, RB)	141	634	4.5(70)	3	15	176	11.7(35)	1	—	—	—	—	—	—	—	—	—	—	k	—	24	805
1997	Arz	14(0)	23	81	3.5(11)	0	3	4	1.3(7)	0	—	—	—	—	—	—	—	—	—	—	—	—	0	109
1999	NYG	16(4)	61	143	2.3(17)	2	12	86	7.2(28)	1	—	—	—	—	—	—	—	—	—	—	—	—	18	211
NFL	5	62(12)	253	955	3.8(70)	5	43	434	10.1(35)	2	—	—	—	—	—	—	—	—	—	—	k	—	42	1400

JOHNSON, LEVI Levi, DB, 6´3˝/196 lbs; Texas A&M-Kingsville; 1973: Det, rnd 3; B10/30/1950 Corpus Christi, TX **[I]** **1973** Det 14 (RCB) **1974** Det 14 (12, RCB) **1975** Det 14 (14, RCB) **1976** Det 14 (14, RCB) **1977** Det 3 **NFL** 59 (40) [5 yrs]

JOHNSON, LONNIE Lonnie Demetrius, TE, 6´3˝/240 lbs; Florida State; 1994: Buf, rnd 2; B2/14/1971 Miami, FL

YEAR	TEAM	G(GS, POS)	RUSH	YD	AVG(LG)	TD	REC	YD	AVG(LG)	TD	PASS	COMP	PCT	YD	AVG(LG)	TD	INT	SK	YD	QBR	KPR	OTD	PTS	TAY
1994	Buf	10(1)	—	—	—	—	3	42	14.0(21)	0	—	—	—	—	—	—	—	—	—	—	—	—	0	21
1995	†Buf	16(16, TE)	—	—	—	—	49	504	10.3(52)	1	—	—	—	—	—	—	—	—	—	—	—	—	6	257
1996	†Buf	16(15, TE)	—	—	—	—	46	457	9.9(33)	0	—	—	—	—	—	—	—	—	—	—	—	—	0	229
1997	Buf	16(16, TE)	1	6	6.0(6)	0	41	340	8.3(62)	2	—	—	—	—	—	—	—	—	—	—	—	—	12	186
1998	†Buf	16(16, TE)	—	—	—	—	14	146	10.4(27)	2	—	—	—	—	—	—	—	—	—	—	k	—	12	56
1999	KC	14(2)	—	—	—	—	10	98	9.8(19)	1	—	—	—	—	—	—	—	—	—	—	k	—	6	50
NFL	6	88(66)	1	6	6.0(6)	0	163	1587	9.7(62)	6	—	—	—	—	—	—	—	—	—	—	k	—	36	799

JOHNSON, LORNE Lorne E., FB-LB, 6´2˝/195 lbs; Temple; B4/19/1909 Orlando, FL, D3/11/1970 Lynn, MA

YEAR	TEAM	G(GS, POS)	RUSH	YD	AVG(LG)	TD	REC	YD	AVG(LG)	TD	PASS	COMP	PCT	YD	AVG(LG)	TD	INT	SK	YD	QBR	KPR	OTD	PTS	TAY
1934	Phi	1(0)	1	0	0.0	0	—	—	—	—	—	—	—	—	—	—	—	—	—	—	—	—	0	0

JOHNSON, M.L. Michael Lamar, LB, 6´3˝/228 lbs; Hawaii; 1987: Sea, rnd 9; B1/26/1964 New York, NY **1987**†Sea 8 (0) **1988**†Sea 16 (1) **1989** Sea 13 (8, ROLB) **NFL** 37 (9) [3 yrs]

JOHNSON, MALCOLM Malcolm Alexander, WR, 6´5˝/215 lbs; Notre Dame; 1999: Pit, rnd 5; B8/27/1977 Washington, DC **2000** Pit 4 (0) **2000** NYJ 1 (0)

YEAR	TEAM	G(GS, POS)	RUSH	YD	AVG(LG)	TD	REC	YD	AVG(LG)	TD	PASS	COMP	PCT	YD	AVG(LG)	TD	INT	SK	YD	QBR	KPR	OTD	PTS	TAY
1999	Pit	6(0)	—	—	—	—	2	23	11.5(18)	0	—	—	—	—	—	—	—	—	—	—	—	—	0	12
NFL	2	11(0)	—	—	—	—	2	23	11.5(18)	0	—	—	—	—	—	—	—	—	—	—	—	—	0	12

JOHNSON, MARCUS Michael Allen, G-T, 6´6˝/321 lbs; Mississippi; 2005: Min, rnd 2; B12/1/1981 Greenville, MS **2005** Min 14 (8, rg)

JOHNSON, MARIO Mario Chavez, DT-G, 6´3˝/292 lbs; Missouri; 1992: NYJ, rnd 10; B1/30/1970 St. Louis, MO **1992** NYJ 14 (0) **1993** NE 6 (0) **NFL** 20 (0) [2 yrs]

JOHNSON, MARK Mark Steven, DE-LB, 6´2˝/240 lbs; Missouri; 1975: Buf, rnd 12; B8/14/1953 Moline, IL **1975** Buf 11 (2) **1976** Buf 13 (1) **1977** Cle 7 **NFL** 31 (3) [3 yrs]

JOHNSON, MARK Mark Anthony, DB, 6´1˝/194 lbs; Western Kentucky; B3/20/1964 Houston, TX **1987** Cin 3 (3)

JOHNSON, MARSHALL Marshall Donell, WR-DB, 6´1˝/191 lbs; Houston; 1975: Bal, rnd 4; B11/1/1952 Jacksonville, FL

YEAR	TEAM	G(GS, POS)	RUSH	YD	AVG(LG)	TD	REC	YD	AVG(LG)	TD	PASS	COMP	PCT	YD	AVG(LG)	TD	INT	SK	YD	QBR	KPR	OTD	PTS	TAY
1975	†Bal	14	—	—	—	—	4	115	28.8(68)	2	—	—	—	—	—	—	—	—	—	—	kp	—	12	97
1977	†Bal	3	—	—	—	—	—	—	—	—	—	—	—	—	—	—	—	—	—	—	k	—	0	0
1978	Bal	15(1)	—	—	—	—	1	22	22.0(22)	0	—	—	—	—	—	—	—	—	—	—	kp	—	0	341
NFL	3	32(1)	—	—	—	—	5	137	27.4(68)	2	—	—	—	—	—	—	—	—	—	—	kp	—	12	438

JOHNSON, MARVIN Marvin L., DB-HB, 5´11˝/183 lbs; San Jose State; B4/13/1927 San Francisco, CA, D2/1981 Los Gatos, CA **1952** LARm 5 **1952** GB 5 **1953** GB 7 (db)

YEAR	TEAM	G(GS, POS)	RUSH	YD	AVG(LG)	TD	REC	YD	AVG(LG)	TD	PASS	COMP	PCT	YD	AVG(LG)	TD	INT	SK	YD	QBR	KPR	OTD	PTS	TAY
1951	†LARm	9	—	—	—	—	2	38	19.0(28)	0	—	—	—	—	—	—	—	—	—	—	—	—	0	19
NFL	3	26	—	—	—	—	2	38	19.0(28)	0	—	—	—	—	—	—	—	—	—	—	i	—	0	50

JOHNSON, MAURICE Maurice Edward, TE, 6´2˝/242 lbs; Temple; B1/9/1967 Washington, DC

YEAR	TEAM	G(GS, POS)	RUSH	YD	AVG(LG)	TD	REC	YD	AVG(LG)	TD	PASS	COMP	PCT	YD	AVG(LG)	TD	INT	SK	YD	QBR	KPR	OTD	PTS	TAY
1991	Phi	12(6, te)	—	—	—	—	6	70	11.7(31)	2	—	—	—	—	—	—	—	—	—	—	—	—	12	45
1992	†Phi	11(3)	—	—	—	—	2	16	8.0(13)	0	—	—	—	—	—	—	—	—	—	—	—	—	0	8
1993	Phi	16(2)	—	—	—	—	10	81	8.1(17)	0	—	—	—	—	—	—	—	—	—	—	k	—	0	33
1994	Phi	16(10, TE)	—	—	—	—	21	204	9.7(22)	2	—	—	—	—	—	—	—	—	—	—	k	—	12	97
NFL	4	55(21)	—	—	—	—	39	371	9.5(31)	4	—	—	—	—	—	—	—	—	—	—	k	—	24	183

JOHNSON, MELVIN Melvin Carlton, DB, 6´0˝/198 lbs; Kentucky; 1995: TB, rnd 2; B4/15/1972 Cincinnati, OH **1995** TB 11 (3) **1996** TB 16 (16, FS) **1997**†TB 16 (7, fs) **1998** KC 7 (1) **NFL** 50 (27) [4 yrs]

JOHNSON, MIKE Michael Alan, DB, 5´11˝/184 lbs; Kansas; 1966: Oak, rnd 14; B10/7/1943 Denver, CO **1966**†Dal 14 **1967**†Dal 14 (RCB) **1968**†Dal 14 (RCB) **1969** Dal 12 **NFL** 54 [4 yrs]

JOHNSON, MIKE Michael, LB, 6´1˝/230 lbs; Virginia Tech; 1984: Cle, rnd S1; B11/26/1962 Southport, NC **1986**†Cle 16 (0) **1987**†Cle 11 (10, RILB) **1988**†Cle 16 (16, LILB) **1989**†Cle★16 (16, MLB) **1990** Cle✧16 (15, MLB) **1991** Cle 5 (4) **1992** Cle 16 (16, MLB) **1993** Cle 16 (16, MLB) **1994**†Det 16 (16, RILB) **1995**†Det 16 (16, RLB) **NFL** 144 (125) [10 yrs]

JOHNSON, MIKE Michael, DE, 6´5˝/253 lbs; Illinois; 1984: Hou, rnd 9; B4/24/1962 Chicago, IL **1984** Hou 16 (0)

JOHNSON, MITCH Mitchell Allen, T-G, 6´4˝/251 lbs; Los Angeles State; UCLA; 1965: Dal, rnd 17; B3/1/1942 Chicago, IL **1965** Dal 12 **1967** Was 14 (14, LT) **1969**†LARm 14 **1971** Cle 11

YEAR	TEAM	G(GS, POS)	RUSH	YD	AVG(LG)	TD	REC	YD	AVG(LG)	TD	PASS	COMP	PCT	YD	AVG(LG)	TD	INT	SK	YD	QBR	KPR	OTD	PTS	TAY
1966	Was	14(14, LT)	—	—	—	—	1	1	1.0(1)	0	—	—	—	—	—	—	—	—	—	—	k	—	0	-8
1970	LARm	14	1	1	1.0(1)	0	—	—	—	—	—	—	—	—	—	—	—	—	—	—	k	—	0	3
NFL	6	79(28)	1	1	1.0(1)	0	1	1	1.0(1)	0	—	—	—	—	—	—	—	—	—	—	k	—	0	-5

JOHNSON, MONTE Monte Charles, LB, 6´4˝/239 lbs; Nebraska; 1973: Oak, rnd 2; B10/26/1951 Denver, CO **1973**†Oak 13 **1974**†Oak 14 **1975**†Oak 14 (13, MLB) **1976**†Oak 14 (RILB) **1977**†Oak 14 (14, LILB) **1978** Oak 14 (13, LILB) **1979** Oak 16 (15, LILB) **NFL** 99 (55) [7 yrs]

JOHNSON, NATE Nathan Elijah, T-DT, 6´3˝/244 lbs; Illinois; B6/18/1920 Dale, IL, D8/24/2004 Freeport, IL **1946**†NYY-A 14 (12) **1947**†NYY-A☆14 (14) **1948** ChiR-A 14 (12) **1949** ChiH-A 12 (0) **AAFC** 54 (38) [4 yrs]

1950 NYY 11 (RT)

JOHNSON, NATE Nathaniel, WR, 5´11˝/192 lbs; Hillsdale; 1980: Pit, rnd 7; B5/12/1957 St. Petersburg, FL **1980** NYG 16 (0)

JOHNSON, NATE Nathaniel James, RB, 6´2˝/224 lbs; Texas Southern; B10/25/1963 Fort Worth, TX **1987** NO 1 (0)

JOHNSON, NORM Norman Douglas, K, 6´2˝/196 lbs; UCLA; B5/31/1960 Inglewood, CA **[K]** **1983**†Sea 16 (0) **1984**†Sea★16 (0) **1985** Sea 16 (0) **1986** Sea 16 (0) **1987**†Sea 13 (0) **1988**†Sea 16 (0) **1989** Sea 16 (0) **1990** Sea 16 (0) **1991**†Atl 14 (0) **1992** Atl 16 (0) **1993** Atl★15 (0) **1994** Atl 16 (0) **1995**†Pit 16 (0) **1996**†Pit 16 (0) **1997**†Pit 16 (0) **1998** Pit 15 (0) **1999** Phi 15 (0)

YEAR	TEAM	G(GS, POS)	RUSH	YD	AVG(LG)	TD	REC	YD	AVG(LG)	TD	PASS	COMP	PCT	YD	AVG(LG)	TD	INT	SK	YD	QBR	KPR	OTD	PTS	TAY
1982	Sea	9(0)	—	—	—	—	—	—	—	—	1	1	100.0	27	27.0(27)	0	0	—	—	—	K	—	43	14
NFL	18	273(0)	—	—	—	—	—	—	—	—	1	1	100.0	27	27.0(27)	0	0	—	—	—	KP	—	1736	14

JOHNSON, OLRICK Olrick, LB, 6´0˝/244 lbs; Florida A&M; B8/20/1977 Miami, FL **1999** NYJ 3 (0) **1999**†Min 5 (0) **2000** NE 12 (0) **NFL** 20 (0) [2 yrs]

JOHNSON, OSCAR Oscar Gotthard, FB, 5´10˝/199 lbs; Vermont; B1901 Lynn, MA, deceased **1924** ChiB 1 (0)

JOHNSON, PAT John Patrick, DB, 6´1˝/204 lbs; Purdue; B6/10/1972 Mineral Point, MO **1995**†Mia 14 (0)

YEAR	TEAM	G (GS, POS)	RUSH	YD	AVG(LG)	TD	REC	YD	AVG(LG)	TD	PASS	COMP	PCT	YD	AVG(LG)	TD	INT	SK	YD	QBR	KPR	OTD	PTS	TAY

JOHNSON, PATRICK   Patrick Jevon, WR, 5´10˝/186 lbs; Oregon; 1998: Bal, rnd 2; B8/10/1976 Gainesville, GA

1998	Bal	13(0)	—	—	—	—	12	159	13.3(35)	1	—	—	—	—	—	—	—	—	—	—	kp	1	12	255
1999	Bal	10(6, wr)	1	12	12.0(12)	0	29	526	18.1(76)	3	—	—	—	—	—	—	—	—	—	—	—	—	18	290
2000	†Bal	12(9, WR)	2	21	10.5(19)	0	12	156	13.0(46)	2	—	—	—	—	—	—	—	—	—	—	—	—	12	109
2001	Bal	4(0)	—	—	—	—	5	57	11.4(25)	1	—	—	—	—	—	—	—	—	—	—	k	—	6	43
2002	Jax	9(6, wr)	1	-9	-9.0(-9)	0	9	187	20.8(79)	2	0	0	0.0	0	—	0	0	1	7	—	—	—	12	95
2003	Was	16(2)	—	—	—	—	15	170	11.3(31)	1	—	—	—	—	—	—	—	—	—	—	kp	—	6	207
2005	Bal	6(0)	—	—	—	—	2	31	15.5(19)	0	—	—	—	—	—	—	—	—	—	—	—	—	0	16
NFL	7	70(23)	4	24	6.0(19)	0	84	1286	15.3(79)	10	0	0	0.0	0	—	0	0	1	7	—	kp	1	66	1013

JOHNSON, PEPPER   Thomas, LB, 6´3˝/250 lbs; Ohio State; 1986: NYG, rnd 2; B7/29/1964 Detroit, MI   **1986**†NYG 16 (0)   **1987** NYG 12 (12, LILB)   **1988** NYG 16 (15, LILB)   **1989**†NYG 14 (4)   **1990**†NYG★16 (16, RILB)   **1991** NYG 16 (16, RILB)   **1992** NYG 16 (16, LILB)   **1993** Cle 16 (11, LLB)   **1994**†Cle★16 (16, MLB)   **1995** Cle 16 (16, MLB)   **1996** Det 15 (12, MLB)   **1997** NYJ 8 (8, lilb)   **1998**†NYJ 16 (16, MLB)   **NFL** 193 (158) [13 yrs]

JOHNSON, PETE   Peter Thomas, DB, 6´2˝/200 lbs; VMI; 1959: ChiB, rnd 3; B8/9/1937 Bedford, VA   **1959** ChiB 7

JOHNSON, PETE   Pete, aka Willie James Hammock, RB, 6´0˝/252 lbs; Ohio State; 1977: Cin, rnd 2; B3/2/1954 Fort Valley, GA

1977	Cin	14(9, FB)	153	585	3.8(65)	4	5	49	9.8(21)	0	—	—	—	—	—	—	—	—	—	—	k	—	24	646
1978	Cin	16(11, FB)	180	762	4.2(50)	7	31	236	7.6(34)	1	—	—	—	—	—	—	—	—	—	—	—	—	42	950
1979	Cin	16(13, FB)	243	865	3.6(35)	14	24	154	6.4(15)	1	—	—	—	—	—	—	—	—	—	—	—	—	90	1087
1980	Cin	12(8, FB)	186	747	4.0(57)	6	21	172	8.2(28)	1	—	—	—	—	—	—	—	—	—	—	—	—	42	898
1981	†Cin★	16(16, FB)	274	1077	3.9(39)	12	46	320	7.0(33)	4	—	—	—	—	—	—	—	—	—	—	—	—	96	1377
1982	†Cin	9(9, FB)	156	622	4.0(21)	7	31	267	8.6(25)	0	—	—	—	—	—	—	—	—	—	—	—	—	42	826
1983	Cin	11(8, FB)	210	763	3.6(16)	14	15	129	8.6(18)	0	—	—	—	—	—	—	—	—	—	—	—	—	84	968
1984	SD	3(0)	19	46	2.4(7)	3	2	7	3.5(7)	0	—	—	—	—	—	—	—	—	—	—	—	—	18	80
1984	†Mia	13(0)	68	159	2.3(9)	9	—	—	—	—	—	—	—	—	—	—	—	—	—	—	—	—	54	249
NFL	8	110(74)	1489	5626	3.8(65)	76	175	1334	7.6(34)	6	—	—	—	—	—	—	—	—	—	—	k	—	492	7079

JOHNSON, PIKE   Frank Leonard, T-G, 5´11˝/185 lbs; Washington & Lee; B9/30/1896 Javia, Sweden, D4/13/1963 Boston, MA   **1920** Akr 10 (9, LT)   **1921** Akr 12 (11, LT)   **NFL** 22 (20) [2 yrs]

JOHNSON, PRESTON   Preston, RB, 6´2˝/230 lbs; Florida A&M; B2/18/1945

| 1968 | Bos-A | 3 | 2 | 6 | 3.0(6) | 1 | — | — | — | — | — | — | — | — | — | — | — | — | — | — | — | — | 0 | 6 |

JOHNSON, RANDY   Randolph Klaus, QB, 6´3˝/205 lbs; Texas A&M-Kingsville; 1966: Atl, rnd 1/Den, rnd 4; B6/17/1944 San Antonio, TX

1966	Atl	14(11, QB)	35	142	4.1(21)	1	—	—	—	—	295	129	43.7	1795	6.1(53)	12	21	26	236	47.8	—	—	24	300
1967	Atl	14(12, QB)	24	144	6.0(17)	1	—	—	—	—	288	142	49.3	1620	5.6(82)	10	21	34	311	47.8	—	—	6	174
1968	Atl	8(7, qb)	11	97	8.8(26)	1	—	—	—	—	156	73	46.8	892	5.7(71)	2	10	20	153	—	—	—	6	163
1969	Atl	6	11	55	5.0(13)	1	—	—	—	—	93	51	54.8	788	8.5(65)	4	5	18	152	—	—	—	6	299
1970	Atl	4	7	21	3.0(14)	1	—	—	—	—	72	40	55.6	443	6.2(34)	2	8	16	148	—	—	—	0	-68
1971	NYG	5	6	29	4.8(17)	0	—	—	—	—	74	41	55.4	477	6.4(45)	3	3	13	116	—	—	—	6	163
1972	NYG	4	9	26	2.9(9)	1	—	—	—	—	17	10	58.8	230	13.5(63)	3	1	2	10	—	—	—	6	46
1973	NYG	9(qb)	4	24	6.0(11)	1	—	—	—	—	177	99	55.9	1279	7.2(48)	7	8	19	134	—	—	—	6	389
1975	Was	8(1)	2	10	5.0(10)	0	—	—	—	—	79	41	51.9	556	7.0(36)	4	10	2	19	—	—	—	0	-92
1976	GB	3(1)	5	25	5.0(11)	1	—	—	—	—	35	21	60.0	249	7.1(45)	0	1	2	23	—	—	—	6	120
NFL	10	75(32)	114	573	5.0(26)	10	—	—	—	—	1286	647	50.3	8329	6.5(82)	51	90	152	1302	55.1	—	—	60	1493

JOHNSON, RANDY   Robert Randall, G, 6´2˝/255 lbs; Georgia; 1976: Sea, rnd 4; B1/2/1953 Floyd County, GA   **1977** TB 12   **1978** TB 10 (1)   **NFL** 22 (1) [2 yrs]

JOHNSON, RAY   Raymond Robert, DB-TB-FB, 6´1˝/195 lbs; Denver; 1937: Cle, rnd 9; B10/16/1914 Denver, CO, D8/20/1989 Topeka, KS

1937	Cle	2(2)	7	28	4.0	0	—	—	—	—	—	—	—	—	—	—	—	—	—	—	—	—	0	28
1938	Cle	1(0)	—	—	—	—	—	—	—	—	5	3	60.0	45	9.0	0	1	—	—	—	—	—	0	-18
1940	ChiC	1(0)	—	—	—	—	—	—	—	—	—	—	—	—	—	—	—	—	—	—	—	—	0	1
NFL	3	4(2)	7	28	4.0	0	—	—	—	—	5	3	60.0	45	9.0	0	1	—	—	—	—	—	0	11

JOHNSON, RAYLEE   Raylee Terrell, DE, 6´3˝/272 lbs; Arkansas; 1993: SD, rnd 4; B6/1/1970 Chicago, IL   **1993** SD 9 (0)   **1994**†SD 15 (0)   **1995** SD 16 (1)   **1996** SD 16 (1)   **1997** SD 16 (0)   **1998** SD 16 (3)   **1999** SD 16 (16, RDE)   **2001** SD 16 (16, RDE)   **2002** SD 16 (16, RDE)   **2003** SD 9 (1)   **2004**†Den 14 (1)   **NFL** 159 (55) [11 yrs]

JOHNSON, REGGIE   Reginald Roosevelt, TE, 6´2˝/256 lbs; Florida State; 1991: Den, rnd 2; B1/27/1968 Pensacola, FL

1991	†Den	16(3)	—	—	—	—	6	73	12.2(31)	1	—	—	—	—	—	—	—	—	—	—	—	—	6	42
1992	Den	15(7, te)	2	7	3.5(8)	0	10	139	13.9(48)	1	—	—	—	—	—	—	—	—	—	—	k	—	6	99
1993	†Den	13(12, TE)	—	—	—	—	20	243	12.1(38)	1	—	—	—	—	—	—	—	—	—	—	—	—	6	127
1994	†GB	9(2)	—	—	—	—	7	79	11.3(24)	0	—	—	—	—	—	—	—	—	—	—	—	—	0	40
1995	†Phi	9(2)	—	—	—	—	5	68	13.6(33)	2	—	—	—	—	—	—	—	—	—	—	—	—	12	44
1996	KC	11(3)	—	—	—	—	18	189	10.5(26)	1	—	—	—	—	—	—	—	—	—	—	—	—	6	100
1997	GB	4(0)	—	—	—	—	—	—	—	—	—	—	—	—	—	—	—	—	—	—	—	—	—	—
NFL	7	77(29)	2	7	3.5(8)	0	66	791	12.0(48)	6	—	—	—	—	—	—	—	—	—	—	k	—	36	450

JOHNSON, RIALL   Riall, LB, 6´3˝/243 lbs; Stanford; 2001: Cin, rnd 6; B4/20/1978 Lynwood, WA   **2001** Cin 7 (0)   **2002** Cin 12 (0)   **2003** Cin 13 (1)   **NFL** 32 (1) [3 yrs]

JOHNSON, RICH   Richard L., RB, 6´1˝/225 lbs; Illinois; 1969: Hou, rnd 3; B5/13/1947 Canton, IL

| 1969 | †Hou-A | 14 | 11 | 42 | 3.8(9) | 0 | 2 | 17 | 8.5(16) | 1 | — | — | — | — | — | — | — | — | — | — | — | — | 6 | 56 |

JOHNSON, RICHARD   Richard Lavon, WR, 5´7˝/182 lbs; Colorado; B10/19/1961 Los Angeles, CA

1987	Was	1(0)	—	—	—	—	1	5	5.0(5)	0	—	—	—	—	—	—	—	—	—	—	—	—	0	3
1989	Det	16(15, WR)	12	38	3.2(14)	0	70	1091	15.6(75)	8	—	—	—	—	—	—	—	—	—	—	—	—	48	624
1990	Det	16(16, WR)	—	—	—	—	64	727	11.4(44)	6	—	—	—	—	—	—	—	—	—	—	—	—	36	394
NFL	3	33(31)	12	38	3.2(14)	0	135	1823	13.5(75)	14	—	—	—	—	—	—	—	—	—	—	—	—	84	1020

JOHNSON, RICHARD   Richard James, DB, 6´1˝/195 lbs; Wisconsin; 1985: Hou, rnd 1; B9/16/1963 Harvey, IL   **1985** Hou 16 (2)   **1986** Hou 16 (0)   **1987** Hou 5 (1)   **1988**†Hou 16 (3)   **1989** Hou 14 (0)   **1990**†Hou 16 (16, RCB)   **1991**†Hou 14 (14, RCB)   **1992** Hou 1 (1)   **NFL** 98 (37) [8 yrs]

JOHNSON, RICK   Richard Lee, T, 6´6˝/255 lbs; Grand Valley State; B12/12/1963 Greenville, MI   **1987** Det 1 (0)

JOHNSON, ROB   Rob Garland, QB, 6´4˝/204 lbs; USC; 1995: Jax, rnd 4; B3/18/1973 Newport Beach, CA

1995	Jax	1(0)	3	17	5.7(7)	0	—	—	—	—	7	3	42.9	24	3.4(19)	0	1	1	13	—	—	—	0	-11
1996	Jax	2(0)	—	—	—	—	—	—	—	—	—	—	—	—	—	—	—	—	—	—	—	—	—	—
1997	Jax	5(1)	10	34	3.4(25)	1	—	—	—	—	28	22	78.6	344	12.3(40)	2	2	6	29	—	—	—	6	146
1998	Buf	8(6, qb)	24	123	5.1(32)	1	—	—	—	—	107	67	62.6	910	8.5(66)	8	3	29	163	—	—	—	6	508
1999	†Buf	2(1)	8	61	7.6(25)	0	—	—	—	—	34	25	73.5	298	8.8(42)	2	0	1	9	—	—	—	0	220
2000	Buf	12(11, QB)	42	307	7.3(23)	1	1	-6	-6.0(-6)	0	306	175	57.2	2125	6.9(74)	12	7	49	292	82.2	—	—	6	1157
2001	Buf	8(8, QB)	36	241	6.7(23)	1	—	—	—	—	216	134	62.0	1465	6.8(61)	5	7	31	196	—	—	—	6	729
2002	†TB	6(2)	14	73	5.2(21)	0	—	—	—	—	88	57	64.8	536	6.1(23)	1	2	19	94	—	—	—	0	266
2003	Was	2(0)	1	6	6.0(6)	0	—	—	—	—	7	5	71.4	39	5.6(14)	0	3	3	15	—	—	—	0	26
2003	Oak	2(0)	2	15	7.5(14)	0	—	—	—	—	13	6	46.2	54	4.2(15)	0	1	1	6	—	—	—	0	2
NFL	9	48(29)	140	877	6.3(32)	4	1	-6	-6.0(-6)	0	806	494	61.3	5795	7.2(74)	30	23	140	817	83.6	—	—	24	3042

JOHNSON, ROBERT   Robert, TE, 6´6˝/270 lbs; Auburn; B6/20/1980 Montgomery, AL   **2003** ChiB 1 (0)

| 2005 | Was | 2(0) | — | — | — | — | 1 | 14 | 14.0(14) | 0 | — | — | — | — | — | — | — | — | — | — | — | — | 0 | 7 |
| NFL | 2 | 3(0) | — | — | — | — | 1 | 14 | 14.0(14) | 0 | — | — | — | — | — | — | — | — | — | — | — | — | 0 | 7 |

JOHNSON, RON   Ronald, DB, 5´10˝/200 lbs; Eastern Michigan; 1978: Pit, rnd 1; B6/8/1956 Detroit, MI   **1978**†Pit 16 (16, LCB)   **1979** Pit 11 (11, LCB)   **1980** Pit 16 (16, LCB)   **1981** Pit 12 (3)   **1982**†Pit 9 (9, FS)   **1983**†Pit 12 (7, fs)   **1984**†Pit 15 (0)   **NFL** 91 (62) [7 yrs]

YEAR	TEAM	G (GS, POS)	RUSH	YD	AVG(LG)	TD	REC	YD	AVG(LG)	TD	PASS	COMP	PCT	YD	AVG(LG)	TD	INT	SK	YD	QBR	KPR	OTD	PTS	TAY

JOHNSON, RON Ron, WR, 6´2˝/225 lbs; Minnesota; 2002: Bal, rnd 4; B5/23/1980 Detroit, MI

2002	Bal	16(4)	—	—	—	—	10	114	11.4(33)	1	—	—	—	—	—	—	—	—	—	—	k	1	12	53
2003	Bal	6(0)	—	—	—	—	1	12	12.0(12)	0	—	—	—	—	—	—	—	—	—	—	—	—	0	6
NFL	2	22(4)	—	—	—	—	11	126	11.5(33)	1	—	—	—	—	—	—	—	—	—	—	k	1	12	59

JOHNSON, RON Ronald, WR, 6´3˝/190 lbs; Long Beach State; 1981: Sea, rnd 7; B9/21/1958 Monterey, CA

1985	Phi	8(0)	—	—	—	—	11	186	16.9(37)	0	—	—	—	—	—	—	—	—	—	—	—	—	0	93
1986	Phi	12(0)	—	—	—	—	11	207	18.8(39)	1	—	—	—	—	—	—	—	—	—	—	—	—	6	109
1987	Phi	3(0)	—	—	—	—	—	—	—	—	—	—	—	—	—	—	—	—	—	—	—	—	—	—
1988	†Phi	10(4)	—	—	—	—	19	417	21.9(54)	2	—	—	—	—	—	—	—	—	—	—	—	—	12	219
1989	†Phi	14(9, WR)	1	3	3.0(3)	0	20	295	14.8(34)	1	—	—	—	—	—	—	—	—	—	—	—	—	6	156
NFL	5	47(13)	1	3	3.0(3)	0	61	1105	18.1(54)	4	—	—	—	—	—	—	—	—	—	—	—	—	24	576

JOHNSON, RON Ronald Adolphis, RB, 6´1˝/205 lbs; Michigan; 1969: Cle, rnd 1; B10/17/1947 Detroit, MI

1969	†Cle	14(HB)	138	472	3.4(48)	7	24	164	6.8(18)	0	1	0	0.0	0	0.0	0	0	—	—	—	k	—	42	640
1970	NYG★	14(RB)	263	1027	3.9(68)	8	48	487	10.1(50)	4	—	—	—	—	—	—	—	—	—	—	—	—	72	**1436**
1971	NYG	2	32	156	4.9(17)	1	6	47	7.8(30)	0	—	—	—	—	—	—	—	—	—	—	—	—	6	190
1972	NYG★	14(RB)	298	1182	4.0(35)	9	45	451	10.0(39)	5	1	0	0.0	0	0.0	0	0	—	—	—	—	—	84	1523
1973	NYG	12(RB)	260	902	3.5(29)	6	32	377	11.8(45)	3	—	—	—	—	—	—	—	—	—	—	—	—	54	1166
1974	NYG	11	97	218	2.2(14)	4	24	171	7.1(21)	2	—	—	—	—	—	—	—	—	—	—	—	—	36	354
1975	NYG	14(RB)	116	351	3.0(23)	5	34	280	8.2(36)	1	—	—	—	—	—	—	—	—	—	—	—	—	36	546
NFL	7	81	1204	4308	3.6(68)	40	213	1977	9.3(50)	15	2	0	0.0	0	0.0	0	0	—	—	—	k	—	330	5853

JOHNSON, RON Ronald Lee, DE, 6´5˝/275 lbs; Shippensburg (PA); B10/23/1979 York, PA   **2003** Phi 3 (0)

JOHNSON, RUDI Rudi Ali, RB, 5´10˝/220 lbs; Auburn; 2001: Cin, rnd 4; B10/1/1979 Petersburg, VA

2001	Cin	2(0)	—	—	—	—	—	—	—	—	—	—	—	—	—	—	—	—	—	—	k	—	0	19
2002	Cin	7(0)	17	67	3.9(13)	0	6	34	5.7(14)	0	—	—	—	—	—	—	—	—	—	—	k	—	0	166
2003	Cin	13(5, RB)	215	957	4.5(54)	9	21	146	7.0(17)	0	—	—	—	—	—	—	—	—	—	—	k	—	54	1113
2004	Cin◇	16(16, RB)	361	1454	4.0(52)	12	15	84	5.6(30)	0	—	—	—	—	—	—	—	—	—	—	—	—	72	1616
2005	†Cin	16(14, RB)	337	1458	4.3(33)	12	23	90	3.9(15)	0	—	—	—	—	—	—	—	—	—	—	—	—	72	1623
NFL	5	54(35)	930	3936	4.2(54)	33	65	354	5.4(30)	0	—	—	—	—	—	—	—	—	—	—	—	—	198	4537

JOHNSON, RUDY Rudolph, HB, 5´11˝/190 lbs; Nebraska; 1964: SF, rnd 5/NYJ, rnd 12; B8/12/1941 Houston, TX

1964	SF	5	16	48	3.0(24)	1	5	21	4.2(12)	0	—	—	—	—	—	—	—	—	—	—	—	—	6	69
1965	SF	14	6	9	1.5(4)	0	3	49	16.3(28)	0	—	—	—	—	—	—	—	—	—	—	k	—	0	45
1966	Atl	1	3	3	1.0(3)	0	—	—	—	—	—	—	—	—	—	—	—	—	—	—	—	—	0	3
NFL	3	20	25	60	2.4(24)	1	8	70	8.8(28)	0	—	—	—	—	—	—	—	—	—	—	k	—	6	116

JOHNSON, SAM Samuel, WR, 5´11˝/180 lbs; Utah State; Prairie View A&M; B9/7/1964 East Los Angeles, CA   **1987** LARm 3 (1)

JOHNSON, SAMMY Samuel Lee, RB, 6´0˝/223 lbs; North Carolina; 1974: SF, rnd 4; B9/22/1952 Burlington, NC

1974	SF	14	44	237	5.4(32)	2	11	106	9.6(23)	0	—	—	—	—	—	—	—	—	—	—	k	—	12	311
1975	SF	14	55	185	3.4(26)	3	23	177	7.7(20)	0	2	0	0.0	0	0.0	0	0	—	—	—	k	—	18	449
1976	SF	6	24	52	2.2(12)	2	5	52	10.4(24)	0	—	—	—	—	—	—	—	—	—	—	—	—	12	98
1976	†Min	8	17	98	5.8(18)	0	2	22	11.0(11)	0	—	—	—	—	—	—	—	—	—	—	k	—	0	114
1977	†Min	14	55	217	3.9(26)	2	4	21	5.3(8)	0	—	—	—	—	—	—	—	—	—	—	—	—	12	248
1978	Min	3	11	41	3.7(17)	0	—	—	—	—	—	—	—	—	—	—	—	—	—	—	—	—	0	41
1979	GB	3	—	—	—	—	—	—	—	—	—	—	—	—	—	—	—	—	—	—	—	—	0	1
NFL	6	62	206	830	4.0(32)	9	45	378	8.4(24)	0	2	0	0.0	0	0.0	0	0	—	—	—	k	—	54	1261

JOHNSON, SIDNEY Sidney, DB, 5´9˝/175 lbs; California; B3/7/1965 Los Angeles, CA   **1988** KC 13 (0) **1990**†Was 10 (1) **1991**†Was 15 (0) **1992** Was 8 (0) **NFL** 46 (1) [4 yrs]

JOHNSON, SMILEY Howard White, G-LB, 5´9˝/198 lbs; Georgia; B9/22/1916 Nashville, TN, D2/26/1945 Iwo Jima   **1940** GB 11 (1) **1941**†GB 11 (0) **NFL** 22 (1) [2 yrs]

JOHNSON, SPENCER Spencer, DT, 6´3˝/286 lbs; Auburn; B12/12/1981 Waynesboro, MS   **2004**†Min 9 (7, ldt) **2005** Min 10 (2) **NFL** 19 (9) [2 yrs]

JOHNSON, SPIDER Robert, T, 6´4˝/210 lbs; Tennessee-Chattanooga; B1908, deceased   **1930** Por 3 (0)

JOHNSON, STAN George Stanley, NT, 6´4˝/275 lbs; Tennessee State; 1978: LA, rnd 2; B6/18/1955 Sandusky, OH   **1978** KC 10

JOHNSON, STEVE Steven Emil, TE, 6´6˝/245 lbs; Virginia Tech; 1988: NE, rnd 6; B6/22/1965 Huntsville, AL

| 1988 | NE | 14(3) | — | — | — | — | 1 | 5 | 5.0(5) | 0 | — | — | — | — | — | — | — | — | — | — | — | — | 0 | 3 |

JOHNSON, TANK Terry, DT, 6´3˝/300 lbs; Washington; 2004: Chi, rnd 2; B12/7/1981 Chandler, AZ   **2004** ChiB 16 (1) **2005**†ChiB 16 (4) **NFL** 32 (5) [2 yrs]

JOHNSON, TED Ted Curtis, LB, 6´4˝/253 lbs; Colorado; 1995: NE, rnd 2; B12/4/1972 Alameda, CA   **1995** NE 12 (12, RILB) **1996**†NE 16 (16, RILB) **1997**†NE 16 (16, MLB) **1998** NE 13 (13, MLB) **1999** NE 5 (5, mlb) **2000** NE 13 (11, RILB) **2001**†NE 12 (5, mlb) **2002** NE 14 (11, MLB) **2003**†NE 8 (2) **2004**†NE 16 (15, LILB) **NFL** 125 (106) [10 yrs]

JOHNSON, TEYO Teyo, TE, 6´5˝/260 lbs; Stanford; 2003: Oak, rnd 2; B11/29/1981 San Diego, CA

2003	Oak	16(5, te)	—	—	—	—	14	128	9.1(21)	1	—	—	—	—	—	—	—	—	—	—	—	—	6	69
2004	Oak	8(1)	—	—	—	—	9	131	14.6(25)	2	—	—	—	—	—	—	—	—	—	—	—	—	12	76
2005	Arz	7(3)	—	—	—	—	3	29	9.7(13)	0	—	—	—	—	—	—	—	—	—	—	—	—	0	15
NFL	3	31(9)	—	—	—	—	26	288	11.1(25)	3	—	—	—	—	—	—	—	—	—	—	—	—	18	159

JOHNSON, THOMAS Thomas, DT-DE, 6´2˝/294 lbs; Middle Tennessee State; B6/24/1981   **2005** Dal 2 (0)

JOHNSON, TIM Timothy, DT-DE, 6´3˝/275 lbs; Penn State; 1987: Pit, rnd 6; B1/29/1965 Sarasota, FL   **1987** Pit 12 (0) **1988** Pit 15 (12, LDE/rde) **1989**†Pit 14 (14, RDE) **1990**†Was 16 (2) **1991**†Was 16 (16, RDT) **1992**†Was 16 (16, RDT) **1993** Was 15 (15, RDT) **1994** Was 14 (13, RDT) **1995** Was 14 (5, rdt) **1996** Cin 14 (13, RDT) **NFL** 146 (106) [10 yrs]

JOHNSON, TIM Tim Maurice, LB, 6´0˝/240 lbs; Youngstown State; B2/7/1978 Birmingham, AL   **2001** Bal 1 (0) **2002**†Oak 6 (0) **2003** Oak 12 (4) **2004** Oak 16 (0) **2005** Oak 16 (0) **NFL** 51 (4) [5 yrs]

JOHNSON, TODD Todd Edward, DB, 6´1˝/200 lbs; Florida; 2003: Chi, rnd 4; B12/18/1979 Sarasota, FL   **2004** ChiB 16 (10, FS) **2005**†ChiB 14 (2) **NFL** 30 (12) [2 yrs]

JOHNSON, TOM Thomas, DT, 6´2˝/230 lbs; Michigan; 1952: GB, rnd 6; B1/19/1931 Chicago, IL   **1952** GB 8

JOHNSON, TOMMY Tommy Postell, DB, 5´10˝/183 lbs; Alabama; B12/5/1971 Rome, GA   **1995** Jax 1 (0)

JOHNSON, TONY Tony Vincent, TE, 6´5˝/255 lbs; Alabama; 1996: Phi, rnd 6; B2/5/1972 Como, MS

1996	NO	9(7, te)	—	—	—	—	7	76	10.9(17)	1	—	—	—	—	—	—	—	—	—	—	—	—	6	43
1997	NO	7(1)	—	—	—	—	1	13	13.0(13)	0	—	—	—	—	—	—	—	—	—	—	—	—	0	7
1998	NO	11(0)	—	—	—	—	1	8	8.0(8)	0	—	—	—	—	—	—	—	—	—	—	—	—	0	4
NFL	3	27(8)	—	—	—	—	9	97	10.8(17)	1	—	—	—	—	—	—	—	—	—	—	—	—	6	54

JOHNSON, TRACY Tracy Illya, RB, 6´0˝/234 lbs; Clemson; 1989: Hou, rnd 10; B11/29/1966 Concord, NC

1989	†Hou	16(0)	4	16	4.0(8)	0	1	8	8.0(8)	0	—	—	—	—	—	—	—	—	—	—	k	—	0	49
1990	Atl	16(4)	30	106	3.5(12)	3	10	79	7.9(16)	1	—	—	—	—	—	—	—	—	—	—	k	—	24	153
1991	†Atl	16(5, rb)	8	26	3.3(6)	0	3	27	9.0(13)	0	—	—	—	—	—	—	—	—	—	—	—	—	0	40
1992	Sea	16(0)	3	26	8.7(19)	0	—	—	—	—	—	—	—	—	—	—	—	—	—	—	k	—	0	26
1993	Sea	16(1)	2	8	4.0(5)	0	3	15	5.0(8)	1	—	—	—	—	—	—	—	—	—	—	—	—	6	21
1994	Sea	16(11, FB)	12	44	3.7(14)	2	10	91	9.1(17)	0	—	—	—	—	—	—	—	—	—	—	—	—	12	110
1995	Sea	15(4)	1	2	2.0(2)	1	1	-2	-2.0(-2)	0	—	—	—	—	—	—	—	—	—	—	—	—	6	11
1996	TB	10(0)	—	—	—	—	—	—	—	—	—	—	—	—	—	—	—	—	—	—	—	—	—	—
NFL	8	121(25)	60	228	3.8(19)	6	28	218	7.8(17)	2	—	—	—	—	—	—	—	—	—	—	k	—	48	408

JOHNSON, TRAVIS Travis, DT, 6´4˝/290 lbs; Florida State; 2005: Hou, rnd 1; B4/26/1982 Sherman Oaks, CA   **2005** Hou 15 (3)

JOHNSON, TRE´ Edward Stanton, G-T, 6´2˝/328 lbs; Temple; 1994: Was, rnd 2; B8/30/1971 New York, NY   **1994** Was 14 (1) **1995** Was 10 (9, RG) **1996** Was 15 (15, LG) **1997** Was 11 (11, RG/lg) **1998** Was 10 (10, LG) **1999**†Was★16 (16, RG) **2000** Was 4 (4) **2001** Cle 3 (3) **2002** Was 10 (3) **NFL** 93 (72) [9 yrs]

YEAR	TEAM	G (GS, POS)	RUSH	YD	AVG (LG)	TD	REC	YD	AVG (LG)	TD	PASS	COMP	PCT	YD	AVG (LG)	TD	INT	SK	YD	QBR	KPR	OTD	PTS	TAY

JOHNSON, TREVOR Trevor, DE, 6´4˝/255 lbs; Nebraska; 2004: NYJ, rnd 7; B2/26/1981 Gordon, NE **2004**†NYJ 16 (0) **2005** NYJ 9 (0) **NFL** 25 (0) [2 yrs]

JOHNSON, TROY Troy Dwan, WR, 6´1˝/180 lbs; Southeastern Louisiana; Southern (LA); B10/20/1962 New Orleans, LA

1986	SL	13(2)	—	—	—		14	203	14.5(39)	0	—	—	—	—	—		—	—	—		k	—	0	103
1987	SL	14(2)	1	9	9.0(9)	0	15	308	20.5(49)	2	—	—	—	—	—		—	—	—		—	—	12	173
1988	Pit	14(0)	—	—	—		10	237	23.7(60)	0	—	—	—	—	—		—	—	—		—	—	0	119
1989	Det	9(2)	—	—	—		2	29	14.5(22)	0	—	—	—	—	—		—	—	—		—	—	0	15
NFL	**4**	50(6)	1	9	9.0(9)	0	41	777	19.0(60)	2	—	—	—	—	—		—	—	—		k	—	12	409

JOHNSON, TROY Troy Antwain, LB-DE, 6´2˝/236 lbs; Oklahoma; 1988: Chi, rnd 5; B11/10/1964 Houston, TX **1988**†ChiB 16 (1) **1989** ChiB 7 (0) **1990** NYJ 16 (4) **1991**†NYJ 16 (0) **1992** Det 9 (0) **NFL** 64 (5) [5 yrs]

JOHNSON, TRUMAINE Trumaine, WR, 6´1˝/196 lbs; Grambling State; 1983: SD, rnd 6; B11/16/1960 Bogalusa, LA

1985	SD	11(2)	—	—	—		4	51	12.8(20)	1	—	—	—	—	—		—	—	—		—	—	6	31
1986	SD	16(4)	—	—	—		30	399	13.3(30)	1	—	—	—	—	—		—	—	—		k	—	6	208
1987	Buf	12(0)	—	—	—		15	186	12.4(26)	2	—	—	—	—	—		—	—	—		—	—	12	103
1988	†Buf	16(10, WR)	—	—	—		37	514	13.9(49)	0	—	—	—	—	—		—	—	—		—	—	0	257
NFL	**4**	55(16)	—	—	—		86	1150	13.4(49)	4	—	—	—	—	—		—	—	—		k	—	24	598

JOHNSON, TYRONE Tyrone Benjamin, WR, 5´11˝/171 lbs; Western State (CO); B9/4/1971 Denver, CO **1994** NO 1 (0)

JOHNSON, UNDRA Undra Jerome, RB, 5´9˝/199 lbs; West Virginia; 1989: Atl, rnd 7; B1/8/1966 Valdosta, GA **1989** NO 5 (0) **1989** Atl 1 (0) **NFL** 6 (0) [1 yr]

JOHNSON, VANCE Vance Edward, WR, 5´11˝/185 lbs; Arizona; 1985: Den, rnd 2; B3/13/1963 Trenton, NJ [R]

1985	Den	16(7, wr)	10	36	3.6(14)	0	51	721	14.1(63)	3	0	0	0.0	0	0	0	—	—	—		kp	—	18	812
1986	†Den	12(7, WR)	5	15	3.0(6)	0	31	363	11.7(34)	2	1	0	0.0	0	0	0	—	—	—		kp	—	12	219
1987	†Den	11(9, WR)	1	-8	-8.0(-8)	0	42	684	16.3(59)	7	1	0	0.0	0	0	0	—	—	—		kp	—	42	408
1988	Den	16(13, WR)	1	1	1.0(1)	0	68	896	13.2(86)	5	—	—	—	—	—		—	—	—		p	—	30	474
1989	†Den	16(16, WR)	—	—	—		76	1095	14.4(69)	7	1	0	0.0	0	0	0	—	—	—		p	—	42	641
1990	Den	16(13, WR)	—	—	—		54	747	13.8(49)	3	—	—	—	—	—		—	—	—		kp	—	18	462
1991	†Den	10(0)	—	—	—		21	208	9.9(22)	3	—	—	—	—	—		—	—	—		p	—	18	173
1992	Den	11(7, WR)	—	—	—		24	294	12.3(40)	2	—	—	—	—	—		—	—	—		—	—	12	157
1993	Den	10(8, wr)	—	—	—		36	517	14.4(56)	5	—	—	—	—	—		—	—	—		—	—	30	284
1995	Den	10(1)	—	—	—		12	170	14.2(23)	0	—	—	—	—	—		—	—	—		—	—	0	85
NFL	**10**	128(81)	17	44	2.6(14)	0	415	5695	13.7(86)	37	4	0	0.0	0	0	0	—	—	—		kp	—	222	3713

JOHNSON, VAUGHAN Vaughan Monroe, LB, 6´3˝/235 lbs; North Carolina State; 1984: NO, rnd S1; B3/24/1962 Morehead City, NC **1986** NO 16 (0) **1987**†NO☆12 (12, RILB) **1988**☆16 (16, RILB) **1989** NO★16 (16, RILB) **1990**†NO★16 (16, RILB) **1991**†NO★13 (11, RILB) **1992**†NO★16 (14, RILB) **1993** NO 15 (13, RILB) **1994** Phi 4 (0) **NFL** 124 (98) [9 yrs]

JOHNSON, WALT Walter, DT, 6´1˝/250 lbs; Pittsburgh; B9/13/1965 **1987** Dal 1 (0)

JOHNSON, WALTER Walter, DT, 6´4˝/265 lbs; New Mexico State; Los Angeles State; 1965: Cle, rnd 2/Den, rnd R2; B11/13/1942 Cincinnati, OH, D6/29/1999 Cleveland, OH **1965**†Cle 14 **1966** Cle 14 (LDT) **1967**†Cle◇14 (LDT/rdt) **1968**†Cle☆14 (LDT) **1969**☆Cle◇14 (LDT) **1970** Cle 14 (LDT) **1971** Cle 14 (LDT) **1972**†Cle 14 (LDT) **1973** Cle 14 (LDT) **1974** Cle 14 (LDT) **1975** Cle 14 (13, LDT) **1976** Cle 14 (LDT) **1977** Cin 14 **NFL** 182 (13) [13 yrs]

JOHNSON, WALTER Walter Ulysses, LB, 6´0˝/241 lbs; Louisiana Tech; 1987: Hou, rnd 2; B11/13/1963 Monroe, LA **1987**†Hou 10 (0) **1988**†Hou 16 (0) **1989** NO 15 (0) **NFL** 41 (0) [3 yrs]

JOHNSON, WALTER Walter Clarke, DE, 6´5˝/235 lbs; Tuskegee; 1967: SF, rnd 8; B11/25/1943 Lithonia, GA **1967** SF 1

JOHNSON, WILL William Alexander, LB, 6´4˝/245 lbs; Louisiana-Monroe; 1987: Chi, rnd 5; B12/4/1964 Monroe, LA **1987**†ChiB 11 (0)

JOHNSOS, LUKE Luke Andrew, E, 6´2˝/195 lbs; Northwestern; B12/6/1905 Chicago, IL, D12/10/1984 Evanston, IL [KC]

1929	ChiB☆	15(13, RE/le)	—	—	—		—	—	—		—	—	—	—	—		—	—	—		—	—	—	—
1930	ChiB☆	14(12, LE)	—	—	—		—	—	—		—	—	—	—	—		—	—	—		—	—	—	—
1931	ChiB☆	13(13, LE)	—	—	—		—	—	—		—	—	—	—	—		—	—	—		—	—	—	—
1932	ChiB☆	14(13, LE)	—	—	—		19	321	**16.9**	2	—	—	—	—	—		—	—	—		K	2	26	181
1933	ChiB	6(6, re)	—	—	—		10	188	18.8	**3**	—	—	—	—	—		—	—	—		K	—	19	109
1934	†ChiB	13(2)	—	—	—		5	57	11.4	1	—	—	—	—	—		—	—	—		—	—	6	34
1935	ChiB	12(2)	1	4	4.0(4)	0	19	298	15.7	4	—	—	—	—	—		—	—	—		—	—	24	173
1936	ChiB	12(3)	—	—	—		5	121	24.2	2	—	—	—	—	—		—	—	—		—	—	12	71
NFL	**8**	99(64)	1	4	4.0(4)	0	58	985	17.0	20	—	—	—	—	—		—	—	—		K	2	146	607

JOHNSTON, BRIAN Joseph Brian, C, 6´3˝/275 lbs; North Carolina; 1985: NYG, rnd 3; B11/26/1962 Highland, MD **1986**†NYG 4 (0) **1987** NYG 5 (0) **NFL** 9 (0) [2 yrs]

JOHNSTON, DARYL Daryl Peter 'Moose', RB, 6´2˝/238 lbs; Syracuse; 1989: Dal, rnd 2; B2/10/1966 Youngstown, NY

1989	Dal	16(10, FB)	67	212	3.2(13)	0	16	133	8.3(28)	3	—	—	—	—	—		—	—	—		—	—	18	294
1990	Dal	16(16)	10	35	3.5(8)	1	14	148	10.6(26)	1	—	—	—	—	—		—	—	—		—	—	12	124
1991	†Dal	16(14, FB)	17	54	3.2(10)	0	28	244	8.7(22)	1	—	—	—	—	—		—	—	—		—	—	6	181
1992	†Dal	16(16, FB)	17	61	3.6(14)	0	32	249	7.8(18)	2	—	—	—	—	—		—	—	—		—	—	12	196
1993	†Dal◇	16(16, FB)	24	74	3.1(11)	3	50	372	7.4(20)	1	—	—	—	—	—		—	—	—		—	—	24	295
1994	†Dal◇	16(16, FB)	40	138	3.5(9)	2	44	325	7.4(24)	2	—	—	—	—	—		—	—	—		—	—	24	331
1995	†Dal	16(16, FB)	25	111	4.4(18)	2	30	248	8.3(24)	1	—	—	—	—	—		—	—	—		—	—	18	260
1996	†Dal	16(15, FB)	22	48	2.2(7)	0	43	278	6.5(23)	1	—	—	—	—	—		—	—	—		—	—	6	192
1997	Dal	6(6, FB)	2	3	1.5(3)	0	18	166	9.2(21)	1	—	—	—	—	—		—	—	—		—	—	6	91
1998	†Dal	16(13, FB)	8	17	2.1(6)	0	18	60	3.3(9)	1	—	—	—	—	—		—	—	—		—	—	6	52
1999	Dal	1(0)	—	—	—		1	4	4.0(4)	0	—	—	—	—	—		—	—	—		—	—	0	2
NFL	**11**	151(122)	232	753	3.2(18)	8	294	2227	7.6(28)	14	—	—	—	—	—		—	—	—		—	—	132	2017

JOHNSTON, JIMMY James Everett, B, 6´1˝/193 lbs; Washington; 1939: Was, rnd 10; B4/16/1917 Parma, ID, D11/27/1973 Caldwell, ID [K]

1939	Was	11(5, WB)	7	47	6.7	0	11	111	10.1	1	—	—	—	—	—		—	—	—		KP	—	7	108
1940	†Was	11(11, FB)	87	256	2.9(65)	3	29	350	12.1(45)	3	—	—	—	—	—		—	—	—		Pi	1	42	546
1946	ChiC	6(0)	6	18	3.0(11)	0	—	—	—		—	—	—	—	—		—	—	—		ki	—	0	25
NFL	**3**	28(16)	100	321	3.2(65)	3	40	461	11.5(45)	4	—	—	—	—	—		—	—	—		KPki	1	49	679

JOHNSTON, MARK Mark Ronald, DB, 6´0˝/203 lbs; Northwestern; B3/4/1938 Sycamore, IL **1960**†Hou-A☆14 (RCB) **1961**†Hou-A★14 (RCB) **1962**†Hou-A 14 (RCB) **1963** Hou-A 14 **1964** Oak-A 1 **1964** NYJ-A 8 (LCB) **NFL** 65 [5 yrs]

JOHNSTON, PRES Luther Preston, HB-FB-LB, 6´0˝/205 lbs; SMU; 1942: GB, rnd 7; B10/12/1921 Newcastle, TX, D1/15/1979 Lubbock, TX [K]

1946	Mia-A	3(2)	30	165	5.5	2	4	35	8.8	0	1	1	100.0	9	9.0(9)	0	0	—	—		KP	—	1	207
1946	Buf-A	8(5, lh)	15	53	3.5	0	2	19	9.5	1	—	—	—	—	—		—	—	—		Pki	—	18	69
AAFC	**1**	11(7)	45	218	4.8	2	6	54	9.0	1	1	1	100.0	9	9.0(9)	0	0	—	—		KPki	—	19	276

JOHNSTON, REX Rex David, HB, 6´1˝/195 lbs; USC; B11/8/1937 Colton, CA

| 1960 | Pit | 12 | 4 | 12 | 3.0(17) | 0 | — | — | — | | — | — | — | — | — | | — | — | — | | kp | — | 0 | 120 |

JOHNSTON, SWEDE Chester Arthur, B, 5´10˝/197 lbs; Marquette; Miami (FL); Elmhurst; B3/7/1910 Appleton, WI, D9/19/2002 St. Louis, MO

1931	GB	2(0)	—	—	—		—	—	—		—	—	—	—	—		—	—	—		—	—	—	—
1933	ChiC	1(0)	—	—	—		—	—	—		—	—	—	—	—		—	—	—		—	—	—	—
1934	GB	1(1)	7	23	3.3		—	—	—		—	—	—	—	—		—	—	—		—	—	0	23
1934	SL	3(2, FB)	35	84	2.4	1	1	25	25.0(25)	0	4	3	75.0	17	4.3	0	0	—	—		—	—	6	115
1935	GB	11(3)	52	176	3.4	0	6	59	9.8	1	—	—	—	—	—		—	—	—		—	—	6	211
1936	†GB	9(2)	42	110	2.6	1	2	11	5.5	0	—	—	—	—	—		—	—	—		—	—	6	126
1937	GB	1(0)	—	—	—		—	—	—		—	—	—	—	—		—	—	—		—	—	—	—
1938	†GB	2(0)	—	—	—		—	—	—		—	—	—	—	—		—	—	—		—	—	—	—
1939	Pit	8(2)	59	220	3.7	2	—	—	—		—	—	—	—	—		—	—	—		P	—	12	240

YEAR	TEAM	G (GS, POS)	RUSH	YD	AVG (LG)	TD	REC	YD	AVG (LG)	TD	PASS	COMP	PCT	YD	AVG (LG)	TD	INT	SK	YD	QBR	KPR	OTD	PTS	TAY
1940	Pit	10 (3)	41	113	2.8	0	—	—	—	—	—	—	—	—	—	—	—	—	—	—	P	—	0	113
NFL	9	48 (13)	236	726	3.1	4	9	95	10.6 (25)	1	4	3	75.0	17	4.3	0	0	—	—	—	P	—	30	827

Johnstone, Lance Lance, DE, 6´4˝/250 lbs; Temple; 1996: Oak, rnd 2; B6/11/1973 Philadelphia, PA **[S]** **1996** Oak 16 (10, LDE) **1997** Oak 14 (6, lde) **1998** Oak 16 (15, RDE) **1999** Oak 16 (16, RDE) **2000**†Oak 14 (9, RDE) **2001** Min 16 (5, rde) **2002** Min 16 (16, RDE) **2003** Min 16 (0) **2004**†Min 16 (1) **2005** Min 15 (1) **NFL** 155 (79) [10 yrs]

Joiner, Charlie Charles, WR, 5´11˝/188 lbs; Grambling State; 1969: Hou, rnd 4; B10/14/1947 Many, LA; HOF 1996

YEAR	TEAM	G (GS, POS)	RUSH	YD	AVG (LG)	TD	REC	YD	AVG (LG)	TD	PASS	COMP	PCT	YD	AVG (LG)	TD	INT	SK	YD	QBR	KPR	OTD	PTS	TAY
1969	Hou-A	7	—	—	—	—	7	77	11.0 (16)	0	—	—	—	—	—	—	—	—	—	—	k	—	0	67
1970	Hou	9 (8, WR)	—	—	—	—	28	416	14.9 (**87**)	3	—	—	—	—	—	—	—	—	—	—	—	—	18	223
1971	Hou	14 (13, WR)	—	—	—	—	31	681	22.0 (70)	7	—	—	—	—	—	—	—	—	—	—	k	—	42	386
1972	Hou	6 (WR)	2	12	6.0 (9)	0	16	306	19.1 (82)	2	—	—	—	—	—	—	—	—	—	—	—	—	12	175
1972	Cin	6	1	2	2.0 (2)	0	8	133	16.6 (25)	0	—	—	—	—	—	—	—	—	—	—	k	—	0	82
1973	†Cin	5 (4)	—	—	—	—	13	214	16.5 (26)	0	—	—	—	—	—	—	—	—	—	—	—	—	0	107
1974	Cin	14 (12, WR)	4	20	5.0 (8)	0	24	390	16.3 (65)	1	—	—	—	—	—	—	—	—	—	—	—	—	6	220
1975	†Cin	14 (11, WR)	—	—	—	—	37	726	19.6 (51)	5	—	—	—	—	—	—	—	—	—	—	—	—	30	388
1976	SD★	14 (14, WR)	—	—	—	—	50	1056	21.1 (81)	7	1	0	0.0	0	0.0	0	0	—	—	—	—	—	42	563
1977	SD	14 (14, WR)	—	—	—	—	35	542	15.5 (32)	6	—	—	—	—	—	—	—	—	—	—	k	—	36	294
1978	SD	16 (15, WR)	—	—	—	—	33	607	18.4 (46)	1	—	—	—	—	—	—	—	—	—	—	—	—	6	309
1979	†SD✧	16 (16, WR)	1	-12	-12.0 (-12)	0	72	1008	14.0 (39)	4	—	—	—	—	—	—	—	—	—	—	—	—	24	512
1980	†SD★	16 (16, WR)	—	—	—	—	71	1132	15.9 (51)	4	—	—	—	—	—	—	—	—	—	—	—	—	24	586
1981	†SD	16 (16, WR)	—	—	—	—	70	1188	17.0 (57)	7	—	—	—	—	—	—	—	—	—	—	—	—	42	629
1982	†SD	9 (9, WR)	—	—	—	—	36	545	15.1 (43)	0	—	—	—	—	—	—	—	—	—	—	—	—	0	273
1983	SD	16 (16, WR)	—	—	—	—	65	960	14.8 (33)	3	—	—	—	—	—	—	—	—	—	—	—	—	18	495
1984	SD	16 (16, WR)	—	—	—	—	61	793	13.0 (41)	6	—	—	—	—	—	—	—	—	—	—	—	—	36	427
1985	SD	16 (14, WR)	—	—	—	—	59	932	15.8 (39)	7	—	—	—	—	—	—	—	—	—	—	—	—	42	501
1986	SD	15 (9, WR)	—	—	—	—	34	440	12.9 (33)	2	—	—	—	—	—	—	—	—	—	—	—	—	12	230
NFL	18	239 (203)	8	22	2.8 (9)	0	750	12146	16.2 (87)	65	1	0	0.0	0	0.0	0	0	—	—	—	k	—	390	6464

Joiner, Tim Timothy Lane, LB, 6´4˝/235 lbs; LSU; 1983: Hou, rnd 3; B1/7/1961 Monrovia, CA **1983** Hou 15 (0) **1984** Hou 11 (0) **1987** Den 3 (3) **NFL** 29 (3) [3 yrs]

Joines, Vernon Vernon Willis, WR, 6´2˝/200 lbs; Maryland; 1989: Cle, rnd 5; B6/20/1965 Charlotte, NC **1989** Cle 4 (0)

YEAR	TEAM	G (GS, POS)	RUSH	YD	AVG (LG)	TD	REC	YD	AVG (LG)	TD	PASS	COMP	PCT	YD	AVG (LG)	TD	INT	SK	YD	QBR	KPR	OTD	PTS	TAY
1990	Cle	16 (0)	—	—	—	—	6	86	14.3 (24)	0	—	—	—	—	—	—	—	—	—	—	—	—	0	43
NFL	2	20 (0)	—	—	—	—	6	86	14.3 (24)	0	—	—	—	—	—	—	—	—	—	—	k	—	0	40

Jolitz, Evan Evan C., LB, 6´2˝/225 lbs; Xavier (OH); Cincinnati; 1974: Cin, rnd 3; B7/26/1951 St. Mary's, OH **1974** Cin 12

Jolley, Al Alvin Jay, T, 6´2˝/220 lbs; Tulsa; Kansas State; Marietta; B9/29/1899 Onago, KS, D8/26/1948 Marietta, OH **[C]** **1922** Akr 10 (8, LT) **1923** Day 1 (1) **1923** Oor 3 (3) **1929** Buf 7 (6, LT) **1930** Bkn 8 (5, lt) **1931** Cle 6 (3) **NFL** 35 (26) [5 yrs]

Jolley, Doug Doug, TE, 6´4˝/250 lbs; Brigham Young; 2002: Oak, rnd 2; B1/2/1979 Sandy, UT

YEAR	TEAM	G (GS, POS)	RUSH	YD	AVG (LG)	TD	REC	YD	AVG (LG)	TD	PASS	COMP	PCT	YD	AVG (LG)	TD	INT	SK	YD	QBR	KPR	OTD	PTS	TAY
2002	†Oak	16 (4)	—	—	—	—	32	409	12.8 (33)	2	—	—	—	—	—	—	—	—	—	—	—	—	12	215
2003	Oak	15 (10, TE)	—	—	—	—	31	250	8.1 (26)	1	—	—	—	—	—	—	—	—	—	—	—	—	6	130
2004	Oak	16 (13, TE)	—	—	—	—	27	313	11.6 (34)	2	—	—	—	—	—	—	—	—	—	—	—	—	12	167
2005	NYJ	16 (7, te)	—	—	—	—	29	324	11.2 (60)	1	—	—	—	—	—	—	—	—	—	—	—	—	6	167
NFL	4	63 (34)	—	—	—	—	119	1296	10.9 (60)	6	—	—	—	—	—	—	—	—	—	—	—	—	36	678

Jolley, Gordon Gordon Harold, G-T, 6´5˝/250 lbs; Utah; 1971: Det, rnd 17; B5/22/1949 Provo, UT **1972** Det 5 **1973** Det 14 **1974** Det 11 (2) **1975** Det 2 (2) **1976** Sea 14 (4) **1977** Sea 13 (11, LG) **NFL** 59 (19) [6 yrs]

Jolley, Lewis Lewis Elman, RB, 5´11˝/210 lbs; North Carolina; 1972: Hou, rnd 3; B11/15/1949 Bostic, NC **1972** Hou 7

YEAR	TEAM	G (GS, POS)	RUSH	YD	AVG (LG)	TD	REC	YD	AVG (LG)	TD	PASS	COMP	PCT	YD	AVG (LG)	TD	INT	SK	YD	QBR	KPR	OTD	PTS	TAY
1973	Hou	10	7	6	0.9 (3)	0	3	56	18.7 (48)	0	—	—	—	—	—	—	—	—	—	—	k	—	0	45
NFL	2	17	7	6	0.9 (3)	0	3	56	18.7 (48)	0	—	—	—	—	—	—	—	—	—	—	k	—	0	147

Jolly, Ken Kenneth Clay, LB, 6´2˝/220 lbs; Park; MidAmerican Nazarene; B2/28/1962 Dallas, TX **1984** KC 16 (0) **1985** KC 16 (12, ROLB) **NFL** 32 (12) [2 yrs]

Jolly, Mike Michael Anthony Joseph, DB, 6´3˝/188 lbs; Michigan; 1980: NO, rnd 4; B3/19/1958 Detroit, MI **1980** GB 16 (0) **1982**†GB 7 (0) **1983** GB 12 (0) **NFL** 35 (0) [3 yrs]

Jonas, Don Donald Walter, HB, 5´11˝/195 lbs; Penn State; 1961: Phi, rnd 13/1962: NYT, rnd 32; B12/3/1938 Scranton, PA **1962** Phi 1

Jonas, Marvin Marvin Frederick, G, 5´11˝/186 lbs; Utah; B4/25/1909 Salt Lake City, UT, D1/15/1987 Burbank, CA **1931** Bkn 2 (0)

Jonasen, Charlie Charles, E, none; B12/20/1892 Minneapolis, MN, D3/9/1989 Minneapolis, MN **1921** Min 1 (0)

Jonasen, Eric Eric Gustav, T, 6´5˝/310 lbs; Penn State; Bloomsburg; 1992: SD, rnd 5; B8/16/1968 Baltimore, MD **1993** SD 16 (2) **1994**†SD 16 (0) **NFL** 32 (2) [2 yrs]

Jones TB, none **1921** Ham 1 (0)

Jones, A.J. Anthony Levine, RB, 6´1˝/202 lbs; Texas; 1982: LARm, rnd 8; B5/30/1959 Youngstown, OH **1982** LARm 6 (0) **1983**†LARm 9 (0) **1984** LARm 13 (0) **1985** LARm 1 (0)

YEAR	TEAM	G (GS, POS)	RUSH	YD	AVG (LG)	TD	REC	YD	AVG (LG)	TD	PASS	COMP	PCT	YD	AVG (LG)	TD	INT	SK	YD	QBR	KPR	OTD	PTS	TAY
1985	Det	8 (0)	1	2	2.0 (2)	0	—	—	—	—	—	—	—	—	—	—	—	—	—	—	k	—	0	78
NFL	4	37 (0)	1	2	2.0 (2)	0	—	—	—	—	—	—	—	—	—	—	—	—	—	—	k	—	0	78

Jones, Aaron Aaron Delmas, DE-LB, 6´5˝/261 lbs; Eastern Kentucky; 1988: Pit, rnd 1; B12/18/1966 Orlando, FL **1988** Pit 15 (12, ROLB/lde) **1989**†Pit 16 (2) **1990** Pit 7 (1) **1991** Pit 16 (7, LDE) **1992**†Pit 13 (0) **1993** NE 11 (1) **1994**†NE 16 (0) **1995** NE 10 (0) **1996** Mia 8 (0) **NFL** 112 (23) [9 yrs]

Jones, Adrian Adrian, T, 6´5˝/265 lbs; Kansas; 2004: NYJ, rnd 4; B6/10/1981 Dallas, TX **2004**†NYJ 12 (0) **2005** NYJ 16 (16, LT) **NFL** 28 (16) [2 yrs]

Jones, Aki Aki, DE-DT, 6´4˝/276 lbs; Fordham; B5/21/1982 Jamaica, NY **2005** Was 4 (0)

Jones, Andre Andre Fitzgerald, LB, 6´2˝/245 lbs; Notre Dame; 1991: Pit, rnd 7; B5/15/1969 Washington, DC **1992** Det 6 (0)

Jones, Andrew Andrew Lee, RB, 6´2˝/216 lbs; Washington State; 1975: NO, rnd 3; B10/23/1951 Jackson, MS

YEAR	TEAM	G (GS, POS)	RUSH	YD	AVG (LG)	TD	REC	YD	AVG (LG)	TD	PASS	COMP	PCT	YD	AVG (LG)	TD	INT	SK	YD	QBR	KPR	OTD	PTS	TAY
1975	NO	13	42	108	2.6 (18)	1	10	52	5.2 (12)	0	—	—	—	—	—	—	—	—	—	—	—	—	6	144
1976	NO	2	1	2	2.0 (2)	0	—	—	—	—	—	—	—	—	—	—	—	—	—	—	—	—	0	2
NFL	2	15	43	110	2.6 (18)	1	10	52	5.2 (12)	0	—	—	—	—	—	—	—	—	—	—	—	—	6	146

Jones, Anthony Anthony Andrew, TE, 6´3˝/248 lbs; Maryland-Eastern Shore; Wichita State; 1984: Was, rnd 11; B5/16/1960 Baltimore, MD **1985** Was 16 (2) **1986** Was 15 (1) **1987**†Was 2 (0)

YEAR	TEAM	G (GS, POS)	RUSH	YD	AVG (LG)	TD	REC	YD	AVG (LG)	TD	PASS	COMP	PCT	YD	AVG (LG)	TD	INT	SK	YD	QBR	KPR	OTD	PTS	TAY
1984	Was	16 (0)	—	—	—	—	1	6	6.0 (6)	0	—	—	—	—	—	—	—	—	—	—	—	—	0	3
1988	Was	8 (3)	—	—	—	—	2	10	5.0 (9)	0	—	—	—	—	—	—	—	—	—	—	—	—	0	5
1988	SD	4 (1)	—	—	—	—	1	11	11.0 (11)	0	—	—	—	—	—	—	—	—	—	—	k	—	0	4
NFL	5	61 (7)	—	—	—	—	4	27	6.8 (11)	0	—	—	—	—	—	—	—	—	—	—	k	—	0	-4

Jones, Arrington Arrington, RB, 6´0˝/225 lbs; Winston-Salem State; 1981: SF, rnd 5; B12/16/1959 Richmond, VA **1981** SF 1 (0)

Jones, Art Arthur Edward, WB-DB-HB-TB, 6´2˝/192 lbs; Richmond; 1941: Phi, rnd 2; B6/13/1919 Farmville, VA, D8/29/1995 Suffolk, VA

YEAR	TEAM	G (GS, POS)	RUSH	YD	AVG (LG)	TD	REC	YD	AVG (LG)	TD	PASS	COMP	PCT	YD	AVG (LG)	TD	INT	SK	YD	QBR	KPR	OTD	PTS	TAY
1941	Pit★	11 (9, WB)	62	239	3.9 (34)	4	4	121	30.3 (59)	1	23	6	26.1	86	3.7 (19)	0	3	—	—	—	Pkpi	—	30	447
1945	Pit	7 (2)	16	64	4.0 (20)	0	5	8	1.6 (6)	0	—	—	—	—	—	—	—	—	—	—	kpi	—	0	128
NFL	2	18 (11)	78	303	3.9 (34)	4	9	129	14.3 (59)	1	23	6	26.1	86	3.7 (19)	0	3	—	—	—	Pkpi	—	30	575

Jones, Ben Benjamin F.H., FB-BB-TB-WB, 5´11˝/205 lbs; Indiana (P); Grove City; B1897 Du Bois, PA, D5/17/1929 Grove City, PA **[K]** **1923** Can☆11 (5, fb), 36 **1924** Cle 8 (6, FB), 25 **1925** Can 6 (6, TB), 12 **1925** Fra 5 (3), 12 **1926** Fra 14 (13, BB), 54 **1927** ChiC 9 (9, BB), 12 **1928** ChiC 5 (4, FB) **NFL** 58 (46), 151 [6 yrs]

Jones, Bert Bertram Hays, QB, 6´3˝/210 lbs; LSU; 1973: Bal, rnd 1; B9/7/1951 Ruston, LA

YEAR	TEAM	G (GS, POS)	RUSH	YD	AVG (LG)	TD	REC	YD	AVG (LG)	TD	PASS	COMP	PCT	YD	AVG (LG)	TD	INT	SK	YD	QBR	KPR	OTD	PTS	TAY
1973	Bal	8 (5, qb)	18	58	3.2 (17)	0	—	—	—	—	108	43	39.8	539	5.0 (51)	4	12	14	126	28.8	—	—	0	-133
1974	Bal	11 (8, QB)	39	279	7.2 (39)	4	—	—	—	—	270	143	53.0	1610	6.0 (57)	8	12	36	328	62.4	—	—	24	684
1975	†Bal	14 (14, QB)	47	321	6.8 (36)	3	—	—	—	—	344	203	59.0	2483	7.2 (90)	18	8	38	325	89.1	—	—	18	1363
1976	†Bal★	14 (14, QB)	38	214	5.6 (17)	2	—	—	—	—	343	207	60.3	**3104**	9.0 (79)	24	9	29	284	102.5	—	—	12	1546
1977	†Bal☆	14 (14, QB)	28	146	5.2 (22)	2	—	—	—	—	393	**224**	57.0	2686	6.8 (78)	17	11	26	221	80.8	—	—	12	1154
1978	Bal	3 (3)	9	38	4.2 (14)	0	—	—	—	—	42	27	64.3	370	8.8 (78)	4	1	6	62	—	—	—	0	203
1979	Bal	4 (4)	10	40	4.0 (25)	1	—	—	—	—	92	43	46.7	643	7.0 (59)	3	3	10	77	—	—	—	6	267

YEAR	TEAM	G(GS, POS)	RUSH	YD	AVG(LG)	TD	REC	YD	AVG(LG)	TD	PASS	COMP	PCT	YD	AVG(LG)	TD	INT	SK	YD	QBR	KPR	OTD	PTS	TAY
1980	Bal	15(15, QB)	27	175	6.5(19)	2	—	—	—	—	446	248	55.6	3134	7.0(47)	23	21	34	262	75.3	—	—	12	1037
1981	Bal	15(15, QB)	20	85	4.3(17)	0	—	—	—	—	426	244	57.3	3094	7.3(67)	21	20	31	263	76.9	—	—	0	937
1982	LARm	4(4, qb)	11	73	6.6(17)	0	—	—	—	—	87	48	55.2	527	6.1(51)	2	4	8	72	—	—	—	0	187
NFL	10	102(96)	247	1429	5.8(39)	14	—	—	—	—	2551	1430	56.1	18190	7.1(90)	124	101	232	2020	78.2	—	—	84	7244

JONES, BILL William, RB, 5´11˝/228 lbs; SMU; Southwest Texas State; 1989: KC, rnd 12; B9/10/1966 Abilene, TX

YEAR	TEAM	G(GS, POS)	RUSH	YD	AVG(LG)	TD	REC	YD	AVG(LG)	TD	PASS	COMP	PCT	YD	AVG(LG)	TD	INT	SK	YD	QBR	KPR	OTD	PTS	TAY
1990	†KC	16(5, rb)	10	47	4.7(14)	0	19	137	7.2(19)	5	—	—	—	—	—	—	—	—	—	—	—	—	30	141
1991	†KC	15(14, rb)	—	—	—	—	14	97	6.9(14)	1	—	—	—	—	—	—	—	—	—	—	—	—	6	54
1992	KC	7(6, fb)	—	—	—	—	2	6	3.0(5)	0	—	—	—	—	—	—	—	—	—	—	—	—	0	3
NFL	3	38(25)	10	47	4.7(14)	0	35	240	6.9(19)	6	—	—	—	—	—	—	—	—	—	—	—	—	36	197

JONES, BILLY William H., G, 6´0˝/220 lbs; Charleston (WV); West Virginia Wesleyan; B1/30/1920 Mannington, WV, D2/1988 Lexington, NC **1947** Bkn-A 7 (1)

JONES, BOB Robert, DB, 6´1˝/194 lbs; Virginia Union; 1973: Cin, rnd 6; B2/10/1951 Boardman, FL **1973** Cin 9 **1974** Cin 14 **1976** Atl 14

YEAR	TEAM	G(GS, POS)	RUSH	YD	AVG(LG)	TD	REC	YD	AVG(LG)	TD	PASS	COMP	PCT	YD	AVG(LG)	TD	INT	SK	YD	QBR	KPR	OTD	PTS	TAY
1975	Atl	14	—	—	—	—	1	25	25.0(25)	0	—	—	—	—	—	—	—	—	—	—	—	—	0	13
NFL	4	51	—	—	—	—	1	25	25.0(25)	0	—	—	—	—	—	—	—	—	—	—	kp	—	0	14

JONES, BOB Robert Thomas, DE, 6´3˝/270 lbs; Penn State; B9/3/1978 Barberton, OH **2002** NYG 11 (0)

JONES, BOB Robert Dean, WR, 6´4˝/196 lbs; San Diego State; 1967: Chi, rnd 2; B8/25/1945 Warren, OH **1968** ChiB 1

YEAR	TEAM	G(GS, POS)	RUSH	YD	AVG(LG)	TD	REC	YD	AVG(LG)	TD	PASS	COMP	PCT	YD	AVG(LG)	TD	INT	SK	YD	QBR	KPR	OTD	PTS	TAY
1967	ChiB	14	—	—	—	—	3	80	26.7(51)	1	—	—	—	—	—	—	—	—	—	—	—	—	6	45
NFL	2	15	—	—	—	—	3	80	26.7(51)	1	—	—	—	—	—	—	—	—	—	—	—	—	6	45

JONES, BOBBY Robert Irven, G, 6´2˝/215 lbs; Indiana; B3/28/1912 Wabash, IN **1934** GB 12 (12, RG)

JONES, BOBBY Robert Ellis, WR, 5´11˝/180 lbs; Youngstown State; Millikin; B7/12/1955 Sharon, PA

YEAR	TEAM	G(GS, POS)	RUSH	YD	AVG(LG)	TD	REC	YD	AVG(LG)	TD	PASS	COMP	PCT	YD	AVG(LG)	TD	INT	SK	YD	QBR	KPR	OTD	PTS	TAY
1978	NYJ	16	—	—	—	—	1	18	18.0(18)	0	—	—	—	—	—	—	—	—	—	—	—	—	0	9
1979	NYJ	10(7, wr)	1	4	4.0(4)	0	19	379	19.9(51)	1	—	—	—	—	—	—	—	—	—	—	kp	—	6	234
1980	NYJ	15(5, wr)	—	—	—	—	14	193	13.8(25)	0	—	—	—	—	—	—	—	—	—	—	kp	—	0	112
1981	†NYJ	16(3)	—	—	—	—	16	239	14.9(36)	1	—	—	—	—	—	—	—	—	—	—	p	1	12	121
1982	†NYJ	9(0)	—	—	—	—	3	32	10.7(17)	0	—	—	—	—	—	—	—	—	—	—	—	—	0	16
1983	Cle	15(11, WR)	1	19	19.0(19)	0	36	507	14.1(32)	4	—	—	—	—	—	—	—	—	—	—	—	—	24	293
NFL	6	81(26)	2	23	11.5(19)	0	89	1368	15.4(51)	6	—	—	—	—	—	—	—	—	—	—	kp	1	42	783

JONES, BOYD Boyd Efram, T, 6´3˝/265 lbs; Texas Southern; B5/30/1961 Galveston, TX **1984** GB 2 (0)

JONES, BRANDON Brandon, WR, 6´1˝/208 lbs; Oklahoma; 2005: Ten, rnd 3; B10/6/1982 Texarkana, TX

YEAR	TEAM	G(GS, POS)	RUSH	YD	AVG(LG)	TD	REC	YD	AVG(LG)	TD	PASS	COMP	PCT	YD	AVG(LG)	TD	INT	SK	YD	QBR	KPR	OTD	PTS	TAY
2005	Ten	10(8, WR)	1	1	1.0(1)	0	23	299	13.0(38)	2	—	—	—	—	—	—	—	—	—	—	p	—	12	211

JONES, BRENT Brent Michael, TE, 6´4˝/230 lbs; Santa Clara; 1986: Pit, rnd 5; B2/12/1963 San Jose, CA

YEAR	TEAM	G(GS, POS)	RUSH	YD	AVG(LG)	TD	REC	YD	AVG(LG)	TD	PASS	COMP	PCT	YD	AVG(LG)	TD	INT	SK	YD	QBR	KPR	OTD	PTS	TAY
1987	†SF	4(0)	—	—	—	—	2	35	17.5(22)	0	—	—	—	—	—	—	—	—	—	—	—	—	0	18
1988	†SF	11(0)	—	—	—	—	8	57	7.1(18)	2	—	—	—	—	—	—	—	—	—	—	—	—	12	39
1989	†SF	16(16, TE)	—	—	—	—	40	500	12.5(36)	4	—	—	—	—	—	—	—	—	—	—	—	—	24	270
1990	†SF	16(16, TE)	—	—	—	—	56	747	13.3(67)	5	—	—	—	—	—	—	—	—	—	—	—	—	30	399
1991	SF	10(9, TE)	—	—	—	—	27	417	15.4(41)	0	—	—	—	—	—	—	—	—	—	—	—	—	0	209
1992	†SF★	15(15, TE)	—	—	—	—	45	628	14.0(43)	4	—	—	—	—	—	—	—	—	—	—	—	—	24	334
1993	†SF★	16(16, TE)	—	—	—	—	68	735	10.8(29)	3	—	—	—	—	—	—	—	—	—	—	—	—	18	383
1994	†SF★	15(15, TE)	—	—	—	—	49	670	13.7(69)	9	—	—	—	—	—	—	—	—	—	—	—	—	56	380
1995	†SF✧	16(16, TE)	—	—	—	—	60	595	9.9(39)	3	—	—	—	—	—	—	—	—	—	—	—	—	18	313
1996	†SF	11(10, TE)	—	—	—	—	33	428	13.0(39)	1	—	—	—	—	—	—	—	—	—	—	—	—	6	219
1997	†SF	13(12, TE)	—	—	—	—	29	383	13.2(33)	2	—	—	—	—	—	—	—	—	—	—	—	—	12	202
NFL	11	143(125)	—	—	—	—	417	5195	12.5(69)	33	—	—	—	—	—	—	—	—	—	—	—	—	200	2763

JONES, BRIAN Brian Keith, LB, 6´1˝/250 lbs; UCLA; Texas; 1991: LARd, rnd 8; B1/22/1968 Iowa City, IA **1991** Ind 11 (1) **1995** NO 16 (7, MLB) **1996** NO 16 (1) **1998** NO 1 (0) **NFL** 44 (9) [4 yrs]

JONES, BRIAN Brian, TE, 6´3˝/235 lbs; Louisiana-Lafayette; Arkansas-Pine Bluff; B8/23/1981 Bastrop, LA

YEAR	TEAM	G(GS, POS)	RUSH	YD	AVG(LG)	TD	REC	YD	AVG(LG)	TD	PASS	COMP	PCT	YD	AVG(LG)	TD	INT	SK	YD	QBR	KPR	OTD	PTS	TAY
2004	Jax	16(0)	—	—	—	—	6	87	14.5(26)	1	—	—	—	—	—	—	—	—	—	—	—	—	8	49
2005	†Jax	13(1)	—	—	—	—	3	49	16.3(41)	0	—	—	—	—	—	—	—	—	—	—	—	—	0	25
NFL	2	29(1)	—	—	—	—	9	136	15.1(41)	1	—	—	—	—	—	—	—	—	—	—	—	—	8	73

JONES, BRUCE Robert Bruce, G, 6´1˝/219 lbs; Alabama; B8/30/1904 Jasper, AL, D12/1974 Evergreen, AL **1927** GB 9 (9, RG) **1928** GB 13 (10, RG), 6 **1930** Nwk 2 (1) **1933** Bkn 8 (1) **1934** Bkn 10 (2)

YEAR	TEAM	G(GS, POS)	RUSH	YD	AVG(LG)	TD	REC	YD	AVG(LG)	TD	PASS	COMP	PCT	YD	AVG(LG)	TD	INT	SK	YD	QBR	KPR	OTD	PTS	TAY
1932	Bkn	12(10, LG)	—	—	—	—	1	10	10.0(10)	0	—	—	—	—	—	—	—	—	—	—	—	—	0	5
NFL	6	54(33)	—	—	—	—	1	10	10.0(10)	0	—	—	—	—	—	—	—	—	—	—	—	1	6	15

JONES, BRUCE Bruce Wayne, DB, 6´1˝/197 lbs; North Alabama; 1986: Chi, rnd 7; B12/26/1962 Courtland, AL **1987** Pit 2 (0)

JONES, BRYANT Bryant LyDell, DB, 5´11˝/186 lbs; Toledo; B12/5/1963 Detroit, MI **1987** Ind 3 (3)

JONES, BUCK Horatio, aka White Cloud, E, 6´0˝/210 lbs; Haskell Indian; B10/23/1888 Cattaraugus Indian Reservation, NY, D9/8/1985 Lewiston, NY **1922** Oor 2 (1)

JONES, CALVIN Calvin, DB, 5´7˝/170 lbs; Washington; 1973: Den, rnd 15; B1/26/1951 San Francisco, CA **1973** Den 14 (14, RCB) **1974** Den 14 (14, RCB) **1975** Den 8 (8, RCB) **1976** Den 10 (8, RCB) **NFL** 46 (44) [4 yrs]

JONES, CALVIN Calvin D'Wayne, RB, 5´11˝/205 lbs; Nebraska; 1994: LARd, rnd 3; B11/27/1970 Omaha, NE

YEAR	TEAM	G(GS, POS)	RUSH	YD	AVG(LG)	TD	REC	YD	AVG(LG)	TD	PASS	COMP	PCT	YD	AVG(LG)	TD	INT	SK	YD	QBR	KPR	OTD	PTS	TAY
1994	LARd	7(0)	22	93	4.2(10)	0	2	6	3.0(4)	0	—	—	—	—	—	—	—	—	—	—	—	—	0	96
1995	Oak	9(0)	5	19	3.8(15)	0	—	—	—	—	—	—	—	—	—	—	—	—	—	—	k	—	0	36
1996	†GB	1(0)	—	—	—	—	—	—	—	—	—	—	—	—	—	—	—	—	—	—	—	—	—	—
NFL	3	17(0)	27	112	4.1(15)	0	2	6	3.0(4)	0	—	—	—	—	—	—	—	—	—	—	k	—	0	132

JONES, CEDRIC Cedric Decorrus, WR, 6´1˝/184 lbs; Duke; 1982: NE, rnd 3; B6/1/1960 Norfolk, VA

YEAR	TEAM	G(GS, POS)	RUSH	YD	AVG(LG)	TD	REC	YD	AVG(LG)	TD	PASS	COMP	PCT	YD	AVG(LG)	TD	INT	SK	YD	QBR	KPR	OTD	PTS	TAY
1982	†NE	2(0)	—	—	—	—	1	5	5.0(5)	0	—	—	—	—	—	—	—	—	—	—	—	—	0	3
1983	NE	15(11, WR)	—	—	—	—	20	323	16.1(30)	1	—	—	—	—	—	—	—	—	—	—	k	—	6	170
1984	NE	14(3)	—	—	—	—	19	244	12.8(22)	2	—	—	—	—	—	—	—	—	—	—	k	1	18	137
1985	†NE	16(3)	—	—	—	—	21	237	11.3(29)	2	—	—	—	—	—	—	—	—	—	—	k	1	18	121
1986	†NE	16(0)	1	-7	-7.0(-7)	0	14	222	15.9(28)	1	—	—	—	—	—	—	—	—	—	—	k	—	6	112
1987	NE	12(4)	—	—	—	—	25	388	15.5(29)	3	1	0	0.0	0	0.0	0	0	—	—	—	—	—	18	209
1988	NE	16(2)	—	—	—	—	22	313	14.2(41)	1	—	—	—	—	—	—	—	—	—	—	—	—	6	162
1989	NE	15(12, WR)	1	3	3.0(3)	0	48	670	14.0(65)	6	—	—	—	—	—	—	—	—	—	—	—	—	36	368
1990	NE	14(2)	—	—	—	—	21	301	14.3(26)	0	—	—	—	—	—	—	—	—	—	—	k	—	0	145
NFL	9	120(37)	2	-4	-2.0(3)	0	191	2703	14.2(65)	16	1	0	0.0	0	0.0	0	0	—	—	—	k	2	108	1425

JONES, CEDRIC Cedric L., DE, 6´4˝/275 lbs; Oklahoma; 1996: NYG, rnd 1; B4/30/1974 Houston, TX **1996** NYG 16 (0) **1997** NYG 9 (2) **1998** NYG 16 (1) **1999** NYG 16 (16, RDE) **2000**†NYG 16 (16, RDE) **NFL** 73 (35) [5 yrs]

JONES, CHARLIE Charles Clifford, DE, 6´1˝/202 lbs; George Washington; B1/24/1929 Summers, AR

YEAR	TEAM	G(GS, POS)	RUSH	YD	AVG(LG)	TD	REC	YD	AVG(LG)	TD	PASS	COMP	PCT	YD	AVG(LG)	TD	INT	SK	YD	QBR	KPR	OTD	PTS	TAY
1955	Was	10	—	—	—	—	4	58	14.5(21)	0	—	—	—	—	—	—	—	—	—	—	—	—	0	29

JONES, CHARLIE Charlie Edward, WR, 5´8˝/175 lbs; Fresno State; 1996: SD, rnd 4; B12/1/1972 Hanford, CA

YEAR	TEAM	G(GS, POS)	RUSH	YD	AVG(LG)	TD	REC	YD	AVG(LG)	TD	PASS	COMP	PCT	YD	AVG(LG)	TD	INT	SK	YD	QBR	KPR	OTD	PTS	TAY
1996	SD	14(4)	—	—	—	—	41	524	12.8(63)	4	—	—	—	—	—	—	—	—	—	—	p	—	24	298
1997	SD	16(11, WR)	4	42	10.5(17)	0	32	423	13.2(44)	1	—	—	—	—	—	—	—	—	—	—	—	—	6	259
1998	SD	16(11, WR)	4	39	9.8(14)	0	46	699	15.2(56)	3	—	—	—	—	—	—	—	—	—	—	k	—	18	399
1999	SD	8(1)	1	-8	-8.0(-8)	0	10	90	9.0(44)	1	—	—	—	—	—	—	—	—	—	—	p	—	6	90
NFL	4	54(27)	9	73	8.1(17)	0	129	1736	13.5(63)	9	—	—	—	—	—	—	—	—	—	—	kp	—	54	1045

JONES, CHRIS Chris Juan, C, 6´3˝/263 lbs; Delaware State; B6/26/1964 Norfolk, VA **1987** NYG 3 (3)

JONES, CHRIS T. Christopher Todd, WR, 6´3˝/209 lbs; Miami (FL); 1995: Phi, rnd 3; B8/7/1971 West Palm Beach, FL

YEAR	TEAM	G (GS, POS)	RUSH	YD	AVG (LG)	TD	REC	YD	AVG (LG)	TD	PASS	COMP	PCT	YD	AVG (LG)	TD	INT	SK	YD	QBR	KPR	OTD	PTS	TAY
1995	†Phi	12(0)	—	—	—	—	5	61	12.2(17)	0	—	—	—	—	—	—	—	—	—	—	k	—	0	47
1996	†Phi	16(16, WR)	—	—	—	—	70	859	12.3(38)	5	—	—	—	—	—	—	—	—	—	—	k	—	30	455
1997	Phi	4(1)	—	—	—	—	5	73	14.6(32)	0	—	—	—	—	—	—	—	—	—	—	—	—	0	37
NFL	3	32(17)	—	—	—	—	80	993	12.4(38)	5	—	—	—	—	—	—	—	—	—	—	k	—	30	538

JONES, CLARENCE Clarence Thomas, T, 6´6˝/280 lbs; Maryland; 1991: NYG, rnd 4; B5/6/1968 Brooklyn, NY **1991** NYG 3 (0) **1992** NYG 3 (0) **1993** NYG 4 (0) **1994** LARm 16 (16, LT) **1995** SL 13 (0) **1996** NO 16 (16, RT) **1997** NO 15 (15, RT) **1998** NO 14 (14, RT) **1999** Car 16 (16, LT) **2000** Car 11 (11, LT) **NFL** 111 (88) [10 yrs]

JONES, CLINT Clinton, RB, 6´0˝/205 lbs; Michigan State; 1967: Min, rnd 1; B5/24/1945 Cleveland, OH **[R]**

YEAR	TEAM	G (GS, POS)	RUSH	YD	AVG (LG)	TD	REC	YD	AVG (LG)	TD	PASS	COMP	PCT	YD	AVG (LG)	TD	INT	SK	YD	QBR	KPR	OTD	PTS	TAY
1967	Min	14	13	23	1.8(9)	0	—	—	—	—	—	—	—	—	—	—	—	—	—	—	k	1	6	255
1968	†Min	12(12, HB)	128	536	4.2(43)	1	4	26	6.5(14)	0	—	—	—	—	—	—	—	—	—	—	k	—	6	559
1969	†Min	14	54	241	4.5(80)	3	3	23	7.7(9)	0	—	—	—	—	—	—	—	—	—	—	k	—	18	472
1970	†Min	14	120	369	3.1(23)	9	9	117	13.0(72)	0	—	—	—	—	—	—	—	—	—	—	k	—	54	685
1971	†Min	14(10, RB)	180	675	3.8(73)	4	9	98	10.9(18)	0	—	—	—	—	—	—	—	—	—	—	k	—	24	913
1972	Min	7	52	164	3.2(33)	2	6	42	7.0(10)	0	—	—	—	—	—	—	—	—	—	—	k	—	12	352
1973	SD	12(5, rb)	55	170	3.1(38)	1	7	125	17.9(37)	0	—	—	—	—	—	—	—	—	—	—	k	—	6	310
NFL	7	87(27)	602	2178	3.6(80)	20	38	431	11.3(72)	0	—	—	—	—	—	—	—	—	—	—	k	1	126	3545

JONES, CODY Cody C., DT-DE, 6´5˝/243 lbs; San Jose State; 1973: LA, rnd 5; B5/3/1951 San Francisco, CA **1974**†LARm 12 (1) **1975**†LARm 14 (6, ldt) **1976**†LARm 14 **1977**†LARm 14 (14, RDT) **1978**†LARm✧16 (16, RDT) **1980**†LARm 15 (15, RDT) **1981** LARm 16 (16, RDE) **1982** LARm 9 (9, RDT) **NFL** 110 (77) [8 yrs]

JONES, CURTIS Curtis Warner, LB, 6´2˝/245 lbs; Missouri Southern State; Missouri; B12/20/1943 Stanton, TN, D7/26/1998 Columbia, MO **1968** SD-A 1

JONES, DALE Marvin Dale, LB, 6´1˝/234 lbs; Tennessee; 1987: Dal, rnd 10; B3/8/1963 Cleveland, TN **1987** Dal 3 (3)

JONES, DAMON Damon, TE, 6´5˝/270 lbs; Michigan; Southern Illinois; 1997: Jax, rnd 5; B9/18/1974 Evanston, IL

YEAR	TEAM	G (GS, POS)	RUSH	YD	AVG (LG)	TD	REC	YD	AVG (LG)	TD	PASS	COMP	PCT	YD	AVG (LG)	TD	INT	SK	YD	QBR	KPR	OTD	PTS	TAY
1997	†Jax	11(3)	—	—	—	—	5	87	17.4(26)	2	—	—	—	—	—	—	—	—	—	—	—	—	12	54
1998	†Jax	16(7, te)	—	—	—	—	8	90	11.3(31)	4	—	—	—	—	—	—	—	—	—	—	k	—	24	34
1999	†Jax	15(8, te)	—	—	—	—	19	221	11.6(31)	4	—	—	—	—	—	—	—	—	—	—	—	—	24	131
2000	Jax	1(0)	—	—	—	—	1	12	12.0(12)	0	—	—	—	—	—	—	—	—	—	—	—	—	0	6
2001	Jax	7(4)	—	—	—	—	8	140	17.5(40)	1	—	—	—	—	—	—	—	—	—	—	—	—	6	75
NFL	5	50(22)	—	—	—	—	41	550	13.4(40)	11	—	—	—	—	—	—	—	—	—	—	k	—	66	299

JONES, DAN Daniel T., T, 6´7˝/298 lbs; Maine; B7/22/1970 Malden, MA **1993** Cin 15 (5, rt) **1994** Cin 14 (0) **1995** Cin 5 (0) **NFL** 34 (5) [3 yrs]

JONES, DANTE Dante Delaneo, LB, 6´1˝/235 lbs; Oklahoma; 1988: Chi, rnd 2; B3/23/1965 Dallas, TX **1988**†ChiB 15 (1) **1989** ChiB 10 (1) **1990**†ChiB 2 (0) **1991**†ChiB 16 (0) **1992** ChiB 13 (0) **1993** ChiB 16 (16, MLB) **1994**†ChiB 15 (10, MLB) **1995** Den 5 (5, mlb) **NFL** 92 (33) [8 yrs]

JONES, DARYL Daryl Lawrence, WR, 5´9˝/175 lbs; Miami (FL); 2002: NYG, rnd 7; B2/2/1979 Dallas, TX **2004** ChiB 2 (0)

YEAR	TEAM	G (GS, POS)	RUSH	YD	AVG (LG)	TD	REC	YD	AVG (LG)	TD	PASS	COMP	PCT	YD	AVG (LG)	TD	INT	SK	YD	QBR	KPR	OTD	PTS	TAY
2002	†NYG	13(6, wr)	1	4	4.0(4)	0	8	90	11.3(32)	0	—	—	—	—	—	—	—	—	—	—	kp	—	0	92
NFL	2	15(6)	1	4	4.0(4)	0	8	90	11.3(32)	0	—	—	—	—	—	—	—	—	—	—	kp	—	0	114

JONES, DARYLL Daryll Keith, DB, 6´0˝/190 lbs; Georgia; 1984: GB, rnd 7; B3/23/1962 Columbia, GA **1984** GB 16 (0) **1985** GB 8 (1) **1987** Den 1 (1) **NFL** 25 (2) [3 yrs]

JONES, DAVE David Ray, WR, 6´2˝/192 lbs; Kansas State; 1969: Cle, rnd 11; B8/10/1947 Goodland, KS

YEAR	TEAM	G (GS, POS)	RUSH	YD	AVG (LG)	TD	REC	YD	AVG (LG)	TD	PASS	COMP	PCT	YD	AVG (LG)	TD	INT	SK	YD	QBR	KPR	OTD	PTS	TAY
1969	†Cle	13	—	—	—	—	2	33	16.5(22)	0	—	—	—	—	—	—	—	—	—	—	—	—	0	17
1970	Cle	14	—	—	—	—	—	—	—	—	—	—	—	—	—	—	—	—	—	—	p	—	0	0
1971	†Cle	14	—	—	—	—	4	66	16.5(21)	0	—	—	—	—	—	—	—	—	—	—	p	—	0	51
NFL	3	41	—	—	—	—	6	99	16.5(22)	0	—	—	—	—	—	—	—	—	—	—	p	—	0	68

JONES, DAVID David Dennison, TE, 6´2˝/220 lbs; Delaware State; 1991: SD, rnd 7; B11/9/1968 East Orange, NJ

YEAR	TEAM	G (GS, POS)	RUSH	YD	AVG (LG)	TD	REC	YD	AVG (LG)	TD	PASS	COMP	PCT	YD	AVG (LG)	TD	INT	SK	YD	QBR	KPR	OTD	PTS	TAY
1992	LARd	16(0)	—	—	—	—	2	29	14.5(25)	0	—	—	—	—	—	—	—	—	—	—	—	—	0	15

JONES, DAVID David Jeffrey, G-C, 6´3˝/262 lbs; Texas; 1984: Det, rnd 8; B10/25/1961 Taipei, Taiwan **1984** Det 10 (0) **1985** Det 9 (8, RG) **1987** Den 3 (1) **1987**†Was 5 (0) **NFL** 27 (9) [3 yrs]

JONES, DEACON David D., DE, 6´5˝/272 lbs; South Carolina State; Mississippi Valley State; 1961: LA, rnd 14; B12/9/1938 Eatonville, FL; HOF 1980 **[K]** **1961** LARm 14 (LDE) **1962** LARm 14 (LDE) **1963** LARm 14 (LDE) **1964** LARm★14 (LDE) **1965** LARm★14 (LDE) **1966** LARm★14 (LDE) **1967**†LARm★14 (LDE) **1968** LARm★14 (14, LDE) **1969**†LARm★14 (14, LDE) **1970** LARm★14 (13, LDE) **1971** LARm 11 (10, LDE) **1972** SD★14 (LDE) **1973** SD 12 (LDE) **1974**†Was 14 (1) **NFL** 191 (52) [14 yrs]

JONES, DHANI Dhani Makalani, LB, 6´1˝/240 lbs; Michigan; 2000: NYG, rnd 6; B2/22/1978 San Diego, CA **2001** NYG 16 (0) **2002**†NYG 15 (14, RLB) **2003** NYG 16 (16, RLB) **2004**†Phi 16 (15, RLB) **2005** Phi 16 (16, LLB) **NFL** 79 (61) [5 yrs]

JONES, DON Donald Ray, LB, 6´0˝/231 lbs; Washington; 1992: NO, rnd 9; B3/26/1969 Lynchburg, VA **1992** NYJ 2 (0) **1993** NYJ 6 (0) **NFL** 8 (0) [2 yrs]

JONES, DONNIE Donald Scott, P, 6´2˝/222 lbs; LSU; 2004: Sea, rnd 7; B7/5/1980 Baton Rouge, LA **2004** Sea 7 (0)

YEAR	TEAM	G (GS, POS)	RUSH	YD	AVG (LG)	TD	REC	YD	AVG (LG)	TD	PASS	COMP	PCT	YD	AVG (LG)	TD	INT	SK	YD	QBR	KPR	OTD	PTS	TAY
2005	Mia	16(0)	1	0	0.0(0)	0	—	—	—	—	—	—	—	—	—	—	—	—	—	—	P	—	0	0
NFL	2	23(0)	1	0	0.0	0	—	—	—	—	—	—	—	—	—	—	—	—	—	—	P	—	0	0

JONES, DONTA Markeysia Donta, LB, 6´2˝/226 lbs; Nebraska; 1995: Pit, rnd 4; B8/27/1972 Washington, DC **1995**†Pit 16 (0) **1996**†Pit 15 (2) **1997**†Pit 16 (4) **1998** Pit 16 (4) **1999** Car 16 (0) **2000**†NO 12 (0) **NFL** 91 (10) [6 yrs]

JONES, DOUG Douglas Charles, DB, 6´2˝/202 lbs; Arizona State; Cal State-Northridge; 1973: KC, rnd 6; B5/31/1950 San Diego, CA **1973** KC 4 **1974** KC 14 **1976** Buf 14 (14, SS) **1977** Buf 14 (14, SS) **1978** Buf 12 (9, SS) **1979** Det 10 **NFL** 68 (37) [6 yrs]

JONES, DUB William Augustus, HB-DB-WB-TB, 6´4˝/202 lbs; Tulane; LSU; 1946: ChiC, rnd 1; B12/29/1924 Arcadia, LA

YEAR	TEAM	G (GS, POS)	RUSH	YD	AVG (LG)	TD	REC	YD	AVG (LG)	TD	PASS	COMP	PCT	YD	AVG (LG)	TD	INT	SK	YD	QBR	KPR	OTD	PTS	TAY
1946	Mia-A	9(3)	24	102	4.3	0	—	—	—	—	—	—	—	—	—	—	—	—	—	—	—	—	0	102
1946	Bkn-A	2(1)	19	62	3.3	0	—	—	—	—	2	1	50.0	0	0.0	0	1	—	—	—	kp	—	0	24
1947	Bkn-A	8(2)	43	136	3.2	1	—	—	—	—	15	3	20.0	37	2.5	0	2	—	—	—	kpi	—	6	213
1948	†Cle-A	12(2)	33	149	4.5	1	9	119	13.2	2	—	—	—	—	—	—	—	—	—	—	k	—	18	234
1949	†Cle-A	11(9, RH)	77	312	4.1	4	12	241	20.1	1	—	—	—	—	—	—	—	—	—	—	k	—	30	562
AAFC	4	42(17)	196	761	3.9	6	21	360	17.1	3	17	4	23.5	37	2.2	0	3	—	—	—	kpi	—	54	1134
1950	†Cle	12(RH)	83	384	4.6(61)	6	31	458	14.8(80)	5	—	—	—	—	—	—	—	—	—	—	—	—	66	698
1951	†Cle★	12(RH)	104	492	4.7(43)	7	30	570	19.0(81)	5	—	—	—	—	—	—	—	—	—	—	—	—	72	872
1952	Cle	12(RH)	65	270	4.2(35)	2	43	651	15.1(63)	4	2	1	50.0	3	1.5(3)	1	0	—	—	—	—	—	36	642
1953	†Cle	12(RH)	31	28	0.9(10)	0	24	373	15.5(58)	0	1	0	0.0	0	0.0	0	0	—	—	—	p	—	0	217
1954	†Cle	12(lh)	51	231	4.5(24)	0	19	347	18.3(48)	2	—	—	—	—	—	—	—	—	—	—	—	—	12	415
1955	†Cle	12(rh)	10	44	4.4(13)	0	3	115	38.3(46)	1	—	—	—	—	—	—	—	—	—	—	—	—	6	107
NFL	6	72	344	1449	4.2(61)	15	150	2514	16.8(81)	17	3	1	33.3	3	1.0(3)	1	0	—	—	—	p	—	192	2950

JONES, E.J. Earnest Christopher, RB, 5´11˝/216 lbs; Kansas; B2/1/1962 Chicago, IL

YEAR	TEAM	G (GS, POS)	RUSH	YD	AVG (LG)	TD	REC	YD	AVG (LG)	TD	PASS	COMP	PCT	YD	AVG (LG)	TD	INT	SK	YD	QBR	KPR	OTD	PTS	TAY
1985	KC	5(0)	12	19	1.6(7)	0	3	31	10.3(15)	0	—	—	—	—	—	—	—	—	—	—	—	—	0	35
1987	Dal	3(0)	2	7	3.5(5)	0	3	16	5.3(10)	0	—	—	—	—	—	—	—	—	—	—	—	—	0	15
NFL	2	8(0)	14	26	1.9(7)	0	6	47	7.8(15)	0	—	—	—	—	—	—	—	—	—	—	—	—	0	50

JONES, EARL Darrel Earl, DB, 6´0˝/178 lbs; Norfolk State; 1980: Atl, rnd 3; B7/19/1957 Tuscaloosa, AL **1980**†Atl 16 (0) **1981** Atl 16 (0) **1982**†Atl 9 (0) **1983** Atl 16 (0) **NFL** 57 (0) [4 yrs]

JONES, ED Ed, DB, 6´0˝/185 lbs; Rutgers; 1975: Dal, rnd 9; B6/29/1952 Long Branch, NJ **1975** Buf 12 (SS)

JONES, EDGAR Edgar Francis 'Special Delivery', HB-DB, 5´10˝/193 lbs; Pittsburgh; 1942: ChiB, rnd 19; B5/6/1920 Scranton, PA, D5/18/2004 Scranton, PA

YEAR	TEAM	G (GS, POS)	RUSH	YD	AVG (LG)	TD	REC	YD	AVG (LG)	TD	PASS	COMP	PCT	YD	AVG (LG)	TD	INT	SK	YD	QBR	KPR	OTD	PTS	TAY
1945	ChiB	1(0)	8	41	5.1(12)	0	1	0	0.0(0)	0	1	0	0.0	0	0.0	0	0	—	—	—	k	—	0	83
1946	†Cle-A	14(13, LH)	77	539	7.0(56)	4	4	120	30.0	1	4	1	25.0	4	1.0(4)	0	0	—	—	—	kpi	1	36	827
1947	†Cle-A	9(5, lh)	69	443	6.4	5	5	92	18.4	1	3	2	66.7	79	26.3	0	0	—	—	—	kp	—	36	629
1948	†Cle-A	13(9, LH)	100	400	4.0	5	14	293	20.9	5	—	—	—	—	—	—	—	—	—	—	—	—	60	622
1949	†Cle-A	7(5, lh)	43	127	3.0	4	9	130	14.4	3	1	0	0.0	0	0.0	0	0	—	—	—	k	—	42	247
AAFC	4	43(32)	289	1509	5.2(56)	18	32	635	19.8	10	8	3	37.5	83	10.4(4)	0	0	—	—	—	kpi	1	174	2324

JONES, ELLIS Ellis Nathaniel, G-LB, 6´0˝/190 lbs; Tulsa; 1945: Bos, rnd 8; B3/16/1921 Abilene, TX, D2/24/2002 Greeley, CO **1945** Bos 8 (0)

Jones, Elmer Elmer John, G-LB, 6´0˝/224 lbs; Franklin & Marshall; Wake Forest; 1946: NYG, rnd 2; B8/4/1920 Buffalo, NY, D2/21/1996 New Smyrna Beach, FL **1946** Buf-A 12 (1) **1947** Det 10 (2) **1948** Det 9 (0) **NFL** 19 (2) [2 yrs]

Jones, Ernest Ernest Lee, DT-DE, 6´2˝/263 lbs; Oregon; 1994: LARm, rnd 3; B4/1/1971 Utica, NY **1995** NO 1 (0) **1996** Den 6 (0) **1997** Den 1 (0) **1998** Den 1 (0) **1998** Car 7 (0) **1999** Car 13 (0) **NFL** 29 (0) [5 yrs]

Jones, Ernie Ernest, DB, 6´3˝/180 lbs; Miami (FL); 1976: Sea, rnd 5; B1/3/1953 Boca Raton, FL **1976** Sea 9 (3) **1977** NYG 14 **1978** NYG 16 (16, FS) **1979** NYG 5 **NFL** 44 (19) [4 yrs]

Jones, Ernie Ernest Lee, WR, 5´11˝/186 lbs; Indiana; 1988: Phx, rnd 7; B12/15/1964 Elkhart, IN

YEAR	TEAM	G (GS, POS)	RUSH	YD	AVG (LG)	TD	REC	YD	AVG (LG)	TD	PASS	COMP	PCT	YD	AVG (LG)	TD	INT	SK	YD	QBR	KPR	OTD	PTS	TAY
1988	Phx	16(0)	—	—	—	—	23	496	21.6(93)	3	—	—	—	—	—	—	—	—	—	—	k	—	18	245
1989	Phx	15(9, WR)	1	18	18.0(18)	0	45	838	18.6(72)	3	—	—	—	—	—	—	—	—	—	—	kp	—	18	479
1990	Phx	15(8, WR)	4	33	8.3(15)	0	43	724	16.8(68)	4	—	—	—	—	—	—	—	—	—	—	—	—	24	415
1991	Phx	16(16, WR)	5	24	4.8(9)	0	61	957	15.7(53)	4	—	—	—	—	—	—	—	—	—	—	—	—	24	523
1992	Phx	11(5, wr)	2	-3	-1.5(1)	0	38	559	14.7(72)	4	—	—	—	—	—	—	—	—	—	—	—	—	24	297
1993	LARm	10(0)	1	4	4.0(4)	0	5	56	11.2(21)	2	—	—	—	—	—	—	—	—	—	—	—	—	12	42
NFL	6	83(38)	13	76	5.8(18)	0	215	3630	16.9(93)	20	—	—	—	—	—	—	—	—	—	—	kp	—	120	2000

Jones, Ezell Ezell M., T, 6´4˝/255 lbs; Minnesota; 1969: NYJ, rnd 4; B7/11/1947 Collierville, TN **1969** Bos-A 14 **1970** Bos 4 **NFL** 18 [2 yrs]

Jones, Fred Frederick Cornelius, WR, 5´9˝/175 lbs; Grambling State; 1990: KC, rnd 4; B3/6/1967 Atlanta, GA

YEAR	TEAM	G (GS, POS)	RUSH	YD	AVG (LG)	TD	REC	YD	AVG (LG)	TD	PASS	COMP	PCT	YD	AVG (LG)	TD	INT	SK	YD	QBR	KPR	OTD	PTS	TAY
1990	†KC	6(0)	1	-1	-1.0(-1)	0	1	5	5.0(5)	0	—	—	—	—	—	—	—	—	—	—	k	—	0	42
1991	†KC	11(0)	—	—	—	—	8	85	10.6(23)	0	—	—	—	—	—	—	—	—	—	—	kp	—	0	101
1992	KC	14(4)	—	—	—	—	18	265	14.7(56)	0	—	—	—	—	—	—	—	—	—	—	k	—	0	139
1993	†KC	10(1)	5	34	6.8(13)	0	9	111	12.3(19)	0	—	—	—	—	—	—	—	—	—	—	k	—	0	111
NFL	4	41(5)	6	33	5.5(13)	0	36	466	12.9(56)	0	—	—	—	—	—	—	—	—	—	—	kp	—	0	391

Jones, Fred Fred Allen, LB, 6´2˝/247 lbs; Colorado; B10/18/1977 Subic Bay, Philippines **2000** Buf 15 (0) **2001** Buf 16 (0) **2003**†KC 11 (0) **2004** KC 16 (0) **NFL** 58 (0) [4 yrs]

Jones, Fred Fredrick Daniel, LB, 6´3˝/240 lbs; Florida State; B9/2/1965 Miami, FL **1987** KC 2 (0)

Jones, Freddie Freddie Ray, TE, 6´4˝/260 lbs; North Carolina; 1997: SD, rnd 2; B9/16/1974 Cheverly, MD

YEAR	TEAM	G (GS, POS)	RUSH	YD	AVG (LG)	TD	REC	YD	AVG (LG)	TD	PASS	COMP	PCT	YD	AVG (LG)	TD	INT	SK	YD	QBR	KPR	OTD	PTS	TAY
1997	SD	13(8, TE)	—	—	—	—	41	505	12.3(62)	2	—	—	—	—	—	—	—	—	—	—	—	—	12	263
1998	SD	16(16, TE)	—	—	—	—	57	602	10.6(28)	3	—	—	—	—	—	—	—	—	—	—	—	—	20	316
1999	SD	16(16, TE)	—	—	—	—	56	670	12.0(36)	2	—	—	—	—	—	—	—	—	—	—	—	—	12	345
2000	SD	16(16, TE)	—	—	—	—	71	766	10.8(44)	5	—	—	—	—	—	—	—	—	—	—	—	—	30	408
2001	SD	14(9, te)	—	—	—	—	35	388	11.1(34)	4	—	—	—	—	—	—	—	—	—	—	—	—	24	214
2002	Arz	16(16, TE)	—	—	—	—	44	358	8.1(24)	1	—	—	—	—	—	—	—	—	—	—	—	—	6	184
2003	Arz	16(16, TE)	—	—	—	—	55	517	9.4(34)	3	—	—	—	—	—	—	—	—	—	—	—	—	18	274
2004	Arz	16(15, TE)	—	—	—	—	45	426	9.5(40)	2	—	—	—	—	—	—	—	—	—	—	—	—	12	223
NFL	8	123(112)	—	—	—	—	404	4232	10.5(62)	22	—	—	—	—	—	—	—	—	—	—	—	—	134	2226

Jones, Gary Gary DeWayne, DB, 6´1˝/210 lbs; Texas A&M; 1990: Pit, rnd 9; B11/30/1967 San Augustine, TX **1990** Pit 16 (1) **1991** Pit 9 (1) **1993**†Pit 13 (2) **1994**†Pit 14 (0) **1995** NYJ 11 (8, fs) **1996** NYJ 15 (15, FS) **NFL** 78 (27) [6 yrs]

Jones, Gene Ray Gene, LB, 6´0˝/200 lbs; Rice; 1959: ChiB, rnd 13; B10/18/1936 Woodson, TX **1961** Hou-A 1

Jones, George George Dee, RB, 5´9˝/204 lbs; San Diego State; 1997: Pit, rnd 5; B12/31/1973 Greenville, SC

YEAR	TEAM	G (GS, POS)	RUSH	YD	AVG (LG)	TD	REC	YD	AVG (LG)	TD	PASS	COMP	PCT	YD	AVG (LG)	TD	INT	SK	YD	QBR	KPR	OTD	PTS	TAY
1997	Pit	16(1)	72	235	3.3(32)	1	16	96	6.0(25)	1	—	—	—	—	—	—	—	—	—	—	—	—	12	298
1998	Jax	12(0)	39	121	3.1(21)	0	1	9	9.0(9)	0	—	—	—	—	—	—	—	—	—	—	k	—	0	132
1999	Cle	6(0)	8	15	1.9(9)	0	—	—	—	—	—	—	—	—	—	—	—	—	—	—	k	—	0	12
NFL	3	34(1)	119	371	3.1(32)	1	17	105	6.2(25)	1	—	—	—	—	—	—	—	—	—	—	k	—	12	442

Jones, Gordon Gordon, WR, 6´0˝/190 lbs; Pittsburgh; 1979: TB, rnd 2; B7/25/1957 Tampa, FL

YEAR	TEAM	G (GS, POS)	RUSH	YD	AVG (LG)	TD	REC	YD	AVG (LG)	TD	PASS	COMP	PCT	YD	AVG (LG)	TD	INT	SK	YD	QBR	KPR	OTD	PTS	TAY
1979	†TB	12(1)	1	12	12.0(12)	0	4	80	20.0(37)	1	—	—	—	—	—	—	—	—	—	—	—	—	6	57
1980	TB	16(14, WR)	1	-10	-10.0(-10)	0	48	669	13.9(41)	5	—	—	—	—	—	—	—	—	—	—	—	—	30	350
1981	†TB	13(4)	—	—	—	—	20	276	13.8(44)	1	—	—	—	—	—	—	—	—	—	—	—	—	6	143
1982	†TB	9(7, WR)	—	—	—	—	14	205	14.6(26)	1	—	—	—	—	—	—	—	—	—	—	—	—	6	108
1983	LARm	11(0)	—	—	—	—	11	172	15.6(46)	0	—	—	—	—	—	—	—	—	—	—	—	—	0	86
NFL	5	61(26)	2	2	1.0(12)	0	97	1402	14.5(46)	8	—	—	—	—	—	—	—	—	—	—	—	—	48	743

Jones, Greg Gregory Martin, RB, 6´1˝/201 lbs; UCLA; 1970: Min, rnd 5; B2/12/1948 San Francisco, CA

YEAR	TEAM	G (GS, POS)	RUSH	YD	AVG (LG)	TD	REC	YD	AVG (LG)	TD	PASS	COMP	PCT	YD	AVG (LG)	TD	INT	SK	YD	QBR	KPR	OTD	PTS	TAY
1970	Buf	10	31	113	3.6(17)	1	8	89	11.1(34)	0	—	—	—	—	—	—	—	—	—	—	k	1	12	235
1971	Buf	14	16	53	3.3(11)	0	16	113	7.1(21)	1	—	—	—	—	—	—	—	—	—	—	k	—	6	124
NFL	2	24	47	166	3.5(17)	1	24	202	8.4(34)	1	—	—	—	—	—	—	—	—	—	—	k	1	18	358

Jones, Greg Gregory Phillip, LB, 6´4˝/238 lbs; Colorado; 1997: Was, rnd 2; B5/22/1974 Denver, CO **1997** Was 16 (3) **1998** Was 16 (5, llb) **1999**†Was 15 (15, LLB) **2000** Was 16 (4) **2001**†ChiB 16 (0) **2002** Arz 3 (1) **NFL** 82 (28) [6 yrs]

Jones, Greg Greg, RB, 6´1˝/248 lbs; Florida State; 2004: Jax, rnd 2; B4/4/1981 Columbia, SC

YEAR	TEAM	G (GS, POS)	RUSH	YD	AVG (LG)	TD	REC	YD	AVG (LG)	TD	PASS	COMP	PCT	YD	AVG (LG)	TD	INT	SK	YD	QBR	KPR	OTD	PTS	TAY
2004	Jax	16(3)	62	162	2.6(12)	3	3	13	4.3(9)	0	—	—	—	—	—	—	—	—	—	—	k	—	18	214
2005	†Jax	14(13, FB)	151	575	3.8(27)	4	10	65	6.5(10)	0	—	—	—	—	—	—	—	—	—	—	k	—	24	633
NFL	2	30(16)	213	737	3.5(27)	7	13	78	6.0(10)	0	—	—	—	—	—	—	—	—	—	—	k	—	42	846

Jones, Harris Harris J., G, 6´5˝/255 lbs; Johnson C. Smith; B10/3/1945 Lake City, SC **1971** SD 11 **1973** Hou 5 **1974** Hou 11 (LG) **NFL** 27 [3 yrs]

Jones, Harry Harry Lee, RB, 6´2˝/205 lbs; Arkansas; 1967: Phi, rnd 1; B7/25/1945 Huntington, WV

YEAR	TEAM	G (GS, POS)	RUSH	YD	AVG (LG)	TD	REC	YD	AVG (LG)	TD	PASS	COMP	PCT	YD	AVG (LG)	TD	INT	SK	YD	QBR	KPR	OTD	PTS	TAY
1967	Phi	11	8	17	2.1(6)	0	3	32	10.7(23)	0	—	—	—	—	—	—	—	—	—	—	k	—	0	35
1968	Phi	4	22	24	1.1(10)	0	5	87	17.4(48)	0	—	—	—	—	—	—	—	—	—	—	k	—	0	71
1969	Phi	12	1	0	0.0(0)	0	—	—	—	—	—	—	—	—	—	—	—	—	—	—	—	—	0	0
1970	Phi	2	13	44	3.4(16)	0	1	12	12.0(12)	0	—	—	—	—	—	—	—	—	—	—	k	—	0	43
NFL	4	29	44	85	1.9(16)	0	9	131	14.6(48)	0	—	—	—	—	—	—	—	—	—	—	k	—	0	149

Jones, Harvey Harvey Mabry, FB-DB-HB, 6´0˝/175 lbs; Baylor; B4/15/1921 Beaumont, TX, D7/21/1993 Clarendon, TX

YEAR	TEAM	G (GS, POS)	RUSH	YD	AVG (LG)	TD	REC	YD	AVG (LG)	TD	PASS	COMP	PCT	YD	AVG (LG)	TD	INT	SK	YD	QBR	KPR	OTD	PTS	TAY
1944	Cle	10(8, FB)	38	133	3.5(36)	1	6	59	9.8(19)	0	—	—	—	—	—	—	—	—	—	—	kpi	—	6	283
1945	Cle	9(2)	8	15	1.9(5)	0	2	36	18.0(44)	1	—	—	—	—	—	—	—	—	—	—	i	—	6	101
1947	Was	4(0)	—	—	—	—	—	—	—	—	—	—	—	—	—	—	—	—	—	—	k	—	0	15
NFL	3	23(10)	46	148	3.2(36)	1	8	95	11.9(44)	1	—	—	—	—	—	—	—	—	—	—	kpi	—	12	399

Jones, Hassan Hassan Ameer, WR, 6´0˝/198 lbs; Florida State; 1986: Min, rnd 5; B7/2/1964 Clearwater, FL

YEAR	TEAM	G (GS, POS)	RUSH	YD	AVG (LG)	TD	REC	YD	AVG (LG)	TD	PASS	COMP	PCT	YD	AVG (LG)	TD	INT	SK	YD	QBR	KPR	OTD	PTS	TAY
1986	Min	16(6, wr)	1	14	14.0(14)	0	28	570	20.4(55)	4	—	—	—	—	—	—	—	—	—	—	—	—	24	319
1987	†Min	12(0)	—	—	—	—	7	189	27.0(58)	2	—	—	—	—	—	—	—	—	—	—	—	—	12	105
1988	†Min	16(15, WR)	1	7	7.0(7)	0	40	778	19.5(68)	5	—	—	—	—	—	—	—	—	—	—	—	—	30	421
1989	†Min	16(13, WR)	1	37	37.0(37)	0	42	694	16.5(50)	1	—	—	—	—	—	—	—	—	—	—	—	—	6	389
1990	Min	15(10, WR)	1	-7	-7.0(-7)	0	51	810	15.9(75)	7	—	—	—	—	—	—	—	—	—	—	—	—	42	433
1991	Min	16(7, wr)	—	—	—	—	32	384	12.0(43)	1	0	0	0.0	0	0.0	0	0	1	0	—	—	—	6	197
1992	†Min	9(5, wr)	1	1	1.0(1)	0	22	308	14.0(43)	4	1	1	100.0	18	18.0(18)	0	0	—	—	—	—	—	24	184
1993	KC	8(0)	—	—	—	—	7	91	13.0(22)	0	—	—	—	—	—	—	—	—	—	—	—	—	0	46
NFL	8	108(56)	5	52	10.4(37)	0	229	3824	16.7(75)	24	1	1	100.0	18	18.0(18)	0	0	1	0	—	—	—	144	2093

Jones, Henry Henry D., RB, 6´2˝/235 lbs; Grambling State; 1969: Den, rnd 9; B2/24/1946 Baton Rouge, LA

YEAR	TEAM	G (GS, POS)	RUSH	YD	AVG (LG)	TD	REC	YD	AVG (LG)	TD	PASS	COMP	PCT	YD	AVG (LG)	TD	INT	SK	YD	QBR	KPR	OTD	PTS	TAY
1969	Den-A	2	1	3	3.0(3)	0	—	—	—	—	—	—	—	—	—	—	—	—	—	—	—	—	0	3

Jones, Henry Henry Louis, DB, 5´11˝/197 lbs; Illinois; 1991: Buf, rnd 1; B12/29/1967 St. Louis, MO **1991**†Buf 15 (0) **1992**†Buf★16 (16, SS) **1993**†Buf 16 (16, SS) **1994** Buf 16 (16, SS) **1995** Buf 13 (13, SS) **1996** Buf 5 (5, ss) **1997** Buf 15 (15, SS) **1998**†Buf 16 (16, SS) **1999**†Buf 16 (16, SS) **2000** Buf 16 (16, SS) **2001** Min 5 (5, ss) **2002** Atl 9 (0) **NFL** 158 (134) [12 yrs]

Jones, Homer Homer Carroll, SE-WR, 6´2˝/215 lbs; Texas Southern; 1963: NYG, rnd 20/Hou, rnd 5; B2/18/1941 Pittsburg, TX

YEAR	TEAM	G(GS, POS)	RUSH	YD	AVG(LG)	TD	REC	YD	AVG(LG)	TD	PASS	COMP	PCT	YD	AVG(LG)	TD	INT	SK	YD	QBR	KPR	OTD	PTS	TAY
1964	NYG	3	—	—	—	—	4	82	20.5(30)	0	—	—	—	—	—	—	—	—	—	—	k	—	0	62
1965	NYG	14	1	17	17.0(17)	0	26	709	27.3(**89**)	6	—	—	—	—	—	—	—	—	—	—	—	—	36	402
1966	NYG	14(SE)	5	43	8.6(11)	0	48	1044	21.8(98)	8	—	—	—	—	—	—	—	—	—	—	—	—	48	605
1967	NYG★	14(SE)	5	60	12.0(46)	1	49	1209	24.7(70)	**13**	—	—	—	—	—	—	—	—	—	—	k	—	84	748
1968	NYG★	14(SE)	3	18	6.0(11)	0	45	1057	23.5(84)	7	—	—	—	—	—	—	—	—	—	—	—	—	42	582
1969	NYG	14(SE)	3	8	2.7(9)	0	42	744	17.7(54)	1	—	—	—	—	—	—	—	—	—	—	—	—	6	385
1970	Cle	14(wr/wr)	—	—	—	—	10	141	14.1(43)	1	—	—	—	—	—	—	—	—	—	—	k	1	12	390
NFL	7	87	17	146	8.6(46)	1	224	4986	22.3(98)	36	—	—	—	—	—	—	—	—	—	—	k	1	228	3172

Jones, Horace Horace Arthur, DE, 6´3˝/255 lbs; Louisville; 1971: Oak, rnd 12; B7/31/1949 Pensacola, FL **1971** Oak 14 (12, LDE) **1972**†Oak 14 (14, RDE) **1973**†Oak 14 (5, rde) **1974**†Oak 14 (14, RDE) **1975**†Oak 14 (14, RDE) **1977** Sea 1 **NFL** 71 (59) [6 yrs]

Jones, Isaac Isaac Douglas, WR, 6´0˝/190 lbs; Purdue; B12/7/1975 Little Rock, AR **2000** Ind 1 (0)

YEAR	TEAM	G(GS, POS)	RUSH	YD	AVG(LG)	TD	REC	YD	AVG(LG)	TD	PASS	COMP	PCT	YD	AVG(LG)	TD	INT	SK	YD	QBR	KPR	OTD	PTS	TAY
1999	Ind	1(1)	—	—	—	—	1	8	8.0(8)	0	—	—	—	—	—	—	—	—	—	—	—	—	0	4
NFL	2	2(1)	—	—	—	—	1	8	8.0(8)	0	—	—	—	—	—	—	—	—	—	—	—	—	0	4

Jones, J.J. John Eddie, QB, 6´1˝/190 lbs; Fisk; B4/16/1952 Memphis, TN

YEAR	TEAM	G(GS, POS)	RUSH	YD	AVG(LG)	TD	REC	YD	AVG(LG)	TD	PASS	COMP	PCT	YD	AVG(LG)	TD	INT	SK	YD	QBR	KPR	OTD	PTS	TAY
1975	NYJ	7(1)	9	59	6.6(19)	0	—	—	—	—	57	16	28.1	181	3.2(20)	1	5	7	64	—	—	—	0	-46

Jones, J.J. Jerry Glenn, LB, 6´1˝/230 lbs; Arkansas; B6/7/1978 Little Rock, AR **2002** NO 13 (0)

Jones, Jamal Jamal, WR, 6´0˝/214 lbs; North Carolina A&T; B4/24/1981 **2005** GB 2 (0)

Jones, James James, RB, 5´10˝/200 lbs; Mississippi State; 1980: Dal, rnd 3; B12/6/1958 Starkville, MS **[R]**

YEAR	TEAM	G(GS, POS)	RUSH	YD	AVG(LG)	TD	REC	YD	AVG(LG)	TD	PASS	COMP	PCT	YD	AVG(LG)	TD	INT	SK	YD	QBR	KPR	OTD	PTS	TAY
1980	†Dal	16(0)	41	135	3.3(9)	0	5	39	7.8(16)	0	—	—	—	—	—	—	—	—	—	—	kp	—	0	673
1981	†Dal	16(0)	34	183	5.4(59)	1	6	37	6.2(16)	0	—	—	—	—	—	—	—	—	—	—	kp	—	6	347
1982	Dal	5(0)	—	—	—	—	—	—	—	—	—	—	—	—	—	—	—	—	—	—	k	—	0	16
1984	Dal	9(0)	8	13	1.6(6)	0	7	57	8.1(19)	1	—	—	—	—	—	—	—	—	—	—	—	—	6	47
1985	†Dal	16(2)	1	0	0.0(0)	0	24	179	7.5(35)	0	2	1	50.0	12	6.0(12)	1	1	—	—	—	k	—	0	87
NFL	5	62(2)	84	331	3.9(59)	1	42	312	7.4(35)	1	2	1	50.0	12	6.0(12)	1	1	—	—	—	kp	—	12	1168

Jones, James James Alfie, DT-NT, 6´2˝/290 lbs; Northern Iowa; 1991: Cle, rnd 3; B2/6/1969 Davenport, IA **1991** Cle 16 (16, LDT) **1995** Den 16 (16, LDT) **1997** Bal 16 (16, LDT) **1998** Bal 16 (16, LDT) **1999**†Det 16 (16, LDT) **2000** Det 16 (16, LDT)

YEAR	TEAM	G(GS, POS)	RUSH	YD	AVG(LG)	TD	REC	YD	AVG(LG)	TD	PASS	COMP	PCT	YD	AVG(LG)	TD	INT	SK	YD	QBR	KPR	OTD	PTS	TAY
1992	Cle	16(16, LDT)	—	—	—	—	1	1	1.0(1)	1	—	—	—	—	—	—	—	—	—	—	S	—	6	6
1993	Cle	16(12, LDT)	2	2	1.0(1)	1	—	—	—	—	—	—	—	—	—	—	—	—	—	—	S	—	6	12
1994	†Cle	16(5, ldt)	1	0	0.0(0)	0	1	1	1.0(1)	0	—	—	—	—	—	—	—	—	—	—	S	—	0	1
1996	Bal	16(11, NT)	—	—	—	—	1	2	2.0(2)	1	—	—	—	—	—	—	—	—	—	—	S	—	6	6
NFL	10	160(140)	3	2	0.7(1)	1	3	4	1.3(2)	2	—	—	—	—	—	—	—	—	—	—	iS	1	26	49

Jones, James James Roosevelt, FB-RB-TB-TE, 6´2˝/229 lbs; Florida; 1983: Det, rnd 1; B3/21/1961 Pompano Beach, FL

YEAR	TEAM	G(GS, POS)	RUSH	YD	AVG(LG)	TD	REC	YD	AVG(LG)	TD	PASS	COMP	PCT	YD	AVG(LG)	TD	INT	SK	YD	QBR	KPR	OTD	PTS	TAY
1983	†Det	14(14, FB)	135	475	3.5(18)	6	46	467	10.2(46)	1	2	0	0.0	0	0.0	0	0	—	—	—	—	—	42	774
1984	Det	16(16, FB)	137	532	3.9(34)	3	77	662	8.6(39)	5	5	3	60.0	62	12.4(27)	1	0	1	3	—	—	—	48	954
1985	Det	14(13, FB)	244	886	3.6(29)	6	45	334	7.4(36)	3	1	0	0.0	0	0.0	0	0	—	—	—	—	—	54	1128
1986	Det	16(16, FB)	252	903	3.6(39)	8	54	334	6.2(21)	1	—	—	—	—	—	—	—	—	—	—	—	—	54	1155
1987	Det	11(11, FB)	96	342	3.6(19)	0	34	262	7.7(35)	0	1	0	0.0	0	0.0	0	1	—	—	—	—	—	0	433
1988	Det	14(14, FB)	96	314	3.3(13)	0	29	259	8.9(40)	0	1	0	0.0	0	0.0	0	0	—	—	—	—	—	0	444
1989	Sea	2(0)	—	—	—	—	1	8	8.0(8)	0	—	—	—	—	—	—	—	—	—	—	—	—	0	4
1990	Sea	16(0)	5	20	4.0(5)	0	1	22	22.0(22)	0	—	—	—	—	—	—	—	—	—	—	k	—	0	22
1991	Sea	16(6, rb)	45	154	3.4(22)	3	10	103	10.3(29)	0	—	—	—	—	—	—	—	—	—	—	—	—	18	236
1992	Sea	16(1)	—	—	—	—	21	190	9.0(30)	0	—	—	—	—	—	—	—	—	—	—	k	—	0	96
NFL	10	135(91)	1010	3626	3.6(39)	26	318	2641	8.3(46)	10	10	3	30.0	62	6.2(27)	1	1	1	3	—	k	—	216	5245

Jones, Jeff Jeffrey Raymond, T, 6´6˝/310 lbs; Texas A&M; B5/30/1972 Killeen, TX **1995** Det 2 (0) **1996** Det 7 (0) **NFL** 9 (0) [2 yrs]

Jones, Jermaine Jermaine, DB, 5´8˝/173 lbs; Northwestern State (LA); 1999: NYJ, rnd 5; B7/25/1976 Morgan City, LA **1999** NYJ 1 (0) **1999** ChiB 1 (0) **2002** Dal 1 (0) **NFL** 3 (0) [2 yrs]

Jones, Jerry Jerald Joseph, G, 6´1˝/205 lbs; Notre Dame; B1894, D6/2/1938 Rochester, MN **1920** Dec 13 (8, RG) **1922** RI 8 (7, RG) **1923** Tol 8 (7, LG) **1924** Cle 5 (5, RG) **NFL** 34 (27) [4 yrs]

Jones, Jerry Gerald Robert, T-DE-DT, 6´4˝/260 lbs; Bowling Green State; 1966: Atl, rnd 2/Den, rnd 7; B2/14/1944 Dayton, OH **1966** Atl 7 **1967** NO 9 (RT) **1968** NO 14 (RT) **1969** NO 14 **NFL** 44 [4 yrs]

Jones, Jim James Alexander, T-DB, 6´0˝/175 lbs; Union (TN); 1943: Det, rnd 6; B12/18/1920 Florence, AL, D12/1979 Sneedville, TN

YEAR	TEAM	G(GS, POS)	RUSH	YD	AVG(LG)	TD	REC	YD	AVG(LG)	TD	PASS	COMP	PCT	YD	AVG(LG)	TD	INT	SK	YD	QBR	KPR	OTD	PTS	TAY
1946	Det	2(0)	3	3	1.0(4)	0	—	—	—	—	4	0	0.0	0	0.0	0	1	—	—	—	Pk	—	0	-38

Jones, Jim James Clyde, SE-FL-WR, 6´3˝/195 lbs; Wisconsin; 1964: Chi, rnd 6/Den, rnd 25; B3/3/1941 Henderson, SC

YEAR	TEAM	G(GS, POS)	RUSH	YD	AVG(LG)	TD	REC	YD	AVG(LG)	TD	PASS	COMP	PCT	YD	AVG(LG)	TD	INT	SK	YD	QBR	KPR	OTD	PTS	TAY
1965	ChiB	13(SE)	2	13	6.5(7)	0	21	350	16.7(54)	4	—	—	—	—	—	—	—	—	—	—	—	—	24	208
1966	ChiB	14(SE)	1	-7	-7.0(-7)	0	28	504	18.0(80)	5	—	—	—	—	—	—	—	—	—	—	—	—	30	270
1967	ChiB	14	4	19	4.8(24)	0	7	138	19.7(34)	0	—	—	—	—	—	—	—	—	—	—	—	—	0	88
1968	Den-A	13(fl)	1	-1	-1.0(-1)	0	13	190	14.6(60)	2	—	—	—	—	—	—	—	—	—	—	—	—	12	104
NFL	4	54	8	24	3.0(24)	0	69	1182	17.1(80)	11	—	—	—	—	—	—	—	—	—	—	—	—	66	670

Jones, Jim James Ray, DB, 6´1˝/204 lbs; Washington; 1958: LA, rnd 3; B5/6/1935, D10/82 **1958** LARm 12 **1961** Oak-A 1 **NFL** 13 [2 yrs]

Jones, Jimmie Jimmie Lee, RB, 5´10˝/205 lbs; UCLA; B6/15/1950 Los Angeles, CA

YEAR	TEAM	G(GS, POS)	RUSH	YD	AVG(LG)	TD	REC	YD	AVG(LG)	TD	PASS	COMP	PCT	YD	AVG(LG)	TD	INT	SK	YD	QBR	KPR	OTD	PTS	TAY
1974	Det	14(2)	32	147	4.6(21)	1	4	35	8.8(15)	0	—	—	—	—	—	—	—	—	—	—	k	—	6	532

Jones, Jimmie Jimmie Sims, DT-DE, 6´4˝/285 lbs; Miami (FL); 1990: Dal, rnd 3; B1/9/1966 Lakeland, FL **1990** Dal 16 (6, ldt) **1991**†Dal 16 (6, rdt) **1992**†Dal 16 (2) **1993**†Dal 15 (2) **1994** LARm 14 (14, LDT) **1995** SL 16 (16, LDT) **1996** SL 14 (14, LDT) **1997** Phi 14 (0) **NFL** 121 (60) [8 yrs]

Jones, Jimmie Jimmie Lee, DE, 6´5˝/220 lbs; Wichita State; 1969: NYJ, rnd 6; B1/17/1947 Columbia, SC **1969** NYJ-A 14 **1970** NYJ 3 **1971**†Was 14 (1) **1972** Was 3 **1973** Was 6 **NFL** 40 (1) [5 yrs]

Jones, Jock Jock Stacy, LB, 6´2˝/235 lbs; Virginia Tech; 1990: Cle, rnd 8; B3/13/1968 Ashland, VA **1990** Cle 11 (0) **1991** Cle 9 (0) **1991** Phx 5 (0) **1992** Phx 14 (2) **1993** Phx 7 (0) **NFL** 46 (2) [4 yrs]

Jones, Joe Joseph Willie, DE, 6´6˝/250 lbs; Tennessee State; 1970: Cle, rnd 2; B1/7/1948 Dallas, TX **1970** Cle 14 (lde) **1971**†Cle 14 (LDE) **1973** Cle 14 (LDE) **1974** Phi 14 (RDE) **1975** Phi 7 (5, rde) **1975** Cle 6 **1976** Cle 14 (LDE) **1977** Cle 14 (14, LDE) **1978** Cle 14 (5, rde) **1979** Was 16 (3) **1980** Was 7 (0) **NFL** 134 (27) [10 yrs]

Jones, Joe Joseph, TE, 6´5˝/255 lbs; Virginia Tech; 1985: Dal, rnd 10; B6/26/1962 Windber, PA

YEAR	TEAM	G(GS, POS)	RUSH	YD	AVG(LG)	TD	REC	YD	AVG(LG)	TD	PASS	COMP	PCT	YD	AVG(LG)	TD	INT	SK	YD	QBR	KPR	OTD	PTS	TAY
1987	Ind	3(2)	—	—	—	—	3	25	8.3(13)	1	—	—	—	—	—	—	—	—	—	—	—	—	6	18

Jones, Joey Joseph Russell, WR, 5´8˝/165 lbs; Alabama; 1984: Atl, rnd S1; B10/29/1962 Mobile, AL

YEAR	TEAM	G(GS, POS)	RUSH	YD	AVG(LG)	TD	REC	YD	AVG(LG)	TD	PASS	COMP	PCT	YD	AVG(LG)	TD	INT	SK	YD	QBR	KPR	OTD	PTS	TAY
1986	Atl	11(2)	1	7	7.0(7)	0	7	141	20.1(41)	0	—	—	—	—	—	—	—	—	—	—	p	—	0	79

Jones, John John, TE, 6´4˝/255 lbs; Pittsburgh; Indiana (PA); B4/4/1975 Cleveland, OH **2000** Bal 8 (0) **2003** Bal 11 (0)

YEAR	TEAM	G(GS, POS)	RUSH	YD	AVG(LG)	TD	REC	YD	AVG(LG)	TD	PASS	COMP	PCT	YD	AVG(LG)	TD	INT	SK	YD	QBR	KPR	OTD	PTS	TAY
2001	†Bal	15(2)	—	—	—	—	2	13	6.5(13)	0	—	—	—	—	—	—	—	—	—	—	—	—	0	7
2002	Bal	15(4)	—	—	—	—	6	47	7.8(18)	1	—	—	—	—	—	—	—	—	—	—	—	—	6	29
NFL	4	49(6)	—	—	—	—	8	60	7.5(18)	1	—	—	—	—	—	—	—	—	—	—	—	—	6	35

Jones, Julian Julian Deon, DB, 6´0˝/190 lbs; Missouri; B6/8/1978 Phoenix, AZ **2002** Phi 2 (0)

Jones, Julius Julius Andre Maurice, RB, 5´10˝/210 lbs; Notre Dame; 2004: Dal, rnd 2; B8/14/1981 Big Stone Gap, VA

YEAR	TEAM	G(GS, POS)	RUSH	YD	AVG(LG)	TD	REC	YD	AVG(LG)	TD	PASS	COMP	PCT	YD	AVG(LG)	TD	INT	SK	YD	QBR	KPR	OTD	PTS	TAY
2004	Dal	8(7, RB)	197	819	4.2(53)	7	17	109	6.4(37)	0	—	—	—	—	—	—	—	—	—	—	—	—	42	944
2005	Dal	13(12, RB)	257	993	3.9(51)	5	35	218	6.2(26)	0	—	—	—	—	—	—	—	—	—	—	—	—	30	1152
NFL	2	21(19)	454	1812	4.0(53)	12	52	327	6.3(37)	0	—	—	—	—	—	—	—	—	—	—	—	—	72	2096

JONES, JUNE June Sheldon, QB, 6´4˝/200 lbs; Oregon; Hawaii; Portland State; B2/19/1953 Portland, OR [C]

YEAR	TEAM	G(GS, POS)	RUSH	YD	AVG(LG)	TD	REC	YD	AVG(LG)	TD	PASS	COMP	PCT	YD	AVG(LG)	TD	INT	SK	YD	QBR	KPR	OTD	PTS	TAY
1977	Atl	1	—	—	—	—	—	—	—	—	1	1	100.0	1	-1.0(-1)	0	0	—	—	—	—	—	0	-1
1978	Atl	7(3)	10	-3	-0.3(17)	0	—	—	—	—	79	34	43.0	394	5.0(38)	1	4	17	132	—	—	—	0	39
1979	Atl	5(2)	6	19	3.2(9)	0	—	—	—	—	83	38	45.8	505	6.1(49)	2	3	13	100	—	—	—	0	162
1981	Atl	4(0)	1	-1	-1.0(-1)	0	—	—	—	—	3	2	66.7	25	8.3(14)	0	0	—	—	—	—	—	0	12
NFL	4	17(5)	17	15	0.9(17)	0	—	—	—	—	166	75	45.2	923	5.6(49)	3	7	30	232	—	—	—	0	212

JONES, K.C. Kirk Cameron, C, 6´1˝/275 lbs; Miami (FL); B3/28/1974 Midland, TX **2000**†Den 16 (0)

JONES, KEITH Keith, RB, 5´9˝/190 lbs; Nebraska; 1988: LARm, rnd 6; B2/5/1966 Omaha, NE

YEAR	TEAM	G(GS, POS)	RUSH	YD	AVG(LG)	TD	REC	YD	AVG(LG)	TD	PASS	COMP	PCT	YD	AVG(LG)	TD	INT	SK	YD	QBR	KPR	OTD	PTS	TAY
1989	†Cle	16(2)	43	160	3.7(15)	1	15	126	8.4(36)	0	—	—	—	—	—	—	—	—	—	—	k	—	6	215

JONES, KEITH Keith Lamar, RB, 6´1˝/210 lbs; Illinois; 1989: Atl, rnd 3; B3/20/1966 Rock Hill, MO

YEAR	TEAM	G(GS, POS)	RUSH	YD	AVG(LG)	TD	REC	YD	AVG(LG)	TD	PASS	COMP	PCT	YD	AVG(LG)	TD	INT	SK	YD	QBR	KPR	OTD	PTS	TAY
1989	Atl	14(9, RB)	52	202	3.9(19)	6	41	396	9.7(46)	0	1	0	0.0	0	0.0	0	0	—	—	—	k	—	36	555
1990	Atl	15(10, FB)	49	185	3.8(22)	0	13	103	7.9(16)	0	1	1	100.0	37	37.0(37)	0	0	—	—	—	k	1	6	381
1991	Atl	5(3)	35	126	3.6(14)	0	6	58	9.7(15)	0	—	—	—	—	—	—	—	—	—	—	—	—	0	155
1992	Atl	16(8, RB)	79	278	3.5(26)	0	12	94	7.8(15)	0	1	0	0.0	0	0.0	0	0	—	—	—	k	—	0	349
NFL	4	50(30)	215	791	3.7(26)	6	72	651	9.0(46)	0	3	1	33.3	37	12.3(37)	0	0	—	—	—	k	1	42	1440

JONES, KEN Kenneth A., WB-E, 6´3˝/185 lbs; Franklin & Marshall; B9/2/1897, D1/3/1983 Solsville, NY **1924** Buf 5 (3)

JONES, KEN Kenneth Eugene, T-DE, 6´5˝/260 lbs; Arkansas State; 1976: Buf, rnd 2; B12/1/1952 St. Louis, MO **1976** Buf 12 (7, LDE) **1977** Buf 14 (2) **1978** Buf 16 (16, LT) **1979** Buf 16 (16, LT) **1980**†Buf☆16 (16, LT) **1981**†Buf 15 (15, LT) **1982** Buf 9 (9, LT) **1983** Buf 16 (16, LT) **1984** Buf 16 (16, LT) **1985** Buf 16 (14, LT) **1986** Buf 12 (12, LT) **1987** NYJ 5 (4) **NFL** 163 (143) [12 yrs]

JONES, KENYATTA Kenyatta Lapoleon, T, 6´3˝/307 lbs; South Florida; 2001: NE, rnd 4; B1/18/1979 Gainesville, FL **2001** NE 5 (0) **2002** NE 13 (12, RT) **2004** Was 3 (2) **NFL** 21 (14) [3 yrs]

JONES, KEVIN Kevin S., RB-TB, 5´11˝/211 lbs; Virginia Tech; 2004: Det, rnd 1; B8/21/1982 Chester, PA

YEAR	TEAM	G(GS, POS)	RUSH	YD	AVG(LG)	TD	REC	YD	AVG(LG)	TD	PASS	COMP	PCT	YD	AVG(LG)	TD	INT	SK	YD	QBR	KPR	OTD	PTS	TAY
2004	Det	15(14, RB)	241	1133	4.7(74)	5	28	180	6.4(34)	1	—	—	—	—	—	—	—	—	—	—	—	—	36	1278
2005	Det	13(13, RB)	186	664	3.6(40)	5	20	109	5.4(28)	0	—	—	—	—	—	—	—	—	—	—	—	—	30	769
NFL	2	28(27)	427	1797	4.2(74)	10	48	289	6.0(34)	1	—	—	—	—	—	—	—	—	—	—	—	—	66	2047

JONES, KIM Kim Richard, RB, 6´4˝/238 lbs; Colorado State; 1975: Bal, rnd 7; B1/19/1952 Waterloo, IA

YEAR	TEAM	G(GS, POS)	RUSH	YD	AVG(LG)	TD	REC	YD	AVG(LG)	TD	PASS	COMP	PCT	YD	AVG(LG)	TD	INT	SK	YD	QBR	KPR	OTD	PTS	TAY
1976	NO	11	6	21	3.5(10)	0	1	14	14.0(14)	0	—	—	—	—	—	—	—	—	—	—	k	—	0	25
1977	NO	14	8	23	2.9(8)	0	1	9	9.0(9)	0	—	—	—	—	—	—	—	—	—	—	k	—	0	21
1978	NO	16	9	31	3.4(8)	0	2	10	5.0(6)	0	—	—	—	—	—	—	—	—	—	—	—	—	0	36
1979	NO	2	3	5	1.7(3)	0	—	—	—	—	—	—	—	—	—	—	—	—	—	—	—	—	0	5
NFL	4	43	26	80	3.1(10)	0	4	33	8.3(14)	0	—	—	—	—	—	—	—	—	—	—	k	—	0	87

JONES, KIRK Nolton Kirk, RB, 5´10˝/210 lbs; UNLV; B1/5/1965 Long Beach, CA, D6/1/2001 **1987** Cle 1 (0)

JONES, LACURTIS LaCurtis Burl, LB, 6´0˝/200 lbs; Baylor; 1996: Mia, rnd 4; B6/23/1972 Waco, TX **1996** TB 10 (0)

JONES, LAM John Wesley, WR, 5´11˝/180 lbs; Texas; 1980: NYJ, rnd 1; B4/4/1958 Lawton, OK

YEAR	TEAM	G(GS, POS)	RUSH	YD	AVG(LG)	TD	REC	YD	AVG(LG)	TD	PASS	COMP	PCT	YD	AVG(LG)	TD	INT	SK	YD	QBR	KPR	OTD	PTS	TAY
1980	NYJ	16(13, WR)	2	5	2.5(7)	0	25	482	19.3(55)	3	—	—	—	—	—	—	—	—	—	—	k	—	18	268
1981	NYJ	15(3)	2	0	0.0(5)	0	20	342	17.1(47)	3	—	—	—	—	—	—	—	—	—	—	k	—	18	177
1982	†NYJ	8(7, WR)	1	2	2.0(2)	0	18	294	16.3(51)	2	—	—	—	—	—	—	—	—	—	—	—	—	12	159
1983	NYJ	14(7, wr)	4	10	2.5(9)	0	43	734	17.1(50)	4	—	—	—	—	—	—	—	—	—	—	—	—	24	397
1984	NYJ	8(8, WR)	—	—	—	—	32	470	14.7(37)	1	—	—	—	—	—	—	—	—	—	—	—	—	6	240
NFL	5	61(38)	9	17	1.9(9)	0	138	2322	16.8(55)	13	—	—	—	—	—	—	—	—	—	—	k	—	78	1241

JONES, LARRY Lawrence Allen, WB-DB, 5´10˝/170 lbs; Truman State; 1974: NYG, rnd 15; B3/4/1951 Lemoore, CA

YEAR	TEAM	G(GS, POS)	RUSH	YD	AVG(LG)	TD	REC	YD	AVG(LG)	TD	PASS	COMP	PCT	YD	AVG(LG)	TD	INT	SK	YD	QBR	KPR	OTD	PTS	TAY
1974	†Was	13	—	—	—	—	—	—	—	—	—	—	—	—	—	—	—	—	—	—	kp	1	6	351
1975	Was	14	—	—	—	—	2	33	16.5(21)	0	—	—	—	—	—	—	—	—	—	—	kp	1	6	550
1976	Was	1	—	—	—	—	—	—	—	—	—	—	—	—	—	—	—	—	—	—	kp	—	0	11
1977	Was	14	1	1	1.0(1)	0	5	55	11.0(15)	0	—	—	—	—	—	—	—	—	—	—	k	—	0	41
1978	SF	9	1	-9	-9.0(-9)	0	1	21	21.0(21)	0	—	—	—	—	—	—	—	—	—	—	p	—	0	38
NFL	5	51	2	-8	-4.0(1)	0	8	109	13.6(21)	0	—	—	—	—	—	—	—	—	—	—	kp	2	12	990

JONES, LENOY Lenoy, LB, 6´1˝/228 lbs; TCU; B9/25/1974 Marlin, TX **1996** Hou 11 (0) **1997** Ten 16 (0) **1998** Ten 9 (0) **1999** Cle 16 (1) **2000** Cle 8 (1) **2001** Cle 7 (1) **2002**†Cle 5 (0) **NFL** 72 (3) [7 yrs]

JONES, LEONARD Leonard Dewayne, DB, 6´2˝/185 lbs; Texas Tech; 1987: Min, rnd 9; B10/28/1964 St. Louis, MO **1987** Den 2 (1)

JONES, LEROY Leroy, DE, 6´8˝/263 lbs; Norfolk State; 1975: LA, rnd 2; B9/29/1950 Greenwood, MS **1976** SD 14 (10, LDE) **1977** SD 14 (13, LDE) **1978** SD 16 (15, LDE) **1979**†SD 16 (15, LDE) **1980**†SD 15 (15, LDE) **1981**†SD 16 (14, LDE) **1982**†SD 8 (8, LDE) **1983** SD 12 (0) **NFL** 111 (90) [8 yrs]

JONES, LEVI Levi J., T, 6´5˝/310 lbs; Arizona State; 2002: Cin, rnd 1; B8/24/1979 Eloy, AZ **2002** Cin 16 (14, LT) **2003** Cin 16 (16, LT) **2004** Cin 16 (16, LT) **2005**†Cin 15 (15, LT) **NFL** 63 (61) [4 yrs]

JONES, LEW Lewis Norten, G-LB, 6´0˝/215 lbs; Texas Tech; B12/15/1912 Cleburne, TX, D9/1970 **1943** Bkn 10 (7, RG)

JONES, LYNDELL Anthony Lydell, DB, 5´9˝/175 lbs; Hawaii; B3/18/1959 Seattle, WA **1987** Atl 3 (2)

JONES, MARCUS Marcus Edward, DE-DT, 6´6˝/286 lbs; North Carolina; 1996: TB, rnd 1; B8/15/1973 Jacksonville, FL **1996** TB 16 (3) **1997** TB 7 (1) **1998** TB 15 (0) **1999**†TB 16 (4) **2000** TB 16 (16, RDE) **2001**†TB 15 (15, LDE) **NFL** 85 (39) [6 yrs]

JONES, MARK Mark Christopher, WR, 5´9˝/185 lbs; Tennessee; 2004: TB, rnd 7; B11/3/1980 Wallingford, PA [R] **2004** NYG 14 (0) **2005**†TB 16 (0) **NFL** 30 (0) [2 yrs]

JONES, MARLON Marlon Anthony, DE-DT, 6´4˝/263 lbs; Central State (OH); B7/1/1964 Baltimore, MD **1987** Cle 1 (0) **1988** Cle 16 (1) **1989** Cle 8 (0) **NFL** 25 (1) [3 yrs]

JONES, MARSHALL Marshall Durell, WB-TB-FB, 5´11˝/165 lbs; North Dakota; B12/10/1894 Fargo, IN, D1/21/1960 Hennepin County, MI **1920** Ham 1 (0) **1920** Det 1 (0) **1921** Akr 7 (1) **NFL** 9 (1) [2 yrs]

JONES, MARVIN Marvin Maurice, LB, 6´2˝/244 lbs; Florida State; 1993: NYJ, rnd 1; B6/28/1972 Miami, FL **1993** NYJ 9 (0) **1994** NYJ 15 (11, MLB) **1995** NYJ 10 (10, MLB) **1996** NYJ 12 (12, MLB) **1997** NYJ 16 (16, RILB) **1999** NYJ 16 (16, RILB) **2000** NYJ 16 (16, RILB) **2001**†NYJ 16 (16, MLB) **2002**†NYJ 16 (16, MLB) **2003** NYJ 16 (16, MLB) **NFL** 142 (129) [10 yrs]

JONES, MATT Matthew, WR, 6´6˝/242 lbs; Arkansas; 2005: Jax, rnd 1; B4/22/1983 Fort Smith, AR

YEAR	TEAM	G(GS, POS)	RUSH	YD	AVG(LG)	TD	REC	YD	AVG(LG)	TD	PASS	COMP	PCT	YD	AVG(LG)	TD	INT	SK	YD	QBR	KPR	OTD	PTS	TAY
2005	†Jax	16(1)	12	51	4.3(25)	0	36	432	12.0(42)	5	3	2	66.7	12	4.0(6)	0	0	—	—	—	—	—	30	298

JONES, MELVIN Melvin Curtis, G, 6´2˝/260 lbs; Houston; 1980: Was, rnd 7; B2/27/1954 Houston, TX **1981** Was 11 (10, RG)

JONES, MIKE Michael, LB, 6´3˝/224 lbs; Alcorn State; Jackson State; B7/12/1954 Chicago, IL **1977** Sea 12

JONES, MIKE Michael Anthony, LB, 6´1˝/233 lbs; Missouri; B4/15/1969 Kansas City, MO **1991**†LARd 16 (0) **1992** LARd 16 (0) **1993**†LARd 16 (2) **1994** LARd 16 (2) **1995** Oak 16 (16, RLB) **1996** Oak 15 (15, RLB) **1997** SL 16 (15, LLB) **1998** SL 16 (15, LLB) **1999**†SL 16 (16, LLB) **2000**†SL 16 (16, LLB) **2001**†Pit 15 (0) **2002**†Oak 3 (0) **2002** Pit 6 (1) **NFL** 183 (98) [12 yrs]

JONES, MIKE Michael, LB, 6´4˝/224 lbs; Brockport State; B8/19/1964 New York, NY **1987** Buf 1 (0)

JONES, MIKE Michael Anthony, WR, 5´11˝/181 lbs; Tennessee State; 1983: Min, rnd 6; B4/14/1960 Chattanooga, TN

YEAR	TEAM	G(GS, POS)	RUSH	YD	AVG(LG)	TD	REC	YD	AVG(LG)	TD	PASS	COMP	PCT	YD	AVG(LG)	TD	INT	SK	YD	QBR	KPR	OTD	PTS	TAY
1983	Min	16(0)	1	9	9.0(9)	0	6	95	15.8(47)	0	—	—	—	—	—	—	—	—	—	—	k	—	0	58
1984	Min	16(14, WR)	4	45	11.3(36)	0	38	591	15.6(70)	1	—	—	—	—	—	—	—	—	—	—	—	—	6	346
1985	Min	16(8, wr)	2	6	3.0(6)	0	46	641	13.9(44)	4	—	—	—	—	—	—	—	—	—	—	—	—	24	347
1986	NO	16(8, WR)	—	—	—	—	48	625	13.0(45)	3	—	—	—	—	—	—	—	—	—	—	—	—	18	328
1987	†NO	12(7, WR)	—	—	—	—	27	420	15.6(43)	3	—	—	—	—	—	—	—	—	—	—	—	—	18	225
1989	NO	3(0)	—	—	—	—	—	—	—	—	—	—	—	—	—	—	—	—	—	—	—	—	—	—
NFL	6	79(37)	7	60	8.6(36)	0	165	2372	14.4(70)	11	—	—	—	—	—	—	—	—	—	—	k	—	66	1302

JONES, MIKE Michael David, DE, 6´4˝/290 lbs; North Carolina State; 1991: Phx, rnd 2; B8/25/1969 Columbia, SC **1991** Phx 16 (1) **1992** Phx 15 (15, RDE/lde) **1993** Phx 16 (3) **1994**†NE 16 (16, RDE) **1995** NE 13 (3) **1996**†NE 16 (12, LDE) **1997**†NE 16 (7, lde) **1998** SL 16 (15, RDE) **1999**†Ten 11 (3) **NFL** 135 (75) [9 yrs]

YEAR	TEAM	G (GS, POS)	RUSH	YD	AVG(LG)	TD	REC	YD	AVG(LG)	TD	PASS COMP	PCT	YD	AVG(LG)	TD	INT	SK	YD	QBR	KPR	OTD	PTS	TAY

JONES, MIKE   Michael Lenere, TE, 6´3˝/255 lbs; Michigan; Texas A&M; 1990: Min, rnd 3; B11/10/1966 Bridgeport, CT

YEAR	TEAM	G (GS, POS)	RUSH	YD	AVG(LG)	TD	REC	YD	AVG(LG)	TD	...	...	OTD	PTS	TAY
1990	Min	11(0)	—	—	—	—	—	—	—	—			—	12	14
1991	Min	16(0)	—	—	—	—	2	8	4.0(5)	2			—	12	14
1992	Sea	4(1)	—	—	—	—	3	18	6.0(7)	0			—	0	9
NFL	3	31(1)	—	—	—	—	5	26	5.2(7)	2			—	12	23

JONES, NATE   Nathan, DB, 5´10˝/180 lbs; Rutgers; 2004: Dal, rnd 7; B6/13/1982 Scotch Plains, NJ   **2004** Dal 16 (1)   **2005** Dal 16 (0)   **NFL** 32 (1) [2 yrs]

JONES, PACMAN   Adam, DB, 5´11˝/187 lbs; West Virginia; 2005: Ten, rnd 1; B9/30/1983 College Park, GA

YEAR	TEAM	G (GS, POS)	...	PASS COMP	PCT	YD	AVG(LG)	TD	INT	SK	YD	QBR	KPR	OTD	PTS	TAY
2005	Ten	15(13, RCB)		0	0.0	0	0.0	0	0	1	13	—	kp	1	6	619

JONES, POTSY   Thomas Clinton, G, 5´11˝/216 lbs; Bucknell; B10/15/1909 Llewellyn, PA, D7/3/1990 Lucama, NC   **1930** Min 2 (1)   **1930** Fra 14 (10, RG/lg)   **1931** Fra 8 (8, RG)   **1932** NYG 9 (5, RG)   **1933**†NYG 7 (7, RG)   **1934**†NYG☆12 (10, LG)   **1935**†NYG☆9 (7, LG)   **1936** NYG 10 (5, RG)   **1938** GB 8 (0)   **NFL** 79 (53) [8 yrs]

JONES, QUINTIN   Quintin, DB, 5´11˝/193 lbs; Pittsburgh; 1988: Hou, rnd 2; B7/28/1966 Miami, FL   **1988** Hou 4 (0)   **1990** Hou 1 (0)   **NFL** 5 (0) [2 yrs]

JONES, RALPH   Ralph Carroll, E-DE, 6´3˝/200 lbs; Union (TN); Alabama; B2/14/1922 Florence, AL

YEAR	TEAM	G (GS, POS)	RUSH	YD	AVG(LG)	TD	REC	YD	AVG(LG)	TD	...	OTD	PTS	TAY
1946	Det	11(0)	—	—	—	—	4	84	21.0(29)	0		—	0	42
1947	Bal-A	6(1)	—	—	—	—	3	23	7.7	0		—	0	12

JONES, RAY   Raymond, DB, 5´11˝/187 lbs; Southern (LA); 1970: Phi, rnd 2; B12/24/1947 Lufkin, TX   **1970** Phi 12 (LCB)   **1971** Mia 2   **1972** SD 14   **1973** NO 2   **NFL** 30 [4 yrs]

JONES, REGGIE   Reginald Moore, DB, 6´1˝/202 lbs; Memphis; 1991: NO, rnd 5; B1/11/1969 Memphis, TN   **1991**†NO 13 (1)   **1992**†NO 15 (15, RCB)   **1993** NO 12 (2)   **1994** NO 1 (1)   **NFL** 41 (19) [4 yrs]

JONES, REGGIE   Reginald Lee, WR, 6´0˝/175 lbs; LSU; B5/8/1971 Kansas City, KS

YEAR	TEAM	G (GS, POS)	RUSH	YD	AVG(LG)	TD	REC	YD	AVG(LG)	TD	...	KPR	OTD	PTS	TAY
1995	Car	1(0)	—	—	—	—	—	—	—	—			—		
2000	SD	11(2)	—	—	—	—	22	253	11.5(34)	0		kp	—	0	131
2001	SD	9(0)	—	—	—	—	5	29	5.8(11)	0		kp	—	0	71
NFL	3	21(2)	—	—	—	—	27	282	10.4(34)	0		kp	—	0	201

JONES, RENO   Reno Victor, G, 6´0˝/195 lbs; Cornell; B2/20/1897 Niles, OH, D1/7/1989 Wykoff, NJ   **1922** Tol 4 (2)

JONES, RICHARD   Richard B., DB, 5´9˝/183 lbs; Texas A&M-Kingsville; B8/4/1973 Waco, TX   **1996**†Ind 3 (0)

JONES, RICKY   Broderick, LB-DB, 6´1˝/211 lbs; Tuskegee; B3/9/1955 Birmingham, AL   **1977** Cle 3   **1978** Cle 15   **1979** Cle 16   **1980** Bal 12 (0)   **1981** Bal 16 (0)   **1982** Bal 9 (0)   **1983** Bal 16 (0)   **NFL** 87 [7 yrs]

JONES, ROBBIE   Robert Washington, LB, 6´2˝/230 lbs; Alabama; 1983: NYG, rnd 12; B12/25/1959 Demopolis, AL   **1984**†NYG 16 (0)   **1985**†NYG 16 (0)   **1986**†NYG 16 (0)   **1987** NYG 12 (0)   **NFL** 60 (0) [4 yrs]

JONES, ROBERT   Robert Lee, LB, 6´3˝/244 lbs; East Carolina; 1992: Dal, rnd 1; B9/27/1969 Blackstone, VA   **1992**†Dal 15 (13, MLB)   **1993**†Dal 13 (3)   **1994**†Dal 16 (16, MLB)   **1995**†Dal 12 (12, MLB)   **1996** SL 16 (13, MLB)   **1997** SL 16 (15, MLB)   **1998** Mia 16 (16, RLB)   **1999** Mia 16 (15, RLB)   **2000**†Mia 16 (16, RLB)   **2001** Was 15 (9, RLB)   **NFL** 151 (128) [10 yrs]

JONES, ROD   Roderick Wayne, DB, 6´0˝/185 lbs; SMU; 1986: TB, rnd 1; B3/31/1964 Dallas, TX   **1986** TB 16 (16, RCB)   **1987** TB 11 (11, RCB)   **1988** TB 14 (1)   **1989** TB 16 (16, RCB)   **1990**†Cin 16 (6, rcb)   **1991** Cin 4 (2)   **1992** Cin 16 (14, LCB)   **1993** Cin 16 (16, RCB)   **1994** Cin 16 (16, RCB)   **1995** Cin 13 (9, RCB)   **1996** Cin 8 (0)   **NFL** 146 (107) [11 yrs]

JONES, ROD   Roderick Earl, TE, 6´4˝/240 lbs; Washington; 1987: NYG, rnd 8; B3/3/1964 Richmond, CA   **1988** KC 2 (0)   **1989** Sea 4 (0)

YEAR	TEAM	G (GS, POS)	RUSH	YD	AVG(LG)	TD	REC	YD	AVG(LG)	TD	...	OTD	PTS	TAY
1987	KC	3(1)	—	—	—	—	8	76	9.5(16)	1		—	6	43
NFL	3	9(1)	—	—	—	—	8	76	9.5(16)	1		—	6	43

JONES, ROD   Rodrek Edward, T, 6´4˝/325 lbs; Kansas; 1996: Cin, rnd 7; B1/11/1974 Detroit, MI   **1996** Cin 5 (1)   **1997** Cin 13 (8, lt)   **1998** Cin 7 (2)   **1999** Cin 16 (15, LT)   **2000** Cin 16 (11, LT)   **2001**†SL 6 (1)   **NFL** 63 (38) [6 yrs]

JONES, ROGER   Roger Carver, DB, 5´9˝/175 lbs; Tennessee State; B4/22/1969 Cleveland, TN   **1991** TB 6 (0)   **1992** TB 9 (1)   **1993** TB 16 (5, cb)   **1994** Cin 16 (0)   **1995** Cin 16 (15, LCB)   **1996** Cin 14 (2)   **1997** Ten 2 (0)   **NFL** 79 (23) [7 yrs]

JONES, RON   Ronald Gene, TE, 6´3˝/220 lbs; Texas-El Paso; 1969: GB, rnd 6; B10/7/1946 Dallas, TX   **1969** GB 6

JONES, RONDELL   Rondell Tony, DB, 6´2˝/210 lbs; North Carolina; 1993: Den, rnd 3; B5/7/1971 Sunderland, MD   **1993**†Den 16 (0)   **1994** Den 16 (3)   **1995** Den 14 (0)   **1996** Den 16 (0)   **1997** Bal 14 (12, FS)   **NFL** 76 (15) [5 yrs]

JONES, RULON   Rulon Kent, DE, 6´6˝/260 lbs; Utah State; 1980: Den, rnd 2; B3/25/1958 Salt Lake City, UT [S]   **1980** Den 16 (2)   **1981** Den 16 (16, RDE)   **1982** Den 9 (9, RDE)   **1983**†Den 12 (12, RDE)   **1984**†Den 16 (16, RDE)   **1985** Den★16 (16, RDE)   **1986**†Den★16 (16, RDE)   **1987**†Den☆12 (12, RDE)   **1988** Den 16 (0)   **NFL** 129 (99) [9 yrs]

JONES, RUSHEN   Rushen, DB, 5´10˝/194 lbs; Vanderbilt; B8/4/1980, HI   **2003** Min 11 (0)   **2004**†Min 5 (0)   **NFL** 16 (0) [2 yrs]

JONES, SCOTT   Robert Scott, T, 6´5˝/281 lbs; Washington; 1989: Cin, rnd 12; B3/20/1966 Portland, OR   **1989** Cin 15 (0)   **1990** NYJ 3 (0)   **1991** GB 2 (1)   **1991** Cin 2 (0)   **NFL** 22 (1) [3 yrs]

JONES, SEAN   Dwight Andre Sean-O'Neil, DE, 6´7˝/270 lbs; Northeastern; 1984: LARd, rnd 2; B12/19/1962 Kingston, Jamaica [S]   **1984**†LARd 16 (0)   **1985**†LARd 15 (4)   **1986** LARd 16 (16, RDE)   **1987** LARd 12 (12, RDE)   **1988**†Hou 16 (0)   **1989**†Hou 16 (5, rde)   **1990**†Hou 16 (16, RDE)   **1991**†Hou 16 (12, RDE)   **1992**†Hou 15 (15, RDE)   **1993**†Hou☆16 (16, RDE)   **1994**†GB☆16 (16, RDE)   **1995**†GB☆16 (15, RDE)   **1996**†GB 15 (15, RDE)   **NFL** 201 (143) [13 yrs]

JONES, SEAN   Sean, DB, 6´2˝/212 lbs; Georgia; 2004: Cle, rnd 2; B3/2/1982 Atlanta, GA   **2005** Cle 16 (0)

JONES, SELWYN   Selwyn Aldridge, DB, 6´0˝/192 lbs; Colorado State; 1992: Cle, rnd 7; B5/13/1970 Houston, TX   **1993** Cle 11 (2)   **1994** NO 5 (1)   **1995** Sea 15 (1)   **1996** Sea 16 (1)   **NFL** 47 (4) [4 yrs]

JONES, SHAWN   Andrew Shawn, DB, 6´1˝/200 lbs; Georgia Tech; B6/16/1970 Thomasville, GA   **1993** Min 1 (0)

JONES, SPIKE   John Amos, P, 6´2˝/197 lbs; Georgia; 1970: Hou, rnd 4; B7/9/1947 Louisville, GA [P]   **1970** Hou 14   **1971** Buf 13   **1974** Buf 8   **1977** Phi 14

YEAR	TEAM	G (GS, POS)	RUSH	YD	AVG(LG)	TD	REC	YD	AVG(LG)	TD	PASS COMP	PCT	YD	AVG(LG)	TD	INT	SK	YD	QBR	OTD	PTS	TAY
1972	Buf	14	2	18	9.0(10)	0	—	—	—	—	2	1	50.0	4	2.0(4)	0	0	—	—	—	P	0	20
1973	Buf	1	1	0	0.0(0)	0	—	—	—	—	—	—	—	—	—	—	—	—	—	—	P	0	0
1975	Phi	12	1	-1	-1.0(-1)	0	—	—	—	—	—	—	—	—	—	—	—	—	—	—	P	0	-1
1976	Phi	14	—	—	—	—	—	—	—	—	1	1	100.0	4	-4.0(-4)	0	0	—	—	—	P	0	-2
NFL	8	103	4	17	4.3(10)	0	—	—	—	—	2	2	66.7	4	0.0(4)	0	0	—	—	—	P	0	17

JONES, STAN   Stanley Paul, G-DT-T, 6´1˝/252 lbs; Maryland; 1953: ChiB, rnd 5; B11/24/1931 Altoona, PA; HOF 1991   **1954** ChiB 12 (RT)   **1955** ChiB★12 (RG)   **1956**†ChiB★11 (RG)   **1957** ChiB★12 (RG)   **1958** ChiB☆12 (RG)   **1959** ChiB★12 (RG)   **1960** ChiB★12 (LG)   **1961** ChiB★14 (LG)   **1962** ChiB 14 (LG)   **1963**†ChiB 13 (LDT)   **1964** ChiB 14 (LDT)   **1965** ChiB 6 (ldt)   **1966** Was 13 (RDT)   **NFL** 157 [13 yrs]

JONES, STEVE   Steven Hunter, RB, 6´0˝/200 lbs; Duke; 1973: LA, rnd 5; B3/6/1951 Sanford, SC

YEAR	TEAM	G (GS, POS)	RUSH	YD	AVG(LG)	TD	REC	YD	AVG(LG)	TD	...	KPR	OTD	PTS	TAY
1973	Buf	11	3	9	3.0(7)	0	—	—	—	—		k	—	0	35
1974	Buf	1													
1974	†SL	7													
1975	†SL	13	54	275	5.1(23)	2	19	194	10.2(21)	1		k	—	18	400
1976	SL	13	113	451	4.0(19)	8	29	152	5.2(15)	1		k	—	54	612
1977	SL	14	24	77	3.2(18)	3	12	66	5.5(16)	0		k	—	18	152
1978	SL	16	105	392	3.7(17)	2	27	217	8.0(38)	0		k	—	12	521
NFL	6	75	299	1204	4.0(23)	15	87	629	7.2(38)	2		k	—	102	1720

JONES, TEBUCKY   Tebucky Shermaine, DB, 6´2˝/218 lbs; Syracuse; 1998: NE, rnd 1; B10/6/1974 New Britain, CT   **1998**†NE 16 (0)   **1999** NE 11 (2)   **2000** NE 15 (9, FS)   **2001**†NE 16 (12, FS)   **2002** NE 14 (12, FS)   **2003** NO 15 (15, FS)   **2004** NO 16 (16, FS)   **2005** Mia 6 (6, ss)   **NFL** 109 (72) [8 yrs]

JONES, TERRY   Terry Wayne, NT-DT, 6´2˝/259 lbs; Alabama; 1978: GB, rnd 11; B11/8/1956 Sandersville, GA   **1978** GB 16   **1979** GB 12 (6, ldt)   **1980** GB 15 (1)   **1981** GB 16 (16, NT)   **1982**†GB 9 (9, NT)   **1983** GB 1 (1)   **1984** GB 16 (16, NT)   **NFL** 85 (49) [7 yrs]

JONES, TERRY   Terry W., TE, 6´3˝/265 lbs; Alabama; 2002: Bal, rnd 5; B12/3/1979 Tuscaloosa, AL

YEAR	TEAM	G (GS, POS)	RUSH	YD	AVG(LG)	TD	REC	YD	AVG(LG)	TD	...	OTD	PTS	TAY
2002	Bal	14(6, TE)	—	—	—	—	11	106	9.6(27)	1		—	6	58
2003	†Bal	16(13, TE)	—	—	—	—	19	159	8.4(25)	3		—	18	95
2004	Bal	15(10, TE)	—	—	—	—	20	152	7.6(19)	1		—	6	81

YEAR	TEAM	G (GS, POS)	RUSH	YD	AVG(LG)	TD	REC	YD	AVG(LG)	TD	PASS	COMP	PCT	YD	AVG(LG)	TD	INT	SK	YD	QBR	KPR	OTD	PTS	TAY
2005	Bal	1(0)	—	—	—	—	—	—	—	—	—	—	—	—	—	—	—	—	—	—	—	—	—	38
2005	SF	7(5, te)	—	—	—	—	9	76	8.4(21)	0	—	—	—	—	—	—	—	—	—	—	—	—	0	38
NFL	4	53(34)	—	—	—	—	59	493	8.4(27)	5	—	—	—	—	—	—	—	—	—	—	—	—	30	272

JONES, THOMAS   Thomas Quinn, RB, 5´10˝/220 lbs; Virginia; 2000: Arz, rnd 1; B8/19/1978 Big Stone Gap, VA

YEAR	TEAM	G (GS, POS)	RUSH	YD	AVG(LG)	TD	REC	YD	AVG(LG)	TD	KPR	OTD	PTS	TAY
2000	Arz	14(4)	112	373	3.3(29)	2	32	208	6.5(20)	0			12	497
2001	Arz	16(2)	112	380	3.4(21)	5	21	151	7.2(18)	0			30	506
2002	Arz	9(9, RB)	138	511	3.7(58)	2	20	113	5.7(17)	0			12	588
2003	TB	16(3)	137	627	4.6(61)	3	24	180	7.5(29)	0	k		18	763
2004	ChiB	14(14, RB)	240	948	4.0(54)	7	56	427	7.6(45)	0			42	1232
2005	†ChiB	15(15, RB)	314	1335	4.3(42)	9	26	143	5.5(41)	0			54	1497
NFL	6	84(47)	1053	4174	4.0(61)	28	179	1222	6.8(45)	0	k		168	5081

JONES, THURMAN   Thurman Lee, FB-DB, 5´10˝/198 lbs; Abilene Christian; B4/6/1918 Wilson, OK, D1/16/1988 Tugwell, TX [K]

YEAR	TEAM	G (GS, POS)	RUSH	YD	AVG(LG)	TD	KPR	OTD	PTS	TAY
1941	Bkn	1(0)	1	3	3.0(3)	0			0	3
1942	Bkn	4(0)	1	2	2.0(2)	0	K		1	2
NFL	2	5(0)	2	5	2.5(3)	0	K		1	5

JONES, TODD   Todd A., T, 6´3˝/295 lbs; Arkansas; Henderson State; 1991: Cle, rnd 11; B7/3/1967 Hope, AR   **1993** NE 4 (0)

JONES, TOM   Thomas Lee, RB, 6´0˝/200 lbs; Kentucky State; Miami (OH); 1954: Cle, rnd 9; B6/22/1931 Cincinnati, OH, D8/28/1978 Port Chevron, Canada   **1955** Cle 2

JONES, TONY   Anthony Bernard, WR, 5´7˝/142 lbs; Texas; 1990: Hou, rnd 6; B12/30/1965 Grapeland, TX

YEAR	TEAM	G (GS, POS)	RUSH	YD	AVG(LG)	TD	REC	YD	AVG(LG)	TD	KPR	OTD	PTS	TAY
1990	†Hou	15(0)	1	-2	-2.0(-2)	0	30	409	13.6(47)	6			36	233
1991	†Hou	16(0)	—	—	—	—	19	251	13.2(68)	2			12	136
1992	Atl	10(4)	—	—	—	—	14	138	9.9(24)	1			6	74
1993	Hou	2(0)	—	—	—	—	—	—	—	—			—	—
NFL	4	43(4)	1	-2	-2.0(-2)	0	63	798	12.7(68)	9			54	442

JONES, TONY   Reginald Antonio, DB, 6´4˝/200 lbs; Syracuse; B2/16/1972 Tampa, FL   **1995** Arz 2 (0)

JONES, TONY   Tony Edward, T-G, 6´5˝/290 lbs; Western Carolina; B5/24/1966 Royston, GA   **1988**†Cle 4 (0)   **1989**†Cle 9 (3)   **1990** Cle 16 (16, RT)   **1991** Cle 16 (16, LT)   **1992** Cle 16 (16, LT)   **1993** Cle 16 (16, LT)   **1994**†Cle☆16 (16, LT)   **1995** Cle 16 (16, LT)   **1996** Bal 15 (15, LT)   **1997**†Den 16 (16, RT/lt)   **1998**†Den◇16 (16, LT)   **1999** Den 12 (12, LT)   **2000**†Den 16 (16, LT)   **NFL** 184 (174) [13 yrs]

JONES, TOO TALL   Edward Lee, DE, 6´9˝/271 lbs; Tennessee State; 1974: Dal, rnd 1; B2/23/1951 Jackson, TN [S]   **1974** Dal 14   **1975**†Dal 14 (LDE)   **1976**†Dal 14 (14, LDE)   **1977**†Dal 14 (LDE)   **1978**†Dal☆16 (LDE)   **1980**†Dal 16 (16, LDE)   **1981**†Dal★16 (16, LDE)   **1982**†Dal★9 (9, LDE)   **1983**†Dal★16 (16, LDE)   **1984** Dal 16 (16, LDE)   **1985**†Dal☆16 (16, LDE)   **1987** Dal 15 (14, LDE)   **1988** Dal 16 (16, LDE)   **1989** Dal 16 (10, LDE)   **NFL** 224 (159) [15 yrs]

JONES, TYRONE   Tyrone, LB, 6´0˝/220 lbs; Southern (LA); B8/3/1961 St. Marys, GA   **1988** Phx 1 (0)

JONES, TYRONE   Earnest Tyrone, DB, 6´4˝/223 lbs; Arkansas State; B11/9/1966 Ruston, LA   **1989** Phi 3 (0)

JONES, VICTOR   Victor Tyrone, RB, 5´8˝/212 lbs; LSU; B12/5/1967 Zachary, LA   **1991** Hou 14 (0)   **1993** Pit 16 (0)   **1994** Pit 10 (0)   **1994** KC 1 (0)

YEAR	TEAM	G (GS, POS)	RUSH	YD	AVG(LG)	TD	REC	YD	AVG(LG)	TD	KPR	OTD	PTS	TAY
1990	Hou	10(0)	14	75	5.4(14)	0	—	—	—	—			0	75
1992	Den	16(1)	—	—	—	—	3	17	5.7(16)	0			0	9
NFL	5	67(1)	14	75	5.4(14)	0	3	17	5.7(16)	0	k		0	76

JONES, VICTOR   Victor Purnell, LB, 6´2˝/250 lbs; Virginia Tech; 1988: TB, rnd 12; B10/19/1966 Rockville, MD   **1988** TB 8 (0)   **1989** Det 11 (9, RILB)   **1990** Det 16 (5, rilb)   **1991**†Det 10 (0)   **1992** Det 16 (0)   **1993**†Det 16 (1)   **1994**†Det 16 (0)   **NFL** 93 (15) [7 yrs]

JONES, WALTER   Walter Junior, T, 6´5˝/300 lbs; Florida State; 1997: Sea, rnd 1; B1/19/1974 Aliceville, AL   **1997** Sea 12 (12, LT)   **1998** Sea 16 (16, LT)   **1999**†Sea◇16 (16, LT)   **2000** Sea 16 (16, LT)   **2001** Sea★16 (16, LT)   **2002** Sea★14 (14, LT)   **2003**†Sea★16 (16, LT)   **2004**†Sea★16 (16, LT)   **2005**†Sea★15 (15, LT)   **NFL** 137 (137) [9 yrs]

JONES, WAYNE   Wayne Walter, G, 6´4˝/270 lbs; Utah; 1982: Mia, rnd 10; B2/10/1960 Grand Island, NE   **1987** Min 6 (0)

JONES, WILLIE   William D., FB, 5´11˝/208 lbs; Purdue; 1961: Min, rnd 17; B8/30/1939 Angleton, TX

YEAR	TEAM	G (GS, POS)	RUSH	YD	AVG(LG)	TD	KPR	OTD	PTS	TAY
1962	Buf-A	10	4	17	4.3(10)	0	k	—	0	94

JONES, WILLIE   Willie Lee, DT-DE, 6´1˝/260 lbs; Kansas State; 1966: SL, rnd 18; B5/28/1942 Moro, AR   **1967** Hou-A 6   **1968** Cin-A 1   **1970**†Cin 10   **1971** Cin 5   **NFL** 22 [4 yrs]

JONES, WILLIE   Willie Lorenzo, DE, 6´4˝/240 lbs; Florida State; 1979: Oak, rnd 2; B11/22/1957 Dublin, GA   **1979** Oak 16 (3)   **1980**†Oak 16 (0)   **1981** Oak 8 (0)   **NFL** 40 (3) [3 yrs]

JONES, WILLIE   Willie J., T, 6´6˝/256 lbs; Central Florida; Morgan State; Grambling State; B12/17/1975 Belle Glade, FL   **2001** KC 12 (0)   **2002** KC 6 (0)   **NFL** 18 (0) [2 yrs]

JORDAN, ANDREW   Andrew, TE, 6´4˝/260 lbs; Western Carolina; 1994: Min, rnd 6; B6/21/1972 Charlotte, NC

YEAR	TEAM	G (GS, POS)	RUSH	YD	AVG(LG)	TD	REC	YD	AVG(LG)	TD	KPR	OTD	PTS	TAY
1994	†Min	16(12, TE)	—	—	—	—	35	336	9.6(25)	0	k	—	2	161
1995	Min	13(7, te)	—	—	—	—	27	185	6.9(17)	2			12	103
1996	†Min	13(9, TE)	—	—	—	—	19	128	6.7(15)	0			2	64
1997	Min	2(0)	—	—	—	—	—	—	—	—			—	—
1997	TB	2(0)	—	—	—	—	1	0	0.0(0)	0			0	0
1998	Phi	3(0)	—	—	—	—	2	9	4.5(8)	0			0	5
1999	Min	11(1)	—	—	—	—	5	40	8.0(11)	1	k		6	10
2000	†Min	16(4)	—	—	—	—	8	63	7.9(12)	0			0	32
2001	Min	16(4)	—	—	—	—	3	11	3.7(4)	1			6	11
NFL	8	92(37)	—	—	—	—	100	772	7.7(25)	4			28	384

JORDAN, ANTONY   Antony, LB, 6´2˝/234 lbs; Vanderbilt; 1998: Ind, rnd 5; B12/19/1974 Sewell, NJ   **1998** Ind 15 (3)   **2000** Atl 8 (0)   **2001** Atl 4 (0)   **NFL** 27 (3) [3 yrs]

JORDAN, BRIAN   Brian O'Neil, DB, 5´11˝/205 lbs; Richmond; 1989: Buf, rnd 7; B3/29/1967 Baltimore, MD   **1989** Atl 4 (0)   **1990** Atl 16 (15, SS)   **1991**†Atl 16 (15, SS)   **NFL** 36 (30) [3 yrs]

JORDAN, BUFORD   Paul Buford, RB, 6´0˝/223 lbs; McNeese State; 1984: GB, rnd S1; B6/26/1962 Lafayette, IN

YEAR	TEAM	G (GS, POS)	RUSH	YD	AVG(LG)	TD	REC	YD	AVG(LG)	TD	KPR	OTD	PTS	TAY
1986	NO	16(9, fb)	68	207	3.0(10)	1	11	127	11.5(37)	0			6	281
1987	†NO	12(4)	12	36	3.0(8)	2	2	13	6.5(11)	0	kp		12	69
1988	NO	14(3)	19	115	6.1(44)	0	5	70	14.0(25)	0		1	6	150
1989	NO	11(7, FB)	38	179	4.7(32)	3	4	53	13.3(17)	0			18	236
1990	†NO	6(0)	—	—	—	—	—	—	—	—			—	—
1991	†NO	14(6, fb)	47	150	3.2(25)	2	15	92	6.1(19)	1	k		18	209
1992	†NO	2(0)	—	—	—	—	—	—	—	—	k		0	3
NFL	7	75(29)	184	687	3.7(44)	8	37	355	9.6(37)	1	kp	1	60	947

JORDAN, CHARLES   Charles Alexander, WR, 5´11˝/182 lbs; Long Beach C.C.; B10/9/1969 Los Angeles, CA

YEAR	TEAM	G (GS, POS)	RUSH	YD	AVG(LG)	TD	REC	YD	AVG(LG)	TD	KPR	OTD	PTS	TAY
1994	†GB	10(0)	1	5	5.0(5)	0	—	—	—	—	kp	—	0	40
1995	GB	6(1)	—	—	—	—	7	117	16.7(35)	2	kp		12	306
1996	Mia	6(0)	—	—	—	—	7	152	21.7(43)	0	k		0	97
1997	†Mia	14(1)	3	12	4.0(16)	0	27	471	17.4(44)	3	kp		18	397
1998	Mia	3(0)	—	—	—	—	2	17	8.5(9)	0	p		0	31
1999	Sea	4(1)	—	—	—	—	1	6	6.0(6)	0	kp		0	42
1999	GB	4(0)	—	—	—	—	2	54	27.0(43)	0	kp		0	36
NFL	6	47(3)	4	17	4.3(16)	0	46	817	17.8(44)	5	kp	—	30	948

JORDAN, CURTIS   Curtis Wayne, DB, 6´2˝/200 lbs; Texas Tech; 1976: TB, rnd 6; B1/25/1954 Lubbock, TX   **1976** TB 11 (9, LCB)   **1977** TB 12 (2)   **1978** TB 16 (5, fs)   **1979**†TB 16 (2)   **1980** TB 16 (16, LCB)   **1981** Was 2 (0)   **1982** Was 9 (0)   **1983**†Was 15 (13, SS)   **1984**†Was 16 (14, FS)   **1985** Was 16 (16, FS)   **1986**†Was 16 (16, FS)   **NFL** 145 (93) [11 yrs]

JORDAN, DARIN   Darin Godfrey, LB-DE, 6´1˝/242 lbs; Northeastern; 1988: Pit, rnd 5; B12/4/1964 Boston, MA   **1988** Pit 15 (2)   **1990**†LARd 0 (0)   **1991** SF 15 (4)   **1992**†SF 15 (1)   **1993** SF 14 (0)   **1994**†SF 0 (0)   **NFL** 59 (7) [6 yrs]

JORDAN, DAVID   David Turner, G, 6´6˝/274 lbs; Auburn; 1984: NYG, rnd 10; B6/14/1962 Birmingham, AL   **1984**†NYG 14 (1)   **1985**†NYG 16 (0)   **1987** TB 3 (3)   **NFL** 33 (4) [3 yrs]

YEAR	TEAM	G (GS, POS)	RUSH	YD	AVG(LG)	TD	REC	YD	AVG(LG)	TD	PASS COMP	PCT	YD	AVG(LG)	TD	INT	SK	YD	QBR	KPR	OTD	PTS	TAY

JORDAN, DONALD Donald Ray, RB, 6´0˝/210 lbs; Houston; 1984: Chi, rnd 12; B2/9/1962 Houston, TX

| 1984 | ChiB | 13(0) | 11 | 70 | 6.4(29) | 0 | 1 | 6 | 6.0(6) | 0 | — | — | — | — | — | — | — | — | — | k | — | 0 | 60 |

JORDAN, FRANK Francis, WB, /168 lbs; Bucknell; Villanova; B12/5/1897 Minneapolis, MN, D9/1980 Tucson, AZ **1920** RI 3 (1) **1923** Mil 1 (0) **NFL** 4 (1) [2 yrs]

JORDAN, HENRY Henry Wendell, DT-DE, 6´2˝/248 lbs; Virginia; 1957: Cle, rnd 5; B1/26/1935 Emporia, VA, D2/21/1977 Milwaukee, WI; HOF 1995 **1957**†Cle 12 **1958**†Cle 12 **1959** GB 12 (RDT) **1960**†GB★14 (RDT) **1961**†GB☆14 (RDT) **1962**†GB☆14 (RDT) **1963** GB★14 (RDT) **1964** GB☆12 (RDT) **1965**†GB 14 (RDT) **1966**†GB★14 (RDT) **1967**†GB☆14 (RDT) **1968** GB 14 (RDT) **1969** GB 5 (RDT) **NFL** 163 [13 yrs]

JORDAN, JAMES James Robert, WR, 6´2˝/225 lbs; Louisiana Tech; B6/11/1978 Los Angeles, CA **2002** SF 6 (0) **2003** SF 1 (0) **NFL** 7 (0) [2 yrs]

JORDAN, JEFF Jeffrey Lincoln, RB, 6´1˝/215 lbs; Washington; B7/12/1945 St. Louis, MO **1971** Was 1 **1972** Was 1

| 1970 | LARm | 9 | 10 | 50 | 5.0(10) | 0 | 1 | -5 | -5.0(-5) | 0 | — | — | — | — | — | — | — | — | — | — | — | 0 | 48 |
| NFL | 3 | | 11 | 10 | 50 | 5.0(10) | 0 | 1 | -5 | -5.0(-5) | 0 | — | — | — | — | — | — | — | — | — | — | 0 | 48 |

JORDAN, JEFF Jeffrey Flynn, DB, 6´3˝/190 lbs; Tulsa; 1965: Min, rnd 8/Den, rnd 15; B11/23/1943 San Antonio, TX **1965** Min 12 **1966** Min 14 **1967** Min 11 **NFL** 37 [3 yrs]

JORDAN, JIMMY James Andrew, RB, 6´1˝/200 lbs; Florida; 1967: Atl, rnd 3; B8/11/1944 Glenville, CA **1967** NO 1

JORDAN, KEN Kenneth Ray, LB, 6´2˝/235 lbs; Tuskegee; B4/29/1964 Birmingham, AL **1987** GB 3 (1)

JORDAN, KEVIN Kevin Michael, WR, 6´1˝/188 lbs; UCLA; B12/14/1972 Washington, DC **1996** Arz 1 (0)

JORDAN, LAMONT Lamont, RB, 5´10˝/230 lbs; Maryland; 2001: NYJ, rnd 2; B11/11/1978 Forestville, MD

2001	†NYJ	16(0)	39	292	7.5(46)	1	7	44	6.3(25)	1	1	0	0.0	0	0	0.0	0	—	—	k	—	12	346
2002	†NYJ	14(0)	84	316	3.8(61)	3	17	160	9.4(27)	0	—	—	—	—	—	—	—	—	—	k	—	18	463
2003	NYJ	16(0)	46	190	4.1(39)	4	11	101	9.2(25)	0	—	—	—	—	—	—	—	—	—	k	—	24	325
2004	†NYJ	16(0)	93	479	5.2(33)	2	15	112	7.5(25)	0	1	0	0.0	0	0	0.0	0	—	—	k	—	12	589
2005	Oak	14(14, RB)	272	1025	3.8(26)	9	70	563	8.0(28)	2	—	—	—	—	—	—	—	—	—	k	—	68	1407
NFL	5	76(14)	534	2302	4.3(61)	19	120	980	8.2(28)	3	2	0	0.0	0	0	0.0	0	—	—	k	—	134	3129

JORDAN, LARRY Lawrence Gene, DE-LB, 6´6˝/230 lbs; Youngstown State; B4/18/1938 Youngstown, OH **1962** Den-A 2 **1964** Den-A 8 **NFL** 10 [2 yrs]

JORDAN, LEANDER Leander James, T-G, 6´4˝/322 lbs; Indiana (PA); 2000: Car, rnd 3; B9/15/1977 Pittsburgh, PA **2001** Car 13 (5, rg) **2003** Jax 6 (0) **2004** SD 5 (0) **2005** SD 13 (9, LT) **NFL** 37 (14) [4 yrs]

JORDAN, LEE ROY Lee Roy, LB, 6´1˝/221 lbs; Alabama; 1963: Dal, rnd 1/Bos, rnd 2; B4/27/1941 Excel, AL [I] **1963** Dal 7 (7, RLB) **1964** Dal 12 (RLB) **1965** Dal 13 **1966**†Dal☆14 (MLB) **1967**†Dal★14 (MLB) **1968**†Dal★14 (MLB) **1969**†Dal★14 (MLB) **1970**†Dal 14 (MLB) **1971**†Dal 14 (MLB) **1972**†Dal 14 (MLB) **1973**†Dal★14 (MLB) **1974** Dal☆14 (MLB) **1975**†Dal☆14 (MLB) **1976** Dal 14 (14, MLB) **NFL** 186 (21) [14 yrs]

JORDAN, OMARI Omari Jammile, DT, 6´4˝/315 lbs; Buffalo; B4/15/1978 Cleveland, OH **2004** Car 4 (0)

JORDAN, RANDY Randy Loment, RB, 5´10˝/207 lbs; North Carolina; B6/6/1970 Henderson, NC

1993	†LARd	10(2)	12	33	2.8(12)	0	4	42	10.5(33)	0	—	—	—	—	—	—	—	—	—	—	—	0	54
1995	Jax	12(3)	21	62	3.0(10)	0	5	89	17.8(71)	1	—	—	—	—	—	—	—	—	—	k	—	6	123
1996	†Jax	15(0)									—	—	—	—	—	—	—	—	—	k	—	0	163
1997	†Jax	7(0)	1	2	2.0(2)	0	—	—	—	—	—	—	—	—	—	—	—	—	—	—	—	0	2
1998	Oak	16(0)	47	159	3.4(23)	1	3	2	0.7(2)	0	—	—	—	—	—	—	—	—	—	—	—	6	170
1999	Oak	16(0)	9	32	3.6(12)	2	8	82	10.3(30)	0	—	—	—	—	—	—	—	—	—	k	—	12	150
2000	†Oak	16(0)	46	213	4.6(43)	3	27	299	11.1(55)	1	—	—	—	—	—	—	—	—	—	—	1	30	398
2001	†Oak	16(0)	13	59	4.5(37)	0	9	63	7.0(19)	0	—	—	—	—	—	—	—	—	—	—	—	0	91
2002	†Oak	14(0)	3	14	4.7(12)	1	2	19	9.5(15)	0	—	—	—	—	—	—	—	—	—	—	—	6	34
NFL	9	122(5)	152	574	3.8(43)	7	58	596	10.3(71)	2	—	—	—	—	—	—	—	—	—	k	—	60	1183

JORDAN, RICHARD Richard Lamont, LB, 6´1˝/245 lbs; Missouri Southern State; 1997: Det, rnd 7; B12/1/1974 Holdenville, OK **1997**†Det 10 (0) **1998** Det 16 (3) **1999** Det 9 (0) **2002** Det 1 (0) **NFL** 36 (3) [4 yrs]

JORDAN, SHELBY Shelby Lewis, T, 6´7˝/260 lbs; Washington-St. Louis; 1973: Hou, rnd 7; B1/23/1952 St. Louis, MO **1975** NE 14 (14, RT) **1977** NE 10 (3) **1978**†NE 16 (16, RT) **1979** NE 14 (12, RT) **1980** NE 16 (16, RT) **1981** NE 16 (16, RT) **1982**†NE 9 (9, RT) **1983**†LARd 13 (0) **1984** LARd 11 (1) **1985**†LARd 16 (2) **1986** LARd 16 (2) **NFL** 151 (91) [11 yrs]

JORDAN, STEVE Steven Russell, TE, 6´3˝/236 lbs; Brown; 1982: Min, rnd 7; B1/10/1961 Phoenix, AZ

1982	†Min	9(1)	—	—	—	—	3	42	14.0(29)	0	—	—	—	—	—	—	—	—	—	—	—	0	21
1983	Min	13(2)	—	—	—	—	15	212	14.1(28)	2	—	—	—	—	—	—	—	—	—	—	—	12	116
1984	Min	14(14, TE)	1	4	4.0(4)	1	38	414	10.9(26)	2	—	—	—	—	—	—	—	—	—	—	—	18	231
1985	Min	16(16, TE)	—	—	—	—	68	795	11.7(32)	0	—	—	—	—	—	—	—	—	—	—	—	0	398
1986	Min★	16(16, TE)	—	—	—	—	58	859	14.8(68)	6	—	—	—	—	—	—	—	—	—	—	—	36	460
1987	†Min★	12(12, TE)	—	—	—	—	35	490	14.0(38)	2	—	—	—	—	—	—	—	—	—	—	—	12	255
1988	†Min★	16(16, TE)	—	—	—	—	57	756	13.3(38)	5	—	—	—	—	—	—	—	—	—	—	—	30	403
1989	†Min★	16(15, TE)	—	—	—	—	35	506	14.5(34)	3	—	—	—	—	—	—	—	—	—	—	—	18	268
1990	†Min★	16(16, TE)	—	—	—	—	45	636	14.1(38)	3	—	—	—	—	—	—	—	—	—	k	—	18	315
1991	Min☆	16(16, TE)	—	—	—	—	57	638	11.2(25)	2	—	—	—	—	—	—	—	—	—	—	—	12	329
1992	†Min	14(12, TE)	—	—	—	—	28	394	14.1(60)	2	—	—	—	—	—	—	—	—	—	—	—	12	207
1993	†Min	14(12, TE)	—	—	—	—	56	542	9.7(53)	1	—	—	—	—	—	—	—	—	—	—	—	6	276
1994	†Min	4(1)	—	—	—	—	3	23	7.7(10)	0	—	—	—	—	—	—	—	—	—	—	—	0	12
NFL	13	176(149)	1	4	4.0(4)	1	498	6307	12.7(68)	28	—	—	—	—	—	—	—	—	—	k	—	174	3290

JORDAN, STEVE Stephen Bernard, K, 5´10˝/205 lbs; USC; B3/20/1963 San Francisco, CA [K] **1987** Ind 3 (0)

JORDAN, TIM Timothy Christopher, LB, 6´3˝/226 lbs; Wisconsin; 1987: NE, rnd 4; B4/26/1964 Madison, WI **1987** NE 5 (0) **1988** NE 16 (6, lolb) **1989** NE 9 (4) **NFL** 30 (10) [3 yrs]

JORDAN, TONY Anthony T., RB, 6´2˝/220 lbs; Kansas State; 1988: Phx, rnd 5; B5/5/1965 Rochester, NY

1988	Phx	9(2)	61	160	2.6(12)	3	4	24	6.0(12)	0	—	—	—	—	—	—	—	—	—	—	—	18	202
1989	Phx	13(8, RB)	83	211	2.5(15)	2	6	20	3.3(8)	0	—	—	—	—	—	—	—	—	—	—	—	12	241
NFL	2	22(10)	144	371	2.6(15)	5	10	44	4.4(12)	0	—	—	—	—	—	—	—	—	—	—	—	30	443

JORDEN, TIM Timothy Robert, TE, 6´3˝/235 lbs; Indiana; B10/30/1966 Lakewood, OH

1990	Phx	16(11, TE)	—	—	—	—	2	10	5.0(6)	0	—	—	—	—	—	—	—	—	—	—	—	0	5
1991	Phx	16(9, TE)	—	—	—	—	15	127	8.5(19)	0	—	—	—	—	—	—	—	—	—	—	—	0	64
1992	†Pit	15(4)	—	—	—	—	6	28	4.7(8)	2	—	—	—	—	—	—	—	—	—	—	—	12	24
1993	†Pit	16(1)	—	—	—	—	1	12	12.0(12)	0	—	—	—	—	—	—	—	—	—	—	—	0	6
NFL	4	63(25)	—	—	—	—	24	177	7.4(19)	2	—	—	—	—	—	—	—	—	—	—	—	12	99

JORGENSEN, BUD Carl Ankerovergaa, T, 6´0˝/205 lbs; St. Mary's (CA); B2/5/1911 Denmark, D7/2/1984 Arcadia, CA [K] **1934** GB 10 (2) **1935** Phi 11 (2) **NFL** 21 (4) [2 yrs]

JORGENSEN, WAGNER Wagner O., C-LB, 6´2˝/215 lbs; St. Mary's (CA); 1936: Bkn, rnd 3; B7/31/1913 Denmark, D7/24/1977 San Mateo, CA **1936** Bkn 8 (0) **1937** Bkn 10 (6, C) **NFL** 18 (6) [2 yrs]

JOSEPH, DWAYNE Dwayne Leonard, DB, 5´9˝/180 lbs; Syracuse; B6/2/1972 Miami, FL **1995** ChiB 16 (1)

JOSEPH, ELVIS Elvis, RB, 6´1˝/216 lbs; Louisiana-Lafayette; Southern (LA); B8/30/1978 St. Michaels, Barbados **2002** Jax 15 (0)

| 2001 | Jax | 14(3) | 68 | 294 | 4.3(27) | 0 | 18 | 183 | 10.2(29) | 2 | — | — | — | — | — | — | — | — | — | k | 1 | 18 | 579 |
| NFL | 2 | 29(3) | 68 | 294 | 4.3(27) | 0 | 18 | 183 | 10.2(29) | 2 | — | — | — | — | — | — | — | — | — | k | 1 | 18 | 736 |

JOSEPH, JAMES James, RB, 6´2˝/222 lbs; Auburn; 1991: Phi, rnd 7; B10/28/1967 Phenix City, AL

1991	Phi	16(3)	135	440	3.3(24)	3	10	64	6.4(13)	0	—	—	—	—	—	—	—	—	—	—	—	18	502
1992	†Phi	16(0)									—	—	—	—	—	—	—	—	—	—	—		
1993	Phi	16(5, fb)	39	140	3.6(12)	0	29	291	10.0(48)	1	—	—	—	—	—	—	—	—	—	—	—	6	291
1994	Phi	14(6, fb)	60	203	3.4(34)	1	43	344	8.0(35)	2	—	—	—	—	—	—	—	—	—	k	—	18	391
1995	Cin	16(1)	16	40	2.5(8)	0	20	118	5.9(10)	0	—	—	—	—	—	—	—	—	—	k	—	0	101
NFL	5	78(15)	250	823	3.3(34)	4	102	817	8.0(48)	3	—	—	—	—	—	—	—	—	—	k	—	42	1285

JOSEPH, KERRY Kerry Tremaine, DB, 6´1˝/205 lbs; McNeese State; B10/4/1973 New Iberia, LA **1998** Sea 16 (0) **1999**†Sea 16 (4) **2000** Sea 16 (10, SS) **2001** Sea 8 (0) **NFL** 56 (14) [4 yrs]

JOSEPH, RED Chalmer Edward, E, 6´3˝/190 lbs; Miami (OH); Ohio State; B11/7/1905, OH, D9/17/1983 Harlingen, TX **1927** Day 8 (8, RE) **1930** Por 12 (7, re), 6 **1931** Cle 1 (0) **NFL** 21 (15) [3 yrs]

JOSEPH, RICOT Ricot, DB, 6´0˝/185 lbs; Central Florida; B3/13/1980 Haiti **2002** Was 6 (0)

JOSEPH, VANCE Vance Desmond, DB, 6´0˝/202 lbs; Colorado; B9/20/1972 Marrero, LA **1995** NYJ 13 (6, rcb) **1996** Ind 4 (0) **NFL** 17 (6) [2 yrs]

JOSEPH, WILLIAM William, DT, 6´5˝/315 lbs; Miami (FL); 2003: NYG, rnd 1; B9/3/1979 Miami, FL **2003** NYG 14 (0) **2004** NYG 15 (4) **2005**†NYG 10 (10, RDT) **NFL** 39 (14) [3 yrs]

JOSEPH, ZIP Zern Carlton, E-G-C, 6´2˝/170 lbs; Miami (OH); B5/31/1903, OH, D11/24/1977 San Diego County, CA **1925** Day 5 (0) **1927** Day 6 (2) **NFL** 11 (2) [2 yrs]

JOSEPHSON, LES Lester Andrew, RB, 6´1˝/207 lbs; Augustana (SD); B7/29/1942 Minneota, MN

YEAR	TEAM	G(GS, POS)	RUSH	YD	AVG(LG)	TD	REC	YD	AVG(LG)	TD	PASS	COMP	PCT	YD	AVG(LG)	TD	INT	SK	YD	QBR	KPR	OTD	PTS	TAY
1964	LARm	14(FB)	96	451	4.7(75)	3	21	269	12.8(58)	1	—	—	—	—	—	—	—	—	—	—	—	—	24	621
1965	LARm	13(HB)	71	225	3.2(18)	0	18	169	9.4(30)	0	2	1	50.0	15	7.5(15)	1	0	—	—	—	—	—	0	322
1966	LARm	14	14	97	6.9(14)	0	2	10	5.0(6)	1	—	—	—	—	—	—	—	—	—	—	—	—	6	107
1967	†LARm✧	14(HB)	178	800	4.5(27)	4	37	400	10.8(48)	4	5	2	40.0	47	9.4(24)	0	1	—	—	—	k	—	48	1060
1969	†LARm	14(14, FB)	124	461	3.7(17)	0	32	295	9.2(51)	2	—	—	—	—	—	—	—	—	—	—	—	—	12	619
1970	LARm	12(12, FB)	150	640	4.3(23)	5	44	427	9.7(30)	0	1	1	100.0	25	25.0(25)	0	0	1	1	—	—	—	30	916
1971	LARm	14(9, FB)	99	449	4.5(57)	3	26	230	8.8(29)	2	—	—	—	—	—	—	—	—	—	—	k	—	30	589
1972	LARm	8	18	75	4.2(13)	0	14	170	12.1(34)	1	—	—	—	—	—	—	—	—	—	—	—	—	6	165
1973	†LARm	14	36	174	4.8(14)	2	—	—	—	—	—	—	—	—	—	—	—	—	—	—	—	—	12	194
1974	†LARm	12	11	35	3.2(8)	0	—	—	—	—	—	—	—	—	—	—	—	—	—	—	—	—	0	35
NFL	10	129(35)	797	3407	4.3(75)	17	194	1970	10.2(58)	11	8	4	50.0	87	10.9(25)	1	1	1	1	—	k	—	168	4627

JOSUE, STEVE Steve, LB, 6´2˝/230 lbs; Carson-Newman; 2003: GB, rnd 7; B4/5/1980 Miami, FL **2004**†GB 4 (0)

JOSWICK, BOB Robert Leonard, DE-DT, 6´5˝/250 lbs; Tulsa; 1968: Mia, rnd 13; B1/12/1946 Uniontown, PA **1968** Mia-A 1 (1) **1969** Mia-A 5 (1) **NFL** 6 (2) [2 yrs]

JOURDAIN, YONEL Yonel, RB, 5´11˝/204 lbs; Southern Illinois; B4/20/1971 Brooklyn, NY

YEAR	TEAM	G(GS, POS)	RUSH	YD	AVG(LG)	TD	REC	YD	AVG(LG)	TD	PASS	COMP	PCT	YD	AVG(LG)	TD	INT	SK	YD	QBR	KPR	OTD	PTS	TAY
1994	Buf	9(0)	17	56	3.3(16)	0	10	56	5.6(18)	0	—	—	—	—	—	—	—	—	—	—	k	—	0	280
1995	†Buf	8(0)	8	31	3.9(19)	0	1	7	7.0(7)	0	—	—	—	—	—	—	—	—	—	—	kp	—	0	93
NFL	2	17(0)	25	87	3.5(19)	0	11	63	5.7(18)	0	—	—	—	—	—	—	—	—	—	—	kp	—	0	373

JOYCE, BILL William Kelly, QB, 5´8˝/180 lbs; Holy Cross; Catholic; B6/3/1895 Pittsfield, MA, D8/29/1974 Camlachie, Canada **1920** Det 1 (1)

JOYCE, DELVIN Delvin, RB, 5´7˝/195 lbs; James Madison; B9/21/1978 Martinsville, VA

YEAR	TEAM	G(GS, POS)	RUSH	YD	AVG(LG)	TD	REC	YD	AVG(LG)	TD	PASS	COMP	PCT	YD	AVG(LG)	TD	INT	SK	YD	QBR	KPR	OTD	PTS	TAY
2002	†NYG	12(0)	2	2	1.0(1)	0	1	5	5.0(5)	0	—	—	—	—	—	—	—	—	—	—	kp	—	0	371
2003	NYG	16(0)	11	39	3.5(8)	0	3	7	2.3(5)	0	—	—	—	—	—	—	—	—	—	—	kp	—	0	126
NFL	2	28(0)	13	41	3.2(8)	0	4	12	3.0(5)	0	—	—	—	—	—	—	—	—	—	—	kp	—	0	496

JOYCE, DON Donald Gilbert, DE-DT, 6´3˝/253 lbs; Tulane; 1951: ChiC, rnd 2; B10/8/1929 Steubenville, OH **1951** ChiC 12 (RDT) **1952** ChiC 12 (RDT) **1953** ChiC 10 (RDT) **1954** Bal 12 (RDE) **1955** Bal 11 (RDE) **1956** Bal 12 (RDE) **1957** Bal 12 (RDE) **1958**†Bal✧12 (RDE) **1959**†Bal 11 (RDE) **1960** Bal 11 **1961** Min 14 (7, RDE) **1962** Den-A 6 **NFL** 135 (7) [12 yrs]

JOYCE, ERIC Eric Torezi, DB, 5´10˝/200 lbs; Tennessee State; B1/21/1978 Nashville, TN **2002** ChiB 3 (0)

JOYCE, MATT Matthew Lodge, G-T, 6´7˝/300 lbs; Richmond; B3/30/1972 La Crosse, WI **1995** Sea 16 (13, LG) **1996** Arz 2 (0) **1997** Arz 9 (6, lg) **1998**†Arz 11 (0) **1999** Arz 15 (15, LT/lg) **2000** Arz 13 (13, LG) **2001** Det 16 (12, RT) **2002** Det 15 (6, rt) **2003** Det 13 (3) **2004** Det 12 (3) **NFL** 122 (71) [10 yrs]

JOYCE, TERRY Terry Patrick, P-TE, 6´6˝/230 lbs; Wichita State; Missouri Southern State; B7/18/1954 Kirksville, MO

YEAR	TEAM	G(GS, POS)	RUSH	YD	AVG(LG)	TD	REC	YD	AVG(LG)	TD	PASS	COMP	PCT	YD	AVG(LG)	TD	INT	SK	YD	QBR	KPR	OTD	PTS	TAY
1976	SL	14	1	0	0.0(0)	0	—	—	—	—	—	—	—	—	—	—	—	—	—	—	P	—	0	0
1977	SL	4	1	-13	-13.0(-13)	0	—	—	—	—	1	1	100.0	1	1.0(1)	0	0	—	—	—	P	—	0	-13
NFL	2	18	2	-13	-6.5	0	—	—	—	—	1	1	100.0	1	1.0(1)	0	0	—	—	—	P	—	0	-13

JOYNER, L.C. L.C., HB, 6´1˝/187 lbs; Contra Costa JC; 1956: SF, rnd 21; B8/15/1930 Los Angeles, CA, D4/22/2001 Fresno, CA **1960** Oak-A 2

JOYNER, LARRY Larry, LB, 6´0˝/207 lbs; Minnesota; B1/22/1964 Memphis, TN **1987** Hou 1 (0)

JOYNER, SETH Seth, LB-DB, 6´2˝/241 lbs; Texas-El Paso; 1986: Phi, rnd 8; B11/18/1964 Spring Valley, NY **[IS]** **1986** Phi 14 (7, rlb) **1987** Phi 12 (12, LLB) **1988**†Phi 16 (16, LLB) **1989**†Phi 14 (14, LLB) **1990**†Phi 16 (16, LLB) **1991** Phi★16 (16, LLB) **1992**†Phi☆16 (16, LLB) **1993** Phi★16 (16, LLB) **1994** Arz★16 (16, LLB) **1995** Arz 16 (16, LLB/ss) **1996** Arz☆16 (16, LLB) **1997**†GB 11 (10, LLB) **1998**†Den 16 (1) **NFL** 195 (172) [13 yrs]

JOYNER, WILLIE Willie, RB, 5´10˝/200 lbs; Maryland; 1984: Hou, rnd 7; B4/2/1962 Brooklyn, NY

YEAR	TEAM	G(GS, POS)	RUSH	YD	AVG(LG)	TD	REC	YD	AVG(LG)	TD	PASS	COMP	PCT	YD	AVG(LG)	TD	INT	SK	YD	QBR	KPR	OTD	PTS	TAY
1984	Hou	10(0)	14	22	1.6(9)	0	—	—	—	—	—	—	—	—	—	—	—	—	—	—	k	—	0	34

JOZWIAK, BRIAN Brian Joseph, G-T, 6´5˝/304 lbs; West Virginia; 1986: KC, rnd 1; B6/20/1963 Baltimore, MD **1986**†KC 15 (1) **1987** KC 10 (1) **1988** KC 3 (1) **NFL** 28 (3) [3 yrs]

JUDD, SAXON Saxon Thomas, E, 6´1˝/190 lbs; Louisiana-Lafayette; Tulsa; 1944: ChiC, rnd 3; B11/29/1919 Pottsboro, TX, D3/31/1990 Tulsa, OK

YEAR	TEAM	G(GS, POS)	RUSH	YD	AVG(LG)	TD	REC	YD	AVG(LG)	TD	PASS	COMP	PCT	YD	AVG(LG)	TD	INT	SK	YD	QBR	KPR	OTD	PTS	TAY
1946	Bkn-A	13(2, re)	—	—	—	—	34	443	13.0	4	—	—	—	—	—	—	—	—	—	—	k	1	30	251
1947	Bkn-A	14(10, RE)	—	—	—	—	18	204	11.3	1	—	—	—	—	—	—	—	—	—	—	k	—	6	82
1948	Bkn-A	14(5, re)	—	—	—	—	32	350	10.9	2	—	—	—	—	—	—	—	—	—	—	—	—	12	185
AAFC	3	41(17)	—	—	—	—	84	997	11.9	7	—	—	—	—	—	—	—	—	—	—	k	1	48	518

JUDIE, ED Edward Charles, LB, 6´2˝/231 lbs; Northern Arizona; B7/6/1959 Tyler, TX **1982** SF 7 (2) **1983** SF 4 (1) **1983** TB 11 (10, LOLB) **1984** Mia 2 (0) **NFL** 24 (13) [3 yrs]

JUDSON, WILLIAM William Thadius, DB, 6´1˝/189 lbs; South Carolina State; 1981: Mia, rnd 8; B3/26/1959 Detroit, MI **[I]** **1982**†Mia 9 (0) **1983**†Mia 16 (16, LCB) **1984**†Mia 16 (16, RCB) **1985**†Mia 16 (16, RCB) **1986** Mia 16 (16, LCB) **1987** Mia 12 (12, RCB) **1988** Mia 16 (16, RCB) **1989** Mia 14 (14, RCB) **NFL** 115 (106) [8 yrs]

JUE, BHAWOH Bhawoh Papi, DB, 6´0˝/200 lbs; Penn State; 2001: GB, rnd 3; B5/24/1979 Monrovia, Liberia **2001**†GB 15 (7, ss) **2002** GB 4 (0) **2003**†GB 16 (0) **2004**†GB 16 (4) **2005** SD 14 (14, FS) **NFL** 65 (25) [5 yrs]

JUENGER, DAVE David William, WR, 6´1˝/195 lbs; Ohio University; 1973: Chi, rnd 14; B2/4/1951 Chillicothe, OH **1973** ChiB 1

JULIAN, FRED Alfred J., DB, 5´9˝/185 lbs; Michigan; B1/27/1938 Detroit, MI **1960** NYT-A 14 (LS)

JULIEN, JARMAR Jarmar Antwion, RB, 5´11˝/240 lbs; San Jose State; B12/11/1979 San Jose, CA **2002** KC 2 (0)

JUMA, KEVIN Kevin Wade, WR, 6´2˝/195 lbs; Idaho; B7/30/1962 Seattle, WA

YEAR	TEAM	G(GS, POS)	RUSH	YD	AVG(LG)	TD	REC	YD	AVG(LG)	TD	PASS	COMP	PCT	YD	AVG(LG)	TD	INT	SK	YD	QBR	KPR	OTD	PTS	TAY
1987	Sea	3(2)	—	—	—	—	7	95	13.6(26)	0	—	—	—	—	—	—	—	—	—	—	—	—	0	48

JUNE, CATO Cato, LB, 6´0˝/227 lbs; Michigan; 2003: Ind, rnd 6; B11/18/1979 Riverside, CA **2003**†Ind 11 (0) **2004**†Ind 16 (16, RLB) **2005**†Ind★13 (13, RLB) **NFL** 40 (29) [3 yrs]

JUNGMICHEL, BUDDY Harold Neve, G, 5´9˝/200 lbs; Texas; 1942: NYG, rnd 15; B10/18/1919 Gonzales, TX, D8/28/1982 Austin, TX **1946** Mia-A☆14 (13, LG)

JUNIOR, E.J. Ester James, LB, 6´3˝/238 lbs; Alabama; 1981: SL, rnd 1; B12/8/1959 Salisbury, MD **1981** SL 16 (13, RLB) **1982**†SL 9 (9, LLB) **1983** SL 12 (11, MLB/llb) **1984** SL★16 (16, RLB/mlb) **1985** SL★16 (16, MLB) **1986** SL 13 (13, LILB) **1987** SL 13 (13, RLB) **1988** Phx 16 (16, RLB) **1989** Mia 16 (12, LOLB) **1990**†Mia 16 (0) **1991** Mia 16 (0) **1992** TB 2 (0) **1992** Sea 5 (0) **1993** Sea 4 (0) **NFL** 170 (119) [13 yrs]

JUNKER, STEVE Steven Norbert, E, 6´3˝/217 lbs; Xavier (OH); 1957: Det, rnd 4; B5/22/1935 Cincinnati, OH

YEAR	TEAM	G(GS, POS)	RUSH	YD	AVG(LG)	TD	REC	YD	AVG(LG)	TD	PASS	COMP	PCT	YD	AVG(LG)	TD	INT	SK	YD	QBR	KPR	OTD	PTS	TAY
1957	†Det	12(LE)	—	—	—	—	22	305	13.9(32)	4	—	—	—	—	—	—	—	—	—	—	—	—	24	173
1959	Det	6	—	—	—	—	—	—	—	—	—	—	—	—	—	—	—	—	—	—	—	—	—	—
1960	Det	12	—	—	—	—	6	55	9.2(14)	0	—	—	—	—	—	—	—	—	—	—	—	—	0	28
1961	Was	11	—	—	—	—	9	130	14.4(38)	0	—	—	—	—	—	—	—	—	—	—	k	—	0	50
1962	Was	14	—	—	—	—	11	149	13.5(35)	2	—	—	—	—	—	—	—	—	—	—	—	—	12	85
NFL	5	55	—	—	—	—	48	639	13.3(38)	6	—	—	—	—	—	—	—	—	—	—	k	—	36	335

JUNKIN, MIKE Michael Wayne, LB, 6´3˝/241 lbs; Duke; 1987: Cle, rnd 1; B11/21/1964 North Little Rock, AR **1987** Cle 4 (0) **1988**†Cle 11 (7, rilb) **1989** KC 5 (0) **NFL** 20 (7) [3 yrs]

JUNKIN, TREY Abner Kirk, TE-LB, 6´2˝/235 lbs; Louisiana Tech; 1983: Buf, rnd 4; B1/23/1961 Conway, AR **1983** Buf 16 (0) **1984** Buf 2 (0) **1984**†Was 12 (0) **1990** Sea 12 (0) **1991** Sea 16 (0) **1993** Sea 16 (1) **1995** Sea 16 (0) **1996** Oak 6 (0) **1996** Arz 10 (0) **1997** Arz 16 (0) **1998**†Arz 16 (0) **1999** Arz 16 (0) **2000** Arz 16 (0) **2001** Arz 16 (0) **2002**†NYG 0 (0)

YEAR	TEAM	G(GS, POS)	RUSH	YD	AVG(LG)	TD	REC	YD	AVG(LG)	TD	PASS	COMP	PCT	YD	AVG(LG)	TD	INT	SK	YD	QBR	KPR	OTD	PTS	TAY
1985	†LARd	16(0)	—	—	—	—	2	8	4.0(5)	1	—	—	—	—	—	—	—	—	—	—	—	—	6	9
1986	LARd	3(0)	—	—	—	—	2	38	19.0(19)	0	—	—	—	—	—	—	—	—	—	—	—	—	0	19
1987	LARd	12(1)	—	—	—	—	2	15	7.5(8)	0	—	—	—	—	—	—	—	—	—	—	—	—	0	8
1988	LARd	16(1)	—	—	—	—	4	25	6.3(9)	2	—	—	—	—	—	—	—	—	—	—	—	—	12	23
1989	LARd	16(0)	—	—	—	—	3	32	10.7(28)	2	—	—	—	—	—	—	—	—	—	—	k	—	12	11
1992	Sea	16(1)	—	—	—	—	3	25	8.3(13)	1	—	—	—	—	—	—	—	—	—	—	—	—	6	18
1994	Sea	16(0)	—	—	—	—	1	1	1.0(1)	1	—	—	—	—	—	—	—	—	—	—	—	—	6	6
NFL	20	281(4)	—	—	—	—	17	144	8.5(28)	7	—	—	—	—	—	—	—	—	—	—	k	—	42	92

JUREVICIUS, JOE Joseph Michael, WR, 6´5˝/230 lbs; Penn State; 1998: NYG, rnd 2; B12/23/1974 Cleveland, OH

YEAR	TEAM	G(GS, POS)	RUSH	YD	AVG(LG)	TD	REC	YD	AVG(LG)	TD	PASS	COMP	PCT	YD	AVG(LG)	TD	INT	SK	YD	QBR	KPR	OTD	PTS	TAY
1998	NYG	14(1)	—	—	—	—	9	146	16.2(59)	0	—	—	—	—	—	—	—	—	—	—	—	—	0	73
1999	NYG	16(1)	—	—	—	—	18	318	17.7(71)	1	—	—	—	—	—	—	—	—	—	—	—	—	6	164
2000	†NYG	14(3)	—	—	—	—	24	272	11.3(43)	1	—	—	—	—	—	—	—	—	—	—	k	—	6	129
2001	NYG	14(9, wr)	—	—	—	—	51	706	13.8(46)	3	—	—	—	—	—	—	—	—	—	—	—	—	18	368
2002	†TB	15(3)	—	—	—	—	37	423	11.4(26)	4	—	—	—	—	—	—	—	—	—	—	—	—	24	232
2003	TB	5(2)	—	—	—	—	12	118	9.8(22)	2	—	—	—	—	—	—	—	—	—	—	—	—	12	69
2004	TB	10(3)	—	—	—	—	27	333	12.3(42)	2	—	—	—	—	—	—	—	—	—	—	—	—	12	177
2005	†Sea	16(11, WR)	—	—	—	—	55	694	12.6(52)	10	—	—	—	—	—	—	—	—	—	—	—	—	60	397
NFL	8	104(33)	—	—	—	—	233	3010	12.9(71)	23	—	—	—	—	—	—	—	—	—	—	k	—	138	1608

JURGENSEN, SONNY Christian Adolph, QB, 5´11˝/202 lbs; Duke; 1957: Phi, rnd 4; B8/23/1934 Wilmington, NC; HOF 1983

YEAR	TEAM	G(GS, POS)	RUSH	YD	AVG(LG)	TD	REC	YD	AVG(LG)	TD	PASS	COMP	PCT	YD	AVG(LG)	TD	INT	SK	YD	QBR	KPR	OTD	PTS	TAY
1957	Phi	10(qb)	10	-3	-0.3(8)	2	—	—	—	—	70	33	47.1	470	6.7(61)	5	8	—	—	—	—	—	12	-43
1958	Phi	12	1	1	1.0(1)	0	—	—	—	—	22	12	54.5	259	11.8(61)	0	1	—	—	—	—	—	0	91
1959	Phi	12	—	—	—	—	—	—	—	—	5	3	60.0	27	5.4(19)	1	0	—	—	—	—	—	0	19
1960	†Phi	12	4	5	1.3(9)	0	—	—	—	—	44	24	54.5	486	11.0(71)	5	1	—	—	—	—	—	0	233
1961	Phi★	14(QB)	20	27	1.4(14)	0	—	—	—	—	416	**235**	56.5	**3723**	8.9(69)	**32**	**24**	—	—	88.1	—	—	0	1089
1962	Phi	14(QB)	17	44	2.6(30)	2	—	—	—	—	366	196	53.6	**3261**	**8.9**(**84**)	22	**26**	—	—	74.3	—	—	12	765
1963	Phi	9(QB)	13	38	2.9(13)	1	—	—	—	—	184	99	53.8	1413	7.7(75)	11	13	13	111	—	—	—	6	290
1964	Was★	14(QB)	27	57	2.1(24)	3	—	—	—	—	385	207	53.8	2934	7.6(80)	24	13	—	—	85.4	—	—	18	1154
1965	Was	13(QB)	17	23	1.4(27)	2	—	—	—	—	356	190	53.4	2367	6.6(55)	15	16	—	—	69.6	—	—	12	662
1966	Was★	14(QB)	12	14	1.2(16)	0	—	—	—	—	**436**	**254**	58.3	**3209**	7.4(86)	28	19	—	—	84.5	—	—	0	999
1967	Was★	14(QB)	15	46	3.1(21)	2	—	—	—	—	**508**	**288**	56.7	**3747**	7.4(86)	**31**	16	—	—	**87.3**	—	—	12	1455
1968	Was	12(QB)	8	21	2.6(11)	1	—	—	—	—	292	167	57.2	1980	6.8(**99**)	17	11	—	—	81.7	—	—	6	666
1969	Was★	14(QB)	17	156	9.2(33)	1	—	—	—	—	**442**	**274**	62.0	**3102**	7.0(88)	22	15	40	322	85.4	—	—	6	1227
1970	Was	14(14, QB)	6	39	6.5(14)	1	—	—	—	—	337	202	**59.9**	2354	7.0(66)	23	10	25	214	91.5	—	—	6	941
1971	†Was	5(1)	3	29	9.7(11)	0	—	—	—	—	28	16	57.1	170	6.1(30)	0	2	1	8	—	—	—	0	34
1972	Was	7(4)	4	-5	-1.3(0)	0	—	—	—	—	59	39	66.1	633	10.7(36)	2	4	2	21	—	—	—	0	162
1973	†Was	14(4)	3	7	2.3(7)	0	1	-3	-3.0(-3)	0	145	87	60.0	904	6.2(36)	6	5	16	114	—	—	—	0	288
1974	†Was	14(4, qb)	4	-6	-1.5(0)	0	—	—	—	—	167	107	**64.1**	1185	7.1(44)	11	5	10	69	—	—	—	0	442
NFL	18	218(27)	181	493	2.7(33)	15	1	-3	-3.0(-3)	0	4262	2433	57.1	32224	7.6(99)	255	189	107	859	82.6	—	—	90	10469

JURICH, MIKE Michael, T, 6´1˝/234 lbs; Denver; 1941: Bkn, rnd 15; B1/7/1919 Ruth, NV, D1/5/1996 Denver, CO **1941** Bkn 4 (0) **1942** Bkn 11 (0) **NFL** 15 (0) [2 yrs]

JURICH, TOM Thomas N., K, 5´10˝/185 lbs; Northern Arizona; 1978: Pit, rnd 10; B7/26/1956 Alhambra, CA **[K]** **1978** NO 1

JURIGA, JIM James Allen, G-T, 6´6˝/269 lbs; Illinois; 1986: Den, rnd 4; B9/12/1964 Fort Wayne, IN **1988** Den 16 (15, LT) **1989**†Den 16 (16, RG) **1990** Den 12 (11, RG) **NFL** 44 (42) [3 yrs]

JURKIEWICZ, WALT Walter Stephen, C, 6´1˝/220 lbs; Indiana; B2/16/1919 Scott Haven, PA, D12/3/2002 Plymouth, IN **1946** Det 11 (1)

JURKOVIC, JOHN Ivan John, DT-NT, 6´2˝/301 lbs; Eastern Illinois; B8/18/1967 Friedrichshafen, Germany **1991** GB 5 (0) **1992** GB 16 (12, NT) **1993**†GB 16 (12, NT) **1994**†GB 16 (15, LDT) **1995**†GB 16 (14, LDT) **1996**†Jax☆16 (14, RDT) **1997** Jax 3 (3) **1998**†Jax 16 (16, RDT/ldt) **1999** Cle 10 (9, RDT) **NFL** 114 (95) [9 yrs]

JURY, BOB Robert Vincent, DB, 6´1˝/188 lbs; Pittsburgh; 1978: Sea, rnd 3; B10/5/1955 Los Angeles, CA **1978** SF 15 (8, ss)

JUSTER, RUBIN Rubin J., T, 6´2˝/230 lbs; Minnesota; B9/9/1923, D1/1985 Chicago, IL **1946** Bos 4 (0)

JUSTICE, CHARLIE Charles Ronald, HB, 5´10˝/176 lbs; North Carolina; 1950: Was, rnd 16; B5/18/1924 Asheville, NC, D10/17/2003 Cherryville, NC

YEAR	TEAM	G(GS, POS)	RUSH	YD	AVG(LG)	TD	REC	YD	AVG(LG)	TD	PASS	COMP	PCT	YD	AVG(LG)	TD	INT	SK	YD	QBR	KPR	OTD	PTS	TAY
1950	Was	8(LH)	59	285	4.8(71)	0	19	180	9.5(37)	2	4	1	25.0	15	3.8(15)	0	0	—	—	—	Pkp	—	12	492
1952	Was	11	36	129	3.6(26)	0	11	106	9.6(15)	1	1	0	0.0	0	0.0	0	1	—	—	—	Pkp	—	6	193
1953	Was	12(LH)	115	616	5.4(43)	2	22	434	19.7(54)	2	—	—	—	—	—	—	—	—	—	—	kp	—	24	854
1954	Was	12(LH)	56	254	4.5(50)	1	11	242	22.0(80)	2	2	0	0.0	0	0.0	0	1	—	—	—	P	—	18	355
NFL	4	43	266	1284	4.8(71)	3	63	962	15.3(80)	7	7	1	14.3	15	2.1(15)	0	2	—	—	—	Pkp	—	60	1894

JUSTICE, ED Edward S., WB-HB, 6´1˝/200 lbs; Gonzaga; B11/19/1912 Post Falls, ID, D10/26/1991 Anacortes, WA

YEAR	TEAM	G(GS, POS)	RUSH	YD	AVG(LG)	TD	REC	YD	AVG(LG)	TD	PASS	COMP	PCT	YD	AVG(LG)	TD	INT	SK	YD	QBR	KPR	OTD	PTS	TAY
1936	†Bos	12(5, wb)	11	10	0.9	0	8	132	16.5	0	—	—	—	—	—	—	—	—	—	—	—	—	0	76
1937	†Was	10(1)	8	35	4.4	0	9	150	16.7	3	—	—	—	—	—	—	—	—	—	—	—	—	18	125
1938	Was	9(3)	10	11	1.1	0	14	173	12.4(41)	1	—	—	—	—	—	—	—	—	—	—	—	—	6	103
1939	Was	8(2)	5	56	11.2	1	7	124	17.7	1	—	—	—	—	—	—	—	—	—	—	—	1	18	133
1940	†Was	7(6, WB)	3	34	11.3	0	15	170	11.3(25)	2	—	—	—	—	—	—	—	—	—	—	i	—	12	138
1941	Was	8(2)	4	-8	-2.0(2)	0	8	149	18.6(36)	1	—	—	—	—	—	—	—	—	—	—	ki	—	6	94
1942	†Was✧	9(7, WB)	3	-1	-0.3(2)	0	9	108	12.0(35)	1	—	—	—	—	—	—	—	—	—	—	i	—	6	55
NFL	7	63(26)	44	137	3.1(2)	1	70	1006	14.4(41)	9	—	—	—	—	—	—	—	—	—	—	ki	1	66	723

JUSTIN, KERRY Kerry August, DB, 5´11˝/175 lbs; Oregon State; B5/3/1955 New Orleans, LA **1978** Sea 16 **1979** Sea 14 (2) **1980** Sea 11 (10, LCB) **1981** Sea 15 (9, rcb) **1982** Sea 9 (1) **1983**†Sea 16 (10, LCB) **1986** Sea 16 (1) **1987** Sea 7 (0) **NFL** 104 (33) [8 yrs]

JUSTIN, PAUL Paul Donald, QB, 6´4˝/211 lbs; Arizona State; 1991: Chi, rnd 7; B5/19/1968 Schaumburg, IL

YEAR	TEAM	G(GS, POS)	RUSH	YD	AVG(LG)	TD	REC	YD	AVG(LG)	TD	PASS	COMP	PCT	YD	AVG(LG)	TD	INT	SK	YD	QBR	KPR	OTD	PTS	TAY
1995	Ind	3(1)	3	1	0.3(2)	0	—	—	—	—	36	20	55.6	212	5.9(20)	0	2	3	22	—	—	—	0	27
1996	†Ind	8(2)	2	7	3.5(6)	0	—	—	—	—	127	74	58.3	839	6.6(38)	2	0	7	58	—	—	—	0	437
1997	Ind	8(4)	6	2	0.3(3)	0	—	—	—	—	140	83	59.3	1046	7.5(44)	5	5	10	86	—	—	—	0	350
1998	Cin	5(3)	1	2	2.0(2)	0	—	—	—	—	63	34	54.0	426	6.8(41)	1	3	7	60	—	—	—	2	100
1999	SL	10(0)	5	-1	-0.2(3)	0	—	—	—	—	14	9	64.3	91	6.5(27)	0	0	1	3	—	—	—	0	45
NFL	5	34(10)	17	11	0.6(6)	0	—	—	—	—	380	220	57.9	2614	6.9(44)	8	10	28	229	—	—	—	2	958

JUSTIN, SID Sidney Arthur, DB, 5´10˝/170 lbs; Long Beach State; B8/14/1954 New Orleans, LA **1979** LARm 13 **1982** Bal 5 (2) **NFL** 18 (2) [2 yrs]

JUZWIK, STEVE Stephen Robert, HB-FB, 5´8˝/186 lbs; Notre Dame; 1942: Was, rnd 21; B6/18/1918 Gary, IN, D6/6/1964 Chicago, IL **[K]**

YEAR	TEAM	G(GS, POS)	RUSH	YD	AVG(LG)	TD	REC	YD	AVG(LG)	TD	PASS	COMP	PCT	YD	AVG(LG)	TD	INT	SK	YD	QBR	KPR	OTD	PTS	TAY
1942	Was	2(1)	15	75	5.0(39)	2	—	—	—	—	—	—	—	—	—	—	—	—	—	—	Kkp	—	15	120
1946	Buf-A☆	13(9, RH)	71	455	6.4(68)	3	23	357	15.5	3	—	—	—	—	—	—	—	—	—	—	kpi	1	42	989
1947	Buf-A	10(3)	26	130	5.0	0	5	35	7.0	1	—	—	—	—	—	—	—	—	—	—	Kkp	—	40	174
1948	ChiR-A	4(1)	13	19	1.5	0	1	5	5.0(5)	0	—	—	—	—	—	—	—	—	—	—	K	—	5	22
AAFC	3	27(13)	110	604	5.5(68)	3	29	397	13.7(5)	4	—	—	—	—	—	—	—	—	—	—	Kkpi	1	87	1184

KAB, VYTO Vyto, TE, 6´5˝/243 lbs; Penn State; 1982: Phi, rnd 3; B12/23/1959 Albany, GA

YEAR	TEAM	G(GS, POS)	RUSH	YD	AVG(LG)	TD	REC	YD	AVG(LG)	TD	PASS	COMP	PCT	YD	AVG(LG)	TD	INT	SK	YD	QBR	KPR	OTD	PTS	TAY
1982	Phi	9(2)	—	—	—	—	4	35	8.8(13)	1	—	—	—	—	—	—	—	—	—	—	—	—	6	23
1983	Phi	14(14, TE)	—	—	—	—	18	195	10.8(25)	1	—	—	—	—	—	—	—	—	—	—	—	—	6	103
1984	Phi	16(5, te)	—	—	—	—	9	102	11.3(26)	3	—	—	—	—	—	—	—	—	—	—	—	—	18	66
1985	Phi	1(1)	—	—	—	—	—	—	—	—	—	—	—	—	—	—	—	—	—	—	—	—	—	—
1985	NYG	11(0)	—	—	—	—	—	—	—	—	—	—	—	—	—	—	—	—	—	—	—	—	—	—
1987	Det	7(2)	—	—	—	—	5	54	10.8(28)	0	—	—	—	—	—	—	—	—	—	—	—	—	0	27
NFL	5	58(24)	—	—	—	—	36	386	10.7(28)	5	—	—	—	—	—	—	—	—	—	—	—	—	30	218

YEAR	TEAM	G(GS, POS)	RUSH	YD	AVG(LG)	TD	REC	YD	AVG(LG)	TD	PASS COMP	PCT	YD	AVG(LG)	TD	INT	SK	YD	QBR	KPR	OTD	PTS	TAY

KABEALO, MIKE   Michael T., HB, 5´8˝/185 lbs; Ohio State; B10/1/1915 Youngstown, OH, D9/24/1993 Centerville, OH

| 1944 | Cle | 10(7, HB) | 47 | 152 | 3.2(11) | 1 | 2 | 20 | 10.0(12) | 0 | 1 | 100.0 | 54 | 54.0(54) | 1 | 0 | — | — | — | kpi | | 6 | 298 |

KACHERSKI, JOHN   John Richard, LB, 6´2˝/240 lbs; Ohio State; B6/27/1967 Oceanside, NY   **1992** Den 7 (0)

KACMAREK, JEFF   Jeffrey Alan, NT, 6´2˝/240 lbs; Western Michigan; B4/12/1963 Oak Lawn, IL   **1987** Det 3 (0)

KACYVENSKI, ISAIAH   Isaiah J., LB, 6´1˝/252 lbs; Harvard; 2000: Sea, rnd 4; B10/3/1977 Syracuse, NY   **2000** Sea 16 (0)   **2001**†Sea 16 (0)   **2002** Sea 9 (9, MLB)   **2003** Sea 14 (0)   **2004**†Sea 16 (13, LLB/rlb)   **2005**†Sea 16 (1)   NFL 87 (23) [6 yrs]

KACZMAREK, MICHAEL   Michael Louis, LB, 6´4˝/235 lbs; Southern Illinois; B10/31/1951 Gary, IN   **1973** Bal 14

KACZUR, NICK   Nicholas Jesse, T-G, 6´4˝/319 lbs; Toledo; 2005: NE, rnd 3; B7/28/1979 Brantford, Canada   **2005**†NE 14 (11, LT)

KADELA, DAVE   David Richard, T, 6´6˝/294 lbs; Virginia Tech; B5/6/1978 Dearborn, MI   **2001** Atl 1 (0)   **2004** Car 1 (0)   NFL 2 (0) [2 yrs]

KADESKY, MAX   Max R., E, 5´11˝/170 lbs; Iowa; B2/8/1901 Winsted, CT, D8/14/1970 Dubuque, IA   **1923** RI 8 (8, LE)

KADISH, MIKE   Michael Scott, DT-NT, 6´5˝/270 lbs; Notre Dame; 1972: Mia, rnd 1; B5/27/1950 Grand Rapids, MI   **1973** Buf 12 (9, LDT)   **1974**†Buf 14 (14, NT)   **1975** Buf 14 (14, NT)   **1976** Buf 14 (14, LDT)   **1977** Buf 14 (6, rdt)   **1978** Buf 11 (6, rdt)   **1979** Buf 16 (13, NT)   **1980**†Buf 16 (0)   **1981**†Buf 16 (0)   NFL 127 (84) [9 yrs]

KADZIEL, RON   Ronald Dennis, LB, 6´4˝/230 lbs; Stanford; 1971: Dal, rnd 5; B2/27/1949 Pomona, CA   **1972** NE 14 (1)

KAEDING, NATE   Nate, K, 6´0˝/187 lbs; Iowa; 2004: SD, rnd 3; B3/26/1982 Iowa City, IA **[K]**   **2004**†SD 16 (0)   **2005** SD 16 (0)   NFL 32 (0) [2 yrs]

KAER, MORT   Morton Armour, TB-QB-HB, 5´11˝/167 lbs; USC; B9/7/1902 Omaha, NE, D1/12/1991 Mt. Shasta, CA   **1931** Fra 8 (6, TB), 6

KAESVIHARN, KEVIN   Kevin Robert, DB, 6´1˝/194 lbs; Augustana (SD); B8/29/1976 Paramount, CA   **2001** Cin 10 (3)   **2002** Cin 16 (6, lcb)   **2003** Cin 16 (7, ss)   **2004** Cin 15 (6, ss)   **2005**†Cin 16 (16, FS)   NFL 73 (38) [5 yrs]

KAFENTZIS, KURT   Kurt Michael, DB, 6´2˝/190 lbs; Hawaii; B12/31/1962 Richland, WA   **1987** Hou 2 (0)

KAFENTZIS, MARK   Mark Kevin, DB, 5´10˝/190 lbs; Hawaii; 1982: Cle, rnd 8; B6/30/1958 Richland, WA   **1982**†Cle 9 (0)   **1983** Bal 15 (1)   **1984** Ind 16 (14, SS)   NFL 40 (15) [3 yrs]

KAHL, CY   Cyrus Paul, B, 6´1˝/194 lbs; North Dakota; B11/29/1904 Heaton, ND, D7/30/1971 Portsmouth, OH   **1930** Por 11 (7, BB)   **1931** Por 1 (0)   NFL 12 (7) [2 yrs]

KAHLER, BOB   Robert William, DB-HB, 6´3˝/201 lbs; Nebraska; B2/13/1917 Grand Island, NE

1942	GB	7(0)	8	4	0.5(13)	0	2	21	10.5(12)	0	—	—	—	—	—	—	—	—	p		—	0	24
1943	GB	4(0)	1	5	5.0(5)	0	—	—	—	—	—	—	—	—	—	—	—	—	—		—	0	5
1944	GB	8(0)	—	—	—	—	—	—	—	—	—	—	—	—	—	—	—	—	—		—		
	NFL	3	19(0)	9	9	1.0(13)	0	2	21	10.5(12)	0	—	—	—	—	—	—	—	p		—	0	29

KAHLER, ROYAL   Royal James, T, 6´2˝/226 lbs; Nebraska; 1941: Phi, rnd 5; B3/22/1918 Grand Island, NE, D2/21/2005 Potter, TX   **1941** Pit 9 (0)   **1942** GB 7 (0)   NFL 16 (0) [2 yrs]

KAHN, EDDIE   Edwin Bernard, G, 5´9˝/194 lbs; North Carolina; B11/9/1911 New York, NY, D2/17/1945 Leyte, Phillipines   **1935** Bos 9 (6, lg)   **1936** Bos☆5 (3)   **1937**†Was 10 (2)   NFL 24 (11) [3 yrs]

KAIMER, KARL   Karl Julius, DE, 6´3˝/230 lbs; Boston University; B11/12/1938 Elizabeth, NJ   **1962** NYT-A 8

KAISER, JASON   Jason, DB, 6´0˝/190 lbs; Culver-Stockton; B11/9/1973 Denver, CO   **1998** KC 1 (0)   **1999** Dal 0 (0)   NFL 1 (0) [2 yrs]

KAISER, JOHN   John Frederick, LB, 6´3˝/227 lbs; Arizona; 1984: Sea, rnd 6; B6/6/1962 Oconomowoc, WI   **1984**†Sea 16 (0)   **1985** Sea 16 (0)   **1986** Sea 16 (0)   **1987** Buf 12 (0)   NFL 60 (0) [4 yrs]

KAKASIC, GEORGE   George John, G, 5´10˝/200 lbs; Duquesne; B4/24/1912 Mingo Junction, OH, D1/1973, **[K]**   **1937** Pit 11 (8, LG)   **1938** Pit 4 (2)   **1939** Pit 10 (6, RG)

| 1936 | Pit | 12(7, RG) | 1 | -8 | -8.0(-8) | 0 | — | — | — | — | — | — | — | — | — | — | — | — | K | | 1 | 13 | -8 |
| | NFL | 4 | 37(23) | 1 | -8 | -8.0(-8) | 0 | — | — | — | — | — | — | — | — | — | — | — | K | | 1 | 16 | -8 |

KAKELA, IKE   Wayne Erland, C-G, 6´2˝/220 lbs; Minnesota; B7/16/1905 Eveleth, MN, D10/16/1981 Grand Forks, ND   **1930** Min 3 (0)

KALAFAT, JIM   James William, LB, 6´0˝/235 lbs; Montana State; B2/21/1962 Great Falls, MT   **1987** LARm 1 (0)

KALINA, DAVE   David, WR, 6´3˝/205 lbs; Miami (FL); B9/2/1947 Braddock, PA   **1970** Pit 2

KALIS, TODD   Todd Alexander, G, 6´6˝/296 lbs; Arizona State; 1988: Min, rnd 4; B5/10/1965 Stillwater, MN   **1988**†Min 14 (0)   **1989**†Min 16 (16, RG)   **1990** Min 15 (14, RG)   **1991** Min 16 (8, RG)   **1993**†Min 16 (7, rg)   **1994** Pit 11 (11, RG)   **1995** Cin 15 (11, RG)   NFL 103 (67) [7 yrs]

KALLINA, ED   Edward Kames, T-G, 6´0˝/205 lbs; Sam Houston State; Southwest Texas State; B10/28/1901 Nada, TX, D5/15/1963 Houston, TX   **1928** ChiB 4 (0)

KALMANIR, TOMMY   Thomas J., HB, 5´8˝/171 lbs; Pittsburgh; Nevada-Reno; 1947: Pit, rnd 25/1949: NYY-A, rnd 20; B3/30/1926 Jerome, PA, D10/12/2004 Fresno, CA

1949	†LARm	12(2)	29	218	7.5(51)	1	2	36	18.0(23)	0	—	—	—	—	—	—	—	—	kp		1	12	483
1950	†LARm	10	20	83	4.2(33)	0	5	58	11.6(41)	0	—	—	—	—	—	—	—	—	kp		—	6	331
1951	†LARm	12	16	61	3.8(23)	0	6	91	15.2(38)	1	—	—	—	—	—	—	—	—	kp		1	12	213
1953	Bal	9	16	53	3.3(32)	0	3	31	10.3(22)	1	—	—	—	—	—	—	—	—	kp		—	6	89
	NFL	4	43(2)	81	415	5.1(51)	1	16	215	13.4(41)	3	—	—	—	—	—	—	—	—	kp		2	36	1115

KALSU, BOB   James Robert, G, 6´3˝/235 lbs; Oklahoma; 1968: Buf, rnd 8; B4/13/1945 Oklahoma City, OK, D7/21/1970 Thua Thien, Vietnam   **1968** Buf-A 14 (9, RG)

KALU, N.D.   Ndukwe Dike, DE, 6´3˝/265 lbs; Rice; 1997: Phi, rnd 5; B8/3/1975 Baltimore, MD   **1997** Phi 3 (0)   **1999**†Was 12 (0)   **1998** Was 13 (1)   **2001**†Phi 14 (1)   **2005** Phi 15 (8, RDE)   **2000** Was 15 (0)   **2002**†Phi 16 (0)   **2003**†Phi 16 (16, RDE)   NFL 104 (26) [8 yrs]

KAMANA, JOHN   John Maia, RB, 6´0˝/230 lbs; USC; B12/3/1961 Honolulu, HI   **1984**†LARm 3 (0)

| 1987 | Atl | 2(1) | — | — | — | — | 7 | 51 | 7.3(15) | 1 | — | — | — | — | — | — | — | — | — | | — | 6 | 31 |
| | NFL | 2 | 5(1) | — | — | — | — | 7 | 51 | 7.3(15) | 1 | — | — | — | — | — | — | — | — | — | | — | 6 | 31 |

KAMANU, LEW   Lewellyn K., DE, 6´4˝/245 lbs; Weber State; 1967: Det, rnd 4; B4/9/1944 Honolulu, HI   **1967** Det 9   **1968** Det 3   NFL 12 [2 yrs]

KAMINSKI, LARRY   Larry Michael, C, 6´2˝/245 lbs; Purdue; B1/6/1945 Cleveland, OH   **1966** Den-A 14 (14, C)   **1967** Den-A☆14 (C)   **1968** Den-A 14 (14, C)   **1969** Den-A 14 (14, C)   **1970** Den 14 (14, C)   **1971** Den 3 (3)   **1972** Den 11 (9, C)   **1973** Den 12   NFL 96 (54) [8 yrs]

KAMMERER, CARL   Carlton Cordell, DE-LB, 6´3˝/243 lbs; San Francisco State; Pacific; 1960: SF, rnd 2; B3/20/1937 Stockton, CA   **1961** SF 14   **1962** SF 14 (7, mlb)   **1963** Was 14 (MLB)   **1964** Was 14 (RDE)   **1966** Was 14 (RDE)   **1967** Was 14 (RDE)   **1969** Was 14 (RDE)   NFL 123 (7) [9 yrs]

KAMP, JIM   James, T-G-E, 6´0˝/210 lbs; Oklahoma City; B12/5/1907 El Reno, OK   **1932** SI 12 (7, lt)   **1933** Bos 10 (3)   NFL 22 (10) [2 yrs]

KAMPA, BOB   Robert Eugene, DT, 6´4˝/252 lbs; California; 1973: Buf, rnd 3; B4/26/1951 San Francisco, CA   **1973** Buf 7   **1974** Buf 2   **1974** Den 4 (1)   NFL 13 (1) [2 yrs]

KAMPMAN, AARON   Aaron Allan, DE-DT, 6´4˝/286 lbs; Iowa; 2002: GB, rnd 5; B11/30/1979 Cedar Rapids, IA   **2002**†GB 12 (6, lde)   **2003**†GB 12 (10, LDE)   **2004**†GB 16 (16, LDE)   **2005** GB 16 (16, LDE)   NFL 56 (48) [4 yrs]

KANE, CARL   Carl Everett, B, 5´11˝/195 lbs; St. Louis; B1/24/1913 Philadelphia, PA, D9/5/1983 Vero Beach, FL   **1936** Phi 1 (0)

KANE, GEORGE   George, G, 5´9˝/195 lbs; Fordham; B7/13/1891, NY, D8/1989 Pinellas County, FL   **1921** NYG 1 (0)

KANE, JIM   Harold James, G, 5´11˝/200 lbs; none; B11/28/1896 Rochester, NY, D4/10/1976 Rochester, NY   **1920** Roc 6 (0)

KANE, HERB   Herbert Russell, T, 6´0˝/220 lbs; East Central (OK); 1944: NYG, rnd 4; B12/24/1920 Carroll, IA, D4/19/1995 Las Vegas, NV   **1944** NYG 6 (0)   **1945** NYG 2 (0)   NFL 8 (0) [2 yrs]

KANE, RICK   Richard James, RB, 5´11˝/200 lbs; Oregon; San Jose State; 1977: Det, rnd 3; B11/12/1954 Lincoln, NE

1977	Det	14(6, RB)	124	421	3.4(35)	4	18	186	10.3(20)	0	—	—	—	—	—	—	—	—	kp		—	24	698
1978	Det	15	44	153	3.5(19)	2	16	161	10.1(26)	0	—	—	—	—	—	—	—	—	k		—	12	290
1979	Det	16(6, rb)	94	332	3.5(26)	4	9	104	11.6(36)	1	—	—	—	—	—	—	—	—	k		—	30	515
1980	Det	16(0)	31	125	4.0(22)	0	5	26	5.2(9)	0	—	—	—	—	—	—	—	—	k		—	0	288
1981	Det	16(2)	77	332	4.3(20)	2	17	181	10.6(40)	1	—	—	—	—	—	—	—	—	k		—	18	448
1982	†Det	6(0)	7	17	2.4(6)	0	3	25	8.3(12)	0	—	—	—	—	—	—	—	—	k		—	0	34
1983	†Det	14(0)	4	19	4.8(9)	0	2	15	7.5(9)	0	—	—	—	—	—	—	—	—	—		—	0	27
1984	†Was	12(0)	17	43	2.5(10)	0	1	7	7.0(7)	0	—	—	—	—	—	—	—	—	—		—	0	45
1985	Det	16(1)	11	44	4.0(7)	0	5	56	11.2(18)	0	—	—	—	—	—	—	—	—	—		—	0	72
	NFL	9	125(15)	409	1486	3.6(35)	12	76	761	10.0(40)	2	—	—	—	—	—	—	—	—	kp		—	84	2415

YEAR	TEAM	G (GS, POS)	RUSH	YD	AVG(LG)	TD	REC	YD	AVG(LG)	TD	PASS COMP	PCT	YD	AVG(LG)	TD	INT	SK	YD	QBR	KPR	OTD	PTS	TAY

KANE, TOMMY Thomas Henry, WR, 5´11˝/180 lbs; Syracuse; 1988: Sea, rnd 3; B1/14/1964 Montreal, Canada

1988	Sea	9(0)	—	—	—	—	6	32	5.3(9)	0	—	—	—	—	—	—	—	—	—	—	—	0	16
1989	Sea	5(0)	—	—	—	—	7	94	13.4(20)	0	—	—	—	—	—	—	—	—	—	—	—	0	47
1990	Sea	16(11, WR)	—	—	—	—	52	776	14.9(63)	4	—	—	—	—	—	—	—	—	—	—	—	24	408
1991	Sea	16(15, WR)	—	—	—	—	50	763	15.3(60)	2	—	—	—	—	—	—	—	—	—	—	—	12	392
1992	Sea	11(11, WR)	—	—	—	—	27	369	13.7(31)	3	—	—	—	—	—	—	—	—	—	—	—	18	200
NFL	5	57(37)	—	—	—	—	142	2034	14.3(63)	9	—	—	—	—	—	—	—	—	—	—	—	54	1062

KANELL, DANNY Daniel Paul, QB, 6´3˝/218 lbs; Florida State; 1996: NYG, rnd 4; B11/21/1973 Fort Lauderdale, FL

1996	NYG	4(0)	7	6	0.9(13)	0	—	—	—	—	60	23	38.3	227	3.8(25)	1	1	7	48	—	—	0	85
1997	†NYG	16(10, QB)	15	2	0.1(8)	0	—	—	—	—	294	156	53.1	1740	5.9(68)	11	9	19	171	70.7	—	0	567
1998	NYG	10(10, QB)	15	36	2.4(10)	0	—	—	—	—	299	160	53.5	1603	5.4(49)	11	10	22	172	67.3	—	0	493
1999	Atl	3(1)	—	—	—	—	—	—	—	—	84	42	50.0	593	7.1(52)	4	5	9	37	—	—	0	157
2000	Atl	5(1)	1	0	0.0(0)	0	—	—	—	—	116	57	49.1	524	4.5(35)	2	5	8	60	—	—	0	72
2003	Den	5(2)	6	5	0.8(9)	0	—	—	—	—	103	53	51.5	442	4.3(26)	2	5	2	24	49.1	—	0	36
NFL	6	43(24)	44	49	1.1(13)	0	—	—	—	—	956	491	51.4	5129	5.4(68)	31	34	63	512	63.2	—	0	1409

KANICKI, JIM James Henry, DT, 6´4˝/270 lbs; Michigan State; 1963: Cle, rnd 2/Buf, rnd 7; B12/17/1941 Bay City, MI **1963** Cle 13 **1964**†Cle 14 (RDT) **1965**†Cle 14 (RDT)
1966 Cle 14 (RDT) **1967**†Cle 14 (RDT/ldt) **1968**†Cle 13 (RDT) **1969**†Cle 6 (rdt) **1970** NYG 14 (RDT) **1971** NYG 14 (LDT) **NFL** 116 [9 yrs]

KANTOR, JOE Joseph John, HB, 6´1˝/218 lbs; Notre Dame; B12/17/1942 Parma Heights, OH

| 1966 | Was | 4 | 1 | 2 | 2.0(2) | 0 | — | — | — | — | — | — | — | — | — | — | — | — | — | — | k | 0 | 7 |

KANYA, AL Albert Joseph, T-E, 6´0˝/200 lbs; Syracuse; B3/7/1908, D10/1985 Queens, NY **1931** SI 11 (11, LT), 6 **1932** SI 12 (9, LT) **NFL** 23 (20) [2 yrs]

KAPELE, JOHN John Kamana, DE-DT-T, 6´0˝/240 lbs; Utah; Brigham Young; 1960: Pit, rnd 10/DalT, rnd 1; B10/19/1937 Honolulu, HI **1960** Pit 12 **1961** Pit 14 **1962** Pit 6
1962 Phi 6 **NFL** 38 [3 yrs]

KAPITANSKY, BERNIE Bernard, G, 6´1˝/212 lbs; Long Island; B1/1/1921 Brooklyn, NY **1942** Bkn 7 (0)

KAPLAN, AVE Avold R., BB-HB-QB, 5´9˝/165 lbs; Hamline; B11/16/1899 Owatonna, MN, D12/28/1989 Birmingham, AL **[K]** **1923** Min 8 (8, BB), 18

KAPLAN, BERNIE Bernard, G, 5´11˝/195 lbs; Western Maryland; B6/8/1913 Philadelphia, PA, D6/14/1992 **1935** NYG 12 (4) **1936** NYG 7 (4) **1942** Phi 3 (0) **NFL** 22 (8) [3 yrs]

KAPLAN, KEN Kenneth Scott, T, 6´4˝/270 lbs; New Hampshire; 1983: TB, rnd 6; B1/12/1960 Boston, MA **1984** TB 16 (2) **1985** TB 16 (0) **1987** NO 3 (3) **NFL** 35 (5) [3 yrs]

KAPLAN, SAM Samuel, E, /166 lbs; Lehigh; Catholic; B1/1899 Washington, DC, D6/29/1970 **1921** Was 1 (1)

KAPLANOFF, CARL Carl George, G-T, 6´0˝/235 lbs; Ohio State; 1939: Bkn, rnd 12; B4/4/1917, D6/6/1991, CA **1939** Bkn 11 (6, RG)

KAPORCH, AL Albert John, T-G, 5´10˝/215 lbs; St. Bonaventure; B10/6/1913 Pittston, PA, D10/14/2004 Plains Township, PA **1943** Det 10 (9, RT) **1944** Det 10 (10, RG)
1945 Det 2 (2) **NFL** 22 (21) [3 yrs]

KAPP, JOE Joseph Robert, QB, 6´2˝/215 lbs; California; 1959: Was, rnd 18; B3/19/1938 Santa Fe, NM

1967	Min	13(12, QB)	27	167	6.2(24)	2	—	—	—	—	214	102	47.7	1386	6.5(85)	8	17	23	200	48.2	—	—	12	240
1968	†Min	14(14, QB)	50	269	5.4(27)	3	—	—	—	—	248	129	52.0	1695	6.8(61)	10	17	31	278	58.8	—	—	18	517
1969	†Min◇	13(13, QB)	22	104	4.7(18)	0	—	—	—	—	237	120	50.6	1726	7.3(83)	19	13	28	198	78.5	—	—	0	542
1970	Bos	11(10, QB)	20	71	3.6(14)	0	—	—	—	—	219	98	44.7	1104	5.0(48)	3	17	27	231	32.6	—	—	0	-42
NFL	4	51(49)	119	611	5.1(27)	5	—	—	—	—	918	449	48.9	5911	6.4(85)	40	64	109	907	55.1	—	—	30	1257

KAPTER, ALEX Alexander Joe, G, 6´0˝/205 lbs; Northwestern; 1944: Det, rnd 21; B3/26/1922 Waukegan, IL, D7/26/2005 Thousand Oaks, CA **1946** Cle-A 6 (0)

KARAMATIC, GEORGE George, FB-DB, 5´8˝/187 lbs; Gonzaga; 1938: NYG, rnd 1; B2/22/1917 Seattle, WA **[K]**

| 1938 | Was | 10(2) | 50 | 185 | 3.7 | 0 | 4 | 99 | 24.8(39) | 1 | — | — | — | — | — | — | — | — | — | — | K | — | 11 | 240 |

KARAS, EMIL Emil, LB, 6´3˝/230 lbs; Dayton; 1959: Was, rnd 3; B12/13/1933 Pittsburgh, PA, D11/25/1974 San Diego, CA **1959** Was 11 (4) **1960**†LAC-A 12 (MLB)
1961†SD-A◇14 (LLB) **1962** SD-A◇14 (LLB) **1963**†SD-A◇14 (LLB) **1964** SD-A 4 **1966** SD-A 2 **NFL** 71 (4) [7 yrs]

KARCH, BOB Robert H., T, 6´1˝/220 lbs; Ohio State; B7/4/1894 Columbus, OH, D11/14/1958 Columbus, OH **1922** Col 4 (4, RT) **1923** Lou 2 (2) **NFL** 6 (6) [2 yrs]

KARCHER, JIM James Norman, G, 6´0˝/207 lbs; Ohio State; B5/2/1914 Forest, OH, D8/19/1997 St. Louis Park, MN **1936**†Bos 10 (7, RG) **1937**†Was 11 (7, RG)
1938 Was☆10 (10, RG) **1939** Was☆11 (9, RG) **NFL** 42 (33) [4 yrs]

KARCHER, KEN Kenneth Paul, QB, 6´3˝/205 lbs; Notre Dame; Tulane; B7/1/1963 Pittsburgh, PA

1987	Den	3(3)	9	3	0.3(8)	0	—	—	—	—	102	56	54.9	628	6.2(49)	5	4	5	45	—	—	—	0	182
1988	Den	1(0)	—	—	—	—	—	—	—	—	12	6	50.0	128	10.7(74)	1	0	—	—	—	—	—	0	69
NFL	2	4(3)	9	3	0.3(8)	0	—	—	—	—	114	62	54.4	756	6.6(74)	6	4	5	45	—	—	—	0	251

KARCIS, BULL John, FB-BB-HB, 5´9˝/223 lbs; Carnegie Mellon; B12/3/1908 Monaca, PA, D9/4/1973 Pittsburgh, PA **[KC]**

1932	Bkn	11(10, BB)	20	68	3.4	1	—	—	—	—	—	—	—	—	—	—	—	—	—	—	—	6	78
1933	Bkn	10(5, BB)	70	232	3.3	0	1	4	4.0(4)	0	—	—	—	—	—	—	—	—	—	—	—	0	234
1934	Bkn	9(8, BB)	51	202	4.0	0	—	—	—	—	—	—	—	—	—	—	—	—	—	—	—	0	202
1935	Bkn	12(7, FB)	68	188	2.8	1	5	58	11.6	0	5	2	40.0	23	4.6	0	0	—	—	—	—	—	6	239
1936	Pit	12(12, FB)	89	272	3.1	2	8	71	8.9	0	4	0	0.0	0	0.0	0	2	—	—	—	K	—	13	248
1937	Pit☆	6(2, fb)	127	513	4.0	3	2	18	9.0	0	3	1	33.3	2	0.7(2)	1	1	—	—	—	—	—	18	518
1938	Pit	3(0)	16	31	1.9	0	—	—	—	—	—	—	—	—	—	—	—	—	—	—	—	0	31
1938	†NYG◇	8(1)	73	181	2.5	4	—	—	—	—	—	—	—	—	—	—	—	—	—	—	1	30	221
1939	NYG	10(0)	31	93	3.0	0	—	—	—	—	—	—	—	—	—	—	—	—	—	—	—	0	93
1943	NYG	8(0)	12	19	1.6(7)	0	1	1	1.0(1)	0	—	—	—	—	—	—	—	—	—	—	k	—	0	26
NFL	9	89(45)	557	1799	3.2(7)	11	17	152	8.9(4)	0	12	3	25.0	25	2.1(2)	1	3	—	—	—	Kk	1	73	1889

KARILIVACZ, CARL Carl E., DB-HB, 6´0˝/188 lbs; Syracuse; 1953: Det, rnd 23; B11/20/1930 Glen Cove, NY, D8/30/1969 Glen Cove, NY **1953**†Det 12 **1954**†Det 11 (DB)
1955 Det 12 (DB) **1956** Det 11 (DB) **1957**†Det 12 (db) **1958**†NYG 12 (DB) **1959** LARm 9 (db) **1960** LARm 9 **NFL** 85 [8 yrs]

KARLIS, RICH Richard John, K, 6´0˝/180 lbs; Cincinnati; B5/23/1959 Salem, OH **[K]** **1982** Den 9 (0) **1983**†Den 16 (0) **1984**†Den 16 (0) **1985** Den 16 (0) **1986**†Den 16 (0)
1987†Den 12 (0) **1988** Den 16 (0) **1989**†Min 13 (0) **1990** Det 6 (0) **NFL** 120 (0) [9 yrs]

KARMAZIN, MIKE Michael Lawrence, G, 5´11˝/210 lbs; Duke; 1946: Bos, rnd 24; B7/16/1919 Manown, PA, D1/21/2004 New Orleans, LA **1946**†NYY-A 10 (0)

KARNEY, MIKE Mike, FB, 5´11˝/254 lbs; Arizona State; 2004: NO, rnd 5; B7/6/1981 San Jose, CA

2004	NO	16(8, FB)	3	7	2.3(4)	0	6	42	7.0(17)	0	—	—	—	—	—	—	—	—	—	—	—	0	28
2005	NO	16(14, FB)	6	12	2.0(3)	0	10	61	6.1(10)	0	—	—	—	—	—	—	—	—	—	—	—	0	43
NFL	2	32(22)	9	19	2.1(4)	0	16	103	6.4(17)	0	—	—	—	—	—	—	—	—	—	—	—	0	71

KARNOFSKY, ABE Abraham Sonny, QB-HB-DB, 5´10˝/175 lbs; Arizona; B9/22/1922 Oxnard, CA

1945	Phi	8(2)	41	134	3.3(19)	2	5	113	22.6(38)	0	—	—	—	—	—	—	—	—	—	—	kpi	—	12	375
1946	Bos	11(7, qb)	36	84	2.3(35)	1	8	139	17.4(56)	1	—	—	—	—	—	—	—	—	—	—	kp	1	18	491
NFL	2	19(9)	77	218	2.8(35)	3	13	252	19.4(56)	1	—	—	—	—	—	—	—	—	—	—	kpi	1	30	865

KARPINSKI, KEITH Keith Carl, LB, 6´3˝/255 lbs; Penn State; 1989: Det, rnd 11; B10/12/1966 Southfield, MI **1989** Det 16 (0)

KARPOWICH, ED Edwin Walter, T, 6´4˝/220 lbs; Catholic; 1936: Pit, rnd 8; B9/28/1912 Duquesne, PA **1938** Pit 8 (6, lt) **1939** Pit 7 (3) **1940** Pit 1 (0)

1936	Pit	11(3)	—	—	—	—	1	-6	-6.0(-6)	0	—	—	—	—	—	—	—	—	—	—	—	0	-3
1937	Pit	9(4)	1	15	15.0(15)	0	—	—	—	—	—	—	—	—	—	—	—	—	—	—	—	0	15
NFL	5	36(16)	1	15	15.0(15)	0	1	-6	-6.0(-6).	0	—	—	—	—	—	—	—	—	—	—	—	0	12

KARR, BILL William Morrison, E, 6´1˝/190 lbs; West Virginia; B3/29/1911 Ripley, WV, D10/29/1979 Clendenin, WV

1933	†ChiB	13(7, RE)	—	—	—	—	9	182	20.2(34)	3	—	—	—	—	—	—	—	—	—	—	—	1	24	106
1934	†ChiB	12(11, RE)	—	—	—	—	3	68	22.7(49)	1	—	—	—	—	—	—	—	—	—	—	—	—	6	39
1935	ChiB☆	10(10, RE)	—	—	—	—	9	220	24.4(42)	6	—	—	—	—	—	—	—	—	—	—	—	—	36	140
1936	ChiB	8(6, RE)	4	11	2.8	1	6	121	20.2(40)	2	—	—	—	—	—	—	—	—	—	—	—	—	18	92
1937	†ChiB☆	10(8, RE)	1	10	10.0(10)	0	7	188	26.9(42)	2	—	—	—	—	—	—	—	—	—	—	—	—	12	114

YEAR	TEAM	G (GS, POS)	RUSH	YD	AVG (LG)	TD	REC	YD	AVG (LG)	TD	PASS	COMP	PCT	YD	AVG (LG)	TD	INT	SK	YD	QBR	KPR	OTD	PTS	TAY
1938	ChiB	10 (4)	1	6	6.0 (6)	0	14	253	18.1	4	—	—	—	—	—	—	—	—	—	—	—	—	24	153
NFL	6	63 (46)	6	27	4.5 (10)	1	48	1032	21.5 (49)	18	—	—	—	—	—	—	—	—	—	—	—	1	120	643

Karras, Alex Alexander George, DT, 6´2˝/248 lbs; Iowa; 1958: Det, rnd 1; B7/15/1935 Gary, IN **1958** Det 12 (LDT) **1959** Det 12 (LDT) **1960** Det★12 (LDT) **1961** Det★14 (LDT) **1962** Det★14 (LDT) **1964** Det☆14 (LDT) **1965** Det★14 (LDT) **1966** Det☆14 (LDT) **1967** Det☆14 (LDT) **1968** Det☆14 (LDT) **1969** Det☆14 (LDT) **1970** Det 13 (LDT) **NFL** 161 [12 yrs]

Karras, Johnny John Bernard, HB, 5´11˝/187 lbs; Illinois; 1952: ChiC, rnd 2; B1/29/1928 Chicago, IL

YEAR	TEAM	G (GS, POS)	RUSH	YD	AVG (LG)	TD	REC	YD	AVG (LG)	TD	PASS	COMP	PCT	YD	AVG (LG)	TD	INT	SK	YD	QBR	KPR	OTD	PTS	TAY
1952	ChiC	10	24	42	1.8 (17)	0	5	63	12.6 (29)	1	—	—	—	—	—	—	—	—	—	—	kp	—	6	115

Karras, Lou Louis George, DT, 6´4˝/241 lbs; Purdue; 1950: Was, rnd 3; B9/19/1927 Gary, IN **1950** Was 12 (LDT) **1951** Was 12 (LDT)

YEAR	TEAM	G (GS, POS)	RUSH	YD	AVG (LG)	TD	REC	YD	AVG (LG)	TD	PASS	COMP	PCT	YD	AVG (LG)	TD	INT	SK	YD	QBR	KPR	OTD	PTS	TAY
1952	Was	2	—	—	—	—	1	-2	-2.0 (-2)	0	—	—	—	—	—	—	—	—	—	—	—	—	0	-1
NFL	3	26	—	—	—	—	1	-2	-2.0 (-2)	0	—	—	—	—	—	—	—	—	—	—	—	—	0	-1

Karras, Ted Theodore George, G-T-LB, 6´1˝/245 lbs; Indiana; B1/31/1934 Gary, IN **1958** Pit 12 (LT) **1959** Pit 12 (LT) **1960** ChiB 12 (RG) **1961** ChiB 14 **1962** ChiB 14 **1963**†ChiB 14 (LG) **1964** ChiB 14 **1965** Det 12 (LG) **1966** LARm 4 **NFL** 108 [9 yrs]

Karras, Ted Theodore George, DT, 6´2˝/265 lbs; Northwestern; B12/10/1964 Gary, IN **1987** Was 1 (1)

Karrs, John John Bernard, BB, 6´1˝/210 lbs; Duquesne; B9/19/1915 Pittsburgh, PA

YEAR	TEAM	G (GS, POS)	RUSH	YD	AVG (LG)	TD	REC	YD	AVG (LG)	TD	PASS	COMP	PCT	YD	AVG (LG)	TD	INT	SK	YD	QBR	KPR	OTD	PTS	TAY
1944	Cle	10 (8, BB)	7	0	0.0 (3)	0	—	—	—	—	10	4	40.0	49	4.9 (23)	0	4	—	—	—	—	—	0	-136

Karstens, George George Jacob, C, 6´4˝/205 lbs; Indiana; B2/9/1924 Chicago, IL **1949** Det 2 (0)

Kartz, Keith Keith Leonard, C-G-T, 6´4˝/270 lbs; California; B5/5/1963 Las Vegas, NV **1987**†Den 12 (3) **1988** Den 13 (12, RG) **1989**†Den 16 (16, C) **1990** Den 16 (16, C) **1991**†Den 16 (16, C) **1992** Den 15 (15, C) **1993**†Den 12 (10, C) **NFL** 100 (88) [7 yrs]

Karwales, Jack John Joseph, E, 6´0˝/215 lbs; Michigan; B6/22/1920 Chicago, IL, D12/31/2004 **1947** ChiC 2 (0)

Kasap, Mike Michael, T, 6´2˝/255 lbs; Illinois; Purdue; 1945: Det, rnd 12; B11/20/1922 Oglesby, IL, D10/20/1994 La Salle, IL **1947** Bal-A 12 (3)

Kasay, John John David, K, 5´10˝/198 lbs; Georgia; 1991: Sea, rnd 4; B10/27/1969 Athens, GA **[K]** **1991** Sea 16 (0) **1992** Sea 16 (0) **1993** Sea 16 (0) **1994** Sea 16 (0) **1995** Car 16 (0) **1996**†Car★16 (0) **1997** Car 16 (0) **1998** Car 16 (0) **1999** Car 13 (0) **2001** Car 16 (0) **2002** Car 2 (0) **2003**†Car 16 (0) **2004** Car 14 (0) **2005**†Car 16 (0) **NFL** 205 (0) [14 yrs]

Kashama, Alain Alain Kaleta Olony T., DE, 6´4˝/270 lbs; Michigan; B12/8/1979 Montreal, Canada **2004** ChiB 3 (0) **2005** Sea 1 (0) **NFL** 4 (0) [2 yrs]

Kaska, Tony Anthony, BB-HB, 5´11˝/193 lbs; Illinois Wesleyan; B7/1/1911 Johnston City, IL, D8/9/1994 Marin County, CA

YEAR	TEAM	G (GS, POS)	RUSH	YD	AVG (LG)	TD	REC	YD	AVG (LG)	TD	PASS	COMP	PCT	YD	AVG (LG)	TD	INT	SK	YD	QBR	KPR	OTD	PTS	TAY
1935	†Det	2 (0)	5	15	3.0	0	—	—	—	—	—	—	—	—	—	—	—	—	—	—	—	—	0	15
1936	Bkn	12 (0)	9	29	3.2	1	1	5	5.0 (5)	0	1	0	0.0	0	0.0	0	1	—	—	—	—	—	6	2
1937	Bkn	10 (6, BB)	1	4	4.0 (4)	0	4	84	21.0	0	—	—	—	—	—	—	—	—	—	—	—	—	0	46
1938	Bkn	11 (4, BB)	2	1	0.5	0	2	77	38.5	0	—	—	—	—	—	—	—	—	—	—	—	—	0	40
NFL	4	35 (10)	17	49	2.9 (4)	1	7	166	23.7 (5)	0	1	0	0.0	0	0.0	0	1	—	—	—	—	—	6	102

Kasky, Ed Edward Thomas, T, 6´1˝/220 lbs; Villanova; B6/22/1919 Brooklyn, NY, D12/27/1997, **[K]** **1942** Phi 10 (3)

Kasper, Kevin Kevin Joseph, WR, 6´1˝/197 lbs; Iowa; 2001: Den, rnd 6; B12/23/1977 Hinsdale, IL **[R]** **2002** Den 4 (0) **2002** Sea 3 (0) **2004** NE 8 (0)

YEAR	TEAM	G (GS, POS)	RUSH	YD	AVG (LG)	TD	REC	YD	AVG (LG)	TD	PASS	COMP	PCT	YD	AVG (LG)	TD	INT	SK	YD	QBR	KPR	OTD	PTS	TAY
2001	Den	10 (5, wr)	3	19	6.3 (27)	0	8	84	10.5 (21)	0	—	—	—	—	—	—	—	—	—	—	k	—	0	223
2002	Arz	6 (4)	3	19	6.3 (9)	0	15	180	12.0 (24)	3	—	—	—	—	—	—	—	—	—	—	k	—	18	366
2003	Arz	7 (0)	1	-4	-4.0 (-4)	0	1	23	23.0 (23)	0	—	—	—	—	—	—	—	—	—	—	k	—	0	69
NFL	4	38 (9)	7	34	4.9 (27)	0	24	287	12.0 (24)	3	—	—	—	—	—	—	—	—	—	—	k	—	18	907

Kasper, Cy Thomas Cyril, HB, 5´10˝/170 lbs; Notre Dame; B5/27/1895 Fairbault, MN, D12/28/1991 Bismarck, ND **1923** Roc 1 (1)

Kasperek, Dick Dick Lee, C, 6´3˝/225 lbs; Iowa State; 1966: SL, rnd 16; B2/6/1943 St. Peter, MN **1966** SL 4 **1967** SL 2 **1968** SL 14 **NFL** 20 [3 yrs]

Kassel, Chuck Charles Edward, E, 6´1˝/191 lbs; Illinois; B1/20/1903 Chicago, IL, D11/1977 Elgin, IL **1927** ChiB 1 (0) **1927** Fra 11 (8, le), 12 **1928** Fra 14 (14, RE), 6 **1929** ChiC 13 (13, RE), 12 **1930** ChiC☆13 (12, RE) **1931** ChiC 9 (9, RE), 12

YEAR	TEAM	G (GS, POS)	RUSH	YD	AVG (LG)	TD	REC	YD	AVG (LG)	TD	PASS	COMP	PCT	YD	AVG (LG)	TD	INT	SK	YD	QBR	KPR	OTD	PTS	TAY
1932	ChiC	10 (8, RE)	—	—	—	—	7	141	20.1	1	—	—	—	—	—	—	—	—	—	—	—	—	6	76
1933	ChiC	8 (7, RE)	2	2	1.0	0	2	44	22.0	0	—	—	—	—	—	—	—	—	—	—	—	—	0	24
NFL	7	79 (71)	2	2	1.0	0	9	185	20.6	7	—	—	—	—	—	—	—	—	—	—	—	1	48	130

Kassell, Brad Brad, LB, 6´3˝/242 lbs; North Texas; B1/7/1980 Llano, TX **2002**†Ten 9 (0) **2003**†Ten 16 (4) **2004** Ten 15 (14, MLB) **2005** Ten 16 (14, MLB) **NFL** 56 (32) [4 yrs]

Kassulke, Karl Karl Otto, DB, 6´0˝/195 lbs; Marquette; Drake; 1963: Det, rnd 11; B3/20/1941 Milwaukee, WI **1963** Min 14 (12, LS) **1964** Min 14 (14, LS) **1965** Min 14 (8, LS) **1966** Min 14 (14, LS) **1967** Min 14 (14, LS) **1968**†Min 14 (14, LS) **1969**†Min☆13 (13, LS) **1970**†Min✧14 (14, SS) **1971**†Min 12 (12, SS) **1972** Min 8 (6, SS) **NFL** 131 (121) [10 yrs]

Katalinas, Leo Leo John, T-G, 6´2˝/240 lbs; Catholic; B2/4/1915 Shenandoah, PA, D7/1977 Teaneck, NJ **1938** GB 8 (0)

Katcavage, Jim James Richard, DE-DT, 6´3˝/237 lbs; Dayton; 1956: NYG, rnd 4; B10/28/1934 Wilkes-Barre, PA, D2/22/1995 Maple Glen, PA **1956**†NYG 12 (LDE) **1957** NYG 10 (RDT) **1958**†NYG 11 (LDE) **1959**†NYG☆12 (LDE) **1960** NYG 8 (LDE) **1961**†NYG★14 (LDE) **1962**†NYG★14 (LDE) **1963**†NYG★14 (LDE) **1964** NYG☆14 (LDE) **1965** NYG 14 (LDE) **1966** NYG☆14 (LDE) **1967** NYG 14 (LDE) **1968** NYG 14 (LDE) **NFL** 165 [13 yrs]

Katchik, Joe Joseph, DT, 6´9˝/290 lbs; Notre Dame; 1954: LA, rnd 10; B1/9/1931 Plymouth, PA **1960** NYT-A 2

Katolin, Mike Michael Ross, C, 6´3˝/255 lbs; San Jose State; B1/30/1958 Pasadena, CA

YEAR	TEAM	G (GS, POS)	RUSH	YD	AVG (LG)	TD	REC	YD	AVG (LG)	TD	PASS	COMP	PCT	YD	AVG (LG)	TD	INT	SK	YD	QBR	KPR	OTD	PTS	TAY
1987	Cle	3 (3)	1	0	0.0 (0)	0	—	—	—	—	—	—	—	—	—	—	—	—	—	—	—	—	0	0

Katrishen, Mike William Michael, G, 6´1˝/214 lbs; Alabama; Southern Mississippi; 1948: Was, rnd 10; B5/7/1922 Hazelton, PA, D3/1980 **1948** Was 12 (3) **1949** Was 11 (6, rg) **NFL** 23 (9) [2 yrs]

Kattus, Eric John Eric, TE, 6´5˝/240 lbs; Michigan; 1986: Cin, rnd 4; B3/4/1963 Cincinnati, OH

YEAR	TEAM	G (GS, POS)	RUSH	YD	AVG (LG)	TD	REC	YD	AVG (LG)	TD	PASS	COMP	PCT	YD	AVG (LG)	TD	INT	SK	YD	QBR	KPR	OTD	PTS	TAY
1986	Cin	16 (1)	—	—	—	—	11	99	9.0 (28)	1	—	—	—	—	—	—	—	—	—	—	—	—	6	55
1987	Cin	11 (0)	—	—	—	—	18	217	12.1 (57)	2	—	—	—	—	—	—	—	—	—	—	k	—	12	111
1988	Cin	4 (0)	—	—	—	—	2	8	4.0 (11)	0	—	—	—	—	—	—	—	—	—	—	—	—	0	4
1989	Cin	16 (1)	—	—	—	—	12	93	7.8 (16)	0	—	—	—	—	—	—	—	—	—	—	—	—	0	47
1990	†Cin	16 (3)	—	—	—	—	11	145	13.2 (31)	2	—	—	—	—	—	—	—	—	—	—	k	—	12	78
1991	Cin	16 (2)	—	—	—	—	12	136	11.3 (24)	0	—	—	—	—	—	—	—	—	—	—	—	—	0	68
1992	NYJ	4 (0)	—	—	—	—	—	—	—	—	—	—	—	—	—	—	—	—	—	—	—	—	—	—
NFL	7	83 (7)	—	—	—	—	66	698	10.6 (57)	5	—	—	—	—	—	—	—	—	—	—	k	—	30	361

Katula, Matt Matt, C, 6´6˝/280 lbs; Wisconsin; B8/22/1982 Brookfield, WI **2005** Bal 16 (0)

Katzenmoyer, Andy Andrew Warren, LB, 6´3˝/255 lbs; Ohio State; 1999: NE, rnd 1; B12/2/1977 Westerville, OH **1999** NE 16 (11, MLB) **2000** NE 8 (3) **NFL** 24 (14) [2 yrs]

Kauahi, Kani Daniel Kani, C, 6´2˝/268 lbs; Arizona State; Hawaii; B9/6/1959 Kekaha, HI **1982** Sea 2 (0) **1983** Sea 10 (2) **1984**†Sea 16 (0) **1985** Sea 16 (0) **1986** Sea 16 (3) **1988** GB 16 (0) **1989** Phx 16 (2) **1990** Phx 15 (0) **1991** Phx 16 (0) **1992**†KC 16 (0) **1993** Phx 1 (0) **NFL** 140 (7) [11 yrs]

Kaufman, Jake Jake, T, none **1925** Fra 1 (0)

Kauffman, John John Richard, T-G, none; B11/27/1906 Miamisburg, OH, D10/19/1982 Englewood, CO **1929** Day 1 (1)

Kaufman, Mel Melvin, LB, 6´2˝/221 lbs; Cal Poly-San Luis Obispo; B2/24/1958 Los Angeles, CA **1981** Was 11 (6, rlb) **1982**†Was 9 (7, LLB) **1983**†Was 16 (16, LLB) **1984**†Was 15 (15, LLB) **1985** Was 15 (15, LLB) **1986** Was 2 (2) **1987**†Was 12 (12, LLB) **1988** Was 11 (6, llb) **NFL** 91 (79) [8 yrs]

Kaufman, Napoleon Napoleon, RB, 5´9˝/185 lbs; Washington; 1995: Oak, rnd 1; B6/7/1973 Kansas City, MO **[R]**

YEAR	TEAM	G (GS, POS)	RUSH	YD	AVG (LG)	TD	REC	YD	AVG (LG)	TD	PASS	COMP	PCT	YD	AVG (LG)	TD	INT	SK	YD	QBR	KPR	OTD	PTS	TAY
1995	Oak	16 (1)	108	490	4.5 (28)	1	9	62	6.9 (18)	0	—	—	—	—	—	—	—	—	—	—	k	1	12	783
1996	Oak	16 (9, RB)	150	874	**5.8 (77)**	1	22	143	6.5 (19)	1	—	—	—	—	—	—	—	—	—	—	k	—	12	1134
1997	Oak	16 (16, RB)	272	1294	4.8 (83)	6	40	403	10.1 (70)	2	1	0	0.0	0	0.0	0	0	—	—	—	—	—	48	1566
1998	Oak	13 (13, RB)	217	921	4.2 (80)	2	25	191	7.6 (39)	0	—	—	—	—	—	—	—	—	—	—	—	—	12	1037
1999	Oak	16 (5, rb)	138	714	5.2 (75)	2	18	181	10.1 (50)	1	—	—	—	—	—	—	—	—	—	—	k	—	18	1031
2000	†Oak	14 (2)	93	499	5.4 (60)	0	13	127	9.8 (25)	1	—	—	—	—	—	—	—	—	—	—	k	—	6	631
NFL	6	91 (46)	978	4792	4.9 (83)	12	127	1107	8.7 (70)	5	1	0	0.0	0	0.0	0	0	—	—	—	k	1	108	6180

YEAR	TEAM	G (GS, POS)	RUSH	YD	AVG(LG)	TD	REC	YD	AVG(LG)	TD	PASS	COMP	PCT	YD	AVG(LG)	TD	INT	SK	YD	QBR	KPR	OTD	PTS	TAY

KAUFUSI, STEVE Sitiveni P., DE-DT, 6´4˝/274 lbs; Brigham Young; 1988: Phi, rnd 12; B10/17/1963 Nuku'Alofa, Tonga **1989**†Phi 16 (0) **1990**†Phi 16 (0) **NFL** 32 (0) [2 yrs]

KAUMEYER, THOM Thomas E., DB, 5´11˝/187 lbs; Oregon; 1989: LARm, rnd 6; B3/17/1967 La Jolla, CA **1989** Sea 1 (0) **1990** Sea 7 (0) **NFL** 8 (0) [2 yrs]

KAURIC, JERRY Jerry, K, 6´0˝/210 lbs; none; B6/28/1963 Windsor, Canada [K]

YEAR	TEAM	G (GS, POS)	RUSH	YD	AVG(LG)	TD	REC	YD	AVG(LG)	TD	PASS	COMP	PCT	YD	AVG(LG)	TD	INT	SK	YD	QBR	KPR	OTD	PTS	TAY
1990	Cle	14(0)	—	—	—	—	1	21	21.0(21)	0	—	—	—	—	—	—	—	—	—	—	K	—	66	11

KAVANAUGH, KEN Kenneth William, E, 6´3˝/207 lbs; LSU; 1940: ChiB, rnd 3; B11/23/1916 Little Rock, AR [K]

YEAR	TEAM	G (GS, POS)	RUSH	YD	AVG(LG)	TD	REC	YD	AVG(LG)	TD	...	KPR	OTD	PTS	TAY
1940	†ChiB◇	11(0)	—	—	—	—	12	276	23.0(74)	3			—	18	153
1941	†ChiB◇	11(0)	—	—	—	—	11	314	28.5(48)	6		Kki	—	37	188
1945	ChiB	10(2)	—	—	—	—	25	543	21.7(64)	6		k	—	36	294
1946	†ChiB☆	10(4, LE)	—	—	—	—	18	337	18.7(38)	5			—	30	194
1947	ChiB☆	12(6, LE)	—	—	—	—	32	818	25.6(81)	13			—	78	474
1948	ChiB☆	12(7, LE)	—	—	—	—	18	352	19.6(64)	6			1	42	206
1949	ChiB	12(10, LE)	—	—	—	—	29	655	22.6(81)	9			—	54	373
1950	†ChiB	12(LE)	—	—	—	—	17	331	19.5(67)	2			1	18	176
NFL	8	90(29)	—	—	—	—	162	3626	22.4(81)	50		Kki	2	313	2056

KAVEL, GEORGE George Charles, HB, 5´11˝/170 lbs; Carnegie Mellon; B3/3/1910 Wendel, PA, D7/17/1995 Sarasota, FL

YEAR	TEAM	G (GS, POS)	RUSH	YD	AVG(LG)	TD	...	OTD	PTS	TAY
1934	Pit	1(1)	5	5	1.0	0		—	0	5
1934	Phi	1(0)	2	5	2.5	0		—	0	5
NFL	1	2(1)	7	10	1.4	0		—	0	10

KAW, EDDIE Edgar Lawrence, TB-HB, 5´11˝/185 lbs; Cornell; B1/18/1897 Houston, TX, D12/13/1971 Walnut Creek, CA **1924** Buf 11 (11, TB), 12

KAWAL, EDDIE Edward Joseph, C, 6´2˝/205 lbs; Illinois; Widener; B10/13/1909 Cicero, IL, D9/26/1960 Oak Park, IL **1931** ChiB 1 (0) **1934**†ChiB☆13 (12, C) **1936** ChiB☆11 (8, C) **1937**†Was 9 (9, C)

YEAR	TEAM	G (GS, POS)	RUSH	YD	AVG(LG)	TD	REC	YD	AVG(LG)	TD	...	OTD	PTS	TAY
1935	ChiB	12(6, C)	—	—	—	—	1	11	11.0(11)			1	6	16
NFL	5	46(35)	—	—	—	—	1	11	11.0(11)	0		1	6	6

KAY, BILL William Henry, DB, 6´1˝/190 lbs; Purdue; 1981: Hou, rnd 6; B1/10/1960 Detroit, MI **1981** Hou 16 (2) **1982** Hou 9 (1) **1983** Hou 16 (6, lcb) **1984** SL 10 (0) **1984** SD 5 (3) **NFL** 56 (12) [4 yrs]

KAY, CLARENCE Clarence Hubert, TE, 6´2˝/237 lbs; Georgia; 1984: Den, rnd 7; B7/30/1961 Seneca, SC

YEAR	TEAM	G (GS, POS)	RUSH	YD	AVG(LG)	TD	REC	YD	AVG(LG)	TD	...	KPR	OTD	PTS	TAY
1984	†Den	16(13, TE)	—	—	—	—	16	136	8.5(21)	3			—	18	83
1985	Den	16(16, TE)	—	—	—	—	29	339	11.7(27)	3			—	18	185
1986	Den	13(12, TE)	—	—	—	—	15	195	13.0(34)	1			—	6	103
1987	†Den	12(12, TE)	—	—	—	—	31	440	14.2(30)	0			—	0	220
1988	Den	14(14, TE)	—	—	—	—	34	352	10.4(27)	4			—	24	196
1989	†Den	16(16, TE)	—	—	—	—	21	197	9.4(20)	2			—	12	109
1990	Den	16(14, TE)	—	—	—	—	29	282	9.7(22)	0		k	—	0	121
1991	†Den	16(16, TE)	—	—	—	—	11	139	12.6(32)	0			—	0	70
1992	Den	16(13, TE)	—	—	—	—	7	56	8.0(15)	0			—	0	28
NFL	9	135(126)	—	—	—	—	193	2136	11.1(34)	13		k	—	78	1113

KAY, RICK Richard Floyd, LB, 6´4˝/235 lbs; Colorado; B11/10/1949 Henderson, NV, D9/3/1998 **1973** †LARm 14 **1975**†LARm 14 **1976** LARm 3 (3) **1977** LARm 5 **1977** Atl 7 **NFL** 43 (3) [4 yrs]

KAZADI, MUADIANVITA Muadianvita Matt, LB, 6´2˝/240 lbs; Tulsa; 1997: SL, rnd 6; B12/20/1973 Kinshasa, Zaire **1997** SL 12 (0)

KEAHEY, DUCE Eulis Duce, T, 6´2˝/215 lbs; George Washington; B1/20/1917 Grand Saline, TX, D4/1/1999 **1942** NYG 1 (0) **1942** Bkn 1 (0) **NFL** 2 (0) [1 yr]

KEANE, JIM James Patrick, E-DE, 6´4˝/217 lbs; Iowa; Northwestern; 1945: ChiB, rnd 18; B1/11/1924 Bellaire, OH

YEAR	TEAM	G (GS, POS)	RUSH	YD	AVG(LG)	TD	REC	YD	AVG(LG)	TD	...	KPR	OTD	PTS	TAY
1946	†ChiB	11(1)	—	—	—	—	14	331	23.6(42)	3		Pp	—	18	199
1947	ChiB☆	12(3)	—	—	—	—	64	910	14.2(50)	10			—	60	505
1948	ChiB	11(4)	—	—	—	—	30	414	13.8(53)	3			—	18	222
1949	ChiB☆	12(6, RE)	—	—	—	—	47	696	14.8(39)	6			—	36	378
1950	†ChiB	12(RE)	—	—	—	—	36	433	12.0(70)	0			—	0	217
1951	ChiB	12(RE)	—	—	—	—	15	247	16.5(37)	1			—	6	129
1952	GB	11	—	—	—	—	18	191	10.6(29)	1			—	6	101
NFL	7	81(13)	—	—	—	—	224	3222	14.4(70)	24		Pp	—	144	1749

KEANE, TOM Thomas Lawrence, DB-E, 6´1˝/192 lbs; Ohio State; West Virginia; 1948: LA, rnd 3; B9/7/1926 Bellaire, OH, D6/19/2001 Miami, FL [KI]

YEAR	TEAM	G (GS, POS)	RUSH	YD	AVG(LG)	TD	REC	YD	AVG(LG)	TD	PASS	COMP	PCT	YD	AVG(LG)	TD	INT	...	QBR/KPR	OTD	PTS	TAY
1948	LARm	11(0)	7	16	2.3(3)	0	11	195	17.7(57)	2	—	—	—	—	—	—	—			—	12	124
1949	†LARm	10(0)	—	—	—	—	4	70	17.5(44)	0	—	—	—	—	—	—	—			—	0	35
1950	†LARm	9(SS)	—	—	—	—	1	19	19.0(19)	0	—	—	—	—	—	—	—		i	1	6	40
1951	†LARm	10	—	—	—	—	12	133	11.1(21)	1	1	0	0.0	0	0.0	0	1		i	—	0	19
1952	DalT	12(1, DB)	—	—	—	—	3	73	24.3(47)	0	—	—	—	—	—	—	—		pi	—	0	83
1953	Bal★	12(DB)	—	—	—	—	3	61	20.3(37)	0	—	—	—	—	—	—	—		Ppi	—	0	92
1954	Bal	12(DB)	—	—	—	—	—	—	—	—	1	1	100.0	0	0.0	0	0		i	—	0	-3
1955	ChiC	11(DB)	—	—	—	—	—	—	—	—	—	—	—	—	—	—	—		Ki	—	0	
NFL	8	87(1)	7	16	2.3(3)	0	34	551	16.2(57)	2	2	1	50.0	0	—	0	1		KPpi	1	18	422

KEARNEY, JIM James Lee, DB, 6´2˝/206 lbs; Prairie View A&M; 1965: Det, rnd 11; B1/21/1943 Wharton, TX [I] **1965** Det 7 **1966** Det 6 **1967** KC-A 3 (3) **1968**†KC-A 14 (14, LS) **1969**†KC-A 14 (LS) **1970** KC 14 (SS) **1971**†KC 14 (SS) **1972** KC 14 (SS) **1973** KC 14 (SS) **1974** KC 14 (SS) **1975** KC 14 (SS) **1976** NO 14 **NFL** 142 (17) [12 yrs]

KEARNEY, TIM Timothy Edward, LB, 6´2˝/227 lbs; Northern Michigan; 1972: Dal, rnd 4; B11/5/1950 Kingsford, MI **1972** Cin 1 **1973**†Cin 14 **1974** Cin 12 **1975** KC 14 **1976** SL 14 (6, MLB) **1977** SL 14 (10, MLB) **1978** SL 15 (LILB) **1979** SL 13 (12, RILB) **1981** SL 6 (6, rilb) **NFL** 106 (34) [10 yrs]

KEARNS, TOM Thomas Norman, T, 6´4˝/247 lbs; Miami (FL); 1942: NYG, rnd 8; B11/26/1920 Bedford, MA **1945** NYG 3 (0) **1946** ChiC 9 (1) **NFL** 12 (1) [2 yrs]

KEARSE, JEVON Jevon 'The Freak', DE, 6´4˝/255 lbs; Florida; 1999: Ten, rnd 1; B9/3/1976 Fort Myers, FL [S] **1999**†Ten★16 (16, LDE) **2000**†Ten◇16 (16, LDE) **2001** Ten◇16 (16, RDE) **2002**†Ten 4 (1) **2003**†Ten 14 (14, RDE) **2004**†Phi 14 (14, LDE) **2005** Phi 15 (15, LDE) **NFL** 95 (92) [7 yrs]

KEARSE, TIM Timothy Allynn, WR, 5´10˝/186 lbs; San Jose State; 1983: SD, rnd 11; B10/24/1959 York, PA

YEAR	TEAM	G (GS, POS)	RUSH	YD	AVG(LG)	TD	REC	YD	AVG(LG)	TD	...	OTD	PTS	TAY
1987	Ind	3(0)	—	—	—	—	3	56	18.7(21)	0		—	0	28

KEASEY, ZAK Zak, LB, 6´0˝/240 lbs; Princeton; B3/19/1982 Clarkston, MI **2005** Was 1 (0)

KEATHLEY, MICHAEL Michael, G, 6´4˝/296 lbs; TCU; B3/9/1978 Arlington, TX **2001** SD 16 (0) **2002** SD 12 (2) **2003** SD 8 (2) **NFL** 36 (4) [3 yrs]

KEATING, BILL William Lawrence, DT-G, 6´2˝/242 lbs; Michigan; B11/22/1944 Chicago, IL **1966** Den-A 14 (rdt) **1967** Den-A 6 **1967** Mia-A 2 **NFL** 22 [2 yrs]

KEATING, CHRIS Christopher Paul, LB, 6´2˝/223 lbs; Maine; B10/12/1957 Boston, MA **1979** Buf 16 **1980** Buf 15 (0) **1981** Buf 2 (2) **1982** Buf 9 (4) **1983** Buf 16 (16, LILB) **1984** Buf 16 (6, rolb) **1985** Was 10 (0) **NFL** 84 (28) [7 yrs]

KEATING, TOM Thomas Arthur, DT, 6´2˝/247 lbs; Michigan; 1964: KC, rnd 5/Min, rnd 4; B9/2/1942 Chicago, IL **1964** Buf-A 3 **1965** Buf-A 6 **1966** Oak-A★14 (RDT) **1967**†Oak-A★14 (RDT) **1969**†Oak-A☆14 (13, RDT) **1970**†Oak☆13 (12, RDT) **1971** Oak 7 **1972** Oak 8 **1973**†Pit 12 **1974** KC 14 (LDT) **1975** KC 9 **NFL** 114 (25) [11 yrs]

KEATON, CURTIS Curtis Isaiah, RB, 5´10˝/212 lbs; West Virginia; James Madison; 2000: Cin, rnd 4; B10/18/1976 Columbus, OH

YEAR	TEAM	G (GS, POS)	RUSH	YD	AVG(LG)	TD	REC	YD	AVG(LG)	TD	...	KPR	OTD	PTS	TAY
2000	Cin	6(0)	6	24	4.0(8)	0	—	—	—	—		k	—	0	34
2001	Cin	13(0)	5	48	9.6(21)	0	1	9	9.0(9)	0		k	—	0	314
2002	NO	6(0)	12	19	1.6(4)	0	—	—	—	—			—	0	19
NFL	3	25(0)	23	91	4.0(21)	0	1	9	9.0(9)	0		k	—	0	367

KECK, STAN James Stanton, G-T, 5´11˝/205 lbs; Princeton; B9/11/1897 Greensburg, PA, D1/20/1951 Pittsburgh, PA [K] **1923** Cle☆3 (2), 7

KECKIN, VAL Valdemar Christian, QB, 6´4˝/215 lbs; Southern Mississippi; 1961: GB, rnd 11; B2/12/1938 Los Angeles, CA

YEAR	TEAM	G (GS, POS)	RUSH	YD	AVG(LG)	TD	REC	YD	AVG(LG)	TD	PASS	COMP	PCT	YD	AVG(LG)	TD	INT	...	OTD	PTS	TAY
1962	SD-A	6	1	3	3.0(3)	0	—	—	—	—	9	5	55.6	64	7.1(25)	0	1		—	0	-5

KECMAN, DAN Daniel S., LB, 6´2˝/230 lbs; Maryland; B6/10/1948 Pittsburgh, PA **1970** Bos 1

YEAR	TEAM	G(GS,POS)	RUSH	YD	AVG(LG)	TD	REC	YD	AVG(LG)	TD	PASS COMP	PCT	YD	AVG(LG)	TD	INT	SK	YD	QBR	KPR	OTD	PTS	TAY

KEEBLE, JERRY Jerry Anthony, LB, 6´3˝/230 lbs; Minnesota; B8/19/1963 St. Louis, MO **1987** SF 3 (1)

KEEBLE, JOE Joseph Bailey, HB-FB, 6´0˝/190 lbs; UCLA; B8/29/1909 Cleburne, TX, D4/27/1984 San Luis Obispo, CA

| 1937 | Cle | 7(2) | 12 | 40 | 3.3 | 0 | 1 | 42 | 42.0(42) | 1 | 9 | 2 | 22.2 | 25 | 2.8 | 0 | 3 | — | — | — | — | 6 | -42 |

KEEFE, EMMETT Emmett Gerald, G, 5´10˝/195 lbs; Notre Dame; B4/28/1893 Raub, IN, D9/11/1965 Chicago, IL **1920** ChiT 8 (7, LG) **1921** RI 7 (7, LG) **1921** GB 1 (0) **1922** RI 5 (2) **1922** Mil 2 (1) **NFL** 23 (18) [3 yrs]

KEEFER, JACK Jackson Milliman, TB-HB-FB, 5´9˝/172 lbs; Michigan; Brown; B5/1/1900 Olney, IL, D8/3/1966 Dayton, OH **[K]** **1926** Pro 11 (5, tb), 15 **1928** Day 3 (2) **NFL** 14 (7) [2 yrs]

KEEL, MARK Mark Anthony, TE, 6´4˝/228 lbs; Arizona; 1983: NE, rnd 9; B10/1/1961 Fort Worth, TX

1987	Sea	3(3)	—	—	—	—	6	88	14.7(24)	1	—	—	—	—	—	—	—	—	—	—	—	6	49
1987	KC	7(2)	—	—	—	—	2	9	4.5(7)	0	—	—	—	—	—	—	—	—	—	—	—	0	5
NFL	1	10(5)	—	—	—	—	8	97	12.1(24)	1	—	—	—	—	—	—	—	—	—	—	—	6	54

KEELING, RAY Raymond Grigsby, T-G, 6´3˝/242 lbs; Texas; B8/24/1915 Dallas, TX, D4/1/1996 Littlefield, TX **1938** Phi 9 (3) **1939** Phi 9 (0) **NFL** 18 (3) [2 yrs]

KEELING, REX Rex George, P, 6´4˝/205 lbs; Samford; 1967: Hou, rnd 16; B9/9/1943 Dallas, TX

| 1968 | Cin-A | 1 | 1 | 10 | 10.0(10) | 0 | — | — | — | — | 1 | 0 | 0.0 | 0 | 0.0 | 0 | 0 | — | — | — | P | — | 0 | 10 |

KEEN, RABBIT Delbert Allen, QB, 5´9˝/170 lbs; Arkansas; B12/10/1914 Stillwell, OK, D6/4/1984 Overland Park, KS

1937	Phi	8(0)	34	154	4.5	0	5	45	9.0	0	5	1	20.0	86	17.2(86)	1	0	—	—	—	—	—	0	225
1938	Phi	1(0)	3	10	3.3	0	—	—	—	—	—	—	—	—	—	—	—	—	—	—	—	—	0	10
NFL	2	9(0)	37	164	4.4	0	5	45	9.0	0	5	1	20.0	86	17.2(86)	1	0	—	—	—	—	—	0	235

KEENAN, ED Edward F., G, 6´4˝/320 lbs; Washington (MD); B10/30/1894, CT, D1/28/1984 Waterbury, CT **1926** Har 10 (10, RG)

KEENAN, JACK John Harvey, T-G, 5´10˝/214 lbs; South Carolina; B6/8/1919 Greensboro, NC, D2/8/1977 Nash, NC **1944** Was 10 (3) **1945** Was 3 (0) **NFL** 13 (3) [2 yrs]

KEENE, BOB Robert, B, 5´10˝/185 lbs; Detroit Mercy; B8/26/1919 Detroit, MI

1943	Det	5(1)	1	1	1.0(1)	0	1	27	27.0(27)	0	—	—	—	—	—	—	—	—	—	—	k	—	0	12
1944	Det	10(2)	9	26	2.9(7)	0	5	91	18.2(46)	2	—	—	—	—	—	—	—	—	—	—	Pkpi	—	12	212
1945	Det	1(0)	2	2	1.0(2)	0	—	—	—	—	—	—	—	—	—	—	—	—	—	—	—	—	0	2
NFL	3	16(3)	12	29	2.4(7)	0	6	118	19.7(46)	2	—	—	—	—	—	—	—	—	—	—	Pkpi	—	12	225

KEENEY, BRAD Brad O'Hara, DT, 6´3˝/294 lbs; The Citadel; B11/20/1973 Augusta, GA **1996** NYJ 1 (0)

KEETON, DURWOOD Durwood Lee, DB, 5´11˝/178 lbs; Oklahoma; 1974: SL, rnd 4; B8/14/1952 Bonham, TX **1975** NE 12

KEEVER, CARL Carl Richmond, LB, 6´2˝/236 lbs; Oregon State; Boise State; B8/17/1961 Reno, NV **1987** SF 3 (0)

KEHOE, SCOTT Scott Anton, T, 6´4˝/282 lbs; Illinois; B9/20/1964 Oak Lawn, IL **1987** Mia 3 (3)

KEHR, RICK Karl Richard, G, 6´3˝/285 lbs; Carthage; B6/18/1959 Phoenixville, PA **1987†**Was 5 (0)

KEIM, MIKE Karl Michael, T, 6´7˝/302 lbs; Brigham Young; B11/12/1965 Anaheim, CA **1992** Sea 1 (0) **1993** Sea 3 (0) **1994** Sea 16 (0) **1995** Sea 7 (0) **NFL** 27 (0) [4 yrs]

KEISEL, BRETT Brett, DE, 6´5˝/269 lbs; Brigham Young; 2002: Pit, rnd 7; B9/19/1978 Provo, UT **2002†**Pit 5 (0) **2004†**Pit 13 (0) **2005†**Pit 16 (0) **NFL** 34 (0) [3 yrs]

KEITH, CRAIG Craig Carlton, TE, 6´3˝/262 lbs; Lenoir-Rhyne; 1993: Pit, rnd 7; B4/27/1971 Raleigh, NC

1993	Pit	1(0)	—	—	—	—	—	—	—	—	—	—	—	—	—	—	—	—	—	—	—	—	—	—
1994	†Pit	16(1)	—	—	—	—	1	2	2.0(2)	0	—	—	—	—	—	—	—	—	—	—	—	—	0	1
1995	Jax	11(3)	—	—	—	—	3	20	6.7(9)	0	—	—	—	—	—	—	—	—	—	—	—	—	0	10
NFL	3	28(4)	—	—	—	—	4	22	5.5(9)	0	—	—	—	—	—	—	—	—	—	—	—	—	0	11

KEITH, JOHN John Martin, DB, 6´0˝/207 lbs; Furman; 2000: SF, rnd 4; B2/4/1977 Newnan, GA **2000** SF 6 (3) **2001** SF 1 (0) **2002†**SF 8 (3) **2003** SF 8 (2) **NFL** 23 (8) [4 yrs]

KEITHLEY, GARY Gary Tom, QB, 6´3˝/210 lbs; Texas; Texas-El Paso; 1973: SL, rnd 2; B1/11/1951 Alvin, TX

| 1973 | SL | 14 | 8 | 29 | 3.6(18) | 0 | — | — | — | — | 73 | 32 | 43.8 | 369 | 5.1(80) | 1 | 5 | 41 | — | P | — | — | 0 | 19 |

KEKERIS, JIM James J., T, 6´1˝/257 lbs; Missouri; 1947: Det, rnd 3/Mia-A, rnd 15; B10/17/1923 St. Louis, MO, D9/15/1997 Columbia, MO **[K]** **1947†**Phi 10 (2) **1948** GB 5 (0) **NFL** 15 (2) [2 yrs]

KELCHER, LOUIE Louis James, DT-NT, 6´5˝/291 lbs; SMU; 1975: SD, rnd 2; B8/23/1953 Beaumont, TX **1975** SD 13 (13, LDT) **1976** SD 14 (14, LDT) **1977** SD★12 (12, LDT) **1978** SD★15 (15, LDT) **1979** SD 1 **1980†**SD★15 (14, LDT) **1981†**SD☆14 (14, LDT) **1982†**SD 8 (7, LDT) **1983** SD 8 (0) **1984†**SF 16 (0) **NFL** 116 (89) [10 yrs]

KELL, PAUL Paul Ernest, T, 6´2˝/217 lbs; Notre Dame; 1939: GB, rnd 8; B7/8/1915 Princeton, IL, D5/1977 Chippewa Falls, WI **1939†**GB✧9 (2) **1940** GB 11 (2) **NFL** 20 (4) [2 yrs]

KELLAGHER, BILL William Michael, FB, 5´11˝/205 lbs; Fordham; B8/13/1920 Locust Gap, PA, D5/11/2003 DeBarry, FL

1946	ChiR-A	12(2)	49	178	3.6(53)	3	2	36	18.0	0	3	2	66.7	15	5.0	0	1	—	—	—	Pk	—	18	197
1947	ChiR-A	14(2)	42	243	5.8	0	3	22	7.3	0	—	—	—	—	—	—	—	—	—	—	i	—	0	301
1948	ChiR-A	12(5, fb)	33	97	2.9	1	—	—	—	—	—	—	—	—	—	—	—	—	—	—	k	—	6	116
AAFC	3	38(9)	124	518	4.2(53)	4	5	58	11.6	0	3	2	66.7	15	5.0	0	1	—	—	—	Pki	—	24	614

KELLAR, BILL William Elden, WR, 5´11˝/187 lbs; Stanford; 1978: KC, rnd 7; B2/8/1956 Longview, WA **1978** KC 5

KELLAR, MARK Mark Peter, RB, 6´0˝/225 lbs; Northern Illinois; 1974: Min, rnd 6; B7/17/1952 Chicago, IL

1976	Min	3	7	25	3.6(11)	0	2	22	11.0(19)	0	—	—	—	—	—	—	—	—	—	—	k	—	0	43
1977	†Min	14	7	15	2.1(9)	0	—	—	—	—	—	—	—	—	—	—	—	—	—	—	k	—	0	7
1978	†Min	16	11	34	3.1(5)	0	3	-5	-1.7(8)	0	—	—	—	—	—	—	—	—	—	—	k	—	0	30
NFL	3	33	25	74	3.0(11)	0	5	17	3.4(19)	0	—	—	—	—	—	—	—	—	—	—	k	—	0	80

KELLAR, SCOTT Scott Jeffery, NT, 6´3˝/282 lbs; Northern Illinois; 1986: Ind, rnd 5; B12/31/1963 Elgin, IL **1986** Ind 14 (8, nt) **1987** Ind 3 (2) **NFL** 17 (10) [2 yrs]

KELLER, KEN Kenneth Ray, HB, 5´10˝/180 lbs; North Carolina; 1956: Phi, rnd 11; B9/12/1934 Salina, PA, D12/10/1997 Youngstown, OH

1956	Phi	11(LH)	112	433	3.9(51)	4	7	36	5.1(13)	0	—	—	—	—	—	—	—	—	—	—	kp	—	24	690
1957	Phi	12	57	195	3.4(15)	0	4	31	7.8(30)	0	—	—	—	—	—	—	—	—	—	—	kp	—	0	320
NFL	2	23	169	628	3.7(51)	4	11	67	6.1(30)	0	—	—	—	—	—	—	—	—	—	—	kp	—	24	1010

KELLER, LARRY Larry Ray, LB, 6´2˝/223 lbs; Houston; 1975: SD, rnd 9; B10/2/1953 San Benito, TX **1976** NYJ 14 **1978** NYJ 16 (8, LOLB)

| 1977 | NYJ | 14(9, RLB) | 1 | 25 | 25.0(25) | 0 | — | — | — | — | — | — | — | — | — | — | — | — | — | — | i | — | 0 | 56 |
| NFL | 3 | 44(17) | 1 | 25 | 25.0(25) | 0 | — | — | — | — | — | — | — | — | — | — | — | — | — | — | i | — | 0 | 81 |

KELLER, MIKE Michael F., LB, 6´4˝/221 lbs; Michigan; 1972: Dal, rnd 3; B12/13/1949 Chicago, IL **1972** Dal 5

KELLERMANN, ERNIE Ernest James, DB, 6´0˝/183 lbs; Miami (OH); 1965: Dal, rnd 12; B12/17/1943 Cleveland, OH **1966** Cle 14 (11, RS/ls) **1967†**Cle 14 (LS/rs) **1968†**Cle✧14 (LS/rs) **1969†**Cle☆11 (LS) **1970** Cle 14 (SS) **1971†**Cle 14 (ss) **1972** Cin 14 **1973** Buf 10 (SS) **NFL** 105 (11) [8 yrs]

KELLERMEYER, DOUG Douglas Arthur, G-T, 6´3˝/275 lbs; Brigham Young; B6/1/1961 Bucyrus, OH **1987** Hou 3 (0)

KELLEY, BILL Billie Rex, E, 6´2˝/195 lbs; Texas Tech; 1949: GB, rnd 23; B8/23/1926 Becton, TX

| 1949 | GB | 12(1) | — | — | — | — | 17 | 222 | 13.1(32) | 1 | — | — | — | — | — | — | — | — | — | — | — | — | 6 | 116 |

KELLEY, BOB Robert, C, 6´2˝/232 lbs; West Texas A&M; 1952: Phi, rnd 25; B5/8/1930 Hereford, TX **1955** Phi 12 (C) **1956** Phi 12 (C) **NFL** 24 [2 yrs]

KELLEY, BRIAN Brian Lee, LB, 6´3˝/230 lbs; California Lutheran; 1973: NYG, rnd 14; B9/1/1951 Dallas, TX **1973** NYG 14 **1974** NYG 13 (13, MLB) **1975** NYG 14 (14, MLB) **1976** NYG 14 (14, RLB) **1977** NYG 13 (12, RLB) **1979** NYG 16 (16, ROLB) **1980** NYG 2 (1) **1981†**NYG 16 (16, LILB) **1982** NYG 9 (9, LILB) **1983** NYG 16 (16, LILB)

| 1978 | NYG | 16(16, RLB) | 1 | 2 | 2.0(2) | 0 | 1 | -1 | -1.0(-1) | 0 | — | — | — | — | — | — | — | — | — | — | i | — | 0 | 17 |
| NFL | 11 | 143(127) | 1 | 2 | 2.0(2) | 0 | 1 | -1 | -1.0(-1) | 0 | — | — | — | — | — | — | — | — | — | — | kiS | — | 0 | 138 |

KELLEY, CHRIS Christopher John, TE, 6´4˝/240 lbs; Akron; 1987: Pit, rnd 7; B11/13/1964 Lorain, OH **[K]** **1987** Cle 2 (0)

KELLEY, DOC Albert James, TB-HB, 5´10˝/170 lbs; Northwestern; B3/1/1902 Chicago, IL, D7/5/1963 **1924** Dul 5 (3) **1925** Dul 3 (2, TB) **1926** Dul 5 (2) **NFL** 13 (7) [3 yrs]

KELLEY, ED Edward Allen, T, 6´4˝/230 lbs; Texas; 1948: NYG, rnd 30; B2/18/1924 Sugar Land, TX, D6/27/2002 Harlingen, TX

| 1949 | LAD-A | 12(2) | 1 | -2 | -2.0(-2) | 0 | — | — | — | — | — | — | — | — | — | — | — | — | — | — | — | — | 0 | -2 |

Kelley, Edward Edward Clemens, DB, 6´2˝/195 lbs; Texas; 1955: LA, rnd 5; B6/8/1933 Gonzales, TX **1961** DalT-A 13 **1962** DalT-A 1 **NFL** 14 [2 yrs]

Kelley, Ethan Ethan Jeffrey Arthur, DT, 6´2˝/310 lbs; Baylor; 2003: NE, rnd 7; B2/12/1980 Sugar Land, TX **2004** NE 1 (0) **2005** Cle 10 (2) **NFL** 11 (2) [2 yrs]

Kelley, Frank Frank Edward, HB, 5´10˝/165 lbs; South Dakota State; B10/1903 Tyndall, SD, deceased **1927** Cle 7 (1), 18

Kelley, Gorden Gorden Bond, LB, 6´3˝/231 lbs; Georgia; 1960: LAC, rnd 2; B6/11/1938 Decatur, IL **1960** SF 12 (9, LLB) **1961** SF 14 (14, LLB) **1962** Was 11 (LLB) **1963** Was 14 **NFL** 51 (23) [4 yrs]

Kelley, Ike Dwight Allen, LB, 5´11˝/225 lbs; Ohio State; 1966: Phi, rnd 17; B7/14/1944 Ludington, MI **1966** Phi 14 **1967** Phi 14 **1969** Phi 14 **1970** Phi 11 **1971** Phi 14 **NFL** 67 [5 yrs]

Kelley, Les Leslie Howard, LB, 6´3˝/233 lbs; Alabama; 1967: NO, rnd 1; B12/9/1944 Decatur, AL **1967** NO 2 **1968** NO 14 **1969** NO 14 **NFL** 30 [3 yrs]

Kelley, Mike Michael Dennis, QB, 6´3˝/195 lbs; Georgia Tech; 1982: Atl, rnd 6; B12/31/1959 Sonora, PA

YEAR	TEAM	G(GS, POS)	RUSH	YD	AVG(LG)	TD	REC	YD	AVG(LG)	TD	PASS	COMP	PCT	YD	AVG(LG)	TD	INT	SK	YD	QBR	KPR	OTD	PTS	TAY
1987	SD	3(1)	4	17	4.3(10)	0	—	—	—	—	29	17	58.6	305	10.5(67)	1	0	1	7	—	—	—	0	175

Kelley, Mike Michael Peter, C-G-T, 6´5˝/273 lbs; Notre Dame; 1985: Hou, rnd 3; B2/27/1962 Westfield, MA **1985** Hou 16 (0) **1987** Hou 1 (0) **NFL** 17 (0) [2 yrs]

Kellin, Kevin Kevin Robert, DT, 6´6˝/267 lbs; Minnesota; B11/16/1959 Hampton, VA **1986** TB 9 (0) **1987** TB 7 (1) **1988** TB 4 (0) **NFL** 20 (1) [3 yrs]

Kellison, John John Snowden, G-T, 6´1˝/210 lbs; West Virginia Wesleyan; B11/3/1886 Buckeye, WV, D5/7/1971 Marlinton, WV **1920** Can 3 (3, RG) **1921** Can 4 (3) **1922** Tol 1 (0) **NFL** 8 (6) [3 yrs]

Kellogg HB, deceased **1921** Mun 1 (1)

Kellogg, Bill William J., HB, 5´10˝/178 lbs; Indiana (PA); Syracuse; B3/3/1897 Pittsburgh, PA, D11/28/1969 Syracuse, NY **1924** Fra 4 (0), 18 **1925** Roc 5 (2), 12 **NFL** 9 (2), 30 [2 yrs]

Kellogg, Bob Robert Francis, TB, 5´8˝/165 lbs; Louisiana-Monroe; Tulane; B8/4/1917 Wynne, AR, D5/9/1985 Columbus, MS

YEAR	TEAM	G(GS, POS)	RUSH	YD	AVG(LG)	TD	REC	YD	AVG(LG)	TD	PASS	COMP	PCT	YD	AVG(LG)	TD	INT	SK	YD	QBR	KPR	OTD	PTS	TAY
1940	ChiC	3(0)	9	31	3.4	0	—	—	—	—	18	6	33.3	42	2.3	0	4	—	—	—	P	—	0	-108

Kellogg, Clarence Clarence, FB, 5´10˝/205 lbs; St. Mary's (CA); B9/8/1911, D9/3/1988 Denver, CO **[K]**

YEAR	TEAM	G(GS, POS)	RUSH	YD	AVG(LG)	TD	REC	YD	AVG(LG)	TD	PASS	COMP	PCT	YD	AVG(LG)	TD	INT	SK	YD	QBR	KPR	OTD	PTS	TAY
1936	ChiC	12(1)	66	164	2.5	0	4	11	2.8	0	—	—	—	—	—	—	—	—	—	—	K	—	9	170

Kellogg, Mike Michael Karl, FB, 6´0˝/220 lbs; Santa Clara; B10/28/1942 Tucson, AZ **1967** Den-A 2

YEAR	TEAM	G(GS, POS)	RUSH	YD	AVG(LG)	TD	REC	YD	AVG(LG)	TD	PASS	COMP	PCT	YD	AVG(LG)	TD	INT	SK	YD	QBR	KPR	OTD	PTS	TAY
1966	Den-A	8	6	3	0.5(5)	0	1	5	5.0(5)	0	—	—	—	—	—	—	—	—	—	—	—	—	0	6
NFL	2	10	6	3	0.5(5)	0	1	5	5.0(5)	0	—	—	—	—	—	—	—	—	—	—	—	—	0	6

Kellum, Marv Marvin Lee, LB, 6´2˝/225 lbs; Wichita State; B6/23/1952 Topeka, KS **1974**†Pit 14 **1975**†Pit 14 **1976**†Pit 14 **1977** SL 14 (4) **NFL** 56 (4) [4 yrs]

Kelly, Ben Benjamin Oliver, DB, 5´9˝/185 lbs; Colorado; 2000: Mia, rnd 3; B9/15/1978 Cleveland, OH **2000** Mia 2 (0) **2001** Mia 2 (0) **2001** NE 2 (0) **2002** NE 7 (0) **NFL** 13 (0) [3 yrs]

Kelly, Bob Robert Joseph, HB-DB, 5´10˝/190 lbs; Notre Dame; Navy; 1947: GB, rnd 10; B6/6/1925 Chicago, IL

YEAR	TEAM	G(GS, POS)	RUSH	YD	AVG(LG)	TD	REC	YD	AVG(LG)	TD	PASS	COMP	PCT	YD	AVG(LG)	TD	INT	SK	YD	QBR	KPR	OTD	PTS	TAY
1947	LAD-A	12(8, RH)	51	205	4.0(50)	2	9	68	7.6	1	—	—	—	—	—	—	—	—	—	—	kpi	—	18	366
1948	LAD-A	4(1)	3	10	3.3	0	—	—	—	—	—	—	—	—	—	—	—	—	—	—	i	—	0	9
1949	Bal-A	10(2)	9	17	1.9	0	2	25	12.5	0	—	—	—	—	—	—	—	—	—	—	ki	—	0	40
AAFC	3	26(11)	63	232	3.7(50)	2	11	93	8.5	1	—	—	—	—	—	—	—	—	—	—	kpi	—	18	415

Kelly, Bob Bob L., T-DT, 6´2˝/270 lbs; New Mexico State; 1961: Hou, rnd 22; B8/18/1940 Carlsbad, NM **1961**†Hou-A 14 **1962** Hou-A 6 **1963** Hou-A 11 **1964** Hou-A 1 **1967** KC-A 3 **1968** Cin-A 4 **NFL** 39 [6 yrs]

Kelly, Brian Brian, DB, 5´11˝/193 lbs; USC; 1998: TB, rnd 2; B1/14/1976 Las Vegas, NV **[I]** **1998** TB 16 (3) **1999**†TB 16 (3) **2000**†TB 16 (3) **2001**†TB 16 (11, LCB) **2002**†TB 16 (16, LCB) **2003** TB 5 (5, lcb) **2004** TB 16 (16, LCB) **2005**†TB 16 (16, LCB) **NFL** 117 (73) [8 yrs]

Kelly, Ellison Ellison Lamar, G, 6´1˝/235 lbs; Michigan State; 1959: NYG, rnd 5; B5/17/1935 Lake City, FL **1959**†NYG 12

Kelly, Elmo Elmo Lee, E, 6´1˝/200 lbs; Wichita State; B2/10/1917 Tipton, OK, D12/28/1996 **1944** ChiB 3 (0)

Kelly, Eric Eric, DB, 5´10˝/201 lbs; Kentucky; 2001: Min, rnd 3; B1/15/1977 Milwaukee, WI **2001** Min 16 (11, RCB) **2002** Min 16 (12, RCB) **2003** Min 16 (0) **NFL** 48 (23) [3 yrs]

Kelly, Jeff Jeff, LB, 5´11˝/242 lbs; Stephen F. Austin State; Kansas State; 1999: Atl, rnd 6; B12/13/1975 La Grange, TX **1999** Atl 16 (1) **2000** Atl 12 (6, mlb) **2002** Atl 1 (0) **NFL** 29 (7) [3 yrs]

Kelly, Jeff Jeff, QB, 6´1˝/212 lbs; Southern Mississippi; 2002: Sea, rnd 7; B9/7/1979 Deerpark, AL **2002** Sea 1 (0)

Kelly, Jim James Harry, TE, 6´2˝/218 lbs; Notre Dame; 1964: Pit, rnd 2/Bos, rnd 2; B4/23/1942 McKeesport, PA

YEAR	TEAM	G(GS, POS)	RUSH	YD	AVG(LG)	TD	REC	YD	AVG(LG)	TD	PASS	COMP	PCT	YD	AVG(LG)	TD	INT	SK	YD	QBR	KPR	OTD	PTS	TAY
1964	Pit	6(te)	—	—	—	—	10	186	18.6(27)	1	—	—	—	—	—	—	—	—	—	—	k	—	6	95
1965	Phi	1	—	—	—	—	—	—	—	—	—	—	—	—	—	—	—	—	—	—	—	—	—	—
1967	Phi	12	—	—	—	—	21	345	16.4(59)	4	—	—	—	—	—	—	—	—	—	—	—	—	24	193
NFL	3	19	—	—	—	—	31	531	17.1(59)	5	—	—	—	—	—	—	—	—	—	—	k	—	30	288

Kelly, Jim James William, TE, 6´4˝/212 lbs; Tennessee State; B8/7/1951 Columbia, TN

YEAR	TEAM	G(GS, POS)	RUSH	YD	AVG(LG)	TD	REC	YD	AVG(LG)	TD	PASS	COMP	PCT	YD	AVG(LG)	TD	INT	SK	YD	QBR	KPR	OTD	PTS	TAY
1974	ChiB	14	—	—	—	—	8	100	12.5(24)	0	—	—	—	—	—	—	—	—	—	—	—	—	0	50

Kelly, Jim James Edward, QB, 6´3˝/217 lbs; Miami (FL); 1983: Buf, rnd 1; B2/14/1960 Pittsburgh, PA; HOF 2002

YEAR	TEAM	G(GS, POS)	RUSH	YD	AVG(LG)	TD	REC	YD	AVG(LG)	TD	PASS	COMP	PCT	YD	AVG(LG)	TD	INT	SK	YD	QBR	KPR	OTD	PTS	TAY
1986	Buf	16(16, QB)	41	199	4.9(20)	0	—	—	—	—	480	285	59.4	3593	7.5(84)	22	17	43	330	83.3	—	—	0	1426
1987	Buf✧	12(12, QB)	29	133	4.6(24)	0	1	35	35.0(35)	0	419	250	59.7	2798	6.7(47)	19	11	27	239	83.8	—	—	0	1205
1988	†Buf	16(16, QB)	35	154	4.4(20)	0	1	5	5.0(5)	0	452	269	59.5	3380	7.5(66)	15	17	30	229	78.2	—	—	0	1242
1989	†Buf	13(13, QB)	29	137	4.7(19)	2	—	—	—	—	391	228	58.3	3130	**8.0(78)**	25	18	30	216	86.2	—	—	12	1127
1990	†Buf★	14(14, QB)	22	63	2.9(15)	0	—	—	—	—	346	219	**63.3**	2829	8.2(71)	24	9	20	158	**101.2**	—	—	0	1238
1991	†Buf★	15(15, QB)	20	45	2.3(12)	1	—	—	—	—	474	304	64.1	3844	**8.1(77)**	**33**	17	31	227	**97.6**	—	—	6	1462
1992	†Buf★	16(16, QB)	31	53	1.7(10)	1	—	—	—	—	462	269	58.2	3457	7.5(65)	23	**19**	20	145	81.2	—	—	6	1147
1993	†Buf	16(16, QB)	36	102	2.8(17)	0	—	—	—	—	470	288	61.3	3382	7.2(65)	18	18	25	171	79.9	—	—	0	1163
1994	Buf	14(14, QB)	25	77	3.1(18)	1	—	—	—	—	448	285	**63.6**	3114	7.0(83)	22	17	34	244	84.6	—	—	6	1074
1995	†Buf	15(15, QB)	17	20	1.2(17)	0	—	—	—	—	458	255	55.7	3130	6.8(77)	22	13	26	181	81.1	—	—	0	1175
1996	†Buf	13(13, QB)	19	66	3.5(22)	2	—	—	—	—	379	222	58.6	2810	7.4(67)	14	19	37	287	73.2	—	—	12	801
NFL	11	160(160)	304	1049	3.5(24)	7	2	40	20.0(35)	0	4779	2874	60.1	35467	7.4(84)	237	175	323	2427	84.4	—	—	42	13058

Kelly, Jimmy James J., TB-HB, 5´9˝/160 lbs; St. Louis; Detroit Mercy; B1890, MI, deceased **1920** Det 6 (3, TB)

Kelly, Joe Joseph Winston, LB, 6´2˝/227 lbs; Washington; 1986: Cin, rnd 1; B12/11/1964 Sun Valley, CA **1986** Cin 16 (7, rilb) **1987** Cin 10 (10, RILB) **1988**†Cin 16 (15, RILB) **1989** Cin 16 (16, RILB) **1990** NYJ 12 (12, RLB) **1991**†NYJ 16 (12, RLB) **1992** NYJ 9 (0) **1993**†LARd 16 (14, MLB) **1994** LARm 16 (14, LLB) **1995** GB 13 (4) **1996**†Phi 16 (1) **NFL** 156 (105) [11 yrs]

Kelly, John John D., T, 6´3˝/250 lbs; Florida A&M; 1966: Was, rnd 20; B3/31/1944 Fort Lauderdale, FL **1966** Was 2 **1967** Was 14 **NFL** 16 [2 yrs]

Kelly, Leroy Leroy, RB, 6´0˝/202 lbs; Morgan State; 1964: Cle, rnd 8; B5/20/1942 Philadelphia, PA; HOF 1994 **[R]**

YEAR	TEAM	G(GS, POS)	RUSH	YD	AVG(LG)	TD	REC	YD	AVG(LG)	TD	PASS	COMP	PCT	YD	AVG(LG)	TD	INT	SK	YD	QBR	KPR	OTD	PTS	TAY
1964	†Cle	14	6	12	2.0(5)	0	—	—	—	—	—	—	—	—	—	—	—	—	—	—	kp	1	6	370
1965	†Cle	13	37	139	3.8(16)	0	9	122	13.6(52)	0	—	—	—	—	—	—	—	—	—	—	kp	2	12	661
1966	Cle★	14(HB)	209	1141	**5.5(70)**	**15**	32	366	11.4(40)	1	1	0	0.0	0	0.0	0	0	—	—	—	kp	—	96	1636
1967	†Cle★	14(HB)	**235**	**1205**	**5.1(42)**	**11**	20	282	14.1(48)	2	1	0	0.0	0	0.0	0	0	—	—	—	Pkp	—	78	**1536**
1968	†Cle★	14(HB)	**248**	**1239**	5.0(65)	**16**	22	297	13.5(68)	4	4	1	25.0	34	8.5(34)	1	0	—	—	—	kp	—	**120**	**1589**
1969	†Cle★	13(FB)	196	817	4.2(31)	9	20	267	13.4(36)	1	5	1	20.0	36	7.2(36)	1	0	—	—	—	kp	—	60	1058
1970	Cle✧	13(RB)	206	656	3.2(33)	6	24	311	13.0(55)	2	—	—	—	—	—	—	—	—	—	—	p	—	48	887
1971	†Cle★	14(RB)	234	865	3.7(35)	**10**	25	252	10.1(29)	2	4	1	25.0	23	5.8(23)	0	0	—	—	—	kp	—	72	1251
1972	†Cle	14(RB)	224	811	3.6(18)	4	23	204	8.9(28)	1	1	0	0.0	0	0.0	0	0	1	7	—	p	—	30	973
1973	Cle	13(RB)	132	389	2.9(19)	3	15	180	12.0(36)	0	—	—	—	—	—	—	—	—	—	—	p	—	18	511
NFL	10	136	1727	7274	4.2(70)	74	190	2281	12.0(68)	13	16	3	18.8	93	5.8(36)	2	0	1	7	—	Pkp	3	540	10470

Kelly, Lewis Lewis, T-G, 6´4˝/306 lbs; South Carolina State; 2000: Min, rnd 7; B4/21/1977 Lithonia, GA **2001** Min 4 (0) **2002** Min 7 (5, lt) **2003** Min 6 (0) **2005** NYG 1 (0) **NFL** 18 (5) [4 yrs]

Kelly, Maurice Maurice, DB, 6´2˝/205 lbs; East Tennessee State; B10/9/1972 Orangeburg, SC **2000** Sea 16 (0) **2001** Sea 8 (3) **NFL** 24 (3) [2 yrs]

KELLY, MIKE Michael Grey, TE, 6´4˝/215 lbs; Davidson; B1/14/1948 Davidson, NC **1970**†Cin 12 **1972** Cin 13 **1973** NO 1

YEAR	TEAM	G (GS, POS)	RUSH	YD	AVG (LG)	TD	REC	YD	AVG (LG)	TD	PASS	COMP	PCT	YD	AVG (LG)	TD	INT	SK	YD	QBR	KPR	OTD	PTS	TAY
1971	Cin	14	—	—	—	—	1	9	9.0(9)	0	—	—	—	—	—	—	—	—	—	—	k	—	0	-11
NFL	4	40	—	—	—	—	1	9	9.0(9)	0	—	—	—	—	—	—	—	—	—	—	k	—	0	-26

KELLY, PAT Patrick Joseph, TE, 6´6˝/252 lbs; Syracuse; 1988: Den, rnd 7; B10/29/1965 Rochester, NY, D3/27/2003 Charlottesville, VA **1990** NYJ 1 (0) **1991**†NYJ 8 (0)

YEAR	TEAM	G (GS, POS)	RUSH	YD	AVG (LG)	TD	REC	YD	AVG (LG)	TD	PASS	COMP	PCT	YD	AVG (LG)	TD	INT	SK	YD	QBR	KPR	OTD	PTS	TAY
1988	Den	16(0)	—	—	—	—	1	4	4.0(4)	0	—	—	—	—	—	—	—	—	—	—	—	—	0	2
1989	†Den	16(1)	—	—	—	—	3	13	4.3(6)	0	—	—	—	—	—	—	—	—	—	—	—	—	0	7
NFL	4	41(1)	—	—	—	—	4	17	4.3(6)	0	—	—	—	—	—	—	—	—	—	—	k	—	0	-3

KELLY, REGGIE Reginald Kuta, TE, 6´4˝/255 lbs; Mississippi State; 1999: Atl, rnd 2; B2/22/1977 Aberdeen, MA

YEAR	TEAM	G (GS, POS)	RUSH	YD	AVG (LG)	TD	REC	YD	AVG (LG)	TD	PASS	COMP	PCT	YD	AVG (LG)	TD	INT	SK	YD	QBR	KPR	OTD	PTS	TAY
1999	Atl	16(2)	—	—	—	—	8	146	18.3(50)	0	—	—	—	—	—	—	—	—	—	—	—	—	0	73
2000	Atl	16(16, TE)	—	—	—	—	31	340	11.0(37)	2	—	—	—	—	—	—	—	—	—	—	—	—	12	180
2001	Atl	14(13, TE)	—	—	—	—	16	142	8.9(25)	0	—	—	—	—	—	—	—	—	—	—	—	—	0	71
2002	†Atl	16(16, TE)	—	—	—	—	14	162	11.6(33)	0	—	—	—	—	—	—	—	—	—	—	—	—	0	81
2003	Cin	12(11, TE)	—	—	—	—	13	81	6.2(13)	1	—	—	—	—	—	—	—	—	—	—	—	—	6	46
2004	Cin	16(15, TE)	—	—	—	—	15	85	5.7(14)	0	—	—	—	—	—	—	—	—	—	—	k	—	0	42
2005	†Cin	15(14, TE)	—	—	—	—	15	90	6.0(16)	1	—	—	—	—	—	—	—	—	—	—	—	—	6	50
NFL	7	105(87)	—	—	—	—	112	1046	9.3(50)	4	—	—	—	—	—	—	—	—	—	—	k	—	24	542

KELLY, ROB Robert James, DB, 6´0˝/199 lbs; Ohio State; 1997: NO, rnd 2; B6/21/1974 Newark, OH **1997** NO 16 (2) **1998** NO 16 (3) **1999** NO 16 (7, fs) **2000**†NO 12 (0) **NFL** 60 (12) [4 yrs]

KELLY, SHIPWRECK John Simms, B, 6´2˝/190 lbs; Kentucky; B7/8/1910 Simmstown, KY, D8/17/1986 Lighthouse Point, FL **[K]**

YEAR	TEAM	G (GS, POS)	RUSH	YD	AVG (LG)	TD	REC	YD	AVG (LG)	TD	PASS	COMP	PCT	YD	AVG (LG)	TD	INT	SK	YD	QBR	KPR	OTD	PTS	TAY
1932	NYG	5(0)	32	133	4.2	0	7	49	7.0	0	7	3	42.9	22	3.1	0	0	—	—	—	—	—	0	169
1933	Bkn☆	10(10, WB)	85	274	3.2	2	**22**	246	11.2(45)	**3**	9	3	33.3	28	3.1	0	3	—	—	—	K	2	43	336
1934	Bkn	9(3)	29	96	3.3(41)	1	—	—	—	—	35	11	31.4	134	3.8	0	5	—	—	—	—	—	6	-27
1937	Bkn	2(1)	16	29	1.8	0	1	7	7.0(7)	0	12	2	16.7	21	1.8	0	3	—	—	—	—	—	0	-77
NFL	4	26(14)	162	532	3.3(41)	3	30	302	10.1(45)	3	63	19	30.2	205	3.3	0	11	—	—	—	K	2	49	401

KELLY, TEX Clarence Ashley, G-T, 6´3˝/220 lbs; none; B10/29/1898 Duncan, OK, D2/4/1978 Shawnee, OK **1922** Tol 7 (4) **1923** Buf 2 (2) **1925** Roc 6 (4) **1926** Buf 1 (0) **1929** Ora 1 (0) **NFL** 17 (10) [5 yrs]

KELLY, TODD Todd Eric, LB-DE, 6´2˝/259 lbs; Tennessee; 1993: SF, rnd 1; B11/27/1970 Hampton, VA **1993**†SF 14 (5, llb) **1994** SF 11 (1) **1995** Cin 16 (0) **1996** Cin 3 (0) **1996** Atl 2 (0) **NFL** 46 (6) [4 yrs]

KELLY, TOMMY Tommy, DE-DT, 6´6˝/300 lbs; Mississippi State; B12/27/1980 Jackson, MS **2004** Oak 10 (3) **2005** Oak 16 (12, rde) **NFL** 26 (15) [2 yrs]

KELLY, WILD BILL William Carl, B, 5´10˝/184 lbs; Montana; B6/24/1905 Denver, CO, D11/14/1931 New York, NY **1927** NYY 12 (9, BB), 18 **1928** NYY 12 (10, TB), 12 **1929** Fra 17 (8, bb), 6 **1930** Bkn 11 (9, BB), 6 **NFL** 52 (36), 42 [4 yrs]

KELM, LARRY Larry Dean, LB, 6´4˝/236 lbs; Texas A&M; 1987: LARm, rnd 4; B11/29/1964 Corpus Christi, TX **1987** LARm 12 (1) **1988**†LARm 16 (1) **1989**†LARm 7 (6, lilb) **1990** LARm 11 (10, LILB) **1991** LARm 16 (15, MLB) **1992** LARm 16 (15, MLB) **1993**†SF 10 (1) **NFL** 88 (49) [7 yrs]

KELSAY, CHAD Chad, LB, 6´2˝/252 lbs; Nebraska; 1999: Pit, rnd 7; B4/9/1977 Auburn, NE **1999** Pit 6 (0)

KELSAY, CHRIS Christopher, DE, 6´4˝/275 lbs; Nebraska; 2003: Buf, rnd 2; B10/31/1979 Auburn, NE **2003** Buf 16 (0) **2004** Buf 16 (10, LDE) **2005** Buf 16 (16, LDE) **NFL** 48 (26) [3 yrs]

KELSCH, MATT Matthew Leroy, E, 5´11˝/190 lbs; Iowa; B10/4/1904 Dougherty, IA, D1/27/1976 Queens, NY **1930** Bkn 2 (0)

KELSCH, MOSE Christian, FB-HB, 5´10˝/223 lbs; none; B1/31/1897 Pittsburgh, PA, D7/13/1935 Pittsburgh, PA **[K]**

YEAR	TEAM	G (GS, POS)	RUSH	YD	AVG (LG)	TD	REC	YD	AVG (LG)	TD	PASS	COMP	PCT	YD	AVG (LG)	TD	INT	SK	YD	QBR	KPR	OTD	PTS	TAY
1933	Pit	8(0)	8	37	4.6	0	—	—	—	—	—	—	—	—	—	—	—	—	—	—	K	—	11	37
1934	Pit	8(0)	3	11	3.7	0	—	—	—	—	—	—	—	—	—	—	—	—	—	—	K	—	5	11
NFL	2	16(0)	11	48	4.4	0	—	—	—	—	—	—	—	—	—	—	—	—	—	—	K	—	16	48

KELSO, MARK Mark Alan, DB, 5´11˝/181 lbs; William & Mary; 1985: Phi, rnd 10; B7/23/1963 Pittsburgh, PA **[I]** **1986** Buf 3 (0) **1987** Buf 12 (12, FS) **1988**†Buf 16 (16, FS) **1989**†Buf 16 (16, FS) **1990**†Buf 6 (5, fs) **1991**†Buf 16 (16, FS) **1992**†Buf 16 (16, FS) **1993**†Buf 14 (14, FS) **NFL** 99 (95) [8 yrs]

KEMOEATU, MA'AKE Ma'ake Tu'Amelie, DT, 6´5˝/335 lbs; Utah; B1/10/1979 Tonga **2002** Bal 16 (1) **2003**†Bal 15 (0) **2004** Bal 14 (3) **2005** Bal 16 (16, LDT) **NFL** 61 (20) [4 yrs]

KEMP, BOBBY Bobby, DB, 6´0˝/189 lbs; Cal State-Fullerton; 1981: Cin, rnd 8; B5/29/1959 Oakland, CA **1981**†Cin 16 (10, SS) **1982**†Cin 9 (9, SS) **1983** Cin 16 (16, SS) **1984** Cin 10 (8, SS) **1985** Cin 16 (16, SS) **1986** Cin 16 (10, FS) **1987** TB 12 (12, SS) **NFL** 95 (81) [7 yrs]

KEMP, JACK John French, QB, 6´1˝/201 lbs; Occidental; 1957: Det, rnd 17; B7/13/1935 Los Angeles, CA

YEAR	TEAM	G (GS, POS)	RUSH	YD	AVG (LG)	TD	REC	YD	AVG (LG)	TD	PASS	COMP	PCT	YD	AVG (LG)	TD	INT	SK	YD	QBR	KPR	OTD	PTS	TAY
1957	Pit	4	3	-1	-0.3(2)	0	—	—	—	—	18	8	44.4	88	4.9(21)	0	2	—	—	—	P	—	0	-37
1960	†LAC-A☆	14(12, QB)	54	238	4.4(8)	8	—	—	—	—	406	211	52.0	3018	**7.4(69)**	20	25	—	—	67.1	—	—	48	927
1961	†SD-A★	14(14, QB)	43	105	2.4(23)	6	—	—	—	—	364	165	45.3	2686	7.4(**91**)	15	22	—	—	59.2	—	—	36	703
1962	SD-A	2(2)	8	28	3.5(19)	1	—	—	—	—	45	13	28.9	292	6.5(67)	2	2	—	—	—	—	—	6	114
1962	Buf-A✧	4	12	56	4.7(28)	1	—	—	—	—	94	51	54.3	636	6.8(31)	3	4	—	—	—	—	—	6	239
1963	†Buf-A★	14(QB)	50	239	4.8(26)	8	—	—	—	—	384	193	50.3	2910	7.6(89)	13	20	—	—	65.1	—	—	48	1039
1964	†Buf-A✧	14(QB)	37	124	3.4(14)	5	—	—	—	—	269	119	44.2	2285	**8.5(94)**	13	26	—	—	50.9	—	—	30	342
1965	†Buf-A★	14(QB)	36	49	1.4(12)	4	1	-9	-9.0(-9)	0	391	179	45.8	2368	6.1(78)	10	18	—	—	54.8	—	—	24	599
1966	†Buf-A★	14(QB)	40	130	3.3(26)	5	—	—	—	—	389	166	42.7	2451	6.3(55)	11	16	—	—	56.2	—	—	30	821
1967	Buf-A	14(QB)	36	58	1.6(14)	2	—	—	—	—	369	161	43.6	2503	6.8(63)	14	26	—	—	50.0	—	—	14	360
1969	Buf-A✧	14(QB)	37	124	3.4(13)	0	—	—	—	—	344	170	49.4	1981	5.8(55)	13	22	21	187	53.2	—	—	0	300
NFL	10	122(28)	356	1150	3.2(28)	40	1	-9	-9.0(-9)	0	3073	1436	46.7	21218	6.9(94)	114	183	21	187	57.3	P	—	242	5405

KEMP, JEFF Jeffrey Allen, QB, 6´0˝/201 lbs; Dartmouth; B7/11/1959 Santa Ana, CA

YEAR	TEAM	G (GS, POS)	RUSH	YD	AVG (LG)	TD	REC	YD	AVG (LG)	TD	PASS	COMP	PCT	YD	AVG (LG)	TD	INT	SK	YD	QBR	KPR	OTD	PTS	TAY
1981	LARm	1(0)	2	9	4.5(7)	0	—	—	—	—	6	2	33.3	25	4.2(19)	0	1	2	13	—	—	—	0	-19
1983	†LARm	4(0)	3	-2	-0.7(0)	0	—	—	—	—	25	12	48.0	135	5.4(21)	1	0	2	12	—	—	—	0	71
1984	†LARm	14(13, QB)	34	153	4.5(23)	1	—	—	—	—	284	143	50.4	2021	7.1(63)	13	7	24	190	78.7	—	—	6	959
1985	LARm	5(1)	5	0	0.0(3)	0	—	—	—	—	38	16	42.1	214	5.6(35)	0	1	6	58	—	—	—	0	67
1986	†SF	10(6, qb)	15	49	3.3(12)	0	—	—	—	—	200	119	59.5	1554	7.8(66)	11	8	8	56	—	—	—	0	561
1987	†Sea	13(1)	5	9	1.8(12)	0	—	—	—	—	33	23	69.7	396	12.0(55)	5	1	3	20	—	—	—	0	192
1988	Sea	11(1)	6	51	8.5(21)	0	—	—	—	—	35	13	37.1	132	3.8(19)	0	5	3	21	—	—	—	0	-83
1989	Sea	9(0)	1	0	0.0(0)	0	—	—	—	—	—	—	—	—	—	—	—	—	—	—	—	—	0	0
1990	Sea	15(0)	—	—	—	—	—	—	—	—	—	—	—	—	—	—	—	—	—	—	—	—	—	—
1991	Sea	7(5, qb)	22	106	4.8(18)	0	—	—	—	—	181	94	51.9	1207	6.7(38)	4	12	8	38	—	—	—	0	250
1991	Phi	7(2)	16	73	4.6(18)	0	—	—	—	—	114	57	50.0	546	4.8(57)	5	5	12	61	—	—	—	0	171
NFL	10	96(29)	109	448	4.1(23)	1	—	—	—	—	916	479	52.3	6230	6.8(66)	39	40	68	469	70.0	—	—	6	2168

KEMP, PERRY Perry Commodore, WR, 5´11˝/170 lbs; California (PA); B12/31/1961 Canonsburg, PA

YEAR	TEAM	G (GS, POS)	RUSH	YD	AVG (LG)	TD	REC	YD	AVG (LG)	TD	PASS	COMP	PCT	YD	AVG (LG)	TD	INT	SK	YD	QBR	KPR	OTD	PTS	TAY
1987	Cle	3(3)	—	—	—	—	12	224	18.7(34)	2	—	—	—	—	—	—	—	—	—	—	—	—	12	122
1988	GB	16(4)	—	—	—	—	48	620	12.9(36)	0	—	—	—	—	—	—	—	—	—	—	—	—	0	310
1989	GB	14(13, WR)	5	43	8.6(14)	0	48	611	12.7(39)	2	—	—	—	—	—	—	—	—	—	—	—	—	12	359
1990	GB	16(16, WR)	1	-1	-1.0(-1)	0	44	527	12.0(29)	2	—	—	—	—	—	—	—	—	—	—	—	—	12	273
1991	GB	16(12, WR)	—	—	—	—	42	583	13.9(39)	2	—	—	—	—	—	—	—	—	—	—	—	—	12	302
NFL	5	65(48)	6	42	7.0(14)	0	194	2565	13.2(39)	8	—	—	—	—	—	—	—	—	—	—	—	—	48	1365

KEMP, RAY Raymond Howard, T, 6´1˝/215 lbs; Duquesne; B4/7/1907 Cecil, PA, D3/26/2002 Ashtabula, OH **1933** Pit 5 (0)

KEMPF, FLORIAN Florian Gerard, K, 5´9˝/170 lbs; Pennsylvania; B5/25/1956 Philadelphia, PA **[K]** **1982** Hou 9 (0) **1984** Hou 9 (0) **1987** NO 1 (0)

YEAR	TEAM	G (GS, POS)	RUSH	YD	AVG (LG)	TD	REC	YD	AVG (LG)	TD	PASS	COMP	PCT	YD	AVG (LG)	TD	INT	SK	YD	QBR	KPR	OTD	PTS	TAY
1983	Hou	16(0)	—	—	—	—	1	7	7.0(7)	0	—	—	—	—	—	—	—	—	—	—	K	—	84	4
NFL	4	35(0)	—	—	—	—	1	7	7.0(7)	0	—	—	—	—	—	—	—	—	—	—	K	—	151	4

KEMPINSKA, CHARLIE Charles Conrad, G, 6´0˝/235 lbs; Mississippi; B10/30/1938 Natchez, MS **1960** LAC-A 10

KEMPTON, HERB Herbert Mayberry, BB-QB, 5´8˝/155 lbs; Yale; B12/8/1892 Malden, MA, D9/23/1970 Ocala, FL **1921** Can 6 (5, BB)

YEAR	TEAM	G (GS, POS)	RUSH	YD	AVG (LG)	TD	REC	YD	AVG (LG)	TD	PASS COMP	PCT	YD	AVG (LG)	TD	INT	SK	YD	QBR	KPR	OTD	PTS	TAY

KENDALL, CHARLIE   Charles Barton, DB, 6′2″/165 lbs; UCLA; B1/4/1935   **1960**†Hou-A 14 (ls)

KENDALL, PETE   Peter Marcus, G-C, 6′5″/279 lbs; Boston College; 1996: Sea, rnd 1; B7/9/1973 Quincy, MA   **1996** Sea 12 (11, LG)   **1997** Sea 16 (16, LG)   **1998** Sea 16 (16, LG)   **1999**†Sea 16 (16, LG)   **2000** Sea 16 (16, LG)   **2001** Arz 11 (11, LG)   **2002** Arz 12 (12, LG)   **2003** Arz 13 (13, C)   **2004**†NYJ 15 (15, LG)   **2005** NYJ 16 (16, C/lg)
NFL 143 (142) [10 yrs]

KENDRICK, JIM   James Marcellus, B-E, 6′0″/195 lbs; Texas A&M; B8/22/1893 Hillside, TX, D11/17/1941 Waco, TX **[KC]**   **1922** Can 4 (3)   **1922** Tol 2 (2)   **1923** Lou 3 (3, LE)   **1924** ChiB 9 (3)   **1925** Ham 2 (2), 4   **1925** Buf 7 (7, WB), 14   **1925** Roc 1 (0)   **1925** RI 1 (1)   **1926** Buf 10 (10, BB), 16   **1927** NYG 8 (0)   **NFL** 47 (31), 34 [6 yrs]

KENDRICK, VINCE   Vincent, RB, 6′0″/231 lbs; Florida; 1974: Atl, rnd 4; B3/18/1952 Miami, FL

1974	Atl	14	17	71	4.2 (17)	0	12	86	7.2 (12)	1	—	—	—	—	—	—	—	—	—	—	—	6	119
1976	TB	1	1	3	3.0 (3)	0	—	—	—	—	—	—	—	—	—	—	—	—	—	—	—	0	3
NFL	2	15	18	74	4.1 (17)	0	12	86	7.2 (12)	1	—	—	—	—	—	—	—	—	—	—	—	6	122

KENELEY, MATT   Matthew Edward, DT, 6′5″/295 lbs; USC; 1997: NYG, rnd 7; B12/1/1973 Santa Ana, CA   **1999** SF 7 (0)

KENERSON, JOHN   John D., DE-DT, 6′3″/255 lbs; Kentucky State; B3/18/1938 Chicago, IL   **1960** LARm 7   **1962** Pit 1   **1962** NYT-A 8   **NFL** 16 [2 yrs]

KENN, MIKE   Michael Lee, T, 6′7″/273 lbs; Michigan; 1978: Atl, rnd 1; B2/9/1956 Evanston, IL   **1978**†Atl 16 (16, LT)   **1979** Atl 16 (16, LT)   **1980**†Atl★16 (16, LT)   **1981** Atl★16 (16, LT)   **1982**†Atl★9 (9, LT)   **1983** Atl★16 (16, LT)   **1984** Atl★14 (14, LT)   **1985** Atl 11 (11, LT)   **1986** Atl 16 (16, LT)   **1987** Atl 12 (12, LT)   **1988** Atl 16 (16, LT)   **1989** Atl 15 (15, LT)   **1990** Atl 16 (16, LT)   **1991**†Atl☆15 (15, LT)   **1992** Atl 16 (16, LT)   **1993** Atl 16 (16, LT)   **1994** Atl 15 (15, LT)   **NFL** 251 (251) [17 yrs]

KENNARD, DEREK   Derek Craig, G-C, 6′3″/285 lbs; Nevada-Reno; 1984: SL, rnd S2; B9/9/1962 Stockton, CA   **1986** SL 15 (10, G)   **1987** SL 12 (11, C)   **1988** Phx 16 (16, C)   **1989** Phx 14 (14, C)   **1990** Phx 16 (16, LG)   **1991** NO 3 (3)   **1992** NO☆16 (16, RG)   **1993** NO 16 (16, RG)   **1995**†Dal 8 (4)   **1996**†Dal 1 (0)

| 1994 | †Dal | 16 (16, RG) | — | — | — | — | 1 | -3 | -3.0 (-3) | 0 | — | — | — | — | — | — | — | — | — | — | — | 0 | -2 |
| **NFL** | 11 | 133 (122) | — | — | — | — | 1 | -3 | -3.0 (-3) | 0 | — | — | — | — | — | — | — | — | k | — | — | 0 | -6 |

KENNARD, GEORGE   George Arthur, G, 6′0″/210 lbs; Kansas; B1/8/1928 Kansas City, MO   **1952** NYG 12 (RG)   **1953** NYG 12 (LG)   **1954** NYG 12 (RG)   **1955** NYG 12
NFL 48 [4 yrs]

KENNARD, KEN   Kenneth Jerome, NT-DE, 6′2″/248 lbs; Angelo State (TX); B10/4/1954 Fort Worth, TX   **1977** Hou 11   **1978**†Hou 16   **1979**†Hou 16   **1980**†Hou 16 (11, NT)   **1981** Hou 16 (16, NT)   **1982** Hou 9 (9, LDE)   **NFL** 84 (36) [6 yrs]

KENNEALLY, GEORGE   George Vincent, E, 6′0″/190 lbs; St. Bonaventure; B4/12/1902 South Boston, MA, D9/3/1968 Boston, MA **[K]**   **1926** Pot 11 (8, le)   **1927** Pot☆13 (13, LE/re), 6   **1928** Pot☆9 (7, LE), 6   **1929** Bos 8 (8, LE), 1   **1930** ChiC 11 (8, LE)   **1932** Bos 10 (8, LE)   **1934** Phi 11 (10, LE)

1933	Phi	8 (8, LE)	—	—	—	—	2	37	18.5	0	—	—	—	—	—	—	—	—	—	—	—	0	19
1935	Phi	8 (2)	3	-4	-1.3	0	—	—	—	—	—	—	—	—	—	—	—	—	—	—	—	0	-4
NFL	9	89 (72)	3	-4	-1.3	0	2	37	18.5	0	—	—	—	—	—	—	—	—	—	K	—	13	25

KENNEDY, ALLAN   Allan Stephen, T, 6′7″/273 lbs; Washington State; 1981: Was, rnd 10; B1/8/1958 Vancouver, Canada   **1981**†SF 2 (0)   **1983**†SF 16 (0)   **1984**†SF 15 (1)
NFL 33 (1) [3 yrs]

KENNEDY, BILL   William James, G, 5′11″/200 lbs; Michigan State; B3/13/1919 Lee, MA, D12/29/1998 Southfield, MI   **1942** Det 11 (3)   **1947** Bos 12 (8, LG)   **NFL** 23 (11) [2 yrs]

KENNEDY, BOB   Robert Henry, B, 5′11″/195 lbs; Washington State; 1943: Phi, rnd 4; B6/29/1921 Sandpoint, ID

1946	†NYY-A	13 (4)	58	179	3.1	2	11	59	5.4	0	6	2	33.3	45	7.5	0	3	—	—	Pkpi	—	12	201
1947	†NYY-A	14 (1)	44	258	5.9	1	—	—	—	—	3	2	66.7	56	18.7	0	0	—	—	Ppi	—	6	366
1948	NYY-A	14 (3)	33	90	2.7	1	5	23	4.6	0	1	0	0.0	0	0.0	0	0	—	—	Pkpi	—	6	140
1949	†NYY-A	12 (10, FB)	118	490	4.2	5	7	55	7.9	1	1	1	100.0	27	27.0 (27)	0	0	—	—	ki	—	36	578
AAFC	4	53 (18)	253	1017	4.0	9	23	137	6.0	1	11	5	45.5	128	11.6 (27)	0	3	—	—	Pkpi	—	60	1285
1950	NYY	5	—	—	—	—	—	—	—	—	—	—	—	—	—	—	—	—	—	ki	—	0	6

KENNEDY, BOB   Robert Michael, DB-HB, 6′0″/178 lbs; North Carolina; 1949: Was, rnd 8; B9/16/1928 Weehauken, NJ

| 1949 | LAD-A | 10 (1) | 2 | 14 | 7.0 | 0 | — | — | — | — | — | — | — | — | — | — | — | — | — | i | — | 0 | 42 |

KENNEDY, CORTEZ   Cortez, DT, 6′3″/298 lbs; Miami (FL); 1990: Sea, rnd 1; B8/23/1968 Osceola, AR **[S]**   **1990** Sea 16 (2)   **1991** Sea★16 (16, RDT)   **1992** Sea★16 (16, RDT)   **1993** Sea★16 (16, RDT)   **1994** Sea★16 (16, RDT)   **1995** Sea★16 (16, RDT)   **1996** Sea★16 (16, RDT)   **1997** Sea 8 (8, rdt)   **1998** Sea◇15 (15, RDT)   **1999**†Sea◇16 (16, RDT)   **2000** Sea 16 (16, RDT)   **NFL** 167 (153) [11 yrs]

KENNEDY, JIMMIE   James Dale, TE, 6′3″/231 lbs; Hiram; Colorado State; 1974: Was, rnd 9; B7/30/1952 Laurel, MS

1975	†Bal	14	—	—	—	—	2	15	7.5 (12)	1	—	—	—	—	—	—	—	—	—	k	—	6	19
1976	†Bal	14	—	—	—	—	1	32	32.0 (32)	0	—	—	—	—	—	—	—	—	—	k	—	0	20
1977	†Bal	9	—	—	—	—	—	—	—	—	—	—	—	—	—	—	—	—	—	k	—	0	-6
NFL	3	37	—	—	—	—	3	47	15.7 (32)	1	—	—	—	—	—	—	—	—	—	k	—	6	33

KENNEDY, JIMMY   James David, FB, 5′9″/160 lbs; Boston College; Holy Cross; B2/16/1901 Somersworth, NH, D8/4/1968 Somersworth, NH   **1925** Buf 1 (1)

KENNEDY, JIMMY   Jimmy Wayne, DT, 6′4″/320 lbs; Penn State; 2003: SL, rnd 1; B11/15/1979 Yonkers, NY   **2003** SL 13 (0)   **2004**†SL 9 (5, rdt)   **2005** SL 15 (9, RDT)
NFL 37 (14) [3 yrs]

KENNEDY, KENOY   Kenoy Wayne, DB, 6′1″/215 lbs; Arkansas; 2000: Den, rnd 2; B11/15/1977 Dallas, TX   **2000**†Den 13 (0)   **2001** Den 16 (16, SS)   **2002** Den 15 (15, SS)   **2003**†Den 13 (12, SS)   **2004**†Den 16 (16, SS)   **2005** Det 16 (16, SS)   **NFL** 89 (75) [6 yrs]

KENNEDY, LINCOLN   Tamerlane Lincoln, T-G, 6′6″/335 lbs; Washington; 1993: Atl, rnd 1; B2/12/1971 York, PA   **1993** Atl 16 (16, LG)   **1994** Atl 16 (3)   **1995**†Atl 16 (4)   **1996** Oak 16 (16, RT)   **1997** Oak 16 (16, RT)   **1998** Oak 16 (16, RT)   **1999** Oak 15 (15, RT)   **2000**†Oak◇16 (16, RT)   **2001**†Oak☆15 (15, RT)   **2002**†Oak★15 (15, RT)   **2003** Oak 12 (10, RT)   **NFL** 169 (142) [11 yrs]

KENNEDY, MIKE   Michael Scott, DB, 6′0″/195 lbs; Toledo; B2/26/1959 Toledo, OH   **1983** Buf 12 (7, SS)   **1984** Hou 11 (0)   **NFL** 23 (7) [2 yrs]

KENNEDY, SAM   Samuel Edward, LB, 6′3″/235 lbs; San Jose State; B7/10/1964 San Mateo, CA   **1988**†SF 16 (0)

KENNEDY, TOM   Thomas Joseph, T, 6′0″/218 lbs; Wayne State (MI); B6/4/1920 Pittsfield, MA   **1944** Det 2 (0)

KENNEDY, TOM   Thomas Patrick, QB, 6′1″/210 lbs; Los Angeles State; B11/27/1939 Maywood, CA

| 1966 | NYG | 6 | 5 | 16 | 3.2 (10) | 0 | — | — | — | — | 100 | 55 | 55.0 | 748 | 7.5 (82) | 7 | 6 | 20 | 150 | — | — | — | 0 | 185 |

KENNEY, BILL   William Patrick, QB, 6′4″/211 lbs; Arizona State; Northern Colorado; 1978: Mia, rnd 12; B1/20/1955 San Francisco, CA

1980	KC	3 (3)	8	8	1.0 (4)	0	—	—	—	—	69	37	53.6	542	7.9 (75)	5	2	5	43	—	—	—	0	224
1981	KC	13 (13, QB)	24	89	3.7 (21)	1	—	—	—	—	274	147	53.6	1983	7.2 (64)	9	16	20	160	63.6	—	—	6	496
1982	KC	7 (6, QB)	13	40	3.1 (12)	0	—	—	—	—	169	95	56.2	1192	7.1 (51)	7	6	23	166	77.3	—	—	0	431
1983	KC◇	16 (16, QB)	23	59	2.6 (11)	3	1	0	0.0 (0)	0	603	346	57.4	4348	7.2 (53)	24	18	41	284	80.8	—	—	18	1663
1984	KC	9 (8, QB)	9	-8	-0.9 (1)	0	—	—	—	—	282	151	53.5	2098	7.4 (65)	15	10	14	136	80.7	—	—	0	716
1985	KC	16 (10, QB)	14	1	0.1 (5)	1	—	—	—	—	338	181	53.6	2536	7.5 (84)	17	9	28	223	83.6	—	—	6	1004
1986	†KC	15 (8, QB)	18	0	0.0 (9)	0	1	0	0.0 (0)	0	308	161	52.3	1922	6.2 (53)	13	11	25	180	70.8	—	—	0	586
1987	KC	11 (8, QB)	12	-2	-0.2 (6)	0	—	—	—	—	273	154	56.4	2107	7.7 (81)	15	9	22	161	85.8	—	—	0	767
1988	KC	2	6	4	2.0 (2)	0	—	—	—	—	114	58	50.9	549	4.8 (25)	0	5	13	107	—	—	—	0	79
NFL	9	106 (77)	123	191	1.6 (21)	5	2	0	0.0	0	2430	1330	54.7	17277	7.1 (84)	105	86	191	1460	77.0	—	—	30	5965

KENNEY, STEVE   Steven Faucette, G-T, 6′4″/266 lbs; Clemson; B12/26/1955 Wilmington, NC   **1980**†Phi 15 (0)   **1981**†Phi 13 (11, LG)   **1982** Phi 9 (9, LG)   **1983** Phi 16 (16, LG)   **1984** Phi 11 (11, LG)   **1985** Phi 16 (16, LG)   **1986** Det 9 (1)   **NFL** 89 (64) [7 yrs]

KENNISON, EDDIE   Eddie Joseph, WR, 6′1″/201 lbs; LSU; 1996: SL, rnd 1; B1/20/1973 Lake Charles, LA **[R]**

1996	SL	15 (14, WR)	—	—	—	—	54	924	17.1 (77)	9	—	—	—	—	—	—	—	—	—	kp	2	66	914
1997	SL	14 (9, WR)	3	13	4.3 (6)	0	25	404	16.2 (76)	0	—	—	—	—	—	—	—	—	—	kp	—	0	291
1998	SL	16 (13, WR)	2	9	4.5 (9)	0	17	234	13.8 (45)	1	—	—	—	—	—	—	—	—	—	p	—	12	356
1999	NO	16 (16, WR)	3	20	6.7 (15)	0	61	835	13.7 (90)	4	—	—	—	—	—	—	—	—	—	p	—	26	541
2000	ChiB	16 (10, WR)	3	72	24.0 (52)	0	55	549	10.0 (26)	2	—	—	—	—	—	—	—	—	—	—	—	12	357
2001	Den	8 (6, WR)	3	9	3.0 (10)	0	15	169	11.3 (36)	1	—	—	—	—	—	—	—	—	—	—	—	6	99
2001	KC	5 (1)	2	13	6.5 (14)	0	16	322	20.1 (55)	0	—	—	—	—	—	—	—	—	—	—	—	0	174
2002	KC	16 (14, WR)	7	58	8.3 (31)	0	53	906	17.1 (64)	2	—	—	—	—	—	—	—	—	—	—	—	12	521
2003	†KC	16 (16, WR)	2	9	4.5 (5)	0	56	853	15.2 (51)	5	—	—	—	—	—	—	—	—	—	p	—	30	516

YEAR	TEAM	G (GS, POS)	RUSH	YD	AVG (LG)	TD	REC	YD	AVG (LG)	TD	PASS	COMP	PCT	YD	AVG (LG)	TD	INT	SK	YD	QBR	KPR	OTD	PTS	TAY
2004	KC	14(14, WR)	2	15	7.5(15)	0	62	1086	17.5(70)	8	—	—	—	—	—	—	—	—	—	—	k	—	50	619
2005	KC	16(16, WR)	7	43	6.1(23)	0	68	1102	16.2(55)	5	—	—	—	—	—	—	—	—	—	—	p	—	30	631
NFL	10	152(129)	34	261	7.7(52)	0	482	7384	15.3(90)	37	—	—	—	—	—	—	—	—	—	—	kp	3	246	5017

KENT, GREG Edward Greg, T-DE, 6´6˝/275 lbs; Wisconsin; Utah; 1965: Oak, rnd R6/Det, rnd 7; B7/18/1943 Elkhorn, WI **1966** Oak-A 7 **1968** Det 5 **NFL** 12 [2 yrs]

KENT, JOEY Joseph Edward, WR, 6´1˝/191 lbs; Tennessee; 1997: Ten, rnd 2; B4/23/1974 Huntsville, AL

YEAR	TEAM	G (GS, POS)	RUSH	YD	AVG (LG)	TD	REC	YD	AVG (LG)	TD	PASS	COMP	PCT	YD	AVG (LG)	TD	INT	SK	YD	QBR	KPR	OTD	PTS	TAY
1997	Ten	12(0)	—	—	—	—	6	55	9.2(19)	1	—	—	—	—	—	—	—	—	—	—	—	—	6	33
1998	Ten	10(0)	—	—	—	—	4	62	15.5(23)	0	—	—	—	—	—	—	—	—	—	—	—	—	0	31
1999	Ten	8(0)	—	—	—	—	3	42	14.0(25)	0	—	—	—	—	—	—	—	—	—	—	k	—	0	15
NFL	3	30(0)	—	—	—	—	13	159	12.2(25)	1	—	—	—	—	—	—	—	—	—	—	k	—	6	79

KENT, RASHOD Rashod, TE, 6´6˝/275 lbs; Rutgers; B6/7/1980 Fairmont, WV **2003** Hou 7 (4)

KENYON, BILL William Curtis, TB, 5´9˝/180 lbs; Georgetown (DC); B12/5/1898 Manchester, NH, D5/5/1952 Orono, ME **1925** NYG 1 (0)

KER, CRAWFORD Crawford Francis, G, 6´3˝/288 lbs; Florida; 1985: Dal, rnd 3; B5/5/1962 Philadelphia, PA **1985** Dal 5 (0) **1986** Dal 16 (16, RG) **1987** Dal 12 (12, RG) **1988** Dal 16 (16, RG) **1989** Dal 16 (16, RG) **1990** Dal 15 (15, LG) **1991**†Den 12 (10, RG) **NFL** 92 (85) [7 yrs]

KERASIOTIS, NICK Nicholas Peter, G, 5´11˝/195 lbs; St. Ambrose; Iowa; B7/4/1918 Chicago, IL, D5/23/2002 Aurora, IL **1942** ChiB 9 (0) **1945** ChiB 1 (0) **NFL** 10 (0) [2 yrs]

KERBOW, RANDY Randall Morris, WR, 6´1˝/190 lbs; Rice; B12/19/1940 Paris, TX

YEAR	TEAM	G (GS, POS)	RUSH	YD	AVG (LG)	TD	REC	YD	AVG (LG)	TD	PASS	COMP	PCT	YD	AVG (LG)	TD	INT	SK	YD	QBR	KPR	OTD	PTS	TAY
1963	Hou-A	8	—	—	—	—	5	61	12.2(30)	0	—	—	—	—	—	—	—	—	—	—	—	—	0	31

KERCHER, BOB Robert Freed, E, 6´2˝/196 lbs; Georgetown (DC); B1/14/1918 Evansville, IN, D1/4/2004 Russell, KS **1944** GB 2 (0)

KERCHER, DICK Richard S., HB-DB, 6´2˝/205 lbs; Tulsa; 1954: Det, rnd 6; B3/11/1932 Evansville, IN

YEAR	TEAM	G (GS, POS)	RUSH	YD	AVG (LG)	TD	REC	YD	AVG (LG)	TD	PASS	COMP	PCT	YD	AVG (LG)	TD	INT	SK	YD	QBR	KPR	OTD	PTS	TAY
1954	Det	7	3	1	0.3(2)	0	—	—	—	—	—	—	—	—	—	—	—	—	—	—	—	—	0	1

KERCHEVAL, RALPH Ralph Godfrey, B, 6´1˝/190 lbs; Kentucky; B12/1/1911 Salt Lick, KY **[K]**

YEAR	TEAM	G (GS, POS)	RUSH	YD	AVG (LG)	TD	REC	YD	AVG (LG)	TD	PASS	COMP	PCT	YD	AVG (LG)	TD	INT	SK	YD	QBR	KPR	OTD	PTS	TAY
1934	Bkn	11(11, WB)	33	128	3.9	0	8	166	20.8(47)	3	12	3	25.0	17	1.4	0	3	—	—	—	K	—	37	115
1935	Bkn☆	12(9, WB)	34	89	2.6	0	7	130	18.6(44)	2	33	13	39.4	203	6.2	1	1	—	—	—	K	—	35	231
1936	Bkn☆	12(12, WB)	66	261	4.0	2	7	63	9.0	0	25	6	24.0	92	3.7	0	3	—	—	—	K	1	37	249
1937	Bkn	9(3, WB)	48	84	1.8	1	5	57	11.4	0	19	11	57.9	154	8.1	1	1	—	—	—	K	—	13	165
1938	Bkn	11(6, WB)	51	86	1.7	1	11	136	12.4	0	9	3	33.3	98	10.9	0	1	—	—	—	K	—	28	173
1939	Bkn	9(8, WB)	34	99	2.9	0	3	8	2.7	0	1	1	100.0	7	7.0(7)	0	0	—	—	—	KP	—	21	107
1940	Bkn	10(0)	11	19	1.7	0	1	17	17.0(17)	0	7	4	57.1	38	5.4	1	0	—	—	—	KP	—	15	52
NFL	7	74(49)	277	766	2.8	4	42	577	13.7(47)	5	106	41	38.7	609	5.7(7)	3	9	—	—	—	KP	1	186	1089

KERKORIAN, GARY Gary Ray, QB, 5´11˝/185 lbs; Stanford; 1952: Pit, rnd 19; B1/14/1930 Los Angeles, CA, D5/22/2000 Fresno, CA **[K]**

YEAR	TEAM	G (GS, POS)	RUSH	YD	AVG (LG)	TD	REC	YD	AVG (LG)	TD	PASS	COMP	PCT	YD	AVG (LG)	TD	INT	SK	YD	QBR	KPR	OTD	PTS	TAY
1952	Pit	12	2	20	10.0(20)	0	—	—	—	—	11	5	45.5	79	7.2(27)	1	3	—	—	—	K	—	47	-56
1954	Bal	10(QB)	22	36	1.6(11)	1	—	—	—	—	217	117	53.9	1515	7.0(78)	9	12	—	—	66.9	K	—	32	369
1955	Bal	7	6	20	3.3(12)	1	—	—	—	—	29	15	51.7	209	7.2(48)	1	3	—	—	—	K	—	9	20
1956	Bal	3	—	—	—	—	—	—	—	—	2	2	100.0	59	29.5(40)	1	0	—	—	—	K	—	1	35
NFL	4	32	30	76	2.5(20)	2	—	—	—	—	259	139	53.7	1862	7.2(78)	12	18	—	—	63.2	K	—	89	367

KERN, BILL William Franklin, T, 6´0˝/187 lbs; Pittsburgh; B9/2/1906 Kingston, PA, D4/5/1985 Pittsburgh, PA **1929** GB☆12 (9, LT) **1930** GB☆6 (3) **NFL** 18 (12) [2 yrs]

KERN, CHRIS Chris, DB, 5´10˝/196 lbs; Mount Union; B5/16/1979 Fairbault, MN **2004** Det 2 (0)

KERN, DON Donald Emit, TE, 6´4˝/228 lbs; Arizona State; 1984: Cin, rnd 6; B8/25/1962 Los Gatos, CA **1985** Cin 8 (0) **1986** Buf 1 (0)

YEAR	TEAM	G (GS, POS)	RUSH	YD	AVG (LG)	TD	REC	YD	AVG (LG)	TD	PASS	COMP	PCT	YD	AVG (LG)	TD	INT	SK	YD	QBR	KPR	OTD	PTS	TAY
1984	Cin	16(0)	—	—	—	—	2	14	7.0(9)	0	—	—	—	—	—	—	—	—	—	—	—	—	0	7
NFL	3	25(0)	—	—	—	—	2	14	7.0(9)	0	—	—	—	—	—	—	—	—	—	—	—	—	0	7

KERN, REX Rex William, DB, 5´11˝/190 lbs; Ohio State; 1971: Bal, rnd 10; B5/28/1949 Lancaster, OH **1971**†Bal 14 **1972** Bal 5 **1973** Bal 14 (LCB) **1974**†Buf 8 **NFL** 41 [4 yrs]

KERNER, MARLON Marlon Lavalle, DB, 5´10˝/187 lbs; Ohio State; 1995: Buf, rnd 3; B3/18/1973 Columbus, OH **1995**†Buf 14 (5, lcb) **1996** Buf 15 (0) **1997** Buf 13 (2) **1998** Buf 1 (0) **NFL** 43 (7) [4 yrs]

KERNEY, PATRICK Patrick Manning, DE, 6´5˝/273 lbs; Virginia; 1999: Atl, rnd 1; B12/30/1976 Trenton, NJ **[S]** **1999** Atl 16 (2) **2000** Atl 16 (16, LDE) **2001** Atl 16 (16, LDE) **2002**†Atl 16 (16, LDE) **2003** Atl 16 (16, LDE) **2004**†Atl★16 (15, LDE) **2005** Atl 16 (16, LDE) **NFL** 112 (97) [7 yrs]

KERNS, JOHN John Emery, T, 6´3˝/245 lbs; Ohio University; Duke; North Carolina; 1946: Phi, rnd 15; B6/17/1923 Ashtabula, OH, D6/1988 Leesburg, FL **1947** Buf-A 14 (3) **1948**†Buf-A 14 (9, RT) **1949**†Buf-A 12 (12, RT) **AAFC** 40 (24) [3 yrs]

KERNWEIN, GRAHAM Graham A., TB-HB, 5´11˝/175 lbs; Chicago; B10/23/1904 Claremont, IL, D1/25/1983 Rochester, NY **1926** Rac 5 (4, TB)

KERR, BILL William Howard, E, 6´0˝/220 lbs; Notre Dame; 1940: GB, rnd 14; B11/10/1915 Tarrytown, NY, D4/9/1965 San Mateo, CA

YEAR	TEAM	G (GS, POS)	RUSH	YD	AVG (LG)	TD	REC	YD	AVG (LG)	TD	PASS	COMP	PCT	YD	AVG (LG)	TD	INT	SK	YD	QBR	KPR	OTD	PTS	TAY
1946	LAD-A	11(1)	1	10	10.0(10)	0	7	122	17.4	0	—	—	—	—	—	—	—	—	—	—	i	—	0	100

KERR, GEORGE George Ropes, T-G, 6´1˝/211 lbs; Catholic; B8/28/1893 Medford, MA, D10/1977 Frazeyburg, OH **1920** Cle 2 (0) **1921** NYG 1 (0) **NFL** 3 (0) [2 yrs]

KERR, JIM James Norman, DB, 6´0˝/195 lbs; Penn State; 1961: Was, rnd 7/NYT, rnd 19; B7/23/1939 Colver, PA **1961** Was 13 (12, LS) **1962** Was 11 (LS) **NFL** 24 (12) [2 yrs]

KERRIGAN, MIKE Michael Joseph, QB, 6´3˝/205 lbs; Northwestern; B4/27/1960 Chicago, IL

YEAR	TEAM	G (GS, POS)	RUSH	YD	AVG (LG)	TD	REC	YD	AVG (LG)	TD	PASS	COMP	PCT	YD	AVG (LG)	TD	INT	SK	YD	QBR	KPR	OTD	PTS	TAY
1983	NE	1(0)	1	14	14.0(14)	0	—	—	—	—	14	6	42.9	72	5.1(19)	0	1	—	—	—	—	—	0	10
1984	NE	1(0)	—	—	—	—	—	—	—	—	1	1	100.0	13	13.0(13)	0	0	—	—	—	—	—	0	7
NFL	2	2(0)	1	14	14.0(14)	0	—	—	—	—	15	7	46.7	85	5.7(19)	0	1	—	—	—	—	—	0	17

KERRIGAN, TOM Thomas Martin, G, 6´2˝/200 lbs; Columbia; B7/7/1906 New York, NY, D7/29/1979 Stamford, CT **1929** Ora 1 (0) **1930** Nwk 4 (2) **NFL** 5 (2) [2 yrs]

KERSEY, MERRITT Merritt Warren, P-RB, 6´1˝/205 lbs; West Chester; B2/22/1950 Alexandria, VA **1975** Phi 2

YEAR	TEAM	G (GS, POS)	RUSH	YD	AVG (LG)	TD	REC	YD	AVG (LG)	TD	PASS	COMP	PCT	YD	AVG (LG)	TD	INT	SK	YD	QBR	KPR	OTD	PTS	TAY
1974	Phi	14	1	2	2.0(2)	0	—	—	—	—	—	—	—	—	—	—	—	—	—	—	P	—	0	2
NFL	2	16	1	2	2.0(2)	0	—	—	—	—	—	—	—	—	—	—	—	—	—	—	P	—	0	2

KERSHAW, GEORGE George Alfred, E, 6´3˝/220 lbs; Colgate; B3/13/1927 Oneonta, NY, D4/20/2002 Titusville, FL **1949** NYG 9 (1)

KERSTEN, WALLY Wallace Todd, T, 6´5˝/270 lbs; Minnesota; 1982: LARm, rnd 5; B12/8/1959 Minneapolis, MN **1982** LARm 3 (0)

KESEDAY, BOB Robert John, TE, 6´4˝/225 lbs; Texas-El Paso; B1/9/1965 Bayonne, NJ **1987** SL 3 (0)

KETZKO, ALEX Alexander Gregorieff, T, 5´11˝/215 lbs; Michigan State; B11/19/1919, IL, D12/23/1944 France **1943** Det 9 (3)

KEUPER, KEN Kenneth Erwin, B, 6´0˝/207 lbs; Georgia; B11/14/1918 Waukesha, WI, D5/23/1997 Houston County, GA **1945** GB 9 (2) **1946** GB 10 (1) **1948** NYG 7 (0)

YEAR	TEAM	G (GS, POS)	RUSH	YD	AVG (LG)	TD	REC	YD	AVG (LG)	TD	PASS	COMP	PCT	YD	AVG (LG)	TD	INT	SK	YD	QBR	KPR	OTD	PTS	TAY
1947	GB	12(1)	6	14	2.3(8)	0	2	37	18.5(26)	0	—	—	—	—	—	—	—	—	—	—	i	—	0	64
NFL	4	38(4)	6	14	2.3(8)	0	2	37	18.5(26)	0	—	—	—	—	—	—	—	—	—	—	Pki	—	0	87

KEUR, JOSH Joshua Jacob, TE, 6´4˝/270 lbs; Michigan State; B9/4/1976 Muskegon, MI **2000** Ind 1 (0)

KEY, DAVID David Russell, DB, 5´10˝/190 lbs; Michigan; 1991: NE, rnd 6; B3/27/1968 Columbus, OH **1991** NE 3 (0)

KEY, WADE Allan Wade, G-T, 6´5˝/245 lbs; Texas; Southwest Texas State; 1969: Phi, rnd 13; B10/14/1946 San Antonio, TX **1970** Phi 14 (LT) **1971** Phi 14 (LT) **1972** Phi 13 (LT) **1973** Phi 12 (9, LG) **1974** Phi 14 (LG) **1975** Phi 2 **1976** Phi 13 (13, LG) **1977** Phi 14 (14, LG) **1978**†Phi 13 (12, LG) **1979**†Phi 12 (LG) **NFL** 121 (48) [10 yrs]

KEYES, BOB Robert, HB, 5´10˝/183 lbs; San Diego State; B1936

YEAR	TEAM	G (GS, POS)	RUSH	YD	AVG (LG)	TD	REC	YD	AVG (LG)	TD	PASS	COMP	PCT	YD	AVG (LG)	TD	INT	SK	YD	QBR	KPR	OTD	PTS	TAY
1960	Oak-A	4	1	7	7.0(7)	0	1	19	19.0(19)	0	—	—	—	—	—	—	—	—	—	—	p	—	0	17

KEYES, JIMMY James Elton, LB-K, 6´2˝/225 lbs; Mississippi; 1968: Mia, rnd 2; B6/16/1944 Laurel, MS **[K]** **1968** Mia-A 12 **1969** Mia-A 5 **NFL** 17 [2 yrs]

KEYES, LEROY Marvin Leroy, DB-RB, 6´3˝/208 lbs; Purdue; 1969: Phi, rnd 1; B2/18/1947 Newport News, VA

YEAR	TEAM	G (GS, POS)	RUSH	YD	AVG (LG)	TD	REC	YD	AVG (LG)	TD	PASS	COMP	PCT	YD	AVG (LG)	TD	INT	SK	YD	QBR	KPR	OTD	PTS	TAY
1969	Phi	14(HB)	121	361	3.0(28)	3	29	276	9.5(35)	0	2	1	50.0	14	7.0(14)	0	0	—	—	—	k	—	18	601
1970	Phi	3	2	7	3.5(5)	0	—	—	—	—	—	—	—	—	—	—	—	—	—	—	—	—	0	7
1971	Phi	14(SS)	—	—	—	—	—	—	—	—	—	—	—	—	—	—	—	—	—	—	i	—	0	1
1972	Phi	14(SS)	—	—	—	—	—	—	—	—	—	—	—	—	—	—	—	—	—	—	i	—	0	-10
1973	KC	3	2	1	0.5(2)	0	1	-6	-6.0(-6)	0	1	0	0.0	0	0.0	0	0	—	—	—	—	—	0	-2
NFL	5	48	125	369	3.0(28)	3	30	270	9.0(35)	0	3	1	33.3	14	4.7(14)	0	0	—	—	—	ki	—	18	597

KEYES, MARCUS Willis Marcus, DT, 6´3˝/303 lbs; North Alabama; 1996: Chi, rnd 7; B10/20/1973 Taylorsville, MS **1996** ChiB 2 (0)

KEYS, BRADY Brady, DB-HB, 6´0˝/185 lbs; Colorado State; 1960: Pit, rnd 14; B5/19/1936 Austin, TX **1962** Pit 14 (RCB) **1963** Pit 11 (RCB) **1964** Pit 14 (RCB) **1965** Pit 14 (RCB) **1966** Pit✧14 (RCB) **1967** Pit 6 **1967** Min 8 **1968** SL 7

YEAR	TEAM	G(GS, POS)	RUSH	YD	AVG(LG)	TD	REC	YD	AVG(LG)	TD	PASS	COMP	PCT	YD	AVG(LG)	TD	INT	SK	YD	QBR	KPR	OTD	PTS	TAY
1961	Pit	12(RCB)	6	14	2.3(11)	0	—	—	—	—	—	—	—	—	—	—	—	—	—	—	kpi	—	0	126
NFL	8	100	6	14	2.3(11)	0	—	—	—	—	—	—	—	—	—	—	—	—	—	—	kpi	—	0	777

KEYS, HOWARD Howard Newton, C-T, 6´3˝/239 lbs; Oklahoma State; 1959: Phi, rnd 12; B1/24/1935 Orlando, OK, D10/21/1971 Philadelphia, PA **1960**†Phi 12 **1961** Phi 14 (4) **1962** Phi 13 **1963** Phi 2 **NFL** 41 (4) [4 yrs]

KEYS, ISAAC Van, LB, 6´3˝/245 lbs; Morehouse; B6/6/1978 St. Louis, MO **2004** Arz 3 (0) **2005** Arz 6 (0) **NFL** 9 (0) [2 yrs]

KEYS, TYRONE Tyrone Paree, DE-LB, 6´7˝/272 lbs; Mississippi State; 1981: NYJ, rnd 5; B10/24/1959 Jackson, MS **1983** ChiB 14 (4) **1984**†ChiB 14 (7, rde) **1985**†ChiB 16 (0) **1986** TB 14 (2) **1987** TB 3 (0) **1988** SD 13 (11, ROLB) **NFL** 74 (24) [6 yrs]

KEYWORTH, JON Jonathan Kimball, RB, 6´3˝/230 lbs; Colorado; 1974: Was, rnd 6; B12/15/1950 San Diego, CA

YEAR	TEAM	G(GS, POS)	RUSH	YD	AVG(LG)	TD	REC	YD	AVG(LG)	TD	PASS	COMP	PCT	YD	AVG(LG)	TD	INT	SK	YD	QBR	KPR	OTD	PTS	TAY
1974	Den	14(5, fb)	81	374	4.6(30)	**10**	12	109	9.1(18)	0	—	—	—	—	—	—	—	—	—	—	k	—	60	554
1975	Den	14(14, FB)	182	725	4.0(34)	3	42	314	7.5(19)	1	—	—	—	—	—	—	—	—	—	—	—	—	24	917
1976	Den	14(13, FB)	122	349	2.9(13)	3	22	201	9.1(31)	1	—	—	—	—	—	—	—	—	—	—	—	—	24	485
1977	†Den	11(9, FB)	83	311	3.7(16)	1	11	48	4.4(14)	0	—	—	—	—	—	—	—	—	—	—	k	—	6	345
1978	†Den	16(16, FB)	112	444	4.0(30)	3	21	166	7.9(20)	1	—	—	—	—	—	—	—	—	—	—	k	—	24	556
1979	†Den	16(9, FB)	81	323	4.0(17)	1	18	132	7.3(18)	0	1	1	100.0	32	32.0(32)	1	0	—	—	—	—	—	6	420
1980	Den	10(3)	38	127	3.3(14)	1	15	87	5.8(22)	0	—	—	—	—	—	—	—	—	—	—	—	—	6	181
NFL	7	95(69)	699	2653	3.8(34)	22	141	1057	7.5(31)	3	1	1	100.0	32	32.0(32)	1	0	—	—	—	k	—	150	3457

KHAYAT, BOB Robert Conrad, G-K-C, 6´2˝/230 lbs; Mississippi; 1960: Cle, rnd 6/Buf, rnd 1; B4/14/1938 Moss Point, MS **[K]** **1960** Was✧12 **1962** Was 14 **1963** Was 14 **NFL** 40 [3 yrs]

KHAYAT, ED Edward Michael, DT-DE-T, 6´3˝/240 lbs; Millsaps; Tulane; B9/14/1935 Moss Point, MS **[C]** **1957** Was 12 **1958** Phi 5 **1959** Phi 9 (RDE) **1960**†Phi 12 (12, RDT) **1961** Phi 14 (12, RDT) **1962** Was 14 (LDE) **1963** Was 10 **1964** Phi 13 **1965** Phi 14 (5, ldt) **1966** Bos-A 14 **NFL** 117 (29) [10 yrs]

KIBLER, BILL William Joel, TB, 5´11˝/180 lbs; Buffalo; B11/3/1901 Tonawanda, NY, D3/12/1983 Tonawanda, NY **1922** Buf 2 (1)

KICHEFSKI, WALT Walter Raymond, E, 6´1˝/212 lbs; Miami (FL); 1940: ChiB, rnd 22; B6/17/1916 Rhinelander, WI, D1/9/1992 Miami, FL

YEAR	TEAM	G(GS, POS)	RUSH	YD	AVG(LG)	TD	REC	YD	AVG(LG)	TD	PASS	COMP	PCT	YD	AVG(LG)	TD	INT	SK	YD	QBR	KPR	OTD	PTS	TAY
1940	Pit	11(3)	—	—	—	—	4	26	6.5	0	—	—	—	—	—	—	—	—	—	—	—	—	0	13
1941	Pit	11(5, re)	—	—	—	—	5	111	22.2(72)	1	—	—	—	—	—	—	—	—	—	—	k	—	6	64
1942	Pit	11(11, RE)	—	—	—	—	15	189	12.6(26)	0	—	—	—	—	—	—	—	—	—	—	—	—	0	95
1944	C-P	10(8, RE)	—	—	—	—	6	85	14.2(34)	0	—	—	—	—	—	—	—	—	—	—	—	—	0	43
NFL	4	43(27)	—	—	—	—	30	411	13.7(72)	1	—	—	—	—	—	—	—	—	—	—	k	—	6	214

KIDD, BILLY William Wayne, C, 6´4˝/270 lbs; Houston; B11/28/1959 Dallas, TX **1987**†Hou 7 (3)

KIDD, CARL Carl Edward, DB, 6´1˝/200 lbs; Arkansas; B6/14/1973 Pine Bluff, AR **1995** Oak 13 (0) **1996** Oak 16 (0) **NFL** 29 (0) [2 yrs]

KIDD, JOHN Max John, P, 6´3˝/210 lbs; Northwestern; 1984: Buf, rnd 5; B8/22/1961 Springfield, IL **[P]** **1984** Buf 16 (0) **1988**†Buf 16 (0) **1989**†Buf 16 (0) **1990** SD 16 (0) **1991** SD 16 (0) **1994** SD 2 (0) **1994**†Mia 4 (0) **1995**†Mia 16 (0) **1998** Det 2 (0) **1998**†NYJ 8 (0)

YEAR	TEAM	G(GS, POS)	RUSH	YD	AVG(LG)	TD	REC	YD	AVG(LG)	TD	PASS	COMP	PCT	YD	AVG(LG)	TD	INT	SK	YD	QBR	KPR	OTD	PTS	TAY
1985	Buf	16(0)	—	—	—	—	—	—	—	—	0	0	0.0	0	0.0	0	0	1	9	—	P	—	0	0
1986	Buf	16(0)	1	0	0.0(0)	0	—	—	—	—	—	—	—	—	—	—	—	—	—	—	P	—	0	0
1987	Buf	12(0)	—	—	—	—	—	—	—	—	1	0	0.0	0	0.0	0	0	—	—	—	P	—	0	0
1992	†SD	16(0)	2	-13	-6.5(0)	0	—	—	—	—	—	—	—	—	—	—	—	—	—	—	P	—	0	-13
1993	SD	14(0)	3	-13	-4.3(2)	1	—	—	—	—	—	—	—	—	—	—	—	—	—	—	P	—	6	-3
1996	Mia☆	16(0)	1	3	3.0(3)	0	—	—	—	—	—	—	—	—	—	—	—	—	—	—	P	—	0	3
1997	†Mia	13(0)	1	4	4.0(4)	0	—	—	—	—	—	—	—	—	—	—	—	—	—	—	P	—	0	4
NFL	15	215(0)	8	-19	-2.4(4)	1	—	—	—	—	1	0	0.0	0	0.0	0	0	1	9	—	P	—	6	-9

KIDD, KEITH Keith Darryl, WR, 6´1˝/195 lbs; Arkansas; 1984: Min, rnd 9; B9/10/1962 Crossett, AR **1987** Min 1 (0)

KIEL, BLAIR Blair Armstrong, QB, 6´0˝/209 lbs; Notre Dame; 1984: TB, rnd 11; B11/29/1961 Columbus, IN

YEAR	TEAM	G(GS, POS)	RUSH	YD	AVG(LG)	TD	REC	YD	AVG(LG)	TD	PASS	COMP	PCT	YD	AVG(LG)	TD	INT	SK	YD	QBR	KPR	OTD	PTS	TAY
1984	TB	10(0)	—	—	—	—	—	—	—	—	—	—	—	—	—	—	—	—	—	—	—	—	—	—
1986	Ind	3(0)	3	20	6.7(9)	0	—	—	—	—	25	11	44.0	236	9.4(50)	2	0	5	42	—	P	—	0	148
1987	Ind	4(1)	4	30	7.5(16)	0	—	—	—	—	33	17	51.5	195	5.9(21)	1	3	—	—	—	P	—	0	13
1988	GB	1(0)	—	—	—	—	—	—	—	—	—	—	—	—	—	—	—	—	—	—	—	—	—	—
1990	GB	3(1)	5	9	1.8(4)	1	—	—	—	—	85	51	60.0	504	5.9(22)	2	2	8	62	—	—	—	6	201
1991	GB	4(1)	4	46	11.5(26)	0	—	—	—	—	50	29	58.0	361	7.2(35)	3	2	2	13	—	—	—	0	162
NFL	6	25(3)	16	105	6.6(26)	1	—	—	—	—	193	108	56.0	1296	6.7(50)	8	7	15	117	—	P	—	6	523

KIEL, TERRENCE Terrence Dewayne, DB, 5´11˝/207 lbs; Texas A&M; 2003: SD, rnd 2; B11/24/1980 Lufkin, TX **2003** SD 16 (7, ss) **2004**†SD 16 (16, SS) **2005** SD 12 (11, SS) **NFL** 44 (34) [3 yrs]

KIELBASA, MAX Maxmi11an, HB, 6´1˝/185 lbs; Duquesne; 1943: Pit, rnd 16; B8/23/1921, PA, D1/12/1980 Pittsburgh, PA

YEAR	TEAM	G(GS, POS)	RUSH	YD	AVG(LG)	TD	REC	YD	AVG(LG)	TD	PASS	COMP	PCT	YD	AVG(LG)	TD	INT	SK	YD	QBR	KPR	OTD	PTS	TAY
1946	Pit	2(0)	2	-2	-1.0(1)	0	—	—	—	—	—	—	—	—	—	—	—	—	—	—	—	—	0	-2

KIELEY, HOWARD Howard, T, 5´8˝/208 lbs; none; B8/1896, MI, deceased **1923** Dul 7 (7, RT) **1924** Dul 6 (6, RT) **1925** Dul 2 (1) **1926** ChiC 6 (0) **NFL** 21 (14) [4 yrs]

KIESLING, WALT Walter Andrew, G-T, 6´3˝/260 lbs; St. Thomas; B3/27/1903 St. Paul, MN, D3/2/1962 Pittsburgh, PA; HOF 1966 **[C]** **1926** Dul 14 (11, RT) **1927** Dul 6 (6, LG) **1928** Pot 10 (10, RG) **1929** ChiC☆12 (12, LG) **1930** ChiC☆11 (9, LG) **1931** ChiC☆9 (9, LG) **1932** ChiC☆10 (10, LG) **1933** ChiC 10 (4) **1934** ChiB 13 (5, rg) **1935** GB 10 (2) **1936**†GB 8 (2) **1937** Pit 6 (1) **1938** Pit 6 (0) **NFL** 125 (81) [13 yrs]

KIEWEL, JEFF Jeffrey Clayton, G, 6´4˝/270 lbs; Arizona; B9/27/1960 Tucson, AZ **1985** Atl 16 (9, LG) **1987** Atl 12 (0) **NFL** 28 (9) [2 yrs]

KIGHT, DANNY Edward Oliver, K, 6´1˝/214 lbs; Augusta State (GA); B8/18/1971 Atlanta, GA **1999**†Ind 12 (0) **2000**†Ind 16 (0) **2001**†Bal 10 (0) **NFL** 38 (0) [3 yrs]

KIGHT, KELVIN Kelvin Jerome, WR, 6´0˝/209 lbs; Florida; B7/2/1982 Atlanta, GA **2004** GB 1 (0)

KIICK, GEORGE George Herman, FB, 6´0˝/200 lbs; Bucknell; 1940: Pit, rnd 3; B9/5/1917 Hanover, PA, D3/21/2002 Pompton Plains, NJ

YEAR	TEAM	G(GS, POS)	RUSH	YD	AVG(LG)	TD	REC	YD	AVG(LG)	TD	PASS	COMP	PCT	YD	AVG(LG)	TD	INT	SK	YD	QBR	KPR	OTD	PTS	TAY
1940	Pit	11(4, FB)	66	212	3.2	0	3	22	7.3	0	2	0	0.0	0	0.0	0	1	—	—	—	—	—	0	183
1945	Pit	6(3)	15	45	3.0(9)	1	1	-2	-2.0(-2)	0	—	—	—	—	—	—	—	—	—	—	k	—	6	58
NFL	2	17(7)	81	257	3.2(9)	1	4	20	5.0	0	2	0	0.0	0	0.0	0	1	—	—	—	k	—	6	241

KIICK, JIM James Forrest, RB, 5´11˝/214 lbs; Wyoming; 1968: Mia, rnd 5; B8/9/1946 Lincoln Park, NJ

YEAR	TEAM	G(GS, POS)	RUSH	YD	AVG(LG)	TD	REC	YD	AVG(LG)	TD	PASS	COMP	PCT	YD	AVG(LG)	TD	INT	SK	YD	QBR	KPR	OTD	PTS	TAY
1968	Mia-A✧	14(13, HB)	165	621	3.8(25)	4	44	422	9.6(38)	0	1	0	0.0	0	0.0	0	0	—	—	—	k	—	24	885
1969	Mia-A✧	14(14, RB)	180	575	3.2(27)	**9**	29	443	15.3(53)	1	—	—	—	—	—	—	—	—	—	—	—	—	60	892
1970	†Mia	14(14, RB)	191	658	3.4(56)	6	42	497	11.8(47)	0	1	1	100.0	25	25.0(25)	0	0	—	—	—	—	—	36	979
1971	†Mia	13(11, RB)	162	738	4.6(34)	3	40	338	8.4(27)	0	—	—	—	—	—	—	—	—	—	—	—	—	18	937
1972	†Mia	14	137	521	3.8(26)	5	21	147	7.0(15)	1	—	—	—	—	—	—	—	—	—	—	—	—	36	650
1973	†Mia	14	76	257	3.4(32)	0	27	208	7.7(22)	0	—	—	—	—	—	—	—	—	—	—	—	—	0	361
1974	†Mia	14(7, RB)	86	274	3.2(15)	1	18	155	8.6(19)	1	1	1	100.0	13	13.0(13)	0	0	—	—	—	—	—	12	373
1976	Den	14	31	114	3.7(19)	1	10	78	7.8(19)	1	—	—	—	—	—	—	—	—	—	—	—	—	12	168
1977	Den	3	1	1	1.0(1)	0	2	14	7.0(11)	0	—	—	—	—	—	—	—	—	—	—	—	—	0	8
1977	Was	1	—	—	—	—	—	—	—	—	—	—	—	—	—	—	—	—	—	—	—	—	—	—
NFL	9	115(59)	1029	3759	3.7(56)	29	233	2302	9.9(53)	4	3	2	66.7	38	12.7(25)	0	0	—	—	—	k	—	198	5252

KILBOURNE, WARREN Warren William, T, 6´3˝/240 lbs; Minnesota; B6/20/1916 St. Paul, MN, D5/16/1967 Ramsey, MN **1939** GB 4 (0)

KILCULLEN, BOB Robert Brian, DT-DE-T, 6´3˝/245 lbs; Texas Tech; 1957: ChiB, rnd 8; B5/13/1936 St. Louis, MI **1957** ChiB 12 **1958** ChiB 12 (RT) **1960** ChiB 4 **1961** ChiB 14 (LDT) **1962** ChiB 14 (LDT) **1963**†ChiB 14 (LDE) **1964** ChiB 12 (RDT) **1965** ChiB 8 **1966** ChiB 14 (ldt) **NFL** 104 [9 yrs]

KILEY, ROGER Roger Joseph, E, 6´0˝/180 lbs; Notre Dame; B10/23/1900 Chicago, IL, D9/9/1974 River Forest, IL **1923** ChiC 11 (11, LE), 6

YEAR	TEAM	G (GS, POS)	RUSH	YD	AVG(LG)	TD	REC	YD	AVG(LG)	TD	PASS	COMP	PCT	YD	AVG(LG)	TD	INT	SK	YD	QBR	KPR	OTD	PTS	TAY

KILGORE, JON   Jon Wilton, P, 6´1˝/205 lbs; Auburn; B12/3/1943 Fort Jackson, SC   **1965** LARm 5   **1967**†LARm 14   **1969** SF 7

1966	LARm	14	—	—	—	—	1	1	100.0	47	47.0(47)	0	0	—	—	—	—	P	—	0	24
1968	ChiB	7	—	—	—	—	1	0	0.0	—	—	—	—	—	—	—	—	P	—	0	0
NFL	5	47	—	—	—	—	2	1	50.0	47	23.5(47)	0	0	—	—	—	—	P	—	0	24

KILLENS, TERRY   Terry Deleon, LB, 6´1˝/235 lbs; Penn State; 1996: Hou, rnd 3; B3/24/1974 Cincinnati, OH   **1996** Hou 14 (0)   **1997** Ten 16 (0)   **1998** Ten 16 (1)   **1999**†Ten 16 (1)
2000†Ten 16 (0)   **2001** SF 16 (2)   **2002** Sea 3 (0)   **2002**†SF 0 (0)   **NFL** 97 (4) [7 yrs]

KILLETT, CHARLIE   Charles William, HB, 6´1˝/205 lbs; Mississippi; Memphis; 1963: NYG, rnd 16/Buf, rnd 29; B11/8/1940 Helena, AR

| 1963 | †NYG | 13 | 11 | 36 | 3.3(8) | 0 | — | — | — | — | — | — | — | — | — | — | — | k | — | 0 | 158 |

KILLIAN, GENE   Lowell Eugene, G, 6´4˝/250 lbs; Tennessee; 1974: Dal, rnd 16; B9/22/1952 Tampa, FL   **1974** Dal 7

KILLIHER, LYONS   Lyons, G, none; B1903, IL, deceased   **1928** ChiC 1 (0)

KILLINGER, GLENN   William Glenn, TB, 5´9˝/167 lbs; Penn State; B9/13/1898 Harrisburg, PA, D1/25/1988 Stanton, DE   **1921** Can 1 (1)   **1926** NYG 1 (1)   **NFL** 2 (2) [2 yrs]

KILLINGS, CEDRIC   Cedric Lapon, DT, 6´2˝/290 lbs; Carson-Newman; B12/14/1977 Miami, FL   **2000** SF 14 (1)   **2001** Car 4 (0)   **2005**†Was 10 (1)   **NFL** 28 (2) [3 yrs]

KILLORIN, PAT   Patrick Michael, C, 6´2˝/220 lbs; Syracuse; 1966: Pit, rnd 3/Mia, rnd 10; B6/11/1944 Watertown, NY   **1966** Pit 5

KILMER, BILLY   William Orland, QB-HB, 6´0˝/204 lbs; UCLA; 1961: SF, rnd 1/SD, rnd 5; B9/5/1939 Topeka, KS

1961	SF	11	96	509	5.3(31)	10	—	—	—	—	34	19	55.9	286	8.4(28)	0	4	—	—	—	P	—	60	592
1962	SF	12(10, LH)	93	478	5.1(35)	5	16	152	9.5(70)	1	13	8	61.5	191	14.7(73)	1	3	—	—	—	—	36	590
1964	SF	10	36	113	3.1(14)	0	11	136	12.4(35)	0	14	8	57.1	92	6.6(24)	1	1	—	—	—	—	0	192
1966	SF	6	3	23	7.7(13)	0	—	—	—	—	16	5	31.3	84	5.3(26)	0	1	—	—	—	P	—	0	25
1967	NO	10(4, qb)	20	142	7.1(31)	1	—	—	—	—	204	97	47.5	1341	6.6(96)	6	11	18	147	56.4	—	6	413
1968	NO	12(QB)	21	97	4.6(22)	2	—	—	—	—	315	167	53.0	2060	6.5(51)	15	17	26	170	66.9	—	12	542
1969	NO	14(QB)	11	18	1.6(12)	0	—	—	—	—	360	193	53.6	2532	7.0(52)	20	17	22	212	74.9	—	0	704
1970	NO	13(QB)	12	42	3.5(15)	0	—	—	—	—	237	135	57.0	1557	6.6(46)	6	17	19	155	55.5	—	0	171
1971	†Was	14(13, QB)	17	5	0.3(3)	2	—	—	—	—	306	166	54.2	2221	7.3(71)	13	13	16	110	74.0	—	12	681
1972	†Was★	12(10, QB)	3	-3	-1.0(1)	0	—	—	—	—	225	120	53.3	1648	7.3(89)	19	11	9	67	**84.8**	—	0	476
1973	†Was	10(10, QB)	9	10	1.1(5)	0	—	—	—	—	227	122	53.7	1656	7.3(64)	14	9	15	88	81.3	—	0	548
1974	†Was	11(10, QB)	6	27	4.5(10)	0	—	—	—	—	234	137	58.5	1632	7.0(51)	10	6	13	96	83.5	—	0	653
1975	Was☆	12(12, QB)	11	34	3.1(11)	1	—	—	—	—	346	178	51.4	2440	7.1(96)	23	16	23	138	77.2	—	6	739
1976	†Was	10(9, QB)	13	-7	-0.5(2)	0	—	—	—	—	206	108	52.4	1252	6.1(53)	12	10	15	125	70.3	—	0	279
1977	Was	8(8, QB)	10	20	2.0(12)	0	—	—	—	—	201	99	49.3	1187	5.9(59)	8	7	22	180	—	—	0	374
1978	Was	5(2)	1	1	1.0(1)	0	—	—	—	—	46	23	50.0	316	6.9(50)	4	3	4	22	—	P	—	0	59
NFL	16	170(88)	362	1509	4.2(35)	21	27	288	10.7(70)	2	2984	1585	53.1	20495	6.9(96)	152	146	202	1510	71.6	P	—	132	7036

KILROY, BUCKO   Francis Joseph, G-MG-T-DT, 6´2˝/243 lbs; Notre Dame; Temple; B5/30/1921 Philadelphia, PA   **1943** P-P 9 (4)   **1944** Phi 10 (4)   **1945** Phi 9 (0)   **1946** Phi 9 (1)
1947†Phi 12 (9, RG)   **1948**†Phi☆12 (12, RG)   **1949**†Phi☆12 (12, RG)   **1950** Phi☆12 (RG)   **1951** Phi☆12 (RT)   **1952** Phi★12 (MG)   **1953** Phi★12 (MG)   **1954** Phi★12 (MG)
1955 Phi 1   **NFL** 134 (42) [13 yrs]

KILSON, DAVID   David Wayne, DB, 6´1˝/200 lbs; Nevada-Reno; B8/11/1960 San Francisco, CA   **1983** Buf 16 (2)

KIMBALL, BOBBY   Robert Lund, WR, 6´1˝/190 lbs; Oklahoma; B3/12/1957 Camarillo, CA   **1979** GB 7   **1980** GB 1 (0)   **NFL** 8 [2 yrs]

KIMBAL, BRUCE   Bruce Michael, G, 6´2˝/260 lbs; Massachusetts; 1979: Pit, rnd 7; B8/19/1959 Beverly, MA   **1982** NYG 1 (1)   **1983**†Was 16 (0)   **1984**†Was 8 (0)   **NFL** 25 (1) [3 yrs]

KIMBER, BILL   William Lee, DE, 6´2˝/192 lbs; Florida State; B1/31/1936 Winter Park, FL   **1959** NYG 1   **1961** Bos-A 4

| 1960 | NYG | 3 | — | — | — | — | 2 | 48 | 24.0(41) | 0 | — | — | — | — | — | — | — | — | — | 0 | 24 |
| NFL | 3 | 8 | — | — | — | — | 2 | 48 | 24.0(41) | 0 | — | — | — | — | — | — | — | — | — | 0 | 24 |

KIMBLE, FRANK   Frank, E, 6´5˝/205 lbs; West Virginia; B11/9/1917 Williamson, WV; D2/12/2001 Williamson, WV

| 1945 | Pit | 9(3) | — | — | — | — | 2 | 16 | 8.0(13) | 0 | — | — | — | — | — | — | — | — | — | 0 | 8 |

KIMBLE, GARRY   Garry Lynn, DB, 5´11˝/184 lbs; Sam Houston State; 1985: Was, rnd 11; B4/5/1963 Lake Charles, LA   **1987** Was 3 (0)

KIMBROUGH, ELBERT   Elbert Leon, DB, 5´11˝/196 lbs; Northwestern; 1961: LA, rnd 2/Oak, rnd 4; B3/24/1938 Galesburg, IL   **1961** LARm 5   **1962** SF 14 (9, LS)
1963 SF 14 (11, LS)   **1964** SF 14 (14, LS)   **1965** SF 14 (14, LS)   **1966** SF 14 (14, LS)   **1968** NO 10   **NFL** 85 (62) [7 yrs]

KIMBROUGH, JOHN   John Alec, FB, 6´2˝/210 lbs; Texas A&M; 1941: ChiC, rnd 1; B6/14/1918 Haskell, TX, D5/9/2006 Haskell, TX

1946	LAD-A	14(7, FB)	122	473	3.9	6	9	162	18.0	1	—	—	—	—	—	—	—	k	—	42	655
1947	LAD-A	14(5, fb)	131	562	4.3	8	16	281	17.6	3	—	—	—	—	—	—	—	k	—	66	834
1948	LAD-A	10(3, FB)	76	189	2.5	3	10	131	13.1	2	—	—	—	—	—	—	—	k	—	30	289
AAFC	3	38(15)	329	1224	3.7	17	35	574	16.4	6	—	—	—	—	—	—	—	k	—	138	1777

KIMBROUGH, JOHN   John, WR, 5´10˝/165 lbs; St. Cloud State; 1977: Buf, rnd 3; B8/12/1954 Mount Vernon, AL

| 1977 | Buf | 14 | — | — | — | — | 10 | 207 | 20.7(42) | 1 | — | — | — | — | — | — | — | kp | 1 | 18 | 349 |

KIMBROUGH, TONY   Antonius, WR, 6´2˝/192 lbs; Jackson State; 1993: Den, rnd 7; B9/17/1970 Weir, MS

1993	†Den	15(0)	—	—	—	—	8	79	9.9(16)	0	—	—	—	—	—	—	—	—	—	0	40
1994	Den	12(0)	—	—	—	—	2	20	10.0(12)	0	—	—	—	—	—	—	—	—	—	0	10
NFL	2	27(0)	—	—	—	—	10	99	9.9(16)	0	—	—	—	—	—	—	—	—	—	0	50

KIMMEL, J.D.   John D., DT, 6´2˝/248 lbs; Army; Houston; 1952: SF, rnd 11; B9/30/1929 Omaha, NE   **1955** Was 12 (RDT)   **1956** Was 12 (RDT)   **1958** GB 12 (RDT)   **NFL** 36 [3 yrs]

KIMMEL, JAMIE   James L., LB, 6´3˝/235 lbs; Syracuse; 1985: LARd, rnd 4; B3/28/1962 Johnson City, NY   **1986** LARd 16 (0)   **1987** LARd 15 (0)   **NFL** 31 (0) [2 yrs]

KIMMEL, JERRY   Jerry M., LB, 6´2˝/240 lbs; Syracuse; 1986: NYG, rnd 10; B7/18/1963 Johnson City, NY   **1987** NYG 2 (2)

KIMMEL, JON   Jon Joseph, LB, 6´4˝/240 lbs; Colgate; B7/21/1960 Binghamton, NY   **1985** Phi 4 (0)   **1987** Was 1 (1)   **NFL** 5 (1) [2 yrs]

KIMRIN, OLA   Ola, K, 6´3˝/230 lbs; Texas-El Paso; B2/29/1972 Malmo, Sweden [K]   **2004** Was 5 (0)

KINARD, BILLY   William Russell, DB-HB, 6´0˝/189 lbs; Mississippi; 1956: Cle, rnd 2; B12/16/1933 Jackson, MS   **1957** GB 12   **1958** GB 12 (DB)   **1960** Buf-A 14 (RCB)

| 1956 | Cle | 7 | 1 | 27 | 27.0(27) | 1 | — | — | — | — | — | — | — | — | — | — | — | k | — | 6 | 128 |
| NFL | 4 | 45 | 1 | 27 | 27.0(27) | 1 | — | — | — | — | — | — | — | — | — | — | — | kpi | — | 6 | 165 |

KINARD, BRUISER   Frank Manning, T, 6´1˝/216 lbs; Mississippi; 1938: Bkn, rnd 3; B10/23/1914 Pelahatchie, MS, D9/7/1985 Jackson, MS; HOF 1971 [K]   **1938** Bkn★11 (11, RT)
1939 Bkn★11 (11, RT)   **1940** Bkn☆9 (8, LT)   **1941** Bkn★11 (11, LT)   **1942** Bkn★11 (11, LT)   **1944** Bkn☆10 (10, LT)

| 1943 | Bkn☆ | 10(10, LT) | — | — | — | — | 5 | 62 | 12.4(36) | 1 | — | — | — | — | — | — | — | K | — | 17 | 36 |
| NFL | 7 | 73(72) | — | — | — | — | 5 | 62 | 12.4(36) | 1 | — | — | — | — | — | — | — | Kki | 1 | 42 | 63 |

1946†NYY-A☆14 (14, LT)   **1947**†NYY-A 14 (3)   **AAFC** 73 (72) [7 yrs]

KINARD, GEORGE   George Truitt, G, 6´1˝/202 lbs; Mississippi; 1941: Bkn, rnd 13; B10/9/1916 Crystal Springs, MS, D3/23/2000 Rnkin, MS   **1941** Bkn 11 (0)   **1942** Bkn 7 (7, LG)
NFL 18 (7) [2 yrs]

1946†NYY-A 11 (5, lg)

KINARD, TERRY   Alfred Terance, DB, 6´1˝/199 lbs; Clemson; 1983: NYG, rnd 1; B11/24/1959 Bitburg, GA [I]   **1983** NYG 16 (10, FS)   **1984**†NYG 15 (15, FS)
1985†NYG 16 (16, FS)   **1986** NYG 14 (14, FS)   **1987** NYG 12 (12, FS)   **1988** NYG◇16 (16, FS)   **1989**†NYG 16 (16, FS)   **1990**†Hou 16 (16, FS)   **NFL** 121 (115) [8 yrs]

KINCAID, JIM   James Davis, DB, 5´11˝/180 lbs; South Carolina; 1954: LA, rnd 3; B8/11/1930 Arnsted, WV [K]   **1954** Was 2

KINCHEN, BRIAN   Brian Douglas, TE, 6´2˝/240 lbs; LSU; 1988: Mia, rnd 12; B8/6/1965 Baton Rouge, LA

1988	Mia	16(0)	—	—	—	—	1	3	3.0(3)	0	—	—	—	—	—	—	—	—	—	0	2
1989	Mia	16(0)	—	—	—	—	1	12	12.0(12)	0	—	—	—	—	—	—	—	k	—	0	2
1990	Mia	4(0)	—	—	—	—	—	—	—	—	—	—	—	—	—	—	—	k	—	0	1
1991	Cle	14(0)	—	—	—	—	—	—	—	—	—	—	—	—	—	—	—	—	—	0	0
1992	Cle	16(0)	—	—	—	—	—	—	—	—	—	—	—	—	—	—	—	—	—	0	0
1993	Cle	16(15, TE)	—	—	—	—	29	347	12.0(40)	2	—	—	—	—	—	—	—	k	—	12	169

YEAR	TEAM	G (GS, POS)	RUSH	YD	AVG (LG)	TD	REC	YD	AVG (LG)	TD	PASS	COMP	PCT	YD	AVG (LG)	TD	INT	SK	YD	QBR	KPR	OTD	PTS	TAY
1994	†Cle	16 (11, TE)	—	—	—	—	24	232	9.7 (38)	1	—	—	—	—	—	—	—	—	—	—	k	—	6	114
1995	Cle	13 (12, TE)	—	—	—	—	20	216	10.8 (41)	0	—	—	—	—	—	—	—	—	—	—	—	—	0	108
1996	Bal	16 (16, TE)	—	—	—	—	55	581	10.6 (29)	1	—	—	—	—	—	—	—	—	—	—	k	—	6	300
1997	Bal	16 (7, te)	—	—	—	—	11	95	8.6 (24)	1	—	—	—	—	—	—	—	—	—	—	—	—	6	53
1998	Bal	16 (5, te)	—	—	—	—	13	110	8.5 (24)	0	—	—	—	—	—	—	—	—	—	—	k	—	0	58
1999	Car	16 (0)	—	—	—	—	5	45	9.0 (26)	2	—	—	—	—	—	—	—	—	—	—	k	—	12	17
2000	Car	16 (0)	—	—	—	—	1	7	7.0 (7)	0	—	—	—	—	—	—	—	—	—	—	—	—	0	4
2003	†NE	2 (0)	—	—	—	—	—	—	—	—	—	—	—	—	—	—	—	—	—	—	—	—	—	—
NFL	14	193 (66)	—	—	—	—	160	1648	10.3 (41)	7	—	—	—	—	—	—	—	—	—	—	k	—	42	825

KINCHEN, TODD Todd Whittington, WR, 5´11˝/187 lbs; LSU; 1992: LARm, rnd 3; B1/7/1969 Baton Rouge, LA **[R]**

YEAR	TEAM	G (GS, POS)	RUSH	YD	AVG (LG)	TD	REC	YD	AVG (LG)	TD	PASS	COMP	PCT	YD	AVG (LG)	TD	INT	SK	YD	QBR	KPR	OTD	PTS	TAY
1992	LARm	14 (0)	—	—	—	—	—	—	—	—	—	—	—	—	—	—	—	—	—	—	kp	2	12	106
1993	LARm	6 (1)	2	10	5.0 (8)	0	8	137	17.1 (35)	1	—	—	—	—	—	—	—	—	—	—	kp	—	6	87
1994	LARm	13 (0)	1	44	44.0 (44)	1	23	352	15.3 (43)	3	—	—	—	—	—	—	—	—	—	—	kp	—	24	518
1995	SL	16 (1)	4	16	4.0 (15)	0	36	419	11.6 (35)	4	1	0	0.0	0	0.0	0	0	—	—	—	kp	—	24	615
1996	Den	7 (0)	—	—	—	—	1	27	27.0 (27)	0	—	—	—	—	—	—	—	—	—	—	p	—	0	184
1997	Atl	16 (0)	—	—	—	—	16	266	16.6 (53)	1	—	—	—	—	—	—	—	—	—	—	kp	—	6	327
1998	Atl	11 (0)	—	—	—	—	11	157	14.3 (32)	1	—	—	—	—	—	—	—	—	—	—	p	—	6	92
NFL	7	83 (2)	7	70	10.0 (44)	1	95	1358	14.3 (53)	10	1	0	0.0	0	0.0	0	0	—	—	—	kp	2	78	1927

KINDER, RANDY Randolph Samuel, RB, 6´1˝/213 lbs; Notre Dame; B4/4/1975 Washington, DC **1997** GB 6 (0) **1997** Phi 6 (0) **NFL** 12 (0) [1 yr]

KINDERDINE, HOBBY George H., C, 5´11˝/181 lbs; none; B8/13/1894 Miamisburg, OH, D6/22/1967 Kettering, OH **1920** Day 8 (7, C) **1921** Day 9 (9, C) **1922** Day 8 (8, C) **1923** Day 8 (8, C) **1924** Day 8 (8, C) **1925** Day 8 (8, C) **1926** Day 6 (6, C) **1927** Day 8 (8, C) **1928** Day 7 (7, C) **1929** Day 6 (6, C) **NFL** 76 (75) [10 yrs]

KINDERDINE, SHINE Harry R., G, 6´0˝/195 lbs; none; B3/1893 Miamisburg, OH, D2/17/1947 Dayton, OH **1924** Day 1 (0)

KINDERDINE, WALT James Walter, B, none; B8/5/1899 Miamisburg, OH, D7/25/1964 **1923** Day 5 (0) **1924** Day 4 (1) **1925** Day 2 (0) **NFL** 11 (1) [3 yrs]

KINDERMAN, KEITH Keith John, FB-DB, 6´0˝/221 lbs; Iowa; Florida State; 1963: SD, rnd 3/GB, rnd 8; B4/16/1940 Chicago, IL **1963** SD-A 3 **1965** Hou-A 4

YEAR	TEAM	G (GS, POS)	RUSH	YD	AVG (LG)	TD	REC	YD	AVG (LG)	TD	PASS	COMP	PCT	YD	AVG (LG)	TD	INT	SK	YD	QBR	KPR	OTD	PTS	TAY
1964	†SD-A	8	24	111	4.6 (22)	0	3	21	7.0 (18)	0	1	0	0.0	0	0.0	0	0	—	—	—	—	—	0	122
NFL	3	15	24	111	4.6 (22)	0	3	21	7.0 (18)	0	1	0	0.0	0	0.0	0	0	—	—	—	k	—	0	134

KINDIG, HOWARD Howard Wayne, DE-T, 6´6˝/265 lbs; Los Angeles State; 1964: SD, rnd 14/Phi, rnd 13; B6/22/1941 Mexico, MO **1965**†SD-A 14 **1966** SD-A 14 (LDE) **1967** SD-A 7 (LDE) **1967** Buf-A 5 (1) **1968** Buf-A 14 **1969** Buf-A 12 **1970** Buf 10 (LT) **1971** Buf 14 **1972**†Mia 14 **1974** NYJ 8 **NFL** 112 (1) [9 yrs]

KINDLE, GREG Gregory Lamarr, G-T, 6´4˝/265 lbs; Tennessee State; 1974: SL, rnd 2; B9/16/1950 Houston, TX **1974** SL 10 (2) **1975** SL 14 **1976** Atl 10 (10, RG) **1977** Atl 1 **NFL** 35 (12) [4 yrs]

KINDRICKS, BILL William Alfred, DT, 6´3˝/268 lbs; Alabama A&M; 1968: Cin, rnd 6; B7/24/1946 Tuskegee, AL **1968** Cin-A 9

KINDT, DON Donald John, DB-FB-HB, 6´1˝/207 lbs; Wisconsin; 1947: ChiB, rnd 1; B7/2/1925 Milwaukee, WI, D5/5/2000 Brookfield, WI **[I]**

YEAR	TEAM	G (GS, POS)	RUSH	YD	AVG (LG)	TD	REC	YD	AVG (LG)	TD	PASS	COMP	PCT	YD	AVG (LG)	TD	INT	SK	YD	QBR	KPR	OTD	PTS	TAY
1947	ChiB	12 (11, LH)	61	266	4.4 (48)	2	2	24	12.0 (14)	0	—	—	—	—	—	—	—	—	—	—	ki	—	12	372
1948	ChiB	12 (6, FB)	54	189	3.5 (66)	2	11	137	12.5 (49)	0	—	—	—	—	—	—	—	—	—	—	i	—	12	294
1949	ChiB	12 (6, FB)	41	118	2.9 (15)	0	12	118	9.8 (38)	0	—	—	—	—	—	—	—	—	—	—	i	—	0	170
1950	†ChiB	12 (DB)	1	4	4.0 (4)	0	3	72	24.0 (42)	1	—	—	—	—	—	—	—	—	—	—	kp	—	6	47
1951	ChiB	12 (DB)	2	5	2.5 (3)	0	4	39	9.8 (12)	1	—	—	—	—	—	—	—	—	—	—	i	—	6	66
1952	ChiB	12 (DB)	3	13	4.3 (6)	0	—	—	—	—	—	—	—	—	—	—	—	—	—	—	pi	—	2	49
1953	ChiB✧	12 (DB)	—	—	—	—	—	—	—	—	—	—	—	—	—	—	—	—	—	—	i	1	6	152
1954	ChiB	12 (DB)	10	-9	-0.9 (10)	0	9	101	11.2 (21)	0	—	—	—	—	—	—	—	—	—	—	kpi	—	0	51
1955	ChiB	12 (DB)	—	—	—	—	2	15	7.5 (10)	0	—	—	—	—	—	—	—	—	—	—	p	—	0	3
NFL	9	108 (23)	172	586	3.4 (66)	4	43	506	11.8 (49)	2	—	—	—	—	—	—	—	—	—	—	kpi	1	44	1202

KINDT, DON Donald John, TE, 6´6˝/242 lbs; Wisconsin-LaCrosse; B5/9/1961 Milwaukee, WI

YEAR	TEAM	G (GS, POS)	RUSH	YD	AVG (LG)	TD	REC	YD	AVG (LG)	TD	PASS	COMP	PCT	YD	AVG (LG)	TD	INT	SK	YD	QBR	KPR	OTD	PTS	TAY
1987	ChiB	3 (2)	—	—	—	—	5	34	6.8 (11)	1	—	—	—	—	—	—	—	—	—	—	—	—	6	22

KINEK, GEORGE George, E, 6´2˝/190 lbs; Tulane; 1951: LA, rnd 4; B1/13/1929 Palmerton, PA, D1/21/1995 Salisbury Township, PA **1954** ChiC 12

KINEK, MICHAEL Michael Kenneth, E, 6´1˝/200 lbs; Michigan State; B8/11/1917 Akron, OH **1940** Cle 2 (0)

KINER, STEVE Steven Albert, LB, 6´1˝/220 lbs; Tennessee; 1970: Dal, rnd 3; B6/12/1947 Sandstone, MN **1971** NE 14 (14, RLB) **1973** NE 14 (14, LLB) **1974** Hou 14 (RILB) **1975** Hou 14 (LILB) **1976** Hou 14 (LILB) **1977** Hou 14 (14, LILB) **1978**†Hou 16 (16, LILB)

YEAR	TEAM	G (GS, POS)	RUSH	YD	AVG (LG)	TD	REC	YD	AVG (LG)	TD	PASS	COMP	PCT	YD	AVG (LG)	TD	INT	SK	YD	QBR	KPR	OTD	PTS	TAY
1970	†Dal	14	—	—	—	—	1	14	14.0 (14)	0	—	—	—	—	—	—	—	—	—	—	ki	—	0	35
NFL	8	114 (58)	—	—	—	—	1	14	14.0 (14)	0	—	—	—	—	—	—	—	—	—	—	ki	—	2	76

KING TB, none; deceased **1920** Det 1 (0)

KING, ANDRE Andre Omar, WR, 5´11˝/195 lbs; Miami (FL); 2001: Cle, rnd 7; B11/26/1973 Kingston, Jamaica

YEAR	TEAM	G (GS, POS)	RUSH	YD	AVG (LG)	TD	REC	YD	AVG (LG)	TD	PASS	COMP	PCT	YD	AVG (LG)	TD	INT	SK	YD	QBR	KPR	OTD	PTS	TAY
2001	Cle	7 (0)	—	—	—	—	11	149	13.5 (48)	0	—	—	—	—	—	—	—	—	—	—	k	—	0	144
2002	†Cle	11 (1)	—	—	—	—	5	41	8.2 (13)	0	—	—	—	—	—	—	—	—	—	—	kp	—	0	66
2003	Cle	15 (0)	—	—	—	—	9	88	9.8 (28)	0	—	—	—	—	—	—	—	—	—	—	k	1	6	81
2004	Cle	9 (2)	—	—	—	—	5	49	9.8 (16)	0	—	—	—	—	—	—	—	—	—	—	k	—	0	45
NFL	4	42 (3)	—	—	—	—	30	327	10.9 (48)	0	—	—	—	—	—	—	—	—	—	—	kp	1	6	335

KING, ANDY Andrew Joel, G, 6´4˝/310 lbs; Illinois State; B11/9/1978 Lincoln, IL **2002** SL 5 (0) **2003** SL 1 (0) **NFL** 6 (0) [2 yrs]

KING, ANGELO Angelo Tyrone, LB, 6´1˝/224 lbs; South Carolina State; B2/10/1958 Columbia, SC **1981**†Dal 15 (0) **1982**†Dal 9 (0) **1983**†Dal 16 (1) **1984** Det 16 (0) **1985** Det 16 (9, ROLB) **1986** Det 11 (5, lolb) **1987** Det 1 (1) **NFL** 84 (16) [7 yrs]

KING, AUSTIN Austin Patrick, C, 6´5˝/303 lbs; Northwestern; 2003: TB, rnd 4; B4/11/1981 Cincinnati, OH **2004**†Atl 4 (0) **2005** Atl 16 (1) **NFL** 20 (1) [2 yrs]

KING, BRUCE Bruce Eric, RB, 6´1˝/219 lbs; Purdue; 1985: KC, rnd 5; B1/7/1963 Clarksville, IN

YEAR	TEAM	G (GS, POS)	RUSH	YD	AVG (LG)	TD	REC	YD	AVG (LG)	TD	PASS	COMP	PCT	YD	AVG (LG)	TD	INT	SK	YD	QBR	KPR	OTD	PTS	TAY
1985	KC	16 (6, fb)	28	83	3.0 (9)	0	7	45	6.4 (8)	0	—	—	—	—	—	—	—	—	—	—	k	—	0	104
1986	KC	4 (0)	—	—	—	—	—	—	—	—	—	—	—	—	—	—	—	—	—	—	—	—	—	—
1986	Buf	5 (1)	4	10	2.5 (7)	0	—	—	—	—	—	—	—	—	—	—	—	—	—	—	—	—	0	10
1987	Buf	3 (2)	9	28	3.1 (8)	0	1	3	3.0 (3)	0	—	—	—	—	—	—	—	—	—	—	—	—	0	30
NFL	3	28 (9)	41	121	3.0 (9)	0	8	48	6.0 (8)	0	—	—	—	—	—	—	—	—	—	—	k	—	0	143

KING, CARLOS Carlos Jermaine, RB, 6´0˝/230 lbs; North Carolina State; 1998: Pit, rnd 4; B11/25/1973 Garden Grove, CA **1998** Pit 1 (0)

KING, CHARLIE Charles Ronnie, DB, 6´0˝/184 lbs; Purdue; 1965: Buf, rnd R8/Bal, rnd 18; B1/7/1943 Canton, OH **1966**†Buf-A 14 **1967** Buf-A 14 **1968** Cin-A 14 (RCB) **1969** Cin-A 9 **NFL** 51 [4 yrs]

KING, CLAUDE Claude Robert, HB, 5´11˝/185 lbs; Houston; 1960: Den, rnd 1/Chi, rnd 18; B12/3/1938

YEAR	TEAM	G (GS, POS)	RUSH	YD	AVG (LG)	TD	REC	YD	AVG (LG)	TD	PASS	COMP	PCT	YD	AVG (LG)	TD	INT	SK	YD	QBR	KPR	OTD	PTS	TAY
1961	†Hou-A	11	12	50	4.2 (17)	2	3	83	27.7 (44)	1	—	—	—	—	—	—	—	—	—	—	kp	—	18	184
1962	Bos-A	14	21	144	6.9 (71)	1	5	42	8.4 (33)	0	—	—	—	—	—	—	—	—	—	—	k	—	6	217
NFL	2	25	33	194	5.9 (71)	3	8	125	15.6 (44)	1	—	—	—	—	—	—	—	—	—	—	kp	—	24	401

KING, DAVID David Joel, DB, 5´8˝/176 lbs; Auburn; 1985: SD, rnd 10; B5/19/1963 Mobile, AL **1985** SD 1 (0) **1987** GB 3 (0) **NFL** 4 (0) [2 yrs]

KING, DICK Richard Stewart Cutter, FB-WB-TB-HB, 5´8˝/175 lbs; Harvard; B2/9/1895 Boston, MA, D10/16/1930 Bogota, Colombia **[K]** **1921** Ham 5 (4, FB) **1922** Mil 4 (4, WB) **1922** Roc 3 (3, TB) **1923** SL 7 (7, FB), 2 **NFL** 19 (18) [3 yrs]

KING, DON Donald William, DE-DT, 6´3˝/260 lbs; Kentucky; B3/11/1929 McBee, SC **1954** Cle 8 **1956** Phi 3 **1956** GB 6 **1960** Den-A 14 (lde) **NFL** 31 [3 yrs]

KING, DON Donald Erwin, DB, 6´0˝/200 lbs; SMU; B2/10/1964 Dallas, TX **1987** GB 1 (0)

KING, ED Edward Joseph, G-DE-DG, 6´0˝/217 lbs; Boston College; B5/10/1925 Chelsea, MA **1948**†Buf-A 14 (1) **1949**†Buf-A 5 (0) **AAFC** 19 (1) [2 yrs] **1950** Bal 12

KING, ED Edward E'Dainia, G-T, 6´4˝/300 lbs; Auburn; 1991: Cle, rnd 2; B12/3/1969 Fort Benning, GA **1991** Cle 16 (15, RG) **1992** Cle 16 (15, RG) **1993** Cle 6 (2) **1995** NO 1 (0) **1996** NO 16 (16, RG) **1997** NO 2 (0) **NFL** 57 (48) [6 yrs]

YEAR	TEAM	G(GS, POS)	RUSH	YD	AVG(LG)	TD	REC	YD	AVG(LG)	TD	PASS	COMP	PCT	YD	AVG(LG)	TD	INT	SK	YD	QBR	KPR	OTD	PTS	TAY

KING, EMANUEL Emanuel, LB, 6´4˝/250 lbs; Alabama; 1985: Cin, rnd 1; B8/15/1963 Leroy, AL **1985** Cin 16 (2) **1986** Cin 16 (16, LOLB) **1987** Cin 12 (12, LOLB) **1988**†Cin 7 (0)
1989 LARd 16 (3) **NFL** 67 (33) [5 yrs]

KING, EMMETT Emmett Eugene, FB-HB, 5´9˝/195 lbs; none; B5/8/1933 Hallettsville, TX, D4/28/1998 Glencoe, IL

| 1954 | ChiC | 12(FB) | 57 | 167 | 2.9(17) | 0 | 6 | 43 | 7.2(17) | 1 | — | — | — | — | — | — | — | — | — | k | — | 6 | 198 |

KING, ERIC Eric, DB, 5´8˝/189 lbs; Wake Forest; 2005: Buf, rnd 5; B5/10/1982 Baltimore, MD **2005** Buf 16 (0)

KING, FAY Lafayette Henry, E, 6´2˝/195 lbs; Georgia; 1946: LA, rnd 7; B3/7/1922 Dothan, AL, D7/1969 Albany, GA

1946	Buf-A	14(0, re)	—	—	—	—	30	466	15.5	6	—	—	—	—	—	—	—	—	—	—	—	36	263
1947	Buf-A	14(2)	—	—	—	—	26	382	14.7	6	—	—	—	—	—	—	—	—	—	—	—	36	221
1948	ChiR-A	14(8, RE)	—	—	—	—	50	647	12.9	7	—	—	—	—	—	—	—	—	—	k	—	42	355
1949	ChiH-A	8(3)	—	—	—	—	9	88	9.8	1	—	—	—	—	—	—	—	—	—	k	—	6	47
AAFC	4	50(13)	—	—	—	—	115	1583	13.8	20	—	—	—	—	—	—	—	—	—	k	—	120	886

KING, FRED Frederick James, HB, 6´2˝/205 lbs; Hobart; B6/3/1913 New York, NY, D3/12/1987 Reading, MA **1937** Bkn 1 (0)

KING, GORDON Gordon David, T-G, 6´6˝/275 lbs; Stanford; 1978: NYG, rnd 1; B2/3/1956 Madison, WI **1978** NYG 11 (3) **1979** NYG 7 **1980** NYG 12 (9, RT)
1981†NYG 16 (16, RT) **1982** NYG 9 (9, RT) **1983** NYG 14 (14, RT) **1985**†NYG 15 (0) **1986**†NYJ 11 (9, rt) **1987** NYJ 2 (0) **NFL** 97 (60) [9 yrs]

KING, GUS Alexander Cook, E-HB, 5´11˝/180 lbs; Centre; B1/11/1900 Flemingsburg, KY, D7/1955 **1922** Tol 3 (2)

KING, HENRY Henry Louis, DB, 6´4˝/205 lbs; Utah State; 1967: NYJ, rnd 3; B1/25/1945 San Francisco, CA **1967** NYJ-A 13

KING, HORACE Horace Edward, RB, 5´10˝/208 lbs; Georgia; 1975: Det, rnd 6; B3/5/1953 Athens, GA

1975	Det	14	61	260	4.3(26)	2	13	81	6.2(22)	0	1	0	0.0	0	0.0	0	0	1	1	—	k	—	12	348
1976	Det	7(7, FB)	93	325	3.5(22)	0	21	163	7.8(19)	0	—	—	—	—	—	—	—	—	—	k	—	0	425
1977	Det	14(13, FB)	155	521	3.4(35)	1	40	238	5.9(30)	0	—	—	—	—	—	—	—	—	—	p	—	6	650
1978	Det	15(15, FB)	155	660	4.3(75)	4	48	396	8.3(34)	2	0	0	0.0	0	0.0	0	0	1	2	—	k	—	36	908
1979	Det	16(4)	39	160	4.1(23)	1	18	150	8.3(30)	0	—	—	—	—	—	—	—	—	—	k	—	6	251
1980	Det	16(0)	18	57	3.2(8)	1	19	184	9.7(29)	1	—	—	—	—	—	—	—	—	—	k	—	12	164
1981	Det	16(0)	7	25	3.6(7)	0	21	217	10.3(41)	1	—	—	—	—	—	—	—	—	—	k	—	6	127
1982	†Det	9(1)	18	67	3.7(25)	0	9	74	8.2(14)	1	—	—	—	—	—	—	—	—	—	k	—	6	102
1983	†Det	16(1)	3	6	2.0(4)	0	9	76	8.4(14)	0	—	—	—	—	—	—	—	—	—	k	—	0	40
NFL	9	123(41)	549	2081	3.8(75)	9	198	1579	8.0(41)	5	1	0	0.0	0	0.0	0	0	2	3	—	kp	—	84	3014

KING, JEROME Jerome Manual, DB, 5´10˝/175 lbs; Purdue; B1/4/1955 Jersey City, NJ **1979** Atl 1 **1980** Atl 2 (0) **1980** NYG 1 (0) **NFL** 4 [2 yrs]

KING, JOE Joe D., DB, 6´2˝/195 lbs; Oklahoma State; B5/7/1968 Dallas, TX **1991** Cin 6 (0) **1991** Cle 7 (0) **1992** TB 14 (2) **1993** TB 15 (10, FS) **1995** Oak 16 (2)
NFL 58 (14) [4 yrs]

KING, KENNY Kenneth Leon, RB, 5´11˝/203 lbs; Oklahoma; 1979: Hou, rnd 3; B3/7/1957 Clarendon, TX

1979	Hou	12	3	9	3.0(4)	0	—	—	—	—	—	—	—	—	—	—	—	—	—	k	—	0	11
1980	†Oak★	15(13, RB)	172	761	4.4(89)	4	22	145	6.6(18)	0	—	—	—	—	—	—	—	—	—	—	—	24	874
1981	Oak	14(14, RB)	170	828	4.9(60)	0	27	216	8.0(30)	0	—	—	—	—	—	—	—	—	—	—	—	0	936
1982	†LARd	9(9, FB)	69	264	3.8(21)	2	9	57	6.3(20)	0	—	—	—	—	—	—	—	—	—	—	—	12	313
1983	†LARd	15(15, FB)	82	294	3.6(16)	1	14	149	10.6(34)	1	—	—	—	—	—	—	—	—	—	—	—	12	384
1984	†LARd	16(16, FB)	67	254	3.8(18)	0	14	99	7.1(15)	0	—	—	—	—	—	—	—	—	—	—	—	0	304
1985	†LARd	16(0)	16	67	4.2(19)	0	3	49	16.3(37)	0	—	—	—	—	—	—	—	—	—	—	—	0	92
NFL	7	97(67)	579	2477	4.3(89)	7	89	715	8.0(37)	1	—	—	—	—	—	—	—	—	—	—	—	48	2912

KING, KENNY Kenny, DE, 6´3˝/285 lbs; Alabama; 2003: Arz, rnd 5; B4/23/1981 Daphne, AL **2003** Arz 11 (1)

KING, LAMAR Lamar, DE, 6´3˝/305 lbs; Saginaw Valley State (MI); 1999: Sea, rnd 1; B8/10/1975 Boston, MA **1999**†Sea 14 (0) **2000** Sea 14 (14, RDE) **2001** Sea 8 (8, RDE)
2002 Sea 12 (12, LDE) **2003**†Sea 9 (3) **NFL** 57 (37) [5 yrs]

KING, LINDEN Linden Keith, LB, 6´4˝/241 lbs; Colorado State; 1977: SD, rnd 3; B6/28/1955 Memphis, TN **1978** SD 14 **1979**†SD 16 (1) **1980**†SD 5 (0) **1981**†SD 16 (16, LLB)
1982†SD 9 (7, LLB) **1983** SD 16 (16, LOLB) **1984** SD 16 (16, LOLB) **1985** SD 16 (16, LOLB) **1986** LARd 16 (0) **1987** LARd 12 (8, LOLB) **1988** LARd 14 (13, LOLB)
1989 LARd 14 (13, LOLB) **NFL** 164 (106) [12 yrs]

KING, PHIL Phillip Edgar, HB-FB, 6´4˝/223 lbs; Vanderbilt; 1958: NYG, rnd 1; B6/22/1936 Nashville, TN, D1/18/1973 Memphis, TN

1958	†NYG	12	83	316	3.8(38)	1	11	132	12.0(35)	0	—	—	—	—	—	—	—	—	—	k	—	6	476
1959	†NYG	12(rh)	72	232	3.2(24)	0	7	98	14.0(35)	1	—	—	—	—	—	—	—	—	—	k	—	6	310
1960	NYG	10	26	97	3.7(30)	0	3	6	2.0(4)	0	—	—	—	—	—	—	—	—	—	k	—	0	143
1961	†NYG	5	4	7	1.8(4)	0	—	—	—	—	—	—	—	—	—	—	—	—	—	—	—	0	7
1962	†NYG	14(LH)	108	460	4.3(20)	2	15	186	12.4(37)	0	—	—	—	—	—	—	—	—	—	k	—	12	580
1963	†NYG	14(LH)	161	613	3.8(50)	3	32	377	11.8(46)	5	—	—	—	—	—	—	—	—	—	k	—	48	857
1964	Pit	8	26	71	2.7(12)	1	4	32	8.0(13)	1	—	—	—	—	—	—	—	—	—	k	—	12	99
1965	Min	14	72	356	4.9(21)	0	12	96	8.0(25)	1	—	—	—	—	—	—	—	—	—	k	—	6	408
1966	Min	14	17	40	2.4(12)	0	2	24	12.0(18)	1	1	1	100.0	9	9.0(9)	0	0	0	0	—	k	—	6	50
NFL	9	103	569	2192	3.9(50)	7	86	951	11.1(46)	9	1	1	100.0	9	9.0(9)	0	0	0	0	—	k	—	96	2929

KING, RALPH Ralph Warren, G, 6´0˝/250 lbs; Chicago; B11/2/1901 Chicago, IL, D2/1978 Fairhope, AL **1924** Rac 9 (8, RG) **1925** ChiB 2 (2) **NFL** 11 (8) [2 yrs]

KING, RIP Andrew V., B, 6´1˝/202 lbs; West Virginia; B10/25/1895 Franklin, TN, D5/4/1950 Reno, NV [K] **1920** Akr☆11 (9, FB) **1921** Akr☆11 (10, FB), 15 **1922** Akr☆6 (5, FB), 21
1923 ChiC 11 (6, RH), 7 **1924** ChiC 2 (2) **1925** Ham 2 (0) **NFL** 43 (32), 43 [6 yrs]

KING, SHAUN Shaun Earl, QB, 6´1˝/215 lbs; Tulane; 1999: TB, rnd 2; B5/29/1977 St. Petersburg, FL

1999	†TB	6(5, qb)	18	38	2.1(8)	0	—	—	—	—	146	89	61.0	875	6.0(68)	7	4	11	78	—	—	—	0	351
2000	†TB	16(16, QB)	73	353	4.8(19)	5	—	—	—	—	428	233	54.4	2769	6.5(75)	18	13	37	240	75.8	—	—	32	1358
2001	TB	3(0)	5	-12	-2.4(0)	0	—	—	—	—	31	21	67.7	210	6.8(42)	0	1	3	29	—	—	—	2	53
2002	TB	3(1)	4	25	6.3(15)	0	—	—	—	—	27	10	37.0	80	3.0(20)	1	1	1	5	—	—	—	0	25
2003	TB	3(0)	4	20	5.0(12)	0	—	—	—	—	22	15	68.2	130	5.9(20)	1	1	3	25	—	—	—	0	50
2004	Arz	3(2)	9	30	3.3(16)	0	—	—	—	—	84	47	56.0	502	6.0(40)	1	4	6	42	—	—	—	0	126
NFL	6	34(24)	113	454	4.0(19)	5	—	—	—	—	738	415	56.2	4566	6.2(75)	27	24	61	419	73.4	—	—	34	1962

KING, SHAWN Shawn Keldric, DE, 6´3˝/278 lbs; LSU; Louisiana-Monroe; 1995: Car, rnd 2; B6/24/1972 West Monroe, LA **1995** Car 13 (0) **1996** Car 16 (0) **1997** Car 9 (2)
1999 Ind 9 (8, LDE) **NFL** 47 (10) [4 yrs]

KING, STEVE George Stephen, LB, 6´4˝/232 lbs; Tulsa; B6/10/1951 McAlester, OK **1973** NE 7 **1974** NE 14 (14, ROLB) **1975** NE 14 (8, rolb) **1976**†NE 11 (7, ROLB)
1977 NE 14 (4) **1978**†NE 16 (5, lolb) **1979** NE 16 (1) **1980** NE 16 (0) **1981** NE 16 (1) **NFL** 124 (40) [9 yrs]

KING, TIM Timothy, DB, 6´2˝/190 lbs; Delaware State; B3/7/1960 New York, NY **1987** TB 3 (2)

KING, TONY Tony Emanuel, DB, 6´1˝/197 lbs; Findlay; 1966: Buf, rnd R3; B5/6/1944 Canton, OH **1967** Buf-A 7

KING, VICK Vick Lee, RB, 5´10˝/215 lbs; Southern (LA); McNeese State; B2/4/1980 Houma, LA

| 2004 | Mia | 2(0) | 4 | 9 | 2.3(3) | 0 | — | — | — | — | — | — | — | — | — | — | — | — | — | — | — | 0 | 13 |

KINGERY, ELLSWORTH Ellsworth Lee, DB, 5´11˝/180 lbs; Tulane; B8/6/1929 Lake Charles, LA **1954** ChiC 9

KINGERY, WAYNE B. Wayne, HB-DB, 5´11˝/175 lbs; LSU; McNeese State; B6/5/1927 Lake Charles, LA

| 1949 | Bal-A | 9(0) | 3 | 3 | 1.0 | 0 | 1 | -2 | -2.0(-2) | 0 | — | — | — | — | — | — | — | — | — | Ppi | — | 0 | 6 |

KINGREA, RICK Richard Owen, LB, 6´1˝/233 lbs; Tulane; 1971: Cle, rnd 14; B7/18/1949 Pearlsburg, VA **1971**†Cle 14 **1972**†Cle 7 **1973** Buf 4 **1973** NO 9 **1974** NO 14
1975 NO 14 (2) **1976** NO 14 **1977** NO 1 **NFL** 91 (2) [8 yrs]

KINGSBURY, KLIFF Kliff, QB, 6´4˝/231 lbs; Texas Tech; 2003: NE, rnd 6; B8/9/1979 San Antonio, TX

| 2005 | NYJ | 1(0) | — | — | — | — | — | — | — | — | 2 | 1 | 50.0 | 17 | 8.5(17) | 0 | 0 | — | — | — | — | — | 0 | 9 |

YEAR	TEAM	G (GS, POS)	RUSH	YD	AVG(LG)	TD	REC	YD	AVG(LG)	TD	PASS	COMP	PCT	YD	AVG(LG)	TD	INT	SK	YD	QBR	KPR	OTD	PTS	TAY

KINGSRITER, DOUG Douglas James, TE, 6′2″/222 lbs; Minnesota; 1973: Min, rnd 6; B1/29/1950 Little Falls, MN

YEAR	TEAM	G (GS, POS)	RUSH	YD	AVG(LG)	TD	REC	YD	AVG(LG)	TD	KPR	OTD	PTS	TAY
1973	†Min	11	—	—	—	—	2	27	13.5(14)	0		—	0	14
1974	†Min	14	—	—	—	—	5	89	17.8(21)	0		—	0	45
1975	Min	3										—		
NFL	3	28	—	—	—	—	7	116	16.6(21)	0		—	0	58

KINLAW, REGGIE Reginald, NT, 6′2″/245 lbs; Oklahoma; 1979: Oak, rnd 12; B1/9/1957 Miami, FL   **1979** Oak 16 (2) **1980**†Oak☆14 (13, NT) **1981** Oak 1 (0) **1982**†LARd 8 (8, NT) **1983**†LARd 16 (16, NT) **1984**†LARd 13 (13, NT) **1985** Sea 16 (0) **1986** Sea 14 (5, nt) **NFL** 98 (57) [8 yrs]

KINNEBREW, LARRY Lawrence D., RB, 6′1″/255 lbs; Tennessee State; 1983: Cin, rnd 6; B6/11/1959 Rome, GA

YEAR	TEAM	G (GS, POS)	RUSH	YD	AVG(LG)	TD	REC	YD	AVG(LG)	TD	KPR	OTD	PTS	TAY
1983	Cin	16(0)	39	156	4.0(17)	3	2	4	2.0(2)	0		—	18	188
1984	Cin	16(4, fb)	154	623	4.0(23)	9	19	159	8.4(22)	1	k	—	60	790
1985	Cin	12(11, FB)	170	714	4.2(29)	9	22	187	8.5(29)	1		—	60	903
1986	Cin	16(9, FB)	131	519	4.0(39)	8	13	136	10.5(31)	1		—	54	672
1987	Cin	11(8, FB)	145	570	3.9(52)	8	9	114	12.7(25)	1		—	48	707
1989	†Buf	15(10, FB)	131	533	4.1(25)	6	5	60	12.0(18)	1		—	36	623
1990	Buf	2(0)	9	18	2.0(4)	1						—	6	28
NFL	7	88(42)	779	3133	4.0(52)	44	70	660	9.4(31)	3	k	—	282	3910

KINNEY, ERRON Erron Quincy, TE, 6′5″/275 lbs; Florida; 2000: Ten, rnd 3; B7/28/1977 Richmond, VA

YEAR	TEAM	G (GS, POS)	RUSH	YD	AVG(LG)	TD	REC	YD	AVG(LG)	TD	KPR	OTD	PTS	TAY
2000	†Ten	16(10, TE)	—	—	—	—	19	197	10.4(19)	1		—	6	104
2001	Ten	13(12, TE)	—	—	—	—	25	263	10.5(24)	1	k	—	6	136
2002	†Ten	15(7, TE)	—	—	—	—	13	173	13.3(31)	0	k	—	0	83
2003	†Ten	16(16, TE)	—	—	—	—	41	381	9.3(28)	3	k	1	24	198
2004	Ten	9(9, TE)	—	—	—	—	25	193	7.7(21)	2	k	—	18	118
2005	Ten	14(14, TE)	—	—	—	—	55	543	9.9(27)	2		—	12	282
NFL	6	83(68)	—	—	—	—	178	1750	9.8(31)	10	k	1	66	918

KINNEY, GEORGE George Raynard, DE, 6′4″/250 lbs; Wiley; 1965: Hou, rnd 9; B11/13/1942 Jackson, MS   **1965** Hou-A 1

KINNEY, JEFF Jeffrey Bruce, RB, 6′2″/215 lbs; Nebraska; 1972: KC, rnd 1; B11/1/1949 Oxford, NE

YEAR	TEAM	G (GS, POS)	RUSH	YD	AVG(LG)	TD	REC	YD	AVG(LG)	TD	KPR	OTD	PTS	TAY
1972	KC	9	38	122	3.2(16)	1	4	45	11.3(19)	0	k	—	6	158
1973	KC	14	50	128	2.6(8)	1	11	126	11.5(25)	0	k	—	6	256
1974	KC	13	63	249	4.0(21)	0	18	105	5.8(16)	1		—	6	307
1975	KC	13(2)	85	304	3.6(20)	2	21	148	7.0(18)	0	k	—	12	407
1976	KC	1	1	7	7.0(7)	0						—	0	7
1976	Buf	12(7, FB)	116	475	4.1(22)	1	14	78	5.6(15)	0		—	6	524
NFL	5	62(9)	353	1285	3.6(22)	5	68	502	7.4(25)	1	k	—	36	1658

KINNEY, KELVIN Kelvin Lamonta, DE, 6′6″/264 lbs; Virginia State; 1996: Was, rnd 6; B12/31/1972 Montgomery, WV   **1997** Was 4 (1) **1998** Was 14 (12, RDE) **NFL** 18 (13) [2 yrs]

KINNEY, STEVE Steven Arthur, T, 6′5″/255 lbs; Utah State; B6/27/1949 San Jose, CA   **1973** ChiB 2 **1974** ChiB 10 **NFL** 12 [2 yrs]

KINNEY, VINCE Vincent Marc, WR, 6′2″/190 lbs; Maryland; 1978: Den, rnd 10; B3/17/1956 Baltimore, MD   **1979**†Den 15

YEAR	TEAM	G (GS, POS)	RUSH	YD	AVG(LG)	TD	REC	YD	AVG(LG)	TD	KPR	OTD	PTS	TAY
1978	†Den	8	—	—	—	—	1	23	23.0(23)	0		—	0	12
NFL	2	23	—	—	—	—	1	23	23.0(23)	0	k	—	0	11

KINSCHERF, CARL Carl Raymond, FB, 6′1″/188 lbs; Colgate; B10/20/1919 Brooklyn, NY

YEAR	TEAM	G (GS, POS)	RUSH	YD	AVG(LG)	TD	REC	YD	AVG(LG)	TD	KPR	OTD	PTS	TAY
1943	NYG	8(2)	49	77	1.6(10)	1	2	4	2.0(2)	0	Pk	—	6	116
1944	†NYG	7(0)	9	21	2.3(4)	0	1	9	9.0(9)	0	i	—	0	24
NFL	2	15(2)	58	98	1.7(10)	1	3	13	4.3(9)	0	Pki	—	6	140

KINZER, MATT Matthew Roy, P, 6′3″/225 lbs; Purdue; B6/17/1963 Indianapolis, IN   **1987** Det 1 (0)

KIRBY, CHARLES Charles Edward, FB, 6′1″/249 lbs; Virginia; B11/27/1974 South View, NC   **2000** TB 6 (2)

KIRBY, JACK Jack Evans, HB-DB, 5′11″/185 lbs; USC; B9/21/1922 Los Angeles, CA

YEAR	TEAM	G (GS, POS)	RUSH	YD	AVG(LG)	TD	KPR	OTD	PTS	TAY
1949	GB	6(0)	3	6	2.0(8)	0	kp		0	119

KIRBY, JOHN John Patrick, LB, 6′3″/230 lbs; Nebraska; 1964: Min, rnd 5/SD, rnd 2; B5/30/1942 David City, NE   **1964** Min 14 **1965** Min 14 **1966** Min 10 (9, RLB) **1967** Min 14 (14, RLB) **1968**†Min 14 (7, RLB) **1969** Min 2 **1969** NYG 12 **1970** NYG 14 **NFL** 94 (30) [7 yrs]

KIRBY, TERRY Terry Gayle, RB, 6′1″/221 lbs; Virginia; 1993: Mia, rnd 3; B1/20/1970 Hampton, VA [R]

YEAR	TEAM	G (GS, POS)	RUSH	YD	AVG(LG)	TD	REC	YD	AVG(LG)	TD	PASS	COMP	PCT	YD	AVG(LG)	TD	INT	KPR	OTD	PTS	TAY
1993	Mia	16(8, rb)	119	390	3.3(20)	3	75	874	11.7(47)	3								k	—	36	897
1994	Mia	4(4)	60	233	3.9(30)	2	14	154	11.0(26)	0									—	14	330
1995	†Mia	16(4)	108	414	3.8(38)	4	66	618	9.4(46)	3	1	1	100.0	31	31.0(31)	1	0		—	42	799
1996	†SF	14(10, RB)	134	559	4.2(31)	3	52	439	8.4(52)	1	2	1	50.0	24	12.0(24)	1	0	kp	—	24	836
1997	†SF	16(3)	125	418	3.3(38)	6	23	279	12.1(82)	1								k	1	52	712
1998	†SF	9(0)	48	258	5.4(31)	3	16	134	8.4(25)	0	1	1	100.0	28	28.0(28)	1	0		—	18	459
1999	Cle	16(10, RB)	130	452	3.5(28)	6	58	528	9.1(78)	3	1	1	100.0	2	2.0(2)	0	0	k	—	54	857
2000	†Oak	2(0)	11	51	4.6(28)	0	3	19	6.3(9)	0									—	0	61
2001	†Oak	11(0)	10	49	4.9(20)	0	9	62	6.9(9)	0								k	1	6	466
2002	Oak	6(0)	16	51	3.2(13)	0	17	115	6.8(24)	1	1	1	0.0	0	0.0(0)	0	0	k	2	18	353
NFL	10	110(39)	761	2875	3.8(38)	27	333	3222	9.7(82)	12	6	4	66.7	85	14.2(31)	3	0	kp	4	264	5768

KIRCHBAUM, KELLY Kelly, LB, 6′2″/240 lbs; Kentucky; 1979: NYJ, rnd 5; B6/14/1957 Fort Knox, KY   **1980** KC 1 (0) **1987** Phi 3 (0) **NFL** 4 (0) [2 yrs]

KIRCHIRO, BILL William John, G, 6′1″/235 lbs; Maryland; 1962: SL, rnd 7; B6/29/1940 Bernardsville, NJ   **1962** Bal 8

KIRCHNER, MARK Mark Steven, G-T, 6′3″/261 lbs; Baylor; 1983: Pit, rnd 7; B10/19/1959 Pasadena, TX   **1983** Pit 3 (0) **1983** KC 5 (1) **1984** Ind 11 (1) **1986** Ind 13 (5, lg) **NFL** 32 (7) [3 yrs]

KIRCUS, DAVID David, WR, 6′1″/185 lbs; Grand Valley State; 2003: Det, rnd 6; B2/19/1980 Mount Clemens, MI

YEAR	TEAM	G (GS, POS)	RUSH	YD	AVG(LG)	TD	REC	YD	AVG(LG)	TD	KPR	OTD	PTS	TAY
2003	Det	5(2)	—	—	—	—	3	53	17.7(19)	0		—	0	27
2004	Det	7(0)	—	—	—	—	3	68	22.7(50)	1		—	6	39
NFL	2	12(2)	—	—	—	—	6	121	20.2(50)	1		—	6	66

KIRK, ERNEST Ernest, DE, 6′2″/265 lbs; Howard Payne; B4/14/1952 Marlin, TX   **1977** Hou 14

KIRK, GEORGE George Asa, C, 6′0″/205 lbs; Baylor; B9/21/1901 Ballinger, TX, D3/20/1996 Austin, TX   **1926** Buf 7 (7, C)

KIRK, KEN Kenneth Henry, LB, 6′2″/230 lbs; Mississippi; 1960: Chi, rnd 9/Buf, rnd 1; B2/26/1938 Tupelo, MS   **1960** ChiB 12 **1961** ChiB 10 **1962** Pit 14 **1963** LARm 8 **NFL** 44 [4 yrs]

KIRK, RANDY Randall Scott, LB, 6′2″/232 lbs; San Diego State; B12/27/1964 San Jose, CA   **1987** SD 13 (1) **1988** SD 16 (0) **1989** Phx 6 (0) **1990** Was 1 (0) **1991** Cle 2 (0) **1991** SD 5 (0) **1992** Cin 15 (0) **1993** Cin 16 (0) **1994** Arz 16 (0) **1995** Arz 16 (0) **1996**†SF 16 (0) **1997**†SF 16 (0) **1998**†SF 3 (0) **NFL** 157 (1) [13 yrs]

KIRKGARD, HEINIE Henry Gotlieb, HB, /165 lbs; Trinity (TX); Centre; SMU; B9/2/1898 Danevang, TX, D2/26/1967 Dallas, TX   **1923** Tol 5 (3)

KIRKLAND, BO B'Ho, G, 6′0″/215 lbs; Alabama; B4/9/1912 Columbia, GA   **1935** Bkn 11 (9, RG) **1936** Bkn 12 (8, LG) **NFL** 23 (17) [2 yrs]

KIRKLAND, LEVON Lorenzo Levon, LB, 6′1″/250 lbs; Clemson; 1992: Pit, rnd 2; B2/17/1969 Lamar, SC   **1992**†Pit 16 (0) **1993**†Pit 16 (13, LILB) **1994**†Pit 16 (15, LILB) **1995**†Pit 16 (16, LILB) **1996**†Pit★16 (16, LILB) **1997**†Pit★16 (16, LILB) **1998** Pit 16 (16, LILB) **1999** Pit 16 (16, LILB) **2000** Pit 16 (16, LILB) **2001** Sea 16 (16, MLB) **2002**†Phi 16 (15, MLB) **NFL** 176 (155) [11 yrs]

KIRKLAND, MIKE Michael Albert, QB, 6′1″/195 lbs; Arkansas; 1976: Bal, rnd 5; B6/29/1954 Pasadena, TX

YEAR	TEAM	G (GS, POS)	RUSH	YD	AVG(LG)	TD	REC	PASS	COMP	PCT	YD	AVG(LG)	TD	INT	SK	YD	OTD	PTS	TAY
1978	Bal	16(2)	8	35	4.4(18)	0	—	41	19	46.3	211	5.1(34)	1	8	11	78	—	0	-175

KIRKLESKI, FRANK Frank William, B, 5′10″/179 lbs; Lafayette; B5/19/1904 Nutley, NJ, D5/6/1980 Chatham, NJ   **1927** Pot 12 (9, TB), 12 **1929** Ora 12 (9, TB), 12 **1930** Nwk 12 (7, TB), 6 **1931** Bkn 3 (0) **NFL** 39 (25), 30 [4 yrs]

KIRKMAN, RED Roger Randolph, B, 6´1˝/195 lbs; Case Western Reserve; Washington & Jefferson; B10/17/1905 Woodland, WV, D11/30/1973 Columbus, OH **[K]**

YEAR	TEAM	G (GS, POS)	RUSH	YD	AVG (LG)	TD	REC	YD	AVG (LG)	TD	PASS	COMP	PCT	YD	AVG (LG)	TD	INT	SK	YD	QBR	KPR	OTD	PTS	TAY
1933	Phi	9 (8, BB)	22	43	2.0	0	4	84	21.0	1	73	22	30.1	354	4.8	2	13	—	—	—	K	—	8	-243
1934	Phi	10 (7, BB)	6	12	2.0	0	8	114	14.3 (54)	1	23	7	30.4	38	1.7	1	2	—	—	—	K	—	11	18
1935	Phi	1 (1)	—	—	—	—	—	—	—	—	1	1	100.0	1	1.0 (1)	1	0	—	—	—	K	—	1	6
NFL	3	20 (16)	28	55	2.0	0	12	198	16.5 (54)	2	97	30	30.9	393	4.1 (1)	4	15	—	—	—	K	—	20	-220

KIRKSEY, JON Jonathan O'Neal, DT, 6´4˝/350 lbs; Sacramento State; 1993: NO, rnd 8; B2/21/1970 Greenville, SC **1996** SL 11 (1)

KIRKSEY, ROY Roy Lewis, G, 6´1˝/235 lbs; Maryland-Eastern Shore; 1971: NYJ, rnd 8; B9/18/1947 Greenville, SC, D9/5/1981, SC **1971** NYJ 4 **1972** NYJ 10 **1973** Phi 7 **1974** Phi 13 **NFL** 34 [4 yrs]

KIRKSEY, WILLIAM William W., LB, 6´2˝/221 lbs; Southern Mississippi; B1/29/1966 Birmingham, AL **1990** Min 9 (0)

KIRNER, GARY Gary Burgess, G-T, 6´3˝/255 lbs; USC; 1964: SD, rnd 5; B6/22/1942 Los Angeles, CA **1964**†SD-A 14 **1965**†SD-A 14 **1966** SD-A 14 **1967** SD-A 14 (LG) **1968** SD-A 14 (LG) **1969** SD-A 7 **NFL** 77 [6 yrs]

KIROUAC, LOU Louis, G-T-K, 6´3˝/248 lbs; Boston College; B5/17/1940 Manchester, NH **[K]** **1963**†NYG 14 **1964**†Bal 14 **1966** Atl 14 **1967** Atl 8 (LG) **NFL** 50 [4 yrs]

KIRSCHKE, TRAVIS Travis, DT-DE, 6´3˝/292 lbs; UCLA; B9/6/1974 Fullerton, CA **1997**†Det 3 (0) **1999**†Det 15 (7, rde) **2000** Det 13 (0) **2001** Det 16 (2) **2002** Det 15 (1) **2003** SF 15 (15, RDT) **2004**†Pit 16 (1) **2005**†Pit 16 (0) **NFL** 109 (26) [8 yrs]

KISELAK, MIKE Michael John, C-G, 6´3˝/295 lbs; Maryland; B3/9/1967 North Tarrytown, NY **1998**†Dal 15 (7, c)

KISER, PAUL Paul David, G, 6´4˝/272 lbs; Wake Forest; 1987: Atl, rnd 6; B11/19/1963 Valdese, NC **1987** Det 1 (0)

KISH, BEN Benjamin Ernest, B, 6´0˝/207 lbs; Pittsburgh; 1940: ChiC, rnd 8; B3/31/1917 Tonawanda, NY, D2/24/1989 Philadelphia, PA **[K]**

YEAR	TEAM	G (GS, POS)	RUSH	YD	AVG (LG)	TD	REC	YD	AVG (LG)	TD	PASS	COMP	PCT	YD	AVG (LG)	TD	INT	SK	YD	QBR	KPR	OTD	PTS	TAY
1940	Bkn	11 (3)	—	—	—	—	9	124	13.8	0	—	—	—	—	—	—	—	—	—	—	Pi	—	0	52
1941	Bkn	5 (0)	—	—	—	—	4	50	12.5 (27)	0	—	—	—	—	—	—	—	—	—	—	Pi	—	0	29
1943	P-P	10 (9, FB)	22	50	2.3 (11)	0	8	67	8.4 (17)	1	—	—	—	—	—	—	—	—	—	—	Pi	1	12	188
1944	Phi	10 (10, FB)	22	96	4.4 (20)	0	5	73	14.6 (45)	1	—	—	—	—	—	—	—	—	—	—	KPki	—	7	176
1945	Phi	9 (5, FB)	9	82	9.1 (22)	0	8	78	9.8 (18)	0	—	—	—	—	—	—	—	—	—	—	i	—	0	116
1946	Phi	10 (2)	6	13	2.2 (4)	0	3	16	5.3 (7)	0	—	—	—	—	—	—	—	—	—	—	Pi	—	0	29
1947	†Phi	12 (8, fb)	3	-1	-0.3 (1)	0	1	12	12.0 (12)	0	—	—	—	—	—	—	—	—	—	—	Pki	—	0	32
1948	Phi	9 (0)	10	106	10.6 (66)	1	—	—	—	—	—	—	—	—	—	—	—	—	—	—	pi	—	6	128
1949	†Phi	7 (0)	2	-2	-1.0 (0)	0	—	—	—	—	—	—	—	—	—	—	—	—	—	—	—	—	0	-2
NFL	9	83 (37)	74	344	4.6 (66)	1	38	420	11.1 (45)	2	—	—	—	—	—	—	—	—	—	—	KPkpi	1	25	747

KISIDAY, GEORGE George John, E, 5´11˝/210 lbs; Duquesne; Columbia; 1948: NYG, rnd 22; B4/16/1923 Ambridge, PA, D11/9/1970

YEAR	TEAM	G (GS, POS)	RUSH	YD	AVG (LG)	TD	REC	YD	AVG (LG)	TD	PASS	COMP	PCT	YD	AVG (LG)	TD	INT	SK	YD	QBR	KPR	OTD	PTS	TAY
1948	†Buf-A	14 (0)	—	—	—	—	1	20	20.0 (20)	0	—	—	—	—	—	—	—	—	—	—	—	—	0	10

KISSELL, ADOLPH Adolph J., HB, 5´11˝/190 lbs; Boston College; 1942: ChiB, rnd 21; B9/11/1920 Nashua, NH, D8/7/1983 Wareham, MA

YEAR	TEAM	G (GS, POS)	RUSH	YD	AVG (LG)	TD	REC	YD	AVG (LG)	TD	PASS	COMP	PCT	YD	AVG (LG)	TD	INT	SK	YD	QBR	KPR	OTD	PTS	TAY
1942	ChiB	4 (0)	2	-1	-0.5 (11)	0	—	—	—	—	—	—	—	—	—	—	—	—	—	—	k	—	0	32

KISSELL, ED Edward John Julius, DB, 6´1˝/193 lbs; Wake Forest; 1952: Pit, rnd 30; B9/29/1929 Nashua, NH **[K]** **1952** Pit 6 (ss) **1954** Pit 7 **NFL** 13 [2 yrs]

KISSELL, JOHN John Jay, DT-T, 6´3˝/245 lbs; Boston College; 1947: LA, rnd 14; B5/14/1923 Nashua, NH, D4/9/1992 Nashua, NH **1948**†Buf-A 14 (1) **1949**†Buf-A☆12 (0) **AAFC** 26 (1) [2 yrs]

1950†Cle 12 (RDT) **1951**†Cle☆12 (RDT) **1952** Cle 12 **1954**†Cle 12 (LDT) **1955**†Cle 12 (LDT) **1956** Cle 12 (LDT) **NFL** 72 [6 yrs]

KISSELL, VITO Vito Joseph, LB-FB, 5´10˝/205 lbs; Holy Cross; 1949: Buf-A, rnd 3/Pit, rnd 17; B6/13/1927 Nashua, NH **[K]**

YEAR	TEAM	G (GS, POS)	RUSH	YD	AVG (LG)	TD	REC	YD	AVG (LG)	TD	PASS	COMP	PCT	YD	AVG (LG)	TD	INT	SK	YD	QBR	KPR	OTD	PTS	TAY
1949	†Buf-A	9 (0)	10	19	1.9	0	3	37	12.3	0	—	—	—	—	—	—	—	—	—	—	ki	—	0	33
1950	Bal	11 (RLB)	2	6	3.0 (7)	0	—	—	—	—	—	—	—	—	—	—	—	—	—	—	Kki	—	11	-8

KITNA, JON Jon, QB, 6´2˝/220 lbs; Central Washington; B9/21/1972 Tacoma, WA

YEAR	TEAM	G (GS, POS)	RUSH	YD	AVG (LG)	TD	REC	YD	AVG (LG)	TD	PASS	COMP	PCT	YD	AVG (LG)	TD	INT	SK	YD	QBR	KPR	OTD	PTS	TAY
1997	Sea	3 (1)	10	9	0.9 (8)	1	—	—	—	—	45	31	68.9	371	8.2 (61)	1	2	3	10	—	—	—	6	130
1998	Sea	6 (5, qb)	20	67	3.3 (21)	1	—	—	—	—	172	98	57.0	1177	6.8 (70)	7	8	11	72	—	—	—	6	381
1999	†Sea	15 (15, QB)	35	56	1.6 (10)	0	—	—	—	—	495	270	54.5	3346	6.8 (51)	23	16	32	198	77.7	—	—	0	1204
2000	Sea	15 (12, QB)	48	127	2.6 (13)	1	—	—	—	—	418	259	62.0	2658	6.4 (71)	18	19	33	166	75.6	—	—	6	796
2001	Cin	16 (15, QB)	27	73	2.7 (20)	1	—	—	—	—	**581**	313	53.9	3216	5.5 (49)	12	22	25	185	61.1	—	—	6	871
2002	Cin	14 (12, QB)	24	57	2.4 (12)	4	—	—	—	—	473	294	62.2	3178	6.7 (72)	16	16	24	159	79.1	—	—	24	1126
2003	Cin	16 (16, QB)	38	113	3.0 (15)	0	—	—	—	—	520	324	62.3	3591	6.9 (82)	26	15	37	249	87.4	—	—	0	1439
2004	Cin	4 (3)	10	42	4.2 (15)	0	—	—	—	—	104	61	58.7	623	6.0 (30)	5	4	6	41	75.9	—	—	0	219
2005	†Cin	3 (0)	2	14	7.0 (11)	0	—	—	—	—	29	17	58.6	99	3.4 (16)	0	2	2	10	—	—	—	0	-17
NFL	9	92 (79)	214	558	2.6 (21)	8	—	—	—	—	2837	1667	58.8	18259	6.4 (82)	108	104	173	1090	75.3	—	—	48	6148

KITSON, SYD Sydney William, G-T, 6´4˝/258 lbs; Wake Forest; 1980: GB, rnd 3; B9/27/1958 Orange, NJ **1980** GB 14 (0) **1981** GB 11 (0) **1984** GB 8 (3) **1984** Dal 1 (0)

YEAR	TEAM	G (GS, POS)	RUSH	YD	AVG (LG)	TD	REC	YD	AVG (LG)	TD	PASS	COMP	PCT	YD	AVG (LG)	TD	INT	SK	YD	QBR	KPR	OTD	PTS	TAY
1983	GB	16 (9, RG)	—	—	—	—	1	9	9.0 (9)	0	—	—	—	—	—	—	—	—	—	—	k	—	0	-11
NFL	4	50 (12)	—	—	—	—	1	9	9.0 (9)	0	—	—	—	—	—	—	—	—	—	—	—	—	0	5

KITTNER, KURT Kurt, QB, 6´2˝/221 lbs; Illinois; 2002: Atl, rnd 5; B1/23/1980 Schaumburg, IL

YEAR	TEAM	G (GS, POS)	RUSH	YD	AVG (LG)	TD	REC	YD	AVG (LG)	TD	PASS	COMP	PCT	YD	AVG (LG)	TD	INT	SK	YD	QBR	KPR	OTD	PTS	TAY
2003	Atl	7 (4)	8	13	1.6 (7)	0	—	—	—	—	114	44	38.6	391	3.4 (31)	2	6	5	30	32.5	—	—	0	-22

KITTREDGE, PAUL Paul John, B, 5´10˝/170 lbs; Holy Cross; B10/9/1904 Clinton, MA, D3/2/1947 Groton, CT **1929** Bos 7 (1), 12

KITTS, JIM James Matthew, RB, 6´2˝/248 lbs; Ferrum; B12/28/1972 Portsmouth, VA **1997**†Mia 10 (0) **1998** Was 3 (0) **1998**†GB 2 (0) **NFL** 15 (0) [2 yrs]

KITZMILLER, DUTCH John Wesley, FB, 5´11˝/170 lbs; Oregon; B11/25/1904 Harrisburg, PA, D4/2/1986 Dallas, OR **[K]** **1931** NYG☆14 (4), 27

KIZZIRE, LEE William Lee, FB, 6´0˝/200 lbs; Wyoming; B1915, WV, D12/5/1943 New Guinea

YEAR	TEAM	G (GS, POS)	RUSH	YD	AVG (LG)	TD	REC	YD	AVG (LG)	TD	PASS	COMP	PCT	YD	AVG (LG)	TD	INT	SK	YD	QBR	KPR	OTD	PTS	TAY
1937	Det	7 (0)	7	20	2.9	0	—	—	—	—	—	—	—	—	—	—	—	—	—	—	—	—	0	20

KLAPSTEIN, EARL Earl Loren, T, 6´0˝/220 lbs; Pacific; 1944: Phi, rnd 24; B3/8/1922 Lodi, CA, D4/28/1997 Lodi, CA **1946** Pit 9 (0)

KLASNIC, JOHN John, WB-DB, 6´0˝/185 lbs; Auburn; B2/23/1927 Port View, PA **1948** Bkn-A 1 (0)

KLAUS, FEE Feryl J., C, 5´9˝/190 lbs; none; B9/26/1902 Green Bay, WI, D2/14/1951 Green Bay, WI **1921** GB 4 (2)

KLAWITTER, DICK Richard Dominic, C, 6´7˝/270 lbs; South Dakota State; 1956: ChiB, rnd 8; B6/29/1929 Chicago, IL, D12/11/1977 Waterloo, IA **1956** ChiB 5

KLECKO, DAN Dan, DT, 5´11˝/283 lbs; Temple; 2003: NE, rnd 4; B1/12/1981 Colts Neck, NJ

YEAR	TEAM	G (GS, POS)	RUSH	YD	AVG (LG)	TD	REC	YD	AVG (LG)	TD	PASS	COMP	PCT	YD	AVG (LG)	TD	INT	SK	YD	QBR	KPR	OTD	PTS	TAY
2003	†NE	13 (1)	2	5	2.5 (5)	0	—	—	—	—	—	—	—	—	—	—	—	—	—	—	kS	—	0	-5
2004	NE	6 (2)	—	—	—	—	3	18	6.0 (11)	0	—	—	—	—	—	—	—	—	—	—	—	—	0	9
2005	NE	11 (0)	—	—	—	—	—	—	—	—	—	—	—	—	—	—	—	—	—	—	S	—	0	0
NFL	3	30 (3)	2	5	2.5 (5)	0	3	18	6.0 (11)	0	—	—	—	—	—	—	—	—	—	—	kS	—	0	4

KLECKO, JOE Joseph Edward, DT-NT-DE, 6´3˝/263 lbs; Temple; 1977: NYJ, rnd 6; B10/15/1953 Chester, PA **1977** NYJ 13 (6, ldt) **1978** NYJ☆16 (16, RDE) **1979** NYJ☆16 (16, RDT) **1980** NYJ 15 (15, RDE) **1981**†NYJ★16 (16, RDE) **1982**†NYJ 2 (0) **1983** NYJ★16 (16, LDT) **1984** NYJ✧12 (11, ldt) **1985**†NYJ★16 (16, NT) **1986** NYJ☆11 (10, NT) **1987** NYJ 7 (7, NT) **1988** Ind 15 (14, NT) **NFL** 155 (143) [12 yrs]

KLEIN, BOB Robert Owen, TE, 6´5˝/235 lbs; USC; 1969: LA, rnd 1; B7/27/1947 South Gate, CA

YEAR	TEAM	G (GS, POS)	RUSH	YD	AVG (LG)	TD	REC	YD	AVG (LG)	TD	PASS	COMP	PCT	YD	AVG (LG)	TD	INT	SK	YD	QBR	KPR	OTD	PTS	TAY
1969	†LARm	14 (1)	—	—	—	—	2	17	8.5 (16)	1	—	—	—	—	—	—	—	—	—	—	k	—	6	-2
1970	LARm	7	—	—	—	—	2	20	10.0 (12)	0	—	—	—	—	—	—	—	—	—	—	—	—	0	10
1971	LARm	14 (14, TE)	3	21	7.0 (13)	0	14	160	11.4 (33)	4	—	—	—	—	—	—	—	—	—	—	—	—	24	121
1972	LARm	14 (13, TE)	1	-7	-7.0 (-7)	0	29	330	11.4 (26)	1	—	—	—	—	—	—	—	—	—	—	—	—	6	163
1973	†LARm	14 (14, TE)	—	—	—	—	21	277	13.2 (23)	2	—	—	—	—	—	—	—	—	—	—	k	—	12	134
1974	†LARm	14 (14, TE)	—	—	—	—	24	336	14.0 (32)	4	—	—	—	—	—	—	—	—	—	—	—	—	24	188
1975	LARm	11 (11, TE)	—	—	—	—	16	237	14.8 (44)	2	—	—	—	—	—	—	—	—	—	—	—	—	12	129
1976	†LARm	14 (14, TE)	—	—	—	—	20	229	11.4 (26)	1	—	—	—	—	—	—	—	—	—	—	—	—	6	120
1977	SD	12 (9, TE)	—	—	—	—	20	244	12.2 (41)	1	—	—	—	—	—	—	—	—	—	—	—	—	6	127
1978	SD	16 (16, TE)	—	—	—	—	34	413	12.1 (24)	2	—	—	—	—	—	—	—	—	—	—	k	—	12	215

YEAR	TEAM	G(GS, POS)	RUSH	YD	AVG(LG)	TD	REC	YD	AVG(LG)	TD	PASS	COMP	PCT	YD	AVG(LG)	TD	INT	SK	YD	QBR	KPR	OTD	PTS	TAY
1979	†SD	15(14, TE)	—	—	—	—	37	424	11.5(54)	5	—	—	—	—	—	—	—	—	—	—	—	—	30	237
NFL	11	145(120)	4	14	3.5(13)	0	219	2687	12.3(54)	23	—	—	—	—	—	—	—	—	—	—	k	—	138	1441
KLEIN, DICK Richard James, T-DT, 6´4˝/254 lbs; Georgia; Iowa; 1955: ChiB, rnd 29; B2/11/1934 Pana, IL **1958** ChiB 12 (2) **1959** ChiB 12 (RT) **1960** Dal 7 (4) **1961** Pit 2 **1961** Bos-A 10 (LDT) **1962** Bos-A✧14 **1963** Oak-A 14 (RT) **1964** Oak-A 14 (RT) **NFL** 85 (6) [7 yrs]																								
KLEIN, PERRY Perry Sandor, QB, 6´2˝/218 lbs; California; C.W. Post; 1994: Atl, rnd 4; B3/25/1971 Santa Monica, CA																								
1994	Atl	2(0)	—	—	—	—	—	—	—	—	1	0	0.0	0	0.0	0	0	2	9	—	—	—	0	0
KLEINSASSER, JIM Jim, TE-FB, 6´3˝/272 lbs; North Dakota; 1999: Min, rnd 2; B1/31/1977 Carrington, ND																								
1999	†Min	13(7, fb)	—	—	—	—	6	13	2.2(11)	0	—	—	—	—	—	—	—	—	—	—	k	—	0	-9
2000	†Min	14(8, FB)	12	43	3.6(7)	0	10	98	9.8(21)	0	—	—	—	—	—	—	—	—	—	—	—	—	0	92
2001	Min	11(11, FB)	23	72	3.1(11)	1	24	184	7.7(18)	0	—	—	—	—	—	—	—	—	—	—	—	—	6	174
2002	Min	14(12, TE)	6	17	2.8(4)	0	37	393	10.6(39)	1	—	—	—	—	—	—	—	—	—	—	—	—	6	219
2003	Min	16(16, TE)	2	15	7.5(12)	0	46	401	8.7(19)	4	—	—	—	—	—	—	—	—	—	—	—	—	24	236
2004	Min	1(1)	—	—	—	—	2	24	12.0(18)	0	—	—	—	—	—	—	—	—	—	—	—	—	0	12
2005	Min	16(16, TE)	—	—	—	—	22	171	7.8(15)	0	—	—	—	—	—	—	—	—	—	—	—	—	0	86
NFL	7	85(71)	43	147	3.4(12)	1	147	1284	8.7(39)	5	—	—	—	—	—	—	—	—	—	—	k	—	36	809
KLEMM, ADRIAN Adrian William, G-T, 6´3˝/310 lbs; Hawaii; 2000: NE, rnd 2; B5/21/1977 Inglewood, CA **2000** NE 5 (4) **2002** NE 16 (3) **2003** NE 3 (3) **2004** NE 2 (0) **2005** GB 16 (8, lg) **NFL** 42 (18) [5 yrs]																								
KLENK, QUENTIN Quentin Earl, T, 6´2˝/225 lbs; USC; 1945: Phi, rnd 18; B2/13/1919 Long Beach, CA, D1/4/1979 San Mateo, CA **1946** Buf-A 2 (2) **1946** ChiR-A 8 (1) **AAFC** 10 (3) [1 yr]																								
KLEVER, ROCKY Victor Kenneth, TE-RB, 6´3˝/225 lbs; Montana; 1982: NYJ, rnd 9; B7/10/1959 Portland, OR																								
1983	NYJ	5(0)	—	—	—	—	—	—	—	—	—	—	—	—	—	—	—	—	—	—	—	—	—	—
1984	NYJ	16(2)	—	—	—	—	3	29	9.7(13)	1	—	—	—	—	—	—	—	—	—	—	—	—	6	20
1985	†NYJ	16(6, te)	—	—	—	—	14	183	13.1(23)	2	—	—	—	—	—	—	—	—	—	—	k	—	12	90
1986	†NYJ	16(11, te)	—	—	—	—	15	150	10.0(21)	0	—	—	—	—	—	—	—	—	—	—	—	—	0	75
1987	NYJ	12(6, TE)	—	—	—	—	14	152	10.9(30)	0	—	—	—	—	—	—	—	—	—	—	k	—	0	86
NFL	5	65(25)	—	—	—	—	46	514	11.2(30)	3	—	—	—	—	—	—	—	—	—	—	k	—	18	270
KLEWICKI, ED Edward Leonard, E, 5´10˝/209 lbs; Michigan State; B5/4/1911 Pittsburgh, PA, D7/20/1997 East Lansing, MI																								
1935	†Det	11(7, LE)	—	—	—	—	4	112	28.0	2	—	—	—	—	—	—	—	—	—	—	—	—	12	66
1936	Det	11(8, LE)	—	—	—	—	4	90	22.5	0	—	—	—	—	—	—	—	—	—	—	—	—	0	45
1937	Det☆	11(11, LE)	10	53	5.3	0	8	134	16.8	0	—	—	—	—	—	—	—	—	—	—	—	1	6	120
1938	Det☆	10(8, LE)	10	76	7.6	0	3	57	19.0	0	—	—	—	—	—	—	—	—	—	—	—	—	0	105
NFL	4	43(34)	20	129	6.4	0	19	393	20.7	2	—	—	—	—	—	—	—	—	—	—	—	1	18	336
KLIEBHAN, ADOLPH Adolph, B, none; B8/14/1897 Milwaukee, WI, D3/1963, WI **1921** GB 1 (1)																								
KLIMEK, TONY Anthony Francis, DE, 5´11˝/200 lbs; Illinois; 1949: ChiC, rnd 14; B11/24/1925 Chicago, IL **1951** ChiC 12 **1952** ChiC 12 **NFL** 24 [2 yrs]																								
KLINE, ALAN Alan Nathan, T, 6´5˝/290 lbs; Ohio State; B5/25/1971 Tiffin, OH **1995** NO 3 (0)																								
KLINE, JIGGS Harry Smethers, E, 6´1˝/196 lbs; Emporia State; B10/22/1913 Elmdale, KS, D7/27/1995 Great Bend, KS **1940** NYG 6 (0) **1942** NYG 10 (0)																								
1939	†NYG	9(0)	—	—	—	—	4	44	11.0	1	—	—	—	—	—	—	—	—	—	—	—	—	6	27
NFL	3	25(0)	—	—	—	—	4	44	11.0	1	—	—	—	—	—	—	—	—	—	—	—	—	6	27
KLINGBEIL, CHUCK Charles E., DT-NT, 6´1˝/288 lbs; Northern Michigan; B11/2/1965 Houghton, MI **1991** Mia 15 (4) **1992**†Mia 15 (15, NT) **1993** Mia 16 (16, RDT) **1994**†Mia 16 (15, RDT) **1995**†Mia 16 (15, RDT) **NFL** 78 (65) [5 yrs]																								
KLINGEL, JOHN John, DE, 6´3˝/267 lbs; Eastern Kentucky; B12/21/1963 Marion, OH **1987** Phi 5 (0) **1988**†Phi 16 (0) **NFL** 21 (0) [2 yrs]																								
KLINGLER, DAVID David R., QB, 6´3˝/210 lbs; Houston; 1992: Cin, rnd 1; B2/17/1969 Houston, TX																								
1992	Cin	4(4)	11	53	4.8(12)	0	—	—	—	—	98	47	48.0	530	5.4(**83**)	3	2	18	146	—	—	—	0	253
1993	Cin	14(13, QB)	41	282	6.9(29)	0	—	—	—	—	343	190	55.4	1935	5.6(51)	6	9	40	202	66.6	—	—	0	920
1994	Cin	10(7, qb)	17	85	5.0(15)	0	1	-6	-6.0(-6)	0	231	131	56.7	1327	5.7(56)	6	9	24	165	—	—	—	0	416
1995	Cin	3(0)	—	—	—	—	—	—	—	—	15	7	46.7	88	5.9(33)	1	1	1	10	—	—	—	0	9
1996	Oak	1(0)	4	36	9.0(14)	0	—	—	—	—	24	10	41.7	87	3.6(20)	0	0	4	16	—	—	—	0	80
1997	Oak	1(0)	1	0	0.0(0)	0	—	—	—	—	7	4	57.1	27	3.9(8)	0	1	—	—	—	—	—	0	-27
NFL	6	33(24)	74	456	6.2(29)	0	1	-6	-6.0(-6)	0	718	389	54.2	3994	5.6(83)	16	22	87	539	65.1	—	—	0	1650
KLOPPENBERG, HARRY William Harry, E-G, 6´1˝/210 lbs; Fordham; B8/30/1908 Bronx, NY **1930** SI 9 (5, re) **1931** Bkn 2 (0) **1933** Bkn 1 (0)																								
1934	Bkn	7(0)	—	—	—	—	3	18	6.0	0	—	—	—	—	—	—	—	—	—	—	—	—	0	9
NFL	4	19(5)	—	—	—	—	3	18	6.0	0	—	—	—	—	—	—	—	—	—	—	—	—	0	9
KLOSTERMAN, BRUCE Bruce Donald, LB, 6´4˝/230 lbs; Iowa; South Dakota State; 1986: Den, rnd 8; B4/17/1963 Dubuque, IA **1987**†Den 9 (0) **1988** Den 12 (5, lilb) **1989**†Den 16 (0) **1990** LARm 5 (1) **NFL** 42 (6) [4 yrs]																								
KLOSTERMAN, DON Donald Clement, QB, 5´10˝/180 lbs; Loyola Marymount; 1952: Cle, rnd 3; B1/18/1930 Le Mars, IA, D6/6/2000 Los Angeles, CA																								
1952	LARm	2	1	-9	-9.0(-9)	0	—	—	—	—	10	3	30.0	47	4.7(30)	0	3	—	—	—	—	—	0	-106
KLOTOVICH, MIKE Michael Joseph, WB, 5´10˝/180 lbs; St. Mary's (CA); B8/15/1917 San Francisco, CA																								
1945	NYG	6(1)	5	26	5.2(15)	0	1	7	7.0(7)	0	—	—	—	—	—	—	—	—	—	—	P	—	0	30
KLOTZ, JACK John Stephen, T, 6´4˝/260 lbs; Widener; 1956: LA, rnd 18; B12/5/1932 Chester, PA **1961** NYT-A 14 (LT) **1962** NYT-A 3 **1962** SD-A 3 **1963** NYJ-A 13 (rt) **1964** Hou-A 8																								
1960	NYT-A	14(LT)	—	—	—	—	0	5	(5)	0	—	—	—	—	—	—	—	—	—	—	k	—	0	-5
NFL	5	55	—	—	—	—	0	5	(5)	0	—	—	—	—	—	—	—	—	—	—	k	—	0	-5
KLUG, AL Alfred W., T-G, 6´1˝/215 lbs; Marquette; 1943: ChiC, rnd 6; B6/1/1920 Milwaukee, WI **1946** Buf-A 12 (5, lt) **1947** Bal-A 11 (6, lt) **1948**†Bal-A 13 (0) **AAFC** 36 (11) [3 yrs]																								
KLUG, DAVE David John, LB, 6´4˝/230 lbs; Concordia (MN); 1980: KC, rnd 4; B5/17/1958 Litchfield, MN **1981** KC 16 (0) **1982** KC 9 (1) **1983** KC 1 (1) **NFL** 26 (2) [3 yrs]																								
KLUMB, JOHN John James, E, 6´3˝/200 lbs; Washington State; B1/22/1916 Aurora, NE, D7/23/1998 Sacramento, CA																								
1939	ChiC	3(0)	—	—	—	—	4	21	5.3	0	—	—	—	—	—	—	—	—	—	—	—	—	0	11
1940	ChiC	6(0)	—	—	—	—	—	—	—	—	—	—	—	—	—	—	—	—	—	—	—	—	—	—
1940	Pit	4(0)	—	—	—	—	3	76	25.3	0	—	—	—	—	—	—	—	—	—	—	—	—	0	38
NFL	2	13(0)	—	—	—	—	7	97	13.9	0	—	—	—	—	—	—	—	—	—	—	—	—	0	49
KLUTKA, NICK Nicholas, E, 5´11˝/198 lbs; Florida; 1946: Bos, rnd 30; B1/21/1921 New Brighton, PA, D4/2/2003 Van Wert, OH																								
1946	Buf-A	11(4)	—	—	—	—	1	9	9.0(9)	0	—	—	—	—	—	—	—	—	—	—	—	—	0	5
KLUWE, CHRIS Chris, P, 6´4˝/215 lbs; UCLA; B12/24/1981 Philadelphia, PA **2005** Min 15 (0)																								
KMETOVIC, PETE Peter George, HB, 5´9˝/175 lbs; Stanford; 1942: Phi, rnd 1; B12/27/1919 San Jose, CA, D2/8/1990 Palo Alto, CA																								
1946	Phi	5(0)	5	30	6.0(27)	0	4	68	17.0(38)	0	—	—	—	—	—	—	—	—	—	—	—	—	0	64
1947	Det	11(1)	14	23	1.6(6)	0	6	143	23.8(53)	2	—	—	—	—	—	—	—	—	—	—	kp	—	12	118
NFL	2	16(1)	19	53	2.8(27)	0	10	211	21.1(53)	2	—	—	—	—	—	—	—	—	—	—	kp	—	12	182
KNAB, SHINER Stanley S., B, 6´1˝/190 lbs; none; B3/25/1894, OH, D11/28/1974 Clermont, FL **1921** Cin 4 (4, FB)																								
KNACK, GLENN Glenn A., G, none; B3/29/1901 Oakfield, NY, D9/1983 Niagara Falls, NY **1922** Buf 1 (0) **1924** Buf 1 (0) **NFL** 2 (0) [2 yrs]																								
KNAFELC, GARY Gary Lee, E, 6´4˝/217 lbs; Colorado; 1954: ChiC, rnd 2; B1/2/1932 Pueblo, CO																								
1954	ChiC	1	—	—	—	—	2	11	5.5(7)	0	—	—	—	—	—	—	—	—	—	—	—	—	0	6
1954	GB	9	—	—	—	—	3	37	12.3(15)	0	—	—	—	—	—	—	—	—	—	—	—	—	0	19
1955	GB	12(LE)	—	—	—	—	40	613	15.3(48)	8	—	—	—	—	—	—	—	—	—	—	—	—	48	347
1956	GB	12(LE)	—	—	—	—	30	418	13.9(38)	6	—	—	—	—	—	—	—	—	—	—	—	—	36	239

YEAR	TEAM	G(GS, POS)	RUSH	YD	AVG(LG)	TD	REC	YD	AVG(LG)	TD	PASS COMP	PCT	YD	AVG(LG)	TD	INT	SK	YD	QBR	KPR	OTD	PTS	TAY
1957	GB	3	—	—	—	—	9	164	18.2(53)	2	—	—	—	—	—	—	—	—	—	—	—	12	92
1958	GB	6	—	—	—	—	8	118	14.8(40)	1	—	—	—	—	—	—	—	—	—	—	—	6	64
1959	GB	12 (RE)	—	—	—	—	27	384	14.2(38)	4	—	—	—	—	—	—	—	—	—	—	—	24	212
1960	†GB	12 (TE)	—	—	—	—	14	164	11.7(23)	0	—	—	—	—	—	—	—	—	—	—	—	0	82
1961	†GB	13	—	—	—	—	3	32	10.7(13)	0	—	—	—	—	—	—	—	—	—	—	—	0	16
1962	GB	11	—	—	—	—	—	—	—	—	—	—	—	—	—	—	—	—	—	—	—	—	—
1963	SF	10 (6, te)	—	—	—	—	18	221	12.3(45)	2	—	—	—	—	—	—	—	—	—	—	—	12	121
NFL	10	101(6)	—	—	—	—	154	2162	14.0(53)	23	—	—	—	—	—	—	—	—	—	—	—	138	1196

KNAFELC, GREG   Gregory Kurt, QB, 6´4˝/220 lbs; Notre Dame; B2/20/1959 Green Bay, WI   **1983** NO 6 (0)

KNAPCZYK, KEN   Kenneth John, WR, 5´11˝/190 lbs; Northern Iowa; B4/21/1963 Mokena, IL

| 1987 | ChiB | 3(3) | — | — | — | — | 4 | 62 | 15.5(22) | 0 | — | — | — | — | — | — | — | — | — | k | — | 0 | 30 |

KNAPP, LINDSAY   Lindsay Haines, G, 6´6˝/300 lbs; Notre Dame; 1993: KC, rnd 5; B2/25/1970 Arlington Heights, IL   **1993**†KC 0 (0)   **1994** KC 1 (0)   **1996**†GB 9 (0) **NFL** 10 (0) [3 yrs]

KNAPPER, JACK   Jack Freeman, B, 6´3˝/190 lbs; Ottawa (KS); B1/12/1910 Kansas City, MO, D4/1953

| 1934 | Phi | 2(0) | 10 | 19 | 1.9 | 0 | — | — | — | — | 7 | 0 | 0.0 | 0 | 0.0 | 0 | 3 | — | — | — | — | 0 | -101 |

KNAPPLE, JEFF   Jeffrey Scott, QB, 6´3˝/200 lbs; UCLA; Colorado; Northern Colorado; B8/27/1956 Wurzburg, Germany

| 1980 | Den | 2(0) | 6 | 0 | 0.0(9) | 0 | — | — | — | — | 4 | 1 | 25.0 | 15 | 3.8(15) | 0 | 0 | — | — | — | — | 0 | 8 |

KNECHT, BILL   William George, T, 6´3˝/205 lbs; Xavier (OH); B7/1899 Cincinnati, OH, deceased   **1925** Day 3 (3)

KNIEF, GAYLE   Gayle C., WR, 6´3˝/205 lbs; Morningside; B12/28/1946 Denison, IA

| 1970 | Bos | 3 | — | — | — | — | 3 | 39 | 13.0(22) | 1 | — | — | — | — | — | — | — | — | — | — | — | 6 | 25 |

KNIGHT, BRYAN   Bryan Jerome, LB, 6´2˝/238 lbs; Pittsburgh; 2002: Chi, rnd 5; B1/22/1979 Buffalo, NY   **2002** ChiB 15 (0)   **2003** ChiB 16 (2) **NFL** 31 (2) [2 yrs]

KNIGHT, CHARLIE   Charles Edward, C-T, 6´2˝/200 lbs; Loyola (IL); B10/1/1899 Chicago, IL, D3/12/1979 Miami, FL   **1920** ChiC 6 (3, C)   **1921** ChiC 4 (2) **NFL** 10 (5) [2 yrs]

KNIGHT, CURT   Luther Curtis, K, 6´2˝/190 lbs; North Texas; Texas; Coast Guard; B4/14/1943 Gulfport, MS **[K]**   **1970** Was 14   **1971**†Was★14   **1972**†Was 14   **1973**†Was 14

| 1969 | Was | 14 | — | — | — | — | — | — | — | — | 1 | 0 | 0.0 | 0 | 0.0 | 0 | 1 | — | — | K | — | 83 | -40 |
| NFL | 5 | 70 | — | — | — | — | — | — | — | — | 1 | 0 | 0.0 | 0 | 0.0 | 0 | 1 | — | — | K | — | 475 | -40 |

KNIGHT, DAVID   David Randle, WR, 6´1˝/182 lbs; William & Mary; 1973: NYJ, rnd 11; B2/1/1951 Trieste, Italy

1973	NYJ	14	—	—	—	—	6	78	13.0(19)	1	—	—	—	—	—	—	—	—	—	p	—	6	44
1974	NYJ	14 (WR)	—	—	—	—	40	579	14.5(42)	4	—	—	—	—	—	—	—	—	—	k	—	24	280
1975	NYJ	6	—	—	—	—	—	—	—	—	—	—	—	—	—	—	—	—	—	—	—	—	—
1976	NYJ	14 (WR)	—	—	—	—	20	403	20.1(42)	2	—	—	—	—	—	—	—	—	—	—	—	12	212
1977	NYJ	10	—	—	—	—	7	129	18.4(39)	0	—	—	—	—	—	—	—	—	—	—	—	0	65
NFL	5	58	—	—	—	—	73	1189	16.3(49)	7	—	—	—	—	—	—	—	—	—	kp	—	42	600

KNIGHT, GEORGE   George F., G, /199 lbs; Loyola (IL); B1898, deceased   **1920** ChiC 2 (0)

KNIGHT, LEANDER   Leander, DB, 6´1˝/193 lbs; Ferrum; Montclair State; B2/16/1963 Newark, NJ   **1987** Atl 1 (0)   **1988** Atl 2 (0)   **1989** NYJ 13 (0)   **1990**†Hou 16 (1) **NFL** 32 (1) [4 yrs]

KNIGHT, MARCUS   Marcus, WR, 6´1˝/180 lbs; Michigan; B6/19/1978 Sylacauga, AL   **2001** Oak 5 (1)

| 2002 | †Oak | 16(1) | — | — | — | — | 3 | 26 | 8.7(12) | 0 | — | — | — | — | — | — | — | — | — | k | — | 0 | 283 |
| NFL | 2 | 21(2) | — | — | — | — | 3 | 26 | 8.7(12) | 0 | — | — | — | — | — | — | — | — | — | — | — | 0 | 13 |

KNIGHT, PAT   Jon Patrick, LB, 6´2˝/204 lbs; SMU; 1952: NYG, rnd 10; B5/14/1929 San Antonio, TX, D10/19/1999 San Antonio, TX   **1952** NYG 2   **1954** NYG 10 (MLB) **1955** NYG 8 (MLB) **NFL** 20 [3 yrs]

KNIGHT, ROGER   Roger Oliver, LB, 6´0˝/245 lbs; Wisconsin; 2001: Pit, rnd 6; B10/11/1978 Queens Village, NY   **2001** NO 1 (0)   **2002** NO 16 (0)   **2003** NO 16 (2)   **2004** NO 15 (0) **NFL** 48 (2) [4 yrs]

KNIGHT, SAMMY   Sammy Dye, DB, 6´0˝/215 lbs; USC; B9/10/1975 Fontana, CA **[I]**   **1997** NO 16 (12, FS)   **1998** NO 14 (13, FS)   **1999** NO 16 (16, SS)   **2000**†NO 16 (16, SS) **2001** NO★16 (16, SS)   **2002** NO 16 (16, FS)   **2003** Mia 16 (16, SS)   **2004** Mia 16 (16, SS)   **2005** KC 16 (16, SS) **NFL** 142 (137) [9 yrs]

KNIGHT, SHAWN   Shawn Matthew, DE, 6´6˝/290 lbs; Brigham Young; 1987: NO, rnd 1; B6/4/1964 Provo, UT   **1987** NO 10 (0)   **1988** Den 14 (0)   **1989** Phx 7 (1) **NFL** 31 (1) [3 yrs]

KNIGHT, STEVE   Steven Paul, G, 6´4˝/298 lbs; Tennessee; B3/13/1961 Abington, VA   **1987** Ind 3 (3)

KNIGHT, SUGE   Marion H., DE, 6´2˝/265 lbs; UNLV; B4/19/1965   **1987** LARm 2 (0)

KNIGHT, TOM   Thomas Lorenzo, DB, 6´0˝/202 lbs; Iowa; 1997: Arz, rnd 1; B12/29/1974 Marlton, NJ   **1997** Arz 15 (14, RCB)   **1998**†Arz 8 (5, rcb)   **1999** Arz 16 (11, RCB) **2000** Arz 16 (15, RCB)   **2001** Arz 8 (8, lcb)   **2003**†Bal 10 (1) **NFL** 73 (54) [6 yrs]

KNOFF, KURT   Kurt L., DB, 6´2˝/191 lbs; Kansas; 1976: Den, rnd 2; B4/6/1954 East Grand Forks, MN   **1977** Hou 3   **1978**†Hou 16   **1979** Min 10 (7, fs)   **1980**†Min 16 (16, FS) **1981** Min 16 (16, FS)   **1982**†Min 9 (4) **NFL** 70 (43) [6 yrs]

KNOLLA, JOHNNY   John Alexander, HB, 5´10˝/180 lbs; Creighton; 1941: Pit, rnd 3; B3/19/1919 Chicago, IL, D1/12/1992

1942	ChiC	11(2)	15	43	2.9(14)	0	8	48	6.0(15)	0	6	1	16.7	16	2.7(16)	0	0	—	—	kpi	—	0	141
1945	ChiC	7(2)	15	36	2.4(8)	0	1	15	15.0(15)	0	1	0	0.0	0	0.0	0	0	—	—	Pkp	—	0	96
NFL	2	18(4)	30	79	2.6(14)	0	9	63	7.0(15)	0	7	1	14.3	16	2.3(16)	0	0	—	—	Pkpi	—	0	237

KNOP, OSCAR   Robert Oscar, B-E, 6´0˝/191 lbs; Illinois; B9/5/1896 Chicago, IL, D11/5/1952 Chicago, IL   **1920** ChiT 8 (6, RE)   **1921** Ham 5 (2)   **1922** Ham 5 (2) **1923** Ham 4 (2)   **1923** ChiB 12 (8, FB)   **1924** ChiB 11 (9, FB)   **1925** ChiB 17 (11, FB)   **1926** ChiB 13 (12, FB), 6   **1927** ChiB 10 (7, FB), 6 **NFL** 85 (61), 42 [8 yrs]

KNORR, LARRY   Lawrence Frank, E, 6´2˝/192 lbs; Alabama; Dayton; B4/22/1917 New York, NY, D11/26/1996, OH   **1945** Det 2 (0)

| 1942 | Det | 8(2) | — | — | — | — | 2 | 18 | 9.0(10) | 0 | — | — | — | — | — | — | — | — | — | — | — | 0 | 9 |
| NFL | 2 | 10(2) | — | — | — | — | 2 | 18 | 9.0(10) | 0 | — | — | — | — | — | — | — | — | — | — | — | 0 | 9 |

KNORR, MICAH   Micah, P, 6´2˝/199 lbs; Utah State; B1/9/1975 Orange, CA **[KP]**   **2000** Dal 14 (0)   **2002** Den 8 (0)   **2004** Den 12 (0)

2001	Dal	16(0)	1	0	0.0(0)	0	—	—	—	—	1	0	0.0	0	0.0	0	0	—	—	P	—	0	0
2002	Dal	7(0)	1	-10	-10.0(-10)	0	—	—	—	—	—	—	—	—	—	—	—	—	—	P	—	0	-10
2003	†Den	16(0)	—	—	—	—	—	—	—	—	1	0	0.0	0	0.0	0	0	—	—	KP	—	5	0
NFL	5	73(0)	2	-10	-5.0	0	—	—	—	—	2	0	0.0	0	0.0	0	0	—	—	KP	—	5	-10

KNOX, BILL   William Robert, DB, 5´9˝/190 lbs; Purdue; B6/19/1951 Elba, AL   **1974** ChiB 14   **1975** ChiB 14   **1976** ChiB 14 **NFL** 42 [3 yrs]

KNOX, CHARLIE   Charles, B, 5´11˝/185 lbs; St. Edmonds   **1937** Phi 1 (0)

KNOX, DARYL   Daryl A., LB, 6´3˝/220 lbs; UNLV; B9/3/1962   **1987** Pit 3 (0)

KNOX, KEVIN   Kevin DeVon, WR, 6´3˝/195 lbs; Florida State; 1994: Buf, rnd 6; B1/30/1971 Niceville, FL   **1994** Arz 2 (0)

KNOX, MIKE   Michael Alan, LB, 6´2˝/240 lbs; Nebraska; B11/21/1962 Boulder, CO   **1987** Den 3 (0)

KNOX, RONNIE   Ronald, QB, 6´1˝/198 lbs; California; UCLA; 1957: ChiB, rnd 3; B2/14/1935 Santa Monica, CA   **1957** ChiB 1

KNOX, SAM   Frank Samuel, G-T, 6´0˝/213 lbs; New Hampshire; Illinois; B3/29/1910 Bow, NH, D5/1981 Bradenton, FL   **1934** Det 11 (2)   **1935**†Det 9 (8, LG)   **1936** Det 11 (7, LG) **NFL** 31 (17) [3 yrs]

KNUTSON, GENE   Eugene Peter, DE, 6´2˝/218 lbs; Michigan; 1954: GB, rnd 10; B11/10/1932 Beloit, WI   **1954** GB 12   **1956** GB 6 **NFL** 18 [2 yrs]

KNUTSON, STEVE   Steven Craig, G-T, 6´3˝/254 lbs; USC; 1975: Atl, rnd 16; B10/5/1951 Bagley, MN   **1976** GB 12   **1977** GB 13 (LG)   **1978** SF 15 (1) **NFL** 40 (1) [3 yrs]

KOART, MATT   Matthew, DE, 6´5˝/257 lbs; USC; 1986: GB, rnd 5; B9/28/1963, CA   **1986** GB 6 (0)

KOBOLINSKI, STEVE   Stephen A., C, 5´8˝/170 lbs; Boston College; B11/19/1903 Boston, MA, D10/11/1976 Fall River, MA   **1926** Bkn 1 (0)

KOBROSKY, MICKEY   Milton Leonard, QB, 6´0˝/187 lbs; Trinity (CT); 1937: NYG, rnd 5; B2/22/1915 Springfield, MA, D5/29/2003 Longmeadow, MA

| 1937 | NYG | 7(0) | 13 | 41 | 3.2 | 0 | — | — | — | — | 13 | 2 | 15.4 | 18 | 1.4 | 0 | 2 | — | — | — | — | 0 | -30 |

YEAR	TEAM	G (GS, POS)	RUSH	YD	AVG (LG)	TD	REC	YD	AVG (LG)	TD	PASS COMP	PCT	YD	AVG (LG)	TD	INT	SK	YD	QBR	KPR	OTD	PTS	TAY

KOCH, AARON Aaron Paul, G-T, 6´3˝/300 lbs; Oregon State; B2/1/1978 Portland, OR **2000** Jax 8 (0) **2001** Jax 16 (1) **NFL** 24 (1) [2 yrs]

KOCH, GEORGE George Theodore, HB, 6´0˝/200 lbs; St. Mary's (TX); Baylor; B7/2/1919 Temple, TX, D9/5/1966 Temple, TX

| 1945 | †Cle | 5 (1) | 12 | 101 | 8.4 (32) | 0 | — | — | — | — | — | — | — | — | — | — | — | — | k | — | 0 | 93 |
| 1947 | Buf-A | 13 (3) | 37 | 149 | 4.0 | 1 | 1 | 10 | 10.0 (10) | 0 | — | — | — | — | — | — | — | — | kpi | — | 6 | 234 |

KOCH, GREG Gregory Michael, T-G, 6´4˝/270 lbs; Arkansas; 1977: GB, rnd 2; B6/14/1955 Bethesda, MD **1977** GB 14 (3) **1978** GB 16 (16, RT) **1979** GB 16 (16, RT) **1980** GB 16 (16, RT) **1981** GB 16 (16, RT) **1982** †GB☆9 (9, RT) **1983** GB 15 (14, RT) **1984** GB 15 (14, RT) **1985** GB 16 (16, RT) **1986** Mia 16 (16, RT) **1987** Mia 1 (1) **1987** †Min 9 (6, RG) **NFL** 159 (143) [11 yrs]

KOCH, MARKUS Markus, DE-DT, 6´5˝/270 lbs; Boise State; 1986: Was, rnd 2; B2/13/1963 Niedermarsberg, Germany **1986** Was 16 (0) **1987** †Was 12 (2) **1988** Was 11 (6, rde) **1989** Was 10 (7, ldt) **1990** †Was 13 (13, RDE) **1991** Was 6 (6, rde) **NFL** 68 (34) [6 yrs]

KOCH, PETE Peter Alan, NT-DE-DT, 6´6˝/270 lbs; Maryland; 1984: Cin, rnd 1; B1/23/1962 Nassau County, NY **1984** Cin 16 (0) **1985** KC 16 (0) **1986** †KC 16 (16, RDE) **1987** KC 6 (6, nt) **1989** LARd 4 (0) **NFL** 58 (22) [5 yrs]

KOCH, POLLY Walter Henry, G-T, 5´11˝/185 lbs; Wisconsin; B1/27/1895 Fond du Lac, WI, D6/22/1976 Hartford, WI **1920** RI 4 (0)

KOCHEL, MIKE Michael Joseph, G, 5´11˝/195 lbs; Fordham; 1939: ChiC, rnd 19; B3/6/1916 Bloomfield, NJ, D8/18/1994 Bellevue, NE **1939** ChiC 8 (3)

KOCHMAN, ROGER Roger, HB, 6´2˝/205 lbs; Penn State; 1962: Buf, rnd 15/SL, rnd 4; B6/16/1941 Pittsburgh, PA

| 1963 | Buf-A | 5 (HB) | 47 | 232 | 4.9 (48) | 0 | 4 | 148 | 37.0 (68) | 1 | — | — | — | — | — | — | — | — | p | — | 6 | 317 |

KOCOUREK, DAVE David Allen, TE-FL, 6´5˝/240 lbs; Wisconsin; 1959: Pit, rnd 19; B8/20/1937 Chicago, IL

1960	†LAC-A	14 (FL)	—	—	—	—	40	662	16.5 (52)	1	—	—	—	—	—	—	—	—	—	—	6	336
1961	†SD-A★	14 (FL)	—	—	—	—	55	1055	19.2 (76)	4	—	—	—	—	—	—	—	—	—	—	24	548
1962	SD-A★	14 (TE)	—	—	—	—	39	688	17.6 (45)	4	—	—	—	—	—	—	—	—	—	—	26	364
1963	†SD-A★	14 (TE)	—	—	—	—	23	359	15.6 (35)	5	—	—	—	—	—	—	—	—	—	—	32	205
1964	†SD-A★	14 (TE)	—	—	—	—	33	593	18.0 (49)	5	—	—	—	—	—	—	—	—	—	—	30	322
1965	†SD-A☆	14 (TE)	—	—	—	—	28	363	13.0 (29)	2	—	—	—	—	—	—	—	—	—	—	12	192
1966	Mia-A	14 (14, TE)	—	—	—	—	27	320	11.9 (43)	2	—	—	—	—	—	—	—	—	—	—	12	170
1967	†Oak-A	10	—	—	—	—	1	4	4.0 (4)	0	—	—	—	—	—	—	—	—	—	—	2	2
1968	†Oak-A	7 (1)	—	—	—	—	3	46	15.3 (18)	1	—	—	—	—	—	—	—	—	—	—	6	28
NFL	9	115 (15)	—	—	—	—	249	4090	16.4 (76)	24	—	—	—	—	—	—	—	—	—	—	150	2165

KOCUREK, KRIS Kris, DT, 6´4˝/293 lbs; Texas Tech; 2001: Sea, rnd 7; B11/15/1978 Rockdale, TX **2001** Ten 1 (0)

KODBA, JOE Joseph Stephen, C-LB, 5´11˝/190 lbs; Butler; Purdue; B2/27/1922, Yugoslavia, D9/7/2005 Swartz Creek, MI **1947** Bal-A 13 (3)

KOEGEL, VIC Victor Aloysius, LB, 6´0˝/215 lbs; Ohio State; 1974: Atl, rnd 12; B11/2/1952 Cincinnati, OH **1974** Cin 6

KOEGEL, WARREN Warren DeWitt, C, 6´3˝/253 lbs; Penn State; 1971: Oak, rnd 3; B11/1/1949 Mineola, NY **1971** Oak 16 **1973** SL 3 **1974** NYJ 2 **NFL** 21 [3 yrs]

KOEHLER, BOB Robert Adam Charles, FB, 5´11˝/185 lbs; Northwestern; B4/7/1894 Chicago, IL, D7/1/1949 Sister Lake, MN [K] **1920** Dec 10 (6, FB) **1921** ChiC 8 (8, FB), 8 **1922** ChiC 10 (10, FB), 12 **1923** ChiC 11 (6, fb), 6 **1924** ChiC 10 (10, FB), 6 **1925** ChiC☆12 (11, FB), 24 **1926** ChiC 10 (7, FB) **NFL** 71 (58), 56 [7 yrs]

KOENEN, MICHAEL Michael, P, 5´11˝/195 lbs; Western Washington; B7/13/1982 Ferndale, WA [K] **2005** Atl 16 (0)

KOENINGER, ART Arthur Frank, C, 6´1˝/202 lbs; Tennessee-Chattanooga; B11/11/1906 Roscoe, PA, D12/16/1990 Chattanooga, TN **1931** Fra 2 (0) **1933** Phi 1 (1)

| 1932 | SI | 10 (5, c) | — | — | — | — | 1 | 17 | 17.0 (17) | 0 | — | — | — | — | — | — | — | — | — | — | 0 | 9 |
| NFL | 3 | 13 (6) | — | — | — | — | 1 | 17 | 17.0 (17) | 0 | — | — | — | — | — | — | — | — | — | — | 0 | 9 |

KOEPER, DICK Richard Manfred, T, 6´4˝/260 lbs; Oregon State; 1965: GB, rnd 6; B7/23/1943 San Francisco, CA **1966** Atl 3

KOEPFER, KARL Karl Justin, G, 6´2˝/230 lbs; Bowling Green State; 1958: Det, rnd 8; B10/7/1934 Swanton, OH **1958** Det 1

KOFLER, MATT Matthew Joseph, QB, 6´3˝/192 lbs; San Diego State; 1982: Buf, rnd 2; B8/30/1959 Longview, WA

1982	Buf	4 (0)	2	21	10.5 (12)	0	—	—	—	—	—	—	—	—	—	—	—	—	—	—	0	21
1983	Buf	16 (0)	4	25	6.3 (11)	0	—	—	—	61	35	57.4	440	7.2 (28)	4	3	10	85	—	—	0	145
1984	Buf	16 (0)	10	80	8.0 (19)	0	—	—	—	93	33	35.5	432	4.6 (70)	2	5	15	111	—	—	0	106
1985	Ind	5 (1)	4	33	8.3 (23)	1	—	—	—	48	23	47.9	284	5.9 (33)	1	3	8	58	—	—	6	70
NFL	4	41 (1)	20	159	7.9 (23)	1	—	—	—	202	91	45.0	1156	5.7 (70)	7	11	33	254	—	—	6	342

KOHL, DUTCH George Henry, E, /185 lbs; none; B9/5/1893 Hammond, IN, deceased **1920** Ham 5 (1, RE) **1922** Ham 5 (1) **NFL** 10 (2) [2 yrs]

KOHLBRAND, JOE Joseph, LB, 6´4˝/242 lbs; Miami (FL); 1985: NO, rnd 8; B3/18/1963 Merritt Island, FL **1985** NO 12 (0) **1986** NO 16 (0) **1987** †NO 12 (0) **1988** NO 16 (2) **1989** NO 16 (0) **NFL** 72 (2) [5 yrs]

KOHRS, BOB Robert Henry, DE-LB, 6´3˝/240 lbs; Arizona State; 1980: Pit, rnd 2; B11/8/1958 Phoenix, AZ **1981** Pit 16 (6, lde) **1982** †Pit 9 (0) **1983** Pit 9 (0) **1984** †Pit 10 (0) **1985** Pit 11 (0) **NFL** 55 (6) [5 yrs]

KOKEN, MIKE Michael Richard, QB-HB, 5´11˝/185 lbs; Notre Dame; B4/5/1909 Butler, PA, D4/15/1962 South Bend, IN [K]

| 1933 | ChiC | 9 (4) | 27 | 65 | 2.4 | 0 | 2 | 44 | 22.0 | 0 | 26 | 9 | 34.6 | 74 | 2.8 | 1 | 2 | — | — | K | — | 1 | 49 |

KOLB, JON Jon Paul, T-C, 6´2˝/262 lbs; Oklahoma State; 1969: Pit, rnd 3; B8/30/1947 Ponca City, OK **1969** Pit 14 **1970** Pit 14 **1971** Pit 14 (14, LT) **1972** †Pit 14 (14, LT) **1973** †Pit 14 (14, LT) **1974** †Pit☆14 (14, LT) **1975** †Pit☆14 (14, LT) **1976** †Pit☆14 (14, LT) **1977** Pit 13 (13, LT) **1978** †Pit☆16 (16, LT) **1979** †Pit☆14 (12, LT) **1980** Pit 7 (7, lt) **1981** Pit 15 (6, lt) **NFL** 177 (138) [13 yrs]

KOLBERG, ELMER Elmer Frank, HB-E, 6´4˝/201 lbs; Oregon State; 1938: Phi, rnd 9; B1/21/1916 Orange, CA, D9/30/1994 Portland, OR

1939	Phi	8 (3)	—	—	—	—	3	33	11.0	0	—	—	—	—	—	—	—	—	—	—	—	0	17
1940	Phi	10 (5, rh)	—	—	—	—	6	43	7.2	0	—	—	—	—	—	—	—	—	Pi	—	0	32
1941	Pit	4 (0)	—	—	—	—	1	2	2.0 (2)	0	—	—	—	—	—	—	—	—	—	—	0	1
NFL	3	22 (8)	—	—	—	—	10	78	7.8 (2)	0	—	—	—	—	—	—	—	—	Pi	—	0	49

KOLEN, MIKE John Michael, LB, 6´2˝/220 lbs; Auburn; 1970: Mia, rnd 12; B1/31/1948 Opelika, AL **1970** †Mia 14 (14, RLB) **1971** †Mia 14 (10, RLB) **1972** †Mia 13 (13, RLB) **1973** †Mia 14 (13, RLB) **1974** †Mia 14 (13, RLB) **1975** Mia 9 (9, MLB) **1977** Mia 6 (4) **NFL** 84 (76) [7 yrs]

KOLESAR, BOB Robert C., G, 5´10˝/200 lbs; Michigan; 1943: Det, rnd 12; B4/5/1921 Cleveland, OH, D1/13/2004 Midland, MI **1946** Cle-A 2 (0)

KOLIC, LARRY Lawrence Vincent, LB, 6´1˝/242 lbs; Ohio State; 1986: Mia, rnd 7; B8/31/1963 Cleveland, OH **1986** Mia 2 (2) **1987** Mia 7 (0) **1988** Mia 7 (0) **NFL** 16 (2) [3 yrs]

KOLLAR, BILL William Wallace, DE-NT-DT, 6´3˝/255 lbs; Montana State; 1974: Cin, rnd 1; B11/27/1952 Warren, OH **1974** Cin 14 **1975** †Cin 14 **1976** Cin 9 **1977** TB 14 **1978** TB 16 (2) **1979** †TB 15 (8, nt) **1980** TB 15 (13, LDE) **1981** TB 12 (12, LDE) **NFL** 109 (35) [8 yrs]

KOLLS, LOUIS Louis C., C, 6´1˝/205 lbs; St. Ambrose; B12/15/1892 Chattanooga, TN, D2/24/1941 Hooppole, IL **1920** ChiC 1 (0) **1920** Ham 4 (1) **1922** RI 6 (5, C) **1923** RI 6 (5, C) **1924** RI 9 (7, C) **1925** RI 11 (10, C) **1927** NYY 2 (1) **NFL** 39 (29) [6 yrs]

KOLMAN, ED Edward Victor, G-T, 6´2˝/232 lbs; Temple; 1940: ChiB, rnd 5; B10/21/1915 Brooklyn, NY, D7/31/1985 New Hyde Park, NY **1940** †ChiB★10 (6) **1941** †ChiB★11 (9, LT) **1942** †ChiB★11 (9, LT) **1946** †ChiB 11 (4) **1947** ChiB 12 (4) **1949** NYG 11 (1) **NFL** 66 (33) [6 yrs]

KOLODZIEJ, ROSS Ross Anthony, DT, 6´2˝/295 lbs; Wisconsin; 2001: NYG, rnd 7; B5/11/1978 Stevens Point, WI **2001** NYG 9 (1) **2002** NYG 1 (0) **2004** Arz 13 (4) **2005** Arz 16 (14, LDT) **NFL** 39 (19) [4 yrs]

KOLODZIEJSKI, CHRIS Christopher James, TE, 6´3˝/231 lbs; Wyoming; 1984: Pit, rnd 2; B2/5/1961 Augsburg, Germany

| 1984 | Pit | 7 (3) | — | — | — | — | 5 | 59 | 11.8 (22) | 1 | — | — | — | — | — | — | — | — | — | — | 0 | 30 |

KOMAN, BILL William John, LB, 6´2˝/229 lbs; North Carolina; 1956: Bal, rnd 8; B9/16/1934 Ambridge, PA **1956** Bal 12 **1957** Phi 11 (11, RLB) **1958** Phi 12 (12, LLB) **1959** ChiC 11 (RLB) **1960** SL 12 (RLB) **1961** SL 14 (RLB) **1962** SL✧14 (RLB) **1963** SL☆14 (RLB) **1964** SL★14 (RLB) **1965** SL 14 (RLB) **1966** SL 14 (RLB) **1967** SL 14 (RLB) **NFL** 156 (23) [12 yrs]

KOMLO, JEFF William Jeffrey, QB, 6´2˝/200 lbs; Delaware; 1979: Det, rnd 9; B7/30/1956 Cheverly, MD

1979	Det	16 (14, QB)	30	107	3.6 (16)	2	—	—	—	368	183	49.7	2238	6.1 (40)	11	23	40	361	52.8	—	12	381
1980	Det	4 (0)	—	—	—	—	—	—	—	4	2	50.0	26	6.5 (20)	0	1	—	—	—	—	0	-27
1981	Det	3 (2)	6	3	0.5 (5)	0	—	—	—	57	29	50.9	290	5.1 (46)	1	3	5	45	—	—	0	33

YEAR	TEAM	G(GS, POS)	RUSH	YD	AVG(LG)	TD	REC	YD	AVG(LG)	TD	PASS	COMP	PCT	YD	AVG(LG)	TD	INT	SK	YD	QBR	KPR	OTD	PTS	TAY
1983	TB	2(0)	2	11	5.5(11)	0	—	—	—	—	8	4	50.0	49	6.1(17)	0	1	3	25	—	—	—	0	-5
NFL	4	25(16)	38	121	3.2(16)	2	—	—	—	—	437	218	49.9	2603	6.0(46)	12	28	48	431	50.9	—	—	12	383

KOMPARA, JOHN John Joseph, DT, 6´2˝/245 lbs; South Carolina; 1959: NYG, rnd 13; B4/12/1936 Canton, OH **1960** LAC-A 7

KONCAR, MARK Mark, T, 6´5˝/271 lbs; Colorado; 1976: GB, rnd 1; B5/5/1953 Murray, UT **1976** GB 14 (14, LT) **1977** GB 13 (13, LT) **1979** GB 12 (12, LT) **1980** GB 1 (1) **1981** GB 13 (11, LT) **1982** Hou 5 (0) **NFL** 58 (51) [6 yrs]

KONDRLA, JOHN John Joseph, T, 6´2˝/195 lbs; St. Vincent; 1945: Pit, rnd 30; B2/23/1921 Republic, PA **1945** Pit 1 (0)

KONECNY, MARK Mark William, RB, 5´11˝/197 lbs; Alma; B4/2/1963 Chicago, IL

1987	Mia	3(0)	6	46	7.7(19)	0	6	26	4.3(10)	0	—	—	—	—	—	—	—	—	—	—	—	—	0	59
1988	Phi	16(0)	—	—	—	—	1	18	18.0(18)	0	—	—	—	—	—	—	—	—	—	—	kp	—	0	98
NFL	2	19(0)	6	46	7.7(19)	0	7	44	6.3(18)	0	—	—	—	—	—	—	—	—	—	—	kp	—	0	157

KONETSKY, FLOYD Floyd Walter, E, 6´0˝/197 lbs; Florida; 1943: Cle, rnd 29; B5/26/1920 Marianna, PA **1944** Cle 8 (6, LE) **1945**†Cle 10 (4) **NFL** 18 (10) [2 yrs]
1947 Bal-A 6 (1)

KONISZEWSKI, JOHN John Edward, T, 6´3˝/243 lbs; George Washington; B8/29/1921 Dickson City, PA, D12/30/2003 Peckville, PA **1945**†Was 8 (3) **1946** Was 9 (7, LT) **1948** Was 12 (4) **NFL** 29 (14) [3 yrs]

KONOPASEK, ED Edward Steven, T, 6´6˝/289 lbs; Ball State; B4/12/1964 Gary, IN **1987** GB 3 (3)

KONOVSKY, BOB Robert Erwin, G-DE, 6´2˝/246 lbs; Wisconsin; 1956: ChiC, rnd 7; B8/19/1934 Chicago, IL, D3/6/1982 Chicago, IL **1956** ChiC 12 **1957** ChiC 12 (RG)
1958 ChiC 12 (RG) **1961** Den-A 13 **NFL** 49 [4 yrs]

KONRAD, ROB Robert L., FB, 6´3˝/255 lbs; Syracuse; 1999: Mia, rnd 2; B11/12/1976 Rochester, NY

1999	†Mia	15(9, FB)	9	16	1.8(5)	0	34	251	7.4(25)	1	—	—	—	—	—	—	—	—	—	—	—	—	6	147
2000	†Mia	15(13, FB)	15	39	2.6(5)	0	14	83	5.9(18)	0	—	—	—	—	—	—	—	—	—	—	—	—	0	81
2001	Mia	12(9, FB)	5	22	4.4(18)	1	5	52	10.4(17)	1	—	—	—	—	—	—	—	—	—	—	—	—	12	63
2002	Mia	16(12, FB)	3	2	0.7(2)	0	34	233	6.9(19)	3	—	—	—	—	—	—	—	—	—	—	k	—	18	137
2003	Mia	14(12, FB)	4	17	4.3(11)	0	16	166	10.4(25)	0	—	—	—	—	—	—	—	—	—	—	—	—	0	100
2004	Mia	10(1)	2	18	9.0(15)	0	8	69	8.6(20)	1	—	—	—	—	—	—	—	—	—	—	—	—	6	58
NFL	6	82(56)	38	114	3.0(18)	1	111	854	7.7(25)	6	—	—	—	—	—	—	—	—	—	—	k	—	42	584

KONZ, KEN Kenneth Earl, DB, 5´10˝/184 lbs; LSU; 1951: Cle, rnd 1; B9/25/1928 Weimar, TX [KI] **1953**†Cle 12 (DB) **1954** Cle 12 (db) **1955**†Cle★12 (DB) **1956** Cle☆12 (DB)
1957†Cle☆12 (DB) **1958** Cle 12 (DB) **1959** Cle 12 **NFL** 84 [7 yrs]

KOOISTRA, SCOTT Daniel Scott, T, 6´6˝/320 lbs; North Carolina State; 2003: Cin, rnd 7; B10/14/1980 Madison, WI **2003** Cin 8 (0) **2004** Cin 16 (0) **2005**†Cin 15 (1)
NFL 39 (1) [3 yrs]

KOONCE, GEORGE George Earl, LB, 6´1˝/245 lbs; Chowan Coll. (NC); East Carolina; B10/15/1968 New Bern, NC **1992** GB 16 (10, LOLB) **1993** GB 15 (15, LILB)
1994†GB 16 (16, RLB) **1995**†GB 16 (16, RLB) **1996**†GB 16 (16, MLB) **1997**†GB 4 (0) **1998**†GB 14 (14, LLB) **1999** GB 15 (15, LLB) **2000** Sea 16 (16, MLB)
NFL 128 (118) [9 yrs]

KOONS, JOE Joseph Leo, C, 6´2˝/195 lbs; Scranton; B1/12/1915 Wilkes-Barre, PA, D10/20/1993 Shelby, MI **1941** Bkn 6 (0)

KOONTZ, ED Edward Larry, LB, 6´2˝/230 lbs; Catawba; 1968: Bos, rnd 17; B6/11/1946 Hanover, PA **1968** Bos-A 6 (1)

KOONTZ, JOE Joseph William, WR, 6´1˝/192 lbs; San Francisco State; 1968: NYG, rnd 9; B8/13/1945 Visalia, CA **1968** NYG 14

KOPAY, DAVE David Marquette, RB, 6´0˝/218 lbs; Washington; B6/28/1942 Chicago, IL

1964	SF	14(5, rh)	75	271	3.6(18)	2	20	135	6.8(30)	2	1	0	0.0	0	0.0	0	0	—	—	—	k	—	12	349
1965	SF	12	28	81	2.9(10)	2	11	147	13.4(44)	1	—	—	—	—	—	—	—	—	—	—	k	1	24	186
1966	SF	14	47	204	4.3(32)	1	10	67	6.7(26)	1	—	—	—	—	—	—	—	—	—	—	kp	—	12	251
1967	SF	8	6	21	3.5(10)	0	2	11	5.5(11)	0	—	—	—	—	—	—	—	—	—	—	k	—	0	33
1968	Det	14(fb)	53	207	3.9(22)	0	18	130	7.2(21)	0	—	—	—	—	—	—	—	—	—	—	k	—	0	271
1969	Was	13	3	4	1.3(3)	0	6	60	10.0(18)	0	—	—	—	—	—	—	—	—	—	—	k	—	0	86
1970	Was	12	13	49	3.8(14)	0	7	24	3.4(9)	0	—	—	—	—	—	—	—	—	—	—	p	—	0	56
1971	NO	10	—	—	—	—	—	—	—	—	—	—	—	—	—	—	—	—	—	—	—	—	0	0
1972	†GB	14	10	39	3.9(20)	0	3	19	6.3(9)	0	—	—	—	—	—	—	—	—	—	—	—	—	0	49
NFL	9	111(5)	235	876	3.7(32)	3	77	593	7.7(44)	4	1	0	0.0	0	0.0	0	0	—	—	—	kp	1	48	1279

KOPCHA, JOE Joseph Edward, G, 6´0˝/221 lbs; Tennessee-Chattanooga; B12/23/1905 Whiting, IN, D7/29/1986 Hobart, IN [K] **1929** ChiB 12 (9, rg) **1932** ChiB☆12 (9, RG)
1933†ChiB☆13 (11, RG) **1936** Det 12 (7, RG)

1934	ChiB☆	11(10, RG)	—	—	—	—	2	24	12.0	0	—	—	—	—	—	—	—	—	—	—	K	—	0	12
1935	ChiB☆	12(10, RG)	—	—	—	—	—	—	—	—	1	0	0.0	0	0.0	0	0	—	—	—	K	—	3	0
NFL	6	72(56)	—	—	—	—	2	24	12.0	0	1	0	0.0	0	0.0	0	0	—	—	—	K	—	3	12

KOPLOW, LOU Louis H., T, 6´3˝/235 lbs; Boston University; B2/1/1904, D8/12/1988 Brookline, MA **1926** Pro 1 (1)

KOPP, JEFF Jeffrey Blair, LB, 6´3˝/244 lbs; USC; 1995: Mia, rnd 6; B7/8/1971 Danville, CA **1995**†Mia 16 (0) **1996** Jax 12 (0) **1997**†Jax 16 (3) **1998** Jax 6 (0) **1998** Bal 7 (0)
1999 NE 6 (0) **NFL** 63 (3) [5 yrs]

KOPPEN, DAN Daniel, C, 6´2˝/296 lbs; Boston College; 2003: NE, rnd 5; B9/12/1979 Dubuque, IA **2003**†NE 16 (15, C) **2004**†NE 16 (16, C) **2005** NE 9 (9, C) **NFL** 41 (40) [3 yrs]

KOPPISCH, WALT Walter Frederic, TB-WB-HB, 5´10˝/180 lbs; Columbia; B6/6/1901 Pendleton, NY, D11/5/1953 New York, NY [C] **1925** Buf 6 (4, TB) **1926** NYG 9 (5, wb)
NFL 15 (9) [2 yrs]

KORFF, MARK Mark Curtis, LB, 6´1˝/230 lbs; Florida; B4/5/1963 Canoga Park, CA **1987** SF 2 (0)

KORISKY, ED Edward A., C, 6´1˝/210 lbs; Villanova; B8/23/1918 Hartford, CT, D7/13/1992 Hartford, CT **1944** Bos 9 (3)

KORS, R.J. Richard James, DB, 6´0˝/195 lbs; USC; Long Beach State; 1989: Sea, rnd 12; B6/27/1966 Santa Monica, CA **1991**†NYJ 16 (0) **1992** NYJ 14 (3) **1993** Cin 7 (0)
NFL 37 (3) [3 yrs]

KORTAS, KEN Kenneth Conrad, DT, 6´4˝/280 lbs; Louisville; 1964: SL, rnd 1/KC, rnd 3; B5/17/1942 Chicago, IL **1964** SL 14 **1965** Pit 14 **1966** Pit 14 (LDT) **1967** Pit 14 (LDT)
1968 Pit 14 (LDT) **1969** ChiB 3 **NFL** 73 [6 yrs]

KORTE, STEVE Steven Jeffrey, C-G, 6´3˝/265 lbs; Arkansas; 1983: NO, rnd 2; B1/15/1960 Denver, CO **1983** NO 16 (0) **1984** NO 15 (15, RG/c) **1985** NO 12 (12, C)
1986 NO 16 (16, C) **1987**†NO 3 (0) **1988** NO 16 (16, C) **1989** NO 5 (4) **NFL** 83 (63) [7 yrs]

KORVER, KELVIN Kelvin Mitchell, DT, 6´6˝/267 lbs; Texas A&M; Northwestern Iowa; 1972: Oak, rnd 2; B2/21/1949 Dallas, TX **1973**†Oak 14 **1974** Oak 14 **1975** Oak 1 (1)
NFL 24 (1) [3 yrs]

KOSAR, BERNIE Bernie Joseph, QB, 6´5˝/210 lbs; Miami (FL); 1985: Cle, rnd S1; B11/25/1963 Boardman, OH

1985	†Cle	12(10, QB)	26	-12	-0.5(10)	1	—	—	—	—	248	124	50.0	1578	6.4(68)	8	7	19	121	69.3	—	—	6	547
1986	†Cle	16(16, QB)	24	19	0.8(17)	0	1	1	1.0(1)	0	531	310	58.4	3854	7.3(72)	17	10	39	274	83.8	—	—	0	1632
1987	†Cle★	15(12, QB)	15	22	1.5(7)	1	—	—	—	—	389	241	62.0	3033	7.8(54)	22	9	22	129	95.4	—	—	6	1299
1988	Cle	9(9, QB)	12	-1	-0.1(13)	1	—	—	—	—	259	156	60.2	1890	7.3(77)	10	7	25	172	84.3	—	—	6	724
1989	†Cle	16(16, QB)	30	70	2.3(23)	1	1	-7	-7.0(-7)	0	513	303	59.1	3533	6.9(97)	18	14	34	192	80.3	—	—	6	1373
1990	Cle	13(13, QB)	10	13	1.3(5)	0	—	—	—	—	423	230	54.4	2562	6.1(50)	10	15	37	220	65.7	—	—	0	744
1991	Cle	16(16, QB)	26	74	2.8(14)	0	1	1	1.0(1)	0	494	307	62.1	3487	7.1(71)	18	9	41	232	87.8	—	—	0	1548
1992	Cle	7(7, qb)	5	12	2.4(8)	0	—	—	—	—	155	103	66.5	1160	7.5(69)	8	7	21	126	—	—	—	0	352
1993	Cle	7(6, qb)	14	11	1.4(10)	0	—	—	—	—	138	79	57.2	807	5.8(38)	5	3	21	128	—	—	—	0	328
1993	†Dal	4(1)	9	7	0.8(4)	0	—	—	—	—	63	36	57.1	410	6.5(86)	3	0	2	4	—	—	—	0	227
1994	Mia	2(0)	1	17	17.0(17)	0	—	—	—	—	12	7	58.3	80	6.7(22)	1	1	—	—	—	—	—	0	22
1995	†Mia	7	19	2.7(14)	1	—	—	—	—	—	108	74	68.5	699	6.5(31)	3	5	28	—	—	—	—	6	194
1996	Mia	3(0)	1	6	6.0(6)	0	—	—	—	—	32	24	75.0	208	6.5(20)	1	0	6	34	—	—	—	0	115
NFL	12	126(108)	180	265	1.5(23)	5	3	-5	-1.7(1)	0	3365	1994	59.3	23301	6.9(97)	124	87	273	1660	81.8	—	—	30	9103

YEAR	TEAM	G(GS, POS)	RUSH	YD	AVG(LG)	TD	REC	YD	AVG(LG)	TD	PASS COMP	PCT	YD	AVG(LG)	TD	INT	SK	YD	QBR	KPR	OTD	PTS	TAY

KOSEL, STAN Stanley Joseph, FB-HB, 5´11˝/190 lbs; Albright; B8/17/1916 Carteret, NJ, D5/1982 Carteret, NJ

1938	Bkn	8(1)	13	43	3.3	0	—	—	—	1	1	0	0.0	0	0.0	0	0	—	—	—	—	0	43
1939	Bkn	5(1)	2	6	3.0	0	2	40	20.0	1	—	—	—	—	—	—	—	—	—	—	—	6	31
NFL	2	13(2)	15	49	3.3	0	2	40	20.0	1	1	0	0.0	0	0.0	0	0	—	—	—	—	6	74

KOSENS, TERRY Theodore James, DB, 6´3˝/195 lbs; Hofstra; 1963: Min, rnd 10; B10/3/1941 Brooklyn, NY, D12/4/2004 Brightwaters, NY **1963** Min 8 (4)

KOSHLAP, JULIE Julius Michael, B, 5´11˝/180 lbs; Georgetown (DC); 1941: Bkn, rnd 21; B12/25/1917 Wallington, NJ, D1/5/2001 Ann Arbor, MI **1945** Pit 1 (0)

KOSIER, KYLE Kyle Blaine, G-T, 6´5˝/293 lbs; Arizona State; 2002: SF, rnd 7; B1/27/1978 Peoria, AZ **2002**†SF 15 (1) **2003** SF 16 (12, LG) **2004** SF 16 (16, LT/rg) **2005** Det 16 (11, LG) **NFL** 63 (40) [4 yrs]

KOSIKOWSKI, FRANK Frank Leon, DE, 6´1˝/200 lbs; Marquette; Notre Dame; B7/23/1926 Cudahy, WI **1948**†Cle-A 12 (0)

KOSINS, GARY Gary James, RB, 6´1˝/215 lbs; Dayton; 1972: Mia, rnd 3; B1/21/1949 Warsaw, IN

1972	ChiB	14	3	5	1.7(3)	0	2	15	7.5(8)	1	—	—	—	—	—	—	—	—	—	—	—	6	18
1973	ChiB	12	24	65	2.7(7)	0	4	8	2.0(10)	0	—	—	—	—	—	—	—	—	—	—	—	0	69
1974	ChiB	14	8	30	3.8(12)	1	1	3	3.0(3)	0	—	—	—	—	—	—	—	—	—	—	—	6	42
NFL	3	40	35	100	2.9(12)	1	7	26	3.7(10)	1	—	—	—	—	—	—	—	—	—	—	—	12	128

KOSS, STEIN Stein Jeffrey, TE, 6´2˝/225 lbs; Arizona State; B8/21/1963 Durango, CO

| 1987 | KC | 2(2) | — | — | — | — | 2 | 25 | 12.5(14) | 0 | — | — | — | — | — | — | — | — | — | — | — | 0 | 13 |

KOSTELNIK, RON Ronald Michael, DT, 6´4˝/260 lbs; Cincinnati; 1961: GB, rnd 2/Buf, rnd 14; B1/14/1940 Colver, PA, D1/29/1993 Scott County, KY **1961** GB 14 **1962** GB 14 **1963** GB 13 (LDT) **1964** GB 14 (LDT) **1965** GB 14 (LDT) **1966** GB 14 (LDT) **1967** GB 14 (LDT) **1968** GB 13 (LDT) **1969** Bal 10 **NFL** 120 [9 yrs]

KOSTIUK, MICHAEL Michael A., T, 6´0˝/212 lbs; Detroit Tech; B8/1/1919 Krydor, Canada, deceased **1941** Cle 1 (0) **1945** Det 6 (3) **NFL** 7 (3) [2 yrs]

KOSTKA, STAN Stanislas Clarence, FB-LB, 5´11˝/225 lbs; Oregon; Minnesota; B7/8/1912 St. Paul, MN, D2/3/1997 Fargo, ND

| 1935 | Bkn | 9(5, fb) | 63 | 249 | 4.0 | 0 | 1 | 9 | 9.0(9) | 0 | 4 | 0 | 0.0 | 0 | 0.0 | 0 | 2 | — | — | — | — | 0 | 174 |

KOSTOS, MARTY Martin V., E, 5´11˝/185 lbs; Schuylkill; B11/11/1901, D9/1961 Sunbury, PA **1929** Fra 6 (2, LE)

KOSTOS, TONY Anthony Joseph, E-C-G-T, 5´11˝/191 lbs; Bucknell; B6/12/1905, PA, D11/16/1984 New Brunswick, NJ [K] **1927** Fra 7 (3) **1928** Fra 16 (14, LE), 2 **1929** Fra 19 (16), 6 **1930** Fra 16 (11, LE), 7 **1930** Min 2 (0) **1931** Fra 6 (3) **NFL** 66 (47), 15 [5 yrs]

KOTAL, EDDIE Edward Louis, B, 5´8˝/170 lbs; Illinois; Lawrence; B9/1/1902, IL, D1/27/1973 North Hollywood, CA **1925** GB 5 (1), 6 **1926** GB 10 (5, hb), 12 **1927** GB 8 (6, TB), 6 **1928** GB☆12 (11, WB), 18 **1929** GB 11 (5, TB), 18 **NFL** 46 (28), 60 [5 yrs]

KOTAR, DOUG Douglas Allan, RB, 5´11˝/205 lbs; Kentucky; B6/11/1951 Canonsburg, PA, D12/16/1983 Pittsburgh, PA

1974	NYG	12(RB)	106	396	3.7(53)	4	10	57	5.7(18)	—	—	—	—	—	—	—	—	—	—	kp	—	24	589
1975	NYG	14	122	378	3.1(46)	6	9	86	9.6(17)	—	—	—	—	—	—	—	—	—	—	kp	—	36	631
1976	NYG	14(RB)	185	731	4.0(24)	3	36	319	8.9(30)	—	—	—	—	—	—	—	—	—	—	k	—	18	915
1977	NYG	12(RB)	132	480	3.6(32)	2	15	73	4.9(13)	—	—	—	—	—	—	—	—	—	—	k	—	12	543
1978	NYG	15(11, RB)	149	625	4.2(46)	1	22	225	10.2(31)	1	—	—	—	—	—	—	—	—	—	k	—	12	759
1979	NYG	16(RB)	160	616	3.8(32)	3	25	230	9.2(37)	0	—	—	—	—	—	—	—	—	—	k	—	18	770
1981	NYG	7(4)	46	154	3.3(18)	1	9	32	3.6(11)	0	—	—	—	—	—	—	—	—	—	—	—	6	180
NFL	7	90(15)	900	3380	3.8(53)	20	126	1022	8.1(37)	1	—	—	—	—	—	—	—	—	—	kp	—	126	4385

KOTITE, RICH Richard Edward, TE, 6´3˝/233 lbs; Miami (FL); Wagner; 1965: Min, rnd 18/NYJ, rnd R9; B10/13/1942 Brooklyn, NY [C]

1967	NYG	4	—	—	—	—	—	—	—	—	—	—	—	—	—	—	—	—	—	—	—	—	—
1968	Pit	12	—	—	—	—	6	65	10.8(20)	2	—	—	—	—	—	—	—	—	—	—	—	12	43
1969	NYG	3	—	—	—	—	1	2	2.0(2)	1	—	—	—	—	—	—	—	—	—	—	—	6	6
1971	NYG	14	—	—	—	—	10	146	14.6(43)	2	—	—	—	—	—	—	—	—	—	—	—	12	83
1972	NYG	2	—	—	—	—	—	—	—	—	—	—	—	—	—	—	—	—	—	—	—	—	—
NFL	5	35	—	—	—	—	17	213	12.5(43)	5	—	—	—	—	—	—	—	—	—	—	—	30	132

KOTTLER, MARTY Martin Albert, FB, 5´9˝/180 lbs; Centre; B5/1/1910 Carnegie, PA, D6/10/1989 Centerbrook, CT **1933** Pit 3 (0)

KOUTOUVIDES, NIKO Niko Stelios, LB, 6´3˝/226 lbs; Purdue; 2004: Sea, rnd 4; B3/25/1981 Plainville, CT **2004**†Sea 16 (2) **2005**†Sea 12 (0) **NFL** 28 (2) [2 yrs]

KOVAC, ED Edward William, HB, 6´0˝/195 lbs; Cincinnati; 1960: Chi, rnd 6/NYT, rnd 1; B4/22/1938 McKeesport, PA

1960	Bal	12	4	1	0.3(5)	0	2	27	13.5(25)	0	—	—	—	—	—	—	—	—	—	k	—	0	8
1962	NYT-A	3	3	5	1.7(3)	0	1	3	3.0(5)	0	—	—	—	—	—	—	—	—	—	ki	—	0	35
NFL	2	15	7	6	0.9(5)	0	3	30	10.0(25)	0	—	—	—	—	—	—	—	—	—	ki	—	0	42

KOVACH, JIM James Joseph, LB, 6´2˝/230 lbs; Kentucky; 1979: NO, rnd 4; B5/1/1956 Parma Heights, OH **1979** NO 16 **1980** NO 11 (2) **1981** NO 15 (15, RILB) **1982** NO 8 (8, LILB) **1983** NO☆16 (16, LILB) **1984** NO 15 (15, RILB) **1985** NO 2 (2) **1985**†SF 4 (0) **NFL** 87 (58) [7 yrs]

KOVACSY, BILL William George, G, /195 lbs; Illinois; B2/15/1901 Bridgeport, CT, D5/30/1980 Hammond, IN **1923** Ham 4 (2)

KOVALESKI, MIKE Michael Aaron, LB, 6´2˝/225 lbs; Notre Dame; B1/30/1965 Union City, NJ **1987** Cle 1 (0)

KOVATCH, JOHN John George, E, 6´3˝/197 lbs; Notre Dame; 1942: Was, rnd 13; B7/21/1920 South Bend, IN

1942	Was	8(0)	—	—	—	—	12	90	7.5(15)	1	—	—	—	—	—	—	—	—	—	k	—	6	48
1946	Was	10(3)	—	—	—	—	6	67	11.2(23)	0	—	—	—	—	—	—	—	—	—	—	—	0	34
1947	GB	3(0)	—	—	—	—	—	—	—	—	—	—	—	—	—	—	—	—	—	—	—	—	—
NFL	3	21(3)	—	—	—	—	18	157	8.7(23)	1	—	—	—	—	—	—	—	—	—	k	—	6	82

KOVATCH, JOHNNY John Paul, E, 5´11˝/172 lbs; Northwestern; 1938: GB, rnd 7; B6/24/1912 South Bend, IN

| 1938 | Cle | 6(0) | — | — | — | — | 8 | 97 | 12.1(42) | 1 | — | — | — | — | — | — | — | — | — | — | — | 6 | 54 |

KOWALCZYK, WALT Walter Joseph, FB-DB, 6´0˝/208 lbs; Michigan State; 1958: Phi, rnd 1; B4/17/1935 Westfield, MA

1958	Phi	12	17	43	2.5(17)	1	8	72	9.0(15)	0	—	—	—	—	—	—	—	—	—	i	—	6	86
1959	Phi	12	26	37	1.4(6)	0	9	33	3.7(13)	0	—	—	—	—	—	—	—	—	—	—	—	0	54
1960	Dal	12(7, FB)	50	156	3.1(34)	1	14	143	10.2(23)	1	—	—	—	—	—	—	—	—	—	k	—	12	228
1961	Oak-A	4	10	28	2.8(18)	0	3	8	2.7(4)	0	—	—	—	—	—	—	—	—	—	k	—	0	36
NFL	4	40(7)	103	264	2.6(34)	2	34	256	7.5(23)	1	—	—	—	—	—	—	—	—	—	ki	—	18	403

KOWALKOWSKI, BOB Robert, G, 6´3˝/240 lbs; Virginia; 1965: Det, rnd 7/Bos, rnd R2; B11/5/1943 Upper Darby, PA **1966** Det 14 (LG) **1967** Det 14 **1968** Det 14 **1969** Det 2 **1970** Det 10 **1971** Det 14 (RG) **1972** Det 14 (14, RG) **1973** Det 14 (14, RG) **1974** Det 14 (14, RG) **1975** Det 14 (14, RG) **1976** Det 14 (14, RG) **1977** GB 4 **NFL** 142 (70) [12 yrs]

KOWALKOWSKI, SCOTT Scott Thomas, LB, 6´2˝/228 lbs; Notre Dame; 1991: Phi, rnd 8; B8/23/1968 Farmington Hills, MI **1991** Phi 16 (0) **1992**†Phi 16 (0) **1994**†Det 16 (0) **1995**†Det 16 (0) **1996** Det 16 (1) **1997**†Det 16 (0) **1998** Det 15 (0) **1999**†Det 16 (3) **2000** Det 16 (2) **2001** Det 15 (0) **NFL** 158 (6) [10 yrs]

KOWALSKI, ADOLPH Adolph Ernest, BB-DB, 6´3˝/205 lbs; Tulsa; 1945: Bkn, rnd 5; B1921 **1947** Bkn-A 10 (0)

KOWALSKI, ANDY Anthony Joseph, E, 6´1˝/199 lbs; Mississippi State; B6/2/1920 Gloucester City, NJ, D12/3/1983 Clinton, MS

1943	Bkn	8(6, RE)	—	—	—	—	11	145	13.2(35)	0	—	—	—	—	—	—	—	—	—	i	—	0	77
1944	Bkn	10(1)	—	—	—	—	9	155	17.2(58)	1	—	—	—	—	—	—	—	—	—	—	—	6	83
1945	Bos	3(0)	—	—	—	—	—	—	—	—	—	—	—	—	—	—	—	—	—	—	—	—	—
NFL	3	21(7)	—	—	—	—	20	300	15.0(58)	1	—	—	—	—	—	—	—	—	—	i	—	6	159

KOWALSKI, GARY Gary Stuart, T-G, 6´6˝/280 lbs; Boston College; 1983: LARm, rnd 6; B7/2/1960 New Haven, CT **1983** LARm 15 (0) **1985** SD 13 (1) **1986** SD 16 (16, RT) **1987** SD 12 (9, RT) **1988** SD 2 (2) **NFL** 58 (28) [5 yrs]

KOWGIOS, NICK Nicholas, RB, 6´0˝/216 lbs; Lafayette; B11/19/1962 Yonkers, NY

| 1987 | Det | 3(0) | 1 | 2 | 2.0(2) | 0 | 1 | 3 | 3.0(3) | 0 | — | — | — | — | — | — | — | — | — | — | — | 0 | 4 |

KOY, ERNIE Ernest Melvin, RB-FL-P, 6´3˝/230 lbs; Texas; 1965: NYG, rnd 11/Hou, rnd 3; B10/22/1942 Bellville, TX

1965	NYG	13	35	174	5.0(27)	4	4	22	5.5(9)	0	2	0	0.0	0	0.0	0	1	—	—	Pk	—	0	231
1966	NYG	13(FL)	66	146	2.2(13)	0	8	43	5.4(26)	0	2	0	0.0	0	0.0	0	1	—	—	Pk	—	0	143
1967	NYG◇	14(HB)	146	704	4.8(61)	4	32	212	6.6(24)	3	4	3	75.0	101	25.3(68)	1	0	—	—	Pk	—	30	914

YEAR	TEAM	G(GS, POS)	RUSH	YD	AVG(LG)	TD	REC	YD	AVG(LG)	TD	PASS	COMP	PCT	YD	AVG(LG)	TD	INT	SK	YD	QBR	KPR	OTD	PTS	TAY
1968	NYG	13(HB)	89	394	4.4(26)	3	12	59	4.9(20)	1	3	2	66.7	13	4.3(11)	0	0	—	—	—	P	—	24	465
1969	NYG	14(HB)	76	300	3.9(24)	2	19	152	8.0(41)	4	1	1	100.0	15	15.0(15)	0	0	—	—	—	P	—	36	424
1970	NYG	12	2	5	2.5(7)	0	1	10	10.0(10)	0	—	—	—	—	—	—	—	—	—	—	P	—	0	10
NFL	6	79	414	1723	4.2(61)	9	76	498	6.6(41)	6	12	6	50.0	129	10.8(68)	1	1	—	—	—	Pk	—	90	2186

Koy, Ted James Theodore, TE-RB-LB, 6´2˝/212 lbs; Texas; 1970: Oak, rnd 2; B9/15/1947 Bellville, TX **1970**†Oak 14 **1973** Buf 13 **1974**†Buf 12

YEAR	TEAM	G(GS, POS)	RUSH	YD	AVG(LG)	TD	REC	YD	AVG(LG)	TD	PASS	COMP	PCT	YD	AVG(LG)	TD	INT	SK	YD	QBR	KPR	OTD	PTS	TAY
1971	Buf	14	—	—	—	—	10	133	13.3(22)	1	—	—	—	—	—	—	—	—	—	—	—	—	6	72
1972	Buf	14	1	9	9.0(9)	0	1	9	9.0(9)	0	—	—	—	—	—	—	—	—	—	—	k	—	0	2
NFL	5	67	1	9	9.0(9)	0	11	142	12.9(22)	1	—	—	—	—	—	—	—	—	—	—	k	—	6	73

Kozak, Scott Scott Allen, LB, 6´3˝/226 lbs; Oregon; 1989: Hou, rnd 2; B11/28/1965 Hillsboro, OR **1989**†Hou 16 (0) **1990**†Hou 16 (0) **1991**†Hou 16 (0) **1992** Hou 16 (0) **1993**†Hou 16 (0) **NFL** 80 (0) [5 yrs]

Kozel, Chet Chester Richard, T-G, 6´2˝/211 lbs; Mississippi; B10/15/1919 Kenosha, WI, D6/27/1982 Kenosha, WI **1947** Buf-A 12 (9, lt) **1948** Buf-A 2 (0) **1948** ChiR-A 5 (1) **AAFC** 19 (10) [2 yrs]

Kozerski, Bruce Bruce W., C-G-T, 6´4˝/287 lbs; Holy Cross; 1984: Cin, rnd 9; B4/2/1962 Plains, PA **1984** Cin 16 (1) **1985** Cin 14 (0) **1986** Cin 16 (15, LG/c) **1987** Cin 8 (4) **1988** Cin 16 (16, C) **1989** Cin 15 (15, C) **1990** Cin 16 (16, C) **1991** Cin 16 (16, C) **1992** Cin 16 (16, LG) **1993** Cin 15 (15, C) **1994** Cin 16 (16, RT) **1995** Cin 8 (8, rg) **NFL** 172 (138) [12 yrs]

Koziak, Mike Michael, G, 5´9˝/185 lbs; none; B1892, deceased **1925** Dul 1 (1)

Kozlowski, Brian Brian Scott, TE, 6´3˝/250 lbs; Connecticut; B10/4/1970 Rochester, NY

YEAR	TEAM	G(GS, POS)	RUSH	YD	AVG(LG)	TD	REC	YD	AVG(LG)	TD	PASS	COMP	PCT	YD	AVG(LG)	TD	INT	SK	YD	QBR	KPR	OTD	PTS	TAY
1994	NYG	16(3)	—	—	—	—	1	5	5.0(5)	0	—	—	—	—	—	—	—	—	—	—	k	—	0	-7
1995	NYG	16(0)	—	—	—	—	2	17	8.5(12)	0	—	—	—	—	—	—	—	—	—	—	k	—	0	9
1996	NYG	5(0)	—	—	—	—	1	4	4.0(4)	1	—	—	—	—	—	—	—	—	—	—	k	—	6	8
1997	Atl	16(5, te)	—	—	—	—	7	99	14.1(29)	1	—	—	—	—	—	—	—	—	—	—	k	—	6	74
1998	†Atl	16(4)	—	—	—	—	10	103	10.3(25)	1	—	—	—	—	—	—	—	—	—	—	k	—	6	54
1999	Atl	16(3)	—	—	—	—	11	122	11.1(26)	2	—	—	—	—	—	—	—	—	—	—	k	—	12	60
2000	Atl	16(3)	—	—	—	—	15	151	10.1(30)	2	—	—	—	—	—	—	—	—	—	—	k	—	12	58
2001	Atl	16(0)	—	—	—	—	15	270	18.0(46)	1	—	—	—	—	—	—	—	—	—	—	kp	—	6	125
2002	†Atl	16(2)	—	—	—	—	6	59	9.8(14)	0	—	—	—	—	—	—	—	—	—	—	k	—	0	35
2003	Atl	16(9, te)	—	—	—	—	10	87	8.7(19)	0	—	—	—	—	—	—	—	—	—	—	k	—	0	26
2004	Was	11(1)	—	—	—	—	3	29	9.7(13)	0	—	—	—	—	—	—	—	—	—	—	k	—	0	4
2005	†Was	16(0)	—	—	—	—	2	26	13.0(18)	0	—	—	—	—	—	—	—	—	—	—	—	—	0	13
NFL	12	176(30)	—	—	—	—	83	972	11.7(46)	8	—	—	—	—	—	—	—	—	—	—	kp	—	48	456

Kozlowski, Glen Glen Allen, WR, 6´1˝/200 lbs; Brigham Young; 1986: Chi, rnd 11; B12/31/1962 Honolulu, HI

YEAR	TEAM	G(GS, POS)	RUSH	YD	AVG(LG)	TD	REC	YD	AVG(LG)	TD	PASS	COMP	PCT	YD	AVG(LG)	TD	INT	SK	YD	QBR	KPR	OTD	PTS	TAY
1987	ChiB	3(3)	—	—	—	—	15	199	13.3(28)	3	—	—	—	—	—	—	—	—	—	—	k	—	18	142
1988	†ChiB	16(0)	1	3	3.0(3)	0	3	92	30.7(50)	0	—	—	—	—	—	—	—	—	—	—	kp	—	0	51
1989	ChiB	15(0)	—	—	—	—	3	74	24.7(55)	0	—	—	—	—	—	—	—	—	—	—	kp	—	0	12
1990	†ChiB	12(0)	—	—	—	—	7	83	11.9(32)	0	—	—	—	—	—	—	—	—	—	—	—	—	0	42
1991	†ChiB	16(0)	—	—	—	—	2	16	8.0(11)	0	—	—	—	—	—	—	—	—	—	—	—	—	0	8
1992	ChiB	4(0)	—	—	—	—	1	7	7.0(7)	0	—	—	—	—	—	—	—	—	—	—	—	—	0	4
NFL	6	66(3)	1	3	3.0(3)	0	31	471	15.2(55)	3	—	—	—	—	—	—	—	—	—	—	kp	—	18	258

Kozlowski, Mike Michael John, DB, 6´0˝/196 lbs; San Diego State; Brigham Young; Colorado; 1979: Mia, rnd 10; B2/24/1956 Newark, NJ **1979**†Mia 16 (1) **1981**†Mia 14 (0) **1982**†Mia 9 (0) **1983**†Mia 16 (0) **1984**†Mia 16 (0) **1985**†Mia 5 (2) **1986** Mia 15 (0) **NFL** 91 (3) [7 yrs]

Kozlowski, Stan Stanley J., FB, 6´1˝/200 lbs; Notre Dame; Holy Cross; 1946: Was, rnd 3; B2/5/1924 Rumford, RI, D8/23/1972 Boxboro, MA

YEAR	TEAM	G(GS, POS)	RUSH	YD	AVG(LG)	TD	REC	YD	AVG(LG)	TD	PASS	COMP	PCT	YD	AVG(LG)	TD	INT	SK	YD	QBR	KPR	OTD	PTS	TAY
1946	Mia-A	5(0)	18	61	3.4	0	2	27	13.5	0	—	—	—	—	—	—	—	—	—	—	kp	—	0	101

Kozlowsky, Joe Joseph Alexander, T-G-E, 5´10˝/201 lbs; Boston College; B8/9/1901 Cambridge, MA, D12/22/1970 Boston, MA **1925** Pro 11 (11, LT) **1926** Pro 10 (8, LT) **1927** Pro☆12 (8, rt) **1929** Bos 8 (8, RT) **1930** Pro 8 (2) **NFL** 49 (37) [5 yrs]

Kraayeveld, Dave David Ray, DE-DT, 6´5˝/255 lbs; Wisconsin-Whitewater; Milton; B10/26/1955 Elkhorn, WI **1978** Sea 12

Kracum, George George Vince, FB, 6´1˝/210 lbs; Pittsburgh; 1941: ChiC, rnd 8; B1/24/1918 Tresckow, PA, D6/7/1981 Minneapolis, MN

YEAR	TEAM	G(GS, POS)	RUSH	YD	AVG(LG)	TD	REC	YD	AVG(LG)	TD	PASS	COMP	PCT	YD	AVG(LG)	TD	INT	SK	YD	QBR	KPR	OTD	PTS	TAY
1941	Bkn	11(0)	52	169	3.3(17)	3	2	17	8.5(13)	0	—	—	—	—	—	—	—	—	—	—	ki	—	18	235

Kraehe, Ollie Oliver Robert, E-G-C, 5´10˝/180 lbs; Washington-St. Louis; B8/22/1898 St. Louis, MO, D11/2/1969 St. Louis, MO **[C]** **1922** RI 3 (0) **1923** SL 7 (6, LE) **NFL** 10 (6) [2 yrs]

Kraemer, Eldred Eldred John, G, 6´2˝/225 lbs; Pittsburgh; 1955: SF, rnd 5; B10/2/1929 St. Cloud, MN, D9/16/1992 Pittsburgh, PA **1955** SF 12

Kraft, Reynold Reynold Rudolph, E, 5´11˝/170 lbs; Illinois; B3/29/1895 Menomonie, WI, D11/7/1951 Chicago, IL **1922** Min 2 (2, RE)

Kraft, Rudy Rudolph George, G-C, 5´10˝/190 lbs; Penn State; B10/21/1896 Wilkes-Barre, PA, D11/20/1978 Buffalo, NY **1921** Ton 1 (1, LG)

Kragen, Greg Greg John, NT-DT, 6´3˝/263 lbs; Utah State; B3/4/1962 Chicago, IL **1985** Den 16 (1) **1986**†Den 16 (14, NT) **1987**†Den 12 (9, NT) **1988** Den 16 (16, NT) **1989**†Den★14 (14, NT) **1990** Den 16 (16, NT) **1991**†Den☆16 (16, NT) **1992** Den☆16 (16, NT) **1993**†Den 14 (14, NT) **1994**†KC 16 (2) **1995** Car 16 (14, NT) **1996**†Car 16 (16, NT) **1997** Car 16 (16, NT) **NFL** 200 (164) [13 yrs]

Krahl, Jim James Kenneth, DT, 6´5˝/252 lbs; Texas Tech; 1978: NYG, rnd 5; B11/19/1953 Houston, TX **1978** NYG 16 (3) **1979** Bal 1 **1980** Bal 2 (0) **1980** SF 2 (0) **NFL** 21 (3) [3 yrs]

Krakau, Merv Mervin Floyd, LB, 6´2˝/242 lbs; Iowa State; 1973: Buf, rnd 14; B5/16/1951 Jefferson, IA **1973** Buf 14 (rlb) **1974**†Buf 11 **1975** Buf 14 (9, RILB) **1976** Buf 14 (14, MLB) **1977** Buf 13 (MLB) **1978** Buf 5 **1978** NE 1 **NFL** 72 (23) [6 yrs]

Kraker, Joe Joseph J., G, 6´1˝/170 lbs; Saskatchewan (Canada); B6/14/1896, MN, D11/14/1958 St. Louis County, MN **1924** RI 5 (4, RG)

Krakoski, Joe Joseph Andrew, DB, 6´2˝/195 lbs; Illinois; 1961: Was, rnd 6/Oak, rnd 18; B12/18/1937 Danville, IL **1961** Was 11 (8, LCB) **1963** Oak-A☆14 (LS) **1964** Oak-A 14 (LS) **1965** Oak-A 12 (LS) **1966** Oak-A 11 (ls) **NFL** 62 (8) [5 yrs]

Krakoski, Joe Joseph Joshua, LB, 6´1˝/224 lbs; Washington; 1985: Hou, rnd 6; B11/11/1962 Aurora, IL **1986** Was 8 (0)

Krall, Gerry Gerald Stanley, DB-HB, 5´10˝/185 lbs; Ohio State; 1949: ChiB, rnd 6/LAD-A, rnd 10; B4/19/1927 Toledo, OH

YEAR	TEAM	G(GS, POS)	RUSH	YD	AVG(LG)	TD	REC	YD	AVG(LG)	TD	PASS	COMP	PCT	YD	AVG(LG)	TD	INT	SK	YD	QBR	KPR	OTD	PTS	TAY
1950	Det	7(DB)	3	0	0.0(6)	0	2	61	30.5(41)	0	—	—	—	—	—	—	—	—	—	—	p	—	0	35

Kramer, Erik William Erik, QB, 6´1˝/200 lbs; North Carolina State; B11/6/1964 Encino, CA

YEAR	TEAM	G(GS, POS)	RUSH	YD	AVG(LG)	TD	REC	YD	AVG(LG)	TD	PASS	COMP	PCT	YD	AVG(LG)	TD	INT	SK	YD	QBR	KPR	OTD	PTS	TAY
1987	Atl	3(2)	2	10	5.0(11)	0	—	—	—	—	92	45	48.9	559	6.1(33)	4	5	10	82	—	—	—	0	110
1991	†Det	13(8, qb)	35	26	0.7(12)	1	—	—	—	—	265	136	51.3	1635	6.2(73)	11	8	14	74	71.8	—	—	6	589
1992	Det	7(3)	12	34	2.8(11)	0	—	—	—	—	106	58	54.7	771	7.3(77)	4	8	15	80	—	—	—	0	120
1993	†Det	5(4)	10	5	0.5(4)	0	—	—	—	—	138	87	63.0	1002	7.3(48)	8	3	5	35	—	—	—	0	426
1994	†ChiB	6(5, qb)	6	-2	-0.3(2)	0	—	—	—	—	158	99	62.7	1129	7.1(85)	8	8	14	87	—	—	—	0	283
1995	ChiB	16(16, QB)	35	39	1.1(11)	1	—	—	—	—	522	315	60.3	3838	7.4(76)	29	10	15	95	93.5	—	—	6	1713
1996	ChiB	4(4, qb)	8	4	0.5(3)	0	—	—	—	—	150	73	48.7	781	5.2(58)	3	6	7	53	—	—	—	0	170
1997	ChiB	15(13, QB)	27	83	3.1(31)	2	—	—	—	—	477	275	57.7	3011	6.3(78)	14	14	25	149	74.0	—	—	12	1119
1998	ChiB	8(8, QB)	13	17	1.3(8)	1	—	—	—	—	250	151	60.4	1823	7.3(79)	9	7	10	71	83.1	—	—	6	704
1999	SD	6(4)	5	1	0.2(3)	0	—	—	—	—	141	78	55.3	788	5.6(41)	2	10	7	62	—	—	—	0	5
NFL	10	83(67)	153	217	1.4(31)	5	—	—	—	—	2299	1317	57.3	15337	6.7(85)	92	79	122	788	76.6	—	—	30	5236

Kramer, Fritz Frederick F., G-C, 6´0˝/230 lbs; Washington State; B5/27/1903, D1/20/1992 Orange, CA **1927** NYY 10 (6, lg)

Kramer, George George Lambert, G-T, 6´2˝/240 lbs; none; B6/2/1894 Joliet, IL, D9/1974 Chicago, IL **1921** Min 3 (1) **1922** Min 3 (3, LG) **1923** Min 7 (3) **1924** Min 6 (3, LG) **NFL** 19 (10) [4 yrs]

Kramer, Jack John Francis, T, 6´0˝/220 lbs; Marquette; 1945: ChiC, rnd 20; B7/26/1919 Milwaukee, WI, D12/15/1978 Milwaukee, WI **1946** Buf-A 13 (2)

Kramer, Jerry Gerald Louis, G, 6´3˝/245 lbs; Idaho; 1958: GB, rnd 4; B1/23/1936 Jordan, MT **[K]** **1958** GB 12 (RG) **1959** GB 12 (RG) **1960**†GB☆12 (RG) **1961** GB☆8 (RG) **1962**†GB★14 (RG) **1963** GB★14 (RG) **1964** GB 2 **1965**†GB 14 (RG) **1966**†GB☆14 (14, RG) **1967**†GB★14 (RG) **1968** GB☆14 (RG) **NFL** 130 (14) [11 yrs]

YEAR	TEAM	G(GS, POS)	RUSH	YD	AVG(LG)	TD	REC	YD	AVG(LG)	TD	PASS	COMP	PCT	YD	AVG(LG)	TD	INT	SK	YD	QBR	KPR	OTD	PTS	TAY
KRAMER, JORDAN Jordan, LB, 6´1˝/230 lbs; Idaho; B12/7/1979 Parma, ID **2003**†Ten 2 (0) **2004** Ten 4 (0) **NFL** 6 (0) [2 yrs]																								
KRAMER, KENT Kent Devlin, TE, 6´4˝/235 lbs; Minnesota; 1966: SF, rnd 9/Mia, rnd 13; B7/21/1944 Los Angeles, CA																								
1966	SF	14	—	—	—	—	5	81	16.2(24)	3	—	—	—	—	—	—	—	—	—	—	—	—	18	56
1967	NO	10(TE)	—	—	—	—	20	207	10.4(17)	2	—	—	—	—	—	—	—	—	—	—	—	—	12	114
1969	†Min	13	—	—	—	—	2	37	18.5(24)	1	—	—	—	—	—	—	—	—	—	—	—	—	6	24
1970	†Min	11	—	—	—	—	1	10	10.0(10)	0	—	—	—	—	—	—	—	—	—	—	—	—	0	5
1971	Phi	10(3, te)	—	—	—	—	6	65	10.8(17)	1	—	—	—	—	—	—	—	—	—	—	k	—	6	23
1972	Phi	14(8, TE)	—	—	—	—	11	176	16.0(29)	1	—	—	—	—	—	—	—	—	—	—	—	—	6	93
1973	Phi	11	—	—	—	—	—	—	—	—	—	—	—	—	—	—	—	—	—	—	—	—	—	—
1974	Phi	14	—	—	—	—	—	—	—	—	—	—	—	—	—	—	—	—	—	—	k	—	0	9
NFL	8	97(11)	—	—	—	—	45	576	12.8(29)	8	—	—	—	—	—	—	—	—	—	—	k	—	48	322
KRAMER, KYLE Kyle Mevoy, DB, 6´3˝/190 lbs; Bowling Green State; 1989: Cle, rnd 5; B1/12/1967 Kansas City, MO **1989**†Cle 14 (0)																								
KRAMER, RON Ronald John, E-TE, 6´3˝/234 lbs; Michigan; 1957: GB, rnd 1; B6/24/1935 Girard, KS																								
1957	GB	11(LE)	—	—	—	—	28	337	12.0(31)	0	1	0	0.0	0	0.0	0	1	—	—	—	—	—	0	129
1959	GB	12	—	—	—	—	—	—	—	—	—	—	—	—	—	—	—	—	—	—	—	—	—	—
1960	†GB	12	—	—	—	—	4	55	13.8(18)	0	—	—	—	—	—	—	—	—	—	—	—	—	0	28
1961	†GB	14(TE)	5	13	2.6(12)	0	35	559	16.0(53)	4	—	—	—	—	—	—	—	—	—	—	—	—	24	313
1962	†GB★	14(TE)	1	-4	-4.0(-4)	0	37	555	15.0(54)	7	—	—	—	—	—	—	—	—	—	—	—	—	42	309
1963	GB☆	12(TE)	—	—	—	—	32	537	16.8(49)	4	—	—	—	—	—	—	—	—	—	—	—	—	24	289
1964	GB	14(TE)	—	—	—	—	34	551	16.2(55)	0	—	—	—	—	—	—	—	—	—	—	—	—	0	276
1965	Det	14(te)	—	—	—	—	18	206	11.4(23)	1	—	—	—	—	—	—	—	—	—	—	—	—	6	108
1966	Det	14(TE)	—	—	—	—	37	432	11.7(68)	0	—	—	—	—	—	—	—	—	—	—	—	—	0	216
1967	Det	11(TE)	—	—	—	—	4	40	10.0(16)	0	—	—	—	—	—	—	—	—	—	—	—	—	0	20
NFL	10	128	6	9	1.5(12)	0	229	3272	14.3(68)	16	1	0	0.0	0	0.0	0	1	—	—	—	—	—	96	1685
KRAMER, TOMMY Thomas Francis, QB, 6´2˝/200 lbs; Rice; 1977: Min, rnd 1; B3/7/1955 San Antonio, TX																								
1977	Min	6(1)	10	3	0.3(8)	0	—	—	—	—	57	30	52.6	425	7.5(69)	5	4	6	45	—	—	—	0	81
1978	Min	4	1	10	10.0(10)	0	—	—	—	—	16	5	31.3	50	3.1(19)	0	1	1	11	—	—	—	0	-5
1979	Min	16(16, QB)	32	138	4.3(20)	1	0	3	(3)	0	566	315	55.7	3397	6.0(55)	23	**24**	36	249	69.3	—	—	6	1003
1980	†Min	15(15, QB)	31	115	3.7(13)	1	—	—	—	—	**522**	299	57.3	3582	6.9(76)	19	23	37	214	72.2	—	—	6	1091
1981	Min	14(14, QB)	10	13	1.3(8)	0	—	—	—	—	**593**	**322**	54.3	**3912**	6.6(63)	26	**24**	19	149	72.6	—	—	0	1139
1982	†Min	9(9, QB)	21	77	3.7(18)	3	—	—	—	—	308	176	57.1	2037	6.6(65)	15	12	21	130	77.3	—	—	18	721
1983	Min	3(3)	8	3	0.4(8)	0	—	—	—	—	82	55	67.1	550	6.7(49)	3	4	3	27	—	—	—	0	133
1984	Min	9(9, QB)	15	9	0.6(14)	0	1	20	20.0(20)	1	236	124	52.5	1678	7.1(70)	9	10	24	145	70.6	—	—	6	508
1985	Min	15(15, QB)	27	54	2.0(11)	0	—	—	—	—	**506**	277	54.7	3522	7.0(57)	19	**26**	39	255	67.8	—	—	0	870
1986	Min★	13(13, QB)	23	48	2.1(13)	1	—	—	—	—	372	208	55.9	3000	**8.1(76)**	**24**	10	31	178	92.6	—	—	6	1278
1987	†Min	6(5, qb)	10	44	4.4(15)	2	—	—	—	—	81	40	49.4	452	5.6(40)	4	3	7	35	—	—	—	12	190
1988	Min	10(6, qb)	14	8	0.6(5)	0	—	—	—	—	173	83	48.0	1264	7.3(47)	5	9	11	62	—	—	—	0	305
1989	†Min	8(4)	12	9	0.8(5)	0	—	—	—	—	136	77	56.6	906	6.7(39)	7	7	12	75	—	—	—	0	217
1990	NO	1(0)	—	—	—	—	—	—	—	—	3	1	33.3	2	0.7(2)	0	1	2	11	—	—	—	0	-39
NFL	14	129(110)	214	531	2.5(20)	8	1	23	23.0(20)	1	3651	2012	55.1	24777	6.8(76)	159	158	249	1586	72.8	—	—	54	7491
KRANCHICK, MATT Matthew Alan, TE, 6´8˝/253 lbs; Penn State; 2004: Pit, rnd 6; B12/13/1979 Carlisle, PA **2004** Pit 2 (0) **2005**†NYG 2 (0)																								
2005	Pit	4(1)	—	—	—	—	1	6	6.0(6)	0	—	—	—	—	—	—	—	—	—	—	—	—	0	3
NFL	2	8(1)	—	—	—	—	1	6	6.0(6)	0	—	—	—	—	—	—	—	—	—	—	—	—	0	3
KRANZ, KEN Kenneth Andrew, DB, 5´10˝/190 lbs; Wisconsin-Milwaukee; 1949: GB, rnd 21; B9/12/1923 Milwaukee, WI **1949** GB 7 (0)																								
KRATCH, BOB Robert Anthony, G, 6´3˝/288 lbs; Iowa; 1989: NYG, rnd 3; B1/6/1966 Brooklyn, NY **1989** NYG 4 (1) **1990**†NYG 14 (10, RG) **1991** NYG 15 (1) **1992** NYG 16 (7, rg) **1993**†NYG 16 (16, RG) **1994**†NE☆16 (16, LG) **1995** NE 16 (16, RG) **1996**†NE 8 (4) **NFL** 105 (71) [8 yrs]																								
KRATZER, DAN Daniel Leon, WR, 6´3˝/192 lbs; Northern Arizona; Missouri Valley; 1972: Cin, rnd 8; B7/7/1949 Kearney, MO **1973** KC 1																								
KRAUS, BABE Francis Lucius, T-G, 6´2˝/220 lbs; Colgate; Hobart; B9/2/1899 Fulton, NY, D9/5/1966 Geneva, NY **1924** Buf 7 (4)																								
KRAUSE, BILL William Edward, G, 6´0˝/210 lbs; Baldwin-Wallace; 1938: Pit, rnd 11; B7/9/1914, D7/1971 **1938** Cle 2 (1)																								
KRAUSE, HENRY Henry J., C-G, 6´1˝/211 lbs; St. Louis; B8/28/1913 St. Louis, MO, D2/20/1987 Beltsville, MD **1936** Bkn 12 (11, C) **1937** Bkn 5 (3) **1937** Was 3 (0) **1938** Was 9 (1) **NFL** 29 (15) [3 yrs]																								
KRAUSE, LARRY Lawrence James, RB, 6´0˝/208 lbs; St. Norbert; 1970: GB, rnd 17; B4/22/1948 Stanley, WI																								
1970	GB	14	2	13	6.5(12)	0	2	22	11.0(11)	0	—	—	—	—	—	—	—	—	—	—	k	1	6	277
1971	GB	9	3	-6	-2.0(2)	0	—	—	—	—	—	—	—	—	—	—	—	—	—	—	k	—	0	20
1973	GB	14	1	8	8.0(8)	0	—	—	—	—	—	—	—	—	—	—	—	—	—	—	k	—	0	87
1974	GB	14	—	—	—	—	—	—	—	—	—	—	—	—	—	—	—	—	—	—	k	—	0	-9
NFL	4	51	6	15	2.5(12)	0	2	22	11.0(11)	0	—	—	—	—	—	—	—	—	—	—	k	1	6	375
KRAUSE, MAX Max Joseph, B, 5´10˝/202 lbs; Gonzaga; B4/5/1909 Spokane, WA, D7/11/1984 Spokane, WA **[K]**																								
1933	NYG	5(2)	16	61	3.8	0	2	28	14.0(14)	1	—	—	—	—	—	—	—	—	—	—	K	—	7	80
1934	NYG	12(4)	26	89	3.4	0	1	4	4.0(4)	0	—	—	—	—	—	—	—	—	—	—	—	—	0	91
1935	NYG	6(2)	32	121	3.8	0	1	5	5.0(5)	0	—	—	—	—	—	—	—	—	—	—	—	—	0	124
1936	NYG	9(2)	11	37	3.4	0	5	47	9.4	1	—	—	—	—	—	—	—	—	—	—	—	—	6	66
1937	Was	8(0)	21	47	2.2	1	2	13	6.5	0	—	—	—	—	—	—	—	—	—	—	—	—	6	64
1938	Was	6(4)	25	214	8.6(71)	2	2	62	31.0(40)	1	—	—	—	—	—	—	—	—	—	—	—	—	18	270
1939	Was	2(0)	3	23	7.7	0	—	—	—	—	—	—	—	—	—	—	—	—	—	—	—	—	0	23
1940	Was	9(8, BB)	4	21	5.3	0	—	—	—	—	—	—	—	—	—	—	—	—	—	—	—	—	0	21
NFL	8	57(22)	138	613	4.4(71)	3	13	159	12.2(40)	3	—	—	—	—	—	—	—	—	—	—	K	—	37	738
KRAUSE, PAUL Paul James, DB-WR, 6´3˝/200 lbs; Iowa; 1964: Was, rnd 2/Den, rnd 12; B2/19/1942 Flint, MI; HOF 1998 **[I]** **1964** Was★14 (RS) **1966** Was 13 (RS) **1967** Was 13 (RS) **1968**†Min☆14 (14, RS) **1969**†Min★14 (14, RS) **1970**†Min☆14 (14, FS) **1971**†Min★14 (14, FS) **1973**†Min★14 (14, FS) **1974**†Min✧14 (10, FS) **1975**†Min★14 (14, FS) **1976**†Min 14 (14, FS) **1978**†Min 16 (2) **1979** Min 16 (8, FS)																								
1965	Was★	14(RS)	—	—	—	—	2	17	8.5(13)	0	—	—	—	—	—	—	—	—	—	—	i	1	6	97
1972	Min★	14(14, FS)	1	0	0.0(0)	0	—	—	—	—	1	0	0.0	0	0.0	0	0	—	—	—	i	2	12	89
1977	†Min	14(14, FS)	—	—	—	—	—	—	—	—	1	1	100.0	11	11.0(11)	1	0	—	—	—	i	—	0	26
NFL	16	226(146)	1	0	0.0	0	2	17	8.5(13)	0	2	1	50.0	11	5.5(11)	1	0	—	—	—	i	6	36	829
KRAUSE, RYAN Ryan, TE, 6´2˝/244 lbs; Nebraska-Omaha; 2004: SD, rnd 6; B6/16/1981 Omaha, NE **2005** SD 3 (0)																								
2004	†SD	1(1)	—	—	—	—	5	81	16.2(29)	1	—	—	—	—	—	—	—	—	—	—	—	—	6	46
NFL	2	4(1)	—	—	—	—	5	81	16.2(29)	1	—	—	—	—	—	—	—	—	—	—	—	—	6	46
KRAUSS, BARRY Richard Barry, LB, 6´3˝/245 lbs; Alabama; 1979: Bal, rnd 1; B3/17/1957 Pompano Beach, FL **1979** Bal 15 (6, mlb) **1980** Bal 16 (7, llb/rlb) **1981** Bal 16 (13, RLB/llb) **1984** Ind 16 (16, RILB) **1985** Ind 16 (16, RILB) **1986** Ind 4 (4) **1987**†Ind 12 (11, RILB) **1988** Ind 16 (15, RILB) **1989** Mia 16 (12, RILB)																								
1982	Bal	9(8, RILB)	—	—	—	—	1	5	5.0(5)	1	—	—	—	—	—	—	—	—	—	—	S	—	6	8
1983	Bal	16(16, RILB)	1	-1	-1.0(-1)	0	—	—	—	—	—	—	—	—	—	—	—	—	—	—	S	—	0	-1
NFL	11	152(124)	1	-1	-1.0(-1)	0	1	5	5.0(5)	1	—	—	—	—	—	—	—	—	—	—	iS	—	6	10
KRAYNAK, RICH Richard Bernard, LB, 6´1˝/227 lbs; Pittsburgh; 1983: Phi, rnd 8; B1/20/1961 Phoenixville, PA **1983** Phi 16 (0) **1984** Phi 14 (0) **1985** Phi 16 (0) **1986** Phi 6 (0) **1987** Atl 9 (8, rolb) **NFL** 61 (8) [5 yrs]																								
KREAMCHECK, JOHN John, DT, 6´5˝/255 lbs; William & Mary; 1953: ChiB, rnd 8; B1/7/1926 Vestaburg, PA **1953** ChiB 12 **1954** ChiB 12 (LDT) **1955** ChiB 12 **NFL** 36 [3 yrs]																								
KREIDER, DAN Dan, FB, 5´11˝/246 lbs; New Hampshire; B3/11/1977 Lancaster, PA																								
2000	Pit	10(7, FB)	2	24	12.0(22)	0	5	42	8.4(14)	0	—	—	—	—	—	—	—	—	—	—	k	—	0	30
2001	†Pit	13(1)	7	29	4.1(12)	1	2	5	2.5(5)	0	—	—	—	—	—	—	—	—	—	—	—	—	6	42

YEAR	TEAM	G (GS, POS)	RUSH	YD	AVG (LG)	TD	REC	YD	AVG (LG)	TD	PASS	COMP	PCT	YD	AVG (LG)	TD	INT	SK	YD	QBR	KPR	OTD	PTS	TAY
2002	†Pit	16 (13, FB)	6	16	2.7 (5)	0	18	122	6.8 (15)	1	—	—	—	—	—	—	—	—	—	—	k	—	8	85
2003	Pit	16 (12, FB)	7	29	4.1 (9)	1	9	107	11.9 (26)	0	—	—	—	—	—	—	—	—	—	—	k	—	6	77
2004	†Pit	16 (9, FB)	4	18	4.5 (6)	0	10	75	7.5 (13)	1	—	—	—	—	—	—	—	—	—	—	—	—	6	61
2005	†Pit	16 (9, FB)	3	21	7.0 (12)	0	7	43	6.1 (9)	0	—	—	—	—	—	—	—	—	—	—	k	—	0	31
NFL	6	87 (51)	29	137	4.7 (22)	2	51	394	7.7 (26)	2	—	—	—	—	—	—	—	—	—	—	k	—	26	324

KREIDER, STEVE Steven Kenneth, WR, 6´3˝/192 lbs; Lehigh; 1979: Cin, rnd 6; B5/12/1958 Reading, PA **[K]**

YEAR	TEAM	G (GS, POS)	RUSH	YD	AVG (LG)	TD	REC	YD	AVG (LG)	TD	PASS	COMP	PCT	YD	AVG (LG)	TD	INT	SK	YD	QBR	KPR	OTD	PTS	TAY
1979	Cin	15	2	0	0.0 (0)	0	3	20	6.7 (8)	0	0	0	0.0	0	0.0	0	0	1	9	—	—	—	0	10
1980	Cin	16 (0)	—	—	—	—	17	272	16.0 (30)	0	1	0	0.0	0	0.0	0	0	—	—	—	k	—	0	140
1981	†Cin	16 (1)	1	21	21.0 (21)	0	37	520	14.1 (46)	5	3	1	33.3	13	4.3 (13)	0	0	—	—	—	—	—	30	313
1982	†Cin	9 (0)	—	—	—	—	16	230	14.4 (28)	1	—	—	—	—	—	—	—	—	—	—	K	—	7	120
1983	Cin	16 (2)	1	2	2.0 (2)	0	42	554	13.2 (54)	1	1	0	0.0	0	0.0	0	0	—	—	—	—	—	6	284
1984	Cin	16 (3)	—	—	—	—	20	243	12.1 (27)	1	—	—	—	—	—	—	—	—	—	—	—	—	6	127
1985	Cin	16 (0)	—	—	—	—	10	184	18.4 (56)	1	1	1	100.0	1	1.0 (1)	0	0	—	—	—	K	—	7	98
1986	Cin	10 (0)	—	—	—	—	5	96	19.2 (23)	0	1	0	0.0	0	0.0	0	1	—	—	—	—	—	0	8
NFL	8	114 (6)	4	23	5.8 (21)	0	150	2119	14.1 (56)	9	7	2	28.6	14	2.0 (13)	0	1	1	9	—	Kk	—	56	1099

KREINHEDER, WALT Walter Roswell, C-G-B, 6´2˝/208 lbs; Michigan; B9/8/1901 Buffalo, NY, D10/12/1960 Boerne, TX **[K]** **1922** Akr 5 (5, c), 4 **1923** SL☆6 (6, C) **1925** Cle 5 (3) **NFL** 16 (14) [3 yrs]

KREITLING, RICH Richard Allen, E, 6´2˝/208 lbs; Auburn; Illinois; 1959: Cle, rnd 1; B3/13/1936 Chicago, IL

YEAR	TEAM	G (GS, POS)	RUSH	YD	AVG (LG)	TD	REC	YD	AVG (LG)	TD	PASS	COMP	PCT	YD	AVG (LG)	TD	INT	SK	YD	QBR	KPR	OTD	PTS	TAY
1959	Cle	12	—	—	—	—	—	—	—	—	—	—	—	—	—	—	—	—	—	—	—	—	—	—
1960	Cle	12 (SE/te)	2	-17	-8.5 (-2)	0	16	316	19.8 (69)	3	—	—	—	—	—	—	—	—	—	—	—	—	18	156
1961	Cle	13 (SE)	0	4	(4)	0	21	229	10.9 (19)	3	—	—	—	—	—	—	—	—	—	—	—	—	18	134
1962	Cle	14 (SE)	—	—	—	—	44	659	15.0 (53)	3	—	—	—	—	—	—	—	—	—	—	—	—	18	345
1963	Cle	14 (SE)	—	—	—	—	22	386	17.5 (45)	6	—	—	—	—	—	—	—	—	—	—	—	—	36	223
1964	ChiB	14 (SE)	—	—	—	—	20	185	9.3 (22)	2	—	—	—	—	—	—	—	—	—	—	—	—	12	103
NFL	6	79	2	-13	-6.5 (4)	0	123	1775	14.4 (69)	17	—	—	—	—	—	—	—	—	—	—	—	—	102	960

KREJCI, JOE Joseph Albert, E, 6´0˝/190 lbs; Peru State; B3/16/1906 Plattsmouth, NE, D8/10/1992 Fort Myers, FL **1934** ChiC 1 (0)

KREMER, KEN James Kendall, NT-DE, 6´4˝/250 lbs; Ball State; 1979: KC, rnd 7; B7/16/1957 Hammond, IN **1979** KC 16 **1980** KC 14 (0) **1981** KC 16 (8, nt) **1982** KC 9 (9, NT) **1983** KC 16 (5, nt) **1984** KC 16 (1) **NFL** 87 (23) [6 yrs]

KREMSER, KARL Karl Friedrich, K, 6´0˝/175 lbs; Army; Tennessee; 1969: Mia, rnd 5; B8/3/1945 Salzwedel, Germany **[K]** **1969** Mia-A 14 **1970** Mia 1 **NFL** 15 [2 yrs]

KRENK, MITCH Mitchell James, TE, 6´2˝/225 lbs; Nebraska; B11/19/1959 Crete, NE

YEAR	TEAM	G (GS, POS)	RUSH	YD	AVG (LG)	TD	REC	YD	AVG (LG)	TD	PASS	COMP	PCT	YD	AVG (LG)	TD	INT	SK	YD	QBR	KPR	OTD	PTS	TAY
1984	†ChiB	8 (0)	—	—	—	—	2	31	15.5 (24)	0	—	—	—	—	—	—	—	—	—	—	—	—	0	16

KRENTLER, TY Walter L., FB, /160 lbs; Detroit Mercy; B4/21/1896 Detroit, MI, D11/30/1971 St. Clair Shores, MI **1920** Det 5 (1)

KRENZEL, CRAIG Craig, QB, 6´4˝/225 lbs; Ohio State; 2004: Chi, rnd 5; B7/1/1981 Sterling Heights, MI

YEAR	TEAM	G (GS, POS)	RUSH	YD	AVG (LG)	TD	REC	YD	AVG (LG)	TD	PASS	COMP	PCT	YD	AVG (LG)	TD	INT	SK	YD	QBR	KPR	OTD	PTS	TAY
2004	ChiB	6 (5, qb)	18	41	2.3 (12)	0	—	—	—	—	127	59	46.5	718	5.7 (49)	3	6	23	158	52.5	—	—	2	175

KREPFLE, KEITH Keith Robert, TE, 6´3˝/227 lbs; Iowa State; 1974: Phi, rnd 5; B2/4/1952 Dubuque, IA

YEAR	TEAM	G (GS, POS)	RUSH	YD	AVG (LG)	TD	REC	YD	AVG (LG)	TD	PASS	COMP	PCT	YD	AVG (LG)	TD	INT	SK	YD	QBR	KPR	OTD	PTS	TAY
1975	Phi	14	—	—	—	—	1	16	16.0 (16)	0	—	—	—	—	—	—	—	—	—	—	—	—	0	8
1976	Phi	10 (1)	—	—	—	—	6	80	13.3 (30)	1	—	—	—	—	—	—	—	—	—	—	—	—	6	45
1977	Phi	14 (14, TE)	—	—	—	—	27	530	19.6 (55)	3	—	—	—	—	—	—	—	—	—	—	—	—	18	280
1978	Phi	10 (10, TE)	—	—	—	—	26	374	14.4 (34)	3	—	—	—	—	—	—	—	—	—	—	—	—	18	202
1979	†Phi☆	16 (16, TE)	—	—	—	—	41	760	18.5 (45)	3	—	—	—	—	—	—	—	—	—	—	—	—	18	395
1980	†Phi	13 (11, TE)	1	2	2.0 (2)	0	30	450	15.0 (27)	4	—	—	—	—	—	—	—	—	—	—	—	—	24	247
1981	†Phi	16 (16, TE)	—	—	—	—	20	210	10.5 (26)	5	—	—	—	—	—	—	—	—	—	—	—	—	30	130
1982	†Atl	4 (0)	—	—	—	—	1	5	5.0 (5)	0	—	—	—	—	—	—	—	—	—	—	—	—	0	3
NFL	8	97 (68)	1	2	2.0 (2)	0	152	2425	16.0 (55)	19	—	—	—	—	—	—	—	—	—	—	—	—	114	1310

KREROWICZ, MARK Mark Thomas, G, 6´3˝/285 lbs; Ohio State; 1985: Cle, rnd 6; B3/1/1963 Toledo, OH **1987** Cle 3 (3)

KRESKY, JOE Joseph Lawrence, G-T, 6´0˝/215 lbs; Wisconsin; B4/27/1906 Marinette, WI, D12/24/1988 Naples, FL **1932** Bos 8 (6, LG) **1933** Phi 9 (9, LG) **1934** Phi 10 (6, lg) **1935** Pit 1 (0) **1935** Phi 9 (8, LG) **NFL** 37 (29) [4 yrs]

KRESSER, ERIC Eric Joel, QB, 6´2˝/209 lbs; Florida; Marshall; B2/6/1973 Cincinnati, OH

YEAR	TEAM	G (GS, POS)	RUSH	YD	AVG (LG)	TD	REC	YD	AVG (LG)	TD	PASS	COMP	PCT	YD	AVG (LG)	TD	INT	SK	YD	QBR	KPR	OTD	PTS	TAY
1998	Cin	2 (0)	1	-1	-1.0 (-1)	0	—	—	—	—	21	10	47.6	164	7.8 (37)	1	2	—	—	—	—	—	0	6

KREUTZ, OLIN Olin George, C, 6´2˝/292 lbs; Washington; 1998: Chi, rnd 3; B6/9/1977 Honolulu, HI **1998** ChiB 9 (1) **1999** ChiB 16 (16, C) **2000** ChiB 7 (7, c) **2001**†ChiB★16 (16, C) **2002** ChiB✧15 (15, C) **2004** ChiB★16 (16, C) **2005**†ChiB★16 (16, C)

YEAR	TEAM	G (GS, POS)	RUSH	YD	AVG (LG)	TD	REC	YD	AVG (LG)	TD	PASS	COMP	PCT	YD	AVG (LG)	TD	INT	SK	YD	QBR	KPR	OTD	PTS	TAY
2003	ChiB✧	16 (16, C)	—	—	—	—	1	-8	-8.0 (-8)	0	—	—	—	—	—	—	—	—	—	—	—	—	0	-4
NFL	8	111 (103)	—	—	—	—	1	-8	-8.0 (-8)	0	—	—	—	—	—	—	—	—	—	—	—	—	0	-4

KREVIS, AL Alvin Raymond, T, 6´5˝/263 lbs; Boston College; 1975: Cin, rnd 2; B7/9/1952 Providence, RI **1975** Cin 3 **1976** NYJ 10 **NFL** 13 [2 yrs]

KRIEG, DAVE David Michael, QB, 6´1˝/193 lbs; Milton; B10/20/1958 Iola, WI

YEAR	TEAM	G (GS, POS)	RUSH	YD	AVG (LG)	TD	REC	YD	AVG (LG)	TD	PASS	COMP	PCT	YD	AVG (LG)	TD	INT	SK	YD	QBR	KPR	OTD	PTS	TAY
1980	Sea	1 (0)	—	—	—	—	—	—	—	—	2	0	0.0	0	0.0	0	0	1	6	—	—	—	0	0
1981	Sea	7 (3)	11	56	5.1 (29)	1	—	—	—	—	112	64	57.1	843	7.5 (57)	7	5	11	85	—	—	—	6	323
1982	Sea	3 (2)	6	-3	-0.5 (4)	0	—	—	—	—	78	49	62.8	501	6.4 (44)	2	2	16	117	—	—	—	0	178
1983	†Sea	9 (8, QB)	16	55	3.4 (10)	2	1	11	11.0 (11)	0	243	147	60.5	2139	**8.8 (50)**	18	11	38	279	95.0	—	—	12	800
1984	†Sea★	16 (16, QB)	46	186	4.0 (37)	3	—	—	—	—	480	276	57.5	3671	7.6 (80)	32	**24**	40	314	83.3	—	—	18	1252
1985	Sea	16 (16, QB)	35	121	3.5 (17)	1	—	—	—	—	532	285	53.6	3602	6.8 (54)	27	20	52	448	76.2	—	—	6	1267
1986	Sea	15 (14, QB)	35	122	3.5 (19)	1	—	—	—	—	375	225	60.0	2921	7.8 (72)	21	11	35	281	91.0	—	—	6	1258
1987	†Sea	12 (12, QB)	36	155	4.3 (17)	2	—	—	—	—	294	178	60.5	2131	7.2 (75)	23	15	27	247	87.6	—	—	12	756
1988	†Sea✧	9 (9, QB)	24	64	2.7 (17)	0	—	—	—	—	228	134	58.8	1741	7.6 (75)	18	8	12	92	94.6	—	—	0	705
1989	Sea✧	15 (14, QB)	40	160	4.0 (18)	0	—	—	—	—	499	286	57.3	3309	6.6 (60)	21	20	37	289	74.8	—	—	0	1120
1990	Sea	16 (16, QB)	32	115	3.6 (25)	0	1	-6	-6.0 (-6)	0	448	265	59.2	3194	7.1 (63)	15	20	40	360	73.6	—	—	0	984
1991	Sea	10 (9, QB)	13	59	4.5 (24)	0	—	—	—	—	285	187	**65.6**	2080	7.3 (60)	11	12	32	216	82.5	—	—	0	674
1992	†KC	16 (16, QB)	37	74	2.0 (17)	2	—	—	—	—	413	230	55.7	3115	7.5 (77)	15	12	48	323	79.9	—	—	12	1247
1993	†KC	12 (5, qb)	21	24	1.1 (20)	0	—	—	—	—	189	105	55.6	1238	6.6 (66)	7	3	22	138	—	—	—	0	558
1994	†Det	14 (7, qb)	23	35	1.5 (15)	0	—	—	—	—	212	131	61.8	1629	7.7 (51)	14	3	14	100	—	—	—	0	800
1995	Arz	16 (16, QB)	19	29	1.5 (17)	0	—	—	—	—	521	304	58.3	3554	6.8 (48)	16	**21**	53	380	72.6	—	—	0	1046
1996	ChiB	13 (12, QB)	16	12	0.8 (2)	1	1	5	5.0 (5)	0	377	226	59.9	2278	6.0 (53)	14	12	14	104	76.3	—	—	6	754
1997	Ten	8 (0)	4	-2	-0.5 (0)	0	—	—	—	—	2	1	50.0	2	1.0 (2)	0	0	—	—	—	—	—	0	-1
1998	Ten	5 (0)	3	-1	-0.3 (0)	0	—	—	—	—	21	12	57.1	199	9.5 (55)	0	0	2	15	—	—	—	0	99
NFL	19	213 (175)	417	1261	3.0 (37)	13	3	10	3.3 (11)	0	5311	3105	58.5	38147	7.2 (80)	261	199	494	3794	81.5	—	—	78	13815

KRIEG, JIM James Leo, WR, 5´9˝/172 lbs; Washington; 1972: Den, rnd 5; B5/29/1949 Buffalo, NY

YEAR	TEAM	G (GS, POS)	RUSH	YD	AVG (LG)	TD	REC	YD	AVG (LG)	TD	PASS	COMP	PCT	YD	AVG (LG)	TD	INT	SK	YD	QBR	KPR	OTD	PTS	TAY
1972	Den	6	1	63	63.0 (63)	0	4	99	24.8 (37)	0	—	—	—	—	—	—	—	—	—	—	kp	—	0	114

KRIEGER, BOB Robert E., E, 6´1˝/190 lbs; Dartmouth; B5/2/1918 Minneapolis, MN, D10/17/1980 Minneapolis, MN

YEAR	TEAM	G (GS, POS)	RUSH	YD	AVG (LG)	TD	REC	YD	AVG (LG)	TD	PASS	COMP	PCT	YD	AVG (LG)	TD	INT	SK	YD	QBR	KPR	OTD	PTS	TAY
1941	Phi	11 (11, LE)	—	—	—	—	19	240	12.6 (33)	2	—	—	—	—	—	—	—	—	—	—	—	—	12	130
1946	Phi	7 (2)	—	—	—	—	2	47	23.5 (35)	0	—	—	—	—	—	—	—	—	—	—	—	—	0	24
NFL	2	18 (13)	—	—	—	—	21	287	13.7 (35)	2	—	—	—	—	—	—	—	—	—	—	—	—	12	154

KRIEGER, EARL Earl Carlton, FB-HB, 5´11˝/185 lbs; Ohio University; B8/31/1896 Columbus, OH, D11/10/1960 Bexley, OH **1921** Det 5 (1) **1922** Col 4 (3, FB) **NFL** 9 (4) [2 yrs]

KRIEL, EMMETT Emmett Karl, G, 6´2˝/199 lbs; Baylor; 1938: Phi, rnd 10; B5/12/1916 Coupland, TX, D11/26/1984 Houston, TX **1939** Phi 1 (0)

KRIEWALD, DOUG Douglas Clark, G, 6´4˝/245 lbs; West Texas A&M; 1967: Chi, rnd 6; B8/30/1945 Seguin, TX **1967** ChiB 2 **1968** ChiB 13 (1) **NFL** 15 (1) [2 yrs]

KRIEWALDT, CLINT Clint, LB, 6´1˝/242 lbs; Wisconsin-Stevens Point; 1999: Det, rnd 6; B3/17/1976 Shiocton, WI **1999**†Det 12 (0) **2000** Det 13 (1) **2001** Det 14 (1) **2002** Det 10 (0) **2003** Pit 15 (0) **2004**†Pit 15 (0) **2005**†Pit 16 (2) **NFL** 95 (4) [7 yrs]

KRIMM, JOHN John Joseph, DB, 6´2˝/190 lbs; Notre Dame; 1982: NO, rnd 3; B5/30/1960 Philadelphia, PA **1982** NO 9 (0)

KRING, FRANK Frank H., LB, 6´0˝/190 lbs; TCU; B12/21/1918 Lampassas, TX **1945** Det 4 (2)

KRISHER, BILLY William Irwin, G, 6´1˝/233 lbs; Oklahoma; 1958: Pit, rnd 3; B9/18/1935 Perry, OK **1958** Pit 8 **1960** DalT-A☆13 (RG) **1961** DalT-A★14 (RG) **NFL** 35 [3 yrs]

KRISS, HOWIE Howard Edwin, HB, 5´9˝/175 lbs; Ohio State; B6/2/1907 Cleveland, OH, D6/13/1992 El Paso, TX **1931** Cle 2 (0)

KRISTUFEK, FRANK Frank Charles, T, 6´0˝/209 lbs; Pittsburgh; B12/12/1915 McKees Rocks, PA, D6/16/1998 Torrance, CA **1940** Bkn 11 (4) **1941** Bkn 11 (5, rt) **NFL** 22 (9) [2 yrs]

KRIVONAK, JOE Joseph, G, 6´2˝/230 lbs; South Carolina; 1942: GB, rnd 6; B1918, PA **1946** Mia-A 4 (0)

KROL, JOE Joseph, HB, 6´0˝/200 lbs; Western Ontario; B12/20/1919 **1945** Det 2 (0)

KROLL, ALEX Alexander Stanley, T-C, 6´3˝/230 lbs; Yale; Rutgers; 1962: NYT, rnd 2; B11/23/1937 Leechburg, PA **1962** NYT-A 14 (LT)

KROLL, BOB Robert Lee, DB, 6´1˝/195 lbs; Northern Michigan; B6/9/1950 Green Bay, WI **1972**†GB 5

KRONER, GARY Gary Lee, DB-K, 6´1˝/200 lbs; Wisconsin; 1963: NYJ, rnd 19/GB, rnd 7; B11/6/1940 Green Bay, WI **[K]** **1965** Den-A 14 **1966** Den-A 14 **1967** Den-A 3 **NFL** 31 [3 yrs]

KROUSE, RAY Raymond Francis, DT-DE-T, 6´3˝/263 lbs; Maryland; 1951: NYG, rnd 2; B3/21/1927 Washington, DC, D4/7/1966 Bethesda, MD **1951** NYG 12 **1952** NYG 12 (RDT) **1953** NYG 10 (RDT) **1954** NYG★12 (LDT) **1955** NYG☆12 (LDT) **1956** Det☆12 (LDT) **1957**†Det 12 **1958**†Bal 12 **1959**†Bal 12 **1960** Was 12 **NFL** 118 [10 yrs]

KRUCZEK, MIKE Michael Francis, QB, 6´1˝/202 lbs; Boston College; 1976: Pit, rnd 2; B3/15/1953 Washington, DC

YEAR	TEAM	G (GS, POS)	RUSH	YD	AVG (LG)	TD	REC	YD	AVG (LG)	TD	PASS	COMP	PCT	YD	AVG (LG)	TD	INT	SK	YD	QBR	KPR	OTD	PTS	TAY
1976	†Pit	10 (6, qb)	18	106	5.9 (22)	2	—	—	—	—	85	51	60.0	758	8.9 (64)	0	3	11	105	—	—	—	12	385
1977	Pit	2	1	0	0.0 (0)	0	—	—	—	—	7	2	28.6	19	2.7 (13)	0	0	—	—	—	—	—	0	10
1978	†Pit	9	5	7	1.4 (8)	0	—	—	—	—	11	5	45.5	46	4.2 (21)	0	2	4	40	—	—	—	0	-50
1979	†Pit	8	4	20	5.0 (22)	0	—	—	—	—	20	13	65.0	153	7.7 (31)	0	1	3	26	—	—	—	0	57
1980	Was	7 (1)	9	5	0.6 (5)	0	—	—	—	—	31	22	71.0	209	6.7 (41)	0	2	5	51	—	—	—	0	30
NFL	5	36 (7)	37	138	3.7 (22)	2	—	—	—	—	154	93	60.4	1185	7.7 (64)	0	8	23	222	—	—	—	12	431

KRUEGER, AL Albert Leroy, T, 5´10˝/180 lbs; Drake; B8/18/1901 Wellman, IA, D2/25/1976 **1924** KC 7 (5, lt)

KRUEGER, AL Alvin John, HB-E, 6´0˝/190 lbs; USC; 1941: Was, rnd 7; B4/3/1919 Orange, CA, D2/20/1999 Lancaster, CA

YEAR	TEAM	G (GS, POS)	RUSH	YD	AVG (LG)	TD	REC	YD	AVG (LG)	TD	PASS	COMP	PCT	YD	AVG (LG)	TD	INT	SK	YD	QBR	KPR	OTD	PTS	TAY
1941	Was	7 (0)	—	—	—	—	7	123	17.6 (35)	1	—	—	—	—	—	—	—	—	—	—	ki	—	6	82
1942	Was✧	11 (0)	—	—	—	—	9	65	7.2 (19)	0	—	—	—	—	—	—	—	—	—	—	k	—	0	37
NFL	2	18 (0)	—	—	—	—	16	188	11.8 (35)	1	—	—	—	—	—	—	—	—	—	—	ki	—	6	118
1946	LAD-A	10 (3)	—	—	—	—	19	213	11.2	1	—	—	—	—	—	—	—	—	—	—	—	—	6	112

KRUEGER, CHARLIE Charles Andrew, DT-DE, 6´4˝/256 lbs; Texas A&M; 1958: SF, rnd 1; B1/28/1937 Caldwell, TX **1959** SF 12 (RDE) **1960** SF★12 (11, RDE) **1961** SF 14 (13, RDE/rdt) **1962** SF 14 (12, RDT) **1963** SF 7 (7, LDT) **1964** SF✧14 (14, LDT) **1965** SF☆14 (14, LDT) **1966** SF 14 (14, LDT) **1967** SF 13 (13, LDT) **1968** SF 14 (14, LDT) **1969** SF 14 (14, LDT) **1970**†SF☆14 (14, LDT) **1971**†SF 14 (LDT) **1972** SF 14 (14, LDT) **1973** SF 14 (14, LDT) **NFL** 198 (168) [15 yrs]

KRUEGER, ROLF Rolf Frank, DE-DT, 6´4˝/253 lbs; Texas A&M; 1969: SL, rnd 2; B12/8/1946 Caldwell, TX **1969** SL 14 (LDE) **1970** SL 14 (LDE) **1971** SL 14 (LDT) **1972**†SF 4 **1973** SF 14 **1974** SF 9 **NFL** 69 [6 yrs]

KRUMM, TODD Todd Alan, DB, 6´0˝/189 lbs; Michigan State; B12/18/1965 Royal Oak, MI **1988**†ChiB 15 (0)

KRUMRIE, TIM Timothy Alan, NT-DT, 6´2˝/270 lbs; Wisconsin; 1983: Cin, rnd 10; B5/20/1960 Eau Claire, WI **1983** Cin 16 (2) **1984** Cin 16 (16, NT) **1985** Cin 16 (16, NT) **1986** Cin 16 (16, NT) **1987** Cin★12 (12, NT) **1988**†Cin★16 (16, NT) **1989** Cin 16 (16, NT) **1990**†Cin 16 (15, NT) **1991** Cin 16 (16, NT) **1992** Cin 16 (16, NT) **1993** Cin 16 (16, NT) **1994** Cin 16 (4) **NFL** 188 (161) [12 yrs]

KRUPA, JOE Joseph Steven, DT, 6´2˝/232 lbs; Purdue; 1956: Pit, rnd 2; B7/6/1933 Chicago, IL **1956** Pit 12 **1957** Pit 12 (LDT) **1958** Pit 12 (RDT) **1959** Pit 9 (LDT) **1960** Pit 12 (RDT) **1961** Pit 14 (RDT) **1962** Pit 14 (RDT) **1963** Pit✧14 (RDT) **1964** Pit 11 **NFL** 110 [9 yrs]

KRUSE, BOB Robert Anthony, G-T, 6´2˝/259 lbs; Colorado State; Wayne State (NE); 1967: Oak, rnd 12; B2/10/1942 Franklin Park, IL **1967**†Oak-A 13 **1968**†Oak-A 12 **1969** Buf-A 3 **NFL** 28 [3 yrs]

KRUTKO, LARRY Lawrence LeRoy, FB, 6´0˝/220 lbs; West Virginia; 1958: Pit, rnd 2; B6/27/1935 Carmichaels, PA

YEAR	TEAM	G (GS, POS)	RUSH	YD	AVG (LG)	TD	REC	YD	AVG (LG)	TD	PASS	COMP	PCT	YD	AVG (LG)	TD	INT	SK	YD	QBR	KPR	OTD	PTS	TAY
1958	Pit	6	4	6	1.5 (5)	0	—	—	—	—	—	—	—	—	—	—	—	—	—	—	—	—	0	6
1959	Pit	12 (FB)	75	226	3.0 (12)	4	13	100	7.7 (27)	0	—	—	—	—	—	—	—	—	—	—	—	—	24	316
1960	Pit	7	17	99	5.8 (18)	0	1	8	8.0 (8)	0	—	—	—	—	—	—	—	—	—	—	—	—	0	103
NFL	3	25	96	331	3.4 (18)	4	14	108	7.7 (27)	0	—	—	—	—	—	—	—	—	—	—	—	—	24	425

KRYSL, JERRY Gerald Charles, T, 5´11˝/200 lbs; Kansas State; B1/26/1905 **1927** Cle 8 (2)

KSIONZYK, JOHN John Lawrence, QB, 5´10˝/190 lbs; St. Bonaventure; B1/28/1919 Binghamton, NY

YEAR	TEAM	G (GS, POS)	RUSH	YD	AVG (LG)	TD	REC	YD	AVG (LG)	TD	PASS	COMP	PCT	YD	AVG (LG)	TD	INT	SK	YD	QBR	KPR	OTD	PTS	TAY
1947	LARm	3 (0)	—	—	—	—	—	—	—	—	7	1	14.3	17	2.4 (17)	0	2	—	—	—	—	—	0	-72

KUBALA, RAY Raymond George, C, 6´5˝/265 lbs; Texas A&M; 1964: Den, rnd 7/Phi, rnd 4; B10/26/1942 West, TX **1964** Den-A 8 **1965** Den-A 14 (C) **1966** Den-A 14 **1967** Den-A 5 **NFL** 41 [4 yrs]

KUBERSKI, BOB Robert Kenneth, DT, 6´4˝/298 lbs; Navy; 1993: GB, rnd 7; B4/5/1971 Chester, PA **1995**†GB 9 (0) **1996** GB 1 (0) **1997**†GB 11 (3) **1998**†GB 16 (0) **1999** NE 5 (0) **NFL** 42 (3) [5 yrs]

KUBIAK, GARY Gary Wayne, QB, 6´0˝/192 lbs; Texas A&M; 1983: Den, rnd 8; B8/15/1961 Houston, TX **[C]**

YEAR	TEAM	G (GS, POS)	RUSH	YD	AVG (LG)	TD	REC	YD	AVG (LG)	TD	PASS	COMP	PCT	YD	AVG (LG)	TD	INT	SK	YD	QBR	KPR	OTD	PTS	TAY
1983	Den	4 (0)	4	17	4.3 (8)	1	—	—	—	—	22	12	54.5	186	8.5 (78)	1	1	2	20	—	—	—	6	85
1984	Den	7 (2)	9	27	3.0 (17)	1	1	20	20.0 (20)	0	75	44	58.7	440	5.9 (41)	4	1	10	86	—	—	—	6	247
1985	Den	16 (0)	1	6	6.0 (6)	0	—	—	—	—	5	2	40.0	61	12.2 (54)	1	0	—	—	—	—	—	0	42
1986	†Den	16 (0)	6	22	3.7 (10)	0	—	—	—	—	38	23	60.5	249	6.6 (26)	1	3	3	23	—	—	—	0	32
1987	†Den	12 (0)	1	3	3.0 (3)	0	—	—	—	—	7	3	42.9	25	3.6 (17)	0	2	2	14	—	—	—	0	-65
1988	Den	16 (1)	17	65	3.8 (15)	0	—	—	—	—	69	43	62.3	497	7.2 (68)	5	3	2	13	—	—	—	0	219
1989	†Den	16 (1)	15	35	2.3 (10)	0	—	—	—	—	55	32	58.2	284	5.2 (22)	2	2	8	53	—	P	—	0	107
1990	Den	16 (0)	9	52	5.8 (18)	0	—	—	—	—	22	11	50.0	145	6.6 (36)	0	4	3	19	—	—	—	0	-36
1991	†Den	16 (0)	3	11	3.7 (12)	0	—	—	—	—	5	3	60.0	33	6.6 (14)	0	0	1	8	—	—	—	0	28
NFL	9	119 (4)	65	238	3.7 (18)	2	1	20	20.0 (20)	0	298	173	58.1	1920	6.4 (78)	14	16	31	236	—	P	—	12	658

KUBIN, LARRY Lawrence William, LB, 6´2˝/234 lbs; Penn State; 1981: Was, rnd 6; B2/26/1959 Union, NJ **1982**†Was 9 (0) **1983**†Was 12 (0) **1984**†Was 16 (0) **1985** Buf 2 (0) **1985** TB 4 (0) **NFL** 43 (0) [4 yrs]

KUCHARSKI, TED Theodore Michael, E, 6´1˝/185 lbs; Holy Cross; B8/26/1907 Exeter, NH, D10/7/1992 Mesa, AZ **1930** Pro 8 (0)

KUCHTA, FRANK Frank William, LB-C, 6´2˝/225 lbs; Notre Dame; 1958: Was, rnd 9; B9/18/1936 Cleveland, OH **1958** Was 2 **1959** Was 12 (2) **1960** Den-A 12 (mlb) **NFL** 26 (2) [3 yrs]

KUCZO, PAUL Paul James, B, 5´9˝/165 lbs; Villanova; B2/4/1903 Stamford, CT, D12/4/1970 Stamford, CT **1929** SI 4 (1)

KUCZYNSKI, BERT Bernard Carl, E, 6´0˝/196 lbs; Pennsylvania; 1943: Det, rnd 19; B1/8/1920 Philadelphia, PA, D1/19/1997 Allentown, PA

YEAR	TEAM	G (GS, POS)	RUSH	YD	AVG (LG)	TD	REC	YD	AVG (LG)	TD	PASS	COMP	PCT	YD	AVG (LG)	TD	INT	SK	YD	QBR	KPR	OTD	PTS	TAY
1943	Det	2 (1)	—	—	—	—	1	4	4.0 (4)	0	—	—	—	—	—	—	—	—	—	—	—	—	0	2
1946	Phi	3 (0)	—	—	—	—	1	9	9.0 (9)	1	—	—	—	—	—	—	—	—	—	—	—	—	6	10
NFL	2	5 (1)	—	—	—	—	2	13	6.5 (9)	1	—	—	—	—	—	—	—	—	—	—	—	—	6	12

KUECHENBERG, BOB Robert John, G-T-C, 6´2˝/253 lbs; Notre Dame; 1969: Phi, rnd 4; B10/14/1947 Gary, IN **1970**†Mia 14 (5, lg) **1971**†Mia 14 (14, LG) **1972**†Mia 14 (14, LG) **1973**†Mia 13 (13, LG) **1974**†Mia★14 (14, LG) **1975** Mia★14 (14, LG) **1976** Mia 10 (10, LG) **1977** Mia★14 (12, LG) **1978**†Mia★16 (15, LG/lt) **1979**†Mia 16 (16, LT) **1980** Mia 16 (16, LG) **1981**†Mia 16 (9, LG) **1982**†Mia✧9 (9, LG) **1983**†Mia★16 (15, LG) **NFL** 196 (176) [14 yrs]

KUECHENBERG, RUDY Rudolph Bernard, LB, 6´0˝/215 lbs; Indiana; B2/7/1943 Hobart, IN **1967** ChiB 14 **1968** ChiB 14 **1969** ChiB 14 (RLB) **1970** Cle 3 **1970** GB 6 **1971** Atl 3 **NFL** 54 [5 yrs]

KUEHL, RYAN Ryan Phillip, DT, 6´5˝/290 lbs; Virginia; B1/18/1972 Washington, DC **1996** Was 2 (0) **1997** Was 12 (5, ldt) **1999** Cle 16 (0) **2000** Cle 16 (0) **2001** Cle 16 (0) **2002**†Cle 16 (0) **2004** NYG 16 (0) **2005**†NYG 16 (0) **NFL** 110 (5) [8 yrs]

KUEHL, WADDY Ray Otto, B, 5´9˝/165 lbs; St. Ambrose; Dubuque; B2/12/1893 Davenport, IA, D7/24/1967 Venice, FL **[K]** **1920** RI 10 (2) **1921** Det 6 (3, WB), 6 **1921** Buf 2 (0), 6 **1922** Buf 10 (9, WB), 19 **1923** RI 8 (7, WB), 24 **1924** Day 3 (3) **NFL** 39 (24), 55 [5 yrs]

YEAR	TEAM	G(GS, POS)	RUSH	YD	AVG(LG)	TD	REC	YD	AVG(LG)	TD	PASS	COMP	PCT	YD	AVG(LG)	TD	INT	SK	YD	QBR	KPR	OTD	PTS	TAY

Kuehn, Art Arthur Bert, C, 6´3˝/257 lbs; San Jose State; UCLA; 1975: Was, rnd 15; B2/12/1953 Victoria, Canada **1976** Sea 14 (7, c) **1977** Sea 14 (14, C) **1978** Sea 16 (3) **1979** Sea 16 (1) **1980** Sea 16 (1) **1981** Sea 16 (7, c) **1982** Sea 6 (0) **1983** NE 2 (0) **NFL** 100 (33) [8 yrs]

Kuehner, Oscar Oscar, T-G-E, 6´0˝/200 lbs; none; B1889, OH, deceased **1920** Col 10 (5, LT) **1921** Col 7 (6, lt) **NFL** 17 (11) [2 yrs]

Kuffel, Ray Raymond Francis, E, 6´3˝/213 lbs; Marquette; Notre Dame; 1947: Buf-A, rnd 3/1944: ChiC, rnd 20; B12/9/1921 Milwaukee, WI, D12/12/1974 Brookfield, WI **1949** ChiH-A 2 (0)

YEAR	TEAM	G(GS, POS)	RUSH	YD	AVG(LG)	TD	REC	YD	AVG(LG)	TD	PASS	COMP	PCT	YD	AVG(LG)	TD	INT	SK	YD	QBR	KPR	OTD	PTS	TAY
1947	Buf-A	7(2)	—	—	—	—	3	37	12.3	0	—	—	—	—	—	—	—	—	—	—	—	—	0	19
1948	ChiR-A	14(7, le)	—	—	—	—	19	365	19.2	3	—	—	—	—	—	—	—	—	—	—	k	—	18	199
AAFC	3	23(9)	—	—	—	—	22	402	18.3	3	—	—	—	—	—	—	—	—	—	—	k	—	18	217

Kugler, Pete Peter David, NT-DE, 6´4˝/255 lbs; Penn State; 1981: SF, rnd 6; B8/9/1959 Philadelphia, PA **1981** SF 13 (0) **1982** SF 7 (4) **1983**†SF 16 (16, NT) **1986**†SF 3 (0) **1987**†SF 11 (8, LDE) **1988**†SF 6 (1) **1989**†SF 14 (6, nt) **1990**†SF 11 (0) **NFL** 81 (35) [8 yrs]

Kuharich, Joe Joseph Lawrence, G, 5´11˝/195 lbs; Notre Dame; 1938: Pit, rnd 12; B4/14/1917 South Bend, IN, D1/25/1981 Philadelphia, PA **[KC]** **1940** ChiC 11 (6, RG) **1941** ChiC★10 (9, RG) **1945** ChiC 6 (6, RG) **NFL** 27 (21) [3 yrs]

Kuhrt, George George, T, 5´11˝/185 lbs; none; B7/1896 Tonawanda, NY, deceased **1921** Ton 1 (1, LT)

Kuick, Stan Stanley Jacob, G, 5´10˝/192 lbs; Beloit; B4/24/1904 Kewaunee, WI, D8/26/1977 Orlando, FL **1926** Mil 9 (9, LG)

Kulbacki, Joe Joseph Vincent, HB, 6´0˝/185 lbs; Purdue; 1960: Bos, rnd 1/Was, rnd 16; B3/1/1938 Ridgway, PA

YEAR	TEAM	G(GS, POS)	RUSH	YD	AVG(LG)	TD	REC	YD	AVG(LG)	TD	PASS	COMP	PCT	YD	AVG(LG)	TD	INT	SK	YD	QBR	KPR	OTD	PTS	TAY
1960	Buf-A	14	41	108	2.6(17)	1	2	9	4.5(7)	0	—	—	—	—	—	—	—	—	—	—	kp	—	6	194

Kulbitski, Vic Victor John, FB, 5´10˝/205 lbs; Minnesota; Notre Dame; 1944: Phi, rnd 7; B6/15/1921 Virginia, MN, D5/23/1998 West St. Paul, MN **[K]**

YEAR	TEAM	G(GS, POS)	RUSH	YD	AVG(LG)	TD	REC	YD	AVG(LG)	TD	PASS	COMP	PCT	YD	AVG(LG)	TD	INT	SK	YD	QBR	KPR	OTD	PTS	TAY
1946	Buf-A	13(8, FB)	97	605	6.2	2	1	0	0.0	0	—	—	—	—	—	—	—	—	—	—	ki	—	12	646
1947	Buf-A	13(7, FB)	56	249	4.4	1	9	117	13.0	4	—	—	—	—	—	—	—	—	—	—	Kkpi	—	31	359
1948	†Buf-A	14(6, fb)	40	152	3.8	0	3	37	12.3	0	—	—	—	—	—	—	—	—	—	—	Kk	1	14	174
AAFC	3	40(21)	193	1006	5.2	3	13	154	11.8	4	—	—	—	—	—	—	—	—	—	—	Kkpi	1	57	1178

Kullman, Mike Michael, DB, 6´1˝/185 lbs; Kutztown; B1/22/1962 Frankfurt, Germany, D7/21/2003 Allentown, PA **1987** Phi 3 (1)

Kumerow, Eric Eric Palmer, DE-LB, 6´7˝/264 lbs; Ohio State; 1988: Mia, rnd 1; B4/17/1965 Chicago, IL **1988** Mia 14 (0) **1989** Mia 12 (0) **1990**†Mia 16 (0) **NFL** 42 (0) [3 yrs]

Kunz, George George James, T, 6´5˝/257 lbs; Notre Dame; 1969: Atl, rnd 1; B7/5/1947 Fort Sheridan, IL **1969** Atl✧14 (14, RT) **1970** Atl 9 (9, RT) **1972** Atl★14 (14, RT) **1973** Atl★14 (14, RT) **1974** Atl★14 (14, RT) **1975**†Bal★12 (12, RT) **1976**†Bal★14 (14, RT) **1977**†Bal★14 (14, RT) **1978** Bal 1 (1) **1980** Bal 9 (6, rt)

YEAR	TEAM	G(GS, POS)	RUSH	YD	AVG(LG)	TD	REC	YD	AVG(LG)	TD	PASS	COMP	PCT	YD	AVG(LG)	TD	INT	SK	YD	QBR	KPR	OTD	PTS	TAY
1971	Atl✧	14(14, RT)	—	—	—	—	1	2	2.0(2)	0	—	—	—	—	—	—	—	—	—	—	—	—	0	1
NFL	11	129(126)	—	—	—	—	1	2	2.0(2)	0	—	—	—	—	—	—	—	—	—	—	k	—	0	-1

Kunz, Lee Lee Roy, LB, 6´2˝/226 lbs; Nebraska; 1979: Chi, rnd 7; B4/21/1957 Golden, CO **1979**†ChiB 16 **1980** ChiB 16 (2) **1981** ChiB 16 (7, mlb) **NFL** 48 (9) [3 yrs]

Kunz, Terry Terry Tim, RB, 6´1˝/215 lbs; Colorado; 1976: Oak, rnd 8; B10/26/1952 Denver, CO

YEAR	TEAM	G(GS, POS)	RUSH	YD	AVG(LG)	TD	REC	YD	AVG(LG)	TD	PASS	COMP	PCT	YD	AVG(LG)	TD	INT	SK	YD	QBR	KPR	OTD	PTS	TAY
1976	Oak	7	4	33	8.3(11)	0	—	—	—	—	—	—	—	—	—	—	—	—	—	—	—	—	0	33

Kupcinet, Irv Irving, QB, 6´1˝/190 lbs; Northwestern; North Dakota; B7/31/1912 Chicago, IL, D11/10/2003 Evanston, IL

YEAR	TEAM	G(GS, POS)	RUSH	YD	AVG(LG)	TD	REC	YD	AVG(LG)	TD	PASS	COMP	PCT	YD	AVG(LG)	TD	INT	SK	YD	QBR	KPR	OTD	PTS	TAY
1935	Phi	2(1)	—	—	—	—	—	—	—	—	5	1	20.0	6	1.2(6)	0	0	—	—	—	—	—	0	3

Kupp, Craig Craig Marion, QB, 6´4˝/215 lbs; Montana Tech; Pacific Lutheran; 1990: NYG, rnd 5; B4/14/1967 Sunnyside, WA

YEAR	TEAM	G(GS, POS)	RUSH	YD	AVG(LG)	TD	REC	YD	AVG(LG)	TD	PASS	COMP	PCT	YD	AVG(LG)	TD	INT	SK	YD	QBR	KPR	OTD	PTS	TAY
1991	Phx	1(0)	1	5	5.0(5)	0	—	—	—	—	7	3	42.9	23	3.3(11)	0	0	2	23	—	—	—	0	17

Kupp, Jake Jacob Ralph, G-TE, 6´3˝/248 lbs; Washington; 1964: Dal, rnd 9; B3/12/1941 Pasadena, CA **1964** Dal 14 (10, LG) **1965** Dal 14 (LG) **1967** NO 5 **1967** Atl 6 **1968** NO 14 (LG) **1969** NO✧14 (LG) **1970** NO 14 (LG) **1971** NO 14 (LG) **1972** NO 3 **1973** NO 14 (LG) **1974** NO 14 (LG) **1975** NO 14 (LG)

YEAR	TEAM	G(GS, POS)	RUSH	YD	AVG(LG)	TD	REC	YD	AVG(LG)	TD	PASS	COMP	PCT	YD	AVG(LG)	TD	INT	SK	YD	QBR	KPR	OTD	PTS	TAY
1966	Was	14	—	—	—	—	4	28	7.0(13)	0	—	—	—	—	—	—	—	—	—	—	—	—	0	14
NFL	12	154(10)	—	—	—	—	4	28	7.0(13)	0	—	—	—	—	—	—	—	—	—	—	—	—	0	14

Kurek, Ralph Ralph Eamer, RB, 6´2˝/210 lbs; Wisconsin; 1965: Chi, rnd 20; B2/23/1943 Milwaukee, WI

YEAR	TEAM	G(GS, POS)	RUSH	YD	AVG(LG)	TD	REC	YD	AVG(LG)	TD	PASS	COMP	PCT	YD	AVG(LG)	TD	INT	SK	YD	QBR	KPR	OTD	PTS	TAY
1965	ChiB	14	1	0	0.0(0)	0	—	—	—	—	—	—	—	—	—	—	—	—	—	—	k	—	0	-4
1966	ChiB	14(fb)	52	179	3.4(12)	1	10	178	17.8(49)	0	—	—	—	—	—	—	—	—	—	—	—	—	6	278
1967	ChiB	14	37	112	3.0(13)	0	5	30	6.0(8)	0	—	—	—	—	—	—	—	—	—	—	k	—	0	133
1968	ChiB	14	17	95	5.6(23)	1	4	50	12.5(23)	0	—	—	—	—	—	—	—	—	—	—	k	—	6	118
1969	ChiB	14	8	24	3.0(6)	0	4	30	7.5(13)	0	—	—	—	—	—	—	—	—	—	—	k	—	0	45
1970	ChiB	11	6	24	4.0(11)	0	3	11	3.7(5)	0	—	—	—	—	—	—	—	—	—	—	—	—	0	30
NFL	6	81	121	434	3.6(23)	2	26	299	11.5(49)	0	—	—	—	—	—	—	—	—	—	—	k	—	12	600

Kurisko, Jamie Jamie A., TE, 6´4˝/236 lbs; Allentown College; Southern Connecticut State; B12/22/1963 Nyack, NY

YEAR	TEAM	G(GS, POS)	RUSH	YD	AVG(LG)	TD	REC	YD	AVG(LG)	TD	PASS	COMP	PCT	YD	AVG(LG)	TD	INT	SK	YD	QBR	KPR	OTD	PTS	TAY
1987	NYJ	3(2)	—	—	—	—	1	41	41.0(41)	1	—	—	—	—	—	—	—	—	—	—	—	—	6	26

Kurnick, Howard Howard Raymond, LB, 6´2˝/219 lbs; Cincinnati; 1979: Cin, rnd 8; B5/13/1957 Cleveland, OH **1979** Cin 15

Kurpeikis, Justin Justin William, LB, 6´3˝/254 lbs; Penn State; B7/17/1977 Allison Park, PA **2001**†Pit 3 (0) **2002** Pit 6 (0) **2004** NE 5 (0) **NFL** 14 (0) [3 yrs]

Kurrasch, Roy Roy William, E, 6´2˝/195 lbs; UCLA; B10/8/1922 Toledo, OH **1948** Pit 9 (0)

YEAR	TEAM	G(GS, POS)	RUSH	YD	AVG(LG)	TD	REC	YD	AVG(LG)	TD	PASS	COMP	PCT	YD	AVG(LG)	TD	INT	SK	YD	QBR	KPR	OTD	PTS	TAY
1947	†NYY-A	10(0)	—	—	—	—	2	53	26.5	0	—	—	—	—	—	—	—	—	—	—	—	—	0	27

Kurth, Joe Joseph James, T, 6´1˝/202 lbs; Wisconsin; Notre Dame; B3/27/1914 Madison, WI, D1/13/1987 Plano, TX **1933** GB 13 (9, RT) **1934** GB 7 (3) **NFL** 20 (12) [2 yrs]

Kush, Rod Rodney Randle, DB, 6´0˝/188 lbs; Nebraska-Omaha; 1979: Buf, rnd 5; B12/29/1956 Omaha, NE **1980** Buf 5 (0) **1982** Buf 9 (0) **1983** Buf 4 (4) **1984** Buf 16 (5, fs) **1985** Hou 16 (0)

YEAR	TEAM	G(GS, POS)	RUSH	YD	AVG(LG)	TD	REC	YD	AVG(LG)	TD	PASS	COMP	PCT	YD	AVG(LG)	TD	INT	SK	YD	QBR	KPR	OTD	PTS	TAY
1981	†Buf	16(0)	1	-6	-6.0(-6)	0	—	—	—	—	—	—	—	—	—	—	—	—	—	—	i	—	0	8
NFL	6	66(9)	1	-6	-6.0(-6)	0	—	—	—	—	—	—	—	—	—	—	—	—	—	—	iS	—	0	14

Kusko, John John, B, 5´11˝/194 lbs; Temple; B3/27/1914 Nesquehoning, PA, D7/1974

YEAR	TEAM	G(GS, POS)	RUSH	YD	AVG(LG)	TD	REC	YD	AVG(LG)	TD	PASS	COMP	PCT	YD	AVG(LG)	TD	INT	SK	YD	QBR	KPR	OTD	PTS	TAY
1936	Phi	12(1)	49	209	4.3(70)	1	—	—	—	—	27	6	22.2	108	4.0	0	8	—	—	—	—	—	6	-47
1937	Phi	10(4)	17	27	1.6	0	2	47	23.5	0	7	2	28.6	11	1.6	0	2	—	—	—	—	—	0	-24
1938	Phi	1(0)	—	—	—	—	—	—	—	—	—	—	—	—	—	—	—	—	—	—	—	—	—	—
NFL	3	23(5)	66	236	3.6(70)	1	2	47	23.5	0	34	8	23.5	119	3.5	0	10	—	—	—	—	—	6	-71

Kusserow, Lou Louis Joseph, LB-FB, 6´1˝/200 lbs; Columbia; 1949: NYY-A, rnd S2/Det, rnd 3; B9/6/1927 Braddock, PA, D6/30/2001 Rancho Mirage, CA

YEAR	TEAM	G(GS, POS)	RUSH	YD	AVG(LG)	TD	REC	YD	AVG(LG)	TD	PASS	COMP	PCT	YD	AVG(LG)	TD	INT	SK	YD	QBR	KPR	OTD	PTS	TAY
1949	NYY-A	11(4)	39	136	3.5	0	—	—	—	—	1	0	0.0	0	0.0	0	0	—	—	—	k	—	0	182
1950	NYY	11(LLB)	1	6	6.0(6)	0	—	—	—	—	—	—	—	—	—	—	—	—	—	—	—	—	0	6

Kutler, Rudy Rudolph John, G, 5´9˝/190 lbs; Ohio State; B11/14/1901, OH, D3/20/1974 Garfield Heights, OH **1925** Cle 1 (0)

Kutner, Mal Malcolm James, E-DB, 6´2˝/197 lbs; Texas; 1942: Pit, rnd 4; B3/27/1921 Dallas, TX, D2/4/2005 Tyler, TX

YEAR	TEAM	G(GS, POS)	RUSH	YD	AVG(LG)	TD	REC	YD	AVG(LG)	TD	PASS	COMP	PCT	YD	AVG(LG)	TD	INT	SK	YD	QBR	KPR	OTD	PTS	TAY
1946	ChiC	11(5, RE)	1	-1	-1.0(-1)	0	27	634	23.5(63)	5	—	—	—	—	—	—	—	—	—	—	ki	—	30	330
1947	†ChiC☆	12(9, RE)	—	—	—	—	43	**944**	22.0(70)	7	—	—	—	—	—	—	—	—	—	—	i	1	48	558
1948	†ChiC☆	12(10, RE)	5	50	10.0(32)	1	41	**943**	23.0(71)	**14**	—	—	—	—	—	—	—	—	—	—	i	—	90	627
1949	ChiC	12(12, RE)	5	10	2.0(4)	0	30	465	15.5(49)	5	—	—	—	—	—	—	—	—	—	—	—	—	30	268
1950	ChiC	9(DB)	—	—	—	—	4	74	18.5(51)	0	—	—	—	—	—	—	—	—	—	—	i	—	0	53
NFL	5	56(36)	11	59	5.4(32)	1	145	3060	21.1(71)	31	—	—	—	—	—	—	—	—	—	—	ki	1	198	1835

Kuusisto, Bill William E., G, 6´0˝/228 lbs; Wisconsin; Minnesota; 1941: GB, rnd 8; B4/26/1918 Herman, MI, D5/28/1973 Paynesville, MN **1941**†GB 9 (3) **1942** GB 11 (9, LG) **1943** GB 10 (8, LG) **1944**†GB 10 (3) **1945** GB 10 (1) **1946** GB 4 (1) **NFL** 54 (25) [6 yrs]

Kuykendall, Fulton Fulton Gerald, LB, 6´4˝/225 lbs; UCLA; 1975: Atl, rnd 6; B6/10/1953 Coronado, CA **1975** Atl 14 **1976** Atl 7 (7, LLB) **1977** Atl 5 (5, llb) **1978**†Atl☆16 (16, LLB) **1979** Atl 16 (16, LLB) **1980**†Atl 10 (8, LILB) **1981** Atl 16 (16, LILB) **1982**†Atl 9 (9, LILB) **1983** Atl 14 (14, MLB) **1984** Atl 16 (0) **1985** SF 1 (0) **NFL** 124 (91) [11 yrs]

Kuziel, Bob Robert Charles, C-T, 6´4˝/255 lbs; Pittsburgh; 1972: NO, rnd 3; B7/24/1950 New Haven, CT **1972** NO 1 **1975** Was 14 **1976**†Was 14 **1977** Was 14 **1978** Was 16 (16, C) **1979** Was 16 (16, C) **1980** Was 15 (13, C) **NFL** 90 (45) [7 yrs]

Kuzman, John John N., T, 6´1˝/232 lbs; Fordham; 1941: ChiC, rnd 7; B6/29/1915 Coaldale, PA **1941** ChiC 5 (0) **1946** SF-A 11 (1) **1947** ChiR-A 13 (7, LT) **AAFC** 24 (8) [2 yrs]

YEAR	TEAM	G (GS, POS)	RUSH	YD	AVG(LG)	TD	REC	YD	AVG(LG)	TD	PASS	COMP	PCT	YD	AVG(LG)	TD	INT	SK	YD	QBR	KPR	OTD	PTS	TAY

KVATERNIK, ZVONIMIR Zvonimir, G, 5´11˝/210 lbs; Kansas; B10/18/1911 Kansas City, KS, D10/19/1994 Shawnee Mission, KS **1934** Pit 1 (0)

KVIST, JOHN John L., T, none; B9/13/1899, D7/1972 Perth Amboy, NJ **1920** Roc 1 (0)

KWALICK, TED Thaddeus John, TE, 6´4˝/226 lbs; Penn State; 1969: SF, rnd 1; B4/15/1947 Pittsburgh, PA

1969	SF	13	—	—	—	—	2	32	16.0(31)	1	—	—	—	—	—	—	—	—	—	—	k	—	6	6
1970	†SF	14	3	65	21.7(45)	0	10	148	14.8(26)	1	—	—	—	—	—	—	—	—	—	—	—	—	6	144
1971	†SF★	14(14, TE)	6	62	10.3(28)	0	52	664	12.8(42)	5	—	—	—	—	—	—	—	—	—	—	k	—	30	398
1972	†SF★	14(14, TE)	5	11	2.2(10)	0	40	751	18.8(81)	9	—	—	—	—	—	—	—	—	—	—	—	—	54	432
1973	SF★	14(14, TE)	5	37	7.4(20)	0	47	729	15.5(48)	5	—	—	—	—	—	—	—	—	—	—	—	—	30	427
1974	SF	14	—	—	—	—	13	231	17.8(36)	2	—	—	—	—	—	—	—	—	—	—	—	—	12	126
1975	†Oak	6	—	—	—	—	—	—	—	—	—	—	—	—	—	—	—	—	—	—	—	—	—	—
1976	Oak	7	—	—	—	—	4	15	3.8(6)	0	—	—	—	—	—	—	—	—	—	—	—	—	0	8
1977	Oak	12	—	—	—	—	—	—	—	—	—	—	—	—	—	—	—	—	—	—	—	—	—	—
NFL	9	108(42)	19	175	9.2(45)	0	168	2570	15.3(81)	23	—	—	—	—	—	—	—	—	—	—	k	—	138	1539

KYLE, AARON Aaron Douglas, DB, 5´11˝/185 lbs; Wyoming; 1976: Dal, rnd 1; B4/6/1954 Detroit, MI **1976**†Dal 14 (1) **1977**†Dal 14 (10, RCB) **1978**†Dal 16 (16, RCB) **1979**†Dal 16 (16, RCB) **1980** Den 10 (9, RCB) **1981** Den 16 (16, RCB) **1982** Den 9 (9, RCB) **NFL** 95 (77) [7 yrs]

KYLE, JASON Jason C., LB, 6´3˝/242 lbs; Arizona State; 1995: Sea, rnd 4; B5/12/1972 Tempe, AZ **1995** Sea 16 (0) **1996** Sea 16 (0) **1998** Sea 16 (0) **2000** SF 2 (0) **2001** Car 16 (0) **2002** Car 16 (0) **2003**†Car 16 (0) **2004** Car 16 (0) **2005**†Car 16 (0) **NFL** 130 (0) [9 yrs]

KYLE, JOHNNY John William, FB, 5´9˝/190 lbs; Indiana; B9/12/1898 Gary, IN, D5/1974 Valparaiso, IN **1923** Cle 7 (5, FB), 6

KYLE, RIP James William, C-T-G, 6´0˝/240 lbs; Gettysburg; B8/20/1899 Mifflintown, PA, D2/10/1967 Palo Alto, CA **1925** Can 4 (3) **1926** Can 11 (10, C) **NFL** 15 (13) [2 yrs]

KYLES, TROY Troy Thomas, WR, 6´1˝/185 lbs; Howard; B8/13/1968 Lorain, OH

| 1990 | †NYG | 9(0) | — | — | — | — | 4 | 77 | 19.3(35) | 0 | — | — | — | — | — | — | — | — | — | — | — | — | 0 | 39 |

KYSAR, JEFF Jeffrey John Charles, T, 6´7˝/320 lbs; Arizona State; 1995: Oak, rnd 5; B6/14/1972 Norman, OK **1995** Oak 1 (0)

LAACK, GALEN Galen William, G, 6´0˝/230 lbs; Pacific; 1957: Was, rnd 9; B4/3/1932 Abbotsford, WI, D12/31/1958 Livermore, CA **1958** Phi 8

LAAKSO, ERIC Eric Henry, T-G, 6´4˝/285 lbs; Tulane; 1978: Mia, rnd 4; B11/29/1956 New York, NY **1978**†Mia 16 **1979**†Mia 10 (2) **1980** Mia 16 (16, RT) **1981** Mia 16 (16, RT) **1982**†Mia 9 (9, RT) **1983**†Mia☆15 (14, RT) **1984** Mia 4 (4) **NFL** 86 (61) [7 yrs]

LAAVEG, PAUL Paul Martin, G, 6´4˝/245 lbs; Iowa; 1970: Was, rnd 4; B10/1/1948 Sioux Falls, SD **1970** Was 11 (RG) **1971**†Was 14 (14, LG) **1972**†Was 14 (14, LG) **1973**†Was 14 (14, LG) **1974**†Was 14 (14, LG) **1975** Was 5 (5, lg) **NFL** 72 (47) [6 yrs]

LaBEAUX, SANDY Sandy, DB, 6´2˝/210 lbs; Cal State-Hayward; B8/22/1961 San Antonio, TX **1983** TB 3 (0)

LABINJO, MIKE Mike, LB, 6´0˝/241 lbs; Michigan State; B7/8/1980 Toronto, Canada **2004**†Phi 3 (0) **2005** Ind 2 (0) **2005** Phi 5 (1) **NFL** 10 (1) [2 yrs]

LaBISSONIERE, TONY Horace C., C-G, 5´9˝/185 lbs; St. Thomas (MN); Michigan; B9/13/1896 St. Paul, MN, D1/1972 St. Paul, MN **1922** Ham 2 (2)

LaBOUNTY, MATT Matthew James, DE-DT, 6´4˝/271 lbs; Oregon; 1992: SF, rnd 12; B1/3/1969 San Francisco, CA **1993** SF 6 (0) **1995**†GB 14 (2) **1996** Sea 3 (0) **1997** Sea 15 (6, rde) **1998** Sea 16 (1) **1999**†Sea 16 (1) **2000** Sea 12 (2) **2001** Sea 2 (0) **NFL** 84 (12) [8 yrs]

LaBOY, TRAVIS Travis, DE, 6´4˝/249 lbs; Utah State, Hawaii; 2004: Ten, rnd 2; B8/10/1981 Honolulu, HI **2004** Ten 13 (2) **2005** Ten 15 (7, rde) **NFL** 28 (9) [2 yrs]

LACEY, BOB Robert Reavil, WR, 6´3˝/205 lbs; North Carolina; 1964: Min, rnd 6/NYJ, rnd 11; B3/30/1942 New York, NY **1964** Min 1

LACH, STEVE Stephen John, WB-FB-HB, 6´2˝/210 lbs; Duke; 1942: ChiC, rnd 1; B8/6/1920 Altoona, PA, D7/12/1961 Altoona, PA **[K]**

1942	ChiC	9(6, WB)	30	97	3.2(9)	0	18	261	14.5(53)	4	—	—	—	—	—	—	—	—	—	—	KPkpi	—	25	432
1946	Pit	11(3)	42	111	2.6(14)	5	3	22	7.3(11)	0	1	0	0.0	0	0.0	0	—	—	—	—	i	—	30	177
1947	†Pit	12(8, FB)	120	372	3.1(19)	8	11	77	7.0(24)	1	5	2	40.0	12	2.4(6)	1	0	—	—	—	k	—	54	521
NFL	3	32(17)	192	580	3.0(19)	13	32	360	11.3(53)	5	6	2	33.3	12	2.0(6)	1	0	—	—	—	KPkpi	—	109	1129

LaCHAPELLE, SEAN Sean Paul, WR, 6´3˝/205 lbs; UCLA; 1993: LARm, rnd 5; B7/29/1970 Sacramento, CA

1993	LARm	10(0)	—	—	—	—	2	23	11.5(14)	0	—	—	—	—	—	—	—	—	—	—	—	—	0	12
1996	KC	12(8, WR)	—	—	—	—	27	422	15.6(69)	2	—	—	—	—	—	—	—	—	—	—	—	—	12	221
NFL	2	22(8)	—	—	—	—	29	445	15.3(69)	2	—	—	—	—	—	—	—	—	—	—	—	—	12	233

LACHEY, JIM James Michael, T, 6´6˝/294 lbs; Ohio State; 1985: SD, rnd 1; B6/4/1963 St. Henry, OH **1985** SD☆16 (16, LT) **1986** SD 16 (15, LT) **1987** SD★12 (12, LT) **1988** LARd 1 (1) **1988** Was 15 (14, RT/lt) **1989** Was☆14 (14, LT) **1990**†Was★16 (16, LT) **1991**†Was★15 (15, LT) **1992**†Was 10 (10, LT) **1994** Was 13 (13, LT) **1995** Was 3 (3) **NFL** 131 (129) [10 yrs]

LACINA, CORBIN Corbin James, G, 6´4˝/302 lbs; Augustana (SD); 1993: Buf, rnd 6; B11/2/1970 Mankato, MN **1994** Buf 11 (10, LG) **1995**†Buf 16 (3) **1996** Buf 12 (2) **1997** Buf 16 (13, RG) **1998** Car 10 (10, RG) **1999**†Min 14 (0) **2000** Min 15 (15, LG) **2001** Min 11 (10, LG) **2002** Min 16 (16, LG) **2003** ChiB 8 (1) **NFL** 129 (80) [10 yrs]

LACKMAN, RICK Richard H., HB, 5´11˝/186 lbs; none; B9/20/1910 Philadelphia, PA, D3/12/1990

1933	Phi	4(0)	17	59	3.5	0	—	—	—	—	1	0	0.0	0	0.0	0	1	—	—	—	—	—	0	19
1934	Phi	8(0)	4	9	2.3	0	4	83	20.8	0	—	—	—	—	—	—	—	—	—	—	—	—	0	51
1935	Phi	11(0)	22	56	2.5	0	5	49	9.8	0	1	0	0.0	0	0.0	0	0	—	—	—	—	—	0	81
NFL	3	23(0)	43	124	2.9	0	9	132	14.7	0	2	0	0.0	0	0.0	0	1	—	—	—	—	—	0	150

LaCROSSE, DAVE David Joseph, LB, 6´3˝/210 lbs; Wake Forest; 1977: Pit, rnd 10; B12/22/1955 Philadelphia, PA **1977**†Pit 14

LACY, KEN Kenneth Wayne, RB, 6´0˝/222 lbs; Tulsa; B11/1/1960 Waco, TX

1984	KC	15(4)	46	165	3.6(24)	2	13	87	6.7(20)	2	—	—	—	—	—	—	—	—	—	—	—	—	24	239
1985	KC	2(0)	6	21	3.5(6)	0	—	—	—	—	—	—	—	—	—	—	—	—	—	—	—	—	0	21
1987	KC	3(1)	14	49	3.5(17)	0	—	—	—	—	—	—	—	—	—	—	—	—	—	—	k	—	0	33
NFL	3	20(5)	66	235	3.6(24)	2	13	87	6.7(20)	2	—	—	—	—	—	—	—	—	—	—	k	—	24	293

LADD, ANTHONY Anthony, WR, 6´1˝/188 lbs; Cincinnati; B12/23/1973 Homestead, FL **1998** NE 3 (0)

LADD, ERNIE Ernest, DT, 6´9˝/290 lbs; Grambling State; 1961: SD, rnd 15/Chi, rnd 4; B11/28/1938 Rayville, LA **1961**†SD-A☆14 (RDT) **1962** SD-A◇4 (RDT) **1963**†SD-A◇14 **1964**†SD-A★14 (LDT) **1965**†SD-A★14 (RDT) **1966** Hou-A 14 (RDT) **1967** Hou-A 4 **1967** KC-A 10 **1968**†KC-A 14 **NFL** 112 [8 yrs]

LADD, JIM James W., E, 6´4˝/205 lbs; Bowling Green State; 1954: ChiB, rnd 20; B7/29/1932 Put-In-Bay, OH, D11/13/1996 Indianapolis, IN

| 1954 | ChiC | 11(RE) | — | — | — | — | 22 | 254 | 11.5(22) | 0 | — | — | — | — | — | — | — | — | — | — | — | — | 0 | 127 |

LADOUCEUR, L.P. L.P., DE, 6´4˝/257 lbs; California; B3/13/1981 Montreal, Canada **2005** Dal 13 (0)

LADORUM, DOC Jules F., FB, none; B6/8/1893 Muncie, IN, D2/1980 **1921** Mun 1 (1)

LADROW, WALLY Walter P., HB, 5´9˝/180 lbs; none; B10/16/1895 Brookside, WI, D7/22/1974 Green Bay, WI **1921** GB 1 (0)

LADSON, TINY Glessie Merritt, G, /254 lbs; none; B12/17/1895 Sullivan County, IN, D11/28/1978 Hanover, IN **1922** Evv 3 (3, LG)

LADYGO, PETE Peter Glenn, G-LB, 6´2˝/218 lbs; Maryland; 1952: Pit, rnd 16; B6/23/1925 West Brownsville, PA **1952** Pit 12 (RG) **1954** Pit 12 (RG) **NFL** 24 [2 yrs]

LAFARY, DAVE David Walter, T-G, 6´7˝/280 lbs; Purdue; 1977: NO, rnd 5; B1/13/1955 Cincinnati, OH **1977** NO 10 **1978** NO 15 (13, RG) **1979** NO 16 **1980** NO 15 (4) **1982** NO 9 (9, LT) **1983** NO 16 (16, LT) **1984** NO 1 (1) **1985** NO 11 (11, LT)

| 1981 | NO | 16(4) | — | — | — | — | 1 | 5 | 5.0(5) | 0 | — | — | — | — | — | — | — | — | — | — | — | — | 0 | 3 |
| NFL | 9 | 109(58) | — | — | — | — | 1 | 5 | 5.0(5) | 0 | — | — | — | — | — | — | — | — | — | — | — | — | 0 | 3 |

LaFAVOR, TRON Tron, DT, 6´2˝/290 lbs; Florida; 2003: Chi, rnd 5; B11/27/1979 Fort Lauderdale, FL **2003** ChiB 4 (0)

LaFITTE, BILL William Sorrells, E, 6´1˝/171 lbs; Ouachita Baptist; B1/23/1926 Stonewall, LA, deceased

| 1944 | Bkn | 4(0) | — | — | — | — | 3 | 45 | 15.0(15) | 0 | — | — | — | — | — | — | — | — | — | — | — | — | 0 | 8 |

LaFLEUR, BILL William, P, 6´0˝/204 lbs; Nebraska; B2/25/1976 Superior, NE **2002**†SF 5 (0)

| 2003 | SF | 16(0) | 1 | 0 | 0.0(0) | 0 | — | — | — | — | — | — | — | — | — | — | — | — | — | — | P | — | 0 | 0 |
| NFL | 2 | 21(0) | 1 | 0 | 0.0 | 0 | — | — | — | — | — | — | — | — | — | — | — | — | — | — | P | — | 0 | 0 |

YEAR	TEAM	G(GS, POS)	RUSH	YD	AVG(LG)	TD	REC	YD	AVG(LG)	TD	PASS	COMP	PCT	YD	AVG(LG)	TD	INT	SK	YD	QBR	KPR	OTD	PTS	TAY

LaFleur, David   David Alan, TE, 6´7˝/272 lbs; LSU; 1997: Dal, rnd 1; B1/29/1974 Lake Charles, LA

1997	Dal	16(5, te)	—	—	—	—	18	122	6.8(17)	2	—	—	—	—	—	—	—	—	—	—	—	—	12	71
1998	†Dal	13(13, TE)	—	—	—	—	20	176	8.8(24)	2	—	—	—	—	—	—	—	—	—	—	k	—	12	95
1999	†Dal	16(16, TE)	—	—	—	—	35	322	9.2(25)	7	—	—	—	—	—	—	—	—	—	—	—	—	42	196
2000	Dal	15(10, TE)	—	—	—	—	12	109	9.1(19)	1	—	—	—	—	—	—	—	—	—	—	k	—	6	51
NFL	4	60(44)	—	—	—	—	85	729	8.6(25)	12	—	—	—	—	—	—	—	—	—	—	k	—	72	413

LaFleur, Greg   Gregory Louis, TE, 6´4˝/236 lbs; LSU; 1981: Phi, rnd 3; B9/16/1958 Lafayette, LA

1981	SL	16(11, TE)	—	—	—	—	14	190	13.6(27)	2	—	—	—	—	—	—	—	—	—	—	—	—	12	105
1982	†SL	9(3)	—	—	—	—	5	67	13.4(20)	1	—	—	—	—	—	—	—	—	—	—	—	—	6	39
1983	SL	16(5, te)	—	—	—	—	12	99	8.3(21)	0	—	—	—	—	—	—	—	—	—	—	—	—	0	50
1984	SL	16(5, te)	—	—	—	—	17	198	11.6(23)	0	—	—	—	—	—	—	—	—	—	—	—	—	0	99
1985	SL	16(4)	—	—	—	—	9	119	13.2(24)	0	—	—	—	—	—	—	—	—	—	—	—	—	0	60
1986	SL	4(0)																						
1986	Ind	9(0)	—	—	—	—	7	56	8.0(11)	0	—	—	—	—	—	—	—	—	—	—	—	—	0	28
NFL	6	86(28)	—	—	—	—	64	729	11.4(27)	3	—	—	—	—	—	—	—	—	—	—	—	—	18	380

LaFleur, Joe   Harry Joseph, G-FB-C-HB, 6´0˝/223 lbs; St. Norbert; Marquette; B3/3/1896 DePere, WI, D10/5/1973 La Crosse, WI   **1922** ChiB 10 (6, rg)   **1923** ChiB 10 (3)
1924 ChiB 7 (3)   **NFL** 27 (12) [3 yrs]

Lage, Dick   Richard Lloyd, E, 6´4˝/228 lbs; Lenoir-Rhyne; 1961: Cle, rnd 12; B8/9/1939 Omaha, NE   **1961** SL 1

Lageman, Jeff   Jeffrey David, DE-LB, 6´6˝/266 lbs; Virginia; 1989: NYJ, rnd 1; B7/18/1967 Fairfax, VA   **1990** NYJ 16 (16, RDE)   **1991**†NYJ☆16 (16, RDE)   **1992** NYJ 2 (2)
1993 NYJ 16 (16, RDE)   **1994** NYJ 16 (16, RDE)   **1995** Jax 11 (11, RDE)   **1996**†Jax 12 (9, lde)   **1997**†Jax 16 (16, LDE)   **1998** Jax 1 (1)

| 1989 | NYJ | 16(15, ROLB) | 1 | -5 | -5.0(-5) | 0 | — | — | — | — | — | — | — | — | — | — | — | — | S | — | — | 0 | -5 |
| NFL | 10 | 122(118) | 1 | -5 | -5.0(-5) | 0 | — | — | — | — | — | — | — | — | — | — | — | — | iS | — | — | 0 | 5 |

Lagod, Chet   Chester Joseph, G, 6´2˝/220 lbs; Tennessee-Chattanooga; 1951: NYG, rnd 25; B1/8/1928 Fairpoint, OH   **1953** NYG 11

LaGrand, Morris   James Morris, RB, 6´1˝/220 lbs; Tampa; 1975: KC, rnd 6; B2/9/1953 Tampa, FL   **1975** NO 2

| 1975 | KC | 11 | 13 | 38 | 2.9(11) | 1 | 1 | -1 | -1.0(-1) | 0 | — | — | — | — | — | — | — | — | — | — | — | — | 6 | 48 |
| NFL | 1 | 13 | 13 | 38 | 2.9(11) | 1 | 1 | -1 | -1.0(-1) | 0 | — | — | — | — | — | — | — | — | — | — | — | — | 6 | 48 |

Lahar, Hal   Harold Wade, G, 6´0˝/225 lbs; Oklahoma; 1941: ChiB, rnd 9; B7/14/1919 Durant, OK, D10/20/2003 Dallas, TX [K]   **1941**†ChiB◇8 (0)
1946 Buf-A 12 (3)   **1947** Buf-A 14 (14, LG)   **1948**†Buf-A 13 (13, LG)   **AAFC** 39 (30) [3 yrs]

Lahey, Pat   Thomas Patrick, E-DE, 6´2˝/218 lbs; John Carroll; B10/21/1919 Dunbridge, OH

1946	ChiR-A	13(10, RE)	1	-2	-2.0(-2)	0	17	203	11.9	0	—	—	—	—	—	—	—	—	—	—	ki	—	0	89
1947	ChiR-A	13(4)	—	—	—	—	13	148	11.4	0	—	—	—	—	—	—	—	—	—	—	k	—	0	62
AAFC	2	26(14)	1	-2	-2.0(-2)	0	30	351	11.7	0	—	—	—	—	—	—	—	—	—	—	ki	—	0	151

LaHood, Mike   Michael James, G, 6´3˝/250 lbs; Wyoming; 1968: LA, rnd 2; B12/11/1944 Peoria, IL   **1969**†LARm 14 (7, rg)   **1970** SL 14   **1971** LARm 9   **1972** LARm 14
NFL 51 (7) [4 yrs]

Lahr, Warren   Warren Emmett, DB, 5´11˝/189 lbs; Case Western Reserve; 1947: Pit, rnd 32; B9/5/1923 Mount Zion, PA, D1/19/1969 Cleveland, OH [I]

| 1949 | Cle-A | 11(0) | 9 | 36 | 4.0 | 1 | 1 | 20 | 20.0(20) | 0 | — | — | — | — | — | — | — | — | Ppi | — | — | 6 | 121 |

1950†Cle 12 (DB)   **1951**†Cle☆12 (DB)   **1952**†Cle☆12 (DB)   **1953**†Cle☆12 (DB)   **1955**†Cle☆12 (DB)   **1956** Cle☆12 (DB)   **1957**†Cle 11 (DB)   **1958**†Cle 7 (DB)   **1959** Cle 12 (DB)

| 1954 | †Cle☆ | 12(DB) | 3 | 18 | 6.0(14) | 0 | — | — | — | — | 1 | 0 | 0.0 | 0 | 0.0 | 0 | 1 | — | — | i | 1 | 6 | 7 |
| NFL | 10 | 114 | 3 | 18 | 6.0(14) | 0 | — | — | — | — | 1 | 0 | 0.0 | 0 | 0.0 | 0 | 1 | — | — | i | 5 | 30 | 358 |

Laidlaw, Scott   Robert Scott, RB, 6´0˝/206 lbs; Stanford; 1975: Dal, rnd 14; B2/17/1953 Hawthorne, CA

1975	Dal	8	3	10	3.3(10)	0	11	100	9.1(25)	0	—	—	—	—	—	—	—	—	—	—	—	—	0	60
1976	†Dal	13(7, FB)	94	424	4.5(28)	3	38	325	8.6(26)	1	—	—	—	—	—	—	—	—	—	—	—	—	24	622
1977	Dal	14	9	15	1.7(8)	0	5	60	12.0(18)	1	—	—	—	—	—	—	—	—	—	—	—	—	6	50
1978	†Dal	16(4)	75	312	4.2(59)	3	6	108	18.0(44)	1	—	—	—	—	—	—	—	—	—	—	—	—	24	401
1979	Dal	16(3)	69	236	3.4(15)	3	12	59	4.9(12)	0	—	—	—	—	—	—	—	—	—	—	—	—	18	296
1980	NYG	7(1)	5	10	2.0(3)	0	2	16	8.0(10)	0	—	—	—	—	—	—	—	—	—	—	k	—	0	21
NFL	6	74(15)	255	1007	3.9(59)	9	74	668	9.0(44)	3	—	—	—	—	—	—	—	—	—	—	k	—	72	1449

Laing, Aaron   Aaron Matthew, TE, 6´3˝/260 lbs; New Mexico State; 1994: SD, rnd 5; B7/19/1971 Houston, TX

1994	SD	5(1)																						
1996	SL	12(8, te)	—	—	—	—	13	116	8.9(22)	1	—	—	—	—	—	—	—	—	—	—	k	—	0	58
1997	SL	15(4)	—	—	—	—	5	31	6.2(11)	1	—	—	—	—	—	—	—	—	—	—	—	—	6	21
NFL	3	32(13)	—	—	—	—	18	147	8.2(22)	1	—	—	—	—	—	—	—	—	—	—	k	—	6	79

Lainhart, Porter   Porter Ward, QB, 6´0˝/180 lbs; Washington State; B11/6/1907, WA, D8/1991 Coquille, OR

| 1933 | Phi | 1(0) | — | — | — | — | 1 | 20 | 20.0(20) | 0 | — | — | — | — | — | — | — | — | — | — | — | — | 0 | 10 |

Laird, Bruce   Bruce Allan, DB, 6´0˝/193 lbs; American International; 1972: Bal, rnd 6; B5/23/1950 Lowell, MA [R]   **1972** Bal◇14 (1)   **1973** Bal 12 (6, lcb)   **1974** Bal 14 (14, SS)
1975†Bal 14 (14, SS)   **1976**†Bal 14 (14, SS)   **1977**†Bal 14 (14, SS)   **1978** Bal 14 (14, SS)   **1979** Bal 15 (15, SS)   **1980** Bal☆15 (15, SS)   **1981** Bal 15 (15, SS)   **1982**†SD 9 (6, SS)
1983 SD 14 (0)   **NFL** 164 (127) [12 yrs]

Laird, Jim   James Tyler, B-G-T, 6´0˝/194 lbs; Colgate; B9/10/1897 Montpelier, VT, D8/16/1970 Lebanon, CT [KC]   **1920** Roc 9 (1, FB)   **1920** Buf 1 (1)   **1921** Buf 1 (0)
1921 Roc 6 (5, FB), 24   **1921** Can 1 (1), 12   **1922** Buf☆10 (9, FB), 24   **1925** Pro 11 (8, FB), 29   **1926** Pro 9 (6, FB)   **1927** Pro 14 (12, RG)   **1928** Pro 8 (0)   **1931** SI 9 (3)
NFL 79 (46), 89 [8 yrs]

Lajousky, Bill   William, G, 5´11˝/200 lbs; Catholic; B4/18/1913 Lithuania, D1/7/1973 Waterville, ME

| 1936 | Pit | 11(5, rg) | 1 | 1 | 1.0(1) | 0 | — | — | — | — | — | — | — | — | — | — | — | — | — | — | — | — | 0 | 1 |

Lake, Antwan   Antwan, DE, 6´4˝/285 lbs; West Virginia; B7/10/1979 Seaford, DE   **2002** Det 9 (0)   **2004**†Atl 16 (2)   **2005** Atl 13 (2)   **NFL** 38 (4) [3 yrs]

Lake, Carnell   Carnell Augustino, DB, 6´1˝/210 lbs; UCLA; 1989: Pit, rnd 2; B7/15/1967 Salt Lake City, UT   **1989**†Pit 15 (15, SS)   **1990** Pit☆16 (16, SS)   **1991** Pit 16 (16, SS)
1992†Pit☆16 (16, SS)   **1993**†Pit 14 (16, SS)   **1994**†Pit★16 (16, SS)   **1995**†Pit★16 (16, RCB/ss)   **1996**†Pit★13 (13, SS)   **1997**†Pit★16 (16, RCB/ss)   **1998** Pit 16 (16, LCB)
1999†Jax★16 (16, FS)   **2001**†Bal 15 (1)   **NFL** 185 (171) [12 yrs]

Lakes, Roland   Roland Hayes, DT-DE-T-DT, 6´4˝/279 lbs; Wichita State; 1961: SF, rnd 2/Bos, rnd 9; B12/25/1939 Vicksburg, MS   **1961** SF. 14 (5, rde)   **1962** SF 14 (8, LT)
1963 SF 14 (14, RDT)   **1964** SF 14 (14, RDT)   **1965** SF 14 (14, RDT)   **1966** SF 14 (14, RDT)   **1967** SF 14 (13, RDT)   **1968** SF 14 (14, RDT)   **1969** SF 14 (14, RDT)
1970†SF 14 (14, RDT)   **1971** NYG 14 (RDT)   **NFL** 154 (124) [11 yrs]

Lally, Bob   Robert Michael, LB, 6´2˝/230 lbs; Cornell; 1974: Mia, rnd 9; B2/12/1952 Hoboken, NJ   **1976** GB 2

LaLonde, Roger   Roger Frederick, DT, 6´3˝/255 lbs; Muskingum; 1964: Det, rnd 15/Bos, rnd 8; B1/6/1942 Antwerp, NY   **1964** Det 14   **1965** NYG 11 (LDT)   **NFL** 25 [2 yrs]

Lamana, Pete   Peter Charles, LB-C-FB, 5´11˝/210 lbs; Boston University; B5/15/1921 Bristol, TN   **1947** ChiR-A 12 (0)   **1948** ChiR-A 13 (3)

| 1946 | ChiR-A | 10(1) | 6 | 21 | 3.5 | 0 | — | — | — | — | — | — | — | — | — | — | — | — | — | — | ki | 1 | 6 | 65 |
| AAFC | 3 | 35(4) | 6 | 21 | 3.5 | 0 | — | — | — | — | — | — | — | — | — | — | — | — | — | — | ki | 1 | 6 | 60 |

Lamar, Jason   Jason James, LB, 6´0˝/228 lbs; Toledo; B11/10/1978 Detroit, MI   **2002** Hou 5 (0)

Lamar, Kevin   Kevin Thomas, G, 6´4˝/260 lbs; Stanford; B11/29/1961 Louisville, KY   **1987** Buf 1 (1)

Lamas, Joe   Joseph Francis, G, 5´10˝/216 lbs; Mount St. Mary's; B1/10/1916 Havana, Cuba, D4/22/1996 Manhasset, NY   **1942** Pit 8 (0)

Lamb, Brad   Bradley, WR, 5´10˝/171 lbs; Anderson (IN); 1991: Buf, rnd 8; B10/7/1967 Springboro, OH   **1993** Buf 1 (0)

| 1992 | †Buf | 7(0) | — | — | — | — | 7 | 139 | 19.9(53) | 0 | — | — | — | — | — | — | — | — | — | — | k | — | 0 | 92 |
| NFL | 2 | 8(0) | — | — | — | — | 7 | 139 | 19.9(53) | 0 | — | — | — | — | — | — | — | — | — | — | k | — | 0 | 102 |

Lamb, Mack   Mack Edward, DB, 6´1˝/188 lbs; Tennessee State; B5/9/1944 Miami, FL   **1967** Mia-A 2   **1968** Mia-A 13 (4)   **NFL** 15 (4) [2 yrs]

YEAR	TEAM	G (GS, POS)	RUSH	YD	AVG(LG)	TD	REC	YD	AVG(LG)	TD	PASS	COMP	PCT	YD	AVG(LG)	TD	INT	SK	YD	QBR	KPR	OTD	PTS	TAY

LAMB, RODDY Roy Elmer, B, 5´6˝/160 lbs; Lombard; B8/20/1899 Garrison, NE, D12/21/1995 Philmorth, OR **[K]**   **1925** RI 9 (8, TB), 27 **1926** ChiC 10 (6, WB), 7
1927 ChiC 9 (3, TB), 6

| 1933 | ChiC | 4(1) | 19 | 46 | 2.4 | 0 | — | — | — | — | 5 | 1 | 20.0 | 8 | 1.6(8) | 0 | 1 | — | — | — | — | — | 0 | 10 |
| NFL | 4 | 32(18) | 19 | 46 | 2.4 | 4 | — | — | — | — | 5 | 1 | 20.0 | 8 | 1.6(8) | 3 | 1 | — | — | — | K | 1 | 40 | 80 |

LAMB, RON Ronald, RB, 6´2˝/225 lbs; South Carolina; 1966: Dal, rnd 13; B2/3/1944 New London, CT

1968	Den-A	3	22	63	2.9(17)	0	3	10	3.3(10)	0	—	—	—	—	—	—	—	—	—	—	—	—	0	68
1968	Cin-A	6	17	44	2.6(17)	0	4	77	19.3(60)	0	—	—	—	—	—	—	—	—	—	—	—	—	0	83
1969	Cin-A	14	5	8	1.6(7)	0	—	—	—	—	—	—	—	—	—	—	—	—	—	—	Pk	—	0	-3
1970	†Cin	14	6	35	5.8(16)	0	—	—	—	—	—	—	—	—	—	—	—	—	—	—	k	—	0	46
1971	Cin	12	5	13	2.6(7)	0	—	—	—	—	—	—	—	—	—	—	—	—	—	—	k	—	0	25
1972	Atl	7	—	—	—	—	1	10	10.0(10)	0	—	—	—	—	—	—	—	—	—	—	—	—	0	5
NFL	5	56	55	163	3.0(17)	0	8	97	12.1(60)	0	—	—	—	—	—	—	—	—	—	—	Pk	—	0	224

LAMB, WALT Walter G., E, 6´1˝/195 lbs; Oklahoma; 1943: ChiB, rnd 10; B12/21/1920 Ardmore, OK, D1/5/1991

| 1946 | †ChiB | 11(3) | — | — | — | — | 1 | 10 | 10.0(10) | 0 | — | — | — | — | — | — | — | — | — | — | — | — | 0 | 5 |

LAMBEAU, CURLY Earl Louis, TB-FB-BB-E, 5´10˝/187 lbs; Wisconsin; Notre Dame; B4/9/1898 Green Bay, WI, D6/1/1965 Sturgeon Bay, WI; HOF 1963 **[KC]**   **1921** GB 6 (5, TB), 28
1922 GB☆8 (6, TB), 30   **1923** GB☆10 (9, TB), 18   **1924** GB☆11 (10, TB), 10   **1925** GB 11 (7, TB), 8   **1926** GB 12 (7, TB), 4   **1927** GB 10 (5, fb), 12   **1928** GB 8 (1)   **1929** GB 1 (0)
NFL 77 (50), 110 [9 yrs]

LAMBERT, DION Dion Adrian, DB, 6´0˝/190 lbs; UCLA; 1992: NE, rnd 4; B2/12/1969 Lakeview Terrace, CA   **1992** NE 16 (0)   **1993** NE 14 (4)   **1994** Sea 1 (1)   **NFL** 31 (5) [3 yrs]

LAMBERT, FRANK Franklin Talley, P, 6´3˝/200 lbs; Mississippi; 1965: NYG, rnd 5/NYJ, rnd 10; B4/17/1943 Hattiesburg, MS   **1965** Pit 14   **1966** Pit 14   **NFL** 28 [2 yrs]

LAMBERT, GORDON Gordon Olaf, LB, 6´5˝/245 lbs; West Virginia; Tennessee-Martin; 1968: Den, rnd 4; B7/5/1945 Leckie, WV   **1968** Den-A 10   **1969** Den-A 4   **NFL** 14 [2 yrs]

LAMBERT, JACK John Harold, LB, 6´4˝/220 lbs; Kent State; 1974: Pit, rnd 2; B7/8/1952 Mantua, OH; HOF 1990 **[I]**   **1974**†Pit 14 (14, MLB)   **1975**†Pit★14 (14, MLB)
1976†Pit★14 (14, MLB)   **1977**†Pit★11 (10, MLB)   **1978**†Pit 16 (16, MLB)   **1979**†Pit★16 (13, MLB)   **1980** Pit★14 (13, MLB)   **1981** Pit★16 (16, MLB)   **1982**†Pit★8 (8, RILB)
1983†Pit★15 (15, RILB)   **1984**†Pit 8 (3)   **NFL** 146 (136) [11 yrs]

LAMBERTI, PAT Pasquale C., LB, 6´2˝/225 lbs; Richmond; 1959: ChiC, rnd 13; B9/1/1937 Woodbridge, NJ   **1961** NYT-A 5   **1961** Den-A 7   **NFL** 12 [1 yr]

LAMBRECHT, MIKE Michael James, DT, 6´1˝/271 lbs; St. Cloud State; B5/2/1963 Watertown, MN   **1987** Mia 5 (3)   **1988** Mia 8 (3)   **1989** Mia 6 (0)   **NFL** 19 (3) [3 yrs]

LAMME, BUCK Emerald Ford, E, 6´2˝/180 lbs; Ohio Wesleyan; B7/2/1905, OH, D9/4/1957 Columbus, OH   **1931** Cle 1 (1)

LAMMONS, PETE Peter Spencer, TE, 6´3˝/230 lbs; Texas; 1966: NYJ, rnd 8/Cle, rnd 14; B10/20/1943 Crockett, TX

1966	NYJ-A	14(TE)	—	—	—	—	41	565	13.8(60)	4	—	—	—	—	—	—	—	—	—	—	—	—	24	303
1967	NYJ-A◇	14(TE)	—	—	—	—	45	515	11.4(61)	2	—	—	—	—	—	—	—	—	—	—	—	—	12	268
1968	†NYJ-A	13(TE)	—	—	—	—	32	400	12.5(27)	2	—	—	—	—	—	—	—	—	—	—	—	—	18	215
1969	†NYJ-A	14(TE)	—	—	—	—	33	400	12.1(25)	2	—	—	—	—	—	—	—	—	—	—	—	—	12	210
1970	NYJ	14(TE)	—	—	—	—	25	316	12.6(30)	2	—	—	—	—	—	—	—	—	—	—	—	—	12	168
1971	NYJ	14(TE)	0	3	(3)	0	8	149	18.6(27)	1	—	—	—	—	—	—	—	—	—	—	—	—	6	83
1972	†GB	12	—	—	—	—	1	19	19.0(19)	0	—	—	—	—	—	—	—	—	—	—	—	—	0	10
NFL	7	95	0	3	(3)	0	185	2364	12.8(61)	14	—	—	—	—	—	—	—	—	—	—	—	—	84	1255

LAMONICA, DARYLE Daryle Pat, QB, 6´3˝/215 lbs; Notre Dame; 1963: Buf, rnd 24/GB, rnd 12; B7/17/1941 Fresno, CA

1963	†Buf-A	14	9	8	0.9(7)	0	—	—	—	—	71	33	46.5	437	6.2(**93**)	3	4	—	—	—	P	—	2	82
1964	†Buf-A	14(qb)	55	289	5.3(28)	**6**	—	—	—	—	128	55	43.0	1137	8.9(80)	6	8	—	—	—	—	—	40	628
1965	†Buf-A◇	14	10	30	3.0(10)	1	—	—	—	—	70	29	41.4	376	5.4(74)	3	6	—	—	—	—	—	6	3
1966	†Buf-A	14	9	6	0.7(14)	1	—	—	—	—	84	33	39.3	549	6.5(55)	4	5	—	—	—	—	—	6	111
1967	†Oak-A★	14(QB)	22	110	5.0(26)	4	—	—	—	—	425	220	51.8	3228	7.6(72)	**30**	20	—	—	80.8	—	—	24	1114
1968	†Oak-A☆	13(13, QB)	19	98	5.2(18)	1	—	—	—	—	416	206	49.5	3245	7.8(82)	25	15	—	—	80.9	—	—	6	**1256**
1969	†Oak-A★	14(14, QB)	13	36	2.8(12)	1	—	—	—	—	**426**	221	51.9	**3302**	7.8(80)	**34**	**25**	11	100	79.8	—	—	6	867
1970	†Oak★	14(14, QB)	8	24	3.0(13)	1	—	—	—	—	**356**	179	50.3	**2516**	7.1(60)	**22**	15	15	127	76.5	—	—	6	792
1971	Oak	14(13, QB)	4	16	4.0(13)	0	—	—	—	—	242	118	48.8	1717	7.1(67)	16	16	18	172	66.8	—	—	0	315
1972	†Oak★	14(13, QB)	10	33	3.3(14)	0	—	—	—	—	281	149	53.0	1998	7.1(70)	18	12	14	136	79.5	—	—	0	642
1973	Oak	8(3)	5	-7	-1.4(6)	0	—	—	—	—	93	42	45.2	614	6.6(48)	2	8	11	87	—	—	—	0	-10
1974	Oak	4	2	-3	-1.5(0)	0	—	—	—	—	9	3	33.3	35	3.9(13)	1	4	3	14	—	—	—	0	-141
NFL	12	151(70)	166	640	3.9(28)	14	—	—	—	—	2601	1288	49.5	19154	7.4(93)	164	138	72	636	72.9	P	—	90	5657

LAMONTAGNE, NOEL Noel Michael, T-G, 6´4˝/301 lbs; Virginia; B3/9/1977 Bethlehem, PA   **2000** Cle 2 (0)

LAMSON, CHUCK Charles Watt, DB, 6´0˝/190 lbs; Iowa State; Wyoming; 1961: Min, rnd 4; B3/14/1939 Webster City, IA   **1962** Min 14 (14, LS)   **1963** Min 12 (7, RS)
1965 LARm 13 (LS)   **1966** LARm 14 (13, LS)   **1967**†LARm 14 (LS)   **NFL** 67 (34) [5 yrs]

LAND, DAN Daniel, DB-RB, 6´0˝/195 lbs; Albany State (GA); B7/3/1965 Donalsonville, GA   **1989** LARd 10 (0)   **1990**†LARd 16 (0)   **1991**†LARd 16 (0)   **1992** LARd 16 (0)
1993†LARd 15 (0)   **1994** LARd 16 (0)   **1995** Oak 15 (3)   **1996** Oak 16 (2)   **1997** Oak 16 (0)

| 1987 | TB | 3(2) | 9 | 20 | 2.2(6) | 0 | — | — | — | — | — | — | — | — | — | — | — | — | — | — | — | — | 0 | 20 |
| NFL | 10 | 139(7) | 9 | 20 | 2.2(6) | 0 | — | — | — | — | — | — | — | — | — | — | — | — | — | — | ki | — | 0 | 20 |

LAND, FRED Frederick N., T-G, 6´1˝/220 lbs; LSU; 1948: SF-A, rnd 6/Det, rnd 11; B5/8/1925 North Little Rock, AR, D3/19/1992 Denham Springs, LA   **1948** SF-A 2 (0)

LAND, MEL Melvin, LB-DE, 6´3˝/243 lbs; Michigan State; 1979: Mia, rnd 3; B11/30/1955 Youngstown, OH   **1979**†Mia 16   **1980** SF 3 (0)   **NFL** 19 [2 yrs]

LANDER, LOWELL Lowell Len, HB, 6´0˝/195 lbs; Westminster (PA); B9/12/1932 Pittsburgh, PA, D2/28/2001 Pittsburgh, PA   **1958** ChiC 1

LANDERS, WALTER Walter James, RB, 6´0˝/214 lbs; Clark Atlanta; B7/4/1953 Lanett, AL

1978	GB	4	7	40	5.7(10)	0	—	—	—	—	—	—	—	—	—	—	—	—	—	—	k	1	6	25
1979	GB	9	17	41	2.4(14)	0	5	60	12.0(55)	1	—	—	—	—	—	—	—	—	—	—	—	—	6	76
NFL	2	13	24	81	3.4(14)	0	5	60	12.0(55)	1	—	—	—	—	—	—	—	—	—	—	k	1	12	101

LANDETA, SEAN Sean Edward, P, 6´0˝/215 lbs; Towson State; B1/6/1962 Baltimore, MD **[P]**   **1986**†NYG★16 (0)   **1987** NYG 12 (0)   **1988** NYG 1 (0)   **1989**†NYG☆16 (0)
1990†NYG★16 (0)   **1991** NYG 15 (0)   **1992** NYG 11 (0)   **1993** NYG 8 (0)   **1993** LARm 8 (0)   **1994** LARm☆16 (0)   **1995** SL 16 (0)   **1997**†TB 10 (0)   **1998**†GB 16 (0)   **1999** Phi 16 (0)
2000†Phi 16 (0)   **2001** Phi 16 (0)   **2003**†SL 16 (0)   **2004** SL 10 (0)   **2005** Phi 5 (0)

1985	†NYG☆	16(0)	—	—	—	—	—	—	—	—	1	0	0.0	0	0	0	0	—	—	—	P	—	0	0
1996	SL	16(0)	2	0	0.0(0)	0	—	—	—	—	—	—	—	—	—	—	—	—	—	—	P	—	0	0
2002	Phi	12(0)	1	0	0.0(0)	0	—	—	—	—	—	—	—	—	—	—	—	—	—	—	P	—	0	0
NFL	21	284(0)	3	0	0.0(0)	0	—	—	—	—	1	0	0.0	0	0	0	0	—	—	—	P	—	0	0

LANDOLT, KEVIN Kevin Joseph, DT, 6´4˝/298 lbs; West Virginia; 1999: Jax, rnd 4; B10/25/1975 Mount Holly, NJ   **1999** Jax 1 (0)

LANDRIGAN, JIM James Montague, T, 6´4˝/235 lbs; Holy Cross; Dartmouth; 1947: Mia-A, rnd 25/1945: Pit, rnd 19; B5/31/1923 Everett, MA, D6/24/1974 San Diego, CA
1947 Bal-A 5 (0)

LANDRUM, MIKE Michael Geddie, TE, 6´2˝/231 lbs; Southern Mississippi; B11/6/1961 Laurel, MS

| 1984 | Atl | 15(0) | — | — | — | — | 6 | 66 | 11.0(30) | 0 | — | — | — | — | — | — | — | — | — | — | — | — | 0 | 33 |

LANDRY, GREG Gregory Paul, QB, 6´4˝/210 lbs; Massachusetts; 1968: Det, rnd 1; B12/18/1946 Nashua, NH

1968	Det	4(4, QB)	7	39	5.6(14)	1	—	—	—	—	48	23	47.9	338	7.0(80)	2	7	—	—	—	—	—	6	-52
1969	Det	10(10, qb)	33	243	7.4(26)	0	—	—	—	—	160	80	50.0	853	5.3(43)	4	10	30	265	—	—	—	6	300
1970	†Det	12(6, qb)	35	350	10.0(76)	1	—	—	—	—	136	83	61.0	1072	7.9(58)	9	5	26	198	—	—	—	6	741
1971	Det★	14(14, QB)	76	530	**7.0**(52)	3	—	—	—	—	261	136	52.1	2237	8.6(76)	16	13	29	232	80.9	—	—	18	1239
1972	Det	14(14, QB)	81	524	6.5(38)	**9**	—	—	—	—	268	134	50.0	2066	7.7(82)	18	17	25	149	71.8	—	—	54	1057
1973	Det	7(7, QB)	42	267	6.4(18)	2	—	—	—	—	128	70	54.7	908	7.1(**84**)	3	10	13	98	—	—	—	12	356
1974	Det	5(3)	22	95	4.3(19)	1	—	—	—	—	82	49	59.8	572	7.0(45)	3	1	11	83	—	—	—	6	286
1975	Det	6(3)	20	92	4.6(14)	0	—	—	—	—	56	31	55.4	403	7.2(36)	1	0	17	129	—	—	—	0	299
1976	Det	14(12, QB)	43	234	5.4(28)	1	—	—	—	—	291	168	57.7	2191	7.5(74)	17	8	55	397	89.6	—	—	6	1105

YEAR	TEAM	G(GS, POS)	RUSH	YD	AVG(LG)	TD	REC	YD	AVG(LG)	TD	PASS	COMP	PCT	YD	AVG(LG)	TD	INT	SK	YD	QBR	KPR	OTD	PTS	TAY
1977	Det	11(11, QB)	25	99	4.0(13)	0	—	—	—	—	240	135	56.3	1359	5.7(39)	6	7	34	302	68.7	—	—	0	529
1978	Det	5(5, qb)	5	29	5.8(19)	0	—	—	—	—	77	48	62.3	452	5.9(20)	1	1	21	205	—	—	—	0	220
1979	Bal	16(12, QB)	31	115	3.7(17)	0	—	—	—	—	457	270	59.1	2932	6.4(67)	15	15	42	326	75.3	—	—	0	1056
1980	Bal	16(1)	7	26	3.7(14)	1	—	—	—	—	47	24	51.1	275	5.9(32)	2	3	2	19	—	—	1	6	64
1981	Bal	11(0)	1	11	11.0(11)	0	—	—	—	—	29	14	48.3	195	6.7(34)	0	1	5	50	—	—	1	6	69
1984	ChiB	1(1)	2	1	0.5(1)	1	—	—	—	—	20	11	55.0	199	9.9(55)	1	3	—	—	—	—	—	6	-5
NFL	15	146(103)	430	2655	6.2(76)	21	—	—	—	—	2300	1276	55.5	16052	7.0(84)	98	103	310	2453	72.9	—	1	132	7261

LANDRY, TOM Thomas Wade, DB-HB-QB, 6´1˝/195 lbs; Texas; 1948: NYY-A, rnd 19/1947: NYG, rnd 20; B9/11/1924 Mission, TX; D2/12/2000 Dallas, TX; HOF 1990 **[PIC]**

| 1949 | †NYY-A | 12(1) | 29 | 91 | 3.1 | 0 | 6 | 109 | 18.2 | 0 | — | — | — | — | — | — | — | — | — | — | Pkpi | — | 0 | 231 |

1950†NYG 10 (DB) **1951** NYG 12 (DB) **1953** NYG 12 (DB) **1954** NYG★12 (DB) **1955** NYG☆12 (DB)

| 1952 | NYG | 12(DB) | 7 | 40 | 5.7(8) | 1 | — | — | — | — | 47 | 11 | 23.4 | 172 | 3.7(70) | 1 | 7 | — | — | — | Pkpi | 1 | 12 | -27 |
| NFL | 6 | 70 | | 7 | 40 | 5.7(8) | 1 | — | — | — | — | 47 | 11 | 23.4 | 172 | 3.7(70) | 1 | 7 | — | — | — | Pkpi | 5 | 36 | 127 |

LANDSBERG, MORT Mortimer William, HB, 5´11˝/180 lbs; Cornell; 1941: Pit, rnd 22; B7/25/1919 New York, NY, D12/31/1970 New York, NY

| 1941 | Phi | 11(7, RH) | 23 | 69 | 3.0(33) | 1 | 5 | 51 | 10.2(19) | 0 | — | — | — | — | — | — | — | — | — | — | kpi | — | 0 | 154 |
| 1947 | LAD-A | 6(0) | 2 | -11 | -5.5 | 0 | 1 | 0 | — | — | — | — | — | — | — | — | — | — | — | — | — | — | 0 | -11 |

LANDSEE, BOB Robert John, C-G, 6´4˝/273 lbs; Wisconsin; 1986: Phi, rnd 6; B3/21/1964 Iron Mountain, MI **1986** Phi 7 (1) **1987** Phi 2 (1) **NFL** 9 (2) [2 yrs]

LANE, BOBBY Bobby Allen, LB, 6´2˝/222 lbs; Baylor; 1961: DalT, rnd 20/LA, rnd 11; B10/30/1939 Wagoner, OK **1963**†SD-A 7 **1964** SD-A 1 **NFL** 8 [2 yrs]

LANE, CLAYTON Clayton Harold, T, 6´0˝/215 lbs; New Hampshire; 1948: Pit, rnd 14; B11/23/1922 Worcester, MA **1948** NYY-A 1 (0)

LANE, ERIC Eric T., RB, 6´0˝/195 lbs; Brigham Young; 1981: Sea, rnd 8; B1/6/1959 Oakland, CA

1981	Sea	14(0)	8	22	2.8(5)	0	7	58	8.3(22)	0	—	—	—	—	—	—	—	—	—	k	—	0	109
1982	Sea	9(0)		—	—	—	—	—	—	—	—	1	0	0.0	0	0.0	0	0	—	—	—	k	—	0	7
1983	†Sea	16(0)	3	1	0.3(7)	0	2	9	4.5(7)	0	—	—	—	—	—	—	—	—	—	k	—	0	4
1984	†Sea	15(7, RB)	80	299	3.7(40)	4	11	101	9.2(55)	1	—	—	—	—	—	—	—	—	—	—	—	30	395
1985	Sea	16(3)	14	32	2.3(12)	0	15	153	10.2(20)	0	—	—	—	—	—	—	—	—	—	k	—	0	95
1986	Sea	15(0)	6	11	1.8(4)	0	3	6	2.0(4)	1	—	—	—	—	—	—	—	—	—	k	1	12	7
1987	†Sea	12(1)	13	43	3.1(7)	0	4	30	7.5(12)	0	—	—	—	—	—	—	—	—	—	k	—	0	59
NFL	7	97(12)	124	405	3.3(40)	4	42	357	8.5(55)	2	1	0	0.0	0	0.0	0	0	—	—	—	k	1	42	675

LANE, ERIC Eric, RB, 6´2˝/240 lbs; Tennessee; B3/17/1974 East Orange, NJ

| 1997 | †NYG | 15(0) | 5 | 13 | 2.6(6) | 0 | — | — | — | — | — | — | — | — | — | — | — | — | — | — | — | — | 0 | 13 |

LANE, FRED Freddie Brown, RB, 5´10˝/205 lbs; Lane; B9/6/1975 Nashville, TN, D7/6/2000 Charlotte, NC

1997	Car	13(7, RB)	182	809	4.4(50)	7	8	27	3.4(7)	0	—	—	—	—	—	—	—	—	—	—	—	42	893
1998	Car	14(11, RB)	205	717	3.5(31)	5	12	85	7.1(16)	0	—	—	—	—	—	—	—	—	—	—	—	30	810
1999	Car	15(5, rb)	115	475	4.1(41)	1	23	163	7.1(23)	0	—	—	—	—	—	—	—	—	—	k	—	6	580
NFL	3	42(23)	502	2001	4.0(50)	13	43	275	6.4(23)	0	—	—	—	—	—	—	—	—	—	k	—	78	2282

LANE, GARCIA Garcia R., DB, 5´9˝/180 lbs; Ohio State; 1984: KC, rnd S3; B12/31/1961 Youngstown, OH **1985** KC 16 (0) **1987** KC 1 (1) **NFL** 17 (1) [2 yrs]

LANE, GARY Gary Owen, QB, 6´1˝/210 lbs; Missouri; 1965: Cle, rnd 9/Buf, rnd R2; B12/21/1942 Alton, IL, D6/27/2003 St. Louis, MO **1966** Cle 8 **1968** NYG 7

| 1967 | Cle | 3(1) | 2 | 21 | 10.5(12) | 0 | — | — | — | — | 43 | 21 | 48.8 | 254 | 5.9(23) | 2 | 1 | 4 | 30 | — | — | — | 0 | 118 |
| NFL | 3 | 18(1) | 2 | 21 | 10.5(12) | 0 | — | — | — | — | 43 | 21 | 48.8 | 254 | 5.9(23) | 2 | 1 | 4 | 30 | — | — | — | 0 | 118 |

LANE, LES Leslie Willard, G, 6´3˝/193 lbs; South Dakota; B4/18/1916 Walthill, NE **1939** Bkn 2 (0)

LANE, LEW Lindley Roedesto, B, 5´10˝/180 lbs; St. Mary's (KS); B1/28/1898 Bucklin, KS, D8/1963 **1924** KC 5 (2)

LANE, MACARTHUR MacArthur, RB, 6´1˝/220 lbs; Utah State; 1968: SL, rnd 1; B3/16/1942 Oakland, CA

1968	SL	14	23	74	3.2(17)	0	—	—	—	—	—	—	—	—	—	—	—	—	—	—	—	0	74
1969	SL	9	25	93	3.7(13)	1	9	61	6.8(14)	0	—	—	—	—	—	—	—	—	—	k	—	6	357
1970	SL★	14(RB)	206	977	4.7(75)	11	32	365	11.4(78)	2	—	—	—	—	—	—	—	—	—	—	—	78	1280
1971	SL	13(FB)	150	592	3.9(40)	3	29	298	10.3(34)	0	—	—	—	—	—	—	—	—	—	—	—	18	771
1972	†GB	14(RB)	177	821	4.6(41)	3	26	285	11.0(49)	0	2	2	100.0	19	9.5(10)	0	0	—	—	—	—	—	18	1003
1973	GB	13(RB)	170	528	3.1(20)	1	27	255	9.4(30)	1	2	1	50.0	23	11.5(23)	1	0	—	—	—	k	—	12	688
1974	GB	14(RB)	137	362	2.6(20)	3	34	315	9.3(68)	3	1	0	0.0	0	0.0	0	0	—	—	—	—	—	36	565
1975	KC	9(3)	79	311	3.9(39)	2	25	202	8.1(31)	0	—	—	—	—	—	—	—	—	—	—	—	12	432
1976	KC	14(14, FB)	162	542	3.3(20)	5	66	686	10.4(44)	1	0	0	0.0	0	0.0	0	0	2	—	—	—	—	36	940
1977	KC	3	25	79	3.2(9)	1	3	40	13.3(21)	0	—	—	—	—	—	—	—	—	—	—	—	6	109
1978	KC	16	52	277	5.3(30)	0	36	279	7.8(44)	0	—	—	—	—	—	—	—	—	—	—	—	0	417
NFL	11	133(17)	1206	4656	3.9(75)	30	287	2786	9.7(78)	7	5	3	60.0	42	8.4(23)	1	0	1	2	—	k	—	222	6634

LANE, MAX Max Aaron, T-G, 6´6˝/301 lbs; Navy; 1994: NE, rnd 6; B2/22/1971 Norbone, MO **1994**†NE 14 (0) **1995** NE 16 (16, RT) **1996**†NE 16 (16, RT) **1997**†NE 16 (16, LG) **1998**†NE 16 (11, LG) **1999** NE 16 (6, lg) **2000** NE 6 (5, rt) **NFL** 100 (70) [7 yrs]

LANE, NIGHT TRAIN Richard, DB-E, 6´1˝/194 lbs; Western Nebraska CC-Scottsbluff; B4/16/1927 Austin, TX, D1/29/2002 Austin, TX; HOF 1974 **[I]** **1952** LARm 12 (DB) **1953** LARm 11 (DB) **1957** ChiC☆8 (DB) **1959** ChiC☆12 (DB) **1960** Det★12 (LCB) **1961** Det★12 (LCB) **1962** Det☆14 (LCB) **1963** Det☆14 (LCB) **1964** Det 7 **1965** Det 7

1954	ChiC★	12(DB)	—	—	—	—	4	58	14.5(26)	0	—	—	—	—	—	—	—	—	—	i	—	0	160
1955	ChiC★	12(DB)	—	—	—	—	2	110	55.0(98)	1	—	—	—	—	—	—	—	—	—	i	—	6	99
1956	ChiC★	12(DB)	—	—	—	—	1	75	75.0(75)	0	—	—	—	—	—	—	—	—	—	pi	1	6	209
1958	ChiC★	12(DB)	—	—	—	—	1	10	10.0(10)	0	—	—	—	—	—	—	—	—	—	i	—	0	-5
NFL	14	157	—	—	—	—	8	253	31.6(98)	1	—	—	—	—	—	—	—	—	—	pi	7	50	1043

LANE, OXIE Francis Charles, T, 6´4˝/222 lbs; Marquette; B1/2/1905 Merrill, WI, D8/19/1977 Merrill, WI **1926** Mil 9 (8, LT)

LANE, SKIP Paul John, DB, 6´1˝/210 lbs; Mississippi; B1/30/1960 Norwalk, CT **1984** NYJ 3 (0) **1984** KC 1 (0) **1987** Was 3 (3) **NFL** 7 (3) [2 yrs]

LANG, CHICK James H., T, /195 lbs; none; B10/3/1901 Fort William, Scotland, D10/25/1976 Mount Aukum, CA **1927** Dul 2 (0) **1929** ChiC 3 (3) **NFL** 5 (3) [2 yrs]

LANG, DAVID David, RB, 5´11˝/213 lbs; Northern Arizona; 1990: LARm, rnd 12; B3/28/1967 Loma Linda, CA, D5/19/2005 Stone Mountain, GA

1991	LARm	16(0)	—	—	—	—	—	—	—	—	—	—	—	—	—	—	—	—	—	k	—	0	14
1992	LARm	16(11, FB)	33	203	6.2(71)	5	18	283	15.7(67)	1	—	—	—	—	—	—	—	—	—	k	—	36	433
1993	LARm	6(0)	9	29	3.2(28)	0	4	45	11.3(21)	0	—	—	—	—	—	—	—	—	—	—	—	0	52
1994	LARm	13(0)	6	34	5.7(17)	0	8	60	7.5(12)	0	—	—	—	—	—	—	—	—	—	—	—	0	285
1995	†Dal	16(0)	1	7	7.0(7)	0	—	—	—	—	—	—	—	—	—	—	—	—	—	—	—	0	7
NFL	5	67(11)	49	273	5.6(71)	5	30	388	12.9(67)	1	—	—	—	—	—	—	—	—	—	—	—	36	790

LANG, GENE Gene Eric, RB, 5´10˝/196 lbs; LSU; 1984: Den, rnd 11; B3/15/1962 Pass Christian, MS

1984	†Den	16(0)	8	42	5.3(15)	2	4	24	6.0(9)	1	—	—	—	—	—	—	—	—	—	—	—	18	198
1985	Den	12(2)	84	318	3.8(26)	5	23	180	7.8(24)	2	—	—	—	—	—	—	—	—	—	—	—	42	574
1986	†Den	15(2)	29	94	3.2(14)	1	13	105	8.1(26)	2	—	—	—	—	—	—	—	—	—	—	—	18	332
1987	†Den	12(6, FB)	89	303	3.4(28)	2	17	130	7.6(24)	2	0	0	0.0	0	0.0	0	0	1	7	—	—	—	24	416
1988	Atl	16(3)	53	191	3.6(19)	0	37	398	10.8(50)	1	—	—	—	—	—	—	—	—	—	—	—	6	392
1989	Atl	15(7, rb)	47	176	3.7(22)	1	39	436	11.2(32)	1	—	—	—	—	—	—	—	—	—	—	—	12	409
1990	Atl	3(0)	9	24	2.7(9)	0	1	7	7.0(7)	0	—	—	—	—	—	—	—	—	—	—	—	0	31
NFL	7	89(20)	319	1148	3.6(28)	11	134	1280	9.6(50)	9	1	0	0.0	0	0.0	0	0	1	7	—	—	—	120	2351

LANG, IZZY Israel Alvin, RB, 6´1˝/232 lbs; Tennessee State; 1964: Phi, rnd 18; B2/2/1942 Tampa, FL

1964	Phi	12	12	37	3.1(20)	0	6	69	11.5(23)	0	—	—	—	—	—	—	—	—	—	kp	—	0	225
1965	Phi	14	10	25	2.5(8)	1	2	30	15.0(24)	0	—	—	—	—	—	—	—	—	—	k	—	6	41
1966	Phi	14(2)	52	239	4.6(39)	1	12	107	8.9(24)	0	3	2	66.7	51	17.0(36)	1	0	—	—	—	—	—	6	328
1967	Phi	14(HB)	101	336	3.3(21)	2	26	201	7.7(19)	2	1	1	100.0	26	26.0(26)	0	0	—	—	—	—	—	30	485

YEAR	TEAM	G (GS, POS)	RUSH	YD	AVG(LG)	TD	REC	YD	AVG(LG)	TD	PASS	COMP	PCT	YD	AVG(LG)	TD	INT	SK	YD	QBR	KPR		OTD	PTS	TAY
1968	Phi	11 (HB)	69	235	3.4(17)	0	17	147	8.6(25)	1	—	—	—	—	—	—	—	—	—	—	—	—	—	6	314
1969	LARm	12	1	1	1.0(1)	0	—	—	—	—	—	—	—	—	—	—	—	—	—	—	k	—	—	0	11
NFL	6	77 (2)	245	873	3.6(39)	4	63	554	8.8(25)	4	4	3	75.0	77	19.3(36)	0	0	—	—	—	kp	—	—	48	1403

LANG, KENARD Kenard Dushun, DE-DT-LB, 6´3˝/280 lbs; Miami (FL); 1997: Was, rnd 1; B1/31/1975 Orlando, FL **1997** Was 11 (11, LDE) **1998** Was 16 (16, LDE) **1999**†Was 16 (9, LDE) **2000** Was 16 (0) **2001** Was 16 (16, RDT) **2002**†Cle 15 (14, LDE) **2003** Cle 15 (15, RDE) **2004** Cle 16 (15, RDE) **2005** Cle 16 (5, lolb) **NFL** 137 (101) [9 yrs]

LANG, LE-LO Le-Lo, DB, 5´11˝/185 lbs; Washington; 1990: Den, rnd 5; B1/23/1967 Los Angeles, CA **1990** Den 6 (0) **1991**†Den 16 (0) **1992** Den 16 (1) **1993**†Den 16 (0) **NFL** 54 (1) [4 yrs]

LANGAS, BOB Robert Frederick, DE, 6´4˝/230 lbs; Wayne State (MI); B1/22/1930 Detroit, MI **1954** Bal 8

LANGE, BILL William Henry, G-LB, 6´1˝/239 lbs; Dayton; 1950: LA, rnd 30; B1/12/1928 Delphos, OH **1951** LARm 12 (RG) **1952**†LARm 10 **1953** Bal☆12 (RG) **1954** ChiC 10 (RG) **1955** ChiC 12 (RG) **NFL** 56 [5 yrs]

LANGER, JIM James John, C-G, 6´2˝/250 lbs; South Dakota State; B5/16/1948 Little Falls, MN; HOF 1987 **1970** Mia 6 **1971**†Mia 14 **1972**†Mia 14 (14, C) **1973**†Mia★14 (14, C) **1974**†Mia★14 (14, C) **1975** Mia★14 (14, C) **1976** Mia★14 (14, C) **1977**†Mia★14 (14, C) **1978**†Mia★16 (16, C) **1979** Mia 9 (9, C) **1980**†Min 13 (0) **1981** Min 9 (1) **NFL** 151 (110) [12 yrs]

LANGFORD, JEVON Jevon Dicorious, DE, 6´3˝/290 lbs; Oklahoma State; 1996: Cin, rnd 4; B2/16/1974 Washington, DC **1996** Cin 12 (3) **1997** Cin 14 (0) **1998** Cin 14 (1) **1999** Cin 12 (7, rde) **2000** Cin 11 (3) **2001** Cin 3 (0) **NFL** 66 (14) [6 yrs]

LANGHAM, ANTONIO Collie Antonio, DB, 6´0˝/181 lbs; Alabama; 1994: Cle, rnd 1; B7/31/1972 Town Creek, AL **1994**†Cle 16 (16, LCB) **1995** Cle 16 (16, LCB) **1996** Bal 15 (14, LCB) **1997** Bal 16 (15, LCB) **1998**†SF 11 (6, lcb) **1999** Cle 13 (2) **2000** NE 15 (7, rcb) **NFL** 102 (76) [7 yrs]

LANGHOFF, IRV John Irvin, B, 5´9˝/158 lbs; Marquette; B8/24/1897 Milwaukee, WI, D1/12/1952 Milwaukee, WI [K] **1922** Rac 11 (9, WB), 8 **1923** Rac 4 (4) **NFL** 15 (13) [2 yrs]

LANGHORNE, REGGIE Reginald Devan, WR, 6´2˝/200 lbs; Elizabeth City State; 1985: Cle, rnd 7; B4/7/1963 Suffolk, VA

1985	†Cle	16 (3)					1	12	12.0(12)	0	—	—	—	—	—	—	—	—	—	—	k	—	—	0	7
1986	†Cle	16 (15, WR)	1	-11	-11.0(-11)	0	39	678	17.4(66)	1	—	—	—	—	—	—	—	—	—	—	k	—	—	6	330
1987	†Cle	12 (12, WR)					20	288	14.4(25)	1	—	—	—	—	—	—	—	—	—	—	k	—	—	6	142
1988	†Cle	16 (16, WR)	2	26	13.0(20)	1	57	780	13.7(77)	7	—	—	—	—	—	—	—	—	—	—		—	—	48	461
1989	†Cle	16 (15, WR)	5	19	3.8(18)	0	60	749	12.5(62)	2	—	—	—	—	—	—	—	—	—	—		—	—	12	404
1990	Cle	12 (11, WR)					45	585	13.0(39)	2	—	—	—	—	—	—	—	—	—	—		—	—	12	303
1991	Cle	14 (9, WR)					39	505	12.9(40)	2	—	—	—	—	—	—	—	—	—	—		—	—	12	263
1992	Ind	16 (12, WR)	1	-7	-7.0(-7)	0	65	811	12.5(34)	1	—	—	—	—	—	—	—	—	—	—		—	—	6	404
1993	Ind	16 (16, WR)					85	1038	12.2(72)	3	—	—	—	—	—	—	—	—	—	—		—	—	18	534
NFL	9	134 (109)	9	27	3.0(20)	1	411	5446	13.3(77)	19	—	—	—	—	—	—	—	—	—	—	k	—	—	120	2846

LANHAM, CHARLIE Charles T., T, /170 lbs; none; B6/1/1891, D5/10/1971 Danville, KY **1922** Lou 1 (0) **1923** Lou 1 (1) **NFL** 2 (1) [2 yrs]

LANIER, KEN Kenneth Wayne, T, 6´3˝/281 lbs; Florida State; 1981: Den, rnd 5; B7/8/1959 Columbus, OH **1981** Den 8 (1) **1982** Den 9 (9, RT) **1983**†Den 16 (16, RT) **1984**†Den 16 (15, RT) **1985** Den 16 (16, RT) **1986**†Den 16 (16, RT) **1987**†Den 12 (12, RT) **1988** Den 16 (16, RT) **1989**†Den 16 (16, RT) **1991**†Den 16 (16, RT) **1992** Den 16 (16, RT) **1993** LARd 2 (2) **1994** Den 4 (0)

| 1990 | Den | 16 (16, RT) | | | | | 1 | -4 | -4.0(-4) | 0 | — | — | — | — | — | — | — | — | — | — | | — | — | 0 | -2 |
| NFL | 14 | 179 (167) | | | | | 1 | -4 | -4.0(-4) | 0 | — | — | — | — | — | — | — | — | — | — | | — | — | 0 | -2 |

LANIER, WILLIE Willie Edward, LB, 6´1˝/245 lbs; Morgan State; 1967: KC, rnd 2; B8/21/1945 Clover, VA; HOF 1986 [I] **1967** KC-A 10 (10, RLB) **1968**†KC-A★14 (14, MLB) **1969**†KC-A★14 (MLB) **1970** KC★14 (MLB) **1971**†KC★14 (MLB) **1972** KC★13 (MLB) **1973** KC★14 (MLB) **1974** KC★14 (MLB) **1975** KC★14 (14, MLB) **1976** KC 14 (11, MLB) **1977** KC 14 (MLB) **NFL** 149 (49) [11 yrs]

LANKAS, JIM James Jarrett, B, 6´2˝/220 lbs; St. Mary's (CA); B8/26/1918 Stratton, NE, D8/9/1978 Edison, KS **1942** Phi 1 (0)

| 1943 | GB | 3 (0) | 2 | 2 | 1.0(1) | 0 | — | — | — | — | — | — | — | — | — | — | — | — | — | — | | — | — | 0 | 2 |
| NFL | 2 | 4 (0) | 2 | 2 | 1.0(1) | 0 | — | — | — | — | — | — | — | — | — | — | — | — | — | — | | — | — | 0 | 2 |

LANKFORD, PAUL Paul Jay, DB, 6´1˝/185 lbs; Penn State; 1982: Mia, rnd 3; B6/15/1958 New York, NY **1982** Mia 7 (0) **1983**†Mia 16 (1) **1984**†Mia 16 (6, lcb) **1985** Mia 16 (15, LCB) **1986** Mia 12 (12, RCB) **1987** Mia 12 (12, LCB) **1988** Mia 13 (10, LCB) **1989** Mia 7 (0) **1991** Mia 15 (0) **NFL** 130 (72) [10 yrs]

LANPHEAR, DAN George Daniel, DE, 6´2˝/230 lbs; Wisconsin; 1960: Pit, rnd 8; B1/24/1938 Madison, WI **1960**†Hou-A 14 **1962** Hou-A 2 (2) **NFL** 16 (2) [2 yrs]

LANSDELL, GRENNY Grenville Archer, HB, 6´0˝/190 lbs; USC; 1940: NYG, rnd 1; B7/16/1918 Great Barrington, MA, D5/14/1984 Long Beach, CA

| 1940 | NYG | 2 (1) | 7 | 9 | 1.3 | 0 | — | — | — | — | 3 | 2 | 66.7 | 23 | 7.7 | 0 | 0 | — | — | — | | — | — | 0 | 21 |

LANSFORD, BUCK Alex John, G-T, 6´2˝/232 lbs; Texas; 1955: Phi, rnd 2; B11/4/1933 Corsicana, TX **1955** Phi 12 (12, LG) **1956** Phi◊12 (12, LT) **1957** Phi 10 (10, LT) **1958** LARm 12 (RG) **1959** LARm 4 **1960** LARm 11 (LG) **NFL** 61 (34) [6 yrs]

LANSFORD, JIM James Albert, T, 6´3˝/235 lbs; Texas; 1952: DalT, rnd 9; B8/19/1930 Jackson County, TX, D1/17/1989 **1952** DalT 12 (10, LT)

LANSFORD, MIKE Michael John, K, 6´0˝/183 lbs; Washington; 1980: NYG, rnd 12; B7/20/1958 Monterey Park, CA [K] **1982** LARm 9 (0) **1983**†LARm 4 (0) **1984**†LARm 16 (0) **1985**†LARm 16 (0) **1986**†LARm 16 (0) **1987** LARm 15 (0) **1988**†LARm 16 (0) **1989** LARm☆16 (0) **1990** LARm 16 (0) **NFL** 124 (0) [9 yrs]

LANTZ, MOSE Montgomery Stoffal, C, 5´11˝/185 lbs; Grove City; B11/24/1903 Pittsburgh, PA, D11/2/1969 Pittsburgh, PA **1933** Pit 10 (0)

LANUM, JAKE Ralph Lewis, B, 6´0˝/190 lbs; Millikin; Illinois; B9/13/1896 Champaign, IL, D3/19/1968 Homewood, IL **1920** Dec 12 (7, RH) **1921** ChiS 7 (1) **1922** ChiB 12 (5, fb) **1923** ChiB 10 (7, RH), 6 **1924** ChiB 7 (2) **NFL** 48 (22) [5 yrs]

LANZA, CHUCK Charles Louis, C, 6´2˝/263 lbs; Notre Dame; 1988: Pit, rnd 3; B9/20/1964 Coraopolis, PA **1988** Pit 16 (0) **1989** Pit 11 (0) **NFL** 27 (0) [2 yrs]

LAPHAM, BILL William Gaius, C, 6´5˝/238 lbs; Drake; Iowa; 1958: Phi, rnd 14; B2/2/1934 Des Moines, IA **1960**†Phi 12 **1961** Min 14 (13, C) **NFL** 26 (13) [2 yrs]

LAPHAM, DAVE David Allan, G-C-T, 6´4˝/259 lbs; Syracuse; 1974: Cin, rnd 3; B6/24/1952 Melrose, MA **1974** Cin 14 **1975**†Cin 13 (RG) **1976** Cin 14 (RG) **1977** Cin 13 (RG) **1978** Cin 16 (RG) **1979** Cin 16 (RG/c) **1981** Cin 13 (10, LG) **1982**†Cin 9 (9, LG) **1983** Cin 16 (16, LG) **NFL** 140 (63) [10 yrs]

LAPKA, MYRON Myron Lynn, NT-DE-DT, 6´4˝/258 lbs; USC; 1980: NYG, rnd 3; B5/10/1956 Van Nuys, CA **1980** NYG 10 (0) **1982** LARm 2 (0) **1983** LARm 4 (0) **NFL** 16 (0) [3 yrs]

LAPKA, TED Theodore Aloysius, E, 6´1˝/193 lbs; DePaul; St. Ambrose; B4/20/1920 Hawthorne, IL

1943	†Was	7 (2)	—	—	—		2	39	19.5(32)	0	—	—	—	—	—	—	—	—	—	—		—	—	0	20
1944	Was	5 (2)	—	—	—		4	61	15.3(42)	1	—	—	—	—	—	—	—	—	—	—		—	—	6	36
1946	Was	7 (0)	—	—	—		3	28	9.3(11)	0	—	—	—	—	—	—	—	—	—	—		1	—	6	14
NFL	3	19 (4)	—	—	—		9	128	14.2(42)	1	—	—	—	—	—	—	—	—	—	—		1	—	12	69

LaPOINTE, RON Ronald Arthur, TE, 6´2˝/235 lbs; Penn State; B2/28/1957 Framingham, MA **1980** Bal 2 (0)

LaPORTA, PHIL Philip Francis, T, 6´4˝/256 lbs; Penn State; 1974: NO, rnd 9; B5/4/1952 Oceanside, NY **1974** NO 6 **1975** NO 14 (6, lt) **NFL** 20 (6) [2 yrs]

LaPRESTA, BENNY Benjamin, B, 5´9˝/185 lbs; St. Louis; B1/22/1909, OH, D8/11/1975 St. Louis, MO [K]

1933	Bos	8 (2)	11	62	5.6		1	23	23.0(23)	0	4	2	50.0	50	12.5	0	0	—	—	—	K	—	—	1	99
1934	SL	1 (0)	—	—	—		1	4	4.0(4)	0	1	0	0.0	0		0	0	—	—	—		—	—	0	2
NFL	2	9 (2)	11	62	5.6	0	2	27	13.5(23)	0	5	2	40.0	50	10.0	0	0	—	—	—	K	—	—	1	101

LARABA, BOB Robert Edward, LB-QB, 6´3˝/195 lbs; Texas-El Paso; 1959: GB, rnd 8; B5/30/1933 Sheldon, VT, D2/16/1962 San Diego, CA [K]

1960	†LAC-A	14	3	13	4.3(16)	0	—	—	—		7	2	28.6	23	3.3(16)	0	2	—	—	—	Pi	—	—	0	-44
1961	†SD-A	14 (rlb)	5	5	1.0(9)	1	—	—	—		—	—	—	—	—	—	—	—	—	—	Ki	2	—	19	161
NFL	28		8	18	2.3(16)	1	—	—	—		7	2	28.6	23	3.3(16)	0	2	—	—	—	KPi	2	—	19	118

LARAWAY, JACK Jack Duane, LB, 6´1˝/220 lbs; Purdue; 1959: Det, rnd 10; B9/20/1935 Erie, PA **1960** Buf-A 12 (LLB) **1961**†Hou-A 10 **NFL** 22 [2 yrs]

LARGENT, STEVE Stephen Michael, WR, 5´11˝/187 lbs; Tulsa; 1976: Hou, rnd 4; B9/28/1954 Tulsa, OK; HOF 1995 [K]

1976	Sea	14 (13, WR)	4	-14	-3.5(7)	0	54	705	13.1(45)	4	1	0	0.0	0	0.0	0	0	—	—	—	kp	—	—	24	411
1977	Sea	14 (14, WR)					33	643	19.5(74)	10	—	—	—	—	—	—	—	—	—	—	p	—	—	60	384
1978	Sea★	16 (16, WR)					71	1168	16.5(57)	8	—	—	—	—	—	—	—	—	—	—		—	—	48	624
1979	Sea★	15 (15, WR)					66	1237	18.7(55)	9	—	—	—	—	—	—	—	—	—	—		—	—	54	664

YEAR	TEAM	G (GS, POS)	RUSH	YD	AVG (LG)	TD	REC	YD	AVG (LG)	TD	PASS	COMP	PCT	YD	AVG (LG)	TD	INT	SK	YD	QBR	KPR	OTD	PTS	TAY
1980	Sea	16(16, WR)	1	2	2.0(2)	0	66	1064	16.1(67)	6	—	—		—	—	—	—				—		—	36	564
1981	Sea★	16(16, WR)	6	47	7.8(15)	1	75	1224	16.3(57)	9	1	0	0.0	0	0.0	0	0				—		—	60	714
1982	Sea	8(8, WR)	1	8	8.0(8)	0	34	493	14.5(45)	3	—	—		—	—	—	—				—		—	18	270
1983	†Sea☆	15(14, WR)	—	—		—	72	1074	14.9(46)	11	1	1	100.0	11	11.0(11)	0	0				—		—	66	598
1984	†Sea	16(16, WR)	2	10	5.0(6)	0	74	1164	15.7(65)	12	—	—		—	—	—	—				—		—	72	652
1985	Sea★	16(16, WR)	—	—		—	79	**1287**	16.3(43)	6	1	0	0.0	0	0.0	0	0				—	K	—	37	674
1986	Sea	16(16, WR)	—	—		—	70	1070	15.3(38)	9	1	1	100.0	18	18.0(18)	0	0				—		—	54	589
1987	†Sea	13(13, WR)	2	33	16.5(21)	0	58	912	15.7(55)	**8**	2	0	0.0	0	0.0	0	0				—		—	48	529
1988	†Sea	15(15, WR)	1	-3	-3.0(-3)	0	39	645	16.5(46)	2	—	—		—	—	—	—				—		—	12	330
1989	Sea	10(9, WR)	—	—		—	28	403	14.4(33)	3	—	—		—	—	—	—				—	K	—	19	217
NFL	14	200(197)	17	83	4.9(21)	1	819	13089	16.0(74)	100	7	2	28.6	29	4.1(18)	0	0				—	Kkp	—	608	7216

LARKIN, ERIC Eric Lenell, DE, 6'4"/265 lbs; Miami (FL); B5/14/1962 **1987** Hou 1 (1)

LARO, GORDON Gordon Edward, TE, 6'3"/253 lbs; Michigan; Boston College; B4/17/1972 Lynn, MA

YEAR	TEAM	G (GS, POS)	RUSH	YD	AVG (LG)	TD	REC	YD	AVG (LG)	TD	PTS	TAY
1995	Jax	2(0)	—	—		—	1	6	6.0(6)	0	0	3

LAROSA, PAUL Paul, E, 5'11"/175 lbs; none; B1890, deceased **1920** ChiC 9 (3, LE) **1921** ChiC 2 (2) **NFL** 11 (5) [2 yrs]

LAROSE, DAN Marvin Daniel, T-DE-G, 6'5"/250 lbs; Missouri; 1961: Det, rnd 2/Bos, rnd 3; B2/8/1939 Crystal City, MO **1961** Det 14 (RT) **1962** Det 14 (RT) **1963** Det 9 **1964** Pit 12 **1965** SF 5 **1966** Den-A 11 (lde) **NFL** 65 [6 yrs]

LARPENTER, CARL Carl James, G-T, 6'4"/235 lbs; Texas; B7/1/1936 Port Arthur, TX **1960** Den-A 14 (lt) **1961** Den-A 14 (RG) **1962** DalT-A 2 **NFL** 30 [3 yrs]

LARRIMORE, KAREEM Kareem Maktrel, DB, 5'11"/190 lbs; West Texas A&M; 2000: Dal, rnd 4; B4/21/1976 Los Angeles, CA **2000** Dal 15 (4) **2001** Dal 4 (2) **NFL** 19 (6) [2 yrs]

LARSCHEID, JACK John Phillip, HB, 5'6"/162 lbs; Pacific; B5/10/1933 Whitefish Bay, WI; D2/5/1970 Sacramento, CA

YEAR	TEAM	G (GS, POS)	RUSH	YD	AVG (LG)	TD	REC	YD	AVG (LG)	TD	PASS	COMP	PCT	YD	AVG (LG)	TD	INT	KPR	PTS	TAY
1960	Oak-A	14(hb)	94	397	4.2(87)	1	22	187	8.5(46)	1	6	3	50.0	71	11.8(38)	0	2	kp	12	909
1961	Oak-A	2	6	3	0.5(7)	0	2	11	5.5(6)	0	1	0	0.0	0	0.0	0	1	k	0	88
NFL	2	16	100	400	4.0(87)	1	24	198	8.3(46)	1	7	3	42.9	71	10.1(38)	0	3	kp	12	997

LARSEN, GARY Gary Lee, DT, 6'5"/261 lbs; Concordia (IL); 1964: LA, rnd 10; B3/13/1940 Fargo, ND **1964** LARm 14 **1965** Min 12 (9, LDT) **1966** Min 14 (14, LDT) **1967** Min 14 **1968**†Min 14 (14, LDT) **1969**†Min✧14 (14, LDT) **1970**†Min✧14 (14, LDT) **1971**†Min 14 (14, LDT) **1972** Min 14 (14, LDT) **1973**†Min✧14 (14, LDT) **1974**†Min 11 **NFL** 149 (107) [11 yrs]

LARSEN, LEIF Leif Olve Dolonen, DT, 6'4"/295 lbs; Texas-El Paso; 2000: Buf, rnd 6; B4/3/1975 Oslo, Norway **2000** Buf 7 (0) **2001** Buf 9 (5, ldt) **NFL** 16 (5) [2 yrs]

LARSON, BILL William, FB, 5'10"/190 lbs; Illinois Wesleyan; B1939 **1960** Bos-A 1

LARSON, BILL William Harry, TE, 6'4"/225 lbs; Colorado State; B10/7/1953 Greenfield, IA **1977** Was 1 **1977** Det 12 **1978**†Phi 5 (1)

YEAR	TEAM	G (GS, POS)	RUSH	YD	AVG (LG)	TD	REC	YD	AVG (LG)	TD	PTS	TAY
1975	SF	14	—	—		—	5	64	12.8(24)	0	0	32
1980	Den	2(0)	—	—		—	1	7	7.0(7)	0	0	4
1980	GB	9(0)	—	—		—	4	37	9.3(21)	1	6	24
NFL	4	43(1)	—	—		—	10	108	10.8(24)	1	6	59

LARSON, GREG Gregory Kenneth, C-G-T, 6'3"/250 lbs; Minnesota; 1961: NYG, rnd 6/SD, rnd 11; B11/15/1939 Minneapolis, MN **1961**†NYG 14 (RT) **1962**†NYG 14 (RG) **1963**†NYG 14 (C) **1964** NYG 13 (C) **1965** NYG 12 **1967** NYG 14 (C) **1969** NYG 14 (C) **1970** NYG 14 (C) **1971** NYG 14 (C) **1972** NYG 14 (C) **1973** NYG 14 (C)

YEAR	TEAM	G (GS, POS)	RUSH	YD	AVG (LG)	TD	REC	YD	AVG (LG)	TD	PTS	TAY
1966	NYG☆	14(C)	0	-2	(-2)	0	—	—		—	0	-2
1968	NYG✧	14(C)	—	—		—	0	1	(1)	0	0	1
NFL	13	179	0	-2	(-2)	0	0	1	(1)	0	0	-2

LARSON, KURT Kurt Arvin, LB, 6'4"/236 lbs; Michigan State; 1989: Ind, rnd 8; B2/25/1966 Waukesha, WI **1989** Ind 13 (0) **1990** Ind 16 (0) **1991** GB 13 (0) **NFL** 42 (0) [3 yrs]

LARSON, KYLE Kyle, P, 6'1"/204 lbs; Nebraska; B9/2/1980 Kearney, NE **2005**†Cin 16 (0)

YEAR	TEAM	G (GS, POS)	RUSH	YD	AVG (LG)	TD	QBR	KPR	PTS	TAY
2004	Cin	16(0)	1	11	11.0(11)	1		P	6	21
NFL	2	32(0)	1	11	11.0(11)	1		P	6	21

LARSON, LOUIE Louis Peter, C-B, /168 lbs; none; B1/5/1898 Reynolds, ND; D5/28/1982 Fort Worth, TX **1926** Dul 7 (4) **1929** ChiC 3 (1, C) **NFL** 10 (5) [2 yrs]

LARSON, LYNN Lyndon Arthur, T, 6'4"/254 lbs; Kansas State; 1970: Chi, rnd 4; B3/9/1948 Phoenix, AZ **1971** Bal 1

LARSON, OJAY Frederic Adolphus, C, 6'1"/199 lbs; Notre Dame; B10/15/1897 Calumet, MI; D5/1/1977 Milwaukee, WI **1922** ChiB 10 (10, C) **1923** Mil 11 (10, C) **1924** Mil 8 (7, C) **1925** GB 13 (12, C) **1929** ChiB 1 (0) **1929** ChiC 9 (8) **NFL** 52 (47) [5 yrs]

LARSON, PAUL Paul Leroy, QB, 5'11"/185 lbs; California; 1954: ChiC, rnd 8; B3/19/1932 Turlock, CA **1960** Oak-A 1

YEAR	TEAM	G (GS, POS)	RUSH	YD	AVG (LG)	TD	PASS	COMP	PCT	YD	AVG (LG)	TD	INT	PTS	TAY
1957	ChiC	5	8	12	1.5(8)	0	14	6	42.9	61	4.4(21)	0	1	0	3
NFL	2	6	8	12	1.5(8)	0	14	6	42.9	61	4.4(21)	0	1	0	3

LARSON, PETE Harry Peter, RB, 6'1"/200 lbs; Cornell; 1967: Was, rnd 9; B5/30/1944 Wilmington, DE

YEAR	TEAM	G (GS, POS)	RUSH	YD	AVG (LG)	TD	REC	YD	AVG (LG)	TD	KPR	PTS	TAY
1967	Was	8	25	84	3.4(34)	1	8	45	5.6(13)	0		6	117
1968	Was	14	44	132	3.0(16)	1	12	146	12.2(25)	1	k	12	281
NFL	2	22	69	216	3.1(34)	2	20	191	9.6(25)	1	k	18	398

LARSON, SWEDE Swede, HB, none; deceased **1920** Ham 1 (0) **1923** Ham 3 (2) **NFL** 4 (2) [2 yrs]

LARY, YALE Robert Yale, DB, 5'11"/185 lbs; Texas A&M; 1952: Det, rnd 3; B11/24/1930 Fort Worth, TX; HOF 1979 [PRI]

YEAR	TEAM	G (GS, POS)	RUSH	YD	AVG (LG)	TD	PASS	COMP	PCT	YD	AVG (LG)	TD	INT	KPR	OTD	PTS	TAY
1952	†Det	12(DB)	—	—		—	—	—		—	—	—	—	Pkpi	1	6	276
1953	†Det✧	11(DB)	1	21	21.0(21)	0	—	—		—	—	—	—	Pkpi	1	6	180
1956	Det★	12(DB)	1	10	10.0(10)	0	—	—		—	—	—	—	Pkpi	1	6	138
1957	Det★	12(DB)	1	32	32.0(32)	0	1	0	0.0	0	0.0	0	0	Ppi	0	0	100
1958	Det★	12(DB)	1	2	2.0(2)	0	1	0	0.0	0	0.0	0	0	Ppi	1	6	128
1959	Det★	10(DB)	1	18	18.0(18)	0	1	0	0.0	0	0.0	0	0	Ppi	1	6	-59
1960	Det★	12(RS)	1	19	19.0(19)	0	—	—		—	—	—	—	Ppi	0	0	48
1961	Det★	14(RS)	1	14	14.0(14)	0	—	—		—	—	—	—	Ppi	0	0	82
1962	Det★	14(RS)	—	—		—	—	—		—	—	—	—	Pi	0	0	11
1963	Det☆	10(RS)	1	26	26.0(26)	0	—	—		—	—	—	—	Pi	1	6	47
1964	Det★	14(RS)	2	11	5.5(9)	0	—	—		—	—	—	—	Pi	0	0	82
NFL	11	133	10	153	15.3(32)	0	4	0	0.0	0	0.0	0	0	Pkpi	6	36	1033

LASCARI, JOHN John Albert, E, 6'2"/210 lbs; Georgetown (DC); B3/5/1918 Lodi, NJ; D7/1971, [K]

YEAR	TEAM	G (GS, POS)	RUSH	YD	AVG (LG)	TD	REC	YD	AVG (LG)	TD	KPR	PTS	TAY
1942	NYG	10(1)	—	—		—	3	38	12.7(15)	0	K	6	24

LASH, JIM James Verle, WR, 6'1"/200 lbs; Northwestern; 1973: Min, rnd 3; B11/12/1951 Akron, OH

YEAR	TEAM	G (GS, POS)	RUSH	YD	AVG (LG)	TD	REC	YD	AVG (LG)	TD	PASS	COMP	PCT	YD	AVG (LG)	TD	INT	OTD	PTS	TAY
1973	†Min	9	—	—		—	2	34	17.0(18)	0	—	—		—	—	—	—		0	17
1974	†Min	14(14, WR)	—	—		—	32	631	19.7(57)	0	—	—		—	—	—	—		0	316
1975	†Min	14(14, WR)	—	—		—	37	535	14.5(45)	3	1	0	0.0	0	0.0	0	0	1	24	283
1976	Min	5	—	—		—	4	52	13.0(18)	0	—	—		—	—	—	—		0	26
1976	SF	8(7, WR)	3	5	1.7(8)	0	13	190	14.6(43)	0	—	—		—	—	—	—		0	100
1977	SF	10	—	—		—	3	22	7.3(16)	0	—	—		—	—	—	—		0	11
NFL	5	60(35)	3	5	1.7(8)	0	91	1464	16.1(57)	3	1	0	0.0	0	0.0	0	0	1	24	752

LASHAR, TIM Timothy Alan, K, 5'9"/160 lbs; Oklahoma; B9/5/1964 Santa Monica, CA [K] **1987** ChiB 3 (0)

LASKER, GREG Gregory Cephus, DB, 6'0"/200 lbs; Arkansas; 1986: NYG, rnd 2; B9/28/1964 St. Louis, MO **1986**†NYG 16 (0) **1987** NYG 11 (0) **1988** NYG 4 (0) **1988** ChiB 1 (0) **1988** Phx 1 (0) **NFL** 33 (0) [3 yrs]

LASKEY, BILL William Grant, LB, 6'3"/235 lbs; Michigan; B2/10/1943 Ann Arbor, MI **1965**†Buf-A✧14 **1966** Oak-A 14 **1967**†Oak-A☆13 (LLB) **1968**†Oak-A 0 **1969**†Oak-A 12 (8, LLB) **1970**†Oak 14 (14, LLB) **1971**†Bal 13 **1972** Bal 14 **1973** Den 11 (11, LLB) **1974** Den 14 (10, LLB) **NFL** 119 (43) [10 yrs]

LASKY, FRANK Francis Joseph, T, 6'2"/265 lbs; Florida; 1963: NYG, rnd 2/SD, rnd 14; B10/4/1941 New York, NY **1964** NYG 4 **1965** NYG 14 (RT) **NFL** 18 [2 yrs]

LASLAVIC, JIM James Edward, LB, 6´2˝/237 lbs; Penn State; 1973: Det, rnd 3; B10/24/1951 Pittsburgh, PA **1973** Det 14 (5, mlb) **1974** Det 14 (14, MLB) **1975** Det 14 (13, MLB) **1976** Det 12 (12, MLB) **1977** Det 14 (4) **1978** SD 16 **1980†**SD 16 (3) **1981†**SD 16 (0) **1982** GB 8 (0) **NFL** 124 (51) [9 yrs]

LASSA, NICK Nicholas Anthony, aka Nick Long Time Sleep, T-C-G-E, 5´10˝/205 lbs; Carlisle Indian; Haskell Indian; B7/11/1898 Flathead Indian Reservation, MT, D9/1964 **1922** Oor 9 (9, RT) **1923** Oor 11 (11, C) **NFL** 20 (20) [2 yrs]

LASSAHN, LOU Louis Kenneth, E, 6´0˝/205 lbs; Western Maryland; B10/1/1915, MD, D10/27/1987 Baltimore, MD **1938** Pit 2 (0)

LASSE, DICK Richard Stephen, LB, 6´2˝/222 lbs; Syracuse; 1958: Pit, rnd 6; B11/13/1935 Quincy, MA **1958** Pit 12 (mlb) **1959** Pit 12 (LLB) **1960** Was 12 (LLB) **1961** Was 14 (llb) **1962** NYG 4 **NFL** 54 [5 yrs]

LASSIC, DERRICK Derrick Owens, RB, 5´10˝/188 lbs; Alabama; 1993: Dal, rnd 4; B1/26/1970 Haverstraw, NY

YEAR	TEAM	G(GS, POS)	RUSH	YD	AVG(LG)	TD	REC	YD	AVG(LG)	TD	PASS	COMP	PCT	YD	AVG(LG)	TD	INT	SK	YD	QBR	KPR	OTD	PTS	TAY
1993	†Dal	10(3)	75	269	3.6(15)	3	9	37	4.1(9)	0	—	—	—	—	—	—	—	—	—	—	—	—	18	318

LASSITER, IKE Isaac Thomas, DE-DT, 6´5˝/270 lbs; St. Augustine's; 1962: LA, rnd 9; B11/15/1940 Wilson, NC **1962** Den-A 14 (ldt) **1963** Den-A 7 **1964** Den-A 2 **1965** Oak-A 14 (LDE) **1966** Oak-A★14 (14, LDE) **1967†**Oak-A 14 (LDE) **1968†**Oak-A☆14 (14, LDE) **1969†**Oak-A☆14 (14, LDE) **1970** Bos 5 (5, lde) **1971** NE 14 (12, LDE) **NFL** 112 (59) [10 yrs]

LASSITER, KWAMIE Kwamie Jerome, DB, 6´0˝/207 lbs; Kansas; B12/3/1969 Newport News, VA [I] **1996** Arz 14 (0) **1997** Arz 16 (1) **1998†**Arz 16 (6, fs) **1999** Arz 16 (16, FS) **2000** Arz 16 (16, FS) **2001** Arz 16 (16, FS) **2002** Arz 16 (16, FS) **2003** SD 10 (10, SS) **2004** SL 4 (0)

YEAR	TEAM	G(GS, POS)	RUSH	YD	AVG(LG)	TD	REC	YD	AVG(LG)	TD	PASS	COMP	PCT	YD	AVG(LG)	TD	INT	SK	YD	QBR	KPR	OTD	PTS	TAY
1995	Arz	5(0)	1	1	1.0(1)	0	—	—	—	—	—	—	—	—	—	—	—	—	—	—	—	—	0	1
NFL	10	129(81)	1	1	1.0(1)	0	—	—	—	—	—	—	—	—	—	—	—	—	—	—	kpiS	2	12	247

LASTER, ART Arthur L., T, 6´5˝/280 lbs; Maryland-Eastern Shore; 1970: Oak, rnd 5; B3/2/1948 Gary, IN **1970** Buf 14

LASTER, DON Anthony Donald, T, 6´5˝/285 lbs; Tennessee State; 1982: Was, rnd 12; B12/13/1958 Albany, GA **1982†**Was 8 (0) **1984** Det 14 (8, LT) **NFL** 22 (8) [2 yrs]

LATHAN, GREG Gregory R., WR, 6´1˝/195 lbs; Cincinnati; B9/2/1964 San Diego, CA

YEAR	TEAM	G(GS, POS)	RUSH	YD	AVG(LG)	TD	REC	YD	AVG(LG)	TD	PASS	COMP	PCT	YD	AVG(LG)	TD	INT	SK	YD	QBR	KPR	OTD	PTS	TAY
1987	LARd	3(0)	—	—	—	—	5	98	19.6(33)	0	—	—	—	—	—	—	—	—	—	—	—	—	0	49

LATHON, LAMAR Lamar Lavantha, LB-DE, 6´3˝/260 lbs; Houston; 1990: Hou, rnd 1; B12/23/1967 Wharton, TX **1990†**Hou 11 (1) **1991†**Hou 16 (16, LLB) **1992†**Hou 11 (11, LLB) **1993†**Hou 13 (1) **1994** Hou 16 (15, RDE) **1995** Car 15 (15, LOLB) **1996†**Car★16 (16, ROLB) **1997** Car 15 (15, ROLB) **1998** Car 2 (2) **NFL** 115 (92) [9 yrs]

LATHROP, KIT Kit Douglas, DE-NT, 6´5˝/255 lbs; Arizona State; B5/10/1956 San Jose, CA **1979** Den 9 **1979** GB 2 **1980** GB 15 (0) **1986†**KC 16 (0) **1987** Was 1 (0) **NFL** 43 [4 yrs]

LATIMER, AL Albert, DB, 5´11˝/176 lbs; Ferrum; Clemson; B10/14/1957 Winter Park, FL **1979** Phi 13 **1982†**Det 4 (2) **1983** Det 8 (8, RCB) **1984** Det 15 (0) **NFL** 40 (10) [4 yrs]

LATIMER, DON Donald Bertsom, NT, 6´3˝/259 lbs; Miami (FL); 1978: Den, rnd 1; B3/1/1955 Fort Pierce, FL **1978** Den 14 **1979†**Den 15 (1) **1980** Den 14 (0) **1981** Den 16 (0) **1982** Den 9 (3) **1983†**Den 12 (3) **NFL** 80 (7) [6 yrs]

LATIN, JERRY Jerry Louis, RB, 5´10˝/190 lbs; Northern Illinois; 1975: SL, rnd 11; B8/25/1953 Prescott, AR

YEAR	TEAM	G(GS, POS)	RUSH	YD	AVG(LG)	TD	REC	YD	AVG(LG)	TD	PASS	COMP	PCT	YD	AVG(LG)	TD	INT	SK	YD	QBR	KPR	OTD	PTS	TAY
1975	†SL	10	35	165	4.7(57)	1	2	25	12.5(16)	0	—	—	—	—	—	—	—	—	—	—	—	—	6	188
1976	SL	11	25	115	4.6(26)	1	4	35	8.8(15)	0	—	—	—	—	—	—	—	—	—	—	k	—	6	260
1977	SL	14(3)	56	208	3.7(17)	2	9	89	9.9(20)	0	—	—	—	—	—	—	—	—	—	—	k	—	12	307
1978	SL	2	6	8	1.3(4)	0	1	3	3.0(3)	0	—	—	—	—	—	—	—	—	—	—	k	—	0	28
1978	†LARm	14	18	64	3.6(11)	0	—	—	—	—	—	—	—	—	—	—	—	—	—	—	k	—	0	201
NFL	4	51(3)	140	560	4.0(57)	4	16	152	9.5(20)	0	—	—	—	—	—	—	—	—	—	—	k	—	24	982

LATONE, TONY Anthony J., B, 5´11˝/195 lbs; none; B4/18/1897 Spring Valley, IL, D11/24/1975 Detroit, MI **1925** Pot 12 (10, WB), 48 **1926** Pot☆12 (5, wb), 24 **1927** Pot 12 (11, WB) **1928** Pot☆10 (9, FB), 18 **1929** Bos 8 (8, FB), 54 **1930** Pro 11 (7, FB), 18 **NFL** 65 (50), 162 [6 yrs]

LATOURETTE, CHUCK Charles Pierre, P-DB, 6´0˝/190 lbs; Rice; B7/21/1945 San Antonio, TX, D12/21/1981 Houston, TX

YEAR	TEAM	G(GS, POS)	RUSH	YD	AVG(LG)	TD	REC	YD	AVG(LG)	TD	PASS	COMP	PCT	YD	AVG(LG)	TD	INT	SK	YD	QBR	KPR	OTD	PTS	TAY
1967	SL	14	2	23	11.5(27)	0	—	—	—	—	—	—	—	—	—	—	—	—	—	—	Pp	—	0	14
1968	SL	14	1	15	15.0(15)	0	—	—	—	—	1	0	0.0	0	0.0	0	0	—	—	—	Pkp	1	6	777
1970	SL	14	2	38	19.0(33)	0	—	—	—	—	—	—	—	—	—	—	—	—	—	—	Pkp	1	6	118
1971	SL	13	3	19	6.3(20)	0	—	—	—	—	—	—	—	—	—	—	—	—	—	—	P	—	0	19
NFL	4	55	8	95	11.9(33)	0	—	—	—	—	1	0	0.0	0	0.0	0	0	—	—	—	Pkp	2	12	928

LATTA, GREG Gregory Edwin, TE, 6´3˝/227 lbs; Morgan State; 1974: Bal, rnd 8; B10/13/1952 Newark, NJ, D9/28/1994

YEAR	TEAM	G(GS, POS)	RUSH	YD	AVG(LG)	TD	REC	YD	AVG(LG)	TD	PASS	COMP	PCT	YD	AVG(LG)	TD	INT	SK	YD	QBR	KPR	OTD	PTS	TAY
1975	ChiB	14(4)	—	—	—	—	16	202	12.6(34)	3	—	—	—	—	—	—	—	—	—	—	—	—	18	116
1976	ChiB	14(14, TE)	2	-8	-4.0(-3)	0	18	254	14.1(58)	0	—	—	—	—	—	—	—	—	—	—	—	—	0	119
1977	†ChiB	14(14, TE)	—	—	—	—	26	335	12.9(37)	4	—	—	—	—	—	—	—	—	—	—	—	—	24	188
1978	ChiB	16(16, TE)	—	—	—	—	15	159	10.6(21)	0	—	—	—	—	—	—	—	—	—	—	k	—	0	64
1979	†ChiB	15	—	—	—	—	15	131	8.7(25)	0	—	—	—	—	—	—	—	—	—	—	k	—	0	59
NFL	5	73(48)	2	-8	-4.0(-3)	0	90	1081	12.0(58)	7	—	—	—	—	—	—	—	—	—	—	k	—	42	545

LATTIMORE, BRIAN Brian Keith, RB, 6´1˝/202 lbs; Southeast Missouri State; B10/29/1966 St. Petersburg, FL **1991** Ind 3 (0)

LATTNER, JOHNNY John Joseph, HB, 6´1˝/195 lbs; Notre Dame; 1954: Pit, rnd 1; B10/24/1932 Chicago, IL

YEAR	TEAM	G(GS, POS)	RUSH	YD	AVG(LG)	TD	REC	YD	AVG(LG)	TD	PASS	COMP	PCT	YD	AVG(LG)	TD	INT	SK	YD	QBR	KPR	OTD	PTS	TAY
1954	Pit✧	12(RH)	69	237	3.4(17)	5	25	305	12.2(43)	2	—	—	—	—	—	—	—	—	—	—	kp	—	42	611

LATZKE, PAUL Pete Lewis, C, 6´4˝/240 lbs; Pacific; B3/22/1942 Los Angeles, CA **1966** SD-A 2 **1967** SD-A 13 **1968** SD-A 7 **NFL** 22 [3 yrs]

LAUER, PETE Albert Lee, FB-QB, 5´6˝/165 lbs; Iowa; B10/14/1897 Muncie, IN, D7/9/1950 Evansville, IN **1922** Evv 1 (1, FB)

LAUER, DUTCH Harold Sebastian, B-E, 5´10˝/185 lbs; Detroit Mercy; B1/8/1898 Monroe, MI, D8/9/1978 Southfield, MI [K] **1922** RI 7 (5, WB), 31 **1922** GB 2 (1) **1923** Tol 7 (7, WB) **1925** Det 11 (9, tb) **1926** Det 10 (7, LE), 6 **NFL** 37 (29), 37 [4 yrs]

LAUER, LARRY Lawrence Gene, C, 6´3˝/232 lbs; Alabama; 1951: NYY, rnd 8; B8/27/1927 Chicago, IL, D1/3/1992 Las Vegas, NV **1956** GB 6 **1957** GB 12 **NFL** 18 [2 yrs]

LAUFENBERG, BABE Brandon Hugh, QB, 6´2˝/198 lbs; Stanford; Missouri; Indiana; 1983: Was, rnd 6; B12/5/1959 Burbank, CA **1986** NO 1 (0) **1989** Dal 3 (0)

YEAR	TEAM	G(GS, POS)	RUSH	YD	AVG(LG)	TD	REC	YD	AVG(LG)	TD	PASS	COMP	PCT	YD	AVG(LG)	TD	INT	SK	YD	QBR	KPR	OTD	PTS	TAY
1988	SD	8(6, qb)	31	120	3.9(23)	0	—	—	—	—	144	69	47.9	778	5.4(47)	4	5	18	155	—	—	—	0	329
1990	Dal	4(1)	2	6	3.0(5)	0	—	—	—	—	67	24	35.8	279	4.2(27)	1	6	4	29	—	—	—	0	-90
NFL	4	16(7)	33	126	3.8(23)	0	—	—	—	—	211	93	44.1	1057	5.0(47)	5	11	22	184	—	—	—	0	240

LAUGHLIN, BUD Henry James, FB, 6´1˝/200 lbs; Kansas; 1952: SF, rnd 25; B1/15/1931 Kansas City, MO, D3/20/1986 Shawnee Mission, KS

YEAR	TEAM	G(GS, POS)	RUSH	YD	AVG(LG)	TD	REC	YD	AVG(LG)	TD	PASS	COMP	PCT	YD	AVG(LG)	TD	INT	SK	YD	QBR	KPR	OTD	PTS	TAY
1955	SF	10	20	58	2.9(14)	0	8	54	6.8(27)	0	—	—	—	—	—	—	—	—	—	—	k	—	0	95

LAUGHLIN, JIM James David, LB, 6´0˝/222 lbs; Ohio State; 1980: Atl, rnd 4; B7/5/1958 Euclid, OH **1980†**Atl 16 (6, lilb) **1981** Atl 14 (7, rolb) **1982†**Atl 9 (0) **1983** GB 15 (1) **1984†**LARm 3 (0) **1985†**LARm 10 (0) **1986†**LARm 16 (2) **1987** Atl 5 (3) **NFL** 88 (19) [8 yrs]

LAUGHTON, JIM James Edward, TE, 6´5˝/225 lbs; San Diego State; B1/18/1960 Salinas, CA **1986** Sea 6 (0)

LAURICELLA, HANK Francis Edward, HB, 5´11˝/175 lbs; Tennessee; 1952: Det, rnd 17; B10/9/1930 Harahan, LA

YEAR	TEAM	G(GS, POS)	RUSH	YD	AVG(LG)	TD	REC	YD	AVG(LG)	TD	PASS	COMP	PCT	YD	AVG(LG)	TD	INT	SK	YD	QBR	KPR	OTD	PTS	TAY
1952	DalT	11	19	55	2.9(13)	0	—	—	—	—	22	11	50.0	177	8.0(34)	4	2	—	—	—	Pk	—	0	95

LAURINAITIS, FRANCIS Francis Ignatius, LB, 5´10˝/200 lbs; Richmond; B12/20/1922 New Philadelphia, PA **1947** Bkn-A 8 (0)

LAURO, LINDY Lindoro L., DB, 5´10˝/195 lbs; Pittsburgh; B6/3/1921 New Castle, PA **1951** ChiC 1

LAUX, TED Theodore, HB-DB, 5´10˝/185 lbs; St. Joseph's (PA); B3/1/1918 Swedesboro, NJ [K]

YEAR	TEAM	G(GS, POS)	RUSH	YD	AVG(LG)	TD	REC	YD	AVG(LG)	TD	PASS	COMP	PCT	YD	AVG(LG)	TD	INT	SK	YD	QBR	KPR	OTD	PTS	TAY
1943	P-P	4(0)	9	23	2.6(12)	0	2	19	9.5(15)	0	—	—	—	—	—	—	—	—	—	—	Kpi	—	2	58
1944	Phi	1(0)	2	-1	-0.5(0)	0	1	6	6.0(6)	0	—	—	—	—	—	—	—	—	—	—	P	—	0	2
NFL	2	5(0)	11	22	2.0(12)	0	3	25	8.3(15)	0	—	—	—	—	—	—	—	—	—	—	KPpi	—	2	60

LAVALAIS, CHAD Chad Douglas, DT, 6´1˝/293 lbs; LSU; 2004: Atl, rnd 5; B4/15/1979 Marksville, LA **2004†**Atl 16 (6, rdt) **2005** Atl 14 (14, RDT) **NFL** 30 (20) [2 yrs]

LAVAN, AL Alton, DB, 6´1˝/202 lbs; Colorado State; 1968: Phi, rnd 8; B9/13/1946 Pierce, FL **1969** Atl 11 **1970** Atl 13 **NFL** 24 [2 yrs]

LAVELLI, DANTE Dante Bert Joseph 'Gluefingers', E-DE, 6´0˝/191 lbs; Ohio State; 1947: LA, rnd 12; B2/23/1923 Hudson, OH; HOF 1975

YEAR	TEAM	G(GS, POS)	RUSH	YD	AVG(LG)	TD	REC	YD	AVG(LG)	TD	PASS	COMP	PCT	YD	AVG(LG)	TD	INT	SK	YD	QBR	KPR	OTD	PTS	TAY
1946	†Cle-A☆	14(8, RE)	1	14	14.0(14)	0	**40**	**843**	**21.1(63)**	8	—	—	—	—	—	—	—	—	—	—	—	—	48	476
1947	†Cle-A☆	13(6, RE)	—	—	—	—	49	799	16.3(72)	9	—	—	—	—	—	—	—	—	—	—	k	—	54	440
1948	†Cle-A☆	8(7, RE)	1	9	9.0(9)	0	25	463	18.5(54)	5	—	—	—	—	—	—	—	—	—	—	k	—	30	251

YEAR	TEAM	G(GS, POS)	RUSH	YD	AVG(LG)	TD	REC	YD	AVG(LG)	TD	PASS	COMP	PCT	YD	AVG(LG)	TD	INT	SK	YD	QBR	KPR	OTD	PTS	TAY
1949	†Cle-A☆	9(7, RE)	—	—	—	—	28	475	17.0(67)	7	—	—	—	—	—	—	—	—	—	—	—	—	42	273
AAFC	4	44(28)	2	23	11.5(14)	0	142	2580	18.2(72)	29	—	—	—	—	—	—	—	—	—	—	k	—	174	1438
1950	†Cle	12(RE)	—	—	—	—	37	565	15.3(43)	5	—	—	—	—	—	—	—	—	—	—	—	—	30	308
1951	†Cle★	12(RE)	—	—	—	—	43	586	13.6(47)	6	—	—	—	—	—	—	—	—	—	—	—	—	36	323
1952	†Cle	8(re)	—	—	—	—	21	336	16.0(41)	4	—	—	—	—	—	—	—	—	—	—	—	—	24	188
1953	†Cle★	12(RE)	—	—	—	—	45	783	17.4(55)	6	—	—	—	—	—	—	—	—	—	—	—	—	36	422
1954	†Cle✧	12(RE)	—	—	—	—	47	802	17.1(64)	7	—	—	—	—	—	—	—	—	—	—	—	—	42	436
1955	†Cle	12(RE)	—	—	—	—	31	492	15.9(49)	4	—	—	—	—	—	—	—	—	—	—	—	—	24	266
1956	Cle	11(RE)	—	—	—	—	20	344	17.2(68)	1	—	—	—	—	—	—	—	—	—	—	—	—	6	177
NFL	7	79	—	—	—	—	244	3908	16.0(72)	33	—	—	—	—	—	—	—	—	—	—	—	—	198	2119

Lavender, Joe Joseph, DB, 6´4˝/190 lbs; San Diego State; 1973: Phi, rnd 12; B2/10/1949 Rayville, LA **[I]** **1973** Phi 13 (RCB) **1974** Phi 14 (RCB) **1975** Phi 13 (RCB) **1976**†Was☆14 (14, RCB) **1977** Was 14 (14, RCB) **1978** Was 16 (16, RCB) **1979** Was★16 (14, RCB) **1980** Was✧16 (16, RCB) **1981** Was 16 (16, RCB) **1982**†Was 7 (1) **NFL** 139 (91) [10 yrs]

Lavette, Robert Robert Lee, RB, 5´11˝/190 lbs; Georgia Tech; 1985: Dal, rnd 4; B9/8/1963 Cartersville, GA **[R]**

YEAR	TEAM	G(GS, POS)	RUSH	YD	AVG(LG)	TD	REC	YD	AVG(LG)	TD	PASS	COMP	PCT	YD	AVG(LG)	TD	INT	SK	YD	QBR	KPR	OTD	PTS	TAY
1985	Dal	12(0)	13	34	2.6(10)	0	1	8	8.0(8)	0	—	—	—	—	—	—	—	—	—	—	k	—	0	210
1986	Dal	16(0)	10	6	0.6(5)	0	5	31	6.2(9)	1	—	—	—	—	—	—	—	—	—	—	kp	—	6	188
1987	Dal	4(0)	—	—	—	—	1	6	6.0(6)	0	—	—	—	—	—	—	—	—	—	—	kp	—	0	15
1987	Phi	1(0)	—	—	—	—	—	—	—	—	—	—	—	—	—	—	—	—	—	—	k	—	0	7
NFL	3	33(0)	23	40	1.7(10)	0	7	45	6.4(9)	1	—	—	—	—	—	—	—	—	—	—	kp	—	6	420

Lavine, Paul Paul, LB, 6´2˝/207 lbs; Utah State; B5/1/1962 San Bernardino, CA **1987** Sea 3 (1)

Law, Dennis Raymond Dennis, WR, 6´1˝/179 lbs; East Tennessee State; 1978: Cin, rnd 4; B4/4/1955 Commerce, GA

YEAR	TEAM	G(GS, POS)	RUSH	YD	AVG(LG)	TD	REC	YD	AVG(LG)	TD	PASS	COMP	PCT	YD	AVG(LG)	TD	INT	SK	YD	QBR	KPR	OTD	PTS	TAY
1978	Cin	14	1	-1	-1.0(-1)	0	5	81	16.2(20)	0	—	—	—	—	—	—	—	—	—	—	kp	—	0	21

Law, Hubbard Hubbard Paul, G, 6´1˝/210 lbs; Sam Houston State; 1942: Pit, rnd 15; B1/27/1921 Houston, TX, D3/29/1995 Mesa, AZ **1945** Pit 6 (0)

YEAR	TEAM	G(GS, POS)	RUSH	YD	AVG(LG)	TD	REC	YD	AVG(LG)	TD	PASS	COMP	PCT	YD	AVG(LG)	TD	INT	SK	YD	QBR	KPR	OTD	PTS	TAY
1942	Pit	11(0)	1	6	6.0(6)	0	—	—	—	—	—	—	—	—	—	—	—	—	—	—	i	—	0	14
NFL	2	17(0)	1	6	6.0(6)	0	—	—	—	—	—	—	—	—	—	—	—	—	—	—	—	—	0	6

Law, John John Brendon, T, 5´9˝/180 lbs; Notre Dame; B2/13/1905 Yonkers, NY, D10/14/1962 Tarrytown, NY **1930** Nwk 1 (1)

Law, Ty Tajuan E., DB, 5´11˝/200 lbs; Michigan; 1995: NE, rnd 1; B2/10/1974 Aliquippa, PA **[I]** **1995** NE 14 (7, rcb) **1996**†NE 13 (12, LCB) **1997**†NE 16 (16, LCB) **1998**†NE★16 (16, LCB) **1999** NE 13 (13, LCB) **2000** NE 15 (15, LCB) **2001**†NE✧16 (16, LCB) **2002** NE✧16 (16, LCB) **2003**†NE★15 (15, LCB) **2004** NE 7 (7, LCB) **2005** NYJ✧16 (15, LCB) **NFL** 157 (148) [11 yrs]

Lawler, Al Allen Gilbert, HB-DB, 5´10˝/175 lbs; Texas; 1947: ChiB, rnd 23; B6/23/1922 Malta, TX **[K]**

YEAR	TEAM	G(GS, POS)	RUSH	YD	AVG(LG)	TD	REC	YD	AVG(LG)	TD	PASS	COMP	PCT	YD	AVG(LG)	TD	INT	SK	YD	QBR	KPR	OTD	PTS	TAY
1948	ChiB	7(0)	9	44	4.9(16)	0	3	40	13.3(26)	0	—	—	—	—	—	—	—	—	—	—	Kkp	—	6	160

Lawless, Burton Richard Burton, G, 6´4˝/253 lbs; Florida; 1975: Dal, rnd 2; B11/1/1953 Dothan, AL **1975**†Dal 14 (10, LG) **1976**†Dal 14 (4) **1977**†Dal 14 (4) **1978**†Dal 16 **1979**†Dal 15 **1980** Det 9 (5, lg) **NFL** 82 (23) [6 yrs]

Lawrence, Amos Amos, RB, 5´11˝/181 lbs; North Carolina; 1981: SD, rnd 4; B1/9/1958 Norfolk, VA

YEAR	TEAM	G(GS, POS)	RUSH	YD	AVG(LG)	TD	REC	YD	AVG(LG)	TD	PASS	COMP	PCT	YD	AVG(LG)	TD	INT	SK	YD	QBR	KPR	OTD	PTS	TAY
1981	†SF	13(0)	13	48	3.7(14)	1	3	10	3.3(5)	0	—	—	—	—	—	—	—	—	—	—	k	1	12	255
1982	SF	8(1)	5	7	1.4(4)	0	2	12	6.0(6)	0	—	—	—	—	—	—	—	—	—	—	k	—	0	68
NFL	2	21(1)	18	55	3.1(14)	1	5	22	4.4(6)	0	—	—	—	—	—	—	—	—	—	—	k	1	12	323

Lawrence, Ben Benjamin J., G, 6´1˝/325 lbs; Indiana (PA); B9/19/1961 Sparta, WI **1987** Pit 1 (0)

Lawrence, Don Donald Jerome, DT-T-G, 6´1˝/245 lbs; Notre Dame; 1959: Was, rnd 7; B6/4/1937 Cleveland, OH **1959** Was 12 (9, LT) **1960** Was 12 (RDT) **1961** Was 11 **NFL** 35 (9) [3 yrs]

Lawrence, Ed Edward James, B, 5´8˝/170 lbs; Brown; B7/14/1905 Fitchburg, MA, D11/21/1961 North Las Vegas, NV **1929** Bos 6 (1) **1930** SI 4 (1) **NFL** 10 (2) [2 yrs]

Lawrence, Henry Henry, T-G, 6´4˝/272 lbs; Florida A&M; 1974: Oak, rnd 1; B9/26/1951 Danville, PA **1974**†Oak 14 (1) **1975**†Oak 14 (1) **1976**†Oak 8 **1977**†Oak 14 (11, RT) **1978** Oak 16 (16, RT) **1979** Oak 16 (16, RT) **1980**†Oak 16 (16, RT) **1981** Oak 16 (16, RT) **1982**†LARd 9 (9, RT) **1983**†LARd★16 (16, RT) **1984**†LARd★16 (16, RT) **1985**†LARd 16 (16, RT) **1986** LARd 16 (14, RT) **NFL** 187 (148) [13 yrs]

Lawrence, Jimmy James Boydston, WB-HB, 5´10˝/190 lbs; TCU; 1936: ChiC, rnd 1; B3/15/1913 Dawson, TX, D5/17/1990

YEAR	TEAM	G(GS, POS)	RUSH	YD	AVG(LG)	TD	REC	YD	AVG(LG)	TD	PASS	COMP	PCT	YD	AVG(LG)	TD	INT	SK	YD	QBR	KPR	OTD	PTS	TAY
1936	ChiC	7(1)	26	84	3.2	0	8	98	12.3	0	2	0	0.0	0	0.0	0	1	—	—	—	—	—	0	93
1937	ChiC	11(1)	19	60	3.2	1	3	32	10.7	0	3	0	0.0	0	0.0	0	0	—	—	—	—	—	6	86
1938	ChiC	11(9, WB)	78	207	2.7	3	14	105	7.5	0	11	3	27.3	65	5.9	0	4	—	—	—	—	—	18	162
1939	ChiC	1(0)	3	6	2.0	0	2	18	9.0	0	—	—	—	—	—	—	—	—	—	—	P	—	0	15
1939	†GB✧	3(0)	4	0	0.0	0	1	21	21.0(21)	0	4	1	25.0	15	3.8(15)	0	1	—	—	—	—	—	0	-22
NFL	4	33(11)	130	357	2.7	4	28	274	9.8(21)	0	20	4	20.0	80	4.0(15)	0	6	—	—	—	P	—	24	334

Lawrence, Kent Norman Kent, WR, 6´0˝/180 lbs; Georgia; 1969: Phi, rnd 9; B6/3/1946 Anderson, SC **1970** Atl 1

YEAR	TEAM	G(GS, POS)	RUSH	YD	AVG(LG)	TD	REC	YD	AVG(LG)	TD	PASS	COMP	PCT	YD	AVG(LG)	TD	INT	SK	YD	QBR	KPR	OTD	PTS	TAY
1969	Phi	9	—	—	—	—	1	10	10.0(10)	0	—	—	—	—	—	—	—	—	—	—	kp	—	0	43
NFL	2	10	—	—	—	—	1	10	10.0(10)	0	—	—	—	—	—	—	—	—	—	—	—	—	0	5

Lawrence, Larry Larry Robert, QB, 6´1˝/208 lbs; Iowa; Miami (FL); B4/11/1949 Mount Pleasant, IA

YEAR	TEAM	G(GS, POS)	RUSH	YD	AVG(LG)	TD	REC	YD	AVG(LG)	TD	PASS	COMP	PCT	YD	AVG(LG)	TD	INT	SK	YD	QBR	KPR	OTD	PTS	TAY
1974	Oak	7(1)	4	39	9.8(19)	0	—	—	—	—	11	4	36.4	29	2.6(17)	0	1	3	22	—	—	—	0	14
1975	Oak	1(1)	2	-3	-1.5(-1)	0	—	—	—	—	15	5	33.3	50	3.3(17)	0	1	2	15	—	—	—	0	-18
1976	TB	1	—	—	—	—	—	—	—	—	5	0	0.0	0	0.0	0	2	1	8	—	—	—	0	-80
NFL	3	9(2)	6	36	6.0(19)	0	—	—	—	—	31	9	29.0	79	2.5(17)	0	4	6	45	—	—	—	0	-85

Lawrence, Marcus Marcus, LB, 6´3˝/236 lbs; South Carolina; B6/21/1982 Aiken, SC **2005**†NYG 0 (0)

Lawrence, Reggie Reginald James, WR, 6´0˝/178 lbs; North Carolina State; B9/4/1969 Camden, NJ

YEAR	TEAM	G(GS, POS)	RUSH	YD	AVG(LG)	TD	REC	YD	AVG(LG)	TD	PASS	COMP	PCT	YD	AVG(LG)	TD	INT	SK	YD	QBR	KPR	OTD	PTS	TAY
1993	Phi	1(0)	—	—	—	—	1	5	5.0(5)	0	—	—	—	—	—	—	—	—	—	—	—	—	0	3

Lawrence, Rolland Rolland Derenfro, DB, 5´10˝/179 lbs; Tabor; B3/24/1951 Franklin, PA **[RI]** **1973** Atl 14 **1974** Atl 14 (14, LCB) **1975** Atl☆14 (14, LCB) **1976** Atl 14 (14, LCB) **1977** Atl★14 (14, LCB) **1978**†Atl☆16 (16, LCB) **1979** Atl☆16 (16, LCB) **1980**†Atl 16 (16, LCB) **NFL** 118 (104) [8 yrs]

Lawrie, Nate Nathan Earl, TE, 6´7˝/265 lbs; Yale; 2004: TB, rnd 6; B10/17/1981 Indianapolis, IN **2005** TB 5 (0)

YEAR	TEAM	G(GS, POS)	RUSH	YD	AVG(LG)	TD	REC	YD	AVG(LG)	TD	PASS	COMP	PCT	YD	AVG(LG)	TD	INT	SK	YD	QBR	KPR	OTD	PTS	TAY
2004	TB	2(0)	—	—	—	—	1	15	15.0(15)	0	—	—	—	—	—	—	—	—	—	—	—	—	0	8
NFL	2	7(0)	—	—	—	—	1	15	15.0(15)	0	—	—	—	—	—	—	—	—	—	—	—	—	0	8

Laws, Joe Joseph Ray, HB, 5´9˝/186 lbs; Iowa; B6/16/1911 Colfax, IA, D8/24/1979 Green Bay, WI

YEAR	TEAM	G(GS, POS)	RUSH	YD	AVG(LG)	TD	REC	YD	AVG(LG)	TD	PASS	COMP	PCT	YD	AVG(LG)	TD	INT	SK	YD	QBR	KPR	OTD	PTS	TAY
1934	GB	13(7, HB)	46	155	3.4	1	9	165	18.3(61)	1	4	0	0.0	0	0.0	0	1	—	—	—	—	—	12	213
1935	GB	11(4)	24	63	2.6	1	4	82	20.5(41)	0	1	1	100.0	8	8.0(8)	0	0	—	—	—	—	—	6	118
1936	†GB	11(4)	50	296	5.9(41)	1	10	132	13.2	2	4	1	25.0	22	5.5(22)	1	0	—	—	—	—	—	18	398
1937	GB	11(9, HB)	74	310	4.2	1	10	121	12.1(19)	0	11	5	45.5	42	3.8	1	2	—	—	—	—	1	12	327
1938	†GB	10(7, HB)	60	253	4.2	0	6	55	9.2(17)	1	5	0	0.0	0	0.0	0	2	—	—	—	—	1	12	216
1939	†GB✧	10(3)	55	162	2.9	2	11	177	16.1(31)	1	1	0	0.0	0	0.0	0	0	—	—	—	—	1	24	286
1940	GB	3(2)	7	21	3.0	0	5	60	12.0(24)	1	—	—	—	—	—	—	—	—	—	—	—	—	6	56
1941	†GB	11(4)	21	58	2.8(10)	0	4	48	12.0(18)	1	—	—	—	—	—	—	—	—	—	—	kpi	—	6	136
1942	GB	10(6, HB)	29	100	3.4(17)	0	6	96	16.0(28)	1	3	2	66.7	76	25.3(62)	1	0	—	—	—	kpi	—	6	275
1943	GB	10(2)	43	232	5.4(31)	0	5	33	6.6(22)	0	—	—	—	—	—	—	—	—	—	—	kpi	—	0	332
1944	†GB	10(4)	45	200	4.4(20)	3	7	61	8.7(29)	1	4	1	25.0	15	3.8(15)	0	1	—	—	—	kpi	—	24	309
1945	GB	10(6, HB)	16	82	5.1(20)	0	2	11	5.5(7)	0	—	—	—	—	—	—	—	—	—	—	kpi	—	0	163
NFL	12	120(58)	470	1932	4.1(41)	9	79	1041	13.2(61)	9	33	10	30.3	163	4.9(62)	3	6	—	—	—	kpi	3	126	2826

Lawson, Al Alphonzo, WR, 5´11˝/190 lbs; Delaware State; B6/6/1941 Washington, DC **1964** NYJ-A 1

Lawson, Jamie Jamie Lee, RB, 5´10˝/240 lbs; LSU; Nicholls State; 1989: TB, rnd 5; B10/2/1965 New Orleans, LA **1989** TB 5 (0) **1990** TB 6 (0) **1990** NE 1 (0) **NFL** 12 (0) [2 yrs]

Lawson, Jerry Jerome Lee, DB, 5´11˝/192 lbs; Utah; 1968: Buf, rnd 10; B10/30/1944 Bakersfield, CA **1968** Buf-A 1

Lawson, Jim James Willmer, E, 5´11˝/190 lbs; Stanford; B3/11/1902 Long Beach, CA, D1/3/1989 Carmel-by-the-Sea, CA **1927** NYY 11 (7, re)

YEAR	TEAM	G (GS, POS)	RUSH	YD	AVG (LG)	TD	REC	YD	AVG (LG)	TD	PASS COMP	PCT	YD	AVG (LG)	TD	INT	SK	YD	QBR	KPR	OTD	PTS	TAY

LAWSON, ODELL   Odell, RB, 6´2˝/218 lbs; Langston; 1970: Bos, rnd 7; B12/20/1948 Ponca City, OK

1970	Bos	14(1)	56	99	1.8(15)	0	11	113	10.3(19)	0	—	—	—	—	—	—	—	—	—	kp	—	0	322
1971	NE	2(1)	8	8	1.0(6)	0	—	—	—	—	—	—	—	—	—	—	—	—	—	k	—	0	25
1973	NO	12	6	23	3.8(11)	0	2	-5	-2.5(4)	0	—	—	—	—	—	—	—	—	—	k	—	0	34
1974	NO	9	—	—	—	—	—	—	—	—	—	—	—	—	—	—	—	—	—	k	—	0	5
NFL	4	37(2)	70	130	1.9(15)	0	13	108	8.3(19)	0	—	—	—	—	—	—	—	—	—	kp	—	0	385

LAWSON, ROGER   Roger Alan, RB, 6´2˝/215 lbs; Western Michigan; 1972: Chi, rnd 15; B9/28/1949 Detroit, MI

1972	ChiB	12	33	106	3.2(14)	1	8	120	15.0(40)	0	—	—	—	—	—	—	—	—	—	—	—	6	176
1973	ChiB	10	24	70	2.9(12)	0	9	60	6.7(21)	0	—	—	—	—	—	—	—	—	—	—	—	0	100
NFL	2	22	57	176	3.1(14)	1	17	180	10.6(40)	0	—	—	—	—	—	—	—	—	—	—	—	6	276

LAWSON, STEVE   Stephen Wendell, G, 6´3˝/265 lbs; Kansas; 1971: Cin, rnd 2; B1/4/1949 Atlanta, GA   **1971** Cin 7   **1972** Cin 3   **1973** Min 2   **1974**†Min 13   **1975**†Min 11
1976 SF 14 (14, LG)   **1977** SF 14 (14, LG)   **NFL** 64 (28) [7 yrs]

LAWTON, LUKE   Luke, RB, 5´11˝/237 lbs; McNeese State; B8/26/1980 Lafayette, LA   **2005** NYJ 4 (0)

LAY, RUSS   Russell M., G-T, 5´11˝/198 lbs; Michigan State; B1/11/1907 Williamston, MI, D11/8/1971 Milwaukee, WI   **1934** Det 2 (0)   **1934** Cin 2 (1)   **1934** SL 1 (1)   **NFL** 5 (2) [1 yr]

LAYDEN, BOB   Robert, E-T, 6´0˝/195 lbs; Southwestern (KS); B1/21/1920, KS, D3/14/1988   **1943** Det 4 (0)

LAYDEN, PETE   John Peter, B, 5´11˝/192 lbs; Texas; 1942: NYG, rnd 14; B12/30/1919 Dallas, TX, D7/18/1982 Edna, TX **[K]**   **1950** NYY 10 (DB)

1948	NYY-A	9(4, tb)	95	576	6.1	3	—	—	—	—	105	43	41.0	816	7.8	9	8	—	—	—	Pkpi	—	18	907
1949	†NYY-A	12(0)	19	96	5.1	0	1	0	0.0	0	10	2	20.0	25	2.5	0	1	—	—	—	Pkpi	1	6	336
AAFC	2	21(4)	114	672	5.9	3	1	0	0.0	0	115	45	39.1	841	7.3	9	9	—	—	—	Pkpi	1	24	1243

LAYMAN, JASON   Jason Todd, G-T, 6´5˝/310 lbs; Tennessee; 1996: Hou, rnd 2; B7/29/1973 Sevierville, TN   **1996** Hou 16 (0)   **1997** Ten 14 (0)   **1998** Ten 16 (15, RG)
1999†Ten 15 (1)   **NFL** 61 (16) [4 yrs]

LAYNE, BOBBY   Robert Lawrence 'Blond Bomber', QB, 6´1˝/201 lbs; Texas; 1948: ChiB, rnd 1/Bal-A, rnd 1; B12/19/1926 Santa Ana, TX, D12/1/1986 Lubbock, TX; HOF 1967 **[K]**

1948	ChiB	11(0)	13	80	6.2(18)	1	—	—	—	—	52	16	30.8	232	4.5(35)	3	2	—	—	—	KP	—	6	141
1949	NYB	12(12, QB)	54	196	3.6(27)	3	—	—	—	—	299	155	51.8	1796	6.0(69)	9	18	—	—	55.3	—	—	18	449
1950	Det	12(QB)	56	250	4.5(30)	4	—	—	—	—	336	152	45.2	2323	6.9(82)	16	18	—	—	62.1	K	—	25	812
1951	Det◊	12(QB)	61	290	4.8(36)	1	—	—	—	—	332	152	45.8	2403	7.2(63)	26	23	—	—	67.6	—	—	6	712
1952	†Det★	12(QB)	94	411	4.4(29)	1	—	—	—	—	287	139	48.4	1999	7.0(77)	19	20	—	—	64.5	K	—	8	716
1953	†Det★	12(QB)	87	343	3.9(23)	0	—	—	—	—	273	125	45.8	2088	7.6(97)	16	21	—	—	59.6	—	—	0	627
1954	†Det☆	12(QB)	30	119	4.0(34)	2	—	—	—	—	246	135	54.9	1818	7.4(55)	14	12	—	—	77.3	—	—	12	638
1955	Det	12(QB)	31	111	3.6(19)	0	—	—	—	—	270	143	53.0	1830	6.8(77)	11	17	—	—	61.8	—	—	0	401
1956	Det★	12(QB)	46	169	3.7(20)	5	—	—	—	—	244	129	52.9	1909	7.8(70)	9	17	—	—	62.0	K	—	99	539
1957	Det	11(QB)	24	99	4.1(21)	0	—	—	—	—	179	87	48.6	1169	6.5(65)	6	12	—	—	53.0	K	—	43	234
1958	Det	2	3	1	0.3(4)	0	—	—	—	—	26	12	46.2	171	6.6(0)	1	2	—	—	—	K	—	1	12
1958	Pit☆	10(QB)	37	153	4.1(21)	3	—	—	—	—	268	133	49.6	2339	8.7(78)	13	10	—	—	80.4	—	—	18	1018
1959	Pit★	12(QB)	33	181	5.5(21)	2	—	—	—	—	297	142	47.8	1986	6.7(48)	20	21	—	—	62.8	K	—	77	454
1960	Pit	12(QB)	19	12	0.6(13)	2	—	—	—	—	209	103	49.3	1814	8.7(70)	13	17	—	—	66.2	K	—	48	324
1961	Pit	8(QB)	8	11	1.4(9)	0	—	—	—	—	149	75	50.3	1205	8.1(53)	11	16	—	—	62.8	K	—	5	29
1962	Pit	13(QB)	15	25	1.7(17)	1	—	—	—	—	233	116	49.8	1686	7.2(62)	9	17	—	—	56.2	—	—	6	243
NFL	15	175(12)	611	2451	4.0(36)	25	—	—	—	—	3700	1814	49.0	26768	7.2(97)	196	243	—	—	63.4	KP	—	372	7345

LAYNE, GEORGE   George Langford, RB, 5´11˝/250 lbs; TCU; 2001: KC, rnd 4; B10/9/1978 Alvin, TX

2001	Atl	2(0)	—	—	—	—	—	—	—	—	—	—	—	—	—	—	—	—	—	—	—	—	—
2002	†Atl	2(0)	1	5	5.0(5)	0	2	11	5.5(6)	0	—	—	—	—	—	—	—	—	—	—	—	0	11
2003	Atl	3(0)	1	15	15.0(15)	0	1	3	3.0(3)	0	—	—	—	—	—	—	—	—	—	—	—	0	17
2004	SD	2(0)	—	—	—	—	—	—	—	—	—	—	—	—	—	—	—	—	—	—	—	—	—
2004	Atl	2(0)	1	12	12.0(12)	0	1	6	6.0(6)	0	—	—	—	—	—	—	—	—	—	—	—	0	15
NFL	4	11(0)	3	32	10.7(15)	0	4	20	5.0(6)	0	—	—	—	—	—	—	—	—	—	—	—	0	42

LAYPORT, JOHN   John Evans, G-T, 5´9˝/170 lbs; Wooster; B3/19/1901 Pataskala, OH, D11/4/1986 Hendersonville, NC   **1924** Col 5 (1)   **1925** Day 4 (3)   **1926** Day 4 (0)
NFL 13 (4) [3 yrs]

LAZETICH, BILL   William Valdemere, WB-DB, 6´0˝/195 lbs; Montana; 1939: Det, rnd 16; B10/16/1916 Anaconda, MT

1939	Cle	6(1)	6	23	3.8	0	8	44	5.5	1	—	—	—	—	—	—	—	—	—	—	—	6	50
1942	Cle	9(0)	3	19	6.3(18)	1	6	65	10.8(49)	1	—	—	—	—	—	—	—	—	—	k	—	12	79
NFL	2	15(1)	9	42	4.7(18)	1	14	109	7.8(49)	2	—	—	—	—	—	—	—	—	—	k	—	18	129

LAZETICH, MIKE   Milan, G-LB, 6´1˝/211 lbs; Montana; Michigan; 1945: Cle, rnd 2; B8/27/1921 Anaconda, MT, D7/9/1969 Silver Bow County, MT   **1945**†Cle 10 (7, RG)
1946 LARm 10 (4)   **1947** LARm 11 (2)   **1948** LARm☆12 (6, RG)   **1949**†LARm☆7 (4)   **1950**†LARm 9 (RLB)   **NFL** 59 (23) [6 yrs]

LAZETICH, PETE   Peter Gary, DE-LB-DT-NT, 6´3˝/245 lbs; Stanford; 1972: SD, rnd 2; B2/4/1950 Billings, MT   **1972** SD 14 (mlb)   **1973** SD 12 (3)   **1974** SD 9 (7, LDE)
1976 Phi 13 (5, rdt)   **1977** Phi 14   **NFL** 62 (15) [5 yrs]

LEA, PAUL   Paul Allison, DT-T, 6´2˝/240 lbs; Tulane; 1951: ChiB, rnd 7; B2/19/1929 New Orleans, LA   **1951** Pit 9 (LDT)

LEACH, BILL   William Kenneth, G-T, 6´5˝/280 lbs; Kentucky; North Carolina State; B7/2/1964 Baltimore, MD   **1987** NO 1 (0)

LEACH, MIKE   Michael, TE, 6´2˝/345 lbs; Boston University; William & Mary; B10/18/1976 Jefferson Township, NJ   **2000**†Ten 15 (0)   **2001** Ten 4 (0)   **2002** Den 8 (0)
2003†Den 16 (0)   **2004**†Den 16 (0)   **2005**†Den 16 (0)   **NFL** 75 (0) [6 yrs]

LEACH, SCOTT   Scott Haywood, LB, 6´2˝/221 lbs; Ohio State; 1987: NO, rnd 9; B9/18/1963 Bridgeport, CT   **1987** NO 3 (2)

LEACH, VONTA   Terzell Vonta, RB, 6´0˝/246 lbs; East Carolina; B11/6/1981 Lumberton, NC   **2004**†GB 6 (0)

| 2005 | GB | 16(5, fb) | — | — | — | — | 5 | 19 | 3.8(9) | 0 | — | — | — | — | — | — | — | — | — | k | — | 0 | 4 |
| NFL | 2 | 22(5) | — | — | — | — | 5 | 19 | 3.8(9) | 0 | — | — | — | — | — | — | — | — | — | — | — | 0 | 10 |

LEAF, GAR   Garfield Robert, T, 6´1˝/195 lbs; Lake Forest; Syracuse; B5/26/1902 Waukegan, IL, D3/20/1990 Colorado Springs, CO   **1926** Lou 3 (3, RT)

LEAF, RYAN   Ryan David, QB, 6´5˝/245 lbs; Washington State; 1998: SD, rnd 1; B5/15/1976 Great Falls, MT

1998	SD	10(9, qb)	27	80	3.0(20)	0	—	—	—	—	245	111	45.3	1289	5.3(67)	2	15	22	140	39.0	—	—	0	135
2000	SD	11(9, QB)	28	54	1.9(14)	0	—	—	—	—	322	161	50.0	1883	5.8(83)	11	18	31	155	56.2	—	—	0	331
2001	Dal	4(3)	4	-7	-1.8(0)	0	—	—	—	—	88	45	51.1	494	5.6(38)	1	3	12	82	—	—	—	0	125
NFL	3	25(21)	59	127	2.2(20)	0	—	—	—	—	655	317	48.4	3666	5.6(83)	14	36	65	377	50.0	—	—	0	590

LEAHY, BERNIE   Bernard Phillip, HB, 5´11˝/180 lbs; Notre Dame; B8/15/1908, IL, D3/12/1978 Walnut Creek, CA

| 1932 | ChiB | 1(0) | 1 | 1 | 1.0(1) | 0 | — | — | — | — | — | — | — | — | — | — | — | — | — | — | — | 0 | 1 |

LEAHY, BOB   Robert V., QB, 6´2˝/205 lbs; Connecticut; Emporia State; B9/5/1947 Lindenhurst, NY

| 1971 | Pit | 1 | 1 | -6 | -6.0(-6) | 0 | — | — | — | — | 11 | 3 | 27.3 | 18 | 1.6(9) | 0 | 1 | 1 | 3 | — | — | — | 0 | -37 |

LEAHY, JERRY   Gerald Leo, T, 6´2˝/220 lbs; Colorado; 1957: Det, rnd 7; B10/15/1934 Bay City, MI   **1957** Pit 1

LEAHY, PAT   Patrick Joseph, K, 6´0˝/194 lbs; St. Louis; B3/19/1951 St. Louis, MO **[K]**   **1974** NYJ 6   **1975** NYJ 14   **1976** NYJ 14   **1977** NYJ 14   **1978** NYJ☆16   **1979** NYJ 6
1980 NYJ 16 (0)   **1981**†NYJ☆16 (0)   **1982**†NYJ 9 (0)   **1983** NYJ 16 (0)   **1984** NYJ 16 (0)   **1985**†NYJ 16 (0)   **1986**†NYJ☆16 (0)   **1987** NYJ☆12 (0)   **1989** NYJ 16 (0)
1990 NYJ 16 (0)   **1991** NYJ 15 (0)

| 1988 | NYJ | 16(0) | 1 | 10 | 10.0(10) | 0 | — | — | — | — | — | — | — | — | — | — | — | — | — | K | — | 112 | 10 |
| NFL | 18 | 250 | 1 | 10 | 10.0(10) | 0 | — | — | — | — | — | — | — | — | — | — | — | — | — | KP | — | 1470 | 10 |

LEAKE, JOHN   John, LB, 6´0˝/228 lbs; Clemson; B8/28/1981 Plano, TX   **2005** Atl 8 (0)   **2005** GB 3 (0)   **NFL** 11 (0) [1 yr]

LEAKS, ROOSEVELT   Roosevelt, RB, 5´10˝/225 lbs; Texas; 1975: Bal, rnd 5; B1/31/1953 Brenham, TX

| 1975 | Bal | 11 | 41 | 175 | 4.3(17) | 1 | 1 | 5 | 5.0(5) | 0 | — | — | — | — | — | — | — | — | — | — | — | 6 | 188 |
| 1976 | †Bal | 13(13, FB) | 118 | 445 | 3.8(42) | 7 | 8 | 43 | 5.4(10) | 0 | — | — | — | — | — | — | — | — | — | — | — | 42 | 537 |

YEAR	TEAM	G (GS, POS)	RUSH	YD	AVG (LG)	TD	REC	YD	AVG (LG)	TD	PASS	COMP	PCT	YD	AVG (LG)	TD	INT	SK	YD	QBR	KPR	OTD	PTS	TAY
1977	†Bal	11 (11, FB)	59	237	4.0 (39)	3	3	39	13.0 (26)	1	—	—	—	—	—	—	—	—	—	—	—	—	24	292
1978	Bal	12 (12, FB)	83	266	3.2 (11)	2	9	111	12.3 (27)	2	—	—	—	—	—	—	—	—	—	—	—	—	24	352
1979	Bal	7 (5, fb)	49	145	3.0 (17)	1	14	119	8.5 (15)	0	—	—	—	—	—	—	—	—	—	—	—	—	6	215
1980	†Buf	16 (0)	67	219	3.3 (15)	2	8	57	7.1 (18)	1	—	—	—	—	—	—	—	—	—	—	—	—	18	273
1981	†Buf	16 (5, fb)	91	357	3.9 (31)	6	7	51	7.3 (13)	0	1	0	0.0	0	0.0	0	0	—	—	—	—	—	36	443
1982	Buf	9 (9, FB)	97	405	4.2 (17)	5	13	91	7.0 (11)	0	—	—	—	—	—	—	—	—	—	—	—	—	30	501
1983	Buf	12 (4)	58	157	2.7 (12)	1	8	74	9.3 (12)	0	—	—	—	—	—	—	—	—	—	—	—	—	6	204
NFL	9	107 (59)	663	2406	3.6 (42)	28	71	590	8.3 (27)	4	1	0	0.0	0	0.0	0	0	—	—	—	—	—	192	3001

LEAPER, WES Wesley Stuart, E, 5´11˝/175 lbs; Wisconsin; B10/23/1900 Green Bay, WI, D1/30/1958 Cleveland, OH **1923** GB 2 (1)

LEAR, LES Leslie, T, 5´11˝/225 lbs; Manitoba; B8/22/1918 Grafton, ND, D1/5/1979 Hollywood, FL **1944** Cle 10 (1) **1945**†Cle 9 (1) **1946** LARm 11 (1) **1947** Det 10 (1) **NFL** 40 (4) [4 yrs]

LEARY, TOM Thomas John, E, 5´11˝/180 lbs; Fordham; B4/15/1904 Springfield, MA, D8/6/1976 Springfield, MA **1927** Fra 1 (0) **1929** SI 10 (8, RE), 12 **1930** Nwk 8 (5, le), 12 **1931** Fra 7 (7, RE) **NFL** 26 (20), 24 [4 yrs]

LEASY, WESLEY Wesley, LB, 6´2˝/234 lbs; Mississippi State; 1995: Arz, rnd 7; B9/7/1971 Vicksburg, MS **1995** Arz 12 (0) **1996** Arz 16 (0) **NFL** 28 (0) [2 yrs]

LEATHERMAN, PAUL Paul Christian, G-C, 5´9˝/200 lbs; Chicago; B8/9/1897 Terre Haute, IN, D4/1956 Palm Beach County, FL **1922** Ham 4 (4, LG)

LEATHERS, MILTON Leon Milton, G, 5´11˝/198 lbs; Georgia; B12/16/1908 Winder, GA **1933** Phi 4 (0)

LEAVITT, ALLAN Allan James, K, 5´11˝/176 lbs; Georgia; 1977: Atl, rnd 4; B10/22/1955 St. Petersburg, FL **[K]** **1977** TB 8

LEAVITT, FRANK Frank Simmons, G-C, /270 lbs; none; B6/30/1891 New York, NY, D5/29/1953 Norcross, GA **1921** NYG 2 (1)

LEBARON, EDDIE Edward Wayne 'The Little General', QB, 5´9˝/168 lbs; Pacific; 1950: Was, rnd 10; B1/7/1930 San Rafael, CA **[K]**

YEAR	TEAM	G (GS, POS)	RUSH	YD	AVG (LG)	TD	REC	YD	AVG (LG)	TD	PASS	COMP	PCT	YD	AVG (LG)	TD	INT	SK	YD	QBR	KPR	OTD	PTS	TAY
1952	Was	12 (QB)	43	164	3.8 (32)	2	—	—	—	—	194	96	49.5	1420	7.3 (70)	14	15	—	—	65.7	KP	—	18	364
1953	Was	12 (QB)	21	95	4.5 (27)	2	—	—	—	—	149	62	41.6	874	5.9 (66)	3	17	—	—	28.3	P	—	12	-113
1955	Was✧	12 (QB)	37	190	5.1 (25)	4	—	—	—	—	178	79	44.4	1270	7.1 (70)	9	15	—	—	50.5	P	—	24	310
1956	Was	10 (qb)	11	6	0.5 (9)	0	—	—	—	—	98	47	48.0	554	5.7 (33)	3	10	—	—	—	P	—	0	-102
1957	Was✧	12 (QB)	20	-12	-0.6 (11)	0	—	—	—	—	167	99	59.3	1508	**9.0** (**82**)	11	10	—	—	86.1	—	—	0	397
1958	Was✧	12 (QB)	12	30	2.5 (13)	0	—	—	—	—	145	79	54.5	1365	**9.4** (**71**)	11	10	—	—	83.3	—	—	0	368
1959	Was	12 (QB)	13	7	0.5 (15)	0	—	—	—	—	173	77	44.5	1077	6.2 (49)	8	11	—	—	54.0	—	—	0	146
1960	Dal	11 (QB)	17	94	5.5 (23)	1	—	—	—	—	225	111	49.3	1736	7.7 (76)	12	**25**	26	205	53.5	P	—	6	32
1961	Dal	14 (10, QB)	20	72	3.6 (21)	0	—	—	—	—	236	120	50.8	1741	7.4 (80)	14	16	11	89	66.7	—	—	0	373
1962	Dal✧	14 (QB)	6	-1	-0.2 (3)	0	—	—	—	—	166	95	57.2	1436	8.7 (85)	16	9	15	119	**95.4**	—	—	0	437
1963	Dal	13	2	5	2.5 (4)	0	—	—	—	—	65	33	50.8	418	6.4 (75)	3	3	9	71	—	—	—	0	109
NFL	11	134 (10)	202	650	3.2 (32)	9	—	—	—	—	1796	898	50.0	13399	7.5 (85)	104	141	61	484	61.4	KP	—	60	2320

LEBEAU, DICK Charles Richard, DB, 6´1˝/185 lbs; Ohio State; 1959: Cle, rnd 5; B9/9/1937 London, OH **[IC]** **1959** Det 6 **1960** Det 12 (RCB) **1961** Det 14 **1962** Det 14 (RCB) **1963** Det 14 (RCB) **1964** Det★14 (LCB) **1965** Det★14 (LCB) **1966** Det✧14 (LCB) **1967** Det 14 (RCB) **1968** Det 14 (RCB) **1969** Det 14 (RCB) **1970**†Det☆14 (RCB) **1971** Det☆13 (RCB) **1972** Det 14 (FS) **NFL** 185 [14 yrs]

LEBEL, HARPER Brian Harper, TE, 6´4˝/250 lbs; Colorado State; 1985: KC, rnd 12; B7/14/1963 Granada Hills, CA **1989** Sea 16 (0) **1991** Atl 3 (0) **1992** Atl 16 (2) **1993** Atl 16 (0) **1994** Atl 16 (0) **1995**†Atl 16 (0) **1996** Atl 16 (0) **1998** Bal 5 (0)

YEAR	TEAM	G (GS, POS)	RUSH	YD	AVG (LG)	TD	REC	YD	AVG (LG)	TD	PASS	COMP	PCT	YD	AVG (LG)	TD	INT	SK	YD	QBR	KPR	OTD	PTS	TAY
1990	†Phi	16 (0)	—	—	—	—	1	9	9.0 (9)	0	—	—	—	—	—	—	—	—	—	—	—	—	0	5
1997	ChiB	16 (0)	1	0	0.0 (0)	0	—	—	—	—	—	—	—	—	—	—	—	—	—	—	—	—	0	0
NFL	10	136 (2)	1	0	0.0	0	1	9	9.0 (9)	0	—	—	—	—	—	—	—	—	—	—	—	—	0	5

LEBENGOOD, FUNGY Howard Edward, HB, 5´11˝/175 lbs; Villanova; B4/23/1902 Pottsville, PA, D1/20/1980 Lakeland, FL **1925** Pot 5 (2)

LEBER, BEN Ben, LB, 6´3˝/244 lbs; Kansas State; 2002: SD, rnd 3; B12/7/1978 Vermillion, SD **2002** SD 16 (14, LLB) **2003** SD 16 (16, LLB) **2004**†SD 16 (16, LOLB) **2005** SD 9 (6, lolb) **NFL** 57 (52) [4 yrs]

LEBERMAN, BOB Robert W., DB, 6´1˝/180 lbs; Syracuse; 1954: Bal, rnd 11; B2/10/1932 **1954** Bal 12

LEBLANC, BOB Robert Leron, LB, 6´2˝/243 lbs; Elon; B11/5/1962 Panama City, FL **1987** Buf 3 (3)

LEBLANC, CLARENCE Clarence, DB, 6´3˝/210 lbs; LSU; B3/26/1977 River Ridge, LA **2003** NYG 4 (0)

LEBLANC, MICHAEL Michael Keith, RB, 5´11˝/199 lbs; Stephen F. Austin State; B5/5/1962 Missouri City, TX

YEAR	TEAM	G (GS, POS)	RUSH	YD	AVG (LG)	TD	REC	YD	AVG (LG)	TD	PASS	COMP	PCT	YD	AVG (LG)	TD	INT	SK	YD	QBR	KPR	OTD	PTS	TAY
1987	NE	4 (2)	49	170	3.5 (42)	1	2	3	1.5 (3)	0	—	—	—	—	—	—	—	—	—	—	k	—	6	183

LECHLER, SHANE Edward Shane, P, 6´2˝/225 lbs; Texas A&M; 2000: Oak, rnd 5; B8/7/1976 Sealy, TX **[KP]** **2000**†Oak☆16 (0) **2002**†Oak 14 (0) **2003** Oak☆16 (0) **2004** Oak★16 (0)

YEAR	TEAM	G (GS, POS)	RUSH	YD	AVG (LG)	TD	REC	YD	AVG (LG)	TD	PASS	COMP	PCT	YD	AVG (LG)	TD	INT	SK	YD	QBR	KPR	OTD	PTS	TAY
2001	†Oak★	16 (0)	1	2	2.0 (2)	0	—	—	—	—	—	—	—	—	—	—	—	—	—	—	P	—	0	2
2005	Oak	16 (0)	1	2	2.0 (2)	0	—	—	—	—	—	—	—	—	—	—	—	—	—	—	P	—	0	2
NFL	6	94 (0)	2	4	2.0 (2)	0	—	—	—	—	—	—	—	—	—	—	—	—	—	—	KP	—	7	4

LECHNER, ED Edgar Henry, G-T, 6´1˝/200 lbs; Minnesota; B12/14/1919 Fessenden, ND **1942** NYG 4 (0)

LECHTHALER, ROY Melvin Roy, G, 5´10˝/198 lbs; Lebanon Valley; B4/1/1908, PA, D12/16/1980 Harrisburg, PA **1933** Phi 4 (1)

LECKEY, NICK Nick, C-G, 6´4˝/265 lbs; Kansas State; 2004: Arz, rnd 6; B3/12/1982 Grapevine, TX **2004** Arz 16 (0) **2005** Arz 14 (9, C) **NFL** 30 (9) [2 yrs]

LECKONBY, BILL William Bader, TB, 6´1˝/185 lbs; St. Lawrence; B9/16/1917 Greenville, OH

YEAR	TEAM	G (GS, POS)	RUSH	YD	AVG (LG)	TD	REC	YD	AVG (LG)	TD	PASS	COMP	PCT	YD	AVG (LG)	TD	INT	SK	YD	QBR	KPR	OTD	PTS	TAY
1939	Bkn	5 (0)	4	-1	-0.3	0	—	—	—	—	1	0	0.0	0	0.0	0	0	—	—	—	—	—	0	-1
1940	Bkn	11 (0)	19	53	2.8	0	1	8	8.0 (8)	1	13	7	53.8	74	5.7	0	0	—	—	—	Pi	1	12	123
1941	Bkn	11 (2)	54	202	3.7 (17)	0	1	9	9.0 (9)	1	64	25	39.1	299	4.7 (32)	1	5	—	—	—	Pkpi	—	6	263
NFL	3	27 (2)	77	254	3.3 (17)	0	2	17	8.5 (9)	2	78	32	41.0	373	4.8 (32)	1	5	—	—	—	Pkpi	1	18	385

LECLAIR, JIM James Michael, LB, 6´3˝/234 lbs; North Dakota; 1972: Cin, rnd 3; B10/30/1950 St. Paul, MN **1972** Cin 14 **1973** Cin 10 **1974** Cin 8 (mlb) **1975** Cin 14 (MLB) **1976** Cin✧14 (MLB) **1977** Cin 14 (MLB) **1978** Cin 16 (MLB) **1979** Cin 16 (MLB) **1980** Cin 16 (16, LILB) **1981** Cin 14 (14, LILB) **1982** Cin☆8 (8, LILB) **1983** Cin 14 (14, LILB) **NFL** 158 (52) [12 yrs]

LECLAIR, JIM James Michael, QB, 6´1˝/200 lbs; C.W. Post; 1966: SF, rnd 16; B3/23/1944 Mount Vernon, NY

YEAR	TEAM	G (GS, POS)	RUSH	YD	AVG (LG)	TD	REC	YD	AVG (LG)	TD	PASS	COMP	PCT	YD	AVG (LG)	TD	INT	SK	YD	QBR	KPR	OTD	PTS	TAY
1967	Den-A	5 (1)	8	6	0.8 (10)	1	—	—	—	—	45	19	42.2	275	6.1 (48)	1	1	—	—	—	—	—	6	119
1968	Den-A	3	12	40	3.3 (12)	0	—	—	—	—	54	27	50.0	401	7.4 (50)	1	5	—	—	—	—	—	0	46
NFL	2	8 (1)	20	46	2.3 (12)	1	—	—	—	—	99	46	46.5	676	6.8 (50)	2	6	—	—	—	—	—	6	164

LECLERC, ROGER Roger Alvin, LB-K-C, 6´3˝/235 lbs; Trinity (CT); 1959: ChiB, rnd 15/1960: Den, rnd 1; B10/1/1936 Springfield, MA **[K]** **1960** ChiB 12 **1961** ChiB 14 **1962** ChiB 14 **1964** ChiB 14 **1965** ChiB 14 **1966** ChiB 14 **1967** Den-A 8

YEAR	TEAM	G (GS, POS)	RUSH	YD	AVG (LG)	TD	REC	YD	AVG (LG)	TD	PASS	COMP	PCT	YD	AVG (LG)	TD	INT	SK	YD	QBR	KPR	OTD	PTS	TAY
1963	†ChiB	14	—	—	—	—	—	—	—	—	1	0	0.0	0	0.0	0	0	—	—	—	Ki	—	39	-3
NFL	8	104	—	—	—	—	—	—	—	—	1	0	0.0	0	0.0	0	0	—	—	—	Kki	—	382	-18

LECOUNT, TERRY Terry Jerome, WR, 5´10˝/178 lbs; Florida; 1978: SF, rnd 4; B7/9/1956 Jacksonville, FL

YEAR	TEAM	G (GS, POS)	RUSH	YD	AVG (LG)	TD	REC	YD	AVG (LG)	TD	PASS	COMP	PCT	YD	AVG (LG)	TD	INT	SK	YD	QBR	KPR	OTD	PTS	TAY
1978	SF	3 (3)	—	—	—	—	10	131	13.1 (30)	0	—	—	—	—	—	—	—	—	—	—	k	—	0	82
1979	SF	2	—	—	—	—	—	—	—	—	—	—	—	—	—	—	—	—	—	—	—	—	—	—
1979	Min	12	—	—	—	—	6	119	19.8 (36)	2	0	0	0.0	0	0.0	0	0	1	9	—	—	—	12	70
1980	†Min	16 (0)	—	—	—	—	13	168	12.9 (21)	0	—	—	—	—	—	—	—	—	—	—	—	—	0	84
1981	Min	16 (2)	3	51	17.0 (38)	0	24	425	17.7 (43)	2	—	—	—	—	—	—	—	—	—	—	—	—	12	274
1982	†Min	9 (3)	1	-3	-3.0 (-3)	0	14	179	12.8 (28)	1	—	—	—	—	—	—	—	—	—	—	—	—	6	92
1983	Min	11 (10, WR)	2	42	21.0 (40)	0	21	318	15.1 (49)	2	1	0	0.0	0	0.0	0	0	—	—	—	—	—	12	211
1984	Min	2 (1)	—	—	—	—	1	14	14.0 (14)	0	—	—	—	—	—	—	—	—	—	—	—	—	0	7
1987	Min	1 (0)	—	—	—	—	—	—	—	—	—	—	—	—	—	—	—	—	—	—	—	—	—	—
NFL	8	72 (19)	6	90	15.0 (40)	0	89	1354	15.2 (49)	7	1	0	0.0	0	0.0	0	0	1	9	—	k	—	42	818

LECTURE, JIM James Wayne, G, 5´10˝/220 lbs; Washington-St. Louis; Northwestern; 1946: Phi, rnd 8; B10/29/1924 Chicago, IL, D12/19/1999 **1946** Buf-A 1 (0)

YEAR	TEAM	G(GS, POS)	RUSH	YD	AVG(LG)	TD	REC	YD	AVG(LG)	TD	PASS	COMP	PCT	YD	AVG(LG)	TD	INT	SK	YD	QBR	KPR	OTD	PTS	TAY

LEDBETTER, DOC Homer Carroll, FB-HB, 5´10˝/190 lbs; Arkansas; B1/25/1910 Huntsville, AR, D1995

1932	SI	8(2)	41	114	2.8	2	2	37	18.5	0	—	—	—	—	—	—	—				—		12	153
1932	ChiC	2(1)	11	35	3.2	0	—	—	—	—	—	—	—	—	—	—	—				—		0	35
1933	ChiC	7(2)	15	21	1.4	0	—	—	—	—	4	2	50.0	12	3.0	0	2	—			—		0	-53
NFL	2	17(5)	67	170	2.5	2	2	37	18.5	0	4	2	50.0	12	3.0	0	2	—			—		12	135

LEDBETTER, MONTE Monte Richards, WR, 6´2˝/185 lbs; Northwestern State (LA); 1966: Hou, rnd 11/Cle, rnd 10; B8/13/1943 Jennings, LA

1967	Hou-A	5	—	—	—		4	43	10.8(16)	1	—	—	—	—	—	—	—				—		6	27
1967	Buf-A	5	—	—	—		9	161	17.9(60)	1	—	—	—	—	—	—	—				—		6	86
1968	Buf-A	7	—	—	—		4	94	23.5(43)	1	—	—	—	—	—	—	—				—		6	70
1969	Buf-A	2	—	—	—		—	—	—	—	—	—	—	—	—	—	—				—			
1969	Atl	2	—	—	—		1	16	16.0(16)	1	—	—	—	—	—	—	—				—		0	8
NFL	3	21	—	—	—		18	314	17.4(60)	3	—	—	—	—	—	—	—				—		18	190

LEDBETTER, TOY Toy W., HB, 5´10˝/198 lbs; Oklahoma State; B10/30/1927 Morris, OK, D1/25/1995 Denver, CO

1950	Phi	10	67	320	4.8(23)	1	4	81	20.3(29)	2	—	—	—	—	—	—	—				—		18	381
1953	Phi	10	41	120	2.9(32)	1	13	137	10.5(34)	2	—	—	—	—	—	—	—				—		18	209
1954	Phi	12(LH)	81	241	3.0(14)	1	15	192	12.8(48)	3	—	—	—	—	—	—	—				k		24	417
1955	Phi	8	21	48	2.3(7)	0	7	88	12.6(37)	1	—	—	—	—	—	—	—				k		6	103
NFL	4	40	210	729	3.5(32)	3	39	498	12.8(48)	8	—	—	—	—	—	—	—				k		66	1109

LEDFORD, DWAYNE Billy Dwayne, C, 6´4˝/300 lbs; East Carolina; B11/2/1976 Morgantown, NC   **2000** SF 1 (0)   **2003** SF 8 (1)   **NFL** 9 (1) [2 yrs]

LEDYARD, COURTNEY Courtney, LB, 6´2˝/250 lbs; Michigan State; B3/9/1977 Shaker Heights, OH   **2000** NYJ 4 (0)

LEDYARD, HAL Harold, QB, 6´0˝/185 lbs; Tennessee-Chattanooga; 1953: SF, rnd 9; B7/7/1931 Montgomery, AL, D4/21/1973 Big Sur, CA

| 1953 | SF | 10 | 1 | 3 | 3.0(3) | 0 | — | — | — | — | 9 | 0 | 0.0 | 0 | — | 0 | 1 | — | | | — | | 0 | -37 |

LEE, AMP Anthonia Wayne, RB, 5´11˝/200 lbs; Florida State; 1992: SF, rnd 2; B10/1/1971 Chipley, FL

1992	†SF	16(3)	91	362	4.0(43)	2	20	102	5.1(17)	2	—	—	—	—	—	—	—				k		24	509
1993	†SF	15(3)	72	230	3.2(13)	1	16	115	7.2(22)	2	—	—	—	—	—	—	—				k		18	318
1994	†Min	13(0)	29	104	3.6(16)	0	45	368	8.2(35)	2	—	—	—	—	—	—	—				k		12	295
1995	Min	16(3)	69	371	5.4(66)	2	71	558	7.9(33)	1	—	—	—	—	—	—	—				kp		18	725
1996	†Min	16(3)	51	161	3.2(12)	0	54	422	7.8(21)	2	—	—	—	—	—	—	—				kp		12	426
1997	SL	16(1)	28	104	3.7(14)	0	61	825	13.5(62)	3	—	—	—	—	—	—	—				kp		18	543
1998	SL	14(1)	44	175	4.0(38)	2	64	667	10.4(44)	2	—	—	—	—	—	—	—				—		26	539
1999	†SL	7(0)	3	3	1.0(4)	0	3	22	7.3(14)	1	—	—	—	—	—	—	—				—		6	19
2000	Phi	3(0)	1	2	2.0(2)	0	1	20	20.0(20)	0	—	—	—	—	—	—	—				—		0	12
NFL	9	116(14)	388	1512	3.9(66)	7	335	3099	9.3(62)	15	—	—	—	—	—	—	—				kp		134	3385

LEE, ANDY Andy Paul, P, 6´2˝/205 lbs; Pittsburgh; 2004: SF, rnd 6; B8/11/1982 Westminster, SC   **2004** SF 16 (0)   **2005** SF 16 (0)   **NFL** 32 (0) [2 yrs]

LEE, BERNIE Bernard Michael, QB, 5´11˝/190 lbs; Villanova; B10/25/1912 Broughton, PA, D5/19/1990 Las Vegas, NV   **1938** Phi 1 (0)   **1938** Pit 4 (1)   **NFL** 5 (1) [1 yr]

LEE, BIFF David Hilary, G, 6´0˝/226 lbs; Missouri; Oklahoma; B1/11/1905 Wolf Island, MO, D5/1981 Troy, AL **[K]**   **1931** Por 1 (0)   **1931** Cle 7 (7, LG)   **1933** Cin 9 (7, LG)
1934 Cin 8 (7, RG)   **NFL** 25 (21) [3 yrs]

LEE, BILL William Earl, T, 6´2˝/231 lbs; Alabama; B10/19/1911 Eutaw, AL   **1935** Bkn☆12 (12, RT)   **1936** Bkn☆12 (12, RT)   **1937** Bkn 5 (4)   **1937** GB 4 (1)   **1938**†GB 11 (10, RT)
1939†GB◊11 (9, RT)   **1940** GB 11 (8, RT)   **1941**†GB 11 (4, rt)   **1942** GB 1 (0)   **1946** GB 4 (0)   **NFL** 82 (60) [9 yrs]

LEE, BIVIAN Bivian Lewis, DB, 6´3˝/200 lbs; Prairie View A&M; 1971: NO, rnd 3; B8/3/1948 Austin, TX, D11/12/1984 New Orleans, LA   **1971** NO 14   **1972** NO 13 (rcb)
1973 NO 14 (RCB)   **1974** NO 13 (rcb)   **1975** NO 11   **NFL** 65 [5 yrs]

LEE, BOB Robert Edward, G, 6´1˝/245 lbs; Missouri; B7/4/1935   **1960** Bos-A 8

LEE, BOB Robert Melville, QB-P, 6´2˝/195 lbs; Arizona State; Pacific; 1968: Min, rnd 17; B8/7/1945 Columbus, OH

1969	†Min	14	3	9	3.0(7)	0	—	—	—	—	11	7	63.6	79	7.2(30)	1	0	—	—		P		0	54
1970	Min	6	10	20	2.0(10)	1	—	—	—	—	79	40	50.6	610	7.7(52)	5	5	6	36		—		6	160
1971	†Min	14	11	14	1.3(4)	1	—	—	—	—	90	45	50.0	598	6.6(51)	2	4	8	91		P		6	173
1972	Min	2	—	—	—		—	—	—	—	6	3	50.0	75	12.5(63)	1	0	—	—		—		0	43
1973	Atl	12(QB)	29	67	2.3(11)	0	—	—	—	—	230	120	52.2	1786	7.8(57)	10	8	28	256	77.9	—		0	690
1974	Atl	9(QB)	19	99	5.2(17)	1	—	—	—	—	172	78	45.3	852	5.0(52)	3	14	31	269		—		6	-10
1975	Min	1	1	0	0.0(0)	0	—	—	—	—	14	5	35.7	103	7.4(33)	1	1	6	—		—		0	22
1976	†Min	4(1)	2	2	1.0(2)	0	—	—	—	—	30	15	50.0	156	5.2(21)	0	2	6	41		—		0	0
1977	†Min	5(4)	12	-8	-0.7(7)	0	—	—	—	—	72	42	58.3	522	7.3(48)	4	4	7	47		—		0	113
1978	Min	3	—	—	—		—	—	—	—	4	2	50.0	10	2.5(6)	0	1	2	20		—		0	-35
1979	LARm	3	4	-5	-1.3(0)	0	—	—	—	—	22	11	50.0	243	11.0(41)	2	1	4	39		—		0	87
1980	†LARm	1(0)	1	-1	-1.0(-1)	0	—	—	—	—	—	—	—	—	—	—	—	—	—		—		0	-1
NFL	12	77(5)	92	197	2.1(17)	3	—	—	—	—	730	368	50.4	5034	6.9(63)	30	40	93	805	63.7	P		18	1294

LEE, BOBBY Bobby Dale, WR, 6´4˝/200 lbs; Minnesota; 1968: SL, rnd 17; B8/26/1945 Montgomery, AL   **1968** SL 4   **1969** Atl 2   **NFL** 6 [2 yrs]

LEE, BYRON Byron Keith, LB, 6´2˝/230 lbs; Ohio State; 1986: Phi, rnd 7; B9/8/1964 Columbus, OH   **1986** Phi 3 (0)   **1987** Phi 3 (3)   **NFL** 6 (3) [2 yrs]

LEE, CARL Carl, DB, 5´11˝/185 lbs; Marshall; 1983: Min, rnd 7; B2/6/1961 South Charleston, WV **[I]**   **1983** Min 16 (3)   **1984** Min 16 (14, FS)   **1985** Min 15 (5, rcb)
1986 Min 16 (16, RCB)   **1987**†Min 12 (12, RCB)   **1988**†Min★16 (16, RCB)   **1989**†Min★16 (16, RCB)   **1990** Min◊16 (16, LCB)   **1991** Min 14 (14, LCB)   **1992**†Min☆16 (16, LCB)
1993†Min 16 (16, LCB)   **1994** NO 12 (8, RCB)   **NFL** 181 (152) [12 yrs]

LEE, CHARLES Charles, WR, 6´2˝/210 lbs; Central Florida; 2000: GB, rnd 7; B11/19/1977 Miami, FL

2000	GB	15(1)	—	—	—		10	134	13.4(38)	0	—	—	—	—	—	—	—				p		0	94
2001	GB	7(0)	—	—	—		3	32	10.7(23)	1	—	—	—	—	—	—	—				p		6	12
2002	TB	1(0)	—	—	—		—	—	—	—	—	—	—	—	—	—	—				—			
2003	TB	8(5, wr)	2	14	7.0(8)	0	33	432	13.1(72)	2	—	—	—	—	—	—	—				—		12	240
2004	TB	7(3)	—	—	—		15	207	13.8(35)	0	—	—	—	—	—	—	—				—		0	104
2005	Arz	6(0)	—	—	—		11	152	13.8(49)	0	—	—	—	—	—	—	—				—		0	76
NFL	6	44(9)	2	14	7.0(8)	0	72	957	13.3(72)	3	—	—	—	—	—	—	—				p		18	526

LEE, DANZELL Danzell Ivan, TE, 6´2˝/235 lbs; Lamar; 1985: Was, rnd 6; B3/16/1963 Corsicana, TX   **1988** Atl 5 (0)

| 1987 | Pit | 13(13, TE) | — | — | — | | 12 | 124 | 10.3(24) | 0 | — | — | — | — | — | — | — | | | | — | | 0 | 62 |
| **NFL** | 2 | 18(13) | — | — | — | | 12 | 124 | 10.3(24) | 0 | — | — | — | — | — | — | — | | | | — | | 0 | 62 |

LEE, DAVID David Allen, P, 6´4˝/230 lbs; Louisiana Tech; B11/8/1943 Shreveport, LA **[P]**   **1966** Bal☆14   **1967** Bal 14   **1969** Bal☆14   **1970**†Bal☆14   **1971**†Bal 14   **1972** Bal 14
1974 Bal 14   **1975**†Bal 14   **1978** Bal 16

1968	†Bal	14	3	12	4.0(21)	0	—	—	—	—	—	—	—	—	—	—	—				P		0	12
1973	Bal	14	2	-16	-8.0(0)	0	—	—	—	—	—	—	—	—	—	—	—				P		0	-16
1976	†Bal	14	1	-12	-12.0(-12)	0	—	—	—	—	—	—	—	—	—	—	—				P		0	-12
1977	†Bal	14	2	-2	-1.0(0)	0	—	—	—	—	—	—	—	—	—	—	—				P		0	-2
NFL	13	184	8	-18	-2.3(21)	0	—	—	—	—	—	—	—	—	—	—	—				P		0	-18

LEE, DELPHFRINE Delphrine, DB, 5´10˝/187 lbs; McNeese State; B1/19/1976 New Orleans, LA   **1999** NYJ 4 (0)

LEE, DONALD Donald Tywon, TE, 6´3˝/255 lbs; Mississippi State; 2003: Mia, rnd 5; B8/31/1980 Maben, MS

2003	Mia	16(5, te)	—	—	—		7	110	15.7(25)	1	—	—	—	—	—	—	—				k		6	45
2004	Mia	16(10, TE)	—	—	—		13	110	8.5(15)	1	—	—	—	—	—	—	—				—		6	60
2005	GB	15(5, te)	—	—	—		33	294	8.9(27)	2	—	—	—	—	—	—	—				—		12	157
NFL	3	47(20)	—	—	—		53	514	9.7(27)	4	—	—	—	—	—	—	—				k		24	262

YEAR	TEAM	G (GS, POS)	RUSH	YD	AVG(LG)	TD	REC	YD	AVG(LG)	TD	PASS	COMP	PCT	YD	AVG(LG)	TD	INT	SK	YD	QBR	KPR	OTD	PTS	TAY

LEE, DWIGHT   Dwight Lionel, RB, 6´2˝/190 lbs; Michigan State; 1968: SF, rnd 5; B9/3/1945 Mount Clemens, MI

1968	SF	2	2	1	0.5(1)	0	—	—	—	—	—	—	—	—	—	—	—	—	—	—	k	—	0	14
1968	Atl	11	4	6	1.5(6)	0	—	—	—	—	—	—	—	—	—	—	—	—	—	—	k	—	0	11
NFL	1	13	6	7	1.2(6)	0	—	—	—	—	—	—	—	—	—	—	—	—	—	—	k	—	0	25

LEE, EDWARD   Edward Preston, WR, 5´11˝/182 lbs; South Carolina State; 1982: Det, rnd 11; B12/8/1959 Washington, DC   **1982**†Det 0 (0)

LEE, GARY   Gary DeWayne, WR, 6´1˝/202 lbs; Georgia Tech; 1987: Det, rnd 12; B2/12/1965 Albany, GA

1987	Det	12(3)	—	—	—	—	19	308	16.2(53)	0	—	—	—	—	—	—	—	—	—	—	k	—	0	393
1988	Det	14(6, wr)	—	—	—	—	22	261	11.9(18)	1	—	—	—	—	—	—	—	—	—	—	k	—	6	221
NFL	2	26(9)	—	—	—	—	41	569	13.9(53)	1	—	—	—	—	—	—	—	—	—	—	k	—	6	614

LEE, GENE   Eugene Orson, C, 6´3˝/226 lbs; Florida; 1943: Bkn, rnd 25; B4/21/1922 Covington, GA   **1946** Bos 11 (0)

LEE, GREG   Gregory Lamont, DB, 6´1˝/207 lbs; Arkansas State; B1/15/1965 Pine Bluff, AR   **1988** Pit 16 (0)

LEE, HERMAN   Willie Herman, T-G, 6´4˝/244 lbs; Florida A&M; 1954: ChiB, rnd 23; B8/29/1931 Phenix City, AL   **1957** Pit 8   **1958** ChiB 12 (LT)   **1959** ChiB 12 (LT)   **1961** ChiB 14 (LT)   **1962** ChiB 14 (LT)   **1963**†ChiB 14 (LT)   **1964** ChiB 14 (LT)   **1965** ChiB 14 (LT)   **1966** ChiB 13 (LT)

| 1960 | ChiB | 12(LT) | — | — | — | — | 1 | 16 | 16.0(16) | 0 | — | — | — | — | — | — | — | — | — | — | — | — | 0 | 8 |
| NFL | 10 | 127 | — | — | — | — | 1 | 16 | 16.0(16) | 0 | — | — | — | — | — | — | — | — | — | — | — | — | 0 | 8 |

LEE, JACK   John, BB, 5´10˝/205 lbs; Carnegie Mellon; 1939: Pit, rnd 10; B3/28/1917, D7/1972

| 1939 | Pit | 5(0) | 1 | -11 | -11.0(-11) | 0 | — | — | — | — | 1 | 0 | 0.0 | 0 | 0.0 | 0 | 0 | — | — | P | — | — | 0 | -11 |

LEE, JACKY   Jack Ross, QB, 6´1˝/189 lbs; Cincinnati; 1960: Hou, rnd 1/SL, rnd 6; B7/11/1939 Minneapolis, MN

1960	†Hou-A	14(2)	6	11	1.8(10)	0	—	—	—	—	77	41	53.2	842	10.9(92)	5	6	—	—	—	—	—	0	217
1961	†Hou-A	14	8	36	4.5(9)	0	—	—	—	—	127	66	52.0	1205	9.5(80)	12	6	—	—	—	—	—	0	459
1962	†Hou-A	14	4	1	0.3(4)	0	—	—	—	—	50	26	52.0	433	8.7(98)	4	5	—	—	—	—	—	0	38
1963	Hou-A	14	2	9	4.5(8)	0	—	—	—	—	75	37	49.3	475	6.3(38)	2	8	—	—	—	—	—	0	-64
1964	Den-A	14(QB)	42	163	3.9(16)	3	—	—	—	—	265	133	50.2	1611	6.1(82)	11	20	—	—	51.6	—	—	18	254
1965	Den-A	4	2	1	0.5(2)	0	—	—	—	—	80	44	55.0	692	8.6(66)	5	3	—	—	—	—	—	0	252
1966	Hou-A	8	1	-3	-3.0(-3)	0	—	—	—	—	8	4	50.0	27	3.4(10)	0	1	—	—	—	—	—	0	-30
1967	Hou-A	4	5	0	0.0(7)	0	1	-1	-1.0(-1)	0	72	36	50.0	309	4.3(53)	2	4	2	12	—	—	—	0	4
1967	KC-A	5	1	-3	-3.0(-3)	0	—	—	—	—	19	6	31.6	105	5.5(29)	1	2	—	—	—	—	—	0	-26
1968	†KC-A	6	—	—	—	—	—	—	—	—	45	25	55.6	383	8.5(61)	3	1	—	—	—	—	—	0	167
1969	KC-A	3(1)	1	3	3.0(3)	0	—	—	—	—	20	12	60.0	109	5.4(31)	1	1	2	38	—	—	—	0	23
NFL	10	100(3)	72	218	3.0(16)	3	1	-1	-1.0(-1)	0	838	430	51.3	6191	7.4(98)	46	57	4	50	65.6	—	—	18	1293

LEE, JAMES   James Franklin, DT, 6´5˝/325 lbs; Oregon State; 2003: GB, rnd 5; B3/12/1980 Salem, OR   **2004** GB 9 (1)

LEE, JEFF   Jeffrey Leroy, WR, 6´2˝/195 lbs; Nebraska; B5/23/1955 Racine, WI

| 1980 | SL | 4(0) | — | — | — | — | 2 | 19 | 9.5(12) | 0 | — | — | — | — | — | — | — | — | — | — | — | — | 0 | 10 |

LEE, JOHN   John Dana, DE, 6´2˝/255 lbs; Nebraska; 1976: SD, rnd 13; B2/17/1953 Fort Monmouth, NJ   **1976** SD 14 (4)   **1977** SD 12 (3)   **1978** SD 1 (1)   **1979** SD 10 (2)   **1980**†SD 11 (0)   **1981** NE 4 (4)   **NFL** 52 (14) [6 yrs]

LEE, JOHN   Min John, K, 5´11˝/182 lbs; UCLA; 1986: SL, rnd 2; B5/19/1964 Seoul, South Korea [K]   **1986** SL 11 (0)

LEE, KEITH   Keith Lamar, DB, 5´11˝/192 lbs; Colorado State; 1980: Buf, rnd 5; B12/22/1957 San Antonio, TX   **1981** NE 15 (6, rcb)   **1982**†NE 9 (2)   **1983** NE 15 (0)   **1984** NE 15 (0)   **1985** Ind 14 (0)   **NFL** 68 (8) [5 yrs]

LEE, KEN   Kenneth Alan, LB, 6´4˝/230 lbs; Washington; 1971: Det, rnd 8; B9/3/1948 Honolulu, HI   **1971** Det 1   **1972** Buf 12 (MLB)   **NFL** 13 [2 yrs]

LEE, KEVIN   Kevin DeWayne, WR, 6´1˝/194 lbs; Alabama; 1994: NE, rnd 2; B1/1/1971 Mobile, AL   **1996** SF 2 (0)

| 1995 | NE | 7(2) | 1 | 4 | 4.0(4) | 0 | 8 | 107 | 13.4(33) | 0 | — | — | — | — | — | — | — | — | — | — | k | — | 0 | 57 |
| NFL | 2 | 9(2) | 1 | 4 | 4.0(4) | 0 | 8 | 107 | 13.4(33) | 0 | — | — | — | — | — | — | — | — | — | — | k | — | 0 | 58 |

LEE, LARRY   Larry Dwayne, G-C, 6´2˝/265 lbs; UCLA; 1981: Det, rnd 5; B9/10/1959 Dayton, OH   **1981** Det 16 (0)   **1982**†Det 9 (0)   **1983**†Det 16 (6, rg)   **1984** Det 15 (6, lg)   **1985** Det 6 (4)   **1985**†Mia 5 (0)   **1986** Mia 16 (5, rg)   **1987**†Den 9 (5, c)   **1988** Den 4 (0)   **NFL** 96 (26) [8 yrs]

LEE, LLOYD   Lloyd Ceyoung, DB, 6´1˝/210 lbs; Dartmouth; B8/10/1976 Minneapolis, MN   **1998** SD 8 (0)

LEE, MARK   Mark Anthony, DB, 5´11˝/187 lbs; Washington; 1980: GB, rnd 2; B3/20/1958 Hanford, CA [I]   **1980** GB 15 (1)   **1981** GB 16 (16, LCB)   **1982**†GB 9 (8, LCB)   **1983** GB 16 (16, LCB)   **1984** GB 16 (16, LCB)   **1985** GB 14 (14, LCB)   **1986** GB 16 (16, LCB)   **1987** GB 12 (12, LCB)   **1988** GB 15 (15, LCB)   **1989** GB 12 (10, LCB)   **1990** GB 16 (16, LCB)   **1991** SF 5 (4)   **1991**†NO 3 (2)   **NFL** 165 (146) [12 yrs]

LEE, MIKE   Michael, LB, 6´0˝/232 lbs; UNLV; B8/31/1951 San Diego, CA   **1974** SD 7

LEE, MONTE   Monte Vern, LB, 6´4˝/225 lbs; Texas; 1960: Phi, rnd 8/1961: Hou, rnd 5; B7/11/1938 Ballinger, TX   **1961** SL 12   **1963** Det 8   **1964** Det 14   **1965** Bal 5   **NFL** 39 [4 yrs]

LEE, OUDIOUS   Oudious, NT, 6´1˝/253 lbs; Nebraska; B6/14/1956 Omaha, NE   **1980** SL 1 (0)

LEE, RESHARD   ReShard, RB, 5´10˝/220 lbs; Middle Tennessee State; B10/12/1980 Brunswick, GA

2004	Dal	14(0)	27	128	4.7(14)	1	4	4	4.0(4)	0	—	—	—	—	—	—	—	—	—	—	k	—	6	489
2005	GB	7(1)	11	16	1.5(4)	0	1	5	5.0(5)	0	—	—	—	—	—	—	—	—	—	—	k	—	0	113
NFL	2	21(1)	38	144	3.8(14)	1	2	9	4.5(5)	0	—	—	—	—	—	—	—	—	—	—	k	—	6	602

LEE, RON   Ronnell, RB, 6´4˝/226 lbs; West Virginia; 1976: Bal, rnd 3; B9/17/1953 Bellaire, OH

1976	†Bal	14	41	220	5.4(69)	1	1	-9	-9.0(-9)	0	—	—	—	—	—	—	—	—	—	—	kp	—	6	200
1977	†Bal	13(4)	84	346	4.1(30)	3	10	60	6.0(15)	0	—	—	—	—	—	—	—	—	—	—	—	—	18	406
1978	Bal	15(4)	81	374	4.6(24)	1	13	109	8.4(24)	1	—	—	—	—	—	—	—	—	—	—	—	—	12	444
NFL	3	42(8)	206	940	4.6(69)	5	24	160	6.7(24)	1	—	—	—	—	—	—	—	—	—	—	kp	—	36	1049

LEE, RONNIE   Ronald Van, T-TE-G, 6´3˝/265 lbs; Baylor; 1979: Mia, rnd 3; B12/24/1956 Pine Bluff, AR   **1983** Atl 14 (0)   **1984**†Mia 16 (0)   **1985**†Mia 15 (13, RG)   **1986** Mia 10 (9, RG)   **1987** Mia 9 (9, RT)   **1988** Mia 16 (16, RT)   **1989** Mia 15 (15, RT)   **1990** Sea 15 (9, RT)   **1991** Sea 10 (7, rt)   **1992** Sea 9 (5, rt)

1979	†Mia	16(2)	—	—	—	—	2	14	7.0(10)	0	—	—	—	—	—	—	—	—	—	—	—	—	0	7
1980	Mia	16(13, TE)	—	—	—	—	7	83	11.9(41)	2	—	—	—	—	—	—	—	—	—	—	—	—	12	52
1981	†Mia	16(16, TE)	—	—	—	—	14	64	4.6(11)	1	—	—	—	—	—	—	—	—	—	—	—	—	6	37
1982	†Mia	9(5, te)	—	—	—	—	2	6	3.0(5)	0	—	—	—	—	—	—	—	—	—	—	—	—	0	3
NFL	14	186(119)	—	—	—	—	25	167	6.7(41)	3	—	—	—	—	—	—	—	—	—	—	—	—	18	99

LEE, SHAWN   Shawn Swaboda, DT-NT-DE, 6´2˝/300 lbs; North Alabama; 1988: TB, rnd 6; B10/24/1966 Brooklyn, NY   **1988** TB 15 (0)   **1989** TB 15 (3)   **1990**†Mia 13 (10, NT)   **1991** Mia 3 (2)   **1992**†SD 9 (1)   **1993** SD 16 (15, LDT)   **1994**†SD 15 (15, LDT)   **1995**†SD 16 (15, LDT)   **1996** SD 15 (7, ldt)   **1997** SD 16 (15, RDT)   **1998** ChiB 15 (14, RDE)   **NFL** 148 (97) [11 yrs]

LEE, WILLIE   Willie, DT, 6´5˝/249 lbs; Bethune-Cookman; 1976: KC, rnd 5; B7/13/1950 Daytona Beach, FL   **1976** KC 14 (3)   **1977** KC 14 (10, LDT)   **NFL** 28 (13) [2 yrs]

LEE, ZEPH   Zephrini, DB-RB, 6´3˝/208 lbs; USC; 1986: LARd, rnd 9; B6/17/1963 San Francisco, CA   **1987** Den 1 (0)   **1987** LARd 2 (0)   **1988** LARd 8 (1)   **1989** LARd 13 (6, ss)   **NFL** 24 (7) [3 yrs]

LEEMANS, TUFFY   Alphonse Emil, FB-TB-DB-QB, 6´0˝/195 lbs; Oregon; George Washington; 1936: NYG, rnd 2; B11/12/1912 Superior, WI, D1/19/1979 Hillsboro Beach, FL; HOF 1978

1936	NYG☆	12(4, FB)	**206**	**830**	4.0	2	4	22	5.5(8)	0	42	13	31.0	258	6.1	3	6	—	—	—	—	—	12	**765**
1937	NYG☆	9(4, FB)	144	429	3.0	0	11	157	14.3(18)	1	20	5	25.0	64	3.2	1	1	—	—	—	—	—	6	510
1938	†NYG★	10(3, FB)	121	463	3.8(75)	4	4	68	17.0(45)	0	42	19	45.2	249	5.9	3	6	—	—	—	—	—	24	437
1939	†NYG☆	10(2, FB)	128	429	3.4	3	8	185	23.1(50)	2	26	12	46.2	198	7.6	0	2	—	—	—	—	—	30	581
1940	NYG☆	10(2, FB)	132	474	3.6	1	—	—	—	—	31	15	48.4	159	5.1	2	3	—	—	—	i	—	6	449
1941	†NYG★	11(11, TB)	100	332	3.3(26)	4	—	—	—	—	66	31	47.0	475	7.2(44)	4	5	—	—	—	kpi	—	24	553
1942	NYG☆	8(6, TB)	51	116	2.3(16)	3	1	-10	-10.0(-10)	0	69	35	50.7	555	8.0(50)	7	4	—	—	—	p	—	18	310
1943	†NYG	10(1, TB)	37	59	1.6(13)	0	—	—	—	—	16	7	43.8	103	6.4(30)	2	5	—	—	—	kp	—	0	114
NFL	8	80(37)	919	3132	3.4(75)	17	28	422	15.1(50)	3	383	167	43.6	2318	6.1(50)	25	32	—	—	—	kpi	—	120	3716

LEETZOW, MAX   Max Arthur, DE-DT, 6´4˝/240 lbs; Idaho; 1965: Den, rnd 5/Min, rnd 14; B9/17/1943 Lodi, CA   **1965** Den-A 14 (RDE)   **1966** Den-A 14 (LDE)   **NFL** 28 [2 yrs]

YEAR	TEAM	G (GS, POS)	RUSH	YD	AVG (LG)	TD	REC	YD	AVG (LG)	TD	PASS	COMP	PCT	YD	AVG (LG)	TD	INT	SK	YD	QBR	KPR	OTD	PTS	TAY

LEEUWENBURG, DICK Richard Peter, T, 6´5˝/242 lbs; Stanford; 1964: Chi, rnd 11/Hou, rnd 17; B3/26/1942 Salt Lake City, UT **1965** ChiB 9

LEEUWENBURG, JAY Jay Robert, G-C-T, 6´3˝/294 lbs; Colorado; 1992: KC, rnd 9; B6/18/1969 St. Louis, MO **1992** ChiB 12 (0) **1993** ChiB 16 (16, RT) **1994**†ChiB 16 (16, RG) **1995** ChiB 16 (16, RG) **1996**†Ind 15 (7, rg) **1997** Ind 16 (16, C) **1998** Ind 16 (16, C) **1999** Cin 14 (9, RG) **2000** Was 16 (12, RG) **NFL** 137 (108) [9 yrs]

LEFEAR, BILLY William Ray, RB-WR, 5´11˝/197 lbs; Henderson State; 1972: Cle, rnd 9; B2/12/1950 Magnolia, AR

YEAR	TEAM	G (GS, POS)	RUSH	YD	AVG (LG)	TD	REC	YD	AVG (LG)	TD	PASS	COMP	PCT	YD	AVG (LG)	TD	INT	SK	YD	QBR	KPR	OTD	PTS	TAY
1972	†Cle	9	3	6	2.0(4)	0	—	—	—	—	—	—	—	—	—	—	—	—	—	—	k	—	0	54
1973	Cle	13(rb)	26	135	5.2(43)	0	5	38	7.6(13)	0	—	—	—	—	—	—	—	—	—	—	kp	—	0	282
1974	Cle	11	6	2	0.3(4)	0	4	21	5.3(8)	0	—	—	—	—	—	—	—	—	—	—	kp	—	0	188
1975	Cle	10	—	—	—	—	1	14	14.0(14)	0	—	—	—	—	—	—	—	—	—	—	kp	—	0	233
NFL	4	43	35	143	4.1(43)	0	10	73	7.3(14)	0	—	—	—	—	—	—	—	—	—	—	kp	—	0	757

LEFEBVRE, GIL Gilbert, B, 5´6˝/155 lbs; none; B3/10/1910 Douglas, AZ, D5/7/1987 Bellflower, CA

YEAR	TEAM	G (GS, POS)	RUSH	YD	AVG (LG)	TD	REC	YD	AVG (LG)	TD	PASS	COMP	PCT	YD	AVG (LG)	TD	INT	SK	YD	QBR	KPR	OTD	PTS	TAY
1933	Cin	10(1)	64	155	2.4	0	2	20	10.0	0	14	5	35.7	75	5.4	0	2	—	—	—	—	1	6	133
1934	Cin	4(0)	13	136	10.5	0	—	—	—	—	9	1	11.1	22	2.4(22)	0	0	—	—	—	—	—	0	147
1935	Det	1(0)	4	4	1.0	0	—	—	—	—	—	—	—	—	—	—	—	—	—	—	—	—	0	4
NFL	3	15(1)	81	295	3.6	0	2	20	10.0	0	23	6	26.1	97	4.2(22)	0	2	—	—	—	—	1	6	284

LEFORCE, CLYDE Clyde J., QB, 5´11˝/176 lbs; Tulsa; 1945: Det, rnd 19/1947: SF-A, rnd 1; B6/4/1923 Pawnee, OK

YEAR	TEAM	G (GS, POS)	RUSH	YD	AVG (LG)	TD	REC	YD	AVG (LG)	TD	PASS	COMP	PCT	YD	AVG (LG)	TD	INT	SK	YD	QBR	KPR	OTD	PTS	TAY
1947	Det	9(2, qb)	18	143	7.9(32)	0	—	—	—	—	175	94	53.7	1384	7.9(79)	13	20	—	—	65.0	kpi	—	0	184
1948	Det	12(2, qb)	28	86	3.1(18)	1	8	122	15.3(44)	3	101	50	49.5	912	9.0(83)	9	8	—	—	77.7	kpi	1	30	347
1949	Det	11(1, qb)	13	58	4.5(27)	1	—	—	—	—	112	53	47.3	665	5.9(40)	3	9	—	—	41.7	—	—	6	56
NFL	3	32(5)	59	287	4.9(32)	2	8	122	15.3(44)	3	388	197	50.8	2961	7.6(83)	25	37	—	—	58.1	kpi	1	36	587

LEFTRIDGE, DICK Jack Richard, FB, 6´2˝/240 lbs; West Virginia; 1966: Pit, rnd 1/Mia, rnd 4; B4/14/1944 Hinton, WV, D2/27/2004 Morgantown, WV

YEAR	TEAM	G (GS, POS)	RUSH	YD	AVG (LG)	TD	REC	YD	AVG (LG)	TD	PASS	COMP	PCT	YD	AVG (LG)	TD	INT	SK	YD	QBR	KPR	OTD	PTS	TAY
1966	Pit	4	8	17	2.1(5)	2	—	—	—	—	—	—	—	—	—	—	—	—	—	—	k	—	12	32

LEFTWICH, BYRON Byron Anton, QB, 6´5˝/245 lbs; Marshall; 2003: Jax, rnd 1; B1/14/1980 Washington, DC

YEAR	TEAM	G (GS, POS)	RUSH	YD	AVG (LG)	TD	REC	YD	AVG (LG)	TD	PASS	COMP	PCT	YD	AVG (LG)	TD	INT	SK	YD	QBR	KPR	OTD	PTS	TAY
2003	Jax	15(13, QB)	25	108	4.3(18)	2	—	—	—	—	418	239	57.2	2819	6.7(**84**)	14	16	19	90	73.0	—	—	12	968
2004	Jax	14(14, QB)	39	148	3.8(17)	2	1	-7	-7.0(-7)	0	441	267	60.5	2941	6.7(65)	15	10	25	114	82.2	—	—	12	1310
2005	†Jax	11(11, QB)	31	67	2.2(9)	2	—	—	—	—	302	175	57.9	2123	7.0(45)	15	5	23	110	89.3	—	—	12	1024
NFL	3	40(38)	95	323	3.4(18)	6	1	-7	-7.0(-7)	0	1161	681	58.7	7883	6.8(84)	44	31	67	314	80.8	—	—	36	3301

LEGETTE, BURNIE Burnie A., RB, 6´1˝/243 lbs; Michigan; B12/5/1970 Colorado Springs, CO **1993** NE 7 (0) **1994** NE 3 (0) **NFL** 10 (0) [2 yrs]

LEGETTE, TYRONE Tyrone Christopher, DB, 5´9˝/179 lbs; Nebraska; 1992: NO, rnd 3; B2/15/1970 Marion, SC **1992** NO 8 (0) **1993** NO 14 (1) **1994** NO 15 (2) **1995** NO 16 (1) **1996** TB 15 (0) **1997**†TB 16 (1) **1998** SF 7 (0) **NFL** 91 (5) [7 yrs]

LEGGETT, BRAD Brad, C, 6´4˝/270 lbs; USC; 1990: Den, rnd 8; B1/16/1966 Vckburg, MS **1991** NO 4 (2)

LEGGETT, DAVE William David, QB-DB, 6´2˝/198 lbs; Ohio State; 1955: ChiC, rnd 7; B9/18/1933 New Philadelphia, OH

YEAR	TEAM	G (GS, POS)	RUSH	YD	AVG (LG)	TD	REC	YD	AVG (LG)	TD	PASS	COMP	PCT	YD	AVG (LG)	TD	INT	SK	YD	QBR	KPR	OTD	PTS	TAY
1955	ChiC	4	—	—	—	—	—	—	—	—	1	0	0.0	0	0.0	0	0	—	—	—	—	—	0	0

LEGGETT, EARL Earl Franklin, DT-DE, 6´3˝/265 lbs; LSU; 1957: ChiB, rnd 1; B3/5/1933 Palatka, FL **1957** ChiB 12 **1958** ChiB 12 **1959** ChiB 12 (LDE) **1960** ChiB 12 (LDT) **1962** ChiB 14 (RDT) **1963** ChiB 12 (RDT) **1964** ChiB 14 **1965** ChiB 14 (RDT) **1966** LARm 10 **1967** NO 6 **1968** NO 14 **NFL** 132 [11 yrs]

LEGGETT, SCOTT Scott Curtis, G-T, 6´3˝/285 lbs; Oklahoma; Central Oklahoma; B9/2/1962 Muskogee, OK **1987** Phi 2 (2)

LEGREE, LANCE Lance, DT-DE, 6´1˝/300 lbs; Notre Dame; B12/22/1977 Charleston, SC **2001** NYG 14 (2) **2002**†NYG 15 (10, RDT) **2003** NYG 16 (2) **2004** NYG 15 (7, lde) **2005** NYJ 16 (4) **NFL** 76 (25) [5 yrs]

LEHAN, MICHAEL Michael, DB, 6´0˝/190 lbs; Minnesota; 2003: Cle, rnd 5; B11/25/1979 Hopkins, MN **2003** Cle 12 (2) **2004** Cle 10 (2) **2005** Cle 10 (0) **NFL** 32 (4) [3 yrs]

LEHMAN, TEDDY Teddy, LB, 6´2˝/243 lbs; Oklahoma; 2004: Det, rnd 2; B11/18/1981 Tulsa, OK **2004** Det 16 (16, MLB) **2005** Det 5 (0) **NFL** 21 (16) [2 yrs]

LEHR, MATT Matthew Steven, C-G, 6´3˝/300 lbs; Virginia Tech; 2001: Dal, rnd 5; B4/25/1979 Jacksonville, FL **2001** Dal 8 (0) **2002** Dal 12 (4) **2003**†Dal 16 (16, C) **2004** Dal 7 (2) **2005** Atl 15 (15, LG) **NFL** 58 (37) [5 yrs]

LEHRER, CHRIS Christopher, HB-FB, /185 lbs; none; B1894, deceased **1922** Roc 2 (1)

LEICHT, JAKE Jacob, HB-DB, 5´9˝/170 lbs; Oregon; 1946: Was, rnd 10; B10/1/1920 Jamestown, ND

YEAR	TEAM	G (GS, POS)	RUSH	YD	AVG (LG)	TD	REC	YD	AVG (LG)	TD	PASS	COMP	PCT	YD	AVG (LG)	TD	INT	SK	YD	QBR	KPR	OTD	PTS	TAY
1948	†Bal-A	14(1)	20	88	4.4	1	12	134	11.2	1	—	—	—	—	—	—	—	—	—	—	kpi	—	12	358
1949	Bal-A	12(6, LH)	6	-7	-1.2	0	1	12	12.0(12)	0	—	—	—	—	—	—	—	—	—	—	kp	—	0	114
AAFC	2	26(7)	26	81	3.1	1	13	146	11.2(12)	1	—	—	—	—	—	—	—	—	—	—	kpi	—	12	472

LEIDING, JEFF Jeffrey James, LB, 6´3˝/232 lbs; Texas; 1984: SL, rnd 5; B10/28/1961 Kansas City, MO **1986** Ind 12 (0) **1987** Ind 9 (3) **NFL** 21 (3) [2 yrs]

LEIGEB, BRIAN Brian, DB, 6´2˝/207 lbs; Central Michigan; B10/2/1978 Midland, MI **2002**†Ind 15 (0)

LEIGH, CHARLIE Charles Irving, RB, 5´11˝/206 lbs; none; B10/29/1945 Halifax, VA

YEAR	TEAM	G (GS, POS)	RUSH	YD	AVG (LG)	TD	REC	YD	AVG (LG)	TD	PASS	COMP	PCT	YD	AVG (LG)	TD	INT	SK	YD	QBR	KPR	OTD	PTS	TAY
1968	†Cle	14	23	144	6.3(20)	1	3	-4	-1.3(4)	0	—	—	—	—	—	—	—	—	—	—	kp	—	6	270
1969	†Cle	13	—	—	—	—	2	-9	-4.5(-4)	0	—	—	—	—	—	—	—	—	—	—	kp	—	0	-36
1971	†Mia	14	5	15	3.0(7)	0	—	—	—	—	—	—	—	—	—	—	—	—	—	—	k	—	0	54
1972	†Mia	14	21	79	3.8(10)	0	—	—	—	—	—	—	—	—	—	—	—	—	—	—	kp	—	0	242
1973	†Mia	14	22	134	6.1(34)	1	4	9	2.3(7)	0	—	—	—	—	—	—	—	—	—	—	kp	—	6	284
1974	Mia	1	—	—	—	—	—	—	—	—	—	—	—	—	—	—	—	—	—	—	k	—	0	20
1974	GB	10	1	0	0.0(0)	0	—	—	—	—	—	—	—	—	—	—	—	—	—	—	k	—	0	66
NFL	6	80	72	372	5.2(34)	2	9	-4	-0.4(7)	0	—	—	—	—	—	—	—	—	—	—	kp	—	12	900

LEIGHTY, DUTCH Orland Freed, HB, 5´11˝/168 lbs; Georgetown (DC); B12/29/1895 Lincoln Township, PA, deceased **1921** Was 2 (1)

LEIKER, TONY Anthony Wade, DE, 6´5˝/250 lbs; Stanford; 1987: GB, rnd 7; B9/26/1964 Hays, KS **1987** GB 1 (1)

LEISK, RUBE Charles Wardell, G, 6´0˝/195 lbs; LSU; B7/12/1915 Shreveport, LA **1937** Bkn 11 (7, LG)

LEISLE, RODNEY Rodney Allen, DT, 6´3˝/294 lbs; UCLA; 2004: NO, rnd 5; B2/5/1981 Fresno, CA **2004** NO 2 (0) **2005** NO 1 (0) **NFL** 3 (0) [2 yrs]

LEITH, AL Alfred, aka AL Leth, BB-QB, 5´9˝/175 lbs; Pennsylvania; B3/14/1903 Brooklyn, NY, D4/12/1969 Media, PA **1926** Bkn 7 (3)

LEJEUNE, NORMAN Norman, DB, 6´0˝/207 lbs; LSU; 2003: Phi, rnd 7; B5/10/1980 Baton Rouge, LA **2005** Mia 5 (0)

LEJEUNE, WALT Walter, aka Walt Jean, G-C-T-B, 6´0˝/231 lbs; Heidelberg; Bethany (WV); B1/2/1898 Chillicothe, OH **1922** Akr 8 (8, LG), 24 **1923** Akr 7 (5, LG) **1924** Mil☆10 (9, LG) **1925** GB 9 (4) **1925** Fra 3 (2) **1926** GB 10 (6, lg) **1927** Pot 3 (1) **NFL** 50 (35) [6 yrs]

LEKKERKERKER, BRAD Brad, T, 6´7˝/330 lbs; California-Davis; B5/8/1978 Chino, CA **2005** Oak 1 (0)

LEKKERKERKER, CORY Cory, T, 6´7˝/324 lbs; California-Davis; B7/25/1981 Chino, CA **2005** SD 1 (0)

LELIE, ASHLEY Ashley Jovon, WR, 6´3˝/200 lbs; Hawaii; 2002: Den, rnd 1; B2/16/1980 Bellflower, CA

YEAR	TEAM	G (GS, POS)	RUSH	YD	AVG (LG)	TD	REC	YD	AVG (LG)	TD	PASS	COMP	PCT	YD	AVG (LG)	TD	INT	SK	YD	QBR	KPR	OTD	PTS	TAY
2002	Den	16(1)	4	40	10.0(24)	0	35	525	15.0(48)	2	—	—	—	—	—	—	—	—	—	—	—	—	12	313
2003	†Den	16(10, WR)	8	43	5.4(13)	0	37	628	17.0(60)	2	—	—	—	—	—	—	—	—	—	—	—	—	12	367
2004	†Den	16(16, WR)	3	5	1.7(8)	0	54	1084	**20.1**(**58**)	7	—	—	—	—	—	—	—	—	—	—	—	—	42	582
2005	†Den	16(13, WR)	5	84	16.8(39)	0	42	770	**18.3**(**56**)	1	—	—	—	—	—	—	—	—	—	—	—	—	6	474
NFL	4	64(40)	20	172	8.6(39)	0	168	3007	17.9(60)	12	—	—	—	—	—	—	—	—	—	—	—	—	72	1736

LEMASTER, FRANK Frank Preston, LB, 6´2˝/232 lbs; Kentucky; 1974: Phi, rnd 4; B3/12/1952 Lexington, KY

YEAR	TEAM	G (GS, POS)	RUSH	YD	AVG (LG)	TD	REC	YD	AVG (LG)	TD	PASS	COMP	PCT	YD	AVG (LG)	TD	INT	SK	YD	QBR	KPR	OTD	PTS	TAY
1974	Phi	14	—	—	—	—	—	—	—	—	—	—	—	—	—	—	—	—	—	—	—	—	—	—
1975	Phi	14(14, LLB)	—	—	—	—	—	—	—	—	—	—	—	—	—	—	—	—	—	—	i	1	6	123
1976	Phi	14(14, LLB)	—	—	—	—	1	-4	-4.0(-4)	0	—	—	—	—	—	—	—	—	—	—	—	—	0	-2
1977	Phi	14(14, RILB)	1	30	30.0(30)	0	—	—	—	—	—	—	—	—	—	—	—	—	—	—	—	—	0	30
1978	†Phi	16(16, RILB)	2	29	14.5(23)	0	—	—	—	—	—	—	—	—	—	—	—	—	—	—	i	1	6	46
1979	†Phi	16(16, RILB)	1	15	15.0(15)	0	—	—	—	—	—	—	—	—	—	—	—	—	—	—	—	—	0	15
1980	†Phi	16(16, RILB)	2	21	10.5(11)	0	—	—	—	—	—	—	—	—	—	—	—	—	—	—	i	—	0	23
1981	†Phi✧	16(16, RILB)	1	7	7.0(7)	0	—	—	—	—	—	—	—	—	—	—	—	—	—	—	i	1	6	25

YEAR	TEAM	G(GS, POS)	RUSH	YD	AVG(LG)	TD	REC	YD	AVG(LG)	TD	PASS COMP	PCT	YD	AVG(LG)	TD	INT	SK	YD	QBR	KPR	OTD	PTS	TAY
1982	Phi	9(9, RILB)	1	-1	-1.0(-1)	0	—	—	—	0	—	—	—	—	—	—	—	—	—	S	—	0	-1
NFL	9	129(115)	8	101	12.6(30)	0	1	-4	-4.0(-4)	0	—	—	—	—	—	—	—	—	—	iS	3	18	259

LEMEK, RAY   Raymond Edward, T-G, 6´0˝/238 lbs; Notre Dame; 1956: Was, rnd 19; B6/28/1934 Sioux City, IA, D9/17/2005 Readfield, ME   **1957** Was 12 (12, RT)
1958 Was 12 (12, RT)   **1959** Was 11 (10, RT)   **1960** Was 12 (12, RT)   **1961** Was◊14 (LG)   **1962** Pit☆14 (RG)   **1963** Pit 14 (RG)   **1964** Pit 14 (RG)   **1965** Pit 14   **NFL** 117 (46) [9 yrs]

LEMMERMAN, BRUCE   Bruce, QB, 6´1˝/206 lbs; Cal State-Northridge; B10/4/1945 Los Angeles, CA

YEAR	TEAM	G(GS, POS)	RUSH	YD	AVG(LG)	TD	REC	YD	AVG(LG)	TD	PASS COMP	PCT	YD	AVG(LG)	TD	INT	SK	YD	QBR	KPR	OTD	PTS	TAY
1968	Atl	4	1	0	0.0(0)	0	—	—	—	—	15	3	20.0	40	2.7(18)	0	1	—	—	—	—	0	-20
1969	Atl	7	10	57	5.7(20)	0	—	—	—	—	62	25	40.3	330	5.3(57)	1	4	14	106	—	—	6	77
NFL	2	11	11	57	5.2(20)	1	—	—	—	—	77	28	36.4	370	4.8(57)	1	5	14	106	—	—	6	57

LEMOINE, JIM   James Douglas, TE-G, 6´2˝/250 lbs; Utah State; 1967: Buf, rnd 2; B4/29/1945 Alameda, CA   **1967** Buf-A 8   **1968** Hou-A 13   **1969**†Hou-A 14   **NFL** 35 [3 yrs]

LEMON, CLEO   Cleo, QB, 6´2˝/215 lbs; Arkansas State; B8/16/1979 Greenwood, MS   **2005** SD 1 (0)

LEMON, CLIFF   Clifton Wilson, E, 5´9˝/190 lbs; Centre; B4/15/1901 Paducah, KY, D11/9/1955 Louisville, KY   **1926** ChiB 2 (0)

LEMON, MIKE   Michael Donald, LB, 6´2˝/218 lbs; Kansas; 1975: NO, rnd 6; B2/26/1951 Topeka, KS   **1975** NO 2   **1975** Den 1   **1976** TB 5 (1)   **1977** TB 14   **NFL** 22 (1) [3 yrs]

LEMONS, DEVIN   Devin Wayne, LB, 6´2˝/232 lbs; Texas Tech; B3/20/1979 Bryan, TX   **2004** Was 1 (0)

LENC, GEORGE   George C., E, 6´3˝/204 lbs; Augustana (IL); 1939: Bkn, rnd 11; B3/17/1917 Chicago, IL, D11/16/1942 Pasco, WA   **1939** Bkn 2 (0)

LENKAITIS, BILL   Bill Edward, C-G, 6´4˝/255 lbs; Penn State; 1968: SD, rnd 2; B6/30/1946 Cleveland, OH   **1968** SD-A 6   **1969** SD-A 14 (9, LG)   **1970** SD 9 (7, LG)
1971 NE 14 (2)   **1972** NE 12 (4)   **1973** NE 12 (12, C)   **1974** NE 14 (14, C)   **1975** NE 11 (11, C)   **1976**†NE 14 (14, C)   **1977** NE 14 (14, C)   **1978**†NE 16 (16, C)   **1979** NE 16 (16, C)
1980 NE 16 (16, C)   **1981** NE 12 (0)   **NFL** 180 (135) [14 yrs]

LENNAN, REID   Reid Burgess, G-C-T, 6´0˝/232 lbs; none; B8/17/1920 Baltimore, MD, D2/10/1979   **1945** Was 10 (0)

1947 LAD-A 7 (2)

LENON, PARIS   Paris Michael, LB, 6´2˝/240 lbs; Richmond; B11/26/1977 Lynchburg, VA   **2002**†GB 16 (0)   **2003**†GB 16 (0)   **2004**†GB 16 (4)   **2005** GB 16 (12, LLB/rlb)
NFL 64 (16) [4 yrs]

LENS, GREG   Gregory Joseph, DT, 6´5˝/261 lbs; Trinity (TX); 1970: SL, rnd 4; B3/11/1945 Marshall, MN   **1970** Atl 14 (LDT)   **1971** Atl 7   **NFL** 21 [2 yrs]

LENSING, VINCE   Vincent H., G-T, 6´0˝/200 lbs; General Motors Institute; B1/26/1901 Evansville, IN, D8/26/1951 Evansville, IN   **1921** Evv 5 (1)

LENTZ, JACK   Henry Edgar, DB, 6´0˝/190 lbs; Holy Cross; 1967: Den, rnd 16; B2/22/1945 Baltimore, MD   **1967** Den-A 14 (RS)   **1968** Den-A 12 (RS)   **NFL** 26 [2 yrs]

LENTZ, PESKY   Lawrence H., FB, 5´10˝/175 lbs; Wittenberg; B10/11/1897, D5/30/1966 Baltimore, MD   **1920** Day 2 (0)

LEO, BOBBY   Robert Samuel, RB-WR, 5´10˝/180 lbs; Harvard; 1967: Bos, rnd 7; B1/19/1945 Everett, MA   **1968** Bos-A 1

YEAR	TEAM	G(GS, POS)	RUSH	YD	AVG(LG)	TD	REC	YD	AVG(LG)	TD	PASS COMP	PCT	YD	AVG(LG)	TD	INT	SK	YD	QBR	KPR	OTD	PTS	TAY
1967	Bos-A	2	1	7	7.0(7)	0	1	25	25.0(25)	1	—	—	—	—	—	—	—	—	—	kp	—	6	121
NFL	2	1	7	7.0(7)	0	1	25	25.0(25)	1	—	—	—	—	—	—	—	—	—	kp	—	6	123

LEO, CHARLEY   Charles James, G, 6´0˝/240 lbs; Indiana; B8/29/1934 Niagara Falls, NY   **1960** Bos-A☆(LG)   **1961** Bos-A★14 (RG)   **1962** Bos-A 7   **1963** Buf-A 4   **NFL** 38 [4 yrs]

LEO, JIM   James Phillip, DE-LB, 6´1˝/225 lbs; Cincinnati; 1960: NYG, rnd 3/Buf, rnd 1; B6/18/1937 Niagara Falls, NY   **1960** NYG 12   **1961** Min 14   **1962** Min 14 (14, LDE)
NFL 40 (14) [3 yrs]

LEON, TONY   Anthony David, G-LB, 5´9˝/203 lbs; Alabama; 1943: Was, rnd 8; B2/18/1917 Follansbee, WV   **1943**†Was 6 (0)   **1944** Bkn 10 (10, RG)   **1945** Bos 10 (8, RG)
1946 Bos 10 (1)   **NFL** 36 (19) [4 yrs]

LEONARD, BILL   William George, DE, 6´2˝/200 lbs; Notre Dame; B4/27/1927 Youngstown, OH   **1949** Bal-A 11 (2)

LEONARD, CECIL   Cecil, DB, 5´11˝/160 lbs; Tuskegee; 1969: NYJ, rnd 8; B7/20/1946 Sylacauga, AL   **1969** NYJ-A 8   **1970** NYJ 5   **NFL** 13 [2 yrs]

LEONARD, JIM   James Michael, T, 6´0˝/205 lbs; Geneseo State; Colgate; B1/2/1899 Geneseo, NY, D2/2/1979 Naples, FL   **1923** Roc 3 (2, LT)

LEONARD, JIM   James Raymond, B, 6´0˝/204 lbs; Notre Dame; B2/14/1910 Pedricktown, NJ, D11/28/1993 Woodbury, NJ **[C]**

YEAR	TEAM	G(GS, POS)	RUSH	YD	AVG(LG)	TD	REC	YD	AVG(LG)	TD	PASS COMP	PCT	YD	AVG(LG)	TD	INT	SK	YD	QBR	KPR	OTD	PTS	TAY
1934	Phi	9(5, bb)	55	207	3.8	1	3	7	2.3	0	10	2	20.0	29	2.9	0	0	—	—	—	—	6	235
1935	Phi	11(11, FB)	74	171	2.3	1	—	—	—	—	32	11	34.4	119	3.7	0	3	—	—	—	—	6	121
1936	Phi	10(10, BB)	33	72	2.2	1	5	46	9.2	1	6	2	33.3	45	7.5	0	2	—	—	—	—	6	43
1937	Phi	2(0)																					
NFL	4	32(26)	162	450	2.8	2	8	53	6.6	1	48	15	31.3	193	4.0	0	5	—	—	—	—	18	398

LEONARD, JIM   James Francis, G-C, 6´3˝/258 lbs; Santa Clara; 1980: TB, rnd 7; B10/19/1957 Santa Cruz, CA   **1980** TB 16 (2)   **1981**†TB 16 (3)   **1982**†TB 9 (3)   **1983** TB 15 (1)
1985 SF 9 (0)   **1985** SD 7 (1)   **1986** SD 15 (5, lg)   **NFL** 87 (17) [6 yrs]

LEONARD, JOHN   John Edward, T, 6´2˝/200 lbs; Indiana; B5/13/1896 Bloomington, IN, D10/2/1980 Neshanic, NJ   **1922** ChiC 5 (2)   **1923** ChiC 6 (6, RT)   **NFL** 11 (8) [2 yrs]

LEONARD, MATT   Molia Matthew, DT, 6´3˝/301 lbs; Stanford; B11/7/1979 Agua Dulce, CA   **2003** Jax 4 (0)

LEONARD, TONY   Anthony, DB, 5´11˝/170 lbs; Virginia Union; 1976: SF, rnd 5; B2/28/1953 Richmond, VA **[R]**   **1976** SF 14 (1)   **1977** SF 13 (13, LCB)   **1978** SF 12 (10, LCB)
1978 Det 3   **1979** Det 1   **NFL** 43 (24) [4 yrs]

LEONETTI, BOB   Robert Phillip, G, 6´0˝/230 lbs; Wake Forest; 1947: SF-A, rnd 9/Phi, rnd 9; B1/1/1923 Mount Carmel, PA, D8/1973   **1948** Buf-A 2 (0)   **1948** Bkn-A 9 (0)
AAFC 11 (0) [1 yr]

LEONHARD, JIM   Jim, DB, 5´8˝/190 lbs; Wisconsin; B10/27/1982 Tony, WI   **2005** Buf 10 (0)

LEOPOLD, BOBBY   Leroy Joseph, LB, 6´1˝/215 lbs; Notre Dame; 1980: SF, rnd 8; B10/18/1957 Port Arthur, TX   **1980** SF 16 (15, RLB/rolb)   **1981**†SF 16 (2)   **1982** SF 6 (0)
1983†SF 16 (3)   **1986** GB 12 (7, rolb)   **NFL** 66 (27) [5 yrs]

LEPPER, BARNEY   Bernard, T, 5´10˝/185 lbs; none; B2/19/1898 Buffalo, NY, D12/1/1985 Miami, FL   **1920** Buf 5 (0)

LEPSIS, MATT   Matthew, T, 6´4˝/290 lbs; Colorado; B1/13/1974 Conroe, TX   **1998**†Den 16 (0)   **1999** Den 16 (16, RT)   **2000**†Den 16 (16, RT)   **2001** Den 16 (16, RT)
2002 Den 16 (15, RT)   **2003**†Den 16 (16, RT)   **2004**†Den 16 (16, LT)   **2005**†Den 16 (16, LT)   **NFL** 128 (111) [8 yrs]

LEROY, EMARLOS   Emarlos S., DT, 6´1˝/304 lbs; Georgia; 1999: Jax, rnd 6; B7/31/1975 Albany, GA   **1999**†Jax 13 (0)   **2000** Jax 9 (1)   **NFL** 22 (1) [2 yrs]

LESANE, JIMMY   James Edwin, DB-HB, 5´10˝/176 lbs; The Citadel; Virginia; 1952: ChiB, rnd 20; B3/8/1930 Raleigh, NC

YEAR	TEAM	G(GS, POS)	RUSH	YD	AVG(LG)	TD	REC	YD	AVG(LG)	TD	PASS COMP	PCT	YD	AVG(LG)	TD	INT	SK	YD	QBR	KPR	OTD	PTS	TAY
1952	ChiB	10(DB)	1	5	5.0(5)	0	—	—	—	—	1	0	0.0	0	0	0	0	—	—	—	p	—	0	-15
1954	ChiB	3	—	—	—	—	—	—	—	—	1	0	0.0	0	0	0	0	—	—	—	kp	—	0	14
1954	Bal	4	—	—	—	—	—	—	—	—	—	—	—	—	—	—	—	—	—	—	—	—	
NFL	2	17	1	5	5.0(5)	0	—	—	—	—	2	0	0.0	0	0	0	0	—	—	—	kp	—	0	-1

LESHINSKI, RON   Ronald F., TE, 6´2˝/248 lbs; Army; B3/6/1974 Sandusky, OH   **1999** Phi 1 (0)

LESTER, DARRELL   Darrell George, C, 6´3˝/220 lbs; TCU; 1936: GB, rnd 5; B4/29/1914 Jacksonboro, TX, D7/30/1993 Temple, TX   **1937** GB 8 (1)   **1938** GB 8 (0)   **NFL** 16 (1) [2 yrs]

LESTER, DARRELL   Marcus Darrell, FB, 6´2˝/228 lbs; LSU; McNeese State; 1964: Min, rnd 9; B11/6/1940 Lake Charles, LA

YEAR	TEAM	G(GS, POS)	RUSH	YD	AVG(LG)	TD	REC	YD	AVG(LG)	TD	PASS COMP	PCT	YD	AVG(LG)	TD	INT	SK	YD	QBR	KPR	OTD	PTS	TAY
1964	Min	6	4	18	4.5(7)	0	—	—	—	—	—	—	—	—	—	—	—	—	—	—	—	0	18
1965	Den-A	12																					
1966	Den-A	11	34	84	2.5(10)	0	2	26	13.0(21)	1	—	—	—	—	—	—	—	—	—	kp	—	6	94
NFL	3	29	38	102	2.7(10)	0	2	26	13.0(21)	1	—	—	—	—	—	—	—	—	—	kp	—	6	112

LESTER, KEITH   Keith, TE, 6´5˝/235 lbs; Florida State; Murray State; 1985: Cin, rnd 6; B5/28/1962   **1987** Ind 1 (0)

LESTER, PINKY   Harold W., E-T, 5´6˝/160 lbs; none; B3/13/1900 New London, CT, D1/1/1972 Providence, RI   **1926** Pro 8 (5, le)

LESTER, TIM   Timothy Lee, RB, 5´10˝/233 lbs; Eastern Kentucky; 1992: LARm, rnd 10; B6/15/1968 Miami, FL

YEAR	TEAM	G(GS, POS)	RUSH	YD	AVG(LG)	TD	REC	YD	AVG(LG)	TD	PASS COMP	PCT	YD	AVG(LG)	TD	INT	SK	YD	QBR	KPR	OTD	PTS	TAY
1992	LARm	11(0)																					
1993	LARm	16(14, FB)	11	74	6.7(26)	0	18	154	8.6(21)	0	—	—	—	—	—	—	—	—	—	—	—	0	151
1994	LARm	14(4)	7	14	2.0(8)	0	1	1	1.0(1)	0	—	—	—	—	—	—	—	—	—	k	—	0	8
1995	†Pit	6(1)	5	9	1.8(3)	1	—	—	—	—	—	—	—	—	—	—	—	—	—	—	—	6	19
1996	†Pit	16(13, FB)	8	20	2.5(5)	1	7	70	10.0(19)	0	—	—	—	—	—	—	—	—	—	—	—	6	65
1997	†Pit	16(13, FB)	2	9	4.5(6)	0	10	51	5.1(14)	0	—	—	—	—	—	—	—	—	—	—	—	0	35

YEAR	TEAM	G (GS, POS)	RUSH	YD	AVG (LG)	TD	REC	YD	AVG (LG)	TD	PASS	COMP	PCT	YD	AVG (LG)	TD	INT	SK	YD	QBR	KPR	OTD	PTS	TAY
1998	Pit	9 (7, fb)	—	—	—	—	9	46	5.1 (9)	0	—	—	—	—	—	—	—	—	—	—	—	—	0	23
1999	Dal	5 (2)	—	—	—	—	2	9	4.5 (6)	0	—	—	—	—	—	—	—	—	—	—	—	—	0	5
NFL	8	93 (54)	33	126	3.8 (26)	2	47	331	7.0 (21)	0	—	—	—	—	—	—	—	—	—	—	k	—	12	305

LeSueur, Jeremy Jeremy, DB, 6´0˝/197 lbs; Michigan; 2004: Den, rnd 3; B10/5/1980 Holly Springs, MS **2005** NYJ 3 (0)

Lethridge, Zebbie Zebbie D., DB, 6´0˝/190 lbs; Texas Tech; B1/31/1975 Lubbock, TX **2001** Mia 2 (0)

Letlow, Russ Willard Russell, G-T, 6´0˝/214 lbs; San Francisco; 1936: GB, rnd 1; B10/5/1913 Dinuba, CA, D10/12/1987 San Luis Obispo County, CA **1936** GB 8 (2) **1937** GB☆11 (5, LG) **1938**†GB★11 (7, LG) **1939**†GB★10 (6, LG) **1940** GB☆11 (7, LG) **1941** GB 4 (0) **1942** GB 11 (2) **1946** GB 5 (1) **NFL** 71 (30) [8 yrs]

Letner, Cotton Robert Gene, LB, 6´1˝/215 lbs; Tennessee; B1/26/1937 Ten Mile, TN **1961** Buf-A 5

Letsinger, Jim John Howard, G, 5´10˝/190 lbs; Purdue; B11/17/1911 Jasonville, IN, D1/31/2002 Bloomington, IN **1933** Pit 1 (1)

Lett, Leon Leon, DT-DE, 6´6˝/290 lbs; Emporia State; 1991: Dal, rnd 7; B10/12/1968 Mobile, AL **1991**†Dal 5 (0) **1992**†Dal 16 (0) **1993**†Dal 11 (6, rdt) **1994**†Dal★16 (16, RDT) **1995**†Dal 12 (12, RDT) **1996** Dal 13 (13, RDT) **1997** Dal 3 (3) **1998**†Dal✧16 (15, LDT) **1999**†Dal 8 (1) **2000** Dal 9 (7, RDT) **2001** Den 12 (0) **NFL** 121 (73) [11 yrs]

Levanitis, Steve Steven Joseph, T, 6´1˝/220 lbs; Boston College; B3/26/1920 Cambridge, MA, D3/28/1997 Easton, MA **1942** Phi 5 (0)

Levanti, Lou Louis Michael, C-LB, 6´1˝/215 lbs; Illinois; 1947: LARm, rnd 23/1948: Bal-A, rnd 25; B4/4/1923 West Frankfort, IL, D11/15/1997 **1952** Pit 6

LeVeck, Jack John Charles, LB, 6´0˝/225 lbs; Ohio University; B2/3/1950 Columbus, OH **1973** SL 11 **1974**†SL 13 **1975** Cle 7 **NFL** 31 [3 yrs]

Levels, Dwayne Dwayne, LB, 6´2˝/248 lbs; Oklahoma State; B5/9/1979 Richardson, TX **2003** Cin 13 (1)

Levenick, Dave David John, LB, 6´3˝/222 lbs; Wisconsin; 1982: Atl, rnd 12; B5/28/1959 Milwaukee, WI **1983** Atl 16 (0) **1984** Atl 8 (0) **NFL** 24 (0) [2 yrs]

Levens, Dorsey Herbert Dorsey, RB, 6´1˝/230 lbs; Notre Dame; Georgia Tech; 1994: GB, rnd 5; B5/21/1970 Syracuse, NY

YEAR	TEAM	G (GS, POS)	RUSH	YD	AVG (LG)	TD	REC	YD	AVG (LG)	TD	PASS	COMP	PCT	YD	AVG (LG)	TD	INT	SK	YD	QBR	KPR	OTD	PTS	TAY
1994	†GB	14 (0)	5	15	3.0 (5)	0	1	9	9.0 (9)	0	—	—	—	—	—	—	—	—	—	—	k	—	0	21
1995	†GB	15 (12, RB)	36	120	3.3 (22)	3	48	434	9.0 (27)	4	—	—	—	—	—	—	—	—	—	—	—	—	42	387
1996	†GB	16 (1)	121	566	4.7 (24)	5	31	226	7.3 (49)	5	—	—	—	—	—	—	—	—	—	—	k	—	60	763
1997	†GB★	16 (16, RB)	329	1435	4.4 (52)	7	53	370	7.0 (56)	5	—	—	—	—	—	—	—	—	—	—	—	—	74	1715
1998	†GB	7 (4)	115	378	3.3 (50)	1	27	162	6.0 (17)	0	—	—	—	—	—	—	—	—	—	—	—	—	6	469
1999	GB	14 (14, RB)	279	1034	3.7 (36)	9	71	573	8.1 (53)	1	—	—	—	—	—	—	—	—	—	—	—	—	60	1416
2000	GB	5 (5, rb)	77	224	2.9 (17)	3	16	146	9.1 (37)	0	—	—	—	—	—	—	—	—	—	—	—	—	18	327
2001	†GB	15 (1)	44	165	3.8 (40)	0	24	159	6.6 (19)	1	—	—	—	—	—	—	—	—	—	—	k	—	6	402
2002	†Phi	16 (0)	75	411	5.5 (47)	1	19	124	6.5 (24)	1	2	0	0.0	0	0.0	0	0	—	—	—	k	—	12	497
2003	NYG	11 (0)	68	197	2.9 (17)	3	5	39	7.8 (11)	0	—	—	—	—	—	—	—	—	—	—	—	—	18	247
2004	†Phi	15 (5, rb)	94	410	4.4 (45)	4	9	92	10.2 (23)	0	—	—	—	—	—	—	—	—	—	—	—	—	24	496
NFL	11	144 (58)	1243	4955	4.0 (52)	36	304	2334	7.7 (56)	17	2	0	0.0	0	0.0	0	0	—	—	—	k	—	320	6738

Levenseller, Mike Michael Thomas, WR, 6´1˝/180 lbs; Washington State; 1978: Oak, rnd 6; B2/21/1956 Bremerton, WA **1978** Buf 2 **1978** TB 2 **1979** Cin 12

YEAR	TEAM	G (GS, POS)	RUSH	YD	AVG (LG)	TD	REC	YD	AVG (LG)	TD	PASS	COMP	PCT	YD	AVG (LG)	TD	INT	SK	YD	QBR	KPR	OTD	PTS	TAY
1980	Cin	8 (0)	1	6	6.0 (6)	0	2	30	15.0 (22)	0	—	—	—	—	—	—	—	—	—	—	—	—	0	21
NFL	3	24	1	6	6.0 (6)	0	2	30	15.0 (22)	0	—	—	—	—	—	—	—	—	—	—	p	—	0	47

Leverette, Otis Otis Catrell, DE, 6´6˝/278 lbs; Alabama-Birmingham; 2001: Mia, rnd 6; B5/31/1978 Americus, GA **2001** Was 4 (0) **2002** Was 1 (0) **2003** SD 7 (0) **2004** SF 5 (1) **NFL** 17 (1) [4 yrs]

Levey, Jim James Julius, B, 5´10˝/156 lbs; none; B9/13/1906 Pittsburgh, PA, D3/14/1970 Dallas, TX

YEAR	TEAM	G (GS, POS)	RUSH	YD	AVG (LG)	TD	REC	YD	AVG (LG)	TD	PASS	COMP	PCT	YD	AVG (LG)	TD	INT	SK	YD	QBR	KPR	OTD	PTS	TAY
1934	Pit	1 (1)	9	69	7.7	0	—	—	—	—	—	—	—	—	—	—	—	—	—	—	—	—	0	69
1935	Pit	8 (1)	42	61	1.5	2	7	112	16.0 (34)	2	4	1	25.0	4	1.0 (4)	0	0	—	—	—	—	—	24	149
1936	Pit	4 (0)	4	3	0.8	0	—	—	—	—	—	—	—	—	—	—	—	—	—	—	—	—	0	3
NFL	3	13 (2)	55	133	2.4	2	7	112	16.0 (34)	2	4	1	25.0	4	1.0 (4)	0	0	—	—	—	—	—	24	221

LeVias, Jerry Jerry, WR, 5´9˝/177 lbs; SMU; 1969: Hou, rnd 2; B9/5/1946 Beaumont, TX **[R]**

YEAR	TEAM	G (GS, POS)	RUSH	YD	AVG (LG)	TD	REC	YD	AVG (LG)	TD	PASS	COMP	PCT	YD	AVG (LG)	TD	INT	SK	YD	QBR	KPR	OTD	PTS	TAY
1969	†Hou-A✧	14 (wr)	6	18	3.0 (10)	0	42	696	16.6 (**86**)	5	2	0	0.0	0	0.0	0	0	—	—	—	kp	—	30	878
1970	Hou	14 (WR)	7	37	5.3 (24)	0	41	529	12.9 (63)	5	1	0	0.0	0	0.0	0	1	—	—	—	kp	—	30	583
1971	SD	14	4	73	18.3 (38)	0	21	265	12.6 (37)	1	—	—	—	—	—	—	—	—	—	—	kp	—	6	445
1972	SD	1	—	—	—	—	1	8	8.0 (8)	0	—	—	—	—	—	—	—	—	—	—	p	—	0	-5
1973	SD	14 (11, WR)	2	33	16.5 (22)	0	30	536	17.9 (69)	3	—	—	—	—	—	—	—	—	—	—	—	—	18	316
1974	SD	13 (5, wr)	—	—	—	—	9	105	11.7 (18)	0	—	—	—	—	—	—	—	—	—	—	kp	—	0	95
NFL	6	70 (16)	19	161	8.5 (38)	0	144	2139	14.9 (86)	14	3	0	0.0	0	0.0	0	1	—	—	—	kp	—	84	2311

Levingston, Bashir Bashir, DB, 5´9˝/180 lbs; Utah State; Eastern Washington; B10/2/1976 Inglewood, CA **1999** NYG 12 (0) **2000** NYG 3 (0) **NFL** 15 (0) [2 yrs]

Levitt, Chad Chad Aaron, RB, 6´1˝/231 lbs; Cornell; 1997: Oak, rnd 4; B11/21/1975 Melrose Park, PA

YEAR	TEAM	G (GS, POS)	RUSH	YD	AVG (LG)	TD	REC	YD	AVG (LG)	TD	PASS	COMP	PCT	YD	AVG (LG)	TD	INT	SK	YD	QBR	KPR	OTD	PTS	TAY
1997	Oak	10 (2)	2	3	1.5 (2)	0	2	24	12.0 (22)	0	—	—	—	—	—	—	—	—	—	—	k	—	0	12

Levy, Chuck Charles, RB, 6´0˝/200 lbs; Arizona; 1994: Arz, rnd 2; B1/7/1972 Torrance, CA **[R]**

YEAR	TEAM	G (GS, POS)	RUSH	YD	AVG (LG)	TD	REC	YD	AVG (LG)	TD	PASS	COMP	PCT	YD	AVG (LG)	TD	INT	SK	YD	QBR	KPR	OTD	PTS	TAY
1994	Arz	11 (0)	3	15	5.0 (22)	0	4	35	8.8 (15)	0	—	—	—	—	—	—	—	—	—	—	k	—	0	156
1997	†SF	14 (0)	16	90	5.6 (24)	0	5	68	13.6 (30)	0	—	—	—	—	—	—	—	—	—	—	kp	1	6	466
1998	†SF	12 (0)	25	112	4.5 (21)	1	15	64	4.3 (13)	0	—	—	—	—	—	—	—	—	—	—	k	—	6	207
NFL	3	37 (0)	44	217	4.9 (24)	1	24	167	7.0 (30)	0	—	—	—	—	—	—	—	—	—	—	kp	1	12	829

Levy, Harvey Harvey Sherwin, T-G, 5´10˝/212 lbs; Syracuse; B6/8/1902 Syracuse, NY, D9/29/1986 North Olmsted, OH **1928** NYY 12 (12, RT)

Levy, Len Leonard Bernard, G, 6´0˝/256 lbs; Minnesota; 1942: Cle, rnd 4; B2/19/1921 Minneapolis, MN, D2/9/1999 Minneapolis, MN **1945**†Cle 7 (1) **1946** LARm 10 (2) **NFL** 17 (3) [2 yrs]

1947 LAD-A☆11 (8, LG) **1948** LAD-A 14 (14, LG) **AAFC** 25 (22) [2 yrs]

Lewellen, Verne Verne C., B, 6´1˝/182 lbs; Nebraska; B9/29/1901 Lincoln, NE, D4/16/1980 Rockville, MD **[K]** **1924** GB 8 (3), 12 **1925** GB☆10 (9, HB), 25 **1926** GB☆13 (9, HB), 42 **1927** GB 10 (9, HB), 30 **1927** NYY☆3 (3) **1928** GB☆13 (13, TB), 54 **1929** GB☆13 (5, tb), 48 **1930** GB 14 (11, TB), 54 **1931** GB 7 (3), 36

YEAR	TEAM	G (GS, POS)	RUSH	YD	AVG (LG)	TD	REC	YD	AVG (LG)	TD	PASS	COMP	PCT	YD	AVG (LG)	TD	INT	SK	YD	QBR	KPR	OTD	PTS	TAY
1932	GB	14 (6, TB)	44	115	2.6	0	3	33	11.0	1	13	3	23.1	67	5.2	0	2	—	—	—	—	—	6	90
NFL	9	105 (71)	44	115	2.6	37	3	33	11.0	12	13	3	23.1	67	5.2	9	2	—	—	—	K	2	307	570

Lewis, Albert Albert Ray, DB, 6´2˝/196 lbs; Grambling State; 1983: KC, rnd 3; B10/6/1960 Mansfield, LA **[I]** **1983** KC 16 (1) **1984** KC 15 (15, LCB) **1985** KC 16 (16, LCB) **1986**†KC☆15 (15, LCB) **1987** KC★12 (12, LCB) **1988** KC★14 (12, LCB) **1989** KC★16 (16, LCB) **1990**†KC★15 (14, LCB) **1991** KC 8 (6, lcb) **1992**†KC 9 (8, rcb) **1993**†KC 14 (13, LCB) **1994** LARd 14 (9, RCB) **1995** Oak 16 (15, RCB) **1996** Oak 16 (14, RCB) **1997** Oak 14 (11, RCB) **1998** Oak 15 (12, FS) **NFL** 225 (189) [16 yrs]

Lewis, Alex Alex, LB, 6´1˝/237 lbs; Wisconsin; 2004: Det, rnd 5; B6/11/1981 Delran, NJ **2004** Det 15 (1) **2005** Det 1 (1) **NFL** 16 (2) [2 yrs]

Lewis, Art Arthur E., T, 6´1˝/ lbs; none; B3/1/1891, IN, D10/17/1972 Lucas County, OH **[K]** **1921** Cin 3 (3, LT), 1

Lewis, Art Arthur Everett, T-G, 6´3˝/226 lbs; Ohio University; 1936: NYG, rnd 1; B2/18/1911 Pomeroy, OH, D6/13/1962 Pittsburgh, PA **[C]** **1936** NYG 12 (9, RT) **1938** Cle 9 (3) **1939** Cle 7 (5, lg) **NFL** 28 (17) [3 yrs]

Lewis, Bill Wilton, BB-DB, 5´11˝/186 lbs; TCU

YEAR	TEAM	G (GS, POS)	RUSH	YD	AVG (LG)	TD	REC	YD	AVG (LG)	TD	PASS	COMP	PCT	YD	AVG (LG)	TD	INT	SK	YD	QBR	KPR	OTD	PTS	TAY
1934	Cin	2 (1)	3	-4	-1.3	0	—	—	—	—	—	—	—	—	—	—	—	—	—	—	—	—	0	-4

Lewis, Bill William Glenn, C-G, 6´6˝/285 lbs; Nebraska; 1986: LARd, rnd 7; B7/12/1963 Sioux City, IA **1986** LARd 4 (0) **1987** LARd 8 (6, LG) **1988** LARd 14 (14, C) **1990** Phx 16 (16, C) **1991** Phx 16 (16, C) **1992** Phx 6 (6, C) **1993** NE 7 (5, c) **NFL** 71 (63) [7 yrs]

Lewis, Chad Chad Wayne, TE, 6´6˝/252 lbs; Brigham Young; B10/5/1971 Fort Dix, NJ

YEAR	TEAM	G (GS, POS)	RUSH	YD	AVG (LG)	TD	REC	YD	AVG (LG)	TD	PASS	COMP	PCT	YD	AVG (LG)	TD	INT	SK	YD	QBR	KPR	OTD	PTS	TAY
1997	Phi	16 (3)	—	—	—	—	12	94	7.8 (17)	4	—	—	—	—	—	—	—	—	—	—	k	—	24	63
1998	Phi	2 (0)	—	—	—	—	—	—	—	—	—	—	—	—	—	—	—	—	—	—	—	—	—	—
1999	Phi	6 (4)	—	—	—	—	7	76	10.9 (21)	3	—	—	—	—	—	—	—	—	—	—	—	—	18	53
1999	SL	6 (0)	—	—	—	—	1	12	12.0 (12)	0	—	—	—	—	—	—	—	—	—	—	—	—	0	6
2000	†Phi★	16 (16, TE)	—	—	—	—	69	735	10.7 (52)	3	—	—	—	—	—	—	—	—	—	—	—	—	18	383
2001	†Phi✧	15 (15, TE)	—	—	—	—	41	422	10.3 (33)	6	—	—	—	—	—	—	—	—	—	—	—	—	36	231
2002	†Phi✧	16 (16, TE)	—	—	—	—	42	398	9.5 (30)	3	—	—	—	—	—	—	—	—	—	—	—	—	22	214
2003	†Phi	16 (14, TE)	—	—	—	—	23	293	12.7 (29)	1	—	—	—	—	—	—	—	—	—	—	—	—	6	152

YEAR	TEAM	G (GS, POS)	RUSH	YD	AVG (LG)	TD	REC	YD	AVG (LG)	TD	PASS	COMP	PCT	YD	AVG (LG)	TD	INT	SK	YD	QBR	KPR	OTD	PTS	TAY
2004	†Phi	15(9, TE)	—	—	—	—	29	267	9.2(21)	3	—	—	—	—	—	—	—	—	—	—	—	—	18	149
2005	Phi	8(0)	—	—	—	—	5	64	12.8(17)	0	—	—	—	—	—	—	—	—	—	—	—	—	0	32
NFL	9	116(77)	—	—	—	—	229	2361	10.3(52)	23	—	—	—	—	—	—	—	—	—	—	k	—	142	1282

Lewis, Cliff Clifford Allen, DB-QB, 5´11˝/167 lbs; Duke; 1946: LA, rnd 21; B3/22/1923 Lakewood, OH, D7/25/2002 Tampa, FL **[RI]**

YEAR	TEAM	G (GS, POS)	RUSH	YD	AVG (LG)	TD	REC	YD	AVG (LG)	TD	PASS	COMP	PCT	YD	AVG (LG)	TD	INT	SK	YD	QBR	KPR	OTD	PTS	TAY
1946	Cle-A	10(2)	24	-34	-1.4	0	—	—	—	—	30	11	36.7	125	4.2	1	1	—	—	—	kpi	—	0	128
1947	†Cle-A	13(5, qb)	11	66	6.0	0	—	—	—	—	11	5	45.5	70	6.4	1	1	—	—	—	kpi	—	0	125
1948	†Cle-A	14(0)	5	44	8.8	0	—	—	—	—	8	4	50.0	69	8.6	1	0	—	—	—	Pkpi	—	0	312
1949	†Cle-A	11(1)	9	-17	-1.9	1	—	—	—	—	10	5	50.0	144	14.4	2	2	—	—	—	pi	—	6	92
AAFC	4	48(8)	49	59	1.2	1	—	—	—	—	59	25	42.4	408	6.9	5	4	—	—	—	Pkpi	—	6	656
1950	†Cle	11(SS)	2	-1	-0.5(2)	0	—	—	—	—	4	1	25.0	38	9.5(38)	1	0	—	—	—	pi	—	0	25
1951	†Cle	12(SS)	3	-10	-3.3(1)	0	—	—	—	—	6	4	66.7	68	11.3(20)	1	1	—	—	—	pi	—	0	-12
NFL	2	23	5	-11	-2.2(2)	0	—	—	—	—	10	5	50.0	106	10.6(38)	2	1	—	—	—	pi	—	0	13

Lewis, Cliff Clifford Sylvester, LB, 6´1˝/226 lbs; Southern Mississippi; 1981: GB, rnd 12; B11/9/1959 Brewton, AL **1981** GB 16 (0) **1982**†GB 9 (0) **1983** GB 16 (1) **1984** GB 16 (0) **NFL** 57 (1) [4 yrs]

Lewis, D.D. Dwight Douglass, LB, 6´1˝/225 lbs; Mississippi State; 1968: Dal, rnd 6; B10/16/1945 Knoxville, TN **1968**†Dal 14 **1970**†Dal 12 **1971**†Dal 14 **1972**†Dal 12 **1973**†Dal 14 (RLB) **1974** Dal 14 (RLB) **1975**†Dal 14 (RLB) **1976**†Dal 14 (RLB) **1977**†Dal 14 (RLB) **1978**†Dal 16 (RLB) **1979**†Dal 16 (RLB) **1980**†Dal 16 (16, RLB) **1981**†Dal 16 (16, RLB) **NFL** 186 (32) [13 yrs]

Lewis, D.D. De'Andre De'Wayne, LB, 6´1˝/241 lbs; Texas; B1/8/1979 Bremerhaven, Germany **2002** Sea 16 (0) **2003**†Sea 15 (6, llb) **2005**†Sea 12 (12, ROLB) **NFL** 43 (18) [3 yrs]

Lewis, Damione Damione Ramon, DT, 6´2˝/301 lbs; Miami (FL); 2001: SL, rnd 1; B3/1/1978 Sulphur Springs, TX **2001** SL 9 (3) **2002** SL 16 (2) **2003**†SL 12 (7, rdt) **2004**†SL 16 (10, RDT) **2005** SL 16 (7, rdt) **NFL** 69 (29) [5 yrs]

Lewis, Dan Daniel Nathan, HB-FB, 6´1˝/199 lbs; Wisconsin; 1958: Det, rnd 6; B2/14/1936 Freehold, NJ

YEAR	TEAM	G (GS, POS)	RUSH	YD	AVG (LG)	TD	REC	YD	AVG (LG)	TD	PASS	COMP	PCT	YD	AVG (LG)	TD	INT	SK	YD	QBR	KPR	OTD	PTS	TAY
1958	Det	11	25	131	5.2(20)	0	1	12	12.0(12)	0	—	—	—	—	—	—	—	—	—	—	k	—	0	157
1959	Det	11	49	199	4.1(20)	2	5	75	15.0(30)	0	—	—	—	—	—	—	—	—	—	—	k	—	12	251
1960	Det	12(LH)	92	438	4.8(74)	1	12	192	16.0(55)	1	—	—	—	—	—	—	—	—	—	—	k	—	12	601
1961	Det	13(LH)	110	451	4.1(27)	4	8	118	14.8(22)	0	—	—	—	—	—	—	—	—	—	—	—	—	24	550
1962	Det	12(LH)	120	488	4.1(64)	6	16	158	9.9(34)	1	1	0	0.0	0	0.0	0	0	—	—	—	—	—	42	632
1963	Det	14(FB)	133	528	4.0(27)	2	15	115	7.7(30)	0	—	—	—	—	—	—	—	—	—	—	—	—	12	606
1964	Det	11	122	463	3.8(28)	1	11	129	11.7(92)	1	1	0	0.0	0	0.0	0	0	—	—	—	—	—	12	543
1965	Was	13(FB)	117	343	2.9(23)	2	25	276	11.0(37)	2	2	1	50.0	26	13.0(26)	1	0	—	—	—	—	—	24	529
1966	NYG	13	32	164	5.1(57)	1	6	87	14.5(25)	0	1	1	100.0	4	4.0(4)	0	0	—	—	—	k	—	6	239
NFL	9	110	800	3205	4.0(74)	19	99	1162	11.7(92)	5	5	2	40.0	30	6.0(26)	1	0	—	—	—	k	—	144	4106

Lewis, Darren Darren, RB, 5´10˝/230 lbs; Texas A&M; 1991: Chi, rnd 6; B11/7/1968 Dallas, TX

YEAR	TEAM	G (GS, POS)	RUSH	YD	AVG (LG)	TD	REC	YD	AVG (LG)	TD	PASS	COMP	PCT	YD	AVG (LG)	TD	INT	SK	YD	QBR	KPR	OTD	PTS	TAY
1991	†ChiB	15(0)	15	36	2.4(9)	0	—	—	—	—	—	—	—	—	—	—	—	—	—	—	k	—	0	19
1992	ChiB	16(5, rb)	90	382	4.2(33)	4	18	175	9.7(30)	0	—	—	—	—	—	—	—	—	—	—	k	1	30	686
1993	ChiB	2(1)	7	13	1.9(3)	0	4	26	6.5(18)	0	—	—	—	—	—	—	—	—	—	—	—	—	0	26
NFL	3	33(6)	112	431	3.8(33)	4	22	201	9.1(30)	0	—	—	—	—	—	—	—	—	—	—	k	1	30	731

Lewis, Darryl Darryl Gerard, TE, 6´6˝/232 lbs; Texas-Arlington; 1983: NE, rnd 5; B4/16/1961 Mount Pleasant, TX **1984** Cle 2 (0)

Lewis, Darryll Darryll Lamont, DB, 5´9˝/188 lbs; Arizona; 1991: Hou, rnd 2; B12/16/1968 West Covina, CA **[I]** **1991**†Hou 16 (1) **1992**†Hou 13 (0) **1993** Hou 4 (4) **1994** Hou 16 (15, RCB) **1995** Hou★16 (15, RCB) **1996** Hou 16 (16, RCB) **1997** Ten 16 (14, RCB) **1998** Ten 16 (15, RCB) **1999** SD 13 (8, LCB) **2000** SD 15 (7, lcb) **NFL** 141 (95) [10 yrs]

Lewis, Dave David Ray, QB-P, 6´2˝/216 lbs; Stanford; 1967: NYG, rnd 5; B10/16/1945 Clovis, CA **[P]**

YEAR	TEAM	G (GS, POS)	RUSH	YD	AVG (LG)	TD	REC	YD	AVG (LG)	TD	PASS	COMP	PCT	YD	AVG (LG)	TD	INT	SK	YD	QBR	KPR	OTD	PTS	TAY
1970	†Cin☆	14	2	8	4.0(7)	0	—	—	—	—	4	3	75.0	39	9.8(18)	0	0	—	—	—	P	—	0	28
1971	Cin☆	14	6	6	1.0(9)	0	—	—	—	—	10	3	30.0	18	1.8(13)	0	0	4	22	—	P	—	0	15
1972	Cin	14	1	15	15.0(15)	0	—	—	—	—	—	—	—	—	—	—	—	—	—	—	Pk	—	0	15
1973	†Cin	14	3	-7	-2.3(5)	0	—	—	—	—	—	—	—	—	—	—	—	—	—	—	Pkp	—	0	0
NFL	4	56	12	22	1.8(15)	0	—	—	—	—	14	6	42.9	57	4.1(18)	0	0	4	22	—	Pkp	—	0	58

Lewis, Dave David Rodney, LB, 6´4˝/240 lbs; USC; 1977: TB, rnd 2; B10/15/1954 San Diego, CA **1977** TB 14 (13, LOLB) **1978** TB 16 (16, LOLB) **1979**†TB☆16 (16, LOLB) **1980** TB✧16 (15, LOLB) **1981**†TB 13 (4) **1982**†SD 9 (4) **1983**†LARm 13 (0) **NFL** 97 (68) [7 yrs]

Lewis, David David Wayne, TE, 6´3˝/234 lbs; California; 1984: Det, rnd 1; B6/8/1961 Portland, OR

YEAR	TEAM	G (GS, POS)	RUSH	YD	AVG (LG)	TD	REC	YD	AVG (LG)	TD	PASS	COMP	PCT	YD	AVG (LG)	TD	INT	SK	YD	QBR	KPR	OTD	PTS	TAY
1984	Det	16(7, te)	—	—	—	—	16	236	14.8(58)	3	—	—	—	—	—	—	—	—	—	—	—	—	18	133
1985	Det	15(15, TE)	—	—	—	—	28	354	12.6(40)	3	—	—	—	—	—	—	—	—	—	—	—	—	18	192
1986	Det	11(7, te)	—	—	—	—	10	88	8.8(16)	1	—	—	—	—	—	—	—	—	—	—	—	—	6	49
1987	Mia	5(3)	—	—	—	—	6	53	8.8(22)	1	—	—	—	—	—	—	—	—	—	—	k	—	6	17
NFL	4	47(32)	—	—	—	—	60	731	12.2(58)	8	—	—	—	—	—	—	—	—	—	—	k	—	48	391

Lewis, Derrick Derrick Lamont, WR, 6´2˝/185 lbs; San Diego State; B10/30/1975 New Orleans, LA **2002** NO 2 (0)

YEAR	TEAM	G (GS, POS)	RUSH	YD	AVG (LG)	TD	REC	YD	AVG (LG)	TD	PASS	COMP	PCT	YD	AVG (LG)	TD	INT	SK	YD	QBR	KPR	OTD	PTS	TAY
2003	NO	3(0)	—	—	—	—	1	7	7.0(7)	0	—	—	—	—	—	—	—	—	—	—	—	—	0	4
NFL	2	5(0)	—	—	—	—	1	7	7.0(7)	0	—	—	—	—	—	—	—	—	—	—	—	—	0	4

Lewis, Eddie Edward Lee, DB, 6´0˝/177 lbs; Kansas; 1976: SF, rnd 2; B12/15/1953 Mobile, AL **1976** SF 14 **1977** SF 14 **1978** SF 16 (16, RCB) **1979** SF 7 **1979** Det 8 **1980** Det 14 (1) **NFL** 73 (17) [5 yrs]

Lewis, Ernie Ernest Clayton, FB-LB, 6´1˝/211 lbs; Colorado; 1946: Phi, rnd 9; B11/20/1923 Boonville, MO

YEAR	TEAM	G (GS, POS)	RUSH	YD	AVG (LG)	TD	REC	YD	AVG (LG)	TD	PASS	COMP	PCT	YD	AVG (LG)	TD	INT	SK	YD	QBR	KPR	OTD	PTS	TAY
1946	ChiR-A	12(9, FB)	57	164	2.9	1	2	26	13.0	0	8	4	50.0	17	2.1	0	1	—	—	—	Pki	—	6	153
1947	ChiR-A	14(0)	13	47	3.6	0	—	—	—	—	—	—	—	—	—	—	—	—	—	—	P	—	0	47
1948	ChiR-A	14(1)	13	54	4.2	0	1	6	6.0(6)	0	—	—	—	—	—	—	—	—	—	—	P	—	0	57
1949	ChiH-A	6(5, FB)	11	43	3.9	1	—	—	—	—	—	—	—	—	—	—	—	—	—	—	P	—	6	53
AAFC	4	46(15)	94	308	3.3	2	3	32	10.7(6)	0	8	4	50.0	17	2.1	0	1	—	—	—	Pki	—	12	310

Lewis, Frank Frank Douglas, WR, 6´1˝/196 lbs; Grambling State; 1971: Pit, rnd 1; B7/4/1947 Houma, LA

YEAR	TEAM	G (GS, POS)	RUSH	YD	AVG (LG)	TD	REC	YD	AVG (LG)	TD	PASS	COMP	PCT	YD	AVG (LG)	TD	INT	SK	YD	QBR	KPR	OTD	PTS	TAY
1971	Pit	9	—	—	—	—	3	44	14.7(22)	0	—	—	—	—	—	—	—	—	—	—	—	—	0	22
1972	Pit	13(13, WR)	3	68	22.7(41)	0	27	391	14.5(52)	5	—	—	—	—	—	—	—	—	—	—	p	—	30	320
1973	†Pit	9(9, WR)	1	-1	-1.0(-1)	0	23	409	17.8(53)	3	—	—	—	—	—	—	—	—	—	—	—	—	18	219
1974	†Pit	12(12, WR)	2	25	12.5(22)	0	30	365	12.2(31)	4	—	—	—	—	—	—	—	—	—	—	—	—	24	228
1975	†Pit	10(10, WR)	2	36	18.0(24)	0	17	308	18.1(40)	2	—	—	—	—	—	—	—	—	—	—	—	—	12	200
1976	†Pit	12(12, WR)	2	24	12.0(16)	1	17	306	18.0(64)	1	—	—	—	—	—	—	—	—	—	—	—	—	12	192
1977	Pit	10	—	—	—	—	11	263	23.9(65)	1	—	—	—	—	—	—	—	—	—	—	—	—	6	137
1978	Buf	15(15, WR)	—	—	—	—	41	735	17.9(**92**)	7	—	—	—	—	—	—	—	—	—	—	—	—	42	403
1979	Buf	15(15, WR)	2	-6	-3.0(-1)	0	54	1082	20.0(55)	2	—	—	—	—	—	—	—	—	—	—	—	—	12	545
1980	†Buf	15(14, WR)	—	—	—	—	40	648	16.2(31)	6	—	—	—	—	—	—	—	—	—	—	—	—	36	354
1981	†Buf★	16(16, WR)	—	—	—	—	70	**1244**	17.8(33)	4	—	—	—	—	—	—	—	—	—	—	—	—	24	642
1982	Buf	8(8, WR)	—	—	—	—	28	443	15.8(39)	2	—	—	—	—	—	—	—	—	—	—	—	—	12	232
1983	Buf	11(11, WR)	—	—	—	—	36	486	13.5(27)	3	—	—	—	—	—	—	—	—	—	—	—	—	18	258
NFL	13	155(135)	12	146	12.2(41)	1	397	6724	16.9(92)	40	—	—	—	—	—	—	—	—	—	—	p	—	246	3749

Lewis, Franklin Franklin A., FB, B8/2/1902, D1/1974 Tampa, FL **1931** Cle 1 (0)

Lewis, Garry Garry, DB, 5´11˝/185 lbs; Alcorn State; 1990: LARd, rnd 7; B8/25/1967 New Orleans, LA **1990**†LARd 12 (5, lcb) **1991** LARd 16 (2) **1992** TB 16 (2) **1993** KC 1 (0) **NFL** 45 (9) [4 yrs]

Lewis, Gary Gary Rogers, RB, 6´3˝/225 lbs; Washington State; Arizona State; 1964: SF, rnd 6/Den, rnd 22; B2/22/1942 New Orleans, LA, D12/12/1986 Daly City, CA

YEAR	TEAM	G (GS, POS)	RUSH	YD	AVG (LG)	TD	REC	YD	AVG (LG)	TD	PASS	COMP	PCT	YD	AVG (LG)	TD	INT	SK	YD	QBR	KPR	OTD	PTS	TAY
1964	SF	8(3)	43	115	2.7(17)	1	7	73	10.4(47)	0	—	—	—	—	—	—	—	—	—	—	k	—	6	147
1965	SF	14	52	256	4.9(60)	3	10	25	2.5(12)	0	—	—	—	—	—	—	—	—	—	—	kp	—	18	427
1966	SF	14	36	130	3.6(15)	2	7	44	6.3(18)	1	—	—	—	—	—	—	—	—	—	—	k	—	18	197

YEAR	TEAM	G(GS, POS)	RUSH	YD	AVG(LG)	TD	REC	YD	AVG(LG)	TD	PASS	COMP	PCT	YD	AVG(LG)	TD	INT	SK	YD	QBR	KPR	OTD	PTS	TAY
1967	SF	13	67	342	5.1(52)	6	21	218	10.4(32)	1	—	—	—	—	—	—	—	—	—	—	kp	—	42	571
1968	SF	14(14, HB)	141	573	4.1(22)	1	27	244	9.0(33)	3	—	—	—	—	—	—	—	—	—	—	—	—	24	720
1969	SF	9	4	5	1.3(4)	0	—	—	—	—	—	—	—	—	—	—	—	—	—	—	k	—	0	85
1970	NO	1	—	—	—	—	—	—	—	—	—	—	—	—	—	—	—	—	—	—	k	—	0	4
NFL	7	73(17)	343	1421	4.1(60)	13	72	604	8.4(47)	5	—	—	—	—	—	—	—	—	—	—	kp	—	108	2150
LEWIS, GARY Gary Wayne, TE-WR, 6´5˝/234 lbs; Texas-Arlington; 1981: GB, rnd 2; B12/30/1958 Mount Pleasant, TX																								
1981	GB	16(0)	—	—	—	—	3	31	10.3(15)	0	—	—	—	—	—	—	—	—	—	—	—	—	0	16
1982	†GB	9(0)	—	—	—	—	3	21	7.0(12)	0	—	—	—	—	—	—	—	—	—	—	—	—	0	11
1983	GB	16(1)	4	16	4.0(15)	1	11	204	18.5(49)	1	—	—	—	—	—	—	—	—	—	—	—	—	12	133
1984	GB	3(2)	—	—	—	—	4	29	7.3(15)	0	—	—	—	—	—	—	—	—	—	—	—	—	0	15
NFL	4	44(3)	4	16	4.0(15)	1	21	285	13.6(49)	1	—	—	—	—	—	—	—	—	—	—	—	—	12	174
LEWIS, GARY Gary L., NT, 6´3˝/260 lbs; Oklahoma State; 1983: NO, rnd 4; B1/14/1961 Oklahoma City, OK **1983** NO 6 (0)																								
LEWIS, GREG Gregory Alan, RB, 5´10˝/214 lbs; Washington; 1991: Den, rnd 5; B8/10/1969 Port St. Joe, FL																								
1991	†Den	16(4)	99	376	3.8(27)	4	2	9	4.5(7)	0	—	—	—	—	—	—	—	—	—	—	k	—	24	426
1992	Den	16(2)	73	268	3.7(22)	4	4	30	7.5(16)	0	1	0	0.0	0	0.0	0	0	—	—	—	—	—	24	323
NFL	2	32(6)	172	644	3.7(27)	8	6	39	6.5(16)	0	1	0	0.0	0	0.0	0	0	—	—	—	k	—	48	749
LEWIS, GREG Gregory Alan, WR, 6´0˝/180 lbs; Illinois; B2/12/1980 Chicago, IL																								
2003	†Phi	11(0)	—	—	—	—	6	95	15.8(25)	0	—	—	—	—	—	—	—	—	—	—	—	—	0	48
2004	†Phi	16(3)	4	16	4.0(11)	0	17	183	10.8(25)	0	—	—	—	—	—	—	—	—	—	—	k	—	0	106
2005	Phi	16(16, WR)	2	13	6.5(8)	0	48	561	11.7(34)	1	—	—	—	—	—	—	—	—	—	—	—	—	6	299
NFL	3	43(19)	6	29	4.8(11)	0	71	839	11.8(34)	1	—	—	—	—	—	—	—	—	—	—	k	—	6	452
LEWIS, H. H., G, 5´8˝/175 lbs; none; B1896, deceased **1921** Lou 1 (0)																								
LEWIS, HAL Harold Lee, FB-HB-DB, 6´0˝/200 lbs; Houston; 1959: Bal, rnd 7; B9/22/1935 Houston, TX																								
1959	†Bal	12	4	2	0.5(2)	0	3	54	18.0(25)	0	—	—	—	—	—	—	—	—	—	—	k	—	0	30
1960	Buf-A	3	—	—	—	—	—	—	—	—	—	—	—	—	—	—	—	—	—	—	kp	—	0	34
1962	Oak-A	11(fb)	9	18	2.0(14)	0	7	53	7.6(13)	0	—	—	—	—	—	—	—	—	—	—	kp	—	0	85
NFL	3	26	13	20	1.5(14)	0	10	107	10.7(25)	0	—	—	—	—	—	—	—	—	—	—	kp	—	0	149
LEWIS, HAL Harold DeWitt, DB, 6´0˝/185 lbs; Arizona State; B8/1/1944 Memphis, TN **1968** Den-A 1																								
LEWIS, JAMAL Jamal Lafitte, RB, 5´11˝/240 lbs; Tennessee; 2000: Bal, rnd 1; B8/29/1979 Atlanta, GA																								
2000	†Bal	16(13, RB)	309	1364	4.4(45)	6	27	296	11.0(45)	0	—	—	—	—	—	—	—	—	—	—	—	—	38	1572
2002	Bal	16(15, RB)	308	1327	4.3(75)	6	47	442	9.4(77)	1	—	—	—	—	—	—	—	—	—	—	—	—	42	1613
2003	†Bal★	16(16, RB)	387	**2066**	5.3(82)	14	26	205	7.9(26)	0	—	—	—	—	—	—	—	—	—	—	—	—	84	**2309**
2004	Bal	12(12, RB)	235	1006	4.3(75)	7	10	116	11.6(46)	0	—	—	—	—	—	—	—	—	—	—	—	—	42	1134
2005	Bal	15(15, RB)	269	906	3.4(25)	3	32	191	6.0(15)	1	—	—	—	—	—	—	—	—	—	—	—	—	24	1037
NFL	5	75(71)	1508	6669	4.4(82)	36	142	1250	8.8(77)	2	—	—	—	—	—	—	—	—	—	—	—	—	230	7664
LEWIS, JEFF Jeffrey Scott, QB, 6´2˝/211 lbs; Northern Arizona; 1996: Den, rnd 4; B4/17/1973 Columbus, OH																								
1996	Den	2(0)	4	39	9.8(18)	0	—	—	—	—	17	9	52.9	58	3.4(11)	0	1	1	7	—	—	—	0	28
1997	Den	3(0)	5	2	0.4(5)	0	—	—	—	—	2	1	50.0	21	10.5(21)	0	0	1	7	—	—	—	0	13
1999	Car	2(0)	4	1	0.3(4)	0	—	—	—	—	3	2	66.7	11	3.7(12)	0	0	1	6	—	—	—	0	7
2000	Car	5(0)	8	36	4.5(19)	0	—	—	—	—	32	16	50.0	120	3.8(16)	0	1	7	51	—	—	—	0	56
NFL	4	12(0)	21	78	3.7(19)	0	—	—	—	—	54	28	51.9	210	3.9(21)	0	2	10	71	—	—	—	0	103
LEWIS, JERMAINE Jermaine Edward, WR, 5´7˝/183 lbs; Maryland; 1996: Bal, rnd 5; B10/16/1974 Lanham, MD **[R]**																								
1996	Bal	16(1)	1	-3	-3.0(-3)	0	5	78	15.6(24)	1	—	—	—	—	—	—	—	—	—	—	kp	—	6	468
1997	Bal	14(7, WR)	3	35	11.7(24)	0	42	648	15.4(42)	6	—	—	—	—	—	—	—	—	—	—	kp	2	48	996
1998	Bal★	13(13, WR)	5	20	4.0(9)	0	41	784	19.1(73)	6	—	—	—	—	—	—	—	—	—	—	kp	2	48	762
1999	Bal	15(6, wr)	5	11	2.2(4)	0	25	281	11.2(46)	2	—	—	—	—	—	—	—	—	—	—	kp	—	12	367
2000	†Bal	15(1)	3	38	12.7(23)	0	19	161	8.5(26)	1	1	1	100.0	3	3.0(3)	0	0	—	—	—	kp	2	18	551
2001	†Bal★	15(2)	9	33	3.7(14)	0	4	32	8.0(12)	0	—	—	—	—	—	—	—	—	—	—	kp	—	0	767
2002	Hou	12(1)	3	8	2.7(5)	0	2	41	20.5(33)	0	—	—	—	—	—	—	—	—	—	—	kp	—	0	400
2003	Jax	2(0)	1	6	6.0(6)	0	4	100	25.0(65)	1	—	—	—	—	—	—	—	—	—	—	kp	—	6	102
2004	Jax	9(0)	—	—	—	—	1	4	4.0(4)	0	—	—	—	—	—	—	—	—	—	—	kp	—	0	185
NFL	9	111(31)	30	148	4.9(24)	0	143	2129	14.9(73)	17	1	1	100.0	3	3.0(3)	0	0	—	—	—	kp	6	138	4597
LEWIS, JESS Jess T., LB, 6´1˝/230 lbs; Oregon State; 1970: Hou, rnd 13; B7/28/1947 Aumsville, OR **1970** Hou 10																								
LEWIS, JOE Joseph, DT, 6´2˝/256 lbs; Compton CC (CA); 1958: Pit, rnd 17; B1/23/1936 Los Angeles, CA **1958** Pit 12 (LDT) **1959** Pit 5 (ldt) **1960** Pit 12 **1961** Bal 11 **1962** Phi 13 (RDT) **NFL** 53 [5 yrs]																								
LEWIS, JOHN John R., DB, 5´10˝/175 lbs; Pittsburgh; B3/8/1962 Levittown, PA **1987** Buf 3 (0)																								
LEWIS, JONAS Jonas W. Allen, LB, 5´9˝/210 lbs; San Diego State; B12/27/1978 Riverside, CA **2001** SF 1 (0)																								
2000	SF	10(0)	1	6	6.0(6)	0	—	—	—	—	—	—	—	—	—	—	—	—	—	—	k	—	0	39
NFL	2	11(0)	1	6	6.0(6)	0	—	—	—	—	—	—	—	—	—	—	—	—	—	—	k	—	0	41
LEWIS, KEITH Keith D'Andre, DB, 6´0˝/202 lbs; Oregon; 2004: SF, rnd 6; B10/20/1981 Sacramento, CA **2004** SF 16 (0) **2005** SF 16 (4) **NFL** 32 (4) [2 yrs]																								
LEWIS, KENNY Kenneth, RB, 6´0˝/190 lbs; Virginia Tech; 1980: Oak, rnd 5; B10/2/1957 Danville, VA																								
1980	NYJ	7(0)	—	—	—	—	1	6	6.0(6)	0	—	—	—	—	—	—	—	—	—	—	—	—	0	3
1981	NYJ	5(0)	6	18	3.0(7)	0	2	14	7.0(8)	0	—	—	—	—	—	—	—	—	—	—	k	—	0	58
1983	NYJ	7(0)	5	25	5.0(7)	0	6	62	10.3(23)	0	—	—	—	—	—	—	—	—	—	—	—	—	0	56
NFL	3	19(0)	11	43	3.9(7)	0	9	82	9.1(23)	0	—	—	—	—	—	—	—	—	—	—	k	—	0	117
LEWIS, KEVIN Kevin, DB, 5´11˝/173 lbs; Northwestern State (LA); B11/14/1966 New Orleans, LA **1990**†SF 10 (0) **1991** SF 16 (3) **NFL** 26 (3) [2 yrs]																								
LEWIS, KEVIN Kevin, LB, 6´1˝/235 lbs; Duke; B10/6/1978 Orlando, FL **2000** NYG 7 (0) **2001** NYG 9 (0) **2002**†NYG 15 (2) **2003** NYG 16 (0) **2004** NYG 16 (16, MLB) **2005**†NYG 1 (1) **NFL** 64 (19) [6 yrs]																								
LEWIS, LEO Leo Everett, WR, 5´8˝/170 lbs; Missouri; B9/17/1956 Columbia, MO **[R]**																								
1981	Min	4(1)	1	16	16.0(16)	0	2	58	29.0(52)	0	—	—	—	—	—	—	—	—	—	—	—	—	0	45
1982	†Min	9(0)	—	—	—	—	8	150	18.8(39)	3	—	—	—	—	—	—	—	—	—	—	—	—	18	90
1983	Min	14(4)	1	2	2.0(2)	0	12	127	10.6(18)	0	—	—	—	—	—	—	—	—	—	—	kp	—	0	113
1984	Min	16(5, wr)	2	11	5.5(6)	0	47	830	17.7(56)	4	—	—	—	—	—	—	—	—	—	—	kp	—	24	473
1985	Min	10(10, WR)	1	2	2.0(2)	0	29	442	15.2(43)	3	—	—	—	—	—	—	—	—	—	—	—	—	18	238
1986	Min	16(16, WR)	3	-16	-5.3(-2)	0	32	600	18.8(76)	2	—	—	—	—	—	—	—	—	—	—	p	—	12	312
1987	†Min	12(12, WR)	5	-7	-1.4(4)	0	24	383	16.0(36)	2	—	—	—	—	—	—	—	—	—	—	p	1	18	370
1988	†Min	16(1)	—	—	—	—	11	141	12.8(46)	1	—	—	—	—	—	—	—	—	—	—	kp	—	6	333
1989	†Min	16(0)	1	11	11.0(11)	0	12	148	12.3(28)	1	—	—	—	—	—	—	—	—	—	—	kp	—	6	316
1990	Cle	3(0)	—	—	—	—	—	—	—	—	—	—	—	—	—	—	—	—	—	—	p	—	0	16
1990	Min	11(0)	—	—	—	—	1	9	9.0(9)	0	—	—	—	—	—	—	—	—	—	—	kp	—	0	54
1991	Min	16(0)	—	—	—	—	4	36	9.0(11)	0	—	—	—	—	—	—	—	—	—	—	p	—	0	93
NFL	11	143(49)	14	19	1.4(16)	0	182	2924	16.1(76)	16	—	—	—	—	—	—	—	—	—	—	kp	1	102	2451
LEWIS, MAC Charles Mac, T, 6´6˝/290 lbs; Iowa; 1959: ChiC, rnd 6; B8/28/1937 Pittsburgh, PA **1959** ChiC 8																								
LEWIS, MARK Mark Joseph, TE, 6´2˝/239 lbs; Texas A&M; 1985: GB, rnd 6; B5/5/1961 Houston, TX **1985** GB 1 (0) **1987** GB 1 (1) **1987** Det 9 (1)																								
1986	GB	16(1)	—	—	—	—	2	7	3.5(4)	2	—	—	—	—	—	—	—	—	—	—	—	—	12	14
1988	Det	3(3)	—	—	—	—	3	32	10.7(23)	1	—	—	—	—	—	—	—	—	—	—	—	—	6	21
NFL	4	30(6)	—	—	—	—	5	39	7.8(23)	3	—	—	—	—	—	—	—	—	—	—	—	—	18	35

YEAR	TEAM	G (GS, POS)	RUSH	YD	AVG(LG)	TD	REC	YD	AVG(LG)	TD	PASS COMP	PCT	YD	AVG(LG)	TD	INT	SK	YD	QBR	KPR	OTD	PTS	TAY

LEWIS, MARVIN Marvin Victor, RB, 6´3˝/208 lbs; Tulane; 1982: NO, rnd 6; B1/15/1960 Texarkana, TX **1982** NO 1 (0)

LEWIS, MICHAEL Michael Lee, WR, 5´8˝/165 lbs; none; B11/14/1971 New Orleans, LA **[R]**

YEAR	TEAM	G (GS, POS)	RUSH	YD	AVG(LG)	TD	REC	YD	AVG(LG)	TD										KPR	OTD	PTS	TAY
2001	NO	8(0)	—	—	—	—	—	—	—	—										kp	—	0	293
2002	NO★	16(0)	1	15	15.0(15)	0	8	200	25.0(59)	0										kp	3	18	1307
2003	NO	13(1)	1	2	2.0(2)	0	12	226	18.8(39)	0										kp	—	6	638
2004	NO	14(1)	—	—	—	—	8	127	15.9(30)	0										kp	1	6	736
2005	NO	2(0)	—	—	—	—	—	—	—	—										kp	—	0	5
NFL	5	53(2)	2	17	8.5(15)	0	28	553	19.8(59)	1										kp	4	30	2979

LEWIS, MICHAEL Michael Milton, DB, 6´1˝/211 lbs; Colorado; 2002: Phi, rnd 2; B4/29/1980 Houston, TX **2002**†Phi 14 (4) **2003**†Phi 16 (16, SS) **2004**†Phi★16 (16, SS) **2005** Phi 16 (16, SS) **NFL** 62 (52) [4 yrs]

LEWIS, MIKE Michael Henry, DT-DE-NT, 6´4˝/261 lbs; Wiley; Arkansas-Pine Bluff; B7/14/1949 Houston, TX **1971** Atl 9 **1972** Atl 14 (RDT) **1973** Atl 14 (RDT) **1974** Atl 14 (RDT) **1975** Atl 14 (RDT) **1976** Atl 12 (RDT) **1977** Atl 14 (RDT) **1978**†Atl 16 (RDT) **1979** Atl 13 **1980** GB 10 (0) **NFL** 130 (12) [10 yrs]

LEWIS, MO Morris Clyde, LB, 6´3˝/258 lbs; Georgia; 1991: NYJ, rnd 3; B10/21/1969 Atlanta, GA **[S]** **1991**†NYJ 16 (16, LLB) **1992** NYJ 16 (16, RLB) **1993** NYJ 16 (16, RLB) **1994** NYJ 16 (16, RLB) **1995** NYJ 16 (16, RLB/mlb) **1996** NYJ 9 (9, RLB) **1997** NYJ 16 (16, LOLB) **1998**†NYJ★16 (16, LLB) **1999** NYJ✧16 (16, LOLB) **2001**†NYJ 16 (16, LLB) **2002**†NYJ 16 (16, LLB) **2003** NYJ 15 (15, LLB)

YEAR	TEAM	G (GS, POS)	RUSH	YD	AVG(LG)	TD	REC	YD	AVG(LG)	TD											OTD	PTS	TAY
2000	NYJ★	16(16, LOLB)	1	3	3.0(3)	0	—	—	—	—									iS		—	0	21
NFL	13	200(200)	1	3	3.0(3)	0	—	—	—	—									iS		5	30	214

LEWIS, NATE Nathaniel, WR, 5´11˝/198 lbs; Georgia; Oregon Tech; 1990: SD, rnd 7; B10/19/1966 Moultrie, GA **[R]**

YEAR	TEAM	G (GS, POS)	RUSH	YD	AVG(LG)	TD	REC	YD	AVG(LG)	TD										KPR	OTD	PTS	TAY
1990	SD	12(3)	4	25	6.3(10)	1	14	192	13.7(40)	1										kp	1	18	326
1991	SD✧	16(9, WR)	3	10	3.3(9)	0	42	554	13.2(49)	3										kp	1	24	579
1992	†SD	15(7, WR)	2	7	3.5(4)	0	34	580	17.1(62)	4										kp	—	24	496
1993	SD	15(9, WR)	3	2	0.7(7)	0	38	463	12.2(47)	4										kp	—	24	445
1994	†ChiB	13(0)	—	—	—	—	2	13	6.5(8)	1										kp	—	6	363
1995	ChiB	11(0)	—	—	—	—	—	—	—	—										k	—	0	274
NFL	6	82(28)	12	44	3.7(10)	1	130	1802	13.9(62)	13										kp	2	96	2482

LEWIS, RAY Ray Anthony, LB, 6´1˝/245 lbs; Miami (FL); 1996: Bal, rnd 1; B5/15/1975 Bartow, FL **[I]** **1996** Bal 14 (13, LILB) **1997** Bal★16 (16, MLB) **1998**†Bal★14 (14, MLB) **1999** Bal★16 (16, MLB) **2000**†Bal★16 (16, MLB) **2001**†Bal★16 (16, MLB) **2002** Bal 5 (5, rilb) **2003**†Bal★16 (16, RILB) **2004** Bal★15 (15, RILB) **2005** Bal 6 (6, mlb) **NFL** 134 (133) [10 yrs]

LEWIS, REGGIE Reginald Anthony, DE, 6´2˝/252 lbs; Oregon; San Diego State; 1976: SF, rnd 16; B1/20/1954 New Orleans, LA **1982** NO 9 (0) **1983** NO 12 (0) **1984** NO 13 (0) **NFL** 34 (0) [3 yrs]

LEWIS, REGGIE Reginald Paul, DE-NT, 6´3˝/200 lbs; North Texas; 1979: TB, rnd 3; B5/6/1956 Port Arthur, TX **1979**†TB 12 **1980** TB 10 (0) **NFL** 22 [2 yrs]

LEWIS, RICH Richard L., LB, 6´3˝/220 lbs; Portland State; B6/8/1950 Portland, OR **1972** Hou 10 **1973** Buf 10 (RLB) **1974** Buf 2 **1975** NYJ 11 (RLB) **NFL** 33 [4 yrs]

LEWIS, RODERICK Roderick Albert, TE, 6´5˝/254 lbs; Arizona; 1994: Hou, rnd 5; B6/9/1971 Washington, DC

YEAR	TEAM	G (GS, POS)	RUSH	YD	AVG(LG)	TD	REC	YD	AVG(LG)	TD										KPR	OTD	PTS	TAY
1994	Hou	3(1)	—	—	—	—	4	48	12.0(19)	0											—	0	24
1995	Hou	16(9, TE)	—	—	—	—	16	116	7.3(16)	0										k	—	0	48
1996	Hou	16(7, TE)	—	—	—	—	7	50	7.1(18)	0											—	0	25
1997	Ten	10(1)	—	—	—	—	1	7	7.0(7)	0											—	0	4
NFL	4	45(18)	—	—	—	—	28	221	7.9(19)	0										k	—	0	101

LEWIS, RODNEY Rodney Earl, DB, 5´11˝/190 lbs; Nebraska; 1982: NO, rnd 3; B4/2/1959 Minneapolis, MN **1982** NO 9 (0) **1983** NO 2 (2) **1984** NO 16 (0) **NFL** 27 (2) [3 yrs]

LEWIS, RON Ronald Alexander, WR, 5´11˝/185 lbs; Florida State; 1990: SF, rnd 3; B3/25/1968 Jacksonville, FL

YEAR	TEAM	G (GS, POS)	RUSH	YD	AVG(LG)	TD	REC	YD	AVG(LG)	TD										KPR	OTD	PTS	TAY
1990	SF	8(0)	—	—	—	—	5	44	8.8(14)	0											—	0	22
1992	SF	5(0)	—	—	—	—	—	—	—	—										p	—	0	3
1992	GB	6(4)	—	—	—	—	13	152	11.7(27)	0											—	0	76
1993	†GB	9(0)	—	—	—	—	2	21	10.5(17)	0											—	0	11
1994	GB	6(1)	—	—	—	—	7	108	15.4(38)	0											—	0	54
NFL	4	34(5)	—	—	—	—	27	325	12.0(38)	0										p	—	0	166

LEWIS, RON Ronald Mack, G, 6´3˝/299 lbs; Washington State; B11/17/1972 Los Angeles, CA **1995** Was 4 (0)

LEWIS, SHERMAN Sherman Paul, DB, 5´9˝/158 lbs; Michigan State; 1964: NYJ, rnd 9/Cle, rnd 18; B6/29/1942 Louisville, KY **1966** NYJ-A 5 **1967** NYJ-A 5 **NFL** 10 [2 yrs]

LEWIS, SID Sidney Scot, DB, 5´11˝/180 lbs; Penn State; 1987: NYJ, rnd 10; B5/30/1964 Canton, OH **1987** NYJ 2 (0)

LEWIS, STAN Stanley, DE, 6´4˝/240 lbs; Wayne State (NE); 1975: Cle, rnd 10; B9/11/1953 Chicago, IL **1975** Cle 6

LEWIS, TAHAUN Tahaun, DB, 5´10˝/175 lbs; Nebraska; 1991: LARd, rnd 9; B9/29/1968 Los Angeles, CA **1992**†KC 9 (0)

LEWIS, TERRY Terence L., DB, 5´11˝/193 lbs; Michigan State; 1985: SD, rnd 6; B12/9/1962 Detroit, MI **1985** SD 10 (0)

LEWIS, THOMAS Thomas A., WR, 6´1˝/191 lbs; Indiana; 1994: NYG, rnd 1; B1/10/1972 Akron, OH

YEAR	TEAM	G (GS, POS)	RUSH	YD	AVG(LG)	TD	REC	YD	AVG(LG)	TD										KPR	OTD	PTS	TAY
1994	NYG	9(0)	—	—	—	—	4	46	11.5(23)	0										kp	—	0	181
1995	NYG	8(2)	—	—	—	—	12	208	17.3(46)	1										kp	1	12	257
1996	NYG	13(10, WR)	—	—	—	—	53	694	13.1(34)	4										kp	—	24	400
1997	NYG	4(2)	—	—	—	—	5	84	16.8(34)	0										k	—	0	196
NFL	4	34(14)	—	—	—	—	74	1032	13.9(46)	5										kp	1	36	1034

LEWIS, TIM Timothy Jay, DB, 5´11˝/194 lbs; Pittsburgh; 1983: GB, rnd 1; B12/18/1961 Quakertown, PA **1983** GB 16 (7, rcb) **1984** GB☆16 (16, RCB) **1985** GB 16 (16, RCB) **1986** GB 3 (3) **NFL** 51 (42) [4 yrs]

LEWIS, TINY Loren Leland, BB-FB-WB, 6´2˝/210 lbs; Northwestern; B10/18/1906 Foosland, IL, D1/17/1954 Michigan City, TN **[K]** **1930** Por 13 (7, bb), 22 **1931** Cle 1 (0) **NFL** 14 (7) [2 yrs]

LEWIS, VERNON Vernon, DB, 5´10˝/192 lbs; Pittsburgh; B10/27/1970 Houston, TX **1993** NE 10 (0) **1994**†NE 11 (0) **1995** NE 16 (2) **1996** NE 7 (0) **NFL** 44 (2) [4 yrs]

LEWIS, WILL William L., DB, 5´9˝/185 lbs; Millersville; B1/16/1958 Quakertown, PA **1980** Sea 16 (0) **1981** Sea 10 (0) **NFL** 26 (0) [2 yrs]

LEWIS, WOODLEY Woodley Carl, DB-E, 6´0˝/185 lbs; Oregon; 1950: LA, rnd 8; B6/14/1925 Los Angeles, CA, D12/29/2000 Los Angeles, CA **[RI]**

YEAR	TEAM	G (GS, POS)	RUSH	YD	AVG(LG)	TD	REC	YD	AVG(LG)	TD										KPR	OTD	PTS	TAY
1950	†LARm✧	12(DB)	—	—	—	—	—	—	—	—										kpi	1	6	227
1951	†LARm☆	12(DB)	—	—	—	—	—	—	—	—										kpi	—	0	33
1952	LARm✧	12(DB)	19	114	6.0(51)	0	—	—	—	—										kpi	2	12	510
1953	LARm☆	12(DB)	2	2	1.0(5)	0	—	—	—	—										kpi	2	12	516
1954	LARm	12	26	72	2.8(18)	0	2	19	9.5(12)	0										kpi	1	6	390
1955	†LARm	12	—	—	—	—	19	199	10.5(19)	0										kp	—	0	210
1956	ChiC	12(DB)	—	—	—	—	—	—	—	—											—	0	-1
1957	ChiC	12(LE)	—	—	—	—	21	424	20.2(53)	5										kpi	—	30	608
1958	ChiC☆	12(LE)	—	—	—	—	46	690	15.0(64)	4										kp	—	24	383
1959	ChiC	12(LE)	—	—	—	—	34	534	15.7(85)	3											—	18	282
1960	Dal	6	—	—	—	—	1	19	19.0(19)	0											—	0	10
NFL	11	126	47	188	4.0(51)	0	123	1885	15.3(85)	12										kpi	6	108	3167

LEYENDECKER, TEX Charles B., T-C-LB, 6´1˝/235 lbs; Vanderbilt; B2/3/1906, D6/24/1988 Columbus, OH **1933** Phi 2 (0)

LEYPOLDT, JOHN John Howard, K, 6´2˝/229 lbs; Northern Virginia CC; B3/31/1946 Washington, DC **[K]** **1971** Buf 8 **1972** Buf 14 **1973** Buf 14 **1974**†Buf☆14 **1975** Buf 14 **1976** Buf 1 **1976** Sea 11 **1977** Sea 13 **1978** NO 2 **1978** Sea 1 **NFL** 92 [8 yrs]

LEYVA, VICTOR Victor Samuel, G, 6´4˝/315 lbs; Arizona State; 2001: Cin, rnd 5; B12/18/1977 Porterville, CA **2002** Cin 10 (0)

LICK, DENNIS Dennis Allen, T, 6´3˝/266 lbs; Wisconsin; 1976: Chi, rnd 1; B4/26/1954 Chicago, IL **1976** ChiB 14 (9, rt) **1977**†ChiB☆14 (14, RT) **1978** ChiB 16 (16, RT) **1979**†ChiB 16 (16, RT) **1980** ChiB 16 (16, RT) **1981** ChiB 3 (3) **NFL** 79 (74) [6 yrs]

Lidberg, Cully Carl leroy, FB, 5´10˝/191 lbs; Hamline; Minnesota; B8/25/1900 Red Wing, MN, D6/26/1987 Minneapolis, MN **1926** GB☆11 (8, FB), 24 **1929** GB 10 (4), 12 **1930** GB 5 (3), 6 **NFL** 26 (15), 42 [3 yrs]

Liddiard, Brody Jon Brody, aka Brody Heffner-Liddiard, TE, 6´4˝/240 lbs; Colorado; B6/12/1977 Salt Lake City, UT **2000**†Mia 5 (0) **2001** Min 16 (0) **2002** Min 16 (0) **2003** Min 16 (0) **NFL** 53 (0) [4 yrs]

Liddick, Dave David LeRoy, DT, 6´2˝/240 lbs; George Washington; 1957: Det, rnd 8; B12/10/1935 Harrisburg, PA **1957** Pit 4 **1958**†Cle 0 **NFL** 4 [2 yrs]

Liebel, Frank Frank Edward, E, 6´1˝/211 lbs; Norwich; B11/19/1919 Erie, PA, D12/26/1996 Erie, PA

YEAR	TEAM	G (GS, POS)	RUSH	YD	AVG (LG)	TD	REC	YD	AVG (LG)	TD	PASS	COMP	PCT	YD	AVG (LG)	TD	INT	SK	YD	QBR	KPR	OTD	PTS	TAY
1942	NYG	5 (0)	—	—	—	—	2	51	25.5 (29)	0	—	—	—	—	—	—	—	—	—	—	—	—	0	26
1943	†NYG	10 (4)	—	—	—	—	11	199	18.1 (56)	3	—	—	—	—	—	—	—	—	—	—	—	—	18	115
1944	†NYG	10 (10, RE)	—	—	—	—	13	292	22.5 (58)	5	—	—	—	—	—	—	—	—	—	—	i	1	36	174
1945	NYG☆	10 (0)	—	—	—	—	22	593	**27.0** (**54**)	**10**	—	—	—	—	—	—	—	—	—	—	i	—	60	359
1946	†NYG☆	11 (0)	—	—	—	—	20	360	18.0 (57)	4	—	—	—	—	—	—	—	—	—	—	i	—	24	292
1947	NYG	11 (0)	—	—	—	—	16	258	16.1 (38)	1	—	—	—	—	—	—	—	—	—	—	k	—	6	131
1948	ChiC	5 (0)	—	—	—	—	—	—	—	—	—	—	—	—	—	—	—	—	—	—	—	—	—	—
NFL	7	62 (14)	—	—	—	—	84	1753	20.9 (58)	23	—	—	—	—	—	—	—	—	—	—	ki	1	144	1096

Liebenstein, Todd Todd E., DE, 6´6˝/253 lbs; UNLV; 1982: Was, rnd 4; B1/9/1960 Las Vegas, NM **1982**†Was 9 (0) **1983**†Was 15 (15, LDE) **1984** Was 1 (1) **1985** Was 4 (0) **NFL** 29 (16) [4 yrs]

Lieberum, Don Donald, WB, 6´0˝/175 lbs; Manchester; B7/3/1918 Pittsburgh, PA, D11/7/1982 Fort Wayne, IN

YEAR	TEAM	G (GS, POS)	RUSH	YD	AVG (LG)	TD	REC	YD	AVG (LG)	TD	PASS	COMP	PCT	YD	AVG (LG)	TD	INT	SK	YD	QBR	KPR	OTD	PTS	TAY
1942	NYG	11 (0)	11	29	2.6 (19)	0	6	65	10.8 (30)	0	—	—	—	—	—	—	—	—	—	—	kp	—	0	54

Liggett, Bob Robert Ellsworth, DT, 6´2˝/255 lbs; Nebraska; 1970: KC, rnd 15; B12/8/1946 Aliquippa, PA **1970** KC 7

Light, Matt Matthew Charles, T, 6´4˝/305 lbs; Purdue; 2001: NE, rnd 2; B6/23/1978 Greenville, OH **2001**†NE 14 (12, LT) **2002** NE 16 (16, LT) **2003**†NE 16 (16, LT) **2004**†NE 16 (16, LT) **2005** NE 3 (3) **NFL** 65 (63) [5 yrs]

Liles, Alva Alva Edison, NT-DT, 6´3˝/255 lbs; Boise State; B3/6/1956 Oklahoma City, OK **1980** Oak 2 (0) **1980** Det 1 (0) **NFL** 3 (0) [1 yr]

Liles, Sonny Elvin Maerle, G-LB, 5´8˝/188 lbs; Oklahoma State; B8/9/1919 Marlow, OK, D7/25/2005 Aspen, CO **1943** Det 5 (0) **1944** Det 9 (0) **1945** Det 1 (0) **1945** Cle 8 (0) **NFL** 23 (0) [3 yrs]

Lilja, George George Vincent, G-C-T, 6´4˝/264 lbs; Michigan; 1981: LA, rnd 4; B3/3/1958 Evergreen Park, IL **1982** LARm 9 (0) **1983** NYJ 1 (0) **1984** NYJ 3 (0) **1984** Cle 4 (1) **1985**†Cle 16 (16, LG) **1986**†Cle 16 (0) **1987** Dal 5 (0) **NFL** 54 (17) [6 yrs]

Lilja, Ryan Ryan Matthew, G, 6´2˝/285 lbs; Kansas State; B10/15/1981 Kansas City, MO **2004** Ind 7 (6, lg) **2005**†Ind 16 (16, LG) **NFL** 23 (22) [2 yrs]

Lillard, Joe Joseph, TB-HB, 6´0˝/185 lbs; Oregon; B6/15/1905 Tulsa, OK, D9/18/1978 New York, NY **[K]**

YEAR	TEAM	G (GS, POS)	RUSH	YD	AVG (LG)	TD	REC	YD	AVG (LG)	TD	PASS	COMP	PCT	YD	AVG (LG)	TD	INT	SK	YD	QBR	KPR	OTD	PTS	TAY
1932	ChiC	7 (5, TB)	52	121	2.3	0	1	10	10.0 (10)	0	28	9	32.1	103	3.7	0	3	—	—	—	K	—	2	58
1933	ChiC	11 (7, TB)	119	373	3.1	1	1	19	19.0 (19)	0	67	18	26.9	269	4.0	2	16	—	—	—	K	1	19	-93
NFL	2	18 (12)	171	494	2.9	1	2	29	14.5 (19)	0	95	27	28.4	372	3.9	2	19	—	—	—	K	1	21	-36

Lilly, Bob Robert Lewis 'Mr. Cowboy', DT-DE, 6´5˝/260 lbs; TCU; 1961: Dal, rnd 1/DalT, rnd 2; B7/26/1939 Olney, TX; HOF 1980 **1961** Dal 14 (LDE) **1962** Dal✧14 (LDE) **1963** Dal 14 (14, LDE/rdt) **1964** Dal★14 (RDT) **1965** Dal★14 (RDT) **1966**†Dal★14 (RDT) **1967**†Dal★14 (RDT) **1968**†Dal★14 (RDT) **1969**†Dal★14 (RDT) **1970**†Dal★14 (RDT) **1971**†Dal★14 (RDT) **1972**†Dal★14 (RDT) **1973**†Dal★14 (RDT) **1974** Dal 14 (RDT) **NFL** 196 (14) [14 yrs]

Lilly, Kevin Kevin Paschal, DE-NT-DT, 6´4˝/265 lbs; Tulsa; B5/14/1963 Tulsa, OK **1988** SF 9 (2) **1989** SF 1 (0) **1989** Dal 1 (0) **NFL** 11 (2) [2 yrs]

Lilly, Sammy Samuel Julius, DB, 5´9˝/178 lbs; Georgia Tech; 1988: NYG, rnd 8; B2/12/1965 Anchorage, AK **1989**†Phi 15 (0) **1990** Phi 8 (0) **1990** SD 2 (0) **1991** LARm 16 (1) **1992** LARm 9 (0) **NFL** 50 (1) [4 yrs]

Lilly, Tony Robert Anthoney, DB, 6´0˝/199 lbs; Florida; 1984: Den, rnd 3; B2/16/1962 Alexandria, VA **1984**†Den 13 (0) **1985** Den 16 (5, fs) **1986**†Den 16 (1) **1987**†Den 13 (9, FS) **NFL** 58 (15) [4 yrs]

Lillywhite, Verl Verl Thomas, HB-LB, 5´10˝/185 lbs; USC; B12/5/1926 Garland, UT

YEAR	TEAM	G (GS, POS)	RUSH	YD	AVG (LG)	TD	REC	YD	AVG (LG)	TD	PASS	COMP	PCT	YD	AVG (LG)	TD	INT	SK	YD	QBR	KPR	OTD	PTS	TAY
1948	SF-A	14 (1)	53	340	6.4	3	1	-1	-1.0 (-1)	0	1	0	0.0	0	0.0	0	1	—	—	—	Ppi	—	18	367
1949	†SF-A	12 (3, RH)	69	263	3.8	2	8	82	10.3	2	—	—	—	—	—	—	—	—	—	—	Pki	—	24	339
AAFC	2	26 (4)	122	603	4.9	5	9	81	9.0	2	1	0	0.0	0	0.0	0	1	—	—	—	Pkpi	—	42	706
1950	SF	9 (LLB)	7	4	0.6 (5)	0	1	6	6.0 (6)	0	—	—	—	—	—	—	—	—	—	—	Pki	—	0	19
1951	SF	12 (LH)	67	397	5.9 (60)	1	11	125	11.4 (29)	1	—	—	—	—	—	—	—	—	—	—	Pi	—	12	507
NFL	2	21	74	401	5.4 (60)	1	12	131	10.9 (29)	1	—	—	—	—	—	—	—	—	—	—	Pki	—	12	526

Limbrick, Garrett Garrett, RB, 6´2˝/240 lbs; Oklahoma State; B11/6/1965 Houston, TX

YEAR	TEAM	G (GS, POS)	RUSH	YD	AVG (LG)	TD	REC	YD	AVG (LG)	TD	PASS	COMP	PCT	YD	AVG (LG)	TD	INT	SK	YD	QBR	KPR	OTD	PTS	TAY
1990	†Mia	7 (2)	5	14	2.8 (5)	0	4	23	5.8 (9)	0	—	—	—	—	—	—	—	—	—	—	—	—	0	26

Lince, Dave David LeRoy, TE, 6´7˝/265 lbs; North Dakota; 1966: Phi, rnd 7/Hou, rnd 14; B5/17/1944 Fargo, ND, D1/2/2002 Laguna Beach, CA **1966** Phi 4 **1967** Phi 14 **NFL** 18 [2 yrs]

Lincoln, Jeremy Jeremy Arlo, DB, 5´10˝/180 lbs; Tennessee; 1992: Chi, rnd 3; B4/7/1969 Toledo, OH **1993** ChiB 16 (7, rcb) **1994**†ChiB 15 (14, RCB) **1995** ChiB 16 (14, RCB) **1996** SL 13 (1) **1997** Sea 13 (3) **1998** NYG 16 (1) **1999** NYG 15 (7, rcb) **2000** Det 3 (0) **NFL** 107 (47) [8 yrs]

Lincoln, Keith Keith Payson, FB-HB, 6´1˝/215 lbs; Washington State; 1961: SD, rnd 2/Chi, rnd 5; B5/8/1939 Reading, MI **[K]**

YEAR	TEAM	G (GS, POS)	RUSH	YD	AVG (LG)	TD	REC	YD	AVG (LG)	TD	PASS	COMP	PCT	YD	AVG (LG)	TD	INT	SK	YD	QBR	KPR	OTD	PTS	TAY
1961	†SD-A	14	41	150	3.7 (17)	0	12	208	17.3 (**91**)	2	—	—	—	—	—	—	—	—	—	—	kp	1	18	427
1962	SD-A✧	14 (HB)	117	574	4.9 (86)	2	16	214	13.4 (29)	1	5	2	40.0	43	8.6 (23)	2	0	—	—	—	kp	1	24	975
1963	†SD-A★	14 (FB)	128	826	**6.5** (**76**)	5	24	325	13.5 (39)	3	1	0	0.0	0	0.0	0	0	—	—	—	kp	—	48	1301
1964	†SD-A★	14 (FB)	155	632	4.1 (25)	4	34	302	8.9 (37)	2	4	2	50.0	61	15.3 (53)	1	0	—	—	—	K	—	67	869
1965	SD-A✧	10 (fb)	74	302	4.1 (24)	3	23	376	16.3 (66)	4	3	2	66.7	65	21.7 (34)	1	1	—	—	—	k	—	42	554
1966	SD-A	14	58	214	3.7 (23)	1	14	264	18.9 (67)	2	4	2	50.0	71	17.8 (36)	1	0	—	—	—	—	—	18	407
1967	Buf-A✧	14 (14, HB)	159	601	3.8 (28)	4	41	558	13.6 (60)	5	—	—	—	—	—	—	—	—	—	—	—	—	54	945
1968	Buf-A	4	26	84	3.2 (24)	0	1	3	3.0 (3)	0	—	—	—	—	—	—	—	—	—	—	—	—	0	86
1968	SD-A	1	—	—	—	—	—	—	—	—	—	—	—	—	—	—	—	—	—	—	k	—	0	7
NFL	8	99 (14)	758	3383	4.5 (86)	19	165	2250	13.6 (91)	19	17	8	47.1	240	14.1 (53)	5	1	—	—	—	Kkp	2	271	5568

Lind, Mike Harry Norman Michael, FB, 6´2˝/220 lbs; Notre Dame; 1962: SF, rnd 5/SD, rnd 19; B2/2/1940 Chicago, IL, D10/25/2002 Chicago, IL

YEAR	TEAM	G (GS, POS)	RUSH	YD	AVG (LG)	TD	REC	YD	AVG (LG)	TD	PASS	COMP	PCT	YD	AVG (LG)	TD	INT	SK	YD	QBR	KPR	OTD	PTS	TAY
1963	SF	11	8	26	3.3 (7)	0	2	13	6.5 (8)	0	—	—	—	—	—	—	—	—	—	—	—	—	0	33
1964	SF	13 (9, FB)	100	256	2.6 (21)	7	25	178	7.1 (26)	0	1	1	100.0	69	69.0 (69)	1	0	—	—	—	—	—	42	455
1965	Pit	14 (FB)	111	375	3.4 (20)	1	25	236	9.4 (39)	1	—	—	—	—	—	—	—	—	—	—	—	—	12	508
1966	Pit	6	3	4	1.3 (3)	0	—	—	—	—	—	—	—	—	—	—	—	—	—	—	k	—	0	4
NFL	4	44 (9)	222	661	3.0 (21)	8	52	427	8.2 (39)	1	1	1	100.0	69	69.0 (69)	1	0	—	—	—	k	—	54	999

Lindahl, Joe Virgil Youngquist, G-E, 6´1˝/197 lbs; Wayne State (NE); Kentucky; B3/14/1919 Tilden, NE

YEAR	TEAM	G (GS, POS)	RUSH	YD	AVG (LG)	TD	REC	YD	AVG (LG)	TD	PASS	COMP	PCT	YD	AVG (LG)	TD	INT	SK	YD	QBR	KPR	OTD	PTS	TAY
1945	NYG	2 (0)	—	—	—	—	1	32	32.0 (32)	0	—	—	—	—	—	—	—	—	—	—	—	—	0	16

Lindell, Rian Rian David, K, 6´3˝/235 lbs; Washington State; B1/20/1977 Vancouver, WA **[K]** **2000** Sea 12 (0) **2001** Sea 16 (0) **2002** Sea 16 (0) **2003** Buf 16 (0) **2004** Buf 16 (0) **2005** Buf 16 (0) **NFL** 92 (0) [6 yrs]

Linden, Errol Errol Joseph, T, 6´5˝/258 lbs; Houston; 1961: Det, rnd 10/Hou, rnd 29; B10/21/1937 New Orleans, LA, D3/10/1983 New Orleans, LA **1961** Cle 10 **1962** Min 12 **1963** Min 14 (14, RT) **1964** Min 14 (14, RT) **1965** Min 14 (14, RT) **1966** Atl 14 (14, RT) **1967** Atl 14 (RT) **1968** Atl 14 (RT) **1969** NO 14 (RT) **1970** NO 14 (RT) **NFL** 134 (56) [10 yrs]

Lindon, Luke Luther W., T, 5´10˝/243 lbs; Kentucky; 1940: Cle, rnd 20; B6/23/1915 Salyerville, KY, D4/21/1988 Blacksburg, VA **1944** Det 10 (10, RT) **1945** Det 4 (1) **NFL** 14 (11) [2 yrs]

Lindow, Al Allen Lapham, B, 6´0˝/165 lbs; Washington-St. Louis; B7/9/1919 Milwaukee, WI, D1/18/1989 Fort Lauderdale, FL **1945** ChiC 1 (0)

Lindquist, Paul Paul August, DT, 6´3˝/265 lbs; New Hampshire; 1961: Min, rnd 8; B4/30/1939 Brockton, MA **1961** Bos-A 2

Lindsay, Everett Everett Eric, T-G, 6´4˝/305 lbs; Mississippi; 1993: Min, rnd 5; B9/18/1970 Burlington, IA **1993** Min 12 (12, LT) **1995** Min 16 (0) **1997**†Min 16 (3) **1998**†Min 16 (3) **1999** Bal 16 (16, RT/lg) **2000** Cle 16 (16, RG) **2001** Min 16 (8, lt) **2002** Min 16 (5, lt) **2003** Min 12 (0) **NFL** 136 (63) [9 yrs]

YEAR	TEAM	G(GS, POS)	RUSH	YD	AVG(LG)	TD	REC	YD	AVG(LG)	TD	PASS	COMP	PCT	YD	AVG(LG)	TD	INT	SK	YD	QBR	KPR	OTD	PTS	TAY

LINDSEY, DALE Phillip Dale, LB, 6´2˝/223 lbs; Kentucky; Western Kentucky; 1965: Cle, rnd 7/NYJ, rnd R6; B1/18/1943 Bedford, IN **1965**†Cle 14 **1966** Cle 13 (mlb) **1967**†Cle 14 (MLB) **1968**†Cle 12 (RLB) **1969**†Cle 14 (MLB/rlb) **1970** Cle 14 (MLB/rlb) **1971**†Cle 14 (MLB/rlb) **1972**†Cle 11 (MLB) **1973** NO 5 **NFL** 111 [9 yrs]

LINDSEY, HUB Hubert Allen, RB, 5´11˝/196 lbs; Wyoming; B3/17/1945 Steubenville, OH

YEAR	TEAM	G(GS, POS)	RUSH	YD	AVG(LG)	TD	REC	YD	AVG(LG)	TD	PASS	COMP	PCT	YD	AVG(LG)	TD	INT	SK	YD	QBR	KPR	OTD	PTS	TAY
1968	Den-A	3	4	17	4.3(7)	0	—	—	—	—	—	—	—	—	—	—	—	—	—	—	k	—	0	44

LINDSEY, JIM James Edgar, RB, 6´2˝/210 lbs; Arkansas; 1966: Min, rnd 2/Buf, rnd 2; B11/24/1944 Caldwell, AR

YEAR	TEAM	G(GS, POS)	RUSH	YD	AVG(LG)	TD	REC	YD	AVG(LG)	TD	PASS	COMP	PCT	YD	AVG(LG)	TD	INT	SK	YD	QBR	KPR	OTD	PTS	TAY
1966	Min	14	57	146	2.6(14)	1	20	250	12.5(46)	2	—	—	—	—	—	—	—	—	—	—	kp	—	18	304
1967	Min	8	4	10	2.5(6)	0	4	36	9.0(21)	0	—	—	—	—	—	—	—	—	—	—	k	—	0	54
1968	†Min	14	53	152	2.9(9)	4	15	148	9.9(22)	0	—	—	—	—	—	—	—	—	—	—	k	—	24	258
1969	†Min	10	6	21	3.5(10)	1	2	45	22.5(30)	1	—	—	—	—	—	—	—	—	—	—	k	—	12	55
1970	†Min	11	11	47	4.3(9)	0	4	94	23.5(49)	1	—	—	—	—	—	—	—	—	—	—	—	—	6	99
1971	†Min	14	46	182	4.0(19)	0	8	31	3.9(9)	0	—	—	—	—	—	—	—	—	—	—	—	1	6	198
1972	Min	13	1	8	8.0(8)	0	3	28	9.3(13)	0	—	—	—	—	—	—	—	—	—	—	k	—	0	24
NFL	7	84	178	566	3.2(19)	6	56	632	11.3(49)	4	—	—	—	—	—	—	—	—	—	—	kp	1	66	991

LINDSEY, MENZ Ellis Menzies, BB-QB, 5´6˝/130 lbs; Wabash; B7/25/1897 Boonville, IN, D9/20/1961 Evansville, IN **1921** Evv 5 (5, BB), 12

LINDSEY, STEVE Steve Kendall, K, 6´1˝/185 lbs; Mississippi; B11/25/1974 Hattiesburg, MS **[K]** **1999**†Jax 16 (0) **2000** Jax 10 (0) **2000**†Den 6 (0) **NFL** 32 (0) [2 yrs]

LINDSKOG, VIC Victor Junior, C, 6´1˝/203 lbs; Stanford; 1942: Phi, rnd 2; B12/3/1914 Roundtop, MT, D2/28/2003 Fort Worth, TX **1944** Phi 7 (4) **1945** Phi 10 (6, C) **1946** Phi 11 (10, C) **1947**†Phi 10 (1) **1948**†Phi 12 (11, C) **1949**†Phi 5 (4) **1950** Phi 12 (C)

YEAR	TEAM	G(GS, POS)	RUSH	YD	AVG(LG)	TD	REC	YD	AVG(LG)	TD	PASS	COMP	PCT	YD	AVG(LG)	TD	INT	SK	YD	QBR	KPR	OTD	PTS	TAY
1951	Phi☆	11(C)	—	—	—	—	0	21	(21)	0	—	—	—	—	—	—	—	—	—	—	—	—	0	11
NFL	8	78(36)	—	—	—	—	0	21	(21)	0	—	—	—	—	—	—	—	—	—	—	i	1	6	113

LINDSTROM, CHRIS Christopher Andrew, DE, 6´7˝/260 lbs; Boston University; 1982: SL, rnd 8; B8/3/1960 Weymouth, MA **1983** Cin 1 (0) **1983**†SF 0 (0) **1985** TB 15 (2) **1987** KC 3 (3) **NFL** 19 (5) [3 yrs]

LINDSTROM, DAVE David Alan, DE, 6´6˝/255 lbs; Boston University; 1977: SD, rnd 6; B11/16/1954 Cambridge, MA **1978** KC 16 **1979** KC 13 **1980** KC 16 (14, RDE) **1981** KC 16 (5, lde) **1982** KC 9 (4) **1983** KC 16 (3) **1984** KC 16 (2) **1985** KC 16 (2) **NFL** 118 (30) [8 yrs]

LINE, BILL Billie Boyd, DT, 6´7˝/260 lbs; Air Force; SMU; B8/11/1948 San Angelo, TX **1972** ChiB 13 (RDT)

LINGENFELTER, BOB Robert Newton, T-G, 6´7˝/277 lbs; Nebraska; 1977: Cle, rnd 7; B9/1/1954 Norfolk, NE **1977** Cle 14 (2) **1978**†Min 5 **NFL** 19 (2) [2 yrs]

LINGMERTH, GORAN Goran R., K, 5´8˝/160 lbs; Northern Arizona; B11/11/1964 Nassjo, Sweden **1987** Cle 1 (0)

LINGNER, ADAM Adam James, C, 6´4˝/268 lbs; Illinois; 1983: KC, rnd 9; B11/2/1960 Indianapolis, IN **1983** KC 16 (1) **1984** KC 16 (0) **1985** KC 16 (0) **1986** KC 12 (0) **1987** Buf 12 (0) **1988** Buf 16 (0) **1989**†Buf 16 (0) **1990**†Buf 16 (0) **1991**†Buf 16 (0) **1992**†Buf 16 (0) **1993**†Buf 16 (0) **1994** Buf 16 (0) **1995**†Buf 16 (0) **NFL** 200 (1) [13 yrs]

LINGREL, CHIM Paul Chalmer, WB-HB-FB, 6´2˝/200 lbs; Miami (OH); B1/21/1899 Ridgeway, OH, D3/11/1962 Kenton, OH **1923** Oor 6 (6, WB)

LINHART, TONI Anton Hansjog, K, 6´0˝/178 lbs; Austria Texh School; B7/24/1942 Donawitz, Austria **[K]** **1972** NO 2 **1974** Bal 14 **1975**†Bal 14 **1976**†Bal★14 **1977**†Bal★14 **1978** Bal 16 **1979** Bal 3 **1979** NYJ 5 **NFL** 82 [7 yrs]

LININGER, JACK Raymond Jack, LB-C, 5´11˝/217 lbs; Ohio State; 1949: Det, rnd 21/Cle-A, rnd 26; B6/27/1927 Van Wert, OH, D8/30/2002 Kennesaw, GA **1950** Det 12 (LLB) **1951** Det 12 **NFL** 24 [2 yrs]

LINN, JACK Jack Laroy, T-G, 6´5˝/295 lbs; West Virginia; 1990: Det, rnd 9; B6/10/1967 Sewickley, PA **1991** Ind 1 (0) **1992** Det 4 (4) **1993** Det 3 (2) **1993** Cin 3 (1) **NFL** 11 (7) [3 yrs]

LINNAN, FRANK Michael Francis, T-G, 6´2˝/198 lbs; Marquette; B2/20/1895 Pochahontas, IA, D6/2/1981 Tequesta, FL **1922** Rac 3 (2) **1926** Rac 2 (1) **NFL** 5 (3) [2 yrs]

LINNE, AUBREY Aubrey Arthur, TE, 6´7˝/235 lbs; TCU; B4/19/1939 **1961** Bal 1

LINNE, LARRY Larry Glen, WR, 6´1˝/185 lbs; Texas; Texas-El Paso; B7/20/1962 Baltimore, MD

YEAR	TEAM	G(GS, POS)	RUSH	YD	AVG(LG)	TD	REC	YD	AVG(LG)	TD	PASS	COMP	PCT	YD	AVG(LG)	TD	INT	SK	YD	QBR	KPR	OTD	PTS	TAY
1987	NE	3(3)	—	—	—	—	11	158	14.4(30)	2	—	—	—	—	—	—	—	—	—	—	p	—	12	86

LINNIN, CHRIS Christopher Bennett, DE, 6´4˝/255 lbs; Washington; 1980: NYG, rnd 7; B5/4/1957 Pasadena, CA **1980** NYG 10 (2)

LINTON, JONATHAN Jonathan C., RB, 6´0˝/248 lbs; North Carolina; 1998: Buf, rnd 5; B11/7/1974 Catasauqua, PA

YEAR	TEAM	G(GS, POS)	RUSH	YD	AVG(LG)	TD	REC	YD	AVG(LG)	TD	PASS	COMP	PCT	YD	AVG(LG)	TD	INT	SK	YD	QBR	KPR	OTD	PTS	TAY
1998	†Buf	14(0)	45	195	4.3(20)	1	1	10	10.0(10)	0	—	—	—	—	—	—	—	—	—	—	—	—	6	210
1999	†Buf	16(2, RB)	205	695	3.4(18)	5	29	228	7.9(28)	1	—	—	—	—	—	—	—	—	—	—	—	—	38	864
2000	Buf	14(2)	38	112	2.9(12)	0	3	8	2.7(4)	1	—	—	—	—	—	—	—	—	—	—	k	—	6	116
NFL	3	44(4)	288	1002	3.5(20)	6	33	246	7.5(28)	2	—	—	—	—	—	—	—	—	—	—	k	—	50	1190

LINTZENICH, JOE Joseph Francis, HB, 5´11˝/187 lbs; St. Louis; B3/26/1908 Webster Grove, MO, D6/23/1985 Creve Coeur, MO **1930** ChiB 13 (13, RH) **1931** ChiB 11 (7, RH), 12 **NFL** 24 (20) [2 yrs]

LIO, AUGIE Agostino Salvatore, G-T, 6´0˝/234 lbs; Georgetown (DC); 1941: Det, rnd 4; B4/30/1918 East Boston, MA, D9/3/1989 Clifton, NJ **[K]** **1942** Det✧10 (8, RG) **1943** Det☆10 (9, LT) **1944** Bos☆10 (10, LG) **1945** Bos☆10 (10, LG) **1946** Phi☆11 (5, lg)

YEAR	TEAM	G(GS, POS)	RUSH	YD	AVG(LG)	TD	REC	YD	AVG(LG)	TD	PASS	COMP	PCT	YD	AVG(LG)	TD	INT	SK	YD	QBR	KPR	OTD	PTS	TAY
1941	Det★	11(7, LG)	1	-4	-4.0(-4)	0	—	—	—	—	—	—	—	—	—	—	—	—	—	—	KPki	1	18	-15
NFL	6	62(49)	1	-4	-4.0(-4)	0	—	—	—	—	—	—	—	—	—	—	—	—	—	—	KPki	2	144	1

1947 Bal-A 10 (9, RG)

LIPINSKI, JIM James Victor, T-DT, 6´4˝/238 lbs; Fairmont State; 1950: ChiC, rnd 22; B2/25/1927 Monongah, WV **1950** ChiC 1

LIPPETT, RONNIE Ronald Leon, DB, 5´11˝/180 lbs; Miami (FL); 1983: NE, rnd 8; B12/10/1960 Melbourne, FL **[I]** **1983** NE 16 (16, LCB) **1984** NE 16 (8, lcb) **1985**†NE 16 (16, LCB) **1986** NE☆15 (15, LCB) **1987** NE☆12 (12, LCB) **1988** NE☆15 (15, LCB) **1990** NE 16 (16, LCB) **1991** NE 16 (13, LCB) **NFL** 122 (111) [8 yrs]

LIPPS, LOUIS Louis Adam, WR, 5´10˝/190 lbs; Southern Mississippi; 1984: Pit, rnd 1; B8/9/1962 New Orleans, LA **[R]**

YEAR	TEAM	G(GS, POS)	RUSH	YD	AVG(LG)	TD	REC	YD	AVG(LG)	TD	PASS	COMP	PCT	YD	AVG(LG)	TD	INT	SK	YD	QBR	KPR	OTD	PTS	TAY
1984	†Pit★	14(8, WR)	3	71	23.7(36)	1	45	860	19.1(80)	9	—	—	—	—	—	—	—	—	—	—	p	1	66	957
1985	Pit★	16(16, WR)	2	16	8.0(15)	1	59	1134	19.2(51)	12	—	—	—	—	—	—	—	—	—	—	kp	2	90	972
1986	Pit	13(12, WR)	4	-3	-0.8(8)	0	38	590	15.5(48)	3	—	—	—	—	—	—	—	—	—	—	p	—	18	308
1987	Pit	4(2)	—	—	—	—	11	164	14.9(27)	0	—	—	—	—	—	—	—	—	—	—	p	—	0	93
1988	Pit	16(16, WR)	6	129	21.5(39)	1	50	973	19.5(**89**)	5	2	1	50.0	13	6.5(13)	1	1	1	6	—	p	—	36	632
1989	†Pit	16(16, WR)	13	180	13.8(58)	1	50	944	18.9(79)	5	—	—	—	—	—	—	—	—	—	—	p	—	36	694
1990	Pit	14(14, WR)	1	-5	-5.0(-5)	0	50	682	13.6(37)	3	—	—	—	—	—	—	—	—	—	—	k	—	18	345
1991	Pit	15(14, WR)	—	—	—	—	55	671	12.2(35)	2	—	—	—	—	—	—	—	—	—	—	—	—	12	346
1992	NO	2(0)	—	—	—	—	1	1	1.0(1)	0	—	—	—	—	—	—	—	—	—	—	p	—	0	-3
NFL	9	110(98)	29	388	13.4(58)	4	359	6019	16.8(89)	39	2	1	50.0	13	6.5(13)	1	1	1	6	—	kp	3	276	4344

LIPSCOMB, GENE Eugene Allen 'Big Daddy', DT, 6´6˝/284 lbs; none; B8/9/1931 Detroit, MI, D5/10/1963 Baltimore, MD **1953** LARm 2 **1954** LARm 11 (RDT) **1955**†LARm 12 (rdt) **1956** Bal 11 **1957** Bal 12 (RDT) **1958**†Bal★12 (RDT) **1959**†Bal★12 (RDT) **1960** Bal☆12 (RDT) **1961** Pit☆14 (LDT) **1962** Pit✧14 (LDT) **NFL** 112 [10 yrs]

LIPSCOMB, PAUL Paul F., T-DT, 6´5˝/246 lbs; Tennessee; B1/13/1923 Benton, IL, D8/20/1964 Elm Grove, IN **1945** GB 10 (10, RT) **1946** GB 11 (11, RT) **1947** GB 12 (10, RT) **1948** GB 12 (11, RT) **1949** GB 12 (12, RT) **1950** Was✧12 (RDT) **1951** Was★12 (RT) **1952** Was✧12 (RDT) **1953** Was✧12 (RDT) **1954** Was 1 **1954** ChiB 11 **NFL** 117 (54) [10 yrs]

LIPSKI, JOHN John J., C, 5´11˝/200 lbs; Temple; B1909, D1/22/1963 Philadelphia, PA **1933** Phi 8 (6, C) **1934** Phi 10 (9, C) **NFL** 18 (15) [2 yrs]

LISBON, DON Donald, HB, 5´10˝/197 lbs; Bowling Green State; 1963: SF, rnd 3; B1/15/1941 Youngstown, OH

YEAR	TEAM	G(GS, POS)	RUSH	YD	AVG(LG)	TD	REC	YD	AVG(LG)	TD	PASS	COMP	PCT	YD	AVG(LG)	TD	INT	SK	YD	QBR	KPR	OTD	PTS	TAY
1963	SF	14(8, LH)	109	399	3.7(25)	0	21	259	12.3(51)	2	2	1	50.0	45	22.5(45)	1	0	—	—	—	—	—	12	566
1964	SF	6(4, LH/rh)	55	162	2.9(14)	0	13	104	8.0(39)	1	—	—	—	—	—	—	—	—	—	—	—	—	6	219
NFL	2	20(12)	164	561	3.4(25)	0	34	363	10.7(51)	3	2	1	50.0	45	22.5(45)	1	0	—	—	—	—	—	18	785

LISCH, RUSTY Russell John, QB, 6´3˝/213 lbs; Notre Dame; 1980: SL, rnd 4; B12/21/1956 Belleville, IL

YEAR	TEAM	G(GS, POS)	RUSH	YD	AVG(LG)	TD	REC	YD	AVG(LG)	TD	PASS	COMP	PCT	YD	AVG(LG)	TD	INT	SK	YD	QBR	KPR	OTD	PTS	TAY
1980	SL	2(0)	—	—	—	—	—	—	—	—	17	6	35.3	68	4.0(23)	0	3	3	36	—	—	—	0	-86
1981	SL	9(1)	—	—	—	—	—	—	—	—	—	—	—	—	—	—	—	—	—	—	—	—	—	—
1982	†SL	8(0)	—	—	—	—	—	—	—	—	—	—	—	—	—	—	—	—	—	—	—	—	—	—
1983	SL	4(0)	2	9	4.5(5)	0	—	—	—	—	13	6	46.2	66	5.1(26)	1	2	3	27	—	—	—	0	-33

YEAR	TEAM	G (GS, POS)	RUSH	YD	AVG (LG)	TD	REC	YD	AVG (LG)	TD	PASS	COMP	PCT	YD	AVG (LG)	TD	INT	SK	YD	QBR	KPR	OTD	PTS	TAY
1984	ChiB	7(1)	18	121	6.7(31)	0	—	—	—	—	85	43	50.6	413	4.9(23)	0	6	13	91	—	—	—	0	88
NFL	5	30(2)	20	130	6.5(31)	0	—	—	—	—	115	55	47.8	547	4.8(26)	1	11	19	154	—	—	—	0	-32

Liscio, Tony Anthony Fred, T-G, 6´5˝/264 lbs; Tulsa; 1963: GB, rnd 3/NYJ, rnd 10; B7/2/1940 Pittsburgh, PA **1963** Dal 7 (5, lt) **1964** Dal 10 (LT) **1966**†Dal☆14 (14, LG/lt) **1967**†Dal 14 (LT) **1968**†Dal 14 (LT) **1969**†Dal 14 (LT) **1970**†Dal 11 (8, LT) **1971**†Dal 5 (5, lt) **NFL** 89 (32) [8 yrs]

Liske, Pete Peter Adrian, QB, 6´3˝/200 lbs; Penn State; 1963: NYJ, rnd 15/Phi, rnd 10; B5/24/1942 Plainfield, NJ

YEAR	TEAM	G (GS, POS)	RUSH	YD	AVG (LG)	TD	REC	YD	AVG (LG)	TD	PASS	COMP	PCT	YD	AVG (LG)	TD	INT	SK	YD	QBR	KPR	OTD	PTS	TAY
1964	NYJ-A	2	1	0	0.0(0)	0	—	—	—	—	18	9	50.0	55	3.1(27)	0	2	—	—	—	—	—	0	-53
1969	Den-A	7(2)	10	50	5.0(19)	0	—	—	—	—	115	61	53.0	845	7.3(71)	9	11	15	103	63.4	—	—	0	78
1970	Den	11(9, QB)	7	42	6.0(14)	1	—	—	—	—	238	112	47.1	1340	5.6(74)	7	11	28	228	55.3	—	—	6	317
1971	Phi	14(QB)	13	29	2.2(9)	1	—	—	—	—	269	143	53.2	1957	7.3(69)	11	15	13	134	67.1	—	—	6	473
1972	Phi	14(7, QB)	7	20	2.9(9)	0	—	—	—	—	138	71	51.4	973	7.1(67)	3	7	11	107	60.4	—	—	0	242
NFL	5	48(18)	38	141	3.7(19)	2	—	—	—	—	778	396	50.9	5170	6.6(74)	30	46	67	572	60.4	—	—	12	1056

Liston, Paul Edward Paul Jones, G, 5´11˝/185 lbs; Georgetown (DC); B7/31/1903, PA, D5/4/1979 Somerville, MA **1930** Nwk 1 (0)

Listopad, Ed Edward George, G, 6´1˝/230 lbs; Wake Forest; 1952: ChiC, rnd 19; B8/28/1929 Baltimore, MD **1952** ChiC 4

Liter, Greg Gregory Paul, DE, 6´6˝/275 lbs; Iowa State; B12/31/1963 Wausau, WI **1987** SF 1 (0) **1987** Phi 1 (0) **NFL** 2 (0) [1 yr]

Litkus, Red Bernard Howard, T-E, /187 lbs; none; B1894, PA, deceased **1921** Was 3 (1)

Little, Dave David Gene, TE, 6´2˝/233 lbs; Middle Tennessee State; B4/18/1961 Selma, CA

YEAR	TEAM	G (GS, POS)	RUSH	YD	AVG (LG)	TD	REC	YD	AVG (LG)	TD	PASS	COMP	PCT	YD	AVG (LG)	TD	INT	SK	YD	QBR	KPR	OTD	PTS	TAY
1984	KC	10(1)	—	—	—	—	1	13	13.0(13)	0	—	—	—	—	—	—	—	—	—	—	—	—	0	7
1985	Phi	15(0)	—	—	—	—	7	82	11.7(28)	0	—	—	—	—	—	—	—	—	—	—	—	1	6	41
1986	Phi	16(5, te)	—	—	—	—	14	132	9.4(26)	0	—	—	—	—	—	—	—	—	—	—	—	—	0	66
1987	Phi	12(0)	—	—	—	—	1	8	8.0(8)	0	—	—	—	—	—	—	—	—	—	—	—	—	0	4
1988	†Phi	10(0)	—	—	—	—	—	—	—	—	—	—	—	—	—	—	—	—	—	—	—	—	—	—
1989	†Phi	16(1)	—	—	—	—	2	8	4.0(7)	1	—	—	—	—	—	—	—	—	—	—	k	—	6	-7
1990	Phx	11(0)	—	—	—	—	—	—	—	—	—	—	—	—	—	—	—	—	—	—	—	—	—	—
1991	†Det	2(0)	—	—	—	—	—	—	—	—	—	—	—	—	—	—	—	—	—	—	—	—	—	—
NFL	8	92(7)	—	—	—	—	25	243	9.7(28)	1	—	—	—	—	—	—	—	—	—	—	k	1	12	111

Little, David David Lamar, LB, 6´1˝/232 lbs; Florida; 1981: Pit, rnd 7; B1/3/1959 Miami, FL, D3/17/2005 Miami, FL **1981** Pit 16 (0) **1982**†Pit 9 (1) **1983**†Pit 16 (1) **1984**†Pit 16 (13, LILB) **1985** Pit 16 (16, LILB) **1986** Pit 16 (16, LILB) **1987** Pit 12 (12, LILB) **1988** Pit 16 (14, LILB) **1989**†Pit 16 (16, LILB) **1990** Pit★16 (14, RILB) **1991** Pit 14 (10, RILB) **1992**†Pit 16 (12, RILB) **NFL** 179 (125) [12 yrs]

Little, Earl Earl Jerome, DB, 6´1˝/200 lbs; Michigan; Miami (FL); B3/10/1973 Miami, FL **1998** NO 16 (0) **1999** NO 1 (0) **1999** Cle 9 (0) **2000** Cle 16 (0) **2001** Cle 16 (16, SS) **2002**†Cle 13 (9, fs) **2003** Cle 16 (16, FS) **2004** Cle 16 (11, FS) **2005** GB 4 (0) **NFL** 107 (52) [8 yrs]

Little, Everett Everett Charles, G, 6´4˝/265 lbs; Houston; 1976: TB, rnd 4; B6/12/1954 Lufkin, TX **1976** TB 10 (1)

Little, Floyd Floyd Douglas, RB, 5´10˝/196 lbs; Syracuse; 1967: Den, rnd 1; B7/4/1942 New Haven, CT **[R]**

YEAR	TEAM	G (GS, POS)	RUSH	YD	AVG (LG)	TD	REC	YD	AVG (LG)	TD	PASS	COMP	PCT	YD	AVG (LG)	TD	INT	SK	YD	QBR	KPR	OTD	PTS	TAY
1967	Den-A	13(HB)	130	381	2.9(14)	1	7	11	1.6(15)	0	—	—	—	—	—	—	—	—	—	—	kp	1	12	1014
1968	Den-A✧	11(HB)	158	584	3.7(55)	3	19	331	17.4(66)	1	2	0	0.0	0	0.0	0	0	—	—	—	kp	1	30	1195
1969	Den-A★	9(9, HB)	146	729	5.0(48)	6	19	218	11.5(67)	1	2	0	0.0	0	0.0	0	0	—	—	—	kp	—	42	979
1970	Den★	14(14, RB)	**209**	**901**	4.3(80)	3	17	161	9.5(39)	0	2	0	0.0	0	0.0	0	0	1	5	—	kp	—	18	1125
1971	Den★	14(13, RB)	**284**	**1133**	4.0(40)	6	26	255	9.8(74)	0	1	0	0.0	0	0.0	0	0	—	—	—	k	—	36	**1415**
1972	Den☆	14(14, RB)	216	859	4.0(55)	9	28	367	13.1(40)	4	2	2	100.0	43	21.5(35)	1	0	—	—	—	kp	—	78	1206
1973	Den★	14(13, RB)	256	979	3.8(47)	**12**	41	423	10.3(50)	1	—	—	—	—	—	—	—	—	—	—	p	—	78	1318
1974	Den	14(9, RB)	117	312	2.7(22)	1	29	344	11.9(72)	0	—	—	—	—	—	—	—	—	—	—	kp	—	6	559
1975	Den	14(10, RB)	125	445	3.6(19)	2	29	308	10.6(66)	2	—	—	—	—	—	—	—	—	—	—	k	—	24	696
NFL	9	117(82)	1641	6323	3.9(80)	43	215	2418	11.2(74)	9	9	2	22.2	43	4.8(35)	1	0	1	5	—	kp	2	324	9505

Little, George George Willard, DE-NT, 6´4˝/278 lbs; Iowa; 1985: Mia, rnd 3; B6/27/1963 Duquesne, PA **1985**†Mia 14 (3) **1986** Mia 16 (16, RDE) **1987** Mia 9 (0) **NFL** 39 (19) [3 yrs]

Little, Jack Jack Harold, T, 6´4˝/235 lbs; Texas A&M; 1953: Bal, rnd 5; B12/31/1931 Corpus Christi, TX **1953** Bal 9 (RT) **1954** Bal 11 (RT) **NFL** 20 [2 yrs]

Little, Jim James W., T, 6´1˝/200 lbs; Kentucky; 1945: NYG, rnd 16; B3/18/1920, D2/22/1995 Beattyville, KY **1945** NYG 3 (0)

Little, John John Dvid, DT-DE-NT, 6´3˝/241 lbs; Oklahoma State; 1970: NYJ, rnd 14; B5/3/1947 Tallulah, LA, D7/9/1997 Hot Coffee, MS **1970** NYJ 14 **1971** NYJ 14 (LDT) **1972** NYJ 14 (LDT) **1973** NYJ 14 (LDT) **1974** NYJ 14 **1975** Hou 14 **1976** Hou 14 **1977** Buf 12 **NFL** 110 [8 yrs]

Little, Larry Lawrence Chatmon, G-T, 6´1˝/265 lbs; Bethune-Cookman; B11/2/1945 Groveland, GA; HOF 1993 **1967** SD-A 10 **1968** SD-A 14 (4) **1969** Mia-A✧12 (10, RG) **1970**†Mia 14 (14, RG) **1971**†Mia★14 (14, RG) **1972**†Mia★14 (14, RG) **1973**†Mia★13 (13, RG) **1974**†Mia★14 (14, RG) **1975** Mia☆14 (14, RG) **1976** Mia 14 (14, RG/rt) **1977** Mia☆14 (14, RG) **1978** Mia☆16 (15, RG) **1979**†Mia 15 (14, RG) **1980** Mia 5 (3) **NFL** 183 (157) [14 yrs]

Little, Leonard Leonard Antonio, DE, 6´3˝/261 lbs; Tennessee; 1998: SL, rnd 3; B10/19/1974 Asheville, NC **[S]** **1998** SL 6 (0) **1999**†SL 6 (0) **2000**†SL 14 (0) **2001**†SL 13 (0) **2002** SL 16 (15, LDE) **2003**†SL★12 (12, LDE) **2004**†SL 16 (16, LDE) **2005** SL 14 (14, LDE) **NFL** 97 (57) [8 yrs]

Little, Lou Louis Lawrence, aka Luigi Piccolo, T, 6´0˝/205 lbs; Vermont; Pennsylvania; B12/6/1891 Boston, MA, D5/28/1979 Boynton Beach, FL **1920** Buf 11 (6, RT) **1921** Buf 6 (6, RT) **NFL** 17 (12) [2 yrs]

Little, Steve Steven Richard, K, 6´0˝/180 lbs; Arkansas; 1978: SL, rnd 1; B2/19/1956 Springfield, IL, D9/6/1999 Little Rock, AR **[K]**

YEAR	TEAM	G (GS, POS)	RUSH	YD	AVG (LG)	TD	REC	YD	AVG (LG)	TD	PASS	COMP	PCT	YD	AVG (LG)	TD	INT	SK	YD	QBR	KPR	OTD	PTS	TAY
1978	SL	11	1	0	0.0(0)	0	—	—	—	—	—	—	—	—	—	—	—	—	—	—	P	—	0	0
1979	SL	16	2	0	0.0(0)	0	—	—	—	—	3	2	66.7	31	10.3(16)	0	0	—	—	—	KP	—	54	16
1980	SL	6(0)	—	—	—	—	—	—	—	—	—	—	—	—	—	—	—	—	—	—	K	—	26	0
NFL	3	33	3	0	0.0	0	—	—	—	—	3	2	66.7	31	10.3(16)	0	0	—	—	—	KP	—	80	16

Littlefield, Carl Carl Lester, B, 6´0˝/200 lbs; Washington State; B8/6/1916 Plymouth, CA, D5/23/1988 Plymouth, CA

YEAR	TEAM	G (GS, POS)	RUSH	YD	AVG (LG)	TD	REC	YD	AVG (LG)	TD	PASS	COMP	PCT	YD	AVG (LG)	TD	INT	SK	YD	QBR	KPR	OTD	PTS	TAY
1938	Cle	9(1)	19	69	3.6	0	1	9	9.0(9)	0	15	1	6.7	23	1.5(23)	0	5	—	—	—	—	1	6	-115
1939	Pit	10(4, FB)	39	141	3.6	0	1	18	18.0(18)	0	—	—	—	—	—	—	—	—	—	—	—	—	0	150
1940	Pit	1(0)	—	—	—	—	—	—	—	—	—	—	—	—	—	—	—	—	—	—	—	—	—	—
NFL	3	20(5)	58	210	3.6	0	2	27	13.5(18)	0	15	1	6.7	23	1.5(23)	0	5	—	—	—	—	1	6	35

Littleton, Jody Jody, LB, 6´1˝/235 lbs; Baylor; B10/23/1974 Denver, CO **2002** ChiB 2 (0) **2003** Det 3 (0) **2004** Det 8 (0) **2005** Cle 5 (0) **NFL** 18 (0) [4 yrs]

Little Twig, Joe Joseph, aka Joseph Johnson, E-T, 5´11˝/183 lbs; Carlisle Indian; B1893, D1937, **[K]** **1922** Oor 2 (2) **1923** Oor 11 (10, LE), 1 **1924** RI☆7 (4), 6 **1925** RI 10 (10, LE), 6 **1926** Can 6 (5, le) **1926** Akr 1 (0) **NFL** 37 (31), 13 [5 yrs]

Livers, Mickey Harold Irving, FB, 5´10˝/180 lbs; Georgetown (DC); B11/30/1895, D9/1977 Hampton, VA **1921** Was 1 (0)

Livers, Virgil Virgil Chester, DB, 5´8˝/176 lbs; Western Kentucky; 1975: Chi, rnd 4; B3/26/1952 Fairfield, KY **[R]** **1975** ChiB 14 (7, RCB) **1976** ChiB 14 (14, RCB) **1977**†ChiB 14 (14, RCB) **1978** ChiB 13 (13, RCB) **1979**†ChiB 13 (12, RCB) **NFL** 68 (60) [5 yrs]

Livingston, Andy Andrew Leon, RB, 6´1˝/236 lbs; Phoenix College (JC); B10/21/1944 Eufaula, OK

YEAR	TEAM	G (GS, POS)	RUSH	YD	AVG (LG)	TD	REC	YD	AVG (LG)	TD	PASS	COMP	PCT	YD	AVG (LG)	TD	INT	SK	YD	QBR	KPR	OTD	PTS	TAY
1964	ChiB	2	2	-3	-1.5(1)	0	1	0	0.0(0)	0	—	—	—	—	—	—	—	—	—	—	k	1	6	84
1965	ChiB	14	63	363	5.8(30)	2	12	134	11.2(30)	0	—	—	—	—	—	—	—	—	—	—	k	—	12	486
1967	ChiB	12	28	41	1.5(6)	0	5	62	12.4(38)	0	—	—	—	—	—	—	—	—	—	—	—	—	0	72
1968	ChiB	4	7	25	3.6(8)	0	—	—	—	—	—	—	—	—	—	—	—	—	—	—	—	—	0	25
1969	NO✧	14(HB)	181	761	4.2(18)	5	28	278	9.9(51)	3	4	3	75.0	38	9.5(14)	1	1	—	—	—	—	—	48	949
1970	NO	1	10	29	2.9(10)	0	—	—	—	—	—	—	—	—	—	—	—	—	—	—	—	—	0	29
NFL	6	47	291	1216	4.2(30)	7	46	474	10.3(51)	3	4	3	75.0	38	9.5(14)	1	1	—	—	—	k	1	66	1645

Livingston, Bruce Bruce, DB, 5´10˝/169 lbs; Arkansas Tech; B8/7/1963 **1987** Dal 3 (0)

Livingston, Cliff Clifford Lyman, LB-DE, 6´3˝/218 lbs; UCLA; B7/2/1930 Compton, CA **1954** NYG 12 (RDE) **1955** NYG 4 **1956**†NYG 12 **1957** NYG 10 **1958**†NYG 12 **1959**†NYG 12 (LLB) **1960** NYG 11 (LLB) **1961**†NYG☆13 (LLB) **1962** Min 12 (11, LLB) **1963** LARm 14 (llb) **1964** LARm 14 (14, RLB) **1965** LARm 10 **NFL** 136 (25) [12 yrs]

LIVINGSTON, DALE Dale Roger, K, 6´0˝/210 lbs; Eastern Michigan; Western Michigan; 1968: Cin, rnd 3; B3/12/1945 Plymouth, MI **[K]**

YEAR	TEAM	G (GS, POS)	RUSH	YD	AVG (LG)	TD	REC	YD	AVG (LG)	TD	PASS	COMP	PCT	YD	AVG (LG)	TD	INT	SK	YD	QBR	KPR	OTD	PTS	TAY
1968	Cin-A	12	1	11	11.0(11)	0	—	—	—	—	—	—	—	—	—	—	—	—	—	—	KP	—	59	11
1969	Cin-A	12	1	18	18.0(18)	0	—	—	—	—	2	2	100.0	15	7.5(17)	0	0	—	—	—	P	—	0	26
1970	GB	14	1	1	1.0(1)	0	—	—	—	—	—	—	—	—	—	—	—	—	—	—	KP	—	64	1
NFL	3	38	3	30	10.0(18)	0	—	—	—	—	2	2	100.0	15	7.5(17)	0	0	—	—	—	KP	—	123	38

LIVINGSTON, HOWIE Howard, FB-WB-HB, 6´1˝/183 lbs; Cal State-Fullerton; B5/15/1922 Los Angeles, CA, D7/16/1994 Yorba Linda, CA **[I]**

YEAR	TEAM	G (GS, POS)	RUSH	YD	AVG (LG)	TD	REC	YD	AVG (LG)	TD	PASS	COMP	PCT	YD	AVG (LG)	TD	INT	SK	YD	QBR	KPR	OTD	PTS	TAY
1944	†NYG	10(3, fb)	84	313	3.7(43)	1	1	12	12.0(12)	1	1	0	0.0	0	0.0	0	1	—	—	—	Pkpi	1	18	509
1945	NYG	10(6, fb)	40	109	2.7(13)	3	14	250	17.9(47)	2	—	—	—	—	—	—	—	—	—	—	Pkpi	—	30	409
1946	†NYG	10(7, WB)	10	38	3.8(18)	0	2	36	18.0(24)	1	—	—	—	—	—	—	—	—	—	—	ki	2	18	125
1947	NYG	10(8, WB)	19	87	4.6(43)	0	12	273	22.8(65)	3	—	—	—	—	—	—	—	—	—	—	ki	—	18	356
1948	Was	7(1)	—	—	—	—	—	—	—	—	—	—	—	—	—	—	—	—	—	—	—	—	—	—
1949	Was	12(7, RH)	1	1	1.0(1)	1	3	41	13.7(29)	0	—	—	—	—	—	—	—	—	—	—	i	—	6	65
1950	Was	4	1	0	0.0(0)	0	5	156	31.2(74)	2	—	—	—	—	—	—	—	—	—	—	pi	—	12	103
1950	SF	7	—	—	—	—	—	—	—	—	—	—	—	—	—	—	—	—	—	—	i	1	6	89
1953	ChiB	2	—	—	—	—	—	—	—	—	—	—	—	—	—	—	—	—	—	—	—	—	—	—
NFL	8	72(32)	155	548	3.5(43)	5	37	768	20.8(74)	9	1	0	0.0	0	0.0	0	1	—	—	—	Pkpi	4	108	1655

LIVINGSTON, MIKE Michael Paul, QB, 6´4˝/212 lbs; SMU; 1968: KC, rnd 2; B11/14/1945 Dallas, TX

YEAR	TEAM	G (GS, POS)	RUSH	YD	AVG (LG)	TD	REC	YD	AVG (LG)	TD	PASS	COMP	PCT	YD	AVG (LG)	TD	INT	SK	YD	QBR	KPR	OTD	PTS	TAY
1968	KC-A	1	2	2	1.0(3)	0	—	—	—	—	—	—	—	—	—	—	—	—	—	—	—	—	0	2
1969	†KC-A✧	9(6, qb)	15	102	6.8(39)	0	—	—	—	—	161	84	52.2	1123	7.0(**93**)	4	6	11	124	67.4	—	—	0	444
1970	KC	4(2)	3	26	8.7(16)	0	—	—	—	—	22	11	50.0	122	5.5(31)	0	1	4	42	—	—	—	0	47
1971	KC	3(1)	5	11	2.2(5)	0	—	—	—	—	28	12	42.9	130	4.6(36)	0	0	4	39	—	—	—	0	76
1972	KC	5(2)	14	133	9.5(51)	0	—	—	—	—	78	41	52.6	480	6.2(36)	7	8	6	42	—	—	—	0	88
1973	KC	8(8, QB)	19	94	4.9(28)	2	—	—	—	—	145	75	51.7	916	6.3(48)	6	7	16	124	—	—	—	12	322
1974	KC	8(6, qb)	9	28	3.1(9)	0	—	—	—	—	141	66	46.8	732	5.2(48)	4	10	10	101	—	—	—	0	14
1975	KC	7(7, QB)	13	68	5.2(28)	1	—	—	—	—	176	88	50.0	1245	7.1(69)	8	6	17	131	74.2	—	1	12	501
1976	KC	14(14, QB)	31	89	2.9(19)	2	—	—	—	—	338	189	55.9	2682	7.9(57)	12	13	31	284	77.6	—	—	12	990
1977	KC	13(11, QB)	19	78	4.1(13)	1	—	—	—	—	282	143	50.7	1823	6.5(49)	9	15	30	285	59.8	—	—	6	445
1978	KC	14(14, QB)	23	49	2.1(18)	1	—	—	—	—	290	159	54.8	1573	5.4(44)	5	13	18	171	57.4	—	—	6	351
1979	KC	5(4)	3	2	0.7(5)	0	—	—	—	—	90	44	48.9	469	5.2(38)	1	4	5	49	—	—	—	0	82
NFL	12	91(75)	156	682	4.4(51)	7	—	—	—	—	1751	912	52.1	11295	6.5(93)	56	83	152	1392	63.3	—	1	48	3360

LIVINGSTON, TED Theodore Alfred, T-G, 6´3˝/219 lbs; Kansas State; Indiana; B2/18/1913 Ellsworth, KS, D6/8/1984 Cleveland, OH **1937** Cle 11 (8, RT) **1938** Cle 10 (6, RT) **1939** Cle 11 (9, LG) **1940** Cle✧9 (9, RG) **NFL** 41 (32) [4 yrs]

LIVINGSTON, WALT Walter, HB, 6´0˝/185 lbs; Heidelberg; 1957: Bal, rnd 20; B9/12/1934 Ravenna, OH

YEAR	TEAM	G (GS, POS)	RUSH	YD	AVG (LG)	TD	REC	YD	AVG (LG)	TD	PASS	COMP	PCT	YD	AVG (LG)	TD	INT	SK	YD	QBR	KPR	OTD	PTS	TAY
1960	Bos-A	3	10	16	1.6(5)	1	1	0	0.0(0)	0	—	—	—	—	—	—	—	—	—	—	k	—	6	14

LIVINGSTON, WARREN Warren, DB, 5´10˝/192 lbs; Arizona; B7/5/1938 Eufaula, OK **1961** Dal 8 (8, LCB) **1962** Dal 3 **1963** Dal 14 (RS) **1964** Dal 14 (7, rcb) **1965** Dal 14 (RCB) **1966**†Dal 14 (RCB) **NFL** 67 (15) [6 yrs]

LIVINGSTONE, BOB Robert Edward, HB-DB, 6´0˝/173 lbs; Notre Dame; 1947: ChiR-A, rnd 14/1945: ChiB, rnd 22; B5/11/1922 Hammond, IN

YEAR	TEAM	G (GS, POS)	RUSH	YD	AVG (LG)	TD	REC	YD	AVG (LG)	TD	PASS	COMP	PCT	YD	AVG (LG)	TD	INT	SK	YD	QBR	KPR	OTD	PTS	TAY
1948	ChiR-A	13(5, LH)	55	174	3.2	0	15	240	16.0	2	—	—	—	—	—	—	—	—	—	—	kp	—	12	389
1949	ChiH-A	6(0)	—	—	—	—	3	80	26.7	0	—	—	—	—	—	—	—	—	—	—	kp	—	0	116
1949	†Buf-A	5(0)	1	0	0.0	0	—	—	—	—	—	—	—	—	—	—	—	—	—	—	kpi	1	6	137
AAFC	2	24(5)	56	174	3.1	0	18	320	17.8	2	—	—	—	—	—	—	—	—	—	—	kpi	1	18	642
1950	Bal	11(DB)	1	-3	-3.0(-3)	0	—	—	—	—	—	—	—	—	—	—	—	—	—	—	kpi	—	0	57

LIWIENSKI, CHRIS Chris, G-T, 6´5˝/325 lbs; Indiana; 1998: Det, rnd 7; B8/2/1975 Sterling Heights, MI **1998** Min 1 (0) **2000**†Min 14 (1) **2001** Min 16 (16, RT) **2002** Min 16 (16, RT) **2003** Min 16 (16, LG) **2004**†Min 16 (16, LG) **2005** Min 15 (9, LG) **NFL** 94 (74) [7 yrs]

LLOYD, BRANDON Brandon Matthew, WR, 6´0˝/184 lbs; Illinois; 2003: SF, rnd 4; B7/5/1981 Kansas City, MO

YEAR	TEAM	G (GS, POS)	RUSH	YD	AVG (LG)	TD	REC	YD	AVG (LG)	TD	PASS	COMP	PCT	YD	AVG (LG)	TD	INT	SK	YD	QBR	KPR	OTD	PTS	TAY
2003	SF	16(1)	—	—	—	—	14	212	15.1(44)	2	—	—	—	—	—	—	—	—	—	—	k	—	14	118
2004	SF	13(13, WR)	—	—	—	—	43	565	13.1(52)	6	—	—	—	—	—	—	—	—	—	—	—	—	38	313
2005	SF	16(15, WR)	—	—	—	—	48	733	15.3(89)	5	—	—	—	—	—	—	—	—	—	—	—	—	30	392
NFL	3	45(29)	—	—	—	—	105	1510	14.4(89)	13	—	—	—	—	—	—	—	—	—	—	k	—	82	822

LLOYD, DAN Daniel D., LB, 6´2˝/225 lbs; Washington; 1976: NYG, rnd 6; B11/9/1953 Heber, UT **1976** NYG 14 **1977** NYG 14 **1978** NYG 16 (2) **1979** NYG 13 (8, LILB) **NFL** 57 (10) [4 yrs]

LLOYD, DAVE David Allen, LB-C, 6´3˝/247 lbs; Texas Tech; Georgia; 1959: Cle, rnd 4; B11/9/1936 Sapulpa, OK **[K]** **1959** Cle 12 **1960** Cle 12 **1961** Cle 14 (MLB) **1962** Det 14 **1963** Phi 14 (14, MLB) **1964** Phi 11 (11, MLB) **1965** Phi 13 (13, MLB) **1966** Phi 14 (14, MLB) **1967** Phi 14 (14, MLB) **1968** Phi 13 (MLB) **1969** Phi✧14 (MLB) **1970** Phi 12 (5, mlb) **NFL** 157 (71) [12 yrs]

LLOYD, DOUG Douglas G., RB, 6´1˝/220 lbs; North Dakota State; 1989: LARd, rnd 6; B8/31/1965 Beaver Dam, IL **1991** LARd 1 (0)

LLOYD, GREG Gregory Lenard, LB, 6´2˝/228 lbs; Fort Valley State; 1987: Pit, rnd 6; B5/26/1965 Miami, FL **[S]** **1988** Pit 9 (4) **1989**†Pit 16 (16, ROLB) **1990** Pit 15 (14, ROLB) **1991** Pit✧16 (16, ROLB) **1992**†Pit✧16 (16, ROLB) **1993**†Pit★15 (15, ROLB) **1994**†Pit★15 (15, ROLB) **1995**†Pit★16 (16, ROLB) **1996** Pit 1 (1) **1997** Pit 12 (12, ROLB) **1998** Car 16 (14, ROLB) **NFL** 147 (139) [11 yrs]

LLOYD, JEFF Jeffrey John, DE-NT, 6´6˝/255 lbs; West Texas A&M; 1976: Sea, rnd 3; B3/14/1954 St. Mary's, PA **1976** Buf 9 **1978** KC 16 (4) **NFL** 25 (4) [2 yrs]

LOBENSTEIN, BILL William Joseph, DE, 6´3˝/261 lbs; Wisconsin; Wisconsin-Whitewater; B5/11/1961 Mauston, WI **1987** Den 3 (0)

LOBERG, GREG Gregory Scott, G-T, 6´4˝/264 lbs; California; B12/7/1961 San Rafael, CA **1987** NO 3 (1)

LOCKETT, CHARLES Charles Edward, WR, 6´0˝/178 lbs; Long Beach State; 1987: Pit, rnd 3; B10/1/1965 Los Angeles, CA

YEAR	TEAM	G (GS, POS)	RUSH	YD	AVG (LG)	TD	REC	YD	AVG (LG)	TD	PASS	COMP	PCT	YD	AVG (LG)	TD	INT	SK	YD	QBR	KPR	OTD	PTS	TAY
1987	Pit	11(1)	—	—	—	—	7	116	16.6(25)	1	—	—	—	—	—	—	—	—	—	—	p	—	6	56
1988	Pit	16(5, wr)	—	—	—	—	22	365	16.6(44)	1	—	—	—	—	—	—	—	—	—	—	—	—	6	188
NFL	2	27(6)	—	—	—	—	29	481	16.6(44)	2	—	—	—	—	—	—	—	—	—	—	p	—	12	244

LOCKETT, DANNY Danny Key, LB, 6´2˝/239 lbs; Arizona; 1987: Det, rnd 6; B7/11/1964 Fort Valley, GA **1987** Det 13 (1) **1988** Det 16 (0) **NFL** 29 (1) [2 yrs]

LOCKETT, FRANK Frank Arthur, WR, 6´0˝/200 lbs; Nebraska; 1979: GB, rnd 10; B6/1/1957 Independence, LA **1985** Mia 3 (0)

LOCKETT, J.W. J.W., FB, 6´2˝/226 lbs; Central Oklahoma; B3/23/1937 Bardwell, TX

YEAR	TEAM	G (GS, POS)	RUSH	YD	AVG (LG)	TD	REC	YD	AVG (LG)	TD	PASS	COMP	PCT	YD	AVG (LG)	TD	INT	SK	YD	QBR	KPR	OTD	PTS	TAY
1961	SF	2	11	18	1.6(9)	1	4	35	8.8(0)	0	—	—	—	—	—	—	—	—	—	—	k	—	6	46
1961	Dal	12(7, fb)	66	280	4.2(21)	0	15	114	7.6(26)	2	2	0	0.0	0	0.0	0	0	—	—	—	k	—	12	333
1962	Dal	14	8	24	3.0(7)	1	7	78	11.1(29)	2	1	0	0.0	0	0.0	0	0	—	—	—	kp	—	18	128
1963	Bal	12(FB)	81	273	3.4(18)	0	16	158	9.9(27)	1	—	—	—	—	—	—	—	—	—	—	k	—	6	364
1964	Was	14(FB)	63	175	2.8(13)	1	20	204	10.2(29)	2	—	—	—	—	—	—	—	—	—	—	k	—	18	324
NFL	4	54(7)	229	770	3.4(21)	3	62	589	9.5(29)	7	3	0	0.0	0	0.0	0	0	—	—	—	kp	—	60	1195

LOCKETT, KEVIN Kevin Eugene, WR, 6´0˝/186 lbs; Kansas State; 1997: KC, rnd 2; B9/8/1974 Tulsa, OK

YEAR	TEAM	G (GS, POS)	RUSH	YD	AVG (LG)	TD	REC	YD	AVG (LG)	TD	PASS	COMP	PCT	YD	AVG (LG)	TD	INT	SK	YD	QBR	KPR	OTD	PTS	TAY
1997	KC	9(0)	—	—	—	—	1	35	35.0(35)	0	—	—	—	—	—	—	—	—	—	—	—	—	0	18
1998	KC	13(3)	—	—	—	—	19	281	14.8(38)	0	—	—	—	—	—	—	—	—	—	—	p	—	0	142
1999	KC	16(1)	—	—	—	—	34	426	12.5(39)	2	—	—	—	—	—	—	—	—	—	—	p	—	12	228
2000	KC	16(2)	—	—	—	—	33	422	12.8(34)	2	—	—	—	—	—	—	—	—	—	—	kp	—	12	309
2001	Was	16(0)	—	—	—	—	22	293	13.3(34)	0	1	1	100.0	31	31.0(31)	1	0	—	—	—	p	—	0	156
2002	Was	6(2)	—	—	—	—	11	129	11.7(26)	2	1	1	100.0	14	14.0(14)	1	0	—	—	—	—	—	12	87
2002	Jax	7(2)	—	—	—	—	5	76	15.2(35)	2	—	—	—	—	—	—	—	—	—	—	k	—	12	31
2003	NYJ	3(0)	—	—	—	—	5	76	15.2(23)	0	—	—	—	—	—	—	—	—	—	—	—	—	0	38
NFL	7	86(10)	—	—	—	—	130	1738	13.4(39)	8	2	2	100.0	45	22.5(31)	2	0	—	—	—	kp	—	48	1008

LOCKETT, WADE Milton Wade, WR, 6´1˝/190 lbs; Cal State-Fullerton; B2/13/1964 Los Angeles, CA **1987** LARd 2 (0)

YEAR	TEAM	G(GS, POS)	RUSH	YD	AVG(LG)	TD	REC	YD	AVG(LG)	TD	PASS COMP	PCT	YD	AVG(LG)	TD	INT	SK	YD	QBR	KPR	OTD	PTS	TAY

LOCKHART, EUGENE   Eugene, LB, 6´2˝/234 lbs; Houston; 1984: Dal, rnd 6; B3/8/1961 Crockett, TX   **1984** Dal 15 (8, mlb)   **1985**†Dal 16 (15, MLB)   **1986** Dal 16 (16, MLB)
1987 Dal 9 (9, MLB)   **1988** Dal 16 (16, MLB)   **1989** Dal☆16 (16, MLB)   **1990** Dal☆16 (16, MLB)   **1991** NE 16 (13, LILB)   **1992** NE 16 (8, rilb)   **NFL** 136 (117) [9 yrs]

LOCKHART, SPIDER   Carl Ford, DB, 6´2˝/175 lbs; North Texas; 1965: NYG, rnd 13; B4/6/1943 Dallas, TX, D7/8/1986 Hackensack, NJ [I]   **1965** NYG 14 (LCB)   **1966** NYG◇14 (LCB)
1967 NYG 12 (RS)   **1968** NYG★14 (RS)   **1969** NYG 11 (RS)   **1970** NYG✩14 (FS)   **1971** NYG 13 (FS)   **1972** NYG 13 (FS)   **1973** NYG 14 (FS)   **1974** NYG 14 (FS)
1975 NYG [11 yrs]

LOCKLEAR, SEAN   Sean, T-G, 6´5˝/296 lbs; North Carolina State; 2004: Sea, rnd 3; B5/29/1981 Lumberton, SC   **2004** Sea 16 (0)   **2005**†Sea 16 (16, RT)   **NFL** 32 (16) [2 yrs]

LOCKLIN, BILLY   Billy Ray, LB, 6´2˝/225 lbs; New Mexico State; 1960: LAC, rnd 1; B8/13/1937 Rockdale, TX   **1960** Oak-A 2

LOCKLIN, KERRY   Kerry Barth, TE, 6´3˝/230 lbs; New Mexico State; 1982: LARm, rnd 6; B9/9/1959 Las Cruces, NM   **1982** LARm 6 (0)   **1987** Den 3 (0)   **NFL** 9 (0) [2 yrs]

LOCKWOOD, SCOTT   Scott Nelson, RB, 5´10˝/196 lbs; USC; 1992: NE, rnd 8; B3/23/1968 Los Angeles, CA   **1993** NE 2 (0)

| 1992 | NE | 4 (0) | 35 | 162 | 4.6(23) | 0 | — | — | — | — | — | — | — | — | — | — | — | — | k | — | 0 | 230 |
| NFL | | 6 (0) | 35 | 162 | 4.6(23) | 0 | — | — | — | — | — | — | — | — | — | — | — | — | | — | 0 | 162 |

LODISH, MIKE   Michael Timothy, NT-DT-DE, 6´3˝/275 lbs; UCLA; 1990: Buf, rnd 10; B8/11/1967 Detroit, MI   **1990**†Buf 12 (0)   **1991**†Buf 16 (6, nt)   **1992**†Buf 16 (0)   **1993**†Buf 15 (1)
1994 Buf 15 (5, nt)   **1995** Den 16 (0)   **1996**†Den 16 (16, LDT)   **1997**†Den 16 (0)   **1998** Den 15 (1)   **1999** Den 13 (2)   **2000**†Den 16 (0)   **NFL** 166 (31) [11 yrs]

LOEFFLER, CULLEN   Cullen, C, 6´5˝/241 lbs; Texas; B1/27/1981 Washington, DC   **2004** Min 16 (0)   **2005** Min 16 (0)   **NFL** 32 (0) [2 yrs]

LOEPFE, DICK   Richard, T, 6´2˝/230 lbs; Wisconsin; 1946: ChiC, rnd 11/1948: SF-A, rnd 21; B1/1/1922 Milwaukee, WI   **1948**†ChiC 7 (0)   **1949** ChiC 6 (4)   **NFL** 13 (4) [2 yrs]

LOEWEN, CHUCK   Charles Duane, T-G, 6´3˝/263 lbs; South Dakota State; 1980: SD, rnd 7; B1/23/1957 Mountain Lake, MN   **1980**†SD 16 (0)   **1981**†SD 9 (0)   **1982**†SD 9 (0)
1984 SD 13 (0)   **NFL** 47 (3) [4 yrs]

LOFTON, JAMES   James David, WR, 6´3˝/192 lbs; Stanford; 1978: GB, rnd 1; B7/5/1956 Fort Ord, CA; HOF 2003

1978	GB◇	16 (16, WR)	3	13	4.3(15)	0	46	818	17.8(58)	6	2		0	0.0		0	0	0.0	0	0	k	—	36	437
1979	GB	16 (16, WR)	1	-1	-1.0(-1)	0	54	968	17.9(52)	4	1	0	0.0		0	0	0.0	0	0	—	—	24	503
1980	GB★	16 (16, WR)	—	—	—	—	71	**1226**	17.3(47)	4										—	—	24	633
1981	GB★	16 (16, WR)	—	—	—	—	71	1294	18.2(75)	8										—	—	48	687
1982	†GB★	9 (9, WR)	4	101	25.3(83)	1	35	696	19.9(80)	4	1	1	100.0		43	43.0(43)	0	0	—	—	30	501
1983	GB★	16 (16, WR)	9	36	4.0(13)	0	58	1300	**22.4**(74)	8										—	—	48	726
1984	GB★	16 (16, WR)	10	82	8.2(26)	0	62	1361	**22.0**(79)	7										—	—	42	798
1985	GB★	16 (16, WR)	4	14	3.5(21)	0	69	1153	16.7(56)	4										—	—	24	611
1986	GB	15 (15, WR)	—	—	—	—	64	840	13.1(36)	4	1	0	0.0		0	0.0	0	0	—	—	24	440
1987	LARd	12 (12, WR)	1	1	1.0(1)	0	41	880	**21.5**(49)	5										—	—	30	466
1988	LARd	16 (16, WR)	—	—	—	—	28	549	19.6(57)	0										—	—	0	275
1989	†Buf	12 (2)	—	—	—	—	8	166	20.8(47)	3										—	—	18	98
1990	†Buf	16 (14, WR)	—	—	—	—	35	712	**20.3**(71)	4										—	—	24	376
1991	†Buf◇	15 (15, WR)	—	—	—	—	57	1072	18.8(77)	8										—	—	48	576
1992	†Buf	16 (15, WR)	—	—	—	—	51	786	15.4(50)	6										—	—	36	423
1993	LARm	1 (0)	—	—	—	—	1	16	16.0(16)	0										—	—	0	8
1993	Phi	9 (2)	—	—	—	—	13	167	12.8(32)	0										—	—	0	84
NFL	16	233 (212)	32	246	7.7(83)	1	764	14004	18.3(80)	75	5	1	20.0		43	8.6(43)	0	0	k	—	456	7640

LOFTON, OSCAR   Oscar W., E, 6´6˝/218 lbs; Southeastern Louisiana; B4/2/1938 McCall Creek, MS

| 1960 | Bos-A | 14 (SE) | — | — | — | — | 19 | 360 | 18.9(39) | 4 | | | | | | | | | | — | — | 24 | 200 |

LOFTON, STEVE   Steven Lynn, DB, 5´9˝/180 lbs; Texas A&M; B11/26/1968 Jacksonville, TX   **1991** Phx 11 (1)   **1992** Phx 4 (0)   **1993** Phx 13 (0)   **1995** Car 10 (2)   **1996** Car 11 (3)
1997 NE 4 (0)   **1998** NE 6 (0)   **1998** Car 10 (7, rcb)   **1999** Car 5 (0)   **NFL** 74 (13) [8 yrs]

LOGAN, ANDY   Andrew L., aka Andrew Wyhomanec, T-C, 6´0˝/230 lbs; Case Western Reserve; B2/17/1918 Connorville, OH, D11/21/1998 Cairo, OH   **1941** Det 9 (1)

LOGAN, CHUCK   Charles Russell, TE, 6´4˝/210 lbs; Northwestern; 1964: Chi, rnd 7/Den, rnd 15; B4/10/1943 Chicago, IL   **1965** SL 4 (3)   **1967** SL 14   **1968** SL 14

| 1964 | Pit | 14 | — | — | — | — | 1 | 7 | 7.0(7) | 0 | | | | | | | | | | — | — | 0 | 4 |
| NFL | 4 | 46 (3) | — | — | — | — | 1 | 7 | 7.0(7) | 0 | | | | | | | | | | — | — | 0 | 4 |

LOGAN, DAVE   David Russell, WR, 6´4˝/219 lbs; Colorado; 1976: Cle, rnd 3; B2/2/1954 Fargo, ND

1976	Cle	14	—	—	—	—	5	104	20.8(52)	0										—	—	0	52
1977	Cle	14 (5, WR)	—	—	—	—	19	284	14.9(42)	1	2	0	0.0		0	0.0	0	0	—	—	6	147
1978	Cle	16 (16, WR)	—	—	—	—	37	585	15.8(44)	4										—	—	24	313
1979	Cle	16 (16, WR)	—	—	—	—	59	982	16.6(46)	7										—	—	42	526
1980	†Cle	16 (16, WR)	—	—	—	—	51	822	16.1(65)	4										—	—	24	431
1981	Cle	14 (14, WR)	—	—	—	—	31	497	16.0(40)	4										i	—	24	264
1982	†Cle	9 (9, WR)	—	—	—	—	23	346	15.0(55)	2										—	—	12	183
1983	Cle	16 (12, WR)	—	—	—	—	37	627	16.9(34)	4										—	—	24	324
1984	Den	4 (0)	—	—	—	—	1	3	3.0(3)	0										—	—	0	2
NFL	9	119 (88)	—	—	—	—	263	4250	16.2(65)	24	2	0	0.0		0	0.0	0	0	i	—	144	2240

LOGAN, DAVID   David, NT, 6´2˝/250 lbs; Pittsburgh; 1979: TB, rnd 12; B10/25/1956 Pittsburgh, PA, D1/12/1999 Tampa, FL   **1979**†TB 5   **1980** TB 16 (14, NT)   **1981**†TB 16 (16, NT)
1982†TB 9 (9, NT)   **1983** TB☆16 (16, NT)   **1984** TB☆16 (16, NT)   **1985** TB 16 (16, NT)   **1986** TB 16 (16, NT)   **1987** GB 2 (0)   **NFL** 112 (103) [9 yrs]

LOGAN, DICK   Richard Leroy, G-DT, 6´2˝/228 lbs; Ohio State; 1952: Cle, rnd 11; B5/4/1930 Mansfield, OH   **1952** GB 7   **1953** GB 12   **NFL** 19 [2 yrs]

LOGAN, ERNIE   Ernest Edward, NT-DE-DT, 6´3˝/283 lbs; East Carolina; 1991: Atl, rnd 9; B5/18/1968 Fort Bragg, NC   **1991** Cle 15 (5, rde)   **1992** Cle 16 (0)   **1993** Atl 8 (1)
1995 Jax 15 (1)   **1996** Jax 4 (0)   **1997** NYJ 15 (14, NT)   **1998**†NYJ 16 (12, RDT)   **1999** NYJ 14 (7, nt)   **2000** NYJ 16 (4)   **NFL** 119 (44) [9 yrs]

LOGAN, JAMES   James Eddie, LB, 6´2˝/222 lbs; Memphis; B12/6/1972 Opp, AL   **1995** Hou 3 (0)   **1995** Cin 1 (0)   **1995** Sea 6 (0)   **1996** Sea 6 (0)   **1997** Sea 14 (1)   **1998** Sea 4 (1)
1999†Sea 16 (2)   **2000** Sea 16 (0)   **NFL** 66 (4) [6 yrs]

LOGAN, JERRY   Jerry Don, DB, 6´1˝/185 lbs; West Texas A&M; 1963: Bal, rnd 4/Oak, rnd 9; B8/27/1941 Graham, TX [I]   **1963** Bal 14 (4)   **1964**†Bal☆14 (14, LS)
1965†Bal◇14 (14, LS)   **1966** Bal 14 (LS)   **1967** Bal 14 (LS)   **1968**†Bal✩14 (LS)   **1969** Bal 14 (LS)   **1970**†Bal★14 (SS)   **1971** Bal★14 (SS)   **1972** Bal 14 (SS)   **NFL** 140 (32) [10 yrs]

LOGAN, JIM   James Zimmerman, G, 5´10˝/190 lbs; Indiana; B12/22/1916 Richmond, IN, D3/27/2004 Richmond, IN   **1943**†ChiB 9 (1)

LOGAN, MARC   Marc Anthony, RB, 6´0˝/217 lbs; Kentucky; 1987: Cin, rnd 5; B5/9/1965 Lexington, KY [R]

1987	Cin	3 (3)	37	203	5.5(51)	1	3	14	4.7(18)	0									k	—	6	206
1988	†Cin	9 (0)	2	10	5.0(9)	0	2	20	10.0(17)	0									k	—	0	40
1989	Mia	10 (4)	57	201	3.5(14)	0	5	34	6.8(11)	0									k	2	12	481
1990	†Mia	16 (0)	79	317	4.0(17)	2	7	54	7.7(12)	0									k	—	12	431
1991	Mia	16 (0)	4	5	1.3(2)	0	—	—	—	—									k	—	0	16
1992	†SF	16 (1)	8	44	5.5(26)	1	2	17	8.5(13)	0									k	—	6	211
1993	†SF	14 (12, FB)	58	280	4.8(45)	7	37	348	9.4(24)	0									—	—	42	524
1994	†SF	10 (5, fb)	33	143	4.3(22)	1	16	97	6.1(15)	1									—	—	12	207
1995	Was	16 (9, FB)	23	72	3.1(13)	1	25	276	11.0(32)	2									—	—	18	230
1996	Was	14 (9, FB)	20	111	5.6(36)	2	23	269	11.7(26)	0									—	—	12	266
1997	Was	15 (1)	4	5	1.3(4)	0	3	6	2.0(5)	0									—	—	0	18
NFL	11	139 (44)	325	1391	4.3(51)	15	123	1135	9.2(32)	3									k	2	120	2629

LOGAN, MIKE   Michael Victor, DB, 6´0˝/212 lbs; West Virginia; 1997: Jax, rnd 2; B9/15/1974 Pittsburgh, PA   **1997**†Jax 11 (0)   **1998** Jax 15 (0)   **1999** Jax 2 (0)   **2000** Jax 15 (11, FS)
2001 Pit 16 (1)   **2002**†Pit 14 (0)   **2003** Pit 16 (15, SS)   **2004** Pit 3 (0)   **2005**†Pit 12 (1)   **NFL** 104 (28) [9 yrs]

LOGAN, OBERT   Obert Clark, DB, 5´10˝/180 lbs; Trinity (TX); B12/6/1941 Yoakum, TX, D1/21/2003 Luling, TX   **1965** Dal 14 (9, LS)   **1966**†Dal 14 (6, rs)   **1967** NO 13 (RS)
NFL 41 (15) [3 yrs]

LOGAN, RANDY   Randolph, DB, 6´1˝/195 lbs; Michigan; 1973: Phi, rnd 3; B5/1/1951 Detroit, MI [I]   **1973** Phi 14 (14, SS)   **1974** Phi 14 (14, SS)   **1975** Phi 14 (13, SS)
1976 Phi 14 (14, SS)   **1977** Phi 14 (14, SS)   **1978**†Phi 16 (16, SS)   **1979**†Phi 16 (16, SS)   **1980**†Phi☆16 (16, SS)   **1981**†Phi☆16 (16, SS)   **1982** Phi 9 (9, SS)   **1983** Phi 16 (12, SS)
NFL 159 (154) [11 yrs]

YEAR	TEAM	G (GS, POS)	RUSH	YD	AVG(LG)	TD	REC	YD	AVG(LG)	TD	PASS	COMP	PCT	YD	AVG(LG)	TD	INT	SK	YD	QBR	KPR	OTD	PTS	TAY

LOGEL, BOB — Robert James, E, 6´3˝/210 lbs; none; B7/29/1928 East Aurora, NY, D7/4/2001 Holland, NY   **1949** Buf-A 1 (0)

LOHMEYER, JOHN — John Carl, DT-DE, 6´4˝/229 lbs; Emporia State; 1973: KC, rnd 4; B1/15/1951 Emporia, KS   **1973** KC 7   **1975** KC 7 (LDT)   **1976** KC 13 (10, LDT)
1977 KC 14 (5, rdt)   **NFL** 41 (15) [4 yrs]

LOHMILLER, CHIP — John McLeod, K, 6´3˝/213 lbs; Minnesota; 1988: Was, rnd 2; B7/16/1966 Woodbury, MN [K]   **1988** Was 16 (0)   **1989** Was 16 (0)   **1990†**Was 16 (0)
1991†Was★16 (0)   **1992†**Was 16 (0)   **1993** Was 16 (0)   **1994** Was 16 (0)   **1995** NO 8 (0)   **1996** SL 15 (0)   **NFL** 135 (0) [9 yrs]

LOKANC, JOE — Joseph Andrew, G, 5´11˝/205 lbs; Northwestern; 1941: ChiC, rnd 14; B3/11/1917 East Chicago, IN

| 1941 | ChiC | 9 (0) | — | — | — | — | 1 | 2 | 2.0(2) | 0 | — | — | — | — | — | — | — | — | — | — | — | — | 0 | 1 |

LOLLAR, SLICK — John Hope, B, 5´11˝/200 lbs; Samford; B1906, deceased   **1928** GB 3 (0)

LOLOTAI, AL — Albert, G, 6´0˝/224 lbs; Weber JC; B6/22/1920 Western Samoa, D9/30/1990 Pago Pago, American Samoa   **1945†**Was 10 (8, LG)
1946 LAD-A 14 (12, LG)   **1947** LAD-A 13 (6, lg)   **1948** LAD-A 14 (0)   **1949** LAD-A 8 (6, LG)   **AAFC** 49 (24) [4 yrs]

LOMACK, TONY — Thomas Jerome, WR, 5´8˝/180 lbs; Florida; 1990: LARm, rnd 9; B4/27/1968 Tallahassee, FL   **1990** LARm 3 (0)   **1991** Phx 1 (0)   **NFL** 4 (0) [2 yrs]

LOMAKOSKI, JOHN — John A., T, 6´4˝/250 lbs; Western Michigan; 1962: Det, rnd 4/NYT, rnd 8; B11/11/1940 Washington, MI, D2/16/1999 Munising, MI   **1962** Det 3

LOMAS, MARK — Mark Arnold, DE-DT, 6´4˝/250 lbs; Northern Arizona; 1970: NYJ, rnd 8; B6/8/1948 Los Angeles, CA   **1970** NYJ 14 (LDT)   **1971** NYJ 14 (RDE)   **1972** NYJ 14 (RDE)
1973 NYJ 14 (RDE)   **1974** NYJ 11 (RDE)   **NFL** 67 [5 yrs]

LOMASNEY, TOM — Thomas Martin, E, 6´0˝/190 lbs; Villanova; B5/11/1906 Salem, MA, D12/29/1976 Salem, MA   **1929** SI 4 (1)

LOMAX, NEIL — Neil Vincent, QB, 6´3˝/215 lbs; Portland State; 1981: SL, rnd 2; B2/17/1959 Portland, OR

1981	SL	14 (7, qb)	19	104	5.5(22)	2	—	—	—	—	236	119	50.4	1575	6.7(75)	4	10	32	286	59.9	—	—	12	532
1982	†SL	9 (9, QB)	28	119	4.3(19)	1	1	10	10.0(10)	0	205	109	53.2	1367	6.7(42)	5	6	31	234	70.1	—	—	6	603
1983	SL	13 (13, QB)	27	127	4.7(35)	2	—	—	—	—	354	209	59.0	2636	7.4(71)	24	11	43	315	92.0	—	—	12	1145
1984	SL★	16 (16, QB)	35	184	5.3(20)	3	—	—	—	—	**560**	**345**	61.6	**4614**	8.2(83)	**28**	16	49	377	92.5	—	—	18	2021
1985	SL	16 (16, QB)	32	125	3.9(23)	1	—	—	—	—	471	265	56.3	3214	6.8(47)	18	12	61	442	79.5	—	—	0	1342
1986	SL	14 (14, QB)	35	148	4.2(18)	1	—	—	—	—	421	240	57.0	2583	6.1(48)	13	12	52	381	73.6	—	—	6	1035
1987	SL★	12 (12, QB)	29	107	3.7(19)	0	—	—	—	—	**463**	**275**	59.4	3387	7.3(57)	24	12	48	350	88.5	—	—	0	1441
1988	Phx	14 (14, QB)	17	55	3.2(13)	1	—	—	—	—	443	255	57.6	3395	7.7(93)	20	11	46	315	86.7	—	—	6	1423
NFL	8	108 (101)	222	969	4.4(35)	10	1	10	10.0(10)	0	3153	1817	57.6	22771	7.2(93)	136	90	362	2700	82.7	—	—	60	9540

LONDON, ANTONIO — Antonio Monte, LB, 6´2˝/238 lbs; Alabama; 1993: Det, rnd 3; B4/14/1971 Tullahoma, TN   **1993†**Det 14 (0)   **1994** Det 16 (0)   **1995†**Det 15 (0)
1996 Det 14 (12, LLB)   **1997†**Det 16 (6, llb)   **1998** GB 1 (0)   **NFL** 76 (18) [6 yrs]

LONDON, MIKE — Michael David, LB, 6´2˝/230 lbs; Wisconsin; 1966: SD, rnd 14; B12/31/1944 Madison, WI   **1966** SD-A 3

LONDON, TOM — Tommy, DB, 6´1˝/197 lbs; North Carolina State; B6/15/1954 Shelby, NC   **1978** Cle 15

LONE STAR, FRANK — Frank, G-T, 5´11˝/200 lbs; Carlisle Indian; B1/27/1887, D9/1984 Pittsburgh, PA   **1920** Col 3 (3, LG)

LONE WOLF, TED — Ted, G-T-B, 6´2˝/212 lbs; none; deceased   **1922** Oor 5 (4)   **1923** Oor 4 (4)   **NFL** 9 (8) [2 yrs]

LONEKER, KEITH — Keith Joseph, G, 6´3˝/330 lbs; Kansas; B6/21/1971 Roselle Park, NJ   **1993** LARm 4 (2)   **1994** LARm 2 (2)   **1995** SL 13 (1)   **NFL** 19 (5) [3 yrs]

LONG, BILL — William Gene, E, 6´1˝/200 lbs; Oklahoma State; 1949: Pit, rnd 5/Bkn-A, rnd 25; B9/11/1926 Lenapah, OK, D7/11/1995

| 1949 | Pit | 10 (0) | 2 | 6 | 3.0(10) | 0 | 2 | 21 | 10.5(13) | 0 | — | — | — | — | — | — | — | — | — | — | P | — | 0 | 17 |

LONG, BOB — Robert Albert, HB, 5´10˝/190 lbs; Tennessee; 1946: Phi, rnd 28; B4/9/1922 Trenton, NJ   **1947** Bos 2 (0)

LONG, BOB — Robert Andrew, FL-WR, 6´3˝/205 lbs; Wichita State; 1964: GB, rnd 4/SD, rnd 10; B6/16/1942 McKeesport, PA

1964	GB	7	—	—	—	—	1	19	19.0(19)	0	—	—	—	—	—	—	—	—	—	—	—	—	0	10
1965	†GB	13	—	—	—	—	13	304	23.4(62)	4	—	—	—	—	—	—	—	—	—	—	—	—	24	172
1966	†GB	5	—	—	—	—	3	68	22.7(42)	0	—	—	—	—	—	—	—	—	—	—	—	—	0	34
1967	†GB	10	—	—	—	—	8	96	12.0(21)	0	—	—	—	—	—	—	—	—	—	—	—	—	0	48
1968	Atl	9	—	—	—	—	22	484	22.0(71)	4	—	—	—	—	—	—	—	—	—	—	—	—	24	262
1969	Was	14 (FL)	—	—	—	—	48	533	11.1(52)	1	—	—	—	—	—	—	—	—	—	—	—	—	6	272
1970	LARm	3	—	—	—	—	3	35	11.7(15)	1	—	—	—	—	—	—	—	—	—	—	—	—	6	23
NFL	7	61	—	—	—	—	98	1539	15.7(71)	10	—	—	—	—	—	—	—	—	—	—	—	—	60	820

LONG, BOB — Robert Wendell, LB, 6´3˝/232 lbs; UCLA; 1955: LA, rnd 2; B2/24/1934 South Pasadena, CA   **1955** LARm 1   **1955** Det 10   **1956** Det 12 (RLB)   **1957†**Det 12 (LLB)
1958 Det 12 (LLB)   **1959** Det 12 (LLB)   **1960** LARm 13   **1961** LARm 13   **1962** Dal 8   **NFL** 89 [8 yrs]

LONG, BUFORD — Burford Eugene, DB-HB-E, 6´1˝/195 lbs; Florida; 1953: NYG, rnd 5; B12/14/1931 Lake Wales, FL

1953	NYG	10 (DB)	20	58	2.9(21)	0	14	220	15.7(55)	2	—	—	—	—	—	—	—	—	—	ki	—	14	315
1954	NYG	12	32	106	3.3(11)	1	13	178	13.7(36)	1	—	—	—	—	—	—	—	—	—	kp	—	12	321
1955	NYG	4	—	—	—	—	6	64	10.7(34)	1	—	—	—	—	—	—	—	—	—	k	—	6	119
NFL	3	26	52	164	3.2(21)	1	33	462	14.0(55)	4	—	—	—	—	—	—	—	—	—	kpi	—	32	755

LONG, CARSON — Carson Gerald, K, 5´10˝/210 lbs; Pittsburgh; 1977: LA, rnd 11; B12/16/1954 Pottsville, PA [K]   **1977** Buf 9

LONG, CHARLEY — Charles B., G-T, 6´4˝/260 lbs; Tennessee-Chattanooga; 1961: Bos, rnd 8; B4/6/1938 DeKalb, AL, D12/16/1989 Framingham, MA   **1961** Bos-A 14 (LT)
1962 Bos-A★14 (LT)   **1963†**Bos-A★14 (LG)   **1964** Bos-A☆14 (LG)   **1965** Bos-A 14 (LG)   **1966** Bos-A 14 (LG)   **1967** Bos-A 14 (LG)   **1968** Bos-A 13   **1969** Bos-A 13 (3)
NFL 124 (3) [9 yrs]

LONG, CHUCK — Charles Franklin, QB, 6´4˝/217 lbs; Iowa; 1986: Det, rnd 1; B2/18/1963 Norman, OK

1986	Det	3 (2)	2	0	0.0(0)	0	—	—	—	—	40	21	52.5	247	6.2(34)	2	2	8	69	—	—	—	0	54
1987	Det	12 (12, QB)	22	64	2.9(15)	0	—	—	—	—	416	232	55.8	2598	6.2(53)	11	20	17	127	63.4	—	—	0	618
1988	Det	7 (7, qb)	7	22	3.1(11)	0	—	—	—	—	141	75	53.2	856	6.1(40)	6	18	134	—	—	—	—	0	240
1989	Det	1 (0)	3	2	0.7(6)	0	—	—	—	—	5	2	40.0	42	8.4(37)	0	0	—	—	—	—	—	0	23
1990	LARm	4 (0)	—	—	—	—	—	—	—	—	5	1	20.0	4	0.8(4)	0	0	—	—	—	—	—	0	2
1991	†Det	0 (0)	—	—	—	—	—	—	—	—	—	—	—	—	—	—	—	—	—	—	—	—	0	0
NFL	6	27 (21)	34	88	2.6(15)	0	—	—	—	—	607	331	54.5	3747	6.2(53)	19	28	43	330	64.5	—	—	0	937

LONG, DARREN — Darren Murrell, TE, 6´3˝/240 lbs; Long Beach State; B7/12/1959 Exeter, CA

| 1986 | †LARm | 4 (0) | — | — | — | — | 5 | 47 | 9.4(13) | 0 | — | — | — | — | — | — | — | — | — | — | — | — | 0 | 24 |

LONG, DAVE — David Frank, DE-DT, 6´4˝/245 lbs; Iowa; 1966: SL, rnd 3/Hou, rnd 6; B9/6/1944 Jefferson, IA   **1966** SL 14   **1967** SL 14 (rde)   **1968** SL 14   **1969** NO 14 (RDE)
1970 NO 12 (RDE)   **1971** NO 14 (RDT)   **1972** NO 14 (RDT)   **NFL** 96 [7 yrs]

LONG, DOUG — Douglas, DB, 6´0˝/189 lbs; Whitworth; B5/24/1955 Spokane, WA   **1977** Sea 1   **1978** Sea 15   **NFL** 16 [2 yrs]

LONG, HARVEY — Harvey John, T-G, 6´0˝/195 lbs; Detroit Mercy; B9/11/1906 St. Croix, WI, D3/1985 Cadillac, MI   **1929** ChiB 4 (3)   **1930** Fra 1 (0)   **NFL** 5 (3) [2 yrs]

LONG, HOWIE — Howard Michael, DE-NT, 6´5˝/268 lbs; Villanova; 1981: Oak, rnd 2; B1/6/1960 Somerville, MA; HOF 2000 [S]   **1981** Oak 16 (0)   **1982†**LARm 9 (5, LDE)
1983†LARd★16 (16, LDE)   **1984†**LARd★16 (16, LDE)   **1985†**LARd★16 (16, LDE)   **1986** LARd 13 (12, LDE)   **1987†**LARd✧14 (14, LDE)   **1988** LARd 7 (6, lde)
1989†LARd★16 (11, LDE)   **1990†**LARd☆12 (11, LDE)   **1991†**LARd 14 (13, LDE)   **1992†**LARd✧16 (16, LDE)   **1993†**LARd 16 (16, LDE)   **NFL** 179 (152) [13 yrs]

LONG, JOHNNY — John Anton, QB-HB, 6´0˝/186 lbs; Colgate; B12/13/1914 South Orange, NJ, D2/3/1975 Pemberton, NJ

1944	ChiB	9 (6, qb)	24	2	0.1(12)	0	—	—	—	—	14	9	64.3	128	9.1(51)	1	1	—	—	—	Pkp	—	0	34
1945	ChiB	3 (2)	2	3	1.5(5)	0	—	—	—	—	—	—	—	—	—	—	—	—	—	Pp	—	0	10
NFL	2	12 (8)	26	5	0.2(12)	0	—	—	—	—	14	9	64.3	128	9.1(51)	1	1	—	—	—	Pkp	—	0	44

LONG, KEN — Kenneth Donald, G, 6´3˝/265 lbs; Purdue; 1976: Det, rnd 2; B7/24/1953 Pittsburgh, PA   **1976** Det 13

LONG, KEVIN — Kevin Fernando, RB, 6´1˝/212 lbs; South Carolina; 1977: NYJ, rnd 7; B1/20/1955 Clinton, SC

1977	NYJ	14 (4)	56	170	3.0(12)	0	5	17	3.4(7)	0	—	—	—	—	—	—	—	—	—	—	—	—	0	179
1978	NYJ	16 (16, FB)	214	954	4.5(27)	10	26	204	7.8(10)	0	—	—	—	—	—	—	—	—	—	—	—	—	60	1156
1979	NYJ	12 (6, fb)	116	442	3.8(25)	7	10	115	11.5(27)	0	—	—	—	—	—	—	—	—	—	—	—	—	42	570
1980	NYJ	15 (7, fb)	115	355	3.1(18)	6	20	137	6.8(16)	0	—	—	—	—	—	—	—	—	—	—	—	—	36	484

YEAR	TEAM	G (GS, POS)	RUSH	YD	AVG(LG)	TD	REC	YD	AVG(LG)	TD	PASS	COMP	PCT	YD	AVG(LG)	TD	INT	SK	YD	QBR	KPR	OTD	PTS	TAY
1981	†NYJ	16(0)	73	269	3.7(19)	2	13	66	5.1(18)	3	—	—	—	—	—	—	—	—	—	—	—	—	30	337
NFL	5	73(33)	574	2190	3.8(27)	25	74	539	7.3(27)	3	—	—	—	—	—	—	—	—	—	—	—	168	2725

LONG, KEVIN   Kevin Dale, C, 6´5˝/296 lbs; Florida State; 1998: Ten, rnd 7; B5/2/1975 Summerville, SC   **1998** Ten 16 (2)   **1999**†Ten 16 (12, C)   **2000**†Ten 16 (16, C)
2001 Ten 15 (5, c)   **NFL** 63 (35) [4 yrs]

LONG, KHARI   Khari Ahmad, DE, 6´4˝/257 lbs; Baylor; 2005: KC, rnd 6; B5/23/1982 Wichita Falls, TX   **2005** KC 1 (0)

LONG, LOUIE   Louis Charles, E, 6´0˝/185 lbs; Texas; SMU; B1/6/1909 Chicago, IL, D4/23/1974 Richmond, VA   **1931** Por 13 (1), 6

LONG, MATT   Matthew Scott, C, 6´3˝/270 lbs; San Diego State; B3/16/1961 Glendale, CA   **1987** Phi 3 (3)

LONG, MEL   Melvin M., LB, 6´0˝/228 lbs; Toledo; 1972: Cle, rnd 11; B11/22/1946 Toledo, OH   **1972**†Cle 14   **1973** Cle 14   **1974** Cle 14   **NFL** 42 [3 yrs]

LONG, MIKE   Michael Stanford, E, 6´0˝/188 lbs; Brandeis; B10/29/1938

| 1960 | Bos-A | 2 | — | — | — | — | 2 | 10 | 5.0(5) | 0 | — | — | — | — | — | — | — | — | — | — | — | 0 | 5 |

LONG, RIEN   Rien Michael, DT, 6´6˝/300 lbs; Washington State; 2003: Ten, rnd 4; B8/7/1981 Los Angeles, CA   **2003**†Ten 8 (0)   **2004** Ten 15 (3)   **2005** Ten 16 (1)   **NFL** 39 (4) [3 yrs]

LONG, TERRY   Terry Luther, G, 5´11˝/272 lbs; East Carolina; 1984: Pit, rnd 4; B7/21/1959 Columbia, SC, D6/7/2005 Pittsburgh, PA   **1984**†Pit 12 (7, rg)   **1985** Pit 15 (14, RG)
1986 Pit 16 (16, RG)   **1987** Pit 13 (13, RG)   **1988** Pit 12 (11, RG)   **1989**†Pit 13 (9, RG)   **1990** Pit 16 (16, RG)   **1991** Pit 8 (3)   **NFL** 105 (89) [8 yrs]

LONG, TIM   Timothy Joe, C, 6´6˝/295 lbs; Memphis; 1985: Min, rnd 3; B4/20/1963 Cleveland, TN   **1987** SF 2 (0)

LONG, TOM   Thomas Noble, G, 6´0˝/205 lbs; Ohio State; B8/7/1899, D7/23/1969 Columbus, OH   **1925** Col 7 (1)

LONGENECKER, KEN   Kenneth Allen, T, 6´4˝/285 lbs; Lebanon Valley; B4/23/1938, D8/15/1991 Annville, PA   **1960** Pit 4

LONGLEY, CLINT   Howard Clinton, QB, 6´1˝/193 lbs; Abilene Christian; 1974: Cin, rnd S1; B7/28/1952 Wichita Falls, TX

1974	Dal	2	4	-13	-3.3(1)	0	—	—	—	—	21	12	57.1	209	10.0(50)	2	0	2	18	—	—	—	0	102
1975	†Dal	4(1)	3	12	4.0(7)	0	—	—	—	—	23	7	30.4	102	4.4(23)	1	1	3	29	—	—	—	0	28
1976	SD	3(1)	4	22	5.5(9)	0	—	—	—	—	24	12	50.0	130	5.4(28)	2	3	7	51	—	—	—	0	-23
NFL	3	9(2)	11	21	1.9(9)	0	—	—	—	—	68	31	45.6	441	6.5(50)	5	4	12	98	—	—	—	0	107

LONGMIRE, SAM   Samuel Robert, DB-WR, 6´3˝/195 lbs; Purdue; B1/3/1943 Birmingham, AL   **1967** KC-A 3   **1968** KC-A 2   **NFL** 5 [2 yrs]

LONGO, TOM   Thomas Victor, DB, 6´1˝/200 lbs; Notre Dame; 1965: Phi, rnd 14/Oak, rnd R11; B2/21/1942 Lyndhurst, NJ   **1969** NYG 13   **1970** NYG 14 (SS)   **1971** SL 2
NFL 29 [3 yrs]

LONGSTREET, ROY   Roy William, C, 5´11˝/185 lbs; Iowa State; B2/24/1901 Sioux Falls, SD, D1/9/1991   **1926** Rac 1 (1)

LONGUA, PAUL   Paul J., E, 5´10˝/175 lbs; Villanova; B4/17/1903 Brooklyn, NY, D6/13/1983 Hightown, NJ   **1929** Ora 11 (8, RE), 6   **1930** Nwk 6 (6, LE)   **NFL** 17 (14) [2 yrs]

LONGWELL, RYAN   Ryan Walker, K, 6´0˝/199 lbs; California; B8/16/1974 Seattle, WA [K]   **1997**†GB 16 (0)   **1998**†GB 16 (0)   **1999** GB 16 (0)   **2000** GB 16 (0)   **2001**†GB 16 (0)
2002†GB 16 (0)   **2003**†GB 16 (0)   **2004**†GB 16 (0)   **2005** GB 16 (0)   **NFL** 144 (0) [9 yrs]

LOOK, DEAN   Dean Zachary, QB, 5´11˝/185 lbs; Michigan State; 1960: Den, rnd 1/Det, rnd 20; B7/23/1937 Lansing, MI

| 1962 | NYT-A | 1 | 2 | 9 | 4.5(8) | 0 | — | — | — | — | 1 | 0 | 0.0 | 0 | 0.0 | 0 | 1 | — | — | — | — | 0 | -31 |

LOOKABAUGH, JOHN   John, E, 6´4˝/216 lbs; Maryland; B9/13/1922 Ridgeley, WV, D5/16/1993 Millville, NJ

1946	Was	3(0)	—	—	—	—	6	67	11.2(19)	0	—	—	—	—	—	—	—	—	—	—	—	0	34
1947	Was	6(3)	—	—	—	—	6	78	13.0(31)	1	—	—	—	—	—	—	—	—	—	—	—	6	44
NFL	2	9(3)	—	—	—	—	12	145	12.1(31)	1	—	—	—	—	—	—	—	—	—	—	—	6	78

LOOKER, DANE   Dane Alan, WR, 6´0˝/194 lbs; Washington; B5/5/1976 Puyallup, WA

2002	SL	3(0)	—	—	—	—	—	—	—	—	—	—	—	—	—	—	—	—	—	—	—		
2003	†SL	16(2)	—	—	—	—	47	495	10.5(41)	3	1	1	100.0	11	11.0(11)	0	0	—	—	p	—	18	305
2004	SL	14(0)	—	—	—	—	13	183	14.1(29)	0	—	—	—	—	—	—	—	—	—	—	—	0	92
2005	SL	16(0)	—	—	—	—	23	237	10.3(23)	0	—	—	—	—	—	—	—	—	—	p	—	0	148
NFL	4	49(2)	—	—	—	—	83	915	11.0(41)	3	1	1	100.0	11	11.0(11)	0	0	—	—	p	—	18	544

LOOMIS, ACE   Ace Darl, DB-HB, 6´1˝/190 lbs; Wisconsin-LaCrosse; 1951: Cle, rnd 5; B6/12/1928 Dubuque, IA, D9/11/2003 Santa Fe, NM   **1952** GB 11 (DB)   **1953** GB 10 (DB)

| 1951 | GB | 12(DB) | — | — | — | — | 1 | 9 | 9.0(9) | 0 | — | — | — | — | — | — | — | — | — | i | — | 0 | 88 |
| NFL | 3 | 33 | — | — | — | — | 1 | 9 | 9.0(9) | 0 | — | — | — | — | — | — | — | — | — | kpi | 1 | 6 | 316 |

LOONEY, DON   John Don, E, 6´2˝/182 lbs; TCU; 1940: Phi, rnd 8; B9/2/1917 Saltillo, TX

1940	Phi★	11(8, RE)	2	-4	-2.0	0	58	707	12.2(47)	4	—	—	—	—	—	—	—	—	—	—	1	30	370
1941	Pit	9(0)	—	—	—	—	10	186	18.6(66)	1	—	—	—	—	—	—	—	—	—	k	—	6	99
1942	Pit	3(1)	—	—	—	—	7	59	8.4(14)	1	—	—	—	—	—	—	—	—	—	—	—	6	35
NFL	3	23(9)	2	-4	-2.0	0	75	952	12.7(66)	6	—	—	—	—	—	—	—	—	—	k	1	42	503

LOONEY, JIM   James, LB, 6´0˝/225 lbs; Purdue; B8/18/1957 Bastrop, LA   **1981** SF 1 (0)

LOONEY, JOE DON   Joe Don, HB-FB, 6´1˝/230 lbs; Cameron; Texas; TCU; Oklahoma; 1964: NYG, rnd 1/KC, rnd 6; B10/10/1942 San Angelo, TX, D9/24/1988 Brewster County, TX

1964	†Bal	13	23	127	5.5(58)	1	1	1	1.0(1)	1	—	—	—	—	—	—	—	—	—	Pk	—	12	278
1965	Det	9(HB)	114	356	3.1(35)	5	12	109	9.1(47)	1	—	—	—	—	—	—	—	—	—	k	—	36	466
1966	Det	3	8	42	5.3(24)	1	4	24	6.0(18)	0	—	—	—	—	—	—	—	—	—	k	—	6	94
1966	Was	10	55	178	3.2(19)	3	8	25	3.1(14)	0	—	—	—	—	—	—	—	—	—	k	—	18	261
1967	Was	4	11	26	2.4(20)	1	1	12	12.0(12)	0	—	—	—	—	—	—	—	—	—	k	—	6	54
1969	NO	3	2	-5	-1.7(4)	0	—	—	—	—	1	0	0.0	0	0.0	0	0	—	—	—	—	0	-5
NFL	5	42	214	724	3.4(58)	11	26	171	6.6(47)	2	1	0	0.0	0	0.0	0	0	—	—	Pk	—	78	1147

LOPASKY, BILL   William Joseph, G, 6´2˝/235 lbs; West Virginia; 1960: LAC, rnd 1; B1/29/1937 Trucksville, PA   **1961** SF 10

LOPIENSKI, TOM   Thomas Joseph, FB, 6´0˝/246 lbs; Notre Dame; B6/12/1979 Parkersburg, WV   **2003**†Ind 4 (0)   **2004** Ind 2 (0)   **NFL** 6 (0) [2 yrs]

LORCH, KARL   Karl P., DE-DT, 6´3˝/258 lbs; USC; 1973: Mia, rnd 9; B6/14/1950 Honolulu, HI   **1976**†Was 13   **1977** Was 14 (3)   **1978** Was 16 (8, lde)   **1979** Was 15 (15, LDE)
1980 Was 16 (16, LDE)   **1981** Was 16 (10, LDE)   **NFL** 90 (52) [6 yrs]

LORD, JACK   John Warner, G-T, 6´0˝/195 lbs; Rutgers; B9/23/1904 Avon, NJ, D3/11/1958 Rye, NY   **1929** SI 8 (2)

LORD, JAMMAL   Jammal, DB, 6´2˝/220 lbs; Nebraska; 2004: Hou, rnd 6; B1/10/1981 Brooklyn, NY   **2004** Hou 1 (0)

LORICK, TONY   William Anthony, RB, 6´1˝/217 lbs; Arizona State; 1964: Bal, rnd 2/Oak, rnd 1; B5/25/1941 Los Angeles, CA

1964	†Bal	14(fb)	100	513	5.1(60)	4	11	164	14.9(59)	0	—	—	—	—	—	—	—	—	—	k	—	24	825
1965	†Bal	14	63	296	4.7(38)	1	15	184	12.3(49)	0	—	—	—	—	—	—	—	—	—	k	—	18	484
1966	Bal	14(FB)	143	524	3.7(41)	3	12	81	6.8(19)	0	—	—	—	—	—	—	—	—	—	k	—	18	659
1967	Bal	14(FB)	133	436	3.3(22)	6	22	189	8.6(34)	0	—	—	—	—	—	—	—	—	—	k	—	36	683
1968	NO	13(FB)	104	344	3.3(36)	1	26	272	10.5(29)	3	—	—	—	—	—	—	—	—	—	P	—	18	495
1969	NO	14	5	11	2.2(6)	0	—	—	—	—	—	—	—	—	—	—	—	—	—	p	—	0	11
NFL	6	83	548	2124	3.9(60)	14	86	890	10.3(59)	5	—	—	—	—	—	—	—	—	—	Pkp	—	114	3156

LOSCH, JACK   John Lee, HB, 6´1˝/205 lbs; Miami (FL); 1956: GB, rnd 1; B8/13/1934 New York, NY, D5/27/2004 Williamsport, PA

| 1956 | GB | 12 | 19 | 43 | 2.3(8) | 0 | 7 | 85 | 12.1(43) | 0 | 1 | 1 | 100.0 | 63 | 63.0(63) | 1 | 0 | — | — | kp | — | 0 | 321 |

LOSMAN, J.P.   Jonathan Paul, QB, 6´3˝/220 lbs; UCLA; Tulane; 2004: Buf, rnd 1; B3/12/1981 Venice, CA

2004	Buf	4(0)	2	15	7.5(10)	0	—	—	—	—	5	3	60.0	32	6.4(17)	0	1	1	—	—	—	0	-9
2005	Buf	9(8, qb)	31	154	5.0(30)	0	—	—	—	—	228	113	49.6	1340	5.9(58)	8	8	26	197	64.9	—	0	544
NFL	2	13(8)	33	169	5.1(30)	0	—	—	—	—	233	116	49.8	1372	5.9(58)	8	9	27	197	63.5	—	0	535

LOTHAMER, ED   Edward Dewey, DT-DE, 6´5˝/270 lbs; Michigan State; 1964: KC, rnd 4/Bal, rnd 5; B5/20/1942 Detroit, MI   **1964** KC-A 11   **1965** KC-A 14 (LDT)   **1966** KC-A 7 (ldt)
1967 KC-A 13 (LDT)   **1968**†KC-A 14 (LDT)   **1969**†KC-A 13   **1971**†KC 14   **1972** KC 2   **NFL** 88 [8 yrs]

YEAR	TEAM	G (GS, POS)	RUSH	YD	AVG(LG)	TD	REC	YD	AVG(LG)	TD	PASS	COMP	PCT	YD	AVG(LG)	TD	INT	SK	YD	QBR	KPR	OTD	PTS	TAY

LOTHRIDGE, BILLY William Lamar, DB-P, 6´1˝/194 lbs; Georgia Tech; 1964: Dal, rnd 6/Oak, rnd 12; B1/1/1942 Cleveland, GA, D2/23/1996 Pensacola, FL **[P]**

1964	Dal	14	2	-6	-3.0(2)	1	—	—	—	—	9	2	22.2	24	2.7(13)	0	2	—	—	—	P	—	6	-64
1965	LARm	9	—	—	—	—	—	—	—	—	—	—	—	—	—	—	—	—	—	—	P	—	0	0
1966	Atl	14	1	22	22.0(22)	0	—	—	—	—	1	0	0.0	0	0.0	0	0	—	—	—	P	—	0	22
1967	Atl	14	1	16	16.0(16)	0	—	—	—	—	—	—	—	—	—	—	—	—	—	—	P	—	0	16
1968	Atl☆	14(RS)	1	-16	-16.0(-16)	0	—	—	—	—	—	—	—	—	—	—	—	—	—	—	Pi	—	0	45
1969	Atl	14	—	—	—	—	—	—	—	—	1	1	100.0	9	9.0(9)	0	0	—	—	—	P	—	0	5
1970	Atl	14	—	—	—	—	—	—	—	—	—	—	—	—	—	—	—	—	—	—	P	—	0	0
1971	Atl	9	—	—	—	—	—	—	—	—	1	1	100.0	27	27.0(27)	0	0	—	—	—	P	—	0	14
1972	Mia	2	—	—	—	—	—	—	—	—	—	—	—	—	—	—	—	—	—	—	P	—	0	0
NFL	9	104	5	16	3.2(22)	1	—	—	—	—	12	4	33.3	60	5.0(27)	0	2	—	—	—	Pi	—	6	37

LOTT, ANDRE Andre Marquette, DB, 5´10˝/196 lbs; Tennessee; 2002: Was, rnd 5; B5/31/1979 Memphis, TN **2002** Was 16 (0) **2003** Was 11 (0) **2004** Was 4 (3) **NFL** 31 (3) [3 yrs]

LOTT, ANTHONE Anthone Vouchan, DB, 5´9˝/194 lbs; Florida; B7/22/1974 Gainesville, FL **1997** Cin 5 (0)

LOTT, BILLY Billy Rex, FB, 6´0˝/203 lbs; Mississippi; 1958: NYG, rnd 6/1960: Oak, rnd 2; B11/8/1934 Sumrall, MS

1958	†NYG	12	4	30	7.5(12)	0	—	—	—	—	—	—	—	—	—	—	—	—	—	—	k	—	0	33
1960	Oak-A	14(FB)	99	520	5.3(40)	5	49	524	10.7(28)	1	—	—	—	—	—	—	—	—	—	—	—	—	38	837
1961	Bos-A	14(FB)	100	461	4.6(38)	5	32	333	10.4(47)	6	—	—	—	—	—	—	—	—	—	—	p	—	66	711
1962	Bos-A	7	8	34	4.3(11)	0	1	1	1.0(1)	0	—	—	—	—	—	—	—	—	—	—	—	—	0	35
1963	†Bos-A	14	35	78	2.2(7)	2	3	61	20.3(55)	1	—	—	—	—	—	—	—	—	—	—	—	—	18	134
NFL	5	61	246	1123	4.6(40)	12	85	919	10.8(55)	8	—	—	—	—	—	—	—	—	—	—	kp	—	122	1749

LOTT, JOHN John, T, none; B11/13/1905, NJ, D1/1970 Kaywood Gardens, MD **1929** Ora 2 (0) **1930** Bkn 2 (0) **NFL** 4 (0) [2 yrs]

LOTT, JOHN John Randall, C-G, 6´2˝/260 lbs; North Texas; B5/9/1964 Denton, TX **1987** Pit 1 (0)

LOTT, RONNIE Ronald Mandel, DB, 6´0˝/203 lbs; USC; 1981: SF, rnd 1; B5/8/1959 Albuquerque, NM; HOF 2000 [I] **1981**†SF★16 (16, LCB) **1982** SF◆9 (9, LCB) **1983**†SF★15 (14, LCB) **1984**†SF★12 (11, LCB) **1985**†SF 16 (16, LCB/fs) **1986**†SF★14 (14, FS) **1987**†SF★12 (12, FS) **1988**†SF★13 (12, FS) **1989**†SF★11 (11, FS) **1990**†SF★11 (11, FS) **1991**†LARd★16 (16, SS) **1992** LARd 16 (16, SS) **1993** NYJ 16 (16, FS) **1994** NYJ 15 (15, FS) **NFL** 192 (189) [14 yrs]

LOTT, THOMAS Thomas Willie, RB, 5´11˝/205 lbs; Oklahoma; 1979: SL, rnd 6; B8/1/1957 San Antonio, TX

| 1979 | SL | 10 | 11 | 50 | 4.5(13) | 0 | 2 | 8 | 4.0(5) | 0 | — | — | — | — | — | — | — | — | — | — | kp | — | 0 | 71 |

LOU, RON Ronald Wayne, C, 6´2˝/240 lbs; Arizona State; 1973: Hou, rnd 14; B7/24/1951 Los Angeles, CA **1973** Hou 9 **1975** Phi 14 (2) **1976** Hou 14 **NFL** 37 (2) [3 yrs]

LOUALLEN, FLETCHER Fletcher Allison, DB, 6´0˝/195 lbs; West Alabama; B9/12/1962 Jefferson, SC **1987** Min 3 (3)

LOUCHIEY, COREY Corey, T, 6´8˝/305 lbs; Tennessee; South Carolina; 1994: Buf, rnd 3; B10/10/1971 Greenville, SC **1995**†Buf 13 (3) **1997** Buf 16 (6, rt)

| 1996 | †Buf | 15(4) | — | — | — | 1 | 0 | 0(0) | — | 1 | — | — | — | — | — | — | — | — | — | — | — | — | 0 | 0 |
| **NFL** | 3 | 44(13) | — | — | — | 1 | 0 | 0.0 | — | 1 | — | — | — | — | — | — | — | — | — | — | k | — | 0 | -2 |

LOUCKS, ALVIN Alvin E., G, /170 lbs; Michigan; B6/15/1895, D4/1973 Hopkins, MN **1920** Det 1 (0)

LOUCKS, ED Edwin Earl, E, 5´9˝/180 lbs; Washington & Jefferson; B9/15/1895, D9/14/1959 **1925** Cle 6 (5, re)

LOUD, KAMIL Kamil Kassam, WR, 6´0˝/190 lbs; Cal Poly-San Luis Obispo; 1998: Buf, rnd 7; B6/25/1976 Richmond, CA **1998**†Buf 5 (0)

| 1999 | Buf | 7(0) | — | — | — | — | 6 | 66 | 11.0(20) | 0 | — | — | — | — | — | — | — | — | — | — | k | — | 0 | 29 |
| **NFL** | 2 | 12(0) | — | — | — | — | 6 | 66 | 11.0(20) | 0 | — | — | — | — | — | — | — | — | — | — | k | — | 0 | 29 |

LOUDD, ROMMIE Rommie Lee, LB, 6´2˝/227 lbs; UCLA; 1956: SF, rnd 26; B6/8/1933 Madisonville, TX, D5/9/1998 Miami, FL **1960**†LAC-A 14 (LLB) **1961** Bos-A 13 (RLB) **1962** Bos-A 14 **NFL** 41 [3 yrs]

LOUDERBACK, TOM Thomas Franklin, LB-C-G, 6´2˝/235 lbs; San Jose State; 1955: Was, rnd 10; B3/5/1933 Petaluma, CA **1958** Phi 12 (RLB) **1959** Phi 12 **1960** Oak-A 14 (MLB) **1961** Oak-A 14 (MLB) **1962** Buf-A 2 **NFL** 54 [5 yrs]

LOUKAS, ANGELO Angelo Cous, G-T, 6´3˝/250 lbs; Northwestern; B2/25/1947 Corinth, Greece **1969** Buf-A 13 (LG) **1970** Bos 2 **NFL** 15 [2 yrs]

LOVE, CLARENCE Clarence Eugene, DB, 5´10˝/180 lbs; Toledo; 1998: Phi, rnd 4; B6/16/1976 Jackson, MI **1998** Phi 6 (0) **2000** Bal 1 (0) **2002**†Oak 11 (3) **2003** Oak 13 (0) **NFL** 31 (3) [4 yrs]

LOVE, DUVAL Duval Lee, G, 6´3˝/275 lbs; UCLA; 1985: LARm, rnd 10; B6/24/1963 Los Angeles, CA **1985** LARm 6 (0) **1986**†LARm 16 (0) **1987** LARm 10 (4) **1988**†LARm 15 (15, RG) **1989**†LARm 16 (16, RG) **1990** LARm 16 (16, RG) **1991** LARm 16 (13, RG) **1992**†Pit 16 (16, LG) **1993**†Pit 16 (16, LG) **1994**†Pit★16 (16, LG) **1995** Arz 16 (16, LG) **1996** Arz 9 (8, LG) **NFL** 167 (121) [12 yrs]

LOVE, JOHN John Louis, WR-K, 5´11˝/185 lbs; North Texas; 1967: Was, rnd 7; B2/24/1944 Linden, TX **[K]**

1967	Was	13	—	—	—	—	17	248	14.6(35)	1	—	—	—	—	—	—	—	—	—	—	Kkp	2	34	246
1972	LARm	5	—	—	—	—	1	19	19.0(19)	1	—	—	—	—	—	—	—	—	—	—	kp	—	6	51
NFL	2	18	—	—	—	—	18	267	14.8(35)	2	—	—	—	—	—	—	—	—	—	—	Kkp	2	40	297

LOVE, RANDY Randy Louis, RB, 6´1˝/208 lbs; Houston; 1979: NE, rnd 8; B9/30/1956 Garland, TX

1979	SL	4	—	—	—	—	—	—	—	—	—	—	—	—	—	—	—	—	—	—	—	—	—	—
1980	SL	16(0)	1	3	3.0(3)	0	—	—	—	—	—	—	—	—	—	—	—	—	—	—	k	—	0	4
1981	SL	16(0)	3	11	3.7(4)	0	—	—	—	—	—	—	—	—	—	—	—	—	—	—	k	—	0	12
1982	†SL	9(0)	—	—	—	—	—	—	—	—	—	—	—	—	—	—	—	—	—	—	k	—	0	9
1983	SL	16(1)	35	103	2.9(16)	2	6	58	9.7(16)	1	—	—	—	—	—	—	—	—	—	—	k	—	18	183
1984	SL	16(1)	25	90	3.6(13)	1	7	33	4.7(16)	1	—	—	—	—	—	—	—	—	—	—	k	—	12	108
1985	SL	12(0)	1	4	4.0(4)	0	2	4	2.0(3)	0	—	—	—	—	—	—	—	—	—	—	k	—	0	6
NFL	7	89(2)	65	211	3.2(16)	3	15	95	6.3(16)	2	—	—	—	—	—	—	—	—	—	—	k	—	30	322

LOVE, SEAN Sean Fitzgerald, G, 6´3˝/304 lbs; Penn State; 1991: Dal, rnd 10; B9/6/1968 Coaldale, PA **1993** TB 2 (0) **1994** TB 6 (0) **1995** Car 11 (1) **NFL** 19 (1) [3 yrs]

LOVE, TERRY Terry Lee, DB, 6´2˝/205 lbs; Murray State; B8/25/1958 Forrest City, AR **1987** Min 1 (0)

LOVE, WALT Walter James, WR, 5´9˝/180 lbs; Westminster (UT); 1973: NYG, rnd 10; B6/4/1950 Cleveland, OH **1973** NYG 12

LOVEALL, CALVIN Calvin Earl, DB, 5´9˝/180 lbs; Idaho; B7/23/1962 Kennewick, WA **1988** Hou 3 (0) **1988** KC 4 (0) **1988** Atl 4 (0) **NFL** 11 (0) [1 yr]

LOVELADY, EDWIN Edwin Patrick, WR, 5´9˝/180 lbs; Memphis; B4/23/1963 Chattanooga, TN

| 1987 | NYG | 3(3) | 2 | 11 | 5.5(8) | 0 | 10 | 125 | 12.5(23) | 2 | — | — | — | — | — | — | — | — | — | — | p | — | 12 | 72 |

LOVELADY, JOSH Josh, G, 6´3˝/330 lbs; Houston; B1/28/1978 Fort Hood, TX **2002** Det 3 (0) **2003** Det 12 (0) **NFL** 15 (0) [2 yrs]

LOVEN, FRITZ Fred Oscar, G, /182 lbs; none; B6/11/1894 Minneapolis, MN, D11/1/1975 Cass County, MN **1929** Min 8 (5, LG), 6

LOVERNE, DAVID David, G, 6´3˝/303 lbs; Idaho; San Jose State; 1999: NYJ, rnd 3; B5/22/1976 Concord, CA **2000** NYJ 16 (0) **2001**†NYJ 16 (0) **2002** Was 15 (11, LG) **2003** SL 1 (0) **2004** Det 15 (13, LG) **NFL** 63 (24) [5 yrs]

LOVETERE, JOHN John Manning, DT, 6´4˝/280 lbs; Compton CC (CA); B5/31/1936 Boston, MA **1959** LARm 12 (RDT) **1960** LARm 12 (RDT) **1961** LARm 13 (RDT) **1962** LARm 14 (RDT) **1963**†NYG◆14 (RDT) **1964** NYG 8 (RDT) **1965** NYG 4 **NFL** 77 [7 yrs]

LOVILLE, DEREK Derek Kevin, RB, 5´10˝/203 lbs; Oregon; B7/4/1968 San Francisco, CA

1990	Sea	11(1)	7	12	1.7(4)	0	—	—	—	—	—	—	—	—	—	—	—	—	—	—	k	—	0	101
1991	Sea	16(0)	22	69	3.1(22)	0	—	—	—	—	—	—	—	—	—	—	—	—	—	—	kp	—	0	212
1994	†SF	14(0)	31	99	3.2(13)	0	2	26	13.0(19)	0	—	—	—	—	—	—	—	—	—	—	k	—	0	116
1995	†SF	16(16, RB)	218	723	3.3(27)	10	87	662	7.6(31)	3	—	—	—	—	—	—	—	—	—	—	—	—	80	1169
1996	†SF	12(6, rb)	70	229	3.3(16)	2	16	138	8.6(44)	2	—	—	—	—	—	—	—	—	—	—	k	—	24	407
1997	†Den	16(0)	25	124	5.0(17)	1	2	10	5.0(7)	0	—	—	—	—	—	—	—	—	—	—	k	—	6	200
1998	†Den	16(0)	53	161	3.0(12)	2	2	29	14.5(15)	0	—	—	—	—	—	—	—	—	—	—	k	—	12	211
1999	Den	10(0)	40	203	5.1(36)	1	11	50	4.5(17)	0	—	—	—	—	—	—	—	—	—	—	k	—	6	230
NFL	8	111(23)	466	1620	3.5(36)	16	120	915	7.6(44)	5	—	—	—	—	—	—	—	—	—	—	kp	—	128	2646

YEAR	TEAM	G (GS, POS)	RUSH	YD	AVG (LG)	TD	REC	YD	AVG (LG)	TD	PASS	COMP	PCT	YD	AVG (LG)	TD	INT	SK	YD	QBR	KPR	OTD	PTS	TAY

LOVING, WARREN Warren Eric, RB, 6´1˝/230 lbs; William Penn; B11/12/1960 Jersey City, NJ **1987** Buf 2 (0)

LoVUOLO, FRANK Frank Anthony, E, 6´2˝/210 lbs; St. Bonaventure; 1949: NYG, rnd 7/SF-A, rnd 3; B5/1/1924 Binghamton, NY

| 1949 | NYG | 11 (1) | — | — | — | — | 2 | 37 | 18.5 (22) | 0 | — | — | — | — | — | — | — | — | — | — | — | — | 1 | 6 | 19 |

LOWDERMILK, KIRK Robert Kirk, C, 6´3˝/269 lbs; Ohio State; 1985: Min, rnd 3; B4/10/1963 Canton, OH **1985** Min 16 (2) **1986** Min 11 (0) **1987**†Min 12 (12, C) **1988**†Min 12 (11, C) **1989**†Min☆16 (16, C) **1990** Min 15 (13, C) **1991** Min 16 (16, C) **1992**†Min☆16 (16, C) **1993** Ind 16 (16, C) **1994** Ind 16 (16, C) **1995**†Ind 16 (16, C) **1996**†Ind 16 (16, C) **NFL** 178 (150) [12 yrs]

LOWE, BULL Henry Louis, E-T, 5´11˝/180 lbs; Lafayette; Fordham; B6/21/1895 Arlington, MA, D2/18/1939 Arlington, MA **1920** Can 10 (6, RE) **1921** Cle☆7 (7, RT) **1925** Pro 2 (1) **1925** Fra 8 (5, le) **1926** Fra 2 (2) **1927** Pro 11 (6, re) **NFL** 40 (27) [5 yrs]

LOWE, GARY Gary Richard, DB-HB, 5´11˝/196 lbs; Michigan State; 1956: Was, rnd 5; B5/4/1934 Trenton, MI [I] **1956** Was 11 **1957** Was 1 **1957**†Det 7 **1958** Det 12 (DB) **1959** Det 12 (DB) **1960** Det 11 (LS) **1961** Det 14 (LS) **1962** Det 13 (LS) **1963** Det 3

| 1964 | Det | 13 | — | — | — | — | — | — | — | — | 1 | 0 | 0.0 | 0 | 0.0 | 0 | 1 | — | — | — | — | — | 0 | -40 |
| NFL | | 9 | 97 | — | — | — | — | — | — | — | 1 | 0 | 0.0 | 0 | 0.0 | 0 | 1 | — | — | pi | — | 2 | 120 |

LOWE, LLOYD Loyd Alvie, DB-HB, 5´10˝/155 lbs; North Texas; B12/18/1928 Prairie Hill, TX **1954** ChiB 1

| 1953 | ChiB | 7 (DB) | — | — | — | — | 4 | 34 | 8.5 (11) | 0 | — | — | — | — | — | — | — | — | — | — | kpi | — | 0 | 5 |
| NFL | | 2 | 8 | — | — | — | — | 4 | 34 | 8.5 (11) | 0 | — | — | — | — | — | — | — | — | — | kpi | — | 0 | -16 |

LOWE, OMARE Omare Gerald, DB, 6´1˝/196 lbs; Washington; 2002: Mia, rnd 5; B4/20/1978 Seattle, WA **2002** Mia 16 (0) **2003** NYJ 2 (0) **2004** NE 3 (0) **2005** Atl 16 (1) **NFL** 22 (1) [4 yrs]

LOWE, PAUL Paul Edward, HB, 6´0˝/205 lbs; Oregon State; B9/27/1936 Homer, LA

1960	†LAC-A☆	14 (HB)	136	855	6.3 (63)	8	23	377	16.4 (63)	2	3	1	33.3	24	8.0 (24)	0	0	—	—	—	kp	—	60	1332
1961	†SD-A☆	14 (HB)	175	767	4.4 (87)	9	17	103	6.1 (17)	0	4	2	50.0	70	17.5 (36)	0	0	—	—	—	kp	—	54	1029
1963	†SD-A★	14 (HB)	177	1010	5.7 (66)	8	26	191	7.3 (31)	2	4	2	50.0	100	25.0 (71)	1	1	—	—	—	k	—	60	1268
1964	†SD-A	14 (HB)	130	496	3.8 (50)	3	14	182	13.0 (41)	2	2	0	0.0	0	0.0	0	0	—	—	—	—	—	30	627
1965	†SD-A★	14 (HB)	222	1121	5.0 (59)	6	17	126	7.4 (45)	1	4	3	75.0	81	20.3 (42)	0	0	—	—	—	—	1	48	1290
1966	SD-A	14 (HB)	146	643	4.4 (57)	3	12	41	3.4 (11)	0	3	1	33.3	25	8.3 (25)	0	0	—	—	—	k	—	18	768
1967	SD-A	7	28	71	2.5 (21)	1	2	25	12.5 (13)	0	1	1	100.0	26	26.0 (26)	0	0	—	—	—	k	—	6	132
1968	SD-A	1	1	9	9.0 (9)	0	—	—	—	—	—	—	—	—	—	—	—	—	—	—	—	—	0	9
1968	KC-A	1	1	-10	-10.0 (-10)	0	—	—	—	—	—	—	—	—	—	—	—	—	—	—	—	—	0	-10
1969	KC-A	7	10	33	3.3 (18)	0	—	—	—	—	—	—	—	—	—	—	—	—	—	—	k	—	0	74
NFL		9	100	1026	4995	4.9 (87)	38	111	1045	9.4 (63)	7	21	10	47.6	326	15.5 (71)	1	1	—	—	kp	—	276	6517

LOWE, REGGIE Reginald James, DE, 6´2˝/250 lbs; Troy State; B6/14/1975 Phenix City, AL **1998** Jax 4 (0)

LOWE, WALTER Walter, B, 5´11˝/180 lbs; Dubuque; Georgetown (DC); B3/6/1899 Blackhawk County, IA, D3/1978 Painesville, OH **1923** RI 5 (1)

LOWE, WOODROW Woodrow, LB, 6´0˝/227 lbs; Alabama; 1976: SD, rnd 5; B6/9/1954 Columbus, GA [I] **1976** SD 14 (14, RLB) **1977** SD 14 (14, RLB) **1978** SD 16 (16, RLB) **1979** SD 16 (14, RLB) **1980**†SD☆16 (16, RLB) **1981**†SD 16 (16, RLB) **1982**†SD 9 (7, RLB) **1983** SD 16 (16, ROLB) **1984** SD 15 (15, ROLB) **1985** SD 16 (14, ROLB) **1986** SD 16 (9, ROLB) **NFL** 164 (151) [11 yrs]

LOWERY, DARBY Darby, G-E-T, 6´0˝/213 lbs; none; B1892 deceased **1920** Roc 9 (1, LE) **1921** Roc 4 (2, LE) **1922** Roc 5 (2) **1923** Roc 4 (4, LG) **1924** Roc 7 (6, RG) **1925** Roc 7 (7, LG) **NFL** 36 (22) [6 yrs]

LOWERY, HUGH Hugh, T, 6´0˝/220 lbs; Indiana; Franklin (IN); B7/19/1892 Cutler, IN, D9/5/1972 Bradenton, FL **1920** Det 7 (3, LT)

LOWERY, MICHAEL Michael Zantel, LB, 6´0˝/232 lbs; Mississippi; B2/14/1974 McComb, MS **1996** ChiB 16 (0) **1997** ChiB 16 (0) **NFL** 32 (0) [2 yrs]

LOWERY, NICK Dominic Gerald, K, 6´4˝/215 lbs; Dartmouth; B5/27/1956 Munich, Germany [K] **1978** NE 2 **1980** KC 16 (0) **1981** KC★16 (0) **1982** KC☆9 (0) **1983** KC 16 (0) **1984** KC 16 (0) **1985** KC☆16 (0) **1986**†KC☆16 (0) **1987** KC 12 (0) **1988** KC☆16 (0) **1989** KC 16 (0) **1990**†KC★16 (0) **1991**†KC 16 (0) **1992**†KC☆15 (0) **1993**†KC 16 (0) **1994** NYJ 16 (0) **1995** NYJ 14 (0) **1996** NYJ 16 (0) **NFL** 260 [18 yrs]

LOWRY, ORLANDO Orlando Dewey, LB, 6´4˝/237 lbs; Ohio State; B8/14/1961 Cleveland, OH **1985** Ind 16 (0) **1986** Ind 16 (0) **1987**†Ind 8 (1) **1988** Ind 16 (2) **1989** Ind 9 (0) **1989** NE 2 (0) **NFL** 67 (4) [5 yrs]

LOWRY, QUENTIN Quentin Ivory, LB, 6´2˝/232 lbs; Youngstown State; 1979: Dal, rnd 12; B11/11/1957 Cleveland, OH **1981** Was 9 (0) **1982**†Was 9 (0) **1983** Was 3 (0) **1983** TB 6 (0) **NFL** 27 (0) [3 yrs]

LOWTHER, JACKIE Jack Russell, B, 5´8˝/165 lbs; Detroit Mercy; 1945: Det, rnd 8; B12/27/1922 Detroit, MI, D9/29/1952 Livonia, MI [K]

1944	Det	8 (0)	9	18	2.0 (11)	0	—	—	—	—	10	7	70.0	54	5.4 (13)	0	2	—	—	Ppi	—	0	10
1945	Pit	2 (2)	15	54	3.6 (17)	0	—	—	—	—	4	0	0.0	0	0.0	0	1	—	—	KPkp	—	0	44
NFL		2	10 (2)	24	72	3.0 (17)	0	—	—	—	—	14	7	50.0	54	3.9 (13)	0	3	—	—	KPkpi	—	0	54

LOYD, ALEX Edgar Alex, E, 6´3˝/198 lbs; Oklahoma State; 1950: Was, rnd 15; B8/7/1927 Stigler, OK, D5/25/1976 Dallas, TX

| 1950 | SF | 12 (LE) | — | — | — | — | 32 | 402 | 12.6 (38) | 0 | — | — | — | — | — | — | — | — | — | — | — | — | 0 | 201 |

LOYD, JEREMY Jeremy, LB, 6´2˝/235 lbs; Iowa State; B7/30/1980 Pittsburg, TX **2003**†SL 10 (0) **2005** SL 4 (0) **NFL** 14 (0) [2 yrs]

LOYD, MIKE Charles Michael, QB, 6´2˝/216 lbs; Kansas; Tulsa; Missouri Southern State; B5/6/1956 Joplin, MO

| 1980 | SL | 5 (1) | 2 | 6 | 0.3 (3) | 0 | — | — | — | — | 28 | 5 | 17.9 | 49 | 1.8 (20) | 0 | 1 | 7 | 48 | — | — | 0 | -14 |

LUBISCHER, STEVE Stephen Anthony, LB, 6´3˝/240 lbs; Boston College; B6/29/1962 Long Branch, NJ **1987** Mia 1 (0)

LUBRATOVICH, LOU Milo Milan, T, 6´2˝/230 lbs; Wisconsin; B5/30/1907 Indian Harbor, IN **1931** Bkn 14 (14, LT) **1932** Bkn 12 (12, LT) **1933** Bkn 10 (9, LT) **1934** Bkn 10 (10, LT) **1935** Bkn 7 (5, lt) **NFL** 53 (50) [5 yrs]

LUCAS, AL Albert, DT, 6´1˝/294 lbs; Troy State; B9/1/1978 Macon, GA, D4/10/2005 Los Angeles, CA **2000** Car 13 (0) **2001** Car 7 (0) **NFL** 20 (0) [2 yrs]

LUCAS, CHAD Chad Dennard, WR, 6´1˝/201 lbs; Alabama State; B11/7/1981 Tuskegee, AL **2005** GB 1 (0)

LUCAS, DICK Richard Albert, E, 6´2˝/213 lbs; Boston College; 1956: ChiB, rnd 10; B1/9/1934 South Boston, MA

1958	Pit	4	—	—	—	—	4	47	11.8 (17)	0	—	—	—	—	—	—	—	—	—	—	—	—	0	24
1960	†Phi	12	—	—	—	—	3	34	11.3 (19)	0	—	—	—	—	—	—	—	—	—	k	—	0	7
1961	Phi	14	—	—	—	—	8	67	8.4 (18)	5	—	—	—	—	—	—	—	—	—	—	—	30	59
1962	Phi	9 (TE)	—	—	—	—	19	236	12.4 (24)	1	—	—	—	—	—	—	—	—	—	—	—	6	123
1963	Phi	3	—	—	—	—	—	—	—	—	—	—	—	—	—	—	—	—	—	—	—	0	
NFL		5	42	—	—	—	—	34	384	11.3 (24)	6	—	—	—	—	—	—	—	—	k	—	36	212

LUCAS, JEFF Jeffrey Alan, T, 6´7˝/288 lbs; West Virginia; B5/30/1964 Hackensack, NJ **1987** Pit 3 (3)

LUCAS, JUSTIN Justin, DB, 5´10˝/211 lbs; Texas A&M; Abilene Christian; B7/15/1976 Victoria, TX **1999** Arz 2 (0) **2000** Arz 16 (0) **2001** Arz 13 (4) **2002** Arz 16 (4) **2003** Arz 11 (0) **2004** SL 7 (0) **NFL** 65 (8) [6 yrs]

LUCAS, KEN Kenyatta C., DB, 6´0˝/205 lbs; Mississippi; 2001: Sea, rnd 2; B1/23/1979 Cleveland, MS **2001** Sea 16 (8, LCB) **2002** Sea 16 (16, RCB) **2003**†Sea 14 (7, rcb) **2004**†Sea 16 (16, RCB) **2005** Car 15 (15, LCB) **NFL** 77 (62) [5 yrs]

LUCAS, RAY Ray, QB, 6´3˝/214 lbs; Rutgers; B8/6/1972 Harrison, NJ

1996	†NE	2 (0)	—	—	—	—	—	—	—	—	—	—	—	—	—	—	—	—	—	—	—	—	0	
1997	NYJ	5 (0)	6	55	9.2 (17)	0	—	—	—	—	4	3	75.0	28	7.0 (19)	0	1	—	—	—	—	0	29
1998	†NYJ	15 (0)	5	23	4.6 (16)	0	—	—	—	—	3	1	33.3	27	9.0 (27)	0	0	—	—	—	—	0	37
1999	NYJ	9 (9, QB)	41	144	3.5 (21)	1	—	—	—	—	272	161	59.2	1678	6.2 (56)	14	6	11	69	85.1	—	6	823
2000	NYJ	7 (0)	6	42	7.0 (17)	0	—	—	—	—	41	21	51.2	206	5.0 (30)	0	4	6	24	—	—	0	-15
2001	†Mia	10 (0)	8	6	0.8 (3)	1	—	—	—	—	3	2	66.7	45	15.0 (28)	0	0	—	—	—	—	6	39
2002	Mia	7 (6, qb)	36	126	3.5 (17)	2	—	—	—	—	160	92	57.5	1045	6.5 (77)	4	6	12	90	—	—	12	449
NFL		7	55 (15)	102	396	3.9 (21)	4	—	—	—	—	483	280	58.0	3029	6.3 (77)	18	17	29	183	74.3	—	24	1361

YEAR	TEAM	G(GS, POS)	RUSH	YD	AVG(LG)	TD	REC	YD	AVG(LG)	TD	PASS	COMP	PCT	YD	AVG(LG)	TD	INT	SK	YD	QBR	KPR	OTD	PTS	TAY

LUCAS, RICHIE   Richard John, QB-DB-HB, 6´0˝/190 lbs; Penn State; 1960: Buf, rnd 1/Was, rnd 1; B4/15/1938 Glassport, PA

1960	Buf-A	14	38	138	3.6(16)	2	5	58	11.6(17)	1	49	23	46.9	314	6.4(36)	2	3	—	—	—	p	—	18	222
1961	Buf-A	8	10	15	1.5(9)	0	6	69	11.5(19)	0	50	20	40.0	282	5.6(45)	2	4	—	—	—	ki	1	12	52
NFL	2	22	48	153	3.2(16)	2	11	127	11.5(19)	1	99	43	43.4	596	6.0(45)	4	7	—	—	—	kpi	1	30	274

LUCAS, TIM   Timothy Brian, LB, 6´3˝/230 lbs; California; 1983: SL, rnd 10; B4/3/1961 Stockton, CA **1987**†Den 11 (3) **1988** Den 16 (0) **1989**†Den 16 (0) **1990** Den 11 (5, rilb) **1991**†Den 5 (3) **1992** Den 9 (0) **1993**†Den 7 (0) **NFL** 75 (11) [7 yrs]

LUCCI, MIKE   Michael Gene, LB, 6´2˝/230 lbs; Pittsburgh; Tennessee; 1961: Cle, rnd 5; B12/29/1939 Ambridge, PA **[I]** **1962** Cle 13 (RLB) **1963** Cle 10 **1964**†Cle 14 **1965** Det 11 (lib) **1966** Det 13 (LLB) **1967** Det 14 (MLB) **1968** Det 12 (MLB) **1969** Det☆14 (MLB) **1970**†Det☆14 (MLB) **1971** Det★14 (MLB) **1972** Det 14 (MLB) **1973** Det 11 (MLB) **NFL** 154 (16)

LUCE, DERREL   Derrel Joe, LB, 6´3˝/226 lbs; Baylor; 1975: Bal, rnd 7; B9/29/1952 Lake Jackson, TX **1975**†Bal 14 **1976**†Bal 14 (14, LLB) **1977**†Bal 12 **1978** Bal 16 (7, llb) **1979** Min 16 **1980** Min 4 (0) **1980** Det 9 (0) **NFL** 85 (21) [6 yrs]

LUCE, LEW   Llewellyn Attsett, HB, 6´1˝/187 lbs; Penn State; B4/3/1938 Washington, DC

| 1961 | Was | 2 | 3 | 1 | 0.3(3) | 0 | — | — | — | — | — | — | — | — | — | — | — | — | — | — | kp | — | 0 | 13 |

LUCENTE, JOHN   John, FB-LB, 5´9˝/200 lbs; West Virginia; B11/4/1922 Clarksburg, WV, D12/25/2002 Dearborn, MI

| 1945 | Pit | 10(5, FB) | 82 | 242 | 3.0(18) | 1 | 11 | 45 | 4.1(23) | 0 | — | — | — | — | — | — | — | — | — | — | k | 1 | 12 | 302 |

LUCHEY, NICK   James Nicolas, aka Nick Williams, FB, 6´2˝/270 lbs; Miami (FL); 1999: Cin, rnd 5; B3/30/1977 Royal Oak, MI

1999	Cin	11(0)	10	30	3.0(8)	0	10	96	9.6(19)	0	—	—	—	—	—	—	—	—	—	—	k	—	0	67
2000	Cin	14(4)	10	54	5.4(13)	0	7	84	12.0(20)	0	—	—	—	—	—	—	—	—	—	—	k	—	0	78
2001	Cin	4(2)	—	—	—	—	—	—	—	—	—	—	—	—	—	—	—	—	—	—		—	0	0
2002	Cin	16(3)	12	59	4.9(10)	2	7	46	6.6(15)	0	—	—	—	—	—	—	—	—	—	—	k	—	12	97
2003	†GB	11(2)	1	3	3.0(3)	0	1	12	12.0(12)	0	—	—	—	—	—	—	—	—	—	—	k	—	0	0
2004	†GB	16(6, fb)	10	24	2.4(4)	0	2	20	10.0(11)	0	—	—	—	—	—	—	—	—	—	—		—	0	34
2005	Cin	3(0)	1	0	0.0(0)	0	—	—	—	—	—	—	—	—	—	—	—	—	—	—		—	0	0
NFL	7	75(17)	44	170	3.9(13)	2	27	258	9.6(20)	0	—	—	—	—	—	—	—	—	—	—	k	—	12	276

LUCIER, WAYNE   Wayne, G-C, 6´3˝/300 lbs; Northwestern; Colorado; 2003: NYG, rnd 7; B12/5/1979 Amesbury, MA **2003** NYG 12 (11, LG/c) **2004** NYG 15 (9, rg) **NFL** 27 (20) [2 yrs]

LUCK, OLIVER   Oliver Francis, QB, 6´2˝/196 lbs; West Virginia; 1982: Hou, rnd 2; B4/5/1960 Cleveland, OH

1983	Hou	7(6, qb)	17	55	3.2(17)	0	—	—	—	—	217	124	57.1	1375	6.3(66)	8	13	16	138	63.4	—	—	0	263
1984	Hou	4(0)	10	75	7.5(18)	1	—	—	—	—	36	22	61.1	256	7.1(27)	2	1	2	11	—	—	—	6	183
1985	Hou	5(2)	15	95	6.3(17)	0	—	—	—	—	100	56	56.0	572	5.7(46)	2	2	8	50	—	—	—	0	311
1986	Hou	4(1)	2	12	6.0(8)	0	—	—	—	—	60	31	51.7	341	5.7(27)	1	5	7	62	—	—	—	0	-13
NFL	4	20(9)	44	237	5.4(18)	1	—	—	—	—	413	233	56.4	2544	6.2(66)	13	21	33	261	64.1	—	—	6	744

LUCK, TERRY   Terry Lee, QB, 6´3˝/205 lbs; Nebraska; B12/4/1952 Fayetteville, NC

| 1977 | Cle | 4(1) | 3 | -2 | -0.7(1) | 0 | 1 | 4 | 4.0(4) | 1 | 50 | 25 | 50.0 | 316 | 6.3(33) | 1 | 7 | 1 | 8 | — | — | — | 6 | -112 |

LUCKHURST, MICK   Michael Christopher Wilbert, K, 6´1˝/180 lbs; St. Cloud State; California; B3/31/1958 Redbourn, England **[K]** **1981** Atl 16 (0) **1982**†Atl 9 (0) **1983** Atl 16 (0) **1984** Atl 16 (0) **1985** Atl 16 (0) **1986** Atl 10 (0) **1987** Atl 12 (0) **NFL** 95 (0) [7 yrs]

LUCKMAN, SID   Sidney, QB-HB-DB, 6´0˝/197 lbs; Columbia; 1939: ChiB, rnd 1; B11/21/1916 Brooklyn, NY, D7/5/1998 North Miami Beach, FL; HOF 1965 **[K]**

1939	ChiB	11(7, LH)	24	42	1.8	0	—	—	—	—	51	23	45.1	636	12.5(85)	5	4	—	—	P	—	1	6	235
1940	†ChiB★	11(7, QB)	23	-65	-2.8	0	—	—	—	—	105	48	45.7	941	9.0(74)	4	9	—	—	54.5	Pi	—	0	68
1941	†ChiB★	11(11, QB)	18	18	1.0(20)	1	—	—	—	—	119	68	**57.1**	1181	**9.9(65)**	9	6	—	—	**95.3**	Pki	—	6	460
1942	†ChiB	11(10, QB)	13	-6	-0.5(9)	0	—	—	—	—	105	57	54.3	1024	9.8(52)	10	13	—	—	76.0	Ppi	1	6	147
1943	†ChiB☆	10(3, QB)	22	-40	-1.8(8)	1	—	—	—	—	202	110	54.5	**2194**	10.9(66)	**28**	12	—	—	**107.6**	Pkpi	—	6	810
1944	ChiB☆	7(0, QB)	20	-96	-4.8(7)	1	—	—	—	—	143	71	49.7	1018	7.1(86)	11	12	—	—	63.8	Ppi	—	6	25
1945	ChiB☆	10(2, QB)	36	-118	-3.3(22)	0	—	—	—	—	217	117	53.9	**1727**	8.0(65)	**14**	10	—	—	82.5	Pk	—	0	417
1946	†ChiB★	11(5, QB)	25	-76	-3.0(25)	0	—	—	—	—	229	110	48.0	**1826**	8.0(48)	17	16	—	—	**71.0**	Pi	—	0	301
1947	ChiB☆	12(7, QB)	10	86	8.6(40)	1	1	15	15.0(15)	0	323	176	54.5	2712	8.4(81)	24	**31**	—	—	67.7	KP	—	7	340
1948	ChiB☆	12(8, QB)	8	11	1.4(18)	0	—	—	—	—	163	89	54.6	1047	6.4(53)	13	14	—	—	65.1	P	—	0	40
1949	ChiB	11(2)	3	4	1.3(14)	0	—	—	—	—	50	22	44.0	200	4.0(34)	1	3	—	—	P	—	—	0	-11
1950	ChiB	11	2	1	0.5(1)	0	—	—	—	—	37	13	35.1	180	4.9(44)	1	2	—	—	—	—	—	0	16
NFL	12	128(62)	204	-239	-1.2(40)	4	1	15	15.0(15)	0	1744	904	51.8	14686	8.4(86)	137	132	—	—	75.0	KPkpi	—	2	37	2846

LUCKY, BILL   William Henry, DT, 6´3˝/250 lbs; Baylor; 1954: Cle, rnd 5; B8/24/1931 Temple, TX **1955** GB 12

LUCKY, MIKE   Michael Thomas, TE, 6´6˝/280 lbs; Arizona; 1999: Dal, rnd 7; B11/23/1975 Antioch, CA

1999	†Dal	14(4)	—	—	—	—	5	25	5.0(8)	0	—	—	—	—	—	—	—	—	—	—	—	—	0	13
2001	Dal	16(5, te)	—	—	—	—	13	96	7.4(16)	1	—	—	—	—	—	—	—	—	—	—	—	—	6	53
2002	Dal	16(0)	—	—	—	—	1	22	22.0(22)	0	—	—	—	—	—	—	—	—	—	—	—	—	0	11
NFL	3	46(9)	—	—	—	—	19	143	7.5(22)	1	—	—	—	—	—	—	—	—	—	—	—	—	6	77

LUECK, BILL   William Melville, G, 6´3˝/250 lbs; Arizona; 1968: GB, rnd 1; B4/7/1946 Buckeye, AZ **1968** GB 11 **1969** GB 14 (LG) **1970** GB 14 (LG) **1971** GB 14 (LG) **1972**†GB 14 (LG) **1973** GB 14 (LG) **1974** GB 9 (LG) **1975** Phi 11 (11, RG) **NFL** 101 (11) [8 yrs]

LUFT, DON   Donald Richard, E, 6´5˝/220 lbs; Indiana; B2/14/1930 Fisk, WI, D6/19/2002 Indianapolis, IN

| 1954 | Phi | 12 | — | — | — | — | 3 | 59 | 19.7(30) | 0 | — | — | — | — | — | — | — | — | — | — | — | — | 0 | 30 |

LUHN, NOLAN   Nolan Harry, E, 6´3˝/200 lbs; Tulsa; 1945: GB, rnd 25; B7/27/1921 Kenney, TX

1945	GB	9(4)	—	—	—	—	10	151	15.1(44)	1	—	—	—	—	—	—	—	—	—	—	—	—	6	81
1946	GB☆	11(8, RE)	—	—	—	—	16	224	14.0(36)	2	—	—	—	—	—	—	—	—	—	—	k	—	14	120
1947	GB	12(9, RE)	—	—	—	—	42	696	16.6(44)	7	—	—	—	—	—	—	—	—	—	—	k	—	42	383
1948	GB	12(8, RE)	—	—	—	—	17	285	16.8(40)	2	—	—	—	—	—	—	—	—	—	—	k	—	12	126
1949	GB	12(9, RE)	—	—	—	—	15	169	11.3(30)	1	—	—	—	—	—	—	—	—	—	—	k	—	6	90
NFL	5	56(38)	—	—	—	—	100	1525	15.3(44)	13	—	—	—	—	—	—	—	—	—	—	k	—	80	799

LUJACK, JOHNNY   John Christopher, QB-DB, 6´0˝/186 lbs; Notre Dame; 1946: ChiB, rnd 1/1947: ChiR-A, rnd S; B1/4/1925 Connellsville, PA **[K]**

1948	ChiB☆	9(3)	15	110	7.3(26)	1	—	—	—	—	66	36	54.5	611	9.3(64)	6	3	—	—	—	Ki	—	50	427
1949	ChiB	8(2, QB)	8	64	8.0(20)	2	—	—	—	—	**312**	162	51.9	**2658**	**8.5(81)**	**23**	22	—	—	76.0	KP	—	57	648
1950	†ChiB★	12(QB)	63	397	**6.3(40)**	**11**	1	16	16.0(16)	0	254	121	47.6	1731	6.8(70)	4	21	—	—	41.0	Ki	—	109	571
1951	ChiB★	12(QB/DB)	47	171	3.6(22)	7	—	—	—	—	176	85	48.3	1295	7.4(78)	8	8	—	—	69.2	Ki	—	52	638
NFL	4	45(11)	133	742	5.6(40)	21	1	16	16.0(16)	0	808	404	50.0	6295	7.8(81)	41	54	—	—	65.3	KPi	—	268	2283

LUKE, STEVE   Steven Norman, DB, 6´2˝/205 lbs; Ohio State; 1975: GB, rnd 4; B9/4/1953 Massillon, OH **1975** GB 14 **1976** GB 14 (13, SS) **1977** GB 14 (14, SS) **1978** GB 16 (16, SS) **1979** GB 16 (16, SS) **1980** GB 16 (16, SS) **NFL** 90 (75) [6 yrs]

LUKE, TOMMY   Tommy Junior, DB, 6´0˝/190 lbs; Mississippi; 1967: Buf, rnd 8; B1/26/1944 Louisville, MS **1968** Den-A 7

LUKE, TRIANDOS   Triandos, WR, 5´10˝/190 lbs; Alabama; 2004: Den, rnd 6; B12/24/1981 Phenix City, AL

| 2004 | Den | 10(0) | — | — | — | — | 6 | 52 | 8.7(12) | 0 | — | — | — | — | — | — | — | — | — | — | kp | — | 0 | 147 |

LUKEN, TOM   Thomas James, G, 6´3˝/253 lbs; Purdue; 1972: Phi, rnd 3; B6/15/1950 Cincinnati, OH **1972** Phi 12 (8, LG) **1973** Phi 3 **1974** Phi 14 **1975** Phi 5 (3) **1977** Phi 14 **1978**†Phi 16 (6, lg) **NFL** 64 (17) [6 yrs]

LUKENS, JIM   James Willie, E, 6´4˝/205 lbs; Washington & Lee; 1948: Bos, rnd 21; B9/6/1924 Chester, PA, D10/21/2002 Wernersville, VA

| 1949 | †Buf-A | 11(10, RE) | — | — | — | — | 24 | 249 | 10.4 | 2 | — | — | — | — | — | — | — | — | — | — | — | — | 12 | 135 |

LUMMUS, JACK   Jack, E, 6´3˝/200 lbs; Baylor; B10/22/1917 Ennis, TX, D3/8/1945 Iwo Jima

| 1941 | †NYG | 9(0) | — | — | — | — | 1 | 5 | 5.0(5) | 0 | — | — | — | — | — | — | — | — | — | — | — | — | 0 | 3 |

YEAR	TEAM	G(GS, POS)	RUSH	YD	AVG(LG)	TD	REC	YD	AVG(LG)	TD	PASS	COMP	PCT	YD	AVG(LG)	TD	INT	SK	YD	QBR	KPR	OTD	PTS	TAY

LUMPKIN, FATHER   Roy Lee, B, 6´2˝/211 lbs; Georgia Tech; B1/27/1907 Jefferson, TX, D3/31/1974 Dallas, TX

1930	Por☆	14(13, FB)	—	—	—	—	—	—	—	—	—	—	—	—	—	—	—	—	—	—	—	—	—	—
1931	Por	14(13, BB)	—	—	—	—	—	—	—	—	—	—	—	—	—	—	—	—	—	—	—	—	—	—
1932	Por☆	12(11, BB)	25	47	1.9	0	6	80	13.3	1	—	—	—	—	—	—	—	—	—	—	—	—	6	92
1933	Por	11(10, BB)	7	26	3.7	0	10	191	19.1	1	1	0	0.0	0	0.0	0	0	—	—	—	—	—	6	127
1934	Det	13(11, BB)	6	44	7.3	1	4	24	6.0	0	—	—	—	—	—	—	—	—	—	—	—	1	12	76
1935	Bkn	12(12, BB)	11	26	2.4	0	4	26	6.5	0	6	3	50.0	58	9.7	0	1	—	—	—	—	—	0	28
1936	Bkn	12(12, BB)	11	29	2.6	0	6	34	5.7	0	—	—	—	—	—	—	—	—	—	—	—	—	0	46
1937	Bkn	5(3)	—	—	—	—	—	—	—	—	—	—	—	—	—	—	—	—	—	—	—	—	—	—
NFL	8	93(85)	60	172	2.9	5	30	355	11.8	2	7	3	42.9	58	8.3	0	3	—	—	—	—	1	48	424

LUMPKIN, JOEY   Joey Lynn, LB, 6´2˝/230 lbs; Arizona State; B2/19/1960 Ardmore, OK   **1982** Buf 6 (0)   **1983** Buf 14 (0)   **NFL** 20 (0) [2 yrs]

LUMPKIN, RON   Ronald, DB, 6´2˝/205 lbs; Arizona State; 1973: NYG, rnd 12; B6/22/1951 Los Angeles, CA   **1973** NYG 1

LUMPKIN, SEAN   Sean Franklin, DB, 6´0˝/206 lbs; Minnesota; 1992: NO, rnd 4; B1/4/1970 Golden Valley, MN   **1992†**NO 16 (0)   **1993** NO 12 (0)   **1994** NO 16 (15, SS)   **1995** NO 16 (16, SS)   **1996** NO 7 (1)   **NFL** 67 (32) [5 yrs]

LUNA, BOBBY   Robert Kendal, DB, 5´11˝/187 lbs; Alabama; 1955: SF, rnd 6; B3/25/1933 Lewisburg, TN   **1955** SF 12 (DB)

| 1959 | Pit | 12(DB) | 3 | 3 | 1.0(10) | 0 | — | — | — | — | 1 | 1 | 100.0 | 55 | 55.0(55) | 0 | 0 | — | — | — | Ppi | — | 0 | 72 |
| NFL | 2 | 24 | 3 | 3 | 1.0(10) | 0 | — | — | — | — | 1 | 1 | 100.0 | 55 | 55.0(55) | 0 | 0 | — | — | — | Ppi | — | 0 | 62 |

LUNCEFORD, DAVE   David Glenn, T-DT, 6´4˝/240 lbs; Baylor; 1956: ChiC, rnd 8; B5/6/1934 Canton, TX   **1957** ChiC 12 (LT)

LUND, BILL   William Harold, HB, 5´10˝/180 lbs; Case Western Reserve; 1945: Cle, rnd 15; B10/27/1924 Akron, OH

1946	Cle-A	10(2)	23	72	3.1	1	4	64	16.0	2	—	—	—	—	—	—	—	—	—	—	kpi	—	18	168
1947	Cle-A	8(0)	14	105	7.5	1	6	110	18.3	1	—	—	—	—	—	—	—	—	—	—	ki	1	18	218
AAFC	2	18(2)	37	177	4.8	2	10	174	17.4	3	—	—	—	—	—	—	—	—	—	—	kpi	1	36	386

LUNDAY, KAYO   Kenneth Levin, G-LB-C, 6´3˝/217 lbs; Arkansas; B8/13/1912 Cleora, OK, D7/13/2005 Durant, OK   **1937** NYG 11 (2)   **1938†**NYG✧11 (6, LG)   **1939†**NYG☆11 (0)   **1940** NYG 10 (0)   **1941†**NYG 11 (0)   **1946** NYG 7 (0)   **1947** NYG 6 (0)   **NFL** 67 (8) [7 yrs]

LUNDELL, BOB   Wilbur Harvey, E, 6´4˝/215 lbs; Gustavus Adolphus; B6/21/1907 Pueblo, CO, D7/7/1993 McAllen, TX   **1929** Min☆10 (8, RE)   **1930** Min 4 (2)   **1930** SI 6 (6, RE), 6   **NFL** 20 (16) [2 yrs]

LUNDY, DENNIS   Dennis Leonard, RB, 5´8˝/187 lbs; Northwestern; B7/6/1972 Tampa, FL   **1995** ChiB 2 (0)

| 1995 | Hou | 7(0) | — | — | — | — | 1 | 11 | 11.0(11) | 0 | — | — | — | — | — | — | — | — | — | — | k | — | 0 | 4 |
| NFL | 1 | 9(0) | — | — | — | — | 1 | 11 | 11.0(11) | 0 | — | — | — | — | — | — | — | — | — | — | kp | — | 0 | -10 |

LUNDY, LAMAR   Lamar, DE-E, 6´7˝/245 lbs; Purdue; 1957: LA, rnd 4; B4/17/1935 Richmond, IN   **1960** LARm 12 (RDE)   **1961** LARm 14 (RDE)   **1962** LARm 14 (RDE)   **1963** LARm 14 (RDE)   **1964** LARm 13 (RDE)   **1965** LARm 12 (RDE)   **1966** LARm 14 (RDE)   **1967†**LARm☆14 (RDE)   **1968** LARm 5 (5, rde)   **1969†**LARm 4

1957	LARm	12(12)	—	—	—	—	6	114	19.0(34)	3	—	—	—	—	—	—	—	—	—	—	k	—	18	57
1958	LARm	12(12, LE)	—	—	—	—	25	396	15.8(32)	3	—	—	—	—	—	—	—	—	—	—	—	—	18	213
1959	LARm✧	12(LDE)	—	—	—	—	4	74	18.5(26)	0	—	—	—	—	—	—	—	—	—	—	—	—	0	37
NFL	13	152(29)	—	—	—	—	35	584	16.7(34)	6	—	—	—	—	—	—	—	—	—	—	ki	3	54	394

LUNGREN, CHARLIE   Charles Howard, B-E, 5´8˝/158 lbs; Swarthmore; B6/23/1894, D3/21/1972 Milwaukee, WI   **1923** RI 4 (2)

LUNSFORD, MEL   Melvin T., DE-DT-NT, 6´3˝/256 lbs; Central State (OH); 1972: Oak, rnd 3; B6/13/1950 Cincinnati, OH   **1973** NE 4   **1974** NE 13 (13, LDE)   **1975** NE 4 (4)   **1976†**NE 14 (1)   **1977** NE 13 (13, LDE)   **1978†**NE 16 (15, LDE)   **1979** NE 16 (16, LDE)   **1980** NE 12 (12, LDE)   **NFL** 92 (74) [8 yrs]

LUNZ, JERRY   Gerald A., G-T, 6´3˝/210 lbs; Marquette; B3/13/1903 Milwaukee, WI, D1/11/1974 Milwaukee, WI   **1925** ChiC 14 (13, LG)   **1926** ChiC 12 (11, LG), 6   **1930** Fra 1 (0)   **NFL** 27 (24) [3 yrs]

LURTH, LADUE   Charles Andrew LaDue, HB, 5´8˝/160 lbs; Gustavus Adolphus; B2/23/1905 LeSueur County, MN, D10/2/1991 Moab, UT   **1929** Min 1 (0)

LURTSEMA, BOB   Robert Ross, DT-DE, 6´6˝/250 lbs; Michigan Tech; Western Michigan; B3/29/1942 Grand Rapids, MI   **1967** NYG 14 (RDT)   **1968** NYG✧14 (RDT)   **1969** NYG 13 (RDT)   **1970** NYG 14 (LDE)   **1971** NYG 7   **1971†**Min 0   **1972** Min 14   **1973†**Min 14   **1974†**Min 12   **1975†**Min 14   **1976** Min 1   **1976** Sea 13 (13, RDE)   **1977** Sea 14 (9, RDT)   **NFL** 144 (22) [11 yrs]

LUSBY, VAUGHN   Alawadra Vaughn, DB, 5´10˝/178 lbs; Arkansas; 1979: Cin, rnd 4; B8/23/1956 Fort Polk, LA   **1979** Cin 16   **1980** ChiB 2 (0)   **NFL** 18 [2 yrs]

LUSCINSKI, JIM   James V., T-G, 6´5˝/275 lbs; Norwich; B12/16/1958 Arlington, MA   **1982†**NYJ 6 (0)

LUSH, MIKE   Michael Stephen, DB, 6´2˝/195 lbs; East Stroudsburg; B4/18/1958 Allentown, PA   **1986** Ind 4 (0)   **1986** Min 6 (0)   **1987** Atl 3 (3)   **NFL** 13 (3) [2 yrs]

LUSK, BOB   Robert Arlen, C, 6´1˝/222 lbs; William & Mary; 1956: Det, rnd 6; B5/18/1932 Williamson, WV   **1956** Det 5

LUSK, HENRY   Hendrick Hamilton, TE, 6´2˝/245 lbs; Utah; 1996: NO, rnd 7; B5/8/1972 Seaside, CA

1996	NO	16(3)	—	—	—	—	27	210	7.8(24)	0	—	—	—	—	—	—	—	—	—	—	k	—	0	106
1998	†Mia	3(1)	1	7	7.0(7)	0	—	—	—	—	—	—	—	—	—	—	—	—	—	—	—	—	0	7
NFL	2	19(4)	1	7	7.0(7)	0	27	210	7.8(24)	0	—	—	—	—	—	—	—	—	—	—	k	—	0	113

LUSK, HERB   Herbert H., RB, 6´0˝/190 lbs; Long Beach State; 1976: Phi, rnd 10; B2/19/1953 Memphis, TN

1976	Phi	14(2)	61	254	4.2(22)	0	13	119	9.2(42)	0	—	—	—	—	—	—	—	—	—	—	k	—	0	364
1977	Phi	11	52	229	4.4(70)	2	5	102	20.4(36)	1	—	—	—	—	—	—	—	—	—	—	k	—	18	313
1978	Phi	3	—	—	—	—	—	—	—	—	—	—	—	—	—	—	—	—	—	—	k	—	0	16
NFL	3	28(2)	113	483	4.3(70)	2	18	221	12.3(42)	1	—	—	—	—	—	—	—	—	—	—	k	—	18	693

LUSTEG, BOOTH   Gerald Booth, K, 5´11˝/190 lbs; Connecticut; B5/8/1939 New Haven, CT [K]   **1966†**Buf-A 14   **1968** Pit 13   **1969** GB 4

| 1967 | Mia-A | 8 | — | — | — | — | — | — | — | — | 1 | 0 | 0.0 | 0 | 0.0 | 0 | 0 | — | — | — | K | — | 39 | 0 |
| NFL | 4 | 39 | — | — | — | — | — | — | — | — | 1 | 0 | 0.0 | 0 | 0.0 | 0 | 0 | — | — | — | K | — | 202 | 0 |

LUTHER, ED   Edward Augustine, QB, 6´3˝/206 lbs; San Jose State; 1980: SD, rnd 4; B1/2/1957 Gardena, CA

1980	SD	5(0)	3	5	1.7(9)	0	—	—	—	—	3	2	66.7	26	8.7(13)	0	1	—	—	—	—	—	0	-22
1981	†SD	16(0)	3	-8	-2.7(-1)	0	—	—	—	—	15	7	46.7	68	4.5(25)	0	1	—	—	—	—	—	0	-14
1982	†SD	9(0)	1	-13	-13.0(-13)	0	—	—	—	—	4	2	50.0	55	13.8(55)	0	1	—	—	—	—	—	0	-26
1983	SD	16(6, qb)	9	-14	-1.6(8)	0	—	—	—	—	287	151	52.6	1875	6.5(46)	7	17	13	120	56.6	—	—	0	279
1984	SD	15(3, qb)	4	11	2.8(7)	0	—	—	—	—	151	83	55.0	1163	7.7(88)	5	3	7	57	—	—	—	0	498
NFL	5	61(9)	20	-19	-0.9(9)	0	—	—	—	—	460	245	53.3	3187	6.9(88)	12	23	20	177	63.2	—	—	0	715

LUTZ, DAVE   David Graham, T-G, 6´6˝/305 lbs; Georgia Tech; 1983: KC, rnd 2; B12/20/1959 Monroe, NC   **1983** KC 16 (16, RT)   **1984** KC 7 (6, RT)   **1985** KC 16 (16, RT)   **1986†**KC 9 (8, RT)   **1987** KC 12 (7, rt)   **1988** KC 15 (7, rt)   **1989** KC 16 (16, RG)   **1990†**KC 16 (15, RG)   **1991†**KC 16 (16, RG)   **1992†**KC 16 (16, RG)   **1993†**Det 16 (15, RT)   **1994†**Det 16 (16, RT)   **1995†**Det 16 (16, RT)   **NFL** 187 (170) [13 yrs]

LUZAR, CHRIS   Christopher Myers, TE, 6´7˝/262 lbs; Virginia; 2002: Jax, rnd 4; B2/12/1979 Newport News, VA

2002	Jax	12(0)	—	—	—	—	1	5	5.0(5)	0	—	—	—	—	—	—	—	—	—	—	k	—	0	-13
2003	Jax	11(1)	—	—	—	—	3	30	10.0(21)	0	—	—	—	—	—	—	—	—	—	—	—	—	0	15
NFL	2	23(1)	—	—	—	—	4	35	8.8(21)	0	—	—	—	—	—	—	—	—	—	—	k	—	0	3

LYDAY, ALLEN   Allen Clark, DB, 5´10˝/190 lbs; Texas Southern; Nebraska; B9/16/1960 Wichita, KS   **1984** Hou 4 (0)   **1985** Hou 13 (0)   **1986** Hou 12 (0)   **1987** Hou 7 (0)   **NFL** 36 (0) [4 yrs]

LYGHT, TODD   Todd William, DB, 6´0˝/190 lbs; Notre Dame; 1991: LARm, rnd 1; B2/9/1969 Kwajelein, Marshall Islands [I]   **1991** LARm 12 (8, lcb)   **1992** LARm 12 (12, LCB)   **1993** LARm 9 (4, RCB)   **1994** LARm 16 (16, RCB)   **1995** SL 16 (16, LCB)   **1996** SL 16 (16, LCB)   **1997** SL 16 (16, LCB)   **1998** SL 16 (16, LCB)   **1999†**SL★16 (16, LCB)   **2000†**SL 14 (12, LCB)   **2001** Det 16 (16, LCB)   **2002** Det 16 (14, LCB)   **NFL** 175 (167) [12 yrs]

LYLE, DEWEY   Dewitt Wagner, G-E-T, 5´11˝/196 lbs; Minnesota; B3/23/1891, MN, D11/27/1980 Paso Robles, CA   **1920** RI☆8 (6, RG)   **1921** RI 7 (6, RG)   **1922** RI 6 (6, LG)   **1922** GB 2 (2)   **1923** GB 9 (8, RE)   **NFL** 32 (28) [4 yrs]

YEAR	TEAM	G (GS, POS)	RUSH	YD	AVG (LG)	TD	REC	YD	AVG (LG)	TD	PASS	COMP	PCT	YD	AVG (LG)	TD	INT	SK	YD	QBR	KPR	OTD	PTS	TAY

LYLE, GARRY Garry Thomas, DB-RB, 6´2˝/198 lbs; George Washington; 1967: Chi, rnd 3; B10/20/1945 New Martinsville, WV   **1971** ChiB 14   **1972** ChiB 3   **1973** ChiB 14 (FS)
1974 ChiB 14 (FS)

1968	ChiB	12	4	28	7.0(26)	0	5	32	6.4(13)	0	—	—	—	—	—	—	—	—	—	—	P	—	0	44
1969	ChiB	13	—	—	—	—	1	11	11.0(11)	0	—	—	—	—	—	—	—	—	—	—	kpi	—	0	112
1970	ChiB	14	—	—	—	—	1	5	5.0(5)	0	0	0	0.0	0	0.0	0	0	1	4	—	Pp	—	0	-6
NFL	7	84	4	28	7.0(26)	0	7	48	6.9(13)	0	0	0	0.0	0	0.0	0	0	1	4	—	Pkpi	—	0	295

LYLE, KEITH Keith Allen, DB, 6´2˝/210 lbs; Virginia; 1994: LARm, rnd 3; B4/17/1972 Washington, DC [I]   **1994** LARm 16 (0)   **1997** SL 16 (16, FS)   **1998** SL 16 (16, FS)
1999†SL 9 (6, FS)   **2001** Was 16 (0)   **2002** SD 15 (6, fs)

1995	SL	16(16, FS)	1	4	4.0(4)	0	—	—	—	—	—	—	—	—	—	—	—	—	—	—	i	—	0	31
1996	SL	16(16, FS)	3	39	13.0(20)	0	—	—	—	—	—	—	—	—	—	—	—	—	—	—	i	—	0	146
2000	†SL	16(16, FS)	1	4	4.0(4)	0	—	—	—	—	—	—	—	—	—	—	—	—	—	—	i	1	6	8
NFL	9	136(95)	5	47	9.4(20)	0	—	—	—	—	—	—	—	—	—	—	—	—	—	—	iS	1	6	254

LYLE, RICK Rick James Earl, DE, 6´5˝/285 lbs; Missouri; B2/26/1971 Monroe, LA   **1994** Cle 3 (0)   **1996** Bal 11 (3)   **1997** NYJ 16 (16, LDE)   **1998**†NYJ 16 (16, LDE)
1999 NYJ 16 (16, LDE)   **2000** NYJ 14 (14, LDE)   **2001**†NYJ 16 (3)   **2002** NE 13 (2)   **2003** NE 8 (1)   **NFL** 113 (71) [9 yrs]

LYLES, LENNY Leonard Everett, DB-HB, 6´2˝/202 lbs; Louisville; 1958: Bal, rnd 1; B1/26/1936 Nashville, TN [R]   **1960** SF 12   **1961** Bal 14   **1962** Bal 6   **1963** Bal 14 (RCB)
1964†Bal 14 (RCB)   **1965**†Bal 11 (RCB)   **1966** Bal◇14 (RCB)   **1967** Bal 12 (RCB)   **1968**†Bal 14 (RCB)   **1969** Bal 14 (rcb)

1958	†Bal	12	22	41	1.9(27)	1	5	24	4.8(11)	1	—	—	—	—	—	—	—	—	—	—	k	2	24	321
1959	SF	12	13	28	2.2(13)	1	3	33	11.0(14)	1	—	—	—	—	—	—	—	—	—	—	k	—	6	245
NFL	12	149	35	69	2.0(27)	2	8	57	7.1(18)	1	—	—	—	—	—	—	—	—	—	—	ki	5	48	1240

LYLES, LESTER Lester Everett, DB-LB, 6´3˝/209 lbs; Virginia; 1985: NYJ, rnd 2; B12/27/1962 Washington, DC   **1985**†NYJ 6 (0)   **1986**†NYJ 16 (14, SS)   **1987** NYJ 4 (1)
1988 Phx 6 (4)   **1989** SD 16 (1)   **1990** SD 15 (3)   **NFL** 63 (23) [6 yrs]

LYLES, ROBERT Robert Damon, LB, 6´1˝/226 lbs; TCU; 1984: Hou, rnd 5; B3/21/1961 Los Angeles, CA   **1984** Hou 6 (0)   **1985** Hou 16 (16, LOLB)   **1986** Hou 16 (16, LOLB)
1987†Hou 12 (12, LOLB)   **1988**†Hou 16 (16, LOLB)   **1989**†Hou 13 (13, LOLB)   **1990** Hou 3 (2)   **1990** Atl 11 (11, LOLB)   **1991**†Atl 16 (14, LOLB)   **NFL** 109 (100) [8 yrs]

LYMAN, DEL Marion Dell, T, 6´3˝/223 lbs; UCLA; 1941: GB, rnd 14; B7/9/1918 Aberdeen, WA, D12/19/1986 Ojai, CA   **1941** GB 5 (0)   **1941** Cle 4 (0)   **1944** Cle 2 (0)
NFL 11 (0) [2 yrs]

LYMAN, DUSTIN Dustin Sheehan, TE, 6´4˝/245 lbs; Wake Forest; 2000: Chi, rnd 3; B8/5/1976 Boulder, CO

2000	ChiB	14(7, te)	—	—	—	—	1	4	4.0(4)	0	—	—	—	—	—	—	—	—	—	—	—	—	0	2
2001	†ChiB	4(0)	—	—	—	—	—	—	—	—	—	—	—	—	—	—	—	—	—	—	—	—	—	—
2002	ChiB	12(3)	—	—	—	—	14	121	8.6(21)	2	—	—	—	—	—	—	—	—	—	—	—	—	12	71
2003	ChiB	9(1)	—	—	—	—	11	80	7.3(12)	0	—	—	—	—	—	—	—	—	—	—	—	—	0	40
2004	ChiB	16(10, TE)	—	—	—	—	11	73	6.6(13)	1	—	—	—	—	—	—	—	—	—	—	—	—	6	42
NFL	5	55(21)	—	—	—	—	37	278	7.5(21)	3	—	—	—	—	—	—	—	—	—	—	—	—	18	154

LYMAN, JEFF Jeffrey Borden, LB, 6´3˝/235 lbs; Brigham Young; 1972: SL, rnd 4; B8/21/1950 Salt Lake City, UT   **1972** SL 2   **1972** Buf 1   **NFL** 3 [1 yr]

LYMAN, LINK William Roy, T, 6´2˝/233 lbs; Nebraska; B11/30/1898 Table Rock, NE, D12/28/1972 Barstow, CA; HOF 1964 [K]   **1922** Can 12 (12, LT)   **1923** Can☆12 (12, LT), 6
1924 Cle☆9 (9, LT), 25   **1925** Can 7 (7, LT)   **1925** Fra☆4 (4)   **1926** ChiB 15 (7, lt)   **1927** ChiB 14 (13, RT)   **1928** ChiB☆13 (10, LT)   **1930** ChiB☆11 (10, LT)   **1931** ChiB☆11 (9, LT), 6
1933†ChiB☆13 (13, LT)   **1934**†ChiB☆12 (11, LT)   **NFL** 133 (117), 37 [11 yrs]

LYNCH, BEN Benjamin John, C, 6´4˝/295 lbs; California; 1996: KC, rnd 7; B11/18/1972 Santa Rosa, CA   **1999** SF 16 (1)   **2000** SF 9 (0)   **2001**†SF 11 (1)   **2002**†SF 16 (0)
NFL 52 (2) [4 yrs]

LYNCH, CARL Carl, G, Ohio Wesleyan; B1893, deceased   **1921** Cin 2 (2, RG)

LYNCH, DICK Richard Dennis, DB, 6´1˝/202 lbs; Notre Dame; 1958: Was, rnd 6; B4/29/1936 Oceanside, NY [I]   **1958** Was 12   **1959**†NYG 12 (DB)   **1960** NYG 12 (RCB)
1961†NYG☆14 (RCB)   **1962**†NYG 13 (RCB)   **1963**†NYG☆14 (RCB)   **1964** NYG 10 (RCB)   **1965** NYG☆14 (RCB)   **1966** NYG 8   **NFL** 109 [9 yrs]

LYNCH, ED Edward James, E-T, 6´0˝/191 lbs; Catholic; B10/4/1896 Northampton, MA, D8/24/1967 Dearborn, MI   **1925** Roc☆6 (6, RE)   **1926** Har 1 (1)   **1926** Det 12 (12, RE)
1927 Pro☆11 (10, LE), 6   **1929** Ora 5 (2)   **NFL** 35 (31) [4 yrs]

LYNCH, ERIC Eric, RB, 5´10˝/224 lbs; Grand Valley State; B5/16/1970 Woodhaven, MI

1992	Det	1(0)	—	—	—	—	—	—	—	—	—	—	—	—	—	—	—	—	—	—	—	—	—	—
1993	Det	4(2)	53	207	3.9(15)	2	13	82	6.3(11)	0	—	—	—	—	—	—	—	—	—	—	k	—	12	275
1994	†Det	12(3)	1	0	0.0(0)	0	2	18	9.0(12)	0	—	—	—	—	—	—	—	—	—	—	k	—	0	-21
1995	†Det	5(0)	—	—	—	—	—	—	—	—	—	—	—	—	—	—	—	—	—	—	—	—	—	—
1996	Det	16(0)	2	2	1.0(2)	0	—	—	—	—	—	—	—	—	—	—	—	—	—	—	k	—	0	2
NFL	5	38(5)	56	209	3.7(15)	2	15	100	6.7(12)	0	—	—	—	—	—	—	—	—	—	—	k	—	12	256

LYNCH, FRAN Francis Xavier, RB, 6´1˝/205 lbs; Hofstra; 1967: Den, rnd 5; B12/3/1945 Bridgeport, CT

1967	Den-A	6	2	7	3.5(7)	0	—	—	—	—	—	—	—	—	—	—	—	—	—	—	k	—	0	19
1968	Den-A	9(hb)	66	221	3.3(19)	4	4	52	13.0(22)	0	2	1	50.0	4	2.0(4)	0	0	0	—	—	—	—	24	289
1969	Den-A	11(7, fb)	96	407	4.2(54)	2	9	86	9.6(19)	0	—	—	—	—	—	—	—	—	—	—	—	—	12	470
1970	Den	14(2)	20	81	4.1(19)	1	7	69	9.9(36)	0	—	—	—	—	—	—	—	—	—	—	—	—	6	137
1971	Den	10(1)	26	162	6.2(23)	0	2	42	21.0(42)	1	—	—	—	—	—	—	—	—	—	—	—	—	8	207
1972	Den	14	34	164	4.8(28)	2	7	75	10.7(17)	0	—	—	—	—	—	—	—	—	—	—	k	—	12	222
1973	Den	9	—	—	—	—	—	—	—	—	—	—	—	—	—	—	—	—	—	—	k	—	0	-1
1974	Den	12	3	-2	-0.7(1)	0	—	—	—	—	—	—	—	—	—	—	—	—	—	—	—	—	0	-2
1975	Den	14(1)	57	218	3.8(20)	3	6	33	5.5(19)	1	—	—	—	—	—	—	—	—	—	—	p	—	24	265
NFL	9	99(11)	304	1258	4.1(54)	12	35	357	10.2(40)	2	2	1	50.0	4	2.0(4)	0	0	0	—	—	kp	—	86	1605

LYNCH, JAMES James, RB, 5´11˝/276 lbs; Maryland; B6/17/1982 Washington, DC   **2004** Cin 1 (0)

LYNCH, JIM James Robert, LB, 6´1˝/235 lbs; Notre Dame; 1967: KC, rnd 2; B8/28/1945 Lima, OH   **1967** KC-A 14 (3)   **1968**†KC-A★14 (14, RLB)   **1969**†KC-A☆14 (RLB)
1970 KC 14 (RLB)   **1971** KC 14 (RLB)   **1972** KC 14 (RLB)   **1973** KC 14 (RLB)   **1974** KC 14 (RLB)   **1975** KC 14 (RLB)   **1976** KC 14 (14, RLB)   **1977** KC 11 (RLB)
NFL 151 (31) [11 yrs]

LYNCH, JOHN John Terence, DB, 6´2˝/220 lbs; Stanford; 1993: TB, rnd 3; B9/25/1971 Hinsdale, IL [I]   **1993** TB 15 (4)   **1994** TB 16 (0)   **1995** TB 9 (6, SS)   **1997**†TB◇16 (16, SS)
1998 TB 15 (15, SS)   **1999**†TB★16 (16, SS)   **2000**†TB★16 (16, SS)   **2001**†TB★16 (16, SS)   **2002**†TB★15 (15, SS)   **2003** TB 14 (14, SS)   **2004**†Den◇15 (15, FS)
2005†Den◇16 (16, FS)

| 1996 | TB | 16(14, SS) | 1 | 40 | 40.0(40) | 0 | — | — | — | — | — | — | — | — | — | — | — | — | — | — | iS | — | 0 | 51 |
| NFL | 13 | 195(163) | 1 | 40 | 40.0(40) | 0 | — | — | — | — | — | — | — | — | — | — | — | — | — | — | iS | — | 0 | 114 |

LYNCH, LORENZO Lorenzo, DB, 5´11˝/200 lbs; Sacramento State; B4/6/1963 Oakland, CA   **1987** ChiB 2 (2)   **1988**†ChiB 9 (0)   **1989** ChiB 16 (2)   **1990** Phx 16 (0)
1991 Phx 16 (14, LCB/cb)   **1992** Phx 16 (9, cb)   **1993** Phx 16 (15, CB)   **1994** Arz 15 (15, SS)   **1995** Arz 12 (11, SS)   **1996** Oak 16 (16, SS)   **1997** Oak 15 (0)   **NFL** 149 (84) [11 yrs]

LYNCH, LYNN Lynn E., G, 6´2˝/225 lbs; Illinois; 1951: ChiC, rnd 5; B8/10/1928 Indianapolis, IN   **1951** ChiC 3

LYNCH, PAUL E. Paul, B, 6´1˝/190 lbs; Ohio Northern; B1901, D9/25/1961   **1925** Col 7 (6, WB)

LYNCH, SHAWN Shawn, C, 6´4˝/294 lbs; Duke; B7/25/1979 West Palm Beach, FL   **2005** Arz 2 (1)

LYNCH, TOM Thomas Frank, G, 6´5˝/256 lbs; Boston College; 1977: Sea, rnd 2; B5/24/1955 Chicago, IL   **1977** Sea 14 (5, lg)   **1978** Sea☆16 (16, LG)   **1979** Sea 15 (15, LG)
1980 Sea 16 (12, LG)   **1981**†Buf 5 (2)   **1982** Buf 8 (0)   **1983** Buf 15 (3)   **1984** Buf 16 (0)   **NFL** 105 (53) [8 yrs]

LYNN, ANTHONY Anthony Ray, RB, 6´3˝/230 lbs; Texas Tech; B12/21/1968 McKinney, TX

1993	†Den	13(0)	—	—	—	—	—	—	—	—	—	—	—	—	—	—	—	—	—	—	—	—	—	—
1995	SF	6(0)	2	11	5.5(6)	0	—	—	—	—	—	—	—	—	—	—	—	—	—	—	—	—	0	11
1996	†SF	16(1)	24	164	6.8(67)	0	2	14	7.0(8)	0	—	—	—	—	—	—	—	—	—	—	—	—	0	171
1997	Den	16(0)	—	—	—	—	1	21	21.0(21)	0	—	—	—	—	—	—	—	—	—	—	—	—	0	11
1998	†Den	16(0)	—	—	—	—	—	—	—	—	—	—	—	—	—	—	—	—	—	—	—	—	—	—
1999	Den	16(0)	2	2	1.0(1)	0	—	—	—	—	—	—	—	—	—	—	—	—	—	—	—	—	0	2
NFL	6	83(1)	28	177	6.3(67)	0	3	35	11.7(21)	0	—	—	—	—	—	—	—	—	—	—	—	—	0	195

LYNN, JOHNNY Johnny Ross, DB, 6´0˝/196 lbs; UCLA; 1979: NYJ, rnd 4; B12/19/1956 Los Angeles, CA **1979** NYJ 16 (14, RCB) **1981**†NYJ 13 (0) **1982**†NYJ 8 (0) **1983** NYJ 16 (1) **1984** NYJ 14 (14, RCB/lcb) **1985**†NYJ 14 (12, lcb) **1986**†NYJ 16 (7, fs) **NFL** 97 (48) [7 yrs]

LYON, BABE George Cardinal, T-G, 6´2˝/235 lbs; Kansas State; B3/30/1907 Jamestown, KS, D12/22/1970 Manhattan, KS **1929** NYG 1 (0) **1930** Por 10 (8, rt) **1931** ChiB 1 (0) **1931** Cle 7 (7, LT) **1932** Bkn 10 (2) **1934** SL 3 (1, RT) **NFL** 32 (18) [5 yrs]

LYON, BILLY William Morton, DE-DT, 6´5˝/295 lbs; Marshall; B12/10/1973 Ashland, KY **1998**†GB 4 (0) **1999** GB 16 (4) **2000** GB 11 (1) **2001**†GB 12 (0) **2002** GB 16 (2) **2003** Min 13 (0) **NFL** 72 (7) [6 yrs]

LYONS, DICKY Richard, DB, 6´0˝/191 lbs; Kentucky; 1969: Atl, rnd 4; B8/11/1947 Louisville, KY **1970** NO 4

LYONS, JOHN John Stacy, E, 6´1˝/185 lbs; Tulsa; B9/10/1911 Coronado, CA, D11/26/1981 Bonita, CA **1933** Bkn 2 (0)

LYONS, LAMAR Lamar Kahlil-Kasim, DB, 6´3˝/210 lbs; Washington; B3/25/1973 Los Angeles, CA **1996** Oak 6 (0) **1997** Bal 1 (0) **NFL** 7 (0) [2 yrs]

LYONS, MARTY Martin Anthony, DE-DT-NT, 6´5˝/269 lbs; Alabama; 1979: NYJ, rnd 1; B1/5/1957 Takoma Park, MD **1979** NYJ 16 (16, RDE) **1980** NYJ 16 (16, RDT) **1981**†NYJ 12 (12, RDT) **1982**†NYJ 7 (7, RDT) **1983** NYJ 16 (16, RDT) **1984** NYJ 13 (10, RDT) **1985**†NYJ 16 (8, lde) **1986**†NYJ 12 (11, LDE) **1987** NYJ 13 (13, LDE) **1988** NYJ 16 (16, RDE) **1989** NYJ 10 (10, RDE) **NFL** 147 (135) [11 yrs]

LYONS, MITCH Mitchell Warren, TE, 6´5˝/265 lbs; Michigan State; 1993: Atl, rnd 6; B5/13/1970 Grand Rapids, MI

YEAR	TEAM	G(GS, POS)	RUSH	YD	AVG(LG)	TD	REC	YD	AVG(LG)	TD	PASS	COMP	PCT	YD	AVG(LG)	TD	INT	SK	YD	QBR	KPR	OTD	PTS	TAY
1993	Atl	16(8, TE)	—	—	—	—	8	63	7.9(14)	0	—	—	—	—	—	—	—	—	—	—	—	—	0	32
1994	Atl	7(2)	—	—	—	—	7	54	7.7(10)	0	—	—	—	—	—	—	—	—	—	—	—	—	0	27
1995	†Atl	14(4)	—	—	—	—	5	83	16.6(34)	0	—	—	—	—	—	—	—	—	—	—	—	—	0	42
1996	Atl	14(4)	—	—	—	—	4	16	4.0(5)	1	—	—	—	—	—	—	—	—	—	—	—	—	6	13
1997	Pit	10(3)	—	—	—	—	4	29	7.3(13)	0	—	—	—	—	—	—	—	—	—	—	—	—	0	15
1998	Pit	15(0)	—	—	—	—	3	19	6.3(11)	0	—	—	—	—	—	—	—	—	—	—	k	—	0	-25
1999	Pit	14(2)	—	—	—	—	8	81	10.1(25)	0	—	—	—	—	—	—	—	—	—	—	k	—	0	38
NFL	7	90(23)	—	—	—	—	39	345	8.8(34)	1	—	—	—	—	—	—	—	—	—	—	k	—	6	141

LYONS, PRATT Pratt Gilbert, DE, 6´5˝/295 lbs; Utah State; Troy State; 1997: Ten, rnd 4; B9/17/1974 Fort Worth, TX **1997** Ten 16 (0) **1998** Ten 16 (11, LDE) **NFL** 32 (11) [2 yrs]

LYONS, ROBERT Robert Louis, DB, 6´2˝/200 lbs; Akron; B5/16/1966 Wheeling, WV **1989**†Cle 9 (0)

LYONS, TOMMY Thomas Lewis, G-C, 6´2˝/230 lbs; Georgia; 1971: Den, rnd 14; B8/7/1948 Atlanta, GA **1971** Den 11 (1) **1972** Den 10 (9, RG) **1973** Den 14 (14, RG) **1974** Den 14 (14, RG/lg) **1975** Den 10 (10, LG)

YEAR	TEAM	G(GS, POS)	RUSH	YD	AVG(LG)	TD	REC	YD	AVG(LG)	TD	PASS	COMP	PCT	YD	AVG(LG)	TD	INT	SK	YD	QBR	KPR	OTD	PTS	TAY
1976	Den	14(14, RG)	—	—	—	—	1	-1	-1.0(-1)	0	—	—	—	—	—	—	—	—	—	—	—	—	0	-1
NFL	6	73(62)	—	—	—	—	1	-1	-1.0(-1)	0	—	—	—	—	—	—	—	—	—	—	—	—	0	-1

LYTLE, MATT Matthew Robert, QB, 6´4˝/225 lbs; Pittsburgh; B9/4/1975 Wyomissing, PA **2000** Sea 1 (0)

YEAR	TEAM	G(GS, POS)	RUSH	YD	AVG(LG)	TD	REC	YD	AVG(LG)	TD	PASS	COMP	PCT	YD	AVG(LG)	TD	INT	SK	YD	QBR	KPR	OTD	PTS	TAY
2001	Car	3(1)	2	8	4.0(4)	0	—	—	—	—	30	17	56.7	133	4.4(28)	1	3	3	24	—	—	—	0	-41
NFL	2	4(1)	2	8	4.0(4)	0	—	—	—	—	30	17	56.7	133	4.4(28)	1	3	3	24	—	—	—	0	-41

LYTLE, ROB Robert William, RB, 6´1˝/198 lbs; Michigan; 1977: Den, rnd 2; B11/12/1954 Fremont, OH

YEAR	TEAM	G(GS, POS)	RUSH	YD	AVG(LG)	TD	REC	YD	AVG(LG)	TD	PASS	COMP	PCT	YD	AVG(LG)	TD	INT	SK	YD	QBR	KPR	OTD	PTS	TAY
1977	†Den	14(4)	104	408	3.9(21)	1	17	198	11.6(47)	1	—	—	—	—	—	—	—	—	—	—	—	—	12	522
1978	†Den	13(7, rb)	81	341	4.2(25)	2	6	37	6.2(10)	0	—	—	—	—	—	—	—	—	—	—	—	—	12	380
1979	Den	15(12, RB)	102	371	3.6(19)	4	13	93	7.2(12)	0	—	—	—	—	—	—	—	—	—	—	—	—	24	458
1980	Den	16(0)	57	223	3.9(35)	1	18	177	9.8(37)	0	—	—	—	—	—	—	—	—	—	—	k	—	6	326
1981	Den	16(0)	30	106	3.5(18)	4	6	47	7.8(14)	1	—	—	—	—	—	—	—	—	—	—	k	—	30	180
1982	Den	9(0)	2	2	1.0(2)	0	1	10	10.0(10)	0	—	—	—	—	—	—	—	—	—	—	—	—	0	7
1983	Den	4(0)	—	—	—	—	—	—	—	—	—	—	—	—	—	—	—	—	—	—	—	—	—	—
NFL	7	87(23)	376	1451	3.9(35)	12	61	562	9.2(47)	2	—	—	—	—	—	—	—	—	—	—	k	—	84	1871

MAACK, HERBERT Herbert Henry, T, 6´2˝/210 lbs; Columbia; B4/6/1917 Union City, NJ **1946** Bkn-A 7 (0)

MAARLEVELD, J.D. John David, T, 6´6˝/300 lbs; Notre Dame; Maryland; 1986: TB, rnd 5; B10/24/1961 Jersey City, NJ **1986** TB 14 (0) **1987** TB 11 (3) **NFL** 25 (3) [2 yrs]

MAAS, BILL William Thomas, NT-DE, 6´5˝/271 lbs; Pittsburgh; 1984: KC, rnd 1; B3/2/1962 Newtown Square, PA **1984** KC 14 (14, NT) **1985** KC 16 (16, NT/lde) **1986**†KC★16 (16, NT) **1987** KC★11 (11, NT) **1988** KC 8 (8, NT) **1989** KC 10 (10, NT) **1990**†KC 16 (15, RDE) **1991**†KC 16 (16, RDE) **1992**†KC 9 (5, rde) **1993**†GB 14 (3) **NFL** 130 (114) [10 yrs]

MABRA, RON Ronald Edwin, DB, 5´10˝/166 lbs; Howard; B6/4/1951 Talladega, AL **1975** Atl 8 **1976** Atl 8 **1977** NYJ 3 (1) **NFL** 19 (1) [3 yrs]

MACAFEE, KEN Kenneth Adams, E, 6´2˝/212 lbs; Alabama; B8/31/1929 North Easton, MA

YEAR	TEAM	G(GS, POS)	RUSH	YD	AVG(LG)	TD	REC	YD	AVG(LG)	TD	PASS	COMP	PCT	YD	AVG(LG)	TD	INT	SK	YD	QBR	KPR	OTD	PTS	TAY
1954	NYG	11(RE)	—	—	—	—	24	438	18.3(72)	8	—	—	—	—	—	—	—	—	—	—	—	—	48	259
1955	NYG	8	—	—	—	—	11	170	15.5(40)	1	—	—	—	—	—	—	—	—	—	—	—	—	6	90
1956	†NYG	12(RE)	—	—	—	—	14	184	13.1(29)	4	—	—	—	—	—	—	—	—	—	—	—	—	24	112
1957	NYG	11	—	—	—	—	16	229	14.3(41)	2	—	—	—	—	—	—	—	—	—	—	—	—	12	125
1958	†NYG	10	—	—	—	—	5	52	10.4(22)	2	—	—	—	—	—	—	—	—	—	—	—	—	12	36
1959	Phi	4	—	—	—	—	5	48	9.6(11)	0	—	—	—	—	—	—	—	—	—	—	—	—	0	24
1959	Was	7	—	—	—	—	4	39	9.8(19)	1	—	—	—	—	—	—	—	—	—	—	k	—	6	22
NFL	6	63	—	—	—	—	79	1160	14.7(72)	18	—	—	—	—	—	—	—	—	—	—	k	—	108	667

MACAFEE, KEN Kenneth Adams, TE, 6´4˝/250 lbs; Notre Dame; 1978: SF, rnd 1; B1/9/1956 Portland, OR

YEAR	TEAM	G(GS, POS)	RUSH	YD	AVG(LG)	TD	REC	YD	AVG(LG)	TD	PASS	COMP	PCT	YD	AVG(LG)	TD	INT	SK	YD	QBR	KPR	OTD	PTS	TAY
1978	SF	13(13, TE)	—	—	—	—	22	205	9.3(22)	1	—	—	—	—	—	—	—	—	—	—	—	—	6	108
1979	SF	16(12, TE)	—	—	—	—	24	266	11.1(50)	4	—	—	—	—	—	—	—	—	—	—	—	—	24	153
NFL	2	29(25)	—	—	—	—	46	471	10.2(50)	5	—	—	—	—	—	—	—	—	—	—	—	—	30	261

MACAULAY, JOHN John Dunn, C, 6´3˝/254 lbs; Stanford; 1982: GB, rnd 11; B4/27/1959 San Diego, CA **1984** SF 3 (0)

MACCOLLUM, MAX Maxwell Speers, E, 5´11˝/165 lbs; Centre; B2/22/1900 Marietta, OH, D9/25/1943 Indianapolis, IN **1922** Lou 1 (1)

MACDONALD, ALLEN Allen J., HB, 5´10˝/169 lbs; none; B3/1896 Duluth, MN, deceased **1924** Dul 6 (1)

MACDONALD, DAN Dante J., LB, 6´2˝/230 lbs; Idaho State; B9/2/1962 San Bernardino, CA **1987** Den 3 (0)

MACDONALD, BUCK George Glover, G, 5´10˝/180 lbs; Lehigh; B5/5/1894 Nova Scotia, Canada, D3/1/1985 Miami Springs, FL **1920** Can 2 (0) **1921** Ton 1 (1, RG) **1921** NYG 1 (1) **NFL** 4 (2) [2 yrs]

MACDONALD, MARK Mark Goodwin, G, 6´4˝/267 lbs; Boston College; 1985: Min, rnd 5; B4/30/1961 West Roxbury, MA **1985** Min 16 (3) **1986** Min 10 (0) **1987**†Min 12 (1) **1988** Min 5 (0) **1988** Phx 1 (0) **NFL** 44 (4) [4 yrs]

MACDONNELL, MICKEY John D., B, 5´8˝/159 lbs; none; B1/1904, deceased **1923** Dul 1 (1) **1925** Dul 3 (2, WB), 6 **1925** ChiC 2 (0) **1926** ChiC 11 (5, wb), 12 **1927** ChiC 9 (5, WB) **1928** ChiC 6 (5, WB) **1929** ChiC 13 (10, WB), 12 **1930** ChiC 8 (3) **1931** Fra 3 (2) **NFL** 56 (33), 30 [8 yrs]

MACDOWELL, JAY Jay Sidney, T-DE, 6´2˝/217 lbs; Washington; 1941: Cle, rnd 3; B9/14/1919 Oak Park, IL, D6/15/1992 Springfield, DE **1947**†Phi 12 (3) **1948**†Phi 12 (10, LT) **1949**†Phi 8 (1) **1950** Phi 12 **1951** Phi 12 (lde)

YEAR	TEAM	G(GS, POS)	RUSH	YD	AVG(LG)	TD	REC	YD	AVG(LG)	TD	PASS	COMP	PCT	YD	AVG(LG)	TD	INT	SK	YD	QBR	KPR	OTD	PTS	TAY
1946	Phi	6(0)	—	—	—	—	1	28	28.0(28)	0	—	—	—	—	—	—	—	—	—	—	—	—	2	14
NFL	6	62(14)	—	—	—	—	1	28	28.0(28)	0	—	—	—	—	—	—	—	—	—	—	—	—	2	14

MACEAU, MEL Melvin Anthony, C, 6´0˝/203 lbs; Marquette; 1944: Cle, rnd 14; B12/25/1921 Milwaukee, WI, D2/1981 Rudolph, OH **1946**†Cle-A 12 (0) **1947** Cle-A 14 (0) **1948**†Cle-A 11 (0) **AAFC** 37 (0) [3 yrs]

MACEK, DON Donald Matthew, C-G, 6´3˝/261 lbs; Boston College; 1976: SD, rnd 2; B7/21/1954 Manchester, NH **1976** SD 14 (14, RG) **1977** SD 14 (13, RG) **1978** SD 14 (9, C) **1979** SD 10 (6, c) **1980**†SD 16 (16, C) **1981**†SD 15 (15, C) **1982**†SD 9 (9, C) **1983** SD 11 (11, C) **1984** SD 13 (13, C) **1985** SD 15 (15, C) **1986** SD 13 (13, C) **1987** SD 11 (11, C) **1988** SD 5 (5, c) **1989** SD 2 (0) **NFL** 162 (150) [14 yrs]

MACERELLI, JOHN John Edward, T-G, 6´2˝/230 lbs; St. Vincent; B11/2/1930 Muse, PA, D10/12/1984 Canonsburg, PA **1956** Cle 12

MACHADO, J.P. J.P., G-C, 6´4˝/300 lbs; Illinois; 1999: NYJ, rnd 6; B1/6/1976 Monmouth, IL **1999** NYJ 5 (0) **2000** NYJ 16 (0) **2001**†NYJ 16 (3) **2002**†NYJ 16 (12, LG) **2003** NYJ 16 (0) **NFL** 69 (15) [5 yrs]

MACHUREK, MIKE Michael Bruce, QB, 6´1˝/205 lbs; Idaho State; 1982: Det, rnd 6; B7/22/1960 Las Vegas, NV

YEAR	TEAM	G(GS, POS)	RUSH	YD	AVG(LG)	TD	REC	YD	AVG(LG)	TD	PASS	COMP	PCT	YD	AVG(LG)	TD	INT	SK	YD	QBR	KPR	OTD	PTS	TAY
1984	Det	4(0)	1	9	9.0(9)	0	—	—	—	—	43	14	32.6	193	4.5(48)	0	6	1	12	—	—	—	0	-135

YEAR	TEAM	G (GS, POS)	RUSH	YD	AVG(LG)	TD	REC	YD	AVG(LG)	TD	PASS	COMP	PCT	YD	AVG(LG)	TD	INT	SK	YD	QBR	KPR	OTD	PTS	TAY

Macioszczyk, Art   Arthur A., FB, 6´0˝/208 lbs; Western Michigan; 1943: Phi, rnd 27; B10/19/1920 Hamtramck, MI, D5/6/1982 Detroit, MI

1944	Phi	10(0)	16	55	3.4(12)	0	3	28	9.3(21)	0	—	—	—	—	—	—	—	—	—	—	kp	—	0	67
1947	†Phi	11(2)	30	104	3.5(11)	0	3	20	6.7(8)	0	—	—	—	—	—	—	—	—	—	—	k	—	0	120
1948	Was	1(0)	—	—	—	—	—	—	—	—	—	—	—	—	—	—	—	—	—	—		—	—	—
NFL	3	22(2)	46	159	3.5(12)	0	6	48	8.0(21)	0	—	—	—	—	—	—	—	—	—	—	kp	—	0	187

Mack, Cedric   Cedric Manuel, DB, 6´0˝/193 lbs; Baylor; 1983: SL, rnd 2; B9/14/1960 Freeport, TX [I]   **1983** SL 16 (5, lcb)   **1986** SL 15 (9, RCB)   **1987** SL 10 (10, RCB)
1988 Phx 16 (14, RCB)   **1989** Phx 16 (16, LCB)   **1990** Phx 16 (16, RCB)   **1991** SD 7 (1)   **1992** KC 1 (0)   **1992** NO 14 (2)   **1993** NO 1 (0)

1984	SL	12(0)	—	—	—	—	5	61	12.2(22)	0	—	—	—	—	—	—	—	—	—	—		—	0	31
1985	SL	16(14, LCB)	—	—	—	—	1	16	16.0(16)	0	—	—	—	—	—	—	—	—	i	—		—	0	8
NFL	11	140(87)	—	—	—	—	6	77	12.8(22)	0	—	—	—	—	—	—	—	—	iS	—		1	6	117

Mack, Kevin   James Kevin, RB, 6´0˝/224 lbs; Clemson; 1984: Cle, rnd S1; B8/9/1962 Kings Mountain, NC

1985	†Cle◇	16(15, FB)	222	1104	5.0(61)	7	29	297	10.2(43)	3	—	—	—	—	—	—	—	—	—	—		—	60	1338
1986	†Cle	12(12, FB)	174	665	3.8(20)	10	28	292	10.4(44)	0	—	—	—	—	—	—	—	—	—	—		—	60	911
1987	†Cle◇	12(12, FB)	201	735	3.7(22)	5	32	223	7.0(17)	1	—	—	—	—	—	—	—	—	—	—		—	36	902
1988	†Cle	11(11, FB)	123	485	3.9(65)	3	11	87	7.9(25)	0	—	—	—	—	—	—	—	—	—	—		—	18	559
1989	†Cle	4(1)	37	130	3.5(12)	1	2	7	3.5(4)	0	—	—	—	—	—	—	—	—	—	—		—	6	144
1990	Cle	14(14, FB)	158	702	4.4(26)	5	42	360	8.6(30)	2	—	—	—	—	—	—	—	—	—	—		—	42	942
1991	Cle	14(11, FB)	197	726	3.7(51)	8	40	255	6.4(22)	2	—	—	—	—	—	—	—	—	—	—		—	60	944
1992	Cle	12(6, fb)	169	543	3.2(37)	6	13	81	6.2(23)	0	—	—	—	—	—	—	—	—	—	—		—	36	644
1993	Cle	4(0)	10	33	3.3(7)	1	—	—	—	—	—	—	—	—	—	—	—	—	—	—		—	6	43
NFL	9	99(82)	1291	5123	4.0(65)	46	197	1602	8.1(44)	8	—	—	—	—	—	—	—	—	—	—		—	324	6424

Mack, Kim   Kimbeflu Evanda, DB, 6´0˝/190 lbs; Florida State; B10/29/1961   **1987** Sea 1 (0)

Mack, Milton   Milton Jerome, DB, 5´11˝/188 lbs; Alcorn State; 1987: NO, rnd 5; B9/20/1963 Jackson, MS   **1987**†NO 13 (0)   **1988** NO 14 (1)   **1989** NO 16 (4)   **1990** NO 16 (2)
1991†NO 8 (3)   **1992** TB 16 (16, RCB)   **1992**†NO 0 (0)   **1993** TB 12 (3)   **1994** Det 16 (3)   **NFL** 111 (32) [8 yrs]

Mack, Red   William Richard, TE-WR-HB, 5´10˝/180 lbs; Notre Dame; 1961: Pit, rnd 10/Buf, rnd 23; B6/19/1937 Oconto, WI

1961	Pit	11	—	—	—	—	8	128	16.0(39)	2	—	—	—	—	—	—	—	—	—	—		—	12	74
1962	Pit	14	2	-2	-1.0(7)	0	8	203	25.4(40)	2	—	—	—	—	—	—	—	—	—	—		—	12	110
1963	Pit	14(TE)	2	1	0.5(1)	0	25	618	24.7(85)	3	—	—	—	—	—	—	—	—	—	—		—	18	325
1964	Phi	8	—	—	—	—	8	169	21.1(53)	1	—	—	—	—	—	—	—	—	—	—		—	6	85
1965	Pit	2	—	—	—	—	3	41	13.7(17)	0	—	—	—	—	—	—	—	—	—	—	p	—	0	21
1966	Atl	1	—	—	—	—	—	—	—	—	—	—	—	—	—	—	—	—	—	—		—	—	—
1966	†GB	8	—	—	—	—	—	—	—	—	—	—	—	—	—	—	—	—	—	—		—	—	—
NFL	6	58	4	-1	-0.3(7)	0	52	1159	22.3(85)	8	—	—	—	—	—	—	—	—	—	—	p	—	48	614

Mack, Rico   Rico Rodrigus, LB, 6´4˝/239 lbs; Appalachian State; B2/22/1971 Stratham, GA   **1993**†Pit 8 (0)

Mack, Stacey   Stacey Lamar, RB, 6´1˝/241 lbs; Temple; B6/26/1975 Orlando, FL

1999	Jax	12(0)	7	40	5.7(19)	0	—	—	—	—	—	—	—	—	—	—	—	—	—	—	k	—	0	62
2000	Jax	6(2)	54	145	2.7(14)	1	—	—	—	—	—	—	—	—	—	—	—	—	—	—	k	—	6	169
2001	Jax	16(11, RB)	213	877	4.1(54)	9	23	165	7.2(25)	1	—	—	—	—	—	—	—	—	—	—	k	—	60	1074
2002	Jax	16(0)	98	436	4.4(23)	9	11	79	7.2(12)	0	—	—	—	—	—	—	—	—	—	—	k	—	54	620
2003	Hou	8(5, rb)	93	253	2.7(13)	4	9	55	6.1(10)	0	1	0	0.0	0	0.0	0	1	—	—	—	k	—	24	281
NFL	5	58(18)	465	1751	3.8(54)	23	43	299	7.0(25)	1	1	0	0.0	0	0.0	0	1	—	—	—	k	—	144	2205

Mack, Terence   Terence Bernard, LB, 6´3˝/240 lbs; Clemson; B7/9/1964 Winnsboro, NC   **1987** SL 5 (0)

Mack, Tom   Thomas Lee, G, 6´3˝/250 lbs; Michigan; 1966: LA, rnd 1; B11/1/1943 Cleveland, OH; HOF 1999   **1966** LARm 14 (8, LG)   **1967**†LARm◇14 (LG)
1968 LARm★14 (14, LG)   **1969**†LARm★14 (14, LG)   **1970** LARm★14 (14, LG)   **1971** LARm★14 (14, LG)   **1972** LARm★14 (12, LG)   **1973**†LARm★14 (14, LG)
1974†LARm★14 (14, LG)   **1975**†LARm★14 (14, LG)   **1976**†LARm☆14 (14, LG)   **1977**†LARm★14 (14, LG)   **1978**†LARm★16 (16, LG)   **NFL** 184 (162) [13 yrs]

Mack, Tremain   Tremain F., DB, 6´0˝/193 lbs; Miami (FL); 1997: Cin, rnd 4; B11/21/1974 Tyler, TX [R]   **1997** Cin 4 (4)   **1998** Cin 12 (0)   **1999** Cin★12 (0)   **2000** Cin 16 (0)
NFL 44 (4) [4 yrs]

Mackbee, Earsell   James Earsell, DB, 6´1˝/195 lbs; Utah State; B1/15/1941 Brookhaven, MS   **1965** Min 10   **1966** Min 14 (14, LCB)   **1967** Min 14 (14, LCB)
1968†Min 14 (14, LCB)   **1969**†Min 14 (14, LCB)   **NFL** 66 (56) [5 yrs]

Mackenroth, Jack   Jack Dakota, C, 6´2˝/215 lbs; North Dakota; B6/29/1916 Minot, ND, D10/27/2000 Bellevue, WA   **1938** Det 2 (0)

MacKenzie, Malaefou   Matthew Mark Maleafou Anesi, FB, 5´10˝/238 lbs; USC; 2003: Jax, rnd 7; B7/24/1979 Apia, Western Samoa   **2003** Jax 1 (0)

Mackert, Roy   Charles Leroy, T, 6´2˝/200 lbs; Lebanon Valley; Maryland; B2/2/1894 Sunbury, PA, deceased   **1925** Roc 2 (1)

Mackey, Dee   Dee Elbert, E-TE, 6´5˝/235 lbs; Texas A&M-Commerce; 1958: SF, rnd 24/1960: Bos, rnd 1; B10/16/1934 Gilmer, TX, D2/26/2001 Gladewater, TX

1960	SF	12(6, te)	—	—	—	—	12	159	13.3(25)	0	—	—	—	—	—	—	—	—	—	—		—	0	80
1961	Bal	14	—	—	—	—	4	66	16.5(19)	0	—	—	—	—	—	—	—	—	—	—	k	—	0	24
1962	Bal	14(TE)	—	—	—	—	25	396	15.8(57)	4	—	—	—	—	—	—	—	—	—	—		—	24	218
1963	NYJ-A	14(te)	—	—	—	—	23	263	11.4(31)	3	—	—	—	—	—	—	—	—	—	—	k	—	18	132
1964	NYJ-A	14(te)	—	—	—	—	14	213	15.2(35)	0	—	—	—	—	—	—	—	—	—	—		—	0	107
1965	NYJ-A	10(TE)	—	—	—	—	16	255	15.9(47)	1	—	—	—	—	—	—	—	—	—	—		—	8	133
NFL	6	78(6)	—	—	—	—	94	1352	14.4(57)	8	—	—	—	—	—	—	—	—	—	—	k	—	50	692

Mackey, John   John, TE, 6´2˝/224 lbs; Syracuse; 1963: Bal, rnd 2/NYJ, rnd 5; B9/24/1941 Queens, NY; HOF 1992

1963	Bal◇	14(14, TE)	1	3	3.0(3)	0	35	726	20.7(61)	7	—	—	—	—	—	—	—	—	—	—	k	—	42	537
1964	†Bal	14(TE)	1	-1	-1.0(-1)	0	22	406	18.5(52)	2	—	—	—	—	—	—	—	—	—	—		—	12	212
1965	†Bal◇	14(TE)	1	7	7.0(7)	0	40	814	20.4(68)	7	—	—	—	—	—	—	—	—	—	—		—	42	449
1966	Bal★	14(TE)	1	-6	-6.0(-6)	0	50	829	16.6(89)	9	—	—	—	—	—	—	—	—	—	—		—	54	454
1967	Bal★	14(TE)	—	—	—	—	55	686	12.5(34)	3	—	—	—	—	—	—	—	—	—	—		—	18	358
1968	†Bal★	14(TE)	10	103	10.3(33)	0	45	644	14.3(45)	5	—	—	—	—	—	—	—	—	—	—		—	30	450
1969	Bal	14(TE)	2	3	1.5(7)	0	34	443	13.0(52)	5	—	—	—	—	—	—	—	—	—	—		—	12	235
1970	†Bal	14(TE)	—	—	—	—	28	435	15.5(54)	0	—	—	—	—	—	—	—	—	—	—		—	18	233
1971	†Bal	14	3	18	6.0(9)	0	11	143	13.0(28)	0	—	—	—	—	—	—	—	—	—	—		—	0	90
1972	SD	13	—	—	—	—	11	110	10.0(21)	0	—	—	—	—	—	—	—	—	—	—		—	0	55
NFL	10	139(14)	19	127	6.7(33)	0	331	5236	15.8(89)	38	—	—	—	—	—	—	—	—	—	—	k	—	228	3071

Mackey, Kyle   Kyle Erickson, QB, 6´3˝/220 lbs; Texas A&M-Commerce; 1984: SL, rnd 11; B3/2/1962 Gladewater, TX

1987	Mia	3(3)	17	98	5.8(17)	2	—	—	—	—	—	109	57	52.3	604	5.5(30)	3	5	4	24	—	—	—	12	235
1989	NYJ	4(1)	2	3	1.5(5)	0	—	—	—	—	—	25	11	44.0	125	5.0(22)	0	1	3	18	—	—	—	0	26
NFL	2	7(4)	19	101	5.3(17)	2	—	—	—	—	—	134	68	50.7	729	5.4(30)	3	6	7	42	—	—	—	12	261

Mackey, Louis   Louis, LB, 6´1˝/225 lbs; Akron; B12/29/1977 Richmond, CA   **2001** Dal 1 (0)   **2002** Dal 15 (0)   **NFL** 16 (0) [2 yrs]

Mackie, Doug   Douglas Brian, T, 6´4˝/280 lbs; Ohio State; B2/18/1957 Malden, MA   **1987** Atl 3 (3)

MacKinnon, Jacque   Jacque Harold, TE-FB, 6´4˝/235 lbs; Colgate; 1962: SD, rnd 33/1961: Phi, rnd 20; B11/10/1938 Dover, NJ, D3/6/1975 San Diego, CA

1961	†SD-A	9	—	—	—	—	3	58	19.3(45)	0	—	—	—	—	—	—	—	—	—	—		—	0	29
1962	SD-A	14	59	240	4.1(24)	0	9	125	13.9(32)	2	—	—	—	—	—	—	—	—	—	—		—	12	313
1963	†SD-A	14	—	—	—	—	11	262	23.8(69)	4	—	—	—	—	—	—	—	—	—	—		—	24	151
1964	†SD-A	14	24	124	5.2(48)	2	10	177	17.7(37)	0	—	—	—	—	—	—	—	—	—	—		—	12	233
1965	†SD-A	14	3	17	5.7(9)	0	6	106	17.7(38)	0	—	—	—	—	—	—	—	—	—	—	k	—	0	55
1966	SD-A◇	14(14, TE)	—	—	—	—	26	477	18.3(46)	6	—	—	—	—	—	—	—	—	—	—		—	36	269
1967	SD-A	14	—	—	—	—	7	176	25.1(71)	2	—	—	—	—	—	—	—	—	—	—		—	12	94
1968	SD-A★	14(TE)	—	—	—	—	33	646	19.6(62)	6	—	—	—	—	—	—	—	—	—	—		—	38	353

YEAR	TEAM	G (GS, POS)	RUSH	YD	AVG (LG)	TD	REC	YD	AVG (LG)	TD	PASS COMP	PCT	YD	AVG (LG)	TD	INT	SK	YD	QBR	KPR	OTD	PTS	TAY
1969	SD-A	7	—	—	—	—	7	82	11.7 (23)	0	—	—	—	—	—	—	—	—	—	—	—	0	41
1970	Oak	4 (1)	—	—	—	—	—	—	—	—	—	—	—	—	—	—	—	—	—	—	—	—	—
NFL	10	118 (15)	86	381	4.4 (48)	2	112	2109	18.8 (71)	20	—	—	—	—	—	—	—	—	—	k	—	134	1541

MACKLIN, DAVID   David Thurman, DB, 5′9″/196 lbs; Penn State; 2000: Ind, rnd 3; B7/14/1978 Newport News, VA   **2000**†Ind 16 (2)   **2001** Ind 16 (16, RCB)   **2002**†Ind 16 (15, RCB)   **2003**†Ind 16 (4)   **2004** Arz 16 (16, RCB)   **2005** Arz 16 (15, RCB)   **NFL** 96 (68) [6 yrs]

MACKORELL, JOHNNY   John Campbell, B, 5′10″/178 lbs; Davidson; B11/3/1912 York, SC, D4/28/1980 Morganton, NC

1935	NYG	2 (0)	2	6	3.0	0	—	—	—	—	—	—	—	—	—	—	—	—	—	—	—	0	6

MACKRIDES, BILL   William, QB, 5′11″/182 lbs; Nevada-Reno; 1947: Phi, rnd 3/ChiR-A, rnd 17; B7/8/1925 Philadelphia, PA

1947	†Phi	8 (0)	7	-15	-2.1 (2)	1	—	—	—	—	17	8	47.1	58	3.4 (15)	2	3	—	—	—	—	6	-86
1948	Phi	10 (1)	7	4	0.6 (9)	0	—	—	—	—	53	18	34.0	276	5.2 (28)	2	4	—	—	—	—	0	-8
1949	Phi	7 (0)	14	17	1.2 (17)	1	—	—	—	—	36	14	38.9	182	5.1 (37)	2	2	—	—	—	—	6	48
1950	Phi	8	21	82	3.9 (18)	0	—	—	—	—	46	14	30.4	228	5.0 (59)	4	6	—	—	—	—	0	-24
1951	Phi	6	7	9	1.3 (3)	0	—	—	—	—	54	23	42.6	333	6.2 (43)	3	5	—	—	—	—	0	-10
1953	NYG	3	1	2	2.0 (2)	0	—	—	—	—	15	6	40.0	53	3.5 (0)	1	3	—	—	—	—	0	-87
1953	Pit	4	13	25	1.9 (4)	1	—	—	—	—	94	48	51.1	453	4.8 (36)	1	5	—	—	—	—	6	67
NFL	46 (1)	70	124	1.8 (18)	3	—	—	—	—	315	131	41.6	1583	5.0 (59)	15	28	—	—	—	—	18	-100

MACLEOD, BOB   Robert Frederick, HB, 6′0″/190 lbs; Dartmouth; 1939: Bkn, rnd 1; B10/15/1917 Glen Ellyn, IL, D1/13/2003 Santa Monica, CA

1939	ChiB	9 (1)	17	88	5.2	1	10	231	23.1 (53)	3	—	—	—	—	—	—	—	—	—	—	1	30	239

MACLEOD, TOM   Thomas William, LB, 6′3″/225 lbs; Minnesota; 1973: GB, rnd 3; B1/10/1951 Proctor, MN   **1973** GB 10 (LLB)   **1974** Bal 14 (LLB)   **1975**†Bal☆14 (14, LLB)   **1977**†Bal 14 (LLB)   **1978** Bal 12 (LLB)   **NFL** 64 (14) [5 yrs]

MACMILLAN, STU   Charles Stuart, G-C, 5′9″/175 lbs; North Dakota; B2/13/1908 McVille, ND, D1/13/1992 Seattle, WA   **1931** Cle 2 (0)

MACMURDO, JIM   James Edward, T-G, 6′1″/209 lbs; Pittsburgh; B9/2/1909 Ellwood City, PA, D8/10/1981 Darby, PA   **1932** Bos 10 (8, LT)   **1934** Phi 11 (11, RT)   **1935** Phi 4 (3)   **1936** Phi☆9 (9, RT)   **1937** Phi 3 (0)

| 1933 | Bos | 10 (10, RG) | 1 | 2 | 2.0 (2) | 0 | — | — | — | — | — | — | — | — | — | — | — | — | — | — | — | 0 | 2 |
| NFL | 6 | 47 (41) | 1 | 2 | 2.0 (2) | 0 | — | — | — | — | — | — | — | — | — | — | — | — | — | — | — | 0 | 2 |

MACMURRAY, RAY   Raymond Stuart, G, Lincoln College; Dartmouth; B7/3/1889 Tuscarawas County, OH, D2/21/1966 Huntington, IN   **1921** Mun 1 (1)

MACON, EDDIE   Edwin Donald, DB-HB, 6′0″/177 lbs; Pacific; 1952: ChiB, rnd 2; B3/7/1927 Stockton, CA

1952	ChiB	11	30	194	6.5 (50)	1	8	25	3.1 (20)	0	—	—	—	—	—	—	—	—	—	kp	1	12	430
1953	ChiB	12	40	130	3.3 (17)	1	6	24	4.0 (10)	2	1	0	0.0	0	0.0	0	0	—	—	kp	—	18	323
1960	Oak-A☆	14 (LCB)	—	—	—	—	—	—	—	—	—	—	—	—	—	—	—	—	—	i	1	6	70
NFL	3	37	70	324	4.6 (50)	2	14	49	3.5 (20)	2	1	0	0.0	0	0.0	0	0	—	—	kpi	2	36	823

MACPHEE, WADDY   Walter Scott, HB-FB, 5′8″/160 lbs; Brooklyn; Princeton; B12/23/1899 Brooklyn, NY, D1/20/1980 Charlotte, NC   **1926** Pro 10 (1)

MACWHERTER, KYLE   William Kile, FB, 5′9″/210 lbs; Bethany (WV); Millikin; B7/19/1892 Decatur, IL, D12/1977 Greeley, CO   **1920** Dec 4 (0)

MACZUZAK, JOHN   John A., DT, 6′5″/250 lbs; Pittsburgh; 1963: KC, rnd 22/SF, rnd 9; B4/4/1941   **1964** KC-A 1

MADAR, ELMER   Elmer F., E, 5′11″/185 lbs; Michigan; 1947: Mia-A, rnd 1/Det, rnd 20; B11/28/1920 Sykesville, PA, D2/9/1972 Detroit, MI

1947	Bal-A	9 (6, RE)	—	—	—	—	8	53	6.6	0	—	—	—	—	—	—	—	—	—	k	—	0	26

MADARIK, ELMER   Elmer Laurence, HB-WB, 5′11″/200 lbs; Detroit Mercy; 1944: Det, rnd 18; B7/15/1922 Joliet, IL, D2/3/1974

1945	Det	1 (0)	2	5	2.5 (4)	0	—	—	—	—	—	—	—	—	—	—	—	—	—	i	—	0	40
1946	Det	10 (6, WB)	8	7	0.9 (4)	0	6	38	6.3 (20)	0	14	7	50.0	104	7.4 (47)	1	0	—	—	kpi	—	0	245
1947	Det	8 (5, RH)	19	29	1.5 (9)	1	4	75	18.8 (26)	0	—	—	—	—	—	—	—	—	—	kp	—	6	83
1948	Det	3 (1)	2	7	3.5 (5)	0	—	—	—	—	—	—	—	—	—	—	—	—	—	k	—	0	12
1948	Was	1 (0)	—	—	—	—	—	—	—	—	—	—	—	—	—	—	—	—	—	—	—	—	—
NFL	4	23 (12)	31	48	1.5 (9)	1	10	113	11.3 (26)	0	14	7	50.0	104	7.4 (47)	1	0	—	—	kpi	—	6	380

MADDEN, LLOYD   Lloyd Willis, WB-DB, 6′1″/195 lbs; Colorado Mines; 1940: ChiC, rnd 3; B8/27/1918 Dodge City, KS

1940	ChiC	9 (4)	29	186	6.4	2	4	90	22.5 (56)	1	—	—	—	—	—	—	—	—	—	—	—	18	256

MADDOCK, BOB   Robert Charles, G, 6′0″/200 lbs; Notre Dame; B8/6/1920 Santa Ana, CA, D10/4/2003 Corona Del Mar, CA   **1942** ChiC 2 (1)   **1946** ChiC 7 (4)   **NFL** 9 (5) [2 yrs]

MADDOX, ANTHONY   Anthony, DT, 6′1″/308 lbs; Delta State; 2004: Jax, rnd 4; B11/22/1978 Funston, GA   **2004** Jax 2 (0)   **2005** Jax 5 (0)   **NFL** 7 (0) [2 yrs]

MADDOX, BOB   Robert Earl, DT-DE, 6′5″/237 lbs; Frostburg State; 1973: Cin, rnd 7; B5/2/1949 Frederick, MD   **1974** Cin 14   **1975** KC 6 (ldt)   **1976** KC 8 (7, RDT)   **NFL** 28 (7) [3 yrs]

MADDOX, BUSTER   George Woodrow, T, 6′3″/225 lbs; Kansas State; B11/4/1911 Greenville, TX, D3/14/1956 McKinney, TX   **1935** GB 1 (1)

MADDOX, MARK   Mark Anthony, LB, 6′1″/233 lbs; Northern Michigan; 1991: Buf, rnd 9; B3/23/1968 Milwaukee, WI   **1992**†Buf 15 (1)   **1993**†Buf 11 (8, RILB)   **1994** Buf 15 (14, RILB)   **1995** Buf 4 (9)   **1996** Buf 14 (14, RILB)   **1997** Buf 8 (1)   **1998**†Arz 14 (3)   **1999** Arz 16 (2)   **2000** Arz 14 (0)   **NFL** 111 (47) [9 yrs]

MADDOX, NICK   Nick, RB, 5′11″/209 lbs; Florida State; B12/11/1980 Shelby, NC   **2003** Cle 1 (0)

MADDOX, TOMMY   Thomas Alfred, QB, 6′4″/220 lbs; UCLA; 1992: Den, rnd 1; B9/2/1971 Shreveport, LA

1992	Den	13 (4)	9	20	2.2 (11)	0	—	—	—	—	121	66	54.5	757	6.3 (38)	5	9	10	60	—	—	0	64
1993	†Den	16 (0)	2	-2	-1.0 (-1)	0	—	—	—	—	1	1	100.0	1	1.0 (1)	1	0	—	—	—	—	0	4
1994	LARm	5 (0)	1	1	1.0 (1)	0	—	—	—	—	19	10	52.6	141	7.4 (39)	0	2	—	—	—	—	0	-9
1995	NYG	16 (0)	1	4	4.0 (4)	0	—	—	—	—	23	6	26.1	49	2.1 (13)	0	3	2	7	—	—	0	-92
2001	Pit	3 (0)	6	9	1.5 (8)	1	—	—	—	—	9	7	77.8	154	17.1 (57)	1	1	1	4	—	—	6	61
2002	†Pit	15 (11, QB)	19	43	2.3 (21)	0	—	—	—	—	377	234	62.1	2836	7.5 (72)	20	16	26	148	85.2	—	0	921
2003	Pit	16 (16, QB)	13	12	0.9 (6)	0	—	—	—	—	519	298	57.4	3414	6.6 (53)	18	17	41	242	75.3	—	0	1129
2004	Pit	4 (3)	9	15	1.7 (10)	0	—	—	—	—	60	30	50.0	329	5.5 (39)	1	2	6	37	—	—	0	105
2005	†Pit	5 (2)	8	26	3.3 (16)	0	—	—	—	—	71	34	47.9	406	5.7 (32)	2	4	8	43	—	—	0	79
NFL	9	93 (36)	68	128	1.9 (21)	1	—	—	—	—	1200	686	57.2	8087	6.7 (72)	48	54	94	541	72.4	—	6	2262

MADEROS, GEORGE   George, DB, 6′1″/187 lbs; Cal State-Chico; 1955: SF, rnd 21; B11/3/1933 Chico, CA   **1955** SF 8 (DB)   **1956** SF 12 (DB)   **NFL** 20 [2 yrs]

MADIGAN, JOHN   John A., C-T, 6′0″/185 lbs; St. Mary's (MN); St. Thomas; B3/12/1899 Madison Lake, MN, D1/5/1976 St. Paul, MN   **1922** Min 2 (2, C)   **1923** Dul 7 (7, C)   **1924** Min 6 (6, C)   **NFL** 15 (15) [3 yrs]

MADISE, ADRIAN   Adrian James, WR, 5′11″/215 lbs; TCU; 2003: Den, rnd 5; B3/23/1980 Lancaster, TX

2003	†Den	11 (0)	1	10	10.0 (10)	0	2	10	5.0 (5)	0	—	—	—	—	—	—	—	—	—	k	—	0	77

MADISON, SAM   Samuel Adolphus, DB, 5′11″/185 lbs; Louisville; 1997: Mia, rnd 2; B4/23/1974 Thomasville, GA [I]   **1997**†Mia 14 (3)   **1998**†Mia☆16 (16, RCB)   **1999**†Mia★16 (16, RCB)   **2000**†Mia★16 (16, RCB)   **2001**†Mia☆13 (13, RCB)   **2002** Mia✛16 (16, RCB)   **2003** Mia 16 (16, RCB)   **2004** Mia 16 (16, RCB)   **2005** Mia 15 (15, RCB)   **NFL** 138 (127) [9 yrs]

MADSEN, LYNN   Lynn Thomas, DT, 6′4″/260 lbs; Washington; 1984: Hou, rnd S3; B8/8/1960 Blair, NE   **1986** Hou 15 (0)

MAEDA, CHET   Chester A., HB-DB, 5′10″/187 lbs; Colorado State; 1943: Det, rnd 18; B10/2/1918 Los Angeles, CA

1945	ChiC	1 (0)	—	—	—	—	—	—	—	—	1	0	0.0	0	0.0	0	0	—	—	—	—	0	0

MAEDER, AL   Albert Raymond, T, 5′9″/185 lbs; Minnesota; B1/25/1906 Minneapolis, MN, D8/25/1984 Eden Prairie, MN   **1929** Min 9 (2)

MAESE, JOE   Joseph Michael, C, 6′0″/241 lbs; New Mexico; 2001: Bal, rnd 6; B12/2/1978 Morenci, NM   **2001** Bal 15 (0)   **2002** Bal 16 (0)   **2003**†Bal 16 (0)   **2004** Bal 15 (0)   **2005** Det 3 (0)   **NFL** 65 (0) [5 yrs]

MAGAC, MIKE   Michael Stephen, G, 6′3″/240 lbs; Missouri; 1960: SF, rnd 2/NYT, rnd 1; B5/25/1938 East St. Louis, IL, D8/25/2003 Belleville, IL   **1960** SF 12 (8, RG)   **1961** SF 6   **1962** SF 14 (14, LG)   **1963** SF 10   **1964** SF 14   **1965** Pit 8 (RG)   **1966** Pit 14 (RG)   **NFL** 78 (22) [7 yrs]

MAGEE, CALVIN   Calvin, TE, 6′3″/240 lbs; Southern (LA); B4/23/1963 New Orleans, LA

| 1985 | TB | 16 (7, te) | — | — | — | — | 26 | 288 | 11.1 (35) | 3 | — | — | — | — | — | — | — | — | — | k | — | 18 | 149 |
| 1986 | TB | 16 (13, TE) | — | — | — | — | 45 | 564 | 12.5 (45) | 5 | — | — | — | — | — | — | — | — | — | k | — | 30 | 298 |

YEAR	TEAM	G (GS, POS)	RUSH	YD	AVG(LG)	TD	REC	YD	AVG(LG)	TD	PASS	COMP	PCT	YD	AVG(LG)	TD	INT	SK	YD	QBR	KPR	OTD	PTS	TAY
1987	TB	11(11, TE)	—	—	—	—	34	424	12.5(37)	3	—	—	—	—	—	—	—	—	—	—	—	—	18	227
1988	TB	13(3)	—	—	—	—	9	103	11.4(25)	0	—	—	—	—	—	—	—	—	—	—	—	—	0	52
NFL	4	56(34)	—	—	—	—	114	1379	12.1(45)	11	—	—	—	—	—	—	—	—	—	—	k	—	66	726

MAGEE, JIM   James J., C-T, 6´1˝/202 lbs; Georgia; Villanova; B11/27/1920 Philadelphia, PA, D1/17/2001 Cape May, NJ   **1944** Bos 10 (4, C)   **1945** Bos 9 (0)   **1946** Bos 11 (0)
NFL 30 (4) [3 yrs]

MAGEE, JOHN   John Wesley, G, 5´10˝/220 lbs; Rice; Louisiana-Lafayette; 1945: Phi, rnd 2; B7/21/1923 Robstown, TX, D11/26/1991 Kaplan, LA   **1948** Phi 12 (8, LG)
1949†Phi 12 (3)   **1950** Phi 12 (RG)   **1952** Phi 12 (RG)   **1953** Phi 12 (RG)   **1954** Phi 12 (RG)   **1955** Phi 7

| 1951 | Phi | 12(RG) | — | — | — | — | 0 | 7 | (7) | 0 | — | — | — | — | — | — | — | — | — | — | — | — | 0 | 4 |
| NFL | 8 | 91(11) | — | — | — | — | 0 | 7 | (7) | 0 | — | — | — | — | — | — | — | — | — | — | — | — | 0 | 4 |

MAGERKURTH, GEORGE   George Levi, T, 6´3˝/210 lbs; none; B12/30/1888, KS, D10/7/1966 Rock Island, IL   **1920** RI 1 (0)

MAGGIOLI, CHICK   Achille Fred, DB-HB, 5´11˝/178 lbs; Indiana; Notre Dame; Illinois; 1946: Was, rnd 11; B5/17/1922 Mishawaka, IN

1948	†Buf-A	7(0)	11	27	2.5	0	3	23	7.7	0	1	1	100.0	0	0.0	0	0	—	—	—	Pkpi	—	0	44
1949	Det	12(0)	—	—	—	—	1	9	9.0(9)	0	—	—	—	—	—	—	—	—	—	i	—	1	6	36
1950	Bal	8(DB)	—	—	—	—	—	—	—	—	—	—	—	—	—	—	—	—	—	i	—	0	125
NFL	2	20	—	—	—	—	1	9	9.0(9)	0	—	—	—	—	—	—	—	—	—	i	—	1	6	161

MAGGS, DON   Donald James, T-G, 6´5˝/287 lbs; Tulane; 1984: Hou, rnd S2; B11/1/1961 Youngstown, OH   **1986** Hou 14 (2)   **1988**†Hou 16 (0)   **1989**†Hou 16 (1)
1990†Hou 16 (16, LT)   **1991**†Hou 16 (15, LT)   **1992**†Hou 16 (14, LT)   **1993**†Den 7 (2)   **1994** Den 9 (1)   **NFL** 110 (51) [8 yrs]

MAGINNES, AL   Albert Bristol, T, 6´1˝/188 lbs; Lehigh; B4/5/1897 Boston, MA, D1/30/1966 New York, NY   **1920** Can 1 (0)   **1921** NYG 2 (0)   **NFL** 3 (0) [2 yrs]

MAGINNES, DAVE   William David, WB-HB, 5´10˝/165 lbs; Lehigh; B11/29/1894 Dorchester, MA, D7/26/1981 Exeter, NH   **1921** NYG 2 (1, WB)

MAGLIOLO, JOE   Joseph S., LB, 6´0˝/210 lbs; Texas; 1948: NYY-A, rnd 15/1944: ChiC, rnd 17; B10/17/1922 Galveston, TX   **1948** NYY-A 13 (0)

MAGLISCEAU, AL   Albert Samuel, T, 6´1˝/210 lbs; Geneva; B5/21/1904 Pittsburgh, PA, D11/5/1985 Sun City Center, FL   **1929** Fra 5 (2)

MAGNANI, DANTE   Dante Alfred, HB-WB, 5´10˝/182 lbs; St. Mary's (CA); 1940: Cle, rnd 19; B3/16/1917 Dalzell, IL, D12/22/1985 Vallejo, CA

1940	Cle	11(4)	7	19	2.7	0	11	119	10.8(25)	1	—	—	—	—	—	—	—	—	—	—	Pi	—	6	128
1941	Cle	9(8, WB)	24	128	5.3(29)	0	14	189	13.5(61)	1	—	—	—	—	—	—	—	—	—	—	kpi	1	12	384
1942	Cle★	11(10, WB)	59	344	**5.8(71)**	1	24	276	11.5(67)	4	1	0	0.0	0	0.0	0	0	—	—	—	kp	—	30	614
1943	†ChiB	10(7, RH)	51	310	6.1(79)	2	6	88	14.7(51)	1	—	—	—	—	—	—	—	—	—	—	kpi	1	24	503
1946	†ChiB	10(7, LH)	68	277	4.1(32)	0	14	156	11.1(38)	1	—	—	—	—	—	—	—	—	—	—	ki	—	6	395
1947	LARm	12(3)	48	178	3.7(27)	0	4	57	14.3(40)	1	—	—	—	—	—	—	—	—	—	—	k	—	6	308
1948	LARm	8(1)	38	144	3.8(15)	0	3	28	9.3(16)	1	—	—	—	—	—	—	—	—	—	—	k	—	6	167
1949	ChiB	6(1)	33	59	1.8(9)	0	3	29	9.7(15)	0	—	—	—	—	—	—	—	—	—	—	—	—	0	74
1950	Det	7	3	7	2.3(5)	0	—	—	—	—	—	—	—	—	—	—	—	—	—	—	—	—	0	7
NFL	9	84(41)	331	1466	4.4(79)	3	79	942	11.9(67)	10	1	0	0.0	0	0.0	0	0	—	—	—	Pkpi	2	90	2578

MAGNER, JAMES   James Edward, B, 6´0˝/165 lbs; Widener; North Carolina; B7/22/1903 Philadelphia, PA, D9/20/1977 Philadelphia, PA   **1931** Fra 2 (0)

MAGNUSSON, GLEN   Glen Edward, G, 5´11˝/225 lbs; Northwestern; B7/30/1899 Salt Lake City, UT, D1/7/1945 Chicago, IL   **1925** Ham 1 (1)

MAGUIRE, PAUL   Paul Leo, LB-P, 6´0˝/228 lbs; The Citadel; 1960: LAC, rnd 1; B8/22/1938 Youngstown, OH [P]   **1960** LAC-A☆11 (RLB)   **1962** SD-A◇14 (RLB)
1963†SD-A 14 (RLB)   **1964**†Buf-A 14   **1966**†Buf-A 14   **1967** Buf-A☆ 14   **1970** Buf 14

1961	†SD-A	14(RLB)	1	-11	-11.0(-11)	0	—	—	—	—	—	—	—	—	—	—	—	—	—	—	Pi	—	0	-14
1965	†Buf-A◇	14	1	21	21.0(21)	0	—	—	—	—	—	—	—	—	—	—	—	—	—	—	Pk	—	0	11
1968	Buf-A	14	1	6	6.0(6)	0	—	—	—	—	—	—	—	—	—	—	—	—	—	—	Pk	—	0	-4
1969	Buf-A☆	14	—	—	—	—	—	—	—	—	1	1	100.0	19	19.0(19)	0	0	—	—	—	P	—	0	10
NFL	11	151	3	16	5.3(21)	0	—	—	—	—	1	1	100.0	19	19.0(19)	0	0	—	—	—	Pki	1	6	20

MAGULICK, GEORGE   George, HB, 5´9˝/150 lbs; St. Francis (PA); B1/10/1919 Spangler, PA, deceased

| 1944 | C-P | 9(6, LH) | 17 | 102 | 6.0(49) | 0 | 6 | 50 | 8.3(21) | 0 | — | — | — | — | — | — | — | — | — | — | kpi | — | 0 | 206 |

MAHALIC, DREW   Drew Alan, LB, 6´4˝/225 lbs; Notre Dame; 1975: Den, rnd 3; B5/22/1953 Albany, NY   **1975** SD 13 (1)   **1976** Phi 13   **1977** Phi 14 (9, RLB)   **1978** Phi 9 (8, ROLB)
NFL 49 (18) [4 yrs]

MAHAN, BOB   Robert Cullen, B-E, 5´9˝/178 lbs; Drake; Washington-St. Louis; B2/6/1904 Emmetsburg, IA, D3/5/2000 Berkeley, CA   **1929** Buf 9 (7, FB)   **1930** Bkn 11 (8, RE)
NFL 20 (15) [2 yrs]

MAHAN, SEAN   Sean Christopher, G-C, 6´3˝/301 lbs; Notre Dame; 2003: TB, rnd 5; B5/28/1980 Tulsa, OK   **2003** TB 9 (0)   **2004** TB 16 (8, c)   **2005**†TB 16 (16, RG)
NFL 41 (24) [3 yrs]

MAHAN, WALTER   Walter Everett, G, 5´10˝/212 lbs; West Virginia; B6/23/1902 Follansbee, WV, D5/10/1990 Wheeling, WV   **1926** Fra 1 (1)

MAHE, RENO   Sateki Reno, RB, 5´10˝/195 lbs; Brigham Young; B6/3/1980 Los Angeles, CA

2003	†Phi	2(0)	—	—	—	—	1	5	5.0(5)	0	—	—	—	—	—	—	—	—	—	—	p	—	0	28
2004	†Phi	11(0)	23	91	4.0(22)	0	14	123	8.8(30)	0	—	—	—	—	—	—	—	—	—	—	kp	—	0	166
2005	Phi☆	15(0)	20	87	4.3(13)	0	12	68	5.7(12)	0	—	—	—	—	—	—	—	—	—	—	kp	—	0	289
NFL	3	43	43	178	4.1(22)	0	27	196	7.3(30)	0	—	—	—	—	—	—	—	—	—	—	kp	—	0	482

MAHER, BIRDIE   Gilbert Thomas, E, 5´8˝/180 lbs; Detroit Mercy; B12/16/1892 County Mayo, Ireland, D12/3/1980 Detroit, MI   **1920** Det 2 (1)

MAHER, BRUCE   Bruce David, DB, 5´11˝/190 lbs; Detroit Mercy; 1959: Det, rnd 15/1960: Hou, rnd 1; B7/25/1937 Detroit, MI [I]   **1960** Det 12   **1961** Det 12 (RCB)   **1963** Det 14 (LS)
1964 Det 14 (LS)   **1965** Det 14 (LS)   **1966** Det 14 (LS)   **1967** Det 14 (LS)   **1968** NYG 14 (LS)   **1969** NYG 14 (LS)

| 1962 | Det | 14 | 3 | 8 | 2.7(7) | 0 | — | — | — | — | — | — | — | — | — | — | — | — | — | — | kp | — | 0 | 37 |
| NFL | 10 | 136 | 3 | 8 | 2.7(7) | 0 | — | — | — | — | — | — | — | — | — | — | — | — | — | — | kpi | — | 6 | 443 |

MAHER, FRANK   Francis Xavier, B, 6´1˝/195 lbs; Toledo; 1940: Phi, rnd 10; B5/8/1918 Detroit, MI, deceased   **1941** Pit 2 (0)   **1941** Cle 2 (0)   **NFL** 4 (0) [1 yr]

MAHLUM, ERIC   Eric Arnold, G, 6´4˝/284 lbs; California; 1994: Ind, rnd 2; B12/6/1970 San Diego, CA   **1994** Ind 16 (2)   **1995**†Ind 7 (7, rg)   **1996** Ind 13 (9, RG)   **NFL** 36 (18) [3 yrs]

MAHONEY, IKE   Frank John, B, 5´9˝/173 lbs; Creighton; B10/25/1901 Omaha, NE, D5/1963, [K]   **1925** ChiC 7 (4), 7   **1926** ChiC 11 (8, bb), 13   **1927** ChiC 9 (3)   **1928** ChiC 5 (2)
1931 ChiC 1 (0)   **NFL** 33 (17), 20 [5 yrs]

MAHONEY, JOHN   John Jacob, B-E, 6´0˝/183 lbs; Canisius; B10/16/1899 Buffalo, NY, D9/23/1980 Clarence, NY   **1923** Buf 7 (3)

MAHONEY, ROGER   Roger Sylvis, C-G-E, 6´0˝/205 lbs; Penn State; B7/19/1906, D3/12/1981 Reading, PA   **1928** Fra 14 (10, C)   **1929** Fra 17 (15, C)   **1930** Fra 10 (4)
1930 Min 1 (1)   **NFL** 42 (30) [3 yrs]

MAHRT, AL   Alphonse Herman, B, 5´11˝/168 lbs; Dayton; B10/12/1893 Dayton, OH, D6/24/1970 Chillicothe, OH   **1920** Day☆9 (8, BB)   **1921** Day 7 (6, BB), 6   **1922** Day 8 (8, BB), 6
NFL 24 (22), 12 [3 yrs]

MAHRT, ARMIN   Armin Richard, TB-BB-HB, 5´11˝/175 lbs; Dayton; West Virginia; B11/9/1897 Dayton, OH, D5/7/1961 Stearns County, MN   **1924** Day 7 (7, TB), 6
1925 Day 8 (8, TB)   **1925** Pot 2 (1), 6   **1926** Day 4 (1, BB)   **NFL** 21 (17), 12 [3 yrs]

MAHRT, JOHNNY   John C., E, 5´9˝/180 lbs; Dayton; B12/22/1899 Dayton, OH, D8/24/1967 Dayton, OH   **1925** Day 1 (0)

MAHRT, LOU   Louis Richard, QB, 5´11˝/178 lbs; Dayton; B7/30/1904, FL, D8/7/1982 Dayton, OH [C]   **1926** Day 6 (6)   **1927** Day 2 (2)   **NFL** 8 (8) [2 yrs]

MAIDLOW, STEVE   Steven Kenneth, LB, 6´2˝/234 lbs; Michigan State; 1983: Cin, rnd 4; B6/6/1960 Lansing, MI   **1983** Cin 16 (0)   **1984** Cin 16 (0)   **1985** Buf 16 (2)   **1987** Buf 2 (0)
NFL 50 (4) [4 yrs]

MAILLARD, RALPH   Ralph Jacob, T, 6´2˝/190 lbs; Creighton; B10/10/1905 Randolph, NE, D5/9/1990 Omaha, NE   **1929** ChiB 4 (1)

MAINS, GIL   Gilbert Lee, DT-DE, 6´2˝/243 lbs; Murray State; 1952: Det, rnd 20; B12/17/1929 Mount Carmel, IL   **1953** Det 3   **1954**†Det 12 (RDT)   **1955** Det 12 (LDE)
1956 Det 8 (RDE)   **1957**†Det 11 (RDT)   **1958** Det 12 (RDT)   **1959** Det 12 (RDT)   **1960** Det 12   **1961** Det 3   **NFL** 85 [9 yrs]

MAITLAND, JACK   John Frederick, RB, 6´2˝/211 lbs; Williams; 1970: Bal, rnd 16; B2/8/1948 Pittsburgh, PA

| 1970 | †Bal | 14 | 74 | 209 | 2.8(24) | 1 | 9 | 67 | 7.4(13) | 1 | — | — | — | — | — | — | — | — | — | — | k | — | 12 | 271 |
| 1971 | NE | 14 | 13 | 25 | 1.9(6) | 1 | 1 | 6 | 6.0(6) | 0 | — | — | — | — | — | — | — | — | — | — | k | — | 6 | 48 |

YEAR	TEAM	G(GS, POS)	RUSH	YD	AVG(LG)	TD	REC	YD	AVG(LG)	TD	PASS	COMP	PCT	YD	AVG(LG)	TD	INT	SK	YD	QBR	KPR	OTD	PTS	TAY
1972	NE	13	13	33	2.5(6)	0	4	33	8.3(9)	0	—	—	—	—	—	—	—	—	—	—	k	—	0	53
NFL	3	41	100	267	2.7(24)	2	14	106	7.6(13)	1	—	—	—	—	—	—	—	—	—	—	k	—	18	371
MAJKOWSKI, DON Donald Vincent, QB, 6´2˝/197 lbs; Virginia; 1987: GB, rnd 10; B2/25/1964 Buffalo, NY																								
1987	GB	7(5, qb)	15	127	8.5(33)	0	—	—	—	—	127	55	43.3	875	6.9(70)	5	3	10	77	—	—	—	0	470
1988	GB	13(9, QB)	47	225	4.8(24)	1	—	—	—	—	336	178	53.0	2119	6.3(56)	9	11	20	148	67.8	—	—	6	900
1989	GB★	16(16, QB)	75	358	4.8(20)	5	—	—	—	—	**599**	**353**	58.9	**4318**	7.2(79)	27	20	47	268	82.3	—	—	30	**1902**
1990	GB	9(8, QB)	29	186	6.4(24)	1	—	—	—	—	264	150	56.8	1925	7.3(76)	10	12	32	178	73.5	—	—	6	729
1991	GB	9(8, QB)	25	108	4.3(15)	2	—	—	—	—	226	115	50.9	1362	6.0(39)	3	8	30	152	59.3	—	—	12	504
1992	GB	14(3)	8	33	4.1(8)	0	—	—	—	—	55	38	69.1	271	4.9(32)	2	2	9	60	—	—	—	0	99
1993	Ind	3(0)	2	4	2.0(4)	0	—	—	—	—	24	13	54.2	105	4.4(17)	0	1	1	5	—	—	—	0	17
1994	Ind	9(6, qb)	24	34	1.4(10)	3	—	—	—	—	152	84	55.3	1010	6.6(29)	6	7	9	76	—	—	—	18	319
1995	†Det	8(0)	9	1	0.1(4)	0	—	—	—	—	20	15	75.0	161	8.1(22)	1	0	1	5	—	—	—	0	87
1996	Det	5(2)	14	38	2.7(12)	0	—	—	—	—	102	55	53.9	554	5.4(27)	3	3	10	61	—	—	—	0	210
NFL	10	93(57)	248	1114	4.5(33)	12	—	—	—	—	1905	1056	55.4	12700	6.7(79)	66	67	169	1030	72.9	—	—	72	5234
MAJORS, BILLY William Bobo, DB, 6´0˝/175 lbs; Tennessee; 1961: Buf, rnd 9/Phi, rnd 12; B11/7/1938 Lynchburg, TN **1961** Buf-A 1																								
MAJORS, BOBBY Robert Owen, DB, 6´1˝/193 lbs; Tennessee; 1972: Phi, rnd 3; B7/7/1949 Lynchburg, TN **1972**†Cle 9																								
MAJORS, JOE Joe Inman, DB, 6´1˝/190 lbs; Florida State; B12/25/1936 Lynchburg, TN **1960** Hou-A 1																								
MAKOVICKA, JOEL Joel, FB, 5´11˝/246 lbs; Nebraska; 1999: Arz, rnd 4; B10/6/1975 Brainard, NE																								
1999	Arz	16(10, FB)	8	7	0.9(7)	0	10	70	7.0(15)	1	—	—	—	—	—	—	—	—	—	—	k	—	6	42
2000	Arz	14(10, FB)	3	8	2.7(7)	0	6	18	3.0(5)	0	—	—	—	—	—	—	—	—	—	—	—	—	0	17
2001	Arz	16(14, FB)	1	19	19.0(19)	0	16	95	5.9(25)	1	—	—	—	—	—	—	—	—	—	—	k	—	6	64
2002	Arz	12(1)	5	54	10.8(22)	0	15	81	5.4(17)	3	—	—	—	—	—	—	—	—	—	—	k	—	18	110
NFL	4	58(35)	17	88	5.2(22)	0	47	264	5.6(25)	5	—	—	—	—	—	—	—	—	—	—	k	—	30	232
MALAMALA, SIUPELI Siupeli, T-G, 6´5˝/310 lbs; Washington; 1992: NYJ, rnd 3; B1/15/1969 Tofoa, Tonga **1992** NYJ 9 (5, lt) **1993** NYJ 15 (15, RT) **1994** NYJ 12 (10, RT) **1995** NYJ 6 (4) **1996** NYJ 4 (1) **1997** NYJ 10 (5, rt) **1999** NYJ 6 (1) **NFL** 62 (41) [7 yrs]																								
MALANCON, RYDELL Rydell Joseph, LB, 6´2˝/227 lbs; LSU; 1984: Atl, rnd 4; B1/10/1962 New Orleans, LA **1984** Atl 7 (0) **1987** GB 3 (3) **NFL** 10 (3) [2 yrs]																								
MALBROUGH, ANTHONY Anthony, DB, 5´10˝/185 lbs; Texas Tech; 2000: Cle, rnd 5; B12/9/1976 Beaumont, TX **2000** Cle 9 (1)																								
MALCOLM, HARRY Harry Elmer, T-G, 6´0˝/195 lbs; Indiana (PA); Washington & Jefferson; B11/25/1905 Indiana County, PA, D9/15/1987 Springfield, PA **1929** Fra 14 (10, RT)																								
MALEY, HOWARD Howard Edward, HB, 5´11˝/187 lbs; Texas-Arlington; SMU; 1944: Bkn, rnd 17; B12/6/1921, D6/20/1987 Dallas, TX																								
1946	Bos	11(0)	13	67	5.2(42)	0	2	35	17.5(33)	0	8	3	37.5	71	8.9(43)	1	2	—	—	—	Pkp	—	0	30
1947	Bos	12(0)	32	132	4.1(27)	0	—	—	—	—	12	6	50.0	144	12.0(63)	1	1	—	—	—	Pk	—	0	177
NFL	2	23(0)	45	199	4.4(42)	0	2	35	17.5(33)	0	20	9	45.0	215	10.8(63)	2	3	—	—	—	Pkp	—	0	207
MALINCHAK, BILL William John, SE-WR, 6´1˝/200 lbs; Indiana; 1966: Det, rnd 3; B4/2/1944 Charleroi, PA **1970** Was 9 **1971**†Was 13 **1972** Was 6 **1973**†Was 14 **1974**†Was 13																								
1966	Det	14	—	—	—	—	5	34	6.8(13)	0	—	—	—	—	—	—	—	—	—	—	—	—	0	17
1967	Det	14(SE)	—	—	—	—	26	397	15.3(43)	4	—	—	—	—	—	—	—	—	—	—	—	—	24	219
1968	Det	14	—	—	—	—	1	41	41.0(41)	0	—	—	—	—	—	—	—	—	—	—	—	—	0	21
1969	Det	6	—	—	—	—	2	24	12.0(21)	0	—	—	—	—	—	—	—	—	—	—	P	—	0	12
1976	†Was	3	—	—	—	—	1	12	12.0(12)	0	—	—	—	—	—	—	—	—	—	—	—	—	0	6
NFL	10	106	—	—	—	—	35	508	14.5(43)	4	—	—	—	—	—	—	—	—	—	—	P	1	32	274
MALINOWSKI, GENE Eugene Paul, B, 6´1˝/210 lbs; Georgia; Detroit Mercy; 1947: Bos, rnd 9/1948: SF-A, rnd 12; B9/26/1923 Hamtramck, MI, D11/24/1993 Clinton Township, MI																								
1948	Bos	12(2)	11	21	1.9(9)	0	3	-10	-3.3(1)	0	54	15	27.8	218	4.0(68)	3	7	—	—	—	i	—	0	-136
MALKOVICH, JOE Joseph N., C, 6´3˝/205 lbs; Duquesne; B1/17/1912 Calumet, MI, D2/17/1981 Camarillo, CA **1935** Pit 2 (1)																								
MALLARD, JOSH Joshua B., DE, 6´5˝/254 lbs; Georgia; 2002: Ind, rnd 7; B3/21/1979 Savannah, GA **2002** Ind 13 (0)																								
MALLARD, WESLY Wesly Allen, LB, 6´1˝/230 lbs; Oregon; 2002: NYG, rnd 6; B11/21/1978 Hinesville, GA **2002**†NYG 15 (0) **2003** NYG 15 (0) **2004** NYG 4 (0) **2005** NE 3 (0) **2005**†TB 6 (0) **NFL** 43 (0) [4 yrs]																								
MALLICK, FRAN Francis J., DE-DT, 6´2˝/245 lbs; none; B2/25/1941 **1965** Pit 6																								
MALLORY, IRVIN Irvin M., DB, 6´1˝/196 lbs; Virginia Union; 1971: Cin, rnd 14; B2/10/1949 Glen Allen, VA **1971** NE 2																								
MALLORY, JOHN John, DB, 6´0˝/184 lbs; West Virginia; 1968: Phi, rnd 10; B7/24/1946 Summit, NJ **1969** Atl 13 (RS) **1970** Atl 14 (SS)																								
1968	Phi	14	—	—	—	—	1	58	58.0(58)	1	—	—	—	—	—	—	—	—	—	—	kp	—	6	64
1971	Atl	14(SS)	—	—	—	—	1	27	27.0(27)	0	—	—	—	—	—	—	—	—	—	—	p	1	6	-9
NFL	4	55	—	—	—	—	2	85	42.5(58)	1	—	—	—	—	—	—	—	—	—	—	kpi	3	24	182
MALLORY, LARRY Larry Montel, DB, 5´11˝/185 lbs; Tennessee State; B7/21/1952 Memphis, TN																								
1976	NYG	14(2)	1	0	0.0(0)	0	—	—	—	—	—	—	—	—	—	—	—	—	—	—	i	—	0	-5
1977	NYG	14	—	—	—	—	—	—	—	—	—	—	—	—	—	—	—	—	—	—	ki	—	0	-11
1978	NYG	16	—	—	—	—	—	—	—	—	1	1	100.0	35	35.0(35)	0	0	—	—	—	—	—	0	18
NFL	3	44(2)	1	0	0.0	0	—	—	—	—	1	1	100.0	35	35.0(35)	0	0	—	—	—	ki	—	0	2
MALLORY, RICK Rick Leroy, G, 6´2˝/265 lbs; Washington; 1984: TB, rnd 9; B10/21/1960 Seattle, WA **1985** TB 13 (8, rg) **1987** TB 12 (12, RG) **1988** TB 16 (16, LG)																								
1986	TB	16(1)	—	—	—	—	1	9	9.0(9)	0	—	—	—	—	—	—	—	—	—	—	—	—	0	5
NFL	4	57(37)	—	—	—	—	1	9	9.0(9)	0	—	—	—	—	—	—	—	—	—	—	—	—	0	5
MALLOUF, RAY Raymond Lucian, QB-TB, 5´11˝/180 lbs; SMU; 1941: ChiC, rnd 10; B7/11/1918 Sayre, OK																								
1941	ChiC	9(5, TB)	43	104	2.4(15)	0	—	—	—	—	96	48	50.0	725	7.6(**80**)	2	4	—	—	—	Pkp	—	0	309
1946	ChiC	5(0)	4	6	1.5(18)	0	—	—	—	—	34	14	41.2	260	7.6(59)	4	2	—	—	—	Pi	—	0	86
1947	†ChiC	11(0)	5	13	2.6(17)	0	—	—	—	—	36	21	58.3	340	9.4(52)	1	2	—	—	—	P	—	0	108
1948	†ChiC	12(5, QB)	13	17	1.3(12)	1	—	—	—	—	143	73	51.0	1160	8.1(54)	13	6	—	—	91.2	P	—	6	432
1949	NYG	11(0)	1	-1	-1.0(-1)	0	—	—	—	—	16	3	18.8	19	1.2(11)	0	2	—	—	—	Pi	—	0	-77
NFL	5	48(10)	66	139	2.1(18)	1	—	—	—	—	325	159	48.9	2504	7.7(80)	20	16	—	—	75.0	Pkpi	—	6	858
MALLOY, LES Leslie A., B, 6´0˝/197 lbs; Loyola (IL); B12/8/1907, MN, D7/1982 Downers Grove, IL																								
1931	ChiC	8(2)	—	—	—	—	—	—	—	—	—	—	—	—	—	—	—	—	—	—	—	—	—	—
1932	ChiC	8(3)	9	32	3.6	0	3	57	19.0	0	11	2	18.2	22	2.0	0	0	—	—	—	—	—	0	72
1933	ChiC	10(8, BB)	9	20	2.2	0	—	—	—	—	—	—	—	—	—	—	—	—	—	—	—	—	0	20
NFL	3	26(13)	18	52	2.9	0	3	57	19.0	1	11	2	18.2	22	2.0	0	0	—	—	—	—	—	6	97
MALONE, ALFRED Alfred, DE, 6´5˝/308 lbs; Troy; B2/21/1982 Frisco City, AL **2005** Hou 2 (0)																								
MALONE, ART Arthur Lee, RB, 5´11˝/211 lbs; Arizona State; 1970: Atl, rnd 2; B3/20/1948 Tyler, TX																								
1970	Atl	14	40	136	3.4(12)	0	9	38	4.2(9)	1	—	—	—	—	—	—	—	—	—	—	k	—	6	151
1971	Atl	13(RB)	120	438	3.7(19)	6	34	380	11.2(46)	2	—	—	—	—	—	—	—	—	—	—	—	—	48	698
1972	Atl	14(RB)	180	798	4.4(27)	8	50	585	11.7(57)	2	—	—	—	—	—	—	—	—	—	—	k	—	60	1188
1973	Atl	10(RB)	76	336	4.4(14)	2	19	177	9.3(33)	1	—	—	—	—	—	—	—	—	—	—	—	—	18	450
1974	Atl	13(RB)	116	410	3.5(13)	2	28	168	6.0(13)	0	—	—	—	—	—	—	—	—	—	—	—	—	12	514
1975	Phi	13(FB)	101	325	3.2(18)	0	20	120	6.0(15)	0	—	—	—	—	—	—	—	—	—	—	—	—	0	385
1976	Phi	3	2	14	7.0(15)	1	1	-3	-3.0(-3)	0	—	—	—	—	—	—	—	—	—	—	—	—	6	23
NFL	7	80	635	2457	3.9(27)	19	161	1465	9.1(57)	6	—	—	—	—	—	—	—	—	—	—	k	—	150	3408
MALONE, BENNY Ben, RB, 5´10˝/193 lbs; Arizona State; 1974: Mia, rnd 2; B2/3/1952 Tyler, TX																								
1974	†Mia	13(3)	117	479	4.1(23)	3	2	26	13.0(13)	0	—	—	—	—	—	—	—	—	—	—	k	—	18	591
1975	Mia	10	65	220	3.4(21)	3	2	47	23.5(43)	0	—	—	—	—	—	—	—	—	—	—	k	—	18	277
1976	Mia	14(12, RB)	186	797	4.3(31)	4	9	103	11.4(36)	0	—	—	—	—	—	—	—	—	—	—	—	—	24	889

YEAR	TEAM	G(GS, POS)	RUSH	YD	AVG(LG)	TD	REC	YD	AVG(LG)	TD	PASS	COMP	PCT	YD	AVG(LG)	TD	INT	SK	YD	QBR	KPR	OTD	PTS	TAY
1977	Mia	14(8, RB)	129	615	**4.8**(**66**)	5	4	58	14.5(35)	0	—	—	—	—	—	—	—	—	—	—	—	—	30	694
1978	Mia	6	6	18	3.0(7)	1	—	—	—	—	—	—	—	—	—	—	—	—	—	—	—	—	6	28
1978	Was	9(1)	27	92	3.4(31)	0	3	29	9.7(19)	0	—	—	—	—	—	—	—	—	—	—	—	—	0	107
1979	Was	16(16, RB)	176	472	2.7(14)	3	13	137	10.5(55)	1	—	—	—	—	—	—	—	—	—	—	—	—	24	576
NFL	6	82(40)	706	2693	3.8(66)	19	33	400	12.1(55)	1	—	—	—	—	—	—	—	—	—	—	k	—	120	3160

Malone, Charley Charles C., E, 6´4˝/206 lbs; Texas A&M; B6/18/1910 Hillsboro, TX, D5/23/1992 Lake San Marcos, CA **[K]**

YEAR	TEAM	G(GS, POS)	RUSH	YD	AVG(LG)	TD	REC	YD	AVG(LG)	TD	PASS	COMP	PCT	YD	AVG(LG)	TD	INT	SK	YD	QBR	KPR	OTD	PTS	TAY
1934	Bos	12(10, LE)	1	30	30.0(30)	0	11	131	11.9	2	—	—	—	—	—	—	—	—	—	—	—	—	12	106
1935	Bos	11(11, LE)	—	—	—	—	22	**433**	19.7(55)	2	—	—	—	—	—	—	—	—	—	—	—	—	12	227
1936	†Bos	12(12, RE)	—	—	—	—	11	167	15.2(35)	1	—	—	—	—	—	—	—	—	—	—	—	—	6	89
1937	†Was	11(11, RE)	—	—	—	—	28	419	15.0(61)	4	—	—	—	—	—	—	—	—	—	—	—	—	24	230
1938	Was	11(8, RE)	—	—	—	—	24	257	10.7	1	—	—	—	—	—	—	—	—	—	—	—	—	6	134
1939	Was	11(8, RE)	—	—	—	—	18	274	15.2(48)	3	—	—	—	—	—	—	—	—	—	—	K	—	18	152
1940	†Was	11(11, RE)	—	—	—	—	20	222	11.1	0	—	—	—	—	—	—	—	—	—	—	—	—	0	111
1942	Was✧	5(0)	—	—	—	—	3	29	9.7(10)	0	—	—	—	—	—	—	—	—	—	—	—	—	0	15
NFL	8	84(71)	1	30	30.0(30)	0	137	1932	14.1(61)	13	—	—	—	—	—	—	—	—	—	—	K	—	78	1061

Malone, Darrell Darrell Kenyatta, DB, 5´10˝/177 lbs; Jacksonville State; 1991: KC, rnd 6; B11/23/1967 Mobile, AL **1992** KC 4 (0) **1992**†Mia 4 (0) **1993** Mia 16 (1) **1994** Mia 5 (2) **NFL** 29 (3) [3 yrs]

Malone, Grover John Grover, HB-WB, 5´8˝/175 lbs; Notre Dame; B11/12/1895 Chicago, IL, D11/26/1985 West Allis, WI **1920** ChiT 6 (3, WB) **1921** GB 6 (6, HB) **1921** RI 3 (1) **1923** Akr 2 (0) **NFL** 17 (10) [3 yrs]

Malone, Mark Mark M., QB-WR, 6´4˝/223 lbs; Arizona State; 1980: Pit, rnd 1; B11/22/1958 San Diego, CA

YEAR	TEAM	G(GS, POS)	RUSH	YD	AVG(LG)	TD	REC	YD	AVG(LG)	TD	PASS	COMP	PCT	YD	AVG(LG)	TD	INT	SK	YD	QBR	KPR	OTD	PTS	TAY
1980	Pit	1(0)	—	—	—	—	—	—	—	—	—	—	—	—	—	—	—	—	—	—	—	—	—	—
1981	Pit	8(3)	16	68	4.3(19)	2	1	90	90.0(90)	1	88	45	51.1	553	6.3(30)	3	5	10	76	—	k	—	18	218
1983	†Pit	2(0)	—	—	—	—	—	—	—	—	20	9	45.0	124	6.2(38)	1	2	1	11	—	—	—	0	-13
1984	†Pit	13(9, QB)	25	42	1.7(13)	3	—	—	—	—	272	147	54.0	2137	7.9(61)	16	17	25	211	73.4	—	—	18	541
1985	Pit	10(8, QB)	15	80	5.3(25)	1	—	—	—	—	233	117	50.2	1428	6.1(45)	13	7	10	80	75.5	—	—	6	589
1986	Pit	14(14, QB)	31	107	3.5(45)	5	—	—	—	—	425	216	50.8	2444	5.8(48)	15	18	13	97	62.5	—	—	30	734
1987	Pit	12(12, QB)	34	162	4.8(42)	3	—	—	—	—	336	156	46.4	1896	5.6(63)	6	**19**	18	151	46.7	—	—	18	410
1988	SD	12(8, QB)	37	169	4.6(36)	4	—	—	—	—	272	147	54.0	1580	5.8(59)	6	13	9	45	58.8	—	—	24	509
1989	NYJ	1(0)	1	0	0.0(0)	0	—	—	—	—	2	2	100.0	13	6.5(11)	0	0	—	—	—	—	—	0	7
NFL	9	73(54)	159	628	3.9(45)	18	1	90	90.0(90)	1	1648	839	50.9	10175	6.2(63)	60	81	86	671	61.9	k	—	114	2994

Malone, Ralph Ralph DeVaughn, DE, 6´5˝/225 lbs; Georgia Tech; B1/12/1964 Huntsville, AL **1986** Cle 16 (0)

Malone, Van Van Buren, DB, 5´11˝/189 lbs; Texas; 1994: Det, rnd 2; B7/1/1970 Houston, TX **1994** Det 16 (0) **1995**†Det 16 (0) **1996** Det 15 (15, FS) **1997** Det 8 (4) **NFL** 55 (19) [4 yrs]

Maloney, Ned Norman Edward, E, 6´1˝/190 lbs; Purdue; 1946: Det, rnd 21; B4/21/1923 Chicago, IL **[K]** **1949**†SF-A 12 (0)

YEAR	TEAM	G(GS, POS)	RUSH	YD	AVG(LG)	TD	REC	YD	AVG(LG)	TD	PASS	COMP	PCT	YD	AVG(LG)	TD	INT	SK	YD	QBR	KPR	OTD	PTS	TAY
1948	SF-A	14(1)	—	—	—	—	1	29	29.0(29)	1	—	—	—	—	—	—	—	—	—	—	K	—	7	20
AAFC	2	26(1)	—	—	—	—	1	29	29.0(29)	1	—	—	—	—	—	—	—	—	—	—	Kp	—	7	20

Maloney, Red Gerald Stack, E, 5´11˝/180 lbs; Dartmouth; B9/5/1901 Ware, MA, D5/16/1976 Waban, MA **[K]** **1925** Pro☆12 (12, RE), 19 **1927** NYY 12 (9, RE), 6 **1929** Bos 8 (7, RE) **NFL** 32 (28), 25 [3 yrs]

Mamula, Mike Michael David, DE-LB, 6´4˝/252 lbs; Boston College; 1995: Phi, rnd 1; B8/14/1973 Lackawanna, NY **1995** Phi 14 (13, RDE) **1996** Phi 16 (16, RDE) **1997** Phi 16 (16, RDE) **1999** Phi 16 (13, RDE) **2000** Phi 15 (6, lde) **NFL** 77 (64) [5 yrs]

Manca, Massimo Massimo, K, 5´10˝/211 lbs; Penn State; B3/18/1964 Sassari, Italy **[K]** **1987** Cin 3 (0)

Mancha, Vaughn Vaughn Hall, C-LB, 6´1˝/230 lbs; Alabama; 1948: Bos, rnd 1/LAD-A, rnd 1; B10/7/1921 Sugar Valley, GA **1948** Bos 12 (0)

Mandarich, Tony Ante Josip, T-G, 6´5˝/311 lbs; Michigan State; 1989: GB, rnd 1; B9/23/1966 Oakville, Canada **1989** GB 14 (0) **1990** GB 16 (16, RT) **1991** GB 15 (15, RT) **1996**†Ind 15 (6, rt) **1997** Ind 16 (16, RT) **1998** Ind 10 (10, RG) **NFL** 86 (63) [6 yrs]

Mandarino, Mike Michael Pascol, T-C-G, 5´11˝/240 lbs; La Salle; B3/16/1921 Philadelphia, PA, D12/7/1985 Media, PA **1944** Phi 8 (0) **1945** Phi 5 (0) **NFL** 13 (0) [2 yrs]

Manders, Dave David Francis, C, 6´2˝/250 lbs; Michigan State; B2/20/1941 Milwaukee, WI **1964** Dal 14 **1965** Dal 14 (C) **1966**†Dal✧14 (C) **1968**†Dal 14 **1969**†Dal 14 **1970**†Dal 14 (C) **1971**†Dal 14 (C) **1972**†Dal 14 (C) **1973**†Dal 13 **1974** Dal 14 **NFL** 139 [10 yrs]

Manders, Jack John Albert 'Automatic Jack', HB-FB, 6´1˝/203 lbs; Minnesota; B1/13/1909 Milbank, SD, D1/28/1977 Chicago, IL **[K]**

YEAR	TEAM	G(GS, POS)	RUSH	YD	AVG(LG)	TD	REC	YD	AVG(LG)	TD	PASS	COMP	PCT	YD	AVG(LG)	TD	INT	SK	YD	QBR	KPR	OTD	PTS	TAY
1933	†ChiB	13(6, rh)	65	234	3.6	0	1	9	9.0(9)	0	15	6	40.0	57	3.8	0	3	—	—	—	K	—	31	147
1934	†ChiB☆	13(2)	57	184	3.2	2	1	12	12.0(12)	0	3	2	66.7	14	4.7	0	0	—	—	—	K	1	**76**	227
1935	ChiB☆	12(7, FB)	93	296	3.2	0	2	16	8.0	0	9	1	11.1	10	1.1(10)	0	1	—	—	—	K	—	19	269
1936	ChiB	12(4)	63	207	3.3	4	1	4	4.0(4)	0	3	2	66.7	52	17.3	0	0	—	—	—	K	—	62	275
1937	†ChiB☆	11(9, RH)	73	319	4.4	0	7	163	23.3(63)	4	—	—	—	—	—	—	—	—	—	—	K	1	**69**	431
1938	ChiB	11(10, RH)	67	263	3.9	2	2	27	13.5(17)	1	1	0	0.0	0	0.0	0	0	—	—	—	K	—	37	302
1939	ChiB	11(2)	25	63	2.5	3	1	29	29.0(29)	1	—	—	—	—	—	—	—	—	—	—	K	—	50	113
1940	†ChiB	10(2)	8	20	2.5	0	—	—	—	—	—	—	—	—	—	—	—	—	—	—	Ki	—	23	42
NFL	8	93(42)	451	1586	3.5	11	15	260	17.3(63)	6	31	11	35.5	133	4.3(10)	0	4	—	—	—	Ki	2	367	1805

Manders, Pug Clarence Edward, FB-HB, 6´0˝/200 lbs; Drake; 1939: Bkn, rnd 2; B5/5/1913 Milbank, SD, D1/20/1985 Des Moines, IA **[K]**

YEAR	TEAM	G(GS, POS)	RUSH	YD	AVG(LG)	TD	REC	YD	AVG(LG)	TD	PASS	COMP	PCT	YD	AVG(LG)	TD	INT	SK	YD	QBR	KPR	OTD	PTS	TAY
1939	Bkn✧	11(9, FB)	114	482	4.2	2	3	22	7.3	0	—	—	—	—	—	—	—	—	—	—	—	—	12	513
1940	Bkn★	11(11, FB)	80	311	3.9	5	1	38	38.0(38)	1	1	0	0.0	0	0.0	0	0	—	—	—	i	—	36	395
1941	Bkn★	11(11, FB)	111	**486**	4.4(46)	5	6	67	11.2(27)	0	—	—	—	—	—	—	—	—	—	—	ki	2	42	656
1942	Bkn	11(11, FB)	93	316	3.4(23)	6	4	53	13.3(22)	0	1	0	0.0	0	0.0	0	0	—	—	—	ki	—	36	491
1943	Bkn	10(9, FB)	89	266	3.0(43)	3	5	68	13.6(48)	1	5	4	80.0	31	6.2(11)	1	0	—	—	—	k	—	24	360
1944	Bkn☆	10(9, FB)	127	430	3.4(13)	5	6	78	13.0(30)	0	34	9	26.5	96	2.8(0)	0	4	—	—	—	Kki	—	30	468
1945	Bos	10(10, FB)	76	238	3.1(34)	6	—	—	—	—	9	5	55.6	42	4.7(12)	0	1	—	—	—	ki	—	36	249
NFL	7	74(70)	690	2529	3.7(46)	32	25	326	13.0(48)	2	50	18	36.0	169	3.4(12)	1	5	—	—	—	Kki	2	216	3131
1946	†NYY-A	13(4)	49	168	3.4	3	3	49	16.3	0	3	2	66.7	14	4.7	0	0	—	—	—	k	—	18	241
1947	Buf-A	3(0)	3	15	5.0	0	—	—	—	—	—	—	—	—	—	—	—	—	—	—	—	—	0	15
AAFC	2	16(4)	52	183	3.5(46)	3	3	49	16.3(48)	0	3	2	66.7	14	4.7(12)	0	0	—	—	—	k	—	18	256

Mandeville, Chris Christopher Scott, DB, 6´1˝/213 lbs; California-Davis; B2/1/1965 Santa Barbara, CA **1987** GB 4 (0) **1988** GB 2 (0) **1989** Was 1 (0) **NFL** 7 (0) [3 yrs]

Mandich, Jim James Michael, TE, 6´2˝/224 lbs; Michigan; 1970: Mia, rnd 2; B7/30/1948 Cleveland, OH

YEAR	TEAM	G(GS, POS)	RUSH	YD	AVG(LG)	TD	REC	YD	AVG(LG)	TD	PASS	COMP	PCT	YD	AVG(LG)	TD	INT	SK	YD	QBR	KPR	OTD	PTS	TAY
1970	†Mia	14	—	—	—	—	1	3	3.0(3)	1	—	—	—	—	—	—	—	—	—	—	k	—	6	-24
1971	†Mia	11	—	—	—	—	3	19	6.3(10)	1	—	—	—	—	—	—	—	—	—	—	—	—	6	15
1972	†Mia	14	—	—	—	—	11	168	15.3(39)	3	—	—	—	—	—	—	—	—	—	—	—	—	18	99
1973	†Mia	14	—	—	—	—	24	302	12.6(28)	4	—	—	—	—	—	—	—	—	—	—	—	—	24	171
1974	†Mia	14(10, TE)	—	—	—	—	33	374	11.3(44)	6	—	—	—	—	—	—	—	—	—	—	—	—	36	217
1975	Mia	14(6, te)	—	—	—	—	21	217	10.3(32)	4	—	—	—	—	—	—	—	—	—	—	—	—	24	129
1976	Mia	14	—	—	—	—	22	260	11.8(31)	4	—	—	—	—	—	—	—	—	—	—	—	—	24	150
1977	Mia	14	—	—	—	—	6	63	10.5(15)	0	—	—	—	—	—	—	—	—	—	—	—	—	0	32
1978	†Pit	10	—	—	—	—	—	—	—	—	—	—	—	—	—	—	—	—	—	—	—	—	—	—
NFL	9	119(16)	—	—	—	—	121	1406	11.6(44)	23	—	—	—	—	—	—	—	—	—	—	k	—	138	788

Mandley, Pete William Henry, WR, 5´10˝/191 lbs; Northern Arizona; 1984: Det, rnd 2; B7/29/1961 Phoenix, AZ **[R]**

YEAR	TEAM	G(GS, POS)	RUSH	YD	AVG(LG)	TD	REC	YD	AVG(LG)	TD	PASS	COMP	PCT	YD	AVG(LG)	TD	INT	SK	YD	QBR	KPR	OTD	PTS	TAY
1984	Det	15(0)	—	—	—	—	3	38	12.7(19)	0	—	—	—	—	—	—	—	—	—	—	kp	—	0	69
1985	Det	16(0)	—	—	—	—	18	316	17.6(37)	0	—	—	—	—	—	—	—	—	—	—	kp	1	6	443
1986	Det	16(0)	—	—	—	—	7	106	15.1(51)	0	—	—	—	—	—	—	—	—	—	—	kp	1	6	275
1987	Det	12(12, WR)	1	3	3.0(3)	0	58	720	12.4(41)	7	—	—	—	—	—	—	—	—	—	—	p	—	42	533
1988	Det	15(14, WR)	6	44	7.3(21)	1	44	617	14.0(56)	4	—	—	—	—	—	—	—	—	—	—	p	—	30	485
1989	KC	13(12, WR)	2	1	0.5(8)	0	35	476	13.6(44)	1	—	—	—	—	—	—	—	—	—	—	kp	—	6	285

YEAR	TEAM	G(GS, POS)	RUSH	YD	AVG(LG)	TD	REC	YD	AVG(LG)	TD	PASS	COMP	PCT	YD	AVG(LG)	TD	INT	SK	YD	QBR	KPR	OTD	PTS	TAY
1990	KC	5(2)	—	—	—	—	7	97	13.9(24)	0	—	—	—	—	—	—	—	—	—	—	k	—	0	40
NFL	7	92(40)	9	48	5.3(21)	1	172	2370	13.8(56)	12	—	—	—	—	—	—	—	—	—	—	kp	2	90	2129

MANESS, JAMES James Lynn, WR, 6´1˝/174 lbs; TCU; 1985: Chi, rnd 3; B5/1/1963 Decatur, TX

YEAR	TEAM	G(GS, POS)	RUSH	YD	AVG(LG)	TD	REC	YD	AVG(LG)	TD	PASS	COMP	PCT	YD	AVG(LG)	TD	INT	SK	YD	QBR	KPR	OTD	PTS	TAY
1985	ChiB	8(0)	—	—	—	—	1	34	34.0(34)	0	—	—	—	—	—	—	—	—	—	—	p	—	0	16

MANFREDA, TONY Anthony Richard, HB, 5´8˝/172 lbs; Holy Cross; B2/19/1904 Meriden, CT, D10/9/1988 Brooksville, FL **1930** Nwk 2 (1)

MANGES, MARK Mark Roy, QB, 6´2˝/210 lbs; Maryland; 1978: LA, rnd 4; B1/10/1956 Cumberland, MD **1978** SL 1

MANGIERO, DINO Dino M., NT-DE, 6´2˝/265 lbs; Rutgers; B12/19/1958 New York, NY **1980** KC 16 (1) **1981** KC 9 (0) **1982** KC 6 (0) **1983** KC 16 (11, NT) **1984**†Sea 15 (0) **1987** NE 2 (0) **NFL** 64 (12) [6 yrs]

MANGUM, JOHN John Wayne, DT, 6´1˝/270 lbs; Mississippi; Southern Mississippi; 1966: Bos, rnd 5; B9/30/1942 Magee, MS, deceased **1966** Bos-A 14 **1967** Bos-A 14 (5, ldt) **NFL** 28 (5) [2 yrs]

MANGUM, JOHN John Wayne, DB, 5´10˝/187 lbs; Alabama; 1990: Chi, rnd 6; B3/16/1967 Magee, MS **1990**†ChiB 10 (0) **1991**†ChiB 16 (1) **1992** ChiB 5 (1) **1993** ChiB 12 (1) **1994**†ChiB 16 (3) **1995** ChiB 11 (1) **1996** ChiB 16 (2) **1997** ChiB 16 (16, FS) **1998** ChiB 3 (0) **NFL** 105 (25) [9 yrs]

MANGUM, KRIS Kristofer Thomas, TE, 6´4˝/249 lbs; Alabama; Mississippi; 1997: Car, rnd 7; B8/15/1973 Magee, MS

YEAR	TEAM	G(GS, POS)	RUSH	YD	AVG(LG)	TD	REC	YD	AVG(LG)	TD	PASS	COMP	PCT	YD	AVG(LG)	TD	INT	SK	YD	QBR	KPR	OTD	PTS	TAY
1997	Car	2(1)	—	—	—	—	4	56	14.0(22)	0	—	—	—	—	—	—	—	—	—	—	—	—	0	28
1998	Car	6(0)	—	—	—	—	1	5	5.0(5)	0	—	—	—	—	—	—	—	—	—	—	—	—	0	3
1999	Car	11(0)	—	—	—	—	1	6	6.0(6)	0	—	—	—	—	—	—	—	—	—	—	k	—	0	-7
2000	Car	15(6, te)	—	—	—	—	19	215	11.3(31)	1	—	—	—	—	—	—	—	—	—	—	—	—	6	113
2001	Car	16(10, TE)	—	—	—	—	15	89	5.9(11)	2	—	—	—	—	—	—	—	—	—	—	—	—	12	55
2002	Car	16(8, te)	—	—	—	—	16	159	9.9(35)	0	—	—	—	—	—	—	—	—	—	—	k	—	0	77
2003	†Car	16(11, TE)	—	—	—	—	17	199	11.7(34)	0	—	—	—	—	—	—	—	—	—	—	—	—	0	100
2004	Car	15(10, TE)	—	—	—	—	34	323	9.5(26)	3	—	—	—	—	—	—	—	—	—	—	—	—	18	177
2005	†Car	14(9, TE)	—	—	—	—	23	202	8.8(24)	2	—	—	—	—	—	—	—	—	—	—	k	—	12	105
NFL	9	111(55)	—	—	—	—	130	1254	9.6(35)	8	—	—	—	—	—	—	—	—	—	—	k	—	48	648

MANGUM, PETE Ernest Glynde, LB, 6´0˝/219 lbs; Mississippi; 1954: NYG, rnd 23; B1/17/1931 Forest, LA **1954** NYG 2 **1960** Den-A 14 (LLB) **NFL** 16 [2 yrs]

MANIACI, JOE Joseph Vincent, B, 6´1˝/212 lbs; Fordham; 1936: Bkn, rnd 6; B1/23/1914 New York, NY **[K]**

YEAR	TEAM	G(GS, POS)	RUSH	YD	AVG(LG)	TD	REC	YD	AVG(LG)	TD	PASS	COMP	PCT	YD	AVG(LG)	TD	INT	SK	YD	QBR	KPR	OTD	PTS	TAY
1936	Bkn	11(5, tb)	35	70	2.0	0	1	30	30.0(30)	0	4	1	25.0	1	0.3(1)	0	0	—	—	—	—	—	0	86
1937	Bkn	11(8, FB)	92	433	4.7	2	3	11	3.7	0	4	1	25.0	0	0.0	0	2	—	—	—	K	—	23	379
1938	Bkn	2(1)	17	57	3.4	0	3	55	18.3	0	2	1	50.0	19	9.5(19)	1	0	—	—	—	—	—	0	99
1938	ChiB	9(1)	71	288	4.1	3	6	72	12.0	0	—	—	—	—	—	—	—	—	—	—	K	—	32	354
1939	ChiB	9(6, FB)	77	544	**7.1**(**75**)	4	—	—	—	—	2	1	50.0	10	5.0(10)	0	0	—	—	—	K	1	37	589
1940	†ChiB✧	11(4, fb)	84	368	4.4	2	1	-5	-5.0(-5)	0	—	—	—	—	—	—	—	—	—	—	Ki	1	19	424
1941	†ChiB✧	7(0)	28	95	3.4(14)	3	2	21	10.5(19)	0	—	—	—	—	—	—	—	—	—	—	K	—	29	136
NFL	6	60(25)	404	1855	4.6(75)	14	16	184	11.5(30)	0	12	4	33.3	30	2.5(19)	1	2	—	—	—	Ki	2	140	2065

MANIECKI, JASON Jason Zbiyniew, DT, 6´4˝/291 lbs; Wisconsin; 1996: TB, rnd 5; B8/15/1972 Rabka, Poland **1996** TB 5 (0) **1997**†TB 10 (0) **1998** TB 3 (0) **NFL** 18 (0) [3 yrs]

MANION, JIMMY James Henry, G, 5´10˝/178 lbs; St. Thomas (MN); B9/20/1904 Jasper, MN, D7/11/1978 Pipestone, MN **1926** Dul 11 (7, lg) **1927** Dul 6 (5, lg) **NFL** 17 (12) [2 yrs]

MANKAT, CARL Carl Robert, E-T-G, 6´3˝/208 lbs; Colgate; B1/13/1904 Dayton, OH, D11/21/1963 Dayton, OH **1928** Day 6 (4, LE) **1929** Day 6 (3) **NFL** 12 (7) [2 yrs]

MANKINS, JIM James Frank, RB, 6´1˝/235 lbs; Oklahoma; Florida State; 1966: GB, rnd 12/Mia, rnd R4; B6/23/1944 Chino, CA, D4/1/2004 Anchorage, AK

YEAR	TEAM	G(GS, POS)	RUSH	YD	AVG(LG)	TD	REC	YD	AVG(LG)	TD	PASS	COMP	PCT	YD	AVG(LG)	TD	INT	SK	YD	QBR	KPR	OTD	PTS	TAY
1967	Atl	11	2	7	3.5(7)	0	1	11	11.0(11)	0	—	—	—	—	—	—	—	—	—	—	k	—	0	10

MANKINS, LOGAN Logan, G, 6´4˝/307 lbs; Fresno State; 2005: NE, rnd 1; B3/10/1982 Catheys Valley, CA **2005**†NE 16 (16, LG)

MANLEY, DEXTER Dexter Keith, DE, 6´3˝/253 lbs; Oklahoma State; 1981: Was, rnd 5; B7/2/1959 Houston, TX **[S]** **1981** Was 16 (9, RDE) **1982**†Was 9 (9, RDE) **1983**†Was 16 (16, RDE) **1984**†Was 15 (14, RDE) **1985** Was 16 (16, RDE) **1986**†Was★16 (16, RDE) **1987**†Was☆11 (10, RDE) **1988** Was 16 (13, RDE) **1989** Was 10 (10, RDE) **1990** Phx 4 (0) **1991** TB 14 (7, lde) **NFL** 143 (120) [11 yrs]

MANLEY, JACK Joseph Jackson, LB-C, 6´3˝/215 lbs; Mississippi State; B9/20/1929 Town Creek, AL **1953** SF 12 (RLB)

MANLEY, JAMES James O., DT, 6´2˝/316 lbs; Vanderbilt; 1996: Min, rnd 2; B7/11/1974 Birmingham, AL **1996**†Min 0 (0)

MANLEY, WILLIE William Leon, T-G, 6´2˝/218 lbs; Oklahoma; 1950: GB, rnd 7; B5/20/1926 Hollis, OK **1951** GB 12 (LT)

YEAR	TEAM	G(GS, POS)	RUSH	YD	AVG(LG)	TD	REC	YD	AVG(LG)	TD	PASS	COMP	PCT	YD	AVG(LG)	TD	INT	SK	YD	QBR	KPR	OTD	PTS	TAY
1950	GB	12	—	—	—	—	5	66	13.2(18)	0	—	—	—	—	—	—	—	—	—	—	—	—	0	33
NFL	2	24	—	—	—	—	5	66	13.2(18)	0	—	—	—	—	—	—	—	—	—	—	—	—	0	33

MANN, BOB Robert, E, 5´11˝/172 lbs; Michigan; B4/8/1924 New Bern, NC

YEAR	TEAM	G(GS, POS)	RUSH	YD	AVG(LG)	TD	REC	YD	AVG(LG)	TD	PASS	COMP	PCT	YD	AVG(LG)	TD	INT	SK	YD	QBR	KPR	OTD	PTS	TAY
1948	Det	12(0, le)	6	46	7.7(23)	0	33	560	17.0(45)	3	—	—	—	—	—	—	—	—	—	—	k	—	18	342
1949	Det	12(11, LE)	—	—	—	—	66	**1014**	15.4(64)	4	—	—	—	—	—	—	—	—	—	—	—	—	24	527
1950	GB	3	—	—	—	—	6	89	14.8(40)	1	—	—	—	—	—	—	—	—	—	—	—	—	6	50
1951	GB	11(LE)	2	9	4.5(9)	0	50	696	13.9(52)	8	—	—	—	—	—	—	—	—	—	—	—	—	48	397
1952	GB	12(LE)	—	—	—	—	30	517	17.2(42)	6	—	—	—	—	—	—	—	—	—	—	—	—	36	289
1953	GB	10(LE)	—	—	—	—	23	327	14.2(45)	2	—	—	—	—	—	—	—	—	—	—	—	—	12	174
1954	GB	2	—	—	—	—	—	—	—	—	—	—	—	—	—	—	—	—	—	—	—	—	—	—
NFL	7	62(11)	8	55	6.9(23)	0	208	3203	15.4(64)	24	—	—	—	—	—	—	—	—	—	—	k	—	144	1778

MANN, CHARLES Charles Andre, DE, 6´6˝/268 lbs; Nevada-Reno; 1983: Was, rnd 3; B4/12/1961 Sacramento, CA **[S]** **1983**†Was 16 (1) **1984**†Was 16 (15, LDE) **1985** Was 16 (16, LDE) **1986**†Was 15 (15, LDE) **1987**†Was★12 (12, LDE) **1988** Was✧14 (13, LDE) **1989** Was★16 (16, LDE) **1990**†Was 15 (15, LDE) **1991**†Was★15 (15, LDE) **1992**†Was 16 (16, LDE) **1993** Was 12 (11, LDE) **1994**†SF 14 (0) **NFL** 177 (145) [12 yrs]

MANN, DAVE David Carl, HB-E, 6´1˝/190 lbs; Oregon State; 1954: ChiC, rnd 7; B6/2/1932 Berkeley, CA **[K]**

YEAR	TEAM	G(GS, POS)	RUSH	YD	AVG(LG)	TD	REC	YD	AVG(LG)	TD	PASS	COMP	PCT	YD	AVG(LG)	TD	INT	SK	YD	QBR	KPR	OTD	PTS	TAY
1955	ChiC	12(RH)	87	336	3.9(65)	4	16	137	8.6(42)	1	10	5	50.0	53	5.3(50)	2	0	—	—	—	KPk	—	33	532
1956	ChiC	12(RH)	45	116	2.6(15)	0	13	170	13.1(23)	1	2	0	0.0	0	0.0	0	1	—	—	—	Pk	—	6	192
1957	ChiC	12	22	92	4.2(25)	0	8	137	17.1(32)	0	1	0	0.0	0	0.0	0	0	—	—	—	Pkp	—	0	164
NFL	3	36	154	544	3.5(65)	4	37	444	12.0(42)	2	13	5	38.5	53	4.1(50)	2	1	—	—	—	KPkp	—	39	888

MANN, ERROL Errol Denis, K, 6´0˝/200 lbs; North Dakota; B6/27/1941 Breckenridge, MN **[K]** **1968** GB 2 **1969** Det 14 **1970**†Det 14 **1971** Det 14 **1972** Det 14 **1973** Det 8 **1974** Det 14 **1975** Det 14 **1976** Det 6 **1976**†Oak 7 **1977**†Oak☆14 **1978** Oak 16 **NFL** 137 [11 yrs]

MANNELLY, PATRICK James Patrick, T, 6´5˝/265 lbs; Duke; 1998: Chi, rnd 6; B4/18/1975 Atlanta, GA **1998** ChiB 16 (0) **1999** ChiB 16 (0) **2000** ChiB 16 (0) **2001**†ChiB 15 (0) **2002** ChiB 14 (0) **2003** ChiB 16 (0) **2004** ChiB 16 (0) **2005**†ChiB 16 (0) **NFL** 125 (0) [8 yrs]

MANNING, AARON Aaron K., DB, 5´10˝/178 lbs; Iowa State; B8/26/1961 Jersey City, NJ **1987** Cin 3 (0)

MANNING, ARCHIE Elisha Archie, QB, 6´3˝/212 lbs; Mississippi; 1971: NO, rnd 1; B5/19/1949 Cleveland, MS

YEAR	TEAM	G(GS, POS)	RUSH	YD	AVG(LG)	TD	REC	YD	AVG(LG)	TD	PASS	COMP	PCT	YD	AVG(LG)	TD	INT	SK	YD	QBR	KPR	OTD	PTS	TAY
1971	NO	12(10, QB)	33	172	5.2(17)	4	1	-7	-7.0(-7)	0	177	86	48.6	1164	6.6(63)	6	9	40	332	60.1	—	—	24	461
1972	NO	14(14, QB)	63	351	5.6(18)	2	—	—	—	—	**448**	**230**	51.3	**2781**	6.2(66)	18	**21**	43	347	64.6	—	—	12	1012
1973	NO	13(13, QB)	63	293	4.7(23)	2	—	—	—	—	267	140	52.4	1642	6.1(65)	10	12	28	177	65.2	—	—	12	704
1974	NO	11(11, QB)	28	204	7.3(26)	1	—	—	—	—	261	134	51.3	1429	5.5(79)	6	16	26	172	49.8	—	—	6	319
1975	NO	13(13, QB)	33	186	5.6(16)	1	—	—	—	—	338	159	47.0	1683	5.0(71)	7	20	49	390	44.3	—	—	6	273
1977	NO	10(9, QB)	39	270	6.9(27)	5	—	—	—	—	205	113	55.1	1284	6.3(59)	8	9	36	288	68.8	—	—	30	642
1978	NO★	16(16, QB)	38	202	5.3(19)	1	—	—	—	—	471	291	**61.8**	3416	7.3(71)	17	16	37	301	81.7	—	—	6	1365
1979	NO✧	16(16, QB)	35	186	5.3(20)	2	—	—	—	—	420	252	60.0	3169	7.5(**85**)	15	20	17	140	75.6	—	—	12	1066
1980	NO	16(16, QB)	23	166	7.2(24)	0	—	—	—	—	509	**309**	60.7	**3716**	7.3(56)	23	20	41	311	81.8	—	—	0	1339
1981	NO	12(11, QB)	2	28	14.0(15)	0	—	—	—	—	232	134	57.8	1447	6.2(55)	5	11	21	164	63.6	—	—	0	337
1982	NO	1(0)	—	—	—	—	—	—	—	—	7	1	14.3	3	0.4(3)	0	2	2	18	—	—	—	0	-79
1982	Hou	6(5, QB)	13	85	6.5(24)	0	—	—	—	—	125	66	52.8	877	7.0(54)	6	6	27	216	71.3	—	—	0	314
1983	Hou	3(3)	2	13	6.5(11)	0	—	—	—	—	88	44	50.0	755	8.6(47)	2	8	11	83	—	—	—	0	81
1983	Min	2(0)	1	-1	-1.0(-1)	0	—	—	—	—	—	—	—	—	—	—	—	—	—	—	—	—	0	-1

YEAR	TEAM	G (GS, POS)	RUSH	YD	AVG (LG)	TD	REC	YD	AVG (LG)	TD	PASS	COMP	PCT	YD	AVG (LG)	TD	INT	SK	YD	QBR	KPR	OTD	PTS	TAY
1984	Min	6(2)	11	42	3.8(16)	0	—	—	—	—	94	52	55.3	545	5.8(56)	2	3	18	153	—	—	—	0	205
NFL	13	151(139)	384	2197	5.7(27)	18	1	-7	-7.0(-7)	0	3642	2011	55.2	23911	6.6(85)	125	173	396	3092	67.1	—	—	108	8034

Manning, Brian Brian Keith, WR, 5´11˝/188 lbs; Stanford; 1997: Mia, rnd 6; B4/22/1975 Kansas City, KS **1998** GB 3 (0)

YEAR	TEAM	G (GS, POS)	RUSH	YD	AVG (LG)	TD	REC	YD	AVG (LG)	TD	PASS	COMP	PCT	YD	AVG (LG)	TD	INT	SK	YD	QBR	KPR	OTD	PTS	TAY
1997	†Mia	7(0)	—	—	—	—	7	85	12.1(21)	0	—	—	—	—	—	—	—	—	—	—	—	—	0	43
NFL	2	10(0)	—	—	—	—	7	85	12.1(21)	0	—	—	—	—	—	—	—	—	—	—	—	—	0	43

Manning, Eli Elisha Nelson, QB, 6´5˝/218 lbs; Mississippi; 2004: SD, rnd 1; B1/3/1981 New Orleans, LA

YEAR	TEAM	G (GS, POS)	RUSH	YD	AVG (LG)	TD	REC	YD	AVG (LG)	TD	PASS	COMP	PCT	YD	AVG (LG)	TD	INT	SK	YD	QBR	KPR	OTD	PTS	TAY
2004	NYG	9(7, qb)	6	35	5.8(15)	0	—	—	—	—	197	95	48.2	1043	5.3(52)	6	9	13	83	55.4	—	—	0	227
2005	†NYG	16(16, QB)	29	80	2.8(14)	1	—	—	—	—	557	294	52.8	3762	6.8(78)	**24**	17	28	184	75.9	—	—	6	1411
NFL	2	25(23)	35	115	3.3(15)	1	—	—	—	—	754	389	51.6	4805	6.4(78)	30	26	41	267	70.5	—	—	6	1638

Manning, Jim James Joseph, TB-HB, 5´11˝/195 lbs; Fordham; B11/20/1900 Holyoke, MA, D8/5/1973 Springfield, MA **1926** Har 6 (5, TB), 18 **1926** Pro 1 (1) **NFL** 7 (6) [1 yr]

Manning, Pete Peter Jonathan, DB, 6´3˝/208 lbs; Wake Forest; 1960: Chi, rnd 8/Bos, rnd 1; B8/11/1937 Hudson, MA **1960** ChiB 6 **1961** ChiB 3 **NFL** 9 [2 yrs]

Manning, Peyton Peyton Williams, QB, 6´5˝/230 lbs; Tennessee; 1998: Ind, rnd 1; B3/24/1976 New Orleans, LA

YEAR	TEAM	G (GS, POS)	RUSH	YD	AVG (LG)	TD	REC	YD	AVG (LG)	TD	PASS	COMP	PCT	YD	AVG (LG)	TD	INT	SK	YD	QBR	KPR	OTD	PTS	TAY
1998	Ind	16(16, QB)	15	62	4.1(15)	0	—	—	—	—	**575**	**326**	56.7	**3739**	6.5(78)	26	**28**	22	109	71.2	—	—	0	942
1999	†Ind★	16(16, QB)	35	73	2.1(13)	2	—	—	—	—	533	**331**	**62.1**	**4135**	**7.8(80)**	**26**	15	14	116	**90.7**	—	—	12	1691
2000	†Ind★	16(16, QB)	37	116	3.1(14)	1	—	—	—	—	571	**357**	62.5	**4413**	7.7(78)	**33**	15	20	131	94.7	—	—	6	1898
2001	Ind	16(16, QB)	35	157	4.5(33)	4	—	—	—	—	547	343	62.7	**4131**	7.6(86)	26	23	29	232	84.1	—	—	24	1473
2002	†Ind✧	16(16, QB)	38	148	3.9(13)	2	—	—	—	—	591	392	66.3	4200	7.1(69)	27	**19**	23	145	88.8	—	—	12	1643
2003	†Ind★	16(16, QB)	28	26	0.9(10)	0	1	-2	-2.0(-2)	0	**566**	**379**	**67.0**	**4267**	7.5(79)	**29**	10	18	107	99.0	—	—	0	1904
2004	†Ind★	16(16, QB)	25	38	1.5(19)	0	—	—	—	—	497	336	**67.6**	4557	**9.2(80)**	**49**	10	13	101	**121.1**	—	—	0	**2162**
2005	†Ind★	16(16, QB)	33	45	1.4(12)	0	—	—	—	—	453	305	67.3	3747	8.3(80)	28	10	17	81	**104.1**	—	—	0	1659
NFL	8	128(128)	246	665	2.7(33)	9	1	-2	-2.0(-2)	0	4333	2769	63.9	33189	7.7(86)	244	130	156	1022	93.5	—	—	54	13369

Manning, Ricky Ricky, DB, 5´9˝/185 lbs; UCLA; 2003: Car, rnd 3; B11/18/1980 Fresno, CA **2003**†Car 16 (7, lcb) **2004** Car 16 (16, LCB) **2005**†Car 16 (3) **NFL** 48 (26) [3 yrs]

Manning, Rosie Roosevelt, DT, 6´5˝/256 lbs; Northeastern State (OK); 1972: Atl, rnd 2; B5/31/1950 Wichita Falls, TX **1972** Atl 3 **1973** Atl 1 **1974** Atl 8 **1975** Atl 2 **1975** Phi 10 **NFL** 24 [4 yrs]

Manning, Roy Roy, LB, 6´2˝/245 lbs; Michigan; B12/4/1981 Saginaw, MI **2005** GB 15 (2)

Manning, Wade Wade Ronald Arthur, WR-DB, 5´11˝/190 lbs; Ohio State; B7/25/1955 Meadville, PA

YEAR	TEAM	G (GS, POS)	RUSH	YD	AVG (LG)	TD	REC	YD	AVG (LG)	TD	PASS	COMP	PCT	YD	AVG (LG)	TD	INT	SK	YD	QBR	KPR	OTD	PTS	TAY
1979	†Dal	9	—	—	—	—	—	—	—	—	—	—	—	—	—	—	—	—	—	—	kp	—	0	45
1981	Den	16(0)	—	—	—	—	3	49	16.3(34)	0	—	—	—	—	—	—	—	—	—	—	kp	—	0	322
1982	Den	9(0)	—	—	—	—	3	46	15.3(30)	0	—	—	—	—	—	—	—	—	—	—	k	—	0	144
NFL	3	34	—	—	—	—	6	95	15.8(34)	0	—	—	—	—	—	—	—	—	—	—	kp	—	0	511

Manoa, Tim Timote Taliai, RB, 6´1˝/227 lbs; Penn State; 1987: Cle, rnd 3; B9/9/1964 Tonga

YEAR	TEAM	G (GS, POS)	RUSH	YD	AVG (LG)	TD	REC	YD	AVG (LG)	TD	PASS	COMP	PCT	YD	AVG (LG)	TD	INT	SK	YD	QBR	KPR	OTD	PTS	TAY
1987	†Cle	12(0)	23	116	5.0(35)	0	1	8	8.0(8)	0	—	—	—	—	—	—	—	—	—	—	k	—	0	104
1988	†Cle	16(4)	99	389	3.9(34)	2	10	54	5.4(9)	0	—	—	—	—	—	—	—	—	—	—	—	—	12	436
1989	†Cle	16(15, FB)	87	289	3.3(22)	3	27	241	8.9(32)	2	—	—	—	—	—	—	—	—	—	—	—	—	30	450
1991	Ind	9(5, rb)	27	144	5.3(44)	1	2	5	2.5(5)	0	—	—	—	—	—	—	—	—	—	—	—	—	6	157
NFL	4	53(24)	236	938	4.0(44)	6	40	308	7.7(32)	2	—	—	—	—	—	—	—	—	—	—	k	—	48	1146

Manor, Brison Brison, DE, 6´4˝/247 lbs; Arkansas; 1975: NYJ, rnd 15; B8/10/1952 Bridgeton, NJ **1977**†Den 13 (1) **1978** Den 16 **1979**†Den 16 (16, RDE) **1980** Den 16 (14, RDE) **1981** Den 16 (0) **1982** Den 9 (0) **1983**†Den 16 (4) **1984** TB 6 (0) **1984** Den 5 (0) **NFL** 113 (35) [8 yrs]

Manos, Sam Samuel John, C, 6´3˝/265 lbs; Marshall; B10/2/1962 New Castle, PA **1987** Cin 3 (3)

Manoukian, Don Donald J., G, 5´9˝/242 lbs; Stanford; B6/9/1934 Merced, CA **1960** Oak-A☆14 (LG)

Mansfield, Jerry Gerald, FB-E-HB, 5´8˝/160 lbs; none; B1894, IA, D10/27/1960 **1920** RI 8 (3) **1921** RI 1 (0) **NFL** 9 (3) [2 yrs]

Mansfield, Ray James Ray, C-DT-LB, 6´3˝/250 lbs; Washington; 1963: Phi, rnd 2/Den, rnd 5; B1/21/1941 Bakersfield, CA, D11/2/1996 Grand Canyon National Park, AZ **1963** Phi 14 **1964** Pit 14 (LDT) **1965** Pit 14 (LDT) **1966** Pit 14 (C) **1967** Pit 14 (C) **1968** Pit 14 (C) **1969** Pit 14 (C) **1970** Pit 14 (C) **1971** Pit 14 (C) **1972**†Pit☆14 (C) **1973**†Pit 14 (C) **1974**†Pit 14 (C) **1975**†Pit☆14 (14, C) **1976**†Pit 14 **NFL** 196 (14) [14 yrs]

Mansfield, Von Edward Von, DB, 5´11˝/185 lbs; Wisconsin; 1982: Atl, rnd 5; B7/12/1960 Anderson, IN **1982** Phi 7 (0) **1987** GB 3 (0) **NFL** 10 (0) [2 yrs]

Manske, Eggs Edgar John, E, 6´0˝/185 lbs; Northwestern; B7/4/1912 Nekoosa, WI, D1/27/2002 Los Angeles, CA

YEAR	TEAM	G (GS, POS)	RUSH	YD	AVG (LG)	TD	REC	YD	AVG (LG)	TD	PASS	COMP	PCT	YD	AVG (LG)	TD	INT	SK	YD	QBR	KPR	OTD	PTS	TAY
1935	Phi☆	10(9, LE)	3	9	3.0	0	9	205	22.8(59)	4	—	—	—	—	—	—	—	—	—	—	—	—	24	132
1936	Phi	12(11, LE)	—	—	—	—	17	325	19.1	0	—	—	—	—	—	—	—	—	—	—	—	—	0	163
1937	†ChiB	11(6, LE)	—	—	—	—	9	225	25.0(64)	3	—	—	—	—	—	—	—	—	—	—	—	1	24	138
1938	Pit	6(4, LE)	5	29	5.8	0	9	113	12.6(23)	1	—	—	—	—	—	—	—	—	—	—	—	1	12	91
1938	ChiB	6(1)	—	—	—	—	10	197	19.7(44)	1	—	—	—	—	—	—	—	—	—	—	—	—	6	104
1939	ChiB	11(1)	—	—	—	—	10	321	32.1(50)	2	—	—	—	—	—	—	—	—	—	—	—	—	12	171
1940	†ChiB✧	9(0)	—	—	—	—	6	81	13.5	0	—	—	—	—	—	—	—	—	—	—	—	—	0	41
NFL	6	65(32)	8	38	4.8	0	70	1467	21.0(64)	11	—	—	—	—	—	—	—	—	—	—	—	2	78	837

Mantell, Joe Joseph, G, none; deceased **1924** Col 1 (1)

Manton, Tilly Taldon, B, 5´11˝/188 lbs; LSU; TCU; B8/24/1909 Ryan, OK, D2/15/1991 Houston, TX **[K]**

YEAR	TEAM	G (GS, POS)	RUSH	YD	AVG (LG)	TD	REC	YD	AVG (LG)	TD	PASS	COMP	PCT	YD	AVG (LG)	TD	INT	SK	YD	QBR	KPR	OTD	PTS	TAY
1936	NYG	12(7, BB)	30	86	2.9	0	5	81	16.2(29)	1	5	3	60.0	27	5.4	0	0	—	—	—	K	—	21	145
1937	NYG	10(0)	8	16	2.0	0	3	15	5.0	0	1	1	100.0	14	14.0(14)	0	0	—	—	—	K	—	27	31
1938	NYG	1(0)	—	—	—	—	—	—	—	—	—	—	—	—	—	—	—	—	—	—	K	—	0	0
1938	Was	7(1)	2	3	1.5	0	—	—	—	—	—	—	—	—	—	—	—	—	—	—	K	—	5	3
1943	Bkn	10(3)	2	-7	-3.5(2)	0	6	26	4.3(8)	0	4	2	50.0	26	6.5(17)	0	0	—	—	—	K	—	0	19
NFL	4	40(11)	42	98	2.3(2)	0	14	122	8.7(29)	1	10	6	60.0	67	6.7(17)	0	0	—	—	—	K	—	53	198

Manucci, Dan Daniel Joseph, QB, 6´2˝/196 lbs; Kansas State; 1979: Buf, rnd 5; B9/3/1957 Erie, PA

YEAR	TEAM	G (GS, POS)	RUSH	YD	AVG (LG)	TD	REC	YD	AVG (LG)	TD	PASS	COMP	PCT	YD	AVG (LG)	TD	INT	SK	YD	QBR	KPR	OTD	PTS	TAY
1979	Buf	14	—	—	—	—	—	—	—	—	—	—	—	—	—	—	—	—	—	—	—	—	—	—
1980	†Buf	2(0)	3	29	9.7(17)	0	—	—	—	—	6	5	83.3	64	10.7(22)	0	0	5	48	—	—	—	0	61
1987	Buf	3(1)	4	6	1.5(9)	0	—	—	—	—	21	7	33.3	68	3.2(15)	0	2	3	27	—	—	—	0	-40
NFL	3	19(1)	7	35	5.0(17)	0	—	—	—	—	27	12	44.4	132	4.9(22)	0	2	8	75	—	—	—	0	21

Manuel, Lionel Lionel, WR, 5´11˝/178 lbs; Pacific; 1984: NYG, rnd 7; B4/13/1962 Rancho Cucamonga, CA

YEAR	TEAM	G (GS, POS)	RUSH	YD	AVG (LG)	TD	REC	YD	AVG (LG)	TD	PASS	COMP	PCT	YD	AVG (LG)	TD	INT	SK	YD	QBR	KPR	OTD	PTS	TAY
1984	†NYG	16(5, wr)	3	2	0.7(11)	0	33	619	18.8(53)	4	—	—	—	—	—	—	—	—	—	—	p	—	24	354
1985	†NYG	12(12, WR)	—	—	—	—	49	859	17.5(51)	5	—	—	—	—	—	—	—	—	—	—	—	—	30	455
1986	†NYG	4(4)	1	25	25.0(25)	0	11	181	16.5(35)	3	—	—	—	—	—	—	—	—	—	—	p	—	18	138
1987	NYG	12(12, WR)	1	-10	-10.0(-10)	0	30	545	18.2(50)	6	—	—	—	—	—	—	—	—	—	—	—	—	36	293
1988	NYG	16(16, WR)	4	27	6.8(14)	0	65	1029	15.8(46)	4	—	—	—	—	—	—	—	—	—	—	—	—	24	562
1989	†NYG	16(12, WR)	—	—	—	—	33	539	16.3(49)	1	—	—	—	—	—	—	—	—	—	—	—	—	6	275
1990	NYG	14(0)	—	—	—	—	11	169	15.4(19)	0	—	—	—	—	—	—	—	—	—	—	—	—	0	85
NFL	7	90(61)	9	44	4.9(25)	0	232	3941	17.0(53)	23	—	—	—	—	—	—	—	—	—	—	p	—	138	2159

Manuel, Marquand Marquand Alexander, DB, 6´0˝/209 lbs; Florida; 2002: Cin, rnd 6; B7/11/1979 Miami, FL **2002** Cin 15 (8, ss) **2003** Cin 13 (1) **2004**†Sea 15 (0) **2005**†Sea 16 (10, FS) **NFL** 59 (19) [4 yrs]

Manuel, Rod Roderick Demond, DE, 6´5˝/290 lbs; Oklahoma; 1997: Pit, rnd 6; B10/8/1974 Fort Worth, TX **1997** Pit 1 (0) **1998** Pit 2 (0) **NFL** 3 (0) [2 yrs]

Manuel, Sean Sandor Lorene, TE, 6´2˝/245 lbs; New Mexico State; 1996: SF, rnd 7; B12/1/1973 Los Gatos, CA

YEAR	TEAM	G (GS, POS)	RUSH	YD	AVG (LG)	TD	REC	YD	AVG (LG)	TD	PASS	COMP	PCT	YD	AVG (LG)	TD	INT	SK	YD	QBR	KPR	OTD	PTS	TAY
1996	SF	11(0)	—	—	—	—	3	18	6.0(7)	0	—	—	—	—	—	—	—	—	—	—	—	—	0	9

Manumaleuga, Frank Toto'a Frank, LB, 6´2˝/245 lbs; UCLA; San Jose State; 1979: KC, rnd 4; B5/9/1956 Salelavalu, Western Samoa **1980** KC 16 (13, LILB) **1981** KC 4 (4)

YEAR	TEAM	G (GS, POS)	RUSH	YD	AVG (LG)	TD	REC	YD	AVG (LG)	TD	PASS	COMP	PCT	YD	AVG (LG)	TD	INT	SK	YD	QBR	KPR	OTD	PTS	TAY
1979	KC	15(LILB)	1	-3	-3.0(-3)	0	—	—	—	—	—	—	—	—	—	—	—	—	—	—	i	—	0	9
NFL	3	35(17)	1	-3	-3.0(-3)	0	—	—	—	—	—	—	—	—	—	—	—	—	—	—	i	1	6	55

YEAR	TEAM	G (GS, POS)	RUSH	YD	AVG (LG)	TD	REC	YD	AVG (LG)	TD	PASS COMP	PCT	YD	AVG (LG)	TD	INT	SK	YD	QBR	KPR	OTD	PTS	TAY

MANUMALEUNA, BRANDON Brandon Michael, TE, 6′2″/288 lbs; Arizona; 2001: SL, rnd 4; B1/4/1980 Torrance, CA

2001	†SL	16(0)	—	—	—	—	1	1	1.0(1)	1	—	—	—	—	—	—	—	—	—	—	—	6	6
2002	SL	16(10, TE)	—	—	—	—	8	106	13.3(27)	1	—	—	—	—	—	—	—	—	—	k	—	6	43
2003	†SL	16(15, TE)	4	15	3.8(8)	0	29	238	8.2(39)	2	—	—	—	—	—	—	—	—	—	—	—	12	144
2004	†SL	16(16, TE)	—	—	—	—	15	174	11.6(48)	1	—	—	—	—	—	—	—	—	—	k	—	6	75
2005	SL	14(14, TE)	1	2	2.0(2)	0	13	129	9.9(33)	1	—	—	—	—	—	—	—	—	—	—	—	6	72
NFL	5	78(55)	5	17	3.4(8)	0	66	648	9.8(48)	6	—	—	—	—	—	—	—	—	—	k	—	36	339

MANUSKY, GREG Gregory, LB, 6′1″/238 lbs; Colgate; B8/12/1966 Wilkes-Barre, PA **1988** Was 7 (0) **1989** Was 16 (7, mlb) **1990**†Was 16 (8, MLB) **1991** Min 16 (0)
1992†Min 11 (0) **1993**†Min 16 (0) **1994**†KC 16 (2) **1995**†KC 16 (1) **1996** KC 16 (1) **1997**†KC 16 (1) **1998** KC 16 (1) **1999** KC 16 (0) **NFL** 178 (21) [12 yrs]

MANUWAI, VINCE Vincent, G, 6′2″/312 lbs; Hawaii; 2003: Jax, rnd 3; B7/12/1980 Honolulu, HI **2003** Jax 15 (14, LG) **2004** Jax 16 (16, LG)

| 2005 | †Jax | 16(16, LG) | — | — | — | — | 1 | -1 | -1.0(-1) | 0 | — | — | — | — | — | — | — | — | — | — | — | 0 | -1 |
| NFL | 3 | 47(46) | — | — | — | — | 1 | -1 | -1.0(-1) | 0 | — | — | — | — | — | — | — | — | — | — | — | 0 | -1 |

MANZINI, BAP Baptiste John, C, 5′11″/195 lbs; St. Vincent; 1943: Phi, rnd 21; B8/27/1920 Treveskyn, PA **1944** Phi 10 (6, C) **1945** Phi 9 (4) **1948** Phi 3 (0) **1948** Det 1 (0)
NFL 23 (10) [3 yrs]

MANZO, JOSEPH Joseph M., T, 6′1″/220 lbs; Boston College; 1941: Det, rnd 8; B2/3/1917 Merced, CA **1945** Det 3 (1)

MAPLE, HOWARD Howard Albert, B, 5′7″/175 lbs; Oregon State; B7/20/1903 Adrian, MO, D11/9/1970 Portland, OR **1930** ChiC 8 (4)

MAPLES, BOBBY Bobby Ray, C-LB, 6′3″/250 lbs; Baylor; 1965: Hou, rnd 4/Cle, rnd 3; B12/28/1942 Mount Vernon, TX, D2/16/1991 Sugar Land, TX **1965** Hou-A 14 (llb)
1966 Hou-A 13 (C) **1967**†Hou-A☆14 (C) **1968** Hou-A☆14 (C) **1969**†Hou-A 14 (C) **1970** Hou 14 (C) **1971** Pit 3 **1972** Den 12 (4) **1973** Den 14 (14, C) **1974** Den☆14 (14, C)
1975 Den 14 (14, C) **1976** Den 14 (14, C) **1977**†Den 14 **1978**†Den 16 (5, c) **NFL** 184 (61) [14 yrs]

MAPLES, BUTCH James Harold, LB, 6′4″/225 lbs; Baylor; 1963: Bal, rnd 12/Den, rnd 13; B1/28/1941 Mount Vernon, TX **1963** Bal 5

MAPLES, TAL Talmadge Robert, C, 6′0″/195 lbs; Tennessee; B12/3/1910 Knoxville, TN, D4/19/1975 Pompano Beach, FL **1934** Cin 4 (0)

MARANGI, GARY Gary Angelo, QB, 6′1″/201 lbs; Boston College; 1974: Buf, rnd 3; B7/29/1952 Rockville Centre, NY

1974	Buf	3	4	20	5.0(16)	0	—	—	—	—	18	9	50.0	140	7.8(44)	2	3	1	1	—	—	0	-20
1975	Buf	5	7	78	11.1(30)	1	—	—	—	—	33	13	39.4	235	7.1(64)	3	2	15	—	—	—	0	131
1976	Buf	11(QB)	39	230	5.9(21)	2	—	—	—	—	232	82	35.3	998	4.3(39)	7	16	22	166	30.8	—	12	144
NFL	3	19	50	328	6.6(30)	2	—	—	—	—	283	104	36.7	1373	4.9(64)	12	21	25	182	36.1	—	12	255

MARAS, JOE Joseph Thomas, C, 6′1″/203 lbs; Duquesne; 1938: Cle, rnd 10; B1/19/1916 Hibbing, MN, D9/17/1990 **1938** Pit 5 (1) **1939** Pit 10 (8, C) **1940** Pit 2 (0)
NFL 17 (9) [3 yrs]

MARCHETTI, GINO Gino John, DE-T-DT, 6′4″/244 lbs; San Francisco; 1952: DalT, rnd 2; B1/2/1927 Smithers, WV; HOF 1972 **1954** Bal◇10 (LDE) **1955** Bal★8 (LDE)
1956 Bal★12 (LDE) **1957** Bal★12 (LDE) **1958**†Bal★12 (LDE) **1959**†Bal★12 (LDE) **1960** Bal★12 (LDE) **1961** Bal★14 (LDE) **1962** Bal★14 (LDE) **1963** Bal★14 (LDE)
1964†Bal★14 (LDE) **1966** Bal 4

1952	DalT	12(2, LDE)	—	—	—	—	1	17	17.0(17)	1	—	—	—	—	—	—	—	—	—	—	—	6	14
1953	Bal	11(RDE)	—	—	—	—	0	19	(19)	0	—	—	—	—	—	—	—	—	—	—	—	0	10
NFL	14	161(2)	—	—	—	—	1	36	36.0(19)	1	—	—	—	—	—	—	—	—	i	—	2	20	19

MARCHI, BASILIO Basilio, G-C, 6′2″/220 lbs; NYU; B7/14/1909 Middleport, OH, deceased **1934** Pit 5 (4) **1942** Phi 7 (1) **NFL** 12 (5) [2 yrs]

MARCHIBRODA, TED Theodore John, QB, 5′10″/178 lbs; St. Bonaventure; Detroit Mercy; 1953: Pit, rnd 1; B3/15/1931 Franklin, PA [C]

1953	Pit	4	1	15	15.0(15)	0	—	—	—	—	22	9	40.9	66	3.0(16)	1	2	—	—	—	k	—	0	-17
1955	Pit	7	6	-1	-0.2(8)	1	—	—	—	—	43	24	55.8	280	6.5(47)	2	3	—	—	—	—	—	6	39
1956	Pit	12(QB)	39	152	3.9(26)	2	—	—	—	—	275	124	45.1	1585	5.8(75)	12	19	—	—	49.4	—	—	12	265
1957	ChiC	7	4	10	2.5(7)	0	—	—	—	—	45	15	33.3	238	5.3(75)	1	5	—	—	—	—	—	0	-66
NFL	4	30	50	176	3.5(26)	3	—	—	—	—	385	172	44.7	2169	5.6(75)	16	29	—	—	45.3	k	—	18	221

MARCHIOL, KEN Kenneth J., LB, 6′2″/248 lbs; Adams State; Mesa; B8/27/1965 Las Vegas, NV **1987** NO 3 (1)

MARCHLEWSKI, FRANK Frank Charles, C, 6′2″/240 lbs; Minnesota; 1965: LA, rnd 5/Buf, rnd 19; B10/14/1943 New Kensington, PA **1965** LARm 14 **1967** Atl 14 (C) **1968** Atl 1
1968 LARm 13 **1969** LARm 5 **1970** Buf 13 (C)

| 1966 | Atl | 14(14, C) | — | — | — | — | 0 | 1 | (1) | 0 | — | — | — | — | — | — | — | — | — | — | — | 0 | 1 |
| NFL | 6 | 74(14) | — | — | — | — | 0 | 1 | (1) | 0 | — | — | — | — | — | — | — | — | — | — | — | 0 | 1 |

MARCINIAK, RON Ronald Joseph, G, 6′1″/218 lbs; Kansas State; 1955: Was, rnd 7; B7/16/1932 Pittsburgh, PA **1955** Was 12

MARCOL, CHESTER Czeslaw Bolesaw, K, 6′0″/190 lbs; Hillsdale; 1972: GB, rnd 2; B10/24/1949 Opole, Poland [K] **1972**†GB★14 **1973** GB 14 **1974** GB★14 **1975** GB 1
1976 GB 14 **1977** GB 14 **1978** GB 16 **1979** GB 10 **1980** GB 5 (0) **1980** Hou 1 (0) **NFL** 103 [9 yrs]

MARCOLINI, HUGO Hugo Francis, B, 6′0″/204 lbs; St. Bonaventure; 1947: Bos, rnd 16; B4/7/1923 Brooklyn, NY, D9/22/1963 Saddle River, NJ

| 1948 | Bkn-A | 10(0) | 5 | 11 | 2.2 | 0 | 2 | 38 | 19.0 | 0 | — | — | — | — | — | — | — | — | — | — | k | — | 0 | 33 |

MARCONI, JOE Joseph George, FB, 6′2″/225 lbs; West Virginia; 1956: LA, rnd 1; B2/6/1934 Fredericktown, PA, D8/22/1992 Chicago, IL

1956	LARm	12	75	298	4.0(23)	7	12	70	5.8(31)	0	—	—	—	—	—	—	—	—	—	—	—	42	403
1957	LARm	10(FB)	104	481	4.6(31)	3	16	171	10.7(61)	1	—	—	—	—	—	—	—	—	—	—	—	24	602
1958	LARm	12(FB)	89	428	4.8(45)	1	10	87	8.7(15)	0	—	—	—	—	—	—	—	—	—	—	—	6	482
1959	LARm	12	52	176	3.4(21)	4	10	81	8.1(80)	0	—	—	—	—	—	—	—	—	—	P	—	30	262
1960	LARm	12(FB)	42	240	5.7(75)	3	9	32	3.6(17)	0	—	—	—	—	—	—	—	—	—	P	—	18	286
1961	LARm	13	36	146	4.1(14)	3	4	20	5.0(8)	1	—	—	—	—	—	—	—	—	—	P	—	24	191
1962	ChiB	13(FB)	89	406	4.6(57)	5	23	306	13.3(63)	1	—	—	—	—	—	—	—	—	—	k	—	36	614
1963	†ChiB◇	14(FB)	118	446	3.8(19)	2	28	335	12.0(63)	2	—	—	—	—	—	—	—	—	—	k	—	24	629
1964	ChiB	13	46	98	2.1(8)	2	20	181	9.1(29)	3	—	—	—	—	—	—	—	—	—	k	—	30	206
1965	ChiB	14	19	47	2.5(10)	0	4	43	10.8(29)	1	—	—	—	—	—	—	—	—	—	—	—	0	69
1966	ChiB	10	3	5	1.7(3)	0	—	—	—	—	—	—	—	—	—	—	—	—	—	—	—	0	5
NFL	11	135	673	2771	4.1(75)	30	136	1326	9.8(80)	9	—	—	—	—	—	—	—	—	—	Pk	—	234	3746

MARCONTELL, ED Edmon Dwight, G, 6′0″/240 lbs; Lamar; 1967: SL, rnd 11; B7/10/1945 Liberty, TX **1967** SL 2 **1967** Hou-A 2 **NFL** 4 [1 yr]

MARCUS, PETE Peter Paul, E, 6′2″/200 lbs; Kentucky; Western Kentucky; B12/17/1917 Rillton, PA, D4/20/1997, OH **1944** Was 3 (0)

MARDERIAN, GREG Gregory John, DT, 6′4″/250 lbs; USC; B1/15/1952 Burbank, CA **1976** Atl 1

MARE, OLINDO Olindo Franco, K, 5′10″/190 lbs; MacMurray; Syracuse; B6/6/1973 Hollywood, FL [K] **1997** Mia 16 (0) **1998**†Mia 16 (0) **1999**†Mia★16 (0) **2000** Mia 16 (0)
2002 Mia 16 (0) **2003** Mia 16 (0) **2004** Mia 11 (0) **2005** Mia 16 (0)

| 2001 | †Mia | 16(0) | 1 | -5 | -5.0(-5) | 0 | — | — | — | — | — | — | — | — | — | — | — | — | — | K | — | 96 | -5 |
| NFL | 9 | 139(0) | 1 | -5 | -5.0(-5) | 0 | — | — | — | — | — | — | — | — | — | — | — | — | — | KP | — | 948 | -5 |

MAREFOS, ANDY Andrew Gust, FB-HB, 6′0″/223 lbs; St. Mary's (CA); 1941: NYG, rnd 12; B7/16/1917 San Francisco, CA, D2/18/1996 Marysville, CA [K]

1941	†NYG	10(0)	60	153	2.6(11)	2	1	5	5.0(5)	0	8	2	25.0	69	8.6(75)	1	1	—	—	—	Ki	—	30	213
1942	NYG	11(4)	48	138	2.9(14)	1	—	—	—	—	29	11	37.9	176	6.1(60)	1	5	—	—	—	Ki	—	6	47
NFL	2	21(4)	108	291	2.7(14)	3	1	5	5.0(5)	0	37	13	35.1	245	6.6(75)	2	6	—	—	—	Ki	—	36	260
1946	LAD-A	13(4)	30	93	3.1	4	1	13	13.0(13)	0	—	—	—	—	—	—	—	—	—	K	—	26	140

MAREK, JODIE Joseph Lee, FB, 5′11″/182 lbs; Texas Tech; B3/7/1916 Temple, TX, D11/19/1986 Temple, TX [K]

| 1943 | Bkn | 8(1) | 2 | 9 | 1.5(7) | 0 | — | — | — | — | — | — | — | — | — | — | — | — | — | K | — | 0 | 9 |

MARELLI, RAY Raymond Charles, G, 5′10″/190 lbs; Notre Dame; B1/23/1901 Rockford, IL, D12/1/1976 Rockford, IL **1928** ChiC 2 (1)

MARGARITA, BOB Henry Robert, HB, 5′11″/178 lbs; Brown; 1944: ChiB, rnd 21; B11/3/1920 Boston, MA

1944	ChiB	10(8, LH)	88	463	5.3(47)	4	15	130	8.7(22)	0	—	—	—	—	—	—	—	—	—	Pkpi	—	24	670
1945	ChiB☆	10(8, LH)	112	497	4.4(38)	3	23	394	17.1(47)	2	—	—	—	—	—	—	—	—	—	Pkpi	—	30	809
1946	†ChiB	1(0)	4	0	0.0(2)	0	—	—	—	—	—	—	—	—	—	—	—	—	—	—	—	0	0
NFL	3	21(16)	204	960	4.7(47)	7	38	524	13.8(48)	2	—	—	—	—	—	—	—	—	—	Pkpi	—	54	1479

YEAR	TEAM	G(GS, POS)	RUSH	YD	AVG(LG)	TD	REC	YD	AVG(LG)	TD	PASS-COMP	PCT	YD	AVG(LG)	TD	INT	SK	YD	QBR	KPR	OTD	PTS	TAY

MARGERUM, KEN Kenneth, WR, 6´0˝/175 lbs; Stanford; 1981: Chi, rnd 3; B10/5/1958 Fountain Valley, CA

1981	ChiB	16(6, wr)	1	11	11.0(11)	0	39	584	15.0(41)	1	—	—	—	—	—	—	—	—	—	—	—	6	308
1982	ChiB	9(9, WR)	—	—	—	—	14	207	14.8(28)	3	—	—	—	—	—	—	—	—	—	—	—	18	119
1983	ChiB	15(9, WR)	1	7	7.0(7)	0	21	336	16.0(60)	2	—	—	—	—	—	—	—	—	—	—	—	12	185
1985	†ChiB	16(2)	1	-7	-7.0(-7)	0	17	190	11.2(20)	2	—	—	—	—	—	—	—	—	—	—	—	12	98
1986	†ChiB	1(1)	—	—	—	—	—	—	—	—	—	—	—	—	—	—	—	—	—	—	—	—	—
1986	SF	5(0)	—	—	—	—	2	12	6.0(6)	0	—	—	—	—	—	—	—	—	—	—	—	0	6
1987	SF	2(0)	—	—	—	—	1	7	7.0(7)	0	—	—	—	—	—	—	—	—	—	—	—	0	4
NFL	6	64(27)	3	11	3.7(11)	0	94	1336	14.2(60)	8	—	—	—	—	—	—	—	—	—	—	—	48	719

MARGUCCI, JOE Joseph Americus, HB-QB, 5´10˝/182 lbs; USC; B9/5/1921 Brooklyn, NY, D4/27/1996 Encino, CA

1947	Det	11(4)	26	97	3.7(26)	1	10	125	12.5(79)	1	31	13	41.9	171	5.5(39)	1	5	—	—	—	kp	—	12	97
1948	Det	11(5, RH)	34	14	0.4(10)	3	36	450	12.5(55)	2	—	—	—	—	—	—	—	—	—	kp	—	30	378
NFL	2	22(9)	60	111	1.9(26)	4	46	575	12.5(79)	3	31	13	41.9	171	5.5(39)	1	5	—	—	—	kp	—	42	475

MARINARO, ED Edward Francis, RB, 6´2˝/212 lbs; Cornell; 1972: Min, rnd 2; B3/31/1950 New York, NY

1972	Min	10(6, FB)	66	223	3.4(19)	0	28	218	7.8(18)	1	—	—	—	—	—	—	—	—	—	—	—	6	337
1973	†Min	13	95	302	3.2(27)	2	26	196	7.5(17)	2	—	—	—	—	—	—	—	—	—	—	—	24	430
1974	†Min	14	44	124	2.8(8)	1	17	132	7.8(20)	1	—	—	—	—	—	—	—	—	—	k	—	12	195
1975	†Min	14(12, FB)	101	358	3.5(14)	1	54	462	8.6(25)	3	—	—	—	—	—	—	—	—	—	k	—	24	610
1976	NYJ	6	77	312	4.1(17)	2	21	168	8.0(35)	0	—	—	—	—	—	—	—	—	—	k	—	12	416
1977	Sea	1	—	—	—	—	—	—	—	—	—	—	—	—	—	—	—	—	—	—	—	—	—
NFL	6	58(18)	383	1319	3.4(27)	6	146	1176	8.1(35)	7	—	—	—	—	—	—	—	—	—	k	—	78	1988

MARINO, DAN Daniel Constantine, QB, 6´4˝/218 lbs; Pittsburgh; 1983: Mia, rnd 1; B9/15/1961 Pittsburgh, PA; HOF 2005

1983	†Mia★	11(9, QB)	28	45	1.6(15)	2	—	—	—	—	296	173	58.4	2210	7.5(85)	20	6	10	80	**96.0**	—	—	12	1030
1984	†Mia★	16(16, QB)	28	-7	-0.3(10)	0	—	—	—	—	564	362	64.2	5084	9.0(80)	48	17	13	120	**108.9**	—	—	0	2095
1985	†Mia★	16(16, QB)	26	-24	-0.9(6)	0	—	—	—	—	567	336	59.3	4137	7.3(73)	30	21	18	157	84.1	—	—	0	1355
1986	Mia★	16(16, QB)	12	-3	-0.3(13)	0	—	—	—	—	623	378	60.7	4746	7.6(85)	44	23	17	119	**92.5**	—	—	0	1670
1987	Mia◇	12(12, QB)	12	-5	-0.4(5)	1	—	—	—	—	444	263	59.2	3245	7.3(59)	26	13	9	77	89.2	—	—	6	1238
1988	Mia☆	16(16, QB)	20	-17	-0.9(6)	0	—	—	—	—	606	354	58.4	4434	7.3(80)	28	23	6	31	80.8	—	—	0	1420
1989	Mia	16(16, QB)	14	-7	-0.5(2)	2	—	—	—	—	550	308	56.0	3997	7.3(78)	24	22	10	86	76.9	—	—	12	1252
1990	†Mia	16(16, QB)	16	29	1.8(15)	0	—	—	—	—	531	306	57.6	3563	6.7(69)	21	11	15	90	82.6	—	—	0	1476
1991	†Mia	16(16, QB)	27	32	1.2(11)	1	—	—	—	—	549	318	57.9	3970	7.2(54)	25	13	27	182	85.8	—	—	6	1632
1992	†Mia☆	16(16, QB)	20	66	3.3(12)	0	—	—	—	—	554	330	59.6	4116	7.4(62)	24	16	28	173	85.1	—	—	0	1604
1993	Mia	5(5, qb)	9	-4	-0.4(4)	1	—	—	—	—	150	91	60.7	1218	8.1(80)	8	3	7	42	—	—	—	6	535
1994	†Mia	16(16, QB)	22	-6	-0.3(10)	1	—	—	—	—	615	385	62.6	4453	7.2(64)	30	17	18	113	89.2	—	—	6	1701
1995	†Mia★	14(14, QB)	11	14	1.3(12)	0	1	-6	-6.0(-6)	0	482	309	64.1	3668	7.6(67)	24	15	22	153	90.8	—	—	0	1365
1996	Mia	13(13, QB)	11	-3	-0.3(7)	0	—	—	—	—	373	221	59.2	2795	7.5(74)	17	9	18	131	87.8	—	—	0	1120
1997	†Mia	16(16, QB)	18	-14	-0.8(1)	0	—	—	—	—	548	319	58.2	3780	6.9(55)	16	11	13	102	80.7	—	—	0	1516
1998	†Mia	16(16, QB)	21	-3	-0.1(10)	1	—	—	—	—	537	310	57.7	3497	6.5(61)	23	15	23	178	80.0	—	—	6	1271
1999	†Mia	11(11, QB)	6	-6	-1.0(0)	0	—	—	—	—	369	204	55.3	2448	6.6(62)	12	17	9	66	67.4	—	—	0	598
NFL	17	242(240)	301	87	0.3(15)	9	1	-6	-6.0(-6)	0	8358	4967	59.4	61361	7.3(85)	420	252	270	1930	86.4	—	—	54	22875

MARINO, VIC Victor Irving, G, 5´8˝/205 lbs; Ohio State; B10/2/1918 Columbus, OH   **1947** Bal-A 13 (4)

MARINOVICH, MARV Marvin Jack, G, 6´3˝/250 lbs; USC; 1962: Oak, rnd 28/LA, rnd 12; B8/6/1939 Watsonville, CA   **1965** Oak-A 1

MARINOVICH, TODD Todd Marvin, QB, 6´4˝/215 lbs; USC; 1991: LARd, rnd 1; B7/4/1969 San Leandro, CA

1991	†LARd	1(1)	3	14	4.7(11)	0	—	—	—	—	40	23	57.5	243	6.1(26)	3	0	—	—	—	—	—	0	151
1992	LARd	7(7, qb)	9	30	3.3(11)	0	—	—	—	—	165	81	49.1	1102	6.7(68)	5	9	20	154	—	—	—	0	246
NFL	2	8(8)	12	44	3.7(11)	0	—	—	—	—	205	104	50.7	1345	6.6(68)	8	9	20	154	—	—	—	0	397

MARION, BROCK Brock Elliot, DB, 5´11˝/200 lbs; Nevada-Reno; 1993: Dal, rnd 7; B6/11/1970 Bakersfield, CA **[RI]**   **1993** †Dal 15 (0)   **1994** †Dal 14 (1)   **1995** †Dal 16 (16, FS)   **1996** Dal 10 (10, FS)   **1997** Dal 16 (16, FS)   **1998** †Mia 16 (16, FS)   **1999** Mia 16 (16, FS)   **2000** †Mia★16 (16, FS)   **2001** †Mia 15 (15, FS)   **2002** Mia◇16 (16, FS)   **2003** Mia◇16 (16, FS)   **2004** Det 16 (16, FS)   **NFL** 182 (154) [12 yrs]

MARION, DUTCH Phillip Eugene, FB, 5´9˝/180 lbs; Washington & Jefferson; Michigan; B6/18/1902, IL, D6/23/1985 Dearborn, MI   **1925** Det 10 (9, FB), 24   **1926** Det 12 (10, FB)   **NFL** 22 (19) [2 yrs]

MARION, FRANK Frank N., LB, 6´3˝/227 lbs; Florida A&M; B3/16/1951 Mount Brook, FL   **1977** NYG 3   **1978** NYG 16 (2)   **1979** NYG 16   **1980** NYG 11 (6, LILB)   **1981** NYG 16 (0)   **1982** NYG 9 (0)   **1983** NYG 10 (0)   **NFL** 81 (8) [7 yrs]

MARION, FRED Fred Donald, DB, 6´2˝/192 lbs; Miami (FL); 1982: NE, rnd 5; B1/2/1959 Gainesville, FL **[I]**   **1982** NE 9 (0)   **1983** NE 16 (0)   **1984** NE 16 (10, FS)   **1985** †NE★16 (16, FS)   **1986** †NE 16 (16, FS)   **1987** NE 12 (12, FS)   **1988** NE 16 (16, FS)   **1989** NE 16 (16, FS)   **1990** NE 16 (16, FS)   **1991** NE 11 (11, FS)   **NFL** 144 (113) [10 yrs]

MARION, JERRY Jerry Richard, WR, 5´10˝/175 lbs; Wyoming; 1966: Pit, rnd 10/Bos, rnd R11; B8/7/1944 Bakersfield, CA

| 1967 | Pit | 7 | — | — | — | — | 1 | 16 | 16.0(16) | 0 | — | — | — | — | — | — | — | — | — | p | — | 0 | 5 |

MARK, GREG Greg, DE-LB, 6´3˝/252 lbs; Miami (FL); 1990: NYG, rnd 3; B7/7/1967 Cherry Hill, NJ   **1990** Mia 4 (0)   **1990** Phi 2 (0)   **NFL** 6 (0) [1 yr]

MARK, LOU Louis, C-E, 6´1˝/210 lbs; North Carolina State; 1938: Bkn, rnd 12; B12/21/1914 New York, NY   **1938** Bkn 11 (9, C)   **1939** Bkn 11 (8, C)   **1940** Bkn 11 (1)   **1945** Bos 6 (1)   **NFL** 39 (19) [4 yrs]

MARKER, CLIFF Clifford Norwell, E-B, 5´10˝/190 lbs; Washington State; B6/13/1903 Tacoma, WA, D7/17/1972 Tacoma, WA   **1926** Can 12 (11, LE), 6   **1927** Fra 2 (2)   **1927** NYG 2 (0)   **NFL** 16 (13) [2 yrs]

MARKER, HARRY Harry J., B, 5´6˝/155 lbs; West Virginia; B9/17/1910 Ligonier, PA, D4/19/1989 Patrick AFB, FL   **1934** Pit 1 (0)

MARKHAM, DALE Dale John, T-DE, 6´8˝/280 lbs; North Dakota; 1980: KC, rnd 11; B7/24/1957 Whitewater, WI   **1980** NYG 1 (0)   **1981** SL 2 (0)   **NFL** 3 (0) [2 yrs]

MARKLAND, JEFF Jeffrey Stuart, TE, 6´3˝/245 lbs; Illinois; B11/16/1965 Los Angeles, CA   **1988** Pit 1 (0)

MARKO, STEVE Stephen, aka Steve Markoe, HB, 6´0˝/200 lbs; none; B5/26/1924 Philadelphia, PA, D5/1985 Cherry Hill, NJ

| 1944 | Bkn | 4(1) | 6 | 10 | 1.7(9) | 0 | — | — | — | — | 7 | 1 | 14.3 | 2 | 0.3(2) | 0 | 2 | — | — | — | k | — | 0 | -34 |

MARKOV, VIC Victor William, T, 6´0˝/215 lbs; Washington; 1938: Cle, rnd 4; B12/18/1915 Chicago, IL, D12/7/1998 Fort Lauderdale, FL   **1938** Cle 10 (4)

MARKOVICH, MARK Mark James, C-G, 6´5˝/256 lbs; Penn State; 1974: SD, rnd 2; B11/7/1952 Latrobe, PA   **1974** SD 9   **1975** SD 14   **1976** Det 14   **1977** Det 4 (4)   **NFL** 41 (4) [4 yrs]

MARKS, LARRY Lawrence Eugene, B, 5´11˝/185 lbs; Indiana; B12/20/1902 Wabash, IN, D1/19/1974 Kalamazoo, MI   **1927** NYY 13 (6, wb)   **1928** GB 11 (2), 12   **NFL** 24 (8), 12 [2 yrs]

MARLER, SETH Michael Seth, K, 6´1˝/200 lbs; Tulane; B3/27/1981 Atlanta, GA **[K]**   **2003** Jax 16 (0)

MARONE, SAL Salvatore John, G, 5´10˝/195 lbs; Manhattan; B8/10/1917 Highland Falls, NJ, D1/12/1975 Walden, NY   **1943** †NYG 8 (0)

MARONIC, DUKE Dusan J., G, 5´9˝/209 lbs; none; B7/13/1921 Steelton, PA, D7/1/1996 Harrisburg, PA   **1944** Phi 9 (0)   **1945** Phi 8 (2)   **1946** Phi 11 (11, RG)   **1947** Phi 4 (0)   **1948** †Phi 12 (1)   **1949** †Phi 11 (2)   **1950** Phi 12 (LG)   **1951** NYG 10   **NFL** 77 (16) [8 yrs]

MARONIC, STEVE Steven Jesse, T, 6´0˝/225 lbs; North Carolina; 1939: Det, rnd 5; B5/30/1917, PA, D5/7/1980 Durham, NC **[K]**   **1939** Det 10 (2)   **1940** Det 5 (1)   **NFL** 15 (3) [2 yrs]

MAROTTI, LOU Louis J., G, 5´10˝/210 lbs; Toledo; B3/28/1915 Chisholm, MN, D10/3/2003 Los Gatos, CA   **1943** ChiC 6 (0)   **1944** C-P 8 (0)   **1945** ChiC 1 (0)   **NFL** 15 (0) [3 yrs]

MARQUARDT, RUBE Reuben Allen, E, 5´9˝/155 lbs; Northwestern; B3/7/1898 Evanston, IL, D2/15/1973 Fort Lauderdale, FL   **1921** ChiC 3 (2), 6

MARQUES, BOB Robert, LB, 6´0˝/220 lbs; Boston University; B5/1/1935   **1960** NYT-A 6

MARRONE, DOUG Douglas Charles, G-C-T, 6´5˝/269 lbs; Syracuse; 1986: LARd, rnd 6; B7/25/1964 Bronx, NY   **1987** Mia 4 (0)   **1989** NO 1 (0)   **NFL** 5 (0) [2 yrs]

MARROW, JOHN Herbert John, G-T, 5´11˝/230 lbs; Nebraska-Kearney; B7/8/1914 Lincoln, NE   **1937** ChiC 11 (0)   **1938** ChiC 5 (0)   **NFL** 16 (0) [2 yrs]

YEAR	TEAM	G(GS, POS)	RUSH	YD	AVG(LG)	TD	REC	YD	AVG(LG)	TD	PASS COMP	PCT	YD	AVG(LG)	TD	INT	SK	YD	QBR	KPR	OTD	PTS	TAY

MARROW, VINCE   Vincent Charles, TE, 6´3˝/251 lbs; Youngstown State; Toledo; 1992: Buf, rnd 11; B8/17/1968 Youngstown, OH

| 1994 | Buf | 10(0) | — | — | — | — | 5 | 44 | 8.8(14) | 0 | | | | | | | | | | — | | 0 | 22 |

MARSALIS, JIM   James J., DB, 5´11˝/194 lbs; Tennessee State; 1969: KC, rnd 1; B10/10/1945 Pascagoula, MS   **1969**†KC-A✧14 (LCB)   **1970** KC★14 (LCB)   **1971**†KC☆14 (LCB)
1972 KC 14 (LCB)   **1973** KC 10   **1974** KC 2   **1975** KC 10 (10, lcb)   **1977** NO 12   **NFL** 90 (10) [8 yrs]

MARSH, AARON   Aaron Washington, WR, 6´1˝/190 lbs; Eastern Kentucky; 1968: Bos, rnd 3; B7/27/1945 Dayton, OH

1968	Bos-A	14(12, WR)	4	8	2.0(11)	0	19	331	17.4(70)	4	—	—	—	—	—	—	—	—	—	k	—	24	208
1969	Bos-A	14(4)	—	—	—	—	8	108	13.5(21)	0	—	—	—	—	—	—	—	—	—	k	—	0	100
NFL	2	28(16)	4	8	2.0(11)	0	27	439	16.3(70)	4	—	—	—	—	—	—	—	—	—	k	—	24	308

MARSH, AMOS   Amos, HB-FB, 6´0˝/218 lbs; Oregon State; B5/7/1939 Williams, AZ; D11/2/1992 San Jose, CA

1961	Dal	14(7, FB)	84	379	4.5(71)	1	21	189	9.0(46)	2	—	—	—	—	—	—	—	—	—	kp	—	18	772
1962	Dal	14(FB)	144	802	**5.6(70)**	6	35	467	13.3(85)	2	—	—	—	—	—	—	—	—	—	kp	1	54	1395
1963	Dal	14(9, HB)	99	483	4.9(41)	5	26	224	8.6(35)	0	—	—	—	—	—	—	—	—	—	k	—	30	677
1964	Dal	12(5, hb)	100	401	4.0(28)	2	15	131	8.7(32)	0	—	—	—	—	—	—	—	—	—	k	—	12	474
1965	Det	13	131	495	3.8(62)	6	17	159	9.4(48)	2	1	0	0.0	0	0.0	0	0	—	—	—	—	48	645
1966	Det	14(HB)	134	433	3.2(27)	3	12	111	9.3(20)	0	—	—	—	—	—	—	—	—	—	—	—	18	519
1967	Det	14(HB)	58	229	3.9(25)	2	7	103	14.7(35)	1	—	—	—	—	—	—	—	—	—	—	—	18	306
NFL	7	95(21)	750	3222	4.3(71)	25	133	1384	10.4(85)	7	1	0	0.0	0	0.0	0	0	—	—	kp	1	198	4785

MARSH, CURT   Curtiss Lane, G, 6´5˝/273 lbs; Washington; 1981: Oak, rnd 1; B8/25/1959 Tacoma, WA   **1981** Oak 11 (11, LG)   **1982**†LARd 9 (9, LG)   **1984**†LARd 16 (7, lg)
1985 LARd 7 (0)   **1986** LARd 2 (2)   **NFL** 45 (29) [5 yrs]

MARSH, CURTIS   Curtiss Joseph, WR, 6´2˝/201 lbs; Utah; 1995: Jax, rnd 7; B11/24/1970 Simi Valley, CA

1995	Jax	9(0)	—	—	—	—	7	127	18.1(34)	0	—	—	—	—	—	—	—	—	—	k	—	0	162
1996	Jax	1(0)	—	—	—	—	—	—	—	—	—	—	—	—	—	—	—	—	—	—	—	—	—
1997	Pit	5(0)	1	2	2.0(2)	0	2	14	7.0(8)	0	—	—	—	—	—	—	—	—	—	—	—	0	9
NFL	3	15(0)	1	2	2.0(2)	0	9	141	15.7(34)	0	—	—	—	—	—	—	—	—	—	k	—	0	171

MARSH, DICK   Victor Burton, G, 6´2˝/210 lbs; Oklahoma; Phillips; B8/29/1906 Sayre, OK, D1/1968   **1933** NYG 1 (0)

MARSH, DOUG   Douglas Walter, TE, 6´3˝/236 lbs; Michigan; 1980: SL, rnd 2; B6/18/1958 Akron, OH

1980	SL	16(16, TE)	—	—	—	—	22	269	12.2(29)	4	—	—	—	—	—	—	—	—	—	—	—	24	155
1981	SL	4(3)	—	—	—	—	6	80	13.3(20)	1	—	—	—	—	—	—	—	—	—	—	—	6	45
1982	†SL	8(8, TE)	—	—	—	—	6	94	15.7(21)	0	—	—	—	—	—	—	—	—	—	—	—	0	47
1983	SL	16(16, TE)	—	—	—	—	32	421	13.2(38)	8	—	—	—	—	—	—	—	—	—	—	—	48	251
1984	SL	16(16, TE)	1	-5	-5.0(-5)	0	39	608	15.6(47)	5	—	—	—	—	—	—	—	—	—	—	—	30	324
1985	SL	16(16, TE)	—	—	—	—	37	355	9.6(23)	1	—	—	—	—	—	—	—	—	—	—	—	6	183
1986	SL	16(15, TE)	1	5	5.0(5)	0	25	313	12.5(27)	0	—	—	—	—	—	—	—	—	—	—	—	0	162
NFL	7	92(90)	2	0	0.0(5)	0	167	2140	12.8(47)	19	—	—	—	—	—	—	—	—	—	—	—	114	1165

MARSH, FRANK   Frank Wayne, DB, 6´2˝/205 lbs; Oregon State; B6/19/1940 LaGrande, OR   **1967** SD-A 1

MARSHALL, AL   Albert Calvin, WR, 6´2˝/190 lbs; Boise State; 1973: Den, rnd 10; B1/7/1951 Monroe, LA

| 1974 | NE | 4 | — | — | — | — | 1 | 17 | 17.0(17) | 1 | — | — | — | — | — | — | — | — | — | — | — | 6 | 14 |

MARSHALL, ALFONSO   Alfonso Lanard, DB, 6´1˝/186 lbs; Miami (FL); 2004: Chi, rnd 7; B1/17/1981 Clewiston, FL   **2004** ChiB 7 (0)

MARSHALL, ANTHONY   Anthony Dewayne, DB, 6´1˝/212 lbs; LSU; B9/16/1970 Mobile, AL   **1994**†ChiB 3 (0)   **1995** ChiB 16 (2)   **1996** ChiB 13 (3)   **1997** ChiB 14 (1)
1998 Phi 16 (0)   **NFL** 62 (6) [5 yrs]

MARSHALL, ARTHUR   Arthur James, WR, 5´11˝/186 lbs; Georgia; B4/29/1969 Fort Gordon, GA

1992	Den	16(1)	11	56	5.1(16)	0	26	493	19.0(80)	1	1	100.0	81	81.0(81)	1	0	—	—	—	kp	—	6	549
1993	†Den	16(9, WR)	—	—	—	—	28	360	12.9(40)	2	1	1	100.0	30	30.0(30)	1	0	—	—	—	—	12	210
1994	NYG	16(0)	2	8	4.0(6)	0	16	219	13.7(34)	0	0	0	0.0	0	0.0	0	0	0	1	8	—	kp	0	138
1995	NYG	15(0)	1	1	1.0(1)	0	17	195	11.5(27)	1	—	—	—	—	—	—	—	—	—	p	—	6	140
1996	NYG	5(0)	—	—	—	—	—	—	—	—	—	—	—	—	—	—	—	—	—	p	—	0	79
NFL	5	68(10)	14	65	4.6(16)	0	87	1267	14.6(80)	4	2	2	100.0	111	55.5(81)	2	0	0	1	8	—	kp	24	1115

MARSHALL, BOBBY   Robert Walls, E, 6´2˝/195 lbs; Minnesota; B3/12/1880 Milwaukee, WI, D8/27/1958 Minneapolis, MN   **1920** RI 9 (7, RE)   **1925** Dul 3 (2, LE)   **NFL** 12 (9) [2 yrs]

MARSHALL, BUD   Richard Arlen, DT-DE, 6´4˝/270 lbs; Baylor; Stephen F. Austin State; 1965: GB, rnd 10/NYJ, rnd R11; B9/12/1941 Carthage, TX   **1965**†GB 14   **1966** Was 6
1966 Atl 6   **1967**†Hou-A 11   **Hou-A** 11   **NFL** 48 [4 yrs]

MARSHALL, CHARLEY   Charles Fred, E, 6´0˝/193 lbs; NYU; B10/17/1906 Richford, NY, D11/1986 Staten Island, NY   **1931** SI 10 (5, RE)   **1932** SI 8 (4)   **NFL** 18 (9) [2 yrs]

MARSHALL, CHUCK   Charles Edward, DB, 6´0˝/180 lbs; Oregon State; B2/13/1939 Hickory, MS   **1962** Den-A 5

MARSHALL, DAVID   David Mark, LB, 6´3˝/220 lbs; Eastern Michigan; B1/3/1961 Cleveland, OH   **1984** Cle 16 (0)   **1987** Mia 2 (0)   **NFL** 18 (0) [2 yrs]

MARSHALL, ED   Edward L., WR, 6´4˝/199 lbs; Cameron; 1971: Cin, rnd 11; B9/23/1947 Corpus Christi, TX

1971	Cin	13	—	—	—	—	2	18	9.0(10)	0	—	—	—	—	—	—	—	—	—	—	—	0	9
1976	NYG	6	—	—	—	—	8	166	20.8(52)	3	—	—	—	—	—	—	—	—	—	—	—	18	98
1977	NYG	14(2)	—	—	—	—	7	178	25.4(82)	0	—	—	—	—	—	—	—	—	—	—	—	0	89
NFL	3	33(2)	—	—	—	—	17	362	21.3(82)	3	—	—	—	—	—	—	—	—	—	—	—	18	196

MARSHALL, GREG   Gregory Edward, DT, 6´3˝/255 lbs; Oregon State; 1978: Phi, rnd 7; B9/9/1956 Beverly, MA   **1978** Bal 2

MARSHALL, HENRY   Henry Howard, WR, 6´2˝/214 lbs; Missouri; 1976: KC, rnd 3; B8/9/1954 Broxton, GA

1976	KC	14(14, WR)	5	101	20.2(59)	1	28	443	15.8(31)	2	—	—	—	—	—	—	—	—	—	k	—	18	328
1977	KC	14(13, WR)	7	11	1.6(7)	0	23	445	19.3(49)	4	—	—	—	—	—	—	—	—	—	—	—	24	254
1978	KC	16(16, WR)	1	-5	-5.0(-5)	0	26	433	16.7(40)	2	—	—	—	—	—	—	—	—	—	—	—	12	222
1979	KC	16(12, WR)	2	34	17.0(23)	1	21	332	15.8(38)	1	—	—	—	—	—	—	—	—	—	—	—	12	215
1980	KC	16(16, WR)	3	22	7.3(9)	0	47	799	17.0(75)	6	—	—	—	—	—	—	—	—	—	—	—	36	452
1981	KC	12(12, WR)	3	69	23.0(34)	0	38	620	16.3(64)	4	1	0	0.0	0	0.0	0	1	—	—	—	—	24	359
1982	KC	9(9, WR)	3	25	8.3(16)	0	40	549	13.7(44)	3	1	0	0.0	0	0.0	0	0	—	—	—	—	18	315
1983	KC	13(9, WR)	—	—	—	—	50	788	15.8(52)	6	0	0	0.0	0	0.0	0	1	9	—	—	—	36	424
1984	KC	16(16, WR)	—	—	—	—	62	912	14.7(37)	4	—	—	—	—	—	—	—	—	—	—	—	24	476
1985	KC	11(9, WR)	—	—	—	—	25	446	17.8(50)	0	—	—	—	—	—	—	—	—	—	—	—	0	223
1986	†KC	16(9, wr)	—	—	—	—	46	652	14.2(31)	1	0	0	0.0	0	0.0	0	0	—	—	—	—	6	331
1987	†KC	12(0)	—	—	—	—	10	126	12.6(19)	0	—	—	—	—	—	—	—	—	—	—	—	0	63
NFL	12	165(135)	24	257	10.7(59)	2	416	6545	15.7(75)	33	3	0	0.0	0	0.0	0	1	9	—	k	—	210	3660

MARSHALL, JAMES   James Carl, DB, 6´0˝/187 lbs; Jackson State; B9/8/1952 Magnolia, MS   **1980** NO 16 (3)

MARSHALL, JIM   James Lawrence, DE, 6´4˝/248 lbs; Ohio State; 1960: Cle, rnd 4/Hou, rnd 2; B12/30/1937 Danville, KY   **1960** Cle 12 (12, RDE)   **1961** Min 14 (14, LDE)
1962 Min 14 (14, RDE)   **1963** Min 14 (14, RDE)   **1964** Min☆14 (14, RDE)   **1965** Min 14 (14, RDE)   **1966** Min 14 (14, RDE)   **1967** Min 14 (14, RDE)   **1968**†Min★14 (14, RDE)
1969†Min★14 (14, RDE)   **1970**†Min 14 (14, RDE)   **1971**†Min☆14 (14, RDE)   **1972** Min 14 (14, RDE)   **1973**†Min 14 (14, RDE)   **1974**†Min 14 (14, RDE)   **1975**†Min 14 (14, RDE)
1976 Min 14 (14, RDE)   **1977**†Min 14 (14, RDE)   **1978**†Min 16 (16, RDE)   **1979** Min 16 (16, RDE)   **NFL** 282 (282) [20 yrs]

MARSHALL, KEYONTA   Keyonta, DT, 6´1˝/290 lbs; Grand Valley State; 2005: Phi, rnd 7; B8/13/1981 Saginaw, MI   **2005** Phi 1 (0)

MARSHALL, LARRY   Lawrence Eugene, DB, 5´10˝/195 lbs; Maryland; 1972: KC, rnd 15; B3/2/1950 Levittown, PA [R]   **1972** KC 11   **1973** KC 10   **1974** Min 5   **1974** Phi 8
1975 Phi 10   **1976** Phi 12   **1977** Phi 14   **1978** KC 2   **1978**†LARm 3   **NFL** 75 [7 yrs]

MARSHALL, LEMAR   Lemar, LB, 6´2˝/227 lbs; Michigan State; B12/17/1976 Cincinnati, OH   **2002** Was 16 (0)   **2003** Was 12 (0)   **2004** Was 16 (14, RLB)   **2005**†Was 16 (16, MLB)
NFL 60 (30) [4 yrs]

YEAR	TEAM	G (GS, POS)	RUSH	YD	AVG (LG)	TD	REC	YD	AVG (LG)	TD	PASS	COMP	PCT	YD	AVG (LG)	TD	INT	SK	YD	QBR	KPR	OTD	PTS	TAY

MARSHALL, LEONARD Leonard Allen, DE-DT, 6´3˝/288 lbs; LSU; 1983: NYG, rnd 2; B10/22/1961 Franklin, LA [S] **1983** NYG 14 (6, rde) **1984**†NYG 16 (11, RDE)
1985†NYG★16 (16, RDE) **1986**†NYG★16 (16, RDE) **1987** NYG 10 (10, RDE) **1988** NYG 15 (14, RDE) **1989**†NYG 16 (16, RDE) **1990**†NYG 16 (6, rde) **1991** NYG 16 (16, RDE)
1992 NYG 14 (12, RDE) **1993** NYJ 12 (12, RDT) **1994** Was 16 (3) **NFL** 177 (138) [12 yrs]

MARSHALL, MARVIN Marvin, WR, 5´10˝/162 lbs; South Carolina State; B6/21/1972 Aschaffenburg, Germany
| 1996 | TB | 5(0) | — | — | — | — | 2 | 27 | 13.5(20) | 0 | — | — | — | — | — | — | — | — | — | — | kp | — | 0 | 128 |

MARSHALL, PHIL Philip Pence, E, 5´8˝/165 lbs; Carnegie Mellon; B3/28/1895 Pittsburgh, PA, D8/9/1962 Kittanning, PA **1920** Cle 1 (1)

MARSHALL, RANDY Randall Donn, DE, 6´5˝/237 lbs; Linfield; 1970: Atl, rnd 6; B12/14/1946 Oregon City, OR **1970** Atl 9 **1971** Atl 6 **NFL** 15 [2 yrs]

MARSHALL, RASHEED Rasheed, WR, 6´0˝/190 lbs; West Virginia; 2005: SF, rnd 5; B7/11/1981 Pittsburgh, PA
| 2005 | SF | 12(0) | 1 | -7 | -7.0(-7) | 0 | 1 | -1 | -1.0(-1) | 0 | — | — | — | — | — | — | — | — | — | — | kp | — | 0 | 93 |

MARSHALL, TANK Charles, DT, 6´4˝/245 lbs; Texas A&M; 1977: NYJ, rnd 3; B1/6/1955 Dallas, TX **1977** NYJ 5

MARSHALL, TORRANCE Torrance James, LB, 6´2˝/255 lbs; Oklahoma; 2001: GB, rnd 3; B6/12/1977 Miami, FL **2001**†GB 14 (1) **2002**†GB 16 (0) **2003**†GB 12 (1) **2004** GB 9 (0)
NFL 51 (2) [4 yrs]

MARSHALL, WARREN Warren Keith, RB, 6´0˝/218 lbs; James Madison; 1987: Den, rnd 6; B7/24/1964 High Point, NC **1987** Den 1 (0)

MARSHALL, WHIT Thomas Whitfield, LB, 6´2˝/247 lbs; Georgia; 1996: Phi, rnd 5; B1/6/1973 Atlanta, GA **1996**†Phi 1 (0) **1999** Atl 15 (0) **NFL** 16 (0) [2 yrs]

MARSHALL, WILBER Wilber Buddhiya, LB, 6´1˝/231 lbs; Florida; 1984: Chi, rnd 1; B4/18/1962 Titusville, FL [I] **1984**†ChiB 15 (1) **1985**†ChiB 16 (15, RLB)
1986†ChiB★16 (15, RLB) **1988** Was 16 (16, RLB) **1989** Was 16 (16, RLB) **1990**†Was 16 (15, RLB) **1991**†Was☆16 (16, LLB) **1992**†Was★16 (16, LLB) **1993** Hou 10 (10, RLB)
1994 Arz 15 (15, RLB) **1995** NYJ 15 (6, rlb)
| 1987 | †ChiB★ | 12(12, RLB) | 1 | 1 | 1.0(1) | 0 | — | — | — | — | — | — | — | — | — | — | — | — | — | S | — | 0 | 1 |
| NFL | 12 | 179(153) | 1 | 1 | 1.0(1) | 0 | — | — | — | — | — | — | — | — | — | — | — | — | — | iS | 4 | 24 | 222 |

MARSTON, RALPH Ralph Fulsom, QB, 5´9˝/170 lbs; Boston University; B2/16/1907 Malden, MA, D12/1967 **1929** Bos 1 (1)

MARTELL, HERMAN Herman Joseph, E, 5´8˝/155 lbs; none; B12/8/1900 Crystal Falls, MI, D10/27/1957 Green Bay, WI **1921** GB 1 (0)

MARTHA, PAUL John Paul, DB-SE-WR-HB, 6´0˝/187 lbs; Pittsburgh; 1964: Pit, rnd 1/Buf, rnd 9; B6/22/1942 Pittsburgh, PA [I] **1966** Pit 12 (RS) **1967** Pit 14 (RS) **1968** Pit 9 (RS)
1969 Pit 14 (RS) **1970** Den 13 (12, FS)
1964	Pit	14(se)	4	12	3.0(10)	0	6	145	24.2(54)	0	—	—	—	—	—	—	—	—	—	—	kp	—	0	95
1965	Pit	12	2	3	1.5(6)	0	11	171	15.5(39)	0	—	—	—	—	—	—	—	—	—	—	—	—	0	89
NFL	7	88(12)	6	15	2.5(10)	0	17	316	18.6(54)	0	—	—	—	—	—	—	—	—	—	—	kpi	1	6	469

MARTIN, AARON Aaron Beamon, DB, 6´0˝/190 lbs; North Carolina Central; B2/10/1942 New Bern, NC **1964** LARm 14 (9, RCB) **1965** LARm 4 (4) **1966** Phi 14
1967 Phi 14 (14, LCB) **1968** Was 14 (RS) **NFL** 60 (27) [5 yrs]

MARTIN, ABE Morris Glenn, B, 6´0˝/185 lbs; Southern Illinois; B1/19/1906 Burnt Prairie, IL, D4/17/1997 Springfield, IL
| 1932 | ChiC | 9(5, WB) | 40 | 152 | 3.8 | 1 | 3 | 99 | 33.0 | 0 | — | — | — | — | — | — | — | — | — | — | — | — | 12 | 217 |

MARTIN, AMOS Anthony Irl, LB, 6´3˝/228 lbs; Louisville; 1972: Min, rnd 6; B1/30/1949 Indianapolis, IN **1972** Min 5 **1973**†Min 14 **1974**†Min 14 **1975** Min 5 **1976**†Min 14
1977 Sea 2 **NFL** 54 [6 yrs]

MARTIN, BILL Jake William, TE, 6´4˝/238 lbs; Georgia Tech; 1964: Chi, rnd 2/KC, rnd 2; B10/27/1942 Gainesville, GA
1964	ChiB	14	—	—	—	—	3	93	31.0(68)	0	—	—	—	—	—	—	—	—	—	—	—	—	0	47
1965	ChiB	14	—	—	—	—	1	-1	-1.0(-1)	0	—	—	—	—	—	—	—	—	—	—	—	—	0	-1
1966	Atl	14(TE)	—	—	—	—	29	330	11.4(35)	0	—	—	—	—	—	—	—	—	—	—	k	—	0	150
1967	Atl	14	—	—	—	—	15	182	12.1(36)	3	—	—	—	—	—	—	—	—	—	—	k	—	18	91
1968	Min	14(7, TE)	—	—	—	—	10	101	10.1(15)	1	—	—	—	—	—	—	—	—	—	—	Pk	—	6	41
NFL	5	70(7)	—	—	—	—	58	705	12.2(68)	4	—	—	—	—	—	—	—	—	—	—	Pk	—	24	328

MARTIN, BILLY William Vance, HB, 5´11˝/197 lbs; Minnesota; 1960: Chi, rnd 4/1961: Buf, rnd 30; B6/6/1938 Chicago, IL, D11/10/1976
1962	ChiB	14	9	28	3.1(12)	1	1	8	8.0(8)	0	—	—	—	—	—	—	—	—	—	—	kp	—	6	159
1963	†ChiB	4	—	—	—	—	—	—	—	—	—	—	—	—	—	—	—	—	—	—	kp	—	0	91
1964	ChiB	14	—	—	—	—	1	9	9.0(9)	0	—	—	—	—	—	—	—	—	—	—	kp	—	0	155
NFL	3	32	9	28	3.1(12)	1	2	17	8.5(9)	0	—	—	—	—	—	—	—	—	—	—	kp	—	6	405

MARTIN, BLANCHE Blanche, FB, 6´0˝/195 lbs; Michigan State; 1960: NYT, rnd 1; B1/16/1937, GA
1960	NYT-A	4	12	35	2.9(14)	0	2	5	2.5(11)	0	—	—	—	—	—	—	—	—	—	—	—	—	0	38
1960	†LAC-A	9	6	23	3.8(10)	0	2	18	9.0(11)	1	—	—	—	—	—	—	—	—	—	—	—	—	6	37
NFL	1	13	18	58	3.2(14)	0	4	23	5.8(11)	1	—	—	—	—	—	—	—	—	—	—	—	—	6	75

MARTIN, BOB Robert A., LB, 6´1˝/217 lbs; Nebraska; 1976: NYJ, rnd 6; B11/14/1953 David City, NE **1976** NYJ 13 (RLB) **1977** NYJ 5 (5, rlb) **1978** NYJ 16 (16, ROLB)
1979 NYJ 2 **1979** SF 13 **NFL** 49 (21) [4 yrs]

MARTIN, CALEB Caleb Snyder, T, 6´4˝/245 lbs; Louisiana Tech; B2/10/1924 Winnsboro, LA, D9/10/1994 Winnsboro, LA **1947** ChiC 10 (0)

MARTIN, CECIL Danyel Cecil, FB, 6´0˝/235 lbs; Wisconsin; 1999: Phi, rnd 6; B7/8/1975 Chicago, IL
1999	Phi	12(5, fb)	3	3	1.0(2)	0	11	22	2.0(9)	0	—	—	—	—	—	—	—	—	—	—	—	—	0	14
2000	†Phi	16(9, FB)	13	77	5.9(23)	0	31	219	7.1(26)	0	—	—	—	—	—	—	—	—	—	—	—	—	0	187
2001	†Phi	16(15, FB)	9	27	3.0(8)	0	24	124	5.2(17)	2	—	—	—	—	—	—	—	—	—	—	—	—	12	99
2002	†Phi	16(9, FB)	1	-4	-4.0(-4)	0	15	126	8.4(53)	0	—	—	—	—	—	—	—	—	—	—	—	—	0	59
2003	TB	1(0)	—	—	—	—	—	—	—	—	—	—	—	—	—	—	—	—	—	—	—	—	—	—
NFL	5	61(38)	26	103	4.0(23)	0	81	491	6.1(53)	2	—	—	—	—	—	—	—	—	—	—	—	—	12	359

MARTIN, CHARLES Charles Milton, NT-DE, 6´4˝/280 lbs; West Alabama; B8/31/1959 Canton, GA, D1/23/2005 Houston, TX **1984** GB 16 (2) **1985** GB 16 (10, NT)
1986 GB 14 (11, NT) **1987** GB 2 (2) **1987**†Hou 12 (3) **1988** Atl 16 (0) **NFL** 76 (28) [5 yrs]

MARTIN, CHRIS Christopher, LB, 6´2˝/236 lbs; Auburn; B12/19/1960 Huntsville, AL **1983** NO 15 (0) **1984** Min 16 (1) **1985** Min 12 (12, ROLB) **1986** Min 16 (10, LLB)
1987†Min 12 (4) **1988** Min 9 (0) **1988** KC 6 (0) **1989** KC 16 (16, LOLB) **1990**†KC 16 (16, LOLB) **1991**†KC 16 (15, LOLB) **1992**†KC 14 (12, LLB/lolb) **1993** LARm 16 (4)
1994 LARm 14 (0) **NFL** 178 (90) [12 yrs]

MARTIN, CHRIS James Christopher, DB, 5´9˝/181 lbs; Northwestern; B9/1/1974 Tampa, FL **1996** ChiB 1 (0)

MARTIN, CURTIS Curtis James, RB, 5´11˝/205 lbs; Pittsburgh; 1995: NE, rnd 3; B5/1/1973 Pittsburgh, PA
1995	NE★	16(15, RB)	**368**	**1487**	4.0(49)	14	30	261	8.7(27)	1	—	—	—	—	—	—	—	—	—	—	—	92	**1763**
1996	†NE★	16(16, RB)	316	1152	3.6(57)	**14**	46	333	7.2(41)	3	—	—	—	—	—	—	—	—	—	—	—	104	1474
1997	NE	13(13, RB)	274	1160	4.2(70)	4	41	296	7.2(22)	0	—	—	—	—	—	—	—	—	—	—	—	30	1353
1998	†NYJ✧	15(15, RB)	369	1287	3.5(60)	8	43	365	8.5(23)	1	—	—	—	—	—	—	—	—	—	—	—	54	1555
1999	NYJ☆	16(16, RB)	367	1464	4.0(50)	5	45	259	5.8(34)	0	—	—	—	—	—	—	—	—	—	—	—	30	1644
2000	NYJ	16(16, RB)	316	1204	3.8(55)	9	70	508	7.3(31)	2	1	1	100.0	18	18.0(18)	1	0	—	—	—	—	66	1572
2001	†NYJ★	16(16, RB)	333	1513	4.5(47)	10	53	320	6.0(27)	0	1	1	100.0	18	18.0(18)	1	0	—	—	—	—	60	1787
2002	†NYJ	16(16, RB)	261	1094	4.2(35)	7	49	362	7.4(28)	0	1	0	0.0	0.0		0	0	0	1	4	—	44	1345
2003	NYJ	16(16, RB)	323	1308	4.0(56)	2	42	262	6.2(29)	0	—	—	—	—	—	—	—	—	—	—	—	12	1459
2004	†NYJ★	16(16, RB)	**371**	**1697**	4.6(25)	12	41	245	6.0(22)	0	—	—	—	—	—	—	—	—	—	—	—	84	1950
2005	NYJ	12(12, RB)	220	735	3.3(49)	5	24	118	4.9(54)	0	—	—	—	—	—	—	—	—	—	—	—	30	844
NFL	11	168(166)	3518	14101	4.0(70)	90	484	3329	6.9(41)	10	2	2	100.0	36	18.0(18)	2	0	1	4	—	—	606	16744

MARTIN, DAVE David Kenneth, LB, 6´0˝/225 lbs; Notre Dame; 1968: Phi, rnd 6; B10/23/1946 Kansas City, KS **1968**†KC-A 2 **1969** ChiB 8 **NFL** 10 [2 yrs]

MARTIN, DAVID David Earl, DB, 5´9˝/191 lbs; Villanova; 1981: Det, rnd 9; B3/15/1959 Philadelphia, PA **1986** SD 4 (0) **1987** Buf 3 (2) **NFL** 7 (2) [2 yrs]

MARTIN, DAVID David Earl, TE, 6´4˝/260 lbs; Tennessee; 2001: GB, rnd 6; B3/13/1979 Fort Campbell, KY
2001	GB	14(1)	—	—	—	—	13	144	11.1(31)	1	—	—	—	—	—	—	—	—	—	—	—	—	6	77
2002	†GB	8(2)	—	—	—	—	8	33	4.1(7)	1	—	—	—	—	—	—	—	—	—	—	—	—	6	22
2003	†GB	16(3)	—	—	—	—	13	79	6.1(14)	2	—	—	—	—	—	—	—	—	—	—	—	—	12	50
2004	GB	9(3)	—	—	—	—	5	88	17.6(35)	0	—	—	—	—	—	—	—	—	—	—	—	—	0	44

YEAR	TEAM	G(GS, POS)	RUSH	YD	AVG(LG)	TD	REC	YD	AVG(LG)	TD	PASS	COMP	PCT	YD	AVG(LG)	TD	INT	SK	YD	QBR	KPR	OTD	PTS	TAY
2005	GB	12(8, TE)	—	—	—	—	27	224	8.3(21)	3	—	—	—	—	—	—	—	—	—	—	—	—	20	127
NFL	5	59(17)	—	—	—	—	66	568	8.6(35)	7	—	—	—	—	—	—	—	—	—	—	—	—	44	319

MARTIN, DEE D'Artagnan Athos, DB, 6´1˝/190 lbs; Kentucky State; 1971: NO, rnd 4; B3/28/1949 New Orleans, LA **1971** NO 14 (LCB)

MARTIN, DERRICK Derrick Roy, DB, 6´0˝/185 lbs; Arizona State; San Jose State; B5/31/1957 Los Angeles, CA **1987** SF 3 (1)

MARTIN, DON Donald Joe, DB, 5´11˝/187 lbs; Yale; 1971: Oak, rnd 7; B9/17/1949 Carrollton, MO **1973** NE 14 (2) **1975** KC 14 **1976** TB 1 **NFL** 29 (2) [3 yrs]

MARTIN, DOUG Douglas, DE-NT, 6´3˝/260 lbs; Washington; 1980: Min, rnd 1; B5/22/1957 Fairfield, CA **[S]** **1980**†Min 11 (1) **1981** Min 16 (9, RDE) **1982**†Min☆9 (9, LDE) **1983** Min 16 (16, LDE) **1984** Min 13 (6, lde) **1985** Min 16 (15, LDE) **1986** Min 15 (15, LDE) **1987**†Min 12 (12, LDE) **1988** Min 11 (10, LDE) **1989**†Min 7 (1) **NFL** 126 (94) [10 yrs]

MARTIN, EMANUEL Emanuel C., DB, 5´11˝/184 lbs; Alabama State; B7/31/1969 Miami, FL **1993** Hou 1 (0) **1996**†Buf 16 (1) **1997** Buf 16 (1) **1998**†Buf 14 (4) **1999** Buf 7 (0) **NFL** 54 (6) [5 yrs]

MARTIN, EMERSON Emerson Floyd, G, 6´3˝/302 lbs; Catawba; Hampton; B5/6/1970 Elizabethtown, NC **1995** Car 2 (1)

MARTIN, ERIC Eric Wayne, WR, 6´1˝/207 lbs; LSU; 1985: NO, rnd 7; B11/8/1961 Van Vleck, TX

YEAR	TEAM	G(GS, POS)	RUSH	YD	AVG(LG)	TD	REC	YD	AVG(LG)	TD	PASS	COMP	PCT	YD	AVG(LG)	TD	INT	SK	YD	QBR	KPR	OTD	PTS	TAY
1985	NO	16(12, WR)	2	-1	-0.5(11)	0	35	522	14.9(50)	4	—	—	—	—	—	—	—	—	—	—	kp	—	24	452
1986	NO	16(11, WR)	—	—	—	—	37	675	18.2(84)	5	—	—	—	—	—	—	—	—	—	—	kp	—	30	489
1987	†NO	15(11, WR)	—	—	—	—	44	778	17.7(67)	7	—	—	—	—	—	—	—	—	—	—	kp	—	42	442
1988	NO✧	16(16, WR)	2	12	6.0(9)	0	85	1083	12.7(40)	7	—	—	—	—	—	—	—	—	—	—	k	—	42	576
1989	NO	16(16, WR)	—	—	—	—	68	1090	16.0(53)	8	—	—	—	—	—	—	—	—	—	—	—	—	48	585
1990	†NO	16(16, WR)	—	—	—	—	63	912	14.5(58)	5	—	—	—	—	—	—	—	—	—	—	—	—	30	481
1991	†NO	16(13, WR)	—	—	—	—	66	803	12.2(30)	4	—	—	—	—	—	—	—	—	—	—	—	—	24	422
1992	†NO	16(11, WR)	—	—	—	—	68	1041	15.3(52)	5	—	—	—	—	—	—	—	—	—	—	—	—	30	546
1993	NO	16(13, WR)	—	—	—	—	66	950	14.4(54)	3	—	—	—	—	—	—	—	—	—	—	—	—	18	490
1994	KC	10(1)	—	—	—	—	21	307	14.6(61)	1	—	—	—	—	—	—	—	—	—	—	—	—	6	159
NFL	10	153(120)	4	11	2.8(11)	0	553	8161	14.8(84)	49	—	—	—	—	—	—	—	—	—	—	kp	—	294	4640

MARTIN, FRANK Frank Hayes, HB, 5´10˝/177 lbs; Alabama; B6/13/1919 Calera, AL, D11/1981 Birmingham, AL

YEAR	TEAM	G(GS, POS)	RUSH	YD	AVG(LG)	TD	REC	YD	AVG(LG)	TD	PASS	COMP	PCT	YD	AVG(LG)	TD	INT	SK	YD	QBR	KPR	OTD	PTS	TAY
1943	Bkn	10(1)	25	50	2.0(22)	0	13	152	11.7(34)	0	4	2	50.0	15	3.8(12)	0	0	—	—	—	pi	—	0	159
1944	Bkn	6(0)	11	18	1.6(10)	0	3	15	5.0(12)	0	1	1	100.0	7	7.0(7)	0	0	—	—	—	Ppi	—	0	25
1945	Bos	3(0, lh)	2	10	5.0(7)	0	1	53	53.0(53)	1	—	—	—	—	—	—	—	—	—	—	—	—	6	42
1945	NYG	3(0)	1	1	1.0(1)	0	3	14	4.7(0)	0	—	—	—	—	—	—	—	—	—	—	kpi	—	0	11
NFL	3	22(1)	39	79	2.0(22)	0	20	234	11.7(53)	1	5	3	60.0	22	4.4(12)	0	0	—	—	—	Pkpi	—	6	236

MARTIN, GEORGE George Dwight, DE, 6´4˝/245 lbs; Oregon; 1975: NYG, rnd 11; B2/16/1953 Greenville, SC **1975** NYG 14 (4) **1976** NYG 14 (LDE) **1977** NYG 10 (LDE) **1978** NYG 16 (16, LDE) **1979** NYG 16 (LDE) **1981**†NYG 16 (6, lde) **1982** NYG 9 (2) **1983** NYG 14 (4) **1984**†NYG 16 (2) **1985**†NYG 16 (0) **1986**†NYG 16 (16, LDE) **1987** NYG 12 (9, LDE) **1988** NYG 16 (0)

YEAR	TEAM	G(GS, POS)	RUSH	YD	AVG(LG)	TD	REC	YD	AVG(LG)	TD	PASS	COMP	PCT	YD	AVG(LG)	TD	INT	SK	YD	QBR	KPR	OTD	PTS	TAY
1980	NYG	16(16, LDE)	—	—	—	—	1	4	4.0(4)	1	—	—	—	—	—	—	—	—	—	—	—	—	6	7
NFL	14	201(75)	—	—	—	—	1	4	4.0(4)	1	—	—	—	—	—	—	—	—	—	—	iS	6	42	186

MARTIN, HARVEY Harvey Banks, DE-DT, 6´5˝/260 lbs; Texas A&M-Commerce; 1973: Dal, rnd 3; B11/16/1950 Dallas, TX, D12/24/2001 Grapevine, TX **1973**†Dal 14 **1974** Dal 14 **1975**†Dal 13 (RDE) **1976**†Dal★14 (14, RDE) **1977**†Dal★14 (RDE) **1978**†Dal✧16 (RDE) **1979**†Dal★16 (RDE) **1980**†Dal 16 (16, RDE) **1981**†Dal 16 (16, RDE) **1982**†Dal☆9 (9, RDE) **1983**†Dal 16 (16, RDE) **NFL** 158 (71) [11 yrs]

MARTIN, HERSH Herschel Herbert, B, 5´11˝/180 lbs; Kansas; B7/16/1906 Springfield, MO, D6/1975 Fort Lauderdale, FL **1929** SI 8 (3) **1930** Nwk 7 (2) **NFL** 15 (5) [2 yrs]

MARTIN, IKE Isaac Roy, TB-HB, 5´11˝/190 lbs; William Jewell; B7/15/1887 Liberty, MO, D7/20/1979 Aurora, OH **1920** Can 7 (3, tb)

MARTIN, JACK John Taber, C, 6´3˝/238 lbs; Princeton; Navy; B4/10/1922 Flint, MI **1947** LARm 11 (0) **1948** LARm 12 (5, c) **1949**†LARm 12 (12, C) **NFL** 35 (17) [3 yrs]

MARTIN, JAMAR Jamar, FB, 5´11˝/256 lbs; Ohio State; 2002: Dal, rnd 4; B4/12/1980 Canton, OH

YEAR	TEAM	G(GS, POS)	RUSH	YD	AVG(LG)	TD	REC	YD	AVG(LG)	TD	PASS	COMP	PCT	YD	AVG(LG)	TD	INT	SK	YD	QBR	KPR	OTD	PTS	TAY
2003	†Dal	14(1)	4	7	1.8(3)	0	2	9	4.5(6)	0	—	—	—	—	—	—	—	—	—	—	—	—	0	12
2004	Mia	9(1)	—	—	—	—	4	15	3.8(7)	0	—	—	—	—	—	—	—	—	—	—	—	—	0	8
NFL	2	23(2)	4	7	1.8(3)	0	6	24	4.0(7)	0	—	—	—	—	—	—	—	—	—	—	—	—	0	19

MARTIN, JAMIE Jamie Blane, QB, 6´2˝/212 lbs; Weber State; B2/8/1970 Orange, CA

YEAR	TEAM	G(GS, POS)	RUSH	YD	AVG(LG)	TD	REC	YD	AVG(LG)	TD	PASS	COMP	PCT	YD	AVG(LG)	TD	INT	SK	YD	QBR	KPR	OTD	PTS	TAY
1996	SL	6(0)	7	14	2.0(11)	0	—	—	—	—	34	23	67.6	241	7.1(22)	3	2	4	34	—	—	—	0	70
1998	Jax	4(1)	5	8	1.6(6)	0	—	—	—	—	45	27	60.0	355	7.9(67)	2	0	2	10	—	—	—	0	196
2000	Jax	5(0)	7	-6	-0.9(2)	0	—	—	—	—	33	22	66.7	307	9.3(65)	2	1	—	—	—	—	—	0	118
2001	SL	5(0)	8	-9	-1.1(-1)	0	—	—	—	—	3	3	100.0	22	7.3(10)	0	0	2	7	—	—	—	0	2
2002	SL	5(2, qb)	5	6	1.2(5)	0	—	—	—	—	195	124	63.6	1216	6.2(33)	7	10	10	77	—	—	—	0	249
2004	SL	1(0)	—	—	—	—	—	—	—	—	30	16	53.3	188	6.3(26)	0	0	2	6	—	—	—	0	94
2005	SL	8(5, qb)	9	6	0.7(9)	0	—	—	—	—	177	124	**70.1**	1277	7.2(83)	5	7	11	78	83.5	—	—	0	390
NFL	7	34(8)	41	19	0.5(11)	0	—	—	—	—	517	339	65.6	3606	7.0(83)	19	20	31	212	81.9	—	—	0	1117

MARTIN, JIM James Richard, G-LB-K, 6´2˝/227 lbs; Notre Dame; 1950: Cle, rnd 2; B4/8/1924 Cleveland, OH, D10/9/2002 Corona, CA **[K]** **1950**†Cle 12 **1952**†Det 12 (LG) **1953**†Det 8 **1954**†Det 12 (RG) **1955** Det 9 **1956** Det 12 **1957**†Det 12 **1958** Det 12 **1959** Det 12 **1960** Det 12 **1961** Det✧13 **1963** Bal 14 **1964** Was 14

YEAR	TEAM	G(GS, POS)	RUSH	YD	AVG(LG)	TD	REC	YD	AVG(LG)	TD	PASS	COMP	PCT	YD	AVG(LG)	TD	INT	SK	YD	QBR	KPR	OTD	PTS	TAY
1951	Det	12	—	—	—	—	0	10	(10)	0	—	—	—	—	—	—	—	—	—	—	—	—	0	5
NFL	14	166	—	—	—	—	0	10	(10)	0	—	—	—	—	—	—	—	—	—	—	Kki	—	434	28

MARTIN, JOE Joseph Peter, HB, none; B2/5/1895 Nashville, TN, D5/6/1965 Louisville, KY **1921** Lou 1 (1)

MARTIN, JOHNNY John Jay, WB-HB, 6´1˝/195 lbs; Oklahoma; 1941: ChiB, rnd 14; B1/8/1916 Nashville, AR, deceased

YEAR	TEAM	G(GS, POS)	RUSH	YD	AVG(LG)	TD	REC	YD	AVG(LG)	TD	PASS	COMP	PCT	YD	AVG(LG)	TD	INT	SK	YD	QBR	KPR	OTD	PTS	TAY
1941	ChiC	9(3)	25	56	2.2(17)	1	4	53	13.3(27)	1	—	—	—	—	—	—	—	—	—	—	Pki	—	12	136
1942	ChiC	11(5, wb)	30	10	0.3(27)	0	22	312	14.2(69)	0	—	—	—	—	—	—	—	—	—	—	Pkpi	—	0	293
1943	ChiC	10(5, WB)	30	98	3.3(15)	0	7	138	19.7(50)	0	—	—	—	—	—	—	—	—	—	—	Pkpi	—	0	272
1944	C-P	1(0)	—	—	—	—	—	—	—	—	—	—	—	—	—	—	—	—	—	—	P	—	0	0
1944	Bos	8(6, RH)	19	-7	-0.4(11)	0	6	56	9.3(16)	0	—	—	—	—	—	—	—	—	—	—	Pkpi	—	0	232
1945	Bos	6(5)	39	191	4.9(76)	1	2	20	10.0(17)	0	—	—	—	—	—	—	—	—	—	—	Pkpi	1	12	310
NFL	5	45(24)	143	348	2.4(76)	2	41	579	14.1(69)	1	—	—	—	—	—	—	—	—	—	—	Pkpi	1	24	1243

MARTIN, KELVIN Kelvin Brian, WR, 5´9˝/163 lbs; Boston College; 1987: Dal, rnd 4; B5/14/1965 San Diego, CA **[R]**

YEAR	TEAM	G(GS, POS)	RUSH	YD	AVG(LG)	TD	REC	YD	AVG(LG)	TD	PASS	COMP	PCT	YD	AVG(LG)	TD	INT	SK	YD	QBR	KPR	OTD	PTS	TAY
1987	Dal	7(0)	—	—	—	—	5	103	20.6(33)	0	—	—	—	—	—	—	—	—	—	—	kp	—	0	215
1988	Dal	16(7, wr)	4	-4	-1.0(11)	0	49	622	12.7(35)	3	—	—	—	—	—	—	—	—	—	—	kp	—	18	492
1989	Dal	11(11, WR)	—	—	—	—	46	644	14.0(46)	2	—	—	—	—	—	—	—	—	—	—	p	—	12	344
1990	Dal	16(16, WR)	4	-2	-0.5(3)	0	64	732	11.4(45)	0	—	—	—	—	—	—	—	—	—	—	p	—	0	385
1991	†Dal	16(0)	—	—	—	—	16	243	15.2(27)	0	—	—	—	—	—	—	—	—	—	—	kp	1	6	273
1992	†Dal☆	16(1)	2	13	6.5(0)	0	32	359	11.2(27)	3	—	—	—	—	—	—	—	—	—	—	kp	2	30	693
1993	Sea	16(14, WR)	1	0	0.0(0)	0	57	798	14.0(53)	5	—	—	—	—	—	—	—	—	—	—	kp	—	30	527
1994	Sea	16(15, WR)	—	—	—	—	56	681	12.2(32)	1	—	—	—	—	—	—	—	—	—	—	kp	—	6	461
1995	Phi	9(1)	—	—	—	—	17	206	12.1(22)	0	—	—	—	—	—	—	—	—	—	—	kp	—	0	320
1996	†Dal	16(1)	—	—	—	—	25	380	15.2(60)	1	—	—	—	—	—	—	—	—	—	—	p	—	6	363
NFL	10	139(66)	11	7	0.6(11)	0	367	4768	13.0(60)	15	—	—	—	—	—	—	—	—	—	—	kp	3	108	4071

MARTIN, LARRY Larry L., DT, 6´2˝/270 lbs; San Diego State; 1965: SD, rnd R2/1966: Min, rnd 13; B4/9/1941 **1966** SD-A 1

MARTIN, MATT Matthew Stuart, G, 6´6˝/272 lbs; Kansas State; B10/12/1979 Long Beach, CA **2002**†Ten 1 (0)

MARTIN, MIKE Michael, WR, 5´10˝/186 lbs; Illinois; 1983: Cin, rnd 8; B11/18/1960 Washington, DC **[R]**

YEAR	TEAM	G(GS, POS)	RUSH	YD	AVG(LG)	TD	REC	YD	AVG(LG)	TD	PASS	COMP	PCT	YD	AVG(LG)	TD	INT	SK	YD	QBR	KPR	OTD	PTS	TAY
1983	Cin	10(0)	2	21	10.5(15)	0	2	22	11.0(12)	0	—	—	—	—	—	—	—	—	—	—	kp	—	0	148
1984	Cin	15(0)	1	3	3.0(3)	0	11	164	14.9(42)	0	—	—	—	—	—	—	—	—	—	—	kp	—	0	442
1985	Cin	16(0)	—	—	—	—	14	187	13.4(28)	0	—	—	—	—	—	—	—	—	—	—	kp	—	0	586
1986	Cin	7(0)	—	—	—	—	3	68	22.7(51)	0	—	—	—	—	—	—	—	—	—	—	kp	—	0	88
1987	Cin	12(0)	—	—	—	—	20	394	19.7(54)	3	—	—	—	—	—	—	—	—	—	—	kp	—	18	355
1988	Cin	4(0)	—	—	—	—	2	22	11.0(15)	1	—	—	—	—	—	—	—	—	—	—	p	—	6	21

YEAR	TEAM	G(GS, POS)	RUSH	YD	AVG(LG)	TD	REC	YD	AVG(LG)	TD	PASS	COMP	PCT	YD	AVG(LG)	TD	INT	SK	YD	QBR	KPR	OTD	PTS	TAY
1989	Cin	12(0)	—	—	—	—	15	160	10.7(21)	2	—	—	—	—	—	—	—	—	—	—	p	—	12	122
NFL	7	76(0)	3	24	8.0(15)	0	67	1017	15.2(54)	6	—	—	—	—	—	—	—	—	—	—	kp	—	36	1762

MARTIN, ROBBIE Robbie Lance, WR, 5´8˝/179 lbs; Cal Poly-San Luis Obispo; 1981: Pit, rnd 4; B12/3/1958 Los Angeles, CA **[R]**

YEAR	TEAM	G(GS, POS)	RUSH	YD	AVG(LG)	TD	REC	YD	AVG(LG)	TD	PASS	COMP	PCT	YD	AVG(LG)	TD	INT	SK	YD	QBR	KPR	OTD	PTS	TAY
1981	Det	16(0)	—	—	—	—	—	—	—	—	—	—	—	—	—	—	—	—	—	—	kp	1	6	334
1982	†Det	9(0)	—	—	—	—	1	18	18.0(18)	0	—	—	—	—	—	—	—	—	—	—	kp	—	0	182
1983	†Det	10(0)	—	—	—	—	—	—	—	—	—	—	—	—	—	—	—	—	—	—	kp	1	6	138
1984	Det	14(0)	1	14	14.0(14)	0	1	9	9.0(9)	0	—	—	—	—	—	—	—	—	—	—	kp	—	0	98
1985	Ind	16(5, wr)	1	23	23.0(23)	0	10	128	12.8(22)	0	—	—	—	—	—	—	—	—	—	—	kp	1	6	498
1986	Ind	7(0)	—	—	—	—	1	41	41.0(41)	0	—	—	—	—	—	—	—	—	—	—	kp	—	0	115
NFL	6	72(5)	2	37	18.5(23)	0	13	196	15.1(41)	0	—	—	—	—	—	—	—	—	—	—	kp	3	18	1364

MARTIN, ROD Roderick Darryl, LB, 6´2˝/218 lbs; USC; 1977: Oak, rnd 12; B4/7/1954 Welch, WV **1977**†Oak 1 **1978** Oak 15 (8, rilb) **1979** Oak 16 (15, ROLB) **1980**†Oak 16 (10, ROLB) **1981** Oak☆16 (16, ROLB) **1982**†LARd☆9 (9, ROLB) **1983**†LARd★16 (16, ROLB) **1984**†LARd★16 (16, ROLB) **1985**†LARd☆16 (16, ROLB) **1986** LARd 16 (16, ROLB) **1987** LARd 12 (12, ROLB) **1988** LARd 16 (13, ROLB) **NFL** 165 (147) [12 yrs]

MARTIN, SALADIN Saladin, DB, 6´0˝/180 lbs; San Diego State; B1/17/1956 San Diego, CA **1980** NYJ 3 (0) **1981**†SF 15 (0) **NFL** 18 (0) [2 yrs]

MARTIN, SAMMY Samson Joseph, WR, 5´11˝/175 lbs; LSU; 1988: NE, rnd 4; B8/21/1965 Gretna, LA **[R]**

YEAR	TEAM	G(GS, POS)	RUSH	YD	AVG(LG)	TD	REC	YD	AVG(LG)	TD	PASS	COMP	PCT	YD	AVG(LG)	TD	INT	SK	YD	QBR	KPR	OTD	PTS	TAY
1988	NE	16(0)	—	—	—	—	4	51	12.8(21)	0	—	—	—	—	—	—	—	—	—	—	k	1	6	306
1989	NE	10(1)	2	20	10.0(13)	0	13	229	17.6(37)	0	—	—	—	—	—	—	—	—	—	—	kp	—	0	428
1990	NE	10(0)	—	—	—	—	4	65	16.3(19)	1	—	—	—	—	—	—	—	—	—	—	kp	—	6	174
1991	NE	4(0)	—	—	—	—	—	—	—	—	—	—	—	—	—	—	—	—	—	—	k	—	0	58
1991	Ind	8(0)	—	—	—	—	5	79	15.8(25)	0	—	—	—	—	—	—	—	—	—	—	k	—	0	165
NFL	4	48(1)	2	20	10.0(13)	0	26	424	16.3(37)	1	—	—	—	—	—	—	—	—	—	—	kp	1	12	1129

MARTIN, STEVE Steven, DE, 6´3˝/260 lbs; Jackson State; B12/24/1964 Angie, LA **1987** Was 3 (3)

MARTIN, STEVE Steven Albert, DT-NT, 6´4˝/292 lbs; Missouri; 1996: Ind, rnd 5; B5/31/1974 St. Paul, MN **1996**†Ind 14 (5, rdt) **1997** Ind 12 (0) **1998** Ind 4 (0) **1998** Phi 9 (3) **1999** Phi 16 (15, RDT) **2000** KC 16 (0) **2001**†NYJ 16 (15, RDT) **2002** NE 14 (6, ldt) **2003** Hou 14 (8, NT) **2004**†Min 12 (0) **NFL** 127 (52) [9 yrs]

MARTIN, TEE Tamaurice Nigel, QB, 6´2˝/225 lbs; Tennessee; 2000: Pit, rnd 5; B7/25/1978 Mobile, AL

YEAR	TEAM	G(GS, POS)	RUSH	YD	AVG(LG)	TD	REC	YD	AVG(LG)	TD	PASS	COMP	PCT	YD	AVG(LG)	TD	INT	SK	YD	QBR	KPR	OTD	PTS	TAY
2001	†Pit	1(0)	1	8	8.0(8)	0	—	—	—	—	—	—	—	—	—	—	—	—	—	—	—	—	0	8
2003	Oak	2(0)	5	28	5.6(8)	0	—	—	—	—	16	6	37.5	69	4.3(17)	0	1	1	5	—	—	—	0	23
NFL	2	3(0)	6	36	6.0(8)	0	—	—	—	—	16	6	37.5	69	4.3(17)	0	1	1	5	—	—	—	0	31

MARTIN, TERRANCE Terrance, DE, 6´2˝/290 lbs; North Carolina State; B7/6/1979 Toano, VA **2003** Hou 12 (1) **2004** Cin 2 (0) **NFL** 14 (1) [2 yrs]

MARTIN, TONY Tony Derick, WR, 6´0˝/181 lbs; Bishop; Mesa; 1989: NYJ, rnd 5; B9/5/1965 Miami, FL

YEAR	TEAM	G(GS, POS)	RUSH	YD	AVG(LG)	TD	REC	YD	AVG(LG)	TD	PASS	COMP	PCT	YD	AVG(LG)	TD	INT	SK	YD	QBR	KPR	OTD	PTS	TAY
1990	†Mia	16(5, wr)	1	8	8.0(8)	0	29	388	13.4(45)	2	—	—	—	—	—	—	—	—	—	—	p	—	12	222
1991	Mia	16(0)	—	—	—	—	27	434	16.1(54)	2	—	—	—	—	—	—	—	—	—	—	p	—	12	232
1992	†Mia	16(3)	1	-2	-2.0(-2)	0	33	553	16.8(55)	2	1	0	0.0	0	0.0	0	0	—	—	—	p	—	12	280
1993	Mia	12(0)	1	6	6.0(6)	0	20	347	17.4(**80**)	3	—	—	—	—	—	—	—	—	—	—	—	—	18	195
1994	†SD	16(1)	2	-9	-4.5(4)	0	50	885	17.7(**99**)	7	1	0	0.0	0	0.0	0	1	—	—	—	k	—	42	476
1995	†SD☆	16(16, WR)	—	—	—	—	90	1224	13.6(51)	6	1	0	0.0	0	0.0	0	0	—	—	—	—	—	36	642
1996	SD★	16(16, WR)	—	—	—	—	85	1171	13.8(55)	**14**	—	—	—	—	—	—	—	—	—	—	—	—	84	656
1997	SD	16(16, WR)	—	—	—	—	63	904	14.3(72)	6	—	—	—	—	—	—	—	—	—	—	—	—	36	482
1998	†Atl	16(16, WR)	—	—	—	—	66	1181	17.9(62)	6	1	0	0.0	0	0.0	0	0	—	—	—	—	—	36	621
1999	†Mia	16(13, WR)	1	-6	-6.0(-6)	0	67	1037	15.5(69)	5	—	—	—	—	—	—	—	—	—	—	—	—	30	538
2000	†Mia	10(5, wr)	—	—	—	—	26	393	15.1(44)	0	—	—	—	—	—	—	—	—	—	—	—	—	0	197
2001	Atl	11(9, WR)	—	—	—	—	37	548	14.8(63)	3	—	—	—	—	—	—	—	—	—	—	—	—	18	289
NFL	12	177(100)	6	-3	-0.5(8)	0	593	9065	15.3(99)	56	4	0	0.0	0	0.0	0	1	—	—	—	kp	—	336	4827

MARTIN, TRACY Tracy Aaron, WR, 6´3˝/205 lbs; North Dakota; 1987: NYJ, rnd 6; B12/4/1964 Minneapolis, MN **1987** NYJ 12 (0)

MARTIN, VERN Vernon Lewis, BB, 5´10˝/195 lbs; Texas; 1942: Pit, rnd 2; B5/2/1920 Amarillo, TX

YEAR	TEAM	G(GS, POS)	RUSH	YD	AVG(LG)	TD	REC	YD	AVG(LG)	TD	PASS	COMP	PCT	YD	AVG(LG)	TD	INT	SK	YD	QBR	KPR	OTD	PTS	TAY
1942	Pit	11(11, BB)	—	—	—	—	7	64	9.1(24)	1	—	—	—	—	—	—	—	—	—	—	—	1	12	37

MARTIN, WAYNE Gerald Wayne, DE-DT, 6´5˝/275 lbs; Arkansas; 1989: NO, rnd 1; B10/26/1965 Forrest City, AR **[S]** **1989** NO 16 (0) **1990** NO 11 (11, LDE) **1991**†NO 16 (16, LDE) **1992**†NO☆16 (16, LDE) **1993** NO 16 (16, LDE) **1994** NO✧16 (16, LDE) **1995** NO 16 (16, RDT) **1996** NO 16 (16, LDT) **1997** NO 16 (16, LDT) **1998** NO 16 (16, LDT) **1999** NO 16 (16, LDT) **NFL** 171 (155) [11 yrs]

MARTINEAU, ROY Daniel Roy, G-FB-T, 6´0˝/210 lbs; Buffalo; Syracuse; B8/20/1900 Syracuse, NY, D10/25/1961 Syracuse, NY **1923** Buf 5 (1), 6 **1924** Roc 5 (5, LG) **1925** Roc 7 (7, RG) **NFL** 17 (13) [3 yrs]

MARTINELLI, PATSY Pasquale Joseph, C, 6´0˝/227 lbs; Scranton; B7/27/1919, D9/7/1992 Rockville, MD **1946** Buf-A 3 (0)

MARTINEZ, GLENN Glenn, WR, 6´1˝/183 lbs; Saginaw Valley State; B11/30/1981 Auburndale, FL

YEAR	TEAM	G(GS, POS)	RUSH	YD	AVG(LG)	TD	REC	YD	AVG(LG)	TD	PASS	COMP	PCT	YD	AVG(LG)	TD	INT	SK	YD	QBR	KPR	OTD	PTS	TAY
2005	Det	5(0)	—	—	—	—	1	11	11.0(11)	0	—	—	—	—	—	—	—	—	—	—	k	—	0	18

MARTINI, RICH Richard William, WR, 6´2˝/185 lbs; California-Davis; 1977: Oak, rnd 7; B11/19/1955 Berkeley, CA

YEAR	TEAM	G(GS, POS)	RUSH	YD	AVG(LG)	TD	REC	YD	AVG(LG)	TD	PASS	COMP	PCT	YD	AVG(LG)	TD	INT	SK	YD	QBR	KPR	OTD	PTS	TAY
1979	Oak	16(4)	—	—	—	—	24	259	10.8(22)	2	—	—	—	—	—	—	—	—	—	—	—	—	12	140
1980	†Oak	16(1)	—	—	—	—	1	36	36.0(36)	0	—	—	—	—	—	—	—	—	—	—	—	—	0	18
1981	NO	12(0)	—	—	—	—	8	72	9.0(15)	0	—	—	—	—	—	—	—	—	—	—	—	—	0	36
NFL	3	44(5)	—	—	—	—	33	367	11.1(36)	2	—	—	—	—	—	—	—	—	—	—	—	—	12	194

MARTINKOVIC, JOHN John George, DE-DT, 6´3˝/241 lbs; Xavier (OH); 1951: Was, rnd 6; B2/4/1927 Hamilton, OH **1951** GB 12 **1952** GB 12 (LDE) **1953** GB✧12 (LDE) **1954** GB★12 (LDE) **1955** GB✧12 (LDE) **1956** GB☆12 (LDE) **1957** NYG 12 (LDE) **NFL** 84 [7 yrs]

MARTINOVICH, PHIL Philip Joseph, FB-G, 5´10˝/220 lbs; Pacific; B2/9/1915 Diamond Springs, CA, D9/22/1964 West Sacramento, CA **[K]** **1939** Det 4 (0) **1940**†ChiB✧2 (0) **NFL** 6 (0) [2 yrs]
1946 Bkn-A 10 (6, fb) **1947** Bkn-A 14 (5, fb) **AAFC** 24 (11) [2 yrs]

MARTS, LONNIE Lonnie, LB, 6´2˝/240 lbs; Tulane; B11/10/1968 New Orleans, LA **1991**†KC 16 (2) **1992**†KC 15 (3) **1993**†KC 16 (15, RILB) **1994** TB 16 (14, LLB) **1995** TB 15 (13, LLB) **1996** TB 16 (13, LLB) **1997** Ten 14 (14, RLB) **1998** Ten 16 (15, RLB) **1999**†Jax 16 (16, MLB) **2000** Jax 7 (3) **NFL** 147 (108) [10 yrs]

MARVASO, TOMMY Thomas Michael, DB, 6´1˝/190 lbs; Cincinnati; 1976: Was, rnd 6; B10/2/1953 Washington, DC **1976** NYJ 12 **1977** NYJ 2 **NFL** 14 [2 yrs]

MARVE, EUGENE Eugene Raymond, LB, 6´2˝/237 lbs; Saginaw Valley State; 1982: Buf, rnd 3; B8/14/1960 Flint, MI **1982** Buf 9 (8, LILB) **1983** Buf 16 (16, RILB) **1984** Buf 16 (16, RILB) **1985** Buf 14 (14, LILB) **1986** Buf 16 (16, LILB) **1987** Buf 5 (4) **1988** TB 16 (16, LILB) **1989** TB 16 (16, LILB) **1990** TB 16 (16, LILB) **1991** TB 16 (4) **1992**†SD 16 (0) **NFL** 156 (126) [11 yrs]

MARVIN, MICKEY Phillip Michael, G, 6´4˝/270 lbs; Tennessee; 1977: Oak, rnd 4; B10/5/1955 Pisgah Forest, NC **1977**†Oak 8 **1978** Oak 14 (14, RG) **1979** Oak 2 (2) **1980**†Oak 16 (16, RG) **1981** Oak 16 (16, RG) **1982**†LARd 9 (9, RG) **1983**†LARd 14 (14, RG) **1984**†LARd 9 (6, rg) **1985**†LARd 15 (15, RG) **1986** LARd 16 (16, RG) **1987** LARd 1 (0) **NFL** 120 (108) [11 yrs]

MARX, GREG Gregory Allen, DE, 6´4˝/260 lbs; Notre Dame; 1973: Atl, rnd 2; B7/18/1950 Detroit, MI **1973** Atl 14

MARYLAND, RUSSELL Russell, DT, 6´1˝/285 lbs; Miami (FL); 1991: Dal, rnd 1; B3/22/1969 Chicago, IL **1991**†Dal 16 (7, RDT) **1992**†Dal 14 (13, RDT) **1993**†Dal✧16 (12, RDT) **1994**†Dal 16 (16, LDT) **1995**†Dal 13 (13, LDT) **1996** Oak 16 (16, LDT) **1997** Oak 16 (16, LDT) **1998** Oak 15 (15, RDT) **1999** Oak 16 (16, LDT) **2000** GB 16 (16, LDT) **NFL** 154 (140) [10 yrs]

MASINI, LEN Leonard Leroy, BB-FB-LB, 6´0˝/225 lbs; Fresno State; B10/6/1922 Firebaugh, CA **1948** SF-A 2 (0)

YEAR	TEAM	G(GS, POS)	RUSH	YD	AVG(LG)	TD	REC	YD	AVG(LG)	TD	PASS	COMP	PCT	YD	AVG(LG)	TD	INT	SK	YD	QBR	KPR	OTD	PTS	TAY
1947	SF-A	11(0)	38	167	4.4	2	—	—	—	—	—	—	—	—	—	—	—	—	—	—	i	—	12	182
1948	LAD-A	11(5, bb)	3	12	4.0	0	1	-1	-1.0(-1)	0	—	—	—	—	—	—	—	—	—	—	—	—	0	12
AAFC	2	24(5)	41	179	4.4	2	1	-1	-1.0(-1)	0	—	—	—	—	—	—	—	—	—	—	i	—	12	194

MASKAS, JOHN John J., G-T, 5´11˝/212 lbs; Virginia Tech; 1947: Buf-A, rnd 10/1944: Bos, rnd 14; B8/15/1920 Chios, Greece, D2/9/1983 Manahawkin, NJ **1947** Buf-A 7 (0) **1949** Buf-A 11 (0) **AAFC** 18 (0) [2 yrs]

YEAR	TEAM	G (GS, POS)	RUSH	YD	AVG (LG)	TD	REC	YD	AVG (LG)	TD	PASS COMP	PCT	YD	AVG (LG)	TD	INT	SK	YD	QBR	KPR	OTD	PTS	TAY

MASLOWSKI, MATT   Matthew Anthony, WR, 6´3˝/210 lbs; San Diego; B9/10/1949 Chicago, IL   **1972** ChiB 1

| 1971 | LARm | 14 | — | — | — | — | 3 | 82 | 27.3(36) | 1 | — | — | — | — | — | — | — | — | — | — | — | 6 | 46 |
| NFL | 2 | 15 | — | — | — | — | 3 | 82 | 27.3(36) | 1 | — | — | — | — | — | — | — | — | — | — | — | 6 | 46 |

MASLOWSKI, MIKE   Michael John, LB, 6´1˝/243 lbs; Wisconsin-LaCrosse; B7/11/1974 Thorp, WI   **1999** KC 15 (0)   **2000** KC 16 (5, llb)   **2001** KC 8 (0)   **2002** KC 16 (16, RLB)
2003 KC 10 (10, MLB)   **NFL** 65 (31) [5 yrs]

MASON, DAVE   David Clayton, DB, 6´0˝/199 lbs; Nebraska; 1973: Min, rnd 10; B11/2/1949 Menomonie, MI   **1973** NE 7 (1)   **1974** GB 12   **NFL** 19 (1) [2 yrs]

MASON, DERRICK   Derrick James, WR, 5´10˝/190 lbs; Michigan State; 1997: Ten, rnd 4; B1/17/1974 Detroit, MI [R]

1997	Ten	16(2)	1	-7	-7.0(-7)	0	14	186	13.3(38)	0	—	—	—	—	—	—	—	—	—	kp	—	0	277
1998	Ten	16(0)	—	—	—	—	25	333	13.3(47)	3	—	—	—	—	—	—	—	—	—	kp	—	18	289
1999	†Ten	13(0)	—	—	—	—	8	89	11.1(31)	0	—	—	—	—	—	—	—	—	—	kp	1	6	340
2000	†Ten★	16(12, WR)	1	1	1.0(1)	0	63	895	14.2(34)	5	—	—	—	—	—	—	—	—	—	kp	1	36	1393
2001	Ten	15(15, WR)	—	—	—	—	73	1128	15.5(71)	9	—	—	—	—	—	—	—	—	—	kp	1	62	885
2002	†Ten	14(14, WR)	—	—	—	—	79	1012	12.8(40)	5	—	—	—	—	—	—	—	—	—	p	—	30	546
2003	†Ten◇	16(16, WR)	3	11	3.7(7)	0	95	1303	13.7(50)	8	—	—	—	—	—	—	—	—	—	kp	—	48	793
2004	Ten	16(16, WR)	1	-3	-3.0(-3)	0	96	1168	12.2(37)	7	—	—	—	—	—	—	—	—	—	p	—	42	589
2005	Bal	16(16, WR)	—	—	—	—	86	1073	12.5(39)	3	—	—	—	—	—	—	—	—	—	—	—	18	552
NFL	9	138(91)	6	2	0.3(7)	0	539	7187	13.3(71)	40	—	—	—	—	—	—	—	—	—	kp	3	260	5662

MASON, EDDIE   Eddie Lee, LB, 6´0˝/245 lbs; North Carolina; 1995: NYJ, rnd 6; B1/9/1972 Siler City, NC   **1995** NYJ 15 (0)   **1998** †Jax 4 (0)   **1999** †Was 14 (0)   **2000** Was 16 (2)
2001 Was 15 (1)   **2002** Was 16 (0)   **NFL** 80 (3) [6 yrs]

MASON, JOEL   Joel Gregory, aka Joel Muleski, E, 6´0˝/199 lbs; Western Michigan; B3/12/1913 Iron River, MI, D10/31/1995 Harper Woods, MI

1939	ChiC	9(5, LE)	—	—	—	—	18	188	10.4	0	—	—	—	—	—	—	—	—	—	—	—	0	94
1942	GB	11(7, LE)	—	—	—	—	7	86	12.3(19)	0	—	—	—	—	—	—	—	—	—	—	—	0	43
1943	GB	10(1)	—	—	—	—	8	107	13.4(21)	2	—	—	—	—	—	—	—	—	—	—	—	12	64
1944	GB	10(2)	—	—	—	—	1	9	9.0(9)	0	—	—	—	—	—	—	—	—	—	—	—	0	5
1945	GB	10(5, RE)	—	—	—	—	—	—	—	—	—	—	—	—	—	—	—	—	—	kp	—	0	15
NFL	5	50(20)	—	—	—	—	34	390	11.5(21)	2	—	—	—	—	—	—	—	—	—	kp	—	12	220

MASON, LARRY   Larry Darnell, RB, 5´11˝/205 lbs; Southern Mississippi; Troy State; B3/21/1961 Birmingham, AL

1987	Cle	3(3)	56	207	3.7(22)	2	5	26	5.2(15)	1	—	—	—	—	—	—	—	—	—	k	—	18	230
1988	GB	15(2)	48	194	4.0(17)	0	8	84	10.5(39)	1	—	—	—	—	—	—	—	—	—	—	—	6	241
NFL	2	18(5)	104	401	3.9(22)	2	13	110	8.5(39)	2	—	—	—	—	—	—	—	—	—	k	—	24	471

MASON, LINDSEY   Lindsey Michael, T, 6´5˝/265 lbs; Kansas; 1978: Oak, rnd 3; B8/1/1955 Baltimore, MD   **1978** Oak 16   **1980** †Oak 16 (0)   **1981** Oak 11 (3)   **1982** SF 9 (8, LT)
1983 Bal 5 (1)   **NFL** 57 (12) [5 yrs]

MASON, SAM   Samuel Anthony, FB, 5´8˝/175 lbs; VMI; B7/21/1899 Hampton, VA, D3/7/1971 Richmond, VA [K]   **1922** Min 2 (1)   **1925** Mil 6 (5, FB), 1   **NFL** 8 (6) [2 yrs]

MASON, TOMMY   Thomas Cyril, RB, 6´1˝/196 lbs; Tulane; 1961: Min, rnd 1/Bos, rnd 1; B7/8/1939 Lake Charles, LA

1961	Min	13	60	226	3.8(21)	3	20	122	6.1(18)	0	1	0	0.0	—	—	—	0	0	—	kp	—	18	621
1962	Min◇	14(11, HB)	167	740	4.4(71)	6	36	603	16.8(74)	6	1	0	0.0	0	0.0	0	0	1	—	kp	—	48	1195
1963	Min★	13(13, HB)	166	763	4.6(70)	7	40	365	9.1(41)	2	—	—	—	—	—	—	—	—	—	kp	—	54	1085
1964	Min★	13(12, HB)	169	691	4.1(51)	4	26	239	9.2(29)	1	1	1	100.0	30	30.0(30)	1	0	—	—	kp	—	30	982
1965	Min	10(9, HB)	141	597	4.2(26)	10	22	321	14.6(72)	1	0	0	0.0	0	0.0	0	1	—	—	kp	—	66	862
1966	Min	7(6, HB)	58	235	4.1(52)	2	7	39	5.6(17)	1	—	—	—	—	—	—	—	—	—	p	—	18	274
1967	†LARm	13	63	213	3.4(16)	0	13	70	5.4(24)	0	3	2	66.7	65	21.7(51)	1	0	—	—	—	—	0	286
1968	LARm	12(7, hb)	108	395	3.7(19)	3	15	144	9.6(31)	0	2	0	0.0	0	—	—	0	—	—	—	—	18	497
1969	†LARm	13	33	135	4.1(17)	1	11	185	16.8(67)	1	0	0	0.0	0	—	—	0	—	—	—	—	12	243
1970	LARm	6	44	123	2.8(13)	0	12	127	10.6(32)	1	—	—	—	—	—	—	—	—	—	—	—	6	192
1971	†Was	10(1)	31	85	2.7(11)	0	12	109	9.1(18)	0	—	—	—	—	—	—	—	—	—	—	—	0	140
NFL	11	124(59)	1040	4203	4.0(71)	32	214	2324	10.9(74)	13	9	3	33.3	95	10.6(51)	2	2	—	—	kp	—	270	6373

MASS, WAYNE   Wayne, T, 6´4˝/240 lbs; Clemson; 1968: Chi, rnd 4; B3/11/1946 Portales, NM   **1968** ChiB 14   **1969** ChiB 11   **1970** ChiB 14 (RT)   **1971** Mia 11   **1972** NE 6
1972 Phi 3   **NFL** 59 [5 yrs]

MASSEY, CARLTON   Carlton, DE, 6´4˝/221 lbs; Southwestern (TX); Texas; 1953: Cle, rnd 8; B1/17/1930 Rockwall, TX, D5/22/1989 Dilley, TX   **1954** †Cle 11 (LDE)
1955 †Cle◇12 (LDE)   **1956** Cle 12 (LDE)   **1957** GB 12 (LDE)   **1958** GB 2   **NFL** 49 [5 yrs]

MASSEY, CHRIS   Christopher Todd, RB, 6´0˝/245 lbs; Marshall; 2002: SL, rnd 7; B8/21/1979 Charleston, WV   **2002** SL 16 (1)   **2004** †SL 16 (0)   **2005** SL 16 (0)

| 2003 | †SL | 16(0) | 1 | -1 | -1.0(-1) | 0 | — | — | — | — | — | — | — | — | — | — | — | — | — | — | — | 0 | -1 |
| NFL | 4 | 64(1) | 1 | -1 | -1.0(-1) | 0 | — | — | — | — | — | — | — | — | — | — | — | — | — | — | — | 0 | -1 |

MASSEY, JIM   James Lee, DB, 5´11˝/198 lbs; Linfield; 1972: LA, rnd 10; B4/24/1948 McMinnville, OR   **1974** NE 1   **1975** NE 14 (1)   **NFL** 15 (1) [2 yrs]

MASSEY, ROBERT   Robert Lee, DB, 5´11˝/200 lbs; North Carolina Central; 1989: NO, rnd 2; B2/27/1967 Rock Hill, SC   **1989** NO 16 (16, LCB)   **1990** †NO 16 (16, LCB)
1991 Phx 12 (5, lcb)   **1992** Phx◇15 (12, LCB)   **1993** Phx 10 (10, RCB)   **1994** †Det 16 (15, RCB)   **1995** †Det 16 (3)   **1996** †Jax 16 (2)   **1997** †NYG 16 (0)   **NFL** 133 (79) [9 yrs]

MASSIE, RICK   Richard Ray, WR, 6´1˝/190 lbs; Kentucky; 1984: Den, rnd S2; B1/16/1960 Paris, KY

1987	Den	9(4)	—	—	—	—	13	244	18.8(39)	4	—	—	—	—	—	—	—	—	—	—	—	24	142
1988	Den	4(0)	—	—	—	—	3	39	13.0(21)	0	—	—	—	—	—	—	—	—	—	—	—	0	20
NFL	2	13(4)	—	—	—	—	16	283	17.7(39)	4	—	—	—	—	—	—	—	—	—	—	—	24	162

MASTERS, BILLY   William Joel, TE-SE, 6´5˝/240 lbs; LSU; 1967: KC, rnd 3; B3/15/1944 Grayson, IA

1967	Buf-A	14(SE)	—	—	—	—	20	274	13.7(28)	2	—	—	—	—	—	—	—	—	—	—	—	12	147
1968	Buf-A	14	6	70	11.7(35)	0	8	101	12.6(21)	0	—	—	—	—	—	—	—	—	—	—	—	0	121
1969	Buf-A	14(TE)	1	-3	-3.0(-3)	0	33	387	11.7(31)	1	—	—	—	—	—	—	—	—	—	—	—	6	196
1970	Den	14(2)	—	—	—	—	9	83	9.2(18)	2	—	—	—	—	—	—	—	—	—	—	—	12	52
1971	Den	14(12, TE)	7	71	10.1(37)	0	27	382	14.1(25)	1	—	—	—	—	—	—	—	—	—	—	—	6	267
1972	Den	14(14, TE)	3	-15	-5.0(0)	0	25	393	15.7(27)	3	—	—	—	—	—	—	—	—	—	—	—	18	197
1973	Den	11	1	-9	-9.0(-9)	0	5	65	13.0(28)	0	—	—	—	—	—	—	—	—	—	—	—	0	24
1974	Den	13(1)	—	—	—	—	—	—	—	—	—	—	—	—	—	—	—	—	—	—	—	0	—
1975	KC	14(TE)	—	—	—	—	24	314	13.1(32)	3	—	—	—	—	—	—	—	—	—	—	—	18	172
1976	KC	10(9, TE)	—	—	—	—	18	269	14.9(30)	3	—	—	—	—	—	—	—	—	—	—	—	18	150
NFL	10	132(38)	18	114	6.3(37)	0	169	2268	13.4(32)	15	—	—	—	—	—	—	—	—	—	—	—	90	1323

MASTERS, BOB   Gregory Robert, HB, 5´11˝/200 lbs; Baylor; B6/26/1911 Comanche, TX, D2/9/1987 Hurst, TX

1937	Phi	9(3)	9	32	3.6	0	4	60	15.0	0	—	—	—	—	—	—	—	—	—	—	—	0	62
1938	Phi	1(1)	—	—	—	—	—	—	—	—	—	—	—	—	—	—	—	—	—	—	—	0	—
1939	Pit	4(1)	9	39	4.3	0	2	12	6.0	0	3	1	33.3	9	3.0(9)	0	1	—	—	—	—	0	10
1942	Phi	3(0)	1	3	3.0(3)	0	—	—	—	—	—	—	—	—	—	—	—	—	—	—	—	0	3
1943	P-P	3(0)	2	6	3.0(0)	0	—	—	—	—	—	—	—	—	—	—	—	—	—	k	—	0	13
1943	ChiB	2(0)	2	10	5.0(10)	0	—	—	—	—	—	—	—	—	—	—	—	—	—	—	—	0	10
1944	ChiB	10(4)	11	9	0.8(6)	0	—	—	—	—	—	—	—	—	—	—	—	—	—	—	—	0	9
NFL	6	32(9)	34	99	2.9(10)	0	6	72	12.0	0	3	1	33.3	9	3.0(9)	0	1	—	—	k	—	0	107

MASTERS, NORM   Norman Donald, T, 6´2˝/249 lbs; Michigan State; 1956: ChiC, rnd 2; B9/19/1933 Detroit, MI   **1957** GB 12 (LT)   **1958** GB 12 (LT)   **1959** GB 12 (LT)   **1960** †GB 12
1961 †GB 14 (rt)   **1962** †GB 14   **1963** GB 14   **1964** GB 14 (LT)   **NFL** 104 [8 yrs]

MASTERS, WALT   Walter Thomas, B, 5´10˝/192 lbs; Pennsylvania; B3/28/1907 Pen Argyl, PA, D7/10/1992 Ottawa, Canada

1936	Phi	2(0)	7	18	2.6	0	—	—	—	—	6	1	16.7	11	1.8(11)	0	1	—	—	—	—	0	-17
1943	ChiC	7(1)	14	-17	-1.2(4)	0	—	—	—	—	45	17	37.8	249	5.5(37)	2	7	—	—	Pkp	—	0	-146
1944	C-P	3(0)	1	-14	-14.0(-14)	0	—	—	—	—	7	1	14.3	13	1.9(13)	0	2	—	—	P	—	0	-88
NFL	3	12(1)	22	-13	-0.6(4)	0	—	—	—	—	58	19	32.8	273	4.7(37)	2	10	—	—	Pkp	—	0	-250

MASTERSON, BERNIE Bernard Edward, QB, 6´3˝/195 lbs; Nebraska; B8/10/1911 Shenandoah, IA, D5/16/1963 Chicago, IL **[K]**

YEAR	TEAM	G (GS, POS)	RUSH	YD	AVG (LG)	TD	REC	YD	AVG (LG)	TD	PASS	COMP	PCT	YD	AVG (LG)	TD	INT	SK	YD	QBR	KPR	OTD	PTS	TAY
1934	†ChiB	9 (0)	4	11	2.8	0	5	89	17.8	1	3	3	100.0	39	13.0	1	0	—	—	—	K	—	7	85
1935	ChiB	12 (11, QB)	21	2	0.1	0	7	99	14.1	1	44	18	40.9	446	10.1	6	4	—	—	—	—	—	6	150
1936	ChiB☆	12 (9, QB)	9	-7	-0.8	2	1	28	28.0 (28)	0	42	10	23.8	292	7.0	3	6	—	—	—	—	—	12	-52
1937	†ChiB	10 (5, QB)	30	-21	-0.7	1	—	—	—	—	72	26	36.1	615	8.5	**9**	7	—	—	—	—	—	6	62
1938	ChiB	11 (3, QB)	13	-16	-1.2	0	1	4	4.0 (4)	0	112	46	41.1	848	**7.6**	5	9	—	—	—	—	—	0	75
1939	ChiB	11 (7, QB)	21	-31	-1.5	2	2	37	18.5	0	113	44	38.9	914	**8.1**	8	9	—	—	—	—	—	12	145
1940	†ChiB✧	7 (2)	10	-7	-0.7	1	—	—	—	—	23	9	39.1	212	9.2	2	3	—	—	—	K	—	7	-1
NFL	7	72 (37)	108	-69	-0.6	6	16	257	16.1 (28)	2	409	156	38.1	3366	8.2	34	38	—	—	—	K	—	50	463

MASTERSON, BOB Robert Patrick, E, 6´1˝/213 lbs; Miami (FL); 1938: ChiB, rnd 6; B1/5/1915 North Branch, NJ, D7/1/1994 Miami, FL **[K]**

YEAR	TEAM	G (GS, POS)	RUSH	YD	AVG (LG)	TD	REC	YD	AVG (LG)	TD	PASS	COMP	PCT	YD	AVG (LG)	TD	INT	SK	YD	QBR	KPR	OTD	PTS	TAY
1938	Was	11 (1)	3	89	29.7	0	10	213	21.3	1	—	—	—	—	—	—	—	—	—	—	K	—	14	201
1939	Was	10 (3)	—	—	—	—	10	114	11.4	1	—	—	—	—	—	—	—	—	—	—	K	—	15	62
1940	†Was	11 (1)	1	0	0.0	0	18	283	15.7	4	—	—	—	—	—	—	—	—	—	—	K	—	42	162
1941	Was	11 (9, LE)	1	3	3.0 (3)	0	11	135	12.3 (25)	1	—	—	—	—	—	—	—	—	—	—	Kki	—	23	61
1942	†Was★	11 (11, LE)	3	12	4.0 (11)	0	22	308	14.0 (33)	2	1	0	0.0	0	0.0	0	0	—	—	—	Kk	—	32	176
1943	†Was☆	10 (8, LE)	—	—	—	—	16	200	12.5 (22)	3	—	—	—	—	—	—	—	—	—	—	Kk	—	41	151
1944	Bkn	10 (9, LE)	—	—	—	—	24	258	10.8 (30)	1	1	1	100.0	1	1.0 (1)	0	0	—	—	—	KP	—	6	135
1945	Bos	10 (5, le)	—	—	—	—	15	186	12.4 (21)	0	—	—	—	—	—	—	—	—	—	—	K	—	0	93
NFL	8	84 (47)	8	104	13.0 (11)	0	126	1697	13.5 (33)	13	2	1	50.0	1	0.5 (1)	0	0	—	—	—	KPki	—	173	1039
1946	†NYY-A	14 (8, LE)	—	—	—	—	10	119	11.9	0	—	—	—	—	—	—	—	—	—	—	Kki	—	0	35

MASTERSON, FORREST Forrest Joseph, C-G, 6´3˝/246 lbs; Iowa; 1945: ChiB, rnd 5; B4/2/1922 Alliance, OH **1945** ChiB 7 (1)

MASTON, LE'SHAI Le'Shai Edwoin, RB, 6´0˝/227 lbs; Baylor; B10/7/1970 Dallas, TX

YEAR	TEAM	G (GS, POS)	RUSH	YD	AVG (LG)	TD	REC	YD	AVG (LG)	TD	PASS	COMP	PCT	YD	AVG (LG)	TD	INT	SK	YD	QBR	KPR	OTD	PTS	TAY
1993	†Hou	10 (0)	1	10	10.0 (10)	0	1	14	14.0 (14)	0	—	—	—	—	—	—	—	—	—	—	—	—	0	17
1994	Hou	5 (1)	—	—	—	—	2	12	6.0 (10)	0	—	—	—	—	—	—	—	—	—	—	—	—	0	6
1995	Jax	16 (10, FB)	41	186	4.5 (21)	0	18	131	7.3 (19)	0	—	—	—	—	—	—	—	—	—	—	k	—	0	242
1996	†Jax	15 (7, FB)	8	22	2.8 (7)	0	6	54	9.0 (17)	0	—	—	—	—	—	—	—	—	—	—	—	—	0	49
1998	Was	1 (0)	—	—	—	—	—	—	—	—	—	—	—	—	—	—	—	—	—	—	—	—	—	—
NFL	5	47 (18)	50	218	4.4 (21)	0	27	211	7.8 (19)	0	—	—	—	—	—	—	—	—	—	—	k	—	0	314

MASTRANGELO, JOHN John Battista, T-G, 6´1˝/228 lbs; Notre Dame; 1947: Buf-A, rnd 5/Pit, rnd 3; B3/10/1926 Vandergriff, PA, D10/2/1987 Vandergriff, PA **1949** NYY-A 12 (0)
1947†Pit 11 (5, rg) **1948** Pit 12 (7, LT) **1950**†NYG☆9 (rt) **NFL** 32 (12) [3 yrs]

MASTROGANY, GUS August Nicholas, E, 6´0˝/180 lbs; Iowa; B10/25/1907 Davenport, IA, D5/12/1992 Northbrook, IL **1931** ChiB 1 (0)

MATAELE, STAN Stanley, NT, 6´2˝/276 lbs; Arizona; 1987: TB, rnd 8; B6/24/1963 Tonga **1987** GB 2 (0)

MATAN, BILL William Douglas, DE, 6´4˝/240 lbs; Kansas State; 1966: NYG, rnd 8/Mia, rnd 9; B12/6/1943 St. Louis, MO **1966** NYG 3

MATAU, CHRIS Christopher Volaga, G, 6´3˝/310 lbs; Brigham Young; B1/22/1964 Torrance, CA **1987** LARm 3 (0)

MATESIC, ED Edward J., TB-HB, 6´1˝/198 lbs; Pittsburgh; B11/6/1907 Marshall County, WV, D6/4/1988 Wheeling, WV

YEAR	TEAM	G (GS, POS)	RUSH	YD	AVG (LG)	TD	REC	YD	AVG (LG)	TD	PASS	COMP	PCT	YD	AVG (LG)	TD	INT	SK	YD	QBR	KPR	OTD	PTS	TAY
1934	Phi	11 (11, TB)	63	181	2.9	0	3	38	12.7	1	60	20	33.3	278	4.6	2	5	—	—	—	—	—	6	154
1935	Phi	11 (11, TB)	50	138	2.8	1	—	—	—	—	64	15	23.4	284	4.4	2	13	—	—	—	—	—	6	-220
1936	Pit	12 (11, TB)	46	58	1.3	0	1	13	13.0 (13)	0	138	64	**46.4**	850	6.2	4	**16**	—	—	36.5	—	—	0	-131
NFL	3	34 (33)	159	377	2.4	1	4	51	12.8 (13)	1	262	99	37.8	1412	5.4	8	34	—	—	26.6	—	—	12	-197

MATESIC, JOE Joseph Thomas, T, 6´4˝/250 lbs; Indiana; Arizona State; 1953: NYG, rnd 12; B11/10/1927 Rankin, PA, D8/19/1989 Burgettstown, PA **1954** Pit 1

MATHESON, BOB Robert Edward, LB, 6´4˝/238 lbs; Duke; 1967: Cle, rnd 1; B11/25/1944 Boone, NC, D9/5/1994 Durham, NC **1967**†Cle 14 **1968**†Cle 14 (MLB)
1969†Cle 14 (mlb) **1970** Cle 13 (mlb) **1971**†Mia 14 (1) **1972**†Mia 14 (1) **1973**†Mia 14 (2) **1974**†Mia 14 (8, LLB) **1975** Mia 14 (13, RLB) **1976** Mia 13 (11, RLB)
1977 Mia 14 (9, RILB) **1978**†Mia 12 (3) **1979**†Mia 16 (3) **NFL** 180 (51) [13 yrs]

MATHESON, JACK John Kenneth, E-G, 6´2˝/221 lbs; Western Michigan; B6/9/1920 Detroit, MI, D2/14/1997

YEAR	TEAM	G (GS, POS)	RUSH	YD	AVG (LG)	TD	REC	YD	AVG (LG)	TD	PASS	COMP	PCT	YD	AVG (LG)	TD	INT	SK	YD	QBR	KPR	OTD	PTS	TAY
1943	Det	9 (3, LG)	—	—	—	—	13	156	12.0 (46)	1	—	—	—	—	—	—	—	—	—	—	k	—	6	87
1944	Det	10 (10, RE)	—	—	—	—	23	361	15.7 (44)	3	—	—	—	—	—	—	—	—	—	—	i	—	18	212
1945	Det	9 (9, RE)	—	—	—	—	19	241	12.7 (34)	1	—	—	—	—	—	—	—	—	—	—	p	1	14	131
1946	Det	11 (10, RE)	—	—	—	—	17	178	10.5 (33)	0	—	—	—	—	—	—	—	—	—	—	ki	—	0	94
1947	ChiB	3 (0)	—	—	—	—	1	8	8.0 (8)	0	—	—	—	—	—	—	—	—	—	—	—	—	0	4
NFL	5	42 (32)	—	—	—	—	73	944	12.9 (46)	5	—	—	—	—	—	—	—	—	—	—	kpi	1	38	527

MATHESON, RILEY Riley, G, 6´2˝/207 lbs; Cameron; Texas-El Paso; B12/12/1914 Shannon, TX, D6/1987, Paraguay **1939** Cle 2 (2) **1940** Cle 11 (0) **1941** Cle☆9 (6, RG)
1942 Cle☆10 (8, LG) **1943** Det☆10 (9) **1944** Cle☆9 (8, LG) **1945**†Cle☆10 (9, LG) **1946** LARm☆11 (7, RG) **1947** LARm☆11 (9, LG) **NFL** 83 (58) [9 yrs]
1948 SF-A☆14 (0)

MATHEWS, BARNEY Frank E., E, 5´8˝/186 lbs; Northwestern; B7/1/1903 St. Louis, MO, D4/17/1970 St. Louis, MO **1926** Rac 5 (5, RE)

MATHEWS, JASON Samuel Jason, T, 6´5˝/285 lbs; Brigham Young; Texas A&M; 1994: Ind, rnd 3; B2/9/1971 Orange, TX **1994** Ind 10 (0) **1995**†Ind 16 (16, RT)
1996†Ind 16 (15, RT/lt) **1997** Ind 16 (0) **1998** Ten 3 (0) **1999** Ten 3 (0) **2000**†Ten 16 (1) **2001** Ten 16 (2) **2002**†Ten 16 (2) **2003**†Ten 15 (0) **2004** Ten 15 (7, lt)
NFL 142 (43) [11 yrs]

MATHEWS, NED Ned Alfred, WB-HB, 5´10˝/187 lbs; UCLA; B8/11/1918 Provo, UT, D9/18/2002 Los Angeles, CA **[C]**

YEAR	TEAM	G (GS, POS)	RUSH	YD	AVG (LG)	TD	REC	YD	AVG (LG)	TD	PASS	COMP	PCT	YD	AVG (LG)	TD	INT	SK	YD	QBR	KPR	OTD	PTS	TAY
1941	Det	9 (1)	31	56	1.8 (16)	0	6	56	9.3 (18)	0	8	3	37.5	59	7.4 (27)	1	0	—	—	—	Pkpi	1	6	328
1942	Det	9 (6, WB)	21	79	3.8 (14)	0	3	38	12.7 (20)	0	22	6	27.3	53	2.4 (18)	1	2	—	—	—	kp	—	0	119
1943	Det	10 (4, WB)	38	124	3.3 (42)	1	9	193	21.4 (36)	1	12	4	33.3	76	6.3 (33)	1	0	—	—	—	kpi	1	18	471
1945	Bos	9 (0)	27	146	5.4 (49)	0	4	56	14.0 (23)	1	1	0	0.0	0	0.0	0	0	—	—	—	ki	—	6	254
NFL	4	37 (11)	117	405	3.5 (49)	1	22	343	15.6 (36)	2	43	13	30.2	188	4.4 (33)	3	2	—	—	—	Pkpi	2	30	1171
1946	ChiR-A	8 (2)	12	15	1.3	1	6	100	16.7	2	—	—	—	—	—	—	—	—	—	—	ki	—	18	118
1946	SF-A	6 (1)	18	94	5.2	0	—	—	—	—	1	1	100.0	26	26.0 (26)	0	0	—	—	—	k	—	0	100
1947	SF-A	12 (0)	39	238	6.1	2	6	51	8.5	2	2	0	0.0	0	0.0	0	0	—	—	—	kpi	1	30	473
AAFC	2	26 (3)	69	347	5.0 (49)	3	12	151	12.6 (36)	4	3	1	33.3	26	8.7 (33)	0	0	—	—	—	kpi	1	48	691

MATHEWS, NEIL Neilson Murray, T, 6´0˝/191 lbs; Pennsylvania; B9/13/1893 Chicago, IL, D7/17/1965 Bryn Mawr, PA **1920** ChiT 6 (5, LT)

MATHEWS, RAY Raymond Dyral, HB-E, 6´0˝/185 lbs; Clemson; 1951: Pit, rnd 7; B2/26/1929 Dayton, PA **[K]**

YEAR	TEAM	G (GS, POS)	RUSH	YD	AVG (LG)	TD	REC	YD	AVG (LG)	TD	PASS	COMP	PCT	YD	AVG (LG)	TD	INT	SK	YD	QBR	KPR	OTD	PTS	TAY
1951	Pit	12	21	37	1.8 (15)	0	—	—	—	—	31	15	48.4	208	6.7 (39)	2	0	—	—	—	kpi	1	6	444
1952	Pit★	12 (LH)	66	315	4.8 (36)	0	33	543	16.5 (50)	5	13	3	23.1	104	8.0 (69)	0	1	—	—	—	Kkp	2	43	1068
1953	Pit	12 (LH)	65	260	4.0 (31)	2	27	346	12.8 (77)	4	2	0	0.0	0	0.0	0	0	—	—	—	kpi	1	44	644
1954	Pit	12 (LH)	80	242	3.0 (24)	2	44	652	14.8 (78)	6	4	0	0.0	0	0.0	0	1	—	—	—	kp	—	48	602
1955	Pit✧	12 (LH)	57	187	3.3 (23)	1	42	762	18.1 (61)	6	—	—	—	—	—	—	—	—	—	—	—	—	42	608
1956	Pit	12 (RE)	3	-11	-3.7 (2)	0	31	540	17.4 (64)	5	—	—	—	—	—	—	—	—	—	—	k	—	30	295
1957	Pit	12 (FL)	3	-1	-0.3 (6)	0	15	369	24.6 (64)	4	—	—	—	—	—	—	—	—	—	—	—	—	24	204
1958	Pit	12 (FL)	4	24	6.0 (14)	0	25	525	21.0 (65)	4	—	—	—	—	—	—	—	—	—	—	—	—	24	307
1959	Pit	12	1	4	4.0 (4)	0	13	182	14.0 (56)	0	1	1	100.0	38	38.0 (38)	0	0	—	—	—	p	—	0	121
1960	Dal	6	—	—	—	—	3	44	14.7 (20)	0	—	—	—	—	—	—	—	—	—	—	—	—	0	22
NFL	10	114	300	1057	3.5 (36)	5	233	3963	17.0 (78)	34	51	19	37.3	350	6.9 (69)	2	2	—	—	—	Kkpi	4	261	4314

MATHEWSON B, none; deceased **1920** Ham 1 (0)

MATHIAS, RIC Ric, DB, 5´10˝/180 lbs; Wisconsin-LaCrosse; B12/10/1975 Monroe, WI **1998** Cin 3 (0)

MATHIS, BILL William Hart, FB-HB, 6´1˝/220 lbs; Clemson; 1960: Den, rnd 1/SF, rnd 8; B12/10/1938 Rocky Mount, NC

YEAR	TEAM	G (GS, POS)	RUSH	YD	AVG (LG)	TD	REC	YD	AVG (LG)	TD	PASS	COMP	PCT	YD	AVG (LG)	TD	INT	SK	YD	QBR	KPR	OTD	PTS	TAY
1960	NYT-A	14 (FB)	92	307	3.3 (17)	2	18	103	5.7 (24)	0	—	—	—	—	—	—	—	—	—	—	—	—	12	379
1961	NYT-A★	14 (FB)	**202**	846	4.2 (30)	7	12	42	3.5 (14)	1	—	—	—	—	—	—	—	—	—	—	—	—	48	942
1962	NYT-A	11 (FB)	71	245	3.5 (41)	3	6	32	5.3 (14)	0	—	—	—	—	—	—	—	—	—	—	—	—	18	291

YEAR	TEAM	G (GS, POS)	RUSH	YD	AVG (LG)	TD	REC	YD	AVG (LG)	TD	PASS	COMP	PCT	YD	AVG (LG)	TD	INT	SK	YD	QBR	KPR	OTD	PTS	TAY
1963	NYJ-A✧	14	107	268	2.5(16)	1	18	177	9.8(33)	1	—	—	—	—	—	—	—	—	—	—	k	—	12	368
1964	NYJ-A	14(HB)	105	305	2.9(31)	4	4	39	9.8(15)	0	—	—	—	—	—	—	—	—	—	—	k	—	24	350
1965	NYJ-A	14(HB)	147	604	4.1(79)	5	17	242	14.2(32)	1	—	—	—	—	—	—	—	—	—	—	—	—	36	780
1966	NYJ-A	14	72	208	2.9(23)	2	22	379	17.2(70)	1	—	—	—	—	—	—	—	—	—	—	—	—	18	423
1967	NYJ-A	14	78	243	3.1(18)	4	25	429	17.2(38)	3	—	—	—	—	—	—	—	—	—	—	—	—	46	513
1968	†NYJ-A	14	74	208	2.8(16)	5	9	149	16.6(31)	1	—	—	—	—	—	—	—	—	—	—	—	—	38	338
1969	†NYJ-A	14	96	355	3.7(27)	4	18	183	10.2(35)	1	—	—	—	—	—	—	—	—	—	—	—	—	30	492
NFL	10	137	1044	3589	3.4(79)	37	149	1775	11.9(70)	9	—	—	—	—	—	—	—	—	—	—	k	—	282	4873

MATHIS, DEDRIC Dedric Ronshell, DB, 5´10˝/188 lbs; Houston; 1996: Ind, rnd 2; B9/26/1973 Cuero, TX **1996**†Ind 16 (6, rcb) **1997** Ind 13 (4) **NFL** 29 (10) [2 yrs]

MATHIS, EVAN Evan, G, 6´5˝/304 lbs; Alabama; 2005: Car, rnd 3; B11/1/1981 Homewood, AL **2005** Car 9 (0)

MATHIS, JEROME Jerome, WR, 5´11˝/181 lbs; Hampton; 2005: Hou, rnd 4; B7/26/1981 Petersburg, VA

YEAR	TEAM	G (GS, POS)	RUSH	YD	AVG (LG)	TD	REC	YD	AVG (LG)	TD	PASS	COMP	PCT	YD	AVG (LG)	TD	INT	SK	YD	QBR	KPR	OTD	PTS	TAY
2005	Hou★	12(0)	—	—	—	—	5	65	13.0(34)	1	—	—	—	—	—	—	—	—	—	—	kp	2	18	798

MATHIS, KEVIN Kevin, DB, 5´9˝/185 lbs; Texas A&M-Commerce; B4/29/1974 Gainesville, TX **1997** Dal 16 (3) **1998**†Dal 13 (4) **1999**†Dal 8 (4) **2000**†NO 16 (16, LCB) **2001** NO 14 (13, LCB) **2002**†Atl 11 (0) **2003** Atl 14 (2) **2004**†Atl 15 (12, RCB/lcb) **NFL** 107 (54) [8 yrs]

MATHIS, MARK Mark E., DB, 5´9˝/178 lbs; Liberty; B8/23/1965 Mount Clemens, MI **1987** SL 2 (1)

MATHIS, RASHEAN Rashean Jamil, DB, 6´1˝/200 lbs; Bethune-Cookman; 2003: Jax, rnd 2; B8/27/1980 Jacksonville, FL **2003** Jax 16 (16, RCB/fs) **2004** Jax 16 (16, LCB) **2005**†Jax 16 (16, LCB) **NFL** 48 (48) [3 yrs]

MATHIS, REGGIE Reginald Levi, LB, 6´2˝/220 lbs; Oklahoma; 1979: NO, rnd 2; B3/18/1956 Chattanooga, TN **1979** NO 16 **1980** NO 16 (16, RLB) **NFL** 32 (16) [2 yrs]

MATHIS, ROBERT Robert Nathan, DE, 6´2˝/235 lbs; Alabama A&M; 2003: Ind, rnd 5; B2/26/1981 Atlanta, GA **2003**†Ind 16 (0) **2004**†Ind 16 (1) **2005**†Ind 13 (0) **NFL** 45 (1) [3 yrs]

MATHIS, TERANCE Terance Paul, WR, 5´10˝/177 lbs; New Mexico; 1990: NYJ, rnd 6; B6/7/1967 Detroit, MI **[R]**

YEAR	TEAM	G (GS, POS)	RUSH	YD	AVG (LG)	TD	REC	YD	AVG (LG)	TD	PASS	COMP	PCT	YD	AVG (LG)	TD	INT	SK	YD	QBR	KPR	OTD	PTS	TAY
1990	NYJ	16(1)	2	9	4.5(10)	0	19	245	12.9(23)	0	—	—	—	—	—	—	—	—	—	—	kp	1	6	394
1991	†NYJ	16(0)	1	19	19.0(19)	0	28	329	11.8(39)	1	—	—	—	—	—	—	—	—	—	—	kp	—	6	395
1992	NYJ	16(0)	3	25	8.3(10)	1	22	316	14.4(55)	3	—	—	—	—	—	—	—	—	—	—	kp	—	24	294
1993	NYJ	16(3)	2	20	10.0(17)	1	24	352	14.7(46)	0	—	—	—	—	—	—	—	—	—	—	kp	—	6	232
1994	Atl★	16(16, WR)	—	—	—	—	111	1342	12.1(81)	11	—	—	—	—	—	—	—	—	—	—	—	—	70	726
1995	†Atl	14(12, WR)	—	—	—	—	78	1039	13.3(54)	9	—	—	—	—	—	—	—	—	—	—	—	—	60	565
1996	Atl	16(16, WR)	—	—	—	—	69	771	11.2(55)	7	—	—	—	—	—	—	—	—	—	—	p	—	44	425
1997	Atl	16(16, WR)	3	35	11.7(16)	0	62	802	12.9(49)	6	—	—	—	—	—	—	—	—	—	—	—	—	36	466
1998	†Atl	16(16, WR)	1	-6	-6.0(-6)	0	64	1136	17.8(78)	11	—	—	—	—	—	—	—	—	—	—	p	—	66	612
1999	Atl	16(16, WR)	1	0	0.0(0)	0	81	1016	12.5(52)	6	—	—	—	—	—	—	—	—	—	—	—	—	36	538
2000	Atl	16(16, WR)	1	-5	-5.0(-5)	0	57	679	11.9(44)	5	—	—	—	—	—	—	—	—	—	—	—	—	30	360
2001	Atl	16(16, WR)	—	—	—	—	51	564	11.1(34)	2	—	—	—	—	—	—	—	—	—	—	—	—	12	292
2002	†Pit	16(0)	—	—	—	—	23	218	9.5(22)	2	—	—	—	—	—	—	—	—	—	—	—	—	12	119
NFL	13	206(128)	14	97	6.9(19)	2	689	8809	12.8(81)	63	—	—	—	—	—	—	—	—	—	—	kp	1	408	5416

MATHISON, BRUCE Bruce Martin, QB, 6´3˝/205 lbs; Nebraska; 1983: SD, rnd 10; B4/25/1959 Superior, WI

YEAR	TEAM	G (GS, POS)	RUSH	YD	AVG (LG)	TD	REC	YD	AVG (LG)	TD	PASS	COMP	PCT	YD	AVG (LG)	TD	INT	SK	YD	QBR	KPR	OTD	PTS	TAY
1983	SD	1(0)	1	0	0.0(0)	0	—	—	—	—	5	3	60.0	41	8.2(25)	0	1	—	—	—	—	—	0	-20
1984	SD	2(0)	—	—	—	—	—	—	—	—	—	—	—	—	—	—	—	—	—	—	—	—	—	—
1985	Buf	10(7, qb)	27	231	8.6(22)	1	—	—	—	—	228	113	49.6	1635	7.2(60)	4	14	22	203	—	—	—	6	519
1986	SD	2(0)	1	-1	-1.0(-1)	0	—	—	—	—	—	—	—	—	—	—	—	—	—	—	—	—	0	-1
1987	Sea	3(2)	5	15	3.0(10)	0	—	—	—	—	76	36	47.4	501	6.6(47)	3	5	6	49	—	—	—	0	81
NFL	5	18(9)	34	245	7.2(22)	1	—	—	—	—	309	152	49.2	2177	7.0(60)	7	20	28	252	—	—	—	6	579

MATHYS, CHARLIE Charles Pater, BB-QB, 5´7˝/165 lbs; Ripon; Indiana; B6/20/1897 Green Bay, WI, D1/18/1983 Ashwaubenon, WI **[K]** **1921** Ham 5 (4, BB), 3 **1922** GB 10 (10, BB), 15 **1923** GB 10 (10, BB), 6 **1924** GB 11 (11, BB), 12 **1925** GB 12 (11, BB) **1926** GB 4 (3) **NFL** 52 (49), 36 [6 yrs]

MATICH, TREVOR Trevor Anthony, C-G-T, 6´4˝/277 lbs; Brigham Young; 1985: NE, rnd 1; B10/9/1961 Sacramento, CA **1985** NE 1 (0) **1986**†NE 11 (1) **1987** NE 6 (4) **1988** NE 8 (6, c) **1989** Det 11 (0) **1990** NYJ 16 (6, c) **1992** Ind 16 (1) **1993** Ind 16 (4) **1994** Was 16 (0) **1995** Was 16 (0) **1996** Was 16 (0)

YEAR	TEAM	G (GS, POS)	RUSH	YD	AVG (LG)	TD	REC	YD	AVG (LG)	TD	PASS	COMP	PCT	YD	AVG (LG)	TD	INT	SK	YD	QBR	KPR	OTD	PTS	TAY
1991	†NYJ	15(0)	—	—	—	—	3	23	7.7(14)	1	—	—	—	—	—	—	—	—	—	—	—	—	6	17
NFL	12	148(22)	—	—	—	—	3	23	7.7(14)	1	—	—	—	—	—	—	—	—	—	—	—	—	6	17

MATISI, JOHN John Benrard, T, 6´2˝/221 lbs; Duquesne; 1943: Bkn, rnd 7; B11/2/1920 New York, NY, D4/29/1997, OH **1943** Bkn 4 (1) **1946** Buf-A 12 (0)

MATISI, TONY Anthony Francis, T, 6´2˝/230 lbs; Pittsburgh; 1938: Pit, rnd 4; B8/23/1914 New York, NY, D8/26/1949 Endicott, NY **1938** Det 5 (1)

MATLOCK, JOHN John James, C, 6´4˝/249 lbs; Miami (FL); B10/19/1944 Louisville, KY **1967** NYJ-A 10 **1968** Cin-A 12 **1970** Atl 14 **1971** Atl 12 **1972** Buf 11 (c) **NFL** 59 [5 yrs]

MATSON, OLLIE Ollie Genoa, RB-FL, 6´2˝/220 lbs; San Francisco; 1952: ChiC, rnd 1; B5/1/1930 Trinity, TX; HOF 1972 **[R]**

YEAR	TEAM	G (GS, POS)	RUSH	YD	AVG (LG)	TD	REC	YD	AVG (LG)	TD	PASS	COMP	PCT	YD	AVG (LG)	TD	INT	SK	YD	QBR	KPR	OTD	PTS	TAY
1952	ChiC★	12(FB)	96	344	3.6(25)	3	11	187	17.0(47)	3	—	—	—	—	—	—	—	—	—	—	kpi	3	54	909
1954	ChiC★	12(LH)	101	506	5.0(79)	4	34	611	18.0(70)	3	2	0	0.0	0	0.0	0	0	—	—	—	kpi	2	54	1121
1955	ChiC★	12(LH)	109	475	4.4(54)	1	17	237	13.9(70)	2	1	1	100.0	43	43.0(43)	0	0	—	—	—	kp	2	30	978
1956	ChiC★	12(LH)	192	924	4.8(79)	5	15	199	13.3(45)	2	3	0	0.0	0	0.0	0	0	—	—	—	kp	1	48	1275
1957	ChiC★	12(LH)	134	577	4.3(56)	6	20	451	22.5(75)	3	5	2	40.0	59	11.8(32)	0	0	—	—	—	kp	—	54	960
1958	ChiC☆	12(LH)	129	505	3.9(55)	5	33	465	14.1(59)	3	2	1	50.0	4	2.0(4)	0	0	—	—	—	k	2	60	1112
1959	LARm☆	12(FB)	161	863	5.4(50)	6	18	130	7.2(49)	0	1	0	0.0	0	0.0	0	1	—	—	—	kp	—	36	1066
1960	LARm	12(FL)	61	170	2.8(27)	1	15	98	6.5(24)	0	—	—	—	—	—	—	—	—	—	—	kp	—	6	305
1961	LARm	14(FL)	24	181	7.5(69)	2	29	537	18.5(96)	3	—	—	—	—	—	—	—	—	—	—	—	—	30	485
1962	LARm	13	3	0	0.0(2)	0	3	49	16.3(20)	1	1	1	100.0	13	13.0(13)	0	0	—	—	—	—	—	6	36
1963	Det	8	13	20	1.5(9)	0	2	20	10.0(17)	0	—	—	—	—	—	—	—	—	—	—	k	—	0	46
1964	Phi	12(hb)	96	404	4.2(63)	4	17	242	14.2(32)	1	—	—	—	—	—	—	—	—	—	—	kp	—	30	629
1965	Phi	14(hb)	22	103	4.7(22)	2	2	29	14.5(20)	1	—	—	—	—	—	—	—	—	—	—	—	—	18	143
1966	Phi	14	29	101	3.5(28)	1	6	30	5.0(11)	1	—	—	—	—	—	—	—	—	—	—	k	—	12	285
NFL	14	171	1170	5173	4.4(79)	40	222	3285	14.8(96)	23	15	5	33.3	119	7.9(43)	0	1	—	—	—	kpi	10	438	9347

MATSON, PAT Patrick William, G, 6´1˝/245 lbs; Oregon; B7/22/1944 Laramie, WY **1966** Den-A 14 **1967** Den-A 14 (RG) **1968** Cin-A 14 (RG) **1969** Cin-A 6 (RG) **1970**†Cin 14 (RG) **1971** Cin 14 (RG) **1972** Cin 14 (RG) **1973**†Cin 14 (RG) **1974** Cin 14 (rg) **1975** GB 14 (rg) **NFL** 132 [10 yrs]

MATSOS, ARCHIE Emil George, LB, 6´0˝/217 lbs; Michigan State; 1958: Bal, rnd 16; B11/22/1934 Detroit, MI **[I]** **1960** Buf-A☆14 (MLB) **1961** Buf-A★14 (MLB) **1962** Buf-A✧14 (MLB) **1963** Oak-A★14 (MLB) **1964** Oak-A☆14 (MLB) **1965** Oak-A 12 (MLB) **1966** Den-A 4 **1966** SD-A 9 **NFL** 95 [7 yrs]

MATSU, ARTHUR Arthur A., aka Ichya Matsu, B, 5´7˝/168 lbs; William & Mary; B4/30/1904 Glasgow, Scotland, D5/28/1987 Prescott, AZ **1928** Day 6 (4, BB)

MATTE, TOM Thomas Roland, RB-QB, 6´0˝/214 lbs; Ohio State; 1961: Bal, rnd 1/NYT, rnd 5; B6/14/1939 Pittsburgh, PA

YEAR	TEAM	G (GS, POS)	RUSH	YD	AVG (LG)	TD	REC	YD	AVG (LG)	TD	PASS	COMP	PCT	YD	AVG (LG)	TD	INT	SK	YD	QBR	KPR	OTD	PTS	TAY
1961	Bal	8	13	54	4.2(11)	0	1	8	8.0(8)	0	—	—	—	—	—	—	—	—	—	—	k	—	0	78
1962	Bal	14	74	226	3.1(29)	2	8	81	10.1(22)	1	13	5	38.5	85	6.5(30)	1	0	—	—	—	k	—	18	547
1963	Bal	14(HB)	133	541	4.1(31)	4	48	466	9.7(49)	1	5	1	20.0	20	4.0(20)	0	0	—	—	—	k	—	30	920
1964	†Bal	14	42	215	5.1(80)	1	10	169	16.9(30)	0	4	3	75.0	58	14.5(22)	1	0	—	—	—	k	—	6	370
1965	†Bal	14	69	235	3.4(20)	1	12	131	10.9(15)	0	7	1	14.3	19	2.7(19)	0	1	1	7	—	k	—	6	371
1966	Bal	14	86	381	4.4(30)	0	23	307	13.3(35)	3	3	0	0.0	0	0.0	0	1	1	14	—	kp	—	18	515
1967	Bal	14(HB)	147	636	4.3(30)	9	35	496	14.2(88)	3	5	1	20.0	18	3.6(18)	0	0	—	—	—	k	—	72	997
1968	†Bal✧	14(HB)	183	662	3.6(23)	9	25	275	11.0(50)	1	1	0	0.0	0	0.0	0	0	—	—	—	k	—	60	902
1969	Bal★	14(HB)	235	909	3.9(26)	**11**	43	513	11.9(49)	2	3	1	33.3	46	15.3(46)	0	0	—	—	—	—	—	78	1309
1970	Bal	2	12	43	3.6(16)	0	1	2	2.0(2)	0	—	—	—	—	—	—	—	—	—	—	—	—	0	44
1971	†Bal	14(RB)	173	607	3.5(26)	8	29	239	8.2(34)	0	1	0	0.0	0	0.0	0	0	1	12	—	k	—	48	792
1972	Bal	6	33	137	4.2(18)	0	14	182	13.0(43)	1	—	—	—	—	—	—	—	—	—	—	—	—	6	233
NFL	12	142	1200	4646	3.9(80)	45	249	2869	11.5(88)	12	42	12	28.6	246	5.9(46)	2	2	3	33	—	kp	—	342	7076

YEAR	TEAM	G (GS, POS)	RUSH	YD	AVG(LG)	TD	REC	YD	AVG(LG)	TD	PASS	COMP	PCT	YD	AVG(LG)	TD	INT	SK	YD	QBR	KPR	OTD	PTS	TAY

MATTEO, FRANK   Francis Pasquale, T-G, 5´11˝/195 lbs; Syracuse; B4/2/1896 Syracuse, NY, D12/19/1983 Oneida, NY   **1922** Roc 4 (3, LT) **1923** Roc 4 (4, RT) **1924** Roc 5 (5, LT) **1925** Roc 4 (4, RT) **NFL** 17 (16) [4 yrs]

MATTERN, JOE   Joseph Peter, B, /155 lbs; Minnesota; Lehigh; B9/9/1892, deceased   **1920** Cle 1 (0) **1922** Min 1 (1) **NFL** 2 (1) [2 yrs]

MATTES, RON   Ronald Anthony, T, 6´6˝/309 lbs; Virginia; 1985: Sea, rnd 7; B8/8/1963 Shenandoah, PA   **1986** Sea 16 (16, LT) **1987**†Sea 12 (12, LT) **1988**†Sea 16 (16, LT) **1989** Sea 16 (8, lt) **1990** Sea 15 (7, rt) **1991**†Ind 5 (1) **NFL** 95 (60) [7 yrs]

MATTHEWS, AL   Alvin Leon, DB, 5´11˝/190 lbs; Texas A&M-Kingsville; 1970: GB, rnd 2; B11/7/1947 Austin, TX   **1970** GB 14 **1971** GB 14 (RCB) **1972**†GB 14 (SS) **1973** GB 14 (SS) **1974** GB 14 (SS) **1975** GB 14 (14, SS) **1976** Sea 14 (14, SS) **1977** SF 1 **NFL** 99 (28) [8 yrs]

MATTHEWS, ALLAMA   Allama Uzair, TE-RB, 6´3˝/230 lbs; Vanderbilt; 1983: Atl, rnd 12; B8/24/1961 Jacksonville, FL

1983	Atl	16 (1)	—	—	—	—	3	37	12.3 (23)	0	—	—	—	—	—	—	—	—	—	—	—	—	0	19
1984	Atl	6 (0)	—	—	—	—	1	7	7.0 (7)	0	—	—	—	—	—	—	—	—	—	—	k	—	0	-9
1985	Atl	15 (2)	—	—	—	—	7	57	8.1 (15)	1	—	—	—	—	—	—	—	—	—	—	k	—	6	30
NFL	3	37 (3)	—	—	—	—	11	101	9.2 (23)	1	—	—	—	—	—	—	—	—	—	—	k	—	6	40

MATTHEWS, AUBREY   Aubrey Derron, WR, 5´7˝/165 lbs; Delta State; B9/15/1962 Pascagoula, MS

1986	Atl	4 (0)	1	12	12.0 (12)	0	1	25	25.0 (25)	0	—	—	—	—	—	—	—	—	—	—	k	—	0	22
1987	Atl	12 (6, wr)	1	-4	-4.0 (-4)	0	32	537	16.8 (57)	3	—	—	—	—	—	—	—	—	—	—	—	—	18	280
1988	Atl	4 (0)	—	—	—	—	5	64	12.8 (21)	0	—	—	—	—	—	—	—	—	—	—	p	—	0	28
1988	GB	7 (2)	3	3	1.0 (4)	0	15	167	11.1 (25)	2	—	—	—	—	—	—	—	—	—	—	—	—	12	97
1989	GB	13 (3)	—	—	—	—	18	200	11.1 (25)	0	—	—	—	—	—	—	—	—	—	—	—	—	0	100
1990	Det	13 (6, wr)	—	—	—	—	30	349	11.6 (52)	1	—	—	—	—	—	—	—	—	—	—	—	—	6	180
1991	†Det	1 (1)	—	—	—	—	3	21	7.0 (11)	0	—	—	—	—	—	—	—	—	—	—	—	—	0	11
1992	Det	13 (0)	—	—	—	—	9	137	15.2 (24)	0	—	—	—	—	—	—	—	—	—	—	—	—	0	69
1993	†Det	14 (2)	2	7	3.5 (9)	0	11	171	15.5 (40)	0	—	—	—	—	—	—	—	—	—	—	—	—	0	93
1994	†Det	14 (3)	—	—	—	—	29	359	12.4 (33)	3	—	—	—	—	—	—	—	—	—	—	—	—	18	195
1995	†Det	12 (0)	—	—	—	—	4	41	10.3 (12)	0	—	—	—	—	—	—	—	—	—	—	—	—	0	21
1996	Det	16 (0)	—	—	—	—	3	41	13.7 (21)	0	—	—	—	—	—	—	—	—	—	—	k	—	0	41
NFL	11	123 (23)	7	18	2.6 (12)	0	160	2112	13.2 (57)	9	—	—	—	—	—	—	—	—	—	—	kp	—	54	1107

MATTHEWS, BILL   William Marvin, LB, 6´2˝/235 lbs; South Dakota State; 1978: NE, rnd 5; B3/12/1956 Santa Monica, CA   **1979** NE 16 (1) **1980** NE 16 (0) **1981** NE 16 (9, RILB) **NFL** 48 (10) [3 yrs]

MATTHEWS, BO   William Pierce, RB, 6´4˝/230 lbs; Colorado; 1974: SD, rnd 1; B11/15/1951 Huntsville, AL

1974	SD	14 (8, FB)	95	328	3.5 (16)	4	12	90	7.5 (23)	0	—	—	—	—	—	—	—	—	—	—	—	—	24	413
1975	SD	13 (12, FB)	71	254	3.6 (24)	3	9	59	6.6 (22)	0	—	—	—	—	—	—	—	—	—	—	—	—	18	314
1976	SD	12 (2)	46	199	4.3 (42)	3	12	81	6.8 (15)	0	—	—	—	—	—	—	—	—	—	—	k	—	1	24	274
1977	SD	12	43	193	4.5 (22)	0	3	41	13.7 (23)	0	—	—	—	—	—	—	—	—	—	—	—	—	0	214
1978	SD	11 (9, fb)	71	286	4.0 (28)	0	11	78	7.1 (13)	0	—	—	—	—	—	—	—	—	—	—	—	—	0	325
1979	†SD	16	30	112	3.7 (22)	1	7	40	5.7 (13)	0	—	—	—	—	—	—	—	—	—	—	k	—	6	131
1980	NYG	15 (7, FB)	64	180	2.8 (18)	0	19	86	4.5 (12)	0	—	—	—	—	—	—	—	—	—	—	—	—	0	223
1981	†NYG	5 (1)	4	14	3.5 (6)	0	2	13	6.5 (11)	0	—	—	—	—	—	—	—	—	—	—	—	—	0	21
1981	Mia	3 (0)	—	—	—	—	—	—	—	—	—	—	—	—	—	—	—	—	—	—	—	—	—	—
NFL	8	101 (39)	424	1566	3.7 (42)	11	75	488	6.5 (23)	0	—	—	—	—	—	—	—	—	—	—	—	1	72	1913

MATTHEWS, BRUCE   Bruce Rankin, G-C-T, 6´5˝/289 lbs; USC; 1983: Hou, rnd 1; B8/8/1961 Raleigh, NC   **1983** Hou 16 (15, RG) **1984** Hou 16 (16, C/rt) **1985** Hou 16 (16, RT) **1986** Hou 16 (16, LT) **1987**†Hou 8 (5, RG) **1988**†Hou★16 (16, RG) **1989**†Hou★16 (16, RG) **1990**†Hou★16 (16, RG) **1991**†Hou★16 (16, C) **1992**†Hou★16 (16, C) **1993**†Hou★16 (16, C) **1994** Hou◇16 (16, C) **1995** Hou★16 (16, LG) **1996** Hou★16 (16, LG) **1997** Ten★16 (16, LG) **1998** Ten★16 (16, LG) **1999**†Ten★16 (16, LG) **2000**†Ten★16 (16, LG) **2001** Ten◇16 (16, LG) **NFL** 296 (292) [19 yrs]

MATTHEWS, CLAY   William Clay, DE-T-DT, 6´3˝/219 lbs; Georgia Tech; 1949: LA, rnd 25; B8/1/1928 Charleston, SC   **1950** SF 12 (RT) **1953** SF 9 (LDE) **1954** SF 12 (LDE) **1955** SF 12 (LDE) **NFL** 45 [4 yrs]

MATTHEWS, CLAY   William Clay, LB, 6´2˝/245 lbs; USC; 1978: Cle, rnd 1; B3/15/1956 Palo Alto, CA [S]   **1978** Cle 15 (2) **1979** Cle 16 (16, RLB/rolb) **1980**†Cle 14 (13, ROLB) **1981** Cle 16 (16, ROLB) **1982**†Cle 2 (1) **1983** Cle 16 (16, ROLB) **1984** Cle☆16 (16, ROLB) **1985**†Cle◇14 (14, ROLB) **1986**†Cle 16 (16, ROLB) **1987**†Cle◇12 (12, ROLB) **1988**†Cle★16 (16, ROLB) **1989**†Cle★16 (16, LLB) **1990** Cle 16 (16, LLB) **1991** Cle 15 (15, RLB) **1992** Cle 16 (16, RLB) **1993** Cle 16 (15, RLB) **1994** Atl 15 (15, LLB) **1995**†Atl 16 (16, LLB) **1996** Atl 15 (1) **NFL** 278 (248) [19 yrs]

MATTHEWS, HENRY   John Henry, RB, 6´3˝/203 lbs; Michigan State; B3/17/1949 Akron, OH   **1972** NE 3 (3) **1973** Atl 3

| 1973 | NO | 6 | 4 | 4 | 1.0 (3) | 0 | 2 | 19 | 9.5 (12) | 0 | — | — | — | — | — | — | — | — | — | — | — | — | 0 | 14 |
| NFL | 2 | 12 (3) | 4 | 4 | 1.0 (3) | 0 | 2 | 19 | 9.5 (12) | 0 | — | — | — | — | — | — | — | — | — | — | k | — | 0 | 43 |

MATTHEWS, IRA   Ira Richard, RB-WR, 5´8˝/175 lbs; Wisconsin; 1979: Oak, rnd 6; B8/23/1957 Rockford, IL [R]

1979	Oak☆	16	2	3	1.5 (3)	0	—	—	—	—	—	—	—	—	—	—	—	—	—	—	kp	1	6	366
1980	†Oak	16 (0)	5	11	2.2 (5)	0	3	33	11.0 (20)	0	—	—	—	—	—	—	—	—	—	—	kp	—	0	359
1981	Oak	5 (0)	—	—	—	—	—	—	—	—	—	—	—	—	—	—	—	—	—	—	kp	—	0	56
NFL	3	37	7	14	2.0 (5)	0	3	33	11.0 (20)	0	—	—	—	—	—	—	—	—	—	—	kp	1	6	781

MATTHEWS, SHANE   Michael Shane, QB, 6´3˝/196 lbs; Florida; B6/1/1970 Pascagoula, MS

1996	ChiB	2 (0)	1	2	2.0 (2)	1	—	—	—	—	17	13	76.5	158	9.3 (26)	1	0	1			—	—	6	96
1999	ChiB	8 (7, QB)	14	31	2.2 (14)	0	—	—	—	—	275	167	60.7	1645	6.0 (56)	10	6	13	79	80.6	—	—	0	664
2000	ChiB	6 (5, qb)	10	35	3.5 (14)	0	—	—	—	—	178	102	57.3	964	5.4 (41)	3	6	5	24		—	—	0	292
2001	†ChiB	5 (3)	4	5	1.3 (3)	0	—	—	—	—	129	84	65.1	694	5.4 (34)	5	6	6	48		—	—	0	137
2002	Was	8 (7, QB)	12	31	2.6 (11)	0	1	-13	-13.0 (-13)	0	237	124	52.3	1251	5.0 (43)	11	6	9	54		—	—	0	465
2004	Buf	3 (0)	2	-3	-1.5 (-1)	0	—	—	—	—	3	2	66.7	44	14.7 (33)	1	0	—	—		—	—	0	24
NFL	6	32 (22)	43	101	2.3 (14)	1	1	-13	-13.0 (-13)	0	839	492	58.6	4756	5.7 (56)	31	24	34	208	75.0	—	—	6	1678

MATTHEWS, STEVE   Stephen Keith, QB, 6´3˝/222 lbs; Tennessee; Memphis; 1994: KC, rnd 7; B10/13/1970 Tullahoma, TN

1997	Jax	2 (1)	1	10	10.0 (10)	0	—	—	—	—	40	26	65.0	275	6.9 (43)	0	0	1			—	—	0	148
1998	Ten	1 (0)	—	—	—	—	—	—	—	—	3	2	66.7	24	8.0 (13)	0	1	—	—		—	—	0	12
NFL	2	3 (1)	1	10	10.0 (10)	0	—	—	—	—	43	28	65.1	299	7.0 (43)	0	1	1			—	—	0	160

MATTHEWS, WES   Wesley Carroll, WR, 5´10˝/180 lbs; Oklahoma State; Northeastern State (OK); B10/10/1943 San Antonio, TX

| 1966 | Mia-A | 4 | — | — | — | — | 1 | 20 | 20.0 (20) | 0 | — | — | — | — | — | — | — | — | — | — | kp | — | 0 | 62 |

MATTIACE, FRANK   Frank Louis, DE-NT, 6´1˝/264 lbs; Holy Cross; B1/20/1961 Paterson, NJ   **1987** Ind 3 (0)

MATTIFORD, JACK   John Blaker, G, 5´11˝/210 lbs; Marshall; B6/24/1916 Peora, WV, D4/6/1960 Guilford, CT

| 1941 | Det | 10 (3) | — | — | — | — | 1 | 21 | 21.0 (21) | 0 | — | — | — | — | — | — | — | — | — | — | — | — | 0 | 11 |

MATTINGLY, FRAN   Francis Edward, G-LB, 5´11˝/212 lbs; Texas A&M; Texas A&M-Kingsville; B12/4/1919, D9/1988 Sand Springs, OK   **1947** ChiR-A 1 (0)

MATTIOLI, FRANK   Francis A., G, 6´0˝/210 lbs; Pittsburgh; 1945: ChiB, rnd 14; B2/14/1923 Brackenridge, PA, D11/26/1998 Natrona Heights, PA   **1946** Pit 11 (2)

MATTOS, GRANT   Grant, WR, 6´2˝/220 lbs; USC; B3/12/1981 Mountain View, CA   **2003** SD 6 (0)

MATTOS, HARRY   Harry Raymond, HB, 6´0˝/198 lbs; St. Mary's (CA); B4/7/1911 Oakland, CA, D2/5/1992 San Jose, CA [K]

1936	GB	2 (0)	1	2	2.0 (2)	0	—	—	—	—	12	4	33.3	32	2.7	0	2	—	—		—	—	0	-62
1937	Cle	6 (1)	26	16	0.6	1	—	—	—	—	22	5	22.7	94	4.3	1	4	—	—		K	—	8	-82
NFL	2	8 (1)	27	18	0.7 (2)	1	—	—	—	—	34	9	26.5	126	3.7	1	6	—	—		K	—	8	-144

MATTOX, JOHN   Jack V., T-DT, 6´4˝/240 lbs; Fresno State; B8/3/1938 Fresno, CA   **1961** Den-A 8 (LT)

MATTOX, MARV   Marvin Bruce, B-G, 5´9˝/190 lbs; Washington & Lee; B2/11/1900 Leesville, VA, D2/5/1996 Salisbury, NC   **1923** Mil 5 (3)

MATTSON, RILEY   Riley Carl, T, 6´4˝/252 lbs; Oregon; 1961: Was, rnd 11; B12/18/1938 Portland, OR   **1961** Was 14 (14, LT) **1962** Was 14 (14, LT) **1963** Was 14 (14, LT) **1964** Was 14 (LT) **1966** ChiB 12 **NFL** 68 (42) [5 yrs]

YEAR	TEAM	G(GS, POS)	RUSH	YD	AVG(LG)	TD	REC	YD	AVG(LG)	TD	PASS	COMP	PCT	YD	AVG(LG)	TD	INT	SK	YD	QBR	KPR	OTD	PTS	TAY

MATUSZAK, JOHN John Daniel 'Tooz', DE-DT, 6´8˝/272 lbs; Missouri; Tampa; 1973: Hou, rnd 1; B10/25/1950 Milwaukee, WI, D6/17/1989 Burbank, CA **1973** Hou 14 (RDT) **1974** KC 8 **1975** KC 14 (14, LDE) **1976**†Oak 13 (LDE) **1977**†Oak 14 (14, LDE) **1978** Oak 16 (16, LDE) **1979** Oak 12 (2) **1980**†Oak 16 (16, LDE) **1981** Oak 16 (16, LDE) **NFL** 123 (78) [9 yrs]

MATUSZAK, MARV Marvin H., LB, 6´3˝/232 lbs; Tulsa; 1953: Pit, rnd 3; B9/12/1931 South Bend, IN, D2/28/2004 South Bend, IN **1953** Pit✧12 (MLB) **1955** Pit 4 **1956** Pit 9 (LLB) **1957**†SF★12 (MLB) **1958** SF 4 (LLB) **1958** GB 3 **1959**†Bal 11 **1960** Bal 12 **1961** Bal 14 (5, mlb) **1962** Buf-A✧14 (LLB) **1963**†Buf-A 14 **1964** Den-A 14 (MLB) **NFL** 123 (5) [11 yrs]

MATUZA, AL Albert Charles, C, 6´2˝/200 lbs; Georgetown (DC); 1941: ChiB, rnd 8; B9/11/1918 Shenandoah, PA, D5/16/2004 Morrisville, PA **1941**†ChiB✧10 (1) **1942**†ChiB 11 (0) **1943**†ChiB 10 (0) **NFL** 31 (1) [3 yrs]

MAUCK, CARL Carl Frey, C, 6´4˝/243 lbs; Southern Illinois; 1969: Bal, rnd 13; B7/7/1947 McLeansboro, IL **1969** Bal 4 **1970**†Mia 3 **1971** SD 13 (C) **1972** SD 14 (C) **1973** SD 14 (14, C) **1974** SD 14 (14, C) **1975** Hou 14 (14, C) **1976** Hou 14 (14, C) **1977** Hou 14 (14, C) **1978**†Hou 16 (16, C) **1979**†Hou☆16 (16, C) **1980**†Hou 16 (16, C) **1981** Hou 14 (4) **NFL** 166 (122) [13 yrs]

MAUCK, MATT Matt, QB, 6´1˝/213 lbs; LSU; 2004: Den, rnd 7; B12/12/1979 Evansville, IN

YEAR	TEAM	G(GS, POS)	RUSH	YD	AVG(LG)	TD	REC	YD	AVG(LG)	TD	PASS	COMP	PCT	YD	AVG(LG)	TD	INT	SK	YD	QBR	KPR	OTD	PTS	TAY
2005	Ten	3(1)	7	39	5.6(12)	0	—	—	—	—	27	15	55.6	136	5.0(17)	0	1	1	8	—	—	—	0	67

MAUL, TUFFY Elmo Alvin, FB, 5´11˝/200 lbs; St. Mary's (CA); B6/20/1902, CA, D3/16/1974 Fresno, CA **[K]** **1926** LA 10 (10, FB), 21

MAULDIN, STAN Stanley Hubert, T, 6´2˝/225 lbs; Texas; 1943: ChiC, rnd 7; B12/27/1920 Amarillo, TX, D9/25/1948 Chicago, IL **1946** ChiC 6 (4) **1947** ChiC☆12 (12, RT) **1948** ChiC 1 (1) **NFL** 19 (17) [3 yrs]

MAUMALANGA, CHRIS Christian Netane, DT, 6´2˝/300 lbs; Kansas; 1994: NYG, rnd 4; B12/15/1971 Redwood City, CA **1994** NYG 7 (0) **1995** Arz 6 (0) **1996** Arz 1 (0) **NFL** 14 (0) [3 yrs]

MAUMAU, VILIAMI Vilami Akau'ola, DT, 6´2˝/302 lbs; Colorado; 1998: Car, rnd 7; B4/3/1975 Fo'ui, Tonga **1999** Car 1 (0)

MAURER, ANDY Andrew Lee, G-T, 6´3˝/265 lbs; Oregon; 1970: Atl, rnd 3; B9/30/1948 Silverton, OR **1970** Atl 14 (LG) **1971** Atl 14 (LG) **1972** Atl 14 (LG) **1973** Atl 14 (LG) **1974** NO 4 **1974**†Min 8 (6, RG) **1975**†Min 14 (7, LG) **1976** SF 13 (9, RG) **1977**†Den 13 (13, LT) **NFL** 108 (35) [8 yrs]

MAUTI, RICH Richard Dominic, WR, 6´0˝/190 lbs; Penn State; B5/25/1954 Queens, NY **[R]**

YEAR	TEAM	G(GS, POS)	RUSH	YD	AVG(LG)	TD	REC	YD	AVG(LG)	TD	PASS	COMP	PCT	YD	AVG(LG)	TD	INT	SK	YD	QBR	KPR	OTD	PTS	TAY
1977	NO	14(4)	—	—	—	—	4	71	17.8(23)	0	—	—	—	—	—	—	—	—	—	—	kp	—	0	336
1978	NO	16(1)	—	—	—	—	8	69	8.6(16)	2	—	—	—	—	—	—	—	—	—	—	kp	—	12	178
1979	NO	15	—	—	—	—	2	64	32.0(61)	0	—	—	—	—	—	—	—	—	—	—	kp	—	0	376
1980	NO☆	9(0)	1	2	2.0(2)	0	1	10	10.0(10)	0	—	—	—	—	—	—	—	—	—	—	kp	—	0	396
1982	NO	9(0)	—	—	—	—	4	70	17.5(37)	0	—	—	—	—	—	—	—	—	—	—	k	—	0	53
1983	NO	16(1)	—	—	—	—	2	30	15.0(23)	0	—	—	—	—	—	—	—	—	—	—	k	—	0	42
1984	†Was	16(0)	—	—	—	—	—	—	—	—	—	—	—	—	—	—	—	—	—	—	kp	—	0	-2
NFL	7	95(6)	1	2	2.0(2)	0	21	314	15.0(61)	2	—	—	—	—	—	—	—	—	—	—	kp	—	12	1378

MAVES, EARL Earl Clifford, WB, 5´9˝/180 lbs; Michigan; Wisconsin; 1947: Det, rnd 26; B4/8/1923 Ladysmith, WI **1948** Det 1 (0)

MAVRAIDES, MENIL Menil, G, 6´1˝/235 lbs; Notre Dame; 1954: Phi, rnd 4; B11/17/1931 Lowell, MA **1954** Phi 12 **1957** Phi 12 **NFL** 24 [2 yrs]

MAWAE, KEVIN Kevin James, C-G, 6´4˝/289 lbs; LSU; 1994: Sea, rnd 2; B1/23/1971 Savannah, GA **1994** Sea 14 (11, RG) **1995** Sea 16 (16, RG) **1996** Sea 16 (16, C) **1997** Sea 16 (16, C) **1998**†NYJ☆16 (16, C) **1999** NYJ★16 (16, C) **2000** NYJ★16 (16, C) **2001**†NYJ★16 (16, C) **2002**†NYJ★16 (16, C) **2003** NYJ✧16 (16, C) **2004**†NYJ★16 (16, C) **2005** NYJ 6 (6, c) **NFL** 180 (177) [12 yrs]

MAXEY, CURTIS Curtis Wilson, DE-DT, 6´3˝/298 lbs; Grambling State; 1988: Cin, rnd 8; B6/28/1965 Indianapolis, IN **1988**†Cin 3 (0) **1989** Atl 2 (0) **NFL** 5 (0) [2 yrs]

MAXIE, BRETT Brett Derrell, DB, 6´2˝/194 lbs; Texas Southern; B1/13/1962 Dallas, TX **[I]** **1985** NO 16 (1) **1986** NO 15 (0) **1987** NO 12 (10, FS) **1988** NO 16 (16, FS) **1989** NO 16 (2) **1990**†NO 16 (16, SS) **1991**†NO 16 (16, SS) **1992** NO 10 (10, SS) **1993** NO 1 (1) **1994** Atl 4 (2) **1995** Car 16 (16, SS) **1996**†Car 13 (13, SS) **1997**†SF 2 (1) **NFL** 153 (104) [13 yrs]

MAXSON, ALVIN Alvin Earl, RB, 5´11˝/205 lbs; SMU; 1974: NO, rnd 8; B11/12/1951 Beaumont, TX

YEAR	TEAM	G(GS, POS)	RUSH	YD	AVG(LG)	TD	REC	YD	AVG(LG)	TD	PASS	COMP	PCT	YD	AVG(LG)	TD	INT	SK	YD	QBR	KPR	OTD	PTS	TAY
1974	NO	14(RB)	165	714	4.3(66)	2	42	294	7.0(22)	1	—	—	—	—	—	—	—	—	—	—	—	—	18	886
1975	NO	13(13, FB)	139	371	2.7(14)	3	41	234	5.7(33)	0	—	—	—	—	—	—	—	—	—	—	k	—	18	531
1976	NO	14	34	120	3.5(16)	1	7	21	3.0(14)	0	—	—	—	—	—	—	—	—	—	—	k	—	6	167
1977	†Pit	7	18	56	3.1(8)	0	5	70	14.0(34)	0	—	—	—	—	—	—	—	—	—	—	k	—	0	136
1978	Pit	5	4	9	2.3(7)	0	—	—	—	—	—	—	—	—	—	—	—	—	—	—	k	—	0	12
1978	TB	1	—	—	—	—	—	—	—	—	—	—	—	—	—	—	—	—	—	—	k	—	0	2
1978	Hou	1	—	—	—	—	—	—	—	—	—	—	—	—	—	—	—	—	—	—	—	—	—	—
1978	NYG	1	—	—	—	—	—	—	—	—	—	—	—	—	—	—	—	—	—	—	—	—	—	—
NFL	5	56(13)	360	1270	3.5(66)	6	95	619	6.5(34)	1	—	—	—	—	—	—	—	—	—	—	k	—	42	1734

MAXWELL, BRUCE Donald Bruxe, RB, 6´1˝/220 lbs; Arkansas; 1970: Det, rnd 10; B3/23/1947 Crossett, AR

YEAR	TEAM	G(GS, POS)	RUSH	YD	AVG(LG)	TD	REC	YD	AVG(LG)	TD	PASS	COMP	PCT	YD	AVG(LG)	TD	INT	SK	YD	QBR	KPR	OTD	PTS	TAY
1970	†Det	11	1	9	9.0(9)	0	—	—	—	—	—	—	—	—	—	—	—	—	—	—	k	—	0	14

MAXWELL, JIM James, LB, 6´4˝/242 lbs; Gardner-Webb; B8/8/1981 Johnsonville, SC **2004** NYG 14 (0) **2005** SF 11 (1) **NFL** 25 (1) [2 yrs]

MAXWELL, JOEY Joseph William, C-E, 6´2˝/197 lbs; Notre Dame; B11/5/1904 Cincinnati, OH, D2/21/1983 Ardsley, PA **1927** Fra 18 (9, c) **1928** Fra 8 (6, c) **1929** Fra☆12 (10, re) **NFL** 38 (25) [3 yrs]

MAXWELL, MARCUS Marcus James, WR, 6´4˝/205 lbs; Oregon; 2005: SF, rnd 7; B7/8/1983 Berkeley, CA **2005** SF 4 (0)

MAXWELL, TOMMY Thomas Marshall, DB, 6´2˝/195 lbs; Texas A&M; 1969: Bal, rnd 2; B5/5/1947 Houston, TX **1969** Bal 13 (RCB) **1970**†Bal 14 (RCB) **1971** Oak 13 **1972** Oak 7 **1973**†Oak 8 **1974** Hou 13 **NFL** 68 [6 yrs]

MAXWELL, VERNON Vernon Leroy, LB, 6´2˝/233 lbs; Arizona State; 1983: Bal, rnd 2; B10/25/1961 Birmingham, AL **1983** Bal 16 (16, ROLB) **1984** Ind 16 (15, ROLB) **1985** Det 9 (2) **1986** Det 15 (15, RILB) **1987** Det 12 (1) **1989** Sea 9 (7, rolb) **NFL** 77 (56) [6 yrs]

MAY, ART Arthur Lee, DE, 6´3˝/255 lbs; Tuskegee; 1971: Cin, rnd 5; B11/16/1948 Bessemer, AL **1971** NE 11 (7, rde)

MAY, BILL William, BB, 5´11˝/188 lbs; LSU; B2/4/1913, **[K]**

YEAR	TEAM	G(GS, POS)	RUSH	YD	AVG(LG)	TD	REC	YD	AVG(LG)	TD	PASS	COMP	PCT	YD	AVG(LG)	TD	INT	SK	YD	QBR	KPR	OTD	PTS	TAY
1937	ChiC	9(3)	4	16	4.0	0	—	—	—	—	—	—	—	—	—	—	—	—	—	—	K	—	10	16
1938	ChiC	1(0)	—	—	—	—	1	16	16.0(16)	0	—	—	—	—	—	—	—	—	—	—	K	—	0	8
NFL	2	10(3)	4	16	4.0	0	1	16	16.0(16)	0	—	—	—	—	—	—	—	—	—	—	K	—	10	24

MAY, DEAN Dean Curtis, QB, 6´5˝/220 lbs; Louisville; 1984: Mia, rnd 5; B5/26/1962 Orlando, FL

YEAR	TEAM	G(GS, POS)	RUSH	YD	AVG(LG)	TD	REC	YD	AVG(LG)	TD	PASS	COMP	PCT	YD	AVG(LG)	TD	INT	SK	YD	QBR	KPR	OTD	PTS	TAY
1984	Phi	2(0)	—	—	—	—	—	—	—	—	1	1	100.0	33	33.0(33)	0	0	—	—	—	—	—	0	17
1987	Den	3(0)	2	-4	-2.0(-2)	0	—	—	—	—	5	0	0.0	0	0.0	0	1	1	7	—	—	—	0	-44
NFL	2	5(0)	2	-4	-2.0(-2)	0	—	—	—	—	6	1	16.7	33	5.5(33)	0	1	1	7	—	—	—	0	-28

MAY, DEEMS Bert Deems, TE, 6´4˝/263 lbs; North Carolina; 1992: SD, rnd 7; B3/6/1969 Lexington, NC **1992**†SD 16 (6, te) **1993** SD 15 (1) **1995** SD 5 (0) **1999**†Sea 15 (0)

YEAR	TEAM	G(GS, POS)	RUSH	YD	AVG(LG)	TD	REC	YD	AVG(LG)	TD	PASS	COMP	PCT	YD	AVG(LG)	TD	INT	SK	YD	QBR	KPR	OTD	PTS	TAY
1994	SD	5(2)	—	—	—	—	2	22	11.0(18)	0	—	—	—	—	—	—	—	—	—	—	—	—	0	11
1996	SD	16(12, TE)	—	—	—	—	19	188	9.9(39)	0	—	—	—	—	—	—	—	—	—	—	—	—	0	94
1997	Sea	16(0)	—	—	—	—	2	21	10.5(11)	0	—	—	—	—	—	—	—	—	—	—	k	—	0	4
1998	Sea	16(1)	—	—	—	—	3	7	2.3(5)	1	—	—	—	—	—	—	—	—	—	—	—	—	6	9
NFL	8	104(22)	—	—	—	—	26	238	9.2(39)	1	—	—	—	—	—	—	—	—	—	—	k	—	6	117

MAY, JACK Francis John, C, 5´10˝/210 lbs; Centenary; B4/16/1915, D11/1969 **1938** Cle 9 (1)

MAY, MARC Marc Edward, TE, 6´4˝/230 lbs; Purdue; B1/1/1958 Chicago, IL

YEAR	TEAM	G(GS, POS)	RUSH	YD	AVG(LG)	TD	REC	YD	AVG(LG)	TD	PASS	COMP	PCT	YD	AVG(LG)	TD	INT	SK	YD	QBR	KPR	OTD	PTS	TAY
1987	Min	3(3)	—	—	—	—	1	22	22.0(22)	0	—	—	—	—	—	—	—	—	—	—	—	—	0	11

MAY, MARK Mark Eric, G-T-C, 6´6˝/295 lbs; Pittsburgh; 1981: Was, rnd 1; B11/2/1959 Oneonta, NY **1981** Was 16 (8, lt) **1982**†Was 9 (9, RG) **1983**†Was 15 (15, RG) **1984**†Was 16 (16, RT/rg) **1985** Was 16 (16, RT) **1986**†Was 16 (16, RT) **1987**†Was 10 (10, RT) **1988** Was★16 (16, RG/rt) **1989** Was 9 (9, RG) **1991** SD 9 (0) **1992** Phx 16 (16, LG) **1993** Phx 11 (11, LG) **NFL** 159 (142) [12 yrs]

MAY, RAY Reginald Raymond, LB, 6´1˝/230 lbs; USC; 1967: Pit, rnd 4; B6/4/1945 Los Angeles, CA **1967** Pit 14 **1968** Pit 12 (MLB) **1969** Pit 14 (MLB) **1970**†Bal 14 **1971**†Bal 14 (LLB) **1972** Bal 14 (RLB) **1973** Bal 3 **1973** Den 11 (10, RLB) **1974** Den 14 (12, MLB) **1975** Den 8 (8, RLB) **NFL** 118 (30) [9 yrs]

YEAR	TEAM	G (GS, POS)	RUSH	YD	AVG (LG)	TD	REC	YD	AVG (LG)	TD	PASS COMP	PCT	YD	AVG (LG)	TD	INT	SK	YD	QBR	KPR	OTD	PTS	TAY

MAY, SHERRIDEN   Sherriden Allen, RB, 6´0˝/215 lbs; Idaho; B8/10/1973 Tacoma, WA   **1996** NYJ 8 (0)

| 1995 | NYJ | 5(1) | 2 | 5 | 2.5(3) | 0 | — | — | — | — | — | — | — | — | — | — | — | — | — | — | — | 0 | 5 |
| NFL | 2 | 13(1) | 2 | 5 | 2.5(3) | 0 | — | — | — | — | — | — | — | — | — | — | — | — | — | — | — | 0 | 5 |

MAY, WALT   Walter Orel, G, 6´1˝/205 lbs; none; B2/27/1894 Taylorville, IL, D8/11/1934 Peoria, IL   **1920** Dec 4 (0)

MAYBERRY, DOUG   Douglas Clark, FB, 6´1˝/220 lbs; California; Utah State; 1961: Min, rnd 10; B3/23/1937 Arbuckle, CA

1961	Min	4	13	40	3.1(13)	0	2	18	9.0(13)	0	—	—	—	—	—	—	—	—	—	—	—	0	49
1962	Min	13(10, FB)	74	274	3.7(17)	1	11	100	9.1(21)	1	—	—	—	—	—	—	—	—	—	—	—	12	339
1963	Oak-A	2	—	—	—	—	—	—	—	—	—	—	—	—	—	—	—	—	—	—	—	—	—
NFL	3	19(10)	87	314	3.6(17)	1	13	118	9.1(21)	1	—	—	—	—	—	—	—	—	—	—	—	12	388

MAYBERRY, JAMES   James Loyd, RB, 5´11˝/210 lbs; Colorado; 1979: Atl, rnd 3; B11/5/1957 Amarillo, TX

1979	Atl	16(1)	45	193	4.3(21)	1	7	48	6.9(19)	0	—	—	—	—	—	—	—	—	—	ki	—	1	12	227
1980	†Atl	16(0)	18	88	4.9(24)	0	3	1	0.3(6)	0	—	—	—	—	—	—	—	—	—	—	—	0	89
1981	Atl	16(0)	18	66	3.7(11)	0	3	4	1.3(6)	0	—	—	—	—	—	—	—	—	—	k	—	0	61
NFL	3	48(1)	81	347	4.3(24)	1	13	53	4.1(19)	0	—	—	—	—	—	—	—	—	—	ki	—	1	12	377

MAYBERRY, JERMANE   Jermane Timothy, G-T, 6´4˝/325 lbs; Texas A&M-Kingsville; 1996: Phi, rnd 1; B8/29/1973 Floresville, TX   **1996**†Phi 3 (1) **1997** Phi 16 (16, LT)
1998 Phi 15 (10, LG) **1999** Phi 13 (5, rt) **2000**†Phi 16 (16, RG) **2001**†Phi 16 (15, RG) **2002**†Phi★16 (16, RG) **2003** Phi 5 (5, rg) **2004**†Phi 12 (12, RG) **2005** NO 11 (8, rg)
NFL 123 (104) [10 yrs]

MAYBERRY, TONY   Eino Anthony, C, 6´4˝/293 lbs; Wake Forest; 1990: TB, rnd 4; B12/8/1967 Wurzburg, Germany   **1990** TB 16 (1) **1991** TB 16 (16, C) **1992** TB 16 (16, C)
1993 TB 16 (16, C) **1994** TB 16 (16, C) **1995** TB 16 (16, C) **1996** TB 16 (16, C) **1997**†TB◇16 (16, C) **1998** TB◇16 (16, C) **1999**†TB◇16 (16, C) **NFL** 160 (145) [10 yrs]

MAYER, EMIL   Emil H., E, 6´0˝/190 lbs; Bethany (WV); Catholic; B7/3/1903 East Liverpool, OH, D1/1/1971 Findlay, OH   **1927** Pot 1 (0) **1930** Por 10 (3) **NFL** 11 (3) [2 yrs]

MAYER, FRANK   Francis George, G-T, 5´11˝/215 lbs; Iowa State; Notre Dame; B6/18/1902 Glencoe, MN, D3/1960   **1927** GB 10 (10, LG)

MAYER, SHAWN   Shawn Arron, DB, 6´0˝/202 lbs; Penn State; B3/4/1979 Hillsborough, NJ   **2003**†NE 9 (0) **2004** NE 3 (0) **NFL** 12 (0) [2 yrs]

MAYES, ADRIAN   Adrian Anthony, DB, 6´1˝/211 lbs; LSU; B11/17/1980 Hattiesburg, MS   **2004** Arz 4 (0) **2005** Arz 3 (0) **NFL** 7 (0) [2 yrs]

MAYES, ALONZO   Alonzo Lewis, TE, 6´4˝/259 lbs; Oklahoma State; 1998: Chi, rnd 4; B6/4/1975 Oklahoma City, OK

1998	ChiB	16(16, TE)	—	—	—	—	21	217	10.3(22)	0	—	—	—	—	—	—	—	—	—	—	—	0	109
1999	ChiB	16(9, TE)	—	—	—	—	8	82	10.3(24)	1	—	—	—	—	—	—	—	—	—	—	—	6	46
2000	ChiB	5(3)	—	—	—	—	4	40	10.0(19)	0	—	—	—	—	—	—	—	—	—	—	—	0	20
NFL	3	37(28)	—	—	—	—	33	339	10.3(24)	1	—	—	—	—	—	—	—	—	—	—	—	6	175

MAYES, BEN   Benjamin Clayton, DE-DT, 6´5˝/265 lbs; Drake; 1969: Buf, rnd 5; B3/16/1945 St. Petersburg, FL   **1969** Hou-A 5

MAYES, CARL   Carl Hazen, HB, 6´0˝/190 lbs; Texas; B3/31/1930 Austin, TX

| 1952 | LARm | 7 | 5 | 2 | 0.4(6) | 0 | — | — | — | — | — | — | — | — | — | — | — | — | — | — | — | 0 | 2 |

MAYES, DERRICK   Derrick Binet, WR, 6´0˝/205 lbs; Notre Dame; 1996: GB, rnd 2; B1/28/1974 Indianapolis, IN

1996	GB	7(0)	—	—	—	—	6	46	7.7(12)	2	—	—	—	—	—	—	—	—	—	—	—	12	33
1997	†GB	12(3)	—	—	—	—	18	290	16.1(74)	0	—	—	—	—	—	—	—	—	—	p	—	0	216
1998	†GB	10(6, wr)	—	—	—	—	30	394	13.1(33)	3	—	—	—	—	—	—	—	—	—	p	—	18	216
1999	†Sea	16(15, WR)	—	—	—	—	62	829	13.4(43)	10	—	—	—	—	—	—	—	—	—	—	—	60	465
2000	Sea	13(8, wr)	—	—	—	—	29	264	9.1(40)	1	—	—	—	—	—	—	—	—	—	—	—	6	137
NFL	5	58(32)	—	—	—	—	145	1823	12.6(74)	16	—	—	—	—	—	—	—	—	—	p	—	96	1067

MAYES, MICHAEL   Michael Oneal, DB, 5´10˝/182 lbs; LSU; 1989: NO, rnd 4; B8/17/1966 De Ridder, LA   **1989** NO 2 (0) **1990** NYJ 16 (2) **1991** Min 9 (0) **NFL** 27 (2) [3 yrs]

MAYES, RUEBEN   Rueben A., RB, 5´11˝/201 lbs; Washington State; 1986: NO, rnd 3; B6/6/1963 North Battleford, Canada

1986	NO★	16(12, RB)	286	1353	4.7(50)	8	17	96	5.6(18)	0	—	—	—	—	—	—	—	—	—	k	—	48	1544
1987	†NO★	12(12, RB)	243	917	3.8(38)	5	15	68	4.5(16)	0	—	—	—	—	—	—	—	—	—	—	—	30	1001
1988	NO	16(9, rb)	170	628	3.7(21)	3	11	103	9.4(25)	0	—	—	—	—	—	—	—	—	—	k	—	18	737
1990	†NO	15(8, RB)	138	510	3.7(18)	7	12	121	10.1(66)	0	—	—	—	—	—	—	—	—	—	k	—	42	650
1992	Sea	16(0)	28	74	2.6(14)	0	2	13	6.5(7)	0	—	—	—	—	—	—	—	—	—	k	—	0	107
1993	Sea	1(0)	1	2	2.0(2)	0	—	—	—	—	—	—	—	—	—	—	—	—	—	—	—	0	2
NFL	6	76(41)	866	3484	4.0(50)	23	57	401	7.0(66)	0	—	—	—	—	—	—	—	—	—	k	—	138	4040

MAYES, RUFUS   Rufus Lee, T-G, 6´5˝/260 lbs; Ohio State; 1969: Chi, rnd 1; B12/5/1947 Clarksdale, AR, D1/9/1990 Bellevue, WA   **1969** ChiB 13 (RT) **1970** Cin 14 (LG)
1971 Cin 14 (lt) **1972** Cin 6 **1973** Cin 13 (LT) **1974** Cin 14 (LT) **1975** Cin 14 (LT) **1976** Cin 14 (LT) **1977** Cin 12 (12, LT) **1978** Cin 9 (lt) **1979** Phi 16 **NFL** 139 (12) [11 yrs]

MAYES, TONY   Anthony Curtis, DB, 6´0˝/200 lbs; Kentucky; 1987: TB, rnd 5; B5/19/1964 Tazewell, TN   **1987** SL 3 (2)

MAYFIELD, COREY   Arthur Corey, DT, 6´3˝/302 lbs; Oklahoma; 1992: SF, rnd 10; B2/25/1970 Tyler, TX   **1992** TB 11 (0) **1995** Jax 16 (4) **NFL** 27 (4) [2 yrs]

MAYHEW, LINDY   Hayden Lowe, G-T, 6´1˝/223 lbs; Texas-El Paso; B8/24/1907, D2/21/1990 Lilburn, GA   **1936** Pit 12 (8, LG) **1937** Pit 9 (3) **1938** Pit 6 (0) **NFL** 27 (11) [3 yrs]

MAYHEW, MARTIN   Martin, DB, 5´8˝/172 lbs; Florida State; 1988: Buf, rnd 10; B10/8/1965 Daytona Beach, FL [I]   **1989** Was 16 (7, lcb) **1990**†Was 16 (15, LCB)
1991†Was 16 (16, LCB) **1992**†Was 10 (10, LCB) **1993** TB 15 (14, LCB) **1994** TB 16 (16, LCB) **1995** TB 13 (13, LCB) **1996** TB 16 (16, LCB) **NFL** 118 (107) [8 yrs]

MAYL, GENE   Eugene Aloysius, E, 6´2˝/198 lbs; Dayton; Notre Dame; B10/23/1901 Dayton, OH, D7/12/1986 Dayton, OH   **1925** Day 8 (8, RE) **1926** Day 4 (4, RE), 12
NFL 12 (12) [2 yrs]

MAYNARD, BRAD   Bradley Alan, P, 6´1˝/186 lbs; Ball State; 1997: NYG, rnd 3; B2/9/1974 Tipton, IN [P]

1997	†NYG	16(0)	—	—	—	—	—	—	—	—	—	—	—	—	—	—	—	—	—	P	—	0	0
1998	NYG	16(0)	1	-5	-5.0(-5)	0	—	—	—	—	1	0	0.0	0	0.0	0	0	—	—	P	—	0	-5
1999	NYG	16(0)	—	—	—	—	—	—	—	—	—	—	—	—	—	—	—	—	—	P	—	0	0
2000	†NYG	16(0)	—	—	—	—	—	—	—	—	—	—	—	—	—	—	—	—	—	P	—	0	0
2001	†ChiB	16(0)	1	-10	-10.0(-10)	0	—	—	—	—	1	1	100.0	27	27.0(27)	1	0	—	—	P	—	0	9
2002	ChiB	16(0)	1	20	20.0(20)	0	—	—	—	—	1	1	100.0	12	12.0(12)	1	0	—	—	P	—	0	31
2003	ChiB	16(0)	1	0	0.0(0)	0	—	—	—	—	—	—	—	—	—	—	—	—	—	P	—	0	0
2004	ChiB☆	16(0)	—	—	—	—	—	—	—	—	—	—	—	—	—	—	—	—	—	P	—	0	0
2005	†ChiB	16(0)	—	—	—	—	—	—	—	—	2	1	50.0	18	9.0(18)	0	0	—	—	P	—	0	9
NFL	9	144(0)	4	5	1.3(20)	0	—	—	—	—	5	3	60.0	57	11.4(27)	2	0	—	—	P	—	0	44

MAYNARD, DON   Donald Rogers, E-FL-HB, 6´0˝/180 lbs; Rice; Texas-El Paso; 1957: NYG, rnd 9; B1/25/1935 Crosbyton, TX; HOF 1987

1958	†NYG	12	12	45	3.8(14)	0	5	84	16.8(31)	0	—	—	—	—	—	—	—	—	—	kp	—	0	203
1960	NYT-A☆	14(FL)	—	—	—	—	72	1265	17.6(65)	6	—	—	—	—	—	—	—	—	—	k	—	36	677
1961	NYT-A	14(FL)	—	—	—	—	43	629	14.6(45)	8	—	—	—	—	—	—	—	—	—	p	—	48	359
1962	NYT-A	14(FL)	—	—	—	—	56	1041	18.6(86)	8	—	—	—	—	—	—	—	—	—	—	—	48	561
1963	NYJ-A	12(FL)	2	6	3.0(8)	0	38	780	20.5(73)	9	—	—	—	—	—	—	—	—	—	p	—	54	442
1964	NYJ-A	14(FL)	3	3	1.0(14)	0	46	847	18.4(68)	8	—	—	—	—	—	—	—	—	—	—	—	48	467
1965	NYJ-A★	14(FL)	1	2	2.0(2)	0	68	1218	17.9(56)	14	—	—	—	—	—	—	—	—	—	—	—	84	681
1966	NYJ-A	14(FL)	—	—	—	—	48	840	17.5(55)	5	—	—	—	—	—	—	—	—	—	—	—	30	445
1967	NYJ-A★	14(FL)	4	18	4.5(7)	0	71	1434	20.2(75)	10	—	—	—	—	—	—	—	—	—	—	—	62	785
1968	†NYJ-A★	13(FL)	—	—	—	—	57	1297	22.8(87)	10	—	—	—	—	—	—	—	—	—	—	—	60	699
1969	†NYJ-A★	11(FL)	1	-6	-6.0(-6)	0	47	938	20.0(60)	6	—	—	—	—	—	—	—	—	—	—	—	38	493
1970	NYJ	10(WR)	—	—	—	—	31	525	16.9(47)	0	—	—	—	—	—	—	—	—	—	—	—	0	263
1971	NYJ	14(WR)	1	2	2.0(2)	0	21	408	19.4(74)	2	—	—	—	—	—	—	—	—	—	—	—	12	216
1972	NYJ	14(WR)	—	—	—	—	29	510	17.6(41)	2	—	—	—	—	—	—	—	—	—	—	—	12	265
1973	SL	2	—	—	—	—	1	18	18.0(18)	0	—	—	—	—	—	—	—	—	—	—	—	0	9
NFL	15	186	24	70	2.9(14)	0	633	11834	18.7(87)	88	—	—	—	—	—	—	—	—	—	kp	—	532	6562

YEAR	TEAM	G(GS, POS)	RUSH	YD	AVG(LG)	TD	REC	YD	AVG(LG)	TD	PASS	COMP	PCT	YD	AVG(LG)	TD	INT	SK	YD	QBR	KPR	OTD	PTS	TAY
MAYNARD, LES Lester, E, 6´3˝/210 lbs; Rider; B1911																								
1932	SI	8(5, LE)	—	—	—	—	3	67	22.3	0	—	—	—	—	—	—	—	—	—	—	—	—	0	34
MAYNE, LEW Lewis Elwood, HB, 6´1˝/190 lbs; Texas; B3/21/1920 Cuero, TX																								
1946	Bkn-A	13(2)	70	191	2.7	1	5	9	1.8	0	25	14	56.0	219	8.8	3	4	—	—	—	Pkp	1	12	217
1947	†Cle-A	13(4)	41	75	1.8	0	6	238	39.7	3	—	—	—	—	—	—	—	—	—	—	k	—	18	236
1948	Bal-A	8(0)	14	26	1.9	0	2	33	16.5	0	—	—	—	—	—	—	—	—	—	—	kp	—	0	73
AAFC	3	34(6)	125	292	2.3	1	13	280	21.5	3	25	14	56.0	219	8.8	3	4	—	—	—	Pkp	1	30	526
MAYO, RON Ronald, TE, 6´2˝/222 lbs; Morgan State; 1973: Hou, rnd 6; B10/11/1950 Washington, DC **1973** Hou 13 **1974** Bal 9 **NFL** 22 [2 yrs]																								
MAYOCK, MIKE Michael Francis, DB, 6´2˝/195 lbs; Boston College; 1981: Pit, rnd 10; B8/14/1958 Philadelphia, PA **1982** NYG 3 (0) **1983** NYG 6 (0) **NFL** 9 (0) [2 yrs]																								
MAYS, ALVOID Alvoid Wilson, DB, 5´9˝/180 lbs; West Virginia; 1989: Hou, rnd 8; B7/10/1966 Palmetto, FL **1990**†Was 15 (1) **1991**†Was 13 (0) **1992**†Was 16 (3) **1993** Was 15 (2) **1994** Was 2 (0) **1995** Pit 13 (6, rcb) **NFL** 74 (12) [6 yrs]																								
MAYS, DAMON Damon, WR, 5´9˝/170 lbs; Missouri; 1991: Dal, rnd 9; B5/20/1968 Phoenix, AZ **1992** Hou 1 (0) **1993** Hou 1 (0) **NFL** 2 (0) [2 yrs]																								
MAYS, DAVE David, QB, 6´1˝/204 lbs; Texas Southern; B6/20/1949 Pine Bluff, AR																								
1976	Cle	4	5	14	2.8(6)	0	—	—	—	—	20	9	45.0	101	5.1(21)	0	1	2	4	—	P	—	0	25
1977	Cle	7(4, qb)	4	2	0.5(2)	0	—	—	—	—	121	67	55.4	797	6.6(60)	6	10	6	67	—	—	—	0	31
1978	Buf	1	—	—	—	—	—	—	—	—	15	4	26.7	39	2.6(19)	1	0	1	11	—	—	—	0	25
NFL	3	12(4)	9	16	1.8(6)	0	—	—	—	—	156	80	51.3	937	6.0(60)	7	11	9	82	—	P	—	0	80
MAYS, JERRY Gerald Avery, DE-DT, 6´4˝/252 lbs; SMU; 1961: DalT, rnd 5/Min, rnd 11; B11/24/1939 Dallas, TX, D7/17/1994 Lake Lewisville, TX **1961** DalT-A 14 **1962**†DalT-A★14 (RDT) **1963** KC-A☆14 (RDT) **1964** KC-A★14 (LDT) **1965** KC-A★14 (LDE) **1966**†KC-A★14 (LDE) **1967** KC-A★14 (LDE) **1968**†KC-A★14 (LDE) **1969**†KC-A☆14 (LDE) **1970** KC★14 (LDE) **NFL** 140 [10 yrs]																								
MAYS, JERRY Jerry Dewayne, RB, 5´7˝/176 lbs; Georgia Tech; B12/8/1967 Augusta, GA **1990** SD 2 (0)																								
MAYS, KIVUUSAMA Kivuusama, LB, 6´3˝/247 lbs; North Carolina; 1998: Min, rnd 4; B1/7/1975 Anniston, AL **1998**†Min 16 (0) **1999** Min 11 (0) **1999** GB 3 (0) **NFL** 30 (0) [2 yrs]																								
MAYS, LEE Lee, WR, 6´2˝/200 lbs; Texas-El Paso; 2002: Pit, rnd 6; B9/18/1979 Houston, TX																								
2002	†Pit	16(0)	—	—	—	—	—	—	—	—	—	—	—	—	—	—	—	—	—	—	k	—	0	191
2003	Pit	16(0)	—	—	—	—	2	17	8.5(9)	0	—	—	—	—	—	—	—	—	—	—	k	—	0	28
2004	†Pit	16(1)	—	—	—	—	9	137	15.2(46)	0	—	—	—	—	—	—	—	—	—	—	—	—	0	69
NFL	3	48(1)	—	—	—	—	11	154	14.0(46)	0	—	—	—	—	—	—	—	—	—	—	k	—	0	287
MAYS, STAFFORD Stafford Earl, DE-DT-NT, 6´2˝/252 lbs; Washington; 1980: SL, rnd 9; B3/13/1958 Lawrence, KS **1980** SL 16 (0) **1981** SL 16 (0) **1982**†SL 8 (0) **1983** SL 16 (1) **1984** SL 16 (0) **1985** SL 16 (1) **1986** SL 16 (6, lde) **1987**†Min 12 (7, rdt) **1988**†Min 3 (1) **NFL** 119 (16) [9 yrs]																								
MAZNICKI, FRANK Francis Stanley, HB, 5´9˝/181 lbs; Boston College; 1942: ChiB, rnd 8; B7/19/1920 West Warwick, RI **[K]**																								
1942	†ChiB✧	11(1)	54	343	6.4(42)	1	2	17	8.5(16)	1	1	0	0.0	0	0.0	0	0	—	—	—	Kkpi	—	45	398
1946	†ChiB	4(3)	19	43	2.3(9)	0	2	38	19.0(22)	0	—	—	—	—	—	—	—	—	—	—	Kkpi	—	37	111
1947	Bos	12(1)	34	77	2.3(17)	0	6	76	12.7(26)	0	1	0	0.0	0	0.0	0	1	—	—	—	Kpi	2	37	139
NFL	3	27(5)	107	463	4.3(42)	1	10	131	13.1(26)	1	2	0	0.0	0	0.0	0	1	—	—	—	Kkpi	2	119	648
MAZUREK, FRED Frederick Henry, WR, 5´11˝/192 lbs; Catholic; Pittsburgh; B3/21/1943 Uniontown, PA **1965** Was 1																								
1966	Was	12(2)	—	—	—	—	2	28	14.0(15)	0	—	—	—	—	—	—	—	—	—	—	kp	—	0	203
NFL	2	13(2)	—	—	—	—	2	28	14.0(15)	0	—	—	—	—	—	—	—	—	—	—	kp	—	0	198
MAZZA, VINCE Vincent L., E, 6´1˝/216 lbs; none; B3/25/1925 Niagara Falls, NY, D12/5/1993 Winona, Canada **1945** Det 5 (1) **1946** Det 1 (0) **NFL** 6 (1) [2 yrs]																								
1948†Buf-A 14 (1) **1949**†Buf-A 12 (0)																								
1947	Buf-A	13(2)	—	—	—	—	2	11	5.5	0	—	—	—	—	—	—	—	—	—	—	i	—	0	27
AAFC	3	39(3)	—	—	—	—	2	11	5.5	0	—	—	—	—	—	—	—	—	—	—	i	1	6	42
MAZZANTI, GENO Geno, HB, 5´11˝/190 lbs; Arkansas; 1950: Bal, rnd 26; B4/1/1929 Lake Village, AR																								
1950	Bal	4	7	22	3.1(7)	1	1	11	11.0(11)	0	—	—	—	—	—	—	—	—	—	—	—	—	6	38
MAZZANTI, JERRY Jerry Edward, DE, 6´3˝/240 lbs; Arkansas; 1962: Phi, rnd 16/1963: SD, rnd 25; B7/13/1940 Lake Village, AR **1963** Phi 5 (lde) **1966** Det 13 **1967** Pit 12 **NFL** 30 [3 yrs]																								
MAZZETTI, TIM Timothy Alan, K, 6´1˝/175 lbs; Pennsylvania; B2/1/1956 Sao Paulo, Brazil **[K]** **1978**†Atl 10 **1979** Atl 16 **1980**†Atl☆16 (0) **NFL** 42 [3 yrs]																								
MCADAMS, BOB Robert Louis, DT, 6´3˝/250 lbs; North Carolina Central; 1963: NYG, rnd 17; B11/1/1939 Durham, NC **1963** NYJ-A 12 **1964** NYJ-A 14 **NFL** 26 [2 yrs]																								
MCADAMS, CARL Carl Lee, DT-LB-DE, 6´3˝/240 lbs; Oklahoma; 1966: NYJ, rnd 3/SL, rnd 1; B4/26/1944 Dumas, TX **1967** NYJ-A 8 (1) **1968**†NYJ-A 14 (ldt) **1969** NYJ-A 4 **NFL** 26 (1) [3 yrs]																								
MCADAMS, DEAN Dean LeRoy, TB-HB, 6´1˝/193 lbs; Washington; 1941: Bkn, rnd 1; B10/3/1917 Caldwell, ID **[K]**																								
1941	Bkn	11(0)	38	99	2.6(39)	0	7	94	13.4(47)	0	27	12	44.4	176	6.5(36)	2	3	—	—	—	KPpi	—	9	120
1942	Bkn	11(10, TB)	110	314	2.9(25)	0	3	11	3.7(8)	0	89	35	39.3	441	5.0(56)	2	15	—	—	—	KPkp	—	2	75
1943	Bkn	8(1, tb)	40	-38	-0.9(14)	0	2	6	3.0(8)	0	75	37	49.3	315	4.2(49)	0	7	—	—	—	Pkpi	—	0	-78
NFL	3	30(11)	188	375	2.0(39)	0	12	111	9.3(47)	0	191	84	44.0	932	4.9(56)	4	25	—	—	—	KPkpi	—	11	118
MCADDLEY, JASON Jason, WR, 6´2˝/200 lbs; Alabama; 2002: Arz, rnd 5; B7/28/1979 Brooklyn, NY																								
2002	Arz	9(8, WR)	—	—	—	—	25	362	14.5(42)	1	—	—	—	—	—	—	—	—	—	—	k	—	6	201
2003	Arz	2(0)	—	—	—	—	4	53	13.3(25)	0	—	—	—	—	—	—	—	—	—	—	—	—	0	27
2004	Ten	11(1)	—	—	—	—	2	38	19.0(36)	0	—	—	—	—	—	—	—	—	—	—	k	—	0	298
2005	SF	12(2)	—	—	—	—	7	125	17.9(38)	0	—	—	—	—	—	—	—	—	—	—	k	—	0	80
NFL	4	34(11)	—	—	—	—	38	578	15.2(42)	1	—	—	—	—	—	—	—	—	—	—	k	—	6	605
MCADOO, DERRICK Derrick Mark, RB, 5´10˝/198 lbs; Baylor; B4/2/1965 Pensacola, FL **1988** TB 5 (0) **1988** Phx 4 (0)																								
1987	SL	15(2)	53	230	4.3(17)	3	2	12	6.0(6)	0	—	—	—	—	—	—	—	—	—	—	k	1	24	365
NFL	2	24(2)	53	230	4.3(17)	3	2	12	6.0(6)	0	—	—	—	—	—	—	—	—	—	—	kp	1	24	476
MCAFEE, FRED Fred Lee, RB, 5´10˝/193 lbs; Mississippi College; 1991: NO, rnd 6; B6/20/1968 Philadelphia, MS **[R]**																								
1991	†NO	9(0)	109	494	4.5(34)	2	1	8	8.0(8)	0	—	—	—	—	—	—	—	—	—	—	k	—	12	517
1992	NO	14(1)	39	114	2.9(19)	1	1	16	16.0(16)	0	—	—	—	—	—	—	—	—	—	—	k	—	6	240
1993	NO	15(4)	51	160	3.1(27)	1	1	3	3.0(3)	0	—	—	—	—	—	—	—	—	—	—	k	—	6	332
1994	Arz	7(0)	2	-5	-2.5(2)	1	1	4	4.0(4)	0	—	—	—	—	—	—	—	—	—	—	k	—	6	15
1994	†Pit	6(0)	16	56	3.5(13)	1	—	—	—	—	—	—	—	—	—	—	—	—	—	—	—	—	6	66
1995	†Pit	16(1)	39	156	4.0(22)	1	15	88	5.9(18)	0	—	—	—	—	—	—	—	—	—	—	k	—	6	191
1996	†Pit	14(0)	7	17	2.4(5)	0	5	21	4.2(9)	0	—	—	—	—	—	—	—	—	—	—	—	—	0	28
1997	†Pit	14(0)	13	41	3.2(9)	0	2	44	22.0(30)	0	—	—	—	—	—	—	—	—	—	—	—	—	0	63
1998	Pit	14(0)	18	111	6.2(14)	0	9	27	3.0(11)	0	—	—	—	—	—	—	—	—	—	—	k	1	6	120
1999	†TB	1(0)	—	—	—	—	—	—	—	—	—	—	—	—	—	—	—	—	—	—	—	—	—	—
2000	†NO	12(0)	2	37	18.5(40)	0	—	—	—	—	—	—	—	—	—	—	—	—	—	—	k	—	0	138
2001	NO	16(0)	1	2	2.0(2)	0	—	—	—	—	—	—	—	—	—	—	—	—	—	—	k	—	0	56
2002	NO★	11(0)	1	11	11.0(11)	0	—	—	—	—	—	—	—	—	—	—	—	—	—	—	k	—	0	50
2003	NO	14(0)	1	13	13.0(13)	0	—	—	—	—	—	—	—	—	—	—	—	—	—	—	k	—	0	18
2004	NO	11(0)	2	54	27.0(53)	0	—	—	—	—	—	—	—	—	—	—	—	—	—	—	k	—	0	71
2005	NO	16(0)	—	—	—	—	—	—	—	—	—	—	—	—	—	—	—	—	—	—	k	—	0	155
NFL	15	190(6)	301	1261	4.2(53)	7	35	211	6.0(30)	0	—	—	—	—	—	—	—	—	—	—	k	1	48	2059
MCAFEE, GEORGE George Anderson, HB-DB, 6´0˝/178 lbs; Duke; 1940: Phi, rnd 1; B3/13/1918 Corbin, KY; HOF 1966 **[RI]**																								
1940	†ChiB☆	10(8, RH)	47	253	5.4	2	7	117	16.7	0	11	4	36.4	50	4.5	2	0	—	—	—	Pi	1	18	407
1941	†ChiB★	11(2)	65	474	**7.3**(**70**)	5	7	144	20.6(39)	3	3	1	33.3	44	14.7(44)	1	0	—	—	—	Pkpi	4	72	**967**
1945	ChiB	3(0)	16	139	8.7(38)	3	3	85	28.3(65)	1	1	0	0.0	0	0.0	0	0	—	—	—	Pkpi	—	24	251

YEAR	TEAM	G (GS, POS)	RUSH	YD	AVG (LG)	TD	REC	YD	AVG (LG)	TD	PASS	COMP	PCT	YD	AVG (LG)	TD	INT	SK	YD	QBR	KPR	OTD	PTS	TAY
1946	†ChiB	3(0)	14	53	3.8(14)	0	10	137	13.7(25)	3	2	1	50.0	0	0.0(0)	0	0	—	—	—	kpi	—	18	210
1947	ChiB	12(0, rh)	63	209	3.3(39)	3	32	492	15.4(53)	1	—	—	—	—	—	—	—	—	—	—	Pkpi	—	24	713
1948	ChiB☆	12(8, RH)	92	392	4.3(23)	5	17	227	13.4(50)	2	4	0	0.0	0	0.0	0	0	—	—	—	Pkpi	1	48	878
1949	ChiB	12(6, RH)	42	161	3.8(23)	3	9	157	17.4(52)	1	—	—	—	—	—	—	—	—	—	—	pi	1	30	490
1950	†ChiB	12(DB)	2	4	2.0(4)	0	—	—	—	—	1	0	0.0	0	0.0	0	1	—	—	—	kpi	—	0	112
NFL	8	75(24)	341	1685	4.9(70)	21	85	1359	16.0(65)	11	22	6	27.3	94	4.3(44)	3	1	—	—	—	Pkpi	7	234	4026
McAfee, Wes Wesley Taylor, HB, 5´11˝/175 lbs; Duke; 1941: Pit, rnd 16; B10/20/1918 Corbin, KY, D1/1984 Myrtle Beach, SC **[K]**																								
1941	Phi	8(1)	9	6	0.7(3)	0	3	30	10.0(13)	1	4	1	25.0	4	1.0(4)	0	0	—	—	—	KPkp	—	8	68
McAleney, Ed Edward P., DE, 6´2˝/235 lbs; Massachusetts; 1976: Pit, rnd 8; B9/21/1953 Portland, ME **1976** TB 2																								
McAlister, Chris Christopher James, DB, 6´1˝/206 lbs; Arizona; 1999: Bal, rnd 1; B6/14/1977 Pasadena, CA **1999** Bal 16 (12, LCB) **2000**†Bal 16 (16, RCB) **2001**†Bal 16 (16, RCB) **2002** Bal 13 (12, LCB) **2003**†Bal★15 (15, LCB) **2004** Bal★15 (14, LCB) **2005** Bal 14 (13, LCB) **NFL** 105 (98) [7 yrs]																								
McAlister, James James Edward, RB, 6´1˝/205 lbs; UCLA; 1974: Oak, rnd 6; B9/5/1951 Little Rock, AR																								
1975	Phi	14	103	335	3.3(18)	1	17	134	7.9(39)	2	—	—	—	—	—	—	—	—	—	—	k	—	18	520
1976	Phi	13	68	265	3.9(20)	0	12	72	6.0(25)	0	—	—	—	—	—	—	—	—	—	—	k	—	0	338
1978	†NE	16	19	77	4.1(16)	2	1	12	12.0(12)	0	—	—	—	—	—	—	—	—	—	—	k	—	12	139
NFL	3	43	190	677	3.6(20)	3	30	218	7.3(39)	2	—	—	—	—	—	—	—	—	—	—	k	—	30	997
McAlister, Ken Kenneth H., LB-DB, 6´5˝/220 lbs; San Francisco; B4/15/1960 Oakland, CA **1982** Sea 9 (0) **1983** Sea 2 (0) **1983** SF 4 (0) **1984** KC 15 (9, LOLB) **1986** KC 3 (3) **1987** KC 1 (0) **NFL** 34 (12) [5 yrs]																								
McAllister, Deuce Dulymus James, RB, 6´1˝/221 lbs; Mississippi; 2001: NO, rnd 1; B12/27/1978 Lena, MS																								
2001	NO	16(4)	16	91	5.7(54)	1	15	166	11.1(22)	1	2	1	50.0	12	6.0(12)	1	0	—	—	—	kp	—	12	620
2002	NO★	15(15, RB)	**325**	**1388**	4.3(62)	13	47	352	7.5(30)	3	0	0	0.0	0	0.0	0	0	1	8	—	—	—	96	1709
2003	NO★	16(16, RB)	351	1641	4.7(76)	8	69	516	7.5(39)	0	2	0	0.0	0	0.0	0	0	—	—	—	—	—	48	1979
2004	NO	14(14, RB)	269	1074	4.0(71)	9	34	228	6.7(20)	0	—	—	—	—	—	—	—	—	—	—	—	—	54	1278
2005	NO	5(5, rb)	93	335	3.6(26)	3	17	117	6.9(22)	0	—	—	—	—	—	—	—	—	—	—	—	—	18	424
NFL	5	66(54)	1054	4529	4.3(76)	34	182	1379	7.6(39)	4	4	1	25.0	12	3.0(12)	1	0	1	8	—	kp	—	228	6010
McArthur, Jack Jackson, C-T-G-E, 5´11˝/211 lbs; St. Mary's (CA); B1/1902 Acampo, CA, deceased **1926** LA 10 (10, C) **1927** Buf 5 (5, C) **1927** NYY 8 (7, c) **1928** NYY 13 (13, C) **1929** Ora 10 (2) **1930** Nwk 1 (1) **1930** Pro 4 (0) **1930** Fra 2 (2) **1930** Bkn 5 (0) **1931** Pro 9 (3) **NFL** 67 (43) [6 yrs]																								
McArthur, Kevin Kevin Lee, LB, 6´2˝/244 lbs; Lamar; B5/11/1962 Cameron, LA **1986**†NYJ 8 (1) **1987** NYJ 12 (3) **1988** NYJ 16 (16, ROLB) **1989** NYJ 9 (1) **NFL** 45 (21) [4 yrs]																								
McAuliffe, Jack JohnTheodore, HB, 5´7˝/155 lbs; Montana; Beloit; B5/21/1901 Butte, MT, D12/17/1971 Butte, MT **1926** GB 8 (4)																								
McBath, Mike Michael Strickler, DE-DT-T, 6´4˝/251 lbs; Penn State; 1968: Buf, rnd 5; B5/29/1946 Woodbury, NJ **1968** Buf-A 9 **1969** Buf-A 14 (RDE) **1970** Buf 12 **1971** Buf 13 (ldt) **1972** Buf 2 **NFL** 50 [5 yrs]																								
McBriar, Mat Mat, P, 6´1˝/210 lbs; Hawaii; B7/8/1979 Melbourne, Australia **2005** Dal 16 (0)																								
2004	Dal	16(0)	—	—	—	—	—	—	—	—	1	0	0.0	0	0.0	0	0	—	—	—	P	—	0	0
NFL	2	32(0)	—	—	—	—	—	—	—	—	1	0	0.0	0	0.0	0	0	—	—	—	P	—	0	0
McBride, Adrian Richard Adrian, WR, 6´0˝/195 lbs; Tennessee; Missouri; B3/23/1963 Zanesville, OH **1987** SL 3 (0)																								
McBride, Charlie Charles Harold, BB, 5´10˝/185 lbs; Washington State; B7/6/1914, D4/1972																								
1936	ChiC	1(0)	2	1	0.5	0	1	38	38.0(38)	1	—	—	—	—	—	—	—	—	—	—	—	—	6	25
McBride, Jack John F., FB-TB-HB, 5´11˝/185 lbs; Syracuse; B11/30/1901 Conshohocken, PA, D10/1966 Conshohocken, PA **[K]** **1925** NYG☆12 (12, FB), 25 **1926** NYG 13 (9, FB), 48 **1927** NYG☆12 (12, FB), 57 **1928** NYG 9 (9, FB), 8 **1929** Pro 12 (6, FB), 6 **1930** Bkn 11 (11, FB), 56 **1931** Bkn 13 (13, FB), 19																								
1932	Bkn	3(0)	3	23	7.7	0	—	—	—	—	—	—	—	—	—	—	—	—	—	—	—	—	0	23
1932	NYG	9(6, TB)	84	302	3.6	1	—	—	—	—	74	36	48.6	363	4.9	6	9	—	—	—	—	—	6	164
1933	†NYG	11(2)	33	87	2.6	0	—	—	—	—	24	11	45.8	138	5.8	2	2	—	—	—	K	—	7	86
1934	NYG	1(0)	4	14	3.5	0	—	—	—	—	3	3	100.0	37	12.3	1	0	—	—	—	K	—	1	38
NFL	10	106(80)	124	426	3.4	26	—	—	—	—	101	50	49.5	538	5.3	31	11	—	—	—	K	—	233	670
McBride, Norm Norman, DE, 6´3˝/245 lbs; Utah; 1969: Mia, rnd 4; B2/21/1947 Los Angeles, CA **1969** Mia-A 8 **1970** Mia 2 **NFL** 10 [2 yrs]																								
McBride, Oscar Oscar Bernard, TE, 6´5˝/266 lbs; Notre Dame; B7/23/1972 Gainesville, FL **1996** Arz 2 (1)																								
1995	Arz	16(10, te)	—	—	—	—	13	112	8.6(24)	2	—	—	—	—	—	—	—	—	—	—	—	—	12	66
NFL	2	18(11)	—	—	—	—	13	112	8.6(24)	2	—	—	—	—	—	—	—	—	—	—	—	—	12	66
McBride, Ron James Ronald, RB, 6´0˝/202 lbs; Missouri; B10/12/1948 Fulton, MO **1973** GB 1																								
McBride, Tod Tod Anthony, DB, 6´1˝/208 lbs; UCLA; B1/26/1976 Los Angeles, CA **1999** GB 15 (0) **2000** GB 15 (6, lcb) **2001** GB 16 (0) **2002** GB 15 (4) **2003** Atl 12 (9, RCB) **2004** SL 2 (0) **NFL** 75 (19) [6 yrs]																								
McBurrows, Gerald Gerald Lance, DB, 5´11˝/208 lbs; Kansas; 1995: SL, rnd 7; B10/7/1973 Detroit, MI **1995** SL 14 (3) **1996** SL 16 (7, ss) **1997** SL 8 (3) **1998** SL 10 (0) **1999** Atl 16 (4) **2000** Atl 16 (4) **2001** Atl 14 (8, SS) **2002**†Atl 15 (14, SS) **2003** Atl 13 (2) **NFL** 122 (45) [9 yrs]																								
McCabe, Jerry Jerome Francis, LB, 6´1˝/225 lbs; Holy Cross; B1/25/1965 Detroit, MI **1987** NE 3 (3) **1988** KC 3 (1) **NFL** 6 (4) [2 yrs]																								
McCabe, Richie Richard Paul, DB, 6´1˝/185 lbs; Pittsburgh; 1955: Pit, rnd 22; B3/12/1933 Pittsburgh, PA, D1/4/1983 Denver, CO **1955** Pit 12 (DB) **1957** Pit 2 **1958** Pit 5 **1959** Was 10 **1960** Buf-A☆14 (RS) **1961** Buf-A 9 (LCB) **NFL** 52 [6 yrs]																								
McCadam, Kevin Kevin Edward, DB, 6´1˝/219 lbs; Virginia Tech; Colorado State; 2002: Atl, rnd 5; B3/6/1979 La Mesa, CA **2002**†Atl 11 (1) **2003** Atl 12 (3) **2004**†Atl 16 (2) **2005** Atl 16 (0) **NFL** 55 (6) [4 yrs]																								
McCafferty, Don Donald William, E, 6´4˝/220 lbs; Ohio State; 1943: NYG, rnd 13; B3/12/1921 Cleveland, OH, D7/28/1974 West Bloomfield Hills, MI **[C]**																								
1946	†NYG	9(0)	—	—	—	—	3	38	12.7(17)	1	—	—	—	—	—	—	—	—	—	—	—	—	6	24
McCaffray, Art Arthur Joseph, T, 5´11˝/190 lbs; Santa Clara; Pacific; 1944: Pit, rnd 4; B12/26/1921 Seattle, WA, D12/5/1994 Seattle, WA **1946** Pit 11 (10, RT)																								
McCaffrey, Bob Robert Alan, C, 6´2˝/245 lbs; USC; 1975: GB, rnd 16; B4/16/1952 Bakersfield, CA **1975** GB 11 (2)																								
McCaffrey, Ed Edward Thomas, WR, 6´5˝/215 lbs; Stanford; 1991: NYG, rnd 3; B8/17/1968 Waynesboro, PA																								
1991	NYG	16(0)	—	—	—	—	16	146	9.1(26)	0	—	—	—	—	—	—	—	—	—	—	—	—	0	73
1992	NYG	16(3)	—	—	—	—	49	610	12.4(44)	5	—	—	—	—	—	—	—	—	—	—	—	—	30	330
1993	†NYG	16(1)	—	—	—	—	27	335	12.4(31)	2	—	—	—	—	—	—	—	—	—	—	—	—	12	178
1994	†SF	16(0)	—	—	—	—	11	131	11.9(32)	2	—	—	—	—	—	—	—	—	—	—	—	—	12	76
1995	Den	16(5, wr)	1	-1	-1.0(-1)	0	39	477	12.2(35)	2	—	—	—	—	—	—	—	—	—	—	—	—	14	248
1996	†Den	15(15, WR)	—	—	—	—	48	553	11.5(39)	7	—	—	—	—	—	—	—	—	—	—	—	—	42	312
1997	†Den	15(15, WR)	—	—	—	—	45	590	13.1(35)	8	—	—	—	—	—	—	—	—	—	—	—	—	48	335
1998	†Den★	15(15, WR)	—	—	—	—	64	1053	16.5(48)	**10**	—	—	—	—	—	—	—	—	—	—	—	—	62	577
1999	Den	15(15, WR)	—	—	—	—	71	1018	14.3(78)	7	—	—	—	—	—	—	—	—	—	—	—	—	42	544
2000	†Den	16(16, WR)	—	—	—	—	101	1317	13.0(61)	9	—	—	—	—	—	—	—	—	—	—	—	—	56	704
2001	Den	1(1)	—	—	—	—	6	94	15.7(28)	1	—	—	—	—	—	—	—	—	—	—	—	—	6	52
2002	Den	16(16, WR)	2	22	11.0(17)	0	69	903	13.1(69)	2	—	—	—	—	—	—	—	—	—	—	—	—	12	484
2003	Den	12(7, wr)	—	—	—	—	19	195	10.3(23)	0	—	—	—	—	—	—	—	—	—	—	—	—	0	98
NFL	13	185(109)	3	21	7.0(17)	0	565	7422	13.1(78)	55	—	—	—	—	—	—	—	—	—	—	—	—	336	4007
McCaffrey, Mike Michael James, LB, 6´3˝/235 lbs; California; 1969: Min, rnd 4; B4/11/1946 Bakersfield, CA **1970** Buf 12 (rlb)																								
McCain, Bob Robert Floyd, E, 5´11˝/195 lbs; Mississippi; 1946: Pit, rnd 14; B8/15/1922 Stewart, MS, D9/30/2001 Pasadena, TX																								
1946	Bkn-A	11(0)	—	—	—	—	3	27	9.0	0	—	—	—	—	—	—	—	—	—	—	—	—	0	14
McCall, Bob Robert Henry, RB, 6´0˝/205 lbs; Arizona; 1973: Cin, rnd 5; B4/26/1950 Sarasota, FL																								
1973	NE	8(1)	10	15	1.5(14)	0	3	18	6.0(14)	0	—	—	—	—	—	—	—	—	—	—	k	—	0	11

YEAR	TEAM	G(GS, POS)	RUSH	YD	AVG(LG)	TD	REC	YD	AVG(LG)	TD	PASS	COMP	PCT	YD	AVG(LG)	TD	INT	SK	YD	QBR	KPR	OTD	PTS	TAY
McCall, Don Donald Charles, RB, 5´11˝/195 lbs; USC; 1967: NO, rnd 5; B9/21/1944 Birmingham, AL																								
1967	NO	14	21	86	4.1(49)	1	4	75	18.8(34)	1	—	—	—	—	—	—	—	—	—	—	k	—	12	232
1968	NO	13(HB)	155	637	4.1(48)	4	26	270	10.4(25)	2	1	0	0.0	0	0.0	0	0	—	—	—	—	—	36	822
1969	Pit	13	30	98	3.3(14)	0	2	2	1.0(5)	0	—	—	—	—	—	—	—	—	—	—	k	1	6	326
1970	NO	2	23	63	2.7(11)	1	5	43	8.6(17)	0	—	—	—	—	—	—	—	—	—	—	k	—	6	106
NFL	4	42	229	884	3.9(49)	6	37	390	10.5(34)	3	1	0	0.0	0	0.0	0	0	—	—	—	k	1	60	1485
McCall, Ed Edward, WR, 6´3˝/205 lbs; Miles; B12/19/1943 **1968** Cin-A 1																								
McCall, Joe Joseph Shepard, RB, 5´11˝/205 lbs; Pittsburgh; 1984: LARd, rnd 3; B2/17/1962 Miami, FL																								
1984	LARd	3(0)	1	3	3.0(3)	0	—	—	—	—	—	—	—	—	—	—	—	—	—	—	—	—	0	3
McCall, Reese Reese, TE, 6´6˝/239 lbs; Auburn; 1978: Bal, rnd 1; B6/16/1956 Bessemer, AL																								
1978	Bal	16(3)	—	—	—	—	11	160	14.5(34)	1	—	—	—	—	—	—	—	—	—	—	p	1	12	117
1979	Bal	14(12, TE)	—	—	—	—	37	536	14.5(36)	4	—	—	—	—	—	—	—	—	—	—	—	—	24	288
1980	Bal	16(15, TE)	—	—	—	—	18	322	17.9(47)	5	—	—	—	—	—	—	—	—	—	—	—	—	30	186
1981	Bal	16(14, TE)	—	—	—	—	21	314	15.0(65)	2	—	—	—	—	—	—	—	—	—	—	—	—	12	167
1982	Bal	7(0)	—	—	—	—	2	6	3.0(4)	0	—	—	—	—	—	—	—	—	—	—	—	—	0	3
1983	†Det	16(5, te)	—	—	—	—	1	6	6.0(6)	0	—	—	—	—	—	—	—	—	—	—	—	—	0	3
1984	Det	16(5, te)	—	—	—	—	3	15	5.0(7)	0	—	—	—	—	—	—	—	—	—	—	—	—	0	8
1985	Det	16(2)	—	—	—	—	1	7	7.0(7)	0	—	—	—	—	—	—	—	—	—	—	—	—	0	4
NFL	8	117(56)	—	—	—	—	94	1366	14.5(65)	12	—	—	—	—	—	—	—	—	—	—	p	1	78	775
McCall, Ron Ronald George, LB, 6´2˝/240 lbs; Utah State; Weber State; 1967: SD, rnd 2; B7/11/1944 San Bernardino, CA **1967** SD-A 2 **1968** SD-A 3 **NFL** 5 [2 yrs]																								
McCallister, Fred Frederick Milton, LB, 6´1˝/250 lbs; Florida; B2/17/1962 Melbourne, FL **1987** TB 3 (3)																								
McCallum, Napoleon Napoleon Ardel, RB, 6´2˝/220 lbs; Navy; 1986: LARd, rnd 4; B10/6/1963 Milford, OH																								
1986	LARd	15(5, rb)	142	536	3.8(18)	1	13	103	7.9(22)	0	—	—	—	—	—	—	—	—	—	—	kp	—	6	670
1990	†LARd	16(0)	10	25	2.5(6)	0	—	—	—	—	—	—	—	—	—	—	—	—	—	—	k	—	0	10
1991	†LARd	16(0)	31	110	3.5(9)	1	—	—	—	—	—	—	—	—	—	—	—	—	—	—	k	—	6	150
1992	LARd	13(0)	—	—	—	—	2	13	6.5(5)	0	—	—	—	—	—	—	—	—	—	—	kp	—	0	70
1993	†LARd	13(1)	37	114	3.1(14)	3	2	5	2.5(3)	0	—	—	—	—	—	—	—	—	—	—	k	—	18	144
1994	LARd	1(0)	3	5	1.7(3)	1	—	—	—	—	—	—	—	—	—	—	—	—	—	—	—	—	6	15
NFL	6	74(6)	223	790	3.5(18)	6	17	121	7.1(22)	0	—	—	—	—	—	—	—	—	—	—	kp	—	36	1058
McCambridge, John John Raymond, DE, 6´4˝/245 lbs; Northwestern; 1967: Det, rnd 6; B8/30/1944 Klamath Falls, OR **1967** Det 6																								
McCanless, Jim James Robert, G, 6´2˝/240 lbs; Clemson; B1/1/1936 **1960** Hou-A 1																								
McCann, Ernie Ernest Harmer, T-E-G, 5´11˝/188 lbs; Penn State; B8/5/1902, PA, D11/25/1971 Acton, CA **1926** Har 9 (4)																								
McCann, Jim James William, P, 6´2˝/163 lbs; Arizona State; 1971: SF, rnd 8; B3/29/1949 Phoenix, AZ **1972**†SF 13 **1973** NYG 2 **1975** KC 3																								
1971	SF	13	2	-15	-7.5(-6)	0	—	—	—	—	—	—	—	—	—	—	—	—	—	—	P	—	0	-15
NFL	4	31	2	-15	-7.5(-6)	0	—	—	—	—	—	—	—	—	—	—	—	—	—	—	P	—	0	-15
McCann, Tim Timothy John, DT, 6´5˝/265 lbs; Princeton; B5/15/1947 Milwaukee, WI **1969** NYG 1																								
McCants, Darnerien Darnerien, WR, 6´3˝/214 lbs; Delaware State; 2001: Was, rnd 5; B8/1/1977 Odenton, MD																								
2002	Was	9(1)	1	9	9.0(9)	0	21	256	12.2(32)	2	—	—	—	—	—	—	—	—	—	—	—	—	12	147
2003	Was	15(1)	—	—	—	—	27	360	13.3(32)	6	—	—	—	—	—	—	—	—	—	—	—	—	40	210
2004	Was	5(1)	—	—	—	—	5	71	14.2(27)	0	—	—	—	—	—	—	—	—	—	—	—	—	0	36
2005	Phi	12(0)	—	—	—	—	5	87	17.4(22)	0	—	—	—	—	—	—	—	—	—	—	—	—	0	44
NFL	4	41(3)	1	9	9.0(9)	0	58	774	13.3(32)	8	—	—	—	—	—	—	—	—	—	—	—	—	52	436
McCants, Keith Alvin Keith, DE, 6´3˝/265 lbs; Alabama; 1990: TB, rnd 1; B4/19/1968 Mobile, AL **1990** TB 15 (4) **1991** TB 16 (16, RDE) **1992** TB 16 (15, RDE) **1993** Hou 13 (0) **1994** Hou 4 (1) **1994** Arz 8 (1) **1995** Arz 16 (2) **NFL** 88 (39) [6 yrs]																								
McCardell, Keenan Keenan Wayne, WR, 6´1˝/191 lbs; UNLV; 1991: Was, rnd 12; B1/6/1970 Houston, TX																								
1992	Cle	2(0)	—	—	—	—	1	8	8.0(8)	0	—	—	—	—	—	—	—	—	—	—	—	—	0	4
1993	Cle	6(3)	—	—	—	—	13	234	18.0(43)	4	—	—	—	—	—	—	—	—	—	—	—	—	24	137
1994	†Cle	13(3)	—	—	—	—	10	182	18.2(34)	0	—	—	—	—	—	—	—	—	—	—	—	—	0	91
1995	Cle	16(5, wr)	—	—	—	—	56	709	12.7(36)	4	—	—	—	—	—	—	—	—	—	—	kp	—	24	429
1996	†Jax◇	16(15, WR)	—	—	—	—	85	1129	13.3(52)	3	—	—	—	—	—	—	—	—	—	—	p	—	22	577
1997	†Jax	16(16, WR)	—	—	—	—	85	1164	13.7(60)	5	—	—	—	—	—	—	—	—	—	—	—	—	30	607
1998	†Jax	15(15, WR)	—	—	—	—	64	892	13.9(43)	6	—	—	—	—	—	—	—	—	—	—	k	—	38	476
1999	†Jax	16(15, WR)	—	—	—	—	78	891	11.4(49)	5	—	—	—	—	—	—	—	—	—	—	kp	—	32	471
2000	Jax	16(16, WR)	—	—	—	—	94	1207	12.8(67)	5	—	—	—	—	—	—	—	—	—	—	p	—	30	639
2001	Jax	16(16, WR)	—	—	—	—	93	1110	11.9(65)	6	—	—	—	—	—	—	—	—	—	—	—	—	38	585
2002	†TB	14(14, WR)	1	3	3.0(3)	0	61	670	11.0(65)	6	—	—	—	—	—	—	—	—	—	—	—	—	36	368
2003	TB◇	16(16, WR)	—	—	—	—	84	1174	14.0(76)	8	—	—	—	—	—	—	—	—	—	—	—	1	54	627
2004	†SD	7(6, wr)	1	3	3.0(3)	0	31	393	12.7(31)	1	1	0	0.0	0	0.0	0	0	—	—	—	—	—	6	205
2005	SD	16(16, WR)	2	6	3.0(3)	0	70	917	13.1(54)	9	0	0	0.0	0	0.0	0	0	1	4	—	p	—	54	526
NFL	14	185(156)	4	12	3.0(3)	0	825	10680	12.9(76)	62	1	0	0.0	0	0.0	0	0	1	4	—	kp	1	388	5739
McCareins, Justin Justin Morgan, WR, 6´2˝/215 lbs; Northern Illinois; 2001: Ten, rnd 4; B12/11/1978 Evanston, IL																								
2001	Ten	4(1)	—	—	—	—	3	88	29.3(56)	0	—	—	—	—	—	—	—	—	—	—	kp	—	0	73
2002	†Ten	16(1)	2	18	9.0(16)	0	19	301	15.8(55)	2	—	—	—	—	—	—	—	—	—	—	kp	—	12	298
2003	†Ten	16(10, WR)	1	13	13.0(13)	0	47	813	17.3(73)	7	—	—	—	—	—	—	—	—	—	—	kp	1	48	711
2004	†NYJ	16(16, WR)	2	-5	-2.5(-2)	0	56	770	13.8(43)	4	—	—	—	—	—	—	—	—	—	—	p	—	24	418
2005	NYJ	16(16, WR)	1	8	8.0(8)	0	43	713	16.6(45)	2	—	—	—	—	—	—	—	—	—	—	p	—	12	378
NFL	5	68(44)	6	34	5.7(16)	0	168	2685	16.0(73)	15	—	—	—	—	—	—	—	—	—	—	kp	1	96	1877
McCarren, Larry Lawrence Anthony, C, 6´3˝/246 lbs; Illinois; 1973: GB, rnd 12; B11/9/1951 Park Forest, IL **1973** GB 5 **1974** GB 14 (13, C) **1975** GB 14 (12, C) **1976** GB 14 (14, C) **1977** GB 14 (14, C) **1978** GB 16 (16, C) **1979** GB 16 (16, C) **1980** GB 16 (16, C) **1981** GB☆16 (16, C) **1982**†GB★9 (9, C) **1983** GB★16 (16, C) **1984** GB☆12 (12, C) **NFL** 162 (154) [12 yrs]																								
McCarthy, Brendan Brendan Barrett, RB, 6´3˝/220 lbs; Boston College; 1968: GB, rnd 4; B8/6/1945 Boston, MA																								
1968	Atl	7	31	86	2.8(18)	1	13	119	9.2(21)	0	—	—	—	—	—	—	—	—	—	—	—	—	6	156
1968	Den-A	7(fb)	28	89	3.2(12)	0	7	69	9.9(40)	2	—	—	—	—	—	—	—	—	—	—	—	—	12	134
1969	Den-A	1	—	—	—	—	—	—	—	—	—	—	—	—	—	—	—	—	—	—	—	—	—	—
NFL	2	15	59	175	3.0(18)	1	20	188	9.4(40)	2	—	—	—	—	—	—	—	—	—	—	—	—	18	289
McCarthy, Don Donald, E, 5´10˝/172 lbs; Lehigh; B1897, deceased **1921** Was 3 (2, RE)																								
McCarthy, Jack John Lacey, T, /186 lbs; California **1927** Dul 8 (8, RT)																								
McCarthy, Jim James Patrick, E, 6´1˝/205 lbs; Illinois; B11/28/1920 Lockport, IL, D12/2/1991 Orland Park, IL **[K]**																								
1946	Bkn-A	14(12, LE)	—	—	—	—	11	296	26.9	3	—	—	—	—	—	—	—	—	—	—	Kki	—	23	154
1947	Bkn-A	14(13, LE)	—	—	—	—	10	147	14.7	0	2	1	50.0	17	8.5(17)	0	1	—	—	—	—	—	0	42
1948	ChiR-A	14(10, LE)	—	—	—	—	3	30	10.0	0	—	—	—	—	—	—	—	—	—	—	K	—	27	15
1949	ChiH-A	12(0)	—	—	—	—	4	58	14.5	0	—	—	—	—	—	—	—	—	—	—	K	—	39	29
AAFC	4	54(35)	—	—	—	—	28	531	19.0	3	2	1	50.0	17	8.5(17)	0	1	—	—	—	Kki	—	89	240
McCarthy, John John Patrick, QB, 5´9˝/160 lbs; St. Francis; B8/9/1916 Philadelphia, PA, D5/12/1998																								
1944	C-P	7(2)	6	-49	-8.2(-8)	0	—	—	—	—	67	20	29.9	250	3.7(38)	0	13	—	—	—	Pp	—	0	-440

McCarthy, Shawn Shawn Michael, P, 6´6˝/227 lbs; Purdue; 1990: Atl, rnd 12; B2/22/1968 Fremont, OH

YEAR	TEAM	G (GS, POS)	RUSH	YD	AVG (LG)	TD	REC	YD	AVG (LG)	TD	PASS	COMP	PCT	YD	AVG (LG)	TD	INT	SK	YD	QBR	KPR	OTD	PTS	TAY
1991	NE	13(0)	—	—	—	—	—	—	—	—	1	1	100.0	11	11.0(11)	0	0	—	—	—	P	—	0	6
1992	NE	16(0)	3	-10	-3.3(0)	0	—	—	—	—	—	—	—	—	—	—	—	—	—	—	P	—	0	-10
NFL	2	29(0)	3	-10	-3.3	0	—	—	—	—	1	1	100.0	11	11.0(11)	0	0	—	—	—	P	—	0	-5

McCarthy, Vince Vincent John, B-E, 5´10˝/165 lbs; St. Viator; B11/3/1899, IL, D11/25/1968 Fort Lauderdale, FL **[K]** **1924** RI 2 (1), 7 **1925** RI 4 (2), 12 **NFL** 6 (3), 19 [2 yrs]

McCartney, Pete Peter Daniel, T, 6´6˝/260 lbs; Louisville; B6/15/1962 **1987** NYJ 3 (1)

McCartney, Ron Ronnie L., LB, 6´1˝/220 lbs; Tennessee; 1976: LA, rnd 2; B7/20/1954 Charleston, WV **1977** Atl 14 **1978**†Atl 15 **1979** Atl 16 **NFL** 45 [3 yrs]

McCarty, Mickey Robert Mickey, TE, 6´5˝/255 lbs; TCU; 1968: KC, rnd 4; B11/15/1946 Jonesboro, AR **1969** KC-A 3

McCaslin, Eugene Eugene William, LB, 6´1˝/226 lbs; Florida; 2000: GB, rnd 7; B7/13/1977 Tampa, FL **2000** GB 1 (0)

McCauley, Don Donald Frederick, RB, 6´1˝/211 lbs; North Carolina; 1971: Bal, rnd 1; B5/12/1949 Worcester, MA

YEAR	TEAM	G (GS, POS)	RUSH	YD	AVG (LG)	TD	REC	YD	AVG (LG)	TD	PASS	COMP	PCT	YD	AVG (LG)	TD	INT	SK	YD	QBR	KPR	OTD	PTS	TAY
1971	†Bal	13	58	246	4.2(19)	2	3	6	2.0(8)	0	—	—	—	—	—	—	—	—	—	—	k	—	12	343
1972	Bal	14(10, RB)	178	675	3.8(36)	2	30	256	8.5(34)	2	—	—	—	—	—	—	—	—	—	—	k	1	30	1025
1973	Bal	13(12, FB)	144	514	3.6(24)	2	25	186	7.4(34)	0	—	—	—	—	—	—	—	—	—	—	k	—	12	624
1974	Bal	13	30	90	3.0(15)	0	17	112	6.6(14)	1	2	1	50.0	11	5.5(11)	1	0	—	—	—	k	—	6	164
1975	†Bal	14	60	196	3.3(18)	10	14	93	6.6(32)	1	—	—	—	—	—	—	—	—	—	—	k	—	66	374
1976	†Bal	13(1)	69	227	3.3(16)	9	34	347	10.2(44)	2	—	—	—	—	—	—	—	—	—	—	k	—	66	503
1977	†Bal	14	83	234	2.8(16)	6	51	495	9.7(34)	2	—	—	—	—	—	—	—	—	—	—	k	—	48	544
1978	Bal	15(1)	44	107	2.4(10)	5	34	296	8.7(21)	0	—	—	—	—	—	—	—	—	—	—	k	—	30	350
1979	Bal	15(1)	59	168	2.8(13)	3	55	575	10.5(35)	3	—	—	—	—	—	—	—	—	—	—	k	—	36	500
1980	Bal	16(1)	35	133	3.8(12)	1	34	313	9.2(19)	4	—	—	—	—	—	—	—	—	—	—	k	—	30	323
1981	Bal	16(0)	10	37	3.7(8)	0	36	347	9.6(31)	2	—	—	—	—	—	—	—	—	—	—	—	—	12	221
NFL	11	156(26)	770	2627	3.4(36)	40	333	3026	9.1(44)	17	2	1	50.0	11	5.5(11)	1	0	—	—	—	k	1	348	4968

McCauley, Tom Thomas Michael, DB, 6´3˝/193 lbs; Wisconsin; 1969: Min, rnd 10; B5/3/1947 Worcester, MA **1970** Atl 14 (FS) **1971** Atl 4

YEAR	TEAM	G (GS, POS)	RUSH	YD	AVG (LG)	TD	REC	YD	AVG (LG)	TD	PASS	COMP	PCT	YD	AVG (LG)	TD	INT	SK	YD	QBR	KPR	OTD	PTS	TAY
1969	Atl	14	2	49	24.5(32)	0	—	—	—	—	—	—	—	—	—	—	—	—	—	—	p	—	0	18
NFL	3	32	2	49	24.5(32)	0	—	—	—	—	—	—	—	—	—	—	—	—	—	—	pi	1	6	121

McCausland, Leo Leo Joseph, C-G-T-E, 6´0˝/195 lbs; Detroit Mercy; B6/14/1895 Akron, OH, D9/1968 Akron, OH **1922** Akr 4 (1)

McCaw, Bill William Glass, G-E, 6´2˝/194 lbs; Indiana; B2/6/1898 St. Paul, MN, D4/19/1942 Bloomington, IN **1923** Rac 3 (2) **1926** Lou 4 (4, LG) **NFL** 7 (6) [2 yrs]

McChesney, Bob Robert Edward, E, 6´2˝/195 lbs; UCLA; B7/12/1912 Los Angeles, CA, D9/1986 Silver City, NM

YEAR	TEAM	G (GS, POS)	RUSH	YD	AVG (LG)	TD	REC	YD	AVG (LG)	TD	PASS	COMP	PCT	YD	AVG (LG)	TD	INT	SK	YD	QBR	KPR	OTD	PTS	TAY
1936	†Bos	9(1)	—	—	—	—	5	62	12.4	0	—	—	—	—	—	—	—	—	—	—	—	—	0	31
1937	Was	10(0)	—	—	—	—	6	50	8.3	0	—	—	—	—	—	—	—	—	—	—	—	—	0	25
1938	Was✧	10(2)	—	—	—	—	3	49	16.3(52)	1	—	—	—	—	—	—	—	—	—	—	—	—	6	30
1939	Was	8(3)	1	5	5.0(5)	0	9	86	9.6	0	—	—	—	—	—	—	—	—	—	—	—	1	6	48
1940	†Was	11(0)	—	—	—	—	9	119	13.2	1	—	—	—	—	—	—	—	—	—	—	—	—	6	65
1941	Was	11(1)	—	—	—	—	19	213	11.2(26)	2	—	—	—	—	—	—	—	—	—	—	—	—	12	117
1942	Was✧	10(2)	2	22	11.0(23)	0	8	100	12.5(33)	2	—	—	—	—	—	—	—	—	—	—	—	—	12	82
NFL	7	69(9)	3	27	9.0(23)	0	59	679	11.5(52)	6	—	—	—	—	—	—	—	—	—	—	—	1	42	397

McChesney, Bob Robert Eugene, E, 6´2˝/190 lbs; Hardin-Simmons; 1950: Phi, rnd 4; B10/27/1926 Van Nuys, CA, D12/19/2002 Granada Hills, CA

YEAR	TEAM	G (GS, POS)	RUSH	YD	AVG (LG)	TD	REC	YD	AVG (LG)	TD	PASS	COMP	PCT	YD	AVG (LG)	TD	INT	SK	YD	QBR	KPR	OTD	PTS	TAY
1950	†NYG	12(RE)	—	—	—	—	19	380	20.0(43)	6	—	—	—	—	—	—	—	—	—	—	—	—	36	220
1951	NYG	12(LE)	—	—	—	—	14	230	16.4(40)	2	—	—	—	—	—	—	—	—	—	—	—	—	12	125
1952	NYG	12(LE)	2	2	1.0(2)	0	21	430	20.5(72)	6	—	—	—	—	—	—	—	—	—	—	k	—	36	230
NFL	3	36	2	2	1.0(2)	0	54	1040	19.3(72)	14	—	—	—	—	—	—	—	—	—	—	k	—	84	575

McChesney, Matt Matt, DT, 6´4˝/290 lbs; Colorado; B11/6/1981 Santa Cruz, CA **2005** NYJ 3 (0)

McClain, Cliff Clifford, RB, 6´0˝/217 lbs; South Carolina State; 1970: NYJ, rnd 5; B12/29/1947 Orlando, FL

YEAR	TEAM	G (GS, POS)	RUSH	YD	AVG (LG)	TD	REC	YD	AVG (LG)	TD	PASS	COMP	PCT	YD	AVG (LG)	TD	INT	SK	YD	QBR	KPR	OTD	PTS	TAY
1970	NYJ	10	—	—	—	—	1	11	11.0(11)	0	—	—	—	—	—	—	—	—	—	—	k	—	0	16
1971	NYJ	11	12	108	9.0(63)	2	—	—	—	—	—	—	—	—	—	—	—	—	—	—	k	—	12	124
1972	NYJ	13	59	305	5.2(30)	0	6	88	14.7(44)	0	1	0	0.0	0	0.0	0	0	—	—	—	k	—	0	364
1973	NYJ	12	8	32	4.0(13)	0	6	52	8.7(14)	0	—	—	—	—	—	—	—	—	—	—	k	—	0	72
NFL	4	46	79	445	5.6(63)	2	13	151	11.6(44)	0	1	0	0.0	0	0.0	0	0	—	—	—	k	—	12	576

McClain, Clint Clinton, HB, 5´9˝/190 lbs; SMU; B6/18/1918 Lufkin, TX, D12/11/1994 Dallas, TX

YEAR	TEAM	G (GS, POS)	RUSH	YD	AVG (LG)	TD	REC	YD	AVG (LG)	TD	PASS	COMP	PCT	YD	AVG (LG)	TD	INT	SK	YD	QBR	KPR	OTD	PTS	TAY
1941	†NYG	6(0)	9	36	4.0(11)	2	—	—	—	—	—	—	—	—	—	—	—	—	—	—	i	—	12	85

McClain, Dewey Dewey Loren, LB, 6´3˝/236 lbs; East Central (OK); B4/25/1954 Okmulgee, OK **1976** Atl 14 (5, llb) **1977** Atl 13 **1978**†Atl 16 **1979** Atl 15 **1980** Atl 15 (0) **NFL** 73 (5) [5 yrs]

McClain, Jimmy Jimmy, LB, 6´0˝/231 lbs; Troy State; B7/23/1980 Enterprise, AL **2002** Hou 15 (0) **2003** Hou 9 (0) **2004** Jax 1 (0) **NFL** 25 (0) [3 yrs]

McClain, Joe Joseph T., T, 6´0˝/200 lbs; St. John's (NY); Canisius; B4/5/1905, D4/24/1967 Pottsville, PA **1928** NYY 7 (4)

McClairen, Jack Jack Forsyth, E, 6´4˝/213 lbs; Bethune-Cookman; 1953: Pit, rnd 26; B3/2/1931 Panama City, FL

YEAR	TEAM	G (GS, POS)	RUSH	YD	AVG (LG)	TD	REC	YD	AVG (LG)	TD	PASS	COMP	PCT	YD	AVG (LG)	TD	INT	SK	YD	QBR	KPR	OTD	PTS	TAY
1955	Pit	12	—	—	—	—	1	13	13.0(13)	0	—	—	—	—	—	—	—	—	—	—	—	—	0	7
1956	Pit	7	—	—	—	—	5	56	11.2(18)	0	—	—	—	—	—	—	—	—	—	—	—	—	0	28
1957	Pit✧	12(RE)	—	—	—	—	46	630	13.7(48)	2	—	—	—	—	—	—	—	—	—	—	—	—	12	325
1958	Pit	12(RE)	—	—	—	—	29	491	16.9(35)	1	—	—	—	—	—	—	—	—	—	—	k	—	6	236
1959	Pit	1	—	—	—	—	3	46	15.3(20)	0	—	—	—	—	—	—	—	—	—	—	—	—	0	23
1960	Pit	1	—	—	—	—	1	17	17.0(17)	0	—	—	—	—	—	—	—	—	—	—	k	—	0	-6
NFL	6	45	—	—	—	—	85	1253	14.7(48)	3	—	—	—	—	—	—	—	—	—	—	k	—	18	613

McClanahan, Brent Brent Anthony, RB, 5´10˝/202 lbs; Arizona State; 1973: Min, rnd 5; B9/21/1951 Bakersfield, CA

YEAR	TEAM	G (GS, POS)	RUSH	YD	AVG (LG)	TD	REC	YD	AVG (LG)	TD	PASS	COMP	PCT	YD	AVG (LG)	TD	INT	SK	YD	QBR	KPR	OTD	PTS	TAY
1973	Min	13	17	69	4.1(10)	0	—	—	—	—	—	—	—	—	—	—	—	—	—	—	k	—	0	239
1974	†Min	14	9	41	4.6(14)	1	3	35	11.7(17)	0	—	—	—	—	—	—	—	—	—	—	k	—	6	273
1975	†Min	12(2)	92	336	3.7(15)	0	18	141	7.8(38)	1	—	—	—	—	—	—	—	—	—	—	k	—	6	517
1976	†Min	13(13, FB)	130	382	2.9(19)	4	40	252	6.3(23)	1	—	—	—	—	—	—	—	—	—	—	—	—	30	553
1977	Min	14(14, FB)	95	324	3.4(18)	1	34	276	8.1(23)	2	—	—	—	—	—	—	—	—	—	—	k	—	18	512
1978	†Min	13	10	26	2.6(22)	0	2	11	5.5(7)	0	—	—	—	—	—	—	—	—	—	—	k	—	0	25
1979	Min	16	14	29	2.1(9)	0	10	57	5.7(9)	0	—	—	—	—	—	—	—	—	—	—	k	—	0	66
NFL	7	95(29)	367	1207	3.3(22)	6	107	772	7.2(38)	4	—	—	—	—	—	—	—	—	—	—	k	—	60	2183

McClanahan, Randy Randall Duane, LB, 6´5˝/225 lbs; Louisiana-Lafayette; B12/12/1954 Lincoln, NE **1977**†Oak 14 **1978** Buf 16 (10, MLB) **1980**†Oak 14 (8, RILB) **1981** Oak 16 (16, RILB) **1982**†LARd 1 (0) **NFL** 61 (34) [5 yrs]

McClard, Bill William Wayne, K, 5´10˝/202 lbs; Arkansas; 1972: SD, rnd 3; B10/15/1949 Purcell, OK **[K]** **1972** SD 9 **1973** NO 8 **1975** NO 3

YEAR	TEAM	G (GS, POS)	RUSH	YD	AVG (LG)	TD	REC	YD	AVG (LG)	TD	PASS	COMP	PCT	YD	AVG (LG)	TD	INT	SK	YD	QBR	KPR	OTD	PTS	TAY
1974	NO	14	—	—	—	—	—	—	—	—	1	0	0.0	0	0.0	0	1	—	—	—	K	—	46	-40
NFL	4	34	—	—	—	—	—	—	—	—	1	0	0.0	0	0.0	0	1	—	—	—	K	—	109	-40

McCleary, Norris Norris Elligton, DT, 6´4˝/305 lbs; East Carolina; B5/10/1977 Shelby, NC **2000** KC 3 (0) **2001** KC 10 (0) **NFL** 13 (0) [2 yrs]

McClellan, Mike William Michael, DB, 6´1˝/185 lbs; Oklahoma; 1961: SF, rnd 6/1962: NYT, rnd 30; B10/10/1939 Stamford, TX **1962** Phi 14 **1963** Phi 10 **NFL** 24 [2 yrs]

McClellion, Central Central Bernard, DB, 6´0˝/190 lbs; Ohio State; B9/15/1975 Delray Beach, FL **2001** Was 6 (0)

McClendon, Skip Kenneth Christopher, DE, 6´6˝/282 lbs; Northwestern; Arizona State; 1987: Cin, rnd 3; B4/9/1964 Detroit, MI **1987** Cin 12 (0) **1988**†Cin 16 (16, LDE) **1989** Cin 16 (5, lde) **1990**†Cin 15 (13, LDE) **1991** Cin 5 (0) **1991** SD 2 (0) **1992** Min 3 (0) **1992** Ind 7 (4) **1993** Ind 16 (14, LDE) **NFL** 92 (52) [7 yrs]

McClendon, Willie Willie Edward, RB, 6´1˝/205 lbs; Georgia; 1979: Chi, rnd 3; B9/13/1957 Brunswick, GA

YEAR	TEAM	G (GS, POS)	RUSH	YD	AVG (LG)	TD	REC	YD	AVG (LG)	TD	PASS	COMP	PCT	YD	AVG (LG)	TD	INT	SK	YD	QBR	KPR	OTD	PTS	TAY
1979	†ChiB	16	37	160	4.3(33)	1	6	27	4.5(13)	0	—	—	—	—	—	—	—	—	—	—	k	—	6	181
1980	ChiB	16(0)	10	88	8.8(48)	1	—	—	—	—	—	—	—	—	—	—	—	—	—	—	k	—	6	94
1981	ChiB	16(0)	30	74	2.5(17)	0	2	4	2.0(4)	0	—	—	—	—	—	—	—	—	—	—	—	—	0	76

YEAR	TEAM	G(GS, POS)	RUSH	YD	AVG(LG)	TD	REC	YD	AVG(LG)	TD	PASS	COMP	PCT	YD	AVG(LG)	TD	INT	SK	YD	QBR	KPR	OTD	PTS	TAY
1982	ChiB	9(0)	17	47	2.8(13)	0	1	7	7.0(7)	0	—	—	—	—	—	—	—	—	—	—	—	—	0	51
NFL	4	57	94	369	3.9(48)	2	9	38	4.2(13)	0	—	—	—	—	—	—	—	—	—	—	k	—	12	401

McCLEON, DEXTER Dexter Keith, DB, 5´10˝/195 lbs; Clemson; 1997: SL, rnd 2; B10/9/1973 Meridian, MS **[I]** **1997** SL 16 (1) **1998** SL 15 (6, rcb) **1999**†SL 15 (15, RCB) **2000**†SL 16 (16, RCB) **2001**†SL 16 (16, RCB) **2002** SL 13 (4) **2003**†KC 16 (16, RCB) **2004** KC 13 (6, rcb) **2005** KC 11 (5, rcb) **NFL** 131 (85) [9 yrs]

McCLESKEY, J.J. Thomas Joseph, DB, 5´8˝/180 lbs; Tennessee; B4/10/1970 Knoxville, TN **1994** NO 13 (0) **1995** NO 14 (1) **1996** NO 5 (0) **1996** Arz 5 (0) **1997** Arz 13 (0) **1998**†Arz 12 (0) **1999** Arz 16 (1) **NFL** 78 (2) [6 yrs]

McCLINTON, CURTIS Curtis Realious, FB-TE, 6´3˝/227 lbs; Kansas; 1961: DalT, rnd 14/1960: LA, rnd 10; B6/25/1939 Muskogee, OK

YEAR	TEAM	G(GS, POS)	RUSH	YD	AVG(LG)	TD	REC	YD	AVG(LG)	TD	PASS	COMP	PCT	YD	AVG(LG)	TD	INT	SK	YD	QBR	KPR	OTD	PTS	TAY
1962	†DalT-A★	14(FB)	111	604	5.4(69)	2	29	333	11.5(28)	0	—	—	—	—	—	—	—	—	—	—	k	—	12	793
1963	KC-A	14(FB)	142	568	4.0(36)	3	27	301	11.1(46)	3	3	1	33.3	33	11.0(33)	1	0	—	—	—	—	—	36	785
1964	KC-A	14(fb)	73	252	3.5(30)	1	13	221	17.0(66)	2	—	—	—	—	—	—	—	—	—	—	—	—	20	383
1965	KC-A☆	14(FB)	175	661	3.8(48)	**6**	37	590	15.9(69)	3	1	0	0.0	0	0.0	0	0	—	—	—	—	—	54	1031
1966	†KC-A✧	14(FB)	140	540	3.9(49)	4	19	285	15.0(68)	5	—	—	—	—	—	—	—	—	—	—	—	—	54	748
1967	KC-A✧	14(FB)	97	392	4.0(34)	2	26	219	8.4(25)	1	—	—	—	—	—	—	—	—	—	—	—	—	20	527
1968	†KC-A	9	24	107	4.5(19)	0	3	-4	-1.3(5)	0	—	—	—	—	—	—	—	—	—	—	—	—	0	105
1969	†KC-A	14	—	—	—	—	—	—	—	—	—	—	—	—	—	—	—	—	—	—	—	—	—	—
NFL	8	107	762	3124	4.1(69)	18	154	1945	12.6(69)	14	4	1	25.0	33	8.3(33)	1	0	—	—	—	k	—	196	4370

McCLOSKEY, MIKE Michael James, TE, 6´5˝/244 lbs; Penn State; 1983: Hou, rnd 4; B2/2/1961 Philadelphia, PA

YEAR	TEAM	G(GS, POS)	RUSH	YD	AVG(LG)	TD	REC	YD	AVG(LG)	TD	PASS	COMP	PCT	YD	AVG(LG)	TD	INT	SK	YD	QBR	KPR	OTD	PTS	TAY
1983	Hou	16(7, te)	—	—	—	—	16	137	8.6(20)	1	—	—	—	—	—	—	—	—	—	—	k	—	6	70
1984	Hou	15(0)	—	—	—	—	9	152	16.9(51)	1	—	—	—	—	—	—	—	—	—	—	—	—	6	81
1985	Hou	16(0)	—	—	—	—	4	29	7.3(24)	1	—	—	—	—	—	—	—	—	—	—	—	—	6	20
1987	Phi	1(0)	—	—	—	—	—	—	—	—	—	—	—	—	—	—	—	—	—	—	—	—	—	—
NFL	4	48(7)	—	—	—	—	29	318	11.0(51)	3	—	—	—	—	—	—	—	—	—	—	k	—	18	170

McCLOUD, TYRUS Tyrus Kamall, LB, 6´1˝/250 lbs; Louisville; 1997: Bal, rnd 4; B11/23/1974 Fort Lauderdale, FL **1997** Bal 16 (0) **1998** Bal 7 (2) **NFL** 23 (2) [2 yrs]

McCLOUGHAN, DAVE David Kent, DB, 6´1˝/186 lbs; Colorado; 1991: Ind, rnd 3; B11/20/1966 San Leandro, CA **1991** Ind 15 (0) **1992** GB 5 (0) **1993** Sea 15 (1) **1994** Sea 13 (2) **NFL** 48 (3) [4 yrs]

McCLOUGHAN, KENT Kent Auburn, DB, 6´1˝/190 lbs; Nebraska; 1965: Hou, rnd 11/Was, rnd 3; B2/12/1940 Scottsbluff, NE **1965** Oak-A 14 (LCB) **1966** Oak-A★14 (LCB) **1967**†Oak-A★14 (LCB) **1968** Oak-A☆8 (8, LCB) **1969**†Oak-A 4 **1970**†Oak☆13 (10, LCB) **NFL** 67 (18) [6 yrs]

McCLOVER, DARRELL Darrell A., LB, 6´2˝/219 lbs; Miami (FL); 2004: NYJ, rnd 7; B8/25/1981 Coconut Creek, FL **2004**†NYJ 16 (0)

McCLUNG, WILLIE William Albert, T-DT, 6´2˝/250 lbs; Florida A&M; B5/9/1930 Marion, AL, D7/28/2002 Pittsburgh, PA **1955** Pit 12 (RDT) **1956** Pit 12 (LDT) **1957** Pit 12 (LT) **1958**†Cle 12 (rt) **1959** Cle 12 (LDT) **1960** Det 11 (RT) **1961** Det 3 **NFL** 74 [7 yrs]

McCLURE, BOB Robert D., G, 6´1˝/224 lbs; Drake; Nevada-Reno; 1946: Bos, rnd 3; B7/8/1924 Dardanelle, AR, D4/17/1999 Graeagle, CA **1947** Bos 10 (3) **1948** Bos 12 (0) **NFL** 22 (3) [2 yrs]

McCLURE, BRIAN Brian Scott, QB, 6´6˝/222 lbs; Bowling Green State; 1986: Buf, rnd 12; B12/28/1963 Ravenna, OH

YEAR	TEAM	G(GS, POS)	RUSH	YD	AVG(LG)	TD	REC	YD	AVG(LG)	TD	PASS	COMP	PCT	YD	AVG(LG)	TD	INT	SK	YD	QBR	KPR	OTD	PTS	TAY
1987	Buf	1(1)	2	4	2.0(3)	0	—	—	—	—	38	20	52.6	181	4.8(30)	0	3	2	17	—	—	—	0	-26

McCLURE, TODD Todd, C, 6´1˝/286 lbs; LSU; 1999: Atl, rnd 7; B2/16/1977 Baton Rouge, LA **2000** Atl 10 (7, C) **2001** Atl 15 (15, C) **2002**†Atl 16 (16, C) **2003** Atl 16 (16, C) **2004**†Atl 16 (16, C) **2005** Atl 16 (16, C) **NFL** 89 (86) [6 yrs]

McCLURE, WAYNE Wayne Leroy, LB, 6´1˝/225 lbs; Mississippi; 1968: KC, rnd 9; B7/2/1942 Merryville, TN, D6/12/2005 Covington, LA **1968** Cin-A 13 **1970**†Cin 14 **NFL** 27 [2 yrs]

McCLUSKEY, DAVID David Eugene, RB, 6´1˝/227 lbs; Georgia; 1987: Cin, rnd 10; B11/5/1963 Rome, GA

YEAR	TEAM	G(GS, POS)	RUSH	YD	AVG(LG)	TD	REC	YD	AVG(LG)	TD	PASS	COMP	PCT	YD	AVG(LG)	TD	INT	SK	YD	QBR	KPR	OTD	PTS	TAY
1987	Cin	3(3)	29	94	3.2(12)	1	1	8	8.0(8)	0	—	—	—	—	—	—	—	—	—	—	—	—	6	108

McCOLL, BILL William Frazer, E, 6´4˝/230 lbs; Stanford; 1952: ChiB, rnd 3; B4/2/1930 San Diego, CA

YEAR	TEAM	G(GS, POS)	RUSH	YD	AVG(LG)	TD	REC	YD	AVG(LG)	TD	PASS	COMP	PCT	YD	AVG(LG)	TD	INT	SK	YD	QBR	KPR	OTD	PTS	TAY
1952	ChiB	12(LE)	—	—	—	—	20	277	13.9(30)	2	—	—	—	—	—	—	—	—	—	—	k	—	12	134
1953	ChiB	12(RE)	—	—	—	—	36	453	12.6(55)	4	—	—	—	—	—	—	—	—	—	—	—	1	30	247
1954	ChiB	12(RE)	—	—	—	—	24	368	15.3(45)	2	—	—	—	—	—	—	—	—	—	—	—	—	12	194
1955	ChiB	12(RE)	—	—	—	—	35	502	14.3(42)	4	2	1	50.0	59	29.5(59)	0	0	—	—	—	—	—	24	301
1956	†ChiB	12(RE)	—	—	—	—	24	322	13.4(69)	4	4	1	25.0	79	19.8(**79**)	1	2	—	—	—	k	—	24	120
1957	ChiB	12(FL)	—	—	—	—	19	282	14.8(30)	1	—	—	—	—	—	—	—	—	—	—	—	—	6	146
1958	ChiB	12(RE)	—	—	—	—	35	517	14.8(67)	8	—	—	—	—	—	—	—	—	—	—	—	—	48	299
1959	ChiB	12(RE)	—	—	—	—	8	94	11.8(26)	0	—	—	—	—	—	—	—	—	—	—	—	—	0	47
NFL	8	96	—	—	—	—	201	2815	14.0(69)	25	6	2	33.3	138	23.0(79)	1	2	—	—	—	k	1	156	1486

McCOLL, MILT Milton Bird, LB, 6´6˝/248 lbs; Stanford; B8/28/1959 Oak Park, IL **1981**†SF 16 (0) **1982** SF 9 (2) **1983**†SF 12 (0) **1984**†SF 16 (0) **1985**†SF 16 (4) **1986**†SF 16 (15, LOLB) **1987**†SF 12 (10, LOLB) **1988** LARd 15 (0) **NFL** 112 (31) [8 yrs]

McCOLLUM, ANDY Andrew John, C-G, 6´4˝/300 lbs; Toledo; B6/2/1970 Akron, OH **1995** NO 11 (9, RG) **1996** NO 16 (16, C) **1997** NO 16 (16, LG) **1998** NO 16 (5, lg) **1999**†SL 16 (2) **2000**†SL 16 (16, C) **2001**†SL 16 (16, C) **2002** SL 16 (16, C) **2003**†SL 16 (16, LG) **2004**†SL 16 (16, C) **2005** SL 16 (16, C) **NFL** 171 (144) [11 yrs]

McCOLLUM, BUBBA James Henry, DT, 6´0˝/250 lbs; Kentucky; B9/13/1952 Louisville, KY **1974** Hou 11

McCOLLUM, HARLEY Harley Raymond, T, 6´4˝/245 lbs; Tulane; 1942: Was, rnd 6; B2/28/1916, D6/1984 Palm Springs, CA **1946** NYY-A 10 (0) **1947** ChiR-A 13 (9, RT) **AAFC** 23 (9) [2 yrs]

McCOMB, DON Donald H., DE, 6´4˝/240 lbs; Villanova; 1956: NYG, rnd 21; B3/24/1934 **1960** Bos-A 1

McCOMBS, NAT Nathaniel Hawthorne, aka Chief Big Twig, G-T, 5´11˝/226 lbs; Haskell Indian; B12/18/1904 Eufaula, OK, D7/15/1965 Eufaula, OK **1926** Akr 8 (6, RG), 6 **1929** Buf 9 (9, LG) **NFL** 17 (15) [2 yrs]

McCOMBS, TONY Antonias Orlando, LB, 6´2˝/246 lbs; Eastern Kentucky; 1997: Arz, rnd 6; B8/24/1974 Hopkinsville, KY **1997** Arz 12 (0) **1998**†Arz 14 (13, RLB) **NFL** 26 (13) [2 yrs]

McCONKEY, PHIL Philip Joseph, WR, 5´10˝/170 lbs; Navy; B2/24/1957 Buffalo, NY **[R]**

YEAR	TEAM	G(GS, POS)	RUSH	YD	AVG(LG)	TD	REC	YD	AVG(LG)	TD	PASS	COMP	PCT	YD	AVG(LG)	TD	INT	SK	YD	QBR	KPR	OTD	PTS	TAY
1984	NYG	13(0)	—	—	—	—	8	154	19.3(39)	0	—	—	—	—	—	—	—	—	—	—	kp	1	6	274
1985	†NYG	16(0)	—	—	—	—	25	404	16.2(48)	1	—	—	—	—	—	—	—	—	—	—	kp	—	6	438
1986	GB	4(0)	—	—	—	—	—	—	—	—	—	—	—	—	—	—	—	—	—	—	—	—	—	—
1986	†NYG	12(0)	—	—	—	—	16	279	17.4(46)	1	—	—	—	—	—	—	—	—	—	—	kp	—	6	349
1987	NYG	12(0)	—	—	—	—	11	186	16.9(31)	0	—	—	—	—	—	—	—	—	—	—	kp	—	0	270
1988	NYG	16(0)	—	—	—	—	5	72	14.4(28)	0	—	—	—	—	—	—	—	—	—	—	kp	—	0	149
1989	Phx	5(0)	—	—	—	—	2	18	9.0(10)	0	—	—	—	—	—	—	—	—	—	—	kp	—	0	27
1989	SD	6(0)	—	—	—	—	—	—	—	—	—	—	—	—	—	—	—	—	—	—	p	—	0	41
NFL	6	84(0)	—	—	—	—	67	1113	16.6(48)	2	—	—	—	—	—	—	—	—	—	—	kp	1	18	1548

McCONNELL, BRIAN Brian Thomas, LB, 6´4˝/220 lbs; Michigan State; 1973: Buf, rnd 7; B1/21/1950 Smoke Rise, NJ **1973** Buf 1 **1973** Hou 7 **NFL** 8 [1 yr]

McCONNELL, DEWEY Dewey L., DB-DE, 6´0˝/190 lbs; Wyoming; 1952: LA, rnd 3; B1/26/1930 Laramie, WY, D2/19/1984 Laramie, WY

YEAR	TEAM	G(GS, POS)	RUSH	YD	AVG(LG)	TD	REC	YD	AVG(LG)	TD	PASS	COMP	PCT	YD	AVG(LG)	TD	INT	SK	YD	QBR	KPR	OTD	PTS	TAY
1954	Pit	9(DB)	—	—	—	—	1	2	2.0(2)	0	—	—	—	—	—	—	—	—	—	—	i	—	0	103

McCONNELL, FRANK William Felton, G, 6´0˝/195 lbs; Virginia; Georgia Tech; B8/23/1900 Carnesville, GA, D11/26/1985 Cincinnati, OH **1927** Buf 5 (5, RG)

McCOO, ERIC Eric Franklin, RB, 5´10˝/210 lbs; Penn State; B9/6/1980 Red Bank, NJ

YEAR	TEAM	G(GS, POS)	RUSH	YD	AVG(LG)	TD	REC	YD	AVG(LG)	TD	PASS	COMP	PCT	YD	AVG(LG)	TD	INT	SK	YD	QBR	KPR	OTD	PTS	TAY
2004	Phi	1(0)	9	54	6.0(12)	0	2	15	7.5(8)	0	—	—	—	—	—	—	—	—	—	—	—	—	0	62

McCORD, DARRIS Darris Paul, DE-DT-T, 6´4˝/250 lbs; Tennessee; 1955: Det, rnd 3; B1/4/1933 Detroit, MI **1955** Det 12 (RDT) **1956** Det 12 (LDE) **1957**†Det✧12 (LDE) **1958** Det 12 (LDE) **1959** Det 12 (LDE) **1960** Det 12 (LDE) **1961** Det 14 (LDE) **1962** Det 14 (LDE) **1963** Det 13 (LDE) **1964** Det 14 (LDE) **1965** Det 14 (LDE) **1966** Det 13 (LDE) **1967** Det 14 (LDE) **NFL** 168 [13 yrs]

McCORD, QUENTIN John Quentin, WR, 5´10˝/188 lbs; Kentucky; 2001: Atl, rnd 7; B6/26/1978 La Grange, GA

YEAR	TEAM	G(GS, POS)	RUSH	YD	AVG(LG)	TD	REC	YD	AVG(LG)	TD	PASS	COMP	PCT	YD	AVG(LG)	TD	INT	SK	YD	QBR	KPR	OTD	PTS	TAY
2001	Atl	7(0)	2	11	5.5(8)	0	3	53	17.7(26)	0	—	—	—	—	—	—	—	—	—	—	k	—	0	47
2002	†Atl	9(0)	—	—	—	—	11	253	23.0(60)	1	—	—	—	—	—	—	—	—	—	—	k	—	6	156

YEAR	TEAM	G (GS, POS)	RUSH	YD	AVG(LG)	TD	REC	YD	AVG(LG)	TD	PASS	COMP	PCT	YD	AVG(LG)	TD	INT	SK	YD	QBR	KPR	OTD	PTS	TAY
2003	Atl	9(2)	2	2	1.0(1)	0	9	121	13.4(33)	0	—	—	—	—	—	—	—	—	—	—	p	—	0	104
NFL	3	25(2)	4	13	3.3(8)	0	23	427	18.6(60)	1	—	—	—	—	—	—	—	—	—	—	kp	—	6	306

McCormack, Hurvin Hurvin Michael, DT, 6´5˝/281 lbs; Indiana; B4/6/1972 Brooklyn, NY **1994**†Dal 3 (0) **1995**†Dal 15 (2) **1996**†Dal 16 (4) **1997** Dal 13 (0) **1998**†Dal 16 (1) **1999** Cle 13 (4) **NFL** 76 (11) [6 yrs]

McCormack, Mike Michael Joseph, T-DG-DT, 6´4˝/246 lbs; Kansas; 1951: NYY, rnd 3; B6/21/1930 Chicago, IL; HOF 1984 **[C]** **1951** NYY✩12 (RT) **1954**†Cle✩12 (MG) **1955**†Cle✩12 (RT) **1956** Cle★12 (RT) **1958**†Cle✩9 (RT) **1959** Cle✩10 (RT) **1960** Cle★12 (RT) **1962** Cle★14 (RT)

1957	†Cle★	12(RT)	0	4	(4)	0	—	—	—	—	—	—	—	—	—	—	—	—	—	—	—	—	0	4
1961	Cle★	14(RT)	0	4	(4)	0	—	—	—	—	—	—	—	—	—	—	—	—	—	—	—	—	0	4
NFL	10	119	0	8	(4)	0	—	—	—	—	—	—	—	—	—	—	—	—	—	ki	—	—	0	2

McCormack, Dave David Oliver, T, 6´6˝/250 lbs; LSU; 1965: SF, rnd 5/Bos, rnd R1; B7/10/1943 Winnsboro, LA **1966** SF 14 **1967** NO 2 **NFL** 16 [2 yrs]

McCormick, Elmer Elmer Francis, C-T-C-B, 5´7˝/220 lbs; Detroit Mercy; Canisius; B10/27/1898 Hartford, CT, D2/4/1951 Springfield, MA **1923** Buf✩8 (4) **1924** Buf✩3 (3) **1925** Buf 8 (4) **1925** Fra 8 (5, c) **1926** Har 3 (2) **NFL** 30 (18) [4 yrs]

McCormick, Felix Felix John, FB-G-HB, 5´7˝/185 lbs; Bucknell; B5/21/1905 Newark, NJ, D3/30/1971 Glen Ridge, NJ **[K]** **1929** Ora 10 (3), 3 **1930** Nwk 3 (1) **NFL** 13 (4) [2 yrs]

McCormick, Frank Frank G., WB-FB, 5´11˝/190 lbs; South Dakota; B11/5/1894 Genoa, NE, D3/24/1976 Fullerton, CA **1920** Akr 11 (8, WB) **1921** Akr 2 (1), 18 **1921** Cin 1 (0) **NFL** 14 (9) [2 yrs]

McCormick, John John Joseph, QB, 6´1˝/208 lbs; Massachusetts; B5/26/1937 Boston, MA

1962	Min	13	2	4	2.0(4)	0	—	—	—	—	18	7	38.9	104	5.8(53)	0	5	3	33	—	P	—	0	-144
1963	Den-A	9	3	-5	-1.7(-2)	0	—	—	—	—	72	28	38.9	417	5.8(72)	4	3	—	—	—	—	—	0	104
1965	Den-A	14(qb)	1	-2	-2.0(-2)	0	—	—	—	—	253	103	40.7	1292	5.1(90)	7	14	—	—	43.5	P	—	0	119
1966	Den-A	14(QB)	4	2	0.5(3)	0	—	—	—	—	193	68	35.2	993	5.1(64)	6	15	—	—	30.9	—	—	0	-72
1968	Den-A	1	—	—	—	—	—	—	—	—	19	8	42.1	89	4.7(18)	0	1	—	—	—	—	—	0	5
NFL	5	51	10	-1	-0.1(4)	0	—	—	—	—	555	214	38.6	2895	5.2(90)	17	38	3	33	37.6	P	—	0	12

McCormick, Len Gardner Len, C-LB, 6´3˝/232 lbs; Schreiner College; Southwestern (TX); Baylor; B10/28/1922 Eldorado, TX **1948**†Bal-A 11 (5, c)

McCormick, Tom Thomas, HB, 5´11˝/185 lbs; Pacific; 1952: LA, rnd 8; B5/16/1930 Waco, TX

1953	LARm	11	20	29	1.5(8)	0	5	72	14.4(20)	0	—	—	—	—	—	—	—	—	—	—	kp	—	0	116
1954	LARm	9	48	173	3.6(16)	0	3	58	19.3(31)	0	—	—	—	—	—	—	—	—	—	—	kp	—	0	179
1955	†LARm	6	16	66	4.1(14)	1	3	-1	-0.3(4)	0	—	—	—	—	—	—	—	—	—	—	k	—	6	88
1956	SF	6	2	4	2.0(2)	0	—	—	—	—	—	—	—	—	—	—	—	—	—	—	k	—	0	7
NFL	4	32	86	272	3.2(16)	1	11	129	11.7(31)	0	—	—	—	—	—	—	—	—	—	—	kp	—	6	390

McCormick, Walter Walter Kendell, C-LB, 6´1˝/215 lbs; Washington; USC; 1948: SF-A, rnd 4/NYG, rnd 24; B9/4/1926 Visalia, CA, D4/3/2005 Visalia, CA **1948** SF-A 9 (0)

McCorvey, Kez Kezarrick Montines, WR, 6´0˝/184 lbs; Florida State; 1995: Det, rnd 5; B1/23/1972 Gautier, MS **1995** Det 2 (0) **1996** Det 1 (0)

| 1997 | †Det | 7(0) | — | — | — | — | 2 | 9 | 4.5(6) | 0 | — | — | — | — | — | — | — | — | — | — | — | — | 0 | 5 |
| NFL | 3 | 10(0) | — | — | — | — | 2 | 9 | 4.5(6) | 0 | — | — | — | — | — | — | — | — | — | — | — | — | 0 | 5 |

McCown, Josh Joshua, QB, 6´4˝/212 lbs; SMU; Sam Houston State; 2002: Arz, rnd 3; B7/4/1979 Jacksonville, TX

2002	Arz	2(0)	1	20	20.0(20)	0	—	—	—	—	18	7	38.9	66	3.7(26)	0	2	5	50	—	—	—	0	-27
2003	Arz	10(3, qb)	28	158	5.6(16)	1	—	—	—	—	166	95	57.2	1018	6.1(60)	5	6	25	174	70.3	—	—	6	462
2004	Arz	14(13, QB)	36	112	3.1(12)	2	1	-5	-5.0(-5)	0	408	233	57.1	2511	6.2(48)	11	10	31	263	74.1	—	—	14	1040
2005	Arz	9(6, qb)	29	139	4.8(12)	0	—	—	—	—	270	163	60.4	1836	6.8(49)	9	11	18	101	74.9	—	1	6	662
NFL	4	35(22)	94	429	4.6(20)	3	1	-5	-5.0(-5)	0	862	498	57.8	5431	6.3(60)	25	29	79	588	72.1	—	1	26	2137

McCown, Luke Luke, QB, 6´3˝/208 lbs; Louisiana Tech; 2004: Cle, rnd 4; B7/12/1981 Jacksonville, TX

| 2004 | Cle | 5(4) | 6 | 25 | 4.2(11) | 0 | — | — | — | — | 98 | 48 | 49.0 | 608 | 6.2(58) | 4 | 7 | 12 | 122 | — | — | — | 0 | 69 |

McCoy T, /175 lbs; none; deceased **1920** Det 1 (0)

McCoy, Joel Joel Lawrence, TB, 5´10˝/170 lbs; Alabama; B8/22/1920 Birmingham, AL

| 1946 | Det | 10(0) | 19 | -29 | -1.5(15) | 0 | — | — | — | — | 18 | 6 | 33.3 | 72 | 4.0(34) | 0 | 4 | — | — | — | kp | — | 0 | -158 |

McCoy, Larry Larry Joe, LB, 6´2˝/240 lbs; Lamar; B8/12/1961 Madisonville, TX **1984** LARd 4 (0) **1987** NO 3 (3) **NFL** 7 (3) [2 yrs]

McCoy, LeRon LeRon, WR, 6´1˝/211 lbs; Indiana (PA); 2005: Arz, rnd 7; B1/24/1982 Harrisburg, PA

| 2005 | Arz | 10(4) | — | — | — | — | 18 | 191 | 10.6(24) | 1 | — | — | — | — | — | — | — | — | — | — | — | — | 6 | 101 |

McCoy, Lloyd Lloyd, G, 6´1˝/245 lbs; San Diego State; B1942 **1964** SD-A 1

McCoy, Matt Matt, LB, 6´0˝/234 lbs; San Diego State; 2005: Phi, rnd 2; B10/14/1982 Orange County, CA **2005** Phi 4 (0)

McCoy, Mike Michael Patrick, DT-NT, 6´5˝/284 lbs; Notre Dame; 1970: GB, rnd 1; B9/6/1948 Erie, PA **1970** GB 14 (14, RDT) **1971** GB 12 (12, LDT) **1972** GB 12 (12, LDT) **1973** GB 14 (14, LDT) **1974** GB 14 (14, LDT) **1975** GB 14 (14, LDT) **1976** GB 14 (LDT) **1977**†Oak 14 **1978** Oak 15 (3) **1979** NYG 3 **1980** NYG 2 (2) **1980** Det 4 (0) **NFL** 132 (85) [11 yrs]

McCoy, Mike Michael Charles, DB, 5´11˝/183 lbs; Colorado; 1976: GB, rnd 3; B8/16/1953 West Memphis, AR **1976** GB 14 (1) **1977** GB 14 (14, RCB) **1978** GB 16 (16, RCB) **1979** GB 16 (16, RCB) **1980** GB 16 (16, RCB) **1981** GB 16 (16, RCB) **1982**†GB 9 (9, RCB) **1983** GB 9 (9, RCB) **NFL** 110 (97) [8 yrs]

McCoy, Tony Anthony Bernard, DT-NT, 6´0˝/282 lbs; Florida; 1992: Ind, rnd 4; B6/10/1969 Orlando, FL **1992** Ind 16 (3) **1993** Ind 6 (0) **1994** Ind 15 (15, LDT) **1995**†Ind 16 (16, LDT) **1996** Ind 15 (15, LDT) **1997** Ind 16 (11, LDT) **1998** Ind 14 (13, LDT) **1999** Ind 10 (0) **2000** Arz 6 (6, ldt) **NFL** 114 (79) [9 yrs]

McCrary, Fred Freddy Demetrius, FB, 6´0˝/247 lbs; Mississippi State; 1995: Phi, rnd 6; B9/19/1972 Naples, FL

1995	Phi	13(4, FB)	3	1	0.3(1)	0	9	60	6.7(11)	0	—	—	—	—	—	—	—	—	—	—	k	—	6	27
1997	NO	7(0)	8	15	1.9(8)	0	4	17	4.3(11)	0	—	—	—	—	—	—	—	—	—	—	k	—	0	20
1999	SD	16(14, FB)	—	—	—	—	37	201	5.4(38)	1	—	—	—	—	—	—	—	—	—	—	k	—	6	95
2000	SD	15(12, FB)	7	8	1.1(4)	0	18	141	7.8(19)	2	—	—	—	—	—	—	—	—	—	—	—	—	12	89
2001	SD	16(12, FB)	2	3	1.5(2)	0	13	71	5.5(12)	0	—	—	—	—	—	—	—	—	—	—	—	—	0	39
2002	SD	16(16, FB)	2	1	0.5(2)	0	22	96	4.4(25)	3	—	—	—	—	—	—	—	—	—	—	—	—	18	64
2003	NE	6(3)	3	3	1.0(4)	0	2	12	6.0(9)	0	—	—	—	—	—	—	—	—	—	—	—	—	0	9
2004	†Atl	3(2)	—	—	—	—	2	23	11.5(14)	0	—	—	—	—	—	—	—	—	—	—	—	—	0	12
2005	Atl	15(0)	—	—	—	—	3	12	4.0(11)	0	—	—	—	—	—	—	—	—	—	—	—	—	0	6
NFL	9	107(63)	25	31	1.2(8)	1	110	633	5.8(38)	6	—	—	—	—	—	—	—	—	—	—	k	—	42	359

McCrary, Greg Gregory Alonza, TE, 6´1˝/233 lbs; Clark Atlanta; 1975: Atl, rnd 5; B3/24/1952 Griffin, GA

1975	Atl	13	—	—	—	—	—	—	—	—	—	—	—	—	—	—	—	—	—	—	k	—	0	3
1977	Atl	13(2)	—	—	—	—	2	48	24.0(49)	1	—	—	—	—	—	—	—	—	—	—	—	—	6	29
1978	Was	5	—	—	—	—	—	—	—	—	—	—	—	—	—	—	—	—	—	—	—	—	0	—
1978	SD	8(1)	2	18	9.0(16)	0	1	29	29.0(29)	1	—	—	—	—	—	—	—	—	—	—	—	—	6	38
1979	†SD	14	—	—	—	—	5	32	6.4(19)	0	—	—	—	—	—	—	—	—	—	—	—	—	2	16
1980	†SD	16(10, te)	—	—	—	—	11	106	9.6(28)	2	—	—	—	—	—	—	—	—	—	—	—	—	12	63
1981	Was	5(0)	—	—	—	—	3	13	4.3(12)	0	—	—	—	—	—	—	—	—	—	—	—	—	0	7
NFL	6	74(13)	2	18	9.0(16)	0	22	228	10.4(49)	4	—	—	—	—	—	—	—	—	—	—	k	—	26	155

McCrary, Herdis Herdis William, B, 6´0˝/207 lbs; Georgia; B6/9/1904 Bicknell, IN, D5/11/1981 Green Bay, WI **1929** GB 13 (5, hb), 24 **1930** GB 14 (5, wb), 36 **1931** GB 12 (9, FB, B), 6

1932	GB	11(4)	42	152	3.6	1	—	—	—	—	—	—	—	—	—	—	—	—	—	—	—	—	6	162
1933	GB	2(1)	6	10	1.7	0	—	—	—	—	—	—	—	—	—	—	—	—	—	—	—	—	0	10
NFL	5	52(24)	48	162	3.4	7	—	—	—	—	—	—	—	—	—	—	—	—	—	—	—	1	72	267

McCrary, Michael Michael Curtis, DE, 6´4˝/266 lbs; Wake Forest; 1993: Sea, rnd 7; B7/7/1970 Vienna, VA **[S]** **1993** Sea 15 (0) **1994** Sea 16 (0) **1995** Sea 11 (0) **1996** Sea 16 (13, RDE) **1997** Bal 15 (15, RDE) **1998** Bal★16 (16, RDE) **1999** Bal✧16 (16, RDE) **2000**†Bal 16 (16, RDE) **2001** Bal 10 (10, RDE) **2002** Bal 5 (2) **NFL** 136 (88) [10 yrs]

McCray, Bobby Bobby L., DE, 6´6˝/245 lbs; Florida; 2004: Jax, rnd 7; B11/1/1981 Miami, FL **2004** Jax 16 (7, lde) **2005**†Jax 16 (1) **NFL** 32 (8) [2 yrs]

McCray, Bruce Bruce Edward, DB, 5´9˝/181 lbs; Western Illinois; B10/27/1963 **1987** ChiB 3 (3)

McCray, Prentice Prentice, DB, 6´1˝/188 lbs; Arizona State; 1973: Det, rnd 8; B3/1/1951 Los Angeles, CA **1974** NE 14 (14, FS) **1975** NE 14 (14, SS) **1976**†NE 14 (14, SS) **1977** NE 14 (14, SS) **1978** NE 8 (3) **1979** NE 14 (5, ss) **1980** NE 3 (0) **1980** Det 7 (0) **NFL** 88 (64) [7 yrs]

McCray, Willie Willie Lee, DE, 6´5˝/234 lbs; Alabama; Troy State; 1978: SF, rnd 11; B7/17/1953 Fort Lee, VA **1978** SF 16

McCreary, Loaird Loaird Arthur, TE-WR, 6´5˝/227 lbs; Tennessee State; 1976: Mia, rnd 2; B3/15/1953 Crawfordsville, GA

YEAR	TEAM	G(GS, POS)	RUSH	YD	AVG(LG)	TD	REC	YD	AVG(LG)	TD	PASS	COMP	PCT	YD	AVG(LG)	TD	INT	SK	YD	QBR	KPR	OTD	PTS	TAY
1976	Mia	14	—	—	—	—	2	51	25.5(30)	0	—	—	—	—	—	—	—	—	—	—	—	—	0	26
1977	Mia	14(4)	—	—	—	—	2	10	5.0(9)	1	—	—	—	—	—	—	—	—	—	—	k	—	6	25
1978	†Mia	16(1)	—	—	—	—	3	27	9.0(12)	2	—	—	—	—	—	—	—	—	—	—	—	—	12	24
1979	NYG	11	—	—	—	—	1	7	7.0(7)	0	—	—	—	—	—	—	—	—	—	—	—	—	0	4
NFL	4	55(5)	—	—	—	—	8	95	11.9(30)	3	—	—	—	—	—	—	—	—	—	—	k	—	18	78

McCreary, Bob Robert Joe, T, 6´5˝/256 lbs; Wake Forest; 1961: SF, rnd 5; B6/20/1939 Lenoir, NC **1961** Dal 9 (4)

McCree, Marlon Marlon Tarron, DB, 5´11˝/196 lbs; Kentucky; 2001: Jax, rnd 7; B3/17/1977 Orlando, FL **2001** Jax 13 (11, FS) **2002** Jax 16 (16, FS) **2003** Jax 2 (0) **2003** Hou 13 (11, FS) **2004** Hou 16 (1) **2005**†Car 16 (14, SS) **NFL** 76 (53) [5 yrs]

McCrillis, Ed Edgar Vincent Frederick, G, 6´0˝/205 lbs; Brown; B9/7/1904 New York, NY, D9/1/1940 Warwick, RI **1926** Pro 1 (0) **1929** Bos 7 (5, RG) **NFL** 8 (5) [2 yrs]

McCrumbly, John John Paul, LB, 6´1˝/245 lbs; Texas A&M; 1975: Buf, rnd 5; B7/28/1952 Dallas, TX **1975** Buf 13 (2)

McCullers, Dale Dale Green, LB, 6´1˝/215 lbs; Florida State; 1969: Mia, rnd 12; B10/11/1947 Lake City, FL **1969** Mia-A 14

McCulloch, Earl Earl Raymond, WR-SE, 5´11˝/175 lbs; USC; 1968: Det, rnd 1; B1/10/1946 Clarksville, TX

YEAR	TEAM	G(GS, POS)	RUSH	YD	AVG(LG)	TD	REC	YD	AVG(LG)	TD	PASS	COMP	PCT	YD	AVG(LG)	TD	INT	SK	YD	QBR	KPR	OTD	PTS	TAY
1968	Det	14(SE)	3	13	4.3(5)	0	40	680	17.0(80)	5	—	—	—	—	—	—	—	—	—	—	—	—	30	378
1969	Det	14(SE)	1	4	4.0(4)	0	33	529	16.0(45)	5	—	—	—	—	—	—	—	—	—	—	—	—	30	294
1970	†Det	10(WR)	1	7	7.0(7)	0	15	278	18.5(44)	4	—	—	—	—	—	—	—	—	—	—	—	—	24	166
1971	Det	13(WR)	1	-7	-7.0(-7)	0	21	552	26.3(76)	3	—	—	—	—	—	—	—	—	—	—	—	—	18	284
1972	Det	10	—	—	—	—	5	96	19.2(33)	1	1	1	100.0	23	23.0(23)	0	0	—	—	—	—	—	6	65
1973	Det	11	2	12	6.0(13)	0	9	179	19.9(42)	1	—	—	—	—	—	—	—	—	—	—	—	—	6	107
1974	NO	3	—	—	—	—	1	5	5.0(5)	0	—	—	—	—	—	—	—	—	—	—	—	—	0	3
NFL	7	75	8	29	3.6(13)	0	124	2319	18.7(80)	19	1	1	100.0	23	23.0(23)	0	0	—	—	—	—	—	114	1295

McCullough, Andy Antwone, WR, 6´3˝/210 lbs; Tennessee; 1998: NO, rnd 7; B11/11/1975 Dayton, OH

YEAR	TEAM	G(GS, POS)	RUSH	YD	AVG(LG)	TD	REC	YD	AVG(LG)	TD	PASS	COMP	PCT	YD	AVG(LG)	TD	INT	SK	YD	QBR	KPR	OTD	PTS	TAY
1999	Arz	2(0)	—	—	—	—	3	45	15.0(31)	0	—	—	—	—	—	—	—	—	—	—	—	—	0	23

McCullough, Bob Robert Vernon, G, 6´2˝/245 lbs; Colorado; B11/18/1940 Helena, MT **1962** Den-A 14 (RG) **1963** Den-A 14 (LG) **1964** Den-A 14 (RG)

YEAR	TEAM	G(GS, POS)	RUSH	YD	AVG(LG)	TD	REC	YD	AVG(LG)	TD	PASS	COMP	PCT	YD	AVG(LG)	TD	INT	SK	YD	QBR	KPR	OTD	PTS	TAY
1965	Den-A	14(RG)	—	—	—	—	1	1	1.0(1)	0	—	—	—	—	—	—	—	—	—	—	—	—	0	1
NFL	4	56	—	—	—	—	1	1	1.0(1)	0	—	—	—	—	—	—	—	—	—	—	—	—	0	1

McCullough, George George Wayne, DB, 5´10˝/187 lbs; Baylor; 1997: Ten, rnd 5; B2/18/1975 Galveston, TX **1997** Ten 2 (0) **1998** Ten 7 (0) **1999**†Ten 5 (0) **2000** Ten 10 (0) **2001**†SF 15 (0) **NFL** 39 (0) [5 yrs]

McCullough, Hal Harold Francis, TB, 5´11˝/170 lbs; Cornell; B4/4/1918 New York, NY, D2/13/1991 Doylestown, PA

YEAR	TEAM	G(GS, POS)	RUSH	YD	AVG(LG)	TD	REC	YD	AVG(LG)	TD	PASS	COMP	PCT	YD	AVG(LG)	TD	INT	SK	YD	QBR	KPR	OTD	PTS	TAY
1942	Bkn	9(0)	21	-17	-0.8(14)	0	—	—	—	—	38	12	31.6	211	5.6(71)	1	3	—	—	—	Pp	—	0	-32

McCullough, Hugh Hugh Warner, TB-HB, 6´0˝/185 lbs; Oklahoma; 1939: Pit, rnd 4; B5/18/1916 Anadarko, OK, D2/11/1999, **[K]**

YEAR	TEAM	G(GS, POS)	RUSH	YD	AVG(LG)	TD	REC	YD	AVG(LG)	TD	PASS	COMP	PCT	YD	AVG(LG)	TD	INT	SK	YD	QBR	KPR	OTD	PTS	TAY
1939	Pit	10(6, TB)	60	96	1.6	1	4	57	14.3	0	100	32	32.0	443	4.4	2	12	—	—	14.3	P	—	6	-114
1940	ChiC	11(7, TB)	57	278	4.9	3	—	—	—	—	116	43	37.1	529	4.6(41)	4	**21**	—	—	23.9	KPi	—	19	-205
1941	ChiC	7(0)	15	22	1.5(14)	0	—	—	—	—	32	12	37.5	133	4.2(35)	0	5	—	—	—	Pkp	—	0	-84
1943	P-P	1(0)	—	—	—	—	—	—	—	—	—	—	—	—	—	—	—	—	—	—	—	—	—	—
1945	Bos	7(0)	2	1	0.5(2)	0	1	17	17.0(17)	0	6	0	0.0	0	0.0	0	3	—	—	—	P	—	0	-111
NFL	5	36(13)	134	397	3.0(14)	4	5	74	14.8(17)	0	254	87	34.3	1105	4.4(41)	6	41	—	—	17.0	KPkpi	—	25	-513

McCullough, Jake Richard Charles, DE, 6´5˝/270 lbs; Clemson; 1989: Den, rnd 4; B7/23/1965 Loris, SC **1989** Den 10 (0) **1990** Den 6 (0) **NFL** 16 (0) [2 yrs]

McCullough, Sultan Sultan, RB, 6´0˝/197 lbs; USC; B2/12/1980 Pasadena, CA

YEAR	TEAM	G(GS, POS)	RUSH	YD	AVG(LG)	TD	REC	YD	AVG(LG)	TD	PASS	COMP	PCT	YD	AVG(LG)	TD	INT	SK	YD	QBR	KPR	OTD	PTS	TAY
2003	Was	1(0)	1	9	9.0(9)	0	3	13	4.3(8)	0	—	—	—	—	—	—	—	—	—	—	—	—	0	16

McCullum, Sam Samuel Charles, WR, 6´2˝/203 lbs; Montana State; 1974: Min, rnd 9; B11/30/1952 McComb, MS

YEAR	TEAM	G(GS, POS)	RUSH	YD	AVG(LG)	TD	REC	YD	AVG(LG)	TD	PASS	COMP	PCT	YD	AVG(LG)	TD	INT	SK	YD	QBR	KPR	OTD	PTS	TAY
1974	†Min	12	—	—	—	—	7	138	19.7(34)	3	—	—	—	—	—	—	—	—	—	—	kp	—	18	229
1975	†Min	9	—	—	—	—	2	25	12.5(20)	0	—	—	—	—	—	—	—	—	—	—	kp	—	0	61
1976	Sea	14(13, WR)	—	—	—	—	32	506	15.8(72)	4	—	—	—	—	—	—	—	—	—	—	—	—	24	273
1977	Sea	13(3)	—	—	—	—	9	198	22.0(65)	1	—	—	—	—	—	—	—	—	—	—	—	—	6	104
1978	Sea	16(16, WR)	—	—	—	—	37	525	14.2(44)	3	—	—	—	—	—	—	—	—	—	—	—	—	18	278
1979	Sea	16(16, WR)	—	—	—	—	46	739	16.1(65)	4	—	—	—	—	—	—	—	—	—	—	—	—	24	390
1980	Sea	16(16, WR)	—	—	—	—	62	874	14.1(58)	6	—	—	—	—	—	—	—	—	—	—	—	—	36	467
1981	Sea	16(14, WR)	—	—	—	—	46	567	12.3(36)	3	—	—	—	—	—	—	—	—	—	—	—	—	18	299
1982	†Min	6(2)	—	—	—	—	12	131	10.9(21)	0	—	—	—	—	—	—	—	—	—	—	—	—	0	66
1983	Min	11(5, wr)	—	—	—	—	21	314	15.0(49)	2	—	—	—	—	—	—	—	—	—	—	—	—	12	167
NFL	10	129(85)	—	—	—	—	274	4017	14.7(72)	26	—	—	—	—	—	—	—	—	—	—	kp	—	156	2332

McCune, Robert Robert, LB, 6´1˝/243 lbs; Louisville; 2005: Was, rnd 5; B3/9/1979 Mobile, AL **2005**†Was 5 (0)

McCurry, Dave David Gene, DB, 6´1˝/187 lbs; Iowa State; 1973: Mia, rnd 5; B2/23/1951 Grinnell, IA **1974** NE 2

McCurry, Mike Michael Lee, G, 6´3˝/258 lbs; Indiana; B3/26/1963 Indianapolis, IN **1987** Min 3 (3)

McCusker, Jim James Brian, T, 6´2˝/246 lbs; Pittsburgh; 1958: ChiC, rnd 2; B5/19/1936 Jamestown, NY **1958** ChiC 11 (RT) **1959** Phi 12 (lt) **1960**†Phi 12 (12, LT) **1961** Phi 13 (LT) **1962** Phi 14 (14, LT) **1963** Cle 7 **1964** NYJ-A 14 **NFL** 83 (26) [7 yrs]

McCutcheon, Daylon Daylon, DB, 5´10˝/190 lbs; USC; 1999: Cle, rnd 3; B12/9/1976 Los Angeles, CA **1999** Cle 16 (15, RCB) **2000** Cle 15 (15, RCB) **2001** Cle 16 (15, RCB) **2002**†Cle 13 (11, RCB) **2003** Cle 15 (14, RCB) **2004** Cle 12 (10, RCB) **2005** Cle 16 (16, LCB) **NFL** 103 (96) [7 yrs]

McCutcheon, Lawrence Lawrence, RB, 6´1˝/205 lbs; Colorado State; 1972: LA, rnd 3; B6/2/1950 Plainview, TX

YEAR	TEAM	G(GS, POS)	RUSH	YD	AVG(LG)	TD	REC	YD	AVG(LG)	TD	PASS	COMP	PCT	YD	AVG(LG)	TD	INT	SK	YD	QBR	KPR	OTD	PTS	TAY
1972	LARm	3	—	—	—	—	—	—	—	—	—	—	—	—	—	—	—	—	—	—	—	—	—	—
1973	†LARm★	12(12, RB)	210	1097	5.2(37)	2	30	289	9.6(31)	3	—	—	—	—	—	—	—	—	—	—	k	—	30	1268
1974	†LARm★	14(14, RB)	236	**1109**	4.7(23)	3	39	408	10.5(50)	2	—	—	—	—	—	—	—	—	—	—	—	—	30	1353
1975	†LARm★	13(13, RB)	213	911	4.3(43)	2	31	230	7.4(24)	1	1	0	0.0	0	0.0	0	0	—	—	—	—	—	18	1051
1976	†LARm★	14(14, RB)	291	1168	4.0(40)	9	28	305	10.9(42)	2	—	—	—	—	—	—	—	—	—	—	—	—	66	1421
1977	†LARm★	14(14, RB)	294	1238	4.2(48)	7	25	274	11.0(30)	2	—	—	—	—	—	—	—	—	—	—	—	—	54	1455
1978	LARm	8(7, rb)	118	420	3.6(18)	0	12	76	6.3(33)	2	1	0	0.0	0	0.0	0	0	—	—	—	—	—	12	468
1979	†LARm	11(4)	73	243	3.3(21)	0	19	101	5.3(11)	0	—	—	—	—	—	—	—	—	—	—	—	—	0	294
1980	Den	6(0)	12	52	4.3(32)	0	1	12	12.0(12)	0	0	0	0.0	0	0.0	0	0	1	4	—	—	—	0	58
1980	Sea	8(1)	40	202	5.1(12)	3	8	64	8.0(17)	1	2	1	50.0	12	6.0(12)	0	0	—	—	—	—	—	24	275
1981	Buf	6(3)	34	138	4.1(12)	0	5	40	8.0(17)	0	—	—	—	—	—	—	—	—	—	—	—	—	0	158
NFL	10	109(82)	1521	6578	4.3(48)	26	198	1799	9.1(50)	13	4	1	25.0	12	3.0(12)	0	0	1	4	—	k	—	234	7800

McDade, Karl Karl Vautrain, C-LB, 6´3˝/195 lbs; Portland; B3/27/1915 Madras, OR **1938** Pit 6 (1)

McDaniel, Ed Edward, LB, 5´11˝/230 lbs; Clemson; 1992: Min, rnd 5; B2/23/1969 Batesburg, SC **1992**†Min 8 (0) **1993**†Min 7 (1) **1994**†Min 16 (16, RLB) **1995** Min 16 (16, RLB) **1997**†Min 16 (16, LLB) **1998**†Min✧16 (16, MLB) **1999**†Min 16 (16, MLB) **2000**†Min 16 (16, RLB) **2001** Min 14 (13, RLB) **NFL** 125 (110) [9 yrs]

McDaniel, Emmanuel Emmanuel, DB, 5´9˝/180 lbs; East Carolina; 1996: Car, rnd 4; B7/27/1972 Griffin, GA **1996** Car 2 (0) **1997** Ind 3 (0) **1999** NYG 7 (2) **2000**†NYG 16 (3) **2001** NYG 16 (0) **2002** Car 16 (5, cb) **2003** Arz 15 (0) **NFL** 75 (10) [7 yrs]

YEAR	TEAM	G (GS, POS)	RUSH	YD	AVG(LG)	TD	REC	YD	AVG(LG)	TD	PASS COMP	PCT	YD	AVG(LG)	TD	INT	SK	YD	QBR	KPR	OTD	PTS	TAY

McDANIEL, JEREMY   Jeremy Dwayne, WR, 6'0"/197 lbs; Arizona; B5/2/1976 New Bern, NC

1999	Buf	1 (0)	—	—	—		—	—	—		—	—	—	—		—	—	—		—		—	—
2000	Buf	16 (6, wr)	—	—	—		43	697	16.2(74)	2	—	—	—	—		—	—	—		—		12	359
2001	Buf	7 (0)	—	—	—		11	129	11.7(22)	0	—	—	—	—		—	—	—		—		0	65
NFL 3		24 (6)	—	—	—		54	826	15.3(74)	2	—	—	—	—		—	—	—		—		12	423

McDANIEL, JOHN   John, WR, 6'1"/193 lbs; Lincoln (MO); 1974: Cin, rnd 8; B9/23/1951 Birmingham, AL

1974	Cin	14	1	5	5.0(5)	0	2	79	39.5(60)	0	—	—	—	—		—	—	—		k		0	64
1975	†Cin	14	1	-2	-2.0(-2)	0	—	—	—		—	—	—	—		—	—	—		k		0	22
1976	Cin	14	—	—	—		12	232	19.3(46)	1	—	—	—	—		—	—	—		—		6	121
1977	Cin	14	—	—	—		12	148	12.3(31)	0	—	—	—	—		—	—	—		—		0	74
1978	Was	15 (11, WR)	2	25	12.5(13)	0	34	577	17.0(52)	4	—	—	—	—		—	—	—		—		24	334
1979	Was	15 (2)	—	—	—		25	357	14.3(62)	2	—	—	—	—		—	—	—		—		12	189
1980	Was	10 (7, wr)	—	—	—		14	154	11.0(18)	0	—	—	—	—		—	—	—		—		0	77
NFL 7		96 (20)	4	28	7.0(13)	0	99	1547	15.6(52)	7	—	—	—	—		—	—	—		k		42	880

McDANIEL, LeCHARLS   LeCharls Barnet, DB, 5'9"/183 lbs; Cal Poly-San Luis Obispo; B10/15/1958 Fort Bragg, NC   **1981** Was 6 (0)   **1982**†Was 8 (0)   **1983** NYG 9 (0)   NFL 23 (0) [3 yrs]

McDANIEL, ORLANDO   Orlando Keith, WR, 6'0"/180 lbs; LSU; 1982: Den, rnd 2; B12/1/1960 Shreveport, LA   **1982** Den 3 (0)

McDANIEL, RANDALL   Randall Cornell, G, 6'3"/276 lbs; Arizona State; 1988: Min, rnd 1; B12/19/1964 Phoenix, AZ   **1988**†Min☆16 (15, LG)   **1989**†Min★14 (13, LG)   **1990** Min★16 (16, LG)   **1991** Min★16 (16, LG)   **1992**†Min★16 (16, LG)   **1993**†Min★16 (16, LG)   **1994** Min★16 (16, LG)   **1995** Min★16 (16, LG)   **1997**†Min★16 (16, LG)   **1998**†Min☆16 (16, LG)   **1999**†Min◇16 (16, LG)   **2001**†TB 16 (16, LG)

1996	†Min★	16 (16, LG)	2	1	0.5(1)	0	—	—	—		—	—	—	—		—	—	—		—		0	1
2000	†TB◇	16 (16, LG)	—	—	—		1	2	2.0(2)	1	—	—	—	—		—	—	—		—		6	6
NFL 14		222 (220)	2	1	0.5(1)	0	1	2	2.0(2)	1	—	—	—	—		—	—	—		—		6	7

McDANIEL, TERRY   Terence Lee, DB, 5'10"/180 lbs; Tennessee; 1988: LARd, rnd 1; B2/8/1965 Mansfield, OH [I]   **1988** LARd 2 (2)   **1989** LARd 16 (15, LCB)   **1990**†LARd 16 (13, LCB)   **1991**†LARd 16 (16, LCB)   **1992** LARd★16 (16, LCB)   **1993**†LARd★16 (16, LCB)   **1994** LARd★16 (16, LCB)   **1995** Oak★16 (16, LCB)   **1996** Oak◇16 (15, LCB)   **1997** Oak 13 (12, LCB)   **1998** Sea 9 (0)   NFL 152 (137) [11 yrs]

McDANIEL, WAHOO   Edward Wahoo, LB, 6'1"/235 lbs; Oklahoma; 1960: LAC, rnd 1; B6/19/1938 Bernice, LA, D4/18/2002 Houston, TX   **1960** Hou-A 7   **1961** Den-A 14 (MLB)   **1962** Den-A 14 (MLB)   **1963** Den-A 14 (MLB)   **1964** NYJ-A 12 (MLB)   **1966** Mia-A 12 (8, RLB)   **1967** Mia-A 14 (6, mlb)   **1968** Mia-A 4

| 1965 | NYJ-A | 14 (MLB) | 1 | 13 | 13.0(13) | 0 | — | — | — | | — | — | — | — | | — | — | — | | i | | 0 | 15 |
| NFL 9 | | 105 (14) | 1 | 13 | 13.0(13) | 0 | — | — | — | | — | — | — | — | | — | — | — | | Pi | 1 | 6 | 109 |

McDANIELS, DAVE   David, WR, 6'4"/200 lbs; Mississippi Valley State; 1968: Dal, rnd 2; B4/9/1945 Miami, FL   **1968** Dal 4

McDANIELS, PELLOM   Pellom, LB-DE, 6'3"/284 lbs; Oregon State; B2/21/1968 San Jose, CA   **1993**†KC 10 (0)   **1994** KC 12 (3)   **1995**†KC 16 (2)   **1996** KC 9 (1)   **1997**†KC 16 (6, lolb)   **1998** KC 11 (2)   **1999** Atl 16 (0)   NFL 90 (14) [7 yrs]

McDERMOTT, GARY   Gary Don, RB, 6'1"/211 lbs; Tulsa; 1968: Buf, rnd 9; B6/9/1948 Longview, TX

1968	Buf-A	14	47	102	2.2(17)	3	20	115	5.8(37)	1	3	2	66.7	35	11.7(27)	0	0	—	—		k		26	213
1969	Atl	4	7	6	0.9(3)	0	—	—	—		—	—	—	—		—	—	—		—		0	6
NFL 2		18	54	108	2.0(17)	3	20	115	5.8(37)	1	3	2	66.7	35	11.7(27)	0	0	—	—		k		26	219

McDERMOTT, LLOYD   Lloyd Ivan, DT, 6'3"/240 lbs; Kentucky; 1950: Phi, rnd 6; B12/20/1925 Covington, KY, D1/16/1964 Covington, KY   **1950** Det 1   **1950** ChiC 11 (LDT)   **1951** ChiC 12   NFL 24 [2 yrs]

McDERMOTT, SEAN   Sean, TE, 6'4"/250 lbs; Kansas; B12/5/1976 Lufkin, TX   **2001**†TB 16 (0)   **2002** Hou 16 (0)   **2003** Mia 5 (0)   **2003** NE 1 (0)   NFL 38 (0) [3 yrs]

McDOLE, MARDYE   Mardye Kepez, WR, 5'11"/198 lbs; Mississippi State; 1981: Min, rnd 2; B5/1/1959 Pensacola, FL   **1981** Min 9 (0)   **1982** Min 2 (0)

| 1983 | Min | 15 (1) | — | — | — | | 3 | 29 | 9.7(10) | 0 | — | — | — | — | | — | — | — | | — | | 0 | 15 |
| NFL 3 | | 26 (1) | — | — | — | | 3 | 29 | 9.7(10) | 0 | — | — | — | — | | — | — | — | | k | | 0 | 31 |

McDOLE, RON   Roland Owen, DE-DT, 6'4"/265 lbs; Nebraska; 1961: SL, rnd 4/Den, rnd 4; B9/9/1939 Chester, OH   **1961** SL 13   **1962** Hou-A 4   **1963**†Buf-A 12 (lde)   **1964**†Buf-A★14 (LDE)   **1965**†Buf-A★14 (LDE)   **1966**†Buf-A☆14 (LDE)   **1967** Buf-A 13 (LDE)   **1968** Buf-A☆14 (LDE)   **1969** Buf-A☆14 (LDE)   **1970** Buf 14 (LDE)   **1971**†Was 14 (14, LDE)   **1972**†Was 14 (14, LDE)   **1973**†Was 14 (14, LDE)   **1974**†Was 14 (13, LDE)   **1975** Was 14 (14, LDE)   **1976**†Was 14 (14, LDE)   **1977** Was 14 (14, LDE)   **1978** Was 16 (10, LDE)   NFL 240 (107) [18 yrs]

McDONALD   E-G, /165 lbs; none   **1925** Ham 4 (1)

McDONALD, 2.   WB, none   **1926** Det 1 (0)

McDONALD, CY   Cyril, G, 6'1"/197 lbs; none; B12/17/1896, D1/1968 New York, NY   **1921** Was 3 (3, LG)

McDONALD, DARNELL   Darnell Ali, WR, 6'3"/190 lbs; Kansas State; 1999: TB, rnd 7; B5/26/1976 Fairfax, VA

| 1999 | †TB | 9 (0) | — | — | — | | 9 | 96 | 10.7(23) | 1 | — | — | — | — | | — | — | — | | — | | 6 | 53 |

McDONALD, DEVON   Devon Linton, LB, 6'2"/240 lbs; Notre Dame; 1993: Ind, rnd 4; B11/8/1969 Kingston, Jamaica   **1993** Ind 16 (0)   **1994** Ind 16 (4)   **1995**†Ind 15 (0)   **1996** Arz 16 (0)   NFL 63 (4) [4 yrs]

McDONALD, DON   Don Kay, DB, 5'11"/185 lbs; Houston; 1958: Phi, rnd 29; B2/5/1937 Sherman, TX   **1961** Buf-A 11

McDONALD, DUSTIN   Dustin C., G, 6'4"/205 lbs; Indiana; B10/3/1908   **1935** GB 1 (0)

McDONALD, DWIGHT   Dwight Vinson, WR, 6'3"/185 lbs; U.S. International; San Diego State; B5/24/1951 Nixon, TX

1975	SD	14 (13, WR)	—	—	—		19	298	15.7(57)	3	—	—	—	—		—	—	—		—		18	164
1976	SD	12 (10, WR)	—	—	—		11	161	14.6(44)	0	—	—	—	—		—	—	—		—		24	101
1977	SD	11 (5, wr)	—	—	—		13	174	13.4(22)	0	—	—	—	—		—	—	—		—		0	87
1978	SD	12	—	—	—		3	84	28.0(37)	1	—	—	—	—		—	—	—		—		6	47
NFL 4		49 (28)	—	—	—		46	717	15.6(57)	8	—	—	—	—		—	—	—		—		48	399

McDONALD, FLIP   Donald Gene, E, 6'2"/200 lbs; Oklahoma; B2/12/1921 Webb City, MO, D2/12/2002 Quapaw, OK

1944	Bkn	2 (0)	—	—	—		—	—	—		—	—	—	—		—	—	—		—			
1944	Phi	5 (0)	—	—	—		4	26	6.5(9)	1	—	—	—	—		—	—	—		i		6	27
1945	Phi	9 (2)	—	—	—		8	75	9.4(21)	1	—	—	—	—		—	—	—		—		6	43
1946	Phi	1 (0)	—	—	—		—	—	—		—	—	—	—		—	—	—		—			
NFL 3		17 (2)	—	—	—		12	101	8.4(21)	2	—	—	—	—		—	—	—		i		12	70
1948	NYY-A	2 (0)	—	—	—		3	30	10.0	0	—	—	—	—		—	—	—		—		0	15

McDONALD, JAMES   James Zell, TE, 6'5"/234 lbs; USC; B3/29/1961 Long Beach, CA

1983	†LARm	16 (0)	—	—	—		1	1	1.0(1)	1	—	—	—	—		—	—	—		—		6	6
1984	†LARm	16 (1)	—	—	—		4	55	13.8(22)	0	—	—	—	—		—	—	—		—		0	28
1985	Det	6 (2)	—	—	—		3	23	7.7(9)	0	—	—	—	—		—	—	—		—		0	12
1985	LARm	9 (0)	—	—	—		2	58	29.0(35)	0	—	—	—	—		—	—	—		—		0	29
1987	LARm	5 (3)	—	—	—		4	31	7.8(13)	2	—	—	—	—		—	—	—		—		12	26
NFL 4		52 (6)	—	—	—		14	168	12.0(35)	3	—	—	—	—		—	—	—		—		18	99

McDONALD, JIM   Edward, HB, 6'0"/195 lbs; Duquesne; B2/27/1911, D2/18/1980 Homestead, PA

| 1936 | Pit | 5 (0) | 9 | 18 | 2.0 | 0 | 1 | 8 | 8.0(8) | 0 | — | — | — | — | | — | — | — | | — | | 0 | 22 |

McDONALD, JIM   James Allen, B, 6'1"/193 lbs; Ohio State; 1938: Phi, rnd 1; B6/9/1915 Springfield, OH, D5/1/1997 Knoxville, TN

1938	Det	11 (4)	—	—	—		2	41	20.5	0	—	—	—	—		—	—	—		—		0	21
1939	Det	9 (0)	25	80	3.2	0	5	71	14.2	0	—	—	—	—		—	—	—		—		0	116
NFL 2		20 (4)	25	80	3.2	0	7	112	16.0	0	—	—	—	—		—	—	—		—		0	136

McDONALD, JOHN   John, T-G, 6'0"/195 lbs; Lawrence; B3/20/1900, deceased   **1921** Evv 1 (1)   **1926** Lou 2 (0)   NFL 3 (1) [2 yrs]

YEAR	TEAM	G (GS, POS)	RUSH	YD	AVG(LG)	TD	REC	YD	AVG(LG)	TD	PASS COMP	PCT	YD	AVG(LG)	TD	INT	SK	YD	QBR	KPR	OTD	PTS	TAY

McDonald, Keith   R. Keith, WR, 5´9˝/170 lbs; San Jose State; B11/7/1963 Los Angeles, CA

1987	Hou	3(0)	—	—	—	—	4	56	14.0(24)	1	—	—	—	—	—	—	—	—	—	—	—	—	6	33
1989	Det	6(4)	1	-2	-2.0(-2)	0	12	138	11.5(24)	0	—	—	—	—	—	—	—	—	—	—	—	—	0	67
NFL	2	9(4)	1	-2	-2.0(-2)	0	16	194	12.1(24)	1	—	—	—	—	—	—	—	—	—	—	—	—	6	100

McDonald, Les   Lester Bruce, E, 6´4˝/200 lbs; Nebraska; 1937: ChiB, rnd 1; B9/19/1914 Grand Island, NE, D7/26/1971 Grand Island, NE **[K]**

1937	†ChiB	8(1)	—	—	—	—	11	179	16.3(42)	4	—	—	—	—	—	—	—	—	—	—	—	—	24	110
1938	ChiB	10(6, RE)	1	0	0.0	0	9	175	19.4(30)	1	—	—	—	—	—	—	—	—	—	—	K	—	7	93
1939	ChiB	11(8, LE)	1	-2	-2.0(-2)	0	16	261	16.3	3	—	—	—	—	—	—	—	—	—	—	—	—	18	144
1940	Phi	9(0)	2	-2	-1.0	0	14	289	20.6	0	—	—	—	—	—	—	—	—	—	—	—	—	0	143
1940	Det	1(0)	—	—	—	—	1	20	20.0(20)	0	—	—	—	—	—	—	—	—	—	—	—	—	0	10
NFL	5	39(15)	4	-4	-1.0	0	51	924	18.1(42)	8	—	—	—	—	—	—	—	—	—	—	K	—	49	498

McDonald, Mike   Michael, LB, 6´2˝/215 lbs; Catawba; 1975: NO, rnd 16; B6/20/1953 St. Augustine, FL   **1976 SL 4**

McDonald, Mike   Michael, LB, 6´1˝/238 lbs; USC; B6/22/1958 North Hollywood, CA   **1983**†LARm 0 (0)   **1984**†LARm 16 (0)   **1986**†LARm 13 (0)   **1987** LARm 10 (0)   **1988**†LARm 16 (0)   **1989**†LARm 16 (0)   **1990** LARm 16 (0)   **1991** LARm 16 (0)   **1992** Det 1 (0)   **NFL** 104 (0) **[9 yrs]**

McDonald, Paul   Paul Brian, QB, 6´2˝/185 lbs; USC; 1980: Cle, rnd 4; B2/23/1958 Montebello, CA

1980	†Cle	15(0)	3	-2	-0.7(0)	0	—	—	—	—	—	—	—	—	—	—	—	—	—	—	—	—	0	-2
1981	Cle	12(0)	2	0	0.0(2)	0	—	—	—	—	57	35	61.4	463	8.1(46)	4	2	6	43	—	—	—	0	172
1982	†Cle	9(3)	7	-13	-1.9(10)	0	—	—	—	—	149	73	49.0	993	6.7(56)	5	8	13	95	—	—	—	0	189
1983	Cle	16(2)	3	17	5.7(10)	0	—	—	—	—	68	32	47.1	341	5.0(27)	1	4	6	38	—	—	—	0	33
1984	Cle	16(16, QB)	22	4	0.2(10)	1	1	-4	-4.0(-4)	0	493	271	55.0	3472	7.0(64)	14	23	53	345	67.3	—	—	6	898
1985	†Cle	16(0)	—	—	—	—	—	—	—	—	—	—	—	—	—	—	—	—	—	—	—	—	—	—
1986	Dal	1(0)	—	—	—	—	—	—	—	—	—	—	—	—	—	—	—	—	—	—	—	—	—	—
NFL	7	85(21)	37	6	0.2(10)	1	1	-4	-4.0(-4)	0	767	411	53.6	5269	6.9(64)	24	37	78	521	65.7	—	—	6	1289

McDonald, Quintus   Quintus Alonzo, LB, 6´3˝/259 lbs; Penn State; 1989: Ind, rnd 6; B12/14/1966 Rockingham, NC   **1989** Ind 15 (2)   **1990** Ind 9 (1)   **1991** Ind 16 (9, lolb/lilb)   **NFL** 40 (12) **[3 yrs]**

McDonald, Ramos   Ramos, DB, 5´11˝/195 lbs; New Mexico; 1998: Min, rnd 3; B4/30/1976 Dallas, TX   **1998**†Min 15 (0)   **1999** Min 5 (5, lcb)   **1999** SF 9 (7, RCB)   **2000**†NYG 3 (0)   **NFL** 32 (12) **[3 yrs]**

McDonald, Ray   Raymond Douglas, RB, 6´4˝/248 lbs; Idaho; 1967: Was, rnd 1; B5/7/1944 McKinney, TX, D5/4/1993 Houston, TX   **1968** Was 1

| 1967 | Was | 12(fb) | 52 | 223 | 4.3(35) | 4 | 10 | 60 | 6.0(18) | 0 | — | — | — | — | — | — | — | — | — | — | k | — | 24 | 278 |
| NFL | 2 | 13 | 52 | 223 | 4.3(35) | 4 | 10 | 60 | 6.0(18) | 0 | — | — | — | — | — | — | — | — | — | — | — | — | 24 | 293 |

McDonald, Ricardo   Ricardo Milton, LB, 6´2˝/240 lbs; Pittsburgh; 1992: Cin, rnd 4; B11/8/1969 Kingston, Jamaica   **1992** Cin 16 (13, LILB)   **1993** Cin 14 (12, RILB)   **1994** Cin 13 (13, RLB)   **1995** Cin 16 (15, RLB)   **1996** Cin 16 (15, RLB)   **1997** Cin 13 (12, RILB)   **1998** ChiB 15 (14, LLB)   **1999** ChiB 16 (16, LLB)   **NFL** 119 (110) **[8 yrs]**

McDonald, Shaun   Shaun Terrance, WR, 5´10˝/183 lbs; Arizona State; 2003: SL, rnd 4; B6/13/1981 Phoenix, AZ

2003	SL	8(1)	2	7	3.5(5)	0	10	62	6.2(13)	0	—	—	—	—	—	—	—	—	—	—	—	—	0	38
2004	†SL	16(0)	4	0	0.0(7)	0	37	494	13.4(52)	3	—	—	—	—	—	—	—	—	—	p	—	—	18	255
2005	SL	16(2)	1	7	7.0(7)	0	46	523	11.4(31)	0	—	—	—	—	—	—	—	—	—	p	—	—	0	262
NFL	3	40(3)	7	14	2.0(7)	0	93	1079	11.6(52)	3	—	—	—	—	—	—	—	—	—	p	—	—	18	555

McDonald, Tim   Timothy, DB, 6´2˝/215 lbs; USC; 1987: SL, rnd 2; B1/6/1965 Fresno, CA **[I]**   **1987** SL 3 (0)   **1988** Phx 16 (15, SS)   **1989** Phx★16 (16, SS)   **1990** Phx☆16 (16, SS)   **1991** Phx★13 (13, SS)   **1992** Phx★16 (16, SS)   **1993**†SF★16 (16, SS)   **1994**†SF★16 (16, SS)   **1995**†SF★16 (16, SS)   **1996**†SF☆16 (16, SS)   **1997**†SF 15 (15, SS)   **1998**†SF 16 (16, SS)   **1999** SF 16 (16, SS)   **NFL** 191 (187) **[13 yrs]**

McDonald, Tommy   Thomas Franklin, FL-HB-SE-WR, 5´9˝/178 lbs; Oklahoma; 1957: Phi, rnd 3; B7/26/1934 Roy, NM; HOF 1998

1957	Phi	12(rh)	12	36	3.0(22)	0	9	228	25.3(61)	3	1	1	100.0	11	11.0(11)	0	0	—	—	—	kp	—	18	307
1958	Phi◇	10(rh)	3	-4	-1.3(5)	0	29	603	20.8(91)	9	—	—	—	—	—	—	—	—	—	—	kp	—	54	440
1959	Phi★	12(RH)	2	-10	-5.0(-4)	0	47	846	18.0(71)	10	—	—	—	—	—	—	—	—	—	—	kp	1	66	567
1960	†Phi★	12(FL)	—	—	—	—	39	801	20.5(64)	13	—	—	—	—	—	—	—	—	—	—	kp	—	78	478
1961	Phi★	14(FL)	—	—	—	—	64	1144	17.9(66)	13	—	—	—	—	—	—	—	—	—	—	—	—	78	637
1962	Phi★	14(FL)	—	—	—	—	58	1146	19.8(60)	10	1	1	100.0	10	10.0(10)	1	0	—	—	—	p	—	60	616
1963	Phi	14(FL)	—	—	—	—	41	731	17.8(75)	8	—	—	—	—	—	—	—	—	—	—	—	—	48	406
1964	Dal	14(SE)	—	—	—	—	46	612	13.3(48)	2	—	—	—	—	—	—	—	—	—	—	p	—	12	323
1965	LARm◇	14(FL)	—	—	—	—	67	1036	15.5(51)	9	—	—	—	—	—	—	—	—	—	—	—	—	54	563
1966	LARm	13(FL)	—	—	—	—	55	714	13.0(62)	2	—	—	—	—	—	—	—	—	—	—	—	—	12	367
1967	Atl	14(FL)	—	—	—	—	33	436	13.2(75)	4	—	—	—	—	—	—	—	—	—	—	—	—	24	238
1968	†Cle	9	—	—	—	—	7	113	16.1(42)	1	—	—	—	—	—	—	—	—	—	—	p	—	6	62
NFL	12	152	17	22	1.3(22)	0	495	8410	17.0(91)	84	2	2	100.0	21	10.5(11)	1	0	—	—	—	kp	1	510	5002

McDonald, Walt   Walter Vincent, B, 6´1˝/210 lbs; Tulane; 1943: Was, rnd 10; B11/5/1920 Lowellville, OH

1946	Mia-A	4(0)	1	-4	-4.0(-4)	0	4	55	13.8	0	3	1	33.3	24	8.0(24)	0	1	—	—	—	—	—	0	-5
1946	Bkn-A	9(8, BB)	3	-7	-2.3	0	8	71	8.9	0	—	—	—	—	—	—	—	—	—	—	ki	—	0	37
1947	Bkn-A	12(10, BB)	1	1	1.0(1)	0	3	30	10.0	0	—	—	—	—	—	—	—	—	—	—	p	—	0	30
1948	Bkn-A	12(6, BB)	6	15	2.5	0	7	41	5.9	1	—	—	—	—	—	—	—	—	—	—	i	—	6	47
1949	ChiH-A	9(2)	1	0	0.0	0	—	—	—	—	—	—	—	—	—	—	—	—	—	—	—	—	0	0
AAFC	4	46(26)	12	5	0.4(1)	0	22	197	9.0	1	3	1	33.3	24	8.0(24)	0	1	—	—	—	kpi	—	6	109

McDonald, Walt   Walter, C-LB, 5´10˝/210 lbs; Utah; B10/22/1911 Worland, WY   **1935** Bkn 11 (2)

McDonnell, Brady   Brady Joe, TE, 6´4˝/265 lbs; Colorado; B7/24/1977 Rapid City, SD   **2002** Buf 6 (0)

McDonough, Bob   Robert Walter, G, 5´11˝/205 lbs; Duke; B5/31/1919 Orange, NJ   **1946** Phi 10 (0)

McDonough, Bob   Robert E., DB, 6´1˝/170 lbs; California (PA); B3/7/1963 Pittsburgh, PA   **1987** Det 3 (0)

McDonough, Coley   Coleman Regis, TB-QB, 6´1˝/189 lbs; North Carolina State; Dayton; B10/10/1915 North Braddock, PA, D7/6/1965 Pittsburgh, PA

1939	ChiC	4(1)	6	12	2.0	0	—	—	—	—	9	2	22.2	73	8.1	0	2	—	—	—	P	—	0	-32
1939	Pit	7(0)	23	63	2.7	0	1	3	3.0(3)	—	38	15	39.5	292	7.7	2	6	—	—	—	P	—	6	-15
1940	Pit	4(0)	15	33	2.2	0	—	—	—	—	14	8	57.1	92	6.6	0	3	—	—	—	P	—	6	-31
1941	Pit	6(1)	20	64	3.2(28)	0	—	—	—	—	41	12	29.3	200	4.9(59)	1	7	—	—	—	Pkp	—	0	-76
1944	C-P	2(0)	3	7	2.3(4)	0	—	—	—	—	23	10	43.5	208	9.0(67)	2	4	—	—	—	—	—	0	-39
NFL	4	23(2)	67	179	2.7(28)	1	1	3	3.0(3)	1	125	47	37.6	865	6.9(67)	5	22	—	—	—	Pkp	—	12	-192

McDonough, Paul   Paul Roy, E, 6´4˝/222 lbs; Utah; 1938: Pit, rnd 9; B12/14/1916 Salt Lake City, UT, D8/11/1960 Salt Lake City, UT

1938	Pit	6(3)	—	—	—	—	6	86	14.3	0	—	—	—	—	—	—	—	—	—	—	—	—	0	43
1939	Cle	10(0)	—	—	—	—	8	73	9.1(19)	1	—	—	—	—	—	—	—	—	—	—	—	—	6	42
1940	Cle	11(7, RE)	2	5	2.5	0	12	315	26.3(65)	1	—	—	—	—	—	—	—	—	—	—	—	—	6	168
1941	Cle	11(8, RE)	—	—	—	—	14	198	14.1(26)	2	—	—	—	—	—	—	—	—	—	—	k	—	12	103
NFL	4	38(18)	2	5	2.5	0	40	672	16.8(65)	4	—	—	—	—	—	—	—	—	—	—	k	—	24	355

McDougal, Bob   Robert Walter, FB, 6´2˝/205 lbs; Duke; Miami (FL); 1947: GB, rnd 9; B3/19/1921 Oconto, WI, D8/10/2003 Oconto, WI   **1947** GB 1 (0)

McDougald, Doug   Douglas Elaine, DE, 6´5˝/271 lbs; Virginia Tech; 1980: NE, rnd 5; B2/6/1957 Fayetteville, NC   **1980** NE 8 (0)

McDougal, Kevin   Kevin John, RB, 5´11˝/203 lbs; Colorado State; B5/18/1977 Denver, CO   **2000** Ind 6 (0)

| 2001 | Ind | 9(0) | 17 | 48 | 2.8(12) | 0 | 10 | 100 | 10.0(10) | 0 | — | — | — | — | — | — | — | — | — | — | k | — | 2 | 175 |
| NFL | 2 | 15(0) | 17 | 48 | 2.8(12) | 0 | 10 | 100 | 10.0(10) | 0 | — | — | — | — | — | — | — | — | — | — | — | — | 2 | 53 |

McDougall, Gerry   Gerald Gordon, FB, 6´3˝/225 lbs; UCLA; B3/21/1935 Long Beach, CA

| 1962 | SD-A | 4 | 43 | 197 | 4.6(24) | 3 | 4 | 27 | 6.8(10) | 0 | — | — | — | — | — | — | — | — | — | — | k | — | 18 | 267 |
| 1963 | †SD-A | 14 | 38 | 199 | 5.2(22) | 1 | 10 | 115 | 11.5(26) | 0 | 1 | 1 | 100.0 | 11 | 11.0(11) | 1 | 0 | — | — | — | k | — | 6 | 309 |

YEAR	TEAM	G(GS, POS)	RUSH	YD	AVG(LG)	TD	REC	YD	AVG(LG)	TD	PASS	COMP	PCT	YD	AVG(LG)	TD	INT	SK	YD	QBR	KPR	OTD	PTS	TAY
1964	SD-A	7	23	73	3.2(24)	2	8	106	13.3(24)	0	—	—	—	—	—	—	—	—	—	—	—	—	14	146
NFL	3	25	104	469	4.5(24)	6	22	248	11.3(26)	0	1	1	100.0	11	11.0(11)	1	0	—	—	—	k	—	38	722

McDougle, Jerome Jerome, DE, 6´2˝/264 lbs; Miami (FL); 2003: Phi, rnd 1; B12/15/1978 Pompano Beach, FL **2003**†Phi 8 (0) **2004**†Phi 11 (0) **NFL** 19 (0) [2 yrs]

McDougle, Stockar Stockar, T, 6´6˝/335 lbs; Oklahoma; 2000: Det, rnd 1; B1/11/1977 Fort Lauderdale, FL **2000** Det 8 (8, lt) **2001** Det 9 (3) **2002** Det 12 (11, RT) **2003** Det 16 (16, RT) **2004** Det 16 (16, RT) **2005** Mia 8 (2) **NFL** 69 (56) [6 yrs]

McDowell, Anthony Anthony Lequinn, RB, 5´11˝/235 lbs; Texas Tech; 1992: TB, rnd 8; B11/12/1968 Augsburg, Germany

YEAR	TEAM	G(GS, POS)	RUSH	YD	AVG(LG)	TD	REC	YD	AVG(LG)	TD	PASS	COMP	PCT	YD	AVG(LG)	TD	INT	SK	YD	QBR	KPR	OTD	PTS	TAY
1992	TB	12(8, FB)	14	81	5.8(23)	0	27	258	9.6(51)	2	—	—	—	—	—	—	—	—	—	—	—	—	12	220
1993	TB	4(3)	2	6	3.0(3)	0	8	26	3.3(9)	1	—	—	—	—	—	—	—	—	—	—	—	—	6	24
1994	TB	14(11, FB)	21	58	2.8(8)	0	29	193	6.7(19)	1	—	—	—	—	—	—	—	—	—	—	—	—	6	160
NFL	3	30(22)	37	145	3.9(23)	0	64	477	7.5(51)	4	—	—	—	—	—	—	—	—	—	—	—	—	24	404

McDowell, Bubba Leonard, DB, 6´1˝/206 lbs; Miami (FL); 1989: Hou, rnd 3; B11/4/1966 Fort Gaines, GA **1989**†Hou 16 (16, SS) **1990**†Hou 15 (15, SS) **1991**†Hou☆16 (16, SS) **1992**†Hou 16 (16, SS) **1993**†Hou 14 (14, SS) **1994** Hou 9 (3) **1995** Car 16 (3) **NFL** 102 (83) [7 yrs]

McDowell, John John Bernard, T-G, 6´3˝/260 lbs; St. John's (MN); 1964: GB, rnd 9; B2/12/1942 St. Paul, MN **1964** GB 12 **1965** NYG 14 **1966** SL 1 **NFL** 27 [3 yrs]

McDuffie, George George Allen, DE, 6´6˝/270 lbs; Salem (NC); Findlay; B1/20/1963 Vicksburg, MS **1987** Det 3 (2)

McDuffie, O.J. Otis James, WR, 5´10˝/194 lbs; Penn State; 1993: Mia, rnd 1; B12/2/1969 Marion, OH **[R]**

YEAR	TEAM	G(GS, POS)	RUSH	YD	AVG(LG)	TD	REC	YD	AVG(LG)	TD	PASS	COMP	PCT	YD	AVG(LG)	TD	INT	SK	YD	QBR	KPR	OTD	PTS	TAY
1993	Mia☆	16(0)	1	-4	-4.0(-4)	0	19	197	10.4(18)	0	—	—	—	—	—	—	—	—	—	—	kp	2	12	567
1994	†Mia	15(3)	5	32	6.4(12)	0	37	488	13.2(30)	3	—	—	—	—	—	—	—	—	—	—	kp	—	18	586
1995	†Mia	16(16, WR)	3	6	2.0(11)	0	62	819	13.2(48)	8	—	—	—	—	—	—	—	—	—	—	kp	—	50	718
1996	Mia	16(16, WR)	2	7	3.5(7)	0	74	918	12.4(36)	8	—	—	—	—	—	—	—	—	—	—	p	—	48	608
1997	†Mia	16(16, WR)	—	—	—	—	76	943	12.4(55)	1	—	—	—	—	—	—	—	—	—	—	p	1	12	471
1998	†Mia	16(16, WR)	3	11	3.7(5)	0	**90**	1050	11.7(61)	7	—	—	—	—	—	—	—	—	—	—	p	—	42	652
1999	†Mia	12(10, WR)	—	—	—	—	43	516	12.0(34)	2	—	—	—	—	—	—	—	—	—	—	kp	—	12	297
2000	†Mia	9(1)	1	-3	-3.0(-3)	0	14	143	10.2(24)	0	—	—	—	—	—	—	—	—	—	—	p	—	0	69
NFL	8	116(78)	15	49	3.3(12)	0	415	5074	12.2(61)	29	—	—	—	—	—	—	—	—	—	—	kp	3	194	3966

McElhenny, Hugh Hugh Edward 'The King', HB, 6´1˝/195 lbs; Washington; 1952: SF, rnd 1; B12/31/1928 Los Angeles, CA; HOF 1970 **[R]**

YEAR	TEAM	G(GS, POS)	RUSH	YD	AVG(LG)	TD	REC	YD	AVG(LG)	TD	PASS	COMP	PCT	YD	AVG(LG)	TD	INT	SK	YD	QBR	KPR	OTD	PTS	TAY
1952	SF★	12(RH)	98	684	**7.0(89)**	6	26	367	14.1(77)	3	—	—	—	—	—	—	—	—	—	—	kp	1	60	**1263**
1953	SF★	12(RH)	112	503	4.5(33)	3	30	474	15.8(71)	2	3	2	66.7	13	4.3(11)	1	0	—	—	—	kp	—	30	964
1954	SF☆	6(RH)	64	515	**8.0(60)**	6	8	162	20.3(53)	0	—	—	—	—	—	—	—	—	—	—	kp	—	36	784
1955	SF	12(RH)	90	327	3.6(44)	4	11	203	18.5(55)	2	—	—	—	—	—	—	—	—	—	—	kp	—	36	508
1956	SF★	12(LH)	185	916	5.0(86)	8	16	193	12.1(22)	0	1	0	0.0	0	0.0	0	1	—	—	—	kp	—	48	1121
1957	†SF★	12(LH)	102	478	4.7(61)	1	37	458	12.4(43)	2	—	—	—	—	—	—	—	—	—	—	p	—	18	718
1958	SF✧	12(LH)	113	451	4.0(34)	6	31	366	11.8(59)	2	2	0	0.0	0	0.0	0	0	—	—	—	kp	—	48	678
1959	SF	10(RH)	18	67	3.7(18)	1	22	329	15.0(62)	3	—	—	—	—	—	—	—	—	—	—	—	—	24	257
1960	SF	9(7, LH)	95	347	3.7(38)	0	14	114	8.1(45)	1	—	—	—	—	—	—	—	—	—	—	—	—	6	409
1961	Min✧	13(13, HB)	120	570	4.8(41)	3	37	283	7.6(26)	3	1	0	0.0	0	0.0	0	0	—	—	—	kp	1	42	911
1962	Min	11	50	200	4.0(27)	0	16	191	11.9(41)	0	—	—	—	—	—	—	—	—	—	—	kp	—	0	369
1963	†NYG	14	55	175	3.2(23)	0	11	91	8.3(24)	2	—	—	—	—	—	—	—	—	—	—	kp	—	12	286
1964	Det	8	22	48	2.2(14)	0	5	16	3.2(27)	0	—	—	—	—	—	—	—	—	—	—	kp	—	0	78
NFL	13	143(20)	1124	5281	4.7(89)	38	264	3247	12.3(77)	20	7	2	28.6	13	1.9(11)	1	1	—	—	—	kp	2	360	8342

McElmurry, Blaine Blaine Richard, DB, 6´0˝/188 lbs; Montana; B10/23/1973 Helena, MT **1997** GB 1 (0) **1998**†Jax 2 (0) **1999**†Jax 16 (0) **NFL** 19 (0) [3 yrs]

McElroy, Bucky William Murry, HB, 5´11˝/195 lbs; Southern Mississippi; 1953: ChiB, rnd 7; B1/23/1929 Monroe, LA **1954** ChiB 1

McElroy, Leeland Leeland Anthony, RB, 5´9˝/212 lbs; Texas A&M; 1996: Arz, rnd 2; B6/25/1974 Beaumont, TX

YEAR	TEAM	G(GS, POS)	RUSH	YD	AVG(LG)	TD	REC	YD	AVG(LG)	TD	PASS	COMP	PCT	YD	AVG(LG)	TD	INT	SK	YD	QBR	KPR	OTD	PTS	TAY
1996	Arz	16(6, rb)	89	305	3.4(32)	1	5	41	8.2(22)	1	—	—	—	—	—	—	—	—	—	—	k	—	12	679
1997	Arz	14(8, RB)	135	424	3.1(18)	2	7	32	4.6(17)	0	—	—	—	—	—	—	—	—	—	—	—	—	12	460
NFL	2	30(14)	224	729	3.3(32)	3	12	73	6.1(22)	1	—	—	—	—	—	—	—	—	—	—	k	—	24	1139

McElroy, Ray Raymond Edward, DB, 5´11˝/207 lbs; Eastern Illinois; 1995: Ind, rnd 4; B7/31/1972 Bellwood, IL **1995**†Ind 16 (0) **1996**†Ind 16 (5, ss) **1997** Ind 16 (4) **1998** Ind 16 (0) **2000** ChiB 13 (0) **2001** Det 4 (0) **NFL** 81 (9) [6 yrs]

McElroy, Reggie Reginald Lee, T-G, 6´6˝/290 lbs; West Texas A&M; 1982: NYJ, rnd 2; B3/4/1960 Beaumont, TX **1983** NYJ 16 (1) **1984** NYJ 16 (16, LT) **1985**†NYJ 13 (11, LT) **1986** NYJ 8 (8, RT) **1987** NYJ 8 (5, rt) **1988** NYJ 16 (16, RT) **1989** NYJ 15 (15, RT) **1991**†LARd 16 (5, rg) **1992** LARd 16 (12, RT) **1993** KC 8 (1) **1994**†Min 10 (0) **1995** Den 16 (0) **1996** Den 7 (0) **NFL** 165 (90) [13 yrs]

McElroy, Vann Vann William, DB, 6´2˝/193 lbs; Baylor; 1982: LARd, rnd 3; B1/13/1960 Birmingham, AL **[I]** **1982**†LARd 7 (1) **1983**†LARd★16 (16, FS) **1984**†LARd★16 (16, FS) **1985**†LARd 12 (12, FS) **1986** LARd☆16 (16, FS) **1987** LARd☆12 (12, FS) **1988** LARd 12 (11, FS) **1989** LARd 7 (4) **1990** LARd 3 (0) **1990** Sea 10 (0) **NFL** 111 (88) [9 yrs]

McElwain, Bill William Thompson, B, 5´10˝/175 lbs; Northwestern; B5/14/1903 Chicago, IL **1924** ChiC 3 (2) **1926** ChiC 8 (1), 6 **NFL** 11 (3) [2 yrs]

McEndoo, Jason Jason Howard, C, 6´5˝/307 lbs; Washington State; 1998: Sea, rnd 7; B2/25/1975 San Diego, CA **1998** Sea 1 (0)

McEnulty, Doug Douglas M., FB-HB, 6´3˝/215 lbs; Wichita State; B1/16/1922 Tonganoxie, KS, D1/12/1991 Everett, WA

YEAR	TEAM	G(GS, POS)	RUSH	YD	AVG(LG)	TD	REC	YD	AVG(LG)	TD	PASS	COMP	PCT	YD	AVG(LG)	TD	INT	SK	YD	QBR	KPR	OTD	PTS	TAY
1943	†ChiB	8(3)	16	45	2.8(9)	0	1	10	10.0(10)	1	—	—	—	—	—	—	—	—	—	—	Pi	—	6	61
1944	ChiB	10(1)	8	11	1.4(7)	0	2	10	5.0(5)	1	—	—	—	—	—	—	—	—	—	—	Pi	—	6	50
NFL	2	18(4)	24	56	2.3(9)	0	3	20	6.7(10)	2	—	—	—	—	—	—	—	—	—	—	Pi	—	12	111

McEvoy, Ed Edward Clarence, WB, 5´11˝/190 lbs; Spring Hill; B11/6/1903 Mobile, AL, D8/7/1976 Houston, TX **1926** Har 7 (2)

McEwen, Craig Craig Eugene, TE-RB, 6´1˝/220 lbs; Utah; B12/16/1965 Northport, NY

YEAR	TEAM	G(GS, POS)	RUSH	YD	AVG(LG)	TD	REC	YD	AVG(LG)	TD	PASS	COMP	PCT	YD	AVG(LG)	TD	INT	SK	YD	QBR	KPR	OTD	PTS	TAY
1987	Was	4(3)	—	—	—	—	12	164	13.7(42)	0	—	—	—	—	—	—	—	—	—	—	—	—	0	82
1988	Was	14(8, RB)	—	—	—	—	23	323	14.0(46)	0	—	—	—	—	—	—	—	—	—	—	—	—	0	162
1989	SD	4(3)	—	—	—	—	7	99	14.1(29)	0	—	—	—	—	—	—	—	—	—	—	—	—	0	50
1990	SD	16(4)	—	—	—	—	29	325	11.2(32)	3	—	—	—	—	—	—	—	—	—	—	—	—	18	178
1991	SD	16(6, te)	—	—	—	—	37	399	10.8(30)	3	—	—	—	—	—	—	—	—	—	—	—	—	18	215
NFL	5	54(24)	—	—	—	—	108	1310	12.1(46)	6	—	—	—	—	—	—	—	—	—	—	—	—	36	685

McFadden, Banks James Banks, HB, 6´2˝/180 lbs; Clemson; 1940: Bkn, rnd 1; B2/7/1917 Fort Lawn, SC, D6/4/2005 Ormond Beach, FL

YEAR	TEAM	G(GS, POS)	RUSH	YD	AVG(LG)	TD	REC	YD	AVG(LG)	TD	PASS	COMP	PCT	YD	AVG(LG)	TD	INT	SK	YD	QBR	KPR	OTD	PTS	TAY
1940	Bkn	11(7, HB)	85	411	4.8(75)	1	9	97	10.8(33)	2	8	3	37.5	103	12.9(71)	1	1	—	—	—	i	—	18	526

McFadden, Bryant Bryant, DB, 5´11˝/190 lbs; Florida State; 2005: Pit, rnd 2; B11/21/1981 Hollywood, FL **2005**†Pit 12 (1)

McFadden, Marques Marques Arthur, G-T, 6´4˝/317 lbs; Arizona; B9/12/1978 St. Louis, MO **2002** Dal 4 (0)

McFadden, Marv Marvin G., G, 6´0˝/223 lbs; Michigan State; 1952: Pit, rnd 12; B1/18/1930 Columbus Junction, MI **1953** Pit 12 (RG) **1956** Pit 12 (RG) **NFL** 24 [2 yrs]

McFadden, Paul Paul Joseph, K, 5´11˝/163 lbs; Youngstown State; 1984: Phi, rnd 12; B9/24/1961 Cleveland, OH **[K]** **1984** Phi☆16 (0) **1985** Phi 16 (0) **1986** Phi 16 (0) **1987** Phi 12 (0) **1988** NYG 10 (0) **1989** Atl 9 (0) **NFL** 79 (0) [6 yrs]

McFadden, Thad Thaddeus Dwayne, WR, 6´2˝/200 lbs; Wisconsin; B8/14/1962 Flint, MI

YEAR	TEAM	G(GS, POS)	RUSH	YD	AVG(LG)	TD	REC	YD	AVG(LG)	TD	PASS	COMP	PCT	YD	AVG(LG)	TD	INT	SK	YD	QBR	KPR	OTD	PTS	TAY
1987	Buf	3(2)	—	—	—	—	4	41	10.3(13)	1	—	—	—	—	—	—	—	—	—	—	kp	—	6	85

McFadin, Bud Lewis Pate, DT-DG-LB-G, 6´3˝/260 lbs; Texas; 1951: LA, rnd 1; B8/21/1928 Rankin, TX, D2/13/2006 Victoria, TX **[K]** **1952**†LARm 0 **1953** LARm☆7 (LLB) **1954** LARm 12 (MG) **1955**†LARm★12 (LDT) **1956** LARm★12 (LDT) **1960** Den-A☆14 (LDT) **1961** Den-A★14 (LDT) **1962** Den-A★14 (LDT) **1963** Den-A★14 (LDT) **1964** Hou-A 14 (LDT) **1965** Hou-A 12 (LDT) **NFL** 125 [11 yrs]

McFarland, Anthony Anthony Darelle, DT, 6´0˝/300 lbs; LSU; 1999: TB, rnd 1; B12/18/1977 Winnsboro, LA **1999**†TB 14 (0) **2000**†TB 16 (16, LDT) **2001**†TB 14 (14, LDT) **2002** TB 10 (10, LDT) **2003** TB 16 (16, LDT) **2004** TB 8 (8, RDT) **2005**†TB 15 (15, RDT) **NFL** 93 (79) [7 yrs]

McFarland, Dylan Dylan, T, 6´6˝/304 lbs; Montana; 2004: Buf, rnd 7; B7/11/1980 Kalispell, MT **2004** Buf 2 (0) **2005** Buf 1 (0) **NFL** 3 (0) [2 yrs]

YEAR	TEAM	G (GS, POS)	RUSH	YD	AVG (LG)	TD	REC	YD	AVG (LG)	TD	PASS COMP	PCT	YD	AVG (LG)	TD	INT	SK	YD	QBR	KPR	OTD	PTS	TAY

McFARLAND, JIM James Darrell, TE, 6′5″/225 lbs; Nebraska; 1970: SL, rnd 7; B10/4/1947 North Platte, NE   **1970** Buf 1 **1970** SL 9 **1972** SL 10 **1974**†SL 14 **1975** Mia 6

1971	SL	14 (te)	—	—	—	—	5	54	10.8(21)	2	—	—	—	—	—	—	—	—	—	—	—	12	37
1973	SL	14	—	—	—	—	2	10	5.0(7)	0	—	—	—	—	—	—	—	—	—	k	1	6	17
NFL	6	68	—	—	—	—	7	64	9.1(21)	2	—	—	—	—	—	—	—	—	—	k	1	18	54

McFARLAND, KAY Russel Kay, WR, 6′2″/186 lbs; Colorado State; 1961: SF, rnd 18; B4/10/1938 Quincy, IL

1962	SF	6	—	—	—	—	3	24	8.0(16)	0	—	—	—	—	—	—	—	—	—	—	—	0	12
1963	SF	12	—	—	—	—	11	126	11.5(33)	1	—	—	—	—	—	—	—	—	—	—	—	6	68
1964	SF	12	—	—	—	—	5	67	13.4(33)	0	—	—	—	—	—	—	—	—	—	—	—	0	34
1965	SF	12	—	—	—	—	8	106	13.3(35)	1	—	—	—	—	—	—	—	—	—	—	—	6	58
1966	SF	12	—	—	—	—	13	219	16.8(43)	1	—	—	—	—	—	—	—	—	—	—	—	6	115
1968	SF	9	—	—	—	—	5	140	28.0(65)	1	—	—	—	—	—	—	—	—	—	—	—	6	75
NFL	6	63	—	—	—	—	45	682	15.2(65)	4	—	—	—	—	—	—	—	—	—	—	—	24	361

McFARLANE, NYLE Hardy Nyle, HB, 6′2″/205 lbs; Brigham Young; B11/25/1935 Lehi, UT

| 1960 | Oak-A | 13 | 4 | 52 | 13.0(23) | 0 | 5 | 89 | 17.8(49) | 2 | — | — | — | — | — | — | — | — | — | k | — | 12 | 103 |

McGAHEE, WILLIS Willie Andrew, RB, 6′0″/200 lbs; Miami (FL); 2003: Buf, rnd 1; B10/20/1981 Miami, FL

2004	Buf	16 (11, RB)	284	1128	4.0(41)	13	22	169	7.7(16)	0	—	—	—	—	—	—	—	—	—	—	—	78	1343
2005	Buf	16 (15, RB)	325	1247	3.8(27)	5	28	178	6.4(19)	0	—	—	—	—	—	—	—	—	—	—	—	30	1386
NFL	2	32 (26)	609	2375	3.9(41)	18	50	347	6.9(19)	0	—	—	—	—	—	—	—	—	—	—	—	108	2729

McGARITY, WANE Wane Keith, WR, 5′8″/197 lbs; Texas; 1999: Dal, rnd 4; B9/30/1976 San Antonio, TX

1999	Dal	5 (1)	—	—	—	—	7	70	10.0(18)	0	—	—	—	—	—	—	—	—	p	—	0	36
2000	Dal	14 (0)	6	49	8.2(22)	1	25	250	10.0(35)	0	—	—	—	—	—	—	—	—	p	—	2	18	407
2001	Dal	3 (1)	—	—	—	—	6	45	7.5(11)	1	—	—	—	—	—	—	—	—	p	—	6	36
2001	NO	9 (0)	—	—	—	—	1	-2	-2.0(-2)	0	—	—	—	—	—	—	—	—	p	—	0	87
NFL	3	31 (2)	6	49	8.2(22)	1	39	363	9.3(25)	1	—	—	—	—	—	—	—	—	p	—	2	24	566

McGARRAHAN, SCOTT John Scott, DB, 6′1″/200 lbs; New Mexico; 1998: GB, rnd 6; B2/12/1974 Arlington, TX   **1998**†GB 15 (0) **1999** GB 13 (0) **2000** GB 16 (0) **2001**†Mia 16 (0) **2002** Mia 14 (0) **2004** Ten 16 (1) **2005** SD 2 (0)

| 2003 | †Ten | 16 (2) | — | — | — | — | 1 | 10 | 10.0(10) | 0 | — | — | — | — | — | — | — | — | S | — | 0 | 5 |
| NFL | 8 | 108 (3) | — | — | — | — | 1 | 10 | 10.0(10) | 0 | — | — | — | — | — | — | — | — | iS | — | 0 | 11 |

McGARRY, BARNEY Bernard Duane, G, 6′1″/203 lbs; Utah; 1939: Cle, rnd 6; B12/24/1917 Park City, UT, D3/25/2001 Provo, UT   **1939** Cle 11 (5, RG) **1940** Cle 11 (11, LG) **1941** Cle 11 (11, LG) **1942** Cle 4 (1) **NFL** 37 (28) [4 yrs]

McGARRY, JOHN John Thomas, G, 6′5″/288 lbs; St. Joseph's (IN); B11/24/1963 Chicago, IL   **1987** GB 2 (1)

McGAW, WALT Raymond Peter, G, /195 lbs; Beloit; B12/27/1899 Rockford, IL, D10/8/1979 Trego, WI   **1926** GB 1 (0)

McGEARY, CLARENCE Clarence Valentine, DT, 6′5″/250 lbs; Minnesota; North Dakota State; 1948: GB, rnd 30/Bkn-A, rnd 30; B8/8/1926 St. Paul, MN, D4/6/1993 Salt Lake City, UT   **1950** GB 12 (RDT)

McGEE, BEN Benjamin, DE-DT, 6′3″/250 lbs; Jackson State; 1964: Pit, rnd 4/NYJ, rnd 5; B1/26/1939 Starkville, MS   **1964** Pit 14 (LDE) **1965** Pit 13 (LDE) **1966** Pit★14 (LDE) **1967** Pit 10 (LDE) **1968** Pit◇14 (RDE) **1969** Pit 14 (RDE) **1970** Pit 14 (RDE) **1971** Pit 13 (rdt) **1972**†Pit 14 (RDT) **NFL** 120 [9 yrs]

McGEE, BOB Robert Joseph, T, 6′0″/210 lbs; Santa Clara; B7/28/1912 San Francisco, CA, D9/1/1963 Burlingame, CA   **1938** ChiC 1 (0)

McGEE, BUFORD Buford Lamar, RB, 6′0″/206 lbs; Mississippi; 1984: SD, rnd 11; B8/16/1960 Durant, MS

1984	SD	16 (0)	67	226	3.4(30)	4	9	76	8.4(43)	2	—	—	—	—	—	—	—	—	k	—	36	419
1985	SD	11 (1)	42	181	4.3(44)	3	3	15	5.0(7)	0	—	—	—	—	—	—	—	—	k	—	18	249
1986	SD	9 (3)	63	187	3.0(20)	7	10	105	10.5(18)	0	1	1	100.0	1	1.0(1)	0	0	—	—	k	—	42	310
1987	LARm	3 (1)	3	6	2.0(2)	1	7	40	5.7(12)	0	—	—	—	—	—	—	—	—	—	—	6	36
1988	†LARm	16 (10, FB)	22	69	3.1(12)	0	16	117	7.3(16)	3	—	—	—	—	—	—	—	—	k	—	18	128
1989	†LARm	16 (13, FB)	21	99	4.7(15)	1	37	303	8.2(25)	4	—	—	—	—	—	—	—	—	—	—	30	281
1990	LARm	16 (15, FB)	44	234	5.3(19)	4	47	388	8.3(25)	4	2	2	100.0	23	11.5(22)	1	0	—	—	—	—	30	475
1991	LARm	16 (4)	19	65	3.4(9)	0	20	160	8.0(20)	0	—	—	—	—	—	—	—	—	—	—	0	145
1992	GB	4 (3)	8	19	2.4(4)	0	6	60	10.0(15)	0	—	—	—	—	—	—	—	—	—	—	0	49
NFL	9	107 (50)	289	1086	3.8(44)	17	155	1264	8.2(43)	13	3	3	100.0	24	8.0(22)	1	0	—	—	k	—	180	2090

McGEE, CARL Carl Demetrius, LB, 6′3″/228 lbs; Duke; 1979: Cle, rnd 9; B7/15/1956 Cincinnati, OH   **1980**†SD 6 (0)

McGEE, DELL Antonio Deleon, DB, 5′8″/180 lbs; Auburn; 1996: Arz, rnd 5; B9/7/1973 Columbus, GA   **1998** Arz 3 (0)

McGEE, ED Edward D., T, 6′1″/224 lbs; Temple; 1940: NYG, rnd 12; B2/26/1916 Fort Edward, NY, D12/1995 Glens Falls, NY   **1940** NYG 3 (0) **1944** Bos 10 (10, RT) **1945** Bos 8 (3) **1946** Bos 11 (0) **NFL** 32 (13) [4 yrs]

McGEE, GEORGE George, T, 6′2″/255 lbs; Southern (LA); 1959: Det, rnd 16; B10/7/1935 Baton Rouge, LA   **1960** Bos-A 14 (LT)

McGEE, HARRY Harry Loyd, C-G, 6′1″/198 lbs; Kansas State; B4/27/1905, D10/1983, FL   **1927** Cle 2 (2) **1929** SI 10 (4) **1930** Nwk 1 (0) **1932** SI 1 (0) **NFL** 14 (6) [4 yrs]

McGEE, MAX William Max, E, 6′3″/205 lbs; Tulane; 1954: GB, rnd 5; B7/16/1932 Saxon City, NV [P]

1954	GB	12 (LE)	1	9	9.0(9)	0	36	614	17.1(82)	9	—	—	—	—	—	—	—	—	P	—	54	361
1957	GB	12 (le)	5	40	8.0(24)	0	17	273	16.1(49)	1	—	—	—	—	—	—	—	—	k	—	6	191
1958	GB	12 (LE)	1	9	9.0(9)	0	37	655	17.7(80)	7	1	0	0.0	0	0.0	0	0	—	—	P	—	42	372
1959	GB	12 (LE)	—	—	—	—	30	695	23.2(81)	5	—	—	—	—	—	—	—	—	P	—	30	373
1960	†GB	12 (SE)	2	11	5.5(16)	0	38	787	20.7(57)	4	—	—	—	—	—	—	—	—	P	—	24	425
1961	†GB◇	13 (SE)	—	—	—	—	51	883	17.3(53)	7	—	—	—	—	—	—	—	—	P	—	42	477
1962	†GB	14 (SE)	3	52	17.3(36)	0	49	820	16.7(64)	3	1	0	0.0	0	0.0	0	1	—	—	P	—	18	437
1963	GB	14 (SE)	—	—	—	—	39	749	19.2(63)	6	—	—	—	—	—	—	—	—	—	—	36	405
1964	GB☆	13 (SE)	—	—	—	—	31	592	19.1(55)	6	—	—	—	—	—	—	—	—	—	1	42	326
1965	GB	12	—	—	—	—	10	154	15.4(37)	1	—	—	—	—	—	—	—	—	—	—	6	82
1966	†GB	12	—	—	—	—	4	91	22.8(39)	1	—	—	—	—	—	—	—	—	—	—	6	51
1967	†GB	10	—	—	—	—	3	33	11.0(13)	0	—	—	—	—	—	—	—	—	—	—	0	17
NFL	12	148	12	121	10.1(36)	0	345	6346	18.4(82)	50	2	0	0.0	0	0.0	0	1	—	—	Pk	1	306	3513

McGEE, MIKE Michael Burnette, G, 6′1″/230 lbs; Duke; 1960: SL, rnd 2/Hou, rnd 1; B12/1/1938 Washington, DC   **1960** SL 11 (LG) **1961** SL 13 (LG) **1962** SL 13 (LG) **NFL** 37 [3 yrs]

McGEE, MOLLY Sylvester, RB, 5′10″/184 lbs; Rhode Island; 1974: Atl, rnd 16; B8/26/1952 Haverstraw, NY

| 1974 | Atl | 10 | 7 | 30 | 4.3(10) | 0 | — | — | — | — | — | — | — | — | — | — | — | — | k | — | 0 | 77 |

McGEE, TERRENCE Terrence Dewayne, DB, 5′9″/195 lbs; Northwestern State (LA); 2003: Buf, rnd 4; B10/14/1980 Athens, TX [R]   **2003** Buf 14 (2) **2004** Buf★16 (13, LCB) **2005** Buf☆15 (14, LCB) **NFL** 45 (29) [3 yrs]

McGEE, TIM Timothy Dwayne Hatchett, WR, 5′10″/183 lbs; Tennessee; 1986: Cin, rnd 1; B8/7/1964 Cleveland, OH

1986	Cin☆	16 (0)	4	10	2.5(8)	0	16	276	17.3(51)	1	—	—	—	—	—	—	—	—	kp	—	6	521
1987	Cin	11 (5, wr)	1	-10	-10.0(-10)	0	23	408	17.7(49)	1	—	—	—	—	—	—	—	—	k	—	6	216
1988	†Cin	16 (15, WR)	—	—	—	—	36	686	19.1(78)	6	—	—	—	—	—	—	—	—	—	—	36	373
1989	Cin	16 (16, WR)	2	36	18.0(25)	0	65	1211	18.6(74)	8	—	—	—	—	—	—	—	—	—	—	48	682
1990	†Cin	16 (15, WR)	—	—	—	—	43	737	17.1(52)	1	—	—	—	—	—	—	—	—	—	—	6	374
1991	Cin	16 (16, WR)	—	—	—	—	51	802	15.7(52)	4	—	—	—	—	—	—	—	—	—	—	24	421
1992	Cin	16 (16, WR)	—	—	—	—	35	408	11.7(36)	3	—	—	—	—	—	—	—	—	iS	—	18	219
1993	Was	13 (14, WR)	—	—	—	—	39	500	12.8(54)	3	—	—	—	—	—	—	—	—	—	—	18	265
1994	Cin	14 (2)	1	-18	-18.0(-18)	0	13	175	13.5(25)	1	—	—	—	—	—	—	—	—	—	—	6	75
NFL	9	134 (97)	8	18	2.3(25)	0	321	5203	16.2(78)	28	—	—	—	—	—	—	—	—	kp	—	168	3145

YEAR	TEAM	G (GS, POS)	RUSH	YD	AVG(LG)	TD	REC	YD	AVG(LG)	TD	PASS COMP	PCT	YD	AVG(LG)	TD	INT	SK	YD	QBR	KPR	OTD	PTS	TAY

McGee, Tony Anthony Eugene, DE-DT, 6´4˝/250 lbs; Wyoming; Bishop; 1971: Chi, rnd 3; B1/18/1949 Battle Creek, MI **1971** ChiB 14 (4) **1972** ChiB 14 (14, LDE)
1973 ChiB 14 (14, LDE) **1974** NE 14 (1) **1975** NE 13 (10, LDE) **1976**†NE 14 (13, LDE) **1977** NE 14 (1) **1978**†NE 16 (1) **1979** NE 16 (2) **1980** NE 16 (0) **1981** NE 16 (9, LDE)
1982†Was 9 (0) **1983**†Was 16 (0) **1984**†Was 16 (0) **NFL** 202 (69) [14 yrs]

McGee, Tony Tony Lamont, TE, 6´3˝/247 lbs; Michigan; 1993: Cin, rnd 2; B4/21/1971 Terre Haute, IN

YEAR	TEAM	G (GS, POS)	RUSH	YD	AVG(LG)	TD	REC	YD	AVG(LG)	TD										KPR		PTS	TAY
1993	Cin	15(15, TE)	—	—	—	—	44	525	11.9(37)	0	—	—	—	—	—	—	—	—	—	—	—	0	263
1994	Cin	16(16, TE)	—	—	—	—	40	492	12.3(54)	1	—	—	—	—	—	—	—	—	—	k	—	6	240
1995	Cin	16(16, TE)	—	—	—	—	55	754	13.7(41)	4	—	—	—	—	—	—	—	—	—	—	—	24	397
1996	Cin	16(16, TE)	—	—	—	—	38	446	11.7(22)	4	—	—	—	—	—	—	—	—	—	—	—	24	243
1997	Cin	16(16, TE)	—	—	—	—	34	414	12.2(37)	6	—	—	—	—	—	—	—	—	—	—	—	38	237
1998	Cin	16(16, TE)	—	—	—	—	22	363	16.5(40)	1	—	—	—	—	—	—	—	—	—	—	—	6	187
1999	Cin	16(16, TE)	—	—	—	—	26	344	13.2(35)	2	—	—	—	—	—	—	—	—	—	—	—	12	182
2000	Cin	14(14, TE)	—	—	—	—	26	309	11.9(39)	1	—	—	—	—	—	—	—	—	—	—	—	6	160
2001	Cin	11(9, TE)	—	—	—	—	14	148	10.6(25)	1	—	—	—	—	—	—	—	—	—	—	—	6	79
2002	Dal	16(16, TE)	—	—	—	—	23	294	12.8(58)	1	—	—	—	—	—	—	—	—	—	—	—	6	152
2003	NYG	4(0)																				—	—
2003	Dal	3(0)																				—	—
NFL	11	159(150)	—	—	—	—	322	4089	12.7(58)	21	—	—	—	—	—	—	—	—	—	k	—	128	2139

McGee, Willie Willie, WR, 5´11˝/179 lbs; Alcorn State; 1973: SD, rnd 5; B5/14/1950 New Orleans, LA

YEAR	TEAM	G (GS, POS)	RUSH	YD	AVG(LG)	TD	REC	YD	AVG(LG)	TD										KPR		PTS	TAY
1973	SD	11	—	—	—	—	3	67	22.3(50)	0	—	—	—	—	—	—	—	—	—	kp	—	0	183
1974	†LARm	14	—	—	—	—	—	—	—	—	—	—	—	—	—	—	—	—	—	k	—	0	108
1975	†LARm	14	—	—	—	—	6	83	13.8(22)	0	—	—	—	—	—	—	—	—	—	k	—	0	191
1976	SF	6(6, wr)	3	12	4.0(19)	0	13	269	20.7(52)	4	—	—	—	—	—	—	—	—	—	—	—	24	167
1977	SF	7	1	-3	-3.0(-3)	0	2	27	13.5(14)	0	—	—	—	—	—	—	—	—	—	—	—	0	11
1978	Det	4	—	—	—	—	—	—	—	—	—	—	—	—	—	—	—	—	—	k	—	0	-15
NFL	6	56(6)	4	9	2.3(19)	0	24	446	18.6(52)	4	—	—	—	—	—	—	—	—	—	kp	—	24	643

McGeever, John John, DB, 6´1˝/195 lbs; Auburn; 1962: Den, rnd 7/Phi, rnd 6; B2/14/1939 Bogalusa, LA **1962** Den-A 14 (LCB) **1963** Den-A 13 (LCB) **1964** Den-A 14 (LS)
1965 Den-A 14 (RCB) **1966** Mia-A 12 **NFL** 67 [5 yrs]

McGeoghan, Phil Phil, WR, 6´2˝/224 lbs; Boston University; Maine; B7/8/1979 Freding Hills, MI **2001** Den 2 (0)

McGeorge, Rich Richard Eugene, TE, 6´4˝/235 lbs; Elon; 1970: GB, rnd 1; B9/14/1948 Roanoke, VA

YEAR	TEAM	G (GS, POS)	RUSH	YD	AVG(LG)	TD	REC	YD	AVG(LG)	TD										KPR		PTS	TAY
1970	GB	14	1	3	3.0(3)	0	2	32	16.0(16)	1	—	—	—	—	—	—	—	—	—	—	—	12	29
1971	GB	14(TE)	—	—	—	—	27	463	17.1(50)	4	—	—	—	—	—	—	—	—	—	—	—	24	252
1972	GB	2	—	—	—	—	4	50	12.5(23)	2	—	—	—	—	—	—	—	—	—	—	—	12	35
1973	GB	14(TE)	—	—	—	—	16	260	16.3(44)	1	—	—	—	—	—	—	—	—	—	—	—	6	135
1974	GB	14(TE)	—	—	—	—	30	440	14.7(51)	0	—	—	—	—	—	—	—	—	—	—	—	0	220
1975	GB	14(TE)	—	—	—	—	32	458	14.3(43)	1	—	—	—	—	—	—	—	—	—	k	—	6	236
1976	GB	14(TE)	—	—	—	—	24	278	11.6(28)	1	—	—	—	—	—	—	—	—	—	—	—	6	144
1977	GB	14(TE)	—	—	—	—	17	142	8.4(18)	1	—	—	—	—	—	—	—	—	—	—	—	6	76
1978	GB	16(TE)	—	—	—	—	23	247	10.7(25)	1	—	—	—	—	—	—	—	—	—	k	—	6	114
NFL	9	116	1	3	3.0(3)	0	175	2370	13.5(51)	13	—	—	—	—	—	—	—	—	—	k	—	78	1240

McGhee, Kanavis Kanavis, LB, 6´4˝/257 lbs; Colorado; 1991: NYG, rnd 2; B10/4/1968 Houston, TX **1991** NYG 16 (0) **1992** NYG 14 (1) **1993**†NYG 10 (1) **1994** Cin 1 (0)
1995 Hou 9 (0) **NFL** 50 (2) [5 yrs]

McGibbony, Charlie Charles William, TB, 5´10˝/160 lbs; Alabama; Central Arkansas; B10/23/1915 Pine Bluff, AR

YEAR	TEAM	G (GS, POS)	RUSH	YD	AVG(LG)	TD	REC	YD	AVG(LG)	TD	PASS COMP	PCT	YD	AVG(LG)	TD	INT				KPR		PTS	TAY
1944	Bkn	7(2)	26	81	3.1(27)	0	—	—	—	—	48	18	37.5	262	5.5(65)	1	10	—	—	Pkpi	—	0	-131

McGilbra, Firpo L. Vance, T-G, 6´1˝/210 lbs; Haskell Indian; B11/5/1906 Eufaula, AL, D5/7/1995 Battle Ground, WA **1926** Buf 4 (4)

McGill, Eddie Edward Hoyt, TE, 6´6˝/225 lbs; Western Carolina; 1982: SL, rnd 10; B7/5/1960 Asheville, NC **1982**†SL 9 (0)

YEAR	TEAM	G (GS, POS)	RUSH	YD	AVG(LG)	TD	REC	YD	AVG(LG)	TD												PTS	TAY
1983	SL	2(0)	—	—	—	—	1	11	11.0(11)	0	—	—	—	—	—	—	—	—	—	—	—	0	6
NFL	2	11(0)	—	—	—	—	1	11	11.0(11)	0	—	—	—	—	—	—	—	—	—	—	—	0	6

McGill, George George J., G, 5´10˝/180 lbs; Marquette; B9/17/1897 Winona, MN, D1/1966 Palm Beach County, FL **1922** Rac 3 (2)

McGill, Karmeeleyah Karmeeleyah, LB, 6´3˝/224 lbs; Notre Dame; B1/11/1971 Clearwater, FL **1993** Cin 4 (0)

McGill, Lenny Charles Leonard, DB, 6´1˝/195 lbs; Arizona State; B5/31/1971 Long Beach, CA **1994** GB 6 (0) **1995**†GB 15 (1) **1996** Atl 16 (8, LCB) **1997** Atl 15 (0)
1998 Car 10 (0) **NFL** 62 (9) [5 yrs]

McGill, Mike Michael Ray, LB, 6´2˝/235 lbs; Notre Dame; 1968: Min, rnd 3; B11/21/1946 Hammond, IN **1968**†Min 14 **1969**†Min 10 **1970**†Min 14 **1971** SL 11 (RLB)
1972 SL 4 **NFL** 53 [5 yrs]

McGill, Ralph Ralph Louis, DB, 5´11˝/183 lbs; Tulsa; 1972: SF, rnd 2; B4/28/1950 Thomasville, GA [R] **1972**†SF 11 **1973** SF 14 **1974** SF 13 (6, rcb) **1975** SF 9 (9, FS)
1976 SF 10 (9, FS) **1977** SF 13 (13, FS) **1978** NO 16 **1979** NO 13 **NFL** 99 (37) [8 yrs]

McGinest, Willie William Lee, DE-LB, 6´5˝/270 lbs; USC; 1994: NE, rnd 1; B12/11/1971 Long Beach, CA [S] **1994**†NE 16 (7, lolb) **1995** NE 16 (16, LOLB)
1996†NE◇16 (16, RDE) **1997** NE 11 (11, RDE) **1998**†NE 9 (8, RDE) **1999** NE 16 (16, RDE) **2000** NE 14 (14, LOLB/lde) **2001**†NE 11 (5, rde) **2002** NE 16 (10, LDE)
2003†NE◇14 (11, RDE) **2004** NE 16 (16, LOLB) **2005**†NE 16 (16, LOLB) **NFL** 171 (146) [12 yrs]

McGinley, Ed Edward Francis, T, 5´11˝/185 lbs; Pennsylvania; B8/8/1899 Chester, PA, D4/16/1985 Point Pleasant, NJ **1925** NYG 2 (2)

McGinnis, Larry James Laurence, G-C-E, 6´1˝/210 lbs; Washburn; Marquette; B7/16/1899 Topeka, KS, D3/1948 **1923** Mil 7 (3) **1924** Mil 13 (12, RG/c) **NFL** 20 (15) [2 yrs]

McGirl, Len Leonard Edward, G, 6´2˝/206 lbs; Missouri; B1909 Washington Township, MO, deceased **1934** SL 3 (3, RG)

McGlasson, Ed Edward Tandy, C, 6´4˝/248 lbs; Maryland; Youngstown State; 1979: NYJ, rnd 10; B7/11/1956 Annapolis, MD **1979** NYJ 7 **1980** LARm 1 (0) **1981**†NYG 16 (0)
NFL 24 [3 yrs]

McGlockton, Chester Chester Morris, DT-DE, 6´3˝/334 lbs; Clemson; 1992: LARd, rnd 1; B9/16/1969 Whiteville, NC [S] **1992** LARd 10 (0) **1993**†LARd 16 (16, LDT)
1994 LARd★16 (16, RDT) **1995** Oak★16 (16, RDT) **1996** Oak★16 (16, RDT) **1997** Oak◇16 (16, RDT) **1998** KC 10 (9, RDE) **1999** KC 16 (16, LDT) **2000** KC 15 (15, LDT)
2001 Den 16 (16, LDT) **2002** Den 16 (15, RDT) **2003** NYJ 16 (0) **NFL** 179 (151) [12 yrs]

McGlone, Joe Joseph Carlton, BB, 5´7˝/150 lbs; Harvard; B9/12/1896 Natick, MA, D1/25/1963 New York, NY **1926** Pro 1 (1)

McGoldrick, Hugh Hugh Francis, T-E, 5´10˝/180 lbs; Lehigh; B11/22/1900 Boston, MA, D10/7/1965 Cotuit, MA **1925** Pro 1 (0)

McGonnigal, Bruce Joseph Bruce, TE, 6´4˝/229 lbs; Virginia; 1991: Pit, rnd 9; B5/1/1968 Cambridge, MA **1991** Cle 2 (0)

McGovern, Rob Robert Patrick, LB, 6´2˝/225 lbs; Holy Cross; 1989: KC, rnd 10; B10/1/1966 Teaneck, NJ **1989** KC 16 (2) **1990**†KC 11 (0) **1991** Pit 15 (0) **1992** NE 4 (0)
NFL 46 (2) [4 yrs]

McGowan, Brandon Brandon, DB, 6´0˝/190 lbs; Maine; B9/16/1983 Jersey City, NJ **2005** ChiB 8 (3)

McGowan, Reggie Reginald, WR, 5´8˝/165 lbs; Abilene Christian; B9/25/1964

YEAR	TEAM	G (GS, POS)	RUSH	YD	AVG(LG)	TD	REC	YD	AVG(LG)	TD												PTS	TAY
1987	NYG	3(0)	—	—	—	—	4	111	27.8(63)	1	—	—	—	—	—	—	—	—	—	—	—	6	61

McGrail, Joe Joseph John, NT, 6´3˝/280 lbs; Delaware; 1987: Buf, rnd 12; B6/6/1964 Philadelphia, PA **1987** Buf 2 (0)

McGrath, Brian Brian Patrick, G, /245 lbs; none; B3/18/1901, Ireland, D1/1985 Bronx, NY **1922** Lou 1 (1)

McGrath, Dick Richard James, C-T, 5´10˝/190 lbs; Holy Cross; B6/30/1901 Winthrop, MA, D10/23/1965 Virginia Beach, VA **1926** Bkn 10 (10, C)

McGrath, Frank Frank LeDuke, E, 5´11˝/192 lbs; Georgetown (DC); B3/13/1904, D3/4/1990 Essexville, MI **1927** Fra 12 (11, LE) **1928** NYY 12 (7, le) **NFL** 24 (18) [2 yrs]

McGrath, Mark Mark Allen, WR, 5´11˝/175 lbs; Montana State; B12/17/1957 San Diego, CA

YEAR	TEAM	G (GS, POS)	RUSH	YD	AVG(LG)	TD	REC	YD	AVG(LG)	TD												PTS	TAY
1981	Sea	6(0)	—	—	—	—	4	47	11.8(16)	0	—	—	—	—	—	—	—	—	—	—	—	0	24
1983	†Was	2(0)	—	—	—	—	1	6	6.0(6)	0	—	—	—	—	—	—	—	—	—	—	—	0	3
1984	†Was	13(2)	—	—	—	—	10	118	11.8(24)	1	—	—	—	—	—	—	—	—	—	—	—	6	64

YEAR	TEAM	G (GS, POS)	RUSH	YD	AVG (LG)	TD	REC	YD	AVG (LG)	TD	PASS COMP	PCT	YD	AVG (LG)	TD	INT	SK	YD	QBR	KPR	OTD	PTS	TAY
1985	Was	5 (0)	—	—	—	—	—	—	—	—	—	—	—	—	—	—	—	—	—	—	—	—	—
NFL	4	26 (2)	—	—	—	—	15	171	11.4 (24)	1	—	—	—	—	—	—	—	—	—	—	—	6	91

McGraw, Jon   Jon, DB, 6′3″/206 lbs; Kansas State; 2002: NYJ, rnd 2; B4/2/1979 Manhattan, KS   **2002**†NYJ 15 (1)   **2003** NYJ 6 (6, fs)   **2004**†NYJ 12 (1)   **2005** Det 8 (2)   **NFL** 41 (10) [4 yrs]

McGraw, Mike   Michael Shane, LB, 6′2″/225 lbs; Wyoming; 1975: SL, rnd 10; B12/27/1953 Denver, CO   **1976** SL 4   **1977** Det 1   **NFL** 5 [2 yrs]

McGraw, Thurman   Thurman Fay, DT-T, 6′5″/235 lbs; Colorado State; 1950: Det, rnd 2; B7/17/1927 Garden City, KS, D9/13/2000 Fort Collins, CO   **1950** Det◇12 (LDT)   **1951** Det 8 (LDT)   **1952**†Det☆12 (LDT)   **1953**†Det☆11 (LDT)   **1954**†Det 6   **NFL** 49 [5 yrs]

McGregor, Keli   Keli Scott, TE, 6′6″/250 lbs; Colorado State; 1985: Den, rnd 4; B1/23/1963 Primghar, IA   **1985** Den 2 (0)   **1985** Ind 6 (0)   **NFL** 8 (0) [1 yr]

McGrew, Dan   Daniel Atwood, C, 6′2″/250 lbs; Purdue; 1959: Det, rnd 20; B4/7/1937 Martins Ferry, OH   **1960** Buf-A☆14 (C)

McGrew, Larry   Lawrence, LB, 6′5″/233 lbs; USC; 1980: NE, rnd 2; B7/23/1957 Berkeley, CA, D4/5/2004 Lancaster, CA   **1980** NE 11 (0)   **1982**†NE 8 (8, LOLB)   **1983** NE 16 (5, lolb)   **1984** NE 16 (15, RILB)   **1985**†NE 13 (13, RILB)   **1986**†NE 14 (14, RILB)   **1987** NE 12 (12, RILB)   **1988** NE 16 (15, ROLB)   **1989** NE 16 (16, ROLB)   **1990**†NYG 11 (1)   **NFL** 133 (99) [10 yrs]

McGrew, Reggie   Regnald Gerard, DT, 6′1″/301 lbs; Florida; 1999: SF, rnd 1; B12/16/1976 Mayo, FL   **2000** SF 10 (0)   **2001**†SF 12 (0)   **2002** Atl 2 (0)   **NFL** 24 (0) [3 yrs]

McGrew, Sylvester   Sylvester Lee, DE, 6′4″/257 lbs; Tulane; B2/27/1960 New Orleans, LA   **1987** GB 3 (2)

McGriff, Curtis   Curtis, DE-NT, 6′5″/270 lbs; Alabama; B5/17/1958 Donalsonville, GA   **1980** NYG 13 (11, NT)   **1981** NYG 14 (14, LDE)   **1982** NYG 9 (8, LDE)   **1983** NYG 8 (8, LDE)   **1984**†NYG 16 (14, LDE)   **1985**†NYG 16 (16, LDE)   **1987** Was 1 (0)   **NFL** 77 (71) [7 yrs]

McGriff, Lee   Lee Colson, WR, 5′9″/165 lbs; Florida; B10/3/1953 Tampa, FL

| 1976 | TB | 6 (3) | — | — | — | — | — | — | — | — | 1 | 1 | 100.0 | 39 | 39.0 (39) | 0 | 0 | — | — | — | — | 0 | 20 |

McGriff, Travis   William Travis, WR, 5′8″/185 lbs; Florida; 1999: Den, rnd 3; B6/24/1976 Gainesville, FL

1999	Den	14 (0)	—	—	—	—	3	37	12.3 (15)	0	—	—	—	—	—	—	—	—	—	p	—	0	34
2000	†Den	15 (0)	—	—	—	—	2	51	25.5 (43)	1	—	—	—	—	—	—	—	—	—	—	—	6	31
2001	Den	5 (0)	—	—	—	—	—	—	—	—	—	—	—	—	—	—	—	—	—	—	—	—	—
NFL	3	34 (0)	—	—	—	—	5	88	17.6 (43)	1	—	—	—	—	—	—	—	—	—	p	—	6	64

McGriff, Tyrone   Tyrone Keith, G, 6′0″/270 lbs; Florida A&M; 1980: Pit, rnd 12; B1/13/1958 Vero Beach, FL, D12/9/2000 Melbourne, FL   **1980** Pit 16 (10, RG)   **1981** Pit 12 (0)   **1982**†Pit 8 (2)   **NFL** 36 (10) [3 yrs]

McGriggs, Lamar   Lamar V., DB, 6′3″/213 lbs; Oklahoma State; Western Illinois; 1991: NYG, rnd 8; B5/9/1968 Chicago, IL   **1991** NYG 16 (0)   **1992** NYG 16 (10, SS)   **1993**†Min 9 (4)   **1994**†Min 16 (1)   **NFL** 57 (15) [4 yrs]

McGrorty, Dusty   Dustin Scott, RB, 5′10″/218 lbs; Southern Oregon; B5/9/1981 Seaside, OR   **2004** SL 1 (0)

McGruder, Michael   Michael J.P., DB, 5′11″/185 lbs; Kent State; B5/6/1964 Cleveland Heights, OH   **1989** GB 2 (0)   **1990** Mia 1 (0)   **1991** Mia 16 (5, lcb)   **1992**†SF 9 (2)   **1993**†SF 16 (5, rcb)   **1994** TB 15 (3)   **1995** TB 16 (2)   **1996**†NE 14 (0)   **1997** NE 3 (0)   **NFL** 92 (17) [9 yrs]

McGuire, Gene   Walter Eugene, C, 6′4″/300 lbs; Notre Dame; 1992: NO, rnd 4; B7/17/1970 Fort Dix, NJ   **1993** ChiB 9 (0)   **1996** GB 8 (0)   **NFL** 17 (0) [2 yrs]

McGuire, Kaipo   Roy Kaiponohea, WR, 5′10″/182 lbs; Brigham Young; B1/16/1974 Honolulu, HI   **1997** Ind 3 (0)   **1998** Ind 1 (0)   **NFL** 4 (0) [2 yrs]

McGuire, Monte   Monte Lin, QB, 6′4″/202 lbs; Texas Tech; B5/7/1964 Abilene, TX

| 1987 | Den | 2 (0) | — | — | — | — | — | — | — | — | 3 | 2 | 66.7 | 23 | 7.7 (13) | 0 | 0 | — | — | — | — | 0 | 12 |

McGuirk, Warren   Warren Pierce, T, 5′11″/200 lbs; Boston College; B1/2/1906 Boston, MA, D2/19/1981 Boston, MA   **1929** Pro 12 (10, RT)   **1930** Pro 11 (8, RT)   **NFL** 23 (18) [2 yrs]

McGwire, Dan   Daniel Scott, QB, 6′8″/240 lbs; Iowa; San Diego State; 1991: Sea, rnd 1; B12/18/1967 Pomona, CA

1991	Sea	1 (1)	—	—	—	—	—	—	—	—	7	3	42.9	27	3.9 (13)	0	1	—	—	—	—	0	-27
1992	Sea	2 (1)	3	13	4.3 (11)	0	—	—	—	—	30	17	56.7	116	3.9 (20)	0	3	7	58	—	—	0	-49
1993	Sea	2 (0)	1	-1	-1.0 (-1)	0	—	—	—	—	5	3	60.0	24	4.8 (17)	1	0	—	—	—	—	0	16
1994	Sea	7 (3)	10	-6	-0.6 (2)	0	—	—	—	—	105	51	48.6	578	5.5 (36)	1	2	13	96	—	—	0	208
1995	Mia	1 (0)	—	—	—	—	—	—	—	—	1	0	0.0	0	0.0	0	0	1	7	—	—	0	0
NFL	5	13 (5)	14	6	0.4 (11)	0	—	—	—	—	148	74	50.0	745	5.0 (36)	2	6	21	161	—	—	0	149

McHale, Joe   Joseph T., LB, 6′2″/227 lbs; Delaware; B9/26/1963 Passaic, NJ   **1987** NE 3 (0)

McHale, Tom   Thomas, G, 6′4″/290 lbs; Cornell; B2/25/1963 Gaithersburg, MD   **1987** TB 3 (0)   **1988** TB 10 (0)   **1989** TB 15 (10, LG)   **1990** TB 7 (7, LG)   **1991** TB 15 (10, LG)   **1992** TB 9 (3)   **1993** Phi 8 (4)   **1994** Phi 13 (2)   **1995** Mia 7 (4)   **NFL** 87 (40) [9 yrs]

McHan, Lamar   Clarence Lamar, QB, 6′1″/201 lbs; Arkansas; 1954: ChiC, rnd 1; B12/16/1932 Lake Village, AR, D11/23/1998 New Orleans, LA [K]

1954	ChiC	12 (QB)	34	152	4.5 (18)	1	—	—	—	—	255	105	41.2	1475	5.8 (70)	6	22	—	—	32.4	P	—	6	50
1955	ChiC	12 (QB)	56	194	3.5 (38)	1	—	—	—	—	207	78	37.7	1085	5.2 (74)	11	19	—	—	34.8	K	—	12	52
1956	ChiC	12 (QB)	58	161	2.8 (17)	5	—	—	—	—	152	72	47.4	1159	7.6 (75)	10	8	—	—	73.3	P	—	30	521
1957	ChiC	12 (QB)	25	82	3.3 (18)	2	—	—	—	—	200	87	43.5	1568	7.8 (83)	11	15	—	—	58.1	—	—	12	341
1958	ChiC	12 (QB)	17	65	3.8 (32)	1	0	1	(1)	0	198	91	46.0	1291	6.5 (71)	12	13	—	—	60.4	P	—	6	261
1959	GB	12 (QB)	16	64	4.0 (19)	0	—	—	—	—	108	48	44.4	805	7.5 (81)	8	9	—	—	—	—	—	0	147
1960	GB	12	8	67	8.4 (35)	1	—	—	—	—	91	33	36.3	517	5.7 (47)	5	5	—	—	—	—	—	6	151
1961	Bal	7	4	1	0.3 (7)	0	—	—	—	—	15	3	20.0	28	1.9 (17)	1	4	—	—	—	—	—	0	-140
1962	Bal	10	4	4	1.0 (5)	0	—	—	—	—	20	10	50.0	278	13.9 (74)	3	2	—	—	—	P	—	0	78
1963	Bal	1	—	—	—	—	—	—	—	—	1	0	0.0	0	0.0	0	0	—	—	—	—	—	0	0
1963	SF	11 (9, QB)	17	59	3.5 (16)	0	—	—	—	—	195	83	42.6	1243	6.4 (68)	8	11	—	—	54.3	—	—	0	281
NFL	10	113 (9)	239	849	3.6 (38)	12	0	1	(1)	0	1442	610	42.3	9449	6.6 (83)	73	108	—	—	50.3	KP	—	72	1739

McHugh, Pat   William Patrick, DB-HB, 5′11″/166 lbs; Georgia Tech; 1946: Phi, rnd 12; B12/21/1919 Selma, AL, D9/19/2004 Ooltewah, TN

1947	†Phi	9 (1)	22	171	7.8 (41)	1	2	16	8.0 (10)	0	—	—	—	—	—	—	—	—	—	—	kpi	1	12	347
1948	†Phi	10 (1)	4	12	3.0 (5)	0	—	—	—	—	—	—	—	—	—	—	—	—	—	pi	—	0	159
1949	†Phi	12 (0)	2	5	2.5 (5)	0	—	—	—	—	—	—	—	—	—	—	—	—	—	pi	1	6	85
1950	Phi	12 (DB)	4	14	3.5 (5)	0	—	—	—	—	—	—	—	—	—	—	—	—	—	ki	—	0	43
1951	Phi	8 (DB)	—	—	—	—	—	—	—	—	—	—	—	—	—	—	—	—	—	i	—	0	14
NFL	5	51 (2)	32	202	6.3 (41)	1	2	16	8.0 (10)	0	—	—	—	—	—	—	—	—	—	kpi	2	18	648

McHugh, Sean   Sean Thomas, FB, 6′3″/284 lbs; Penn State; 2004: Ten, rnd 7; B9/4/1983 Chagrin Falls, OH   **2004** GB 1 (0)   **2005** Det 3 (0)   **NFL** 4 (0) [2 yrs]

McIlhany, Danny   Joseph Daniel, DB, 6′1″/195 lbs; Texas A&M; B1/12/1943 Brownwood, TX   **1965** LARm 10 (RCB)

McIlhenny, Don   Donald Brookes, HB, 6′0″/197 lbs; SMU; 1956: Det, rnd 3; B11/22/1934 Cleveland, OH

1956	Det	9 (rh)	87	372	4.3 (30)	3	8	70	8.8 (21)	2	1	0	0.0	0	0.0	0	—	—	—	—	—	—	30	447
1957	GB	12 (LH)	100	384	3.8 (40)	1	18	210	11.7 (28)	2	—	—	—	—	—	—	—	—	—	—	k	—	18	661
1958	GB	12 (RH)	74	239	3.2 (36)	1	20	154	7.7 (55)	1	—	—	—	—	—	—	—	—	—	—	kp	—	12	367
1959	GB	12	47	231	4.9 (46)	1	8	95	11.9 (30)	1	—	—	—	—	—	—	—	—	—	—	k	—	12	299
1960	Dal	11 (7, HB)	96	321	3.3 (21)	1	15	120	8.0 (64)	1	—	—	—	—	—	—	—	—	—	—	—	—	12	396
1961	Dal	3	2	4	2.0 (4)	0	1	6	6.0 (6)	0	—	—	—	—	—	—	—	—	—	—	—	—	0	7
1961	SF	5	8	30	3.8 (15)	0	—	—	—	—	—	—	—	—	—	—	—	—	—	—	k	—	0	129
NFL	6	64 (7)	414	1581	3.8 (46)	7	70	655	9.4 (64)	7	1	0	0.0	0	0.0	0	—	—	—	—	kp	—	84	2306

McIlwain, Wally   Wallace Wesley, WB, 5′9″/173 lbs; Illinois; B1/20/1903 Chicago, IL, D6/30/1963 Evanston, IL [C]   **1926** Rac 5 (5, WB)

McInally, Pat   Patrick John, WR-P, 6′6″/210 lbs; Harvard; 1975: Cin, rnd 5; B5/7/1953 Villa Park, CA [P]

1976	Cin	14	—	—	—	—	—	—	—	—	—	—	—	—	—	—	—	—	—	—	P	—	0	0
1977	Cin☆	14	1	4	4.0 (4)	0	17	258	15.2 (43)	3	1	1	100.0	4	4.0 (4)	0	0	—	—	—	P	—	18	150
1978	Cin☆	16	—	—	—	—	15	189	12.6 (49)	0	—	—	—	—	—	—	—	—	—	—	P	—	0	95
1979	Cin	16	1	18	18.0 (18)	0	1	24	24.0 (24)	0	—	—	—	—	—	—	—	—	—	—	P	—	0	30

YEAR	TEAM	G (GS, POS)	RUSH	YD	AVG (LG)	TD	REC	YD	AVG (LG)	TD	PASS	COMP	PCT	YD	AVG (LG)	TD	INT	SK	YD	QBR	KPR	OTD	PTS	TAY
1980	Cin	16 (7, wr)	1	0	0.0 (0)	0	18	269	14.9 (59)	2	—	—	—	—	—	—	—	—	—	—	P	—	12	145
1981	†Cin★	16 (1)	1	-27	-27.0 (-27)	0	6	68	11.3 (20)	0	—	—	—	—	—	—	—	—	—	—	P	—	0	7
1982	†Cin	9 (0)	—	—	—	—	—	—	—	—	—	—	—	—	—	—	—	—	—	—	P	—	0	0
1983	Cin	16 (0)	—	—	—	—	—	—	—	—	—	—	—	—	—	—	—	—	—	—	P	—	0	0
1984	Cin	16 (0)	—	—	—	—	—	—	—	—	2	2	100.0	77	38.5 (43)	0	0	—	—	—	P	—	0	39
1985	Cin	16 (0)	1	-2	-2.0 (-2)	0	—	—	—	—	1	0	0.0	0	0.0	0	0	—	—	—	P	—	0	-2
NFL	10	149 (8)	5	-7	-1.4 (18)	0	57	808	14.2 (59)	5	4	3	75.0	81	20.3 (43)	0	0	—	—	—	P	—	30	463

McIndoe, Mac George R., E, none; B12/6/1896 Pitcairn, PA, D1/1958 **1921** Mun 2 (2, LE)

McInerney, Nick Nicholas, C-E-T-FB-G, 6´2˝/201 lbs; none; B4/27/1896 Chicago, IL, D8/1984 **1920** ChiC 8 (5, FB) **1921** ChiC 6 (5, RT) **1922** ChiC 11 (11, C) **1923** ChiC 11 (11, C) **1924** ChiC 9 (8, C) **1925** ChiC 10 (5, le) **1926** ChiC 11 (8, RE) **1927** ChiC 8 (1) **NFL** 74 (54) [8 yrs]

McInerney, Sean Sean Mallan, DE, 6´3˝/255 lbs; Frostburg State; B12/27/1960 **1987** ChiB 3 (3)

McInnis, Hugh Hugh Allen, TE, 6´3˝/228 lbs; Southern Mississippi; 1960: SL, rnd 3/Hou, rnd 1; B9/18/1938 Mobile, AL

YEAR	TEAM	G (GS, POS)	RUSH	YD	AVG (LG)	TD	REC	YD	AVG (LG)	TD	PASS	COMP	PCT	YD	AVG (LG)	TD	INT	SK	YD	QBR	KPR	OTD	PTS	TAY
1960	SL	12 (TE)	—	—	—	—	13	260	20.0 (51)	0	—	—	—	—	—	—	—	—	—	—	—	—	0	130
1961	SL	3 (te)	4	30	7.5 (16)	0	7	107	15.3 (22)	0	—	—	—	—	—	—	—	—	—	—	—	—	0	84
1962	SL	9	—	—	—	—	1	10	10.0 (10)	0	—	—	—	—	—	—	—	—	—	—	—	—	0	5
1964	Det	14	—	—	—	—	1	15	15.0 (15)	0	—	—	—	—	—	—	—	—	—	—	—	—	0	8
NFL	4	38	4	30	7.5 (16)	0	22	392	17.8 (51)	0	—	—	—	—	—	—	—	—	—	—	—	—	0	226

McIntosh, Al Ira Daniel, WB, 5´9˝/180 lbs; Rhode Island; B4/12/1903 Providence, RI, D10/13/1973, CA **1925** Pro 9 (7, WB) **1926** Pro 2 (0) **NFL** 11 (7) [2 yrs]

McIntosh, Chris Chris, T, 6´6˝/315 lbs; Wisconsin; 2000: Sea, rnd 1; B2/20/1977 Pewaukee, WI **2000** Sea 14 (10, RT) **2001** Sea 10 (3) **NFL** 24 (13) [2 yrs]

McIntosh, Damion Damion Alexis, T, 6´4˝/325 lbs; Kansas State; 2000: SD, rnd 3; B3/25/1977 Kingston, Jamaica **2000** SD 3 (0) **2001** SD 15 (14, LT) **2002** SD 10 (10, LT) **2003** SD 13 (13, LT) **2004** Mia 14 (14, LT) **2005** Mia 16 (16, LT) **NFL** 71 (67) [6 yrs]

McIntosh, Joe Joseph Ellison, RB, 5´10˝/192 lbs; North Carolina State; 1985: Det, rnd 5; B12/9/1962 Lexington, NC

YEAR	TEAM	G (GS, POS)	RUSH	YD	AVG (LG)	TD	REC	YD	AVG (LG)	TD	PASS	COMP	PCT	YD	AVG (LG)	TD	INT	SK	YD	QBR	KPR	OTD	PTS	TAY
1987	Atl	2 (0)	5	11	2.2 (5)	0	3	15	5.0 (9)	1	—	—	—	—	—	—	—	—	—	—	k	—	6	87

McIntosh, Toddrick Toddrick Poole, DE, 6´3˝/270 lbs; Florida State; 1994: Dal, rnd 7; B1/22/1972 Tallahassee, FL **1994** TB 4 (0) **1995** TB 11 (1) **NFL** 15 (1) [2 yrs]

McIntyre, Corey Corey, FB, 6´0˝/245 lbs; West Virginia; B1/25/1979 Stuart, FL **2005** Cle 15 (1)

McIntyre, Guy Guy Maurice, G, 6´3˝/275 lbs; Georgia; 1984: SF, rnd 3; B2/17/1961 Thomasville, GA **1984**†SF 15 (0) **1985**†SF 15 (2) **1986**†SF 16 (2) **1987** SF 3 (3) **1989**†SF✧16 (13, LG) **1990**†SF★16 (16, LG) **1991** SF★16 (16, LG) **1992**†SF★16 (16, LG) **1993**†SF✧16 (16, LG) **1994**†GB 10 (10, LG) **1995**†Phi 16 (16, LG)

YEAR	TEAM	G (GS, POS)	RUSH	YD	AVG (LG)	TD	REC	YD	AVG (LG)	TD	PASS	COMP	PCT	YD	AVG (LG)	TD	INT	SK	YD	QBR	KPR	OTD	PTS	TAY
1988	†SF	16 (12, RG)	—	—	—	—	1	17	17.0 (17)	1	—	—	—	—	—	—	—	—	—	—	—	—	6	14
1996	†Phi	15 (2)	—	—	—	—	1	4	4.0 (4)	0	—	—	—	—	—	—	—	—	—	—	—	—	0	2
NFL	13	186 (124)	—	—	—	—	2	21	10.5 (17)	1	—	—	—	—	—	—	—	—	—	—	k	1	12	1

McIntyre, Jeff Jeffrey Glenn, LB, 6´3˝/232 lbs; Arizona State; 1979: Den, rnd 6; B9/20/1955 Beaumont, TX **1979** SF 14 (3) **1980** SL 10 (2) **NFL** 24 (5) [2 yrs]

McIntyre, Secdrick Secdrick, RB, 5´10˝/190 lbs; Auburn; B6/2/1954 Montgomery, AL

YEAR	TEAM	G (GS, POS)	RUSH	YD	AVG (LG)	TD	REC	YD	AVG (LG)	TD	PASS	COMP	PCT	YD	AVG (LG)	TD	INT	SK	YD	QBR	KPR	OTD	PTS	TAY
1977	Atl	6	13	65	5.0 (11)	0	1	27	27.0 (27)	1	—	—	—	—	—	—	—	—	—	—	k	—	6	84

McIver, Everett Everett Allen, G, 6´5˝/318 lbs; Elizabeth City State; B8/5/1970 Cumberland, NC **1994** NYJ 4 (0) **1995** NYJ 14 (4) **1996** Mia 7 (5, rg) **1997**†Mia 14 (14, RG) **1998** Dal 6 (6, rg) **1999**†Dal 14 (14, RG) **NFL** 59 (43) [6 yrs]

McIvor, Rick Richard E., QB, 6´4˝/210 lbs; Texas; 1984: SL, rnd 3; B9/26/1960 Fort Davis, TX **1985** SL 2 (0)

YEAR	TEAM	G (GS, POS)	RUSH	YD	AVG (LG)	TD	REC	YD	AVG (LG)	TD	PASS	COMP	PCT	YD	AVG (LG)	TD	INT	SK	YD	QBR	KPR	OTD	PTS	TAY
1984	SL	4 (0)	3	5	1.7 (6)	0	—	—	—	—	4	0	0.0	0	0.0	0	0	—	—	—	—	—	0	5
NFL	2	6 (0)	3	5	1.7 (6)	0	—	—	—	—	4	0	0.0	0	0.0	0	0	—	—	—	—	—	0	5

McJulien, Paul Paul Dorien, P, 5´10˝/190 lbs; Jackson State; B2/24/1965 Chicago, IL

YEAR	TEAM	G (GS, POS)	RUSH	YD	AVG (LG)	TD	REC	YD	AVG (LG)	TD	PASS	COMP	PCT	YD	AVG (LG)	TD	INT	SK	YD	QBR	KPR	OTD	PTS	TAY
1991	GB	16 (0)	1	0	0.0 (0)	0	—	—	—	—	—	—	—	—	—	—	—	—	—	—	P	—	0	0
1992	GB	9 (0)	—	—	—	—	—	—	—	—	1	0	0.0	0	0.0	0	0	—	—	—	P	—	0	0
1993	LARm	5 (0)	—	—	—	—	—	—	—	—	—	—	—	—	—	—	—	—	—	—	P	—	0	0
NFL	3	30 (0)	1	0	0.0	0	—	—	—	—	1	0	0.0	0	0.0	0	0	—	—	—	P	—	0	0

McKalip, Bill William Ward, E-WB, 6´1˝/195 lbs; Oregon State; B6/5/1907 Pittsburgh, PA, D7/11/1993 Corvallis, OR

YEAR	TEAM	G (GS, POS)	RUSH	YD	AVG (LG)	TD	REC	YD	AVG (LG)	TD	PASS	COMP	PCT	YD	AVG (LG)	TD	INT	SK	YD	QBR	KPR	OTD	PTS	TAY
1931	Por☆	14 (8, LE)	—	—	—	—	—	—	—	—	—	—	—	—	—	—	—	—	—	—	—	—	—	—
1932	Por	12 (12, LE)	—	—	—	—	5	105	21.0	0	—	—	—	—	—	—	—	—	—	—	—	—	0	53
1934	Det☆	13 (7, LE)	19	63	3.3	0	6	97	16.2	0	—	—	—	—	—	—	—	—	—	—	—	—	0	112
1936	Det	10 (4)	7	39	5.6	0	1	10	10.0 (10)	0	—	—	—	—	—	—	—	—	—	—	—	—	0	44
NFL	4	49 (31)	26	102	3.9	0	12	212	17.7 (10)	4	—	—	—	—	—	—	—	—	—	—	—	—	24	228

McKay, Bob Robert Charles, T-G, 6´5˝/260 lbs; Texas; 1970: Cle, rnd 1; B12/27/1947 Seminole, TX **1970** Cle 8 **1971**†Cle 14 (RT) **1972**†Cle 10 (RT) **1973** Cle 14 (RT) **1974** Cle 14 (lg/rt) **1975** Cle 7 (7, RG) **1976**†NE 14 (14, RT) **1977** NE 12 (3) **1978** NE 12 **NFL** 105 (24) [9 yrs]

McKay, John John Kenneth, WR, 5´11˝/182 lbs; USC; 1975: Cle, rnd 16; B3/28/1953 Eugene, OR

YEAR	TEAM	G (GS, POS)	RUSH	YD	AVG (LG)	TD	REC	YD	AVG (LG)	TD	PASS	COMP	PCT	YD	AVG (LG)	TD	INT	SK	YD	QBR	KPR	OTD	PTS	TAY
1976	TB	14 (13, WR)	—	—	—	—	20	302	15.1 (49)	1	—	—	—	—	—	—	—	—	—	—	—	—	6	156
1977	TB	14 (10, WR)	—	—	—	—	12	164	13.7 (26)	0	—	—	—	—	—	—	—	—	—	—	—	—	0	82
1978	TB	15 (7, WR)	—	—	—	—	9	166	18.4 (28)	1	—	—	—	—	—	—	—	—	—	—	—	—	6	88
NFL	3	43 (30)	—	—	—	—	41	632	15.4 (49)	2	—	—	—	—	—	—	—	—	—	—	—	—	12	326

McKay, Roy Roy Dale, TB-HB-FB, 6´0˝/193 lbs; Texas; 1943: GB, rnd 5; B2/2/1920 Mason City, TX, D5/29/1969 Sutton County, TX **[K]**

YEAR	TEAM	G (GS, POS)	RUSH	YD	AVG (LG)	TD	REC	YD	AVG (LG)	TD	PASS	COMP	PCT	YD	AVG (LG)	TD	INT	SK	YD	QBR	KPR	OTD	PTS	TAY
1944	GB	3 (1)	5	12	2.4 (11)	0	—	—	—	—	14	6	42.9	72	5.1 (26)	1	2	—	—	—	Pp	—	0	-18
1945	GB	10 (1, tb)	71	231	3.3 (41)	2	—	—	—	—	89	32	36.0	520	5.8 (59)	5	9	—	—	—	Pkpi	—	12	232
1946	GB	11 (0)	21	34	1.6 (9)	1	—	—	—	—	—	—	—	—	—	—	—	—	—	—	KPki	—	8	70
1947	GB	11 (1)	3	11	3.7 (5)	0	—	—	—	—	—	—	—	—	—	—	—	—	—	—	KP	—	1	11
NFL	4	35 (3)	100	288	2.9 (41)	3	—	—	—	—	103	38	36.9	592	5.7 (59)	6	11	—	—	—	KPkpi	—	21	295

McKee, Paul Paul Melvin, E, 6´3˝/217 lbs; Rochester; Syracuse; 1945: Was, rnd 12; B4/26/1923 Beaver Falls, PA

YEAR	TEAM	G (GS, POS)	RUSH	YD	AVG (LG)	TD	REC	YD	AVG (LG)	TD	PASS	COMP	PCT	YD	AVG (LG)	TD	INT	SK	YD	QBR	KPR	OTD	PTS	TAY
1947	Was	11 (3, LE)	—	—	—	—	16	242	15.1 (29)	2	—	—	—	—	—	—	—	—	—	—	—	—	12	131
1948	Was	12 (6, LE)	—	—	—	—	14	171	12.2 (22)	0	—	—	—	—	—	—	—	—	—	—	—	—	0	86
NFL	2	23 (9)	—	—	—	—	30	413	13.8 (29)	2	—	—	—	—	—	—	—	—	—	—	—	—	12	217

McKeehan, James James Bell, TE, 6´3˝/251 lbs; Texas A&M; B8/9/1973 Houston, TX **1996** Hou 14 (0) **1997** Ten 10 (0) **NFL** 24 (0) [2 yrs]

McKeever, Marlin Marlin Thomas, LB-TE, 6´1˝/235 lbs; USC; 1961: LA, rnd 1/SD, rnd 3; B1/1/1940 Cheyenne, WY **1961** LARm 3 **1962** LARm 14 (LLB) **1968** Was 14 **1969** Was 12 **1970** Was 14 (12, MLB) **1971** LARm 14 (14, MLB) **1972** LARm 14 (14, MLB) **1973** Phi 13 (MLB)

YEAR	TEAM	G (GS, POS)	RUSH	YD	AVG (LG)	TD	REC	YD	AVG (LG)	TD	PASS	COMP	PCT	YD	AVG (LG)	TD	INT	SK	YD	QBR	KPR	OTD	PTS	TAY
1963	LARm	13 (LLB/te)	—	—	—	—	11	152	13.8 (29)	0	—	—	—	—	—	—	—	—	—	—	k	—	0	54
1964	LARm	14 (TE)	—	—	—	—	41	582	14.2 (46)	1	—	—	—	—	—	—	—	—	—	—	—	—	6	296
1965	LARm	12 (TE)	—	—	—	—	44	542	12.3 (47)	4	—	—	—	—	—	—	—	—	—	—	—	—	24	291
1966	LARm✧	11	—	—	—	—	23	277	12.0 (31)	1	—	—	—	—	—	—	—	—	—	—	k	—	6	137
1967	Min	14 (14, TE)	—	—	—	—	14	184	13.1 (42)	0	—	—	—	—	—	—	—	—	—	—	—	—	0	92
NFL	13	162 (54)	—	—	—	—	133	1737	13.1 (47)	6	—	—	—	—	—	—	—	—	—	—	ki	—	36	867

McKeever, Vito Juan Devito, DB, 6´0˝/180 lbs; Florida; B10/8/1961 Inverness, FL **1986** TB 16 (8, LCB) **1987** TB 1 (0) **NFL** 17 (8) [2 yrs]

McKeller, Keith Terrell Keith, TE-WR, 6´6˝/240 lbs; Jacksonville State; 1987: Buf, rnd 9; B7/9/1964 Birmingham, AL

YEAR	TEAM	G (GS, POS)	RUSH	YD	AVG (LG)	TD	REC	YD	AVG (LG)	TD	PASS	COMP	PCT	YD	AVG (LG)	TD	INT	SK	YD	QBR	KPR	OTD	PTS	TAY
1987	Buf	1 (1)	—	—	—	—	9	80	8.9 (22)	0	—	—	—	—	—	—	—	—	—	—	—	—	0	40
1988	†Buf	12 (0)	—	—	—	—	—	—	—	—	—	—	—	—	—	—	—	—	—	—	—	—	—	—
1989	†Buf	16 (7, WR)	—	—	—	—	20	341	17.0 (39)	2	—	—	—	—	—	—	—	—	—	—	—	—	12	181
1990	†Buf	16 (14, TE)	—	—	—	—	34	464	13.6 (43)	5	—	—	—	—	—	—	—	—	—	—	—	—	30	257
1991	†Buf	16 (14, TE)	—	—	—	—	44	434	9.9 (29)	3	—	—	—	—	—	—	—	—	—	—	—	—	18	232
1992	†Buf	11 (8, TE)	—	—	—	—	14	110	7.9 (26)	0	—	—	—	—	—	—	—	—	—	—	—	—	0	55
1993	†Buf	8 (1)	—	—	—	—	3	35	11.7 (13)	1	—	—	—	—	—	—	—	—	—	—	—	—	6	23
NFL	7	80 (45)	—	—	—	—	124	1464	11.8 (43)	11	—	—	—	—	—	—	—	—	—	—	—	—	66	787

YEAR	TEAM	G (GS, POS)	RUSH	YD	AVG(LG)	TD	REC	YD	AVG(LG)	TD	PASS	COMP	PCT	YD	AVG(LG)	TD	INT	SK	YD	QBR	KPR	OTD	PTS	TAY

McKENZIE, CHRIS Chris, DB, 5´8˝/182 lbs; Arizona State; B3/17/1982 New York, NY   **2005** Hou 3 (0)

McKENZIE, KAREEM Kareem Michael, T, 6´6˝/327 lbs; Penn State; 2001: NYJ, rnd 3; B5/24/1979 Willingboro, NJ   **2001** NYJ 8 (0)   **2002**†NYJ 16 (16, RT)   **2003** NYJ 16 (16, RT)   **2004**†NYJ 16 (16, RT)   **2005**†NYG 14 (14, RT)   **NFL** 70 (62) [5 yrs]

McKENZIE, KEITH Keith Derrick, DE, 6´3˝/267 lbs; Ball State; 1996: GB, rnd 7; B10/17/1973 Detroit, MI   **1996**†GB 10 (0)   **1997**†GB 16 (16)   **1998**†GB 16 (0)   **1999** GB 16 (2)   **2000** Cle 16 (16, RDE)   **2001** Cle 7 (6, RDE)   **2002** ChiB 4 (3)   **2002** GB 4 (0)   **2003** Buf 6 (0)   **NFL** 95 (27) [8 yrs]

McKENZIE, KEVIN Kevin Eugene, WR, 5´9˝/187 lbs; Washington State; B9/20/1975 Los Angeles, CA

| 1999 | Mia | — | — | — | — | — | 2 | 18 | 9.0(13) | 0 | — | — | — | — | — | — | — | — | — | — | — | — | 0 | 9 |

McKENZIE, MIKE Michael Terrence, DB, 6´0˝/194 lbs; Memphis; 1999: GB, rnd 3; B4/26/1976 Miami, FL [I]   **1999** GB 16 (16, LCB)   **2000** GB 10 (8, LCB)   **2001**†GB 16 (16, LCB)   **2002**†GB 13 (13, LCB)   **2003**†GB 14 (14, LCB)   **2004** GB 1 (0)   **2004** NO 10 (10, LCB)   **2005** NO 15 (15, LCB)   **NFL** 95 (92) [7 yrs]

McKENZIE, RALEIGH Raleigh, G-C-T, 6´2˝/283 lbs; Tennessee; 1985: Was, rnd 11; B2/8/1963 Knoxville, TN   **1985** Was 6 (0)   **1986**†Was 15 (5, rg)   **1987**†Was 12 (12, LG)   **1988** Was 16 (14, LG/c)   **1989** Was 15 (8, lg)   **1990**†Was 16 (12, RG)   **1991**†Was☆16 (14, LG)   **1992**†Was 16 (16, C)   **1993** Was 16 (16, RG/c)   **1994** Was 16 (16, RG)   **1995**†Phi 16 (16, C)   **1996**†Phi 16 (16, RG/rt)   **1999** SD 16 (16, C)   **NFL** 226 (184) [16 yrs]

McKENZIE, REGGIE Reginald, G, 6´4˝/255 lbs; Michigan; 1972: Buf, rnd 2; B7/27/1950 Detroit, MI   **1972** Buf 14 (14, LG)   **1973** Buf☆14 (14, LG)   **1974**†Buf☆14 (14, LG)   **1975** Buf☆14 (14, LG)   **1976** Buf☆14 (14, LG)   **1977** Buf 14 (14, LG)   **1978** Buf 16 (16, LG)   **1979** Buf 16 (16, LG)   **1980**†Buf☆16 (16, LG)   **1981** Buf 6 (6, lg)   **1982** Buf 9 (9, LG)   **1983** Sea 14 (14, LG)   **1984** Sea 10 (8, LG)   **NFL** 171 (169) [13 yrs]

McKENZIE, REGGIE Reginald, LB, 6´1˝/240 lbs; Tennessee; 1985: LARd, rnd 10; B2/8/1963 Knoxville, TN   **1985**†LARd 16 (16, RILB)   **1986** LARd 16 (16, RILB)   **1987** LARd 10 (5, rilb)   **1988** LARd 16 (3)   **1992** SF 2 (0)   **NFL** 60 (40) [5 yrs]

McKENZIE, RICH Richard Anthony, LB, 6´2˝/258 lbs; Penn State; 1993: Cle, rnd 6; B4/15/1971 Fort Lauderdale, FL   **1995** Cle 8 (0)

McKETES, JACK Jack, BB, none   **1926** Ham 1 (0)

McKIBBEN, MIKE Michael Wayne, LB, 6´3˝/228 lbs; Kent State; B9/3/1956 Mount Carmel, IL   **1979** NYJ 16 (10, RLB)   **1980** NYJ 9 (1)   **NFL** 25 (11) [2 yrs]

McKIE, JASON Jason, FB, 5´11˝/231 lbs; Temple; B5/22/1980 Gulf Breeze, FL

2002	Dal	1(1)	—	—	—	—	1	7	7.0(7)	0	—	—	—	—	—	—	—	—	—	—	—	—	0	4
2003	ChiB	6(0)	—	—	—	—	—	—	—	—	—	—	—	—	—	—	—	—	—	—	—	—		
2004	ChiB	15(2)	1	1	1.0(1)	0	13	70	5.4(15)	2	—	—	—	—	—	—	—	—	—	—	k	—	12	66
2005	†ChiB	8(2)	3	22	7.3(13)	0	4	15	3.8(11)	0	—	—	—	—	—	—	—	—	—	—	k	—	0	14
NFL	4	30(5)	4	23	5.8(13)	0	18	92	5.1(15)	2	—	—	—	—	—	—	—	—	—	—	k	—	12	83

McKINLEY, ALVIN Alvin Jerome, DE-DT, 6´3˝/310 lbs; Mississippi State; 2000: Car, rnd 4; B6/9/1978 Kosciusko, MS   **2000** Car 7 (0)   **2001** Cle 7 (0)   **2002**†Cle 13 (0)   **2003** Cle 9 (0)   **2004** Cle 16 (2)   **2005** Cle 16 (16, RDE)   **NFL** 68 (18) [6 yrs]

McKINLEY, BILL William James, DE-LB, 6´2˝/240 lbs; Arizona; 1971: Buf, rnd 6; B1/14/1949 Vincennes, IN   **1971** Buf 7

McKINLEY, DENNIS Dennis L., FB, 6´2˝/250 lbs; Mississippi State; 1999: Arz, rnd 6; B11/3/1976 Kosciusko, MS

1999	Arz	16(0)	—	—	—	—	1	4	4.0(4)	0	—	—	—	—	—	—	—	—	—	—	—	—	0	2
2000	Arz	16(0)	—	—	—	—	2	13	6.5(9)	0	—	—	—	—	—	—	—	—	—	—	k	—	0	12
2001	Arz	14(0)	1	1	1.0(1)	0	1	10	10.0(10)	0	—	—	—	—	—	—	—	—	—	—	k	—	0	2
2002	Arz	12(1)	—	—	—	—	—	—	—	—	—	—	—	—	—	—	—	—	—	—	—	—	0	0
NFL	4	58(1)	1	1	1.0(1)	0	4	27	6.8(10)	0	—	—	—	—	—	—	—	—	—	—	k	—	0	16

McKINNELY, PHIL Philip Byron, T-G-TE, 6´4˝/248 lbs; UCLA; 1976: Atl, rnd 9; B7/8/1954 Oakland, CA   **1976** Atl 12   **1977** Atl 14   **1978**†Atl 14 (4)   **1979** Atl 15   **1980**†Atl 7 (0)   **1981** LARm 7 (0)   **1982** ChiB 8 (8, LT)   **NFL** 77 (12) [7 yrs]

McKINNEY, BILL William C., LB, 6´1˝/226 lbs; West Texas A&M; 1972: Chi, rnd 16; B7/14/1945 Borger, TX   **1972** ChiB 8

McKINNEY, JEREMY Jeremy Adam, G, 6´6˝/301 lbs; Iowa; B1/6/1976 Huntington Park, CA   **2001** Cle 15 (9, RG)   **2002** Dal 3 (2)   **NFL** 18 (11) [2 yrs]

McKINNEY, ODIS Odis, DB, 6´2˝/187 lbs; Colorado; 1978: NYG, rnd 2; B5/19/1957 Detroit, MI   **1978** NYG 14 (6, ss)   **1979** NYG 15   **1980**†Oak 16 (0)   **1981** Oak 16 (14, SS)   **1982**†LARd 9 (1)   **1983**†LARd 16 (0)   **1984**†LARd 16 (1)   **1985** KC 5 (1)   **1986** LARd 2 (0)   **NFL** 119 (26) [9 yrs]

McKINNEY, ROYCE Royce William, DB, 6´1˝/190 lbs; Kentucky State; 1975: Bal, rnd 9; B11/3/1953 River Rouge, MI   **1975** Buf 9 (1)

McKINNEY, SETH Seth Alan, C, 6´3˝/305 lbs; Texas A&M; 2002: Mia, rnd 3; B6/12/1979 Buffalo, TX   **2002** Mia 16 (2)   **2003** Mia 16 (3)   **2004** Mia 16 (16, C)   **2005** Mia 13 (13, C)   **NFL** 61 (34) [4 yrs]

McKINNEY, STEVE Stephen Michael, C-G, 6´4˝/295 lbs; Texas A&M; 1998: Ind, rnd 4; B10/15/1975 Galveston, TX   **1998** Ind 16 (16, LG)   **1999**†Ind 14 (14, LG)   **2000**†Ind 16 (16, LG)   **2002** Hou 16 (16, C)   **2003** Hou 16 (16, C)   **2004** Hou 16 (16, C)   **2005** Hou 16 (16, C)

| 2001 | Ind | 14(14, LG) | — | — | — | — | 1 | 5 | 5.0(5) | 0 | — | — | — | — | — | — | — | — | — | — | — | — | 0 | 3 |
| NFL | 8 | 124(124) | — | — | — | — | 1 | 5 | 5.0(5) | 0 | — | — | — | — | — | — | — | — | — | — | — | — | 0 | 3 |

McKINNEY, ZION Zion Bailus, WR, 6´0˝/200 lbs; South Carolina; B2/10/1958 Pickens, SC   **1980** Was 10 (0)

McKINNIE, BRYANT Bryant Douglas, T, 6´8˝/346 lbs; Miami (FL); 2002: Min, rnd 1; B9/23/1979 Woodbury, NJ   **2002** Min 8 (7, LT)   **2003** Min 16 (16, LT)   **2004** Min 16 (16, LT)   **2005** Min 16 (16, LT)   **NFL** 56 (55) [4 yrs]

McKINNIS, HUGH Hugh Lee, RB, 6´0˝/225 lbs; Arizona State; 1972: Cle, rnd 8; B6/9/1948 Sharon, PA

1973	Cle	14	28	77	2.8(12)	0	3	11	3.7(12)	0	—	—	—	—	—	—	—	—	—	—	—	—	0	83
1974	Cle	13(FB)	124	519	4.2(44)	2	32	258	8.1(55)	0	—	—	—	—	—	—	—	—	—	—	—	—	12	668
1975	Cle	14(FB)	71	259	3.6(14)	4	17	155	9.1(20)	0	—	—	—	—	—	—	—	—	—	—	k	—	24	371
1976	Sea	11(5, fb)	46	105	2.3(14)	4	13	148	11.4(22)	0	—	—	—	—	—	—	—	—	—	—	—	—	24	219
NFL	4	52(5)	269	960	3.6(44)	10	65	572	8.8(55)	0	—	—	—	—	—	—	—	—	—	—	k	—	60	1340

McKINNON, DENNIS Dennis Lewis, WR, 6´1˝/185 lbs; Florida State; B8/22/1961 Quitman, GA [R]

1983	ChiB	16(3)	—	—	—	—	20	326	16.3(49)	4	—	—	—	—	—	—	—	—	—	—	kp	1	30	351
1984	†ChiB	12(12, WR)	2	12	6.0(21)	0	29	431	14.9(32)	3	—	—	—	—	—	—	—	—	—	—	p	—	18	280
1985	†ChiB	14(13, WR)	1	0	0.0(0)	0	31	555	17.9(48)	7	—	—	—	—	—	—	—	—	—	—	kp	—	42	338
1987	ChiB	12(0)	—	—	—	—	27	406	15.0(33)	1	—	—	—	—	—	—	—	—	—	—	p	2	18	433
1988	†ChiB	15(15, WR)	3	25	8.3(12)	1	45	704	15.6(76)	3	—	—	—	—	—	—	—	—	—	—	p	—	24	509
1989	ChiB	16(10, WR)	3	5	1.7(3)	0	28	418	14.9(41)	3	—	—	—	—	—	—	—	—	—	—	p	—	18	246
1990	Dal	9(7, wr)	1	-8	-8.0(-8)	0	14	172	12.3(28)	1	—	—	—	—	—	—	—	—	—	—	p	—	6	93
NFL	7	94(60)	10	34	3.4(21)	1	194	3012	15.5(76)	22	—	—	—	—	—	—	—	—	—	—	kp	3	156	2249

McKINNON, DON Donald Bruce, LB-C, 6´3˝/230 lbs; Dartmouth; 1963: Bos, rnd 10/NYG, rnd 11; B8/28/1941 Arlington, MA   **1963**†Bos-A 14   **1964** Bos-A 3   **NFL** 17 [2 yrs]

McKINNON, RONALD Ronald, LB, 6´0˝/246 lbs; North Alabama; B9/20/1973 Fort Rucker, AL   **1998**†Arz 13 (13, MLB)   **1999** Arz 16 (16, MLB)   **2000** Arz 16 (16, MLB)   **2001** Arz 16 (16, MLB)   **2002** Arz 16 (16, MLB)   **2003** Arz 16 (16, MLB)   **2004** Arz 16 (10, MLB)   **2005** NO 16 (9, MLB)

1996	Arz	16(0)	1	-4	-4.0(-4)	0	—	—	—	—	—	—	—	—	—	—	—	—	—	—	iS	—	0	-4
1997	Arz	16(16, RLB/mlb)	1	3	3.0(3)	0	—	—	—	—	—	—	—	—	—	—	—	—	—	—	iS	—	0	28
NFL	10	157(128)	2	-1	-0.5(3)	0	—	—	—	—	—	—	—	—	—	—	—	—	—	—	kiS	2	12	42

McKISSACK, DICK James Richard, DB, 6´2˝/208 lbs; SMU; 1950: LA, rnd 5; B2/10/1926 San Antonio, TX, D8/28/1982 Dallas, TX   **1952** DalT 1 (1)

McKNIGHT, DENNIS Dennis Neal, G-C, 6´3˝/273 lbs; Drake; B9/12/1959 Dallas, TX   **1982**†SD 7 (0)   **1983** SD 16 (9, c)   **1984** SD 16 (16, RG)   **1985** SD 16 (16, RG)   **1986** SD 16 (16, RG)   **1987** SD 12 (12, RG)   **1988** SD 16 (16, RG)   **1990** Det 14 (10, RG)   **1991** Phi 16 (13, LG)   **1992** Det 12 (2)   **NFL** 141 (100) [10 yrs]

McKNIGHT, JAMES James, WR, 6´1˝/198 lbs; Liberty; B6/17/1972 Orlando, FL

1994	Sea	2(0)	—	—	—	—	1	25	25.0(25)	1	—	—	—	—	—	—	—	—	—	—	—	—	6	18
1995	Sea	16(0)	—	—	—	—	6	91	15.2(24)	0	—	—	—	—	—	—	—	—	—	—	k	—	0	35
1996	Sea	16(0)	—	—	—	—	1	73	73.0(73)	0	—	—	—	—	—	—	—	—	—	—	—	—	0	78
1997	Sea	12(6, wr)	—	—	—	—	34	637	18.7(60)	6	—	—	—	—	—	—	—	—	—	—	k	—	36	348
1998	Sea	14(3)	—	—	—	—	21	346	16.5(59)	2	—	—	—	—	—	—	—	—	—	—	—	—	12	183
2000	Dal	16(15, WR)	—	—	—	—	52	926	17.8(48)	2	—	—	—	—	—	—	—	—	—	—	—	—	12	473
2001	†Mia	16(15, WR)	6	39	6.5(18)	0	55	684	12.4(40)	3	—	—	—	—	—	—	—	—	—	—	—	—	20	396

YEAR	TEAM	G(GS, POS)	RUSH	YD	AVG(LG)	TD	REC	YD	AVG(LG)	TD	PASS	COMP	PCT	YD	AVG(LG)	TD	INT	SK	YD	QBR	KPR	OTD	PTS	TAY
2002	Mia	15(9, WR)	7	58	8.3(19)	0	29	528	18.2(77)	2	—	—	—	—	—	—	—	—	—	—	—	—	12	358
2003	Mia	15(1)	2	75	37.5(68)	1	23	285	12.4(80)	2	—	—	—	—	—	—	—	—	—	—	—	—	18	266
NFL	9	122(49)	15	172	11.5(68)	1	222	3595	16.2(80)	18	—	—	—	—	—	—	—	—	—	—	k	—	116	2153

McKnight, Ted Theodore Robert, RB, 6´1˝/209 lbs; Minnesota-Duluth; 1977: Oak, rnd 2; B2/26/1954 Duluth, MN

YEAR	TEAM	G(GS, POS)	RUSH	YD	AVG(LG)	TD	REC	YD	AVG(LG)	TD	PASS	COMP	PCT	YD	AVG(LG)	TD	INT	SK	YD	QBR	KPR	OTD	PTS	TAY
1977	KC	13	11	74	6.7(19)	0	1	11	11.0(11)	0	—	—	—	—	—	—	—	—	—	—	k	—	0	205
1978	KC	16(16, RH)	104	627	6.0(41)	6	14	83	5.9(19)	1	—	—	—	—	—	—	—	—	—	—	k	—	42	754
1979	KC	15(14, FB)	153	755	4.9(84)	8	38	226	5.9(24)	0	—	—	—	—	—	—	—	—	—	—	k	—	48	952
1980	KC	16(16, FB)	206	693	3.4(25)	3	38	320	8.4(26)	0	—	—	—	—	—	—	—	—	—	—	—	—	18	883
1981	KC	5(5, rb)	54	195	3.6(26)	5	8	77	9.6(23)	0	—	—	—	—	—	—	—	—	—	—	—	—	30	284
1982	Buf	3(0)	—	—	—	—	—	—	—	—	—	—	—	—	—	—	—	—	—	—	k	—	0	-11
NFL	6	68(51)	528	2344	4.4(84)	22	99	717	7.2(26)	1	—	—	—	—	—	—	—	—	—	—	k	—	138	3066

McKoy, Bill William Edmond, LB, 6´3˝/235 lbs; Purdue; 1970: Den, rnd 5; B7/17/1948 Winston-Salem, NC **1970** Den 2 **1971** Den 14 **1972** Den 14 (9, mlb) **1974** SF 14 **NFL** 44 (9) [4 yrs]

McKyer, Tim Timothy Bernard, DB, 6´0˝/174 lbs; Texas-Arlington; 1986: SF, rnd 3; B9/5/1963 Orlando, FL **[I]** **1986†**SF 16 (16, LCB) **1987†**SF 12 (12, LCB) **1988†**SF☆16 (16, LCB) **1989†**SF 7 (1) **1990†**Mia☆16 (16, LCB) **1991†**Atl 16 (16, LCB) **1992** Atl 16 (16, LCB) **1993†**Det 15 (3) **1994†**Pit 16 (2) **1995** Car 16 (16, RCB/lcb) **1996** Atl 8 (7, lcb) **1997†**Den 16 (1) **NFL** 170 (122) [12 yrs]

McLain, Chief Mayes Watt, FB-HB, 6´3˝/225 lbs; Haskell Indian; Iowa; B4/16/1905 Pryor, OK, D3/6/1983 Marietta, GA **1930** Por 14 (4), 42 **1931** Por 1 (1) **1931** SI 9 (5, fb), 12 **NFL** 24 (10), 54 [2 yrs]

McLain, Kevin Kevin Wayne, LB, 6´2˝/230 lbs; Colorado State; 1976: LA, rnd 1; B9/15/1954 Tulsa, OK **1976†**LARm 14 **1977** LARm 8 **1978†**LARm 16 **1979** LARm 10 **NFL** 48 [4 yrs]

McLaughlin, Charlie Charles Edward, TB, 6´0˝/183 lbs; Wichita State; B3/11/1910, D2/1983 Pamplin, VA

YEAR	TEAM	G(GS, POS)	RUSH	YD	AVG(LG)	TD	REC	YD	AVG(LG)	TD	PASS	COMP	PCT	YD	AVG(LG)	TD	INT	SK	YD	QBR	KPR	OTD	PTS	TAY
1934	SL	1(1)	6	22	3.7	0	—	—	—	—	4	2	50.0	18	4.5	0	1	—	—	—	—	—	0	-9

McLaughlin, Joe Joseph James, LB, 6´1˝/235 lbs; Massachusetts; B7/1/1957 Stoneham, MA **1979** GB 3 **1980** NYG 8 (3) **1981†**NYG 16 (0) **1982** NYG 8 (0) **1983** NYG 7 (1) **1984†**NYG 16 (5, lilb) **NFL** 58 (9) [6 yrs]

McLaughlin, John John Raymond, DE, 6´4˝/247 lbs; Notre Dame; California; 1999: TB, rnd 5; B11/13/1975 Cleveland, OH **1999†**TB 12 (0) **2000†**TB 6 (0) **NFL** 18 (0) [2 yrs]

McLaughlin, Lee Lee Massey, G, 6´1˝/225 lbs; Virginia; B2/28/1917 Brownsburg, VA, D8/13/1968 Lexington, VA **1941†**GB 8 (8, LG)

McLaughlin, Leon Leon Clifford, C, 6´2˝/228 lbs; UCLA; 1947: LARm, rnd 21/1948: LAD-A, rnd 29; B5/30/1925 San Diego, CA **1951†**LARm 12 (C) **1952†**LARm 12 (C) **1953** LARm 12 (C) **1954** LARm✧12 (C) **1955†**LARm 12 (C) **NFL** 60 [5 yrs]

McLaughlin, Steve Steven John, K, 6´0˝/167 lbs; Arizona; 1995: SL, rnd 3; B10/2/1971 Tucson, AZ **[K]** **1995** SL 8 (0)

McLaughlin, Tom Thomas Flynn, FB, 5´10˝/185 lbs; Notre Dame; B1/22/1889, Ireland, D6/1964, NY **1921** Ton 1 (1, FB)

McLaughry, John John Jackson, BB, 6´1˝/205 lbs; Brown; 1940: NYG, rnd 3; B4/8/1917 New Wilmington, PA

YEAR	TEAM	G(GS, POS)	RUSH	YD	AVG(LG)	TD	REC	YD	AVG(LG)	TD	PASS	COMP	PCT	YD	AVG(LG)	TD	INT	SK	YD	QBR	KPR	OTD	PTS	TAY
1940	NYG	9(0)	—	—	—	—	1	-1	-1.0(-1)	0	—	—	—	—	—	—	—	—	—	—	—	—	0	-1

McLean, Ray Raymond, FB-HB, 5´7˝/155 lbs; none; B9/13/1897, D10/1967 Detroit, MI **1921** GB 3 (0)

McLean, Ray Raymond 'Scooter', HB, 5´10˝/168 lbs; St. Anselm; 1940: ChiB, rnd 21; B12/6/1915 Lowell, MA, D3/4/1964 Ann Arbor, MI **[KC]**

YEAR	TEAM	G(GS, POS)	RUSH	YD	AVG(LG)	TD	REC	YD	AVG(LG)	TD	PASS	COMP	PCT	YD	AVG(LG)	TD	INT	SK	YD	QBR	KPR	OTD	PTS	TAY
1940	†ChiB✧	10(0)	14	10	0.7(5)	1	6	138	23.0	2	—	—	—	—	—	—	—	—	—	—	Ki	1	25	109
1941	†ChiB✧	10(0)	13	78	6.0(21)	1	5	84	16.8(40)	1	—	—	—	—	—	—	—	—	—	—	kpi	1	18	294
1942	†ChiB☆	11(2)	26	63	2.4(15)	0	19	571	30.1(68)	8	—	—	—	—	—	—	—	—	—	—	kpi	1	54	592
1943	†ChiB	10(0)	35	127	3.6(34)	1	18	435	24.2(66)	2	—	—	—	—	—	—	—	—	—	—	Kkpi	—	18	469
1944	ChiB	8(1)	29	25	0.9(8)	1	19	414	21.8(**86**)	5	—	—	—	—	—	—	—	—	—	—	kpi	1	42	375
1945	ChiB	5(1)	9	22	2.4(15)	0	8	117	14.6(43)	0	—	—	—	—	—	—	—	—	—	—	kpi	—	0	148
1946	†ChiB	10(3)	16	29	1.8(11)	1	17	348	20.5(48)	2	—	—	—	—	—	—	—	—	—	—	kpi	—	18	299
1947	ChiB	12(0)	10	58	5.8(24)	0	11	125	11.4(19)	1	—	—	—	—	—	—	—	—	—	—	Kkpi	—	50	171
NFL	8	76(7)	152	412	2.7(34)	5	103	2232	21.7(86)	21	—	—	—	—	—	—	—	—	—	—	Kkpi	4	225	2455

McLean, Ron Ronald James, NT-DE, 6´3˝/270 lbs; Cal State-Fullerton; 1987: NYJ, rnd 9; B4/13/1963 Everett, WA **1987** Den 3 (0) **1988** KC 6 (0) **NFL** 9 (0) [2 yrs]

McLean, Scott Robert Scott, LB, 6´4˝/231 lbs; Florida State; B12/16/1960 Clermont, FL **1983** Dal 4 (0)

McLemore, Chris Christopher Clark, RB, 6´1˝/232 lbs; Colorado; Arizona; 1987: LARd, rnd 11; B12/31/1963 Las Vegas, NV **1987** LARd 3 (0) **1988** LARd 7 (0)

YEAR	TEAM	G(GS, POS)	RUSH	YD	AVG(LG)	TD	REC	YD	AVG(LG)	TD	PASS	COMP	PCT	YD	AVG(LG)	TD	INT	SK	YD	QBR	KPR	OTD	PTS	TAY
1987	Ind	2(2)	17	58	3.4(9)	0	2	9	4.5(5)	0	—	—	—	—	—	—	—	—	—	—	—	—	0	63
NFL	2	12(2)	17	58	3.4(9)	0	2	9	4.5(5)	0	—	—	—	—	—	—	—	—	—	—	—	—	0	63

McLemore, Dana Dana, DB, 5´10˝/183 lbs; Hawaii; 1982: SF, rnd 10; B7/1/1960 Los Angeles, CA **[R]** **1982** SF 8 (0) **1983†**SF 14 (0) **1984†**SF 16 (0) **1985†**SF 16 (0) **1986** SF 3 (0) **1986** NO 3 (0) **1987†**SF 12 (2) **NFL** 72 (2) [6 yrs]

McLemore, Emmett Emmett, aka Red Fox, BB, 5´7˝/163 lbs; Haskell Indian; Pittsburg State; B9/12/1899 Lyons, OK, D5/1973 Stillwell, OK **[K]** **1923** Oor 9 (8, BB), 8 **1924** KC 4 (3) **NFL** 13 (11) [2 yrs]

McLemore, Thomas Thomas Tyree, TE, 6´5˝/245 lbs; Southern (LA); 1992: Det, rnd 3; B3/14/1970 Shreveport, LA **1993** Cle 4 (0) **1994** Cle 2 (1) **1995** Ind 1 (0)

YEAR	TEAM	G(GS, POS)	RUSH	YD	AVG(LG)	TD	REC	YD	AVG(LG)	TD	PASS	COMP	PCT	YD	AVG(LG)	TD	INT	SK	YD	QBR	KPR	OTD	PTS	TAY
1992	Det	11(1)	—	—	—	—	2	12	6.0(6)	0	—	—	—	—	—	—	—	—	—	—	—	—	0	6
NFL	4	18(2)	—	—	—	—	2	12	6.0(6)	0	—	—	—	—	—	—	—	—	—	—	—	—	0	6

McLenna, Bruce Bruce Oliver, HB, 6´3˝/225 lbs; Michigan; Hillsdale; 1965: Det, rnd 9/KC, rnd R9; B12/23/1941 Holly, MI

YEAR	TEAM	G(GS, POS)	RUSH	YD	AVG(LG)	TD	REC	YD	AVG(LG)	TD	PASS	COMP	PCT	YD	AVG(LG)	TD	INT	SK	YD	QBR	KPR	OTD	PTS	TAY
1966	Det	9	16	51	3.2(19)	0	3	13	4.3(8)	0	—	—	—	—	—	—	—	—	—	—	—	—	0	58

McLeod, Bob Robert Don, TE, 6´4˝/240 lbs; Abilene Christian; 1961: Hou, rnd 12/Chi, rnd 13; B11/10/1938 Sweetwater, TX

YEAR	TEAM	G(GS, POS)	RUSH	YD	AVG(LG)	TD	REC	YD	AVG(LG)	TD	PASS	COMP	PCT	YD	AVG(LG)	TD	INT	SK	YD	QBR	KPR	OTD	PTS	TAY
1961	†Hou-A✧	14(te)	—	—	—	—	14	172	12.3(18)	2	—	—	—	—	—	—	—	—	—	—	k	—	12	94
1962	†Hou-A	14(TE)	—	—	—	—	33	578	17.5(55)	6	—	—	—	—	—	—	—	—	—	—	k	—	36	304
1963	Hou-A	14(TE)	—	—	—	—	33	530	16.1(38)	5	—	—	—	—	—	—	—	—	—	—	—	—	30	290
1964	Hou-A	14	—	—	—	—	8	81	10.1(20)	2	—	—	—	—	—	—	—	—	—	—	—	—	12	51
1965	Hou-A	14	—	—	—	—	15	226	15.1(49)	1	—	—	—	—	—	—	—	—	—	—	—	—	6	118
1966	Hou-A	14(TE)	—	—	—	—	23	339	14.7(41)	3	—	—	—	—	—	—	—	—	—	—	—	—	18	185
NFL	6	84	—	—	—	—	126	1926	15.3(55)	19	—	—	—	—	—	—	—	—	—	—	k	—	114	1041

McLeod, Kevin Kevin Aston, FB, 6´0˝/250 lbs; Auburn; 1998: Jax, rnd 6; B10/17/1974 Montego Bay, Jamaica **2003** Cle 1 (1)

YEAR	TEAM	G(GS, POS)	RUSH	YD	AVG(LG)	TD	REC	YD	AVG(LG)	TD	PASS	COMP	PCT	YD	AVG(LG)	TD	INT	SK	YD	QBR	KPR	OTD	PTS	TAY
1999	†TB	7(0)	—	—	—	—	2	5	2.5(3)	1	—	—	—	—	—	—	—	—	—	—	—	—	6	8
NFL	2	8(1)	—	—	—	—	2	5	2.5(3)	1	—	—	—	—	—	—	—	—	—	—	—	—	6	8

McLeod, Mike Michael James, DB, 6´0˝/180 lbs; Montana State; B5/4/1958 Bozeman, MT **1984** GB 12 (0) **1985** GB 8 (0) **NFL** 20 (0) [2 yrs]

McLeod, Russ Russell Ferguson, C, 6´0˝/190 lbs; St. Louis; B7/29/1906 Cypress River, Canada, D4/4/1977 Los Angeles, CA **1934** SL 3 (1)

McLinton, Harold Harold Lucious, LB, 6´2˝/235 lbs; Southern (LA); 1969: Was, rnd 6; B7/1/1947 Fort Valley, GA, D10/31/1980 Washington, DC **1969** Was 7 (llb) **1970** Was 14 (13, LLB) **1971†**Was 14 **1972†**Was 13 (8, MLB) **1973** Was 8 (8, MLB) **1974** Was 13 (13, MLB) **1975** Was 14 (14, MLB) **1976†**Was 14 (14, MLB) **1977** Was 14 (14, MLB) **1978** Was 16 (15, MLB) **NFL** 127 (99) [10 yrs]

McMahon, Art Arthur John, DB, 6´0˝/190 lbs; North Carolina State; 1968: Bos, rnd 15; B2/24/1946 Newark, NJ **1968** Bos-A 12 (5, rs) **1969** Bos-A 10 **1970** Bos 7 (2) **1972** NE 14 **NFL** 43 (7) [4 yrs]

McMahon, Harry Harry John, BB, 5´7˝/150 lbs; Holy Cross; B10/25/1898 Tampa, FL, D1/12/1984 Southbridge, MA **1926** Har 2 (0)

McMahon, Jim James Robert 'Punky QB', QB, 6´1˝/195 lbs; Brigham Young; 1982: Chi, rnd 1; B8/21/1959 Jersey City, NJ

YEAR	TEAM	G(GS, POS)	RUSH	YD	AVG(LG)	TD	REC	YD	AVG(LG)	TD	PASS	COMP	PCT	YD	AVG(LG)	TD	INT	SK	YD	QBR	KPR	OTD	PTS	TAY
1982	ChiB	8(7, QB)	24	105	4.4(11)	1	—	—	—	—	210	120	57.1	1501	7.1(50)	9	7	27	196	79.9	P	—	6	631
1983	ChiB	14(13, QB)	55	307	5.6(32)	2	1	18	18.0(18)	1	295	175	59.3	2184	7.4(**87**)	12	13	42	266	77.6	P	—	18	973
1984	ChiB	9(9, QB)	39	276	7.1(30)	2	1	42	42.0(42)	0	143	85	59.4	1146	8.0(61)	8	2	10	48	—	—	—	12	850
1985	†ChiB★	13(11, QB)	47	252	5.4(19)	3	1	13	13.0(13)	1	313	178	56.9	2392	7.6(70)	15	11	26	125	82.6	—	—	24	1125
1986	ChiB	6(6, qb)	22	152	6.9(23)	1	—	—	—	—	150	77	51.3	995	6.6(58)	5	8	6	40	—	—	—	6	365
1987	†ChiB	7(6, QB)	22	88	4.0(13)	2	—	—	—	—	210	125	59.5	1639	7.8(59)	12	8	22	136	87.4	—	—	12	668

YEAR	TEAM	G(GS, POS)	RUSH	YD	AVG(LG)	TD	REC	YD	AVG(LG)	TD	PASS	COMP	PCT	YD	AVG(LG)	TD	INT	SK	YD	QBR	KPR	OTD	PTS	TAY
1988	†ChiB	9(9, QB)	26	104	4.0(16)	4	—	—	—	—	192	114	59.4	1346	7.0(63)	6	7	13	79	—	—	—	24	567
1989	SD	12(11, QB)	29	141	4.9(15)	0	1	4	4.0(4)	0	318	176	55.3	2132	6.7(69)	10	10	28	167	73.5	—	—	0	859
1990	†Phi	5(0)	3	1	0.3(3)	0	—	—	—	—	9	6	66.7	63	7.0(21)	0	0	1	7	—	—	—	0	33
1991	Phi	12(11, QB)	22	55	2.5(12)	1	1	-5	-5.0(-5)	0	311	187	60.1	2239	7.2(75)	12	11	21	128	80.3	—	—	6	802
1992	Phi	4(1)	6	23	3.8(11)	0	—	—	—	—	43	22	51.2	279	6.5(42)	1	2	4	25	—	—	—	0	88
1993	†Min	12(12, QB)	33	96	2.9(16)	0	—	—	—	—	331	200	60.4	1968	5.9(58)	9	8	23	104	76.2	—	—	0	805
1994	Arz	3(1)	6	32	5.3(17)	0	—	—	—	—	43	23	53.5	219	5.1(33)	1	3	3	23	—	—	—	0	27
1995	GB	1(0)	—	—	—	—	—	—	—	—	1	1	100.0	6	6.0(6)	0	0	—	—	—	—	—	0	3
1996	†GB	5(0)	4	-1	-0.3(2)	0	—	—	—	—	4	3	75.0	39	9.8(24)	0	0	—	—	—	—	—	0	19
NFL	15	120(97)	338	1631	4.8(32)	16	5	72	14.4(42)	2	2573	1492	58.0	18148	7.1(87)	100	90	226	1344	78.2	P	—	108	7811

McMahon, Mike Michael Edward, QB, 6´2˝/208 lbs; Rutgers; 2001: Det, rnd 5; B2/8/1979 Pittsburgh, PA

YEAR	TEAM	G(GS, POS)	RUSH	YD	AVG(LG)	TD	REC	YD	AVG(LG)	TD	PASS	COMP	PCT	YD	AVG(LG)	TD	INT	SK	YD	QBR	KPR	OTD	PTS	TAY
2001	Det	8(3)	27	145	5.4(22)	1	—	—	—	—	115	53	46.1	671	5.8(69)	3	1	21	122	—	—	—	8	466
2002	Det	8(4)	14	96	6.9(22)	3	1	7	7.0(7)	0	147	62	42.2	874	5.9(49)	7	9	12	99	—	—	—	18	242
2003	Det	3(0)	5	32	6.4(12)	0	—	—	—	—	31	9	29.0	87	2.8(26)	0	2	2	9	—	—	—	0	-5
2004	Det	1(0)	2	18	9.0(14)	0	—	—	—	—	15	11	73.3	77	5.1(19)	0	1	1	12	—	—	—	0	17
2005	Phi	9(7, qb)	34	118	3.5(19)	3	—	—	—	—	207	94	45.4	1158	5.6(48)	5	8	19	96	55.2	—	—	18	432
NFL	5	29(14)	82	409	5.0(22)	7	1	7	7.0(7)	0	515	229	44.5	2867	5.6(69)	15	21	55	338	55.1	—	—	44	1151

McMahon, Tommy Thomas Francis, HB, 5´11˝/200 lbs; Denison; B5/19/1891, D11/22/1962 Newark, OH **1921** Cin 3 (2)

McMakin, John John Garvin, TE, 6´3˝/232 lbs; Clemson; 1972: Pit, rnd 3; B9/24/1950 Spartanburg, SC

YEAR	TEAM	G(GS, POS)	RUSH	YD	AVG(LG)	TD	REC	YD	AVG(LG)	TD	PASS	COMP	PCT	YD	AVG(LG)	TD	INT	SK	YD	QBR	KPR	OTD	PTS	TAY
1972	†Pit	14(TE)	1	0	0.0(0)	0	21	277	13.2(78)	1	—	—	—	—	—	—	—	—	—	—	k	—	6	129
1973	†Pit	14(TE)	—	—	—	—	13	195	15.0(44)	1	—	—	—	—	—	—	—	—	—	—	—	—	6	103
1974	†Pit	8	—	—	—	—	—	—	—	—	—	—	—	—	—	—	—	—	—	—	—	—	0	0
1975	Det	11(2)	—	—	—	—	2	43	21.5(30)	0	—	—	—	—	—	—	—	—	—	—	—	—	0	22
1976	Sea	13(1)	—	—	—	—	9	158	17.6(37)	2	—	—	—	—	—	—	—	—	—	—	—	—	12	89
NFL	5	60(3)	1	0	0.0	0	45	673	15.0(78)	4	—	—	—	—	—	—	—	—	—	—	k	—	24	342

McManus, Tom Thomas Edward, LB, 6´2˝/252 lbs; Boston College; B7/30/1970 Buffalo Grove, IL **1995** Jax 14 (2) **1996**†Jax 16 (11, MLB) **1998**†Jax 16 (4) **1999** Jax 2 (2) **NFL** 48 (19) [4 yrs]

McMath, Herb Herbert Louis, DT-DE, 6´4˝/248 lbs; Morningside; 1976: Oak, rnd 4; B9/6/1954 Coahoma, MS **1976**†Oak 14 **1977** GB 8 **NFL** 22 [2 yrs]

McMichael, Randy Randy Montez, TE, 6´3˝/250 lbs; Georgia; 2002: Mia, rnd 4; B6/28/1979 Griffin, GA

YEAR	TEAM	G(GS, POS)	RUSH	YD	AVG(LG)	TD	REC	YD	AVG(LG)	TD	PASS	COMP	PCT	YD	AVG(LG)	TD	INT	SK	YD	QBR	KPR	OTD	PTS	TAY
2002	Mia	16(16, TE)	1	8	8.0(8)	0	39	485	12.4(45)	4	—	—	—	—	—	—	—	—	—	—	—	—	24	271
2003	Mia	16(16, TE)	—	—	—	—	49	598	12.2(46)	2	—	—	—	—	—	—	—	—	—	—	—	1	18	309
2004	Mia	16(16, TE)	—	—	—	—	73	791	10.8(42)	4	—	—	—	—	—	—	—	—	—	—	—	—	26	416
2005	Mia	16(16, TE)	—	—	—	—	60	582	9.7(30)	5	—	—	—	—	—	—	—	—	—	—	—	—	30	316
NFL	4	64(64)	1	8	8.0(8)	0	221	2456	11.1(46)	15	—	—	—	—	—	—	—	—	—	—	—	1	98	1311

McMichael, Steve Steve Douglas, DT-NT, 6´2˝/270 lbs; Texas; 1980: NE, rnd 3; B10/17/1957 Houston, TX **[S]** **1980** NE 6 (0) **1981** ChiB 10 (0) **1982** ChiB 9 (0) **1983** ChiB 16 (10, RDT) **1984**†ChiB 16 (16, LDT) **1985**†ChiB☆16 (16, LDT) **1986**†ChiB★16 (16, LDT) **1987**†ChiB★12 (12, LDT) **1988**†ChiB☆16 (16, LDT) **1989** ChiB 16 (16, LDT) **1990**†ChiB 16 (7, rdt) **1991**†ChiB☆16 (16, LDT) **1992** ChiB 16 (16, LDT) **1993** ChiB 16 (16, LDT) **1994**†GB 16 (14, RDT) **NFL** 213 (171) [15 yrs]

McMichaels, John John Richard, TB, 5´11˝/190 lbs; Birmingham-Southern; B12/14/1917 Cordova, AL, D12/25/1991 Birmingham, AL

YEAR	TEAM	G(GS, POS)	RUSH	YD	AVG(LG)	TD	REC	YD	AVG(LG)	TD	PASS	COMP	PCT	YD	AVG(LG)	TD	INT	SK	YD	QBR	KPR	OTD	PTS	TAY
1944	Bkn	1(0)	3	1	0.3(2)	0	—	—	—	—	1	0	0.0	0	0.0	0	1	—	—	—	Pp	—	0	-39

McMillan, Chuck Charles David, DB, 6´3˝/175 lbs; John Carroll; 1954: Bal, rnd 13; B11/16/1931 Cleveland, OH **1954** Bal 6

McMillan, David David, DE, 6´3˝/246 lbs; Kansas; 2005: Cle, rnd 5; B9/20/1981 Hinesville, GA **2005** Cle 4 (0)

McMillan, Eddie Edward Alexander, DB, 6´0˝/189 lbs; Florida State; 1973: LA, rnd 4; B11/25/1951 Tampa, FL **1973**†LARm 14 (14, LCB) **1974**†LARm 14 (9, LCB) **1975**†LARm 14 (14, LCB) **1976** Sea 14 (14, LCB) **1977** Sea 14 (14, LCB) **1978** Buf 14 **NFL** 84 (65) [6 yrs]

McMillan, Erik Erik Charles, DB, 6´2˝/200 lbs; Missouri; 1988: NYJ, rnd 3; B5/3/1965 St. Louis, MO **[I]** **1988** NYJ★13 (13, FS) **1989** NYJ★16 (16, FS) **1990** NYJ 16 (16, FS) **1991**†NYJ 16 (6, fs) **1992** NYJ 15 (0) **1993** Phi 6 (0) **1993** Cle 3 (0) **1993**†KC 1 (0) **NFL** 86 (51) [6 yrs]

McMillan, Ernie Ernest Charles, T, 6´5˝/275 lbs; Illinois; 1961: SL, rnd 13/Bos, rnd 29; B2/21/1938 Chicago Heights, IL **1961** SL 6 (RT) **1962** SL 14 (RT) **1963** SL 14 (RT) **1964** SL☆14 (RT) **1965** SL✧14 (RT) **1966** SL☆14 (RT) **1967** SL★14 (RT) **1968** SL☆14 (RT) **1969** SL★14 (RT) **1970** SL★14 (RT) **1971** SL☆14 (RT) **1972** SL 14 **1973** SL 7 (RT) **1974** SL 11 (11, LT) **1975** GB 12 (LT) **NFL** 190 (11) [15 yrs]

McMillan, Randy Lewis Lorando, RB, 6´0˝/219 lbs; Pittsburgh; 1981: Bal, rnd 1; B12/17/1958 Havre de Grace, MD

YEAR	TEAM	G(GS, POS)	RUSH	YD	AVG(LG)	TD	REC	YD	AVG(LG)	TD	PASS	COMP	PCT	YD	AVG(LG)	TD	INT	SK	YD	QBR	KPR	OTD	PTS	TAY
1981	Bal	16(16, FB)	149	597	4.0(42)	3	50	466	9.3(31)	1	—	—	—	—	—	—	—	—	—	—	—	—	24	865
1982	Bal	9(9, FB)	101	305	3.0(13)	1	15	90	6.0(17)	0	—	—	—	—	—	—	—	—	—	—	—	—	6	360
1983	Bal	16(16, FB)	198	802	4.1(39)	5	24	195	8.1(27)	1	—	—	—	—	—	—	—	—	—	—	—	—	36	955
1984	Ind	16(16, FB)	163	705	4.3(31)	5	19	201	10.6(44)	0	—	—	—	—	—	—	—	—	—	—	—	—	30	856
1985	Ind	15(15, FB)	190	858	4.5(38)	7	22	115	5.2(17)	0	—	—	—	—	—	—	—	—	—	—	—	—	42	986
1986	Ind	16(16, FB)	189	609	3.2(28)	3	34	289	8.5(45)	0	—	—	—	—	—	—	—	—	—	—	—	—	18	784
NFL	6	88(88)	990	3876	3.9(42)	24	164	1356	8.3(45)	2	—	—	—	—	—	—	—	—	—	—	—	—	156	4804

McMillen, Dan Daniel A., DE, 6´4˝/240 lbs; Colorado; 1986: Phi, rnd 5; B2/23/1964 Wiesbaden, Germany **1987** LARd 1 (1) **1987** Phi 1 (0) **NFL** 2 (1) [1 yr]

McMillen, Jim James Willard, G, 6´1˝/215 lbs; Illinois; B10/23/1902 Grays Lake, IL, D1/26/1964 Antioch, IL **1924** ChiB☆10 (10, RG) **1925** ChiB☆17 (17, RG) **1926** ChiB☆16 (15, RG) **1927** ChiB☆13 (11, RG) **1928** ChiB☆13 (13, RG) **NFL** 69 (66) [5 yrs]

McMillian, Audray Audray Glenn, DB, 5´11˝/190 lbs; Houston; 1985: NE, rnd 3; B8/13/1962 Carthage, TX **1985** Hou 16 (0) **1986** Hou 16 (0) **1987**†Hou 12 (2) **1989**†Min 16 (2) **1990** Min 15 (2) **1991** Min 16 (7, rcb) **1992**†Min★16 (16, RCB) **1993**†Min 16 (16, RCB) **NFL** 123 (45) [8 yrs]

McMillian, Henry Henry James, DT, 6´3˝/275 lbs; Florida; 1995: Sea, rnd 6; B10/17/1971 Folkston, GA **1995** Sea 1 (0) **1996** Sea 2 (0) **NFL** 3 (0) [2 yrs]

McMillian, Mark Mark D., DB, 5´7˝/154 lbs; Alabama; 1992: Phi, rnd 10; B4/29/1970 Los Angeles, CA **[I]** **1992**†Phi 16 (3) **1993** Phi 16 (12, LCB) **1994** Phi 16 (16, LCB) **1995**†Phi 16 (16, LCB) **1996** NO 16 (16, LCB) **1997**†KC 16 (2) **1998** KC 16 (10, LCB) **1999** SF 6 (6, rcb) **1999**†Was 9 (0) **NFL** 127 (81) [8 yrs]

McMillin, Bo Alvin Nugent, B, 5´9˝/163 lbs; Centre; B1/12/1895 Prairie Hill, TX, D3/31/1952 Bloomington, IN **[C]** **1922** Mil 2 (1), 6 **1923** Mil 2 (2) **1923** Cle 1 (1) **NFL** 5 (4), 6 [2 yrs]

McMillin, Jim James Robert, DB, 6´0˝/190 lbs; Colorado State; B9/18/1939 Pleasant Hill, CA **1961** Den-A 14 (RCB) **1962** Den-A 14 (RCB) **1963** Oak-A 14 (rcb) **1964** Oak-A 1 **1964** Den-A 7 **1965** Den-A 12 (lcb) **NFL** 62 [5 yrs]

McMillon, Todd Todd, DB, 5´11˝/198 lbs; Northern Arizona; B9/26/1974 Bellflower, CA **2000** ChiB 3 (0) **2001**†ChiB 8 (0) **2002** ChiB 10 (1) **2003** ChiB 13 (0) **2004** ChiB 14 (1) **NFL** 48 (2) [5 yrs]

McMullan, John John Gerald, G, 6´0˝/245 lbs; Notre Dame; 1956: NYG, rnd 14; B6/28/1933 Brooklyn, NY, D4/1/1994 **1960** NYT-A 14 (RG) **1961** NYT-A 14 (RG) **NFL** 28 [2 yrs]

McMullen, Billy Wilbur Anthony, WR, 6´4˝/210 lbs; Virginia; 2003: Phi, rnd 3; B3/8/1980 Richmond, VA

YEAR	TEAM	G(GS, POS)	RUSH	YD	AVG(LG)	TD	REC	YD	AVG(LG)	TD	PASS	COMP	PCT	YD	AVG(LG)	TD	INT	SK	YD	QBR	KPR	OTD	PTS	TAY
2003	Phi	5(0)	—	—	—	—	1	2	2.0(2)	0	—	—	—	—	—	—	—	—	—	—	—	—	0	1
2004	†Phi	8(0)	—	—	—	—	3	24	8.0(15)	0	—	—	—	—	—	—	—	—	—	—	—	—	0	12
2005	Phi	16(0)	—	—	—	—	18	268	14.9(38)	1	—	—	—	—	—	—	—	—	—	—	—	—	6	139
NFL	3	29(0)	—	—	—	—	22	294	13.4(38)	1	—	—	—	—	—	—	—	—	—	—	—	—	6	152

McMullen, Danny Daniel Edward, G, 5´8˝/231 lbs; Nebraska; B5/8/1906 Belleville, KS, D8/22/1983 St. Francis, KS **1929** NYG 12 (7, LG) **1930** ChiB 10 (6, rg) **1931** ChiB 11 (5, rg) **1932** Por 2 (0) **NFL** 35 (18) [4 yrs]

McMullen, Kirk Kirk Lawrence, TE, 6´4˝/255 lbs; Pittsburgh; B7/19/1977 Imperial, PA

YEAR	TEAM	G(GS, POS)	RUSH	YD	AVG(LG)	TD	REC	YD	AVG(LG)	TD	PASS	COMP	PCT	YD	AVG(LG)	TD	INT	SK	YD	QBR	KPR	OTD	PTS	TAY
2001	Cin	7(2)	—	—	—	—	2	15	7.5(11)	0	—	—	—	—	—	—	—	—	—	—	—	—	0	8

McMurtry, Chuck Charles, DT, 6´0˝/280 lbs; Whittier; 1960: Buf, rnd 1; B2/15/1937 Chaneller, OK **1960** Buf-A☆14 (LDT) **1961** Buf-A★14 (LDT) **1962** Oak-A 11 (RDT) **1963** Oak-A 14 (LDT) **NFL** 53 [4 yrs]

McMurtry, Greg Gregory Wendell, WR, 6´2˝/207 lbs; Michigan; 1990: NE, rnd 3; B10/15/1967 Brockton, MA

YEAR	TEAM	G (GS, POS)	RUSH	YD	AVG (LG)	TD	REC	YD	AVG (LG)	TD	PASS	COMP	PCT	YD	AVG (LG)	TD	INT	SK	YD	QBR	KPR	OTD	PTS	TAY
1990	NE	13 (5, wr)	—	—	—	—	22	240	10.9 (26)	0	—	—	—	—	—	—	—	—	—	—	—	—	0	120
1991	NE	15 (13, WR)	—	—	—	—	41	614	15.0 (40)	2	—	—	—	—	—	—	—	—	—	—	—	—	12	317
1992	NE	16 (15, WR)	2	3	1.5 (2)	0	35	424	12.1 (65)	1	1	0	0.0	0	0.0	0	0	—	—	—	—	—	6	220
1993	NE	14 (8, wr)	—	—	—	—	22	241	11.0 (20)	1	—	—	—	—	—	—	—	—	—	—	—	—	6	126
1994	ChiB	9 (4)	—	—	—	—	8	112	14.0 (30)	1	—	—	—	—	—	—	—	—	—	—	—	—	6	61
NFL	5	67 (45)	2	3	1.5 (2)	0	128	1631	12.7 (65)	5	1	0	0.0	0	0.0	0	0	—	—	—	—	—	30	844

McNabb, Dexter Dexter Eugene, FB, 6´2˝/250 lbs; Florida; 1992: GB, rnd 5; B7/9/1969 DeFuniak Springs, FL **1993**†GB 16 (0) **1995** Phi 1 (0)

YEAR	TEAM	G (GS, POS)	RUSH	YD	AVG (LG)	TD	REC	YD	AVG (LG)	TD	PASS	COMP	PCT	YD	AVG (LG)	TD	INT	SK	YD	QBR	KPR	OTD	PTS	TAY
1992	GB	16 (0)	2	11	5.5 (8)	0	—	—	—	—	—	—	—	—	—	—	—	—	—	—	—	—	0	11
NFL	3	33 (0)	2	11	5.5 (8)	0	—	—	—	—	—	—	—	—	—	—	—	—	—	—	k	—	0	11

McNabb, Donovan Donovan Jamal, QB, 6´2˝/240 lbs; Syracuse; 1999: Phi, rnd 1; B11/25/1976 Chicago, IL

YEAR	TEAM	G (GS, POS)	RUSH	YD	AVG (LG)	TD	REC	YD	AVG (LG)	TD	PASS	COMP	PCT	YD	AVG (LG)	TD	INT	SK	YD	QBR	KPR	OTD	PTS	TAY
1999	Phi	12 (6, qb)	47	313	6.7 (27)	0	1	-6	-6.0 (-6)	0	216	106	49.1	948	4.4 (63)	8	7	28	204	—	—	—	2	544
2000	†Phi✧	16 (16, QB)	86	629	**7.3 (54)**	6	2	5	2.5 (3)	0	569	330	58.0	3365	5.9 (70)	21	13	45	262	77.8	—	—	36	1959
2001	†Phi✧	16 (16, QB)	82	482	**5.9 (33)**	2	—	—	—	—	493	285	57.8	3233	6.6 (64)	25	12	39	273	84.3	—	—	12	1764
2002	†Phi✧	10 (10, QB)	63	460	7.3 (40)	6	—	—	—	—	361	211	58.4	2289	6.3 (59)	17	6	28	166	86.0	—	—	36	1510
2003	†Phi✧	16 (16, QB)	71	355	5.0 (34)	3	1	-7	-7.0 (-7)	0	478	275	57.5	3216	6.7 (59)	16	11	43	253	79.6	—	—	18	1630
2004	†Phi✧	15 (15, QB)	41	220	5.4 (28)	3	—	—	—	—	469	300	64.0	3875	8.3 (80)	31	8	32	192	104.7	—	—	18	2023
2005	Phi	9 (9, QB)	25	55	2.2 (11)	1	—	—	—	—	357	211	59.1	2507	7.0 (**91**)	16	9	19	112	85.0	—	—	6	1039
NFL	7	94 (88)	415	2514	6.1 (54)	21	4	-8	-2.0 (3)	0	2943	1718	58.4	19433	6.6 (91)	134	66	234	1462	84.1	—	—	128	10467

McNair, Steve Steve LaTreal 'Air', QB, 6´2˝/235 lbs; Alcorn State; 1995: Hou, rnd 1; B2/14/1973 Mt. Olive, MS

YEAR	TEAM	G (GS, POS)	RUSH	YD	AVG (LG)	TD	REC	YD	AVG (LG)	TD	PASS	COMP	PCT	YD	AVG (LG)	TD	INT	SK	YD	QBR	KPR	OTD	PTS	TAY
1995	Hou	4 (2)	11	38	3.5 (13)	0	—	—	—	—	80	41	51.3	569	7.1 (53)	3	1	6	63	—	—	—	0	298
1996	Hou	9 (4)	31	169	5.5 (24)	2	—	—	—	—	143	88	61.5	1197	8.4 (83)	6	4	9	45	—	—	—	12	658
1997	Ten	16 (16, QB)	101	674	**6.7 (47)**	8	—	—	—	—	415	216	52.0	2665	6.4 (55)	14	13	31	190	70.4	—	—	48	1637
1998	Ten	16 (16, QB)	77	559	7.3 (71)	4	—	—	—	—	492	289	58.7	3228	6.6 (47)	15	10	33	176	80.1	—	—	24	1888
1999	†Ten	11 (11, QB)	72	337	4.7 (38)	8	—	—	—	—	331	187	56.5	2179	6.6 (65)	12	8	16	74	78.6	—	—	48	1247
2000	†Ten✧	16 (15, QB)	72	403	5.6 (25)	0	—	—	—	—	396	248	62.6	2847	7.2 (56)	15	13	24	141	83.2	—	—	0	1382
2001	Ten	15 (15, QB)	75	414	5.5 (24)	5	—	—	—	—	431	264	61.3	3350	**7.8 (71)**	21	12	37	251	90.2	—	—	30	1764
2002	†Ten	16 (16, QB)	82	440	5.4 (26)	3	—	—	—	—	492	301	61.2	3387	6.9 (55)	22	15	21	121	84.0	—	—	20	1674
2003	†Ten★	14 (14, QB)	38	138	3.6 (23)	4	1	4	4.0 (4)	0	400	250	62.5	3215	**8.0 (73)**	24	7	19	108	**100.4**	—	—	26	1628
2004	Ten	8 (8, QB)	23	128	5.6 (23)	1	—	—	—	—	215	129	60.0	1343	6.2 (37)	8	9	13	95	73.1	—	—	8	490
2005	Ten✧	14 (14, QB)	32	139	4.3 (19)	1	—	—	—	—	476	292	61.3	3161	6.6 (57)	16	11	20	134	82.4	—	—	6	1370
NFL	11	139 (131)	614	3439	5.6 (71)	36	1	4	4.0 (4)	0	3871	2305	59.5	27141	7.0 (83)	156	103	229	1398	83.3	—	—	222	14032

McNair, Todd Todd Darren, RB, 6´1˝/202 lbs; Temple; 1989: KC, rnd 8; B10/7/1965 Camden, NJ

YEAR	TEAM	G (GS, POS)	RUSH	YD	AVG (LG)	TD	REC	YD	AVG (LG)	TD	PASS	COMP	PCT	YD	AVG (LG)	TD	INT	SK	YD	QBR	KPR	OTD	PTS	TAY
1989	KC	14 (0)	23	121	5.3 (25)	0	34	372	10.9 (24)	1	—	—	—	—	—	—	—	—	—	—	k	—	6	374
1990	†KC	15 (1)	14	61	4.4 (13)	0	40	507	12.7 (65)	2	—	—	—	—	—	—	—	—	—	—	k	—	12	342
1991	†KC	14 (0)	10	51	5.1 (11)	0	37	342	9.2 (36)	1	—	—	—	—	—	—	—	—	—	—	k	—	6	233
1992	†KC	16 (0)	21	124	5.9 (30)	1	44	380	8.6 (36)	1	—	—	—	—	—	—	—	—	—	—	k	—	12	319
1993	†KC	15 (0)	51	278	5.5 (47)	2	10	74	7.4 (24)	0	—	—	—	—	—	—	—	—	—	—	k	—	12	348
1994	Hou	16 (1)	—	—	—	—	8	78	9.8 (21)	0	—	—	—	—	—	—	—	—	—	—	k	—	0	175
1995	Hou	15 (7, fb)	19	136	7.2 (22)	0	60	501	8.4 (25)	1	—	—	—	—	—	—	—	—	—	—	—	—	6	392
1996	KC	16 (0)	9	32	3.6 (9)	0	21	181	8.6 (29)	1	—	—	—	—	—	—	—	—	—	—	k	—	6	119
NFL	8	121 (9)	147	803	5.5 (47)	3	254	2435	9.6 (65)	7	—	—	—	—	—	—	—	—	—	—	k	—	60	2301

McNally, Frank Frank James, C-T-G, 6´1˝/203 lbs; St. Mary's (CA); B3/19/1907, NV, D2/5/1993 Delray Beach, FL **1931** ChiC☆8 (5, C) **1932** ChiC 7 (5, c) **1933** ChiC 11 (6, C) **1934** ChiC 10 (5, c) **NFL** 36 (21) [4 yrs]

McNally, John see Johnny Blood

McNamara, Bob Robert John, DB-FL-HB, 6´0˝/190 lbs; Minnesota; 1953: Cle, rnd 9; B8/12/1931 Hastings, MN **1961** Den-A 14 (LCB)

YEAR	TEAM	G (GS, POS)	RUSH	YD	AVG (LG)	TD	REC	YD	AVG (LG)	TD	PASS	COMP	PCT	YD	AVG (LG)	TD	INT	SK	YD	QBR	KPR	OTD	PTS	TAY
1960	Den-A	14 (FL/ls)	17	33	1.9 (7)	1	7	143	20.4 (55)	1	—	—	—	—	—	—	—	—	—	—	kpi	—	12	233
NFL	2	28	17	33	1.9 (7)	1	7	143	20.4 (55)	1	—	—	—	—	—	—	—	—	—	—	kpi	—	12	300

McNamara, Ed Edmund Leo, T, 6´2˝/225 lbs; Holy Cross; 1943: NYG, rnd 27; B4/13/1920 Clinton, MA, D2/20/2000 West Roxbury, MA **1945** Pit 1 (0)

McNamara, Tom Edward A., G-FB, 5´10˝/210 lbs; Tufts; Detroit Mercy; B8/31/1897 Worcester, MA, D3/13/1966 Worcester, MA **[K]** **1923** Tol 8 (8, RG), 3 **1925** Det 12 (11, LG) **1926** Det 11 (11, RG) **NFL** 31 (30) [3 yrs]

McNanie, Sean Sean Lawrence, DE, 6´5˝/265 lbs; Arizona State; San Diego State; 1984: Buf, rnd 3; B9/9/1961 Rockford, IL **1984** Buf 15 (1) **1985** Buf 16 (0) **1986** Buf 16 (16, LDE) **1987** Buf 12 (12, LDE) **1988** Phx 12 (1) **1990** Ind 1 (0) **NFL** 72 (30) [6 yrs]

McNeal, Don Donald, DB, 5´11˝/190 lbs; Alabama; 1980: Mia, rnd 1; B5/6/1958 Atmore, AL **1980** Mia 13 (13, LCB) **1981**†Mia 12 (12, LCB) **1982**†Mia 9 (9, LCB) **1984**†Mia 11 (10, LCB) **1985**†Mia 10 (0) **1986** Mia 15 (1) **1987** Mia 12 (0) **1988** Mia 16 (3) **1989** Mia 12 (0) **NFL** 110 (48) [9 yrs]

McNeal, Travis Travis S., TE, 6´3˝/248 lbs; Tennessee-Chattanooga; 1989: Sea, rnd 4; B1/10/1967 Birmingham, AL

YEAR	TEAM	G (GS, POS)	RUSH	YD	AVG (LG)	TD	REC	YD	AVG (LG)	TD	PASS	COMP	PCT	YD	AVG (LG)	TD	INT	SK	YD	QBR	KPR	OTD	PTS	TAY
1989	Sea	16 (6, te)	—	—	—	—	9	147	16.3 (48)	0	—	—	—	—	—	—	—	—	—	—	k	—	0	76
1990	Sea	16 (14, TE)	1	2	2.0 (2)	0	10	143	14.3 (30)	0	—	—	—	—	—	—	—	—	—	—	k	—	0	73
1991	Sea	16 (4)	—	—	—	—	17	208	12.2 (36)	1	—	—	—	—	—	—	—	—	—	—	k	—	6	79
1992	LARm	12 (0)	—	—	—	—	4	79	19.8 (38)	0	—	—	—	—	—	—	—	—	—	—	—	—	0	40
1993	LARm	16 (6, te)	—	—	—	—	8	75	9.4 (22)	1	—	—	—	—	—	—	—	—	—	—	—	—	6	43
NFL	5	76 (30)	1	2	2.0 (2)	0	48	652	13.6 (48)	2	—	—	—	—	—	—	—	—	—	—	k	—	12	309

McNeil, Charlie Charles Edis, DB, 5´11˝/180 lbs; Compton CC (CA); B8/8/1936 Caldwell, TX, D1/7/1994 Houston, TX **1960**†LAC-A 9 (RS) **1961**†SD-A★14 (RS) **1962** SD-A 4 **1963** SD-A 10 **1964** SD-A 6 **NFL** 43 [5 yrs]

McNeil, Clifton Clifton Anthony, WR-FL-SE, 6´2˝/187 lbs; Grambling State; 1962: Cle, rnd 11; B5/25/1940 Mobile, AL

YEAR	TEAM	G (GS, POS)	RUSH	YD	AVG (LG)	TD	REC	YD	AVG (LG)	TD	PASS	COMP	PCT	YD	AVG (LG)	TD	INT	SK	YD	QBR	KPR	OTD	PTS	TAY
1964	†Cle	14	—	—	—	—	4	69	17.3 (28)	1	—	—	—	—	—	—	—	—	—	—	—	—	6	40
1965	Cle	13 (se)	—	—	—	—	3	69	23.0 (32)	0	—	—	—	—	—	—	—	—	—	—	—	—	0	35
1966	Cle	14	—	—	—	—	2	94	47.0 (50)	2	—	—	—	—	—	—	—	—	—	—	—	—	12	57
1967	Cle	2	—	—	—	—	3	33	11.0 (23)	2	—	—	—	—	—	—	—	—	—	—	—	—	12	27
1968	SF★	14 (14, FL)	1	-1	-1.0 (-1)	0	**71**	994	14.0 (65)	7	2	1	50.0	43	21.5 (43)	1	1	—	—	—	—	—	42	518
1969	SF	11 (7, fl)	—	—	—	—	17	255	15.0 (80)	3	—	—	—	—	—	—	—	—	—	—	—	—	18	143
1970	NYG☆	14 (WR)	4	7	1.8 (9)	0	50	764	15.3 (59)	4	—	—	—	—	—	—	—	—	—	—	—	1	30	409
1971	NYG	6 (wr)	—	—	—	—	16	209	13.1 (24)	1	—	—	—	—	—	—	—	—	—	—	—	—	6	110
1971	†Was	8 (1)	—	—	—	—	14	244	17.4 (32)	2	—	—	—	—	—	—	—	—	—	—	—	—	12	132
1972	†Was	6	—	—	—	—	—	—	—	—	—	—	—	—	—	—	—	—	—	—	—	—	—	—
1973	Hou	3	—	—	—	—	1	3	3.0 (3)	0	—	—	—	—	—	—	—	—	—	—	—	—	0	2
NFL	10	105 (22)	5	6	1.2 (9)	0	181	2734	15.1 (80)	22	2	1	50.0	43	21.5 (43)	1	1	—	—	—	—	1	138	1470

McNeil, Emanuel Emanuel, NT, 6´3˝/285 lbs; Tennessee-Martin; 1989: NE, rnd 10; B6/9/1967 Richmond, VA **1989** NE 1 (0) **1990** NYJ 2 (0) **NFL** 3 (0) [2 yrs]

McNeil, Frank Francis Kenneth, E, 6´0˝/185 lbs; Washington & Jefferson; B12/23/1909, D10/3/1971 Dade County, FL

YEAR	TEAM	G (GS, POS)	RUSH	YD	AVG (LG)	TD	REC	YD	AVG (LG)	TD	PASS	COMP	PCT	YD	AVG (LG)	TD	INT	SK	YD	QBR	KPR	OTD	PTS	TAY
1932	Bkn	7 (0)	—	—	—	—	3	18	6.0	0	—	—	—	—	—	—	—	—	—	—	—	—	0	9

McNeil, Freeman Freeman, RB, 5´11˝/216 lbs; UCLA; 1981: NYJ, rnd 1; B4/22/1959 Jackson, MS

YEAR	TEAM	G (GS, POS)	RUSH	YD	AVG (LG)	TD	REC	YD	AVG (LG)	TD	PASS	COMP	PCT	YD	AVG (LG)	TD	INT	SK	YD	QBR	KPR	OTD	PTS	TAY
1981	†NYJ	11 (6, RB)	137	623	4.5 (43)	2	18	171	9.5 (18)	1	—	—	—	—	—	—	—	—	—	—	—	—	18	734
1982	†NYJ★	9 (9, RB)	151	**786**	**5.2 (48)**	6	16	187	11.7 (32)	1	—	—	—	—	—	—	—	—	—	—	—	—	42	945
1983	NYJ	9 (9, RB)	160	654	4.1 (19)	1	21	172	8.2 (21)	3	1	1	100.0	5	5.0 (5)	1	0	—	—	—	—	—	24	773
1984	NYJ★	12 (12, RB)	229	1070	4.7 (53)	5	25	294	11.8 (32)	1	—	—	—	—	—	—	—	—	—	—	—	—	36	1272
1985	†NYJ★	14 (13, RB)	294	1331	4.5 (69)	3	38	427	11.2 (25)	2	—	—	—	—	—	—	—	—	—	—	—	—	30	1585
1986	†NYJ	12 (11, RB)	214	856	4.0 (40)	5	49	410	8.4 (26)	1	—	—	—	—	—	—	—	—	—	—	—	—	36	1116
1987	NYJ	9 (8, RB)	121	530	4.4 (30)	0	24	262	10.9 (57)	1	—	—	—	—	—	—	—	—	—	—	—	—	6	666

YEAR	TEAM	G (GS, POS)	RUSH	YD	AVG (LG)	TD	REC	YD	AVG (LG)	TD	PASS	COMP	PCT	YD	AVG (LG)	TD	INT	SK	YD	QBR	KPR	OTD	PTS	TAY
1988	NYJ	16(16, RB)	219	944	4.3(28)	6	34	288	8.5(25)	1	—	—	—	—	—	—	—	—	—	—	—	—	42	1153
1989	NYJ	11(7, rb)	80	352	4.4(19)	2	31	310	10.0(25)	1	—	—	—	—	—	—	—	—	—	—	—	—	18	532
1990	NYJ	16(4)	99	458	4.6(29)	6	16	230	14.4(59)	0	—	—	—	—	—	—	—	—	—	—	—	—	36	633
1991	†NYJ	13(1)	51	300	5.9(58)	2	7	56	8.0(13)	0	—	—	—	—	—	—	—	—	—	—	—	—	12	348
1992	NYJ	12(1)	43	170	4.0(18)	0	16	154	9.6(32)	0	—	—	—	—	—	—	—	—	—	—	—	—	0	247
NFL	12	144(97)	1798	8074	4.5(69)	38	295	2961	10.0(59)	12	1	1	100.0	5	5.0(5)	1	0	—	—	—	—	—	300	10002

McNeil, Gerald Gerald Lynn, WR, 5´7˝/145 lbs; Baylor; 1984: Cle, rnd S2; B3/27/1962 Frankfurt, Germany **[R]**

YEAR	TEAM	G (GS, POS)	RUSH	YD	AVG (LG)	TD	REC	YD	AVG (LG)	TD	PASS	COMP	PCT	YD	AVG (LG)	TD	INT	SK	YD	QBR	KPR	OTD	PTS	TAY
1986	†Cle	16(0)	1	12	12.0(12)	0	1	9	9.0(9)	0	—	—	—	—	—	—	—	—	—	—	kp	2	12	477
1987	†Cle✧	12(0)	1	17	17.0(17)	0	8	120	15.0(39)	2	—	—	—	—	—	—	—	—	—	—	kp	—	12	343
1988	†Cle	16(0)	—	—	—	—	5	74	14.8(23)	0	—	—	—	—	—	—	—	—	—	—	kp	—	0	170
1989	†Cle	16(0)	2	32	16.0(18)	0	10	114	11.4(32)	0	—	—	—	—	—	—	—	—	—	—	kp	—	0	341
1990	†Hou	16(0)	—	—	—	—	5	63	12.6(16)	0	—	—	—	—	—	—	—	—	—	—	kp	—	0	200
NFL	5	76(0)	4	61	15.3(18)	0	29	380	13.1(39)	2	—	—	—	—	—	—	—	—	—	—	kp	2	24	1530

McNeil, Pat Patrick Lamont, RB, 5´9˝/208 lbs; Baylor; 1976: KC, rnd 17; B2/28/1954 Pittsburg, CA **1977** KC 1

YEAR	TEAM	G (GS, POS)	RUSH	YD	AVG (LG)	TD	REC	YD	AVG (LG)	TD	PASS	COMP	PCT	YD	AVG (LG)	TD	INT	SK	YD	QBR	KPR	OTD	PTS	TAY
1976	KC	12	8	26	3.3(7)	0	2	33	16.5(18)	0	—	—	—	—	—	—	—	—	—	—	k	—	0	34
NFL	2	13	8	26	3.3(7)	0	2	33	16.5(18)	0	—	—	—	—	—	—	—	—	—	—	—	—	0	43

McNeil, Ryan Ryan Darrell, DB, 6´2˝/210 lbs; Miami (FL); 1993: Det, rnd 2; B10/4/1970 Fort Pierce, FL **[I]** **1993**†Det 16 (2) **1994**†Det 14 (13, LCB) **1995**†Det 16 (16, LCB) **1996** Det 16 (16, LCB) **1997** SL 16 (16, RCB) **1998** SL 16 (12, RCB) **1999** Cle 16 (14, LCB) **2000** Dal 16 (16, RCB) **2001** SD✧16 (16, RCB) **2002** SD 15 (15, RCB) **2003**†Den 4 (0) **NFL** 161 (136) [11 yrs]

McNeill, Fred Frederick Arnold, LB, 6´2˝/229 lbs; UCLA; 1974: Min, rnd 1; B5/6/1952 Durham, NC **1974**†Min 14 **1975**†Min 14 (5, llb) **1976**†Min 13 (1) **1977**†Min 14 (14, RLB) **1978**†Min 16 (15, RLB) **1979** Min 16 (15, RLB) **1980**†Min 16 (16, RLB) **1981** Min 16 (16, ROLB) **1982**†Min 9 (9, ROLB) **1983** Min 16 (15, ROLB) **1984** Min 13 (13, ROLB) **1985** Min 10 (3) **NFL** 167 (122) [12 yrs]

McNeill, Rod Rodney Carlyle, RB, 6´2˝/219 lbs; USC; 1974: NO, rnd 4; B3/26/1951 Durham, NC

YEAR	TEAM	G (GS, POS)	RUSH	YD	AVG (LG)	TD	REC	YD	AVG (LG)	TD	PASS	COMP	PCT	YD	AVG (LG)	TD	INT	SK	YD	QBR	KPR	OTD	PTS	TAY
1974	NO	11	22	90	4.1(24)	1	5	64	12.8(30)	0	—	—	—	—	—	—	—	—	—	—	p	—	6	127
1975	NO	14(2)	61	206	3.4(17)	2	18	138	7.7(17)	2	—	—	—	—	—	—	—	—	—	—	k	—	24	431
1976	TB	11	27	135	5.0(17)	0	7	33	4.7(9)	0	—	—	—	—	—	—	—	—	—	—	k	—	0	281
NFL	3	36(2)	110	431	3.9(24)	3	30	235	7.8(30)	2	—	—	—	—	—	—	—	—	—	—	kp	—	30	839

McNeill, Tom Thomas Gregg, P, 6´1˝/195 lbs; Stephen F. Austin State; B8/12/1942 Rockford, IL **[P]** **1969** NO 2 **1970**†Min 14 **1971** Phi☆14 **1972** Phi 2 **1973** Phi 10

YEAR	TEAM	G (GS, POS)	RUSH	YD	AVG (LG)	TD	REC	YD	AVG (LG)	TD	PASS	COMP	PCT	YD	AVG (LG)	TD	INT	SK	YD	QBR	KPR	OTD	PTS	TAY
1967	NO	14	4	38	9.5(25)	0	—	—	—	—	1	1	100.0	24	24.0(24)	0	0	—	—	—	P	—	0	50
1968	NO	10	2	1	0.5(15)	0	—	—	—	—	—	—	—	—	—	—	—	—	—	—	P	—	0	1
NFL	7	66	6	39	6.5(25)	0	—	—	—	—	1	1	100.0	24	24.0(24)	0	0	—	—	—	P	—	0	51

McNellis, Bill William, WB, 5´11˝/177 lbs; St. Mary's (MN); B1902 Duluth, MN, D1942 **1927** Dul 2 (1)

McNorton, Bruce Bruce Edward, DB, 5´11˝/175 lbs; Georgetown (KY); 1982: Det, rnd 4; B2/28/1959 Daytona Beach, FL **[I]** **1982**†Det 4 (0) **1983**†Det 16 (8, rcb) **1984** Det 16 (16, RCB) **1985** Det 16 (16, RCB) **1986** Det 16 (16, RCB) **1987** Det 12 (12, RCB) **1988** Det 16 (16, RCB) **1989** Det 8 (0) **1990** Det 12 (8, LCB) **NFL** 116 (92) [9 yrs]

McNown, Cade Cade B., QB, 6´1˝/208 lbs; UCLA; 1999: Chi, rnd 1; B1/12/1977 Portland, OR

YEAR	TEAM	G (GS, POS)	RUSH	YD	AVG (LG)	TD	REC	YD	AVG (LG)	TD	PASS	COMP	PCT	YD	AVG (LG)	TD	INT	SK	YD	QBR	KPR	OTD	PTS	TAY
1999	ChiB	15(6, qb)	32	160	5.0(18)	0	—	—	—	—	235	127	54.0	1465	6.2(80)	8	10	18	94	—	—	—	2	533
2000	ChiB	10(9, QB)	50	326	6.5(30)	3	—	—	—	—	280	154	55.0	1646	5.9(68)	8	9	27	169	68.5	—	—	18	859
NFL	2	25(15)	82	486	5.9(30)	3	—	—	—	—	515	281	54.6	3111	6.0(80)	16	19	45	263	67.7	—	—	20	1392

McNulty, Paul Paul Davis, E, 6´0˝/180 lbs; Michigan; Notre Dame; B8/9/1902 Chicago, IL, D9/27/1985 Chicago, IL **1924** ChiC 9 (6, LE) **1925** ChiC 1 (1), 6 **NFL** 10 (7) [2 yrs]

McPeak, Bill William Patrick, DE, 6´1˝/208 lbs; Notre Dame; Pittsburgh; 1948: Pit, rnd 16; B7/24/1926 New Castle, PA, D5/7/1991 Foxboro, MA **[C]** **1949** Pit 12 (2) **1950** Pit 11 (RDE) **1951** Pit 12 (RDE) **1952** Pit✧12 (RDE) **1953** Pit★12 (RDE) **1954** Pit 12 (RDE) **1955** Pit 10 (RDE) **1956** Pit✧12 (RDE) **1957** Pit 12 (RDE) **NFL** 105 (2) [9 yrs]

McPhail, Buck Coleman Howard, FB-K, 6´1˝/195 lbs; Oklahoma; 1953: Bal, rnd 3; B12/25/1929 Oklahoma City, OK, D3/4/2005 Costa Mesa, CA **[K]**

YEAR	TEAM	G (GS, POS)	RUSH	YD	AVG (LG)	TD	REC	YD	AVG (LG)	TD	PASS	COMP	PCT	YD	AVG (LG)	TD	INT	SK	YD	QBR	KPR	OTD	PTS	TAY
1953	Bal	12	53	138	2.6(30)	0	10	38	3.8(45)	0	—	—	—	—	—	—	—	—	—	—	K	—	27	157

McPhail, Hal Harold Thomas, FB, 6´1˝/230 lbs; Army; Xavier (OH); B10/26/1912 Columbus, OH, D8/30/1977 Newport, KY **[K]**

YEAR	TEAM	G (GS, POS)	RUSH	YD	AVG (LG)	TD	REC	YD	AVG (LG)	TD	PASS	COMP	PCT	YD	AVG (LG)	TD	INT	SK	YD	QBR	KPR	OTD	PTS	TAY
1934	Bos	12(8, FB)	94	356	3.8	1	—	—	—	—	22	9	40.9	96	4.4	0	0	—	—	—	K	2	22	414
1935	Bos	7(4)	45	105	2.3	0	—	—	—	—	2	0	0.0	0	0.0	0	1	—	—	—	—	—	0	65
NFL	2	19(12)	139	461	3.3	1	—	—	—	—	24	9	37.5	96	4.0	0	1	—	—	—	K	2	22	479

McPhail, Jerris Jerris Cornelius, RB, 5´11˝/198 lbs; Wake Forest; East Carolina; 1996: Mia, rnd 5; B6/26/1972 Clinton, NC

YEAR	TEAM	G (GS, POS)	RUSH	YD	AVG (LG)	TD	REC	YD	AVG (LG)	TD	PASS	COMP	PCT	YD	AVG (LG)	TD	INT	SK	YD	QBR	KPR	OTD	PTS	TAY
1996	Mia	9(1)	6	28	4.7(10)	0	20	282	14.1(52)	0	—	—	—	—	—	—	—	—	—	—	k	—	0	279
1997	†Mia	14(1)	17	146	8.6(71)	1	34	262	7.7(19)	1	—	—	—	—	—	—	—	—	—	—	k	—	12	381
1998	Det	3(0)	—	—	—	—	—	—	—	—	—	—	—	—	—	—	—	—	—	—	k	—	0	-19
NFL	3	26(2)	23	174	7.6(71)	1	54	544	10.1(52)	1	—	—	—	—	—	—	—	—	—	—	k	—	12	641

McPhee, Frank Frank Melvin, DB-E, 6´3˝/195 lbs; Princeton; 1953: ChiC, rnd 13; B3/19/1931 Youngstown, OH **1955** ChiC 7

McPherson, Forrest Forrest Winfield, G-C-T, 5´11˝/233 lbs; Nebraska; B10/22/1911 Fairbury, NE, D10/7/1989 Centralia, WA **1935** ChiB 1 (0) **1935** Phi 7 (3) **1936** Phi 12 (11, RG) **1937** Phi 3 (0) **1943** GB 5 (1) **1944** GB 4 (0) **1945** GB 5 (0) **NFL** 37 (15) [6 yrs]

McPherson, Miles Miles Gregory, DB, 5´11˝/184 lbs; New Haven; 1982: LARm, rnd 10; B3/30/1960 Queens, NY **1982**†SD 6 (0) **1983** SD 11 (0) **1984** SD 9 (4) **1985** SD 9 (0) **NFL** 35 (4) [4 yrs]

McQuade, Johnny John Doyle, B, 5´10˝/176 lbs; Georgetown (DC); B6/4/1895, D12/24/1980 Bradford Woods, PA **1922** Can 5 (1)

McQuaid, Dan Daniel James, T-G, 6´7˝/278 lbs; UNLV; B10/4/1960 Cortland, CA **1985** Was 16 (3) **1986**†Was 13 (0) **1987** Was 1 (0) **1988** Min 3 (0) **1988** Ind 1 (0) **NFL** 34 (3) [4 yrs]

McQuarters, Ed Eddie Lee, DT, 6´1˝/255 lbs; Oklahoma; 1965: SL, rnd 18; B4/16/1943 Tulsa, OK **1965** SL 1

McQuarters, R.W. Robert William, DB, 5´10˝/198 lbs; Oklahoma State; 1998: SF, rnd 1; B12/21/1976 Tulsa, OK **[R]** **1998**†SF 16 (7, RCB) **1999** SF 11 (4) **2000** ChiB 15 (2) **2001**†ChiB 16 (16, RCB) **2002** ChiB 9 (9, LCB) **2003** ChiB 16 (6, lcb) **2004** ChiB 16 (14, LCB/rcb) **2005** Det 16 (11, rcb/lcb) **NFL** 115 (69) [8 yrs]

McQuary, Jack John Edward, HB-DB, 6´1˝/208 lbs; California; B6/20/1920 Tacoma, WA, D12/20/1986 Monterey, CA **1946** LAD-A 1 (0)

McQuay, Leon Leon, RB, 5´9˝/200 lbs; Tampa; 1973: NYG, rnd 5; B3/19/1950 Tampa, FL, D11/29/1995 Tampa, FL

YEAR	TEAM	G (GS, POS)	RUSH	YD	AVG (LG)	TD	REC	YD	AVG (LG)	TD	PASS	COMP	PCT	YD	AVG (LG)	TD	INT	SK	YD	QBR	KPR	OTD	PTS	TAY
1974	NYG	13	55	240	4.4(21)	1	5	59	11.8(25)	0	—	—	—	—	—	—	—	—	—	—	kp	—	6	640
1975	NE	13	33	47	1.4(9)	0	4	27	6.8(16)	0	—	—	—	—	—	—	—	—	—	—	k	—	0	88
1976	NO	4	—	—	—	—	—	—	—	—	—	—	—	—	—	—	—	—	—	—	kp	—	0	26
NFL	3	30	88	287	3.3(21)	1	9	86	9.6(25)	0	—	—	—	—	—	—	—	—	—	—	kp	—	6	753

McQuilken, Kim Kim Evan, QB, 6´2˝/203 lbs; Lehigh; 1974: Atl, rnd 3; B2/26/1951 Allentown, PA

YEAR	TEAM	G (GS, POS)	RUSH	YD	AVG (LG)	TD	REC	YD	AVG (LG)	TD	PASS	COMP	PCT	YD	AVG (LG)	TD	INT	SK	YD	QBR	KPR	OTD	PTS	TAY
1974	Atl	5	2	1	0.5(1)	0	—	—	—	—	79	34	43.0	373	4.7(26)	0	9	9	113	—	—	—	0	-173
1975	Atl	3(2)	4	26	6.5(14)	0	—	—	—	—	61	20	32.8	253	4.1(31)	1	9	5	45	—	—	—	0	-203
1976	Atl	8	9	26	2.9(17)	0	—	—	—	—	121	48	39.7	450	3.7(39)	2	10	17	164	—	—	—	0	-139
1977	Atl	7	2	-1	-0.5(0)	0	—	—	—	—	7	5	71.4	47	6.7(14)	1	0	—	—	—	—	—	0	28
1979	Was	3	2	-3	-1.5(-1)	0	—	—	—	—	4	1	25.0	12	3.0(12)	0	1	—	—	—	—	—	0	-37
NFL	5	26(2)	19	49	2.6(17)	0	—	—	—	—	272	108	39.7	1135	4.2(39)	4	29	31	322	—	—	—	0	-524

McRae, Bennie Benjamin Prince, DB, 6´0˝/180 lbs; Michigan; 1962: Chi, rnd 2/Bos, rnd 8; B12/8/1939 Pinehurst, NC **[I]** **1962** ChiB 14 **1963**†ChiB 14 (LCB) **1964** ChiB 14 (LCB) **1965** ChiB☆14 (LCB) **1966** ChiB 14 (LCB) **1967** ChiB 14 (LCB) **1968** ChiB 14 (LCB) **1969** ChiB 14 (LCB) **1970** ChiB 13 (LCB) **1971** NYG 8 **NFL** 133 [10 yrs]

McRae, Charles Charles Edward, T-G, 6´7˝/305 lbs; Tennessee; 1991: TB, rnd 1; B9/16/1968 Clinton, TN **1991** TB 16 (4) **1992** TB 16 (16, RT) **1993** TB 13 (4) **1994** TB 15 (10, LG) **1995** TB 11 (4) **1996** Oak 12 (1) **NFL** 83 (39) [6 yrs]

McRae, Frank Franklin, DT, 6´7˝/270 lbs; Tennessee State; 1966: Chi, rnd 6/Oak, rnd 7; B3/18/1944 Memphis, TN **1967** ChiB 6

YEAR	TEAM	G (GS, POS)	RUSH	YD	AVG(LG)	TD	REC	YD	AVG(LG)	TD	PASS	COMP	PCT	YD	AVG(LG)	TD	INT	SK	YD	QBR	KPR	OTD	PTS	TAY

McRae, Jerrold   Jerrold Elisha, WR, 6´1˝/194 lbs; Tennessee State; 1978: KC, rnd 5; B4/9/1955 Laurel, MS **1978** KC 4

| 1979 | †Phi | 5 | — | — | — | — | 1 | -2 | -2.0(-2) | 0 | — | — | — | — | — | — | — | — | — | — | — | — | 0 | -1 |
| NFL | 2 | 9 | — | — | — | — | 1 | -2 | -2.0(-2) | 0 | — | — | — | — | — | — | — | — | — | — | — | — | 0 | -1 |

McRaven, Bill   Claude Coy, WB, 5´11˝/170 lbs; Murray State; B2/23/1914 East St. Louis, MO

| 1939 | Cle | 9(4) | 7 | 29 | 4.1 | 0 | 2 | 14 | 7.0 | 0 | — | — | — | — | — | — | — | — | — | — | — | — | 0 | 36 |

McRoberts, Bob   Robert Alan, HB, 5´11˝/190 lbs; Wisconsin-Stout; B4/28/1924 Eau Galle, WI **1944** Bos 1 (0)

McRoberts, Wade   Wade Edward, C, 6´0˝/210 lbs; Westminster (PA); B1/7/1901 Niles, OH, D11/1941 **1925** Can 4 (4, C) **1926** Can 8 (3) **NFL** 12 (7) [2 yrs]

McShane, Charles   Charles Dean, LB, 6´3˝/230 lbs; California Lutheran; 1976: Dal, rnd 12; B1/4/1954 Long Beach, CA **1977** Sea 14 **1978** Sea 14 **1979** Sea 1 **NFL** 29 [3 yrs]

McShea, Joe   John Maurice, G, 5´8˝/185 lbs; Rochester; B12/13/1899, D12/21/1985 Rochester, NY **1923** Roc 1 (1)

McSwain, Chuck   Anthony, RB, 6´0˝/193 lbs; Clemson; 1983: Dal, rnd 5; B2/21/1961 Rutherford, NC **1983** Dal 1 (0) **1984** Dal 15 (0)

| 1987 | NE | 3(1) | 9 | 23 | 2.6(9) | 0 | — | — | — | — | — | — | — | — | — | — | — | — | — | — | k | — | 0 | 25 |
| NFL | 3 | 19(1) | 9 | 23 | 2.6(9) | 0 | — | — | — | — | — | — | — | — | — | — | — | — | — | — | k | — | 0 | 130 |

McSwain, Rod   Rodney, DB, 6´1˝/198 lbs; Clemson; 1984: Atl, rnd 3; B1/28/1962 Caroleen, NC **1984** NE 15 (0) **1985**†NE 16 (0) **1986**†NE 9 (0) **1987** NE 12 (0)
1988 NE 16 (1) **1989** NE 9 (4) **1990** NE 13 (12, SS) **NFL** 90 (17) [7 yrs]

McTyer, Tim   Timothy Thomas, DB, 5´11˝/181 lbs; Brigham Young; B12/14/1975 Los Angeles, CA **1997** Phi 10 (0) **1998** Phi 16 (0) **1999** Cle 2 (2) **NFL** 28 (3) [3 yrs]

McVea, Warren   Warren Douglas, RB-SE-WR, 5´9˝/182 lbs; Houston; 1968: Cin, rnd 4; B7/30/1946 San Antonio, TX

1968	Cin-A	12(SE)	9	133	14.8(80)	1	21	264	12.6(55)	2	—	—	—	—	—	—	—	—	—	—	k	—	18	385
1969	†KC-A	11(hb)	106	500	4.7(80)	7	7	71	10.1(22)	0	3	1	33.3	50	16.7(50)	1	0	—	—	—	k	—	42	759
1970	KC	14	61	260	4.3(34)	0	5	26	5.2(15)	0	1	0	0.0	0	0.0	0	0	—	—	—	k	—	0	285
1971	†KC	12	68	288	4.2(19)	3	5	-3	-0.6(10)	0	—	—	—	—	—	—	—	—	—	—	k	—	18	359
1973	KC	7	4	5	1.3(2)	0	—	—	—	—	—	—	—	—	—	—	—	—	—	—	k	—	0	31
NFL	5	56	248	1186	4.8(80)	11	38	358	9.4(55)	2	4	1	25.0	50	12.5(50)	1	0	—	—	—	k	—	78	1818

McVeigh, John   John Bosco, LB, 6´1˝/226 lbs; Miami (FL); Kentucky; 1986: Sea, rnd 12; B10/19/1962 **1987** Sea 3 (3)

McWatters, Bill   Billie Pittman, FB, 6´0˝/225 lbs; North Texas; 1964: Min, rnd 8; B8/1/1942 Donie, TX

| 1964 | Min | 11 | 14 | 60 | 4.3(16) | 1 | 2 | -1 | -0.5(1) | 0 | — | — | — | — | — | — | — | — | — | — | k | — | 6 | 62 |

McWilliams, Bill   William Henry, WB, 6´1˝/205 lbs; Iowa; B11/28/1910 Dubuque, IA

| 1934 | Det | 5(0) | 6 | 16 | 2.7 | — | — | — | — | — | — | — | — | — | — | — | — | — | — | — | — | — | 0 | 16 |

McWilliams, Johnny   Johnny E., TE, 6´4˝/271 lbs; USC; 1996: Arz, rnd 3; B12/14/1972 Ontario, CA

1996	Arz	12(0)	—	—	—	—	7	80	11.4(21)	1	—	—	—	—	—	—	—	—	—	—	—	—	6	45
1997	Arz	16(7, te)	—	—	—	—	7	75	10.7(15)	0	—	—	—	—	—	—	—	—	—	—	—	—	0	38
1998	†Arz	16(15, TE)	—	—	—	—	26	284	10.9(26)	4	—	—	—	—	—	—	—	—	—	—	—	—	24	162
1999	Arz	15(4)	—	—	—	—	11	71	6.5(19)	1	—	—	—	—	—	—	—	—	—	—	—	—	6	41
2000	†Min	15(7, te)	—	—	—	—	22	180	8.2(20)	3	—	—	—	—	—	—	—	—	—	—	—	—	18	105
NFL	5	74(33)	—	—	—	—	73	690	9.5(26)	9	—	—	—	—	—	—	—	—	—	—	—	—	54	390

McWilliams, Shorty   Thomas Edward, DB-HB, 5´11˝/185 lbs; Mississippi State; Army; 1948: LAD-A, rnd 16/ChiB, rnd 8; B5/12/1926 Newton, MS, D1/9/1997 Meridian, MS

| 1949 | LAD-A | 12(2) | 3 | 15 | 5.0 | 0 | — | — | — | — | 2 | 0 | 0.0 | 0 | 0.0 | 0 | 0 | — | — | — | pi | — | 0 | 112 |
| 1950 | Pit | 10(DB) | 14 | 39 | 3.9(12) | 0 | — | — | — | — | 8 | 5 | 62.5 | 113 | 14.1(63) | 0 | 1 | — | — | — | Pkpi | — | 0 | 178 |

Mead, Jack   John Michael, E, 6´3˝/213 lbs; Wisconsin; 1945: NYG, rnd 7; B4/18/1921 Appleton, WI

1946	†NYG	10(0)	—	—	—	—	3	36	12.0(19)	0	—	—	—	—	—	—	—	—	—	—	i	—	0	46
1947	NYG	10(0)	—	—	—	—	6	91	15.2(41)	0	—	—	—	—	—	—	—	—	—	—	—	—	0	46
NFL	2	20(0)	—	—	—	—	9	127	14.1(41)	0	—	—	—	—	—	—	—	—	—	—	i	—	0	92

Meade, Jim   James Gordon, HB, 6´1˝/195 lbs; Maryland; B2/28/1914 Philadelphia, PA, D8/7/1977 Peachtree City, GA

1939	Was	8(0)	13	34	2.6	0	1	1	1.0(1)	0	—	—	—	—	—	—	—	—	—	—	P	—	0	35
1940	†Was	10(4)	48	115	2.4	0	4	39	9.8	0	—	—	—	—	—	—	—	—	—	—	Pi	—	0	130
NFL	2	18(4)	61	149	2.4	0	5	40	8.0(1)	0	—	—	—	—	—	—	—	—	—	—	Pi	—	0	164

Meade, Mike   Michael Lee, RB, 5´11˝/228 lbs; Penn State; 1982: GB, rnd 5; B2/12/1960 Dover, DE

1982	GB	2(1)	14	42	3.0(19)	0	3	-5	-1.7(-1)	0	—	—	—	—	—	—	—	—	—	—	k	—	0	41
1983	GB	16(7, fb)	55	201	3.7(15)	1	16	110	6.9(31)	2	—	—	—	—	—	—	—	—	—	—	—	—	18	276
1984	Det	15(0)	—	—	—	—	—	—	—	—	—	—	—	—	—	—	—	—	—	—	k	—	0	-28
1985	Det	16(0)	3	18	6.0(9)	0	2	21	10.5(14)	0	—	—	—	—	—	—	—	—	—	—	—	—	0	29
NFL	4	49(8)	72	261	3.6(19)	1	21	126	6.0(31)	2	—	—	—	—	—	—	—	—	—	—	k	—	18	317

Meador, Eddie   Edward Doyle, DB, 5´11˝/193 lbs; Arkansas Tech; 1959: LA, rnd 7; B8/10/1937 Dallas, TX [I]

1959	LARm	12(DB)	—	—	—	—	—	—	—	—	—	—	—	—	—	—	—	—	—	—	pi	—	0	-17
1960	LARm★	12(LCB)	—	—	—	—	—	—	—	—	—	—	—	—	—	—	—	—	—	—	pi	1	6	31
1961	LARm☆	14(LCB)	—	—	—	—	—	—	—	—	—	—	—	—	—	—	—	i	—	—	—	—	0	29
1962	LARm	14(LCB)	—	—	—	—	—	—	—	—	—	—	—	—	—	—	—	i	—	—	—	—	0	-5
1963	LARm☆	14(LCB)	1	1	1.0(1)	0	—	—	—	—	—	—	—	—	—	—	—	i	—	—	—	—	0	9
1964	LARm★	14(RS)	—	—	—	—	—	—	—	—	1	0	0.0	0	0.0	0	—	—	—	—	kpi	—	0	92
1965	LARm★	14(RS)	2	35	17.5(24)	1	—	—	—	—	1	0	0.0	0	0.0	0	—	—	—	—	i	—	6	92
1966	LARm★	14(RS)	1	7	7.0(7)	0	—	—	—	—	1	0	0.0	0	0.0	0	—	—	—	—	i	—	0	42
1967	†LARm☆	14(RS)	—	—	—	—	—	—	—	—	1	1	100.0	18	18.0(18)	1	0	—	—	—	pi	2	12	123
1968	LARm☆	14(14, RS)	1	11	11.0(11)	0	—	—	—	—	—	—	—	—	—	—	—	—	—	—	kpi	—	0	74
1969	†LARm☆	14(14, RS)	1	5	5.0(5)	0	—	—	—	—	1	0	0.0	0	0.0	0	—	—	—	—	pi	2	12	91
1970	LARm	13(FS)	—	—	—	—	—	—	—	—	—	—	—	—	—	—	—	—	—	—	—	—	0	12
NFL	12	163(28)	6	59	9.8(24)	1	—	—	—	—	5	1	20.0	18	3.6(18)	1	0	—	—	—	kpi	5	36	573

Meadow, Ralph   Ralph, E, 6´2˝/195 lbs; none; deceased **1920** Can 1 (1)

Meadows, Adam   Adam Jonathan, T, 6´5˝/290 lbs; Georgia; 1997: Ind, rnd 2; B1/25/1974 Powder Springs, GA **1997** Ind 16 (16, LT) **1998** Ind 14 (14, RT) **1999**†Ind 16 (16, RT)
2000†Ind 16 (16, RT) **2001** Ind 15 (15, RT) **2002**†Ind 14 (14, RT) **2003** Ind 12 (5, rt) **NFL** 103 (96) [7 yrs]

Meadows, Darryl   Darryl Scott, DB, 6´1˝/202 lbs; Toledo; B2/15/1961 Cincinnati, OH **1983** Hou 16 (0) **1984** Hou 13 (0) **NFL** 29 (0) [2 yrs]

Meadows, Ed   Edward Allen, DE-E, 6´2˝/221 lbs; Duke; 1954: ChiB, rnd 3; B2/19/1932 Oxford, NC, D10/22/1974 Morehead City, NC **1954** ChiB 12 **1955** Pit 12 (LDE)
1956†ChiB☆12 (RDE) **1957** ChiB 12 (LDE) **1958** Phi 12 (LDE) **1959** Was 5 **NFL** 65 [6 yrs]

Meads, Johnny   Johnny Sand, LB, 6´2˝/231 lbs; Nicholls State; 1984: Hou, rnd 3; B6/25/1961 Labadieville, LA **1984** Hou 16 (0) **1985** Hou 5 (5, rolb) **1986** Hou 16 (13, ROLB)
1987†Hou 12 (12, ROLB) **1988**†Hou 16 (16, ROLB) **1989**†Hou 16 (16, ROLB) **1990**†Hou 16 (16, RLB) **1991**†Hou 16 (16, RLB) **1992** Hou 4 (3) **1992** Was 2 (0)
NFL 119 (97) [9 yrs]

Meagher, Jack   John Francis, E, 5´10˝/178 lbs; Notre Dame; B10/1/1896 Chicago, IL, D11/7/1968 San Francisco, CA **[C]** **1920** ChiT 4 (3)

Mealey, Rondell   Rondell Christopher, RB, 6´0˝/224 lbs; LSU; 2000: GB, rnd 7; B2/24/1977 New Orleans, LA

2001	GB	11(0)	11	37	3.4(9)	0	2	31	15.5(19)	0	—	—	—	—	—	—	—	—	—	—	k	1	6	56
2002	GB	3(1)	11	36	3.3(18)	1	7	45	6.4(11)	0	—	—	—	—	—	—	—	—	—	—	—	—	6	69
NFL	2	14(1)	22	73	3.3(18)	1	9	76	8.4(19)	0	—	—	—	—	—	—	—	—	—	—	k	1	12	124

Meamber, Tim   Timothy Frederick, LB, 6´3˝/231 lbs; Washington; 1985: Min, rnd 3; B10/29/1962 Yreka, CA **1985** Min 4 (0)

Means, Dave   David Mitchell, DE, 6´4˝/235 lbs; Southeast Missouri State; 1974: Buf, rnd 3; B1/23/1952 Hopkinsville, KY **1974**†Buf 9

Means, Natrone   Natrone Jermaine, RB, 5´10˝/245 lbs; North Carolina; 1993: SD, rnd 2; B4/26/1972 Harrisburg, NC

| 1993 | SD | 16(0, rb) | 160 | 645 | 4.0(65) | 8 | 10 | 59 | 5.9(11) | 0 | 1 | 0 | 0.0 | 0 | 0.0 | 0 | 0 | — | — | — | k | — | 48 | 747 |
| 1994 | †SD★ | 16(16, RB) | 343 | 1350 | 3.9(25) | 12 | 39 | 235 | 6.0(22) | 0 | 1 | 0 | 0.0 | 0 | 0.0 | 0 | 0 | — | — | — | — | — | 72 | 1588 |

YEAR	TEAM	G (GS, POS)	RUSH	YD	AVG (LG)	TD	REC	YD	AVG (LG)	TD	PASS	COMP	PCT	YD	AVG (LG)	TD	INT	SK	YD	QBR	KPR	OTD	PTS	TAY
1995	†SD	10 (9, RB)	186	730	3.9 (36)	5	7	46	6.6 (14)	0	—	—	—	—	—	—	—	—	—	—	—	—	30	803
1996	†Jax	14 (4, rb)	152	507	3.3 (35)	2	7	45	6.4 (11)	1	—	—	—	—	—	—	—	—	—	—	—	—	18	555
1997	†Jax	14 (11, RB)	244	823	3.4 (20)	9	15	104	6.9 (21)	0	—	—	—	—	—	—	—	—	—	—	—	—	54	965
1998	SD	10 (10, RB)	212	883	4.2 (72)	5	16	91	5.7 (22)	0	—	—	—	—	—	—	—	—	—	—	—	—	30	979
1999	SD	7 (5, RB)	112	277	2.5 (15)	4	9	51	5.7 (12)	1	—	—	—	—	—	—	—	—	—	—	—	—	30	348
2000	Car	1 (0)	—	—	—	—	—	—	—	—	—	—	—	—	—	—	—	—	—	—	—	—	—	—
NFL	8	88 (55)	1409	5215	3.7 (72)	45	103	631	6.1 (22)	2	2	0	0.0	0	0.0	0	0	—	—	—	k	—	282	5983

MECHAM, CURT Curtis William, TB, 6´0˝/180 lbs; Oregon; 1942: Bkn, rnd 3; B3/2/1920 Bakersfield, CA

YEAR	TEAM	G (GS, POS)	RUSH	YD	AVG (LG)	TD	REC	YD	AVG (LG)	TD	PASS	COMP	PCT	YD	AVG (LG)	TD	INT	SK	YD	QBR	KPR	OTD	PTS	TAY
1942	Bkn	8 (0)	3	0	0.0 (5)	0	—	—	—	—	4	1	25.0	9	2.3 (9)	0	1	—	—	—	—	—	0	-36

MECKLENBURG, KARL Karl Bernard, LB-DE, 6´3˝/240 lbs; Augustana (SD); Minnesota; 1983: Den, rnd 12; B9/1/1960 Seattle, WA **[S]** **1983**†Den 16 (0) **1984**†Den 16 (1) **1985** Den★16 (9, LILB) **1986**†Den★16 (16, LILB) **1987**†Den★12 (12, LILB) **1988** Den 9 (9, LILB) **1989**†Den★15 (15, LILB) **1990** Den 16 (16, LILB) **1991**†Den★16 (16, LILB) **1992** Den 16 (16, LILB) **1993**†Den✧16 (16, LILB) **1994** Den 16 (15, MLB) **NFL** 180 (141) [12 yrs]

MEDLIN, DAN Daniel Ellis, G, 6´3˝/260 lbs; North Carolina State; 1972: Oak, rnd 6; B10/12/1949 High Point, NC **1974** Oak 6 **1975**†Oak 14 **1976**†Oak 13 **1977** TB 14 (14, RG) **1978** TB 14 (8, rg) **1979** Oak 15 (4) **NFL** 76 (26) [6 yrs]

MEDVED, RON Ronald George, DB-LB, 6´1˝/210 lbs; Washington; 1966: Phi, rnd 14; B5/27/1944 Tacoma, WA **1966** Phi 14 **1967** Phi 8 (3) **1968** Phi 14 (LLB) **1969** Phi 3 **1970** Phi 12 (ss) **NFL** 51 (3) [5 yrs]

MEEHAN, GREG Gregory Allen, WR, 6´0˝/191 lbs; Bowling Green State; B4/27/1963 Otis AFB, MA

YEAR	TEAM	G (GS, POS)	RUSH	YD	AVG (LG)	TD	REC	YD	AVG (LG)	TD	PASS	COMP	PCT	YD	AVG (LG)	TD	INT	SK	YD	QBR	KPR	OTD	PTS	TAY
1987	Cin	3 (3)	4	19	4.8 (17)	0	3	25	8.3 (12)	0	—	—	—	—	—	—	—	—	—	—	k	—	0	26

MEEKER, BUTCH Herbert Lawrence, B, 5´3˝/143 lbs; Washington State; B7/14/1904, WA, D4/1980 Brandon, FL **[K]** **1930** Pro 11 (3), 16 **1931** Pro 9 (3), 1 **NFL** 20 (6), 17 [2 yrs]

MEEKS, BOB Robert Earl, C, 6´2˝/279 lbs; Auburn; 1992: Den, rnd 10; B5/28/1969 Andalusia, AL **1993** Den 8 (0)

MEEKS, BRYANT Bryant Adams, C-LB, 6´2˝/193 lbs; Georgia; South Carolina; 1947: Pit, rnd 7/SF-A, rnd 18; B1/16/1926 Jacksonville, FL **1947** Pit 8 (0) **1948** Pit 10 (3) **NFL** 18 (3) [2 yrs]

MEEKS, EDDIE John Edward, WB, 5´7˝/155 lbs; Louisville; B9/30/1897 Louisville, KY, D10/15/1963 Louisville, KY **1922** Lou 3 (1)

MEESE, WARD Ward King, E, 5´10˝/175 lbs; Wabash; B7/28/1898, deceased **1922** Mil 4 (2) **1923** SL 5 (5, RE) **1924** Ham 1 (0) **1925** Ham 1 (0) **NFL** 11 (7) [4 yrs]

MEESTER, BRAD Brad Ley, C-G, 6´3˝/300 lbs; Northern Iowa; 2000: Jax, rnd 2; B3/23/1977 Iowa Falls, IA **2000** Jax 16 (16, LG) **2001** Jax 16 (16, LG) **2002** Jax 16 (16, LG) **2003** Jax 16 (16, C) **2004** Jax 16 (16, C) **2005** Jax 12 (12, C) **NFL** 92 (92) [6 yrs]

MEGGETT, DAVE David Lee, RB, 5´7˝/190 lbs; Morgan State; Towson State; 1989: NYG, rnd 5; B4/30/1966 Charleston, SC **[R]**

YEAR	TEAM	G (GS, POS)	RUSH	YD	AVG (LG)	TD	REC	YD	AVG (LG)	TD	PASS	COMP	PCT	YD	AVG (LG)	TD	INT	SK	YD	QBR	KPR	OTD	PTS	TAY
1989	†NYG★	16 (2)	28	117	4.2 (18)	0	34	531	15.6 (62)	4	—	—	—	—	—	—	—	—	—	—	kp	1	30	937
1990	†NYG☆	16 (1)	22	164	7.5 (51)	0	39	410	10.5 (38)	1	—	—	—	—	—	—	—	—	—	—	kp	1	12	813
1991	NYG	16 (2)	29	153	5.3 (30)	1	50	412	8.2 (22)	3	1	0	0.0	0	0.0	0	0	1	0	—	kp	1	30	680
1992	NYG	16 (0)	32	167	5.2 (30)	0	38	229	6.0 (24)	2	—	—	—	—	—	—	—	—	—	—	kp	1	18	562
1993	†NYG	16 (1)	69	329	4.8 (23)	0	38	319	8.4 (50)	0	2	2	100.0	63	31.5 (42)	2	0	—	—	—	kp	1	6	754
1994	NYG	16 (3)	91	298	3.3 (26)	4	32	293	9.2 (34)	0	2	1	50.0	16	8.0 (16)	1	0	1	7	—	kp	2	36	824
1995	NE	16 (0)	60	250	4.2 (25)	2	52	334	6.4 (19)	0	1	0	0.0	0	0.0	0	0	—	—	—	kp	—	16	989
1996	†NE★	16 (1)	40	122	3.1 (12)	0	33	292	8.8 (26)	0	1	0	0.0	0	0.0	0	0	—	—	—	kp	1	6	877
1997	†NE	16 (2)	20	60	3.0 (10)	1	19	203	10.7 (49)	1	1	1	100.0	35	35.0 (35)	1	0	—	—	—	kp	—	12	762
1998	†NYJ	2 (0)	7	24	3.4 (18)	0	1	15	15.0 (15)	0	—	—	—	—	—	—	—	—	—	—	kp	—	0	48
NFL	10	146 (12)	398	1684	4.2 (51)	8	336	3038	9.0 (62)	11	8	4	50.0	114	14.3 (42)	4	0	2	7	—	kp	8	166	7244

MEGGYESY, DAVE David Michael, LB, 6´2˝/220 lbs; Syracuse; 1963: SL, rnd 17; B11/1/1941 Cleveland, OH **1963** SL 6 **1964** SL 14 **1965** SL 14 (llb) **1966** SL 14 **1967** SL 14 **1968** SL 12 (RLB) **1969** SL 8 (rlb) **NFL** 82 [7 yrs]

MEGNA, MARC Marc, LB, 6´2˝/245 lbs; Richmond; 1999: NYJ, rnd 6; B7/30/1976 Fall River, MA **2000** Cin 2 (0) **2000** NE 4 (0) **NFL** 6 (0) [1 yr]

MEHELICH, CHARLEY Charles J., DE-E, 6´1˝/199 lbs; Duquesne; 1945: Pit, rnd 5; B8/4/1922 Oakmont, PA, D12/2/1984 Willow Grove, PA

YEAR	TEAM	G (GS, POS)	RUSH	YD	AVG (LG)	TD	REC	YD	AVG (LG)	TD	PASS	COMP	PCT	YD	AVG (LG)	TD	INT	SK	YD	QBR	KPR	OTD	PTS	TAY
1946	Pit	10 (4)	—	—	—	—	10	116	11.6 (35)	0	—	—	—	—	—	—	—	—	—	—	—	—	0	58
1947	†Pit☆	11 (4)	—	—	—	—	3	38	12.7 (13)	0	—	—	—	—	—	—	—	—	—	—	—	—	0	19
1948	Pit	12 (6, LE)	—	—	—	—	—	—	—	—	2	0	0.0	0	0.0	0	0	—	—	—	k	—	0	-13
1949	Pit	9 (2)	—	—	—	—	—	—	—	—	—	—	—	—	—	—	—	—	—	—	—	—	—	—
1950	Pit	12 (LDE)	—	—	—	—	2	18	9.0 (10)	0	—	—	—	—	—	—	—	—	—	—	k	—	0	-5
1951	Pit	5 (lde)	—	—	—	—	—	—	—	—	—	—	—	—	—	—	—	—	—	—	—	—	2	0
NFL	6	59 (16)	—	—	—	—	15	172	11.5 (35)	0	2	0	0.0	0	0.0	0	0	—	—	—	k	—	2	59

MEHELICH, TONY Thomas Tony, G, 5´11˝/195 lbs; St. Mary's (MN); B8/4/1906 Grand Rapids, MN, D5/20/1972 Coleraine, MN **1929** Min 8 (4)

MEHL, LANCE Lance Alan, LB, 6´3˝/235 lbs; Penn State; 1980: NYJ, rnd 3; B2/14/1958 Bellaire, OH **1980** NYJ 14 (1) **1981**†NYJ 15 (15, RLB) **1982**†NYJ☆9 (9, RLB) **1983** NYJ☆16 (16, RLB) **1984** NYJ 16 (15, RLB) **1985**†NYJ★16 (16, RILB) **1986** NYJ 8 (7, RILB) **1987** NYJ 3 (2) **NFL** 97 (81) [8 yrs]

MEHRE, HARRY Harry James, C, 6´1˝/190 lbs; Notre Dame; B9/18/1901 Huntington, IN, D9/27/1978 Atlanta, GA **[C]** **1922** Min 3 (2) **1923** Min☆9 (9, C) **NFL** 12 (11) [2 yrs]

MEHRINGER, PETE Peter Joseph, T-G, 6´2˝/206 lbs; Kansas; B7/15/1910 Jetmore, KS, D8/27/1987 Pullman, WA **1934** ChiC 8 (1) **1935** ChiC 8 (0) **1936** ChiC 3 (0) **NFL** 19 (1) [3 yrs]

MEIER, ROB Robert Jack Daniel, DE-DT, 6´5˝/293 lbs; Washington State; 2000: Jax, rnd 7; B8/29/1977 Vancouver, Canada **2000** Jax 16 (0) **2001** Jax 16 (0) **2002** Jax 16 (7, RDE) **2003** Jax 16 (0) **2004** Jax 11 (8, LDE) **2005**†Jax 16 (2) **NFL** 91 (17) [6 yrs]

MEIER, SHAD Shadley Benjamin, TE, 6´4˝/255 lbs; Kansas State; 2001: Ten, rnd 3; B6/7/1978 St. Louis, MO

YEAR	TEAM	G (GS, POS)	RUSH	YD	AVG (LG)	TD	REC	YD	AVG (LG)	TD	PASS	COMP	PCT	YD	AVG (LG)	TD	INT	SK	YD	QBR	KPR	OTD	PTS	TAY
2001	Ten	11 (1)	—	—	—	—	3	31	10.3 (18)	0	—	—	—	—	—	—	—	—	—	—	—	—	0	16
2002	†Ten	12 (0)	—	—	—	—	1	17	17.0 (17)	1	—	—	—	—	—	—	—	—	—	—	—	—	6	14
2003	†Ten	15 (6, te)	—	—	—	—	13	159	12.2 (27)	0	—	—	—	—	—	—	—	—	—	—	k	—	0	74
2004	Ten	14 (7, te)	—	—	—	—	25	127	5.1 (29)	2	—	—	—	—	—	—	—	—	—	—	—	—	12	74
2005	NO	1 (0)	—	—	—	—	—	—	—	—	—	—	—	—	—	—	—	—	—	—	—	—	—	—
NFL	5	53 (14)	—	—	—	—	42	334	8.0 (29)	3	—	—	—	—	—	—	—	—	—	—	k	—	18	176

MEILINGER, STEVE Stephen Frank, E, 6´2˝/227 lbs; Kentucky; 1954: Was, rnd 1; B12/12/1930 Bethlehem, PA

YEAR	TEAM	G (GS, POS)	RUSH	YD	AVG (LG)	TD	REC	YD	AVG (LG)	TD	PASS	COMP	PCT	YD	AVG (LG)	TD	INT	SK	YD	QBR	KPR	OTD	PTS	TAY
1956	Was	12 (RE)	—	—	—	—	24	395	16.5 (51)	5	—	—	—	—	—	—	—	—	—	—	—	—	30	223
1957	Was	12 (RE)	—	—	—	—	13	183	14.1 (34)	2	—	—	—	—	—	—	—	—	—	—	—	—	12	102
1958	GB	12	—	—	—	—	13	139	10.7 (19)	1	—	—	—	—	—	—	—	—	—	—	—	—	6	75
1960	†GB	12	—	—	—	—	2	43	21.5 (23)	0	—	—	—	—	—	—	—	—	—	—	k	—	0	7
1961	Pit	4	1	6	6.0 (6)	0	8	103	12.9 (17)	0	—	—	—	—	—	—	—	—	—	—	—	—	0	58
NFL	5	52	1	6	6.0 (6)	0	60	863	14.4 (51)	8	—	—	—	—	—	—	—	—	—	—	k	—	48	463

MEINERT, DALE Dale Herman, LB-G, 6´2˝/220 lbs; Oklahoma State; 1955: Bal, rnd 8; B12/18/1933 Lone Wolf, OK, D5/10/2004 Clinton, OK **1958** ChiC 12 (LG) **1959** ChiC 12 (LG) **1960** SL 12 (MLB) **1961** SL 14 (MLB) **1962** SL 5 (mlb) **1963** SL✧14 (MLB) **1964** SL☆14 (MLB) **1965** SL✧14 (MLB) **1966** SL 14 (MLB) **1967** SL★14 (MLB) **NFL** 125 [10 yrs]

MEINHARDT, GEORGE George Michael, C-G, 5´9˝/200 lbs; St. Louis; B11/24/1897 St. Louis, MO, D4/1/1971 Dt. Louis, MO **1923** SL 6 (2)

MEISENHEIMER, DARREL Darrel David, DB, 5´10˝/195 lbs; Oklahoma State; 1951: Det, rnd 17; B4/30/1927 Wellsford, KS **1951** NYY 9

MEISNER, BILL William L., WB, 5´11˝/185 lbs; Syracuse; B2/19/1893, D2/1968 North Tonawanda, NY **1921** Ton 1 (1, WB)

MEISNER, GREG Gregory Paul, NT-DE, 6´3˝/257 lbs; Pittsburgh; 1981: LA, rnd 3; B4/23/1959 New Kensington, PA **1981** LARm 9 (0) **1982** LARm 6 (1) **1983**†LARm 16 (10, NT) **1984**†LARm 16 (16, NT) **1985**†LARm 14 (0) **1986**†LARm 15 (0) **1987** LARm 15 (15, NT) **1988**†LARm 12 (0) **1989** KC 12 (0) **1990** KC 16 (0) **1991** NYG 4 (0) **NFL** 135 (42) [11 yrs]

MEIXLER, ED Edward, LB, 6´3˝/245 lbs; Boston University; 1965: Bos, rnd 18; B10/11/1943 **1965** Bos-A 4

MELANDER, JON Jon James, G-T, 6´7˝/280 lbs; Minnesota; 1990: NE, rnd 5; B12/27/1966 Fridley, MN **1991** NE 10 (3) **1992** Cin 15 (7, RG) **1993**†Den 14 (7, lg) **1994** Den 15 (15, LG) **NFL** 54 (32) [4 yrs]

MELINKOVICH, MIKE Michael Joseph, DE, 6´4˝/245 lbs; Washington; 1965: SL, rnd 17; B1/7/1942 Tonasket, WA **1965** SL 14 **1966** SL 10 **1967** Det 7 **NFL** 31 [3 yrs]

YEAR	TEAM	G (GS, POS)	RUSH	YD	AVG(LG)	TD	REC	YD	AVG(LG)	TD	PASS	COMP	PCT	YD	AVG(LG)	TD	INT	SK	YD	QBR	KPR	OTD	PTS	TAY

MELKA, JIM   James David, LB, 6´1˝/235 lbs; Wisconsin; 1985: TB, rnd 12; B1/15/1962 West Allis, WI   **1987** GB 1 (0)

MELLEKAS, JOHN   John Stavros, C-DT-T, 6´3˝/255 lbs; Arizona; 1956: ChiB, rnd 4; B6/14/1933 Newport, RI   **1956**†ChiB 12   **1958** ChiB 12 (c)   **1959** ChiB 12 (C)   **1960** ChiB 12 (C)
1961 ChiB 14   **1962** SF 11   **1963** Phi 11 (9, RDT)   **NFL** 84 (9) [7 yrs]

MELLO, JIM   James Anthony, DB-FB-LB, 5´10˝/190 lbs; Notre Dame; 1945: Bos, rnd 6; B11/8/1920 Warwick, RI

1947	Bos	9(4)	33	62	1.9(9)	0	2	26	13.0(23)	0	—	—	—	—	—	—	—	—	—	—	i	—	0	70
1948	LARm	3(0)	7	3	0.4(4)	0	1	17	17.0(17)	0	—	—	—	—	—	—	—	—	—	—	—	—	0	12
1949	Det	10(0)									—	—	—	—	—	—	—	—	—	—	ki	—	0	38
NFL	3	22(4)	40	65	1.6(9)	0	3	43	14.3(23)	0	—	—	—	—	—	—	—	—	—	—	ki	—	0	120
1948	ChiR-A	6(2)	50	243	4.9	1	3	38	12.7	0	—	—	—	—	—	—	—	—	—	—	k	—	6	272

MELLODY, DUTCH   Walter, WB-C, 5´8˝/188 lbs; none; deceased   **1920** Roc 4 (0)

MELLUS, JOHN   John G., T, 6´0˝/214 lbs; Villanova; 1938: NYG, rnd 9; B6/16/1917 Plymouth, PA, D11/28/2005 Plymouth, PA **[K]**   **1938**†NYG✧11 (0)   **1939**†NYG☆11 (8, RT)
1940 NYG☆8 (8, RT)   **1941**†NYG★11 (11, LT)   **NFL** 41 (27) [4 yrs]

1946 SF-A 14 (10, LT)   **1948**†Bal-A 14 (0)   **1949** Bal-A 12 (1)

| 1947 | Bal-A | 14(9, LT) | | | | | 0 | 5 | (5) | 0 | — | — | — | — | — | — | — | — | — | — | — | — | 0 | 3 |
| **AAFC** | 4 | 54(20) | | | | | 0 | 5 | (5) | 0 | — | — | — | — | — | — | — | — | — | — | K | — | 1 | 3 |

MELONTREE, ANDREW   Andrew Richard, LB, 6´4˝/228 lbs; Baylor; 1980: Cin, rnd 6; B12/1/1957 Tyler, TX   **1980** Cin 16 (0)

MELTON, TERRENCE   Terrence, LB, 6´1˝/235 lbs; Rice; B1/1/1977 Miami, FL   **2004** Atl 1 (0)   **2004** NO 2 (0)   **2005** NO 15 (2)   **NFL** 18 (2) [2 yrs]

MELVILLE, DAN   Daniel Lee, P, 6´0˝/185 lbs; California; B3/4/1956 San Diego, CA

| 1979 | SF | 16 | 3 | 0 | 0.0(0) | 0 | — | — | — | — | — | — | — | — | — | — | — | — | — | — | P | — | 0 | 0 |

MELVIN, TOM   Thomas, E-WB, 6´1˝/185 lbs; none; deceased   **1921** Cin 3 (2), 6

MEMMELAAR, DALE   Dale Edward, G-T, 6´2˝/247 lbs; Wyoming; 1959: ChiC, rnd 21; B1/15/1937 Goshen, NY   **1959** ChiC 12 (LT)   **1960** SL 12   **1961** SL 8   **1962** Dal 14 (RG)
1963 Dal 14 (RG)   **1964**†Cle 14   **1965**†Cle 14   **1966** Bal 12   **1967** Bal 7   **NFL** 107 (9 yrs]

MENASCO, DON   Donald Dean, DB, 6´0˝/185 lbs; Texas; 1952: NYG, rnd 4; B10/18/1929 Hyman, TX   **1952** NYG 12 (DB)   **1953** NYG 8   **1954** Was 6   **NFL** 26 [3 yrs]

MENDENHALL, JOHN   John Rufus, DT-NT, 6´1˝/255 lbs; Grambling State; 1972: NYG, rnd 3; B12/3/1948 Cullen, LA   **1972** NYG 14 (RDT)   **1973** NYG 8 (RDT)
1974 NYG☆13 (RDT)   **1975** NYG 9 (RDT)   **1976** NYG 14 (RDT)   **1977** NYG 14 (LDT)   **1978** NYG 16 (16, LDT)   **1979** NYG 13 (NT)   **1980** Det 15 (12, RDT)   **NFL** 116 (28) [9 yrs]

MENDENHALL, KEN   Kenneth Ernest, C, 6´3˝/242 lbs; Oklahoma; 1970: Atl, rnd 5; B8/11/1948 Enid, OK   **1971**†Bal 14   **1972** Bal 12   **1973** Bal 13 (13, C)   **1974** Bal 14 (14, C)
1975†Bal 14 (14, C)   **1976**†Bal 14 (14, C)   **1977** Bal 16 (16, C)   **1979** Bal 16 (16, C)   **1980** Bal 16 (16, C)   **NFL** 143 (117) [10 yrs]

MENDENHALL, MAT   Matthew W., DE, 6´6˝/254 lbs; Brigham Young; 1980: Was, rnd 2; B5/14/1957 Salt Lake City, UT   **1981** Was 14 (11, lde/rde)   **1982**†Was 9 (9, LDE)
NFL 23 (20) [2 yrs]

MENDENHALL, TERRY   Terry L., LB, 6´1˝/210 lbs; San Diego State; B4/16/1949 Los Angeles, CA   **1971** Oak 14   **1972** Oak 3   **NFL** 17 [2 yrs]

MENDEZ, MARIO   Mario, HB, 5´11˝/200 lbs; San Diego State; B1942 San Diego, CA   **1964** SD-A 1

MENDOZA, RUBEN   Ruben Edward, G, 6´4˝/290 lbs; Yankton; Wayne State (NE); B5/10/1963 Crystal City, TX   **1986** GB 6 (0)

MENEFEE, PEP   Hartwell, WR, 6´1˝/198 lbs; Cameron; New Mexico State; 1966: Hou, rnd 7; B1/1/1943 Fort Worth, TX

| 1966 | NYG | 7 | | | | | 1 | 11 | 11.0(11) | 0 | — | — | — | — | — | — | — | — | — | — | — | — | 0 | 6 |

MENEFEE, VIC   Victor E., E, 6´0˝/185 lbs; Morningside; B1898, deceased   **1921** RI 2 (0)

MERCEIN, CHUCK   Charles Schley, RB, 6´2˝/225 lbs; Yale; 1965: NYG, rnd 3/Buf, rnd 10; B4/9/1943 Milwaukee, WI **[K]**

1965	NYG	13	18	55	3.1(15)	2	3	14	4.7(5)	0	—	—	—	—	—	—	—	—	—	—	Kk	—	12	71
1966	NYG	13(FB)	94	327	3.5(22)	0	27	152	5.6(20)	0	—	—	—	—	—	—	—	—	—	—	—	—	0	403
1967	NYG	1					—	—	—	—	—	—	—	—	—	—	—	—	—	—	K	—	2	0
1967	†GB	6	14	56	4.0(15)	1	1	6	6.0(6)	0	—	—	—	—	—	—	—	—	—	—	—	—	6	69
1968	GB	11	17	49	2.9(8)	1	3	6	2.0(9)	0	—	—	—	—	—	—	—	—	—	—	K	—	19	62
1969	GB	5					—	—	—	—	—	—	—	—	—	—	—	—	—	—	—	—	0	—
1970	NYJ	9	20	44	2.2(10)	0	3	27	9.0(15)	1	—	—	—	—	—	—	—	—	—	—	k	—	6	35
NFL	6	58	163	531	3.3(22)	4	37	205	5.5(20)	1	—	—	—	—	—	—	—	—	—	—	Kk	—	45	640

MERCER, GIRADIE   Giradie, DT, 6´2˝/285 lbs; Marshall; B3/19/1976 Washington, DC   **2002** NYJ 2 (0)

MERCER, KEN   Kenneth Ernest, B, 5´11˝/183 lbs; Simpson; B6/9/1903 Albia, IA, D2/1970 Asbury, IA **[K]**   **1927** Fra 17 (11, TB), 39   **1928** Fra☆14 (11, BB), 38
1929 Fra 13 (7, wb), 18   **NFL** 44 (29), 95 [3 yrs]

MERCER, MIKE   Michael, K, 6´0˝/220 lbs; Minnesota; Florida State; Hardin-Simmons; Arizona State; 1961: Min, rnd 15; B11/21/1935 Algona, IA **[KP]**   **1962** Min 4   **1964** Oak-A 14
1966 Oak-A 2   **1966**†KC-A 10   **1967** Buf-A✧14   **1968** Buf-A 3   **1968** GB 6   **1969** GB 10   **1970** SD 14

1961	Min	14	1	-32	-32.0(-32)	0	—	—	—	—	—	—	—	—	—	—	—	—	—	—	KP	—	63	-32
1963	Oak-A	14	1	-5	-5.0(-5)	0	—	—	—	—	—	—	—	—	—	—	—	—	—	—	KP	—	71	-5
1965	Oak-A	14	1	-1	-1.0(-1)	0	—	—	1	1	100.0	14	14.0(14)	0	0	—	—	—	—	KP	—	62	6
NFL	119	3	-38	-12.7(-1)	0	—	—	—	1	1	100.0	14	14.0(14)	0	0	—	—	—	—	KP	—	594	-31

MEREDITH, DON   Joseph Don 'Dandy Don', QB, 6´3˝/210 lbs; SMU; 1960: Chi, rnd 3/DalT, rnd 1; B4/10/1938 Mount Vernon, TX

1960	Dal	6	3	4	1.3(8)	0	—	—	—	—	68	29	42.6	281	4.1(23)	2	5	3	40	34.0	—	—	0	-46
1961	Dal	8(4, qb)	22	176	8.0(28)	1	—	—	—	—	182	94	51.6	1161	6.4(56)	9	11	16	147	—	—	—	6	372
1962	Dal	13	21	74	3.5(14)	0	—	—	—	—	212	105	49.5	1679	7.9(69)	15	8	14	113	84.2	—	—	0	669
1963	Dal	14(QB)	41	185	4.5(26)	3	—	—	—	—	310	167	53.9	2381	7.7(55)	17	18	35	260	73.1	—	—	18	771
1964	Dal	12(10, QB)	32	81	2.5(17)	4	—	—	—	—	323	158	48.9	2143	6.6(49)	9	16	58	416	59.1	—	—	24	598
1965	Dal	14(QB)	35	247	7.1(22)	1	—	—	—	—	305	141	46.2	2415	7.9(65)	22	13	38	257	79.9	—	—	6	1055
1966	†Dal★	13(QB)	38	242	6.4(22)	5	—	—	—	—	344	177	51.5	2805	8.2(95)	24	12	37	261	87.7	—	—	30	1359
1967	†Dal✧	11(11, QB)	28	84	3.0(16)	2	—	—	—	—	255	128	50.2	1834	7.2(60)	16	16	21	143	68.7	—	—	0	441
1968	†Dal★	22	123	5.6(16)	1	—	—	—	—	309	171	55.3	2500	8.1(95)	21	12	30	180	88.4	—	—	6	1098
NFL	9	104(25)	242	1216	5.0(28)	15	—	—	—	—	2308	1170	50.7	17199	7.5(95)	135	111	252	1817	74.8	—	—	90	6201

MEREDITH, DUDLEY   Cecil Dudley, DT, 6´4˝/280 lbs; Florida; Midwestern State; Lamar; 1957: Det, rnd 21; B1/16/1935 Smithwick, TX, D12/22/1987 Jacksonville Beach, FL
1963 Hou-A 14 (LDT)   **1964**†Buf-A 11   **1965**†Buf-A✧14   **1966**†Buf-A 14   **1967** Buf-A 14   **1968** Buf-A 5   **1968** Hou-A 5   **NFL** 77 [6 yrs]

MEREDITH, RUSSELL   Russell Delmar, T-G, 5´11˝/200 lbs; West Virginia; B6/27/1897 Fairmont, WV, D5/22/1989 Fairmont, WV   **1923** Lou 1 (0)   **1925** Cle 9 (7, LT)   **NFL** 10 (7) [2 yrs]

MERGEN, MIKE   Michael John, T-DT, 6´5˝/245 lbs; Illinois Wesleyan; San Francisco; 1952: ChiC, rnd 16; B2/13/1929 Cicero, IL   **1952** ChiC 12 (LT)

MERGENTHAL, ART   Arthur, G, 5´11˝/215 lbs; Tennessee; Xavier (OH); Bowling Green State; Notre Dame; B3/21/1921 Bellevue, KY, D5/20/2001 Bellevue, KY   **1945**†Cle 10 (2)
1946 LARm 9 (1)   **NFL** 19 (3) [2 yrs]

MERILLAT, LOU   Louis Alfred, E, 5´9˝/165 lbs; Illinois Tech; Army; B6/9/1892 Chicago, IL, D4/26/1948 Chicago, IL   **1925** Can 6 (4)

MERKEL, MONTE   Monte John, G, 5´10˝/215 lbs; Kansas; B11/6/1916 Keystone, IA, D7/22/1981 Missoula, MT   **1943** ChiB 1 (1)

MERKENS, GUIDO   Guido Albert, WR-QB-DB, 6´1˝/200 lbs; Sam Houston State; B8/14/1955 San Antonio, TX

1978	†Hou	12					1	6	6.0(6)	0	—	—	—	—	—	—	—	—	—	—	p	—	0	70
1979	†Hou	16					3	44	14.7(20)	1	—	—	—	—	—	—	—	—	—	—	kp	—	6	15
1980	Hou	3(0)					—	—	—	—	—	—	—	—	—	—	—	—	—	—	—	—	0	—
1980	NO	1(1)					—	—	—	—	—	—	—	—	—	—	—	—	—	—	—	—	0	0
1981	NO	16(11, WR)	2	-1	-0.5(2)	0	29	458	15.8(50)	1	2	1	50.0	20	10.0(20)	1	2	—	—	—	kp	—	6	234
1982	NO	9(1)	9	30	3.3(19)	0	—	—	—	—	49	18	36.7	186	3.8(37)	1	2	8	49	—	—	—	0	48
1983	NO	16(0)	1	16	16.0(16)	0	—	—	—	—	—	—	—	—	—	—	—	—	—	—	P	—	0	16
1984	NO	16(0)					—	—	—	—	—	—	—	—	—	—	—	—	—	—	—	—	0	—
1985	NO	16(0)	1	-2	-2.0(-2)	0	3	61	20.3(39)	1	1	1	100.0	7	7.0(7)	1	0	1	10	—	—	k	—	6	27

YEAR	TEAM	G (GS, POS)	RUSH	YD	AVG(LG)	TD	REC	YD	AVG(LG)	TD	PASS	COMP	PCT	YD	AVG(LG)	TD	INT	SK	YD	QBR	KPR	OTD	PTS	TAY
1987	Phi	3(0)	3	-8	-2.7(1)	0	—	—	—	—	14	7	50.0	70	5.0(17)	0	0	10	62	—	P		0	27
NFL	9	108(13)	16	35	2.2(19)	0	36	569	15.8(50)	3	66	27	40.9	283	4.3(37)	2	2	20	123	—	Pkp	—	18	437

MERKLE, ED Edward Lee, G, 5´10˝/215 lbs; Oklahoma State; B7/3/1917 Windsor, MO, D11/27/1987 Los Angeles County, CA **1944** Was 10 (4, RG)

MERKOVSKY, ELMER Albert J., G-T, 6´1˝/239 lbs; Pittsburgh; B4/13/1917 North Braddock, PA, D6/28/1982 Long Beach, CA **1944** C-P 9 (1) **1945** Pit 10 (10, LG) **1946** Pit 4 (1) **NFL** 23 (12) [3 yrs]

MERLIN, ED Edward, G, 5´10˝/210 lbs; Vanderbilt; 1938: Bkn, rnd 5; B12/31/1916 Spartanburg, SC **1938** Bkn 11 (3) **1939** Bkn 5 (3) **NFL** 16 (6) [2 yrs]

MERLO, JIM James Louis, LB, 6´1˝/221 lbs; Stanford; 1973: NO, rnd 4; B10/3/1951 Sanger, CA **1973** NO 14 (llb) **1974** NO 14 (LLB) **1976** NO 14 (13, LLB) **1977** NO 14 (14, LLB) **1978** NO 16 (16, LLB) **1979** NO 16 **NFL** 88 (43) [6 yrs]

MERRIL, THAN Nathaniel, DB, 6´2˝/212 lbs; Stanford; Yale; 2001: TB, rnd 7; B12/12/1977 Fresno, CA **2001** ChiB 15 (0)

MERRILL, CASEY Richard Casey, DE-DT, 6´4˝/254 lbs; California-Davis; 1979: Cin, rnd 5; B7/16/1957 Oakland, CA **1979** GB 13 **1980** GB 16 (1) **1981** GB 16 (13, RDE) **1982**†GB 9 (2) **1983** GB 5 (2) **1983** NYG 10 (0) **1984**†NYG 16 (0) **1985** NYG 11 (0) **1986** NO 1 (0) **NFL** 97 (16) [8 yrs]

MERRILL, MARK Mark Christopher, LB, 6´4˝/237 lbs; Minnesota; 1978: NYJ, rnd 2; B5/5/1955 St. Paul, MN **1978** NYJ 16 (4) **1979** NYJ 6 (4) **1979**†ChiB 9 **1981** Den 15 (0) **1982** Den 2 (0) **1982**†GB 4 (0) **1983** Buf 12 (0) **1984** Buf 2 (0) **1984**†LARd 2 (0) **NFL** 68 (8) [6 yrs]

MERRILL, WALT Walter O., T, 6´2˝/217 lbs; Alabama; 1940: Bkn, rnd 5; B8/7/1917 Andalusia, AL, D3/12/1953 Covington County, AL **1940** Bkn 11 (5, RT) **1941** Bkn 6 (6, RT) **1942** Bkn 11 (11, RT) **NFL** 28 (22) [3 yrs]

MERRIMAN, SAM Sam, LB, 6´3˝/229 lbs; Idaho; 1983: Sea, rnd 7; B5/5/1961 Tucson, AZ **1983**†Sea 16 (0) **1984**†Sea 16 (0) **1985** Sea 14 (0) **1986** Sea 16 (1) **1987**†Sea 9 (0) **NFL** 71 (1) [5 yrs]

MERRIMAN, SHAWNE Shawne DeAndre, LB, 6´4˝/253 lbs; Maryland; 2005: SD, rnd 1; B5/25/1984 Upper Marlboro, MD **2005** SD★15 (10, LOLB)

MERRITT, AHMAD Ahmad, WR, 5´10˝/195 lbs; Wisconsin; B2/5/1977 Chicago, IL

2001	†ChiB	2(0)	—	—	—	—	2	20	10.0(13)	0	—	—	—	—	—	—	—	—	—	—	—		0	10
2002	ChiB	12(3)	1	5	5.0(5)	0	14	100	7.1(25)	0	—	—	—	—	—	—	—	—	—	—	kp		0	430
2003	ChiB	15(1)	—	—	—	—	3	50	16.7(25)	0	—	—	—	—	—	—	—	—	—	—	k		0	130
NFL	3	29(4)	1	5	5.0(5)	0	19	170	8.9(25)	0	—	—	—	—	—	—	—	—	—	—	kp	—	0	570

MERRITT, DAVID David Lee, LB, 6´1˝/237 lbs; North Carolina State; 1993: Mia, rnd 7; B9/8/1971 Raleigh, NC **1993** Mia 4 (0) **1993** Phx 3 (0) **1994** Arz 16 (0) **1995** Arz 15 (0) **NFL** 38 (0) [3 yrs]

MERRITTS, JIM James Clystis, DE-NT, 6´3˝/255 lbs; Connecticut; West Virginia; B3/22/1961 Roaring Springs, PA **1987** Ind 1 (0)

MERRIWEATHER, MIKE Michael Lamar, LB, 6´2˝/230 lbs; Pacific; 1982: Pit, rnd 3; B11/26/1960 Albany, NY **1982**†Pit 9 (0) **1983**†Pit 16 (16, LOLB) **1984**†Pit★16 (16, LOLB) **1985** Pit★16 (16, LOLB) **1986** Pit◇16 (16, LOLB) **1987** Pit☆12 (12, LOLB) **1989** Min 15 (15, RLB) **1990** Min 16 (16, RLB) **1991** Min 16 (16, RLB) **1992**†Min 16 (16, RLB) **1993** NYJ 1 (0) **1993**†GB 0 (0) **NFL** 149 (139) [11 yrs]

MERROW, JEFF Jeffrey Colin, DE-DT-LB, 6´4˝/236 lbs; West Virginia; 1975: Atl, rnd 11; B7/12/1953 Akron, OH **1975** Atl 12 (12, LDE) **1976** Atl 14 (14, RDE) **1977** Atl 14 (14, RDE) **1978**†Atl 14 (14, RDE) **1979** Atl 3 (2) **1980**†Atl 16 (10, RDE) **1981** Atl 11 (10, RDE) **1982**†Atl 8 (7, RDE) **1983** Atl 16 (12, RDE) **NFL** 108 (101) [9 yrs]

MERSEREAU, SCOTT Scott Robert, DT-NT-DE, 6´4˝/275 lbs; Southern Connecticut State; 1987: LARm, rnd 5; B4/8/1965 Riverhead, NY **1987** NYJ 13 (4) **1988** NYJ 16 (15, NT) **1989** NYJ 16 (15, NT) **1990** NYJ 16 (16, NT) **1991**†NYJ 13 (13, LDT) **1992** NYJ 15 (15, LDT) **1993** NYJ 13 (13, LDT) **NFL** 102 (91) [7 yrs]

MERTENS, JERRY Jerome William, DB, 6´0˝/184 lbs; Drake; 1958: SF, rnd 20; B11/12/1934 Racine, WI **1958** SF◇12 (DB) **1959** SF 12 (DB) **1960** SF 12 (12, LCB) **1961** SF 14 (9, LCB) **1962** SF 14 (12, LCB) **1964** SF 14 **1965** SF 13 (9, RCB) **NFL** 91 (42) [7 yrs]

MERTENS, JIM James Frederick, TE, 6´3˝/240 lbs; Fairmont State; 1969: Mia, rnd 10; B5/25/1947 Cumberland, MD

1969	Mia-A	14	—	—	—	—	2	26	13.0(15)	0	—	—	—	—	—	—	—	—	—	—	k	—	0	-16

MERTES, BUS Bernard James, B, 6´0˝/201 lbs; Iowa; B10/6/1921 Chicago, IL, D1/17/2002 St. Louis Park, MN

1945	ChiC	8(3)	24	111	4.6(52)	0	2	1	0.5(1)	0	—	—	—	—	—	—	—	—	—	—	kp	—	0	111
1949	NYG	8(1)	16	46	2.9(19)	0	2	14	7.0(13)	0	—	—	—	—	—	—	—	—	—	—	—	—	0	53
NFL	2	16(4)	40	157	3.9(52)	0	4	15	3.8(13)	0	—	—	—	—	—	—	—	—	—	—	kp	—	0	164
1946	LAD-A	9(3)	40	111	2.8	0	5	61	12.2	1	—	—	—	—	—	—	—	—	—	—	ki	—	6	161
1947	Bal-A	14(10, FB)	95	321	3.4	2	2	28	14.0	0	—	—	—	—	—	—	—	—	—	—	—	—	12	355
1948	†Bal-A	14(12, FB)	155	680	4.4	4	6	56	9.3	0	—	—	—	—	—	—	—	—	—	—	k	—	24	748
1949	Bal-A	2(2)	11	8	0.7	0	2	22	11.0	1	—	—	—	—	—	—	—	—	—	—	—	—	6	24
AAFC	4	39(27)	301	1120	3.7(52)	6	15	167	11.1(13)	2	—	—	—	—	—	—	—	—	—	—	ki	—	48	1288

MERZ, CURT Curtis Carl, G-DE, 6´4˝/267 lbs; Iowa; 1960: NYT, rnd 1/Phi, rnd 3; B4/17/1938 Newark, NJ **1962**†DalT-A 14 (LDE) **1963** KC-A 14 (rg) **1964** KC-A 14 (rg) **1965** KC-A 14 (RG) **1966**†KC-A 14 (RG) **1967** KC-A 8 (RG) **1968**†KC-A 14 **NFL** 92 [7 yrs]

MESAK, DICK Richard H., T, 6´2˝/225 lbs; St. Mary's (CA); B3/1/1919 San Francisco, CA **1945** Det 6 (1)

MESEROLL, MARK Mark Steven, T, 6´5˝/270 lbs; Wesley; Florida State; B7/22/1955 Piscataway, NJ **1978** NO 16

MESNER, BRUCE Bruce M., NT, 6´5˝/280 lbs; Maryland; 1987: Buf, rnd 8; B3/21/1964 New York, NY **1987** Buf 11 (0)

MESSER, DALE Lyndy Dale, HB-WR-DB, 5´10˝/175 lbs; Fresno State; 1961: SF, rnd 4/SD, rnd 13; B8/6/1937 Lemoore, CA

1961	SF	4	3	13	4.3(6)	0	3	33	11.0(14)	0	—	—	—	—	—	—	—	—	—	—	kp	—	0	22
1962	SF	13	—	—	—	—	3	30	10.0(15)	0	—	—	—	—	—	—	—	—	—	—	kpi	—	0	89
1963	SF	14	—	—	—	—	—	—	—	—	—	—	—	—	—	—	—	—	—	—	p	—	0	-21
1964	SF	6	—	—	—	—	4	72	18.0(28)	0	—	—	—	—	—	—	—	—	—	—	—	—	0	36
1965	SF	9	—	—	—	—	2	41	20.5(37)	0	—	—	—	—	—	—	—	—	—	—	k	—	0	33
NFL	5	46	3	13	4.3(6)	0	12	176	14.7(37)	0	—	—	—	—	—	—	—	—	—	—	kpi	—	0	158

MESSNER, MARK Mark W., LB, 6´2˝/256 lbs; Michigan; 1989: LARm, rnd 6; B12/29/1965 Riverview, MI **1989**†LARm 4 (0)

MESSNER, MAX Max Carlton, LB, 6´3˝/225 lbs; Cincinnati; 1960: Det, rnd 9/Hou, rnd 1; B10/13/1938 Ashland, OH, D3/13/1996 Ashland, OH **1960** Det 1 **1961** Det 14 **1962** Det 14 **1963** Det 14 (LLB) **1964** NYG 6 **1964** Pit 7 (LLB) **1965** Pit 14 **NFL** 70 [6 yrs]

MESTNIK, FRANK Frank Gerald, FB, 6´2˝/200 lbs; Marquette; 1960: SL, rnd 15/Bos, rnd 1; B2/23/1938 Cleveland, OH

1960	SL	9	104	429	4.1(55)	3	3	24	8.0(15)	0	—	—	—	—	—	—	—	—	—	—	k	—	18	465
1961	SL	13(FB)	95	334	3.5(26)	1	12	29	2.4(15)	1	—	—	—	—	—	—	—	—	—	—	k	—	12	361
1963	GB	11	1	4	4.0(4)	0	—	—	—	—	—	—	—	—	—	—	—	—	—	—	k	—	0	-11
NFL	3	33	200	767	3.8(55)	4	15	53	3.5(15)	1	—	—	—	—	—	—	—	—	—	—	k	—	30	815

METCALF, BO Isaac Scott, DB, 6´2˝/193 lbs; Baylor; 1983: Pit, rnd 4; B4/18/1961 Waco, TX **1984** Ind 1 (0)

METCALF, ERIC Eric Quinn, RB-WR, 5´10˝/188 lbs; Texas; 1989: Cle, rnd 1; B1/23/1968 Seattle, WA [R]

1989	†Cle	16(11, RB)	187	633	3.4(43)	6	54	397	7.4(68)	4	2	1	50.0	32	16.0(32)	1	0	—	—	—	k	—	60	1186
1990	Cle	16(10, RB)	80	248	3.1(17)	1	57	452	7.9(35)	1	—	—	—	—	—	—	—	—	—	—	k	2	24	781
1991	Cle	8(3)	30	107	3.6(15)	0	29	294	10.1(45)	0	0	0	0.0	0	0.0	0	0	—	11	—	kp	—	0	300
1992	Cle	16(5, rb)	73	301	4.1(31)	1	47	614	13.1(69)	5	1	0	0.0	0	0.0	0	0	—	—	—	kp	1	42	884
1993	Cle★	16(9, RB)	129	611	4.7(55)	1	63	539	8.6(49)	2	—	—	—	—	—	—	—	—	—	—	kp	2	30	1298
1994	†Cle★	16(8, RB)	93	329	3.5(37)	2	47	436	9.3(57)	4	1	0	0.0	0	0.0	0	0	—	—	—	kp	2	42	850
1995	†Atl	16(15, WR)	28	133	4.8(23)	0	104	1189	11.4(62)	8	1	0	0.0	0	0.0	0	0	—	—	—	kp	1	60	1074
1996	Atl	16(11, WR)	3	8	2.7(4)	0	54	599	11.1(67)	6	—	—	—	—	—	—	—	—	—	—	kp	—	36	798
1997	SD★	16(1)	3	-5	-1.7(2)	0	40	576	14.4(62)	2	—	—	—	—	—	—	—	—	—	—	kp	3	30	702
1998	†Arz	16(3)	—	—	—	—	29	324	10.5(29)	0	—	—	—	—	—	—	—	—	—	—	kp	—	0	605
1999	Car	16(1)	2	20	10.0(17)	0	11	133	12.1(33)	0	0	0	0.0	0	0.0	0	0	—	—	—	kp	1	6	151
2001	Was	10(0)	—	—	—	—	4	19	4.8(9)	0	—	—	—	—	—	—	—	—	—	—	kp	1	6	277
2002	†GB	1(0)	2	7	3.5(5)	0	—	—	—	—	—	—	—	—	—	—	—	—	—	—	kp	—	0	2
NFL	13	179(77)	630	2392	3.8(55)	12	541	5572	10.3(69)	31	5	1	20.0	32	6.4(32)	1	0	2	13	—	kp	12	330	8905

YEAR	TEAM	G (GS, POS)	RUSH	YD	AVG (LG)	TD	REC	YD	AVG (LG)	TD	PASS	COMP	PCT	YD	AVG (LG)	TD	INT	SK	YD	QBR	KPR	OTD	PTS	TAY

METCALF, TERRENCE Terrence Orlando, G-T, 6´3˝/325 lbs; Mississippi; 2002: Chi, rnd 3; B1/28/1978 Clarksdale, MS **2002** ChiB 5 (0) **2003** ChiB 9 (2) **2004** ChiB 13 (5, lg) **2005** ChiB 13 (13, RG) **NFL** 40 (20) [4 yrs]

METCALF, TERRY Terrence Randolph, RB-WR, 5´10˝/185 lbs; Long Beach State; 1973: SL, rnd 3; B9/24/1951 Seattle, WA **[R]**

YEAR	TEAM	G (GS, POS)	RUSH	YD	AVG (LG)	TD	REC	YD	AVG (LG)	TD	PASS	COMP	PCT	YD	AVG (LG)	TD	INT	SK	YD	QBR	KPR	OTD	PTS	TAY
1973	SL	12	148	628	4.2 (50)	2	37	316	8.5 (35)	0	—	—	—	—	—	—	—	—	—	—	k	—	12	870
1974	†SL★	14 (13, RB)	152	718	**4.7** (**75**)	6	50	377	7.5 (22)	1	2	0	0.0	0	0.0	0	0	—	—	—	kp	1	48	**1515**
1975	†SL★	13 (RB)	165	816	4.9 (52)	9	43	378	8.8 (30)	2	2	1	50.0	51	25.5 (51)	1	0	—	—	—	kp	2	78	**1761**
1976	SL	12 (RB)	134	537	4.0 (36)	3	33	388	11.8 (48)	4	1	0	0.0	0	0.0	0	0	—	—	—	kp	—	42	969
1977	SL✧	14 (RB)	149	739	5.0 (62)	4	34	403	11.9 (68)	2	5	3	60.0	27	5.4 (11)	1	1	1	9	—	kp	—	36	1299
1981	Was	16 (2)	18	60	3.3 (12)	0	48	595	12.4 (52)	0	—	—	—	—	—	—	—	—	—	—	kp	—	0	426
NFL	6	81 (15)	766	3498	4.6 (75)	24	245	2457	10.0 (68)	9	10	4	40.0	78	7.8 (51)	2	1	1	9	—	kp	3	216	6839

METHOD, RUSS Russell G., B, 5´10˝/192 lbs; none; B6/27/1897 Duluth, MN, D9/17/1971 Two Harbors, MN **1923** Dul 7 (6, WB) **1924** Dul 5 (4, WB), 6 **1925** Dul 3 (2) **1926** Dul 12 (11, WB), 6 **1927** Dul 8 (5, WB), 6 **1929** ChiC 10 (6, wb) **NFL** 45 (34), 18 [6 yrs]

METZELAARS, PETE Peter Henry, TE, 6´7˝/254 lbs; Wabash; 1982: Sea, rnd 3; B5/24/1960 Three Rivers, MI

YEAR	TEAM	G (GS, POS)	RUSH	YD	AVG (LG)	TD	REC	YD	AVG (LG)	TD	PASS	COMP	PCT	YD	AVG (LG)	TD	INT	SK	YD	QBR	KPR	OTD	PTS	TAY
1982	Sea	9 (2)	—	—	—	—	15	152	10.1 (26)	0	—	—	—	—	—	—	—	—	—	—	—	—	0	76
1983	†Sea	16 (7, TE)	—	—	—	—	7	72	10.3 (17)	1	—	—	—	—	—	—	—	—	—	—	k	—	6	26
1984	†Sea	9 (4)	—	—	—	—	5	80	16.0 (25)	0	—	—	—	—	—	—	—	—	—	—	—	—	0	40
1985	Buf	16 (8, te)	—	—	—	—	12	80	6.7 (13)	1	—	—	—	—	—	—	—	—	—	—	—	—	6	45
1986	Buf	16 (16, TE)	—	—	—	—	49	485	9.9 (44)	3	—	—	—	—	—	—	—	—	—	—	—	1	24	258
1987	Buf	12 (12, TE)	—	—	—	—	28	290	10.4 (34)	0	—	—	—	—	—	—	—	—	—	—	—	—	0	145
1988	†Buf	16 (16, TE)	—	—	—	—	33	438	13.3 (35)	1	—	—	—	—	—	—	—	—	—	—	—	—	6	224
1989	†Buf	16 (16, TE)	—	—	—	—	18	179	9.9 (23)	2	—	—	—	—	—	—	—	—	—	—	—	—	12	100
1990	†Buf	16 (4)	—	—	—	—	10	60	6.0 (12)	1	—	—	—	—	—	—	—	—	—	—	—	—	6	35
1991	†Buf	16 (1)	—	—	—	—	5	54	10.8 (51)	2	—	—	—	—	—	—	—	—	—	—	—	—	12	37
1992	†Buf	16 (7, te)	—	—	—	—	30	298	9.9 (53)	6	—	—	—	—	—	—	—	—	—	—	—	—	36	179
1993	†Buf	16 (16, TE)	—	—	—	—	68	609	9.0 (51)	4	—	—	—	—	—	—	—	—	—	—	—	—	24	325
1994	Buf	16 (16, TE)	—	—	—	—	49	428	8.7 (35)	5	—	—	—	—	—	—	—	—	—	—	—	—	30	239
1995	Car	14 (14, TE)	—	—	—	—	20	171	8.6 (27)	3	—	—	—	—	—	—	—	—	—	—	—	—	18	101
1996	Det	15 (11, TE)	—	—	—	—	17	146	8.6 (20)	0	—	—	—	—	—	—	—	—	—	—	k	—	0	59
1997	†Det	16 (6, te)	—	—	—	—	17	144	8.5 (22)	0	—	—	—	—	—	—	—	—	—	—	—	—	0	72
NFL	16	235 (156)	—	—	—	—	383	3686	9.6 (53)	29	—	—	—	—	—	—	—	—	—	—	k	1	180	1959

METZGER, LOU Louis Eugene, FB-WB, 5´9˝/170 lbs; Georgetown (DC); B2/13/1904 Chicago, IL, D5/25/1953 Evanston, IL **1926** Lou 3 (1)

MEUTH, KEVIN Kevin Karl, T, 6´5˝/270 lbs; Southwest Texas State; B5/4/1964 Richmond, TX **1987** NYG 3 (1)

MEYER, DENNIS John Dennis, DB, 5´11˝/186 lbs; Arkansas State; 1972: Pit, rnd 6; B4/8/1950 Jefferson City, MO **1973**†Pit 11

MEYER, EDDIE Clarence Edwin, T, 6´2˝/240 lbs; West Texas A&M; 1960: NYT, rnd 1; B10/17/1936 **1960** Buf-A 9

MEYER, ERNIE Ernest Henry, G, 6´2˝/200 lbs; Geneva; B6/23/1904 West Bridgewater, PA, D1/23/1979 Paoli, PA **1930** Por 9 (5, LG)

MEYER, FRED Frederic D., E-DE, 6´2˝/190 lbs; Stanford; 1942: Phi, rnd 12; B9/29/1919 Mount Sterling, IL

YEAR	TEAM	G (GS, POS)	RUSH	YD	AVG (LG)	TD	REC	YD	AVG (LG)	TD	PASS	COMP	PCT	YD	AVG (LG)	TD	INT	SK	YD	QBR	KPR	OTD	PTS	TAY
1942	Phi	10 (10, RE)	2	13	6.5 (10)	0	16	324	20.3 (60)	1	—	—	—	—	—	—	—	—	—	—	k	—	6	179
1945	Phi	8 (0)	—	—	—	—	11	135	12.3 (27)	1	—	—	—	—	—	—	—	—	—	—	—	—	6	73
NFL	2	18 (10)	2	13	6.5 (10)	0	27	459	17.0 (60)	2	—	—	—	—	—	—	—	—	—	—	k	—	12	252

MEYER, GIL Gilbert P., E-DE, 6´2˝/200 lbs; Wake Forest; B11/25/1920 Baltimore, MD

YEAR	TEAM	G (GS, POS)	RUSH	YD	AVG (LG)	TD	REC	YD	AVG (LG)	TD	PASS	COMP	PCT	YD	AVG (LG)	TD	INT	SK	YD	QBR	KPR	OTD	PTS	TAY
1947	Bal-A	13 (1)	—	—	—	—	1	3	3.0 (3)	0	—	—	—	—	—	—	—	—	—	—	—	—	0	2

MEYER, JIM James David, T, 6´5˝/290 lbs; Illinois State; 1986: Cle, rnd 7; B6/9/1963 Glenview, IL **1987** GB 2 (0)

MEYER, JOHN John Edwin, LB, 6´1˝/225 lbs; Notre Dame; 1965: Buf, rnd 15/SL, rnd 8; B2/20/1942 Chicago, IL **1966** Hou-A 14 (RLB)

MEYER, RON Ronald Allen, QB, 6´4˝/205 lbs; South Dakota State; 1966: Chi, rnd 7; B8/27/1944 Austin, MN

YEAR	TEAM	G (GS, POS)	RUSH	YD	AVG (LG)	TD	REC	YD	AVG (LG)	TD	PASS	COMP	PCT	YD	AVG (LG)	TD	INT	SK	YD	QBR	KPR	OTD	PTS	TAY
1966	Pit	4	1	-2	-2.0 (-2)	0	—	—	—	—	19	7	36.8	59	3.1 (19)	0	1	—	—	—	—	—	0	-13

MEYERS, BOB Robert Ellis, HB, 6´2˝/184 lbs; Stanford; 1952: SF, rnd 16; B10/12/1930 Los Angeles, CA, D4/19/1993 Morro Bay, CA

YEAR	TEAM	G (GS, POS)	RUSH	YD	AVG (LG)	TD	REC	YD	AVG (LG)	TD	PASS	COMP	PCT	YD	AVG (LG)	TD	INT	SK	YD	QBR	KPR	OTD	PTS	TAY
1952	SF	1	1	2	2.0 (2)	0	—	—	—	—	—	—	—	—	—	—	—	—	—	—	—	—	0	2

MEYERS, JERRY Jerry Edward, DE-DT, 6´4˝/249 lbs; Northern Illinois; 1976: Chi, rnd 15; B2/21/1954 Chicago, IL **1976** ChiB 12 **1977**†ChiB 13 **1978** ChiB 16 **1979** ChiB 6 **1980** KC 2 (0) **NFL** 49 [5 yrs]

MEYERS, JOHN John Douglas, DT, 6´6˝/276 lbs; Washington; 1962: LA, rnd 3/Oak, rnd 4; B1/16/1940 Forest City, IA **1962** Dal 14 (RDT) **1963** Dal 14 (7, RDT) **1964** Phi 14 (14, RDT) **1965** Phi 14 (14, RDT) **1966** Phi 14 (RDT) **1967** Phi 14 (RDT) **NFL** 84 (35) [6 yrs]

MEYERS, KLINKS Stanton Wade, BB, none; B10/23/1893 Indianapolis, IN, D10/1964 **1920** Ham 3 (2, BB)

MEYERS, PAUL Paul Duncan, E, 5´11˝/170 lbs; Wisconsin-Milwaukee; Wisconsin; B12/3/1894, D10/1970 Akron, OH **1921** NYG 1 (1, LE) **1922** Roc 1 (0) **1923** Rac 9 (8, LE), 6 **NFL** 11 (9) [3 yrs]

MEYLAN, WAYNE Wayne A., LB, 6´1˝/237 lbs; Nebraska; 1968: Cle, rnd 4; B3/2/1946 Bay City, MI, D6/26/1987 Ludington, MI **1968**†Cle 14 **1969**†Cle 13 **1970** Min 2 **NFL** 29 [3 yrs]

MIALIK, LARRY Lawrence George, TE, 6´2˝/226 lbs; Wisconsin; 1972: Atl, rnd 12; B5/15/1950 Passaic, NJ **1972** Atl 14 **1974** Atl 14 **1976** SD 7

YEAR	TEAM	G (GS, POS)	RUSH	YD	AVG (LG)	TD	REC	YD	AVG (LG)	TD	PASS	COMP	PCT	YD	AVG (LG)	TD	INT	SK	YD	QBR	KPR	OTD	PTS	TAY
1973	Atl	14	—	—	—	—	2	30	15.0 (17)	0	—	—	—	—	—	—	—	—	—	—	—	—	0	15
NFL	4	49	—	—	—	—	2	30	15.0 (17)	0	—	—	—	—	—	—	—	—	—	—	—	—	0	15

MIANO, RICH Richard James, DB, 6´1˝/200 lbs; Hawaii; 1985: NYJ, rnd 6; B9/3/1962 Newton, MA **1985**†NYJ 16 (1) **1986**†NYJ 14 (1) **1987** NYJ 12 (11, SS) **1988** NYJ 16 (16, SS) **1989** NYJ 2 (2) **1991** Phi 16 (1) **1992**†Phi 16 (11, SS) **1993** Phi 16 (14, FS) **1994** Phi 16 (0) **1995** Atl 11 (0) **NFL** 135 (57) [10 yrs]

MICECH, PHIL Philip John, DE, 6´5˝/265 lbs; Wisconsin-Platteville; B8/11/1961 Milwaukee, WI **1987** Min 3 (3)

MICHAEL, BILL Paul William, G, 6´2˝/240 lbs; Ohio State; 1957: Pit, rnd 2; B12/24/1935 Hamilton, OH **1957** Pit 3

MICHAEL, RICH Richard John, T, 6´3˝/242 lbs; Ohio State; B11/15/1938 Hamilton, OH **1960**†Hou-A☆10 (RT) **1961** Hou-A 14 (RT) **1962**†Hou-A✧14 (RT) **1963** Hou-A✧14 (RT) **1965** Hou-A 14 **1966** Hou-A 14 **NFL** 80 [6 yrs]

MICHAELS, AL Alton Court, TB-FB, 6´0˝/190 lbs; Heidelberg; Ohio State; B4/1/1900 Tiffin, OH, D10/21/1972 Gadsden, AL **[K]** **1923** Akr☆7 (7, FB), 3 **1924** Akr 7 (7, TB), 6 **1925** Cle 14 (12, TB) **NFL** 28 (26), 9 [3 yrs]

MICHAELS, EDDIE Edward Joseph, aka Ed Mikolajewski, G, 5´11˝/205 lbs; Villanova; 1936: ChiB, rnd 2; B6/11/1914 Wilmington, DE, D1/21/1976 Wilmington, DE **1936** ChiB 12 (7, LG) **1937**†Was 11 (3) **1943** P-P 10 (9, RG) **1944** Phi 10 (6, rg) **1945** Phi 9 (8, LG) **1946** Phi 10 (5, LG) **NFL** 62 (38) [6 yrs]

MICHAELS, LOU Louis Andrew, DE-K, 6´2˝/243 lbs; Kentucky; 1958: LA, rnd 1; B9/28/1935 Swoyersville, PA **[K]** **1958** LARm☆12 (RDE) **1959** LARm☆12 (RDE) **1960** LARm 11 **1961** Pit 14 (LDE) **1962** Pit★14 (LDE) **1963** Pit✧14 (LDE) **1964**†Bal 14 **1965**†Bal 14 (LDE) **1966** Bal 14 (LDE) **1967** Bal 14 (lde) **1968**†Bal 14 **1969** Bal 14 **1971** GB 10 **NFL** 171 [13 yrs]

MICHAELS, WALT Walter Edward, LB, 6´0˝/231 lbs; Washington & Lee; 1951: Cle, rnd 7; B10/16/1929 Swoyersville, PA **[KC]** **1951** GB 12 **1952**†Cle 11 (LLB) **1953**†Cle 12 (LLB) **1954**†Cle 12 (RLB) **1955**†Cle✧12 (RLB) **1956** Cle✧12 (MLB) **1957**†Cle★12 (RLB) **1958**†Cle★12 (RLB) **1959** Cle★12 (RLB) **1960** Cle☆11 (RLB) **1961** Cle☆14 (RLB) **1963** NYJ-A 1 **NFL** 133 [12 yrs]

MICHALIK, ART Arthur E., MG-LB-G, 6´2˝/229 lbs; St. Ambrose; 1951: SF, rnd 17; B1/31/1930, **[K]** **1953** SF★12 (MG) **1954** SF 2 **1955** Pit 12 **1956** Pit 12 **NFL** 38 [4 yrs]

MICHALSKE, MIKE August Mike 'Iron Mike', G-T-LB-BB, 6´0˝/210 lbs; Penn State; B4/24/1903 Cleveland, OH, D10/26/1983 Green Bay, WI; HOF 1964 **1927** NYY☆14 (12, LG) **1928** NYY☆13 (13, LG) **1929** GB☆13 (11, LG) **1930** GB☆14 (12, LG) **1931** GB☆13 (8, LG), 6 **1932** GB 13 (9, LG), 8 **1933** GB 13 (8, LG) **1934** GB☆13 (12, LG) **1935** GB☆10 (8, LG) **1937** GB 6 (1) **NFL** 122 (94), 14 [10 yrs]

YEAR	TEAM	G (GS, POS)	RUSH	YD	AVG (LG)	TD	REC	YD	AVG (LG)	TD	PASS COMP	PCT	YD	AVG (LG)	TD	INT	SK	YD	QBR	KPR	OTD	PTS	TAY

MICHEL, MIKE   Michael Walter, P-K, 5´10˝/177 lbs; Stanford; 1977: Mia, rnd 5; B8/4/1954 Ventura, CA **[K]**

1977	Mia	13	1	-2	-2.0(-2)	0	—	—	—	—	—	—	—	—	—	—	—	—	—	KP	—	0	-2
1978	†Phi	10	1	0	0.0(0)	0	—	—	—	—	—	—	—	—	—	—	—	—	—	KP	—	9	0
NFL	2	23	2	-2	-1.0	0	—	—	—	—	—	—	—	—	—	—	—	—	—	KP	—	9	-2

MICHEL, TOM   William Thomas, HB, 5´11˝/215 lbs; East Carolina; 1964: Min, rnd 14/Oak, rnd 19; B12/7/1940 Oakland, CA, D3/21/2005 Greenville, NC

| 1964 | Min | 11(4) | 39 | 129 | 3.3(14) | 0 | 1 | 14 | 14.0(14) | 0 | — | — | — | — | — | — | — | — | — | k | — | 0 | 208 |

MICHELS, JOHN   John Joseph, G, 5´11˝/200 lbs; Tennessee; 1953: Phi, rnd 25; B2/15/1931 Philadelphia, PA   **1953** Phi 11

MICHELS, JOHN   John Spiegel, T, 6´7˝/300 lbs; USC; 1996: GB, rnd 1; B3/19/1973 La Jolla, CA   **1996**†GB 15 (9, LT)   **1997** GB 9 (5, lt)   **NFL** 24 (14) [2 yrs]

MICHO, BOBBY   Robert Anthony, TE-FB, 6´3˝/236 lbs; Texas; 1984: Den, rnd 10; B3/7/1962 Omaha, NE   **1984** SD 6 (0)   **1986**†Den 5 (0)

| 1987 | †Den | 15(3) | 4 | 8 | 2.0(5) | 0 | 25 | 242 | 9.7(26) | 2 | — | — | — | — | — | — | — | — | — | — | — | 12 | 139 |
| NFL | 3 | 26(3) | 4 | 8 | 2.0(5) | 0 | 25 | 242 | 9.7(26) | 2 | — | — | — | — | — | — | — | — | — | — | — | 12 | 139 |

MICKA, MIKE   Michael, FB-HB-QB, 6´0˝/188 lbs; Colgate; 1944: Was, rnd 1; B6/18/1921 Clairton, PA, D1/4/1989 Gaithersburg, MD

1944	Was	10(3)	25	94	3.8(14)	0	2	16	8.0(10)	0	—	—	—	—	—	—	—	—	—	Pi	—	0	102
1945	Was	6(1)	18	57	3.2(6)	0	2	74	37.0(64)	0	—	—	—	—	—	—	—	—	—	k	—	0	89
1945	Bos	3(0)	1	5	5.0(5)	0	—	—	—	—	—	—	—	—	—	—	—	—	—	ki	—	0	6
1946	Bos	11(6, RH)	20	76	3.8(19)	0	—	—	—	—	—	—	—	—	—	—	—	—	—	i	1	6	116
1947	Bos	12(5, qb)	1	-4	-4.0(-4)	0	2	11	5.5(6)	0	—	—	—	—	—	—	—	—	—	i	—	0	38
1948	Bos	12(6, FB)	4	3	0.8(3)	0	—	—	—	—	—	—	—	—	—	—	—	—	—	i	—	0	11
NFL	5	54(21)	69	231	3.3(19)	0	6	101	16.8(64)	0	—	—	—	—	—	—	—	—	—	Pki	1	6	362

MICKEL, JEFF   Arthur Jeffery, T, 6´6˝/300 lbs; Eastern Washington; 1989: Min, rnd 6; B8/4/1966 Limestone, NE   **1990** LARm 1 (0)

MICKELL, DARREN   Darren, DE, 6´4˝/285 lbs; Florida; 1992: KC, rnd S2; B8/3/1970 Miami, FL   **1992**†KC 1 (0)   **1993**†KC 16 (1)   **1994**†KC 16 (13, RDE)   **1995**†KC 12 (6, rde)   **1996** NO 12 (12, LDE)   **1997** NO 14 (13, LDE)   **1999** NO 1 (0)   **2000** SD 16 (16, RDE)   **2001** Oak 1 (0)   **NFL** 89 (61) [9 yrs]

MICKENS, ARNOLD   Arnold Lee, RB, 5´11˝/217 lbs; Indiana; Butler; B10/12/1972 Indianapolis, IN   **1996** Ind 3 (0)

MICKENS, RAY   William Ray, DB, 5´8˝/180 lbs; Texas A&M; 1996: NYJ, rnd 3; B1/4/1973 Frankfurt, Germany   **1996** NYJ 15 (10, RCB)   **1997** NYJ 16 (0)   **1998**†NYJ 16 (3)   **1999** NYJ 15 (5, rcb)   **2000** NYJ 16 (0)   **2001**†NYJ 16 (4)   **2002**†NYJ 16 (1)   **2003** NYJ 16 (14, LCB)   **2005** Cle 16 (0)   **NFL** 142 (37) [9 yrs]

MICKENS, TERRY   Terry KaJuan, WR, 6´0˝/201 lbs; Florida A&M; 1994: GB, rnd 5; B2/21/1971 Tallahassee, FL

1994	†GB	12(0)	—	—	—	—	4	31	7.8(11)	0	—	—	—	—	—	—	—	—	—	—	—	0	16
1995	†GB	16(0)	—	—	—	—	3	50	16.7(24)	0	—	—	—	—	—	—	—	—	—	k	—	0	10
1996	†GB	8(5, wr)	—	—	—	—	18	161	8.9(19)	2	—	—	—	—	—	—	—	—	—	—	—	12	91
1997	†GB	11(0)	—	—	—	—	1	2	2.0(2)	1	—	—	—	—	—	—	—	—	—	k	—	6	-9
1998	Oak	16(2)	—	—	—	—	24	346	14.4(32)	1	—	—	—	—	—	—	—	—	—	—	—	6	178
1999	Oak	16(3)	—	—	—	—	20	261	13.1(30)	0	—	—	—	—	—	—	—	—	—	—	—	0	131
NFL	6	79(10)	—	—	—	—	70	851	12.2(32)	4	—	—	—	—	—	—	—	—	—	k	—	24	416

MICKEY, JOEY   Joey, TE, 6´5˝/274 lbs; Oklahoma; 1993: Phi, rnd 7; B11/29/1970 Oklahoma City, OK   **1993** Dal 5 (0)

MICKLES, JOE   Joseph Nathan, RB, 5´10˝/221 lbs; Mississippi; 1989: Was, rnd 12; B12/25/1965 Birmingham, AL   **1989** Was 9 (0)   **1990** SD 1 (0)   **NFL** 10 (0) [2 yrs]

MIDDENDORF, DAVE   David Warren, G, 6´3˝/260 lbs; Washington State; 1968: Cin, rnd 5; B11/23/1945 Seattle, WA   **1968** Cin-A 14 (LG)   **1969** Cin-A 12   **1970** NYJ 8   **NFL** 34 [3 yrs]

MIDDLEBROOK, OREN   Oren James, WR, 6´2˝/185 lbs; Arkansas State; 1977: Den, rnd 10; B1/23/1953 Aberdeen, MS   **1978**†Phi 16

MIDDLEBROOKS, WILLIE   Willie Frank, DB, 6´1˝/200 lbs; Minnesota; 2001: Den, rnd 1; B2/12/1979 Miami, FL   **2001** Den 8 (0)   **2002** Den 15 (0)   **2003**†Den 16 (0)   **2004** Den 12 (2)   **2005** SF 5 (0)   **NFL** 56 (2) [5 yrs]

MIDDLETON, DAVE   David Hinton, E-HB-FL, 6´1˝/194 lbs; Auburn; 1955: Det, rnd 1; B11/23/1933 Birmingham, AL

1955	Det	12(RH)	59	201	3.4(16)	2	44	663	15.1(77)	3	—	—	—	—	—	—	—	—	—	k	—	30	591
1956	Det	12(RE)	3	9	3.0(10)	0	39	606	15.5(56)	5	—	—	—	—	—	—	—	—	—	—	—	30	337
1957	†Det	8	—	—	—	—	18	294	16.3(56)	2	—	—	—	—	—	—	—	—	—	—	—	12	157
1958	Det	12(RE)	2	1	0.5(2)	0	29	506	17.4(46)	3	—	—	—	—	—	—	—	—	—	k	—	18	269
1959	Det	12(RE)	—	—	—	—	18	402	22.3(79)	2	—	—	—	—	—	—	—	—	—	p	—	12	226
1960	Det	7	3	-1	-0.3(1)	0	5	51	10.2(20)	0	—	—	—	—	—	—	—	—	—	—	—	0	25
1961	Min	12(11, WR)	—	—	—	—	30	444	14.8(57)	2	—	—	—	—	—	—	—	—	—	—	—	12	232
NFL	7	75(11)	67	210	3.1(16)	2	183	2966	16.2(79)	17	—	—	—	—	—	—	—	—	—	kp	—	114	1836

MIDDLETON, FRANK   Franklin, RB, 5´11˝/205 lbs; Florida A&M; B10/28/1960 Savannah, GA

1984	Ind	16(5, rb)	92	275	3.0(20)	1	15	112	7.5(15)	1	—	—	—	—	—	—	—	—	—	k	—	12	342
1985	Ind	5(2)	13	35	2.7(13)	1	5	54	10.8(34)	0	—	—	—	—	—	—	—	—	—	k	—	6	77
1987	SD	3(2)	28	74	2.6(21)	1	8	43	5.4(17)	0	—	—	—	—	—	—	—	—	—	—	—	6	106
NFL	3	24(9)	133	384	2.9(21)	3	28	209	7.5(34)	1	—	—	—	—	—	—	—	—	—	k	—	24	525

MIDDLETON, FRANK   Frank, G, 6´4˝/330 lbs; Arizona; 1997: TB, rnd 3; B10/25/1974 Beaumont, TX   **1997**†TB 15 (2)   **1998** TB 16 (16, RG)   **1999**†TB 16 (16, RG)   **2000**†TB 16 (16, RG)   **2001** Oak 13 (12, RG)   **2002** Oak 16 (16, RG)   **2003** Oak 10 (8, LG)   **2004** Oak 7 (7, lg)   **NFL** 109 (93) [8 yrs]

MIDDLETON, KELVIN   Kelvin Bernard, DB, 6´0˝/186 lbs; Wichita State; B9/8/1961 Macon, GA   **1987** Pit 2 (0)

MIDDLETON, RICK   Richard Ray, LB, 6´2˝/228 lbs; Ohio State; 1974: NO, rnd 1; B11/28/1951 Columbus, OH   **1974** NO 14   **1975** NO 14 (14, RLB)   **1976** SD 10   **1977** SD 14   **1978** SD 12 (2)   **NFL** 64 (16) [5 yrs]

MIDDLETON, RON   Ronald Allen, TE, 6´2˝/262 lbs; Auburn; B7/17/1965 Atmore, AL

1986	Atl	16(3)	—	—	—	—	6	31	5.2(8)	0	—	—	—	—	—	—	—	—	—	—	—	0	16
1987	Atl	12(4)	—	—	—	—	1	1	1.0(1)	0	—	—	—	—	—	—	—	—	—	—	—	0	1
1988	Was	2(0)	—	—	—	—	—	—	—	—	—	—	—	—	—	—	—	—	—	—	—	—	—
1989	†Cle	9(0)	—	—	—	—	1	5	5.0(5)	0	—	—	—	—	—	—	—	—	—	—	—	0	8
1990	†Was	16(5, te)	—	—	—	—	—	—	—	—	—	—	—	—	—	—	—	—	—	k	—	0	-8
1991	†Was	12(12, TE)	—	—	—	—	3	25	8.3(11)	0	—	—	—	—	—	—	—	—	—	—	—	0	13
1992	†Was	16(12, TE)	—	—	—	—	7	50	7.1(16)	0	—	—	—	—	—	—	—	—	—	—	—	0	25
1993	Was	16(16, TE)	—	—	—	—	24	154	6.4(18)	2	—	—	—	—	—	—	—	—	—	—	—	12	87
1994	LARm	16(3)	—	—	—	—	—	—	—	—	—	—	—	—	—	—	—	—	—	—	—	—	—
1995	SD	3(1)	—	—	—	—	—	—	—	—	—	—	—	—	—	—	—	—	—	—	—	—	—
NFL	10	118(56)	—	—	—	—	42	266	6.3(18)	3	—	—	—	—	—	—	—	—	—	k	—	18	140

MIDDLETON, TERDELL   Terdell, RB, 6´0˝/198 lbs; Memphis; 1977: SL, rnd 3; B4/8/1955 Memphis, TN

1977	GB	14(1)	35	97	2.8(16)	0	1	27	27.0(27)	0	—	—	—	—	—	—	—	—	—	k	1	6	202
1978	GB★	16(16, RB)	284	1116	3.9(76)	11	34	332	9.8(50)	1	—	—	—	—	—	—	—	—	—	k	—	72	1404
1979	GB	14(12, RB)	131	495	3.8(28)	2	18	155	8.6(29)	1	—	—	—	—	—	—	—	—	—	—	—	18	598
1980	GB	13(0)	56	155	2.8(15)	2	13	59	4.5(17)	0	—	—	—	—	—	—	—	—	—	—	—	12	205
1981	GB	14(3)	53	181	3.4(34)	1	12	86	7.2(27)	1	—	—	—	—	—	—	—	—	—	k	—	6	239
1982	†TB	2(0)	—	—	—	—	—	—	—	—	—	—	—	—	—	—	—	—	—	—	—	—	—
1983	TB	7(0)	2	4	2.0(2)	0	—	—	—	—	—	—	—	—	—	—	—	—	—	k	—	0	-1
NFL	7	80(32)	561	2048	3.7(76)	15	78	659	8.4(50)	3	—	—	—	—	—	—	—	—	—	k	1	114	2646

MIDLER, LOU   Louis Thomas, G-T, 6´1˝/223 lbs; Minnesota; 1938: Pit, rnd 5; B7/21/1915 St. Paul, MN, D8/29/1992 Marine on Sr. Croix, MN   **1939** Pit 11 (4)   **1940** GB 7 (1)   **NFL** 18 (5) [2 yrs]

MIELZINER, SAUL   Saul Robert, C-G-T-LB, 6´1˝/245 lbs; Carnegie Mellon; B6/1/1905 Cleveland, OH, D10/13/1985 Levittown, PA   **1929** NYG 12 (4)   **1930** NYG 16 (6, lg)   **1931** Bkn 9 (6, c)   **1932** Bkn 11 (10, C)   **1933** Bkn 7 (2)   **1934** Bkn 5 (1)   **NFL** 60 (29) [6 yrs]

YEAR	TEAM	G (GS, POS)	RUSH	YD	AVG(LG)	TD	REC	YD	AVG(LG)	TD	PASS COMP	PCT	YD	AVG(LG)	TD	INT	SK	YD	QBR	KPR	OTD	PTS	TAY

MIESZKOWSKI, ED　Edward Thomas, T, 6´3˝/220 lbs; Notre Dame; 1946: Bos, rnd 7; B10/14/1925 Chicago, IL, D2/15/2004 Lombard, IL　**1946** Bkn-A 13 (7, RT)　**1947** Bkn-A 10 (0)　**AAFC** 23 (7) [2 yrs]

MIGLIAZZO, PAUL　Paul Salvatore, LB, 6´1˝/228 lbs; Oklahoma; 1987: Chi, rnd 8; B3/11/1964 Kansas City, MO　**1987** ChiB 3 (0)

MIHAJLOVICH, LOU　Louis, DE, 5´11˝/175 lbs; Indiana; B2/19/1925 Detroit, MI　**1954** GB 3

| 1948 | LAD-A | 9 (0) | — | — | — | — | 4 | 42 | 10.5 | 0 | — | — | — | — | — | — | — | — | — | — | — | 0 | 21 |

MIHAL, JOE　Joseph, T, 6´2˝/234 lbs; Purdue; 1939: Phi, rnd 3; B4/2/1916 Homestead, PA, D9/18/1979 Dallas County, TX　**1940**†ChiB◇11 (1)　**1941**†ChiB◇9 (0)　**NFL** 20 (1) [2 yrs]　**1946** LAD-A 12 (0)　**1947** ChiR-A 1 (0)　**AAFC** 13 (0) [2 yrs]

MIKE, BOB　Robert Melvin, T, 6´1˝/220 lbs; Florida A&M; UCLA; B10/29/1923　**1948** SF-A 14 (0)　**1949**†SF-A 12 (8, LT)　**AAFC** 26 (8) [2 yrs]

MIKELL, QUINTIN　Quintin, DB, 5´10˝/206 lbs; Boise State; B9/16/1980 New Orleans, LA　**2003**†Phi 16 (0)　**2004**†Phi 14 (0)　**2005** Phi 16 (0)　**NFL** 46 (0) [3 yrs]

MIKE-MAYER, NICK　Nicholas, K, 5´8˝/186 lbs; Temple; 1973: Atl, rnd 10; B3/1/1950 Bologna, Italy **[K]**　**1973** Atl★14　**1974** Atl 14　**1975** Atl 14　**1976** Atl 14　**1977** Atl 7　**1977** Phi 3　**1978** Phi 12　**1980**†Buf 16 (0)　**1982** Buf 2 (0)

1979	Buf	13	1	4	4.0(4)	0	—	—	—	—	—	—	—	—	—	—	—	—	—	K	—	77	4
1981	†Buf	16 (0)	—	—	—	—	—	1	0	0.0	0	0	0.0	0	0	—	—	—	K	—	79	0
NFL	10	125	1	4	4.0(4)	0	—	—	—	—	1	0	0.0	0	0	—	—	—	KP	—	571	4

MIKE-MAYER, STEVE　Istvan, K, 6´0˝/180 lbs; Maryland; 1975: SF, rnd 3; B9/8/1947 Budapest, Hungary **[K]**　**1975** SF 14　**1976** SF 14　**1977** Det 14　**1978** NO 9　**1979** Bal 13　**1980** Bal 16 (0)　**NFL** 80 [6 yrs]

MIKESKA, RUSS　Russell E., TE, 6´3˝/225 lbs; Texas A&M; B9/10/1955 Temple, TX

1979	Atl	16	—	—	—	—	1	14	14.0(14)	0	—	—	—	—	—	—	—	—	—	—	—	0	7
1980	†Atl	16 (2)	—	—	—	—	1	4	4.0(4)	0	—	—	—	—	—	—	—	—	—	—	—	0	2
1981	Atl	16 (0)	—	—	—	—	2	16	8.0(11)	0	—	—	—	—	—	—	—	—	—	—	—	0	8
1982	†Atl	5 (0)	—	—	—	—	2	19	9.5(12)	0	—	—	—	—	—	—	—	—	—	—	—	0	10
NFL	4	53 (2)	—	—	—	—	6	53	8.8(14)	0	—	—	—	—	—	—	—	—	—	—	—	0	27

MIKETA, ANDY　Andrew John, C, 6´2˝/210 lbs; North Carolina; B11/1/1929 Girard, OH　**1954**†Det 12 (C)　**1955** Det 12 (C)　**NFL** 24 [2 yrs]

MIKLICH, BILL　William John, LB-BB-C, 6´0˝/208 lbs; Idaho; B4/3/1919 Greenwood, WI　**1948** NYG 4 (0)　**1948** Det 7 (0)

| 1947 | NYG | 7 (1) | — | — | — | — | 1 | -5 | -5.0(-5) | 0 | — | — | — | — | — | — | — | — | — | k | — | 0 | -15 |
| NFL | 2 | 18 (1) | — | — | — | — | 1 | -5 | -5.0(-5) | 0 | — | — | — | — | — | — | — | — | — | — | — | 0 | -3 |

MIKOLAJCZYK, RON　Ronald, T-G, 6´3˝/275 lbs; Marshall; Tampa; 1973: Oak, rnd 5; B6/2/1950 Passaic, NJ　**1976** NYG 9 (8, lg)　**1977** NYG 14 (RT)　**1978** NYG 8 (8, RT)　**1979** NYG 1　**NFL** 32 (16) [4 yrs]

MIKOLAJEWSKI, PETE　Peter James, QB, 6´1˝/210 lbs; Kent State; B2/26/1943 Portsmouth, VA

| 1969 | SD-A | 1 | — | — | — | — | — | — | — | — | 0 | 0 | 0.0 | 0 | 0 | 0.0 | 0 | 0 | 10 | — | — | 0 | 0 |

MIKOLAS, DOUG　Doug Adolph, NT, 6´1˝/270 lbs; Portland State; B6/7/1962 Manteca, CA　**1987** SF 8 (2)　**1988** SF 1 (0)　**1988** Hou 1 (0)　**NFL** 10 (2) [2 yrs]

MIKULA, TOM　Thomas Michael, FB-LB, 5´10˝/200 lbs; William & Mary; B9/26/1926 Johnstown, PA　**1948** Bkn-A 1 (0)

MIKULAK, MIKE　Michael Nicholas, B, 6´1˝/210 lbs; Oregon; B12/2/1912 Minneapolis, MN, D6/4/1999 Woodland, CA

1934	ChiC	11 (11, FB)	74	308	4.2	3	5	47	9.4	0	10	2	20.0	21	2.1	0	2	—	—	—	—	18	292
1935	ChiC☆	11 (10, FB)	68	82	1.2	1	8	93	11.6	0	—	—	—	—	—	0	—	—	—	—	—	6	139
1936	ChiC	12 (10, BB)	24	56	2.3	0	6	62	10.3	0	—	—	—	—	—	0	—	—	—	—	—	0	87
NFL	3	34 (31)	166	446	2.7	4	19	202	10.6	0	10	2	20.0	21	2.1	0	2	—	—	—	—	24	518

MILAM, BARNES　Israel Barnes, G-T, 6´2˝/190 lbs; Austin; B3/4/1906 Hagerman, TX, D12/18/1979 Austin, TX　**1934** Phi 2 (0)

MILAM, JOE　Joseph Baker, G-E-T, 5´11˝/180 lbs; Phillips; B3/13/1899 Amorita, OK, D11/25/1971 Victoria, TX　**1925** KC 7 (3)

MILAN, DON　Sonald Lee, QB, 6´3˝/200 lbs; Cal Poly-San Luis Obispo; B1/12/1949 Glendale, CA

| 1975 | GB | 7 (1) | 4 | 41 | 10.3(15) | 0 | — | — | — | — | 32 | 15 | 46.9 | 181 | 5.7(56) | 1 | 1 | 7 | 44 | — | — | 0 | 97 |

MILANO, ARCHIE　Archie, E, 6´0˝/197 lbs; St. Francis (PA); B5/26/1918, D8/12/1991　**1945** Det 1 (0)

MILANOVICH, SCOTT　Scott Stewart, QB, 6´3˝/227 lbs; Maryland; B1/25/1973 Butler, PA

| 1996 | TB | 1 (0) | — | — | — | — | — | — | — | — | 3 | 2 | 66.7 | 9 | 3.0(8) | 0 | 0 | — | — | — | — | 0 | 5 |

MILBURN, DARRYL　Darryl Wayne, DE, 6´3˝/260 lbs; Grambling State; 1991: Det, rnd 9; B10/25/1968 Baton Rouge, LA　**1991**†Det 2 (0)

MILBURN, GLYN　Glyn Curt, RB-WR, 5´8˝/177 lbs; Oklahoma; Stanford; 1993: Den, rnd 2; B2/19/1971 Santa Monica, CA **[R]**

1993	†Den	16 (2)	52	231	4.4(26)	0	38	300	7.9(50)	3	—	—	—	—	—	—	—	—	—	kp	—	18	629
1994	Den	16 (3, rb)	58	201	3.5(20)	1	77	549	7.1(33)	3	—	—	—	—	—	—	—	—	—	kp	—	24	913
1995	Den★	16 (1)	49	266	5.4(29)	0	22	191	8.7(23)	0	—	—	—	—	—	—	—	—	—	kp	—	0	1125
1996	Det	16 (0)	—	—	—	—	—	—	—	—	—	—	—	—	—	—	—	—	—	kp	—	0	781
1997	†Det	16 (1)	—	—	—	—	5	77	15.4(43)	0	—	—	—	—	—	—	—	—	—	kp	—	0	727
1998	ChiB	16 (0)	4	8	2.0(3)	0	4	37	9.3(13)	0	—	—	—	—	—	—	—	—	—	kp	3	18	843
1999	ChiB★	16 (1)	16	102	6.4(49)	1	20	151	7.6(22)	0	—	—	—	—	—	—	—	—	—	kp	—	6	895
2000	ChiB	16 (0)	1	6	6.0(6)	0	1	8	8.0(8)	0	—	—	—	—	—	—	—	—	—	kp	—	0	658
2001	ChiB	4 (0)	3	3	1.0(4)	0	3	9	3.0(7)	0	—	—	—	—	—	—	—	—	—	kp	—	0	83
2001	SD	6 (0)	—	—	—	—	—	—	—	—	—	—	—	—	—	—	—	—	—	p	—	0	54
NFL	9	138 (8)	183	817	4.5(49)	2	170	1322	7.8(50)	6	—	—	—	—	—	—	—	—	—	kp	3	66	6705

MILDREN, JACK　Larry Jack, DB, 6´1˝/200 lbs; Oklahoma; 1972: Bal, rnd 2; B10/16/1949 Kingsville, TX

1972	Bal	14	3	8	2.7(5)	0	—	—	—	—	1	0	0.0	0	0.0	0	0	—	—	k	—	0	-6
1973	Bal	14 (SS)	2	14	7.0(10)	0	—	—	—	—	—	—	—	—	—	—	—	—	—	k	—	0	14
1974	NE	14 (10, SS)	—	—	—	—	—	—	—	—	—	—	—	—	—	—	—	—	—	i	—	0	36
NFL	3	42 (10)	5	22	4.4(10)	0	—	—	—	—	1	0	0.0	0	0.0	0	0	—	—	ki	—	0	44

MILEM, JOHN　John Ray, DE, 6´7˝/290 lbs; Lenoir-Rhyne; 2000: SF, rnd 5; B6/9/1975 Concord, NC　**2000** SF 16 (0)　**2001** SF 2 (0)　**2001** Car 2 (0)　**NFL** 20 (0) [2 yrs]

MILES, BUCK　Mark Robert, FB, /195 lbs; Washington & Lee; B12/1888 Brooklyn, NY, deceased　**1920** Akr 1 (0)

MILES, EDDIE　Eddie, LB, 6´1˝/233 lbs; Minnesota; 1990: Pit, rnd 10; B9/13/1968 Miami, FL　**1990** Pit 1 (0)

MILES, LEO　Leo Fidelis, DB, 6´0˝/200 lbs; Virginia State; B5/21/1931 Washington, DC, D9/21/1995 Washington, DC　**1953** NYG 3

MILES, OSTELL　Ostell Shawn, RB, 6´0˝/236 lbs; Houston; 1992: Cin, rnd 9; B8/6/1970 Denver, CO

1992	Cin	11 (0)	8	22	2.8(9)	0	—	—	—	—	—	—	—	—	—	—	—	—	—	k	—	0	30
1993	Cin	15 (2)	22	56	2.5(15)	1	6	89	14.8(27)	0	—	—	—	—	—	—	—	—	—	k	—	6	116
NFL	2	26 (2)	30	78	2.6(15)	1	6	89	14.8(27)	0	—	—	—	—	—	—	—	—	—	k	—	6	146

MILI, ITULA　Itula, TE, 6´4˝/260 lbs; Brigham Young; 1997: Sea, rnd 6; B4/20/1973 Kahuku, HI

1998	Sea	7 (0)	—	—	—	—	1	20	20.0(20)	0	—	—	—	—	—	—	—	—	—	—	—	0	10
1999	†Sea	16 (1)	—	—	—	—	6	28	5.6(8)	1	—	—	—	—	—	—	—	—	—	—	—	6	19
2000	Sea	16 (6, te)	—	—	—	—	28	288	10.3(34)	0	—	—	—	—	—	—	—	—	—	k	—	18	163
2001	Sea	16 (5, te)	—	—	—	—	8	98	12.3(41)	2	—	—	—	—	—	—	—	—	—	—	—	12	59
2002	Sea	16 (12, TE)	—	—	—	—	43	508	11.8(49)	2	—	—	—	—	—	—	—	—	—	—	—	12	264
2003	†Sea	16 (12, TE)	—	—	—	—	46	492	10.7(46)	4	—	—	—	—	—	—	—	—	—	—	—	24	266
2004	†Sea	15 (4)	—	—	—	—	23	240	10.4(20)	1	—	—	—	—	—	—	—	—	—	k	—	6	122
2005	Sea	2 (0)	—	—	—	—	—	—	—	—	—	—	—	—	—	—	—	—	—	—	—	0	—
NFL	8	104 (40)	—	—	—	—	154	1674	10.9(49)	13	—	—	—	—	—	—	—	—	—	k	—	78	903

MILINCHIK, JOE　Joseph Michael, G-T, 6´5˝/290 lbs; North Carolina State; 1986: Det, rnd 3; B3/30/1963 Allentown, PA　**1987** Det 11 (0)　**1988** Det 15 (15, RG)　**1989** Det 15 (1)　**1990** LARm 8 (0)　**1991** LARm 5 (5, rg)　**1992** LARm 16 (16, RG)　**1993** SD 10 (10, RG)　**1994** SD 16 (16, RG)　**NFL** 96 (63) [8 yrs]

MILKS, JOHN John, LB, 6´0˝/222 lbs; San Diego State; B10/17/1943 **1966** SD-A 3

MILLARD, BRYAN Bryan James, G-T, 6´5˝/282 lbs; Texas; B12/2/1960 Sioux City, IA **1984** Sea 14 (0) **1985** Sea 16 (9, lt) **1986** Sea 16 (16, RG) **1988**†Sea☆15 (14, RG) **1989** Sea 16 (16, RG) **1990** Sea 16 (16, RG) **1991** Sea 16 (16, RG)

YEAR	TEAM	G (GS, POS)	RUSH	YD	AVG (LG)	TD	REC	YD	AVG (LG)	TD	PASS	COMP	PCT	YD	AVG (LG)	TD	INT	SK	YD	QBR	KPR	OTD	PTS	TAY
1987	†Sea	12 (12, RG)	—	—	—	—	1	-5	-5.0 (-5)	0	—	—	—	—	—	—	—	—	—	—	—	—	0	-3
NFL	8	121 (99)	—	—	—	—	1	-5	-5.0 (-5)	0	—	—	—	—	—	—	—	—	—	—	—	—	0	-3

MILLARD, KEITH Keith Joseph, DT-NT-DE, 6´6˝/260 lbs; Washington State; 1984: Min, rnd 1; B3/18/1962 Pleasanton, CA **[S]** **1985** Min 16 (5, nt) **1986** Min☆15 (15, RDT) **1987**†Min☆9 (8, RDT) **1988**†Min★15 (15, RDT) **1989**†Min★16 (16, RDT) **1990** Min 4 (4) **1992** Sea 2 (0) **1992** GB 2 (0) **1993** Phi 14 (6, rdt) **NFL** 93 (69) [8 yrs]

MILLEN, HUGH Hugh B., QB, 6´5˝/216 lbs; Washington; 1986: LARm, rnd 3; B11/22/1963 Des Moines, IA

YEAR	TEAM	G (GS, POS)	RUSH	YD	AVG (LG)	TD	REC	YD	AVG (LG)	TD	PASS	COMP	PCT	YD	AVG (LG)	TD	INT	SK	YD	QBR	KPR	OTD	PTS	TAY
1987	LARm	1 (0)	—	—	—	—	—	—	—	—	1	1	100.0	0	0.0 (0)	0	0	1	6	—	—	—	0	0
1988	Atl	3 (0)	1	7	7.0 (7)	0	—	—	—	—	31	17	54.8	215	6.9 (38)	0	2	4	29	—	—	—	0	35
1989	Atl	5 (1)	1	0	0.0 (0)	0	—	—	—	—	50	31	62.0	432	8.6 (47)	1	2	10	71	—	—	—	0	141
1990	Atl	3 (2)	7	-12	-1.7 (2)	0	—	—	—	—	63	34	54.0	427	6.8 (53)	-1	0	11	43	—	—	—	0	207
1991	NE	13 (13, QB)	31	92	3.0 (14)	1	—	—	—	—	409	246	60.1	3073	7.5 (60)	9	18	54	379	72.5	—	—	6	964
1992	NE	7 (7, QB)	17	108	6.4 (26)	0	—	—	—	—	203	124	61.1	1203	5.9 (39)	8	10	33	204	—	—	—	0	350
1994	Den	5 (2)	5	57	11.4 (24)	0	—	—	—	—	131	81	61.8	893	6.8 (76)	2	3	9	63	—	—	—	0	394
1995	Den	3 (0)	3	8	2.7 (7)	0	—	—	—	—	40	26	65.0	197	4.9 (18)	1	0	4	35	—	—	—	0	112
NFL	8	40 (25)	65	260	4.0 (26)	1	—	—	—	—	928	560	60.3	6440	6.9 (76)	22	35	126	830	73.5	—	—	6	2200

MILLEN, MATT Matthew George, LB, 6´2˝/250 lbs; Penn State; 1980: Oak, rnd 2; B3/12/1958 Hokendauqua, PA **1980**†Oak 16 (16, LILB) **1981** Oak 16 (16, LILB) **1982**†LARd 9 (9, LILB) **1983**†LARd 16 (15, LILB) **1984**†LARd☆16 (12, LILB) **1985**†LARd☆16 (16, LILB) **1986** LARd 16 (16, LILB) **1987** LARd 12 (12, LILB) **1988** LARd✧16 (15, LILB) **1989**†SF 15 (9, LILB) **1990**†SF 16 (16, LILB) **1991** Was 16 (14, MLB) **NFL** 180 (166) [12 yrs]

MILLER, AL Alfred Henry, WB-HB-FB-BB, 5´11˝/210 lbs; Harvard; B3/17/1904 Boston, MA, D12/20/1967 Detroit, MI **1929** Bos 7 (4, WB)

MILLER, AL Allen, LB, 6´0˝/228 lbs; Ohio University; 1962: Was, rnd 17/NYT, rnd 17; B4/18/1940 Fostoria, OH **1962** Was 14 (mlb) **1963** Was 11 **NFL** 25 [2 yrs]

MILLER, ALAN Alan Roger, FB, 6´0˝/219 lbs; Boston College; 1959: Phi, rnd 19; B6/19/1937 Mount Kisco, NY

YEAR	TEAM	G (GS, POS)	RUSH	YD	AVG (LG)	TD	REC	YD	AVG (LG)	TD	PASS	COMP	PCT	YD	AVG (LG)	TD	INT	SK	YD	QBR	KPR	OTD	PTS	TAY
1960	Bos-A	14 (FB)	101	416	4.1 (33)	2	29	284	9.8 (48)	2	—	—	—	—	—	—	—	—	—	—	—	—	24	588
1961	Oak-A★	14 (FB)	85	255	3.0 (15)	3	36	315	8.8 (55)	4	—	—	—	—	—	—	—	—	—	—	k	—	42	439
1962	Oak-A	14 (FB)	65	182	2.8 (11)	1	20	259	12.9 (71)	0	—	—	—	—	—	—	—	—	—	—	k	—	6	277
1963	Oak-A	14 (FB)	62	270	4.4 (35)	3	34	404	11.9 (44)	2	—	—	—	—	—	—	—	—	—	—	—	—	30	512
1965	Oak-A	14 (FB)	73	272	3.7 (26)	1	21	208	9.9 (39)	3	—	—	—	—	—	—	—	—	—	—	—	—	24	401
NFL	5	70	386	1395	3.6 (35)	10	140	1470	10.5 (71)	11	—	—	—	—	—	—	—	—	—	—	k	—	126	2216

MILLER, ANTHONY Lawrence Anthony, WR, 5´11˝/190 lbs; San Diego State; Tennessee; 1988: SD, rnd 1; B4/15/1965 Los Angeles, CA

YEAR	TEAM	G (GS, POS)	RUSH	YD	AVG (LG)	TD	REC	YD	AVG (LG)	TD	PASS	COMP	PCT	YD	AVG (LG)	TD	INT	SK	YD	QBR	KPR	OTD	PTS	TAY
1988	SD	16 (15, WR)	7	45	6.4 (20)	0	36	526	14.6 (49)	3	—	—	—	—	—	—	—	—	—	—	k	1	24	606
1989	SD★	16 (16, WR)	4	21	5.3 (24)	0	75	1252	16.7 (69)	**10**	—	—	—	—	—	—	—	—	—	—	k	1	66	925
1990	SD★	16 (16, WR)	3	13	4.3 (10)	0	63	933	14.8 (31)	7	—	—	—	—	—	—	—	—	—	—	k	—	42	513
1991	SD	13 (12, WR)	—	—	—	—	44	649	14.8 (58)	3	—	—	—	—	—	—	—	—	—	—	—	—	18	340
1992	†SD★	16 (16, WR)	1	-1	-1.0 (-1)	0	72	**1060**	14.7 (67)	7	—	—	—	—	—	—	—	—	—	—	k	1	48	582
1993	SD★	16 (16, WR)	1	0	0.0 (0)	0	84	1162	13.8 (66)	7	—	—	—	—	—	—	—	—	—	—	k	—	42	628
1994	Den	16 (14, WR)	1	3	3.0 (3)	0	60	1107	18.5 (76)	5	—	—	—	—	—	—	—	—	—	—	—	—	32	582
1995	Den✧	14 (14, WR)	1	5	5.0 (5)	0	59	1079	18.3 (62)	14	—	—	—	—	—	—	—	—	—	—	—	—	84	615
1996	†Den	16 (16, WR)	3	39	13.0 (26)	1	56	735	13.1 (46)	3	—	—	—	—	—	—	—	—	—	—	—	—	24	432
1997	Dal	16 (16, WR)	1	6	6.0 (6)	0	46	645	14.0 (54)	4	—	—	—	—	—	—	—	—	—	—	—	—	24	349
NFL	10	155 (151)	22	131	6.0 (26)	1	595	9148	15.4 (76)	63	—	—	—	—	—	—	—	—	—	—	k	3	404	5569

MILLER, ARNOLD Arnold, DE, 6´3˝/239 lbs; LSU; B1/3/1975 New Orleans, LA **1999** Cle 9 (0) **2000** Cle 12 (0) **NFL** 21 (0) [2 yrs]

MILLER, BILL William Joseph, SE-WR, 6´1˝/195 lbs; Miami (FL); 1962: DalT, rnd 2/Min, rnd 3; B4/17/1940 McKeesport, PA

YEAR	TEAM	G (GS, POS)	RUSH	YD	AVG (LG)	TD	REC	YD	AVG (LG)	TD	PASS	COMP	PCT	YD	AVG (LG)	TD	INT	SK	YD	QBR	KPR	OTD	PTS	TAY
1962	†DalT-A	14	—	—	—	—	23	277	12.0 (39)	0	—	—	—	—	—	—	—	—	—	—	—	—	0	139
1963	†Buf-A☆	14 (SE)	—	—	—	—	69	860	12.5 (36)	3	—	—	—	—	—	—	—	—	—	—	—	—	18	445
1964	Oak-A	12	—	—	—	—	2	29	14.5 (16)	0	—	—	—	—	—	—	—	—	—	—	—	—	0	15
1966	Oak-A	5	—	—	—	—	—	—	—	—	—	—	—	—	—	—	—	—	—	—	—	—	—	—
1967	†Oak-A	12 (SE)	—	—	—	—	38	537	14.1 (38)	6	—	—	—	—	—	—	—	—	—	—	—	—	36	299
1968	†Oak-A	9 (2)	—	—	—	—	9	176	19.6 (42)	1	—	—	—	—	—	—	—	—	—	—	—	—	6	93
NFL	6	66 (2)	—	—	—	—	141	1879	13.3 (42)	10	—	—	—	—	—	—	—	—	—	—	—	—	60	990

MILLER, BILL William C., DT, 6´4˝/270 lbs; New Mexico Highlands; 1962: Hou, rnd 17/1958: ChiB, rnd 21; B11/17/1936 Raleigh County, WV, D11/24/2003 Fayetteville, NC **1962** Hou-A 4

MILLER, BILLY Billy RoShawn, TE, 6´3˝/230 lbs; USC; 1999: Den, rnd 7; B4/24/1977 Los Angeles, CA

YEAR	TEAM	G (GS, POS)	RUSH	YD	AVG (LG)	TD	REC	YD	AVG (LG)	TD	PASS	COMP	PCT	YD	AVG (LG)	TD	INT	SK	YD	QBR	KPR	OTD	PTS	TAY
1999	Den	10 (0)	—	—	—	—	5	59	11.8 (26)	0	—	—	—	—	—	—	—	—	—	—	k	—	0	49
2000	Den	12 (0)	—	—	—	—	1	7	7.0 (7)	0	—	—	—	—	—	—	—	—	—	—	k	—	0	2
2002	Hou	16 (7, te)	—	—	—	—	51	613	12.0 (42)	3	—	—	—	—	—	—	—	—	—	—	—	—	18	322
2003	Hou	16 (6, te)	—	—	—	—	40	355	8.9 (25)	3	—	—	—	—	—	—	—	—	—	—	—	—	18	193
2004	Hou	16 (8, te)	—	—	—	—	17	178	10.5 (27)	1	—	—	—	—	—	—	—	—	—	—	—	—	6	94
2005	Cle	3 (1)	—	—	—	—	—	—	—	—	—	—	—	—	—	—	—	—	—	—	—	—	—	—
NFL	6	73 (22)	—	—	—	—	114	1212	10.6 (42)	7	—	—	—	—	—	—	—	—	—	—	k	—	42	658

MILLER, BING John Edward, T, 6´1˝/188 lbs; NYU; B12/6/1903 Syracuse, NY, D10/12/1964 Bronx, NY **1929** SI 10 (10, RT) **1930** SI 10 (8, RT) **1931** SI 9 (8, RT) **NFL** 29 (26) [3 yrs]

MILLER, BLAKE William Blake, WB-E, 5´7˝/170 lbs; Michigan State; B5/3/1889 Tonawanda, NY, D1/9/1987 Lansing, MI **1920** Det 2 (0) **1921** Det 3 (2) **NFL** 5 (2) [2 yrs]

MILLER, BLAKE Blake Randolph, C, 6´1˝/282 lbs; LSU; 1991: NE, rnd 7; B8/23/1968 Alexandria, LA **1992** Det 14 (5, c)

MILLER, BOB Robert Marguesse, DT-T, 6´3˝/242 lbs; Virginia; 1952: Det, rnd 5; B12/11/1929 Norwalk, CT **1952**†Det 11 (rt) **1953**†Det 12 **1954**†Det 12 (LDT) **1955** Det 12 (LDT) **1956** Det☆12 (RDT) **1957**†Det 12 (LDT) **1958** Det 10 **NFL** 81 [7 yrs]

MILLER, BRETT Brett Kolste, T, 6´7˝/293 lbs; Iowa; 1983: Atl, rnd 5; B10/2/1958 Lynwood, CA **1983** Atl 16 (0) **1984** Atl 15 (13, RT) **1985** Atl 12 (12, RT) **1986** Atl 8 (7, RT) **1987** Atl 2 (0) **1988** Atl 15 (4) **1989** SD 14 (11, RT) **1990** NYJ 16 (16, RT) **1991** NYJ 15 (0) **1992** NYJ 5 (0) **NFL** 118 (63) [10 yrs]

MILLER, BRONZELL Bronzell LaJames, DE, 6´4˝/247 lbs; Utah; 1995: SL, rnd 7; B10/12/1971 Federal Way, WA **1995** Jax 3 (0)

MILLER, BUBBA Stephen DeJuan, C, 6´1˝/305 lbs; Tennessee; B1/24/1973 Nashville, TN **1997** Phi 13 (3) **1999** Phi 14 (0)

YEAR	TEAM	G (GS, POS)	RUSH	YD	AVG (LG)	TD	REC	YD	AVG (LG)	TD	PASS	COMP	PCT	YD	AVG (LG)	TD	INT	SK	YD	QBR	KPR	OTD	PTS	TAY
1998	Phi	15 (4)	—	—	—	—	1	11	11.0 (11)	0	—	—	—	—	—	—	—	—	—	—	—	—	0	6
2000	†Phi	16 (16, C)	—	—	—	—	1	9	9.0 (9)	0	—	—	—	—	—	—	—	—	—	—	—	—	0	5
NFL	4	58 (23)	—	—	—	—	2	20	10.0 (11)	0	—	—	—	—	—	—	—	—	—	—	—	—	0	10

MILLER, CALEB Caleb, LB, 6´3˝/225 lbs; Arkansas; 2004: Cin, rnd 3; B9/3/1980 Guadalupe County, TX **2004** Cin 13 (3) **2005**†Cin 7 (0) **NFL** 20 (3) [2 yrs]

MILLER, CALVIN Calvin, NT-DT-DE, 6´2˝/260 lbs; Oklahoma State; B8/31/1953 Gulfport, MS **1979** NYG 11 **1980** Atl 2 (0) **NFL** 13 [2 yrs]

MILLER, CANDY Raymond Frederick, T-E, 6´3˝/215 lbs; Purdue; B6/7/1898 Fulton County, IN, D11/3/1986 Frankfort, IN **1922** Can 3 (3), 6 **1922** Rac 8 (8, RT) **1923** Rac 6 (4) **NFL** 17 (15) [2 yrs]

MILLER, CHRIS Christopher James, QB, 6´2˝/204 lbs; Oregon; 1987: Atl, rnd 1; B8/9/1965 Pomona, CA **[K]**

YEAR	TEAM	G (GS, POS)	RUSH	YD	AVG (LG)	TD	REC	YD	AVG (LG)	TD	PASS	COMP	PCT	YD	AVG (LG)	TD	INT	SK	YD	QBR	KPR	OTD	PTS	TAY
1987	Atl	3 (2)	4	21	5.3 (11)	0	—	—	—	—	92	39	42.4	552	6.0 (57)	1	9	5	37	—	—	—	0	-58
1988	Atl	13 (13, QB)	31	138	4.5 (29)	1	—	—	—	—	351	184	52.4	2133	6.1 (68)	11	12	24	207	67.3	—	—	6	790
1989	Atl	15 (15, QB)	10	20	2.0 (7)	0	—	—	—	—	526	280	53.2	3459	6.6 (72)	16	10	41	318	76.1	K	—	3	1430
1990	Atl	12 (12, QB)	26	99	3.8 (18)	1	—	—	—	—	388	222	57.2	2735	7.0 (75)	17	14	26	167	78.7	—	—	6	1002
1991	†Atl✧	15 (14, QB)	32	229	7.2 (20)	0	—	—	—	—	413	220	53.3	3103	7.5 (80)	26	18	23	145	80.6	—	—	0	1191
1992	Atl	8 (8, QB)	23	89	3.9 (16)	0	—	—	—	—	253	152	60.1	1739	6.9 (**89**)	15	6	16	103	90.7	—	—	0	794
1993	Atl	3 (2)	2	11	5.5 (6)	0	—	—	—	—	66	32	48.5	345	5.2 (32)	1	3	8	62	—	—	—	0	69
1994	LARm	13 (10, QB)	20	100	5.0 (16)	0	—	—	—	—	317	173	54.6	2104	6.6 (54)	16	14	28	193	73.6	—	—	0	672

YEAR	TEAM	G(GS, POS)	RUSH	YD	AVG(LG)	TD	REC	YD	AVG(LG)	TD	PASS	COMP	PCT	YD	AVG(LG)	TD	INT	SK	YD	QBR	KPR	OTD	PTS	TAY
1995	SL	13(13, QB)	22	67	3.0(13)	0	—	—	—	—	405	232	57.3	2623	6.5(72)	18	15	31	244	76.2	—	—	0	869
1999	Den	3(3)	8	40	5.0(13)	0	—	—	—	—	81	46	56.8	527	6.5(42)	2	1	7	51	—	—	—	0	274
NFL	10	98(92)	178	814	4.6(29)	2	—	—	—	—	2892	1580	54.6	19320	6.7(89)	123	102	209	1527	74.9	K	—	15	7029

Miller, Chuckie Charles Elliot, DB, 5´8˝/180 lbs; UCLA; 1987: Ind, rnd 8; B5/9/1965 Anniston, AL **1988** Ind 3 (1)

Miller, Clark Franklin Clark, DE, 6´5˝/245 lbs; Utah State; 1961: SF, rnd 5/Oak, rnd 14; B8/11/1938 Oakland, CA **1962** SF 10 (10, RDE) **1963** SF 14 (14, RDE) **1964** SF 14 (13, RDE) **1965** SF 14 (14, RDE) **1966** SF 14 (14, RDE) **1967** SF 13 (13, RDE) **1968** SF 10 (10, RDE) **1969** Was 2 **1970** LARm 6 **NFL** 97 (88) [9 yrs]

Miller, Clay Clay, T-G, 6´4˝/275 lbs; Michigan; 1986: TB, rnd 12; B8/27/1963 Columbus, OH **1987** Hou 3 (2)

Miller, Cleo Cleophus, RB, 5´11˝/207 lbs; Arkansas-Pine Bluff; B9/5/1952 Gould, AR

YEAR	TEAM	G(GS, POS)	RUSH	YD	AVG(LG)	TD	REC	YD	AVG(LG)	TD	PASS	COMP	PCT	YD	AVG(LG)	TD	INT	SK	YD	QBR	KPR	OTD	PTS	TAY
1974	KC	14	40	186	4.7(47)	0	14	149	10.6(34)	0	—	—	—	—	—	—	—	—	—	—	k	—	0	361
1975	KC	6	7	20	2.9(10)	0	—	—	—	—	—	—	—	—	—	—	—	—	—	—	k	—	0	56
1975	Cle	5	6	3	0.5(6)	1	2	20	10.0(10)	0	—	—	—	—	—	—	—	—	—	—	k	—	6	48
1976	Cle	12(12, FB)	153	613	4.0(21)	4	16	145	9.1(38)	0	—	—	—	—	—	—	—	—	—	—	k	—	24	734
1977	Cle	14(14, FB)	163	756	4.6(38)	4	41	291	7.1(28)	1	—	—	—	—	—	—	—	—	—	—	—	—	30	947
1978	Cle	15(9, rb)	89	336	3.8(18)	1	20	152	7.6(23)	0	—	—	—	—	—	—	—	—	—	—	k	—	6	422
1979	Cle	16(3)	39	213	5.5(39)	1	26	251	9.7(33)	0	—	—	—	—	—	—	—	—	—	—	k	—	6	348
1980	†Cle	16(0)	28	139	5.0(50)	3	2	8	4.0(7)	0	—	—	—	—	—	—	—	—	—	—	k	—	18	165
1981	Cle	12(3)	52	165	3.2(13)	2	16	139	8.7(17)	0	—	—	—	—	—	—	—	—	—	—	k	—	12	245
1982	†Cle	5(0)	16	61	3.8(17)	0	3	20	6.7(11)	0	—	—	—	—	—	—	—	—	—	—	—	—	0	71
NFL	9	115(41)	593	2492	4.2(50)	16	140	1175	8.4(38)	1	—	—	—	—	—	—	—	—	—	—	k	—	102	3395

Miller, Corey Corey James, LB, 6´2˝/252 lbs; South Carolina; 1991: NYG, rnd 6; B10/25/1968 Pageland, SC **1991** NYG 16 (1) **1992** NYG 16 (7, rolb) **1993**†NYG 16 (14, LOLB) **1994** NYG 15 (13, RLB) **1995** NYG 14 (9, RLB) **1996** NYG 14 (13, RLB) **1997**†NYG 14 (13, RLB) **1999**†Min 5 (3) **NFL** 110 (73) [8 yrs]

Miller, Craig Craig, DB, 5´11˝/199 lbs; Utah State; B10/4/1977 Bakersfield, CA **2000** Jax 4 (2)

Miller, Dan Daniel Scott, K, 5´10˝/172 lbs; Miami (FL); 1982: Was, rnd 11; B12/30/1960 West Palm Beach, FL **[K]** **1982** NE 2 (0) **1982** Bal 3 (0) **NFL** 5 (0) [1 yr]

Miller, Darrin Darrin James, LB, 6´1˝/227 lbs; Tennessee; B3/24/1965 Flemington, NJ **1988**†Sea 16 (0) **1989** Sea 16 (0) **NFL** 32 (0) [2 yrs]

Miller, Don Donald Charles, HB, 5´11˝/170 lbs; Notre Dame; B3/29/1902 Defiance, OH, D7/28/1979 Cleveland, OH **1925** Pro 1 (1)

Miller, Don Don Jack, HB, 6´2˝/195 lbs; SMU; 1954: Cle, rnd 7; B5/24/1932 Houston, TX **1954** GB 1 **1954** Phi 2 **NFL** 3 [1 yr]

Miller, Donald Donald, LB, 6´2˝/223 lbs; Utah State; Idaho State; B4/9/1964 Chicago, IL **1990** Sea 7 (0)

Miller, Doug Doug Alan, LB, 6´3˝/237 lbs; South Dakota State; 1993: SD, rnd 7; B10/29/1969 Cheyenne, WY, D7/21/1998 Dotsero, CO **1993** SD 8 (0) **1994**†SD 15 (0) **NFL** 23 (0) [2 yrs]

Miller, Dub Milford William, G-T, 6´0˝/218 lbs; Chadron State; B9/28/1911 Litchfield, NE, D4/8/1981 Chadron, NE **1935** ChiB 11 (3) **1936** ChiC 4 (1) **1937** ChiC 8 (0) **NFL** 23 (4) [3 yrs]

Miller, Dutch John Robert, C, 6´1˝/212 lbs; Wittenburg; B2/23/1906 Dover, OH, D7/6/1987 Roswell, NM **1931** Por 1 (0)

Miller, Eddie Edward, TB-QB-DB, 5´10˝/165 lbs; New Mexico State; B2/17/1916 Muskogee, OK, D11/9/2000 Roswell, NM

YEAR	TEAM	G(GS, POS)	RUSH	YD	AVG(LG)	TD	REC	YD	AVG(LG)	TD	PASS	COMP	PCT	YD	AVG(LG)	TD	INT	SK	YD	QBR	KPR	OTD	PTS	TAY
1939	†NYG	8(0)	30	99	3.3	1	—	—	—	—	23	13	56.5	195	8.5	2	2	—	—	—	P	—	6	137
1940	NYG	8(6, TB)	65	206	3.2	1	—	—	—	—	73	35	47.9	505	6.9(60)	4	7	—	—	—	Pi	—	6	204
NFL	2	16(6)	95	305	3.2	2	—	—	—	—	96	48	50.0	700	7.3(60)	6	9	—	—	—	Pi	—	12	340

Miller, Eddie Edward, WR, 6´0˝/185 lbs; South Carolina; 1992: Ind, rnd 9; B6/20/1969 Tumison, GA **1992** Ind 14 (0) **1993** Ind 1 (0) **NFL** 15 (0) [2 yrs]

Miller, Fred Frederick Louis, T, 6´3˝/225 lbs; Pacific; B8/30/1931 San Francisco, CA **1955** Was 12 (RT)

Miller, Fred Frederick David, DT, 6´3˝/250 lbs; LSU; 1962: Bal, rnd 7/Oak, rnd 26; B8/8/1940 Homer, LA **1963** Bal 13 (12, RDT) **1964**†Bal 14 (LDT) **1965**†Bal 12 (LDT) **1966** Bal 14 (RDT) **1967** Bal★14 (LDT) **1968**†Bal★14 (RDT) **1969** Bal✧14 (RDT) **1970**†Bal 12 (RDT) **1971**†Bal 14 (RDT) **1972** Bal 12 (LDT) **NFL** 133 (12) [10 yrs]

Miller, Fred Fred J., T-G, 6´7˝/320 lbs; Baylor; 1996: SL, rnd 5; B2/6/1973 Houston, TX **1996** SL 14 (0) **1997** SL 15 (7, lt) **1998** SL 15 (15, LG) **1999**†SL 16 (16, RT) **2000**†Ten 16 (16, RT) **2001** Ten 16 (16, RT) **2002**†Ten 16 (16, RT) **2003**†Ten 16 (16, RT) **2004** Ten 16 (16, RT) **2005**†ChiB 15 (15, RT) **NFL** 155 (133) [10 yrs]

Miller, Hal Hal Maurice, T, 6´4˝/230 lbs; Georgia Tech; 1953: SF, rnd 5; B2/4/1930 Kingsport, TN **1953** SF 12

Miller, Heath Earl Heath, TE, 6´5˝/265 lbs; Virginia; 2005: Pit, rnd 1; B12/22/1982 Richlands, VA

YEAR	TEAM	G(GS, POS)	RUSH	YD	AVG(LG)	TD	REC	YD	AVG(LG)	TD	PASS	COMP	PCT	YD	AVG(LG)	TD	INT	SK	YD	QBR	KPR	OTD	PTS	TAY
2005	†Pit	16(14, TE)	—	—	—	—	39	459	11.8(50)	6	—	—	—	—	—	—	—	—	—	—	—	—	36	260

Miller, Heinie Henry John, E-G, 5´10˝/185 lbs; Pennsylvania; B1/1/1893 Williamsport, PA, D6/9/1964 Longport, NJ **1920** Buf 11 (6, RE) **1921** Buf 7 (7, RE), 18 **1925** Mil 1 (1) **NFL** 19 (14) [3 yrs]

Miller, Jamir Jamir Malik, LB, 6´5˝/252 lbs; UCLA; 1994: Arz, rnd 1; B11/19/1973 Philadelphia, PA **1994** Arz 16 (0) **1995** Arz 10 (9, RLB) **1996** Arz 16 (16, RLB) **1997** Arz 16 (16, LLB) **1998**†Arz 16 (16, LLB) **1999** Cle 15 (15, RLB) **2000** Cle 16 (16, LLB) **2001** Cle★16 (16, LLB) **NFL** 121 (104) [8 yrs]

Miller, Jim Henry F., HB, 5´11˝/195 lbs; West Virginia Wesleyan; B2/19/1908 Sharpsburg, PA, D2/10/1965 Pittsburgh, PA **1930** Bkn 4 (0), 6

Miller, Jim James Robert, G, 6´3˝/240 lbs; Iowa; B7/24/1949 Iowa City, IA **1971** Atl 14 **1972** Atl 2 **1974** Atl 14 (LG) **NFL** 30 [3 yrs]

Miller, Jim James Gordon, P, 5´11˝/183 lbs; Mississippi; 1980: SF, rnd 3; B7/5/1957 Ripley, MS **1981**†SF 16 (0) **1982** SF 9 (0) **1983** Dal 2 (0) **1984** Dal 1 (0) **1987** NYG 1 (0)

YEAR	TEAM	G(GS, POS)	RUSH	YD	AVG(LG)	TD	REC	YD	AVG(LG)	TD	PASS	COMP	PCT	YD	AVG(LG)	TD	INT	SK	YD	QBR	KPR	OTD	PTS	TAY
1980	SF	16(0)	2	-12	-6.0(0)	0	—	—	—	—	—	—	—	—	—	—	—	—	—	—	P	—	0	-12
NFL	6	45(0)	2	-12	-6.0	0	—	—	—	—	—	—	—	—	—	—	—	—	—	—	P	—	0	-12

Miller, Jim James Donald, QB, 6´2˝/226 lbs; Michigan State; 1994: Pit, rnd 6; B2/9/1971 Grosse Pointe, MI

YEAR	TEAM	G(GS, POS)	RUSH	YD	AVG(LG)	TD	REC	YD	AVG(LG)	TD	PASS	COMP	PCT	YD	AVG(LG)	TD	INT	SK	YD	QBR	KPR	OTD	PTS	TAY
1995	Pit	3(0)	1	2	2.0(2)	0	—	—	—	—	56	32	57.1	397	7.1(42)	2	5	2	8	—	—	—	0	11
1996	Pit	2(1)	2	-4	-2.0(0)	0	—	—	—	—	25	13	52.0	123	4.9(17)	0	0	2	7	—	—	—	0	58
1999	ChiB	5(3, qb)	3	9	3.0(9)	0	—	—	—	—	174	110	63.2	1242	7.1(77)	7	6	7	43	—	—	—	0	425
2000	ChiB	3(2)	7	5	0.7(3)	0	—	—	—	—	82	47	57.3	382	4.7(34)	1	1	2	7	—	—	—	0	161
2001	†ChiB	14(13, QB)	29	-19	-0.7(3)	0	—	—	—	—	395	228	57.7	2299	5.8(66)	13	10	11	72	74.9	—	—	0	796
2002	ChiB	10(8, QB)	13	11	0.8(5)	0	—	—	—	—	314	180	57.3	1944	6.2(54)	13	9	16	101	77.5	—	—	0	688
NFL	6	37(27)	55	4	0.1(9)	0	—	—	—	—	1046	610	58.3	6387	6.1(77)	36	31	40	238	75.2	—	—	0	2138

Miller, John John Milton, FB, 6´0˝/188 lbs; Notre Dame; B3/31/1893, D3/1968 **1921** Day 1 (0)

Miller, John John Thomas, DB, 6´1˝/195 lbs; Michigan State; B6/22/1966 Detroit, MI **1989** Det 9 (0) **1990** Det 4 (0) **NFL** 13 (0) [2 yrs]

Miller, John John Frank, LB, 6´2˝/218 lbs; Mississippi State; B9/22/1960 Oberlin, OH **1987** GB 1 (0)

Miller, Johnny John Joseph, T-DT-DE, 6´5˝/253 lbs; Boston College; 1955: Was, rnd 9; B2/1/1934 Lowell, MA **1956** Was 12 (12, RT) **1958** Was 12 (3) **1959** Was 12 (5, lt) **1960**†GB 5 **NFL** 41 (20) [4 yrs]

Miller, Johnny Johnny, G, 6´1˝/247 lbs; Livingstone; 1976: SF, rnd 14; B2/3/1954 Ellerbe, NC **1977** SF 6

Miller, Josh Joshua Harris, P, 6´4˝/225 lbs; Arizona; B7/14/1970 Queens, NY **[P]** **1996**†Pit 12 (0) **1998** Pit 16 (0) **2002** Pit 14 (0) **2004**†NE 16 (0) **2005**†NE 16 (0)

YEAR	TEAM	G(GS, POS)	RUSH	YD	AVG(LG)	TD	REC	YD	AVG(LG)	TD	PASS	COMP	PCT	YD	AVG(LG)	TD	INT	SK	YD	QBR	KPR	OTD	PTS	TAY
1997	†Pit	16(0)	1	-7	-7.0(-7)	0	—	—	—	—	—	—	—	—	—	—	—	—	—	—	P	—	0	-7
1999	Pit	16(0)	2	-9	-4.5(0)	0	—	—	—	—	—	—	—	—	—	—	—	—	—	—	P	—	0	-9
2000	Pit	16(0)	1	0	0.0(0)	0	—	—	—	—	—	—	—	—	—	—	—	—	—	—	P	—	0	0
2001	†Pit	16(0)	1	0	0.0(0)	0	—	—	—	—	—	—	—	—	—	—	—	—	—	—	P	—	0	0
2003	Pit	16(0)	—	—	—	—	—	—	—	—	1	1	100.0	81	81.0(81)	1	0	—	—	—	P	—	0	46
NFL	10	154(0)	5	-16	-3.2	0	—	—	—	—	1	1	100.0	81	81.0(81)	1	0	—	—	—	P	—	0	30

Miller, Junior Selvia, TE, 6´4˝/239 lbs; Nebraska; 1980: Atl, rnd 1; B11/26/1957 Midland, TX

YEAR	TEAM	G(GS, POS)	RUSH	YD	AVG(LG)	TD	REC	YD	AVG(LG)	TD	PASS	COMP	PCT	YD	AVG(LG)	TD	INT	SK	YD	QBR	KPR	OTD	PTS	TAY
1980	†Atl★	16(14, TE)	2	-2	-1.0(0)	0	46	584	12.7(36)	9	—	—	—	—	—	—	—	—	—	—	—	—	54	335
1981	Atl✧	16(16, TE)	—	—	—	—	32	398	12.4(37)	3	—	—	—	—	—	—	—	—	—	—	—	—	18	214
1982	Atl	9(9, TE)	—	—	—	—	20	221	11.1(39)	1	—	—	—	—	—	—	—	—	—	—	—	—	6	116
1983	Atl	15(6, te)	1	2	2.0(2)	0	16	125	7.8(19)	0	—	—	—	—	—	—	—	—	—	—	—	—	0	65

YEAR	TEAM	G (GS, POS)	RUSH	YD	AVG (LG)	TD	REC	YD	AVG (LG)	TD	PASS	COMP	PCT	YD	AVG (LG)	TD	INT	SK	YD	QBR	KPR	OTD	PTS	TAY
1984	NO	15(0)	—	—	—	—	8	81	10.1(22)	1	—	—	—	—	—	—	—	—	—	—	—	—	6	46
NFL	5	71(45)	3	0	0.0(2)	0	122	1409	11.5(39)	14	—	—	—	—	—	—	—	—	—	—	—	—	84	775
MILLER, JUSTIN Justin, DB, 5´10˝/202 lbs; Clemson; 2005: NYJ, rnd 2; B2/14/1984 Owensboro, KY **2005** NYJ 16 (8, rcb)																								
MILLER, KEITH Keith McLaughlin, LB, 6´1˝/238 lbs; California; B7/9/1976 San Diego, CA **2000**†SL 16 (0) **2002** Sea 7 (0) **NFL** 23 (0) [2 yrs]																								
MILLER, KEVIN Kevin Von, WR, 5´10˝/180 lbs; Louisville; B3/21/1955 Weirton, WV **1979** Min 3 **1980** Min 4 (0)																								
1978	†Min	16	—	—	—	—	1	35	35.0(35)	1	—	—	—	—	—	—	—	—	—	—	kp	—	6	276
NFL	3	23	—	—	—	—	1	35	35.0(35)	1	—	—	—	—	—	—	—	—	—	—	kp	—	6	271
MILLER, LARRY Lawrence, QB, 6´4˝/220 lbs; Northern Iowa; B2/8/1962 Chicago, IL																								
1987	Min	2(0)	1	-1	-1.0(-1)	0	—	—	—	—	6	1	16.7	2	0.3(2)	0	1	1	10	—	—	—	0	-40
MILLER, LES Leslie Paul, NT-DE-DT, 6´7˝/292 lbs; Kansas State; Fort Hays State; B3/1/1965 Arkansas City, KS **1987** SD 9 (4) **1988** SD 13 (0) **1989** SD 14 (0) **1990** SD 14 (9, NT) **1991**†NO 16 (0) **1992**†NO 16 (2) **1993** NO 13 (11, NT) **1994** NO 8 (5, nt) **1994**†SD 4 (0) **1996**†Car 15 (5, lde) **1997** Car 16 (11, LDE) **1998** Car 14 (3) **NFL** 152 (50) [11 yrs]																								
MILLER, MARK Mark George, QB, 6´2˝/176 lbs; Bowling Green State; 1978: Cle, rnd 3; B8/13/1956 Canton, OH																								
1978	Cle	8	7	63	9.0(17)	1	—	—	—	—	39	13	33.3	212	5.4(44)	1	4	5	47	—	—	—	6	24
1979	Cle	2	1	-2	-2.0(-2)	0	—	—	—	—	8	2	25.0	31	3.9(17)	0	1	—	—	—	—	—	0	-27
NFL	2	10	8	61	7.6(17)	1	—	—	—	—	47	15	31.9	243	5.2(44)	1	5	5	47	—	—	—	6	-3
MILLER, MARK Mark Allen, QB, 6´2˝/210 lbs; Colorado State; Mesa; B11/6/1962 Grand Junction, CO																								
1987	Buf	1(0)	—	—	—	—	—	—	—	—	3	1	33.3	9	3.0(9)	0	1	—	—	—	—	—	0	-36
MILLER, MATT Matthew Peter, T-G, 6´6˝/270 lbs; Colorado; 1979: Cle, rnd 4; B7/30/1956 Durango, CO **1979** Cle 16 **1981** Cle 16 (0) **1982**†Cle 9 (0) **NFL** 41 [3 yrs]																								
MILLER, MIKE Michael Duane, WR, 5´11˝/182 lbs; Tennessee; 1983: GB, rnd 4; B12/29/1959 Flint, MI **1985** NO 3 (0)																								
1983	NYG	13(0)	1	2	2.0(2)	0	7	170	24.3(54)	0	—	—	—	—	—	—	—	—	—	—	k	—	0	88
NFL	2	16(0)	1	2	2.0(2)	0	7	170	24.3(54)	0	—	—	—	—	—	—	—	—	—	—	—	—	0	87
MILLER, NATE Nathan Udell, G, 6´3˝/310 lbs; LSU; B10/8/1971 Tuscaloosa, AL **1997** Atl 13 (0)																								
MILLER, NICK Nicholas Galen, LB, 6´2˝/238 lbs; Arkansas; 1986: Cle, rnd 5; B10/26/1963 Brunswick, ME **1987**†Cle 9 (1)																								
MILLER, OOKIE Charles Lewis, C-G-LB, 6´0˝/209 lbs; Purdue; B11/11/1909 Marion, IN, D8/7/2002 Hudson, FL **1932** ChiB 13 (11, C) **1933**†ChiB☆13 (12, C) **1934**†ChiB 12 (0) **1935** ChiB 11 (0) **1936** ChiB 11 (4) **1937** Cle 11 (5, rg) **1938**†GB 11 (7, C) **NFL** 82 (39) [7 yrs]																								
MILLER, PAT Leon Patrick, LB, 6´1˝/206 lbs; Florida; 1986: SF, rnd 5; B6/24/1964 Panama City, FL **1987** SD 1 (0) **1988** SD 8 (3) **NFL** 9 (3) [2 yrs]																								
MILLER, PAUL Paul William, HB, 5´11˝/180 lbs; South Dakota State; B1/23/1913 Platte, SD, D6/2/1994 Tucson, AZ																								
1936	†GB	12(0)	52	227	4.4	1	8	113	14.1(34)	2	1	0	0.0	0	0.0	0	1	—	—	—	—	—	18	264
1937	GB	10(1)	71	262	3.7	0	6	66	11.0	1	—	—	—	—	—	—	—	—	—	—	—	—	6	300
1938	†GB	10(0)	20	48	2.4	0	4	36	9.0(12)	0	—	—	—	—	—	—	—	—	—	—	—	—	0	66
NFL	3	32(1)	143	537	3.8	1	18	215	11.9(34)	3	1	0	0.0	0	0.0	0	1	—	—	—	—	—	24	630
MILLER, PAUL Paul William, DE, 6´2˝/226 lbs; LSU; 1953: LA, rnd 6; B11/8/1930 Mandeville, LA **1954** LARm 12 **1955**†LARm✧12 (LDE) **1956** LARm✧12 (LDE) **1957** LARm 12 (LDE) **1960** DalT-A☆14 (LDE) **1961** DalT-A 14 (LDE) **1962** SD-A 2 **NFL** 78 [7 yrs]																								
MILLER, PRIMO Ralph Edward, T, 6´2˝/220 lbs; Rice; B4/9/1916 San Antonio, TX, D10/3/1979 Denton County, TX **1937** Cle 11 (7, LT) **1938** Cle 8 (3) **NFL** 19 (10) [2 yrs]																								
MILLER, RALPH Ralph, G, 6´3˝/260 lbs; California Lutheran; Alabama State; B8/13/1948 Hartford, AL **1972** Hou 6 **1973** Hou 1 **NFL** 7 [2 yrs]																								
MILLER, ROBERT Robert Laverne, RB, 5´11˝/204 lbs; Kansas; 1975: Min, rnd 5; B1/9/1953 Houston, TX																								
1975	†Min	14	30	93	3.1(10)	1	4	35	8.8(32)	0	—	—	—	—	—	—	—	—	—	—	k	—	6	139
1976	†Min	14	67	286	4.3(36)	0	23	181	7.9(19)	1	—	—	—	—	—	—	—	—	—	—	k	—	6	384
1977	†Min	14	46	152	3.3(14)	0	27	246	9.1(25)	0	—	—	—	—	—	—	—	—	—	—	k	—	0	266
1978	†Min	15(2)	70	213	3.0(19)	3	22	230	10.5(29)	0	—	—	—	—	—	—	—	—	—	—	kp	—	18	351
1979	Min	16	35	109	3.1(20)	2	9	60	6.7(14)	0	—	—	—	—	—	—	—	—	—	—	k	—	12	152
1980	†Min	16(0)	27	98	3.6(27)	1	10	19	1.9(13)	0	—	—	—	—	—	—	—	—	—	—	k	—	6	126
NFL	6	89(2)	275	951	3.5(36)	7	95	771	8.1(32)	1	—	—	—	—	—	—	—	—	—	—	kp	—	48	1417
MILLER, RON Ronald William, E, 6´4˝/200 lbs; USC; B4/17/1933																								
1956	LARm	7	—	—	—	—	11	129	11.7(21)	0	—	—	—	—	—	—	—	—	—	—	—	—	0	65
MILLER, RON Ronald Rudolph, QB, 6´0˝/190 lbs; Wisconsin; 1961: LA, rnd 3/Hou, rnd 21; B8/19/1939 Lyons, IL																								
1962	LARm	6	3	27	9.0(13)	0	—	—	—	—	43	17	39.5	250	5.8(55)	1	1	—	—	—	—	—	0	117
MILLER, SCOTT Scott Patrick, WR, 5´11˝/181 lbs; UCLA; 1991: Mia, rnd 9; B10/20/1968 Phoenix, AZ																								
1991	Mia	16(0)	—	—	—	—	4	49	12.3(15)	0	—	—	—	—	—	—	—	—	—	—	p	—	0	133
1992	†Mia	15(0)	—	—	—	—	—	—	—	—	—	—	—	—	—	—	—	—	—	—	p	—	0	55
1993	Mia	3(0)	—	—	—	—	2	15	7.5(8)	0	—	—	—	—	—	—	—	—	—	—	k	—	0	-1
1994	†Mia	9(0)	—	—	—	—	6	94	15.7(27)	1	—	—	—	—	—	—	—	—	—	—	kp	—	6	58
1996	Mia	12(1)	—	—	—	—	9	116	12.9(22)	0	—	—	—	—	—	—	—	—	—	—	p	1	6	68
NFL	5	55(1)	—	—	—	—	21	274	13.0(27)	1	—	—	—	—	—	—	—	—	—	—	kp	1	12	313
MILLER, SHAWN Shawn Vernon, DE-NT-DT, 6´4˝/255 lbs; Utah State; B3/14/1961 Ogden, UT **1984** LARm 8 (0) **1985**†LARm 16 (3) **1986**†LARm 16 (16, NT/lde) **1987** LARm 6 (6, rde) **1988**†LARm 16 (16, RDE) **1989**†LARm 16 (11, RDE) **NFL** 78 (52) [6 yrs]																								
MILLER, SOLOMON Solomon, WR, 6´1˝/185 lbs; Utah State; 1986: NYG, rnd 6; B12/6/1964 Los Angeles, CA																								
1986	†NYG	16(2)	1	3	3.0(3)	0	9	144	16.0(32)	2	—	—	—	—	—	—	—	—	—	—	k	—	12	91
1987	TB	8(0)	—	—	—	—	5	97	19.4(33)	0	—	—	—	—	—	—	—	—	—	—	k	—	0	72
NFL	2	24(2)	1	3	3.0(3)	0	14	241	17.2(33)	2	—	—	—	—	—	—	—	—	—	—	k	—	12	163
MILLER, TERRY Robert Terry, LB, 6´2˝/225 lbs; Illinois; 1968: Det, rnd 8; B4/11/1946 Mattoon, IL **1970**†Det 1 **1971** SL 9 **1972** SL 12 (RLB) **1973** SL 14 **1974**†SL 5 **NFL** 41 [5 yrs]																								
MILLER, TERRY Terry, RB, 5´10˝/196 lbs; Oklahoma State; 1978: Buf, rnd 1; B1/7/1956 Columbus, GA																								
1978	Buf	16(RB)	238	1060	4.5(60)	7	22	246	11.2(52)	0	—	—	—	—	—	—	—	—	—	—	k	—	42	1255
1979	Buf	16(RB)	139	484	3.5(75)	1	10	111	11.1(52)	0	—	—	—	—	—	—	—	—	—	—	k	—	6	590
1980	Buf	15(0)	12	35	2.9(6)	0	3	25	8.3(15)	0	—	—	—	—	—	—	—	—	—	—	k	—	0	111
1981	Sea	1(0)	2	4	2.0(2)	0	—	—	—	—	—	—	—	—	—	—	—	—	—	—	—	—	0	4
NFL	4	48	391	1583	4.0(75)	8	35	382	10.9(52)	0	—	—	—	—	—	—	—	—	—	—	k	—	48	1959
MILLER, TOM Thomas Marshall, DE-E, 6´2˝/202 lbs; Hampden-Sydney; B5/23/1918 Milton, PA, D12/2/2005 Green Bay, WI																								
1943	P-P	8(1)	—	—	—	—	3	60	20.0(32)	1	—	—	—	—	—	—	—	—	—	—	i	—	6	30
1944	Phi	10(3)	1	-2	-2.0(-2)	0	8	135	16.9(49)	0	—	—	—	—	—	—	—	—	—	—	ki	1	6	99
1945	Was	9(1)	—	—	—	—	11	84	7.6(11)	0	—	—	—	—	—	—	—	—	—	—	—	—	0	42
1946	GB	2(0)	—	—	—	—	—	—	—	—	—	—	—	—	—	—	—	—	—	—	—	—	—	—
NFL	4	29(5)	1	-2	-2.0(-2)	0	22	279	12.7(49)	1	—	—	—	—	—	—	—	—	—	—	ki	1	12	171
MILLER, VERNE Verne L., HB, 5´8˝/152 lbs; Carleton; St. Mary's (MN); B5/11/1908 Grand Rapids, MI, D10/8/1982 Milltown, WI **1930** Min 5 (2)																								
MILLER, WILLIE Willie T., WR, 5´9˝/172 lbs; Colorado State; 1975: Hou, rnd 12; B4/26/1947 Birmingham, AL																								
1975	Cle	14	1	-2	-2.0(-2)	0	7	57	8.1(17)	0	1	1	100.0	26	26.0(26)	1	0	—	—	—	kp	1	6	76
1976	Cle	6	—	—	—	—	—	—	—	—	—	—	—	—	—	—	—	—	—	—	kp	—	0	-18
1978	†LARm	16(14, WR)	1	-7	-7.0(-7)	0	50	767	15.3(52)	5	—	—	—	—	—	—	—	—	—	—	—	—	30	402
1979	LARm	3(3)	1	4	4.0(4)	0	8	111	13.9(23)	1	—	—	—	—	—	—	—	—	—	—	—	—	6	65
1980	†LARm	16(1)	1	-2	-2.0(-2)	0	22	358	16.3(45)	8	—	—	—	—	—	—	—	—	—	—	—	—	48	217
1981	LARm	13(1)	—	—	—	—	10	147	14.7(20)	0	—	—	—	—	—	—	—	—	—	—	—	—	0	74

YEAR	TEAM	G (GS, POS)	RUSH	YD	AVG(LG)	TD	REC	YD	AVG(LG)	TD	PASS COMP	PCT	YD	AVG(LG)	TD	INT	SK	YD	QBR	KPR	OTD	PTS	TAY
1982	LARm	9(8, WR)	1	5	5.0(5)	0	15	346	23.1(85)	1												6	183
NFL	7	77(27)	5	-2	-0.4(5)	0	112	1786	15.9(85)	15	1	1 100.0	26	26.0(26)	1	0	—	—	—	kp	1	96	997

MILLIGAN, HANIK   Hanik, DB, 6'3"/200 lbs; Houston; 2003: SD, rnd 6; B11/3/1979 St. Croix, Virgin Islands   **2004**†SD 14 (0)   **2005** SD★16 (0)   **NFL** 30 (0) [2 yrs]

MILLING, BERT   Bert William, G, 5'10"/185 lbs; Richmond; B11/4/1921 Mobile, AL   **1942** Phi 2 (0)

MILLING, JAMES   James Thomas, WR, 5'9"/156 lbs; Maryland; 1988: Atl, rnd 11; B2/14/1965 Winnsboro, SC

YEAR	TEAM	G (GS, POS)	RUSH	YD	AVG(LG)	TD	REC	YD	AVG(LG)	TD	PASS COMP	PCT	YD	AVG(LG)	TD	INT	SK	YD	QBR	KPR	OTD	PTS	TAY
1988	Atl	6(0)	—	—	—	—	5	66	13.2(34)	0												0	33
1990	Atl	13(0)	—	—	—	—	18	161	8.9(24)	1												6	86
1992	Atl	5(0)	—	—	—	—	3	25	8.3(15)	0												0	13
NFL	3	24(0)	—	—	—	—	26	252	9.7(34)	1												6	131

MILLION, TED   Tedder Clark, G, 6'4"/260 lbs; Duke; B5/9/1963   **1987** Min 1 (0)

MILLMAN, BOB   Robert Dent, HB, 5'11"/178 lbs; Lafayette; B5/17/1903 Cumberland, MD, D3/19/1963 Trenton, NJ   **1925** Pot 2 (0)   **1926** Pot 7 (1), 6   **1927** Pot 3 (1)   **NFL** 12 (2) [3 yrs]

MILLNER, WAYNE   Wayne Vernal, E-DE, 6'1"/189 lbs; Notre Dame; 1936: Bos, rnd 8; B1/31/1913 Boston, MA, D11/19/1976 Arlington, VA; HOF 1968 **[C]**

YEAR	TEAM	G (GS, POS)	RUSH	YD	AVG(LG)	TD	REC	YD	AVG(LG)	TD	PASS COMP	PCT	YD	AVG(LG)	TD	INT	SK	YD	QBR	KPR	OTD	PTS	TAY
1936	†Bos	12(11, LE)	—	—	—	—	18	211	11.7	0												0	106
1937	†Was☆	11(11, LE)	2	6	3.0	0	14	216	15.4(78)	2											1	18	124
1938	Was	11(10, LE)	3	5	1.7	0	18	232	12.9	1												6	126
1939	Was	11(8, LE)	4	12	3.0	0	19	294	15.5(56)	4												24	179
1940	†Was	10(10, LE)	3	31	10.3	0	22	233	10.6(41)	3												18	163
1941	Was☆	11(1)	2	8	4.0(8)	0	20	262	13.1(55)	0												0	139
1945	†Was	10(1)	—	—	—	—	13	130	10.0(27)	2												12	75
NFL	7	76(52)	14	62	4.4(8)	0	124	1578	12.7(78)	12											1	78	911

MILLOY, LAWYER   Lawyer Marzell, DB, 6'0"/210 lbs; Washington; 1996: NE, rnd 2; B11/14/1973 St. Louis, MO **[I]**   **1996**†NE 16 (10, SS)   **1997**†NE 16 (16, SS)   **1998**†NE★16 (16, SS)   **1999** NE★16 (16, SS)   **2000** NE 16 (16, SS)   **2001**†NE★16 (16, SS)   **2002** NE❖16 (16, SS)   **2003** Buf 16 (16, SS)   **2004** Buf 11 (11, SS)   **2005** Buf 16 (16, SS)   **NFL** 155 (149) [10 yrs]

MILLS, CHARLIE   Charles, FB-BB, Maryland; deceased   **1920** Buf 5 (0)

MILLS, DENVER   Denver Burton, LB, 6'3"/225 lbs; William & Mary; B8/29/1925 Crockett, VA, D11/4/1997 Richmond, VA   **1952** ChiC 1

MILLS, DICK   Richard J., G, 6'3"/240 lbs; Pittsburgh; 1961: Det, rnd 3/DalT, rnd 9; B3/6/1939 Indiana, PA   **1961** Det 14   **1962** Det 8   **NFL** 22 [2 yrs]

MILLS, ERNIE   Ernest Lee, WR, 5'11"/192 lbs; Florida; 1991: Pit, rnd 3; B10/28/1968 Dunnellon, FL **[R]**

YEAR	TEAM	G (GS, POS)	RUSH	YD	AVG(LG)	TD	REC	YD	AVG(LG)	TD	PASS COMP	PCT	YD	AVG(LG)	TD	INT	SK	YD	QBR	KPR	OTD	PTS	TAY
1991	Pit	16(2)	—	—	—	—	3	79	26.3(35)	1										kp	1	12	169
1992	†Pit	16(4)	1	20	20.0(20)	0	30	383	12.8(22)	3										k		18	223
1993	†Pit	14(5, wr)	3	12	4.0(19)	0	29	386	13.3(30)	1												6	210
1994	†Pit	15(6, wr)	3	18	6.0(17)	0	19	384	20.2(43)	1										k		6	191
1995	†Pit	16(4)	5	39	7.8(20)	0	39	679	17.4(62)	8										k		48	915
1996	†Pit	9(3)	2	24	12.0(15)	0	7	92	13.1(22)	1										k		6	101
1997	Car	10(5, wr)	—	—	—	—	11	127	11.5(37)	1										k		6	74
1998	Dal	11(1)	3	9	3.0(5)	0	28	479	17.1(43)	4												24	269
1999	Dal	11(6, WR)	1	-1	-1.0(-1)	0	30	325	10.8(36)	0												0	162
NFL	9	118(36)	18	121	6.7(20)	0	196	2934	15.0(62)	20										kp	1	126	2311

MILLS, JAVOR   Javor Irvin, DE, 6'5"/271 lbs; Auburn; B5/11/1979 Wilmington, DE   **2002** Jax 8 (0)

MILLS, JEFF   Jeff Jonathan, LB, 6'3"/244 lbs; Nebraska; 1990: SD, rnd 3; B10/8/1968 Montclair, NJ   **1990** SD 5 (0)   **1990** Den 2 (0)   **1991**†Den 12 (3)   **1992** Den 14 (0)   **1993** Den 13 (0)   **NFL** 46 (3) [4 yrs]

MILLS, JIM   James Anthony, T, 6'9"/276 lbs; Hawaii; 1983: Bal, rnd 9; B9/23/1961 Vancouver, Canada   **1983** Bal 7 (7, rt)   **1984** Ind 14 (13, RT)   **NFL** 21 (20) [2 yrs]

MILLS, JIM   James Gary, G-T, 6'4"/290 lbs; Idaho; 1996: SD, rnd 6; B3/30/1973 Everett, WA   **1996** SD 1 (0)   **1997** SD 1 (0)   **NFL** 2 (0) [2 yrs]

MILLS, JOE   Joseph Edward, C-E-TB-G-WB, 6'3"/212 lbs; Carnegie Mellon; B9/3/1897 Knoxville, OH, D5/31/1967 Alliance, OH **[K]**   **1922** Akr 7 (4, TB), 7   **1923** Akr 6 (5, C)   **1924** Akr 4 (1, RE)   **1925** Akr 5 (2)   **1926** Akr 6 (1)   **NFL** 28 (16) [5 yrs]

MILLS, JOHN HENRY   John Henry, LB, 6'0"/226 lbs; Wake Forest; 1993: Hou, rnd 5; B10/31/1969 Jacksonville, FL   **1993**†Hou 16 (0)   **1995** Hou 16 (0)   **1996** Hou★16 (0)   **1997** Oak 16 (0)   **1998** Oak 5 (0)

YEAR	TEAM	G (GS, POS)	RUSH	YD	AVG(LG)	TD	REC	YD	AVG(LG)	TD	PASS COMP	PCT	YD	AVG(LG)	TD	INT	SK	YD	QBR	KPR	OTD	PTS	TAY
1994	Hou	16(1)	—	—	—	—	1	4	4.0(4)	0										k		0	59
1999	Min	15(0)	—	—	—	—	3	30	10.0(14)	0												0	15
NFL	7	100(1)	—	—	—	—	4	34	8.5(14)	0										k		0	139

MILLS, LAMAR   Franciscus Lamar, DE, 6'5"/270 lbs; Indiana; B1/26/1971 Detroit, MI   **1994** Was 13 (4)

MILLS, PETE   Sullivan, WR, 5'10"/180 lbs; Wichita State; 1965: Buf, rnd 12; B5/29/1942 Calvert, TX   **1966** Buf-A 1

YEAR	TEAM	G (GS, POS)	RUSH	YD	AVG(LG)	TD	REC	YD	AVG(LG)	TD	PASS COMP	PCT	YD	AVG(LG)	TD	INT	SK	YD	QBR	KPR	OTD	PTS	TAY
1965	†Buf-A❖	2	—	—	—	—	1	43	43.0(43)	0												0	22
NFL	2	3	—	—	—	—	1	43	43.0(43)	0										k		0	38

MILLS, SAM   Samuel Davis, LB, 5'9"/229 lbs; Montclair State; B6/3/1959 Neptune, NJ, D4/18/2005 Charlotte, NC   **1986** NO 16 (13, LILB)   **1987**†NO❖12 (12, LILB)   **1988** NO❖16 (16, LILB)   **1989** NO 16 (15, LILB)   **1990**†NO 16 (14, LILB)   **1991**†NO★16 (16, LILB)   **1992**†NO❖16 (16, LILB)   **1993** NO 9 (7, lilb)   **1994** NO 16 (16, LILB)   **1995** Car☆16 (16, LILB)   **1996**†Car★16 (16, LILB)   **1997** Car 16 (16, LILB)   **NFL** 181 (173) [12 yrs]

MILLS, STAN   Stanley, FB-HB-E, 5'9"/180 lbs; Penn State; B12/3/1893 Andalusia, PA, D6/1973 Andalusia, PA   **1922** GB 8 (8, FB)   **1923** GB 9 (6, hb), 18   **1924** Akr 5 (4), 6   **NFL** 22 (18), 24 [3 yrs]

MILNE, BRIAN   Brian Fitzsimons, RB, 6'3"/255 lbs; Penn State; 1996: Ind, rnd 4; B1/7/1973 Waterford, PA

YEAR	TEAM	G (GS, POS)	RUSH	YD	AVG(LG)	TD	REC	YD	AVG(LG)	TD	PASS COMP	PCT	YD	AVG(LG)	TD	INT	SK	YD	QBR	KPR	OTD	PTS	TAY
1996	Cin	6(4)	8	22	2.8(5)	1	3	29	9.7(15)	0												6	47
1997	Cin	16(16, FB)	13	32	2.5(5)	2	23	138	6.0(20)	0												12	121
1998	Cin	14(14, FB)	10	41	4.1(10)	1	26	124	4.8(18)	0												6	113
1999	Cin	1(1)	3	30	10.0(26)	0																	2	30
1999	†Sea	10(0)																						
2000	†NO	16(2)	2	1	0.5(1)	0	5	33	6.6(15)	1												6	23
NFL	5	63(37)	36	126	3.5(26)	4	57	324	5.7(20)	1												32	333

MILNER, BILL   Charles Edgar, LB-G-DE, 6'1"/228 lbs; South Carolina; Duke; 1944: ChiB, rnd 15/1947: Bkn-A, rnd 10; B3/7/1919 Waynesville, NC   **1947** ChiB 12 (4)   **1948** ChiB 12 (2)   **1949** ChiB 12 (0)   **1950**†NYG 12   **NFL** 48 (6) [4 yrs]

MILNER, BILLY   Willie Perry, T, 6'5"/304 lbs; Houston; 1995: Mia, rnd 1; B6/21/1972 Atlanta, GA   **1995**†Mia 16 (9, RT)   **1996** Mia 4 (0)   **1996** SL 9 (0)   **NFL** 29 (9) [2 yrs]

MILO, RAY   Raymond Wesley, DB, 5'11"/178 lbs; New Mexico State; 1978: KC, rnd 11; B2/19/1954 Conroe, TX   **1978** KC 1

MILOT, RICH   Richard Paul, LB, 6'4"/234 lbs; Penn State; 1979: Was, rnd 7; B5/28/1957 Coraopolis, PA   **1979** Was 14 (7, rlb)   **1980** Was 16 (5, mlb)   **1981** Was 11 (6, rlb)   **1982**†Was 9 (9, RLB)   **1983**†Was 16 (16, RLB)   **1984** Was 14 (12, RLB)   **1985** Was 16 (16, RLB)   **1986**†Was 16 (15, RLB)   **1987** Was 9 (5, mlb)   **NFL** 121 (91) [9 yrs]

MILSTEAD, CENTURY   Century Allen, T, 6'1"/213 lbs; Wabash; Yale; B1/1/1900 Rock Island, IL, D6/1/1963 Pleasantville, NY   **1925** NYG☆12 (12, LT)   **1927** NYG☆7 (7, RT)   **1928** NYG 11 (5, rt)   **NFL** 30 (24) [3 yrs]

MILSTEAD, CHARLIE   Charles Frank, QB-DB, 6'2"/190 lbs; Texas A&M; 1960: LAC, rnd 1/Was, rnd 14; B11/21/1937 Tyler, TX **[K]**   **1961** Hou-A 8

YEAR	TEAM	G (GS, POS)	RUSH	YD	AVG(LG)	TD	REC	YD	AVG(LG)	TD	PASS COMP	PCT	YD	AVG(LG)	TD	INT	SK	YD	QBR	KPR	OTD	PTS	TAY
1960	†Hou-A	14	3	3	1.0(7)	0	—	—	—	—	7	4 57.1	43	6.1(30)	0	0	—	—	P	—		0	25
NFL	2	22	3	3	1.0(7)	0	—	—	—	—	7	4 57.1	43	6.1(30)	0	0	—	—	KPi	—	1	40

MILSTEAD, ROD   Roderick Leon, G, 6'2"/290 lbs; Delaware State; 1992: Dal, rnd 5; B11/10/1969 Washington, DC   **1994** SF 5 (0)   **1995**†SF 16 (12, RG)   **1996** SF 11 (0)   **1997** SF 4 (0)   **1998** Was 14 (11, RG)   **1999**†SF 6 (0)   **NFL** 56 (23) [6 yrs]

MILTON, ELDRIDGE   Eldridge Dennis, LB, 6'1"/235 lbs; Clemson; B12/8/1962 Folkston, GA   **1987** ChiB 3 (0)

YEAR	TEAM	G (GS, POS)	RUSH	YD	AVG(LG)	TD	REC	YD	AVG(LG)	TD	PASS	COMP	PCT	YD	AVG(LG)	TD	INT	SK	YD	QBR	KPR	OTD	PTS	TAY

MILTON, GENE　Eugene, WR, 5´10˝/185 lbs; Florida A&M; B9/28/1944 Ocala, FL

1968	Mia-A	13	2	46	23.0(34)	0	9	143	15.9(38)	1	—	—	—	—	—	—	—	—	—	—	kp	—	6	286
1969	Mia-A	14	7	62	8.9(27)	0	12	179	14.9(49)	0	—	—	—	—	—	—	—	—	—	—	kp	1	6	197
NFL	2	27	9	108	12.0(34)	0	21	322	15.3(49)	1	—	—	—	—	—	—	—	—	—	—	kp	1	12	482

MILTON, JOHNNY　John William, E-B, 5´8˝/175 lbs; USC; B1899, deceased　**1923** Mil 1 (0)　**1923** SL 6 (4)　**1924** KC 8 (6, RE)　**NFL** 15 (10) [2 yrs]

MIMS, CHRIS　Christopher Eddie, DE-DT, 6´5˝/288 lbs; Tennessee; 1992: SD, rnd 1; B9/29/1970 Los Angeles, CA　**1992**†SD 16 (4)　**1993** SD 16 (7, lde)　**1994**†SD 16 (16, LDE)　**1995**†SD 15 (15, LDE)　**1996** SD 15 (15, LDE)　**1997** Was 11 (7, LDT)　**1998** SD 6 (0)　**1999** SD 9 (0)　**NFL** 104 (64) [8 yrs]

MIMS, DAVID　David James, WR, 5´8˝/191 lbs; Baylor; B7/7/1970 Daingerfield, TX

1993	Atl	15(2)	1	3	3.0(3)	0	12	107	8.9(19)	1	—	—	—	—	—	—	—	—	—	—	k	—	6	69
1994	Atl	2(2)	—	—	—	—	3	14	4.7(6)	0	—	—	—	—	—	—	—	—	—	—	—	—	0	7
NFL	2	17(4)	1	3	3.0(3)	0	15	121	8.1(19)	1	—	—	—	—	—	—	—	—	—	—	k	—	6	76

MINARIK, HENRY　Henry John, E, 6´2˝/200 lbs; Michigan State; 1951: Pit, rnd 8; B9/1/1927 Flint, MI

| 1951 | Pit | 11(LE) | — | — | — | — | 35 | 459 | 13.1(37) | 1 | — | — | — | — | — | — | — | — | — | — | — | — | 6 | 235 |

MINCY, CHARLES　Charles Anthony, DB, 6´0˝/195 lbs; Washington; 1991: KC, rnd 5; B12/16/1969 Los Angeles, CA [I]　**1991**†KC 0 (0)　**1992**†KC 16 (16, FS)　**1993**†KC 16 (4)　**1994**†KC 16 (8, ss)　**1995** Min 16 (9, fs)　**1996** TB 2 (0)　**1997**†TB 16 (9, FS)　**1998** TB 16 (16, FS)　**1999** Oak 16 (6, fs)　**NFL** 114 (68) [9 yrs]

MINER, TOM　Thomas Earl, K, 6´3˝/235 lbs; Tulsa; 1954: Pit, rnd 3; B5/14/1932 Checotah, OK, D1/1/1988 Tucson, AZ [K]　**1958** Pit 12

MINGO, GENE　Eugene, HB-K, 6´2˝/216 lbs; none; B9/22/1938 Akron, OH [K]

1960	Den-A	14(hb)	83	323	3.9(39)	4	19	156	8.2(18)	1	7	1	14.3	46	6.6(46)	0	0	—	—	—	Kkp	1	**123**	630
1961	Den-A	10	18	51	2.8(15)	0	8	110	13.8(69)	2	8	4	50.0	136	17.0(52)	2	0	—	—	—	Kkp	—	32	250
1962	Den-A★	14(hb)	54	287	5.3(82)	4	14	107	7.6(34)	0	2	1	50.0	18	9.0(18)	0	1	—	—	—	Kkp	—	**137**	360
1963	Den-A	14	24	90	3.8(17)	0	3	11	3.7(27)	0	1	0	0.0	0	0.0(0)	0	0	—	—	—	Kkp	—	83	192
1964	Den-A	7	6	26	4.3(9)	0	3	15	5.0(8)	0	—	—	—	—	—	—	—	—	—	—	Kk	—	33	77
1964	Oak-A	7	—	—	—	—	1	10	10.0(10)	0	—	—	—	—	—	—	—	—	—	—	Kk	—	6	10
1965	Oak-A	14	—	—	—	—	1	5	5.0(5)	0	—	—	—	—	—	—	—	—	—	—	K	—	24	3
1966	Mia-A	14	—	—	—	—	3	40	13.3(34)	0	—	—	—	—	—	—	—	—	—	—	K	—	53	20
1967	Mia-A	6	—	—	—	—	—	—	—	—	—	—	—	—	—	—	—	—	—	—	K	—	12	0
1967	Was	6	—	—	—	—	—	—	—	—	—	—	—	—	—	—	—	—	—	—	K	—	32	0
1969	Pit	14	—	—	—	—	—	—	—	—	—	—	—	—	—	—	—	—	—	—	K	—	62	0
1970	Pit	10	—	—	—	—	—	—	—	—	—	—	—	—	—	—	—	—	—	—	K	—	32	0
NFL	10	130	185	777	4.2(82)	8	52	454	8.7(69)	4	18	6	33.3	200	11.1(52)	2	1	—	—	—	Kkp	1	629	1540

MINICK, PAUL　Paul Daniel, G-E, 6´0˝/195 lbs; Iowa; B12/17/1899 Villisca, IA, D12/22/1978 Springfield, MO　**1927** Buf 5 (5, LG)　**1928** GB 12 (7, lg)　**1929** GB 6 (1)　**NFL** 23 (13) [3 yrs]

MINIEFIELD, KEVIN　Kevin Lamar, DB, 5´9˝/182 lbs; Arizona State; 1993: Det, rnd 8; B3/2/1970 Phoenix, AZ　**1993** ChiB 8 (0)　**1994**†ChiB 12 (0)　**1995** ChiB 15 (7, lcb)　**1996** ChiB 13 (3)　**1997** Arz 3 (0)　**NFL** 51 (10) [5 yrs]

MININI, FRANK　Frank David, HB-BB, 6´1˝/209 lbs; San Jose State; 1947: ChiB, rnd 3; B12/23/1921 Paso Robles, CA

1947	ChiB	12(9, RH)	26	132	5.1(33)	2	2	23	11.5(12)	0	—	—	—	—	—	—	—	—	—	—	ki	—	12	258
1948	ChiB	12(3)	24	79	3.3(18)	2	1	14	14.0(14)	1	—	—	—	—	—	—	—	—	—	—	k	2	30	311
1949	Pit	12(7, bb)	1	5	5.0(5)	0	—	—	—	—	—	—	—	—	—	—	—	—	—	—	k	—	0	155
NFL	3	36(19)	51	216	4.2(33)	4	3	37	12.3(14)	1	—	—	—	—	—	—	—	—	—	—	ki	2	42	724

MINISI, SKIPPY　Anthony Salvatore, HB, 5´11˝/190 lbs; Navy; Pennsylvania; 1948: NYG, rnd 1/ChiR-A, rnd 1; B9/18/1926 Newark, NJ, D5/5/2005 Paoli, PA

| 1948 | NYG | 12(9, RH) | 36 | 160 | 4.4(19) | 1 | 13 | 123 | 9.5(23) | 1 | 3 | 0 | 0.0 | 0 | 0.0(0) | 0 | 2 | — | — | — | kpi | — | 12 | 189 |

MINNIEAR, RANDY　Randall Harry, RB, 6´1˝/210 lbs; Purdue; 1966: NYG, rnd 20; B12/27/1943 Indianapolis, IN

1967	NYG	6	35	98	2.8(13)	1	8	49	6.1(21)	1	—	—	—	—	—	—	—	—	—	—	kp	—	12	139
1968	NYG	2	14	38	2.7(9)	2	4	32	8.0(18)	0	—	—	—	—	—	—	—	—	—	—	kp	—	12	74
1969	NYG	11	35	141	4.0(16)	1	6	68	11.3(21)	0	—	—	—	—	—	—	—	—	—	—	Pkp	—	6	193
1970	Cle	8	12	39	3.3(9)	1	1	-1	-1.0(-1)	0	—	—	—	—	—	—	—	—	—	—	P	—	6	49
NFL	4	27	96	316	3.3(16)	5	19	148	7.8(21)	1	—	—	—	—	—	—	—	—	—	—	P	—	36	454

MINNIFIELD, FRANK　Frank LyDale, DB, 5´9˝/180 lbs; Louisville; B1/1/1960 Lexington, KY [I]　**1984** Cle 15 (12, LCB)　**1985**†Cle 16 (16, LCB)　**1986**†Cle★15 (15, LCB)　**1987**†Cle★12 (12, LCB)　**1988**†Cle★15 (15, LCB)　**1989**†Cle★16 (16, LCB)　**1990** Cle 9 (8, LCB)　**1991** Cle 14 (11, LCB)　**1992** Cle 10 (8, LCB)　**NFL** 122 (113) [9 yrs]

MINNIS, SNOOP　Marvin Dwayne, WR, 6´1˝/172 lbs; Florida State; 2001: KC, rnd 3; B2/6/1977 Miami, FL

2001	KC	13(11, WR)	—	—	—	—	33	511	15.5(56)	1	—	—	—	—	—	—	—	—	—	—	—	—	6	261
2002	KC	2(0)	—	—	—	—	1	4	4.0(4)	0	—	—	—	—	—	—	—	—	—	—	—	—	0	2
NFL	2	15(11)	—	—	—	—	34	515	15.1(56)	1	—	—	—	—	—	—	—	—	—	—	—	—	6	263

MINOR, CLAUDIE　Claudie Dee, T, 6´4˝/280 lbs; San Diego State; 1974: Den, rnd 3; B4/21/1951 Pomona, CA　**1974** Den 14 (14, LT)　**1975** Den 14 (14, LT)　**1976** Den 14 (14, RT)　**1977**†Den 14 (14, RT)　**1978**†Den 16 (16, LT)　**1979**†Den 16 (16, LT)　**1980** Den 15 (15, LT)　**1981** Den 13 (13, LT)　**1982** Den 9 (7, LT)　**NFL** 125 (123) [9 yrs]

MINOR, KORY　Kory DeShaun, LB, 6´1˝/247 lbs; Notre Dame; 1999: SF, rnd 7; B12/14/1976 Inglewood, CA　**2000** Car 15 (0)　**2001** Car 11 (2)　**2002** Car 4 (0)　**NFL** 30 (2) [3 yrs]

MINOR, LINCOLN　Lincoln, RB, 6´2˝/211 lbs; New Mexico State; B1/22/1950 New Orleans, LA

| 1973 | NO | 9 | 3 | 10 | 3.3(8) | 0 | 1 | 1 | 1.0(1) | 0 | — | — | — | — | — | — | — | — | — | — | — | — | 0 | 13 |

MINOR, TRAVIS　Travis D., RB, 5´10˝/205 lbs; Florida State; 2001: Mia, rnd 3; B6/30/1979 New Orleans, LA [R]

2001	†Mia	16(0)	59	281	4.8(56)	2	29	263	9.1(29)	1	—	—	—	—	—	—	—	—	—	—	—	1	24	438
2002	Mia	16(0)	44	180	4.1(23)	2	—	—	—	—	—	—	—	—	—	—	—	—	—	—	k	—	12	581
2003	Mia	16(0)	41	193	4.7(26)	1	4	13	3.3(12)	0	—	—	—	—	—	—	—	—	—	—	k	—	6	427
2004	Mia	11(4)	109	388	3.6(34)	3	13	75	5.8(20)	0	—	—	—	—	—	—	—	—	—	—	k	—	18	456
2005	Mia	16(0)	5	17	3.4(9)	0	1	0	0.0(0)	0	—	—	—	—	—	—	—	—	—	—	—	—	0	9
NFL	5	75(4)	258	1059	4.1(56)	8	47	351	7.5(29)	1	—	—	—	—	—	—	—	—	—	—	k	1	60	1910

MINOR, VIC　Victor Wayne, DB, 6´0˝/198 lbs; Louisiana-Monroe; 1980: Sea, rnd 8; B11/28/1958 Shreveport, LA　**1980** Sea 16 (0)　**1981** Sea 4 (0)　**NFL** 20 (0) [2 yrs]

MINTER, BARRY　Barry Antoine, LB, 6´2˝/242 lbs; Tulsa; 1993: Dal, rnd 6; B1/28/1970 Mount Pleasant, TX　**1993** ChiB 2 (0)　**1994**†ChiB 13 (1)　**1995** ChiB 16 (3)　**1996** ChiB 16 (7, mlb)　**1997** ChiB 16 (16, RLB)　**1998** ChiB 16 (16, MLB)　**1999** ChiB 16 (16, RLB/mlb)　**2000** ChiB 15 (2)　**2001** Cle 1 (0)　**NFL** 111 (61) [9 yrs]

MINTER, CEDRIC　Cedric Alywyn, RB, 5´10˝/200 lbs; Boise State; B11/13/1958 Charleston, SC

1984	NYJ	8(2)	34	136	4.0(14)	1	10	109	10.9(39)	1	—	—	—	—	—	—	—	—	—	—	kp	—	12	304
1985	NYJ	3(0)	8	23	2.9(11)	0	1	13	13.0(13)	0	—	—	—	—	—	—	—	—	—	—	kp	—	0	44
NFL	2	11(2)	42	159	3.8(14)	1	11	122	11.1(39)	1	—	—	—	—	—	—	—	—	—	—	kp	—	12	347

MINTER, MICHAEL　Michael Jerome, NT, 6´3˝/275 lbs; North Texas; B8/13/1965 Mount Pleasant, TX　**1987** Pit 3 (2)

MINTER, MIKE　Michael Christopher, DB, 5´10˝/188 lbs; Nebraska; 1997: Car, rnd 2; B1/15/1974 Cleveland, OH　**1997** Car 16 (11, FS)　**1998** Car 6 (4)　**1999** Car 16 (16, FS)　**2000** Car 16 (16, SS)　**2001** Car 14 (14, SS)　**2002** Car 16 (16, SS)　**2003**†Car 16 (16, SS)　**2004** Car 16 (16, SS)　**2005**†Car 16 (16, FS)　**NFL** 132 (125) [9 yrs]

MINTER, TOM　Tommie Earl, DB, 5´10˝/178 lbs; Baylor; 1962: Min, rnd 9/Min, rnd 19; B7/18/1939 Henderson, TX　**1962** Den-A 7　**1962** Buf-A 5　**NFL** 12 [1 yr]

MINTUN, JOHN　John F., C, 5´11˝/191 lbs; none; B7/12/1894, D2/25/1976 Decatur, IL　**1920** Dec 5 (0)　**1921** ChiS 3 (1)　**1922** Rac 7 (7, C)　**1923** Rac 10 (10, C)　**1924** Rac 10 (10, C)　**1925** KC 8 (8, C)　**1926** Rac 2 (2)　**NFL** 45 (38) [7 yrs]

MIODUSZEWSKI, ED　Edward Thomas, aka Ed Meadows, QB-DB, 5´10˝/185 lbs; William & Mary; 1953: Det, rnd 18; B10/28/1931 Cliffside Park, NJ

| 1953 | Bal | 12 | 3 | 33 | 11.0(25) | 0 | — | — | — | — | 30 | 11 | 36.7 | 113 | 3.8(17) | 2 | 2 | — | — | — | kpi | — | 0 | 18 |

MIOTKE, FRANK　Frank, WR, 6´0˝/175 lbs; Grand Valley State; B12/22/1965 Dearborn, MI　**1991** Hou 8 (0)

MIRA, GEORGE　George Ignacio, QB, 6´0˝/190 lbs; Miami (FL); 1964: SF, rnd 2/Den, rnd 18; B1/11/1942 Key West, FL

| 1964 | SF | 7 | 18 | 177 | 9.8(37) | 0 | — | — | — | — | 53 | 23 | 43.4 | 331 | 6.2(79) | 2 | 5 | — | — | — | — | — | 0 | 153 |
| 1965 | SF | 10 | 5 | 64 | 12.8(25) | 0 | — | — | — | — | 58 | 28 | 48.3 | 460 | 7.9(46) | 4 | 3 | — | — | — | — | — | 0 | 194 |

YEAR	TEAM	G (GS, POS)	RUSH	YD	AVG (LG)	TD	REC	YD	AVG (LG)	TD	PASS	COMP	PCT	YD	AVG (LG)	TD	INT	SK	YD	QBR	KPR	OTD	PTS	TAY
1966	SF	14	10	103	10.3(38)	0	—	—	—	—	53	22	41.5	284	5.4(29)	5	2	—	—	—	—	—	0	190
1967	SF	3(2)	7	23	3.3(9)	0	—	—	—	—	65	35	53.8	592	9.1(58)	5	3	—	—	—	—	—	0	224
1968	SF	13	1	5	5.0(5)	0	—	—	—	—	11	4	36.4	44	4.0(43)	1	1	—	—	—	—	—	0	-8
1969	Phi	7	3	16	5.3(6)	0	—	—	—	—	76	25	32.9	240	3.2(35)	1	5	8	70	—	—	—	0	-59
1971	Mia	6	6	-9	-1.5(3)	0	—	—	—	—	30	11	36.7	159	5.3(43)	1	1	2	17	—	—	—	0	36
NFL	7	60(2)	50	379	7.6(38)	0	—	—	—	—	346	148	42.8	2110	6.1(79)	19	20	10	87	—	—	—	0	729

MIRALDI, DEAN Dean Martin, T-G, 6´5˝/266 lbs; Long Beach State; Utah; 1981: Phi, rnd 2; B4/8/1958 Culver City, CA **1982** Phi 1 (0) **1983** Phi 13 (6, lt) **1984** Phi 16 (16, LT) **1985** Den 10 (0) **1987** LARd 10 (10, RG) **NFL** 50 (32) [5 yrs]

MIRANDA, PAUL Paul Nathaniel, DB, 5´10˝/182 lbs; Central Florida; 1999: Ind, rnd 4; B5/2/1976 Thomasville, GA **1999**†Ind 5 (0) **2000** Sea 3 (0) **2001** Sea 8 (2) **NFL** 16 (2) [3 yrs]

MIRER, RICK Rick Franklin, QB, 6´3˝/210 lbs; Notre Dame; 1993: Sea, rnd 1; B3/19/1970 Elkhart, IN

YEAR	TEAM	G (GS, POS)	RUSH	YD	AVG (LG)	TD	REC	YD	AVG (LG)	TD	PASS	COMP	PCT	YD	AVG (LG)	TD	INT	SK	YD	QBR	KPR	OTD	PTS	TAY
1993	Sea	16(16, QB)	68	343	5.0(33)	3	—	—	—	—	486	274	56.4	2833	5.8(53)	12	17	47	235	67.0	—	—	18	1170
1994	Sea	13(13, QB)	34	153	4.5(14)	0	—	—	—	—	381	195	51.2	2151	5.6(51)	11	7	27	145	70.2	—	—	0	1004
1995	Sea	15(13, QB)	43	193	4.5(24)	1	—	—	—	—	391	209	53.5	2564	6.6(59)	13	**20**	42	255	63.7	—	—	6	750
1996	Sea	11(9, QB)	33	191	5.8(33)	2	—	—	—	—	265	136	51.3	1546	5.8(60)	5	12	22	84	56.6	—	—	12	529
1997	ChiB	7(3)	20	78	3.9(20)	1	—	—	—	—	103	53	51.5	420	4.1(34)	0	6	16	89	—	—	—	8	58
1999	NYJ	8(6, qb)	21	89	4.2(12)	1	—	—	—	—	176	95	54.0	1062	6.0(50)	5	9	22	102	—	—	—	6	295
2000	SF	1(0)	3	0	0.0(3)	0	—	—	—	—	20	10	50.0	126	6.3(26)	1	0	1	6	—	—	—	0	68
2003	Oak	9(8, QB)	20	83	4.2(20)	1	—	—	—	—	221	116	52.5	1267	5.7(47)	3	5	22	122	64.8	—	—	6	542
NFL	8	80(68)	242	1130	4.7(33)	9	—	—	—	—	2043	1088	53.3	11969	5.9(60)	50	76	199	1038	63.5	—	—	56	4415

MIRICH, REX Rex L., DT-DE, 6´4˝/250 lbs; Arizona State; 1963: Oak, rnd 20/Min, rnd 16; B3/11/1941 Florence, AZ **1964** Oak-A 14 (LDT) **1965** Oak-A 14 (LDT) **1966** Oak-A 14 **1967** Den-A 13 (LDE) **1968** Den-A 14 (ldt) **1969** Den-A 7 (2) **1970** Bos 7 (2) **NFL** 83 (4) [7 yrs]

MISCHAK, BOB Robert Michael, G-TE, 6´0˝/237 lbs; Army; 1954: Cle, rnd 23; B10/25/1932 Newark, NJ **1960** NYT-A☆4 (LG) **1961** NYT-A★14 (LG) **1962** NYT-A★14 (LG) **1964** Oak-A☆13 (LG) **1965** Oak-A 8

YEAR	TEAM	G (GS, POS)	RUSH	YD	AVG (LG)	TD	REC	YD	AVG (LG)	TD	PASS	COMP	PCT	YD	AVG (LG)	TD	INT	SK	YD	QBR	KPR	OTD	PTS	TAY
1958	†NYG	12(rg)	—	—	—	—	1	27	27.0(27)	0	—	—	—	—	—	—	—	—	—	—	—	—	0	14
1963	Oak-A	14(te)	—	—	—	—	2	25	12.5(15)	0	—	—	—	—	—	—	—	—	—	—	—	—	0	13
NFL	7	79	—	—	—	—	3	52	17.3(27)	0	—	—	—	—	—	—	—	—	—	—	—	—	0	26

MISHEL, DAVE David, B, 5´9˝/179 lbs; Brown; B7/6/1905 Lynn, MA, D3/11/1975 Newton, MA **[K]** **1927** Pro 4 (3) **1931** Cle 6 (3), 1 **NFL** 10 (6) [2 yrs]

MISKO, JOHN John Charles, P, 6´5˝/207 lbs; Oregon State; B10/1/1954 Highland Park, MI **1982** LARm 9 (0) **1983**†LARm 16 (0) **1984**†LARm 16 (0) **1987** Det 1 (0) **NFL** 42 (0) [4 yrs]

MISSOURI, DWAYNE Dwayne Anthony, DE, 6´5˝/260 lbs; Northwestern; 2001: Bal, rnd 7; B12/23/1978 Frankfurt, Germany **2001** Dal 3 (0)

MISTLER, JOHN John Andrew, WR, 6´2˝/186 lbs; Arizona State; 1981: NYG, rnd 3; B10/28/1958 Columbia, MO

YEAR	TEAM	G (GS, POS)	RUSH	YD	AVG (LG)	TD	REC	YD	AVG (LG)	TD	PASS	COMP	PCT	YD	AVG (LG)	TD	INT	SK	YD	QBR	KPR	OTD	PTS	TAY
1981	†NYG	16(0)	—	—	—	—	8	119	14.9(31)	1	—	—	—	—	—	—	—	—	—	—	—	—	6	65
1982	NYG	9(1)	—	—	—	—	18	191	10.6(24)	2	—	—	—	—	—	—	—	—	—	—	—	—	12	106
1983	NYG	16(9, WR)	—	—	—	—	45	422	9.4(24)	0	1	0	0.0	0	0.0	0	0	—	—	—	—	—	0	211
1984	Buf	3(0)	—	—	—	—	—	—	—	—	—	—	—	—	—	—	—	—	—	—	—	—	—	—
1984	†NYG	1(0)	—	—	—	—	1	5	5.0(5)	0	—	—	—	—	—	—	—	—	—	—	—	—	0	3
NFL	4	45(10)	—	—	—	—	72	737	10.2(31)	3	1	0	0.0	0	0.0	0	0	—	—	—	—	—	18	384

MITCHAM, GENE Eugene Gale, E, 6´2˝/206 lbs; Arizona State; 1955: LA, rnd 17; B5/18/1932 Phoenix, AZ

YEAR	TEAM	G (GS, POS)	RUSH	YD	AVG (LG)	TD	REC	YD	AVG (LG)	TD	PASS	COMP	PCT	YD	AVG (LG)	TD	INT	SK	YD	QBR	KPR	OTD	PTS	TAY
1958	Phi	2	—	—	—	—	3	39	13.0(20)	1	—	—	—	—	—	—	—	—	—	—	—	—	6	25

MITCHELL, AARON Aaron Templeton, DB, 6´1˝/196 lbs; Morris Brown; UNLV; 1979: Dal, rnd 2; B12/15/1956 Los Angeles, CA **1979**†Dal 16 (1) **1980**†Dal 15 (15, RCB) **1981** TB 13 (0) **NFL** 44 (16) [3 yrs]

MITCHELL, AL Albert Edwin, T-C-E, 6´1˝/180 lbs; Thiel; B8/30/1897 Greenville, PA, D5/12/1967 Livonia, NY **1924** Buf 6 (2)

MITCHELL, ALVIN Alvin Eugene, DB, 6´3˝/195 lbs; Morgan State; 1968: Cle, rnd 10; B10/18/1943 Philadelphia, PA **1968**†Cle 12 **1969**†Cle 14 **1970** Den 2 (1) **NFL** 28 (1) [3 yrs]

MITCHELL, ALVIN Alvin Jerome, RB, 6´0˝/235 lbs; Auburn; B8/20/1964 Venice, FL

YEAR	TEAM	G (GS, POS)	RUSH	YD	AVG (LG)	TD	REC	YD	AVG (LG)	TD	PASS	COMP	PCT	YD	AVG (LG)	TD	INT	SK	YD	QBR	KPR	OTD	PTS	TAY
1989	TB	5(0)	—	—	—	—	1	11	11.0(11)	0	—	—	—	—	—	—	—	—	—	—	—	—	0	6

MITCHELL, ANTHONY Anthony Maurice, DB, 6´1˝/198 lbs; Tuskegee; B12/13/1974 Youngstown, OH **2000**†Bal 16 (0) **2002** Bal 16 (6, fs) **2003** Jax 16 (1) **2004** Cin 12 (0) **2005**†Cin 16 (0)

YEAR	TEAM	G (GS, POS)	RUSH	YD	AVG (LG)	TD	REC	YD	AVG (LG)	TD	PASS	COMP	PCT	YD	AVG (LG)	TD	INT	SK	YD	QBR	KPR	OTD	PTS	TAY
2001	†Bal	16(0)	—	—	—	—	1	-11	-11.0(-11)	0	—	—	—	—	—	—	—	—	—	—	—	—	0	-6
NFL	6	92(7)	—	—	—	—	1	-11	-11.0(-11)	0	—	—	—	—	—	—	—	—	—	—	iS	—	0	42

MITCHELL, BASIL Basil Mucktar, RB, 5´10˝/200 lbs; TCU; B9/7/1975 Pittsburgh, TX

YEAR	TEAM	G (GS, POS)	RUSH	YD	AVG (LG)	TD	REC	YD	AVG (LG)	TD	PASS	COMP	PCT	YD	AVG (LG)	TD	INT	SK	YD	QBR	KPR	OTD	PTS	TAY
1999	GB	16(2)	29	117	4.0(15)	0	6	48	8.0(20)	0	—	—	—	—	—	—	—	—	—	—	kp	1	6	290
2000	GB	1(0)	2	8	4.0(4)	0	—	—	—	—	—	—	—	—	—	—	—	—	—	—	k	—	0	19
NFL	2	17(2)	31	125	4.0(15)	0	6	48	8.0(20)	0	—	—	—	—	—	—	—	—	—	—	kp	1	6	309

MITCHELL, BOB Robert Stanley, HB-QB-DB, 5´11˝/195 lbs; Stanford; B1/27/1921 Turlock, CA

YEAR	TEAM	G (GS, POS)	RUSH	YD	AVG (LG)	TD	REC	YD	AVG (LG)	TD	PASS	COMP	PCT	YD	AVG (LG)	TD	INT	SK	YD	QBR	KPR	OTD	PTS	TAY
1946	LAD-A	11(3)	8	-12	-1.5	0	1	1	1.0(1)	0	10	3	30.0	19	1.9	0	2	—	—	—	Pi	—	0	-55
1947	LAD-A	12(3)	32	85	2.7	0	3	36	12.0	1	—	—	—	—	—	—	—	—	—	—	ki	—	6	151
1948	LAD-A	14(1)	2	-2	-1.0	0	—	—	—	—	2	1	50.0	15	7.5(15)	0	1	—	—	—	i	—	0	-49
AAFC	3	37(7)	42	71	1.7	0	4	37	9.3(1)	1	12	4	33.3	34	2.8(15)	0	3	—	—	—	Pki	—	6	48

MITCHELL, BOBBY Robert Cornelius, FL-HB-WR, 6´0˝/192 lbs; Illinois; 1958: Cle, rnd 7; B6/6/1935 Hot Springs, AR; HOF 1983 **[R]**

YEAR	TEAM	G (GS, POS)	RUSH	YD	AVG (LG)	TD	REC	YD	AVG (LG)	TD	PASS	COMP	PCT	YD	AVG (LG)	TD	INT	SK	YD	QBR	KPR	OTD	PTS	TAY
1958	†Cle	12(LH)	80	500	6.3(63)	1	16	131	8.2(25)	3	—	—	—	—	—	—	—	—	—	—	kp	2	36	890
1959	Cle☆	12(LH)	131	743	5.7(90)	5	35	351	10.0(76)	4	—	—	—	—	—	—	—	—	—	—	kp	1	60	1162
1960	Cle★	12(HB)	111	506	4.6(60)	5	45	612	13.6(69)	6	1	1	100.0	23	23.0(23)	1	0	—	—	—	kp	1	72	1152
1961	Cle	14(HB)	101	548	5.4(56)	5	32	368	11.5(52)	3	—	—	—	—	—	—	—	—	—	—	kp	2	60	1099
1962	Was★	14(RH)	1	5	5.0(5)	0	**72**	**1384**	19.2(81)	11	—	—	—	—	—	—	—	—	—	—	kp	1	72	972
1963	Was★	14(FL)	3	24	8.0(21)	0	69	**1436**	20.8(**99**)	7	—	—	—	—	—	—	—	—	—	—	kp	1	48	1014
1964	Was★	14(FL)	2	33	16.5(19)	0	60	904	15.1(60)	**10**	—	—	—	—	—	—	—	—	—	—	k	—	60	548
1965	Was	14(FL)	—	—	—	—	60	867	14.4(80)	6	—	—	—	—	—	—	—	—	—	—	kp	—	36	505
1966	Was	14(FL)	13	141	10.8(48)	1	58	905	15.6(70)	9	1	1	100.0	21	21.0(21)	0	0	—	—	—	p	—	60	660
1967	Was	14(FL)	61	189	3.1(16)	1	60	866	14.4(65)	6	1	1	100.0	17	17.0(17)	0	0	—	—	—	—	—	42	671
1968	Was	14(fl)	10	46	4.6(13)	0	14	130	9.3(18)	0	—	—	—	—	—	—	—	—	—	—	kp	—	0	176
NFL	11	148	513	2735	5.3(90)	18	521	7954	15.3(99)	65	3	3	100.0	61	20.3(23)	1	0	—	—	—	kp	8	546	8847

MITCHELL, BRANDON Brandon Pete, DE-DT, 6´3˝/290 lbs; Texas A&M; 1997: NE, rnd 2; B6/19/1975 Abbeville, LA **1997**†NE 11 (0) **1998** NE 7 (1) **1999** NE 16 (16, LDE) **2000** NE 11 (9, LDE) **2001**†NE 16 (11, LDT) **2002** Sea 5 (2) **2003**†Sea 14 (6, lde) **2004**†Sea 15 (0) **NFL** 95 (45) [8 yrs]

MITCHELL, BRIAN Brian Keith, RB, 5´11˝/225 lbs; Louisiana-Lafayette; 1990: Was, rnd 5; B8/18/1968 Fort Polk, LA **[R]**

YEAR	TEAM	G (GS, POS)	RUSH	YD	AVG (LG)	TD	REC	YD	AVG (LG)	TD	PASS	COMP	PCT	YD	AVG (LG)	TD	INT	SK	YD	QBR	KPR	OTD	PTS	TAY
1990	†Was	15(0)	15	81	5.4(21)	1	2	5	2.5(5)	0	6	3	50.0	40	6.7(18)	0	0	1	3	—	kp	—	6	256
1991	†Was☆	16(0)	3	14	4.7(8)	0	—	—	—	—	—	—	—	—	—	—	—	—	—	—	kp	2	12	557
1992	†Was	16(0)	6	70	11.7(33)	0	3	30	10.0(17)	0	1	0	0.0	0	0.0	0	0	—	—	—	kp	1	6	368
1993	Was	16(4)	63	246	3.9(29)	3	20	157	7.8(18)	0	2	1	50.0	50	25.0(50)	0	1	—	—	—	kp	—	18	571
1994	Was☆	16(7, fb)	78	311	4.0(33)	0	26	236	9.1(46)	1	1	0	0.0	0	0.0	0	1	—	—	—	kp	2	20	1314
1995	Was★	16(1)	46	301	6.5(36)	1	38	324	8.5(22)	1	—	—	—	—	—	—	—	—	—	—	kp	1	18	1261
1996	Was	16(2)	39	193	4.9(32)	0	32	286	8.9(20)	0	1	0	0.0	0	0.0	0	0	—	—	—	kp	—	0	897
1997	Was	16(1)	23	107	4.7(26)	1	36	438	12.2(69)	1	—	—	—	—	—	—	—	—	—	—	kp	2	24	1002
1998	Was	16(0)	39	208	5.3(22)	2	44	306	7.0(24)	0	2	1	50.0	0	0.0(0)	0	0	—	—	—	kp	1	18	1129
1999	†Was	16(0)	40	220	5.5(16)	1	31	305	9.8(36)	0	—	—	—	—	—	—	—	—	—	—	kp	—	6	763
2000	†Phi	16(1)	25	187	7.5(85)	2	13	89	6.8(21)	1	4	1	25.0	21	5.3(21)	0	0	—	—	—	kp	2	30	881
2001	†Phi	16(0)	7	9	1.3(11)	0	6	122	20.3(56)	0	—	—	—	—	—	—	—	—	—	—	kp	1	6	762

YEAR	TEAM	G (GS, POS)	RUSH	YD	AVG (LG)	TD	REC	YD	AVG (LG)	TD	PASS	COMP	PCT	YD	AVG (LG)	TD	INT	SK	YD	QBR	KPR	OTD	PTS	TAY
2002	†Phi	16 (0)	—	—	—	—	—	—	—	—	1	1	100.0	57	57.0 (57)	1	0	—	—	—	kp	1	6	898
2003	NYG	16 (0)	4	20	5.0 (18)	1	4	38	9.5 (11)	0	—	—	—	—	—	—	—	—	—	—	kp	—	6	350
NFL	14	223 (16)	388	1967	5.1 (85)	12	255	2336	9.2 (69)	4	18	7	38.9	168	9.3 (57)	1	2	1	3	—	kp	13	176	11007

MITCHELL, BRIAN Brian Keith, DB, 5´9˝/164 lbs; Brigham Young; 1991: Atl, rnd 7; B12/13/1968 Indianapolis, IN **1991**†Atl 15 (0) **1992** Atl 16 (0) **1993** Atl 5 (0) **NFL** 36 (0) [3 yrs]

MITCHELL, BUSTER Granville Myrick, E-T, 6´0˝/205 lbs; Davis & Elkins; B2/16/1906 Irene, TX, D3/4/1964 Sweetwater, TX

YEAR	TEAM	G (GS, POS)	RUSH	YD	AVG (LG)	TD	REC	YD	AVG (LG)	TD	PASS	COMP	PCT	YD	AVG (LG)	TD	INT	SK	YD	QBR	KPR	OTD	PTS	TAY
1931	Por	13 (6, le)	—	—	—	—	—	—	—	—	—	—	—	—	—	—	—	—	—	—	—	—	—	—
1932	Por	10 (4)	—	—	—	—	2	31	15.5	0	—	—	—	—	—	—	—	—	—	—	—	—	0	16
1933	Por	11 (9, LT)	—	—	—	—	—	—	—	—	—	—	—	—	—	—	—	—	—	—	—	—	—	—
1934	Det☆	13 (6, le)	7	48	6.9	0	—	—	—	—	—	—	—	—	—	—	—	—	—	—	—	—	0	48
1935	†Det	3 (2)	—	—	—	—	—	—	—	—	—	—	—	—	—	—	—	—	—	—	—	—	—	—
1935	NYG	2 (1)	—	—	—	—	1	11	11.0 (11)	0	—	—	—	—	—	—	—	—	—	—	—	—	0	6
1936	NYG	8 (2)	—	—	—	—	2	10	5.0 (10)	0	—	—	—	—	—	—	—	—	—	—	—	—	0	5
1937	Bkn	11 (6, le)	2	4	2.0	0	8	115	14.4 (15)	1	—	—	—	—	—	—	—	—	—	—	—	—	6	67
NFL	7	71 (36)	9	52	5.8	0	13	167	12.8 (15)	1	—	—	—	—	—	—	—	—	—	—	—	—	6	141

MITCHELL, CHARLEY Charles Howard, HB-DB, 5´11˝/185 lbs; Washington; 1963: Den, rnd 18/Chi, rnd 4; B5/25/1940 McNary, AZ

YEAR	TEAM	G (GS, POS)	RUSH	YD	AVG (LG)	TD	REC	YD	AVG (LG)	TD	PASS	COMP	PCT	YD	AVG (LG)	TD	INT	SK	YD	QBR	KPR	OTD	PTS	TAY
1963	Den-A	14 (RCB)	24	41	1.7 (7)	0	8	71	8.9 (20)	0	—	—	—	—	—	—	—	—	—	—	kpi	1	6	562
1964	Den-A	14 (HB)	177	590	3.3 (33)	5	33	225	6.8 (58)	1	1	0	0.0	0	0.0	0	0	—	—	—	kp	—	36	894
1965	Den-A	1	—	—	—	—	—	—	—	—	—	—	—	—	—	—	—	—	—	—	—	—	—	—
1966	Den-A	13 (hb)	70	199	2.8 (21)	0	14	239	17.1 (79)	2	—	—	—	—	—	—	—	—	—	—	k	—	12	339
1967	Den-A	14 (hb)	82	308	3.8 (35)	0	7	15	2.1 (15)	0	—	—	—	—	—	—	—	—	—	—	k	—	0	360
1968	Buf-A	3	—	—	—	—	—	—	—	—	—	—	—	—	—	—	—	—	—	—	k	—	0	23
NFL	6	59	353	1138	3.2 (35)	5	62	550	8.9 (79)	3	1	0	0.0	0	0.0	0	0	—	—	—	kpi	1	54	2176

MITCHELL, CHARLIE Charles E., HB-G, 6´0˝/188 lbs; Southwest Missouri State; Tulsa; 1944: ChiB, rnd 28; B12/28/1920 Oilton, OK, D4/2/1999 **1945** ChiB 8 (1) **1946** GB 2 (0) **NFL** 10 (1) [2 yrs]

MITCHELL, DALE Dale James, LB, 6´3˝/223 lbs; USC; 1975: SF, rnd 13; B9/1/1953 Oceanside, CA **1976** SF 13 **1977** SF 4 **NFL** 17 [2 yrs]

MITCHELL, DERRELL Derrell Lavoice, WR, 5´9˝/189 lbs; Texas Tech; 1994: NO, rnd 6; B9/16/1971 Miami, FL

YEAR	TEAM	G (GS, POS)	RUSH	YD	AVG (LG)	TD	REC	YD	AVG (LG)	TD	PASS	COMP	PCT	YD	AVG (LG)	TD	INT	SK	YD	QBR	KPR	OTD	PTS	TAY
1994	NO	14 (0)	—	—	—	—	1	13	13.0 (13)	0	—	—	—	—	—	—	—	—	—	—	kp	—	0	40

MITCHELL, DEVON Devon Dermott, DB, 6´1˝/194 lbs; Iowa; 1986: Det, rnd 4; B12/30/1962 Kingston, Jamaica **1986** Det 16 (16, FS) **1988** Det 10 (9, FS) **NFL** 26 (25) [2 yrs]

MITCHELL, DONALD Donald Roosevelt, DB, 5´10˝/182 lbs; SMU; 1999: Ten, rnd 4; B12/14/1976 Beaumont, TX **1999**†Ten 16 (0) **2001** Ten 12 (3) **2002**†Ten 16 (10, CB) **NFL** 44 (13) [3 yrs]

MITCHELL, ED Edwin Levine, G, 6´2˝/285 lbs; Southern (LA); 1964: SD, rnd 15/Cle, rnd 12; B9/5/1942 Galveston, TX **1965**†SD-A 3 **1966** SD-A 14 (LG) **1967** SD-A 4 **NFL** 21 [3 yrs]

MITCHELL, FONDREN Fondren Lack, HB, 6´0˝/185 lbs; Florida; 1943: ChiC, rnd 10; B7/19/1921 Tallahassee, FL, D9/24/1952 Tampa, FL

YEAR	TEAM	G (GS, POS)	RUSH	YD	AVG (LG)	TD	REC	YD	AVG (LG)	TD	PASS	COMP	PCT	YD	AVG (LG)	TD	INT	SK	YD	QBR	KPR	OTD	PTS	TAY
1946	Mia-A	7 (0)	5	17	3.4	0	8	131	16.4	0	—	—	—	—	—	—	—	—	—	—	ki	—	0	72

MITCHELL, FREDDIE Freddie Lee, WR, 5´11˝/184 lbs; UCLA; 2001: Phi, rnd 1; B11/28/1978 Lakeland, FL

YEAR	TEAM	G (GS, POS)	RUSH	YD	AVG (LG)	TD	REC	YD	AVG (LG)	TD	PASS	COMP	PCT	YD	AVG (LG)	TD	INT	SK	YD	QBR	KPR	OTD	PTS	TAY
2001	†Phi	15 (1)	2	-4	-2.0 (12)	0	21	283	13.5 (29)	1	1	0	0.0	0	0.0	0	0	—	—	—	—	—	6	143
2002	†Phi	16 (1)	—	—	—	—	12	105	8.8 (18)	0	1	0	0.0	0	0.0	0	0	—	—	—	—	—	0	53
2003	†Phi	16 (6, wr)	—	—	—	—	35	498	14.2 (39)	2	1	1	100.0	25	25.0 (25)	1	0	—	—	—	k	—	12	254
2004	†Phi	16 (9, WR)	—	—	—	—	22	377	17.1 (60)	2	—	—	—	—	—	—	—	—	—	—	—	—	12	199
NFL	4	63 (17)	2	-4	-2.0 (12)	0	90	1263	14.0 (60)	5	3	1	33.3	25	8.3 (25)	1	0	—	—	—	k	—	30	647

MITCHELL, HAL Harold Dwayne, T-G, 6´1˝/225 lbs; UCLA; 1952: NYG, rnd 14; B8/11/1930 **1952** NYG 11

MITCHELL, JEFF Jeffery Clay, C, 6´4˝/300 lbs; Florida; 1997: Bal, rnd 5; B1/29/1974 Dallas, TX **1998** Bal 11 (10, C) **1999** Bal 16 (16, C) **2000**†Bal 14 (14, C) **2001** Car 15 (15, C) **2002** Car 16 (16, C) **2003**†Car 15 (15, C) **2004** Car 16 (16, C) **2005**†Car 16 (16, C) **NFL** 119 (118) [8 yrs]

MITCHELL, JIM James Halcot, DE-DT, 6´3˝/245 lbs; Virginia State; 1970: Det, rnd 3; B9/15/1948 Danville, VA **1970**†Det 14 (LDE) **1971** Det 13 (LDE) **1972** Det 14 (LDE) **1973** Det 9 **1974** Det 14 (14, RDT) **1975** Det 14 (2) **1976** Det 14 (14, LDT) **1977** Det 9 (6, RDE) **NFL** 101 (36) [8 yrs]

MITCHELL, JIM James Robert, TE, 6´1˝/234 lbs; Prairie View A&M; 1969: Atl, rnd 4; B10/19/1947 Shelbyville, TN

YEAR	TEAM	G (GS, POS)	RUSH	YD	AVG (LG)	TD	REC	YD	AVG (LG)	TD	PASS	COMP	PCT	YD	AVG (LG)	TD	INT	SK	YD	QBR	KPR	OTD	PTS	TAY
1969	Atl✧	14 (TE)	5	77	15.4 (40)	0	22	339	15.4 (42)	4	—	—	—	—	—	—	—	—	—	—	—	—	24	267
1970	Atl	14 (TE)	5	23	4.6 (12)	1	44	650	14.8 (51)	6	—	—	—	—	—	—	—	—	—	—	—	—	42	388
1971	Atl	13 (TE)	4	25	6.3 (24)	0	33	593	18.0 (43)	5	—	—	—	—	—	—	—	—	—	—	—	1	36	347
1972	Atl★	14 (TE)	2	19	9.5 (18)	0	28	470	16.8 (40)	4	—	—	—	—	—	—	—	—	—	—	—	—	24	274
1973	Atl	14 (TE)	5	34	6.8 (13)	0	32	420	13.1 (50)	0	—	—	—	—	—	—	—	—	—	—	—	—	0	244
1974	Atl	14 (TE)	3	21	7.0 (15)	0	30	479	16.0 (52)	1	—	—	—	—	—	—	—	—	—	—	—	—	6	266
1975	Atl	14 (TE)	—	—	—	—	34	536	15.8 (32)	4	—	—	—	—	—	—	—	—	—	—	—	1	30	288
1976	Atl	14 (TE)	1	-6	-6.0 (-6)	0	17	209	12.3 (39)	0	—	—	—	—	—	—	—	—	—	—	—	—	0	99
1977	Atl	12 (TE)	1	-6	-6.0 (-6)	0	17	178	10.5 (17)	0	—	—	—	—	—	—	—	—	—	—	—	—	0	83
1978	†Atl	16 (TE)	—	—	—	—	32	366	11.4 (24)	2	—	—	—	—	—	—	—	—	—	—	k	—	12	192
1979	Atl	16 (TE)	—	—	—	—	16	118	7.4 (14)	2	—	—	—	—	—	—	—	—	—	—	—	—	12	69
NFL	11	155	26	187	7.2 (40)	1	305	4358	14.3 (52)	28	—	—	—	—	—	—	—	—	—	—	k	2	186	2515

MITCHELL, JOHNNY Johnnie, TE, 6´3˝/241 lbs; Nebraska; 1992: NYJ, rnd 1; B1/20/1971 Chicago, IL

YEAR	TEAM	G (GS, POS)	RUSH	YD	AVG (LG)	TD	REC	YD	AVG (LG)	TD	PASS	COMP	PCT	YD	AVG (LG)	TD	INT	SK	YD	QBR	KPR	OTD	PTS	TAY
1992	NYJ	11 (3)	—	—	—	—	16	210	13.1 (37)	1	—	—	—	—	—	—	—	—	—	—	—	—	6	110
1993	NYJ	14 (14, TE)	—	—	—	—	39	630	16.2 (65)	6	—	—	—	—	—	—	—	—	—	—	—	—	36	345
1994	NYJ	16 (14, TE)	—	—	—	—	58	749	12.9 (55)	4	—	—	—	—	—	—	—	—	—	—	—	—	24	395
1995	NYJ	12 (11, te)	—	—	—	—	45	497	11.0 (43)	5	—	—	—	—	—	—	—	—	—	—	—	—	30	274
1996	†Dal	4 (1)	—	—	—	—	1	17	17.0 (17)	0	—	—	—	—	—	—	—	—	—	—	—	—	0	9
NFL	5	57 (43)	—	—	—	—	159	2103	13.2 (65)	16	—	—	—	—	—	—	—	—	—	—	—	—	96	1132

MITCHELL, KAWIKA Kawika Uilani, LB, 6´0˝/253 lbs; Georgia; South Florida; 2003: KC, rnd 2; B10/10/1979 Winter Springs, FL **2003**†KC 12 (6, mlb) **2004** KC 15 (12, MLB) **2005** KC 16 (16, MLB) **NFL** 43 (34) [3 yrs]

MITCHELL, KEITH Clarence Marquis, LB, 6´2˝/236 lbs; Texas A&M; B7/24/1974 Garland, TX **1997** NO 16 (2) **1998** NO 16 (15, LLB) **1999** NO 16 (16, LLB) **2000**†NO★16 (16, LLB) **2001** NO 15 (14, LLB) **2002** Hou 11 (7, rolb) **2003** Jax 3 (2) **NFL** 93 (72) [7 yrs]

MITCHELL, KEN Kenneth Wayne, LB, 6´2˝/224 lbs; UNLV; B11/14/1948 Denio, NV **1973** Atl 14 **1974** Atl 14 **NFL** 28 [2 yrs]

MITCHELL, KEVIN Kevin Danyelle, LB, 6´1˝/258 lbs; Syracuse; 1994: SF, rnd 2; B1/1/1971 Harrisburg, PA **1994**†SF 16 (0) **1995**†SF 15 (0) **1996**†SF 12 (3) **1997**†SF 16 (0) **1998** NO 8 (8, MLB) **1999** NO 16 (1) **2000** Was 16 (0) **2001** Was 13 (13, MLB) **2002** Was 16 (3) **2003** Was 16 (0) **NFL** 144 (28) [10 yrs]

MITCHELL, LANCE Lance, LB, 6´2˝/247 lbs; Oklahoma; 2005: Arz, rnd 5; B10/9/1981 Los Banos, CA **2005** Arz 12 (0)

MITCHELL, LEONARD Leonard Boyd, T, 6´7˝/290 lbs; Houston; 1981: Phi, rnd 1; B10/12/1958 Houston, TX **1981**†Phi 16 (0) **1982** Phi 9 (0) **1983** Phi 10 (3) **1984** Phi 16 (14, RT) **1985** Phi 16 (16, RT) **1986** Phi 10 (10, RT) **1987** Atl 12 (12, RT) **NFL** 89 (55) [7 yrs]

MITCHELL, LEROY Leroy, DB, 6´1˝/190 lbs; Texas Southern; 1967: Bos, rnd 11; B9/22/1944 Wharton, TX **1967** Bos-A 14 (14, LCB) **1968** Bos-A★14 (14, LCB) **1970** Hou 14 (LCB) **1971** Den 14 (14, LCB) **1972** Den 14 (14, LCB) **1973** Den 12 (12, LCB) **NFL** 82 (68) [6 yrs]

MITCHELL, LYDELL Lydell Douglas, RB, 5´11˝/204 lbs; Penn State; 1972: Bal, rnd 2; B5/30/1949 Salem, NJ

YEAR	TEAM	G (GS, POS)	RUSH	YD	AVG (LG)	TD	REC	YD	AVG (LG)	TD	PASS	COMP	PCT	YD	AVG (LG)	TD	INT	SK	YD	QBR	KPR	OTD	PTS	TAY
1972	Bal	11 (1)	45	215	4.8 (14)	1	18	147	8.2 (26)	1	—	—	—	—	—	—	—	—	—	—	—	—	12	304
1973	Bal	14 (11, RB)	253	963	3.8 (36)	2	17	113	6.6 (14)	0	—	—	—	—	—	—	—	—	—	—	—	—	12	1040
1974	Bal	14 (14, RB)	214	757	3.5 (31)	5	**72**	544	7.6 (24)	2	—	—	—	—	—	—	—	—	—	—	—	—	42	1089
1975	†Bal★	14 (14, RB)	289	1193	4.1 (70)	11	**60**	544	9.1 (35)	4	—	—	—	—	—	—	—	—	—	—	—	—	90	1595
1976	†Bal★	14 (14, RB)	289	1200	4.2 (43)	5	60	555	9.3 (40)	3	—	—	—	—	—	—	—	—	—	—	—	—	48	1543
1977	†Bal★	14 (14, RB)	301	1159	3.9 (64)	3	**71**	620	8.7 (38)	4	—	—	—	—	—	—	—	—	—	—	—	—	42	**1519**
1978	SD	16 (11, RB)	214	820	3.8 (25)	3	57	500	8.8 (55)	2	—	—	—	—	—	—	—	—	—	—	—	—	30	1110
1979	†SD	12 (5, rb)	63	211	3.3 (15)	0	19	159	8.4 (24)	1	—	—	—	—	—	—	—	—	—	—	k	—	6	296

YEAR	TEAM	G (GS, POS)	RUSH	YD	AVG (LG)	TD	REC	YD	AVG (LG)	TD	PASS	COMP	PCT	YD	AVG (LG)	TD	INT	SK	YD	QBR	KPR	OTD	PTS	TAY
1980	†LARm	2(0)	7	16	2.3(5)	0	2	21	10.5(13)	0	—	—	—	—	—	—	—	—	—	—	—	—	0	27
NFL	9	111(84)	1675	6534	3.9(70)	30	376	3203	8.5(55)	17	—	—	—	—	—	—	—	—	—	—	k	—	282	8521

MITCHELL, MACK Mack Henry, DE, 6´8˝/246 lbs; Houston; 1975: Cle, rnd 1; B8/16/1952 Diboli, TX **1975** Cle 14 (14, RDE) **1976** Cle 14 (10, RDE) **1977** Cle 14 (5, rde) **1978** Cle 14 (14, RDE) **1979** Cin 13 (1) **NFL** 69 (44) [5 yrs]

MITCHELL, MARK Martin, DB, 6´1˝/180 lbs; Tulane; 1977: Phi, rnd 6; B1/10/1954 Lake Charles, LA **1977** Phi 14

MITCHELL, MEL Melvin, DB, 6´1˝/220 lbs; Western Kentucky; 2002: NO, rnd 5; B2/10/1979 Rockledge, FL **2002** NO 16 (0) **2004** NO 15 (0) **2005** NO 13 (0) **NFL** 44 (0) [3 yrs]

MITCHELL, MELVIN Melvin, G-C-T, 6´3˝/260 lbs; Tennessee State; 1976: Mia, rnd 4; B2/21/1953 Dallas, TX **1976** Mia 12 **1977** Mia 3 **1977** Det 9 **1978**†Mia 4 **1980**†Min 6 (0) **NFL** 34 [4 yrs]

MITCHELL, MICHAEL Michael George, DB, 5´10˝/180 lbs; Howard Payne; B10/18/1961 Waco, TX **1987** Was 3 (3) **1989** NYJ 5 (0) **NFL** 8 (3) [2 yrs]

MITCHELL, PAUL Paul Anthony, DT-T, 6´3˝/235 lbs; Minnesota; 1944: ChiC, rnd 2; B8/10/1920 Minneapolis, MN **1946** LAD-A 10 (3) **1947** LAD-A 11 (4) **1948** LAD-A 4 (0) **1948** NYY-A 8 (0) **1949**†NYY-A 12 (0) **AAFC** 45 (7) [4 yrs]

1950 NYY 12 (RDT) **1951** NYY 12 (LT) **NFL** 24 [2 yrs]

MITCHELL, PETE Peter Clark, TE, 6´2˝/243 lbs; Boston College; 1995: Mia, rnd 4; B10/9/1971 Royal Oak, MI

YEAR	TEAM	G (GS, POS)	RUSH	YD	AVG (LG)	TD	REC	YD	AVG (LG)	TD	PASS	COMP	PCT	YD	AVG (LG)	TD	INT	SK	YD	QBR	KPR	OTD	PTS	TAY
1995	Jax	16(4)	—	—	—	—	41	527	12.9(35)	2	—	—	—	—	—	—	—	—	—	—	—	—	12	274
1996	†Jax	16(6, te)	—	—	—	—	52	575	11.1(30)	1	—	—	—	—	—	—	—	—	—	—	—	—	6	293
1997	†Jax	16(12, TE)	—	—	—	—	35	380	10.9(33)	4	—	—	—	—	—	—	—	—	—	—	k	—	24	197
1998	†Jax	16(16, TE)	—	—	—	—	38	363	9.6(38)	2	—	—	—	—	—	—	—	—	—	—	k	—	12	189
1999	NYG	15(6, te)	—	—	—	—	58	520	9.0(25)	3	—	—	—	—	—	—	—	—	—	—	—	—	18	275
2000	†NYG	14(5, te)	—	—	—	—	25	245	9.8(22)	1	—	—	—	—	—	—	—	—	—	—	—	—	6	128
2001	Det	5(1)	—	—	—	—	5	29	5.8(12)	0	—	—	—	—	—	—	—	—	—	—	—	—	0	15
2002	Jax	16(11, TE)	—	—	—	—	25	246	9.8(45)	2	—	—	—	—	—	—	—	—	—	—	—	—	12	133
NFL	8	114(61)	—	—	—	—	279	2885	10.3(45)	15	—	—	—	—	—	—	—	—	—	—	k	—	90	1502

MITCHELL, QASIM Qasim, T-G, 6´6˝/355 lbs; North Carolina A&T; B12/3/1979 Jacksonville, NC **2003** ChiB 2 (2) **2004** ChiB 16 (14, LT) **2005** ChiB 3 (0) **NFL** 21 (16) [3 yrs]

MITCHELL, RANDALL Randall Evans, NT, 6´1˝/275 lbs; Tennessee-Chattanooga; B9/19/1963 Savannah, GA **1987** Phi 3 (3)

MITCHELL, ROLAND Roland Earl, DB, 5´11˝/195 lbs; Texas Tech; 1987: Buf, rnd 2; B3/15/1964 Columbus, TX **1987** Buf 11 (0) **1988** Buf 3 (0) **1988** Phx 11 (0) **1989** Phx 3 (1) **1990** Atl 13 (2) **1991** GB 16 (0) **1992** GB 15 (8, rcb) **1993**†GB 16 (16, RCB) **1994** GB 1 (1) **NFL** 89 (28) [8 yrs]

MITCHELL, RUSSELL Russell Bryan, C, 6´5˝/288 lbs; Mississippi; B12/28/1960 El Campo, TX **1987** NYG 3 (0)

MITCHELL, SCOTT William Scott, QB, 6´6˝/230 lbs; Utah; 1990: Mia, rnd 4; B1/2/1968 Salt Lake City, UT

YEAR	TEAM	G (GS, POS)	RUSH	YD	AVG (LG)	TD	REC	YD	AVG (LG)	TD	PASS	COMP	PCT	YD	AVG (LG)	TD	INT	SK	YD	QBR	KPR	OTD	PTS	TAY
1991	Mia	2(0)	—	—	—	—	—	—	—	—	—	—	—	—	—	—	—	—	—	—	—	—	—	—
1992	†Mia	16(0)	8	10	1.3(8)	0	—	—	—	—	8	2	25.0	32	4.0(18)	0	1	—	—	—	—	—	0	-14
1993	Mia	13(7, QB)	21	89	4.2(32)	0	—	—	—	—	233	133	57.1	1773	7.6(77)	12	8	7	49	84.2	—	—	0	716
1994	Det	9(9, QB)	15	24	1.6(7)	1	—	—	—	—	246	119	48.4	1456	5.9(34)	10	11	12	63	62.0	—	—	6	372
1995	†Det	16(16, QB)	36	104	2.9(18)	4	—	—	—	—	583	346	59.3	4338	7.4(91)	32	12	31	145	92.3	—	—	24	1993
1996	Det	14(14, QB)	37	83	2.2(9)	4	—	—	—	—	437	253	57.9	2917	6.7(62)	17	17	36	199	74.9	—	—	24	987
1997	†Det	16(16, QB)	37	83	2.2(13)	1	—	—	—	—	509	293	57.6	3484	6.8(79)	19	14	41	271	79.6	—	—	6	1370
1998	Det	2(2)	7	30	4.3(17)	0	—	—	—	—	75	38	50.7	452	6.0(44)	1	3	4	28	—	—	—	0	141
1999	Bal	2(2)	1	1	1.0(1)	0	—	—	—	—	56	24	42.9	236	4.2(28)	1	4	6	30	—	—	—	0	-36
2000	Cin	8(5, qb)	10	61	6.1(12)	1	—	—	—	—	187	89	47.6	966	5.2(38)	3	8	16	82	—	—	—	6	249
2001	Cin	1(0)	—	—	—	—	—	—	—	—	12	4	33.3	38	3.2(16)	0	3	2	15	—	—	—	0	-101
NFL	11	99(71)	172	485	2.8(32)	11	—	—	—	—	2346	1301	55.5	15692	6.7(91)	95	81	155	882	75.3	—	—	66	5676

MITCHELL, SHANNON Shannon Lamont, TE, 6´2˝/245 lbs; Georgia; B3/28/1972 Alcoa, TN

YEAR	TEAM	G (GS, POS)	RUSH	YD	AVG (LG)	TD	REC	YD	AVG (LG)	TD	PASS	COMP	PCT	YD	AVG (LG)	TD	INT	SK	YD	QBR	KPR	OTD	PTS	TAY
1994	†SD	16(6, te)	—	—	—	—	11	105	9.5(36)	0	—	—	—	—	—	—	—	—	—	—	k	—	0	56
1995	†SD	15(2)	—	—	—	—	3	31	10.3(24)	1	—	—	—	—	—	—	—	—	—	—	—	—	6	21
1996	SD	16(13, TE)	—	—	—	—	10	57	5.7(25)	0	—	—	—	—	—	—	—	—	—	—	—	—	0	29
1997	SD	4(1)	—	—	—	—	1	14	14.0(14)	0	—	—	—	—	—	—	—	—	—	—	—	—	0	7
NFL	4	51(22)	—	—	—	—	25	207	8.3(36)	1	—	—	—	—	—	—	—	—	—	—	k	—	6	112

MITCHELL, STAN Stanton Earl, RB, 6´2˝/210 lbs; Tennessee; 1966: Was, rnd 8; B8/17/1944 Wayne, MI

YEAR	TEAM	G (GS, POS)	RUSH	YD	AVG (LG)	TD	REC	YD	AVG (LG)	TD	PASS	COMP	PCT	YD	AVG (LG)	TD	INT	SK	YD	QBR	KPR	OTD	PTS	TAY
1966	Mia-A	2	—	—	—	—	—	—	—	—	—	—	—	—	—	—	—	—	—	—	—	—	—	—
1967	Mia-A	14(6, fb)	83	269	3.2(22)	3	18	133	7.4(38)	1	—	—	—	—	—	—	—	—	—	—	k	—	24	398
1968	Mia-A	9(5, fb)	54	176	3.3(30)	1	8	190	23.8(48)	3	—	—	—	—	—	—	—	—	—	—	—	—	24	296
1969	Mia-A	3	28	80	2.9(12)	0	10	125	12.5(34)	0	—	—	—	—	—	—	—	—	—	—	—	—	0	143
1970	†Mia	14	8	23	2.9(9)	0	6	85	14.2(36)	1	—	—	—	—	—	—	—	—	—	—	k	—	6	46
NFL	5	42(11)	173	548	3.2(30)	4	42	533	12.7(48)	5	—	—	—	—	—	—	—	—	—	—	k	—	54	882

MITCHELL, STUMP Lyvonia Albert, RB, 5´9˝/188 lbs; The Citadel; 1981: SL, rnd 9; B3/15/1959 St. Marys, GA **[R]**

YEAR	TEAM	G (GS, POS)	RUSH	YD	AVG (LG)	TD	REC	YD	AVG (LG)	TD	PASS	COMP	PCT	YD	AVG (LG)	TD	INT	SK	YD	QBR	KPR	OTD	PTS	TAY
1981	SL	16(0)	31	175	5.6(43)	0	6	35	5.8(16)	1	—	—	—	—	—	—	—	—	—	—	kp	1	12	910
1982	†SL	9(1)	39	189	4.8(32)	1	11	149	13.5(30)	0	—	—	—	—	—	—	—	—	—	—	kp	—	6	428
1983	SL	15(1)	68	373	5.5(46)	3	7	54	7.7(17)	0	—	—	—	—	—	—	—	—	—	—	kp	—	18	815
1984	SL☆	16(1)	81	434	5.4(39)	9	26	318	12.2(44)	2	1	1	100.0	20	20.0(20)	0	0	—	—	—	kp	—	66	1125
1985	SL	16(8, rb)	183	1006	**5.5(64)**	7	47	502	10.7(46)	3	2	1	50.0	31	15.5(31)	0	0	—	—	—	kp	—	60	1460
1986	SL	15(13, RB)	174	800	4.6(44)	5	41	276	6.7(24)	0	3	1	33.3	15	5.0(15)	1	0	—	—	—	k	—	30	1114
1987	SL	12(12, RB)	203	781	3.8(42)	3	45	397	8.8(39)	2	3	1	33.3	17	5.7(17)	0	0	—	—	—	—	—	30	1028
1988	Phx	14(14, RB)	164	726	4.4(47)	4	25	214	8.6(28)	1	—	—	—	—	—	—	—	—	—	—	k	—	30	949
1989	Phx	3(3)	43	165	3.8(14)	0	1	10	10.0(10)	0	—	—	—	—	—	—	—	—	—	—	—	—	0	170
NFL	9	116(53)	986	4649	4.7(64)	32	209	1955	9.4(46)	9	9	4	44.4	83	9.2(31)	1	0	—	—	—	kp	1	252	7997

MITCHELL, TED Frederick Brice, C, 5´10˝/195 lbs; Bucknell; B8/4/1905 Madison, NJ, D10/11/1985 Toms River, NJ **1929** Ora 12 (12, C) **1930** Nwk 11 (9, C) **NFL** 23 (21) [2 yrs]

MITCHELL, TOM Thomas Gordon, TE-WR, 6´2˝/215 lbs; Bucknell; 1966: Oak, rnd 3; B8/22/1944 Newport, RI

YEAR	TEAM	G (GS, POS)	RUSH	YD	AVG (LG)	TD	REC	YD	AVG (LG)	TD	PASS	COMP	PCT	YD	AVG (LG)	TD	INT	SK	YD	QBR	KPR	OTD	PTS	TAY
1966	Oak-A	14(te)	—	—	—	—	23	301	13.1(24)	1	—	—	—	—	—	—	—	—	—	—	—	—	6	156
1968	†Bal	14	—	—	—	—	6	117	19.5(41)	4	—	—	—	—	—	—	—	—	—	—	—	—	24	79
1969	Bal	8	—	—	—	—	9	199	22.1(51)	3	—	—	—	—	—	—	—	—	—	—	—	—	18	115
1970	†Bal	14	—	—	—	—	20	261	13.1(44)	4	—	—	—	—	—	—	—	—	—	—	—	—	24	151
1971	†Bal	14(TE)	2	9	4.5(13)	0	33	402	12.2(35)	0	—	—	—	—	—	—	—	—	—	—	k	—	0	195
1972	Bal	14(TE)	0	7	(7)	0	40	494	12.4(34)	4	—	—	—	—	—	—	—	—	—	—	—	—	24	274
1973	Bal	13	—	—	—	—	25	313	12.5(33)	4	—	—	—	—	—	—	—	—	—	—	—	—	24	177
1974	SF	14(13, TE)	1	-2	-2.0(-2)	0	19	262	13.8(25)	0	—	—	—	—	—	—	—	—	—	—	—	—	0	129
1975	SF	13(12, TE)	—	—	—	—	25	366	14.6(60)	3	—	—	—	—	—	—	—	—	—	—	—	—	18	198
1976	SF	14(14, TE)	—	—	—	—	20	240	12.0(27)	1	—	—	—	—	—	—	—	—	—	—	k	—	6	102
1977	SF	13(13, TE)	—	—	—	—	19	226	11.9(31)	0	—	—	—	—	—	—	—	—	—	—	—	—	0	113
NFL	11	145(52)	3	14	4.7(13)	0	239	3181	13.3(60)	24	—	—	—	—	—	—	—	—	—	—	k	—	144	1687

MITCHELL, TYWAN Tywan, WR, 6´5˝/245 lbs; Mankato State; B12/10/1975 Crete, IL

YEAR	TEAM	G (GS, POS)	RUSH	YD	AVG (LG)	TD	REC	YD	AVG (LG)	TD	PASS	COMP	PCT	YD	AVG (LG)	TD	INT	SK	YD	QBR	KPR	OTD	PTS	TAY
2000	Arz	11(1)	—	—	—	—	5	80	16.0(42)	0	—	—	—	—	—	—	—	—	—	—	—	—	0	40
2001	Arz	16(4)	—	—	—	—	25	196	7.8(24)	2	—	—	—	—	—	—	—	—	—	—	—	—	12	108
NFL	2	27(5)	—	—	—	—	30	276	9.2(42)	2	—	—	—	—	—	—	—	—	—	—	—	—	12	148

MITCHELL, WILLIE William Anderson, DB, 6´0˝/185 lbs; Tennessee State; B8/28/1940 San Antonio, TX **1964** KC-A 9 **1965** KC-A☆14 (RCB) **1966**†KC-A 14 (RCB) **1967** KC-A 9 (RCB) **1968**†KC-A 13 (RCB) **1969**†KC-A 14 **1970** KC 14 **NFL** 87 [7 yrs]

MITINGER, BOB Robert Bray, LB, 6´2˝/232 lbs; Penn State; 1962: SD, rnd 5/Was, rnd 3; B2/13/1940 Greensburg, PA, D9/25/2004 State College, PA **1962** SD-A 14 **1963**†SD-A 14 **1964**†SD-A 9 **1966** SD-A 2 **1968** SD-A 3 **NFL** 42 [5 yrs]

MITRIONE, MATT Matthew Steven, DT, 6´2˝/295 lbs; Purdue; B7/15/1978 Springfield, IL **2002** NYG 9 (0)

MITZ, ALONZO Alonzo Loqwone, DE-LB, 6´3˝/275 lbs; Florida; 1986: Sea, rnd 8; B6/5/1963 Henderson, NC **1986** Sea 6 (0) **1987** Sea 6 (0) **1988**†Sea 16 (4) **1989** Sea 12 (3) **1991** Cin 15 (13, LDE) **1992** Cin 16 (14, RDE) **NFL** 71 (34) [6 yrs]

MIX, BRYANT Bryant Lee, DE, 6´3˝/291 lbs; Alcorn State; 1996: Hou, rnd 2; B7/28/1972 Water Valley, MS **1996** Hou 6 (2) **1997** Ten 1 (0) **NFL** 7 (2) [2 yrs]

MIX, RON Ronald Jack 'The Intellectual Assassin', T-G, 6´4˝/250 lbs; USC; 1960: Bos, rnd 1/Bal, rnd 1; B3/10/1938 Los Angeles, CA; HOF 1979 **1960**†LAC-A☆14 (RT) **1961**†SD-A★10 (RT) **1962** SD-A★14 (RG) **1963**†SD-A★14 (RT) **1964**†SD-A★14 (RT) **1965**†SD-A★14 (RT) **1966** SD-A★14 (RT) **1967** SD-A★14 (RT) **1968** SD-A★14 (RT) **1969** SD-A 8 **1971** Oak 12 (4) **NFL** 142 (4) [11 yrs]

MIXON, BILLY Billy Raymond, HB-DB, 5´11˝/191 lbs; Georgia; 1951: SF, rnd 3; B5/24/1929 Tifton, GA

YEAR	TEAM	G(GS, POS)	RUSH	YD	AVG(LG)	TD	REC	YD	AVG(LG)	TD	PASS	COMP	PCT	YD	AVG(LG)	TD	INT	SK	YD	QBR	KPR	OTD	PTS	TAY
1953	SF	12	25	176	7.0(33)	1	1	7	7.0(7)	0	—	—	—	—	—	—	—	—	—	—	—	—	6	190
1954	SF	10	7	19	2.7(7)	0	—	—	—	—	—	—	—	—	—	—	—	—	—	—	i	—	0	15
NFL	2	22	32	195	6.1(33)	1	1	7	7.0(7)	0	—	—	—	—	—	—	—	—	—	—	i	—	6	205

MIXON, KENNY Kenneth Jermaine, DE, 6´4˝/271 lbs; LSU; 1998: Mia, rnd 2; B5/31/1975 Sun Valley, CA **1998**†Mia 16 (16, LDE) **1999**†Mia 11 (2) **2000**†Mia 16 (16, LDE) **2001**†Mia 16 (16, LDE) **2002** Min 16 (16, LDE) **2003** Min 16 (16, RDE) **2004**†Min 14 (14, LDE) **NFL** 105 (96) [7 yrs]

MIZELL, WARNER Lawrence Warner, B, 5´10˝/188 lbs; Georgia Tech; B10/8/1907, D5/1971 Newport News, VA **1931** Bkn 5 (1) **1931** Fra 3 (0) **NFL** 8 (1) [1 yr]

MOAN, KELLY Emmett Auto, TB-DB, 6´0˝/193 lbs; West Virginia; 1938: NYG, rnd 7; B10/20/1912 Long Beach, CA, D8/3/1954 Wheeling, WV **[K]**

YEAR	TEAM	G(GS, POS)	RUSH	YD	AVG(LG)	TD	REC	YD	AVG(LG)	TD	PASS	COMP	PCT	YD	AVG(LG)	TD	INT	SK	YD	QBR	KPR	OTD	PTS	TAY
1939	Cle	2(0)	2	-15	-7.5	0	—	—	—	—	9	3	33.3	77	8.6(50)	1	2	—	—	—	K	—	1	-52

MOATS, RYAN Ryan, RB, 5´8˝/210 lbs; Louisiana Tech; 2005: Phi, rnd 3; B12/17/1982 Dallas, TX

YEAR	TEAM	G(GS, POS)	RUSH	YD	AVG(LG)	TD	REC	YD	AVG(LG)	TD	PASS	COMP	PCT	YD	AVG(LG)	TD	INT	SK	YD	QBR	KPR	OTD	PTS	TAY
2005	Phi	7(1)	55	278	5.1(59)	3	4	7	1.8(9)	0	—	—	—	—	—	—	—	—	—	—	k	—	18	308

MOBLEY, JOHN John Ulysses, LB, 6´1˝/236 lbs; Kutztown State; 1996: Den, rnd 1; B10/10/1973 Chester, PA **1996**†Den 16 (16, RLB) **1997**†Den☆16 (16, RLB) **1998**†Den 16 (15, RLB) **1999** Den 2 (2) **2000**†Den 15 (14, RLB) **2001** Den 16 (16, RLB) **2002** Den 16 (16, LLB) **2003** Den 8 (7, llb) **NFL** 105 (102) [8 yrs]

MOBLEY, ORSON Orson Odell, TE, 6´5˝/256 lbs; Florida State; Salem; 1986: Den, rnd 6; B3/4/1963 Brooksville, FL

YEAR	TEAM	G(GS, POS)	RUSH	YD	AVG(LG)	TD	REC	YD	AVG(LG)	TD	PASS	COMP	PCT	YD	AVG(LG)	TD	INT	SK	YD	QBR	KPR	OTD	PTS	TAY
1986	†Den	14(3)	1	-1	-1.0(-1)	0	22	332	15.1(32)	1	—	—	—	—	—	—	—	—	—	—	—	—	6	170
1987	†Den	10(6, te)	—	—	—	—	16	228	14.3(28)	1	—	—	—	—	—	—	—	—	—	—	—	—	6	119
1988	Den	16(9, te)	—	—	—	—	21	218	10.4(28)	2	—	—	—	—	—	—	—	—	—	—	—	—	12	119
1989	†Den	12(5, te)	—	—	—	—	17	200	11.8(36)	0	—	—	—	—	—	—	—	—	—	—	—	—	0	100
1990	Den	9(8, TE)	—	—	—	—	8	41	5.1(9)	0	—	—	—	—	—	—	—	—	—	—	k	—	0	15
NFL	5	61(31)	1	-1	-1.0(-1)	0	84	1019	12.1(36)	4	—	—	—	—	—	—	—	—	—	—	k	—	24	523

MOBLEY, RUDY Rudolph Hamilton, HB-DB, 5´7˝/155 lbs; Hardin-Simmons; 1947: Mia-A, rnd 12/1945: Phi, rnd 11; B12/8/1921 Paducah, TX, D9/8/2003

YEAR	TEAM	G(GS, POS)	RUSH	YD	AVG(LG)	TD	REC	YD	AVG(LG)	TD	PASS	COMP	PCT	YD	AVG(LG)	TD	INT	SK	YD	QBR	KPR	OTD	PTS	TAY
1947	Bal-A	14(2)	26	90	3.5	1	11	121	11.0	1	—	—	—	—	—	—	—	—	—	—	kpi	—	12	216

MOBLEY, SINGOR Singor A., DB, 5´11˝/195 lbs; Washington State; B10/12/1972 Tacoma, WA **1997** Dal 12 (0) **1998**†Dal 16 (0) **1999**†Dal 16 (0) **NFL** 44 (0) [3 yrs]

MOBLEY, STACEY Stacey Lance, WR, 5´8˝/168 lbs; Jackson State; B9/15/1965 Daytona Beach, FL

YEAR	TEAM	G(GS, POS)	RUSH	YD	AVG(LG)	TD	REC	YD	AVG(LG)	TD	PASS	COMP	PCT	YD	AVG(LG)	TD	INT	SK	YD	QBR	KPR	OTD	PTS	TAY
1987	LARm	3(1)	—	—	—	—	8	107	13.4(40)	1	—	—	—	—	—	—	—	—	—	—	p	—	6	66
1989	Det	10(5, wr)	—	—	—	—	13	158	12.2(30)	0	—	—	—	—	—	—	—	—	—	—	—	—	0	79
NFL	2	13(6)	—	—	—	—	21	265	12.6(40)	1	—	—	—	—	—	—	—	—	—	—	p	—	6	145

MOCK, MIKE Michael Earl, LB, 6´1˝/225 lbs; Texas Tech; 1978: NYJ, rnd 8; B2/25/1955 Trondheim, Norway **1978** NYJ 15

MOCKMORE, CHARLIE Charles A., G, 5´11˝/192 lbs; Iowa; B11/7/1891 Platte County, NE, D4/1953 **1920** RI 7 (1)

MODESITT, JEFF Jeffrey A., TE, 6´5˝/245 lbs; Delaware; B1/1/1964 Terre Haute, IN, D8/3/1990 Atlanta, GA **1987** TB 1 (0)

MODZELEWSKI, DICK Richard Blair 'Little Mo', DT, 6´0˝/250 lbs; Maryland; 1953: Was, rnd 2; B2/16/1931 West Natrona, PA **[C]** **1953** Was 12 (LDT) **1954** Was 12 **1955** Pit 12 (LDT) **1956**†NYG 12 (LDT) **1957** NYG☆12 (LDT) **1958**†NYG 12 (LDT) **1959**†NYG 12 (LDT) **1960** NYG 12 (LDT) **1961**†NYG☆14 (LDT) **1962**†NYG 14 (LDT) **1963**†NYG☆14 (LDT) **1964**†Cle✧14 (LDT) **1965**†Cle 14 (LDT) **1966** Cle 14 **NFL** 180 [14 yrs]

MODZELEWSKI, ED Edward Walter 'Big Mo', FB, 6´0˝/217 lbs; Maryland; 1952: Pit, rnd 1; B1/13/1929 West Natrona, PA

YEAR	TEAM	G(GS, POS)	RUSH	YD	AVG(LG)	TD	REC	YD	AVG(LG)	TD	PASS	COMP	PCT	YD	AVG(LG)	TD	INT	SK	YD	QBR	KPR	OTD	PTS	TAY
1952	Pit	10(fb)	82	195	2.4(14)	3	11	109	9.9(23)	0	—	—	—	—	—	—	—	—	—	—	—	—	18	280
1955	†Cle	12(FB)	185	619	3.3(25)	6	13	113	8.7(28)	2	—	—	—	—	—	—	—	—	—	—	—	—	48	746
1956	Cle	8(FB)	107	431	4.0(23)	2	10	27	2.7(6)	0	—	—	—	—	—	—	—	—	—	—	—	—	12	465
1957	†Cle	12	10	21	2.1(5)	0	—	—	—	—	—	—	—	—	—	—	—	—	—	—	k	—	0	20
1958	†Cle	12	3	8	2.7(3)	0	1	10	10.0(10)	0	—	—	—	—	—	—	—	—	—	—	—	—	0	13
1959	Cle	12	6	18	3.0(5)	0	3	18	6.0(13)	1	—	—	—	—	—	—	—	—	—	—	k	—	6	9
NFL	6	66	393	1292	3.3(25)	11	38	277	7.3(28)	3	—	—	—	—	—	—	—	—	—	—	k	—	84	1532

MOE, HAL Harold William, WB, 5´10˝/182 lbs; Oregon State; B3/28/1910 Spokane, WA, D5/26/2001 Corvallis, OR

YEAR	TEAM	G(GS, POS)	RUSH	YD	AVG(LG)	TD	REC	YD	AVG(LG)	TD	PASS	COMP	PCT	YD	AVG(LG)	TD	INT	SK	YD	QBR	KPR	OTD	PTS	TAY
1933	ChiC	10(8, WB)	27	48	1.8	0	7	95	13.6	2	1	0	0.0	0	0.0	0	0	—	—	—	—	—	12	106

MOEGLE, DICKY Richard Lee, DB-HB-FB, 6´0˝/195 lbs; Rice; 1955: SF, rnd 1; B9/14/1934 Taylor, TX **[I]**

YEAR	TEAM	G(GS, POS)	RUSH	YD	AVG(LG)	TD	REC	YD	AVG(LG)	TD	PASS	COMP	PCT	YD	AVG(LG)	TD	INT	SK	YD	QBR	KPR	OTD	PTS	TAY
1955	SF✧	11(DB/lh)	41	235	5.7(39)	5	4	94	23.5(53)	0	1	0	0.0	0	0.0	0	0	—	—	—	kpi	—	30	447
1956	SF☆	12(DB)	7	18	2.6(12)	0	3	79	26.3(37)	0	—	—	—	—	—	—	—	—	—	—	kpi	1	6	122
1957	†SF☆	12(DB)	9	48	5.3(18)	1	—	—	—	—	—	—	—	—	—	—	—	—	—	—	pi	—	6	120
1958	SF	4	—	—	—	—	—	—	—	—	—	—	—	—	—	—	—	—	—	—	—	—	—	—
1959	SF	8	3	9	3.0(4)	0	1	12	12.0(12)	0	1	0	0.0	0	0.0	0	0	—	—	—	—	—	0	15
1960	Pit	12(RS)	—	—	—	—	—	—	—	—	—	—	—	—	—	—	—	—	—	—	kpi	—	0	88
1961	Dal	14(RS)	—	—	—	—	—	—	—	—	—	—	—	—	—	—	—	—	—	—	i	—	0	21
NFL	7	73	60	310	5.2(39)	6	8	185	23.1(53)	0	2	0	0.0	0	0.0	0	0	—	—	—	kpi	1	42	813

MOEGLE, EDDIE Edgar L., WB, 5´9˝/186 lbs; Detroit Mercy; B7/11/1896, D6/1983 Romeo, MI **1920** Det 1 (0) **1921** Det 4 (2) **NFL** 5 (2) [2 yrs]

MOFFETT, TIM Timothy, WR, 6´2˝/180 lbs; Mississippi; 1985: LARd, rnd 3; B2/8/1962 Laurel, MS

YEAR	TEAM	G(GS, POS)	RUSH	YD	AVG(LG)	TD	REC	YD	AVG(LG)	TD	PASS	COMP	PCT	YD	AVG(LG)	TD	INT	SK	YD	QBR	KPR	OTD	PTS	TAY
1985	†LARd	13(0)	—	—	—	—	5	90	18.0(34)	0	—	—	—	—	—	—	—	—	—	—	—	—	0	45
1986	LARd	16(1)	—	—	—	—	6	77	12.8(17)	0	—	—	—	—	—	—	—	—	—	—	—	—	0	39
1987	SD	3(1)	1	1	1.0(1)	0	5	80	16.0(25)	1	—	—	—	—	—	—	—	—	—	—	—	—	6	46
NFL	3	32(2)	1	1	1.0(1)	0	16	247	15.4(34)	1	—	—	—	—	—	—	—	—	—	—	—	—	6	130

MOFFITT, MIKE Michael Jerome, TE, 6´4˝/215 lbs; Fresno State; B7/28/1963 Los Angeles, CA

YEAR	TEAM	G(GS, POS)	RUSH	YD	AVG(LG)	TD	REC	YD	AVG(LG)	TD	PASS	COMP	PCT	YD	AVG(LG)	TD	INT	SK	YD	QBR	KPR	OTD	PTS	TAY
1986	GB	4(0)	—	—	—	—	4	87	21.8(34)	0	—	—	—	—	—	—	—	—	—	—	—	—	0	44

MOHARDT, JOHNNY John Henry, B, 5´10˝/166 lbs; Notre Dame; B1/21/1898 Pittsburgh, PA, D11/24/1961 La Jolla, CA **1922** ChiC 10 (8, RH), 6 **1923** ChiC 10 (6, rh), 6 **1924** Rac 8 (6, wb) **1925** ChiB 14 (5, lh), 6 **NFL** 42 (25), 18 [4 yrs]

MOHR, CHRIS Christopher Garrett, P, 6´5˝/215 lbs; Alabama; 1989: TB, rnd 6; B5/11/1966 Atlanta, GA **[KP]**

YEAR	TEAM	G(GS, POS)	RUSH	YD	AVG(LG)	TD	REC	YD	AVG(LG)	TD	PASS	COMP	PCT	YD	AVG(LG)	TD	INT	SK	YD	QBR	KPR	OTD	PTS	TAY
1989	TB	16(0)	—	—	—	—	—	—	—	—	—	—	—	—	—	—	—	—	—	—	KP	—	1	0
1991	†Buf	16(0)	—	—	—	—	—	—	—	—	1	1	100.0	9	-9.0(-9)	0	0	—	—	—	P	—	0	-5
1992	†Buf	15(0)	1	11	11.0(11)	0	—	—	—	—	—	—	—	—	—	—	—	—	—	—	P	—	0	11
1993	†Buf	16(0)	—	—	—	—	—	—	—	—	—	—	—	—	—	—	—	—	—	—	P	—	0	0
1994	Buf	16(0)	1	-9	-9.0(-9)	0	—	—	—	—	—	—	—	—	—	—	—	—	—	—	P	—	0	-9
1995	†Buf	16(0)	—	—	—	—	—	—	—	—	—	—	—	—	—	—	—	—	—	—	P	—	0	0
1996	†Buf	16(0)	—	—	—	—	—	—	—	—	—	—	—	—	—	—	—	—	—	—	P	—	0	0
1997	Buf	16(0)	1	0	0.0(0)	0	—	—	—	—	1	1	100.0	29	29.0(29)	0	0	—	—	—	P	—	0	15
1998	†Buf	16(0)	—	—	—	—	—	—	—	—	—	—	—	—	—	—	—	—	—	—	P	—	0	0
1999	†Buf	16(0)	1	0	0.0(0)	0	—	—	—	—	—	—	—	—	—	—	—	—	—	—	P	—	0	0
2000	Buf	16(0)	—	—	—	—	—	—	—	—	1	1	100.0	44	44.0(44)	0	0	—	—	—	P	—	0	22
2001	Atl	16(0)	—	—	—	—	—	—	—	—	2	2	100.0	40	20.0(42)	0	0	—	—	—	P	—	0	20
2002	†Atl	16(0)	—	—	—	—	—	—	—	—	1	0	0.0	0	0.0	0	1	—	—	—	P	—	0	-40
2003	Atl	16(0)	—	—	—	—	—	—	—	—	1	0	0.0	0	0.0	0	0	—	—	—	P	—	0	0

YEAR	TEAM	G (GS, POS)	RUSH	YD	AVG(LG)	TD	REC	YD	AVG(LG)	TD	PASS	COMP	PCT	YD	AVG(LG)	TD	INT	SK	YD	QBR	KPR	OTD	PTS	TAY
2004	†Atl	16(0)	—	—	—	—	—	—	—	—	3	2	66.7	24	8.0(26)	0	0	—	—	—	P	—	0	12
NFL	15	239(0)	4	2	0.5(11)	0	—	—	—	—	10	7	70.0	128	12.8(44)	0	1	—	—	—	KP	—	1	26

MOHRING, JOHN John Dennis, LB, 6´3˝/240 lbs; C.W. Post; 1979: Det, rnd 8; B11/14/1956 Glen Cove, NY **1980** Det 1 (0) **1980**†Cle 14 (0) **NFL** 15 (0) [1 yr]

MOHRING, MIKE Michael Joseph, DT, 6´5˝/295 lbs; Pittsburgh; B3/22/1974 Glen Cove, NY **1997** SD 2 (0) **1998** SD 10 (0) **1999** SD 16 (1) **2000** SD 7 (0) **2001** SD 9 (0) **NFL** 44 (1) [5 yrs]

MOHS, LOUIE Louis M., E-G-T, 6´2˝/220 lbs; St. Thomas; B1/1896 St. Cloud, MN, D8/1967 **1922** Min 1 (1) **1923** Min 9 (7, LE), 6 **1924** Min 5 (5, LE) **NFL** 15 (13) [3 yrs]

MOJE, DICK Richard Louis, E, 6´2˝/210 lbs; Loyola Marymount; B5/8/1927 Los Angeles, CA, D6/22/1989 Los Angeles County, CA

| 1951 | GB | 2 | — | — | — | — | 1 | 11 | 11.0(11) | 0 | — | — | — | — | — | — | — | — | — | — | — | — | 0 | 6 |

MOJSIEJENKO, RALF Ralf, P, 6´3˝/209 lbs; Michigan State; 1985: SD, rnd 4; B1/28/1963 Satzgitter, Germany [P] **1986** SD 16 (0) **1987** SD★12 (0) **1988** SD☆16 (0) **1989** Was 16 (0) **1991** SF 5 (0)

1985	SD	16(0)	1	0	0.0(0)	0	—	—	—	—	—	—	—	—	—	—	—	—	—	—	P	—	0	0
1990	Was	12(0)	1	0	0.0(0)	0	—	—	—	—	—	—	—	—	—	—	—	—	—	—	P	—	0	0
NFL	7	93(0)	2	0	0.0	0	—	—	—	—	—	—	—	—	—	—	—	—	—	—	P	—	0	0

MOLDEN, ALEX Alex M., DB, 5´10˝/190 lbs; Oregon; 1996: NO, rnd 1; B8/4/1973 Detroit, MI **1996** NO 14 (2) **1997** NO 16 (15, LCB) **1998** NO 16 (15, LCB) **1999** NO 13 (0) **2000**†NO 15 (6, lcb) **2001** SD 6 (3) **2002** SD 16 (16, LCB) **2003** Det 2 (0) **NFL** 98 (57) [8 yrs]

MOLDEN, FRANK William Francis, DT, 6´5˝/276 lbs; Jackson State; 1965: Pit, rnd 11/Hou, rnd 5; B7/28/1942 Town, MS **1965** LARm 11 **1968** Phi 13 (ldt) **1969** NYG 7 **NFL** 31 [3 yrs]

MOLDEN, FRED Frederick, DT, 6´2˝/272 lbs; Southern Mississippi; Jackson State; B8/12/1963 Singing River, MS **1987** Min 2 (0)

MOLENDA, BO John J., FB-BB-HB, 5´10˝/210 lbs; Michigan; B2/20/1905 Oglesby, IL, D7/20/1986 Banning, CA [K] **1927** NYY 10 (9, FB), 7 **1928** NYY 8 (6, fb), 3 **1928** GB 4 (2) **1929** GB 12 (9, FB), 21 **1930** GB 13 (9, FB), 22 **1931** GB☆14 (4), 21

1932	GB	2(1)	10	20	2.0	0	—	—	—	—	—	—	—	—	—	—	—	—	—	—	—	—	0	20
1932	NYG	10(6, BB)	24	46	1.9	0	1	15	15.0(15)	0	15	7	46.7	106	7.1	1	1	—	—	—	K	—	3	72
1933	†NYG	13(11, BB)	77	240	3.1	3	—	—	—	—	2	1	50.0	8	4.0(8)	0	0	—	—	—	K	—	18	274
1934	†NYG	13(9, BB)	28	99	3.5	0	3	55	18.3(35)	0	—	—	—	—	—	—	—	—	—	—	K	—	2	127
1935	NYG	12(4)	4	23	5.8(14)	0	—	—	—	—	—	—	—	—	—	—	—	—	—	—	K	1	11	33
NFL	9	111(70)	143	428	3.0(14)	12	4	70	17.5(35)	1	17	8	47.1	114	6.7(8)	7	1	—	—	—	K	1	108	650

MOLESWORTH, KEITH Keith Frank, HB-QB, 5´10˝/167 lbs; Monmouth (IL); B10/20/1905 Washington, IA, D3/12/1966 Baltimore, MD [KC]

1931	ChiB	11(2)	—	—	—	—	—	—	—	—	—	—	—	—	—	—	—	—	—	—	—	—	—	276
1932	ChiB☆	14(14, QB)	65	213	3.3	2	3	19	6.3	1	64	25	39.1	346	5.4	3	4	—	—	—	—	—	18	286
1933	†ChiB	13(9, LH)	61	145	2.4	0	11	118	10.7	1	50	19	38.0	433	8.7	4	4	—	—	—	—	—	6	280
1934	†ChiB	12(3)	61	125	2.0	1	1	6	6.0(6)	0	39	13	33.3	249	6.4	3	4	—	—	—	—	—	6	118
1935	ChiB	11(4)	81	293	3.6	4	7	154	22.0	0	36	13	36.1	266	7.4	3	3	—	—	—	—	—	24	438
1936	ChiB	11(0)	60	276	4.6	0	9	146	16.2	0	31	15	48.4	188	6.1	4	4	—	—	—	—	—	0	303
1937	†ChiB	9(3)	20	53	2.7	0	4	21	5.3	0	6	1	16.7	4	0.7(4)	0	0	—	—	—	K	—	1	66
NFL	7	81(35)	348	1105	3.2	8	35	464	13.3(6)	2	226	86	38.1	1486	6.6(4)	18	19	—	—	—	K	—	61	1500

MOLINARO, JIM James Anthony, T, 6´6˝/301 lbs; Notre Dame; 2004: Was, rnd 6; B4/27/1981 Hatfield, PA **2004** Was 11 (0) **2005**†Was 3 (0) **NFL** 14 (0) [2 yrs]

MOLINET, LOU Ignacio Saturnino, FB, 5´11˝/195 lbs; Cornell; B11/30/1904 Chaparra, Cuba, D8/27/1977 West Palm Beach, FL **1927** Fra 9 (2), 6

MOMSEN, BOB Robert Edward, MG-G-LB, 6´3˝/225 lbs; Ohio State; 1951: Det, rnd 7; B5/28/1929 Toledo, OH **1951** Det☆12 **1952** SF 10 (MG) **NFL** 22 [2 yrs]

MOMSEN, TONY Anton, C, 6´1˝/215 lbs; Michigan; 1951: LA, rnd 5; B1/29/1928 Toledo, OH, D3/6/1994 Columbus, OH **1951** Pit 11 **1952** Was 2 **NFL** 13 [2 yrs]

MONACHINO, JIM James, HB-FB-DB, 5´10˝/187 lbs; California; 1951: SF, rnd 12; B7/9/1929 Cleveland, OH

1951	SF	8	21	74	3.5(7)	2	1	6	6.0(6)	0	—	—	—	—	—	—	—	—	—	—	—	—	12	97
1953	SF	5	4	10	2.5(5)	0	2	9	4.5(9)	0	—	—	—	—	—	—	—	—	—	—	—	—	0	15
1955	Was	7	46	207	4.5(34)	2	8	74	9.3(24)	0	—	—	—	—	—	—	—	—	—	—	p	—	12	260
NFL	3	20	71	291	4.1(34)	4	11	89	8.1(24)	0	—	—	—	—	—	—	—	—	—	—	p	—	24	372

MONACO, RAY Raymond William, G, 5´10˝/212 lbs; Holy Cross; B2/10/1918 Providence, RI, D12/7/2002 North Providence, RI **1944** Was 5 (0) **1945** Cle 1 (0) **NFL** 6 (0) [2 yrs]

MONACO, ROB Robin Gabriel, C, 6´3˝/283 lbs; Vanderbilt; 1985: SL, rnd 8; B9/5/1961 Hamden, CT **1985** SL 6 (0)

MONACO, RON Ronnie Carl, LB, 6´1˝/225 lbs; San Diego State; Vanderbilt; South Carolina; B5/3/1963 New Haven, CT **1986** SL 15 (2) **1987** GB 2 (1) **NFL** 17 (3) [2 yrs]

MONAHAN, REGIS John Regis, G-T, 5´10˝/216 lbs; Ohio State; B11/15/1908 Pittsburgh, PA, D4/23/1979 Detroit, MI [K] **1935**†Det 12 (3) **1936** Det 10 (1) **1937** Det 11 (3) **1938** Det 9 (1) **1939** ChiC 2 (1) **NFL** 44 (9) [5 yrs]

MONDS, MARIO Mario, DT, 6´3˝/325 lbs; Cincinnati; 2001: Was, rnd 6; B11/10/1976 Fort Pierce, FL **2001** Cin 2 (0) **2004** Mia 5 (0) **NFL** 7 (0) [2 yrs]

MONDS, WONDER Wonderful, DB, 6´3˝/215 lbs; Nebraska; 1976: Pit, rnd 4; B5/3/1952 Fort Pierce, FL **1978** SF 16

MONFORT, AVERY William Avery, WB, 5´10˝/178 lbs; New Mexico; B12/19/1918 Copan, OK, D4/19/2005 Grass Valley, CA

| 1941 | ChiC | 4(0) | 3 | 8 | 2.7(11) | 0 | — | — | — | — | — | — | — | — | — | — | — | — | — | — | — | — | 0 | 8 |

MONGER, MATT Matthew L., LB, 6´1˝/235 lbs; Oklahoma State; 1985: NYJ, rnd 8; B11/15/1961 Denver, CO **1985**†NYJ 15 (0) **1986**†NYJ 16 (1) **1987** NYJ 12 (0) **1989**†Buf 9 (0) **1990** Buf 4 (0) **NFL** 56 (1) [5 yrs]

MONK, ART James Arthur, WR, 6´3˝/210 lbs; Syracuse; 1980: Was, rnd 1; B12/5/1957 White Plains, NY

1980	Was	16(10, WR)	—	—	—	—	58	797	13.7(54)	3	—	—	—	—	—	—	—	—	—	—	k	—	18	409
1981	Was	16(16, WR)	1	-5	-5.0(-5)	0	56	894	16.0(79)	6	—	—	—	—	—	—	—	—	—	—	—	—	36	472
1982	Was	9(9, WR)	7	21	3.0(14)	0	35	447	12.8(43)	1	—	—	—	—	—	—	—	—	—	—	—	—	6	250
1983	†Was	12(11, WR)	3	-19	-6.3(2)	0	47	746	15.9(43)	5	1	1	100.0	46	46.0(46)	0	0	—	—	—	—	—	30	402
1984	†Was★	16(16, WR)	2	18	9.0(18)	0	106	1372	12.9(72)	7	—	—	—	—	—	—	—	—	—	—	—	—	42	739
1985	Was★	15(14, WR)	7	51	7.3(16)	0	91	1226	13.5(53)	2	—	—	—	—	—	—	—	—	—	—	—	—	12	674
1986	†Was★	16(16, WR)	4	27	6.8(21)	0	73	1068	14.6(69)	4	—	—	—	—	—	—	—	—	—	—	—	—	24	581
1987	†Was	9(9, WR)	6	63	10.5(26)	0	38	483	12.7(62)	6	—	—	—	—	—	—	—	—	—	—	—	—	36	335
1988	†Was	16(13, WR)	7	46	6.6(23)	0	72	946	13.1(46)	5	1	0	0.0	0	0.0	0	0	—	—	—	—	—	30	544
1989	Was	16(12, WR)	3	8	2.7(14)	0	86	1186	13.8(60)	8	—	—	—	—	—	—	—	—	—	—	—	—	48	641
1990	†Was	16(16, WR)	7	59	8.4(26)	0	68	770	11.3(44)	5	—	—	—	—	—	—	—	—	—	—	—	—	30	469
1991	†Was	16(16, WR)	9	19	2.1(14)	0	71	1049	14.8(64)	8	—	—	—	—	—	—	—	—	—	—	—	—	48	584
1992	Was	16(14, WR)	6	45	7.5(16)	0	46	644	14.0(49)	3	—	—	—	—	—	—	—	—	—	—	—	—	18	282
1993	Was	16(5, wr)	1	-1	-1.0(-1)	0	41	398	9.7(29)	2	—	—	—	—	—	—	—	—	—	—	—	—	12	208
1994	NYJ	16(15, WR)	—	—	—	—	46	581	12.6(69)	3	—	—	—	—	—	—	—	—	—	—	—	—	18	306
1995	Phi	3(1)	—	—	—	—	6	114	19.0(36)	0	—	—	—	—	—	—	—	—	—	—	—	—	0	57
NFL	16	224(193)	63	332	5.3(26)	0	940	12721	13.5(79)	68	2	1	50.0	46	23.0(46)	0	0	—	—	—	k	—	408	7051

MONK, QUINCY Quincy Omar, LB, 6´3˝/250 lbs; North Carolina; 2002: NYG, rnd 7; B1/30/1979 Jacksonville, NC **2002** NYG 9 (0) **2003** NYG 4 (0) **2004** Hou 2 (0) **NFL** 15 (0) [3 yrs]

MONNETT, BOB Robert C., TB-HB-QB, 5´9˝/182 lbs; Michigan State; B2/27/1910 Bucyrus, OH, D8/1/1978 Galion, OH [K]

1933	GB	10(6, TB)	108	413	3.8	3	6	44	7.3	0	46	23	50.0	325	7.1	3	3	—	—	—	K	1	34	533
1934	GB	11(5, tb)	68	129	1.9	2	2	27	13.5(26)	0	43	16	37.2	223	5.2	2	4	—	—	—	K	—	29	124
1935	GB	11(3, tb)	68	336	4.9	1	1	8	8.0(8)	0	65	31	47.7	354	5.4	2	5	—	—	—	K	—	11	337
1936	GB	12(8, HB)	104	224	2.2	0	13	169	13.0	0	52	20	38.5	280	5.4	4	3	—	—	—	K	—	3	389
1937	GB	10(9, TB)	87	161	1.9	1	4	32	8.0(13)	0	73	37	50.7	580	7.9	8	8	—	—	—	K	—	6	197
1938	†GB	8(5, TB)	75	225	3.0	0	1	23	23.0(23)	0	57	31	54.4	465	8.2	9	4	—	—	—	K	1	7	354
NFL	6	62(36)	510	1488	2.9	7	27	303	11.2(26)	0	336	158	47.0	2227	6.6	28	26	—	—	—	K	1	90	1933

YEAR	TEAM	G (GS, POS)	RUSH	YD	AVG (LG)	TD	REC	YD	AVG (LG)	TD	PASS	COMP	PCT	YD	AVG (LG)	TD	INT	SK	YD	QBR	KPR	OTD	PTS	TAY
MONROE, CARL	Carl, RB, 5´8˝/166 lbs; Utah; B2/20/1960 Pittsburgh, PA, D4/26/1989 San Jose, CA **[R]**																							
1983	†SF	5(0)	10	23	2.3(5)	0	2	61	30.5(50)	0	—	—	—	—	—	—	—	—	—	—	k	—	0	86
1984	†SF	16(0)	3	13	4.3(7)	0	11	139	12.6(47)	1	—	—	—	—	—	—	—	—	—	—	k	—	6	244
1985	†SF	14(0)	—	—	—	—	10	51	5.1(9)	0	—	—	—	—	—	—	—	—	—	—	k	1	6	333
1986	SF	5(0)	—	—	—	—	2	6	3.0(5)	0	—	—	—	—	—	—	—	—	—	—	k	—	0	22
1987	SF	3(2)	2	26	13.0(17)	0	3	66	22.0(39)	1	—	—	—	—	—	—	—	—	—	—	k	—	6	80
NFL	5	43(2)	15	62	4.1(17)	0	28	323	11.5(50)	2	—	—	—	—	—	—	—	—	—	—	k	1	18	764
MONROE, HENRY	Henry Evans, DB, 5´11˝/180 lbs; Mississippi State; 1979: GB, rnd 7; B12/30/1956 Mobile, AL **1979** GB 3 **1979**†Phi 3 **NFL** 6 [1 yr]																							
MONROE, RODRICK	Rodrick, TE, 6´5˝/254 lbs; Cincinnati; 1998: Dal, rnd 7; B7/30/1975 Hearne, TX **2001** Cle 7 (3)																							
1999	Atl	2(0)	—	—	—	—	1	8	8.0(8)	0	—	—	—	—	—	—	—	—	—	—	—	—	0	4
NFL	2	9(3)	—	—	—	—	1	8	8.0(8)	0	—	—	—	—	—	—	—	—	—	—	—	—	0	4
MONT, TOMMY	Thomas Allison, QB-HB, 6´0˝/194 lbs; Maryland; 1944: NYG, rnd 12/1947: Mia-A, rnd 3; B6/20/1922 Mount Savage, MD																							
1947	Was	4(0)	1	7	7.0(7)	0	2	14	7.0(7)	0	—	—	—	—	—	—	—	—	—	—	pi	—	0	38
1948	Was	11(2)	11	103	9.4(33)	1	—	—	—	—	28	12	42.9	157	5.6(35)	2	2	—	—	—	i	—	6	133
1949	Was	12(0)	14	75	5.4(27)	0	8	105	13.1(30)	2	7	3	42.9	44	6.3(31)	0	0	—	—	—	k	—	12	167
NFL	3	27(2)	26	185	7.1(33)	1	10	119	11.9(30)	2	35	15	42.9	201	5.7(35)	2	2	—	—	—	kpi	—	18	337
MONTAGNE, DAVE	David Andrew, WR, 6´2˝/184 lbs; Oregon State; B4/18/1964 Berkeley, CA																							
1987	KC	3(2)	—	—	—	—	5	47	9.4(16)	0	—	—	—	—	—	—	—	—	—	—	p	—	0	27
MONTALBO, MEL	Melvin James, DB, 6´1˝/190 lbs; Utah State; B3/29/1938 **1962** Oak-A 2																							
MONTANA, JOE	Joseph Clifford 'Joe Cool', QB, 6´2˝/200 lbs; Notre Dame; 1979: SF, rnd 3; B6/11/1956 New Eagle, PA; HOF 2000																							
1979	SF	16(1)	3	22	7.3(13)	0	—	—	—	—	23	13	56.5	96	4.2(18)	1	0	—	—	—	—	—	0	75
1980	SF	15(7, qb)	32	77	2.4(11)	2	—	—	—	—	273	176	**64.5**	1795	6.6(71)	15	9	15	100	87.8	—	—	12	710
1981	†SF★	16(16, QB)	25	95	3.8(20)	2	—	—	—	—	488	311	**63.7**	3565	7.3(78)	19	12	26	193	**88.4**	—	—	12	1513
1982	SF	9(9, QB)	30	118	3.9(21)	1	—	—	—	—	**346**	**213**	61.6	**2613**	7.6(55)	**17**	11	20	166	88.0	—	—	6	**1080**
1983	†SF★	16(16, QB)	61	284	4.7(18)	2	—	—	—	—	515	332	**64.5**	3910	7.6(77)	26	12	33	224	94.6	—	—	12	1909
1984	†SF★	16(15, QB)	39	118	3.0(15)	2	—	—	—	—	432	279	64.6	3630	**8.4(80)**	**28**	10	22	138	**102.9**	—	—	12	1693
1985	†SF★	15(15, QB)	42	153	3.6(16)	3	—	—	—	—	494	**303**	**61.3**	3653	7.4(73)	**27**	13	35	246	91.3	—	—	18	1625
1986	†SF	8(8, QB)	17	38	2.2(17)	0	—	—	—	—	307	191	62.2	2236	7.3(48)	8	9	12	95	80.7	—	—	0	836
1987	†SF★	13(11, QB)	35	141	4.0(20)	1	—	—	—	—	398	266	**66.8**	3054	7.7(57)	**31**	13	22	158	**102.1**	—	—	6	1313
1988	†SF	14(13, QB)	38	132	3.5(15)	3	—	—	—	—	397	238	59.9	2981	7.5(**96**)	18	10	34	223	87.9	—	—	18	1343
1989	†SF★	13(13, QB)	49	227	4.6(19)	3	—	—	—	—	386	271	**70.2**	3521	**9.1(95)**	26	8	33	198	**112.4**	—	—	18	1828
1990	†SF★	15(15, QB)	40	162	4.1(20)	1	—	—	—	—	520	**321**	**61.7**	3944	7.6(78)	26	16	29	153	89.0	—	—	6	1634
1992	SF	1(0)	3	28	9.3(16)	0	—	—	—	—	21	15	71.4	126	6.0(17)	2	0	1	8	—	—	—	0	101
1993	†KC✧	11(11, QB)	25	64	2.6(17)	0	—	—	—	—	298	181	60.7	2144	7.2(50)	13	7	12	61	87.4	—	—	0	921
1994	†KC	14(14, QB)	18	17	0.9(13)	0	—	—	—	—	493	299	60.6	3283	6.7(57)	16	9	19	132	83.6	—	—	0	1379
NFL	15	192(164)	457	1676	3.7(21)	20	—	—	—	—	5391	3409	63.2	40551	7.5(96)	273	139	313	2095	92.3	—	—	120	17957
MONTGOMERY, ALTON	Alton, DB, 6´0˝/205 lbs; Houston; 1990: Den, rnd 2; B6/16/1968 Griffin, GA **1990** Den 15 (4) **1991**†Den 16 (0) **1992** Den 12 (1) **1993** Atl 8 (0) **1994** Atl 2 (1) **1995**†Atl 15 (0) **NFL** 68 (6) [6 yrs]																							
MONTGOMERY, BILL	William A., G-T, 5´9˝/200 lbs; St. Louis; B5/4/1909 St. Louis, MO, D7/1978 Camdenton, MD **1934** SL 3 (1, LG)																							
MONTGOMERY, BILL	William N., HB, 6´0˝/205 lbs; LSU; 1945: Phi, rnd 15; B6/3/1923, D8/21/2003																							
1946	ChiC	3(0)	8	11	1.4(6)	0	—	—	—	—	—	—	—	—	—	—	—	—	—	—	—	—	0	11
MONTGOMERY, BLANCHARD	Blanchard, LB, 6´2˝/236 lbs; UCLA; 1983: SF, rnd 3; B2/17/1961 Los Angeles, CA **1983** SF 11 (3) **1984**†SF 16 (0) **NFL** 27 (3) [2 yrs]																							
MONTGOMERY, CLEO	Cleotha, WR, 5´8˝/183 lbs; Abilene Christian; B7/1/1955 Greenville, MS **[R]** **1981** Cle 4 (0) **1981** Oak 1 (0) **1982**†LARd 9 (0) **1985** LARd 4 (0)																							
1980	Cin	14(0)	1	12	12.0(12)	0	—	—	—	—	—	—	—	—	—	—	—	—	—	—	kp	—	0	263
1983	†LARd	14(0)	2	7	3.5(5)	0	2	29	14.5(15)	0	—	—	—	—	—	—	—	—	—	—	k	—	0	171
1984	†LARd	16(0)	1	1	1.0(1)	0	—	—	—	—	—	—	—	—	—	—	—	—	—	—	kp	1	6	300
NFL	6	62(0)	4	20	5.0(12)	0	2	29	14.5(15)	0	—	—	—	—	—	—	—	—	—	—	kp	1	6	1043
MONTGOMERY, CLIFF	Clifford Earl, TB, 5´9˝/165 lbs; Columbia; B9/17/1910 Pittsburgh, PA, D4/21/2005 Mineola, NY																							
1934	Bkn	11(3)	47	70	1.5	0	2	21	10.5	0	32	7	21.9	93	2.9	1	6	—	—	—	—	—	0	-108
MONTGOMERY, GLENN	Glenn Steven, DT, 6´0˝/282 lbs; Houston; 1989: Hou, rnd 5; B3/31/1967 New Orleans, LA, D6/28/1998 Dallas, TX **1989**†Hou 15 (0) **1990**†Hou 15 (0) **1991**†Hou 16 (0) **1992**†Hou 16 (0) **1993**†Hou 16 (11, RDT) **1994** Hou 14 (14, RDT) **1995** Hou 15 (14, RDT) **1996** Sea 7 (2) **NFL** 114 (41) [8 yrs]																							
MONTGOMERY, GREG	Gregory Hugh, P, 6´4˝/215 lbs; Penn State; Michigan State; 1988: Hou, rnd 3; B10/29/1964 Morristown, NJ **[P]** **1988**†Hou 16 (0) **1990**†Hou 16 (0) **1991**†Hou 15 (0) **1993**†Hou★15 (0) **1994**†Det 16 (0)																							
1989	†Hou☆	16(0)	3	17	5.7(11)	0	—	—	—	—	—	—	—	—	—	—	—	—	—	—	P	—	0	17
1992	†Hou☆	16(0)	2	-14	-7.0(0)	0	—	—	—	—	—	—	—	—	—	—	—	—	—	—	P	—	0	-14
1996	Bal	16(0)	1	0	0.0(0)	0	—	—	—	—	—	—	—	—	—	—	—	—	—	—	P	—	0	0
1997	Bal	16(0)	1	11	11.0(11)	0	—	—	—	—	—	—	—	—	—	—	—	—	—	—	P	—	0	11
NFL	9	142(0)	7	14	2.0(11)	0	—	—	—	—	—	—	—	—	—	—	—	—	—	—	P	—	0	14
MONTGOMERY, JIM	James Brown, T, 6´4˝/235 lbs; Texas A&M; B3/18/1922 Breckenridge, TX, D8/14/1992 Dallas, TX **1946** Det 11 (0)																							
MONTGOMERY, JOE	Joe, RB, 5´10˝/230 lbs; Ohio State; 1999: NYG, rnd 2; B6/8/1976 Robbins, IL																							
1999	NYG	7(5, RB)	115	348	3.0(14)	3	—	—	—	—	—	—	—	—	—	—	—	—	—	—	—	—	20	378
2000	†NYG	3(0)	1	4	4.0(4)	1	—	—	—	—	—	—	—	—	—	—	—	—	—	—	—	—	6	14
2002	Car	3(0)	7	20	2.9(5)	0	—	—	—	—	—	—	—	—	—	—	—	—	—	—	—	—	0	20
NFL	3	13(5)	123	372	3.0(14)	4	—	—	—	—	—	—	—	—	—	—	—	—	—	—	—	—	26	412
MONTGOMERY, MARV	Marvin, T, 6´6˝/255 lbs; USC; 1971: Den, rnd 1; B2/8/1948 Torrance, CA **1971** Den 12 **1972** Den 14 (14, LT) **1973** Den 10 (10, LT) **1974** Den 4 **1975** Den 14 (7, rt) **1976** Den 3 (1) **1976** NO 9 (7, lt) **1977** NO 14 (14, LT) **1978** Atl 1 **NFL** 81 (53) [8 yrs]																							
MONTGOMERY, MIKE	James Michael, RB-WR, 6´2˝/210 lbs; Kansas State; 1971: SD, rnd 3; B7/10/1949 Wichita Falls, TX																							
1971	SD	11	60	226	3.8(26)	1	28	361	12.9(39)	2	6	3	50.0	80	13.3(33)	1	0	—	—	—	—	—	18	472
1972	†Dal	12	35	81	2.3(10)	1	8	131	16.4(46)	1	3	1	33.3	31	10.3(31)	0	0	—	—	—	k	1	18	177
1973	†Dal	9	1	-10	-10.0(-10)	0	14	164	11.7(32)	3	1	0	0.0	0	0.0	0	0	—	—	—	Pkp	—	18	164
1974	Hou	5	—	—	—	—	9	179	19.9(65)	1	—	—	—	—	—	—	—	—	—	—	—	—	6	95
NFL	4	37	96	297	3.1(26)	2	59	835	14.2(65)	7	10	4	40.0	111	11.1(33)	1	0	—	—	—	Pkp	1	60	907
MONTGOMERY, MIKE	Michael Lewis, DT, 6´5˝/276 lbs; Texas A&M; 2005: GB, rnd 6; B8/18/1983 Carthage, TX **2005** GB 12 (0)																							
MONTGOMERY, MONTY	Delmonico Lamont, DB, 5´11˝/197 lbs; Houston; 1997: Ind, rnd 4; B12/8/1973 Dallas, TX **1997** Ind 16 (3) **1998** Ind 16 (5, lcb) **1999** Ind 3 (0) **1999** SF 4 (2) **2000** SF 15 (9, rcb) **2004** NO 5 (0) **NFL** 59 (19) [5 yrs]																							
MONTGOMERY, RANDY	Randle John, DB, 5´11˝/182 lbs; Weber State; 1970: Den, rnd 7; B8/12/1947 Houston, TX **1971** Den 3 **1972** Den 14 (8, RCB) **1973** Den 9 (2) **1974** ChiB 14 **NFL** 40 (10) [4 yrs]																							
MONTGOMERY, ROSS	Ross Eliott, RB, 6´3˝/220 lbs; TCU; 1969: Chi, rnd 3; B12/10/1946 Detroit, MI																							
1969	ChiB	12	15	52	3.5(6)	0	2	8	4.0(6)	0	—	—	—	—	—	—	—	—	—	—	—	—	0	56
1970	ChiB	14(RB)	62	229	3.7(38)	0	14	75	5.4(17)	0	—	—	—	—	—	—	—	—	—	—	k	—	0	276
NFL	2	26	77	281	3.6(38)	0	16	83	5.2(17)	0	—	—	—	—	—	—	—	—	—	—	k	—	0	332
MONTGOMERY, SCOTTIE	Scottie Austin, WR, 6´1˝/195 lbs; Duke; B5/26/1978 Shelby, NC																							
2000	†Den	4(0)	—	—	—	—	1	10	10.0(10)	0	—	—	—	—	—	—	—	—	—	—	—	—	0	5
2001	Den	8(0)	1	5	5.0(5)	0	11	99	9.0(23)	0	—	—	—	—	—	—	—	—	—	—	—	—	0	55
2002	Den	15(0)	4	27	6.8(28)	0	4	51	12.8(21)	1	—	—	—	—	—	—	—	—	—	—	k	—	6	203
NFL	3	27(0)	5	32	6.4(28)	0	16	160	10.0(23)	1	—	—	—	—	—	—	—	—	—	—	k	—	6	262

YEAR	TEAM	G (GS, POS)	RUSH	YD	AVG(LG)	TD	REC	YD	AVG(LG)	TD	PASS COMP	PCT	YD	AVG(LG)	TD	INT	SK	YD	QBR	KPR	OTD	PTS	TAY

MONTGOMERY, SULLY James Ralph, T-C, 6′3″/213 lbs; Centre; B1/12/1901, TX, D9/5/1970 Fort Worth, TX **1923** ChiC 11 (11, LT) **1927** Fra 4 (0) **NFL** 15 (11) [2 yrs]

MONTGOMERY, TYRONE Tyrone, RB, 6′0″/190 lbs; Mississippi; B8/3/1970 Greenville, MS

1993	†LARd	12(0)	37	106	2.9(15)	0	10	43	4.3(9)	0	—	—	—	—	—	—	—	—	—	—	—	0	128
1994	LARd	6(6, rb)	36	97	2.7(15)	0	8	126	15.8(65)	1	—	—	—	—	—	—	—	—	—	—	—	6	165
NFL	2	18(6)	73	203	2.8(15)	0	18	169	9.4(65)	1	—	—	—	—	—	—	—	—	—	—	—	6	293

MONTGOMERY, WILBERT Wilbert, RB, 5′10″/196 lbs; Jackson State; Abilene Christian; 1977: Phi, rnd 6; B9/16/1954 Greenville, MS

1977	Phi	14(1)	45	183	4.1(27)	2	3	18	6.0(8)	0	—	—	—	—	—	—	—	—	—	k	1	18	496
1978	†Phi★	14(14, RB)	259	1220	**4.7(47)**	9	34	195	5.7(23)	1	—	—	—	—	—	—	—	—	—	k	—	60	1477
1979	†Phi★	16(16, RB)	338	1512	4.5(62)	9	41	494	12.0(53)	5	—	—	—	—	—	—	—	—	—	k	—	84	1865
1980	†Phi	12(12, RB)	193	778	4.0(72)	8	50	407	8.1(31)	2	1	0	0.0	0	0.0	0	0	—	—	k	—	60	1080
1981	†Phi	15(15, RB)	286	1402	**4.9(41)**	8	49	521	10.6(35)	2	—	—	—	—	—	—	—	—	—	—	—	60	1753
1982	Phi	8(8, RB)	114	515	**4.5(90)**	7	20	258	12.9(42)	2	—	—	—	—	—	—	—	—	—	k	—	54	721
1983	Phi	5(1)	29	139	4.8(32)	0	9	53	5.9(13)	0	—	—	—	—	—	—	—	—	—	—	—	0	166
1984	Phi	16(14, RB)	201	789	3.9(27)	2	60	501	8.4(28)	0	2	0	0.0	0	0.0	0	0	.1	10	—	—	12	1060
1985	Det	7(6, RB)	75	251	3.3(22)	0	7	55	7.9(28)	0	—	—	—	—	—	—	—	—	—	—	—	0	279
NFL	9	107(87)	1540	6789	4.4(90)	45	273	2502	9.2(53)	12	3	0	0.0	0	0.0	0	0	1	10	k	1	348	8894

MONTLER, MIKE Michael Russell, C-G-T, 6′5″/254 lbs; Colorado; 1969: Bos, rnd 2; B1/10/1944 Columbus, OH **1969** Bos-A 14 (11, LG) **1970** Bos 11 (11, LG/lt) **1971** NE 14 (14, LT) **1972** NE 14 (14, LG) **1973** Buf 10 (7, c) **1974**†Buf 14 (14, C) **1975** Buf 14 (14, C) **1977**†Den 14 (14, C) **1978** Det 4 (4)

| 1976 | Buf | 14(14, C) | — | — | — | — | 1 | 6 | 6.0(6) | 0 | — | — | — | — | — | — | — | — | — | — | — | 0 | 3 |
| NFL | 10 | 123(117) | — | — | — | — | 1 | 6 | 6.0(6) | 0 | — | — | — | — | — | — | — | — | — | — | — | 0 | 3 |

MONTOUTE, SANKAR Sankar Jerome, LB, 6′3″/230 lbs; Wisconsin; St. Leo; B2/2/1961 Trinidad **1987** TB 3 (3)

MONTOYA, MAX Max, G, 6′5″/282 lbs; UCLA; 1979: Cin, rnd 7; B5/12/1956 Montebello, CA **1979** Cin 11 (9, rg) **1980** Cin 16 (16, RG) **1981**†Cin 16 (16, RG) **1982** Cin 9 (9, RG) **1983** Cin 16 (16, RG) **1984** Cin 16 (15, RG) **1985** Cin 16 (16, RG) **1986** Cin★16 (16, RG) **1987** Cin 10 (9, RG) **1988**†Cin★15 (15, RG) **1989** Cin★16 (15, RG) **1990**†LARd 16 (16, RG) **1991**†LARd 11 (10, RG) **1992** LARd 10 (9, RG) **1993**†LARd◇16 (16, RG) **1994** LARd 13 (0) **NFL** 223 (203) [16 yrs]

MONTREUIL, MARK Mark Allen, DB, 6′2″/200 lbs; Concordia (QB); 1995: SD, rnd 7; B12/29/1971 Montreal, Canada **1995**†SD 16 (0) **1996** SD 13 (0) **1997** SD 6 (1) **NFL** 35 (1) [3 yrs]

MONTY, PETE Peter Charles, LB, 6′2″/250 lbs; Wisconsin; 1997: NYG, rnd 4; B7/13/1974 Ft. Collins, CO **1997** NYG 3 (0) **1998** NYG 11 (0) **1999** NYG 16 (3) **2000**†NYG 16 (1) **2001** Min 6 (0) **NFL** 52 (4) [5 yrs]

MOODY, KEITH Keith M., DB, 5′11″/171 lbs; Syracuse; 1976: Buf, rnd 10; B6/13/1953 Salisbury, NC [R] **1976** Buf 14 (2) **1977** Buf 14 (3) **1978** Buf 14 **1979** Buf 16 **1980**†Oak 5 (0) **NFL** 63 (5) [5 yrs]

MOODY, WILKIE Wilkie Osgood, B, 5′7″/183 lbs; Linfield; Denison; B5/12/1897 Irabo, Congo, D2/22/1976 Granville, OH **1920** Col 9 (2) **1921** Day 1 (1) **1924** Col 3 (1) **1925** Col 2 (1) **NFL** 15 (5) [4 yrs]

MOOERS, DOUG Douglas F., DT-DE, 6′6″/265 lbs; Whittier; B3/11/1947 Seattle, WA **1971** NO 4 **1972** NO 14 (rdt) **NFL** 18 [2 yrs]

MOOG, AARON Aaron John, DE, 6′4″/260 lbs; UNLV; B2/3/1962 Loma Linda, CA **1987** Cle 3 (0)

MOON, WARREN Harold Warren, QB, 6′3″/212 lbs; Washington; B11/18/1956 Los Angeles, CA; HOF 2006

1984	Hou	16(16, QB)	58	211	3.6(31)	1	—	—	—	—	450	259	57.6	3338	7.4(76)	12	14	47	371	76.9	—	—	6	1390
1985	Hou	14(14, QB)	39	130	3.3(17)	0	—	—	—	—	377	200	53.1	2709	7.2(80)	15	19	46	366	68.5	—	—	0	800
1986	Hou	15(15, QB)	42	157	3.7(19)	2	—	—	—	—	488	256	52.5	3489	7.1(81)	13	26	41	332	62.3	—	—	12	947
1987	†Hou	12(12, QB)	34	112	3.3(20)	3	—	—	—	—	368	184	50.0	2806	7.6(**83**)	21	18	25	198	74.2	—	—	18	930
1988	†Hou★	11(11, QB)	33	88	2.7(14)	5	—	—	—	—	294	160	54.4	2327	7.9(57)	17	8	12	120	88.4	—	—	30	1067
1989	†Hou★	16(16, QB)	70	268	3.8(19)	4	—	—	—	—	464	280	60.3	3631	7.8(55)	23	14	35	267	88.9	—	—	24	1679
1990	Hou◇	15(15, QB)	55	215	3.9(17)	2	—	—	—	—	**584**	**362**	62.0	**4689**	8.0(87)	**33**	13	36	252	96.8	—	—	12	**2225**
1991	†Hou◇	16(16, QB)	33	68	2.1(12)	2	—	—	—	—	**655**	**404**	61.7	**4690**	7.2(61)	23	**21**	23	174	81.7	—	—	12	1708
1992	†Hou◇	11(11, QB)	27	147	5.4(23)	1	—	—	—	—	346	224	64.7	2521	7.3(72)	18	12	16	105	**89.3**	—	—	6	1028
1993	†Hou◇	15(14, QB)	48	145	3.0(35)	1	—	—	—	—	520	303	58.3	3485	6.7(80)	21	**21**	34	218	75.2	—	—	6	1163
1994	†Min◇	15(14, QB)	27	55	2.0(12)	0	—	—	—	—	**601**	**371**	61.7	**4264**	7.1(65)	18	**19**	29	235	79.9	—	—	0	1517
1995	Min◇	16(16, QB)	33	82	2.5(16)	0	—	—	—	—	**606**	**377**	62.2	**4228**	7.0(85)	33	14	38	277	91.5	—	—	0	1801
1996	Min	8(8, QB)	9	6	0.7(5)	0	—	—	—	—	247	134	54.3	1610	6.5(54)	7	9	19	122	68.7	—	—	0	486
1997	Sea◇	15(14, QB)	17	40	2.4(17)	1	—	—	—	—	528	313	59.3	3678	7.0(60)	25	16	30	192	83.7	—	—	6	1374
1998	Sea	10(10, QB)	16	10	0.6(9)	0	—	—	—	—	258	145	56.2	1632	6.3(45)	11	8	22	140	76.6	—	—	0	561
1999	KC	1(0)	—	—	—	—	—	—	—	—	3	1	33.3	20	6.7(20)	0	0	—	—	—	—	—	0	10
2000	KC	2(1)	2	2	1.0(2)	0	—	—	—	—	34	15	44.1	208	6.1(41)	1	1	5	46	—	—	—	0	71
NFL	17	208(203)	543	1736	3.2(35)	22	—	—	—	—	6823	3988	58.4	49325	7.2(87)	291	233	458	3415	80.9	—	—	132	18754

MOONEY, ED Edward John, LB, 6′2″/225 lbs; Texas Tech; 1968: Det, rnd 4; B2/26/1945 Brooklyn, NY **1968** Det 14 **1969** Det 14 **1970**†Det 14 **1971** Det 14 **1973** Bal 13 **NFL** 69 [5 yrs]

MOONEY, GEORGE George, B, 5′8″/163 lbs; none; B2/22/1896 Chicago, IL, D2/10/1985 Glendale, CA **1922** Mil 5 (1) **1923** Mil 7 (2) **1924** Mil 5 (0) **NFL** 17 (3) [3 yrs]

MOONEY, JIM James L., E-T-G, 5′11″/200 lbs; Georgetown (DC); B9/16/1907 Chicago, IL, D8/12/1944 France, [K] **1930** Nwk 12 (12, RT), 2 **1930** Bkn☆3 (2) **1931** Bkn 14 (8, RT), 1 **1935** ChiC 4 (1)

1933	Cin	7(6, LE)	3	27	9.0(1)	0	3	47	15.7	—	—	—	—	—	—	—	—	—	—	—	—	—	2	51
1934	Cin	8(8, LE)	2	-7	-3.5	0	6	36	6.0	0	6	4	66.7	27	4.5	0	0	—	—	—	—	—	0	25
NFL	5	48(37)	5	20	4.0(1)	0	9	83	9.2	0	6	4	66.7	27	4.5	0	0	—	—	—	K	—	5	75

MOONEY, MIKE Michael Paul, T, 6′6″/320 lbs; Georgia Tech; 1992: Hou, rnd 4; B5/31/1969 Baltimore, MD **1993** SD 1 (0)

MOONEY, TEX Orrin Thomas, aka Orin T. Schupbach Jr., T, 6′5″/280 lbs; West Texas A&M; B3/8/1917 El Paso, TX, D5/19/1956 Riverside County, CA **1942** Cle 1 (0) **1943** Bkn 2 (0) **NFL** 3 (0) [2 yrs]

MOONEY, TIM Timothy Michael, DE, 6′2″/265 lbs; Anderson (IN); Western Kentucky; B1/25/1962 Evansville, IN **1987** Phi 2 (0)

MOONEY, TIPP Bow Tipp, B, 5′10″/187 lbs; Abilene Christian; B4/19/1919 Shamrock, TX, D5/1/1999 Carrollton, TX

1944	ChiB	10(1)	29	88	3.0(14)	0	2	74	37.0(61)	1	—	—	—	—	—	—	—	—	—	kpi	—	6	221
1945	ChiB	7(4)	17	105	6.2(64)	0	2	10	5.0(6)	0	—	—	—	—	—	—	—	—	—	k	—	0	116
NFL	2	17(5)	46	193	4.2(64)	0	4	84	21.0(61)	1	—	—	—	—	—	—	—	—	—	kpi	—	6	337

MOOR, BUDDY Morris Howard, DE, 6′5″/250 lbs; Eastern Kentucky; B12/1/1958 Greenville, MS **1987** Atl 3 (1)

MOORE T **1921** Cle 1 (1)

MOORE, AL Albert Bennett, HB, 5′9″/185 lbs; Northwestern; B4/17/1908 Portland, OR, D3/23/1991 Crawford, CO

| 1932 | ChiB | 2(0) | 6 | 17 | 2.8 | 0 | — | — | — | — | — | — | — | — | — | — | — | — | — | — | — | 0 | 17 |

MOORE, ALEX Alexander Lee, RB, 6′0″/195 lbs; Norfolk State; 1968: SF, rnd 14; B5/22/1945 West Point, GA

| 1968 | Den-A | 3 | 4 | 22 | 5.5(10) | 0 | 3 | 35 | 11.7(16) | 0 | — | — | — | — | — | — | — | — | — | k | — | 0 | 54 |

MOORE, ALLEN Allen A., DE, 6′2″/218 lbs; Texas A&M; B3/12/1909 Burkburnett, TX, D9/1968 **1939**†GB◇5 (0)

MOORE, ALVIN Alvin, RB, 6′0″/194 lbs; Arizona State; 1983: Bal, rnd 7; B5/3/1959 Randolph, AZ

1983	Bal	15(0)	57	205	3.6(13)	1	6	38	6.3(16)	0	—	—	—	—	—	—	—	—	—	k	—	6	244
1984	Ind	13(2)	38	127	3.3(18)	2	9	52	5.8(12)	0	1	0	0.0	0	0.0	0	0	—	—	k	—	12	162
1985	Det	16(5, rb)	80	221	2.8(18)	4	19	154	8.1(14)	1	1	0	0.0	0	0.0	0	0	—	—	k	—	30	378
1986	Det	13(0)	19	73	3.8(18)	0	8	47	5.9(8)	0	—	—	—	—	—	—	—	—	—	—	—	0	97
1987	Sea	1(0)	3	15	5.0(13)	0	—	—	—	—	—	—	—	—	—	—	—	—	—	—	—	0	15
NFL	5	58(7)	197	641	3.3(18)	7	42	291	6.9(16)	1	2	0	0.0	0	0.0	0	0	—	—	k	—	48	896

MOORE, ARTHUR Arthur Clark, NT-DT, 6′5″/253 lbs; Tulsa; 1973: SF, rnd 6; B4/4/1951 Daingerfield, TX **1973** NE 13 **1974** NE 11 **1976** NE 4 **1977** NE 1 **NFL** 29 [4 yrs]

YEAR	TEAM	G(GS, POS)	RUSH	YD	AVG(LG)	TD	REC	YD	AVG(LG)	TD	PASS COMP	PCT	YD	AVG(LG)	TD	INT	SK	YD	QBR	KPR	OTD	PTS	TAY

MOORE, BILL William Julius, E-DE, 6'1"/195 lbs; North Carolina; B2/4/1912, D5/25/1973

| 1939 | Det | 9(0) | 1 | 7 | 7.0(7) | 0 | 6 | 82 | 13.7 | 1 | — | — | — | — | — | — | — | — | — | — | — | 6 | 53 |

MOORE, BLAKE Edward Blake, C-G-T, 6'5"/267 lbs; Wooster; B5/8/1958 Durham, NC **1980** Cin 16 (3) **1981**†Cin 14 (0) **1982** Cin 4 (0) **1983** Cin 16 (5, c)

1984	GB	11(4)	—	—	—	—	1	3	3.0(3)	1	—	—	—	—	—	—	—	—	—	—	—	6	7
1985	GB	16(0)	—	—	—	—	1	3	3.0(3)	1	—	—	—	—	—	—	—	—	—	—	—	6	7
NFL	6	77(13)	—	—	—	—	2	6	3.0(3)	2	—	—	—	—	—	—	—	—	—	—	—	12	13

MOORE, BOB Robert Rory, TE, 6'3"/220 lbs; Stanford; 1971: Oak, rnd 5; B2/12/1949 Baltimore, MD

1971	Oak	14(1)	—	—	—	—	2	26	13.0(14)	0	—	—	—	—	—	—	—	—	—	—	—	0	13
1972	Oak	14(3)	—	—	—	—	6	49	8.2(17)	1	—	—	—	—	—	—	—	—	—	—	—	6	30
1973	†Oak	14(14, TE)	—	—	—	—	34	375	11.0(33)	4	—	—	—	—	—	—	—	—	—	—	—	24	208
1974	†Oak	14(14, TE)	—	—	—	—	30	356	11.9(32)	2	—	—	—	—	—	—	—	—	—	—	—	12	188
1975	†Oak	14(14, TE)	—	—	—	—	19	175	9.2(21)	0	—	—	—	—	—	—	—	—	—	—	—	0	88
1976	TB	12(11, TE)	2	23	11.5(22)	0	23	281	12.2(31)	0	—	—	—	—	—	—	—	—	—	—	—	0	164
1977	TB	3	—	—	—	—	—	—	—	—	—	—	—	—	—	—	—	—	—	—	—	—
1978	†Den	8(2)	—	—	—	—	—	—	—	—	—	—	—	—	—	—	—	—	—	—	—	—
NFL	8	93(59)	2	23	11.5(22)	0	114	1262	11.1(33)	7	—	—	—	—	—	—	—	—	—	—	—	42	689

MOORE, BOBBY see Ahmad Rashad

MOORE, BOOKER Booker Thomas, RB, 5'11"/224 lbs; Penn State; 1981: Buf, rnd 1; B6/23/1959 Flint, MI

1982	Buf	5(0)	16	38	2.4(9)	0	1	8	8.0(8)	0	—	—	—	—	—	—	—	—	—	—	—	0	42
1983	Buf	15(11, FB)	60	275	4.6(21)	1	34	199	5.9(21)	1	—	—	—	—	—	—	—	—	—	—	—	6	380
1984	Buf	15(15, FB)	24	84	3.5(21)	0	33	172	5.2(14)	0	—	—	—	—	—	—	—	—	—	—	—	0	170
1985	Buf	16(6, fb)	15	23	1.5(4)	1	7	44	6.3(9)	0	—	—	—	—	—	—	—	—	—	k	—	6	41
NFL	4	51(32)	115	420	3.7(21)	1	75	423	5.6(21)	1	—	—	—	—	—	—	—	—	—	k	—	12	633

MOORE, BRANDON Brandon, G, 6'3"/295 lbs; Illinois; B6/3/1980 Gary, IN **2003** NYJ 3 (1) **2004**†NYJ 13 (13, RG) **2005** NYJ 16 (16, RG) **NFL** 32 (30) [3 yrs]

MOORE, BRANDON Brandon Christopher, T, 6'6"/290 lbs; Duke; B6/21/1970 Ardmore, PA **1993** NE 11 (0) **1994** NE 4 (0) **1995** NE 6 (0) **NFL** 21 (0) [3 yrs]

MOORE, BRANDON Brandon T., LB, 6'1"/242 lbs; Oklahoma; B1/16/1979 East Meadow, NY **2002**†SF 13 (2) **2003** SF 15 (1) **2004** SF 12 (1) **2005** SF 16 (10, LILB) **NFL** 56 (14) [4 yrs]

MOORE, BRENT Brent Allen, LB, 6'5"/242 lbs; USC; 1986: GB, rnd 9; B1/9/1963 Novato, CA **1987** GB 4 (0)

MOORE, BUCKY William E., DB-HB-WB, 5'11"/185 lbs; Loyola (LA); B1906, deceased

1932	ChiC	4(4)	21	42	2.0	1	2	8	4.0	0	—	—	—	—	—	—	—	—	—	—	—	6	56
1933	Pit	5(3)	16	42	2.6	0	—	—	—	—	—	—	—	—	—	—	—	—	—	—	—	0	42
NFL	2	9(7)	37	84	2.3	1	2	8	4.0	0	—	—	—	—	—	—	—	—	—	—	—	6	98

MOORE, CHARLIE Charles Dewell, G, 6'5"/237 lbs; Arkansas; B1/3/1940 Marianna, AR **1962** Was 14

MOORE, CLARENCE Clarence Kelly, WR, 6'5"/211 lbs; Northern Arizona; 2004: Bal, rnd 6; B9/24/1982 Bellflower, CA

2004	Bal	15(6, wr)	—	—	—	—	24	293	12.2(52)	4	—	—	—	—	—	—	—	—	—	—	—	26	167
2005	Bal	4(1)	—	—	—	—	3	59	19.7(24)	0	—	—	—	—	—	—	—	—	—	—	—	0	30
NFL	2	19(7)	—	—	—	—	27	352	13.0(52)	4	—	—	—	—	—	—	—	—	—	—	—	26	196

MOORE, CLIFF Clifford, WB-DB, 6'1"/202 lbs; Penn State **1934** Cin 1 (0)

MOORE, COREY Corey Antonio, LB, 5'11"/225 lbs; Virginia Tech; 2000: Buf, rnd 3; B3/20/1977 Brownsville, TN **2000** Buf 9 (4) **2001** Mia 1 (0) **NFL** 10 (4) [2 yrs]

MOORE, DAMON Damon, DB, 5'11"/215 lbs; Ohio State; 1999: Phi, rnd 4; B9/15/1976 Fostoria, OH **1999** Phi 16 (1) **2000**†Phi 16 (16, SS) **2001**†Phi 16 (16, SS) **2002** ChiB 6 (1) **NFL** 54 (34) [4 yrs]

MOORE, DANA Dana Earl, P, 5'11"/180 lbs; Mississippi State; B9/7/1961 Baton Rouge, LA **1987** NYG 2 (0)

MOORE, DARRYL Darryl Jerome, G, 6'2"/292 lbs; Texas-El Paso; 1992: Was, rnd 8; B1/27/1969 Minden, LA **1993** Was 2 (0)

MOORE, DAVE David Edward, TE, 6'2"/250 lbs; Pittsburgh; 1992: Mia, rnd 7; B11/11/1969 Morristown, NJ

1992	Mia	1(0)	—	—	—	—	—	—	—	—	—	—	—	—	—	—	—	—	—	—	—	—	—
1992	TB	4(2)	—	—	—	—	1	10	10.0(10)	0	—	—	—	—	—	—	—	—	—	—	—	0	5
1993	TB	15(1)	—	—	—	—	4	47	11.8(19)	1	1	0	0.0	0	0.0	0	0	—	—	—	—	—	6	29
1994	TB	15(5, te)	—	—	—	—	4	57	14.3(18)	0	—	—	—	—	—	—	—	—	—	k	—	0	26
1995	TB	16(8, TE)	1	4	4.0(4)	0	13	102	7.8(21)	0	—	—	—	—	—	—	—	—	—	—	—	0	55
1996	TB	16(8, te)	—	—	—	—	27	237	8.8(23)	3	—	—	—	—	—	—	—	—	—	—	—	18	134
1997	†TB	16(7, te)	—	—	—	—	19	217	11.4(28)	4	—	—	—	—	—	—	—	—	—	—	—	24	129
1998	TB	16(16, TE)	—	—	—	—	24	255	10.6(44)	4	—	—	—	—	—	—	—	—	—	—	—	24	148
1999	†TB	16(16, TE)	—	—	—	—	23	276	12.0(35)	5	—	—	—	—	—	—	—	—	—	—	—	30	163
2000	†TB	16(16, TE)	—	—	—	—	29	288	9.9(28)	3	—	—	—	—	—	—	—	—	—	—	—	18	159
2001	†TB	16(16, TE)	—	—	—	—	35	285	8.1(29)	4	—	—	—	—	—	—	—	—	—	—	—	24	163
2002	Buf	14(5, te)	—	—	—	—	16	141	8.8(19)	2	—	—	—	—	—	—	—	—	—	—	—	12	81
2003	Buf	15(6, te)	—	—	—	—	7	82	11.7(28)	2	—	—	—	—	—	—	—	—	—	—	—	12	51
2004	Buf	15(0)	—	—	—	—	3	17	5.7(10)	0	—	—	—	—	—	—	—	—	—	—	—	0	9
2005	†TB	16(1)	—	—	—	—	1	5	5.0(5)	0	—	—	—	—	—	—	—	—	—	—	—	0	3
NFL	14	207(107)	1	4	4.0(4)	0	206	2019	9.8(44)	28	1	0	0.0	0	0.0	0	0	—	—	—	k	—	168	1151

MOORE, DEAN Irvin Dean, LB, 6'2"/210 lbs; Iowa; 1978: SF, rnd 9; B1/26/1955 Birmingham, AL **1978** SF 16

MOORE, DENIS James Denis, DT-DE, 6'5"/255 lbs; USC; 1966: Det, rnd 14/KC, rnd R11; B7/18/1944 Berkeley, CA, D5/27/1995 Spokane, WA **1967** Det 5 **1968** Det 12 **1969** Det 14 **1970** Phi 2 **NFL** 33 [4 yrs]

MOORE, DERLAND Derland Paul, DT-NT-DE, 6'4"/250 lbs; Oklahoma; 1973: NO, rnd 2; B10/7/1951 Malden, MO **1973** NO 13 **1974** NO 14 (14, RDT) **1975** NO 14 (12, RDT) **1976** NO 14 (14, RDT) **1977** NO 10 (10, RDT) **1978** NO 15 (14, RDT) **1979** NO 15 (15, RDT) **1980** NO 16 (15, RDT) **1981** NO 16 (16, LDE) **1982** NO 9 (9, NT) **1983** NO 16 (16, NT) **1984** NO 16 (11, NT) **1985** NO 6 (0) **1986**†NYJ 1 (0) **NFL** 171 (146) [14 yrs]

MOORE, DERRICK Derrick, RB, 6'0"/229 lbs; Troy State; Northeastern State (OK); 1992: Atl, rnd 8; B10/13/1967 Albany, GA

1993	†Det	13(3)	88	405	4.6(48)	3	21	169	8.0(20)	1	—	—	—	—	—	—	—	—	—	k	—	24	578
1994	†Det	16(0)	27	52	1.9(12)	4	1	10	10.0(10)	0	—	—	—	—	—	—	—	—	—	k	—	24	60
1995	Car	13(10, RB)	195	740	3.8(53)	4	4	12	3.0(5)	0	—	—	—	—	—	—	—	—	—	—	—	24	786
NFL	3	42(13)	310	1197	3.9(53)	11	26	191	7.3(20)	1	—	—	—	—	—	—	—	—	—	k	—	72	1424

MOORE, DINTY Walter Stanley, WB-BB, 5'8"/160 lbs; Lafayette; B9/30/1903 New York, NY, deceased **1927** Pot 7 (3), 12

MOORE, EDDIE Eddie Deon, LB, 6'0"/230 lbs; Tennessee; 2003: Mia, rnd 2; B7/5/1980 South Pittsburgh, TN **2004** Mia 13 (3) **2005** Mia 5 (0) **NFL** 18 (3) [2 yrs]

MOORE, ERIC Eric Patrick, G-T, 6'5"/293 lbs; Indiana; 1988: NYG, rnd 1; B1/21/1965 Berkeley, MO **1988** NYG 11 (10, RG) **1989**†NYG 16 (13, RG) **1990**†NYG 15 (14, LT/rg) **1991** NYG 16 (16, RG) **1992** NYG 10 (10, RG) **1993**†NYG 7 (5, lt) **1994** Cin 6 (6, rg) **1995** Cle 1 (0) **1995**†Mia 2 (0) **NFL** 84 (74) [8 yrs]

MOORE, ERIC Eric, DB, 6'4"/255 lbs; Florida State; 2005: NYG, rnd 6; B2/28/1981 Pahokee, FL **2005** NYG 8 (0)

MOORE, FRED Frederick Wallace, DT-DE, 6'3"/255 lbs; Oklahoma; Memphis; 1962: SD, rnd 15/Bal, rnd 10; B12/18/1939 Sulligent, AL **1964**†SD-A 4 **1965**†SD-A 12 **1966** SD-A 13 **NFL** 29 [3 yrs]

MOORE, GENE Eugene Robert, C-LB, 6'3"/205 lbs; Colorado; 1938: Bkn, rnd 4; B12/16/1912 **1938** Bkn 7 (1)

MOORE, GENE Eugene Ralph, RB, 6'1"/208 lbs; Occidental; 1969: SF, rnd 4; B5/12/1947 San Diego, CA

| 1969 | SF | 5(1) | 2 | 4 | 2.0(2) | 0 | 2 | 28 | 14.0(24) | 0 | — | — | — | — | — | — | — | — | — | — | — | 0 | 18 |

MOORE, GREG Gregory Herring, LB, 6'1"/240 lbs; Tennessee-Chattanooga; B3/28/1965 Cartersville, GA **1987** NE 3 (3)

YEAR	TEAM	G (GS, POS)	RUSH	YD	AVG(LG)	TD	REC	YD	AVG(LG)	TD	PASS COMP	PCT	YD	AVG(LG)	TD	INT	SK	YD	QBR	KPR	OTD	PTS	TAY

MOORE, HENRY   Henry Dewell, DB-HB, 6´1˝/195 lbs; Arkansas; 1956: NYG, rnd 2; B4/3/1934 Little Rock, AR   **1957** Bal 11

| 1956 | †NYG | 5 | 2 | -2 | -1.0(0) | 0 | — | — | — | — | — | — | — | — | — | — | — | — | — | — | — | 0 | -2 |
| NFL | 2 | 16 | 2 | -2 | -1.0 | 0 | — | — | — | — | — | — | — | — | — | — | — | — | — | ki | — | 0 | -6 |

MOORE, HERMAN   Herman Joseph, WR, 6´4˝/210 lbs; Virginia; 1991: Det, rnd 1; B10/20/1969 Danville, VA

1991	†Det	13(1)	—	—	—	—	11	135	12.3(21)	0	—	—	—	—	—	—	—	—	—	—	—	0	68
1992	Det	12(11, WR)	—	—	—	—	51	966	**18.9(77)**	4	—	—	—	—	—	—	—	—	—	—	—	24	503
1993	†Det	15(15, WR)	—	—	—	—	61	935	15.3(93)	6	—	—	—	—	—	—	—	—	—	—	—	36	498
1994	†Det◇	16(16, WR)	—	—	—	—	72	1173	16.3(51)	11	—	—	—	—	—	—	—	—	—	—	—	66	642
1995	†Det★	16(16, WR)	—	—	—	—	**123**	1686	13.7(69)	14	—	—	—	—	—	—	—	—	—	—	—	84	913
1996	Det★	16(16, WR)	—	—	—	—	106	1296	12.2(50)	9	—	—	—	—	—	—	—	—	—	—	—	56	693
1997	†Det★	16(16, WR)	—	—	—	—	**104**	1293	12.4(79)	8	—	—	—	—	—	—	—	—	—	—	—	50	687
1998	Det	15(15, WR)	—	—	—	—	82	983	12.0(36)	5	—	—	—	—	—	—	—	—	—	—	—	30	517
1999	†Det	8(4)	—	—	—	—	16	197	12.3(26)	2	—	—	—	—	—	—	—	—	—	—	—	12	109
2000	Det	15(11, WR)	—	—	—	—	40	434	10.9(30)	3	—	—	—	—	—	—	—	—	—	—	—	18	232
2001	Det	3(1)	—	—	—	—	4	76	19.0(25)	0	—	—	—	—	—	—	—	—	—	—	—	0	38
2002	NYG	1(0)																					
NFL	12	146(122)	—	—	—	—	670	9174	13.7(93)	62	—	—	—	—	—	—	—	—	—	—	—	376	4897

MOORE, JASON   Jason Dwayne, DB, 5´10˝/191 lbs; San Diego State; B1/15/1976 San Bernardino, CA   **1999** Den 6 (0)   **2000** GB 3 (0)   **2000** SF 5 (0)   **2002** SF 9 (0)
NFL 23 (0) [3 yrs]

MOORE, JEFF   Jeffrey Dwayne, RB, 6´0˝/195 lbs; Jackson State; 1979: Sea, rnd 12; B8/20/1956 Kosciusko, MS

1979	Sea	16(1)	44	168	3.8(18)	2	14	128	9.1(24)	0	—	—	—	—	—	—	—	—	—	kp	—	12	468
1980	Sea	14(2)	60	202	3.4(20)	0	25	231	9.2(34)	0	—	—	—	—	—	—	—	—	—	k	—	0	314
1981	Sea	2(0)	1	15	15.0(15)	0	3	18	6.0(10)	0	—	—	—	—	—	—	—	—	—	—	—	0	24
1982	SF	9(4, RB)	85	281	3.3(19)	4	37	405	10.9(55)	4	—	—	—	—	—	—	—	—	—	k	—	48	544
1983	†SF	15(0)	15	43	2.9(14)	1	19	206	10.8(34)	0	—	—	—	—	—	—	—	—	—	k	—	6	168
1984	Was	7(0)	3	13	4.3(5)	0	17	115	6.8(18)	2	—	—	—	—	—	—	—	—	—	—	—	12	81
NFL	6	63(7)	208	722	3.5(20)	7	115	1103	9.6(55)	6	—	—	—	—	—	—	—	—	—	kp	—	78	1598

MOORE, JEFF   Jeffrey Bernard, WR, 6´1˝/194 lbs; Tennessee; 1979: LA, rnd 3; B3/2/1957 Memphis, TN

1980	†LARm	14(0)	—	—	—	—	10	168	16.8(37)	1	—	—	—	—	—	—	—	—	—	—	—	6	89
1981	LARm	10(0)	—	—	—	—	7	105	15.0(35)	0	—	—	—	—	—	—	—	—	—	—	—	0	53
NFL	2	24(0)	—	—	—	—	17	273	16.1(37)	1	—	—	—	—	—	—	—	—	—	—	—	6	142

MOORE, JERALD   Jerald Christopher, RB, 5´9˝/225 lbs; Oklahoma; 1996: SL, rnd 3; B11/20/1974 Houston, TX

1996	SL	11(4)	11	32	2.9(14)	0	3	13	4.3(7)	0	—	—	—	—	—	—	—	—	—	—	—	0	39
1997	SL	9(5, rb)	104	380	3.7(26)	3	8	69	8.6(19)	0	—	—	—	—	—	—	—	—	—	—	—	18	445
1998	SL	11(4)	55	137	2.5(18)	2	9	60	6.7(14)	0	—	—	—	—	—	—	—	—	—	—	—	12	187
2000	†NO	11(1)	37	156	4.2(40)	1	—	—	—	—	—	—	—	—	—	—	—	—	—	—	—	6	166
NFL	4	42(14)	207	705	3.4(40)	6	20	142	7.1(19)	0	—	—	—	—	—	—	—	—	—	—	—	36	836

MOORE, JERRY   Jerry Porter, DB, 6´3˝/208 lbs; Arkansas; 1971: Chi, rnd 4; B3/16/1949 Belleville, IL   **1971** ChiB 11 (FS)   **1972** ChiB 13 (FS)   **1973** NO 10 (ss)   **1974** NO 9
NFL 43 [4 yrs]

MOORE, JIMMY   Jimmy Lee, G, 6´5˝/268 lbs; Ohio State; 1979: Bal, rnd 6; B1/28/1957 Pittsburgh, PA   **1981** Bal 4 (1)

MOORE, JOE   Joseph Lee, RB, 6´1˝/205 lbs; Missouri; 1971: Chi, rnd 1; B6/29/1949 St. Louis, MO

1971	ChiB	9	29	90	3.1(12)	0	2	22	11.0(18)	0	—	—	—	—	—	—	—	—	—	—	—	0	101
1973	ChiB	14	58	191	3.3(25)	0	3	17	5.7(6)	0	—	—	—	—	—	—	—	—	—	p	—	0	195
NFL	2	23	87	281	3.2(25)	0	5	39	7.8(18)	0	—	—	—	—	—	—	—	—	—	p	—	0	296

MOORE, KELVIN   Kelvin, DB, 6´0˝/210 lbs; Iowa State; Morgan State; B3/7/1975 Los Angeles, CA   **1998** Cin 4 (0)

MOORE, KEN   Kenneth Charles, G, 6´0˝/212 lbs; West Virginia Wesleyan; B5/22/1917 Clarksburg, WV, D12/1/2003 Jupiter FL   **1940** NYG 8 (0)

MOORE, KEN   Kenneth Earl, TE, 6´4˝/232 lbs; Northern Illinois; 1977: Min, rnd 5; B7/25/1954 Merigold, MS   **1978** Atl 6

MOORE, LANGSTON   Langston, DT, 6´1˝/303 lbs; South Carolina; 2003: Cin, rnd 6; B7/17/1981 Charleston, SC   **2004** Cin 15 (8, RDT)   **2005** Arz 8 (1)   **NFL** 23 (9) [2 yrs]

MOORE, LARRY   Larry Maceo, C-G, 6´2˝/309 lbs; Brigham Young; B6/1/1975 San Diego, CA   **1998** Ind 6 (5, rg)   **1999**†Ind 16 (16, C)   **2000**†Ind 16 (16, RG)   **2001** Ind 16 (11, RG)
2002 Was 16 (16, C)   **2003** Was 9 (8, C)   **2004** Cin 13 (1)   **2005** Cin 4 (0)   **NFL** 96 (73) [8 yrs]

MOORE, LENNY   Leonard Edward 'Reading Comet', HB-FL, 6´1˝/191 lbs; Penn State; 1956: Bal, rnd 1; B11/25/1933 Reading, PA; HOF 1975

1956	Bal★	12(RH)	86	649	**7.5(79)**	8	11	102	9.3(27)	1	4	1	25.0	4	2.0(8)	1	1	—	—	—	kp	—	54	731
1957	Bal☆	12(RH)	98	488	5.0(55)	3	40	687	17.2(82)	7	2	0	0.0	0	0.0	0	0	—	—	—	p	1	66	989
1958	†Bal★	12(RH)	82	598	**7.3(73)**	7	50	938	18.8(77)	7	—	—	—	—	—	—	—	—	—	—	kp	—	84	1204
1959	†Bal★	12(RH)	92	422	4.6(31)	2	47	846	18.0(71)	6	3	2	66.7	25	8.3(13)	1	0	—	—	—	—	—	48	913
1960	Bal★	12(FL)	91	374	4.1(57)	4	45	936	20.8(80)	9	1	0	0.0	0	0.0	0	0	—	—	—	k	—	78	935
1961	Bal★	13(FL)	92	648	**7.0(54)**	7	49	728	14.9(72)	8	2	0	0.0	0	0.0	0	1	—	—	—	—	—	90	1082
1962	Bal◇	10(HB)	106	470	4.4(25)	2	18	215	11.9(80)	2	—	—	—	—	—	—	—	—	—	—	—	—	24	608
1963	Bal	7(hb)	27	136	5.0(25)	2	21	288	13.7(34)	2	—	—	—	—	—	—	—	—	—	—	p	—	24	307
1964	†Bal★	14(HB)	157	584	3.7(32)	**16**	21	472	22.5(74)	3	—	—	—	—	—	—	—	—	—	—	—	1	**120**	995
1965	†Bal	12(12, HB)	133	464	3.5(28)	5	27	414	15.3(52)	3	—	—	—	—	—	—	—	—	—	—	—	—	48	736
1966	Bal	13(HB)	63	209	3.3(18)	3	21	260	12.4(36)	1	—	—	—	—	—	—	—	—	—	—	k	—	18	552
1967	Bal	14	42	132	3.1(21)	4	13	153	11.8(37)	0	—	—	—	—	—	—	—	—	—	—	k	—	24	401
NFL	12	143(12)	1069	5174	4.8(79)	63	363	6039	16.6(82)	48	12	3	25.0	33	2.8(13)	2	2	—	—	—	kp	2	678	9451

MOORE, LEONARD   Leonard Calvin, RB, 6´0˝/222 lbs; Jackson State; B1/27/1963 Cartersville, GA

| 1987 | Min | 1(1) | 4 | 11 | 2.8(4) | 0 | 1 | 8 | 8.0(8) | 0 | — | — | — | — | — | — | — | — | — | — | — | 0 | 15 |

MOORE, LEROY   Leroy Franklin, DE, 6´2˝/240 lbs; Fort Valley State; B9/16/1935 Pontiac, MI   **1960** Buf-A 1   **1961** Bos-A 14   **1962** Bos-A 5   **1962** Buf-A 6 (LDE)   **1963** Buf-A 2
1964 Den-A 12 (rde)   **1965** Den-A 14 (rde)   **NFL** 54 [6 yrs]

MOORE, MACK   Mack Henry, DE, 6´4˝/258 lbs; Texas A&M; 1981: Mia, rnd 6; B3/4/1959 Monroe, LA   **1985**†Mia 16 (2)   **1986** Mia 7 (0)   **1986** SD 3 (0)   **NFL** 26 (2) [2 yrs]

MOORE, MALCOLM   Malcolm Grady, WR, 6´3˝/240 lbs; USC; 1984: Dal, rnd S2; B6/24/1961 Los Angeles, CA

| 1987 | LARm | 3(1) | — | — | — | — | 6 | 107 | 17.8(26) | 1 | — | — | — | — | — | — | — | — | — | — | — | 6 | 59 |

MOORE, MANFRED   Manfred, RB, 6´1˝/197 lbs; USC; 1974: SF, rnd 9; B12/20/1950 Martinez, CA [R]

1974	SF	14	10	24	2.4(8)	1	2	29	14.5(26)	0	—	—	—	—	—	—	—	—	—	kp	1	12	311
1975	SF	14	3	10	3.3(4)	0	1	11	11.0(11)	0	—	—	—	—	—	—	—	—	—	kp	—	0	356
1976	TB	10	7	4	0.6(7)	0	6	54	9.0(23)	0	—	—	—	—	—	—	—	—	—	kp	—	0	96
1976	†Oak	1																		kp	—	0	61
1977	†Min	12	—	—	—	—	—	—	—	—	—	—	—	—	—	—	—	—	—	kp	—	0	206
NFL	4	51	20	38	1.9(8)	1	9	94	10.4(26)	0	—	—	—	—	—	—	—	—	—	kp	1	12	1029

MOORE, MARK   Mark Quentin, DB, 6´0˝/194 lbs; Oklahoma State; 1987: Sea, rnd 4; B9/3/1964 Nacogdoches, TX   **1987**†Sea 5 (0)

MOORE, MARTY   Martin Neff, LB, 6´1˝/244 lbs; Kentucky; 1994: NE, rnd 7; B3/19/1971 Phoenix, AZ   **1994**†NE 16 (4)   **1995** NE 16 (3)   **1996**†NE 16 (0)   **1997**†NE 16 (0)
1998†NE 14 (2)   **1999** NE 15 (2)   **2000** Cle 16 (9, RLB)   **2001** NE 3 (0)   **NFL** 112 (20) [8 yrs]

MOORE, MAULTY   Maulty James, DT, 6´5˝/265 lbs; Bethune-Cookman; B8/12/1946 Milligan, FL   **1972**†Mia 14   **1973**†Mia 12   **1974**†Mia 14   **1975**†Cin 13   **1976** TB 5 (1)
NFL 58 (1) [5 yrs]

MOORE, McNEIL   Ernest McNeil, DB, 6´0˝/185 lbs; Rice; Sam Houston State; 1954: ChiB, rnd 18; B6/26/1933 Center, TX   **1954** ChiB 12 (DB)   **1956**†ChiB 11 (DB)
1957 ChiB 12 (DB)   **NFL** 35 [3 yrs]

YEAR	TEAM	G (GS, POS)	RUSH	YD	AVG (LG)	TD	REC	YD	AVG (LG)	TD	PASS COMP	PCT	YD	AVG (LG)	TD	INT	SK	YD	QBR	KPR	OTD	PTS	TAY

MOORE, MEWELDE Mewelde Jaem Cadere, RB, 6´1˝/210 lbs; Tulane; 2004: Min, rnd 4; B7/24/1982 Hammond, LA

2004	†Min	10(3)	65	379	5.8(33)	0	27	238	8.8(26)	0	1	0	0.0		0	0	—	—	—	kp	—	0	592
2005	Min	16(8, RB)	155	662	4.3(33)	1	37	339	9.2(29)	2	—	—	—	—	—	—	—	—	—	kp	1	24	1014
NFL	2	26(11)	220	1041	4.7(33)	1	64	577	9.0(29)	2	1	0	0.0		0	0	—	—	—	kp	1	24	1606

MOORE, MICHAEL Michael, G, 6´2˝/318 lbs; Alabama; Troy State; 2000: Was, rnd 4; B11/1/1976 Fayette, AL   **2000** Was 5 (1) **2003** Atl 2 (0) **2004** Atl 1 (1) **NFL** 8 (2) [3 yrs]

MOORE, NAT Nathaniel, WR-RB, 5´9˝/184 lbs; Florida; 1974: Mia, rnd 3; B9/19/1951 Tallahassee, FL

1974	†Mia	13(7, WR)	3	16	5.3(15)	0	37	605	16.4(48)	2	1	1	100.0	31	31.0(31)	0	0	—	—	—	kp	—	12	692
1975	Mia	14(14, WR)	8	69	8.6(36)	0	40	705	17.6(79)	4	—	—	—	—	—	—	—	—	—	kp	—	24	590
1976	Mia	9(9, WR)	4	36	9.0(21)	0	33	625	18.9(67)	4	—	—	—	—	—	—	—	—	—	kp	—	24	399
1977	Mia★	14(14, WR)	14	89	6.4(24)	1	52	765	14.7(73)	12	—	—	—	—	—	—	—	—	—		—	78	542
1978	†Mia	16(15, WR)	4	-3	-0.8(3)	0	48	645	13.4(47)	10	—	—	—	—	—	—	—	—	—	p	—	60	376
1979	†Mia☆	16(14, WR)	3	22	7.3(18)	0	48	840	17.5(53)	6	—	—	—	—	—	—	—	—	—	p	—	36	472
1980	Mia	16(16, WR)	1	3	3.0(3)	0	47	564	12.0(33)	7	1	0	0.0		0	0.0	0	0	—	—	—	42	320
1981	†Mia	13(11, WR)	1	3	3.0(3)	0	26	452	17.4(52)	2	—	—	—	—	—	—	—	—	—		—	12	239
1982	†Mia	9(0)	—	—	—	—	8	82	10.3(23)	1	—	—	—	—	—	—	—	—	—		—	6	46
1983	†Mia	16(15, WR)	—	—	—	—	39	558	14.3(66)	6	—	—	—	—	—	—	—	—	—		—	36	309
1984	†Mia	16(1)	1	3	3.0(3)	0	43	573	13.3(37)	6	—	—	—	—	—	—	—	—	—		—	36	320
1985	†Mia	15(7, wr)	1	11	11.0(11)	0	51	701	13.7(69)	7	—	—	—	—	—	—	—	—	—		—	42	397
1986	Mia	16(1)	—	—	—	—	38	431	11.3(38)	7	—	—	—	—	—	—	—	—	—	p	—	42	244
NFL	13	183(124)	40	249	6.2(36)	1	510	7546	14.8(79)	74	2	1	50.0	31	15.5(31)	0	0	—	—	—	kp	—	450	4943

MOORE, PAUL Paul Neely, BB-LB, 5´9˝/208 lbs; Presbyterian; B1/23/1918 Okeechobee, FL, D5/7/1975 Okeechobee, FL   **1941** Det 8 (0)

| 1940 | Det | 7(0) | 2 | 4 | 2.0 | 0 | 4 | 29 | 7.3(14) | 1 | — | — | — | — | — | — | — | — | — | | — | 6 | 24 |
| NFL | 2 | 15(0) | 2 | 4 | 2.0 | 0 | 4 | 29 | 7.3(14) | 1 | — | — | — | — | — | — | — | — | — | | — | 6 | 24 |

MOORE, RANDY Randall Kay, DT, 6´2˝/241 lbs; Arizona State; 1976: Den, rnd 12; B4/5/1954 Johnstown, PA   **1976** Den 8 (8, rdt)

MOORE, RASHAD Glenn Rashad, DT, 6´3˝/324 lbs; Tennessee; 2003: Sea, rnd 6; B3/16/1979 Huntsville, AL   **2003**†Sea 13 (6, rdt) **2004**†Sea 16 (12, RDT) **NFL** 29 (18) [2 yrs]

MOORE, RED William Roy, G, 5´11˝/248 lbs; Penn State; 1947: Pit, rnd 14/LAD-A, rnd 12; B12/14/1922 Pittsburgh, PA   **1947**†Pit☆12 (12, LG) **1948** Pit 12 (12, LG) **1949** Pit 12 (12, LG) **NFL** 36 (36) [3 yrs]

MOORE, REYNAUD Reynaud Eric, DB, 6´2˝/190 lbs; UCLA; B10/17/1949 Los Angeles, CA   **1971** NO 14

MOORE, RICH Richard Clifton, DT, 6´6˝/280 lbs; Villanova; 1969: GB, rnd 1; B4/26/1947 Cleveland, OH   **1969** GB 14 (LDT) **1970** GB 6 (ldt) **NFL** 20 [2 yrs]

MOORE, RICKY Ricky Delano, RB, 5´11˝/234 lbs; Alabama; 1985: SF, rnd 3; B4/7/1963 Huntsville, AL

1986	Buf	11(8, FB)	33	104	3.2(14)	1	23	184	8.0(27)	0	—	—	—	—	—	—	—	—	—		—	6	206
1987	Hou	3(3)	7	22	3.1(11)	0	3	21	7.0(10)	0	—	—	—	—	—	—	—	—	—		—	0	33
1988	Phx	8(0)	—	—	—	—	1	15	15.0(15)	0	—	—	—	—	—	—	—	—	—		—	0	8
NFL	3	22(11)	40	126	3.2(14)	1	27	220	8.1(27)	0	—	—	—	—	—	—	—	—	—		—	6	246

MOORE, ROB Robert Sean, WR, 6´3˝/203 lbs; Syracuse; 1990: NYJ, rnd S1; B9/27/1968 New York, NY

1990	NYJ	15(14, WR)	2	-4	-2.0(4)	0	44	692	15.7(69)	6	—	—	—	—	—	—	—	—	—		—	36	372
1991	†NYJ	16(16, WR)	—	—	—	—	70	987	14.1(53)	5	—	—	—	—	—	—	—	—	—		—	30	519
1992	NYJ	16(16, WR)	1	21	21.0(21)	0	50	726	14.5(48)	4	—	—	—	—	—	—	—	—	—		—	24	404
1993	NYJ	13(13, WR)	1	-6	-6.0(-6)	0	64	843	13.2(51)	1	—	—	—	—	—	—	—	—	—		—	6	421
1994	NYJ◇	16(16, WR)	1	-3	-3.0(-3)	0	78	1010	12.9(41)	6	—	—	—	—	—	—	—	—	—		—	40	532
1995	Arz	15(15, WR)	—	—	—	—	63	907	14.4(45)	5	2	1	50.0	33	16.5(33)	0	1	—	—	—		—	32	455
1996	Arz	16(16, WR)	—	—	—	—	58	1016	17.5(69)	4	—	—	—	—	—	—	—	—	—		—	26	528
1997	Arz★	16(16, WR)	—	—	—	—	97	1584	16.3(47)	8	—	—	—	—	—	—	—	—	—		—	50	832
1998	†Arz	16(16, WR)	—	—	—	—	67	982	14.7(57)	5	—	—	—	—	—	—	—	—	—		—	30	516
1999	Arz	14(10, WR)	—	—	—	—	37	621	16.8(71)	5	—	—	—	—	—	—	—	—	—		—	30	336
NFL	10	153(147)	5	8	1.6(21)	0	628	9368	14.9(71)	49	2	1	50.0	33	16.5(33)	0	1	—	—	—		—	304	4914

MOORE, ROBERT Robert Anthony, DB, 5´11˝/190 lbs; Northwestern State (LA); B8/15/1964 Shreveport, LA   **1986** Atl 16 (9, SS) **1987** Atl 12 (12, SS) **1988** Atl 16 (16, SS) **1989** Atl 16 (6, fs) **NFL** 60 (43) [4 yrs]

MOORE, ROCCO Rocco Ray, G-T, 6´5˝/276 lbs; Western Michigan; 1977: Phi, rnd 11; B3/31/1955 Charlotte, MI   **1980** ChiB 7 (0)

MOORE, RON Ronald Demon, DT, 6´2˝/316 lbs; Northwestern Oklahoma State; 2000: GB, rnd 7; B8/10/1977 Sanford, FL   **2001** Atl 1 (0)

MOORE, RONALD Ronald Lynn, RB, 5´10˝/220 lbs; Pittsburg State; 1993: Phx, rnd 4; B1/26/1970 Spencer, OK

1993	Phx	16(11, RB)	263	1018	3.9(20)	9	3	16	5.3(6)	0	—	—	—	—	—	—	—	—	—	k	—	54	1110
1994	Arz	16(16, RB)	232	780	3.4(24)	4	8	52	6.5(18)	1	1	0	0.0		0	0.0	0	0	—	k	—	32	851
1995	NYJ	15(3)	43	121	2.8(14)	0	8	50	6.3(13)	0	—	—	—	—	—	—	—	—	—	k	—	0	192
1996	NYJ	16(0)	1	1	1.0(1)	0	—	—	—	—	—	—	—	—	—	—	—	—	—	k	—	0	-1
1997	SL	7(2)	24	103	4.3(27)	1	4	34	8.5(13)	0	—	—	—	—	—	—	—	—	—	k	—	6	132
1997	Arz	6(2)	57	175	3.1(16)	0	—	—	—	—	—	—	—	—	—	—	—	—	—	k	—	0	175
1998	Mia	1(1)	4	12	3.0(4)	0	1	1	1.0(1)	0	—	—	—	—	—	—	—	—	—		—	0	13
NFL	6	77(35)	624	2210	3.5(27)	14	24	153	6.4(18)	1	1	0	0.0		0	0.0	0	0	—	k	—	92	2472

MOORE, SHAWN Shawn Levique, QB, 6´2˝/213 lbs; Virginia; 1991: Den, rnd 11; B4/4/1968 Martinsville, VA

| 1992 | Den | 3(0) | 8 | 39 | 4.9(11) | 0 | — | — | — | — | 34 | 17 | 50.0 | 232 | 6.8(40) | 0 | 3 | 6 | 50 | — | | — | 0 | 35 |

MOORE, STEVE Stephen Elliott, T, 6´4˝/293 lbs; Tennessee State; 1983: NE, rnd 3; B10/1/1960 Memphis, TN, D10/25/1989 Memphis, TN   **1983** NE 4 (0) **1984** NE 16 (0) **1985**†NE 16 (16, RT) **1986** NE 11 (11, RT) **1987** NE 5 (4) **NFL** 52 (31) [5 yrs]

MOORE, STEVON Stevon Nathaniel, DB, 5´11˝/210 lbs; Mississippi; 1989: NYJ, rnd 7; B2/9/1967 Wiggins, MS   **1990**†Mia 7 (0) **1992** Cle 13 (3) **1993** Cle 16 (16, SS) **1994**†Cle 16 (16, SS) **1995** Cle 16 (16, SS) **1996** Bal 16 (16, SS) **1997** Bal 13 (13, SS) **1998** Bal 16 (16, SS) **1999** Bal 8 (0) **NFL** 121 (96) [9 yrs]

MOORE, TOM Thomas Marshall, HB-FB, 6´2˝/215 lbs; Vanderbilt; 1960: GB, rnd 1/DalT, rnd 1; B7/17/1938 Goodlettsville, TN

1960	†GB	12	45	237	5.3(59)	4	5	40	8.0(12)	1	—	—	—	—	—	—	—	—	—	k	—	30	519
1961	†GB	13	61	302	5.0(69)	1	8	41	5.1(11)	1	2	2	100.0	42	21.0(22)	1	0	—	—	—	k	—	12	548
1962	†GB◇	14	112	377	3.4(32)	7	11	100	9.1(34)	0	5	2	40.0	70	14.0(45)	2	1	—	—	—	k	—	42	591
1963	GB☆	12(HB)	132	658	5.0(77)	6	23	237	10.3(45)	2	4	3	75.0	99	24.8(49)	1	0	1	6	—	—	—	48	901
1964	GB	14	102	371	3.6(35)	2	17	140	8.2(33)	2	3	1	33.3	28	9.3(28)	0	0	—	—	—	k	—	24	676
1965	†GB	13	51	124	2.4(13)	1	9	87	12.4(31)	1	2	1	100.0	22	11.0(13)	0	0	—	—	—	k	—	6	320
1966	LARm	14(14, HB)	104	272	2.6(18)	1	60	433	7.2(30)	3	1	1	100.0	20	20.0(20)	0	0	—	—	—	k	—	24	524
1967	Atl	10(FB)	53	104	2.0(18)	0	10	74	7.4(21)	0	2	1	50.0	51	51.0(75)	1	0	—	—	—	k	—	0	197
NFL	8	102(14)	660	2445	3.7(77)	21	141	1152	8.2(45)	10	19	13	68.4	383	20.2(75)	5	1	1	6	—	k	—	186	4275

MOORE, WAYNE Solomon Wayne, T, 6´6˝/265 lbs; Lamar; B8/17/1945 Beaumont, TX, D8/19/1989 Miami, FL   **1970**†Mia 14 **1971** Mia 1 **1972** Mia 9 **1973**†Mia◇13 (12, LT) **1974**†Mia 3 (3) **1975** Mia 14 (14, LT) **1976** Mia 14 (14, LT) **1977** Mia 14 (14, LT) **1978**†Mia 16 (9, LT) **NFL** 98 (66) [9 yrs]

MOORE, WILBUR Wilbur John, WB-HB-DB-FB, 5´11˝/187 lbs; Minnesota; 1939: Was, rnd 9; B4/22/1916 Austin, MN, D8/9/1965 Takoma Park, MD

1939	Was	10(3)	27	100	3.7	0	1	2	2.0(2)	0	—	—	—	—	—	—	—	—	—		—	0	101
1940	†Was	10(0)	15	89	5.9(23)	2	2	26	13.0(21)	1	—	—	—	—	—	—	—	—	—	i	—	18	122
1941	Was	6(5, WB)	10	48	4.8(42)	1	2	6	3.0(5)	0	—	—	—	—	—	—	—	—	—	k	—	6	67
1942	†Was◇	11(4)	10	25	2.5(18)	0	10	114	11.4(30)	2	—	—	—	—	—	—	—	—	—	kpi	—	12	107
1943	†Was☆	9(9, WB)	40	231	5.8(47)	2	30	537	17.9(72)	7	—	—	—	—	—	—	—	—	—	kpi	—	54	586
1944	Was	10(10, RH)	37	140	3.8(75)	2	33	424	12.8(59)	5	—	—	—	—	—	—	—	—	—	kpi	—	42	455
1945	Was	7(5, rh)	29	206	7.1(57)	1	13	115	8.8(32)	1	—	—	—	—	—	—	—	—	—	p	—	12	284
1946	Was	9(1)	15	62	4.1(19)	0	—	—	—	—	—	—	—	—	—	—	—	—	—	pi	—	0	94
NFL	8	72(37)	183	901	4.9(75)	8	91	1224	13.5(72)	16	—	—	—	—	—	—	—	—	—	kpi	—	144	1815

YEAR	TEAM	G (GS, POS)	RUSH	YD	AVG(LG)	TD	REC	YD	AVG(LG)	TD	PASS COMP	PCT	YD	AVG(LG)	TD	INT	SK	YD	QBR	KPR	OTD	PTS	TAY

MOORE, WILL Will Henry, WR, 6´1˝/184 lbs; Texas Southern; B2/21/1970 Dallas, TX

1995	NE	14(13, WR)	—	—	—	—	43	502	11.7(33)	1	—	—	—	—	—	—	—	—	—	—	—	6	256
1996	†NE	2(1)	—	—	—	—	3	37	12.3(16)	0	—	—	—	—	—	—	—	—	—	—	—	0	19
1997	Jax	11(0)	—	—	—	—	1	10	10.0(10)	0	—	—	—	—	—	—	—	—	—	k	—	0	26
1998	†Jax	16(0)	—	—	—	—	1	9	9.0(9)	0	—	—	—	—	—	—	—	—	—	—	—	0	15
NFL	4	43(14)	—	—	—	—	48	558	11.6(33)	1	—	—	—	—	—	—	—	—	—	—	—	6	315

MOORE, ZEKE Ezekiel, DB, 6´3˝/198 lbs; Lincoln (MO); 1967: Hou, rnd 5; B12/2/1943 Tuskegee, AL [I] **1967**†Hou-A 14 **1968** Hou-A 14 **1969**†Hou-A◊13 (RCB) **1970** Hou◊14 (RCB) **1971** Hou 13 (LCB) **1972** Hou 8 **1973** Hou 13 (LCB) **1974** Hou 14 (RCB) **1975** Hou 14 (RCB) **1976** Hou 14 (RCB) **1977** Hou 14 (RCB) **NFL** 145 [11 yrs]

MOOREHEAD, AARON Aaron Matthew, WR, 6´3˝/200 lbs; Illinois; B11/5/1980 Aurora, CO

2003	Ind	7(0)	—	—	—	—	7	101	14.4(35)	0	—	—	—	—	—	—	—	—	—	—	—	0	51
2004	Ind	7(0)	—	—	—	—	1	7	7.0(7)	0	—	—	—	—	—	—	—	—	—	p	—	0	33
2005	Ind	2(0)	—	—	—	—	7	75	10.7(24)	0	—	—	—	—	—	—	—	—	—	—	—	0	38
NFL	3	16(0)	—	—	—	—	15	183	12.2(35)	0	—	—	—	—	—	—	—	—	—	p	—	0	121

MOOREHEAD, EMERY Emery Matthew, TE-WR, 6´2˝/218 lbs; Colorado; 1977: NYG, rnd 6; B3/22/1954 Evanston, IL

1977	NYG	13(7, WR)	1	5	5.0(5)	0	12	143	11.9(20)	1	—	—	—	—	—	—	—	—	—	k	—	6	87
1978	NYG	10	—	—	—	—	3	45	15.0(25)	0	—	—	—	—	—	—	—	—	—	k	—	0	45
1979	NYG	13(4)	36	95	2.6(11)	0	9	62	6.9(19)	0	—	—	—	—	—	—	—	—	—	k	—	0	127
1980	Den	16(0)	2	7	3.5(4)	0	—	—	—	—	—	—	—	—	—	—	—	—	—	k	—	0	10
1981	ChiB	9(0)	—	—	—	—	—	—	—	—	—	—	—	—	—	—	—	—	—	k	—	0	131
1982	ChiB	9(9, TE)	2	3	1.5(6)	0	30	363	12.1(50)	5	—	—	—	7	—	—	—	—	—	—	—	30	210
1983	ChiB	16(15, TE)	5	6	1.2(5)	0	42	597	14.2(36)	3	—	—	—	—	—	—	—	—	—	—	—	18	320
1984	†ChiB	16(9, TE)	1	-2	-2.0(-2)	0	29	497	17.1(50)	1	—	—	—	—	—	—	—	—	—	—	—	6	252
1985	†ChiB	15(14, TE)	—	—	—	—	35	481	13.7(25)	1	—	—	—	—	—	—	—	—	—	—	—	6	246
1986	†ChiB	16(16, TE)	—	—	—	—	26	390	15.0(**85**)	1	—	—	—	—	—	—	—	—	—	—	—	6	200
1987	†ChiB	12(12, TE)	—	—	—	—	24	269	11.2(27)	1	—	—	—	—	—	—	—	—	—	—	—	6	140
1988	†ChiB	13(4)	—	—	—	—	14	133	9.5(28)	2	—	—	—	—	—	—	—	—	—	—	—	12	77
NFL	12	158(90)	47	114	2.4(11)	0	224	2980	13.3(85)	15	—	—	—	—	—	—	—	—	—	—	—	90	1841

MOOREHEAD, KINDAL Kindal Jerome, DT, 6´2˝/285 lbs; Alabama; 2003: Car, rnd 5; B10/14/1978 Memphis, TN **2003** Car 14 (0) **2004** Car 14 (12, RDT) **2005**†Car 15 (0) **NFL** 43 (12) [3 yrs]

MOORING, JOHN John Franklin, T-C, 6´6˝/255 lbs; Tampa; 1971: NYJ, rnd 2; B5/8/1947 Falfurrias, TX **1971** NYJ 14 **1972** NYJ 14 **1973** NYJ 14 **1974** NO 11 **NFL** 53 [4 yrs]

MOORMAN, BRIAN Brian Donald, P, 6´0˝/175 lbs; Pittsburg State; B2/5/1976 Wichita, KS [P]

2001	Buf	16(0)	1	0	0.0(0)	0	—	—	—	—	1	0	0.0	0	0.0	0	0	—	—	—	P	—	0	0
2002	Buf	16(0)	1	-6	-6.0(-6)	0	—	—	—	—	—	—	—	—	—	—	—	—	—	—	P	—	0	-6
2003	Buf	16(0)	1	21	21.0(21)	0	—	—	—	—	—	—	—	—	—	—	—	—	—	—	P	—	0	21
2004	Buf	16(0)	2	23	11.5(34)	0	—	—	—	—	3	1	33.3	24	8.0(24)	0	0	—	—	—	P	—	0	35
2005	Buf★	16(0)	—	—	—	—	—	—	—	—	—	—	—	—	—	—	—	—	—	—	P	—	0	0
NFL	5	80(0)	5	38	7.6(34)	0	—	—	—	—	4	1	25.0	24	6.0(24)	0	0	—	—	—	P	—	0	50

MOORMAN, MO Maurice F., G, 6´5˝/252 lbs; Kentucky; Texas A&M; 1968: KC, rnd 1; B7/24/1944 Louisville, KY **1968**†KC-A 13 (13, RG) **1969**†KC-A☆11 (RG) **1970** KC 13 (RG) **1971**†KC 9 (RG) **1972** KC 13 (RG)

| 1973 | KC | 13(6) | — | — | — | — | 1 | -1 | -1.0(-1) | 0 | — | — | — | — | — | — | — | — | — | — | — | 0 | -1 |
| NFL | 6 | 72(13) | — | — | — | — | 1 | -1 | -1.0(-1) | 0 | — | — | — | — | — | — | — | — | — | — | — | 0 | -1 |

MOOTY, JIM James W., DB, 5´11˝/177 lbs; Arkansas; 1960: NYT, rnd 1; B6/15/1937 **1960** Dal 7

MORABITO, TIM Timothy Robert, DT-NT, 6´3˝/296 lbs; Boston College; B10/12/1973 Garnerville, NY **1996** Cin 7 (1) **1997** Car 8 (0) **1998** Car 8 (8, NT) **1999** Car 16 (16, LDT) **2000** Car 16 (13, LDT) **NFL** 55 (38) [5 yrs]

MORALES, GONZALO Gonzalo, HB, 6´0˝/185 lbs; St. Mary's (CA); 1945: Phi, rnd 7; B6/10/1922 San Francisco, CA, D4/2/2002 San Francisco, CA

1947	Pit	8(1)	29	96	3.3(18)	0	—	—	—	—	27	8	29.6	78	2.9(23)	1	4	—	—	—	kpi	—	0	76
1948	Pit	10(3)	13	29	2.2(8)	0	—	—	—	—	4	3	75.0	30	7.5(14)	0	0	—	—	—	kpi	1	6	116
NFL	2	18(4)	42	125	3.0(18)	0	—	—	—	—	31	11	35.5	108	3.5(23)	1	4	—	—	—	kpi	1	6	192

MORAN, ERIC Eric Michael, T-G, 6´5˝/285 lbs; Washington; 1983: Dal, rnd 10; B6/10/1960 Spokane, WA **1984** Hou 8 (1) **1985** Hou 15 (3) **1986** Hou 14 (4) **NFL** 37 (8) [3 yrs]

MORAN, FRANK Frank C., C-T, 6´4˝/285 lbs; none; B3/18/1987, D12/14/1967 Hollywood, CA **1920** Ham 2 (2, C) **1920** Akr 1 (0) **NFL** 3 (2) [1 yr]

MORAN, HAP Francis Dale, B, 6´1˝/190 lbs; Carnegie Mellon; Grinnell; B7/31/1901 Belleplaine, IA, D12/30/1994 New Milford, CT [K] **1926** Fra 14 (7, TB), 33 **1927** Fra 6 (5, tb), 21 **1927** ChiC 4 (3), 6 **1928** Pot 10 (7, tb) **1928** NYG 1 (1) **1929** NYG 14 (1), 30 **1930** NYG 16 (3), 27 **1931** NYG☆14 (10, WB), 35

1932	NYG	11(5, fb)	82	262	3.2	1	6	47	7.8	0	20	12	60.0	91	4.6	0	0	—	—	—	K	—	8	341
1933	NYG	9(2)	4	8	2.0	0	3	114	38.0	1	1	0	0.0	0	0.0	0	0	—	—	—	—	—	6	70
NFL	8	99(44)	86	270	3.1	13	9	161	17.9	9	21	12	57.1	91	4.3	7	0	—	—	—	K	—	166	606

MORAN, JIM James Patrick, G, 6´1˝/207 lbs; Holy Cross; B9/27/1912 South Boston, MA, D8/18/1983 Natick, MA **1935** Bos 11 (0) **1936** Bos 5 (2) **NFL** 16 (2) [2 yrs]

MORAN, JIM James Henry, DT, 6´5˝/275 lbs; Idaho; 1964: NYG, rnd 10; B5/4/1942 Spokane, WA, D6/9/1999 Pleasanton, CA **1964** NYG 8 **1966** NYG 10 **1967** NYG 10 (LDT) **NFL** 28 [3 yrs]

MORAN, RICH Richard James, G-C, 6´3˝/276 lbs; San Diego State; 1985: GB, rnd 3; B3/19/1962 Boise, ID **1985** GB 16 (9, LG) **1986** GB 5 (1) **1987** GB 12 (12, LG) **1988** GB 16 (16, LG) **1989** GB☆16 (16, LG) **1990** GB 16 (1) **1991** GB 16 (16, LG) **1992** GB 8 (8, lg) **1993** GB 3 (3) **NFL** 108 (82) [9 yrs]

MORAN, SEAN Sean Farrell, LB-DE, 6´4˝/275 lbs; Colorado State; 1996: Buf, rnd 4; B6/5/1973 Denver, CO **1996**†Buf 16 (0) **1997** Buf 16 (7, lilb) **1998**†Buf 9 (2) **1999** Buf 16 (0) **2000**†SL 15 (3) **2001**†SL 16 (1) **2002**†SF 16 (0) **2003** SF 16 (0) **NFL** 120 (13) [8 yrs]

MORAN, TOM Thomas McGee, BB, 5´8˝/175 lbs; Centre; B1898, deceased **1925** NYG 1 (0)

MORANT, JOHNNIE Johnnie E., WR, 6-4˝/229 lbs; Syracuse; 2004: Oak, rnd 5; B12/7/1981 Newark, NJ **2005** Oak 1 (0)

| 2004 | Oak | 4(0) | — | — | — | — | 1 | 20 | 20.0(20) | 0 | — | — | — | — | — | — | — | — | — | — | — | 0 | 10 |
| NFL | 2 | 5(0) | — | — | — | — | 1 | 20 | 20.0(20) | 0 | — | — | — | — | — | — | — | — | — | — | — | 0 | 10 |

MOREAU, DOUG Douglas Paul, TE-K, 6´1˝/215 lbs; LSU; 1966: Mia, rnd 19; B2/15/1945 Thibodeaux, LA [K]

1966	Mia-A	3	—	—	—	—	2	15	7.5(9)	0	—	—	—	—	—	—	—	—	—	—	—	0	8
1967	Mia-A	14(14, TE)	1	-2	-2.0(-2)	0	34	410	12.1(43)	3	—	—	—	—	—	—	—	—	—	—	—	18	218
1968	Mia-A	11(10, TE)	—	—	—	—	27	365	13.5(28)	3	—	—	—	—	—	—	—	—	—	k	—	27	198
1969	Mia-A	5(5, te)	—	—	—	—	10	136	13.6(35)	0	—	—	—	—	—	—	—	—	—	—	—	0	68
NFL	4	33(29)	1	-2	-2.0(-2)	0	73	926	12.7(43)	6	—	—	—	—	—	—	—	—	—	k	—	45	491

MOREAU, FRANK Franklin H., RB, 6´0˝/223 lbs; Louisville; 2000: KC, rnd 4; B9/9/1976 Elizabeth, KY

2000	KC	11(0)	67	179	2.7(22)	4	—	—	—	—	—	—	—	—	—	—	—	—	—	—	—	24	219
2001	Jax	4(1)	8	27	3.4(14)	1	—	—	—	—	—	—	—	—	—	—	—	—	—	—	—	6	37
NFL	2	15(1)	75	206	2.7(22)	5	—	—	—	—	—	—	—	—	—	—	—	—	—	—	—	30	256

MOREINO, JOE Joseph P., NT-DE, 6´6˝/246 lbs; Idaho State; B4/4/1955 Providence, RI **1978** NYJ 1

MORELAND, EARTHWIND Earthwind C., DB, 5´11˝/185 lbs; Georgia Southern; B6/13/1977 Atlanta, GA **2000** NYJ 1 (0) **2001** Cle 2 (0) **2004** NE 9 (2) **NFL** 12 (2) [3 yrs]

MORELAND, JAKE Jake, FB-TE, 6´3˝/255 lbs; Western Michigan; B1/18/1977 Milwaukee, WI **2000** NYJ 7 (0)

| 2001 | Cle | 4(0) | — | — | — | — | 3 | 15 | 5.0(6) | 0 | — | — | — | — | — | — | — | — | — | k | — | 0 | 7 |
| NFL | 2 | 11(0) | — | — | — | — | 3 | 15 | 5.0(6) | 0 | — | — | — | — | — | — | — | — | — | — | — | 0 | 8 |

MORELLI, FRAN Francis Paul, T, 6´2˝/258 lbs; Colgate; B1/15/1939 Medford, MA **1962** NYT-A 12

MORELLI, JOHN John, G-T, 5´10˝/191 lbs; Georgetown (DC); 1945: Bos, rnd 28; B6/11/1923 Revere, MA, D1/26/2004 Greensboro, NC **1944** Bos 10 (3) **1945** Bos 9 (0) **NFL** 19 (3) [2 yrs]

YEAR	TEAM	G (GS, POS)	RUSH	YD	AVG (LG)	TD	REC	YD	AVG (LG)	TD	PASS COMP	PCT	YD	AVG (LG)	TD	INT	SK	YD	QBR	KPR	OTD	PTS	TAY

MORENCY, VERNAND   Vernand, RB, 5′9″/212 lbs; Oklahoma State; 2005: Hou, rnd 3; B2/4/1980 Miami, FL

| 2005 | Hou | 13 (1) | 46 | 184 | 4.0 (25) | 2 | 10 | 87 | 8.7 (16) | 0 | — | — | — | — | — | — | — | — | — | k | — | 12 | 385 |

MORENO, MOSES   Moses Nathaniel, QB, 6′1″/205 lbs; Colorado State; 1998: Chi, rnd 7; B9/5/1975 Chula Vista, CA

1998	ChiB	2 (1)	4	9	2.3 (9)	0	—	—	—	—	43	19	44.2	166	3.9 (21)	1	0	2	16	—	—	—	0	97
1999	SD	1 (0)	—	—	—	—	—	—	—	—	7	5	71.4	78	11.1 (45)	0	0	1	3	—	—	—	0	39
2000	SD	6 (2)	5	20	4.0 (13)	0	—	—	—	—	53	27	50.9	241	4.5 (26)	0	2	8	51	—	—	—	0	61
NFL	3	9 (3)	9	29	3.2 (13)	0	—	—	—	—	103	51	49.5	485	4.7 (45)	1	2	11	70	—	—	—	0	197

MORENO, ZEKE   Ezekiel Aaron, LB, 6′2″/246 lbs; USC; 2001: SD, rnd 5; B10/10/1978 Chula Vista, CA   **2001** SD 16 (0)   **2002** SD 16 (3)   **2003** SD 16 (13, MLB)   **2004** SD 9 (0)
2005 Phi 4 (0)   **NFL** 61 (16) [5 yrs]

MORESCO, TIM   Timothy John, DB, 5′11″/176 lbs; Syracuse; 1977: GB, rnd 6; B10/3/1954 Ithaca, NY   **1977** GB 14   **1978** NYJ 11   **1979** NYJ 16   **1980** NYJ 11 (2)
NFL 52 (2) [4 yrs]

MOREY, SEAN   Sean Joseph, WR, 5′11″/200 lbs; Brown; 1999: NE, rnd 7; B2/26/1976 Marshfield, MA   **1999** NE 2 (0)   **2001**†Phi 0 (0)   **2003**†Phi 16 (0)   **2005**†Pit 15 (0)

| 2004 | †Pit | 16 (0) | — | — | — | — | 1 | 8 | 8.0 (8) | 0 | — | — | — | — | — | — | — | — | — | — | — | 0 | 4 |
| NFL | 5 | 49 (0) | — | — | — | — | 1 | 8 | 8.0 (8) | 0 | — | — | — | — | — | — | — | — | — | k | — | 0 | -8 |

MORGADO, ARNOLD   Arnold Theodore, RB, 6′0″/210 lbs; Michigan State; Hawaii; B3/27/1952 Honolulu, HI

1977	KC	14	3	12	4.0 (9)	0	2	21	10.5 (12)	0	—	—	—	—	—	—	—	—	—	—	—	0	23
1978	KC	16 (FB)	160	593	3.7 (18)	7	7	47	6.7 (15)	0	—	—	—	—	—	—	—	—	—	k	—	42	712
1979	KC	11	75	231	3.1 (19)	4	5	55	11.0 (22)	0	—	—	—	—	—	—	—	—	—	k	—	24	284
1980	KC	11 (0)	47	120	2.6 (11)	4	5	27	5.4 (10)	1	—	—	—	—	—	—	—	—	—	k	—	30	182
NFL	4	52	285	956	3.4 (19)	15	19	150	7.9 (22)	1	—	—	—	—	—	—	—	—	—	k	—	96	1199

MORGAN, ANTHONY   Anthony Eugene, WR, 6′1″/200 lbs; Tennessee; 1991: Chi, rnd 5; B11/15/1967 Cleveland, OH

1991	ChiB	14 (2)	3	18	6.0 (13)	0	13	211	16.2 (84)	2	—	—	—	—	—	—	—	—	—	kp	—	12	151
1992	ChiB	12 (4)	3	68	22.7 (35)	0	14	323	23.1 (83)	2	—	—	—	—	—	—	—	—	—	kp	—	12	257
1993	ChiB	1 (0)	—	—	—	—	—	—	—	—	—	—	—	—	—	—	—	—	—	—	—	0	—
1993	GB	2 (0)	—	—	—	—	1	8	8.0 (8)	0	—	—	—	—	—	—	—	—	—	—	—	0	4
1994	†GB	16 (0)	—	—	—	—	28	397	14.2 (47)	4	—	—	—	—	—	—	—	—	—	—	—	24	219
1995	†GB	16 (8, wr)	—	—	—	—	31	344	11.1 (29)	4	—	—	—	—	—	—	—	—	—	k	—	24	193
1996	GB	3 (0)	—	—	—	—	—	—	—	—	—	—	—	—	—	—	—	—	—	—	—	0	—
NFL	6	64 (14)	6	86	14.3 (35)	0	87	1283	14.7 (84)	12	—	—	—	—	—	—	—	—	—	kp	—	72	823

MORGAN, BILL   Elmer William, T, 6′2″/232 lbs; Oregon; B5/8/1910 Portland, OR, D7/10/1985 Canby, OR   **1933** NYG 13 (5)   **1934**†NYG☆13 (6, lt)   **1935** NYG☆12 (10, LT)
1936 NYG 10 (8, LT)   **NFL** 48 (29) [4 yrs]

MORGAN, BOB   Robert Francis, DT, 6′0″/235 lbs; Maryland; 1953: LA, rnd 8; B6/28/1930 Freeport, PA, D10/10/1991 Westminster, CO   **1954** Was 10 (RDT)

MORGAN, BOBBY   Robert Bernard, DB, 6′0″/205 lbs; New Mexico; B8/7/1940 Warnego, KS   **1967** Pit 5

MORGAN, BOYD   Boyd F., B, 6′0″/198 lbs; USC; 1939: Was, rnd 18; B10/24/1915 Comanche, OK, D6/8/1988 Los Angeles, CA   **1940**†Was 6 (0)

| 1939 | Was | 5 (3) | 1 | 0 | 0.0 | 0 | 1 | 4 | 4.0 (4) | 0 | — | — | — | — | — | — | — | — | — | — | — | 0 | 2 |
| NFL | 2 | 11 (3) | 1 | 0 | 0.0 | 0 | 1 | 4 | 4.0 (4) | 0 | — | — | — | — | — | — | — | — | — | — | — | 0 | 2 |

MORGAN, DAN   Daniel Scott, G, 6′6″/285 lbs; Penn State; 1987: Den, rnd 8; B2/2/1964 Wheeling, WV   **1987** NYG 2 (2)

MORGAN, DAN   Daniel Thomas, LB, 6′2″/233 lbs; Miami (FL); 2001: Car, rnd 1; B12/19/1978 Coral Springs, FL   **2001** Car 11 (11, LLB)   **2002** Car 8 (8, MLB)
2003†Car 11 (11, MLB)   **2004** Car★12 (12, MLB)   **2005**†Car 13 (13, MLB)   **NFL** 55 (55) [5 yrs]

MORGAN, DENNIS   Dennis, RB, 5′11″/200 lbs; Western Illinois; 1974: Dal, rnd 10; B6/26/1952 White Plains, NY   **1974** Dal 13   **1975** Phi 4   **NFL** 17 [2 yrs]

MORGAN, DON   Don, DB, 5′11″/202 lbs; Nevada-Reno; B9/18/1975 Stockton, CA   **1999**†Min 2 (0)   **2000**†Min 2 (0)   **2001** Min 16 (2)   **2002** Arz 7 (0)   **NFL** 27 (2) [4 yrs]

MORGAN, DONOVAN   Donovan, WR, 6′2″/187 lbs; Louisiana-Lafayette; B7/29/1982 New Orleans, LA

| 2005 | Hou | 3 (0) | — | — | — | — | 4 | 42 | 10.5 (14) | 0 | — | — | — | — | — | — | — | — | — | p | — | 0 | 36 |

MORGAN, DWAYNE   Dwayne, T, 6′4″/300 lbs; Clemson; B5/3/1974 Griffin, GA   **2003** Atl 5 (0)

MORGAN, JOE   Joe Winfred, T, 6′1″/245 lbs; McNeese State; Southern Mississippi; 1949: LA, rnd 16; B10/23/1928 De Ridder, LA

| 1949 | †SF-A | 8 (0) | 0 | -1 | (-1) | 0 | — | — | — | — | — | — | — | — | — | — | — | — | — | — | — | 0 | -1 |

MORGAN, KARL   Michael Karl, NT, 6′1″/255 lbs; UCLA; B2/23/1961 Houma, LA   **1984** TB 13 (0)   **1985** TB 16 (0)   **1986** TB 12 (0)   **1986** Hou 1 (0)   **NFL** 42 (0) [3 yrs]

MORGAN, MATT   Matt, T, 6′6″/304 lbs; Pittsburgh; B12/3/1980 Pittsburgh, PA   **2005** SL 1 (0)

MORGAN, MELVIN   Melvin, DB, 6′0″/183 lbs; Mississippi Valley State; 1976: Cin, rnd 11; B3/31/1953 Gulfport, MS   **1976** Cin 14   **1977** Cin 12   **1978** Cin 15   **1979** SF 8 (5, fs)
1980 SF 6 (5, lcb)   **NFL** 55 (10) [5 yrs]

MORGAN, MIKE   Michael Lee, LB, 6′4″/242 lbs; LSU; 1964: Phi, rnd 17; B1/31/1942 Shreveport, LA, D12/2/1996 Baker, LA   **1964** Phi 14 (LLB)   **1965** Phi 14 (14, LLB)
1966 Phi 9 (9, LLB)   **1967** Phi 13 (LLB)   **1968** Was 14   **1969** NO 14 (LLB)   **1970** NO 9 (LLB)   **NFL** 87 (23) [7 yrs]

MORGAN, MIKE   Michael Lee, RB, 5′11″/207 lbs; Wisconsin; B1/19/1956 Tallassee, AL   **1978** ChiB 5

MORGAN, QUINCY   Quincy, WR, 6′1″/210 lbs; Kansas State; 2001: Cle, rnd 2; B9/23/1977 Garland, TX

2001	Cle	16 (10, WR)	2	27	13.5 (23)	0	30	432	14.4 (78)	2	—	—	—	—	—	—	—	—	—	k	—	12	323
2002	†Cle	16 (16, WR)	3	7	2.3 (11)	0	56	964	17.2 (78)	7	—	—	—	—	—	—	—	—	—	—	—	44	524
2003	Cle	16 (15, WR)	3	-4	-1.3 (2)	0	38	516	13.6 (71)	3	—	—	—	—	—	—	—	—	—	k	—	18	306
2004	Cle	6 (5, wr)	—	—	—	—	9	144	16.0 (46)	3	—	—	—	—	—	—	—	—	—	—	—	18	87
2004	Dal	9 (7, WR)	2	23	11.5 (24)	0	22	260	11.8 (53)	0	—	—	—	—	—	—	—	—	—	k	—	0	148
2005	†Pit	16 (0)	—	—	—	—	9	150	16.7 (31)	2	—	—	—	—	—	—	—	—	—	k	—	12	323
NFL	5	79 (53)	10	53	5.3 (24)	0	164	2466	15.0 (78)	17	—	—	—	—	—	—	—	—	—	k	—	104	1711

MORGAN, STANLEY   Stanley Douglas 'Stanley Steamer', WR, 5′11″/181 lbs; Tennessee; 1977: NE, rnd 1; B2/17/1955 Easley, SC **[R]**

1977	NE	14 (14, WR)	1	10	10.0 (10)	0	21	443	21.1 (64)	3	—	—	—	—	—	—	—	—	—	p	—	18	387
1978	†NE	16 (16, WR)	2	11	5.5 (6)	0	34	820	24.1 (75)	5	—	—	—	—	—	—	—	—	—	kp	—	30	623
1979	NE◇	16 (16, WR)	7	39	5.6 (17)	0	44	1002	22.8 (63)	12	—	—	—	—	—	—	—	—	—	kp	1	78	751
1980	NE★	16 (16, WR)	4	36	9.0 (16)	0	45	991	22.0 (71)	6	—	—	—	—	—	—	—	—	—	—	—	36	562
1981	NE	13 (13, WR)	2	21	10.5 (13)	0	44	1029	23.4 (76)	6	—	—	—	—	—	—	—	—	—	p	—	36	607
1982	†NE	9 (9, WR)	2	3	1.5 (3)	0	28	584	20.9 (75)	3	—	—	—	—	—	—	—	—	—	—	—	18	310
1983	NE	16 (16, WR)	1	13	13.0 (13)	0	58	863	14.9 (50)	2	—	—	—	—	—	—	—	—	—	—	—	12	455
1984	NE	13 (12, WR)	—	—	—	—	38	709	18.7 (76)	5	—	—	—	—	—	—	—	—	—	—	—	30	380
1985	†NE	15 (13, WR)	1	0	0.0 (0)	0	39	760	19.5 (50)	5	—	—	—	—	—	—	—	—	—	—	—	30	405
1986	†NE★	16 (16, WR)	—	—	—	—	84	1491	17.8 (44)	10	—	—	—	—	—	—	—	—	—	—	—	60	796
1987	NE◇	10 (9, WR)	—	—	—	—	40	672	16.8 (45)	3	—	—	—	—	—	—	—	—	—	—	—	18	351
1988	NE	16 (14, WR)	1	-6	-6.0 (-6)	0	31	502	16.2 (32)	4	—	—	—	—	—	—	—	—	—	—	—	24	265
1989	NE	10 (10, WR)	—	—	—	—	28	486	17.4 (55)	3	—	—	—	—	—	—	—	—	—	—	—	18	258
1990	Ind	16 (6, wr)	—	—	—	—	23	364	15.8 (42)	5	—	—	—	—	—	—	—	—	—	—	—	30	207
NFL	14	196 (180)	21	127	6.0 (17)	0	557	10716	19.2 (76)	72	—	—	—	—	—	—	—	—	—	kp	1	438	6354

MORIARTY, LARRY   Larry Scott, RB, 6′1″/240 lbs; Notre Dame; 1983: Hou, rnd 5; B4/24/1958 Santa Barbara, CA

1983	Hou	16 (7, FB)	65	321	4.9 (80)	3	4	32	8.0 (12)	0	—	—	—	—	—	—	—	—	—	k	—	18	362
1984	Hou	14 (9, RB)	189	785	4.2 (51)	6	31	206	6.6 (24)	1	1	1	100.0	16	16.0 (16)	0	0	—	—	—	—	—	42	961
1985	Hou	15 (12, FB)	106	381	3.6 (18)	3	17	112	6.6 (16)	0	—	—	—	—	—	—	—	—	—	—	—	18	467
1986	Hou	5 (4)	55	137	2.5 (9)	1	2	16	8.0 (17)	0	—	—	—	—	—	—	—	—	—	—	—	6	155
1986	†KC	10 (1)	35	115	3.3 (11)	0	7	51	7.3 (19)	0	—	—	—	—	—	—	—	—	—	k	—	0	161
1987	KC	12 (4)	30	107	3.6 (11)	0	10	37	3.7 (8)	1	—	—	—	—	—	—	—	—	—	k	—	6	143

YEAR	TEAM	G (GS, POS)	RUSH	YD	AVG (LG)	TD	REC	YD	AVG (LG)	TD	PASS	COMP	PCT	YD	AVG (LG)	TD	INT	SK	YD	QBR	KPR	OTD	PTS	TAY
1988	KC	9 (3)	20	62	3.1 (9)	0	6	40	6.7 (12)	0	—	—	—	—	—	—	—	—	—	—	—	—	0	82
NFL	6	81 (40)	500	1908	3.8 (80)	13	77	494	6.4 (24)	2	1	1	100.0	16	16.0 (16)	0	0	—	—	—	k	—	90	2330

MORIARTY, PAT Patrick John, RB, 6´0˝/195 lbs; Georgia Tech; B5/19/1955 Cleveland, OH

YEAR	TEAM	G (GS, POS)	RUSH	YD	AVG (LG)	TD	REC	YD	AVG (LG)	TD	PASS	COMP	PCT	YD	AVG (LG)	TD	INT	SK	YD	QBR	KPR	OTD	PTS	TAY
1979	Cle	16	14	11	0.8 (8)	2	1	17	17.0 (17)	0	—	—	—	—	—	—	—	—	—	—	k	—	12	25

MORIARTY, TOM Thomas E., DB, 6´0˝/185 lbs; Bowling Green State; B4/7/1953 Lima, OH **1977** Atl 14 **1978**†Atl 14 **1979** Atl 16 **1980** Pit 4 (0) **1981** Atl 9 (0) **NFL** 57 [5 yrs]

MORIN, MILT Milton Denis, TE, 6´4˝/238 lbs; Massachusetts; 1966: Cle, rnd 1/SD, rnd 3; B10/15/1942 Leominster, MA

YEAR	TEAM	G (GS, POS)	RUSH	YD	AVG (LG)	TD	REC	YD	AVG (LG)	TD	PASS	COMP	PCT	YD	AVG (LG)	TD	INT	SK	YD	QBR	KPR	OTD	PTS	TAY
1966	Cle	11 (TE)	—	—	—	—	23	333	14.5 (32)	3	—	—	—	—	—	—	—	—	—	—	—	—	18	182
1967	†Cle	6	—	—	—	—	7	90	12.9 (21)	0	—	—	—	—	—	—	—	—	—	—	—	—	0	45
1968	†Cle★	14 (TE)	1	8	8.0 (8)	0	43	792	18.4 (87)	5	—	—	—	—	—	—	—	—	—	—	—	—	30	429
1969	†Cle	14 (TE)	2	30	15.0 (22)	0	37	495	13.4 (35)	0	—	—	—	—	—	—	—	—	—	—	—	—	0	278
1970	Cle	14 (TE)	1	2	2.0 (2)	0	37	611	16.5 (36)	1	—	—	—	—	—	—	—	—	—	—	k	—	6	298
1971	†Cle★	14 (TE)	1	1	1.0 (1)	0	40	581	14.5 (31)	2	—	—	—	—	—	—	—	—	—	—	—	—	12	302
1972	†Cle	14 (TE)	—	—	—	—	30	540	18.0 (36)	1	—	—	—	—	—	—	—	—	—	—	—	—	6	275
1973	Cle☆	14 (TE)	—	—	—	—	26	417	16.0 (51)	1	—	—	—	—	—	—	—	—	—	—	—	—	6	214
1974	Cle	14 (TE)	—	—	—	—	27	330	12.2 (32)	3	—	—	—	—	—	—	—	—	—	—	—	—	18	180
1975	Cle	14	—	—	—	—	1	19	19.0 (19)	0	—	—	—	—	—	—	—	—	—	—	—	—	0	10
NFL	10	129	5	41	8.2 (22)	0	271	4208	15.5 (87)	16	—	—	—	—	—	—	—	—	—	—	k	—	96	2210

MORITZ, BRETT Brett, G, 6´5˝/250 lbs; Army; Nebraska; 1978: TB, rnd 2; B7/15/1955 Lincoln, NE **1978** TB 6

MORLEY, SAM Samuel Robertson, E, 6´2˝/182 lbs; Stanford; 1954: Was, rnd 20; B5/12/1932 Pasadena, CA **1954** Was 1

MORLEY, STEVE Steve, T, 6´7˝/330 lbs; St. Mary's (Canada); B8/18/1981 Halifax, NS **2005** NYJ 7 (0)

MORLOCK, JACK Jack, WB, 5´10˝/165 lbs; Marshall; 1940: Det, rnd 14; B4/7/1916 McKeesport, PA, D1/7/1976 Huntington, WV

YEAR	TEAM	G (GS, POS)	RUSH	YD	AVG (LG)	TD	REC	YD	AVG (LG)	TD	PASS	COMP	PCT	YD	AVG (LG)	TD	INT	SK	YD	QBR	KPR	OTD	PTS	TAY
1940	Det	4 (0)	1	0	0.0	0	—	—	—	—	—	—	—	—	—	—	—	—	—	—	—	—	0	0

MOROSKI, MIKE Michael Henry, QB, 6´4˝/200 lbs; California-Davis; 1979: Atl, rnd 6; B9/4/1957 Bakersfield, CA

YEAR	TEAM	G (GS, POS)	RUSH	YD	AVG (LG)	TD	REC	YD	AVG (LG)	TD	PASS	COMP	PCT	YD	AVG (LG)	TD	INT	SK	YD	QBR	KPR	OTD	PTS	TAY
1979	Atl	2	3	31	10.3 (19)	1	—	—	—	—	15	8	53.3	97	6.5 (23)	0	0	2	12	—	—	—	6	90
1980	Atl	3 (0)	—	—	—	—	—	—	—	—	3	2	66.7	24	8.0 (18)	0	0	—	—	—	—	—	0	12
1981	Atl	3 (0)	3	17	5.7 (14)	0	—	—	—	—	26	12	46.2	132	5.1 (22)	0	1	—	—	—	—	—	0	43
1982	†Atl	9 (0)	—	—	—	—	—	—	—	—	13	10	76.9	87	6.7 (15)	1	0	4	31	—	—	—	0	49
1983	Atl	16 (2)	2	12	6.0 (7)	0	—	—	—	—	70	45	64.3	575	8.2 (50)	2	4	4	41	—	—	—	0	150
1984	Atl	16 (5, qb)	21	98	4.7 (17)	0	—	—	—	—	191	102	53.4	1207	6.3 (48)	2	9	20	151	—	—	—	0	352
1985	Hou	5 (0)	2	2	1.0 (2)	0	—	—	—	—	34	20	58.8	249	7.3 (46)	1	1	4	25	—	—	—	0	92
1986	†SF	15 (2)	6	22	3.7 (12)	1	—	—	—	—	73	42	57.5	493	6.8 (52)	2	3	6	52	—	—	—	6	169
NFL	8	69 (9)	37	182	4.9 (19)	2	—	—	—	—	425	241	56.7	2864	6.7 (52)	8	18	40	312	—	—	—	12	954

MORRALL, EARL Earl Edwin, QB, 6´1˝/205 lbs; Michigan State; 1956: SF, rnd 1; B5/17/1934 Muskegon, MI

YEAR	TEAM	G (GS, POS)	RUSH	YD	AVG (LG)	TD	REC	YD	AVG (LG)	TD	PASS	COMP	PCT	YD	AVG (LG)	TD	INT	SK	YD	QBR	KPR	OTD	PTS	TAY
1956	SF	12	6	10	1.7 (8)	0	—	—	—	—	78	38	48.7	621	8.0 (37)	1	6	—	—	—	P	—	0	86
1957	Pit✧	12 (QB)	41	81	2.0 (35)	2	—	—	—	—	289	139	48.1	1900	6.6 (64)	11	12	—	—	64.9	—	—	12	626
1958	Pit	2	4	39	9.8 (22)	0	—	—	—	—	46	16	34.8	275	6.0 (66)	1	7	—	—	—	—	—	0	-99
1958	Det	9	7	41	5.9 (40)	0	—	—	—	—	32	9	28.1	188	5.9 (66)	4	2	—	—	—	P	—	0	75
1959	Det	12 (qb)	26	112	4.3 (22)	0	—	—	—	—	137	65	47.4	1102	8.0 (79)	5	6	—	—	—	P	—	0	448
1960	Det	12	10	37	3.7 (17)	1	—	—	—	—	49	32	65.3	423	8.6 (65)	4	3	—	—	94.2	—	—	6	159
1961	Det	13 (qb)	20	86	4.3 (25)	0	—	—	—	—	150	69	46.0	909	6.1 (61)	7	9	—	—	—	P	—	0	216
1962	Det	14	17	65	3.8 (29)	1	—	—	—	—	52	32	61.5	449	8.6 (53)	4	4	—	—	—	P	—	6	160
1963	Det	14 (QB)	26	105	4.0 (18)	1	—	—	—	—	328	174	53.0	2621	8.0 (75)	24	14	—	—	86.2	P	—	6	986
1964	Det	6	10	70	7.0 (25)	0	—	—	—	—	91	50	54.9	588	6.5 (48)	4	3	—	—	—	P	—	0	264
1965	NYG	14 (QB)	17	52	3.1 (14)	0	—	—	—	—	302	155	51.3	2446	8.1 (**89**)	22	12	27	214	86.3	—	—	0	905
1966	NYG	7 (QB)	5	12	2.4 (9)	0	—	—	—	—	151	71	47.0	1105	7.3 (98)	7	12	18	152	54.1	—	—	0	120
1967	NYG	8	4	11	2.8 (10)	1	—	—	—	—	24	13	54.2	181	7.5 (27)	3	1	8	59	—	P	—	6	87
1968	†Bal★	14 (QB)	11	18	1.6 (11)	1	—	—	—	—	317	182	57.4	2909	9.2 (84)	**26**	17	24	180	93.2	—	—	6	933
1969	Bal	9	—	—	—	—	—	—	—	—	99	46	46.5	755	7.6 (42)	5	7	7	63	—	—	—	0	123
1970	†Bal	14	2	6	3.0 (5)	0	—	—	—	—	93	51	54.8	792	8.5 (44)	9	4	14	131	—	—	—	0	287
1971	†Bal	14 (QB)	6	13	2.2 (16)	0	—	—	—	—	167	84	50.3	1210	7.2 (64)	7	12	11	89	58.2	—	—	0	173
1972	†Mia☆	14 (9, QB)	17	67	3.9 (31)	1	—	—	—	—	150	83	55.3	1360	**9.1** (**49**)	11	7	14	114	**91.0**	—	—	6	532
1973	†Mia	14	1	9	9.0 (9)	0	—	—	—	—	38	17	44.7	253	6.7 (53)	0	4	2	18	—	—	—	0	-25
1974	†Mia	14	1	11	11.0 (11)	0	—	—	—	—	27	17	63.0	301	11.1 (46)	2	3	3	16	—	—	—	0	52
1975	Mia	13 (4)	4	33	8.3 (16)	0	—	—	—	—	43	26	60.5	273	6.3 (31)	3	2	4	27	—	—	—	0	105
1976	Mia	14	—	—	—	—	—	—	—	—	26	10	38.5	148	5.7 (67)	1	1	3	29	—	—	—	0	39
NFL	21	255 (13)	235	878	3.7 (40)	8	—	—	—	—	2689	1379	51.3	20809	7.7 (98)	161	148	135	1092	74.1	P	—	48	6248

MORRELL, KYLE Kyle Dougals, DB, 6´1˝/190 lbs; Brigham Young; 1985: Min, rnd 4; B10/9/1963 Scottsdale, AZ **1986** Min 5 (1)

MORRIS, ARIC Aric Termain, DB, 5´10˝/210 lbs; Michigan State; 2000: Ten, rnd 5; B7/22/1977 Winston-Salem, NC **2000**†Ten 15 (0) **2001** Ten 16 (10, SS) **2002**†Ten 16 (0) **2003** NE 4 (0) **NFL** 51 (10) [4 yrs]

MORRIS, BAM Byron, RB, 6´0˝/244 lbs; Texas Tech; 1994: Pit, rnd 3; B1/13/1972 Cooper, TX

YEAR	TEAM	G (GS, POS)	RUSH	YD	AVG (LG)	TD	REC	YD	AVG (LG)	TD	PASS	COMP	PCT	YD	AVG (LG)	TD	INT	SK	YD	QBR	KPR	OTD	PTS	TAY
1994	†Pit	15 (6, rb)	198	836	4.2 (20)	7	22	204	9.3 (49)	0	—	—	—	—	—	—	—	—	—	—	k	—	42	1062
1995	†Pit	13 (4)	148	559	3.8 (30)	9	8	36	4.5 (13)	0	—	—	—	—	—	—	—	—	—	—	—	—	54	667
1996	Bal	11 (7, rb)	172	737	4.3 (19)	4	25	242	9.7 (52)	1	—	—	—	—	—	—	—	—	—	—	k	—	30	891
1997	Bal	11 (8, RB)	204	774	3.8 (25)	4	29	176	6.1 (15)	0	—	—	—	—	—	—	—	—	—	—	k	—	24	910
1998	ChiB	2 (0)	3	8	2.7 (6)	0	—	—	—	—	—	—	—	—	—	—	—	—	—	—	—	—	0	8
1998	KC	10 (5, rb)	129	481	3.7 (38)	8	12	95	7.9 (29)	0	—	—	—	—	—	—	—	—	—	—	—	—	48	609
1999	KC	12 (9, RB)	120	414	3.5 (24)	3	7	37	5.3 (9)	0	—	—	—	—	—	—	—	—	—	—	—	—	18	463
NFL	6	74 (39)	974	3809	3.9 (38)	35	103	790	7.7 (52)	1	—	—	—	—	—	—	—	—	—	—	k	—	216	4609

MORRIS, BOB Robert, G, 5´10˝/200 lbs; Cornell; B12/15/1903 Newark, NJ, D11/1985 North Miami Beach, FL **1926** Bkn 6 (5, LG)

MORRIS, BOB Robert William, HB, 5´11˝/180 lbs; USC; 1946: NYG, rnd 18; B3/9/1925 **1947** NYG 1 (0)

MORRIS, CHRIS Christopher Steven, T, 6´3˝/250 lbs; Indiana; 1971: Min, rnd 10; B10/7/1949 Indianapolis, IN **1972**†Cle 14 **1973** Cle 2 **1975** NO 6 **NFL** 22 [3 yrs]

MORRIS, DENNIT Dennit Elton, LB, 6´1˝/228 lbs; Oklahoma; 1958: SF, rnd 18; B4/15/1936 Hanna, OK **1958** SF 12 **1960**†Hou-A☆14 (MLB) **1961**†Hou-A✧14 (MLB) **NFL** 40 [3 yrs]

MORRIS, DONNIE JOE Donnie Joe, RB, 5´11˝/195 lbs; North Texas; B2/16/1950 Amarillo, TX **1974** KC 3

MORRIS, DWAINE Dwaine, NT-DT, 6´2˝/260 lbs; Louisiana-Lafayette; B8/24/1963 Independence, LA **1985** Phi 1 (0) **1987** Atl 3 (2) **NFL** 4 (2) [2 yrs]

MORRIS, FRANK Francis Michael, FB, 6´2˝/215 lbs; Boston University; B5/25/1918 Newton, MA, D10/16/1988 North Kensington, RI

YEAR	TEAM	G (GS, POS)	RUSH	YD	AVG (LG)	TD	REC	YD	AVG (LG)	TD	PASS	COMP	PCT	YD	AVG (LG)	TD	INT	SK	YD	QBR	KPR	OTD	PTS	TAY
1942	ChiB	6 (0)	3	7	2.3 (6)	0	3	24	8.0 (17)	0	—	—	—	—	—	—	—	—	—	—	—	—	0	19

MORRIS, GEORGE George William, HB, 5´11˝/189 lbs; Baldwin-Wallace; B2/24/1919 East Palestine, OH, D9/13/1999 Palm Beach Gardens, FL

YEAR	TEAM	G (GS, POS)	RUSH	YD	AVG (LG)	TD	REC	YD	AVG (LG)	TD	PASS	COMP	PCT	YD	AVG (LG)	TD	INT	SK	YD	QBR	KPR	OTD	PTS	TAY
1941	Cle	10 (3)	24	69	2.9 (20)	0	9	17	1.9 (6)	0	—	—	—	—	—	—	—	—	—	—	kp	—	0	84
1942	Cle	9 (1)	22	65	3.0 (28)	0	—	—	—	—	—	—	—	—	—	—	—	—	—	—	kpi	—	0	59
NFL	2	19 (4)	46	134	2.9 (28)	0	9	17	1.9 (6)	0	—	—	—	—	—	—	—	—	—	—	kpi	—	0	143

MORRIS, GEORGE George Augustus, C-LB, 6´2˝/220 lbs; Georgia Tech; 1953: SF, rnd 2; B3/19/1931 Vicksburg, MS **1956** SF 12

MORRIS, GLEN Glen Edgar, E, 6´0˝/200 lbs; Colorado State; B6/8/1912 St. Louis, MO, D1/31/1974 San Mateo, CA **1940** Det 4 (2)

MORRIS, JACK John Bradley, DB, 6´0˝/189 lbs; Oregon; 1956: LA, rnd 7; B11/1/1931 White City, KS **[K]** **1958** LARm 12 (DB) **1959** LARm 12 (DB) **1960** LARm 3 **1960** Pit 4 **1961** Min 14 (14, LCB) **NFL** 45 (14) [4 yrs]

MORRIS, JAMIE — James Walter, RB, 5′7″/188 lbs; Michigan; 1988: Was, rnd 4; B6/6/1965 Southern Pines, NC

YEAR	TEAM	G(GS, POS)	RUSH	YD	AVG(LG)	TD	REC	YD	AVG(LG)	TD	PASS	COMP	PCT	YD	AVG(LG)	TD	INT	SK	YD	QBR	KPR	OTD	PTS	TAY
1988	Was	16(4)	126	437	3.5(27)	2	1	3	3.0(3)	0	—	—	—	—	—	—	—	—	—	—	k	—	12	557
1989	Was	12(3)	124	336	2.7(12)	2	8	65	8.1(17)	0	—	—	—	—	—	—	—	—	—	—	—	—	12	389
1990	NE	5(0)	2	4	2.0(3)	0	—	—	—	—	—	—	—	—	—	—	—	—	—	—	k	—	0	41
NFL	3	33(7)	252	777	3.1(27)	4	9	68	7.6(17)	0	—	—	—	—	—	—	—	—	—	—	k	—	24	986

MORRIS, JIM BOB — James Robert, DB, 6′3″/211 lbs; Kansas State; B5/17/1961 Burbank, CA **1987** GB 11 (2)

MORRIS, JOE — Joseph Edward, RB, 5′7″/195 lbs; Syracuse; 1982: NYG, rnd 2; B9/15/1960 Fort Bragg, NC

YEAR	TEAM	G(GS, POS)	RUSH	YD	AVG(LG)	TD	REC	YD	AVG(LG)	TD	KPR	OTD	PTS	TAY
1982	NYG	5(0)	15	48	3.2(7)	1	8	34	4.3(13)	0	—	—	6	75
1983	NYG	15(0)	35	145	4.1(16)	0	2	1	0.5(6)	1	k	—	6	196
1984	†NYG	16(8, RB)	133	510	3.8(28)	4	12	124	10.3(26)	0	k	—	24	591
1985	NYG★	16(16, RB)	294	1336	4.5(65)	21	22	212	9.6(17)	0	k	—	126	1647
1986	†NYG★	15(15, RB)	341	1516	4.4(54)	14	21	233	11.1(23)	1	—	—	90	1778
1987	NYG	11(10, RB)	193	658	3.4(34)	3	11	114	10.4(25)	0	—	—	18	745
1988	NYG	16(15, RB)	307	1083	3.5(27)	5	22	166	7.5(24)	0	—	—	30	1216
1991	Cle	16(4)	93	289	3.1(15)	2	13	76	5.8(13)	0	k	—	12	387
NFL	8	110(68)	1411	5585	4.0(65)	50	111	960	8.6(26)	2	k	—	312	6634

MORRIS, JOHNNY — Johnny Edward, FL-HB, 5′10″/180 lbs; California-Santa Barbara; 1958: ChiB, rnd 12; B9/26/1935 Long Beach, CA [R]

YEAR	TEAM	G(GS, POS)	RUSH	YD	AVG(LG)	TD	REC	YD	AVG(LG)	TD	KPR	OTD	PTS	TAY
1958	ChiB	12(RH)	52	239	4.6(32)	2	11	170	15.5(51)	0	kp	—	12	529
1959	ChiB	12(LH)	87	312	3.6(33)	0	13	197	15.2(51)	2	kp	1	18	715
1960	ChiB◇	12(RH)	73	417	5.7(61)	3	20	224	11.2(66)	3	kp	—	36	683
1961	ChiB	14(FL)	8	49	6.1(21)	0	36	548	15.2(80)	4	kp	—	24	399
1962	ChiB	14(FL)	2	7	3.5(7)	0	58	889	15.3(73)	5	p	—	30	585
1963	†ChiB	13(FL)	1	10	10.0(10)	0	47	705	15.0(51)	2	p	—	12	457
1964	ChiB☆	14(FL)	—	—	—	—	93	1200	12.9(63)	10	—	—	60	650
1965	ChiB	14(FL)	—	—	—	—	53	846	16.0(80)	1	—	—	24	443
1966	ChiB	2					5	49	9.8(15)	0	—	—	0	25
1967	ChiB	14(FL)	1	6	6.0(6)	0	20	231	11.6(31)	1	p	—	6	131
NFL	10	121	224	1040	4.6(61)	5	356	5059	14.2(80)	31	kp	1	222	4615

MORRIS, JON — Jon Nicholson, C, 6′4″/254 lbs; Holy Cross; 1964: Bos, rnd 4/GB, rnd 2; B4/5/1942 Washington, DC **1964** Bos-A★14 (C) **1965** Bos-A★14 (C) **1966** Bos-A★14 (C) **1967** Bos-A★14 (C) **1968** Bos-A★14 (14, C) **1969** Bos-A★14 (14, C) **1970** Bos◇14 (14, C) **1971** NE 14 (13, C) **1972** NE 13 (13, C) **1973** NE 2 (1) **1974** NE 3 **1975** Det 14 (14, C) **1976** Det 14 (14, C) **1977** Det 14 (14, C) **1978** ChiB 10 **NFL** 182 (112) [15 yrs]

MORRIS, LARRY — Lawrence Cleo, LB-FB-HB, 6′2″/226 lbs; Georgia Tech; 1955: LA, rnd 1; B12/10/1933 Decatur, GA **1956** LARm 7 (RLB) **1957** LARm 6 **1959** ChiB 12 (LLB) **1960** ChiB 12 (RLB) **1961** ChiB 14 (RLB) **1962** ChiB 14 (RLB) **1963**†ChiB☆14 (RLB) **1964** ChiB 9 (RLB) **1965** ChiB 12 (RLB) **1966** Atl 12

YEAR	TEAM	G(GS, POS)	RUSH	YD	AVG(LG)	TD	KPR	OTD	PTS	TAY
1955	†LARm	12(rlb/fb)	40	148	3.7(22)	1	—	—	6	158
NFL	11	124	40	148	3.7(22)	1	kpi	1	12	153

MORRIS, LARRY — Calvin Larry, RB, 5′7″/207 lbs; Syracuse; B2/27/1962, NC

YEAR	TEAM	G(GS, POS)	RUSH	YD	AVG(LG)	TD	OTD	PTS	TAY
1987	GB	2(0)	8	18	2.3(10)	0	—	0	18

MORRIS, LEE — Lee A., WR, 5′11″/180 lbs; Oklahoma; B7/14/1964 Oklahoma City, OK

YEAR	TEAM	G(GS, POS)	RUSH	YD	AVG(LG)	TD	REC	YD	AVG(LG)	KPR	OTD	PTS	TAY
1987	GB	5(3)	2		1.0(4)	0	16	259	16.2(46)	kp	—	6	147

MORRIS, MAURICE — Maurice Autora, RB, 5′11″/202 lbs; Oregon; 2002: Sea, rnd 2; B12/1/1979 Chester, SC [R]

YEAR	TEAM	G(GS, POS)	RUSH	YD	AVG(LG)	TD	REC	YD	AVG(LG)	TD	KPR	OTD	PTS	TAY
2002	Sea	11(0)	32	153	4.8(24)	0	3	25	8.3(12)	1	k	1	6	487
2003	†Sea	16(1)	38	239	6.3(43)	0	4	32	8.0(13)	1	k	—	6	562
2004	Sea	15(0)	30	126	4.2(12)	0	9	53	5.9(12)	0	k	—	0	442
2005	†Sea	16(1)	71	288	4.1(49)	1	5	48	9.6(20)	0	k	—	6	328
NFL	4	58(2)	171	806	4.7(49)	1	21	158	7.5(20)	1	kp	1	18	1818

MORRIS, MAX — Glen Max, E-DE, 6′2″/200 lbs; Illinois; Northwestern; 1947: ChiB, rnd 26; B3/13/1925 Norris City, IL, D1/8/1998 Reno, NV

YEAR	TEAM	G(GS, POS)	RUSH	YD	AVG(LG)	TD	REC	YD	AVG(LG)	TD	KPR	OTD	PTS	TAY
1946	ChiR-A	11(1)	1	20	20.0(20)	0	3	66	22.0	0	—	—	0	53
1947	ChiR-A	14(8, LE)	—	—	—	—	22	239	10.9	1	k	1	12	123
1948	Bkn-A	13(7, le)	—	—	—	—	28	372	13.3	1	k	—	6	190
AAFC	3	38(16)	1	20	20.0(20)	0	53	677	12.8	2	k	1	18	366

MORRIS, MERCURY — Eugene E., RB, 5′10″/190 lbs; West Texas A&M; 1969: Mia, rnd 3; B1/5/1947 Pittsburgh, PA [R]

YEAR	TEAM	G(GS, POS)	RUSH	YD	AVG(LG)	TD	REC	YD	AVG(LG)	TD	KPR	OTD	PTS	TAY
1969	Mia-A	14	23	110	4.8(37)	1	6	65	10.8(29)	0	kp	1	12	701
1970	†Mia	12	60	409	6.8(40)	0	12	149	12.4(50)	0	kp	1	6	875
1971	†Mia◇	14	57	315	5.5(51)	1	5	16	3.2(11)	0	k	1	12	541
1972	†Mia◇	14(11, RB)	190	1000	5.3(33)	12	15	168	11.2(34)	0	k	—	72	1328
1973	†Mia★	13(11, RB)	149	954	6.4(70)	10	4	51	12.8(36)	0	k	—	60	1157
1974	Mia	5(3)	56	214	3.8(17)	1	2	27	13.5(24)	1	—	—	12	243
1975	Mia	14(14, RB)	219	875	4.0(49)	4	2	15	7.5(10)	0	—	—	24	923
1976	SD	13	50	256	5.1(30)	2	8	52	6.5(20)	0	—	—	12	302
NFL	8	99(39)	804	4133	5.1(70)	31	54	543	10.1(50)	1	k	3	210	6068

MORRIS, MIKE — Michael Stephen, C-G, 6′5″/276 lbs; Truman State; B2/22/1961 Centerville, IA **1987** SL 14 (0) **1989** KC 5 (0) **1989** NE 11 (0) **1990** Sea 4 (0) **1990** Cle 10 (0) **1991** Min 16 (0) **1992**†Min 16 (0) **1993**†Min 16 (0) **1994**†Min 16 (0) **1995** Min 16 (0) **1996**†Min 16 (0) **1997**†Min 16 (0) **1998**†Min 16 (0) **1999**†Min 16 (0) **NFL** 188 (0) [12 yrs]

MORRIS, RANDALL — Randall, RB, 6′0″/195 lbs; Tennessee; 1984: Sea, rnd 10; B4/22/1961 Anniston, AL [R]

YEAR	TEAM	G(GS, POS)	RUSH	YD	AVG(LG)	TD	REC	YD	AVG(LG)	TD	PASS	COMP	PCT	YD	AVG(LG)	TD	INT	SK	YD	QBR	KPR	OTD	PTS	TAY
1984	†Sea	10(2)	58	189	3.3(16)	0	9	61	6.8(18)	0	0	0	0.0	0		0		1	6	—	k	—	0	253
1985	Sea	16(0)	55	236	4.3(21)	0	6	14	2.3(6)	0	0	0	0.0	0		0	0			—	k	—	6	414
1986	Sea	16(0)	19	149	7.8(49)	1	—				1	0	0.0	0		0	0			—	k	—	6	279
1987	†Sea	10(0)	21	71	3.4(13)	0	—	—	—												k	—	0	85
1988	Sea	9(0)	3	6	2.0(5)	0	—	—	—												k	—	0	59
1988	Det	3(0)	—	—	—																k	—	0	11
NFL	5	64(2)	156	651	4.2(49)	1	15	75	5.0(18)	0	2	0	0.0	0		0		1	6	—	k	—	6	1101

MORRIS, RAYMOND — Raymond Willie, LB, 5′10″/222 lbs; Texas-El Paso; B6/8/1961 Crane, TX **1987** ChiB 3 (0)

MORRIS, RILEY — Riley D., LB-DE, 6′2″/230 lbs; Florida A&M; B3/22/1935 **1960** Oak-A 14 (RLB) **1961** Oak-A 14 (RLB) **1962** Oak-A 4 **NFL** 32 [3 yrs]

MORRIS, ROB — Robert Samuel, LB, 6′2″/243 lbs; Brigham Young; 2000: Ind, rnd 1; B1/18/1975 Nampa, ID **2000** Ind 7 (0) **2001** Ind 14 (14, MLB) **2002**†Ind 16 (16, MLB) **2003**†Ind 16 (16, MLB) **2004**†Ind 15 (14, MLB) **2005** Ind 14 (0) **NFL** 82 (60) [6 yrs]

MORRIS, RON — Ronald Wayne, WR, 6′1″/190 lbs; SMU; 1987: Chi, rnd 2; B11/4/1964 Cooper, TX

YEAR	TEAM	G(GS, POS)	RUSH	YD	AVG(LG)	TD	REC	YD	AVG(LG)	TD	OTD	PTS	TAY
1987	ChiB	12(12, WR)	—	—	—		20	379	19.0(42)	1	—	6	195
1988	†ChiB	16(1)	3	40	13.3(21)	0	28	498	17.8(63)	4	—	24	309
1989	ChiB	16(9, WR)	1	-14	-14.0(-14)	0	30	486	16.2(58)	0	—	6	234
1990	†ChiB	15(15, WR)	2	26	13.0(16)	0	31	437	14.1(67)	3	—	18	260
1991	ChiB	3(1)	—	—			8	147	18.4(33)	0	—	0	74
1992	ChiB	4(0)	—	—			4	44	11.0(26)	0	—	0	22
NFL	6	66(38)	6	52	8.7(21)	0	121	1991	16.5(67)	9	—	54	1093

MORRIS, SAMMY — Samuel, RB, 6′0″/220 lbs; Texas Tech; 2000: Buf, rnd 5; B3/23/1977 San Antonio, TX

YEAR	TEAM	G(GS, POS)	RUSH	YD	AVG(LG)	TD	REC	YD	AVG(LG)	TD	PASS	COMP	SK	YD	KPR	OTD	PTS	TAY
2000	Buf	7(2, RB)	93	341	3.7(32)	5	37	268	7.2(24)	1					k	—	36	532
2001	Buf	16(1)	20	72	3.6(10)	0	7	36	5.1(11)	0					—	—	0	90
2002	Buf	16(0)	2	5	2.5(5)	0	9	48	16.0(18)	0					—	—	0	14
2003	Buf	9(0)	19	70	3.7(12)	1	14	100	7.1(24)	0					—	—	6	186
2004	Mia	13(8, RB)	132	523	4.0(35)	6	22	144	5.6(24)	0	0	0	1	9	k	—	36	657

YEAR	TEAM	G (GS, POS)	RUSH	YD	AVG(LG)	TD	REC	YD	AVG(LG)	TD	PASS	COMP	PCT	YD	AVG(LG)	TD	INT	SK	YD	QBR	KPR	OTD	PTS	TAY
2005	Mia	16(2)	16	58	3.6(9)	1	8	54	6.8(18)	0	—	—	—	—	—	—	—	—	—	—	—	—	6	95
NFL	6	82(19)	282	1069	3.8(35)	13	91	630	6.9(24)	1	0	0	0.0	0	0.0	0	0	1	9	—	k	—	84	1574

MORRIS, SYLVESTER Sylvester, WR, 6´3˝/206 lbs; Jackson State; 2000: KC, rnd 1; B10/6/1977 New Orleans, LA

| 2000 | KC | 15(14, WR) | — | — | — | — | 48 | 678 | 14.1(47) | 3 | 1 | 1 | 100.0 | 31 | 31.0(31) | 0 | 0 | — | — | — | — | — | 18 | 370 |

MORRIS, TOM Thomas Lewis, DB, 5´11˝/175 lbs; Michigan State; 1982: TB, rnd 7; B4/2/1960 Anniston, AL **1982**†TB 8 (0) **1983** TB 12 (0) **NFL** 20 (0) [2 yrs]

MORRIS, VICTOR Victor Fitzgerald, LB, 6´1˝/243 lbs; Miami (FL); B1/25/1964 Boynton Beach, FL **1987** Mia 3 (3)

MORRIS, WAYNE Wayne Lee, RB, 6´0˝/207 lbs; SMU; 1976: SL, rnd 5; B5/3/1954 Dallas, TX

1976	SL	14(1)	64	292	4.6(27)	3	8	75	9.4(19)	1	—	—	—	—	—	—	—	—	—	—	k	—	24	411
1977	SL	12(7, FB)	165	661	4.0(35)	8	24	222	9.3(34)	1	—	—	—	—	—	—	—	—	—	—	k	—	54	866
1978	SL	13(13, RB)	174	631	3.6(27)	1	33	298	9.0(33)	1	—	—	—	—	—	—	—	—	—	—	k	—	12	816
1979	SL	15(15, FB)	106	387	3.7(16)	8	15	237	6.8(20)	1	—	—	—	—	—	—	—	—	—	—	—	—	54	591
1980	SL	16(16, FB)	117	456	3.9(24)	6	15	110	7.3(24)	1	—	—	—	—	—	—	—	—	—	—	—	—	42	576
1981	SL	16(13, FB)	109	417	3.8(14)	5	19	165	8.7(21)	0	—	—	—	—	—	—	—	—	—	—	—	—	30	550
1982	†SL	9(8, FB)	84	274	3.3(11)	4	3	8	2.7(11)	0	—	—	—	—	—	—	—	—	—	—	k	—	24	317
1983	SL	15(11, FB)	75	257	3.4(17)	2	14	55	3.9(11)	0	—	—	—	—	—	—	—	—	—	—	—	—	12	305
1984	SD	10(3)	5	12	2.4(5)	1	5	20	4.0(9)	0	—	—	—	—	—	—	—	—	—	—	—	—	6	32
NFL	9	120(87)	899	3387	3.8(35)	38	156	1190	7.6(34)	5	—	—	—	—	—	—	—	—	—	—	k	—	258	4462

MORRISON, DARRYL Darryl Lamon, DB, 5´11˝/196 lbs; Arizona; 1993: Was, rnd 6; B5/19/1971 Phoenix, AZ **1993** Was 4 (0) **1994** Was 16 (16, FS) **1995** Was 16 (0) **1996** Was 12 (12, SS) **NFL** 48 (28) [4 yrs]

MORRISON, DENNIS Dennis Charles, QB, 6´3˝/211 lbs; Kansas State; 1973: SF, rnd 14; B5/18/1951 Pico Rivera, CA

| 1974 | SF | 3 | 1 | 0 | 0.0(0) | 0 | — | — | — | — | 51 | 21 | 41.2 | 227 | 4.5(26) | 1 | 5 | — | — | — | — | — | 0 | -82 |

MORRISON, DOC Maynard Davis, C, 5´11˝/210 lbs; Michigan; B6/17/1909, D10/20/1993 Monrovia, CA **1933** Bkn 10 (10, C) **1934** Bkn 11 (11, C) **NFL** 21 (21) [2 yrs]

MORRISON, DON Don Alan, T-C, 6´5˝/255 lbs; Texas-Arlington; 1971: NO, rnd 4; B12/16/1949 Fort Worth, TX **1971** NO 14 (LT) **1972** NO 14 (LT) **1973** NO 14 (RT) **1974** NO 11 (RT) **1975** NO 13 (13, RT) **1976** NO 14 (14, RT) **1977** NO 14 (14, RT) **1978** Bal 14 **1979** Det 15 **NFL** 123 (41) [9 yrs]

MORRISON, FRED Fred Liew, FB-HB, 6´2˝/215 lbs; Ohio State; 1950: ChiB, rnd 1; B10/7/1926 Columbus, OH **[P]**

1950	†ChiB	12(FB)	66	252	3.8(25)	1	13	86	6.6(15)	0	—	—	—	—	—	—	—	—	—	—	Pk	—	6	416
1951	ChiB	12	29	96	3.3(26)	0	1	-3	-3.0(-3)	0	1	1	100.0	7	7.0(7)	0	0	—	—	—	Pk	—	0	256
1952	ChiB	12(FB)	95	367	3.9(57)	3	10	129	12.9(39)	0	—	—	—	—	—	—	—	—	—	—	Pk	—	24	448
1953	ChiB	12(FB)	95	307	3.2(17)	2	16	214	13.4(44)	0	—	—	—	—	—	—	—	—	—	—	Pk	—	12	417
1954	†Cle	12(fb)	54	234	4.3(26)	2	12	81	6.8(14)	0	—	—	—	—	—	—	—	—	—	—	k	—	12	288
1955	†Cle★	12(LH)	156	824	5.3(56)	3	9	185	20.6(49)	0	—	—	—	—	—	—	—	—	—	—	—	—	18	947
1956	Cle	12(lh)	83	340	4.1(41)	1	6	29	4.8(10)	1	—	—	—	—	—	—	—	—	—	—	Pk	—	12	372
NFL	7	84	578	2420	4.2(57)	12	67	721	10.8(49)	1	1	1	100.0	7	7.0(7)	0	0	—	—	—	Pk	—	84	3142

MORRISON, JOE Joseph R., HB-FL-FB, 6´1˝/210 lbs; Cincinnati; 1959: NYG, rnd 3; B8/21/1937 Lima, OH, D2/5/1989 Columbia, SC

1959	†NYG	12	62	165	2.7(14)	1	17	183	10.8(37)	1	2	1	50.0	14	7.0(14)	0	0	—	—	—	kp	—	12	375
1960	NYG	12(RH)	103	346	3.4(19)	2	29	367	12.7(51)	3	1	0	0.0	0	0.0	0	1	—	—	—	—	—	30	525
1961	NYG	13(RH)	33	48	1.5(14)	1	11	67	6.1(16)	1	—	—	—	—	—	—	—	—	—	—	kpi	—	12	110
1962	†NYG	14	35	146	4.2(14)	0	6	107	17.8(36)	2	—	—	—	—	—	—	—	—	—	—	kp	—	18	255
1963	†NYG	14(fb)	119	568	4.8(70)	3	31	284	9.2(57)	7	2	1	50.0	18	9.0(18)	0	0	—	—	—	k	—	60	799
1964	NYG	14	45	138	3.1(15)	1	40	505	12.6(70)	2	—	—	—	—	—	—	—	—	—	—	k	—	18	426
1965	NYG	13(FL)	3	20	6.7(11)	0	41	574	14.0(46)	4	—	—	—	—	—	—	—	—	—	—	—	—	30	337
1966	NYG	14(HB)	67	275	4.1(20)	2	46	724	15.7(49)	5	—	—	—	—	—	—	—	—	—	—	k	—	48	687
1967	NYG	13	36	161	4.5(11)	2	37	524	14.2(59)	7	1	1	100.0	12	12.0(12)	0	0	—	—	—	—	—	54	484
1968	NYG	14(FL)	9	28	3.1(11)	0	37	425	11.5(68)	6	—	—	—	—	—	—	—	—	—	—	—	—	36	271
1969	NYG	14(FB)	107	387	3.6(13)	4	44	647	14.7(65)	6	—	—	—	—	—	—	—	—	—	—	k	—	66	786
1970	NYG	10	11	25	2.3(7)	0	11	136	12.4(25)	0	—	—	—	—	—	—	—	—	—	—	—	—	0	93
1971	NYG	13	38	131	3.4(20)	1	40	411	10.3(45)	1	—	—	—	—	—	—	—	—	—	—	—	—	6	342
1972	NYG	14	9	36	4.0(45)	0	5	39	7.8(13)	0	—	—	—	—	—	—	—	—	—	—	—	—	0	56
NFL	14	184	677	2474	3.7(70)	18	354	4993	14.0(70)	47	6	3	50.0	44	7.3(18)	0	1	—	—	—	kpi	—	390	5542

MORRISON, KIRK Kirk, LB, 6´1˝/238 lbs; San Diego State; 2005: Oak, rnd 3; B2/19/1982 Oakland, CA **2005** Oak 16 (15, LLB)

MORRISON, PAT Patrick Anthony, DB, 6´2˝/194 lbs; Southern Connecticut State; B3/21/1965 London, England **1987** NYG 1 (1)

MORRISON, POP Stewart E., T, 6´3˝/205 lbs; none; B3/2/1892, D4/28/1980 Rochester, NY **1920** Roc 2 (0)

MORRISON, REECE Reece Earsal, RB, 6´0˝/207 lbs; Southwest Texas State; 1968: Cle, rnd 3; B10/21/1945 Tulsa, OK

1968	†Cle	14	18	39	2.2(11)	1	2	40	20.0(29)	1	—	—	—	—	—	—	—	—	—	—	k	—	12	99
1969	†Cle	14(hb)	59	300	5.1(54)	1	6	71	11.8(26)	0	1	1	100.0	16	16.0(16)	0	0	—	—	—	kp	—	6	368
1970	†Cle	14(rb)	73	175	2.4(18)	0	5	95	19.0(53)	1	—	—	—	—	—	—	—	—	—	—	kp	—	6	334
1971	†Cle	8	5	-2	-0.4(4)	0	—	—	—	—	—	—	—	—	—	—	—	—	—	—	k	—	0	130
1972	Cle	4	—	—	—	—	—	—	—	—	—	—	—	—	—	—	—	—	—	—	k	—	0	22
1972	Cin	6	1	2	2.0(2)	0	—	—	—	—	—	—	—	—	—	—	—	—	—	—	—	—	0	2
1973	Cin	3	3	11	3.7(8)	0	1	4	4.0(4)	0	—	—	—	—	—	—	—	—	—	—	—	—	0	13
NFL	6	63	159	525	3.3(54)	2	14	210	15.0(53)	2	1	1	100.0	16	16.0(16)	0	0	—	—	—	kp	—	24	967

MORRISON, RON Ronald Vern, DT, 6´4˝/250 lbs; New Mexico; 1960: Hou, rnd 2; B9/10/1938 Lansing, MI **1960** Hou-A 1

MORRISON, STEVE Steven Craig, LB, 6´3˝/246 lbs; Michigan; B12/28/1971 Birmingham, AL **1995** Ind 10 (0) **1996**†Ind 16 (8, RLB) **1997** Ind 16 (9, llb) **1998** Ind 16 (12, LLB) **NFL** 58 (29) [4 yrs]

MORRISON, TIM Timothy, DB, 6´1˝/195 lbs; North Carolina; B4/3/1963 Raeford, NC **1986**†Was 16 (5, rcb) **1987**†Was 7 (0) **NFL** 23 (5) [2 yrs]

MORRISS, GUY Guy Walker, C, 6´4˝/255 lbs; TCU; 1973: Phi, rnd 2; B5/13/1951 Colorado City, TX **1973** Phi 14 (9, C) **1974** Phi 14 (14, C) **1975** Phi 14 (12, C) **1976** Phi 14 (14, C) **1977** Phi 13 (13, C) **1978**†Phi 16 (16, C) **1979**†Phi 16 (16, C) **1980** Phi 16 (16, C) **1981**†Phi☆16 (16, C) **1982** Phi 9 (9, C) **1983** Phi 16 (16, C) **1984** NE 16 (5, c) **1985**†NE 16 (10, c) **1986**†NE 16 (0) **1987** NE 11 (7, C) **NFL** 217 (173) [15 yrs]

MORRISSEY, FRANK Francis J., G-T, 6´1˝/203 lbs; Boston College; B3/11/1899, D11/19/1968 Wynnewood, PA **[K]** **1921** Roc 5 (5, RG) **1922** Buf 10 (10, RT), 14 **1923** Buf☆12 (10, LG), 31 **1924** Buf 2 (2), 6 **1924** Mil 2 (1) **NFL** 31 (28), 51 [4 yrs]

MORRISSEY, JIM James Michael, LB, 6´3˝/223 lbs; Michigan State; 1985: Chi, rnd 11; B12/24/1962 Flint, MI **1985**†ChiB 15 (0) **1986**†ChiB 16 (0) **1987**†ChiB 10 (0) **1988**†ChiB 11 (11, RLB) **1989** ChiB 6 (4) **1990**†ChiB 16 (16, LLB) **1991**†ChiB 16 (11, LLB) **1992** ChiB 16 (14, LLB) **1993** ChiB 2 (0) **1993**†GB 6 (0) **NFL** 114 (56) [9 yrs]

MORROW, BOB Robert Edward, B, 6´0˝/222 lbs; Illinois Wesleyan; 1941: ChiB, rnd 12; B5/5/1918 Madison, WI, D7/9/2003 Stuart, FL

1941	ChiC	9(0)	37	128	3.5(15)	1	—	—	—	—	—	—	—	—	—	—	—	—	—	—	i	—	6	133
1942	ChiC	10(1)	45	145	3.2(16)	1	—	—	—	—	—	—	—	—	—	—	—	—	—	—	—	—	6	155
1943	ChiC	10(4)	38	129	3.4(9)	2	3	20	6.7(14)	0	—	—	—	—	—	—	—	—	—	—	ki	—	12	219
1945	NYG	1(0)	—	—	—	—	—	—	—	—	—	—	—	—	—	—	—	—	—	—	—	—	0	0
NFL	4	30(5)	120	402	3.3(16)	4	3	20	6.7(14)	0	—	—	—	—	—	—	—	—	—	—	ki	—	24	507
1946	†NYY-A	13(6, bb)	8	54	6.8	0	1	6	6.0(6)	0	—	—	—	—	—	—	—	—	—	—	—	—	0	57

MORROW, HAROLD Harold, FB, 5´11˝/232 lbs; Auburn; B2/24/1973 Maplesville, AL **1996** Min 8 (0) **1997**†Min 16 (0) **2002** Min 16 (0) **2003**†Bal 14 (0) **2004** Bal 15 (0) **2005** Arz 14 (0)

1998	†Min	11(0)	3	7	2.3(8)	0	—	—	—	—	—	—	—	—	—	—	—	—	—	—	—	—	0	7
1999	†Min	16(0)	2	1	0.5(5)	0	—	—	—	—	—	—	—	—	—	—	—	—	—	—	k	—	0	6
2000	†Min	16(0)	—	—	—	—	1	2	2.0(2)	0	—	—	—	—	—	—	—	—	—	—	k	—	0	3
2001	Min	16(2)	12	67	5.6(15)	0	13	142	10.9(28)	0	—	—	—	—	—	—	—	—	—	—	k	—	0	157
NFL	10	142(2)	17	75	4.4(15)	0	14	144	10.3(28)	0	—	—	—	—	—	—	—	—	—	—	k	—	0	224

Morrow, Jim James Thomas, B, 5′10″/170 lbs; Pittsburgh; B2/5/1895 Crafton, PA, D8/9/1975 Fort Lauderdale, FL **[K]** **1921** Can 5 (3), 7 **1922** Buf 1 (0) **NFL** 6 (3) [2 yrs]

Morrow, John John Melville, C-G, 6′3″/244 lbs; Michigan; 1956: LA, rnd 28; B4/27/1933 Port Huron, MI **1956** LARm 12 **1958** LARm 12 (C) **1959** LARm 11 (C) **1960** Cle 12 (C) **1961** Cle✧14 (C) **1962** Cle 14 (C) **1963** Cle✧14 (C) **1964**†Cle 14 (C) **1965**†Cle☆14 (C) **1966** Cle 8 (C) **NFL** 125 [10 yrs]

Morrow, Russ Russell Lee, C, 6′7″/210 lbs; Tennessee; 1945: Det, rnd 24; B9/7/1924 St. Louis, MO, D7/18/2004 Westwood, MA **1947** Bkn-A 1 (0)

YEAR	TEAM	G (GS, POS)	RUSH	YD	AVG (LG)	TD	REC	YD	AVG (LG)	TD	PASS	COMP	PCT	YD	AVG (LG)	TD	INT	SK	YD	QBR	KPR	OTD	PTS	TAY
1946	Bkn-A	9(2)	0	22	(22)	1	1	8	8.0(8)	1	—	—	—	—	—	—	—	—	—	—	—	—	12	41
AAFC	2	10(2)	0	22	(22)	1	1	8	8.0(8)	1	—	—	—	—	—	—	—	—	—	—	—	—	12	41

Morrow, Tommy Thomas Alvin, DB-P, 6′0″/187 lbs; Southern Mississippi; B6/3/1938 Georgiana, AL **[I]** **1962** Oak-A 14 (RS) **1963** Oak-A☆14 (RS) **1964** Oak-A 14 (RS) **NFL** 42 [3 yrs]

Morse, Bobby Robert J., RB, 5′10″/207 lbs; Michigan State; 1987: Phi, rnd 12; B10/3/1965 Muskegon, MI

YEAR	TEAM	G (GS, POS)	RUSH	YD	AVG (LG)	TD	REC	YD	AVG (LG)	TD	PASS	COMP	PCT	YD	AVG (LG)	TD	INT	SK	YD	QBR	KPR	OTD	PTS	TAY
1987	Phi	11(0)	6	14	2.3(7)	0	1	8	8.0(8)	0	—	—	—	—	—	—	—	—	—	—	kp	—	0	65
1989	NO	11(0)	2	43	21.5(39)	0	—	—	—	—	—	—	—	—	—	—	—	—	—	—	kp	1	6	160
1990	NO	10(0)	—	—	—	—	—	—	—	—	—	—	—	—	—	—	—	—	—	—	kp	—	0	51
1991	NO	6(0)	3	7	2.3(8)	0	—	—	—	—	—	—	—	—	—	—	—	—	—	—	kp	—	0	19
NFL	4	38(0)	11	64	5.8(39)	0	1	8	8.0(8)	0	—	—	—	—	—	—	—	—	—	—	kp	1	6	295

Morse, Butch Raymond Joseph, E, 6′2″/199 lbs; Oregon; B12/5/1910 Cleveland, OH, D5/22/1995 Corvallis, OR

YEAR	TEAM	G (GS, POS)	RUSH	YD	AVG (LG)	TD	REC	YD	AVG (LG)	TD	PASS	COMP	PCT	YD	AVG (LG)	TD	INT	SK	YD	QBR	KPR	OTD	PTS	TAY
1935	†Det	12(3)	—	—	—	—	6	63	10.5	0	—	—	—	—	—	—	—	—	—	—	—	—	0	32
1936	Det	12(3)	—	—	—	—	5	83	16.6	0	—	—	—	—	—	—	—	—	—	—	—	—	0	42
1937	Det	10(6, RE)	1	-3	-3.0(-3)	0	8	131	16.4(38)	1	—	—	—	—	—	—	—	—	—	—	—	—	6	68
1938	Det	8(4)	—	—	—	—	3	55	18.3	0	—	—	—	—	—	—	—	—	—	—	—	—	0	28
1940	Det	2(0)	—	—	—	—	1	13	13.0(13)	0	—	—	—	—	—	—	—	—	—	—	—	—	0	7
NFL	5	44(16)	1	-3	-3.0(-3)	0	23	345	15.0(38)	1	—	—	—	—	—	—	—	—	—	—	—	—	6	175

Morse, Red Wilbur, G, 5′10″/198 lbs; none; B1899, MN, deceased **1923** Dul 1 (1)

Morse, Steve Steven Bryan, RB, 5′11″/211 lbs; Virginia; B5/28/1963 Mobile, AL

YEAR	TEAM	G (GS, POS)	RUSH	YD	AVG (LG)	TD	REC	YD	AVG (LG)	TD	PASS	COMP	PCT	YD	AVG (LG)	TD	INT	SK	YD	QBR	KPR	OTD	PTS	TAY
1985	Pit	16(0)	8	17	2.1(9)	0	—	—	—	—	—	—	—	—	—	—	—	—	—	—	—	—	0	17

Mortell, Emmett Emmett Francis, B, 6′1″/181 lbs; Notre Dame; Wisconsin; B4/8/1916 Appleton, WI, D1/12/2000 Warminster, PA

YEAR	TEAM	G (GS, POS)	RUSH	YD	AVG (LG)	TD	REC	YD	AVG (LG)	TD	PASS	COMP	PCT	YD	AVG (LG)	TD	INT	SK	YD	QBR	KPR	OTD	PTS	TAY
1937	Phi	11(11, TB)	100	312	3.1	0	1	0	0.0	0	71	18	25.4	320	4.5	2	8	—	—	—	—	—	0	162
1938	Phi	11(7, TB)	110	296	2.7	0	—	—	—	—	57	12	21.1	201	3.5	6	7	—	—	—	—	—	0	147
1939	Phi	8(2)	37	88	2.4	0	—	—	—	—	41	12	29.3	134	3.3	1	0	—	—	—	P	—	0	160
NFL	3	30(20)	247	696	2.8	0	1	0	0.0	0	169	42	24.9	655	3.9	9	15	—	—	—	P	—	0	469

Morton, Chad Chad, RB, 5′8″/203 lbs; USC; 2000: NO, rnd 5; B4/4/1977 Torrance, CA **[R]** **2001**†NYJ 9 (0) **2004** Was 6 (0) **2005**†NYG 16 (0)

YEAR	TEAM	G (GS, POS)	RUSH	YD	AVG (LG)	TD	REC	YD	AVG (LG)	TD	PASS	COMP	PCT	YD	AVG (LG)	TD	INT	SK	YD	QBR	KPR	OTD	PTS	TAY
2000	†NO	16(3)	36	136	3.8(16)	0	30	213	7.1(35)	0	—	—	—	—	—	—	—	—	—	—	kp	—	0	740
2002	†NYJ☆	16(0)	4	8	2.0(6)	0	3	19	6.3(8)	0	—	—	—	—	—	—	—	—	—	—	kp	2	12	708
2003	Was	15(2)	48	216	4.5(27)	0	15	187	12.5(36)	1	—	—	—	—	—	—	—	—	—	—	kp	1	12	787
NFL	6	78(5)	88	360	4.1(27)	0	48	419	8.7(36)	1	—	—	—	—	—	—	—	—	—	—	kp	4	30	2909

Morton, Christian Christian, DB, 6′1″/180 lbs; Illinois; 2004: NE, rnd 7; B4/28/1981 St. Louis, MO **2004**†Atl 2 (0) **2005** Atl 4 (1) **2005** Was 1 (0) **NFL** 7 (1) [2 yrs]

Morton, Craig Larry Craig, QB, 6′4″/214 lbs; California; 1965: Dal, rnd 1/Oak, rnd 10; B2/5/1943 Flint, MI

YEAR	TEAM	G (GS, POS)	RUSH	YD	AVG (LG)	TD	REC	YD	AVG (LG)	TD	PASS	COMP	PCT	YD	AVG (LG)	TD	INT	SK	YD	QBR	KPR	OTD	PTS	TAY
1965	Dal	4(1)	3	-8	-2.7(5)	0	—	—	—	—	34	17	50.0	173	5.1(49)	2	4	10	68	—	—	—	0	-72
1966	Dal	6	7	50	7.1(12)	0	—	—	—	—	27	13	48.1	225	8.3(41)	3	1	1	8	—	—	—	0	138
1967	†Dal	9(3)	15	42	2.8(11)	0	—	—	—	—	137	69	50.4	978	7.1(64)	10	10	17	125	—	—	—	0	181
1968	†Dal	13(1)	4	28	7.0(12)	2	—	—	—	—	85	44	51.8	752	8.8(53)	4	6	4	39	—	—	—	12	204
1969	†Dal	13(13, QB)	16	62	3.9(15)	1	—	—	—	—	302	162	53.6	2619	8.7(67)	21	15	30	246	85.4	—	—	6	887
1970	†Dal	12(11, QB)	16	37	2.3(11)	0	—	—	—	—	207	102	49.3	1819	**8.8**(**89**)	15	7	20	166	89.8	—	—	0	742
1971	Dal	10(4)	4	9	2.3(4)	1	—	—	—	—	143	78	54.5	1131	7.9(76)	7	8	9	76	73.5	—	—	6	300
1972	†Dal	14(14, QB)	8	26	3.3(12)	2	—	—	—	—	339	185	54.6	2396	7.1(46)	15	**21**	23	179	65.9	—	—	12	479
1973	†Dal	14	1	0	0.0(0)	0	—	—	—	—	32	13	40.6	174	5.4(53)	3	1	—	—	—	—	—	0	62
1974	Dal	2	—	—	—	—	—	—	—	—	2	2	100.0	12	6.0(15)	0	0	—	—	—	—	—	0	6
1974	NYG	8(8, QB)	4	5	1.3(2)	0	—	—	—	—	237	122	51.5	1510	6.4(72)	9	13	13	97	61.3	—	—	0	285
1975	NYG	14(14, QB)	22	72	3.3(11)	0	—	—	—	—	363	186	51.2	2359	6.5(56)	11	16	47	331	63.6	—	—	0	667
1976	NYG	12(12, QB)	15	48	3.2(10)	0	—	—	—	—	284	153	53.9	1865	6.6(63)	9	20	39	285	55.6	—	—	0	226
1977	†Den☆	14(14, QB)	31	125	4.0(15)	4	—	—	—	—	254	131	51.6	1929	7.6(81)	14	8	43	338	82.0	—	—	24	880
1978	†Den	14(13, QB)	17	71	4.2(12)	0	—	—	—	—	267	146	54.7	1802	6.7(42)	11	8	36	238	77.0	—	—	0	707
1979	†Den	14(10, QB)	23	13	0.6(7)	1	—	—	—	—	370	204	55.1	2626	7.1(64)	16	19	30	241	70.6	—	—	6	656
1980	Den	12(9, QB)	21	29	1.4(9)	1	—	—	—	—	301	183	60.8	2150	7.1(41)	12	13	26	190	77.8	—	—	6	654
1981	Den	15(15, QB)	8	18	2.3(5)	0	—	—	—	—	376	225	59.8	3195	8.5(**95**)	21	14	54	394	90.5	—	—	0	1161
1982	Den	3(3)	—	—	—	—	—	—	—	—	26	18	69.2	193	7.4(20)	0	3	3	19	—	—	—	0	-24
NFL	18	203(145)	215	627	2.9(15)	12	—	—	—	—	3786	2053	54.2	27908	7.4(95)	183	187	405	3040	73.5	—	—	72	8136

Morton, Dave David Byron, LB, 6′2″/224 lbs; UCLA; B5/13/1955 Fresno, CA **1979** SF 3

Morton, Greg Gregory Alan, DE, 6′1″/230 lbs; Michigan; 1977: Buf, rnd 8; B10/8/1953 Akron, OH **1977** Buf 9

Morton, Jack John Joseph, E-DE-DB, 6′0″/197 lbs; Missouri; Purdue; 1944: ChiB, rnd 9; B7/22/1922 East St. Louis, IL, D12/17/1983 Manteno, IL **1947** Buf-A 2 (0)

YEAR	TEAM	G (GS, POS)	RUSH	YD	AVG (LG)	TD	REC	YD	AVG (LG)	TD	PASS	COMP	PCT	YD	AVG (LG)	TD	INT	SK	YD	QBR	KPR	OTD	PTS	TAY
1946	LAD-A	12(1)	—	—	—	—	4	44	11.0	1	—	—	—	—	—	—	—	—	—	—	i	—	6	33
AAFC	2	14(1)	—	—	—	—	4	44	11.0(18)	1	—	—	—	—	—	—	—	—	—	—	—	—	6	27
1945	ChiB	8(1)	—	—	—	—	1	18	18.0(18)	0	—	—	—	—	—	—	—	—	—	—	—	—	0	9

Morton, John John Jay, LB, 6′2″/220 lbs; TCU; B9/1/1929 Compton, CA **1953** SF 10 (LLB)

Morton, Johnnie Johnnie James, WR, 6′0″/190 lbs; USC; 1994: Det, rnd 1; B10/7/1971 Inglewood, CA

YEAR	TEAM	G (GS, POS)	RUSH	YD	AVG (LG)	TD	REC	YD	AVG (LG)	TD	PASS	COMP	PCT	YD	AVG (LG)	TD	INT	SK	YD	QBR	KPR	OTD	PTS	TAY
1994	Det	14(0)	—	—	—	—	3	39	13.0(18)	1	—	—	—	—	—	—	—	—	—	—	k	1	12	118
1995	†Det	16(13, WR)	3	33	11.0(18)	0	44	590	13.4(32)	8	—	—	—	—	—	—	—	—	—	—	kp	—	48	501
1996	Det	16(15, WR)	9	35	3.9(18)	0	55	714	13.0(62)	6	—	—	—	—	—	—	—	—	—	—	—	—	36	422
1997	†Det	16(16, WR)	3	33	11.0(20)	0	80	1057	13.2(73)	6	—	—	—	—	—	—	—	—	—	—	—	—	36	592
1998	Det	16(16, WR)	1	11	11.0(11)	0	69	1028	14.9(**98**)	2	—	—	—	—	—	—	—	—	—	—	—	—	12	535
1999	†Det	16(12, WR)	—	—	—	—	80	1129	14.1(48)	5	—	—	—	—	—	—	—	—	—	—	k	—	30	597
2000	Det	16(16, WR)	4	25	6.3(27)	0	61	788	12.9(42)	3	—	—	—	—	—	—	—	—	—	—	—	—	20	434
2001	Det	16(16, WR)	1	6	6.0(6)	0	77	1154	15.0(76)	4	—	—	—	—	—	—	—	—	—	—	k	—	24	592
2002	KC	14(14, WR)	10	124	12.4(36)	0	29	397	13.7(30)	1	—	—	—	—	—	—	—	—	—	—	—	—	6	328
2003	†KC	16(16, WR)	8	94	11.8(39)	0	50	740	14.8(50)	4	—	—	—	—	—	—	—	—	—	—	—	—	24	484
2004	KC	13(12, WR)	7	43	6.1(14)	0	55	795	14.5(52)	3	—	—	—	—	—	—	—	—	—	—	—	—	18	456
2005	SF	13(10, WR)	—	—	—	—	21	288	13.7(30)	0	—	—	—	—	—	—	—	—	—	—	—	—	0	144
NFL	12	182(156)	46	404	8.8(39)	0	624	8719	14.0(98)	43	—	—	—	—	—	—	—	—	—	—	kp	1	266	5201

Morton, Michael Michael Da'mond, RB, 5′8″/180 lbs; UNLV; 1982: TB, rnd 12; B2/6/1960 Birmingham, AL **[R]**

YEAR	TEAM	G (GS, POS)	RUSH	YD	AVG (LG)	TD	REC	YD	AVG (LG)	TD	PASS	COMP	PCT	YD	AVG (LG)	TD	INT	SK	YD	QBR	KPR	OTD	PTS	TAY
1982	†TB	9(0)	2	3	1.5(2)	0	1	5	5.0(5)	0	—	—	—	—	—	—	—	—	—	—	k	—	0	52
1983	TB	16(0)	13	28	2.2(5)	0	1	9	9.0(9)	0	—	—	—	—	—	—	—	—	—	—	k	—	0	272
1984	TB	16(0)	16	27	1.7(8)	0	—	—	—	—	—	—	—	—	—	—	—	—	—	—	k	—	0	292
1985	Was	1(0)	—	—	—	—	—	—	—	—	—	—	—	—	—	—	—	—	—	—	k	—	0	41
1987	Sea	2(0)	19	52	2.7(10)	1	—	—	—	—	—	—	—	—	—	—	—	—	—	—	—	—	6	62
NFL	5	44(0)	50	110	2.2(10)	1	2	14	7.0(9)	0	—	—	—	—	—	—	—	—	—	—	k	—	6	718

Morton, Mike Michael Anthony, LB, 6′4″/325 lbs; North Carolina; 1995: Oak, rnd 4; B3/28/1972 Kannapolis, NC **1995** Oak 12 (0) **1996** Oak 16 (6, lolb) **1997** Oak 11 (11, RLB) **1998** Oak 16 (0) **1999**†SL 16 (0) **2000** GB 16 (0) **2001** Ind 16 (0) **NFL** 103 (17) [7 yrs]

YEAR	TEAM	G (GS, POS)	RUSH	YD	AVG(LG)	TD	REC	YD	AVG(LG)	TD	PASS	COMP	PCT	YD	AVG(LG)	TD	INT	SK	YD	QBR	KPR	OTD	PTS	TAY

MORZE, FRANK Frank Joseph, C-T, 6′4″/270 lbs; Boston College; 1955: SF, rnd 2; B3/21/1933 Gardner, MA **1957**†SF☆12 (C) **1958** SF 4 **1959** SF 12 (C) **1960** SF 12 (C)
1961 SF 14 (12, C) **1962** Cle 2 **1963** Cle 14 **1964** SF 14 **NFL** 84 (12) [8 yrs]

MOSCRIP, MONK James Henderson, E, 6′0″/195 lbs; Stanford; 1936: Bkn, rnd 9; B9/17/1913 Adena, OH, D10/11/1980 Atherton, CA **[K]**

1938	Det	11(6, RE)	—	—	—	—	6	118	19.7	1	—	—	—	—	—	—	—	—	—	—	K	—	12	64
1939	Det	11(10, LE)	1	8	8.0(8)	0	14	176	12.6	0	—	—	—	—	—	—	—	—	—	—	K	1	15	96
NFL	2	22(16)	1	8	8.0(8)	0	20	294	14.7	1	—	—	—	—	—	—	—	—	—	—	K	1	27	160

MOSEBAR, DON Donald Howard, C-T-G, 6′6″/285 lbs; USC; 1983: LARd, rnd 1; B9/11/1961 Yakima, WA **1983**†LARd 14 (0) **1984** LARd 10 (10, RG) **1985**†LARd 16 (14, C)
1986 LARd◇16 (16, C) **1987** LARd 12 (12, C) **1988** LARd 13 (13, LT) **1989** LARd 12 (11, C) **1990**†LARd★16 (16, C) **1991**†LARd★16 (16, C) **1992** LARd 16 (16, C)
1993†LARd 16 (16, C) **1994** LARd 16 (16, C) **NFL** 173 (156) [12 yrs]

MOSELEY, MARK Mark Dewayne, K, 5′11″/202 lbs; Texas A&M; Stephen F. Austin State; 1970: Phi, rnd 14; B3/12/1948 Laneville, TX **[K]** **1970** Phi 14 **1971** Hou 12
1972 Hou 1 **1974** Was 13 **1975** Was 14 **1976**†Was 14 **1977** Was☆14 **1978** Was☆16 **1979** Was★16 **1980** Was 16 (0) **1981** Was 16 (0) **1982**†Was★9 (0) **1983**†Was☆16 (0)
1984†Was 16 (0) **1985** Was 16 (0) **1986**†Was 6 (0) **1986** Cle 4 (0) **NFL** 213 [16 yrs]

MOSELLE, DOM Dominic Angelo, DB-HB, 6′0″/192 lbs; Wisconsin-Superior; 1950: Cle, rnd 23; B6/23/1926 Gile, WI

1950	†Cle	11	5	39	7.8(15)	0	—	—	—	—	—	—	—	—	—	—	—	—	—	—	kp	—	0	162
1951	GB	12	12	23	1.9(7)	1	14	233	16.6(85)	2	—	—	—	—	—	—	—	—	—	—	kpi	—	18	437
1952	GB	8(1)	—	—	—	—	—	—	—	—	—	—	—	—	—	—	—	—	—	—	kpi	—	0	37
1954	Phi	12	29	114	3.9(14)	1	17	242	14.2(38)	2	—	—	—	—	—	—	—	—	—	—	k	—	18	299
NFL	4	43(1)	46	176	3.8(15)	2	31	475	15.3(85)	4	—	—	—	—	—	—	—	—	—	—	kpi	—	36	935

MOSER, BOB Robert Joseph, C, 6′3″/240 lbs; Pacific; 1951: ChiB, rnd 4; B12/26/1928 Modesto, CA **1951** ChiB 12 **1952** ChiB 12 **1953** ChiB 6 **NFL** 30 [3 yrs]

MOSER, RICK Richard Avery, RB, 6′0″/210 lbs; Rhode Island; 1978: Pit, rnd 8; B12/18/1956 White Plains, NY **1980** Mia 4 (0) **1981** KC 1 (0) **1982** Pit 6 (0) **1982**†TB 1 (0)

1978	†Pit	15	42	153	3.6(15)	0	1	-1	-1.0(-1)	0	—	—	—	—	—	—	—	—	—	—	k	—	0	146
1979	Pit	16	11	33	3.0(8)	1	1	6	6.0(6)	0	—	—	—	—	—	—	—	—	—	—	k	—	6	37
1981	Pit	6(0)	1	4	4.0(4)	0	1	5	5.0(5)	1	—	—	—	—	—	—	—	—	—	—	k	—	6	43
NFL	5	49	54	190	3.5(15)	1	3	10	3.3(6)	1	—	—	—	—	—	—	—	—	—	—	k	—	12	228

MOSER, TED Theodore F., G, 5′9″/195 lbs; none; B6/14/1897 Louisville, KY, D8/1986 Dayton, OH **1921** Lou 1 (1)

MOSES, DON Donald Clyde, BB, 5′11″/185 lbs; USC; B1906, D6/15/1965 Arcadia, CA

| 1933 | Cin | 3(0) | 7 | 20 | 2.9 | 0 | — | — | — | — | — | — | — | — | — | — | — | — | — | — | — | — | 0 | 20 |

MOSES, HAVEN Haven Christopher, WR-SE, 6′2″/208 lbs; San Diego State; 1968: Buf, rnd 1; B7/27/1946 Los Angeles, CA

1968	Buf-A	14(SE)	5	-4	-0.8(19)	0	42	633	15.1(55)	2	—	—	—	—	—	—	—	—	—	—	—	—	12	323
1969	Buf-A◇	14(SE)	—	—	—	—	39	752	19.3(55)	5	—	—	—	—	—	—	—	—	—	—	—	—	30	401
1970	Buf	14(WR)	—	—	—	—	39	726	18.6(45)	2	—	—	—	—	—	—	—	—	—	—	—	—	12	373
1971	Buf	12(WR)	—	—	—	—	23	470	20.4(73)	2	—	—	—	—	—	—	—	—	—	—	—	—	12	245
1972	Buf	5	—	—	—	—	3	60	20.0(25)	1	—	—	—	—	—	—	—	—	—	—	—	—	6	35
1972	Den	8(6, wr)	2	11	5.5(14)	0	15	224	14.9(33)	5	—	—	—	—	—	—	—	—	—	—	—	—	30	148
1973	Den◇	14(14, WR)	3	25	8.3(22)	1	28	518	18.5(76)	8	—	—	—	—	—	—	—	—	—	—	—	—	54	334
1974	Den	14(14, WR)	2	16	8.0(11)	0	34	559	16.4(42)	2	—	—	—	—	—	—	—	—	—	—	—	—	12	306
1975	Den	13(13, WR)	—	—	—	—	29	505	17.4(42)	2	—	—	—	—	—	—	—	—	—	—	—	—	12	263
1976	Den	14(14, WR)	1	-4	-4.0(-4)	0	25	498	19.9(71)	7	—	—	—	—	—	—	—	—	—	—	—	—	42	280
1977	†Den	14(14, WR)	5	-1	-0.2(8)	0	27	539	20.0(35)	4	—	—	—	—	—	—	—	—	—	—	—	—	24	289
1978	†Den	16(16, WR)	—	—	—	—	37	744	20.1(42)	5	—	—	—	—	—	—	—	—	—	—	—	—	30	397
1979	†Den	16(16, WR)	—	—	—	—	54	943	17.5(64)	6	—	—	—	—	—	—	—	—	—	—	—	—	36	502
1980	Den	15(14, WR)	—	—	—	—	38	674	17.7(33)	4	—	—	—	—	—	—	—	—	—	—	—	—	24	357
1981	Den	16(6, wr)	—	—	—	—	15	246	16.4(30)	1	—	—	—	—	—	—	—	—	—	—	—	—	6	128
NFL	14	199(127)	18	43	2.4(22)	1	448	8091	18.1(76)	56	—	—	—	—	—	—	—	—	—	—	—	—	342	4379

MOSES, J.J. Jerry James, WR, 5′6″/178 lbs; Iowa State; B9/12/1979 Waterloo, IA **[R]** **2002** GB 2 (0) **2003** Hou 15 (0) **2004** Hou 15 (0) **2005** Arz 2 (0) **NFL** 34 (0) [4 yrs]

MOSES, KELVIN Kelvin, LB, 6′0″/239 lbs; Wake Forest; B9/3/1976 Hartsville, SC **2001**†NYJ 16 (0) **2002**†NYJ 16 (0) **NFL** 32 (0) [2 yrs]

MOSHER, CLURE Clure Harrison, C-G-LB, 6′1″/215 lbs; Louisville; 1942: Pit, rnd 14; B1/11/1920 Fort Worth, TX, D7/23/1966 New York, NY **1942** Pit 2 (0)

MOSIER, JOHN John Paul, TE, 6′3″/220 lbs; Kansas; 1970: Den, rnd 6; B3/1/1948 Wichita Falls, TX

1971	Den	11(1)	4	31	7.8(29)	0	3	36	12.0(19)	0	—	—	—	—	—	—	—	—	—	—	—	—	0	49
1972	Bal	14	—	—	—	—	1	53	53.0(53)	0	—	—	—	—	—	—	—	—	—	—	—	—	0	27
NFL	2	25(1)	4	31	7.8(29)	0	4	89	22.3(53)	0	—	—	—	—	—	—	—	—	—	—	—	—	0	76

MOSLEY, ANTHONY Anthony Lewis, RB, 5′9″/205 lbs; Fresno State; B6/17/1965 Selma, CA

| 1987 | ChiB | 2(2) | 18 | 80 | 4.4(16) | 0 | 2 | 8 | 4.0(16) | 0 | — | — | — | — | — | — | — | — | — | — | k | 1 | 6 | 90 |

MOSLEY, C.J. Calvin Michael, DT, 6′3″/305 lbs; Missouri; 2005: Min, rnd 6; B8/6/1983 Fort Knox, KY **2005** Min 12 (2)

MOSLEY, HENRY Henry, HB, 6′2″/210 lbs; Morris Brown; 1955: ChiB, rnd 6; B2/10/1931 Chattanooga, TN

| 1955 | ChiB | 1 | 3 | 10 | 3.3(4) | 0 | — | — | — | — | — | — | — | — | — | — | — | — | — | — | k | — | 0 | 9 |

MOSLEY, MIKE Michael Gene, WR, 6′2″/192 lbs; Texas A&M; 1981: Buf, rnd 3; B6/6/1958 Hillsboro, TX

1982	Buf	9(0)	—	—	—	—	9	96	10.7(31)	0	—	—	—	—	—	—	—	—	—	—	kp	—	0	271
1983	Buf	7(2)	—	—	—	—	14	180	12.9(35)	3	—	—	—	—	—	—	—	—	—	—	k	—	18	206
1984	Buf	4(0)	—	—	—	—	4	38	9.5(17)	0	1	0	0.0	0	0.0	0	0	0	0	—	—	—	0	19
NFL	3	20(2)	—	—	—	—	27	314	11.6(35)	3	1	0	0.0	0	0.0	0	0	0	0	—	kp	—	18	496

MOSLEY, NORM Norman S., TB, 5′9″/185 lbs; Alabama; 1945: Phi, rnd 23/1948: Bal-A, rnd 19; B1/4/1922 Blytheville, AR

| 1948 | Pit | 5(1) | 13 | 39 | 3.0(8) | 1 | — | — | — | — | 2 | 0 | 0.0 | 0 | 0.0(16) | 0 | 0 | — | — | — | kp | — | 6 | 82 |

MOSLEY, RUSS Russell Clinton, HB, 5′10″/170 lbs; Alabama; B7/22/1918 Puxico, MO, D8/2/1997 **1946** GB 2 (0)

| 1945 | GB | 6(0) | 16 | 49 | 3.1(9) | 0 | 1 | 10 | 10.0(10) | 0 | 1 | 0 | 0.0 | 0 | 0.0 | 0 | 1 | — | — | — | pi | — | 0 | 37 |
| NFL | 2 | 8(0) | 16 | 49 | 3.1(9) | 0 | 1 | 10 | 10.0(10) | 0 | 1 | 0 | 0.0 | 0 | 0.0 | 0 | 1 | — | — | — | pi | — | 0 | 52 |

MOSLEY, WAYNE Wayne, RB, 6′0″/190 lbs; Alabama A&M; B10/6/1952 Decatur, AL

| 1974 | Buf | 3 | 2 | 6 | 3.0(4) | 0 | — | — | — | — | — | — | — | — | — | — | — | — | — | — | — | — | 0 | 6 |

MOSS, BRENT Brent, RB, 5′9″/211 lbs; Wisconsin; B1/30/1972 Racine, WI

| 1995 | SL | 4(0) | 22 | 90 | 4.1(18) | 0 | 1 | -3 | -3.0(-3) | 0 | — | — | — | — | — | — | — | — | — | — | — | — | 0 | 89 |

MOSS, EDDIE Eddie B., RB, 6′0″/215 lbs; Southeast Missouri State; 1972: Buf, rnd 13; B9/27/1948 Dell, AR

1973	SL	5	14	41	2.9(13)	0	—	—	—	—	—	—	—	—	—	—	—	—	—	—	k	—	0	59
1974	†SL	11	4	13	3.3(5)	0	—	—	—	—	—	—	—	—	—	—	—	—	—	—	k	—	0	26
1975	SL	8	4	12	3.0(5)	1	—	—	—	—	—	—	—	—	—	—	—	—	—	—	k	—	6	28
1976	SL	2	—	—	—	—	—	—	—	—	—	—	—	—	—	—	—	—	—	—	—	—	0	0
1977	Was	9	—	—	—	—	—	—	—	—	—	—	—	—	—	—	—	—	—	—	k	—	0	5
NFL	5	35	22	66	3.0(13)	1	—	—	—	—	—	—	—	—	—	—	—	—	—	—	k	—	6	118

MOSS, GARY Gary James, DB, 5′10″/192 lbs; Georgia; B7/18/1964 Habersham County, GA **1987** Atl 3 (3)

MOSS, JOE Joseph Charles, T, 6′1″/221 lbs; Maryland; 1952: LA, rnd 14; B4/9/1930 Elkins, WV **1952** Was 12 (RT)

MOSS, MARTIN Martin, DE, 6′4″/250 lbs; UCLA; 1982: Det, rnd 8; B12/16/1958 San Diego, CA **1982**†Det 5 (0) **1983**†Det 15 (0) **1984** Det 16 (0) **1985** Det 6 (0)
NFL 42 (0) [4 yrs]

MOSS, PAUL Paul, E, 6′2″/200 lbs; Purdue; B10/2/1908 Brazil, IN, D5/25/1999

1933	Pit	10(7, LE)	—	—	—	—	13	283	21.8(30)	2	—	—	—	—	—	—	—	—	—	—	—	—	12	152
1934	SL	3(2, LE)	—	—	—	—	6	131	21.8(56)	1	—	—	—	—	—	—	—	—	—	—	—	—	6	71
NFL	2	13(9)	—	—	—	—	19	414	21.8(56)	3	—	—	—	—	—	—	—	—	—	—	—	—	18	222

YEAR	TEAM	G (GS, POS)	RUSH	YD	AVG(LG)	TD	REC	YD	AVG(LG)	TD	PASS	COMP	PCT	YD	AVG(LG)	TD	INT	SK	YD	QBR	KPR	OTD	PTS	TAY

Moss, Perry   Perry Lee, QB, 5´10˝/170 lbs; Tulsa; Illinois; 1948: GB, rnd 13/SF-A, rnd 27; B8/4/1926 Tulsa, OK

| 1948 | GB | 6(1) | 5 | 2 | 0.4(3) | 0 | — | — | — | — | 17 | 4 | 23.5 | 20 | 1.2(10) | 0 | 0 | — | — | — | — | — | 0 | 12 |

Moss, Randy   Randy Gene 'The Freak', WR, 6´4˝/200 lbs; Florida State; Marshall; 1998: Min, rnd 1; B2/13/1977 Rand, WV

1998	†Min★	16(11, WR)	1	4	4.0(4)	0	69	1313	**19.0(61)**	17	—	—	—	—	—	—	—	—	—	p	—	106	741	
1999	†Min◇	16(16, WR)	4	43	10.8(15)	0	80	**1413**	17.7(67)	11	1	1	100.0	27	27.0(27)	1	0	—	—	p	1	72	910	
2000	†Min★	16(16, WR)	3	5	1.7(9)	0	77	1437	18.7(78)	15	—	—	—	—	—	—	—	—	—	p	—	92	799	
2001	Min	16(16, WR)	3	38	12.7(18)	0	82	1233	15.0(73)	10	1	1	100.0	29	29.0(29)	0	0	—	—	—	—	60	719	
2002	Min★	16(16, WR)	6	51	8.5(25)	0	**106**	**1347**	12.7(60)	7	3	1	33.3	13	4.3(13)	1	0	—	—	k	—	42	767	
2003	Min★	16(16, WR)	6	18	3.0(11)	0	111	1632	14.7(72)	17	1	0	0.0	0	0.0	0	0	—	—	k	—	102	926	
2004	†Min	13(13, WR)	—	—	—	—	49	767	15.7(**82**)	13	2	1	50.0	37	18.5(37)	0	1	—	—	p	—	78	427	
2005	Oak	16(15, WR)	—	—	—	—	60	1005	16.8(79)	8	—	—	—	—	—	—	—	—	—	—	—	48	543	
NFL	8	125(119)	23	159	6.9(25)	0	634	10147	16.0(82)	98	8	4	50.0	106	13.3(37)	2	1	—	—	kp	1	600	5831	

Moss, Roland   Roland, TE, 6´3˝/215 lbs; Toledo; 1969: Bal, rnd 7; B9/20/1946 St. Matthews, SC   **1969** Bal 6   **1970** SD 2

1970	Buf	4	—	—	—	—	2	31	15.5(22)	0	—	—	—	—	—	—	—	—	—	k	—	0	57	
1971	NE	14(6, te)	—	—	—	—	9	124	13.8(20)	1	—	—	—	—	—	—	—	—	—	—	1	12	67	
NFL	3	26(6)	—	—	—	—	11	155	14.1(22)	1	—	—	—	—	—	—	—	—	—	k	1	12	109	

Moss, Santana   Santana Terrell, WR, 5´10˝/185 lbs; Miami (FL); 2001: NYJ, rnd 1; B6/1/1979 Miami, FL **[R]**

2001	†NYJ	5(0)	1	-6	-6.0(-6)	0	2	40	20.0(33)	0	—	—	—	—	—	—	—	—	—	p	—	0	66	
2002	†NYJ☆	15(1)	7	48	6.9(14)	0	30	433	14.4(47)	4	—	—	—	—	—	—	—	—	—	p	2	36	593	
2003	NYJ	16(12, WR)	10	67	6.7(25)	0	74	1105	14.9(65)	10	—	—	—	—	—	—	—	—	—	p	—	60	852	
2004	†NYJ	15(14, WR)	6	18	3.0(12)	0	45	838	18.6(69)	5	—	—	—	—	—	—	—	—	—	p	—	30	552	
2005	†Was★	16(16, WR)	3	-3	-1.0(3)	0	84	1483	17.7(78)	9	—	—	—	—	—	—	—	—	—	p	—	54	789	
NFL	5	67(43)	27	124	4.6(25)	0	235	3899	16.6(78)	28	—	—	—	—	—	—	—	—	—	p	2	180	2851	

Moss, Winston   Winston N., LB, 6´3˝/245 lbs; Miami (FL); 1987: TB, rnd 2; B12/24/1965 Miami, FL   **1987** TB 12 (6, rolb)   **1988** TB 16 (15, ROLB)   **1989** TB 16 (16, ROLB)   **1990** TB 16 (15, RILB/rolb)   **1991**†LARd 16 (16, LLB)   **1992** LARd 15 (15, RLB)   **1993**†LARd 16 (16, RLB)   **1994** LARd 16 (14, RLB)   **1995** Sea 16 (16, RLB)   **1996** Sea 16 (16, RLB)   **1997** Sea 14 (14, LLB)   **NFL** 169 (159) [11 yrs]

Moss, Zefross   Zafross, T, 6´6˝/325 lbs; Alabama State; B8/17/1966 Tuscaloosa, AL   **1989** Ind 16 (0)   **1990** Ind 16 (16, LT)   **1991** Ind 11 (10, LT)   **1992** Ind 13 (13, LT)   **1993** Ind 16 (16, RT)   **1994** Ind 11 (11, RT)   **1995**†Det 14 (14, RT)   **1996** Det 15 (15, RT)   **1997**†NE 15 (15, RT)   **1998**†NE 14 (14, RT)   **1999** NE 13 (13, RT)   **NFL** 154 (137) [11 yrs]

Mostardo, Rich   Richard Albert, DB, 5´11˝/188 lbs; Charleston (WV); Kent State; 1960: Cle, rnd 12/Oak, rnd 2; B7/1/1938 Bryn Mawr, PA   **1960** Cle 10 (RS)   **1961** Min 11 (9, LS)   **1962** Oak-A 5   **NFL** 26 (9) [3 yrs]

Mote, Kelley   Kelley Henry, E-DE-DB, 6´2˝/189 lbs; South Carolina; Duke; 1946: Det, rnd 16; B4/27/1923 Hapeville, GA

1947	Det	12(1)	—	—	—	—	16	180	11.3(46)	1	—	—	—	—	—	—	—	—	—	ki	—	6	92	
1948	Det	12(10, LE)	—	—	—	—	13	212	16.3(28)	0	—	—	—	—	—	—	—	—	—	k	—	0	88	
1949	Det	12(1)	—	—	—	—	4	58	14.5(22)	0	—	—	—	—	—	—	—	—	—	—	—	0	29	
1950	†NYG	9	—	—	—	—	4	72	18.0(41)	1	—	—	—	—	—	—	—	—	—	i	—	6	46	
1951	NYG	12	—	—	—	—	11	187	17.0(39)	4	—	—	—	—	—	—	—	—	—	—	—	24	114	
1952	NYG	12	—	—	—	—	4	45	11.3(19)	0	—	—	—	—	—	—	—	—	—	—	—	0	23	
NFL	6	69(12)	—	—	—	—	52	754	14.5(46)	6	—	—	—	—	—	—	—	—	—	ki	—	36	391	

Moten, Bobby   Robert Earl, WR, 6´4˝/212 lbs; Bishop; 1967: Atl, rnd 9; B1/29/1943 Clarksville, TX   **1968** Den-A 3

Moten, Eric   Eric Dean, G, 6´3˝/306 lbs; Michigan State; 1991: SD, rnd 2; B4/11/1968 Cleveland, OH   **1991** SD 16 (11, LG)   **1992**†SD 16 (16, LG)   **1993** SD 4 (4)   **1995**†SD 16 (15, LG)   **1996** SD 15 (15, LG)   **NFL** 67 (61) [5 yrs]

Moten, Gary   Gary Kim, LB, 6´1˝/210 lbs; SMU; 1983: SF, rnd 7; B4/3/1961 Galveston, TX   **1983**†SF 6 (0)   **1987** KC 1 (0)   **NFL** 7 (0) [2 yrs]

Moten, Mike   Michael Edward, DT, 6´5˝/266 lbs; Florida; B3/12/1974 Daytona Beach, FL   **1998**†Arz 1 (0)

Motl, Bob   Robert Joseph, E, 6´3˝/195 lbs; Northwestern; 1943: Was, rnd 9; B7/26/1920 Chicago, IL

| 1946 | ChiR-A | 14(1) | — | — | — | — | 9 | 124 | 13.8 | 1 | — | — | — | — | — | — | — | — | — | — | — | 6 | 67 | |

Motley, Marion   Marion, FB-LB, 6´1˝/232 lbs; South Carolina State; UNLV; B6/5/1920 Leesburg, GA, D6/27/1999 Cleveland, OH; HOF 1968

1946	†Cle-A☆	13(10, FB)	73	601	**8.2(76)**	5	10	188	18.8(63)	1	—	—	—	—	—	—	—	—	—	kpi	—	36	748	
1947	†Cle-A☆	14(12, FB)	146	889	6.1(50)	8	7	73	10.4	1	—	—	—	—	—	—	—	—	—	ki	1	60	1191	
1948	†Cle-A☆	14(14, FB)	157	**964**	6.1	5	13	192	14.8(78)	2	1	0	0.0	0	0.0	0	0	—	—	k	—	42	1247	
1949	†Cle-A☆	11(10, FB)	113	570	5.0	**8**	15	191	12.7	0	—	—	—	—	—	—	—	—	—	k	—	48	828	
AAFC	4	52(46)	489	3024	6.2(76)	26	45	644	14.3(78)	4	1	0	0.0	0	0.0	0	0	—	—	kpi	1	186	4013	
1950	†Cle★	12(FB)	140	**810**	5.8(69)	3	11	151	13.7(41)	1	—	—	—	—	—	—	—	—	—	—	—	24	921	
1951	†Cle	11(FB)	61	273	4.5(26)	1	10	52	5.2(34)	0	—	—	—	—	—	—	—	—	—	k	—	6	309	
1952	†Cle	12(FB)	104	444	4.3(59)	1	13	213	16.4(68)	2	0	0	0.0	0	0.0	0	0	—	—	k	—	18	614	
1953	†Cle	12(fb)	32	161	5.0(34)	0	6	47	7.8(23)	0	—	—	—	—	—	—	—	—	—	k	—	0	200	
1955	Pit	7	2	8	4.0(8)	0	—	—	—	—	—	—	—	—	—	—	—	—	—	—	—	0	8	
NFL	5	54	339	1696	5.0(76)	5	40	463	11.6(78)	3	2	0	0.0	0	0.0	0	0	—	—	k	—	48	2051	

Mott, Buster   Norman Howard, B, 5´8˝/193 lbs; Georgia; B6/21/1909 Atlanta, GA, deceased

1933	GB	3(1)	5	13	2.6	0	—	—	—	—	—	—	—	—	—	—	—	—	—	—	—	0	13	
1934	Cin	1(0)	—	—	—	—	1	12	12.0(12)	0	—	—	—	—	—	—	—	—	—	—	—	0	6	
1934	Pit	1(0)	5	24	4.8	0	—	—	—	—	—	—	—	—	—	—	—	—	—	—	—	0	24	
NFL	2	5(1)	10	37	3.7	0	1	12	12.0(12)	0	—	—	—	—	—	—	—	—	—	—	—	0	43	

Mott, Joe   John Christopher, LB, 6´4˝/253 lbs; Iowa; 1989: NYJ, rnd 3; B10/6/1965 Endicott, NY   **1989** NYJ 16 (0)   **1990** NYJ 16 (14, LLB)   **1993**†GB 2 (0)   **NFL** 34 (14) [3 yrs]

Mott, Steve   Walter Stephen, C, 6´3˝/266 lbs; Alabama; 1983: Det, rnd 5; B3/24/1961 New Orleans, LA   **1983**†Det 13 (12, C)   **1984** Det 6 (6, c)   **1985** Det 16 (16, C)   **1986** Det 14 (14, C)   **1987** Det 11 (11, C)   **1988** Det 16 (16, C)   **NFL** 76 (75) [6 yrs]

Moulds, Eric   Eric Shannon, WR, 6´2˝/210 lbs; Mississippi State; 1996: Buf, rnd 1; B7/17/1973 Lucedale, MS **[R]**

1996	†Buf	16(5, wr)	12	44	3.7(11)	0	20	279	13.9(47)	2	—	—	—	—	—	—	—	—	—	k	1	18	629	
1997	Buf	16(8, WR)	4	59	14.8(29)	0	29	294	10.1(32)	0	—	—	—	—	—	—	—	—	—	kp	—	2	492	
1998	†Buf★	16(15, WR)	—	—	—	—	67	**1368**	20.4(84)	9	—	—	—	—	—	—	—	—	—	—	—	54	729	
1999	†Buf	14(14, WR)	1	1	1.0(1)	0	65	994	15.3(54)	7	—	—	—	—	—	—	—	—	—	—	—	42	533	
2000	Buf◇	16(16, WR)	2	24	12.0(20)	0	94	1326	14.1(52)	5	—	—	—	—	—	—	—	—	—	—	—	30	712	
2001	Buf	16(16, WR)	3	3	1.0(6)	0	67	904	13.5(80)	5	—	—	—	—	—	—	—	—	—	—	—	32	480	
2002	Buf★	16(15, WR)	1	7	7.0(7)	0	100	1292	12.9(70)	10	—	—	—	—	—	—	—	—	—	—	—	60	703	
2003	Buf	13(13, WR)	—	—	—	—	64	780	12.2(49)	1	—	—	—	—	—	—	—	—	—	—	—	6	395	
2004	Buf	16(16, WR)	5	19	3.8(12)	0	88	1043	11.9(49)	5	—	—	—	—	—	—	—	—	—	k	—	30	553	
2005	Buf	15(15, WR)	—	—	—	—	81	816	10.1(55)	4	—	—	—	—	—	—	—	—	—	—	—	24	428	
NFL	10	154(133)	28	157	5.6(29)	0	675	9096	13.5(84)	48	—	—	—	—	—	—	—	—	—	kp	1	298	5653	

Mowatt, Zeke   Ezekiel, TE, 6´3˝/238 lbs; Florida State; B3/5/1961 Wauchula, FL

1983	NYG	16(14, TE)	—	—	—	—	21	280	13.3(46)	1	—	—	—	—	—	—	—	—	—	—	—	6	145	
1984	†NYG	16(16, TE)	—	—	—	—	48	698	14.5(34)	6	—	—	—	—	—	—	—	—	—	—	—	36	379	
1986	†NYG	16(5, te)	—	—	—	—	10	119	11.9(30)	1	—	—	—	—	—	—	—	—	—	—	—	12	70	
1987	NYG	12(1)	—	—	—	—	3	39	13.0(29)	1	—	—	—	—	—	—	—	—	—	—	—	6	25	
1988	NYG	16(3)	—	—	—	—	15	196	13.1(38)	1	—	—	—	—	—	—	—	—	—	—	—	6	103	
1989	†NYG	16(11, TE)	—	—	—	—	27	288	10.7(31)	0	—	—	—	—	—	—	—	—	—	—	—	0	144	
1990	NE	10(0)	—	—	—	—	6	67	11.2(16)	0	—	—	—	—	—	—	—	—	—	—	—	0	34	
1991	NYG	16(8, te)	—	—	—	—	5	78	15.6(33)	1	—	—	—	—	—	—	—	—	—	—	—	6	44	
NFL	8	118(58)	—	—	—	—	135	1765	13.1(46)	12	—	—	—	—	—	—	—	—	—	—	—	72	943	

Moyer, Alex Alexander, LB, 6´1˝/221 lbs; Northwestern; 1985: Mia, rnd 3; B10/25/1963 Detroit, MI **1985**†Mia 10 (0) **1986** Mia 3 (0) **NFL** 13 (0) [2 yrs]

Moyer, Ken Kenneth Wayne, G-T-C, 6´7˝/297 lbs; Toledo; B11/19/1966 Canoga Park, CA **1989** Cin 8 (0) **1990**†Cin 16 (16, RG) **1991** Cin 15 (10, RG) **1993** Cin 16 (14, LG) **1994** Cin 16 (14, RG) **NFL** 71 (54) [5 yrs]

Moyer, Paul Paul Stewart, DB, 6´1˝/201 lbs; Cal State-Fullerton; Arizona State; B7/26/1961 Villa Park, CA **1983**†Sea 16 (1) **1984**†Sea 16 (0) **1985** Sea 11 (3) **1986** Sea 16 (6, ss) **1987** Sea 12 (1) **1988**†Sea 16 (16, SS) **1989** Sea 11 (3) **NFL** 98 (30) [7 yrs]

Moynihan, Dick Richard A., BB-FB, 5´8˝/160 lbs; Villanova; B1/9/1902 Haverhill, MA **[K]** **1927** Fra 9 (4), 3

Moynihan, Tim Timothy Anthony, C, 6´1˝/204 lbs; Notre Dame; B9/21/1906 Chicago, IL, D4/3/1952 Orange, CA **1932** ChiC☆10 (5, C) **1933** ChiC 8 (3) **NFL** 18 (8) [2 yrs]

Mraz, Mark Mark David, DE, 6´4˝/258 lbs; Utah State; 1987: Atl, rnd 5; B2/9/1965 Glendale, CA **1987** Atl 11 (0) **1989** LARd 11 (0) **NFL** 22 (0) [2 yrs]

Mrkonic, George George Ralph, T-DT, 6´2˝/225 lbs; Kansas; 1953: Phi, rnd 4; B12/17/1929 McKeesport, PA **1953** Phi 10

Mrosko, Bob Robert Allen, TE, 6´6˝/265 lbs; Penn State; 1989: Hou, rnd 9; B11/13/1965 Cleveland, OH

YEAR	TEAM	G (GS, POS)	RUSH	YD	AVG (LG)	TD	REC	YD	AVG (LG)	TD	PASS	COMP	PCT	YD	AVG (LG)	TD	INT	SK	YD	QBR	KPR	OTD	PTS	TAY
1989	†Hou	15 (14, TE)	—	—	—	—	3	28	9.3 (14)	0	—	—	—	—	—	—	—	—	—	—	k	—	0	15
1990	†NYG	16 (2)	—	—	—	—	3	27	9.0 (16)	1	—	—	—	—	—	—	—	—	—	—	—	—	6	19
1991	Ind	11 (4)	—	—	—	—	8	90	11.3 (20)	0	—	—	—	—	—	—	—	—	—	—	k	—	0	39
NFL	3	42 (20)	—	—	—	—	14	145	10.4 (20)	1	—	—	—	—	—	—	—	—	—	—	k	—	6	73

Mruczkowski, Gene Gene Vincent, G, 6´2˝/305 lbs; Purdue; B6/6/1980 Cleveland, OH **2004**†NE 10 (0) **2005**†NE 7 (0) **NFL** 17 (0) [2 yrs]

Mruczkowski, Scott Scott Allen, C, 6´4˝/321 lbs; Bowling Green; 2005: SD, rnd 7; B4/5/1982 Garfield Heights, OH **2005** SD 6 (0)

Mucha, Rudy Rudolph J., G-C, 6´1˝/236 lbs; Washington; 1941: Cle, rnd 1; B7/22/1918 Chicago, IL, D9/7/1982 Dolton, IL **1945** Cle 3 (0) **1945** ChiB 4 (2)

YEAR	TEAM	G (GS, POS)	RUSH	YD	AVG (LG)	TD	REC	YD	AVG (LG)	TD	PASS	COMP	PCT	YD	AVG (LG)	TD	INT	SK	YD	QBR	KPR	OTD	PTS	TAY
1941	Cle	10 (3)	1	0	0.0 (0)	0	1	3	3.0 (3)	0	—	—	—	—	—	—	—	—	—	—	P	—	0	2
1946	†ChiB	5 (1)	1	-1	-1.0 (-1)	0	—	—	—	—	—	—	—	—	—	—	—	—	—	—	P	—	0	-1
NFL	3	22 (6)	2	-1	-0.5	0	1	3	3.0 (3)	0	—	—	—	—	—	—	—	—	—	—	P	—	0	1

Muckensturm, Jerry Jerry Ray, LB, 6´4˝/223 lbs; Arkansas State; 1976: Chi, rnd 7; B10/13/1953 Belleville, IL **1976** ChiB 13 **1977**†ChiB 14 **1978** ChiB 16 **1979**†ChiB 16 (16, LLB) **1980** ChiB 15 (15, LLB) **1982** ChiB 6 (0) **1983** ChiB 1 (0) **NFL** 81 (31) [7 yrs]

Mucker, Larry Larry Donnell, WR, 5´11˝/190 lbs; Arizona State; 1977: TB, rnd 9; B12/15/1954 Fresno, CA

YEAR	TEAM	G (GS, POS)	RUSH	YD	AVG (LG)	TD	REC	YD	AVG (LG)	TD	PASS	COMP	PCT	YD	AVG (LG)	TD	INT	SK	YD	QBR	KPR	OTD	PTS	TAY
1977	TB	14	—	—	—	—	4	59	14.8 (23)	0	—	—	—	—	—	—	—	—	—	—	—	—	0	30
1978	TB	16 (7, wr)	5	35	7.0 (13)	0	13	271	20.8 (48)	0	—	—	—	—	—	—	—	—	—	—	kp	—	0	164
1979	†TB	16 (4)	4	16	4.0 (16)	0	14	268	19.1 (42)	5	—	—	—	—	—	—	—	—	—	—	—	—	30	175
1980	TB	7 (0)	—	—	—	—	2	37	18.5 (19)	0	—	—	—	—	—	—	—	—	—	—	—	—	0	19
NFL	4	53 (11)	9	51	5.7 (16)	0	33	635	19.2 (48)	5	—	—	—	—	—	—	—	—	—	—	kp	—	30	387

Mudd, Howard Howard Edward, G, 6´2˝/254 lbs; Michigan State; Hillsdale; 1964: SF, rnd 9; B2/10/1942 Midland, MI **1964** SF 14 **1965** SF 14 (14, RG) **1966** SF✧14 (14, RG) **1967** SF★14 (14, RG) **1968** SF★14 (14, RG) **1969** SF 5 **1969** ChiB 8 **1970** ChiB 10 **NFL** 93 (56) [7 yrs]

Muehlheuser, Frank Frank Paul, FB-LB, 6´2˝/215 lbs; Colgate; 1947: NYG, rnd 8/LAD-A, rnd 15; B7/2/1926 Irvington, NJ

YEAR	TEAM	G (GS, POS)	RUSH	YD	AVG (LG)	TD	REC	YD	AVG (LG)	TD	PASS	COMP	PCT	YD	AVG (LG)	TD	INT	SK	YD	QBR	KPR	OTD	PTS	TAY
1948	Bos	12 (4)	38	169	4.4 (35)	1	3	19	6.3 (12)	0	—	—	—	—	—	—	—	—	—	—	Pk	—	6	201
1949	NYB	8 (2)	9	10	1.1 (3)	1	2	26	13.0 (10)	0	—	—	—	—	—	—	—	—	—	—	Pk	—	6	58
NFL	2	20 (6)	47	179	3.8 (35)	2	5	45	9.0 (12)	0	—	—	—	—	—	—	—	—	—	—	Pk	—	12	259

Muelhaupt, Chuck Edward Charles, G, 6´3˝/230 lbs; Iowa State; 1957: Det, rnd 26; B12/11/1935 Canton, OH **1960** Buf-A 14 (RG) **1961** Buf-A 14 (RG) **NFL** 28 [2 yrs]

Mueller, Jamie Jamie F., RB, 6´1˝/225 lbs; Benedictine; 1987: Buf, rnd 3; B10/4/1964 Cleveland, OH

YEAR	TEAM	G (GS, POS)	RUSH	YD	AVG (LG)	TD	REC	YD	AVG (LG)	TD	PASS	COMP	PCT	YD	AVG (LG)	TD	INT	SK	YD	QBR	KPR	OTD	PTS	TAY
1987	Buf	12 (6, fb)	82	354	4.3 (20)	2	3	13	4.3 (11)	0	—	—	—	—	—	—	—	—	—	—	k	—	12	380
1988	†Buf	15 (15, FB)	81	296	3.7 (20)	0	8	42	5.3 (17)	0	—	—	—	—	—	—	—	—	—	—	—	—	0	317
1989	†Buf	14 (3)	16	44	2.8 (9)	0	1	8	8.0 (8)	0	—	—	—	—	—	—	—	—	—	—	k	—	0	52
1990	†Buf	16 (8, FB)	59	207	3.5 (20)	2	16	106	6.6 (30)	1	—	—	—	—	—	—	—	—	—	—	—	—	18	285
NFL	4	57 (32)	238	901	3.8 (20)	4	28	169	6.0 (30)	1	—	—	—	—	—	—	—	—	—	—	k	—	30	1034

Mueller, Vance Vance Alan, RB, 6´0˝/210 lbs; Occidental; 1986: LARd, rnd 4; B5/5/1964 Tucson, AZ

YEAR	TEAM	G (GS, POS)	RUSH	YD	AVG (LG)	TD	REC	YD	AVG (LG)	TD	PASS	COMP	PCT	YD	AVG (LG)	TD	INT	SK	YD	QBR	KPR	OTD	PTS	TAY
1986	LARd	15 (1)	13	30	2.3 (8)	0	6	54	9.0 (20)	0	—	—	—	—	—	—	—	—	—	—	k	—	0	100
1987	LARd	12 (0)	37	175	4.7 (35)	1	11	95	8.6 (14)	0	—	—	—	—	—	—	—	—	—	—	k	—	6	416
1988	LARd	14 (1)	17	60	3.5 (13)	0	5	63	12.6 (28)	0	—	—	—	—	—	—	—	—	—	—	k	—	0	114
1989	LARd	16 (2)	48	161	3.4 (19)	2	18	240	13.3 (29)	2	—	—	—	—	—	—	—	—	—	—	k	—	24	356
1990	†LARd	16 (1)	13	43	3.3 (12)	0	—	—	—	—	—	—	—	—	—	—	—	—	—	—	—	—	0	43
NFL	5	73 (5)	128	469	3.7 (35)	3	40	452	11.3 (29)	2	—	—	—	—	—	—	—	—	—	—	k	—	30	1028

Muellner, Bill William Clarence, E, 5´11˝/175 lbs; DePaul; B9/30/1914 Chicago, IL **1937** ChiC 1 (0)

Mugg, Garvin Garvin Bray, T, 6´1˝/215 lbs; North Texas; B2/19/1918 Weston, TX, D10/27/1990 Tallapoosa, GA **1945** Det 3 (0)

Mughelli, Ovie Ovie Phillip, FB, 6´1˝/260 lbs; Wake Forest; 2003: Bal, rnd 4; B6/10/1980 Boston, MA **2003**†Bal 6 (0) **2004** Bal 3 (0)

YEAR	TEAM	G (GS, POS)	RUSH	YD	AVG (LG)	TD	REC	YD	AVG (LG)	TD	PASS	COMP	PCT	YD	AVG (LG)	TD	INT	SK	YD	QBR	KPR	OTD	PTS	TAY
2005	Bal	13 (5, FB)	—	—	—	—	3	13	4.3 (6)	0	—	—	—	—	—	—	—	—	—	—	—	—	0	7
NFL	3	22 (5)	—	—	—	—	3	13	4.3 (6)	0	—	—	—	—	—	—	—	—	—	—	—	—	0	7

Muha, Joe Joseph George, FB-LB, 6´1˝/205 lbs; VMI; 1943: Phi, rnd 1; B4/28/1921 Central City, PA, D3/31/1993 Hemet, CA **[K]**

YEAR	TEAM	G (GS, POS)	RUSH	YD	AVG (LG)	TD	REC	YD	AVG (LG)	TD	PASS	COMP	PCT	YD	AVG (LG)	TD	INT	SK	YD	QBR	KPR	OTD	PTS	TAY
1946	Phi	10 (8, FB)	12	41	3.4 (16)	0	—	—	—	—	—	—	—	—	—	—	—	—	—	—	Pki	—	0	52
1947	†Phi	12 (9, FB)	27	107	4.0 (28)	1	1	10	10.0 (10)	0	—	—	—	—	—	—	—	—	—	—	KPk	1	15	132
1948	†Phi☆	11 (11, FB)	25	90	3.6 (14)	0	2	22	11.0 (20)	1	—	—	—	—	—	—	—	—	—	—	KP	—	6	106
1949	†Phi	12 (11, FB)	3	19	6.3 (13)	0	1	10	10.0 (10)	0	—	—	—	—	—	—	—	—	—	—	KPkpi	1	11	57
1950	Phi☆	11 (LLB)	—	—	—	—	—	—	—	—	—	—	—	—	—	—	—	—	—	—	KPki	1	6	38
NFL	5	56 (39)	67	257	3.8 (28)	1	4	42	10.5 (20)	1	—	—	—	—	—	—	—	—	—	—	KPkpi	3	38	385

Muhammad, Calvin Calvin Saleem, aka Calvin Vincent Rainey, WR, 5´11˝/190 lbs; Texas Southern; 1980: Oak, rnd 12; B12/10/1958 Jacksonville, FL

YEAR	TEAM	G (GS, POS)	RUSH	YD	AVG (LG)	TD	REC	YD	AVG (LG)	TD	PASS	COMP	PCT	YD	AVG (LG)	TD	INT	SK	YD	QBR	KPR	OTD	PTS	TAY
1982	†LARd	8 (0)	—	—	—	—	3	92	30.7 (43)	1	—	—	—	—	—	—	—	—	—	—	—	—	6	51
1983	†LARd	15 (4)	—	—	—	—	13	252	19.4 (45)	2	—	—	—	—	—	—	—	—	—	—	—	—	12	136
1984	†Was	10 (8, WR)	—	—	—	—	42	729	17.4 (80)	4	—	—	—	—	—	—	—	—	—	—	—	—	24	385
1985	Was	12 (5, wr)	—	—	—	—	9	116	12.9 (32)	1	—	—	—	—	—	—	—	—	—	—	—	—	6	63
1987	SD	2 (0)	—	—	—	—	2	87	43.5 (67)	0	—	—	—	—	—	—	—	—	—	—	—	—	0	44
NFL	5	47 (17)	—	—	—	—	69	1276	18.5 (80)	8	—	—	—	—	—	—	—	—	—	—	—	—	48	678

Muhammad, Muhsin Muhsin, aka Steve Wilson, WR, 6´2˝/217 lbs; Michigan State; 1996: Car, rnd 2; B5/5/1973 Lansing, MI

YEAR	TEAM	G (GS, POS)	RUSH	YD	AVG (LG)	TD	REC	YD	AVG (LG)	TD	PASS	COMP	PCT	YD	AVG (LG)	TD	INT	SK	YD	QBR	KPR	OTD	PTS	TAY
1996	†Car	9 (5, wr)	1	-1	-1.0 (-1)	0	25	407	16.3 (54)	1	—	—	—	—	—	—	—	—	—	—	—	—	6	208
1997	Car	13 (5, wr)	—	—	—	—	27	317	11.7 (38)	0	—	—	—	—	—	—	—	—	—	—	—	—	2	159
1998	Car	16 (16, WR)	—	—	—	—	68	941	13.8 (72)	6	—	—	—	—	—	—	—	—	—	—	—	—	38	501
1999	Car✧	15 (15, WR)	—	—	—	—	**96**	1253	13.1 (60)	8	—	—	—	—	—	—	—	—	—	—	—	—	48	667
2000	Car	16 (16, WR)	2	12	6.0 (8)	0	**102**	1183	11.6 (36)	6	—	—	—	—	—	—	—	—	—	—	—	—	36	634
2001	Car	11 (11, WR)	—	—	—	—	50	585	11.7 (43)	1	—	—	—	—	—	—	—	—	—	—	—	—	6	298
2002	Car	14 (14, WR)	3	40	13.3 (20)	0	63	823	13.1 (42)	3	—	—	—	—	—	—	—	—	—	—	—	—	18	467
2003	†Car	15 (15, WR)	2	-2	-1.0 (0)	0	54	837	15.5 (60)	3	—	—	—	—	—	—	—	—	—	—	k	—	18	419
2004	Car★	16 (16, WR)	3	15	5.0 (13)	0	93	**1405**	15.1 (51)	**16**	—	—	—	—	—	—	—	—	—	—	—	—	96	798
2005	†ChiB	15 (15, WR)	—	—	—	—	64	750	11.7 (33)	4	—	—	—	—	—	—	—	—	—	—	—	—	24	395
NFL	10	140 (128)	11	64	5.8 (20)	0	642	8501	13.2 (72)	48	—	—	—	—	—	—	—	—	—	—	k	—	292	4542

Muhammad, Mustafah Mustafah Jaleel, DB, 5´9˝/180 lbs; Fresno State; B10/19/1973 Los Angeles, CA **1999** Ind 11 (1) **2000**†Ind 13 (3) **NFL** 24 (4) [2 yrs]

Muhlbach, Don Don Lynn, C, 6´5˝/262 lbs; Texas A&M; B8/17/1981 Newark, OH **2004** Det 8 (0) **2005** Det 13 (0) **NFL** 21 (0) [2 yrs]

Muhlmann, Horst Horst Herbert Erich, K, 6´1˝/215 lbs; none; B1/2/1940 Dortmund, Germany, D11/17/1991 Selm, Germany **[K]** **1969** Cin-A 14 **1970**†Cin 14 **1971** Cin 14 **1972** Cin 14 **1973**†Cin 14 **1974** Cin 14 **1975** Phi 14 **1976** Phi 14 **1977** Phi 9 **NFL** 121 [9 yrs]

Muirhead, Stan Stanley Nelson, G-T, 6´0˝/180 lbs; Michigan; B8/29/1902 Calumet, MI, D9/14/1992 Detroit, MO **1924** Day 5 (5, RG) **1924** Cle☆3 (3) **NFL** 8 (8) [1 yr]

YEAR	TEAM	G(GS, POS)	RUSH	YD	AVG(LG)	TD	REC	YD	AVG(LG)	TD	PASS	COMP	PCT	YD	AVG(LG)	TD	INT	SK	YD	QBR	KPR	OTD	PTS	TAY

MULARKEY, MIKE Michael Rene, TE, 6´4˝/245 lbs; Florida; 1983: SF, rnd 9; B11/19/1961 Miami, FL

1983	Min	3(3)	—	—	—	—	—	—	—	—	—	—	—	—	—	—	—	—	—	—	—	—	—	—
1984	Min	16(2)	—	—	—	—	14	134	9.6(26)	2	—	—	—	—	—	—	—	—	—	—	—	—	12	77
1985	Min	15(5, te)	—	—	—	—	13	196	15.1(51)	1	—	—	—	—	—	—	—	—	—	—	—	—	6	112
1986	Min	16(1)	—	—	—	—	11	89	8.1(20)	2	—	—	—	—	—	—	—	—	—	—	—	—	12	55
1987	Min	9(0)	—	—	—	—	1	6	6.0(6)	0	—	—	—	—	—	—	—	—	—	—	k	—	0	4
1988	†Min	16(0)	1	-6	-6.0(-6)	0	3	39	13.0(19)	0	—	—	—	—	—	—	—	—	—	—	—	—	0	14
1989	†Pit	14(14, TE)	—	—	—	—	22	326	14.8(34)	1	—	—	—	—	—	—	—	—	—	—	—	—	6	168
1990	Pit	16(15, TE)	—	—	—	—	32	365	11.4(28)	3	—	—	—	—	—	—	—	—	—	—	—	—	18	198
1991	Pit	9(6, te)	—	—	—	—	6	67	11.2(21)	0	—	—	—	—	—	—	—	—	—	—	—	—	0	34
NFL	9	114(46)	1	-6	-6.0(-6)	0	102	1222	12.0(51)	9	—	—	—	—	—	—	—	—	—	—	k	—	54	660

MULBARGER, JOE Joseph G., T-G, 5´9˝/221 lbs; none; B1895, OH, deceased   **1920** Col 9 (3, RT) **1921** Col 8 (8, RT), 6 **1922** Col 8 (8, LT) **1923** Col 10 (8, RT) **1924** Col 8 (8, RG) **1925** Col 9 (8, RG) **1926** Col 7 (7, RG) **NFL** 59 (50) [7 yrs]

MULITALO, EDWIN Edwin Moliki, G, 6´3˝/345 lbs; Arizona; 1999: Bal, rnd 4; B9/1/1974 Daly City, CA   **1999** Bal 10 (8, LG) **2000**†Bal 16 (16, LG) **2001**†Bal 14 (14, LG) **2002** Bal 16 (15, LG) **2003**†Bal 15 (15, LG) **2004** Bal 15 (15, LG) **2005** Bal 16 (15, LG) **NFL** 102 (98) [7 yrs]

MUL-KEY, HERB Herbert Felton, RB, 6´0˝/190 lbs; none; B11/15/1949 Atlanta, GA

1972	†Was	2(1)	33	155	4.7(35)	1	4	66	16.5(28)	0	—	—	—	—	—	—	—	—	—	—	k	—	6	287
1973	†Was◇	14	8	20	2.5(7)	0	—	—	—	—	—	—	—	—	—	—	—	—	—	—	kp	1	6	549
1974	Was	7	1	3	3.0(3)	0	—	—	—	—	—	—	—	—	—	—	—	—	—	—	kp	—	0	213
NFL	3	23(1)	42	178	4.2(35)	1	4	66	16.5(28)	0	—	—	—	—	—	—	—	—	—	—	kp	1	12	1049

MULLADY, TOM Thomas Francis, TE-WR, 6´3˝/232 lbs; Rhodes; 1979: Buf, rnd 7; B1/30/1957 Dayton, OH

1979	NYG	2	—	—	—	—	—	—	—	—	—	—	—	—	—	—	—	—	—	—	—	—	—	—
1980	NYG	16(3)	—	—	—	—	28	391	14.0(42)	2	—	—	—	—	—	—	—	—	—	—	—	—	12	206
1981	†NYG	16(3)	—	—	—	—	14	136	9.7(21)	1	—	—	—	—	—	—	—	—	—	—	—	—	6	73
1982	NYG	9(9, TE)	—	—	—	—	27	287	10.6(32)	0	—	—	—	—	—	—	—	—	—	—	—	—	0	144
1983	NYG	16(3)	—	—	—	—	13	184	14.2(35)	1	—	—	—	—	—	—	—	—	—	—	—	—	6	97
1984	†NYG	16(0)	—	—	—	—	2	35	17.5(22)	0	—	—	—	—	—	—	—	—	—	—	—	—	0	18
NFL	6	75(18)	—	—	—	—	84	1033	12.3(42)	4	—	—	—	—	—	—	—	—	—	—	—	—	24	537

MULLANEY, MARK Mark Alan, DE, 6´6˝/242 lbs; Colorado State; 1975: Min, rnd 1; B4/30/1953 Denver, CO   **1975**†Min 14 **1976**†Min 12 (1) **1977**†Min 14 **1978**†Min 15 (9, LDE) **1979** Min 16 (16, LDE) **1980**†Min 16 (15, LDE) **1981** Min 15 (15, LDE) **1982**†Min 9 (9, RDE) **1983** Min 7 (4) **1984** Min 7 (6, RDE) **1985** Min 15 (13, RDE) **1986** Min 11 (9, RDE) **NFL** 151 (111) [12 yrs]

MULLEN, CHIEF Samuel, WB, /165 lbs; Haskell Indian; B1/9/1894 Lawton, OK, D5/25/1976 Lawton, OK   **1921** Evv 2 (0)

MULLEN, DAVLIN Davlin, DB, 6´1˝/175 lbs; Western Kentucky; 1983: NYJ, rnd 8; B2/17/1960 McKeesport, PA   **1983** NYJ 11 (0) **1984** NYJ 15 (6, LCB) **1985**†NYJ 11 (1) **1986** NYJ 5 (0) **NFL** 42 (7) [4 yrs]

MULLEN, GARY Gary, WR, 5´11˝/174 lbs; West Virginia; B2/1/1963 McKeesport, PA

| 1987 | ChiB | 3(0) | — | — | — | — | 2 | 33 | 16.5(20) | 0 | — | — | — | — | — | — | — | — | — | — | — | — | 0 | 17 |

MULLEN, RODERICK Roderick Louis, DB, 6´1˝/202 lbs; Grambling State; 1995: NYG, rnd 5; B12/5/1972 Baton Rouge, LA   **1995**†GB 8 (0) **1996**†GB 14 (0) **1997**†GB 16 (1) **1999** Car 15 (0) **NFL** 53 (1) [4 yrs]

MULLEN, TOM Thomas Patrick, G-T, 6´3˝/248 lbs; Southwest Missouri State; 1974: NYG, rnd 2; B11/11/1951 St. Louis, MO   **1974** NYG 11 (LG) **1975** NYG 12 (LG) **1976** NYG 12 (12, LT) **1977** NYG 8 **1978** SL 7 **NFL** 50 (12) [5 yrs]

MULLEN, VERN Vern Elmo, E-HB, 6´0˝/186 lbs; Illinois; West Virginia Wesleyan; B2/27/1900 Taylorville, IL, D9/14/1980 Taft, CA   **1923** Can 4 (4) **1924** ChiB 11 (1) **1925** ChiB 16 (0) **1926** ChiB 16 (4), 6 **1927** ChiC 1 (0) **1927** Pot 8 (8, RE) **NFL** 56 (17) [5 yrs]

MULLENEAUX, CARL Carl Kenneth, E, 6´3˝/209 lbs; Utah State; B9/16/1914 Phoenix, AZ, D1/23/1995 Chico, CA

1938	†GB	9(2)	—	—	—	—	4	97	24.3(36)	2	—	—	—	—	—	—	—	—	—	—	—	—	12	59
1939	†GB◇	11(6, RE)	—	—	—	—	12	218	18.2(48)	1	—	—	—	—	—	—	—	—	—	—	—	—	6	114
1940	GB★	10(3)	—	—	—	—	16	288	18.0(47)	6	—	—	—	—	—	—	—	—	—	—	—	1	42	174
1941	†GB	10(0)	—	—	—	—	9	216	24.0(56)	2	—	—	—	—	—	—	—	—	—	—	—	—	12	118
1945	GB	5(1)	—	—	—	—	3	31	10.3(13)	0	—	—	—	—	—	—	—	—	—	—	—	—	0	16
1946	GB	1(0)	—	—	—	—	—	—	—	—	—	—	—	—	—	—	—	—	—	—	—	—	—	—
NFL	6	46(12)	—	—	—	—	44	850	19.3(56)	11	—	—	—	—	—	—	—	—	—	—	—	1	72	480

MULLENEAUX, LEE Cecil Lee, C-WB, 6´2˝/221 lbs; Northern Arizona; B4/1/1908, D11/14/1985 Whittier, CA   **1934** SL 2 (2, C) **1935** Pit 7 (5, c) **1936** Pit 12 (12, C) **1938** ChiC 4 (4) **1938**†GB 5 (3)

1932	NYG	6(4)	3	1	0.3	0	—	—	—	—	—	—	—	—	—	—	—	—	—	—	—	—	0	1
1933	Cin	9(7, WB)	19	62	3.3	0	2	13	6.5	0	—	—	—	—	—	—	—	—	—	—	—	—	0	69
1934	Cin	8(3, c)	3	7	2.3	0	1	5	5.0(5)	0	—	—	—	—	—	—	—	—	—	—	—	—	0	10
NFL	6	53(40)	25	70	2.8	0	3	18	6.0(5)	0	—	—	—	—	—	—	—	—	—	—	—	—	0	79

MULLER, BRICK Harold Powers, E, 6´2˝/195 lbs; California; B6/12/1901 Dunsmuir, CA, D5/17/1962 Berkeley, CA [C]   **1926** LA☆10 (10, RE), 6

MULLIGAN, GEORGE George Edward, E, 6´1˝/198 lbs; Catholic; B6/7/1914 Waterbury, CT, deceased

| 1936 | Phi | 9(0) | — | — | — | — | 1 | 3 | 3.0(3) | 0 | — | — | — | — | — | — | — | — | — | — | — | — | 0 | 2 |

MULLIGAN, WAYNE Wayne Eugene, C-T, 6´3˝/250 lbs; Clemson; 1969: SL, rnd 8; B5/5/1947 Baltimore, MD   **1969** SL 14 **1970** SL 14 (C) **1971** SL 7 (c) **1972** SL 12 (RT/c) **1973** SL 13 (C) **1974** NYJ 13 (C) **1975** NYJ 14 (14, C) **NFL** 87 (14) [7 yrs]

MULLINS, DON Don Ray, DB, 6´1˝/195 lbs; Houston; B3/31/1939 Shreveport, LA   **1961** ChiB 4 **1962** ChiB 9 **NFL** 13 [2 yrs]

MULLINS, ERIC Eric Dwayne, WR, 5´11˝/181 lbs; Stanford; 1984: Hou, rnd 6; B7/30/1962 Houston, TX

| 1984 | Hou | 13(2) | 1 | 0 | 0.0(0) | 0 | 6 | 85 | 14.2(25) | 1 | — | — | — | — | — | — | — | — | — | — | — | — | 6 | 48 |

MULLINS, GERRY Gerald Blaine, G-T, 6´3˝/244 lbs; USC; 1971: Pit, rnd 4; B8/24/1949 Fullerton, CA   **1971** Pit 14 **1973**†Pit 13 **1975**†Pit 14 (14, RG) **1976**†Pit 14 (RT) **1977** Pit 12 (5, lg) **1978**†Pit 16 (RG) **1979**†Pit☆15 (rg)

1972	†Pit	14(RT)	—	—	—	—	1	3	3.0(3)	1	—	—	—	—	—	—	—	—	—	—	—	—	6	7
1974	†Pit	12(RG)	—	—	—	—	1	7	7.0(7)	1	—	—	—	—	—	—	—	—	—	—	—	—	6	9
NFL	9	124(19)	—	—	—	—	2	10	5.0(7)	2	—	—	—	—	—	—	—	—	—	—	k	1	18	0

MULLINS, NOAH Noah Walker, HB, 5´11˝/182 lbs; Kentucky; 1942: ChiB, rnd 10; B5/23/1918 Midway, KY, D10/31/1998 Versailles, KY

1946	ChiB	10(3)	20	102	5.1(45)	0	—	—	—	1	1	100.0	16	16.0(16)	0	0	—	—	—	—	kpi	—	0	228
1947	ChiB	12(2)	9	55	6.1(41)	0	1	4	4.0(4)	0	—	—	—	—	—	—	—	—	—	—	pi	—	0	228
1948	ChiB	12(2)	36	208	5.8(74)	1	9	127	14.1(26)	4	1	0	0.0	—	—	—	—	—	—	—	Pkpi	1	36	420
1949	NYG	11(1)	2	-3	-1.5(4)	0	2	45	22.5(24)	1	—	—	—	—	—	—	—	—	—	—	i	—	6	36
NFL	4	45(8)	67	362	5.4(74)	1	12	176	14.7(26)	5	2	1	50.0	16	8.0(16)	0	0	—	—	—	Pkpi	1	42	911

MULREADY, JERRY John Jerome, E-DE, 6´1˝/205 lbs; Minnesota; North Dakota State; 1947: Pit, rnd 19; B1/5/1923 Fargo, ND, D6/3/1976 Fargo, ND

| 1947 | ChiR-A | 9(6, RE) | — | — | — | — | 7 | 108 | 15.4 | 0 | — | — | — | — | — | — | — | — | — | — | — | — | 0 | 54 |

MULVEY, VINCE Vincent James, B, /155 lbs; Syracuse; B10/6/1891 Geneva, NY, D2/25/1988 Rochester, NY   **1923** Buf 3 (1)

MUMFORD, TONY Anthony Vincent, RB, 6´0˝/215 lbs; Penn State; 1985: NE, rnd 12; B6/14/1963 Philadelphia, PA   **1985** SL 2 (0)

MUMLEY, NICK Nicholas, DE-T, 6´4˝/255 lbs; Purdue; 1959: Phi, rnd 5; B1/26/1937 Wheeling, WV   **1960** NYT-A 14 (RDE) **1961** NYT-A 14 (LDE) **1962** NYT-A 14 **NFL** 42 [3 yrs]

MUMPHORD, LLOYD Lloyd N., DB, 5´10˝/176 lbs; Texas Southern; 1969: Mia, rnd 16; B12/20/1946 Los Angeles, CA [I]   **1969** Mia-A 11 (7, RCB) **1970**†Mia 14 (14, RCB) **1971**†Mia 14 **1972**†Mia 14 **1973**†Mia 11 **1974** Mia 13 **1975**†Bal 14 (10, LCB) **1976**†Bal 13 (LCB) **1977** Bal 2 **1978** Bal 16 (5, lcb) **NFL** 122 (36) [10 yrs]

MUMPHREY, LLOYD Lloyd Ellis, DE-LB, 6´3˝/260 lbs; Mississippi Valley State; B2/14/1961 Memphis, TN   **1987** KC 3 (2)

YEAR	TEAM	G(GS, POS)	RUSH	YD	AVG(LG)	TD	REC	YD	AVG(LG)	TD	PASS	COMP	PCT	YD	AVG(LG)	TD	INT	SK	YD	QBR	KPR	OTD	PTS	TAY

MUNCHAK, MIKE Michael Anthony, G, 6´3˝/281 lbs; Penn State; 1982: Hou, rnd 1; B3/5/1960 Scranton, PA; HOF 2001 **1982** Hou 4 (3) **1983** Hou☆16 (16, LG) **1984** Hou★16 (16, LG) **1985** Hou★16 (16, LG) **1986** Hou 6 (6, LG) **1987**†Hou★12 (12, LG) **1988**†Hou★16 (16, LG) **1989**†Hou★16 (16, LG) **1990**†Hou★16 (16, LG) **1991**†Hou★13 (13, LG) **1992**†Hou★15 (14, LG) **1993**†Hou★13 (12, LG) **NFL** 159 (156) [12 yrs]

MUNCIE, CHUCK Harry Vance, RB, 6´3˝/227 lbs; California; 1976: NO, rnd 1; B3/17/1953 Uniontown, PA

1976	NO	12(11, FB)	149	659	4.4(51)	2	31	272	8.8(33)	0	—	—	—	—	—	—	—	—	—	—	k	—	12	839
1977	NO	14(11, RB)	201	811	4.0(36)	6	21	248	11.8(35)	1	—	—	—	—	—	—	—	—	—	—	k	—	42	1004
1978	NO	13(11, RB)	160	557	3.5(28)	7	26	233	9.0(34)	0	1	0	0.0	0	0.0	0	0	—	—	—	—	—	42	744
1979	NO★	16(15, RB)	238	1198	5.0(69)	11	40	308	7.7(28)	0	2	1	50.0	40	20.0(40)	1	0	—	—	—	—	—	66	1487
1980	NO	4(3)	40	168	4.2(24)	2	7	25	3.6(8)	0	—	—	—	—	—	—	—	—	—	—	—	—	12	201
1980	†SD	11(5, fb)	135	659	4.9(53)	4	24	234	9.8(19)	0	—	—	—	—	—	—	—	—	—	—	k	—	24	920
1981	†SD★	15(14, RB)	251	1144	4.6(73)	**19**	43	362	8.4(32)	0	1	1	100.0	3	3.0(3)	1	0	—	—	—	—	—	114	1522
1982	†SD★	9(9, RB)	138	569	4.1(27)	8	25	207	8.3(39)	1	3	2	66.7	83	27.7(66)	2	0	—	—	—	—	—	54	809
1983	SD	15(12, RB)	235	886	3.8(34)	12	42	396	9.4(27)	1	—	—	—	—	—	—	—	—	—	—	—	—	78	1209
1984	SD	1(1)	14	51	3.6(11)	0	4	38	9.5(20)	0	—	—	—	—	—	—	—	—	—	—	—	—	0	70
NFL	9	110(92)	1561	6702	4.3(73)	71	263	2323	8.8(39)	3	7	4	57.1	126	18.0(66)	4	0	—	—	—	k	—	444	8804

MUNDAY, GEORGE George, T-G, 6´2˝/215 lbs; Emporia State; B6/13/1907 Climax, KS, D10/17/1975 Miami Beach, FL **1931** Cle 1 (0) **1931** NYG 1 (0) **1932** NYG 4 (1) **1933** Cin 10 (9, LT) **1934** Cin 8 (8, LT) **1934** SL 2 (1) **NFL** 26 (19) [4 yrs]

MUNDEE, FRED Frederick William, C-LB, 6´1˝/220 lbs; Notre Dame; B5/20/1913 Youngstown, OH, D1/15/1990 Chicago, IL **1943**†ChiB 5 (0) **1944** ChiB 10 (1) **1945** ChiB 6 (1) **NFL** 21 (2) [3 yrs]

MUNFORD, MARC Marc Christopher, LB, 6´2˝/231 lbs; Nebraska; 1987: Den, rnd 4; B2/14/1965 Lincoln, NE **1987** Den 12 (0) **1988** Den 7 (0) **1989**†Den 16 (6, rilb) **1990** Den 13 (10, RILB) **NFL** 48 (16) [4 yrs]

MUNGAVIN, JOCK James Francis, E, 5´10˝/175 lbs; Wisconsin-Superior; Wisconsin; B9/12/1893 Superior, WI, D10/26/1977 Washburn, WI **1920** ChiT 3 (2)

MUNGER T, none **1924** ChiC 1 (1)

MUNGRO, JAMES James Alevia, RB, 5´9˝/214 lbs; Syracuse; B2/13/1978 East Stroudsburg, PA

2002	†Ind	9(1)	97	336	3.5(49)	8	13	81	6.2(11)	0	—	—	—	—	—	—	—	—	—	—	—	—	48	457
2003	Ind	7(0)	24	60	2.5(9)	2	1	-4	-4.0(-4)	0	—	—	—	—	—	—	—	—	—	—	k	—	14	55
2004	†Ind	15(0)	5	19	3.8(8)	0	7	36	5.1(16)	3	—	—	—	—	—	—	—	—	—	—	k	—	18	58
2005	†Ind	12(0)	7	15	2.1(7)	0	3	28	9.3(17)	0	—	—	—	—	—	—	—	—	—	—	k	—	0	38
NFL	4	43(1)	133	430	3.2(49)	10	24	141	5.9(17)	3	—	—	—	—	—	—	—	—	—	—	k	—	80	608

MUNN, LYLE Lyle Smith, E, 6´0˝/186 lbs; Kansas State; B4/13/1902 Fairbury, NE, D1/12/1984 Topeka, KS **[K]** **1925** KC 7 (7, RE) **1926** KC 11 (11, RE), 6 **1927** Cle 10 (6, re) **1928** Det 10 (9, LE) **1929** NYG 15 (11, RE), 1 **NFL** 53 (44), 7 [5 yrs]

MUNNS, GEORGE George Francis, QB-TB, 5´9˝/170 lbs; Miami (OH); B6/25/1898 Oxford, OH, D8/25/1972, **[K]** **1921** Cin 4 (4, QB), 1

MUNOZ, ANTHONY Michael Anthony, T, 6´6˝/278 lbs; USC; 1980: Cin, rnd 1; B8/19/1958 Ontario, CA; HOF 1998 **1981**†Cin★16 (16, LT) **1982**†Cin★9 (9, LT) **1983** Cin★16 (15, LT) **1988**†Cin★16 (16, LT) **1989** Cin★16 (16, LT) **1990**†Cin★16 (16, LT) **1991** Cin★13 (13, LT) **1992** Cin 8 (7, lt)

1980	Cin	16(16, LT)	—	—	—	—	1	-6	-6.0(-6)	0	—	—	—	—	—	—	—	—	—	—	—	—	0	-3
1984	Cin★	16(16, LT)	—	—	—	—	1	1	1.0(1)	1	—	—	—	—	—	—	—	—	—	—	—	—	6	6
1985	Cin★	16(16, LT)	—	—	—	—	1	1	1.0(1)	0	—	—	—	—	—	—	—	—	—	—	—	—	0	1
1986	Cin★	16(16, LT)	—	—	—	—	2	7	3.5(5)	2	—	—	—	—	—	—	—	—	—	—	—	—	12	14
1987	Cin★	11(11, LT)	—	—	—	—	2	15	7.5(12)	1	—	—	—	—	—	—	—	—	—	—	—	—	6	13
NFL	13	185(183)	—	—	—	—	7	18	2.6(12)	4	—	—	—	—	—	—	—	—	—	—	—	—	24	29

MUNSEY, NELSON Nelson Emory, DB, 6´1˝/188 lbs; Wyoming; B7/2/1948 Uniontown, PA **1972** Bal 9 **1973** Bal 14 (RCB) **1974** Bal 14 (RCB) **1975**†Bal 14 (14, RCB) **1976** Bal 8 (8, RCB) **1977**†Bal 13 (RCB) **NFL** 72 (22) [6 yrs]

MUNSON, BILL William Alan, QB, 6´2˝/203 lbs; Utah State; 1964: LA, rnd 1/Hou, rnd 16; B8/11/1941 Sacramento, CA, D7/10/2000 Lodi, CA

1964	LARm	11(8, QB)	19	150	7.9(33)	0	—	—	—	—	223	108	48.4	1533	6.9(**95**)	9	15	—	—	56.5	—	—	0	362
1965	LARm	10(10, qb)	26	157	6.0(38)	1	—	—	—	—	267	144	53.9	1701	6.4(47)	10	14	—	—	64.2	—	—	6	508
1966	LARm	5	4	3	0.8(2)	0	—	—	—	—	50	30	60.0	284	5.7(25)	2	1	—	—	—	—	—	0	115
1967	†LARm	5	2	-22	-11.0(0)	0	—	—	—	—	10	5	50.0	38	3.8(18)	1	2	—	—	—	—	—	0	-78
1968	Det	12(11, QB)	25	109	4.4(20)	1	—	—	—	—	329	181	55.0	2311	7.0(86)	15	8	—	—	82.3	—	—	6	1030
1969	Det	8(7, QB)	7	31	4.4(13)	0	—	—	—	—	166	84	50.6	1062	6.4(62)	7	8	12	93	64.9	—	—	0	277
1970	†Det	8(8, QB)	9	33	3.7(11)	0	—	—	—	—	158	84	53.2	1049	6.6(56)	10	7	10	66	76.7	—	—	0	328
1971	Det	4	3	9	3.0(6)	0	—	—	—	—	38	21	55.3	216	5.7(34)	1	1	1	5	—	—	—	0	82
1972	Det	2	1	0	0.0(0)	0	—	—	—	—	35	20	57.1	194	5.5(29)	1	1	1	0	—	—	—	0	62
1973	Det	10(7, qb)	10	33	3.3(11)	0	—	—	—	—	187	95	50.8	1129	6.0(54)	9	8	14	94	67.8	—	—	0	323
1974	Det	11(11, QB)	18	40	2.2(9)	1	1	-6	-6.0(-6)	0	292	166	56.8	1874	6.4(56)	8	7	24	172	75.3	—	—	6	744
1975	Det	5(3)	4	-3	-0.8(2)	0	—	—	—	—	109	65	59.6	626	5.7(32)	5	2	8	65	—	—	—	0	255
1976	Sea	5	1	6	6.0(6)	0	—	—	—	—	37	20	54.1	295	8.0(44)	1	3	3	29	—	—	—	0	39
1977	SD	4	1	2	2.0(2)	0	—	—	—	—	31	20	64.5	225	7.3(28)	1	1	1	11	—	—	—	0	80
1978	Buf	4	—	—	—	—	—	—	—	—	43	24	55.8	328	7.6(43)	4	2	—	—	—	—	—	0	104
1979	Buf	3	—	—	—	—	—	—	—	—	7	3	42.9	31	4.4(16)	0	0	—	—	—	—	—	0	16
NFL	16	107(65)	130	548	4.2(38)	3	1	-6	-6.0(-6)	0	1982	1070	54.0	12896	6.5(95)	84	80	74	535	71.5	—	—	18	4243

MURAKOWSKI, ART Arthur Raymond, FB-LB, 6´0˝/195 lbs; Northwestern; 1950: Det, rnd 3; B5/15/1925 East Chicago, IN, D9/13/1985 Hammond, IN **1951** Det 12

MURANSKY, ED Edward William, T, 6´7˝/277 lbs; Michigan; 1982: LARd, rnd 4; B1/20/1960 Youngstown, OH **1982**†LARd 5 (0) **1983** LARd 16 (0) **1984** LARd 3 (0) **NFL** 24 (0) [3 yrs]

MURCHISON, LEE Ola Lee, WR, 6´3˝/205 lbs; Pacific; 1960: SF, rnd 6/DalT, rnd 1; B4/16/1938, AR **1961** Dal 14

MURDOCK, GUY Guy Boyd, C, 6´2˝/245 lbs; Michigan; 1972: Hou, rnd 16; B6/27/1950 Chicago, IL **1972** Hou 14

MURDOCK, JESSE Jesse, HB, 6´2˝/203 lbs; California Western; B9/17/1938 Oakland, CA **1963** Oak-A 1 **1963**†Buf-A 6 **NFL** 7 [1 yr]

MURDOCK, LES Leslie Ray, K, 6´3˝/245 lbs; Florida State; B6/6/1941 Boston, MA **[K]** **1967** NYG 4

MURLEY, DICK Richard Allen, T, 6´0˝/247 lbs; Purdue; 1956: Pit, rnd 4; B8/1/1933 Richmond, IN **1956** Pit 2 **1956** Phi 5 **NFL** 7 [1 yr]

MURPHY, BILL William Leslie, G, 6´0˝/203 lbs; Washington-St. Louis; B4/7/1914 Owensboro, KY **1940** ChiC 8 (2) **1941** ChiC 4 (0) **NFL** 12 (2) [2 yrs]

MURPHY, BILL William Joseph, WR, 6´1˝/185 lbs; Cornell; B3/26/1946 Montclair, NJ

1968	Bos-A	6(5, wr)	—	—	—	—	18	268	14.9(26)	0	—	—	—	—	—	—	—	—	—	—	—	—	0	134

MURPHY, DENNIS Alvin Dennis, DT, 6´2˝/250 lbs; Florida; 1965: Chi, rnd 10/Hou, rnd 6; B3/9/1943 Cairo, GA **1965** ChiB 2

MURPHY, FRANK Frank, WR, 6´0˝/206 lbs; Kansas State; 2000: Chi, rnd 6; B2/11/1977 Jacksonville, FL **2000**†TB 1 (0) **2002** Hou 5 (0) **2004** TB 3 (0)

2001	†TB	11(0)	—	—	—	—	8	71	8.9(20)	1	—	—	—	—	—	—	—	—	—	—	k	—	6	186
NFL	4	20(0)	—	—	—	—	8	71	8.9(20)	1	—	—	—	—	—	—	—	—	—	—	k	—	6	253

MURPHY, FRED Fred Joe, E, 6´3˝/205 lbs; Georgia Tech; B2/20/1938 Atlanta, GA **1961** Min 13

1960	Cle	9(se)	—	—	—	—	2	36	18.0(23)	0	—	—	—	—	—	—	—	—	—	—	—	—	0	18
NFL	2	22	—	—	—	—	2	36	18.0(23)	0	—	—	—	—	—	—	—	—	—	—	—	—	0	18

MURPHY, GEORGE George Patrick, BB, 6´0˝/200 lbs; USC; B5/10/1926 Santa Monica, CA, D8/25/1987 Chula Vista, CA

1949	LAD-A	11(7, BB)	1	0	0.0	0	1	17	17.0(17)	0	—	—	—	—	—	—	—	—	—	—	—	—	0	9

MURPHY, HARVEY Harvey Allen, E, 5´10˝/194 lbs; Mississippi; B8/24/1915, D5/25/1992 Harvey, LA **1940** Cle 2 (0)

MURPHY, JAMES James Jessie, WR, 5´10˝/177 lbs; Utah State; 1981: Min, rnd 10; B10/10/1959 Deland, FL

1981	KC	10(0)	—	—	—	—	2	36	18.0(22)	0	—	—	—	—	—	—	—	—	—	—	k	—	0	175

MURPHY, JIM James Thomas, B-E-C, 6´0˝/184 lbs; St. Thomas; B11/3/1904 Russell, MN, D12/17/1993 Denton, TX **1926** Rac 5 (0) **1926** Dul 2 (2) **1928** ChiC 1 (0) **NFL** 8 (2) [2 yrs]

MURPHY, JOE Joseph Thomas, G, 5´9˝/215 lbs; Harvard; Dartmouth; B5/15/1897 Concord, NH, D5/21/1940 Manchester, NH **1920** Can 2 (0) **1921** Cle 6 (6, RG) **NFL** 8 (6) [2 yrs]

MURPHY, KEVIN Kevin Dion, LB, 6´2˝/233 lbs; Oklahoma; 1986: TB, rnd 2; B9/8/1963 Plano, TX **1986** TB 16 (0) **1987** TB 9 (0) **1988** TB 16 (16, LOLB) **1989** TB 16 (16, LOLB) **1990** TB 15 (7, ROLB) **1991** TB 16 (14, LLB) **1992**†SD 14 (1) **1993** Sea 14 (10, RLB) **NFL** 116 (64) [8 yrs]

MURPHY, MARK Mark Steven, DB, 6´2˝/200 lbs; West Liberty State; B4/22/1958 Canton, OH **[I]** **1980** GB 1 (0) **1981** GB 16 (7, ss) **1982**†GB 9 (0) **1983** GB 16 (12, FS) **1984** GB 16 (16, SS) **1985** GB 15 (14, SS) **1987** GB 12 (12, SS) **1988** GB 14 (13, SS) **1989** GB 16 (16, SS) **1990** GB 16 (16, SS) **1991** GB 16 (16, SS) **NFL** 147 (122) [11 yrs]

MURPHY, MARK Mark Hodge, DB, 6´4˝/210 lbs; Colgate; B7/13/1955 Fulton, NY **[I]** **1977** Was 14 **1979** Was 16 (16, FS) **1980** Was 16 (16, FS) **1981** Was 16 (16, FS) **1982**†Was 9 (9, FS) **1983**†Was★15 (15, FS) **1984**†Was 7 (2)

YEAR	TEAM	G (GS, POS)	RUSH	YD	AVG (LG)	TD	REC	YD	AVG (LG)	TD	PASS	COMP	PCT	YD	AVG (LG)	TD	INT	SK	YD	QBR	KPR	OTD	PTS	TAY
1978	Was	16	—	—	—	—	1	13	13.0(13)	0	—	—	—	—	—	—	—	—	—	—	—	—	0	7
NFL	8	109(74)	—	—	—	—	1	13	13.0(13)	0	—	—	—	—	—	—	—	—	—	—	kiS	—	0	153

MURPHY, MATT Matthew Jarrid, TE, 6´5˝/260 lbs; Maryland; 2002: Det, rnd 7; B2/23/1980 New Haven, MI **2003** Hou 1 (0) **2004** Hou 11 (1)

YEAR	TEAM	G (GS, POS)	RUSH	YD	AVG (LG)	TD	REC	YD	AVG (LG)	TD	PASS	COMP	PCT	YD	AVG (LG)	TD	INT	SK	YD	QBR	KPR	OTD	PTS	TAY
2002	Det	3(0)	—	—	—	—	1	8	8.0(8)	0	—	—	—	—	—	—	—	—	—	—	—	—	0	4
2005	Hou	9(2)	—	—	—	—	2	26	13.0(14)	0	—	—	—	—	—	—	—	—	—	—	—	—	0	13
NFL	4	24(3)	—	—	—	—	3	34	11.3(14)	0	—	—	—	—	—	—	—	—	—	—	—	—	0	17

MURPHY, MIKE Michael William, LB, 6´2˝/222 lbs; Southwest Missouri State; 1979: Hou, rnd 6; B1/14/1957 St. Louis, MO **1979** Hou 3

MURPHY, NICK Nicholas Jon, P, 5´11˝/188 lbs; Arizona State; B10/22/1979 St. Louis, MO **2004** Bal 3 (0) **2004** KC 2 (0) **2005** Phi 1 (0) **NFL** 6 (0) [2 yrs]

MURPHY, PHIL Philip John, DT, 6´5˝/290 lbs; South Carolina State; 1980: LA, rnd 3; B9/26/1957 New London, CT **1980**†LARm 16 (0) **1981** LARm 16 (0) **NFL** 32 (0) [2 yrs]

MURPHY, ROB Robert Donald, C, 6´5˝/310 lbs; Ohio State; B1/18/1977 Buffalo, NY **2002** Ind 10 (0) **2003** SF 2 (0) **2004** SF 15 (0) **NFL** 27 (0) [3 yrs]

MURPHY, TERRENCE Terrence Cardene, WR, 6´1˝/202 lbs; Texas A&M; 2005: GB, rnd 2; B12/15/1982 Tyler, TX

YEAR	TEAM	G (GS, POS)	RUSH	YD	AVG (LG)	TD	REC	YD	AVG (LG)	TD	PASS	COMP	PCT	YD	AVG (LG)	TD	INT	SK	YD	QBR	KPR	OTD	PTS	TAY
2005	GB	3(0)	—	—	—	—	5	36	7.2(12)	0	—	—	—	—	—	—	—	—	—	—	k	—	0	34

MURPHY, TOM Thomas, TB-HB, 5´8˝/165 lbs; Wisconsin-Superior; B1/22/1900 Minneapolis, MN, D12/1986 Tacoma, WA **1926** Mil 8 (4)

MURPHY, TOM Thomas Benjamin, B, 5´11˝/170 lbs; Arkansas; B12/7/1906 Jonesboro, AR, D10/19/1981 Dallas, TX

YEAR	TEAM	G (GS, POS)	RUSH	YD	AVG (LG)	TD	REC	YD	AVG (LG)	TD	PASS	COMP	PCT	YD	AVG (LG)	TD	INT	SK	YD	QBR	KPR	OTD	PTS	TAY
1934	ChiC	5(0)	12	37	3.1	0	1	-2	-2.0(-2)	0	9	3	33.3	8	0.9	0	1	—	—	—	—	—	0	0

MURPHY, TOMMY Thomas B., BB-HB, 5´10˝/187 lbs; St. Mary's (KS); B5/2/1899 Norwood, OH, D4/29/1961 Cleveland, OH **1926** KC 1 (0) **1926** Col 6 (5, BB) **NFL** 7 (5) [1 yr]

MURPHY, YO Llewellyn, WR, 5´10˝/187 lbs; Idaho; B5/11/1973 San Pedro, CA **1999** Min 1 (0) **2001**†SL 16 (0)

YEAR	TEAM	G (GS, POS)	RUSH	YD	AVG (LG)	TD	REC	YD	AVG (LG)	TD	PASS	COMP	PCT	YD	AVG (LG)	TD	INT	SK	YD	QBR	KPR	OTD	PTS	TAY
1999	TB	7(0)	—	—	—	—	4	28	7.0(9)	0	—	—	—	—	—	—	—	—	—	—	k	—	0	111
2002	SL	11(1)	—	—	—	—	5	23	4.6(8)	0	—	—	—	—	—	—	—	—	—	—	k	—	0	18
NFL	3	35(1)	—	—	—	—	9	51	5.7(9)	0	—	—	—	—	—	—	—	—	—	—	kp	—	0	202

MURRAH, WILLIAM William Ervin, C-G, 5´10˝/215 lbs; Texas A&M; B9/5/1900 Plano, TX, deceased **1922** Can 6 (5, C) **1923** SL 7 (5, LG) **NFL** 13 (10) [2 yrs]

MURRAY, BILL Earl William, G-T, 6´2˝/240 lbs; Purdue; 1950: Bal, rnd 4; B7/16/1926 Dayton, KY, D7/14/1994 Midlothian, VA **1950** Bal 12 (11, LG) **1952** Pit 11 (lt)

YEAR	TEAM	G (GS, POS)	RUSH	YD	AVG (LG)	TD	REC	YD	AVG (LG)	TD	PASS	COMP	PCT	YD	AVG (LG)	TD	INT	SK	YD	QBR	KPR	OTD	PTS	TAY
1951	NYG	12(RG)	—	—	—	—	1	-4	-4.0(-4)	0	—	—	—	—	—	—	—	—	—	—	k	—	0	-17
NFL	3	35(11)	—	—	—	—	1	-4	-4.0(-4)	0	—	—	—	—	—	—	—	—	—	—	k	—	0	-18

MURRAY, CALVIN Leon Calvin, RB, 5´11˝/185 lbs; Ohio State; 1981: Phi, rnd 4; B10/18/1958 Middle Township, NJ **1982** Phi 1 (0)

YEAR	TEAM	G (GS, POS)	RUSH	YD	AVG (LG)	TD	REC	YD	AVG (LG)	TD	PASS	COMP	PCT	YD	AVG (LG)	TD	INT	SK	YD	QBR	KPR	OTD	PTS	TAY
1981	†Phi	7(0)	23	134	5.8(20)	0	1	7	7.0(7)	0	—	—	—	—	—	—	—	—	—	—	k	—	0	137
NFL	2	8(0)	23	134	5.8(20)	0	1	7	7.0(7)	0	—	—	—	—	—	—	—	—	—	—	k	—	0	134

MURRAY, DAN Daniel Francis, LB, 6´1˝/240 lbs; East Stroudsburg; 1988: Buf, rnd 6; B10/20/1966 Teaneck, NJ **1989** Ind 2 (0) **1990** NYJ 2 (0) **NFL** 4 (0) [2 yrs]

MURRAY, EDDIE Edward Peter, K, 5´10˝/177 lbs; Tulane; 1980: Det, rnd 7; B8/29/1956 Halifax, Canada **[K]** **1980** Det★16 (0) **1981** Det☆16 (0) **1982**†Det☆7 (0) **1983**†Det 16 (0) **1984** Det 16 (0) **1985** Det 16 (0) **1986** Det 16 (0) **1987** Det 12 (0) **1988** Det☆16 (0) **1989** Det★16 (0) **1990** Det 11 (0) **1991**†Det 16 (0) **1992** KC 1 (0) **1992** TB 7 (0) **1993**†Dal 14 (0) **1994** Phi☆16 (0) **1995** Was 16 (0) **1997**†Min 12 (0) **1999**†Dal 4 (0) **2000** Was 6 (0) **NFL** 250 (0) [19 yrs]

MURRAY, FRAN Francis Thomas, B, 6´0˝/200 lbs; Pennsylvania; 1937: Phi, rnd 2; B7/21/1915 Glenolden, PA, D6/28/1998 Boca Raton, FL **[K]**

YEAR	TEAM	G (GS, POS)	RUSH	YD	AVG (LG)	TD	REC	YD	AVG (LG)	TD	PASS	COMP	PCT	YD	AVG (LG)	TD	INT	SK	YD	QBR	KPR	OTD	PTS	TAY
1939	Phi	11(6, RH)	49	137	2.8	1	13	144	11.1	1	—	—	—	—	—	—	—	—	—	—	KP	—	26	224
1940	Phi	11(6, RH)	8	7	0.9	0	12	125	10.4	0	—	—	—	—	—	—	—	—	—	—	KPi	—	6	70
NFL	2	22(12)	57	144	2.5	1	25	269	10.8	1	—	—	—	—	—	—	—	—	—	—	KPi	—	32	294

MURRAY, JAB Richard John, E-C-G-T, 6´1˝/219 lbs; Marquette; B10/28/1892 Oconto, WI, deceased **[K]** **1921** GB 6 (5, C) **1922** GB 3 (3) **1922** Rac 8 (8, RG), 1 **1923** GB 9 (5, re) **1924** GB 4 (2) **NFL** 30 (23) [4 yrs]

MURRAY, JOE Joseph Andrew, G, 6´4˝/265 lbs; USC; B11/7/1960 Los Angeles, CA **1987** LARm 3 (3)

MURRAY, JOCK John T., E-G, 6´1˝/201 lbs; St. Thomas; B2/19/1904 Duluth, MN, D7/17/1969 Minneapolis, MN **1926** Dul 7 (5, le)

MURRAY, MARK Mark Allen, LB, 6´2˝/240 lbs; Florida; B10/15/1967 Orlando, FL **1991** Den 6 (0)

MURRAY, WALTER Walter Clyde, WR, 6´4˝/200 lbs; Hawaii; 1986: Was, rnd 2; B12/13/1962 Berkeley, CA

YEAR	TEAM	G (GS, POS)	RUSH	YD	AVG (LG)	TD	REC	YD	AVG (LG)	TD	PASS	COMP	PCT	YD	AVG (LG)	TD	INT	SK	YD	QBR	KPR	OTD	PTS	TAY
1986	Ind	5(0)	—	—	—	—	2	34	17.0(24)	0	—	—	—	—	—	—	—	—	—	—	—	—	0	17
1987	†Ind	14(3)	—	—	—	—	20	339	17.0(43)	3	—	—	—	—	—	—	—	—	—	—	—	—	18	185
NFL	2	19(3)	—	—	—	—	22	373	17.0(43)	3	—	—	—	—	—	—	—	—	—	—	—	—	18	202

MURRELL, ADRIAN Adrian Bryan, RB, 5´11˝/211 lbs; West Virginia; 1993: NYJ, rnd 5; B10/16/1970 Fayetteville, NC

YEAR	TEAM	G (GS, POS)	RUSH	YD	AVG (LG)	TD	REC	YD	AVG (LG)	TD	PASS	COMP	PCT	YD	AVG (LG)	TD	INT	SK	YD	QBR	KPR	OTD	PTS	TAY
1993	NYJ	16(0)	34	157	4.6(37)	1	5	12	2.4(8)	0	—	—	—	—	—	—	—	—	—	—	k	—	6	170
1994	NYJ	10(1)	33	160	4.8(19)	0	7	76	10.9(20)	0	—	—	—	—	—	—	—	—	—	—	k	—	0	256
1995	NYJ	15(9, RB)	192	795	4.1(30)	1	71	465	6.5(43)	2	—	—	—	—	—	—	—	—	—	—	k	—	18	1038
1996	NYJ	16(16, RB)	301	1249	4.1(78)	6	17	81	4.8(30)	1	—	—	—	—	—	—	—	—	—	—	—	—	42	1355
1997	NYJ	16(15, RB)	300	1086	3.6(43)	7	27	106	3.9(23)	0	—	—	—	—	—	—	—	—	—	—	—	—	42	1209
1998	†Arz	15(14, RB)	274	1042	3.8(32)	8	18	169	9.4(30)	2	—	—	—	—	—	—	—	—	—	—	—	—	60	1217
1999	Arz	16(12, RB)	193	553	2.9(22)	0	49	335	6.8(23)	0	—	—	—	—	—	—	—	—	—	—	—	—	0	721
2000	Was	15(0)	20	50	2.5(13)	0	16	93	5.8(12)	0	—	—	—	—	—	—	—	—	—	—	k	—	0	131
2003	Dal	3(0)	28	107	3.8(17)	0	4	32	8.0(14)	0	—	—	—	—	—	—	—	—	—	—	—	—	0	123
NFL	9	122(67)	1375	5199	3.8(78)	23	214	1369	6.4(43)	5	—	—	—	—	—	—	—	—	—	—	k	—	168	6218

MURRELL, BILL William Ellis, TE, 6´3˝/220 lbs; Winston-Salem State; 1979: Pit, rnd 6; B6/14/1956 Walnut Cove, NC

YEAR	TEAM	G (GS, POS)	RUSH	YD	AVG (LG)	TD	REC	YD	AVG (LG)	TD	PASS	COMP	PCT	YD	AVG (LG)	TD	INT	SK	YD	QBR	KPR	OTD	PTS	TAY
1979	SL	12	—	—	—	—	2	20	10.0(14)	0	—	—	—	—	—	—	—	—	—	—	—	—	0	10

MURRY, DON Donald Franklin, T-E-G, 6´2˝/191 lbs; Wisconsin; B1900 Taylorville, IL, D7/1951 **1922** Rac 4 (3) **1924** Rac 10 (10, LT) **1925** ChiB 17 (15, RT), 6 **1926** ChiB 15 (15, RT) **1927** ChiB 11 (4) **1928** ChiB☆12 (12, RT) **1929** ChiB 14 (13, RT) **1930** ChiB 11 (2) **1931** ChiB 13 (0) **1932** ChiB 5 (1) **NFL** 112 (75) [10 yrs]

MURTAGH, MICKEY George Augustus, C-G-E-B, 6´1˝/189 lbs; Georgetown (DC); B4/8/1904 Jersey City, NJ, D2/10/1993 Richmond, VA **1926** NYG 11 (10, C) **1927** NYG 13 (11, C) **1928** NYG 10 (10, C) **1929** NYG 13 (0), 6 **1930** NYG 11 (5, c) **1931** NYG 7 (4) **1932** NYG 6 (1) **NFL** 71 (41) [7 yrs]

MURTHA, GREG Gregory Thomas, T, 6´6˝/268 lbs; Minnesota; 1980: Phi, rnd 6; B4/23/1957 Minneapolis, MN **1982** Bal 5 (0)

MURTHA, TED Ted, G-FB, 5´11˝/205 lbs; none; B1901, deceased **1921** Col 2 (2)

MUSGRAVE, BILL William Scott, QB, 6´2˝/199 lbs; Oregon; 1991: Dal, rnd 4; B11/11/1967 Grand Junction, CO

YEAR	TEAM	G (GS, POS)	RUSH	YD	AVG (LG)	TD	REC	YD	AVG (LG)	TD	PASS	COMP	PCT	YD	AVG (LG)	TD	INT	SK	YD	QBR	KPR	OTD	PTS	TAY
1991	SF	1(0)	—	—	—	—	—	—	—	—	5	4	80.0	33	6.6(15)	1	0	—	—	—	—	—	0	22
1993	SF	1(0)	3	-3	-1.0(-1)	0	—	—	—	—	—	—	—	—	—	—	—	—	—	—	—	—	0	-3
1994	†SF	0(0)	—	—	—	—	—	—	—	—	—	—	—	—	—	—	—	—	—	—	—	—	0	0
1995	Den	4(0)	4	-4	-1.0(0)	0	—	—	—	—	12	8	66.7	93	7.8(23)	0	0	—	—	—	—	—	0	43
1996	Den	6(1)	12	-4	-0.3(6)	-0	—	—	—	—	52	31	59.6	276	5.3(46)	0	2	4	32	—	—	—	0	54
NFL	5	12(1)	19	-11	-0.6(6)	0	—	—	—	—	69	43	62.3	402	5.8(46)	1	2	4	32	—	—	—	0	115

MUSGROVE, SPAIN Spain, DE-DT, 6´4˝/275 lbs; Utah State; 1967: Was, rnd 2; B7/30/1945 Kansas City, MO **1967** Was 6 **1968** Was 14 (LDE) **1969** Was 10 **1970** Hou 7 **NFL** 37 [4 yrs]

YEAR	TEAM	G (GS, POS)	RUSH	YD	AVG(LG)	TD	REC	YD	AVG(LG)	TD	PASS COMP	PCT	YD	AVG(LG)	TD	INT	SK	YD	QBR	KPR	OTD	PTS	TAY

MUSICK, JIM James Andrew, FB, 5′11″/195 lbs; USC; B5/5/1910 Santa Ana, CA, D12/15/1992 Santa Ana, CA **[K]**

1932	Bos	10(10, FB)	88	316	3.6	1	—	—	—	—	2	1	50.0	7	3.5(7)	0	1	—	—	—	—	—	6	290
1933	Bos☆	12(11, FB)	**173**	**809**	4.7	5	3	78	26.0	0	36	11	30.6	151	4.2	0	14	—	—	—	K	—	45	414
1935	Bos	5(5, FB)	60	174	2.9	2	—	—	—	—	1	0	0.0	0	0.0	0	0	—	—	—	K	—	14	194
1936	Bos	6(0)	6	14	2.3	0	—	—	—	—	1	1	100.0	9	9.0(9)	0	0	—	—	—	K	—	0	19
NFL	4	33(26)	327	1313	4.0	8	3	78	26.0	0	40	13	32.5	167	4.2(9)	0	15	—	—	—	K	—	65	916

MUSSER, NEAL James Neal, LB, 6′2″/220 lbs; North Carolina State; B3/20/1957 Elon, NC   **1981** Atl 7 (0)   **1982**†Atl 8 (0)   **NFL** 15 (0) [2 yrs]

MUSSO, GEORGE George Francis 'Moose', G-T, 6′2″/262 lbs; Millikin; B4/8/1910 Collinsville, IL, D9/5/2000 Edwardsville, IL; HOF 1982   **1933**†ChiB☆12 (5, RT)
1934†ChiB 12 (11, RT)   **1935** ChiB☆12 (12, RT)   **1936** ChiB 12 (9, RT)   **1937**†ChiB☆11 (10, RG)   **1938** ChiB☆11 (11, RG)   **1939** ChiB★11 (11, RG)   **1940**†ChiB◇6 (6, RG)
1941†ChiB◇10 (0)   **1942**†ChiB 11 (0)   **1943**†ChiB 10 (10, RG)   **1944** ChiB 10 (0)   **NFL** 128 (84) [12 yrs]

MUSSO, JOHNNY John, RB, 5′11″/201 lbs; Alabama; 1972: Chi, rnd 3; B3/6/1950 Birmingham, AL

1975	ChiB	2	6	33	5.5(16)	0	—	—	—	—	—	—	—	—	—	—	—	—	—	—	—	—	0	33
1976	ChiB	14	57	200	3.5(11)	4	4	26	6.5(9)	0	—	—	—	—	—	—	—	—	—	—	k	—	26	241
1977	†ChiB	14	37	132	3.6(13)	2	3	13	4.3(21)	0	—	—	—	—	—	—	—	—	—	—	k	—	12	184
NFL	3	30	100	365	3.7(16)	6	7	39	5.6(21)	0	—	—	—	—	—	—	—	—	—	—	k	—	38	458

MUSTAFAA, NAJEE Najee, aka Reggie Rutland, DB, 6′1″/190 lbs; Georgia Tech; 1987: Min, rnd 4; B6/20/1964 East Point, GA   **1987**†Min 7 (0)   **1988**†Min 16 (7, lcb)
1989†Min 16 (16, LCB)   **1990** Min 16 (16, RCB)   **1991** Min 13 (12, RCB)   **1993** Cle 14 (14, RCB)   **1995** Oak 15 (1)   **NFL** 97 (66) [7 yrs]

MUSTARD, CHAD Chad, TE, 6′6″/288 lbs; North Dakota; B10/8/1977 Central City, NE

2003	Cle	10(0)	—	—	—	—	4	29	7.3(12)	0	—	—	—	—	—	—	—	—	—	—	k	—	0	6
2004	Cle	7(0)	—	—	—	—	1	9	9.0(9)	0	—	—	—	—	—	—	—	—	—	—	k	—	0	-13
NFL	2	17(0)	—	—	—	—	5	38	7.6(12)	0	—	—	—	—	—	—	—	—	—	—	k	—	0	-7

MUSTER, BRAD Brad William, RB, 6′3″/235 lbs; Stanford; 1988: Chi, rnd 1; B4/11/1965 Novato, CA

1988	†ChiB	16(0)	44	197	4.5(15)	0	21	236	11.2(40)	1	—	—	—	—	—	—	—	—	—	—	k	—	6	308
1989	ChiB	16(16, FB)	82	327	4.0(20)	5	32	259	8.1(25)	3	—	—	—	—	—	—	—	—	—	—	—	—	48	522
1990	†ChiB	16(15, FB)	141	664	4.7(28)	6	47	452	9.6(48)	0	—	—	—	—	—	—	—	—	—	—	—	—	36	950
1991	†ChiB	11(11, FB)	90	412	4.6(24)	6	35	287	8.2(21)	1	—	—	—	—	—	—	—	—	—	—	—	—	42	621
1992	ChiB	16(16, FB)	98	414	4.2(35)	3	34	389	11.4(44)	2	1	0	0.0	0	0.0	0	0	—	—	—	—	—	30	609
1993	NO	13(11, FB)	64	214	3.3(18)	2	23	195	8.5(31)	0	—	—	—	—	—	—	—	—	—	—	—	—	18	342
1994	NO	7(1)	1	3	3.0(3)	0	10	88	8.8(21)	0	—	—	—	—	—	—	—	—	—	—	—	—	6	57
NFL	7	95(70)	520	2231	4.3(35)	24	202	1906	9.4(48)	7	1	0	0.0	0	0.0	0	1	—	—	—	k	—	186	3407

MUTRYN, CHET Chester A., HB-DB, 5′9″/179 lbs; Xavier (OH); 1943: Phi, rnd 20; B3/12/1921 Cleveland, OH, D3/24/1995 Cleveland, OH **[K]**

1946	Buf-A	14(8, LH)	57	289	5.1	3	7	168	24.0(54)	3	—	—	—	—	—	—	—	—	—	—	kp	1	30	449
1947	Buf-A☆	14(14, LH)	`140	868	6.2(50)	9	10	176	17.6(58)	2	—	—	—	—	—	—	—	—	—	—	Kkpi	1	73	1570
1948	†Buf-A☆	14(14, LH)	147	823	5.6(68)	**10**	39	794	20.4(71)	5	6	2	33.3	21	3.5	0	0	—	—	—	kp	1	**96**	**1702**
1949	†Buf-A☆	11(11, LH)	131	696	5.3	5	29	333	11.5	0	—	—	—	—	—	—	—	—	—	—	kp	—	30	1029
AAFC	4	53(47)	475	2676	5.6(68)	25	85	1471	17.3(71)	10	6	2	33.3	21	3.5	0	0	—	—	—	Kkpi	3	229	4749
1950	Bal	12(LH)	108	355	3.3(34)	2	36	379	10.5(30)	2	1	1	100.0	—	—	—	—	—	—	—	kp	—	24	715

MUTSCHELLER, JIM James Francis, E-DE, 6′1″/205 lbs; Notre Dame; 1952: DalT, rnd 12; B3/31/1930 Beaver Falls, PA

1954	Bal	12	—	—	—	—	1	49	49.0(49)	0	—	—	—	—	—	—	—	—	—	—	—	—	0	25
1955	Bal	12(RE)	—	—	—	—	33	518	15.7(48)	7	—	—	—	—	—	—	—	—	—	—	—	—	42	294
1956	Bal	12(RE)	—	—	—	—	44	715	16.3(53)	6	—	—	—	—	—	—	—	—	—	—	—	—	36	388
1957	Bal★	12(RE)	—	—	—	—	32	558	17.4(66)	**8**	—	—	—	—	—	—	—	—	—	—	—	—	48	319
1958	†Bal	12(RE)	—	—	—	—	28	504	18.0(54)	7	—	—	—	—	—	—	—	—	—	—	—	—	42	287
1959	†Bal	12(RE)	—	—	—	—	44	699	15.9(40)	8	—	—	—	—	—	—	—	—	—	—	—	—	48	390
1960	Bal	11(TE)	—	—	—	—	18	271	15.1(43)	2	—	—	—	—	—	—	—	—	—	—	—	—	12	146
1961	Bal	12(TE)	—	—	—	—	20	370	18.5(45)	2	—	—	—	—	—	—	—	—	—	—	—	—	12	195
NFL	8	95	—	—	—	—	220	3684	16.7(66)	40	—	—	—	—	—	—	—	—	—	—	—	—	240	2042

MYER, STEVE Steven Paul, QB, 6′2″/191 lbs; New Mexico; 1976: Sea, rnd 4; B7/17/1954 Covina, CA

1977	Sea	7(4)	6	1	0.2(4)	0	—	—	—	—	130	70	53.8	729	5.6(45)	6	12	9	80	—	—	—	0	-85
1978	Sea	4	2	10	5.0(5)	0	—	—	—	—	22	11	50.0	94	4.3(17)	0	2	—	—	—	—	—	0	-23
1979	Sea	1	1	0	0.0(0)	0	—	—	—	—	8	2	25.0	28	3.5(18)	0	0	—	—	—	—	—	0	14
NFL	3	12(4)	9	11	1.2(5)	0	—	—	—	—	160	83	51.9	851	5.3(45)	6	14	9	80	—	—	—	0	-94

MYERS, BOB Robert Clarence, DT, 6′0″/260 lbs; Ohio State; 1955: Bal, rnd 28; B1/31/1933 Springfield, OH   **1955** Bal 1

MYERS, BOBBY Bobby Jermaine, DB, 6′1″/189 lbs; Wisconsin; 2000: Ten, rnd 4; B10/11/1976 New Haven, CT   **2000**†Ten 16 (1)   **2001** Ten 1 (1)   **NFL** 17 (2) [2 yrs]

MYERS, BRAD Bradford James, B-E, 6′1″/197 lbs; Bucknell; 1953: LA, rnd 9; B2/14/1929 Lancaster, PA

1953	LARm	12	40	124	3.1(31)	3	4	13	3.3(9)	0	—	—	—	—	—	—	—	—	—	—	p	—	18	157
1956	LARm	5	6	33	5.5(12)	0	—	—	—	—	—	—	—	—	—	—	—	—	—	—	kp	—	0	66
1958	Phi	9	9	23	2.6(15)	0	4	25	6.3(13)	0	—	—	—	—	—	—	—	—	—	—	—	—	0	36
NFL	3	26	55	180	3.3(31)	3	8	38	4.8(13)	0	—	—	—	—	—	—	—	—	—	—	kp	—	18	258

MYERS, CHIP Phillip Leon, WR, 6′4″/203 lbs; Northwestern Oklahoma State; 1967: SF, rnd 10; B8/9/1945 Panama City, FL, D2/23/1999 Minneapolis, MN

1967	SF	12	—	—	—	—	2	13	6.5(8)	0	—	—	—	—	—	—	—	—	—	—	—	—	0	7
1969	Cin-A	14(5, wr)	—	—	—	—	10	205	20.5(50)	2	—	—	—	—	—	—	—	—	—	—	—	—	12	113
1970	†Cin	14(5, wr)	—	—	—	—	32	542	16.9(50)	1	—	—	—	—	—	—	—	—	—	—	—	—	6	276
1971	Cin	10(7, wr)	—	—	—	—	27	286	10.6(20)	1	—	—	—	—	—	—	—	—	—	—	—	—	6	148
1972	Cin◇	14(14, WR)	—	—	—	—	57	792	13.9(42)	3	—	—	—	—	—	—	—	—	—	—	—	—	18	411
1973	Cin	5(4)	—	—	—	—	7	77	11.0(18)	0	—	—	—	—	—	—	—	—	—	—	—	—	0	39
1974	Cin	14(3)	—	—	—	—	32	383	12.0(22)	1	—	—	—	—	—	—	—	—	—	—	—	—	6	197
1975	†Cin	13(2)	—	—	—	—	36	527	14.6(34)	3	—	—	—	—	—	—	—	—	—	—	—	—	18	279
1976	Cin	12(4)	—	—	—	—	17	267	15.7(63)	1	—	—	—	—	—	—	—	—	—	—	—	—	6	139
NFL	9	108(44)	—	—	—	—	220	3092	14.1(63)	12	—	—	—	—	—	—	—	—	—	—	—	—	72	1606

MYERS, CHRIS Chris, G, 6′5″/300 lbs; Miami (FL); 2005: Den, rnd 6; B9/15/1981 Miami, FL   **2005**†Den 9 (0)

MYERS, DAVE David W., G-B, 5′11″/177 lbs; NYU; B11/11/1906 Brooklyn, NY, D3/1972 New York, NY   **1930** SI 6 (5, rg)   **1931** Bkn☆7 (6, LG)   **NFL** 13 (11) [2 yrs]

MYERS, DENNY Dennis Edward, G, 6′1″/206 lbs; Iowa; B11/10/1905 Algona, IA, D5/30/1957 Newton, MA   **1931** ChiB 2 (0)

MYERS, FRANK Frank, T, 6′5″/255 lbs; Texas A&M; 1978: Bal, rnd 5; B1/4/1956 San Bernardino, CA   **1978**†Min 12 (11, LT)   **1979** Min 14   **NFL** 26 (11) [2 yrs]

MYERS, GREG Gregory Jay, DB, 6′1″/202 lbs; Colorado State; 1996: Cin, rnd 5; B9/30/1972 Tampa, FL   **1996** Cin 14 (0)   **1997** Cin 16 (14, FS)   **1998** Cin 16 (16, FS)
1999 Cin 12 (4)   **2000** Dal 6 (4)   **NFL** 64 (38) [5 yrs]

MYERS, JACK John Melvin, FB-QB-LB, 6′2″/200 lbs; UCLA; 1948: Phi, rnd 5; B10/8/1924 St. Louis, MO

1948	†Phi	12(7, qb)	21	118	5.6(29)	1	7	57	8.1(31)	0	—	—	—	—	—	—	—	—	—	—	i	—	6	156
1949	†Phi	12(3)	48	182	3.8(12)	1	7	98	14.0(26)	0	—	—	—	—	—	—	—	—	—	—	k	—	6	238
1950	Phi	12(FB)	29	159	5.5(42)	0	12	204	17.0(39)	0	—	—	—	—	—	—	—	—	—	—	k	—	0	256
1952	†LARm	12	27	82	3.0(14)	1	2	1	0.5(3)	0	—	—	—	—	—	—	—	—	—	—	—	—	6	93
NFL	4	48(10)	125	541	4.3(42)	3	28	360	12.9(39)	0	—	—	—	—	—	—	—	—	—	—	ki	—	18	742

MYERS, LEONARD Leonard Bernard, DB, 5′10″/196 lbs; Miami (FL); 2001: NE, rnd 6; B12/18/1978 Fort Lauderdale, FL   **2001** NE 7 (0)   **2002** NE 8 (1)   **2003** NYJ 1 (0)
2003 Det 1 (0)   **NFL** 17 (1) [3 yrs]

MYERS, MICHAEL Michael Dewayne, DT-DE, 6′2″/292 lbs; Alabama; 1998: Dal, rnd 4; B1/20/1976 Vicksburg, MS   **1998**†Dal 16 (1)   **1999**†Dal 6 (0)   **2000** Dal 13 (7, rdt)
2001 Dal 16 (16, RDT)   **2002** Dal 16 (0)   **2003** Dal 1 (1)   **2003** Cle 7 (1)   **2004** Cle 16 (7, lde)   **2005**†Den 16 (15, LDT)   **NFL** 107 (48) [8 yrs]

YEAR	TEAM	G (GS, POS)	RUSH	YD	AVG(LG)	TD	REC	YD	AVG(LG)	TD	PASS	COMP	PCT	YD	AVG(LG)	TD	INT	SK	YD	QBR	KPR	OTD	PTS	TAY

MYERS, RYAN Ryan, LB, 6´2˝/245 lbs; Akron; B2/27/1980 Oberlin, OH **2005** NYJ 15 (0)

MYERS, TOM Thomas William, QB, 6´1˝/188 lbs; Northwestern; 1965: Det, rnd 4/Den, rnd 12; B8/13/1943 Piqua, OH

1965	Det	1	—	—	—	—	—	—	—	—	5	3	60.0	16	3.2(8)	0	1	—	—	—	—	—	0	-32
1966	Det	1	—	—	—	—	—	—	—	—	1	0	0.0	0	0.0	0	1	—	—	—	—	—	0	-40
NFL	2	2	—	—	—	—	—	—	—	—	6	3	50.0	16	2.7(8)	0	2	—	—	—	—	—	0	-72

MYERS, TOM Thomas Patrick, DB, 5´11˝/184 lbs; Syracuse; 1972: NO, rnd 3; B10/24/1950 Cohoes, NY [I] **1972** NO 13 (6, fs) **1974** NO 12 (12, FS) **1975** NO 9 (8, SS) **1976** NO 14 (12, FS) **1977** NO 12 (10, FS) **1978** NO 16 (16, FS) **1979** NO★15 (15, FS) **1980** NO 16 (15, FS)

1973	NO	13 (12, FS)	1	8	8.0(8)	0	—	—	—	—	—	—	—	—	—	—	—	—	—	pi	—	0	26
1981	NO	16 (15, FS)	2	-3	-1.5(6)	0	—	—	—	—	2	1	50.0	8	4.0(8)	1	0	—	—	—	i	—	0	66
NFL	10	136 (121)	3	5	1.7(8)	0	—	—	—	—	2	1	50.0	8	4.0(8)	1	0	—	—	—	pi	5	30	505

MYERS, TOMMY Thomas Edward, B, 5´8˝/170 lbs; Fordham; B2/9/1901 New Britain, CT, D7/1/1944 **1925** NYG 2 (0) **1926** Bkn 2 (1) **NFL** 4 (1) [2 yrs]

MYERS, TRUCK Cyril Edward, E-T, 6´0˝/177 lbs; Ohio State; B4/16/1897 Bucyrus, OH, D7/19/1969 Winter Garden, FL [K] **1922** Tol 9 (7, LE), 1 **1923** Cle 5 (3) **1925** Cle 2 (1) **NFL** 16 (11) [3 yrs]

MYERS, WILBUR Wilbur Lee, DB, 5´11˝/195 lbs; Delta State; B8/17/1961 Bassfield, MS **1983**†Den 16 (0)

MYHRA, STEVE Steven Murray, G-LB-K, 6´1˝/237 lbs; Minnesota; North Dakota; 1956: Bal, rnd 12; B4/2/1934 Wahpeton, ND, D8/4/1994 Detroit Lakes, MN [K] **1958**†Bal 12 **1959**†Bal 12 **1960** Bal 12 **1961** Bal 14

| 1957 | Bal | 12 | 1 | 1 | 1.0(1) | 0 | — | — | — | — | — | — | — | — | — | — | — | — | — | Kk | — | 26 | 5 |
| NFL | 5 | 62 | 1 | 1 | 1.0(1) | 0 | — | — | — | — | — | — | — | — | — | — | — | — | — | Kk | — | 312 | 5 |

MYLES, DESHONE DeShone, LB, 6´2˝/235 lbs; Nevada-Reno; 1998: Sea, rnd 4; B10/31/1974 Las Vegas, NV **1998** Sea 12 (7, mlb) **1999** Sea 5 (0) **2001** NO 1 (0) **NFL** 18 (7) [3 yrs]

MYLES, GODFREY Godfrey Clarence, LB, 6´1˝/240 lbs; Florida; 1991: Dal, rnd 3; B9/22/1968 Miami, FL **1991** Dal 3 (0) **1992**†Dal 16 (0) **1993**†Dal 10 (0) **1994**†Dal 15 (0) **1995**†Dal 16 (11, RLB) **1996**†Dal 16 (0) **NFL** 76 (11) [6 yrs]

MYLES, HARRY Harry Seig, E-T-G, 6´0˝/190 lbs; Hampden-Sydney; B9/1/1904 Lewisburg, WV, D11/30/1978 Orange Park, FL **1929** Buf 5 (2) **1930** Nwk 1 (0) **NFL** 6 (2) [2 yrs]

MYLES, JESSE Jesse James, RB, 5´10˝/210 lbs; LSU; B9/28/1960 New Orleans, LA

1983	†Den	16 (0)	8	52	6.5(16)	0	7	119	17.0(33)	1	—	—	—	—	—	—	—	—	—	—	—	6	117
1984	Den	7 (0)	5	7	1.4(2)	0	2	22	11.0(12)	0	—	—	—	—	—	—	—	—	—	—	—	0	18
NFL	2	23 (0)	13	59	4.5(16)	0	9	141	15.7(33)	1	—	—	—	—	—	—	—	—	—	—	—	6	135

MYLES, REGGIE Reggie, DB, 5´11˝/185 lbs; Alabama; B10/10/1979 Pascagoula, MS **2002** Cin 9 (0) **2003** Cin 16 (0) **2004** Cin 16 (0) **2005** Cin 10 (0) **NFL** 51 (0) [4 yrs]

MYLES, TOBY Toby, T, 6´5˝/320 lbs; Mississippi State; Jackson State; 1998: NYG, rnd 5; B7/23/1975 Jackson, MS **1999** NYG 8 (0) **2001** Oak 1 (0) **2001** Cle 2 (0) **NFL** 11 (0) [2 yrs]

MYRTLE, CHIP Charles Joseph, LB, 6´2˝/225 lbs; Maryland; B2/6/1945 Hyattsville, MD **1967** Den-A 14 (RLB) **1969** Den-A 12 (9, RLB) **1970** Den 14 (2) **1971** Den 14 (14, RLB) **1972** Den 14 (14, RLB) **1974** SD 8

| 1968 | Den-A | 13 (rlb) | — | — | — | — | 1 | 18 | 18.0(18) | 0 | — | — | — | — | — | — | — | — | — | — | — | 2 | 9 |
| NFL | 7 | 89 (39) | — | — | — | — | 1 | 18 | 18.0(18) | 0 | — | — | — | — | — | — | — | — | — | ki | — | 2 | 25 |

MYSLINSKI, TOM Thomas Joseph, G, 6´3˝/283 lbs; Tennessee; 1992: Dal, rnd 4; B12/7/1968 Rome, NY **1992** Was 1 (0) **1993** Buf 1 (0) **1993** ChiB 1 (0) **1994** ChiB 4 (0) **1995** Jax 9 (9, RG) **1996**†Pit 8 (6, rg) **1997**†Pit 16 (7, rg) **1998** Ind 1 (0) **1999**†Dal 10 (2) **2000** Pit 6 (0) **NFL** 57 (24) [9 yrs]

NABORS, ROLAND Roland Richard, LB-C, 6´2˝/200 lbs; Texas Tech; 1947: NYY-A, rnd 7/Bos, rnd 18; B7/22/1924 Meadow, TX **1948** NYY-A 10 (0)

NACRELLI, ANDY Andrew Frank, E, 6´1˝/190 lbs; Fordham; 1955: Phi, rnd 12; B8/15/1933 Chester, PA, D9/23/1991 Lake Oswego, OR

| 1958 | Phi | 2 | — | — | — | — | 2 | 15 | 7.5(11) | 0 | — | — | — | — | — | — | — | — | — | — | — | 0 | 8 |

NADOLNEY, PEACHES Romanus Frank, G-T, 5´11˝/211 lbs; Notre Dame; B5/23/1899, WI, D2/21/1963 Houston, TX **1922** GB 8 (2) **1923** Mil 3 (1) **1924** Mil 3 (2) **1925** Mil 6 (5, LG) **NFL** 20 (10) [4 yrs]

NAEOLE, CHRIS Chris Kealoha, G, 6´3˝/317 lbs; Colorado; 1997: NO, rnd 1; B12/25/1974 Kailua, HI **1997** NO 4 (0) **1998** NO 16 (16, RG) **1999** NO 15 (15, RG) **2000**†NO 16 (16, RG) **2001** NO 16 (16, RG) **2002** Jax 16 (16, RG) **2003** Jax 16 (16, RG) **2004** Jax 16 (16, RG) **2005**†Jax 15 (15, RG) **NFL** 130 (126) [9 yrs]

NAFZIGER, DANA Dana Albert, TE-LB, 6´1˝/220 lbs; Cal Poly-San Luis Obispo; B10/26/1953 Woodstock, IL **1978** TB 14 (1) **1979**†TB 16 (2) **1981**†TB 16 (0) **1982** TB 8 (0)

| 1977 | TB | 14 (10, TE) | — | — | — | — | 9 | 119 | 13.2(38) | 0 | — | — | — | — | — | — | — | — | — | k | — | 0 | 49 |
| NFL | 5 | 68 (13) | — | — | — | — | 9 | 119 | 13.2(38) | 0 | — | — | — | — | — | — | — | — | — | k | — | 0 | 55 |

NAGEL, RAY Raymond Robert, QB, 5´11˝/177 lbs; UCLA; B5/18/1927 Los Angeles, CA

| 1953 | ChiC | 4 | 2 | 0.2(6) | 0 | — | — | — | — | 62 | 30 | 48.4 | 192 | 3.1(27) | 0 | 5 | — | — | — | — | — | 0 | -96 |

NAGEL, ROSS Ross Otto, DT-T, 6´4˝/234 lbs; St. Louis; B6/12/1923 St. Louis, MO, D2/12/1997 Waco, TX **1942** ChiC 1 (0) **1951** NYY 9 **NFL** 10 [2 yrs]

NAGIDA, BILL William, BB, /180 lbs; none **1926** Ham 1 (0)

NAGLE, BROWNING Browning Kenneth, QB, 6´3˝/225 lbs; West Virginia; Louisville; 1991: NYJ, rnd 2; B4/29/1968 Philadelphia, PA

1991	NYJ	1 (0)	1	-1	-1.0(-1)	0	—	—	—	—	2	1	50.0	10	5.0(10)	0	0	—	—	—	—	—	0	4
1992	NYJ	14 (13, QB)	24	57	2.4(20)	0	—	—	—	—	387	192	49.6	2280	5.9(51)	7	17	27	215	—	—	—	0	552
1993	NYJ	3 (0)	—	—	—	—	—	—	—	—	14	6	42.9	71	5.1(18)	0	0	3	21	—	—	—	0	36
1994	Ind	1 (1)	1	12	12.0(12)	0	—	—	—	—	21	8	38.1	69	3.3(23)	0	1	2	18	—	—	—	0	7
1996	Atl	5 (0)	—	—	—	—	—	—	—	—	13	6	46.2	59	4.5(17)	1	2	4	20	—	—	—	0	-46
NFL	5	24 (14)	26	68	2.6(20)	0	—	—	—	—	437	213	48.7	2489	5.7(51)	8	20	36	274	—	—	—	0	553

NAGLE, JOHNNY John C., E, 5´9˝/175 lbs; none; B8/4/1893 Reading, PA, D11/5/1974 Erasmus, PA **1921** NYG 1 (0)

NAGLER, GERN Robert Gern, E, 6´2˝/190 lbs; Santa Clara; 1953: Cle, rnd 14; B2/23/1932 Yuba City, CA

1953	ChiC	11 (LE)	—	—	—	—	43	610	14.2(41)	6	—	—	—	—	—	—	—	—	—	—	—	36	335
1955	ChiC	11 (RE)	—	—	—	—	7	218	31.1(74)	3	—	—	—	—	—	—	—	—	—	—	—	18	124
1956	ChiC	8 (RE)	—	—	—	—	14	268	19.1(49)	4	—	—	—	—	—	—	—	—	—	—	—	24	154
1957	ChiC	12 (RE)	—	—	—	—	27	475	17.6(83)	4	—	—	—	—	—	—	—	—	—	—	—	24	258
1958	ChiC◊	12 (RE)	—	—	—	—	36	469	13.0(47)	5	—	—	—	—	—	—	—	—	—	—	—	30	260
1959	Pit	12	—	—	—	—	14	222	15.9(35)	2	—	—	—	—	—	—	—	—	—	—	—	12	121
1960	Cle	12 (TE)	—	—	—	—	36	616	17.1(53)	3	—	—	—	—	—	—	—	—	—	—	—	18	323
1961	Cle	13 (TE)	—	—	—	—	19	241	12.7(21)	1	—	—	—	—	—	—	—	—	—	—	—	6	126
NFL	8	91	—	—	—	—	196	3119	15.9(83)	28	—	—	—	—	—	—	—	—	—	—	—	168	1700

NAGURSKI, BRONKO Bronislaw, FB-LB-T, 6´2˝/226 lbs; Minnesota; B11/3/1908 Rainy River, Canada, D1/7/1990 International Falls, MN; HOF 1963 [K]

1930	ChiB☆	13 (13, FB)	—	—	—	—	—	—	—	—	—	—	—	—	—	—	—	—	—	—	—	—	—
1931	ChiB☆	10 (8, FB)	—	—	—	—	—	—	—	—	—	—	—	—	—	—	—	—	—	—	—	—	—
1932	ChiB☆	14 (14, FB)	121	533	4.4	4	6	67	11.2	0	26	11	42.3	150	5.8	3	2	—	—	—	—	—	24	617
1933	†ChiB☆	13 (10, FB)	128	533	4.2	1	1	23	23.0(23)	0	27	14	51.9	233	8.6	0	3	—	—	—	K	—	7	551
1934	†ChiB☆	13 (11, FB)	123	586	4.8	7	3	32	10.7	0	14	5	35.7	48	3.4	2	1	—	—	—	K	—	44	666
1935	ChiB	5 (3)	50	170	3.4	1	—	—	—	0	3	0	0.0	0	0.0	0	0	—	—	—	—	—	6	140
1936	ChiB☆	11 (8, FB)	122	529	4.3	3	1	12	12.0(12)	0	5	1	20.0	8	1.6(8)	1	2	—	—	—	K	—	19	494
1937	ChiB	10 (8, FB)	73	343	4.7	1	—	—	—	0	2	1	50.0	35	17.5(35)	0	1	—	—	—	—	—	6	376
1943	†ChiB	8 (0)	16	84	5.3(11)	1	—	—	—	0	—	—	—	—	—	—	—	—	—	—	—	6	94
NFL	9	97 (75)	633	2778	4.4(11)	25	11	134	12.2(23)	0	77	32	41.6	474	6.2(35)	7	9	—	—	—	K	—	154	3007

NAILS, JAMIE Jamie Marcellus, G, 6´6˝/335 lbs; Florida A&M; 1997: Buf, rnd 4; B6/3/1977 Baxley, GA **1997** Buf 2 (0) **1998**†Buf 15 (3) **1999**†Buf 16 (3) **2000** Buf 16 (16, RG) **2002** Mia 14 (14, LG) **2003** Mia 15 (15, LG) **NFL** 78 (51) [6 yrs]

NAIOTI, JOHN John F., HB, 5´10˝/180 lbs; St. Francis (PA); B11/6/1921 Fulton, NY, D9/5/1990, [K] **1942** Pit 1 (0)

| 1945 | Pit | 6 (1) | 1 | -17 | -17.0(-17) | 0 | 2 | 14 | 7.0(8) | 0 | — | — | — | — | — | — | — | — | — | K | — | 4 | -10 |
| NFL | 2 | 7 (1) | 1 | -17 | -17.0(-17) | 0 | 2 | 14 | 7.0(8) | 0 | — | — | — | — | — | — | — | — | — | K | — | 4 | -10 |

YEAR	TEAM	G(GS, POS)	RUSH	YD	AVG(LG)	TD	REC	YD	AVG(LG)	TD	PASS	COMP	PCT	YD	AVG(LG)	TD	INT	SK	YD	QBR	KPR	OTD	PTS	TAY

NAIRAN, RALPH Roger, E-WB, 5´11˝/185 lbs; Trinity (TX); B1902 **1926** Buf 3 (0)

NAIRNE, ROB Robert Carlton, LB, 6´4˝/223 lbs; Oregon State; B3/24/1954 Redding, CA **1977**†Den 13 **1978**†Den 16 (1) **1979**†Den 10 (4) **1980** Den 16 (16, LOLB)
1981 NO 16 (13, ROLB) **1982** NO 9 (9, ROLB) **1983** NO 16 (1) **NFL** 96 (44) [7 yrs]

NAJARIAN, PETER Peter Michael, LB, 6´2˝/233 lbs; Minnesota; B12/22/1963 San Francisco, CA **1987** Min 5 (3) **1988** TB 1 (0) **1989** TB 12 (0) **NFL** 18 (3) [3 yrs]

NALEN, TOM Thomas Andrew, C, 6´3˝/286 lbs; Boston College; 1994: Den, rnd 7; B5/13/1971 Foxboro, MA **1994** Den 7 (1) **1995** Den 15 (15, C) **1996**†Den 16 (16, C)
1998†Den✧16 (16, C) **1999** Den★16 (16, C) **2000**†Den★16 (16, C) **2001** Den 16 (16, C) **2002** Den 7 (7, c) **2003**†Den★16 (16, C) **2004**†Den 16 (16, C) **2005**†Den 16 (16, C)

| 1997 | †Den✧ | 16 (16, C) | — | — | — | — | 1 | -1 | -1.0(-1) | 0 | — | — | — | — | — | — | — | — | — | — | — | — | 0 | -1 |
| NFL | 12 | 173 (167) | — | — | — | — | 1 | -1 | -1.0(-1) | 0 | — | — | — | — | — | — | — | — | — | — | — | — | 0 | -1 |

NALL, CRAIG Craig Matthew, QB, 6´3˝/230 lbs; LSU; Northwestern State (LA); 2002: GB, rnd 5; B4/21/1979 Alexandria, LA

2003	GB	1 (0)	2	-2	-1.0(-1)	0	—	—	—	—	—	—	—	—	—	—	—	—	—	—	—	—	0	-2
2004	GB	5 (0)	3	7	2.3(9)	0	—	—	—	—	33	23	69.7	314	9.5(43)	4	0	2	8	—	—	—	0	184
NFL	2	6 (0)	5	5	1.0(9)	0	—	—	—	—	33	23	69.7	314	9.5(43)	4	0	2	8	—	—	—	0	182

NAMATH, JOE Joseph William 'Broadway Joe', QB, 6´2˝/200 lbs; Alabama; 1965: NYJ, rnd 1/SL, rnd 1; B5/31/1943 Beaver Falls, PA; HOF 1985

1965	NYJ-A✧	13 (9, QB)	8	19	2.4(14)	0	—	—	—	—	340	164	48.2	2220	6.5(62)	18	15	—	—	68.8	—	—	0	619
1966	NYJ-A☆	14 (14, QB)	6	42	7.0(39)	2	—	—	—	—	**471**	**232**	49.3	**3379**	7.2(77)	19	**27**	—	—	62.6	—	—	12	767
1967	NYJ-A★	14 (14, QB)	6	14	2.3(13)	0	—	—	—	—	**491**	**258**	52.5	**4007**	8.2(75)	26	28	26	261	73.8	—	1	6	1028
1968	†NYJ-A★	14 (14, QB)	5	11	2.2(4)	2	—	—	—	—	380	187	49.2	3147	8.3(87)	15	17	15	112	72.1	—	—	12	1000
1969	†NYJ-A★	14 (QB)	11	33	3.0(16)	2	—	—	—	—	361	185	51.2	2734	7.6(60)	19	17	13	117	74.3	—	—	12	835
1970	NYJ	5 (qb)	1	-1	-1.0(-1)	0	—	—	—	—	179	90	50.3	1259	7.0(72)	5	12	6	63	54.7	—	—	0	174
1971	NYJ	4	3	-1	-0.3(1)	0	—	—	—	—	59	28	47.5	537	9.1(74)	5	6	—	—	—	—	—	0	53
1972	NYJ★	13 (QB)	6	8	1.3(2)	0	—	—	—	—	324	162	50.0	**2816**	8.7(83)	**19**	21	11	101	72.5	—	—	0	671
1973	NYJ	6 (qb)	1	-2	-2.0(-2)	0	—	—	—	—	133	68	51.1	966	7.3(63)	5	6	10	97	—	—	—	0	266
1974	NYJ	14 (QB)	8	1	0.1(3)	1	—	—	—	—	**361**	191	52.9	2616	7.2(89)	20	**22**	19	195	69.4	—	—	6	539
1975	NYJ	14 (13, QB)	10	6	0.6(6)	0	—	—	—	—	326	157	48.2	2286	7.0(91)	15	28	27	253	51.0	—	—	0	104
1976	NYJ	11 (QB)	2	5	2.5(5)	0	—	—	—	—	230	114	49.6	1090	4.7(35)	4	16	16	150	39.9	—	—	0	-70
1977	LARm	4	4	5	1.3(7)	0	—	—	—	—	107	50	46.7	606	5.7(42)	3	5	7	76	—	—	—	0	123
NFL	13	140 (64)	71	140	2.0(39)	7	—	—	—	—	3762	1886	50.1	27663	7.4(91)	173	220	150	1425	65.5	—	1	48	6107

NANCE, JIM James Solomon, RB, 6´1˝/235 lbs; Syracuse; 1965: Bos, rnd 19/Chi, rnd 4; B12/30/1942 Indiana, PA, D6/16/1992 Quincy, MA

1965	Bos-A	14 (FB)	111	321	2.9(20)	5	12	83	6.9(22)	0	—	—	—	—	—	—	—	—	—	—	kp	—	30	419
1966	Bos-A★	14 (FB)	**299**	**1458**	4.9(65)	**11**	8	103	12.9(45)	0	—	—	—	—	—	—	—	—	—	—	—	—	66	**1620**
1967	Bos-A★	14 (14, FB)	**269**	**1216**	4.5(53)	7	22	196	8.9(36)	1	—	—	—	—	—	—	—	—	—	—	—	—	48	1389
1968	Bos-A	12 (12, FB/hb)	177	593	3.4(30)	4	14	51	3.6(13)	0	—	—	—	—	—	—	—	—	—	—	—	—	24	659
1969	Bos-A☆	14 (14, FB/hb)	**193**	750	3.9(43)	6	29	168	5.8(27)	0	—	—	—	—	—	—	—	—	—	—	—	—	36	894
1970	Bos	13 (13, FB/rb)	145	522	3.6(21)	7	26	148	5.7(16)	0	—	—	—	—	—	—	—	—	—	—	—	—	42	666
1971	NE	13 (13, FB)	129	463	3.6(50)	5	18	95	5.3(12)	0	—	—	—	—	—	—	—	—	—	—	—	—	30	561
1973	NYJ	7	18	78	4.3(18)	0	4	26	6.5(9)	0	—	—	—	—	—	—	—	—	—	—	—	—	0	91
NFL	8	101 (66)	1341	5401	4.0(65)	45	133	870	6.5(45)	1	—	—	—	—	—	—	—	—	—	—	kp	—	276	6297

NAPIER, WALTER Walter, DT, 6´4˝/270 lbs; Paul Quinn; B8/27/1932 Waco, TX **1960** DalT-A 14 (LDT) **1961** DalT-A 6 **NFL** 20 [2 yrs]

NAPONIC, BOB Robert Andrew, QB, 6´0˝/190 lbs; Illinois; 1969: Hou, rnd 10; B3/9/1947 Greensburg, PA

| 1970 | Hou | 2 | 3 | 12 | 4.0(11) | 0 | — | — | — | — | 20 | 6 | 30.0 | 85 | 4.3(21) | 0 | 2 | 8 | 53 | — | — | — | 0 | -26 |

NAPOSKI, ERIC Eric Andrew, LB, 6´2˝/230 lbs; Connecticut; B12/20/1966 New York, NY **1988** NE 3 (0) **1989** NE 1 (0) **NFL** 5 (0) [2 yrs]

NARDACCI, NICK Nicholas James, B, 5´10˝/160 lbs; West Virginia; B10/8/1903 Youngstown, OH, D8/30/1961 Youngstown, OH **1925** Cle 2 (1)

NARDI, DICK Richard Louis, B, 5´10˝/200 lbs; Ohio State; 1938: Det, rnd 8; B9/25/1915 Cleveland, OH, D12/1972

1938	Det	8 (1)	20	109	5.4	0	—	—	—	—	—	—	—	—	—	—	—	—	—	—	—	—	0	109
1939	Pit	3 (2)	8	10	1.3	0	—	—	—	—	5	2	40.0	12	2.4	0	1	—	—	P	—	—	0	-24
1939	Bkn	3 (0)	2	5	2.5	0	1	3	3.0(3)	0	—	—	—	—	—	—	—	—	—	—	—	—	0	7
NFL	2	14 (3)	30	124	4.1	0	1	3	3.0(3)	0	5	2	40.0	12	2.4	0	1	—	—	P	—	—	0	92

NASH, BOB Robert Arthur, T-E, 6´1˝/205 lbs; Cornell; Rutgers; B12/16/1892 County Meathe, Ireland, D2/1/1977 Winsted, CT **1920** Akr 9 (7, LE) **1921** Buf☆11 (11, LT), 6
1922 Buf 2 (2) **1923** Buf 6 (6, LT) **1924** Roc 2 (2) **1925** NYG 3 (3) **NFL** 33 (31) [6 yrs]

NASH, DAMIEN Damien Darnell, RB, 5´11˝/215 lbs; Missouri; 2005: Ten, rnd 5; B4/14/1982 St. Louis, MO

| 2005 | Ten | 3 | 6 | 32 | 5.3(8) | 0 | 3 | 14 | 4.7(7) | 0 | — | — | — | — | — | — | — | — | — | — | — | — | 0 | 39 |

NASH, JOE Joseph Andrew, NT-DT, 6´3˝/278 lbs; Boston College; B10/11/1960 Boston, MA **1982** Sea 7 (1) **1983**†Sea 16 (8, NT) **1984**†Sea★16 (16, NT)
1985 Sea☆16 (16, NT) **1986** Sea 16 (11, NT) **1987**†Sea 12 (12, NT) **1988**†Sea 15 (15, NT) **1989** Sea 16 (16, NT) **1990** Sea 16 (16, LDT) **1991** Sea 16 (0)
1992 Sea 16 (16, LDT) **1993** Sea 16 (16, LDT) **1994** Sea 16 (15, LDT) **1995** Sea 16 (11, LDT) **1996** Sea 8 (0) **NFL** 218 (169) [15 yrs]

NASH, KENNY Kenneth, WR, 6´2˝/193 lbs; San Jose State; B10/28/1962 Los Angeles, CA

| 1987 | KC | 1 (0) | — | — | — | — | 2 | 22 | 11.0(14) | 0 | — | — | — | — | — | — | — | — | — | — | — | — | 0 | 11 |

NASH, KEYON Keyon, DB, 6´3˝/215 lbs; Albany State (GA); 2002: Oak, rnd 6; B3/11/1979 Colquitt, GA **2004** Oak 2 (0)

NASH, MARCUS Marcus DeLando, WR, 6´3˝/195 lbs; Tennessee; 1998: Den, rnd 1; B2/1/1976 Tulsa, OK **1999** Den 2 (1) **1999** Bal 1 (0)

| 1998 | †Den | 8 (0) | — | — | — | — | 4 | 76 | 19.0(31) | 0 | — | — | — | — | — | — | — | — | — | — | — | — | 0 | 38 |
| NFL | 2 | 11 (1) | — | — | — | — | 4 | 76 | 19.0(31) | 0 | — | — | — | — | — | — | — | — | — | — | — | — | 0 | 38 |

NASH, TOM Thomas Acton, E, 6´3˝/208 lbs; Georgia; B11/21/1905 Lincoln County, GA, D8/24/1972 Washington, GA **1928** GB 8 (6, re) **1929** GB 10 (5, re), 6
1930 GB☆12 (7, re), 6 **1931** GB☆13 (9, RE), 6 **1934** Bkn 3 (2)

1932	GB☆	10 (2)	—	—	—	—	3	50	16.7	0	—	—	—	—	—	—	—	—	—	—	—	—	4	25
1933	Bkn	9 (7, RE)	—	—	—	—	9	184	20.4(61)	2	—	—	—	—	—	—	—	—	—	—	—	—	12	102
NFL	7	65 (38)	—	—	—	—	12	234	19.5(61)	4	—	—	—	—	—	—	—	—	—	—	—	1	34	137

NASON, ED Edward Earl, aka Running Deer, T-WB, 5´8˝/185 lbs; none; B4/8/1899, D3/9/1977 Wichita, KS **1922** Oor 4 (1) **1923** Oor 6 (3) **NFL** 10 (4) [2 yrs]

NATHAN, TONY Tony Curtis, RB, 6´0˝/206 lbs; Alabama; 1979: Mia, rnd 3; B12/14/1956 Birmingham, AL

1979	†Mia☆	16	16	68	4.3(18)	0	17	213	12.5(35)	2	—	—	—	—	—	—	—	—	—	—	kp	1	18	702
1980	Mia	16 (6, rb)	60	327	5.4(18)	5	57	588	10.3(61)	5	1	0	0.0	0	0.0	0	0	0	0	—	kp	—	36	746
1981	Mia	13 (11, RB)	147	782	**5.3(46)**	5	50	452	9.0(31)	5	—	—	—	—	—	—	—	—	—	—	—	—	48	1073
1982	†Mia	8 (7, RB)	66	233	3.5(15)	1	16	114	7.1(16)	0	2	1	50.0	15	7.5(15)	1	0	—	—	—	—	—	6	313
1983	†Mia	16 (12, RB)	151	685	4.5(40)	3	52	461	8.9(25)	1	4	3	75.0	46	11.5(22)	0	0	—	—	—	k	—	24	944
1984	†Mia	16 (12, RB)	118	558	4.7(22)	1	61	579	9.5(26)	2	—	—	—	—	—	—	—	—	—	—	—	—	18	868
1985	†Mia	16 (15, RB)	143	667	4.7(45)	5	72	651	9.0(73)	1	—	—	—	—	—	—	—	—	—	—	—	—	36	1048
1986	Mia	16 (0)	27	203	7.5(20)	0	48	457	9.5(23)	2	—	—	—	—	—	—	—	—	—	—	—	—	12	442
1987	Mia	6 (0)	4	20	5.0(8)	0	10	77	7.7(14)	0	—	—	—	—	—	—	—	—	—	—	—	—	0	59
NFL	9	123 (63)	732	3543	4.8(46)	16	383	3592	9.4(73)	16	8	4	50.0	61	7.6(22)	1	0	—	—	—	kp	1	198	6192

NATKIN, BRIAN Brian Jay, TE, 6´2˝/250 lbs; Texas-El Paso; B1/3/1978 San Antonio, TX

| 2001 | Ten | 3 (1) | — | — | — | — | 2 | 42 | 21.0(27) | 0 | — | — | — | — | — | — | — | — | — | — | — | — | 0 | 21 |

NATOWICH, ANDY Andrew, HB, 5´10˝/175 lbs; Holy Cross; B12/11/1918 Derby, CT **1944** Was 1 (0)

NATTIEL, MIKE Michael Dondril, LB, 6´0˝/227 lbs; Florida; 2003: Min, rnd 6; B11/8/1980 Gainesville, FL **2003** Min 16 (0) **2004**†Min 16 (0) **NFL** 32 (0) [2 yrs]

NATTIEL, RICKY Ricky Rennard, WR, 5´9˝/180 lbs; Florida; 1987: Den, rnd 1; B1/25/1966 Gainesville, FL

1987	†Den	12 (3)	2	13	6.5(10)	0	31	630	20.3(54)	2	—	—	—	—	—	—	—	—	—	—	kp	—	12	369
1988	Den	15 (11, WR)	5	51	10.2(29)	0	46	574	12.5(74)	1	1	0	0.0	0	0.0	0	0	—	—	—	kp	—	6	485
1989	†Den	8 (0)	—	—	—	—	10	183	18.3(43)	1	—	—	—	—	—	—	—	—	—	—	p	—	6	129

YEAR	TEAM	G (GS, POS)	RUSH	YD	AVG (LG)	TD	REC	YD	AVG (LG)	TD	PASS	COMP	PCT	YD	AVG (LG)	TD	INT	SK	YD	QBR	KPR	OTD	PTS	TAY
1990	Den	15(3)	—	—	—	—	18	297	16.5(52)	2	—	—	—	—	—	—	—	—	—	—	kp	—	12	144
1991	†Den	16(0)	—	—	—	—	16	288	18.0(70)	2	—	—	—	—	—	—	—	—	—	—	p	—	12	147
1992	Den	4(0)	—	—	—	—	—	—	—	—	—	—	—	—	—	—	—	—	—	—	—	—		
NFL	6	70(17)	7	64	9.1(29)	0	121	1972	16.3(74)	8	1	0	0.0	0	0.0	0	0	—	—	—	kp	—	48	1273

NAUMETZ, FRED   Frederick, C, 6´1˝/222 lbs; Boston College; 1943: Cle, rnd 3; B3/28/1922 Newburyport, MA, D1/2/1998 Thousand Oaks, CA   **1946** LARm 11 (4)
1947 LARm☆12 (12, C)   **1948** LARm☆11 (7, C)   **1949**†LARm☆12 (0)   **1950**†LARm☆12 (C)   **NFL** 58 (23) [5 yrs]

NAUMOFF, PAUL   Paul Peter, LB, 6´1˝/215 lbs; Tennessee; 1967: Det, rnd 3; B7/3/1945 Columbus, OH   **1967** Det 14 (2)   **1968** Det 14 (LLB)   **1969** Det 14 (LLB)
1970 Det★14 (14, LLB)   **1971** Det 14 (14, LLB)   **1972** Det 14 (14, LLB)   **1973** Det 14 (14, LLB)   **1974** Det 14 (14, LLB)   **1975** Det☆14 (14, LLB)   **1976** Det 14 (12, LLB)
1977 Det 13 (12, LLB)   **1978** Det 15 (13, LLB)   **NFL** 168 (123) [12 yrs]

NAUMU, JOHNNY   John Punualii, HB, 5´8˝/175 lbs; Hawaii; USC; B9/30/1919 Hooevha, HI, D9/ 1982

| 1948 | LAD-A | 9(0) | 1 | 0 | 0.0 | 0 | — | — | — | — | — | — | — | — | — | — | — | — | — | — | Pk | — | 0 | 41 |

NAVARRE, JOHN   John Robert, QB, 6´6˝/236 lbs; Michigan; 2004: Arz, rnd 7; B9/9/1980 Cudahy, WI

2004	Arz	1(1)	—	—	—	—	—	—	—	—	40	18	45.0	168	4.2(33)	1	4	1	8	—	—	—	0	-71
2005	Arz	1(1)	—	—	—	—	—	—	—	—	24	14	58.3	174	7.3(43)	1	1	4	27	—	—	—	0	52
NFL	2	2(1)	—	—	—	—	—	—	—	—	64	32	50.0	342	5.3(43)	2	5	5	35	—	—	—	0	-19

NAVE, STEVE   Steven Lewis, LB, 6´2˝/250 lbs; Kansas; B8/29/1963 Nowata, OK   **1987** Cle 2 (1)

NAVIES, HANNIBAL   Hannibal Carter, LB, 6´3˝/247 lbs; Colorado; 1999: Car, rnd 4; B7/19/1977 Chicago, IL   **1999** Car 9 (0)   **2000** Car 13 (1)   **2001** Car 5 (5, llb)
2002 Car 12 (9, RLB)   **2003**†GB 16 (16, LLB)   **2004**†GB 15 (14, LLB)   **2005**†Cin 15 (1)   **NFL** 85 (46) [7 yrs]

NEACY, CLEM   Clement Francis, E-T, 6´3˝/206 lbs; Wisconsin-Milwaukee; Colgate; B7/19/1898 Milwaukee, WI, D3/19/1968 Palos Verde Estates, CA   **1924** Mil 13 (13, LE), 12
1925 Mil 6 (5, LE), 6   **1926** Mil 9 (8, RE)   **1927** Dul 6 (4)   **1927** ChiB 2 (2)   **1928** ChiC 6 (4, RE)   **NFL** 42 (36), 18 [5 yrs]

NEAD, SPENCER   Spencer, FB, 6´4˝/259 lbs; Brigham Young; 2003: NE, rnd 7; B11/3/1977 Tacoma, WA

| 2003 | SL | 10(0) | — | — | — | — | 1 | 6 | 6.0(6) | 0 | — | — | — | — | — | — | — | — | — | — | k | — | 0 | 0 |

NEAL, DAN   Thomas Daniel, C-G, 6´4˝/250 lbs; Kentucky; 1973: Bal, rnd 11; B8/30/1949 Corbin, KY   **1973** Bal 5   **1974** Bal 14   **1975** ChiB 6 (3)   **1976** ChiB 14 (10, C)
1977†ChiB 14   **1978** ChiB 16 (16, C)   **1979**†ChiB 16 (16, C)   **1980** ChiB 16 (16, C)   **1982** ChiB 9 (9, C)   **1983** ChiB 8 (8, C)

| 1981 | ChiB | 16(16, C) | 1 | -6 | -6.0(-6) | 0 | — | — | — | — | — | — | — | — | — | — | — | — | — | — | — | — | 0 | -6 |
| NFL | 11 | 134(94) | 1 | -6 | -6.0(-6) | 0 | — | — | — | — | — | — | — | — | — | — | — | — | — | — | — | — | 0 | -6 |

NEAL, ED   William Henry Edward, MG-C-G-T, 6´4˝/285 lbs; LSU; Tulane; Ouachita Baptist; B12/31/1918 Wichita Falls, TX, D12/27/1984 Euless, TX   **1945** GB 9 (0)   **1946** GB 10 (2)
1947 GB 12 (0)   **1948** GB 12 (0)   **1949** GB 12 (2)   **1950** GB★12 (MG/c)   **1951** GB 1   **1951** ChiB 4   **NFL** 72 (4) [7 yrs]

NEAL, FRANKIE   Frankie Leon, WR, 6´1˝/202 lbs; Florida; Fort Hays State; 1987: GB, rnd 3; B10/1/1965 Sebring, FL

| 1987 | GB | 12(3) | 1 | 0 | 0.0(0) | 0 | 36 | 420 | 11.7(38) | 3 | 1 | 0 | 0.0 | 0 | — | 0 | 0 | — | — | — | k | — | 18 | 209 |

NEAL, LEON   Leon Kamil, RB, 5´9˝/185 lbs; Washington; 1996: Buf, rnd 6; B9/11/1972 St. Paul, MN   **1997** Ind 1 (0)

NEAL, LORENZO   Lorenzo LaVonne, FB, 5´11˝/245 lbs; Fresno State; 1993: NO, rnd 4; B12/27/1970 Hanford, CA

1993	NO	2(2)	21	175	8.3(74)	1	—	—	—	—	—	—	—	—	—	—	—	—	—	—	—	—	6	185
1994	NO	16(7, fb)	30	90	3.0(12)	1	2	9	4.5(5)	0	—	—	—	—	—	—	—	—	—	—	k	—	6	107
1995	NO	16(7, fb)	5	3	0.6(3)	0	12	123	10.3(69)	1	—	—	—	—	—	—	—	—	—	—	k	—	6	68
1996	NO	16(11, FB)	21	58	2.8(11)	0	31	194	6.3(23)	1	—	—	—	—	—	—	—	—	—	—	k	—	12	170
1997	NYJ	16(10, FB)	10	28	2.8(8)	0	8	40	5.0(14)	1	—	—	—	—	—	—	—	—	—	—	k	—	6	45
1998	TB	16(1)	5	25	5.0(12)	0	5	14	2.8(5)	1	—	—	—	—	—	—	—	—	—	—	k	—	6	37
1999	†Ten	16(14, FB)	2	1	0.5(1)	1	7	27	3.9(8)	2	—	—	—	—	—	—	—	—	—	—	k	—	18	20
2000	†Ten	16(5, fb)	1	-2	-2.0(-2)	0	9	31	3.4(8)	2	—	—	—	—	—	—	—	—	—	—	k	—	12	24
2001	Cin	16(10, FB)	5	10	2.0(4)	0	19	101	5.3(12)	1	—	—	—	—	—	—	—	—	—	—	k	—	6	66
2002	Cin◇	16(8, FB)	9	31	3.4(9)	0	21	133	6.3(15)	1	—	—	—	—	—	—	—	—	—	—	k	—	6	80
2003	SD	16(15, FB)	18	40	2.2(7)	1	16	62	3.9(11)	0	—	—	—	—	—	—	—	—	—	—	k	—	6	67
2004	†SD	16(10, FB)	16	53	3.3(8)	0	13	66	5.1(12)	0	—	—	—	—	—	—	—	—	—	—	k	—	0	83
2005	SD★	16(15, FB)	29	98	3.4(9)	0	24	145	6.0(21)	1	—	—	—	—	—	—	—	—	—	—	k	—	6	176
NFL	13	194(115)	172	610	3.5(74)	5	167	945	5.7(69)	11	—	—	—	—	—	—	—	—	—	—	k	—	96	1125

NEAL, LOUIS   Louis Charles, WR, 6´4˝/215 lbs; Prairie View A&M; 1973: Oak, rnd 5; B1/10/1951 San Francisco, CA

1973	Atl	5	—	—	—	—	5	131	26.2(50)	1	—	—	—	—	—	—	—	—	—	—	—	—	6	71
1974	Atl	10	1	-1	-1.0(-1)	0	8	99	12.4(21)	0	—	—	—	—	—	—	—	—	—	—	—	—	0	49
NFL	2	15	1	-1	-1.0(-1)	0	13	230	17.7(50)	1	—	—	—	—	—	—	—	—	—	—	—	—	6	119

NEAL, RANDY   Randy Peter, LB, 6´3˝/236 lbs; Virginia; B12/29/1972 Hackensack, NJ   **1995** Cin 3 (0)   **1996** Cin 1 (0)   **1998** SF 1 (0)   **NFL** 5 (0) [3 yrs]

NEAL, RAY   Raymond Robert, T-G, 5´9˝/211 lbs; Wabash; Washington & Jefferson; B11/1/1897 Mellott, IN, D11/25/1977 Greencastle, IN   **1922** Akr 10 (6, lg)   **1924** Ham 5 (5, LT)
1925 Ham 5 (5, LT), 6   **1926** Ham 2 (2, LG)   **NFL** 22 (18) [4 yrs]

NEAL, RICHARD   Richard, DE-DT, 6´3˝/260 lbs; Southern (LA); 1969: NO, rnd 2; B9/27/1947 Minden, LA, D4/3/1983 St. Louis, MO   **1969** NO 14   **1970** NO 12 (LDE)
1971 NO 14 (LDE)   **1972** NO 14 (LDE)   **1973** NYJ 14   **1974** NYJ 14 (rde)   **1975** NYJ 9 (9, RDE)   **1976** NYJ 13 (RDE)   **1977** NYJ 14 (RDE)   **1978** NO 2   **NFL** 120 (9) [10 yrs]

NEAL, SPEEDY   Robert, RB, 6´2˝/254 lbs; Miami (FL); 1984: Buf, rnd 3; B8/26/1962 Key West, FL

| 1984 | Buf | 12(1) | 49 | 175 | 3.6(10) | 1 | 9 | 76 | 8.4(18) | 0 | — | — | — | — | — | — | — | — | — | — | — | — | 6 | 223 |

NEAL, STEVE   Stephen, G-T, 6´4˝/305 lbs; Cal State-Bakersfield; B10/9/1976 San Diego, CA   **2002** NE 2 (1)   **2004**†NE 16 (14, RG)   **2005**†NE 16 (16, RG)   **NFL** 34 (31) [3 yrs]

NEALY, RAY   Ray T., RB, 5´11˝/220 lbs; Arkansas-Pine Bluff; B4/30/1975 Little Rock, AR

| 1997 | Mia | 1(0) | 1 | 2 | 2.0(2) | 0 | — | — | — | — | — | — | — | — | — | — | — | — | — | — | — | — | 0 | 2 |

NEASE, MIKE   Michael Ray, G, 6´3˝/272 lbs; Tennessee-Chattanooga; B10/30/1961 Morristown, TN   **1987** Phi 2 (1)

NECE, RYAN   Ryan Clint, LB, 6´3˝/224 lbs; UCLA; B2/24/1979 San Bernardino, CA   **2002** TB 8 (0)   **2003** TB 15 (10, LLB)   **2004** TB 16 (0)   **2005**†TB 16 (14, LLB)
NFL 55 (24) [4 yrs]

NECK, TOMMY   Thomas Ulric, DB, 5´11˝/190 lbs; LSU; 1962: Chi, rnd 18/Bos, rnd 20; B1/10/1939 Marksville, LA   **1962** ChiB 1

NED, DERRICK   Derrick Deyone, FB, 6´1˝/220 lbs; Grambling State; B1/5/1969 Eunice, LA

1993	NO	14(1)	9	71	7.9(35)	1	9	54	6.0(14)	0	—	—	—	—	—	—	—	—	—	—	—	—	6	108
1994	NO	16(1)	11	36	3.3(15)	0	13	86	6.6(19)	0	—	—	—	—	—	—	—	—	—	—	k	—	0	51
1995	NO	12(0)	3	1	0.3(5)	0	3	9	3.0(9)	0	—	—	—	—	—	—	—	—	—	—	k	—	0	9
NFL	3	42(2)	23	108	4.7(35)	1	25	149	6.0(19)	0	—	—	—	—	—	—	—	—	—	—	k	—	6	168

NED, LARRY   Larry Lee, RB, 5´11˝/217 lbs; San Diego State; 2002: Oak, rnd 6; B8/23/1978 Eunice, LA   **2003** Min 3 (0)

| 2004 | †Min | 16(0) | — | — | — | — | 1 | 9 | 9.0(9) | 0 | — | — | — | — | — | — | — | — | — | — | — | — | 0 | 5 |
| NFL | 2 | 19(0) | — | — | — | — | 1 | 9 | 9.0(9) | 0 | — | — | — | — | — | — | — | — | — | — | — | — | 0 | 5 |

NEDNEY, JOE   Joseph Thomas, K, 6´5˝/225 lbs; San Jose State; B3/22/1973 San Jose, CA [K]   **1996** Mia 16 (0)   **1997** Arz 10 (0)   **1998** Arz 12 (0)   **1999** Arz 1 (0)   **1999** Oak 3 (0)
2000 Den 3 (0)   **2000** Car 12 (0)   **2001** Ten 16 (0)   **2002**†Ten 16 (0)   **2003** Ten 1 (0)   **2005** SF 15 (0)   **NFL** 105 (0) [9 yrs]

NEELY, BOBBY   Robert Lee, TE, 6´3˝/255 lbs; Virginia; B3/22/1974 Atlanta, GA

| 1996 | ChiB | 11(5, te) | — | — | — | — | 9 | 92 | 10.2(21) | 0 | — | — | — | — | — | — | — | — | — | — | — | — | 0 | 46 |

NEELY, RALPH   Ralph Eugene, T-G, 6´6˝/265 lbs; Oklahoma; 1965: Bal, rnd 2/Hou, rnd 2; B9/12/1943 Little Rock, AR   **1965** Dal 14 (14, RT)   **1966**†Dal☆14 (RT)
1967 Dal★14 (RT)   **1968** Dal☆14 (RT)   **1969**†Dal☆12 (11, RT)   **1970**†Dal 14 (10, lt/rg)   **1971** Dal 7 (7, LT)   **1973**†Dal 14 (LT)   **1974** Dal 14 (LT)   **1975**†Dal☆14 (LT)
1976†Dal 14 (14, LT)   **1977**†Dal 14 (LT)

| 1972 | †Dal | 13(LT) | 1 | 10 | 10.0(10) | 0 | — | — | — | — | — | — | — | — | — | — | — | — | — | — | — | — | 0 | 10 |
| NFL | 13 | 172(56) | 1 | 10 | 10.0(10) | 0 | — | — | — | — | — | — | — | — | — | — | — | — | — | — | — | — | 0 | -47 |

NEFF, BOB   Robert Milan, DB, 5´11˝/180 lbs; Stephen F. Austin State; B3/5/1944 Hearne, TX   **1966** Mia-A 14   **1967** Mia-A 14 (9, RS)   **1968** Mia-A 5   **NFL** 33 (9) [3 yrs]

NEGUS, FRED Frederick Wilson, C-LB, 6´1˝/208 lbs; Michigan; Wisconsin; 1945: Cle, rnd 7; B11/7/1923 Colerain, OH, D4/18/2005 Fort Atkinson, WI **1947** ChiR-A 12 (9, C)
1948 ChiR-A 14 (5, C) **1949** ChiH-A 12 (5, c) **AAFC** 38 (19) [3 yrs]

1950†ChiB 11 (RLB)

NEHEMIAH, RENALDO Renaldo, WR, 6´1˝/181 lbs; Maryland; B3/24/1959 Newark, NJ

YEAR	TEAM	G(GS, POS)	RUSH	YD	AVG(LG)	TD	REC	YD	AVG(LG)	TD	PASS	COMP	PCT	YD	AVG(LG)	TD	INT	SK	YD	QBR	KPR	OTD	PTS	TAY
1982	SF	8(3)	1	-1	-1.0(-1)	0	8	161	20.1(55)	1	—											—	6	85
1983	†SF	16(1)	—				17	236	13.9(27)	1	—											—	6	123
1984	†SF	16(0)	—				18	357	19.8(59)	2	—											—	12	189
NFL		40(4)	1	-1	-1.0(-1)	0	43	754	17.5(59)	4	—											—	24	396

NEIDERT, JOHN John Thomas, LB, 6´2˝/230 lbs; Louisville; 1968: Cin, rnd 6; B6/18/1946 Akron, OH **1968** Cin-A 8 **1968**†NYJ-A 5 **1969**†NYJ-A 14 **1970** ChiB 3 **NFL** 30 [3 yrs]

NEIGHBORS, BILLY William Wesley, G, 6´0˝/250 lbs; Alabama; 1962: Bos, rnd 6/Was, rnd 4; B2/4/1940 Tuscaloosa, AL **1962** Bos-A☆14 (14, RG) **1963**†Bos-A☆14 (RG)
1964 Bos-A☆14 (RG) **1965** Bos-A 14 (RG) **1966** Mia-A 14 (10, RG) **1967** Mia-A 14 (14, RG) **1968** Mia-A 14 (13, RG) **1969** Mia-A 14 (5, rg) **NFL** 112 (56) [8 yrs]

NEIL, DALLAS Dallas, TE, 6´1˝/235 lbs; Montana; B9/30/1976 Great Falls, MT **2000** Atl 6 (0)

NEIL, DAN Daniel P., G, 6´2˝/285 lbs; Texas; 1997: Den, rnd 3; B10/21/1973 Houston, TX **1997** Den 3 (0) **1998**†Den 16 (16, RG) **1999** Den 15 (15, RG) **2000**†Den 16 (16, RG)
2001 Den 15 (15, RG) **2002** Den 16 (16, RG) **2003**†Den 14 (14, RG) **2004** Den 13 (12, RG) **NFL** 108 (104) [8 yrs]

NEIL, KENNY Kenny, DE-DT, 6´4˝/244 lbs; Iowa State; 1981: NYJ, rnd 7; B1/8/1959 Cincinnati, OH **1981**†NYJ 16 (0) **1982**†NYJ 9 (7, RDE) **1983** NYJ 16 (16, RDE)
1987 Hou 1 (0) **NFL** 42 (23) [4 yrs]

NEILL, BILL William M., NT, 6´4˝/258 lbs; Pittsburgh; 1981: NYG, rnd 5; B3/15/1959 Gaterford, PA **1981**†NYG 16 (16, NT) **1982** NYG 7 (5, NT) **1983** NYG 1 (1) **1984** GB 16 (0)
NFL 40 (22) [4 yrs]

NEILL, JIM James Hubert, FB-WB, 6´2˝/190 lbs; Texas Tech; B5/9/1913 Brownfield, TX, D7/1988 **1939** ChiC 1 (0)

YEAR	TEAM	G(GS, POS)	RUSH	YD	AVG(LG)	TD	REC	YD	AVG(LG)	TD	PASS	COMP	PCT	YD	AVG(LG)	TD	INT	SK	YD	QBR	KPR	OTD	PTS	TAY
1937	NYG	3(0)	7	55	7.9	0	—					3	1	33.3	0	0.0	0	1	—	—	—	—	—	0	15
NFL	2	4(0)	7	55	7.9	0	—					3	1	33.3	0	0.0	0	1	—	—	—	—	—	0	15

NEILS, STEVE Steven Lynn, LB, 6´2˝/217 lbs; Minnesota; 1974: SL, rnd 5; B5/2/1951 St. Peter, MN **1974**†SL 14 **1975**†SL 14 **1976** SL 7 **1977** SL 14 (6, llb) **1978** SL 16 (LOLB)
1979 SL 9 (LILB) **1980** SL 14 (14, LOLB) **NFL** 88 (20) [7 yrs]

NELMS, MIKE Michael Craig, DB, 6´1˝/188 lbs; Sam Houston State; Baylor; 1977: Buf, rnd 7; B4/8/1955 Fort Worth, TX [R] **1980** Was◇16 (0) **1981** Was★16 (0) **1982**†Was★8 (0)
1983†Was☆12 (0) **1984**†Was 16 (0) **NFL** 68 (0) [5 yrs]

NELSEN, BILL William Keith, QB, 6´0˝/195 lbs; USC; 1963: Pit, rnd 10; B1/29/1941 Los Angeles, CA

YEAR	TEAM	G(GS, POS)	RUSH	YD	AVG(LG)	TD	REC	YD	AVG(LG)	TD	PASS	COMP	PCT	YD	AVG(LG)	TD	INT	SK	YD	QBR	KPR	OTD	PTS	TAY
1963	Pit	2	1	-6	-6.0(-6)	0	—					2	0	0.0	0	0.0	0	0	—	—	—	—	—	0	-6
1964	Pit	5	3	17	5.7(13)	0	—					42	16	38.1	276	6.6(44)	2	3	—	—	—	—	—	0	45
1965	Pit	12(QB)	26	84	3.2(21)	1	1	-5	-5.0(-5)	0		270	121	44.8	1917	7.1(87)	8	17	—	—	52.7	—	—	6	410
1966	Pit	5(qb)	6	18	3.0(9)	1	—					112	63	56.3	1122	10.0(68)	7	1	—	—	65.3	—	—	0	574
1967	Pit	8(qb)	9	-19	-2.1(11)	0	—					165	74	44.8	1125	6.8(58)	10	9	—	—	65.3	—	—	0	234
1968	†Cle☆	14(10, QB)	13	30	2.3(18)	1	—					293	152	51.9	2366	8.1(87)	19	10	11	102	86.4	—	—	6	918
1969	†Cle◇	14(QB)	5	-11	-2.2(9)	0	—					352	190	54.0	2743	7.8(82)	23	19	17	164	78.8	—	—	0	716
1970	Cle	12(QB)	7	-4	-0.6(2)	0	—					313	159	50.8	2156	6.9(78)	16	16	8	79	68.9	—	—	0	514
1971	Cle	14(QB)	13	-18	-1.4(1)	0	—					325	174	53.5	2319	7.1(53)	13	23	22	222	60.3	—	—	0	287
1972	†Cle	4	1	-2	-2.0(-2)	0	—					31	14	45.2	141	4.5(26)	0	3	3	29	—	—	—	0	-52
NFL	10	90(10)	84	89	1.1(21)	2	1	-5	-5.0(-5)	0		1905	963	50.6	14165	7.4(87)	98	101	61	596	70.2	—	—	12	3639

NELSON, AL Albert, DB, 5´11˝/186 lbs; Cincinnati; 1965: Phi, rnd 3/Buf, rnd 9; B10/27/1943 Cincinnati, OH [R] **1965** Phi 14 (14, LCB) **1966** Phi 13 (13, LCB) **1967** Phi 1
1968 Phi 14 (LCB) **1969** Phi 14 (LCB) **1970** Phi 14 (RCB) **1971** Phi 14 (LCB) **1972** Phi 14 (LCB) **1973** Phi 8 **NFL** 105 (27) [9 yrs]

NELSON, ANDY Andrew Vaughn, DB, 6´1˝/180 lbs; Memphis; 1957: Bal, rnd 11; B5/27/1933 Athens, AK [I] **1957** Bal 12 (DB) **1958**†Bal☆12 (DB) **1959**†Bal☆12 (DB)
1960 Bal★12 (LS) **1961** Bal☆14 (LS) **1962** Bal 14 (LS) **1963** Bal 13 (LS) **1964** NYG 14 **NFL** 103 [8 yrs]

NELSON, BEN Ben, WR, 6´2˝/185 lbs; St. Cloud State; B8/21/1979 Coon Rapids, MN **2004** Min 3 (0)

NELSON, BENNY James Benny, DB, 6´0˝/185 lbs; Alabama; 1964: Hou, rnd 12/Det, rnd 5; B4/1/1941 Gadsden, AL **1964** Hou-A 14

NELSON, BILL William Howard, DT, 6´7˝/270 lbs; Oregon State; 1970: LA, rnd 7; B3/9/1948 Berkeley, CA **1971** LARm 6 (6, rdt) **1972** LARm 7 **1973**†LARm 12 **1974**†LARm 14
1975 LARm 8 **NFL** 47 (6) [5 yrs]

NELSON, BOB Robert Lee, LB, 6´4˝/232 lbs; Nebraska; 1975: Buf, rnd 2; B6/30/1953 Stillwater, MN **1976** Buf 14 **1977** Buf 11 **1979** SF 1 (1) **1980**†Oak 9 (8, rilb)
1982†LARd 9 (8, RILB) **1983**†LARd 16 (16, RILB) **1984** LARd 12 (11, RILB) **NFL** 72 (44) [7 yrs]

NELSON, BOB Robert William, NT-DE, 6´4˝/272 lbs; Miami (FL); 1982: Mia, rnd 5; B3/3/1959 Baltimore, MD **1986** TB 16 (10, LDE) **1988** GB 14 (7, nt) **1989** GB 16 (16, NT)
1990 GB 16 (16, NT) **NFL** 62 (49) [4 yrs]

NELSON, BRUCE Bruce Edward, G, 6´5˝/301 lbs; Iowa; 2003: Car, rnd 2; B5/12/1979 Emmetsburg, IA **2003**†Car 14 (1)

NELSON, CHUCK Charles LaVerne, K, 5´11˝/175 lbs; Washington; 1983: LARm, rnd 4; B2/23/1960 Seattle, WA [K] **1983**†LARm 12 (0) **1984** Buf 7 (0) **1986** Min 16 (0)
1987†Min 12 (0) **1988**†Min☆16 (0) **NFL** 63 (0) [5 yrs]

NELSON, DARRELL Darrell Maurice, TE, 6´2˝/235 lbs; Memphis; B10/27/1961 Memphis, TN **1985** Pit 5 (5, te)

YEAR	TEAM	G(GS, POS)	RUSH	YD	AVG(LG)	TD	REC	YD	AVG(LG)	TD	PASS	COMP	PCT	YD	AVG(LG)	TD	INT	SK	YD	QBR	KPR	OTD	PTS	TAY
1984	†Pit	11(9, TE)	—				2	31	15.5(19)	0													—	0	16
NFL	2	16(14)	—				2	31	15.5(19)	0													—	0	16

NELSON, DARRIN Darrin Milo, RB, 5´9˝/184 lbs; Stanford; 1982: Min, rnd 1; B1/2/1959 Sacramento, CA [R]

YEAR	TEAM	G(GS, POS)	RUSH	YD	AVG(LG)	TD	REC	YD	AVG(LG)	TD	PASS	COMP	PCT	YD	AVG(LG)	TD	INT	SK	YD	QBR	KPR	OTD	PTS	TAY
1982	†Min	7(4, RB)	44	136	3.1(18)	0	9	100	11.1(22)	0	—										k	—	0	228
1983	Min	15(9, RB)	154	642	4.2(56)	1	51	618	12.1(68)	0	—										k	—	6	1136
1984	Min	15(8, rb)	80	406	5.1(39)	3	27	162	6.0(17)	1	—										kp	—	24	893
1985	Min	16(10, RB)	200	893	4.5(37)	5	43	301	7.0(25)	1	—										kp	—	36	1158
1986	Min	16(16, RB)	191	793	4.2(42)	4	53	593	11.2(34)	1	—										k	—	42	1205
1987	Min	10(9, RB)	131	642	4.9(72)	2	26	129	5.0(13)	0	—										k	—	12	786
1988	†Min	13(11, RB)	112	380	3.4(27)	1	16	105	6.6(27)	0	—										k	—	6	518
1989	Min	5(0)	31	124	4.0(24)	0	7	52	7.4(11)	0	—										k	—	0	257
1989	SD	9(0)	36	197	5.5(28)	0	31	328	10.6(49)	0	—											—	0	361
1990	SD	14(0)	3	14	4.7(5)	0	4	29	7.3(10)	0	—										kp	—	0	34
1991	Min	16(0)	28	210	7.5(29)	2	19	142	7.5(13)	0	1	1	100.0	25	25.0(25)	1	0				k	—	12	536
1992	†Min	16(0)	10	5	0.5(9)	0	—														k	—	0	196
NFL	11	152(67)	1020	4442	4.4(72)	18	286	2559	8.9(68)	5	1	1	100.0	25	25.0(25)	1	0				kp	—	138	7305

NELSON, DAVID David Leon, RB, 6´2˝/230 lbs; Heidelberg; B11/23/1963 Miami, FL

YEAR	TEAM	G(GS, POS)	RUSH	YD	AVG(LG)	TD	REC	YD	AVG(LG)	TD	PASS	COMP	PCT	YD	AVG(LG)	TD	INT	SK	YD	QBR	KPR	OTD	PTS	TAY
1984	Min	14(0)	1	3	3.0(3)	0	—														k	—	0	-12

NELSON, DENNIS Dennis Ray, T, 6´5˝/260 lbs; Illinois State; 1969: Bal, rnd 3; B2/2/1946 Kewanee, IL **1970** Bal 6 **1971**†Bal 14 (RT) **1972** Bal 13 (RT) **1974** Bal 14 (RT)
1976 Phi 14 **1977** Phi 2

YEAR	TEAM	G(GS, POS)	RUSH	YD	AVG(LG)	TD	REC	YD	AVG(LG)	TD	PASS	COMP	PCT	YD	AVG(LG)	TD	INT	SK	YD	QBR	KPR	OTD	PTS	TAY
1973	Bal	14(RT)	0	3	(3)	0	—															—	0	3
NFL	7	77	0	3	(3)	0	—															—	0	3

NELSON, DERRIE Derald Lawrence, LB, 6´2˝/236 lbs; Nebraska; 1981: Dal, rnd 4; B2/8/1958 York, NE **1983** SD 15 (0) **1984** SD 6 (0) **1985** SD 16 (1) **1986** SD 11 (0)
NFL 48 (1) [4 yrs]

NELSON, DON Donald Roswell, T-C, 6´1˝/210 lbs; Ohio Wesleyan; B2/10/1903 Cambridge, MA, D10/26/1980 Larkspur, CA **1926** Ham 1 (1) **1926** Can 6 (6, LT) **NFL** 7 (7) [1 yr]

NELSON, DON Donald Fritz, G, 5´10˝/200 lbs; Iowa; B5/12/1915 Moline, IL, D10/25/1996 Ames, IA **1937** Bkn 11 (4, RG)

NELSON, EDMUND Edmund Clau-Von, DE-NT-DT, 6´3˝/272 lbs; Auburn; 1982: Pit, rnd 7; B4/30/1960 Live Oak, FL **1982**†Pit 8 (2) **1983**†Pit 16 (5, nt) **1984**†Pit 16 (5, rde)
1985 Pit 6 (6, rde) **1986** Pit 16 (16, RDE) **1987** Pit 10 (8, RDE) **1988** NE 12 (1) **NFL** 84 (43) [7 yrs]

NELSON, FRANK Dewey Frank, B, 5´9˝/166 lbs; Utah; 1948: Bos, rnd 20/NYY-A, rnd 29; B5/28/1923 Salt Lake City, UT, D2/19/2002 Phoenix, AZ

YEAR	TEAM	G (GS, POS)	RUSH	YD	AVG (LG)	TD	REC	YD	AVG (LG)	TD	PASS	COMP	PCT	YD	AVG (LG)	TD	INT	SK	YD	QBR	KPR	OTD	PTS	TAY
1948	Bos	12(4)	18	60	3.3(19)	0	1	10	10.0(10)	0	17	8	47.1	71	4.2(29)	0	2	—	—	—	kpi	—	0	50
1949	NYB	4(0)	8	26	3.3(25)	0	—	—	—	—	—	—	—	—	—	—	—	—	—	—	kpi	—	0	37
NFL	2	16(4)	26	86	3.3(25)	0	1	10	10.0(10)	0	17	8	47.1	71	4.2(29)	0	2	—	—	—	kpi	—	0	87

NELSON, HERB Herbert Russell, E-T, 6´4˝/219 lbs; Pennsylvania; B4/25/1921 Hartford, CT, D7/18/2004 Westwood, MA **1948** Bkn-A 4 (1)

YEAR	TEAM	G (GS, POS)	RUSH	YD	AVG (LG)	TD	REC	YD	AVG (LG)	TD	PASS	COMP	PCT	YD	AVG (LG)	TD	INT	SK	YD	QBR	KPR	OTD	PTS	TAY
1946	Buf-A	12(7, RE)	1	1	1.0(1)	0	4	47	11.8	0	—	—	—	—	—	—	—	—	—	—	—	—	0	25
1947	Bkn-A	14(4, re)	—	—	—	—	2	17	8.5	0	—	—	—	—	—	—	—	—	—	—	—	—	0	9
AAFC	3	30(12)	1	1	1.0(1)	0	6	64	10.7	0	—	—	—	—	—	—	—	—	—	—	—	—	0	33

NELSON, JIM James Robert, LB, 6´1˝/234 lbs; Penn State; B4/16/1975 Riverside, CA **1998**†GB 0 (0) **1999** GB 16 (0) **2000**†Min 16 (0) **2001** Min 16 (2) **2002** Min 16 (1) **2003**†Ind 7 (0) **2004** Ind 15 (1) **2005** Bal 2 (0) **NFL** 88 (4) [8 yrs]

NELSON, JIMMY Jimmy Guess, B, 5´11˝/180 lbs; Alabama; 1942: ChiC, rnd 19; B7/26/1919 Live Oak, FL, D12/24/1986 Encinitas, CA

YEAR	TEAM	G (GS, POS)	RUSH	YD	AVG (LG)	TD	REC	YD	AVG (LG)	TD	PASS	COMP	PCT	YD	AVG (LG)	TD	INT	SK	YD	QBR	KPR	OTD	PTS	TAY
1946	Mia-A	14(5, rh)	39	163	4.2	2	4	20	5.0	0	24	8	33.3	135	5.6	0	4	—	—	—	Pkpi	—	12	177

NELSON, KARL Karl Stuart, T, 6´6˝/285 lbs; Iowa State; 1983: NYG, rnd 3; B6/14/1960 DeKalb, IL **1984**†NYG 16 (16, RT) **1985**†NYG 16 (16, RT) **1986**†NYG 16 (16, RT) **1988** NYG 9 (3) **NFL** 57 (51) [4 yrs]

NELSON, LEE Lee Martin, DB, 5´10˝/185 lbs; Florida State; 1976: SL, rnd 15; B1/30/1954 Kissimmee, FL **1976** SL 9 (2) **1977** SL 10 (8, LCB) **1978** SL 16 (1) **1979** SL 16 **1980** SL 16 (10, SS) **1981** SL 15 (15, SS) **1982**†SL 8 (7, SS) **1983** SL 16 (16, SS) **1984** SL 16 (6, ss) **1985** SL 13 (0) **NFL** 135 (65) [10 yrs]

NELSON, MARK Mark David, T, 6´4˝/270 lbs; Iowa State; Bowling Green State; B6/22/1964 Grand Forks, ND **1987** KC 1 (0)

NELSON, PACKIE Everett Fritchof, T, 5´11˝/205 lbs; Illinois; B2/18/1907 Chicago, IL, D12/1/1992 Gaithersburg, MD **1929** ChiB 7 (7, LT)

NELSON, RALPH Ralph, RB, 6´2˝/195 lbs; None; B1/23/1953 Los Angeles, CA

YEAR	TEAM	G (GS, POS)	RUSH	YD	AVG (LG)	TD	REC	YD	AVG (LG)	TD	PASS	COMP	PCT	YD	AVG (LG)	TD	INT	SK	YD	QBR	KPR	OTD	PTS	TAY
1975	Was	14	31	139	4.5(16)	0	5	58	11.6(27)	1	—	—	—	—	—	—	—	—	—	—	k	—	6	205
1976	Sea	8(3)	52	173	3.3(25)	1	12	96	8.0(18)	0	—	—	—	—	—	—	—	—	—	—	—	—	6	231
NFL	2	22(3)	83	312	3.8(25)	1	17	154	9.1(27)	1	—	—	—	—	—	—	—	—	—	—	k	—	12	436

NELSON, REGGIE Reginald DeWayne, T, 6´3˝/321 lbs; McNeese State; 1999: SD, rnd 5; B6/23/1976 Alexandria, LA **1999** SD 2 (0) **2000** Jax 1 (0) **NFL** 3 (0) [2 yrs]

NELSON, RHETT Rhett, DB, 6´0˝/200 lbs; Colorado State; B2/16/1980 Minneapolis, MN **2003** Min 3 (0) **2004**†Min 4 (0) **NFL** 7 (0) [2 yrs]

NELSON, ROBERT Robert Cole, C-T-DT-LB, 6´1˝/214 lbs; Baylor; 1941: Det, rnd 5; B1/30/1920 Paris, TX, D11/3/1986 Granbury, TX **[K]** **1946** LAD-A☆10 (6, C) **1949** LAD-A☆12 (11, C)

YEAR	TEAM	G (GS, POS)	RUSH	YD	AVG (LG)	TD	REC	YD	AVG (LG)	TD	PASS	COMP	PCT	YD	AVG (LG)	TD	INT	SK	YD	QBR	KPR	OTD	PTS	TAY
1947	LAD-A☆	14(12, C)	—	—	—	—	3	61	20.3	1	—	—	—	—	—	—	—	—	—	—	i	1	12	88
1948	LAD-A☆	14(14, C)	1	-7	-7.0(-7)	0	—	—	—	—	—	—	—	—	—	—	—	—	—	—	i	—	0	-12
AAFC	4	50(43)	1	-7	-7.0(-7)	0	3	61	20.3	1	—	—	—	—	—	—	—	—	—	—	Kki	1	64	61

1941 Det 9 (2) **1945** Det 9 (7, C) **1950** Bal 3 **NFL** 21 (9) [3 yrs]

NELSON, SHANE Curtis Shane, LB, 6´1˝/226 lbs; Baylor; B5/25/1955 Mathis, TX **1977** Buf 14 (14, LLB) **1978** Buf 16 (16, LLB) **1979** Buf 16 (16, RILB) **1980**†Buf 16 (16, RILB) **1981** Buf 10 (10, RILB) **1982** Buf 1 (1) **NFL** 73 (73) [6 yrs]

NELSON, STEVE Steven Lee, LB, 6´2˝/230 lbs; Augsburg; North Dakota State; 1974: NE, rnd 2; B4/26/1951 Farmington, MN **1974** NE 11 (9, LILB) **1975** NE 14 (14, LILB) **1976**†NE 10 (10, LILB) **1977** NE 13 (13, LILB) **1978**†NE☆14 (14, LILB) **1979** NE☆15 (15, LILB) **1980** NE★16 (16, LILB) **1981** NE 12 (12, LILB) **1982**†NE 9 (9, LILB) **1983** NE 8 (7, lilb) **1984** NE★16 (16, LILB) **1985**†NE★15 (15, LILB) **1986** NE 10 (10, LILB) **1987** NE 11 (11, LILB) **NFL** 174 (171) [14 yrs]

NELSON, TEDDY Theodore R., DB, 5´10˝/203 lbs; UNLV; B1/1/1965 Pittsburgh, PA **1987** KC 3 (3)

NELSON, TERRY Terry Louis, TE, 6´2˝/233 lbs; Arkansas-Pine Bluff; 1973: LA, rnd 4; B5/20/1951 Arkadelphia, AR

YEAR	TEAM	G (GS, POS)	RUSH	YD	AVG (LG)	TD	REC	YD	AVG (LG)	TD	PASS	COMP	PCT	YD	AVG (LG)	TD	INT	SK	YD	QBR	KPR	OTD	PTS	TAY
1973	LARm	2	—	—	—	—	—	—	—	—	—	—	—	—	—	—	—	—	—	—	—	—	—	—
1974	†LARm	10	1	3	3.0(3)	0	—	—	—	—	—	—	—	—	—	—	—	—	—	—	—	—	0	3
1975	†LARm	14(3)	—	—	—	—	1	5	5.0(5)	0	—	—	—	—	—	—	—	—	—	—	—	—	0	3
1976	†LARm	14	—	—	—	—	4	48	12.0(16)	0	—	—	—	—	—	—	—	—	—	—	—	—	0	25
1977	†LARm	14(14, TE)	3	31	10.3(18)	0	31	401	12.9(46)	3	—	—	—	—	—	—	—	—	—	—	—	—	18	247
1978	†LARm	13(13, TE)	6	67	11.2(17)	1	23	344	15.0(52)	0	—	—	—	—	—	—	—	—	—	—	—	—	6	249
1979	†LARm	16(16, TE)	2	-16	-8.0(-6)	0	25	293	11.7(26)	3	—	—	—	—	—	—	—	—	—	—	—	—	18	146
1980	†LARm	4(2)	—	—	—	—	3	22	7.3(12)	0	—	—	—	—	—	—	—	—	—	—	—	—	0	11
NFL	8	87(48)	12	85	7.1(18)	1	87	1113	12.8(52)	6	—	—	—	—	—	—	—	—	—	—	—	—	42	683

NEMECEK, ANDY Andrew James, C-G-T, 6´4˝/215 lbs; Ohio State; B5/6/1896 Lorain, OH, D5/8/1984 Mayfield Heights, OH **1923** Col 10 (10, RG) **1924** Col☆8 (8, C) **1925** Col 9 (9, C) **NFL** 27 (27) [3 yrs]

NEMECEK, JERRY Jerald Cyrill, E, 6´0˝/185 lbs; NYU; B1/1/1907 New York, NY, D5/5/1987 Pittsford, NY **1931** Bkn 9 (5, RE), 6

NEMETH, STEVE Steve Joseph, QB-HB, 5´10˝/174 lbs; Notre Dame; B12/10/1922 South Bend, IN, D3/27/1998 South Bend, IN **[K]**

YEAR	TEAM	G (GS, POS)	RUSH	YD	AVG (LG)	TD	REC	YD	AVG (LG)	TD	PASS	COMP	PCT	YD	AVG (LG)	TD	INT	SK	YD	QBR	KPR	OTD	PTS	TAY
1945	†Cle	9(4)	—	—	—	—	—	—	—	—	1	0	0.0	0	0.0	0	0	—	—	—	—	—	0	0
1946	ChiR-A	13(1)	4	10	2.5	0	—	—	—	—	23	5	21.7	68	3.0	0	0	—	—	—	KPp	—	59	53
1947	Bal-A	4(1)	1	1	1.0(1)	0	—	—	—	—	6	2	33.3	18	3.0	0	2	—	—	—	KP	—	1	-70
AAFC	2	17(2)	5	11	2.2(1)	0	—	—	—	—	29	7	24.1	86	3.0	0	2	—	—	—	KPp	—	60	-17

NEMZEK, TED Theodore C., T, /205 lbs; Moorhead State (MN); B2/11/1906 Moorhead, MN, D5/21/1968 North Arlington, NJ **1930** Min 4 (3)

NERY, CARL Carl N., G, 6´0˝/214 lbs; Duquesne; 1940: Pit, rnd 8; B6/17/1917 Lawrenceville, PA **1940** Pit 11 (4) **1941** Pit 11 (0) **NFL** 22 (4) [2 yrs]

NERY, RON Ronald Duane, DE, 6´6˝/247 lbs; Kansas State; 1956: NYG, rnd 7; B12/30/1934 New Kensington, PA, D4/2/2002 Topeka, KS **1960**†LAC-A☆14 (RDE) **1961**†SD-A☆14 (RDE) **1962** SD-A 14 (RDE) **1963** Den-A 4 **1963** Hou-A 4 **NFL** 50 [4 yrs]

NESBIT, JAMAR Jamar Kendric, G-C, 6´4˝/329 lbs; South Carolina; B12/17/1976 Heidelberg, Germany **1999** Car 7 (0) **2000** Car 16 (16, RG) **2001** Car 16 (16, LG) **2002** Car 14 (13, LG) **2003** Jax 16 (2) **2004** NO 16 (4) **2005** NO 16 (4) **NFL** 101 (55) [7 yrs]

NESBITT, DICK Richard Jackson, HB-FB, 6´0˝/204 lbs; Drake; B11/12/1907 Des Moines, IA, D3/5/1962 Minneapolis, MN

YEAR	TEAM	G (GS, POS)	RUSH	YD	AVG (LG)	TD	REC	YD	AVG (LG)	TD	PASS	COMP	PCT	YD	AVG (LG)	TD	INT	SK	YD	QBR	KPR	OTD	PTS	TAY
1930	ChiB	8(1)	—	—	—	—	—	—	—	—	—	—	—	—	—	—	—	—	—	—	—	—	—	—
1931	ChiB☆	13(6, rh)	—	—	—	—	—	—	—	—	—	—	—	—	—	—	—	—	—	—	—	—	—	—
1932	ChiB	14(14, RH)	92	295	3.2	2	2	5	2.5	0	4	2	50.0	14	3.5	0	0	—	—	—	—	—	12	325
1933	ChiB	4(0)	21	78	3.7	0	1	15	15.0(15)	0	3	1	33.3	23	7.7(23)	0	0	—	—	—	—	—	0	97
1933	ChiC	5(3)	67	173	2.6	1	5	21	4.2	0	15	1	6.7	11	0.7(22)	0	4	—	—	—	—	—	8	39
1934	Bkn	9(0)	25	58	2.3	0	—	—	—	—	1	1	100.0	46	46.0(46)	0	0	—	—	—	—	—	0	81
NFL	5	53(24)	205	604	2.9	5	8	41	5.1(15)	0	23	5	21.7	94	4.1(46)	1	4	—	—	—	—	1	38	577

NESSER, AL Alfred L., G-E-C, 6´0˝/195 lbs; none; B6/6/1893 Columbus, OH, D3/11/1967 Akron, OH **[C]** **1920** Akr 11 (5, re) **1921** Akr☆12 (12, RG), 6 **1922** Akr☆9 (9, RG), 6 **1923** Akr 7 (7, RE), 6 **1924** Akr 7 (7, LG) **1925** Akr 6 (6, LG) **1925** Cle 7 (7, LG), 6 **1926** Akr 3 (3) **1926** NYG 5 (4) **1927** NYG 13 (11, RG) **1928** NYG 4 (3) **1931** Cle 9 (1) **NFL** 93 (75), 24 [10 yrs]

NESSER, CHARLIE Charles T., B, 6´2˝/182 lbs; none; B1902 Columbus, OH, D2/26/1970 Franklin County, OH **1921** Col 9 (6, TB)

NESSER, FRANK Frank B., FB-G-T, 6´1˝/245 lbs; none; B6/3/1899 Columbus, OH, D11/1/1953 Columbus, OH **[K]** **1920** Col 10 (5, FB) **1921** Col 9 (8, FB), 7 **1922** Col 8 (7, RG), 6 **1925** Col 6 (4, FB) **1926** Col 7 (2) **NFL** 40 (26), 13 [5 yrs]

NESSER, FRED Frederick W., T-E-FB, 6´5˝/250 lbs; none; B9/10/1897 Columbus, OH, D7/2/1967 Columbus, OH **1921** Col 7 (7, LT)

NESSER, JOHN John, G-T, 5´11˝/195 lbs; none; B4/25/1876 Triere, Germany, deceased **1921** Col 2 (1)

NESSER, PHIL Phillip G., G-T-WB, 6´0˝/225 lbs; none; B12/10/1880 Triere, Germany, D5/9/1959 Columbus, OH **1920** Col 1 (1) **1921** Col 6 (3) **NFL** 7 (4) [2 yrs]

NESSER, TED Theodore, C-T-G, 5´10˝/230 lbs; none; B4/5/1883 Denison, OH, D6/7/1941 Columbus, OH **[C]** **1920** Col 5 (1) **1921** Col 9 (9, C) **NFL** 14 (10) [2 yrs]

NETHERTON, BILL William Jackson, E, 5´11˝/180 lbs; Kentucky; B3/2/1898 Worthington, KY, D8/9/1984 Louisville, KY **1921** Lou 1 (1, RE) **1922** Lou 1 (1) **NFL** 2 (2) [2 yrs]

NETTLES, DOUG Gordon Douglas, DB, 6´0˝/179 lbs; Vanderbilt; 1974: Bal, rnd 5; B8/13/1951 Panama City, FL **1974** Bal 13 (4) **1975**†Bal 13 (5, lcb) **1977**†Bal 14 (1) **1978** Bal 16 (14, RCB) **1979** Bal 15 (13, LCB) **1980** NYG 2 (0) **NFL** 73 (37) [6 yrs]

YEAR	TEAM	G (GS, POS)	RUSH	YD	AVG (LG)	TD	REC	YD	AVG (LG)	TD	PASS	COMP	PCT	YD	AVG (LG)	TD	INT	SK	YD	QBR	KPR	OTD	PTS	TAY

NETTLES, JIM James Arthur, DB, 5´10˝/177 lbs; Wisconsin; B2/15/1942 Muncie, IN [I] **1965** Phi 14 **1966** Phi 14 (10, RCB) **1967** Phi 12 (RCB) **1968** Phi 14 **1969**†LARm 13 (5, rcb) **1970** LARm 14 **1971** LARm 14 (14, LCB) **1972** LARm 14 (14, FS) **NFL** 109 (43) [8 yrs]

NEUBERT, KEITH Keith Robert, TE, 6´5˝/250 lbs; Nebraska; 1988: NYJ, rnd 8; B9/13/1964 Fort Atkinson, WI **1988** NYJ 1 (0)

YEAR	TEAM	G (GS, POS)	RUSH	YD	AVG (LG)	TD	REC	YD	AVG (LG)	TD	PASS	COMP	PCT	YD	AVG (LG)	TD	INT	SK	YD	QBR	KPR	OTD	PTS	TAY
1989	NYJ	16 (2)	—	—	—	—	28	302	10.8 (35)	1	—	—	—	—	—	—	—	—	—	—	—	—	6	156
NFL	2	17 (2)	—	—	—	—	28	302	10.8 (35)	1	—	—	—	—	—	—	—	—	—	—	—	—	6	156

NEUFELD, RYAN Ryan Matthew, TE, 6´4˝/250 lbs; UCLA; B11/22/1975 Morgan Hill, CA

YEAR	TEAM	G (GS, POS)	RUSH	YD	AVG (LG)	TD	REC	YD	AVG (LG)	TD	PASS	COMP	PCT	YD	AVG (LG)	TD	INT	SK	YD	QBR	KPR	OTD	PTS	TAY
1999	†Dal	6 (0)	—	—	—	—	—	—	—	—	—	—	—	—	—	—	—	—	—	—	—	—	—	—
2000	Jax	3 (0)	—	—	—	—	—	—	—	—	—	—	—	—	—	—	—	—	—	—	—	—	—	—
2003	Buf	16 (1)	1	14	14.0 (14)	0	3	41	13.7 (25)	0	—	—	—	—	—	—	—	—	—	—	—	—	0	35
2004	Buf	16 (5, te)	—	—	—	—	6	61	10.2 (29)	0	—	—	—	—	—	—	—	—	—	—	k	—	0	19
2005	Buf	13 (0)	—	—	—	—	1	9	9.0 (9)	0	—	—	—	—	—	—	—	—	—	—	k	—	0	-2
NFL	5	54 (6)	1	14	14.0 (14)	0	10	111	11.1 (29)	0	—	—	—	—	—	—	—	—	—	—	k	—	0	52

NEUHEISEL, RICK Richard Gerald, QB, 6´1˝/190 lbs; UCLA; B2/7/1961 Madison, WI [K]

YEAR	TEAM	G (GS, POS)	RUSH	YD	AVG (LG)	TD	REC	YD	AVG (LG)	TD	PASS	COMP	PCT	YD	AVG (LG)	TD	INT	SK	YD	QBR	KPR	OTD	PTS	TAY
1987	SD	3 (2)	6	41	6.8 (18)	1	—	—	—	—	59	40	67.8	367	6.2 (32)	1	1	10	89	—	K	—	7	200

NEUJAHR, QUENTIN Quentin Troy, C, 6´4˝/297 lbs; Kansas State; B1/30/1971 Seward, NE **1996** Bal 5 (0) **1997** Bal 9 (7, c) **1998**†Jax 16 (16, C) **1999**†Jax 16 (0) **2000** Jax 16 (2) **NFL** 62 (25) [5 yrs]

NEUMAN, BOB Robert John, E, 6´0˝/198 lbs; Illinois Wesleyan; B1/18/1912 Mendota, IL, D1/17/1984 Normal, IL

YEAR	TEAM	G (GS, POS)	RUSH	YD	AVG (LG)	TD	REC	YD	AVG (LG)	TD	PASS	COMP	PCT	YD	AVG (LG)	TD	INT	SK	YD	QBR	KPR	OTD	PTS	TAY
1934	ChiC	5 (0)	1	0	0.0	0	—	—	—	—	—	—	—	—	—	—	—	—	—	—	—	—	0	0
1935	ChiC	11 (5, re)	—	—	—	—	3	52	17.3	0	—	—	—	—	—	—	—	—	—	—	—	1	6	26
1936	ChiC	8 (1)	1	3	3.0 (3)	0	3	41	13.7	0	—	—	—	—	—	—	—	—	—	—	—	—	0	24
NFL	3	24 (6)	2	3	1.5 (3)	0	6	93	15.5	0	—	—	—	—	—	—	—	—	—	—	—	1	6	50

NEUMANN, TOM Thomas James, HB, 5´11˝/205 lbs; Wisconsin; Northen Michigan; 1963: Bos, rnd 17; B3/4/1940 Menomonie, WI

YEAR	TEAM	G (GS, POS)	RUSH	YD	AVG (LG)	TD	REC	YD	AVG (LG)	TD	PASS	COMP	PCT	YD	AVG (LG)	TD	INT	SK	YD	QBR	KPR	OTD	PTS	TAY
1963	†Bos-A	10	44	148	3.4 (17)	0	10	48	4.8 (16)	1	—	—	—	—	—	—	—	—	—	—	—	—	6	177

NEVERS, ERNIE Ernest Alonzo, FB, 6´0˝/204 lbs; Stanford; B6/11/1903 Willow River, MN, D5/3/1976 San Rafael, CA; HOF 1963 [KC] **1926** Dul☆14 (13, FB), 71 **1927** Dul☆9 (9, FB), 31 **1929** ChiC☆11 (10, FB), 85 **1930** ChiC☆11 (8, FB), 48 **1931** ChiC☆9 (9, FB), 66 **NFL** 54 (49), 301 [5 yrs]

NEVETT, ELIJAH Elijah, DB-WR, 6´0˝/185 lbs; Clark Atlanta; B4/28/1944 Bessemer, AL **1967** NO 2 **1968** NO 10 **1969** NO 14 (RCB) **1970** NO 11 **NFL** 37 [4 yrs]

NEVILLE, TOM Thomas Oliver, T, 6´4˝/260 lbs; Mississippi State; 1965: Bos, rnd 7/Pit, rnd 9; B8/12/1943 Montgomery, AL **1965** Bos-A 14 (RT) **1966** Bos-A✧14 (RT) **1967** Bos-A 14 (RT) **1968** Bos-A 14 (13, RT) **1969** Bos-A 14 (14, RT) **1970** Bos 13 (13, RT) **1972** NE 13 (13, RT) **1973** NE 8 (8, RT) **1974** NE 14 (14, RT) **1976**†NE 14 (rt) **1977** NE 14 (13, RT) **1978**†Den 16 (15, RT) **1979** NYG 14 (RT)

YEAR	TEAM	G (GS, POS)	RUSH	YD	AVG (LG)	TD	REC	YD	AVG (LG)	TD	PASS	COMP	PCT	YD	AVG (LG)	TD	INT	SK	YD	QBR	KPR	OTD	PTS	TAY
1971	NE	14 (14, RT)	0	-8	(-8)	0	—	—	—	—	—	—	—	—	—	—	—	—	—	—	—	—	0	-8
NFL	14	190 (117)	0	-8	(-8)	0	—	—	—	—	—	—	—	—	—	—	—	—	—	—	—	—	0	-8

NEVILLE, TOM Thomas Lee, G-T, 6´5˝/300 lbs; Weber State; Fresno State; B9/4/1961 Great Falls, MN, D5/9/1998 Fresno, CA **1986** GB 16 (15, LG) **1987** GB 12 (0) **1988** GB 2 (0) **1991** SF 12 (0) **1992** GB 8 (0) **NFL** 50 (15) [5 yrs]

NEWASHE, BILL William, T, 5´11˝/200 lbs; Carlisle Indian; B1890, deceased **1923** Oor 5 (5, RT)

NEWBERRY, JEREMY Jeremy David, C-G, 6´5˝/310 lbs; California; 1998: SF, rnd 2; B3/23/1976 Antioch, CA **1999** SF 16 (16, RG) **2000** SF 16 (16, C) **2001**†SF✧15 (15, C) **2002**†SF★16 (16, C) **2003** SF 16 (16, C) **2004** SF 1 (1) **2005** SF 10 (10, C) **NFL** 90 (90) [7 yrs]

NEWBERRY, TOM Thomas J., G-C, 6´2˝/285 lbs; Wisconsin-LaCrosse; 1986: LARm, rnd 2; B12/20/1962 Onalaska, WI **1986**†LARm 16 (14, LG) **1987** LARm☆12 (12, LG) **1988**†LARm★16 (16, LG) **1989**†LARm★16 (16, LG) **1990** LARm☆15 (15, LG) **1991** LARm 16 (16, C/lg) **1992** LARm 16 (16, LG) **1993** LARm 9 (9, LG) **1994** LARm 15 (14, LG/c) **1995**†Pit 16 (15, LG) **NFL** 147 (143) [10 yrs]

NEWBILL, RICHARD Richard Arthur, LB, 6´1˝/240 lbs; Miami (FL); 1990: Hou, rnd 5; B2/8/1968 Camden, NJ **1990** Min 2 (0) **1990** Sea 1 (0) **1991** Sea 1 (0) **1992** Sea 7 (0) **NFL** 11 (0) [3 yrs]

NEWELL, STEVE Stephen Eugene, WR, 6´1˝/186 lbs; Long Beach State; 1967: SD, rnd 9; B12/27/1944 Springfield, IL

YEAR	TEAM	G (GS, POS)	RUSH	YD	AVG (LG)	TD	REC	YD	AVG (LG)	TD	PASS	COMP	PCT	YD	AVG (LG)	TD	INT	SK	YD	QBR	KPR	OTD	PTS	TAY
1967	SD-A	7 (1)	—	—	—	—	7	68	9.7 (14)	0	—	—	—	—	—	—	—	—	—	—	—	—	0	34

NEWHOUSE, REGGIE Reggie, WR, 6´1˝/191 lbs; Baylor; B2/16/1981 Dallas, TX

YEAR	TEAM	G (GS, POS)	RUSH	YD	AVG (LG)	TD	REC	YD	AVG (LG)	TD	PASS	COMP	PCT	YD	AVG (LG)	TD	INT	SK	YD	QBR	KPR	OTD	PTS	TAY
2004	Arz	3 (0)	—	—	—	—	1	5	5.0 (5)	0	—	—	—	—	—	—	—	—	—	—	—	—	0	3
2005	Arz	3 (1)	—	—	—	—	4	45	11.3 (17)	0	—	—	—	—	—	—	—	—	—	—	—	—	0	23
NFL	2	6 (1)	—	—	—	—	5	50	10.0 (17)	0	—	—	—	—	—	—	—	—	—	—	—	—	0	25

NEWHOUSE, ROBERT Robert Fulton, RB, 5´10˝/209 lbs; Houston; 1972: Dal, rnd 2; B1/9/1950 Longview, TX

YEAR	TEAM	G (GS, POS)	RUSH	YD	AVG (LG)	TD	REC	YD	AVG (LG)	TD	PASS	COMP	PCT	YD	AVG (LG)	TD	INT	SK	YD	QBR	KPR	OTD	PTS	TAY
1972	†Dal	14	28	116	4.1 (19)	1	1	8	8.0 (8)	0	—	—	—	—	—	—	—	—	—	—	k	—	6	242
1973	†Dal	14 (6, rb)	84	436	5.2 (54)	1	9	87	9.7 (38)	1	—	—	—	—	—	—	—	—	—	—	k	—	12	512
1974	Dal	14	124	501	4.0 (23)	3	9	67	7.4 (21)	0	—	—	—	—	—	—	—	—	—	—	—	—	18	565
1975	†Dal	14 (FB)	209	930	4.4 (29)	2	34	275	8.1 (23)	0	2	1	50.0	46	23.0 (46)	1	0	—	—	—	—	—	12	1116
1976	†Dal	14 (7, fb)	116	450	3.9 (24)	3	15	86	5.7 (16)	0	—	—	—	—	—	—	—	—	—	—	—	—	18	523
1977	†Dal	14 (FB)	180	721	4.0 (29)	3	16	106	6.6 (41)	1	—	—	—	—	—	—	—	—	—	—	—	—	24	809
1978	†Dal	13 (12, FB)	140	584	4.2 (24)	8	20	176	8.8 (24)	2	—	—	—	—	—	—	—	—	—	—	—	—	60	762
1979	†Dal	14 (12, FB)	124	449	3.6 (21)	3	7	55	7.9 (21)	1	—	—	—	—	—	—	—	—	—	—	—	—	24	512
1980	†Dal	16 (10, FB)	118	451	3.8 (29)	6	8	75	9.4 (18)	0	—	—	—	—	—	—	—	—	—	—	—	—	36	549
1981	†Dal	16 (0)	14	33	2.4 (6)	0	1	21	21.0 (21)	0	—	—	—	—	—	—	—	—	—	—	k	—	0	33
1982	†Dal	9 (0)	14	79	5.6 (27)	1	—	—	—	—	—	—	—	—	—	—	—	—	—	—	—	—	6	89
1983	†Dal	16 (0)	9	34	3.8 (8)	0	—	—	—	—	—	—	—	—	—	—	—	—	—	—	p	—	0	29
NFL	12	168 (47)	1160	4784	4.1 (54)	31	120	956	8.0 (41)	5	2	1	50.0	46	23.0 (46)	1	0	—	—	—	kp	—	216	5738

NEWKIRK, ROBERT Robert, DT, 6´3˝/290 lbs; Michigan State; B3/6/1977 Belle Glade, FL **1999** NO 5 (0) **2000** ChiB 5 (0) **2001** ChiB 10 (1) **NFL** 20 (1) [3 yrs]

NEWLAND, BOB Robert Vaughn, WR, 6´2˝/190 lbs; Oregon; 1971: NO, rnd 7; B10/27/1948 Medford, OR

YEAR	TEAM	G (GS, POS)	RUSH	YD	AVG (LG)	TD	REC	YD	AVG (LG)	TD	PASS	COMP	PCT	YD	AVG (LG)	TD	INT	SK	YD	QBR	KPR	OTD	PTS	TAY
1971	NO	14	—	—	—	—	21	319	15.2 (44)	0	—	—	—	—	—	—	—	—	—	—	—	—	0	160
1972	NO	14 (WR)	—	—	—	—	47	579	12.3 (42)	2	—	—	—	—	—	—	—	—	—	—	k	—	12	291
1973	NO	14 (WR)	1	6	6.0 (6)	0	29	489	16.9 (42)	4	—	—	—	—	—	—	—	—	—	—	—	—	24	271
1974	NO	14 (WR)	—	—	—	—	27	490	18.1 (79)	2	—	—	—	—	—	—	—	—	—	—	—	—	12	255
NFL	4	56	1	6	6.0 (6)	0	124	1877	15.1 (79)	8	—	—	—	—	—	—	—	—	—	—	k	—	48	976

NEWLAND, HARRY Harry Edward, E, none; B3/12/1892 Stanford, KY, D10/17/1974 Brownsville, OR **1921** Lou 1 (1)

NEWMAN, ANTHONY Anthony Q., DB, 6´0˝/203 lbs; Oregon; 1988: LARm, rnd 2; B11/21/1965 Bellingham, WA [I] **1988**†LARm 16 (0) **1989** LARm 15 (1) **1990** LARm 16 (6, fs) **1991** LARm 16 (1) **1992** LARm 16 (16, SS/fs) **1993** LARm 16 (16, FS) **1994** LARm 16 (14, FS) **1996** NO 16 (16, SS) **1997** NO 12 (12, SS) **1998** Oak 11 (11, SS) **1999** Oak 16 (13, SS)

YEAR	TEAM	G (GS, POS)	RUSH	YD	AVG (LG)	TD	REC	YD	AVG (LG)	TD	PASS	COMP	PCT	YD	AVG (LG)	TD	INT	SK	YD	QBR	KPR	OTD	PTS	TAY
1995	NO	12 (1)	—	—	—	—	1	18	18.0 (18)	0	—	—	—	—	—	—	—	—	—	—	—	—	0	9
NFL	12	178 (107)	—	—	—	—	1	18	18.0 (18)	0	—	—	—	—	—	—	—	—	—	—	iS	2	12	170

NEWMAN, ED Edward Kenneth, G, 6´2˝/245 lbs; Florida Atlantic; Duke; 1973: Mia, rnd 6; B6/4/1951 New York, NY **1973**†Mia 11 (1) **1974**†Mia 14 (4) **1975** Mia 14 **1976** Mia 14 (8, rg/lg) **1977** Mia 14 (3) **1978** Mia 12 (9, lg) **1979**†Mia 16 (16, LG) **1980** Mia 16 (16, RG) **1981**†Mia★16 (16, RG) **1982** Mia★8 (8, RG) **1983**†Mia★16 (16, RG) **1984**†Mia★16 (16, RG) **NFL** 167 (113) [12 yrs]

NEWMAN, HARRY Harry F., G-T, 5´6˝/150 lbs; Ohio University; B1/24/1897, D12/10/1973 Shaker Heights, OH **1924** Akr 6 (6, RG)

NEWMAN, HARRY Harry Lawrence, TB, 5´8˝/179 lbs; Michigan; B9/5/1909 Detroit, MI, D5/2/2000 Las Vegas, NV [K]

YEAR	TEAM	G (GS, POS)	RUSH	YD	AVG (LG)	TD	REC	YD	AVG (LG)	TD	PASS	COMP	PCT	YD	AVG (LG)	TD	INT	SK	YD	QBR	KPR	OTD	PTS	TAY
1933	†NYG☆	14 (12, TB)	130	437	3.4	3	4	136	34.0 (**78**)	1	**136**	**53**	39.0	**973**	**7.2**	**11**	**17**	—	—	51.7	K	—	33	402
1934	NYG☆	10 (10, TB)	141	483	3.4	3	4	55	13.8	0	93	35	37.6	391	4.2	1	12	—	—	—	K	1	37	271
1935	†NYG	8 (4)	65	166	2.6	0	2	12	6.0 (7)	0	29	9	31.0	132	4.6	0	7	—	—	—	K	—	9	-42
NFL	3	32 (26)	336	1086	3.2	6	10	203	20.3 (78)	1	258	97	37.6	1496	5.8	12	36	—	—	33.5	K	1	79	631

NEWMAN, KEITH Keith Anthony, LB, 6´2˝/248 lbs; North Carolina; 1999: Buf, rnd 4; B1/19/1977 Tampa, FL **1999** Buf 3 (0) **2000** Buf 16 (16, LOLB) **2001** Buf 16 (16, LLB) **2002** Buf 16 (10, LLB) **2003** Atl 12 (11, LOLB) **2004**†Min 15 (14, LLB) **2005** Min 13 (10, LLB) **NFL** 91 (77) [7 yrs]

YEAR	TEAM	G (GS, POS)	RUSH	YD	AVG (LG)	TD	REC	YD	AVG (LG)	TD	PASS	COMP	PCT	YD	AVG (LG)	TD	INT	SK	YD	QBR	KPR	OTD	PTS	TAY

NEWMAN, OBIE Olin Berris, E-TB-WB, 6´2˝/199 lbs; Carnegie Mellon; B1900, D6/4/1949, **[K]** **1925** Akr 8 (6, RE), 7 **1926** Akr 8 (5, TB) **1926** Ham 1 (1) **NFL** 17 (12) [2 yrs]

NEWMAN, PAT Edward Patrick, WR, 5´11˝/189 lbs; Utah State; 1990: Min, rnd 10; B9/10/1968 Memphis, TN

YEAR	TEAM	G (GS, POS)	RUSH	YD	AVG (LG)	TD	REC	YD	AVG (LG)	TD	PASS	COMP	PCT	YD	AVG (LG)	TD	INT	SK	YD	QBR	KPR	OTD	PTS	TAY
1991	†NO	7 (0)	—	—	—	—	3	33	11.0 (14)	0	—	—	—	—	—	—	—	—	—	—	—	—	0	17
1992	†NO	10 (0)	—	—	—	—	3	21	7.0 (8)	0	—	—	—	—	—	—	—	—	—	—	kp	—	0	71
1993	NO	16 (0)	—	—	—	—	8	121	15.1 (32)	1	—	—	—	—	—	—	—	—	—	—	p	—	6	75
1994	Cle	1 (0)	—	—	—	—	—	—	—	—	—	—	—	—	—	—	—	—	—	—	—	—	—	—
NFL	4	34 (0)	—	—	—	—	14	175	12.5 (32)	1	—	—	—	—	—	—	—	—	—	—	kp	—	6	162

NEWMAN, TERENCE Terence, DB, 5´11˝/188 lbs; Kansas State; 2003: Dal, rnd 1; B9/4/1978 Salina, KS **2003**†Dal 16 (16, LCB) **2004** Dal 16 (16, LCB)

YEAR	TEAM	G (GS, POS)	RUSH	YD	AVG (LG)	TD	REC	YD	AVG (LG)	TD	PASS	COMP	PCT	YD	AVG (LG)	TD	INT	SK	YD	QBR	KPR	OTD	PTS	TAY
2005	Dal	16 (16, LCB)	1	4	4.0 (4)	0	—	—	—	—	—	—	—	—	—	—	—	—	—	—	piS	—	0	10
NFL	3	48 (48)	1	4	4.0 (4)	0	—	—	—	—	—	—	—	—	—	—	—	—	—	—	piS	—	0	27

NEWMAN, TIM Timothy, RB, 6´0˝/220 lbs; Johnson C. Smith; B6/11/1964 Charlotte, NC **1987** NYJ 1 (0)

NEWMEYER, DON Donald Charles, T, 6´2˝/205 lbs; California; B2/13/1902 Cleveland, OH, D6/25/1992 Napa, CA **[K]** **1926** LA 10 (10, RT), 2

NEWSOM, TONY Anthony Edwin, DB, 5´8˝/175 lbs; Stephen F. Austin State; B7/20/1965 Jacksonville, FL **1987** Hou 5 (3)

NEWSOME, BILLY William Ray, DE-DT, 6´4˝/250 lbs; Grambling State; 1970: Bal, rnd 5; B3/2/1948 Jacksonville, TX **1970**†Bal 14 **1971**†Bal 14 (LDT) **1972** Bal 14 (LDE) **1973** NO 14 (LDE) **1974** NO 13 (LDE) **1975** NYJ 14 (14, LDE) **1976** NYJ 2 **1977**†ChiB 14 (RDE) **NFL** 99 (14) [8 yrs]

NEWSOME, CRAIG Craig, DB, 6´0˝/190 lbs; Arizona State; 1995: GB, rnd 1; B8/10/1971 San Bernardino, CA **1995**†GB 16 (16, LCB) **1996**†GB 16 (16, LCB) **1997** GB 1 (1) **1998**†GB 13 (13, LCB) **1999** SF 7 (2) **NFL** 53 (48) [5 yrs]

NEWSOME, HARRY Harry Kent, P, 6´0˝/192 lbs; Wake Forest; 1985: Pit, rnd 8; B1/25/1963 Cheraw, SC **[P]**

YEAR	TEAM	G (GS, POS)	RUSH	YD	AVG (LG)	TD	REC	YD	AVG (LG)	TD	PASS	COMP	PCT	YD	AVG (LG)	TD	INT	SK	YD	QBR	KPR	OTD	PTS	TAY
1985	Pit	16 (0)	—	—	—	—	—	—	—	—	—	—	—	—	—	—	—	—	—	—	P	—	0	0
1986	Pit	16 (0)	—	—	—	—	—	—	—	—	2	1	50.0	12	6.0 (12)	1	0	—	—	—	P	—	0	11
1987	Pit	12 (0)	2	16	8.0 (16)	0	—	—	—	—	—	—	—	—	—	—	—	—	—	—	P	—	0	16
1988	Pit	16 (0)	2	0	0.0 (0)	0	—	—	—	—	—	—	—	—	—	—	—	—	—	—	P	—	0	0
1989	†Pit	16 (0)	2	-8	-4.0 (0)	0	—	—	—	—	—	—	—	—	—	—	—	—	—	—	P	—	0	-8
1990	Min	16 (0)	2	-2	-1.0 (0)	0	—	—	—	—	—	—	—	—	—	—	—	—	—	—	P	—	0	-2
1991	Min	16 (0)	—	—	—	—	—	—	—	—	—	—	—	—	—	—	—	—	—	—	P	—	0	0
1992	†Min	16 (0)	—	—	—	—	—	—	—	—	1	0	0.0	0	0.0	0	0	—	—	—	P	—	0	0
1993	†Min	16 (0)	—	—	—	—	—	—	—	—	—	—	—	—	—	—	—	—	—	—	P	—	0	0
NFL	9	140 (0)	8	6	0.8 (16)	0	—	—	—	—	3	1	33.3	12	4.0 (12)	1	0	—	—	—	P	—	0	17

NEWSOME, OZZIE Ozzie, TE, 6´2˝/232 lbs; Alabama; 1978: Cle, rnd 1; B3/16/1956 Muscle Shoals, AL; HOF 1999

YEAR	TEAM	G (GS, POS)	RUSH	YD	AVG (LG)	TD	REC	YD	AVG (LG)	TD	PASS	COMP	PCT	YD	AVG (LG)	TD	INT	SK	YD	QBR	KPR	OTD	PTS	TAY
1978	Cle	16 (16, TE)	13	96	7.4 (33)	2	38	589	15.5 (47)	2	—	—	—	—	—	—	—	—	—	—	p	—	24	440
1979	Cle☆	16 (16, TE)	1	6	6.0 (6)	0	55	781	14.2 (74)	9	—	—	—	—	—	—	—	—	—	—	p	—	54	442
1980	†Cle☆	16 (16, TE)	2	13	6.5 (9)	0	51	594	11.6 (44)	3	—	—	—	—	—	—	—	—	—	—	—	—	18	325
1981	Cle★	16 (16, TE)	2	20	10.0 (14)	0	69	1002	14.5 (62)	6	—	—	—	—	—	—	—	—	—	—	—	—	36	551
1982	†Cle☆	9 (9, TE)	—	—	—	—	49	633	12.9 (54)	3	—	—	—	—	—	—	—	—	—	—	—	—	18	332
1983	Cle☆	16 (16, TE)	—	—	—	—	89	970	10.9 (66)	6	—	—	—	—	—	—	—	—	—	—	—	—	36	515
1984	Cle★	16 (15, TE)	—	—	—	—	**89**	1001	11.2 (52)	5	—	—	—	—	—	—	—	—	—	—	—	—	30	526
1985	†Cle★	16 (16, TE)	—	—	—	—	62	711	11.5 (38)	5	—	—	—	—	—	—	—	—	—	—	—	—	30	381
1986	†Cle	16 (16, TE)	—	—	—	—	39	417	10.7 (31)	3	—	—	—	—	—	—	—	—	—	—	—	—	18	224
1987	†Cle	13 (13, TE)	—	—	—	—	34	375	11.0 (25)	0	—	—	—	—	—	—	—	—	—	—	—	—	0	188
1988	†Cle	16 (14, TE)	—	—	—	—	35	343	9.8 (28)	2	—	—	—	—	—	—	—	—	—	—	—	—	12	182
1989	†Cle	16 (13, TE)	—	—	—	—	29	324	11.2 (31)	1	—	—	—	—	—	—	—	—	—	—	—	—	6	167
1990	Cle	16 (15, TE)	—	—	—	—	23	240	10.4 (38)	2	—	—	—	—	—	—	—	—	—	—	—	—	12	130
NFL	13	198 (191)	18	135	7.5 (33)	2	662	7980	12.1 (74)	47	—	—	—	—	—	—	—	—	—	—	p	—	294	4399

NEWSOME, RICHARD Richard Lawrence, DB, 5´11˝/202 lbs; Michigan State; B12/6/1977 Lima, OH **2001** NO 11 (0)

NEWSOME, TIMMY Timothy Arthur, RB, 6´1˝/232 lbs; Winston-Salem State; 1980: Dal, rnd 6; B5/17/1958 Ahoskie, NC

YEAR	TEAM	G (GS, POS)	RUSH	YD	AVG (LG)	TD	REC	YD	AVG (LG)	TD	PASS	COMP	PCT	YD	AVG (LG)	TD	INT	SK	YD	QBR	KPR	OTD	PTS	TAY
1980	†Dal	16 (1)	25	79	3.2 (23)	2	4	43	10.8 (16)	0	—	—	—	—	—	—	—	—	—	—	k	—	12	234
1981	†Dal	15 (0)	13	38	2.9 (7)	0	—	—	—	—	—	—	—	—	—	—	—	—	—	—	k	—	0	86
1982	†Dal	9 (0)	15	98	6.5 (25)	1	6	118	19.7 (46)	1	—	—	—	—	—	—	—	—	—	—	k	—	12	171
1983	†Dal	16 (0)	44	185	4.2 (20)	2	18	250	13.9 (52)	4	—	—	—	—	—	—	—	—	—	—	k	—	36	363
1984	Dal	15 (4)	66	268	4.1 (30)	5	26	263	10.1 (29)	0	—	—	—	—	—	—	—	—	—	—	—	—	30	450
1985	†Dal	14 (13, FB)	88	252	2.9 (15)	2	46	361	7.8 (24)	1	—	—	—	—	—	—	—	—	—	—	—	—	18	458
1986	Dal	16 (12, FB)	34	110	3.2 (13)	2	48	421	8.8 (30)	3	—	—	—	—	—	—	—	—	—	—	k	—	30	358
1987	Dal	11 (8, FB)	25	121	4.8 (24)	2	34	274	8.1 (30)	2	—	—	—	—	—	—	—	—	—	—	k	—	24	280
1988	Dal	9 (8, FB)	32	75	2.3 (8)	3	30	236	7.9 (32)	0	—	—	—	—	—	—	—	—	—	—	—	—	18	223
NFL	9	121 (46)	342	1226	3.6 (30)	19	212	1966	9.3 (52)	11	—	—	—	—	—	—	—	—	—	—	k	—	180	2621

NEWSOME, VINCE Vincent Karl, DB, 6´1˝/180 lbs; Washington; 1983: LARm, rnd 4; B1/22/1961 Braintree, England **1983**†LARm 16 (3) **1984**†LARm 16 (7, ss) **1985**†LARm 16 (1) **1986**†LARm☆16 (12, FS) **1987** LARm 8 (8, SS) **1988** LARm 6 (6, ss) **1989**†LARm 16 (16, FS) **1990** LARm 16 (16, SS) **1991** Cle 15 (15, FS) **1992** Cle 16 (16, FS) **NFL** 141 (100) [10 yrs]

NEWSON, KENDALL Kendall Montrae, WR, 6´1˝/197 lbs; Middle Tennessee State; 2002: Jax, rnd 7; B3/5/1980 Decatur, GA

YEAR	TEAM	G (GS, POS)	RUSH	YD	AVG (LG)	TD	REC	YD	AVG (LG)	TD	PASS	COMP	PCT	YD	AVG (LG)	TD	INT	SK	YD	QBR	KPR	OTD	PTS	TAY
2003	Mia	6 (0)	—	—	—	—	2	55	27.5 (37)	0	—	—	—	—	—	—	—	—	—	—	p	—	0	23

NEWSON, TONY Tony Roderick, LB, 6´1˝/247 lbs; Utah State; B9/11/1979 Las Vegas, NV **2002** KC 4 (0) **2004** SL 3 (0) **NFL** 7 (0) [2 yrs]

NEWTON, BOB Robert Lee, G-T, 6´4˝/257 lbs; Nebraska; 1971: Chi, rnd 3; B8/16/1949 Pomona, CA **1971** ChiB 12 **1972** ChiB 14 (RG) **1973** ChiB 13 (12, RG) **1974** ChiB 14 (14, RG) **1975** ChiB 6 (1) **1976** Sea 12 (7, rg) **1977** Sea 13 (1) **1978** Sea 16 (16, RG) **1979** Sea 11 (11, RG) **1980** Sea 16 (16, RG) **1981** Sea 15 (15, RG) **NFL** 142 (93) [11 yrs]

NEWTON, CAM Cam, DB, 6´1˝/203 lbs; Furman; B5/19/1982 Darlington, SC **2005** Atl 6 (0)

NEWTON, CHUCK Charles Edward, FB-HB, 6´0˝/204 lbs; Washington; 1939: Phi, rnd 2; B11/15/1916 Randolph Township, IN, D4/4/1994 Seattle, WA

YEAR	TEAM	G (GS, POS)	RUSH	YD	AVG (LG)	TD	REC	YD	AVG (LG)	TD	PASS	COMP	PCT	YD	AVG (LG)	TD	INT	SK	YD	QBR	KPR	OTD	PTS	TAY
1939	Phi	9 (7, FB)	1	0	0.0	0	9	123	13.7 (22)	1	—	—	—	—	—	—	—	—	—	—	—	—	6	67
1940	Phi	3 (2)	—	—	—	—	1	22	22.0 (22)	0	—	—	—	—	—	—	—	—	—	—	i	—	0	18
NFL	2	12 (9)	1	0	0.0	0	10	145	14.5 (22)	1	—	—	—	—	—	—	—	—	—	—	i	—	6	85

NEWTON, JIM James Christopher, T, 6´9˝/297 lbs; Utah State; B10/13/1978 Omaha, NE **2003** Ind 3 (0)

NEWTON, NATE Nathaniel 'The Kitchen', G-T, 6´3˝/318 lbs; Florida A&M; B12/20/1961 Orlando, FL **1986** Dal 11 (0) **1987** Dal 11 (11, LG) **1989** Dal 16 (16, LG) **1990** Dal 16 (16, RT) **1991**†Dal 14 (14, RT) **1992**†Dal★15 (15, LG) **1993**†Dal★16 (16, LG) **1994**†Dal★16 (16, LG) **1995**†Dal★16 (16, LG) **1996**†Dal★16 (16, LG) **1997** Dal 13 (13, LG) **1998**†Dal✧16 (16, LG) **1999** Car 7 (0)

YEAR	TEAM	G (GS, POS)	RUSH	YD	AVG (LG)	TD	REC	YD	AVG (LG)	TD	PASS	COMP	PCT	YD	AVG (LG)	TD	INT	SK	YD	QBR	KPR	OTD	PTS	TAY
1988	Dal	15 (15, LG)	—	—	—	—	1	2	2.0 (2)	0	—	—	—	—	—	—	—	—	—	—	—	—	0	1
NFL	14	198 (180)	—	—	—	—	1	2	2.0 (2)	0	—	—	—	—	—	—	—	—	—	—	—	—	0	1

NEWTON, TIM Timothy Reginald, DT-NT, 6´0˝/280 lbs; Florida; 1985: Min, rnd 6; B3/23/1963 Orlando, FL **1985** Min 16 (14, NT) **1986** Min 14 (9, LDT) **1987**†Min 9 (0) **1988** Min 14 (1) **1989** Min 9 (2) **1990** TB 14 (5, nt) **1991** TB 16 (16, LDT/rdt) **1993**†KC 16 (0) **NFL** 108 (47) [8 yrs]

NEWTON, TOM Thomas Richard, RB, 6´0˝/212 lbs; California; B3/8/1954 Carmel, FL

YEAR	TEAM	G (GS, POS)	RUSH	YD	AVG (LG)	TD	REC	YD	AVG (LG)	TD	PASS	COMP	PCT	YD	AVG (LG)	TD	INT	SK	YD	QBR	KPR	OTD	PTS	TAY
1977	NYJ	14 (1)	8	39	4.9 (8)	0	5	33	6.6 (9)	0	—	—	—	—	—	—	—	—	—	—	—	—	0	56
1978	NYJ	16	11	45	4.1 (7)	2	5	48	9.6 (14)	0	—	—	—	—	—	—	—	—	—	—	—	—	12	89
1979	NYJ	16	37	145	3.9 (51)	6	4	33	8.3 (11)	0	—	—	—	—	—	—	—	—	—	—	k	—	36	207
1980	NYJ	16 (4)	59	299	5.1 (23)	0	20	144	7.2 (18)	0	—	—	—	—	—	—	—	—	—	—	—	—	0	371
1981	†NYJ	16 (7, fb)	73	244	3.3 (13)	1	17	104	6.1 (13)	0	—	—	—	—	—	—	—	—	—	—	—	—	6	306
1982	†NYJ	9 (0)	—	—	—	—	1	7	7.0 (7)	0	—	—	—	—	—	—	—	—	—	—	—	—	0	4
NFL	6	87 (12)	188	772	4.1 (51)	9	52	369	7.1 (18)	0	—	—	—	—	—	—	—	—	—	—	k	—	54	1032

NGUYEN, DAT Dat, LB, 5´11˝/243 lbs; Texas A&M; 1999: Dal, rnd 3; B9/25/1975 Saigon, Vietnam **1999**†Dal 16 (0) **2000** Dal 10 (5, mlb) **2001** Dal 16 (16, MLB) **2002** Dal 8 (8, MLB) **2003**†Dal☆16 (16, MLB) **2004** Dal 16 (16, MLB) **2005** Dal 8 (4) **NFL** 90 (65) [7 yrs]

NICCOLAI, ARMAND Armand, T-G, 6´2˝/226 lbs; Duquesne; B11/8/1911 Vesta, PA, D12/2/1988 Pittsburgh, PA **[K]** **1934** Pit 12 (12, RT) **1936** Pit☆11 (4, RT) **1937** Pit 11 (5, RT) **1938** Pit 11 (10, RT) **1939** Pit 11 (8, RT) **1940** Pit 11 (11, RT) **1941** Pit 8 (0) **1942** Pit 10 (0)

YEAR	TEAM	G (GS, POS)	RUSH	YD	AVG (LG)	TD	REC	YD	AVG (LG)	TD	PASS	COMP	PCT	YD	AVG (LG)	TD	INT	SK	YD	QBR	KPR	OTD	PTS	TAY
1935	Pit☆	12 (10, RT)	—	—	—	—	1	0	0.0	0	—	—	—	—	—	—	—	—	—	—	K	—	28	0
NFL	9	97 (60)	—	—	—	—	1	0	0.0	0	—	—	—	—	—	—	—	—	—	—	Ki	—	173	0

NICELY, JIM James Harris, T, 5´10˝/185 lbs; Gettysburg; B10/7/1898 Montoursville, PA, deceased **1930** SI 1 (0)

NICHELINI, AL Allen James, WB-HB, 6´0˝/207 lbs; St. Mary's (CA); B11/23/1909 St. Helena, CA, D1/3/1992 Fresno, CA

YEAR	TEAM	G (GS, POS)	RUSH	YD	AVG (LG)	TD	REC	YD	AVG (LG)	TD	PASS	COMP	PCT	YD	AVG (LG)	TD	INT	SK	YD	QBR	KPR	OTD	PTS	TAY
1935	ChiC	11 (7, WB)	94	234	2.5	4	1	0	0.0	0	1	1	100.0	16	16.0 (16)	0	0	—	—	—	—	—	24	282
1936	ChiC	12 (11, WB)	55	189	3.4	0	9	133	14.8	0	—	—	—	—	—	—	—	—	—	—	—	1	6	256
NFL	2	23 (18)	149	423	2.8	4	10	133	13.3	0	1	1	100.0	16	16.0 (16)	0	0	—	—	—	—	1	30	538

NICHOLAS, CALVIN Calvin Lewis, WR, 6´4˝/208 lbs; Grambling State; 1987: SF, rnd 11; B6/11/1964 Baton Rouge, LA

YEAR	TEAM	G (GS, POS)	RUSH	YD	AVG (LG)	TD	REC	YD	AVG (LG)	TD	PASS	COMP	PCT	YD	AVG (LG)	TD	INT	SK	YD	QBR	KPR	OTD	PTS	TAY
1988	SF	7 (0)	—	—	—	—	1	14	14.0 (14)	0	—	—	—	—	—	—	—	—	—	—	—	—	0	7

NICHOLS, ALLEN Allen, FB, 5´10˝/205 lbs; Temple; B10/28/1916, D6/1981

YEAR	TEAM	G (GS, POS)	RUSH	YD	AVG (LG)	TD	REC	YD	AVG (LG)	TD	PASS	COMP	PCT	YD	AVG (LG)	TD	INT	SK	YD	QBR	KPR	OTD	PTS	TAY
1945	Pit	1 (1)	10	5	0.5 (9)	0	—	—	—	—	—	—	—	—	—	—	—	—	—	—	—	—	0	5

NICHOLS, BOB Robert Gordon, T, 6´3˝/250 lbs; Stanford; 1964: Pit, rnd 9/Hou, rnd 18; B7/18/1943 Los Angeles, CA **1965** Pit 14 **1966** LARm 13 **1967**†LARm 14 **NFL** 41 [3 yrs]

NICHOLS, BOBBY Robert P., TE, 6´2˝/220 lbs; Boston University; 1967: Bos, rnd 17; B1/30/1943 **1968** Bos-A 6 (1)

YEAR	TEAM	G (GS, POS)	RUSH	YD	AVG (LG)	TD	REC	YD	AVG (LG)	TD	PASS	COMP	PCT	YD	AVG (LG)	TD	INT	SK	YD	QBR	KPR	OTD	PTS	TAY
1967	Bos-A	9	—	—	—	—	1	19	19.0 (19)	0	—	—	—	—	—	—	—	—	—	—	—	—	0	10
NFL	2	15 (1)	—	—	—	—	1	19	19.0 (19)	0	—	—	—	—	—	—	—	—	—	—	—	—	0	10

NICHOLS, GERALD Gerald William, DT-NT-DE, 6´2˝/261 lbs; Florida State; 1987: NYJ, rnd 7; B2/10/1964 St. Louis, MO **1987** NYJ 13 (5, nt) **1988** NYJ 16 (2) **1989** NYJ 16 (0) **1990** NYJ 15 (0) **1991** TB 16 (5, ldt) **1993** Phi 7 (3) **1993** Was 2 (0) **NFL** 85 (15) [6 yrs]

NICHOLS, HAMILTON Hamilton James, G-LB, 5´11˝/209 lbs; Rice; 1946: ChiC, rnd 4/1947: Buf-A, rnd 21; B10/18/1924 Houston, TX **1947**†ChiC 11 (4) **1948**†ChiC 12 (2) **1949** ChiC 11 (3) **1951** GB 9 (RG) **NFL** 43 (9) [4 yrs]

NICHOLS, JOHN John Howard, G-T, 6´0˝/200 lbs; Ohio State; B7/30/1904, D6/16/1978 Cleveland, OH **1926** Can 13 (10, LG)

NICHOLS, MARK Mark Stephen, WR, 6´2˝/210 lbs; San Jose State; 1981: Det, rnd 1; B10/29/1959 Bakersfield, CA

YEAR	TEAM	G (GS, POS)	RUSH	YD	AVG (LG)	TD	REC	YD	AVG (LG)	TD	PASS	COMP	PCT	YD	AVG (LG)	TD	INT	SK	YD	QBR	KPR	OTD	PTS	TAY
1981	Det	12 (0)	3	50	16.7 (30)	0	10	222	22.2 (59)	1	—	—	—	—	—	—	—	—	—	—	k	—	6	180
1982	Det	7 (3)	1	3	3.0 (3)	0	8	153	19.1 (48)	2	—	—	—	—	—	—	—	—	—	—	—	—	12	90
1983	†Det	16 (11, WR)	1	13	13.0 (13)	0	29	437	15.1 (46)	1	—	—	—	—	—	—	—	—	—	—	—	—	6	237
1984	Det	15 (9, WR)	3	27	9.0 (13)	0	34	744	21.9 (77)	1	—	—	—	—	—	—	—	—	—	—	—	—	6	404
1985	Det	14 (12, WR)	1	15	15.0 (15)	0	36	592	16.4 (43)	4	—	—	—	—	—	—	—	—	—	—	—	—	24	331
1987	Det	12 (1)	—	—	—	—	7	87	12.4 (23)	0	—	—	—	—	—	—	—	—	—	—	—	—	0	44
NFL	6	76 (36)	9	108	12.0 (30)	0	124	2235	18.0 (77)	9	—	—	—	—	—	—	—	—	—	—	k	—	54	1285

NICHOLS, MARK Mark Robe, LB, 6´3˝/225 lbs; Colorado State; 1978: Oak, rnd 8; B10/23/1956 Columbus, OH **1978** SF 15

NICHOLS, MIKE Lee Michael, C, 6´3˝/225 lbs; Arkansas-Monticello; B7/29/1938 College Heights, AR **1961** Den-A 14 (C)

YEAR	TEAM	G (GS, POS)	RUSH	YD	AVG (LG)	TD	REC	YD	AVG (LG)	TD	PASS	COMP	PCT	YD	AVG (LG)	TD	INT	SK	YD	QBR	KPR	OTD	PTS	TAY
1960	Den-A	14 (C)	0	3	(3)	0	—	—	—	—	—	—	—	—	—	—	—	—	—	—	—	—	0	3
NFL	2	28	0	3	(3)	0	—	—	—	—	—	—	—	—	—	—	—	—	—	—	—	—	0	3

NICHOLS, RALPH Ralph Dale, T-G, 6´0˝/210 lbs; Kansas State; B8/2/1899, deceased **1926** Har 10 (7, RT)

NICHOLS, RICKY Ricky Antonio, WR, 5´10˝/176 lbs; East Carolina; 1985: Ind, rnd 8; B7/27/1962 Norfolk, VA **1985** Ind 3 (0)

NICHOLS, ROBBIE Robert B., LB, 6´3˝/220 lbs; Tulsa; B11/17/1946 Cleveland, OK **1970**†Bal 14 **1971** Bal 4 **NFL** 18 [2 yrs]

NICHOLS, SID Sidney Warren, BB, 5´7˝/177 lbs; Illinois; B4/15/1895 Creston, IA, D3/23/1971 Paso Robles, CA **1920** RI 7 (3) **1921** RI 7 (3), 6 **NFL** 14 (6) [2 yrs]

NICHOLSON, CALVIN Calvin T., DB, 5´9˝/183 lbs; Oregon State; 1989: NO, rnd 11; B7/9/1967 Los Angeles, CA **1989** NO 1 (0) **1991** NO 8 (0) **NFL** 9 (0) [2 yrs]

NICHOLSON, DONTE Donte Lamar, DB, 6´1˝/216 lbs; Oklahoma; 2005: TB, rnd 5; B12/18/1981 Los Angeles, CA **2005**†TB 9 (0)

NICHOLSON, FRANK Frank, LB, 6´2˝/205 lbs; Delaware State; B3/6/1961 **1987** NYG 3 (1)

NICHOLSON, JIM James Burton, T, 6´6˝/269 lbs; Michigan State; 1973: LA, rnd 9; B2/28/1949 Honolulu, HI **1974** KC 13 (RT) **1975** KC 12 (12, RT) **1976** KC 14 (14, RT) **1977** KC 12 (12, RT) **1978** KC 6 **1979** KC 15 (RT) **NFL** 72 (38) [6 yrs]

NICKEL, ELBIE Elbert Everett, E-DE, 6´1˝/196 lbs; Cincinnati; 1947: Pit, rnd 17; B12/28/1922 Fullerton, KY

YEAR	TEAM	G (GS, POS)	RUSH	YD	AVG (LG)	TD	REC	YD	AVG (LG)	TD	PASS	COMP	PCT	YD	AVG (LG)	TD	INT	SK	YD	QBR	KPR	OTD	PTS	TAY
1947	†Pit	11 (1)	—	—	—	—	1	10	10.0 (10)	0	—	—	—	—	—	—	—	—	—	—	—	—	0	5
1948	Pit	12 (7, RE)	—	—	—	—	22	324	14.7 (35)	1	—	—	—	—	—	—	—	—	—	—	—	—	6	167
1949	Pit	12 (10, RE)	—	—	—	—	26	633	**24.3** (**52**)	3	—	—	—	—	—	—	—	—	—	—	k	—	18	337
1950	Pit	12 (RE)	—	—	—	—	22	527	24.0 (65)	4	—	—	—	—	—	—	—	—	—	—	—	—	24	284
1951	Pit	12 (RE)	—	—	—	—	28	447	16.0 (77)	3	—	—	—	—	—	—	—	—	—	—	—	—	18	239
1952	Pit✧	12 (RE)	—	—	—	—	55	884	16.1 (54)	9	—	—	—	—	—	—	—	—	—	—	—	—	54	487
1953	Pit✧	12 (RE)	—	—	—	—	62	743	12.0 (40)	4	—	—	—	—	—	—	—	—	—	—	—	—	24	392
1954	Pit	12 (RE)	—	—	—	—	40	584	14.6 (52)	5	—	—	—	—	—	—	—	—	—	—	—	—	30	317
1955	Pit	12 (RE)	—	—	—	—	36	488	13.6 (30)	2	—	—	—	—	—	—	—	—	—	—	—	—	12	254
1956	Pit✧	12 (FL)	—	—	—	—	27	376	13.9 (47)	5	—	—	—	—	—	—	—	—	—	—	—	—	30	213
1957	Pit	12	—	—	—	—	10	115	11.5 (31)	1	—	—	—	—	—	—	—	—	—	—	—	—	6	63
NFL	11	131 (18)	—	—	—	—	329	5131	15.6 (77)	37	—	—	—	—	—	—	—	—	—	—	k	—	222	2756

NICKERSON, HARDY Hardy Otto, LB, 6´2˝/230 lbs; California; 1987: Pit, rnd 5; B9/1/1965 Compton, CA **1987** Pit 12 (0) **1988** Pit 15 (10, RILB) **1989**†Pit 10 (8, RILB) **1990** Pit 16 (14, LILB) **1991** Pit 16 (14, LILB) **1992**†Pit 15 (15, LILB) **1993** TB★16 (16, MLB) **1994** TB 14 (14, MLB) **1995** TB 16 (16, MLB) **1996** TB★16 (16, MLB) **1997**†TB★16 (16, MLB) **1998** TB✧10 (10, MLB) **1999**†TB★16 (16, MLB) **2000** Jax 6 (6, mlb) **2001** Jax 15 (14, MLB) **2002**†GB 16 (15, MLB) **NFL** 225 (200) [16 yrs]

NICKEY, DONNIE Donnie Orvin, DB, 6´2˝/215 lbs; Ohio State; 2003: Ten, rnd 5; B4/25/1980 Akron, OH **2003**†Ten 12 (0) **2004** Ten 15 (6, ss)

YEAR	TEAM	G (GS, POS)	RUSH	YD	AVG (LG)	TD	REC	YD	AVG (LG)	TD	PASS	COMP	PCT	YD	AVG (LG)	TD	INT	SK	YD	QBR	KPR	OTD	PTS	TAY
2005	Ten	16 (0)	—	—	—	—	1	26	26.0 (26)	0	—	—	—	—	—	—	—	—	—	—	—	—	0	13
NFL	3	43 (6)	—	—	—	—	1	26	26.0 (26)	0	—	—	—	—	—	—	—	—	—	—	—	—	0	13

NICKLA, ED Edward Michael, T, 6´3˝/240 lbs; Tennessee; Maryland; 1955: ChiB, rnd 14; B8/11/1933 New York, NY **1959** ChiB 12

NICKLAS, PETE Peter Lawrence, T, 6´4˝/240 lbs; Baylor; 1962: Oak, rnd 30/1961: Bal, rnd 9; B7/24/1939 **1962** Oak-A 14

NICKSICH, GEORGE George, MG-LB-G, 6´0˝/225 lbs; St. Bonaventure; B5/5/1928 Monessen, PA, D1/1985 Greensburg, PA **1950** Pit 12 (MG)

NICOLAS, SCOTT Scott Stephen, LB, 6´3˝/226 lbs; Miami (FL); 1982: Cle, rnd 12; B8/7/1960 Wichita Falls, TX **1982**†Cle 9 (0) **1983** Cle 16 (8, LILB) **1984** Cle 16 (0) **1985**†Cle 16 (1) **1986**†Cle 16 (0) **1987** Mia 12 (0) **NFL** 85 (9) [6 yrs]

NIEDZIELA, BRUNO Bruno Joseph, T, 6´2˝/225 lbs; Iowa; 1947: ChiR-A, rnd 16/1945: ChiB, rnd 19; B4/12/1923 Chicago, IL **1947** ChiR-A 12 (9)

NIEHAUS, FANNY Francis W., WB-BB, 6´0˝/170 lbs; Washington & Jefferson; B3/16/1902, D3/1985 Wadsworth, OH **1925** Akr 7 (4), 6 **1926** Pot 4 (2) **NFL** 11 (6) [2 yrs]

NIEHAUS, RALPH Ralph H., T, 6´4˝/220 lbs; Dayton; 1939: Det, rnd 17; B11/18/1917 Cincinnati, OH **1939** Cle 6 (2)

NIEHAUS, STEVE Steven Gerard, DT-DE, 6´4˝/263 lbs; Notre Dame; 1976: Sea, rnd 1; B9/25/1954 Cincinnati, OH **1976** Sea 14 (14, LDT) **1977** Sea 8 **1978** Sea 14 (6, rdt) **1979** Min 3 **NFL** 39 (20) [4 yrs]

NIEHOFF, ROBERT Robert Thomas, DB, 6´2˝/205 lbs; Cincinnati; B5/9/1964 Cincinnati, OH **1987** Cin 3 (0)

NIELSEN, GIFFORD Gifford Gifford, QB, 6´4˝/205 lbs; Brigham Young; 1978: Hou, rnd 3; B10/25/1954 Provo, UT

YEAR	TEAM	G (GS, POS)	RUSH	YD	AVG (LG)	TD	REC	YD	AVG (LG)	TD	PASS	COMP	PCT	YD	AVG (LG)	TD	INT	SK	YD	QBR	KPR	OTD	PTS	TAY
1978	†Hou	2	—	—	—	—	—	—	—	—	4	2	50.0	0	0.0 (0)	0	0	2	12	—	—	—	0	0
1979	†Hou	16 (1)	5	7	1.4 (7)	0	—	—	—	—	61	32	52.5	404	6.6 (41)	3	3	3	26	—	—	—	0	104
1980	†Hou	16 (0)	1	0	0.0 (0)	0	—	—	—	—	4	2	50.0	12	3.0 (8)	1	0	—	—	—	—	—	0	11
1981	Hou	5 (2)	6	2	0.3 (4)	0	—	—	—	—	93	60	64.5	709	7.6 (44)	5	3	8	61	—	—	—	0	262
1982	Hou	9 (4, qb)	9	37	4.1 (9)	0	—	—	—	—	161	87	54.0	1005	6.2 (46)	6	8	12	92	—	—	—	0	250

YEAR	TEAM	G (GS, POS)	RUSH	YD	AVG(LG)	TD	REC	YD	AVG(LG)	TD	PASS	COMP	PCT	YD	AVG(LG)	TD	INT	SK	YD	QBR	KPR	OTD	PTS	TAY
1983	Hou	7 (7, QB)	8	43	5.4(20)	0	—	—	—	—	175	90	51.4	1125	6.4(48)	5	8	22	163	—	—	—	0	311
NFL	6	55 (14)	29	89	3.1(20)	0	—	—	—	—	498	273	54.8	3255	6.5(48)	20	22	47	354	—	—	—	0	937

NIELSEN, HANS   Hans Jorgen, K, 5´11˝/165 lbs; Michigan State; B11/18/1952 Vejle, Denmark **[K]**   **1981** ChiB 3 (0)

NIELSEN, WALT   Walter Ring, FB, 6´3˝/220 lbs; Arizona; 1939: NYG, rnd 1; B2/4/1917

| 1940 | NYG | 9 (5, fb) | 73 | 269 | 3.7 | 1 | 2 | 17 | 8.5(18) | 0 | 1 | 0 | 0.0 | 0 | 0.0 | 0 | 0 | — | — | — | P | — | 6 | 288 |

NIELSON   WB, none   **1924** Roc 1 (1)

NIEMANN, WALLY   Walter Albright, C, 5´11˝/180 lbs; Michigan; B4/21/1894 Hermansville, MI, D12/5/1967 Menomonie, MI   **1922** GB 8 (8, C)   **1923** GB 10 (9, C)   **1924** GB 4 (1)   **NFL** 22 (18) [3 yrs]

NIEMI, LAURIE   Laurie Jack, T-DT, 6´1˝/251 lbs; Washington State; 1949: Was, rnd 2; B3/19/1925 Red Lodge, MT, D2/19/1968 Spokane, WA   **1949** Was 12 (4)   **1950** Was 8 (LT)   **1951** Was◇12 (LT)   **1952** Was◇12 (LT)   **1953** Was 12   **NFL** 56 (4) [5 yrs]

NIENHUIS, DOUG   Doug, T, 6´6˝/307 lbs; Oregon State; 2005: Sea, rnd 7; B2/16/1982 Long Beach, CA   **2005** NYJ 7 (0)

NIES, JOHN   John Richard, P, 6´2˝/199 lbs; Arizona; 1990: Buf, rnd 6; B2/13/1967 Jersey City, NJ   **1990** Buf 4 (0)

NIGHSWANDER, NICK   Nicholas M., C, 6´0˝/232 lbs; Morehead State; B11/3/1952   **1974**†Buf 7

NILAND, JOHN   John Hugh, G, 6´3˝/245 lbs; Iowa; 1966: Dal, rnd 1/Oak, rnd 13; B2/29/1944 Quincy, MA   **1966**†Dal 13 (lg)   **1967** Dal 14 (LG)   **1968**†Dal◇14 (LG)   **1969** Dal★14 (LG)   **1970**†Dal★14 (LG)   **1971**†Dal★14 (LG)   **1972** Dal★14 (LG)   **1973**†Dal★13 (LG)   **1974** Dal☆14 (LG)   **1975** Phi 14 (13, LG)   **NFL** 138 (13) [10 yrs]

NILES, JERRY   Jerry Maynard, QB, 6´1˝/195 lbs; Iowa; B5/1/1919 East Moline, IL, D12/27/1950

| 1947 | NYG | 4 (0) | 8 | 24 | 3.0(20) | 0 | — | — | — | — | 57 | 19 | 33.3 | 269 | 4.7(64) | 1 | 7 | — | — | — | k | — | 0 | -120 |

NILSEN, REED   Reed Elfin, C, 6´0˝/230 lbs; Brigham Young; 1947: Det, rnd 16/Bkn-A, rnd 14; B1/13/1921 Provo, UT   **1947** Det 2 (0)

NINOWSKI, JIM   James, QB, 6´1˝/206 lbs; Michigan State; 1958: Cle, rnd 4; B3/26/1936 Detroit, MI

1958	†Cle	4	2	1	0.5(7)	0	—	—	—	—	17	8	47.1	139	8.2(34)	1	3	—	—	—	—	—	0	-45
1959	Cle	2	1	11	11.0(11)	0	—	—	—	—	10	3	30.0	41	4.1(20)	0	1	—	—	—	—	—	0	-9
1960	Det	11 (QB)	32	81	2.5(14)	5	—	—	—	—	283	134	47.3	1599	5.7(55)	2	18	—	—	40.9	—	—	30	221
1961	Det	13 (QB)	33	238	7.2(40)	5	—	—	—	—	247	117	47.4	1921	7.8(84)	7	18	—	—	53.0	—	—	30	564
1962	Cle	7 (qb)	9	15	1.7(7)	0	—	—	—	—	173	87	50.3	1178	6.8(53)	7	8	—	—	66.6	—	—	0	319
1963	Cle	4	5	-19	-3.8(2)	0	—	—	—	—	61	29	47.5	423	6.9(70)	2	6	4	45	—	—	—	0	-38
1964	Cle	3	1	-8	-8.0(-8)	0	—	—	—	—	9	6	66.7	125	13.9(41)	2	0	1	12	—	—	—	0	65
1965	Cle	6	4	46	11.5(17)	0	—	—	—	—	83	40	48.2	549	6.6(32)	4	3	8	70	—	—	—	0	221
1966	Cle	14	3	-11	-3.7(4)	0	—	—	—	—	18	11	61.1	175	9.7(44)	4	1	1	14	—	—	—	0	57
1967	Was	14	—	—	—	—	—	—	—	—	18	12	66.7	123	6.8(31)	0	1	—	—	—	—	—	0	22
1968	Was	7	2	13	6.5(8)	0	—	—	—	—	95	49	51.6	633	6.7(56)	4	6	—	—	—	—	—	0	110
1969	NO	4	—	—	—	—	—	—	—	—	34	17	50.0	227	6.7(70)	1	2	1	11	—	—	—	0	39
NFL	12	89	92	367	4.0(40)	10	—	—	—	—	1048	513	49.0	7133	6.8(84)	34	67	15	152	55.4	—	—	60	1524

NIPP, MAURY   Maurice Herman, G, 6´0˝/219 lbs; Loyola Marymount; 1952: Phi, rnd 9; B3/21/1930 Yankton, SD   **1952** Phi 10 (LG)   **1953** Phi 12 (LG)   **1956** Phi 3   **NFL** 25 [3 yrs]

NISBET, DAVE   David McLean, E, 6´1˝/190 lbs; Washington; B8/29/1910, D12/1976 Seattle, WA

| 1933 | ChiC | 10 (6, re) | — | — | — | — | 1 | 25 | 25.0(25) | 0 | 3 | 1 | 33.3 | 36 | 12.0(36) | 0 | 1 | — | — | — | — | — | 0 | -10 |

NISBY, JOHN   John Edward, G, 6´1˝/235 lbs; Pacific; 1957: GB, rnd 6; B9/9/1936 San Francisco, CA   **1957** Pit 11 (RG)   **1958** Pit 12 (RG)   **1959** Pit★12 (RG)   **1960** Pit☆12 (RG)   **1961** Pit★13 (RG)   **1962** Was◇14 (LG)   **1963** Was 14 (LG)   **1964** Was 14 (LG)   **NFL** 102 [8 yrs]

NITSCHKE, RAY   Raymond Ernest, LB, 6´3˝/235 lbs; Illinois; 1958: GB, rnd 3; B12/29/1936 Elmwood Park, IL, D3/8/1998 Venice, FL; HOF 1978 **[I]**   **1958** GB 12 (MLB)   **1959** GB 12 (MLB)   **1960**†GB 12 (6, MLB)   **1961**†GB 12 (MLB)   **1962**†GB☆14 (MLB)   **1963** GB☆12 (MLB)   **1964** GB★14 (MLB)   **1965**†GB☆12 (MLB)   **1966**†GB☆14 (MLB)   **1967**†GB☆14 (MLB)   **1968** GB 14 (MLB)   **1969** GB☆14 (MLB)   **1970** GB 14 (MLB)   **1971** GB 9

| 1972 | †GB | 11 | — | — | — | — | 1 | 34 | 34.0(34) | 0 | — | — | — | — | — | — | — | — | — | — | — | — | 0 | 17 |
| NFL | 15 | 190 (6) | — | — | — | — | 1 | 34 | 34.0(34) | — | — | — | — | — | — | — | — | — | — | — | ki | — | 2 | 12 | 260 |

NITTMO, BJORN   Bjorn Arne, K, 5´11˝/185 lbs; Appalachian State; B7/26/1966 Lomma, Sweden **[K]**   **1989** NYG 6 (0)

NIX, DOYLE   Doyle Edward, DB, 6´1˝/191 lbs; SMU; 1955: GB, rnd 18; B5/30/1933 Texarkana, TX   **1955** GB 12 (DB)   **1958** Was 11 (DB)   **1959** Was 8 (DB)   **1960**†LAC-A 12 (LCB)   **1961** DalT-A 11 (LS)   **NFL** 54 [5 yrs]

NIX, EMERY   Kenneth Emery, TB-QB, 5´11˝/180 lbs; TCU; B12/1/1919 Chillicothe, OH, D12/6/2005 Blanco, TX

1943	†NYG	10 (6, tb)	19	26	1.4(25)	0	—	—	—	—	53	24	45.3	396	7.5(56)	3	3	—	—	—	kpi	—	0	149
1946	NYG	4 (0)	8	-25	-3.1(3)	0	—	—	—	—	19	10	52.6	156	8.2(35)	2	0	—	—	—	—	—	0	63
NFL	2	14 (6)	27	1	0.0(25)	0	—	—	—	—	72	34	47.2	552	7.7(56)	5	3	—	—	—	kpi	—	0	212

NIX, GEORGE   George Augustus, G, 5´11˝/195 lbs; Haskell Indian; B3/18/1895 Howkan, AK, D10/5/1978 Tacoma, WA   **1926** Buf 2 (0)

NIX, JACK   Jack Clarence, WB, 6´0˝/175 lbs; Mississippi State; 1940: Cle, rnd 17; B11/9/1917 Moselle, MS, D12/29/1990 Starkville, MS   **1940** Cle 1 (0)

NIX, JACK   Jack Louis, E, 6´2˝/200 lbs; USC; 1950: SF, rnd 20; B5/7/1928 Gary, IN **[K]**

| 1950 | SF | 9 | — | — | — | — | 9 | 114 | 12.7(50) | 0 | — | — | — | — | — | — | — | — | — | — | K | — | 1 | 57 |

NIX, JOHN   John, DT, 6´1˝/313 lbs; Southern Mississippi; 2001: Dal, rnd 7; B11/24/1976 Lucedale, MS   **2001** Dal 16 (0)   **2002** Dal 14 (0)   **2004** Arz 1 (0)   **NFL** 31 (0) [3 yrs]

NIX, KENT   Alvin Kent, QB, 6´2˝/195 lbs; TCU; B3/12/1944 Corpus Christi, TX

1967	Pit	12 (QB)	15	45	3.0(15)	2	—	—	—	—	268	136	50.7	1587	5.9(66)	8	19	—	—	49.5	—	—	12	139
1968	Pit	8	6	15	2.5(12)	0	—	—	—	—	130	56	43.1	720	5.5(61)	4	8	—	—	—	—	—	0	75
1969	Pit	5	10	70	7.0(20)	0	—	—	—	—	53	25	47.2	290	5.5(47)	2	6	7	39	—	—	—	0	-15
1970	ChiB	1	—	—	—	—	—	—	—	—	1	0	0.0	0	0.0	0	0	1	2	—	—	—	0	0
1971	ChiB	8	9	12	1.3(14)	0	—	—	—	—	137	51	37.2	760	5.5(45)	6	10	10	91	—	—	—	0	22
1972	Hou	12	3	3	1.0(5)	0	—	—	—	—	63	33	52.4	287	4.6(19)	3	6	6	45	—	—	—	0	-79
NFL	6	46	43	145	3.4(20)	2	—	—	—	—	652	301	46.2	3644	5.6(66)	23	49	24	177	44.3	—	—	12	142

NIX, ROOSEVELT   Roosevelt, DE, 6´6˝/299 lbs; Central State (OH); 1992: Cin, rnd 8; B4/17/1967 Toledo, OH   **1992** Cin 6 (0)   **1993** Cin 10 (0)   **1994** Min 2 (0)   **NFL** 18 (0) [3 yrs]

NIXON, FRED   Frederick Lenar, WR, 5´11˝/191 lbs; Oklahoma; 1980: GB, rnd 4; B9/22/1958 Camilla, GA

1980	GB	15 (0)	—	—	—	—	4	78	19.5(32)	0	—	—	—	—	—	—	—	—	—	—	kp	—	0	139
1981	GB	8 (1)	—	—	—	—	2	27	13.5(19)	0	—	—	—	—	—	—	—	—	—	—	kp	—	0	99
NFL	2	23 (1)	—	—	—	—	6	105	17.5(32)	0	—	—	—	—	—	—	—	—	—	—	kp	—	0	238

NIXON, JEFF   Jeffrey Allen, DB, 6´3˝/190 lbs; Richmond; 1979: Buf, rnd 4; B10/13/1956 Furstenfeldbruck, Germany   **1979** Buf 16 (4)   **1980** Buf 7 (5, fs)   **1981**†Buf 13 (0)   **1982** Buf 7 (0)   **NFL** 43 (9) [4 yrs]

NIXON, MIKE   Michael Regis, aka Michael Regis Nicksick, HB, 5´11˝/181 lbs; Pittsburgh; B11/21/1911 Masontown, PA, D9/22/2000 Schaumburg, IL **[C]**   **1942** Bkn 3 (0)

| 1935 | Pit | 3 (0) | 7 | 5 | 0.7 | 0 | — | — | — | — | 3 | 0 | 0.0 | 0 | 0.0 | 0 | 1 | — | — | — | — | — | 0 | -35 |
| NFL | 2 | 6 (0) | 7 | 5 | 0.7 | 0 | — | — | — | — | 3 | 0 | 0.0 | 0 | 0.0 | 0 | 1 | — | — | — | — | — | 0 | -35 |

NIXON, TORY   Torran Blake, DB, 5´11˝/186 lbs; Arizona State; San Diego State; 1985: Was, rnd 2; B2/24/1962 Eugene, OR   **1985**†SF 16 (0)   **1986**†SF 16 (0)   **1987**†SF 12 (0)   **1988**†SF 6 (0)   **NFL** 50 (0) [4 yrs]

NIZIOLEK, BOB   Robert Craig, TE, 6´4˝/220 lbs; Colorado; 1981: Det, rnd 8; B6/30/1958 Chicago, IL   **1981** Det 4 (0)

NKWENTI, MATHIAS   Mathias Fru, T, 6´3˝/300 lbs; Temple; 2001: Pit, rnd 4; B5/11/1978 Yaounde, Cameroon   **2001** Pit 1 (0)   **2003** Pit 1 (0)   **NFL** 2 (0) [2 yrs]

NOBILE, LEO   Leo Anthony, G, 5´10˝/213 lbs; Penn State; B9/22/1922 Ambridge, PA   **1947** Was 9 (1)   **1948** Pit 12 (1)   **1949** Pit 12 (0)   **NFL** 33 (2) [3 yrs]

NOBIS, TOMMY   Thomas Henry, LB, 6´2˝/240 lbs; Texas; 1966: Atl, rnd 1/Hou, rnd 1; B9/20/1943 San Antonio, TX   **1966** Atl☆14 (MLB)   **1967** Atl★14 (MLB)   **1968** Atl★14 (MLB)   **1969** Atl 5   **1970** Atl★14 (MLB)   **1971** Atl 4   **1972** Atl☆14 (MLB)   **1973** Atl 14 (MLB)   **1974** Atl 14 (MLB)   **1975** Atl 13 (MLB)   **1976** Atl 13 (MLB)   **NFL** 133 [11 yrs]

NOBLE, BRANDON   Brandon Patrick, DT, 6´2˝/285 lbs; Penn State; B4/10/1974 San Rafael, CA   **1999**†Dal 16 (0)   **2000** Dal 16 (9, LDT)   **2001** Dal 16 (16, LDT)   **2002** Dal 16 (16, LDT)   **2004** Was 16 (7, ldt)   **NFL** 80 (48) [5 yrs]

Noble, Brian Brian David, LB, 6´3˝/250 lbs; Arizona State; 1985: GB, rnd 5; B9/6/1962 Anaheim, CA **1985** GB 16 (15, RILB) **1986** GB 16 (16, ROLB/rilb) **1987** GB☆12 (12, LILB) **1988** GB 12 (10, LILB) **1989** GB 16 (16, LILB) **1990** GB 14 (14, LILB) **1991** GB 16 (16, LILB) **1992** GB 13 (9, LILB) **1993** GB 2 (2) **NFL** 117 (110) [9 yrs]

Noble, Dave David Gordon, WB, 6´2˝/195 lbs; Wisconsin; Nebraska; B7/29/1900 Omaha, NE, D1/24/1983 Omaha, NE **1924** Cle☆9 (8, WB), 36 **1925** Cle☆13 (13, WB), 36 **NFL** 22 (21), 72 [2 yrs]

Noble, Dick Richard Brown, G, /178 lbs; Trinity (CT); B12/4/1902 Hartford, CT, D5/14/1973 Milford, CT **1926** Har 1 (0)

Noble, Don Donald LaWayne, TE, 6´2˝/253 lbs; California; B10/11/1965 Los Angeles, CA **1987** LARm 2 (0)

Noble, James James Brown, WR, 6´0˝/193 lbs; Stephen F. Austin State; B8/14/1963 Jacksonville, FL **1986** Was 6 (0)

YEAR	TEAM	G (GS, POS)	RUSH	YD	AVG (LG)	TD	REC	YD	AVG (LG)	TD	PASS	COMP	PCT	YD	AVG (LG)	TD	INT	SK	YD	QBR	KPR	OTD	PTS	TAY
1987	Ind	3(2)	—	—	—	—	10	78	7.8(18)	2	—	—	—	—	—	—	—	—	—	—	k	—	12	54
NFL	2	9(2)	—	—	—	—	10	78	7.8(18)	2	—	—	—	—	—	—	—	—	—	—	—	—	12	49

Noble, Jim James E., E, 6´1˝/190 lbs; Syracuse; B10/10/1901, D9/30/1959 Willowick, OH **1925** Buf 9 (9, LE)

Noble, Mike Michael Wayne, LB, 6´4˝/220 lbs; Stanford; B10/31/1963 Santa Ana, CA **1987** LARd 1 (1)

Nocera, John John Stanley, LB, 6´1˝/220 lbs; Iowa; 1957: Phi, rnd 16; B5/4/1934 Youngstown, OH, D5/17/1981 Youngstown, OH **1959** Phi 12 **1960** Phi 10 **1961** Phi 12 (LLB) **1962** Phi 14 (llb) **1963** Den-A 9 (LLB) **NFL** 57 [5 yrs]

Nock, George George Verdell, RB, 5´11˝/200 lbs; Morgan State; 1969: NYJ, rnd 16; B3/4/1946 Baltimore, MD

YEAR	TEAM	G (GS, POS)	RUSH	YD	AVG (LG)	TD	REC	YD	AVG (LG)	TD	PASS	COMP	PCT	YD	AVG (LG)	TD	INT	SK	YD	QBR	KPR	OTD	PTS	TAY
1969	†NYJ-A	2	3	-5	-1.7(4)	0	—	—	—	—	—	—	—	—	—	—	—	—	—	—	—	—	0	-5
1970	NYJ	14(RB)	135	402	3.0(19)	5	18	146	8.1(21)	1	—	—	—	—	—	—	—	—	—	—	k	—	36	533
1971	NYJ	14	48	137	2.9(17)	3	6	44	7.3(19)	2	—	—	—	—	—	—	—	—	—	—	k	—	30	195
1972	Was	7	6	22	3.7(6)	0	—	—	—	—	—	—	—	—	—	—	—	—	—	—	—	—	0	22
NFL	4	37	192	556	2.9(19)	8	24	190	7.9(21)	3	—	—	—	—	—	—	—	—	—	—	k	—	66	745

Nofsinger, Terry William Terry, QB, 6´4˝/215 lbs; Utah; 1961: Pit, rnd 17; B7/13/1938 Salt Lake City, UT

YEAR	TEAM	G (GS, POS)	RUSH	YD	AVG (LG)	TD	REC	YD	AVG (LG)	TD	PASS	COMP	PCT	YD	AVG (LG)	TD	INT	SK	YD	QBR	KPR	OTD	PTS	TAY
1961	Pit	5	6	6	1.0(3)	0	—	—	—	—	11	7	63.6	78	7.1(23)	0	0	—	—	—	—	—	0	45
1962	Pit	1	—	—	—	—	—	—	—	—	—	—	—	—	—	—	—	—	—	—	—	—	—	—
1963	Pit	2	—	—	—	—	—	—	—	—	3	2	66.7	46	15.3(27)	0	0	—	—	—	—	—	0	23
1964	Pit	1	—	—	—	—	—	—	—	—	4	3	75.0	35	8.8(22)	0	1	—	—	—	—	—	0	-23
1965	SL	1	4	1	0.3(2)	1	—	—	—	—	20	8	40.0	47	2.3(12)	1	1	—	—	—	—	—	6	-1
1966	SL	7(5, qb)	18	25	1.4(12)	2	—	—	—	—	162	68	42.0	799	4.9(49)	2	8	—	—	41.2	—	—	12	135
1967	Atl	7	3	33	11.0(31)	0	—	—	—	—	60	30	50.0	352	5.9(38)	1	2	5	45	—	—	—	0	134
NFL	7	24(5)	31	65	2.1(31)	3	—	—	—	—	260	118	45.4	1357	5.2(49)	4	12	5	45	47.5	—	—	18	314

Noga, Al Alapati, DE-DT, 6´1˝/265 lbs; Hawaii; 1988: Min, rnd 3; B9/16/1965 American Samoa **1988**†Min 9 (1) **1989**†Min 16 (15, LDE) **1990** Min 16 (16, LDE) **1991** Min 16 (8, LDE) **1992**†Min 16 (16, LDE) **1993** Was 16 (4) **1994** Ind 4 (0) **NFL** 93 (60) [7 yrs]

Noga, Niko Falaniko, LB, 6´1˝/234 lbs; Hawaii; 1984: SL, rnd 8; B3/1/1962 American Samoa **1984** SL 16 (0) **1985** SL 16 (11, LLB) **1986** SL 16 (16, RILB) **1987** SL 12 (12, MLB) **1988** Phx 16 (16, MLB) **1989** Det 14 (1) **1990** Det 16 (0) **1991**†Det 16 (0) **NFL** 122 (56) [8 yrs]

Noga, Pete Petelo, LB, 6´0˝/212 lbs; Hawaii; B6/24/1964 American Samoa **1987** SL 3 (3)

Nolan, Dick Richard Charles, DB, 6´1˝/185 lbs; Maryland; 1954: NYG, rnd 4; B3/26/1932 Pittsburgh, PA **[IC]** **1954** NYG 12 (DB) **1955** NYG 10 (DB) **1956**†NYG 12 (DB) **1957** NYG 11 (DB) **1958** ChiC 12 (DB) **1959**†NYG 12 (DB) **1960** NYG 10 (LS) **1961** NYG 9 (LS) **1962** Dal 11 (RS) **NFL** 99 [9 yrs]

Nolan, Earl Michael Earl, T, 6´1˝/205 lbs; Arizona; B3/8/1914, D3/23/1981 Long Beach, CA **1937** ChiC 8 (3) **1938** ChiC 4 (2) **NFL** 12 (5) [2 yrs]

Nolan, John John Ervin, G, 5´10˝/185 lbs; Santa Clara; B7/10/1900 Los Angeles, CA, D10/21/1971 San Diego, CA **1926** LA 10 (10, RG)

Nolan, John John Joseph, T, 6´2˝/232 lbs; Holy Cross; Penn State; 1948: Bos, rnd 3/ChiR-A, rnd 3; B2/26/1926 Glens Falls, NY, D7/14/1996 Glens Falls, NY **1948** Bos 12 (2) **1949** NYB 12 (12, LT) **1950** NYY 12 **NFL** 36 (14) [3 yrs]

Nolander, Don Donald Austin, C, 6´1˝/210 lbs; Minnesota; 1945: Was, rnd 32; B9/14/1921 Minneapolis, MN, D4/24/1999 Bonita Springs, FL **1946** LAD-A 11 (7, c)

Noll, Ben Benjamin Richard, G, 6´4˝/300 lbs; Pennsylvania; B11/14/1981 Minneapolis, MN **2004** Dal 1 (1) **2005** Dal 4 (0) **NFL** 5 (1) [2 yrs]

Noll, Chuck Charles Henry, LB-G-C, 6´1˝/220 lbs; Dayton; 1953: Cle, rnd 20; B1/5/1932 Cleveland, OH; HOF 1993 **[C]** **1953**†Cle 12 (RG) **1954**†Cle 12 (rg) **1955**†Cle 12 (LLB) **1956** Cle 12 (LLB) **1957** Cle 5 (llb) **1958**†Cle 12 (RG) **1959** Cle 12 **NFL** 77 [7 yrs]

Nolting, Ray Raymond Albert, HB, 5´11˝/185 lbs; Cincinnati; B11/8/1913 Cincinnati, OH, D7/5/1995 Cincinnati, OH

YEAR	TEAM	G (GS, POS)	RUSH	YD	AVG (LG)	TD	REC	YD	AVG (LG)	TD	PASS	COMP	PCT	YD	AVG (LG)	TD	INT	SK	YD	QBR	KPR	OTD	PTS	TAY
1936	ChiB	11(6, RH)	76	352	4.6	0	2	50	25.0	1	13	3	23.1	30	2.3	2	1	—	—	—	—	—	6	367
1937	†ChiB☆	11(4, rh)	106	424	4.0	2	4	64	16.0	0	4	0	0.0	0	0.0	0	1	—	—	—	—	—	12	436
1938	ChiB	11(9, LH)	63	297	4.7	1	4	90	22.5	1	11	0	0.0	0	0.0	0	3	—	—	—	—	—	12	237
1939	ChiB	11(9, RH)	50	216	4.3	2	6	87	14.5	1	—	—	—	—	—	—	—	—	—	—	P	1	24	295
1940	†ChiB✧	11(11, LH)	78	373	4.8	1	3	36	12.0	0	2	1	50.0	38	19.0(38)	0	0	—	—	—	Pi	1	12	433
1941	†ChiB✧	9(5, LH)	40	169	4.2(28)	1	4	68	17.0(25)	0	5	3	60.0	71	14.2(53)	1	0	—	—	—	kp	—	6	297
1942	†ChiB	11(3)	57	245	4.3(39)	2	2	23	11.5(15)	0	—	—	—	—	—	—	—	—	—	—	kp	1	18	280
1943	†ChiB	7(0)	38	209	5.5(22)	1	5	90	18.0(48)	0	—	—	—	—	—	—	—	—	—	—	kpi	—	6	277
NFL	8	82(47)	508	2285	4.5(39)	10	30	508	16.9(48)	3	35	7	20.0	139	4.0(53)	3	5	—	—	—	Pkpi	3	96	2621

Nomellini, Leo Leo Joseph 'The Lion', DT-T, 6´3˝/259 lbs; Minnesota; 1950: SF, rnd 1; B6/19/1924 Lucca, Italy, D10/17/2000 Stanford, CA; HOF 1969 **1950** SF✧12 (12, LDT) **1951** SF★12 (12, RT/LDT) **1953** SF★12 (12, LDT) **1954** SF☆12 (12, LDT) **1955** SF 12 (12, LT) **1956** SF✧12 (12, LDT) **1957**†SF★12 (12, LDT) **1958** SF✧12 (12, LDT) **1959** SF★12 (12, LDT) **1960** SF★12 (11, LDT) **1961** SF★14 (14, LDT) **1962** SF☆14 (14, LDT) **1963** SF 14 (7, ldt)

YEAR	TEAM	G (GS, POS)	RUSH	YD	AVG (LG)	TD	REC	YD	AVG (LG)	TD	PASS	COMP	PCT	YD	AVG (LG)	TD	INT	SK	YD	QBR	KPR	OTD	PTS	TAY
1952	SF★	12(12, RT/LDT)	1	5	5.0(5)	0	—	—	—	—	—	—	—	—	—	—	—	—	—	—	k	—	0	8
NFL	14	174(166)	1	5	5.0(5)	0	—	—	—	—	—	—	—	—	—	—	—	—	—	—	kp	1	10	20

Nomina, Tom Thomas John, DT-G, 6´3˝/260 lbs; Miami (OH); 1963: Den, rnd 2/LA, rnd 2; B12/27/1941 Delphos, OH **1963** Den-A 14 **1964** Den-A 11 (lg) **1965** Den-A 12 (lg) **1966** Mia-A 11 (11, LDT) **1967** Mia-A 5 **1968** Mia-A 14 (13, LDT) **NFL** 67 (24) [6 yrs]

Nonnemaker, Ike Clarence Frederick, E-BB, 5´8˝/175 lbs; Ohio State; Wittenberg; B12/11/1901 Columbus, OH, D11/29/1988 Lockbourne, OH **1926** Col 7 (3)

Noonan, Danny Daniel Nicholas, DT-DE, 6´4˝/270 lbs; Nebraska; 1987: Dal, rnd 1; B7/14/1965 Lincoln, NE **1987** Dal 11 (0) **1988** Dal 16 (16, RDT) **1989** Dal 7 (5, lde) **1990** Dal 16 (15, RDT) **1991**†Dal 15 (3) **1992** Dal 2 (2) **1992** GB 6 (0) **NFL** 73 (41) [6 yrs]

Noonan, Jerry Gerald Michael, B-E, 6´1˝/189 lbs; Notre Dame; Fordham; B10/13/1898, D11/1967 San Francisco, CA **1921** Roc 5 (4, BB), 12 **1921** NYG 1 (0) **1923** Roc 1 (0) **1924** Roc 5 (5, TB), 6 **NFL** 12 (9), 18 [3 yrs]

Noonan, Karl Karl Paul, SE-FL-WR, 6´2˝/198 lbs; Iowa; B2/17/1944 Dubuque, IA

YEAR	TEAM	G (GS, POS)	RUSH	YD	AVG (LG)	TD	REC	YD	AVG (LG)	TD	PASS	COMP	PCT	YD	AVG (LG)	TD	INT	SK	YD	QBR	KPR	OTD	PTS	TAY
1966	Mia-A	14(7, se)	—	—	—	—	17	224	13.2(35)	1	—	—	—	—	—	—	—	—	—	—	—	—	6	140
1967	Mia-A	14	—	—	—	—	12	141	11.8(32)	1	—	—	—	—	—	—	—	—	—	—	—	—	6	76
1968	Mia-A★	14(14, SE)	—	—	—	—	58	760	13.1(50)	**11**	—	—	—	—	—	—	—	—	—	—	—	—	66	435
1969	Mia-A	14(14, FL/se)	1	-11	-11.0(-11)	0	29	307	10.6(27)	3	—	—	—	—	—	—	—	—	—	—	—	—	18	158
1970	†Mia	14	1	-9	-9.0(-9)	0	10	186	18.6(51)	1	—	—	—	—	—	—	—	—	—	—	—	—	6	89
1971	†Mia	14	—	—	—	—	10	180	18.0(43)	0	—	—	—	—	—	—	—	—	—	—	—	—	0	90
NFL	6	84(35)	2	-20	-10.0(-9)	0	136	1798	13.2(51)	17	—	—	—	—	—	—	—	—	—	—	—	—	102	987

Noppenberg, John John Louis, B, 6´0˝/196 lbs; Miami (FL); 1940: Pit, rnd 13; B9/8/1917 Wallace, MI

YEAR	TEAM	G (GS, POS)	RUSH	YD	AVG (LG)	TD	REC	YD	AVG (LG)	TD	PASS	COMP	PCT	YD	AVG (LG)	TD	INT	SK	YD	QBR	KPR	OTD	PTS	TAY
1940	Pit	9(4)	2	4	2.0	0	4	74	18.5	0	—	—	—	—	—	—	—	—	—	—	Pi	—	0	63
1941	Pit	4(2)	10	21	2.1(8)	0	—	—	—	—	3	0	0.0	0	0.0	0	0	—	—	—	P	—	0	21
1941	Det	2(0)	1	-5	-5.0(-5)	0	—	—	—	—	—	—	—	—	—	—	—	—	—	—	k	—	0	4
NFL	2	15(6)	13	20	1.5(8)	0	4	74	18.5	0	3	0	0.0	0	0.0	0	0	—	—	—	Pki	—	0	88

Norbeck, John John W., G-B, /195 lbs; none; B7/25/1898 Minneapolis, MN, D10/23/1984 Santa Ana, CA **1921** Min 2 (0)

YEAR	TEAM	G (GS, POS)	RUSH	YD	AVG(LG)	TD	REC	YD	AVG(LG)	TD	PASS	COMP	PCT	YD	AVG(LG)	TD	INT	SK	YD	QBR	KPR	OTD	PTS	TAY

NORBERG, HANK   Henry Francis, E, 6'2"/225 lbs; Stanford; 1943: ChiB, rnd 18; B12/22/1920, D12/4/1974

YEAR	TEAM	G (GS, POS)	RUSH	YD	AVG(LG)	TD	REC	YD	AVG(LG)	TD	...	KPR	OTD	PTS	TAY
1946	SF-A	14(0)	—	—	—	—	3	29	9.7	0		i	—	0	32
1947	SF-A	11(0)	—	—	—	—	2	31	15.5	0		i	—	0	16
AAFC	2	25(0)	—	—	—	—	5	60	12.0	0		i	—	0	47
1948	ChiB	10(0)	—	—	—	—	1	4	4.0(4)	0			—	0	2

NORBY, JOHN   John Heyerdahl, HB, 6'0"/195 lbs; Idaho; B8/30/1910 Rupert, ID, D9/19/1998 Spokane, WA

YEAR	TEAM	G (GS, POS)	RUSH	YD	AVG(LG)	TD	REC	YD	AVG(LG)	TD	...	OTD	PTS	TAY
1934	NYG	3(0)	1	4	4.0(4)	0	1	6	6.0(6)	0		—	0	7
1934	Phi	1(0)												
1934	SL	1(0)	1	1	1.0(1)	0	1	34	34.0(34)	0		—	0	18
1935	Bkn	6(0)	—	—	—	—	1	3	3.0(3)	0		—	0	2
NFL	2		2	5	2.5(4)	0	3	43	14.3(34)	0		—	0	27

NORD, KEITH   Keith Sterling, DB, 6'0"/197 lbs; St. Cloud State; B3/3/1957 Minneapolis, MN   **1979** Min 16   **1980**†Min 16 (0)   **1981** Min 16 (0)   **1982**†Min 9 (0)   **1983** Min 3 (0)   **1985** Min 15 (13, FS)   NFL 75 (13) [6 yrs]

NORDGREN, FRED   Frederic Marvin, NT, 6'0"/240 lbs; Portland State; B12/11/1959 Hillsboro, OR   **1987** TB 3 (3)

NORDQUIST, MARK   Mark Allan, G-C, 6'4"/246 lbs; Pacific; 1968: Phi, rnd 5; B11/3/1945 Long Beach, CA   **1968** Phi 14 (RG)   **1969** Phi 14   **1970** Phi 14   **1971** Phi 14 (RG)   **1972** Phi 14 (RG)   **1973** Phi 14 (RG)   **1974** Phi 12 (RG)   **1975** ChiB 14 (13, RG)   **1976** ChiB 1   NFL 111 (13) [9 yrs]

NORDSTROM, SWEDE   Harry William, G-T, 6'2"/238 lbs; Trinity (CT); B10/11/1896 Brooklyn, NY, D2/13/1963 Toms River, NJ   **1925** NYG 4 (0)   **1926** Bkn 4 (1)   NFL 8 (1) [2 yrs]

NORGARD, AL   Alvar Alfred, E, 6'1"/194 lbs; Stanford; B11/3/1907 Fort Bragg, CA, D11/20/1975 Aptos, CA

YEAR	TEAM	G (GS, POS)	RUSH	YD	AVG(LG)	TD	REC	YD	AVG(LG)	TD	...	OTD	PTS	TAY
1934	GB	10(8, RE)	—	—	—	—	3	29	9.7(22)	0		—	0	15

NORGARD, ERIK   Erik Christian, G-C, 6'1"/282 lbs; Colorado; B11/4/1965 Bellevue, WA   **1990**†Hou 16 (0)   **1992**†Hou 15 (0)   **1994** Hou 16 (7, rg)   **1995** Hou 12 (0)   **1998** Ten 1 (1)

YEAR	TEAM	G (GS, POS)	RUSH	YD	AVG(LG)	TD	REC	YD	AVG(LG)	TD	...	KPR	OTD	PTS	TAY
1993	†Hou	16(4)	—	—	—	—	1	13	13.0(13)	0			—	0	7
1996	Hou	13(0)	—	—	—	—	1	1	1.0(1)	1			—	6	6
1997	Ten	16(0)	—	—	—	—	1	2	2.0(2)	1			—	6	6
NFL	8	105(12)	—	—	—	—	3	16	5.3(13)	2		k	—	12	-12

NORI, REINO   Reino Oscar, QB, 5'7"/165 lbs; Northern Illinois; B2/26/1913 DeKalb, IL, D10/8/1988 DeKalb, IL

YEAR	TEAM	G (GS, POS)	RUSH	YD	AVG(LG)	TD	REC	YD	AVG(LG)	TD	PASS	COMP	PCT	YD	AVG(LG)	TD	INT	...	OTD	PTS	TAY
1937	Bkn	6(1)	26	81	3.1	0	—	—	—	—	23	11	47.8	168	7.3(60)	1	3		—	0	50
1938	ChiB	1(0)	1	1	1.0(1)	0	—	—	—	—									—	0	1
NFL	2	7(1)	27	82	3.0(1)	0	—	—	—	—	23	11	47.8	168	7.3(60)	1	3		—	0	51

NORMAN, BEN   Benjamin Lee, RB, 6'1"/212 lbs; Colorado State; B12/16/1955 Elkin, NC   **1980** Den 3 (0)

NORMAN, BOB   Robert H., C, 6'1"/185 lbs; none; B4/23/1919 Marion, IL, D4/25/1982 Marion, IL   **1945** ChiC 1 (0)

NORMAN, CHRIS   Christopher Cooper, P, 6'2"/198 lbs; South Carolina; B5/25/1962 Albany, GA

YEAR	TEAM	G (GS, POS)	RUSH	YD	AVG(LG)	TD	REC	YD	PASS	COMP	PCT	YD	AVG(LG)	TD	INT	...	QBR	OTD	PTS	TAY
1984	†Den	16(0)															P	—	0	0
1985	Den	16(0)	1	0	0.0(0)	0	—	—	1	0	0.0	0	0.0	0	0		P	—	0	0
1986	Den	6(0)	1	-11	-11.0(-11)	0	—	—	1	1	100.0	43	43.0(43)	1	0		P	—	0	16
NFL	3	38(0)	2	-11	-5.5	0	—	—	2	1	50.0	43	21.5(43)	1	0		P	—	0	16

NORMAN, DENNIS   Dennis M., C-T, 6'5"/312 lbs; Princeton; 2001: Sea, rnd 7; B1/26/1980 Philadelphia, PA   **2003**†Sea 1 (0)   **2005**†Jax 16 (4)   NFL 17 (4) [2 yrs]

NORMAN, DICK   Richard Michael, QB, 6'3"/209 lbs; Stanford; 1960: Chi, rnd 5/1961: Oak, rnd 5; B9/14/1938 Downey, CA   **1961** ChiB 3

NORMAN, JIM   James Thomas, DT-T, 6'2"/248 lbs; none; B1/2/1934 Fortress Monroe, VA   **1955** Was 7

NORMAN, JOE   Joseph Dennison, LB, 6'1"/220 lbs; Indiana; 1979: Sea, rnd 2; B10/15/1956 Millersburg, OH   **1979**†Sea 15 (1)   **1980** Sea 16 (1)   **1981** Sea 8 (7, MLB)   **1983**†Sea 11 (1)   NFL 50 (10) [4 yrs]

NORMAN, JOSH   Josh, TE, 6'2"/236 lbs; Oklahoma; B7/27/1980 Midland, TX

YEAR	TEAM	G (GS, POS)	RUSH	YD	AVG(LG)	TD	REC	YD	AVG(LG)	TD	...	OTD	PTS	TAY
2002	SD	11(1)	—	—	—	—	16	201	12.6(29)	1		—	6	106
2003	SD	7(1)	—	—	—	—	6	72	12.0(21)	1		—	6	41
NFL	2	18(2)	—	—	—	—	22	273	12.4(29)	2		—	12	147

NORMAN, PETTIS   Pettis Burch, TE-SE, 6'3"/222 lbs; Johnson C. Smith; 1962: DalT, rnd 16; B1/4/1939 Lincolnton, GA

YEAR	TEAM	G (GS, POS)	RUSH	YD	AVG(LG)	TD	REC	YD	AVG(LG)	TD	...	KPR	OTD	PTS	TAY
1962	Dal	14	—	—	—	—	2	34	17.0(29)	0		k	—	0	-8
1963	Dal	14(5, se)	—	—	—	—	18	341	18.9(49)	3		p	—	18	181
1964	Dal	14(TE)	—	—	—	—	24	311	13.0(37)	2			—	12	166
1965	Dal	14	—	—	—	—	11	110	10.0(21)	3			—	18	70
1966	†Dal	14(TE)	—	—	—	—	12	144	12.0(29)	0			—	0	72
1967	†Dal	14(TE)	9	91	10.1(28)	0	20	220	11.0(39)	2			—	12	211
1968	†Dal	13(TE)	4	51	12.8(26)	0	18	204	11.3(34)	1		k	—	6	143
1969	†Dal	10(10, TE)	5	20	4.0(21)	0	13	238	18.3(31)	3			—	18	154
1970	†Dal	14(TE)	2	16	8.0(22)	0	6	70	11.7(23)	0			—	0	51
1971	SD	14(TE)	1	1	1.0(1)	0	27	358	13.3(30)	1			—	6	185
1972	SD	13(TE)	1	9	9.0(9)	0	19	262	13.8(30)	0			—	0	140
1973	SD	14(12, TE)	1	10	10.0(10)	0	13	200	15.4(24)	0			—	0	110
NFL	12	162(27)	23	198	8.6(28)	0	183	2492	13.6(49)	15		kp	—	90	1474

NORMAN, TIM   Timothy Scott, T, 6'6"/270 lbs; Illinois; B7/10/1959 Winfield, IL   **1983** ChiB 1 (0)

NORMAN, TONY   Anthony Alexander, DE, 6'5"/270 lbs; Iowa State; B1/27/1955 Atlanta, GA   **1987** Min 2 (0)

NORMAN, WILL   Willard Patterson, WB-TB, 6'0"/175 lbs; Washington & Jefferson; B9/22/1903, D7/1964, WA   **1928** Pot 10 (6, WB), 6

NORRIE, DAVID   David Doherty, QB, 6'4"/220 lbs; UCLA; 1986: Sea, rnd 11; B11/30/1963 Boston, MA

YEAR	TEAM	G (GS, POS)	RUSH	YD	AVG(LG)	TD	REC	YD	PASS	COMP	PCT	YD	AVG(LG)	TD	INT	SK	YD	...	OTD	PTS	TAY
1987	NYJ	2(2)	5	5	1.0(2)	0	—	—	68	35	51.5	376	5.5(41)	1	4	15	72		—	0	38

NORRIS, HAL   Harold, LB-DB, 5'11"/194 lbs; California; 1955: Was, rnd 16; B11/4/1931 Baton Rouge, LA   **1955** Was 12   **1956** Was 1   NFL 13 [2 yrs]

NORRIS, JACK   John Clayton, E, 6'3"/185 lbs; Western Maryland; Maryland; B5/18/1909 Lancaster, PA   **1932** SI 2 (1)

NORRIS, JEROME   Jerome, DB, 6'0"/187 lbs; Furman; B1/31/1964   **1987** Atl 3 (0)

NORRIS, JIM   James Arthur, DT-T, 6'4"/238 lbs; Houston; 1962: Oak, rnd 7/LA, rnd 10; B10/14/1939 Houston, TX   **1962** Oak-A 7   **1963** Oak-A 14   **1964** Oak-A 1   NFL 22 [3 yrs]

NORRIS, JIMMY   James Najee, DB, 5'11"/188 lbs; Upsala; B3/12/1964 Asheville, NC   **1987** NYG 3 (0)

NORRIS, JON   Jonathan Clayton, DE-DT, 6'3"/260 lbs; American International; B11/1/1962 Lancaster, Wales   **1987** ChiB 3 (3)

NORRIS, MORAN   Torrance Moran, FB, 6'1"/250 lbs; Kansas; 2001: NO, rnd 4; B6/16/1978 Houston, TX

YEAR	TEAM	G (GS, POS)	RUSH	YD	AVG(LG)	TD	REC	YD	AVG(LG)	TD	...	KPR	OTD	PTS	TAY
2001	NO	5(0)													
2002	Hou	13(0)	—	—	—	—						k	—	0	-19
2003	Hou	16(9, FB)	—	—	—	—	7	40	5.7(11)	0		k	—	0	16
2004	Hou	12(4)	1	0	0.0(0)	0	4	13	3.3(7)	0		k	—	0	2
2005	Hou	16(5, FB)	—	—	—	—	1	4	4.0(4)	1		k	—	6	-6
NFL	5	62(18)	1	0	0.0	0	12	57	4.8(11)	1		k	—	6	-8

NORRIS, TRUSSE   Trusse Rupert Brown, E, 6'1"/194 lbs; UCLA; B8/10/1937 Houston, TX   **1960**†LAC-A 2

NORRIS, ULYSSES   Ulysses, TE, 6'4"/230 lbs; Georgia; 1979: Det, rnd 4; B1/15/1957 Monticello, GA

YEAR	TEAM	G (GS, POS)	RUSH	YD	AVG(LG)	TD	REC	YD	AVG(LG)	TD	...	KPR	OTD	PTS	TAY
1979	Det	16(1)	—	—	—	—	4	43	10.8(34)	1			—	6	27
1980	Det	16(1)											—	0	0
1981	Det	12(2)	—	—	—	—	8	132	16.5(34)	0			—	0	66
1982	†Det	9(6, te)	—	—	—	—	3	44	14.7(30)	0			—	0	22
1983	†Det	15(15, TE)	—	—	—	—	26	291	11.2(41)	7		k	—	42	166

YEAR	TEAM	G (GS, POS)	RUSH	YD	AVG (LG)	TD	REC	YD	AVG (LG)	TD	PASS	COMP	PCT	YD	AVG (LG)	TD	INT	SK	YD	QBR	KPR	OTD	PTS	TAY
1984	Buf	14(0)	—	—	—	—	—	—	—	—	—	—	—	—	—	—	—	—	—	—	—	—	—	—
1985	Buf	2(1)	—	—	—	—	2	30	15.0(18)	0	—	—	—	—	—	—	—	—	—	—	—	—	0	15
NFL	7	84(27)	—	—	—	—	43	540	12.6(41)	8	—	—	—	—	—	—	—	—	—	—	k	—	48	295
NORSETH, MIKE Michael Adam, QB, 6´2˝/200 lbs; Kansas; 1986: Cle, rnd 7; B8/22/1964 Los Angeles, CA																								
1988	Cin	1(0)	1	5	5.0(5)	0	—	—	—	—	—	—	—	—	—	—	—	—	—	—	—	—	0	5
NORTH, JIM James Morris, T, 6´3˝/235 lbs; Central Washington; B8/11/1919 Tukwila, WA, D2/4/2003 Seattle, WA **1944** Was 7 (6, RT)																								
NORTH, JOHN John Puckett, E-DB, 6´2˝/199 lbs; Vanderbilt; 1947: Mia-A, rnd 16/1945: Was, rnd 6; B6/17/1921 Gilliam, LA **[C]**																								
1948	†Bal-A	14(13, RE)	—	—	—	—	8	204	25.5(**80**)	1	—	—	—	—	—	—	—	—	—	—	i	1	12	127
1949	Bal-A	11(6, RE)	—	—	—	—	25	490	19.6(**80**)	4	—	—	—	—	—	—	—	—	—	—	—	—	24	265
AAFC	2	25(19)	—	—	—	—	33	694	21.0(80)	5	—	—	—	—	—	—	—	—	—	—	i	1	36	392
1950	Bal	4(3)	—	—	—	—	5	90	18.0(39)	0	—	—	—	—	—	—	—	—	—	—	—	—	0	45
NORTHCUTT, DENNIS Dennis LaMont, WR, 5´11˝/175 lbs; Arizona; 2000: Cle, rnd 2; B12/22/1977 Los Angeles, CA **[R]**																								
2000	Cle	15(8, wr)	9	33	3.7(13)	0	39	422	10.8(37)	0	—	—	—	—	—	—	—	—	—	—	p	—	0	398
2001	Cle	11(7, wr)	3	26	8.7(12)	0	18	211	11.7(26)	0	—	—	—	—	—	—	—	—	—	—	kp	—	0	154
2002	†Cle	13(0)	8	104	13.0(36)	1	38	601	15.8(43)	5	—	—	—	—	—	—	—	—	—	—	p	2	50	702
2003	Cle	15(6, wr)	12	83	6.9(23)	0	62	729	11.8(44)	2	1	0	0.0	0	0.0	0	0	—	—	—	p	—	12	573
2004	Cle	16(11, WR)	8	19	2.4(8)	0	55	806	14.7(58)	2	—	—	—	—	—	—	—	—	—	—	p	—	12	684
2005	Cle	16(7, WR)	2	33	16.5(31)	0	42	441	10.5(58)	2	—	—	—	—	—	—	—	—	—	—	p	1	18	467
NFL	6	86(39)	42	298	7.1(36)	1	254	3210	12.6(58)	11	1	0	0.0	0	0.0	0	0	—	—	—	kp	3	92	2976
NORTHERN, GABE Gabriel O'Kara, LB-DE, 6´2˝/240 lbs; LSU; 1996: Buf, rnd 2; B6/8/1974 Baton Rouge, LA **1996** Buf 16 (2) **1997** Buf 16 (1) **1998**†Buf 16 (16, ROLB) **1999**†Buf 16 (16, ROLB) **2000** Min 9 (2) **NFL** 73 (37) [5 yrs]																								
NORTON, DON Donald Farris, E, 6´1˝/190 lbs; Iowa; 1960: Oak, rnd 1/Phi, rnd 5; B3/13/1938 Iowa City, IA, D6/23/1997 Cedar Rapids, IA																								
1960	†LAC-A	14	1	2	2.0(2)	0	25	414	16.6(69)	5	—	—	—	—	—	—	—	—	—	—	k	—	30	267
1961	†SD-A✧	14(SE)	—	—	—	—	47	816	17.4(52)	6	—	—	—	—	—	—	—	—	—	—	—	—	36	438
1962	SD-A✧	14(SE)	—	—	—	—	48	771	16.1(47)	7	—	—	—	—	—	—	—	—	—	—	—	—	42	421
1963	†SD-A	7(SE)	—	—	—	—	21	281	13.4(36)	1	1	1	100.0	15	15.0(15)	0	0	—	—	—	—	—	6	153
1964	†SD-A	14(SE)	—	—	—	—	49	669	13.7(58)	6	—	—	—	—	—	—	—	—	—	—	k	—	36	350
1965	†SD-A	14(SE)	1	-5	-5.0(-5)	0	34	485	14.3(61)	2	—	—	—	—	—	—	—	—	—	—	—	—	12	248
1966	SD-A	14	—	—	—	—	4	50	12.5(18)	0	—	—	—	—	—	—	—	—	—	—	—	—	0	25
NFL	7	91	2	-3	-1.5(2)	0	228	3486	15.3(69)	27	1	1	100.0	15	15.0(15)	0	0	—	—	—	k	—	162	1901
NORTON, JERRY Jerry Ray, DB-HB, 5´11˝/195 lbs; SMU; 1954: Phi, rnd 7; B5/16/1931 Gilmer, TX **[PI]**																								
1954	Phi	12(DB)	1	-3	-3.0(-3)	0	—	—	—	—	—	—	—	—	—	—	—	—	—	—	pi	1	6	76
1955	Phi	12(db/rh)	36	144	4.0(23)	1	11	125	11.4(36)	1	1	0	0.0	0	0.0	0	0	—	—	—	kpi	1	18	321
1956	Phi	6(db)	—	—	—	—	—	—	—	—	—	—	—	—	—	—	—	—	—	—	ki	—	0	40
1957	Phi✧	12(DB)	2	73	36.5(61)	0	—	—	—	—	1	0	0.0	0	0.0	0	0	—	—	—	Pkpi	1	6	229
1958	Phi★	9(DB)	—	—	—	—	—	—	—	—	—	—	—	—	—	—	—	—	—	—	pi	—	0	-2
1959	ChiC★	12(DB)	2	41	20.5(24)	0	—	—	—	—	—	—	—	—	—	—	—	—	—	—	Pkpi	—	0	75
1960	SL☆	12(LS)	2	47	23.5(26)	0	—	—	—	—	—	—	—	—	—	—	—	—	—	—	Pi	—	0	93
1961	SL★	14(LS)	1	15	15.0(15)	0	—	—	—	—	—	—	—	—	—	—	—	—	—	—	Pi	2	12	136
1962	Dal✧	14(LS)	—	—	—	—	—	—	—	—	—	—	—	—	—	—	—	—	—	—	i	1	6	11
1963	GB	14	2	0	0.0(4)	0	—	—	—	—	—	—	—	—	—	—	—	—	—	—	P	—	0	0
1964	GB	14	1	24	24.0(24)	0	—	—	—	—	—	—	—	—	—	—	—	—	—	—	P	—	0	24
NFL	11	131	47	341	7.3(61)	1	11	125	11.4(36)	1	2	0	0.0	0	0.0	0	0	—	—	—	Pkpi	6	48	1003
NORTON, JIM James Charles, DB-P, 6´3˝/190 lbs; Idaho; 1960: DalT, rnd 1/Det, rnd 7; B10/20/1938 Glendale, CA **[PI]** **1961**†Hou-A☆14 (LS) **1962**†Hou-A★14 (LS) **1964** Hou-A 14 **1965** Hou-A 14 (LS) **1966** Hou-A 14 (RS)																								
1960	†Hou-A	13(LCB)	—	—	—	—	1	5	5.0(5)	0	—	—	—	—	—	—	—	—	—	—	i	—	0	-3
1963	Hou-A✧	14(LS)	1	15	15.0(15)	0	—	—	—	—	—	—	—	—	—	—	—	—	—	—	Pi	—	0	71
1967	†Hou-A★	14(RS)	1	-7	-7.0(-7)	0	—	—	—	—	—	—	—	—	—	—	—	—	—	—	Pi	1	6	46
1968	Hou-A	14	1	20	20.0(20)	0	—	—	—	—	—	—	—	—	—	—	—	—	—	—	Pi	—	0	10
NFL	9	125	3	28	9.3(20)	0	1	5	5.0(5)	0	—	—	—	—	—	—	—	—	—	—	Pi	1	6	408
NORTON, JIM James Alfred, DE-DT-T-E, 6´4˝/254 lbs; Washington; 1965: SF, rnd 3; B11/18/1942 Wilmington, NC **1965** SF 14 **1966** SF 14 (11, LDE) **1967** Atl 14 (LDE) **1968** Atl 7 **1968** Phi 6 **1969** Was 5 **1970** NYG 4 **NFL** 64 (11) [6 yrs]																								
NORTON, KEN Kenneth Howard, LB, 6´2˝/241 lbs; UCLA; 1988: Dal, rnd 2; B9/29/1966 Lincoln, IL **1988** Dal 3 (0) **1989** Dal 13 (13, RLB) **1990** Dal 15 (15, RLB) **1991**†Dal 16 (16, LLB) **1992**†Dal 16 (16, RLB) **1993**†Dal★16 (16, MLB) **1994**†SF 16 (16, RLB) **1995**†SF★16 (16, MLB) **1996**†SF 16 (16, MLB) **1997**†SF✧16 (16, RLB) **1998**†SF 16 (16, RLB) **1999** SF 16 (16, MLB) **2000** SF 16 (16, MLB) **NFL** 191 (188) [13 yrs]																								
NORTON, MARTY Martin, B, 5´6˝/178 lbs; Hamline; B1903, deceased **1922** Min 3 (3, TB), 12 **1924** Min 6 (4, TB), 12 **1925** GB 10 (7, hb), 36 **NFL** 19 (14), 60 [3 yrs]																								
NORTON, RAY Raymond, WB, none; B1900, NY, deceased **1925** Cle 1 (0)																								
NORTON, RAY Raymond, HB, 6´2˝/184 lbs; San Jose State; 1960: SF, rnd 4/Den, rnd 1; B9/22/1937																								
1960	SF	3	2	2	1.0(9)	0	—	—	—	—	—	—	—	—	—	—	—	—	—	—	—	—	0	2
1961	SF	6	2	-2	-1.0(2)	0	—	—	—	—	—	—	—	—	—	—	—	—	—	—	k	—	0	43
NFL	2	9	4	0	0.0(9)	0	—	—	—	—	—	—	—	—	—	—	—	—	—	—	k	—	0	45
NORTON, RICK Richard Eugene, QB, 6´2˝/200 lbs; Kentucky; 1966: Mia, rnd 1/Cle, rnd 2; B11/16/1943 Louisville, KY																								
1966	Mia-A	7	3	2	0.7(3)	0	—	—	—	—	55	21	38.2	192	3.5(43)	3	6	2	13	—	—	—	0	-127
1967	Mia-A	14	7	14	2.0(13)	0	—	—	—	—	133	53	39.8	596	4.5(32)	1	9	15	156	—	—	—	0	-43
1968	Mia-A	3	1	9	9.0(9)	0	—	—	—	—	41	17	41.5	254	6.2(65)	0	4	7	58	—	—	—	0	-24
1969	Mia-A	7(5, qb)	8	16	2.0(9)	0	—	—	—	—	148	65	43.9	709	4.8(29)	2	11	18	175	—	—	—	0	-60
1970	GB	1	—	—	—	—	—	—	—	—	5	3	60.0	64	12.8(29)	1	0	2	16	—	—	—	0	37
NFL	5	32(5)	19	41	2.2(13)	0	—	—	—	—	382	159	41.6	1815	4.8(65)	7	30	44	418	—	—	—	0	-217
NORTON, ZACH Zach, DB, 5´11˝/183 lbs; Cincinnati; B11/19/1981 Fort Lauderdale, FL **2005** Bal 3 (0)																								
NORVELL, JAY Merritt Jay, LB, 6´2˝/232 lbs; Iowa; B3/28/1963 Madison, WI **1987** ChiB 6 (3)																								
NORWOOD, RALPH Ralph E., T, 6´7˝/285 lbs; LSU; 1989: Atl, rnd 2; B1/23/1966 New Orleans, LA, D11/24/1989 Suwanee, GA **1989** Atl 11 (1)																								
NORWOOD, SCOTT Scott Allen, K, 6´0˝/207 lbs; James Madison; B7/17/1960 Alexandria, VA **[K]** **1985** Buf 16 (0) **1986** Buf 16 (0) **1987** Buf 12 (0) **1988**†Buf★16 (0) **1989**†Buf 16 (0) **1990**†Buf 16 (0) **1991**†Buf 16 (0) **NFL** 108 (0) [7 yrs]																								
NOSICH, JOHN John Anthony, T, 6´3˝/230 lbs; Duquesne; B10/12/1915 Clairton, PA, D7/24/1985 McKeesport, PA **1938** Pit 2 (0)																								
NOTT, DOUG Douglas N., TB, 5´11˝/195 lbs; Detroit Mercy; B6/14/1911 Pontiac, MI, D5/25/1991 Detroit, MI																								
1935	Bos	4(2)	45	95	2.1	0	—	—	—	—	24	7	29.2	134	5.6	1	3	—	—	—	—	—	0	47
1935	Det	5(2)	3	3	1.0	0	—	—	—	—	10	2	20.0	35	3.5	0	2	—	—	—	—	—	0	-60
NFL	1	9(4)	48	98	2.0	0	—	—	—	—	34	9	26.5	169	5.0	1	5	—	—	—	—	—	0	-13
NOTT, MIKE Wesley Michael, QB, 6´3˝/203 lbs; Santa Clara; B5/19/1952 Eureka, CA																								
1976	KC	1	—	—	—	—	—	—	—	—	10	4	40.0	46	4.6(23)	0	0	1	9	—	P	—	0	23
NOTTAGE, DEXTER Dexter Alexander, DE, 6´4˝/287 lbs; Florida A&M; 1994: Was, rnd 6; B11/14/1970 Miami, FL **1994** Was 15 (1) **1995** Was 16 (0) **1996** Was 16 (4) **1997** KC 1 (0) **NFL** 48 (5) [4 yrs]																								
NOTTINGHAM, DON Donald Ray, RB, 5´10˝/210 lbs; Kent State; 1971: Bal, rnd 17; B6/28/1949 Widen, WV																								
1971	†Bal	14	95	388	4.1(36)	5	15	88	5.9(35)	0	—	—	—	—	—	—	—	—	—	—	—	1	36	482
1972	Bal	14(FB)	123	466	3.8(25)	3	25	191	7.6(27)	0	—	—	—	—	—	—	—	—	—	—	k	—	18	600
1973	Bal	3	28	118	4.2(20)	1	2	10	5.0(5)	0	—	—	—	—	—	—	—	—	—	—	k	—	6	135

YEAR	TEAM	G (GS, POS)	RUSH	YD	AVG(LG)	TD	REC	YD	AVG(LG)	TD	PASS	COMP	PCT	YD	AVG(LG)	TD	INT	SK	YD	QBR	KPR	OTD	PTS	TAY
1973	†Mia	11	24	134	5.6(30)	0	1	16	16.0(16)	0	—	—	—	—	—	—	—	—	—	—	—	—	0	142
1974	†Mia	14	66	273	4.1(24)	8	3	40	13.3(20)	0	—	—	—	—	—	—	—	—	—	—	—	—	48	373
1975	Mia	14(13, FB)	168	718	4.3(56)	12	9	66	7.3(18)	0	—	—	—	—	—	—	—	—	—	—	k	—	72	906
1976	Mia	14(8, FB)	63	185	2.9(13)	3	4	33	8.3(29)	0	—	—	—	—	—	—	—	—	—	—	k	—	18	249
1977	Mia	14	44	214	4.9(13)	2	8	58	7.3(16)	0	—	—	—	—	—	—	—	—	—	—	k	—	12	269
NFL	**7**	98(21)	611	2496	4.1(56)	34	67	502	7.5(35)	0	—	—	—	—	—	—	—	—	—	—	k	1	210	3155

NOVACEK, JAY Jay McKinley, TE, 6´4˝/234 lbs; Wyoming; 1985: SL, rnd 6; B10/24/1962 Martin, SD

YEAR	TEAM	G (GS, POS)	RUSH	YD	AVG(LG)	TD	REC	YD	AVG(LG)	TD	KPR	OTD	PTS	TAY
1985	SL	16(0)	—	—	—	—	1	4	4.0(4)	0	k	—	0	7
1986	SL	8(0)	—	—	—	—	1	2	2.0(2)	0	—	—	0	1
1987	SL	7(4)	—	—	—	—	20	254	12.7(25)	3	—	—	18	142
1988	Phx	16(1)	1	10	10.0(10)	0	38	569	15.0(42)	4	—	—	24	315
1989	Phx	16(1)	—	—	—	—	23	225	9.8(30)	1	—	—	6	118
1990	Dal☆	16(15, TE)	—	—	—	—	59	657	11.1(41)	4	—	—	24	349
1991	†Dal★	16(12, TE)	—	—	—	—	59	664	11.3(49)	4	—	—	24	352
1992	†Dal★	16(16, TE)	—	—	—	—	68	630	9.3(34)	6	—	—	36	345
1993	†Dal◇	16(16, TE)	1	2	2.0(2)	1	44	445	10.1(30)	1	k	—	12	224
1994	†Dal★	16(14, TE)	—	—	—	—	47	475	10.1(27)	2	—	—	12	248
1995	†Dal★	15(15, TE)	2	12	6.0(10)	0	62	705	11.4(33)	5	—	—	32	378
NFL	**11**	158(94)	4	22	—	—	422	4630	11.0(49)	30	k	—	188	2476

NOVAK, EDDIE Edward, B, 5´9˝/175 lbs; none; B8/3/1897 Webster, MN, D7/1984 Webster, MN [K] **1920** RI☆9 (5, WB), **1921** RI 7 (7, WB), 6 **1922** RI 1 (0) **1922** Min 1 (1) **1924** Min 5 (4), 1 **1925** RI 11 (8, FB), 6 **NFL** 34 (25), 13 [5 yrs]

NOVAK, JACK Clarence John, TE, 6´4˝/242 lbs; Wisconsin; 1975: Cin, rnd 12; B6/6/1953 Kewaunee, WI

YEAR	TEAM	G (GS, POS)	RUSH	YD	AVG(LG)	TD	REC	YD	AVG(LG)	TD	OTD	PTS	TAY
1975	†Cin	14	—	—	—	—	2	34	17.0(19)	0	—	0	17
1976	TB	12(2)	—	—	—	—	8	130	16.3(30)	1	—	6	70
1977	TB	9(2)	—	—	—	—	2	24	12.0(15)	0	—	0	12
NFL	**3**	35(4)	—	—	—	—	12	188	15.7(30)	1	—	6	99

NOVAK, JEFF Jeffrey Ladd, G-T, 6´6˝/297 lbs; Southwest Texas State; 1990: SD, rnd 7; B7/27/1967 Arlington Heights, IL **1994** Mia 7 (0) **1995** Jax 16 (13, lg) **1996** Jax 6 (0) **1997**†Jax 7 (2) **1998** Jax 4 (0) **NFL** 40 (15) [5 yrs]

NOVAK, KEN Kenneth, DT, 6´7˝/268 lbs; Purdue; 1976: Bal, rnd 1; B7/3/1954 Willowick, OH **1976**†Bal 11 **1977** Bal 12 **NFL** 23 [2 yrs]

NOVAK, NICK Nick, K, 6´1˝/191 lbs; Maryland; B8/21/1981 Charlottesville, VA [K] **2005** Was 5 (0) **2005** Arz 5 (0) **NFL** 10 (0) [1 yr]

NOVITSKY, CRAIG Craig Aaron, G, 6´5˝/295 lbs; UCLA; 1994: NO, rnd 5; B5/12/1971 Washington, DC **1994** NO 9 (1) **1995** NO 16 (3) **1996** NO 16 (6, lg) **NFL** 41 (10) [3 yrs]

NOVOSELSKY, BRENT Brent Howard, TE, 6´2˝/232 lbs; Pennsylvania; B1/8/1966 Skokie, IL

YEAR	TEAM	G (GS, POS)	RUSH	YD	AVG(LG)	TD	REC	YD	AVG(LG)	TD	KPR	OTD	PTS	TAY
1988	ChiB	8(0)	—	—	—	—	—	—	—	—	—	—	—	—
1989	†Min	15(3)	—	—	—	—	4	11	2.8(6)	2	—	—	12	16
1990	Min	16(3)	—	—	—	—	—	—	—	—	—	—	0	0
1991	Min	16(0)	—	—	—	—	4	27	6.8(8)	0	—	—	0	14
1992	†Min	16(1)	—	—	—	—	4	63	15.8(34)	0	—	—	0	32
1993	†Min	15(0)	—	—	—	—	—	—	—	—	—	—	0	0
1994	Min	12(0)	—	—	—	—	2	7	3.5(4)	0	k	—	0	-17
NFL	**7**	98(7)	—	—	—	—	14	108	7.7(34)	2	k	—	12	44

NOVOTNY, RAY Raymond John, B, 5´10˝/165 lbs; Ashland University; B10/12/1907 Cleveland, OH, D5/30/1995 Welches, OR **1930** Por 11 (1), 6 **1931** Cle 10 (7, WB)

YEAR	TEAM	G (GS, POS)	RUSH	YD	AVG(LG)	TD	REC	YD	AVG(LG)	TD	PASS	COMP	PCT	YD	AVG(LG)	TD	INT	PTS	TAY
1932	Bkn	10(4)	6	4	0.7	0	3	72	24.0	0	15	5	33.3	50	3.3	0	1	0	25
NFL	**3**	31(12)	6	4	0.7	1	3	72	24.0	0	15	5	33.3	50	3.3	1	1	6	40

NOVSEK, JOE Joseph John, DE, 6´4˝/237 lbs; Tulsa; 1961: Oak, rnd 17/Bal, rnd 19; B5/29/1939 **1962** Oak-A 14

NOWAK, GARY Gary William, DT, 6´5˝/258 lbs; Michigan State; 1971: SD, rnd 10; B12/8/1948 St. Clair Shores, MI **1971** SD 5

NOWAK, WALT Walter Ignatius, E, 5´11˝/185 lbs; Villanova; B6/2/1915 Camden, NJ, D11/12/1993 Westmont, NJ **1944** Phi 2 (0)

NOWASKEY, BOB Robert John, E-DE, 6´0˝/205 lbs; George Washington; 1940: Cle, rnd 7; B2/3/1918 Everson, PA, D3/21/1971 Arlington Heights, IL [K]

YEAR	TEAM	G (GS, POS)	RUSH	YD	AVG(LG)	TD	REC	YD	AVG(LG)	TD	KPR	OTD	PTS	TAY
1946	LAD-A	14(5, le)	3	14	4.7	0	19	198	10.4	3	pi	1	24	168
1947	LAD-A	14(1)	—	—	—	—	8	106	13.3	0	pi	0	—	75
1948	LAD-A	1(0)	—	—	—	—	—	—	—	—	—	—	—	—
1948	†Bal-A	13(3)	—	—	—	—	1	31	31.0(31)	0	—	—	0	16
1949	Bal-A	12(2)	—	—	—	—	—	—	—	—	i	—	0	4
AAFC	**4**	54(11)	3	14	4.7	0	28	335	12.0(31)	3	pi	1	24	263
1940	†ChiB◇	10(2)	1	4	4.0(4)	0	5	105	21.0	0	—	—	12	67
1941	†ChiB★	11(5, le)	3	5	1.7(3)	0	12	199	16.6(40)	1	K	1	13	110
1942	†ChiB	11(6, LE)	1	3	3.0(3)	0	6	128	21.3(29)	0	—	—	0	67
1950	Bal	9(LDE)	—	—	—	—	—	—	—	—	—	—	—	—
NFL	**4**	41(13)	5	12	2.4(4)	0	23	432	18.8(40)	3	K	1	25	243

NOWATZKE, TOM Thomas Matthew, FB-LB, 6´3˝/230 lbs; Indiana; 1965: Det, rnd 1/NYJ, rnd 1; B9/30/1942 La Porte, IN

YEAR	TEAM	G (GS, POS)	RUSH	YD	AVG(LG)	TD	REC	YD	AVG(LG)	TD	KPR	OTD	PTS	TAY
1965	Det	14	27	73	2.7(14)	1	5	45	9.0(22)	1	k	—	12	93
1966	Det	14(FB)	151	512	3.4(21)	6	54	316	5.9(25)	1	—	—	42	735
1967	Det	14	70	288	4.1(15)	4	21	145	6.9(25)	2	—	—	36	411
1968	Det	14	36	116	3.2(11)	1	4	6	1.5(5)	0	k	—	6	118
1969	Det	9	—	—	—	—	—	—	—	—	k	—	0	-1
1970	†Bal	11(fb)	73	248	3.4(14)	1	16	93	5.8(17)	0	k	—	6	293
1971	†Bal	14	1	1	1.0(1)	0	—	—	—	—	ki	—	0	11
1972	Bal	6	3	11	3.7(6)	0	—	—	—	—	ki	—	0	11
NFL	**8**	96	361	1249	3.5(21)	13	100	605	6.1(25)	4	ki	—	102	1670

NOYES, LEN Leonard William, G, 6´0˝/214 lbs; Montana; 1938: Bkn, rnd 8; B7/12/1914 Butte, MT, D12/24/1985 Winston-Salem, NC **1938** Bkn 5 (0)

NUGENT, CLEM Earl Clement, FB-WB, 5´9˝/155 lbs; Iowa; B11/9/1899 Algona, IA, deceased **1924** Roc 1 (0)

NUGENT, DAN Daniel Lawrence, G, 6´3˝/250 lbs; Auburn; 1975: LA, rnd 3; B8/22/1953 Mount Clemens, MI, D10/18/2001 Boca Raton, FL **1976**†Was 14 (5, rg) **1977** Was 14 (2) **1978** Was 16 (16, RG) **1980** Was 14 (1) **NFL** 58 (24) [4 yrs]

NUGENT, DAVID David Michael, DE, 6´4˝/300 lbs; Purdue; 2000: NE, rnd 6; B10/27/1977 Cincinnati, OH **2000** NE 6 (0) **2001** NE 9 (1) **2002** Bal 9 (0) **NFL** 24 (1) [3 yrs]

NUGENT, MIKE Michael, K, 5´10˝/182 lbs; Ohio State; 2005: NYJ, rnd 2; B3/2/1982 Centerville, OH [K] **2005** NYJ 16 (0)

NUGENT, PHIL Philip Harper, DB, 6´2˝/195 lbs; Tulane; 1961: Den, rnd 9/GB, rnd 3; B8/16/1939 Lafayette, LA **1961** Den-A 12 (LS)

NUGENT, TERRY Terence John, QB, 6´4˝/218 lbs; Colorado State; 1984: Cle, rnd 6; B12/5/1961 Merced, CA

YEAR	TEAM	G (GS, POS)	RUSH	YD	AVG(LG)	TD	REC	YD	AVG(LG)	TD	PASS	COMP	PCT	YD	AVG(LG)	TD	INT	SK	OTD	PTS	TAY
1987	Ind	1(0)	2	1	0.5(2)	0	—	—	—	—	5	3	60.0	47	9.4(21)	0	0	1	9	—	—	—	0	25

NUNAMAKER, JULIAN Julian Francis, DE-DT, 6´3˝/252 lbs; Tennessee-Martin; 1969: Buf, rnd 3; B2/13/1946 Charleston, SC, D2/25/1995 Jackson, TN **1969** Buf-A 10 **1970** Buf 8 **NFL** 18 [2 yrs]

NUNLEY, FRANK Frank Hembre, LB, 6´2˝/229 lbs; Michigan; 1967: SF, rnd 3; B10/1/1945 Florence, AL **1967** SF 14 (1) **1968** SF 14 **1969** SF 14 (10, MLB) **1970**†SF 14 (14, MLB) **1971**†SF 14 (14, MLB) **1972**†SF 13 (9, MLB) **1973** SF 14 (13, MLB) **1975** SF 14 (14, MLB) **1976** SF 13 (12, MLB) **NFL** 137 (86) [10 yrs]

NUNLEY, JEREMY Jody Jeremy, DE, 6´5˝/278 lbs; Alabama; 1994: Hou, rnd 2; B9/19/1971 Winchester, TN **1994** Hou 12 (0)

NUNN, FREDDIE JOE Freddie Joe, DE-LB, 6´5˝/262 lbs; Mississippi; 1985: SL, rnd 1; B4/9/1962 Noxubee County, MS [S] **1985** SL 16 (16, RLB) **1986** SL 16 (16, LOLB) **1987** SL 12 (12, LDE) **1988** Phx☆16 (16, RDE) **1989** Phx 12 (12, LDE) **1990** Phx 16 (16, LDE) **1991** Phx 16 (16, LOLB) **1992** Phx 11 (9, LOLB) **1993** Phx 16 (9, lde/rde) **1994** Ind 11 (6, lde) **1995**†Ind 10 (1) **1996** Ind 5 (0) **NFL** 157 (129) [12 yrs]

YEAR	TEAM	G (GS, POS)	RUSH	YD	AVG(LG)	TD	REC	YD	AVG(LG)	TD	PASS	COMP	PCT	YD	AVG(LG)	TD	INT	SK	YD	QBR	KPR	OTD	PTS	TAY

NUNNERY, R.B.   Robert Brock, T, 6´4˝/275 lbs; LSU; 1956: Det, rnd 12; B12/28/1933 McComb, MS   **1960** DalT-A 6

NUSSBAUMER, BOB   Robert John, HB, 5´11˝/172 lbs; Michigan; 1946: GB, rnd 3; B4/23/1924 Oak Park, IL, D7/26/1997 Moreland Hills, OH   **1949** ChiC 12 (0)   **1950** ChiC 1 (1)

1951 GB 4

1946	GB	10(3)	29	43	1.5(16)	0	10	143	14.3(35)	0	1	1	100.0	10	10.0(10)	0	0	—	—	—	kpi	—	0	232
1947	Was	12(1)	43	136	3.2(12)	4	47	597	12.7(55)	4	—	—	—	—	—	—	—	—	—	—	kpi	—	24	489
1948	Was	10(2)	23	59	2.6(16)	0	19	252	13.3(37)	1	—	—	—	—	—	—	—	—	—	—	kp	—	6	185
NFL	6	49(7)	95	238	2.5(47)	0	76	992	13.1(55)	5	1	1	100.0	10	10.0(10)	0	0	—	—	—	kpi	—	30	1011

NUSSMEIER, DOUG   Douglas Keith, QB, 6´3˝/211 lbs; Idaho; 1994: NO, rnd 4; B12/11/1970 Portland, OR

1996	NO	3(1)	3	6	2.0(6)	0	—	—	—	—	50	28	56.0	272	5.4(57)	1	1	3	17	—	—	—	0	107
1997	NO	5(2)	8	30	3.8(15)	0	—	—	—	—	32	18	56.3	183	5.7(24)	0	3	6	32	—	—	—	0	2
NFL	2	8(3)	11	36	3.3(15)	0	—	—	—	—	82	46	56.1	455	5.5(57)	1	4	9	49	—	—	—	0	109

NUTTEN, TOM   Thomas R., G-C, 6´4˝/280 lbs; Western Michigan; 1995: Buf, rnd 7; B6/8/1971 Magog, Canada   **1995** Buf 1 (0)   **1998** SL 4 (2)   **1999**†SL 14 (14, LG)
2000†SL 16 (16, LG)   **2001** SL 15 (14, LG)   **2002** SL 11 (11, LG)   **2004**†SL 8 (6, LG)   **2005** SL 8 (6, lg)   **NFL** 77 (69) [8 yrs]

NUTTER, BUZZ   Madison Monroe, C-LB, 6´4˝/230 lbs; Virginia Tech; 1953: Was, rnd 12; B2/16/1931 Summersville, WV   **1954** Bal 12 (C)   **1955** Bal 12   **1956** Bal 12 (C)
1957 Bal 12 (C)   **1958**†Bal 12 (12, C)   **1959**†Bal 12 (C)   **1960** Bal 12 (C)   **1961** Pit 14 (C)   **1962** Pit★14 (C)   **1963** Pit☆14 (C)   **1964** Pit 14 (C)   **1965**†Bal 13 (c)   **NFL** 153 (12) [12 yrs]

NUTTING, ED   John Edward, T, 6´4˝/246 lbs; Georgia Tech; 1961: Cle, rnd 2/DalT, rnd 15; B2/8/1939 Washington, DC   **1961** Cle 4   **1963** Dal 14 (7, RT)   **NFL** 18 (7) [2 yrs]

NUZUM, JERRY   Jerry Hanson, HB-FB, 6´1˝/199 lbs; New Mexico State; 1948: Pit, rnd 3; B9/8/1923 Clovis, NM, D4/23/1997 Monroeville, PA

1948	Pit	10(1)	26	109	4.2(20)	0	2	37	18.5(32)	0	—	—	—	—	—	—	—	—	—	—	kpi	—	0	160
1949	Pit	12(3, HB)	139	611	4.4(64)	5	4	81	20.3(63)	2	1	1	100.0	21	21.0(21)	0	0	—	—	—	k	—	42	724
1950	Pit	12	57	154	2.7(32)	1	6	142	23.7(68)	1	—	—	—	—	—	—	—	—	—	—	k	—	12	240
1951	Pit	11 (fb)	27	56	2.1(9)	1	2	43	21.5(39)	0	—	—	—	—	—	—	—	—	—	—	—	—	6	88
NFL	4	45(4)	249	930	3.7(64)	7	14	303	21.6(68)	3	1	1	100.0	21	21.0(21)	0	0	—	—	—	kpi	—	60	1211

NUZUM, RICK   Frederick Merril, C, 6´4˝/238 lbs; Kentucky; 1975: LA, rnd 5; B6/30/1952 Charleston, WV   **1977**†LARm 14   **1978** GB 16   **NFL** 30 [2 yrs]

NUZZO, CHIP   Anthony Chris, DB, 5´11˝/190 lbs; Princeton; B7/26/1965 Olean, NY   **1987** Buf 3 (0)

NWOKORIE, CHUKIE   Chijoka Obinna, DE, 6´3˝/288 lbs; Purdue; B7/10/1975 Tuskegee, AL   **1999** Ind 1 (0)   **2000** Ind 2 (0)   **2001** Ind 16 (5, lde)   **2002** Ind 3 (0)   **2003** GB 14 (0)
NFL 36 (5) [5 yrs]

NYDALL, MALLY   Melvin John, B, 5´11˝/163 lbs; Minnesota; B11/24/1906 Minneapolis, MN, D5/1979 Sun City, AZ **[K]**   **1929** Min 10 (8, BB), 14   **1930** Min 9 (6, WB), 1
1930 Fra 4 (3), 12   **1931** Fra 4 (2)   **NFL** 27 (19), 27 [3 yrs]

NYE, BLAINE   Blaine Francis, G, 6´4˝/251 lbs; Stanford; 1968: Dal, rnd 5; B3/29/1946 Ogden, UT   **1968** Dal 13   **1969**†Dal 14   **1970**†Dal 14 (10, RG)   **1971** Dal 14 (RG)
1972†Dal☆14 (RG)   **1973**†Dal 14 (RG)   **1974** Dal✧14 (RG)   **1975**†Dal☆14 (RG)   **1976**†Dal★14 (RG)   **NFL** 125 (10) [9 yrs]

NYERS, DICK   Charles Richard, DB-HB, 5´11˝/177 lbs; Indianapolis; B9/8/1934 Indianapolis, IN   **1956** Bal 5

| 1957 | Bal | 7 | 1 | -4 | -4.0(-4) | 0 | — | — | — | — | — | — | — | — | — | — | — | — | — | — | k | — | 0 | 91 |
| NFL | 2 | 12 | 1 | -4 | -4.0(-4) | 0 | — | — | — | — | — | — | — | — | — | — | — | — | — | — | kp | — | 0 | 121 |

NYGREN, BERNIE   Bernard Clifford, HB-DB, 5´9˝/193 lbs; Gustavus Adolphus; San Jose State; B11/14/1918 Minneapolis, MN, D12/26/1984 San Jose, CA   **1947** Bkn-A 1 (0)

| 1946 | LAD-A | 14(5, RH) | 26 | 111 | 4.3 | 0 | 13 | 170 | 13.1 | 1 | — | — | — | — | — | — | — | — | — | — | ki | — | 6 | 249 |
| AAFC | 2 | 15(5) | 26 | 111 | 4.3 | 0 | 13 | 170 | 13.1 | 1 | — | — | — | — | — | — | — | — | — | — | — | — | 6 | 201 |

NYSTROM, LEE   Lee Allen, T, 6´5˝/260 lbs; Macalester; B10/30/1951 Worthington, MN   **1974** GB 13

NYVALL, VIC   Victor A., RB, 5´10˝/185 lbs; Northwestern State (LA); B4/29/1948

| 1970 | NO | 2 | 5 | 6 | 1.2(6) | 0 | 2 | -1 | -0.5(1) | 0 | — | — | — | — | — | — | — | — | — | — | — | — | 0 | 6 |

OAKES, DON   Donald Sherman, T-DT, 6´4˝/255 lbs; Virginia Tech; 1961: Phi, rnd 3/Bos, rnd 21; B7/22/1938 Roanoke, VA   **1961** Phi 8   **1962** Phi 14   **1963**†Bos-A 14 (LT)
1964 Bos-A 13 (LT)   **1965** Bos-A 14 (LT)   **1966** Bos-A 14 (LT)   **1967** Bos-A✧14 (LT)   **1968** Bos-A 13 (3)   **NFL** 104 (3) [8 yrs]

OAKLEY, CHARLEY   Charles Lynn, DB, 5´10˝/170 lbs; LSU; 1954: ChiC, rnd 23; B7/1/1931 Montgomery, AL   **1954** ChiC 1

OAS, BEN   Bernard, C-BB, 6´0˝/195 lbs; St. Mary's (MN); B4/27/1901, MN, D2/1976 Chicago, IL   **1929** Min 7 (4)

OATES, BART   Bart Steven, C, 6´4˝/275 lbs; Brigham Young; B12/16/1958 Mesa, AZ   **1985**†NYG 16 (14, C)   **1986**†NYG 16 (16, C)   **1987** NYG☆12 (12, C)   **1988** NYG 16 (16, C)
1989†NYG 16 (16, C)   **1990**†NYG✧16 (16, C)   **1991** NYG✧16 (16, C)   **1992** NYG 16 (15, C)   **1993**†NYG✧16 (15, C)   **1994**†SF★16 (15, C)   **1995**†SF★16 (14, C)
NFL 172 (165) [11 yrs]

OATES, BRAD   Robert Bradley, T-G, 6´6˝/274 lbs; Duke; Brigham Young; 1976: SL, rnd 3; B9/30/1953 Mesa, AZ   **1976** SL 14   **1977** SL 9   **1978** Det 16 (15, RT)   **1979** SL 11
1980 SL 10 (5, lt)   **1980** KC 1 (0)   **1981** Cin 5 (2)   **1981** GB 1 (0)   **NFL** 67 (20) [6 yrs]

OATIS, VICTOR   Victor Hugo, WR, 6´0˝/177 lbs; Northwestern State (LA); 1983: Phi, rnd 6; B1/6/1959 Monroe, LA

| 1983 | Bal | 9(0) | — | — | — | — | 6 | 93 | 15.5(25) | 0 | — | — | — | — | — | — | — | — | — | — | — | — | 0 | 47 |

OATS, CARLETON   Carleton, DT-DE, 6´3˝/260 lbs; Florida A&M; 1964: Oak, rnd 21/Min, rnd 16; B4/24/1942 Tampa, FL   **1965** Oak-A 14   **1966** Oak-A 14   **1967**†Oak-A 9
1968†Oak-A 14 (14, RDT)   **1969**†Oak-A 13 (13, LDT)   **1970**†Oak 13 (13, LDT)   **1971** Oak 12 (8, RDT)   **1972**†Oak 14   **1973** GB 8   **NFL** 111 (48) [9 yrs]

O'BARD, RONNIE   Ronald Alexander, DB, 5´9˝/190 lbs; Idaho; Brigham Young; B6/11/1958 San Diego, CA   **1985** SD 16 (0)

OBECK, VIC   Victor Francis Joseph, G, 6´0˝/225 lbs; Springfield; B3/28/1917 Audobon, NJ, D4/21/1979 New York, NY   **1945** ChiC 10 (3)

1946 Bkn-A 12 (0)

OBEE, DUNC   Duncan Francis, C, 5´11˝/215 lbs; Dayton; B7/9/1918 Battle Creek, MI, D11/27/1998, OH   **1941** Det 3 (0)

OBEE, TERRY   Terry Lamar, WR, 5´10˝/190 lbs; Oregon; B6/15/1968 Vallejo, CA   **1991** Min 1 (0)

| 1993 | ChiB | 16(5, wr) | — | — | — | — | 26 | 351 | 13.5(48) | 3 | — | — | — | — | — | — | — | — | — | — | kp | — | 18 | 329 |
| NFL | 2 | 17(5) | — | — | — | — | 26 | 351 | 13.5(48) | 3 | — | — | — | — | — | — | — | — | — | — | — | — | 18 | 191 |

OBEN, ROMAN   Roman Dissake, T, 6´4˝/305 lbs; Louisville; 1996: NYG, rnd 3; B10/9/1972 Cameroon, West Africa   **1996** NYG 2 (0)   **1997**†NYG 16 (16, LT)   **1998** NYG 16 (16, LT)
1999 NYG 16 (16, LT)   **2000** Cle 16 (16, LT)   **2001** Cle 16 (14, LT)   **2002**†TB 16 (16, LT)   **2003** TB 15 (13, LT)   **2004**†SD 16 (16, LT)   **2005** SD 8 (8, lt)   **NFL** 137 (131) [10 yrs]

OBERBROEKLING, RAY   Raymond Joseph, T, 5´8˝/198 lbs; Loras; B12/31/1898 New Vienna, IA, D3/1972 New Vienna, IA   **1924** Ken 2 (0)

OBERG, TOM   Thomas Harvey, DB, 6´0˝/185 lbs; Oregon State; Portland State; B8/7/1945 Portland, OR   **1968** Den-A 9   **1969** Den-A 7 (7, ls)   **NFL** 16 (7) [2 yrs]

O'BERRY, HERMAN   Herman Lee, DB, 5´9˝/185 lbs; Oregon; 1995: SL, rnd 7; B7/11/1971 Sacramento, CA   **1996** SL 9 (0)

O'BOYLE, HARRY   Harry William, B, 5´9˝/178 lbs; Notre Dame; B10/31/1904 Des Moines, IA, D5/5/1994 Wheeling, IL **[K]**

1928	GB	10(8, FB)	—	—	—	—	—	—	—	—	—	—	—	—	—	—	—	—	—	—	K	—	23	0
1932	GB	11(6, BB)	9	14	1.6	0	—	—	—	—	7	1	14.3	8	1.1(8)	0	2	—	—	—	K	—	7	-62
1933	Phi	2(0)	2	4	2.0	0	—	—	—	—	2	0	0.0	0	0.0(—)	0	1	—	—	—	K	—	0	-36
NFL	3	23(14)	11	18	1.6	0	—	—	—	—	9	1	11.1	8	0.9(8)	0	3	—	—	—	K	—	30	-98

O'BRADOVICH, ED   Edward, DE, 6´3˝/255 lbs; Illinois; 1962: Chi, rnd 7; B5/21/1940 Hillside, IL   **1962** ChiB 14 (LDE)   **1963**†ChiB 6 (lde)   **1964** ChiB 7   **1965** ChiB 13
1966 ChiB 14 (LDE)   **1967** ChiB 14 (LDE)   **1968** ChiB 14 (LDE)   **1969** ChiB 14 (RDE)   **1970** ChiB 14 (RDE)   **1971** ChiB 14 (RDE)   **NFL** 124 [10 yrs]

OBRADOVICH, JIM   James Robert, TE, 6´2˝/225 lbs; USC; 1975: NYG, rnd 7; B4/2/1953 Los Angeles, CA

1975	NYG	14(1)	—	—	—	—	7	65	9.3(28)	1	—	—	—	—	—	—	—	—	—	—	k	—	6	46
1976	SF	14	—	—	—	—	1	11	11.0(11)	0	—	—	—	—	—	—	—	—	—	—	—	—	0	6
1977	SF	12	—	—	—	—	2	16	8.0(11)	0	—	—	—	—	—	—	—	—	—	—	—	—	0	2
1978	TB	16(9, te)	—	—	—	—	14	219	15.6(28)	3	—	—	—	—	—	—	—	—	—	—	k	—	18	128
1979	†TB	16(2)	—	—	—	—	6	63	10.5(19)	1	—	—	—	—	—	—	—	—	—	—	k	—	6	37
1980	TB	16(1)	—	—	—	—	11	152	13.8(24)	0	—	—	—	—	—	—	—	—	—	—	k	—	0	47
1981	†TB	16(3)	—	—	—	—	4	42	10.5(16)	1	—	—	—	—	—	—	—	—	—	—	k	—	6	25
1982	†TB	9(3)	—	—	—	—	2	22	11.0(15)	0	—	—	—	—	—	—	—	—	—	—	k	—	0	8

YEAR	TEAM	G (GS, POS)	RUSH	YD	AVG (LG)	TD	REC	YD	AVG (LG)	TD	PASS	COMP	PCT	YD	AVG (LG)	TD	INT	SK	YD	QBR	KPR	OTD	PTS	TAY
1983	TB	16 (5, te)	—	—	—	—	9	71	7.9 (19)	1	—	—	—	—	—	—	—	—	—	—	k	—	6	26
NFL	9	129 (24)	—	—	—	—	56	661	11.8 (28)	7	—	—	—	—	—	—	—	—	—	—	k	—	42	323

O'Brien, Con Cornelius, T, 6´2˝/195 lbs; Boston College; B2/13/1898, Ireland, D5/9/1973 Medford, WA **1921** NYG 1 (1)

O'Brien, Bill William George, HB, 6´0˝/180 lbs; none; B8/25/1924 Detroit, MI, D5/8/2005 Eastport, MI

YEAR	TEAM	G (GS, POS)	RUSH	YD	AVG (LG)	TD	REC	YD	AVG (LG)	TD	PASS	COMP	PCT	YD	AVG (LG)	TD	INT	SK	YD	QBR	KPR	OTD	PTS	TAY
1947	Det	9 (1)	1	2	2.0 (2)	0	—	—	—	—	—	—	—	—	—	—	—	—	—	—	—	—	0	2

O'Brien, Dave David Hyde, T-DT-G, 6´3˝/247 lbs; Boston College; 1963: Min, rnd 13/Bos, rnd 18; B6/13/1941 Cambridge, MA **1963** Min 14 **1964** Min 14 **1965** NYG 10 **1966** SL 14 **1967** SL 8 **NFL** 60 [5 yrs]

O'Brien, Davey Robert David, QB-TB, 5´7˝/151 lbs; TCU; 1939: Phi, rnd 1; B6/22/1917 Dallas, TX, D11/18/1977 Fort Worth, TX

YEAR	TEAM	G (GS, POS)	RUSH	YD	AVG (LG)	TD	REC	YD	AVG (LG)	TD	PASS	COMP	PCT	YD	AVG (LG)	TD	INT	SK	YD	QBR	KPR	OTD	PTS	TAY
1939	Phi★	11 (8, QB)	108	-14	-0.1	1	—	—	—	—	201	99	49.3	**1324**	6.6 (85)	6	**17**	—	—	45.3	P	—	6	8
1940	Phi☆	11 (11, QB)	100	-180	-1.8	1	—	—	—	—	**277**	**124**	44.8	1290	4.7 (47)	5	17	—	—	39.2	Pi	—	6	-108
NFL	2	22 (19)	208	-194	-0.9	2	—	—	—	—	478	223	46.7	2614	5.5 (85)	11	34	—	—	41.8	Pi	—	12	-100

O'Brien, Fran Francis Joseph, T, 6´1˝/253 lbs; Michigan State; 1959: Cle, rnd 3; B4/17/1936 Springfield, MA, D10/21/1999 Washington, DC **1959** Cle 12 (rt) **1960** Was 12 (12, LT) **1961** Was 14 (14, RT) **1962** Was 14 (RT) **1963** Was 13 (RT) **1964** Was 14 (RT) **1965** Was 14 (RT) **1966** Was 2 **1966** Pit 11 **1967** Pit 4 **1968** Pit 14 (LT) **NFL** 124 (26) [10 yrs]

O'Brien, Gail Joseph Gail, T, 6´1˝/219 lbs; Nebraska; B11/14/1911 Cheyenne, WY, D7/7/1978 Los Angeles County, CA **1934** Bos 10 (6, rt) **1935** Bos 11 (10, RT) **1936**†Bos 11 (4) **NFL** 32 (20) [3 yrs]

O'Brien, Jack John Joseph, HB, 5´10˝/170 lbs; Minnesota; B8/8/1899 Minneapolis, MN, D1971 **1929** Min 1 (1)

O'Brien, Jack Jack Edward, E, 6´2˝/213 lbs; Florida; 1954: Pit, rnd 7; B10/21/1932 Jeannette, PA

YEAR	TEAM	G (GS, POS)	RUSH	YD	AVG (LG)	TD	REC	YD	AVG (LG)	TD	PASS	COMP	PCT	YD	AVG (LG)	TD	INT	SK	YD	QBR	KPR	OTD	PTS	TAY
1954	Pit	7	—	—	—	—	1	9	9.0 (9)	0	—	—	—	—	—	—	—	—	—	—	—	—	0	5
1955	Pit	12	—	—	—	—	9	105	11.7 (38)	2	—	—	—	—	—	—	—	—	—	—	—	—	12	63
1956	Pit	12	—	—	—	—	6	71	11.8 (25)	0	—	—	—	—	—	—	—	—	—	—	—	—	0	36
NFL	3	31	—	—	—	—	16	185	11.6 (38)	2	—	—	—	—	—	—	—	—	—	—	—	—	12	103

O'Brien, Jim James Eugene, WR-K, 6´0˝/195 lbs; Cincinnati; 1970: Bal, rnd 3; B2/2/1947 El Paso, TX **[K]**

YEAR	TEAM	G (GS, POS)	RUSH	YD	AVG (LG)	TD	REC	YD	AVG (LG)	TD	PASS	COMP	PCT	YD	AVG (LG)	TD	INT	SK	YD	QBR	KPR	OTD	PTS	TAY
1970	†Bal	14	—	—	—	—	1	28	28.0 (28)	0	—	—	—	—	—	—	—	—	—	—	K	—	93	14
1971	†Bal	14	—	—	—	—	—	—	—	—	—	—	—	—	—	—	—	—	—	—	K	—	95	0
1972	Bal	14 (WR)	3	9	3.0 (7)	0	11	263	23.9 (44)	2	—	—	—	—	—	—	—	—	—	—	K	—	75	151
1973	Det	10	—	—	—	—	2	14	7.0 (9)	0	—	—	—	—	—	—	—	—	—	—	K	—	38	7
NFL	4	52	3	9	3.0 (7)	0	14	305	21.8 (44)	2	—	—	—	—	—	—	—	—	—	—	K	—	301	172

O'Brien, Ken Kenneth John, QB, 6´4˝/210 lbs; Sacramento State; California-Davis; 1983: NYJ, rnd 1; B11/27/1960 Rockville Centre, NY

YEAR	TEAM	G (GS, POS)	RUSH	YD	AVG (LG)	TD	REC	YD	AVG (LG)	TD	PASS	COMP	PCT	YD	AVG (LG)	TD	INT	SK	YD	QBR	KPR	OTD	PTS	TAY
1984	NYJ	10 (5, qb)	16	29	1.8 (7)	0	—	—	—	—	203	116	57.1	1402	6.9 (49)	6	7	22	168	—	—	—	0	480
1985	†NYJ✧	16 (16, QB)	25	58	2.3 (22)	0	—	—	—	—	488	297	60.9	3888	8.0 (**96**)	25	8	62	399	**96.2**	—	—	0	1807
1986	†NYJ	15 (14, QB)	17	46	2.7 (11)	0	—	—	—	—	482	300	**62.2**	3690	7.7 (83)	25	20	40	353	85.8	—	—	0	1216
1987	NYJ	12 (12, QB)	30	61	2.0 (11)	0	—	—	—	—	393	234	59.5	2696	6.9 (59)	13	8	50	364	82.8	—	—	0	1154
1988	NYJ	14 (12, QB)	21	25	1.2 (17)	0	—	—	—	—	424	236	55.7	2567	6.1 (50)	15	7	37	267	78.6	—	—	0	1104
1989	NYJ	15 (12, QB)	9	18	2.0 (5)	0	—	—	—	—	477	288	60.4	3346	7.0 (57)	12	18	50	391	74.3	—	—	0	1031
1990	NYJ	16 (16, QB)	21	72	3.4 (15)	0	—	—	—	—	411	226	55.0	2855	6.9 (69)	13	10	34	262	77.3	P	—	0	1165
1991	†NYJ✧	16 (16, QB)	23	60	2.6 (13)	0	1	27	27.0 (27)	0	489	287	58.7	3300	6.7 (53)	10	11	33	273	76.6	—	—	0	1334
1992	NYJ	10 (3)	8	8	1.0 (7)	0	—	—	—	—	98	55	56.1	642	6.6 (55)	5	6	10	61	—	—	—	0	114
1993	Phi	5 (4)	4	17	4.3 (11)	0	—	—	—	—	137	71	51.8	708	5.2 (41)	4	3	15	116	—	—	—	0	271
NFL	10	129 (110)	174	394	2.3 (22)	0	1	27	27.0 (27)	0	3602	2110	58.6	25094	7.0 (96)	128	98	353	2654	80.4	P	—	0	9675

O'Brien, Mike Michael Patrick, DB, 6´1˝/195 lbs; California; B4/25/1956 Kirkland, WA **1979** Sea 3

Obrovac, Mike Michael Louis, T-G, 6´6˝/275 lbs; Bowling Green State; B10/11/1955 Canton, OH **1981**†Cin 6 (1) **1982**†Cin 9 (0) **1983** Cin 10 (1) **NFL** 25 (2) [3 yrs]

Obst, Henry Henry D., G, 5´11˝/192 lbs; Syracuse; B12/23/1906, D8/27/1975 Brooklyn, NY **1931** SI 2 (2) **1933** Phi 1 (0) **NFL** 3 (2) [2 yrs]

O'Callaghan, John John James, TE, 6´4˝/245 lbs; Long Beach State; San Diego State; B5/15/1964 **1987** Sea 1 (1)

O'Connell, Grat John Grattan, E, 5´11˝/185 lbs; Boston College; B10/27/1902 Thomaston, CT, D3/14/1942 Simsbury, CT **1926** Har 10 (10, RE), 6 **1927** Pro 2 (2) **NFL** 12 (12) [2 yrs]

O'Connell, Harry Harold F., T, 6´1˝/190 lbs; Chicago; B2/13/1904 Chicago, IL, D5/1965, IL **1924** ChiB 1 (0)

O'Connell, Milt Milton Timothy, E, 6´0˝/175 lbs; Lafayette; B11/12/1900 Nutley, NJ, D5/18/1928 Wilmington, DE **1924** Fra 13 (8, RE), 6 **1925** Fra 2 (1) **NFL** 15 (9) [2 yrs]

O'Connell, Tommy Thomas Bernard, QB, 5´11˝/187 lbs; Notre Dame; Illinois; 1952: ChiB, rnd 18; B9/26/1930 Chicago, IL

YEAR	TEAM	G (GS, POS)	RUSH	YD	AVG (LG)	TD	REC	YD	AVG (LG)	TD	PASS	COMP	PCT	YD	AVG (LG)	TD	INT	SK	YD	QBR	KPR	OTD	PTS	TAY
1953	ChiB	12	7	16	2.3 (17)	0	—	—	—	—	67	33	49.3	437	6.5 (40)	1	4	—	—	—	—	—	0	80
1956	Cle	7 (5, QB)	24	40	1.7 (11)	2	—	—	—	—	96	42	43.8	551	5.7 (46)	4	8	—	—	—	—	—	12	36
1957	†Cle	11 (QB)	14	-5	-0.4 (7)	1	—	—	—	—	110	63	57.3	1229	11.2 (65)	9	8	—	—	—	—	—	6	345
1960	Buf-A	14 (qb)	16	21	1.3 (12)	1	—	—	—	—	145	65	44.8	1033	7.1 (64)	7	13	—	—	—	—	—	8	63
1961	Buf-A	1	—	—	—	—	—	—	—	—	5	1	20.0	11	2.2 (11)	0	1	—	—	—	—	—	0	-35
NFL	5	45 (5)	61	72	1.2 (17)	4	—	—	—	—	423	204	48.2	3261	7.7 (65)	21	34	—	—	—	—	—	26	488

O'Connor, Bill William Francis, E-DE, 6´4˝/220 lbs; Notre Dame; 1948: Buf-A, rnd 4/LARm, rnd 18; B5/2/1926 New York, NY, D9/13/1990 Oklahoma City, OK **1949**†Cle-A 9 (1)

YEAR	TEAM	G (GS, POS)	RUSH	YD	AVG (LG)	TD	REC	YD	AVG (LG)	TD	PASS	COMP	PCT	YD	AVG (LG)	TD	INT	SK	YD	QBR	KPR	OTD	PTS	TAY
1948	†Buf-A	14 (4, re)	—	—	—	—	31	301	9.7	2	—	—	—	—	—	—	—	—	—	—	k	—	12	146
AAFC	2	23 (5)	—	—	—	—	31	301	9.7	2	—	—	—	—	—	—	—	—	—	—	—	—	12	161
1951	NYY	12	—	—	—	—	14	192	13.7 (33)	0	—	—	—	—	—	—	—	—	—	—	k	—	0	91

O'Connor, Bob Robert Charles, G-T-BB, 6´1˝/220 lbs; Stanford; B1/27/1910 Elmira, NY **1935** GB 7 (1)

O'Connor, Dan Daniel Gerald, T-G, 6´2˝/210 lbs; Boston College; Georgetown (DC); B1/1894 Manchester, NH, D6/9/1964 Boston, MA **1920** Can 10 (4) **1921** Cle 7 (5, LT) **NFL** 17 (9) [2 yrs]

O'Connor, Frank Francis Stephen, T, 6´1˝/210 lbs; Holy Cross; B12/14/1897 Melrose, MA, D12/15/1965 Worcester, MA **1926** Har 2 (0)

O'Connor, Paul Paul, G, 6´3˝/270 lbs; Miami (FL); 1987: NYG, rnd 5; B11/7/1962 Summit, NJ **1987** TB 2 (2)

O'Connor, Red Red, E, 5´8˝/170 lbs; DePaul; deceased **1920** ChiC 3 (1) **1921** ChiC 5 (4, RE) **1922** ChiC 5 (4) **1924** ChiC 3 (3) **NFL** 16 (12) [4 yrs]

O'Connor, Tom Thomas L., P, 6´1˝/190 lbs; South Carolina; B11/8/1963 Patchoge, NY **1987** NYJ 3 (0)

Odegard, Don Don Boyd, DB, 6´0˝/180 lbs; Oregon State; UNLV; 1990: Cin, rnd 6; B11/22/1966 Seattle, WA **1990** NYJ 14 (0) **1991**†NYJ 16 (1) **NFL** 30 (1) [2 yrs]

O'Dell, Stu Stewart Harry, LB, 6´1˝/220 lbs; Indiana; 1974: Was, rnd 13; B11/27/1951 Linton, IN **1974**†Was 8 **1976**†Was 14 **1977** Was 3 **1978** Bal 14 **NFL** 39 [4 yrs]

O'Delli, Mel Melvin J., HB, 5´8˝/176 lbs; Duquesne; 1945: Pit, rnd 14; B1923 **1945** Pit 2 (0)

Oden, Curly Olof Gustave Hazard, B, 5´6˝/163 lbs; Brown; B5/10/1899 Stockholm, Sweden, D8/31/1978 Cranston, RI **[K]** **1925** Pro 8 (7, BB) **1926** Pro☆13 (12, BB), 60 **1927** Pro 13 (11, BB), 12 **1928** Pro☆11 (9, BB), 27 **1930** Pro 10 (6, BB), 1 **1931** Pro 11 (4), 6 **1932** Bos 1 (0) **NFL** 67 (49), 106 [7 yrs]

Oden, Derrick Derrick, LB, 5´11˝/230 lbs; Alabama; 1993: Phi, rnd 6; B9/29/1970 Los Angeles, CA **1993** Phi 12 (0) **1994** Phi 11 (0) **1995**†Phi 12 (0) **NFL** 35 (0) [3 yrs]

Oden, McDonald McDonald, TE, 6´4˝/234 lbs; Tennessee State; B3/28/1958 Franklin, TN

YEAR	TEAM	G (GS, POS)	RUSH	YD	AVG (LG)	TD	REC	YD	AVG (LG)	TD	PASS	COMP	PCT	YD	AVG (LG)	TD	INT	SK	YD	QBR	KPR	OTD	PTS	TAY
1980	†Cle	16 (0)	—	—	—	—	3	18	6.0 (8)	0	—	—	—	—	—	—	—	—	—	—	—	—	0	9
1981	Cle	16 (0)	—	—	—	—	1	6	6.0 (6)	0	—	—	—	—	—	—	—	—	—	—	—	—	0	3
1982	†Cle	9 (0)	—	—	—	—	1	4	4.0 (4)	0	—	—	—	—	—	—	—	—	—	—	—	—	0	2
NFL	3	41 (0)	—	—	—	—	5	28	5.6 (8)	0	—	—	—	—	—	—	—	—	—	—	—	—	0	14

Odle, Phil Phillip Morris, WR, 5´11˝/195 lbs; Brigham Young; 1968: Det, rnd 5; B11/23/1942 Macdonia, IL

YEAR	TEAM	G (GS, POS)	RUSH	YD	AVG (LG)	TD	REC	YD	AVG (LG)	TD	PASS	COMP	PCT	YD	AVG (LG)	TD	INT	SK	YD	QBR	KPR	OTD	PTS	TAY
1968	Det	14	—	—	—	—	6	71	11.8 (18)	0	—	—	—	—	—	—	—	—	—	—	—	—	0	36
1969	Det	13	—	—	—	—	2	24	12.0 (14)	0	—	—	—	—	—	—	—	—	—	—	—	—	0	12
1970	Det	4	—	—	—	—	—	—	—	—	—	—	—	—	—	—	—	—	—	—	—	—	—	—
NFL	3	31	—	—	—	—	8	95	11.9 (18)	0	—	—	—	—	—	—	—	—	—	—	—	—	0	48

YEAR	TEAM	G (GS, POS)	RUSH	YD	AVG(LG)	TD	REC	YD	AVG(LG)	TD	PASS COMP	PCT	YD	AVG(LG)	TD	INT	SK	YD	QBR	KPR	OTD	PTS	TAY

ODOM, ANTWAN   Antwan, DE, 6´4˝/277 lbs; Alabama; 2004: Ten, rnd 2; B9/24/1981 Mobile, AL   **2004** Ten 16 (8, LDE)   **2005** Ten 16 (9, RDE)   **NFL** 32 (17) [2 yrs]

ODOM, CLIFF   Clifton Louis, LB, 6´2˝/237 lbs; Texas-Arlington; 1980: Cle, rnd 3; B8/15/1958 Beaumont, TX   **1980** Cle 8 (0)   **1982** Bal 8 (2)   **1983** Bal 15 (5, lilb)
1984 Ind 16 (15, LILB)   **1985** Ind 16 (16, LILB)   **1986** Ind 16 (16, LILB)   **1987**†Ind 12 (12, LILB)   **1988** Ind 13 (7, lilb)   **1989** Ind 16 (3)   **1990**†Mia 16 (16, RILB)   **1991** Mia 14 (11, LILB)
1992†Mia 3 (0)   **1993** Mia 14 (1)   **NFL** 167 (104) [13 yrs]

ODOM, HENRY   Henry Collins, RB, 5´10˝/200 lbs; South Carolina State; 1983: Pit, rnd 8; B2/12/1959 Bamberg, SC

| 1983 | †Pit | 16(0) | 2 | 7 | 3.5(4) | 0 | — | — | — | — | — | — | — | — | — | — | — | — | k | — | 0 | 178 |

ODOM, JASON   Jason Brian, T, 6´5˝/307 lbs; Florida; 1996: TB, rnd 4; B3/31/1974 Winter Haven, FL   **1996** TB 12 (7, rt)   **1997**†TB 16 (16, RT)   **1998** TB 15 (15, RT)   **1999** TB 3 (3)
NFL 46 (41) [4 yrs]

ODOM, JOE   Joe Edward, LB, 6´1˝/238 lbs; Purdue; 2003: Chi, rnd 6; B12/14/1979 Alton, IL   **2003** ChiB 10 (3)   **2004** ChiB 16 (5, llb)   **2005** ChiB 2 (0)   **NFL** 28 (8) [3 yrs]

ODOM, RICKY   Ricky L., DB, 6´0˝/183 lbs; USC; 1978: KC, rnd 7; B9/16/1956 Jonesboro, LA   **1978** KC 8   **1978** SF 3 (3)   **1979** LARm 3   **NFL** 14 (3) [2 yrs]

ODOM, SAMMY   Sammy Joe, DT, 6´2˝/235 lbs; Northwestern State (LA); 1964: Hou, rnd 10/Cle, rnd 7; B11/13/1941 Shreveport, LA, D1/18/2001 Mansfield, LA   **1964** Hou-A 14

ODOM, STEVE   Stephen Talmage, WR, 5´8˝/173 lbs; Utah; 1974: GB, rnd 5; B9/5/1952 Oakland, CA [R]

1974	GB	14	6	66	11.0(28)	1	15	249	16.6(57)	1	—	—	—	—	—	—	—	—	kp	1	18	580
1975	GB◇	14(WR)	5	55	11.0(27)	0	15	299	19.9(56)	4	—	—	—	—	—	—	—	—	kp	1	30	634
1976	GB	12(WR)	4	78	19.5(28)	0	23	456	19.8(66)	2	—	—	—	—	—	—	—	—	k	—	12	491
1977	GB	14(WR)	1	6	6.0(6)	0	27	549	20.3(**95**)	3	—	—	—	—	—	—	—	—	k	—	18	419
1978	GB	12	—	—	—	—	4	60	15.0(18)	1	—	—	—	—	—	—	—	—	kp	1	12	480
1979	GB	9	—	—	—	—	—	—	—	—	—	—	—	—	—	—	—	—	kp	—	0	192
1979	NYG	6	—	—	—	—	—	—	—	—	—	—	—	—	—	—	—	—	kp	—	0	83
NFL	6	81	16	205	12.8(28)	1	84	1613	19.2(95)	11	—	—	—	—	—	—	—	—	kp	3	90	2878

ODOMES, NATE   Nathaniel Bernard, DB, 5´9˝/188 lbs; Wisconsin; 1987: Buf, rnd 2; B8/25/1965 Columbus, GA [I]   **1987** Buf 12 (12, RCB)   **1988**†Buf 16 (16, RCB)
1989†Buf☆16 (16, RCB)   **1990**†Buf 16 (16, RCB)   **1991**†Buf☆16 (16, RCB)   **1992**†Buf◇16 (16, RCB)   **1993**†Buf★16 (15, RCB)   **1996** Atl 7 (4)   **NFL** 115 (111) [8 yrs]

ODOMS, RILEY   Riley Mackey, TE, 6´4˝/230 lbs; Houston; 1972: Den, rnd 1; B3/1/1950 Luling, TX

1972	Den	14	5	72	14.4(27)	0	21	320	15.2(48)	1	—	—	—	—	—	—	—	—	—	—	6	237
1973	Den★	14(14, TE)	5	53	10.6(21)	0	43	629	14.6(47)	7	—	—	—	—	—	—	—	—	—	—	42	403
1974	Den★	14(14, TE)	4	25	6.3(31)	0	42	639	15.2(41)	6	—	—	—	—	—	—	—	—	—	—	36	375
1975	Den★	14(14, TE)	5	27	5.4(12)	0	40	544	13.6(43)	3	—	—	—	—	—	—	—	—	—	1	24	314
1976	Den☆	14(14, TE)	3	36	12.0(15)	2	30	477	15.9(47)	3	—	—	—	—	—	—	—	—	—	—	30	310
1977	†Den☆	14(14, TE)	—	—	—	—	37	429	11.6(33)	3	—	—	—	—	—	—	—	—	—	—	18	230
1978	†Den◇	16(16, TE)	2	5	2.5(7)	0	54	829	15.4(42)	6	—	—	—	—	—	—	—	—	—	—	36	450
1979	†Den	13(12, TE)	1	-7	-7.0(-7)	0	40	638	15.9(45)	1	—	—	—	—	—	—	—	—	—	—	6	317
1980	Den	15(15, TE)	—	—	—	—	39	590	15.1(30)	6	—	—	—	—	—	—	—	—	—	—	36	325
1981	Den	15(15, TE)	—	—	—	—	38	516	13.6(28)	5	—	—	—	—	—	—	—	—	—	—	30	283
1982	Den	8(6, TE)	—	—	—	—	8	82	10.3(18)	0	—	—	—	—	—	—	—	—	—	—	0	41
1983	†Den	2(0)	—	—	—	—	4	62	15.5(21)	0	—	—	—	—	—	—	—	—	—	—	0	31
NFL	12	153(134)	25	211	8.4(31)	2	396	5754	14.5(48)	41	—	—	—	—	—	—	—	—	—	1	264	3314

O'DONAHUE, PAT   James Patrick Michael, DE, 6´1˝/215 lbs; Wisconsin; 1952: SF, rnd 5; B10/7/1930 Eau Claire, WI [K]   **1952** SF 8 (RDE)   **1955** GB 12   **NFL** 20 [2 yrs]

O'DONNELL, DICK   Richard, E, 6´0˝/190 lbs; Minnesota; B1900, deceased   **1923** Dul 7 (6, LE), 6   **1924** GB 9 (9, LE)   **1925** GB 12 (12, LE), 6   **1926** GB 11 (11, LE), 12
1927 GB 9 (9, RE)   **1928** GB 13 (8, RE), 6   **1929** GB 10 (8, RE)   **1930** GB 10 (8, RE)   **1931** Bkn 11 (6, le), 6   **NFL** 92 (77), 36 [9 yrs]

O'DONNELL, JOE   Joseph Raymond, G-T, 6´2˝/262 lbs; Michigan; 1964: Buf, rnd 13/GB, rnd 3; B8/31/1941 Ann Arbor, MI   **1964**†Buf-A 14 (RG)   **1965**†Buf-A◇14   **1967** Buf-A 14 (RG)
1969 †Buf-A 14 (RG)   **1970** Buf 14 (RG)   **1971** Buf 7 (RG)

| 1966 | †Buf-A | 14 (RG) | — | — | — | — | 1 | 2 | 2.0(2) | 0 | — | — | — | — | — | — | — | — | — | — | 0 | 4 |
| NFL | 7 | 91 | — | — | — | — | 1 | 2 | 2.0(2) | 0 | — | — | — | — | — | — | — | — | — | — | 0 | 4 |

O'DONNELL, NEIL   Neil Kennedy, QB, 6´3˝/228 lbs; Maryland; 1990: Pit, rnd 3; B7/3/1966 Morristown, NJ

1991	Pit	12(8, QB)	18	82	4.6(22)	1	—	—	—	—	286	156	54.5	1963	6.9(**89**)	11	7	30	214	78.8	—	—	6	849
1992	†Pit◇	12(12, QB)	27	5	0.2(9)	0	—	—	—	—	313	185	59.1	2283	7.3(51)	13	9	27	208	83.6	—	—	6	862
1993	†Pit	16(15, QB)	26	111	4.3(27)	0	—	—	—	—	486	270	55.6	3208	6.6(71)	14	7	41	331	79.5	—	—	0	1505
1994	†Pit	14(14, QB)	31	80	2.6(18)	1	—	—	—	—	370	212	57.3	2443	6.6(60)	13	9	35	250	78.9	—	—	6	1017
1995	†Pit	12(12, QB)	24	45	1.9(14)	0	—	—	—	—	416	246	59.1	2970	7.1(71)	17	7	15	126	87.7	—	—	0	1335
1996	NYJ	6(6, qb)	6	30	5.0(17)	0	—	—	—	—	188	110	58.5	1147	6.1(78)	4	7	18	127	—	—	—	0	344
1997	NYJ	15(14, QB)	32	36	1.1(19)	1	—	—	—	—	460	259	56.3	2796	6.1(70)	17	7	45	289	80.3	—	—	6	1249
1998	Cin	13(11, QB)	13	34	2.6(10)	0	—	—	—	—	343	212	**61.8**	2216	6.5(76)	15	4	30	217	90.2	—	—	0	1057
1999	Ten	8(5, qb)	19	1	0.1(4)	0	—	—	—	—	195	116	59.5	1382	7.1(54)	10	5	9	63	—	—	—	0	542
2000	†Ten	6(1)	9	-2	-0.2(4)	0	—	—	—	—	64	36	56.3	530	8.3(67)	2	3	3	23	—	—	—	0	153
2001	Ten	5(1)	6	28	4.7(15)	0	—	—	—	—	76	42	55.3	496	6.5(35)	2	2	6	58	—	—	—	0	206
2002	†Ten	4(0)	3	-3	-1.0(-1)	0	—	—	—	—	5	3	60.0	24	4.8(15)	0	0	—	—	—	—	—	0	9
2003	Ten	1(1)	1	-1	-1.0(-1)	0	—	—	—	—	27	18	66.7	232	8.6(34)	2	1	—	—	—	—	—	0	85
NFL	13	124(100)	215	446	2.1(27)	4	—	—	—	—	3229	1865	57.8	21690	6.7(89)	120	68	259	1906	81.8	—	—	24	9211

O'DONOGHUE, NEIL   Cornelius Joseph Dennis, K, 6´6˝/208 lbs; St. Bernard; Auburn; 1977: Buf, rnd 5; B1/18/1953 Dublin, Ireland [K]   **1977** Buf 5   **1978** TB 15   **1979**†TB 16
1980 SL 10 (0)   **1981** SL 16 (0)   **1982**†SL 8 (0)   **1983** SL 16 (0)   **1984** SL 16 (0)   **1985** SL 8 (0)   **NFL** 110 [9 yrs]

ODSON, URBAN   Urban Leroy, T, 6´3˝/251 lbs; Minnesota; 1942: GB, rnd 1; B11/17/1918 Clark, SD, D6/22/1986 Rapid City, SD   **1946** GB 6 (0)   **1947** GB 11 (0)   **1948** GB 12 (0)
1949 GB 10 (0)   **NFL** 39 (0) [4 yrs]

O'DWYER, MATT   Matthew Phillip, G, 6´5˝/305 lbs; Northwestern; 1995: NYJ, rnd 2; B9/1/1972 Lincolnshire, IL   **1995** NYJ 12 (2)   **1996** NYJ 16 (16, RG)   **1997** NYJ 16 (16, RG)
1998†NYJ 16 (16, RG)   **1999** Cin 16 (16, LG)   **2000** Cin 10 (10, LG)   **2001** Cin 12 (12, LG)   **2002** Cin 16 (16, LG)   **2003** Cin 4 (1)   **2004** TB 4 (0)   **NFL** 122 (105) [10 yrs]

OECH, VERNE   Vernon Milton, G, 6´1˝/207 lbs; Montana; Minnesota; 1936: ChiB, rnd 5; B5/31/1913 Beach, ND   **1936** ChiB 7 (0)   **1937** ChiB 1 (0)   **NFL** 8 (0) [2 yrs]

OEHLER, CAP   John Walter, C-LB, 6´0˝/204 lbs; Purdue; B8/5/1910 Queens, NY   **1933** Pit 11 (11, C)   **1935** Bkn 12 (10, C)   **1936** Bkn 5 (1)

| 1934 | Pit☆ | 12(12, C) | 2 | 14 | 7.0 | 0 | — | — | — | — | — | — | — | — | — | — | — | — | — | — | 0 | 14 |
| NFL | 4 | 40(34) | 2 | 14 | 7.0 | 0 | — | — | — | — | — | — | — | — | — | — | — | — | — | — | 2 | 14 |

OEHLRICH, ARNIE   Arnold Henry, WB-BB, 5´11˝/190 lbs; Nebraska; B11/24/1905 Clarks, NE   **1928** Fra 16 (15, WB), 12   **1929** Fra 17 (14, WB), 6   **NFL** 33 (29), 18 [2 yrs]

OELERICH, JOHN   John Herman, HB, 6´0˝/192 lbs; St. Ambrose; B2/7/1916 Davenport, IA

1938	ChiB	2(0)	2	2	1.0	0	—	—	—	—	1	1	100.0	10	10.0(10)	0	0	—	—	—	—	0	7
1938	Pit	3(1)	21	21	1.8	0	2	23	11.5	0	—	—	—	—	—	—	0	—	—	—	—	0	33
NFL	1	5(1)	14	23	1.6	0	2	23	11.5	0	1	1	100.0	10	10.0(10)	0	0	—	—	—	—	0	40

OFFERDAHL, JOHN   John Arnold, LB, 6´3˝/232 lbs; Western Michigan; 1986: Mia, rnd 2; B8/17/1964 Wisconsin Rapids, WI   **1986** Mia★15 (15, RILB)   **1987** Mia★9 (9, RILB)
1988 Mia★16 (16, RILB)   **1989** Mia★10 (8, LILB)   **1990**†Mia★16 (16, LILB)   **1991** Mia 6 (6, rilb)   **1992** Mia 8 (8, RILB)   **1993** Mia 9 (8, MLB)   **NFL** 89 (86) [8 yrs]

OFFICE, KENDRICK   Kendrick LaShawn, DE, 6´5˝/270 lbs; West Alabama; B8/2/1978 Butler, AL   **2001** Buf 8 (1)   **2002** Buf 10 (1)   **NFL** 18 (2) [2 yrs]

OFFICE, TONY   Anthony Lee, LB, 6´2˝/250 lbs; Illinois State; B2/24/1960 Tifton, GA   **1987** Det 3 (2)

OFFORD, WILLIE   Willie, DB, 6´1˝/216 lbs; South Carolina; 2002: Min, rnd 3; B12/22/1978 Palatka, FL   **2002** Min 12 (6, ss)   **2003** Min 16 (0)   **2004**†Min 16 (0)   **2005** Min 3 (1)
NFL 47 (7) [4 yrs]

OFODILE, A.J.   Anselm Aniagboso, TE, 6´6˝/260 lbs; Missouri; 1994: Buf, rnd 5; B10/9/1973 Detroit, MI   **1997** Bal 12 (0)   **1998** Bal 5 (0)

| 1999 | Bal | 7(3) | — | — | — | — | 4 | 25 | 6.3(9) | 0 | — | — | — | — | — | — | — | — | — | — | 0 | 13 |
| NFL | 3 | 24(3) | — | — | — | — | 4 | 25 | 6.3(9) | 0 | — | — | — | — | — | — | — | — | — | — | 0 | 13 |

OGAS, DAVE   David H., LB, 6´1˝/225 lbs; San Diego State; B7/23/1946 Silver City, NM   **1968** Oak-A 6   **1969** Buf-A 14   **NFL** 20 [2 yrs]

YEAR	TEAM	G (GS, POS)	RUSH	YD	AVG(LG)	TD	REC	YD	AVG(LG)	TD	PASS	COMP	PCT	YD	AVG(LG)	TD	INT	SK	YD	QBR	KPR	OTD	PTS	TAY

OGBOGU, ERIC Eric, DE, 6'4"/270 lbs; Maryland; 1998: NYJ, rnd 6; B7/18/1975 Irvington, NY **1998**†NYJ 12 (0) **1999** NYJ 14 (0) **2001** NYJ 15 (0) **2002** Cin 12 (0) **2003**†Dal 16 (3) **2004** Dal 15 (1) **2005** Dal 6 (0) **NFL** 90 (4) [7 yrs]

OGDEN, JEFF Jeffrey Matthew, WR, 6'0"/190 lbs; Eastern Washington; B2/22/1975 Snohomish, WA

YEAR	TEAM	G (GS, POS)	RUSH	YD	AVG(LG)	TD	REC	YD	AVG(LG)	TD	KPR	OTD	PTS	TAY
1998	†Dal	16(0)	1	12	12.0(12)	0	8	63	7.9(12)	0	k	—	0	64
1999	†Dal	16(0)	—	—	—	—	12	144	12.0(25)	0	kp	—	0	152
2000	†Mia	16(0)	—	—	—	—	2	24	12.0(12)	0	p	1	6	250
2001	†Mia	16(0)	—	—	—	—	6	73	12.2(18)	1	p	—	6	259
2002	Bal	3(0)	—	—	—	—	—	—	—	—	p	—	0	11
NFL	5	67(0)	1	12	12.0(12)	0	28	304	10.9(25)	1	kp	1	12	735

OGDEN, JONATHAN Jonathan Phillip, T-G, 6'9"/340 lbs; UCLA; 1996: Bal, rnd 1; B7/31/1974 Washington, DC **1997** Bal★16 (16, LT) **1998** Bal★13 (13, LT) **1999** Bal★16 (16, LT) **2000** Bal★15 (15, LT) **2001** Bal★16 (16, LT) **2002** Bal★16 (16, LT) **2004** Bal★12 (12, LT) **2005** Bal◇16 (16, LT)

YEAR	TEAM	G (GS, POS)	RUSH	YD	AVG(LG)	TD	REC	YD	AVG(LG)	TD	OTD	PTS	TAY
1996	Bal	16(16, LG)	—	—	—	—	1	1	1.0(1)	1	—	6	6
2003	†Bal★	16(16, LT)	—	—	—	—	1	1	1.0(1)	1	—	6	6
NFL	10	152(152)	—	—	—	—	2	2	1.0(1)	2	—	12	11

OGDEN, RAY Raymond Douglas, TE, 6'5"/225 lbs; Alabama; 1965: SL, rnd 3/Hou, rnd 8; B9/2/1942 Jessup, GA

YEAR	TEAM	G (GS, POS)	RUSH	YD	AVG(LG)	TD	REC	YD	AVG(LG)	TD	KPR	OTD	PTS	TAY
1965	SL	3	—	—	—	—	—	—	—	—	k	—	0	25
1966	SL	14	—	—	—	—	—	—	—	—	k	—	0	-15
1967	NO	2	—	—	—	—	1	19	19.0(19)	0	—	—	0	10
1967	Atl	11(TE)	—	—	—	—	19	308	16.2(82)	1	k	—	6	155
1968	Atl	14(TE)	1	12	12.0(12)	0	25	452	18.1(60)	2	k	—	12	248
1969	ChiB	11	—	—	—	—	7	100	14.3(21)	0	—	—	0	50
1970	ChiB	9	—	—	—	—	1	6	6.0(6)	1	—	—	6	8
1971	ChiB	6	—	—	—	—	—	—	—	—	—	—	0	
NFL	7	70	1	12	12.0(12)	0	53	885	16.7(82)	4	k	—	24	481

OGLE, KENDALL Kendell, LB, 6'0"/231 lbs; Maryland; 1999: Cle, rnd 6; B11/25/1975 Hillside, NJ **1999** Cle 2 (0)

OGLE, RICK Richard James, LB, 6'3"/230 lbs; Colorado; 1971: SL, rnd 11; B1/14/1949 Bozeman, MT **1971** SL 6 (rlb) **1972** Det 4 **NFL** 10 [2 yrs]

OGLESBY, ALFRED Alfred Lee, NT-DE-DT, 6'4"/290 lbs; Houston; 1990: Mia, rnd 3; B1/27/1967 Weimar, TX **1990**†Mia 13 (6, nt) **1991** Mia 12 (12, NT/lde) **1992** Mia 6 (0) **1992** GB 7 (0) **1994** NYJ 15 (1) **1995** Cin 6 (0) **NFL** 59 (19) [5 yrs]

OGLESBY, CEDRIC Cedric, K, 5'11"/175 lbs; South Carolina; B7/26/1977 Decatur, GA [K] **2001** Arz 3 (0)

OGLESBY, EVAN Evan, DB, 5'10"/185 lbs; North Alabama; B12/18/1981 Toccoa, GA **2005** Bal 3 (0)

OGLESBY, PAUL Paul William, T-DT, 6'4"/235 lbs; UCLA; 1960: Hou, rnd 2/SL, rnd 10; B1/9/1939 San Francisco, CA, D9/25/1994 Riverside, CA **1960** Oak-A 14 (RT)

OGLETREE, CRAIG Craig Algemon, LB, 6'2"/236 lbs; Auburn; 1990: Cin, rnd 7; B4/2/1968 Barnesville, GA **1990**†Cin 11 (0)

OGRIN, PAT Patrick John, DT, 6'5"/265 lbs; Wyoming; B2/10/1958 Butte, MT **1981** Was 5 (0) **1982**†Was 3 (0) **NFL** 8 (0) [2 yrs]

OGUNLEYE, ADEWALE Adewale, DE, 6'4"/260 lbs; Indiana; B8/9/1977 Brooklyn, NY **2001** Mia 7 (0) **2002** Mia 16 (16, LDE) **2003** Mia★16 (16, LDE) **2004** ChiB 12 (12, LDE) **2005**†ChiB 15 (15, LDE) **NFL** 66 (59) [5 yrs]

OHALETE, IFEANYI Ifeanyi, DB, 6'2"/222 lbs; USC; B5/22/1979 Springfield, IL **2001** Was 16 (0) **2002** Was 16 (10, SS) **2004** Arz 16 (13, FS) **2005**†Cin 15 (12, SS)

YEAR	TEAM	G (GS, POS)	RUSH	YD	AVG(LG)	TD	REC	YD	AVG(LG)	TD	QBR	OTD	PTS	TAY
2003	Was	15(14, SS)	—	—	—	—	1	3	3.0(3)	0	i	—	0	47
NFL	5	78(49)	—	—	—	—	1	3	3.0(3)	0	iS	1	6	173

O'HANLEY, ROSS Ross A., DB, 6'0"/183 lbs; Boston College; B2/16/1939 Everett, WA, D4/2/1972 Needham, MA **1960** Bos-A☆14 (RS) **1961** Bos-A☆7 **1962** Bos-A 14 (LS) **1963**†Bos-A 14 (LS) **1964** Bos-A 14 (LS) **1965** Bos-A 14 (LS) **NFL** 77 [6 yrs]

O'HARA, SHAUN Shaun, G-C, 6'3"/306 lbs; Rutgers; B6/23/1977 Chicago, IL **2000** Cle 8 (4) **2002**†Cle 16 (16, RG) **2003** Cle 14 (14, LG/rg) **2004** NYG 12 (12, C) **2005**†NYG 16 (16, C)

YEAR	TEAM	G (GS, POS)	RUSH	YD	AVG(LG)	TD	REC	YD	AVG(LG)	TD	OTD	PTS	TAY
2001	Cle	16(4)	—	—	—	—	1	2	2.0(2)	1	—	6	6
NFL	6	82(66)	—	—	—	—	1	2	2.0(2)	1	—	6	6

O'HEARN, ED Edmund Francis, T-G, 5'10"/185 lbs; Boston College; Lehigh; B12/1/1898 Brookline, MA, D4/25/1972 Boston, MA **1920** Cle 2 (0) **1921** NYG 2 (2, LT) **NFL** 4 (2) [2 yrs]

O'HEARN, JACK John Ewing, WB, 5'10"/180 lbs; Cornell; B7/28/1893 Brookline, MA, D7/22/1977 Boston, MA **1920** Cle 5 (1) **1921** Buf 2 (1) **NFL** 7 (2) [2 yrs]

OHLGREN, EARL Earl August, E, 6'2"/210 lbs; Minnesota; B2/21/1918 Cokato, MN, D1/1/1963 Hubbard County, MN **1942** GB 2 (2)

OHMER WB, none; deceased **1921** Cin 1 (1)

OKANLAWON, TONY Anthony A., DB, 5'11"/187 lbs; Maryland; B3/4/1979 Lagos, Nigeria **2003** SD 1 (0)

OKEAFOR, CHIKE Chikeze Russell, DE, 6'4"/265 lbs; Purdue; 1999: SF, rnd 3; B3/27/1976 Grand Rapids, MI **1999** SF 12 (0) **2000** SF 15 (0) **2001** SF 14 (3) **2002**†SF 16 (16, RDE) **2003**†Sea 16 (16, RDE) **2004** Sea 16 (16, LDE) **2005** Arz 16 (16, LDE) **NFL** 105 (67) [7 yrs]

OKOBI, CHUKKY Chukwunweze Sonume, C-G, 6'1"/310 lbs; Purdue; 2001: Pit, rnd 5; B10/18/1978 Pittsburgh, PA **2001** Pit 1 (0) **2002** Pit 13 (5, c) **2003** Pit 16 (0) **2004**†Pit 16 (0) **2005**†Pit 16 (0) **NFL** 62 (5) [5 yrs]

OKONIEWSKI, STEVE John Stephen, DT-DE, 6'3"/257 lbs; Washington; Montana; 1972: Atl, rnd 2; B8/22/1949 Bremerton, WA **1972** Buf 10 **1973** Buf 5 **1974** GB 14 (RDT) **1975** GB 14 **1976** SL 8 **1977** SL 1 **NFL** 52 [6 yrs]

OKOYE, CHRISTIAN Christian Emeka 'The Nigerian Nightmare', RB, 6'1"/253 lbs; Azusa Pacific; 1987: KC, rnd 2; B8/16/1961 Enugu, Nigeria

YEAR	TEAM	G (GS, POS)	RUSH	YD	AVG(LG)	TD	REC	YD	AVG(LG)	TD	OTD	PTS	TAY
1987	KC	12(12, FB)	157	660	4.2(43)	3	24	169	7.0(22)	0	—	18	775
1988	KC	9(9, FB)	105	473	4.5(48)	3	8	51	6.4(12)	0	—	18	529
1989	KC★	15(14, FB)	370	1480	4.0(59)	12	2	12	6.0(8)	0	—	72	1606
1990	†KC	14(13, FB)	245	805	3.3(32)	7	4	23	5.8(8)	0	—	42	887
1991	†KC★	14(12, FB)	225	1031	4.6(48)	9	3	34	11.3(13)	0	—	54	1138
1992	KC	15(5, FB)	144	448	3.1(22)	6	1	5	5.0(5)	0	—	36	511
NFL	6	79(65)	1246	4897	3.9(59)	40	42	294	7.0(22)	0	—	240	5444

OLANDER, CLIFF Clifford Valmore, QB, 6'5"/191 lbs; New Mexico State; 1977: SD, rnd 5; B5/15/1955 Hartford, CT [K]

YEAR	TEAM	G (GS, POS)	RUSH	YD	AVG(LG)	TD	PASS	COMP	PCT	YD	AVG(LG)	TD	INT	SK	YD	KPR	OTD	PTS	TAY
1977	SD	2(1)	7	30	4.3(17)	0	16	7	43.8	76	4.8(15)	0	2	1	4	—	—	0	-12
1978	SD	9	1	-3	-3.0(-3)	0	8	5	62.5	49	6.1(22)	0	1	2	18	—	—	0	-19
1979	SD	4	—	—	—	—	—	—	—	—	—	—	—	—	—	K	—	1	0
NFL	3	15(1)	8	27	3.4(17)	0	24	12	50.0	125	5.2(22)	0	3	3	22	K	—	1	-31

OLDERMAN, BOB Robert Bruce, G, 6'5"/262 lbs; Virginia; 1985: KC, rnd 4; B6/5/1962 Brookville, PA, D10/20/1993 Atlanta, GA **1985** KC 16 (14, RG)

OLDERSHAW, DOUG Douglas C., G-E, 6'0"/195 lbs; California-Santa Barbara; 1938: NYG, rnd 11; B7/6/1915 Bakersfield, CA, D10/30/1995 Laguna Beach, CA **1939**†NYG 10 (0) **1940** NYG★11 (4) **1941** NYG☆10 (9) **NFL** 31 (10) [3 yrs]

OLDHAM, CHRIS Christopher Martin, DB, 5'9"/193 lbs; Oregon; 1990: Det, rnd 4; B10/26/1968 Sacramento, CA **1990** Det 16 (0) **1991** Buf 2 (0) **1991** Phx 2 (0) **1992** Phx 1 (0) **1993** Phx 16 (6, ss) **1994** Arz 11 (1) **1995**†Pit 15 (0) **1996**†Pit 16 (0) **1997**†Pit 16 (0) **1998** Pit 16 (1) **1999** Pit 15 (0) **2000**†NO 13 (1) **2001** NO 16 (1) **NFL** 155 (10) [12 yrs]

OLDHAM, JIM James R., E-B, 5'10"/183 lbs; Arizona; B1905, deceased **1926** Rac 5 (3, LE), 6

OLDHAM, RAY Donnil Ray, DB, 6'0"/200 lbs; Middle Tennessee State; 1973: Bal, rnd 8; B2/23/1951 Gallatin, TN, D7/25/2005 Chattanooga, TN **1973** Bal 11 (2) **1974** Bal 14 (10, LCB) **1975**†Bal 14 **1976**†Bal 14 (6, rcb) **1977**†Bal 14 **1978** Bal 2 **1978**†Pit 4 **1979** NYG 15 (11, FS) **1980** Det 16 (12, FS) **1981** Det 16 (16, SS) **1982** Det 5 (5, SS) **NFL** 125 (62) [10 yrs]

OLDS, BILL William Henry, RB, 6'1"/224 lbs; Nebraska; 1973: Bal, rnd 3; B2/21/1951 Kansas City, KS

YEAR	TEAM	G (GS, POS)	RUSH	YD	AVG(LG)	TD	REC	YD	AVG(LG)	TD	KPR	OTD	PTS	TAY
1973	Bal	13	26	100	3.8(17)	2	2	-4	-2.0(-1)	0	k	—	12	87
1974	Bal	13(FB)	129	475	3.7(34)	1	21	153	7.3(18)	2	—	18	572
1975	†Bal	14(FB)	94	281	3.0(14)	2	30	194	6.5(28)	2	—	24	408

YEAR	TEAM	G(GS, POS)	RUSH	YD	AVG(LG)	TD	REC	YD	AVG(LG)	TD	PASS	COMP	PCT	YD	AVG(LG)	TD	INT	SK	YD	QBR	KPR	OTD	PTS	TAY
1976	Sea	1(1)	2	9	4.5(6)	0	—	—	—	—	—	—	—	—	—	—	—	—	—	—	—	—	0	9
1976	Phi	11(3)	36	120	3.3(11)	1	9	29	3.2(14)	0	—	—	—	—	—	—	—	—	—	—	k	—	6	141
NFL	4	52(4)	287	985	3.4(34)	6	62	372	6.0(28)	4	—	—	—	—	—	—	—	—	—	—	k	—	60	1216

O'Leary, Dan Daniel Edward, TE, 6´3˝/248 lbs; Notre Dame; 2001: Buf, rnd 6; B9/1/1977 Cleveland, OH **2001** Buf 8 (0) **2002** Pit 4 (0) **2002** NYG 5 (0) **NFL** 17 (0) [2 yrs]

Olejniczak, Stan Stanley Joseph, aka Stan Olenn, T, 6´0˝/220 lbs; Pittsburgh; B5/21/1912 Nefts, OH, D3/11/1982 Buffalo, NY **1935** Pit 12 (6, rt)

Olenchalk, John John Hunt, LB-C, 6´0˝/228 lbs; Stanford; B11/27/1955 Stockton, CA **1981** KC 1 (0) **1982** KC 9 (0) **NFL** 10 (0) [2 yrs]

Olenski, Mitch Mitchell Joseph, T, 6´3˝/222 lbs; Alabama; 1944: Bkn, rnd 9; B1/14/1920 Benton, IL, D6/13/2000 **1946** Mia-A 14 (10, LT) **1947** Det 12 (8, RT)

Olerich, Dave David Byron, LB-TE, 6´1˝/220 lbs; San Francisco; B11/14/1944 Elmhurst, IL **1968** SF 14 **1969** SL 14 **1970** SL 11 **1971** Hou 14 **1972**†SF 12 **1973** SF 14

YEAR	TEAM	G(GS, POS)	RUSH	YD	AVG(LG)	TD	REC	YD	AVG(LG)	TD	PASS	COMP	PCT	YD	AVG(LG)	TD	INT	SK	YD	QBR	KPR	OTD	PTS	TAY
1967	SF	6	—	—	—	—	1	2	2.0(2)	0	—	—	—	—	—	—	—	—	—	—	—	—	0	1
NFL	7	85	—	—	—	—	1	2	2.0(2)	0	—	—	—	—	—	—	—	—	—	—	k	—	0	-51

Oliker, Aaron Aaron Earl, E, 5´11˝/170 lbs; West Virginia; B12/5/1903 Clarksburg, WV, D9/8/1965 Clarksburg, WV **1926** Pot 1 (1)

Oliphant, Elmer Elmer Quillen, WB-TB, 5´7˝/175 lbs; Purdue; Army; B7/9/1892 Bloomfield, IN, D7/3/1975 New Canaan, CT **[K]** **1920** Roc 1 (0) **1921** Buf☆10 (10, WB), 47 **NFL** 11 (10) [2 yrs]

Oliphant, Mike Michael Nathaniel, RB, 5´10˝/183 lbs; Puget Sound; 1988: Was, rnd 3; B5/19/1963 Jacksonville, FL

YEAR	TEAM	G(GS, POS)	RUSH	YD	AVG(LG)	TD	REC	YD	AVG(LG)	TD	PASS	COMP	PCT	YD	AVG(LG)	TD	INT	SK	YD	QBR	KPR	OTD	PTS	TAY
1988	Was	8(0)	8	30	3.8(20)	0	15	111	7.4(16)	0	—	—	—	—	—	—	—	—	—	—	kp	—	0	97
1989	†Cle	14(0)	15	97	6.5(21)	1	3	22	7.3(9)	0	—	—	—	—	—	—	—	—	—	—	k	—	6	112
1991	Cle	4(0)	—	—	—	—	—	—	—	—	—	—	—	—	—	—	—	—	—	—	—	—	—	—
NFL	3	26(0)	23	127	5.5(21)	1	18	133	7.4(16)	0	—	—	—	—	—	—	—	—	—	—	kp	—	6	209

Olive, Bobby Bobby Lee, WR, 6´0˝/167 lbs; Ohio State; 1991: KC, rnd 11; B4/22/1969 Paris, TN **1995** Ind 1 (0) **1996** Ind 1 (0) **NFL** 2 (0) [2 yrs]

Olivea, Shane Shane, T, 6´3˝/312 lbs; Ohio State; 2004: SD, rnd 7; B10/7/1981 Cedarhurst, NY **2004**†SD 16 (16, RT) **2005** SD 15 (15, RT) **NFL** 31 (31) [2 yrs]

Oliver, Bill William Seth, G, 5´11˝/180 lbs; Alabama; B2/16/1902 Panola, AL, D5/1/1932 Birmingham, AL **1927** NYY 13 (12, RG)

Oliver, Bob Robert Lee, DE, 6´3˝/240 lbs; Abilene Christian; 1969: Cle, rnd 17; B6/17/1947 Olney, TX **1969** Cle 8

Oliver, Chip Ralph, LB, 6´2˝/220 lbs; USC; 1968: Oak, rnd 11; B4/24/1944 Winona, MS **1968**†Oak-A 14 (10, LLB) **1969**†Oak-A 14 (6, llb) **NFL** 28 (16) [2 yrs]

Oliver, Clancy Clarence H., DB, 6´1˝/183 lbs; San Diego State; B11/17/1947 Bakersfield, CA **1969** Pit 9 **1970** Pit 14 (fs) **1973** SL 2 **NFL** 25 [3 yrs]

Oliver, Darryl Darryl Hiram, RB, 5´10˝/195 lbs; Miami (FL); 1987: Sea, rnd 11; B7/13/1964 Palatka, FL

YEAR	TEAM	G(GS, POS)	RUSH	YD	AVG(LG)	TD	REC	YD	AVG(LG)	TD	PASS	COMP	PCT	YD	AVG(LG)	TD	INT	SK	YD	QBR	KPR	OTD	PTS	TAY
1987	Atl	2(0)	1	0	0.0(0)	0	1	2	2.0(2)	0	—	—	—	—	—	—	—	—	—	—	k	—	0	16

Oliver, Frank Franklin Justice, DB, 6´1˝/194 lbs; Kentucky State; 1975: SF, rnd 4; B3/3/1952 Wetumpka, AL **1975** Buf 14 (2) **1976** TB 4 **NFL** 18 (2) [2 yrs]

Oliver, Greg Gregory Curtis, RB, 6´0˝/192 lbs; Trinity (TX); 1973: Phi, rnd 17; B1/15/1949 San Antonio, TX

YEAR	TEAM	G(GS, POS)	RUSH	YD	AVG(LG)	TD	REC	YD	AVG(LG)	TD	PASS	COMP	PCT	YD	AVG(LG)	TD	INT	SK	YD	QBR	KPR	OTD	PTS	TAY
1973	Phi	11	1	6	6.0(6)	0	1	9	9.0(9)	0	—	—	—	—	—	—	—	—	—	—	k	—	0	13
1974	Phi	14	7	19	2.7(7)	0	—	—	—	—	—	—	—	—	—	—	—	—	—	—	—	—	0	19
NFL	2	25	8	25	3.1(7)	0	1	9	9.0(9)	0	—	—	—	—	—	—	—	—	—	—	k	—	0	32

Oliver, Hubie Hubert, RB, 5´10˝/215 lbs; Arizona; 1981: Phi, rnd 10; B11/12/1957 Elyria, OH

YEAR	TEAM	G(GS, POS)	RUSH	YD	AVG(LG)	TD	REC	YD	AVG(LG)	TD	PASS	COMP	PCT	YD	AVG(LG)	TD	INT	SK	YD	QBR	KPR	OTD	PTS	TAY
1981	†Phi	13(10, FB)	75	329	4.4(39)	1	10	37	3.7(27)	0	—	—	—	—	—	—	—	—	—	—	—	—	6	358
1983	Phi	16(16, FB)	121	434	3.6(24)	1	49	421	8.6(25)	2	—	—	—	—	—	—	—	—	—	—	—	—	18	665
1984	Phi	16(15, FB)	72	263	3.7(17)	0	32	142	4.4(21)	0	—	—	—	—	—	—	—	—	—	—	—	—	0	334
1985	Phi	1(0)	1	3	3.0(3)	0	1	4	4.0(4)	0	—	—	—	—	—	—	—	—	—	—	—	—	0	5
1986	Ind	4(0)	—	—	—	—	—	—	—	—	—	—	—	—	—	—	—	—	—	—	—	—	—	—
1986	Hou	2(0)	1	1	1.0(1)	0	1	-2	-2.0(-2)	0	—	—	—	—	—	—	—	—	—	—	—	—	0	0
NFL	5	52(41)	270	1030	3.8(39)	2	93	602	6.5(27)	2	—	—	—	—	—	—	—	—	—	—	—	—	24	1361

Oliver, Jack John Gerald, T, 6´3˝/281 lbs; Texas-El Paso; Memphis; 1985: NYG, rnd 6; B2/3/1962 Washington, DC **1987** ChiB 3 (3)

Oliver, Jeff Jeffrey Peter, T-G, 6´4˝/292 lbs; Boston College; B7/28/1965 Delhi, NY **1989** NYJ 1 (0)

Oliver, Louis Louis, DB, 6´2˝/224 lbs; Florida; 1989: Mia, rnd 1; B3/9/1966 Belle Glade, FL **[I]** **1989** Mia 15 (13, FS) **1990**†Mia☆16 (16, FS) **1991** Mia 16 (16, FS) **1992**†Mia☆16 (16, FS) **1993** Mia 11 (11, FS) **1994** Cin 12 (12, SS) **1995**†Mia 15 (5, fs) **1996** Mia 16 (12, SS) **NFL** 117 (101) [8 yrs]

Oliver, Maurice Julius Maurice, LB, 6´3˝/235 lbs; Southern Mississippi; B6/14/1967 Birmingham, AL **1991** TB 3 (0)

Oliver, Muhammad Muhammad Ramadan, DB, 5´11˝/185 lbs; Oregon; 1992: Den, rnd 9; B3/12/1969 Brooklyn, NY **1992** Den 3 (0) **1993** KC 2 (0) **1993** GB 2 (0) **1994**†Mia 13 (2) **1995** Was 1 (0) **NFL** 21 (2) [4 yrs]

Oliver, Vince Vincent James, QB, 5´11˝/180 lbs; Indiana; B12/28/1915 Whiting, IN, D8/28/1985 Chicago, IL

YEAR	TEAM	G(GS, POS)	RUSH	YD	AVG(LG)	TD	REC	YD	AVG(LG)	TD	PASS	COMP	PCT	YD	AVG(LG)	TD	INT	SK	YD	QBR	KPR	OTD	PTS	TAY
1945	ChiC	3(1)	11	-3	-0.3(15)	0	—	—	—	—	10	4	40.0	22	2.2(10)	0	0	—	—	—	—	—	0	8

Oliver, Winslow Winslow Paul, RB, 5´7˝/180 lbs; New Mexico; 1996: Car, rnd 3; B3/3/1973 Houston, TX **[R]**

YEAR	TEAM	G(GS, POS)	RUSH	YD	AVG(LG)	TD	REC	YD	AVG(LG)	TD	PASS	COMP	PCT	YD	AVG(LG)	TD	INT	SK	YD	QBR	KPR	OTD	PTS	TAY
1996	†Car	16(0)	47	183	3.9(16)	0	15	144	9.6(29)	0	—	—	—	—	—	—	—	—	—	—	kp	1	6	658
1997	Car	6(0)	1	0	0.0(0)	0	6	47	7.8(11)	0	—	—	—	—	—	—	—	—	—	—	p	—	0	65
1998	Car	16(0)	—	—	—	—	—	—	—	—	—	—	—	—	—	—	—	—	—	—	kp	—	0	257
1999	Atl	14(0)	8	32	4.0(10)	0	8	74	9.3(14)	0	—	—	—	—	—	—	—	—	—	—	kp	1	6	252
2000	Atl	12(0)	—	—	—	—	—	—	—	—	—	—	—	—	—	—	—	—	—	—	kp	—	0	4
NFL	5	64(0)	56	215	3.8(16)	0	29	265	9.1(29)	0	—	—	—	—	—	—	—	—	—	—	kp	2	12	1236

Olivo, Brock Brock James, RB, 6´0˝/226 lbs; Missouri; B6/24/1976 St. Louis, MO

YEAR	TEAM	G(GS, POS)	RUSH	YD	AVG(LG)	TD	REC	YD	AVG(LG)	TD	PASS	COMP	PCT	YD	AVG(LG)	TD	INT	SK	YD	QBR	KPR	OTD	PTS	TAY
1998	Det	1(0)	—	—	—	—	—	—	—	—	—	—	—	—	—	—	—	—	—	—	—	—	—	—
1999	Det	14(0)	1	1	1.0(1)	0	4	24	6.0(12)	0	—	—	—	—	—	—	—	—	—	—	k	—	0	46
2000	Det	13(0)	—	—	—	—	3	50	16.7(19)	0	—	—	—	—	—	—	—	—	—	—	k	—	0	5
2001	Det	16(0)	1	6	6.0(6)	0	—	—	—	—	—	—	—	—	—	—	—	—	—	—	k	—	0	31
NFL	4	44(0)	2	7	3.5(6)	0	7	74	10.6(19)	0	—	—	—	—	—	—	—	—	—	—	k	—	0	82

Olkewicz, Neal Neal, LB, 6´0˝/230 lbs; Maryland; B1/30/1957 Phoenixville, PA **1979** Was 16 (9, MLB) **1980** Was 12 (11, MLB) **1981** Was 14 (14, MLB) **1982**†Was 9 (9, MLB) **1983**†Was 16 (16, MLB) **1984**†Was 16 (16, MLB) **1985** Was 16 (16, MLB) **1986**†Was 16 (16, MLB) **1987**†Was 10 (6, MLB) **1988** Was 16 (16, MLB) **1989** Was 9 (8, MLB) **NFL** 150 (137) [11 yrs]

Olmstead, Charlie Charles Howard, G, none; B3/21/1898 Louisville, KY, D12/16/1970 Louisville, KY **1922** Lou 3 (2) **1923** Lou 3 (3, RG) **NFL** 6 (5) [2 yrs]

Olsavsky, Jerry Jerome Daniel, LB, 6´1˝/221 lbs; Pittsburgh; 1989: Pit, rnd 10; B3/29/1967 Youngstown, OH **1989**†Pit 16 (8, rilb) **1990** Pit 15 (0) **1991** Pit 16 (4) **1992**†Pit 7 (0) **1993** Pit 7 (7, rilb) **1994** Pit 1 (0) **1995**†Pit 15 (5, rilb) **1996**†Pit 15 (13, RILB) **1997**†Pit 16 (0) **1998** Bal 9 (0) **NFL** 117 (37) [10 yrs]

Olsen, Hans Hans Christian, DT, 6´4˝/304 lbs; Brigham Young; B7/31/1977 Caldwell, ID **2001** Ind 2 (0)

Olsen, Merlin Merlin Jay, DT, 6´5˝/270 lbs; Utah State; 1962: LA, rnd 1/Den, rnd 1; B9/15/1940 Logan, UT; HOF 1982 **1962** LARm✧12 (12, LDT) **1963** LARm★14 (LDT) **1964** LARm★14 (LDT) **1965** LARm★14 (LDT) **1966** LARm★14 (LDT) **1967**†LARm★14 (LDT) **1968** LARm★14 (14, LDT) **1969**†LARm★14 (14, LDT) **1970** LARm★14 (14, LDT) **1971** LARm★14 (14, LDT) **1972** LARm★14 (14, LDT) **1973**†LARm★14 (14, RDT) **1974**†LARm★14 (14, RDT) **1975**†LARm★14 (14, RDT) **1976**†LARm 14 (14, RDT) **NFL** 208 (138) [15 yrs]

Olsen, Norm Norman E., T, 6´2˝/220 lbs; Alabama; B12/1/1921 New York, NY **1944** Cle 10 (0)

Olsen, Orrin Orrin James, C, 6´1˝/245 lbs; Brigham Young; 1976: KC, rnd 8; B7/7/1953 Logan, UT **1976** KC 14

Olsen, Phil Phil Vernor, DT-C, 6´5˝/265 lbs; Utah State; 1970: Bos, rnd 1; B4/26/1948 Logan, UT **1971** LARm 10 (8, RDT) **1972** LARm 14 **1973**†LARm 14 **1974**†LARm 14 **1975** Den 14 **1976** Den 13 (1) **NFL** 79 (9) [6 yrs]

Olsen, Ralph Ralph Kenneth, DE, 6´4˝/220 lbs; Utah; 1947: GB, rnd 32; B4/10/1924 Salt Lake City, UT, D11/28/1994 Fruit Heights, UT **1949** GB 4 (0)

Olshansky, Igor Igor, DE-DT, 6´6˝/309 lbs; Oregon; 2004: SD, rnd 2; B5/3/1982 Dnepropetrovsk, Ukraine **2004**†SD 16 (16, RDE) **2005** SD 14 (12, RDE) **NFL** 30 (28) [2 yrs]

YEAR	TEAM	G(GS, POS)	RUSH	YD	AVG(LG)	TD	REC	YD	AVG(LG)	TD	PASS	COMP	PCT	YD	AVG(LG)	TD	INT	SK	YD	QBR	KPR	OTD	PTS	TAY

OLSON, BENJI Benjamin Dempsey, G, 6´4˝/320 lbs; Washington; 1998: Ten, rnd 5; B6/5/1975 Bremerton, WA **1998** Ten 13 (1) **1999**†Ten 16 (16, RG) **2000**†Ten 16 (16, RG) **2001** Ten 16 (16, RG) **2002**†Ten 16 (16, RG) **2003**†Ten 16 (16, RG) **2004** Ten 15 (15, RG) **2005** Ten 16 (16, RG) **NFL** 124 (112) [8 yrs]

OLSON, CARL Carl Virgil, T, 6´2˝/206 lbs; UCLA; B1/16/1917 San Francisco, CA **1942** ChiC 2 (0)

OLSON, ERIK Erik Kames, DB, 6´1˝/210 lbs; Colorado State; 2000: Jax, rnd 7; B1/4/1977 Ventura, CA **2000** Jax 14 (0)

OLSON, FORREST Forrest Morten, G-FB, 6´0˝/200 lbs; Iowa; B11/15/1902 Vermillion, SD, D12/13/1979 Sioux City, IA **1927** NYY 3 (0)

OLSON, GLENN Glenn Earl, BB, 6´0˝/195 lbs; Iowa; B3/14/1915 Colo, IA, D5/1973 **1940** Cle 2 (0)

OLSON, HAROLD Harold Vincent, T, 6´2˝/255 lbs; Clemson; 1960: Buf, rnd 1/SL, rnd 2; B1/19/1938 Asheville, NC **1960** Buf-A 14 (LT) **1961** Buf-A✧14 (RT) **1962** Buf-A☆14 (RT) **1963** Den-A 14 (LT) **1964** Den-A 14 (LT) **NFL** 70 [5 yrs]

OLSONOSKI, LARRY Lawrence Rodney, G, 6´2˝/214 lbs; Minnesota; 1948: GB, rnd 6/SF-A, rnd 15; B9/10/1925 Lancaster, MN, D3/6/1991 Edina, MN **1948** GB 12 (2) **1949** GB 4 (0) **1949** NYB 8 (2) **NFL** 24 (4) [2 yrs]

OLSSEN, LANCE Lance Everett, T-C, 6´5˝/257 lbs; Purdue; 1968: SF, rnd 3; B4/17/1947 Boston, MA **1968** SF 7 **1969** SF 2 **NFL** 9 [2 yrs]

OLSSON, LES Carl Lester, G, 6´0˝/232 lbs; Mercer; B8/18/1909 Akron, OH, D7/3/1972 Barberton, OH **1934** Bos 12 (9, RG) **1935** Bos 11 (10, RG) **1936**†Bos☆12 (10, LG) **1937**†Was☆11 (9, LG) **1938** Was☆11 (9, LG) **NFL** 57 (47) [5 yrs]

OLSZEWSKI, AL Albert Frank, E, 6´2˝/185 lbs; Penn State; Pittsburgh; B11/14/1920

| 1945 | Pit | 1 (0) | — | — | — | — | 2 | 28 | 14.0 (22) | 0 | — | — | — | — | — | — | — | — | — | | | — | 0 | 14 |

OLSZEWSKI, JOHNNY John Peter 'Johnny O', FB-HB, 5´11˝/200 lbs; California; 1953: ChiC, rnd 1; B12/21/1930 Washington, DC, D12/8/1996

1953	ChiC★	12 (FB)	106	386	3.6 (34)	4	21	210	10.0 (77)	1	1	0	0.0	0	0.0	0	—	—	—		kp	—	30	493
1954	ChiC	11 (RH)	106	352	3.3 (23)	1	12	133	11.1 (25)	1	—	—	—	—	—	—	—	—	—		k	—	12	440
1955	ChiC✧	11 (FB)	84	326	3.9 (41)	1	9	37	4.1 (9)	0	—	—	—	—	—	—	—	—	—		k	—	6	351
1956	ChiC☆	11 (FB)	157	598	3.8 (34)	2	17	182	10.7 (31)	0	—	—	—	—	—	—	—	—	—		k	—	12	689
1957	ChiC	11 (FB)	83	271	3.3 (38)	2	3	36	12.0 (24)	0	—	—	—	—	—	—	—	—	—		—	—	12	322
1958	Was	10 (FB)	98	505	5.2 (45)	2	11	102	9.3 (36)	0	—	—	—	—	—	—	—	—	—		kp	—	12	553
1959	Was	10 (LH)	65	432	**6.6 (65)**	1	7	62	8.9 (15)	0	—	—	—	—	—	—	—	—	—		p	—	6	468
1960	Was	11 (LH)	75	227	3.0 (15)	3	10	62	6.2 (31)	0	—	—	—	—	—	—	—	—	—		kp	—	18	327
1961	Det	14	30	109	3.6 (15)	0	1	14	14.0 (14)	0	—	—	—	—	—	—	—	—	—		k	—	0	115
1962	Den-A	12	33	114	3.5 (46)	0	13	150	11.5 (26)	1	—	—	—	—	—	—	—	—	—		k	—	6	215
NFL	10	113	837	3320	4.0 (65)	16	104	988	9.5 (77)	3	1	0	0.0	0	0.0	0	—	0	1		kp	—	114	3972

OLTZ, RUSS Russell Manning, C-G-T-FB, 6´0˝/210 lbs; Illinois; B3/18/1899 Beloit, WI, D6/2/1956 **1920** Ham 5 (2, LG) **1921** Ham 5 (5, RG), 6 **1923** Ham 7 (7, C) **1924** Ham 5 (4, RT) **1925** Ham 5 (5, C) **NFL** 27 (23) [5 yrs]

O'MAHONEY, JIM James John, LB, 6´1˝/228 lbs; Miami (FL); 1963: Min, rnd 8; B3/29/1941 Pittsburgh, PA **1965** NYJ-A 14 **1966** NYJ-A 12 **NFL** 26 [2 yrs]

O'MALLEY, JIM James John, LB, 6´1˝/229 lbs; Notre Dame; 1973: Den, rnd 12; B7/24/1951 Youngstown, OH **1973** Den 12 **1974** Den 14 (5, rlb) **1975** Den 14 **NFL** 40 (5) [3 yrs]

O'MALLEY, JOE Joseph Patrick, DE, 6´2˝/218 lbs; Georgia; 1955: ChiB, rnd 4; B1/1/1933 Scranton, PA **1955** Pit 10 **1956** Pit 12 (LDE) **NFL** 22 [2 yrs]

O'MALLEY, TOM Thomas Louis, QB, 5´11˝/185 lbs; Cincinnati; B7/23/1925

| 1950 | GB | 1 | 1 | -9 | -9.0 (-9) | 0 | — | — | — | — | 15 | 4 | 26.7 | 31 | 2.1 (20) | 0 | 6 | — | — | | — | — | 0 | -234 |

OMENSKY G, none **1926** Lou 1 (1)

O'NEAL, ANDRE Andre T., LB, 6´1˝/235 lbs; Marshall; B12/12/1975 Decatur, GA **2000** KC 10 (0) **2001** KC 3 (0) **2001** GB 2 (0) **2001** Min 4 (1) **NFL** 19 (1) [2 yrs]

O'NEAL, BRIAN Brian Louis, FB, 6´0˝/233 lbs; Penn State; B2/25/1970 Cincinnati, OH **1994** Phi 14 (0) **1995**†SF 3 (0) **NFL** 17 (0) [2 yrs]

O'NEAL, CALVIN Calvin, LB, 6´1˝/235 lbs; Michigan; 1977: Bal, rnd 6; B10/6/1954 Osceola, AR **1978** Bal 15

O'NEAL, DELTHA Deltha Lee, DB, 5´10˝/196 lbs; California; 2000: Den, rnd 1; B1/30/1977 Palo Alto, CA **[RI]** **2000**†Den 16 (0) **2001** Den★16 (16, LCB) **2002** Den 16 (14, LCB) **2004** Cin 12 (10, LCB) **2005**†Cin★15 (14, LCB)

| 2003 | Den | 13 (6, rcb) | 1 | 0 | 0.0 (0) | 0 | 2 | 4 | 2.0 (3) | 0 | — | — | — | — | — | — | — | — | — | | kpi | 1 | 6 | 171 |
| NFL | 6 | 88 (60) | 1 | 0 | 0.0 | 0 | 2 | 4 | 2.0 (3) | 0 | — | — | — | — | — | — | — | — | — | | kpiS | 6 | 36 | 1373 |

O'NEAL, JIM James C. Summer, G, 6´1˝/230 lbs; TCU; Texas-El Paso; Southwestern (TX); B2/13/1924 Anna, TX **1946** ChiR-A 12 (5, rg) **1947** ChiR-A 12 (5, rg) **AAFC** 24 (7) [2 yrs]

O'NEAL, KEN Kenneth Adrian, TE, 6´3˝/240 lbs; Idaho State; B6/21/1962 San Francisco, CA

| 1987 | NO | 2 (0) | — | — | — | — | 3 | 10 | 3.3 (5) | 1 | — | — | — | — | — | — | — | — | — | | — | — | 6 | 10 |

O'NEAL, LESLIE Leslie Claudis, DE-LB, 6´4˝/264 lbs; Oklahoma State; 1986: SD, rnd 1; B5/7/1964 Pulaski County, AR **[S]** **1986** SD 13 (13, RDE) **1988** SD 9 (1) **1989** SD★16 (16, ROLB) **1990** SD★16 (16, ROLB) **1991** SD 16 (16, ROLB) **1992**†SD★15 (15, RDE) **1993** SD✧16 (16, RDE) **1994**†SD★16 (16, RDE) **1995**†SD★16 (16, RDE) **1996** SL 16 (16, RDE) **1997** SL 15 (14, RDE) **1998** KC 16 (13, LDE/lolb) **1999** KC 10 (10, RDE) **NFL** 196 (178) [13 yrs]

O'NEAL, ROBERT Robert Oliver, DB, 6´1˝/199 lbs; Clemson; 1993: Mia, rnd 6; B2/1/1971 Atlanta, GA **1994** Ind 2 (0)

O'NEAL, STEVE Stephen James, P, 6´3˝/185 lbs; Texas A&M; 1969: NYJ, rnd 13; B2/4/1946 Hearne, TX **[P]**

1969	†NYJ-A	14	—	—	—	—	—	—	—	—	—	—	—	—	—	—	—	—	—		P	—	0	0
1970	NYJ	14	1	16	16.0 (16)	0	—	—	—	—	1	1	100.0	2	2.0 (2)	0	0	—	—		P	—	0	17
1971	NYJ	14	—	—	—	—	—	—	—	—	1	0	0.0	0	0.0	0	0	—	—		P	—	0	0
1972	NYJ	14	—	—	—	—	—	—	—	—	—	—	—	—	—	—	—	—	—		P	—	0	0
1973	NO	14	2	-1	-0.5 (6)	0	—	—	—	—	—	—	—	—	—	—	—	—	—		P	—	0	-1
NFL	5	70	3	15	5.0 (16)	0	—	—	—	—	2	1	50.0	2	1.0 (2)	0	0	—	—		P	—	0	16

O'NEIL, BOB Robert Maioli, G-DE-LB, 6´1˝/229 lbs; Duquesne; Notre Dame; 1953: Pit, rnd 15; B2/21/1931 **1956** Pit 12 (LG) **1957** Pit 12 (LDE)

| 1961 | NYT-A | 14 | — | — | — | — | 1 | -13 | -13.0 (-13) | 0 | — | — | — | — | — | — | — | — | — | | — | — | 0 | -7 |
| NFL | 3 | 38 | — | — | — | — | 1 | -13 | -13.0 (-13) | 0 | — | — | — | — | — | — | — | — | — | | — | 1 | 6 | -7 |

O'NEIL, CHUCK Charles Leo, E-B, 5´10˝/180 lbs; Phillips; B3/25/1898, D11/1951 **1921** Evv 5 (5, RE) **1922** Evv 1 (1) **1922** Tol 1 (0) **1923** Tol 2 (0) **NFL** 9 (6) [3 yrs]

O'NEIL, ED Edward William, LB, 6´3˝/236 lbs; Penn State; 1974: Det, rnd 1; B9/8/1952 Warren, PA **1974** Det 14 **1975** Det 14 (6, rlb) **1977** Det 14 (11, MLB) **1980** GB 12 (11, LILB)

1976	Det	14 (4)	—	—	—	—	1	32	32.0 (32)	1	—	—	—	—	—	—	—	—	—		i	—	6	32
1978	Det	16 (16, MLB)	1	25	25.0 (25)	0	—	—	—	—	—	—	—	—	—	—	—	—	—		i	—	0	54
1979	Det	16 (12, LLB)	1	0	0.0 (0)	0	—	—	—	—	—	—	—	—	—	—	—	—	—		i	—	0	0
NFL	7	100 (60)	2	25	12.5 (25)	0	1	32	32.0 (32)	1	—	—	—	—	—	—	—	—	—		i	2	18	86

O'NEIL, KEITH Keith, LB, 6´0˝/230 lbs; Northern Arizona; B8/26/1980 Rochester, MN **2003**†Dal 15 (0) **2004** Dal 16 (0) **2005** Ind 11 (0) **NFL** 42 (0) [3 yrs]

O'NEIL, RED Charles, C, 5´10˝/190 lbs; Connecticut; B12/1899 New Haven, CT, D1955 **1926** Har 9 (7, C), 6

O'NEILL, BILL William James, B, 6´0˝/187 lbs; Detroit Mercy; B4/25/1910 Chicago, IL **1935** Det 1 (0)

| 1937 | Cle | 1 (0) | 4 | 12 | 3.0 | 0 | — | — | — | — | 2 | 1 | 50.0 | 20 | 10.0 (20) | 0 | 1 | — | — | | — | — | 0 | -18 |
| NFL | 2 | 2 (0) | 4 | 12 | 3.0 | 0 | — | — | — | — | 2 | 1 | 50.0 | 20 | 10.0 (20) | 0 | 1 | — | — | | — | — | 0 | -18 |

O'NEILL, KEVIN Kevin Christopher, LB, 6´2˝/239 lbs; Bowling Green State; B4/14/1975 Twinsburg, OH **1998** Det 11 (0) **1999**†Det 4 (0) **2000** Det 11 (0) **NFL** 26 (0) [3 yrs]

O'NEILL, PAT Patrick James, P, 6´1˝/200 lbs; Syracuse; 1994: NE, rnd 5; B2/9/1971 Scott AFB, IL **[K]** **1994**†NE 16 (0) **1995** NE 8 (0) **1995** ChiB 1 (0) **NFL** 25 (0) [2 yrs]

O'NEILL, TIP Gerald Raphael, WB, 5´10˝/170 lbs; St. Norbert; Detroit Mercy; B10/24/1898 Sault Saint Marie, MI, D12/6/1984 Boynton Beach, FL **1922** Day 4 (0), 6

O'NEILL, WALLY Richard Wallace, E-G-T, 6´0˝/195 lbs; Wisconsin-Superior; B3/27/1899, MI, D1/1973 Aberdeen, SD **1925** Dul 3 (1)

ONESTI, LARRY Lawrence Joseph, LB, 6´0˝/195 lbs; Northwestern; 1962: Hou, rnd 9/Chi, rnd 8; B11/12/1938 Chicago, IL **1962**†Hou-A 4 **1963** Hou-A 14 **1964** Hou-A 6 (mlb) **1965** Hou-A 14 **NFL** 38 [4 yrs]

ONKOTZ, DENNIS Dennis Henry, LB, 6´1˝/220 lbs; Penn State; 1970: NYJ, rnd 3; B2/6/1948 Northampton, PA **1970** NYJ 9

ONTKO, BOB Robert Paul, LB, 6´3˝/237 lbs; Penn State; 1987: Ind, rnd 9; B3/21/1964 Kingston, PA **1987** Ind 3 (3)

YEAR	TEAM	G (GS, POS)	RUSH	YD	AVG(LG)	TD	REC	YD	AVG(LG)	TD	PASS COMP	PCT	YD	AVG(LG)	TD	INT	SK	YD	QBR	KPR	OTD	PTS	TAY
OPALEWSKI, ED	Edward L., T, 6´3˝/230 lbs; Eastern Michigan; B11/11/1919 Detroit, MI, D3/4/1993 Novi, MI																			**1943** Det 2 (0)	**1944** Det 9 (5, lt)	**NFL** 11 (5) [2 yrs]	
OPFAR, DAVE	David Louis, NT, 6´4˝/270 lbs; Penn State; B1/16/1960 McKeesport, PA																			**1987** Pit 3 (1)			
OPPERMAN, JIM	James Jay, LB, 6´3˝/220 lbs; Colorado State; B12/18/1953 Waterbury, CT																			**1975** Phi 10			
O'QUINN, RED	John William, DB-E, 6´2˝/195 lbs; Wake Forest; 1949: ChiB, rnd 3/Bal-A, rnd 16; B9/7/1925 Bluett Falls, NC, D4/21/2002 Ottawa, Canada																			**1950** ChiB 12 (DB)			
1951 ChiB 2																							
1951	Phi	5	—	—	—	—	3	58	19.3(34)	0	—	—	—	—	—	—	—	—	—	—	—	0	29
NFL	2	19	—	—	—	—	3	58	19.3(34)	0	—	—	—	—	—	—	—	—	—	i	1	6	97
ORDUNA, JOE	Joseph Manuel, RB, 6´0˝/195 lbs; Nebraska; 1971: SF, rnd 2; B11/6/1948 Omaha, NE																						
1972	NYG	11	36	129	3.6(17)	1	4	6	1.5(6)	1	—	—	—	—	—	—	—	—	—	k	—	12	211
1973	NYG	14	36	104	2.9(25)	1	6	44	7.3(17)	0	—	—	—	—	—	—	—	—	—	k	—	6	150
1974	Bal	14	2	3	1.5(2)	1	1	8	8.0(8)	0	—	—	—	—	—	—	—	—	—	k	—	6	40
NFL	3	39	74	236	3.2(25)	3	11	58	5.3(17)	1	—	—	—	—	—	—	—	—	—	k	—	24	401
ORI, FRANK	Frank, G, 6´2˝/244 lbs; Northern Iowa; B3/20/1964 Highland Park, IL																			**1987** Min 3 (3)			
ORIARD, MIKE	Michael Vincent, C-G, 6´4˝/223 lbs; Notre Dame; 1970: KC, rnd 5; B5/26/1948 Spokane, WA																			**1970** KC 1	**1971**†KC 14 **1972** KC 14 **1973** KC 13	**NFL** 42 [4 yrs]	
ORISTAGLIO, BOB	Robert Peter, DE-E, 6´2˝/214 lbs; Pennsylvania; B4/6/1924 Philadelphia, PA, D2/14/1995 York, PA																						
1949	†Buf-A	12(0)	—	—	—	—	1	14	14.0(14)	0	—	—	—	—	—	—	—	—	—	—	—	0	7
1950	Bal	12(3)	—	—	—	—	14	134	9.6(16)	0	—	—	—	—	—	—	—	—	—	k	—	0	69
1951	†Cle	12(lde)	—	—	—	—	1	20	20.0(20)	1	—	—	—	—	—	—	—	—	—	—	—	6	15
1952	Phi	4	—	—	—	—	—	—	—	—	—	—	—	—	—	—	—	—	—	—	—	0	0
NFL	3	28(3)	—	—	—	—	15	154	10.3(20)	1	—	—	—	—	—	—	—	—	—	k	—	6	84
ORLANDO, BO	Joseph John, DB, 5´10˝/180 lbs; West Virginia; 1989: Hou, rnd 6; B4/3/1966 Berwick, PA																			**1990**†Hou 16 (0)	**1991**†Hou 16 (16, FS)	**1992**†Hou 6 (1)	
1993†Hou 16 (3) **1994** Hou 16 (0) **1995**†SD 16 (16, FS) **1996** Cin 16 (16, FS) **1997** Cin 16 (2) **1998** Pit 11 (1) **NFL** 129 (55) [9 yrs]																							
ORLICH, DAN	Daniel E., DE-E, 6´5˝/215 lbs; Northwestern; Penn State; UNLV; 1949: GB, rnd 8; B12/21/1924 Chisholm, MN																						
1949	GB	12(2)	—	—	—	—	4	39	9.8(12)	0	—	—	—	—	—	—	—	—	—	—	—	0	20
1950	GB	12(LDE)	—	—	—	—	—	—	—	—	—	—	—	—	—	—	—	—	—	i	1	6	-5
1951	GB	12(LDE)	—	—	—	—	1	9	9.0(9)	0	—	—	—	—	—	—	—	—	—	—	—	0	5
NFL	3	36(2)	—	—	—	—	5	48	9.6(12)	0	—	—	—	—	—	—	—	—	—	i	1	6	19
ORLOVSKY, DAN	Daniel John, QB, 6´4˝/238 lbs; Connecticut; 2005: Det, rnd 5; B8/18/1983 Bridgeport, CT																						
2005	Det	2(0)	—	—	—	—	—	—	—	—	17	7	41.2	63	3.7(20)	0	0	1	3	—	—	0	32
ORMSBEE, ELLIOTT	Ezra Elliott, HB, 5´11˝/185 lbs; Bradley; 1944: Phi, rnd 11; B9/19/1921 Hamilton, IL																						
1946	Phi	4(0)	4	12	3.0(11)	0	—	—	—	—	—	—	—	—	—	—	—	—	—	k	—	0	2
ORNS, FRED	Frederick Karl, LB, 6´2˝/230 lbs; Chapman; B5/24/1962																			**1987** Sea 2 (0)			
OROSZ, TOM	Thomas Paul, P, 6´1˝/204 lbs; Ohio State; B9/26/1959 Painesville, PA																			**1982**†Mia 9 (0)	**1984** SF 2 (0)		
1981	†Mia	16(0)	1	13	13.0(13)	0	—	—	—	—	—	—	—	—	—	—	—	—	—	P	—	0	13
1983	†SF	16(0)	2	39	19.5(23)	0	—	—	—	—	—	—	—	—	—	—	—	—	—	P	—	0	39
NFL	4	43(0)	3	52	17.3(23)	0	—	—	—	—	—	—	—	—	—	—	—	—	—	P	—	0	52
O'ROURKE, CHARLIE	Charles Christopher, QB, 5´11˝/175 lbs; Boston College; 1941: ChiB, rnd 5; B5/10/1917 Montreal, Canada, D4/14/2000 Brockton, MA																						
1942	†ChiB	11(1, qb)	18	-17	-0.9(17)	1	—	—	—	—	88	37	42.0	951	10.8(68)	11	—	—	—	Ppi	—	6	-119
1946	LAD-A	14(8, QB)	47	50	1.1	1	—	—	—	—	182	105	57.7	1250	6.9(68)	12	14	—	—	Pk	—	6	205
1947	LAD-A	14(9, QB)	24	55	2.3	1	—	—	—	—	178	89	50.0	1449	8.1(54)	13	16	—	—	k	—	6	224
1948	†Bal-A	14(1)	7	15	2.1	1	—	—	—	—	51	24	47.1	377	7.4	3	4	—	—	P	—	6	69
1949	Bal-A	5(0)	—	—	—	—	—	—	—	—	7	1	14.3	12	1.7(12)	1	1	—	—	P	—	0	-34
AAFC	4	47(18)	78	120	1.5(17)	3	—	—	—	—	418	219	52.4	3088	7.4(68)	28	35	—	—	Pk	—	18	463
ORR, JIMMY	James Edward, FL-E-SE-WR, 5´11˝/185 lbs; Wake Forest; Clemson; Georgia; 1957: LA, rnd 25; B10/4/1935 Seneca, SC																						
1958	Pit☆	12(LE)	1	8	8.0(8)	0	33	910	27.6(78)	7	—	—	—	—	—	—	—	—	—	P	—	42	498
1959	Pit★	12(RE)	5	43	8.6(29)	0	35	604	17.3(43)	5	1	0	0.0	0	0.0	0	0	—	—	P	—	30	370
1960	Pit	12(FL)	8	57	7.1(19)	0	29	541	18.7(51)	4	—	—	—	—	—	—	—	—	—	—	—	24	348
1961	Bal	13	—	—	—	—	18	357	19.8(64)	4	—	—	—	—	—	—	—	—	—	—	—	24	199
1962	Bal	14(FL)	1	14	14.0(14)	0	55	974	17.7(80)	11	—	—	—	—	—	—	—	—	—	—	—	66	556
1963	Bal	12(FL)	—	—	—	—	41	708	17.3(60)	5	—	—	—	—	—	—	—	—	—	—	—	30	379
1964	†Bal	14(FL)	—	—	—	—	40	867	21.7(69)	6	—	—	—	—	—	—	—	—	—	—	—	36	464
1965	†Bal★	14(FL)	—	—	—	—	45	847	18.8(57)	10	—	—	—	—	—	—	—	—	—	—	—	60	474
1966	Bal	13(FL)	—	—	—	—	37	618	16.7(61)	3	—	—	—	—	—	—	—	—	—	—	—	18	324
1967	Bal	5	—	—	—	—	3	72	24.0(55)	1	—	—	—	—	—	—	—	—	—	—	—	6	41
1968	†Bal	13(SE)	—	—	—	—	29	743	25.6(84)	6	—	—	—	—	—	—	—	—	—	—	—	36	402
1969	Bal	7(SE)	—	—	—	—	25	474	19.0(47)	2	—	—	—	—	—	—	—	—	—	—	—	12	247
1970	†Bal	8	—	—	—	—	10	199	19.9(29)	2	—	—	—	—	—	—	—	—	—	—	—	12	110
NFL	13	149	15	122	8.1(29)	0	400	7914	19.8(84)	66	1	0	0.0	0	0.0	0	0	—	—	P	—	396	4409
ORR, RAHEEM	Raheem, LB, 6´3˝/258 lbs; Rutgers; 2004: Hou, rnd 7; B11/8/1980 Elizabeth, NJ																			**2004** NYG 2 (0)			
ORR, SHANTEE	Shantee DeShJuan, LB, 6´0˝/250 lbs; Michigan; B5/28/1981 Detroit, MI																			**2003** Hou 6 (0) **2004** Hou 4 (0) **2005** Hou 16 (12, LOLB)	**NFL** 26 (12) [3 yrs]		
ORR, TERRY	Terrance, TE, 6´3˝/231 lbs; Texas; 1985: Was, rnd 10; B9/27/1961 Savannah, GA																						
1986	†Was	16(1)	—	—	—	—	3	45	15.0(22)	1	—	—	—	—	—	—	—	—	—	k	—	6	29
1987	†Was	10(1)	—	—	—	—	3	35	11.7(23)	0	—	—	—	—	—	—	—	—	—	k	—	0	20
1988	Was	16(3)	—	—	—	—	11	222	20.2(58)	2	—	—	—	—	—	—	—	—	—	kp	—	12	112
1989	Was	16(1)	—	—	—	—	3	80	26.7(48)	0	—	—	—	—	—	—	—	—	—	—	—	0	25
1990	Was	2(0)	—	—	—	—	—	—	—	—	—	—	—	—	—	—	—	—	—	—	—	0	—
1990	SD	9(0)	—	—	—	—	—	—	—	—	—	—	—	—	—	—	—	—	—	k	—	0	-2
1991	†Was	16(6, te)	—	—	—	—	10	201	20.1(47)	4	—	—	—	—	—	—	—	—	—	—	—	24	121
1992	†Was	16(7, te)	—	—	—	—	22	356	16.2(58)	3	—	—	—	—	—	—	—	—	—	k	—	18	181
1993	Was	4(0)	—	—	—	—	—	—	—	—	—	—	—	—	—	—	—	—	—	—	—	0	—
NFL	8	105(19)	—	—	—	—	52	939	18.1(58)	10	—	—	—	—	—	—	—	—	—	kp	—	60	485
ORTEGA, RALPH	Ralph, LB, 6´2˝/220 lbs; Florida; 1975: Atl, rnd 2; B7/6/1953 Havana, Cuba																			**1975** Atl 14 **1976** Atl 14 (4) **1977** Atl 14 (MLB) **1978** Atl 15 **1979** Mia 8			
1980 Mia 16 (6, lilb) **NFL** 81 (10) [6 yrs]																							
ORTEGO, KEITH	Bryant Keith, WR, 6´0˝/180 lbs; McNeese State; B8/30/1963 Eunice, LA																			**1985**†ChiB 7 (0)	**1987**†ChiB 8 (0)		
1986	†ChiB	16(13, WR)	—	—	—	—	23	430	18.7(58)	2	—	—	—	—	—	—	—	—	—	—	—	12	225
NFL	3	31(13)	—	—	—	—	23	430	18.7(58)	2	—	—	—	—	—	—	—	—	—	p	—	12	298
ORTH, HENRY	Henry William, G, 6´0˝/180 lbs; Miami (OH); B11/20/1897 Chillicothe, OH, D3/25/1980 Zanesville, OH																			**1921** Cin 1 (1)			
ORTMANN, CHUCK	Charles H., B, 6´1˝/190 lbs; Michigan; 1951: Pit, rnd 2; B6/1/1929 Milwaukee, WI																						
1951	Pit	12(TB)	59	327	5.5(32)	0	4	62	15.5(22)	0	139	56	40.3	671	4.8(37)	3	13	—	—	24.0	Pi	0	246
1952	DalT	3(1)	8	24	3.0(15)	0	—	—	—	—	15	5	33.3	73	4.9(54)	0	1	—	—	—	—	0	21
NFL	2	15(1)	67	351	5.2(32)	0	4	62	15.5(22)	0	154	61	39.6	744	4.8(54)	3	14	—	—	23.8	Pi	0	266
ORTON, GREG	Gregory Jay, G, 6´1˝/265 lbs; Nebraska; B8/9/1962 Nebraska City, NE																			**1987** Det 3 (3)			
ORTON, KYLE	Kyle Raymond, QB, 6´4˝/226 lbs; Purdue; 2005: Chi, rnd 4; B11/14/1982 Altoona, IA																						
2005	ChiB	15(15, QB)	24	44	1.8(15)	0	—	—	—	—	368	190	51.6	1869	5.1(54)	9	13	30	190	59.7	—	—	0	504

Orvis, Herb Herbert Vaughn, DT-DE, 6´5˝/248 lbs; Colorado; 1972: Det, rnd 1; B10/17/1946 Petoskey, MI **1972** Det 14 (2) **1973** Det 14 (14, LDT) **1974** Det 14 (14, LDT) **1975** Det☆14 (14, LDT) **1976** Det 2 (2) **1977** Det 14 (14, LDT) **1978** Bal 2 (2) **1979** Bal 16 (13, RDT) **1980** Bal 16 (16, RDT) **1981** Bal 16 (15, LDT) **NFL** 122 (106) [10 yrs]

Orwoll, Ossie Oswald Christian, HB, 5´11˝/165 lbs; Luther; B11/17/1900 Portland, OR, D5/8/1967 Decorah, IA **1926** Mil 3 (1)

Osborn, Dave David Vance, RB, 6´0˝/208 lbs; North Dakota; 1965: Min, rnd 13; B3/18/1943 Everett, WA

YEAR	TEAM	G(GS, POS)	RUSH	YD	AVG(LG)	TD	REC	YD	AVG(LG)	TD	PASS	COMP	PCT	YD	AVG(LG)	TD	INT	SK	YD	QBR	KPR	OTD	PTS	TAY
1965	Min	14	20	106	5.3(21)	2	1	4	4.0(4)	0	—	—	—	—	—	—	—	—	—	—	k	—	12	280
1966	Min	14	87	344	4.0(25)	1	15	141	9.4(38)	2	—	—	—	—	—	—	—	—	—	—	k	—	18	439
1967	Min☆	14(14, HB)	215	972	4.5(73)	2	34	272	8.0(29)	1	—	—	—	—	—	—	—	—	—	—	—	—	18	1133
1968	†Min	4	42	140	3.3(23)	0	—	—	—	—	—	—	—	—	—	—	—	—	—	—	—	—	0	140
1969	†Min	14(14, HB)	186	643	3.5(58)	7	22	236	10.7(31)	1	—	—	—	—	—	—	—	—	—	—	—	—	48	836
1970	†Min✧	14(10, RB)	207	681	3.3(16)	5	23	202	8.8(28)	1	—	—	—	—	—	—	—	—	—	—	—	—	36	837
1971	†Min	11(10, FB)	123	349	2.8(15)	5	25	195	7.8(25)	1	—	—	—	—	—	—	—	—	—	—	—	—	36	502
1972	Min	14	82	261	3.2(14)	2	20	166	8.3(18)	1	—	—	—	—	—	—	—	—	—	—	—	—	18	369
1973	†Min	11	48	216	4.5(14)	0	3	4	1.3(5)	0	—	—	—	—	—	—	—	—	—	—	—	—	0	218
1974	†Min	13(10, RB)	131	514	3.9(17)	4	29	196	6.8(25)	0	—	—	—	—	—	—	—	—	—	—	k	—	24	651
1975	†Min	14	32	94	2.9(9)	1	1	-4	-4.0(-4)	0	—	—	—	—	—	—	—	—	—	—	k	—	6	125
1976	GB	6	6	16	2.7(6)	0	—	—	—	—	—	—	—	—	—	—	—	—	—	—	k	—	0	-10
NFL	12	143(58)	1179	4336	3.7(73)	29	173	1412	8.2(38)	7	—	—	—	—	—	—	—	—	—	—	k	—	216	5519

Osborn, Duke Robert Duke, G-C, 5´10˝/188 lbs; Penn State; B2/1/1897 Falls Creek, PA **1921** Can 10 (8, RG) **1922** Can☆12 (12, RG) **1923** Can☆10 (9, RG) **1924** Cle 9 (9, C) **1925** Pot☆11 (11, RG) **1926** Pot 14 (14, RG) **1927** Pot 8 (7, rg) **1928** Pot 8 (0) **NFL** 82 (70) [8 yrs]

Osborn, Mike Michael Joseph, LB, 6´5˝/235 lbs; Kansas State; B11/19/1955 San Antonio, TX **1978**†Phi 16 (1)

Osborne, Chuck Charles Wayne, DT, 6´2˝/290 lbs; Arizona; 1996: SL, rnd 7; B11/2/1973 Los Angeles, CA **1996** SL 15 (1) **1998** Oak 6 (0) **1999** Oak 16 (0) **NFL** 37 (1) [3 yrs]

Osborne, Clancy Clarence Dewitt, LB, 6´3˝/218 lbs; Arizona State; 1957: LA, rnd 27; B11/23/1934 Lubbock, TX **1959** SF 8 (llb) **1960** SF 8 (llb) **1961** Min 14 (11, LLB) **1962** Min 14 (11, RLB) **1963** Oak-A 14 (RLB) **1964** Oak-A 14 (RLB) **NFL** 72 (22) [6 yrs]

Osborne, Eldonta Eldonta R., LB, 6´0˝/226 lbs; Louisiana Tech; B8/12/1967 **1990** Phx 12 (0)

Osborne, Jim James Henry, DT, 6´3˝/250 lbs; Southern (LA); 1972: Chi, rnd 7; B9/7/1949 Sylvania, GA **1972** ChiB 14 (13, LDT) **1973** ChiB 14 (14, LDT) **1974** ChiB 14 (14, LDT) **1975** ChiB 12 (3) **1976** ChiB 14 (14, LDT) **1977**†ChiB 14 (12, LDT) **1978** ChiB 15 (15, LDT) **1979**†ChiB 16 (16, LDT) **1980** ChiB 16 (16, LDT) **1981** ChiB 16 (16, LDT) **1982** ChiB 9 (9, LDT) **1983** ChiB 16 (12, LDT) **1984**†ChiB 16 (0) **NFL** 186 (154) [13 yrs]

Osborne, Richard Richard Arlen, TE, 6´3˝/230 lbs; Texas A&M; 1976: Phi, rnd 9; B10/31/1953 Wichita, KS

YEAR	TEAM	G(GS, POS)	RUSH	YD	AVG(LG)	TD	REC	YD	AVG(LG)	TD	PASS	COMP	PCT	YD	AVG(LG)	TD	INT	SK	YD	QBR	KPR	OTD	PTS	TAY
1976	Phi	4	—	—	—	—	—	—	—	—	—	—	—	—	—	—	—	—	—	—	—	—	—	—
1976	NYJ	9	—	—	—	—	2	9	4.5(7)	1	—	—	—	—	—	—	—	—	—	—	k	—	6	3
1977	Phi	14(1)	—	—	—	—	1	6	6.0(6)	0	—	—	—	—	—	—	—	—	—	—	—	—	0	3
1978	†Phi	16(7, te)	—	—	—	—	13	145	11.2(48)	0	—	—	—	—	—	—	—	—	—	—	—	—	0	73
1979	SL	7	—	—	—	—	7	37	5.3(10)	0	—	—	—	—	—	—	—	—	—	—	—	—	0	19
NFL	4	50(8)	—	—	—	—	23	197	8.6(48)	1	—	—	—	—	—	—	—	—	—	—	k	—	6	97

Osborne, Tom Thomas William, WR, 6´3˝/190 lbs; Hastings; 1959: SF, rnd 19; B2/23/1937 Hastings, NE

YEAR	TEAM	G(GS, POS)	RUSH	YD	AVG(LG)	TD	REC	YD	AVG(LG)	TD	PASS	COMP	PCT	YD	AVG(LG)	TD	INT	SK	YD	QBR	KPR	OTD	PTS	TAY
1960	Was	10	—	—	—	—	7	46	6.6(10)	0	—	—	—	—	—	—	—	—	—	—	—	—	0	23
1961	Was	14	—	—	—	—	22	297	13.5(60)	2	—	—	—	—	—	—	—	—	—	—	—	—	12	159
NFL	2	24	—	—	—	—	29	343	11.8(60)	2	—	—	—	—	—	—	—	—	—	—	—	—	12	182

Osby, Vince Vincent Lee, LB, 5´11˝/220 lbs; Illinois; B7/8/1961 Los Angeles, CA **1984** SD 16 (0) **1985** SD 7 (0) **NFL** 23 (0) [2 yrs]

Osgood, Kassim Kassim, WR, 6´5˝/209 lbs; San Diego State; B5/20/1980 Boston, MA

YEAR	TEAM	G(GS, POS)	RUSH	YD	AVG(LG)	TD	REC	YD	AVG(LG)	TD	PASS	COMP	PCT	YD	AVG(LG)	TD	INT	SK	YD	QBR	KPR	OTD	PTS	TAY
2003	SD	16(2)	—	—	—	—	13	278	21.4(57)	2	—	—	—	—	—	—	—	—	—	—	—	—	12	149
2004	†SD	16(7, WR)	—	—	—	—	15	308	20.5(65)	2	—	—	—	—	—	—	—	—	—	—	—	—	12	164
2005	SD	12(3)	1	4	4.0(4)	0	2	21	10.5(15)	0	—	—	—	—	—	—	—	—	—	—	—	—	0	15
NFL	3	44(12)	1	4	4.0(4)	0	30	607	20.2(65)	4	—	—	—	—	—	—	—	—	—	—	—	—	24	328

O'Shea, Terry Terence William, TE, 6´4˝/236 lbs; California (PA); B12/3/1966 Pittsburgh, PA

YEAR	TEAM	G(GS, POS)	RUSH	YD	AVG(LG)	TD	REC	YD	AVG(LG)	TD	PASS	COMP	PCT	YD	AVG(LG)	TD	INT	SK	YD	QBR	KPR	OTD	PTS	TAY
1989	†Pit	16(2)	—	—	—	—	1	8	8.0(8)	0	—	—	—	—	—	—	—	—	—	—	—	—	0	4
1990	Pit	16(0)	—	—	—	—	1	13	13.0(13)	0	—	—	—	—	—	—	—	—	—	—	—	—	0	7
NFL	2	32(2)	—	—	—	—	2	21	10.5(13)	0	—	—	—	—	—	—	—	—	—	—	—	—	0	11

Oshodin, Willie William Ehizela, DE, 6´4˝/265 lbs; Villanova; B9/16/1969 Benin City, Nigeria **1993**†Den 15 (5, rde) **1994** Den 13 (0) **1995** Den 2 (0) **NFL** 30 (5) [3 yrs]

Osiecki, Sandy Stanley Eugene, QB, 6´5˝/202 lbs; Arizona State; B5/18/1960 Ansonia, CT

YEAR	TEAM	G(GS, POS)	RUSH	YD	AVG(LG)	TD	REC	YD	AVG(LG)	TD	PASS	COMP	PCT	YD	AVG(LG)	TD	INT	SK	YD	QBR	KPR	OTD	PTS	TAY
1984	KC	4(0)	1	-2	-2.0(-2)	0	—	—	—	—	17	7	41.2	64	3.8(19)	0	1	1	2	—	—	—	0	-10

Osika, Craig Craig, G-C, 6´3˝/293 lbs; Indiana; B12/4/1979 Hobart, IN **2002** SF 1 (0) **2003** Cle 1 (0) **NFL** 2 (0) [2 yrs]

Osley, Willie Willie Glenn, DB, 6´0˝/195 lbs; Illinois; 1973: KC, rnd 10; B4/10/1951 Detroit, MI **1974** NE 7 (4) **1974** KC 3 **NFL** 10 (4) [1 yr]

Osmanski, Bill William Thomas, FB, 5´11˝/197 lbs; Holy Cross; 1939: ChiB, rnd 1; B12/29/1915 Providence, RI, D12/25/1996 Chicago, IL

YEAR	TEAM	G(GS, POS)	RUSH	YD	AVG(LG)	TD	REC	YD	AVG(LG)	TD	PASS	COMP	PCT	YD	AVG(LG)	TD	INT	SK	YD	QBR	KPR	OTD	PTS	TAY
1939	ChiB★	10(3, fb)	121	**699**	5.8(86)	7	3	65	21.7	1	—	—	—	—	—	—	—	—	—	—	—	—	48	807
1940	†ChiB✧	8(6, FB)	50	192	3.8(68)	3	1	13	13.0(13)	0	—	—	—	—	—	—	—	—	—	—	—	—	18	229
1941	†ChiB★	10(7, FB)	70	371	5.3(23)	4	4	52	13.0(27)	0	1	0	0.0	0	0.0	0	0	—	—	—	ki	—	24	441
1942	†ChiB	1(1)	2	9	4.5(14)	0	—	—	—	—	—	—	—	—	—	—	—	—	—	—	—	—	0	9
1943	ChiB	4(3)	37	102	2.8(9)	1	—	—	—	—	—	—	—	—	—	—	—	—	—	—	—	—	6	112
1946	†ChiB☆	9(4)	78	343	4.4(20)	5	4	40	10.0(28)	0	—	—	—	—	—	—	—	—	—	—	kpi	—	30	509
1947	ChiB	4(0)	10	37	3.7(15)	0	—	—	—	—	—	—	—	—	—	—	—	—	—	—	k	—	0	59
NFL	7	46(24)	368	1753	4.8(86)	20	12	170	14.2(28)	1	1	0	0.0	0	0.0	0	0	—	—	—	kpi	—	126	2165

Osmanski, Joe Joseph Charles, FB, 6´2˝/218 lbs; Holy Cross; 1941: Was, rnd 18; B12/26/1917 Providence, RI, D12/24/1993 Chicago, IL

YEAR	TEAM	G(GS, POS)	RUSH	YD	AVG(LG)	TD	REC	YD	AVG(LG)	TD	PASS	COMP	PCT	YD	AVG(LG)	TD	INT	SK	YD	QBR	KPR	OTD	PTS	TAY
1946	†ChiB	8(6, FB)	55	201	3.7(19)	2	2	14	7.0(14)	0	—	—	—	—	—	—	—	—	—	—	k	—	12	237
1947	ChiB	12(3)	64	328	5.1(24)	1	7	134	19.1(39)	0	—	—	—	—	—	—	—	—	—	—	—	—	6	405
1948	ChiB	12(1)	74	341	4.6(32)	1	9	43	4.8(19)	0	—	—	—	—	—	—	—	—	—	—	k	—	6	369
1949	ChiB	2(0)	15	45	3.0(0)	0	1	3	3.0(3)	0	—	—	—	—	—	—	—	—	—	—	—	—	0	47
1949	NYB	8(8, FB)	66	267	4.0(48)	2	17	135	7.9(42)	0	—	—	—	—	—	—	—	—	—	—	k	—	12	341
NFL	4	42(18)	274	1182	4.3(48)	6	36	329	9.1(42)	0	—	—	—	—	—	—	—	—	—	—	k	—	36	1398

Ossowski, Ted Theodore Leroy, T, 6´0˝/218 lbs; USC; Oregon State; 1947: NYY-A, rnd 9/1944: Was, rnd 16; B5/12/1922 Beatrice, NE, deceased **1947** NYY-A 3 (0)

O'Steen, Dwayne Dwayne Philip, DB, 6´1˝/193 lbs; California; San Jose State; B12/20/1954 Los Angeles, CA, D9/15/2001 San Jose, CA **1978** LARm 13 **1979**†LARm 16 (12, LCB) **1980**†Oak 15 (6, rcb) **1981** Oak 16 (6, rcb) **1982** Bal 3 (2) **1982**†TB 0 (0) **1983** TB 3 (0) **1983** GB 7 (0) **1984** GB 4 (0) **NFL** 77 (26) [7 yrs]

Ostendarp, Jim James Elmore, HB, 5´8˝/178 lbs; Bucknell; B2/15/1923 Baltimore, MD, D12/15/2005 Holyoke, MA **1951** NYG 2

YEAR	TEAM	G(GS, POS)	RUSH	YD	AVG(LG)	TD	REC	YD	AVG(LG)	TD	PASS	COMP	PCT	YD	AVG(LG)	TD	INT	SK	YD	QBR	KPR	OTD	PTS	TAY
1950	†NYG	7	18	144	8.0(55)	2	—	—	—	—	—	—	—	—	—	—	—	—	—	—	kp	—	12	212
NFL	2	9	18	144	8.0(55)	2	—	—	—	—	—	—	—	—	—	—	—	—	—	—	kp	—	12	259

Ostroski, Jerry Gerald, G-T-C, 6´4˝/310 lbs; Tulsa; 1992: KC, rnd 10; B7/12/1970 Collegeville, PA **1994** Buf 4 (3) **1995**†Buf 16 (13, RG) **1996**†Buf 16 (16, RG) **1997** Buf 16 (16, RT) **1998**†Buf 16 (16, RT) **1999**†Buf 15 (15, C) **2000** Buf 16 (16, C) **2001** Buf 7 (7, rg) **NFL** 106 (102) [8 yrs]

Ostroski, Phil Phillip Lucas, G, 6´4˝/291 lbs; Penn State; 1998: SF, rnd 5; B9/23/1975 Wilkes-Barre, PA **1999** SF 15 (0) **2000** SF 13 (0) **NFL** 28 (0) [2 yrs]

Ostrowski, Chet Chester Casmir, DE, 6´1˝/232 lbs; Notre Dame; 1952: Was, rnd 10; B4/8/1930 Chicago, IL, D10/10/2001 Orland Park, IL **1954** Was 12 (12, RDE) **1955** Was 11 (11, RDE) **1956** Was 12 (12, RDE) **1957** Was 12 (12, RDE) **1958** Was 12 (12, RDE) **1959** Was 9 **NFL** 68 (59) [6 yrs]

O'Sullivan, Dennis Dennis, C, 6´3˝/300 lbs; Tulane; B1/28/1976 Suffern, NY **2002** NYJ 3 (0)

O'Sullivan, J.T. John Thomas, QB, 6´2˝/220 lbs; California-Davis; 2002: NO, rnd 6; B8/25/1979 Burbank, CA

YEAR	TEAM	G(GS, POS)	RUSH	YD	AVG(LG)	TD	REC	YD	AVG(LG)	TD	PASS	COMP	PCT	YD	AVG(LG)	TD	INT	SK	YD	QBR	KPR	OTD	PTS	TAY
2004	GB	1(0)	2	-2	-1.0(-1)	0	—	—	—	—	—	—	—	—	—	—	—	—	—	—	—	—	0	-2

Oswald, Paul Paul Eugene, C-G, 6´3˝/273 lbs; Kansas; 1987: Pit, rnd 11; B4/9/1964 Topeka, KS **1987** Pit 2 (0) **1988** Dal 1 (0) **1988** Atl 3 (1) **NFL** 6 (1) [2 yrs]

YEAR	TEAM	G (GS, POS)	RUSH	YD	AVG (LG)	TD	REC	YD	AVG (LG)	TD	PASS COMP	PCT	YD	AVG (LG)	TD	INT	SK	YD	QBR	KPR	OTD	PTS	TAY

OTIS, JIM James Lloyd, RB, 6´0˝/220 lbs; Ohio State; 1970: NO, rnd 9; B4/29/1948 Celina, OH

1970	NO	13 (FB)	71	211	3.0 (15)	0	20	124	6.2 (22)	0	—	—	—	—	—	—	—	—	—	k	—	0	265
1971	†KC	13	49	184	3.8 (14)	0	13	81	6.2 (26)	2	—	—	—	—	—	—	—	—	—	—	—	12	235
1972	KC	10	29	92	3.2 (12)	0	12	76	6.3 (13)	0	—	—	—	—	—	—	—	—	—	—	—	0	130
1973	SL	10 (FB)	55	234	4.3 (19)	1	2	19	9.5 (14)	0	—	—	—	—	—	—	—	—	—	—	—	6	254
1974	†SL	14 (10, FB)	158	664	4.2 (23)	1	19	109	5.7 (13)	0	—	—	—	—	—	—	—	—	—	—	—	6	729
1975	†SL✧	14 (FB)	269	1076	4.0 (30)	5	12	69	5.8 (12)	1	—	—	—	—	—	—	—	—	—	—	—	36	1166
1976	SL	14 (FB)	233	891	3.8 (23)	2	2	15	7.5 (8)	0	—	—	—	—	—	—	—	—	—	—	—	12	919
1977	SL	13 (6, fb)	99	334	3.4 (25)	2	2	18	9.0 (9)	0	—	—	—	—	—	—	—	—	—	k	—	12	364
1978	SL	15 (FB)	197	664	3.4 (17)	8	8	38	4.8 (12)	0	—	—	—	—	—	—	—	—	—	—	—	48	763
NFL	9	116 (16)	1160	4350	3.8 (30)	19	90	549	6.1 (26)	3	—	—	—	—	—	—	—	—	—	k	—	132	4823

O'TOOLE, BILL Milton Timothy, G, none; B1898, MN, deceased   **1924** Dul 1 (0)

OTTE, LOWELL Frederic Lowell, E, 6´2˝/180 lbs; Iowa; B7/20/1904 Fremont County, IA, D7/20/1936 Sidney, IA   **1927** Buf 5 (5, RE)

OTTELE, DICK Ricard G., BB-DB, 6´3˝/210 lbs; Washington; 1948: NYY-A, rnd 13/NYG, rnd 9; B12/8/1926 Yuma, CO, D9/20/1985 Bremerton, WA

| 1948 | LAD-A | 8 (0) | 2 | 11 | 5.5 | 0 | — | — | — | — | — | — | — | — | — | — | — | — | k | — | 0 | 13 |

OTTIS, BRAD Brad Allen, DE, 6´5˝/281 lbs; Wayne State (NE); 1994: LARm, rnd 2; B2/8/1972 Wahoo, NE   **1994** LARm 13 (0)   **1995** SL 12 (0)   **1996** Arz 11 (1)   **1997** Arz 16 (4)   **1999** Arz 14 (7, lde)   **2000** Arz 15 (11, LDE)   **NFL** 81 (23) [6 yrs]

OTTO, BO Albert Henry, C-G-T, /182 lbs; none; B8/16/1903 Louisville, KY, D1/6/2001 Arlington Heights, IL   **1922** Lou 4 (4, RG)   **1923** Lou 3 (3, C)   **NFL** 7 (7) [2 yrs]

OTTO, BOB Robert, DE, 6´6˝/251 lbs; Idaho State; 1985: Sea, rnd 9; B12/16/1962 Sacramento, CA   **1986** Dal 4 (0)   **1987** Hou 3 (0)   **NFL** 7 (0) [2 yrs]

OTTO, GUS August Joseph, LB, 6´1˝/220 lbs; Missouri; 1965: Oak, rnd 4; B12/8/1943 St. Louis, MO   **1965** Oak-A 14 (14, RLB)   **1966** Oak-A 14 (14, RLB)   **1967**†Oak-A☆14 (14, RLB)   **1968**†Oak-A☆13 (12, RLB)   **1969**†Oak-A★14 (14, RLB)   **1970**†Oak☆14 (14, RLB)   **1971** Oak 8 (8, RLB)   **1972**†Oak 11 (5, rlb)   **NFL** 102 (95) [8 yrs]

OTTO, JIM James Edwin 'Double O', C, 6´2˝/255 lbs; Miami (FL); 1960: Oak, rnd 1; B1/5/1938 Wausau, WI; HOF 1980   **1960** Oak-A☆14 (C)   **1961** Oak-A★14 (C)   **1962** Oak-A★14 (C)   **1963** Oak-A★14 (C)   **1964** Oak-A★14 (C)   **1965** Oak-A★14 (C)   **1966** Oak-A★14 (C)   **1967**†Oak-A★14 (14, C)   **1968**†Oak-A★14 (14, C)   **1969**†Oak-A★14 (14, C)   **1970**†Oak★14 (14, C)   **1971** Oak★14 (14, C)   **1972**†Oak★14 (14, C)   **1973**†Oak 14 (14, C)   **1974**†Oak 14 (14, C)   **NFL** 210 (98) [15 yrs]

OUBRE, LOUIS Louis Byron, G, 6´4˝/262 lbs; Oklahoma; 1981: NO, rnd 5; B5/15/1958 New Orleans, LA   **1982** NO 9 (9, RG)   **1983** NO 16 (16, RG)   **1984** NO 12 (5, lg)   **1987** Mia 3 (1)   **NFL** 40 (31) [4 yrs]

OURS, GREG Gregory William, C, 6´5˝/279 lbs; Muskingum; B10/29/1963 Hebron, OH   **1987** Mia 3 (3)

OURS, WES John Wesley, RB, 6´0˝/284 lbs; West Virginia; B12/30/1977 Christian, KY

| 2001 | Ten | 3 (1) | — | — | — | — | 1 | 3 | 3.0 (3) | 0 | — | — | — | — | — | — | — | — | — | — | — | 0 | 2 |

OUTLAW, JOHN John L., DB, 5´10˝/180 lbs; Jackson State; 1968: Bos, rnd 10; B1/8/1945 Clarksdale, MS   **1969** Bos-A 9 (1)   **1970** Bos 5   **1971** NE 14 (14, RCB)   **1972** NE 6 (5, RCB)   **1973** Phi 7 (LCB)   **1974** Phi 14 (LCB)   **1975** Phi 14 (8, LCB)   **1976** Phi 13 (LCB)   **1977** Phi 14 (LCB)   **1978**†Phi 14 (8, LCB)   **NFL** 110 (36) [10 yrs]

OVERHAUSER, CHAD Chad Michael, T, 6´4˝/314 lbs; UCLA; 1998: Chi, rnd 7; B6/17/1975 Sacramento, CA   **2002** Hou 3 (0)

OVERMYER, BILL William Lee, LB, 6´3˝/220 lbs; Ashland University; 1972: Phi, rnd 14; B6/16/1949 Fremont, OH   **1972** Phi 6

OVERSTREET, DAVID David Arthur, RB, 5´11˝/208 lbs; Oklahoma; 1981: Mia, rnd 1; B9/20/1958 Big Sandy, TX, D6/24/1984 Winona, TX

| 1983 | †Mia | 14 (0) | 85 | 392 | 4.6 (44) | 4 | 13 | 85 | 6.9 (20) | 2 | — | — | — | — | — | — | — | — | — | — | — | 18 | 440 |

OVERSTREET, WILL William Sparkman, LB, 6´2˝/259 lbs; Tennessee; 2002: Atl, rnd 3; B10/7/1979 Jackson, MS   **2002** Atl 2 (0)   **2003** Atl 4 (2)   **NFL** 6 (2) [2 yrs]

OVERTON, DON Donald Eugene, RB, 6´0˝/221 lbs; Fairmont State; B9/24/1967 Columbus, OH

1990	NE	7 (0)	5	8	1.6 (6)	0	2	19	9.5 (15)	0	—	—	—	—	—	—	—	—	—	k	—	0	56
1991	†Det	14 (0)	14	59	4.2 (9)	0	4	38	9.5 (14)	0	—	—	—	—	—	—	—	—	—	k	—	0	89
1992	Det	1 (0)	—	—	—	—	—	—	—	—	—	—	—	—	—	—	—	—	—	—	—	—	—
NFL	3	22 (0)	19	67	3.5 (9)	0	6	57	9.5 (14)	0	—	—	—	—	—	—	—	—	—	k	—	0	145

OVERTON, JERRY Jerry Lee, DB, 6´2˝/190 lbs; Utah; 1963: Dal, rnd 15; B1/24/1941 El Dorado Springs, MO   **1963** Dal 10

OWEN, AL Herbert Alton, HB, 6´0˝/194 lbs; Mercer; B2/16/1913 Glen Ridge, NJ, D6/11/1992 Sarasota County, FL

1939	†NYG	8 (1)	8	11	1.4	0	2	45	22.5 (39)	1	—	—	—	—	—	—	—	—	—	—	—	6	39
1940	NYG	5 (0)	2	10	5.0 (5)	0	1	5	5.0 (5)	0	—	—	—	—	—	—	—	—	—	—	—	0	13
1942	NYG	7 (1)	8	27	3.4 (6)	0	1	20	20.0 (20)	0	—	—	—	—	—	—	—	—	—	p	—	0	47
NFL	3	20 (2)	18	48	2.7 (6)	0	4	70	17.5 (39)	1	—	—	—	—	—	—	—	—	—	p	—	6	98

OWEN, BILL William Criswell, T-G, 6´0˝/211 lbs; Oklahoma State; Phillips; B9/29/1903 Aline, OK, D3/1975 Kinsley, KS   **1926** KC 11 (8, RT)   **1927** Cle 13 (13, RT)   **1928** Det☆10 (9, RT)   **1929** NYG 15 (14, RT)   **1930** NYG☆16 (12, RT)   **1931** NYG☆14 (14, RT)   **1932** NYG 11 (9, RT)   **1933** NYG 13 (9, RT)   **1934**†NYG 12 (7, RT)   **1935**†NYG 12 (4)   **1936** NYG 11 (0)   **NFL** 138 (99) [11 yrs]

OWEN, STEVE Stephen Joseph 'Stout Steve', T-G, 5´10˝/237 lbs; Phillips; B4/21/1898 Cleo Springs, OK, D5/17/1964 New York, NY; HOF 1966 [C]   **1924** KC 9 (8, RG)   **1925** KC 8 (8, LT)   **1925** Cle 1 (1)   **1926** NYG☆13 (13, LT/rt)   **1927** NYG☆13 (13, LT)   **1928** NYG 12 (12, LT)   **1929** NYG☆15 (14, LT)   **1930** NYG 17 (13, LT)   **1931** NYG 8 (1)   **1933**†NYG 1 (0)   **NFL** 97 (83) [9 yrs]

OWEN, TOM Willis Thomas, QB, 6´1˝/195 lbs; Wichita State; 1974: SF, rnd 13; B9/1/1952 Shreveport, LA

1974	SF	10 (7, QB)	16	36	2.3 (7)	1	—	—	—	—	—	184	88	47.8	1327	7.2 (68)	10	15	25	202	—	—	—	6	160
1975	SF	4	1	1	1.0 (1)	0	—	—	—	—	—	51	24	47.1	318	6.2 (24)	1	2	6	57	—	—	—	0	85
1976	NE	2	—	—	—	—	—	—	—	—	—	5	1	20.0	7	1.4 (7)	0	—	—	—	—	—	—	0	4
1978	†NE	2	—	—	—	—	—	—	—	—	—	26	15	57.7	182	7.0 (23)	0	2	3	22	—	—	—	0	11
1979	NE	6	2	-1	-0.5 (0)	0	—	—	—	—	—	47	27	57.4	248	5.3 (32)	2	3	4	41	—	—	—	0	13
1981	NE	2 (1)	—	—	—	—	—	—	—	—	—	36	15	41.7	218	6.1 (28)	1	4	2	19	—	—	—	0	-46
NFL	6	26 (8)	19	36	1.9 (7)	1	—	—	—	—	—	349	170	48.7	2300	6.6 (68)	14	26	40	341	—	—	—	6	226

OWENS, ARTIE Arthur Gene, WR-RB, 5´10˝/176 lbs; West Virginia; 1976: SD, rnd 4; B1/14/1953 Montgomery, AL [R]

1976	SD	14	—	—	—	—	3	54	18.0 (28)	1	—	—	—	—	—	—	—	—	—	k	—	6	208
1977	SD	14 (1)	1	3	3.0 (3)	0	—	—	—	—	—	—	—	—	—	—	—	—	—	k	—	0	15
1978	SD	13 (2)	—	—	—	—	9	188	20.9 (41)	0	—	—	—	—	—	—	—	—	—	kp	—	0	333
1979	†SD	16 (2)	40	151	3.8 (23)	1	15	176	11.7 (32)	1	—	—	—	—	—	—	—	—	—	k	—	12	520
1980	Buf	4 (0)	—	—	—	—	—	—	—	—	—	—	—	—	—	—	—	—	—	k	—	0	37
1980	NO	3 (0)	—	—	—	—	—	—	—	—	—	—	—	—	—	—	—	—	—	—	—	—	—
NFL	5	64 (5)	41	154	3.8 (23)	1	27	418	15.5 (41)	2	—	—	—	—	—	—	—	—	—	kp	—	18	1113

OWENS, BILLY Billy Joe, DB, 6´1˝/207 lbs; Pittsburgh; 1988: Dal, rnd 10; B12/2/1965 Syracuse, NY   **1988** Dal 16 (0)

OWENS, BRIG Brigman, DB, 5´11˝/190 lbs; Cincinnati; 1965: Dal, rnd 7; B2/16/1943 Linden, TX [KI]   **1966** Was 14 (14, LS)   **1967** Was 14 (LS)   **1968** Was 14 (LS)   **1969** Was 14 (LS)   **1970** Was 14 (14, SS)   **1971**†Was 14 (14, FS)   **1972**†Was 14 (11, SS)   **1973**†Was☆14 (14, FS)   **1974**†Was 14 (14, FS)   **1975** Was 14 (3)   **1976**†Was 14 (2)   **1977** Was 4   **NFL** 158 (86) [12 yrs]

OWENS, BURGESS Clarence Burgess, DB, 6´2˝/200 lbs; Miami (FL); 1973: NYJ, rnd 1; B8/2/1951 Columbus, OH [I]   **1973** NYJ 14 (SS)   **1974** NYJ 14 (SS)   **1975** NYJ 11 (11, SS)   **1976** NYJ 14 (FS)   **1977** NYJ 14 (14, FS)   **1978** NYJ 14 (14, FS)   **1979** NYJ 16 (FS)   **1980** Oak 16 (16, FS)   **1981** Oak 16 (16, FS)   **1982**†LARd 8 (8, FS)   **NFL** 137 (79) [10 yrs]

OWENS, CHAD Chad, WR, 5´7˝/183 lbs; Hawaii; 2005: Jax, rnd 6; B4/3/1982 Honolulu, HI   **2005** Jax 1 (0)

OWENS, DAN Daniel William, DE-DT-NT, 6´3˝/280 lbs; USC; 1990: Det, rnd 2; B3/16/1967 Whittier, CA   **1990** Det 16 (12, LDE)   **1991**†Det 16 (16, RDE)   **1992** Det 16 (4)   **1993**†Det 15 (11, RDE)   **1994**†Det 16 (8, nt)   **1995**†Det 16 (0)   **1996** Atl 16 (9, rdt)   **1997** Atl 15 (15, RDT)   **1998** Det 11 (11, LDT)   **1999**†Det 8 (0)   **NFL** 145 (86) [10 yrs]

OWENS, DARRICK Darrick Alfred, WR, 6´2˝/195 lbs; Mississippi; B11/5/1970 Boynton Beach, FL   **1992** Pit 3 (0)

OWENS, DENNIS Dennis Ray, NT, 6´1˝/257 lbs; North Carolina State; B2/24/1960 Clinton, NC   **1982**†NE 9 (0)   **1983** NE 16 (14, NT)   **1984** NE 16 (16, NT)   **1985**†NE 14 (13, NT)   **1986**†NE 16 (1)   **NFL** 71 (44) [5 yrs]

OWENS, DON Donald Fred, DT-T, 6´5˝/255 lbs; Southern Mississippi; 1957: Pit, rnd 3; B4/3/1932 St. Louis, MO, D8/17/1997 Jefferson City, MO **1957** Was 10 (RDT) **1958** Phi 12 (RDT) **1959** Phi 12 (RDT) **1960** Phi 3 **1960** SL 9 (LDT) **1961** SL 14 (LDT) **1962** SL 14 (LDT) **1963** SL 13 (LDT) **NFL** 87 [7 yrs]

OWENS, IKE Isiah Hudson, DE, 6´1˝/190 lbs; Illinois; B1/8/1920 Columbus, GA, D1/14/1980 Gary, IN **1948** ChiR-A 8 (0)

OWENS, JAMES James Earl, RB-WR-DB, 5´11˝/192 lbs; UCLA; 1979: SF, rnd 2; B7/5/1955 Sacramento, CA **[R]**

YEAR	TEAM	G (GS, POS)	RUSH	YD	AVG (LG)	TD	REC	YD	AVG (LG)	TD	PASS	COMP	PCT	YD	AVG (LG)	TD	INT	SK	YD	QBR	KPR	OTD	PTS	TAY
1979	SF	16	7	33	4.7(11)	0	10	121	12.1(17)	0	—	—	—	—	—	—	—	—	—	—	k	1	6	491
1980	SF	14(6, wr)	—	—	—	—	9	133	14.8(29)	0	—	—	—	—	—	—	—	—	—	—	k	1	6	338
1981	†TB	16(1)	91	406	4.5(35)	3	12	145	12.1(35)	0	—	—	—	—	—	—	—	—	—	—	k	—	18	622
1982	†TB	8(6, RB)	76	238	3.1(14)	0	8	42	5.3(12)	1	—	—	—	—	—	—	—	—	—	—	k	—	6	271
1983	TB	12(5, rb)	96	266	2.8(15)	5	15	81	5.4(11)	1	—	—	—	—	—	—	—	—	—	—	k	—	36	442
1984	TB	4(0)	1	1	1.0(1)	0	2	13	6.5(9)	1	—	—	—	—	—	—	—	—	—	—	k	—	6	61
NFL	6	70(18)	271	944	3.5(35)	8	56	535	9.6(35)	3	—	—	—	—	—	—	—	—	—	—	k	2	78	2223

OWENS, JIM James Donald, E-DE, 6´3˝/205 lbs; Oklahoma; 1949: Pit, rnd 23/Bal-A, rnd 12; B3/6/1927 Oklahoma City, OK

YEAR	TEAM	G (GS, POS)	RUSH	YD	AVG (LG)	TD	REC	YD	AVG (LG)	TD	PASS	COMP	PCT	YD	AVG (LG)	TD	INT	SK	YD	QBR	KPR	OTD	PTS	TAY
1950	Bal	9(4)	—	—	—	—	19	188	9.9(43)	0	—	—	—	—	—	—	—	—	—	—	ki	1	6	123

OWENS, JOE Joseph T., DE, 6´2˝/245 lbs; Alcorn State; 1969: NO, rnd 9; B11/8/1946 Columbia, MS **1970** SD 14 (LDE) **1971** NO 14 (RDE) **1972** NO 14 (RDE) **1973** NO 14 (RDE) **1974** NO 14 (rde) **1975** NO 14 **1976** Hou 3 **NFL** 87 [7 yrs]

OWENS, JOHN John Wesley, TE, 6´3˝/266 lbs; Notre Dame; 2002: Det, rnd 5; B1/10/1980 Washington, DC **2003** Det 7 (1) **2004** ChiB 2 (0)

YEAR	TEAM	G (GS, POS)	RUSH	YD	AVG (LG)	TD	REC	YD	AVG (LG)	TD	PASS	COMP	PCT	YD	AVG (LG)	TD	INT	SK	YD	QBR	KPR	OTD	PTS	TAY
2002	Det	15(8, te)	—	—	—	—	5	49	9.8(13)	0	—	—	—	—	—	—	—	—	—	—	—	—	0	25
NFL	3	24(9)	—	—	—	—	5	49	9.8(13)	0	—	—	—	—	—	—	—	—	—	—	—	—	0	25

OWENS, LUKE Luke, DE-DT-T, 6´2˝/254 lbs; Kent State; 1957: Bal, rnd 3; B10/19/1933 Cleveland, OH **1957** Bal 11 **1958** ChiC 11 (RDE) **1959** ChiC 12 (RDE) **1960** SL 14 (RDE) **1961** SL 12 (rde) **1962** SL 14 (RDE) **1963** SL☆14 (RDT) **1964** SL 14 (RDT) **1965** SL 13 (RDT) **NFL** 115 [9 yrs]

OWENS, MARV Marvin Duane, WR, 5´11˝/203 lbs; San Diego State; 1972: Min, rnd 14; B6/16/1950 Orange, CA **1973** SL 8 **1974** NYJ 2 **NFL** 10 [2 yrs]

OWENS, MEL Mel Tyrae, LB, 6´2˝/224 lbs; Michigan; 1981: LA, rnd 1; B12/7/1958 Detroit, MI **1981** LARm 16 (0) **1982** LARm 7 (1) **1983**†LARm 16 (16, LOLB) **1984**†LARm 16 (16, LOLB) **1985**†LARm 16 (15, LOLB) **1986**†LARm 16 (16, LOLB) **1987** LARm 12 (12, LOLB) **1988** LARm 7 (4) **1989**†LARm 16 (11, LILB) **NFL** 122 (91) [9 yrs]

OWENS, MORRIS Morris Lamar, WR, 6´0˝/190 lbs; Arizona State; 1975: Mia, rnd 5; B2/14/1953 Oakland, CA

YEAR	TEAM	G (GS, POS)	RUSH	YD	AVG (LG)	TD	REC	YD	AVG (LG)	TD	PASS	COMP	PCT	YD	AVG (LG)	TD	INT	SK	YD	QBR	KPR	OTD	PTS	TAY
1975	Mia	2	—	—	—	—	—	—	—	—	—	—	—	—	—	—	—	—	—	—	—	—	—	—
1976	Mia	2	—	—	—	—	—	—	—	—	—	—	—	—	—	—	—	—	—	—	—	—	—	—
1976	TB	12(11, WR)	2	2	1.0(18)	0	30	390	13.0(27)	6	—	—	—	—	—	—	—	—	—	—	—	—	36	227
1977	TB	14(14, WR)	2	-2	-1.0(5)	0	34	655	19.3(67)	3	—	—	—	—	—	—	—	—	—	—	—	—	18	341
1978	TB	16(11, WR)	—	—	—	—	32	640	**20.0(66)**	5	—	—	—	—	—	—	—	—	—	—	—	—	30	345
1979	†TB	16(12, WR)	—	—	—	—	20	377	18.9(64)	0	—	—	—	—	—	—	—	—	—	—	—	—	0	189
NFL	5	62(48)	4	0	0.0(18)	0	116	2062	17.8(67)	14	—	—	—	—	—	—	—	—	—	—	—	—	84	1101

OWENS, PETE Floyd Russell, G-C, 5´11˝/205 lbs; Texas Tech; B2/11/1917 Littlefield, TX, D11/3/1962 Fort Worth, TX **1943** Bkn 5 (2)

OWENS, R.C. Raleigh C. 'Alley Oop', HB-E, 6´3˝/197 lbs; College of Idaho; 1956: SF, rnd 14; B11/12/1933 Shreveport, LA

YEAR	TEAM	G (GS, POS)	RUSH	YD	AVG (LG)	TD	REC	YD	AVG (LG)	TD	PASS	COMP	PCT	YD	AVG (LG)	TD	INT	SK	YD	QBR	KPR	OTD	PTS	TAY
1957	†SF	12(RH)	—	—	—	—	27	395	14.6(46)	5	—	—	—	—	—	—	—	—	—	—	—	—	30	223
1958	SF	12(RH)	—	—	—	—	40	620	15.5(48)	1	—	—	—	—	—	—	—	—	—	—	—	—	6	315
1959	SF	12	1	0	0.0(0)	0	17	347	20.4(75)	3	—	—	—	—	—	—	—	—	—	—	—	—	18	189
1960	SF☆	12(10, RH)	—	—	—	—	37	532	14.4(42)	6	—	—	—	—	—	—	—	—	—	—	—	—	36	296
1961	SF	14(14, RH)	0	23	(23)	1	55	1032	18.8(54)	5	—	—	—	—	—	—	—	—	—	—	—	—	36	574
1962	Bal	14	—	—	—	—	25	307	12.3(26)	2	—	—	—	—	—	—	—	—	—	—	—	—	12	164
1963	Bal	3	—	—	—	—	1	7	7.0(7)	0	—	—	—	—	—	—	—	—	—	—	—	—	0	4
1964	NYG	11	—	—	—	—	4	45	11.3(14)	0	—	—	—	—	—	—	—	—	—	—	—	—	0	23
NFL	8	90(24)	1	23	23.0(23)	1	206	3285	15.9(75)	22	—	—	—	—	—	—	—	—	—	—	—	—	138	1786

OWENS, RICH Ritchie Darryl, DE-DT, 6´6˝/274 lbs; Lehigh; 1995: Was, rnd 5; B5/22/1972 Philadelphia, PA **1995** Was 10 (3) **1996** Was 16 (16, RDE) **1997** Was 16 (15, RDE) **1999**†Mia 16 (14, LDE) **2000** Mia 12 (3) **2001** KC 16 (1) **2002** KC 8 (0) **2002** Sea 3 (0) **NFL** 97 (52) [7 yrs]

OWENS, RICHARD Richard, TE, 6´4˝/273 lbs; Louisville; B11/4/1980 Gainesville, FL

YEAR	TEAM	G (GS, POS)	RUSH	YD	AVG (LG)	TD	REC	YD	AVG (LG)	TD	PASS	COMP	PCT	YD	AVG (LG)	TD	INT	SK	YD	QBR	KPR	OTD	PTS	TAY
2004	Min	7(2)	—	—	—	—	8	69	8.6(18)	0	—	—	—	—	—	—	—	—	—	—	—	—	0	35
2005	Min	16(2)	—	—	—	—	2	18	9.0(12)	0	—	—	—	—	—	—	—	—	—	—	k	—	0	-11
NFL	2	23(4)	—	—	—	—	10	87	8.7(18)	0	—	—	—	—	—	—	—	—	—	—	k	—	0	24

OWENS, RIP Ralph B., G, 5´10˝/220 lbs; Nebraska; Lawrence; B12/9/1894, WI, D8/1970 Lakeview, AR **1922** GB 3 (2)

OWENS, STEVE Loren Everett, RB, 6´2˝/215 lbs; Oklahoma; 1970: Det, rnd 1; B12/9/1947 Gore, OK

YEAR	TEAM	G (GS, POS)	RUSH	YD	AVG (LG)	TD	REC	YD	AVG (LG)	TD	PASS	COMP	PCT	YD	AVG (LG)	TD	INT	SK	YD	QBR	KPR	OTD	PTS	TAY
1970	Det	6	36	122	3.4(23)	2	4	21	5.3(11)	0	—	—	—	—	—	—	—	—	—	—	k	—	12	164
1971	Det★	14(FB)	246	1035	4.2(23)	8	32	350	10.9(74)	2	—	—	—	—	—	—	—	—	—	—	—	—	60	1300
1972	Det	10(FB)	143	519	3.6(18)	4	15	100	6.7(15)	0	—	—	—	—	—	—	—	—	—	—	—	—	24	609
1973	Det	12(FB)	113	401	3.5(16)	3	24	232	9.7(30)	0	—	—	—	—	—	—	—	—	—	—	—	—	18	547
1974	Det	11(7, FB)	97	374	3.9(27)	3	24	158	6.6(13)	0	—	—	—	—	—	—	—	—	—	—	—	—	18	483
NFL	5	53(7)	635	2451	3.9(27)	20	99	861	8.7(74)	2	—	—	—	—	—	—	—	—	—	—	k	—	132	3103

OWENS, TERRELL Terrell Eldorado, WR, 6´3˝/226 lbs; Tennessee-Chattanooga; 1996: SF, rnd 3; B12/7/1973 Alexander City, AL

YEAR	TEAM	G (GS, POS)	RUSH	YD	AVG (LG)	TD	REC	YD	AVG (LG)	TD	PASS	COMP	PCT	YD	AVG (LG)	TD	INT	SK	YD	QBR	KPR	OTD	PTS	TAY
1996	†SF	16(10, WR)	—	—	—	—	35	520	14.9(46)	4	—	—	—	—	—	—	—	—	—	—	k	—	24	282
1997	†SF	16(15, WR)	—	—	—	—	60	936	15.6(56)	8	—	—	—	—	—	—	—	—	—	—	k	—	48	509
1998	†SF	16(10, wr)	4	53	13.3(21)	1	67	1097	16.4(79)	14	—	—	—	—	—	—	—	—	—	—	—	—	92	682
1999	SF	14(14, WR)	—	—	—	—	60	754	12.6(36)	4	—	—	—	—	—	—	—	—	—	—	—	—	24	397
2000	SF★	14(13, WR)	3	11	3.7(5)	0	97	1451	15.0(69)	13	—	—	—	—	—	—	—	—	—	—	—	—	80	802
2001	†SF★	16(16, WR)	4	21	5.3(12)	0	93	1412	15.2(60)	**16**	—	—	—	—	—	—	—	—	—	—	—	—	96	807
2002	†SF★	14(14, WR)	7	79	11.3(38)	1	100	1300	13.0(76)	**13**	—	—	—	—	—	—	—	—	—	—	—	—	84	804
2003	SF✧	15(15, WR)	3	-2	-0.7(3)	0	80	1102	13.8(75)	9	—	—	—	—	—	—	—	—	—	—	—	—	54	594
2004	†Phi★	14(14, WR)	3	-5	-1.7(6)	0	77	1200	15.6(59)	14	—	—	—	—	—	—	—	—	—	—	—	—	84	665
2005	Phi	7(7, wr)	1	2	2.0(2)	0	47	763	16.2(**91**)	6	—	—	—	—	—	—	—	—	—	—	—	—	36	414
NFL	10	142(128)	25	159	6.4(38)	2	716	10535	14.7(91)	101	—	—	—	—	—	—	—	—	—	—	k	—	622	5955

OWENS, TERRY Terry Woodrow, T, 6´0˝/260 lbs; Jacksonville State; 1966: SD, rnd 11/Chi, rnd 11; B7/5/1944 Jasper, AL **1966** SD-A 14 (1) **1967** SD-A 14 (4) **1968** SD-A 14 (14, LT) **1969** SD-A 14 (LT) **1970** SD 14 (LT) **1971** SD 14 (LT) **1972** SD☆14 (LT) **1973** SD 14 (14, LT) **1974** SD 13 (13, LT) **1975** SD 7 (LT) **NFL** 132 (46) [10 yrs]

OWENS, TINKER Charles Wayne, WR, 5´11˝/170 lbs; Oklahoma; 1976: NO, rnd 4; B10/3/1954 Miami, OK

YEAR	TEAM	G (GS, POS)	RUSH	YD	AVG (LG)	TD	REC	YD	AVG (LG)	TD	PASS	COMP	PCT	YD	AVG (LG)	TD	INT	SK	YD	QBR	KPR	OTD	PTS	TAY
1976	NO	14(1)	—	—	—	—	12	241	20.1(74)	1	—	—	—	—	—	—	—	—	—	—	p	—	6	126
1978	NO	14(10, WR)	—	—	—	—	40	446	11.1(47)	2	—	—	—	—	—	—	—	—	—	—	—	—	12	233
1979	NO	13(2)	—	—	—	—	7	72	10.3(21)	1	—	—	—	—	—	—	—	—	—	—	k	—	6	36
1980	NO	7(0)	—	—	—	—	1	26	26.0(26)	0	—	—	—	—	—	—	—	—	—	—	—	—	0	13
NFL	4	48(13)	—	—	—	—	60	785	13.1(74)	4	—	—	—	—	—	—	—	—	—	—	kp	—	24	408

OXENDINE, KEN Ken Qwarious, RB, 6´0˝/228 lbs; Virginia Tech; 1998: Atl, rnd 7; B10/4/1975 Richmond, VA

YEAR	TEAM	G (GS, POS)	RUSH	YD	AVG (LG)	TD	REC	YD	AVG (LG)	TD	PASS	COMP	PCT	YD	AVG (LG)	TD	INT	SK	YD	QBR	KPR	OTD	PTS	TAY
1998	†Atl	9(0)	18	50	2.8(21)	0	1	11	11.0(11)	0	—	—	—	—	—	—	—	—	—	—	—	—	0	56
1999	Atl	12(9, RB)	141	452	3.2(20)	1	17	172	10.1(32)	1	—	—	—	—	—	—	—	—	—	—	—	—	12	553
NFL	2	21(9)	159	502	3.2(21)	1	18	183	10.2(32)	1	—	—	—	—	—	—	—	—	—	—	—	—	12	609

OZDOWSKI, MIKE Michael Thomas, DE, 6´5˝/243 lbs; Virginia; 1977: Bal, rnd 2; B9/24/1955 Cleveland, OH **1978** Bal 16 (3) **1979** Bal 11 (4) **1980** Bal 15 (10, RDE) **1981** Bal 12 (12, RDE) **NFL** 54 (29) [4 yrs]

PACE, CALVIN Calvin, DE, 6´4˝/262 lbs; Wake Forest; 2003: Arz, rnd 1; B10/28/1980 Detroit, MI **2003** Arz 16 (16, RDE) **2004** Arz 14 (0) **2005** Arz 5 (1) **NFL** 35 (17) [3 yrs]

PACE, JAMES James E., HB, 6´0˝/195 lbs; Michigan; 1958: SF, rnd 1; B1/1/1936 Little Rock, AR

YEAR	TEAM	G (GS, POS)	RUSH	YD	AVG (LG)	TD	REC	YD	AVG (LG)	TD	PASS	COMP	PCT	YD	AVG (LG)	TD	INT	SK	YD	QBR	KPR	OTD	PTS	TAY
1958	SF	12	52	161	3.1(34)	2	10	59	5.9(24)	0	—	—	—	—	—	—	—	—	—	—	kp	—	12	215

YEAR	TEAM	G (GS, POS)	RUSH	YD	AVG(LG)	TD	REC	YD	AVG(LG)	TD	PASS	COMP	PCT	YD	AVG(LG)	TD	INT	SK	YD	QBR	KPR	OTD	PTS	TAY

PACE, ORLANDO Orlando Lamar, T, 6'7"/325 lbs; Ohio State; 1997: SL, rnd 1; B11/4/1975 Sandusky, OH   **1997** SL 13 (9, LT)   **1998** SL 16 (16, LT)   **1999**†SL★16 (16, LT) **2000**†SL★16 (16, LT)   **2001**†SL★16 (16, LT)   **2002** SL✧10 (10, LT)   **2003**†SL★16 (16, LT)   **2004**†SL★16 (16, LT)   **2005** SL★16 (16, LT)   **NFL** 135 (131) [9 yrs]

PACELLA, DAVE David Wade, C-G, 6'2"/266 lbs; Maryland; B2/7/1960 Sewickley, PA   **1984** Phi 16 (0)

PACEWIC, VINCE Vincent C., HB, 6'1"/205 lbs; Loyola Marymount; San Francisco; 1943: Was, rnd 27; B5/28/1920 Collinsville, IL, D4/1/1990 Los Angeles, CA

| 1947 | Was | 2(0) | — | — | — | — | 5 | 42 | 8.4(15) | 0 | — | — | — | — | — | — | — | — | — | — | — | — | 0 | 21 |

PACHECO, CHRIS Christopher Luis, NT, 6'0"/250 lbs; Cal State-Northridge; Fresno State; B1/22/1964 Los Angeles, CA   **1987** LARm 3 (0)

PACKER, WALTER Walter, DB, 5'10"/174 lbs; Mississippi State; 1977: Atl, rnd 8; B11/7/1955 Leakesville, MS   **1977** TB 10   **1977** Sea 1   **NFL** 11 [1 yr]

PADAN, BOB Robert Samuel, TB-WB, /165 lbs; Ohio State; Otterbein; B8/1893 Portsmouth, OH, deceased   **1922** Lou 3 (3, TB)

PADJEN, GARY Gary Anthony, LB, 6'2"/244 lbs; Arizona State; 1980: Dal, rnd 11; B7/2/1958 Salt Lake City, UT   **1982** Bal 8 (3)   **1983** Bal 16 (0)   **1984** Ind 16 (0)   **1987** Ind 1 (0) **NFL** 41 (3) [4 yrs]

PADLOW, MAX Max, E, 6'1"/199 lbs; Ohio State; B8/15/1912, Russia, D8/8/1971 Dayton, OH   **1935** Phi 4 (0)   **1936** Phi 1 (0)   **NFL** 5 (0) [2 yrs]

PAFFRATH, BOB Robert William, B, 5'8"/190 lbs; Minnesota; 1941: GB, rnd 3; B7/13/1918 Mankato, MN, D5/21/2005 Beaverton, OR

1946	Bkn-A	5(0)	8	19	2.4	1	2	-3	-1.5	0	1	0	0.0	0	0	0	0	0	—	—	—	—	6	28
1946	Mia-A	7(2)	23	81	3.5	1	2	-3	-1.5	0	—	—	—	—	—	—	—	—	—	Pkp	—	6	102
AAFC	1	12(2)	31	100	3.2	2	4	-6	-1.5	0	1	0	0.0	0	0.0	0	0	0	—	Pkp	—	12	129

PAGAC, FRED Frederick, TE, 6'0"/222 lbs; Ohio State; B4/26/1952 Brownsville, PA

1974	ChiB	14(TE)	1	-1	-1.0(-1)	0	6	79	13.2(24)	0	—	—	—	—	—	—	—	—	—	k	—	0	47
1976	TB	14(3)	1	4	4.0(4)	0	2	15	7.5(10)	0	—	—	—	—	—	—	—	—	—	k	—	0	17
NFL	2	28(3)	2	3	1.5(4)	0	8	94	11.8(24)	0	—	—	—	—	—	—	—	—	—	k	—	0	63

PAGE, ALAN Alan Cedric, DT, 6'4"/245 lbs; Notre Dame; 1967: Min, rnd 1; B8/7/1945 Canton, OH; HOF 1988   **1967** Min 14 (11, LDT)   **1968**†Min★14 (14, RDT) **1969**†Min★14 (14, RDT)   **1970**†Min★14 (14, RDT)   **1971**★Min★14 (14, RDT)   **1972** Min★14 (14, RDT)   **1973**†Min★14 (14, RDT)   **1974**†Min★14 (14, RDT)   **1975**†Min★14 (14, RDT) **1976**†Min★14 (14, RDT)   **1977**†Min✩14 (14, rdt)   **1978** Min 6 (6, rdt)   **1978** ChiB 10 (10, RDT)   **1979**†ChiB 16 (16, RDT)   **1980** ChiB✩16 (16, RDT)   **1981** ChiB 16 (16, RDT) **NFL** 218 (215) [15 yrs]

PAGE, CRAIG Warren Craig, C, 6'3"/303 lbs; Georgia Tech; B1/17/1976 Jupiter, FL   **2000** Dal 2 (0)

PAGE, PAUL Paul Eugene, HB-DB, 6'0"/180 lbs; SMU; 1949: Bal-A, rnd 11/NYG, rnd 1; B9/16/1927 Eldorado, TX

| 1949 | Bal-A | 8(2) | 25 | 81 | 3.2 | 0 | 4 | 62 | 15.5 | 0 | — | — | — | — | — | — | — | — | — | kp | — | 0 | 171 |

PAGE, SOLOMON Solomon, G-T, 6'4"/325 lbs; West Virginia; 1999: Dal, rnd 2; B2/27/1976 Pittsburgh, PA   **1999**†Dal 14 (6, lg)   **2000** Dal 16 (16, RG)   **2001** Dal 14 (14, RT) **2002** Dal 15 (15, RT/rg)   **2003** SD 8 (7, rg)   **NFL** 67 (58) [5 yrs]

PAGEL, DEREK Derek, DB, 6'1"/206 lbs; Iowa; 2003: NYJ, rnd 5; B10/24/1979 Plainfield, IA   **2003** NYJ 14 (0)   **2004** NYJ 5 (0)   **NFL** 19 (0) [2 yrs]

PAGEL, MIKE Michael Jonathan, QB, 6'2"/206 lbs; Arizona State; 1982: Bal, rnd 4; B9/13/1960 Douglas, AZ

1982	Bal	9(9, QB)	19	82	4.3(32)	1	—	—	—	—	221	111	50.2	1281	5.8(53)	5	7	16	129	62.4	—	—	6	478
1983	Bal	15(15, QB)	54	441	8.2(33)	0	—	—	—	—	328	163	49.7	2353	7.2(72)	12	17	40	278	64.0	—	—	0	998
1984	Ind	11(9, QB)	26	149	5.7(23)	1	—	—	—	—	212	114	53.8	1426	6.7(54)	8	8	28	201	71.8	—	—	6	592
1985	Ind	16(14, QB)	25	160	6.4(29)	2	1	6	6.0(6)	0	393	199	50.6	2414	6.1(80)	14	15	25	180	65.8	—	—	12	860
1986	Cle	1(0)	2	0	0.0(0)	0	—	—	—	—	3	2	66.7	53	17.7(45)	0	0	—	—	—	—	—	0	27
1987	†Cle	4(0)	—	—	—	—	—	—	—	—	—	—	—	—	—	—	—	—	—	—	—	—	—	—
1988	†Cle	5(4)	4	1	0.3(5)	0	—	—	—	—	134	71	53.0	736	5.5(28)	3	4	1	9	—	—	—	0	224
1989	†Cle	16(0)	2	-1	-0.5(4)	0	—	—	—	—	14	5	35.7	60	4.3(18)	1	1	—	—	—	—	—	0	-6
1990	Cle	16(3)	3	-1	-0.3(0)	0	—	—	—	—	148	69	46.6	819	5.5(32)	3	8	5	40	—	—	—	0	104
1991	LARm	16(0)	—	—	—	—	—	—	—	—	27	11	40.7	150	5.6(30)	2	0	—	—	—	—	—	0	85
1992	LARm	16(0)	1	0	0.0(0)	0	—	—	—	—	20	8	40.0	99	4.9(22)	1	2	—	—	—	—	—	0	-26
1993	LARm	7(0)	—	—	—	—	—	—	—	—	9	3	33.3	23	2.6(10)	0	1	—	—	—	—	—	0	-29
NFL	12	132(54)	136	831	6.1(33)	4	1	6	6.0(6)	0	1509	756	50.1	9414	6.2(80)	49	63	115	837	63.3	—	—	24	3306

PAGLIEI, JOE Joseph Anthony, FB, 6'0"/220 lbs; Clemson; B4/12/1934 Clairton, PA

1959	Phi	7	2	-5	-2.5(1)	0	2	9	4.5(11)	0	—	—	—	—	—	—	—	—	—	P	—	0	-1
1960	NYT-A	11	17	69	4.1(25)	1	1	13	13.0(13)	0	—	—	—	—	—	—	—	—	—	P	—	6	86
NFL	2	18	19	64	3.4(25)	1	3	22	7.3(13)	0	—	—	—	—	—	—	—	—	—	P	—	6	85

PAHL, LOUIE Louis, WB-FB, 5'8"/185 lbs; none; B1898, deceased   **1923** Min 8 (7, WB), 6   **1924** Min 3 (3)   **NFL** 11 (10) [2 yrs]

PAHUKOA, JEFF Jeff Kalani, G-T, 6'2"/268 lbs; Washington; 1991: LARm, rnd 12; B2/9/1969 Vancouver, WA   **1991** LARm 7 (0)   **1992** LARm 16 (0)   **1993** LARm 16 (5, lg) **1995** Atl 6 (2)   **1996** Atl 14 (8)   **NFL** 59 (10) [5 yrs]

PAHUKOA, SHANE Shane Kapualani, DB, 6'2"/202 lbs; Washington; B11/25/1970 Vancouver, WA   **1995** NO 15 (2)

PAIGE, LEE Lee E., DB, 6'0"/197 lbs; Florida State; B10/16/1960 Jackson, MS   **1987** TB 3 (0)

PAIGE, STEPHONE Stephone, WR, 6'2"/184 lbs; Fresno State; B10/15/1961 Long Beach, CA

1983	KC	16(0)	—	—	—	—	30	528	17.6(43)	6	—	—	—	—	—	—	—	—	—	—	—	36	294
1984	KC	16(1)	3	19	6.3(9)	0	30	541	18.0(65)	4	—	—	—	—	—	—	—	—	—	k	—	24	449
1985	KC	16(8, wr)	1	15	15.0(15)	0	43	943	21.9(84)	10	—	—	—	—	—	—	—	—	—	k	—	60	543
1986	†KC	16(15, WR)	2	-2	-1.0(12)	0	52	829	15.9(51)	11	—	—	—	—	—	—	—	—	—	—	—	66	468
1987	KC	12(11, WR)	—	—	—	—	43	707	16.4(51)	4	—	—	—	—	—	—	—	—	—	—	—	24	374
1988	KC	16(16, WR)	—	—	—	—	61	902	14.8(49)	7	—	—	—	—	—	—	—	—	—	—	—	42	486
1989	KC	14(12, WR)	—	—	—	—	44	759	17.3(50)	2	—	—	—	—	—	—	—	—	—	—	—	12	390
1990	†KC	16(16, WR)	—	—	—	—	65	1021	15.7(86)	5	—	—	—	—	—	—	—	—	—	—	—	30	536
1991	KC	3(2)	—	—	—	—	9	111	12.3(26)	0	—	—	—	—	—	—	—	—	—	—	—	0	56
NFL	9	125(81)	6	32	5.3(15)	0	377	6341	16.8(86)	49	—	—	—	—	—	—	—	—	—	k	—	294	3593

PAIGE, TONY Anthony Ricardo, RB, 5'10"/225 lbs; Virginia Tech; 1984: NYJ, rnd 6; B10/14/1962 Washington, SC

1984	NYJ	16(3)	35	130	3.7(24)	7	6	31	5.2(10)	1	—	—	—	—	—	—	—	—	—	k	—	48	183
1985	†NYJ	16(9, FB)	55	158	2.9(30)	8	18	120	6.7(19)	2	—	—	—	—	—	—	—	—	—	—	—	60	308
1986	†NYJ	16(7, FB)	47	109	2.3(9)	2	18	121	6.7(18)	0	—	—	—	—	—	—	—	—	—	—	—	12	190
1987	Det	5(0)	4	13	3.3(6)	0	2	1	0.5(3)	0	—	—	—	—	—	—	—	—	—	—	—	0	14
1988	Det	16(2)	52	207	4.0(20)	0	11	100	9.1(15)	0	—	—	—	—	—	—	—	—	—	—	—	0	257
1989	Det	16(4)	30	105	3.5(16)	0	2	27	13.5(15)	0	—	—	—	—	—	—	—	—	—	—	—	0	119
1990	†Mia	13(13, FB)	32	95	3.0(11)	2	35	247	7.1(17)	4	—	—	—	—	—	—	—	—	—	k	—	36	262
1991	Mia	16(16, FB)	10	25	2.5(6)	0	57	469	8.2(30)	2	—	—	—	—	—	—	—	—	—	—	—	6	266
1992	†Mia	16(16, FB)	7	11	1.6(6)	1	48	399	8.3(30)	1	—	—	—	—	—	—	—	—	—	—	—	12	225
NFL	9	130(70)	272	853	3.1(30)	20	197	1515	7.7(30)	9	—	—	—	—	—	—	—	—	—	k	—	174	1821

PAINE, HOMER Homer, T, 6'0"/235 lbs; Tulsa; Oklahoma; 1948: Bkn-A, rnd 7/1946: Phi, rnd 14; B9/20/1923 Hennessey, OK   **1949** ChiH-A 12 (10, LT)

PAINE, JEFF Jeffrey Franklin, LB, 6'2"/224 lbs; Texas A&M; 1984: KC, rnd 5; B8/19/1961 Garland, TX   **1984** KC 14 (3)   **1985** KC 12 (4)   **1986** Was 2 (0)   **1987** SL 1 (0) **NFL** 29 (7) [4 yrs]

PAINTER, CARL Carl Drew, RB, 5'9"/184 lbs; Hampton; 1988: Det, rnd 6; B5/10/1964 Norfolk, VA

1988	Det	12(0)	17	42	2.5(13)	0	1	5	1.0(1)	0	—	—	—	—	—	—	—	—	—	k	—	0	135
1989	Det	15(0)	15	64	4.3(19)	0	3	41	13.7(27)	0	—	—	—	—	—	—	—	—	—	k	—	0	84
NFL	2	27(0)	32	106	3.3(13)	0	4	42	10.5(27)	0	—	—	—	—	—	—	—	—	—	k	—	0	218

PALATELLA, LOU Louis, G-LB, 6'2"/230 lbs; Pittsburgh; 1955: SF, rnd 12; B7/28/1933 Vandergrift, PA   **1955** SF 9 (RG)   **1956** SF 10   **1957**†SF 12 (LG)   **1958** SF 12   **NFL** 43 [4 yrs]

PALAZZI, LOU Louis Joseph, C, 6'0"/198 lbs; Penn State; 1943: NYG, rnd 7; B6/26/1921 Groton, CT   **1946** NYG 5 (0)   **1947** NYG 11 (0)   **NFL** 16 (0) [2 yrs]

PALELEI, LONNIE Si'ulagi Jack, G-T, 6´3˝/310 lbs; Purdue; UNLV; 1993: Pit, rnd 5; B10/15/1970 Nu'uuli, American Samoa **1993** Pit 3 (0) **1995** Pit 1 (0) **1997** NYJ 15 (14, LG) **1998** NYG 9 (0) **1999** Phi 16 (12, RT) **NFL** 44 (26) [5 yrs]

PALEPOI, ANTON Anton Charles, DE, 6´3˝/283 lbs; UNLV; 2002: Sea, rnd 2; B11/19/1978 American Samoa **2002** Sea 13 (1) **2003** Sea 7 (0) **2004†**Sea 1 (0) **2004** Den 11 (0) **2005** Arz 3 (0) **NFL** 35 (1) [4 yrs]

PALERMO, JIM James Vincent, G-C, 5´9˝/180 lbs; Missouri; B3/31/1902 Kansas City, KS, D10/26/1983 Shawnee Mission, KS **1925** KC 2 (0) **1926** KC 1 (0) **NFL** 3 (0) [2 yrs]

PALEWICZ, AL Albert Paul, LB, 6´1˝/215 lbs; Miami (FL); 1973: KC, rnd 8; B3/23/1950 Fort Worth, TX **1973** KC 14 **1974** KC 13 **1975** KC 9 **1977** NYJ 14 (1) **NFL** 50 (1) [4 yrs]

PALM, MIKE Myron Herrick, BB-WB, 5´10˝/170 lbs; Penn State; B11/26/1899 St. James, MN, D4/8/1974 Washington, DC **[C]** **1925** NYG 2 (1) **1926** NYG 1 (1), 6

YEAR	TEAM	G(GS, POS)	RUSH	YD	AVG(LG)	TD	REC	YD	AVG(LG)	TD	PASS	COMP	PCT	YD	AVG(LG)	TD	INT	SK	YD	QBR	KPR	OTD	PTS	TAY
1933	Cin	6(3)	14	6	0.4	0	—	—	—	—	8	3	37.5	51	6.4	0	2	—	—	—	—	—	0	-49
NFL	3	9(5)	14	6	0.4	0	—	—	—	—	8	3	37.5	51	6.4	0	2	—	—	—	—	—	6	-49

PALMER, CARSON Carson, QB, 6´5˝/230 lbs; USC; 2003: Cin, rnd 1; B12/27/1979 Fresno, CA

YEAR	TEAM	G(GS, POS)	RUSH	YD	AVG(LG)	TD	REC	YD	AVG(LG)	TD	PASS	COMP	PCT	YD	AVG(LG)	TD	INT	SK	YD	QBR	KPR	OTD	PTS	TAY
2004	Cin	13(13, QB)	18	47	2.6(14)	1	—	—	—	—	432	263	60.9	2897	6.7(76)	18	18	25	178	77.3	—	—	6	876
2005	†Cin✧	16(16, QB)	34	41	1.2(14)	1	—	—	—	—	509	**345**	**67.8**	3836	7.5(70)	**32**	12	19	105	101.1	—	—	6	1649
NFL	2	29(29)	52	88	1.7(14)	2	—	—	—	—	941	608	64.6	6733	7.2(76)	50	30	44	283	90.2	—	—	12	2525

PALMER, CHUCK Charles William, BB-WB, 5´10˝/185 lbs; Northwestern; B2/15/1901 Chicago, IL, D2/10/1974 Littleton, CO **1924** Rac 3 (2) **1926** Lou 4 (4, BB) **NFL** 7 (6) [2 yrs]

PALMER, DAVID David Lee, WR, 5´8˝/173 lbs; Alabama; 1994: Min, rnd 2; B11/19/1972 Birmingham, AL **[R]**

YEAR	TEAM	G(GS, POS)	RUSH	YD	AVG(LG)	TD	REC	YD	AVG(LG)	TD	PASS	COMP	PCT	YD	AVG(LG)	TD	INT	SK	YD	QBR	KPR	OTD	PTS	TAY
1994	†Min	13(1)	1	1	1.0(1)	0	6	90	15.0(39)	0	—	—	—	—	—	—	—	—	—	—	p	—	0	89
1995	Min	14(0)	7	15	2.1(9)	0	12	100	8.3(19)	0	—	—	—	—	—	—	—	—	—	—	kp	1	6	386
1996	†Min	11(1)	2	9	4.5(8)	0	6	40	6.7(20)	0	—	—	—	—	—	—	—	—	—	—	kp	1	6	242
1997	†Min☆	16(0)	11	36	3.3(10)	1	26	193	7.4(23)	1	—	—	—	—	—	—	—	—	—	—	kp	—	12	653
1998	†Min	16(0)	10	52	5.2(15)	0	18	185	10.3(33)	0	0	0	0.0	0	0.0	0	0	1	2	—	kp	1	6	730
1999	Min	8(2)	3	12	4.0(7)	0	4	25	6.3(13)	0	—	—	—	—	—	—	—	—	—	—	kp	—	0	274
2000	Min	6(0)	—	—	—	—	1	-2	-2.0(-2)	0	—	—	—	—	—	—	—	—	—	—	kp	—	0	12
NFL	7	84(4)	34	125	3.7(15)	1	73	631	8.6(39)	1	0	0	0.0	0	0.0	0	0	1	2	—	kp	3	30	2385

PALMER, DERRELL Derrell Franklin, DT-T, 6´2˝/240 lbs; TCU; 1943: ChiB, rnd 6; B8/27/1922 Breckenridge, TX **1946†**NYY-A 13 (1) **1947†**NYY-A 14 (11, LT) **1948** NYY-A 14 (10, lt) **1949†**Cle-A 11 (1) **AAFC** 52 (23) [4 yrs]

1950†Cle 12 (lt/ldt) **1951†**Cle 10 **1952†**Cle 11 (RDT) **1953†**Cle 11 (RDT) **NFL** 44 [4 yrs]

PALMER, DICK Richard Harry, LB, 6´2˝/232 lbs; Kentucky; 1970: Bal, rnd 10; B4/9/1947 Lexington, KY **1970** Mia 9 **1972** Buf 4 **1972** NO 6 **1973** NO 10 **1974** Atl 14 **NFL** 43 [4 yrs]

PALMER, EMILE Emile, DT, 6´3˝/320 lbs; Syracuse; B4/5/1973 Landover, MD **1996** NO 1 (0)

PALMER, GERY Gary Dean, T, 6´4˝/255 lbs; Kansas; 1973: Bal, rnd 4; B12/25/1950 Weimar, TX **1975** KC 2

PALMER, JESSE Jesse James, QB, 6´2˝/225 lbs; Florida; 2001: NYG, rnd 4; B10/5/1978 Toronto, Canada

YEAR	TEAM	G(GS, POS)	RUSH	YD	AVG(LG)	TD	REC	YD	AVG(LG)	TD	PASS	COMP	PCT	YD	AVG(LG)	TD	INT	SK	YD	QBR	KPR	OTD	PTS	TAY
2002	NYG	2(0)	1	-3	-3.0(-3)	0	—	—	—	—	4	3	75.0	30	7.5(14)	0	0	—	—	—	—	—	0	12
2003	NYG	6(3)	4	23	5.8(26)	0	—	—	—	—	116	60	51.7	532	4.6(40)	3	4	16	95	58.5	—	—	0	144
NFL	2	8(3)	5	20	4.0(26)	0	—	—	—	—	120	63	52.5	562	4.7(40)	3	4	16	95	59.8	—	—	0	156

PALMER, LES Leslie Hatfield, HB, 6´0˝/190 lbs; North Carolina State; B12/15/1923 Cedar Grove, WV **1948** Phi 5 (0)

PALMER, MIKE Major O., T, 5´10˝/210 lbs; none; B2/2/1890, WI, D3/16/1972 Ceylon, MN **1921** Min 4 (4, LT)

PALMER, MITCH Richard Mitchell, LB, 6´4˝/245 lbs; Colorado State; B9/2/1973 Oceanside, CA **1998** TB 16 (0) **1999** TB 4 (0) **2000†**Min 16 (0) **NFL** 36 (0) [3 yrs]

PALMER, PAUL Paul Woodrow, RB, 5´9˝/184 lbs; Temple; 1987: KC, rnd 1; B10/14/1964 Bethesda, MD

YEAR	TEAM	G(GS, POS)	RUSH	YD	AVG(LG)	TD	REC	YD	AVG(LG)	TD	PASS	COMP	PCT	YD	AVG(LG)	TD	INT	SK	YD	QBR	KPR	OTD	PTS	TAY
1987	KC☆	12(1)	24	155	6.5(35)	0	4	27	6.8(10)	0	1	0	0.0	0	0.0	0	0	—	—	—	k	2	12	542
1988	KC	15(11, RB)	134	452	3.4(26)	2	53	611	11.5(71)	4	—	—	—	—	—	—	—	—	—	—	k	—	36	817
1989	Det	5(0)	—	—	—	—	—	—	—	—	—	—	—	—	—	—	—	—	—	—	k	—	0	90
1989	Dal	9(8, RB)	112	446	4.0(63)	2	17	93	5.5(13)	0	—	—	—	—	—	—	—	—	—	—	—	—	12	513
NFL	3	41(20)	270	1053	3.9(63)	4	74	731	9.9(71)	4	1	0	0.0	0	0.0	0	0	—	—	—	k	2	60	1961

PALMER, RANDY Randy, TE, 6´4˝/235 lbs; Texas A&M-Kingsville; B11/12/1975 Pleasanton, TX **1999** Cle 3 (0)

PALMER, SCOTT Darrell Scott, DT, 6´3˝/245 lbs; Texas; 1971: NYJ, rnd 7; B9/15/1948 Cleburne, TX **1971** NYJ 2 **1972** SL 5 **NFL** 7 [2 yrs]

PALMER, STERLING Sterling Lanard, DE, 6´5˝/256 lbs; Florida State; 1993: Was, rnd 4; B2/4/1971 Fort Lauderdale, FL **1993** Was 14 (10, RDE) **1994** Was 16 (16, RDE) **1995** Was 13 (13, RDE) **1996** Was 6 (5, lde) **NFL** 49 (44) [4 yrs]

PALMER, TOM Thomas, DT, 6´2˝/240 lbs; Wake Forest; 1950: ChiC, rnd 17; B8/12/1929, D2/1980 Kingsport, TN **1953** Pit 11 **1954** Pit 7 **NFL** 18 [2 yrs]

PALUCK, JOHN John Joseph, DE, 6´2˝/241 lbs; Pittsburgh; 1956: Was, rnd 2; B5/23/1935 Swoyersville, PA, D4/22/2003 Fairfax, VA **1956** Was 12 **1959** Was 12 (12, LDE) **1960** Was☆12 (12, LDE) **1961** Was 13 (LDE) **1962** Was 14 **1963** Was 14 (LDE) **1964** Was★14 (LDE) **1965** Was 14 (rde) **NFL** 105 (24) [8 yrs]

PALUMBO, SAM Samuel Frank, LB-C, 6´2˝/226 lbs; Notre Dame; 1955: Cle, rnd 4; B6/7/1932 Cleveland, OH **1955†**Cle 9 **1956** Cle 12 **1957** GB 9 (MLB) **1960** Buf-A 1 **NFL** 31 [4 yrs]

PANACCION, TONY Victor Samuel, T, 6´1˝/212 lbs; Penn State; B9/11/1908, D3/26/1986 Bryn Mawr, PA **1930** Fra 4 (3)

PANCIERA, DON Donald Matthew, QB-DB, 6´1˝/192 lbs; Boston College; San Francisco; 1949: NYY-A, rnd 6/Phi, rnd 4; B6/23/1927 Westerly, RI

YEAR	TEAM	G(GS, POS)	RUSH	YD	AVG(LG)	TD	REC	YD	AVG(LG)	TD	PASS	COMP	PCT	YD	AVG(LG)	TD	INT	SK	YD	QBR	KPR	OTD	PTS	TAY
1949	†NYY-A	12(12, QB)	10	-4	-0.4	0	—	—	—	—	150	51	34.0	801	5.3	5	16	—	—	—	—	—	0	-219
1950	Det	4	—	—	—	—	—	—	—	—	—	—	—	—	—	—	—	—	—	—	i	—	0	-4
1952	ChiC	10	4	6	1.5(8)	0	—	—	—	—	96	35	36.5	582	6.1(47)	5	9	—	—	—	—	—	0	-38
NFL	2	14	4	6	1.5(8)	0	—	—	—	—	96	35	36.5	582	6.1(47)	5	9	—	—	—	i	—	0	-42

PANE, CHRIS Chris Albert, DB, 5´11˝/184 lbs; New Mexico; Cal State-Chico; B5/19/1953 Berkeley, CA **1976** Den 4 **1977** Den 11 (1) **1978†**Den 5 **1979†**Den 16 **NFL** 36 (1) [4 yrs]

PANELLI, JOHN John Rocco, LB-FB, 5´11˝/200 lbs; Notre Dame; 1949: Det, rnd 2/NYY-A, rnd 2; B5/7/1926 Morristown, NJ

YEAR	TEAM	G(GS, POS)	RUSH	YD	AVG(LG)	TD	REC	YD	AVG(LG)	TD	PASS	COMP	PCT	YD	AVG(LG)	TD	INT	SK	YD	QBR	KPR	OTD	PTS	TAY
1949	Det	11(1)	10	37	3.7(9)	0	1	13	13.0(13)	0	—	—	—	—	—	—	—	—	—	—	ki	—	0	42
1950	Det	8	32	82	2.6(14)	0	2	9	4.5(7)	0	—	—	—	—	—	—	—	—	—	—	k	—	0	105
1951	ChiC	12	13	38	2.9(18)	0	1	5	5.0(5)	0	—	—	—	—	—	—	—	—	—	—	k	—	0	68
1952	ChiC	9	—	—	—	—	—	—	—	—	—	—	—	—	—	—	—	—	—	—	i	—	0	-10
1953	ChiC	11	—	—	—	—	—	—	—	—	—	—	—	—	—	—	—	—	—	—	i	—	0	17
NFL	5	51(1)	55	157	2.9(18)	0	4	27	6.8(13)	0	—	—	—	—	—	—	—	—	—	—	ki	—	0	221

PANEPINTO, MIKE Michael Gino, RB, 5´7˝/180 lbs; Canisius; B11/17/1965 Buffalo, NY **1987** Buf 1 (0)

PANFIL, KEN Kenneth Charles, T, 6´6˝/262 lbs; Purdue; 1954: LA, rnd 6; B9/16/1930 Chicago, IL, D4/28/2002 Palos Heights, IL **1956** LARm 6 **1957** LARm 12 (RT) **1958** LARm 12 (RT) **1959** ChiC✧12 (RT) **1960** SL 12 (RT) **1961** SL 3 **1962** SL 1 **NFL** 58 [7 yrs]

PANGLE, HAL Harold James, B, 5´10˝/200 lbs; Oregon State; B5/4/1912 Huntington Beach, CA, D1/1/1968 Los Angeles County, CA

YEAR	TEAM	G(GS, POS)	RUSH	YD	AVG(LG)	TD	REC	YD	AVG(LG)	TD	PASS	COMP	PCT	YD	AVG(LG)	TD	INT	SK	YD	QBR	KPR	OTD	PTS	TAY
1935	ChiC	9(3)	18	50	2.8	0	1	5	5.0(5)	0	4	1	25.0	15	3.8(15)	0	2	—	—	—	—	—	0	-20
1936	ChiC	12(4)	38	101	2.7	1	9	195	21.7	0	2	0	0.0	0	0.0	0	0	—	—	—	—	—	6	209
1937	ChiC	11(8, FB)	61	203	3.3	2	5	58	11.6	0	2	0	0.0	0	0.0	0	1	—	—	—	—	—	12	212
1938	ChiC	4(1)	2	3	1.5	0	2	14	7.0	0	—	—	—	—	—	—	—	—	—	—	—	—	0	10
NFL	4	36(16)	119	357	3.0	3	17	272	16.0(5)	0	8	1	12.5	15	1.9(15)	0	3	—	—	—	—	—	18	411

PANKEY, IRV Irvin Lee, T, 6´4˝/277 lbs; Penn State; 1980: LA, rnd 2; B2/15/1958 Aberdeen, MD **1980†**LARm 16 (1) **1981** LARm 13 (12, LT) **1982** LARm 9 (9, LT) **1984†**LARm 16 (9, RT) **1985†**LARm 16 (12, LT) **1986†**LARm 16 (16, LT) **1987** LARm 12 (12, LT) **1988†**LARm☆16 (16, LT) **1989†**LARm 14 (14, LT) **1990** LARm 16 (16, LT) **1991** Ind 3 (3) **1992** Ind 3 (2) **NFL** 150 (122) [12 yrs]

PANNELL, ERNIE Ernest Woodrow, T, 6´2˝/220 lbs; Texas A&M; 1941: GB, rnd 16; B2/2/1917 Manor, TX, D9/24/1998 Houston, TX **1941†**GB 10 (3) **1942** GB 5 (5, lt) **1945** GB 7 (3) **NFL** 22 (11) [3 yrs]

YEAR	TEAM	G (GS, POS)	RUSH	YD	AVG(LG)	TD	REC	YD	AVG(LG)	TD	PASS	COMP	PCT	YD	AVG(LG)	TD	INT	SK	YD	QBR	KPR	OTD	PTS	TAY

PANOS, JOE Zois, aka Zois Panagiotopoulos, G-C, 6´2˝/293 lbs; Wisconsin-Whitewater; Wisconsin; 1994: Phi, rnd 3; B1/24/1971 Brookfield, WI   **1994** Phi 16 (2)   **1995** Phi 9 (9, RG)   **1996**†Phi 16 (16, LG)   **1997** Phi 13 (13, LG)   **1998**†Buf 16 (16, RG)   **2000** Buf 13 (0)   **NFL** 83 (56) [6 yrs]

PAOLUCCI, BEN Ben John, DT, 6´2˝/240 lbs; Wayne State (MI); 1958: Det, rnd 9; B3/5/1937 Cleveland, OH   **1959** Det 4

PAPAC, NICK Nicholas Robert, QB, 5´11˝/190 lbs; Fresno State; B5/18/1935 Fresno, CA

| 1961 | Oak-A | 14 | 6 | 28 | 4.7(11) | 1 | — | — | — | — | 44 | 13 | 29.5 | 173 | 3.9(43) | 2 | 7 | — | — | — | — | — | 6 | -146 |

PAPACH, GEORGE George Martin, FB, 6´2˝/208 lbs; Purdue; 1948: Pit, rnd 12; B4/27/1925 Youngstown, OH

1948	Pit	10(3)	60	324	**5.4(42)**	2	4	72	18.0(31)	1	—	—	—	—	—	—	—	—	—	—	k	—	18	386
1949	Pit	12(9, FB)	99	407	4.1(25)	0	6	18	3.0(11)	0	1	0	0.0	0	0.0	0	0	—	—	—	k	—	0	428
NFL	2	22(12)	159	731	4.6(42)	2	10	90	9.0(31)	1	1	0	0.0	0	0.0	0	0	—	—	—	k	—	18	814

PAPALE, VINCE Vincent Francis, WR, 6´2˝/195 lbs; St. Joseph's (PA); B2/9/1946 Chester, PA   **1976** Phi 14   **1978**†Phi 13

| 1977 | Phi | 14 | — | — | — | — | 1 | 15 | 15.0(15) | 0 | — | — | — | — | — | — | — | — | — | — | — | — | 0 | 8 |
| NFL | 3 | 41 | — | — | — | — | 1 | 15 | 15.0(15) | 0 | — | — | — | — | — | — | — | — | — | — | — | — | 0 | 8 |

PAPE, ORAN Oran Henry, B, 5´11˝/180 lbs; Iowa; B3/10/1904 Waupeton, IA, D4/29/1936 Muscatine, IA   **1930** Min 6 (3), 12   **1930** GB 2 (1)   **1931** Pro 11 (7, WB), 18

1932	Bos	5(0)	9	148	16.4	0	—	—	—	—	2	1	50.0	5	2.5(5)	0	1	—	—	—	—	1	6	121
1932	SI	2(0)	6	12	2.0	0	—	—	—	—	7	1	14.3	26	3.7(26)	1	1	—	—	—	—	—	0	-10
NFL	3	26(11)	15	160	10.7	3	—	—	—	—	9	2	22.2	31	3.4(26)	1	2	—	—	—	—	1	36	151

PAPIT, JOHNNY John Michael, HB, 6´0˝/190 lbs; Virginia; 1951: Was, rnd 7; B7/25/1928 Philadelphia, PA

1951	Was	11	44	175	4.0(33)	0	3	43	14.3(24)	0	—	—	—	—	—	—	—	—	—	—	—	—	0	197
1952	Was	11	34	102	3.0(13)	0	3	71	23.7(39)	1	—	—	—	—	—	—	—	—	—	—	k	—	6	153
1953	GB	4	6	44	7.3(21)	1	—	—	—	—	—	—	—	—	—	—	—	—	—	—	k	—	6	62
1953	Was	3	11	58	5.3(15)	0	1	9	9.0(9)	0	—	—	—	—	—	—	—	—	—	—	k	—	0	63
NFL	3	29	95	379	4.0(33)	1	7	123	17.6(39)	1	—	—	—	—	—	—	—	—	—	—	k	—	12	474

PAPPIO, JOE Joseph, G-E-T-BB, 6´0˝/189 lbs; Haskell Indian; B1903, deceased   **1923** Oor 1 (0)   **1930** ChiC 4 (0)   **NFL** 5 (0) [2 yrs]

PARDEE, JACK John Perry, LB, 6´2˝/225 lbs; Texas A&M; 1957: LA, rnd 2; B4/19/1936 Exira, IA [IC]   **1957** LARm 12   **1958** LARm 12 (LLB)   **1959** LARm 12 (LLB)
1960 LARm 8 (LLB)   **1961** LARm 13 (LLB)   **1962** LARm 14 (RLB)   **1963** LARm★14 (RLB)   **1964** LARm 14 (LLB)   **1966** LARm 14 (13, LLB)   **1967**†LARm 14 (LLB)
1968 LARm 14 (14, LLB)   **1969**†LARm 14 (14, LLB)   **1970** LARm 14 (14, LLB)   **1971**†Was☆14 (14, LLB)   **1972**†Was 13 (13, LLB)   **NFL** 196 (82) [15 yrs]

PARDONNER, PAUL Paul F., BB, 5´8˝/170 lbs; Purdue; B4/29/1910 Ingomar, OH, D2/14/1989 Columbus, OH [K]

1934	ChiC	6(3)	—	—	—	—	1	1	1.0(1)	0	—	—	—	—	—	—	—	—	—	—	K	—	3	1
1935	ChiC	9(5, bb)	4	-14	-3.5	0	2	44	22.0	0	5	1	20.0	6	1.2(6)	0	3	—	—	—	K	—	4	-109
NFL	2	15(8)	4	-14	-3.5	0	3	45	15.0(1)	0	5	1	20.0	6	1.2(6)	0	3	—	—	—	K	—	7	-109

PARDRIDGE, CURT Curtis Lynn, WR, 5´10˝/175 lbs; Northern Illinois; 1986: SD, rnd 6; B3/12/1964 DeKalb, IL

| 1987 | Sea | 3(0) | — | — | — | — | 8 | 145 | 18.1(47) | 1 | — | — | — | — | — | — | — | — | — | — | k | — | 6 | 77 |

PAREMORE, BOB Robert Cero, HB, 5´11˝/190 lbs; Florida A&M; 1963: SL, rnd 6/Den, rnd 17; B12/5/1939 Tallahassee, FL, D7/22/2004 Tallahassee, FL   **1964** SL 4

| 1963 | SL | 14 | 36 | 107 | 3.0(14) | 0 | 6 | 89 | 14.8(32) | 1 | — | — | — | — | — | — | — | — | — | — | kp | 1 | 12 | 272 |
| NFL | 2 | 18 | 36 | 107 | 3.0(14) | 0 | 6 | 89 | 14.8(32) | 1 | — | — | — | — | — | — | — | — | — | — | kp | 1 | 12 | 329 |

PARILLI, BABE Vito, QB, 6´1˝/196 lbs; Kentucky; 1952: GB, rnd 1; B5/7/1930 Rochester, PA

1952	GB	12(QB)	32	106	3.3(19)	1	—	—	—	—	177	77	43.5	1416	8.0(**90**)	13	17	—	—	56.6	P	—	6	209
1953	GB	12(QB)	42	171	4.1(19)	4	—	—	—	—	166	74	44.6	830	5.0(45)	4	19	—	—	28.5	P	—	24	-114
1956	Cle	5(qb)	18	65	3.6(19)	0	—	—	—	—	49	24	49.0	409	8.3(68)	3	7	—	—	—		—	0	5
1957	GB	12(qb)	24	83	3.5(20)	2	—	—	—	—	102	39	38.2	669	6.6(75)	4	12	—	—	34.8		—	12	-23
1958	GB	8	15	1.9(5)		0	—	—	—	—	157	68	43.3	1068	6.8(80)	10	13	—	—	53.3		—	0	79
1960	Oak-A	14(qb)	21	131	6.2(16)	1	1	0	0.0(0)	0	187	87	46.5	1003	5.4(49)	5	11	—	—	47.6		—	6	228
1961	Bos-A	14(QB)	38	183	4.8(24)	4	—	—	—	—	198	104	**52.5**	1314	6.6(53)	13	9	—	—	76.5		1	32	585
1962	Bos-A	10(QB)	28	169	6.0(33)	2	—	—	—	—	253	140	55.3	1988	7.9(67)	18	8	—	—	91.5		—	12	953
1963	†Bos-A◊	14(QB)	36	126	3.5(19)	5	—	—	—	—	337	153	45.4	2345	7.0(77)	13	24	—	—	52.1		—	30	454
1964	Bos-A★	14(QB)	34	168	4.9(32)	2	—	—	—	—	473	228	48.2	**3465**	7.3(80)	**31**	**27**	27	279	70.8	P	—	12	996
1965	Bos-A	14(QB)	50	200	4.0(17)	0	—	—	—	—	426	173	40.6	2597	6.1(73)	18	26	—	—	50.0		—	0	549
1966	Bos-A◊	14(QB)	28	42	1.5(17)	1	—	—	—	—	382	181	47.4	2721	7.1(63)	20	20	—	—	66.9		—	6	713
1967	Bos-A	14(11, QB)	14	61	4.4(18)	0	—	—	—	—	344	161	46.8	2317	6.7(**79**)	19	24	29	250	58.5		—	0	355
1968	†NYJ-A	14	7	-2	-0.3(10)	1	—	—	—	—	55	29	52.7	401	7.3(40)	5	2	3	23	—		—	6	154
1969	NYJ-A	14	3	4	1.3(2)	0	—	—	—	—	24	14	58.3	138	5.8(29)	2	1	—	—	—		—	0	43
NFL	15	189(11)	383	1522	4.0(33)	23	1	0	0.0	0	3330	1552	46.6	22681	6.8(90)	178	220	59	552	59.6	P	1	146	5183

PARIS, BUBBA William H., T-G, 6´6˝/300 lbs; Michigan; 1982: SF, rnd 2; B10/6/1960 Louisville, KY   **1983**†SF 16 (16, LT)   **1984**†SF 16 (15, LT)   **1985**†SF 16 (16, LT)
1986†SF 10 (9, LT)   **1987**†SF 11 (8, LT)   **1988**†SF 16 (1)   **1989**†SF 16 (16, LT)   **1990**†SF 16 (16, LT)   **1991** Ind 13 (8, lg)   **1991**†Det 0 (0)   **NFL** 130 (105) [9 yrs]

PARISH, DON Donald Edward, LB, 6´1˝/220 lbs; Stanford; 1970: SL, rnd 4; B1/4/1948 Paso Robles, CA   **1970** SL 14 (RLB)   **1971** SL 1   **1971** LARm 1   **1972** SL 2   **1972** Den 1 (1)
NFL 19 (1) [3 yrs]

PARK, ERNIE Ernest Carol, G-T, 6´3˝/253 lbs; McMurry; 1963: SD, rnd 19; B10/22/1940 San Angelo, TX   **1963**†SD-A 7   **1964**†SD-A 14   **1965**†SD-A 14 (LG)
1966 Mia-A 14 (11, LG)   **1967** Den-A 14   **1969** Cin-A 11 (LG)   **NFL** 74 (11) [6 yrs]

PARK, KAULANA Kaulana Hnr, RB, 6´2˝/230 lbs; Stanford; B6/16/1962 Honolulu, HI

| 1987 | NYG | 2(2) | 6 | 11 | 1.8(4) | 0 | 1 | 6 | 6.0(6) | 0 | — | — | — | — | — | — | — | — | — | — | — | — | 0 | 14 |

PARKER, ACE Clarence McKay, TB-DB-QB, 6´0˝/178 lbs; Duke; 1937: Bkn, rnd 2; B5/17/1912 Portsmouth, VA; HOF 1972 [K]

1937	Bkn☆	4(4, TB)	34	26	0.8	1	—	—	—	—	61	28	45.9	514	8.4	1	7	—	—	—	K	1	13	28
1938	Bkn☆	11(11, TB)	93	253	2.7	2	1	19	19.0(19)	1	**148**	63	42.6	**865**	5.8	5	7	—	—	53.5	K	1	29	475
1939	Bkn☆	11(10, TB)	104	271	2.6	5	1	5	5.0(5)	0	157	72	45.9	977	6.2(66)	4	13	—	—	40.2	KP	—	33	312
1940	Bkn☆	11(10, TB)	89	306	3.4	2	3	139	46.3(71)	2	111	49	44.1	817	7.4	10	7	—	—	73.3	KPi	1	49	**710**
1941	Bkn	11(9, TB)	85	301	3.5(60)	0	3	66	22.0(36)	0	102	51	50.0	639	6.3(47)	2	8	—	—	43.7	Pkpi	—	0	443
1945	Bos	8(1)	18	-49	-2.7(7)	0	—	—	—	—	24	10	41.7	123	5.1(41)	0	5	—	—	—	P	—	0	-188
NFL	6	56(45)	423	1108	2.6	10	8	229	28.6(71)	4	603	273	45.3	3935	6.5(66)	22	47	—	—	46.7	KPkpi	3	124	1780
1946	†NYY-A☆	12(4, tb)	75	184	2.5	3	—	—	—	—	115	62	53.9	763	6.6(75)	8	3	—	—	—	Pkp	1	24	558

PARKER, ANDY Andrew James, TE, 6´5˝/244 lbs; Utah; 1984: LARd, rnd 5; B9/8/1961 Redlands, CA   **1984** LARd 9 (0)   **1985**†LARd 16 (0)   **1987** LARd 12 (0)   **1990** LARd 5 (0)

1986	LARd	13(0)	—	—	—	—	2	8	4.0(6)	1	—	—	—	—	—	—	—	—	—	—	—	—	6	9
1988	LARd	16(11, TE)	—	—	—	—	4	33	8.3(12)	0	—	—	—	—	—	—	—	—	—	—	—	—	0	17
1989	SD	10(6, te)	—	—	—	—	2	5	2.5(4)	1	—	—	—	—	—	—	—	—	—	—	—	—	6	8
NFL	7	81(17)	—	—	—	—	8	46	5.8(12)	2	—	—	—	—	—	—	—	—	—	—	—	—	12	33

PARKER, ANTHONY Will Anthony, DB, 5´10˝/181 lbs; Arizona State; B2/11/1966 Sylacauga, AL   **1989** Ind 1 (0)   **1991**†KC 2 (0)   **1992**†Min 16 (3)   **1993**†Min 14 (0)
1994†Min 15 (15, LCB)   **1995** SL 16 (16, RCB)   **1996** SL 14 (14, RCB)   **1997**†TB 15 (14, RCB)   **1998** TB 11 (7, rcb)   **NFL** 104 (69) [9 yrs]

PARKER, ANTHONY Anthony E., DB, 6´1˝/200 lbs; Weber State; 1999: SF, rnd 4; B12/4/1975 Denver, CO   **2000** SF 16 (0)   **2001** SF 5 (0)   **NFL** 21 (0) [2 yrs]

PARKER, ARTIMUS Artimus L., DB, 6´3˝/208 lbs; USC; 1974: Phi, rnd 12; B1/16/1952 Winston-Salem, NC, D5/31/2004 Sacramento, CA   **1974** Phi 14   **1975** Phi 14 (5, fs)
1976 Phi 14 (1)   **1977** NYJ 11 (4)   **NFL** 53 (10) [4 yrs]

PARKER, BUDDY Raymond Klein, BB-FB, 6´0˝/193 lbs; North Texas; Centenary; B12/16/1913 Slaton, TX, D3/22/1982 Kaufman, TX [KC]

1935	†Det	11(2)	59	156	2.6	0	1	12	12.0(12)	0	1	0	0.0	0	0.0	0	1	—	—	—	—	—	0	122
1936	Det	10(5, bb)	6	21	3.5	0	1	15	15.0(15)	0	1	0	0.0	0	0.0	0	0	—	—	—	—	—	0	29
1937	ChiC	11(3)	50	115	2.3	1	2	14	7.0	0	0	0	0.0	0	0.0	0	0	—	—	—	K	—	7	132
1938	ChiC	10(10, FB)	45	144	3.2	2	16	142	8.9	0	2	2	100.0	21	10.5	0	0	—	—	—		—	12	246
1939	ChiC	9(1)	12	37	3.1	0	5	33	6.6	0	—	—	—	—	—	—	—	—	—	—		—	0	74
1940	ChiC	10(4)	6	8	1.3	1	6	45	7.5	0	—	—	—	—	—	—	—	—	—	—	Ki	—	9	51

YEAR	TEAM	G(GS, POS)	RUSH	YD	AVG(LG)	TD	REC	YD	AVG(LG)	TD	PASS	COMP	PCT	YD	AVG(LG)	TD	INT	SK	YD	QBR	KPR	OTD	PTS	TAY
1941	ChiC	11(7, BB)	1	-1	-1.0(-1)	0	7	122	17.4(44)	0	—	—	—	—	—	—	—	—	—	—	Ki	—	0	58
1942	ChiC	11(8, BB)	1	9	9.0(9)	0	2	7	3.5(4)	0	—	—	—	—	—	—	—	—	—	—	—	—	0	13
1943	ChiC	4(0)	—	—	—	—	—	—	—	—	—	—	—	—	—	—	—	—	—	—	—	—	—	—
NFL	9	87(40)	180	489	2.7(9)	4	40	390	9.8(44)	0	5	2	40.0	21	4.2	0	1	—	—	—	Ki	—	28	703

Parker, Carl Carl Wayne, WR, 6´2˝/201 lbs; Vanderbilt; 1988: Cin, rnd 12; B2/5/1965 Columbus, GA **1988**†Cin 3 (0)

YEAR	TEAM	G(GS, POS)	RUSH	YD	AVG(LG)	TD	REC	YD	AVG(LG)	TD	PASS	COMP	PCT	YD	AVG(LG)	TD	INT	SK	YD	QBR	KPR	OTD	PTS	TAY
1989	Cin	3(0)	—	—	—	—	1	45	45.0(45)	0	—	—	—	—	—	—	—	—	—	—	—	—	0	23
NFL	2	6(0)	—	—	—	—	1	45	45.0(45)	0	—	—	—	—	—	—	—	—	—	—	—	—	0	23

Parker, Charlie Charles Ruffing, G, 6´1˝/245 lbs; Southern Mississippi; 1964: Den, rnd 13/Bal, rnd 13; B6/19/1941 Greenville, MS **1965** Den-A 14

Parker, Chris Christopher Lee, RB, 5´11˝/213 lbs; Marshall; B12/31/1972 Lynchburg, VA **1997**†Jax 1 (0)

Parker, Daren Daren Roger, P, 6´0˝/185 lbs; South Carolina; B4/10/1968 **1992** Den 3 (0)

Parker, Dave David A., E, 6´3˝/200 lbs; Hardin-Simmons; 1941: Bkn, rnd 19; B1/30/1918 Novice, TX, D2/12/1991 Stephenville, TX

YEAR	TEAM	G(GS, POS)	RUSH	YD	AVG(LG)	TD	REC	YD	AVG(LG)	TD	PASS	COMP	PCT	YD	AVG(LG)	TD	INT	SK	YD	QBR	KPR	OTD	PTS	TAY
1941	Bkn	7(0)	—	—	—	—	1	10	10.0(10)	0	—	—	—	—	—	—	—	—	—	—	—	—	0	5

Parker, De'Mond De'Mond Keith, RB, 5´10˝/185 lbs; Oklahoma; 1999: GB, rnd 5; B12/24/1976 Tulsa, OK

YEAR	TEAM	G(GS, POS)	RUSH	YD	AVG(LG)	TD	REC	YD	AVG(LG)	TD	PASS	COMP	PCT	YD	AVG(LG)	TD	INT	SK	YD	QBR	KPR	OTD	PTS	TAY
1999	GB	11(0)	36	184	5.1(26)	2	4	15	3.8(7)	0	—	—	—	—	—	—	—	—	—	—	k	—	12	255
2000	GB	8(0)	18	85	4.7(24)	0	9	50	5.6(10)	0	—	—	—	—	—	—	—	—	—	—	—	—	0	110
NFL	2	19(0)	54	269	5.0(26)	2	13	65	5.0(10)	0	—	—	—	—	—	—	—	—	—	—	k	—	12	365

Parker, Don Donald Martin, G, 6´3˝/258 lbs; Virginia; 1966: SF, rnd 4/NYJ, rnd R1; B8/9/1944 Honolulu, HI **1967** SF 12

Parker, Eric Eric Samuel, WR, 6´0˝/180 lbs; Tennessee; B4/14/1979 Shorewood, IL

YEAR	TEAM	G(GS, POS)	RUSH	YD	AVG(LG)	TD	REC	YD	AVG(LG)	TD	PASS	COMP	PCT	YD	AVG(LG)	TD	INT	SK	YD	QBR	KPR	OTD	PTS	TAY
2002	SD	9(2)	—	—	—	—	17	268	15.8(31)	1	—	—	—	—	—	—	—	—	—	—	—	—	6	139
2003	SD	8(4)	3	21	7.0(13)	0	18	244	13.6(33)	3	—	—	—	—	—	—	—	—	—	—	p	—	18	250
2004	†SD	15(13, WR)	4	53	13.3(38)	0	47	690	14.7(79)	4	—	—	—	—	—	—	—	—	—	—	p	—	24	520
2005	SD	16(9, WR)	4	55	13.8(30)	0	57	725	12.7(49)	3	—	—	—	—	—	—	—	—	—	—	kp	—	18	450
NFL	4	48(28)	11	129	11.7(38)	0	139	1927	13.9(79)	11	—	—	—	—	—	—	—	—	—	—	kp	—	66	1359

Parker, Ervin Ervin, LB, 6´4˝/236 lbs; South Carolina State; 1980: Buf, rnd 4; B8/19/1958 Georgetown, SC **1980**†Buf 16 (0) **1981**†Buf 16 (0) **1982** Buf 9 (9, LOLB) **1983** Buf 16 (16, ROLB) **NFL** 57 (25) [4 yrs]

Parker, Frank William Frank, DT, 6´5˝/270 lbs; Oklahoma State; 1961: Cle, rnd 6/1962: NYT, rnd 29; B10/16/1939 Broken Bow, OK **1962** Cle 14 **1963** Cle 14 (RDT) **1964** Cle 8 **1966** Cle 12 (rdt) **1967**†Cle 12 **1968** Pit 10 (rdt) **1969** NYG 8 **NFL** 78 [7 yrs]

Parker, Freddie Freddie R., RB, 5´10˝/215 lbs; Mississippi Valley State; B7/6/1962 Heidelberg, MS

YEAR	TEAM	G(GS, POS)	RUSH	YD	AVG(LG)	TD	REC	YD	AVG(LG)	TD	PASS	COMP	PCT	YD	AVG(LG)	TD	INT	SK	YD	QBR	KPR	OTD	PTS	TAY
1987	GB	1(0)	8	33	4.1(17)	0	3	22	7.3(13)	0	—	—	—	—	—	—	—	—	—	—	—	—	0	44

Parker, Glenn Glenn Andrew, G-T, 6´5˝/305 lbs; Arizona; 1990: Buf, rnd 3; B4/22/1966 Westminster, CA **1990**†Buf 16 (3) **1991**†Buf 16 (5, rg) **1992**†Buf 13 (13, RG) **1993**†Buf 16 (9, lg) **1994** Buf 16 (16, RT) **1995**†Buf 13 (13, RT) **1996**†Buf 14 (13, RT) **1997**†KC 15 (15, RT) **1998** KC 15 (15, LG) **1999** KC 12 (11, LT) **2000**†NYG 13 (13, LG) **2001** NYG 15 (15, LG) **NFL** 174 (141) [12 yrs]

Parker, Howie Howard Ingram, BB, 6´2˝/220 lbs; SMU; B8/23/1926 Greenville, TX

YEAR	TEAM	G(GS, POS)	RUSH	YD	AVG(LG)	TD	REC	YD	AVG(LG)	TD	PASS	COMP	PCT	YD	AVG(LG)	TD	INT	SK	YD	QBR	KPR	OTD	PTS	TAY
1948	NYY-A	3(0)	—	—	—	—	1	17	17.0(17)	0	—	—	—	—	—	—	—	—	—	—	—	—	0	9

Parker, Jeff Jeffrey, WR, 5´10˝/185 lbs; Bethune-Cookman; B7/16/1969 Daytona Beach, FL

YEAR	TEAM	G(GS, POS)	RUSH	YD	AVG(LG)	TD	REC	YD	AVG(LG)	TD	PASS	COMP	PCT	YD	AVG(LG)	TD	INT	SK	YD	QBR	KPR	OTD	PTS	TAY
1992	TB	3(0)	—	—	—	—	1	12	12.0(12)	0	—	—	—	—	—	—	—	—	—	—	—	—	0	6

Parker, Jeremiah Jeremiah, DE, 6´5˝/250 lbs; California; 2000: NYG, rnd 7; B11/15/1977 Franklin, LA **2000** NYG 4 (0)

Parker, Jerry Jerry Lynn, LB, 6´0˝/227 lbs; Central State (OH); B9/13/1964 **1987** Cle 2 (0)

Parker, Jim James Thomas, T-G, 6´3˝/273 lbs; Ohio State; 1957: Bal, rnd 1; B4/3/1934 Macon, GA, D7/18/2004 Columbia, MD; HOF 1973 **1957** Bal☆12 (LT) **1958**†Bal★12 (LT) **1959**†Bal★12 (LT) **1960** Bal★12 (LT) **1961** Bal★14 (LT) **1962** Bal★14 (LG/lt) **1963** Bal★14 (LG) **1964**†Bal★14 (LG) **1965**†Bal★14 (14, LG) **1966** Bal☆14 (RT) **1967** Bal 3 **NFL** 135 (14) [11 yrs]

Parker, Joe Joseph Jackson, E, 6´1˝/220 lbs; Texas; 1944: Phi, rnd 5; B7/11/1923 Wichita Falls, TX **1947**†ChiC 12 (1)

YEAR	TEAM	G(GS, POS)	RUSH	YD	AVG(LG)	TD	REC	YD	AVG(LG)	TD	PASS	COMP	PCT	YD	AVG(LG)	TD	INT	SK	YD	QBR	KPR	OTD	PTS	TAY
1946	ChiC	8(1)	—	—	—	—	2	17	8.5(11)	0	—	—	—	—	—	—	—	—	—	—	k	—	0	-7
NFL	2	20(2)	—	—	—	—	2	17	8.5(11)	0	—	—	—	—	—	—	—	—	—	—	k	—	0	-7

Parker, Joel Joseph Lee, WR, 6´5˝/212 lbs; Florida; 1974: NO, rnd 5; B4/23/1952 Louisville, KY

YEAR	TEAM	G(GS, POS)	RUSH	YD	AVG(LG)	TD	REC	YD	AVG(LG)	TD	PASS	COMP	PCT	YD	AVG(LG)	TD	INT	SK	YD	QBR	KPR	OTD	PTS	TAY
1974	NO	14(WR)	2	2	1.0(6)	0	41	455	11.1(58)	4	1	0	0.0	0	0.0	0	0	1	6	—	—	—	24	250
1975	NO	7(WR)	—	—	—	—	9	123	13.7(32)	2	—	—	—	—	—	—	—	—	—	—	—	—	12	72
1977	NO	1	—	—	—	—	1	7	7.0(7)	0	—	—	—	—	—	—	—	—	—	—	—	—	0	4
NFL	3	22	2	2	1.0(6)	0	51	585	11.5(58)	6	1	0	0.0	0	0.0	0	0	1	6	—	—	—	36	325

Parker, J'Vonne J'Vonne, DT, 6´4˝/310 lbs; Rutgers; B6/7/1982 Newark, NJ **2005** Cle 4 (0)

Parker, Kenny Kenneth, DB, 6´1˝/190 lbs; Fordham; 1968: NYG, rnd 16; B7/22/1946 Paterson, NJ **1970** NYG 14

Parker, Kerry Kerry Anthony, DB, 6´1˝/192 lbs; Grambling State; B10/3/1955 New Orleans, LA **1984** KC 15 (0) **1987** Buf 2 (2) **NFL** 17 (2) [2 yrs]

Parker, Larry Larry, WR, 6´1˝/205 lbs; USC; 1999: KC, rnd 4; B7/14/1976 Bakersfield, CA

YEAR	TEAM	G(GS, POS)	RUSH	YD	AVG(LG)	TD	REC	YD	AVG(LG)	TD	PASS	COMP	PCT	YD	AVG(LG)	TD	INT	SK	YD	QBR	KPR	OTD	PTS	TAY
1999	KC	10(0)	—	—	—	—	—	—	—	—	—	—	—	—	—	—	—	—	—	—	kp	—	0	35
2000	KC	16(0)	1	-7	-7.0(-7)	0	3	41	13.7(27)	0	—	—	—	—	—	—	—	—	—	—	kp	—	0	108
2001	KC	12(4)	3	6	2.0(7)	0	15	199	13.3(44)	2	—	—	—	—	—	—	—	—	—	—	kp	—	12	159
NFL	3	38(4)	4	-1	-0.3(7)	0	18	240	13.3(44)	2	—	—	—	—	—	—	—	—	—	—	kp	—	12	301

Parker, Orlando Orlando Lateef, WR, 5´11˝/190 lbs; Troy State; 1994: NYJ, rnd 4; B3/7/1972 Montgomery, AL

YEAR	TEAM	G(GS, POS)	RUSH	YD	AVG(LG)	TD	REC	YD	AVG(LG)	TD	PASS	COMP	PCT	YD	AVG(LG)	TD	INT	SK	YD	QBR	KPR	OTD	PTS	TAY
1994	NYJ	2(0)	—	—	—	—	1	7	7.0(7)	0	—	—	—	—	—	—	—	—	—	—	—	—	0	4

Parker, Ricky Ricky Duwayne, DB, 6´0˝/194 lbs; San Diego State; 1997: Chi, rnd 6; B12/4/1974 Burlington, VT **1997** Jax 12 (0)

Parker, Riddick Riddick Thurston, DT-DE, 6´3˝/295 lbs; North Carolina; B11/20/1972 Emporia, VA **1997** Sea 12 (0) **1998** Sea 8 (0) **1999**†Sea 16 (3) **2000** Sea 16 (16, LDT) **2001**†NE 13 (0) **2002** Bal 11 (0) **2003**†Bal 6 (1) **NFL** 82 (20) [7 yrs]

Parker, Robert Robert Lewis, RB, 6´1˝/201 lbs; Brigham Young; B1/7/1963 Alexander City, AL

YEAR	TEAM	G(GS, POS)	RUSH	YD	AVG(LG)	TD	REC	YD	AVG(LG)	TD	PASS	COMP	PCT	YD	AVG(LG)	TD	INT	SK	YD	QBR	KPR	OTD	PTS	TAY
1987	KC	3(2)	47	150	3.2(10)	1	7	44	6.3(14)	0	—	—	—	—	—	—	—	—	—	—	k	—	6	186

Parker, Rodney Rodney, WR, 6´1˝/190 lbs; Tennessee State; 1978: Atl, rnd 6; B7/18/1953 Mobile, AL

YEAR	TEAM	G(GS, POS)	RUSH	YD	AVG(LG)	TD	REC	YD	AVG(LG)	TD	PASS	COMP	PCT	YD	AVG(LG)	TD	INT	SK	YD	QBR	KPR	OTD	PTS	TAY
1980	†Phi	8(0)	—	—	—	—	9	148	16.4(30)	1	—	—	—	—	—	—	—	—	—	—	—	—	6	79
1981	Phi	11(0)	—	—	—	—	8	168	21.0(55)	2	—	—	—	—	—	—	—	—	—	—	—	—	12	94
NFL	2	19(0)	—	—	—	—	17	316	18.6(55)	3	—	—	—	—	—	—	—	—	—	—	—	—	18	173

Parker, Samie Samie Jabar, WR, 5´11˝/177 lbs; Oregon; 2004: KC, rnd 4; B3/25/1981 Long Beach, CA

YEAR	TEAM	G(GS, POS)	RUSH	YD	AVG(LG)	TD	REC	YD	AVG(LG)	TD	PASS	COMP	PCT	YD	AVG(LG)	TD	INT	SK	YD	QBR	KPR	OTD	PTS	TAY
2004	KC	4(0)	—	—	—	—	9	137	15.2(48)	1	—	—	—	—	—	—	—	—	—	—	—	—	6	74
2005	KC	12(8, WR)	—	—	—	—	36	533	14.8(49)	3	—	—	—	—	—	—	—	—	—	—	—	—	18	282
NFL	2	16(8)	—	—	—	—	45	670	14.9(49)	4	—	—	—	—	—	—	—	—	—	—	—	—	24	355

Parker, Sirr Sirr Eluan, WR, 5´11˝/196 lbs; Texas A&M; B10/31/1977 Los Angeles, CA **2000** Cin 2 (0)

Parker, Steve Steven Franklin, DE, 6´6˝/265 lbs; Washington; Idaho; B12/8/1956 Spokane, WA **1980** NO 4 (1)

Parker, Steve Steven Royce, DE, 6´4˝/256 lbs; East Tennessee State; B9/21/1959 Evanston, IL **1983** Bal 16 (15, RDE) **1984** Ind 9 (1) **NFL** 25 (16) [2 yrs]

Parker, Vaughn Vaughn Antoine, T, 6´3˝/300 lbs; UCLA; 1994: SD, rnd 2; B6/5/1971 Buffalo, NY **1994**†SD 6 (0) **1995**†SD 15 (7, rt) **1996** SD 16 (16, LT) **1997** SD 16 (16, LT) **1998** SD 6 (6, RT) **1999** SD 15 (15, RT) **2000** SD 16 (16, RT) **2001** SD 16 (16, RT) **2002** SD 12 (12, RT) **2003** SD 3 (3) **2004** Was 1 (0) **NFL** 122 (107) [11 yrs]

Parker, Willie William Nolen, C-G, 6´3˝/245 lbs; North Texas; 1971: SF, rnd 3; B12/28/1948 Baytown, TX **1973** Buf 14 **1974**†Buf 14 **1975** Buf 14 **1976** Buf 2 **1977** Buf 14 (14, C) **1978** Buf 16 (16, C) **1979** Buf 16 (16, C) **1980** Det 4 (1) **NFL** 94 (47) [8 yrs]

YEAR	TEAM	G(GS, POS)	RUSH	YD	AVG(LG)	TD	REC	YD	AVG(LG)	TD	PASS COMP	PCT	YD	AVG(LG)	TD	INT	SK	YD	QBR	KPR	OTD	PTS	TAY

PARKER, WILLIE Willie Everette, RB, 5'10"/209 lbs; North Carolina; B11/11/1980 Clinton, NC

YEAR	TEAM	G(GS, POS)	RUSH	YD	AVG(LG)	TD	REC	YD	AVG(LG)	TD	OTD	PTS	TAY
2004	Pit	8(0)	32	186	5.8(58)	0	3	16	5.3(12)	0	—	0	194
2005	†Pit	15(15, RB)	255	1202	4.7(80)	4	18	218	12.1(48)	1	—	30	1356
NFL	2	23(15)	287	1388	4.8(80)	4	21	234	11.1(48)	1	—	30	1550

PARKER, WILLIE Willie David, DT, 6'3"/275 lbs; Arkansas-Pine Bluff; 1967: Hou, rnd 5; B3/12/1945 Bastrop, LA **1967**†Hou-A 14 (10, LDT) **1968** Hou-A 14 (LDT) **1969**†Hou-A 12 **1970** Hou 14 (LDT) **NFL** 54 (10) [4 yrs]

PARKIN, DAVE David Rodney, DB, 6'0"/191 lbs; Utah State; 1979: Atl, rnd 9; B1/7/1956 Salt Lake City, UT **1979** Det 9

PARKINSON, DOC Thomas H., FB-HB, 6'1"/205 lbs; Pittsburgh; B3/16/1907 Fayette City, PA, D12/28/1976 Pittsburgh, PA **1931** SI 11 (11, FB)

PARKS, BILLY William James, WR, 6'1"/185 lbs; Long Beach State; 1970: SD, rnd 6; B1/1/1948 Santa Monica, CA

YEAR	TEAM	G(GS, POS)	RUSH	YD	AVG(LG)	TD	REC	YD	AVG(LG)	TD	OTD	PTS	TAY
1971	SD	10(WR)	5	77	15.4(54)	0	41	609	14.9(56)	4	—	24	402
1972	†Dal	12(7, wr)	—	—	—	—	18	298	16.6(38)	1	—	6	154
1973	Hou	14(WR)	—	—	—	—	43	581	13.5(66)	1	—	6	296
1974	Hou	14(WR)	—	—	—	—	20	330	16.5(59)	1	—	6	170
1975	Hou	10	—	—	—	—	1	8	8.0(8)	0	—	0	4
NFL	5	60(7)	5	77	15.4(54)	0	123	1826	14.8(66)	7	—	42	1025

PARKS, DAVE David Wayne, SE-TE-WR, 6'2"/220 lbs; Texas Tech; 1964: SF, rnd 1/SD, rnd 4; B12/25/1941 Muenster, TX

YEAR	TEAM	G(GS, POS)	RUSH	YD	AVG(LG)	TD	REC	YD	AVG(LG)	TD	PASS COMP	PCT	YD	AVG(LG)	TD	INT	OTD	PTS	TAY
1964	SF◇	14(14, SE)	—	—	—	—	36	703	19.5(43)	8							—	48	392
1965	SF★	14(14, SE)	—	—	—	—	80	1344	16.8(53)	12							—	72	732
1966	SF★	13(13, SE)	1	-1	-1.0(-1)	0	66	974	14.8(65)	5							—	30	511
1967	SF	9(9, SE)	—	—	—	—	26	313	12.0(43)	2							—	12	167
1968	NO	10(SE)	—	—	—	—	25	258	10.3(41)	0	1	0	0	0.0	0	0	—	0	129
1969	NO	14(TE/se)	—	—	—	—	31	439	14.2(40)	3							—	18	235
1970	NO	13(TE)	—	—	—	—	26	447	17.2(38)	2							—	12	234
1971	NO	14(TE)	2	-2	-1.0(10)	0	35	568	16.2(40)	5							—	30	307
1972	NO	12(TE)	1	-7	-7.0(-7)	0	32	542	16.9(66)	6							—	36	294
1973	NO	5	—	—	—	—	3	31	10.3(12)	1							—	6	21
NFL	10	118(50)	4	-10	-2.5(10)	0	360	5619	15.6(83)	44	1	0	0.0	0	0.0	0	—	264	3020

PARKS, JEFF Jeffrey Dupree, TE, 6'4"/238 lbs; Auburn; 1986: Hou, rnd 5; B9/14/1964 Columbia, SC **1986** Hou 5 (0) **1987**†Hou 7 (0)

YEAR	TEAM	G(GS, POS)	RUSH	YD	AVG(LG)	TD	REC	YD	AVG(LG)	TD	OTD	PTS	TAY
1988	TB	3(1)	—	—	—	—	1	22	22.0(22)	0	—	0	11
NFL	3	15(1)	—	—	—	—	1	22	22.0(22)	0	—	0	11

PARKS, LIMBO Lemuel Tyrone, G, 6'3"/265 lbs; Arkansas; B3/21/1965 Kansas City, MO **1987** SF 3 (0)

PARKS, MICKEY Edward Harry, C-LB, 6'0"/225 lbs; Oklahoma; 1938: Was, rnd 9; B12/4/1915 Shawnee, OK, D9/27/1976 Yountville, CA [K] **1938** Was 8 (3) **1939** Was 10 (8, C) **1940**†Was 6 (0) **NFL** 24 (11) [3 yrs]

1946 ChiR-A 13 (2)

PARKS, NATHAN Nathan Jacob, T, 6'5"/303 lbs; Stanford; 1997: KC, rnd 7; B10/25/1974 Chico, CA **1999** Oak 2 (0)

PARKS, RICKEY Richard, WR, 6'1"/179 lbs; Arkansas-Pine Bluff; B2/19/1964

YEAR	TEAM	G(GS, POS)	RUSH	YD	AVG(LG)	TD	REC	YD	AVG(LG)	TD	OTD	PTS	TAY
1987	Min	2(1)	—	—	—	—	3	46	15.3(19)	0	—	0	23

PARKS, TOMMY Thomas E., P, 6'2"/225 lbs; Mississippi State; B10/14/1968 Okolona, MS **2001** NYJ 1 (0)

PARLAVECCHIO, CHET Chester Louis, LB, 6'2"/225 lbs; Penn State; 1982: GB, rnd 6; B2/14/1960 Newark, NJ **1983** GB 3 (0) **1983** SL 9 (0) **NFL** 12 (0) [1 yr]

PARMALEE, BERNIE Bernard, RB, 5'11"/201 lbs; Ball State; B9/16/1967 Jersey City, NJ

YEAR	TEAM	G(GS, POS)	RUSH	YD	AVG(LG)	TD	REC	YD	AVG(LG)	TD	KPR	OTD	PTS	TAY
1992	†Mia	10(0)	6	38	6.3(20)	0	—	—	—	—	k	—	0	117
1993	Mia	16(0)	4	16	4.0(12)	0	1	1	1.0(1)	0		—	0	17
1994	†Mia	15(10, RB)	216	868	4.0(47)	6	34	249	7.3(22)	1	k	—	44	1028
1995	†Mia	16(12, RB)	236	878	3.7(40)	9	39	345	8.8(35)	1		—	60	1146
1996	Mia	16(0)	25	80	3.2(17)	0	21	189	9.0(17)	0		—	0	175
1997	†Mia	16(4)	18	59	3.3(12)	0	28	301	10.8(29)	1		—	6	215
1998	†Mia	15(0)	8	20	2.5(10)	0	21	221	10.5(23)	0		—	0	131
1999	NYJ	16(0)	27	133	4.9(18)	0	15	113	7.5(23)	0		—	0	190
2000	NYJ	14(0)	27	87	3.2(18)	2	9	66	7.3(18)	0		—	12	140
NFL	9	134(26)	567	2179	3.8(47)	17	168	1485	8.8(35)	3	k	—	122	3156

PARMER, JIM James Richard, FB-HB, 6'0"/193 lbs; Texas A&M; Oklahoma State; 1948: Phi, rnd 25; B4/25/1926 Dallas, TX, D4/20/2005 Lubbock, TX

YEAR	TEAM	G(GS, POS)	RUSH	YD	AVG(LG)	TD	REC	YD	AVG(LG)	TD	KPR	OTD	PTS	TAY
1948	Phi	11(2)	30	167	5.6(42)	3	—	—	—	—	ki	—	18	197
1949	†Phi	12(1)	66	234	3.5(34)	5	5	33	6.6(30)	0	i	—	30	303
1950	Phi	10	60	203	3.4(27)	7	6	103	17.2(59)	1		—	48	330
1951	Phi	11(FB)	92	316	3.4(15)	2	13	80	6.2(16)	0		—	12	376
1952	Phi	6	12	23	1.9(8)	0	2	10	5.0(8)	0	k	—	0	31
1953	Phi	12(FB)	38	158	4.2(15)	2	14	89	6.4(45)	0	k	—	12	226
1954	Phi	10(FB)	119	408	3.4(24)	0	12	40	3.3(16)	0		—	0	428
1955	Phi	12	34	129	3.8(36)	1	1	-4	-4.0(-4)	0		—	6	137
1956	Phi	4	1	-2	-2.0(-2)	0	—	—	—	—		—	0	-2
NFL	9	88(3)	452	1636	3.6(42)	20	53	351	6.6(59)	1	ki	—	126	2025

PARNELL, BABE Frederick Anthony, T-G, 6'3"/205 lbs; Colgate; Allegheny; B1/9/1901 Ashtabula, OH, D5/29/1982 Kingsville, OH **1925** NYG 11 (9, RT) **1926** NYG 4 (3) **1927** NYG 2 (0) **1928** NYG 1 (0) **NFL** 18 (12) [4 yrs]

PARRELLA, JOHN John Lorin, DT, 6'3"/300 lbs; Nebraska; 1993: Buf, rnd 2; B11/22/1969 Topeka, KS **1993** Buf 10 (0) **1994**†SD 13 (1) **1995**†SD 16 (1) **1996** SD 16 (9, LDT) **1997** SD 16 (16, LDT) **1998** SD 16 (16, RDT) **1999** SD 16 (16, RDT) **2000** SD 16 (16, RDT) **2001** SD 16 (16, RDT) **2002**†Oak 16 (15, RDT) **2003** Oak 5 (5, rdt) **2004** Oak 16 (0) **NFL** 172 (111) [12 yrs]

PARRIOTT, BILL William Wright, FB, 5'10"/165 lbs; West Virginia; B4/11/1911 Newburgh, WV, D1/24/1984 Morgantown, WV **1934** Cin 1 (0)

PARRIS, GARY Gary Thomas, TE, 6'2"/226 lbs; Florida State; 1973: SD, rnd 15; B6/13/1950 East St. Louis, IL [K]

YEAR	TEAM	G(GS, POS)	RUSH	YD	AVG(LG)	TD	REC	YD	AVG(LG)	TD	KPR	OTD	PTS	TAY
1973	SD	9												
1974	SD	14(1)	—	—	—	—	3	36	12.0(17)	0	k	—	0	2
1975	Cle	14	—	—	—	—	1	12	12.0(12)	0		—	0	6
1976	Cle	14	—	—	—	—	5	73	14.6(20)	0		—	0	37
1977	Cle	14(6, te)	—	—	—	—	21	213	10.1(26)	5		—	30	132
1978	Cle	16	—	—	—	—	1	4	4.0(4)	0		—	0	2
1979	SL	9(TE)	—	—	—	—	14	174	12.4(39)	0	K	—	1	87
1980	SL	1(0)	—	—	—	—	—	—	—	—		—	0	
NFL	8	91(7)	—	—	—	—	45	512	11.4(39)	5	Kk	—	31	265

PARRISH, BERNIE Bernard Paul, DB, 5'11"/194 lbs; Florida; 1958: Cle, rnd 9; B4/29/1936 Long Beach, CA [I] **1959** Cle 12 (DB) **1960** Cle◇12 (LCB) **1961** Cle 14 (LCB) **1962** Cle 13 (LCB) **1963** Cle☆14 (LCB) **1964**†Cle☆14 (LCB) **1965**†Cle 14 (LCB) **1966** Cle 1 **1966** Hou-A 11 **NFL** 105 [8 yrs]

PARRISH, DON Donald, NT-DE, 6'2"/255 lbs; Pittsburgh; 1977: Atl, rnd 12; B4/6/1955 Tallahassee, FL **1978** KC 15 (12, NT) **1979** KC 16 (16, NT) **1980** KC 16 (15, NT) **1981** KC 16 (8, NT) **1982** KC 8 (0) **NFL** 71 (51) [5 yrs]

PARRISH, JAMES James Herbert, T, 6'6"/310 lbs; Temple; B5/19/1968 Baltimore, MD; D3/10/2004 Plano, TX **1993** SF 1 (0) **1995**†Pit 16 (1) **1996** NYJ 1 (0) **NFL** 18 (1) [3 yrs]

PARRISH, LEMAR Lemar, DB, 5'11"/185 lbs; Lincoln (MO); 1970: Cin, rnd 7; B12/13/1947 West Palm Beach, FL [RI] **1970**†Cin◇14 (14, LCB) **1971** Cin◇14 (14, LCB) **1972** Cin☆14 (14, LCB) **1973**†Cin☆14 (14, LCB) **1974** Cin★13 (13, LCB) **1975**†Cin★11 (11, LCB) **1976** Cin★14 (14, LCB) **1977** Cin★11 (11, LCB) **1978** Was 11 (11, LCB) **1979** Was★16 (16, LCB) **1980** Was☆15 (15, LCB) **1981** Was 12 (8, LCB) **1982** Buf 7 (0) **NFL** 166 (155) [13 yrs]

YEAR	TEAM	G (GS, POS)	RUSH	YD	AVG (LG)	TD	REC	YD	AVG (LG)	TD	PASS	COMP	PCT	YD	AVG (LG)	TD	INT	SK	YD	QBR	KPR	OTD	PTS	TAY

PARRISH, ROSCOE Roscoe, WR, 5´10˝/168 lbs; Miami (FL); 2005: Buf, rnd 2; B7/16/1982 Miami, FL

| 2005 | Buf | 10(1) | 2 | -2 | -1.0(4) | 0 | 15 | 148 | 9.9(28) | 1 | 1 | 1 | 100.0 | 3 | 3.0(3) | 0 | 0 | — | — | — | kp | — | 6 | 306 |

PARRISH, TONY Tony, DB, 6´0˝/210 lbs; Washington; 1998: Chi, rnd 2; B11/23/1975 Los Angeles, CA [I] **1998** ChiB 16 (16, FS) **1999** ChiB 16 (16, SS) **2000** ChiB 16 (16, SS) **2001**†ChiB 16 (16, SS) **2002**†SF 16 (16, SS) **2003** SF☆16 (16, SS) **2004** SF 16 (16, SS) **2005** SF 9 (9, SS) **NFL** 121 (121) [8 yrs]

PARROS, RICK Rick U., RB, 5´11˝/200 lbs; Utah State; 1980: Den, rnd 4; B6/14/1958 Brooklyn, NY

1981	Den	16(16, FB)	176	749	4.3(25)	2	25	216	8.6(26)	1	—	—	—	—	—	—	—	—	—	—	—	—	18	882
1982	Den	9(9, FB)	77	277	3.6(14)	1	37	259	7.0(24)	2	—	—	—	—	—	—	—	—	—	—	—	—	18	427
1983	Den	6(5, fb)	30	96	3.2(13)	1	12	126	10.5(33)	2	—	—	—	—	—	—	—	—	—	—	—	—	18	179
1984	†Den	15(2)	46	208	4.5(25)	2	6	25	4.2(9)	0	—	—	—	—	—	—	—	—	—	—	—	—	12	241
1985	Sea	4(0)	8	19	2.4(6)	0	1	27	27.0(27)	0	—	—	—	—	—	—	—	—	—	—	—	—	0	33
1987	†Sea	1(1)	13	32	2.5(7)	1	1	7	7.0(7)	0	—	—	—	—	—	—	—	—	—	—	—	—	6	46
NFL	6	51(33)	350	1381	3.9(25)	7	82	660	8.0(33)	5	—	—	—	—	—	—	—	—	—	—	—	—	72	1806

PARRY, JOSH Joshua David, RB, 6´2˝/250 lbs; San Jose State; B4/5/1978 Sonora, CA

2004	†Phi	13(4)	—	—	—	—	9	75	8.3(22)	0	—	—	—	—	—	—	—	—	—	—	k	—	0	32
2005	Phi	15(11, FB)	—	—	—	—	13	89	6.8(13)	0	—	—	—	—	—	—	—	—	—	—	—	—	0	45
NFL	2	28(15)	—	—	—	—	22	164	7.5(22)	0	—	—	—	—	—	—	—	—	—	—	k	—	0	76

PARRY, OX Owen Lloyd, T, 6´4˝/230 lbs; Baylor; B11/17/1914 San Antonio, TX, D3/2/1976 Henrietta, TX **1937** NYG 11 (2) **1938**†NYG✧10 (7, RT) **1939**†NYG 11 (3) **NFL** 32 (12) [3 yrs]

PARSEGHIAN, ARA Ara Raoul, HB, 5´10˝/194 lbs; Akron; Miami (OH); 1948: Cle-A, rnd 25/1947: Pit, rnd 13; B5/21/1923 Akron, OH

1948	†Cle-A	12(1)	32	135	4.2	1	2	31	15.5	1	—	—	—	—	—	—	—	—	—	—	ki	—	12	228
1949	Cle-A	2(1)	12	31	2.6	0	1	2	2.0(2)	0	—	—	—	—	—	—	—	—	—	—	—	—	0	32
AAFC	2	14(2)	44	166	3.8	1	3	33	11.0(2)	1	—	—	—	—	—	—	—	—	—	—	ki	—	12	260

PARSLEY, CLIFF Clifford Donald, P, 6´1˝/211 lbs; Oklahoma State; 1977: NO, rnd 6; B12/26/1954 Kansas City, MO [P] **1977** Hou 14 **1978**†Hou 16 **1979**†Hou 16 **1980**†Hou 16 (0) **1982** Hou 4 (0)

| 1981 | Hou | 16(0) | — | — | — | — | — | — | — | — | 2 | 2 | 100.0 | 43 | 21.5(31) | 0 | 0 | — | — | — | P | — | 0 | 22 |
| NFL | 6 | 82 | — | — | — | — | — | — | — | — | 2 | 2 | 100.0 | 43 | 21.5(31) | 0 | 0 | — | — | — | P | — | 0 | 22 |

PARSON, RAY Ray A., T, 6´4˝/245 lbs; Minnesota; 1970: Det, rnd 2; B5/30/1947 Uniontown, PA **1971** Det 14

PARSONS, BOB Robert Herber, TE-P, 6´4˝/234 lbs; Penn State; 1972: Chi, rnd 5; B6/29/1950 Bethlehem, PA [P]

1972	ChiB	13	1	0	0.0(0)	0	1	6	6.0(6)	1	—	—	—	—	—	—	—	—	—	—	—	—	6	8
1973	ChiB	14	2	2	1.0(5)	0	2	23	11.5(17)	1	—	—	—	—	—	—	—	—	—	Pk	—	6	4
1974	ChiB	14	—	—	—	—	2	9	4.5(5)	0	1	0	0.0	0	0.0	0	0	—	—	P	—	6	10
1975	ChiB	14(TE)	—	—	—	—	13	184	14.2(38)	0	1	0	0.0	0	0.0	0	0	—	—	P	—	6	97
1976	ChiB	14	1	2	2.0(2)	0	1	9	9.0(9)	0	2	2	100.0	48	24.0(25)	0	0	—	—	P	—	0	31
1977	†ChiB☆	14	—	—	—	—	—	—	—	—	4	4	100.0	61	15.3(32)	0	0	—	—	P	—	0	31
1978	ChiB	16	1	0	0.0(0)	0	—	—	—	—	1	0	0.0	0	0.0	0	0	—	—	P	—	0	0
1979	†ChiB	16	—	—	—	—	—	—	—	—	2	1	50.0	22	11.0(22)	0	0	—	—	P	—	0	11
1980	ChiB	16(0)	2	4	2.0(4)	0	—	—	—	—	1	0	0.0	0	0.0	0	0	—	—	P	—	0	4
1981	ChiB	16(0)	1	-6	-6.0(-6)	0	—	—	—	—	—	—	—	—	—	—	—	—	—	P	—	0	-6
1982	ChiB	9(0)	—	—	—	—	—	—	—	—	—	—	—	—	—	—	—	—	—	P	—	0	0
1983	ChiB	14(0)	1	27	27.0(27)	0	—	—	—	—	—	—	—	—	—	—	—	—	—	P	—	0	27
NFL	12	170	9	29	3.2(27)	0	19	231	12.2(38)	4	13	7	53.8	131	10.1(32)	0	0	—	—	Pk	—	24	215

PARSONS, EARLE Earle O., HB, 6´0˝/180 lbs; USC; 1944: Phi, rnd 12; B1920

1946	SF-A	10(2)	74	362	4.9	2	8	52	6.5	0	—	—	—	—	—	—	—	—	—	—	kp	—	12	565
1947	SF-A	11(0)	33	125	3.8	0	9	163	18.1	2	—	—	—	—	—	—	—	—	—	—	kp	—	12	312
AAFC	2	21(2)	107	487	4.6	2	17	215	12.6	2	—	—	—	—	—	—	—	—	—	—	kp	—	24	877

PARSONS, LLOYD Lloyd Marion, B, 5´11˝/200 lbs; Minnesota; Gustavus Adolphus; B6/10/1918 Minneapolis, MN, D11/24/1986 Hennepin County, MN

| 1941 | Det | 7(0) | 5 | 9 | 1.8(4) | 0 | 1 | 3 | 3.0(3) | 0 | — | — | — | — | — | — | — | — | — | — | — | — | 0 | 11 |

PARSON, RICH Rich, WR, 5´10˝/183 lbs; Maryland; B5/16/1980 Newark, DE **2005** Was 1 (0)

PARTEE, DENNIS Dennis Franklin, K, 6´1˝/229 lbs; SMU; 1968: SD, rnd 11; B9/1/1946 Cameron, TX [KP] **1968** SD-A 14 **1969** SD-A☆14 **1970** SD 13 **1972** SD 14 **1973** SD 14 **1974** SD 14 **1975** SD 14

| 1971 | SD | 14 | 1 | 7 | 7.0(7) | 0 | — | — | — | — | — | — | — | — | — | — | — | — | — | KP | — | 87 | 7 |
| NFL | 8 | 111 | 1 | 7 | 7.0(7) | 0 | — | — | — | — | — | — | — | — | — | — | — | — | — | KP | — | 380 | 7 |

PARTEN, TY Ty Daniel, DE-DT, 6´5˝/278 lbs; Arizona; 1993: Cin, rnd 3; B10/13/1969 Washington, DC **1993** Cin 11 (1) **1994** Cin 14 (4) **1995** Cin 1 (1) **1997** KC 2 (0) **1998** KC 16 (6, lde) **1999** KC 16 (0) **2000** KC 2 (0) **NFL** 62 (12) [7 yrs]

PARTLOW, LOU Louis Jerald, FB-TB-WB-HB, 6´1˝/185 lbs; none; B10/9/1892 Miamisburg, OH, D4/14/1981 Burbank, CA **1920** Day 9 (8, FB) **1921** Day 6 (6, FB), 6 **1922** Day 6 (5, TB), 6 **1923** Day 8 (8, TB) **1923** Cle 1 (0) **1924** Day 8 (6, WB), 12 **1925** Day 3 (1) **1926** Day 4 (2) **1927** Day 5 (3) **1929** Day 1 (0) **NFL** 51 (37), 24 [9 yrs]

PARTRIDGE, RICK Richard Blake, P, 6´1˝/175 lbs; Utah; 1979: GB, rnd 8; B8/26/1957 Orange, CA

1979	NO	13	—	—	—	—	—	—	—	—	—	—	—	—	—	—	—	—	—	P	—	0	0
1980	†SD	16(0)	3	0	0.0(0)	0	—	—	—	—	—	—	—	—	—	—	—	—	—	P	—	0	0
1987	Buf	3(0)	1	13	13.0(13)	0	—	—	—	—	—	—	—	—	—	—	—	—	—	P	—	0	13
NFL	3	32	4	13	3.3(13)	0	—	—	—	—	—	—	—	—	—	—	—	—	—	P	—	0	13

PASCHAL, BILL William Avner, FB-HB, 6´0˝/201 lbs; Georgia Tech; B5/28/1921 Atlanta, GA, D5/26/2003 Marietta, GA

1943	†NYG☆	9(3, FB)	147	572	3.9(54)	10	9	74	8.2(24)	2	—	—	—	—	—	—	—	—	—	Pkp	—	72	844
1944	†NYG☆	10(6, FB)	196	737	3.8(68)	9	—	—	—	—	8	2	25.0	31	3.9(19)	0	2	—	—	Pkp	—	54	955
1945	NYG☆	4(1)	59	247	4.2(77)	2	2	11	5.5(6)	0	1	0	0.0	0	0.0	0	0	—	—	k	—	12	286
1946	NYG	10(1, FB)	117	362	3.1(30)	4	9	78	8.7(35)	2	—	—	—	—	—	—	—	—	—	Pkp	—	36	564
1947	NYG	4(1)	41	139	3.4(23)	1	1	3	3.0(3)	0	1	0	0.0	0	0.0	0	0	—	—	p	—	6	157
1947	Bos	8(4)	37	124	3.4(0)	1	3	67	22.3(30)	0	—	—	—	—	—	—	—	—	—	k	—	6	196
1948	Bos	12(6, LH)	80	249	3.1(20)	1	8	93	11.6(22)	2	—	—	—	—	—	—	—	—	—	Pkp	—	30	528
NFL	6	57(21)	677	2430	3.6(77)	28	32	326	10.2(35)	8	10	2	20.0	31	3.1(19)	0	2	—	—	Pkp	—	216	3528

PASCHAL, DOUG Douglas Clyde, RB, 6´2˝/217 lbs; North Carolina; 1980: Min, rnd 5; B3/5/1958 Greenville, NC

| 1980 | †Min | 16(0) | 15 | 53 | 3.5(10) | 1 | 2 | 18 | 9.0(11) | 0 | — | — | — | — | — | — | — | — | — | k | — | 6 | 78 |

PASCHKA, GORDON Gordon F., FB-G, 6´0˝/220 lbs; Minnesota; 1942: Phi, rnd 4; B3/6/1920 Chaska, MN, D6/9/1964 Rainy Lake, CA [K] **1943** P-P 10 (1)

| 1947 | NYG | 6(0) | 48 | 143 | 3.0(15) | 2 | 1 | -6 | -6.0(-6) | 0 | — | — | — | — | — | — | — | — | — | k | — | 12 | 165 |
| NFL | 2 | 16(1) | 48 | 143 | 3.0(15) | 2 | 1 | -6 | -6.0(-6) | 0 | — | — | — | — | — | — | — | — | — | Kk | — | 14 | 165 |

PASHE, BILL William Thomas, DB, 5´11˝/185 lbs; George Washington; 1963: NYG, rnd 18; B8/5/1940 New York, NY **1964** NYJ-A 4

PASHOS, TONY Anthony George, T, 6´6˝/337 lbs; Illinois; 2003: Bal, rnd 5; B8/3/1980 Palos Heights, IL **2004** Bal 6 (0) **2005** Bal 16 (7, rt) **NFL** 22 (7) [2 yrs]

PASKETT, KEITH Keith Paxton, WR, 5´11˝/180 lbs; Western Kentucky; B12/7/1964 Nashville, TN

| 1987 | GB | 12(0) | — | — | — | — | 12 | 188 | 15.7(47) | 1 | — | — | — | — | — | — | — | — | — | — | — | — | 6 | 99 |

PASKVAN, GEORGE George Oscar, FB, 6´0˝/190 lbs; Wisconsin; 1941: GB, rnd 1; B4/28/1918 McCook, IL

| 1941 | †GB | 7(3) | 38 | 116 | 3.1(12) | 0 | — | — | — | — | — | — | — | — | — | — | — | — | — | i | — | 0 | 112 |

PASQUA, JOE Joseph Bernard, T, 6´1˝/225 lbs; SMU; B7/31/1918 Dallas, TX, D12/10/1998 Muenster, TX [K] **1942** Cle 11 (11, RT) **1943**†Was 9 (5, RT) **1946** LARm 4 (0) **NFL** 24 (16) [3 yrs]

PASQUALE, RON Ronald R., G, 6´2˝/266 lbs; Akron; B2/28/1964 Youngstown, OH **1987** SL 1 (0)

YEAR	TEAM	G (GS, POS)	RUSH	YD	AVG (LG)	TD	REC	YD	AVG (LG)	TD	PASS	COMP	PCT	YD	AVG (LG)	TD	INT	SK	YD	QBR	KPR	OTD	PTS	TAY

PASQUARIELLO, RALPH   Ralph Angelo, FB, 6'2"/237 lbs; Villanova; 1950: LA, rnd 1; B5/30/1926 Brighton, MA, D1/15/1999 Peabody, MA

1950	†LARm	9	7	31	4.4(14)	1	1	2	2.0(2)	0	—	—	—	—	—	—	—	—	—	—	k	—	6	41
1951	ChiC	10(FB)	53	251	4.7(28)	1	2	-9	-4.5(-4)	0	—	—	—	—	—	—	—	—	—	—		—	6	257
1952	ChiC	10	48	129	2.7(13)	0	7	46	6.6(10)	0	—	—	—	—	—	—	—	—	—	—	k	—	0	150
NFL	3	29	108	411	3.8(28)	2	10	39	3.9(10)	0	—	—	—	—	—	—	—	—	—	—	k	—	12	448

PASQUESI, TONY   Anthony Leonard, DT-MG-LB, 6'4"/250 lbs; Notre Dame; 1955: ChiC, rnd 3; B6/13/1933 Chicago, IL   **1955** ChiC 7 (MG)   **1956** ChiC 11 (LDT)   **1957** ChiC 11
NFL 29 [3 yrs]

PASS, PATRICK   Patrick D., FB, 5'10"/217 lbs; Georgia; 2000: NE, rnd 7; B12/31/1977 Scottsdale, GA

2000	NE	5(2)	18	58	3.2(11)	0	4	17	4.3(15)	0	—	—	—	—	—	—	—	—	—	—		—	0	67
2001	†NE	16(0)	1	7	7.0(7)	0	6	66	11.0(23)	1	—	—	—	—	—	—	—	—	—	—	k	—	6	117
2002	NE	15(0)	4	27	6.8(13)	0	—	—	—	—	—	—	—	—	—	—	—	—	—	—	k	—	0	45
2003	†NE	13(1)	6	27	4.5(11)	0	4	21	5.3(11)	0	—	—	—	—	—	—	—	—	—	—	k	—	0	127
2004	†NE	14(4)	39	141	3.6(19)	0	28	215	7.7(22)	0	—	—	—	—	—	—	—	—	—	—	k	—	0	274
2005	†NE	12(4)	54	245	4.5(31)	3	22	227	10.3(39)	0	—	—	—	—	—	—	—	—	—	—	k	—	18	390
NFL	6	75(11)	122	505	4.1(31)	3	64	546	8.5(39)	1	—	—	—	—	—	—	—	—	—	—	k	—	24	1018

PASSUELO, BILL   William, T-G, 6'2"/230 lbs; none; B12/23/1897, D1/1965, MI   **1923** Col 3 (0)

PASTIN, FRANK   Frank Andrew, G, 5'10"/197 lbs; Waynesburg; B12/16/1920 Pittsburgh, PA   **1942** Pit 1 (0)

PASTORINI, DAN   Dante Anthony, QB, 6'2"/208 lbs; Santa Clara; 1971: Hou, rnd 1; B5/26/1949 Sonora, CA [KP]

1971	Hou	14(QB)	26	140	5.4(27)	3	—	—	—	—	270	127	47.0	1702	6.3(62)	7	21	20	152	43.8	P	—	18	216
1972	Hou	14(QB)	38	205	5.4(17)	2	—	—	—	—	299	144	48.2	1711	5.7(82)	7	12	37	310	57.1	P	—	12	636
1973	Hou	14(QB)	31	102	3.3(17)	0	—	—	—	—	290	154	53.1	1482	5.1(50)	5	17	30	313	49.0	P	—	0	188
1974	Hou	11(10, QB)	24	-6	-0.3(7)	0	—	—	—	—	247	140	56.7	1571	6.4(65)	10	10	23	225	72.4	—	—	0	430
1975	Hou✧	14(14, QB)	23	97	4.2(19)	1	—	—	—	—	342	163	47.7	2053	6.0(77)	14	16	24	210	61.0	P	—	6	564
1976	Hou	13(13, QB)	11	45	4.1(11)	0	—	—	—	—	309	167	54.0	1795	5.8(67)	10	10	24	234	68.6	P	—	0	593
1977	Hou	14(QB)	18	39	2.2(15)	2	—	—	—	—	319	169	53.0	1987	6.2(85)	13	18	20	198	62.3	K	—	12	398
1978	†Hou	16(QB)	18	11	0.6(11)	0	—	—	—	—	368	199	54.1	2473	6.7(80)	16	17	15	123	70.4	—	—	0	648
1979	†Hou	15(QB)	15	23	1.5(14)	0	—	—	—	—	324	163	50.3	2090	6.5(55)	14	18	29	212	62.1	—	—	0	418
1980	Oak	5(5, qb)	4	24	6.0(10)	0	—	—	—	—	130	66	50.8	932	7.2(56)	5	8	10	103		—	—	0	195
1981	LARm	7(5, qb)	7	5	0.7(13)	0	—	—	—	—	152	64	42.1	719	4.7(46)	2	14	14	149		—	—	0	-186
1983	Phi	3(0)	1	0	0.0(0)	0	—	—	—	—	5	0	0.0	0	0.0	0	0	—	—	—	—	—	0	0
NFL	12	140(57)	216	685	3.2(27)	8	—	—	—	—	3055	1556	50.9	18515	6.1(85)	103	161	246	2229	59.1	KP	—	48	4098

PASTRANA, CHUCK   Charles Alan, QB, 6'1"/190 lbs; Maryland; 1969: Den, rnd 11; B11/20/1944 Annapolis, MD

1969	Den-A	2	—	—	—	—	1	15	15.0(15)	0	—	—	—	—	—	—	—	—	—	—		—	0	8
1970	Den	5(3)	14	89	6.4(14)	1	—	—	—	—	75	29	38.7	420	5.6(58)	1	9	8	60		—	—	6	-46
NFL	2	7(3)	14	89	6.4(14)	1	1	15	15.0(15)	0	75	29	38.7	420	5.6(58)	1	9	8	60		—	—	6	-39

PATANELLI, MIKE   Michael Joseph, DE, 6'2"/218 lbs; Manchester; Bowling Green State; Ball State; B8/12/1922 Elkhart, IN   **1947** Bkn-A 2 (0)

PATE, LLOYD   Lloyd Robert, RB, 6'1"/205 lbs; Cincinnati; 1969: Buf, rnd 12; B3/11/1946 Columbus, OH

| 1970 | Buf | 9(rb) | 46 | 162 | 3.5(18) | 1 | 19 | 103 | 5.4(21) | 0 | — | — | — | — | — | — | — | — | — | — | k | — | 6 | 230 |

PATE, RUPERT   Rupert George, G, 6'1"/205 lbs; Wake Forest; 1940: ChiC, rnd 20; B9/6/1917 Goldsboro, NC   **1940** ChiC 1 (0)   **1941** Phi 1 (0)   **1942** Phi 7 (0)   **NFL** 9 (0) [3 yrs]

PATERA, DENNIS   Dennis Allen, K, 6'0"/214 lbs; Brigham Young; 1968: SF, rnd 17; B10/17/1945 Portland, OR [K]   **1968** SF 5

PATERA, JACK   John Arlen, LB, 6'1"/234 lbs; Oregon; 1955: Bal, rnd 4; B8/1/1933 Bismarck, ND [C]   **1955** Bal 12   **1956** Bal 12   **1957** Bal 12 (MLB)   **1958** ChiC 9 (MLB)
1959 ChiC 12   **1960** Dal 3   **1961** Dal 1   **NFL** 61 [7 yrs]

PATERRA, GREG   Greg Richard, RB, 5'11"/211 lbs; Slippery Rock; 1989: Atl, rnd 11; B5/12/1967 McKeesport, PA

| 1989 | Atl | 10(0) | 9 | 32 | 3.6(8) | 0 | 5 | 42 | 8.4(20) | 0 | — | — | — | — | — | — | — | — | — | — | k | — | 0 | 62 |

PATERRA, HERB   Herbert E., LB, 6'1"/232 lbs; Michigan State; 1963: Buf, rnd 18; B11/8/1940 Glassport, PA   **1963**†Buf-A 10

PATHON, JEROME   Jerome, WR, 6'0"/183 lbs; Acadia (Canada); Washington; 1998: Ind, rnd 2; B12/16/1975 Capetown, South Africa

1998	Ind	16(15, WR)	3	-2	-0.7(4)	0	50	511	10.2(45)	1	—	—	—	—	—	—	—	—	—	—		—	6	259
1999	†Ind	10(2)	—	—	—	—	14	163	11.6(38)	0	—	—	—	—	—	—	—	—	—	—	kp	—	0	115
2000	†Ind	16(10, WR)	1	3	3.0(3)	0	50	646	12.9(38)	3	—	—	—	—	—	—	—	—	—	—	k	—	18	534
2001	Ind	4(3)	1	-8	-8.0(-8)	0	24	330	13.8(60)	2	—	—	—	—	—	—	—	—	—	—	k	—	12	165
2002	NO	14(13, WR)	—	—	—	—	43	523	12.2(64)	4	—	—	—	—	—	—	—	—	—	—		—	24	282
2003	NO	16(12, WR)	—	—	—	—	44	578	13.1(40)	4	—	—	—	—	—	—	—	—	—	—		—	24	309
2004	NO	15(7, wr)	—	—	—	—	34	581	17.1(38)	1	—	—	—	—	—	—	—	—	—	—		—	6	296
2005	Atl	8(0)	—	—	—	—	1	18	18.0(18)	0	—	—	—	—	—	—	—	—	—	—	k	—	0	18
NFL	8	99(62)	5	-7	-1.4(4)	0	260	3350	12.9(64)	15	—	—	—	—	—	—	—	—	—	—	kp	—	90	1976

PATMON, DeWAYNE   Dewayne, DB, 6'0"/202 lbs; Michigan; B4/25/1979 San Diego, CA   **2001** NYG 7 (0)   **2002**†NYG 15 (0)   **NFL** 22 (0) [2 yrs]

PATRICK, FRANK   Frank W., B, 5'11"/190 lbs; Pittsburgh; 1938: ChiC, rnd 3; B1/16/1916 East Chicago, IN, D9/26/1992, [K]

1938	ChiC	7(5, BB)	1	1	1.0(1)	0	1	21	21.0(21)	1	1	0	0.0	—	—	0	0	—	—	—	K	—	17	17
1939	ChiC	8(5, TB)	30	84	2.8	1	—	—	—	—	79	22	27.8	291	3.7(60)	1	13	—	—	—	KP	—	7	-276
NFL	2	15(10)	31	85	2.7(1)	1	1	21	21.0(21)	1	80	22	27.5	291	3.6(60)	1	13	—	—	—	KP	—	24	-259

PATRICK, FRANK   Frank Andrew, QB, 6'7"/225 lbs; Nebraska; 1970: GB, rnd 10; B3/11/1947 Derry, PA

1970	GB	1	2	5	2.5(3)	0	—	—	—	—	14	6	42.9	59	4.2(16)	0	1	6	55	—	—	—	0	-6
1971	GB	1	—	—	—	—	—	—	—	—	5	1	20.0	39	7.8(39)	0	1	—	—	—	—	—	0	-21
1972	GB	2	—	—	—	—	—	—	—	—	4	1	25.0	9	2.3(9)	0	0	1	11	—	—	—	0	5
NFL	3	4	2	5	2.5(3)	0	—	—	—	—	23	8	34.8	107	4.7(39)	0	2	7	66	—	—	—	0	-22

PATRICK, GARIN   Garin James, C, 6'3"/269 lbs; Louisville; B8/31/1971 Canton, OH   **1995** Ind 5 (0)

PATRICK, JOHN   John Raymond, BB-QB-FB, 6'0"/202 lbs; Penn State; 1941: Phi, rnd 12; B1/16/1918 Central City, PA, D4/29/2000 Johnstown, PA   **1945** Pit 3 (0)   **1946** Pit 4 (0)

| 1941 | Pit | 11(8, BB) | — | — | — | — | 1 | 12 | 12.0(12) | 0 | — | — | — | — | — | — | — | — | — | — | ki | — | 0 | 23 |
| NFL | 3 | 18(8) | — | — | — | — | 1 | 12 | 12.0(12) | 0 | — | — | — | — | — | — | — | — | — | — | | — | 0 | 6 |

PATRICK, MIKE   Charles Michael, P, 6'0"/209 lbs; Mississippi State; B9/6/1952 Austin, TX   **1975** NE 14   **1977** NE 14   **1978** NE 1

| 1976 | †NE | 14 | 1 | -16 | -16.0(-16) | 0 | — | — | — | — | — | — | — | — | — | — | — | — | — | — | P | — | 0 | -16 |
| NFL | 4 | 43 | 1 | -16 | -16.0(-16) | 0 | — | — | — | — | — | — | — | — | — | — | — | — | — | — | P | — | 0 | -16 |

PATRICK, WAYNE   Wayne Allen, RB, 6'2"/254 lbs; Louisville; 1968: Cin, rnd 10; B9/1/1946 Gainesville, FL

1968	Buf-A	3	1	2	2.0(2)	0	1	5	5.0(5)	0	—	—	—	—	—	—	—	—	—	—		—	0	5
1969	Buf-A	14(FB)	83	361	4.3(72)	3	35	229	6.5(19)	0	—	—	—	—	—	—	—	—	—	—		—	18	506
1970	Buf	9(FB)	66	259	3.9(20)	1	16	142	8.9(38)	0	—	—	—	—	—	—	—	—	—	—	k	—	6	333
1971	Buf	14(FB)	79	332	4.2(41)	1	36	327	9.1(62)	0	—	—	—	—	—	—	—	—	—	—		—	6	506
1972	Buf	13	35	130	3.7(9)	0	8	42	5.3(10)	1	—	—	—	—	—	—	—	—	—	—		—	6	156
NFL	5	53	264	1084	4.1(72)	5	96	745	7.8(62)	1	—	—	—	—	—	—	—	—	—	—	k	—	36	1505

PATT, MAURY   Maurice Howard, E, 6'2"/205 lbs; Carnegie Mellon; 1937: Det, rnd 5; B1/31/1915 Altoona, PA, D4/2/1961 Altoona, PA

1938	Det	10(2)	3	30	10.0	0	7	80	11.4	0	—	—	—	—	—	—	—	—	—	—		—	0	70
1939	Cle	10(0)	6	20	3.3	0	15	165	11.0	0	—	—	—	—	—	—	—	—	—	—		—	0	103
1940	Cle	10(1)	1	0	0.0	0	2	52	26.0	0	—	—	—	—	—	—	—	—	—	—		—	6	31
1941	Cle	11(5, LE)	5	16	3.2(11)	0	17	163	9.6(25)	2	—	—	—	—	—	—	—	—	—	—		—	6	103
1942	Cle	7(0)	—	—	—	—	—	—	—	—	—	—	—	—	—	—	—	—	—	—		—	0	
NFL	5	48(8)	15	66	4.4(11)	0	41	460	11.2(25)	2	—	—	—	—	—	—	—	—	—	—		—	12	306

PATTEN, DAVID David, WR, 5´10˝/190 lbs; Western Carolina; B8/19/1974 Hopkins, SC **[R]**

YEAR	TEAM	G(GS, POS)	RUSH	YD	AVG(LG)	TD	REC	YD	AVG(LG)	TD	PASS	COMP	PCT	YD	AVG(LG)	TD	INT	SK	YD	QBR	KPR	OTD	PTS	TAY
1997	†NYG	16(3)	1	2	2.0(2)	0	13	226	17.4(40)	2	—	—	—	—	—	—	—	—	—	—	k	—	12	128
1998	NYG	12(0)	—	—	—	—	11	119	10.8(39)	1	—	—	—	—	—	—	—	—	—	—	k	1	12	358
1999	NYG	16(0)	1	27	27.0(27)	0	9	115	12.8(19)	0	—	—	—	—	—	—	—	—	—	—	k	—	0	263
2000	Cle	14(11, WR)	—	—	—	—	38	546	14.4(65)	1	—	—	—	—	—	—	—	—	—	—	k	—	6	417
2001	†NE	16(14, WR)	5	67	13.4(29)	1	51	749	14.7(**91**)	4	2	1	50.0	60	30.0(60)	1	1	—	—	—	k	—	30	481
2002	NE	16(14, WR)	2	6	3.0(7)	0	61	824	13.5(39)	5	1	0	0.0	0	0.0	0	0	—	—	—	—	—	30	443
2003	NE	6(5, wr)	1	4	4.0(4)	0	9	140	15.6(42)	0	—	—	—	—	—	—	—	—	—	—	—	—	0	74
2004	†NE	16(11, WR)	1	5	5.0(5)	0	44	800	18.2(48)	7	—	—	—	—	—	—	—	—	—	—	k	—	42	441
2005	Was	9(7, WR)	—	—	—	—	22	217	9.9(32)	0	—	—	—	—	—	—	—	—	—	—	—	—	0	109
NFL	9	121(65)	11	111	10.1(29)	1	258	3736	14.5(91)	20	3	1	33.3	60	20.0(60)	1	1	—	—	—	k	1	132	2712

PATTEN, JOEL John Lawrence, T, 6´7˝/310 lbs; Duke; B2/7/1958 Augsburg, Germany **1980**†Cle 8 (0) **1987**†Ind 12 (0) **1988** Ind 15 (13, RT) **1989** SD 14 (14, LT) **1990** SD 8 (0) **1991** LARd 1 (0) **NFL** 58 (27) [6 yrs]

PATTERSON BB-G, none; deceased **1921** Cle 2 (2)

PATTERSON, BILLY Joseph William, B, 5´10˝/167 lbs; Baylor; 1939: Pit, rnd 3; B8/20/1918 Hillsboro, TX, D7/8/1998 McAllen, TX **[K]**

YEAR	TEAM	G(GS, POS)	RUSH	YD	AVG(LG)	TD	REC	YD	AVG(LG)	TD	PASS	COMP	PCT	YD	AVG(LG)	TD	INT	SK	YD	QBR	KPR	OTD	PTS	TAY
1939	ChiB	8(1)	14	34	2.4	0	—	—	—	—	38	14	36.8	227	6.0	3	4	—	—	—	KP	—	1	3
1940	Pit	11(9, TB)	87	171	2.0	0	—	—	—	—	117	34	29.1	529	4.5	3	15	—	—	14.9	P	—	0	-150
NFL	2	19(10)	101	205	2.0	0	—	—	—	—	155	48	31.0	756	4.9	6	19	—	—	21.5	KP	—	1	-147

PATTERSON, CLETE Clitus Henry, G, 5´10˝/205 lbs; Ohio University; B3/18/1902 Wellsville, OH, deceased **1924** Ken 3 (1)

PATTERSON, CRAIG Craig Allan, DE-NT, 6´4˝/314 lbs; Brigham Young; B7/18/1964 Santa Cruz, CA **1991** Phx 16 (13, RDE)

PATTERSON, DIMITRI Dimitri, DB, 5´11˝/196 lbs; Southeast Missouri State; B6/18/1983 Orlando, FL **2005** Was 2 (0)

PATTERSON, DON Donald Ray, DB, 5´11˝/175 lbs; Georgia Tech; B10/31/1957 Gray, GA **1979** Det 2 **1980** NYG 3 (1) **NFL** 5 (1) [2 yrs]

PATTERSON, ELTON Elton, DE, 6´2˝/271 lbs; Central Florida; 2003: Cin, rnd 7; B6/13/1981 Tallahassee, FL **2004** Cin 2 (0) **2004** Jax 6 (0) **NFL** 8 (0) [1 yr]

PATTERSON, ELVIS Elvis Vernell, DB, 5´11˝/193 lbs; Kansas; B10/21/1960 Bryan, TX **1984**†NYG 15 (0) **1985**†NYG 16 (15, LCB) **1986**†NYG 15 (7, lcb) **1987** NYG 1 (1) **1987** SD 13 (11, LCB) **1988** SD 14 (6, lcb) **1989** SD 16 (3) **1990**†LARd 16 (1) **1992** LARd 15 (0) **1993** LARd 3 (0) **1993**†Dal 11 (0)

YEAR	TEAM	G(GS, POS)	RUSH	YD	AVG(LG)	TD	REC	YD	AVG(LG)	TD	PASS	COMP	PCT	YD	AVG(LG)	TD	INT	SK	YD	QBR	KPR	OTD	PTS	TAY
1991	†LARd	16(0)	—	—	—	—	1	34	34.0(34)	0	—	—	—	—	—	—	—	—	—	—	—	1	6	17
NFL	10	151(44)	—	—	—	—	1	34	34.0(34)	0	—	—	—	—	—	—	—	—	—	—	iS	4	24	210

PATTERSON, GORDON Gordon, E, /165 lbs; none; B3/1900 St. Johnsbury, VT, deceased **1921** Was 3 (3, LE)

PATTERSON, MIKE Michael, DT, 5´11˝/292 lbs; USC; 2005: Phi, rnd 1; B9/1/1983 Sacramento, CA **2005** Phi 16 (7, rdt)

PATTERSON, PAUL Paul L., WB-DB, 5´9˝/185 lbs; Illinois; B2/16/1927 Aurora, IL, D6/11/1982 Chicago, IL

YEAR	TEAM	G(GS, POS)	RUSH	YD	AVG(LG)	TD	REC	YD	AVG(LG)	TD	PASS	COMP	PCT	YD	AVG(LG)	TD	INT	SK	YD	QBR	KPR	OTD	PTS	TAY
1949	ChiH-A	12(0)	2	0	0.0	0	16	304	19.0	4	—	—	—	—	—	—	—	—	—	—	pi	—	24	274

PATTERSON, RENO Reno, NT, 6´3˝/275 lbs; Bethune-Cookman; B4/22/1961 Chicago, IL **1987** SF 1 (0)

PATTERSON, SHAWN Kenneth Shawn, DE-NT, 6´5˝/267 lbs; Arizona State; 1988: GB, rnd 2; B6/13/1964 Tempe, AZ **1988** GB 15 (4) **1989** GB 6 (6, rde) **1990** GB 11 (0) **1991** GB 11 (0) **1993** GB 5 (3) **NFL** 48 (13) [5 yrs]

PATTILLO, DARRELL Darrell Lester, DB, 5´10˝/194 lbs; San Diego State; Long Beach State; B9/28/1960 Los Angeles, CA **1983** SD 1 (0)

PATTISON, MARK Mark Lester, WR, 6´2˝/190 lbs; Washington; 1985: LARd, rnd 7; B12/13/1961 Seattle, WA

YEAR	TEAM	G(GS, POS)	RUSH	YD	AVG(LG)	TD	REC	YD	AVG(LG)	TD	PASS	COMP	PCT	YD	AVG(LG)	TD	INT	SK	YD	QBR	KPR	OTD	PTS	TAY
1986	LARm	1(0)	—	—	—	—	—	—	—	—	—	—	—	—	—	—	—	—	—	—	—	—	—	—
1986	LARd	2(0)	—	—	—	—	2	12	6.0(6)	0	—	—	—	—	—	—	—	—	—	—	—	—	0	6
1987	†NO	9(4)	—	—	—	—	9	132	14.7(36)	0	—	—	—	—	—	—	—	—	—	—	—	—	0	66
1988	NO	6(0)	—	—	—	—	1	8	8.0(8)	0	—	—	—	—	—	—	—	—	—	—	—	—	0	4
NFL	3	18(4)	—	—	—	—	12	152	12.7(36)	0	—	—	—	—	—	—	—	—	—	—	—	—	0	76

PATTON, BOB Robert Thomas, C, 6´1˝/245 lbs; Delaware; B10/21/1954 Camp Lejeune, NC **1976** Buf 12

PATTON, CLIFF John Clifton, G-LB, 6´2˝/243 lbs; TCU; B7/29/1923 Clyde, TX, D11/9/2002 Comanche, TX **[K]** **1946** Phi 4 (0) **1947**†Phi 12 (12, LG) **1948**†Phi 12 (2) **1949**†Phi☆12 (7, LG) **1950** Phi 12 **1951** ChiC 12 (LLB) **NFL** 64 (21) [6 yrs]

PATTON, JAMES James Gregory, NT-DE, 6´3˝/287 lbs; Texas; 1992: Buf, rnd 2; B1/5/1970 Houston, TX **1993** Buf 2 (0) **1994** Buf 11 (0) **NFL** 13 (0) [2 yrs]

PATTON, JERRY Jerry Ampstead, DT, 6´3˝/261 lbs; Nebraska; B5/27/1946 Saginaw, MI, D5/20/1983 Shreveport, LA **1971** Min 3 **1972** Buf 14 (RDT) **1973** Buf 14 (RDT) **1974** Phi 14 (RDT) **1975** NE 3 (3) **NFL** 48 (3) [5 yrs]

PATTON, JIMMY James Russell, DB, 5´11˝/183 lbs; Mississippi; 1955: NYG, rnd 8; B9/29/1933 Greenville, MS, D12/22/1972 Villa Rica, GA **[I]** **1955** NYG 11 **1957** NYG 12 (DB) **1958**†NYG★12 (DB) **1959**†NYG★11 (DB) **1960** NYG★12 (RS) **1961**†NYG★14 (RS) **1962**†NYG★14 (RS) **1963**†NYG☆14 (RS) **1964** NYG 14 (LS) **1965** NYG 14 (RS) **1966** NYG 13

YEAR	TEAM	G(GS, POS)	RUSH	YD	AVG(LG)	TD	REC	YD	AVG(LG)	TD	PASS	COMP	PCT	YD	AVG(LG)	TD	INT	SK	YD	QBR	KPR	OTD	PTS	TAY
1956	†NYG	12(DB)	2	-1	-0.5(0)	0	—	—	—	—	—	—	—	—	—	—	—	—	—	—	kpi	—	0	41
NFL	12	153	2	-1	-0.5	0	—	—	—	—	—	—	—	—	—	—	—	—	—	—	kpi	4	24	764

PATTON, JOE Joseph Cephus, T-G, 6´5˝/306 lbs; Alabama A&M; 1994: Was, rnd 3; B1/15/1972 Birmingham, AL **1994** Was 2 (0) **1995** Was 16 (13, LT) **1996** Was 16 (15, LT) **1997** Was 16 (16, LG/lt) **1998** Was 11 (10, rt/rg) **NFL** 61 (54) [5 yrs]

PATTON, MARVCUS Marvcus Raymond, LB, 6´2˝/236 lbs; UCLA; 1990: Buf, rnd 8; B5/1/1967 Los Angeles, CA **1990**†Buf 16 (0) **1991**†Buf 16 (2) **1992**†Buf 16 (4) **1993**†Buf 16 (16, LILB) **1994** Buf 16 (16, LILB) **1995** Was 16 (16, RLB) **1996** Was 16 (16, RLB) **1997** Was 16 (16, MLB) **1998** Was 16 (16, MLB) **1999** KC 16 (16, MLB) **2000** KC 16 (15, MLB) **2001** KC 16 (15, MLB) **2002** KC 16 (15, MLB) **NFL** 208 (163) [13 yrs]

PATTON, RICKY Ricky Riccardo, RB, 5´11˝/190 lbs; Ferris State; Michigan; Jackson State; 1978: Atl, rnd 10; B4/6/1954 Flint, MI

YEAR	TEAM	G(GS, POS)	RUSH	YD	AVG(LG)	TD	REC	YD	AVG(LG)	TD	PASS	COMP	PCT	YD	AVG(LG)	TD	INT	SK	YD	QBR	KPR	OTD	PTS	TAY
1978	†Atl	16(1)	68	206	3.0(15)	1	10	90	9.0(32)	1	—	—	—	—	—	—	—	—	—	—	—	—	12	266
1979	Atl	4	3	1	0.3(1)	0	—	—	—	—	—	—	—	—	—	—	—	—	—	—	—	—	0	1
1979	GB	6(1)	37	134	3.6(14)	0	6	41	6.8(9)	0	—	—	—	—	—	—	—	—	—	—	—	—	0	155
1980	SF	9(0)	1	1	1.0(1)	0	—	—	—	—	—	—	—	—	—	—	—	—	—	—	k	—	0	-16
1981	†SF	16(15, RB)	152	543	3.6(28)	4	27	195	7.2(31)	1	—	—	—	—	—	—	—	—	—	—	k	—	30	671
1982	SF	1(0)	—	—	—	—	—	—	—	—	—	—	—	—	—	—	—	—	—	—	—	—	—	—
NFL	5	52(17)	261	885	3.4(28)	5	43	326	7.6(32)	2	—	—	—	—	—	—	—	—	—	—	k	—	42	1076

PATTON, ROBERT Robert Harold, G, 6´0˝/226 lbs; Clemson; 1952: NYG, rnd 5; B8/25/1927 Oakland, CA, deceased **1952** NYG 12

PATULSKI, WALT Walter George, DE, 6´6˝/259 lbs; Notre Dame; 1972: Buf, rnd 1; B2/3/1950 Fulton, NY **1972** Buf 14 (LDE) **1973** Buf 14 (LDE) **1974**†Buf 14 (LDE) **1975** Buf 14 (LDE) **1977** SL 14 **NFL** 70 [5 yrs]

PAUL, DON Donald, LB-MG-C, 6´1˝/228 lbs; UCLA; 1947: LARm, rnd 3/LAD-A, rnd 8; B3/18/1925 Fresno, CA **1948** LARm 11 (0) **1949**†LARm 12 (0) **1950**†LARm 10 (MLB) **1951**†LARm✧12 (RLB) **1952**†LARm★12 (RLB) **1953** LARm★10 (RLB) **1954** LARm☆12 (RLB) **1955**†LARm 8 (MG) **NFL** 87 [8 yrs]

PAUL, DON Donald Ray, DB-HB, 6´0˝/187 lbs; Washington State; 1950: ChiC, rnd 4; B7/23/1926 Tacoma, WA, D9/7/2001 Eugene, OR **[RI]** **1954**†Cle 12 (DB) **1955**†Cle☆11 (DB) **1956** Cle✧12 (DB) **1957**†Cle★12 (DB) **1958**†Cle★12 (DB)

YEAR	TEAM	G(GS, POS)	RUSH	YD	AVG(LG)	TD	REC	YD	AVG(LG)	TD	PASS	COMP	PCT	YD	AVG(LG)	TD	INT	SK	YD	QBR	KPR	OTD	PTS	TAY
1950	ChiC	12(DB)	14	80	5.7(18)	0	5	93	18.6(35)	1	—	—	—	—	—	—	—	—	—	—	kpi	1	12	589
1951	ChiC	12(DB)	37	247	6.7(68)	3	23	398	17.3(53)	3	—	—	—	—	—	—	—	—	—	—	kpi	—	36	775
1952	ChiC	5(DB)	6	28	4.7(16)	0	4	32	8.0(11)	1	—	—	—	—	—	—	—	—	—	—	kp	—	6	105
1953	ChiC✧	12(DB)	16	114	7.1(36)	0	16	167	10.4(27)	2	2	1	50.0	13	6.5(13)	0	0	—	—	—	kpi	—	12	292
NFL	9	100	73	469	6.4(68)	3	48	690	14.4(53)	7	2	1	50.0	13	6.5(13)	0	0	—	—	—	kpi	4	84	2238

PAUL, HAROLD Harold, T, 6´5˝/245 lbs; Texas Southern; Oklahoma; B11/8/1949 Galveston, TX **1974** SD 1

PAUL, MARKUS Markus Dwayne, DB, 6´2˝/200 lbs; Syracuse; 1989: Chi, rnd 4; B4/1/1966 Orlando, FL **1989** ChiB 16 (2) **1990**†ChiB 16 (0) **1991**†ChiB 14 (7, ss) **1992** ChiB 16 (5, ss) **1993** ChiB 8 (0) **1993** TB 1 (0) **NFL** 71 (14) [5 yrs]

PAUL, TITO Tito Jermaine, DB, 6´0˝/195 lbs; Ohio State; 1995: Arz, rnd 5; B12/7/1972 Kissimmee, FL **1995** Arz 14 (4) **1996** Arz 16 (3) **1997** Arz 1 (0) **1997** Cin 14 (5, rcb) **1998**†Den 16 (0) **1999** Was 6 (0) **NFL** 67 (12) [5 yrs]

YEAR	TEAM	G (GS, POS)	RUSH	YD	AVG(LG)	TD	REC	YD	AVG(LG)	TD	PASS COMP	PCT	YD	AVG(LG)	TD	INT	SK	YD	QBR	KPR	OTD	PTS	TAY

PAUL, WHITNEY   Whitney, LB-DE, 6′3″/220 lbs; Colorado; 1976: KC, rnd 10; B10/8/1953 Galveston, TX   **1976** KC 14 (8, LDE)   **1977** KC 14 (13, LDE)   **1978** KC 16 (16, LOLB)   **1979** KC 15 (15, LOLB)   **1980** KC 12 (10, ROLB)   **1981** KC 16 (10, LOLB)   **1982** NO 9 (0)   **1983** NO 16 (15, ROLB)   **1984** NO 16 (16, ROLB)   **1985** NO 14 (8, ROLB)   **1986**†KC 13 (1)   **NFL** 155 (112) [11 yrs]

PAULEKAS, TONY   Anthony J., G-C-LB, 5′10″/207 lbs; Washington & Jefferson; B8/9/1912 Cherry Hill, PA, D9/18/1995 Farrell, PA   **1936**†GB 10 (3)

PAULK, JEFF   Jeffrey Howard, FB, 6′0″/240 lbs; Arizona State; 1999: Atl, rnd 3; B4/26/1976 Phoenix, AZ   **1999** Atl 1 (0)   **2000** NE 1 (0)   **NFL** 2 (0) [2 yrs]

PAULSON, DAINARD   Dainard Alexander, DB, 6′0″/190 lbs; Oregon State; B5/15/1937 Los Angeles, CA [I]   **1961** NYT-A 14 (RCB)   **1962** NYT-A 14 (LCB)   **1963** NYJ-A 14 (LS)   **1964** NYJ-A★14 (LS)   **1965** NYJ-A★14 (LS)   **1966** NYJ-A 14   **NFL** 84 [6 yrs]

PAULY, FRANK   Frank George, T, 6′1″/270 lbs; Washington & Jefferson; B1/24/1904, D6/10/1968   **1930** ChiB 6 (5, rt)

PAUP, BRYCE   Bryce Eric, LB, 6′5″/247 lbs; Northern Iowa; 1990: GB, rnd 6; B2/29/1968 Jefferson, IA [S]   **1990** GB 5 (0)   **1991** GB 12 (1)   **1992** GB 16 (10, lolb)   **1993**†GB 15 (14, ROLB/lolb)   **1994**†GB★16 (16, LLB)   **1995**†Buf★15 (15, LOLB)   **1996**†Buf★12 (11, LOLB)   **1997** Buf◇16 (16, LOLB)   **1998**†Jax 16 (16, LLB)   **1999**†Jax 15 (14, LLB)   **2000**†Min 10 (0)   **NFL** 148 (113) [11 yrs]

PAVELEC, TED   Theodore Charles, G-T, 6′0″/218 lbs; Detroit Mercy; 1941: Det, rnd 10; B11/4/1918 Kalamazoo, MI [K]   **1941** Det 10 (2)   **1942** Det 10 (9, LG)   **1943** Det 5 (3)   **NFL** 25 (14) [3 yrs]

PAVKOV, STAN   Stonko S., G-T, 6′0″/212 lbs; Idaho; B10/23/1916 Gooding, ID, D2/8/2002 Modesto, CA   **1939** Pit 2 (0)   **1940** Pit 9 (2)   **NFL** 11 (2) [2 yrs]

PAVLICH, CHARLES   Charles J., G-T, 6′2″/210 lbs; none; B1/15/1921, D3/6/1999 Los Angeles, CA   **1946** SF-A 10 (0)

PAXTON, LONIE   Leonidas E., C, 6′2″/260 lbs; Sacramento State; B3/13/1978 Anaheim, CA   **2000** NE 16 (0)   **2001**†NE 16 (0)   **2002** NE 16 (0)   **2003** NE 13 (0)   **2004**†NE 16 (0)   **2005**†NE 16 (0)   **NFL** 93 (0) [6 yrs]

PAYMAH, KARL   Karl, DB, 6′0″/204 lbs; Washington State; 2005: Den, rnd 3; B11/29/1982 Culver City, CA   **2005**†Den 13 (0)

PAYNE, CHARLIE   Charles Martin, WB, 5′11″/185 lbs; Detroit Mercy; B10/27/1914   **1937** Det 1 (0)

PAYNE, KEN   Kenneth Eugene, WR, 6′1″/185 lbs; Langston; 1974: GB, rnd 6; B10/6/1950 Oklahoma City, OK

1974	GB	12	—	—	—	—	5	63	12.6(18)	0	—	—	—	—	—	—	—	—	—	—	0	32
1975	GB☆	14 (wr)	1	-2	-2.0(-2)	0	58	766	13.2(54)	0	—	—	—	—	—	—	—	—	—	—	0	381
1976	GB	14 (WR)	—	—	—	—	33	467	14.2(57)	4	—	—	—	—	—	—	—	—	—	—	24	254
1977	GB	4	—	—	—	—	7	99	14.1(45)	1	—	—	—	—	—	—	—	—	—	—	6	55
1978	†Phi	16 (9, WR)	1	17	17.0(17)	0	13	238	18.3(50)	1	—	—	—	—	—	—	—	—	—	—	6	141
NFL	5	60 (9)	2	15	7.5(17)	0	116	1633	14.1(57)	6	—	—	—	—	—	—	—	—	—	—	36	862

PAYNE, ROD   Reginald Gerald, C, 6′4″/305 lbs; Michigan; 1997: Cin, rnd 3; B6/14/1974 Miami, FL   **1998** Cin 6 (0)

PAYNE, RUSSELL   William Russell, TE, 6′1″/240 lbs; Appalachian State; B3/21/1965 Virginia Beach, VA

| 1987 | Den | 1 (0) | — | — | — | — | 1 | 8 | 8.0(8) | 0 | — | — | — | — | — | — | — | — | — | — | 0 | 4 |

PAYNE, SETH   Seth Copeland, DT-NT, 6′4″/303 lbs; Cornell; 1997: Jax, rnd 4; B2/12/1975 Clifton Springs, NY   **1997**†Jax 12 (5, rdt)   **1998** Jax 6 (1)   **1999**†Jax 16 (16, RDT)   **2000** Jax 16 (16, RDT)   **2001** Jax 16 (16, RDT)   **2002** Hou 16 (16, NT)   **2003** Hou 2 (2)   **2004** Hou 16 (12, NT)   **2005** Hou 16 (14, NT)   **NFL** 116 (96) [9 yrs]

PAYTON, EDDIE   Edward, RB, 5′8″/175 lbs; Jackson State; B8/3/1951 Columbia, MS [R]   **1977** Cle 2   **1978** KC 14   **1981** Min 16 (0)   **1982** Min 9 (0)

1977	Det	8	4	13	3.3(14)	0	2	10	5.0(14)	0	1	0	0.0	0	0.0	0	0	—	—	kp	2	12	363
1980	†Min	16 (0)	2	15	7.5(8)	0	—	—	—	—	—	—	—	—	—	—	—	—	—	kp	—	0	485
NFL	5	65	6	28	4.7(14)	0	2	10	5.0(14)	0	1	0	0.0	0	0.0	0	0	—	—	kp	3	18	2006

PAYTON, JARRETT   Jarrett, RB, 6′0″/220 lbs; Miami (FL); B2/5/1983 Arlington, IL

| 2005 | Ten | 13 (0) | 33 | 105 | 3.2(15) | 2 | 6 | 30 | 5.0(9) | 0 | — | — | — | — | — | — | — | — | — | k | — | 12 | 134 |

PAYTON, SEAN   Patrick Sean, QB, 5′11″/200 lbs; Eastern Illinois; B12/29/1963 Naperville, IL [C]

| 1987 | ChiB | 3 (0) | 1 | 28 | 28.0(28) | 0 | — | — | — | — | 23 | 8 | 34.8 | 79 | 3.4(20) | 0 | 1 | 7 | 47 | — | — | 0 | 28 |

PAYTON, WALTER   Walter Jerry 'Sweetness', RB, 5′10″/200 lbs; Jackson State; 1975: Chi, rnd 1; B7/25/1954 Columbia, MS, D11/1/1999 South Barrington, IL; HOF 1993

1975	ChiB	13 (7, RB)	196	679	3.5(54)	7	33	213	6.5(40)	0	1	0	0.0	0	0.0	0	1	—	—	Pk	—	42	1050
1976	ChiB★	14 (14, RB)	311	1390	4.5(60)	13	15	149	9.9(34)	0	—	—	—	—	—	—	—	—	—	k	—	78	1580
1977	†ChiB★	14 (14, RB)	339	1852	5.5(73)	14	27	269	10.0(75)	2	—	—	—	—	—	—	—	—	—	k	—	96	2202
1978	ChiB★	16 (16, RB)	333	1395	4.2(76)	11	50	480	9.6(61)	0	—	—	—	—	—	—	—	—	—	—	—	66	1745
1979	†ChiB★	16 (16, RB)	369	1610	4.4(43)	14	31	313	10.1(65)	2	1	1	100.0	54	54.0(54)	1	0	—	—	—	—	96	1949
1980	ChiB★	16 (16, RB)	317	1460	4.6(69)	6	46	367	8.0(54)	1	3	0	0.0	0	0.0	0	0	—	—	—	—	42	1709
1981	ChiB	16 (16, RB)	339	1222	3.6(39)	6	41	379	9.2(30)	2	2	0	0.0	0	0.0	0	0	—	—	—	—	48	1482
1982	ChiB	9 (9, RB)	148	596	4.0(26)	1	32	311	9.7(40)	0	3	1	33.3	39	13.0(39)	1	0	—	—	—	—	6	786
1983	ChiB★	16 (16, RB)	314	1421	4.5(49)	6	53	607	11.5(74)	2	6	3	50.0	95	15.8(56)	3	0	—	—	—	—	48	1777
1984	†ChiB★	16 (16, RB)	381	1684	4.4(72)	11	45	368	8.2(31)	0	8	3	37.5	47	5.9(42)	2	1	—	—	—	—	66	1972
1985	†ChiB★	16 (16, RB)	324	1551	4.8(40)	9	49	483	9.9(65)	2	5	3	60.0	96	19.2(50)	1	0	—	—	—	—	66	1946
1986	†ChiB★	16 (16, RB)	321	1333	4.2(41)	8	37	382	10.3(57)	3	4	0	0.0	0	0.0	0	1	—	—	—	—	66	1579
1987	†ChiB	12 (12, RB)	146	533	3.7(17)	4	33	217	6.6(16)	1	1	0	0.0	0	0.0	0	0	—	—	—	—	30	647
NFL	13	190 (184)	3838	16726	4.4(76)	110	492	4538	9.2(75)	15	34	11	32.4	331	9.7(56)	8	6	—	—	Pk	—	750	20420

PEABODY, DWIGHT   Dwight Van Dorn, E-BB, 5′11″/170 lbs; Ohio State; B1/26/1894 Oberlin, OH, D1/3/1972 Venice, CA   **1920** Col 1 (0)   **1922** Tol 7 (5, RE)   **NFL** 8 (5) [2 yrs]

PEACE, LARRY   Lawrence, HB, 5′11″/185 lbs; Pittsburgh; B2/13/1917 Bradford, PA [K]

| 1941 | Bkn | 7 (0) | 4 | 2 | 0.5(2) | 0 | — | — | — | — | — | — | — | — | — | — | — | — | — | K | — | 1 | 2 |

PEACOCK, ELVIS   Elvis Zaring, RB, 6′1″/212 lbs; Oklahoma; 1978: LA, rnd 1; B11/7/1956 Miami, FL

1979	LARm	11	52	224	4.3(15)	0	21	261	12.4(49)	0	—	—	—	—	—	—	—	—	—	k	—	0	356
1980	LARm	13 (9, RB)	164	777	4.7(36)	7	25	213	8.5(59)	2	—	—	—	—	—	—	—	—	—	—	—	54	964
1981	Cin	3 (0)	—	—	—	—	—	—	—	—	—	—	—	—	—	—	—	—	—	—	—	—	—
NFL	3	27 (9)	216	1001	4.6(36)	7	46	474	10.3(59)	2	—	—	—	—	—	—	—	—	—	k	—	54	1319

PEACOCK, JOHNNY   John Byron, DB, 6′1″/200 lbs; Houston; 1969: Hou, rnd 5; B3/2/1947 Austin, TX   **1969**†Hou-A 14 (rs)   **1970** Hou 14 (FS)   **NFL** 28 [2 yrs]

PEAKS, CLARENCE   Clarence Earl, FB, 6′1″/218 lbs; Michigan State; 1957: Phi, rnd 1; B9/23/1935 Greenville, MS

1957	Phi	12 (FB)	125	495	4.0(35)	1	11	99	9.0(53)	0	3	2	66.7	56	18.7(37)	0	1	—	—	k	—	6	566
1958	Phi	11 (FB)	115	386	3.4(23)	3	29	248	8.6(33)	2	—	—	—	—	—	—	—	—	—	—	—	30	550
1959	Phi	12 (FB)	124	451	3.6(34)	3	28	209	7.5(23)	0	—	—	—	—	—	—	—	—	—	—	—	18	586
1960	Phi	7 (fb)	86	465	5.4(57)	3	14	116	8.3(34)	0	—	—	—	—	—	—	—	—	—	—	—	18	553
1961	Phi	13 (FB)	135	471	3.5(33)	5	32	472	14.8(48)	0	1	0	0.0	0	0.0	0	0	—	—	k	—	30	756
1962	Phi	14 (FB)	137	447	3.3(48)	3	39	347	8.9(27)	0	—	—	—	—	—	—	—	—	—	—	—	18	651
1963	Phi	14 (fb)	64	212	3.3(26)	1	22	167	7.6(23)	1	—	—	—	—	—	—	—	—	—	—	—	12	311
1964	Pit	12 (fb)	118	503	4.3(70)	2	12	113	9.4(41)	0	—	—	—	—	—	—	—	—	—	k	—	12	726
1965	Pit	10	47	230	4.9(36)	0	3	22	7.3(21)	0	—	—	—	—	—	—	—	—	—	k	—	0	370
NFL	9	105	951	3660	3.8(70)	21	190	1793	9.4(53)	3	4	2	50.0	56	14.0(37)	0	1	—	—	k	—	144	5067

PEAR, DAVE   David Louis, NT-DT, 6′2″/250 lbs; Washington; 1975: Bal, rnd 3; B6/1/1953 Vancouver, WA   **1975**†Bal 13   **1976** TB 13 (13, LDT)   **1977** TB☆14 (14, NT)   **1978** TB★16 (16, NT)   **1979** Oak 16 (16, NT)   **1980**†Oak 7 (3)   **NFL** 79 (62) [6 yrs]

PEARCE, HARLEY   Harley Charles, E-B, 5′10″/180 lbs; Ohio Wesleyan; B3/24/1901 Hillsboro, OH, D5/13/1979 Columbus, OH   **1926** Col 7 (6, LE), 6

PEARCE, PARD   Walter Irving, QB-BB, 5′5″/150 lbs; Pennsylvania; B10/23/1896 Providence, RI, D5/24/1974 Newport, RI   **1920** Dec 13 (8, QB)   **1921** ChiS 11 (8, QB), 12   **1922** ChiB 8 (1), 6   **1924** Ken 2 (1)   **1925** Pro 8 (1)   **NFL** 42 (19), 18 [5 yrs]

PEARCY, JIM   James Wheeler, G, 5′11″/210 lbs; Marshall; B7/26/1918 Harrisville, WV, D3/15/2005 Hendersonville, NC   **1946** ChiR-A (3)   **1947** ChiR-A 14 (11, LG)   **1948** ChiR-A 14 (13, LG)   **1949** ChiH-A 8 (3)   **AAFC** 49 (30) [4 yrs]

PEARLMAN, RED   Isador Ralph, T-G, 6′0″/195 lbs; Pittsburgh; B7/29/1898 Pittsburgh, PA, D11/28/1985 Hollywood, FL   **1920** Cle 8 (6, RT)   **1921** Cle 8 (8, LG)   **1924** Roc 2 (1)   **NFL** 18 (15) [3 yrs]

PEARMAN, ALVIN Francis Alvin, RB, 5´9˝/208 lbs; Virginia; 2005: Jax, rnd 4; B8/10/1982 Princeton, NJ

YEAR	TEAM	G (GS, POS)	RUSH	YD	AVG (LG)	TD	REC	YD	AVG (LG)	TD	PASS	COMP	PCT	YD	AVG (LG)	TD	INT	SK	YD	QBR	KPR	OTD	PTS	TAY
2005	†Jax	16(0)	39	149	3.8(45)	1	32	240	7.5(19)	0	—	—	—	—	—	—	—	—	—	—	kp	—	6	511

PEARS, MORGAN Morgan T., T, 6´6˝/332 lbs; Colorado State; B5/4/1980 Los Angeles, CA **2004** NYG 2 (0)

PEARSON, AARON Aaron Dantianto, LB, 6´0˝/239 lbs; Mississippi State; 1986: KC, rnd 11; B8/22/1964 Gadsden, AL **1986**†KC 15 (0) **1987** KC 12 (9, LILB) **1988** KC 16 (10, LILB) **NFL** 43 (19) [3 yrs]

PEARSON, BARRY Barry Lynn, WR, 5´11˝/185 lbs; Northwestern; B2/4/1950 Geneseo, IL

YEAR	TEAM	G (GS, POS)	RUSH	YD	AVG (LG)	TD	REC	YD	AVG (LG)	TD	PASS	COMP	PCT	YD	AVG (LG)	TD	INT	SK	YD	QBR	KPR	OTD	PTS	TAY
1972	†Pit	0	—	—	—	—	—	—	—	—	—	—	—	—	—	—	—	—	—	—	—	—	0	0
1973	†Pit	13	—	—	—	—	23	317	13.8(46)	3	—	—	—	—	—	—	—	—	—	—	—	—	18	174
1974	KC	14	1	1	1.0(1)	0	27	387	14.3(48)	1	—	—	—	—	—	—	—	—	—	—	—	—	6	200
1975	KC	14(WR)	—	—	—	—	36	608	16.9(45)	3	—	—	—	—	—	—	—	—	—	—	p	—	18	340
1976	KC	8	—	—	—	—	—	—	—	—	—	—	—	—	—	—	—	—	—	—	—	—	—	—
NFL	5	49	1	1	1.0(1)	0	86	1312	15.3(48)	7	—	—	—	—	—	—	—	—	—	—	p	—	42	713

PEARSON, BERT Madison B., C-G, 6´0˝/206 lbs; Kansas State; B3/22/1905 Manhattan, KS, D5/1/1945 **1929** ChiB 12 (7, c) **1930** ChiB 14 (10, C) **1931** ChiB☆13 (12, C) **1932** ChiB 9 (2) **1933** ChiB 5 (1) **1934**†ChiB 4 (1) **1935** ChiC 10 (5, c) **1936** ChiC 10 (0) **NFL** 77 (38) [8 yrs]

PEARSON, DENNIS Dennis Mack, WR, 5´11˝/177 lbs; Washington; San Diego State; 1978: Atl, rnd 5; B2/9/1955 Gordo, AL

YEAR	TEAM	G (GS, POS)	RUSH	YD	AVG (LG)	TD	REC	YD	AVG (LG)	TD	PASS	COMP	PCT	YD	AVG (LG)	TD	INT	SK	YD	QBR	KPR	OTD	PTS	TAY
1978	Atl	13	1	1	1.0(1)	0	5	71	14.2(23)	0	—	—	—	—	—	—	—	—	—	—	k	1	6	334
1979	Atl	16	—	—	—	—	7	119	17.0(40)	0	—	—	—	—	—	—	—	—	—	—	kp	—	0	235
NFL	2	29	1	1	1.0(1)	0	12	190	15.8(40)	0	—	—	—	—	—	—	—	—	—	—	kp	1	6	568

PEARSON, DREW Drew 'Mr. Clutch', WR, 6´0˝/184 lbs; Tulsa; B1/12/1951 South River, NJ

YEAR	TEAM	G (GS, POS)	RUSH	YD	AVG (LG)	TD	REC	YD	AVG (LG)	TD	PASS	COMP	PCT	YD	AVG (LG)	TD	INT	SK	YD	QBR	KPR	OTD	PTS	TAY
1973	†Dal	14(6, wr)	—	—	—	—	22	388	17.6(40)	2	—	—	—	—	—	—	—	—	—	—	kp	—	12	257
1974	Dal★	14(WR)	3	6	2.0(22)	0	62	**1087**	17.5(50)	2	1	1	100.0	46	46.0(46)	1	0	—	—	—	—	1	18	588
1975	†Dal☆	14(WR)	1	11	11.0(11)	0	46	822	17.9(46)	8	—	—	—	—	—	—	—	—	—	—	—	—	48	462
1976	†Dal★	14(WR)	2	20	10.0(11)	0	**58**	806	13.9(40)	6	1	1	100.0	39	39.0(39)	1	0	—	—	—	—	1	42	478
1977	†Dal★	14(WR)	2	22	11.0(11)	0	48	**870**	18.1(67)	2	—	—	—	—	—	—	—	—	—	—	—	—	12	467
1978	†Dal☆	16(WR)	3	29	9.7(33)	0	44	714	16.2(53)	3	—	—	—	—	—	—	—	—	—	—	—	—	18	401
1979	†Dal	15(WR)	3	27	9.0(16)	0	55	1026	**18.7(56)**	8	—	—	—	—	—	—	—	—	—	—	—	—	48	580
1980	†Dal	16(15, WR)	2	30	15.0(32)	0	43	568	13.2(30)	6	—	—	—	—	—	—	—	—	—	—	—	—	36	344
1981	†Dal	16(16, WR)	3	31	10.3(25)	0	38	614	16.2(42)	3	2	2	100.0	81	40.5(59)	1	0	—	—	—	—	—	18	399
1982	†Dal	9(8, WR)	—	—	—	—	26	382	14.7(48)	3	2	1	50.0	26	13.0(26)	0	1	—	—	—	—	—	18	179
1983	†Dal	14(13, WR)	2	13	6.5(10)	0	47	545	11.6(32)	5	1	0	0.0	0	0.0	0	1	—	—	—	—	—	30	271
NFL	11	156(58)	21	189	9.0(33)	0	489	7822	16.0(67)	48	7	5	71.4	192	27.4(59)	3	2	—	—	—	kp	2	300	4424

PEARSON, DUDLEY Dudley Lester, BB, 5´9˝/165 lbs; Notre Dame; B2/8/1896 Outagamie County, WI, D9/3/1982 Milwaukee, WI **1922** Rac 4 (2)

PEARSON, J.C. Jayice, DB, 5´11˝/187 lbs; Cal Poly-Pomona; Washington; B8/17/1963, Japan **1986**†KC 8 (0) **1987** KC 12 (2) **1988** KC 16 (6, lcb) **1989** KC 16 (3) **1990**†KC 16 (5, lcb) **1991**†KC 15 (12, LCB) **1992** KC 7 (0) **1993**†Min 13 (0) **NFL** 103 (28) [8 yrs]

PEARSON, KALVIN Kalvin, DB, 5´10˝/190 lbs; Morehouse; Grambling State; B10/22/1978 Town Creek, AL **2002** Cle 5 (0) **2005**†TB 14 (1) **NFL** 19 (1) [2 yrs]

PEARSON, LINDY Lindell Eugene, HB, 6´0˝/198 lbs; Oklahoma; B3/6/1929 Oklahoma City, OK

YEAR	TEAM	G (GS, POS)	RUSH	YD	AVG (LG)	TD	REC	YD	AVG (LG)	TD	PASS	COMP	PCT	YD	AVG (LG)	TD	INT	SK	YD	QBR	KPR	OTD	PTS	TAY
1950	Det	11	31	82	2.6(11)	2	1	4	4.0(4)	0	3	0	0.0	0	0.0	0	3	—	—	—	kp	—	12	0
1951	Det	12	22	88	4.0(25)	0	5	43	8.6(14)	0	—	—	—	—	—	—	—	—	—	—	—	—	0	110
1952	Det	3(1)	3	0	0.0(0)	0	—	—	—	—	—	—	—	—	—	—	—	—	—	—	—	—	0	0
1952	GB	2	2	2	1.0(2)	0	1	16	16.0(16)	0	—	—	—	—	—	—	—	—	—	—	—	—	0	10
NFL	3	28(1)	58	172	3.0(25)	2	7	63	9.0(16)	0	3	0	0.0	0	0.0	0	3	—	—	—	kp.	—	12	120

PEARSON, MIKE Michael Wayne, T, 6´7˝/297 lbs; Florida; 2002: Jax, rnd 2; B8/22/1980 Tampa, FL **2002** Jax 16 (11, LT) **2003** Jax 16 (16, LT) **2004** Jax 4 (4) **2005** Jax 4 (2) **NFL** 40 (33) [4 yrs]

PEARSON, PRESTON Preston James, RB, 6´1˝/205 lbs; Illinois; 1967: Bal, rnd 12; B1/17/1945 Freeport, IL **[R]**

YEAR	TEAM	G (GS, POS)	RUSH	YD	AVG (LG)	TD	REC	YD	AVG (LG)	TD	PASS	COMP	PCT	YD	AVG (LG)	TD	INT	SK	YD	QBR	KPR	OTD	PTS	TAY
1967	Bal	7	—	—	—	—	—	—	—	—	—	—	—	—	—	—	—	—	—	—	—	—	—	—
1968	†Bal	14	19	78	4.1(13)	0	2	70	35.0(61)	2	—	—	—	—	—	—	—	—	—	—	k	2	24	445
1969	Bal	14	24	81	3.4(10)	0	4	64	16.0(37)	0	—	—	—	—	—	—	—	—	—	—	kp	—	0	361
1970	Pit	14(RB)	173	503	2.9(30)	2	6	71	11.8(18)	0	—	—	—	—	—	—	—	—	—	—	k	—	12	613
1971	Pit	14(RB)	131	605	4.6(29)	0	20	246	12.3(41)	2	—	—	—	—	—	—	—	—	—	—	k	1	18	838
1972	†Pit	11	67	264	3.9(21)	0	11	79	7.2(15)	0	—	—	—	—	—	—	—	—	—	—	kp	—	0	399
1973	†Pit	14(FB)	132	554	4.2(47)	2	11	173	15.7(36)	2	—	—	—	—	—	—	—	—	—	—	k	—	24	739
1974	†Pit	9	70	317	4.5(53)	4	11	118	10.7(31)	0	—	—	—	—	—	—	—	—	—	—	k	—	24	494
1975	†Dal	14(10, RB)	133	509	3.8(32)	2	27	351	13.0(49)	2	—	—	—	—	—	—	—	—	—	—	k	—	24	866
1976	†Dal	10(2)	68	233	3.4(21)	1	23	316	13.7(30)	2	—	—	—	—	—	—	—	—	—	—	—	—	18	411
1977	†Dal	14(10, rb)	89	341	3.8(22)	1	46	535	11.6(36)	4	—	—	—	—	—	—	—	—	—	—	—	—	30	639
1978	†Dal	16	25	104	4.2(18)	0	47	526	11.2(34)	0	—	—	—	—	—	—	—	—	—	—	—	—	0	367
1979	†Dal	14	7	14	2.0(11)	1	26	333	12.8(26)	1	—	—	—	—	—	—	—	—	—	—	—	—	12	196
1980	†Dal	11(0)	3	6	2.0(2)	0	20	213	10.6(20)	2	—	—	—	—	—	—	—	—	—	—	—	—	12	123
NFL	14	176(22)	941	3609	3.8(53)	13	254	3095	12.2(61)	17	—	—	—	—	—	—	—	—	—	—	kp	3	198	6488

PEARSON, WILLIE Willie, DB, 6´0˝/190 lbs; North Carolina A&T; 1969: Mia, rnd 5; B5/9/1947 Bennettsville, SC **1969** Mia-A 5

PEASE, BRENT Brent Richard, QB, 6´2˝/201 lbs; Montana; 1987: Min, rnd 11; B10/8/1964 Moscow, ID

YEAR	TEAM	G (GS, POS)	RUSH	YD	AVG (LG)	TD	REC	YD	AVG (LG)	TD	PASS	COMP	PCT	YD	AVG (LG)	TD	INT	SK	YD	QBR	KPR	OTD	PTS	TAY
1987	Hou	7(3)	15	33	2.2(8)	1	—	—	—	—	113	56	49.6	728	6.4(51)	3	5	5	36	—	—	—	6	222
1988	†Hou	13(0)	8	-2	-0.3(4)	1	—	—	—	—	22	6	27.3	64	2.9(21)	0	4	2	18	—	—	—	6	-120
NFL	2	20(3)	23	31	1.3(8)	2	—	—	—	—	135	62	45.9	792	5.9(51)	3	9	7	54	—	—	—	12	102

PEASE, GEORGE George Gregory, BB-TB, 5´8˝/185 lbs; Columbia; B6/18/1903 Brooklyn, NY, D10/26/1984 Dallas, TX **1929** Ora☆10 (9, BB), 6

PEAT, TODD Marion Todd, G, 6´2˝/300 lbs; Northern Illinois; 1987: SL, rnd 11; B5/20/1964 Champaign, IL **1987** SL 12 (8, LG) **1988** Phx 15 (15, LG) **1989** Phx 4 (4) **1990**†LARd 16 (1) **1992** LARd 16 (8, rg) **1993**†LARd 16 (0) **NFL** 79 (36) [6 yrs]

PEAVEY, JACK John A., C, 6´2˝/260 lbs; Springfield; Troy State; B6/6/1963 Attleboro, MA **1987** Den 3 (1)

PEAY, FRANCIS Francis G., T, 6´5˝/250 lbs; Arizona; Cameron; Missouri; 1966: NYG, rnd 1/KC, rnd 2; B5/23/1944 Pittsburgh, PA **1966** NYG 9 (RT) **1967** NYG 13 **1968** GB 14 **1969** GB 14 (LT) **1970** GB 14 (LT) **1971** GB 14 (LT) **1972** GB 6 **1973** KC 9 (RT) **1974** KC 10 **NFL** 103 [9 yrs]

PECK, JARED Jared, T, 6´5˝/290 lbs; North Dakota State; B5/6/1979 Bloomington, MN **2004** Atl 1 (0)

PEDERSEN, WIN Windidge Christian, T, 6´3˝/223 lbs; Minnesota; 1940: NYG, rnd 8; B6/9/1915 Chicago, IL, D1/16/1983 Hopkins, MN **[K]** **1941** NYG 9 (5, RT) **1945** NYG 4 (0) **1946** Bos 10 (2) **NFL** 23 (7) [3 yrs]

PEDERSON, DOUG Douglas Irvin, QB, 6´3˝/220 lbs; Louisiana-Monroe; B1/31/1968 Bellingham, WA

YEAR	TEAM	G (GS, POS)	RUSH	YD	AVG (LG)	TD	REC	YD	AVG (LG)	TD	PASS	COMP	PCT	YD	AVG (LG)	TD	INT	SK	YD	QBR	KPR	OTD	PTS	TAY
1993	Mia	7(0)	2	-1	-0.5(0)	0	—	—	—	—	8	4	50.0	41	5.1(12)	0	0	1	4	—	—	—	0	20
1996	GB	1(0)	—	—	—	—	—	—	—	—	—	—	—	—	—	—	—	—	—	—	—	—	—	—
1997	GB	1(0)	3	-4	-1.3(-1)	0	—	—	—	—	—	—	—	—	—	—	—	—	—	—	—	—	0	-4
1998	†GB	12(0)	8	-4	-0.5(1)	0	—	—	—	—	24	14	58.3	128	5.3(29)	2	0	1	7	—	—	—	0	70
1999	Phi	16(9, QB)	20	33	1.6(19)	0	—	—	—	—	227	119	52.4	1276	5.6(84)	7	9	20	109	—	—	—	0	346
2000	Cle	11(8, QB)	18	68	3.8(15)	0	—	—	—	—	210	117	55.7	1047	5.0(67)	2	8	17	116	—	—	—	0	282
2001	†GB	16(0)	1	-1	-1.0(-1)	0	—	—	—	—	—	—	—	—	—	—	—	—	—	—	—	—	0	-1
2002	†GB	16(0)	1	-1	-1.0(-1)	0	—	—	—	—	28	19	67.9	134	4.8(20)	1	0	1	8	—	—	—	0	71
2003	†GB	16(0)	6	-5	-0.8(0)	0	—	—	—	—	2	2	100.0	16	8.0(14)	0	0	—	—	—	—	—	0	3
2004	GB	4(0)	2	15	7.5(9)	0	—	—	—	—	23	11	47.8	120	5.2(24)	0	2	—	—	—	—	—	0	-5
NFL	10	100(17)	61	100	1.6(19)	0	—	—	—	—	522	286	54.8	2762	5.3(84)	12	19	40	244	62.3	—	—	0	781

YEAR	TEAM	G (GS, POS)	RUSH	YD	AVG (LG)	TD	REC	YD	AVG (LG)	TD	PASS COMP	PCT	YD	AVG (LG)	TD	INT	SK	YD	QBR	KPR	OTD	PTS	TAY

PEDERSON, JIM　James Palmer, B, 5´9˝/189 lbs; Augsburg; B10/19/1907 Harvey, ND, D8/14/1978 Pawtucket, RI　**1930** Min 7 (5, BB)　**1930** Fra 4 (3)　**1931** Fra 8 (7, WB)

YEAR	TEAM	G (GS, POS)	RUSH	YD	AVG (LG)	TD																OTD	PTS	TAY
1932	ChiB	1(0)	1	2	2.0(2)	0	—	—	—	—	—	—	—	—	—	—	—	—	—	—	—	—	0	2
NFL	3	20(15)	1	2	2.0(2)	0	—	—	—	—	—	—	—	—	—	—	—	—	—	—	—	0	2

PEEBLES, DANNY　Daniel Percy, WR, 5´11˝/180 lbs; North Carolina State; 1989: TB, rnd 2; B5/30/1966 Raleigh, NC

1989	TB	13(1)	2	-6	-3.0(1)	0	11	180	16.4(32)	0											—	0	84
1990	TB	10(0)	—	—	—	—	6	50	8.3(18)	1										k	—	6	129
1991	Cle	7(1)	—	—	—	—	—	—	—	—										k	—	0	29
NFL	3	30(2)	2	-6	-3.0(1)	0	17	230	13.5(32)	1										k	—	6	242

PEEBLES, JIM　James McAden, E-T-DE, 6´4˝/231 lbs; Vanderbilt; B8/27/1920 Culleoka, TN, D7/19/1997 Nashville, TN **[K]**

1946	Was	11(7, LE)	—	—	—	—	9	164	18.2(31)	1										K	—	6	87
1947	Was	12(11, RT)	—	—	—	—	4	26	6.5(11)	0										Kk	—	0	11
1948	Was	11(4)	—	—	—	—	—	—	—	—										K	—	1	0
1949	Was	11(2)	1	-3	-3.0(-3)	0	—	—	—	—											—	0	-3
1951	Was	12	—	—	—	—	—	—	—	—											—	—	—
NFL	5	57(24)	1	-3	-3.0(-3)	0	13	190	14.6(35)	1										Kk	—	7	95

PEED, ART　Arthur, T, /205 lbs; none　**1929** Buf 1 (0)

PEEK, ANTWAN　Antwan, LB, 6´1˝/230 lbs; Cincinnati; 2003: Hou, rnd 3; B10/29/1979 Cincinnati, OH　**2003** Hou 10 (4)　**2004** Hou 14 (1)　**2005** Hou 16 (16, ROLB)　NFL 40 (21) [3 yrs]

PEELLE, JUSTIN　Justin Morris, TE, 6´4˝/255 lbs; Oregon; 2002: SD, rnd 4; B3/15/1979 Fresno, CA

2002	SD	15(2)	—	—	—	—	3	15	5.0(10)	0											—	0	8
2003	SD	15(9, TE)	—	—	—	—	16	133	8.3(24)	1										k	—	6	71
2004	†SD	16(4)	—	—	—	—	10	84	8.4(17)	2											—	12	52
2005	SD	16(4)	—	—	—	—	11	38	3.5(11)	1											—	6	24
NFL	4	62(19)	—	—	—	—	40	270	6.8(24)	4										k	—	24	154

PEERY, GORDON　Gordon George, BB, 5´10˝/155 lbs; Oklahoma State; B1/12/1904 Stillwater, OK, D5/21/1994 El Reno, OK　**1927** Cle 4 (3)

PEETE, RODNEY　Rodney, QB, 6´0˝/230 lbs; USC; 1989: Det, rnd 6; B3/16/1966 Mesa, AZ

YEAR	TEAM	G (GS, POS)	RUSH	YD	AVG (LG)	TD					PASS COMP	PCT	YD	AVG (LG)	TD	INT	SK	YD	QBR		OTD	PTS	TAY
1989	Det	8(8, QB)	33	148	4.5(14)	4	—	—	—	—	195	103	52.8	1479	7.6(69)	5	9	27	164	—	—	24	593
1990	Det	11(11, QB)	47	363	7.7(37)	6	—	—	—	—	271	142	52.4	1974	7.3(68)	13	8	27	173	79.8	—	36	1155
1991	Det	8(8, QB)	25	125	5.0(26)	2	—	—	—	—	194	116	59.8	1339	6.9(68)	5	9	11	42	—	—	12	480
1992	Det	10(10, QB)	21	83	4.0(12)	0	—	—	—	—	213	123	57.7	1702	8.0(78)	9	9	28	170	—	—	0	619
1993	Det	10(10, QB)	45	165	3.7(28)	1	—	—	—	—	252	157	62.3	1670	6.6(93)	6	14	34	174	66.4	—	6	480
1994	†Dal	7(1)	9	-2	-0.2(2)	0	—	—	—	—	56	33	58.9	470	8.4(65)	4	1	4	21	—	—	0	213
1995	†Phi	15(12, QB)	32	147	4.6(18)	1	—	—	—	—	375	215	57.3	2326	6.2(37)	8	14	33	166	67.3	—	6	800
1996	Phi	5(5, qb)	20	31	1.5(11)	0	—	—	—	—	134	80	59.7	992	7.4(62)	3	5	11	53	—	—	6	352
1997	Phi	5(3)	8	37	4.6(16)	0	—	—	—	—	118	68	57.6	869	7.4(38)	4	4	17	85	—	—	0	332
1998	Phi	5(4)	5	30	6.0(19)	1	—	—	—	—	129	71	55.0	758	5.9(25)	2	4	16	103	—	—	6	269
1999	Was	3(0)	2	-1	-0.5(0)	0	—	—	—	—	17	8	47.1	107	6.3(30)	2	1	2	9	—	—	0	23
2001	Oak	1(0)	—	—	—	—	—	—	—	—	—	—	—	—	—	—	—	—	—	—	—	0	—
2002	Car	14(14, QB)	22	14	0.6(10)	0	—	—	—	—	381	223	58.5	2630	6.9(69)	15	14	31	192	77.4	—	0	844
2003	Car	1(1)	—	—	—	—	—	—	—	—	10	4	40.0	19	1.9(8)	0	0	3	20	—	—	0	10
2004	Car	1(0)	1	-1	-1.0(-1)	0	—	—	—	—	1	1	100.0	3	3.0(3)	0	0	—	—	—	—	0	1
NFL	15	104(87)	270	1139	4.2(37)	16	—	—	—	—	2346	1344	57.3	16338	7.0(93)	76	92	244	1372	73.3	—	96	6168

PEETS, BRIAN　Brian Canvin, TE, 6´4˝/225 lbs; Pacific; B7/15/1956 Stockton, CA

1978	Sea	8	—	—	—	—	1	14	14.0(14)	0	—	—	—	—	—	—	—	—	—	—	—	0	7
1979	Sea	16(14, TE)	—	—	—	—	25	293	11.7(28)	1	—	—	—	—	—	—	—	—	—	—	—	6	152
1981	SF	5(0)	—	—	—	—	1	5	5.0(5)	0	—	—	—	—	—	—	—	—	—	—	—	0	3
NFL	3	29(14)	—	—	—	—	27	312	11.6(28)	1	—	—	—	—	—	—	—	—	—	—	—	6	161

PEGRAM, ERRIC　Erric Dermont, RB, 5´10˝/195 lbs; North Texas; 1991: Atl, rnd 6; B1/7/1969 Dallas, TX **[R]**

1991	†Atl	16(7, RB)	101	349	3.5(34)	1	1	-1	-1.0(-1)	0										k	—	6	379
1992	Atl	16(1)	21	89	4.2(15)	0	2	25	12.5(19)	0										k	—	0	128
1993	Atl	16(14, RB)	292	1185	4.1(29)	3	33	302	9.2(30)	0										k	—	18	1369
1994	Atl	13(5, rb)	103	358	3.5(25)	1	16	99	6.2(28)	0										k	—	6	428
1995	†Pit	15(11, RB)	213	813	3.8(38)	5	26	206	7.9(22)	1										k	—	38	996
1996	Pit	12(4)	97	509	5.2(27)	1	17	112	6.6(14)	0										k	1	12	749
1997	SD	4(0)	9	23	2.6(18)	1	2	7	3.5(4)	0											—	6	37
1997	NYG	11(0)	19	72	3.8(6)	1	19	83	4.4(14)	0										k	—	6	176
NFL	7	103(42)	855	3398	4.0(38)	13	116	833	7.2(30)	1										k	1	92	4260

PEGUESE, WILLIS　Willis, DE, 6´4˝/273 lbs; Miami (FL); 1990: Hou, rnd 3; B12/18/1966 Miami, FL　**1990** Hou 2 (0)　**1991** Hou 7 (0)　**1992** Hou 1 (1)　**1992** Ind 12 (0)　**1993** Ind 13 (4)　**NFL** 35 (5) [4 yrs]

PEIFFER, DAN　Daniel William, C, 6´3˝/252 lbs; Southeast Missouri State; 1973: SL, rnd 14; B3/29/1951 Sigourney, IA　**1975** ChiB 11 (11, C)　**1976** ChiB 4 (4)　**1977**†ChiB 14 (C)　**1980** Was 8 (3)　**NFL** 37 (18) [4 yrs]

PEKO, TUPE　Situpe, G-C, 6´4˝/305 lbs; Michigan State; 2001: NYJ, rnd 7; B9/19/1978 Whittier, CA　**2003**†Ind 16 (1)　**2004**†Ind 11 (8, rg)　**NFL** 27 (9) [2 yrs]

PELFREY, DOUG　William Douglas, K, 5´11˝/185 lbs; Kentucky; 1993: Cin, rnd 8; B9/25/1970 Fort Thomas, KY **[K]**　**1993** Cin 15 (0)　**1994** Cin 16 (0)　**1995** Cin 16 (0)　**1996** Cin 16 (0)　**1997** Cin 16 (0)　**1999** Cin 16 (0)

1998	Cin	16(0)	—	—	—	—	—	—	—	—	1	0	0.0	0	0.0	0	0	1	4	—	K	—	78	0
NFL	7	111(0)	—	—	—	—	—	—	—	—	1	0	0.0	0	0.0	0	0	1	4	—	KP	—	660	0

PELFREY, RAY　Raymond Harrison, E-HB, 6´0˝/190 lbs; Auburn; Eastern Kentucky; 1951: GB, rnd 17; B1/11/1928 Sardinia, OH

1951	GB	12(RE)	3	44	14.7(24)	0	38	462	12.2(49)	5	—	—	—	—	—	—	—	—	—	—	P	—	30	300
1952	GB	1	—	—	—	—	1	10	10.0(10)	0	—	—	—	—	—	—	—	—	—	—	k	—	0	16
1952	ChiC	1	—	—	—	—	1	11	11.0(11)	0	—	—	—	—	—	—	—	—	—	—	k	—	0	-2
1952	DalT	6(6, RE)	—	—	—	—	18	243	13.5(48)	2	—	—	—	—	—	—	—	—	—	—		—	12	132
1953	NYG	12	—	—	—	—	17	233	13.7(60)	3	—	—	—	—	—	—	—	—	—	—		—	18	132
NFL	3	32(6)	3	44	14.7(24)	0	75	959	12.8(60)	10	—	—	—	—	—	—	—	—	—	—	Pk	—	60	578

PELLEGRINI, BOB　Robert Francis, LB-G, 6´2˝/233 lbs; Maryland; 1956: Phi, rnd 1; B11/13/1934 Williamsport, PA　**1956** Phi 12 (RG)　**1958** Phi 12 (MLB)　**1959** Phi 12 (LLB)　**1960** Phi 9 (8, LLB)　**1961** Phi 14　**1962** Was 9 (MLB)　**1963** Was 14 (LLB)　**1964** Was 12　**1965** Was 13 (RLB)　**NFL** 107 (8) [9 yrs]

PELLEGRINI, JOE　Joseph, DT-NT, 6´2˝/270 lbs; Idaho; B8/9/1956 Aberdeen, WA　**1978** NYJ 9　**1979** NYJ 4　**NFL** 13 [2 yrs]

PELLEGRINI, JOSEPH　Joseph Anthony, G-C, 6´4˝/265 lbs; Harvard; B4/8/1957 Boston, MA　**1982**†NYJ 9 (0)　**1983** NYJ 16 (9, LG)　**1984** Atl 15 (3)　**1985** Atl 5 (2)　**1986** Atl 8 (1)　**NFL** 53 (15) [5 yrs]

PELLINGTON, BILL　William, LB, 6´2˝/234 lbs; Defiance; Rutgers; B9/25/1927 Ramsey, NJ, D4/25/1994 Baltimore, MD **[I]**　**1953** Bal 12 (LLB)　**1954** Bal 12 (LLB)　**1956** Bal 12 (LLB)　**1957** Bal 1　**1959**†Bal 12 (LLB)　**1960** Bal☆12 (LLB)　**1961** Bal 14 (MLB/llb)　**1962** Bal☆14 (LLB)　**1963** Bal 14 (MLB)　**1964**†Bal☆14 (MLB)

1955	Bal	12(LLB)	—	—	—	—	1	10	10.0(10)	0	—	—	—	—	—	—	—	—	—	—	kpi	—	0	19
1958	†Bal☆	12(MLB)	—	—	—	—	1	-1	-1.0(-1)	0	—	—	—	—	—	—	—	—	—	—	i	—	0	24
NFL	12	141	—	—	—	—	2	9	4.5(10)	0	—	—	—	—	—	—	—	—	—	—	kpi	1	6	127

PELLUER, SCOTT　Scott John, LB, 6´2˝/219 lbs; Washington State; 1981: Dal, rnd 4; B4/28/1959 Yakima, WA　**1981** NO 16 (0)　**1982** NO 6 (1)　**1983** NO 16 (0)　**1984** NO 16 (0)　**1985** NO 11 (5, rilb)　**NFL** 65 (6) [5 yrs]

YEAR	TEAM	G(GS, POS)	RUSH	YD	AVG(LG)	TD	REC	YD	AVG(LG)	TD	PASS	COMP	PCT	YD	AVG(LG)	TD	INT	SK	YD	QBR	KPR	OTD	PTS	TAY
PELLUER, STEVE Steven Carl, QB, 6´4˝/209 lbs; Washington; 1984: Dal, rnd 5; B7/29/1962 Yakima, WA																								
1984	Dal	1(0)	—	—	—	—	—	—	—	—	—	—	—	—	—	—	—	—	—	—	—	—	—	—
1985	Dal	2(0)	3	-2	-0.7(1)	0	—	—	—	—	8	5	62.5	47	5.9(28)	0	0	—	—	—	—	—	0	22
1986	Dal	16(9, QB)	41	255	6.2(21)	1	—	—	—	—	378	215	56.9	2727	7.2(84)	8	17	47	362	67.9	—	—	6	989
1987	Dal	12(4)	25	142	5.7(21)	1	—	—	—	—	101	55	54.5	642	6.4(44)	3	2	5	35	—	—	—	6	408
1988	Dal	16(14, QB)	51	314	6.2(27)	2	—	—	—	—	435	245	56.3	3139	7.2(61)	17	19	21	112	73.9	—	—	12	1229
1989	KC	5(3)	17	143	8.4(27)	2	—	—	—	—	47	26	55.3	301	6.4(24)	1	0	8	61	—	—	—	12	319
1990	†KC	13(0)	5	6	1.2(5)	0	—	—	—	—	5	2	40.0	14	2.8(11)	0	1	—	—	—	—	—	0	-27
NFL	7	65(30)	142	858	6.0(27)	6	—	—	—	—	974	548	56.3	6870	7.1(84)	29	39	81	570	71.6	—	—	36	2938
PELSHAK, TROY Zenret, LB, 6´2˝/242 lbs; North Carolina A&T; B3/6/1977 Charlotte, NC **1999** SL 9 (0) **2000** SL 3 (0) **2000** Jax 1 (0) **NFL** 13 (0) [2 yrs]																								
PENA, BUBBA Robert B., G, 6´2˝/250 lbs; Massachusetts; 1971: Cle, rnd 4; B8/8/1949 Wareham, MA **1972** Cle 2																								
PENARANDA, JAIRO Jairo Alonso, RB, 5´11˝/217 lbs; UCLA; 1981: LA, rnd 12; B6/15/1958 Barranquilla, Colombia **1981** LARm 16 (0) **1985** Phi 4 (0) **NFL** 20 (0) [2 yrs]																								
PENCHION, BOB Robert Earl, G-C, 6´5˝/265 lbs; Alcorn State; 1972: Buf, rnd 5; B8/11/1949 Town Creek, AL **1972** Buf 12 (RG) **1973** Buf 5 **1974** SF 8 **1975** SF 9 (8, LG) **1976** Sea 14 (13, LG) **NFL** 48 (21) [5 yrs]																								
PENN, CHRIS Christopher Anthony, WR, 6´0˝/198 lbs; Tulsa; 1994: KC, rnd 3; B4/20/1971 Nowata, OK																								
1994	KC	8(0)	—	—	—	—	3	24	8.0(13)	0	—	—	—	—	—	—	—	—	—	—	k	—	0	71
1995	KC	2(0)	—	—	—	—	1	12	12.0(12)	0	—	—	—	—	—	—	—	—	—	—	kp	—	0	-6
1996	KC	16(16, WR)	—	—	—	—	49	628	12.8(22)	5	—	—	—	—	—	—	—	—	—	—	p	—	30	417
1997	ChiB	14(4)	1	-1	-1.0(-1)	0	47	576	12.3(33)	3	—	—	—	—	—	—	—	—	—	—	—	—	18	302
1998	ChiB	14(1)	—	—	—	—	31	448	14.5(37)	3	—	—	—	—	—	—	—	—	—	—	—	—	20	239
1999	SD	16(3)	—	—	—	—	17	257	15.1(43)	1	—	—	—	—	—	—	—	—	—	—	p	—	6	177
NFL	6	70(24)	1	-1	-1.0(-1)	0	148	1945	13.1(43)	12	—	—	—	—	—	—	—	—	—	—	kp	—	74	1200
PENN, JESSE Jesse Andrew, LB, 6´3˝/220 lbs; Virginia Tech; 1985: Dal, rnd 2; B9/6/1962 Martinsville, VA **1985**†Dal 16 (0) **1986** Dal 15 (0) **1987** Dal 11 (1) **NFL** 42 (1) [3 yrs]																								
PENNINGTON, CHAD James Chad, QB, 6´3˝/225 lbs; Marshall; 2000: NYJ, rnd 1; B6/26/1976 Knoxville, TN																								
2000	NYJ	1(0)	1	0	0.0(0)	0	—	—	—	—	5	2	40.0	67	13.4(62)	1	0	1	4	—	—	—	0	39
2001	NYJ	2(0)	1	11	11.0(11)	0	—	—	—	—	20	10	50.0	92	4.6(24)	1	0	1	8	—	—	—	0	62
2002	†NYJ	15(12, QB)	29	49	1.7(14)	2	—	—	—	—	399	275	**68.9**	3120	7.8(47)	22	6	22	135	**104.2**	—	—	12	1499
2003	NYJ	10(9, QB)	21	42	2.0(10)	2	—	—	—	—	297	189	63.6	2139	7.2(65)	13	12	25	160	82.9	—	—	12	717
2004	†NYJ	13(13, QB)	34	126	3.7(16)	1	—	—	—	—	370	242	65.4	2673	7.2(48)	16	9	18	103	91.0	—	—	6	1193
2005	NYJ	3(3)	6	27	4.5(14)	0	—	—	—	—	83	49	59.0	530	6.4(37)	2	3	9	52	—	—	—	0	182
NFL	6	44(37)	92	255	2.8(16)	5	—	—	—	—	1174	767	65.3	8621	7.3(65)	55	30	76	462	92.1	—	—	30	3691
PENNINGTON, LEON Leon Tyrone, LB, 6´1˝/225 lbs; Florida; B12/25/1963 **1987** TB 3 (0)																								
PENNINGTON, TOM Thomas Durward, K, 6´2˝/210 lbs; Georgia; 1962: Buf, rnd 11/GB, rnd 12; B11/26/1939 Albany, GA **[K]** **1962** DalT-A 3																								
PENNISON, JAY Jay Leslie, C, 6´1˝/276 lbs; Nicholls State; B9/9/1961 Houma, LA **1986** Hou 16 (12, C) **1987**†Hou 12 (12, C) **1988**†Hou 16 (16, C) **1989**†Hou 12 (12, C) **1990** Hou 15 (15, C) **NFL** 71 (67) [5 yrs]																								
PENNYWELL, CARLOS Carlos Jerome, WR, 6´2˝/180 lbs; Grambling State; 1978: NE, rnd 3; B3/18/1956 Crowley, LA																								
1978	NE	16	—	—	—	—	1	28	28.0(28)	0	—	—	—	—	—	—	—	—	—	—	—	—	0	14
1979	NE	6	—	—	—	—	4	35	8.8(13)	1	—	—	—	—	—	—	—	—	—	—	—	—	6	23
1980	NE	11(0)	—	—	—	—	4	31	7.8(16)	1	—	—	—	—	—	—	—	—	—	—	k	—	6	6
1981	NE	5(2)	1	3	3.0(3)	0	3	49	16.3(22)	1	—	—	—	—	—	—	—	—	—	—	—	—	6	33
NFL	4	38(2)	1	3	3.0(3)	0	12	143	11.9(28)	3	—	—	—	—	—	—	—	—	—	—	k	—	18	75
PENNYWELL, ROBERT Robert, LB, 6´1˝/222 lbs; Grambling State; 1976: SF, rnd 6; B11/6/1954 Crowley, LA **1977** Atl 14 (9, LLB) **1978**†Atl 15 (15, MLB) **1979** Atl 16 (16, MLB) **1980**†Atl 16 (2) **NFL** 61 (42) [4 yrs]																								
PENROSE, CRAIG Craig R., QB, 6´3˝/211 lbs; Colorado; San Diego State; 1976: Den, rnd 4; B7/25/1953 Woodland, CA																								
1976	Den	4(2)	2	-3	-1.5(-1)	0	—	—	—	—	36	16	44.4	265	7.4(41)	3	3	—	—	—	—	—	0	25
1977	Den	8	4	24	6.0(17)	0	—	—	—	—	39	21	53.8	217	5.6(35)	0	4	5	49	—	—	—	0	-28
1978	Den	4(2)	1	0	0.0(0)	0	—	—	—	—	37	16	43.2	185	5.0(29)	2	4	—	—	—	—	—	0	-58
1979	Den	2	—	—	—	—	—	—	—	—	5	2	40.0	44	8.8(29)	0	1	—	—	—	—	—	0	-18
NFL	4	18(4)	7	21	3.0(17)	0	—	—	—	—	117	55	47.0	711	6.1(41)	5	12	5	49	—	—	—	0	-79
PENSE, LEON James Leon, BB, 6´0˝/170 lbs; Arkansas; 1945: Pit, rnd 9; B2/5/1922 Chewey, OK																								
1945	Pit	10(8, BB)	6	1	0.2(1)	0	1	32	32.0(32)	0	—	—	—	—	—	—	—	—	—	—	ki	—	0	47
PENTECOST, JOHN John Mathew, G, 6´2˝/251 lbs; UCLA; B12/23/1943 Lawndale, CA **1967** Min 4																								
PEOPLES, GEORGE George Evans, RB, 6´0˝/211 lbs; Auburn; 1982: Dal, rnd 8; B8/25/1960 Tampa, FL, D11/23/2003 Tampa, FL **1983** NE 16 (0) **1985** TB 2 (0)																								
1982	†Dal	8(0)	7	22	3.1(7)	0	—	—	—	—	—	—	—	—	—	—	—	—	—	—	—	—	0	22
1984	TB	6(0)	1	2	2.0(2)	0	—	—	—	—	—	—	—	—	—	—	—	—	—	—	—	—	0	2
NFL	4	32(0)	8	24	3.0(7)	0	—	—	—	—	—	—	—	—	—	—	—	—	—	—	—	—	0	24
PEOPLES, WOODY Woodrow, G, 6´2˝/252 lbs; Grambling State; B8/16/1943 Birmingham, AL **1968** SF 13 **1969** SF 14 (14, RG) **1970**†SF 14 (14, RG) **1971**†SF☆14 (14, RG) **1972**†SF★14 (14, RG) **1973** SF✧14 (14, RG) **1974** SF 10 (9, RG) **1975** SF 14 (14, RG) **1977** SF 14 (14, RG) **1978**†Phi 15 (14, RG) **1979**†Phi 16 (16, RG) **1980**†Phi 16 (16, RG) **NFL** 168 (153) [12 yrs]																								
PEPPER G, none; deceased **1920** Roc 1 (0)																								
PEPPER, GENE Eugene Francis, G-T-DT-LB, 6´2˝/239 lbs; Missouri; 1950: Was, rnd 6; B9/22/1927 Overland, MO **1950** Was 12 **1951** Was 11 **1952** Was 12 (LG) **1953** Was 6 **1954** Bal 3 **NFL** 44 [5 yrs]																								
PEPPERS, JULIUS Julius Frazier, DE, 6´6˝/283 lbs; North Carolina; 2002: Car, rnd 1; B1/18/1980 Wilson, NC **2002** Car 12 (12, LDE) **2003**†Car 16 (16, LDE) **2004** Car★16 (16, LDE) **2005**†Car✧16 (16, LDE) **NFL** 60 (60) [4 yrs]																								
PERANTONI, FRANK Francis Joseph, C, 6´0˝/220 lbs; Princeton; B9/13/1923 Raritan, NJ, D9/11/1991 Somerville, NJ **1948** NYY-A 14 (3) **1949**†NYY-A 12 (1) **AAFC** 26 (4) [2 yrs]																								
PERCIVAL, MAC Mac, K, 6´4˝/220 lbs; Texas Tech; B2/26/1940 Lubbock, TX **[K]** **1967** ChiB 14 **1968** ChiB☆14 **1969** ChiB 14 **1971** ChiB 14 **1972** ChiB 14 **1973** ChiB 4 **1974** Dal 3																								
1970	ChiB	14	—	—	—	—	1	19	19.0(19)	0	—	—	—	—	—	—	—	—	—	—	K	—	88	10
NFL	8	91	—	—	—	—	1	19	19.0(19)	0	—	—	—	—	—	—	—	—	—	—	K	—	466	10
PERDUE, BOLO Charles Willard, DE-E, 5´10˝/170 lbs; Duke; Arkansas; 1940: Was, rnd 16; B5/10/1916 Thomasville, NC, D3/31/1988 **1946** Bkn-A 10 (1)																								
1940	NYG	10(0)	—	—	—	—	2	28	14.0	0	—	—	—	—	—	—	—	—	—	—	—	—	0	14
PEREZ, PETE Peter J., G, 5´9˝/220 lbs; Illinois; B4/23/1924 Aurora, IL **1945** ChiB 3 (0)																								
PERGINE, JOHN John Samuel, LB, 6´1˝/225 lbs; Notre Dame; 1968: LA, rnd 11; B9/13/1946 Norristown, PA **1969**†LARm 14 **1970** LARm 12 **1971** LARm 12 **1972** LARm 12 **1973**†Was 14 **1974**†Was 12																								
1975	Was	14	—	—	—	—	2	41	20.5(30)	1	—	—	—	—	—	—	—	—	—	—	—	—	6	26
NFL	7	90	—	—	—	—	2	41	20.5(30)	1	—	—	—	—	—	—	—	—	—	—	kp	—	6	22
PERINA, BOB Robert Ian, DB-TB-HB, 6´1˝/205 lbs; Princeton; B1/16/1921 Irvington, NJ, D8/2/1991 Madison, WI																								
1946	†NYY-A	13(2)	45	135	3.0	1	—	—			48	21	43.8	279	5.8	1	4	—	—	—	Pkpi	—	6	295
1947	Bkn-A	14(4)	67	116	1.7	3	9	67	7.4	1	24	11	45.8	91	3.8	0	2	—	—	—	Pkpi	—	24	199
1948	ChiR-A	13(1)	6	1	0.2	0	2	13	6.5	0	—	—	—	—	—	—	—	—	—	—	kpi	—	0	76
AAFC	3	40(7)	118	252	2.1	4	11	80	7.3	1	72	32	44.4	370	5.1	1	6	—	—	—	Pkpi	—	30	569
1949	ChiB	12(1)	4	4	1.0(2)	0	3	33	11.0(14)	0	—	—	—	—	—	—	—	—	—	—	ki	—	0	9
1950	Bal	1	—	—	—	—	—	—	—	—	—	—	—	—	—	—	—	—	—	—	—	—	—	—
NFL	2	13(1)	4	4	1.0(2)	0	3	33	11.0(14)	0	—	—	—	—	—	—	—	—	—	—	—	—	0	21

YEAR	TEAM	G (GS, POS)	RUSH	YD	AVG(LG)	TD	REC	YD	AVG(LG)	TD	PASS	COMP	PCT	YD	AVG(LG)	TD	INT	SK	YD	QBR	KPR	OTD	PTS	TAY

PERINI, PETE Evo Peter, FB-LB, 6´0˝/225 lbs; Ohio State; B2/10/1928 New Village, NJ **[K]**

1954	ChiB	12	4	11	2.8(4)	0	5	56	11.2(20)	0	—	—	—	—	—	—	—	—	—	Kk	—	1	38
1955	ChiB	2	2	0	0.0(1)	0	1	3	3.0(3)	0	—	—	—	—	—	—	—	—	—	—	—	0	2
1955	†Cle	6	—	—	—	—	—	—	—	—	—	—	—	—	—	—	—	—	—	—	—	—	—
NFL	**2**	20	6	11	1.8(4)	0	6	59	9.8(20)	0	—	—	—	—	—	—	—	—	—	Kk	—	1	40

PERKINS, ANTONIO Antonio D., DB, 5´11˝/188 lbs; Oklahoma; 2005: Cle, rnd 4; B1/9/1982 Lawton, OK   **2005** Cle 1 (0)

PERKINS, ART Arthur Ray, FB, 6´0˝/225 lbs; North Texas; 1962: LA, rnd 4/Hou, rnd 18; B5/1/1940 Fort Worth, TX

1962	LARm	13	48	181	3.8(20)	2	14	83	5.9(13)	0	—	—	—	—	—	—	—	—	—	—	—	12	243
1963	LARm	13	37	70	1.9(8)	4	8	61	7.6(17)	0	—	—	—	—	—	—	—	—	—	k	—	24	141
NFL	**2**	26	85	251	3.0(20)	6	22	144	6.5(17)	0	—	—	—	—	—	—	—	—	—	k	—	36	383

PERKINS, BILL William Osborne, HB, 6´2˝/225 lbs; Iowa; 1963: Dal, rnd 12; B1/12/1941 Jersey City, NJ

| 1963 | NYJ-A | 4 | 3 | 8 | 2.7(8) | 0 | — | — | — | — | — | — | — | — | — | — | — | — | — | k | — | 0 | 3 |

PERKINS, BRUCE Bruce Kerry, RB, 6´2˝/230 lbs; Arizona State; B8/14/1967 Waterloo, IA

1990	TB	16(3)	13	36	2.8(9)	0	8	85	10.6(34)	2	—	—	—	—	—	—	—	—	—	—	—	12	89
1991	Ind	14(1)	4	11	2.8(4)	0	3	-2	-0.7(3)	0	—	—	—	—	—	—	—	—	—	—	—	0	10
NFL	**2**	30(4)	17	47	2.8(9)	0	11	83	7.5(34)	2	—	—	—	—	—	—	—	—	—	—	—	12	99

PERKINS, DON Donald E., B, 6´0˝/196 lbs; Wisconsin-Platteville; B9/18/1917 Dodgeville, WI, D9/24/1998 Branson, MO

1944	†GB	10(2)	58	207	3.6(26)	0	1	1	1.0(1)	0	—	—	—	—	—	—	—	—	—	Pki	2	12	345
1945	GB	7(0)	35	175	5.0(49)	1	2	11	5.5(10)	0	—	—	—	—	—	—	—	—	—	P	—	6	191
1945	ChiB	2(2)	11	98	8.9(38)	1	—	—	—	—	—	—	—	—	—	—	—	—	—	—	—	6	108
1946	†ChiB	8(0)	34	105	3.1(36)	0	2	41	20.5(21)	0	—	—	—	—	—	—	—	—	—	kp	—	0	145
NFL	**3**	27(4)	138	585	4.2(49)	2	5	53	10.6(21)	0	—	—	—	—	—	—	—	—	—	Pkpi	2	24	788

PERKINS, DON Donald Anthony, FB-HB, 5´10˝/204 lbs; New Mexico; 1960: Bal, rnd 9/NYT, rnd 1; B3/4/1938 Waterloo, IA

1961	Dal★	14(HB)	200	815	4.1(47)	4	32	298	9.3(38)	1	—	—	—	—	—	—	—	—	—	kp	—	30	1125
1962	Dal★	14(HB)	222	945	4.3(35)	7	13	104	8.0(21)	0	—	—	—	—	—	—	—	—	—	—	—	42	1067
1963	Dal◇	11(10, FB)	149	614	4.1(19)	7	14	84	6.0(19)	0	—	—	—	—	—	—	—	—	—	—	—	42	726
1964	Dal	13(FB)	174	768	4.4(59)	6	15	155	10.3(37)	0	—	—	—	—	—	—	—	—	—	—	—	36	906
1965	Dal	13(FB)	177	690	3.9(43)	0	14	142	10.1(27)	0	—	—	—	—	—	—	—	—	—	—	—	0	761
1966	†Dal◇	14(14, FB)	186	726	3.9(24)	8	23	231	10.0(39)	0	—	—	—	—	—	—	—	—	—	—	—	48	922
1967	†Dal★	14(FB)	201	823	4.1(30)	6	18	116	6.4(15)	0	—	—	—	—	—	—	—	—	—	—	—	36	941
1968	†Dal★	14(FB)	191	836	4.4(28)	4	17	180	10.6(24)	2	—	—	—	—	—	—	—	—	—	—	—	36	976
NFL	**8**	107(24)	1500	6217	4.1(59)	42	146	1310	9.0(39)	3	—	—	—	—	—	—	—	—	—	kp	—	270	7423

PERKINS, HORACE Horace Alonzo, DB, 5´11˝/180 lbs; Colorado; 1977: Mia, rnd 8; B3/15/1954 El Campo, TX   **1979** KC 16

PERKINS, JIM James William, T-G, 6´2˝/250 lbs; Colorado; 1962: Den, rnd 21/Phi, rnd 7; B6/16/1939 Loyalton, CA, D7/24/1992   **1962** Den-A 14 (lt)   **1963** Den-A 14 (lt)
1964 Den-A 14 (LG)   **NFL** 42 [3 yrs]

PERKINS, JOHNNY John Eugene, WR, 6´2˝/205 lbs; Abilene Christian; 1977: NYG, rnd 2; B4/21/1953 Franklin, TX

1977	NYG	13	—	—	—	—	20	279	13.9(54)	0	—	—	—	—	—	—	—	—	—	—	—	0	140
1978	NYG	14(12, WR)	1	3	3.0(3)	0	32	514	16.1(67)	3	—	—	—	—	—	—	—	—	—	—	—	18	275
1979	NYG	13	—	—	—	—	20	337	16.9(38)	4	—	—	—	—	—	—	—	—	—	—	—	24	189
1980	NYG	6(4)	—	—	—	—	14	193	13.8(58)	3	—	—	—	—	—	—	—	—	—	—	—	18	112
1981	†NYG	16(14, WR)	2	-1	-0.5(10)	0	51	858	16.8(80)	6	—	—	—	—	—	—	—	—	—	—	—	36	458
1982	NYG	8(7, WR)	—	—	—	—	26	430	16.5(35)	2	—	—	—	—	—	—	—	—	—	—	—	12	225
1983	NYG	1(0)	—	—	—	—	—	—	—	—	—	—	—	—	—	—	—	—	—	—	—	—	—
NFL	**7**	71(37)	3	2	0.7(10)	0	163	2611	16.0(80)	18	—	—	—	—	—	—	—	—	—	—	—	108	1398

PERKINS, RAY Walter Ray, WR-SE, 6´3˝/183 lbs; Alabama; 1966: Bal, rnd 7/Bos, rnd R5; B12/6/1941 Mount Olive, MS **[C]**

1967	Bal	8(se)	—	—	—	—	16	302	18.9(57)	2	—	—	—	—	—	—	—	—	—	—	—	12	161
1968	†Bal	14	—	—	—	—	15	227	15.1(29)	1	—	—	—	—	—	—	—	—	—	—	—	6	119
1969	Bal	14	3	36	12.0(18)	0	28	391	14.0(47)	3	—	—	—	—	—	—	—	—	—	—	—	18	247
1970	†Bal	11	2	6	3.0(4)	0	10	194	19.4(41)	1	—	—	—	—	—	—	—	—	—	—	—	6	108
1971	†Bal	11(WR)	5	35	7.0(18)	0	24	424	17.7(64)	4	—	—	—	—	—	—	—	—	—	—	—	24	267
NFL	**5**	58	10	77	7.7(18)	0	93	1538	16.5(64)	11	—	—	—	—	—	—	—	—	—	—	—	66	901

PERKINS, RAY Rayotis, DE, 6´5˝/242 lbs; Virginia; B9/25/1964 Richmond, VA   **1987** Dal 2 (1)

PERKINS, WILLIS Willis LaFran, DE-G, 6´0˝/260 lbs; Texas Southern; B2/14/1934 Columbus, TX   **1961** Bos-A 1   **1961** Hou-A 1   **1963** Hou-A 3   **NFL** 5 [2 yrs]

PERKO, JOHN John Joseph, G, 6´1˝/207 lbs; Duquesne; B2/20/1915 Hibbing, MN, D5/9/1973 Hibbing, MN   **1938** Pit 10 (8, RG)   **1939** Pit 8 (3)   **1940** Pit 11 (9, RG)
1944 C-P 10 (8, RG)   **1945** Pit 10 (10, RG)   **1946** Pit 9 (0)   **1947** Pit 7 (0)

| 1937 | Pit | 10(8, RG) | 1 | 5 | 5.0(5) | 0 | — | — | — | — | — | — | — | — | — | — | — | — | — | — | — | 0 | 5 |
| **NFL** | **8** | 75(46) | 1 | 5 | 5.0(5) | 0 | — | — | — | — | — | — | — | — | — | — | — | — | — | ki | — | 0 | -2 |

PERKO, JOHN John Francis, G, 6´1˝/225 lbs; Minnesota; Notre Dame; 1944: Phi, rnd 10; B4/8/1918 Ely, MN, D6/7/1994 Hibbing, MN   **1946** Buf-A 14 (10, LG)

PERKO, MIKE Michael John, NT, 6´4˝/235 lbs; Gonzaga; Utah State; 1982: Pit, rnd 6; B3/30/1957 Seattle, WA   **1982** Atl 9 (2)

PERKO, TOM Thomas Patrick, LB, 6´3˝/233 lbs; Pittsburgh; 1976: GB, rnd 4; B6/17/1954 Steubenville, OH, D2/2/1980 Ambridge, PA   **1976** GB 14 (4)

PERLO, PHIL Phillip Donald, LB, 6´0˝/220 lbs; Maryland; B12/6/1935 Washington, DC, D12/11/1993 Houston, TX   **1960** Hou-A 7

PEROT, PETEY Edward Joseph, G, 6´2˝/261 lbs; Northwestern State (LA); 1979: Phi, rnd 2; B4/28/1957 Natchitoches, LA   **1979** †Phi 14 (6, lg)   **1980** †Phi 16 (15, LG)
1981 †Phi 16 (5, lg)   **1982** Phi 9 (0)   **1984** Phi 12 (5, lg)   **1985** NO 7 (7, lg)   **NFL** 74 (38) [6 yrs]

PERPICH, GEORGE George Rudolph, T, 6´2˝/223 lbs; Georgetown (DC); 1943: Was, rnd 11; B6/22/1920 Croatia, D5/26/1993 Hibbing, MN   **1946** Bkn-A 13 (0)
1947 Bal-A 14 (10, RT)   **AAFC** 27 (10) [2 yrs]

PERREAULT, PETE Peter Wayne, G-T, 6´3˝/248 lbs; Boston University; B3/1/1939 Shrewsbury, MA   **1963** NYJ-A 3   **1964** NYJ-A 14   **1965** NYJ-A 3   **1966** NYJ-A 6   **1967** NYJ-A 9
1968 Cin-A 14   **1969** †NYJ-A 14   **1970** NYJ 13   **1971** Min 10   **NFL** 86 [9 yrs]

PERRETTA, RALPH Ralph Joseph, C-G, 6´2˝/252 lbs; Purdue; 1975: SD, rnd 8; B1/30/1953 Rockville Centre, MD   **1975** SD 5   **1976** SD 13 (3)   **1977** SD 14 (14, C)
1978 SD 15 (8, c)   **1979** †SD 16   **1980** NYG 5 (0)   **1980** †SD 5 (0)   **NFL** 73 (25) [6 yrs]

PERRIE, MIKE Michael, QB, 5´11˝/197 lbs; St. Mary's (CA); 1939: Cle, rnd 17; B10/1916 Spokane, WA   **1939** Cle 2 (0)

PERRIMAN, BRETT Brett, WR, 5´9˝/180 lbs; Miami (FL); 1988: NO, rnd 2; B10/10/1965 Miami, FL

1988	NO	16(0)	3	17	5.7(17)	0	16	215	13.4(33)	2	—	—	—	—	—	—	—	—	—	—	—	12	135
1989	NO	14(1)	1	-10	-10.0(-10)	0	20	356	17.8(47)	0	—	—	—	—	—	—	—	—	p	—	—	0	173
1990	†NO	16(15, WR)	—	—	—	—	36	382	10.6(29)	2	—	—	—	—	—	—	—	—	—	—	—	12	201
1991	†Det	15(14, WR)	4	10	2.5(6)	0	52	668	12.8(42)	1	—	—	—	—	—	—	—	—	—	—	—	6	349
1992	Det	16(16, WR)	—	—	—	—	69	810	11.7(40)	4	—	—	—	—	—	—	—	—	—	k	—	24	424
1993	†Det	15(15, WR)	4	16	4.0(16)	0	49	496	10.1(34)	2	—	—	—	—	—	—	—	—	—	—	—	12	274
1994	†Det	16(14, WR)	9	86	9.6(25)	0	56	761	13.6(39)	4	1	0	0.0	0	0.0	0	—	—	—	—	—	28	487
1995	†Det	16(16, WR)	5	48	9.6(16)	0	108	1488	13.8(91)	9	—	—	—	—	—	—	—	—	—	kp	—	56	852
1996	Det	16(16, WR)	1	13	13.0(13)	0	94	1021	10.9(44)	5	—	—	—	—	—	—	—	—	—	—	—	30	549
1997	KC	5(4)	—	—	—	—	6	83	13.8(27)	0	—	—	—	—	—	—	—	—	—	—	—	0	42
1997	†Mia	8(5, wr)	—	—	—	—	19	309	16.3(26)	1	—	—	—	—	—	—	—	—	—	—	—	6	160
NFL	**10**	153(116)	27	180	6.7(25)	0	525	6589	12.6(91)	30	1	0	0.0	0	0.0	0	—	—	—	kp	—	186	3644

PERRIMAN, DEAN Dean, G-T, 6´3˝/260 lbs; Washington; B11/19/1959   **1987** Sea 1 (0)

YEAR	TEAM	G(GS, POS)	RUSH	YD	AVG(LG)	TD	REC	YD	AVG(LG)	TD	PASS	COMP	PCT	YD	AVG(LG)	TD	INT	SK	YD	QBR	KPR	OTD	PTS	TAY
PERRIN, BENNY Jesse Bennett, DB, 6´2˝/178 lbs; Alabama; 1982: SL, rnd 3; B10/20/1959 Orange County, CA **1982**†SL 9 (9, FS) **1985** SL 7 (6, fs)																								
1983	SL	16(16, FS)	1	0	0.0(0)	0	—	—	—	—	1	1	100.0	4	4.0(4)	0	0	—	—	—	iS	1	6	32
1984	SL	16(16, FS)	—	—	—	—	—	—	—	—	1	1	100.0	0	0.0(0)	0	0	—	—	—	i	—	0	2
NFL	4	48(47)	1	0	0.0	0	—	—	—	—	2	2	100.0	4	2.0(4)	0	0	—	—	—	iS	1	6	64
PERRIN, JACK John Stephenson, BB, 5´9˝/160 lbs; Michigan; B2/4/1898 Escanaba, MI, D6/24/1969 Detroit, MI **[K]** **1926** Har 6 (2), 6																								
PERRIN, LONNIE William D., RB, 6´1˝/222 lbs; Illinois; 1976: Den, rnd 5; B2/3/1952 Norfolk, VA																								
1976	Den	14	37	118	3.2(14)	2	4	35	8.8(15)	0	—	—	—	—	—	—	—	—	—	—	k	—	12	337
1977	†Den	14(5, fb)	110	456	4.1(62)	3	6	106	17.7(41)	1	—	—	—	—	—	—	—	—	—	—	k	—	24	571
1978	†Den	16	108	455	4.2(28)	4	10	54	5.4(13)	1	—	—	—	—	—	—	—	—	—	—	k	—	30	603
1979	Was	5	2	4	2.0(3)	0	—	—	—	—	—	—	—	—	—	—	—	—	—	—	k	—	0	32
1979	†ChiB	9	5	14	2.8(5)	0	1	27	27.0(27)	0	—	—	—	—	—	—	—	—	—	—	k	—	0	26
NFL	4	58(5)	262	1047	4.0(62)	9	21	222	10.6(41)	2	—	—	—	—	—	—	—	—	—	—	k	—	66	1568
PERRINO, MIKE Michael Nicholas, T, 6´5˝/285 lbs; Notre Dame; 1986: SD, rnd 8; B3/2/1964 Chicago, IL **1987** Phi 3 (3)																								
PERROTTI, MIKE Michael Anthony, T, 6´3˝/243 lbs; Ohio State; Cincinnati; B6/12/1923 Cleveland, OH, D11/1974 **1949** LAD-A 12 (3)																								
1948	LAD-A	14(0)	—	—	—	—	0	7	(7)	0	—	—	—	—	—	—	—	—	—	—	—	—	0	4
AAFC	2	26(3)	—	—	—	—	0	7	(7)	0	—	—	—	—	—	—	—	—	—	—	—	—	0	4
PERRY, BRUCE Bruce, RB, 5´10˝/200 lbs; Maryland; 2004: Phi, rnd 7; B3/22/1981 Philadelphia, PA																								
2005	Phi	2(1)	16	74	4.6(11)	0	—	—	—	—	—	—	—	—	—	—	—	—	—	—	k	—	0	197
PERRY, CHRIS Raymond Christopher, RB, 6´1˝/235 lbs; Michigan; 2004: Cin, rnd 1; B12/27/1981 Advance, NC																								
2004	Cin	2(0)	2	1	0.5(1)	0	3	33	11.0(13)	0	—	—	—	—	—	—	—	—	—	—	—	—	0	18
2005	†Cin	14(2)	61	279	4.6(30)	0	51	328	6.4(28)	2	—	—	—	—	—	—	—	—	—	—	—	—	12	453
NFL	2	16(2)	63	280	4.4(30)	0	54	361	6.7(28)	2	—	—	—	—	—	—	—	—	—	—	—	—	12	471
PERRY, CLAUDE Claude, T-G-E, 6´1˝/210 lbs; Alabama; B10/31/1901 Walker, AL, D7/17/1975 Goodsprings, AL **1927** GB 9 (5, rt) **1928** GB 13 (7, LT) **1929** GB 12 (5, lt) **1930** GB 9 (2) **1931** GB 5 (3) **1931** Bkn 4 (2) **1932** GB 13 (3) **1933** GB 11 (6, rt) **1935** GB 5 (0)																								
1934	GB	12(5, lt)	1	2	2.0(2)	0	—	—	—	—	—	—	—	—	—	—	—	—	—	—	—	—	0	2
NFL	9	93(38)	1	2	2.0(2)	0	—	—	—	—	—	—	—	—	—	—	—	—	—	—	—	—	0	2
PERRY, DARREN Darren, DB, 5´11˝/196 lbs; Penn State; 1992: Pit, rnd 8; B12/29/1968 Chesapeake, VA **[I]** **1992**†Pit 16 (16, FS) **1993**†Pit 16 (16, FS) **1994**†Pit☆16 (16, FS) **1995**†Pit 16 (16, FS) **1996**†Pit 16 (16, FS) **1997**†Pit 16 (16, FS) **1998** Pit 14 (14, FS) **2000**†NO 16 (16, FS) **NFL** 126 (126) [8 yrs]																								
PERRY, ED Edwin Lewis, TE, 6´4˝/255 lbs; James Madison; 1997: Mia, rnd 6; B9/1/1974 Richmond, VA **2000** Mia 9 (0) **2001**†Mia 16 (0) **2002** Mia 16 (0) **2004** Mia 16 (0) **2005** KC 6 (0)																								
1997	†Mia	16(4)	—	—	—	—	11	45	4.1(10)	1	—	—	—	—	—	—	—	—	—	—	k	—	6	20
1998	†Mia	14(5, te)	—	—	—	—	25	255	10.2(46)	0	—	—	—	—	—	—	—	—	—	—	—	—	0	128
1999	†Mia	16(1)	—	—	—	—	3	8	2.7(5)	1	—	—	—	—	—	—	—	—	—	—	—	—	6	9
NFL	8	109(10)	—	—	—	—	39	308	7.9(46)	2	—	—	—	—	—	—	—	—	—	—	k	—	12	141
PERRY, GERALD Gerald, T-G, 6´6˝/290 lbs; Southern (LA); 1988: Den, rnd 2; B11/12/1964 Columbia, SC **1988** Den 16 (6, lg) **1989**†Den 16 (15, LT) **1990** Den 8 (8, LT) **1991** LARm 11 (9, LT) **1992** LARm 16 (16, LT) **1993**†LARd 15 (15, LT) **1994** LARd 12 (12, LT) **1995** Oak 3 (3) **NFL** 97 (84) [8 yrs]																								
PERRY, GERRY Gerald Edward, T-DT-DE-G, 6´4˝/237 lbs; Pepperdine; California; 1952: LA, rnd 29; B7/17/1930 Ballston Spa, NY **[K]** **1954**†Det 11 **1956** Det 12 **1957**†Det 12 **1958** Det 12 **1959** Det 10 **1960** SL 12 **1961** SL 13 (rt) **1962** SL 14 **NFL** 96 [8 yrs]																								
PERRY, JASON Jason Robert, DB, 6´0˝/200 lbs; North Carolina State; 1999: SD, rnd 4; B8/1/1976 Passaic, NJ **1999** SD 16 (5, fs) **2000** SD 1 (0) **2001** SD 14 (3) **2002** Min 3 (0) **2002** Cin 2 (0) **NFL** 36 (8) [4 yrs]																								
PERRY, JOE Fletcher Joseph 'The Jet', FB, 6´0˝/200 lbs; Compton CC (CA); B1/22/1927 Stevens, AR; HOF 1969 **[K]**																								
1948	SF-A	14(0)	77	562	**7.3**(**57**)	**10**	8	79	9.9	1	—	—	—	—	—	—	—	—	—	—	ki	1	72	821
1949	†SF-A☆	11(5, fb)	115	**783**	**6.8**(**59**)	**8**	11	146	13.3	3	2	0	0.0	0	0.0	0	0	—	—	—	k	—	66	1078
AAFC	2	25(5)	192	1345	7.0(59)	18	19	225	11.8	4	2	0	0.0	0	0.0	0	0	—	—	—	ki	1	138	1899
1950	SF	12(FB)	124	647	5.2(78)	5	13	69	5.3(16)	1	—	—	—	—	—	—	—	—	—	—	k	—	36	780
1951	SF	11(FB)	136	677	5.0(58)	3	18	167	9.3(35)	1	1	1	100.0	31	31.0(31)	1	0	—	—	—	k	—	24	833
1952	SF✧	12(FB)	158	725	4.6(78)	8	15	81	5.4(17)	0	2	0	0.0	0	0.0	0	0	—	—	—	—	—	48	846
1953	SF★	12(FB)	**192**	**1018**	5.3(51)	**10**	19	191	10.1(60)	3	1	1	100.0	14	14.0(14)	0	0	—	—	—	Kk	—	78	1227
1954	SF★	12(FB)	**173**	**1049**	6.1(58)	8	26	203	7.8(70)	0	1	1	100.0	34	34.0(34)	0	0	—	—	—	K	—	57	**1248**
1955	SF	11(FB)	156	701	4.5(42)	2	19	55	2.9(19)	1	2	0	0.0	0	0.0	0	0	—	—	—	—	—	18	754
1956	SF	11(FB)	115	520	4.5(39)	3	18	104	5.8(20)	0	—	—	—	—	—	—	—	—	—	—	—	—	18	602
1957	†SF	8	97	454	4.7(34)	3	15	130	8.7(17)	0	1	0	0.0	0	0.0	0	0	—	—	—	—	—	18	549
1958	SF☆	12(FB)	125	758	6.1(73)	4	23	218	9.5(64)	1	—	—	—	—	—	—	—	—	—	—	—	—	30	912
1959	SF	11(FB)	139	602	4.3(40)	3	12	53	4.4(15)	0	—	—	—	—	—	—	—	—	—	—	—	—	18	659
1960	SF	10	36	95	2.6(21)	1	3	-3	-1.0(3)	0	—	—	—	—	—	—	—	—	—	—	—	—	6	104
1961	Bal	13(FB)	168	675	4.0(27)	3	34	322	9.5(27)	1	—	—	—	—	—	—	—	—	—	—	—	—	24	871
1962	Bal	12(FB)	94	359	3.8(21)	0	22	194	8.8(32)	0	—	—	—	—	—	—	—	—	—	—	—	—	0	456
1963	SF	9	24	98	4.1(16)	0	4	12	3.0(8)	0	1	0	0.0	0	0.0	0	0	—	—	—	—	—	0	104
NFL	1 4	156	1737	8378	4.8(78)	53	241	1796	7.5(70)	8	9	3	33.3	79	8.8(34)	1	0	—	—	—	Kk	—	375	9942
PERRY, LEON Leon, RB, 5´11˝/224 lbs; Mississippi; B8/14/1957 Gloster, MS																								
1980	NYG	10(5, fb)	59	272	4.6(17)	1	8	84	10.5(25)	1	—	—	—	—	—	—	—	—	—	—	—	—	12	329
1981	†NYG	16(8, RB)	72	257	3.6(23)	0	13	140	10.8(24)	1	—	—	—	—	—	—	—	—	—	—	—	—	6	332
1982	NYG	2(1)	3	14	4.7(15)	0	1	-1	-1.0(-1)	0	—	—	—	—	—	—	—	—	—	—	—	—	0	14
NFL	3	28(14)	134	543	4.1(23)	1	22	223	10.1(25)	2	—	—	—	—	—	—	—	—	—	—	—	—	18	675
PERRY, LOWELL Lowell Wesley, E, 6´1˝/190 lbs; Michigan; 1953: Pit, rnd 8; B12/5/1931 Ypsilanti, MI, D1/7/2001 Southfield, MI																								
1956	Pit	6(LE)	2	37	18.5(23)	0	14	334	23.9(75)	2	—	—	—	—	—	—	—	—	—	—	kp	—	12	370
PERRY, MARIO Romauro Ron, TE, 6´6˝/240 lbs; Mississippi; 1987: LARd, rnd 11; B12/20/1963 Chicago, IL																								
1987	LARd	3(2)	—	—	—	—	1	3	3.0(3)	1	—	—	—	—	—	—	—	—	—	—	—	—	6	7
PERRY, MARLO Malcolm Marlo, LB, 6´4˝/250 lbs; Jackson State; 1994: Buf, rnd 3; B8/25/1972 Forest, MS **1994** Buf 2 (0) **1995**†Buf 16 (11, LILB) **1996**†Buf 13 (0) **1997** Buf 13 (0) **1998** Buf 16 (1) **1999**†Buf 16 (0) **NFL** 76 (12) [6 yrs]																								
PERRY, MICHAEL DEAN Michael Dean, DT-DE, 6´1˝/285 lbs; Clemson; 1988: Cle, rnd 2; B8/27/1965 Aiken, SC **[S]** **1988**†Cle 16 (2) **1989**†Cle★16 (16, RDT) **1990** Cle★16 (16, RDT) **1991** Cle★16 (15, RDT) **1992** Cle☆14 (14, RDT) **1993** Cle★16 (13, RDT) **1994**†Cle★15 (14, RDT) **1995** Den☆14 (14, RDT) **1996**†Den★15 (15, RDT) **1997** Den 9 (9, RDT) **1997** KC 1 (1) **NFL** 148 (129) [10 yrs]																								
PERRY, ROD Rodney Cornell, DB, 5´9˝/178 lbs; Colorado; 1975: LA, rnd 4; B9/11/1953 Fresno, CA **[I]** **1975**†LARm 9 **1976**†LARm 14 (14, LCB) **1977**†LARm 5 (2) **1978**†LARm★16 (16, RCB) **1979**†LARm 9 (7, RCB) **1980**†LARm★16 (16, RCB) **1981** LARm 16 (16, RCB) **1982** LARm 9 (9, RCB) **1983** Cle 16 (4) **1984** Cle 8 (0) **NFL** 118 (84) [10 yrs]																								
PERRY, SCOTT Scott Endecott, DB, 6´0˝/180 lbs; Williams; 1976: Cin, rnd 5; B3/11/1954 Pleasanton, CA **1976** Cin 12 **1977** Cin 9 **1978** Cin 13 (FS) **1979** Cin 14 **1980** SF 11 (0) **1980**†SD 4 (0) **NFL** 63 [5 yrs]																								
PERRY, TAB Ted Wilson, WR, 6´2˝/229 lbs; UCLA; 2005: Cin, rnd 6; B1/20/1982 Milpitas, CA																								
2005	†Cin	16(0)	3	9	3.0(7)	1	4	21	5.3(13)	1	—	—	—	—	—	—	—	—	—	—	k	—	12	637
PERRY, TODD Todd Joseph, G, 6´5˝/310 lbs; Kentucky; 1993: Chi, rnd 4; B11/28/1970 Elizabethtown, KY **1993** ChiB 13 (3) **1994**†ChiB 15 (4) **1995** ChiB 15 (15, LG) **1996** ChiB 16 (16, LG) **1997** ChiB 11 (11, LG) **1998** ChiB 16 (16, LG) **1999** ChiB 16 (16, LG) **2000** ChiB 16 (16, LG) **2001** Mia 16 (16, RG) **2002** Mia 16 (16, RG) **2003** Mia 15 (15, RG) **NFL** 165 (144) [11 yrs]																								
PERRY, VERNON Vernon, DB, 6´2˝/211 lbs; Jackson State; B9/22/1953 Jackson, MS **1979**†Hou 16 (16, SS) **1980**†Hou☆16 (16, SS) **1981** Hou 16 (16, SS) **1982** Hou 7 (6, SS) **1983** NO 12 (0) **NFL** 67 (54) [5 yrs]																								

YEAR	TEAM	G(GS, POS)	RUSH	YD	AVG(LG)	TD	REC	YD	AVG(LG)	TD	PASS COMP	PCT	YD	AVG(LG)	TD	INT	SK	YD	QBR	KPR	OTD	PTS	TAY

PERRY, VICTOR   Victor Antonio, T, 6′5″/278 lbs; Georgia; B2/26/1964 Fitzgerald, GA   **1987** SL 1 (0)

PERRY, WILLIAM   William Anthony 'The Refrigerator', DT-DE, 6′2″/235 lbs; Clemson; 1985: Chi, rnd 1; B12/16/1962 Aiken, SC   **1988** ChiB 3 (3)   **1989** ChiB 13 (9, RDT)
1991†ChiB 16 (16, RDT)   **1992** ChiB 15 (14, RDT)   **1993** ChiB 7 (0)   **1993** Phi 8 (8, RDT)   **1994** Phi 16 (16, RDT)

1985	†ChiB	16 (9, RDT)	5	7	1.4(2)	2	1	4	4.0(4)	1	—	—	—	—	—	—	—	—	S	—	18	34	
1986	†ChiB	16 (16, RDT)	1	-1	-1.0(-1)	0	—	—	—	—	—	—	—	—	—	—	—	—	S	—	0	-1	
1987	†ChiB	12 (11, RDT)	1	0	0.0(0)	0	—	—	—	—	—	—	—	—	—	—	—	—	S	—	0	0	
1990	†ChiB	16 (16, LDT)	1	-1	-1.0(-1)	0	—	—	—	—	—	—	—	—	—	—	—	—	S	—	0	-1	
NFL	10	138 (118)	8	5	0.6(2)	2	1	4	4.0(4)	1	—	—	—	—	—	—	—	—	S	—	18	32	

PERRY, WILMONT   Wilmont Darnell, RB, 6′1″/230 lbs; Livingstone; 1998: NO, rnd 5; B2/24/1975 Franklinton, NC

1998	NO	6 (2)	30	122	4.1(19)	0	1	2	2.0(2)	0	—	—	—	—	—	—	—	—	—	—	0	123	
1999	NO	7 (3)	48	180	3.8(22)	0	4	26	6.5(11)	0	—	—	—	—	—	—	—	—	—	k	0	169	
NFL	2	13 (5)	78	302	3.9(22)	0	5	28	5.6(11)	0	—	—	—	—	—	—	—	—	—	k	0	292	

PERRYMAN, BOB   Robert Lewis, RB, 6′1″/233 lbs; Michigan; 1987: NE, rnd 3; B10/16/1964 Raleigh, NC

1987	NE	9 (1)	41	187	4.6(48)	0	3	13	4.3(7)	0	—	—	—	—	—	—	—	—	—	k	—	0	192
1988	NE	16 (16, FB)	146	448	3.1(16)	6	17	134	7.9(18)	0	—	—	—	—	—	—	—	—	—	—	—	36	575
1989	NE	16 (14, FB)	150	562	3.7(18)	2	29	195	6.7(16)	0	—	—	—	—	—	—	—	—	—	—	—	12	680
1990	NE	8 (7, FB)	32	97	3.0(13)	1	15	88	5.9(15)	0	—	—	—	—	—	—	—	—	—	—	—	6	151
1991	Den	15 (7, rb)	21	45	2.1(6)	0	17	171	10.1(24)	0	—	—	—	—	—	—	—	—	—	—	—	0	131
1992	Den	4 (1)	3	-1	-0.3(1)	0	2	15	7.5(9)	0	—	—	—	—	—	—	—	—	—	—	—	0	7
NFL	6	68 (46)	393	1338	3.4(48)	9	83	616	7.4(24)	0	—	—	—	—	—	—	—	—	—	k	—	54	1734

PERRYMAN, JIM   James T., DB, 6′0″/180 lbs; Millikin; B12/23/1960 Oakland, CA   **1985** Buf 11 (0)   **1987**†Ind 14 (3)   **NFL** 25 (3) [2 yrs]

PERRYMAN, RAY   Raymond, DB, 6′0″/204 lbs; Northern Arizona; 2001: Oak, rnd 5; B11/27/1978 Phoenix, AZ   **2002** Bal 2 (0)   **2003** Jax 4 (0)   **2004** Jax 4 (0)   **NFL** 10 (0) [3 yrs]

PERSON, ARA   Ara, TE, 6′4″/225 lbs; Morgan State; 1970: Bal, rnd 3; B9/23/1948 Baltimore, MD   **1972** SL 4

PESONEN, DICK   Richard Martin, DB, 6′0″/190 lbs; Minnesota; Minnesota-Duluth; B6/10/1938 Grand Rapids, MI   **1960**†GB 12   **1961** Min 11 (11, RCB)   **1962**†NYG 13
1963†NYG 14   **1964** NYG 5 (RS)   **NFL** 55 (11) [5 yrs]

PESSOLANO, LOUIE   Louis Carl, T-G-E, 6′0″/215 lbs; Villanova; B2/23/1907 New Kensington, PA, D2/8/1983 Augusta, GA   **1929** SI 3 (1)

PESUIT, WALLY   Walter George, G-C-T-DE, 6′4″/252 lbs; Kentucky; 1976: Dal, rnd 5; B3/4/1954 Steubenville, OH   **1976** Atl 1   **1977** Mia 14   **1978** Mia 16   **1979** Det 16
1980 Det 1 (0)   **NFL** 48 [5 yrs]

PETCHEL, JOHN   John, BB, 5′11″/185 lbs; Duquesne; B5/27/1919 Freeland, PA, D1/25/1988 Beaver, PA

1942	Cle	7 (1)	1	-2	-2.0(-2)	0	1	16	16.0(16)	0	—	—	—	—	—	—	—	—	—	k	—	0	2
1944	Cle	10 (2)	5	11	2.2(6)	0	1	43	43.0(43)	1	3	2	66.7	27	9.0(14)	0	0	—	—	ki	—	6	73
1945	Pit	9 (2)	2	2	1.0(15)	0	2	25	12.5(21)	0	1	1	100.0	8	8.0(8)	0	0	—	—	i	—	0	18
NFL	3	26 (5)	8	11	1.4(15)	0	4	84	21.0(43)	1	4	3	75.0	35	8.8(14)	0	0	—	—	ki	—	6	93

PETCOFF, BONI   Boni Eli, T, 5′10″/223 lbs; Ohio State; B2/1/1900, D8/5/1965 Toledo, OH   **1924** Col☆8 (8, RT)   **1925** Col 9 (9, RT)   **1926** Col 4 (3, RT)   **NFL** 21 (20) [3 yrs]

PETE, LAWRENCE   Lawrence, NT-DT, 6′0″/286 lbs; Nebraska; 1989: Det, rnd 5; B1/18/1966 Wichita, KS   **1989** Det 16 (0)   **1990** Det 6 (1)   **1991**†Det 14 (3)   **1992** Det 13 (4)
1993 Det 12 (12, NT)   **NFL** 61 (20) [5 yrs]

PETER, CHRISTIAN   Christian, DT, 6′3″/300 lbs; Nebraska; 1996: NE, rnd 5; B10/5/1972 Locust, NJ   **1997** NYG 7 (0)   **1998** NYG 16 (6, ldt)   **1999** NYG 16 (10, LDT)
2000†NYG 16 (15, LDT)   **2001** Ind 14 (0)   **2002** ChiB 12 (3)   **NFL** 81 (34) [6 yrs]

PETER, JASON   Jason Michael, DE, 6′4″/295 lbs; Nebraska; 1998: Car, rnd 1; B9/13/1974 Locust, NJ   **1998** Car 14 (11, LDE)   **1999** Car 9 (9, LDE)   **2000** Car 9 (0)   **2001** Car 6 (0)
NFL 38 (20) [4 yrs]

PETERMAN, STEPHEN   Stephen Frederick, G, 6′4″/318 lbs; LSU; 2004: Dal, rnd 3; B1/11/1982 Gulfport, MS   **2005** Dal 3 (0)

PETERS, ANTON   Anton Berdette, DT, 6′4″/245 lbs; Florida; 1963: Den, rnd 6/LA, rnd 8; B2/3/1941 Fort Myers, FL   **1963** Den-A 10

PETERS, FLOYD   Floyd Charles, DT, 6′4″/254 lbs; San Francisco State; 1958: Bal, rnd 8; B5/21/1936 Council Bluffs, IA   **1959** Cle 12   **1960** Cle 12 (RDT)   **1961** Cle 13 (RDT)
1962 Cle 14 (RDT)   **1963** Det 14 (LDT)   **1964** Phi★14 (14, LDT)   **1965** Phi 9 (9, LDT)   **1966** Phi★14 (LDT)   **1967** Phi★14 (LDT)   **1968** Phi 5 (ldt)   **1969** Phi 14 (LDT)
1970 Was 10 (9, LDT)   **NFL** 145 (32) [12 yrs]

PETERS, FRANK   Frank D., T, 6′4″/250 lbs; Ohio University; 1969: NYJ, rnd 9; B7/17/1947 Lockbourne, OH   **1969** Cin-A 3

PETERS, FROSTY   Forrest Ingman, B, 5′10″/183 lbs; Montana; Illinois; B4/22/1904 Creston, IA, D4/17/1980 Decatur, IL **[K]**   **1930** Pro 12 (8, TB), 25   **1930** Por 3 (2)
1931 Bkn 9 (5, tb), 2   **1932** ChiC 1 (1)   **NFL** 25 (16), 27 [3 yrs]

PETERS, JASON   Jason, T, 6′4″/328 lbs; Arkansas; B1/22/1982 Queen City, TX   **2004** Buf 5 (1)

| 2005 | Buf | 16 (10, RT) | — | — | — | — | 2 | 5 | 2.5(4) | 1 | — | — | — | — | — | — | — | — | — | — | — | 6 | 8 |
| NFL | 2 | 21 (11) | — | — | — | — | 2 | 5 | 2.5(4) | 1 | — | — | — | — | — | — | — | — | — | — | 1 | 12 | 8 |

PETERS, SCOTT   Scott Thomas, C-G, 6′3″/300 lbs; Arizona State; 2002: Phi, rnd 4; B11/23/1978 Arcadia, CA   **2003** NYG 7 (4)

PETERS, TONY   Anthony Lemont, DB, 6′1″/187 lbs; Oklahoma; 1975: Cle, rnd 4; B4/28/1953 Oklahoma City, OK   **1975** Cle 14 (12, RCB)   **1976** Cle 14 (10, rcb)
1977 Cle 14 (14, SS)   **1978** Cle 16 (15, SS)   **1979** Was 16 (5, ss/fs)   **1980** Was 16 (11, SS)   **1981** Was 16 (16, SS)   **1982**†Was★9 (9, SS)   **1984** Was 8 (6, ss)   **1985** Was 10 (10, SS)
NFL 133 (108) [10 yrs]

PETERS, TYRELL   Tyrell Jermain, LB, 6′0″/230 lbs; Oklahoma; B8/4/1974 Oklahoma City, OK   **1997** Bal 4 (0)   **1998** Bal 10 (0)   **1999** Bal 13 (0)   **NFL** 27 (0) [3 yrs]

PETERS, VOLNEY   Volney Monroe, DT-T-DE, 6′4″/237 lbs; USC; 1951: ChiC, rnd 13; B1/1/1928 Minneapolis, MN   **1953** ChiC 12 (LDT)   **1954** Was 8 (LDT)   **1955** Was◇12 (LDT)
1956 Was 12 (LDT)   **1957** Was 12 (LDT)   **1958** Phi 10   **1960**†LAC-A☆14 (LDT)   **1961** Oak-A 12 (ldt)

| 1952 | ChiC | 12 (LDT) | 1 | -7 | -7.0(-7) | 0 | — | — | — | — | — | — | — | — | — | — | — | — | — | kp | 1 | 6 | -23 |
| NFL | 9 | 104 | 1 | -7 | -7.0(-7) | 0 | — | — | — | — | — | — | — | — | — | — | — | — | — | kp | 1 | 6 | -23 |

PETERSEN, KEN   Thornton Kenneth, G, 6′2″/235 lbs; Utah; 1961: Min, rnd 14; B3/26/1939 Logan, UT   **1961** Min 12

PETERSEN, KURT   Kurt David, G, 6′4″/264 lbs; Missouri; 1980: Dal, rnd 4; B6/17/1957 St. Louis, MO   **1980**†Dal 16 (0)   **1981**†Dal 16 (14, RG)   **1982**†Dal☆9 (9, RG)
1983 Dal 14 (14, RG)   **1984** Dal 13 (13, RG)   **1985**†Dal 16 (16, RG)   **NFL** 84 (66) [6 yrs]

PETERSEN, TED   Theodore Hans, T-C-G, 6′5″/244 lbs; Eastern Illinois; 1977: Pit, rnd 4; B2/7/1955 Kankakee, IL   **1977**†Pit 14   **1978**†Pit 15   **1979**†Pit 16 (6, lt)   **1980** Pit 16 (9, LT)
1981 Pit 2 (0)   **1982**†Pit 7 (0)   **1983** Pit 13 (13, LT)   **1984** Cle 4 (0)   **1984** Ind 5 (4)   **1987** Pit 2 (2)   **NFL** 94 (34) [9 yrs]

PETERSMARK, BRETT   Robert Brett, C, 6′3″/280 lbs; Eastern Michigan; B3/5/1964   **1987** Hou 3 (0)

PETERSON, ADRIAN   Adrian, RB, 5′10″/210 lbs; Georgia Southern; 2002: Chi, rnd 6; B7/1/1979 Gainesville, FL

2002	ChiB	9 (0)	19	101	5.3(14)	1	3	18	6.0(10)	0	—	—	—	—	—	—	—	—	—	k	—	6	127
2003	ChiB	6 (1)	22	70	3.2(10)	0	1	5	5.0(5)	0	—	—	—	—	—	—	—	—	—	k	—	0	73
2004	ChiB	14 (0)	6	19	3.2(13)	0	2	30	15.0(30)	0	—	—	—	—	—	—	—	—	—	k	—	0	46
2005	†ChiB	16 (0)	76	391	5.1(36)	2	7	48	6.9(18)	0	—	—	—	—	—	—	—	—	—	k	—	12	437
NFL	4	45 (1)	123	581	4.7(36)	3	13	101	7.8(30)	0	—	—	—	—	—	—	—	—	—	k	—	18	683

PETERSON, ANDREW   Andrew Scott, T, 6′5″/308 lbs; Washington; 1995: Car, rnd 5; B6/11/1972 Greenock, Scotland   **1995** Car 4 (2)

PETERSON, BEN   Ben, LB, 6′3″/250 lbs; Pittsburg State; B3/28/1977 Clay Center, KS   **1999** Cin 3 (0)

PETERSON, BILL   William Wallace, LB-TE, 6′3″/230 lbs; San Jose State; B6/6/1945 San Jose, CA   **1969** Cin-A 14 (RLB)   **1970**†Cin 14   **1971** Cin 14   **1972** Cin 14
1975 KC 14 (9, LLB)

| 1968 | Cin-A | 7 | — | — | — | — | 1 | 10 | 10.0(10) | 0 | — | — | — | — | — | — | — | — | — | k | — | 0 | 40 |
| NFL | 6 | 77 (9) | — | — | — | — | 1 | 10 | 10.0(10) | 0 | — | — | — | — | — | — | — | — | — | ki | — | 0 | 47 |

PETERSON, CAL   Calvin Elston, LB, 6′3″/220 lbs; UCLA; 1974: Dal, rnd 3; B10/16/1952 Los Angeles, CA   **1974** Dal 14   **1975**†Dal 14   **1976** TB 5 (4)   **1979** KC 16
1980 KC 16 (6, rolb)   **1981** KC 11 (7, rolb)   **1982** LARd 4 (0)   **NFL** 80 (17) [7 yrs]

PETERSON, CARL   Carl John, C-E, 5′11″/175 lbs; Nebraska; B3/26/1897 Salt Lake City, UT, D7/1964, KS   **1924** KC 9 (9, C)

Peterson, Ike Kenneth, B, 5´9˝/185 lbs; Gonzaga; B7/8/1909 Berill, ID

YEAR	TEAM	G(GS, POS)	RUSH	YD	AVG(LG)	TD	REC	YD	AVG(LG)	TD	PASS	COMP	PCT	YD	AVG(LG)	TD	INT	SK	YD	QBR	KPR	OTD	PTS	TAY
1935	ChiC	11(4)	95	297	3.1	0	2	37	18.5	0	17	5	29.4	92	5.4	1	3	—	—	—	—	—	0	247
1936	Det	11(2)	41	278	6.8(84)	3	8	38	4.8	0	6	0	0.0	0	0.0	0	1	—	—	—	—	—	18	287
NFL	2	22(6)	136	575	4.2(84)	3	10	75	7.5	0	23	5	21.7	92	4.0	1	4	—	—	—	—	—	18	534

Peterson, Jerry Gerald Ray, DT, 6´3˝/290 lbs; Texas; 1955: Bal, rnd 15; B10/8/1934 El Campo, CA **1956** Bal 1

Peterson, Jim James A., LB, 6´5˝/235 lbs; San Diego State; 1973: LA, rnd 6; B1/20/1950 San Diego, CA **1974**†LARm 14 **1975**†LARm 14 **1976** TB 3 (2) **NFL** 31 (2) [3 yrs]

Peterson, Joe Joseph, DB, 5´10˝/185 lbs; Nevada-Reno; B8/15/1964 San Francisco, CA **1987** NE 3 (3)

Peterson, Julian Julian Thomas, LB, 6´3˝/235 lbs; Michigan State; 2000: SF, rnd 1; B7/28/1978 Temple Hills, MD **2000** SF 13 (7, llb) **2001**†SF 14 (14, LLB) **2002**†SF★16 (16, LLB) **2003** SF★16 (16, LLB) **2004** SF 5 (5, llb) **2005** SF 15 (14, LOLB) **NFL** 79 (72) [6 yrs]

Peterson, Kenny James Kenneth, DT-DE, 6´3˝/300 lbs; Ohio State; 2003: GB, rnd 3; B11/21/1978 Canton, OH **2003**†GB 9 (0) **2004**†GB 9 (0) **2005** GB 16 (0) **NFL** 34 (0) [3 yrs]

Peterson, Les Lester Carl, E-T, 6´3˝/206 lbs; Texas; B11/27/1909, D1/25/1993 Big Spring, TX

YEAR	TEAM	G(GS, POS)	RUSH	YD	AVG(LG)	TD	REC	YD	AVG(LG)	TD	PASS	COMP	PCT	YD	AVG(LG)	TD	INT	SK	YD	QBR	KPR	OTD	PTS	TAY
1931	Por	10(0)	—	—	—	—	—	—	—	—	—	—	—	—	—	—	—	—	—	—	—	—	—	—
1932	GB	9(5, re)	—	—	—	—	1	23	23.0(23)	0	—	—	—	—	—	—	—	—	—	—	—	—	0	12
1932	SI	5(4)	—	—	—	—	1	26	26.0(26)	0	—	—	—	—	—	—	—	—	—	—	—	—	0	13
1933	Bkn	9(2)	—	—	—	—	13	170	13.1	0	—	—	—	—	—	—	—	—	—	—	—	—	0	85
1934	GB	11(4)	1	0	0.0	0	6	139	23.2	0	—	—	—	—	—	—	—	—	—	—	—	—	0	70
NFL	4	44(15)	1	0	0.0	0	21	358	17.0(26)	0	—	—	—	—	—	—	—	—	—	—	—	—	0	179

Peterson, Mike Porter Michael, LB, 6´1˝/230 lbs; Florida; 1999: Ind, rnd 2; B6/17/1976 Gainesville, FL **1999**†Ind 16 (13, RLB) **2000**†Ind 16 (16, RLB) **2001** Ind 9 (9, RLB) **2002**†Ind 16 (16, LLB) **2003** Jax 16 (16, MLB) **2004** Jax 16 (16, MLB) **2005**†Jax☆16 (16, MLB) **NFL** 105 (102) [7 yrs]

Peterson, Nels Nelson Lane, B, 5´8˝/179 lbs; West Virginia Wesleyan; B9/22/1913 Weston, WV, D12/4/1990, **[K]**

YEAR	TEAM	G(GS, POS)	RUSH	YD	AVG(LG)	TD	REC	YD	AVG(LG)	TD	PASS	COMP	PCT	YD	AVG(LG)	TD	INT	SK	YD	QBR	KPR	OTD	PTS	TAY
1937	Was	2(0)	2	8	4.0	0	—	—	—	—	—	—	—	—	—	—	—	—	—	—	—	—	0	8
1938	Cle	7(2)	21	70	3.3(32)	1	4	43	10.8	1	6	0	0.0	0	0.0	0	2	—	—	—	K	—	20	27
NFL	2	9(2)	23	78	3.4(32)	1	4	43	10.8	1	6	0	0.0	0	0.0	0	2	—	—	—	K	—	20	35

Peterson, Phil Phillip, E, 5´11˝/195 lbs; Wisconsin; B3/29/1906, D3/1981 St. Croix Falls, WI **1934** Bkn 3 (0)

Peterson, Ray Raymond, TB, 6´0˝/190 lbs; San Francisco; B1/18/1916, D7/1977 Seattle, WA

YEAR	TEAM	G(GS, POS)	RUSH	YD	AVG(LG)	TD	REC	YD	AVG(LG)	TD	PASS	COMP	PCT	YD	AVG(LG)	TD	INT	SK	YD	QBR	KPR	OTD	PTS	TAY
1937	GB	2(0)	—	—	—	—	—	—	—	—	6	3	50.0	47	7.8	0	0	—	—	—	—	—	0	24

Peterson, Russ Russell Harold, TB, 6´3˝/216 lbs; Montana; B8/25/1905 Midale, Canada, D10/1971 **1932** Bos 3 (0)

Peterson, Todd Joseph Todd, K, 5´10˝/177 lbs; Navy; Georgia; 1993: NYG, rnd 7; B2/4/1970 Washington, DC **[K]** **1994** Arz 2 (0) **1995** Sea 16 (0) **1996** Sea 16 (0) **1997** Sea 16 (0) **1998** Sea 16 (0) **1999**†Sea 16 (0) **2000** KC 11 (0) **2001** KC 16 (0) **2002** Pit 10 (0) **2003** SF 8 (0) **2004** SF 16 (0) **2005** Atl 16 (0) **NFL** 159 (0) [12 yrs]

Peterson, Tony Anthony Wayne, LB, 6´1˝/223 lbs; Notre Dame; 1994: SF, rnd 5; B1/23/1972 Cleveland, OH **1994**†SF 15 (0) **1995**†SF 15 (0) **1996** SF 13 (0) **1997** ChiB 16 (0) **1998**†SF 16 (1) **1999** SF 12 (0) **NFL** 87 (1) [6 yrs]

Peterson, Will William James, DB, 6´0˝/200 lbs; Michigan; Western Illinois; 2001: NYG, rnd 3; B6/15/1979 Uniontown, PA **2001** NYG 16 (5, rcb) **2002**†NYG 12 (12, RCB) **2003** NYG 5 (5, rcb) **2004** NYG 16 (15, RCB) **2005** NYG 2 (2) **NFL** 51 (39) [5 yrs]

Petitbon, Johnny John Ellis, DB-HB, 5´11˝/186 lbs; Notre Dame; 1952: DalT, rnd 7; B6/4/1931 New Orleans, LA **1956** Cle 12 (DB) **1957** GB 12 (DB)

YEAR	TEAM	G(GS, POS)	RUSH	YD	AVG(LG)	TD	REC	YD	AVG(LG)	TD	PASS	COMP	PCT	YD	AVG(LG)	TD	INT	SK	YD	QBR	KPR	OTD	PTS	TAY
1952	DalT	11(DB)	—	—	—	—	1	11	11.0(11)	0	—	—	—	—	—	—	—	—	—	—	ki	—	0	19
1955	†Cle	12(DB)	3	10	3.3(7)	0	—	—	—	—	—	—	—	—	—	—	—	—	—	—	i	—	0	11
NFL	4	47	3	10	3.3(7)	0	1	11	11.0(11)	0	—	—	—	—	—	—	—	—	—	—	ki	—	0	25

Petitbon, Richie Richard Alvin, DB, 6´3˝/206 lbs; Tulane; 1959: ChiB, rnd 2; B4/18/1938 New Orleans, LA **[IC]** **1959** ChiB 12 (DB) **1960** ChiB 12 (LS) **1961** ChiB 14 (LS) **1962** ChiB★14 (LS) **1963**†ChiB★14 (LS) **1964** ChiB 14 (LS) **1965** ChiB 14 (LS) **1966** ChiB★14 (LS) **1968** ChiB 14 (LS) **1969**†LARm 12 (12, LS) **1972** Was 3 (3)

YEAR	TEAM	G(GS, POS)	RUSH	YD	AVG(LG)	TD	REC	YD	AVG(LG)	TD	PASS	COMP	PCT	YD	AVG(LG)	TD	INT	SK	YD	QBR	KPR	OTD	PTS	TAY
1967	ChiB★	14(LS)	—	—	—	—	—	—	—	—	0	0	0.0	0	0.0	0	0	1	7	—	i	—	0	48
1970	LARm	14(SS)	1	3	3.0(3)	0	—	—	—	—	—	—	—	—	—	—	—	—	—	—	i	—	0	8
1971	†Was☆	14(13, SS)	1	-2	-2.0(-2)	0	—	—	—	—	—	—	—	—	—	—	—	—	—	—	i	—	0	75
NFL	14	179(28)	2	1	0.5(3)	0	—	—	—	—	0	0	0.0	0	0.0	0	0	1	7	—	kpi	3	18	628

Petitgout, Luke Lucas George, T-G, 6´6˝/310 lbs; Notre Dame; 1999: NYG, rnd 1; B6/16/1976 Milford, DE **1999** NYG 15 (8, LG) **2000**†NYG 16 (16, RT) **2001** NYG 16 (16, RT) **2002**†NYG 16 (16, LT) **2003** NYG 10 (10, LT) **2004** NYG 16 (16, LT) **2005**†NYG 16 (15, LT) **NFL** 105 (97) [7 yrs]

Petitti, Rob Rod Christopher, T, 6´6˝/347 lbs; Pittsburgh; 2005: Dal, rnd 6; B5/21/1982 Clark, NJ **2005** Dal 16 (16, RT)

Petree, Leo Leo Harley, HB, /200 lbs; Truman State; B1/1893 Union Star, MO, D1971 Toledo, OH **1920** Cle 2 (1) **1922** Tol 5 (3), 6 **NFL** 7 (4) [2 yrs]

Petrella, Bob Robert Francis, DB, 5´11˝/190 lbs; Tennessee; 1966: Mia, rnd 8/Min, rnd 12; B11/7/1944 Philadelphia, PA **1966** Mia-A 3 **1967** Mia-A 9 **1968** Mia-A 9 (7, LS) **1969** Mia-A 14 (6, ls) **1970**†Mia 14 **1971**†Mia 12 **NFL** 61 (13) [6 yrs]

Petrella, Pepper John Anton, HB, 5´7˝/160 lbs; Penn State; B5/7/1920 Downington, PA, D12/21/1991 Azusa, CA

YEAR	TEAM	G(GS, POS)	RUSH	YD	AVG(LG)	TD	REC	YD	AVG(LG)	TD	PASS	COMP	PCT	YD	AVG(LG)	TD	INT	SK	YD	QBR	KPR	OTD	PTS	TAY
1945	Pit	3(1)	15	33	2.2(11)	0	—	—	—	—	—	—	—	—	—	—	—	—	—	—	kpi	—	0	98

Petrich, Bob Robert Marl, DE, 6´4˝/252 lbs; West Texas A&M; 1963: SD, rnd 11/NYG, rnd 6; B3/15/1941 Long Beach, CA **1963**†SD-A 14 (RDE) **1964**†SD-A 14 (RDE) **1965**†SD-A 14 (RDE) **1966** SD-A 14 (RDE) **1967** Buf-A 6 **NFL** 62 [5 yrs]

Petrilas, Bill William A., HB-E, 6´1˝/195 lbs; none; B9/28/1915 New Haven, CT, D11/4/1976 Middletown, CT **1945** NYG 5 (2)

YEAR	TEAM	G(GS, POS)	RUSH	YD	AVG(LG)	TD	REC	YD	AVG(LG)	TD	PASS	COMP	PCT	YD	AVG(LG)	TD	INT	SK	YD	QBR	KPR	OTD	PTS	TAY
1944	†NYG	9(1)	12	29	2.4(12)	0	—	—	—	—	—	—	—	—	—	—	—	—	—	—	pi	2	12	206
NFL	2	14(3)	12	29	2.4(12)	0	—	—	—	—	—	—	—	—	—	—	—	—	—	—	pi	2	12	197

Petro, Steve Stephen Lawrence, G, 5´10˝/195 lbs; Pittsburgh; 1939: Pit, rnd 9; B10/21/1914 Johnstown, PA, D8/15/1994 Pittsburgh, PA **1940** Bkn 11 (6, LG) **1941** Bkn 6 (0) **NFL** 17 (6) [2 yrs]

Petrovich, George George John, G-T-DT, 6´2˝/225 lbs; Texas; 1948: ChiC, rnd 15; B3/22/1926 Palestine, TX **1949** ChiC 12 (5, LG) **1950** ChiC 10 (10, LG) **NFL** 22 (15) [2 yrs]

Petry, Stan Stanley Edward, DB, 5´11˝/174 lbs; TCU; 1989: KC, rnd 4; B8/14/1966 Alvin, TX **1989** KC 16 (0) **1990**†KC 16 (2) **1991** KC 2 (0) **1991**†NO 2 (0) **NFL** 36 (2) [3 yrs]

Pettey, Phil Philip Edward, G, 6´4˝/274 lbs; Missouri; B4/17/1961 Kenosha, WI **1987** Was 3 (3)

Petties, Neal Cornelius, E, 6´2˝/198 lbs; San Diego State; 1963: Bal, rnd 14/Oak, rnd 21; B9/16/1940 San Diego, CA **1965**†Bal 9 **1966** Bal 10

YEAR	TEAM	G(GS, POS)	RUSH	YD	AVG(LG)	TD	REC	YD	AVG(LG)	TD	PASS	COMP	PCT	YD	AVG(LG)	TD	INT	SK	YD	QBR	KPR	OTD	PTS	TAY
1964	†Bal	14	—	—	—	—	2	20	10.0(15)	1	—	—	—	—	—	—	—	—	—	—	k	—	6	9
NFL	3	33	—	—	—	—	2	20	10.0(15)	1	—	—	—	—	—	—	—	—	—	—		—	6	15

Pettigrew, Gary Gary Louis, DT-DE, 6´5˝/255 lbs; Stanford; 1966: Phi, rnd 2/SD, rnd 6; B10/10/1944 Vancouver, Canada **1966** Phi 14 (RDE) **1967** Phi 13 (10, RDE) **1968** Phi 14 (RDT) **1969** Phi 7 (rdt) **1970** Phi 14 (RDT) **1971** Phi 13 (6, rdt) **1972** Phi 13 **1973** Phi 14 (LDT) **1974** Phi 4 **1974** NYG 5 (LDT) **NFL** 111 (16) [9 yrs]

Pettitt, Duane Duane Edward, DE, 6´4˝/265 lbs; San Diego State; B11/2/1964 Long Beach, CA **1987** SD 3 (0)

Petty, John John, FB, 6´1˝/228 lbs; Purdue; 1942: ChiB, rnd 9; B10/3/1919 Lebanon, PA, D4/6/1979 Wilmington, OH

YEAR	TEAM	G(GS, POS)	RUSH	YD	AVG(LG)	TD	REC	YD	AVG(LG)	TD	PASS	COMP	PCT	YD	AVG(LG)	TD	INT	SK	YD	QBR	KPR	OTD	PTS	TAY
1942	†ChiB✧	10(2)	41	149	3.6(14)	2	4	53	13.3(16)	0	—	—	—	—	—	—	—	—	—	—	Pi	—	12	198

Petty, Larry Otis Lawrence, G, Illinois State; Illinois; B11/1893 Sumner, IL, deceased **1920** Can 2 (0)

Petty, Ross Manley Ross, G, 6´1˝/180 lbs; Illinois; B9/11/1892 Sumner, IL, D3/13/1966 Milwaukee, WI **1920** Dec 10 (5, LG)

Pettyjohn, Barry Barry Glen, C-T, 6´5˝/285 lbs; Pittsburgh; B3/29/1964 Cincinnati, OH **1987** Hou 2 (0)

Petway, David David Lawrence, DB, 6´1˝/207 lbs; Northern Illinois; B10/17/1955 Chicago, IL **1981** GB 6 (0)

Peviani, Bob Robert Angelo, LB, 6´1˝/210 lbs; USC; 1953: NYG, rnd 6; B9/15/1931 Los Angeles, CA **1953** NYG 12 (LLB)

Peyton, Leo Leo, WB-BB-FB, 5´11˝/190 lbs; none; deceased **1923** Roc 2 (1) **1924** Roc 4 (3, WB) **NFL** 6 (4) [2 yrs]

PFOHL, BOB Robert Stormont, B, 6´0˝/200 lbs; Kings Point; Purdue; 1948: Bal-A, rnd 24/NYG, rnd 7; B5/21/1926 Vincennes, IN, D5/11/1997 Lafayette, IN

YEAR	TEAM	G(GS, POS)	RUSH	YD	AVG(LG)	TD	REC	YD	AVG(LG)	TD	PASS	COMP	PCT	YD	AVG(LG)	TD	INT	SK	YD	QBR	KPR	OTD	PTS	TAY
1948	†Bal-A	14(14, RH)	107	455	4.3	4	13	134	10.3	1	—	—	—	—	—	—	—	—	—	—	kp	1	36	780
1949	Bal-A	12(7, RH)	67	205	3.1	2	7	62	8.9	0	—	—	—	—	—	—	—	—	—	—	k	—	12	294
AAFC	2	26(21)	174	660	3.8	6	20	196	9.8	1	—	—	—	—	—	—	—	—	—	—	kp	1	48	1074

PHARMER, ART Charles Arthur, B, 5´10˝/186 lbs; Minnesota; B7/21/1908, D2/1970, **[K]** **1930** Min 8 (5, TB), 8 **1930** Fra 5 (5, tb), 4 **1931** Fra 2 (2) **NFL** 15 (12), 12 [2 yrs]

PHARR, TOMMY Tommy Lee, DB, 5´10˝/187 lbs; Mississippi State; B7/31/1947 Canton, GA **1970** Buf 10

PHELAN, BOB Robert Richard, B, 5´11˝/185 lbs; Notre Dame; B6/20/1898 Charleston, IA, D8/1973 Fort Madison, IA **1922** Tol 8 (8, TB), 12 **1923** RI 7 (6, FB) **1924** RI 6 (2) **NFL** 21 (16) [3 yrs]

PHELPS, DON Donald Cooper, HB-DB, 5´11˝/185 lbs; Kentucky; 1950: Cle, rnd 5; B1/7/1924 Richmond, KY, D6/11/1982 Frankford, KY

YEAR	TEAM	G(GS, POS)	RUSH	YD	AVG(LG)	TD	REC	YD	AVG(LG)	TD	PASS	COMP	PCT	YD	AVG(LG)	TD	INT	SK	YD	QBR	KPR	OTD	PTS	TAY
1950	†Cle	12	39	198	5.1(33)	2	1	28	28.0(28)	0	—	—	—	—	—	—	—	—	—	—	kpi	1	18	500
1951	Cle	4	16	65	4.1(10)	1	—	—	—	—	—	—	—	—	—	—	—	—	—	—	kp	—	6	94
1952	Cle	1	—	—	—	—	—	—	—	—	—	—	—	—	—	—	—	—	—	—	p	—	0	-10
NFL	3	17	55	263	4.8(33)	3	1	28	28.0(28)	0	—	—	—	—	—	—	—	—	—	—	kpi	1	24	584

PHENIX, PERRY Perry Lee, DB, 5´11˝/210 lbs; Southern Mississippi; B11/14/1974 Dallas, TX **1998** Ten 15 (3) **1999**†Ten 16 (1) **2000**†Ten 16 (0) **2001** Car 2 (0) **2001** Ten 12 (11, FS) **NFL** 61 (15) [4 yrs]

PHIFER, ROMAN Roman Zubinsky, LB, 6´2˝/248 lbs; UCLA; 1991: LARm, rnd 2; B3/5/1968 Plattsburgh, NY **1991** LARm 12 (5, rlb) **1992** LARm 16 (14, RLB) **1993** LARm 16 (16, RLB) **1994** LARm 16 (16, RLB) **1995** SL 16 (16, RLB) **1996** SL 15 (15, RLB) **1997** SL 16 (15, RLB) **1998** SL 13 (13, RLB) **1999** NYJ 16 (12, ROLB) **2000** NYJ 16 (10, ROLB) **2001**†NE 16 (16, RLB) **2002** NE 14 (14, RLB) **2003**†NE 16 (15, LLB) **2004**†NE 13 (1) **2005** NYG 2 (0) **NFL** 213 (178) [15 yrs]

PHILBIN, GERRY Gerald John, DE, 6´2˝/245 lbs; Buffalo; 1964: NYJ, rnd 3/Det, rnd 3; B7/31/1941 Pawtucket, RI **1964** NYJ-A 6 **1965** NYJ-A 14 (LDE) **1966** NYJ-A 14 (LDE) **1967** NYJ-A☆14 (LDE) **1968**†NYJ-A★14 (LDE) **1969**†NYJ-A★13 (LDE) **1970** NYJ 11 (LDE) **1971** NYJ 10 (LDE) **1972** NYJ 14 (LDE) **1973** Phi 13 (6, lde) **NFL** 123 (6) [10 yrs]

PHILCOX, TODD Todd Stuart, QB, 6´4˝/218 lbs; Syracuse; B9/25/1966 Norwalk, CT

YEAR	TEAM	G(GS, POS)	RUSH	YD	AVG(LG)	TD	REC	YD	AVG(LG)	TD	PASS	COMP	PCT	YD	AVG(LG)	TD	INT	SK	YD	QBR	KPR	OTD	PTS	TAY
1990	Cin	2(0)	—	—	—	—	—	—	—	—	2	0	0.0	0	0.0	0	1	2	9	—	—	—	0	-40
1991	Cle	4(0)	1	-1	-1.0(-1)	0	—	—	—	—	8	4	50.0	49	6.1(28)	0	1	—	—	—	—	—	0	-17
1992	Cle	2(1)	—	—	—	—	—	—	—	—	27	13	48.1	217	8.0(69)	3	1	1	6	—	—	—	0	84
1993	Cle	5(4)	2	3	1.5(3)	1	—	—	—	—	108	52	48.1	699	6.5(56)	4	7	7	60	—	—	—	6	103
1997	SD	2(0)	1	3	3.0(3)	0	—	—	—	—	28	16	57.1	173	6.2(29)	0	1	8	44	—	—	—	0	50
NFL	5	15(5)	4	5	1.3(3)	1	—	—	—	—	173	85	49.1	1138	6.6(69)	7	11	18	119	—	—	—	6	179

PHILION, ED Edmond Paul, DT, 6´2˝/277 lbs; Ferris State; B3/27/1970 Windsor, Canada **1994** Buf 4 (0) **1995**†Buf 2 (0) **NFL** 6 (0) [2 yrs]

PHILLIPS, ANTHONY Anthony Dwayne, DB, 6´2˝/209 lbs; Texas A&M-Kingsville; 1994: Atl, rnd 3; B10/5/1970 Galveston, TX **1994** Atl 5 (0) **1995** Atl 6 (4) **1996** Atl 7 (5, rcb) **1998** Min 2 (0) **NFL** 20 (9) [4 yrs]

PHILLIPS, BOBBY Bobby, RB, 5´9˝/187 lbs; Virginia Union; B12/8/1969 Richmond, VA

YEAR	TEAM	G(GS, POS)	RUSH	YD	AVG(LG)	TD	REC	YD	AVG(LG)	TD	PASS	COMP	PCT	YD	AVG(LG)	TD	INT	SK	YD	QBR	KPR	OTD	PTS	TAY
1995	Min	8(0)	14	26	1.9(7)	0	—	—	—	—	—	—	—	—	—	—	—	—	—	—	k	—	0	26

PHILLIPS, CHARLIE Charles W., DB, 6´2˝/215 lbs; USC; 1975: Oak, rnd 2; B12/22/1952 Greenville, MS **1975**†Oak 14 (1) **1976**†Oak 14 **1977** Oak 7 (3) **1978** Oak 16 (16, SS) **1979** Oak 16 (3) **NFL** 67 (23) [5 yrs]

PHILLIPS, EWELL Ewell Ivan, G, 5´11˝/210 lbs; Oklahoma Baptist; B4/20/1909 Comanche, OK, D12/31/1990 Lancaster, NC

YEAR	TEAM	G(GS, POS)	RUSH	YD	AVG(LG)	TD	REC	YD	AVG(LG)	TD	PASS	COMP	PCT	YD	AVG(LG)	TD	INT	SK	YD	QBR	KPR	OTD	PTS	TAY
1936	NYG	12(5, lg)	—	—	—	—	1	5	5.0(5)	0	—	—	—	—	—	—	—	—	—	—	—	—	0	3

PHILLIPS, GEORGE George Cannady, LB, 6´3˝/215 lbs; UCLA; 1944: Phi, rnd 8; B1921 **1945** Cle 1 (0)

PHILLIPS, IRVIN Irvin Jerome, DB, 6´1˝/192 lbs; Arkansas Tech; 1981: SD, rnd 3; B1/23/1960 Leesburg, FL **1981**†SD 15 (0) **1983** LARd 5 (0) **NFL** 20 (0) [2 yrs]

PHILLIPS, JASON Jason Howell, WR, 5´7˝/166 lbs; Houston; 1989: Det, rnd 10; B10/11/1966 Crowley, LA

YEAR	TEAM	G(GS, POS)	RUSH	YD	AVG(LG)	TD	REC	YD	AVG(LG)	TD	PASS	COMP	PCT	YD	AVG(LG)	TD	INT	SK	YD	QBR	KPR	OTD	PTS	TAY
1989	Det	16(6, WR)	—	—	—	—	30	352	11.7(55)	1	—	—	—	—	—	—	—	—	—	—	—	—	6	181
1990	Det	13(2)	—	—	—	—	8	112	14.0(29)	0	—	—	—	—	—	—	—	—	—	—	k	—	0	69
1991	†Atl	11(0)	—	—	—	—	6	73	12.2(24)	0	—	—	—	—	—	—	—	—	—	—	—	—	0	37
1992	Atl	12(0)	—	—	—	—	4	26	6.5(8)	1	—	—	—	—	—	—	—	—	—	—	p	—	6	18
1993	Atl	6(0)	—	—	—	—	1	15	15.0(15)	0	—	—	—	—	—	—	—	—	—	—	k	—	0	16
NFL	5	58(8)	—	—	—	—	49	578	11.8(55)	2	—	—	—	—	—	—	—	—	—	—	kp	—	12	320

PHILLIPS, JERMAINE Jermaine, DB, 6´1˝/214 lbs; Georgia; 2002: TB, rnd 5; B3/27/1979 Roswell, GA **2002**†TB 16 (0) **2003** TB 14 (8, FS) **2004** TB 9 (9, FS) **2005**†TB 13 (13, SS) **NFL** 52 (30) [4 yrs]

PHILLIPS, JESS Jess Willard, RB-DB, 6´1˝/210 lbs; Michigan State; 1968: Cin, rnd 4; B2/28/1947 Beaumont, TX

YEAR	TEAM	G(GS, POS)	RUSH	YD	AVG(LG)	TD	REC	YD	AVG(LG)	TD	PASS	COMP	PCT	YD	AVG(LG)	TD	INT	SK	YD	QBR	KPR	OTD	PTS	TAY
1968	Cin-A	14(LS)	1	7	7.0(7)	0	—	—	—	—	—	—	—	—	—	—	—	—	—	—	kpi	—	0	32
1969	Cin-A	14(FB)	118	578	4.9(83)	3	13	128	9.8(31)	0	—	—	—	—	—	—	—	—	—	—	k	—	18	679
1970	†Cin☆	14(FB)	163	648	4.0(76)	4	31	124	4.0(17)	1	—	—	—	—	—	—	—	—	—	—	—	—	30	755
1971	Cin	14(RB)	94	420	4.5(31)	0	22	125	5.7(19)	1	—	—	—	—	—	—	—	—	—	—	k	—	6	507
1972	Cin	13	48	207	4.3(20)	1	10	50	5.0(15)	0	—	—	—	—	—	—	—	—	—	—	—	—	6	242
1973	NO	14(RB)	198	663	3.3(20)	0	22	169	7.7(34)	0	—	—	—	—	—	—	—	—	—	—	—	—	0	748
1974	NO	14(FB)	174	556	3.2(14)	2	11	55	5.0(17)	0	—	—	—	—	—	—	—	—	—	—	k	—	12	623
1975	†Oak	14(2)	63	298	4.7(66)	1	4	25	6.3(22)	0	—	—	—	—	—	—	—	—	—	—	k	—	6	451
1976	†NE	13	24	164	6.8(46)	1	1	18	18.0(18)	0	—	—	—	—	—	—	—	—	—	—	k	—	6	370
1977	NE	14	5	27	5.4(13)	1	—	—	—	—	—	—	—	—	—	—	—	—	—	—	k	—	6	40
NFL	10	138(2)	888	3568	4.0(83)	13	114	694	6.1(34)	2	—	—	—	—	—	—	—	—	—	—	kpi	—	90	4445

PHILLIPS, JOE Joseph Gordon, NT-DT-DE, 6´5˝/298 lbs; Oregon State; SMU; 1986: Min, rnd 4; B7/15/1963 Portland, OR **1986** Min 16 (1) **1987** SD 13 (7, RDE) **1988** SD 16 (16, RDE) **1989** SD 16 (15, NT) **1990** SD 3 (3) **1991** SD 16 (16, NT) **1992**†KC 12 (10, LDT) **1993**†KC 16 (16, NT) **1994**†KC 16 (16, LDT) **1995**†KC 16 (16, LDT) **1996** KC 16 (16, LDT) **1997**†KC 15 (15, NT) **1998** SL 13 (4) **1999**†Min 16 (1) **NFL** 200 (152) [14 yrs]

PHILLIPS, JOE Joseph, WR, 5´9˝/188 lbs; Kentucky; B5/12/1963 Franklin, KY **1985** Was 4 (0) **1987** Was 2 (0) **NFL** 6 (0) [2 yrs]

PHILLIPS, KIM Kim Darnell, DB, 5´9˝/188 lbs; North Texas; 1989: NO, rnd 3; B10/28/1966 New Boston, TX **1989** NO 5 (0) **1990** Buf 1 (0) **NFL** 6 (0) [2 yrs]

PHILLIPS, KIRK Kirk Douglas, WR, 6´1˝/202 lbs; Tulsa; B7/31/1960 Poteau, OK

YEAR	TEAM	G(GS, POS)	RUSH	YD	AVG(LG)	TD	REC	YD	AVG(LG)	TD	PASS	COMP	PCT	YD	AVG(LG)	TD	INT	SK	YD	QBR	KPR	OTD	PTS	TAY
1984	Dal	8(0)	—	—	—	—	1	6	6.0(6)	0	—	—	—	—	—	—	—	—	—	—	—	—	0	3

PHILLIPS, LAWRENCE Lawrence Lamond, RB, 6´0˝/223 lbs; Nebraska; 1996: SL, rnd 1; B5/12/1975 Little Rock, AR

YEAR	TEAM	G(GS, POS)	RUSH	YD	AVG(LG)	TD	REC	YD	AVG(LG)	TD	PASS	COMP	PCT	YD	AVG(LG)	TD	INT	SK	YD	QBR	KPR	OTD	PTS	TAY
1996	SL	15(11, RB)	193	632	3.3(38)	4	8	28	3.5(11)	1	0	0	0.0	0	0.0	0	0	1	12	—	k	—	30	705
1997	SL	10(9, RB)	183	633	3.5(28)	8	10	33	3.3(17)	0	—	—	—	—	—	—	—	—	—	—	—	—	48	730
1997	Mia	2(0)	18	44	2.4(8)	0	1	6	6.0(6)	0	—	—	—	—	—	—	—	—	—	—	—	—	0	47
1999	SF	8(0)	30	144	4.8(68)	2	15	152	10.1(47)	0	—	—	—	—	—	—	—	—	—	—	k	—	12	370
NFL	3	35(20)	424	1453	3.4(68)	14	34	219	6.4(47)	1	0	0	0.0	0	0.0	0	0	1	12	—	k	—	90	1852

PHILLIPS, LOYD Loyd Wade, DE, 6´3˝/240 lbs; Arkansas; 1967: Chi, rnd 1; B5/2/1945 Fort Worth, TX **1967** ChiB 7 **1968** ChiB 13 (RDE) **1969** ChiB 12 **NFL** 32 [3 yrs]

PHILLIPS, MEL Melvin, DB, 6´2˝/198 lbs; North Carolina A&T; 1966: SF, rnd 5/Buf, rnd 19; B1/6/1942 Shelby, NC **1966** SF 11 **1967** SF 14 **1968** SF 13 **1969** SF 11 (10, RS) **1970**†SF 14 (14, SS) **1971**†SF 13 (SS) **1972** SF 14 (14, SS) **1973** SF 14 (13, SS) **1974** SF 6 (6, SS) **1975** SF 9 (8, SS) **1976** SF 14 (14, SS) **1977** SF 14 (14, SS) **NFL** 147 (93) [12 yrs]

PHILLIPS, MIKE Michael, C-LB, 6´0˝/208 lbs; Western Maryland; B11/22/1921 Clifton Heights, PA **1947** Bal-A 12 (9, C)

PHILLIPS, RAY Ray Charles, LB, 6´4˝/224 lbs; Nebraska; 1977: Cin, rnd 5; B3/18/1954 Fordyce, AR **1977** Cin 14 **1978** Cin 2 **1978**†Phi 10 (4) **1979**†Phi 11 **1980**†Phi 16 (0) **1981**†Phi 16 (1) **NFL** 69 (5) [5 yrs]

PHILLIPS, RAY Raymond Thomas, LB-DE, 6´3˝/243 lbs; North Carolina State; 1986: Den, rnd 7; B7/24/1964 Mooresville, NC **1986** Atl 1 (0) **1987** Phi 3 (2) **NFL** 4 (2) [2 yrs]

PHILLIPS, RED James Jackson, E, 6´1˝/197 lbs; Auburn; 1958: LA, rnd 1; B2/5/1936 Alexander City, AL

YEAR	TEAM	G(GS, POS)	RUSH	YD	AVG(LG)	TD	REC	YD	AVG(LG)	TD	PASS	COMP	PCT	YD	AVG(LG)	TD	INT	SK	YD	QBR	KPR	OTD	PTS	TAY
1958	LARm	12(11, RE)	—	—	—	—	35	524	15.0(**93**)	2	—	—	—	—	—	—	—	—	—	—	—	—	12	272
1959	LARm	9(9, FL)	—	—	—	—	37	541	14.6(64)	4	—	—	—	—	—	—	—	—	—	—	—	—	24	291

YEAR	TEAM	G(GS, POS)	RUSH	YD	AVG(LG)	TD	REC	YD	AVG(LG)	TD	PASS	COMP	PCT	YD	AVG(LG)	TD	INT	SK	YD	QBR	KPR	OTD	PTS	TAY
1960	LARm★	12(SE)	—	—	—	—	52	883	17.0(61)	8	—	—	—	—	—	—	—	—	—	—	—	—	48	482
1961	LARm★	14(SE)	—	—	—	—	**78**	1092	14.0(69)	5	—	—	—	—	—	—	—	—	—	—	—	—	30	571
1962	LARm✧	14(SE)	—	—	—	—	60	875	14.6(65)	5	—	—	—	—	—	—	—	—	—	—	—	—	30	463
1963	LARm	14(SE)	—	—	—	—	54	793	14.7(52)	1	—	—	—	—	—	—	—	—	—	—	—	—	6	402
1964	LARm	7(SE)	—	—	—	—	17	245	14.4(33)	2	—	—	—	—	—	—	—	—	—	—	—	—	12	133
1965	Min	12(9, WR)	—	—	—	—	15	185	12.3(43)	1	—	—	—	—	—	—	—	—	—	—	—	—	6	98
1966	Min	12(10, WR)	—	—	—	—	32	554	17.3(68)	3	—	—	—	—	—	—	—	—	—	—	—	—	18	292
1967	Min	13(9, WR)	—	—	—	—	21	352	16.8(42)	3	—	—	—	—	—	—	—	—	—	—	—	—	18	191
NFL	10	119(48)	—	—	—	—	401	6044	15.1(93)	34	—	—	—	—	—	—	—	—	—	—	—	—	204	3192

PHILLIPS, REGGIE Reginald Keith, DB, 5´10˝/170 lbs; SMU; 1985: Chi, rnd 2; B12/12/1960 Houston, TX **1985**†ChiB 16 (1) **1986**†ChiB 16 (8, rcb) **1987**†ChiB 12 (5, lcb) **1988** Phx 16 (0) **NFL** 60 (14) [4 yrs]

PHILLIPS, ROD Rodney Augustus, RB, 6´0˝/220 lbs; Cincinnati; Jackson State; B12/23/1952 Meridian, MS

YEAR	TEAM	G(GS, POS)	RUSH	YD	AVG(LG)	TD	REC	YD	AVG(LG)	TD	PASS	COMP	PCT	YD	AVG(LG)	TD	INT	SK	YD	QBR	KPR	OTD	PTS	TAY
1975	†LARm	14(1)	17	69	4.1(20)	0	2	10	5.0(8)	0	—	—	—	—	—	—	—	—	—	—	—	—	0	74
1976	†LARm	14	34	206	6.1(33)	1	4	23	5.8(15)	0	—	—	—	—	—	—	—	—	—	—	—	—	6	228
1977	†LARm	14	37	183	4.9(25)	1	1	5	5.0(5)	0	—	—	—	—	—	—	—	—	—	—	k	—	6	191
1978	†LARm	15(2)	28	81	2.9(11)	0	7	48	6.9(16)	0	—	—	—	—	—	—	—	—	—	—	k	—	0	112
1979	SL	11	3	50	16.7(17)	1	—	—	—	—	—	—	—	—	—	—	—	—	—	—	—	—	6	60
1980	SL	16(0)	2	6	3.0(4)	0	—	—	—	—	—	—	—	—	—	—	—	—	—	—	k	—	0	4
NFL	6	84(3)	121	595	4.9(33)	3	14	86	6.1(16)	0	—	—	—	—	—	—	—	—	—	—	k	—	18	668

PHILLIPS, RYAN Richard Ryan, LB, 6´4˝/252 lbs; Idaho; 1997: NYG, rnd 3; B2/7/1974 Renton, WA **1997** NYG 10 (0) **1998** NYG 16 (3) **1999** NYG 16 (16, LLB) **2000**†NYG 16 (16, LLB) **2001** Ind 13 (6, rlb) **NFL** 71 (41) [5 yrs]

PHILLIPS, SHAUN Shaun Jamal, DE, 6´3˝/260 lbs; Purdue; 2004: SD, rnd 4; B5/13/1981 Willingboro, NJ **2004**†SD 16 (0) **2005** SD 15 (3) **NFL** 31 (3) [2 yrs]

PHILLIPS, WES Wesley Alan, T, 6´5˝/275 lbs; Lenoir-Rhyne; B8/1/1953 Atlanta, GA **1979** Hou 8

PHILPOTT, DEAN Dean Earnest, FB, 6´0˝/200 lbs; Fresno State; 1958: ChiC, rnd 11; B11/11/1935 Mesa, AR

YEAR	TEAM	G(GS, POS)	RUSH	YD	AVG(LG)	TD	REC	YD	AVG(LG)	TD	PASS	COMP	PCT	YD	AVG(LG)	TD	INT	SK	YD	QBR	KPR	OTD	PTS	TAY
1958	ChiC	9	12	44	3.7(7)	0	4	30	7.5(12)	0	—	—	—	—	—	—	—	—	—	—	k	—	0	32

PHILPOTT, ED Edward Leigh, LB, 6´3˝/240 lbs; Miami (OH); 1967: Bos, rnd 4; B9/14/1945 Wichita, KS **1967** Bos-A 13 (13, LLB) **1968** Bos-A 14 (14, LLB) **1969** Bos-A 14 (14, LLB) **1970** Bos 14 (12, LLB) **1971** NE 13 (4) **NFL** 68 (57) [5 yrs]

PHILYAW, CHARLES Charles Henry, DE, 6´9˝/276 lbs; Texas Southern; 1976: Oak, rnd 2; B2/25/1954 Shreveport, LA **1976**†Oak 14 (lde) **1977** Oak 3 **1978** Oak 15 (3) **1979** Oak 12 **NFL** 44 (3) [4 yrs]

PHILYAW, DINO Delvic Dyvon, RB, 5´10˝/205 lbs; Oregon; 1995: NE, rnd 6; B10/30/1970 Dudley, NC

YEAR	TEAM	G(GS, POS)	RUSH	YD	AVG(LG)	TD	REC	YD	AVG(LG)	TD	PASS	COMP	PCT	YD	AVG(LG)	TD	INT	SK	YD	QBR	KPR	OTD	PTS	TAY
1995	Car	1(0)	—	—	—	—	—	—	—	—	—	—	—	—	—	—	—	—	—	—	k	—	0	8
1996	Car	9(0)	12	38	3.2(8)	1	—	—	—	—	—	—	—	—	—	—	—	—	—	—	—	—	6	48
1999	NO	13(0)	4	16	4.0(18)	0	2	23	11.5(14)	0	—	—	—	—	—	—	—	—	—	—	k	—	0	398
NFL	3	23(0)	16	54	3.4(18)	1	2	23	11.5(14)	0	—	—	—	—	—	—	—	—	—	—	k	—	6	454

PHILYAW, MARENO Mareno, WR, 6´2˝/208 lbs; Troy State; 2000: Atl, rnd 6; B12/19/1977 Atlanta, GA **2000** Atl 1 (0)

PHIPPS, MIKE Michael Elston, QB, 6´3˝/208 lbs; Purdue; 1970: Cle, rnd 1; B11/19/1947 Shelbyville, IN

YEAR	TEAM	G(GS, POS)	RUSH	YD	AVG(LG)	TD	REC	YD	AVG(LG)	TD	PASS	COMP	PCT	YD	AVG(LG)	TD	INT	SK	YD	QBR	KPR	OTD	PTS	TAY
1970	Cle	14(qb)	11	94	8.5(26)	0	—	—	—	—	60	29	48.3	529	8.8(53)	1	5	7	86	—	—	—	0	164
1971	†Cle	14	6	35	5.8(15)	0	—	—	—	—	47	13	27.7	179	3.8(39)	1	4	—	—	—	—	—	0	-31
1972	†Cle	14(QB)	60	256	4.3(18)	5	—	—	—	—	305	144	47.2	1994	6.5(80)	13	16	23	183	61.0	—	—	30	728
1973	Cle	14(QB)	60	395	6.6(27)	5	—	—	—	—	299	148	49.5	1719	5.7(51)	9	**20**	44	362	49.4	—	—	30	550
1974	Cle	14(QB)	39	279	7.2(19)	1	—	—	—	—	256	117	45.7	1384	5.4(55)	9	17	33	280	46.7	—	—	6	346
1975	Cle	14(12, QB)	18	70	3.9(12)	0	—	—	—	—	313	162	51.8	1749	5.6(48)	4	19	28	261	47.5	—	—	0	205
1976	Cle	4(1)	4	26	6.5(24)	0	—	—	—	—	37	20	54.1	146	3.9(23)	3	0	1	6	—	—	—	0	114
1977	ChiB	3	—	—	—	—	—	—	—	—	5	3	60.0	5	1.0(10)	0	0	3	26	—	—	—	0	3
1978	ChiB	6(4)	13	34	2.6(10)	0	—	—	—	—	83	44	53.0	465	5.6(35)	2	10	6	55	—	—	—	0	-124
1979	†ChiB	12(10, QB)	27	51	1.9(12)	0	—	—	—	—	255	134	52.5	1535	6.0(68)	9	8	15	145	69.6	—	—	0	544
1980	ChiB	7(6, qb)	15	38	2.5(9)	2	—	—	—	—	122	61	50.0	630	5.2(56)	2	9	7	69	—	—	—	12	23
1981	ChiB	3(0)	1	0	0.0(0)	0	—	—	—	—	17	11	64.7	171	10.1(43)	2	0	5	41	—	—	—	0	96
NFL	12	119(33)	254	1278	5.0(27)	13	—	—	—	—	1799	886	49.2	10506	5.8(80)	55	108	172	1514	52.6	—	—	78	2616

PIASECKY, ALEX Alexander, E, 6´2˝/197 lbs; Duke; B2/1/1917 Greensburg, PA, D9/16/1992 Orange City, FL

YEAR	TEAM	G(GS, POS)	RUSH	YD	AVG(LG)	TD	REC	YD	AVG(LG)	TD	PASS	COMP	PCT	YD	AVG(LG)	TD	INT	SK	YD	QBR	KPR	OTD	PTS	TAY
1943	†Was	9(0)	—	—	—	—	3	17	5.7(7)	1	—	—	—	—	—	—	—	—	—	—	ki	—	6	11
1944	Was	10(6, RE)	—	—	—	—	8	77	9.6(18)	0	—	—	—	—	—	—	—	—	—	—	—	—	0	39
1945	†Was	9(0)	—	—	—	—	1	18	18.0(18)	0	—	—	—	—	—	—	—	—	—	—	—	—	0	9
NFL	3	28(6)	—	—	—	—	12	112	9.3(18)	1	—	—	—	—	—	—	—	—	—	—	ki	—	6	58

PICARD, BOB Robert, WR, 6´1˝/195 lbs; Eastern Washington; 1973: Phi, rnd 6; B11/24/1949 Omak, WA **1973** Phi 14 **1974** Phi 14 **1975** Phi 14 **1976** Phi 4 **1976** Det 8 **NFL** 54 [4 yrs]

PICCOLO, BILL William James, C, 5´11˝/185 lbs; Canisius; 1943: NYG, rnd 10; B5/1/1920 Buffalo, NY, D2/26/2005 Ravenna, OH **1943**†NYG 10 (3) **1944** NYG 4 (2) **1945** NYG 4 (0) **NFL** 18 (5) [3 yrs]

PICCOLO, BRIAN Louis Brian, RB, 6´0˝/205 lbs; Wake Forest; B10/31/1943 Pittsfield, MA, D6/6/1970 New York, NY

YEAR	TEAM	G(GS, POS)	RUSH	YD	AVG(LG)	TD	REC	YD	AVG(LG)	TD	PASS	COMP	PCT	YD	AVG(LG)	TD	INT	SK	YD	QBR	KPR	OTD	PTS	TAY
1966	ChiB	14	3	12	4.0(5)	0	—	—	—	—	—	—	—	—	—	—	—	—	—	—	—	—	0	12
1967	ChiB	14(FB)	87	317	3.6(31)	0	13	103	7.9(25)	0	—	—	—	—	—	—	—	—	—	—	—	—	0	369
1968	ChiB	14	123	450	3.7(19)	2	28	291	10.4(44)	0	—	—	—	—	—	—	—	—	—	—	—	—	12	616
1969	ChiB	9	45	148	3.3(15)	2	17	143	8.4(25)	1	—	—	—	—	—	—	—	—	—	—	p	—	18	243
NFL	4	51	258	927	3.6(31)	4	58	537	9.3(44)	1	—	—	—	—	—	—	—	—	—	—	p	—	30	1239

PICCONE, LOU Louis James, WR, 5´9˝/175 lbs; West Liberty State; B7/17/1949 Vineland, NJ **[R]**

YEAR	TEAM	G(GS, POS)	RUSH	YD	AVG(LG)	TD	REC	YD	AVG(LG)	TD	PASS	COMP	PCT	YD	AVG(LG)	TD	INT	SK	YD	QBR	KPR	OTD	PTS	TAY
1974	NYJ	14	—	—	—	—	—	—	—	—	—	—	—	—	—	—	—	—	—	—	kp	—	0	406
1975	NYJ	13	—	—	—	—	7	79	11.3(21)	0	—	—	—	—	—	—	—	—	—	—	kp	—	0	271
1976	NYJ	14(7, WR)	1	11	11.0(11)	0	12	147	12.3(23)	0	—	—	—	—	—	—	—	—	—	—	kp	1	6	397
1977	Buf	14(10, WR)	1	6	6.0(6)	0	17	240	14.1(25)	2	—	—	—	—	—	—	—	—	—	—	kp	—	12	165
1978	Buf	16(1)	—	—	—	—	7	71	10.1(15)	2	—	—	—	—	—	—	—	—	—	—	kp	—	14	70
1979	Buf	16(4)	—	—	—	—	33	556	16.8(49)	2	—	—	—	—	—	—	—	—	—	—	kp	—	12	284
1980	†Buf	9(0)	—	—	—	—	7	82	11.7(16)	0	—	—	—	—	—	—	—	—	—	—	p	—	0	46
1981	†Buf	14(0)	—	—	—	—	5	65	13.0(16)	0	—	—	—	—	—	—	—	—	—	—	kp	—	0	46
1982	Buf	8(2)	—	—	—	—	12	140	11.7(29)	0	—	—	—	—	—	—	—	—	—	—	k	—	0	75
NFL	9	118(24)	2	17	8.5(11)	0	100	1380	13.8(49)	6	—	—	—	—	—	—	—	—	—	—	kp	1	44	1758

PICKARD, BOB Robert Harry, WR, 6´0˝/190 lbs; Xavier (OH); B9/3/1952 Canton, OH

YEAR	TEAM	G(GS, POS)	RUSH	YD	AVG(LG)	TD	REC	YD	AVG(LG)	TD	PASS	COMP	PCT	YD	AVG(LG)	TD	INT	SK	YD	QBR	KPR	OTD	PTS	TAY
1974	Det	14(2)	1	5	5.0(5)	0	8	88	11.0(18)	1	—	—	—	—	—	—	—	—	—	—	—	—	6	54

PICKEL, BILL William George, NT-DT-DE, 6´5˝/265 lbs; Rutgers; 1983: LARd, rnd 2; B11/5/1959 Queens, NY **[S]** **1983**†LARd 16 (1) **1984**†LARd 16 (3) **1985**†LARd 16 (16, NT) **1986** LARd☆15 (15, NT) **1987** LARd 12 (11, NT) **1988** LARd 16 (16, NT) **1989** LARd 16 (3) **1990**†LARd 14 (3) **1991**†NYJ 15 (1) **1992** NYJ 11 (1) **1993** NYJ 11 (3) **1994** NYJ 16 (0) **NFL** 174 (73) [12 yrs]

PICKENS, BOB Robert James, T, 6´4˝/258 lbs; Wisconsin; Nebraska; 1966: Chi, rnd 3/KC, rnd R2; B2/2/1943 Chicago, IL **1967** ChiB 12 **1968** ChiB 5 **1969** ChiB 3 **NFL** 20 [3 yrs]

PICKENS, BRUCE Bruce Evon, DB, 5´11˝/190 lbs; Nebraska; 1991: Atl, rnd 1; B5/9/1968 Kansas City, MO **1991** Atl 7 (0) **1992** Atl 16 (4) **1993** Atl 4 (4) **1993** GB 2 (0) **1993**†KC 3 (0) **1995** Oak 16 (1) **NFL** 48 (9) [4 yrs]

PICKENS, CARL Carl McNally, WR, 6´2˝/206 lbs; Tennessee; 1992: Cin, rnd 2; B3/23/1970 Murphy, NC

YEAR	TEAM	G(GS, POS)	RUSH	YD	AVG(LG)	TD	REC	YD	AVG(LG)	TD	PASS	COMP	PCT	YD	AVG(LG)	TD	INT	SK	YD	QBR	KPR	OTD	PTS	TAY
1992	Cin	16(10, WR)	—	—	—	—	26	326	12.5(38)	1	—	—	—	—	—	—	—	—	—	—	p	1	12	317
1993	Cin	13(12, WR)	—	—	—	—	43	565	13.1(36)	6	1	0	0.0	0	0.0	0	0	—	—	—	p	—	36	309
1994	Cin☆	15(15, WR)	—	—	—	—	71	1127	15.9(70)	**11**	—	—	—	—	—	—	—	—	—	—	p	—	66	636

YEAR	TEAM	G (GS, POS)	RUSH	YD	AVG (LG)	TD	REC	YD	AVG (LG)	TD	PASS	COMP	PCT	YD	AVG (LG)	TD	INT	SK	YD	QBR	KPR	OTD	PTS	TAY
1995	Cin★	16 (15, WR)	1	6	6.0 (6)	0	**99**	1234	12.5 (68)	**17**	—	—	—	—	—	—	—	—	—	—	p	—	102	681
1996	Cin★	16 (16, WR)	2	2	1.0 (2)	0	**100**	1180	11.8 (61)	12	1	1	100.0	12	12.0 (12)	0	0	—	—	—	p	—	74	655
1997	Cin	12 (12, WR)	1	-6	-6.0 (-6)	0	52	695	13.4 (50)	5	—	—	—	—	—	—	—	—	—	—	—	—	30	367
1998	Cin	16 (16, WR)	2	4	2.0 (4)	0	82	1023	12.5 (67)	5	—	—	—	—	—	—	—	—	—	—	—	—	32	541
1999	Cin	16 (14, WR)	—	—	—	—	57	737	12.9 (75)	6	1	1	100.0	6	6.0 (6)	0	0	—	—	—	—	—	36	402
2000	†Ten	9 (6, wr)	—	—	—	—	10	242	24.2 (67)	0	—	—	—	—	—	—	—	—	—	—	—	—	0	121
NFL	9	129 (116)	6	6	1.0 (6)	0	540	7129	13.2 (75)	63	3	2	66.7	18	6.0 (12)	0	0	—	—	—	p	1	388	4027

PICKENS, LYLE Lyle Edward, DB, 5´10˝/175 lbs; Colorado; 1986: Det, rnd 9; B9/5/1964 New Orleans, LA **1987** Den 1 (0)

PICKERING, CLAY Clayton Floyd, WR, 6´5˝/215 lbs; Maine; B6/2/1961 Jacksonville, FL **1984** Cin 3 (0) **1985** Cin 1 (0) **1986** ChiB 4 (0)

YEAR	TEAM	G (GS, POS)	RUSH	YD	AVG (LG)	TD	REC	YD	AVG (LG)	TD	PASS	COMP	PCT	YD	AVG (LG)	TD	INT	SK	YD	QBR	KPR	OTD	PTS	TAY
1987	NE	1 (0)	—	—	—	—	1	10	10.0 (10)	0	—	—	—	—	—	—	—	—	—	—	—	—	0	5
NFL	4	9 (0)	—	—	—	—	1	10	10.0 (10)	0	—	—	—	—	—	—	—	—	—	—	—	—	0	5

PICKETT, CODY Cody, QB, 6´4˝/220 lbs; Washington; 2004: SF, rnd 7; B6/30/1980 Caldwell, ID

YEAR	TEAM	G (GS, POS)	RUSH	YD	AVG (LG)	TD	REC	YD	AVG (LG)	TD	PASS	COMP	PCT	YD	AVG (LG)	TD	INT	SK	YD	QBR	KPR	OTD	PTS	TAY
2004	SF	2 (0)	1	5	5.0 (5)	0	—	—	—	—	10	4	40.0	55	5.5 (18)	0	2	2	14	—	—	—	0	-48
2005	SF	5 (2)	13	42	3.2 (12)	0	—	—	—	—	35	14	40.0	140	4.0 (28)	0	2	3	16	—	—	—	0	32
NFL	2	7 (2)	14	47	3.4 (12)	0	—	—	—	—	45	18	40.0	195	4.3 (28)	0	4	5	30	—	—	—	0	-16

PICKETT, RYAN Ryan Lamont, DT, 6´2˝/310 lbs; Ohio State; 2001: SL, rnd 1; B10/8/1979 Zephyrhills, FL **2001**†SL 11 (0) **2002** SL 16 (14, LDT) **2003**†SL 16 (13, LDT) **2004**†SL 16 (16, LDT) **2005** SL 16 (16, LDT) **NFL** 75 (59) [5 yrs]

PIDGEON, TIM Timothy Charles, LB, 6´0˝/233 lbs; Syracuse; 1987: Mia, rnd 9; B9/20/1964 Oneonta, NY **1987** Mia 3 (3)

PIEL, MIKE Michael Lloyd, DE-NT, 6´4˝/268 lbs; Illinois; 1988: LARm, rnd 3; B9/21/1965 Carmel, CA **1989**†LARm 13 (6, rde) **1990** LARm 16 (11, RDE) **1991** LARm 6 (3) **1992** LARm 15 (5, rde) **NFL** 50 (25) [4 yrs]

PIEPUL, MILT Milton John, FB, 6´1˝/215 lbs; Notre Dame; 1941: Det, rnd 11; B9/14/1918 Springfield, MA, D3/19/1994 Northampton, MA

YEAR	TEAM	G (GS, POS)	RUSH	YD	AVG (LG)	TD	REC	YD	AVG (LG)	TD	PASS	COMP	PCT	YD	AVG (LG)	TD	INT	SK	YD	QBR	KPR	OTD	PTS	TAY
1941	Det	11 (2)	20	56	2.8 (13)	0	—	—	—	—	1	1	100.0	23	23.0 (23)	0	0	—	—	—	P	—	0	68

PIERCE, AARON Aaron R., TE, 6´5˝/252 lbs; Washington; 1992: NYG, rnd 3; B9/6/1969 Seattle, WA

YEAR	TEAM	G (GS, POS)	RUSH	YD	AVG (LG)	TD	REC	YD	AVG (LG)	TD	PASS	COMP	PCT	YD	AVG (LG)	TD	INT	SK	YD	QBR	KPR	OTD	PTS	TAY
1992	NYG	1 (0)	—	—	—	—	—	—	—	—	—	—	—	—	—	—	—	—	—	—	—	—	—	—
1993	†NYG	13 (6, te)	—	—	—	—	12	212	17.7 (54)	0	—	—	—	—	—	—	—	—	—	—	—	—	0	106
1994	NYG	16 (11, TE)	—	—	—	—	20	214	10.7 (29)	4	—	—	—	—	—	—	—	—	—	—	—	—	24	127
1995	NYG	16 (11, TE)	1	6	6.0 (6)	0	33	310	9.4 (26)	0	—	—	—	—	—	—	—	—	—	—	—	—	0	161
1996	NYG	10 (4)	1	1	1.0 (1)	1	11	144	13.1 (30)	1	—	—	—	—	—	—	—	—	—	—	—	—	12	88
1997	†NYG	16 (4)	—	—	—	—	10	47	4.7 (14)	0	—	—	—	—	—	—	—	—	—	—	k	—	0	19
1999	Bal	10 (8, TE)	—	—	—	—	11	102	9.3 (26)	0	—	—	—	—	—	—	—	—	—	—	k	—	0	43
NFL	7	82 (44)	2	7	3.5 (6)	1	97	1029	10.6 (54)	5	—	—	—	—	—	—	—	—	—	—	k	—	36	544

PIERCE, ANTONIO Antonio, LB, 6´1˝/240 lbs; Arizona; B10/26/1978 Ontario, CA **2001** Was 16 (7, rlb) **2002** Was 8 (1) **2003** Was 15 (0) **2004** Was 16 (16, MLB) **2005** NYG 13 (13, MLB) **NFL** 68 (37) [5 yrs]

PIERCE, BRETT Brett Clayton, TE, 6´5˝/250 lbs; Stanford; B1/7/1981 Vancouver, WA **2004** Dal 8 (1)

YEAR	TEAM	G (GS, POS)	RUSH	YD	AVG (LG)	TD	REC	YD	AVG (LG)	TD	PASS	COMP	PCT	YD	AVG (LG)	TD	INT	SK	YD	QBR	KPR	OTD	PTS	TAY
2005	Dal	10 (1)	—	—	—	—	2	15	7.5 (10)	0	—	—	—	—	—	—	—	—	—	—	—	—	0	8
NFL	2	18 (2)	—	—	—	—	2	15	7.5 (10)	0	—	—	—	—	—	—	—	—	—	—	k	—	0	6

PIERCE, DANNY John Daniel, RB, 6´3˝/216 lbs; Mississippi State; Memphis; 1970: Was, rnd 5; B1/17/1948 Laurel, MS

YEAR	TEAM	G (GS, POS)	RUSH	YD	AVG (LG)	TD	REC	YD	AVG (LG)	TD	PASS	COMP	PCT	YD	AVG (LG)	TD	INT	SK	YD	QBR	KPR	OTD	PTS	TAY
1970	Was	2	5	6	1.2 (8)	0	1	6	6.0 (6)	0	—	—	—	—	—	—	—	—	—	—	—	—	0	9

PIERCE, DICK Richard, G, 5´11˝/185 lbs; Michigan; B3/1/1896, D9/1966 Detroit, MI **1920** ChiT 4 (2)

PIERCE, DON Donald Hite, C, 6´1˝/186 lbs; Kansas; B2/7/1919 Topeka, KS, D1/2/1965 Kansas City, KS **1942** Bkn 2 (0) **1943** ChiC 1 (0) **NFL** 3 (0) [2 yrs]

PIERCE, STEVE Stephen Nathan, WR, 5´10˝/190 lbs; Illinois; B12/12/1963

YEAR	TEAM	G (GS, POS)	RUSH	YD	AVG (LG)	TD	REC	YD	AVG (LG)	TD	PASS	COMP	PCT	YD	AVG (LG)	TD	INT	SK	YD	QBR	KPR	OTD	PTS	TAY
1987	Cle	2 (0)	—	—	—	—	2	21	10.5 (13)	0	—	—	—	—	—	—	—	—	—	—	—	—	0	11

PIERCE, TERRY Terry DeWayne, LB, 6´1˝/251 lbs; Kansas State; 2003: Den, rnd 2; B6/21/1981 Fort Worth, TX **2003** Den 3 (0) **2004**†Den 15 (0) **NFL** 18 (0) [2 yrs]

PIERI, DAMON Mark Damon, DB, 6´0˝/186 lbs; San Diego State; B9/25/1970 Phoenix, AZ **1993** NYJ 5 (0) **1996**†Car 16 (1) **1997** Car 16 (0) **NFL** 37 (1) [3 yrs]

PIEROTTI, AL Albert Felix, C-G-T-B, 5´10˝/204 lbs; Washington & Lee; B10/24/1895 Boston, MA, D2/12/1964 Revere, MA **[C]** **1920** Akr 1 (0) **1920** Cle 5 (3, C) **1921** NYG 2 (2, C) **1922** Mil 9 (9, C) **1923** Rac 1 (0) **1923** Mil 3 (3) **1924** Mil 4 (2) **1927** Pro 14 (11, C) **1929** Bos 7 (6, C) **NFL** 46 (36) [7 yrs]

PIERRE, JOE Joseph Nick, E, 6´0˝/185 lbs; Pittsburgh; B10/15/1920 South Fork, PA, D11/19/2003 Bel Air, MD **1945** Pit 10 (7, RE)

PIERSON, PETE Peter Samuel, T, 6´5˝/295 lbs; Washington; 1994: TB, rnd 5; B2/4/1971 Portland, OR **1995** TB 12 (4) **1996** TB 11 (2) **1997**†TB 15 (0) **1998** TB 16 (0) **1999**†TB 15 (0) **2000**†TB 15 (15, LT) **2001**†TB 16 (0) **2002** Ind 1 (0) **NFL** 101 (21) [8 yrs]

PIERSON, REGGIE Reginald Lee, DB, 5´11˝/185 lbs; Oklahoma State; B12/13/1952 Los Angeles, CA **1976** Det 4 **1976** TB 5 (1) **NFL** 9 (1) [1 yr]

PIERSON, SHURRON Shurron Torian, DE-LB, 6´2˝/250 lbs; South Florida; 2003: Oak, rnd 4; B5/31/1982 Inverness, FL **2003** Oak 6 (0) **2004** ChiB 6 (0) **NFL** 12 (0) [2 yrs]

PIETROSANTE, NICK Nicholas Vincent, FB, 6´2˝/225 lbs; Notre Dame; 1959: Det, rnd 1; B9/10/1937 Ansonia, CT, D2/6/1988 Royal Oak, MI

YEAR	TEAM	G (GS, POS)	RUSH	YD	AVG (LG)	TD	REC	YD	AVG (LG)	TD	PASS	COMP	PCT	YD	AVG (LG)	TD	INT	SK	YD	QBR	KPR	OTD	PTS	TAY
1959	Det	10 (FB)	76	447	5.9 (37)	3	16	140	8.8 (20)	0	—	—	—	—	—	—	—	—	—	—	k	—	18	570
1960	Det✧	12 (FB)	161	872	5.4 (57)	8	13	129	9.9 (28)	0	—	—	—	—	—	—	—	—	—	—	k	—	48	1045
1961	Det✧	14 (FB)	201	841	4.2 (42)	5	26	315	12.1 (76)	0	—	—	—	—	—	—	—	—	—	—	—	—	30	1049
1962	Det	13 (FB)	134	445	3.3 (22)	2	26	251	9.7 (26)	2	—	—	—	—	—	—	—	—	—	—	—	—	24	601
1963	Det	12	112	418	3.7 (22)	5	16	173	10.8 (24)	0	1	1	100.0	37	37.0 (37)	0	0	—	—	—	—	—	30	573
1964	Det	14 (FB)	147	536	3.6 (21)	4	19	152	8.0 (20)	0	1	0	0.0	0	0.0	0	1	—	—	—	—	—	24	612
1965	Det	14 (FB)	107	374	3.5 (12)	1	18	163	9.1 (54)	0	—	—	—	—	—	—	—	—	—	—	—	—	6	466
1966	Cle	13	7	20	2.9 (8)	0	1	12	12.0 (12)	0	—	—	—	—	—	—	—	—	—	—	k	—	0	5
1967	†Cle	14	10	73	7.3 (31)	0	6	56	9.3 (23)	0	—	—	—	—	—	—	—	—	—	—	—	—	0	101
NFL	9	116	955	4026	4.2 (57)	28	141	1391	9.9 (76)	2	2	1	50.0	37	18.5 (37)	0	1	—	—	—	k	—	180	5020

PIETRZAK, JIM James Michael, C-DT-T, 6´5˝/260 lbs; Eastern Michigan; 1974: NYG, rnd 6; B2/21/1953 Detroit, MI **1974** NYG 14 **1975** NYG 14 **1977** NYG 14 **1978** NYG 16 **1979** NYG 3 **1979** NO 11 **1980** NO 15 (2) **1981** NO 16 (5, c) **1982** NO 9 (0) **1983** NO 16 (0) **1984** NO 10 (0) **1987** KC 2 (2) **NFL** 140 (9) [11 yrs]

PIFFERINI, BOB Robert Marico, C, 6´0˝/210 lbs; San Jose State; 1949: Det, rnd 15; B10/1/1922 Oakdale, CA **1949** Det 12 (1)

PIFFERINI, BOB Robert Marico, LB, 6´2˝/226 lbs; UCLA; 1972: Chi, rnd 6; B6/27/1950 San Jose, CA **1972** ChiB 14 **1973** ChiB 12 (RLB) **1974** ChiB 12 **1975** ChiB 14 **1977**†LARm 5 **NFL** 57 [5 yrs]

PIGGOTT, BERT Bert Coley, RB, 6´2˝/195 lbs; Illinois; B3/5/1921 Hinsdale, IL

YEAR	TEAM	G (GS, POS)	RUSH	YD	AVG (LG)	TD	REC	YD	AVG (LG)	TD	PASS	COMP	PCT	YD	AVG (LG)	TD	INT	SK	YD	QBR	KPR	OTD	PTS	TAY
1947	LAD-A	13 (2)	46	161	3.5	0	7	63	9.0	1	—	—	—	—	—	—	—	—	—	—	kpi	—	6	249

PIGNATELLI, CARL Carlo Arthur, HB-BB, 6´0˝/210 lbs; Iowa; B11/26/1907 Rock Falls, IL, D6/14/1964, IL **1931** Cle 7 (3)

PIHOS, PETE Peter Louis, E-DE, 6´1˝/210 lbs; Indiana; 1945: Phi, rnd 5; B10/22/1923 Orlando, FL; HOF 1970

YEAR	TEAM	G (GS, POS)	RUSH	YD	AVG (LG)	TD	REC	YD	AVG (LG)	TD	PASS	COMP	PCT	YD	AVG (LG)	TD	INT	SK	YD	QBR	KPR	OTD	PTS	TAY
1947	†Phi☆	12 (12, RE)	—	—	—	—	23	382	16.6 (66)	7	—	—	—	—	—	—	—	—	—	—	kp	1	48	259
1948	†Phi☆	12 (11, RE)	8	-3	-0.4 (5)	0	46	766	16.7 (48)	11	—	—	—	—	—	—	—	—	—	—	k	—	66	429
1949	†Phi☆	11 (9, RE)	—	—	—	—	34	484	14.2 (49)	4	—	—	—	—	—	—	—	—	—	—	k	—	24	247
1950	Phi★	12 (RE)	—	—	—	—	38	447	11.8 (43)	6	—	—	—	—	—	—	—	—	—	—	—	—	36	254
1951	Phi✧	12 (RE/LDE)	—	—	—	—	35	536	15.3 (38)	5	—	—	—	—	—	—	—	—	—	—	ki	—	30	308
1952	Phi★	12 (lde/re)	—	—	—	—	12	219	18.3 (47)	1	—	—	—	—	—	—	—	—	—	—	—	1	12	115
1953	Phi★	12 (RE)	—	—	—	—	**63**	**1049**	16.7 (59)	**10**	—	—	—	—	—	—	—	—	—	—	—	—	60	575
1954	Phi★	12 (RE)	1	-1	-1.0 (-1)	0	**60**	872	14.5 (34)	10	—	—	—	—	—	—	—	—	—	—	—	—	60	485
1955	Phi★	12 (RE)	—	—	—	—	**62**	**864**	13.9 (40)	7	—	—	—	—	—	—	—	—	—	—	—	—	42	467
NFL	9	107 (32)	9	-4	-0.4 (5)	0	373	5619	15.1 (66)	61	—	—	—	—	—	—	—	—	—	—	kpi	2	378	3138

PIKE, CHRIS Christopher Holtz, DT, 6´8˝/280 lbs; North Carolina; Tulsa; 1987: Phi, rnd 6; B1/13/1964 Washington, DC **1989**†Cle 12 (0) **1990** Cle 12 (11, LDT) **1991** LARm 8 (4) **NFL** 32 (15) [3 yrs]

YEAR	TEAM	G (GS, POS)	RUSH	YD	AVG (LG)	TD	REC	YD	AVG (LG)	TD	PASS	COMP	PCT	YD	AVG (LG)	TD	INT	SK	YD	QBR	KPR	OTD	PTS	TAY

Pike, Mark Mark Harold, DE-LB, 6´4˝/272 lbs; Georgia Tech; 1986: Buf, rnd 7; B12/27/1963 Elizabethtown, KY **1987** Buf 3 (0) **1988**†Buf 16 (0) **1989**†Buf 16 (0) **1990**†Buf 16 (0) **1991**†Buf 16 (1) **1992**†Buf 16 (0) **1993**†Buf 14 (0) **1994** Buf 16 (0) **1995**†Buf 16 (0) **1996**†Buf 16 (0) **1997** Buf 15 (0) **1998**†Buf 13 (0) **NFL** 173 (1) [12 yrs]

Pilconis, Joe Joseph George, E, 6´1˝/189 lbs; Temple; B10/9/1911 Shenandoah, PA, D6/29/1993 New Ringgold, PA

YEAR	TEAM	G (GS, POS)	RUSH	YD	AVG (LG)	TD	REC	YD	AVG (LG)	TD	PASS	COMP	PCT	YD	AVG (LG)	TD	INT	SK	YD	QBR	KPR	OTD	PTS	TAY
1934	Phi	9(2)	1	5	5.0(5)	0	1	3	3.0(3)	0	—	—	—	—	—	—	—	—	—	—	—	—	0	7
1936	Phi	12(4)	—	—	—	—	4	51	12.8	1	—	—	—	—	—	—	—	—	—	—	—	—	6	31
1937	Phi	11(3)	2	21	10.5	0	6	59	9.8	0	—	—	—	—	—	—	—	—	—	—	—	1	6	51
NFL	3	32(9)	3	26	8.7(5)	0	11	113	10.3(3)	1	—	—	—	—	—	—	—	—	—	—	—	1	12	88

Pile, Willie Willie Marquis, DB, 6´2˝/206 lbs; Virginia Tech; 2003: KC, rnd 7; B5/25/1980 New York, NY **2004** KC 16 (5, ss) **2005** Dal 16 (1) **NFL** 32 (6) [2 yrs]

Pilgrim, Evan Evan Boyd, G, 6´4˝/304 lbs; Brigham Young; 1995: Chi, rnd 3; B8/14/1972 Pittsburg, CA **1996** ChiB 6 (0) **1997** ChiB 13 (6, lg) **1998** Ten 2 (0) **1999** Atl 3 (1) **2000** Atl 7 (1) **NFL** 31 (8) [5 yrs]

Pillath, Roger Roger Allen, T, 6´4˝/242 lbs; Wisconsin; 1964: LA, rnd 3/Buf, rnd 7; B12/21/1941 Marinette, WI **1965** LARm 14 **1966** Pit 6 **NFL** 20 [2 yrs]

Piller, Zach Zachary Paul, G, 6´5˝/321 lbs; Georgia Tech; Florida; 1999: Ten, rnd 3; B5/2/1976 St. Petersburg, FL **1999** Ten 8 (0) **2000**†Ten 16 (0) **2001** Ten 14 (9, LG) **2002**†Ten 13 (13, LG) **2003**†Ten 16 (16, LG) **2004** Ten 1 (1) **2005** Ten 16 (16, LG) **NFL** 84 (55) [7 yrs]

Pillers, Lawrence Lawrence Dwight, DE-DT-NT, 6´4˝/255 lbs; Alcorn State; 1976: NYJ, rnd 11; B11/4/1952 Hazelhurst, MS **1976** NYJ 14 (13, LDE) **1977** NYJ 13 (13, LDE) **1978** NYJ 16 (16, LDE) **1979** NYJ 16 (15, LDE) **1980** NYJ 3 (1) **1980** SF 13 (10, RDE) **1981**†SF 14 (6, rde) **1982** SF 9 (5, RDE) **1983**†SF 16 (13, LDE) **1984**†SF 16 (7, lde) **1985** Atl 9 (0) **NFL** 139 (99) [10 yrs]

Pillman, Brian Brian William, LB, 5´10˝/228 lbs; Miami (OH); B5/22/1962 Cincinnati, OH, D10/5/1997 Bloomington, MN **1984** Cin 6 (0)

Pillow, Frank William Frank, WR, 5´10˝/170 lbs; Tennessee State; 1988: TB, rnd 11; B3/11/1965 Nashville, TN

YEAR	TEAM	G (GS, POS)	RUSH	YD	AVG (LG)	TD	REC	YD	AVG (LG)	TD	PASS	COMP	PCT	YD	AVG (LG)	TD	INT	SK	YD	QBR	KPR	OTD	PTS	TAY
1988	TB	15(0)	—	—	—	—	15	206	13.7(34)	1	—	—	—	—	—	—	—	—	—	—	k	—	6	101
1989	TB	3(0)	—	—	—	—	—	—	—	—	—	—	—	—	—	—	—	—	—	—	k	—	0	2
1990	TB	16(2)	—	—	—	—	8	118	14.8(23)	0	—	—	—	—	—	—	—	—	—	—	—	—	0	59
NFL	3	34(2)	—	—	—	—	23	324	14.1(34)	1	—	—	—	—	—	—	—	—	—	—	k	—	6	162

Pinckert, Ernie Erny, B, 6´0˝/197 lbs; USC; B5/1/1907 Medford, WI, D8/30/1977 Los Angeles, CA

YEAR	TEAM	G (GS, POS)	RUSH	YD	AVG (LG)	TD	REC	YD	AVG (LG)	TD	PASS	COMP	PCT	YD	AVG (LG)	TD	INT	SK	YD	QBR	KPR	OTD	PTS	TAY
1932	Bos	9(6, WB)	16	72	4.5	0	3	42	14.0	0	—	—	—	—	—	—	—	—	—	—	—	—	0	93
1933	Bos	12(12, WB)	53	216	4.1	0	4	71	17.8	0	2	0	0.0	0	0.0	0	0	—	—	—	—	1	6	262
1934	Bos	12(11, WB)	34	102	3.0	1	1	9	9.0(9)	0	—	—	—	—	—	—	—	—	—	—	—	—	6	117
1935	Bos	11(9, WB)	16	32	2.0	0	5	60	12.0	0	—	—	—	—	—	—	—	—	—	—	—	—	0	62
1936	†Bos	12(8, WB)	18	80	4.4	0	1	17	17.0(17)	0	—	—	—	—	—	—	—	—	—	—	—	—	0	89
1937	†Was	11(10, WB)	2	10	5.0	0	10	145	14.5	1	—	—	—	—	—	—	—	—	—	—	—	—	6	88
1938	Was✧	9(7, WB)	3	7	2.3	0	3	20	6.7	0	—	—	—	—	—	—	—	—	—	—	—	—	0	17
1939	Was✧	10(9, BB)	5	17	3.4	0	—	—	—	—	—	—	—	—	—	—	—	—	—	—	—	—	0	17
1940	†Was	11(0)	—	—	—	—	2	27	13.5	0	—	—	—	—	—	—	—	—	—	—	i	—	0	30
NFL	9	97(72)	147	536	3.6	1	29	391	13.5(17)	1	2	0	0.0	0	0.0	0	0	—	—	—	i	1	18	773

Pincura, Stan Stanley, BB, 5´11˝/175 lbs; Ohio State; B5/2/1913 Lorain, OH, D2/13/1979 Lorain, OH

YEAR	TEAM	G (GS, POS)	RUSH	YD	AVG (LG)	TD	REC	YD	AVG (LG)	TD	PASS	COMP	PCT	YD	AVG (LG)	TD	INT	SK	YD	QBR	KPR	OTD	PTS	TAY
1937	Cle	11(7, BB)	5	-22	-4.4	0	12	139	11.6	0	27	9	33.3	92	3.4	0	3	—	—	—	—	—	0	-27
1938	Cle	11(1)	2	-6	-3.0	0	6	72	12.0	1	33	13	39.4	240	7.3	1	7	—	—	—	—	—	6	-120
NFL	2	22(8)	7	-28	-4.0	0	18	211	11.7	1	60	22	36.7	332	5.5	1	10	—	—	—	—	—	6	-147

Pinder, Cyril Cyril Calvin, RB, 6´2˝/210 lbs; Illinois; 1968: Phi, rnd 2; B11/13/1946 Fort Lauderdale, FL

YEAR	TEAM	G (GS, POS)	RUSH	YD	AVG (LG)	TD	REC	YD	AVG (LG)	TD	PASS	COMP	PCT	YD	AVG (LG)	TD	INT	SK	YD	QBR	KPR	OTD	PTS	TAY
1968	Phi	14(fb)	40	117	2.9(21)	0	16	166	10.4(48)	0	—	—	—	—	—	—	—	—	—	—	—	—	0	200
1969	Phi	14	60	309	5.2(50)	1	12	77	6.4(20)	0	—	—	—	—	—	—	—	—	—	—	k	—	6	354
1970	Phi	14(RB)	166	657	4.0(40)	2	28	249	8.9(27)	0	—	—	—	—	—	—	—	—	—	—	—	—	12	802
1971	ChiB	12	63	311	4.9(40)	1	10	51	5.1(14)	0	—	—	—	—	—	—	—	—	—	—	—	—	6	347
1972	ChiB	13(RB)	87	300	3.4(19)	3	1	13	13.0(13)	0	—	—	—	—	—	—	—	—	—	—	k	—	18	336
1973	Dal	5	12	15	1.3(5)	0	—	—	—	—	—	—	—	—	—	—	—	—	—	—	—	—	0	15
NFL	6	72	428	1709	4.0(50)	7	67	556	8.3(48)	0	—	—	—	—	—	—	—	—	—	—	k	—	42	2052

Pine, Ed Edward Harry, LB, 6´4˝/235 lbs; Utah; 1962: SF, rnd 2/Oak, rnd 3; B7/13/1940 Reno, NV **1962** SF 14 (13, LLB) **1963** SF 14 (14, LLB) **1964** SF 14 **1965** Pit 8 **NFL** 50 (27) [4 yrs]

Pingel, Johnny John Spencer, TB-QB-HB, 6´0˝/176 lbs; Michigan State; 1939: Det, rnd 1; B11/6/1916 Mount Clemens, MI, D8/14/1999 Palm Beach Gardens, FL

YEAR	TEAM	G (GS, POS)	RUSH	YD	AVG (LG)	TD	REC	YD	AVG (LG)	TD	PASS	COMP	PCT	YD	AVG (LG)	TD	INT	SK	YD	QBR	KPR	OTD	PTS	TAY
1939	Det	9(8, tb)	74	301	4.1	1	—	—	—	—	48	27	56.3	343	7.1	3	4	—	—	—	P	—	6	338

Pinkett, Allen Allen Jerome, RB, 5´9˝/190 lbs; Notre Dame; 1986: Hou, rnd 3; B1/25/1964 Washington, DC **[R]**

YEAR	TEAM	G (GS, POS)	RUSH	YD	AVG (LG)	TD	REC	YD	AVG (LG)	TD	PASS	COMP	PCT	YD	AVG (LG)	TD	INT	SK	YD	QBR	KPR	OTD	PTS	TAY
1986	Hou	16(3)	77	225	2.9(14)	2	35	248	7.1(20)	1	—	—	—	—	—	—	—	—	—	—	kp	—	18	497
1987	†Hou	8(0)	31	149	4.8(22)	2	1	7	7.0(7)	0	—	—	—	—	—	—	—	—	—	—	k	—	12	240
1988	†Hou	16(2)	122	513	4.2(27)	7	12	114	9.5(51)	2	—	—	—	—	—	—	—	—	—	—	k	—	54	682
1989	†Hou	16(6, rb)	94	449	4.8(60)	1	31	239	7.7(23)	1	—	—	—	—	—	—	—	—	—	—	—	—	12	584
1990	†Hou	15(0)	66	268	4.1(19)	0	11	85	7.7(38)	0	—	—	—	—	—	—	—	—	—	—	k	—	0	342
1991	†Hou	16(16, RB)	171	720	4.2(32)	9	29	228	7.9(36)	1	—	—	—	—	—	—	—	—	—	—	k	—	60	1047
NFL	6	87(27)	561	2324	4.1(60)	21	119	921	7.7(51)	5	—	—	—	—	—	—	—	—	—	—	kp	—	156	3391

Pinkney, Cleveland Cleveland, DT, 6´1˝/300 lbs; South Carolina; B9/14/1977 Sumter, SC **2003** TB 4 (0) **2004** Atl 3 (0) **2004** Car 2 (0) **NFL** 9 (0) [2 yrs]

Pinkney, Lovell Lovell, TE, 6´4˝/248 lbs; Texas; 1995: SL, rnd 4; B8/18/1972 Washington, DC

YEAR	TEAM	G (GS, POS)	RUSH	YD	AVG (LG)	TD	REC	YD	AVG (LG)	TD	PASS	COMP	PCT	YD	AVG (LG)	TD	INT	SK	YD	QBR	KPR	OTD	PTS	TAY
1995	SL	8(0)	—	—	—	—	1	13	13.0(13)	0	—	—	—	—	—	—	—	—	—	—	k	—	0	18

Pinkney, Reggie Vernon Reginald, DB, 5´11˝/190 lbs; East Carolina; 1977: Det, rnd 6; B5/27/1955 St. Louis, MA **1977** Det 11 (1) **1978** Det 13 **1979** Bal 16 (1) **1980** Bal 16 (1) **1981** Bal 16 (3) **NFL** 72 (6) [5 yrs]

Pinkston, Todd Todd, WR, 6´2˝/174 lbs; Southern Mississippi; 2000: Phi, rnd 2; B4/23/1977 Forest, MS

YEAR	TEAM	G (GS, POS)	RUSH	YD	AVG (LG)	TD	REC	YD	AVG (LG)	TD	PASS	COMP	PCT	YD	AVG (LG)	TD	INT	SK	YD	QBR	KPR	OTD	PTS	TAY
2000	†Phi	16(1)	—	—	—	—	10	181	18.1(45)	0	—	—	—	—	—	—	—	—	—	—	—	—	0	91
2001	†Phi	15(15, WR)	1	5	5.0(5)	0	42	586	14.0(62)	4	—	—	—	—	—	—	—	—	—	—	—	—	24	318
2002	†Phi	15(15, WR)	1	-15	-15.0(-15)	0	60	798	13.3(42)	7	—	—	—	—	—	—	—	—	—	—	—	—	42	419
2003	†Phi	16(15, WR)	1	-11	-11.0(-11)	0	36	575	16.0(59)	2	—	—	—	—	—	—	—	—	—	—	—	—	12	287
2004	†Phi	16(16, WR)	—	—	—	—	36	676	**18.8**(**80**)	1	—	—	—	—	—	—	—	—	—	—	—	—	6	343
NFL	5	78(62)	3	-21	-7.0(5)	0	184	2816	15.3(80)	14	—	—	—	—	—	—	—	—	—	—	—	—	84	1457

Pinner, Artose Artose Deonce, RB, 5´10˝/229 lbs; Kentucky; 2003: Det, rnd 4; B1/5/1978 Hopkinsville, KY

YEAR	TEAM	G (GS, POS)	RUSH	YD	AVG (LG)	TD	REC	YD	AVG (LG)	TD	PASS	COMP	PCT	YD	AVG (LG)	TD	INT	SK	YD	QBR	KPR	OTD	PTS	TAY
2003	Det	3(2)	39	99	2.5(12)	0	5	40	8.0(21)	0	—	—	—	—	—	—	—	—	—	—	—	—	0	119
2004	Det	9(2)	57	174	3.1(14)	2	11	72	6.5(26)	0	—	—	—	—	—	—	—	—	—	—	—	—	12	230
2005	Det	16(2)	106	349	3.3(19)	3	21	181	8.6(24)	0	—	—	—	—	—	—	—	—	—	—	—	—	18	470
NFL	3	28(6)	202	622	3.1(19)	5	37	293	7.9(26)	0	—	—	—	—	—	—	—	—	—	—	—	—	30	819

Pinney, Ray Raymond Earl, T-G-C, 6´4˝/251 lbs; Washington; 1976: Pit, rnd 2; B6/29/1954 Seattle, WA **1976**†Pit 14 (1) **1977**†Pit 14 **1978**†Pit 13 (11, RT) **1980** Pit 16 (16, LG) **1985** Pit 15 (11, LT) **1986** Pit 16 (15, LT) **1987** Pit 12 (6, LT)

YEAR	TEAM	G (GS, POS)	RUSH	YD	AVG (LG)	TD	REC	YD	AVG (LG)	TD	PASS	COMP	PCT	YD	AVG (LG)	TD	INT	SK	YD	QBR	KPR	OTD	PTS	TAY
1981	Pit	16(11, LT)	—	—	—	—	1	1	1.0(1)	1	—	—	—	—	—	—	—	—	—	—	—	—	6	6
1982	†Pit	9(9, LT)	—	—	—	—	1	3	3.0(3)	1	—	—	—	—	—	—	—	—	—	—	—	—	6	7
NFL	9	125(80)	—	—	—	—	2	4	2.0(3)	2	—	—	—	—	—	—	—	—	—	—	—	—	12	12

Pinnock, Andrew Andrew, FB, 5´10˝/260 lbs; South Carolina; 2003: SD, rnd 7; B3/12/1980 Hartford, CT

YEAR	TEAM	G (GS, POS)	RUSH	YD	AVG (LG)	TD	REC	YD	AVG (LG)	TD	PASS	COMP	PCT	YD	AVG (LG)	TD	INT	SK	YD	QBR	KPR	OTD	PTS	TAY
2003	SD	16(0)	—	—	—	—	—	—	—	—	—	—	—	—	—	—	—	—	—	—	k	—	0	20
2004	SD	1(0)	9	26	2.9(11)	0	3	26	8.7(14)	0	—	—	—	—	—	—	—	—	—	—	—	—	0	39
2005	SD	11(0)	1	4	4.0(4)	0	—	—	—	—	—	—	—	—	—	—	—	—	—	—	k	—	0	13
NFL	3	28(0)	10	30	3.0(11)	0	3	26	8.7(14)	0	—	—	—	—	—	—	—	—	—	—	k	—	0	72

Piper, Scott Scott Cameron, WR, 6´1˝/180 lbs; Arizona; 1976: Buf, rnd 6; B6/18/1954 Philadelphia, PA **1976** Atl 13

YEAR	TEAM	G (GS, POS)	RUSH	YD	AVG(LG)	TD	REC	YD	AVG(LG)	TD	PASS COMP	PCT	YD	AVG(LG)	TD	INT	SK	YD	QBR	KPR	OTD	PTS	TAY

PIPKIN, JOYCE Joyce Clarence, E-DE-BB, 6´1˝/204 lbs; Arkansas; B1/9/1924 Lono, AR   **1949** LAD-A 11 (0)

| 1948 | NYG | 8(0) | | | | | 2 | 28 | 14.0(17) | 0 | — | — | — | — | — | — | — | — | — | — | — | — | 0 | 14 |

PIPPENS, JERRELL Jerrell, DB, 6´2˝/195 lbs; Nebraska; B6/30/1980 Philadelphia, PA   **2004** SD 7 (0) **2004** ChiB 2 (0) **2005** SD 2 (0) **NFL** 11 (0) [2 yrs]

PIPPENS, WOODIE A. Woodrow, RB, 5´11˝/225 lbs; Thiel; B2/7/1963 Cleveland, OH

| 1987 | KC | 2(0) | 3 | 16 | 5.3(11) | 0 | 2 | 12 | 6.0(7) | 0 | — | — | — | — | — | — | — | — | — | — | — | — | 0 | 22 |

PIRO, HANK Henry William, E, 6´0˝/186 lbs; Syracuse; B12/20/1917 Northoltz, Germany

| 1941 | Phi | 10(1) | | | | | 10 | 141 | 14.1(26) | 1 | — | — | — | — | — | — | — | — | — | — | ki | — | 6 | 89 |

PIRRO, ROCCO Rocco A., G-B-T, 6´0˝/226 lbs; Catholic; 1940: Pit, rnd 12; B6/30/1916 Syracuse, NY, D1/26/1995 Solvay, NY   **1940** Pit 9 (0)

| 1941 | Pit | 11(1) | 1 | 1 | 1.0(1) | 0 | 2 | 31 | 15.5(19) | 0 | — | — | — | — | — | — | — | — | — | — | i | — | 0 | 14 |
| NFL | 2 | 20(1) | 1 | 1 | 1.0(1) | 0 | 2 | 31 | 15.5(19) | 0 | — | — | — | — | — | — | — | — | — | — | — | — | 0 | 17 |

1946 Buf-A 13 (11, RG) **1947** Buf-A 13 (12, RG) **1948**†Buf-A 14 (14, RG) **1949**†Buf-A 11 (11, RG) **AAFC** 20 (1) [2 yrs]

PISARCIK, JOE Joseph Anthony, QB, 6´4˝/220 lbs; New Mexico State; B7/2/1952 Kingston, PA

1977	NYG	13(11, QB)	27	57	2.1(14)	2	—	—	—	—	241	103	42.7	1346	5.6(82)	4	14	32	262	42.3	—	—	12	210
1978	NYG	15(12, QB)	17	68	4.0(11)	1	—	—	—	—	301	143	47.5	2096	7.0(67)	12	23	28	205	52.1	—	—	6	266
1979	NYG	4(4)	1	6	6.0(6)	0	—	—	—	—	108	43	39.8	537	5.0(48)	2	6	17	123	—	—	—	0	45
1980	Phi	9(0)	3	-3	-1.0(0)	0	—	—	—	—	22	15	68.2	187	8.5(46)	0	0	5	34	—	—	—	0	91
1981	Phi	7(0)	7	1	0.1(10)	0	—	—	—	—	15	8	53.3	154	10.3(44)	2	2	1	8	—	—	—	0	8
1982	Phi	1(0)	—	—	—	—	—	—	—	—	1	1	100.0	24	24.0(24)	0	0	—	—	—	—	—	0	12
1983	Phi	5(0)	3	-1	-0.3(0)	0	—	—	—	—	34	16	47.1	172	5.1(33)	1	0	.4	30	—	—	—	0	90
1984	Phi	7(3, qb)	7	19	2.7(16)	2	—	—	—	—	176	96	54.5	1036	5.9(40)	3	3	25	183	—	—	—	12	452
NFL	8	61(30)	65	147	2.3(16)	5	—	—	—	—	898	425	47.3	5552	6.2(82)	24	48	112	845	53.9	—	—	30	1173

PISARKIEWICZ, STEVE Stephen John, QB, 6´2˝/205 lbs; Missouri; 1977: SL, rnd 1; B11/10/1953 Florissant, MO

1978	SL	3	5	-1	-0.2(1)	0	—	—	—	—	29	10	34.5	164	5.7(40)	0	3	2	20	—	—	—	0	-39
1979	SL	6	11	20	1.8(12)	0	—	—	—	—	109	52	47.7	621	5.7(39)	3	4	14	85	—	—	—	0	186
1980	GB	1(0)	—	—	—	—	—	—	—	—	5	2	40.0	19	3.8(16)	0	0	1	7	—	—	—	0	10
NFL	3	10	16	19	1.2(12)	0	—	—	—	—	143	64	44.8	804	5.6(78)	3	7	17	112	—	—	—	0	156

PISKOR, ROMAN Roman J., G-T, 6´0˝/245 lbs; Niagara; B8/9/1917 North Tonawanda, NY, D8/1981 North Tonawanda, NY   **1946** NYY-A 12 (7, LG) **1947**†Cle-A 10 (1)
1948 ChiR-A 12 (2) **AAFC** 34 (10) [3 yrs]

PITCOCK, CHUCK Charles Clayton, C, 6´4˝/272 lbs; Tulane; B2/20/1958 Homestead, FL   **1987** TB 2 (2)

PITTMAN, BRYAN Bryan, C, 6´4˝/255 lbs; Washington; B1/20/1977 Tacoma, WA   **2003** Hou 16 (0) **2004** Hou 16 (0) **2005** Hou 16 (0) **NFL** 48 (0) [3 yrs]

PITTMAN, CHARLIE Charles Vernon, RB, 6´1˝/200 lbs; Penn State; 1970: SL, rnd 3; B1/22/1948 Baltimore, MD

1970	SL	8	2	4	2.0(2)	0	—	—	—	—	—	—	—	—	—	—	—	—	—	—	k	—	0	91
1971	†Bal	10	2	3	1.5(3)	0	—	—	—	—	—	—	—	—	—	—	—	—	—	—	k	—	0	123
NFL	2	18	4	7	1.8(3)	0	—	—	—	—	—	—	—	—	—	—	—	—	—	—	k	—	0	214

PITTMAN, DANNY Danny Ray, WR, 6´2˝/205 lbs; Wyoming; 1980: NYG, rnd 4; B4/3/1958 Memphis, TN

1980	NYG	11(7, WR)	1	-7	-7.0(-7)	0	25	308	12.3(22)	0	—	—	—	—	—	—	—	—	—	—	k	—	0	158
1981	†NYG	8(0)	—	—	—	—	1	8	8.0(8)	0	—	—	—	—	—	—	—	—	—	—	kp	—	0	56
1982	NYG	8(0)	—	—	—	—	1	21	21.0(21)	0	—	—	—	—	—	—	—	—	—	—	kp	—	0	63
1983	NYG	8(0)	—	—	—	—	7	154	22.0(40)	1	—	—	—	—	—	—	—	—	—	—	kp	—	6	99
1983	SL	4(0)	—	—	—	—	2	21	10.5(11)	0	—	—	—	—	—	—	—	—	—	—	kp	—	0	11
1984	SL	10(0)	—	—	—	—	10	145	14.5(50)	0	—	—	—	—	—	—	—	—	—	—	kp	—	0	172
NFL	5	49(7)	1	-7	-7.0(-7)	0	46	657	14.3(50)	1	—	—	—	—	—	—	—	—	—	—	kp	—	6	558

PITTMAN, JULIAN Julian, DE, 6´4˝/286 lbs; Florida State; 1998: NO, rnd 4; B4/22/1975 Niceville, FL   **1998** NO 2 (0)

PITTMAN, KAVIKA Kavika Charles, DE, 6´6˝/273 lbs; McNeese State; 1996: Dal, rnd 2; B10/9/1974 Frankfurt, Germany   **1996**†Dal 15 (0) **1997** Dal 15 (0) **1998** Dal 15 (15, LDE)
1999†Dal 16 (16, LDE) **2000**†Den 15 (15, RDE) **2001** Den 14 (14, RDE) **2002** Den 16 (15, RDE) **2003** Car 2 (0) **NFL** 108 (75) [8 yrs]

PITTMAN, MICHAEL Michael, RB, 6´0˝/218 lbs; Fresno State; 1998: Arz, rnd 4; B8/14/1975 New Orleans, LA

1998	†Arz	15(0)	29	91	3.1(11)	0	—	—	—	—	—	—	—	—	—	—	—	—	—	—	k	—	0	115
1999	Arz	10(2)	64	289	4.5(58)	2	16	196	12.3(46)	0	1	1	100.0	26	26.0(26)	0	0	—	—	—	kp	—	12	417
2000	Arz	16(11, RB)	184	719	3.9(29)	4	73	579	7.9(36)	2	—	—	—	—	—	—	—	—	—	—	—	—	36	699
2001	Arz	15(14, RB)	241	846	3.5(42)	5	42	264	6.3(27)	0	—	—	—	—	—	—	—	—	—	—	k	—	30	1099
2002	†TB	16(15, RB)	204	718	3.5(21)	1	59	477	8.1(64)	0	—	—	—	—	—	—	—	—	—	—	—	—	6	967
2003	TB	16(13, RB)	187	751	4.0(17)	0	75	597	8.0(68)	2	—	—	—	—	—	—	—	—	—	—	—	—	12	1060
2004	TB	13(13, RB)	219	926	4.2(78)	7	41	391	9.5(68)	3	—	—	—	—	—	—	—	—	—	—	—	—	60	1207
2005	†TB	16(4)	70	436	6.2(64)	1	36	300	8.3(41)	1	—	—	—	—	—	—	—	—	—	—	k	—	12	641
NFL	8	117(72)	1198	4776	4.0(78)	20	342	2804	8.2(68)	8	1	1	100.0	26	26.0(26)	0	0	—	—	—	kp	—	168	6563

PITTMAN, RALPH Ralph Dale, BB-WB, 5´10˝/200 lbs; Baylor; B12/23/1901 DeLeon, TX, D7/5/1977 DeLeon, TX   **1926** Buf 5 (4)

PITTMAN, SWEDE Melvin Osroe, C-LB, 6´0˝/215 lbs; Hardin-Simmons; B2/23/1906 Abilene, TX, D12/24/1975 Ennis, TX   **1935** Pit 2 (0)

PITTS, ALABAMA Edwin Collins, HB, 5´10˝/185 lbs; none; B1908 Opelika, AL, D6/7/1941 Valdese, NC

| 1935 | Phi | 3(0) | — | — | — | — | 2 | 21 | 10.5 | — | — | — | — | — | — | — | — | — | — | — | — | — | 0 | 11 |

PITTS, CHESTER Chester Morise, T-G, 6´4˝/320 lbs; San Diego State; 2002: Hou, rnd 2; B6/26/1979 Inglewood, CA   **2002** Hou 16 (16, LT) **2003** Hou 16 (16, LT)
2004 Hou 16 (16, LG) **2005** Hou 16 (16, LT) **NFL** 64 (64) [4 yrs]

PITTS, ELIJAH Elijah Eugene, HB, 6´1˝/204 lbs; Philander Smith; 1961: GB, rnd 13; B2/3/1938 Mayflower, AR, D7/10/1998 Buffalo, NY **[R]**

1961	†GB	14	23	75	3.3(17)	1	1	5	5.0(5)	0	—	—	—	—	—	—	—	—	—	—	k	—	6	87
1962	†GB	14	22	110	5.0(28)	2	3	44	14.7(29)	0	2	0	0.0	0	0.0	0	0	—	—	—	p	—	12	134
1963	GB	14	54	212	3.9(34)	5	9	54	6.0(21)	1	2	2	100.0	41	20.5(21)	1	0	—	—	—	p	—	36	345
1964	GB	14	27	127	4.7(27)	1	6	38	6.3(22)	0	—	—	—	—	—	—	—	—	—	—	p	1	12	282
1965	†GB	14(1)	54	122	2.3(12)	4	11	182	16.5(80)	1	2	1	50.0	51	25.5(51)	0	0	—	—	—	kp	—	30	367
1966	†GB	14(hb)	115	393	3.4(20)	7	26	460	17.7(80)	3	2	0	0.0	0	0.0	0	0	—	—	—	kp	—	60	667
1967	GB	8(HB)	77	247	3.2(30)	6	15	210	14.0(84)	0	1	1	100.0	21	21.0(21)	0	0	—	—	—	p	—	36	394
1968	GB	14	72	264	3.7(14)	2	17	142	8.4(19)	0	—	—	—	—	—	—	—	—	—	—	kp	—	12	361
1969	GB	14	35	134	3.8(13)	0	9	47	5.2(21)	1	—	—	—	—	—	—	—	—	—	—	kp	—	6	150
1970	LARm	2	3	8	2.7(3)	0	—	—	—	—	—	—	—	—	—	—	—	—	—	—	k	—	0	8
1970	NO	6	32	96	3.0(11)	0	7	63	9.0(12)	0	—	—	—	—	—	—	—	—	—	—	k	—	0	135
1971	GB	6	—	—	—	—	—	—	—	—	—	—	—	—	—	—	—	—	—	—	—	—	0	-1
NFL	11	134(1)	514	1788	3.5(34)	28	104	1245	12.0(84)	6	9	4	44.4	113	12.6(51)	1	0	—	—	—	kp	1	210	2926

PITTS, FRANK Frank H., WR-SE, 6´3˝/199 lbs; Southern (LA); 1965: KC, rnd 4/Chi, rnd 16; B11/12/1943 Atlanta, GA

1965	KC-A	7	—	—	—	—	1	11	11.0(11)	0	—	—	—	—	—	—	—	—	—	—	kp	—	0	30
1966	†KC-A	14	—	—	—	—	1	11	11.0(11)	0	—	—	—	—	—	—	—	—	—	—	—	1	6	44
1967	KC-A	14	3	19	6.3(15)	1	4	131	32.8(59)	1	—	—	—	—	—	—	—	—	—	—	—	—	12	109
1968	†KC-A	13(SE)	11	107	9.7(28)	0	30	655	21.8(90)	6	—	—	—	—	—	—	—	—	—	—	—	—	36	465
1969	†KC-A	14(SE)	5	28	5.6(11)	0	31	470	15.2(51)	2	—	—	—	—	—	—	—	—	—	—	—	—	12	273
1970	KC	12(WR)	5	84	16.8(42)	0	11	172	15.6(54)	2	—	—	—	—	—	—	—	—	—	—	—	—	12	180
1971	†Cle	13(wr)	—	—	—	—	27	487	18.0(53)	4	—	—	—	—	—	—	—	—	—	—	k	—	24	367
1972	†Cle	14(WR)	3	29	9.7(13)	0	36	620	17.2(80)	4	—	—	—	—	—	—	—	—	—	—	—	—	48	379
1973	Cle	13(WR)	—	—	—	—	31	317	10.2(51)	4	—	—	—	—	—	—	—	—	—	—	—	—	24	179
1974	†Oak	13	1	-10	-10.0(-10)	0	3	23	7.7(11)	0	—	—	—	—	—	—	—	—	—	—	—	—	0	2
NFL	10	127	28	257	9.2(42)	1	175	2897	16.6(90)	27	—	—	—	—	—	—	—	—	—	—	kp	1	174	2025

YEAR	TEAM	G (GS, POS)	RUSH	YD	AVG(LG)	TD	REC	YD	AVG(LG)	TD	PASS COMP	PCT	YD	AVG(LG)	TD	INT	SK	YD	QBR	KPR	OTD	PTS	TAY

PITTS, HUGH Hugh Lynn, LB-C, 6´2˝/223 lbs; TCU; 1956: LA, rnd 2; B4/8/1934 Woodville, TX **1956** LARm 9 (LLB) **1960**†Hou-A 12 (c) **NFL** 21 [2 yrs]

PITTS, JOHN John Martin, DB, 6´4˝/218 lbs; Arizona State; 1967: Buf, rnd 1; B2/28/1945 Birmingham, AL **1967** Buf-A 14 **1968** Buf-A 14 (7, ls) **1969** Buf-A 14 (LS) **1970** Buf 14 (SS) **1971** Buf 14 (SS) **1972** Buf 14 (FS) **1973** Buf 3 **1973** Den 7 **1974** Den 14 (4) **1975** Den 1 **1975** Cle 6 **NFL** 115 (11) [9 yrs]

PITTS, MIKE Michael Anthony, DT-DE, 6´5˝/277 lbs; Alabama; 1983: Atl, rnd 1; B9/25/1960 Baltimore, MD **1983** Atl 16 (4) **1984** Atl 14 (13, LDE) **1985** Atl 16 (16, LDT) **1986** Atl 16 (0) **1987** Phi 12 (6, rdt) **1988**†Phi 16 (16, LDT) **1989**†Phi 16 (16, LDT) **1990**†Phi 4 (3) **1991** Phi 16 (15, LDT) **1992**†Phi 11 (3) **1993** NE 16 (15, LDE) **1994**†NE 16 (16, LDE) **NFL** 169 (123) [12 yrs]

PITTS, RON Ronald Dewayne, DB, 5´10˝/175 lbs; UCLA; 1985: Buf, rnd 7; B10/14/1962 Detroit, MI **1986** Buf 10 (0) **1987** Buf 12 (3) **1988** GB 14 (1) **1989** GB 14 (2) **1990** GB 16 (0) **NFL** 66 (6) [5 yrs]

PIVARNIK, JOE Joseph John, G, 5´9˝/217 lbs; Notre Dame; B2/18/1912 Bridgeport, CT, D1/22/1976 Middletown, CT **1936** Phi 6 (0)

PIVEC, DAVE David John, TE, 6´3˝/240 lbs; Notre Dame; 1965: Chi, rnd 14; B9/25/1943 Baltimore, MD

1966	LARm	3	—	—	—	—	—	—	—	—	—	—	—	—	—	—	—	—	—	—	—	—	—	—
1967	†LARm	14	—	—	—	—	2	2	1.0(2)	1	—	—	—	—	—	—	—	—	—	—	—	—	6	6
1968	LARm	14	—	—	—	—	3	27	9.0(12)	0	—	—	—	—	—	—	—	—	—	—	k	—	2	-17
1969	Den-A	14 (5, te)	—	—	—	—	9	117	13.0(18)	0	—	—	—	—	—	—	—	—	—	—	—	—	0	59
NFL		4	45 (5)	—	—	—	—	14	146	10.4(18)	1	—	—	—	—	—	—	—	—	—	k	—	8	48

PLANANSKY, JOE Joe, TE, 6´4˝/254 lbs; Chadron State (NE); B10/21/1971 Hemingford, NE **1995** Mia 2 (0)

PLANK, DOUG Douglas Michael, DB, 6´0˝/200 lbs; Ohio State; 1975: Chi, rnd 12; B3/4/1953 Greensburg, PA **1975** ChiB 14 (14, SS) **1976** ChiB 14 (14, SS) **1977**†ChiB 11 (11, FS) **1978** ChiB 14 (FS) **1979**†ChiB 16 (16, FS) **1980** ChiB 15 (15, FS) **1981** ChiB 16 (12, FS) **1982** ChiB 1 (1) **NFL** 101 (83) [8 yrs]

PLANK, EARL Earl A., E, /174 lbs; none; B7/28/1905 Columbus, OH, D9/30/1952 Bellefontaine, OH **1926** Col 1 (0) **1929** Buf 2 (1) **1930** Bkn 7 (3) **NFL** 10 (4) [3 yrs]

PLANSKY, TONY Anthony Joseph, B, 6´2˝/215 lbs; Georgetown (DC); B6/20/1900 South Boston, MA, D2/10/1979 North Adams, MA **[K]** **1928** NYG 6 (3), 6 **1929** NYG☆11 (9, FB), 62 **1932** Bos 1 (1) **NFL** 18 (13), 68 [3 yrs]

PLANTZ, RON Ronald Anthony, C, 6´4˝/272 lbs; Notre Dame; B7/27/1964 Chicago, IL **1987** Ind 3 (3)

PLANUTIS, JERRY Gerald Robert, HB, 5´9˝/175 lbs; Michigan State; 1956: Was, rnd 12; B5/18/1930 Detroit, MI

| 1956 | Was | 3 | 2 | 6 | 3.0(3) | 0 | 1 | 5 | 5.0(5) | 0 | — | — | — | — | — | — | — | — | — | — | — | — | 0 | 9 |

PLASMAN, DICK Herbert G., E-T, 6´3˝/218 lbs; Vanderbilt; 1937: ChiB, rnd 3; B4/6/1914 Metcalf, AZ, D6/20/1981 Naples, FL **[K]**

1937	†ChiB	9 (2)	—	—	—	—	3	18	6.0	1	—	—	—	—	—	—	—	—	—	K	—	8	14
1938	ChiB	8 (6, LE)	—	—	—	—	8	117	14.6	1	—	—	—	—	—	—	—	—	—	K	—	6	64
1939	ChiB☆	11 (3)	—	—	—	—	19	403	21.2	3	1	0	0	0	0.0	0	0	—	—	K	—	21	217
1940	†ChiB◇	11 (8, LE)	—	—	—	—	11	245	22.3	0	—	—	—	—	—	—	—	—	—	K	—	15	133
1941	†ChiB★	10 (5, LE)	1	1	1.0(1)	0	14	283	20.2(42)	2	—	—	—	—	—	—	—	—	—	K	—	6	143
1944	ChiB	3 (0)	—	—	—	—	1	17	17.0(17)	0	—	—	—	—	—	—	—	—	—	k	—	0	-8
1946	ChiC	3 (0)	—	—	—	—	—	—	—	—	—	—	—	—	—	—	—	—	—	—	—	—	—	—
1947	†ChiC	4 (1)	—	—	—	—	—	—	—	—	—	—	—	—	—	—	—	—	—	—	—	—	—	—
NFL		8	59 (25)	1	1	1.0(1)	0	56	1083	19.3(42)	7	1	0	0	0	0.0	0	0	—	—	Kk	—	56	562

PLATUKIS, GEORGE George Paul, E-DE, 6´0˝/196 lbs; Duquesne; 1938: Pit, rnd 6; B3/15/1915 West Hazleton, PA, D5/17/1973 Benton, PA

1938	Pit	5 (2)	3	6	2.0	0	4	82	20.5	0	—	—	—	—	—	—	—	—	—	—	—	—	0	47
1939	Pit	11 (6, LE)	—	—	—	—	7	170	24.3(63)	3	—	—	—	—	—	—	—	—	—	—	—	—	18	100
1940	Pit	11 (11, LE)	—	—	—	—	15	290	19.3(45)	2	—	—	—	—	—	—	—	—	—	—	—	—	12	155
1941	Pit	11 (7, LE)	—	—	—	—	2	15	7.5(11)	0	—	—	—	—	—	—	—	—	—	—	—	—	0	8
1942	Cle	9 (2)	—	—	—	—	5	64	12.8(22)	1	—	—	—	—	—	—	—	—	—	i	—	1	12	44
NFL		5	47 (28)	3	6	2.0	0	33	621	18.8(63)	6	—	—	—	—	—	—	—	—	—	i	—	1	42	354

PLAYER, SCOTT Scott Darwin, P, 6´1˝/213 lbs; Flager; Florida State; B12/17/1969 St. Augustine, FL **[P]** **1998**†Arz 16 (0) **2003** Arz 16 (0) **2004** Arz 16 (0) **2005** Arz 16 (0)

1999	Arz	16 (0)	1	-18	-18.0(-18)	0	—	—	—	—	—	—	—	—	—	—	—	—	—	P	—	0	-18
2000	Arz★	16 (0)	1	-11	-11.0(-11)	0	—	—	—	—	—	—	—	—	—	—	—	—	—	P	—	0	-11
2001	Arz	12 (0)	1	0	0.0(0)	0	—	—	—	—	—	—	—	—	—	—	—	—	—	P	—	0	0
2002	Arz	16 (0)	1	0	0.0(0)	0	—	—	—	—	—	—	—	—	—	—	—	—	—	P	—	0	0
NFL		8	124 (0)	4	-29	-7.3	0	—	—	—	—	—	—	—	—	—	—	—	—	P	—	0	-29

PLEASANT, ANTHONY Anthony Devon, DE-DT, 6´5˝/280 lbs; Tennessee State; 1990: Cle, rnd 3; B1/27/1968 Century, FL **[S]** **1990** Cle 16 (7, rde) **1991** Cle 16 (7, RDE) **1992** Cle 16 (14, RDE) **1993** Cle 16 (14, RDE) **1994**†Cle 14 (14, RDE) **1995** Cle 16 (16, RDE) **1996** Bal 12 (12, RDE) **1997** Atl 11 (0) **1998**†NYJ 16 (15, RDE) **1999** NYJ 16 (16, RDE) **2000** SF 16 (16, LDE) **2001**†NE 16 (16, RDT) **2002** NE 14 (11, RDT) **2003** NE 7 (0) **NFL** 202 (157) [14 yrs]

PLEASANT, MARQUIS Marquis Anthony, WR, 6´2˝/172 lbs; SMU; B6/28/1965 Dallas, TX

| 1987 | Cin | 3 (0) | — | — | — | — | 2 | 45 | 22.5(35) | 0 | — | — | — | — | — | — | — | — | — | — | — | 0 | 23 |

PLEASANT, MIKE Michael Ricardo, WR, 6´2˝/193 lbs; Oklahoma; B8/16/1955 Muskogee, OK **1984**†LARm 5 (0)

PLEASANT, REGGIE Regnald Lecarno, DB, 5´9˝/175 lbs; Clemson; 1985: Atl, rnd 6; B5/2/1962 Sumter, SC **1985** Atl 3 (0)

PLISKA, JOE Joseph Stanley, BB, 5´10˝/185 lbs; Notre Dame; B10/17/1890 Chicago, IL, D8/25/1940 Chicago, IL **1920** Ham 4 (0) **1921** Ham 1 (1) **NFL** 5 (1) [2 yrs]

PLOEGER, KURT Kurt Alan, DE-DT, 6´5˝/259 lbs; Gustavus Adolphus; 1985: Dal, rnd 6; B12/1/1962 Iowa Falls, IA **1986** Dal 3 (0) **1986** GB 1 (0) **1987** Min 1 (1) **NFL** 5 (1) [2 yrs]

PLUM, MILT Milton Ross, QB, 6´1˝/205 lbs; Penn State; 1957: Cle, rnd 2; B1/20/1935 Westville, NJ **[K]**

1957	†Cle	9 (qb)	26	118	4.5(30)	0	—	—	—	—	76	41	53.9	590	7.8(58)	2	5	—	—	—	—	0	223
1958	†Cle	12 (QB)	37	107	2.9(22)	4	—	—	—	—	189	102	54.0	1619	8.6(74)	11	11	—	—	77.9	K	—	26	572
1959	Cle	12 (QB)	21	20	1.0(17)	1	1	20	20.0(20)	0	266	156	58.6	1992	7.5(76)	14	8	—	—	87.2	—	—	6	786
1960	Cle★	12 (QB)	17	-24	-1.4(7)	2	—	—	—	—	250	151	**60.4**	2297	**9.2(86)**	21	5	—	—	**110.4**	—	—	12	1050
1961	Cle◇	14 (QB)	24	-17	-0.7(14)	0	—	—	—	—	302	177	58.6	2416	8.0(77)	18	10	—	—	90.3	—	—	6	891
1962	Det	14 (QB)	29	170	5.9(45)	1	—	—	—	—	325	179	55.1	2378	7.3(80)	15	20	—	—	68.2	K	—	21	644
1963	Det	10	9	26	2.9(13)	0	—	—	—	—	77	27	35.1	339	4.4(39)	2	11	—	—	—	K	—	16	-275
1964	Det	12 (QB)	12	28	2.3(18)	0	—	—	—	—	287	154	53.7	2241	7.8(92)	18	15	—	—	78.5	—	—	6	649
1965	Det	14 (QB)	21	37	1.8(15)	3	—	—	—	—	308	143	46.4	1710	5.6(55)	12	**19**	—	—	51.2	—	—	18	222
1966	Det	6 (6, qb)	12	59	4.9(15)	0	—	—	—	—	146	82	56.2	943	6.5(63)	4	13	—	—	47.8	K	—	1	31
1967	Det	9 (qb)	6	5	0.8(10)	0	—	—	—	—	172	86	50.0	925	5.4(43)	4	8	—	—	54.5	—	—	0	168
1968	LARm	4	2	3	1.5(2)	0	—	—	—	—	12	5	41.7	49	4.1(25)	1	1	—	—	—	—	—	0	-8
1969	NYG	1	1	-1	-1.0(-1)	0	—	—	—	—	9	3	33.3	37	4.1(23)	0	0	1	12	—	—	—	0	18
NFL		13	129 (6)	217	531	2.4(45)	13	1	20	20.0(20)	0	2419	1306	54.0	17536	7.2(92)	122	127	1	12	72.2	K	—	112	4969

PLUMMER, AHMED Ahmed Kamil, DB, 6´0˝/191 lbs; Ohio State; 2000: SF, rnd 1; B3/26/1976 Wyoming, OH **2000** SF 16 (14, LCB) **2001**†SF 15 (15, LCB) **2002**†SF 15 (15, LCB) **2003** SF 15 (15, LCB) **2004** SF 6 (6, LCB) **2005** SF 3 (3) **NFL** 70 (68) [6 yrs]

PLUMMER, BRUCE Bruce Elliott, DB, 6´0˝/190 lbs; Mississippi State; 1987: Den, rnd 9; B9/1/1964 Bogalusa, LA **1987**†Den 11 (0) **1988** Den 8 (0) **1988** Mia 3 (0) **1989** Ind 16 (2) **1990** Den 7 (0) **1990** SF 1 (0) **1991** Phi 6 (0) **NFL** 52 (2) [5 yrs]

PLUMMER, CHAD Chad, WR, 6´2˝/223 lbs; Cincinnati; 1999: Den, rnd 6; B11/30/1975 Delray Beach, FL **1999** Ind 1 (0) **2000** Ind 3 (0) **NFL** 4 (0) [2 yrs]

PLUMMER, GARY Gary Lee, LB, 6´2˝/244 lbs; California; B1/26/1960 Fremont, CA **1986** SD 15 (13, LILB) **1987** SD 8 (7, LILB) **1988** SD 16 (12, RILB) **1991** SD 16 (15, LILB) **1992**†SD 16 (13, MLB) **1993** SD 16 (15, MLB) **1994**†SF 16 (16, MLB) **1995**†SF 16 (15, RLB) **1996** SF 13 (11, RLB) **1997**†SF 16 (16, MLB)

1989	SD	16 (16, LILB)	1	6	6.0(6)	0	—	—	—	—	—	—	—	—	—	—	—	—	—	—	—	0	6
1990	SD	16 (15, LILB)	2	3	1.5(2)	0	1	2	2.0(2)	1	—	—	—	—	—	—	—	—	—	—	—	12	19
NFL		12	180 (164)	3	9	3.0(6)	1	1	2	2.0(2)	1	—	—	—	—	—	—	—	—	—	kiS	—	12	30

PLUMMER, JAKE Jason Steven 'Jake the Snake', QB, 6´2˝/212 lbs; Arizona State; 1997: Arz, rnd 2; B12/19/1974 Boise, ID

1997	Arz	10 (9, QB)	39	216	5.5(31)	2	1	2	2.0(2)	0	296	157	53.0	2203	7.4(70)	15	15	52	291	73.1	—	—	14	814
1998	†Arz	16 (16, QB)	51	217	4.3(27)	4	—	—	—	—	547	324	59.2	3737	6.8(57)	17	20	49	280	75.0	—	—	24	1411
1999	Arz	12 (11, QB)	39	121	3.1(17)	2	—	—	—	—	381	201	52.8	2111	5.5(63)	9	**24**	27	152	50.8	—	—	12	282

YEAR	TEAM	G (GS, POS)	RUSH	YD	AVG (LG)	TD	REC	YD	AVG (LG)	TD	PASS	COMP	PCT	YD	AVG (LG)	TD	INT	SK	YD	QBR	KPR	OTD	PTS	TAY
2000	Arz	14 (14, QB)	37	183	4.9 (24)	0	—	—	—	—	475	270	56.8	2946	6.2 (70)	13	**21**	22	151	—	—	—	0	881
2001	Arz	16 (16, QB)	35	163	4.7 (21)	0	—	—	—	—	525	304	57.9	3653	7.0 (68)	18	14	29	204	79.6	—	—	2	1520
2002	Arz	16 (16, QB)	46	283	6.2 (34)	2	1	2	2.0 (2)	0	530	284	53.6	2972	5.6 (80)	18	20	36	248	65.7	—	—	12	1080
2003	†Den	11 (11, QB)	37	205	5.5 (40)	3	—	—	—	—	302	189	62.6	2182	7.2 (60)	15	7	14	73	91.2	—	—	18	1121
2004	†Den	16 (16, QB)	62	202	3.3 (22)	1	—	—	—	—	521	303	58.2	4089	7.8 (85)	27	**20**	15	90	84.5	—	—	6	1592
2005	†Den✧	16 (16, QB)	46	151	3.3 (22)	2	—	—	—	—	456	277	60.7	3366	7.4 (72)	18	7	22	135	90.2	—	—	12	1664
NFL	9	127 (125)	392	1741	4.4 (40)	16	2	4	2.0 (2)	0	4033	2309	57.3	27259	6.8 (85)	150	148	266	1624	75.1	—	—	100	10363

Plummer, Tony Tony Lamont, DB, 5´11˝/188 lbs; Pacific; 1970: SL, rnd 10; B1/21/1947 Dallas, TX **1970** SL 1 **1971** Atl 7 **1972** Atl 14 **1973** Atl 14 **1974**†LARm 5 **NFL** 41 [5 yrs]

Plump, Dave David, DB, 6´1˝/200 lbs; Fresno State; 1965: SD, rnd R10/SF, rnd 12; B12/13/1942 Vicksburg, MS **1966** SD-A 14

Plumridge, Ted Theodore Earle, C, 6´2˝/205 lbs; Colgate; St. John's (NY); B9/1/1901 Brooklyn, NY, D10/6/1962 Brooklyn, NY **1926** Bkn 2 (2)

Plunkett WB, 5´7˝/160 lbs; none; deceased **1920** ChiC 1 (0)

Plunkett, Art Arthur Scott, T, 6´7˝/269 lbs; UNLV; 1981: LA, rnd 8; B3/8/1959 Chicago, IL **1981** SL 8 (0) **1982**†SL 9 (0) **1983** SL 16 (4) **1984** SL 16 (0) **1985**†NE 15 (0) **1987** NE 7 (1) **NFL** 71 (5) [6 yrs]

Plunkett, Jim James William, QB, 6´3˝/220 lbs; Stanford; 1971: NE, rnd 1; B12/5/1947 San Jose, CA

YEAR	TEAM	G (GS, POS)	RUSH	YD	AVG (LG)	TD	REC	YD	AVG (LG)	TD	PASS	COMP	PCT	YD	AVG (LG)	TD	INT	SK	YD	QBR	KPR	OTD	PTS	TAY
1971	NE	14 (14, QB)	45	210	4.7 (16)	0	—	—	—	—	328	158	48.2	2158	6.6 (88)	19	16	36	319	68.6	—	—	0	744
1972	NE	14 (14, QB)	36	230	6.4 (21)	1	—	—	—	—	355	169	47.6	2196	6.2 (62)	8	25	39	385	45.7	—	—	6	378
1973	NE	14 (14, QB)	44	209	4.8 (20)	5	—	—	—	—	**376**	**193**	51.3	**2550**	6.8 (64)	13	17	37	350	65.8	—	—	30	919
1974	NE	14 (14, QB)	30	161	5.4 (37)	2	—	—	—	—	352	173	49.1	2457	7.0 (69)	19	**22**	21	174	64.1	—	—	12	625
1975	NE	5 (5, qb)	4	7	1.8 (5)	1	—	—	—	—	92	36	39.1	571	6.2 (76)	3	7	13	89	—	—	—	6	38
1976	SF	12 (12, QB)	19	95	5.0 (12)	0	—	—	—	—	243	126	51.9	1592	6.6 (**85**)	13	16	26	249	63.0	—	—	0	316
1977	SF	14 (14, QB)	28	71	2.5 (9)	1	—	—	—	—	248	128	51.6	1693	6.8 (47)	9	14	30	242	62.1	—	—	6	413
1979	Oak	4	3	18	6.0 (15)	0	—	—	—	—	15	7	46.7	89	5.9 (39)	1	1	2	9	—	—	—	0	28
1980	†Oak	13 (11, QB)	28	141	5.0 (17)	2	—	—	—	—	320	165	51.6	2299	7.2 (**86**)	18	16	36	285	72.9	—	—	12	761
1981	Oak	9 (7, qb)	12	38	3.2 (13)	1	—	—	—	—	179	94	52.5	1045	5.8 (42)	4	9	22	184	—	—	—	6	231
1982	†LARd	9 (9, QB)	15	6	0.4 (10)	0	—	—	—	—	261	152	58.2	2035	7.8 (52)	14	15	23	211	77.0	—	—	0	494
1983	†LARd	14 (13, QB)	26	78	3.0 (20)	0	—	—	—	—	379	230	60.7	2935	7.7 (**99**)	20	18	42	363	82.7	—	—	0	926
1984	†LARd	8 (6, qb)	16	14	0.9 (9)	1	—	—	—	—	198	108	54.5	1473	7.4 (73)	6	10	13	103	—	—	—	6	391
1985	LARd	3 (3)	5	12	2.4 (7)	0	—	—	—	—	103	71	68.9	803	7.8 (41)	3	3	13	101	—	—	—	0	309
1986	LARd	10 (8, QB)	12	47	3.9 (11)	0	—	—	—	—	252	133	52.8	1986	7.9 (81)	14	9	27	215	82.5	—	—	0	750
NFL	15	157 (144)	323	1337	4.1 (37)	14	—	—	—	—	3701	1943	52.5	25882	7.0 (99)	164	198	380	3279	67.5	—	—	84	7318

Plunkett, Sherman Sherman Eugene, T, 6´4˝/290 lbs; Maryland-Eastern Shore; 1956: Cle, rnd 6; B4/17/1933 Oklahoma City, OK, D11/18/1989 Baltimore, MD **1958**†Bal 12 **1959**†Bal 12 **1960** Bal 12 **1961**†SD-A 12 **1962** SD-A 14 (RT) **1963** NYJ-A 14 (RT) **1964** NYJ-A✧14 (RT) **1965** NYJ-A☆14 (RT) **1966** NYJ-A★14 (RT) **1967** NYJ-A☆14 (RT) **NFL** 132 [10 yrs]

Plunkett, Warren Warren Francisco, BB, 6´0˝/200 lbs; Minnesota; B8/4/1920 St. Paul, MN

YEAR	TEAM	G (GS, POS)	RUSH	YD	AVG (LG)	TD	REC	YD	AVG (LG)	TD	PASS	COMP	PCT	YD	AVG (LG)	TD	INT	SK	YD	QBR	KPR	OTD	PTS	TAY
1942	Cle	10 (2)	—	—	—	—	2	16	8.0 (18)	0	—	—	—	—	—	—	—	—	—	—	k	—	0	-3

Ply, Bobby Robert Vernon, DB, 6´1˝/190 lbs; Baylor; 1962: NYT, rnd 5/Pit, rnd 16; B8/13/1940 Mission, TX **1962**†DalT-A 14 **1963** KC-A 14 **1964** KC-A 14 **1965** KC-A 14 **1966**†KC-A 14 **1967** KC-A 3 **1967** Buf-A 3 **1967** Den-A 1 (1) **NFL** 77 (1) [6 yrs]

Poage, Ray Raymond Coy, TE-SE-FL-WR, 6´4˝/208 lbs; Texas; 1963: Min, rnd 3/Den, rnd 2; B11/14/1940 Plainview, TX, D9/23/1997 Brazoria County, TX

YEAR	TEAM	G (GS, POS)	RUSH	YD	AVG (LG)	TD	REC	YD	AVG (LG)	TD	PASS	COMP	PCT	YD	AVG (LG)	TD	INT	SK	YD	QBR	KPR	OTD	PTS	TAY
1963	Min	7 (6, TE)	—	—	—	—	15	354	23.6 (67)	2	—	—	—	—	—	—	—	—	—	—	—	—	12	187
1964	Phi	14 (14, SE)	—	—	—	—	37	479	12.9 (42)	1	—	—	—	—	—	—	—	—	—	—	—	—	6	245
1965	Phi	13 (SE)	—	—	—	—	31	612	19.7 (63)	5	1	0	0.0	0	0.0	0	0	—	—	—	—	—	30	331
1967	NO	12 (FL)	—	—	—	—	24	380	15.8 (65)	0	—	—	—	—	—	—	—	—	—	—	—	—	0	190
1968	NO	10	1	22	22.0 (22)	0	1	11	11.0 (11)	0	—	—	—	—	—	—	—	—	—	—	—	—	0	28
1969	NO	14 (te)	1	-3	-3.0 (-3)	0	18	236	13.1 (29)	4	—	—	—	—	—	—	—	—	—	—	—	—	24	135
1970	NO	12	1	13	13.0 (13)	0	15	166	11.1 (36)	1	—	—	—	—	—	—	—	—	—	—	k	—	6	92
1971	Atl	4	—	—	—	—	4	71	17.8 (31)	0	—	—	—	—	—	—	—	—	—	—	—	—	0	36
NFL	8	86 (20)	3	32	10.7 (22)	0	145	2309	15.9 (67)	13	1	0	0.0	0	0.0	0	0	—	—	—	k	—	78	1243

Pochman, Owen Owen, K, 6´0˝/180 lbs; Brigham Young; 2001: NE, rnd 7; B8/2/1977 Renton, WA **[K]** **2001** NYG 10 (0) **2003** SF 6 (0) **NFL** 16 (0) [2 yrs]

Podmajersky, Paul Paul, G, 5´11˝/220 lbs; Michigan State; Wyoming; Iowa; Illinois; B11/17/1916 Chicago, IL, D10/12/1993 Roseburg, OR **1944** ChiB 1 (0)

Podolak, Ed Edward Joseph, RB, 6´1˝/204 lbs; Iowa; 1969: KC, rnd 2; B9/1/1947 Atlantic, IA **[R]**

YEAR	TEAM	G (GS, POS)	RUSH	YD	AVG (LG)	TD	REC	YD	AVG (LG)	TD	PASS	COMP	PCT	YD	AVG (LG)	TD	INT	SK	YD	QBR	KPR	OTD	PTS	TAY
1969	†KC-A	4	—	—	—	—	—	—	—	—	—	—	—	—	—	—	—	—	—	—	kp	—	0	60
1970	KC☆	14 (RB)	168	749	4.5 (65)	3	26	307	11.8 (59)	1	2	2	100.0	40	20.0 (24)	0	0	—	—	—	kp	—	24	**1247**
1971	†KC	13 (RB)	184	708	3.8 (25)	9	36	252	7.0 (23)	0	2	2	100.0	42	21.0 (23)	0	0	—	—	—	kp	—	54	979
1972	KC	13 (RB)	171	615	3.6 (30)	4	46	345	7.5 (27)	2	—	—	—	—	—	—	—	—	—	—	kp	—	36	823
1973	KC	14 (RB)	210	721	3.4 (25)	3	55	445	8.1 (25)	0	1	0	0.0	0	0.0	0	0	—	—	—	p	—	18	1009
1974	KC	9 (RB)	101	386	3.8 (14)	2	43	306	7.1 (26)	1	—	—	—	—	—	—	—	—	—	—	p	—	18	623
1975	KC	14 (13, RB)	102	351	3.4 (25)	3	37	332	9.0 (21)	2	1	0	0.0	0	0.0	0	1	2	13	—	p	—	30	548
1976	KC	10 (4, rb)	88	371	4.2 (22)	5	13	156	12.0 (23)	0	—	—	—	—	—	—	—	—	—	—	—	—	30	499
1977	KC	13 (rb)	133	550	4.1 (41)	5	32	313	9.8 (23)	0	—	—	—	—	—	—	—	—	—	—	p	—	30	760
NFL	9	104 (17)	1157	4451	3.8 (65)	34	288	2456	8.5 (59)	6	6	4	66.7	82	13.7 (24)	0	1	2	13	—	kp	—	240	6546

Podoley, Jim James, HB-E, 6´2˝/200 lbs; Central Michigan; 1957: Was, rnd 4; B9/16/1933 Mount Morris, MI

YEAR	TEAM	G (GS, POS)	RUSH	YD	AVG (LG)	TD	REC	YD	AVG (LG)	TD	PASS	COMP	PCT	YD	AVG (LG)	TD	INT	SK	YD	QBR	KPR	OTD	PTS	TAY
1957	Was✧	12 (RH)	114	442	3.9 (33)	2	27	554	**20.5** (**82**)	4	—	—	—	—	—	—	—	—	—	—	k	—	36	770
1958	Was	10 (RH)	48	169	3.5 (9)	0	16	381	23.8 (66)	4	—	—	—	—	—	—	—	—	—	—	—	—	24	380
1959	Was	11	18	83	4.6 (25)	0	18	282	15.7 (48)	2	1	0	0.0	0	0.0	0	0	—	—	—	k	—	12	285
1960	Was	10	29	52	1.8 (9)	0	17	244	14.4 (41)	1	—	—	—	—	—	—	—	—	—	—	kp	—	6	194
NFL	4	43	209	746	3.6 (33)	2	78	1461	18.7 (82)	11	1	0	0.0	0	0.0	0	0	—	—	—	kp	—	78	1629

Poe, Billy Billy Gene, G, 6´3˝/280 lbs; Morehead State; B4/26/1964 Ironton, OH **1987** Cin 3 (3)

Poe, Johnnie Johnnie Edward, DB, 6´1˝/190 lbs; Missouri; 1981: NO, rnd 6; B8/29/1959 St. Louis, MO **1981** NO 15 (15, RCB) **1982** NO 9 (9, RCB) **1983** NO☆16 (16, RCB) **1984** NO 16 (16, RCB) **1985** NO 16 (16, RCB) **1986** NO 16 (16, RCB) **1987**†NO 12 (2) **NFL** 100 (90) [7 yrs]

Pohlman, John John Theodore, FB, 5´9˝/178 lbs; Brown; B9/18/1902 New Haven, CT, D5/8/1957 Milford, CT **1925** Pro 2 (0)

Poillon, Dick Richard Charles, B, 6´0˝/193 lbs; Canisius; B8/13/1920 Astoria, NY, D11/14/1994 Palm Beach County, **[K]**

YEAR	TEAM	G (GS, POS)	RUSH	YD	AVG (LG)	TD	REC	YD	AVG (LG)	TD	PASS	COMP	PCT	YD	AVG (LG)	TD	INT	SK	YD	QBR	KPR	OTD	PTS	TAY
1942	Was✧	7 (2)	55	148	2.7 (13)	0	—	—	—	—	15	2	13.3	52	3.5 (33)	0	3	—	—	—	KPkp	—	5	69
1946	Was	11 (2)	25	45	1.8 (8)	1	7	114	16.3 (33)	0	—	—	—	—	—	—	—	—	—	—	Kkp	—	45	131
1947	Was	12 (10, QB)	28	104	3.7 (21)	2	20	250	12.5 (30)	4	—	—	—	—	—	—	—	—	—	—	KPkpi	—	85	272
1948	Was	12 (11, lh)	71	233	3.3 (14)	1	9	105	11.7 (21)	1	—	—	—	—	—	—	—	—	—	—	KP	1	66	301
1949	Was	12 (3, FB)	7	5	0.7 (5)	0	1	8	8.0 (8)	0	—	—	—	—	—	—	—	—	—	—	KP	—	46	9
NFL	5	54 (28)	186	535	2.9 (21)	4	37	477	12.9 (33)	5	15	2	13.3	52	3.5 (33)	0	3	—	—	—	KPkpi	1	247	782

Poimbeouf, Lance Lance Joseph, G, 6´3˝/225 lbs; Louisiana-Lafayette; B11/10/1940 **1963** Dal 1

Poindexter, Anthony Anthony Scott, DB, 6´0˝/220 lbs; Virginia; 1999: Bal, rnd 7; B7/28/1976 Lynchburg, VA **2000**†Bal 12 (0)

Pointer, John John Leslie, LB, 6´2˝/225 lbs; Vanderbilt; B1/16/1958 Columbia, TN **1987** GB 3 (3)

Pokorny, Frank Frank Edward, WR, 6´0˝/198 lbs; Youngstown State; B5/13/1963 Uniontown, PA **1985** Pit 4 (0)

Polamalu, Troy Trou Aumua, DB, 5´10˝/213 lbs; USC; 2003: Pit, rnd 1; B4/19/1981 Garden Grove, CA **2003** Pit 16 (0) **2004**†Pit★16 (16, SS) **2005**†Pit★16 (16, SS) **NFL** 48 (32) [3 yrs]

Polanski, John John B., FB, 6´2˝/211 lbs; Wake Forest; 1942: Det, rnd 11; B9/6/1918 Buffalo, NY, deceased

YEAR	TEAM	G (GS, POS)	RUSH	YD	AVG (LG)	TD	REC	YD	AVG (LG)	TD	PASS	COMP	PCT	YD	AVG (LG)	TD	INT	SK	YD	QBR	KPR	OTD	PTS	TAY
1942	Det	3 (1)	17	67	3.9 (13)	0	—	—	—	—	—	—	—	—	—	—	—	—	—	—	ki	—	0	101

YEAR	TEAM	G(GS, POS)	RUSH	YD	AVG(LG)	TD	REC	YD	AVG(LG)	TD	PASS	COMP	PCT	YD	AVG(LG)	TD	INT	SK	YD	QBR	KPR	OTD	PTS	TAY
1946	LAD-A	13(3)	28	77	2.8	1	2	15	7.5	1	—	—	—	—	—	—	—	—	—	—	i	—	12	145

POLISKY, JOHN John, G-T, 6´0˝/225 lbs; St. Edward's; Notre Dame; B1/15/1901 Pittsburgh, PA, D4/1978 Wellsville, OH **1929** ChiB 9 (6, RG)

POLITE, LOUSAKA Lousaka Romon, RB, 6´0˝/246 lbs; Pittsburgh; B9/14/1981 North Braddock, PA

YEAR	TEAM	G(GS, POS)	RUSH	YD	AVG(LG)	TD	REC	YD	AVG(LG)	TD	PASS	COMP	PCT	YD	AVG(LG)	TD	INT	SK	YD	QBR	KPR	OTD	PTS	TAY
2004	Dal	1(0)	—	—	—	—	1	4	4.0(4)	0	—	—	—	—	—	—	—	—	—	—	—	—	0	2
2005	Dal	14(3)	2	8	4.0(6)	0	9	72	8.0(15)	1	—	—	—	—	—	—	—	—	—	—	—	—	6	49
NFL	2	15(3)	2	8	4.0(6)	0	10	76	7.6(15)	1	—	—	—	—	—	—	—	—	—	—	—	—	6	51

POLK, CARLOS Carlos Devonn, LB, 6´2˝/250 lbs; Nebraska; 2001: SD, rnd 4; B2/22/1977 Memphis, TN **2001** SD 6 (0) **2002** SD 15 (0) **2003** SD 16 (0) **2004** SD 1 (0) **NFL** 38 (0) [4 yrs]

POLK, DASHON DeShon Lamor, LB, 6´2˝/242 lbs; Arizona; 2000: Buf, rnd 7; B3/13/1977 Pacoima, CA **2000** Buf 5 (0) **2001** Buf 16 (1) **2002** Buf 16 (0) **2003** Buf 16 (0) **2004** Hou 16 (4) **2005** Hou 16 (11, LILB) **NFL** 85 (16) [6 yrs]

POLLACK, DAVID David M., LB, 6´2˝/261 lbs; Georgia; 2005: Cin, rnd 1; B6/19/1982 Snellville, GA **2005**†Cin 14 (5, llb)

POLLACK, FRANK Frank Steven, T-G, 6´5˝/285 lbs; Northern Arizona; 1990: SF, rnd 6; B11/5/1967 Camp Springs, MD **1990**†SF 15 (0) **1991** SF 15 (0) **1994**†SF 12 (4) **1995**†SF 15 (0) **1996**†SF 16 (2) **1997**†SF 16 (0) **NFL** 89 (6) [6 yrs]

POLLARD, AL Alfred Lee, HB-FB, 6´0˝/196 lbs; Loyola Marymount; Army; 1951: NYY, rnd 21; B9/7/1928 Los Angeles, CA, D3/3/2002 Devon, PA **[K]**

YEAR	TEAM	G(GS, POS)	RUSH	YD	AVG(LG)	TD	REC	YD	AVG(LG)	TD	PASS	COMP	PCT	YD	AVG(LG)	TD	INT	SK	YD	QBR	KPR	OTD	PTS	TAY
1951	Phi	6	24	119	5.0(28)	0	3	17	5.7(8)	0	—	—	—	—	—	—	—	—	—	—	kp	—	0	283
1951	NYY	6	2	2	1.0(3)	0	0	18	(18)	0	—	—	—	—	—	—	—	—	—	—	kp	—	0	93
1952	Phi	12(lh)	55	186	3.4(23)	1	8	59	7.4(14)	0	—	—	—	—	—	—	—	—	—	—	k	—	6	439
1953	Phi	12(fb)	23	44	1.9(11)	0	7	33	4.7(24)	0	—	—	—	—	—	—	—	—	—	—	Kkp	—	1	173
NFL	3	36	104	351	3.4(28)	1	18	127	7.1(24)	0	—	—	—	—	—	—	—	—	—	—	Kkp	—	7	987

POLLARD, BOB Robert Lee, DE-DT, 6´3˝/250 lbs; Texas Southern; Weber State; 1971: NO, rnd 11; B12/30/1948 Beaumont, TX **1971** NO 14 (14, LDT) **1972** NO 14 (14, LDT) **1973** NO 14 (14, LDT) **1974** NO 14 (14, RDE) **1975** NO 14 (14, LDT) **1976** NO 8 (8, LDE) **1977** NO 14 (12, RDE) **1978** SL 15 (LDE) **1979** SL 16 (LDE) **1980** SL 16 (16, LDE) **1981** SL 15 (15, LDE) **NFL** 154 (121) [11 yrs]

POLLARD, DARRYL Cedric Darryl, DB, 5´11˝/187 lbs; Weber State; B5/11/1964 Ellsworth, ME **1987** SF 3 (2) **1988**†SF 14 (0) **1989**†SF 16 (14, LCB) **1990**†SF 16 (16, LCB) **1992** TB 16 (2) **NFL** 65 (34) [5 yrs]

POLLARD, FRANK Frank D., RB, 5´10˝/218 lbs; Baylor; 1980: Pit, rnd 11; B6/15/1957 Clifton, TX

YEAR	TEAM	G(GS, POS)	RUSH	YD	AVG(LG)	TD	REC	YD	AVG(LG)	TD	PASS	COMP	PCT	YD	AVG(LG)	TD	INT	SK	YD	QBR	KPR	OTD	PTS	TAY
1980	Pit	16(0)	4	16	4.0(12)	0	—	—	—	—	—	—	—	—	—	—	—	—	—	—	kp	—	0	180
1981	Pit	14(10, RB)	123	570	4.6(29)	2	19	156	8.2(26)	0	—	—	—	—	—	—	—	—	—	—	—	—	12	668
1982	†Pit	9(8, RB)	62	238	3.8(18)	2	6	39	6.5(11)	0	—	—	—	—	—	—	—	—	—	—	—	—	12	278
1983	†Pit	16(3)	135	608	4.5(32)	4	16	127	7.9(17)	0	—	—	—	—	—	—	—	—	—	—	—	—	24	712
1984	†Pit	15(15, FB)	213	851	4.0(52)	6	21	186	8.9(18)	0	—	—	—	—	—	—	—	—	—	—	—	—	36	1004
1985	Pit	16(16, FB)	233	991	4.3(56)	3	24	250	10.4(20)	0	—	—	—	—	—	—	—	—	—	—	—	—	18	1146
1986	Pit	3(3)	24	86	3.6(12)	0	2	15	7.5(10)	0	—	—	—	—	—	—	—	—	—	—	—	—	0	94
1987	Pit	12(7, fb)	128	536	4.2(33)	3	14	77	5.5(17)	0	—	—	—	—	—	—	—	—	—	—	—	—	18	605
1988	Pit	10(3)	31	93	3.0(7)	0	2	22	11.0(19)	0	—	—	—	—	—	—	—	—	—	—	—	—	0	104
NFL	9	111(65)	953	3989	4.2(56)	20	104	872	8.4(26)	0	—	—	—	—	—	—	—	—	—	—	kp	—	120	4789

POLLARD, FRITZ Frederick Douglass, TB-BB-WB, 5´9˝/165 lbs; Bates; Brown; B1/27/1894 Chicago, IL, D5/11/1986 Silver Spring, MD; HOF 2005 **[KC]** **1920** Akr☆11 (9, TB) **1921** Akr 12 (11, TB), 42 **1922** Mil 7 (5, TB), 20 **1923** Ham 2 (2, BB), 1 **1925** Ham 1 (0) **1925** Akr 8 (5, TB), 12 **1925** Pro 4 (0) **1926** Akr 4 (4, BB) **NFL** 49 (36), 75 [6 yrs]

POLLARD, MARCUS Marcus LaJuan, TE, 6´3˝/247 lbs; Bradley; B2/8/1972 Valley, AL

YEAR	TEAM	G(GS, POS)	RUSH	YD	AVG(LG)	TD	REC	YD	AVG(LG)	TD	PASS	COMP	PCT	YD	AVG(LG)	TD	INT	SK	YD	QBR	KPR	OTD	PTS	TAY
1995	†Ind	8(0)	—	—	—	—	—	—	—	—	—	—	—	—	—	—	—	—	—	—	—	—	—	—
1996	†Ind	16(4)	—	—	—	—	6	86	14.3(48)	1	—	—	—	—	—	—	—	—	—	—	—	—	6	48
1997	Ind	16(6, te)	—	—	—	—	10	116	11.6(28)	0	—	—	—	—	—	—	—	—	—	—	—	—	2	58
1998	Ind	16(11, TE)	—	—	—	—	24	309	12.9(44)	4	—	—	—	—	—	—	—	—	—	—	k	—	28	164
1999	†Ind	16(10, TE)	—	—	—	—	34	374	11.0(33)	4	—	—	—	—	—	—	—	—	—	—	—	—	24	207
2000	†Ind	16(14, TE)	—	—	—	—	30	439	14.6(50)	3	—	—	—	—	—	—	—	—	—	—	—	—	20	235
2001	Ind	16(16, TE)	—	—	—	—	47	739	15.7(86)	8	—	—	—	—	—	—	—	—	—	—	—	—	48	410
2002	†Ind	15(15, TE)	—	—	—	—	43	478	11.1(41)	6	—	—	—	—	—	—	—	—	—	—	—	—	38	269
2003	†Ind	14(13, TE)	—	—	—	—	40	541	13.5(70)	3	—	—	—	—	—	—	—	—	—	—	k	—	18	280
2004	†Ind	13(13, TE)	—	—	—	—	29	309	10.7(31)	6	—	—	—	—	—	—	—	—	—	—	—	—	36	185
2005	Det	16(16, TE)	—	—	—	—	46	516	11.2(86)	3	—	—	—	—	—	—	—	—	—	—	—	—	18	273
NFL	11	162(118)	—	—	—	—	309	3907	12.6(86)	38	—	—	—	—	—	—	—	—	—	—	k	—	238	2127

POLLARD, ROBERT Robert, DE, 6´2˝/278 lbs; TCU; B6/28/1981 Metairie, LA **2004**†SD 1 (0)

POLLARD, TRENT Trent Deshawn, T, 6´4˝/304 lbs; Eastern Washington; 1994: Cin, rnd 5; B11/20/1972 Seattle, WA **1994** Cin 8 (0) **1995** Cin 9 (0) **NFL** 17 (0) [2 yrs]

POLLEY, TOM Thomas Craig, LB, 6´3˝/246 lbs; UNLV; 1985: Phi, rnd 8; B2/17/1962 Minneapolis, MN **1985** Phi 2 (0) **1987** Cle 2 (2) **NFL** 4 (2) [2 yrs]

POLLEY, TOMMY Tommy William, LB, 6´3˝/240 lbs; Florida State; 2001: SL, rnd 2; B1/18/1978 Baltimore, MD **2001**†SL 16 (11, LLB) **2002** SL 12 (11, RLB) **2003**†SL 14 (14, RLB) **2004**†SL 15 (13, LLB) **2005** Bal 16 (15, MLB/rlb) **NFL** 73 (64) [5 yrs]

POLLOCK, RED William Henry, HB-E, 6´2˝/194 lbs; Widener; B12/5/1911 Philadelphia, PA, D8/7/1993 Freeport, NY

YEAR	TEAM	G(GS, POS)	RUSH	YD	AVG(LG)	TD	REC	YD	AVG(LG)	TD	PASS	COMP	PCT	YD	AVG(LG)	TD	INT	SK	YD	QBR	KPR	OTD	PTS	TAY
1935	ChiB	11(5, rh)	45	254	5.6	3	7	135	19.3	1	12	1	8.3	18	1.5(18)	0	2	—	—	—	—	—	24	286
1936	ChiB	7(2)	—	—	—	—	1	15	15.0(15)	0	—	—	—	—	—	—	—	—	—	—	—	—	0	8
NFL	2	18(7)	45	254	5.6	3	8	150	18.8(15)	1	12	1	8.3	18	1.5(18)	0	2	—	—	—	—	—	24	293

POLOFSKY, GORDON Gordon Zelig, LB-G, 6´1˝/219 lbs; Tennessee; 1952: LA, rnd 5; B1/10/1931 Providence, RI **1952** ChiC 10 (LLB) **1953** ChiC 4 **1954** ChiC 12 (RLB) **NFL** 26 [3 yrs]

POLOWSKI, LARRY Larry Robert, LB, 6´3˝/235 lbs; Boise State; 1979: Sea, rnd 7; B9/15/1957 Three Rivers, MI **1979** Sea 14

POLSFOOT, FRAN Francis Charles, E, 6´3˝/203 lbs; Washington State; 1950: ChiC, rnd 3; B4/19/1927 Montessano, WA, D4/5/1985 Denver, CO

YEAR	TEAM	G(GS, POS)	RUSH	YD	AVG(LG)	TD	REC	YD	AVG(LG)	TD	PASS	COMP	PCT	YD	AVG(LG)	TD	INT	SK	YD	QBR	KPR	OTD	PTS	TAY
1950	ChiC	12(10, LE)	—	—	—	—	38	653	17.2(81)	6	—	—	—	—	—	—	—	—	—	—	—	—	36	357
1951	ChiC★	12(LE)	—	—	—	—	57	796	14.0(80)	4	—	—	—	—	—	—	—	—	—	—	P	—	24	418
1952	ChiC	3	—	—	—	—	—	—	—	—	—	—	—	—	—	—	—	—	—	—	—	—	—	—
1953	Was	10	—	—	—	—	11	164	14.9(66)	0	—	—	—	—	—	—	—	—	—	—	—	—	0	82
NFL	4	37(10)	—	—	—	—	106	1613	15.2(81)	10	—	—	—	—	—	—	—	—	—	—	P	—	60	857

POLTL, RANDY Randall Patrick, DB, 6´3˝/190 lbs; Stanford; 1974: Min, rnd 12; B3/26/1952 Long Beach, CA **1974**†Min 5 **1975** Den 13 (1) **1976** Den 12 **1977**†Den 14 (1) **NFL** 44 (2) [4 yrs]

PONDER, DAVID David Earl, DT, 6´3˝/248 lbs; Florida State; B6/27/1962 Dade City, FL **1985** Dal 4 (0)

PONDER, WILLIE Willie Columbus, WR, 6´0˝/205 lbs; Tulsa; Southeast Missouri State; 2003: NYG, rnd 6; B2/14/1980 Tulsa, OK

YEAR	TEAM	G(GS, POS)	RUSH	YD	AVG(LG)	TD	REC	YD	AVG(LG)	TD	PASS	COMP	PCT	YD	AVG(LG)	TD	INT	SK	YD	QBR	KPR	OTD	PTS	TAY
2003	NYG	4(0)	—	—	—	—	7	35	5.0(16)	0	—	—	—	—	—	—	—	—	—	—	—	—	0	18
2004	NYG	11(0)	1	-4	-4.0(-4)	0	1	3	3.0(3)	0	—	—	—	—	—	—	—	—	—	—	k	1	6	435
2005	NYG	11(0)	1	4	4.0(4)	0	—	—	—	—	—	—	—	—	—	—	—	—	—	—	k	1	6	394
NFL	3	26(0)	2	0	0.0(4)	0	8	38	4.8(16)	0	—	—	—	—	—	—	—	—	—	—	k	2	12	846

PONDS, ANTWAUNE Antwaune, LB, 6´2˝/252 lbs; Syracuse; 1998: Was, rnd 7; B6/29/1975 Harrisburg, PA **1998** Was 3 (0)

PONTBRIAND, RYAN Ryan David, C, 6´2˝/255 lbs; Rice; 2003: Cle, rnd 5; B10/1/1979 Houston, TX **2003** Cle 16 (0) **2004** Cle 16 (0) **2005** Cle 11 (0) **NFL** 43 (0) [3 yrs]

POOL, BRODNEY Brodney, DB, 6´2˝/208 lbs; Oklahoma; 2005: Cle, rnd 2; B5/24/1984 Houston, TX **2005** Cle 13 (0)

POOL, DAVID David Allen, DB, 5´9˝/188 lbs; Tennessee State; Carson-Newman; 1990: SD, rnd 6; B12/20/1966 Cincinnati, OH **1990** Buf 9 (1) **1991** NE 15 (3) **1992** NE 16 (14, LCB) **1993**†Buf 2 (0) **1994** Mia 1 (0) **NFL** 43 (18) [5 yrs]

POOL, HAMPTON Hampton John, E, 6´3˝/221 lbs; California; Army; Stanford; 1940: ChiB, rnd 9; B3/11/1915 San Miguel, CA, D5/26/2000 Mariposa, CA **[C]**

YEAR	TEAM	G(GS, POS)	RUSH	YD	AVG(LG)	TD	REC	YD	AVG(LG)	TD	PASS	COMP	PCT	YD	AVG(LG)	TD	INT	SK	YD	QBR	KPR	OTD	PTS	TAY
1940	†ChiB✧	5(4)	—	—	—	—	2	55	27.5(35)	0	—	—	—	—	—	—	—	—	—	—	—	—	0	28
1941	†ChiB✧	7(0)	—	—	—	—	5	101	20.2(56)	1	—	—	—	—	—	—	—	—	—	—	—	—	6	56

YEAR	TEAM	G(GS, POS)	RUSH	YD	AVG(LG)	TD	REC	YD	AVG(LG)	TD	PASS	COMP	PCT	YD	AVG(LG)	TD	INT	SK	YD	QBR	KPR	OTD	PTS	TAY
1942	†ChiB	11(0)	—	—	—	—	10	321	32.1(64)	5	—	—	—	—	—	—	—	—	—	—	—	—	30	186
1943	†ChiB	10(0)	—	—	—	—	18	363	20.2(42)	5	—	—	—	—	—	—	—	—	—	—	—	—	30	207
NFL	4	33(4)	—	—	—	—	35	840	24.0(64)	11	—	—	—	—	—	—	—	—	—	—	—	—	66	475
1946	Mia-A	4(0)	—	—	—	—	3	63	21.0	0	—	—	—	—	—	—	—	—	—	—	—	—	0	32

Poole, Barney George Barney, DE-E, 6´2˝/231 lbs; Mississippi; North Carolina; Army; 1948: NYY-A, rnd 9/1945: NYG, rnd 6; B10/29/1923 Gloster, MS, D4/12/2005 Jackson, MS

YEAR	TEAM	G(GS, POS)	RUSH	YD	AVG(LG)	TD	REC	YD	AVG(LG)	TD	PASS	COMP	PCT	YD	AVG(LG)	TD	INT	SK	YD	QBR	KPR	OTD	PTS	TAY
1949	†NYY-A	11(0)	—	—	—	—	6	83	13.8	0	—	—	—	—	—	—	—	—	—	—	pi	—	0	38

1951 NYY 11 (RDE) **1953** Bal 12 (LDE) **1954** NYG 11 (LDE)

YEAR	TEAM	G(GS, POS)	RUSH	YD	AVG(LG)	TD	REC	YD	AVG(LG)	TD	PASS	COMP	PCT	YD	AVG(LG)	TD	INT	SK	YD	QBR	KPR	OTD	PTS	TAY
1950	NYY	12(RDE)	—	—	—	—	4	82	20.5(52)	1	—	—	—	—	—	—	—	—	—	—	k	—	6	24
1952	DalT	12(RDE)	—	—	—	—	2	23	11.5(15)	0	—	—	—	—	—	—	—	—	—	—	—	—	0	12
NFL	5	58	—	—	—	—	6	105	17.5(52)	1	—	—	—	—	—	—	—	—	—	—	k	—	6	30

Poole, Bob Robert Edward, TE, 6´4˝/225 lbs; Clemson; 1964: SF, rnd 8; B10/5/1941 Paducah, KY

YEAR	TEAM	G(GS, POS)	RUSH	YD	AVG(LG)	TD	REC	YD	AVG(LG)	TD	PASS	COMP	PCT	YD	AVG(LG)	TD	INT	SK	YD	QBR	KPR	OTD	PTS	TAY
1964	SF	13	—	—	—	—	1	8	8.0(8)	0	—	—	—	—	—	—	—	—	—	—	—	—	0	4
1965	SF	9	—	—	—	—	2	29	14.5(15)	0	—	—	—	—	—	—	—	—	—	—	—	—	0	15
1966	Hou-A	14(te)	—	—	—	—	12	131	10.9(19)	0	—	—	—	—	—	—	—	—	—	—	—	—	0	66
1967	†Hou-A	14	—	—	—	—	4	55	13.8(18)	0	—	—	—	—	—	—	—	—	—	—	—	—	0	28
NFL	4	50	—	—	—	—	19	223	11.7(19)	0	—	—	—	—	—	—	—	—	—	—	—	—	0	112

Poole, Jim James Eugene, E, 6´2˝/218 lbs; Mississippi; 1937: NYG, rnd 7; B9/9/1915 Gloster, MS, D11/16/1994 Oxford, MS

YEAR	TEAM	G(GS, POS)	RUSH	YD	AVG(LG)	TD	REC	YD	AVG(LG)	TD	PASS	COMP	PCT	YD	AVG(LG)	TD	INT	SK	YD	QBR	KPR	OTD	PTS	TAY
1937	NYG	11(9, LE)	—	—	—	—	5	79	15.8(38)	2	—	—	—	—	—	—	—	—	—	—	—	—	12	50
1938	†NYG★	11(10, LE)	—	—	—	—	7	98	14.0	1	—	—	—	—	—	—	—	—	—	—	—	—	6	54
1939	†NYG★	11(11, LE)	—	—	—	—	7	99	14.1	0	—	—	—	—	—	—	—	—	—	—	—	—	0	50
1940	NYG★	11(11, LE)	—	—	—	—	10	156	15.6(38)	3	—	—	—	—	—	—	—	—	—	—	—	—	18	93
1941	†NYG	11(11, LE)	—	—	—	—	6	74	12.3(16)	2	—	—	—	—	—	—	—	—	—	—	i	1	18	58
1945	ChiC	9(4)	—	—	—	—	6	82	13.7(29)	2	—	—	—	—	—	—	—	—	—	—	i	—	12	74
1945	NYG	3(1)	—	—	—	—	—	—	—	—	—	—	—	—	—	—	—	—	—	—	—	—	—	—
1946	†NYG☆	11(11, LE)	—	—	—	—	24	307	12.8(31)	3	—	—	—	—	—	—	—	—	—	—	—	—	18	169
NFL	7	78(68)	—	—	—	—	65	895	13.8(38)	13	—	—	—	—	—	—	—	—	—	—	i	1	84	547

Poole, Keith Keith Robert Strohmaier, WR, 6´0˝/188 lbs; Arizona State; 1997: NO, rnd 4; B6/18/1974 San Jose, CA

YEAR	TEAM	G(GS, POS)	RUSH	YD	AVG(LG)	TD	REC	YD	AVG(LG)	TD	PASS	COMP	PCT	YD	AVG(LG)	TD	INT	SK	YD	QBR	KPR	OTD	PTS	TAY
1997	NO	3(0)	—	—	—	—	4	98	24.5(49)	2	—	—	—	—	—	—	—	—	—	—	—	—	12	59
1998	NO	15(4)	—	—	—	—	24	509	21.2(82)	2	—	—	—	—	—	—	—	—	—	—	—	—	12	265
1999	NO	15(15, WR)	1	14	14.0(14)	0	42	796	19.0(67)	6	—	—	—	—	—	—	—	—	—	—	—	—	36	442
2000	†NO	15(4)	—	—	—	—	21	293	14.0(49)	1	—	—	—	—	—	—	—	—	—	—	—	—	6	152
2001	Den	6(3)	—	—	—	—	5	38	7.6(10)	0	—	—	—	—	—	—	—	—	—	—	—	—	0	19
NFL	5	54(26)	1	14	14.0(14)	0	96	1734	18.1(82)	11	—	—	—	—	—	—	—	—	—	—	—	—	66	936

Poole, Ken Kenneth Dawayne, DE, 6´3˝/251 lbs; Louisiana-Monroe; 1981: Mia, rnd 5; B10/20/1958 Hermitage, AR **1981**†Mia 16 (0)

Poole, Larry Larry Eugene, RB, 6´1˝/195 lbs; Kent State; 1975: Cle, rnd 9; B7/31/1952 Akron, OH

YEAR	TEAM	G(GS, POS)	RUSH	YD	AVG(LG)	TD	REC	YD	AVG(LG)	TD	PASS	COMP	PCT	YD	AVG(LG)	TD	INT	SK	YD	QBR	KPR	OTD	PTS	TAY
1975	Cle	3	17	114	6.7(26)	0	1	5	5.0(5)	0	—	—	—	—	—	—	—	—	—	—	kp	—	0	157
1976	Cle	13(rb)	78	356	4.6(26)	1	14	70	5.0(21)	0	—	—	—	—	—	—	—	—	—	—	k	—	6	418
1977	Cle	13	38	118	3.1(12)	1	17	137	8.1(21)	3	—	—	—	—	—	—	—	—	—	—	—	—	24	212
1978	†Hou	9	—	—	—	—	—	—	—	—	—	—	—	—	—	—	—	—	—	—	k	—	0	47
NFL	4	38	133	588	4.4(26)	2	32	212	6.6(21)	3	—	—	—	—	—	—	—	—	—	—	kp	—	30	833

Poole, Nate Nathan, WR, 6´2˝/210 lbs; Marshall; B2/1/1977 Danville, VA

YEAR	TEAM	G(GS, POS)	RUSH	YD	AVG(LG)	TD	REC	YD	AVG(LG)	TD	PASS	COMP	PCT	YD	AVG(LG)	TD	INT	SK	YD	QBR	KPR	OTD	PTS	TAY
2002	Arz	5(1)	—	—	—	—	13	108	8.3(15)	1	—	—	—	—	—	—	—	—	—	—	—	—	6	59
2003	Arz	15(1)	—	—	—	—	13	177	13.6(37)	1	—	—	—	—	—	—	—	—	—	—	—	—	6	94
2004	Arz	9(1)	—	—	—	—	5	70	14.0(24)	0	—	—	—	—	—	—	—	—	—	—	—	—	0	35
2005	NO	7(0)	—	—	—	—	3	63	21.0(42)	0	—	—	—	—	—	—	—	—	—	—	—	—	0	32
NFL	4	36(3)	—	—	—	—	34	418	12.3(42)	2	—	—	—	—	—	—	—	—	—	—	—	—	12	219

Poole, Nathan Nathan Lewis, RB, 5´9˝/210 lbs; Louisville; 1979: Cin, rnd 10; B12/17/1956 Alexander City, AL

YEAR	TEAM	G(GS, POS)	RUSH	YD	AVG(LG)	TD	REC	YD	AVG(LG)	TD	PASS	COMP	PCT	YD	AVG(LG)	TD	INT	SK	YD	QBR	KPR	OTD	PTS	TAY
1979	Cin	16	1	-3	-3.0(-3)	0	1	-10	-10.0(-10)	0	—	—	—	—	—	—	—	—	—	—	k	—	0	15
1980	Cin	16(0)	5	6	1.2(7)	0	2	-4	-2.0(3)	0	—	—	—	—	—	—	—	—	—	—	k	—	0	-3
1982	Den	9(0)	7	36	5.1(20)	0	—	—	—	—	—	—	—	—	—	—	—	—	—	—	k	—	0	21
1983	†Den	16(10, FB)	81	246	3.0(19)	4	20	184	9.2(23)	0	—	—	—	—	—	—	—	—	—	—	—	—	24	378
1985	Den	3(0)	4	12	3.0(6)	0	—	—	—	—	—	—	—	—	—	—	—	—	—	—	—	—	0	12
1987	Den	2(0)	28	126	4.5(15)	1	1	9	9.0(9)	0	—	—	—	—	—	—	—	—	—	—	—	—	6	141
NFL	6	62(10)	126	423	3.4(20)	5	24	179	7.5(23)	0	—	—	—	—	—	—	—	—	—	—	k	—	30	564

Poole, Ollie Oliver Lamar, DE-E, 6´3˝/220 lbs; North Carolina; Mississippi; 1944: NYG, rnd 15; B4/18/1922 Gloster, MS **1949** Det 8 (0)

YEAR	TEAM	G(GS, POS)	RUSH	YD	AVG(LG)	TD	REC	YD	AVG(LG)	TD	PASS	COMP	PCT	YD	AVG(LG)	TD	INT	SK	YD	QBR	KPR	OTD	PTS	TAY
1947	NYY-A	5(0)	—	—	—	—	1	19	19.0(19)	0	—	—	—	—	—	—	—	—	—	—	p	—	0	10
1948	Bal-A	9(1)	—	—	—	—	1	2	2.0(2)	0	—	—	—	—	—	—	—	—	—	—	—	—	0	1
AAFC	2	14(1)	—	—	—	—	2	21	10.5(19)	0	—	—	—	—	—	—	—	—	—	—	p	—	0	11

Poole, Ray Ray Smith, DE-E, 6´2˝/215 lbs; North Carolina; Mississippi; 1944: NYG, rnd 13; B4/15/1921 Gloster, MS **[K]** **1950** NYG☆12 (RDE) **1951** NYG 11 (RDE) **1952** NYG 12 (RDE)

YEAR	TEAM	G(GS, POS)	RUSH	YD	AVG(LG)	TD	REC	YD	AVG(LG)	TD	PASS	COMP	PCT	YD	AVG(LG)	TD	INT	SK	YD	QBR	KPR	OTD	PTS	TAY
1947	NYG	12(12, RE)	—	—	—	—	23	395	17.2(61)	4	—	—	—	—	—	—	—	—	—	—	i	—	24	213
1948	NYG	12(12, RE)	—	—	—	—	35	492	14.1(51)	3	—	—	—	—	—	—	—	—	—	—	—	1	26	261
1949	NYG	12(11, RE)	—	—	—	—	25	277	11.1(40)	1	—	—	—	—	—	—	—	—	—	—	k	—	6	132
NFL	6	71(35)	—	—	—	—	83	1164	14.0(61)	8	—	—	—	—	—	—	—	—	—	—	Kki	1	223	606

Poole, Shelley Shelley O'Neal, RB, 6´4˝/225 lbs; Temple; B12/3/1964 Button Gwinnett, GA **1987** Atl 1 (0)

Poole, Steve Steven Albert, LB, 6´1˝/232 lbs; Tennessee; B8/25/1952 Fort Oglethorpe, GA **1976** NYJ 9

Poole, Tyrone Tyrone, DB, 5´8˝/188 lbs; Fort Valley State (GA); 1995: Car, rnd 1; B2/3/1972 La Grange, GA **1995** Car 16 (13, LCB) **1996**†Car 15 (15, RCB) **1997** Car 16 (16, RCB) **1998** Ind 15 (15, RCB) **1999**†Ind 15 (14, RCB) **2000**†Ind 15 (12, RCB) **2002** Den 16 (4) **2003**†NE 16 (16, RCB) **2004** NE 5 (4) **2005** NE 1 (1) **NFL** 130 (110) [10 yrs]

Poole, Will William Starling, DB, 5´10˝/190 lbs; Boston College; USC; 2004: Mia, rnd 4; B7/24/1981 St. Albans, NY **2004** Mia 15 (1)

Popa, Eli Eli Charles, LB, 5´10˝/202 lbs; Illinois; B11/4/1930 Massillon, OH **1952** ChiC 4

Pope, Bucky Frank Buckley, FL-WR, 6´5˝/195 lbs; Duke; Catawba; 1964: LA, rnd 8; B3/23/1941 Pittsburgh, PA

YEAR	TEAM	G(GS, POS)	RUSH	YD	AVG(LG)	TD	REC	YD	AVG(LG)	TD	PASS	COMP	PCT	YD	AVG(LG)	TD	INT	SK	YD	QBR	KPR	OTD	PTS	TAY
1964	LARm	14(FL)	2	11	5.5(17)	0	25	786	31.4(**95**)	**10**	—	—	—	—	—	—	—	—	—	—	—	—	60	454
1966	LARm	3	—	—	—	—	1	14	14.0(14)	1	—	—	—	—	—	—	—	—	—	—	—	—	6	12
1967	LARm	13	—	—	—	—	8	152	19.0(48)	2	—	—	—	—	—	—	—	—	—	—	—	—	12	86
1968	GB	3(1)	—	—	—	—	—	—	—	—	—	—	—	—	—	—	—	—	—	—	—	—	—	—
NFL	4	33(1)	2	11	5.5(17)	0	34	952	28.0(95)	13	—	—	—	—	—	—	—	—	—	—	—	—	78	552

Pope, Daniel Daniel, P, 5´10˝/203 lbs; Alabama; B3/28/1975 Alpharetta, GA

YEAR	TEAM	G(GS, POS)	RUSH	YD	AVG(LG)	TD	REC	YD	AVG(LG)	TD	PASS	COMP	PCT	YD	AVG(LG)	TD	INT	SK	YD	QBR	KPR	OTD	PTS	TAY
1999	KC	16(0)	1	0	0.0(0)	0	—	—	—	—	—	—	—	—	—	—	—	—	—	—	P	—	0	0
2000	Cin	16(0)	2	22	11.0(22)	0	—	—	—	—	—	—	—	—	—	—	—	—	—	—	P	—	0	22
2001	NYJ	1(0)	—	—	—	—	—	—	—	—	—	—	—	—	—	—	—	—	—	—	P	—	0	0
NFL	3	33(0)	3	22	7.3(22)	0	—	—	—	—	—	—	—	—	—	—	—	—	—	—	P	—	0	22

Pope, Derrick Derrick, LB, 6´1˝/223 lbs; Alabama; 2004: Mia, rnd 7; B5/4/1982 Galveston, TX **2004** Mia 16 (3) **2005** Mia 12 (2) **NFL** 28 (5) [2 yrs]

Pope, Kendyll Kendyll, LB, 6´2˝/220 lbs; Florida State; 2004: Ind, rnd 4; B5/9/1981 Ft. White, FL **2004** Ind 2 (0)

Pope, Ken Kenith Van, DB, 5´11˝/200 lbs; Oklahoma; 1974: Oak, rnd 9; B12/28/1951 Galveston, TX **1974** NE 4

YEAR	TEAM	G(GS, POS)	RUSH	YD	AVG(LG)	TD	REC	YD	AVG(LG)	TD	PASS	COMP	PCT	YD	AVG(LG)	TD	INT	SK	YD	QBR	KPR	OTD	PTS	TAY

POPE, LEW Lewis Lawrence, B, 6´0˝/196 lbs; Purdue; B2/18/1908 West Lafayette, IN, D2/5/1964

1931	Pro	8(3)																				—		177
1933	Cin	10(10, TB)	56	179	3.2	1	1	20	20.0(20)	0	21	5	23.8	115	5.5	0	2	—	—	—	—	—	6	177
1934	Cin	8(5, WB)	40	163	4.1	0	1	17	17.0(17)	0	42	10	23.8	115	2.7	0	10	—	—	—	—	—	0	-171
NFL	3	26(18)	96	342	3.6	1	2	37	18.5(20)	0	63	15	23.8	230	3.7	0	12	—	—	—	—	—	6	6

POPE, MARQUEZ Marquez Phillips, DB, 5´11˝/193 lbs; Fresno State; 1992: SD, rnd 2; B10/29/1970 Nashville, TN   **1992**†SD 7 (0)   **1993** SD 16 (1)   **1994** LARm 16 (16, SS)
1995†SF 16 (16, RCB)   **1996**†SF 16 (16, RCB)   **1997**†SF 5 (5, rcb)   **1998**†SF 6 (3)   **1999** Cle 16 (15, SS)   **2000**†Oak 15 (14, SS)   **2001**†Oak 16 (12, SS)   **NFL** 129 (98) [10 yrs]

POPE, MONSANTO Monsanto Leshawn, DT, 6´3˝/300 lbs; Virginia; 2002: Den, rnd 7; B1/27/1978 Norfolk, VA   **2002** Den 14 (1)   **2003**†Den 16 (5, ldt)   **2004**†Den 16 (15, RDT)
2005 Den 2 (0)   **NFL** 48 (21) [4 yrs]

POPE, SPENCER Gordon Spencer, E, 5´10˝/170 lbs; Indiana; B3/9/1893 Linton, IN, D9/9/1976 Pottsville, PA   **1920** Mun 1 (0)

POPOVICH, JOHN John, HB, 5´8˝/160 lbs; St. Vincent; B3/6/1918 Monessen, PA, D2/3/2004 Charleroi, PA

1944	C-P	6(1)	8	29	3.6(9)	0	3	-1	-0.3(1)	0	—	—	—	—	—	—	—	—	—	—	k	—	0	59
1945	Pit	1(0)	4	-8	-2.0(4)	0	—	—	—	—	—	—	—	—	—	—	—	—	—	—	k	—	0	16
NFL	2	7(1)	12	21	1.8(9)	0	3	-1	-0.3(1)	0	—	—	—	—	—	—	—	—	—	—	k	—	0	75

POPOVICH, MILT Milton John, B, 5´11˝/196 lbs; Montana; 1938: ChiC, rnd 2; B12/29/1913 Butte, MT, D6/23/2005 Butte, MT

1938	ChiC	7(0)	6	13	2.2	0	1	8	8.0(8)	0	—	—	—	—	—	—	—	—	—	—	—	—	0	17
1939	ChiC	10(4, WB)	26	78	3.0	0	2	10	5.0	0	6	5	83.3	52	8.7	0	0	—	—	—	P	1	6	109
1940	ChiC	10(1)	41	138	3.4	0	5	32	6.4	0	—	—	—	—	—	—	—	—	—	—	P	—	0	154
1941	ChiC	6(1)	5	4	0.8(4)	0	—	—	—	—	—	—	—	—	—	—	—	—	—	—	—	—	0	4
1942	ChiC	10(1)	—	—	—	—	2	21	10.5(12)	0	—	—	—	—	—	—	—	—	—	—	Pi	—	0	12
NFL	5	43(7)	78	233	3.0(4)	0	10	71	7.1(12)	0	6	5	83.3	52	8.7	0	0	—	—	—	Pi	1	6	296

POPPINGA, BRADY Brady, LB, 6´3˝/259 lbs; Brigham Young; 2005: GB, rnd 4; B9/21/1979 Evanston, WY   **2005** GB 12 (1)

POPSON, TED Theodore Paul, TE, 6´4˝/250 lbs; Portland State; 1991: NYG, rnd 11; B9/10/1966 Granada Hills, CA

1994	†SF	16(1)	—	—	—	—	13	141	10.8(24)	0	—	—	—	—	—	—	—	—	—	—	—	—	0	71
1995	†SF	12(0)	—	—	—	—	16	128	8.0(16)	0	—	—	—	—	—	—	—	—	—	—	—	—	0	64
1996	SF	15(6, te)	—	—	—	—	26	301	11.6(39)	6	—	—	—	—	—	—	—	—	—	—	—	—	36	181
1997	†KC	13(12, TE)	—	—	—	—	35	320	9.1(21)	2	—	—	—	—	—	—	—	—	—	—	—	—	12	170
1998	KC	12(1)	—	—	—	—	13	90	6.9(17)	0	—	—	—	—	—	—	—	—	—	—	—	—	0	45
NFL	5	68(20)	—	—	—	—	103	980	9.5(39)	8	—	—	—	—	—	—	—	—	—	—	—	—	48	530

PORCHER, ROBERT Robert, DE-DT, 6´3˝/266 lbs; South Carolina State; 1992: Det, rnd 1; B7/30/1969 Wando, SC **[S]**   **1992** Det 16 (1)   **1993**†Det 16 (4)   **1994**†Det 15 (15, LDE)
1995†Det 16 (16, RDT)   **1996** Det 16 (16, LDE)   **1997**†Det 16 (16, LDE)   **1998** Det 16 (15, LDE)   **1999**†Det★15 (14, LDE)   **2000** Det 16 (16, LDE)   **2001** Det★16 (16, LDE)
2002 Det 15 (15, LDE)   **2003** Det 14 (14, LDE)   **NFL** 187 (158) [12 yrs]

PORELL, TOM Thomas Reardon, NT, 6´3˝/275 lbs; Boston College; B9/23/1964 Cambridge, MA   **1987** NE 1 (1)

PORT, CHRIS Christopher Charles, G-T, 6´5˝/295 lbs; Duke; 1990: NO, rnd 12; B11/2/1967 Wanaque, NJ   **1991**†NO 14 (11, RG)   **1992**†NO 16 (16, RG)   **1993** NO 15 (15, LG)
1994 NO 16 (16, RG)   **1995** NO 8 (8, rg)   **NFL** 69 (50) [5 yrs]

PORTER, ALVIN Alvin Guy, DB, 5´11˝/175 lbs; Oklahoma State; B5/10/1977 Shreveport, LA   **2001**†Bal 16 (0)   **2002** Bal 16 (5, lcb)   **2003** Bal 1 (0)   **NFL** 33 (5) [3 yrs]

PORTER, DARYL Daryl Maurice, DB, 5´9˝/188 lbs; Boston College; 1997: Pit, rnd 6; B1/16/1974 Fort Lauderdale, FL   **1997** Det 7 (0)   **1998**†Buf 2 (0)   **1999**†Buf 16 (0)
2001 Ten 14 (3)

| 2000 | Buf | 16(0) | — | — | — | — | 1 | 44 | 44.0(44) | 0 | — | — | — | — | — | — | — | — | — | — | i | 1 | 6 | 17 |
| NFL | 5 | 55(3) | — | — | — | — | 1 | 44 | 44.0(44) | 0 | — | — | — | — | — | — | — | — | — | — | ki | 1 | 6 | 28 |

PORTER, JACK Jack David, C, 6´3˝/255 lbs; Oklahoma; 1970: NYJ, rnd 8; B7/27/1948 Kingfisher, OK   **1971** SD 1

PORTER, JERRY Jerry, WR, 6´2˝/220 lbs; West Virginia; 2000: Oak, rnd 2; B7/14/1978 Washington, DC

2000	†Oak	12(0)	—	—	—	—	1	6	6.0(6)	0	—	—	—	—	—	—	—	—	—	—	—	—	0	3
2001	†Oak	15(1)	2	13	6.5(7)	0	19	220	11.6(21)	0	—	—	—	—	—	—	—	—	—	—	—	—	0	135
2002	†Oak	16(13, WR)	4	6	1.5(4)	0	51	688	13.5(36)	9	—	—	—	—	—	—	—	—	—	—	—	—	58	395
2003	Oak	10(1)	1	10	10.0(10)	0	28	361	12.9(35)	1	—	—	—	—	—	—	—	—	—	—	—	—	6	196
2004	Oak	16(16, WR)	1	-4	-4.0(-4)	0	64	998	15.6(52)	9	—	—	—	—	—	—	—	—	—	—	k	—	54	531
2005	Oak	16(14, WR)	1	-8	-8.0(-8)	0	76	942	12.4(49)	5	—	—	—	—	—	—	—	—	—	—	—	—	30	488
NFL	6	85(45)	9	17	1.9(10)	0	239	3215	13.5(52)	24	—	—	—	—	—	—	—	—	—	—	k	—	148	1748

PORTER, JOEY Joey Eugene, LB, 6´2˝/250 lbs; Colorado State; 1999: Pit, rnd 3; B3/22/1977 Bakersfield, CA **[S]**   **1999** Pit 16 (0)   **2000** Pit 16 (16, ROLB)   **2001**†Pit 15 (15, ROLB)
2002†Pit★16 (16, ROLB)   **2003** Pit 14 (14, ROLB)   **2004**†Pit★15 (15, ROLB)   **2005**†Pit★16 (16, ROLB)   **NFL** 108 (92) [7 yrs]

PORTER, KERRY Kerry, RB, 6´1˝/215 lbs; Washington State; 1987: Buf, rnd 7; B9/23/1964 Vicenza, Italy

1987	Buf	6(0)	2	0	0.0(1)	0	—	—	—	—	—	—	—	—	—	—	—	—	—	—	—	—	0	0
1989	LARd	16(0)	13	54	4.2(23)	0	—	—	—	—	—	—	—	—	—	—	—	—	—	—	—	—	0	54
1990	Den	13(3)	1	3	3.0(3)	0	4	44	11.0(16)	0	—	—	—	—	—	—	—	—	—	—	—	—	0	25
NFL	3	35(3)	16	57	3.6(23)	0	4	44	11.0(16)	0	—	—	—	—	—	—	—	—	—	—	—	—	0	79

PORTER, KEVIN Kevin James, DB, 5´10˝/215 lbs; Auburn; 1988: KC, rnd 3; B4/11/1966 Bronx, NY   **1988** KC 15 (7, ss)   **1989** KC 16 (16, SS)   **1990**†KC 16 (14, SS)
1991†KC 16 (15, SS)   **1992** KC 13 (0)   **1992** NYJ 2 (0)   **NFL** 78 (52) [5 yrs]

PORTER, LEW Lewis, WR, 5´11˝/178 lbs; Southern (LA); 1970: Den, rnd 8; B3/7/1947 Clarksville, MS

| 1970 | KC | 5 | 2 | 21 | 10.5(14) | 0 | 1 | 29 | 29.0(29) | 0 | — | — | — | — | — | — | — | — | — | — | kp | — | 0 | 35 |

PORTER, RICKY Richard Anthony, RB, 5´10˝/198 lbs; Slippery Rock; 1982: Det, rnd 12; B1/14/1960 Sylacauga, AL   **1982** Det 1 (0)   **1983** Bal 14 (0)

| 1987 | Buf | 9(0) | 47 | 177 | 3.8(13) | 0 | 9 | 70 | 7.8(26) | 0 | — | — | — | — | — | — | — | — | — | — | k | — | 0 | 311 |
| NFL | 3 | 24(0) | 47 | 177 | 3.8(13) | 0 | 9 | 70 | 7.8(26) | 0 | — | — | — | — | — | — | — | — | — | — | kp | — | 0 | 415 |

PORTER, ROB Robert Bryant, DB, 6´2˝/210 lbs; Holy Cross; B5/9/1962 Suffern, NY   **1987** NYG 3 (1)

PORTER, RON Ronald Dean, LB, 6´3˝/232 lbs; Idaho; 1967: Bal, rnd 5; B7/27/1945 Columbus, GA   **1967** Bal 14 (LLB)   **1968**†Bal 14   **1969** Bal 2   **1969** Phi 10 (RLB)
1970 Phi 14 (RLB)   **1971** Phi 12 (RLB)   **1972** Phi 14 (LLB)   **1973**†Min 13   **NFL** 93 [7 yrs]

PORTER, RUFUS Rufus, LB-DE, 6´1˝/228 lbs; Southern (LA); B5/18/1965 Amite, LA   **1988**†Sea★16 (0)   **1989** Sea★16 (3)   **1990** Sea 12 (12, RLB)   **1991** Sea 15 (15, RLB)
1992 Sea 16 (16, RLB)   **1993** Sea 7 (6, rlb)   **1994** Sea 15 (15, RLB)   **1995** NO 14 (12, LLB)   **1996** NO 13 (9, LLB)   **1997**†TB 11 (10, LLB)   **NFL** 135 (98) [10 yrs]

PORTER, TRACY Tracy Randolph, WR, 6´2˝/196 lbs; LSU; 1981: Det, rnd 4; B6/1/1959 Baton Rouge, LA

1981	Det	12(0)	—	—	—	—	3	63	21.0(27)	1	—	—	—	—	—	—	—	—	—	—	p	—	6	37
1982	†Det	8(0)	—	—	—	—	9	124	13.8(23)	0	1	0	0.0	0	0.0	0	0	—	—	—	—	—	0	62
1983	Bal	16(7, wr)	—	—	—	—	28	384	13.7(38)	0	—	—	—	—	—	—	—	—	—	—	—	—	0	192
1984	Ind	16(12, WR)	—	—	—	—	39	590	15.1(63)	2	—	—	—	—	—	—	—	—	—	—	—	—	12	305
NFL	4	52(19)	—	—	—	—	79	1161	14.7(63)	3	1	0	0.0	0	0.0	0	0	—	—	—	p	—	18	596

PORTER, WILLIE Willie Church, DB, 5´11˝/190 lbs; Texas Southern; B3/25/1946 Victoria, TX   **1968** Bos-A 13

PORTERFIELD, GARRY Garry Mark, DE, 6´3˝/231 lbs; Tulsa; 1965: Dal, rnd 14/Oak, rnd 17; B8/4/1943 Pawnee, OK   **1965** Dal 2

PORTILLA, JOSE Jose Casiano, T, 6´6˝/320 lbs; Arizona; B9/11/1972 Zaragoza, Mexico   **1998**†Atl 16 (0)   **1999** Atl 4 (0)   **NFL** 20 (0) [2 yrs]

PORTIS, CLINTON Clinton Earl, RB, 5´11˝/205 lbs; Miami (FL); 2002: Den, rnd 2; B9/1/1981 Laurel, MS

2002	Den	16(12, RB)	273	1508	**5.5(59)**	15	33	364	11.0(66)	2	—	—	—	—	—	—	—	—	—	—	—	—	102	1850
2003	†Den◇	13(13, RB)	290	1591	**5.5(65)**	14	38	314	8.3(72)	0	—	—	—	—	—	—	—	—	—	—	—	—	86	1888
2004	Was	15(15, RB)	343	1315	3.8(64)	5	40	235	5.9(18)	2	2	1	50.0	15	7.5(15)	1	0	—	—	—	—	—	42	1505
2005	†Was	16(16, RB)	352	1516	4.3(47)	11	30	216	7.2(23)	0	2	1	50.0	17	8.5(17)	1	0	—	—	—	—	—	68	1748
NFL	4	60(56)	1258	5930	4.7(65)	45	141	1129	8.0(72)	4	4	2	50.0	32	8.0(17)	2	0	—	—	—	—	—	298	6991

PORTIS, MARICO Marico Jermond, G, 6´2˝/313 lbs; Alabama; B11/29/1979 Birmingham, AL   **2004** Ten 1 (0)

POSEY, DAVID David Ellsworth, K, 5´11˝/167 lbs; Florida; 1977: SF, rnd 9; B4/1/1956 Painesville, OH **[K]** **1978**†NE 11

POSEY, JEFF Jeff, LB-DE, 6´4˝/241 lbs; Southern Mississippi; B8/14/1975 Bassfield, MS **1998**†SF 16 (0) **1999** SF 16 (6, LDE) **2000** SF 16 (9, LLB) **2001** Car 4 (0) **2001** Jax 7 (5, llb) **2002** Hou 16 (9, ROLB) **2003** Buf 16 (16, LLB) **2004** Buf 16 (15, LLB) **2005** Buf 16 (16, LLB) **NFL** 123 (76) [8 yrs]

POST, BOBBY Robert Kent, DB, 6´1˝/195 lbs; Kings Point; B1/12/1944 Twin Falls, ID **1967** NYG 5

POST, DICKIE Richard Marvin, RB, 5´9˝/190 lbs; Houston; 1967: SD, rnd 4; B9/27/1945 San Pedro, CA

YEAR	TEAM	G (GS, POS)	RUSH	YD	AVG (LG)	TD	REC	YD	AVG (LG)	TD	PASS	COMP	PCT	YD	AVG (LG)	TD	INT	SK	YD	QBR	KPR	OTD	PTS	TAY
1967	SD-A★	13 (HB)	161	663	4.1 (67)	7	32	278	8.7 (66)	1	6	1	16.7	9	1.5 (9)	0	0	1	9	—	k	—	48	1028
1968	SD-A☆	13 (HB)	151	758	5.0 (62)	3	18	165	9.2 (23)	0	4	1	25.0	23	5.8 (23)	0	0	1	17	—	k	—	18	931
1969	SD-A★	14 (HB)	182	**873**	4.8 (60)	6	24	235	9.8 (46)	0	2	1	50.0	4	2.0 (4)	0	0	—	—	—	k	—	36	1067
1970	SD	9 (RB)	74	225	3.0 (18)	1	13	113	8.7 (30)	0	—	—	—	—	—	—	—	—	—	—	—	—	6	292
1971	Den	6 (1)	18	44	2.4 (16)	0	4	46	11.5 (15)	1	—	—	—	—	—	—	—	—	—	—	k	—	6	113
1971	Hou	7	22	42	1.9 (10)	0	5	66	13.2 (28)	0	—	—	—	—	—	—	—	—	—	—	—	—	0	75
NFL	5	62 (1)	608	2605	4.3 (67)	17	96	903	9.4 (66)	2	12	3	25.0	36	3.0 (23)	0	0	2	26	—	k	—	114	3505

POSTUS, AL Albert Michael, TB-DB, 5´10˝/180 lbs; Villanova; 1944: Phi, rnd 22; B9/21/1920 Philadelphia, PA

YEAR	TEAM	G (GS, POS)	RUSH	YD	AVG (LG)	TD	REC	YD	AVG (LG)	TD	PASS	COMP	PCT	YD	AVG (LG)	TD	INT	SK	YD	QBR	KPR	OTD	PTS	TAY
1945	Pit	2 (0)	2	4	2.0 (12)	0	—	—	—	—	5	2	40.0	73	14.6 (52)	0	1	—	—	—	k	—	0	-1

POTEAT, HANK Henry Major, DB, 5´9˝/192 lbs; Pittsburgh; 2000: Pit, rnd 3; B8/30/1977 Harrisburg, PA **[R]** **2000** Pit 15 (0) **2001** Pit 13 (0) **2002**†Pit 13 (0) **2003** TB 1 (0) **2004**†NE 0 (0) **2005**†NE 10 (1) **NFL** 52 (1) [6 yrs]

POTH, PHIL Phillip J., G, 5´11˝/195 lbs; Gonzaga; B5/2/1911 Seattle, WA, D9/24/1998 Seattle, WA **1934** Phi 1 (0)

POTO, JOHN John P., HB, 5´10˝/194 lbs; none; B4/10/1926 Boston, MA, D11/1965

YEAR	TEAM	G (GS, POS)	RUSH	YD	AVG (LG)	TD	REC	YD	AVG (LG)	TD	PASS	COMP	PCT	YD	AVG (LG)	TD	INT	SK	YD	QBR	KPR	OTD	PTS	TAY
1947	Bos	6 (1)	6	27	4.5 (11)	1	—	—	—	—	—	—	—	—	—	—	—	—	—	—	kp	—	6	83
1948	Bos	12 (0)	13	32	2.5 (12)	0	10	101	10.1 (29)	0	—	—	—	—	—	—	—	—	—	—	kp	—	0	82
NFL	2	18 (1)	19	59	3.1 (12)	1	10	101	10.1 (29)	0	—	—	—	—	—	—	—	—	—	—	kp	—	6	165

POTTEIGER, EARL William Earl, B, 5´7˝/170 lbs; Ursinus; B1/11/1891 Reading, PA, D8/25/1962 Reading, PA **[C]** **1920** Buf 2 (1) **1921** ChiC 1 (1) **1922** Mil 3 (1) **1924** Ken 3 (2) **1925** NYG 2 (0) **1926** NYG 1 (0) **1927** NYG 2 (0) **1928** NYG 7 (0) **NFL** 21 (5) [8 yrs]

POTTER, KEVIN Kevin Craig, DB, 5´10˝/188 lbs; Missouri; 1983: Hou, rnd 9; B12/19/1959 St. Louis, MO **1983** ChiB 8 (0) **1984**†ChiB 1 (0) **NFL** 9 (0) [2 yrs]

POTTER, STEVE Stephen John, LB, 6´3˝/235 lbs; Virginia; B11/6/1957 Bradford, PA **1981**†Mia 16 (0) **1982**†Mia 9 (0) **1983** KC 16 (1) **1984** Buf 10 (0) **NFL** 51 (1) [4 yrs]

POTTIOS, MYRON Myron Joseph, LB, 6´2˝/232 lbs; Notre Dame; 1961: Pit, rnd 2; B1/18/1939 Van Voorhis, PA **1961** Pit✧14 (MLB) **1963** Pit★14 (MLB) **1964** Pit✧7 (MLB) **1965** Pit 6 (MLB) **1966** LARm 12 **1967**†LARm 11 (MLB) **1968** LARm 14 (14, MLB) **1969**†LARm 5 **1970** LARm 14 (14, MLB) **1971**†Was 14 (14, MLB) **1972**†Was 12 (7, mlb) **1973**†Was 6 (6, mlb) **NFL** 129 (55) [12 yrs]

POTTS, CHARLIE Charles, DB, 6´3˝/210 lbs; Purdue; 1972: Det, rnd 6; B4/29/1949 Chicago, IL **1972** Det 10

POTTS, DADDY Robert Crockett, T, 6´1˝/235 lbs; Clemson; B8/16/1898 York County, SC, D8/11/1981 Columbia, SC **1926** Fra 16 (9, LT)

POTTS, ROOSEVELT Roosevelt Bernard, RB, 6´0˝/250 lbs; Louisiana-Monroe; 1993: Ind, rnd 2; B1/8/1971 Rayville, LA

YEAR	TEAM	G (GS, POS)	RUSH	YD	AVG (LG)	TD	REC	YD	AVG (LG)	TD	PASS	COMP	PCT	YD	AVG (LG)	TD	INT	SK	YD	QBR	KPR	OTD	PTS	TAY
1993	Ind	16 (15, RB)	179	711	4.0 (34)	0	26	189	7.3 (24)	0	—	—	—	—	—	—	—	—	—	—	—	—	0	806
1994	Ind	16 (15, FB)	77	336	4.4 (52)	1	26	251	9.7 (30)	1	—	—	—	—	—	—	—	—	—	—	—	—	12	477
1995	Ind	15 (15, FB)	65	309	4.8 (37)	0	21	228	10.9 (52)	1	—	—	—	—	—	—	—	—	—	—	—	—	6	428
1997	Ind	2 (0)	1	1	1.0 (1)	0	—	—	—	—	—	—	—	—	—	—	—	—	—	—	—	—	0	1
1997	†Mia	6 (1)	1	3	3.0 (3)	0	3	27	9.0 (13)	0	—	—	—	—	—	—	—	—	—	—	k	—	0	18
1998	Bal	16 (15, FB)	36	115	3.2 (33)	0	30	168	5.6 (18)	2	—	—	—	—	—	—	—	—	—	—	k	—	12	197
NFL	5	71 (61)	359	1475	4.1 (52)	1	106	863	8.1 (52)	4	—	—	—	—	—	—	—	—	—	—	k	—	30	1926

POTTS, BILL William, HB, /200 lbs; Villanova; B1910 **1934** Pit 1 (0)

POUGH, ERNEST Ernest Leon, WR, 6´1˝/174 lbs; Texas Southern; 1976: Pit, rnd 3; B5/17/1952 Jacksonville, FL

YEAR	TEAM	G (GS, POS)	RUSH	YD	AVG (LG)	TD	REC	YD	AVG (LG)	TD	PASS	COMP	PCT	YD	AVG (LG)	TD	INT	SK	YD	QBR	KPR	OTD	PTS	TAY
1976	†Pit	14	2	8	4.0 (6)	0	8	161	20.1 (50)	1	—	—	—	—	—	—	—	—	—	—	k	—	6	193
1977	†Pit	14	—	—	—	—	1	3	3.0 (3)	0	—	—	—	—	—	—	—	—	—	—	k	—	0	8
1978	NYG	12	3	33	11.0 (25)	0	1	2	2.0 (2)	0	—	—	—	—	—	—	—	—	—	—	k	—	0	122
NFL	3	40	5	41	8.2 (25)	0	10	166	16.6 (50)	1	—	—	—	—	—	—	—	—	—	—	k	—	6	322

POUHA, SIONE Sione Sonasi, DT, 6´3˝/330 lbs; Utah; 2005: NYJ, rnd 3; B2/3/1979 Salt Lake City, UT **2005** NYJ 14 (0)

POUNDS, DARRYL Daryl Lamont, DB, 5´10˝/185 lbs; Nicholls State; 1995: Was, rnd 3; B7/21/1972 Fort Worth, TX **1995** Was 9 (0) **1996** Was 12 (1) **1997** Was 16 (0) **1998** Was 16 (3) **1999**†Was 16 (0) **2000** Den 9 (0) **NFL** 78 (4) [6 yrs]

POURDANESH, SHAR Shariar, T, 6´6˝/312 lbs; UNLV; B7/19/1970 Teheran, Iran **1996** Was 16 (8, rt) **1997** Was 16 (14, LT) **1998** Was 16 (15, RT) **1999** Pit 4 (2) **2000** Pit 5 (2) **NFL** 57 (41) [5 yrs]

POWE, KARL Karl Alonzo, WR, 6´2˝/175 lbs; Alabama State; 1985: Dal, rnd 7; B1/17/1962 Mobile, AL **1986** Dal 1 (0)

YEAR	TEAM	G (GS, POS)	RUSH	YD	AVG (LG)	TD	REC	YD	AVG (LG)	TD	PASS	COMP	PCT	YD	AVG (LG)	TD	INT	SK	YD	QBR	KPR	OTD	PTS	TAY
1985	†Dal	15 (1)	—	—	—	—	14	237	16.9 (34)	0	—	—	—	—	—	—	—	—	—	—	k	—	0	121
NFL	2	16 (1)	—	—	—	—	14	237	16.9 (34)	0	—	—	—	—	—	—	—	—	—	—	—	—	0	119

POWE, KEITH Keith, DE, 6´3˝/285 lbs; Lamar; Texas-El Paso; B6/5/1969 Biloxi, MS **1994** TB 5 (0) **1995** TB 3 (0) **NFL** 8 (0) [2 yrs]

POWELL, ALVIN Alvin Robert, G, 6´5˝/294 lbs; Winston-Salem State; 1984: Sea, rnd S2; B11/19/1959 Panama City, Panama **1987**†Sea 12 (0) **1988** Sea 6 (0) **1989** Mia 2 (0) **NFL** 20 (0) [3 yrs]

POWELL, ANDRE Andre Maurice, LB, 6´1˝/226 lbs; Penn State; 1992: Mia, rnd 8; B6/5/1969 York, PA **1993**†NYG 15 (1) **1994** NYG 1 (0) **NFL** 16 (1) [2 yrs]

POWELL, ART Arthur Louis, SE-DB-WR, 6´3˝/211 lbs; San Jose State; 1959: Phi, rnd 11; B2/25/1937 Dallas, TX

YEAR	TEAM	G (GS, POS)	RUSH	YD	AVG (LG)	TD	REC	YD	AVG (LG)	TD	PASS	COMP	PCT	YD	AVG (LG)	TD	INT	SK	YD	QBR	KPR	OTD	PTS	TAY
1959	Phi	12 (DB)	—	—	—	—	—	—	—	—	—	—	—	—	—	—	—	—	—	—	kpi	1	6	230
1960	NYT-A☆	14 (SE)	—	—	—	—	69	1167	16.9 (76)	**14**	—	—	—	—	—	—	—	—	—	—	k	—	84	687
1961	NYT-A	14 (SE)	—	—	—	—	71	881	12.4 (48)	5	—	—	—	—	—	—	—	—	—	—	—	—	30	466
1962	NYT-A☆	14 (SE)	—	—	—	—	64	**1130**	17.7 (80)	8	—	—	—	—	—	—	—	—	—	—	—	—	48	605
1963	Oak-A★	14 (SE)	—	—	—	—	73	**1304**	17.9 (85)	**16**	—	—	—	—	—	—	—	—	—	—	—	—	96	732
1964	Oak-A★	14 (SE)	—	—	—	—	76	1361	17.9 (77)	11	—	—	—	—	—	—	—	—	—	—	—	—	66	736
1965	Oak-A★	14 (SE)	—	—	—	—	52	800	15.4 (66)	12	—	—	—	—	—	—	—	—	—	—	—	—	72	460
1966	Oak-A★	14 (SE)	—	—	—	—	53	1026	19.4 (46)	11	—	—	—	—	—	—	—	—	—	—	—	—	66	568
1967	Buf-A	6 (se)	—	—	—	—	20	346	17.3 (37)	4	—	—	—	—	—	—	—	—	—	—	—	—	24	193
1968	Min	1	—	—	—	—	1	31	31.0 (31)	0	—	—	—	—	—	—	—	—	—	—	—	—	0	16
NFL	10	117	—	—	—	—	479	8046	16.8 (85)	81	—	—	—	—	—	—	—	—	—	—	kpi	1	492	4691

POWELL, CARL Carl Demetris, DE, 6´2˝/285 lbs; Louisville; 1997: Ind, rnd 5; B1/4/1974 Detroit, MI **1997** Ind 11 (0) **2000** Bal 2 (0) **2001**†ChiB 16 (0) **2002** Was 15 (4) **2003** Cin 16 (3) **2004** Cin 10 (2) **2005**†Cin 11 (1) **NFL** 81 (10) [7 yrs]

POWELL, CHARLEY Charles Elvin, DE-LB-E, 6´3˝/226 lbs; none; B4/4/1932, TX **1952** SF 7 **1953** SF 12 (RDE) **1955** SF 12 (RDE) **1956** SF 12 (RDE) **1960** Oak-A 14 (RDE) **1961** Oak-A 14 (RDE)

YEAR	TEAM	G (GS, POS)	RUSH	YD	AVG (LG)	TD	REC	YD	AVG (LG)	TD	PASS	COMP	PCT	YD	AVG (LG)	TD	INT	SK	YD	QBR	KPR	OTD	PTS	TAY
1957	†SF	12 (RLB)	—	—	—	—	1	27	27.0 (27)	0	—	—	—	—	—	—	—	—	—	—	—	—	0	14
NFL	7	83	—	—	—	—	1	27	27.0 (27)	0	—	—	—	—	—	—	—	—	—	—	k	—	2	8

POWELL, CRAIG Craig Steven, LB, 6´4˝/230 lbs; Ohio State; 1995: Cle, rnd 1; B11/13/1971 Youngstown, OH **1995** Cle 3 (3) **1996** Bal 9 (0) **1998** NYJ 2 (0) **NFL** 14 (3) [3 yrs]

POWELL, DARNELL Darnell, RB, 6´0˝/197 lbs; Tennessee-Chattanooga; 1976: Buf, rnd 6; B5/31/1954 Atlanta, GA

YEAR	TEAM	G (GS, POS)	RUSH	YD	AVG (LG)	TD	REC	YD	AVG (LG)	TD	PASS	COMP	PCT	YD	AVG (LG)	TD	INT	SK	YD	QBR	KPR	OTD	PTS	TAY
1976	Buf	11	11	40	3.6 (20)	0	1	6	6.0 (6)	0	—	—	—	—	—	—	—	—	—	—	k	—	0	84
1978	NYJ	14 (1)	20	77	3.8 (17)	1	—	—	—	—	—	—	—	—	—	—	—	—	—	—	k	—	6	92
NFL	2	25 (1)	31	117	3.8 (20)	1	1	6	6.0 (6)	0	—	—	—	—	—	—	—	—	—	—	k	—	6	176

POWELL, DICK Richard Lee, E, 6´2˝/215 lbs; Davis & Elkins; B5/21/1904 Gilmer County, WV, D4/29/1986 Martinsville, VA **1932** NYG 2 (0) **1933** Cin 3 (1) **NFL** 5 (1) [2 yrs]

POWELL, JEMEEL Jemeel, DB, 6´0˝/185 lbs; California; B8/29/1980 Los Angeles, CA **2003**†Dal 3 (0)

POWELL, JEFF Jeffrey O'Neal, RB, 5´10˝/185 lbs; William & Mary; Tennessee; 1986: Chi, rnd 6; B5/27/1963 Nashville, TN **1987** SD 1 (0)

YEAR	TEAM	G (GS, POS)	RUSH	YD	AVG (LG)	TD	REC	YD	AVG (LG)	TD	PASS COMP	PCT	YD	AVG (LG)	TD	INT	SK	YD	QBR	KPR	OTD	PTS	TAY

POWELL, JESSE   Jesse Loy, LB, 6´2˝/220 lbs; West Texas A&M; 1969: Mia, rnd 9; B4/14/1947 Matador, TX   **1969** Mia-A 14   **1970** Mia 11   **1971**†Mia 14   **1972**†Mia 14   **1973** Mia 3   **NFL** 56 [5 yrs]

POWELL, MARVIN   Marvin, T, 6´5˝/268 lbs; USC; 1977: NYJ, rnd 1; B8/30/1955 Fort Bragg, NC   **1977** NYJ 11 (10, RT)   **1978** NYJ 14 (14, RT)   **1979** NYJ★16 (16, RT)   **1980** NYJ★15 (15, RT)   **1981**†NYJ★14 (14, RT)   **1982**†NYJ★8 (8, RT)   **1983** NYJ★16 (16, RT)   **1984** NYJ 16 (16, RT)   **1985**†NYJ 14 (14, RT)   **1986** TB 3 (3)   **1987** TB 6 (4)   **NFL** 133 (130) [11 yrs]

POWELL, MARVIN   Marvin, FB, 6´2˝/235 lbs; USC; B6/6/1976 Los Angeles, CA

| 1999 | NO | 9(0) | 1 | 1 | 1.0(1) | 0 | — | — | — | — | — | — | — | — | — | — | — | — | — | — | — | 0 | 1 |

POWELL, PRESTON   Preston, FB, 6´2˝/225 lbs; Grambling State; 1961: Cle, rnd 7/Oak, rnd 20; B9/23/1936 Winnfield, LA

| 1961 | Cle | 12 | 1 | 5 | 5.0(5) | 0 | — | — | — | — | — | — | — | — | — | — | — | — | — | k | — | 0 | 86 |

POWELL, ROGER   Roger Mills, WB, 6´0˝/180 lbs; Texas A&M; B8/17/1894 Austin, TX, D1/28/1988 Waco, TX   **1926** Buf 1 (0)

POWELL, RONNIE   Ronnie, WR, 5´10˝/174 lbs; Arkansas Tech; Northwestern State (LA); B11/3/1974 Hope, AR

| 1999 | Cle | 14(0) | 1 | -14 | -14.0(-14) | 0 | 1 | 45 | 45.0(45) | 0 | — | — | — | — | — | — | — | — | — | k | — | 0 | 335 |

POWELL, STAN   Stancil, aka Wrinkle Meat, G, 5´11˝/185 lbs; Carlisle Indian; Haskell Indian; B1890, deceased   **1923** Oor 8 (7, LG)

POWELL, STEVE   Steven Orville, RB, 5´11˝/186 lbs; Truman State; 1978: Buf, rnd 7; B1/2/1956 St. Louis, MO   **1978** Buf 10

| 1979 | Buf | 15 | 10 | 29 | 2.9(9) | 0 | — | — | — | — | — | — | — | — | — | — | — | — | — | k | — | 0 | 36 |
| NFL | 2 | 25 | 10 | 29 | 2.9(9) | 0 | — | — | — | — | — | — | — | — | — | — | — | — | — | k | — | 0 | 44 |

POWELL, TIM   Tim Arden, DE, 6´4˝/248 lbs; Northwestern; B9/2/1942 North Canton, OH   **1965** LARm 8   **1966** Pit 4   **NFL** 12 [2 yrs]

POWERS, CLYDE   Clyde Joseph, DB, 6´1˝/195 lbs; Oklahoma; 1974: NYG, rnd 5; B8/19/1951 Pascagoula, MS   **1974** NYG 14 (7, ss)   **1975** NYG 14 (7, SS)   **1976** NYG 14 (SS)   **1977** NYG 14 (14, SS)   **1978** KC 1   **NFL** 57 (28) [5 yrs]

POWERS, JIM   James W., DB-LB-QB, 6´0˝/185 lbs; USC; 1950: SF, rnd 26; B2/29/1928

1950	SF	10(SS)	3	4	1.3(3)	0	—	—	—	—	20	9	45.0	108	5.4(50)	0	2	—	—	i	—	0	-5
1951	SF	12(DB)	—	—	—	—	—	—	—	—	—	—	—	—	—	—	—	—	—	i	—	0	53
1952	SF	12(LLB)	—	—	—	—	—	1	0	0.0	—	0	0	0	0	—	—	—	—	i	—	0	27
1953	SF	12	3	-10	-3.3(0)	0	—	—	—	—	49	22	44.9	259	5.3(28)	1	2	—	—	P	—	0	45
NFL	4	46	6	-6	-1.0(3)	0	—	—	—	—	70	31	44.3	367	5.2(50)	1	4	—	—	Pi	—	0	120

POWERS, JOHN   John Paul, TE, 6´2˝/215 lbs; Notre Dame; 1962: Pit, rnd 9; B6/15/1940 Harvard, IL   **1963** Pit 14   **1965** Pit 2   **1966** Min 5

1962	Pit	14	—	—	—	—	1	16	16.0(16)	0	—	—	—	—	—	—	—	—	—	—	—	0	8
1964	Pit	14(TE)	2	10	5.0(9)	0	8	193	24.1(42)	0	—	—	—	—	—	—	—	—	—	—	—	0	107
NFL	5	49	2	10	5.0(9)	0	9	209	23.2(42)	0	—	—	—	—	—	—	—	—	—	—	—	0	115

POWERS, RICKY   Richard, RB, 6´0˝/213 lbs; Michigan; B11/30/1970 Akron, OH

| 1995 | Cle | 3(0) | 14 | 51 | 3.6(15) | 0 | 1 | 6 | 6.0(6) | 0 | — | — | — | — | — | — | — | — | — | k | — | 0 | 63 |

POWERS, SAMMY   Sam, G-T, 5´10˝/170 lbs; none; B1901, deceased   **1921** GB 4 (1)

POWERS, WARREN   Warren Anthony, DB, 6´0˝/185 lbs; Nebraska; B2/19/1941 Kansas City, MO [I]   **1963** Oak-A 5   **1964** Oak-A 10 (Is)   **1965** Oak-A 12 (Is)   **1966** Oak-A 14 (LS)   **1967**†Oak-A 14 (rs)   **1968**†Oak-A 8 (4)   **NFL** 63 (4) [6 yrs]

POWERS, WARREN   Warren, DE, 6´6˝/287 lbs; Maryland; 1989: Den, rnd 2; B2/4/1965 Baltimore, MD   **1989**†Den 15 (1)   **1990** Den 16 (16, LDE)   **1991**†Den 13 (11, LDE)   **1992** LARm 7 (0)   **NFL** 51 (28) [4 yrs]

POZDERAC, PHIL   Philip Maurice, T, 6´9˝/277 lbs; Notre Dame; 1982: Dal, rnd 5; B12/19/1959 Cleveland, OH   **1982** Dal 7 (0)   **1983** Dal 16 (2)   **1985**†Dal 14 (9, LT)   **1986** Dal 16 (10, RT)   **1987** Dal 2 (2)

| 1984 | Dal | 15(14, LT/rt) | — | — | — | — | 1 | 1 | 1.0(1) | 0 | — | — | — | — | — | — | — | — | — | — | — | 0 | 1 |
| NFL | 6 | 70(37) | — | — | — | — | 1 | 1 | 1.0(1) | 0 | — | — | — | — | — | — | — | — | — | — | — | 0 | 1 |

PRATER, DEAN   Troy Dean, DE, 6´5˝/225 lbs; Oklahoma State; 1981: Cle, rnd 10; B9/28/1958 Altus, OK, D3/14/1996 Horseheads, NY   **1982** KC 2 (0)   **1983** KC 16 (1)   **1984** Buf 13 (0)   **1985** Buf 16 (0)   **1986** Buf 16 (0)   **1987** Buf 10 (0)   **1988** Buf 4 (0)   **NFL** 77 (1) [7 yrs]

PRATHER, DALE   Dale Lambert, E-T, 6´2˝/190 lbs; George Washington; B9/19/1910, D9/7/1973   **1938** Cle 6 (1)

PRATHER, GUY   Guy Tyrone, LB, 6´2˝/230 lbs; Grambling State; B3/28/1958 Gaithersburg, MD   **1981** GB 16 (0)   **1982**†GB 9 (0)   **1983** GB 16 (0)   **1984** GB 16 (0)

| 1985 | GB | 16(1) | 1 | 0 | 0.0(0) | 0 | — | — | — | — | — | — | — | — | — | — | — | — | — | S | — | 0 | 0 |
| NFL | 5 | 73(1) | 1 | 0 | 0.0 | 0 | — | — | — | — | — | — | — | — | — | — | — | — | — | kS | — | 0 | -8 |

PRATT, ROBERT   Robert Henry, G, 6´3˝/255 lbs; North Carolina; 1974: Bal, rnd 3; B5/25/1951 Richmond, VA   **1974** Bal 13   **1975**†Bal 14 (9, LG)   **1976**†Bal 14 (14, LG)   **1977**†Bal 14 (14, LG)   **1978** Bal 16 (15, LG)   **1979** Bal 16 (16, LG)   **1980** Bal 16 (16, LG)   **1981** Bal 15 (15, LG)   **1982** Sea 9 (9, RG)   **1983**†Sea 15 (15, RG)   **1985** Sea 12 (12, RG)

| 1984 | †Sea | 16(16, RG) | — | — | — | — | 1 | 30 | 30.0(30) | 0 | — | — | — | — | — | — | — | — | — | — | — | 0 | 15 |
| NFL | 12 | 170(151) | — | — | — | — | 1 | 30 | 30.0(30) | 0 | — | — | — | — | — | — | — | — | — | k | — | 1 | 6 | 25 |

PRCHLIK, JOHN   John George, DT-T, 6´4˝/234 lbs; Yale; 1947: Bos, rnd 30; B7/20/1925 Cleveland, OH, D12/31/2003 Fairfield Grade, TN   **1949** Det 12 (2)   **1950** Det 12 (RDT)   **1951** Det 12 (RDT)   **1952**†Det 12 (RDT)   **1953**†Det 11 (RDT)   **NFL** 59 (2) [5 yrs]

PREAS, GEORGE   George Robert, T-G-LB, 6´2˝/244 lbs; Virginia Tech; 1955: Bal, rnd 5; B6/25/1933 Roanoke, VA   **1955** Bal 12 (RT)   **1956** Bal 12 (RT)   **1957** Bal 10 (RT)   **1958**†Bal 12 (RT)   **1959**†Bal 12 (RT)   **1960** Bal 12 (RT)   **1961** Bal 14 (RT)   **1962** Bal 14 (RT)   **1963** Bal 14 (RT)   **1964**†Bal☆14 (RT)   **1965**†Bal 14 (RT)   **NFL** 140 [11 yrs]

PREBOLA, GENE   Eugene Nicholas, TE, 6´3˝/225 lbs; Boston University; 1960: Hou, rnd 1/Det, rnd 19; B6/30/1938 Bronx, NY

1960	Oak-A	14(TE)	—	—	—	—	33	404	12.2(36)	2	—	—	—	—	—	—	—	—	—	—	—	12	212
1961	Den-A	14(TE)	—	—	—	—	29	349	12.0(54)	1	—	—	—	—	—	—	—	—	—	k	—	8	173
1962	Den-A	14(TE)	—	—	—	—	41	599	14.6(55)	1	—	—	—	—	—	—	—	—	—	—	—	8	305
1963	Den-A	14(TE)	—	—	—	—	30	471	15.7(57)	2	—	—	—	—	—	—	—	—	—	—	—	14	246
NFL	4	56	—	—	—	—	133	1823	13.7(57)	6	—	—	—	—	—	—	—	—	—	k	—	42	935

PREECE, STEVE   Steven Packer, DB, 6´1˝/195 lbs; Oregon State; B2/15/1947 Idaho Falls, ID   **1969** NO 14 (Is)   **1970** Phi 14 (FS)   **1971** Phi 7   **1972** Phi 1   **1972** Den 13 (8, FS)   **1975**‡LARm 14

1973	†LARm	14(14, FS)	1	11	11.0(11)	1	—	—	—	—	—	—	—	—	—	—	—	—	—	i	—	6	36
1974	†LARm	14(10, FS)	1	-4	-4.0(-4)	0	—	—	—	—	—	—	—	—	—	—	—	—	—	i	—	0	19
1976	†LARm	14	1	0	0.0(0)	0	—	—	—	—	—	—	—	—	—	—	—	—	—	—	—	0	1
1977	Sea	14(14, FS)	—	—	—	—	1	0	0.0	—	—	0	0	—	—	—	—	—	—	—	—	0	35
NFL	9	119(46)	3	7	2.3(11)	1	1	0	0.0	—	—	0	0	0	0	—	—	—	—	ki	—	2	18	96

PREGULMAN, MERV   Mervin, C-G, 6´3˝/215 lbs; Michigan; 1944: GB, rnd 1; B10/10/1922 Lansing, MI [K]   **1946** GB 11 (7, RG)   **1947** Det 12 (9, C)   **1948** Det 12 (8, C)   **1949** NYB 12 (0)   **NFL** 47 (24) [4 yrs]

PRENTICE, TRAVIS   Travis Jason, RB, 5´11˝/221 lbs; Miami (OH); 2000: Cle, rnd 3; B12/8/1976 Louisville, KY

2000	Cle	16(11, RB)	173	512	3.0(17)	7	37	191	5.2(13)	1	—	—	—	—	—	—	—	—	—	—	—	48	683
2001	Min	14(0)	14	13	0.9(6)	2	1	10	10.0(10)	0	—	—	—	—	—	—	—	—	—	k	—	12	25
NFL	2	30(11)	187	525	2.8(17)	9	38	201	5.3(13)	1	—	—	—	—	—	—	—	—	—	k	—	60	708

PRESCOTT, HAL   Harold Dougald, E, 6´1˝/199 lbs; Hardin-Simmons; 1943: GB, rnd 19; B10/18/1920 Abilene, TX, D5/1/2002 Cisco, TX   **1948** Phi 11 (0)   **1949** Phi 3 (0)   **1949** Det 1 (0)

1946	GB	2(0)	—	—	—	—	1	8	8.0(8)	0	—	—	—	—	—	—	—	—	—	—	—	0	4
1947	†Phi	11(2)	—	—	—	—	1	15	15.0(15)	0	—	—	—	—	—	—	—	—	—	i	—	0	-3
1949	NYB	5(1)	—	—	—	—	10	162	16.2(41)	1	—	—	—	—	—	—	—	—	—	—	—	6	86
NFL	4	33(3)	—	—	—	—	12	185	15.4(41)	1	—	—	—	—	—	—	—	—	—	i	—	6	88

PRESIDENT, ANDRE   Andre, TE, 6´3˝/255 lbs; Angelo State (TX); B6/16/1971 Fort Worth, TX   **1995** NE 1 (0)   **1995** ChiB 2 (0)   **NFL** 3 (0) [1 yr]

PRESLEY, LEE   Leo Grady, FB-C, 6´2˝/230 lbs; Oklahoma; B3/16/1922 El Campo, TX, D9/1975

| 1945 | Was | 8(3) | 1 | 1 | 1.0(1) | 0 | — | — | — | — | — | — | — | — | — | — | — | — | — | — | — | 0 | 1 |

YEAR	TEAM	G (GS, POS)	RUSH	YD	AVG(LG)	TD	REC	YD	AVG(LG)	TD	PASS	COMP	PCT	YD	AVG(LG)	TD	INT	SK	YD	QBR	KPR	OTD	PTS	TAY

PRESNELL, GLENN Glenn Emery, B, 5'10"/195 lbs; Nebraska; B7/28/1905 Gilead, NE, D9/13/2004 Ironton, OH **[K]**

1931	Por☆	14 (11, TB)																			K	—	13	254
1932	Por☆	12 (7, tb)	68	232	3.4		4	54	13.5		1	46	17	37.0	259	5.6	2	4	—	—	K	—	13	254
1933	Por☆	11 (9, TB)	118	522	4.4	6	3	23	7.7	0	125	50	40.0	774	6.2	6	12	—	—	37.6	K	—	64	531
1934	Det☆	13 (3, tb)	108	413	3.8	7	3	42	14.0	0	57	13	22.8	223	3.9	2	8	—	—		K	—	63	306
1935	†Det	12 (6, tb)	71	225	3.2	0	3	73	24.3(48)	1	45	15	33.3	193	4.3	0	6	—	—		K	1	28	133
1936	Det	12 (5, tb)	48	201	4.2	1	—	—	—		36	15	41.7	221	6.1	2	7	—	—		K	—	15	52
NFL	6	74 (41)	413	1593	3.9	18	13	192	14.8(48)	2	309	110	35.6	1670	5.4	17	37	—	—	33.0	K	2	218	1339

PRESTEL, JIM James Francis, DT, 6'5"/275 lbs; Idaho; 1959: Cle, rnd 6/1960: Bos, rnd 1; B6/28/1937 Indianapolis, IN **1960** Cle 6 **1961** Min 14 (14, LDT) **1962** Min 14 (14, LDT) **1963** Min 14 (14, LDT) **1964** Min 14 (14, LDT) **1965** Min 13 **1966** NYG 13 (LDT) **1967** Was 8 **NFL** 96 (56) [8 yrs]

PRESTON, BILL William, T, none; deceased **1920** Akr 1 (0)

PRESTON, DAVE Richard David, RB, 5'10"/195 lbs; Bowling Green State; 1977: NE, rnd 12; B5/29/1955 Dayton, OH

1978	†Den	16	66	296	4.5(16)	1	24	199	8.3(21)	1	—	—	—	—	—						kp	—	12	478
1979	†Den	10 (3)	43	169	3.9(18)	1	19	137	7.2(19)	1	1	0	0.0	0	0.0	0	0	—	—		kp	—	12	437
1980	Den	12 (10, RB)	111	385	3.5(19)	4	35	309	8.8(36)	0	—	—	—	—	—						kp	—	24	613
1981	Den	16 (14, RB)	183	640	3.5(23)	3	52	507	9.8(37)	0	—	—	—	—	—						k	—	18	910
1982	Den	8 (5, RB)	19	81	4.3(13)	0	14	134	9.6(20)	0	—	—	—	—	—							—	0	148
1983	†Den	14 (3)	57	222	3.9(28)	1	17	137	8.1(25)	1	—	—	—	—	—							—	12	306
NFL	6	76 (35)	479	1793	3.7(28)	10	161	1423	8.8(37)	3	1	0	0.0	0	0.0	0	0	—	—		kp	—	78	2890

PRESTON, DUKE Raymond Newton, C, 6'5"/311 lbs; Illinois; 2005: Buf, rnd 4; B6/12/1982 San Diego, CA **2005** Buf 15 (1)

PRESTON, JOHN John Stanley, DB, 6'0"/207 lbs; TCU; Central Oklahoma; B8/28/1962 Dallas, TX **1987** SL 5 (0)

PRESTON, PAT Paddison Wade, G, 6'2"/216 lbs; Wake Forest; Duke; 1943: ChiB, rnd 17; B6/15/1921 Kernersville, NC, D6/23/2002 Mount Airy, NC **1946**†ChiB 11 (6, RG) **1947** ChiB 3 (2) **1948** ChiB 12 (2) **1949** ChiB 12 (4) **NFL** 38 (14) [4 yrs]

PRESTON, RAY Raymond Newton, LB, 6'0"/218 lbs; Syracuse; 1976: SD, rnd 11; B1/25/1954 Lawrence, MA **1976** SD 14 **1977** SD 11 **1978** SD 16 (1) **1979**†SD 16 (16, LLB) **1980**†SD 14 (13, LLB) **1981** SD 16 (0) **1982**†SD 9 (0) **1983** SD 16 (0) **1984** SD 10 (0) **NFL** 122 (30) [9 yrs]

PRESTON, ROELL Roell, WR, 5'10"/187 lbs; Mississippi; 1995: Atl, rnd 5; B6/23/1972 Miami, FL **[R]** **1997** GB 1 (0) **1999**†Ten 2 (0) **1999** Mia 1 (0) **1999** SF 4 (0)

1995	Atl	14 (0)	—	—	—		7	129	18.4(61)	1	—	—	—	—	—						k	—	6	247
1996	Atl	15 (2)	—	—	—		21	208	9.9(17)	1	—	—	—	—	—						k	—	6	310
1998	†GB★	16 (0)	—	—	—		2	23	11.5(13)	0	—	—	—	—	—						kp	3	18	862
NFL	5	53 (2)	—	—	—		30	360	12.0(61)	2	—	—	—	—	—						kp	3	30	1626

PRESTRIDGE, LUKE Luke Earl, P, 6'4"/235 lbs; Baylor; 1979: Den, rnd 7; B9/17/1956 Houston, TX **[P]** **1980** Den☆16 (0) **1981** Den 16 (0) **1982** Den★9 (0) **1984** NE 9 (0)

1979	†Den	16	1	29	29.0(29)	0	—	—	—		1	0	0.0	0	0.0	0	0	—	—		P	—	0	29
1983	†Den	16 (0)	1	7	7.0(7)	0	—	—	—		—	—	—	—	—						P	—	0	7
NFL	6	82	2	36	18.0(29)	0	—	—	—		1	0	0.0	0	0.0	0	0	—	—		P	—	0	36

PREWITT, FELTO Felton Winters, C-LB, 5'11"/207 lbs; Tulsa; 1946: Phi, rnd 6; B5/17/1924 Corsicana, TX, D3/15/1998 Reno, NV **1946** Buf-A 14 (8, C) **1947** Buf-A 13 (10, C) **1948**†Buf-A 7 (5, c) **1949** Bal-A 12 (7, C) **AAFC** 46 (30) [4 yrs]

PRIATKO, BILL William Daniel, LB, 6'2"/220 lbs; Pittsburgh; B10/16/1931 North Braddock, PA **1957** Pit 2

PRICE, ART Arthur Brennan, LB, 6'3"/227 lbs; Wisconsin; B5/17/1962 Hampton, VA **1987** Atl 3 (0)

PRICE, COTTON Charles Walemon, TB-DB-QB, 6'1"/180 lbs; Texas A&M; B5/31/1918 Bridgeport, TX **[K]**

1940	Det◇	9 (1)	42	122	2.9	2	—	—	—		66	33	50.0	456	6.9	3	7	—	—		KP	—	16	105
1941	Det	11 (2)	16	36	2.3(13)	0	1	6	6.0(6)	0	33	9	27.3	118	3.6(19)	0	4	—	—		Pkp	—	0	-8
1945	Det	8 (3)	24	71	3.0(14)	0	—	—	—		52	16	30.8	256	4.9(63)	3	8	—	—		Pkpi	—	0	-59
NFL	3	28 (6)	82	229	2.8(14)	2	1	6	6.0(6)	0	151	58	38.4	830	5.5(63)	6	19	—	—		KPkpi	—	16	38
1946	Mia-A	7 (2)	15	-55	-3.7	0	2	17	8.5		74	36	48.6	484	6.5	2	5	—	—		Pk	—	0	8

PRICE, DARYL Daryl, DE, 6'3"/274 lbs; Colorado; 1996: SF, rnd 4; B10/23/1972 Galveston, TX **1996**†SF 13 (0) **1997** SF 5 (0) **NFL** 18 (0) [2 yrs]

PRICE, DENNIS Dennis Sean, DB, 6'1"/175 lbs; UCLA; 1988: LARd, rnd 5; B6/14/1965 Los Angeles, CA **1988** LARd 12 (4) **1989** LARd 5 (0) **1991**†NYJ 0 (0) **1992** NYJ 14 (0) **NFL** 31 (4) [4 yrs]

PRICE, DEREK Derek Christopher, TE, 6'3"/240 lbs; Iowa; B8/12/1972 Tempe, AZ

| 1996 | Det | 13 (1) | — | — | — | | 1 | 14 | 14.0(14) | 0 | — | — | — | — | — | | | | | | | — | 0 | 7 |

PRICE, EDDIE Edward J., FB, 5'11"/190 lbs; Tulane; 1950: NYG, rnd 2/1949: Bkn-A, rnd 20; B9/2/1925 New Orleans, LA, D7/21/1979 New Orleans, LA

1950	†NYG	10 (FB)	126	703	5.6(74)	4	4	30	7.5(21)	0	—	—	—	—	—							—	24	758
1951	NYG★	12 (FB)	271	971	3.6(80)	7	5	19	3.8(8)	0	—	—	—	—	—							—	42	1051
1952	NYG★	11 (FB)	183	748	4.1(75)	5	11	36	3.3(14)	0	—	—	—	—	—						k	—	30	822
1953	NYG	12 (FB)	101	206	2.0(15)	2	26	233	9.0(31)	1	—	—	—	—	—							—	18	348
1954	NYG◇	12 (FB)	135	555	4.1(47)	2	28	352	12.6(83)	3	—	—	—	—	—							—	30	766
1955	NYG	6	30	109	3.6(29)	0	1	2	2.0(2)	0	—	—	—	—	—							—	0	110
NFL	6	63	846	3292	3.9(80)	20	75	672	9.0(83)	4	—	—	—	—	—						k	—	144	3854

PRICE, ELEX Elex Drummond, DT, 6'3"/260 lbs; Alcorn State; B8/11/1950 Yazoo City, MS **1973** NO 14 (RDT) **1974** NO 14 (LDT) **1975** NO 14 **1976** NO 14 (13, LDT) **1977** NO 11 (9, LDT) **1978** NO 16 (16, LDT) **1979** NO 6 **1980** NO 14 **NFL** 103 (39) [8 yrs]

PRICE, ERNIE Ernest R., DE, 6'4"/248 lbs; Texas A&M-Kingsville; 1973: Det, rnd 1; B9/20/1950 Corpus Christi, TX, D2/5/2004 Houston, TX **1973** Det 12 (3) **1974** Det 11 (6, lde) **1975** Det 13 **1976** Det 14 **1977** Det 12 (6, rde) **1978** Det 3 (1) **1978** Sea 12 (11, LDE) **1979** Sea 4 (4) **NFL** 81 (31) [7 yrs]

PRICE, JIM James Bluford, LB, 6'2"/225 lbs; Auburn; 1963: NYJ, rnd 6/Dal, rnd 3; B9/17/1940 Nettleton, MS **1963** NYJ-A 14 (LLB) **1964** Den-A 6 **NFL** 20 [2 yrs]

PRICE, JIM James, TE, 6'4"/247 lbs; Stanford; B10/2/1966 Englewood, NJ

1991	LARm	12 (6, TE)	—	—	—		35	410	11.7(27)	2	—	—	—	—	—							—	12	215
1992	LARm	15 (3)	—	—	—		34	324	9.5(25)	2	—	—	—	—	—							—	12	172
1993	Dal	3 (0)	—	—	—		1	4	4.0(4)	0	—	—	—	—	—							—	0	2
1995	SL	13 (0)	—	—	—		4	29	7.3(24)	0	—	—	—	—	—							—	0	15
NFL	4	43 (9)	—	—	—		74	767	10.4(27)	4	—	—	—	—	—							—	24	404

PRICE, KENNY Kenneth James, LB, 6'2"/225 lbs; Iowa; B4/7/1949 Houston, TX **1971** NE 1

PRICE, MARCUS Marcus Raymond, T, 6'4"/310 lbs; LSU; 1995: Jax, rnd 6; B3/3/1972 Port Arthur, TX **1997** SD 2 (0) **1998** SD 10 (0) **2000** NO 7 (0) **2001** NO 12 (0) **2002** Buf 16 (3) **2003** Buf 16 (4) **2004** Buf 14 (3) **NFL** 77 (10) [7 yrs]

PRICE, MITCHELL Mitchell Labraie, DB, 5'9"/181 lbs; SMU; Tulane; 1990: Cin, rnd 9; B5/10/1967 Jacksonville, FL **1990**†Cin 16 (1) **1991** Cin 13 (2) **1992** Phx 2 (1) **1992** Cin 4 (0) **1993** Cin 1 (0) **1993** LARm 5 (0) **NFL** 41 (4) [4 yrs]

PRICE, PEERLESS Peerless LeCross, WR, 5'11"/190 lbs; Tennessee; 1999: Buf, rnd 2; B10/27/1976 Dayton, OH

1999	†Buf	16 (4)	1	-7	-7.0(-7)	0	31	393	12.7(45)	3	—	—	—	—	—						kp	—	18	228
2000	Buf	16 (9)	2	32	16.0(27)	0	52	762	14.7(42)	3	—	—	—	—	—						p	—	18	430
2001	Buf	16 (16, WR)	6	97	16.2(31)	0	55	895	16.3(70)	7	—	—	—	—	—						p	—	42	595
2002	Buf	16 (16, WR)	3	-13	-4.3(1)	0	94	1252	13.3(73)	3	—	—	—	—	—							—	54	658
2003	Atl	16 (15, WR)	2	3	1.5(5)	0	64	838	13.1(49)	3	—	—	—	—	—							—	18	437
2004	†Atl	16 (15, WR)	3	34	11.3(16)	0	45	575	12.8(50)	3	1	1	100.0	25	25.0(25)	0	0	—	—			—	18	349
2005	Dal	7 (1)	1	9	9.0(9)	0	6	96	16.0(58)	0	—	—	—	—	—						p	—	0	60
NFL	7	103 (83)	18	155	8.6(31)	0	347	4811	13.9(73)	28	1	1	100.0	25	25.0(25)	0	0	—	—		kp	—	168	2756

YEAR	TEAM	G (GS, POS)	RUSH	YD	AVG(LG)	TD	REC	YD	AVG(LG)	TD	PASS COMP	PCT	YD	AVG(LG)	TD	INT	SK	YD	QBR	KPR	OTD	PTS	TAY

PRICE, SAMMY   Samuel Lee, RB, 5´11˝/215 lbs; Illinois; 1966: Mia, rnd 11/NYG, rnd 16; B10/1/1943 Margaret, AL

1966	Mia-A	14	31	107	3.5(14)	0	2	14	7.0(9)	0	—	—	—	—	—	—	—	—	—	—	—	0	114
1967	Mia-A	9(8, FB)	46	179	3.9(38)	1	8	56	7.0(27)	1	—	—	—	—	—	—	—	—	—	—	—	12	222
1968	Mia-A	13	5	27	5.4(15)	0	—	—	—	—	—	—	—	—	—	—	—	—	—	k	—	0	34
NFL	3	36(8)	82	313	3.8(38)	1	10	70	7.0(27)	1	—	—	—	—	—	—	—	—	—	k	—	12	370

PRICE, SHAWN   Shawn Sterling, DE-DT, 6´5˝/268 lbs; Pacific; B3/28/1970 Van Nuys, CA   **1993** TB 9 (6, rde)   **1994** TB 6 (0)   **1995** Car 16 (0)   **1996†**Buf 15 (0)   **1997** Buf 10 (0)   **1998** Buf 14 (2)   **1999†**Buf 15 (1)   **2000** Buf 13 (6, lde)   **2001** Buf 11 (11, LDT)   **2002** SD 2 (0)   **NFL** 111 (26) [10 yrs]

PRICE, STACY   Stacy, LB, 6´2˝/194 lbs; Arkansas State; B3/24/1962   **1987** SD 3 (0)

PRICE, TERRY   Terrence Todd, DE, 6´4˝/272 lbs; Texas A&M; 1990: Chi, rnd 10; B4/5/1968 Atlanta, GA   **1990†**ChiB 2 (0)

PRICER, BILLY   Billy Carol, FB, 5´10˝/208 lbs; Oklahoma; 1957: Bal, rnd 6; B9/3/1934 Perry, OK, D9/24/1999 Oklahoma City, OK

1957	Bal	12	2	18	9.0(14)	0	—	—	—	—	—	—	—	—	—	—	—	—	—	k	—	0	28
1958	†Bal	12	10	26	2.6(4)	1	3	14	4.7(6)	0	—	—	—	—	—	—	—	—	—	k	—	6	76
1959	†Bal	12	34	128	3.8(16)	0	2	3	1.5(4)	0	—	—	—	—	—	—	—	—	—	k	—	0	106
1960	Bal	12	46	131	2.8(11)	1	8	77	9.6(21)	1	—	—	—	—	—	—	—	—	—	k	—	12	183
1961	DalT-A	6	5	13	2.6(5)	0	2	21	10.5(11)	0	—	—	—	—	—	—	—	—	—	k	—	0	28
NFL	5	54	97	316	3.3(16)	2	15	115	7.7(21)	1	—	—	—	—	—	—	—	—	—	k	—	18	420

PRIDE, DAN   Daniel M., LB, 6´3˝/225 lbs; Tennessee State; Jackson State; 1966: SD, rnd 10; B6/7/1942 Ironton, OH   **1968** ChiB 3   **1969** ChiB 3   **NFL** 6 [2 yrs]

PRIDEMORE, TOM   Lawrence Thomas, DB, 5´10˝/186 lbs; West Virginia; 1978: Atl, rnd 9; B4/29/1956 Oak Hill, WV [I]   **1978†**Atl 16 (14, FS)   **1979** Atl 16 (5, fs)   **1980†**Atl 16 (16, FS)   **1981** Atl 16 (16, FS)   **1982†**Atl 9 (9, FS)   **1983** Atl 16 (16, SS)

1984	Atl	16(16, FS)	1	7	7.0(7)	0	—	—	—	—	—	—	—	—	—	—	—	—	—	i	—	0	-3
1985	Atl	16(5, fs)	1	48	48.0(48)	0	—	—	—	—	—	—	—	—	—	—	—	—	—	i	—	0	83
NFL	8	121(97)	2	55	27.5(48)	0	—	—	—	—	—	—	—	—	—	—	—	—	—	kpi	1	6	308

PRIESTLEY, BOB   Robert Bagley, E, 5´11˝/192 lbs; Brown; B1/5/1920 Everett, MA

| 1942 | Phi | 9(0) | — | — | — | — | 4 | 47 | 11.8(15) | 0 | — | — | — | — | — | — | — | — | — | — | — | 0 | 24 |

PRIMEAU, FRANK   Francis E., BB, 5´11˝/170 lbs; none; B2/1895 North Tonawanda, NY, deceased   **1921** Ton 1 (1, BB)

PRIMUS, GREG   Gregory Lamar, WR, 5´11˝/190 lbs; Colorado State; B10/20/1970 Denver, CO   **1995** ChiB 4 (0)

| 1994 | ChiB | 3(1) | — | — | — | — | 3 | 25 | 8.3(12) | 0 | — | — | — | — | — | — | — | — | — | — | — | 0 | 13 |
| NFL | 2 | 7(1) | — | — | — | — | 3 | 25 | 8.3(12) | 0 | — | — | — | — | — | — | — | — | — | k | — | 0 | 22 |

PRIMUS, JAMES   James Dewitt, RB, 5´11˝/196 lbs; UCLA; 1988: Atl, rnd 9; B5/18/1964 Yuma, AZ   **1989** Atl 5 (0)

| 1988 | Atl | 16(6, rb) | 35 | 95 | 2.7(29) | 1 | 8 | 42 | 5.3(8) | 0 | — | — | — | — | — | — | — | — | — | k | — | 6 | 124 |
| NFL | 2 | 21(6) | 35 | 95 | 2.7(29) | 1 | 8 | 42 | 5.3(8) | 0 | — | — | — | — | — | — | — | — | — | k | — | 6 | 125 |

PRINCE, RYAN   Ryan Scott, TE, 6´4˝/265 lbs; Weber State; B5/16/1977 Farmington, UT   **2001** Jax 8 (2)

PRINCIPE, DOM   Dominic Alfred, B-LB, 6´0˝/205 lbs; Fordham; 1940: NYG, rnd 9; B2/9/1917 Brockton, MA

1940	NYG	6(1)	11	8	0.7	0	—	—	—	—	—	—	—	—	—	—	—	—	—	i	—	0	15
1941	†NYG	8(0)	1	5	5.0(5)	0	4	54	13.5(28)	0	—	—	—	—	—	—	—	—	—	—	—	0	32
1942	NYG	11(1)	—	—	—	—	2	33	16.5(17)	0	—	—	—	—	—	—	—	—	—	P	—	0	17
NFL	3	25(2)	12	13	1.1(5)	0	6	87	14.5(28)	0	—	—	—	—	—	—	—	—	—	Pi	—	0	64
1946	Bkn-A	10(7, FB)	39	139	3.6	2	3	25	8.3	0	—	—	—	—	—	—	—	—	—	k	—	12	199

PRINDLE, MIKE   Michael John, K, 5´9˝/160 lbs; Western Michigan; B11/12/1963 Grand Rapids, MI [K]   **1987** Det 3 (0)

PRINGLE, ALAN   Alan Keith, K, 6´0˝/195 lbs; Rice; 1975: Hou, rnd 10; B1/20/1952 Los Taques, Venezuela   **1975** Det 1

PRINGLE, MIKE   Michael A., RB, 5´8˝/186 lbs; Washington State; Cal State-Fullerton; 1990: Atl, rnd 6; B10/1/1967 Los Angeles, CA

| 1990 | Atl | 3(0) | 2 | 9 | 4.5(9) | 0 | — | — | — | — | — | — | — | — | — | — | — | — | — | k | — | 0 | 8 |

PRINGLEY, MIKE   Michael Charles, DE, 6´4˝/277 lbs; North Carolina; 1999: Det, rnd 7; B5/22/1976 Linden, NJ   **1999** Det 9 (0)   **2000** SD 2 (0)   **2001** SD 1 (0)   **NFL** 12 (0) [3 yrs]

PRINT, BOB   Robert Thomas, LB, 6´0˝/230 lbs; Dayton; B1/16/1944 Cleveland, OH   **1967** SD-A 7   **1968** SD-A 8   **NFL** 15 [2 yrs]

PRIOLEAU, PIERSON   Pierson Olin, DB, 5´11˝/188 lbs; Virginia Tech; 1999: SF, rnd 4; B8/6/1977 Charleston, SC   **1999** SF 14 (5, rcb)   **2000** SF 14 (6, fs)   **2001** Buf 6 (2)   **2002** Buf 16 (16, FS)   **2003** Buf 16 (6, fs)   **2004** Buf 16 (2)   **2005†**Was 15 (6, ss)   **NFL** 97 (43) [7 yrs]

PRIOR, ANTHONY   Anthony Eugene, DB, 5´11˝/185 lbs; Washington State; 1992: NYG, rnd 9; B3/27/1970 Lowell, MA   **1993** NYJ 16 (0)   **1994** NYJ 13 (0)   **1995** NYJ 11 (0)   **1996†**Min 3 (0)   **1997** Min 12 (0)   **1998** Oak 4 (0)   **NFL** 59 (0) [6 yrs]

PRIOR, MIKE   Michael Robert, DB, 6´0˝/208 lbs; Illinois State; 1985: TB, rnd 7; B11/14/1963 Chicago Heights, IL [I]   **1985** TB 16 (0)   **1987†**Ind 13 (7, fs)   **1988** Ind 16 (16, FS)   **1989** Ind 16 (16, FS)   **1991** Ind 9 (7, fs)   **1993†**GB 16 (4)   **1994†**GB 16 (0)   **1995†**GB 16 (2)   **1996†**GB 16 (0)   **1997†**GB 16 (0)   **1998†**GB 16 (1)

1990	Ind	16(16, FS)	—	—	—	—	1	40	40.0(40)	0	—	—	—	—	—	—	—	—	—	pi	—	0	61
1992	Ind	16(16, FS)	—	—	—	—	1	17	17.0(17)	0	—	—	—	—	—	—	—	—	—	pi	—	0	25
NFL	13	198(85)	—	—	—	—	2	57	28.5(40)	0	—	—	—	—	—	—	—	—	—	kpiS	1	6	440

PRISBY, ERROL   Errol Dwain, DB, 5´10˝/184 lbs; Cincinnati; B1/24/1943 Ravenna, OH   **1967** Den-A 5

PRISCO, NICK   Nicholas Anthony, TB, 5´8˝/193 lbs; Rutgers; B1/12/1909 Edgewater, NJ, D6/13/1981 Tarpon Springs, FL

| 1933 | Phi | 2(0) | 6 | 6 | 0.9 | 0 | 2 | 9 | 4.5(8) | 0 | 0 | 0 | 0 | — | — | — | — | — | — | — | — | 0 | 10 |

PRITCHARD, BILL   William England, B, 5´10˝/185 lbs; Penn State; B12/23/1901 Frostburg, MD, D4/10/1978 Buffalo, NY [K]   **1927** Pro 12 (9, FB), 9   **1928** NYY 13 (11, FB), 7   **NFL** 25 (20), 16 [2 yrs]

PRITCHARD, BOSH   Abisha Collins, HB, 5´11˝/164 lbs; VMI; Georgia Tech; B9/10/1919 Windsor, NC, D11/8/1996 Fort Myers, FL [R]

1942	Cle	1(0)	3	-27	-9.0(0)	0	—	—	—	—	—	—	—	—	—	—	—	—	—	Pk	—	0	-18
1942	Phi◇	6(4)	35	193	5.5(36)	0	2	4	2.0(4)	0	—	—	—	—	—	—	—	—	—	Pkpi	1	6	354
1946	Phi	11(5, RH)	42	218	5.2(68)	3	14	309	22.1(59)	3	1	0.0	0	0.0	0	0	0	—	—	Pkpi	—	36	560
1947	†Phi	11(5, RH)	69	294	4.3(31)	1	16	315	19.7(69)	3	—	—	—	—	—	—	—	—	—	Pkpi	—	24	663
1948	Phi	12(9, RH)	117	517	4.4(65)	4	27	252	9.3(34)	2	—	—	—	—	—	—	—	—	—	kp	2	48	979
1949	†Phi	8(7, RH)	84	506	6.0(77)	3	8	185	23.1(75)	2	1	0.0	0	0.0	0	0	1	—	—	kp	—	30	657
1951	Phi	6	31	6	0.2(0)	0	8	103	12.9(38)	0	—	—	—	—	—	—	—	—	—	kp	—	0	79
1951	NYG	5	11	23	2.1(9)	0	—	—	—	—	—	—	—	—	—	—	—	—	—	kp	1	6	119
NFL	6	60(30)	392	1730	4.4(77)	11	75	1168	15.6(75)	10	2	0.0	0	0.0	0	0	1	—	—	Pkpi	4	150	3391

PRITCHARD, MIKE   Michael Robert, WR, 5´10˝/188 lbs; Colorado; 1991: Atl, rnd 1; B10/25/1969 Shaw AFB, SC

1991	†Atl	16(11, WR)	—	—	—	—	50	624	12.5(29)	2	—	—	—	—	—	—	—	—	—	k	—	12	325
1992	Atl	16(15, WR)	5	37	7.4(22)	0	77	827	10.7(38)	5	—	—	—	—	—	—	—	—	—	—	—	30	476
1993	Atl	15(14, WR)	2	4	2.0(4)	0	74	736	9.9(34)	7	—	—	—	—	—	—	—	—	—	—	—	42	407
1994	Den	3(0)	—	—	—	—	19	271	14.3(50)	1	—	—	—	—	—	—	—	—	—	—	—	6	141
1995	Den	15(13, WR)	6	17	2.8(9)	0	33	441	13.4(45)	3	—	—	—	—	—	—	—	—	—	—	—	18	253
1996	Sea	16(5, wr)	2	13	6.5(7)	0	21	328	15.6(44)	1	—	—	—	—	—	—	—	—	—	—	—	6	182
1997	Sea	16(15, WR)	1	14	14.0(14)	0	64	843	13.2(61)	2	—	—	—	—	—	—	—	—	—	—	—	12	446
1998	Sea	16(16, WR)	1	17	17.0(17)	0	58	742	12.8(50)	3	—	—	—	—	—	—	—	—	—	—	—	20	403
1999	†Sea	14(5, wr)	—	—	—	—	26	375	14.4(51)	2	—	—	—	—	—	—	—	—	—	—	—	12	198
NFL	9	127(94)	17	102	6.0(22)	0	422	5187	12.3(61)	26	—	—	—	—	—	—	—	—	—	k	—	158	2829

PRITCHARD, RON   Ronald David, LB, 6´1˝/235 lbs; Arizona State; 1969: Hou, rnd 1; B4/9/1947 Chicago, IL   **1969** Hou-A 14   **1970** Hou☆14 (RLB)   **1971** Hou☆14 (RLB)   **1972** Hou 6 (MLB)   **1972** Cin 7   **1973†**Cin 10 (RLB)   **1974** Cin 14 (RLB)   **1975†**Cin 14 (RLB)   **1976** Cin 6   **1977** Cin 6   **NFL** 105 [9 yrs]

PRITCHETT, BILLY   Billy Ray, RB, 6´3˝/230 lbs; West Texas A&M; 1974: Cle, rnd 6; B2/22/1951 Mart, TX

| 1975 | Cle | 14(rb) | 75 | 199 | 2.7(19) | 0 | 16 | 109 | 6.8(18) | 0 | — | — | — | — | — | — | — | — | — | — | — | 0 | 254 |
| 1976 | Atl | 6(1) | 14 | 74 | 5.3(16) | 1 | 1 | 1 | 1.0(1) | 0 | — | — | — | — | — | — | — | — | — | — | — | 6 | 85 |

YEAR	TEAM	G(GS, POS)	RUSH	YD	AVG(LG)	TD	REC	YD	AVG(LG)	TD	PASS	COMP	PCT	YD	AVG(LG)	TD	INT	SK	YD	QBR	KPR	OTD	PTS	TAY
1977	Atl	9	3	7	2.3(6)	0	—	—	—	—	—	—	—	—	—	—	—	—	—	—	—	—	0	7
NFL	3	29(1)	92	280	3.0(19)	1	17	110	6.5(18)	0	—	—	—	—	—	—	—	—	—	—	—	—	6	345
Pritchett, Kelvin Kelvin Bratodd, DT-DE, 6´3˝/322 lbs; Mississippi; 1991: Dal, rnd 1; B10/24/1969 Atlanta, GA **1991**†Det 16 (0) **1992** Det 16 (15, RDE) **1993**†Det 16 (5, rde) **1994**†Det 16 (15, RDE) **1995** Jax 16 (16, LDT) **1996**†Jax 13 (4) **1997** Jax 8 (5, ldt) **1998**†Jax 15 (9, LDT) **1999**†Det 16 (2) **2000** Det 15 (0) **2001** Det 16 (1) **2002** Det 16 (3) **2003** Det 13 (0) **2004** Det 16 (0) **NFL** 208 (75) [14 yrs]																								
Pritchett, Stanley Stanley Jerome, FB, 6´2˝/250 lbs; South Carolina; 1996: Mia, rnd 4; B12/22/1973 Atlanta, GA																								
1996	Mia	16(16, FB)	7	27	3.9(16)	0	33	354	10.7(74)	2	—	—	—	—	—	—	—	—	—	—	—	—	12	214
1997	†Mia	6(5, FB)	3	7	2.3(4)	0	5	35	7.0(17)	0	—	—	—	—	—	—	—	—	—	—	—	—	0	25
1998	†Mia	16(12, FB)	6	19	3.2(11)	1	17	97	5.7(24)	0	—	—	—	—	—	—	—	—	—	—	—	—	6	78
1999	†Mia	14(7, fb)	47	158	3.4(25)	1	43	312	7.3(30)	4	—	—	—	—	—	—	—	—	—	—	—	—	30	344
2000	†Phi	16(2)	58	225	3.9(18)	1	25	193	7.7(17)	0	—	—	—	—	—	—	—	—	—	—	k	—	6	332
2001	†ChiB	7(0)	—	—	—	—	—	—	—	—	—	—	—	—	—	—	—	—	—	—	—	—	—	—
2002	ChiB	16(2)	1	2	2.0(2)	0	19	165	8.7(24)	1	—	—	—	—	—	—	—	—	—	—	—	—	6	90
2003	ChiB	16(11, FB)	21	93	4.4(18)	2	18	83	4.6(20)	0	—	—	—	—	—	—	—	—	—	—	—	—	12	155
2004	Atl	14(2)	6	18	3.0(8)	0	2	5	2.5(4)	1	—	—	—	—	—	—	—	—	—	—	k	—	6	13
NFL	9	121(57)	149	549	3.7(25)	5	162	1244	7.7(74)	8	—	—	—	—	—	—	—	—	—	—	k	—	78	1248
Pritchett, Wes Wesley Andrew, LB, 6´2˝/234 lbs; Notre Dame; 1989: Mia, rnd 6; B7/7/1966 Atlanta, GA **1991** Atl 3 (0)																								
Pritko, Steve Stephen, E-DE, 6´2˝/209 lbs; Villanova; 1943: Cle, rnd 28; B12/21/1920 Northampton, PA																								
1943	†NYG	10(2)	—	—	—	—	1	12	12.0(12)	0	—	—	—	—	—	—	—	—	—	—	—	1	6	6
1944	Cle	10(10, RE)	—	—	—	—	18	296	16.4(53)	3	—	—	—	—	—	—	—	—	—	—	i	—	18	161
1945	†Cle☆	10(10, RE)	—	—	—	—	19	255	13.4(35)	4	—	—	—	—	—	—	—	—	—	—	—	—	24	148
1946	LARm	11(4)	—	—	—	—	18	185	10.3(29)	2	—	—	—	—	—	—	—	—	—	—	—	—	12	103
1947	LARm	11(0)	—	—	—	—	10	101	10.1(20)	0	—	—	—	—	—	—	—	—	—	—	—	—	0	51
1948	Bos	12(5, re)	—	—	—	—	3	42	14.0(29)	0	—	—	—	—	—	—	—	—	—	—	k	1	6	14
1949	NYB	2(1)	—	—	—	—	1	4	4.0(4)	0	—	—	—	—	—	—	—	—	—	—	—	—	0	2
1949	GB	8(2)	—	—	—	—	6	94	15.7(24)	2	—	—	—	—	—	—	—	—	—	—	—	—	12	57
1950	GB	12(RDE)	—	—	—	—	17	125	7.4(14)	2	—	—	—	—	—	—	—	—	—	—	—	—	12	73
NFL	8	86(34)	—	—	—	—	93	1114	12.0(53)	13	—	—	—	—	—	—	—	—	—	—	ki	2	90	613
Proby, Bryan Brian Craig, DT, 6´5˝/285 lbs; Arizona State; 1995: KC, rnd 6; B11/30/1971 Compton, CA **1995** KC 3 (0)																								
Prochaska, Ray Raymond Edward, E, 6´3˝/200 lbs; Nebraska; 1941: Cle, rnd 7; B8/9/1919 Ulysses, NE, D3/9/1997 Orange County, CA [C]																								
1941	Cle	8(0)	—	—	—	—	4	29	7.3(11)	0	—	—	—	—	—	—	—	—	—	—	—	—	0	15
Proctor, Dewey Dewey Michael, FB-LB, 5´11˝/215 lbs; Furman; 1943: NYG, rnd 3; B7/1/1921 Lake View, SC																								
1946	†NYY-A	4(0)	23	76	3.3	1	3	32	10.7	1	—	—	—	—	—	—	—	—	—	—	—	—	12	107
1947	NYY-A	11(1)	15	15	1.0	1	1	4	4.0(4)	0	1	0	0.0	0	0.0	0	0	—	—	—	ki	—	6	54
1948	ChiR-A	9(4, FB)	47	190	4.0	1	2	18	9.0	0	—	—	—	—	—	—	—	—	—	—	—	—	6	209
1949	NYY-A	1(0)	1	-1	-1.0(-1)	0	—	—	—	—	—	—	—	—	—	—	—	—	—	—	—	—	0	-1
AAFC	4	25(5)	86	280	3.3	3	6	54	9.0(4)	1	1	0	0.0	0	0.0	0	0	—	—	—	ki	—	24	369
Proctor, Rex Rex Gardner, DB, 5´10˝/180 lbs; Rice; B12/1/1929 Sour Lake, TX, D11/28/1970 Fort Worth, TX **1953** ChiB 3																								
Proehl, Ricky Richard Scott, WR, 6´0˝/190 lbs; Wake Forest; 1990: Phx, rnd 3; B3/7/1968 Bronx, NY																								
1990	Phx	16(2)	1	4	4.0(4)	0	56	802	14.3(45)	4	—	—	—	—	—	—	—	—	—	—	kp	—	24	415
1991	Phx	16(16, WR)	3	21	7.0(17)	0	55	766	13.9(62)	2	—	—	—	—	—	—	—	—	—	—	p	—	12	420
1992	Phx	16(15, WR)	3	23	7.7(10)	0	60	744	12.4(63)	3	1	0	0.0	0	0.0	0	1	—	—	—	—	—	18	370
1993	Phx	16(16, WR)	8	47	5.9(17)	0	65	877	13.5(51)	7	—	—	—	—	—	—	—	—	—	—	—	—	42	521
1994	Arz	16(16, WR)	—	—	—	—	51	651	12.8(63)	5	—	—	—	—	—	—	—	—	—	—	—	—	30	351
1995	Sea	8(0)	—	—	—	—	5	29	5.8(9)	0	—	—	—	—	—	—	—	—	—	—	—	—	0	15
1996	Sea	16(7, wr)	—	—	—	—	23	309	13.4(56)	2	—	—	—	—	—	—	—	—	—	—	—	—	12	165
1997	ChiB	15(10, WR)	—	—	—	—	58	753	13.0(78)	7	—	—	—	—	—	—	—	—	—	—	p	—	44	431
1998	SL	16(11, WR)	1	14	14.0(14)	0	60	771	12.9(47)	3	—	—	—	—	—	—	—	—	—	—	—	—	20	415
1999	†SL	15(2)	—	—	—	—	33	349	10.6(30)	0	—	—	—	—	—	—	—	—	—	—	p	—	0	175
2000	†SL	12(4)	—	—	—	—	31	441	14.2(29)	4	—	—	—	—	—	—	—	—	—	—	k	—	24	228
2001	†SL	16(3)	1	5	5.0(5)	0	40	563	14.1(37)	5	—	—	—	—	—	—	—	—	—	—	—	—	32	312
2002	SL	16(2)	—	—	—	—	43	466	10.8(33)	4	1	0	0.0	0	0.0	0	0	1	1	—	—	—	24	253
2003	†Car	16(2)	—	—	—	—	27	389	14.4(66)	4	—	—	—	—	—	—	—	—	—	—	k	—	24	219
2004	Car	16(3)	1	9	9.0(9)	0	34	497	14.6(34)	0	1	0	0.0	0	0.0	0	0	—	—	—	k	—	0	277
2005	†Car	16(0)	1	-8	-8.0(-8)	0	25	441	17.6(69)	4	—	—	—	—	—	—	—	—	—	—	—	—	24	233
NFL	16	242(109)	19	115	6.1(17)	0	666	8848	13.3(78)	54	3	0	0.0	0	0.0	0	1	1	1	—	kp	—	330	4794
Profit, Gene Eugene Anthony, DB, 5´10˝/168 lbs; Yale; B11/11/1964 Baton Rouge, LA **1986**†NE 4 (0) **1987** NE 7 (0) **1988** NE 1 (0) **NFL** 12 (0) [3 yrs]																								
Profit, Joe Joseph, RB, 6´0˝/213 lbs; Louisiana-Monroe; 1971: Atl, rnd 1; B8/13/1949 Lake Providence, LA																								
1971	Atl	4	3	10	3.3(4)	1	—	—	—	—	—	—	—	—	—	—	—	—	—	—	k	—	6	117
1972	Atl	8	40	132	3.3(14)	0	3	22	7.3(14)	0	—	—	—	—	—	—	—	—	—	—	—	—	0	143
1973	Atl	3	18	55	3.1(9)	2	—	—	—	—	—	—	—	—	—	—	—	—	—	—	k	—	12	60
1973	NO	8(FB)	72	274	3.8(22)	0	11	108	9.8(26)	0	—	—	—	—	—	—	—	—	—	—	k	—	0	367
NFL	3	23	133	471	3.5(22)	3	14	130	9.3(26)	0	—	—	—	—	—	—	—	—	—	—	k	—	18	687
Prokop, Eddie Edward Stanley, B, 5´11˝/200 lbs; Georgia Tech; 1945: Bos, rnd 1; B2/11/1922 Cleveland, OH, D5/30/1955 Cleveland, OH																								
1946	†NYY-A	12(3, FB)	65	236	3.6	1	5	52	10.4	1	11	4	36.4	72	6.5	0	0	—	—	—	kpi	1	18	445
1947	†NYY-A	13(4, fb)	76	324	4.3(52)	4	3	79	26.3	1	8	4	50.0	137	17.1	2	1	—	—	—	kpi	—	30	615
1948	ChiR-A	9(7, RH)	54	266	4.9	1	7	223	31.9	3	1	0	0.0	0	0.0	0	0	—	—	—	kp	—	24	551
1949	NYY-A	6(1)	31	109	3.5	2	1	7	7.0(7)	0	—	—	—	—	—	—	—	—	—	—	k	—	12	150
AAFC	4	40(15)	226	935	4.1(52)	8	16	361	22.6(7)	5	20	8	40.0	209	10.4	2	1	—	—	—	kpi	1	84	1760
Prokop, Joe Joseph Michael, HB, 6´2˝/170 lbs; Notre Dame; Bradley; B1/9/1921 Cleveland, OH **1948** ChiR-A 2 (0)																								
Prokop, Joe Joseph Michael, P, 6´2˝/230 lbs; Cal Poly-Pomona; B7/7/1960 St. Paul, MN [P] **1985** GB 9 (0) **1987** SD 3 (0) **1988** NYJ 16 (0) **1992** Mia 7 (0) **1992** NYG 1 (0)																								
1989	NYJ	16(0)	1	17	17.0(17)	1	—	—	—	—	—	—	—	—	—	—	—	—	—	—	P	—	6	27
1990	NYJ	16(0)	3	2	0.7(8)	0	—	—	—	—	—	—	—	—	—	—	—	—	—	—	P	—	0	2
1991	SF	11(0)	1	-10	-10.0(-10)	0	—	—	—	—	—	—	—	—	—	—	—	—	—	—	P	—	0	-10
NFL	7	79(0)	5	9	1.8(17)	1	—	—	—	—	—	—	—	—	—	—	—	—	—	—	P	—	6	19
Promuto, Vince Vincent Louis, G, 6´1˝/245 lbs; Holy Cross; 1960: Was, rnd 4/Buf, rnd 1; B6/8/1938 New York, NY **1960** Was 12 (12, RG) **1961** Was 14 (14, RG) **1962** Was 14 (14, RG) **1963** Was✧14 (14, RG) **1964** Was✧13 (RG) **1965** Was 14 (RG) **1966** Was 14 (RG) **1967** Was 14 (RG) **1968** Was 4 **1969** Was 14 (RG) **1970** Was 3 (2) **NFL** 130 (56) [11 yrs]																								
Protz, Jack John Michael, LB, 6´1˝/218 lbs; North Carolina; Syracuse; 1970: SD, rnd 11; B4/14/1948 Jersey City, NJ **1970** SD 14																								
Prout, Bob Robert Alan, DB, 6´1˝/190 lbs; Knox; B5/11/1951 Chicago, IL **1974** Oak 2 **1975** NYJ 7 **NFL** 9 [2 yrs]																								
Provence, Andrew Andrew Clark, DT-DE, 6´3˝/265 lbs; South Carolina; 1983: Atl, rnd 3; B3/8/1961 Savannah, GA **1983** Atl 16 (12, LDT) **1984** Atl 16 (3) **1985** Atl 16 (0) **1986** Atl 16 (0) **1987** Atl 5 (1) **NFL** 69 (16) [5 yrs]																								
Provencial, Ken Joseph Kenneth, E, 6´2˝/190 lbs; Georgetown (DC); B1908, NY, deceased **1930** Fra 1 (0)																								
Provo, Fred Frederick Lewis, HB, 5´9˝/185 lbs; Washington; 1948: GB, rnd 14/ChiR-A, rnd 21; B4/17/1922 Seattle, WA																								
1948	GB	9(0)	29	90	3.1(28)	0	4	-9	-2.3(3)	0	1	1	100.0	20	20.0(20)	1	0	—	—	—	kp	—	0	274
Provost, Ted Ted R., DB, 6´2˝/195 lbs; Ohio State; 1970: LA, rnd 7; B7/26/1948 Navarre, OH **1970**†Min 7 **1971** SL 2 **NFL** 9 [2 yrs]																								

PRUDHOMME, REMI Joseph Remi, C-DE-G-DT, 6´4˝/250 lbs; LSU; 1964: Buf, rnd 14/SL, rnd 3; B4/24/1942 Opelousas, LA, D12/6/1990 New Orleans, LA **1966**†Buf-A 14 **1967** Buf-A 10 (RDE) **1968**†KC-A 14 **1969**†KC-A 14 **1971** NO 14 **1972** NO 5 **1972** Buf 8 (C) **NFL** 79 [6 yrs]

PRUETT, PERRY Perry W., DB, 6´0˝/185 lbs; North Texas; B3/7/1949 Dallas, TX **1971** NE 11 (1)

PRUITT, ETRIC Etric, DB, 6´0˝/197 lbs; Southern Mississippi; 2004: Atl, rnd 6; B8/16/1981 Theodore, AL **2004** Atl 3 (0) **2005**†Sea 6 (0) **NFL** 9 (0) [2 yrs]

PRUITT, GREG Gregory Donald, RB, 5´10˝/190 lbs; Oklahoma; 1973: Cle, rnd 2; B8/18/1951 Houston, TX **[R]**

YEAR	TEAM	G (GS, POS)	RUSH	YD	AVG (LG)	TD	REC	YD	AVG (LG)	TD	PASS	COMP	PCT	YD	AVG (LG)	TD	INT	SK	YD	QBR	KPR	OTD	PTS	TAY
1973	Cle✧	13	61	369	6.0(65)	4	9	110	12.2(42)	1	1	0	0.0	0	0.0	0	0	—	—	—	kp	—	30	782
1974	Cle✧	14(RB)	126	540	4.3(54)	3	21	274	13.0(43)	1	2	2	100.0	115	57.5(60)	2	0	—	—	—	kp	1	30	1280
1975	Cle	14(14, RB)	217	1067	4.9(50)	8	44	299	6.8(48)	1	—	—	—	—	—	—	—	—	—	—	kp	—	54	1459
1976	Cle★	14(RB)	209	1000	4.8(64)	4	45	341	7.6(27)	1	3	2	66.7	39	13.0(29)	1	0	—	—	—	k	—	30	1252
1977	Cle★	14(14, RB)	236	1086	4.6(78)	3	37	471	12.7(60)	1	9	4	44.4	28	3.1(13)	3	0	1	10	—	—	—	24	1386
1978	Cle	12(12, RB)	176	960	5.5(70)	3	38	292	7.7(26)	2	3	0	0.0	0	0.0	0	2	—	—	—	k	—	30	1082
1979	Cle	6(rb)	62	233	3.8(27)	0	14	155	11.1(27)	1	—	—	—	—	—	—	—	—	—	—	k	—	6	323
1980	†Cle	16(9, RB)	40	117	2.9(19)	0	50	444	8.9(43)	5	—	—	—	—	—	—	—	—	—	—	—	—	30	364
1981	Cle	15(5, rb)	31	124	4.0(15)	0	65	636	9.8(33)	4	—	—	—	—	—	—	—	—	—	—	k	—	24	499
1982	†LARd	9(0)	4	22	5.5(13)	0	2	29	14.5(23)	1	—	—	—	—	—	—	—	—	—	—	kp	—	6	277
1983	†LARd★	16(0)	26	154	5.9(18)	2	1	6	6.0(6)	0	1	0	0.0	0	0.0	0	0	—	—	—	kp	1	18	702
1984	†LARd	15(0)	8	0	0.0(3)	0	2	12	6.0(8)	0	—	—	—	—	—	—	—	—	—	—	kp	—	0	185
NFL	12	158(54)	1196	5672	4.7(78)	27	328	3069	9.4(60)	18	19	8	42.1	182	9.6(60)	6	2	1	10	—	kp	2	282	9589

PRUITT, JAMES James Bouvias, WR, 6´3˝/199 lbs; Cal State-Fullerton; 1986: Mia, rnd 4; B1/29/1964 Los Angeles, CA

YEAR	TEAM	G (GS, POS)	RUSH	YD	AVG (LG)	TD	REC	YD	AVG (LG)	TD	PASS	COMP	PCT	YD	AVG (LG)	TD	INT	SK	YD	QBR	KPR	OTD	PTS	TAY
1986	Mia	16(0)	—	—	—	—	15	235	15.7(27)	2	—	—	—	—	—	—	—	—	—	—	p	1	18	233
1987	Mia	12(1)	—	—	—	—	26	404	15.5(37)	3	—	—	—	—	—	—	—	—	—	—	—	—	18	217
1988	Mia	11(0)	—	—	—	—	2	38	19.0(19)	0	—	—	—	—	—	—	—	—	—	—	—	—	0	19
1988	Ind	1(0)	—	—	—	—	—	—	—	—	—	—	—	—	—	—	—	—	—	—	—	—	—	—
1989	Ind	16(3)	—	—	—	—	5	71	14.2(40)	1	—	—	—	—	—	—	—	—	—	—	k	—	6	118
1990	†Mia	6(0)	—	—	—	—	13	235	18.1(35)	3	—	—	—	—	—	—	—	—	—	—	—	—	18	133
1991	Mia	5(0)	—	—	—	—	2	30	15.0(24)	0	—	—	—	—	—	—	—	—	—	—	—	—	0	15
NFL	6	67(4)	—	—	—	—	63	1013	16.1(40)	9	—	—	—	—	—	—	—	—	—	—	kp	1	60	734

PRUITT, MICKEY Mickey Aaron, LB-DB, 6´1˝/206 lbs; Colorado; B1/10/1965 Bamberg, IL **1988**†ChiB 14 (3) **1989** ChiB 14 (1) **1990**†ChiB 16 (2) **1991**†Dal 12 (1) **1992**†Dal 6 (0) **NFL** 62 (7) [5 yrs]

PRUITT, MIKE Michael, RB, 6´0˝/222 lbs; Purdue; 1976: Cle, rnd 1; B4/3/1954 Chicago, IL

YEAR	TEAM	G (GS, POS)	RUSH	YD	AVG (LG)	TD	REC	YD	AVG (LG)	TD	PASS	COMP	PCT	YD	AVG (LG)	TD	INT	SK	YD	QBR	KPR	OTD	PTS	TAY
1976	Cle	13(2)	52	138	2.7(18)	0	8	26	3.3(15)	0	—	—	—	—	—	—	—	—	—	—	k	—	0	167
1977	Cle	13	47	205	4.4(21)	1	3	12	4.0(6)	0	—	—	—	—	—	—	—	—	—	—	k	—	6	262
1978	Cle	16(9, FB)	135	560	4.1(71)	5	20	112	5.6(15)	0	—	—	—	—	—	—	—	—	—	—	—	—	30	666
1979	Cle★	16(16, FB)	264	1294	4.9(77)	9	41	372	9.1(50)	2	—	—	—	—	—	—	—	—	—	—	—	—	66	1580
1980	†Cle★	16(16, FB)	249	1034	4.2(56)	6	63	471	7.5(28)	0	—	—	—	—	—	—	—	—	—	—	—	—	36	1330
1981	Cle	16(15, FB)	247	1103	4.5(21)	7	63	442	7.0(21)	1	—	—	—	—	—	—	—	—	—	—	—	—	48	1399
1982	†Cle	9(9, FB)	143	516	3.6(17)	3	22	140	6.4(13)	0	—	—	—	—	—	—	—	—	—	—	—	—	18	616
1983	Cle☆	15(14, RB)	293	1184	4.0(27)	10	30	157	5.2(21)	2	—	—	—	—	—	—	—	—	—	—	—	—	72	1373
1984	Cle	10(7, rb)	163	506	3.1(14)	6	5	29	5.8(9)	0	—	—	—	—	—	—	—	—	—	—	—	—	36	581
1985	Buf	4(2)	7	24	3.4(7)	0	—	—	—	—	—	—	—	—	—	—	—	—	—	—	—	—	0	24
1985	KC	9(7, FB)	105	366	3.5(54)	2	7	43	6.1(9)	0	—	—	—	—	—	—	—	—	—	—	—	—	12	408
1986	KC	15(15, FB)	139	448	3.2(16)	2	8	56	7.0(13)	0	—	—	—	—	—	—	—	—	—	—	—	—	12	496
NFL	11	152(112)	1844	7378	4.0(77)	51	270	1860	6.9(50)	5	—	—	—	—	—	—	—	—	—	—	k	—	336	8900

PRYCE, TREVOR Trevor, DT-DE, 6´5˝/295 lbs; Michigan; Clemson; 1997: Den, rnd 1; B8/3/1975 Brooklyn, NY **[S]** **1997**†Den 8 (3) **1998**†Den 16 (15, RDT) **1999** Den★15 (15, RDT) **2000**†Den★16 (16, RDT) **2001** Den★16 (16, RDT) **2002** Den✧16 (16, LDE) **2003**†Den 16 (16, LDE) **2004** Den 2 (1) **2005**†Den 16 (16, RDE) **NFL** 121 (114) [9 yrs]

PRYOR, BARRY Barry L., RB, 6´0˝/215 lbs; Boston University; B3/4/1946 Pittsburgh, PA

YEAR	TEAM	G (GS, POS)	RUSH	YD	AVG (LG)	TD	REC	YD	AVG (LG)	TD	PASS	COMP	PCT	YD	AVG (LG)	TD	INT	SK	YD	QBR	KPR	OTD	PTS	TAY
1969	Mia-A	14	—	—	—	—	2	-3	-1.5(0)	0	—	—	—	—	—	—	—	—	—	—	—	—	0	-2
1970	Mia	2	2	0	0.0(5)	0	—	—	—	—	—	—	—	—	—	—	—	—	—	—	—	—	0	0
NFL	2	16	2	0	0.0(5)	0	2	-3	-1.5	0	—	—	—	—	—	—	—	—	—	—	—	—	0	-2

PSALTIS, JIM David James, DB, 6´1˝/190 lbs; San Jose State; USC; 1953: ChiC, rnd 2; B12/14/1927 Chicago, IL **1953** ChiC 12 (DB) **1954** GB 11 (DB) **1955** ChiC 12 (DB) **NFL** 35 [3 yrs]

PTACEK, BOB Robert J., QB, 6´1˝/205 lbs; Michigan; 1959: Cle, rnd 8; B4/23/1937 Cleveland, OH

YEAR	TEAM	G (GS, POS)	RUSH	YD	AVG (LG)	TD	REC	YD	AVG (LG)	TD	PASS	COMP	PCT	YD	AVG (LG)	TD	INT	SK	YD	QBR	KPR	OTD	PTS	TAY
1959	Cle	12	3	13	4.3(6)	0	—	—	—	—	—	—	—	—	—	—	—	—	—	—	—	—	0	13

PUCCI, BEN Benito Modesto, T, 6´4˝/255 lbs; none; B1/26/1925 St. Louis, MO **1946** Buf-A 12 (1) **1947** ChiR-A 13 (3) **1948**†Cle-A 12 (0) **AAFC** 37 (4) [3 yrs]

PUCILLO, MIKE Michael, G, 6´4˝/311 lbs; Auburn; 2002: Buf, rnd 7; B7/14/1979 Cleveland, OH **2003** Buf 13 (12, RG) **2004** Buf 2 (0) **2005** Cle 10 (6, lg) **NFL** 25 (18) [3 yrs]

PUDDY, HAL Marvin Harold, T, 6´3˝/220 lbs; Oregon State; B8/18/1924 Hood River, OR, D1/31/1975 Port Angeles, WA **1948** SF-A 4 (0)

PUDLOSKI, CHET Chester E., T, 6´1˝/210 lbs; Villanova; B8/3/1915 Wilkes-Barre, PA, D8/1990 **1944** Cle 10 (10, LT)

PUETZ, GARRY Garry Spencer, G-T, 6´3˝/263 lbs; Valparaiso; 1973: NYJ, rnd 12; B3/14/1952 Elmhurst, IL **1973** NYJ 7 (4) **1974** NYJ 14 (14, RG) **1975** NYJ 14 (14, RG) **1976** NYJ 14 (14, RT/rg) **1977** NYJ 14 (14, LT) **1978** NYJ 6 **1978** TB 10 (8, RG) **1979** Phi 2 **1979** NE 5 (4) **1980** NE 16 (0) **1981** NE 15 (1) **1982**†Was 2 (0) **NFL** 119 (73) [10 yrs]

PUGH, DAVID David Winston, DT, 6´2˝/270 lbs; Virginia Tech; 2002: Ind, rnd 6; B7/24/1979 Madison Heights, VA **2002** Ind 4 (1)

PUGH, JETHRO Jethro, DT-DE, 6´6˝/260 lbs; Elizabeth City State; 1965: Dal, rnd 11; B7/3/1944 Windsor, NC **1965** Dal 12 **1966**†Dal 14 **1967**†Dal 14 (LDT) **1968**†Dal☆13 (LDT) **1969**†Dal 12 (11, LDT) **1970**†Dal 14 (LDT) **1971**†Dal 12 (LDT) **1972**†Dal 14 (LDT) **1973**†Dal 13 (LDT) **1974** Dal 14 (LDT) **1975**†Dal 13 (LDT) **1976**†Dal 13 (13, LDT) **1977**†Dal 12 (LDT) **1978**†Dal 13 (LDT) **NFL** 183 (24) [14 yrs]

PUGH, MARION Marion C., B, 6´1˝/187 lbs; Texas A&M; 1941: Phi, rnd 3; B9/6/1919 Fort Worth, TX, D11/20/1976 College Station, TX **[K]**

YEAR	TEAM	G (GS, POS)	RUSH	YD	AVG (LG)	TD	REC	YD	AVG (LG)	TD	PASS	COMP	PCT	YD	AVG (LG)	TD	INT	SK	YD	QBR	KPR	OTD	PTS	TAY
1941	NYG	5(0)	24	50	2.1(45)	0	—	—	—	—	24	12	50.0	161	6.7(53)	1	0	—	—	—	Kp	—	0	136
1945	NYG	5(2)	24	-52	-2.2(8)	0	—	—	—	—	58	27	46.6	390	6.7(47)	3	3	—	—	—	—	—	0	38
NFL	2	10(2)	48	-2	-0.0(45)	0	—	—	—	—	82	39	47.6	551	6.7(53)	4	3	—	—	—	Kp	—	0	174
1946	Mia-A	14(10, QB)	29	-125	-4.3	2	4	43	10.8	0	118	55	46.6	608	5.2(63)	5	12	—	—	—	k	—	12	-226

PUKI, CRAIG Craig Alan, LB, 6´1˝/231 lbs; Tennessee; 1980: SF, rnd 3; B1/18/1957 Deadwood, SD **1980** SF 16 (0) **1981**†SF 16 (6, rilb) **1982**†SL 7 (0) **NFL** 39 (6) [3 yrs]

PUMPHREY, DON Donald Anson, G, 6´4˝/275 lbs; Valdosta State; B11/22/1963 Tallahassee, FL **1987** TB 3 (3)

PUPLIS, ANDY Andrew Joseph, WB, 5´9˝/180 lbs; Notre Dame; B2/1/1915 Chicago, IL, D1/25/1990 Maywood, IL **1943** ChiC 8 (0)

PUPUNU, ALFRED Alfred Sione, TE, 6´2˝/260 lbs; Weber State; B10/17/1969 Tonga

YEAR	TEAM	G (GS, POS)	RUSH	YD	AVG (LG)	TD	REC	YD	AVG (LG)	TD	PASS	COMP	PCT	YD	AVG (LG)	TD	INT	SK	YD	QBR	KPR	OTD	PTS	TAY
1992	†SD	15(2)	—	—	—	—	—	—	—	—	—	—	—	—	—	—	—	—	—	—	—	—	—	—
1993	SD	16(7, te)	—	—	—	—	13	142	10.9(28)	0	—	—	—	—	—	—	—	—	—	—	—	—	0	71
1994	†SD	13(10, TE)	—	—	—	—	21	214	10.2(25)	2	—	—	—	—	—	—	—	—	—	—	—	—	12	117
1995	†SD	15(14, TE)	—	—	—	—	35	315	9.0(26)	0	—	—	—	—	—	—	—	—	—	—	—	—	0	158
1996	SD	9(8, te)	—	—	—	—	24	271	11.3(41)	1	—	—	—	—	—	—	—	—	—	—	k	—	6	141
1997	SD	8(1)	—	—	—	—	1	7	7.0(7)	0	—	—	—	—	—	—	—	—	—	—	—	—	0	4
1997	KC	1(0)	—	—	—	—	—	—	—	—	—	—	—	—	—	—	—	—	—	—	—	—	—	—
1997	†NYG	0(0)	—	—	—	—	—	—	—	—	—	—	—	—	—	—	—	—	—	—	—	—	0	0
1998	NYG	9(0)	—	—	—	—	1	2	2.0(2)	0	—	—	—	—	—	—	—	—	—	—	—	—	0	1
1999	SD	8(0)	—	—	—	—	4	17	4.3(11)	0	—	—	—	—	—	—	—	—	—	—	—	—	0	9
2000	Det	9(0)	—	—	—	—	3	32	10.7(17)	0	—	—	—	—	—	—	—	—	—	—	—	—	0	16
NFL	9	103(42)	—	—	—	—	102	1000	9.8(41)	3	—	—	—	—	—	—	—	—	—	—	k	—	18	515

YEAR TEAM	G(GS, POS)	RUSH	YD	AVG(LG)	TD	REC	YD	AVG(LG)	TD	PASS COMP	PCT	YD	AVG(LG)	TD	INT	SK	YD	QBR	KPR	OTD	PTS	TAY

PURDIN, CAL   Calvin O'Neal, B, 6'2"/188 lbs; Tulsa; 1943: ChiC, rnd 25; B2/22/1921 Jefferson, OK, D12/1982 Augusta, KS

1943 ChiC	4(2)	9	20	2.2(13)	0	3	35	11.7(20)	0	2	1	50.0	7	3.5(7)	0	0	—	—	—	Pkp	—	0	51
1946 Bkn-A	7(3)	8	11	1.4	0	10	107	10.7	0	1	1	100.0	2	-2.0(-2)	0	0	—	—	—	kp	—	0	117
1946 Mia-A	2(1)	2	1	0.5	0	2	1	0.5	0	—	—	—	—	—	—	—	—	—	—	k	—	0	-3
AAFC 2	9(4)	10	12	1.2(13)	0	12	108	9.0(20)	0	1	1	100.0	2	-2.0(7)	0	0	—	—	—	kp	—	0	114

PURDY, MIKE   Clair Joseph, BB-WB, 5'10"/179 lbs; Brown; B1895 Auburn, NY, D1/10/1950 Auburn, NY   **1920** Roc 3 (1, BB) **1921** NYG 1 (1) **1922** Mil 9 (8, BB), 6 **NFL** 13 (10) [3 yrs]

PURDY, PID   Everett Virgil, BB, 5'6"/145 lbs; Beloit; B6/15/1904 Beatrice, NE, D1/16/1951 Ingleside, NE [K]   **1926** GB 11 (8, BB), 20 **1927** GB 6 (4), 10 **NFL** 17 (12), 30 [2 yrs]

PUREIFORY, DAVE   David Lee, DE-DT, 6'1"/260 lbs; Eastern Michigan; 1972: GB, rnd 6; B7/12/1949 Pensacola, FL [K]   **1972** GB 14 **1973** GB 13 **1974** GB 13 (rdt) **1975** GB 14 (14, RDT) **1976** GB 12 (8, RDT) **1977** GB 12 (RDT) **1978** Cin 7 **1978** Det 8 (8, LDE) **1979** Det 15 (15, LDE) **1980** Det 16 (16, LDE) **1981** Det 15 (15, LDE) **1982**†Det 9 (9, LDE) **NFL** 148 (85) [11 yrs]

PURLING, DAVE   David Alan, DT, 6'5"/240 lbs; USC; B6/26/1962 Long Beach, CA   **1987** LARm 1 (0)

PURNELL, FRANK   Frank, FB, 5'11"/230 lbs; Alcorn State; B4/5/1933 Sweatman, MS

| 1957 GB | 9 | 5 | 22 | 4.4(7) | 0 | 2 | 16 | 8.0(15) | 0 | — | — | — | — | — | — | — | — | — | — | — | — | 0 | 30 |

PURNELL, JIM   James Fred, LB, 6'2"/229 lbs; Wisconsin; B12/12/1941 La Porte, IN, D11/4/2003 Evanston, IL   **1964** ChiB 6 **1965** ChiB 12 **1966** ChiB 14 (RLB) **1967** ChiB 14 (RLB) **1968** ChiB 14 (RLB) **1969** LARm 14 **1970** LARm 14 (6, rlb) **1971** LARm 14 (14, LLB) **1972** LARm 13 (12, LLB) **NFL** 115 (32) [9 yrs]

PURNELL, LOVETT   Lovett Shaizer, TE, 6'3"/245 lbs; West Virginia; 1996: NE, rnd 7; B4/7/1972 Seaford, DE

1996 NE	2(0)	—	—	—	—	—	—	—	—	—	—	—	—	—	—	—	—	—	—	—	—	—	—
1997 †NE	16(2)	—	—	—	—	5	57	11.4(20)	3	—	—	—	—	—	—	—	—	—	—	—	—	18	44
1998 †NE	16(5, te)	—	—	—	—	12	92	7.7(22)	2	—	—	—	—	—	—	—	—	—	—	—	—	12	56
1999 Bal	2(0)	—	—	—	—	2	10	5.0(5)	0	—	—	—	—	—	—	—	—	—	—	—	—	0	5
NFL 4	36(7)	—	—	—	—	19	159	8.4(22)	5	—	—	—	—	—	—	—	—	—	—	—	—	30	105

PURVIS, ANDRE   Andre Lamont, DT, 6'4"/310 lbs; North Carolina; 1997: Cin, rnd 5; B7/14/1973 Jacksonville, NC   **1997** Cin 7 (1) **1998** Cin 9 (0) **1999** Cin 5 (0) **NFL** 21 (1) [3 yrs]

PURVIS, VIC   James Victor, DB, 5'11"/190 lbs; Southern Mississippi; B11/17/1943 Brandon, MS   **1966** Bos-A 14 **1967** Bos-A 2 **NFL** 16 [2 yrs]

PUTMAN, EARL   Earl Robert, C, 6'6"/308 lbs; Arizona State; 1954: NYG, rnd 5; B1/10/1932 Cincinnati, OH   **1957** ChiC 11 (C)

PUTNAM, DUANE   Duane, G, 6'0"/228 lbs; Pacific; B9/5/1928 Pollack, SD   **1952**†LARm 6 **1953** LARm 9 (LG) **1954** LARm★11 (LG) **1955**†LARm★12 (12, LG) **1956** LARm☆12 (12, LG) **1957** LARm★12 (LG) **1958** LARm★12 (LG) **1959** LARm★10 (LG) **1960** Dal 12 (LG) **1961** Cle 14 **1962** LARm 11 (RG) **NFL** 121 (24) [11 yrs]

PUTZIER, FRED   Frederick James, E-WB, 5'9"/174 lbs; St. Olaf; B6/11/1899 Bird Island, MN, D9/17/1986 Prescott, WI   **1924** Min 3 (1)

PUTZIER, JEB   Jebediah Lee, TE, 6'4"/256 lbs; Boise State; 2002: Den, rnd 6; B1/20/1979 Eagle, ID

2002 Den	3(1)	—	—	—	—	—	—	—	—	—	—	—	—	—	—	—	—	—	—	—	—	—	—
2003 Den	4(0)	—	—	—	—	4	34	8.5(13)	0	—	—	—	—	—	—	—	—	—	—	k	—	0	18
2004 †Den	16(5, TE)	—	—	—	—	36	572	15.9(39)	2	—	—	—	—	—	—	—	—	—	—	—	—	12	296
2005 †Den	16(4)	—	—	—	—	37	481	13.0(32)	0	—	—	—	—	—	—	—	—	—	—	—	—	2	241
NFL 4	39(10)	—	—	—	—	77	1087	14.1(39)	2	—	—	—	—	—	—	—	—	—	—	k	—	14	555

PUTZIER, ROLLIN   Rollin William, DT-NT, 6'4"/279 lbs; Oregon; 1988: GB, rnd 4; B12/10/1965 Coeur d'Alene, ID   **1988** Pit 5 (0) **1989** SF 11 (0) **NFL** 16 (0) [2 yrs]

PUZZUOLI, DAVE   Phillip David, NT, 6'3"/260 lbs; Pittsburgh; 1983: Cle, rnd 6; B1/12/1961 Greenwich, CT   **1983** Cle 16 (0) **1984** Cle 16 (1) **1985**†Cle 16 (0) **1986**†Cle 16 (0) **1987**†Cle 12 (1) **NFL** 76 (2) [5 yrs]

PYATT, BRAD   Bradley James, WR, 5'11"/195 lbs; Kentucky; Northern Colorado; B4/16/1980 Arvada, CO

2003 Ind	8(0)	—	—	—	—	1	2	2.0(2)	0	—	—	—	—	—	—	—	—	—	—	kp	—	0	310
2004 Ind	8(0)	—	—	—	—	2	12	6.0(7)	0	—	—	—	—	—	—	—	—	—	—	kp	—	0	93
NFL 2	16(0)	—	—	—	—	3	14	4.7(7)	0	—	—	—	—	—	—	—	—	—	—	kp	—	0	403

PYBURN, JACK   Jack Harris, T, 6'6"/250 lbs; Texas A&M; 1967: Mia, rnd 11; B12/28/1944 Shreveport, LA   **1967** Mia-A 10 **1968** Mia-A 13 **NFL** 23 [2 yrs]

PYEATT, JOHNNY   John Joseph, DB, 6'3"/204 lbs; none; B9/16/1933 Florence, AZ   **1960** Den-A 14 (RCB) **1961** Den-A 3 **NFL** 17 [2 yrs]

PYLE, MIKE   Michael Johnson, C, 6'3"/250 lbs; Yale; 1961: Chi, rnd 7; B7/18/1939 Keokuk, IA   **1961** ChiB 14 (14, C) **1962** ChiB 14 (14, C) **1963**†ChiB★14 (14, C) **1964** ChiB 11 (11, C) **1965** ChiB☆13 (13, C) **1966** ChiB 13 (13, C) **1967** ChiB 14 (14, C) **1968** ChiB 14 (14, C) **1969** ChiB 14 (C) **NFL** 121 (107) [9 yrs]

PYLE, PALMER   William Palmer, G, 6'3"/247 lbs; Michigan State; 1959: Bal, rnd 6/1960: Hou, rnd 1; B6/12/1937 Keokuk, IA   **1960** Bal 11 **1961** Bal 14 (LG) **1962** Bal 6 (6, lg) **1963** Bal 7 **1964** Min 10 (9, LG) **1966** Oak-A 13 **NFL** 61 (15) [6 yrs]

PYLES, DAVID   Robert David, T, 6'5"/275 lbs; Miami (OH); B9/3/1960 Portsmouth, OH   **1987** LARd 2 (0)

PYLMAN, BOB   Robert William, T, 6'4"/214 lbs; South Dakota State; B10/30/1913 Ellendale, ND, D4/9/1971   **1939** Phi 10 (2)

| 1938 Phi | 11(1) | — | — | — | — | 1 | 1 | 1.0(1) | 0 | — | — | — | — | — | — | — | — | — | — | 1 | 6 | 1 |
| NFL 2 | 21(3) | — | — | — | — | 1 | 1 | 1.0(1) | 0 | — | — | — | — | — | — | — | — | — | — | 1 | 6 | 1 |

PYNE, GEORGE   George Francis, T, 5'11"/218 lbs; Holy Cross; B10/17/1909 Marlboro, MA, D6/1974   **1931** Pro 2 (1)

PYNE, GEORGE   George Francis, DT, 6'4"/285 lbs; Olivet; 1965: Bos, rnd 16; B7/12/1941 Milford, MA   **1965** Bos-A 14

PYNE, JIM   James M., G-C, 6'2"/290 lbs; Virginia Tech; 1994: TB, rnd 7; B11/23/1971 Milford, MA   **1995** TB 15 (13, LG) **1996** TB 12 (11, LG) **1997**†TB 15 (14, LG) **1998** Det 16 (16, C) **1999** Cle 16 (16, LG) **2000** Cle 2 (2) **2001** Phi 5 (1) **NFL** 81 (73) [7 yrs]

QUAERNA, JERRY   Jerold Oscar, T, 6'6"/275 lbs; Michigan; B10/9/1963 Janesville, WI   **1987** Det 3 (3)

QUAM, RED   Arthur Charles, BB, /165 lbs; none; B7/10/1896 Minneapolis, MN, D5/1/1973 Hibbing, MN   **1926** Dul 1 (0)

QUARLES, BERNARD   Bernard Darwin, QB, 6'2"/215 lbs; UCLA; Hawaii; B1/4/1960 Los Angeles, CA

| 1987 LARm | 1(0) | 1 | 8 | 8.0(8) | 0 | — | — | — | — | 3 | 1 | 33.3 | 40 | 13.3(40) | 1 | 1 | — | — | — | — | — | 0 | -7 |

QUARLES, SHELTON   Shelton Eugene, LB, 6'1"/225 lbs; Vanderbilt; B9/11/1971 Nashville, TN   **1997**†TB 16 (0) **1998** TB 16 (0) **1999**†TB 16 (14, LLB) **2000**†TB 14 (13, LLB) **2001**†TB 16 (16, LLB) **2002**†TB◇16 (16, MLB) **2003** TB 11 (11, MLB) **2004** TB 15 (15, MLB) **2005**†TB 16 (16, MLB) **NFL** 136 (101) [9 yrs]

QUAST, JOHN   John Henry, E, 5'10"/165 lbs; Purdue; B4/4/1900 Louisville, KY, D8/9/1966 Louisville, KY   **1923** Lou 1 (1, RE)

QUATSE, JESS   Jesse, T, 5'11"/226 lbs; Pittsburgh; B4/4/1908 Rillton, PA, D12/27/1977 Lakeland, FL   **1933** GB 9 (3) **1933** Pit 1 (1) **1935**†NYG 10 (2)

| 1934 Pit | 12(12, LT) | — | — | — | — | 1 | 0 | 0.0 | 0 | 0.0 | 0 | 0 | — | 0 | 0 | 0 | 0 |
| NFL 3 | 32(18) | — | — | — | — | 1 | 0 | 0.0 | 0 | 0.0 | 0 | 0 | — | 0 | 0 | 0 | 0 |

QUAYLE, FRANK   Frank Joseph, RB, 5'10"/195 lbs; Virginia; 1969: Den, rnd 5; B1/15/1947 Brooklyn, NY

| 1969 Den-A | 11(2) | 57 | 183 | 3.2(17) | 0 | 11 | 167 | 15.2(71) | 0 | — | — | — | — | — | — | — | — | — | — | — | — | 0 | 267 |

QUEEN, JEFF   Jeffrey Richard, RB-TE, 6'1"/217 lbs; Morgan State; 1968: SD, rnd 12; B8/15/1946 Boston, MA

1969 SD-A	14(te)	—	—	—	—	10	148	14.8(42)	0	—	—	—	—	—	—	—	—	—	—	—	—	0	74
1970 SD	14(FB)	77	261	3.4(19)	1	20	236	11.8(65)	1	—	—	—	—	—	—	—	—	—	—	k	—	12	391
1971 SD	14(FB)	95	318	3.3(41)	4	23	270	11.7(54)	3	—	—	—	—	—	—	—	—	—	—	—	—	42	508
1972 Oak	14	4	10	2.5(10)	0	—	—	—	—	—	—	—	—	—	—	—	—	—	—	—	—	0	10
1973 Oak	9	—	—	—	—	—	—	—	—	—	—	—	—	—	—	—	—	—	—	—	—	—	—
1974 Hou	11	2	7	3.5(4)	0	1	4	4.0(4)	1	—	—	—	—	—	—	—	—	—	—	—	—	6	14
NFL 6	76	178	596	3.3(41)	5	54	658	12.2(65)	5	—	—	—	—	—	—	—	—	—	—	k	—	60	997

QUERY, JEFF   Jeffrey Lee, WR, 6'0"/165 lbs; Millikin; 1989: GB, rnd 5; B3/7/1967 Decatur, IL [R]

1989 GB	16(0)	—	—	—	—	23	350	15.2(45)	2	—	—	—	—	—	—	—	—	—	—	kp	—	12	317
1990 GB	16(0)	3	39	13.0(18)	0	34	458	13.5(47)	2	—	—	—	—	—	—	—	—	—	—	p	1	18	426
1991 GB	16(0)	—	—	—	—	7	94	13.4(26)	0	—	—	—	—	—	—	—	—	—	—	p	—	0	134
1992 Cin	10(2)	1	1	1.0(1)	0	16	265	16.6(83)	3	—	—	—	—	—	—	—	—	—	—	k	—	18	147
1993 Cin	16(16, WR)	2	13	6.5(8)	0	56	654	11.7(51)	4	—	—	—	—	—	—	—	—	—	—	—	—	24	360

YEAR	TEAM	G(GS, POS)	RUSH	YD	AVG(LG)	TD	REC	YD	AVG(LG)	TD	PASS	COMP	PCT	YD	AVG(LG)	TD	INT	SK	YD	QBR	KPR	OTD	PTS	TAY
1994	Cin	10(3)	—	—	—	—	5	44	8.8(14)	0	—	—	—	—	—	—	—	—	—	—	—	—	0	22
1995	Cin	1(0)	—	—	—	—	—	—	—	—	—	—	—	—	—	—	—	—	—	—	p	—	0	0
1995	Was	1(0)	—	—	—	—	—	—	—	—	—	—	—	—	—	—	—	—	—	—	—	—	—	—
NFL	7	86(21)	6	53	8.8(18)	0	141	1865	13.2(83)	11	—	—	—	—	—	—	—	—	—	—	kp	1	72	1406

Quick, Greg Gregory, T, 6´4˝/280 lbs; Catawba; B4/26/1964 **1987** Atl 1 (0)

Quick, Jerry Jerry Dean, T, 6´5˝/279 lbs; Kansas; Wichita State; B12/30/1963 Anthony, KS **1987** Pit 1 (0)

Quick, Mike Michael Anthony, WR, 6´2˝/190 lbs; North Carolina State; 1982: Phi, rnd 1; B5/14/1959 Hamlet, NC

YEAR	TEAM	G(GS, POS)	RUSH	YD	AVG(LG)	TD	REC	YD	AVG(LG)	TD	PASS	COMP	PCT	YD	AVG(LG)	TD	INT	SK	YD	QBR	KPR	OTD	PTS	TAY
1982	Phi	9(0)	—	—	—	—	10	156	15.6(49)	1	—	—	—	—	—	—	—	—	—	—	—	—	6	83
1983	Phi★	16(16, WR)	—	—	—	—	69	**1409**	20.4(83)	13	—	—	—	—	—	—	—	—	—	—	—	—	78	770
1984	Phi✧	14(14, WR)	1	-5	-5.0(-5)	0	61	1052	17.2(**90**)	9	—	—	—	—	—	—	—	—	—	—	—	—	54	566
1985	Phi★	16(15, WR)	—	—	—	—	73	**1247**	17.1(**99**)	**11**	—	—	—	—	—	—	—	—	—	—	—	—	66	679
1986	Phi★	16(16, WR)	—	—	—	—	60	939	15.6(75)	9	—	—	—	—	—	—	—	—	—	—	k	—	54	491
1987	Phi★	12(12, WR)	—	—	—	—	46	790	17.2(61)	11	—	—	—	—	—	—	—	—	—	—	—	—	66	450
1988	†Phi	8(8, WR)	—	—	—	—	22	508	23.1(55)	4	—	—	—	—	—	—	—	—	—	—	—	—	24	274
1989	Phi	6(5, wr)	—	—	—	—	13	228	17.5(40)	2	—	—	—	—	—	—	—	—	—	—	—	—	12	124
1990	Phi	4(4)	—	—	—	—	9	135	15.0(39)	1	—	—	—	—	—	—	—	—	—	—	—	—	6	73
NFL	9	101(90)	1	-5	-5.0(-5)	0	363	6464	17.8(99)	61	—	—	—	—	—	—	—	—	—	—	k	—	366	3508

Quigley, Red Gerald, TB-BB, 5´9˝/155 lbs; none; B12/18/1895 Rochester, NY, D9/21/1966 Rochester, NY **1920** Roc 9 (1, TB)

Quillan, Fred Frederick David, C, 6´5˝/261 lbs; Oregon; 1978: SF, rnd 7; B1/27/1956 West Palm Beach, FL **1978** SF 14 (7, c) **1979** SF 16 (16, C) **1980** SF 16 (16, C) **1981**†SF 16 (16, C) **1982** SF 9 (9, C) **1983**†SF 14 (14, C) **1984**†SF★16 (16, C) **1985**†SF★15 (15, C) **1986**†SF 16 (16, C) **1987**†SF 11 (4) **NFL** 143 (129) [10 yrs]

Quillen, Frank Frank Harris, E-DE, 6´5˝/225 lbs; Pennsylvania; B12/18/1920 Ridley Park, PA, D9/21/1990 Hockessin, DE

YEAR	TEAM	G(GS, POS)	RUSH	YD	AVG(LG)	TD	REC	YD	AVG(LG)	TD	PASS	COMP	PCT	YD	AVG(LG)	TD	INT	SK	YD	QBR	KPR	OTD	PTS	TAY
1946	ChiR-A	14(4)	—	—	—	—	13	143	11.0	2	—	—	—	—	—	—	—	—	—	—	ki	—	12	84
1947	ChiR-A	6(2)	—	—	—	—	7	113	16.1	1	—	—	—	—	—	—	—	—	—	—	—	—	6	62
AAFC	2	20(6)	—	—	—	—	20	256	12.8	3	—	—	—	—	—	—	—	—	—	—	ki	—	18	145

Quilter, Charley Charles Rew, T-DT, 6´1˝/240 lbs; Tyler JC (TX); B5/8/1926 Shreveport, LA **1949**†SF-A 12 (1)

1950 SF 8

Quinlan, Bill William David, DE, 6´3˝/248 lbs; Michigan State; 1956: Cle, rnd 3; B6/19/1932 Lawrence, MA **1957**†Cle☆12 (LDE) **1958** Cle 10 (RDE) **1959** GB 12 (RDE) **1960**†GB☆12 (RDE) **1961**†GB 14 (RDE) **1962**†GB 14 (RDE) **1963** Phi 11 **1964** Det 12 **1965** Was 14 **NFL** 111 [9 yrs]

Quinlan, Skeets Volney Ralph, HB, 5´11˝/173 lbs; TCU; San Diego State; 1952: LA, rnd 4; B6/22/1928 San Angelo, TX, D1/18/1998 Okeechobee, FL

YEAR	TEAM	G(GS, POS)	RUSH	YD	AVG(LG)	TD	REC	YD	AVG(LG)	TD	PASS	COMP	PCT	YD	AVG(LG)	TD	INT	SK	YD	QBR	KPR	OTD	PTS	TAY
1952	†LARm	12(LH)	52	224	4.3(38)	1	14	265	18.9(80)	2	4	0	0.0	0	0.0	0	0	—	—	—	kp	—	18	659
1953	LARm	12(LH)	97	705	**7.3**(**74**)	4	17	260	15.3(59)	2	4	2	50.0	60	15.0(40)	0	1	—	—	—	k	—	36	883
1954	LARm✧	11(LH)	82	490	6.0(35)	4	18	324	18.0(80)	2	2	1	50.0	34	17.0(34)	0	1	—	—	—	kp	—	36	687
1955	†LARm	6	15	70	4.7(12)	0	19	245	12.9(46)	0	—	—	—	—	—	—	—	—	—	—	p	1	6	253
1956	LARm	2	10	21	2.1(9)	0	3	24	8.0(0)	0	—	—	—	—	—	—	—	—	—	—	kp	—	0	46
1956	Cle	6	2	4	2.0(3)	0	4	63	15.8(31)	0	—	—	—	—	—	—	—	—	—	—	kp	—	0	79
NFL	5	49	258	1514	5.9(74)	9	75	1181	15.7(80)	6	10	3	30.0	94	9.4(40)	0	2	—	—	—	kp	1	96	2606

Quinn, Ivan Ivan W., G, Carroll (WI); B5/26/1899, NE, D8/7/1969 San Diego, CA **1924** KC 1 (1)

Quinn, Jonathan Jonathan Ryan, QB, 6´6˝/243 lbs; Tulane; Middle Tennessee State; 1998: Jax, rnd 3; B2/27/1975 Turlock, CA

YEAR	TEAM	G(GS, POS)	RUSH	YD	AVG(LG)	TD	REC	YD	AVG(LG)	TD	PASS	COMP	PCT	YD	AVG(LG)	TD	INT	SK	YD	QBR	KPR	OTD	PTS	TAY
1998	Jax	4(2)	11	77	7.0(17)	1	—	—	—	—	64	34	53.1	387	6.0(64)	2	3	9	49	—	—	—	6	171
2000	Jax	1(0)	2	-2	-1.0(-1)	0	—	—	—	—	—	—	—	—	—	—	—	—	—	—	—	—	0	-2
2001	Jax	6(1)	8	42	5.3(27)	0	—	—	—	—	61	32	52.5	361	5.9(45)	1	1	6	43	—	—	—	0	188
2002	KC	1(0)	1	-1	-1.0(-1)	0	—	—	—	—	—	—	—	—	—	—	—	—	—	—	—	—	0	-1
2004	ChiB	5(3)	3	35	11.7(23)	0	—	—	—	—	98	51	52.0	413	4.2(32)	1	3	15	109	—	—	—	0	127
NFL	5	17(6)	25	151	6.0(27)	1	—	—	—	—	223	117	52.5	1161	5.2(64)	4	7	30	201	—	—	—	6	482

Quinn, Kelly Kelly B., LB, 6´1˝/220 lbs; Michigan State; B8/20/1963 Thomaston, GA **1987** Min 3 (2)

Quinn, Marcus Marcus, DB, 6´1˝/205 lbs; LSU; B6/27/1959 Tylertown, MS **1987** TB 3 (3)

Quinn, Mike Michael Patrick, QB, 6´4˝/216 lbs; Stephen F. Austin State; B4/15/1974 Las Vegas, NV

YEAR	TEAM	G(GS, POS)	RUSH	YD	AVG(LG)	TD	REC	YD	AVG(LG)	TD	PASS	COMP	PCT	YD	AVG(LG)	TD	INT	SK	YD	QBR	KPR	OTD	PTS	TAY
1997	Pit	1(0)	—	—	—	—	—	—	—	—	2	1	50.0	10	5.0(10)	0	0	—	—	—	—	—	0	5
1998	Dal	3(0)	5	-6	-1.2(-1)	0	—	—	—	—	1	1	100.0	10	10.0(10)	0	0	—	—	—	—	—	0	-1
NFL	2	4(0)	5	-6	-1.2(-1)	0	—	—	—	—	3	2	66.7	20	6.7(10)	0	0	—	—	—	—	—	0	4

Quinn, Paddy Patrick George, HB, 5´7˝/170 lbs; none; B2/5/1890, IA, D2/1963, IL **1920** RI 3 (0) **1921** RI 1 (0) **NFL** 4 (0) [2 yrs]

Quinn, Steve Stephen Timothy, C, 6´1˝/225 lbs; Notre Dame; B2/11/1946 Pittsburg, KS **1968** Hou-A 9

Quirk, Ed Edward George, FB-MG-LB, 6´1˝/231 lbs; Missouri; 1948: Was, rnd 15; B2/27/1925 St. Louis, MO, deceased **1950** Was 12 (MG) **1951** Was 6

YEAR	TEAM	G(GS, POS)	RUSH	YD	AVG(LG)	TD	REC	YD	AVG(LG)	TD	PASS	COMP	PCT	YD	AVG(LG)	TD	INT	SK	YD	QBR	KPR	OTD	PTS	TAY
1948	Was	12(6, FB)	77	328	4.3(24)	4	9	40	4.4(11)	0	—	—	—	—	—	—	—	—	—	—	—	—	24	388
1949	Was	8(4)	40	139	3.5(13)	1	5	33	6.6(15)	0	—	—	—	—	—	—	—	—	—	—	k	—	6	170
NFL	4	38(10)	117	467	4.0(24)	5	14	73	5.2(15)	0	—	—	—	—	—	—	—	—	—	—	ki	—	30	553

Raab, Marc Marc, C, 6´3˝/265 lbs; USC; B1/26/1969 San Diego, CA **1993** Was 2 (0) **1998** SD 1 (0) **NFL** 3 (0) [2 yrs]

Raba, Bob Robert William, TE, 6´1˝/222 lbs; Maryland; B4/23/1955 Washington, DC **1977** NYJ 14 **1978** NYJ 4 **1980** Bal 3 (0) **1981** Was 8 (0)

YEAR	TEAM	G(GS, POS)	RUSH	YD	AVG(LG)	TD	REC	YD	AVG(LG)	TD	PASS	COMP	PCT	YD	AVG(LG)	TD	INT	SK	YD	QBR	KPR	OTD	PTS	TAY
1979	NYJ	8	—	—	—	—	2	9	4.5(6)	0	—	—	—	—	—	—	—	—	—	—	k	—	0	8
NFL	5	37	—	—	—	—	2	9	4.5(6)	0	—	—	—	—	—	—	—	—	—	—	k	—	0	12

Rabach, Casey Casey Edward, C-G, 6´4˝/301 lbs; Wisconsin; 2001: Bal, rnd 3; B9/24/1977 Sturgeon Bay, WI **2002** Bal 12 (5, lg) **2003**†Bal 14 (2) **2004** Bal 16 (16, C) **2005**†Was 16 (16, C) **NFL** 58 (39) [4 yrs]

Rabb, Warren Samuel Warren, QB, 6´3˝/204 lbs; LSU; 1960: Det, rnd 2/DalT, rnd 1; B12/12/1937 Baton Rouge, LA

YEAR	TEAM	G(GS, POS)	RUSH	YD	AVG(LG)	TD	REC	YD	AVG(LG)	TD	PASS	COMP	PCT	YD	AVG(LG)	TD	INT	SK	YD	QBR	KPR	OTD	PTS	TAY
1960	Det	7	—	—	—	—	—	—	—	—	—	—	—	—	—	—	—	—	—	—	—	—	—	—
1961	Buf-A	9	13	47	3.6(19)	0	—	—	—	—	74	34	45.9	586	7.9(76)	5	2	—	—	—	—	—	2	285
1962	Buf-A	14(QB)	37	77	2.1(14)	3	—	—	—	—	177	67	37.9	1196	6.8(76)	10	14	—	—	47.7	—	—	20	195
NFL	3	30	50	124	2.5(19)	3	—	—	—	—	251	101	40.2	1782	7.1(76)	15	16	—	—	58.6	—	—	22	480

Rabold, Mike Michael John, G, 6´2˝/239 lbs; Indiana; 1959: Det, rnd 2; B3/12/1937 Chicago, IL, D10/13/1970 Greenwood, IN **1959** Det 12 **1960** SL 12 **1961** Min 14 (14, RG) **1962** Min 14 (14, RG) **1964** ChiB 14 (LG) **1965** ChiB 14 (LG) **1966** ChiB 14 (LG) **1967** ChiB 11 **NFL** 105 (28) [8 yrs]

Raborn, Buster Carroll M., C-LB, 6´0˝/198 lbs; SMU; B3/28/1913, D12/21/1991 Fortuna, CA **1936** Pit 10 (0) **1937** Pit 11 (1) **NFL** 21 (1) [2 yrs]

Rachal, Latario Latorio Deshawn, WR, 5´11˝/183 lbs; Fresno State; B1/31/1973 Lynwood, CA **1997** SD 14 (0) **1998** SD 11 (0) **NFL** 25 (0) [2 yrs]

Racis, Frank Frank J., G-T-E, 6´0˝/200 lbs; none; B11/9/1899 Shenandoah, PA, D8/19/1982 Shenandoah, PA **1925** Pot 12 (11, LG) **1926** Pot☆14 (14, LT), 6 **1927** Pot 13 (13, LG), 6 **1928** Pot 10 (10, LG) **1928** NYY 1 (1) **1929** Bos☆7 (7, LG) **1930** Pro 11 (6, lg), 6 **1931** Fra 8 (7, LT) **NFL** 76 (69), 18 [7 yrs]

Rackers, Neil Neil W., K, 6´0˝/205 lbs; Illinois; 2000: Cin, rnd 6; B8/16/1976 St. Louis, MO **[K]** **2001** Cin 16 (0) **2002** Cin 16 (0) **2003** Arz 7 (0) **2004** Arz 16 (0) **2005** Arz★15 (0)

YEAR	TEAM	G(GS, POS)	RUSH	YD	AVG(LG)	TD	REC	YD	AVG(LG)	TD	PASS	COMP	PCT	YD	AVG(LG)	TD	INT	SK	YD	QBR	KPR	OTD	PTS	TAY
2000	Cin	16(0)	1	-5	-5.0(-5)	0	—	—	—	—	—	—	—	—	—	—	—	—	—	—	K	—	57	-5
NFL	6	86(0)	1	-5	-5.0(-5)	0	—	—	—	—	—	—	—	—	—	—	—	—	—	—	KP	—	475	-5

Rackley, David David Henry, WR, 5´9˝/172 lbs; Texas Southern; B2/2/1961 Miami, FL **1985** NO 7 (0)

Rackley, Derek Derek, TE, 6´4˝/250 lbs; Minnesota; B7/18/1977 Apple Valley, MN **2000** Atl 16 (0) **2002**†Atl 16 (0) **2003** Atl 16 (1) **2004**†Atl 16 (0) **2005** Atl 16 (0)

YEAR	TEAM	G(GS, POS)	RUSH	YD	AVG(LG)	TD	REC	YD	AVG(LG)	TD	PASS	COMP	PCT	YD	AVG(LG)	TD	INT	SK	YD	QBR	KPR	OTD	PTS	TAY
2001	Atl	16(0)	—	—	—	—	1	1	1.0(1)	1	—	—	—	—	—	—	—	—	—	—	—	—	6	6
NFL	6	96(1)	—	—	—	—	1	1	1.0(1)	1	—	—	—	—	—	—	—	—	—	—	—	—	6	6

Radachowsky, George George Joseph, DB, 5´11˝/186 lbs; Boston College; 1984: LARm, rnd 7; B9/7/1962 Danbury, CT **1984** Ind 16 (0) **1985** Ind 3 (0) **1987** NYJ 8 (3) **1988** NYJ 9 (3) **1989** NYJ 16 (13, SS) **NFL** 52 (19) [5 yrs]

YEAR	TEAM	G (GS, POS)	RUSH	YD	AVG (LG)	TD	REC	YD	AVG (LG)	TD	PASS	COMP	PCT	YD	AVG (LG)	TD	INT	SK	YD	QBR	KPR	OTD	PTS	TAY

RADE, JOHN John Anthony, LB, 6´1˝/232 lbs; Boise State; 1983: Atl, rnd 8; B8/31/1960 Ceres, CA **1983** Atl 16 (11, LLB) **1984** Atl 7 (7, llb) **1985** Atl 16 (14, LLB) **1986** Atl 15 (15, RILB) **1987** Atl 11 (11, RILB) **1988** Atl 15 (15, LILB) **1989** Atl 15 (14, LILB) **1990** Atl 16 (15, RILB) **1991**†Atl 11 (10, LILB) **NFL** 122 (112) [9 yrs]

RADECIC, KEITH J. Keith, C, 6´1˝/260 lbs; Penn State; B12/24/1963 Pittsburgh, PA **1987** SL 3 (3)

RADECIC, SCOTT J. Scott, LB, 6´3˝/243 lbs; Penn State; 1984: KC, rnd 2; B6/14/1962 Pittsburgh, PA **1984** KC 16 (2) **1985** KC 16 (16, LILB) **1986**†KC 16 (13, RILB) **1987** Buf 12 (9, RILB) **1988**†Buf 16 (3) **1989**†Buf 16 (12, LILB) **1990** Ind 15 (1) **1991** Ind 14 (9, LILB) **1992** Ind 16 (9, LILB) **1993** Ind 16 (4) **1994** Ind 16 (1) **1995**†Ind 13 (0) **NFL** 182 (79) [12 yrs]

RADEMACHER, BILL William Stiles, WR-DB, 6´1˝/190 lbs; Northern Michigan; B5/13/1942 Menomonie, MI

YEAR	TEAM	G (GS, POS)	RUSH	YD	AVG (LG)	TD	REC	YD	AVG (LG)	TD	PASS	COMP	PCT	YD	AVG (LG)	TD	INT	SK	YD	QBR	KPR	OTD	PTS	TAY
1964	NYJ-A	6	—	—	—	—	—	—	—	—	—	—	—	—	—	—	—	—	—	—	pi	—	0	9
1965	NYJ-A	4	—	—	—	—	—	—	—	—	—	—	—	—	—	—	—	—	—	—	—	—	—	—
1966	NYJ-A	4	—	—	—	—	1	3	3.0(3)	0	—	—	—	—	—	—	—	—	—	—	—	—	0	2
1967	NYJ-A	3	—	—	—	—	—	—	—	—	—	—	—	—	—	—	—	—	—	—	—	—	—	—
1968	†NYJ-A	14	1	-13	-13.0(-13)	0	2	11	5.5(6)	0	—	—	—	—	—	—	—	—	—	—	k	—	0	-23
1969	Bos-A	13(4)	—	—	—	—	17	217	12.8(40)	3	—	—	—	—	—	—	—	—	—	—	—	—	18	124
1970	Bos	14(1)	—	—	—	—	4	51	12.8(16)	0	—	—	—	—	—	—	—	—	—	—	—	—	0	26
NFL	7	58(5)	1	-13	-13.0(-13)	0	24	282	11.8(40)	3	—	—	—	—	—	—	—	—	—	—	kpi	—	18	137

RADFORD, BRUCE Bruce E., NT-DE, 6´5˝/257 lbs; Grambling State; 1979: Den, rnd 3; B10/5/1955 Pineville, LA **1979** Den 16 **1980** TB 12 (0) **1981** SL 9 (1) **NFL** 37 (1) [3 yrs]

RADICK, KEN Kenneth Milton, E-G-T, 5´10˝/210 lbs; Indiana; Marquette; B6/17/1907 Green Bay, WI, D8/25/1987 Oshkosh, WI **1930** GB 4 (1) **1931** GB 1 (1) **1931** Bkn 2 (1) **NFL** 7 (3) [2 yrs]

RADLOFF, WAYNE Wayne Richard, C-G, 6´5˝/274 lbs; Georgia; B5/17/1961 London, England **1985** Atl 16 (0) **1986** Atl 16 (16, C) **1987** Atl 12 (12, C) **1988** Atl 10 (10, C) **1989** Atl 11 (4) **NFL** 65 (42) [5 yrs]

RADO, ALEX Alexander, HB-DB, 6´1˝/200 lbs; West Virginia Tech; B7/19/1911 Dayton, OH, D8/30/1995 Dayton, OH

YEAR	TEAM	G (GS, POS)	RUSH	YD	AVG (LG)	TD	REC	YD	AVG (LG)	TD	PASS	COMP	PCT	YD	AVG (LG)	TD	INT	SK	YD	QBR	KPR	OTD	PTS	TAY
1934	Pit	8(4, HB)	38	210	5.5	0	5	93	18.6	0	24	8	33.3	179	7.5	0	2	—	—	—	—	—	0	266

RADO, GEORGE George, G-DE, 5´9˝/194 lbs; Duquesne; B10/24/1912 Youngstown, OH, D4/30/1992 New Cumberland, WV **1935** Pit 11 (8, LG) **1936** Pit☆12 (6, lg) **1937** Pit 1 (0) **1937** Phi 9 (1) **1938** Phi 10 (6, RG) **NFL** 43 (21) [4 yrs]

RADOSEVICH, GEORGE George, T-C, 6´2˝/228 lbs; Pittsburgh; B1/25/1928 Brentwood, PA **1954** Bal 10 **1955** Bal 12 (LT) **1956** Bal 8 **NFL** 30 [3 yrs]

RADOVICH, BILL William Alex, G, 5´10˝/238 lbs; USC; B6/24/1915 Chicago, IL, D3/6/2002 Newport Beach, CA **1938** Det✧10 (4) **1939** Det 11 (1) **1940** Det 10 (2) **1941** Det 11 (4) **1945** Det☆9 (8, RG) **NFL** 51 (19) [5 yrs]

1946 LAD-A☆14 (12, RG) **1947** LAD-A 14 (3) **AAFC** 28 (15) [2 yrs]

RADZIEVITCH, VIC Victor John, B-G-FB, 5´10˝/165 lbs; Connecticut; B6/8/1903 Torrington, CT, D6/1974 Torrington, **[K]** **1926** Har 8 (0), 5

RAE, MIKE Michael John, QB, 6´0˝/193 lbs; USC; 1973: Oak, rnd 8; B7/26/1951 Long Beach, CA

YEAR	TEAM	G (GS, POS)	RUSH	YD	AVG (LG)	TD	REC	YD	AVG (LG)	TD	PASS	COMP	PCT	YD	AVG (LG)	TD	INT	SK	YD	QBR	KPR	OTD	PTS	TAY
1976	†Oak	7(2)	10	37	3.7(12)	1	—	—	—	—	65	35	53.8	417	6.4(37)	6	1	8	71	—	—	—	6	246
1977	Oak	10(1)	13	75	5.8(21)	1	—	—	—	—	30	15	50.0	162	5.4(30)	1	4	9	88	—	—	—	6	11
1978	TB	6(5, qb)	20	186	9.3(42)	0	—	—	—	—	118	57	48.3	705	6.0(33)	4	7	37	288	—	—	—	0	279
1979	†TB	5	1	2	2.0(2)	0	—	—	—	—	36	17	47.2	252	7.0(29)	1	2	5	31	—	—	—	0	53
NFL	4	28(8)	44	300	6.8(42)	2	—	—	—	—	249	124	49.8	1536	6.2(37)	12	14	59	478	—	—	—	12	588

RAEMER, NORBERT Norbert LaVerne, G, 5´11˝/210 lbs; Kansas State; B7/3/1920 Herkimer, KS **1942** Bkn 1 (0)

RAFFEL, BILL William, E, 5´11˝/195 lbs; Pennsylvania; B8/26/1907 Ashland, KY, D7/24/1982 Wynnewood, PA

YEAR	TEAM	G (GS, POS)	RUSH	YD	AVG (LG)	TD	REC	YD	AVG (LG)	TD	PASS	COMP	PCT	YD	AVG (LG)	TD	INT	SK	YD	QBR	KPR	OTD	PTS	TAY
1932	Bkn	4(2)	—	—	—	—	1	15	15.0(15)	0	—	—	—	—	—	—	—	—	—	—	—	—	0	8

RAFFERTY, IAN Ian, T-G, 6´6˝/300 lbs; North Carolina State; B9/2/1976 Summerville, SC **1999** NYJ 5 (0)

RAFFERTY, TOM Thomas Michael, C-G, 6´3˝/256 lbs; Penn State; 1976: Dal, rnd 4; B8/2/1954 Syracuse, NY **1976**†Dal 13 **1977**†Dal 14 (14, RG) **1978**†Dal 16 (16, RG) **1979**†Dal 16 (16, RG) **1980**†Dal 16 (16, RG) **1981**†Dal 16 (15, C) **1982**†Dal 9 (9, C) **1984** Dal 16 (16, C) **1985**†Dal 16 (16, C) **1986** Dal 16 (16, C) **1987** Dal 12 (12, C) **1988** Dal 15 (13, C) **1989** Dal 12 (8, C)

YEAR	TEAM	G (GS, POS)	RUSH	YD	AVG (LG)	TD	REC	YD	AVG (LG)	TD	PASS	COMP	PCT	YD	AVG (LG)	TD	INT	SK	YD	QBR	KPR	OTD	PTS	TAY
1983	†Dal	16(15, C)	—	—	—	—	1	8	8.0(8)	0	—	—	—	—	—	—	—	—	—	—	—	—	0	4
NFL	14	203(182)	—	—	—	—	1	8	8.0(8)	0	—	—	—	—	—	—	—	—	—	—	—	—	0	4

RAFFERTY, VINCE Vincent Edward, C-G, 6´4˝/285 lbs; Colorado; B8/6/1961 Manhattan, KS **1987** GB 3 (3)

RAFTER, BILLY William John, B, 5´6˝/155 lbs; Syracuse; B10/7/1895 Troy, NY, D6/28/1966 Syracuse, NY **1921** Roc 1 (0) **1924** Roc 2 (0) **NFL** 3 (0) [2 yrs]

RAGAZZO, PHIL Philip John, T-G, 6´0˝/216 lbs; Case Western Reserve; 1938: GB, rnd 8; B6/24/1915 Niles, OH, D10/3/1994 Niles, OH **1938** Cle 10 (6, LG) **1939** Cle 11 (3) **1940** Cle 1 (0) **1940** Phi 6 (5, rt) **1941** Phi☆10 (10, RT) **1945** NYG 5 (5, RT) **1946**†NYG 11 (1) **1947** NYG 9 (1) **NFL** 63 (31) [7 yrs]

RAGLIN, FLOYD Floyd C., WR, 5´9˝/180 lbs; UNLV; Southern (LA); B2/10/1961 Alton, IL **1987** Mia 2 (0)

RAGONE, DAVE Dave Patrick, QB, 6´3˝/245 lbs; Louisville; 2003: Hou, rnd 3; B10/3/1979 Middleburg Heights, OH

YEAR	TEAM	G (GS, POS)	RUSH	YD	AVG (LG)	TD	REC	YD	AVG (LG)	TD	PASS	COMP	PCT	YD	AVG (LG)	TD	INT	SK	YD	QBR	KPR	OTD	PTS	TAY
2003	Hou	2(2)	6	51	8.5(14)	0	1	-5	-5.0(-5)	0	40	20	50.0	135	3.4(24)	0	1	8	39	—	—	—	0	76

RAGSDALE, GEORGE George Ellis, RB-WR, 5´11˝/185 lbs; North Carolina A&T; 1976: TB, rnd 12; B12/4/1952 Dinwiddie, VA

YEAR	TEAM	G (GS, POS)	RUSH	YD	AVG (LG)	TD	REC	YD	AVG (LG)	TD	PASS	COMP	PCT	YD	AVG (LG)	TD	INT	SK	YD	QBR	KPR	OTD	PTS	TAY
1977	TB	9	3	21	7.0(15)	0	2	17	8.5(10)	0	—	—	—	—	—	—	—	—	—	—	k	—	0	53
1978	TB	15	25	121	4.8(18)	1	3	41	13.7(31)	1	—	—	—	—	—	—	—	—	—	—	k	—	12	352
1979	†TB	15	6	5	0.8(3)	0	3	28	9.3(19)	0	—	—	—	—	—	—	—	—	—	—	k	—	0	184
NFL	3	39	34	147	4.3(18)	1	8	86	10.8(31)	1	—	—	—	—	—	—	—	—	—	—	k	—	12	588

RAGUNAS, VINCENT Vincent Joseph, B, 5´11˝/200 lbs; VMI; B7/12/1924 Plymouth, PA, D3/19/2001 Richmond, VA **1949** Pit 3 (0)

RAGUSA, PAT Patrick A., K, 5´8˝/180 lbs; St. John's (NY); B3/17/1963 Caracas, Venezuela **[K]** **1987** NYJ 3 (0)

RAIBLE, STEVE Steven Carl, WR, 6´2˝/195 lbs; Georgia Tech; 1976: Sea, rnd 2; B6/2/1954 Louisville, KY

YEAR	TEAM	G (GS, POS)	RUSH	YD	AVG (LG)	TD	REC	YD	AVG (LG)	TD	PASS	COMP	PCT	YD	AVG (LG)	TD	INT	SK	YD	QBR	KPR	OTD	PTS	TAY
1976	Sea	13	1	2	2.0(2)	0	4	126	31.5(80)	1	—	—	—	—	—	—	—	—	—	—	—	1	12	70
1977	Sea	14(3)	—	—	—	—	5	79	15.8(22)	0	—	—	—	—	—	—	—	—	—	—	k	—	0	29
1978	Sea	16	2	13	6.5(13)	0	22	316	14.4(38)	1	—	—	—	—	—	—	—	—	—	—	—	—	8	176
1979	Sea	16(4)	—	—	—	—	20	252	12.6(41)	1	—	—	—	—	—	—	—	—	—	—	—	—	6	131
1980	Sea	16(0)	—	—	—	—	16	232	14.5(40)	0	—	—	—	—	—	—	—	—	—	—	—	—	0	116
1981	Sea	9(0)	—	—	—	—	1	12	12.0(12)	0	—	—	—	—	—	—	—	—	—	—	—	—	0	6
NFL	6	84(7)	3	15	5.0(13)	0	68	1017	15.0(80)	3	—	—	—	—	—	—	—	—	—	—	k	1	26	528

RAIFF, JIM James Herman, T, 5´10˝/235 lbs; Dayton; B12/21/1930, D9/17/1994 Dayton, OH **1954** Bal 3

RAIMEY, DAVE David E., DB, 5´10˝/195 lbs; Michigan; 1963: Cle, rnd 9; B11/18/1940 Dayton, OH **1964** Cle 5

RAIMONDI, BEN Benjamin Louis, TB, 5´10˝/175 lbs; William & Mary; Indiana; 1947: NYY-A, rnd 1/ChiC, rnd 6; B1/23/1925 Brooklyn, NY

YEAR	TEAM	G (GS, POS)	RUSH	YD	AVG (LG)	TD	REC	YD	AVG (LG)	TD	PASS	COMP	PCT	YD	AVG (LG)	TD	INT	SK	YD	QBR	KPR	OTD	PTS	TAY
1947	NYY-A	7(0)	6	11	1.8	0	—	—	—	—	15	3	20.0	54	3.6	0	0	—	—	—	—	—	0	38

RAINER, WALI Wali Rashid, LB, 6´2˝/247 lbs; Virginia; 1999: Cle, rnd 4; B4/19/1977 Rockingham, NC **1999** Cle 16 (15, MLB) **2000** Cle 16 (16, MLB) **2001** Cle 14 (14, MLB) **2002** Jax 16 (14, MLB) **2003** Det 16 (0) **2004** Det 16 (0) **2005** Det 16 (5, llb) **NFL** 110 (64) [7 yrs]

RAINES, MIKE Vaughn Michael, DT-DE, 6´5˝/255 lbs; Alabama; 1974: SF, rnd 6; B2/14/1953 Montgomery, AL **1974** SF 2

RAINEY, CALVIN see Calvin Muhammad

RAINS, DAN Daniel Paul, LB, 6´1˝/224 lbs; Cincinnati; B4/26/1956 Rochester, PA **1982** ChiB 2 (0) **1983** ChiB 15 (5, rlb) **1984**†ChiB 16 (0) **1986** ChiB 9 (0) **NFL** 42 (5) [4 yrs]

RAIOLA, DOMINIC Dominic, C, 6´1˝/295 lbs; Nebraska; 2001: Det, rnd 2; B12/30/1978 Honolulu, HI **2001** Det 16 (0) **2002** Det 16 (16, C) **2003** Det 16 (16, C) **2004** Det 16 (16, C) **2005** Det 16 (16, C) **NFL** 80 (64) [5 yrs]

RAJKOVICH, PETER Peter Joseph, FB-LB, 5´10˝/190 lbs; Detroit Mercy; B1/17/1911 Austria, D11/14/1979 Caro, MI

YEAR	TEAM	G (GS, POS)	RUSH	YD	AVG (LG)	TD	REC	YD	AVG (LG)	TD	PASS	COMP	PCT	YD	AVG (LG)	TD	INT	SK	YD	QBR	KPR	OTD	PTS	TAY
1934	Pit	3(3)	39	140	3.6	0	—	—	—	—	—	—	—	—	—	—	—	—	—	—	—	—	0	140

RAKESTRAW, LARRY Lawrence Clyde, QB, 6'2"/195 lbs; Georgia; 1964: Chi, rnd 8/Oak, rnd 11; B4/22/1942 Mableton, GA

YEAR	TEAM	G (GS, POS)	RUSH	YD	AVG (LG)	TD	REC	YD	AVG (LG)	TD	PASS	COMP	PCT	YD	AVG (LG)	TD	INT	SK	YD	QBR	KPR	OTD	PTS	TAY
1966	ChiB	1	1	-5	-5.0(-5)	0	—	—	—	0	0	0	0.0	0	0.0	0	0	3	33	—	—	—	0	-5
1967	ChiB	5	11	42	3.8(20)	2	—	—	—	—	44	21	47.7	228	5.2(34)	3	2	15	—	—	—	—	12	111
1968	ChiB	7	9	12	1.3(7)	0	—	—	—	—	67	30	44.8	361	5.4(80)	1	7	6	49	—	—	—	0	-83
NFL	3	13	21	49	2.3(20)	2	—	—	—	—	111	51	45.9	589	5.3(80)	4	9	11	97	—	—	—	12	24

RAKOCZY, GREGG Gregg Adam, C-G-T, 6'6"/290 lbs; Miami (FL); 1987: Cle, rnd 2; B5/18/1965 Medford Lakes, NJ   **1987**†Cle 12 (0)   **1988**†Cle 16 (16, C)   **1989**†Cle 16 (16, C)   **1990** Cle 16 (12, RG)   **1991** NE 5 (2)   **1992** NE 16 (2)   **NFL** 81 (48) [6 yrs]

RALPH, DAN Daniel Ray, DT, 6'4"/260 lbs; Colorado; Oregon; 1984: Atl, rnd 6; B3/9/1961 Denver, CO   **1984** StL 6 (0)

RAMBO, KEN-YON Ken-Yon, WR, 6'1"/195 lbs; Ohio State; 2001: Oak, rnd 7; B10/4/1978 Cerritos, CA

YEAR	TEAM	G (GS, POS)	RUSH	YD	AVG (LG)	TD	REC	YD	AVG (LG)	TD	KPR	OTD	PTS	TAY
2001	Dal	13(0)	—	—	—	—	3	28	9.3(14)	0	kp	—	0	19
2002	Dal	16(0)	—	—	—	—	14	211	15.1(47)	0	kp	—	0	106
NFL	2	29(0)	—	—	—	—	17	239	14.1(47)	0	kp	—	0	125

RAMEY, JIM James Edward, DE, 6'4"/261 lbs; Kentucky; 1979: Cle, rnd 3; B3/9/1957 Louisville, KY   **1979** StL 7   **1987** TB 3 (0)   **NFL** 10 [2 yrs]

RAMIREZ, TONY Tony, T, 6'6"/296 lbs; Northern Colorado; 1997: Det, rnd 6; B1/26/1973 Lincoln, NE   **1997** Det 2 (0)   **1998** Det 16 (7, rt)   **1999**†Det 12 (3)   **NFL** 30 (10) [3 yrs]

RAMONA, JOE Joe Louis, G-DG, 6'1"/210 lbs; Santa Clara; 1953: NYG, rnd 28; B7/11/1931 San Jose, CA   **1953** NYG 8

RAMSEY, BUSTER Garrard Sliger, G-LB, 6'1"/219 lbs; William & Mary; 1943: ChiC, rnd 14; B3/16/1920 Townsend, TN [C]   **1947**†ChiC☆8 (7, RG)   **1948**†ChiC☆12 (10, RG)   **1949** ChiC☆12 (11, RG)   **1950** ChiC☆12 (12, RG)   **1951** ChiC 2

YEAR	TEAM	G (GS, POS)	RUSH	YD	AVG (LG)	TD	KPR	OTD	PTS	TAY
1946	ChiC☆	11(11, RG)	1	5	5.0(5)	0	i	—	0	6
NFL	6	57(51)	1	5	5.0(5)	0	ki	—	2	3

RAMSEY, CHUCK Lowell Wallace, P, 6'2"/191 lbs; Wake Forest; 1974: NE, rnd 6; B2/24/1952 Rock Hill, SC [P]   **1977** NYJ 12   **1978** NYJ 16   **1982**†NYJ 9 (0)   **1983** NYJ 16 (0)   **1984** NYJ 16 (0)

YEAR	TEAM	G (GS, POS)	RUSH	YD	AVG (LG)	TD	PASS	COMP	PCT	YD	AVG (LG)	TD	INT	KPR	OTD	PTS	TAY
1979	NYJ	16	2	0	0.0(0)	0	—	—	—	—	—	—	—	P	—	0	0
1980	NYJ	16(0)	1	-15	-15.0(-15)	0	2	1	50.0	6	3.0(6)	0	0	P	—	0	-12
1981	†NYJ	16(0)	3	0	0.0(0)	0	—	—	—	—	—	—	—	P	—	0	0
NFL	8	117	6	-15	-2.5	0	2	1	50.0	6	3.0(6)	0	0	P	—	0	-12

RAMSEY, DERRICK Derrick Kent, TE, 6'4"/230 lbs; Kentucky; 1978: Oak, rnd 5; B12/23/1956 Hastings, FL

YEAR	TEAM	G (GS, POS)	REC	YD	AVG (LG)	TD	KPR	OTD	PTS	TAY
1978	Oak	16	—	—	—	—	k	—	0	20
1979	Oak	16(3)	13	161	12.4(40)	3	—	—	18	96
1980	†Oak	16(0)	5	117	23.4(58)	0	k	—	0	54
1981	Oak	16(12, TE)	52	674	13.0(66)	4	—	—	24	357
1982	†LARd	9(0)	—	—	—	—	—	—	—	—
1983	LARd	2(0)	—	—	—	—	—	—	—	—
1983	NE	14(7, te)	24	335	14.0(39)	6	—	—	36	198
1984	NE	16(13, TE)	66	792	12.0(34)	7	—	—	42	431
1985	†NE	16(3)	28	285	10.2(26)	1	—	—	6	148
1987	Det	1(0)	—	—	—	—	—	—	—	—
NFL	9	122(38)	188	2364	12.6(66)	21	k	—	126	1302

RAMSEY, FRANK Harold Frank, T, 6'1"/240 lbs; Oregon State; 1938: ChiB, rnd 7; B5/16/1916 Corvallis, OR, D1/1985 Corvallis, OR   **1945** ChiB 9 (2)

RAMSEY, GREG Gregory Scott, DE, 6'3"/244 lbs; Fresno State; B12/19/1963 San Francisco, CA   **1987** Sea 2 (0)

RAMSEY, KNOX Knox Wagner, G, 6'1"/216 lbs; William & Mary; 1948: LAD-A, rnd 9/ChiB, rnd 5; B2/13/1926 Speed, IN, D3/19/2005 Richmond, VA   **1948** LAD-A 13 (7, RG)   **1949** LAD-A 12 (8, RG)   **AAFC** 25 (15) [2 yrs]
1950 ChiC 12   **1951** ChiC 10 (RG)   **1952** Phi 3   **1952** Was 8   **1953** Was 11 (LG)   **NFL** 44 [4 yrs]

RAMSEY, NATE Nathan Lee, DB, 6'1"/200 lbs; Indiana State; 1963: Phi, rnd 14; B7/12/1941 Neptune, NJ [I]   **1963** Phi 14   **1964** Phi 13 (LCB)   **1965** Phi 14 (14, LS)   **1966** Phi 12 (LS)   **1967** Phi 14 (LS)   **1968** Phi 14 (LS)   **1969** Phi 14 (LS)   **1970** Phi 11 (SS)   **1971** Phi 14 (RCB)   **1972** Phi 14 (RCB)   **1973** NO 4   **NFL** 138 (14) [11 yrs]

RAMSEY, PATRICK Patrick Allen, QB, 6'2"/217 lbs; Tulane; 2002: Was, rnd 1; B2/14/1979 Ruston, LA

YEAR	TEAM	G (GS, POS)	RUSH	YD	AVG (LG)	TD	PASS	COMP	PCT	YD	AVG (LG)	TD	INT	SK	YD	QBR	OTD	PTS	TAY
2002	Was	10(5, qb)	13	-1	-0.1(3)	1	227	117	51.5	1539	6.8(62)	9	8	18	132	—	—	6	504
2003	Was	11(11, QB)	15	62	4.1(24)	1	337	179	53.1	2166	6.4(64)	14	9	30	206	75.8	—	6	865
2004	Was	9(7, qb)	10	19	1.9(17)	0	272	169	62.1	1665	6.1(51)	10	11	23	137	74.8	—	0	462
2005	Was	4(1)	7	3	0.4(5)	0	25	15	60.0	279	11.2(72)	1	1	4	27	—	—	0	108
NFL	4	34(24)	45	83	1.8(24)	2	861	480	55.7	5649	6.6(72)	34	29	75	502	75.0	—	12	1938

RAMSEY, RAY Raymond Leroy, B, 6'2"/166 lbs; Bradley; 1947: ChiC, rnd 10; B7/18/1921 Springfield, IL [I]

YEAR	TEAM	G (GS, POS)	RUSH	YD	AVG (LG)	TD	REC	YD	AVG (LG)	TD	PASS	COMP	PCT	YD	AVG (LG)	TD	INT	KPR	OTD	PTS	TAY
1947	ChiR-A	14(10, RH)	70	433	6.2	2	35	768	21.9(80)	8	—	—	—	—	—	—	—	kpi	—	60	1160
1948	Bkn-A	11(6, wb)	22	48	2.2	0	13	315	24.2(50)	2	1	0	0.0	0	0.0	0	0	kpi	—	18	455
1949	ChiH-A	12(10, WB)	32	43	1.3	0	17	366	21.5(77)	4	—	—	—	—	—	—	—	kpi	—	24	536
AAFC	3	37(26)	124	524	4.2	2	65	1449	22.3(80)	14	1	0	0.0	0	0.0	0	0	kpi	1	102	2151
1950	ChiC	6(DB)	—	—	—	—	—	—	—	—	—	—	—	—	—	—	—	i	—	0	-5
1951	ChiC	10(DB)	—	—	—	—	8	135	16.9(35)	0	—	—	—	—	—	—	—	i	—	0	133
1952	ChiC	12(DB)	—	—	—	—	3	27	9.0(13)	0	—	—	—	—	—	—	—	i	—	0	56
1953	ChiC	12(DB)	—	—	—	—	12	118	9.8(20)	0	—	—	—	—	—	—	—	i	1	6	256
NFL	4	37	—	—	—	—	23	280	12.2(80)	0	—	—	—	—	—	—	—	i	1	6	439

RAMSEY, RED Herschel Randolph, E, 6'0"/196 lbs; Texas Tech; 1938: Phi, rnd 6; B4/9/1911 Chillicothe, TX, D4/19/1984 Kaufman County, TX

YEAR	TEAM	G (GS, POS)	REC	YD	AVG (LG)	TD	KPR	OTD	PTS	TAY
1938	Phi	11(0)	5	122	24.4(40)	1	—	—	6	66
1939	Phi	11(6, LE)	31	359	11.6(85)	1	—	—	6	185
1940	Phi	11(8, LE)	17	143	8.4	0	i	—	0	72
1945	Phi	2(0)	—	—	—	—	—	—	—	—
NFL	4	35(14)	53	624	11.8(85)	2	i	—	12	322

RAMSEY, STEVE Stephen Wayne, QB, 6'2"/210 lbs; North Texas; 1970: NO, rnd 5; B4/22/1948 Dallas, TX, D10/15/1999 Meridian, TX

YEAR	TEAM	G (GS, POS)	RUSH	YD	AVG (LG)	TD	PASS	COMP	PCT	YD	AVG (LG)	TD	INT	SK	YD	QBR	OTD	PTS	TAY
1970	NO	1	—	—	—	—	2	1	50.0	6	6.0	0	0	—	—	—	—	0	0
1971	Den	9(5, qb)	3	6	2.0(6)	0	178	84	47.2	1120	6.3(47)	5	13	13	105	—	—	0	71
1972	Den	9(5, qb)	6	15	2.5(8)	2	137	65	47.4	1050	7.7(75)	3	9	26	184	—	—	12	215
1973	Den	5	—	—	—	—	27	10	37.0	194	7.2(76)	2	—	—	—	—	—	0	27
1974	Den	7(2)	5	-2	-0.4(1)	0	74	41	55.4	580	7.8(43)	5	7	9	55	—	—	0	33
1975	Den	11(7, QB)	6	38	6.3(17)	0	233	128	54.9	1562	6.7(60)	9	14	23	187	63.6	—	0	304
1976	Den	12(12, QB)	13	51	3.9(15)	0	270	128	47.4	1931	7.2(71)	11	13	39	261	64.9	—	0	552
NFL	7	54(31)	33	108	3.3(17)	2	921	456	49.5	6437	7.0(76)	35	58	110	792	58.9	—	12	1202

RAMSEY, TOM Thomas Lloyd, QB, 6'1"/189 lbs; UCLA; 1983: NE, rnd 10; B7/9/1961 Encino, CA

YEAR	TEAM	G (GS, POS)	RUSH	YD	AVG (LG)	TD	PASS	COMP	PCT	YD	AVG (LG)	TD	INT	SK	YD	QBR	OTD	PTS	TAY
1986	NE	5(0)	1	-6	-6.0(-6)	0	3	1	33.3	7	2.3(7)	0	0	0	0	—	—	0	-3
1987	NE	9(3)	13	75	5.8(19)	1	134	71	53.0	898	6.7(40)	6	6	14	90	—	—	6	324
1988	NE	7(1)	3	8	2.7(9)	0	27	12	44.4	100	3.7(23)	0	2	6	40	—	—	0	-62
1989	Ind	7(1)	4	5	1.3(3)	0	50	24	48.0	280	5.6(47)	1	1	4	26	—	—	0	110
NFL	4	28(5)	21	82	3.9(19)	1	214	108	50.5	1285	6.0(47)	7	10	20	122	—	—	6	370

RAMSON, EASON Eason Lloyd, TE, 6'2"/232 lbs; Washington State; 1978: GB, rnd 12; B4/30/1956 Sacramento, CA

YEAR	TEAM	G (GS, POS)	RUSH	YD	AVG (LG)	TD	REC	YD	AVG (LG)	TD	KPR	OTD	PTS	TAY
1978	StL	15(7, te)	2	8	4.0(5)	0	23	238	10.3(26)	1	—	—	6	132
1979	SF	2	—	—	—	—	—	—	—	—	—	—	—	—
1980	SF	16(3)	2	-2	-1.0(4)	0	21	179	8.5(22)	2	k	—	12	101
1981	†SF	11(0)	—	—	—	—	4	45	11.3(16)	0	k	—	0	20
1982	SF	9(0)	—	—	—	—	2	27	13.5(21)	0	k	—	0	4

YEAR	TEAM	G(GS, POS)	RUSH	YD	AVG(LG)	TD	REC	YD	AVG(LG)	TD	PASS	COMP	PCT	YD	AVG(LG)	TD	INT	SK	YD	QBR	KPR	OTD	PTS	TAY
1983	†SF	16(4)	1	3	3.0(3)	0	17	125	7.4(16)	1	—	—	—	—	—	—	—	—	—	—	—	—	6	71
1985	Buf	16(12, TE)	—	—	—	—	37	369	10.0(43)	1	—	—	—	—	—	—	—	—	—	—	—	—	6	190
NFL	7	85(26)	5	9	1.8(5)	0	104	983	9.5(43)	5	—	—	—	—	—	—	—	—	—	—	k	—	30	516

RANDALL, CURTIS Curtis Mandell, LB, 6´3˝/225 lbs; Louisiana Tech; B8/6/1979 Columbus, GA **2004** Sea 4 (0)

RANDALL, DENNIS Dennis Allen, DE-DT, 6´7˝/250 lbs; Oklahoma State; 1967: NYJ, rnd 3; B7/7/1945 Tulsa, OK **1967** NYJ-A 7 **1968** Cin-A 13 **NFL** 20 [2 yrs]

RANDALL, GREG Greg, aka Greg Robinson-Randall, T, 6´5˝/322 lbs; Michigan State; 2000: NE, rnd 4; B6/23/1978 Galveston, TX **2000** NE 12 (4) **2001**†NE 16 (16, RT) **2002** NE 7 (3) **2003** Hou 16 (16, RT) **NFL** 51 (39) [4 yrs]

RANDALL, MARCUS Marcus, DB, 6´2˝/219 lbs; LSU; B3/14/1982 Baton Rouge, LA **2005** Ten 3 (0)

RANDALL, TOM Thomas Gene, G, 6´5˝/245 lbs; Iowa State; 1978: Dal, rnd 7; B8/3/1956 Mason City, IA **1978**†Dal 11 **1979**†Hou 13 **NFL** 24 [2 yrs]

RANDELS, PROC Horace Malvern, E, 6´0˝/180 lbs; Kansas State; B8/5/1900, KS, D1/17/1933 Salt lake County, UT **1926** KC 11 (11, LE) **1927** Cle 5 (2), 12 **1928** Det 10 (3), 6 **NFL** 26 (16), 18 [3 yrs]

RANDLE EL, ANTWAAN Atwaan, WR, 5´10˝/186 lbs; Indiana; 2002: Pit, rnd 2; B8/17/1979 Riverdale, IL **[R]**

YEAR	TEAM	G(GS, POS)	RUSH	YD	AVG(LG)	TD	REC	YD	AVG(LG)	TD	PASS	COMP	PCT	YD	AVG(LG)	TD	INT	SK	YD	QBR	KPR	OTD	PTS	TAY
2002	†Pit	16(0)	19	134	7.1(24)	0	47	489	10.4(36)	2	8	7	87.5	45	5.6(25)	0	0	1	10	—	kp	1	18	746
2003	Pit	16(1)	15	75	5.0(32)	0	37	364	9.8(32)	1	4	3	75.0	6	1.5(9)	0	0	—	—	—	kp	2	18	708
2004	†Pit	16(7, wr)	8	34	4.3(12)	0	43	601	14.0(39)	3	1	1	100.0	10	10.0(10)	1	0	—	—	—	kp	—	18	709
2005	†Pit☆	16(15, WR)	12	73	6.1(43)	0	35	558	15.9(63)	1	3	3	100.0	67	22.3(51)	1	0	—	—	—	kp	2	18	645
NFL	4	64(23)	54	316	5.9(43)	0	162	2012	12.4(63)	7	16	14	87.5	128	8.0(51)	2	0	1	10	—	kp	5	72	2807

RANDLE, ERVIN Ervin, LB, 6´1˝/250 lbs; Baylor; 1985: TB, rnd 3; B10/12/1962 Hearne, TX **1985** TB 16 (7, LOLB) **1986** TB 16 (0) **1987** TB☆12 (12, RILB) **1988** TB 9 (6, rilb) **1989** TB 16 (16, RILB) **1990** TB 16 (7, rilb) **1991**†KC 12 (1) **1992** KC 8 (8, lilb) **NFL** 105 (57) [8 yrs]

RANDLE, JOHN John Anthony, DT-DE, 6´1˝/290 lbs; Texas A&M-Kingsville; B12/12/1967 Hearne, TX **[S]** **1990** Min 16 (0) **1991** Min 16 (8, lde) **1992**†Min 16 (14, RDT) **1993**†Min★16 (16, RDT) **1994**†Min★16 (16, RDT) **1995** Min★16 (16, RDT) **1996**†Min★16 (16, RDT) **1997**†Min★16 (16, RDT) **1998**†Min★16 (16, RDE) **1999**†Min 16 (16, LDE/rdt) **2000**†Min 16 (16, LDE) **2001** Sea★15 (14, RDT) **2002** Sea 12 (12, RDT) **2003**†Sea 16 (9, RDT) **NFL** 219 (185) [14 yrs]

RANDLE, SONNY Ulmo Shannon, E-WR, 6´2˝/189 lbs; Virginia; 1958: ChiC, rnd 19; B1/6/1936 Cohasset, VA

YEAR	TEAM	G(GS, POS)	RUSH	YD	AVG(LG)	TD	REC	YD	AVG(LG)	TD	PASS	COMP	PCT	YD	AVG(LG)	TD	INT	SK	YD	QBR	KPR	OTD	PTS	TAY
1959	ChiC	8(re)	—	—	—	—	15	202	13.5(31)	1	—	—	—	—	—	—	—	—	—	—	k	—	6	109
1960	SL★	12(SE)	—	—	—	—	62	893	14.4(57)	**15**	—	—	—	—	—	—	—	—	—	—	—	—	90	522
1961	SL✧	14(SE)	—	—	—	—	44	591	13.4(41)	9	—	—	—	—	—	—	—	—	—	—	—	—	54	341
1962	SL★	14(SE)	—	—	—	—	63	1158	18.4(86)	7	—	—	—	—	—	—	—	—	—	—	—	—	42	614
1963	SL☆	14(SE)	—	—	—	—	51	1014	19.9(68)	12	—	—	—	—	—	—	—	—	—	—	—	—	72	567
1964	SL	7(SE)	—	—	—	—	25	517	20.7(50)	5	—	—	—	—	—	—	—	—	—	—	—	—	30	284
1965	SL✧	14(SE)	—	—	—	—	51	845	16.6(72)	9	—	—	—	—	—	—	—	—	—	—	—	—	54	468
1966	SL	14(SE)	—	—	—	—	17	218	12.8(45)	2	—	—	—	—	—	—	—	—	—	—	—	—	12	119
1967	SF	14(10, se/fl)	—	—	—	—	33	502	15.2(58)	4	—	—	—	—	—	—	—	—	—	—	—	—	24	271
1968	SF	3	—	—	—	—	3	44	14.7(29)	1	—	—	—	—	—	—	—	—	—	—	—	—	6	27
1968	†Dal	6	—	—	—	—	1	12	12.0(12)	0	—	—	—	—	—	—	—	—	—	—	—	—	0	6
NFL	10	120(10)	—	—	—	—	365	5996	16.4(86)	65	—	—	—	—	—	—	—	—	—	—	k	—	390	3326

RANDLE, TATE Ernest Tate, DB, 6´0˝/202 lbs; Texas Tech; 1982: Mia, rnd 8; B8/15/1959 Fredericksburg, TX **1982** Hou 7 (0) **1983** Hou 2 (0) **1983** Bal 10 (6, rcb) **1984** Ind 16 (6, lcb) **1985** Ind 16 (4) **1986** Ind 15 (6, fs) **1987** Mia 3 (1) **NFL** 69 (23) [6 yrs]

RANDOLPH, AL Alvin Chester, DB, 6´2˝/205 lbs; Iowa; 1966: SF, rnd 3; B7/8/1944 East St. Louis, IL **1966** SF 13 (5, rs) **1967** SF 14 (14, LS) **1968** SF 14 (14, LS) **1969** SF 14 (11, LS) **1970**†SF 14 **1971** GB 14 (ss) **1972** Cin 2 **1972** Det 6 **1973** Min 11 **1974** SF 6 **1974**†Buf 3 **NFL** 111 (44) [9 yrs]

RANDOLPH, CLARE Clare Loring, C-G-LB-E, 6´2˝/204 lbs; Indiana; B5/2/1907 Chicago, IL, D12/24/1972 Glendale, CA **1930** ChiC 9 (3) **1931** Por 14 (9, C) **1932** Por 10 (6, c) **1933** Por 10 (9, C) **1934** Det 12 (8, C) **1935**†Det☆12 (11, C) **1936** Det 11 (4) **NFL** 78 (50) [7 yrs]

RANDOLPH, HARRY Harry Fitz, HB, 5´11˝/195 lbs; Bethany (WV); B4/10/1900 Dickerson Run, PA, D12/3/1957 Harrison, NJ **1923** Col 2 (0)

RANDOLPH, TERRY Terry Allen, DB, 6´0˝/184 lbs; American International; 1977: GB, rnd 11; B7/17/1955 Brooklyn, NY **1977** GB 14

RANDOLPH, THOMAS Thomas Carl, DB, 5´9˝/180 lbs; Kansas State; 1994: NYG, rnd 2; B10/5/1970 Norfolk, VA **1994** NYG 16 (10, RCB) **1995** NYG 16 (16, RCB) **1996** NYG 16 (2) **1997**†NYG 16 (4) **1998** Cin 16 (1) **1999**†Ind 15 (0) **NFL** 95 (33) [6 yrs]

RANKIN, WALT Walter Velpo, QB-FB, 5´11˝/197 lbs; Texas Tech; B1/28/1919 Laverty, OK, D12/7/1993 Lubbock, TX

YEAR	TEAM	G(GS, POS)	RUSH	YD	AVG(LG)	TD	REC	YD	AVG(LG)	TD	PASS	COMP	PCT	YD	AVG(LG)	TD	INT	SK	YD	QBR	KPR	OTD	PTS	TAY
1941	ChiC	1(0)	—	—	—	—	—	—	—	—	—	—	—	—	—	—	—	—	—	—	—	—	—	—
1943	ChiC	10(8, QB)	2	1	0.5(1)	0	10	44	4.4(17)	0	—	—	—	—	—	—	—	—	—	—	ki	—	0	35
1944	C-P	10(8, QB)	4	13	3.3(6)	0	4	18	4.5(8)	0	—	—	—	—	—	—	—	—	—	—	i	—	0	21
1945	ChiC	6(3)	8	11	1.4(5)	0	3	25	8.3(9)	0	—	—	—	—	—	—	—	—	—	—	ki	—	0	18
1946	ChiC	11(4)	5	1	0.2(5)	0	—	—	—	—	—	—	—	—	—	—	—	—	—	—	ki	—	0	1
1947	†ChiC	12(0)	3	4	1.3(2)	0	—	—	—	—	—	—	—	—	—	—	—	—	—	—	—	—	0	4
NFL	6	50(23)	22	30	1.4(6)	0	17	87	5.1(17)	0	—	—	—	—	—	—	—	—	—	—	ki	—	0	79

RANSOM, DERRICK Derrick Wayne, DT, 6´3˝/306 lbs; Cincinnati; 1998: KC, rnd 6; B9/13/1976 Indianapolis, IN **1998** KC 7 (0) **1999** KC 10 (0) **2000** KC 10 (0) **2001** KC 16 (16, RDT) **2002** KC 13 (10, RDT) **2003** Arz 5 (0) **2004** Jax 10 (0) **NFL** 71 (26) [7 yrs]

RANSPOT, KEITH Edgar Keith, E, 6´3˝/205 lbs; SMU; B12/11/1913 Weatherford, TX, D10/11/1991 Dallas, TX **[K]**

YEAR	TEAM	G(GS, POS)	RUSH	YD	AVG(LG)	TD	REC	YD	AVG(LG)	TD	PASS	COMP	PCT	YD	AVG(LG)	TD	INT	SK	YD	QBR	KPR	OTD	PTS	TAY
1940	ChiC	1(0)	—	—	—	—	—	—	—	—	—	—	—	—	—	—	—	—	—	—	—	—	—	—
1942	Det	1(0)	—	—	—	—	—	—	—	—	—	—	—	—	—	—	—	—	—	—	—	—	—	—
1942	GB	5(0)	—	—	—	—	1	25	25.0(25)	1	—	—	—	—	—	—	—	—	—	—	—	—	6	18
1943	Bkn	9(2)	—	—	—	—	7	80	11.4(28)	0	—	—	—	—	—	—	—	—	—	—	—	—	0	40
1944	Bos	10(10, LE)	—	—	—	—	19	269	14.2(40)	3	—	—	—	—	—	—	—	—	—	—	Kk	—	18	142
1945	Bos	9(7, LE)	—	—	—	—	8	117	14.6(30)	0	—	—	—	—	—	—	—	—	—	—	—	—	0	59
NFL	5	35(19)	—	—	—	—	35	491	14.0(40)	4	—	—	—	—	—	—	—	—	—	—	Kk	—	24	258

RAPACZ, JOHN John Joseph, C-LB, 6´4˝/252 lbs; Western Michigan; Oklahoma; 1947: Cle-A, rnd 7/Bos, rnd 3; B5/25/1924 Rosedale, OH, D1/2/1991 Midwest City, OK **1948** ChiR-A 10 (3) **1949** ChiH-A☆12 (7, C) **AAFC** 22 (10) [2 yrs]

1950†NYG☆10 (C) **1951** NYG☆12 (C) **1952** NYG 8 (C) **1953** NYG 12 (C) **1954** NYG 12 **NFL** 54 [5 yrs]

RAPP, BOB Joseph Robert, WB-BB-HB-QB, 5´8˝/159 lbs; none; B2/18/1898 Columbus, OH, D2/1968 Columbus, OH **1922** Col 7 (4), 6 **1923** Col☆10 (7, WB), 30 **1924** Col 8 (8, WB), 30 **1925** Col 9 (9, BB), 12 **1926** Col 6 (6, WB) **1929** Buf 3 (1) **NFL** 43 (35), 78 [6 yrs]

RAPP, HERB Herbert Leo, C, 6´0˝/195 lbs; Xavier (OH); B7/21/1905 Hamilton, OH, D7/21/1983 Los Altos Hills, CA **1930** Sl 8 (3) **1931** Sl 11 (6, C) **NFL** 19 (9) [2 yrs]

RAPP, MANNY Manuel Warren, TB-FB, 6´0˝/215 lbs; St. Louis; B9/17/1908 Peverly, MO, D5/17/1965 St. Louis, MO **1942** Cle 1 (0)

YEAR	TEAM	G(GS, POS)	RUSH	YD	AVG(LG)	TD	REC	YD	AVG(LG)	TD	PASS	COMP	PCT	YD	AVG(LG)	TD	INT	SK	YD	QBR	KPR	OTD	PTS	TAY
1934	SL	3(3, TB)	15	67	4.5	0	—	—	—	—	16	6	37.5	175	10.9	1	6	—	—	—	—	—	0	-81
NFL	2	4(3)	15	67	4.5	0	—	—	—	—	16	6	37.5	175	10.9	1	6	—	—	—	—	—	0	-81

RASBY, WALTER Walter Herbert, TE, 6´3˝/252 lbs; Wake Forest; B9/7/1972 Washington, DC

YEAR	TEAM	G(GS, POS)	RUSH	YD	AVG(LG)	TD	REC	YD	AVG(LG)	TD	PASS	COMP	PCT	YD	AVG(LG)	TD	INT	SK	YD	QBR	KPR	OTD	PTS	TAY
1994	†Pit	2(0)	—	—	—	—	—	—	—	—	—	—	—	—	—	—	—	—	—	—	—	—	—	—
1995	Car	9(2)	—	—	—	—	5	47	9.4(15)	0	—	—	—	—	—	—	—	—	—	—	—	—	2	24
1996	†Car	16(1)	—	—	—	—	—	—	—	—	—	—	—	—	—	—	—	—	—	—	—	—	0	0
1997	Car	14(2)	—	—	—	—	1	1	1.0(1)	0	—	—	—	—	—	—	—	—	—	—	k	—	0	-13
1998	Det	16(16, TE)	—	—	—	—	15	119	7.9(17)	1	—	—	—	—	—	—	—	—	—	—	—	—	6	65
1999	†Det	16(6, te)	—	—	—	—	3	19	6.3(13)	1	—	—	—	—	—	—	—	—	—	—	—	—	6	15
2000	Det	16(8, te)	—	—	—	—	10	78	7.8(17)	1	—	—	—	—	—	—	—	—	—	—	—	—	6	44
2001	Was	16(11, TE)	—	—	—	—	10	128	12.8(27)	2	—	—	—	—	—	—	—	—	—	—	—	—	12	74
2002	Was	13(9, TE)	—	—	—	—	9	85	9.4(18)	0	—	—	—	—	—	—	—	—	—	—	—	—	0	43
2003	NO	16(7, te)	—	—	—	—	6	55	9.2(17)	0	—	—	—	—	—	—	—	—	—	—	k	—	0	7
2004	Was	6(6, te)	—	—	—	—	5	52	10.4(13)	0	—	—	—	—	—	—	—	—	—	—	—	—	0	26

YEAR	TEAM	G (GS, POS)	RUSH	YD	AVG (LG)	TD	REC	YD	AVG (LG)	TD	PASS	COMP	PCT	YD	AVG (LG)	TD	INT	SK	YD	QBR	KPR	OTD	PTS	TAY
2004	†Pit	4(2)	—	—	—	—	—	—	—	—	—	—	—	—	—	—	—	—	—	—	—	—	—	—
NFL	11	144(70)	—	—	—	—	64	584	9.1(27)	5	—	—	—	—	—	—	—	—	—	—	k	—	32	283

Rascher, Am Ambrose Henry, T-G, 6´2˝/210 lbs; St. Viator; Indiana; B11/3/1908 Cedar Lake, IN, D3/6/1988 **1932** Por 7 (1)

Rash, Lou Louis Clyde, DB, 5´9˝/180 lbs; Mississippi Valley State; B6/5/1960 Cleveland, MS **1984** Phi 4 (0) **1987** GB 3 (3) **NFL** 7 (3) [2 yrs]

Rashad, Ahmad Ahmad, aka Bobby Moore, WR, 6´2˝/205 lbs; Oregon; 1972: SL, rnd 1; B11/19/1949 Portland, OR

YEAR	TEAM	G (GS, POS)	RUSH	YD	AVG (LG)	TD	REC	YD	AVG (LG)	TD	PASS	COMP	PCT	YD	AVG (LG)	TD	INT	SK	YD	QBR	KPR	OTD	PTS	TAY
1972	SL	14(WR)	9	44	4.9(15)	0	29	500	17.2(**98**)	3	—	—	—	—	—	—	—	—	—	—	k	—	18	446
1973	SL	13(WR)	—	—	—	—	30	409	13.6(65)	3	—	—	—	—	—	—	—	—	—	—	—	—	18	220
1974	†Buf☆	14(WR)	—	—	—	—	36	433	12.0(29)	4	—	—	—	—	—	—	—	—	—	—	k	2	36	222
1976	†Min	13(11, WR)	—	—	—	—	53	671	12.7(47)	3	—	—	—	—	—	—	—	—	—	—	—	—	18	351
1977	†Min	14(14, WR)	—	—	—	—	**51**	681	13.4(48)	2	—	—	—	—	—	—	—	—	—	—	—	—	12	351
1978	†Min★	16(16, WR)	—	—	—	—	66	769	11.7(58)	8	—	—	—	—	—	—	—	—	—	—	—	—	48	425
1979	Min★	16(16, WR)	—	—	—	—	**80**	**1156**	14.4(52)	9	—	—	—	—	—	—	—	—	—	—	—	—	54	623
1980	†Min★	16(16, WR)	1	8	8.0(8)	0	69	1095	15.9(76)	5	—	—	—	—	—	—	—	—	—	—	—	—	30	581
1981	Min★	16(15, WR)	—	—	—	—	58	884	15.2(53)	7	—	—	—	—	—	—	—	—	—	—	—	—	42	477
1982	Min	7(6, WR)	—	—	—	—	23	233	10.1(21)	0	—	—	—	—	—	—	—	—	—	—	—	—	0	117
NFL	10	139(94)	10	52	5.2(15)	0	495	6831	13.8(98)	44	—	—	—	—	—	—	—	—	—	—	k	2	276	3810

Rasheed, Kenyon Kenyon, FB, 5´10˝/235 lbs; Oklahoma; B8/23/1970 Kansas City, MO

YEAR	TEAM	G (GS, POS)	RUSH	YD	AVG (LG)	TD	REC	YD	AVG (LG)	TD	PASS	COMP	PCT	YD	AVG (LG)	TD	INT	SK	YD	QBR	KPR	OTD	PTS	TAY
1993	NYG	5(3)	9	42	4.7(23)	1	1	3	3.0(3)	0	—	—	—	—	—	—	—	—	—	—	—	—	6	54
1994	NYG	16(7, fb)	17	44	2.6(6)	0	10	97	9.7(22)	0	—	—	—	—	—	—	—	—	—	—	—	—	0	93
1995	NYJ	3(0)	1	3	3.0(3)	0	2	15	7.5(9)	0	—	—	—	—	—	—	—	—	—	—	—	—	0	11
NFL	3	24(10)	27	89	3.3(23)	1	13	115	8.8(22)	0	—	—	—	—	—	—	—	—	—	—	—	—	6	157

Rasheed, Saleem Saleen, LB, 6´2˝/229 lbs; Alabama; 2002: SF, rnd 3; B6/15/1981 Birmingham, AL **2002**†SF 6 (0) **2003** SF 16 (1) **2004** SF 14 (2) **2005** SF 9 (1) **NFL** 45 (4) [4 yrs]

Raskowski, Leo Leo Thomas, T, 6´3˝/219 lbs; Ohio State; B3/28/1906 Cleveland, OH, deceased **1932** SI 11 (9, RT) **1933** Bkn 3 (1) **1933** Pit 3 (0) **1935** Phi 2 (0) **NFL** 19 (10) [3 yrs]

Rasley, Rocky Rocky, G, 6´3˝/250 lbs; Oregon State; 1969: Det, rnd 9; B4/27/1947 Bakersfield, CA **1969** Det 12 **1970** Det 8 **1972** Det 14 **1973** Det 14 **1974** NO 14 **1975** KC 11 (LG) **1976** SF 1 **NFL** 74 [7 yrs]

Rasmussen, Kemp Kemp Alan, DE, 6´3˝/255 lbs; Indiana; B5/25/1979 Rochester, MN **2002** Car 10 (0) **2003**†Car 13 (0) **2004** Car 12 (0) **2005**†Car 15 (0) **NFL** 50 (0) [4 yrs]

Rasmussen, Randy Randall Lee, G, 6´2˝/255 lbs; Nebraska-Kearney; 1967: NYJ, rnd 12; B5/10/1945 St. Paul, NE **1967** NYJ-A 14 (14, LG) **1968**†NYJ-A 14 (7, lg) **1969**†NYJ-A 13 (13, LG) **1970** NYJ 13 (13, LG) **1971** NYJ 14 (14, LG) **1972** NYJ☆14 (14, LG) **1973** NYJ 14 (14, LG) **1974** NYJ 14 (14, LG) **1975** NYJ 14 (14, LG) **1976** NYJ 14 (14, LG) **1977** NYJ 14 (14, LG) **1978** NYJ 16 (16, LG) **1979** NYJ☆16 (16, LG) **1980** NYJ 8 (8, LG) **1981**†NYJ 15 (15, LG) **NFL** 207 (198) [15 yrs]

Rasmussen, Randy Randy Robert, C-G, 6´7˝/253 lbs; Minnesota; 1984: Pit, rnd 8; B9/27/1960 Minneapolis, MN **1984**†Pit 16 (0) **1985** Pit 11 (0) **1986** Pit 4 (3) **1987**†Min 5 (0) **1988**†Min 7 (0) **NFL** 43 (3) [5 yrs]

Rasmussen, Wayne Wayne Floyd, DB, 6´2˝/175 lbs; South Dakota State; 1964: Det, rnd 9; B6/7/1942 Chicago, IL **1964** Det 11 **1965** Det 14 (RS) **1966** Det 14 **1967** Det 10 **1968** Det 14 **1969** Det 14 **1970** Det 14 (FS) **1971** Det 14 **1972** Det 7 **NFL** 112 [9 yrs]

Rassas, Nick Nicholas Charles, DB, 6´0˝/190 lbs; Notre Dame; 1966: Atl, rnd 2/SD, rnd 2; B1/13/1944 Baltimore, MD **1966** Atl 8 **1967** Atl 5 (RS) **1968** Atl 14 (LS) **NFL** 27 [3 yrs]

Rate, Ed Edwin Schellhase, BB, 5´9˝/170 lbs; Purdue; B5/27/1899 Canton, OH, D3/31/1990 **1923** Mil 1 (1)

Ratekin, Roy Ralph Roy, E, 5´10˝/180 lbs; Colorado State; B9/24/1899 Surface Creek, CO, D10/1984 Red Oak, IA **1921** Akr 4 (1)

Rather, Bo David Elmer, WR, 6´1˝/184 lbs; Michigan; 1973: Mia, rnd 4; B10/7/1950 Sandusky, OH

YEAR	TEAM	G (GS, POS)	RUSH	YD	AVG (LG)	TD	REC	YD	AVG (LG)	TD	PASS	COMP	PCT	YD	AVG (LG)	TD	INT	SK	YD	QBR	KPR	OTD	PTS	TAY
1973	Mia	6	—	—	—	—	—	—	—	—	—	—	—	—	—	—	—	—	—	—	—	—	—	—
1974	ChiB	13(WR)	2	10	5.0(14)	0	29	400	13.8(59)	3	1	0	0.0	0	0.0	0	0	—	—	—	—	—	18	225
1975	ChiB	14(14, WR)	4	24	6.0(18)	0	39	685	17.6(54)	2	—	—	—	—	—	—	—	—	—	—	k	—	12	368
1976	ChiB	9(2)	1	4	4.0(4)	0	5	33	6.6(7)	0	—	—	—	—	—	—	—	—	—	—	—	—	0	21
1977	†ChiB	13(9, WR)	2	8	4.0(10)	0	17	294	17.3(42)	2	—	—	—	—	—	—	—	—	—	—	—	—	12	165
1978	ChiB	6(2)	—	—	—	—	1	16	16.0(16)	0	—	—	—	—	—	—	—	—	—	—	—	—	0	8
1978	†Mia	3	—	—	—	—	1	39	39.0(39)	0	—	—	—	—	—	—	—	—	—	—	—	—	0	20
NFL	6	64(27)	9	46	5.1(18)	0	92	1467	15.9(59)	7	1	0	0.0	0	0.0	0	0	—	—	—	k	—	42	806

Rathman, Tom Thomas Dean, RB, 6´1˝/230 lbs; Nebraska; 1986: SF, rnd 3; B10/7/1962 Grand Island, NE

YEAR	TEAM	G (GS, POS)	RUSH	YD	AVG (LG)	TD	REC	YD	AVG (LG)	TD	PASS	COMP	PCT	YD	AVG (LG)	TD	INT	SK	YD	QBR	KPR	OTD	PTS	TAY
1986	†SF	16(1)	33	138	4.2(29)	1	13	121	9.3(14)	0	—	—	—	—	—	—	—	—	—	—	k	—	6	230
1987	†SF	12(7, FB)	62	257	4.1(35)	1	30	329	11.0(29)	3	—	—	—	—	—	—	—	—	—	—	k	—	24	454
1988	†SF	16(16, FB)	102	427	4.2(26)	2	42	382	9.1(24)	0	—	—	—	—	—	—	—	—	—	—	—	—	12	638
1989	†SF	16(16, FB)	79	305	3.9(13)	1	73	616	8.4(36)	1	—	—	—	—	—	—	—	—	—	—	—	—	12	628
1990	†SF	16(16, FB)	101	318	3.1(22)	7	48	327	6.8(28)	0	—	—	—	—	—	—	—	—	—	—	—	—	42	552
1991	SF	16(16, FB)	63	183	2.9(16)	6	34	286	8.4(32)	0	—	—	—	—	—	—	—	—	—	—	—	—	36	386
1992	†SF	15(15, FB)	57	194	3.4(17)	5	44	343	7.8(27)	4	—	—	—	—	—	—	—	—	—	—	—	—	54	436
1993	†SF	8(4)	19	80	4.2(19)	3	10	86	8.6(17)	0	—	—	—	—	—	—	—	—	—	—	—	—	18	153
1994	LARd	16(16, FB)	28	118	4.2(14)	0	26	194	7.5(18)	0	—	—	—	—	—	—	—	—	—	—	—	—	0	215
NFL	9	131(107)	544	2020	3.7(35)	26	320	2684	8.4(36)	8	—	—	—	—	—	—	—	—	—	—	k	—	204	3690

Ratica, Joe Joseph H., C-LB, 6´0˝/205 lbs; St. Vincent; B8/4/1914 Dembo, PA, D10/21/1942 **1939** Bkn 7 (4)

Ratigan, Brian Brian Lee, LB, 6´4˝/241 lbs; Notre Dame; B12/27/1970 Council Bluffs, IA **1994** Ind 14 (0)

Ratkowski, Ray Raymond James, HB, 6´0˝/195 lbs; Notre Dame; 1961: Bos, rnd 17/GB, rnd 20; B11/10/1939 New York, NY **1961** Bos-A 1

Ratliff, Don Donald Eugene, DE, 6´5˝/250 lbs; Maryland; B7/18/1950 Baltimore, MD **1975** Phi 6 (2)

Ratliff, Jay Jeremiah J., DE, 6´3˝/293 lbs; Auburn; 2005: Dal, rnd 7; B8/29/1981 St. Petersburg, FL **2005** Dal 4 (1)

Ratliff, Keiwan Keiwan Jevar, DB, 5´10˝/178 lbs; Florida; 2004: Cin, rnd 2; B4/19/1981 Columbus, OH **2004** Cin 16 (5, lcb) **2005**†Cin 16 (3) **NFL** 32 (8) [2 yrs]

Rattay, Tim Tim, QB, 6´0˝/200 lbs; Louisiana Tech; 2000: SF, rnd 7; B3/15/1977 Elyria, OH

YEAR	TEAM	G (GS, POS)	RUSH	YD	AVG (LG)	TD	REC	YD	AVG (LG)	TD	PASS	COMP	PCT	YD	AVG (LG)	TD	INT	SK	YD	QBR	KPR	OTD	PTS	TAY
2000	SF	1(0)	2	-1	-0.5(0)	0	—	—	—	—	1	1	100.0	4	-4.0(-4)	0	0	—	—	—	—	—	0	-3
2001	SF	3(0)	5	-3	-0.6(1)	0	—	—	—	—	2	2	100.0	21	10.5(20)	0	0	—	—	—	—	—	0	8
2002	SF	4(0)	5	0	0.0(5)	0	—	—	—	—	43	26	60.5	232	5.4(27)	2	0	5	26	—	—	—	0	126
2003	SF	11(3)	8	0	0.0(6)	0	—	—	—	—	118	73	61.9	856	7.3(61)	7	2	7	54	**96.6**	—	—	0	383
2004	SF	9(9, QB)	12	55	4.6(15)	0	—	—	—	—	325	198	60.9	2169	6.7(65)	10	10	37	211	78.1	—	—	2	790
2005	SF	4(4)	7	18	2.6(13)	0	—	—	—	—	97	56	57.7	667	6.9(89)	5	6	10	63	—	—	—	0	137
NFL	6	32(16)	39	69	1.8(15)	0	—	—	—	—	586	356	60.8	3941	6.7(89)	24	18	59	354	81.6	—	—	2	1440

Ratterman, Fred Lawrence Frederick, HB, /160 lbs; Michigan; B8/9/1912 Cincinnati, OH, D3/6/1988 Cincinnati, OH

YEAR	TEAM	G (GS, POS)	RUSH	YD	AVG (LG)	TD	REC	YD	AVG (LG)	TD	PASS	COMP	PCT	YD	AVG (LG)	TD	INT	SK	YD	QBR	KPR	OTD	PTS	TAY
1934	Cin	1(0)	2	1	0.5	0	—	—	—	—	3	0	0.0	0	0.0	0	0	—	—	—	—	—	0	1

Ratterman, George George William, QB, 6´0˝/192 lbs; Notre Dame; 1948: Bos, rnd 16; B11/12/1926 Cincinnati, OH **[K]**

YEAR	TEAM	G (GS, POS)	RUSH	YD	AVG (LG)	TD	REC	YD	AVG (LG)	TD	PASS	COMP	PCT	YD	AVG (LG)	TD	INT	SK	YD	QBR	KPR	OTD	PTS	TAY
1947	Buf-A☆	14(4, QB)	17	-49	-2.9	1	—	—	—	—	244	124	50.8	1840	7.5(61)	22	**20**	—	—	—	K	—	6	191
1948	†Buf-A	14(13, QB)	12	-18	-1.5	3	—	—	—	—	335	168	50.1	2577	7.7(71)	16	**22**	—	—	—	—	—	18	501
1949	†Buf-A	11(11, QB)	36	85	2.4	4	—	—	—	—	252	146	**57.9**	1777	7.1	14	13	—	—	—	—	—	24	564
AAFC	3	39(28)	65	18	0.3	8	—	—	—	—	831	438	52.7	6194	7.5(71)	52	55	—	—	70.3	K	—	48	1255
1950	NYY☆	12(QB)	11	0	0.0(3)	3	—	—	—	—	294	140	47.6	2251	7.7(69)	**22**	**24**	—	—	64.6	—	—	18	306
1951	NYY	6	3	9	3.0(7)	0	—	—	—	—	67	31	46.3	340	5.1(36)	2	6	—	—	—	—	—	0	-51
1952	Cle	6	1	2	2.0(2)	0	—	—	—	—	6	2	33.3	20	3.3(11)	1	2	—	—	—	—	—	0	-63
1953	†Cle	9	2	6	3.0(3)	0	—	—	—	—	41	23	56.1	301	7.3(45)	4	0	—	—	—	—	—	0	177
1954	†Cle	6	8	-13	-1.6(2)	1	—	—	—	—	53	32	60.4	465	8.8(48)	3	3	—	—	—	—	—	6	125

YEAR	TEAM	G (GS, POS)	RUSH	YD	AVG(LG)	TD	REC	YD	AVG(LG)	TD	PASS	COMP	PCT	YD	AVG(LG)	TD	INT	SK	YD	QBR	KPR	OTD	PTS	TAY
1955	†Cle	10	6	8	1.3(10)	1	—	—	—	—	47	32	68.1	504	10.7(35)	6	3	—	—	—	—	—	6	180
1956	Cle	4(qb)	10	19	1.9(11)	1	—	—	—	—	57	39	68.4	398	7.0(46)	1	3	—	—	—	—	—	6	113
NFL	7	53	41	31	0.8(11)	6	—	—	—	—	565	299	52.9	4279	7.6(71)	39	41	—	—	70.5	—	—	36	786

RAUCH, DICK Richard Harvie, C-G-T, 5´9˝/178 lbs; Penn State; B7/15/1893 Harrisburg, PA, D10/9/1970 Harrisburg, PA [C] **1925** Pot 6 (2) **1928** NYY 2 (0) **1929** Bos 1 (1) **NFL** 9 (3) [3 yrs]

RAUCH, JOHN John, QB-DB, 6´1˝/195 lbs; Georgia; 1949: Det, rnd 1/NYY-A, rnd S2; B8/20/1927 Philadelphia, PA [C]

1949	NYB	9(0)	3	46	15.3(17)	1	—	—	—	—	25	11	44.0	169	6.8(61)	1	3	—	—	—	i	—	6	20
1950	NYY	8	2	12	6.0(7)	0	—	—	—	—	51	29	56.9	502	9.8(82)	6	2	—	—	—	—	—	0	213
1951	NYY	6	1	5	5.0(5)	0	—	—	—	—	82	25	30.5	237	2.9(39)	1	3	—	—	—	—	—	0	9
1951	Phi	4	6	21	3.5(11)	0	—	—	—	—	12	5	41.7	51	4.3(18)	0	1	—	—	—	—	—	0	7
NFL	3	27	12	84	7.0(17)	1	—	—	—	—	170	70	41.2	959	5.6(82)	8	9	—	—	—	i	—	6	248

RAVENSBERG, BOB Robert Alexander, E, 6´0˝/190 lbs; Indiana; 1947: ChiC, rnd 17/1948: SF-A, rnd 17; B10/20/1925 Bellevue, KY **1948**†ChiC 11 (1)

| 1949 | ChiC | 12(2) | 2 | 8 | 4.0(6) | 0 | 10 | 203 | 20.3(48) | 3 | — | — | — | — | — | — | — | — | — | — | — | — | 18 | 125 |
| NFL | 2 | 23(3) | 2 | 8 | 4.0(6) | 0 | 10 | 203 | 20.3(48) | 3 | — | — | — | — | — | — | — | — | — | — | i | — | 18 | 120 |

RAVOTTI, ERIC Eric Allen, LB, 6´3˝/250 lbs; Penn State; 1994: Pit, rnd 6; B3/16/1971 Freeport, PA **1994** Pit 2 (0) **1995** Pit 6 (1) **1996**†Pit 15 (2) **NFL** 23 (3) [3 yrs]

RAWLINGS, BOB Robert, B, none; deceased **1922** Buf 6 (0)

RAY, BABY Buford Garfield, T, 6´6˝/249 lbs; Vanderbilt; B9/30/1915 Una, TN, D1/21/1986 Nashville, TN **1938**†GB 11 (0) **1939**†GB★11 (8, LT) **1940** GB 11 (8, LT) **1941**†GB☆11 (8, LT) **1942** GB 11 (6, LT) **1943** GB☆8 (8, LT) **1944**†GB☆9 (8) **1945** GB 10 (5, LT) **1946** GB 11 (10, LT) **1947** GB 11 (10, LT) **1948** GB 12 (0) **NFL** 116 (66) [11 yrs]

RAY, DARROL Darrol Anthony, DB, 6´1˝/200 lbs; Oklahoma; 1980: NYJ, rnd 2; B6/25/1958 San Francisco, CA [I] **1980** NYJ 16 (16, FS) **1981**†NYJ☆16 (16, FS) **1982**†NYJ☆9 (9, FS) **1983** NYJ 16 (16, FS) **1984** NYJ 15 (12, FS) **NFL** 72 (69) [5 yrs]

RAY, DAVID David Eugene, K, 6´0˝/195 lbs; Alabama; 1966: Cle, rnd 16; B9/19/1944 Phenix City, AL [K] **1969**†LARm 1 **1971** LARm 14 **1972** LARm 14 **1973**†LARm 14 **1974**†LARm 13

| 1970 | LARm | 14 | — | — | — | — | 1 | 11 | 11.0(11) | 0 | — | — | — | — | — | — | — | — | — | — | K | — | 121 | 6 |
| NFL | 6 | 70 | — | — | — | — | 1 | 11 | 11.0(11) | 0 | — | — | — | — | — | — | — | — | — | — | K | — | 497 | 6 |

RAY, EDDIE Edward Brown, RB-TE, 6´2˝/240 lbs; LSU; 1970: Bos, rnd 4; B4/5/1947 Vicksburg, MS

1970	Bos	5(1)	5	13	2.6(4)	0	—	—	—	—	—	—	—	—	—	—	—	—	—	—	—	—	0	13
1971	SD	4	2	15	7.5(8)	0	—	—	—	—	—	—	—	—	—	—	—	—	—	—	—	—	0	15
1972	Atl	7	8	34	4.3(9)	0	1	14	14.0(14)	0	—	—	—	—	—	—	—	—	—	—	—	—	0	41
1973	Atl	14	96	434	4.5(17)	9	19	192	10.1(39)	2	—	—	—	—	—	—	—	—	—	—	—	—	66	630
1974	Atl	11	46	139	3.0(17)	0	10	43	4.3(10)	0	—	—	—	—	—	—	—	—	—	—	—	—	0	161
1976	Buf	7	24	56	2.3(7)	0	3	26	8.7(15)	0	—	—	—	—	—	—	—	—	—	—	—	—	0	69
NFL	6	48(1)	181	691	3.8(17)	9	33	275	8.3(39)	2	—	—	—	—	—	—	—	—	—	—	—	—	66	929

RAY, JOHN John William, T, 6´8˝/350 lbs; West Virginia; B4/26/1969 Charleston, WV **1993** Ind 2 (0)

RAY, MARCUS Marcus Kenyon, DB, 5´11˝/215 lbs; Michigan; B8/14/1976 Columbus, OH **1999** Oak 8 (0)

RAY, RICKY Ricky Lee, DB, 5´11˝/180 lbs; Norfolk State; 1979: NO, rnd 6; B5/30/1957 Waynesboro, VA **1979** NO 6 **1980** NO 13 (9, lcb) **1981** NO 4 (4) **1981**†Mia 8 (0) **NFL** 31 (13) [3 yrs]

RAY, TERRY Terry, DB, 6´1˝/205 lbs; Oklahoma; 1992: Atl, rnd 6; B10/12/1969 Shape, Belgium **1992** Atl 10 (2) **1993** NE 15 (1) **1994**†NE 16 (0) **1995** NE 16 (16, SS) **1996**†NE 16 (7, ss) **NFL** 73 (26) [5 yrs]

RAYAM, THOMAS Thomas Leon, G-DT, 6´6˝/297 lbs; Alabama; 1990: Was, rnd 10; B1/3/1968 Orlando, FL **1992** Cin 10 (5, rg) **1993** Cin 10 (8, RG) **NFL** 20 (13) [2 yrs]

RAYBON, ISRAEL Israel Deshon, DE, 6´6˝/300 lbs; North Alabama; 1996: Pit, rnd 5; B2/5/1973 Huntsville, AL **1996**†Pit 3 (0) **1997** Car 9 (0) **NFL** 12 (0) [2 yrs]

RAYBURN, SAM Sam Branson, DT, 6´3˝/303 lbs; Tulsa; B10/20/1980 Chickasha, OK **2003**†Phi 10 (0) **2004** Phi 16 (2) **2005** Phi 16 (2) **NFL** 42 (4) [3 yrs]

RAYBURN, VAN Virgil Homer, E, 6´1˝/180 lbs; Tennessee; B8/4/1910 Pulaski, TN, D6/15/1991 Osceola, AR

| 1933 | Bkn | 9(3) | — | — | — | — | 2 | 15 | 7.5 | 0 | — | — | — | — | — | — | — | — | — | — | — | — | 0 | 8 |

RAYE, JIMMY James Arthur, DB, 6´0˝/185 lbs; Michigan State; 1968: LA, rnd 16; B3/26/1946 Fayetteville, NC **1969** Phi 2

RAYE, JIMMY James Arthur, WR, 5´9˝/165 lbs; San Diego State; B11/24/1968 Fayetteville, NC

| 1991 | LARm | 2(0) | — | — | — | — | 1 | 19 | 19.0(19) | 0 | — | — | — | — | — | — | — | — | — | — | k | — | 0 | 37 |

RAYHLE, FRED Frederick, TE, 6´5˝/217 lbs; Tennessee-Chattanooga; B4/9/1954 Covington, KY **1977** Sea 2

RAYMER, CORY Cory Gene, C, 6´3˝/300 lbs; Wisconsin; 1995: Was, rnd 2; B3/3/1973 Fond du Lac, WI **1995** Was 3 (2) **1996** Was 6 (5, c) **1997** Was 6 (3) **1998** Was 16 (16, C) **1999**†Was 16 (16, C) **2001** Was 16 (16, C) **2002** SD 3 (3) **2003** SD 15 (8, c) **2004** Was 15 (14, C) **2005**†Was 2 (0) **NFL** 98 (83) [10 yrs]

RAYMOND, COREY Corey, DB, 5´11˝/185 lbs; LSU; B7/28/1969 New Iberia, LA **1992** NYG 16 (0) **1993**†NYG 16 (8, RCB) **1994** NYG 16 (12, rcb/lcb) **1995**†Det 16 (15, RCB) **1996** Det 13 (13, RCB) **1997** Det 13 (12, RCB) **NFL** 90 (60) [6 yrs]

RAYNER, DAVE Dave, K, 6´2˝/209 lbs; Michigan State; 2005: Ind, rnd 6; B10/26/1982 Oxford, MI [K] **2005** Ind 14 (0)

RAZZANO, RICK Richard Anthony, LB, 5´11˝/227 lbs; Virginia Tech; B11/15/1955 New Castle, PA **1980** Cin 14 (0) **1981**†Cin 16 (2) **1982**†Cin 9 (1) **1983** Cin 16 (2) **1984** Cin 10 (5, lilb) **NFL** 65 (10) [5 yrs]

REACH, KEVIN Kevin Thaddeus, G-C, 6´3˝/270 lbs; Utah; B10/24/1963 Atlanta, GA **1987** SF 3 (3)

READ, JACK Jack, G-T, none; deceased **1921** Akr 3 (0)

READER, JAMIE Jamieson Jordan, FB, 6´0˝/238 lbs; Akron; B5/4/1974 Washington, DC

| 2001 | †Phi | 16(0) | — | — | — | — | — | — | — | — | — | — | — | — | — | — | — | — | — | — | — | — | 0 | 7 |

READER, RUSS Russell Burton, DB, 6´0˝/185 lbs; Michigan; Michigan State; 1947: ChiB, rnd 21; B6/26/1923 Ypsilanti, MI **1947** ChiB 2 (0)

READON, IKE Isaac, NT, 6´0˝/273 lbs; Hampton; 1986: KC, rnd 10; B5/16/1963 Miami, FL **1987** Mia 3 (0)

REAGAN, FRANK Francis Xavier, B, 5´11˝/182 lbs; Pennsylvania; 1941: NYG, rnd 3; B7/28/1919 Philadelphia, PA, D11/20/1972 Philadelphia, PA [I]

1941	NYG	5(2)	35	146	4.2(21)	4	—	—	—	—	6	1	16.7	16	2.7(16)	0	0	—	—	—	Pkpi	—	24	320
1946	†NYG	6(0)	62	246	4.0(52)	2	4	71	17.8(36)	0	6	3	50.0	32	5.3(22)	0	0	—	—	—	Pkp	—	12	388
1947	NYG	10(4)	14	22	1.6(20)	0	—	—	—	—	25	12	48.0	191	7.6(88)	1	2	—	—	—	Pkpi	—	0	247
1948	NYG	11(6, qb)	—	—	—	—	—	—	—	—	—	—	—	—	—	—	—	—	—	—	Pi	—	0	100
1949	†Phi	12(0)	—	—	—	—	—	—	—	—	—	—	—	—	—	—	—	—	—	—	Ppi	1	6	282
1950	Phi	12(DB)	3	55	18.3(40)	0	—	—	—	—	—	—	—	—	—	—	—	—	—	—	Ppi	1	6	185
1951	Phi	12(DB)	—	—	—	—	—	—	—	—	—	—	—	—	—	—	—	—	—	—	Pi	—	0	40
NFL	7	68(12)	114	469	4.1(52)	6	4	71	17.8(36)	0	37	16	43.2	239	6.5(88)	1	2	—	—	—	Pkpi	2	48	1561

REAGEN, ED Edward J., T, none; B4/7/1900 Bethayres, PA, D10/15/1983 Paoli, PA **1926** Bkn 1 (0)

REAGOR, MONTAE Willie Montae, DT, 6´3˝/285 lbs; Texas Tech; 1999: Den, rnd 2; B6/29/1977 Waxahachie, TX **1999** Den 9 (0) **2000** Den 13 (0) **2001** Den 8 (0) **2002** Den 15 (1) **2003**†Ind 13 (12, RDT) **2004** Ind 16 (16, LDT) **2005**†Ind 13 (12, RDT) **NFL** 87 (41) [7 yrs]

REAM, CHARLES Charles Daniel, T, 6´2˝/225 lbs; Ohio State; 1938: Cle, rnd 9; B12/12/1913 Youngstown, OH **1938** Cle 10 (3)

REAMON, TOMMY Thomas Waverly, RB, 5´10˝/192 lbs; Missouri; 1974: Pit, rnd 9; B3/12/1952 Virgilnia, VA

| 1976 | KC | 11(4, rb) | 103 | 314 | 3.0(14) | 4 | 10 | 136 | 13.6(49) | 1 | — | — | — | — | — | — | — | — | — | — | kp | — | 30 | 561 |

REARDON, KERRY Kerry Edward, DB, 5´11˝/180 lbs; Iowa; 1971: KC, rnd 6; B5/6/1949 Kansas City, MO **1971**†KC 6 **1972** KC 7 **1973** KC 12 **1974** KC 11 **1975** KC 8 (8, LCB) **1976** KC 14 (14, LCB) **NFL** 58 (22) [6 yrs]

REASONS, GARY Gary Phillip, LB, 6´4˝/235 lbs; Northwestern State (LA); 1984: NYG, rnd 4; B2/18/1962 Crowley, TX **1984**†NYG 16 (11, LILB) **1985**†NYG 16 (15, LILB) **1986**†NYG 16 (16, LILB) **1987** NYG 10 (0) **1988** NYG 16 (7, rilb) **1990**†NYG 16 (3) **1991** NYG 16 (15, LILB) **1992** Cin 12 (9, RILB)

YEAR	TEAM	G (GS, POS)	RUSH	YD	AVG (LG)	TD	REC	YD	AVG (LG)	TD	PASS	COMP	PCT	YD	AVG (LG)	TD	INT	SK	YD	QBR	KPR	OTD	PTS	TAY
1989	†NYG	16 (12, LILB)	1	2	2.0 (2)	0	—	—	—	—	—	—	—	—	—	—	—	—	—	—	iS	—	2	37
NFL	9	134 (88)	1	2	2.0 (2)	0	—	—	—	—	—	—	—	—	—	—	—	—	—	—	iS	—	2	89

REAVES, JOHN Thomas Johnson, QB, 6´3˝/210 lbs; Florida; 1972: Phi, rnd 1; B3/2/1950 Anniston, AL

YEAR	TEAM	G (GS, POS)	RUSH	YD	AVG (LG)	TD	REC	YD	AVG (LG)	TD	PASS	COMP	PCT	YD	AVG (LG)	TD	INT	SK	YD	QBR	KPR	OTD	PTS	TAY
1972	Phi	11 (qb)	18	109	6.1 (16)	1	—	—	—	—	224	108	48.2	1508	6.7 (77)	7	12	38	322	58.4	—	—	6	428
1973	Phi	1	2	2	1.0 (3)	0	—	—	—	—	19	5	26.3	17	0.9 (6)	0	1	3	19	—	—	—	0	-30
1974	Phi	4	1	8	8.0 (8)	0	—	—	—	—	20	5	25.0	84	4.2 (29)	0	2	3	21	—	—	—	0	-30
1975	Cin	7	6	13	2.2 (9)	2	—	—	—	—	51	25	49.0	297	5.8 (51)	2	3	2	9	—	—	—	12	72
1976	Cin	3	—	—	—	—	—	—	—	—	22	8	36.4	76	3.5 (19)	2	1	3	17	—	—	—	0	8
1977	Cin	9	5	0	0.0 (0)	0	—	—	—	—	59	24	40.7	383	6.5 (40)	0	5	2	17	—	—	—	0	-9
1978	Cin	9 (4)	6	50	8.3 (20)	0	—	—	—	—	144	74	51.4	790	5.5 (51)	3	8	8	61	—	—	—	0	140
1981	Hou	5 (2)	6	13	2.2 (13)	0	—	—	—	—	61	31	50.8	379	6.2 (51)	2	2	3	27	—	—	—	0	133
1987	TB	2 (2)	—	—	—	—	—	—	—	—	16	6	37.5	83	5.2 (26)	1	0	1	12	—	—	—	0	47
NFL	9	51 (8)	44	195	4.4 (20)	3	—	—	—	—	616	286	46.4	3617	5.9 (77)	17	34	63	505	51.4	—	—	18	759

REAVES, KEN Kenneth Milton, DB, 6´3˝/210 lbs; Norfolk State; 1966: Atl, rnd 4; B10/29/1944 Braddock, PA **[I]** **1966** Atl 14 **1967** Atl 14 (LCB) **1968** Atl 14 (LCB) **1969** Atl✧14 (LCB) **1970** Atl 14 (LCB) **1971** Atl 14 (LCB) **1972** Atl 14 (LCB) **1973** Atl 14 (LCB) **1974** NO 4 **1974** SL 6 (6, ss) **1975**†SL 14 (SS) **1976** SL 14 (SS) **1977** SL 14 (SS) **NFL** 164 (6) [12 yrs]

REAVES, WILLARD Willard Sheldon, RB, 5´11˝/200 lbs; Northern Arizona; B8/17/1959 Flagstaff, AZ **1989** Mia 2 (0)

YEAR	TEAM	G (GS, POS)	RUSH	YD	AVG (LG)	TD	REC	YD	AVG (LG)	TD	PASS	COMP	PCT	YD	AVG (LG)	TD	INT	SK	YD	QBR	KPR	OTD	PTS	TAY
1989	Was	1 (0)	1	-1	-1.0 (-1)	0	—	—	—	—	—	—	—	—	—	—	—	—	—	—		—	0	-1
NFL	1	3 (0)	1	-1	-1.0 (-1)	0	—	—	—	—	—	—	—	—	—	—	—	—	—	—	k	—	0	-7

REAVIS, DAVE David Craig, T-G, 6´5˝/257 lbs; Arkansas; 1973: Pit, rnd 5; B6/19/1950 Nashville, TN **1974**†Pit 14 **1975**†Pit 10 **1976** TB 1 (1) **1977** TB 14 (14, LT) **1978** TB 16 (16, LT) **1979**†TB 16 (16, LT) **1980** TB 16 (16, LT) **1981** TB 12 (5, lt) **1982**†TB 7 (7, LT) **1983** TB 15 (11, LT) **NFL** 121 (86) [10 yrs]

REBOWE, RUSTY Rusty, LB, 5´10˝/213 lbs; Nicholls State; B1/17/1956 Destrehan, LA **1978** NO 1

REBSAMEN, PAUL Paul Meyer, C, 6´0˝/188 lbs; Centenary; B1905 Fort Smith, AR, D3/13/1947 Hot Springs, AR **1927** Pot 4 (1)

RECHER, DAVE David Eugene, C, 6´1˝/245 lbs; Iowa; B12/30/1942 Chicago, IL **1965** Phi 14 **1966** Phi 10 **1967** Phi 14 **1968** Phi 8 **NFL** 46 [4 yrs]

RECHICHAR, BERT Albert Daniel, DB-LB-HB-E, 6´1˝/209 lbs; Tennessee; 1952: Cle, rnd 1; B7/16/1930 Belle Vernon, PA **[KRI]** **1952**†Cle 12 (SS) **1954** Bal 12 (DB) **1955** Bal★12 (DB) **1957** Bal✧12 (DB) **1959** Bal 10 **1960** Pit 6 **1961** NYT-A 2

YEAR	TEAM	G (GS, POS)	RUSH	YD	AVG (LG)	TD	REC	YD	AVG (LG)	TD	PASS	COMP	PCT	YD	AVG (LG)	TD	INT	SK	YD	QBR	KPR	OTD	PTS	TAY
1953	Bal☆	11 (DB)	—	—	—	—	3	151	50.3 (66)	2	—	—	—	—	—	—	—	—	—	—	Kkpi	1	33	133
1956	Bal✧	10 (DB)	1	-1	-1.0 (-1)	0	—	—	—	—	—	—	—	—	—	—	—	—	—	—	KPpi	—	17	27
1958	†Bal	12	—	—	—	—	4	34	8.5 (12)	1	—	—	—	—	—	—	—	—	—	—	Kkp	—	9	21
NFL	10	99	1	-1	-1.0 (-1)	0	7	185	26.4 (66)	3	—	—	—	—	—	—	—	—	—	—	KPkpi	1	179	336

RECKMACK, RAY Raymond P., E-HB, 6´0˝/198 lbs; Syracuse; B8/26/1914, CT, D5/1/1982 Emmaus, PA **1937** Det 1 (0) **1937** Bkn 1 (0) **NFL** 2 (0) [1 yr]

RECTOR, RON Ronny S., RB, 6´0˝/200 lbs; Northwestern; 1966: GB, rnd 9; B5/29/1944 Akron, OH, D12/4/1980 Barberton, OH

YEAR	TEAM	G (GS, POS)	RUSH	YD	AVG (LG)	TD	REC	YD	AVG (LG)	TD	PASS	COMP	PCT	YD	AVG (LG)	TD	INT	SK	YD	QBR	KPR	OTD	PTS	TAY
1966	Was	6	5	8	1.6 (4)	0	2	9	4.5 (6)	0	—	—	—	—	—	—	—	—	—	—	k	—	0	33
1966	Atl	4	4	32	8.0 (20)	0	—	—	—	—	—	—	—	—	—	—	—	—	—	—	—	—	0	32
1967	Atl	10	24	127	5.3 (16)	0	4	13	3.3 (9)	0	—	—	—	—	—	—	—	—	—	—	—	—	0	134
NFL	2	20	33	167	5.1 (20)	0	6	22	3.7 (9)	0	—	—	—	—	—	—	—	—	—	—	k	—	0	198

REDD, GLEN Glen Herrscher, LB, 6´1˝/229 lbs; Brigham Young; 1981: NO, rnd 6; B6/17/1958 Ogden, UT **1981** NO 16 (16, LILB) **1983** NO 16 (0) **1984** NO 16 (1) **1985** NO 16 (16, LILB) **1986** NO 4 (3) **1986** Ind 8 (0) **NFL** 76 (36) [5 yrs]

REDDEN, BARRY Barry Dwayne, RB, 5´10˝/210 lbs; Richmond; 1982: LARm, rnd 1; B7/21/1960 Sarasota, FL

YEAR	TEAM	G (GS, POS)	RUSH	YD	AVG (LG)	TD	REC	YD	AVG (LG)	TD	PASS	COMP	PCT	YD	AVG (LG)	TD	INT	SK	YD	QBR	KPR	OTD	PTS	TAY
1982	LARm	9 (0)	8	24	3.0 (7)	0	4	16	4.0 (11)	0	—	—	—	—	—	—	—	—	—	—	k	—	0	204
1983	†LARm	15 (0)	75	372	5.0 (40)	2	4	30	7.5 (9)	0	—	—	—	—	—	—	—	—	—	—	k	—	12	480
1984	†LARm	14 (0)	45	247	5.5 (35)	0	4	39	9.8 (6)	0	—	—	—	—	—	—	—	—	—	—	k	—	0	452
1985	†LARm	14 (1)	87	380	4.4 (41)	0	16	162	10.1 (32)	0	—	—	—	—	—	—	—	—	—	—	—	—	0	461
1986	†LARm	15 (14, FB)	110	467	4.2 (41)	4	28	217	7.8 (24)	1	—	—	—	—	—	—	—	—	—	—	—	—	30	621
1987	SD	12 (0)	11	36	3.3 (7)	0	7	46	6.6 (13)	0	—	—	—	—	—	—	—	—	—	—	—	—	0	59
1988	SD	8 (2)	19	30	1.6 (5)	3	1	11	11.0 (11)	0	—	—	—	—	—	—	—	—	—	—	—	—	18	66
1989	†Cle	16 (1)	40	180	4.5 (38)	1	6	34	5.7 (8)	0	—	—	—	—	—	—	—	—	—	—	k	—	6	179
1990	Cle	5 (0)	1	-1	-1.0 (-1)	0	—	—	—	—	—	—	—	—	—	—	—	—	—	—	—	—	0	-1
NFL	9	108 (18)	396	1735	4.4 (41)	10	70	555	7.9 (32)	1	—	—	—	—	—	—	—	—	—	—	k	—	66	2520

REDDING, CORY Cory B., DE, 6´4˝/285 lbs; Texas; 2003: Det, rnd 3; B11/15/1980 Houston, TX **2003** Det 9 (0) **2004** Det 16 (16, LDE) **2005** Det 16 (14, LDE) **NFL** 41 (30) [3 yrs]

REDDING, REGGIE Reginald J., G-T, 6´3˝/298 lbs; Cal State-Fullerton; 1990: Atl, rnd 5; B9/22/1968 Cincinnati, OH **1991**†Atl 13 (0) **1992** NE 14 (14, LG) **NFL** 27 (14) [2 yrs]

REDEEN, SHEEPY Clarence Elmer, E, /185 lbs; none; B10/7/1891 Minneapolis, MN, D9/2/1971 Minneapolis, MN **1921** Min 4 (4, RE)

REDICK, CORN Cornelius, WR, 5´11˝/185 lbs; Cal State-Fullerton; 1986: Phi, rnd 7; B1/7/1964 Los Angeles, CA

YEAR	TEAM	G (GS, POS)	RUSH	YD	AVG (LG)	TD	REC	YD	AVG (LG)	TD	PASS	COMP	PCT	YD	AVG (LG)	TD	INT	SK	YD	QBR	KPR	OTD	PTS	TAY
1987	GB	1 (0)	—	—	—	—	1	18	18.0 (18)	0	—	—	—	—	—	—	—	—	—	—	—	—	0	9

REDINGER, RUEL Otis Ruel, B, 5´10˝/185 lbs; Colgate; Penn State; B12/31/1898, D9/26/1969 Valley City, OH **1925** Can 7 (5, WB)

REDMAN, CHRIS Chris James, QB, 6´3˝/223 lbs; Louisville; 2000: Bal, rnd 3; B7/7/1977 Louisville, KY

YEAR	TEAM	G (GS, POS)	RUSH	YD	AVG (LG)	TD	REC	YD	AVG (LG)	TD	PASS	COMP	PCT	YD	AVG (LG)	TD	INT	SK	YD	QBR	KPR	OTD	PTS	TAY
2000	†Bal	2 (0)	1	0	0.0 (0)	0	—	—	—	—	3	2	66.7	19	6.3 (12)	0	0	—	—	—	—	—	0	10
2001	†Bal	0 (0)	—	—	—	—	—	—	—	—	—	—	—	—	—	—	—	—	—	—	—	—	0	0
2002	Bal	6 (6, qb)	10	8	0.8 (6)	0	—	—	—	—	182	97	53.3	1034	5.7 (36)	7	3	11	68	—	—	—	0	440
2003	Bal	2 (0)	2	4	2.0 (4)	0	—	—	—	—	13	7	53.8	58	4.5 (16)	0	2	6	45	—	—	—	0	-47
NFL	4	10 (6)	13	12	0.9 (6)	0	—	—	—	—	198	106	53.5	1111	5.6 (36)	7	5	17	113	—	—	—	0	403

REDMAN, GUS Augustus A., B, 5´11˝/170 lbs; Norwich; Purdue; B12/1896 Methuen, MA, D7/19/1949 Lowell, MA **1921** Mun 2 (2, WB) **1921** Day 5 (5, WB) **1922** Day 3 (1), 6 **1924** Day 6 (5, bb) **NFL** 16 (13) [3 yrs]

REDMAN, RICK Richard Clark, LB-P, 6´1˝/220 lbs; Washington; 1965: SD, rnd 5/Phi, rnd 10; B3/7/1943 Portland, OR **1965** SD-A 10 **1968** SD-A 1 **1969** SD-A 14 (MLB) **1970** SD 14 **1971** SD 12 (LLB) **1972** SD 10 (RLB) **1973** SD 11 (RLB)

YEAR	TEAM	G (GS, POS)	RUSH	YD	AVG (LG)	TD	REC	YD	AVG (LG)	TD	PASS	COMP	PCT	YD	AVG (LG)	TD	INT	SK	YD	QBR	KPR	OTD	PTS	TAY
1966	SD-A	14 (MLB/llb)	2	14	7.0 (32)	0	—	—	—	—	—	—	—	—	—	—	—	—	—	—	Pi	1	6	11
1967	SD-A✧	14 (MLB)	1	-13	-13.0 (-13)	0	—	—	—	—	—	—	—	—	—	—	—	—	—	—	Pi	—	0	3
NFL	9	100	3	1	0.3 (32)	0	—	—	—	—	—	—	—	—	—	—	—	—	—	—	Pi	1	6	18

REDMON, ANTHONY Kendrick Anthony, G, 6´5˝/308 lbs; Auburn; 1994: Arz, rnd 5; B4/9/1971 Brewton, AL **1994** Arz 6 (5, rg) **1995** Arz 12 (9, RG) **1996** Arz 16 (16, RG) **1997** Arz 16 (16, RG) **1998** Car 10 (4) **1999** Car 15 (15, RG) **2000** Atl 4 (4) **NFL** 79 (69) [7 yrs]

REDMOND, J.R. Joseph Robert, RB, 5´11˝/215 lbs; Arizona State; 2000: NE, rnd 3; B9/28/1977 Los Angeles, CA

YEAR	TEAM	G (GS, POS)	RUSH	YD	AVG (LG)	TD	REC	YD	AVG (LG)	TD	PASS	COMP	PCT	YD	AVG (LG)	TD	INT	SK	YD	QBR	KPR	OTD	PTS	TAY
2000	NE	12 (5, rb)	125	406	3.2 (20)	1	20	126	6.3 (20)	2	—	—	—	—	—	—	—	—	—	—	k	—	18	499
2001	†NE	12 (0)	35	119	3.4 (16)	0	13	132	10.2 (17)	0	—	—	—	—	—	—	—	—	—	—	k	—	0	212
2002	NE	9 (0)	4	2	0.5 (5)	0	2	5	2.5 (3)	0	—	—	—	—	—	—	—	—	—	—	k	—	0	2
2003	Oak	1 (0)	9	30	3.3 (9)	0	1	6	6.0 (6)	0	—	—	—	—	—	—	—	—	—	—	—	—	0	33
2004	Oak	16 (1)	21	119	5.7 (18)	0	32	233	7.3 (22)	0	—	—	—	—	—	—	—	—	—	—	k	—	0	269
NFL	5	50 (6)	194	676	3.5 (20)	1	68	502	7.4 (22)	2	—	—	—	—	—	—	—	—	—	—	k	—	18	1014

REDMOND, JIMMY James Louis, WR, 6´0˝/190 lbs; Ohio State; McNeese State; B8/18/1977 Kansas City, MO **2002** Jax 14 (0)

YEAR	TEAM	G (GS, POS)	RUSH	YD	AVG (LG)	TD	REC	YD	AVG (LG)	TD	PASS	COMP	PCT	YD	AVG (LG)	TD	INT	SK	YD	QBR	KPR	OTD	PTS	TAY
2003	Jax	12 (0)	—	—	—	—	3	67	22.3 (29)	0	—	—	—	—	—	—	—	—	—	—	k	—	0	40
NFL	2	26 (0)	—	—	—	—	3	67	22.3 (29)	0	—	—	—	—	—	—	—	—	—	—	k	—	0	57

REDMOND, RUDY Rudolph Cruzette, DB, 6´1˝/196 lbs; Pacific; 1969: Chi, rnd 4; B8/25/1947 Spokane, WA **1969** Atl 14 (RCB) **1970** Atl 14 (RCB) **1971** Atl 8 **1972** Det 14 (RCB) **NFL** 50 [4 yrs]

YEAR	TEAM	G (GS, POS)	RUSH	YD	AVG(LG)	TD	REC	YD	AVG(LG)	TD	PASS	COMP	PCT	YD	AVG(LG)	TD	INT	SK	YD	QBR	KPR	OTD	PTS	TAY

REDMOND, TOM Thomas Benjamin, DE-G-T, 6´5˝/250 lbs; Vanderbilt; 1959: ChiC, rnd 6; B9/21/1937 Atlanta, GA **1960** SL 12 **1961** SL 10 **1962** SL 14 **1963** SL 9 **1964** SL 14
1965 SL 1 **NFL** 60 [6 yrs]

REDWINE, JARVIS Jarvis John, RB, 5´10˝/203 lbs; Oregon State; Nebraska; 1981: Min, rnd 2; B5/16/1957 Los Angeles, CA

1981	Min	3(0)	5	20	4.0(8)	0	—	—	—	—	—	—	—	—	—	—	—	—	—	—	—	—	0	20
1982	†Min	7(0)	2	2	1.0(2)	0	—	—	—	—	—	—	—	—	—	—	—	—	—	—	k	—	0	108
1983	Min	16(1)	10	48	4.8(21)	0	1	4	4.0(4)	0	—	—	—	—	—	—	—	—	—	—	k	—	0	318
NFL	3	26(1)	17	70	4.1(21)	0	1	4	4.0(4)	0	—	—	—	—	—	—	—	—	—	—	k	—	0	446

REEBERG, LUCIEN Lucien Henry, T, 6´4˝/285 lbs; Hampton; 1963: Det, rnd 19; B2/21/1942 Bronx, NY, D1/31/1964 Detroit, MI **1963** Det 14 (RT)

REECE, BEASLEY Beasley Young, DB, 6´1˝/193 lbs; North Texas; 1976: Dal, rnd 9; B3/18/1954 Waco, TX **1977** NYG 10 **1978** NYG 8 (8, SS) **1979** NYG 16 (16, SS)
1980 NYG 16 (14, SS) **1981**†NYG 16 (16, FS) **1982** NYG 9 (9, FS) **1983** NYG 7 (6, fs) **1983** TB 9 (8, FS) **1984** TB 16 (14, FS/ss)

| 1976 | †Dal | 10 | — | — | — | — | 1 | 6 | 6.0(6) | 0 | — | — | — | — | — | — | — | — | — | — | — | — | 0 | 3 |
| NFL | 9 | 117(91) | — | — | — | — | 1 | 6 | 6.0(6) | 0 | — | — | — | — | — | — | — | — | — | — | kpi | 1 | 6 | 291 |

REECE, DANNY Daniel Louis, DB, 5´11˝/190 lbs; USC; 1976: Cin, rnd 3; B1/28/1955 Los Angeles, CA [R] **1976** TB 11 (10, RCB) **1979**†TB 16 (1) **1980** TB 16 (1)

1977	TB	14	—	—	—	—	2	59	29.5(45)	0	—	—	—	—	—	—	—	—	—	—	kp	—	0	176
1978	TB	15	—	—	—	—	1	25	25.0(25)	0	—	—	—	—	—	—	—	—	—	—	kpi	—	0	269
NFL	5	72(12)	—	—	—	—	3	84	28.0(45)	0	—	—	—	—	—	—	—	—	—	—	kpi	1	6	632

REECE, DON Donald Miles, FB-LB-T, 6´1˝/230 lbs; Missouri; 1943: Bkn, rnd 22; B12/1/1919 Marysville, OH, D8/26/1992 Marysville, OH

| 1946 | Mia-A | 13(4, FB) | 30 | 109 | 3.6 | 2 | 1 | 5 | 5.0(5) | 0 | — | — | — | — | — | — | — | — | — | — | i | — | 12 | 144 |

REECE, GEOFF Geoffrey Robert, C, 6´4˝/247 lbs; Washington State; 1975: LA, rnd 3; B5/16/1952 Everett, WA **1976**†LARm 14 **1977** Sea 3 **NFL** 17 [2 yrs]

REECE, JOHN John L., DB, 6´0˝/203 lbs; Nebraska; 1994: Arz, rnd 4; B1/24/1971 Crowell, TX **1995** SL 5 (0)

REECE, TRAVIS Travis, RB, 6´3˝/252 lbs; Michigan State; B4/3/1975 Detroit, MI **1998** Det 3 (0) **1999**†Det 4 (0) **NFL** 7 (0) [2 yrs]

REED, ALVIN Alvin D., TE, 6´5˝/235 lbs; Prairie View A&M; B8/1/1944 Kilgore, TX

1967	†Hou-A	14(TE)	—	—	—	—	11	144	13.1(20)	1	—	—	—	—	—	—	—	—	—	—	k	—	6	62
1968	Hou-A★	14(TE)	—	—	—	—	46	747	16.2(60)	5	—	—	—	—	—	—	—	—	—	—	—	—	30	399
1969	†Hou-A★	14(TE)	—	—	—	—	51	664	13.0(43)	2	—	—	—	—	—	—	—	—	—	—	—	—	12	297
1970	Hou☆	13(TE)	—	—	—	—	47	604	12.9(34)	2	—	—	—	—	—	—	—	—	—	—	k	—	12	297
1971	Hou	14(TE)	—	—	—	—	25	408	16.3(36)	1	—	—	—	—	—	—	—	—	—	—	k	—	6	209
1972	Hou	14(TE)	—	—	—	—	19	251	13.2(29)	0	—	—	—	—	—	—	—	—	—	—	—	—	0	126
1973	Was	5(5, te)	—	—	—	—	9	124	13.8(34)	0	—	—	—	—	—	—	—	—	—	—	—	—	0	62
1974	†Was	14	—	—	—	—	4	36	9.0(11)	1	—	—	—	—	—	—	—	—	—	—	—	—	6	23
1975	Was	14	—	—	—	—	2	5	2.5(4)	2	—	—	—	—	—	—	—	—	—	—	—	—	12	13
NFL	9	116(5)	—	—	—	—	214	2983	13.9(60)	14	—	—	—	—	—	—	—	—	—	—	k	—	84	1487

REED, ANDRE Andre Darnell, WR, 6´2˝/190 lbs; Kutztown State; 1985: Buf, rnd 4; B1/29/1964 Allentown, PA

1985	Buf	16(15, WR)	3	-1	-0.3(14)	1	48	637	13.3(32)	4	—	—	—	—	—	—	—	—	—	—	p	—	30	335
1986	Buf	15(15, WR)	3	-8	-2.7(4)	0	53	739	13.9(55)	7	—	—	—	—	—	—	—	—	—	—	—	—	42	397
1987	Buf	12(12, WR)	1	1	1.0(1)	0	57	752	13.2(40)	5	—	—	—	—	—	—	—	—	—	—	—	—	30	402
1988	†Buf◇	15(14, WR)	6	64	10.7(36)	0	71	968	13.6(65)	6	—	—	—	—	—	—	—	—	—	—	—	—	36	578
1989	†Buf★	16(16, WR)	2	31	15.5(23)	0	88	1312	14.9(78)	9	—	—	—	—	—	—	—	—	—	—	—	—	54	732
1990	†Buf★	16(16, WR)	3	23	7.7(26)	0	71	945	13.3(56)	8	—	—	—	—	—	—	—	—	—	—	—	—	48	536
1991	†Buf★	16(16, WR)	12	136	11.3(46)	0	81	1113	13.7(55)	10	—	—	—	—	—	—	—	—	—	—	—	—	60	743
1992	†Buf◇	16(16, WR)	8	65	8.1(24)	0	65	913	14.0(51)	3	—	—	—	—	—	—	—	—	—	—	—	—	18	537
1993	†Buf◇	15(15, WR)	9	21	2.3(15)	0	52	854	16.4(65)	6	—	—	—	—	—	—	—	—	—	—	—	—	36	478
1994	Buf★	16(16, WR)	10	87	8.7(20)	0	90	1303	14.5(83)	8	1	1	100.0	32	32.0(32)	0	0	—	—	—	—	—	48	795
1995	†Buf	6(6, wr)	7	48	6.9(14)	0	24	312	13.0(41)	3	—	—	—	—	—	—	—	—	—	—	—	—	18	219
1996	†Buf	16(16, WR)	8	22	2.8(13)	0	66	1036	15.7(67)	6	—	—	—	—	—	—	—	—	—	—	—	—	36	570
1997	Buf	15(15, WR)	3	11	3.7(9)	0	60	880	14.7(77)	5	0	0	0.0	0	0.0	0	0	1	20	—	—	—	30	476
1998	†Buf	15(13, WR)	—	—	—	—	63	795	12.6(67)	5	—	—	—	—	—	—	—	—	—	—	—	—	30	423
1999	†Buf	16(16, WR)	—	—	—	—	52	536	10.3(30)	1	—	—	—	—	—	—	—	—	—	—	—	—	6	273
2000	Was	13(0)	—	—	—	—	10	103	10.3(21)	1	—	—	—	—	—	—	—	—	—	—	—	—	6	57
NFL	16	234(217)	75	500	6.7(46)	1	951	13198	13.9(83)	87	1	1	100.0	32	32.0(32)	0	0	1	20	—	p	—	528	7547

REED, BEN Henry Benton, DE, 6´5˝/265 lbs; Mississippi; 1986: TB, rnd 10; B5/7/1963 Baton Rouge, LA **1987** NE 3 (3)

REED, BOBBY Robert, HB, 5´11˝/187 lbs; Pacific; B11/14/1939 New Orleans, LA

1962	Min	6	6	22	3.7(11)	0	4	37	9.3(37)	1	—	—	—	—	—	—	—	—	—	—	kp	—	6	225
1963	Min	10	21	88	4.2(16)	0	13	137	10.5(45)	0	—	—	—	—	—	—	—	—	—	—	kp	—	0	375
NFL	2	27	110	4.1(16)	0	17	174	10.2(45)	1	—	—	—	—	—	—	—	—	—	—	kp	—	6	599

REED, DOUG Douglas Nathaniel, DE-DT, 6´3˝/254 lbs; San Diego State; 1983: LARm, rnd 4; B7/16/1960 San Diego, CA **1984**†LARm 9 (1) **1985**†LARm 16 (16, LDE)
1986†LARm 16 (10, LDE) **1987** LARm 12 (12, LDE) **1988**†LARm 16 (15, LDE) **1989** LARm 11 (11, LDE) **1990** LARm 16 (16, LDE) **NFL** 96 (81) [7 yrs]

REED, ED Edward Earl, DB, 5´11˝/200 lbs; Miami (FL); 2002: Bal, rnd 1; B9/11/1978 St. Rose, LA [I] **2002** Bal 16 (16, SS) **2003**†Bal★ 16 (15, SS) **2004** Bal★ 16 (16, SS)
2005 Bal 10 (10, SS) **NFL** 58 (57) [4 yrs]

REED, FRANK Frank Rodney, DB, 5´11˝/193 lbs; Washington; 1976: Atl, rnd 8; B5/13/1954 Seattle, WA **1976** Atl 14 (14, RCB) **1977** Atl 14 (3) **1978**†Atl 16 (16, SS)
1979 Atl 11 (13, SS) **1980**†Atl 16 (7, ss) **NFL** 71 (51) [5 yrs]

REED, HENRY Henry Elax, DE-LB, 6´3˝/230 lbs; Weber State; 1971: NYG, rnd 10; B1/15/1948 Detroit, MI **1971** NYG 14 (LDE) **1972** NYG 14 (LDE) **1973** NYG 10 **1974** NYG 13
NFL 51 [4 yrs]

REED, J.R. Herbert Lee, DB, 5´11˝/190 lbs; South Florida; 2004: Phi, rnd 4; B2/11/1982 Tampa, FL **2004**†Phi 14 (1)

REED, JAKE Willie, WR, 6´3˝/216 lbs; Grambling State; 1991: Min, rnd 3; B9/28/1967 Covington, GA

1991	Min	1(0)	—	—	—	—	—	—	—	—	—	—	—	—	—	—	—	—	—	—	—	—	—	—
1992	†Min	16(0)	—	—	—	—	6	142	23.7(51)	0	—	—	—	—	—	—	—	—	—	—	k	—	0	57
1993	†Min	10(1)	—	—	—	—	5	65	13.0(18)	0	—	—	—	—	—	—	—	—	—	—	—	—	0	33
1994	†Min	16(16, WR)	—	—	—	—	85	1175	13.8(59)	4	—	—	—	—	—	—	—	—	—	—	—	—	24	608
1995	Min	16(16, WR)	—	—	—	—	72	1167	16.2(55)	9	—	—	—	—	—	—	—	—	—	—	—	—	54	629
1996	†Min	16(15, WR)	—	—	—	—	72	1320	18.3(82)	7	—	—	—	—	—	—	—	—	—	—	—	—	42	695
1997	†Min	16(16, WR)	—	—	—	—	68	1138	16.7(56)	6	—	—	—	—	—	—	—	—	—	—	—	—	36	599
1998	†Min	11(11, WR)	—	—	—	—	34	474	13.9(56)	4	—	—	—	—	—	—	—	—	—	—	—	—	24	257
1999	†Min	16(8, WR)	—	—	—	—	44	643	14.6(50)	2	—	—	—	—	—	—	—	—	—	—	—	—	12	332
2000	†NO	7(6, wr)	—	—	—	—	16	206	12.9(22)	0	—	—	—	—	—	—	—	—	—	—	—	—	0	103
2001	Min	16(0)	—	—	—	—	27	309	11.4(27)	1	—	—	—	—	—	—	—	—	—	—	—	—	8	160
2002	NO	14(1)	—	—	—	—	21	360	17.1(54)	3	—	—	—	—	—	—	—	—	—	—	—	—	18	195
NFL	12	155(90)	—	—	—	—	450	6999	15.6(82)	36	—	—	—	—	—	—	—	—	—	—	k	—	218	3666

REED, JAMES James Curtis, LB, 6´2˝/230 lbs; California; B10/10/1955 Corpus Christi, TX **1977** Phi 4

REED, JAMES James, DT, 6´0˝/286 lbs; Iowa State; 2001: NYJ, rnd 7; B2/3/1977 Saginaw, MI **2001**†NYJ 16 (2) **2002**†NYJ 16 (0) **2003** NYJ 16 (0) **2004**†NYJ 16 (0)
2005 NYJ 16 (16, LDT) **NFL** 80 (18) [5 yrs]

REED, JEFF Jeffrey Montgomery, K, 5´11˝/226 lbs; North Carolina; B4/9/1979 Charlotte, NC [K] **2002**†Pit 6 (0) **2003** Pit 16 (0) **2004**†Pit 16 (0) **2005**†Pit 16 (0)
NFL 54 (0) [4 yrs]

REED, JOE Joseph Butler, QB, 6´1˝/195 lbs; Baylor; Mississippi State; 1971: SF, rnd 11; B1/8/1948 Newport, RI

| 1972 | †SF | 9 | 4 | 22 | 5.5(22) | 0 | — | — | — | — | — | — | — | — | — | — | — | — | — | — | — | — | 0 | 22 |
| 1973 | SF | 6 | 15 | 85 | 5.7(20) | 0 | — | — | — | 114 | 51 | 44.7 | 589 | 5.2(38) | 2 | 6 | 10 | 56 | — | — | — | — | 0 | 150 |

YEAR	TEAM	G(GS, POS)	RUSH	YD	AVG(LG)	TD	REC	YD	AVG(LG)	TD	PASS	COMP	PCT	YD	AVG(LG)	TD	INT	SK	YD	QBR	KPR	OTD	PTS	TAY
1974	SF	6(4)	16	107	6.7(27)	0	—	—	—	—	74	29	39.2	316	4.3(58)	2	7	7	50	—	—	—	0	-5
1975	Det	10(8, QB)	34	193	5.7(22)	1	—	—	—	—	191	86	45.0	1181	6.2(65)	9	10	14	119	59.3	—	—	6	439
1976	Det	13(2)	11	63	5.7(14)	1	—	—	—	—	62	32	51.6	425	6.9(57)	3	3	12	93	—	—	—	6	181
1977	Det	3(1)	1	3	3.0(3)	0	—	—	—	—	40	13	32.5	150	3.8(26)	0	4	11	75	—	—	—	0	-82
1978	Det	1	1	0	0.0(0)	0	—	—	—	—	—	—	—	—	—	—	—	—	—	—	—	—	0	0
1979	Det	2	2	11	5.5(11)	0	—	—	—	—	32	14	43.8	164	5.1(50)	2	1	5	27	—	—	—	0	63
NFL	8	50(15)	84	484	5.8(27)	2	—	—	—	—	513	225	43.9	2825	5.5(65)	18	31	59	420	48.1	—	—	12	767

Reed, Josh Joshua Blake, WR, 5´10˝/208 lbs; LSU; 2002: Buf, rnd 2; B5/1/1980 Lafayette, LA

YEAR	TEAM	G(GS, POS)	RUSH	YD	AVG(LG)	TD	REC	YD	AVG(LG)	TD	PASS	COMP	PCT	YD	AVG(LG)	TD	INT	SK	YD	QBR	KPR	OTD	PTS	TAY
2002	Buf	16(2)	—	—	—	—	37	509	13.8(42)	2	—	—	—	—	—	—	—	—	—	—	—	—	12	265
2003	Buf	16(16, WR)	3	38	12.7(16)	0	58	588	10.1(26)	2	—	—	—	—	—	—	—	—	—	—	—	—	12	342
2004	Buf	12(1)	2	-1	-0.5(6)	0	16	153	9.6(20)	0	—	—	—	—	—	—	—	—	—	—	p	—	0	78
2005	Buf	16(6, wr)	1	-3	-3.0(-3)	0	32	449	14.0(51)	2	—	—	—	—	—	—	—	—	—	—	k	—	12	241
NFL	4	60(25)	6	34	5.7(16)	0	143	1699	11.9(51)	6	—	—	—	—	—	—	—	—	—	—	kp	—	36	925

Reed, Leo Leo Tautua, T-G, 6´4˝/240 lbs; Colorado State; 1961: SL, rnd 20; B1/3/1940 Kahuku, HI **1961** Hou-A 5 **1961** Den-A 4 **NFL** 9 [1 yr]

Reed, Mark Mark, QB, 6´3˝/201 lbs; Moorhead State (MN); 1981: NYG, rnd 8; B2/21/1959 Moorhead, MN

YEAR	TEAM	G(GS, POS)	RUSH	YD	AVG(LG)	TD	REC	YD	AVG(LG)	TD	PASS	COMP	PCT	YD	AVG(LG)	TD	INT	SK	YD	QBR	KPR	OTD	PTS	TAY
1983	Bal	1(0)	2	27	13.5(18)	0	—	—	—	—	10	6	60.0	34	3.4(16)	0	1	—	—	—	—	—	0	4

Reed, Michael Michael Jerome, DB, 5´9˝/180 lbs; Boston College; 1995: Car, rnd 7; B8/16/1972 Wilmington, DE **1995** Car 1 (0) **1996** Car 2 (0) **NFL** 3 (0) [2 yrs]

Reed, Mike Michael, RB, 6´0˝/215 lbs; Washington; B1/6/1975 Woodbridge, England **1998** Phi 4 (0)

Reed, Max John Maxwell, C, 5´8˝/185 lbs; Bucknell; B5/15/1902 Lewisburg, PA, D6/27/1973 Lewisburg, PA **1925** Buf 9 (9, C) **1926** Fra 13 (13, C), 6 **1927** Fra 10 (9, C) **1928** NYG 3 (1) **NFL** 35 (32) [4 yrs]

Reed, Oscar Oscar Lee, RB, 6´0˝/222 lbs; Colorado State; 1968: Min, rnd 7; B3/24/1944 Jonestown, MS

YEAR	TEAM	G(GS, POS)	RUSH	YD	AVG(LG)	TD	REC	YD	AVG(LG)	TD	PASS	COMP	PCT	YD	AVG(LG)	TD	INT	SK	YD	QBR	KPR	OTD	PTS	TAY
1968	Min	7	2	6	3.0(5)	0	—	—	—	—	—	—	—	—	—	—	—	—	—	—	—	—	0	6
1969	†Min	14	83	393	4.7(23)	1	7	59	8.4(16)	2	—	—	—	—	—	—	—	—	—	—	k	—	18	466
1970	†Min	12	42	132	3.1(21)	1	6	53	8.8(19)	0	—	—	—	—	—	—	—	—	—	—	k	—	6	165
1971	†Min	13	50	182	3.6(18)	1	15	138	9.2(26)	0	—	—	—	—	—	—	—	—	—	—	—	—	6	261
1972	Min	14(14, RB)	151	639	4.2(43)	2	30	205	6.8(37)	0	—	—	—	—	—	—	—	—	—	—	—	—	12	762
1973	†Min	12(8, RB)	100	401	4.0(30)	3	19	122	6.4(13)	0	—	—	—	—	—	—	—	—	—	—	k	—	18	491
1974	†Min	7	62	215	3.5(15)	0	15	99	6.6(12)	1	—	—	—	—	—	—	—	—	—	—	—	—	6	270
1975	Atl	7	14	40	2.9(7)	0	2	1	0.5(1)	0	—	—	—	—	—	—	—	—	—	—	k	—	0	28
NFL	8	86(22)	504	2008	4.0(43)	8	94	677	7.2(37)	3	—	—	—	—	—	—	—	—	—	—	k	—	66	2447

Reed, Rayshun Brandon Rayshun, DB, 5´10˝/185 lbs; Troy State; B4/10/1981 Columbus, GA **2004** SF 7 (1)

Reed, Robert Robert, G, 6´3˝/250 lbs; Tennessee State; 1965: Was, rnd 16/Hou, rnd 12; B2/23/1943 Longview, TX **1965** Was 8

Reed, Robert Robert E., WR, 6´1˝/203 lbs; Mississippi; Arkansas; Lambuth; B1/14/1975 Hinds County, MS

YEAR	TEAM	G(GS, POS)	RUSH	YD	AVG(LG)	TD	REC	YD	AVG(LG)	TD	PASS	COMP	PCT	YD	AVG(LG)	TD	INT	SK	YD	QBR	KPR	OTD	PTS	TAY
1999	SD	3(0)	—	—	—	—	1	1	1.0(1)	0	0	0	0.0	0	0.0	0	0	1	11	—	kp	—	0	32

Reed, Rock Joseph T., HB, 5´8˝/173 lbs; LSU; B8/7/1914 Bald Knob, AR

YEAR	TEAM	G(GS, POS)	RUSH	YD	AVG(LG)	TD	REC	YD	AVG(LG)	TD	PASS	COMP	PCT	YD	AVG(LG)	TD	INT	SK	YD	QBR	KPR	OTD	PTS	TAY
1937	ChiC	8(0)	10	33	3.3	0	2	26	13.0	0	1	0	0.0	0	0.0	0	0	—	—	—	—	1	6	46
1939	ChiC	4(3)	5	-6	-1.2	0	3	67	22.3	0	1	1	100.0	2	2.0(2)	0	0	—	—	—	—	—	0	29
NFL	2	12(3)	15	27	1.8	0	5	93	18.6	0	2	1	50.0	2	1.0(2)	0	0	—	—	—	—	1	6	75

Reed, Smith Smith Wayne, HB, 6´0˝/215 lbs; Alcorn State; 1965: NYG, rnd 19/KC, rnd 5; B6/25/1942 Vicksburg, MS **1966** NYG 1

YEAR	TEAM	G(GS, POS)	RUSH	YD	AVG(LG)	TD	REC	YD	AVG(LG)	TD	PASS	COMP	PCT	YD	AVG(LG)	TD	INT	SK	YD	QBR	KPR	OTD	PTS	TAY
1965	NYG	10	19	70	3.7(17)	0	6	42	7.0(16)	0	—	—	—	—	—	—	—	—	—	—	—	—	0	91
NFL	2	11	19	70	3.7(17)	0	6	42	7.0(16)	0	—	—	—	—	—	—	—	—	—	—	—	—	0	91

Reed, Taft Taft, DB, 6´2˝/200 lbs; Jackson State; 1966: Phi, rnd 19/SD, rnd 9; B6/12/1942 Hattiesburg, MS **1967** Phi 6

Reed, Tony Anthony Wayne, RB, 5´11˝/197 lbs; Colorado; 1977: KC, rnd 2; B3/30/1955 San Francisco, CA

YEAR	TEAM	G(GS, POS)	RUSH	YD	AVG(LG)	TD	REC	YD	AVG(LG)	TD	PASS	COMP	PCT	YD	AVG(LG)	TD	INT	SK	YD	QBR	KPR	OTD	PTS	TAY
1977	KC	14(8, RB)	126	505	4.0(59)	2	12	125	10.4(20)	0	—	—	—	—	—	—	—	—	—	—	k	—	12	662
1978	KC	16(16, LH)	206	1053	5.1(62)	5	48	483	10.1(44)	1	—	—	—	—	—	—	—	—	—	—	—	—	36	1350
1979	KC	11(11, RB)	113	446	3.9(23)	1	34	352	10.4(40)	0	—	—	—	—	—	—	—	—	—	—	—	—	6	632
1980	KC	15(7, RB)	68	180	2.6(24)	0	44	422	9.6(34)	1	—	—	—	—	—	—	—	—	—	—	—	—	6	396
1981	Den	15(0)	68	156	2.3(10)	0	34	317	9.3(33)	0	1	0	0.0	0	0.0	0	1	—	—	—	—	—	0	275
NFL	5	71(42)	581	2340	4.0(62)	8	172	1699	9.9(44)	2	1	0	0.0	0	0.0	0	1	—	—	—	k	—	60	3314

Reeder, Dan Daniel Robert, RB, 5´11˝/235 lbs; Boston College; Delaware; 1985: LARd, rnd 5; B3/18/1961 Shamokin, PA

YEAR	TEAM	G(GS, POS)	RUSH	YD	AVG(LG)	TD	REC	YD	AVG(LG)	TD	PASS	COMP	PCT	YD	AVG(LG)	TD	INT	SK	YD	QBR	KPR	OTD	PTS	TAY
1986	Pit	11(0)	6	20	3.3(6)	0	2	4	2.0(3)	0	—	—	—	—	—	—	—	—	—	—	k	—	0	14
1987	Pit	2(0)	2	8	4.0(4)	0	—	—	—	—	—	—	—	—	—	—	—	—	—	—	—	—	0	8
NFL	2	13(0)	8	28	3.5(6)	0	2	4	2.0(3)	0	—	—	—	—	—	—	—	—	—	—	k	—	0	22

Reese, Albert Albert, DT, 6´6˝/275 lbs; Grambling State; B4/29/1973 Mobile, AL **1997**†SF 5 (0)

Reese, Allen Allen Bernard, DT, 5´10˝/294 lbs; Kansas State; B10/10/1980 Bartow, FL **2003** KC 2 (0)

Reese, Archie Archie Ronald Bernard, DE-NT-DT, 6´3˝/267 lbs; Clemson; 1978: SF, rnd 5; B2/4/1956 Mayesville, SC **1978** SF 16 (13, LDE) **1979** SF 16 (16, LDE) **1980** SF 16 (16, LDT/nt) **1981**†SF 16 (16, NT) **1982**†LARd 9 (0) **1983** LARd 10 (0) **NFL** 83 (61) [6 yrs]

Reese, Booker Booker Ted, DE, 6´0˝/260 lbs; Bethune-Cookman; 1982: TB, rnd 2; B9/20/1959 Jacksonville, FL **1982**†TB 7 (0) **1983** TB 16 (7, lde) **1984** TB 1 (0) **1984** LARm 9 (0) **1985** LARm 2 (0) **NFL** 35 (7) [4 yrs]

Reese, Dave David E., E, 6´0˝/176 lbs; Denison; B11/19/1892 Massillon, OH, D6/26/1978 Dayton, OH **1920** Day 9 (7, RE) **1921** Day 9 (9, RE), 6 **1922** Day 8 (8, RE) **1923** Day 8 (8, RE) **NFL** 34 (32) [4 yrs]

Reese, Don Donald Francis, DT-DE, 6´6˝/254 lbs; Jackson State; 1974: Mia, rnd 1; B9/4/1951 Mobile, AL, D9/18/2003 Prichard, AL **1974**†Mia 13 **1975** Mia 14 (11, RDT) **1976** Mia 14 (9, RDT) **1978** NO 14 **1979** NO 16 (12, RDE) **1980** NO 12 (3) **1981** SD 5 (2) **NFL** 88 (37) [7 yrs]

Reese, Guy Guy Price, DT, 6´5˝/258 lbs; SMU; 1962: Dal, rnd 15/DalT, rnd 11; B9/22/1939 Dallas, TX **1962** Dal 14 (LDT) **1963** Dal 14 (14, LDT) **1964**†Bal 14 **1965**†Bal 13 **1966** Atl 2 **NFL** 57 (14) [5 yrs]

Reese, Hank Henry L., C-G, 5´11˝/214 lbs; Temple; B10/24/1909 Scranton, PA, D8/3/1975 Ocean City, NJ **[K]** **1933** NYG 11 (5, c) **1934** NYG 13 (6, lg) **1935** Phi 11 (11, C) **1936** Phi 10 (10, C) **1937** Phi 11 (8, C) **1938** Phi 11 (2) **1939** Phi 5 (3) **NFL** 72 (45) [7 yrs]

Reese, Ike Isaiah, LB, 6´2˝/222 lbs; Michigan State; 1998: Phi, rnd 5; B10/16/1973 Jacksonville, NC **1998** Phi 16 (0) **1999** Phi 16 (0) **2000**†Phi 16 (0) **2001** Phi 16 (0) **2002**†Phi 16 (3) **2003**†Phi 16 (1) **2004**†Phi★16 (1) **2005** Atl 16 (0) **NFL** 128 (5) [8 yrs]

Reese, Izell Izell, DB, 6´2˝/195 lbs; Alabama-Birmingham; 1998: Dal, rnd 6; B5/7/1974 Dothan, AL **1998**†Dal 16 (0) **1999** Dal 8 (4) **2000** Dal 16 (7, fs) **2001** Dal 16 (4) **2002** Den 15 (15, FS) **2003** Buf 13 (9, FS) **2004** Buf 9 (9, FS) **NFL** 93 (48) [7 yrs]

Reese, Jerry Jerry, DE, 6´2˝/267 lbs; Kentucky; 1988: Pit, rnd 5; B7/11/1964 Hopkinsville, KY **1988** Pit 15 (0)

Reese, Jerry Jerry Maurice, WR, 5´11˝/190 lbs; San Jose State; B3/18/1973 Berkeley, CA

YEAR	TEAM	G(GS, POS)	RUSH	YD	AVG(LG)	TD	REC	YD	AVG(LG)	TD	PASS	COMP	PCT	YD	AVG(LG)	TD	INT	SK	YD	QBR	KPR	OTD	PTS	TAY
1997	Buf	5(0)	—	—	—	—	1	13	13.0(13)	0	—	—	—	—	—	—	—	—	—	—	—	—	0	7

Reese, Jerry Jerry Louis, DB, 6´3˝/192 lbs; Oklahoma; B1/7/1955 New Orleans, LA **1979** KC 7 (SS) **1980** KC 14 (0) **NFL** 21 [2 yrs]

Reese, Ken Kenneth Earl, HB-QB, 5´11˝/175 lbs; Alabama; 1945: Phi, rnd 31; B4/30/1921 El Dorado, AR, D3/1978 Tuscaloosa, AL

YEAR	TEAM	G(GS, POS)	RUSH	YD	AVG(LG)	TD	REC	YD	AVG(LG)	TD	PASS	COMP	PCT	YD	AVG(LG)	TD	INT	SK	YD	QBR	KPR	OTD	PTS	TAY
1947	Det	4(0)	3	1	0.3(5)	0	—	—	—	—	—	—	—	—	—	—	—	—	—	—	k	—	0	11

Reese, Lloyd Lloyd George, B, 6´2˝/240 lbs; Tennessee; B6/17/1920 New Philadelphia, OH, D10/28/1981 Dover, OH

YEAR	TEAM	G(GS, POS)	RUSH	YD	AVG(LG)	TD	REC	YD	AVG(LG)	TD	PASS	COMP	PCT	YD	AVG(LG)	TD	INT	SK	YD	QBR	KPR	OTD	PTS	TAY
1946	ChiB	3(0)	18	84	4.7(16)	2	—	—	—	—	—	—	—	—	—	—	—	—	—	—	—	—	12	104

Reese, Marcus Marcus Harrison, LB, 6´1˝/233 lbs; UCLA; B6/15/1981 San Jose, CA **2004** ChiB 11 (2)

Reese, Steve Stephen, LB, 6´2˝/229 lbs; Louisville; B1/7/1952 Columbus, GA **1974** NYJ 11 **1975** NYJ 12 **1976** TB 12 (10, MLB) **NFL** 35 (10) [3 yrs]

Reeve, Lew Lew Parks, T, 5´10˝/193 lbs; Iowa State; B10/16/1890 Hampton, IA, D5/11/1960 Austin, MN **1920** ChiT 3 (2)

YEAR	TEAM	G (GS, POS)	RUSH	YD	AVG(LG)	TD	REC	YD	AVG(LG)	TD	PASS	COMP	PCT	YD	AVG(LG)	TD	INT	SK	YD	QBR	KPR	OTD	PTS	TAY

REEVES, BRYAN — Bryan, WR, 5´11˝/195 lbs; Arizona State; Nevada-Reno; B7/10/1970 Los Angeles, CA

1994	Arz	14(0)	1	-1	-1.0(-1)	0	14	202	14.4(33)	1	—	—	—	—	—	—	—	—	—	—	kp	—	6	139
1995	Arz	5(0)	—	—	—	—	6	62	10.3(22)	0	—	—	—	—	—	—	—	—	—	—	p	—	0	52
NFL	2	19(0)	1	-1	-1.0(-1)	0	20	264	13.2(33)	1	—	—	—	—	—	—	—	—	—	—	kp	—	6	191

REEVES, CARL — Carl Don Mark, DE, 6´4˝/270 lbs; North Carolina State; 1995: Chi, rnd 6; B12/17/1971 Durham, NC   **1996** ChiB 5 (0)   **1997** ChiB 15 (10, RDE)   **1998** ChiB 11 (0)   **NFL** 31 (10) [3 yrs]

REEVES, DAN — Daniel Edward, RB, 6´1˝/200 lbs; South Carolina; B1/19/1944 Rome, GA; HOF 1967 [KC]

1965	Dal	13(4)	33	102	3.1(13)	2	9	210	23.3(47)	1	2	1	50.0	11	5.5(11)	0	0	—	—	—	k	—	18	253
1966	†Dal☆	14(HB)	175	757	4.3(67)	8	41	557	13.6(51)	8	6	3	50.0	48	8.0(29)	0	0	—	—	—	kp	—	96	1180
1967	†Dal	14(HB)	173	603	3.5(32)	5	39	490	12.6(60)	6	7	4	57.1	195	27.9(74)	2	1	—	—	—	—	—	66	996
1968	†Dal	4(4)	40	178	4.4(25)	4	7	84	12.0(21)	1	4	2	50.0	43	10.8(24)	0	0	—	—	—	—	—	30	287
1969	†Dal	13	59	173	2.9(14)	4	18	187	10.4(29)	1	3	1	33.3	35	11.7(35)	0	1	2	14	—	—	—	30	289
1970	†Dal	14	35	84	2.4(8)	2	12	140	11.7(23)	0	3	1	33.3	14	4.7(14)	0	1	—	—	—	p	—	12	141
1971	†Dal	14	17	79	4.6(22)	0	3	25	8.3(11)	0	5	2	40.0	24	4.8(14)	0	1	—	—	—	K	—	1	64
1972	Dal	14	3	14	4.7(14)	0	—	—	—	—	2	0	0.0	0	—	0	0	—	—	—	—	—	0	14
NFL	8	100(8)	535	1990	3.7(67)	25	129	1693	13.1(60)	17	32	14	43.8	370	11.6(74)	2	4	2	14	—	Kkp	—	253	3222

REEVES, JACQUES — Jacques D., DB, 6´1˝/183 lbs; Purdue; 2004: Dal, rnd 7; B10/8/1982 Lancaster, TX   **2004** Dal 15 (1)   **2005** Dal 16 (0)   **NFL** 31 (1) [2 yrs]

REEVES, JOHN — John Edwin, LB, 6´3˝/245 lbs; Purdue; B2/23/1975 Bradenton, FL   **1999** SD 5 (0)   **2000** SD 9 (0)   **NFL** 14 (0) [2 yrs]

REEVES, KEN — Kenneth Wayne, T-G, 6´5˝/270 lbs; Texas A&M; 1985: Phi, rnd 6; B10/4/1961 Pittsburg, TX   **1985** Phi 15 (13, LT)   **1986** Phi 15 (15, LG/lt)   **1987** Phi 10 (0)   **1988** †Phi 15 (1)   **1989** Phi 14 (3)   **1990** Cle 16 (0)   **NFL** 85 (32) [6 yrs]

REEVES, MARION — Marion Francis, DB, 6´1˝/195 lbs; Clemson; B2/23/1952 Lexington, SC   **1974** Phi 14

REEVES, ROY — Roy Don, WR, 6´0˝/182 lbs; South Carolina; 1969: Hou, rnd 14; B2/8/1946 Americus, GA   **1969** Buf-A 2

REEVES, WALTER — Walter James, TE, 6´4˝/270 lbs; Auburn; 1989: Phx, rnd 2; B12/16/1965 Eufaula, AL

1989	Phx	16(3)	—	—	—	—	1	5	5.0(5)	0	—	—	—	—	—	—	—	—	—	—	k	—	0	-8
1990	Phx	16(16, TE)	—	—	—	—	18	126	7.0(16)	0	—	—	—	—	—	—	—	—	—	—	—	—	0	63
1991	Phx	15(13, TE)	—	—	—	—	8	45	5.6(13)	0	—	—	—	—	—	—	—	—	—	—	—	—	0	23
1992	Phx	16(16, TE)	—	—	—	—	6	28	4.7(12)	0	—	—	—	—	—	—	—	—	—	—	—	—	0	14
1993	Phx	16(15, TE)	—	—	—	—	9	67	7.4(18)	1	—	—	—	—	—	—	—	—	—	—	—	—	6	39
1994	Cle	5(5, te)	—	—	—	—	6	61	10.2(12)	1	—	—	—	—	—	—	—	—	—	—	—	—	6	36
1995	Cle	5(3)	—	—	—	—	6	12	2.0(3)	1	—	—	—	—	—	—	—	—	—	—	—	—	6	11
1996	SD	9(1)	—	—	—	—	1	3	3.0(3)	0	—	—	—	—	—	—	—	—	—	—	—	—	0	2
NFL	8	98(72)	—	—	—	—	55	347	6.3(22)	4	—	—	—	—	—	—	—	—	—	—	k	—	18	179

REGAN, JIM — James, BB, /172 lbs; Still   **1925** Col 3 (3)

REGENT, SHAWN — Shawn Michael, C, 6´5˝/280 lbs; Boston College; B4/14/1963 Buffalo, NY   **1987** LARd 3 (3)

REGER, JOHN — John George, LB-G, 6´0˝/225 lbs; Pittsburgh; B9/11/1931 Wheeling, WV   **1955** Pit 12 (RLB)   **1956** Pit 12 (RLB)   **1957** Pit 12 (RLB)   **1958** Pit 12 (RLB)   **1959** Pit★12 (RLB)   **1960** Pit★12 (RLB)   **1961** Pit★14 (RLB)   **1962** Pit 9 (RLB)   **1963** Pit 9   **1964** Was 14 (14, LLB)   **1965** Was 12 (LLB)   **1966** Was 14 (LLB)   **NFL** 144 (14) [12 yrs]

REGNER, TOM — Thomas Eugene, G, 6´1˝/235 lbs; Notre Dame; 1967: Hou, rnd 1; B4/19/1944 Kenosha, WI   **1967** †Hou-A 14 (3)   **1968** Hou-A 14 (LG)   **1969** †Hou-A 14 (LG)   **1970** Hou 3   **1971** Hou 8   **1972** Hou 14 (LG)   **NFL** 67 (3) [6 yrs]

REGNIER, PETE — Pierre Norman, WB-HB, /170 lbs; Minnesota; B9/1896 Marshall, MN, deceased   **1921** Min 4 (4, WB)   **1922** GB 5 (4)   **NFL** 9 (8) [2 yrs]

REGULAR, MOSES — Moses, LB, 6´3˝/255 lbs; Missouri Valley; B10/30/1971 Kissimmee, FL   **1996** NYG 3 (0)

REHAGE, STEVE — Stephen Michael, DB, 6´1˝/190 lbs; LSU; B11/6/1963 New Orleans, LA   **1987** NYG 3 (3)

REHBERG, SCOTT — Scott Joseph, G-T, 6´8˝/325 lbs; Central Michigan; 1997: NE, rnd 7; B11/17/1973 Kalamazoo, MI   **1997** NE 6 (0)   **1998** NE 2 (0)   **1999** Cle 15 (13, RG)   **2000** Cin 10 (6, lg)   **2001** Cin 14 (4)   **2002** Cin 16 (3)   **2003** Cin 16 (1)   **NFL** 79 (27) [7 yrs]

REHDER, TOM — Thomas Bernard, T-G, 6´7˝/280 lbs; Notre Dame; 1988: NE, rnd 3; B1/27/1965 Sacramento, CA   **1988** NE 16 (0)   **1989** NE 16 (0)   **1990** NYG 8 (0)   **NFL** 40 (0) [3 yrs]

REHNQUIST, MILT — Milton, G-C-T, 6´0˝/229 lbs; Bethany (KS); B1897, deceased   **1924** KC 3 (0)   **1925** KC 7 (5, LG)   **1925** Cle 4 (4)   **1926** KC 10 (9, RG)   **1927** Cle☆13 (12, LG)   **1928** Pro☆11 (11, LG)   **1929** Pro☆8 (7, C)   **1930** Pro 10 (7, LG)   **1931** Pro 2 (0)   **1931** NYG 8 (1)   **1932** Bos 1 (0)   **NFL** 77 (56) [9 yrs]

REICH, FRANK — Frank Michael, QB, 6´4˝/210 lbs; Maryland; 1985: Buf, rnd 3; B12/4/1961 Freeport, NY

1985	Buf	1(0)	—	—	—	—	—	—	—	—	1	1	100.0	19	19.0(19)	0	0	—	—	—	—	—	0	10
1986	Buf	3(0)	1	0	0.0(0)	0	—	—	—	—	19	9	47.4	104	5.5(37)	0	2	2	4	—	—	—	0	-28
1988	Buf	3(0)	3	-3	-1.0(-1)	0	—	—	—	—	—	—	—	—	—	—	—	—	—	—	—	—	0	-3
1989	Buf	7(3)	9	30	3.3(9)	0	—	—	—	—	87	53	60.9	701	8.1(63)	7	2	4	24	—	—	—	0	336
1990	†Buf	16(2)	15	24	1.6(9)	0	—	—	—	—	63	36	57.1	469	7.4(43)	2	0	6	41	—	—	—	0	269
1991	†Buf	16(1)	13	6	0.5(8)	0	—	—	—	—	41	27	65.9	305	7.4(29)	6	2	4	42	—	—	—	0	109
1992	†Buf	16(0)	9	-9	-1.0(0)	0	—	—	—	—	47	24	51.1	221	4.7(21)	0	2	9	76	—	—	—	0	22
1993	†Buf	15(0)	6	-6	-1.0(-1)	0	—	—	—	—	26	16	61.5	153	5.9(30)	2	0	6	47	—	—	—	0	81
1994	Buf	16(2)	6	3	0.5(5)	0	—	—	—	—	93	56	60.2	568	6.1(47)	1	4	7	57	—	—	—	0	132
1995	Car	3(3)	1	3	3.0(3)	0	—	—	—	—	84	37	44.0	441	5.3(46)	2	2	12	100	—	—	—	0	154
1996	NYJ	11(7, QB)	18	31	1.7(10)	0	—	—	—	—	331	175	52.9	2205	6.7(52)	15	16	14	94	68.9	—	—	0	569
1997	†Det	6(0)	4	-4	-1.0(4)	0	—	—	—	—	30	11	36.7	121	4.0(27)	0	2	—	—	—	—	—	0	-24
1998	Det	6(2)	6	3	0.5(5)	0	—	—	—	—	110	63	57.3	768	7.0(41)	5	4	4	18	—	—	—	0	252
NFL	13	119(20)	91	78	0.9(10)	0	—	—	—	—	932	508	54.5	6075	6.5(63)	40	36	68	503	72.9	—	—	0	1876

REICHARDT, BILL — William John, FB, 5´11˝/210 lbs; Iowa; 1952: GB, rnd 7; B6/24/1930 Iowa City, IA, D6/1/2004 Des Moines, IA [K]

| 1952 | GB | 12 | 39 | 121 | 3.1(14) | 1 | 5 | 18 | 3.6(12) | 0 | — | — | — | — | — | — | — | — | — | — | Kk | — | 26 | 144 |

REICHEL, LOU — Louis John, C, 5´11˝/180 lbs; Butler; B1902, deceased [K]   **1926** Col 7 (7, C), 2

REICHENBACH, MIKE — John Michael, LB, 6´2˝/235 lbs; East Stroudsburg; B9/14/1961 Fort Meade, MD   **1984** Phi 12 (1)   **1985** Phi 16 (16, LILB)   **1986** Phi 16 (16, MLB)   **1987** Phi 16 (9, MLB)   **1988** †Phi 11 (11, MLB)   **1990** Mia 16 (0)   **1991** Mia 16 (15, RILB/lilb)

| 1989 | †Phi | 16(4) | 1 | 30 | 30.0(30) | 0 | — | — | — | — | — | — | — | — | — | — | — | — | — | — | — | — | 0 | 30 |
| NFL | 8 | 119(72) | 1 | 30 | 30.0(30) | 0 | — | — | — | — | — | — | — | — | — | — | — | — | — | — | iS | — | 0 | 32 |

REICHLE, DICK — Richard Wendell, E, 6´0˝/190 lbs; Illinois; B11/23/1896 Lincoln, IL, D6/13/1967 Richmond Heights, MO   **1923** Mil☆6 (6, RE)

REICHOW, CHUCK — Charles J., B, 5´9˝/183 lbs; St. Thomas; B3/19/1901 St. Paul, MN, D3/29/1993 Peoria, AZ   **1925** Mil 2 (0)   **1926** Rac 5 (5, FB)   **NFL** 7 (5) [2 yrs]

REICHOW, JERRY — Garret Neal, E-QB, 6´2˝/217 lbs; Iowa; 1956: Det, rnd 4; B5/19/1934 Decorah, IA

1956	Det	8	1	1	1.0(1)	0	4	63	15.8(41)	1	6	3	50.0	19	3.2(14)	0	1	—	—	—	k	—	6	1
1957	†Det	12	2	9	4.5(7)	0	17	215	12.6(32)	3	2	0	0.0	0	0.0	0	0	—	—	—	—	—	18	132
1959	Det	9	13	98	7.5(46)	0	7	118	16.9(32)	1	27	9	33.3	168	6.2(41)	0	2	—	—	—	—	—	6	166
1960	†Phi	12	—	—	—	—	—	—	—	—	—	—	—	—	—	—	—	—	—	—	—	—	0	-32
1961	Min☆	14(10, WR)	3	9	3.0(21)	0	50	859	17.2(51)	11	3	0	0.0	0	0.0	0	1	—	—	—	—	—	66	454
1962	Min	12(12, WR)	—	—	—	—	39	561	14.4(41)	3	—	—	—	—	—	—	—	—	—	—	—	—	18	296
1963	Min	14(14, WR)	1	-12	-12.0(-12)	0	35	479	13.7(57)	3	—	—	—	—	—	—	—	—	—	—	—	—	18	243
1964	Min	14(14, WR)	—	—	—	—	20	284	14.2(51)	2	—	—	—	—	—	—	—	—	—	—	—	—	12	152
NFL	8	95(48)	20	105	5.3(46)	0	172	2579	15.0(57)	24	38	12	31.6	187	4.9(41)	0	4	—	—	—	k	—	144	1410

REID, ALAN — Alan DeWitt, RB, 5´8˝/190 lbs; TCU; Minnesota; B9/6/1960 Wurzburg, Germany   **1987** Phi 1 (0)

REID, ANDY — Andrew Barton, RB, 6´0˝/194 lbs; Georgia; 1976: Sea, rnd 13; B2/26/1954 Hamilton, OH   **1976** Buf 1

REID, BILL — William John, C, 6´1˝/242 lbs; Stanford; B5/2/1952 Long Beach, CA   **1975** SF 13 (13, C)

YEAR	TEAM	G(GS, POS)	RUSH	YD	AVG(LG)	TD	REC	YD	AVG(LG)	TD	PASS	COMP	PCT	YD	AVG(LG)	TD	INT	SK	YD	QBR	KPR	OTD	PTS	TAY

REID, BREEZY Floyd, HB, 5'10"/187 lbs; Georgia; 1950: ChiB, rnd 9; B9/14/1927 Bridgeton, NJ, D3/15/1994 Cincinnati, OH

1950	GB	11(LH)	87	394	4.5(57)	1	11	120	10.9(44)	2	—	—	—	—	—	—	—	—	—	—	—	—	18	474
1951	GB	12	23	73	3.2(33)	0	9	115	12.8(29)	0	1	0	0.0	0	0.0	0	0	0	—	—	—	—	0	131
1952	GB	12(RH)	58	156	2.7(14)	2	12	250	20.8(81)	2	—	—	—	—	—	—	—	—	—	—	—	—	24	311
1953	GB	12(LH)	95	492	5.2(43)	3	10	100	10.0(26)	0	—	—	—	—	—	—	—	—	—	—	k	—	18	594
1954	GB	12(LH)	99	507	5.1(69)	5	14	129	9.2(25)	0	—	—	—	—	—	—	—	—	—	—	—	—	30	622
1955	GB	12(LH)	83	303	3.7(28)	2	13	138	10.6(60)	1	—	—	—	—	—	—	—	—	—	—	k	—	18	388
1956	GB	7	14	39	2.8(11)	0	3	16	5.3(12)	0	—	—	—	—	—	—	—	—	—	—	p	—	0	42
NFL	7	78	459	1964	4.3(69)	13	72	868	12.1(81)	5	1	0	0.0	0	0.0	0	0	0	—	—	kp	—	108	2561

REID, DARRELL Darrell, DE, 6'2"/288 lbs; Minnesota; B6/20/1982 Farmingdale, NJ **2005**†Ind 8 (1)

REID, DEXTER Dexter Devon, DB, 5'11"/200 lbs; North Carolina; 2004: NE, rnd 4; B3/18/1981 Norfolk, VA **2004**†NE 13 (2) **2005**†Ind 16 (0) **NFL** 29 (2) [2 yrs]

REID, GABE Gabriel, TE, 6'4"/260 lbs; Brigham Young; B5/28/1977 Pago Pago, American Samoa **2003** ChiB 1 (0)

| 2005 | †ChiB | 16(3) | — | — | — | — | 3 | 20 | 6.7(10) | 0 | — | — | — | — | — | — | — | — | — | — | — | — | 0 | 10 |
| NFL | 2 | 17(3) | — | — | — | — | 3 | 20 | 6.7(10) | 0 | — | — | — | — | — | — | — | — | — | — | — | — | 0 | 10 |

REID, JIM James Varrett, T-G, 6'6"/306 lbs; Virginia; 1994: Hou, rnd 5; B2/13/1971 Newport News, VA **1995** Hou 6 (0)

REID, JOE Joseph Edmondson, LB-C-DG, 6'3"/225 lbs; LSU; 1951: LA, rnd 13; B3/18/1929 Meridian, MS **1951**†LARm 11 **1952** DalT 11 (RLB) **NFL** 22 [2 yrs]

REID, LAMONT Lamont, DB, 6'0"/187 lbs; North Carolina State; B5/4/1982 Concord, NC **2005** Arz 10 (1)

REID, MICHAEL Michael Edward, LB, 6'2"/226 lbs; Wisconsin; 1987: Atl, rnd 7; B6/25/1964 Albany, GA **1987** Atl 11 (0) **1988** Atl 16 (3) **1989** Atl 16 (3) **1990** Atl 6 (4) **1991**†Atl 2 (0) **1992** Atl 16 (1) **NFL** 67 (11) [6 yrs]

REID, MIKE Michael Barry, DT, 6'3"/255 lbs; Penn State; 1970: Cin, rnd 1; B5/24/1947 Altoona, PA **1970**†Cin 9 (LDT) **1971** Cin☆14 (LDT) **1972** Cin★14 (LDT) **1973**†Cin★13 (LDT) **1974** Cin★14 (LDT) **NFL** 64 [5 yrs]

REID, MIKE Michael Fitzgerald, DB, 6'1"/218 lbs; North Carolina State; 1993: Phi, rnd 3; B11/24/1970 Spartanburg, SC **1993** Phi 9 (0) **1994** Phi 3 (0) **NFL** 12 (0) [2 yrs]

REID, SPENCER Spencer Eldon Karene, LB, 6'1"/247 lbs; Brigham Young; B2/8/1976 Pago Pago, American Samoa **1998** Car 16 (0) **1999**†Ind 12 (0) **NFL** 28 (0) [2 yrs]

REIFSNYDER, BOB Robert Harland, DE, 6'2"/250 lbs; Navy; 1959: LA, rnd 4; B6/18/1937 Brooklyn, NY **1960** NYT-A 14 (LDE) **1961** NYT-A 2 **NFL** 16 [2 yrs]

REIHNER, GEORGE George Arthur, G, 6'4"/263 lbs; Penn State; 1977: Hou, rnd 2; B4/27/1955 Pittsburgh, PA **1977** Hou 13 (LG) **1978**†Hou 9 (LG) **1979**†Hou 2 **1982** Hou 3 (1) **NFL** 27 (1) [4 yrs]

REILLY, DAMEON Dameon Elliott, WR, 5'11"/180 lbs; Rhode Island; B5/10/1963 Bronx, NY

| 1987 | Mia | 3(1) | — | — | — | — | 5 | 70 | 14.0(20) | 0 | — | — | — | — | — | — | — | — | — | — | — | — | 0 | 35 |

REILLY, JIM James Christopher, G, 6'2"/260 lbs; Notre Dame; 1970: Buf, rnd 3; B2/8/1948 Yonkers, NY, D8/10/1994 Greenburgh, NY **1970** Buf 13 (lg) **1971** Buf 14 (LG) **NFL** 27 [2 yrs]

REILLY, KEVIN Kevin Patrick, LB, 6'2"/220 lbs; Villanova; 1973: Mia, rnd 7; B4/10/1951 Wilmington, DE **1973** Phi 7 **1974** Phi 14 **1975** NE 4 (1) **NFL** 25 (1) [3 yrs]

REILLY, MIKE Charles Michael, LB, 6'3"/225 lbs; Iowa; 1964: Chi, rnd 4/Buf, rnd 5; B3/17/1942 Dubuque, IA **1964** ChiB 8 **1965** ChiB 14 **1966** ChiB 14 **1967** ChiB 14 **1968** ChiB 14 **1969**†Min 10 **NFL** 74 [6 yrs]

REILLY, MIKE Michael Dennis, LB, 6'4"/217 lbs; Oklahoma; 1982: LARm, rnd 8; B2/14/1959 Miami, FL **1982** LARm 9 (2)

REIMERS, BRUCE Bruce Michael, G-T, 6'7"/285 lbs; Iowa State; 1984: Cin, rnd 8; B9/28/1960 Algona, IA **1984** Cin 15 (0) **1985** Cin 14 (0) **1986** Cin 16 (5, lg) **1987** Cin 10 (8, LG) **1988**†Cin 16 (16, LG) **1989** Cin 15 (15, LG) **1990**†Cin 12 (12, LG) **1991** Cin 10 (8, LG) **1992** TB 16 (16, LG) **1993** TB 11 (10, LG) **NFL** 135 (90) [10 yrs]

REINFELDT, MIKE Michael Ray, DB, 6'2"/192 lbs; Wisconsin-Milwaukee; B5/6/1953 Baraboo, WI [I] **1976** Oak 2 **1976** Hou 11 (11, SS) **1977** Hou 14 (14, FS) **1978**†Hou 16 (16, FS) **1979**†Hou★16 (16, FS) **1980**†Hou☆16 (16, FS) **1981** Hou 16 (16, FS) **1982** Hou 9 (9, FS) **1983** Hou 4 (4) **NFL** 104 (102) [8 yrs]

REINHARD, BILL William Carl, B, 5'10"/168 lbs; California; 1944: Was, rnd 23; B5/17/1922 Los Angeles, CA

1947	LAD-A	8(0)	1	2	2.0(2)	—	2	0	0.0	0	—	—	0.0	0	0.0	0	0	—	—	—	pi	—	6	26
1948	LAD-A	14(1)	6	31	5.2	0	5	48	9.6	0	5	0	0.0	0	0.0	0	0	—	—	—	kpi	2	12	314
AAFC	2	22(1)	7	33	4.7(2)	1	5	48	9.6	0	7	0	0.0	0	0.0	0	0	—	—	—	kpi	2	18	340

REINHARD, BOB Robert Richard, T-FB, 6'4"/234 lbs; California; 1942: ChiC, rnd 5; B10/17/1920 Hollywood, CA, D8/2/1996 Eugene, OR

1946	LAD-A☆	14(14, LT)	1	-30	-30.0(-30)	—	—	1	1	100.0	7	7.0(7)	0	0	—	—	—	P	1	6	-27
1947	LAD-A	14(11, FB)	41	150	3.7	0	3	34	11.3	1	4	2	50.0	21	5.3	0	0	—	—	—	Pki	—	6	175
1948	LAD-A	14(14, LT)	1	21	21.0(21)	0	4	54	13.5	0	—	—	—	—	—	—	—	—	—	—	Pkp	—	0	72
1949	LAD-A☆	12(12, LT)	—	—	—	—	1	2	2.0(2)	0	—	—	—	—	—	—	—	—	—	—	Pkp	—	0	1
AAFC	4	54(51)	43	141	3.3(21)	0	8	90	11.3(2)	1	5	3	60.0	28	5.6(7)	0	0	—	—	—	Pkpi	1	12	221
1950	†LARm☆	12(RT)	—	—	—	—	1	11	11.0(11)	0	—	—	—	—	—	—	—	—	—	—	—	—	6	11

REINKE, JEFF Jeffrey Jay, DE, 6'4"/262 lbs; Mankato State; 1986: LARd, rnd 10; B9/12/1962 Granite Falls, MN **1987** Cin 1 (1)

REISER, EARL Earl, BB-WB, /160 lbs; none; B1899, deceased **1923** Lou 2 (2, BB)

REISSIG, BILL William George, BB-LB-DE, 6'0"/195 lbs; Fort Hays State; B11/2/1915 Bunker Hill, KS, D7/8/1996 St. John, KS [K] **1938** Bkn 11 (4) **1939** Bkn 11 (0) **NFL** 22 (4) [2 yrs]

REISZ, ALBIE Albert Harry, TB-HB-QB, 5'10"/175 lbs; Southeastern Louisiana; B11/29/1917 Lorain, OH, D5/1/1985 New Orleans, LA

1944	Cle	10(2, tb)	69	134	1.9(46)	2	—	—	—	—	113	49	43.4	777	6.9(70)	8	10	—	—	53.6	Pkpi	—	12	388
1945	†Cle	10(0)	12	-2	-0.2(16)	0	1	11	11.0(11)	0	21	8	38.1	146	7.0(44)	2	3	—	—	—	Ppi	—	0	50
1946	LARm	2(1)	—	—	—	—	—	—	—	—	—	—	—	—	—	—	—	—	—	—	—	—	—	—
NFL	3	22(3)	81	132	1.6(46)	2	1	11	11.0(11)	0	134	57	42.5	923	6.9(70)	10	13	—	—	51.5	Pkpi	—	12	437
1947	Buf-A	13(0)	2	32	16.0	0	—	—	—	—	—	—	—	—	—	—	—	—	—	—	P	—	0	32

REITER, PECK Herbert Gustave, G-E, 5'9"/185 lbs; Miami (OH); Marietta; B2/15/1899 Dayton, OH, D5/15/1968 Los Angeles, CA **1926** Day 6 (6, RG) **1927** Day 2 (1) **NFL** 8 (7) [2 yrs]

REMBERT, JOHNNY John Lee, LB, 6'3"/234 lbs; Clemson; 1983: NE, rnd 4; B1/19/1961 Hollandale, MS **1983** NE 15 (8, LILB) **1984** NE 7 (0) **1985**†NE 16 (6, rilb) **1986**†NE 16 (10, rilb) **1987** NE 11 (1) **1988** NE★16 (15, RILB) **1989** NE◇16 (16, LOLB/rilb) **1990** NE 5 (5, lilb) **1991** NE 12 (1) **1992** NE 12 (10, RILB) **NFL** 126 (72) [10 yrs]

REMBERT, REGGIE Reginald Bernard, WR, 6'5"/200 lbs; West Virginia; 1990: NYJ, rnd 2; B12/25/1966 Okeechobee, FL

1991	Cin	16(0)	—	—	—	—	9	117	13.0(23)	1	—	—	—	—	—	—	—	—	—	—	—	—	6	64
1992	Cin	9(4)	—	—	—	—	19	219	11.5(27)	0	—	—	—	—	—	—	—	—	—	—	—	—	0	110
1993	Cin	3(0)	—	—	—	—	8	101	12.6(21)	0	—	—	—	—	—	—	—	—	—	—	—	—	0	51
NFL	3	28(4)	—	—	—	—	36	437	12.1(27)	1	—	—	—	—	—	—	—	—	—	—	—	—	6	224

REMINGTON, BILL Joseph William, C-LB, 6'1"/185 lbs; Washington State; 1943: Det, rnd 24; B11/2/1920 **1946** SF-A 9 (1)

REMMERT, DENNIS Dennis, LB, 6'3"/215 lbs; Northern Iowa; B1939 Traer, IA **1960** Buf-A 2

REMO, ROGER Roger M., LB, 6'3"/237 lbs; Syracuse; B8/7/1964 **1987** Ind 3 (0)

REMSBERG, DAN Daniel Lloyd, T, 6'6"/275 lbs; Abilene Christian; 1985: SD, rnd 9; B4/7/1962 Temple, TX **1986**†Den 16 (1) **1987** Den 5 (0) **NFL** 21 (1) [2 yrs]

RENFRO, DEAN Weldon Eugene, HB, 5'11"/180 lbs; North Texas; 1955: Cle, rnd 2; B6/15/1932 Whitesboro, TX

| 1955 | Bal | 7 | 4 | 13 | 3.3(5) | 0 | — | — | — | — | — | — | — | — | — | — | — | — | — | — | k | — | 0 | 18 |

RENFRO, DICK Golie Richard, FB-LB, 5'10"/200 lbs; Washington State; 1943: Det, rnd 11; B1/25/1919 Fort Worth, TX, D10/11/1998 Eureka, CA

| 1946 | SF-A | 3(3) | 18 | 85 | 4.7 | 3 | — | — | — | — | — | — | — | — | — | — | — | — | — | — | k | — | 18 | 120 |

RENFRO, LEONARD Leonard Andrew, DT, 6'2"/291 lbs; Colorado; 1993: Phi, rnd 1; B6/29/1970 Detroit, MI **1993** Phi 14 (2) **1994** Phi 9 (0) **NFL** 23 (2) [2 yrs]

YEAR	TEAM	G (GS, POS)	RUSH	YD	AVG(LG)	TD	REC	YD	AVG(LG)	TD	PASS COMP	PCT	YD	AVG(LG)	TD	INT	SK	YD	QBR	KPR	OTD	PTS	TAY

RENFRO, MEL Melvin Lacy, DB-RB, 6´0˝/190 lbs; Oregon; 1964: Dal, rnd 2/Oak, rnd 10; B12/30/1941 Houston, TX; HOF 1996 [RI]   **1964** Dal★14 (RS)   **1965** Dal★14 (RS)
1967†Dal★9 (8, RS)   **1968**†Dal★14 (8, RS)   **1969**†Dal★14 (RS)   **1970**†Dal★14 (RCB)   **1971**†Dal★14 (RCB)   **1972**†Dal★14 (RCB)   **1973**†Dal★14 (RCB)   **1974** Dal 11 (11, RCB)
1975†Dal 11 (RCB)   **1976** Dal 9 (9, RCB)   **1977**†Dal 11

| 1966 | †Dal★ | 11 (8, RS) | 8 | 52 | 6.5(27) | 0 | 4 | 65 | 16.3(42) | 0 | — | — | — | — | — | — | — | — | — | kpi | 1 | 6 | 362 |
| NFL | 14 | 174 (44) | 8 | 52 | 6.5(27) | 0 | 4 | 65 | 16.3(42) | 0 | — | — | — | — | — | — | — | — | — | kpi | 6 | 36 | 1779 |

RENFRO, MIKE Michael Ray, WR, 6´0˝/184 lbs; TCU; 1978: Hou, rnd 4; B6/19/1955 Fort Worth, TX

1978	Hou	14 (10, WR)	1	9	9.0(9)	0	26	339	13.0(58)	2	—	—	—	—	—	—	—	—	—	—	—	12	189
1979	†Hou	15 (2)	—	—	—	—	16	323	20.2(49)	2	—	—	—	—	—	—	—	—	—	—	—	12	172
1980	†Hou	16 (16, WR)	1	12	12.0(12)	0	35	459	13.1(42)	1	—	—	—	—	—	—	—	—	—	—	—	6	247
1981	Hou	12 (12, WR)	—	—	—	—	39	451	11.6(43)	1	—	—	—	—	—	—	—	—	—	—	—	6	231
1982	Hou	9 (4)	—	—	—	—	21	295	14.0(54)	3	—	—	—	—	—	—	—	—	—	—	—	18	163
1983	Hou	9 (7, WR)	1	3	3.0(3)	0	23	316	13.7(38)	2	—	—	—	—	—	—	—	—	—	—	—	12	171
1984	Dal	16 (11, WR)	—	—	—	—	35	583	16.7(60)	2	2	1	50.0	49	24.5(49)	1	0	—	—	—	—	12	331
1985	†Dal	16 (16, WR)	—	—	—	—	60	955	15.9(58)	8	—	—	—	—	—	—	—	—	—	—	—	48	518
1986	Dal	12 (6, WR)	—	—	—	—	22	325	14.8(30)	3	1	1	100.0	23	23.0(23)	0	0	—	—	—	—	18	189
1987	Dal	14 (11, WR)	—	—	—	—	46	662	14.4(43)	4	—	—	—	—	—	—	—	—	—	—	—	24	351
NFL	10	133 (95)	3	24	8.0(12)	0	323	4708	14.6(60)	28	3	2	66.7	72	24.0(49)	1	0	—	—	—	—	168	2559

RENFRO, RAY Raymond Austin, HB-FL, 6´1˝/190 lbs; North Texas; 1952: Cle, rnd 4; B11/7/1930 Whitesboro, TX, D8/5/1997 Fort Worth, TX

1952	†Cle	11	10	26	2.6(11)	0	8	8.0(8)		0	—	—	—	—	—	—	—	—	—	kp	—	0	99
1953	†Cle◇	12 (lh)	60	352	5.9(58)	4	39	722	18.5(70)	4	3	1	33.3	36	12.0(36)	1	0	—	—	—	p	1	54	764
1954	†Cle	7 (LH)	29	151	5.2(35)	0	13	249	17.5(64)	1	1	0	0.0	0	0.0	0	1	—	—	—	k	—	6	239
1955	†Cle☆	12 (RH)	29	90	3.1(14)	0	29	603	**20.8(61)**	8	2	0	0.0	0	0.0	0	0	—	—	—	p	—	48	430
1956	Cle	12 (RH)	4	24	6.0(10)	0	17	325	19.1(46)	4	—	—	—	—	—	—	—	—	—	—	—	24	207
1957	†Cle	12 (RH)	2	22	11.0(16)	0	21	589	28.0(65)	6	—	—	—	—	—	—	—	—	—	—	—	36	347
1958	†Cle	12 (RH)	3	17	5.7(12)	0	24	573	23.9(52)	6	—	—	—	—	—	—	—	—	—	—	—	36	334
1959	Cle☆	12 (RH)	—	—	—	—	30	528	17.6(70)	6	—	—	—	—	—	—	—	—	—	—	—	36	294
1960	Cle◇	12 (FL)	—	—	—	—	24	378	15.8(66)	4	—	—	—	—	—	—	—	—	—	—	—	24	209
1961	Cle	14 (FL)	—	—	—	—	48	834	17.4(57)	6	—	—	—	—	—	—	—	—	—	—	—	36	447
1962	Cle	14 (FL)	—	—	—	—	31	638	20.6(65)	4	—	—	—	—	—	—	—	—	—	—	—	24	339
1963	Cle	12	—	—	—	—	4	82	20.5(39)	1	—	—	—	—	—	—	—	—	—	—	—	6	46
NFL	12	142	137	682	5.0(58)	4	281	5508	19.6(70)	50	6	1	16.7	36	6.0(36)	1	1	—	—	—	kp	1	330	3753

RENFRO, WILL William Ellis, DT-DE-T, 6´5˝/233 lbs; Memphis; 1954: Was, rnd 24; B3/15/1932 Crowder, MS   **1957** Was 11   **1958** Was 12 (12, RDT)   **1959** Was 11   **1960** Pit 12
1961 Phi 14 (rde)   **NFL** 60 (12) [5 yrs]

RENGEL, MIKE Michael James, DT, 6´5˝/260 lbs; Air Force; Minnesota; Hawaii; B12/1/1946 Minneapolis, MN   **1969** NO 5

RENGEL, NEIL Neil Albert, FB, 5´9˝/205 lbs; Minnesota; St. Cloud State; B4/9/1906 St. Cloud, MN   **1930** Fra 11 (4)

RENN, BOB Robert Clifton, HB, 6´0˝/180 lbs; Florida State; 1958: Cle, rnd 22; B5/25/1934 Henderson, NC

| 1961 | NYT-A | 12 | 14 | 14.0(14) | | 0 | 18 | 268 | 14.9(67) | 1 | — | — | — | — | — | — | — | — | — | k | — | 6 | 204 |

RENNAKER, TERRY Terry Lewis, LB, 6´6˝/225 lbs; Stanford; B5/1/1958 Newport, RI   **1980** Sea 15 (0)

RENNER, BILL William Arthur, P, 6´0˝/198 lbs; Virginia Tech; B5/23/1959 Quantico, VA   **1987** GB 3 (0)

| 1986 | GB | 3 (0) | 1 | 0 | 0.0(0) | 0 | — | — | — | — | — | — | — | — | — | — | — | — | — | P | — | 0 | 0 |
| NFL | 2 | 6 (0) | 1 | 0 | 0.0(0) | 0 | — | — | — | — | — | — | — | — | — | — | — | — | — | P | — | 0 | 0 |

RENO, JESS Jessie Harry, E, 5´9˝/165 lbs; none; B1890, deceased   **1920** Mun 1 (1, LE)   **1922** Evv 2 (2, LE)   **NFL** 3 (3) [2 yrs]

RENTIE, CAESAR Caeser Harris, T, 6´3˝/293 lbs; Oklahoma; 1988: Chi, rnd 7; B11/10/1964 Hartshorne, OK   **1988** ChiB 5 (0)

RENTNER, PUG Ernest John, B, 6´1˝/187 lbs; Northwestern; B9/18/1910 Joliet, IL, D8/24/1978 Glencoe, IL [K]

1934	Bos	10 (2)	23	96	4.2	0	1	35	35.0(35)	1	11	2	18.2	13	1.2	0	3	—	—	—	—	6	5
1935	Bos	11 (6, bb)	81	243	3.0	1	1	9	9.0(9)	0	50	9	18.0	148	3.0	1	15	—	—	K	1	13	-254
1936	†Bos	12 (3)	95	404	4.3	1	4	33	8.3	0	39	15	38.5	198	5.1	0	6	—	—	—	2	18	310
1937	†ChiB	10 (2)	21	70	3.3	0	6	101	16.8	1	—	—	—	—	—	—	—	—	—	—	—	6	126
NFL	4	43 (13)	220	813	3.7	2	12	178	14.8(35)	2	100	26	26.0	359	3.6	1	24	—	—	K	3	43	187

RENTZ, LARRY Ralph Lawrence, DB, 6´1˝/170 lbs; Florida; 1969: SD, rnd 17; B8/1/1947 Miami, FL   **1969** SD-A 2

RENTZEL, LANCE Thomas Lance, WR-FL, 6´2˝/202 lbs; Oklahoma; 1965: Min, rnd 2/Buf, rnd 6; B10/14/1943 Queens, NY

1965	Min	11	1	-1	-1.0(-1)	0	—	—	—	—	—	—	—	—	—	—	—	—	—	kp	1	6	255
1966	Min	9	—	—	—	—	2	10	5.0(8)	0	—	—	—	—	—	—	—	—	—	kp	0	12
1967	†Dal	14 (FL)	—	—	—	—	58	996	17.2(74)	8	—	—	—	—	—	—	—	—	—	p	—	48	553
1968	†Dal☆	14 (FL)	—	—	—	—	54	1009	18.7(65)	6	—	—	—	—	—	—	—	—	—	p	—	36	558
1969	†Dal☆	14 (FL)	2	11	5.5(14)	0	43	960	**22.3(75)**	12	—	—	—	—	—	—	—	—	—	p	1	78	545
1970	Dal	11 (WR)	1	11	11.0(11)	0	28	556	19.9(86)	5	1	1	100.0	58	58.0(58)	1	0	—	—	—	—	30	348
1971	LARm	14 (14, WR)	14	113	8.1(50)	1	38	534	14.1(41)	5	—	—	—	—	—	—	—	—	—	p	—	36	410
1972	LARm	14 (14, WR)	7	71	10.1(18)	1	27	365	13.5(40)	1	—	—	—	—	—	—	—	—	—	—	—	12	269
1974	†LARm	14	1	-9	-9.0(-9)	0	18	396	22.0(38)	1	—	—	—	—	—	—	—	—	—	—	—	6	194
NFL	9	115 (28)	26	196	7.5(50)	2	268	4826	18.0(86)	38	1	1	100.0	58	58.0(58)	1	0	—	—	—	kp	2	252	3143

REPKO, JAY Jay Kevin, TE, 6´3˝/240 lbs; Ursinus; Pennsylvania; B6/12/1958 Pottstown, PA

| 1987 | Phi | 3 (0) | — | — | — | — | 5 | 46 | 9.2(12) | 0 | — | — | — | — | — | — | — | — | — | — | — | 0 | 23 |

REPKO, JOE Joseph Stephen, T, 6´0˝/236 lbs; Seton Hall; Boston College; 1943: Pit, rnd 12; B3/15/1920 Lansford, PA, D3/13/1997   **1946** Pit 9 (0)   **1947** Pit 8 (0)
1948 LARm 12 (0)   **1949** LARm 8 (0)   **NFL** 37 (0) [4 yrs]

REPPOND, MIKE Michael Gene, WR, 5´11˝/179 lbs; Arkansas; 1973: Buf, rnd 9; B11/24/1951 San Diego, CA   **1973** ChiB 2

RESSLER, GLENN Glenn Emanuel, G-C-T-DT, 6´3˝/250 lbs; Penn State; 1965: Bal, rnd 3/Den, rnd 3; B5/21/1943 Dornsife, PA   **1965**†Bal 12   **1966** Bal 13   **1967** Bal 14 (LG)
1968†Bal☆14 (LG)   **1969** Bal 8 (LG)   **1970**†Bal 13 (LG)   **1971**†Bal 14 (LG)   **1972** Bal 9 (LG)   **1973** Bal 14 (LG)   **1974** Bal 14 (LG)   **NFL** 125 [10 yrs]

RESTIC, JOE Joseph William, E, 6´2˝/180 lbs; St. Francis (PA); Villanova; B7/21/1927 Hastings, PA   **1952** Phi 3

RETZLAFF, PETE Palmer Edward 'The Baron', E-HB-TE, 6´1˝/211 lbs; South Dakota State; 1953: Det, rnd 22; B8/21/1931 Ellendale, ND

1956	Phi	10	—	—	—	—	12	159	13.3(20)	0	—	—	—	—	—	—	—	—	—	—	—	0	80
1957	Phi	12 (RH)	—	—	—	—	10	120	12.0(28)	0	—	—	—	—	—	—	—	—	—	—	—	0	60
1958	Phi★	12 (RH)	1	-4	-4.0(-4)	0	56	766	13.7(49)	2	—	—	—	—	—	—	—	—	—	—	—	12	389
1959	Phi	10 (RE)	2	-11	-5.5(-5)	0	34	595	17.5(45)	1	—	—	—	—	—	—	—	—	—	—	—	6	292
1960	†Phi★	12 (SE)	2	3	1.5(7)	0	46	826	18.0(57)	5	—	—	—	—	—	—	—	—	—	—	—	30	441
1961	Phi	14 (SE)	1	8	8.0(8)	0	50	769	15.4(61)	8	—	—	—	—	—	—	—	—	—	—	—	48	433
1962	Phi	8 (SE)	—	—	—	—	30	584	19.5(84)	3	—	—	—	—	—	—	—	—	—	—	—	18	307
1963	Phi	14 (TE)	—	—	—	—	57	895	15.7(46)	4	—	—	—	—	—	—	—	—	—	—	—	24	468
1964	Phi★	12 (TE)	—	—	—	—	51	855	16.8(44)	8	—	—	—	—	—	—	—	—	—	—	—	48	468
1965	Phi★	14 (TE)	—	—	—	—	66	1190	18.0(78)	10	—	—	—	—	—	—	—	—	—	—	—	60	645
1966	Phi☆	14 (TE)	—	—	—	—	40	653	16.3(40)	6	—	—	—	—	—	—	—	—	—	—	—	36	357
NFL	11	132	6	-4	-0.7(8)	0	452	7412	16.4(84)	47	—	—	—	—	—	—	—	—	—	—	—	282	3937

REUBER, ALAN Alan Michael, T, 6´6˝/323 lbs; Texas A&M; B1/26/1981 Plano, TX   **2004** Arz 3 (0)

REUTER, VIC Victor John, C, 6´0˝/215 lbs; Lafayette; B12/1/1909 Elizabeth, NJ, D1/11/1998 Hackettstown, NJ   **1932** SI 2 (1)

REUTERSHAN, RANDY Randy, WR, 5´10˝/182 lbs; Pittsburgh; 1978: Pit, rnd 6; B6/30/1955 New York, NY   **1978** Pit 11

REUTT, RAY Raymond Francis, E, 6´0˝/195 lbs; VMI; B3/4/1917 Norfolk, VA, D8/18/2004 Hollywood, FL   **1943** P-P 2 (0)

YEAR	TEAM	G (GS, POS)	RUSH	YD	AVG(LG)	TD	REC	YD	AVG(LG)	TD	PASS COMP	PCT	YD	AVG(LG)	TD	INT	SK	YD	QBR	KPR	OTD	PTS	TAY

REVEIZ, FUAD Fuad, K, 5´11˝/225 lbs; Tennessee; 1985: Mia, rnd 7; B2/24/1963 Bogota, Colombia **[K]**   **1985**†Mia 16 (0)   **1986** Mia 16 (0)   **1987** Mia 11 (0)   **1988** Mia 11 (0) **1990** SD 4 (0)   **1990** Min 9 (0)   **1991** Min 16 (0)   **1992**†Min 16 (0)   **1993**†Min 16 (0)   **1994**†Min★16 (0)   **1995** Min 16 (0)   **NFL** 147 (0) [10 yrs]

REXER, FREEMAN Freeman Riley, E, 6´1˝/211 lbs; Tulane; B6/18/1918 Houston, TX   **1944** Bos 2 (0)   **1944** Det 6 (0)   **1945** ChiC 1 (0)

| 1943 | ChiC | 10(2) | — | — | — | — | 1 | 14 | 14.0(14) | 0 | — | — | — | — | — | — | — | — | — | — | — | 0 | 7 |
| NFL | 3 | 19(2) | — | — | — | — | 1 | 14 | 14.0(14) | 0 | — | — | — | — | — | — | — | — | — | — | — | 0 | 7 |

REYES, TUTAN Tutankhamen Marques, G-T, 6´3˝/299 lbs; Mississippi; 2000: NO, rnd 5; B10/28/1977 Queens, NY   **2001** NO 1 (0)   **2004** Car 14 (12, RG/lg)   **2005**†Car 16 (16, RG)   **NFL** 31 (28) [3 yrs]

REYNOLDS, AL Allan F., G, 6´3˝/250 lbs; Tarkio; B2/15/1938 Winchester, KS   **1960** DalT-A 6   **1961** DalT-A 14   **1962**†DalT-A 14 (RG)   **1963** KC-A 9 (RG)   **1964** KC-A 13 (RG) **1965** KC-A 14   **1966**†KC-A 14   **1967** KC-A 14   **NFL** 98 [8 yrs]

REYNOLDS, BILL William, HB, 5´8˝/183 lbs; Mississippi; B10/10/1918 Chicago, IL

1944	Bkn	5(1)	11	71	6.5(29)	1	—	—	—	—	—	—	—	—	—	—	—	—	kp	—	6	91
1945	ChiC	9(1)	7	10	1.4(4)	0	—	—	—	—	—	—	—	—	—	—	—	—	P	—	0	10
NFL	2	14(2)	18	81	4.5(29)	1	—	—	—	—	—	—	—	—	—	—	—	—	Pkp	—	6	101

REYNOLDS, BILLY William Dean, HB, 5´11˝/195 lbs; Pittsburgh; 1953: Cle, rnd 2; B7/10/1931 St. Marys, WV, D12/2/2002 Bedford, OH **[R]**

1953	†Cle	12(rh)	72	313	4.3(16)	3	9	120	13.3(55)	0	—	—	—	—	—	—	—	—	kp	—	18	438
1954	†Cle	12(RH)	64	180	2.8(33)	2	10	76	7.6(22)	0	—	—	—	—	—	—	—	—	kp	—	12	454
1957	†Cle	12(lh)	29	57	2.0(8)	1	1	12	12.0(12)	0	—	—	—	—	—	—	—	—	kp	—	6	114
1958	Pit	12	10	29	2.9(11)	1	1	1	1.0(1)	0	—	—	—	—	—	—	—	—	kp	—	6	179
1960	Oak-A	6	1	6	6.0(6)	0	3	43	14.3(24)	0	—	—	—	—	—	—	—	—	p	—	0	17
NFL	5	54	176	585	3.3(33)	7	24	252	10.5(55)	0	—	—	—	—	—	—	—	—	kp	—	42	1201

REYNOLDS, BOB Robert O'Dell, T, 6´4˝/221 lbs; Stanford; 1936: GB, rnd 6; B3/30/1914 Norris, OK, D2/8/1994 San Rafael, CA   **1937** Det 9 (8, RT)   **1938** Det 11 (8, RT) **NFL** 20 (16) [2 yrs]

REYNOLDS, BOB Robert Louis, T, 6´5˝/265 lbs; Bowling Green State; 1963: SL, rnd 2/Bos, rnd 4; B1/22/1939 Nashville, TN, D10/10/1996 Naperville, IL   **1963** SL 14 **1964** SL 10 (LT)   **1965** SL 14 (LT)   **1966** SL◇14 (LT)   **1967** SL 13 (LT)   **1968** SL◇14 (LT)   **1969** SL◇14 (LT)   **1970** SL 14 (LT)   **1972** NE 12 (10, LT)   **1973** NE 4 (4)   **1973** SL 1

| 1971 | SL | 14(LT) | — | — | — | — | 1 | 4 | -4.0(-4) | 0 | — | — | — | — | — | — | — | — | — | — | 0 | -2 |
| NFL | 11 | 138(14) | — | — | — | — | 1 | 4 | -4.0(-4) | 0 | — | — | — | — | — | — | — | — | — | — | 0 | -2 |

REYNOLDS, CHUCK Charles Robert, C-G, 6´2˝/240 lbs; TCU; Tulsa; 1969: Cle, rnd 8; B10/5/1946 Fort Worth, TX   **1969**†Cle 11   **1970** Cle 14   **NFL** 25 [2 yrs]

REYNOLDS, ED Edward Rannell, LB, 6´5˝/238 lbs; Virginia; B9/23/1961 Stuttgart, Germany   **1983** NE 12 (0)   **1984** NE 16 (0)   **1985**†NE 12 (0)   **1986**†NE 16 (3)   **1987** NE 12 (1) **1988** NE 14 (14, LILB)   **1989** NE 16 (16, LILB)   **1990** NE 12 (12, RILB)   **1991** NE 9 (0)   **1992** NYG 16 (5, rilb)   **NFL** 135 (51) [10 yrs]

REYNOLDS, HOMER Homer, G, 5´10˝/190 lbs; Tulsa; B10/31/1913, D2/7/1988 Woodstock, VA   **1934** SL 2 (1)

REYNOLDS, JACK John Sumner 'Hacksaw', LB, 6´1˝/232 lbs; Tennessee; 1970: LA, rnd 1; B11/22/1947 Cincinnati, OH   **1970** LARm 14   **1971** LARm 4   **1972** LARm 14 **1973**†LARm 14 (14, MLB)   **1974**†LARm 14 (14, MLB)   **1975**†LARm 14 (14, MLB)   **1976**†LARm 14 (14, MLB)   **1977**†LARm 9 (6, mlb)   **1978**†LARm 16 (16, MLB) **1979**†LARm☆16 (16, MLB)   **1980**†LARm◇16 (16, MLB)   **1981**†SF☆16 (16, RILB)   **1982** SF 9 (9, LILB)   **1983**†SF 13 (13, RILB)   **1984** SF 15 (14, RILB)   **NFL** 198 (162) [15 yrs]

REYNOLDS, JAMAL Idris Jamal, DE, 6´3˝/260 lbs; Florida State; 2001: GB, rnd 1; B2/20/1979 Augusta, GA   **2001**†GB 6 (0)   **2002**†GB 7 (0)   **2003**†GB 5 (0)   **NFL** 18 (0) [3 yrs]

REYNOLDS, JERRY Jerry Bradford, T-C, 6´6˝/320 lbs; UNLV; 1994: Cin, rnd 6; B4/2/1970 Fort Thomas, KY   **1996** NYG 8 (0)   **1997** NYG 5 (0)   **1998** NYG 12 (2)   **NFL** 25 (2) [3 yrs]

REYNOLDS, JIM James Albert, FB-LB, 6´1˝/190 lbs; Auburn; 1943: NYG, rnd 6; B1/8/1920 La Grange, GA

| 1946 | Mia-A | 7(2) | 32 | 96 | 3.0 | 0 | 1 | 32 | 32.0(32) | 0 | — | — | — | — | — | — | — | — | Pki | — | 0 | 133 |

REYNOLDS, JIM James Stephen, DB, 6´0˝/193 lbs; Oklahoma State; B8/21/1921 Bethany, OK, deceased   **1946** Pit 2 (0)

REYNOLDS, JOFFREY Joffrey Roy, RB, 5´10˝/221 lbs; Houston; B11/26/1979 Houston, TX   **2003** SL 4 (0)

REYNOLDS, JOHN John Duke, C, 5´10˝/185 lbs; Baylor; 1937: ChiC, rnd 8; B4/20/1914 Tyler, TX   **1937** ChiC 5 (0)

REYNOLDS, M.C. Mack Charles, QB, 6´0˝/193 lbs; LSU; B2/11/1935 Mansfield, LA, D9/8/1991 Shreveport, LA

1958	ChiC	11(qb)	48	252	5.3(50)	0	—	—	—	—	195 105	53.8	1422	7.3(91)	11	11	—	—	72.6	—	—	0	578
1959	ChiC	7	5	-4	-0.8(11)	0	—	—	—	—	39 19	48.7	329	8.4(85)	4	1	—	—	—	—	—	0	141
1960	Was	8	4	20	5.0(12)	0	—	—	—	—	30 13	43.3	154	5.1(31)	0	3	—	—	—	—	—	0	-23
1961	Buf-A	12(QB)	30	142	4.7(20)	4	—	—	—	—	181 83	45.9	1004	5.5(52)	2	13	—	—	37.2	—	—	24	174
1962	Oak-A	1	1	9	9.0(9)	0	—	—	—	—	5	2	40.0	23	4.6(15)	0	0	—	—	—	—	0	21
NFL	5	39	88	419	4.8(50)	4	—	—	—	—	450 222	49.3	2932	6.5(91)	17	28	—	—	57.0	—	—	24	890

REYNOLDS, OWEN Owen Gaston, E-FB, 6´3˝/212 lbs; Georgia; B1/12/1900 Douglasville, GA, D3/10/1993 Spring Lake, MI   **1925** NYG 9 (0)   **1926** Bkn 9 (6, le)   **NFL** 18 (6) [2 yrs]

REYNOLDS, QUENTIN Quentin James, G-T, 6´1˝/205 lbs; Brown; B4/11/1902 Bronx, NY, D3/17/1965 Travis AFB, CA   **1926** Bkn 8 (2)

REYNOLDS, RICKY Derrick Scott, DB, 5´11˝/190 lbs; Washington State; 1987: TB, rnd 2; B1/19/1965 Sacramento, CA **[I]**   **1987** TB 12 (12, LCB)   **1988** TB 16 (16, LCB) **1989** TB 16 (15, LCB)   **1990** TB 15 (15, LCB)   **1991** TB 16 (16, LCB)   **1992** TB☆16 (16, LCB)   **1993** TB 14 (13, RCB)   **1994**†NE 15 (10, LCB)   **1995** NE 16 (16, LCB) **1996** NE 12 (9, RCB)   **NFL** 148 (138) [10 yrs]

REYNOLDS, ROBERT Robert, LB, 6´3˝/242 lbs; Ohio State; 2004: Ten, rnd 5; B5/20/1981 Bowling Green, KY   **2004** Ten 14 (1)   **2005** Ten 15 (1)   **NFL** 29 (2) [2 yrs]

REYNOLDS, TOM Raoul Thomas, WR, 6´3˝/200 lbs; San Diego State; 1972: NE, rnd 2; B4/11/1949 Pasadena, CA

1972	NE	12	—	—	—	—	8	152	19.0(36)	2	—	—	—	—	—	—	—	—	—	—	12	86
1973	ChiB	9	—	—	—	—	7	127	18.1(30)	0	—	—	—	—	—	—	—	—	—	—	0	64
NFL	2	21	—	—	—	—	15	279	18.6(36)	2	—	—	—	—	—	—	—	—	—	—	12	150

RHEA, FLOYD Floyd Mack, G, 6´0˝/218 lbs; Oregon; 1943: Bkn, rnd 15; B9/21/1920 Rhea's Mills, AR   **1943** ChiC 1 (0)   **1944** Bkn 8 (7, LG)   **1945** Bos 8 (0)   **1947** Det 2 (0) **NFL** 19 (7) [4 yrs]

RHEA, HUGH Hugh McCall, G, 6´3˝/225 lbs; Nebraska; B9/9/1909 Arlington, NE, D10/18/1973   **1933** Bkn 2 (1)

RHEAMS, LEONTA Leonta DeMarkel, DT, 6´2˝/303 lbs; Houston; 1998: NE, rnd 4; B8/1/1976 Tyler, TX   **1998** NE 6 (0)

RHEM, STEVE Steve Lamar, WR, 6´2˝/212 lbs; Minnesota; Louisiana-Monroe; Arkansas-Monticello; Rowan College; B11/9/1971 Ocala, FL   **1994** NO 7 (0)

| 1995 | NO | 8(0) | — | — | — | — | 4 | 50 | 12.5(20) | 0 | — | — | — | — | — | — | — | — | — | — | 0 | 25 |
| NFL | 2 | 15(0) | — | — | — | — | 4 | 50 | 12.5(20) | 0 | — | — | — | — | — | — | — | — | — | — | 0 | 25 |

RHENSTROM, ELMER Elmer Gustaf, E, 5´10˝/185 lbs; Beloit; B8/18/1895 Beaver Dam, WI, D12/27/1967 Ontario, CA   **1922** Rac 6 (3)

RHETT, ERRICT Errict Undra, RB, 5´11˝/210 lbs; Florida; 1994: TB, rnd 2; B12/11/1970 Pembroke Pines, FL

1994	TB	16(8, RB)	284	1011	3.6(27)	7	22	119	5.4(12)	0	—	—	—	—	—	—	—	—	—	—	44	1141
1995	TB	16(16, RB)	332	1207	3.6(21)	11	14	110	7.9(18)	0	—	—	—	—	—	—	—	—	—	—	66	1372
1996	TB	9(7, RB)	176	539	3.1(35)	3	4	11	2.8(5)	1	—	—	—	—	—	—	—	—	—	—	24	580
1997	†TB	11(0)	31	96	3.1(21)	3	—	—	—	—	—	—	—	—	—	—	—	—	k	—	18	127
1998	Bal	13(1)	44	180	4.1(46)	0	11	65	5.9(16)	0	—	—	—	—	—	—	—	—	—	—	0	213
1999	Bal	16(10, RB)	236	852	3.6(52)	5	24	169	7.0(20)	2	—	—	—	—	—	—	—	—	—	—	42	997
2000	Cle	5(4)	71	258	3.6(42)	0	14	78	5.6(16)	0	—	—	—	—	—	—	—	—	—	—	0	297
NFL	7	86(46)	1174	4143	3.5(52)	29	89	552	6.2(20)	3	—	—	—	—	—	—	—	—	k	—	194	4725

RHINEHART, COBY Jacoby M., DB, 5´11˝/198 lbs; SMU; 1999: Arz, rnd 6; B2/7/1977 Dallas, TX   **1999** Arz 16 (0)   **2001** Arz 13 (0)   **2002** Arz 16 (2)   **2003** Arz 16 (2) **NFL** 61 (4) [4 yrs]

RHODEMYRE, JAY Jay E., C-LB, 6´1˝/210 lbs; Kentucky; 1948: GB, rnd 7/ChiR-A, rnd 7; B12/16/1922 Ashland, KY, D6/7/1968 Lexington, KY   **1948** GB 9 (7, C)   **1949** GB 12 (10, C) **1951** GB☆12 (C)   **1952** GB 12 (C)   **NFL** 45 (17) [4 yrs]

RHODES, BRUCE Bruce, DB, 6´0˝/187 lbs; San Francisco State; B4/17/1952 San Francisco, CA, D2/23/1981 San Francisco, CA   **1976** SF 14 (5, fs)   **1978** Det 15 (5, ss) **NFL** 29 (10) [2 yrs]

RHODES, DANNY Danny Boylet, LB, 6´2˝/220 lbs; Arkansas; 1974: Bal, rnd 6; B3/18/1951 Lake Jackson, TX   **1974** Bal 14

YEAR	TEAM	G (GS, POS)	RUSH	YD	AVG(LG)	TD	REC	YD	AVG(LG)	TD	PASS	COMP	PCT	YD	AVG(LG)	TD	INT	SK	YD	QBR	KPR	OTD	PTS	TAY

RHODES, DOMINIC Dominic Dondrell, RB, 5'9"/203 lbs; Midwestern State; B1/17/1979 Waco, TX **[R]**

2001	Ind	15(10, RB)	233	1104	4.7(77)	9	34	224	6.6(19)	0	—	—	—	—	—	—	—	—	—	—	k	1	60	1462
2003	†Ind	11(0)	37	157	4.2(25)	0	6	62	10.3(27)	1	—	—	—	—	—	—	—	—	—	—	k	—	6	364
2004	†Ind	16(0)	53	254	4.8(55)	1	2	24	12.0(20)	0	—	—	—	—	—	—	—	—	—	—	k	1	12	754
2005	†Ind	13(1)	40	118	3.0(24)	4	12	88	7.3(15)	0	—	—	—	—	—	—	—	—	—	—	k	—	24	442
NFL	4	55(11)	363	1633	4.5(77)	14	54	398	7.4(27)	1	—	—	—	—	—	—	—	—	—	—	k	2	102	3022

RHODES, DON Donald Nelson, T, 6'2"/225 lbs; Washington & Jefferson; B7/9/1909, D1/1968 **1933** Pit 7 (5, LT)

RHODES, KERRY Kerry, DB, 6'2"/209 lbs; Louisville; 2005: NYJ, rnd 4; B8/2/1982 Birmingham, AL **2005** NYJ 16 (16, FS)

RHODES, RAY Raymond Earl, DB-WR, 5'11"/185 lbs; TCU; Tulsa; 1974: NYG, rnd 10; B10/20/1950 Mexia, TX **[C]** **1977** NYG 14 (RCB) **1978** NYG 13 (10, RCB) **1979** NYG 15 (RCB) **1980** SF 14 (7, LCB)

1974	NYG	14	1	-6	-6.0(-6)	0	9	138	15.3(25)	0	—	—	—	—	—	—	—	—	—	—	kp	—	0	149
1975	NYG	14(WR)	3	-4	-1.3(14)	0	26	537	20.7(56)	6	—	—	—	—	—	—	—	—	—	—	—	—	36	295
1976	NYG	13(WR)	2	10	5.0(16)	0	16	305	19.1(63)	1	—	—	—	—	—	—	—	—	—	—	—	—	6	168
NFL	7	97(17)	6	0	0.0(16)	0	51	980	19.2(63)	7	—	—	—	—	—	—	—	—	—	—	kpi	—	42	729

RHOME, JERRY Gerald Byron, QB, 6'0"/190 lbs; SMU; Tulsa; 1964: Dal, rnd 13/NYJ, rnd 25; B3/6/1942 Dallas, TX

1965	Dal	11	4	11	2.8(16)	0	—	—	—	—	21	9	42.9	157	7.5(82)	1	1	7	44	—	—	—	0	55
1966	†Dal	7	7	37	5.3(11)	0	—	—	—	—	36	21	58.3	253	7.0(47)	0	1	4	39	—	—	—	0	124
1967	†Dal	14	2	-11	-5.5(-2)	0	—	—	—	—	18	9	50.0	86	4.8(19)	0	1	4	26	—	—	—	0	-8
1968	†Dal	1	—	—	—	—	—	—	—	—	—	—	—	—	—	—	—	—	—	—	—	—	—	—
1969	†Cle	11	1	0	0.0(0)	0	—	—	—	—	19	7	36.8	35	1.8(22)	0	2	3	26	—	—	—	0	-63
1970	Hou	13(4, qb)	9	54	6.0(11)	1	—	—	—	—	168	88	52.4	1031	6.1(87)	5	8	10	85	61.4	—	—	6	285
1971	LARm	14	3	0	0.0(0)	0	—	—	—	—	18	5	27.8	66	3.7(43)	1	1	1	10	—	—	—	0	-2
NFL	7	71(4)	26	91	3.5(16)	1	—	—	—	—	280	139	49.6	1628	5.8(87)	7	14	29	230	55.2	—	—	6	390

RHONE, EARNEST Earnest Calvin, LB, 6'2"/220 lbs; Henderson State; B8/20/1953 Ogden, AR **1975** Mia 14 (4) **1977** Mia 4 **1978**†Mia 16 (2) **1979** Mia 16 **1980** Mia 14 (1) **1981**†Mia 16 (16, RILB) **1982**†Mia 9 (9, RILB) **1983**†Mia 12 (12, RILB) **1984**†Mia 15 (10, rilb) **NFL** 116 (54) [9 yrs]

RHYMES, BUSTER George, WR, 6'2"/217 lbs; Oklahoma; 1985: Min, rnd 4; B1/27/1962 Miami, FL

1985	Min	15(0)	—	—	—	—	5	124	24.8(36)	0	—	—	—	—	—	—	—	—	—	—	k	—	0	612
1986	Min	5(0)	—	—	—	—	3	25	8.3(12)	0	—	—	—	—	—	—	—	—	—	—	k	—	0	91
NFL	2	20(0)	—	—	—	—	8	149	18.6(36)	0	—	—	—	—	—	—	—	—	—	—	k	—	0	703

RIBAR, FRANK Frank Andrew, G-LB, 6'1"/190 lbs; Duke; 1940: Det, rnd 18; B1/15/1915 Wickhaven, PA, D10/1976 **1943**†Was 2 (0)

RIBBLE, DAVE Loran Thomas, G-T, 6'1"/225 lbs; Hardin-Simmons; B3/28/1907 Brownwood, TX, D1944 **1932** Por 1 (0) **1933** ChiC 1 (0) **1934** Pit 10 (8, RG) **1935** Pit 3 (2) **NFL** 15 (10) [4 yrs]

RIBLETT, PAUL Paul Gerald, E, 5'10"/184 lbs; Pennsylvania; B5/23/1908 Youngwood, PA, D3/1/1976 Cherry Hill, NJ

1932	Bkn	11(10, LE)	2	4	2.0	0	10	110	11.0	1	—	—	—	—	—	—	—	—	—	—	—	—	6	64
1933	Bkn	10(8, LE)	—	—	—	—	12	173	14.4	1	—	—	—	—	—	—	—	—	—	—	—	—	6	92
1934	Bkn	11(10, LE)	1	19	19.0(19)	0	8	154	19.3	1	—	—	—	—	—	—	—	—	—	—	—	—	6	101
1935	Bkn	12(12, LE)	2	16	8.0	0	6	86	14.3	0	—	—	—	—	—	—	—	—	—	—	—	—	0	59
1936	Bkn	12(5, le)	2	4	2.0	0	4	49	12.3	0	—	—	—	—	—	—	—	—	—	—	—	—	0	29
NFL	5	56(45)	7	43	6.1(19)	0	40	572	14.3	3	—	—	—	—	—	—	—	—	—	—	—	—	18	344

RICARD, ALAN Alan, FB, 5'11"/237 lbs; Louisiana-Monroe; B1/17/1977 Independence, LA

2001	Bal	5(0)	—	—	—	—	—	—	—	—	—	—	—	—	—	—	—	—	—	—	—	—	—	—
2002	Bal	16(8, FB)	14	58	4.1(19)	2	10	60	6.0(17)	0	—	—	—	—	—	—	—	—	—	—	—	1	18	108
2003	†Bal	16(13, FB)	19	79	4.2(30)	0	9	62	6.9(15)	0	—	—	—	—	—	—	—	—	—	—	—	1	6	110
2004	Bal	16(9, FB)	10	36	3.6(14)	0	11	39	3.5(8)	0	—	—	—	—	—	—	—	—	—	—	—	—	0	56
2005	Bal	2(2)	—	—	—	—	2	18	9.0(11)	0	—	—	—	—	—	—	—	—	—	—	—	—	0	9
NFL	5	55(32)	43	173	4.0(30)	2	32	179	5.6(17)	0	—	—	—	—	—	—	—	—	—	—	—	2	24	283

RICARDO, BENNY Benito Concepcion, K, 5'10"/175 lbs; San Diego State; B1/4/1954 Asuncion, Paraguay **[K]** **1976** Buf 2 **1976** Det 8 **1978** Det 16 **1979** Det 16 **1980** NO 14 (0) **1981** NO 16 (0) **1983** Min 16 (0) **1984** SD 2 (0) **NFL** 90 [7 yrs]

RICCA, JIM James Emanuel, MG-T-G-DT, 6'4"/270 lbs; Georgetown (DC); B10/8/1927 Rockville Centre, NY **1951** Was 11 (MG) **1952** Was 12 (MG) **1953** Was 12 (MG) **1954** Was 12 (MG) **1955** Det 6 **1955** Phi 6 (MG) **1956** Phi 1 **NFL** 60 [6 yrs]

RICE WB, none; deceased **1921** Ham 1 (0)

RICE, ALLEN Allen Troy, RB, 5'10"/203 lbs; Baylor; 1984: Min, rnd 5; B4/5/1962 Houston, TX

1984	Min	14(0)	14	58	4.1(16)	1	4	59	14.8(24)	1	—	—	—	—	—	—	—	—	—	—	k	—	12	92
1985	Min	14(1)	31	104	3.4(15)	3	9	61	6.8(13)	1	—	—	—	—	—	—	—	—	—	—	k	—	24	180
1986	Min	14(8, fb)	73	220	3.0(19)	2	30	391	13.0(32)	3	1	0	0.0	0	0.0	0	—	—	—	—	kp	—	30	459
1987	†Min	12(2)	51	131	2.6(13)	1	19	201	10.6(24)	1	—	—	—	—	—	—	—	—	—	—	k	—	12	246
1988	†Min	16(4)	110	322	2.9(24)	6	30	279	9.3(38)	0	—	—	—	—	—	—	—	—	—	—	k	—	36	507
1989	Min	4(0)	6	25	4.2(10)	0	4	29	7.3(14)	0	0	0	0.0	0	0.0	0	0	1	10	—	k	—	0	38
1990	Min	15(0)	22	74	3.4(15)	0	4	46	11.5(24)	0	—	—	—	—	—	—	—	—	—	—	k	—	0	93
1991	GB	6(3)	30	100	3.3(21)	0	2	10	5.0(7)	0	—	—	—	—	—	—	—	—	—	—	k	—	0	96
NFL	8	95(18)	337	1034	3.1(24)	13	102	1076	10.5(38)	6	1	0	0.0	0	0.0	0	0	1	10	—	kp	—	114	1708

RICE, ANDY Andrew, DT, 6'2"/268 lbs; Texas Southern; B9/6/1940 Hallettsville, TX **1966**†KC-A 14 (LDT) **1967** KC-A 4 **1967**†Hou-A 7 **1968** Cin-A 14 (LDT) **1969** Cin-A 14 (LDT) **1970** SD 9 (rdt) **1971** SD 12 **1972** ChiB 14 **1973** ChiB 14 **NFL** 102 [8 yrs]

RICE, DAN Daniel Jerome, RB, 6'1"/241 lbs; Michigan; B11/9/1963 Boston, MA

| 1987 | Cin | 3(0) | 18 | 59 | 3.3(8) | 0 | — | — | — | — | — | — | — | — | — | — | — | — | — | — | — | — | 0 | 59 |

RICE, FLOYD Floyd Elliott, LB-TE, 6'3"/223 lbs; Alcorn State; 1971: Hou, rnd 9; B8/31/1949 Natchez, MS **1971** Hou 14 **1972** Hou 14 (LLB) **1973** Hou 5 (LLB) **1973** SD 5 (rlb) **1974** SD 12 (12, RLB) **1975** SD 14 (8, RLB) **1976**†Oak 10 **1977**†Oak 13 (11, LOLB) **1978** NO 15 **NFL** 102 (31) [8 yrs]

RICE, GEORGE George Gaylen, DT, 6'3"/260 lbs; LSU; 1966: Hou, rnd 3/Chi, rnd 1; B6/10/1944 Liberty, MO **1966** Hou-A 5 **1967**†Hou-A 14 (RDT) **1968** Hou-A 11 (RDT) **1969** Hou-A 7 **NFL** 37 [4 yrs]

RICE, HAROLD Harold Thurston, DE, 6'2"/235 lbs; Tennessee State; 1969: Oak, rnd 11; B6/23/1945 Nashville, TN **1971** Oak 12

RICE, JERRY Jerry Lee, WR, 6'2"/200 lbs; Mississippi Valley State; 1985: SF, rnd 1; B10/13/1962 Crawford, MS

1985	†SF	16(4)	6	26	4.3(15)	1	49	927	18.9(66)	3	—	—	—	—	—	—	—	—	—	—	k	—	24	506
1986	†SF★	16(15, WR)	10	72	7.2(18)	1	86	1570	18.3(66)	15	2	1	50.0	16	8.0(16)	0	0	—	—	—	—	—	96	950
1987	†SF★	12(12, WR)	8	51	6.4(17)	1	65	1078	16.6(57)	22	—	—	—	—	—	—	—	—	—	—	—	—	138	710
1988	†SF★	16(16, WR)	13	107	8.2(29)	1	64	1306	20.4(96)	9	3	1	33.3	14	4.7(14)	0	1	—	—	—	—	—	60	782
1989	†SF★	16(16, WR)	5	33	6.6(17)	0	82	1483	18.1(68)	17	—	—	—	—	—	—	—	—	—	—	—	—	102	860
1990	†SF★	16(16, WR)	2	0	0.0(2)	0	100	1502	15.0(64)	13	—	—	—	—	—	—	—	—	—	—	—	—	78	816
1991	SF★	16(16, WR)	1	2	2.0(2)	0	80	1206	15.1(73)	14	—	—	—	—	—	—	—	—	—	—	—	—	84	675
1992	†SF★	16(16, WR)	9	58	6.4(26)	1	84	1201	14.3(80)	10	—	—	—	—	—	—	—	—	—	—	—	—	66	719
1993	†SF★	16(16, WR)	3	69	23.0(43)	1	98	1503	15.3(80)	15	—	—	—	—	—	—	—	—	—	—	—	—	96	906
1994	†SF☆	16(16, WR)	7	93	13.3(28)	2	112	1499	13.4(69)	13	—	—	—	—	—	—	—	—	—	—	—	—	92	928
1995	†SF★	16(16, WR)	5	36	7.2(20)	1	122	1848	15.1(81)	15	1	1	100.0	41	41.0(41)	1	0	—	—	—	—	1	104	1071
1996	†SF★	16(16, WR)	11	77	7.0(38)	1	108	1254	11.6(39)	8	1	0	0.0	0	0.0	0	0	—	—	—	—	—	54	754
1997	SF	2(1)	1	-10	-10.0(-10)	0	7	78	11.1(16)	1	—	—	—	—	—	—	—	—	—	—	—	—	6	34
1998	†SF◇	16(16, WR)	—	—	—	—	82	1157	14.1(75)	9	—	—	—	—	—	—	—	—	—	—	—	—	58	624
1999	SF	16(16, WR)	2	13	6.5(11)	0	67	830	12.4(62)	5	—	—	—	—	—	—	—	—	—	—	—	—	30	453
2000	SF	16(16, WR)	1	-2	-2.0(-2)	0	75	805	10.7(68)	7	—	—	—	—	—	—	—	—	—	—	—	—	42	436

YEAR	TEAM	G(GS, POS)	RUSH	YD	AVG(LG)	TD	REC	YD	AVG(LG)	TD	PASS	COMP	PCT	YD	AVG(LG)	TD	INT	SK	YD	QBR	KPR	OTD	PTS	TAY
2001	†Oak	16(15, WR)	—	—	—	—	83	1139	13.7(40)	9	—	—	—	—	—	—	—	—	—	—	—	—	54	615
2002	†Oak★	16(16, WR)	3	20	6.7(12)	0	92	1211	13.2(75)	7	—	—	—	—	—	—	—	—	—	—	—	—	42	661
2003	Oak	16(15, WR)	—	—	—	—	63	869	13.8(47)	2	1	0	0.0	0	0.0	0	0	—	—	—	—	—	12	445
2004	Oak	6(5, wr)	—	—	—	—	5	67	13.4(18)	0	—	—	—	—	—	—	—	—	—	—	—	—	0	34
2004	†Sea	11(9, WR)	—	—	—	—	25	362	14.5(56)	3	—	—	—	—	—	—	—	—	—	—	—	—	18	196
NFL	20	303(284)	87	645	7.4(43)	10	1549	22895	14.8(96)	197	10	3	30.0	71	7.1(41)	1	1	—	—	—	k	1	1256	13169

RICE, KEN Kenneth Earl, T-G, 6´2˝/240 lbs; Auburn; 1961: Buf, rnd 1/SL, rnd 1; B9/14/1939 Bainbridge, GA **1961** Buf-A★14 (LT) **1963** †Buf-A 14 (RT) **1964** Oak-A 14 (LT) **1965** Oak-A 14 (LG) **1966** Mia-A 14 **1967** Mia-A 9 (4) **NFL** 79 (4) [6 yrs]

RICE, ORIAN Orian Earl, BB-C, 6´0˝/165 lbs; Syracuse; Muhlenberg; B3/21/1900 Binghamton, NY, D5/1968 Roselle, NJ **1929** NYG 2 (0)

RICE, RODNEY Rodney Donadrain, DB, 5´8˝/180 lbs; Brigham Young; 1989: NE, rnd 8; B6/18/1966 Albany, GA **1989** NE 10 (0) **1990** TB 16 (1) **NFL** 26 (1) [2 yrs]

RICE, RON Ronald Wilson, DB, 6´1˝/206 lbs; Eastern Michigan; B11/9/1972 Detroit, MI **1996** Det 13 (2) **1997** †Det 12 (8, SS) **1998** Det 16 (16, SS) **1999** †Det 16 (16, SS) **2000** Det 14 (14, SS) **2001** Det 8 (8, ss) **NFL** 79 (64) [6 yrs]

RICE, SIMEON Simeon James, DE, 6´5˝/268 lbs; Illinois; 1996: Arz, rnd 1; B2/24/1974 Chicago, IL [S] **1996** Arz☆16 (15, RDE) **1997** Arz 16 (15, RDE) **1998** †Arz 16 (16, RDE) **1999** Arz★16 (16, RDE) **2000** Arz 15´(11, RDE) **2001** †TB 16 (16, RDE) **2002** †TB★16 (16, RDE) **2003** TB★16 (16, RDE) **2004** TB 16 (16, RDE) **2005** †TB 15 (15, RDE) **NFL** 158 (152) [10 yrs]

RICH, HERB DB, 5´11˝/181 lbs; Vanderbilt; 1950: Bal, rnd 6; B10/7/1928 Newark, NJ [I] **1951** †LARm 7 (DB) **1952** LARm☆11 (DB) **1953** LARm 7 (DB) **1954** NYG 11 (DB) **1955** NYG 11 (DB) **1956** NYG 5

| 1950 | Bal | 12(DB) | 2 | 6 | 3.0(5) | 0 | — | — | — | — | — | — | — | — | — | — | — | — | — | kpi | 2 | 12 | 451 |
| NFL | 7 | 64 | 2 | 6 | 3.0(5) | 0 | — | — | — | — | — | — | — | — | — | — | — | — | — | kpi | 4 | 24 | 760 |

RICH, RANDY Randall Wayne, DB, 5´10˝/178 lbs; New Mexico; B12/28/1953 Bakersfield, CA **1977** Det 2 **1977** †Den 0 **1978** Oak 2 **1978** Cle 9 **1979** Cle 16 **NFL** 29 [3 yrs]

RICHARD, GARY Gary Ross, DB, 5´9˝/171 lbs; Pittsburgh; 1988: GB, rnd 7; B10/9/1965 Denver, CO **1988** GB 10 (0)

RICHARD, KRIS Kris, DB, 5´11˝/190 lbs; USC; 2002: Sea, rnd 3; B10/28/1978 Los Angeles, CA **2002** Sea 7 (0) **2003** Sea 15 (1) **2004** †Sea 16 (0) **2005** SF 1 (0) **NFL** 39 (1) [4 yrs]

RICHARD, STANLEY Stanley Palmer, DB, 6´2˝/198 lbs; Texas; 1991: SD, rnd 1; B10/21/1967 Mineola, TX [I] **1991** SD 15 (14, FS) **1992** †SD 14 (14, FS) **1993** SD 16 (16, FS) **1994** †SD☆16 (16, FS) **1995** Was 16 (16, FS) **1997** Was 15 (15, FS) **1998** Was 15 (15, FS) **NFL** 124 (122) [8 yrs]

RICHARDS, BOBBY Robert Griffin, DE-DT, 6´2˝/245 lbs; LSU; 1961: Phi, rnd 15/1962: Oak, rnd 32; B10/2/1938 Columbus, MS **1962** Phi 14 (RDE) **1963** Phi 14 (RDE/ldt) **1964** Phi 14 (12, RDE) **1965** Phi 14 (12, RDE) **1966** Atl 14 (LDE) **1967** Atl 14 **NFL** 84 (24) [6 yrs]

RICHARDS, CURVIN Curvin Stephen, RB, 5´9˝/195 lbs; Pittsburgh; 1991: Dal, rnd 4; B12/26/1968 Port of Spain, Trinidad

1991	Dal	2(0)	2	4	2.0(3)	0	—	—	—	—	—	—	—	—	—	—	—	—	—	—	—	0	4
1992	Dal	9(0)	49	176	3.6(15)	1	3	8	2.7(6)	—	—	—	—	—	—	—	—	—	—	—	—	6	190
1993	Det	1(0)	4	1	0.3(1)	0	—	—	—	—	—	—	—	—	—	—	—	—	—	—	—	0	1
NFL	3	12(0)	55	181	3.3(15)	1	3	8	2.7(6)	—	—	—	—	—	—	—	—	—	—	—	—	6	195

RICHARDS, DAVID David Reed, G-T, 6´5˝/315 lbs; SMU; UCLA; 1988: SD, rnd 4; B4/11/1966 Staten Island, NY **1988** SD 16 (16, RT) **1989** SD 16 (16, RG) **1990** SD 16 (16, RG) **1991** SD 16 (16, RG) **1992** †SD☆16 (16, RG) **1993** †SD 15 (15, LG) **1994** Atl 15 (14, LG) **1995** †Atl 14 (12, RT) **1996** Atl 6 (6, rt) **1996** NE 5 (0) **NFL** 135 (127) [9 yrs]

RICHARDS, DICK Richard, FB-WB, 6´0˝/194 lbs; Kentucky; B11/17/1907, D11/12/1996 Riverside, CA

| 1933 | Bkn | 9(4, FB) | 14 | 40 | 2.9 | 0 | 2 | 22 | 11.0 | 0 | — | — | — | — | — | — | — | — | — | — | — | 0 | 51 |

RICHARDS, GOLDEN John Golden, WR, 6´1˝/181 lbs; Hawaii; Brigham Young; 1973: Dal, rnd 2; B12/31/1950 Salt Lake City, UT

1973	†Dal	12	1	2	2.0(2)	0	6	91	15.2(53)	1	—	—	—	—	—	—	—	—	—	kp	—	6	86
1974	Dal	14(WR)	1	-5	-5.0(-5)	0	26	467	18.0(58)	5	—	—	—	—	—	—	—	—	—	p	—	30	263
1975	†Dal	14(WR)	3	18	6.0(11)	0	21	451	21.5(62)	4	—	—	—	—	—	—	—	—	—	p	1	30	422
1976	†Dal	11(9, WR)	—	—	—	—	19	414	21.8(56)	3	—	—	—	—	—	—	—	—	—	—	—	18	222
1977	†Dal	14(WR)	—	—	—	—	17	225	13.2(50)	3	—	—	—	—	—	—	—	—	—	—	—	18	128
1978	Dal	1	—	—	—	—	1	2	2.0(2)	0	—	—	—	—	—	—	—	—	—	—	—	0	1
1978	ChiB	15(14, WR)	—	—	—	—	27	379	14.0(52)	0	—	—	—	—	—	—	—	—	—	—	—	0	190
1979	ChiB	5	—	—	—	—	5	107	21.4(52)	1	—	—	—	—	—	—	—	—	—	—	—	6	59
NFL	7	86(23)	5	15	3.0(11)	0	122	2136	17.5(62)	17	—	—	—	—	—	—	—	—	—	kp	1	108	1368

RICHARDS, HOWARD Howard Glenn, G-T, 6´6˝/263 lbs; Missouri; 1981: Dal, rnd 1; B8/7/1959 St. Louis, MO **1981** †Dal 16 (0) **1982** †Dal 8 (8, LG) **1983** †Dal 16 (2) **1984** Dal 11 (4) **1985** †Dal 7 (0) **1986** Dal 9 (2) **1987** Sea 2 (2) **NFL** 69 (18) [7 yrs]

RICHARDS, JIM James Buis, DB, 6´1˝/190 lbs; Virginia Tech; 1968: NYJ, rnd 8; B10/28/1946 Charlotte, NC **1968** †NYJ-A 12 **1969** †NYJ-A 14 (LS) **NFL** 26 [2 yrs]

RICHARDS, KINK Elvin C., B, 5´11˝/195 lbs; Simpson; B12/27/1910 Garden Grove, IL, D7/21/1976 Oakland, CA [K]

1933	†NYG	8(0)	41	277	6.8	4	7	127	18.1(60)	3	—	—	—	—	—	—	—	—	—	K	—	43	396
1934	†NYG	13(1)	48	173	3.6	1	6	56	9.3(20)	1	1	1	100.0	9	9.0(9)	0	0	—	—	—	K	—	13	221
1935	†NYG☆	12(3, fb)	153	449	2.9	4	8	41	5.1	0	—	—	—	—	—	—	—	—	—	K	—	28	510
1936	NYG	11(8, fb)	114	421	3.7	1	7	146	20.9(59)	1	—	—	—	—	—	—	—	—	—	—	—	12	509
1937	NYG	11(4)	87	329	3.8	1	10	149	14.9(50)	2	—	—	—	—	—	—	—	—	—	—	—	18	424
1938	†NYG◇	9(0)	25	111	4.4	0	1	8	8.0(8)	0	1	0	0.0	0	0.0	0	1	—	—	—	K	—	2	75
1939	†NYG	9(2)	40	117	2.9	1	2	8	4.0(8)	0	—	—	—	—	—	—	—	—	—	P	—	6	131
NFL	7	73(18)	508	1877	3.7	12	41	535	13.0(60)	7	2	1	50.0	9	4.5(9)	0	1	—	—	—	KP	—	122	2264

RICHARDS, PERRY Perry Walter, E, 6´2˝/205 lbs; Detroit Mercy; 1957: Pit, rnd 5; B1/14/1934 Detroit, MI

1957	Pit	7	—	—	—	—	1	15	15.0(15)	0	—	—	—	—	—	—	—	—	—	—	—	0	8
1958	Det	3	—	—	—	—	7	90	12.9(30)	0	—	—	—	—	—	—	—	—	—	—	—	0	45
1959	ChiC	4	—	—	—	—	5	89	17.8(25)	1	—	—	—	—	—	—	—	—	—	p	—	6	57
1960	SL	8	—	—	—	—	1	10	10.0(10)	0	—	—	—	—	—	—	—	—	—	—	—	0	5
1961	Buf-A	11	—	—	—	—	19	285	15.0(43)	3	—	—	—	—	—	—	—	—	—	k	—	18	153
1962	NYT-A	14	—	—	—	—	6	69	11.5(22)	0	—	—	—	—	—	—	—	—	—	—	—	0	35
NFL	6	47	—	—	—	—	39	558	14.3(43)	4	—	—	—	—	—	—	—	—	—	kp	—	24	301

RICHARDS, PETE J. Peter, C, 5´10˝/190 lbs; Swarthmore; B1905 **1927** Fra 3 (1)

RICHARDS, RAY Ray William, T-G-E, 6´1˝/230 lbs; Nebraska; B7/16/1906 Lincoln, NE, D9/18/1974 La Habra, CA [C] **1930** Fra 13 (10, LT) **1933** †ChiB 12 (5, rt) **1934** Det 6 (0) **1935** ChiB 12 (7, LG) **1936** ChiB 1 (1) **NFL** 44 (23) [5 yrs]

RICHARDS, TED Edward John, E, 5´9˝/174 lbs; Illinois; B11/7/1901 Oshkosh, WI, D12/1/1978 Stanwood, WA **1929** ChiB 1 (0)

RICHARDSON, AL Alpette, LB, 6´2˝/211 lbs; Georgia Tech; 1980: Atl, rnd 8; B9/23/1957 Abbeville, AL **1980** †Atl☆16 (16, LOLB) **1981** †Atl 16 (16, LOLB) **1982** †Atl 8 (8, LOLB) **1983** Atl 5 (5, llb) **1984** Atl 16 (14, RLB) **1985** Atl 16 (11, RLB) **NFL** 77 (70) [6 yrs]

RICHARDSON, AL Alvin, DE, 6´3˝/250 lbs; Grambling State; 1957: Phi, rnd 26; B2/1/1935 New Orleans, LA **1960** Bos-A 3

RICHARDSON, BOB Robert George, DB, 6´1˝/180 lbs; UCLA; B2/24/1944 Minneapolis, MN **1966** Den-A 9

RICHARDSON, BUCKY John Powell, QB, 6´1˝/228 lbs; Texas A&M; 1992: Hou, rnd 8; B2/7/1969 Baton Rouge, LA

1992	Hou	7(0)	1	-1	-1.0(-1)	0	—	—	—	—	5	0	0.0	0	0.0	0	0	1	7	—	—	0	-1
1993	Hou	2(0)	2	9	4.5(11)	0	—	—	—	—	4	3	75.0	55	13.8(34)	0	0	1	8	—	—	0	37
1994	Hou	7(4, qb)	30	217	7.2(18)	1	—	—	—	—	181	94	51.9	1202	6.6(76)	6	6	23	136	—	—	6	618
NFL	3	16(4)	33	225	6.8(18)	1	—	—	—	—	185	97	52.4	1257	6.8(76)	6	6	25	151	—	—	6	654

RICHARDSON, C.J. Carl Ray, DB, 5´10˝/209 lbs; Miami (FL); 1995: Hou, rnd 7; B6/10/1972 Dallas, TX **1995** Arz 1 (0) **1997** Sea 14 (0) **NFL** 15 (0) [2 yrs]

RICHARDSON, CHARLIE Charles A., BB, /143 lbs; none; B9/12/1906, IL, D1/11/2000 Huntington Beach, CA **1925** Mil 1 (0)

RICHARDSON, DAMIEN Damien A., DB, 6´1˝/210 lbs; Arizona State; 1998: Car, rnd 6; B4/3/1976 Los Angeles, CA **1998** Car 14 (7, SS) **1999** Car 15 (0) **2000** Car 16 (1) **2001** Car 16 (2) **2002** Car 16 (0) **NFL** 77 (10) [5 yrs]

YEAR	TEAM	G (GS, POS)	RUSH	YD	AVG (LG)	TD	REC	YD	AVG (LG)	TD	PASS COMP	PCT	YD	AVG (LG)	TD	INT	SK	YD	QBR	KPR	OTD	PTS	TAY

RICHARDSON, DAVID   David, DB, 6′0″/202 lbs; Cal Poly-San Luis Obispo; B9/9/1981 Inglewood, CA   **2004** Jax 2 (0)   **2005**†Jax 7 (0)   **NFL** 9 (0) [2 yrs]

RICHARDSON, ERIC   Eric, WR, 6′1″/183 lbs; San Jose State; 1984: Buf, rnd 2; B4/18/1962 San Francisco, CA

1985	Buf	16(1)	—	—	—	—	12	201	16.8(27)	0	—	—	—	—	—	—	—	—	—	k	—	0	125
1986	Buf	14(1)	—	—	—	—	3	49	16.3(32)	0	—	—	—	—	—	—	—	—	—	kp	—	0	53
NFL	2	30(2)	—	—	—	—	15	250	16.7(32)	0	—	—	—	—	—	—	—	—	—	kp	—	0	177

RICHARDSON, ERNIE   Ernest, TE, 6′5″/225 lbs; Jackson State; B7/17/1950 Greenville, MS   **1974** Cle 2

RICHARDSON, GLOSTER   Gloster Van, WR-FL, 6′2″/200 lbs; Jackson State; 1965: KC, rnd 7; B7/18/1942 Greenville, MS

1967	KC-A	13	—	—	—	—	12	312	26.0(56)	2	—	—	—	—	—	—	—	—	—	—	—	12	166
1968	†KC-A	13(fl)	1	-3	-3.0(-3)	0	22	494	22.5(92)	6	—	—	—	—	—	—	—	—	—	—	—	36	274
1969	†KC-A	13(fl)	—	—	—	—	23	381	16.6(39)	2	—	—	—	—	—	—	—	—	—	—	—	12	201
1970	KC	12	1	4	4.0(4)	0	5	171	34.2(61)	2	—	—	—	—	—	—	—	—	—	—	—	12	100
1971	Dal	11(3)	—	—	—	—	8	170	21.3(45)	3	—	—	—	—	—	—	—	—	—	—	—	18	100
1972	†Cle	7	—	—	—	—	1	7	7.0(7)	0	—	—	—	—	—	—	—	—	—	—	—	0	4
1973	Cle	14(wr)	3	-10	-3.3(4)	0	12	175	14.6(32)	1	—	—	—	—	—	—	—	—	—	—	—	6	83
1974	Cle	9(wr)	—	—	—	—	9	266	29.6(60)	2	—	—	—	—	—	—	—	—	—	—	—	12	143
NFL	8	92(3)	5	-9	-1.8(4)	0	92	1976	21.5(92)	18	—	—	—	—	—	—	—	—	—	—	—	108	1069

RICHARDSON, GRADY   Grady Gene, TE, 6′4″/225 lbs; Cal State-Fullerton; B4/2/1952 Houston, TX   **1979** Was 3   **1980** Was 1 (0)   **NFL** 4 [2 yrs]

RICHARDSON, GREG   Gregory Lamar, WR, 5′7″/171 lbs; Alabama; 1987: Min, rnd 6; B10/6/1964 Mobile, AL   **1987** Min 2 (0)   **1988** TB 2 (0)   **NFL** 4 (0) [2 yrs]

RICHARDSON, HUEY   Huey L., LB-DE, 6′5″/238 lbs; Florida; 1991: Pit, rnd 1; B2/2/1968 Atlanta, GA   **1991** Pit 5 (0)   **1992** Was 4 (0)   **1992** NYJ 7 (0)   **NFL** 16 (0) [2 yrs]

RICHARDSON, JEFF   Jeffrey, T-G-C, 6′3″/250 lbs; Michigan State; 1967: NYJ, rnd 6; B9/1/1944 Johnstown, PA   **1967** NYJ-A 11   **1968**†NYJ-A 14   **1969** Mia-A 3   **NFL** 28 [3 yrs]

RICHARDSON, JERRY   Jerome Johnson, FL-HB, 6′3″/185 lbs; Wofford; 1958: Bal, rnd 13; B7/11/1936 Spring Hope, NC

1959	†Bal	11	—	—	—	—	7	81	11.6(15)	3	—	—	—	—	—	—	—	—	—	—	—	18	56
1960	Bal	11	—	—	—	—	8	90	11.3(23)	1	—	—	—	—	—	—	—	—	—	—	—	6	50
NFL	2	22	—	—	—	—	15	171	11.4(23)	4	—	—	—	—	—	—	—	—	—	—	—	24	106

RICHARDSON, JERRY   Jerome J., DB, 6′3″/190 lbs; West Texas A&M; 1964: LA, rnd 3/Den, rnd 7; B11/13/1941 Los Angeles, CA   **1964** LARm 14 (LCB)   **1965** LARm 14   **1966** Atl 14 (14, LS)   **1967** Atl 13   **NFL** 55 (14) [4 yrs]

RICHARDSON, JESS   Jesse William, DT, 6′2″/261 lbs; Alabama; 1953: Phi, rnd 8; B8/18/1930 Philadelphia, PA, D6/17/1975 Philadelphia, PA   **1953** Phi 12   **1954** Phi 12 (LDT)   **1955** Phi 12 (LDT)   **1956** Phi 11 (LDT)   **1958** Phi 12 (LDT)   **1959** Phi★12 (LDT)   **1960**†Phi☆12 (LDT)   **1961** Phi☆14 (LDT)   **1962** Bos-A 14 (LDT)   **1963**†Bos-A 14 (LDT)   **1964** Bos-A 14 (ldt)   **NFL** 139 [11 yrs]

RICHARDSON, JOHN   John Edward, DT, 6′3″/245 lbs; UCLA; 1967: Mia, rnd 9; B5/25/1945 Minneapolis, MN   **1967** Mia-A 14 (8, RDT)   **1968** Mia-A 11 (3)   **1969** Mia-A 14 (14, RDT)   **1970**†Mia 14 (14, RDT)   **1971** Mia 10 (5, rdt)   **1972** SL 11 (LDT)   **1973** SL 14 (LDT)   **NFL** 88 (44) [7 yrs]

RICHARDSON, KYLE   Kyle Davis, P, 6′2″/210 lbs; Arkansas State; B3/2/1973 Farmington, MO [P]   **1997** Mia 3 (0)   **1999** Bal 16 (0)   **2000**†Bal 16 (0)   **2003** Cin 11 (0)   **2005** Cle 16 (0)

1997	Sea	2(0)	1	0	0.0(0)	0	—	—	—	—	—	—	—	—	—	—	—	—	—	P	—	0	0
1998	Bal	16(0)	1	0	0.0(0)	0	—	—	—	—	—	—	—	—	—	—	—	—	—	P	—	0	0
2001	†Bal	16(0)	1	0	0.0(0)	0	—	—	—	—	1	1	100.0	11	-11.0(-11)	0	0	—	—	P	—	0	-6
2002	Min	16(0)	1	0	0.0(0)	0	—	—	—	—	—	—	—	—	—	—	—	—	—	P	—	0	0
NFL	8	112(0)	4	0	0.0	0	—	—	—	—	1	1	100.0	11	-11.0(-11)	0	0	—	—	P	—	0	-6

RICHARDSON, MIKE   Michael Wayne, RB, 5′11″/196 lbs; SMU; 1969: Hou, rnd 7; B12/8/1946 Fort Worth, TX

1969	†Hou-A	14	5	51	10.2(28)	0	—	—	—	—	—	—	—	—	—	—	—	—	—	p	—	2	109
1970	Hou	14(RB)	103	368	3.6(34)	2	34	381	11.2(67)	1	—	—	—	—	—	—	—	—	—	p	—	18	564
1971	Hou	7	17	33	1.9(13)	0	4	17	4.3(9)	0	—	—	—	—	—	—	—	—	—	kp	—	0	53
NFL	3	35	125	452	3.6(34)	2	38	398	10.5(67)	1	—	—	—	—	—	—	—	—	—	kp	—	20	725

RICHARDSON, MIKE   Michael Calvin, DB, 6′0″/187 lbs; Arizona State; 1983: Chi, rnd 2; B5/23/1961 Compton, CA [I]   **1983** ChiB 16 (14, LCB)   **1984**†ChiB 15 (15, LCB)   **1985**†ChiB 14 (14, LCB)   **1986**†ChiB☆16 (16, LCB)   **1987**†ChiB 11 (6, LCB)   **1988**†ChiB 16 (15, LCB)   **1989** SF 3 (0)   **NFL** 91 (80) [7 yrs]

RICHARDSON, PAUL   Paul P., WR, 6′3″/204 lbs; UCLA; B2/25/1969 Chicago, IL   **1993** Phi 1 (0)

RICHARDSON, PETE   E.C., DB, 6′0″/193 lbs; Dayton; 1968: Buf, rnd 7; B10/17/1946 Youngstown, OH   **1969** Buf-A 14 (rs)   **1970** Buf 12 (FS)   **1971** Buf 13 (fs)   **NFL** 39 [3 yrs]

RICHARDSON, REGGIE   Reginald Eugene, DB, 6′0″/180 lbs; Utah; B4/13/1963 Houston, TX   **1987** LARm 3 (3)

RICHARDSON, TERRY   Terry J., RB, 6′0″/204 lbs; Syracuse; B10/8/1971 Fort Lauderdale, FL

| 1996 | †Pit | 1(0) | 5 | 17 | 3.4(8) | 0 | — | — | — | — | — | — | — | — | — | — | — | — | — | — | — | 0 | 17 |

RICHARDSON, TOM   Thomas Edward, WR, 6′2″/195 lbs; Jackson State; B10/15/1944 Greenville, MS   **1970** Bos 1

| 1969 | Bos-A | 14 | — | — | — | — | 1 | 5 | 5.0(5) | 0 | — | — | — | — | — | — | — | — | — | — | — | 0 | 3 |
| NFL | 2 | 15 | — | — | — | — | 1 | 5 | 5.0(5) | 0 | — | — | — | — | — | — | — | — | — | — | — | 0 | 3 |

RICHARDSON, TONY   Antonio, FB, 6′1″/232 lbs; Auburn; B12/17/1971 Frankfurt, Germany

1995	†KC	14(1)	8	18	2.3(5)	0	—	—	—	—	—	—	—	—	—	—	—	—	—	—	—	0	18
1996	KC	13(0)	4	10	2.5(4)	0	2	18	9.0(17)	1	—	—	—	—	—	—	—	—	—	—	—	6	24
1997	†KC	14(0)	2	11	5.5(6)	0	3	6	2.0(3)	3	—	—	—	—	—	—	—	—	—	—	—	18	29
1998	KC	14(1)	20	45	2.3(6)	2	2	13	6.5(15)	0	—	—	—	—	—	—	—	—	—	p	—	12	67
1999	KC	16(16, FB)	84	387	4.6(26)	1	24	141	5.9(29)	0	—	—	—	—	—	—	—	—	—	—	—	6	468
2000	KC	16(16, FB)	147	697	4.7(33)	3	58	468	8.1(24)	3	—	—	—	—	—	—	—	—	—	—	—	36	976
2001	KC	14(7, FB)	66	191	2.9(19)	7	30	265	8.8(47)	0	—	—	—	—	—	—	—	—	—	—	—	42	394
2002	KC	14(12, FB)	22	81	3.7(14)	2	18	125	6.9(23)	1	—	—	—	—	—	—	—	—	—	—	—	18	169
2003	†KC◇	16(10, FB)	24	60	2.5(8)	0	12	76	6.3(14)	0	—	—	—	—	—	—	—	—	—	—	—	0	98
2004	KC★	12	56	4.7(13)		0	19	118	6.2(21)	0	—	—	—	—	—	—	—	—	—	—	—	0	115
2005	KC	16(16, FB)	6	20	3.3(8)	0	9	68	7.6(22)	1	—	—	—	—	—	—	—	—	—	—	—	6	59
NFL	11	163(95)	395	1576	4.0(33)	15	177	1298	7.3(47)	9	—	—	—	—	—	—	—	—	—	p	—	144	2415

RICHARDSON, WALLY   Wallace Herman, QB, 6′4″/225 lbs; Penn State; 1997: Bal, rnd 7; B2/11/1974 Orangeburg, SC

| 1998 | Bal | 1(0) | 1 | 0 | 0.0(0) | 0 | — | — | — | — | 2 | 1 | 50.0 | 1 | 0.5(1) | 0 | 0 | — | — | — | — | 0 | 1 |

RICHARDSON, WILLIE   Willie Louis, FL-WR, 6′1″/198 lbs; Jackson State; 1963: Bal, rnd 7/NYJ, rnd 3; B11/17/1939 Clarksdale, MS

1963	Bal	13(3)	—	—	—	—	17	204	12.0(22)	0	—	—	—	—	—	—	—	—	—	kp	—	0	121
1964	Bal	10	—	—	—	—	3	42	14.0(16)	0	—	—	—	—	—	—	—	—	—	—	—	0	21
1965	Bal	9	—	—	—	—	1	14	14.0(14)	1	—	—	—	—	—	—	—	—	—	—	—	6	12
1966	Bal	13	—	—	—	—	14	246	17.6(69)	2	—	—	—	—	—	—	—	—	—	—	—	12	133
1967	Bal★	14(FL)	—	—	—	—	63	860	13.7(31)	8	—	—	—	—	—	—	—	—	—	—	—	48	470
1968	Bal★	14(FL)	—	—	—	—	37	698	18.9(79)	8	—	—	—	—	—	—	—	—	—	—	—	48	389
1969	Bal	14(FL)	—	—	—	—	43	646	15.0(39)	3	—	—	—	—	—	—	—	—	—	—	—	18	338
1970	†Mia	10	—	—	—	—	7	67	9.6(27)	1	—	—	—	—	—	—	—	—	—	—	—	6	39
1971	†Bal	12	2	27	13.5(24)	0	10	173	17.3(49)	2	—	—	—	—	—	—	—	—	—	—	—	12	124
NFL	9	109(3)	2	27	13.5(24)	0	195	2950	15.1(79)	25	—	—	—	—	—	—	—	—	—	kp	—	150	1646

RICHESON, RAY   Thomas Ray, G, 6′0″/235 lbs; Alabama; 1948: Bkn-A, rnd 26/Phi, rnd 10; B9/27/1923 Russellville, AL, D4/1/2003 Birmingham, AL   **1949** ChiH-A 12 (1)

RICHEY, MIKE   James Michael, T, 6′4″/263 lbs; North Carolina; 1969: Buf, rnd 4; B1/30/1947 Washington, DC   **1969** Buf-A 14 (LT)   **1970** NO 5   **NFL** 19 [2 yrs]

RICHEY, TOM   Thomas John, T, 6′4″/274 lbs; Kentucky; B6/13/1961 Euclid, OH   **1987** Cin 3 (0)

RICHEY, WADE   Wade Edward, K, 6′3″/205 lbs; LSU; B5/19/1976 Lafayette, LA [K]   **1998**†SF 16 (0)   **1999** SF 16 (0)   **2000** SF 16 (0)   **2001** SD 16 (0)   **2002** SD 12 (0)   **2003**†Bal 15 (0)   **2004** Bal 12 (0)   **NFL** 103 (0) [7 yrs]

YEAR	TEAM	G(GS, POS)	RUSH	YD	AVG(LG)	TD	REC	YD	AVG(LG)	TD	PASS	COMP	PCT	YD	AVG(LG)	TD	INT	SK	YD	QBR	KPR	OTD	PTS	TAY

RICHIE, DAVID David James, NT, 6´4˝/280 lbs; Washington; B9/26/1973 Orange, CA **1997** Den 2 (0) **1998**†SF 8 (0) **1999** SF 1 (0) **2000** Jax 1 (0) **NFL** 12 (0) [4 yrs]

RICHINS, ALDO Aldo, WB, 5´9˝/188 lbs; Utah; B11/2/1910 Colonia Diaz, Mexico **1935** Det 1 (0)

RICHMAN, HARRY Harry Eugene, G, 5´11˝/186 lbs; Illinois; B1/9/1907 Chicago, IL, D5/1967 Champaign, IL **1929** ChiB 1 (0)

RICHMOND, ROCK Rodney, DB, 5´10˝/180 lbs; Oregon; B1/7/1958 Los Angeles, CA **1987** Pit 2 (0)

RICHTER, FRANK Frank Ashton, LB, 6´3˝/235 lbs; Georgia; 1967: Den, rnd 7; B12/24/1944 Toccoa, GA **1967** Den-A 9 **1968** Den-A 11 **1969** Den-A 14 (5, rlb) **NFL** 34 (5) [3 yrs]

RICHTER, LES Leslie Alan, LB-MG, 6´3˝/238 lbs; California; 1952: DalT, rnd 1; B10/6/1930 Fresno, CA [K] **1954** LARm✧12 **1955**†LARm★12 (LLB) **1956** LARm★12 (MG) **1957** LARm★12 (MG) **1958** LARm★12 (MLB) **1959** LARm★12 (MLB) **1960** LARm★12 (MLB) **1961** LARm✧14 (MLB)

YEAR	TEAM	G(GS, POS)	RUSH	YD	AVG(LG)	TD	REC	YD	AVG(LG)	TD	PASS	COMP	PCT	YD	AVG(LG)	TD	INT	SK	YD	QBR	KPR	OTD	PTS	TAY
1962	LARm	14	0	8	(8)	0	—	—	—	—	—	—	—	—	—	—	—	—	—	—	—	—	0	8
NFL	9	112	0	8	(8)	0	—	—	—	—	—	—	—	—	—	—	—	—	—	—	Kki	—	193	123

RICHTER, PAT Hugh Vernon, TE-SE-P, 6´5˝/229 lbs; Wisconsin; 1963: Was, rnd 1/Den, rnd 10; B9/9/1941 Madison, WI [P]

YEAR	TEAM	G(GS, POS)	RUSH	YD	AVG(LG)	TD	REC	YD	AVG(LG)	TD	PASS	COMP	PCT	YD	AVG(LG)	TD	INT	SK	YD	QBR	KPR	OTD	PTS	TAY
1963	Was	14(SE)	—	—	—	—	27	383	14.2(34)	3	—	—	—	—	—	—	—	—	—	—	P	—	18	207
1964	Was	14	1	-9	-9.0(-9)	0	4	49	12.3(16)	0	—	—	—	—	—	—	—	—	—	—	P	—	0	16
1965	Was	11(SE)	—	—	—	—	16	189	11.8(35)	2	—	—	—	—	—	—	—	—	—	—	P	—	12	105
1966	Was	14(te)	—	—	—	—	7	100	14.3(20)	0	—	—	—	—	—	—	—	—	—	—	P	—	0	50
1967	Was	14	—	—	—	—	1	31	31.0(31)	0	—	—	—	—	—	—	—	—	—	—	P	—	0	16
1968	Was	14(TE)	—	—	—	—	42	533	12.7(40)	9	—	—	—	—	—	—	—	—	—	—	—	—	54	312
1969	Was	11	—	—	—	—	—	—	—	—	—	—	—	—	—	—	—	—	—	—	k	—	0	-15
1970	Was	11(1)	—	—	—	—	2	30	15.0(26)	0	—	—	—	—	—	—	—	—	—	—	k	—	0	-15
NFL	8	103(1)	1	-9	-9.0(-9)	0	99	1315	13.3(40)	14	—	—	—	—	—	—	—	—	—	—	Pk	—	84	674

RICKARDS, PAUL Paul E., QB, 6´1˝/193 lbs; Pittsburgh; B6/30/1926 Wheeling, WV, D7/26/1999

YEAR	TEAM	G(GS, POS)	RUSH	YD	AVG(LG)	TD	REC	YD	AVG(LG)	TD	PASS	COMP	PCT	YD	AVG(LG)	TD	INT	SK	YD	QBR	KPR	OTD	PTS	TAY
1948	LARm	3(0)	2	21	10.5(11)	0	—	—	—	—	2	2	100.0	4	2.0(3)	0	0	—	—	—	—	—	0	23

RICKETTS, TOM Thomas Gordon, G-T, 6´5˝/296 lbs; Pittsburgh; 1989: Pit, rnd 1; B11/21/1965 Pittsburgh, PA **1989**†Pit 12 (2) **1990** Pit 16 (3) **1991** Pit 14 (8, LG) **1992** Ind 8 (2) **1993** KC 3 (0) **NFL** 53 (15) [5 yrs]

RICKS, HAROLD Harold, RB, 5´10˝/200 lbs; Tennessee-Chattanooga; B12/26/1962

YEAR	TEAM	G(GS, POS)	RUSH	YD	AVG(LG)	TD	REC	YD	AVG(LG)	TD	PASS	COMP	PCT	YD	AVG(LG)	TD	INT	SK	YD	QBR	KPR	OTD	PTS	TAY
1987	TB	3(1)	24	76	3.2(14)	1	1	12	12.0(12)	0	—	—	—	—	—	—	—	—	—	—	k	—	6	103

RICKS, LAWRENCE Lawrence Talmadge, RB, 5´9˝/194 lbs; Michigan; 1983: Dal, rnd 8; B6/4/1961 Barberton, OH

YEAR	TEAM	G(GS, POS)	RUSH	YD	AVG(LG)	TD	REC	YD	AVG(LG)	TD	PASS	COMP	PCT	YD	AVG(LG)	TD	INT	SK	YD	QBR	KPR	OTD	PTS	TAY
1983	KC	12(0)	21	28	1.3(10)	0	3	5	1.7(7)	0	—	—	—	—	—	—	—	—	—	—	—	—	0	31
1984	KC	5(0)	2	1	0.5(1)	0	—	—	—	—	—	—	—	—	—	—	—	—	—	—	k	—	0	9
NFL	2	17(0)	23	29	1.3(10)	0	3	5	1.7(7)	0	—	—	—	—	—	—	—	—	—	—	k	—	0	40

RICKS, MIKHAEL Mikhael Roy, TE-WR, 6´5˝/260 lbs; Stephen F. Austin State; 1998: SD, rnd 2; B11/14/1974 Galveston, TX

YEAR	TEAM	G(GS, POS)	RUSH	YD	AVG(LG)	TD	REC	YD	AVG(LG)	TD	PASS	COMP	PCT	YD	AVG(LG)	TD	INT	SK	YD	QBR	KPR	OTD	PTS	TAY
1998	SD	16(9, wr)	—	—	—	—	30	450	15.0(39)	2	—	—	—	—	—	—	—	—	—	—	—	—	12	235
1999	SD	16(15, WR)	2	11	5.5(7)	0	40	429	10.7(50)	0	1	0	0.0	0	0.0	0	0	—	—	—	—	—	2	226
2000	SD	3(1)	—	—	—	—	3	35	11.7(23)	0	—	—	—	—	—	—	—	—	—	—	—	—	0	18
2000	KC	1(0)	—	—	—	—	—	—	—	—	—	—	—	—	—	—	—	—	—	—	—	—	—	—
2001	KC	16(0)	—	—	—	—	18	252	14.0(40)	1	—	—	—	—	—	—	—	—	—	—	—	—	8	131
2002	Det	14(12, TE)	—	—	—	—	27	339	12.6(49)	3	—	—	—	—	—	—	—	—	—	—	—	—	18	185
2003	Det	16(6, te)	—	—	—	—	37	434	11.7(38)	2	—	—	—	—	—	—	—	—	—	—	—	—	12	227
NFL	6	82(43)	2	11	5.5(7)	0	155	1939	12.5(50)	8	1	0	0.0	0	0.0	0	0	—	—	—	—	—	52	1021

RIDDELL, SPEED Ted Eugene, E, 5´10˝/185 lbs; Nebraska; B6/17/1896 Beatrice, NE, D12/8/1968 Scottsbluff, NE **1920** RI 1 (0)

RIDDICK, LOUIS Louis Angelo, DB, 6´2˝/215 lbs; Pittsburgh; 1991: SF, rnd 9; B3/15/1969 Quakertown, PA **1992** Atl 16 (4) **1993** Cle 15 (0) **1994**†Cle 16 (0) **1996** Atl 16 (1) **1998** Oak 15 (3)

YEAR	TEAM	G(GS, POS)	RUSH	YD	AVG(LG)	TD	REC	YD	AVG(LG)	TD	PASS	COMP	PCT	YD	AVG(LG)	TD	INT	SK	YD	QBR	KPR	OTD	PTS	TAY
1995	Cle	16(0)	—	—	—	—	1	25	25.0(25)	0	—	—	—	—	—	—	—	—	—	—	—	—	0	13
NFL	6	94(8)	—	—	—	—	1	25	25.0(25)	0	—	—	—	—	—	—	—	—	—	—	S	—	2	13

RIDDICK, RAY Raymond Ernest, E, 6´1˝/211 lbs; Fordham; B10/17/1917 Lowell, MA, D7/14/1976 Hampton, NH

YEAR	TEAM	G(GS, POS)	RUSH	YD	AVG(LG)	TD	REC	YD	AVG(LG)	TD	PASS	COMP	PCT	YD	AVG(LG)	TD	INT	SK	YD	QBR	KPR	OTD	PTS	TAY
1940	GB	10(7, RE)	—	—	—	—	11	148	13.5	0	—	—	—	—	—	—	—	—	—	—	—	—	0	74
1941	†GB☆	11(9, RE)	—	—	—	—	3	33	11.0(45)	0	—	—	—	—	—	—	—	—	—	—	k	—	0	16
1942	GB	3(1)	—	—	—	—	6	104	17.3(24)	1	—	—	—	—	—	—	—	—	—	—	—	—	6	57
1946	GB	2(0)	—	—	—	—	—	—	—	—	—	—	—	—	—	—	—	—	—	—	—	—	—	—
NFL	4	26(17)	—	—	—	—	20	285	14.3(45)	1	—	—	—	—	—	—	—	—	—	—	k	—	6	147

RIDDICK, ROBB Robbert Lee, RB, 6´0˝/195 lbs; Millersville; 1981: Buf, rnd 9; B4/26/1957 Quakertown, PA

YEAR	TEAM	G(GS, POS)	RUSH	YD	AVG(LG)	TD	REC	YD	AVG(LG)	TD	PASS	COMP	PCT	YD	AVG(LG)	TD	INT	SK	YD	QBR	KPR	OTD	PTS	TAY
1981	†Buf	10(0)	3	29	9.7(12)	0	—	—	—	—	—	—	—	—	—	—	—	—	—	—	kp	—	0	104
1983	Buf	16(0)	4	18	4.5(12)	0	3	43	14.3(24)	0	—	—	—	—	—	—	—	—	—	—	kp	—	0	219
1984	Buf	16(0)	3	3	1.0(6)	0	23	276	12.0(38)	0	—	—	—	—	—	—	—	—	—	—	—	—	0	141
1986	Buf	15(8, RB)	150	632	4.2(41)	4	49	468	9.6(31)	1	—	—	—	—	—	—	—	—	—	—	k	—	30	991
1987	Buf	6(1)	59	221	3.7(25)	5	15	96	6.4(17)	3	1	1	100.0	35	35.0(35)	0	0	—	—	—	k	—	50	398
1988	†Buf	15(0)	111	438	3.9(21)	12	30	282	9.4(26)	1	2	2	100.0	31	15.5(26)	0	0	—	—	—	k	1	84	730
NFL	6	78(9)	330	1341	4.1(41)	21	120	1165	9.7(38)	5	3	3	100.0	66	22.0(35)	0	0	—	—	—	kp	1	164	2582

RIDDLE, RYAN Ryan, DE, 6´2˝/251 lbs; California; 2005: Oak, rnd 6; B7/5/1981 Los Angeles, CA **2005** Oak 12 (0)

RIDGE, HOUSTON Houston Robert, DE-DT, 6´4˝/270 lbs; San Diego State; 1966: SD, rnd 13; B7/18/1944 Madera, CA **1966** SD-A 11 **1967** SD-A 14 (LDT) **1968** SD-A 14 (LDE) **1969** SD-A 5 **NFL** 44 [4 yrs]

RIDGEWAY, DANTE Dante DeAndre, WR, 5´11˝/212 lbs; Ball State; 2005: SL, rnd 6; B4/18/1984 Chicago, IL

YEAR	TEAM	G(GS, POS)	RUSH	YD	AVG(LG)	TD	REC	YD	AVG(LG)	TD	PASS	COMP	PCT	YD	AVG(LG)	TD	INT	SK	YD	QBR	KPR	OTD	PTS	TAY
2005	NYJ	7(0)	—	—	—	—	2	26	13.0(17)	0	—	—	—	—	—	—	—	—	—	—	—	—	0	13

RIDGLE, ELSTON Elston Albert, DE, 6´6˝/265 lbs; Northern Arizona; Nevada-Reno; B8/24/1963 Los Angeles, CA **1987** SF 3 (2) **1989** Buf 1 (0) **1989** Sea 2 (0) **1990** Phx 10 (0) **1992** Cin 7 (0) **NFL** 23 (2) [4 yrs]

RIDGWAY, COLIN Colin, P, 6´5˝/211 lbs; Lamar; B2/19/1937 Melbourne, Australia, D5/13/1993 University Park, TX **1965** Dal 3

RIDLEHUBER, PRESTON Howard Preston, RB, 6´2˝/217 lbs; Georgia; 1966: SF, rnd 11/NYJ, rnd 19; B11/2/1943 Greenwood, SC

YEAR	TEAM	G(GS, POS)	RUSH	YD	AVG(LG)	TD	REC	YD	AVG(LG)	TD	PASS	COMP	PCT	YD	AVG(LG)	TD	INT	SK	YD	QBR	KPR	OTD	PTS	TAY
1966	Atl	3	4	23	5.8(12)	0	4	84	21.0(53)	2	—	—	—	—	—	—	—	—	—	—	—	—	12	75
1968	†Oak-A	10	4	7	1.8(10)	0	—	—	—	—	—	—	—	—	—	—	—	—	—	—	—	1	6	7
1969	Buf-A	9	4	25	6.3(11)	0	—	—	—	—	1	1	100.0	45	45.0(45)	1	0	—	—	—	p	—	0	51
NFL	3	22	12	55	4.6(12)	0	4	84	21.0(53)	2	1	1	100.0	45	45.0(45)	1	0	—	—	—	p	1	18	133

RIDLER, DON Donald George, T, 6´0˝/210 lbs; Michigan State; B1907 Detroit, MI, D1963 **1931** Cle 1 (1)

RIDLON, JIMMY James Arthur, DB, 6´1˝/181 lbs; Syracuse; 1957: SF, rnd 4; B7/11/1934 Nanuet, NY **1957**†SF 12 **1958** SF 12 (DB) **1959** SF 12 **1960** SF 12 **1961** SF 11 **1962** SF 9 (6, ls) **1963** Dal 7 (4) **1964** Dal☆14 (10, LS) **NFL** 89 (20) [8 yrs]

RIEHM, CHRIS Christopher Alan, G-T, 6´6˝/275 lbs; Ohio State; B4/14/1961 Columbus, OH **1986** LARd 12 (2) **1987** LARd 1 (0) **1988** LARd 8 (4) **NFL** 21 (6) [3 yrs]

RIEMERSMA, JAY Allen Jay, TE, 6´5˝/255 lbs; Michigan; 1996: Buf, rnd 7; B5/17/1973 Evansville, IN

YEAR	TEAM	G(GS, POS)	RUSH	YD	AVG(LG)	TD	REC	YD	AVG(LG)	TD	PASS	COMP	PCT	YD	AVG(LG)	TD	INT	SK	YD	QBR	KPR	OTD	PTS	TAY
1997	Buf	16(8, te)	—	—	—	—	26	208	8.0(22)	2	—	—	—	—	—	—	—	—	—	—	—	—	14	114
1998	†Buf	16(4)	—	—	—	—	25	288	11.5(28)	6	—	—	—	—	—	—	—	—	—	—	k	—	36	168
1999	†Buf	14(11, TE)	—	—	—	—	37	496	13.4(38)	4	—	—	—	—	—	—	—	—	—	—	—	—	24	268
2000	Buf	12(12, TE)	—	—	—	—	31	372	12.0(35)	5	—	—	—	—	—	—	—	—	—	—	—	—	30	211
2001	Buf	16(15, TE)	—	—	—	—	53	590	11.1(36)	3	—	—	—	—	—	—	—	—	—	—	—	—	18	310
2002	Buf	16(15, TE)	—	—	—	—	32	350	10.9(29)	0	—	—	—	—	—	—	—	—	—	—	—	—	0	175
2003	Pit	11(7, te)	—	—	—	—	10	138	13.8(24)	1	—	—	—	—	—	—	—	—	—	—	—	—	6	74
2004	Pit	11(2)	—	—	—	—	7	82	11.7(26)	2	—	—	—	—	—	—	—	—	—	—	—	—	12	51
NFL	8	112(74)	—	—	—	—	221	2524	11.4(38)	23	—	—	—	—	—	—	—	—	—	—	k	—	140	1371

YEAR	TEAM	G (GS, POS)	RUSH	YD	AVG (LG)	TD	REC	YD	AVG (LG)	TD	PASS	COMP	PCT	YD	AVG (LG)	TD	INT	SK	YD	QBR	KPR	OTD	PTS	TAY

RIENSTRA, JOHN John William, G, 6´5˝/273 lbs; Temple; 1986: Pit, rnd 1; B3/22/1963 Grand Rapids, MI **1986** Pit 4 (4) **1987** Pit 12 (2) **1988** Pit 5 (4) **1989**†Pit 15 (14, LG) **1990** Pit 6 (3) **1991** Cle 16 (16, LG) **1992** Cle 7 (5, lg) **NFL** 65 (48) [7 yrs]

RIESENBERG, DOUG Douglas John, T, 6´5˝/280 lbs; California; 1987: NYG, rnd 6; B7/22/1965 Moscow, ID **1987** NYG 8 (0) **1988** NYG 16 (11, RT) **1989**†NYG 16 (16, RT) **1990**†NYG 16 (16, RT) **1991** NYG 15 (15, RT) **1992** NYG 16 (16, RT) **1993**†NYG 16 (16, RT) **1994** NYG 16 (16, RT) **1995** NYG 16 (16, RT) **1996** TB 10 (10, RT) **NFL** 145 (132) [10 yrs]

RIETH, BILL William John, G-C, 5´11˝/203 lbs; Carnegie Mellon; B6/20/1916 Cleveland, OH, D10/15/1999 Lorain, OH **1941** Cle 6 (1) **1942** Cle 10 (4) **1944** Cle 9 (3) **1945** Cle 1 (0) **NFL** 26 (8) [4 yrs]

RIEVES, CHARLIE Charles Ernest, LB, 6´1˝/218 lbs; Alabama; Houston; B1/6/1939 Stuttgart, AR **1962** Oak-A 14 (RLB) **1963** Oak-A 9 **1964** Hou-A 8 **1965** Hou-A 7 **NFL** 38 [4 yrs]

RIFENBURG, DICK Richard Gale, E, 6´3˝/195 lbs; Michigan; 1948: Phi, rnd 15; B8/21/1926 Petoskey, MI, D12/5/1994 Cheektowaga, NY

YEAR	TEAM	G (GS, POS)	RUSH	YD	AVG (LG)	TD	REC	YD	AVG (LG)	TD	PASS	COMP	PCT	YD	AVG (LG)	TD	INT	SK	YD	QBR	KPR	OTD	PTS	TAY
1950	Det	12	—	—	—	—	10	96	9.6 (19)	1	—	—	—	—	—	—	—	—	—	—	—	—	6	53

RIFFLE, CHARLEY Charles Francis, G, 6´0˝/212 lbs; Notre Dame; B1/6/1918 Dillonvale, OH, D2/28/2002 Sun City West, AZ **1944** Cle 8 (1) **1946**†NYY-A 14 (13, RG) **1947**†NYY-A 14 (4) **1948** NYY-A 14 (0) **AAFC** 42 (17) [3 yrs]

RIFFLE, DICK Fred Richard, B, 6´1˝/200 lbs; Albright; 1938: Phi, rnd 2; B2/2/1915 Wellsboro, PA, D4/29/1981 Corning, NY **[K]**

YEAR	TEAM	G (GS, POS)	RUSH	YD	AVG (LG)	TD	REC	YD	AVG (LG)	TD	PASS	COMP	PCT	YD	AVG (LG)	TD	INT	SK	YD	QBR	KPR	OTD	PTS	TAY
1938	Phi	11 (4)	65	227	3.5	1	—	—	—	—	31	9	29.0	178	5.7 (39)	2	4	—	—	—	—	—	6	176
1939	Phi	10 (3)	18	61	3.4	0	6	57	9.5	0	4	1	25.0	2	0.5 (2)	0	1	—	—	—	P	—	0	51
1940	Phi	11 (6, FB)	81	238	2.9	4	8	58	7.3	1	—	—	—	—	—	—	—	—	—	—	P	—	30	312
1941	Pit✧	10 (7, FB)	109	388	3.6 (54)	1	2	24	12.0 (14)	1	39	8	20.5	88	2.3 (22)	1	9	—	—	—	Pkpi	—	12	292
1942	Pit	11 (11, FB)	115	467	4.1 (44)	4	3	50	16.7 (31)	0	8	3	37.5	64	8.0 (27)	0	1	—	—	—	KPkpi	—	25	598
NFL	5	53 (31)	388	1381	3.6 (54)	10	19	189	9.9 (31)	2	82	21	25.6	332	4.0 (39)	3	15	—	—	—	KPkpi	—	73	1429

RIGGINS, CHARLES Charles LaCarda, DE, 6´5˝/295 lbs; Bethune-Cookman; 1982: GB, rnd 9; B11/9/1959 Sanford, FL **1987** TB 3 (0)

RIGGINS, JOHN Robert John 'Diesel', RB, 6´2˝/230 lbs; Kansas; 1971: NYJ, rnd 1; B8/4/1949 Centralia, KS; HOF 1992

YEAR	TEAM	G (GS, POS)	RUSH	YD	AVG (LG)	TD	REC	YD	AVG (LG)	TD	PASS	COMP	PCT	YD	AVG (LG)	TD	INT	SK	YD	QBR	KPR	OTD	PTS	TAY
1971	NYJ	14 (14, FB)	180	769	4.3 (25)	1	36	231	6.4 (32)	2	—	—	—	—	—	—	—	—	—	—	—	—	18	905
1972	NYJ	12 (8, FB)	207	944	4.6 (40)	7	21	230	11.0 (67)	1	—	—	—	—	—	—	—	—	—	—	—	—	48	1134
1973	NYJ	11 (11, FB)	134	482	3.6 (15)	4	23	158	6.9 (19)	0	—	—	—	—	—	—	—	—	—	—	—	—	24	601
1974	NYJ	10 (9, FB)	169	680	4.0 (34)	5	19	180	9.5 (32)	2	—	—	—	—	—	—	—	—	—	—	—	—	42	830
1975	NYJ★	14 (14, FB)	238	1005	4.2 (42)	8	30	363	12.1 (34)	1	—	—	—	—	—	—	—	—	—	—	—	—	54	1272
1976	†Was	14 (14, FB)	162	572	3.5 (15)	3	21	172	8.2 (18)	1	—	—	—	—	—	—	—	—	—	—	—	—	24	693
1977	Was	5 (5, fb)	68	203	3.0 (12)	0	7	95	13.6 (53)	2	—	—	—	—	—	—	—	—	—	—	—	—	12	261
1978	Was	15 (15, FB)	248	1014	4.1 (31)	5	31	299	9.6 (33)	0	—	—	—	—	—	—	—	—	—	—	—	—	30	1214
1979	Was	16 (15, FB)	260	1153	4.4 (66)	9	28	163	5.8 (23)	3	—	—	—	—	—	—	—	—	—	—	—	—	72	1340
1981	Was	15 (4, rb)	195	714	3.7 (24)	**13**	6	59	9.8 (22)	0	—	—	—	—	—	—	—	—	—	—	—	—	78	874
1982	†Was	8 (8, RB)	**177**	553	3.1 (19)	3	10	50	5.0 (11)	0	—	—	—	—	—	—	—	—	—	—	—	—	18	608
1983	†Was☆	15 (15, RB)	375	1347	3.6 (44)	**24**	5	29	5.8 (14)	0	1	0	0.0	0	0.0	0	0	—	—	—	—	—	144	1602
1984	†Was	14 (14, RB)	327	1239	3.8 (24)	**14**	7	43	6.1 (11)	0	—	—	—	—	—	—	—	—	—	—	—	—	84	1401
1985	Was	12 (11, RB)	176	677	3.8 (51)	8	6	18	3.0 (8)	0	1	0	0.0	0	0.0	0	0	—	—	—	—	—	48	766
NFL	14	175 (157)	2916	11352	3.9 (66)	104	250	2090	8.4 (67)	12	2	0	0.0	0	0.0	0	0	—	—	—	—	—	696	13497

RIGGLE, BOB Robert Dunbar, DB, 6´1˝/200 lbs; Penn State; 1966: Atl, rnd 20; B2/5/1944 Washington, PA **1966** Atl 14 (RS) **1967** Atl 11 **NFL** 25 [2 yrs]

RIGGS, GERALD Gerald Antonio, RB, 6´1˝/230 lbs; Arizona State; 1982: Atl, rnd 1; B11/6/1960 Tullos, LA

YEAR	TEAM	G (GS, POS)	RUSH	YD	AVG (LG)	TD	REC	YD	AVG (LG)	TD	PASS	COMP	PCT	YD	AVG (LG)	TD	INT	SK	YD	QBR	KPR	OTD	PTS	TAY
1982	†Atl	9 (0)	78	299	3.8 (37)	5	23	185	8.0 (15)	0	—	—	—	—	—	—	—	—	—	—	—	—	30	442
1983	Atl	14 (0)	100	437	4.4 (40)	8	17	149	8.8 (25)	0	—	—	—	—	—	—	—	—	—	—	k	—	48	667
1984	Atl☆	15 (14, RB)	353	1486	4.2 (57)	13	42	277	6.6 (21)	0	—	—	—	—	—	—	—	—	—	—	—	—	78	1755
1985	Atl★	16 (16, RB)	**397**	**1719**	4.3 (50)	10	33	267	8.1 (44)	0	—	—	—	—	—	—	—	—	—	—	—	—	60	**1953**
1986	Atl✧	16 (15, RB)	343	1327	3.9 (31)	9	24	136	5.7 (11)	0	1	0	0.0	0	0.0	0	0	—	—	—	—	—	54	1485
1987	Atl✧	12 (12, RB)	203	875	4.3 (44)	2	25	199	8.0 (48)	0	—	—	—	—	—	—	—	—	—	—	—	—	12	995
1988	Atl	9 (9, RB)	113	488	4.3 (34)	1	22	171	7.8 (30)	0	—	—	—	—	—	—	—	—	—	—	—	—	6	584
1989	Was	12 (7, rb)	201	834	4.1 (58)	4	7	67	9.6 (13)	0	—	—	—	—	—	—	—	—	—	—	—	—	24	908
1990	†Was	10 (0)	123	475	3.9 (20)	6	7	60	8.6 (18)	0	—	—	—	—	—	—	—	—	—	—	—	—	36	565
1991	†Was	16 (0)	78	248	3.2 (32)	11	1	5	5.0 (5)	0	—	—	—	—	—	—	—	—	—	—	—	—	66	361
NFL	10	129 (73)	1989	8188	4.1 (58)	69	201	1516	7.5 (48)	0	1	0	0.0	0	0.0	0	0	—	—	—	k	—	414	9711

RIGGS, JIM James Thomas, TE, 6´5˝/245 lbs; Clemson; 1987: Cin, rnd 4; B9/23/1963 Fort Knox, KY

YEAR	TEAM	G (GS, POS)	RUSH	YD	AVG (LG)	TD	REC	YD	AVG (LG)	TD	PASS	COMP	PCT	YD	AVG (LG)	TD	INT	SK	YD	QBR	KPR	OTD	PTS	TAY
1987	Cin	9 (0)	—	—	—	—	—	—	—	—	—	—	—	—	—	—	—	—	—	—	—	—	—	—
1988	†Cin	16 (1)	—	—	—	—	9	82	9.1 (16)	0	—	—	—	—	—	—	—	—	—	—	—	—	0	41
1989	Cin	10 (1)	—	—	—	—	5	29	5.8 (9)	0	—	—	—	—	—	—	—	—	—	—	—	—	0	15
1990	†Cin	16 (0)	—	—	—	—	8	79	9.9 (21)	0	—	—	—	—	—	—	—	—	—	—	k	—	0	32
1991	Cin	16 (1)	—	—	—	—	4	14	3.5 (7)	0	—	—	—	—	—	—	—	—	—	—	k	—	0	5
1992	Cin	12 (2)	—	—	—	—	11	70	6.4 (17)	0	—	—	—	—	—	—	—	—	—	—	—	—	0	35
1993	Was	3 (0)	—	—	—	—	—	—	—	—	—	—	—	—	—	—	—	—	—	—	—	—	—	—
NFL	7	82 (5)	—	—	—	—	37	274	7.4 (21)	0	—	—	—	—	—	—	—	—	—	—	k	—	0	127

RIGGS, THRON Thron, T, 6´1˝/225 lbs; Washington; B4/25/1921 Buckley, WA **1944** Bos 10 (1)

RIGHETTI, JOE Joseph William, DT, 6´2˝/253 lbs; Waynesburg; 1969: Cle, rnd 6; B12/31/1947 Fredericktown, PA **1969**†Cle 14 **1970** Cle 9 **NFL** 23 [2 yrs]

RILEY G, 5´11˝/195 lbs; none; B1902, deceased **1924** Rac 1 (1)

RILEY, AVON Avon Gabrielle, LB, 6´3˝/230 lbs; UCLA; 1981: Hou, rnd 9; B2/10/1958 Savannah, GA **1981** Hou 16 (0) **1982** Hou 9 (8, LOLB) **1983** Hou 16 (16, LOLB) **1984** Hou 16 (16, LOLB) **1985** Hou 15 (15, LILB) **1986** Hou 16 (6, lilb) **1987** Pit 3 (0) **NFL** 91 (61) [7 yrs]

RILEY, BOB Robert Henry, T, 6´5˝/276 lbs; Indiana; 1987: Min, rnd 10; B6/23/1964 Pittsburgh, PA **1987** Cin 3 (3)

RILEY, BOBBY Robert, WR, 5´8˝/168 lbs; Oklahoma State; B10/17/1964 **1987** NYJ 1 (0)

RILEY, BUTCH Thomas Mitchem, LB, 6´2˝/220 lbs; Texas A&M-Kingsville; 1969: Bal, rnd 12; B3/13/1947 Ingleside, TX **1969** Bal 11

RILEY, CAMERON Cameron, DB, 6´1˝/195 lbs; Missouri; B5/13/1964 Metroplois, IL **1987** Pit 2 (2)

RILEY, EARL Earl, DB, 6´1˝/205 lbs; Washington State; B1/13/1977 Dos Palos, CA **2000** Dal 1 (0)

RILEY, ERIC Eric, TE, 6´3˝/230 lbs; Eastern Washington; B10/10/1964 Snoquamie, WA

YEAR	TEAM	G (GS, POS)	RUSH	YD	AVG (LG)	TD	REC	YD	AVG (LG)	TD	PASS	COMP	PCT	YD	AVG (LG)	TD	INT	SK	YD	QBR	KPR	OTD	PTS	TAY
1987	NYJ	2 (1)	—	—	—	—	4	42	10.5 (16)	0	—	—	—	—	—	—	—	—	—	—	—	—	0	21

RILEY, EUGENE Milton Eugene, TE, 6´2˝/236 lbs; Ball State; B10/9/1966 Cincinnati, OH **1990** Ind 1 (0)

YEAR	TEAM	G (GS, POS)	RUSH	YD	AVG (LG)	TD	REC	YD	AVG (LG)	TD	PASS	COMP	PCT	YD	AVG (LG)	TD	INT	SK	YD	QBR	KPR	OTD	PTS	TAY
1991	Det	5 (1)	—	—	—	—	1	3	3.0 (3)	0	—	—	—	—	—	—	—	—	—	—	—	—	0	2
NFL	2	6 (1)	—	—	—	—	1	3	3.0 (3)	0	—	—	—	—	—	—	—	—	—	—	—	—	0	2

RILEY, JIM James Glen, DE, 6´4˝/250 lbs; Oklahoma; 1967: Mia, rnd 2; B7/6/1945 Galveston, TX **1967** Mia-A 14 **1968** Mia-A 13 (9, LDE) **1969** Mia-A 14 (14, LDE) **1970**†Mia 14 (14, LDE) **1971**†Mia 13 (13, LDE) **NFL** 68 (50) [5 yrs]

RILEY, JACK John Horn, T-G, 6´3˝/220 lbs; Northwestern; B6/13/1909 Chicago, IL, D3/22/1993 Kenilworth, IL **1933** Bos 12 (12, RT)

RILEY, KARON Karon, LB, 6´2˝/268 lbs; SMU; Minnesota; 2001: Chi, rnd 4; B8/23/1978 Detroit, MI **2001** ChiB 5 (0) **2002** Atl 3 (0) **2003** Atl 16 (0) **2004** Atl 1 (0) **NFL** 25 (0) [4 yrs]

RILEY, KEN Kenneth Jerome, DB, 5´11˝/181 lbs; Florida A&M; 1969: Cin, rnd 6; B8/6/1947 Bartow, FL **[I]** **1970**†Cin 14 (RCB) **1971** Cin 13 (RCB) **1972** Cin 12 (RCB) **1973**†Cin 14 (RCB) **1974** Cin 14 (RCB) **1975**†Cin☆14 (RCB) **1976** Cin☆14 (RCB) **1977** Cin 14 (RCB) **1978** Cin 16 (RCB) **1979** Cin 13 (RCB) **1980** Cin 16 (16, RCB) **1981**†Cin☆16 (16, RCB) **1982**†Cin 9 (9, RCB) **1983** Cin☆14 (14, RCB)

YEAR	TEAM	G (GS, POS)	RUSH	YD	AVG (LG)	TD	REC	YD	AVG (LG)	TD	PASS	COMP	PCT	YD	AVG (LG)	TD	INT	SK	YD	QBR	KPR	OTD	PTS	TAY
1969	Cin-A	14 (RCB)	—	—	—	—	2	15	7.5 (17)	0	—	—	—	—	—	—	—	—	—	—	ki	—	0	178
NFL	15	207 (55)	—	—	—	—	2	15	7.5 (17)	0	—	—	—	—	—	—	—	—	—	—	ki	5	30	453

YEAR	TEAM	G (GS, POS)	RUSH	YD	AVG (LG)	TD	REC	YD	AVG (LG)	TD	PASS	COMP	PCT	YD	AVG (LG)	TD	INT	SK	YD	QBR	KPR	OTD	PTS	TAY

Riley, Larry Lawrence, DB, 5´10˝/192 lbs; Salem (NC); B11/21/1954 Eustis, FL **1977** Den 5 **1978** NYJ 4 **NFL** 9 [2 yrs]

Riley, Lee Leon Francis, DB, 6´1˝/192 lbs; Detroit Mercy; 1955: Det, rnd 4; B8/24/1932 Omaha, NE **[I]** **1955** Det 12 **1958** Phi 12 (DB) **1959** Phi 12 (DB) **1960** NYG 12 **1961** NYT-A 12 (RS) **1962** NYT-A 14 (RS)

YEAR	TEAM	G (GS, POS)	RUSH	YD	AVG (LG)	TD	REC	YD	AVG (LG)	TD	PASS	COMP	PCT	YD	AVG (LG)	TD	INT	SK	YD	QBR	KPR	OTD	PTS	TAY
1956	Phi	9(DB)	—	—	—	—	1	10	10.0(10)	0	—	—	—	—	—	—	—	—	—	—	kpi	—	0	191
NFL	7	83	—	—	—	—	1	10	10.0(10)	0	—	—	—	—	—	—	—	—	—	—	kpi	—	0	469

Riley, Pat Patrick Joseph, DE, 6´5˝/286 lbs; Miami (FL); 1995: Chi, rnd 2; B3/8/1972 Marrero, LA **1995** ChiB 1 (0)

Riley, Phillip Phillip Shayon, WR, 5´11˝/189 lbs; Florida State; 1996: Phi, rnd 6; B9/24/1972 Orlando, FL **1996** NYJ 1 (0)

Riley, Preston Preston Troy, WR, 6´0˝/180 lbs; Memphis; 1970: SF, rnd 9; B10/30/1947 Vicksburg, MS

YEAR	TEAM	G (GS, POS)	RUSH	YD	AVG (LG)	TD	REC	YD	AVG (LG)	TD	PASS	COMP	PCT	YD	AVG (LG)	TD	INT	SK	YD	QBR	KPR	OTD	PTS	TAY
1970	†SF	14	—	—	—	—	7	136	19.4(68)	0	—	—	—	—	—	—	—	—	—	—	kp	—	0	53
1971	†SF	11	—	—	—	—	3	39	13.0(24)	0	—	—	—	—	—	—	—	—	—	—	p	—	0	17
1972	†SF	14(8, WR)	—	—	—	—	11	156	14.2(28)	1	—	—	—	—	—	—	—	—	—	—	—	—	6	83
1973	NO	1	—	—	—	—	—	—	—	—	—	—	—	—	—	—	—	—	—	—	—	—	—	—
NFL	4	40(8)	—	—	—	—	21	331	15.8(68)	1	—	—	—	—	—	—	—	—	—	—	kp	—	6	153

Riley, Steve Steven Bruce, T, 6´5˝/258 lbs; USC; 1974: Min, rnd 1; B11/23/1952 Chula Vista, CA **1974** Min 2 **1975**†Min 14 **1976**†Min 14 (14, LT) **1977**†Min 14 (14, LT) **1978** Min 5 (5, lt) **1979** Min 16 (16, LT) **1980**†Min 16 (16, LT) **1981** Min 16 (16, LT) **1982**†Min 9 (9, LT) **1983** Min 16 (15, LT) **1984** Min 16 (16, LT) **NFL** 138 (121) [11 yrs]

Riley, Victor Victor Allan, T-G, 6´5˝/328 lbs; Auburn; 1998: KC, rnd 1; B11/4/1974 Lexington, SC **1998** KC 16 (15, RT) **1999** KC 16 (16, RT) **2000** KC 16 (16, RT) **2001** KC 7 (5, rt) **2002** NO 14 (2) **2003** NO 16 (16, RT) **2004** NO 16 (15, RT) **2005** Hou 10 (8, rg/lt) **NFL** 111 (93) [8 yrs]

Rimington, Dave David Brian, C, 6´3˝/288 lbs; Nebraska; 1983: Cin, rnd 1; B5/22/1960 Omaha, NE **1983** Cin 12 (11, C) **1984** Cin 16 (16, C) **1985** Cin 16 (16, C) **1986** Cin 12 (12, C) **1987** Cin 8 (8, C) **1988**†Phi 16 (16, C) **1989**†Phi 6 (1) **NFL** 86 (80) [7 yrs]

Rimpf, Brian Brian, G-T, 6´6˝/318 lbs; East Carolina; 2004: Bal, rnd 7; B2/11/1981 Raleigh, NC **2004** Bal 1 (0) **2005** Bal 15 (7, rg) **NFL** 16 (7) [2 yrs]

Rindy, Stuart Stuart, T, 6´5˝/266 lbs; Wisconsin-Whitewater; B5/22/1964 Milwaukee, WI **1987** ChiB 2 (0)

Ring, Bill William Thomas, RB, 5´10˝/208 lbs; Brigham Young; B12/13/1956 Des Moines, IA

YEAR	TEAM	G (GS, POS)	RUSH	YD	AVG (LG)	TD	REC	YD	AVG (LG)	TD	PASS	COMP	PCT	YD	AVG (LG)	TD	INT	SK	YD	QBR	KPR	OTD	PTS	TAY
1981	†SF	12(0)	22	106	4.8(16)	0	3	28	9.3(21)	1	—	—	—	—	—	—	—	—	—	—	k	—	6	192
1982	SF	8(3)	48	183	3.8(11)	1	13	94	7.2(15)	0	—	—	—	—	—	—	—	—	—	—	kp	—	6	295
1983	†SF	16(5, fb)	64	254	4.0(25)	2	23	182	7.9(24)	0	—	—	—	—	—	—	—	—	—	—	k	—	12	373
1984	†SF	16(1)	38	162	4.3(34)	3	3	10	3.3(15)	0	—	—	—	—	—	—	—	—	—	—	k	—	18	209
1985	†SF	10(0)	8	23	2.9(9)	1	2	14	7.0(8)	0	—	—	—	—	—	—	—	—	—	—	—	—	6	40
1986	†SF	7(0)	3	4	1.3(4)	0	1	8	8.0(8)	0	—	—	—	—	—	—	—	—	—	—	k	—	0	8
NFL	6	69(9)	183	732	4.0(34)	7	45	336	7.5(24)	1	—	—	—	—	—	—	—	—	—	—	kp	—	48	1117

Ringo, Jim James Stephen, C, 6´1˝/232 lbs; Syracuse; 1953: GB, rnd 7; B11/21/1931 Orange, NJ; HOF 1981 **[C]** **1953** GB 5 (c) **1954** GB 12 (12, C) **1955** GB 12 (12, C) **1956** GB 12 (12, C) **1957** GB★12 (12, C) **1959** GB★12 (12, C) **1960**†GB★12 (12, C) **1961**†GB★14 (14, C) **1962**†GB★14 (14, C) **1963** GB★14 (14, C) **1964** Phi★14 (14, C) **1965** Phi✧14 (14, C) **1966** Phi☆14 (14, C) **1967** Phi✧14 (C)

YEAR	TEAM	G (GS, POS)	RUSH	YD	AVG (LG)	TD	REC	YD	AVG (LG)	TD	PASS	COMP	PCT	YD	AVG (LG)	TD	INT	SK	YD	QBR	KPR	OTD	PTS	TAY
1958	GB★	12(12, C)	0	13	(13)	0	—	—	—	—	—	—	—	—	—	—	—	—	—	—	—	—	0	13
NFL	15	187(168)	0	13	(13)	0	—	—	—	—	—	—	—	—	—	—	—	—	—	—	—	—	0	13

Ringwalt, Carroll Carroll Walter, C-G, 6´0˝/210 lbs; Indiana; B12/15/1907 Bedford, IN, D6/26/1990 Indianapolis, IN **1930** Por 3 (1) **1931** Fra 7 (3) **NFL** 10 (4) [2 yrs]

Riopel, Hop Albert Didace, TB, 5´8˝/165 lbs; Holy Cross; B10/11/1900 Worcester, MA, D9/4/1966 Worcester, MA **1925** Pro 4 (1)

Riordan, Mike Charles J., E-BB, 5´11˝/195 lbs; NYU; B12/8/1905, D5/1976 Trenton, NJ **1929** SI 9 (6, le)

Riordan, Tim Timothy P., QB, 6´1˝/185 lbs; Temple; 1984: SL, rnd S3; B7/15/1960 New London, CT

YEAR	TEAM	G (GS, POS)	RUSH	YD	AVG (LG)	TD	REC	YD	AVG (LG)	TD	PASS	COMP	PCT	YD	AVG (LG)	TD	INT	SK	YD	QBR	KPR	OTD	PTS	TAY
1987	NO	1(0)	1	3	3.0(3)	0	—	—	—	—	1	0	0.0	0	0.0	0	0	—	—	—	—	—	0	3

Risher, Alan Alan David, QB, 6´2˝/190 lbs; LSU; B5/6/1961 New Orleans, LA

YEAR	TEAM	G (GS, POS)	RUSH	YD	AVG (LG)	TD	REC	YD	AVG (LG)	TD	PASS	COMP	PCT	YD	AVG (LG)	TD	INT	SK	YD	QBR	KPR	OTD	PTS	TAY
1985	TB	16(0)	1	10	10.0(10)	0	—	—	—	—	—	—	—	—	—	—	—	—	—	—	—	—	0	10
1987	GB	3(3)	11	64	5.8(15)	1	—	—	—	—	74	44	59.5	564	7.6(46)	3	3	12	77	—	—	—	6	251
NFL	2	19(3)	12	74	6.2(15)	1	—	—	—	—	74	44	59.5	564	7.6(46)	3	3	12	77	—	—	—	6	261

Risien, Cody Cody Lewis, T-G, 6´7˝/269 lbs; Texas A&M; 1979: Cle, rnd 7; B3/22/1957 Bryan, TX **1979** Cle 16 (10, LG) **1980**†Cle 16 (16, RT) **1981** Cle 16 (16, RT) **1982**†Cle 9 (9, RT) **1983** Cle☆16 (16, RT) **1985**†Cle 12 (12, RT) **1986**†Cle★16 (16, RT) **1987**†Cle★13 (13, RT) **1988**†Cle 16 (16, RT) **1989**†Cle 16 (16, RT) **NFL** 146 (140) [10 yrs]

Risk, Ed Edward, DB, 5´11˝/180 lbs; Purdue; B4/5/1908 Terre Haute, IN, D1/22/1969 Jacksonville, FL **1932** ChiC 2 (0)

Risley, Elliott Elliott Clarence, T, 6´0˝/207 lbs; Indiana; B1/24/1896 Compton, IL, D8/23/1942 Dixon, IL **[K]** **1921** Ham 5 (5, LT), 2 **1922** Ham 2 (2) **1923** Ham 2 (2) **NFL** 9 (9) [3 yrs]

Rison, Andre Andre Previn, WR, 6´1˝/188 lbs; Michigan State; 1989: Ind, rnd 1; B3/18/1967 Flint, MI

YEAR	TEAM	G (GS, POS)	RUSH	YD	AVG (LG)	TD	REC	YD	AVG (LG)	TD	PASS	COMP	PCT	YD	AVG (LG)	TD	INT	SK	YD	QBR	KPR	OTD	PTS	TAY
1989	Ind	16(13, WR)	3	18	6.0(18)	0	52	820	15.8(61)	4	—	—	—	—	—	—	—	—	—	—	kp	—	24	488
1990	Atl★	16(15, WR)	—	—	—	—	82	1208	14.7(75)	10	—	—	—	—	—	—	—	—	—	—	p	—	60	654
1991	†Atl★	16(15, WR)	1	-9	-9.0(-9)	0	81	976	12.0(39)	12	—	—	—	—	—	—	—	—	—	—	—	—	72	539
1992	Atl★	15(13, WR)	—	—	—	—	93	1119	12.0(71)	11	—	—	—	—	—	—	—	—	—	—	—	—	66	615
1993	Atl★	16(16, WR)	—	—	—	—	86	1242	14.4(53)	**15**	—	—	—	—	—	—	—	—	—	—	—	—	90	696
1994	Atl	15(14, WR)	—	—	—	—	81	1088	13.4(69)	8	—	—	—	—	—	—	—	—	—	—	—	—	50	584
1995	Cle	16(14, WR)	2	0	0.0(5)	0	47	701	14.9(59)	3	—	—	—	—	—	—	—	—	—	—	—	—	18	366
1996	Jax	10(9, wr)	—	—	—	—	34	458	13.5(61)	2	—	—	—	—	—	—	—	—	—	—	—	—	12	239
1996	†GB	5(4)	—	—	—	—	13	135	10.4(22)	1	—	—	—	—	—	—	—	—	—	—	—	—	6	73
1997	†KC✧	16(16, WR)	1	2	2.0(2)	0	72	1092	15.2(45)	7	—	—	—	—	—	—	—	—	—	—	—	—	42	583
1998	KC	14(13, WR)	2	12	6.0(11)	0	40	542	13.6(80)	5	—	—	—	—	—	—	—	—	—	—	—	—	30	308
1999	KC	15(14, WR)	—	—	—	—	21	218	10.4(20)	0	—	—	—	—	—	—	—	—	—	—	—	—	0	109
2000	†Oak	16(0)	—	—	—	—	41	606	14.8(49)	6	—	—	—	—	—	—	—	—	—	—	—	—	36	333
NFL	12	186(156)	9	23	2.6(18)	0	743	10205	13.7(80)	84	—	—	—	—	—	—	—	—	—	—	kp	—	506	5586

Rissmiller, Ray Raymond Harold, T, 6´4˝/250 lbs; Georgia; 1965: Phi, rnd 2/Buf, rnd 8; B7/22/1942 Easton, PA **1966** Phi 1 **1967** NO 11 (11, LT) **1968** Buf-A 4 **NFL** 16 (11) [3 yrs]

Risvold, Ray Raymond T., B, /170 lbs; none; B3/27/1902, WI, D10/2/1984 Quincy, FL **1927** ChiC 7 (3) **1928** ChiC 3 (0) **NFL** 10 (3) [2 yrs]

Ritcher, Jim James Alexander, G, 6´3˝/273 lbs; North Carolina State; 1980: Buf, rnd 1; B5/21/1958 Hinckley, OH **1980**†Buf 14 (0) **1981**†Buf 14 (3) **1982** Buf 9 (0) **1983** Buf 16 (16, LG) **1984** Buf 14 (14, LG) **1985** Buf 16 (16, LG) **1986** Buf 16 (16, LG) **1987** Buf 12 (12, LG) **1988**†Buf 16 (16, LG) **1989**†Buf 16 (16, LG) **1990**†Buf☆16 (16, LG) **1991**†Buf★16 (16, LG) **1992**†Buf✧16 (16, LG) **1993**†Buf 12 (10, LG) **1994** Atl 2 (0) **1995**†Atl 13 (0) **NFL** 218 (167) [16 yrs]

Ritchey, James James Alan, QB, 6´2˝/220 lbs; Stephen F. Austin State; B7/10/1973 Honolulu, HI

YEAR	TEAM	G (GS, POS)	RUSH	YD	AVG (LG)	TD	REC	YD	AVG (LG)	TD	PASS	COMP	PCT	YD	AVG (LG)	TD	INT	SK	YD	QBR	KPR	OTD	PTS	TAY
1997	Ten	1(0)	1	6	6.0(6)	0	—	—	—	—	2	2	100.0	15	7.5(11)	0	0	1	9	—	—	—	0	14

Ritchhart, Del Delbert Bush, C, 6´0˝/195 lbs; Colorado; B11/2/1910, D3/1981 Denver, CO **1936** Det 11 (8, C) **1937** Det 10 (3) **NFL** 21 (11) [2 yrs]

Ritchie, Jon Jon David, FB, 6´2˝/250 lbs; Michigan; Stanford; 1998: Oak, rnd 3; B9/4/1974 Mechanicsburg, PA

YEAR	TEAM	G (GS, POS)	RUSH	YD	AVG (LG)	TD	REC	YD	AVG (LG)	TD	PASS	COMP	PCT	YD	AVG (LG)	TD	INT	SK	YD	QBR	KPR	OTD	PTS	TAY
1998	Oak	15(10, FB)	9	23	2.6(14)	0	29	225	7.8(31)	0	—	—	—	—	—	—	—	—	—	—	—	—	0	136
1999	Oak	16(14, FB)	5	12	2.4(5)	0	45	408	9.1(20)	1	—	—	—	—	—	—	—	—	—	—	—	—	6	221
2000	†Oak	13(11, FB)	—	—	—	—	26	173	6.7(17)	0	—	—	—	—	—	—	—	—	—	—	—	—	0	87
2001	†Oak	15(10, FB)	—	—	—	—	19	154	8.1(17)	2	—	—	—	—	—	—	—	—	—	—	—	—	12	87
2002	†Oak	16(2)	—	—	—	—	10	66	6.6(14)	1	—	—	—	—	—	—	—	—	—	—	—	—	6	38
2003	†Phi	16(7, FB)	1	1	1.0(1)	0	17	86	5.1(12)	3	—	—	—	—	—	—	—	—	—	—	—	—	18	59
2004	Phi	3(0)	—	—	—	—	4	36	9.0(11)	0	—	—	—	—	—	—	—	—	—	—	—	—	0	18
NFL	7	94(54)	15	36	2.4(14)	0	150	1148	7.7(31)	7	—	—	—	—	—	—	—	—	—	—	—	—	42	645

Ritzmann, Constantin Constantin, DE, 6´3˝/254 lbs; Tennessee; B12/20/1979 Mellensee, Germany **2005** Atl 1 (0)

Rivera, Gabe Adrian Gabriel, NT, 6´2˝/293 lbs; Texas Tech; 1983: Pit, rnd 1; B4/7/1961 Crystal City, TX **1983** Pit 6 (0)

RIVERA, HANK Henry Charles, DB, 5´11˝/180 lbs; Oregon State; 1962: Oak, rnd 10/Cle, rnd 5; B12/25/1938 Los Angeles, CA **1962** Oak-A 9 (ls) **1963**†Buf-A 3 **NFL** 12 [2 yrs]

RIVERA, MARCO Marco Anthony, G, 6´4˝/310 lbs; Penn State; 1996: GB, rnd 6; B4/26/1972 Brooklyn, NY **1997**†GB 14 (0) **1998**†GB 15 (15, LG) **1999** GB 16 (16, RG) **2000** GB 16 (16, RG) **2001**†GB 16 (16, RG) **2002**†GB✧16 (16, RG) **2003**†GB★16 (16, RG) **2004**†GB★16 (16, RG) **2005** Dal 14 (14, RG) **NFL** 139 (125) [9 yrs]

RIVERA, RON Ronald Eugene, LB, 6´3˝/239 lbs; California; 1984: Chi, rnd 2; B1/7/1962 Fort Ord, CA **1984**†ChiB 15 (0) **1985**†ChiB 16 (0) **1986**†ChiB 16 (2) **1987**†ChiB 12 (5, llb) **1988**†ChiB 16 (16, LLB) **1989** ChiB 16 (14, LLB) **1990**†ChiB 14 (14, RLB) **1991**†ChiB 16 (5, llb) **1992** ChiB 16 (0) **NFL** 137 (56) [9 yrs]

RIVERA, STEVE Steven Jose, WR, 5´11˝/184 lbs; California; 1976: SF, rnd 4; B8/5/1954 Pensacola, FL

YEAR	TEAM	G (GS, POS)	RUSH	YD	AVG (LG)	TD	REC	YD	AVG (LG)	TD	PASS	COMP	PCT	YD	AVG (LG)	TD	INT	SK	YD	QBR	KPR	OTD	PTS	TAY
1976	SF	11(1)	—	—	—	—	1	7	7.0(7)	0	—	—	—	—	—	—	—	—	—	—	p	—	0	2
1977	SF	1	—	—	—	—	—	—	—	—	—	—	—	—	—	—	—	—	—	—	p	—	0	-8
1977	†ChiB	3	—	—	—	—	1	7	7.0(7)	0	—	—	—	—	—	—	—	—	—	—	—	—	0	4
NFL	2	15(1)	—	—	—	—	2	14	7.0(7)	0	—	—	—	—	—	—	—	—	—	—	p	—	0	-3

RIVERS, GARLAND Garland A., DB, 6´1˝/181 lbs; Michigan; 1987: Det, rnd 4; B11/3/1964 **1987** ChiB 2 (0)

RIVERS, JAMIE James Albert, LB, 6´2˝/245 lbs; Bowling Green State; 1967: SL, rnd 5; B9/22/1945 Youngstown, OH **1968** SL 9 (MLB) **1969** SL 10 (MLB) **1970** SL 14 (MLB) **1971** SL 12 (MLB) **1972** SL 2 **1973** SL 10 **1974** NYJ 13 (MLB) **1975** NYJ 6 (2) **NFL** 76 (2) [8 yrs]

RIVERS, MARCELLUS Marcellus, TE, 6´4˝/250 lbs; Oklahoma State; B10/26/1978 Oklahoma City, OK

YEAR	TEAM	G (GS, POS)	RUSH	YD	AVG (LG)	TD	REC	YD	AVG (LG)	TD	PASS	COMP	PCT	YD	AVG (LG)	TD	INT	SK	YD	QBR	KPR	OTD	PTS	TAY
2001	NYG	16(0)	—	—	—	—	3	11	3.7(8)	2	—	—	—	—	—	—	—	—	—	—	k	—	12	12
2002	†NYG	15(0)	—	—	—	—	2	25	12.5(17)	1	—	—	—	—	—	—	—	—	—	—	—	—	8	18
2003	NYG	12(6, te)	—	—	—	—	17	155	9.1(27)	0	—	—	—	—	—	—	—	—	—	—	k	—	0	75
2004	NYG	16(3)	—	—	—	—	5	36	7.2(13)	1	—	—	—	—	—	—	—	—	—	—	k	—	6	16
2005	Hou	16(5, te)	—	—	—	—	24	168	7.0(20)	0	—	—	—	—	—	—	—	—	—	—	—	—	0	84
NFL	5	75(14)	—	—	—	—	51	395	7.7(27)	4	—	—	—	—	—	—	—	—	—	—	k	—	26	204

RIVERS, NATE Nathan, RB, 6´3˝/215 lbs; South Carolina State; 1980: Phi, rnd 5; B8/31/1955 Wadmalaw Island, SC **1980** NYG 3 (0)

RIVERS, PHILIP Philip, QB, 6´5˝/236 lbs; North Carolina State; 2004: NYG, rnd 1; B12/8/1981 Decatur, AL

YEAR	TEAM	G (GS, POS)	RUSH	YD	AVG (LG)	TD	REC	YD	AVG (LG)	TD	PASS	COMP	PCT	YD	AVG (LG)	TD	INT	SK	YD	QBR	KPR	OTD	PTS	TAY
2004	SD	2(0)	4	-5	-1.3(0)	0	—	—	—	—	8	5	62.5	33	4.1(13)	1	0	—	—	—	—	—	0	17
2005	SD	2(0)	1	-1	-1.0(-1)	0	—	—	—	—	22	12	54.5	115	5.2(22)	0	1	3	16	—	—	—	0	17
NFL	2	4(0)	5	-6	-1.2	0	—	—	—	—	30	17	56.7	148	4.9(22)	1	1	3	16	—	—	—	0	33

RIVERS, REGGIE Reginald C., RB, 6´1˝/206 lbs; Southwest Texas State; B2/22/1968 Dayton, OH

YEAR	TEAM	G (GS, POS)	RUSH	YD	AVG (LG)	TD	REC	YD	AVG (LG)	TD	PASS	COMP	PCT	YD	AVG (LG)	TD	INT	SK	YD	QBR	KPR	OTD	PTS	TAY
1991	†Den	16(0)	2	5	2.5(3)	0	—	—	—	—	—	—	—	—	—	—	—	—	—	—	—	—	0	5
1992	Den	16(3)	74	282	3.8(48)	3	45	449	10.0(37)	1	—	—	—	—	—	—	—	—	—	—	—	—	24	542
1993	†Den	16(2)	15	50	3.3(14)	1	6	59	9.8(17)	1	—	—	—	—	—	—	—	—	—	—	—	—	14	95
1994	Den	16(1)	43	83	1.9(11)	2	20	136	6.8(25)	0	1	0	0.0	0	0.0	0	0	—	—	—	—	—	12	171
1995	Den	16(0)	2	2	1.0(1)	0	3	32	10.7(23)	0	—	—	—	—	—	—	—	—	—	—	—	—	0	18
1996	†Den	16(0)	2	6	3.0(3)	0	1	-1	-1.0(-1)	0	—	—	—	—	—	—	—	—	—	—	—	—	0	6
NFL	6	96(6)	138	428	3.1(48)	6	75	675	9.0(37)	2	1	0	0.0	0	0.0	0	0	—	—	—	—	—	50	836

RIVERS, RON Ronald Leroy, RB, 5´8˝/205 lbs; Fresno State; B11/13/1971 Elizabeth, NJ

YEAR	TEAM	G (GS, POS)	RUSH	YD	AVG (LG)	TD	REC	YD	AVG (LG)	TD	PASS	COMP	PCT	YD	AVG (LG)	TD	INT	SK	YD	QBR	KPR	OTD	PTS	TAY
1995	†Det	16(0)	18	73	4.1(19)	1	1	5	5.0(5)	0	—	—	—	—	—	—	—	—	—	—	k	—	6	221
1996	Det	15(0)	19	86	4.5(26)	0	2	28	14.0(19)	0	—	—	—	—	—	—	—	—	—	—	k	—	0	93
1997	†Det	16(0)	29	166	5.7(31)	1	—	—	—	—	—	—	—	—	—	—	—	—	—	—	k	—	6	180
1998	Det	15(0)	19	102	5.4(36)	1	3	58	19.3(38)	0	—	—	—	—	—	—	—	—	—	—	k	—	6	126
1999	†Det	7(6, rb)	82	295	3.6(37)	0	22	173	7.9(31)	1	—	—	—	—	—	—	—	—	—	—	—	—	6	387
2000	Atl	6(0)	8	27	3.4(10)	0	—	—	—	—	—	—	—	—	—	—	—	—	—	—	—	—	0	27
NFL	6	75(6)	175	749	4.3(37)	3	28	264	9.4(38)	1	—	—	—	—	—	—	—	—	—	—	k	—	24	1033

RIVES, DON Donald Earl, LB, 6´2˝/225 lbs; Texas Tech; 1973: Chi, rnd 15; B8/30/1951 Wheeler, TX **1973** ChiB 14 (4) **1975** ChiB 2 (1) **1976** ChiB 14 (14, MLB) **1977**†ChiB 14 **1978** ChiB 16 (7, mlb)

YEAR	TEAM	G (GS, POS)	RUSH	YD	AVG (LG)	TD	REC	YD	AVG (LG)	TD	PASS	COMP	PCT	YD	AVG (LG)	TD	INT	SK	YD	QBR	KPR	OTD	PTS	TAY
1974	ChiB	14(7, MLB)	1	2	2.0(2)	0	—	—	—	—	—	—	—	—	—	—	—	—	—	—	—	—	0	2
NFL	6	74(33)	1	2	2.0(2)	0	—	—	—	—	—	—	—	—	—	—	—	—	—	—	i	—	0	0

RIZZO, JACK John Ralph, RB, 5´10˝/195 lbs; Lehigh; B6/15/1949 Boston, MA

YEAR	TEAM	G (GS, POS)	RUSH	YD	AVG (LG)	TD	REC	YD	AVG (LG)	TD	PASS	COMP	PCT	YD	AVG (LG)	TD	INT	SK	YD	QBR	KPR	OTD	PTS	TAY
1973	NYG	6	1	3	3.0(3)	0	1	11	11.0(11)	0	—	—	—	—	—	—	—	—	—	—	k	—	0	35

RIZZO, JOE Joseph Vincent, LB, 6´1˝/220 lbs; Kings Point; 1973: Buf, rnd 15; B12/17/1950 New York, NY **1974** Den 11 **1975** Den 14 (6, rlb) **1976** Den 12 (12, LILB/llb) **1977**†Den 13 (12, LILB) **1978**†Den 14 (14, LILB) **1979**†Den 13 (12, LILB) **1980** Den 4 (4) **NFL** 81 (60) [7 yrs]

ROACH, JOHN John Gipson, QB-DB, 6´4˝/197 lbs; SMU; 1956: ChiC, rnd 3; B3/26/1933 Dallas, TX

YEAR	TEAM	G (GS, POS)	RUSH	YD	AVG (LG)	TD	REC	YD	AVG (LG)	TD	PASS	COMP	PCT	YD	AVG (LG)	TD	INT	SK	YD	QBR	KPR	OTD	PTS	TAY
1956	ChiC	8	—	—	—	—	—	—	—	—	—	—	—	—	—	—	—	—	—	—	P	—	0	0
1959	ChiC	12	9	20	2.2(7)	0	—	—	—	—	57	22	38.6	340	6.0(62)	2	4	—	—	—	—	—	0	40
1960	SL	12(QB)	19	39	2.1(19)	1	—	—	—	—	188	87	46.3	1423	7.6(57)	17	19	—	—	62.7	—	—	6	86
1961	†GB	7	2	-5	-2.5(1)	1	—	—	—	—	4	0	0.0	0	0.0	0	0	—	—	—	—	—	6	5
1962	GB	8	1	5	5.0(5)	0	—	—	—	—	12	3	25.0	33	2.8(18)	0	0	—	—	—	—	—	0	22
1963	GB	8	3	31	10.3(22)	0	—	—	—	—	84	38	45.2	620	7.4(45)	4	8	7	53	—	—	—	0	41
1964	Dal	9(4)	8	9	1.1(11)	0	—	—	—	—	68	32	47.1	349	5.1(37)	1	6	10	87	—	—	—	0	-52
NFL	7	64(4)	42	99	2.4(22)	2	—	—	—	—	413	182	44.1	2765	6.7(62)	24	37	17	140	48.7	P	—	12	142

ROACH, ROLLIN Rollin, FB-WB, 5´6˝/145 lbs; TCU; B12/20/1902 **1927** ChiC 1 (1), 6

ROACH, TRAVIS Travis Morgan, G, 6´2˝/260 lbs; Texas; 1973: NYJ, rnd 6; B3/18/1950 Hamilton, TX, D5/30/1988 Austin, TX **1974** NYJ 14

ROACHES, CARL Carl Edward, WR, 5´8˝/168 lbs; Texas A&M; 1976: TB, rnd 14; B10/2/1953 Houston, TX **[R]** **1980**†Hou 16 (0) **1981** Hou★16 (0) **1982** Hou 9 (0) **1983** Hou 16 (0) **1985** NO 3 (0)

YEAR	TEAM	G (GS, POS)	RUSH	YD	AVG (LG)	TD	REC	YD	AVG (LG)	TD	PASS	COMP	PCT	YD	AVG (LG)	TD	INT	SK	YD	QBR	KPR	OTD	PTS	TAY
1984	Hou	16(0)	—	—	—	—	4	69	17.3(24)	0	—	—	—	—	—	—	—	—	—	—	kp	—	0	286
NFL	6	76(0)	—	—	—	—	4	69	17.3(24)	0	—	—	—	—	—	—	—	—	—	—	kp	2	12	1438

ROAF, WILLIE William Layton, T, 6´5˝/320 lbs; Louisiana Tech; 1993: NO, rnd 1; B4/18/1970 Pine Bluff, AR **1993** NO 16 (16, RT) **1994** NO★16 (16, LT) **1995** NO★16 (16, LT) **1996** NO★13 (13, LT) **1997** NO★16 (16, LT) **1998** NO✧15 (15, LT) **1999** NO★16 (16, LT) **2000**†NO★16 (16, LT) **2001** NO 7 (7, lt) **2002** KC★16 (16, LT) **2003**†KC★16 (16, LT) **2004** KC★16 (16, LT) **2005** KC★10 (10, LT) **NFL** 189 (189) [13 yrs]

ROAN, MICHAEL Michael Phillip, TE, 6´3˝/251 lbs; Wisconsin; 1995: Hou, rnd 4; B8/29/1972 Iowa City, IA

YEAR	TEAM	G (GS, POS)	RUSH	YD	AVG (LG)	TD	REC	YD	AVG (LG)	TD	PASS	COMP	PCT	YD	AVG (LG)	TD	INT	SK	YD	QBR	KPR	OTD	PTS	TAY
1995	Hou	5(2)	—	—	—	—	8	46	5.8(11)	0	—	—	—	—	—	—	—	—	—	—	—	—	0	23
1996	Hou	15(1)	—	—	—	—	—	—	—	—	—	—	—	—	—	—	—	—	—	—	k	—	0	-2
1997	Ten	14(13, TE)	—	—	—	—	12	159	13.3(26)	0	—	—	—	—	—	—	—	—	—	—	k	—	0	70
1998	Ten	16(1)	—	—	—	—	13	93	7.2(16)	0	—	—	—	—	—	—	—	—	—	—	k	1	6	36
1999	Ten	11(1)	—	—	—	—	9	93	10.3(24)	3	—	—	—	—	—	—	—	—	—	—	—	—	18	62
2000	Ten	1(1)	—	—	—	—	3	12	4.0(6)	0	—	—	—	—	—	—	—	—	—	—	—	—	0	6
NFL	6	62(19)	—	—	—	—	45	403	9.0(26)	3	—	—	—	—	—	—	—	—	—	—	k	1	24	194

ROAN, OSCAR Oscar Bennie, TE, 6´6˝/215 lbs; UCLA; SMU; 1975: Cle, rnd 3; B10/17/1951 Dallas, TX

YEAR	TEAM	G (GS, POS)	RUSH	YD	AVG (LG)	TD	REC	YD	AVG (LG)	TD	PASS	COMP	PCT	YD	AVG (LG)	TD	INT	SK	YD	QBR	KPR	OTD	PTS	TAY
1975	Cle	14(TE)	—	—	—	—	41	463	11.3(31)	3	—	—	—	—	—	—	—	—	—	—	—	—	18	247
1976	Cle	11(TE)	—	—	—	—	15	174	11.6(23)	4	—	—	—	—	—	—	—	—	—	—	—	—	24	107
1977	Cle	10(8, TE)	—	—	—	—	13	136	10.5(27)	2	—	—	—	—	—	—	—	—	—	—	—	—	12	78
1978	Cle	14	—	—	—	—	—	—	—	—	—	—	—	—	—	—	—	—	—	—	—	—	—	—
NFL	4	49(8)	—	—	—	—	69	773	11.2(31)	9	—	—	—	—	—	—	—	—	—	—	—	—	54	432

ROBB, HARRY Harry Duplein, B, 5´10˝/186 lbs; Penn State; Columbia; B5/11/1897, D12/1971 Greenville, PA **[KC]** **1921** Can 5 (5, bb), 6 **1922** Can☆9 (9, TB), 18 **1923** Can☆11 (10, BB), 6 **1925** Can 8 (7, BB), 18 **1926** Can 13 (10, BB), 13 **NFL** 46 (41), 61 [5 yrs]

ROBB, JOE Alvis Joe, DE-LB, 6´3˝/238 lbs; TCU; 1959: ChiB, rnd 14; B3/15/1937 Lufkin, TX, D4/18/1987 Houston, TX **1959** Phi 12 (LDE) **1960** Phi 12 (LDE) **1961** SL 12 (LDE) **1962** SL 14 (LDE) **1963** SL 14 (LDE) **1964** SL 13 (LDE) **1965** SL 14 (LDE) **1966** SL★14 (LDE) **1967** SL 11 (LDE) **1968** Det 9 (RDE) **1969** Det 14 (LDE) **1970** Det 6 (lde) **1971** Det 14 **NFL** 159 [13 yrs]

YEAR TEAM	G (GS, POS)	RUSH	YD	AVG (LG)	TD	REC	YD	AVG (LG)	TD	PASS COMP	PCT	YD	AVG (LG)	TD	INT	SK	YD	QBR	KPR	OTD	PTS	TAY

ROBB, LOYAL Loyal Vestus, T, 5´9˝/184 lbs; none; B7/11/1890 Fillmore County, NE, D6/7/1966 Kansas City, MO **1920** RI 1 (0)

ROBB, STAN Stanley, E, 6´0˝/185 lbs; Centre; B1901, deceased **1926** Can 3 (3), 6

ROBBINS, AUSTIN Austin Dion, DT, 6´6˝/290 lbs; North Carolina; 1994: LARd, rnd 4; B3/1/1971 Washington, DC **1994** LARd 2 (0) **1995** Oak 16 (0) **1996** NO 15 (7, RDT) **1997** NO 12 (6) **1998** NO 16 (1) **1999** NO 14 (3) **2000** Oak 3 (0) **2000** GB 2 (0) **NFL** 80 (11) [7 yrs]

ROBBINS, BARRET Barrett G., C, 6´3˝/320 lbs; TCU; 1995: Oak, rnd 2; B8/26/1973 Houston, TX **1995** Oak 16 (0) **1996** Oak 14 (14, C) **1997** Oak 16 (16, C) **1998** Oak 16 (16, C) **1999** Oak 16 (16, C) **2000**†Oak 16 (16, C) **2001** Oak 2 (2) **2002**†Oak★16 (16, C) **2003** Oak 9 (9, C) **NFL** 121 (105) [9 yrs]

ROBBINS, FRED Frederick, DT, 6´4˝/306 lbs; Wake Forest; 2000: Min, rnd 2; B3/25/1977 Pensacola, FL **2000** Min 8 (0) **2001** Min 16 (12, LDT) **2002** Min 16 (15, LDT) **2003** Min 16 (12, LDT) **2004** NYG 15 (15, RDT) **2005** NYG 16 (6, rdt) **NFL** 87 (60) [6 yrs]

ROBBINS, JACK Jack William, TB, 6´2˝/183 lbs; Arkansas; 1938: ChiC, rnd 1; B1/23/1916 Little Rock, AR, D1/1983 Lafayette, LA

1938 ChiC	9 (3)	63	213	3.4	0	—	—	—	—	97	52	53.6	577	5.9	2	9	—	—	—	—	—	0	152
1939 ChiC	8 (0)	38	97	2.6	0	2	12	6.0	0	85	36	42.4	499	5.9	4	10	—	—	P	—	—	0	-28
NFL 2	17 (3)	101	310	3.1	0	2	12	6.0	0	182	88	48.4	1076	5.9	6	19	—	—	P	—	—	0	124

ROBBINS, KEVIN Kevin Avery, T-G, 6´5˝/286 lbs; Wichita State; Michigan State; 1989: LARm, rnd 3; B12/12/1966 Washington, DC **1989** Cle 1 (0) **1990** Cle 6 (4) **1993** LARm 1 (0) **NFL** 8 (4) [3 yrs]

ROBBINS, RANDY Randy, DB, 6´2˝/189 lbs; Arizona; 1984: Den, rnd 4; B9/14/1962 Casa Grande, AZ **1984**†Den 16 (1) **1985** Den 10 (1) **1986**†Den 16 (2) **1987**†Den 10 (4) **1988** Den 16 (5, ss) **1989**†Den 16 (2) **1990** Den 16 (9, LCB) **1991**†Den 16 (2) **1992** NE 15 (15, FS/ss) **NFL** 131 (41) [9 yrs]

ROBBINS, TOOTIE James Elbert, T, 6´5˝/303 lbs; East Carolina; 1982: SL, rnd 4; B6/2/1958 Windsor, NC **1982**†SL 9 (9, RT) **1983** SL 13 (11, RT) **1984** SL 16 (16, RT) **1985** SL 12 (11, RT) **1986** SL 12 (5, rt) **1987** SL 14 (14, RT) **1988** Phx 15 (15, RT) **1989** Phx 9 (9, RT) **1990** Phx 16 (16, RT) **1991** Phx 16 (16, RT) **1992** GB 15 (15, RT) **1993** GB 12 (11, RT) **NFL** 159 (148) [12 yrs]

ROBERG, MIKE Michael, TE, 6´4˝/263 lbs; Idaho; 2001: Car, rnd 7; B9/18/1977 Kent, WA **2001**†TB 1 (0)

| 2002 †Ind | 12 (1) | — | — | — | — | 2 | 17 | 8.5 (15) | 1 | — | — | — | — | — | — | — | — | — | — | — | — | 6 | 14 |
| NFL 2 | 13 (1) | — | — | — | — | 2 | 17 | 8.5 (15) | 1 | — | — | — | — | — | — | — | — | — | — | — | — | 6 | 14 |

ROBERSON, BO Irvin, FL-HB-WR, 6´1˝/195 lbs; Cornell; B7/23/1935 Blakely, GA **[R]**

1961 †SD-A	14	58	275	4.7 (59)	3	6	81	13.5 (24)	0	—	—	—	—	—	—	—	—	—	k	—	18	358
1962 Oak-A	14 (hb)	89	270	3.0 (63)	3	29	583	20.1 (72)	3	6	0	0.0	0	0.0	0	0	—	—	k	1	44	960
1963 Oak-A	19 (FL)	19	47	2.5 (11)	0	25	407	16.3 (52)	3	—	—	—	—	—	—	—	—	—	kp	—	18	529
1964 Oak-A	14 (FL)	1	-4	-4.0 (-4)	0	44	624	14.2 (54)	1	—	—	—	—	—	—	—	—	—	kp	—	6	763
1965 Oak-A	6 (fl)	1	-4	-4.0 (-4)	0	15	220	14.7 (55)	0	—	—	—	—	—	—	—	—	—	k	—	0	185
1965 †Buf-A◇	8 (FL)	—	—	—	—	31	483	15.6 (74)	3	—	—	—	—	—	—	—	—	—	k	—	18	256
1966 Mia-A	11 (8, FL)	—	—	—	—	26	519	20.0 (80)	2	—	—	—	—	—	—	—	—	—	k	—	12	270
NFL 6	81 (8)	168	584	3.5 (63)	6	176	2917	16.6 (80)	12	6	0	0.0	0	0.0	0	0	—	—	kp	1	116	3319

ROBERSON, CHRIS Christopher Robert, DB, 5´11˝/185 lbs; Eastern Michigan; 2005: Buf, rnd 7; B6/3/1983 Farmington Hills, MI **2005** Jax 6 (0)

ROBERSON, JAMES James Earl, DE, 6´3˝/275 lbs; Florida State; B5/3/1971 Bartow, FL **1996** Hou 15 (5, rde) **1997** Ten 15 (11, RDE) **1998** Ten 10 (5, rde) **1999** Jax 2 (0) **NFL** 42 (21) [4 yrs]

ROBERSON, LAKE James Lake, DE, 6´1˝/210 lbs; Mississippi; B8/5/1918 Clarksdale, MS, D12/11/1984 Lyon, MS **1945** Det 4 (0)

ROBERSON, VERN Vernon Lee, DB, 6´1˝/195 lbs; Grambling State; B8/3/1952 Natchitoches, LA **1977** Mia 14 (9, FS) **1978** SF 16 (12, FS) **NFL** 30 (21) [2 yrs]

ROBERTS, ALFREDO Alfredo, TE-WR, 6´3˝/250 lbs; Miami (FL); 1988: KC, rnd 8; B3/1/1965 Fort Lauderdale, FL

1988 KC	16 (7, te)	—	—	—	—	10	104	10.4 (20)	0	—	—	—	—	—	—	—	—	—	—	—	0	52
1989 KC	16 (2)	—	—	—	—	8	55	6.9 (25)	1	—	—	—	—	—	—	—	—	—	—	—	6	33
1990 †KC	16 (13, TE)	—	—	—	—	11	119	10.8 (27)	0	—	—	—	—	—	—	—	—	—	k	—	0	45
1991 †Dal	16 (10, WR)	—	—	—	—	16	136	8.5 (21)	1	—	—	—	—	—	—	—	—	—	—	—	6	73
1992 Dal	16 (4)	—	—	—	—	3	36	12.0 (18)	0	—	—	—	—	—	—	—	—	—	—	—	0	18
NFL 5	80 (36)	—	—	—	—	48	450	9.4 (27)	2	—	—	—	—	—	—	—	—	—	k	—	12	220

ROBERTS, ARCHIE Arthur James, QB, 6´0˝/190 lbs; Columbia; 1965: NYJ, rnd 7; B11/4/1942 Holyoke, MA

| 1967 Mia-A | 1 | — | — | — | — | — | — | — | — | 10 | 5 | 50.0 | 11 | 1.1 (9) | 0 | 1 | 1 | 9 | — | — | — | 0 | -35 |

ROBERTS, BILL William, HB, 6´0˝/200 lbs; Dartmouth; B9/11/1929 Dubuque, IA

| 1956 GB | 4 | — | — | — | — | 1 | 14 | 14.0 (14) | 0 | — | — | — | — | — | — | — | — | — | — | — | 0 | 7 |

ROBERTS, C.R. Cornelius R., FB, 6´3˝/202 lbs; USC; 1958: NYG, rnd 14; B2/29/1936 Los Angeles, CA

1959 SF	1	10	67	6.7 (46)	1	—	—	—	—	—	—	—	—	—	—	—	—	—	—	—	6	77
1960 SF	12 (fb)	73	213	2.9 (30)	2	9	49	5.4 (27)	0	—	—	—	—	—	—	—	—	—	k	—	12	273
1961 SF	12 (10, FB)	63	338	5.4 (54)	1	10	83	8.3 (19)	0	—	—	—	—	—	—	—	—	—	—	—	6	390
1962 SF	2	9	19	2.1 (12)	0	2	0	0.0 (1)	0	—	—	—	—	—	—	—	—	—	—	—	0	19
NFL 4	27 (10)	155	637	4.1 (54)	4	21	132	6.3 (27)	0	—	—	—	—	—	—	—	—	—	k	—	24	758

ROBERTS, CLIFF Clifford, T, 6´3˝/260 lbs; Illinois; 1961: SD, rnd 6; B1938 **1961** Oak-A 10

ROBERTS, FRED Fred Everett, G, 6´1˝/200 lbs; Iowa; B3/18/1907 Knoxville, IA, D1/17/1982 Kansas City, KS **1930** Por 12 (10, RG/lg) **1931** Por 13 (5, rg) **1932** Por 1 (1) **NFL** 26 (16) [3 yrs]

ROBERTS, GARY Gary Lee, G, 6´2˝/242 lbs; Purdue; 1969: NYJ, rnd 11; B11/30/1946 Parkersburg, WV **1970** Atl 11

ROBERTS, GENE Eugene O., HB-FB, 5´11˝/188 lbs; Kansas; Tennessee-Chattanooga; 1946: NYG, rnd 8/1947: Bkn-A, rnd S; B1/20/1923

1947 NYG	9 (0)	86	296	3.4 (46)	1	4	58	14.5 (30)	0	—	—	—	—	—	—	—	—	—	k	—	6	356
1948 NYG	11 (1, FB)	145	491	3.4 (27)	0	14	222	15.9 (49)	1	—	—	—	—	—	—	—	—	—	kp	—	18	677
1949 NYG☆	12 (10, LH)	152	634	4.2 (63)	9	35	711	20.3 (85)	8	1	0	0.0	0	0.0	0	1	—	—	k	—	102	1081
1950 †NYG◇	12 (LH)	116	483	4.2 (62)	4	11	144	13.1 (47)	1	—	—	—	—	—	—	—	—	—	k	—	32	598
NFL 4	44 (11)	499	1904	3.8 (63)	14	64	1135	17.7 (85)	12	1	0	0.0	0	0.0	0	1	—	—	kp	—	158	2712

ROBERTS, GEORGE George William, P, 6´0˝/181 lbs; Virginia Tech; B6/10/1955 Lynchburg, VA **[P]** **1979**†Mia 16 **1980** Mia 16 (0) **1982**†Atl 3 (0)

1978 †Mia	16	1	-7	-7.0 (-7)	0	—	—	—	—	—	—	—	—	—	—	—	—	—	P	—	—	0	-7
1981 †SD	16 (0)	1	2	2.0 (2)	0	—	—	—	—	—	—	—	—	—	—	—	—	—	P	—	—	0	2
NFL 5	67	2	-5	-2.5 (2)	0	—	—	—	—	—	—	—	—	—	—	—	—	—	P	—	—	0	-5

ROBERTS, GREG Gregory Lafayette, G, 6´3˝/260 lbs; Oklahoma; 1979: TB, rnd 2; B1/19/1956 Nacogdoches, TX **1979**†TB 16 (16, RG) **1980** TB 6 (6, rg) **1981**†TB☆16 (14, RG) **1982** TB 7 (6, RG) **NFL** 45 (42) [4 yrs]

ROBERTS, GUY Guy Thomas, B, 5´8˝/175 lbs; Iowa State; B5/10/1900 Schaler, IA, D6/8/1993 Los Altos, CA **1926** Can 3 (3) **1927** Pot 8 (3) **NFL** 11 (6) [2 yrs]

ROBERTS, GUY Guy Michael, LB, 6´1˝/217 lbs; Maryland; 1972: Hou, rnd 8; B6/12/1950 North Babylon, NY **1972** Hou 7 **1973** Hou 14 (RLB) **1974** Hou 14 **1975** Hou 14 **1976** Atl 14 (3) **1977** Mia 4 **NFL** 67 (3) [6 yrs]

ROBERTS, HAL Hal Lynn, P, 6´1˝/180 lbs; Houston; B8/25/1952 Dallas, TX **1974**†SL 14

ROBERTS, JACK James Thomas, B, 6´0˝/210 lbs; Georgia; B9/27/1910 Pine Log, GA, D10/29/1981 St. Matthews, KY

1932 Bos	5 (0)	6	21	3.5	0	—	—	—	—	—	—	—	—	—	—	—	—	—	—	—	—	0	21
1932 SI	3 (0)	14	59	4.2	0	—	—	—	—	—	—	—	—	—	—	—	—	—	—	—	—	0	59
1933 Phi	9 (6, HB)	91	261	2.9	1	1	6	6.0 (6)	0	10	4	40.0	97	9.7	1	3	—	—	—	—	—	6	208
1934 Phi	1 (1)	10	28	2.8	0	—	—	—	—	—	—	—	—	—	—	—	—	—	—	—	—	0	28
1934 Pit	6 (0)	24	55	2.3	0	—	—	—	—	—	—	—	—	—	—	—	—	—	—	—	—	0	55
NFL 3	24 (7)	145	424	2.9	1	1	6	6.0 (6)	0	10	4	40.0	97	9.7	1	3	—	—	—	—	—	6	371

ROBERTS, LARRY Larry P., DE, 6´3˝/270 lbs; Alabama; 1986: SF, rnd 2; B6/2/1963 Dothan, AL **1986**†SF 16 (2) **1987**†SF 11 (2) **1988**†SF 16 (16, LDE) **1989**†SF 15 (5, lde) **1990**†SF 6 (0) **1991** SF 16 (9, RDE) **1992** SF 3 (0) **1993**†SF 6 (0) **NFL** 89 (34) [8 yrs]

YEAR	TEAM	G (GS, POS)	RUSH	YD	AVG(LG)	TD	REC	YD	AVG(LG)	TD	PASS	COMP	PCT	YD	AVG(LG)	TD	INT	SK	YD	QBR	KPR	OTD	PTS	TAY

ROBERTS, MACE Mason W., E-G-T, 6´0˝/185 lbs; none; B6/25/1896, IL, D1/7/1971 Hammond, IN **1920** Ham 5 (0) **1921** Ham 1 (0) **1922** Ham 2 (1) **1924** Ham 4 (1)
NFL 12 (2) [4 yrs]

ROBERTS, RAY Richard Ray, T, 6´6˝/308 lbs; Virginia; 1992: Sea, rnd 1; B6/3/1969 Asheville, NC **1992** Sea 16 (16, LT) **1994** Sea 14 (14, LT) **1995** Sea 11 (0)
1997†Det 14 (14, LT) **1998** Det 16 (16, LT) **1999** Det 14 (14, LT) **2000** Det 10 (10, LT)

1993	Sea	16(16, LT)	—	—	—		1	4	4.0(4)	0	—	—	—	—	—	—					—	—	0	2
1996	Det	16(16, LT)	—	—	—		1	5	(5)	0	—	—	—	—	—	—					—	—	0	3
NFL		9	127(116)	—	—	—		1	9	9.0(5)	0	—	—	—	—	—	—					—	—	0	5

ROBERTS, RED James Madison, T-E-TB-G, 6´1˝/235 lbs; Centre; B8/23/1900 Somerset, KY, D6/27/1945 Middlesboro, KY **1922** Tol 2 (2) **1923** Akr 1 (1) **NFL** 3 (3) [2 yrs]

ROBERTS, TERRELL Terrell, DB, 5´10˝/197 lbs; Oregon State; B4/7/1981 Berkeley, CA **2003** Cin 12 (0) **2004** Cin 11 (1) **NFL** 23 (1) [2 yrs]

ROBERTS, TIM Tim, DE, 6´6˝/318 lbs; Southern Mississippi; 1992: Hou, rnd 5; B4/14/1969 Atlanta, GA **1992**†Hou 6 (0) **1993** Hou 6 (0) **1994** Hou 12 (0) **1995** NE 13 (12, LDE)
NFL 37 (14) [4 yrs]

ROBERTS, TOM Thomas Albert, T-G, 6´1˝/215 lbs; DePaul; 1939: NYG, rnd 10; B4/1/1916 New Troy, MI, D4/8/1990 Chicago, IL **1943**†NYG 9 (0) **1944** ChiB 7 (2) **1945** ChiB 9 (1)
NFL 25 (3) [3 yrs]

ROBERTS, WALTER Walter 'The Flea', WR-SE, 5´9˝/163 lbs; San Jose State; B2/15/1942 Texarkana, TX **[R]**

1964	†Cle	14	—	—	—		1	24	24.0(24)	1	—	—	—	—	—	—					kp	—	6	400
1965	†Cle	14(SE)	3	30	10.0(14)	0	16	314	19.6(80)	4	—	—	—	—	—	—					kp	—	24	502
1966	Cle	14	—	—	—		2	19	9.5(10)	0	—	—	—	—	—	—					kp	—	0	151
1967	NO	13	—	—	—		17	384	22.6(96)	3	—	—	—	—	—	—					kp	2	30	529
1969	Was	14	—	—	—		4	66	16.5(22)	0	—	—	—	—	—	—					kp	—	0	133
1970	Was	14(12, WR)	2	15	7.5(21)	0	27	411	15.2(66)	1	—	—	—	—	—	—					p	—	6	204
NFL		6	83(12)	5	45	9.0(21)	0	67	1218	18.2(96)	9	—	—	—	—	—	—					kp	2	66	1918

ROBERTS, WES Wesley Lee, DE, 6´6˝/253 lbs; TCU; 1980: Bal, rnd 7; B8/1/1957 Dodge City, KS **1980** NYJ 6 (0)

ROBERTS, WILLIAM William Harold, G-T, 6´5˝/291 lbs; Ohio State; 1984: NYG, rnd 1; B8/5/1962 Miami, FL **1984**†NYG 11 (8, LT) **1986**†NYG 16 (0) **1987** NYG 12 (12, RT)
1988 NYG 16 (13, LT) **1989**†NYG 16 (16, LG) **1990**†NYG✩16 (16, LG) **1991** NYG 16 (16, LG) **1992** NYG 16 (15, LG) **1993**†NYG 16 (16, LG) **1994** NYG 16 (15, LG)
1995 NE 16 (11, LG) **1996**†NE 16 (16, LG) **1997** NYJ 12 (0) **NFL** 195 (154) [13 yrs]

ROBERTS, WILLIE Willie Lee, DB, 6´1˝/190 lbs; Houston; 1972: Hou, rnd 13; B6/28/1948 Colquitt, GA **1973** ChiB 4

ROBERTS, WOOKY Wolcott, BB-TB, 5´7˝/160 lbs; Colgate; Navy; B9/1/1897 Elmwood, IL, D8/27/1951 Drexel Hill, PA **[K]** **1922** Can 11 (9, BB), 6 **1923** Can 8 (3), 6
1924 Cle 9 (9, BB), 25 **1925** Cle 2 (2) **1926** Fra 6 (5, bb), 6 **NFL** 36 (28), 43 [5 yrs]

ROBERTSON, BERNARD Bernard H., T, 6´3˝/310 lbs; Tulane; 2001: Chi, rnd 5; B6/9/1979 New Orleans, LA **2002** ChiB 15 (5, lt)

ROBERTSON, BOB John Robert, T, 6´4˝/246 lbs; Illinois; 1968: Hou, rnd 9; B12/24/1946 Pittsfield, IL **1968** Hou-A 14

ROBERTSON, BOBBY Robert James, C-HB-DB, 5´11˝/185 lbs; USC; St. Mary's (CA); 1942: Bkn, rnd 1; B6/18/1917 Pine Ridge, SD

| 1942 | Bkn | 11(1, C) | 46 | 132 | 2.9(34) | 0 | 5 | 61 | 12.2(26) | 0 | 3 | 1 | 33.3 | 1 | 0.3(1) | 0 | 1 | — | — | Ppi | | — | 0 | 142 |

ROBERTSON, DEWAYNE Dewayne, DT, 6´1˝/317 lbs; Kentucky; 2003: NYJ, rnd 1; B10/16/1981 Memphis, TN **2003** NYJ 16 (16, LDT) **2004**†NYJ 16 (16, LDT)
2005 NYJ 13 (12, RDT) **NFL** 45 (44) [3 yrs]

ROBERTSON, HARRY Harold J., T, 5´10˝/185 lbs; Syracuse; B3/4/1896 Chambly, Canada, deceased **1922** Roc 1 (1)

ROBERTSON, ISIAH Isiah B., LB, 6´3˝/225 lbs; Southern (LA); 1971: LA, rnd 1; B8/17/1949 New Orleans, LA **[I]** **1971** LARm★14 (12, RLB) **1972** LARm✩14 (14, RLB)
1973†LARm★14 (14, RLB) **1974**†LARm★14 (14, RLB) **1975**†LARm★14 (14, RLB) **1976**†LARm★14 (14, RLB) **1977**†LARm★14 (14, RLB) **1978**†LARm 13 (6, rlb)
1979 Buf 16 (16, LOLB) **1980**†Buf 16 (16, ROLB) **1981**†Buf 16 (16, ROLB) **1982** Buf 9 (9, ROLB) **NFL** 168 (159) [12 yrs]

ROBERTSON, JAMAL Jamal, RB, 5´10˝/210 lbs; Ohio Northern; B1/10/1977 Washington, DC

2002	SF	6(0)	—	—	—		—	—	—		—	—	—	—	—	—					k	—	0	77
2003	SF	9(0)	32	136	4.3(23)	0	—	—	—		—	—	—	—	—	—					k	—	0	136
2004	SF	7(0)	16	71	4.4(16)	1	4	34	8.5(14)	0	—	—	—	—	—	—					k	—	6	283
2004	Car	5(0)	—	—	—		—	—	—		—	—	—	—	—	—					k	—	0	90
2005	†Car	6(0)	14	41	2.9(11)	1	—	—	—		—	—	—	—	—	—					k	—	6	154
NFL		4	33(0)	62	248	4.0(23)	2	4	34	8.5(14)	0	—	—	—	—	—	—					k	—	12	740

ROBERTSON, JAMES James A., B, 5´8˝/160 lbs; Carnegie Mellon; B3/8/1901, D12/1974 Cuyahoga Falls, OH **1924** Akr 8 (4) **1925** Akr✩8 (8, BB), 12 **NFL** 16 (12) [2 yrs]

ROBERTSON, MARCUS Marcus Aaron, DB, 5´11˝/198 lbs; Iowa State; 1991: Hou, rnd 4; B10/2/1969 Pasadena, CA **[I]** **1991**†Hou 16 (0) **1992**†Hou 16 (14, FS)
1993 Hou✩13 (13, FS) **1994** Hou 16 (16, FS) **1995** Hou 2 (2) **1996** Hou 16 (16, FS) **1997** Ten 14 (14, FS) **1998** Ten 12 (12, FS) **1999**†Ten 15 (15, FS) **2000**†Ten 15 (15, FS)
2001 Sea 12 (12, FS) **2002** Sea 15 (15, FS) **NFL** 162 (144) [12 yrs]

ROBERTSON, TOM Thomas Blane, C, 6´0˝/199 lbs; Kansas; LSU; Tulsa; B7/25/1917 Lawton, OK, D5/3/1998 Tulsa, OK **1941** Bkn 11 (0) **1942** Bkn 9 (8) **NFL** 20 (8) [2 yrs]

1946†NYY-A 14 (13, C)

ROBERTSON, TYRONE Julius Tyrone, DT, 6´4˝/295 lbs; Georgia; 2001: Buf, rnd 7; B8/15/1979 Danville, VA **2001** Buf 12 (0)

ROBESON, PAUL Paul Leroy, E-T, 6´3˝/219 lbs; Rutgers; B4/8/1898 Princeton, NJ, D1/23/1976 Philadelphia, PA **1921** Akr 8 (6, le) **1922** Mil 7 (7, RE), 12 **NFL** 15 (13) [2 yrs]

ROBINSON, BILL William Andrew, HB, 6´0˝/195 lbs; Lincoln (MO); 1952: Pit, rnd 25; B9/29/1929 **1960** NYT-A 1

| 1952 | GB | 2 | 3 | 4 | 1.3(4) | 0 | — | — | — | | — | — | — | — | — | — | | | | | k | — | 0 | 23 |
| NFL | | 2 | 3 | 3 | 4 | 1.3(4) | 0 | — | — | — | | — | — | — | — | — | — | | | | | — | 0 | 4 |

ROBINSON, BILLY John William, DB, 6´1˝/200 lbs; Arizona State; B2/13/1963 Wichita, KS **1987** Cle 3 (0)

ROBINSON, BO Melvin Dell, RB-TE, 6´2˝/228 lbs; West Texas A&M; 1979: Det, rnd 3; B5/27/1956 La Mesa, TX

1979	Det	14(12, FB)	87	302	3.5(29)	2	14	118	8.4(14)	0	—	—	—	—	—	—					k	—	12	374
1980	Det	14(0)	3	2	0.7(4)	0	—	—	—		—	—	—	—	—	—					—	—	0	2
1981	Atl	15(0)	9	24	2.7(5)	0	—	—	—		—	—	—	—	—	—					—	—	0	24
1982	†Atl	9(0)	19	108	5.7(16)	0	7	55	7.9(29)	2	—	—	—	—	—	—					—	—	12	146
1983	Atl	12(9, TE)	3	-9	3.0(7)	0	12	100	8.3(15)	0	—	—	—	—	—	—					—	—	0	59
1984	NE	16(1)	—	—	—		4	32	8.0(17)	1	—	—	—	—	—	—					k	—	6	14
NFL		6	80(22)	121	445	3.7(29)	2	37	305	8.2(29)	3	—	—	—	—	—	—					k	—	30	619

ROBINSON, BRYAN Bryan Keith, DT-DE, 6´4˝/305 lbs; Fresno State; B6/22/1974 Toledo, OH **1997** SL 11 (0) **1998** ChiB 11 (5, lde) **1999** ChiB 16 (16, LDE)
2000 ChiB 16 (16, LDE) **2001**†ChiB 16 (16, LDE) **2002** ChiB 15 (13, LDT) **2003** ChiB 16 (16, RDT) **2004** Mia 16 (13, LDT) **2005**†Cin 10 (9, LDT) **NFL** 127 (104) [9 yrs]

ROBINSON, CHARLEY Charles Rogers, G-LB, 5´11˝/240 lbs; Morgan State; B5/30/1927 Lester Manor, VA **1951** GB 2 **1954** Bal 6 **NFL** 8 [2 yrs]

ROBINSON, CRAIG Joe Craig, T, 6´4˝/250 lbs; Houston; 1971: NO, rnd 16; B12/23/1948 Austin, TX **1972** NO 8 **1973** NO 11 **NFL** 19 [2 yrs]

ROBINSON, DAMIEN Damien Dion, DB, 6´2˝/223 lbs; Iowa; 1997: Phi, rnd 4; B12/23/1973 Dallas, TX **1998** TB 7 (0) **2001**†NYJ 14 (14, FS) **2002**†NYJ 15 (15, FS)
2003†Sea 15 (4)

1999	†TB	16(16, FS)	—	—	—		1	17	17.0(17)	0	—	—	—	—	—	—					iS	—	0	35
2000	†TB	16(16, FS)	—	—	—		1	36	36.0(36)	0	—	—	—	—	—	—					i	—	0	-11
NFL		6	83(65)	—	—	—		2	53	26.5(36)	0	—	—	—	—	—	—					piS	—	0	90

ROBINSON, DAVE Richard David, LB, 6´3˝/245 lbs; Penn State; 1963: GB, rnd 1/SD, rnd 3; B5/3/1941 Mount Holly, NJ **[I]** **1963** GB 14 **1964** GB 11 (LLB) **1965**†GB 14 (LLB)
1966†GB★14 (LLB) **1967**†GB★14 (LLB) **1968** GB✩14 (LLB) **1969** GB★14 (LLB) **1970** GB 4 (llb) **1971** GB 14 (LLB) **1972**†GB 14 (LLB) **1973**†Was 14 (14, LLB)
1974†Was 14 (14, LLB) **NFL** 155 (28) [12 yrs]

ROBINSON, DEJUAN DeJuan Fitzgerald, DB, 5´10˝/185 lbs; Northern Arizona; B6/3/1965 Selma, AL **1987** Cle 3 (3)

ROBINSON, DERRECK Derreck, DE, 6´4˝/289 lbs; Iowa; B3/3/1982 Minneapolis, MN **2005** SD 3 (0)

ROBINSON, DON Don Kanary, T, 6´5˝/280 lbs; Baylor; B2/5/1965 Dallas, TX **1987** Atl 2 (0)

ROBINSON, DUNTA Dunta, DB, 6´0˝/180 lbs; South Carolina; 2004: Hou, rnd 1; B4/11/1982 Athens, GA **2004** Hou 16 (16, RCB) **2005** Hou 16 (16, RCB/lcb) **NFL** 32 (32) [2 yrs]

YEAR	TEAM	G(GS, POS)	RUSH	YD	AVG(LG)	TD	REC	YD	AVG(LG)	TD	PASS	COMP	PCT	YD	AVG(LG)	TD	INT	SK	YD	QBR	KPR	OTD	PTS	TAY

ROBINSON, ED Eldred, B, 5´8˝/155 lbs; none; B8/26/1904, D9/1986 Hoagland, IN [K] **1923** Ham 3 (2), 7 **1924** Ham 4 (3) **1925** Ham 5 (4, WB), 7 **1926** Ham 1 (0) **1926** Lou 4 (4, WB) **NFL** 17 (13), 14 [4 yrs]

ROBINSON, ED Edward, LB, 6´0˝/228 lbs; Florida; B12/7/1970 DeFuniak Springs, FL **1994**†Pit 16 (0)

ROBINSON, EDDIE Eddie Joseph, LB, 6´1˝/240 lbs; Alabama State; 1992: Hou, rnd 2; B4/13/1970 New Orleans, LA **1992**†Hou 16 (11, RLB) **1993**†Hou 16 (15, LLB) **1994** Hou 15 (15, LLB) **1995** Hou 16 (16, LLB) **1996**†Jax 16 (15, LLB) **1997**†Jax 16 (14, RLB) **1998** Ten 16 (16, LLB) **1999**†Ten 16 (16, LLB) **2000**†Ten 16 (16, RLB) **2001** Ten 16 (16, RLB) **2002** Buf 16 (15, RLB) **NFL** 175 (165) [11 yrs]

ROBINSON, EUGENE Eugene Keefe, DB, 6´1˝/190 lbs; Colgate; B5/28/1963 Hartford, CT [I] **1985** Sea 16 (0) **1986** Sea 16 (16, FS) **1987**†Sea 12 (12, FS) **1988**†Sea 16 (16, FS) **1989** Sea 16 (14, FS) **1990** Sea 16 (16, FS) **1991** Sea 16 (16, FS) **1992** Sea✧16 (16, FS) **1993** Sea★16 (16, FS) **1994** Sea 14 (14, FS) **1995** Sea 16 (16, FS) **1996**†GB 16 (16, FS) **1997**†GB 16 (16, FS) **1998**†Atl★16 (16, FS) **1999** Atl 16 (16, FS) **2000** Car 16 (16, FS) **NFL** 250 (232) [16 yrs]

ROBINSON, FRANK Frank Lawson, DB, 5´11˝/175 lbs; Boise State; 1992: Den, rnd 5; B1/11/1969 Newark, NJ **1992** Cin 3 (0) **1992** Den 12 (0) **1993**†Den 16 (2) **NFL** 31 (2) [2 yrs]

ROBINSON, FRED Frederick Leroy, G, 6´1˝/242 lbs; Washington; 1955: Cle, rnd 14; B9/2/1930 West Haven, CT **1957**†Cle 12 (RG)

ROBINSON, FRED Fred Lee, LB-DE, 6´4˝/240 lbs; Miami (FL); 1984: TB, rnd 8; B10/22/1961 Miami, FL **1984** SD 16 (0) **1985** SD 16 (1) **1986** SD 10 (5, rolb) **1986** Mia 4 (0) **NFL** 46 (6) [3 yrs]

ROBINSON, FREDDIE Freddie O'Neal, DB, 6´1˝/191 lbs; Alabama; 1987: Ind, rnd 6; B2/1/1964 Mobile, AL **1987**†Ind 9 (9, FS) **1988** Ind 13 (10, SS) **NFL** 22 (19) [2 yrs]

ROBINSON, GERALD Gerald, DE-DT, 6´3˝/262 lbs; Auburn; 1986: Min, rnd 1; B5/4/1963 Tuskegee, AL **1986** Min 12 (4) **1987**†Min 4 (0) **1989** SD 2 (0) **1990** SD 11 (1) **1991** LARm 15 (4) **1992** LARm 16 (16, LDE) **1993** LARm 16 (3) **1994** LARm 13 (0) **NFL** 89 (28) [8 yrs]

ROBINSON, GIL Gilmer George, E, 6´0˝/180 lbs; Catawba; B4/18/1910 Spencer, NC, D7/11/1985 Hemet, CA **1933** Pit 1 (0)

ROBINSON, GLENN Glenn William, DE-LB, 6´6˝/242 lbs; Oklahoma State; 1974: Bal, rnd 3; B10/20/1951 Killeen, TX **1975**†Bal 11 **1976** TB 14 (3) **1977** TB 14 **NFL** 39 (3) [3 yrs]

ROBINSON, GREG Greg, RB, 5´10˝/205 lbs; Louisiana-Monroe; 1993: LARd, rnd 8; B8/7/1969 Grenada, MS

YEAR	TEAM	G(GS, POS)	RUSH	YD	AVG(LG)	TD	REC	YD	AVG(LG)	TD	PASS	COMP	PCT	YD	AVG(LG)	TD	INT	SK	YD	QBR	KPR	OTD	PTS	TAY
1993	†LARd	12(12, RB)	156	591	3.8(16)	1	15	142	9.5(58)	0	—	—	—	—	—	—	—	—	—	—	k	—	6	669
1995	SL	6(1)	40	165	4.1(37)	0	2	12	6.0(6)	0	—	—	—	—	—	—	—	—	—	—	—	—	0	171
1996	SL	11(0)	32	134	4.2(24)	1	1	6	6.0(6)	0	—	—	—	—	—	—	—	—	—	—	—	—	6	147
NFL	3	29(13)	228	890	3.9(37)	2	18	160	8.9(58)	0	—	—	—	—	—	—	—	—	—	—	k	—	12	987

ROBINSON, GREG Gregory louis, T, 6´5˝/280 lbs; Nevada-Reno; Sacramento State; 1986: NE, rnd 5; B12/25/1962 Sacramento, CA **1986** TB 3 (0) **1987** NE 3 (3) **NFL** 6 (3) [2 yrs]

ROBINSON, GREGG Gregg Alan, DE-NT, 6´6˝/255 lbs; Dartmouth; 1978: NYJ, rnd 6; B8/16/1956 Palmer, MA **1978** NYJ 16

ROBINSON, JACK John, T, 6´2˝/220 lbs; Truman State; B6/18/1911 Miami, NM, D4/27/2001 Springer, NM **1935** Bkn 8 (0) **1936** Bkn 3 (0) **1936** ChiC 8 (0) **1937** ChiC 11 (10, RT) **1938** Pit 2 (1) **1938** Cle 6 (1) **NFL** 38 (12) [4 yrs]

ROBINSON, JACQUE Jacque, FB, 5´11˝/215 lbs; Washington; 1985: Buf, rnd 8; B3/5/1963 Oakland, CA

YEAR	TEAM	G(GS, POS)	RUSH	YD	AVG(LG)	TD	REC	YD	AVG(LG)	TD	PASS	COMP	PCT	YD	AVG(LG)	TD	INT	SK	YD	QBR	KPR	OTD	PTS	TAY
1987	Phi	3(3)	24	114	4.8(18)	0	2	9	4.5(5)	0	—	—	—	—	—	—	—	—	—	—	—	—	0	119

ROBINSON, JEFF Jeffrey William, TE, 6´4˝/264 lbs; Idaho; 1993: Den, rnd 4; B2/20/1970 Spokane, WA

YEAR	TEAM	G(GS, POS)	RUSH	YD	AVG(LG)	TD	REC	YD	AVG(LG)	TD	PASS	COMP	PCT	YD	AVG(LG)	TD	INT	SK	YD	QBR	KPR	OTD	PTS	TAY
1993	†Den	16(0)	—	—	—	—	—	—	—	—	—	—	—	—	—	—	—	—	—	—	S	—	0	0
1994	Den	16(0)	—	—	—	—	—	—	—	—	—	—	—	—	—	—	—	—	—	—	S	—	0	0
1995	Den	16(0)	—	—	—	—	—	—	—	—	—	—	—	—	—	—	—	—	—	—	kS	—	0	-1
1996	Den	16(0)	—	—	—	—	—	—	—	—	—	—	—	—	—	—	—	—	—	—	S	—	0	0
1997	SL	16(0)	—	—	—	—	—	—	—	—	—	—	—	—	—	—	—	—	—	—	S	—	0	0
1998	SL	16(0)	—	—	—	—	1	4	4.0(4)	1	—	—	—	—	—	—	—	—	—	—	—	—	6	7
1999	†SL	16(9, TE)	—	—	—	—	6	76	12.7(30)	2	—	—	—	—	—	—	—	—	—	—	—	—	12	48
2000	†SL	16(2)	—	—	—	—	5	52	10.4(27)	0	—	—	—	—	—	—	—	—	—	—	—	—	0	26
2001	†SL	16(6, te)	—	—	—	—	11	108	9.8(26)	1	—	—	—	—	—	—	—	—	—	—	—	—	6	59
2003	†Dal	16(0)	—	—	—	—	2	8	4.0(5)	2	—	—	—	—	—	—	—	—	—	—	—	—	12	14
2004	Dal	16(0)	—	—	—	—	2	2	1.0(1)	2	—	—	—	—	—	—	—	—	—	—	—	—	12	11
2005	SL	5(1)	—	—	—	—	1	28	28.0(28)	0	—	—	—	—	—	—	—	—	—	—	—	—	0	14
NFL	12	181(18)	—	—	—	—	28	278	9.9(30)	8	—	—	—	—	—	—	—	—	—	—	kS	—	48	178

ROBINSON, JEROY Jeroy, LB, 6´1˝/241 lbs; Texas A&M; 1990: Den, rnd 4; B6/14/1968 Houston, TX **1990** Den 3 (0) **1990** Phx 3 (0) **NFL** 6 (0) [1 yr]

ROBINSON, JERRY Gerald, FL-WR, 5´11˝/190 lbs; Grambling State; 1962: SD, rnd 8/Chi, rnd 11; B3/9/1939 Jonesboro, LA

YEAR	TEAM	G(GS, POS)	RUSH	YD	AVG(LG)	TD	REC	YD	AVG(LG)	TD	PASS	COMP	PCT	YD	AVG(LG)	TD	INT	SK	YD	QBR	KPR	OTD	PTS	TAY
1962	SD-A	14(FL)	2	10	5.0(7)	0	21	391	18.6(72)	3	—	—	—	—	—	—	—	—	—	—	k	—	18	489
1963	†SD-A	14	—	—	—	—	18	315	17.5(36)	2	—	—	—	—	—	—	—	—	—	—	k	—	12	165
1964	†SD-A	14	1	10	10.0(10)	0	10	93	9.3(21)	0	—	—	—	—	—	—	—	—	—	—	kp	—	0	88
1965	NYJ-A	4	—	—	—	—	—	—	—	—	—	—	—	—	—	—	—	—	—	—	kp	—	0	80
NFL	4	46	3	20	6.7(10)	0	49	799	16.3(72)	5	—	—	—	—	—	—	—	—	—	—	kp	—	30	821

ROBINSON, JERRY Jerry Dewayne, LB, 6´2˝/223 lbs; UCLA; 1979: Phi, rnd 1; B12/18/1956 San Francisco, CA **1979**†Phi 16 (6, lilb) **1980**†Phi☆16 (16, ROLB) **1981**†Phi★15 (15, ROLB) **1982** Phi 9 (9, LILB) **1983** Phi☆16 (16, LILB) **1984** Phi 15 (15, LILB) **1985**†LARd 11 (0) **1986** LARd 16 (16, LOLB) **1987** LARd 12 (12, RILB) **1988** LARd 15 (15, RILB) **1989** LARd 11 (11, RILB) **1990**†LARd 16 (16, LLB) **1991**†LARd 16 (0) **NFL** 184 (147) [13 yrs]

ROBINSON, JIM James Peter, WR, 5´9˝/170 lbs; Georgia Tech; 1975: Atl, rnd 15; B1/3/1953 New York, NY

YEAR	TEAM	G(GS, POS)	RUSH	YD	AVG(LG)	TD	REC	YD	AVG(LG)	TD	PASS	COMP	PCT	YD	AVG(LG)	TD	INT	SK	YD	QBR	KPR	OTD	PTS	TAY
1976	NYG	12(7, WR)	—	—	—	—	18	249	13.8(30)	1	—	—	—	—	—	—	—	—	—	—	kp	—	6	260
1977	NYG	14(14, WR)	—	—	—	—	22	422	19.2(80)	3	—	—	—	—	—	—	—	—	—	—	p	—	18	278
1978	NYG	16(16, WR)	—	—	—	—	32	620	19.4(52)	2	—	—	—	—	—	—	—	—	—	—	p	—	12	331
1979	NYG	11(7, WR)	—	—	—	—	13	146	11.2(31)	0	—	—	—	—	—	—	—	—	—	—	kp	—	0	107
1980	SF	5(0)	—	—	—	—	—	—	—	—	—	—	—	—	—	—	—	—	—	—	p	—	0	21
NFL	5	58(44)	—	—	—	—	85	1437	16.9(80)	6	—	—	—	—	—	—	—	—	—	—	kp	—	36	997

ROBINSON, JOHNNIE John, DB, 6´3˝/205 lbs; Tennessee State; 1966: Det, rnd 7/Buf, rnd R2; B11/6/1944 Mobile, AL **1966** Det 14

ROBINSON, JOHNNY Johnny Nolan, DB-FL-HB, 6´1˝/205 lbs; LSU; 1960: DalT, rnd 1/Det, rnd 1; B9/9/1938 Delhi, LA [I] **1963** KC-A★14 (RS) **1964** KC-A✧10 (RS) **1965** KC-A★14 (RS) **1966**†KC-A★14 (RS) **1967** KC-A★14 (RS) **1968**†KC-A★14 (RS) **1969**†KC-A☆14 (RS) **1970** KC★14 (FS) **1971**†KC☆14 (FS)

YEAR	TEAM	G(GS, POS)	RUSH	YD	AVG(LG)	TD	REC	YD	AVG(LG)	TD	PASS	COMP	PCT	YD	AVG(LG)	TD	INT	SK	YD	QBR	KPR	OTD	PTS	TAY
1960	DalT-A	14(FL)	98	458	4.7(49)	4	41	611	14.9(74)	4	1	0	0.0	0	0.0	0	1	—	—	—	kp	1	54	940
1961	DalT-A	14(FL)	52	200	3.8(45)	2	35	601	17.2(71)	5	—	—	—	—	—	—	—	—	—	—	p	—	42	540
1962	†DalT-A	14(RS)	—	—	—	—	1	16	16.0(16)	0	—	—	—	—	—	—	—	—	—	—	i	—	0	13
NFL	12	164	150	658	4.4(49)	6	77	1228	15.9(74)	9	1	0	0.0	0	0.0	0	1	—	—	—	kpi	3	108	1989

ROBINSON, JOHNNY Johnny Dean, NT, 6´2˝/260 lbs; Louisiana Tech; 1981: Oak, rnd 4; B2/14/1959 Jonesboro, LA **1981** Oak 16 (16, NT) **1982**†LARd 7 (0) **1983**†LARd 4 (0) **NFL** 27 (16) [3 yrs]

ROBINSON, JUNIOR David Lee, DB, 5´9˝/181 lbs; East Carolina; 1990: NE, rnd 5; B2/3/1968 High Point, NC, D9/30/1995 Winston-Salem, NC **1990** NE 16 (0) **1992** Det 10 (0) **NFL** 26 (0) [2 yrs]

ROBINSON, KOREN Koren, WR, 6´1˝/205 lbs; North Carolina State; 2001: Sea, rnd 1; B3/19/1980 Belmont, NC

YEAR	TEAM	G(GS, POS)	RUSH	YD	AVG(LG)	TD	REC	YD	AVG(LG)	TD	PASS	COMP	PCT	YD	AVG(LG)	TD	INT	SK	YD	QBR	KPR	OTD	PTS	TAY
2001	Sea	16(13, WR)	4	13	3.3(6)	0	39	536	13.7(42)	1	—	—	—	—	—	—	—	—	—	—	—	—	6	286
2002	Sea	16(16, WR)	8	56	7.0(20)	0	78	1240	15.9(83)	5	—	—	—	—	—	—	—	—	—	—	—	—	30	701
2003	†Sea	15(15, WR)	4	15	3.8(16)	0	65	896	13.8(38)	4	—	—	—	—	—	—	—	—	—	—	—	1	30	483
2004	†Sea	10(8, wr)	1	3	3.0(3)	0	31	495	16.0(33)	2	—	—	—	—	—	—	—	—	—	—	—	—	12	261
2005	Min★	14(5, wr)	4	27	6.8(13)	1	22	347	15.8(80)	1	—	—	—	—	—	—	—	—	—	—	kp	1	18	732
NFL	5	71(57)	21	114	5.4(20)	1	235	3514	15.0(83)	13	—	—	—	—	—	—	—	—	—	—	kp	2	96	2462

ROBINSON, LARRY Lawrence Cordill, RB, 6´4˝/210 lbs; Ferrum; Tennessee; B4/6/1951 Appomattox, VA

YEAR	TEAM	G(GS, POS)	RUSH	YD	AVG(LG)	TD	REC	YD	AVG(LG)	TD	PASS	COMP	PCT	YD	AVG(LG)	TD	INT	SK	YD	QBR	KPR	OTD	PTS	TAY
1973	Dal	4	2	17	8.5(11)	0	—	—	—	—	—	—	—	—	—	—	—	—	—	—	k	—	0	43

ROBINSON, LARRY Lawrence Wayne, DB, 5´9˝/194 lbs; Northwestern State (LA); B4/30/1962 Shreveport, LA **1987** NYJ 3 (2)

ROBINSON, LYBRANT Lybrant, DE, 6´4˝/250 lbs; Delaware State; 1989: Was, rnd 5; B8/31/1964 Salisbury, MD **1989** Was 5 (0)

ROBINSON, MARCUS Marcus Antonio, WR, 6´3˝/215 lbs; South Carolina; 1997: Chi, rnd 4; B2/27/1975 Ft. Valley, GA

YEAR	TEAM	G (GS, POS)	RUSH	YD	AVG (LG)	TD	REC	YD	AVG (LG)	TD	PASS	COMP	PCT	YD	AVG (LG)	TD	INT	SK	YD	QBR	KPR	OTD	PTS	TAY
1998	ChiB	3 (0)	—	—	—	—	4	44	11.0 (20)	1	—	—	—	—	—	—	—	—	—	—	—	—	6	27
1999	ChiB	16 (11, WR)	—	—	—	—	84	1400	16.7 (80)	9	—	—	—	—	—	—	—	—	—	—	—	—	54	745
2000	ChiB	11 (11, WR)	1	9	9.0 (9)	0	55	738	13.4 (68)	5	—	—	—	—	—	—	—	—	—	—	—	—	30	403
2001	ChiB	5 (4)	—	—	—	—	23	269	11.7 (34)	2	—	—	—	—	—	—	—	—	—	—	—	—	12	145
2002	ChiB	16 (2)	—	—	—	—	21	244	11.6 (45)	3	—	—	—	—	—	—	—	—	—	—	—	—	18	137
2003	†Bal	15 (5, wr)	—	—	—	—	31	451	14.5 (50)	6	—	—	—	—	—	—	—	—	—	—	—	—	36	256
2004	†Min	16 (7, wr)	—	—	—	—	47	657	14.0 (50)	8	—	—	—	—	—	—	—	—	—	—	—	—	48	369
2005	Min	15 (8, wr)	—	—	—	—	31	515	16.6 (68)	5	—	—	—	—	—	—	—	—	—	—	—	—	32	283
NFL	8	97 (48)	1	9	9.0 (9)	0	296	4318	14.6 (80)	39	—	—	—	—	—	—	—	—	—	—	—	—	236	2363

ROBINSON, MARK Mark Leon, DB, 5´11˝/206 lbs; Penn State; 1984: KC, rnd 4; B9/13/1962 Washington, DC **1984** KC 16 (0) **1985** KC 11 (1) **1986**†KC 9 (3) **1987** KC 12 (4) **1988** TB 9 (9, SS) **1989** TB 15 (15, SS) **1990** TB 16 (16, SS) **NFL** 88 (48) [7 yrs]

ROBINSON, MATT Matthew Gillette, QB, 6´2˝/196 lbs; Georgia; 1977: NYJ, rnd 9; B6/28/1955 Farmington, MI

YEAR	TEAM	G (GS, POS)	RUSH	YD	AVG (LG)	TD	REC	YD	AVG (LG)	TD	PASS	COMP	PCT	YD	AVG (LG)	TD	INT	SK	YD	QBR	KPR	OTD	PTS	TAY
1977	NYJ	4 (1)	5	45	9.0 (19)	0	—	—	—	—	54	20	37.0	310	5.7 (58)	2	8	7	57	—	—	—	0	-110
1978	NYJ	16 (11, QB)	28	23	0.8 (15)	0	—	—	—	—	266	124	46.6	2002	7.5 (77)	13	16	28	228	63.5	—	—	0	449
1979	NYJ	15 (1)	3	4	1.3 (10)	1	—	—	—	—	31	17	54.8	191	6.2 (33)	0	2	5	30	—	—	—	6	30
1980	Den	14 (7, qb)	21	47	2.2 (22)	3	—	—	—	—	162	78	48.1	942	5.8 (52)	2	12	17	136	—	—	—	18	78
1981	†Buf	15 (0)	1	-2	-2.0 (-2)	0	—	—	—	—	2	0	0.0	0	0.0	0	0	1	9	—	—	—	0	-2
1982	Buf	5 (0)	—	—	—	—	—	—	—	—	8	5	62.5	74	9.3 (31)	1	0	1	10	—	—	—	0	42
NFL	6	69 (20)	58	117	2.0 (22)	4	—	—	—	—	523	244	46.7	3519	6.7 (77)	18	38	59	470	50.2	—	—	24	487

ROBINSON, MIKE Michael Bruce, DE, 6´4˝/265 lbs; Oklahoma State; Arizona; 1981: Cle, rnd 4; B8/19/1956 Cleveland, OH **1981** Cle 10 (0) **1982**†Cle 8 (8, RDE) **NFL** 18 (8) [2 yrs]

ROBINSON, MIKE Michael F., DB, 6´1˝/192 lbs; Hampton; B6/24/1973 Richmond, VA **1996** GB 6 (0)

ROBINSON, PATRICK Patrick Lavel, WR, 5´8˝/176 lbs; Tennessee State; 1993: Hou, rnd 7; B10/3/1969 Memphis, TN **[R]**

YEAR	TEAM	G (GS, POS)	RUSH	YD	AVG (LG)	TD	REC	YD	AVG (LG)	TD	PASS	COMP	PCT	YD	AVG (LG)	TD	INT	SK	YD	QBR	KPR	OTD	PTS	TAY
1993	Cin	15 (3)	1	6	6.0 (6)	0	8	72	9.0 (14)	0	—	—	—	—	—	—	—	—	—	—	kp	—	0	249
1994	Arz	15 (0)	—	—	—	—	1	5	5.0 (5)	0	—	—	—	—	—	—	—	—	—	—	kp	—	0	134
NFL	2	30 (3)	1	6	6.0 (6)	0	9	77	8.6 (14)	0	—	—	—	—	—	—	—	—	—	—	kp	—	0	383

ROBINSON, PAUL Paul Harvey, RB, 6´0˝/198 lbs; Arizona; 1968: Cin, rnd 3; B12/19/1944 Tucson, AZ

YEAR	TEAM	G (GS, POS)	RUSH	YD	AVG (LG)	TD	REC	YD	AVG (LG)	TD	PASS	COMP	PCT	YD	AVG (LG)	TD	INT	SK	YD	QBR	KPR	OTD	PTS	TAY
1968	Cin-A★	14 (HB)	**238**	**1023**	4.3 (87)	**8**	24	128	5.3 (68)	1	—	—	—	—	—	—	—	—	—	—	kp	—	54	1181
1969	Cin-A✧	14 (HB)	160	489	3.1 (24)	4	20	104	5.2 (25)	0	—	—	—	—	—	—	—	—	—	—	k	—	24	674
1970	†Cin	14 (RB)	149	622	4.2 (26)	6	17	175	10.3 (27)	1	—	—	—	—	—	—	—	—	—	—	kp	—	42	923
1971	Cin	14	49	213	4.3 (17)	1	8	47	5.9 (16)	0	—	—	—	—	—	—	—	—	—	—	k	—	6	312
1972	Cin	4	21	94	4.5 (15)	0	—	—	—	—	—	—	—	—	—	—	—	—	—	—	—	—	0	94
1972	Hou	8 (RB)	86	355	4.1 (30)	3	14	112	8.0 (24)	0	—	—	—	—	—	—	—	—	—	—	—	—	18	441
1973	Hou	11	34	151	4.4 (22)	2	7	46	6.6 (19)	0	—	—	—	—	—	—	—	—	—	—	—	—	12	194
NFL	6	79	737	2947	4.0 (87)	24	90	612	6.8 (68)	2	—	—	—	—	—	—	—	—	—	—	kp	—	156	3818

ROBINSON, RAFAEL Eugene Rafael, DB, 5´11˝/200 lbs; Wisconsin; B6/19/1969 Marshall, TX **1992** Sea 6 (0) **1993** Sea 16 (1) **1994** Sea 16 (1) **1995** Sea 13 (3) **1996** Hou 16 (2) **1997** Ten 3 (0) **NFL** 70 (7) [6 yrs]

ROBINSON, REX Noble Rexford, K, 5´11˝/205 lbs; Georgia; 1981: Cin, rnd 6; B3/17/1959 Marietta, GA **[K]** **1982** NE 3 (0)

ROBINSON, SHELTON Sheldon Derrick, LB, 6´2˝/233 lbs; North Carolina; B9/14/1960 Goldsboro, NC **1982** Sea 9 (1) **1983**†Sea 16 (15, LILB) **1984**†Sea 16 (16, LILB) **1985** Sea 15 (3) **1986** Det 16 (4) **1987** Det 12 (12, LILB) **1988** Det 12 (0) **NFL** 96 (51) [7 yrs]

ROBINSON, STACY Stacy Laddell, WR, 5´11˝/186 lbs; Prairie View A&M; North Dakota State; 1985: NYG, rnd 2; B2/19/1962 St. Paul, MN

YEAR	TEAM	G (GS, POS)	RUSH	YD	AVG (LG)	TD	REC	YD	AVG (LG)	TD	PASS	COMP	PCT	YD	AVG (LG)	TD	INT	SK	YD	QBR	KPR	OTD	PTS	TAY
1985	NYG	4 (0)	—	—	—	—	—	—	—	—	—	—	—	—	—	—	—	—	—	—	—	—	—	—
1986	†NYG	12 (10, WR)	—	—	—	—	29	494	17.0 (49)	2	—	—	—	—	—	—	—	—	—	—	—	—	12	257
1987	NYG	5 (4)	—	—	—	—	6	58	9.7 (14)	2	—	—	—	—	—	—	—	—	—	—	—	—	12	39
1988	NYG	11 (0)	—	—	—	—	7	143	20.4 (62)	3	—	—	—	—	—	—	—	—	—	—	—	—	18	87
1989	†NYG	6 (0)	—	—	—	—	4	41	10.3 (16)	0	—	—	—	—	—	—	—	—	—	—	—	—	0	21
1990	†NYG	5 (0)	—	—	—	—	2	13	6.5 (7)	0	—	—	—	—	—	—	—	—	—	—	—	—	0	7
NFL	6	43 (14)	—	—	—	—	48	749	15.6 (62)	7	—	—	—	—	—	—	—	—	—	—	—	—	42	410

ROBINSON, TERRENCE Terrence, LB, 6´0˝/240 lbs; Oklahoma State; B3/12/1980 Tyler, TX **2003** Atl 1 (0)

ROBINSON, TONY Kevin Altona, QB, 6´3˝/200 lbs; Tennessee; B1/22/1964 Monticello, FL

YEAR	TEAM	G (GS, POS)	RUSH	YD	AVG (LG)	TD	REC	YD	AVG (LG)	TD	PASS	COMP	PCT	YD	AVG (LG)	TD	INT	SK	YD	QBR	KPR	OTD	PTS	TAY
1987	Was	1 (0)	2	0	0.0 (2)	0	—	—	—	—	18	11	61.1	152	8.4 (42)	0	2	2	12	—	—	—	0	-4

ROBINSON, TRAVARIS Travaris Jerod, DB, 5´10˝/193 lbs; Auburn; B9/1/1981 Miami, FL **2003** TB 4 (0) **2003** Atl 5 (1) **NFL** 9 (1) [1 yr]

ROBINSON, VIRGIL Virgil, RB, 5´11˝/195 lbs; Grambling State; 1971: GB, rnd 2; B11/2/1947 Inverness, MS

YEAR	TEAM	G (GS, POS)	RUSH	YD	AVG (LG)	TD	REC	YD	AVG (LG)	TD	PASS	COMP	PCT	YD	AVG (LG)	TD	INT	SK	YD	QBR	KPR	OTD	PTS	TAY
1971	NO	11	29	96	3.3 (12)	1	12	53	4.4 (17)	1	—	—	—	—	—	—	—	—	—	—	k	—	12	296
1972	NO	3	5	1	0.2 (5)	0	—	—	—	—	—	—	—	—	—	—	—	—	—	—	—	—	0	1
NFL	2	14	34	97	2.9 (12)	1	12	53	4.4 (17)	1	—	—	—	—	—	—	—	—	—	—	k	—	12	297

ROBINSON, WAYNE Wayne Lavern, LB-C, 6´2˝/225 lbs; Minnesota; 1952: Phi, rnd 8; B1/14/1930 Minneapolis, MN **1952** Phi 12 (LLB) **1953** Phi 11 (LLB) **1954** Phi✧12 (LLB) **1955** Phi★12 (LLB) **1956** Phi☆11 (LLB) **NFL** 58 [5 yrs]

ROBISKIE, TERRY Terry Joseph, RB, 6´1˝/210 lbs; LSU; 1977: Oak, rnd 8; B11/12/1954 New Orleans, LA **[C]**

YEAR	TEAM	G (GS, POS)	RUSH	YD	AVG (LG)	TD	REC	YD	AVG (LG)	TD	PASS	COMP	PCT	YD	AVG (LG)	TD	INT	SK	YD	QBR	KPR	OTD	PTS	TAY
1977	†Oak	14	22	100	4.5 (10)	1	—	—	—	—	—	—	—	—	—	—	—	—	—	—	k	—	6	103
1978	Oak	7 (5, rb)	49	189	3.9 (18)	2	5	51	10.2 (21)	0	—	—	—	—	—	—	—	—	—	—	k	—	12	248
1979	Oak	3 (1)	10	14	1.4 (16)	0	5	36	7.2 (11)	0	—	—	—	—	—	—	—	—	—	—	k	—	0	23
1980	Mia	8 (5, fb)	78	250	3.2 (36)	2	13	60	4.6 (15)	0	—	—	—	—	—	—	—	—	—	—	—	—	12	300
1981	Mia	1 (0)	—	—	—	—	—	—	—	—	—	—	—	—	—	—	—	—	—	—	—	—	—	—
NFL	5	33 (11)	159	553	3.5 (36)	5	23	147	6.4 (21)	0	—	—	—	—	—	—	—	—	—	—	k	—	30	674

ROBISON, BURLE Burle Hoover, E-C, 6´4˝/197 lbs; Brigham Young; B2/17/1910 Provo, UT, D12/8/1962 Reno, NV

YEAR	TEAM	G (GS, POS)	RUSH	YD	AVG (LG)	TD	REC	YD	AVG (LG)	TD	PASS	COMP	PCT	YD	AVG (LG)	TD	INT	SK	YD	QBR	KPR	OTD	PTS	TAY
1935	Phi	7 (0)	—	—	—	—	1	18	18.0 (18)	0	—	—	—	—	—	—	—	—	—	—	—	—	0	9

ROBISON, GEORGE George Alfred, G, 6´2˝/215 lbs; VMI; B2/14/1931 Jackson County, MO **1952** DalT 4 (1)

ROBISON, TOMMY Tommy L., LB, 6´4˝/290 lbs; Texas A&M; 1984: Cle, rnd S2; B11/17/1961 Merkel, TX **1987** GB 3 (0) **1989** Atl 9 (4) **NFL** 12 (4) [2 yrs]

ROBL, HAL Harold, LB, 6´0˝/227 lbs; Wisconsin-Oshkosh; B1918 Oshkosh, WI **1945** ChiC 2 (0)

ROBNETT, ED William Edward, FB-LB, 5´8˝/205 lbs; Texas A&M; Texas Tech; 1947: SF-A, rnd 12/1946: Was, rnd 18; B3/7/1920 Klondike, TX, D9/20/1990 Lubbock, TX

YEAR	TEAM	G (GS, POS)	RUSH	YD	AVG (LG)	TD	REC	YD	AVG (LG)	TD	PASS	COMP	PCT	YD	AVG (LG)	TD	INT	SK	YD	QBR	KPR	OTD	PTS	TAY
1947	SF-A	4 (0)	7	18	2.6	0	—	—	—	—	—	—	—	—	—	—	—	—	—	—	—	—	0	18

ROBNETT, MARSHALL Marshall Foch, C-G, 6´0˝/205 lbs; Texas A&M-Commerce; Texas A&M; 1941: ChiC, rnd 6; B3/8/1918 Klondike, TX, D11/28/1967 Lisbon, TX **[K]** **1943** ChiC 9 (2) **1944** C-P 8 (7, C) **1945** ChiC 5 (2) **NFL** 22 (11) [3 yrs]

ROBOTTI, FRANK Frank P., LB, 6´0˝/220 lbs; Boston College; B1939 **1961** Bos-A 12

ROBUSTELLI, ANDY Andrew Richard, DE, 6´1˝/230 lbs; Arnold; 1951: LA, rnd 19; B12/6/1925 Stamford, CT; HOF 1971 **1951**†LARm 11 (RDE) **1952**†LARm☆12 (RDE) **1953** LARm★12 (RDE) **1955**†LARm★12 (RDE) **1956** NYG★12 (RDE) **1957** NYG★12 (RDE) **1958**†NYG☆12 (RDE) **1959**†NYG★12 (RDE) **1960** NYG★12 (RDE) **1961**†NYG★14 (RDE) **1963**†NYG 14 (RDE) **1964** NYG 14 (RDE)

YEAR	TEAM	G (GS, POS)	RUSH	YD	AVG (LG)	TD	REC	YD	AVG (LG)	TD	PASS	COMP	PCT	YD	AVG (LG)	TD	INT	SK	YD	QBR	KPR	OTD	PTS	TAY
1954	LARm☆	12 (RDE)	—	—	—	—	1	49	49.0 (49)	1	—	—	—	—	—	—	—	—	—	—	k	—	6	15
1962	†NYG☆	14 (RDE)	—	—	—	—	1	26	26.0 (26)	0	—	—	—	—	—	—	—	—	—	—	—	—	0	13
NFL	14	175	—	—	—	—	2	75	37.5 (49)	1	—	—	—	—	—	—	—	—	—	—	ki	4	32	62

ROBY, COURTNEY Courtney, WR, 6´0˝/189 lbs; Indiana; 2005: Ten, rnd 3; B1/10/1983 Indianapolis, IN

YEAR	TEAM	G (GS, POS)	RUSH	YD	AVG (LG)	TD	REC	YD	AVG (LG)	TD	PASS	COMP	PCT	YD	AVG (LG)	TD	INT	SK	YD	QBR	KPR	OTD	PTS	TAY
2005	Ten	13 (6, wr)	2	16	8.0 (11)	0	21	289	13.8 (32)	1	—	—	—	—	—	—	—	—	—	—	k	—	6	331

ROBY, DOUG Douglas Fergusson, TB, 5´10˝/190 lbs; Phillips; Michigan; B3/24/1898 Port Tobacco, MD, D3/31/1992 Ann Arbor, MI **[K]** **1923** Cle 7 (7, TB), 7

ROBY, REGGIE Reginald Henry, P, 6´3˝/249 lbs; Iowa; 1983: Mia, rnd 6; B7/30/1961 Waterloo, IA, D2/22/2005 Nashville, TN [P] **1983**†Mia 16 (0) **1984**†Mia★16 (0) **1985**†Mia☆16 (0) **1988** Mia 15 (0) **1990**†Mia 16 (0) **1991** Mia☆16 (0) **1992**†Mia 9 (0) **1994** Was★16 (0) **1996** Hou 16 (0)

YEAR	TEAM	G (GS, POS)	RUSH	YD	AVG (LG)	TD	REC	YD	AVG (LG)	TD	PASS	COMP	PCT	YD	AVG (LG)	TD	INT	SK	YD	QBR	KPR	OTD	PTS	TAY
1986	Mia☆	15(0)	2	-8	-4.0(0)	0	—	—	—	—	—	—	—	—	—	—	—	—	—	—	P	—	0	-8
1987	Mia☆	10(0)	1	0	0.0(0)	0	—	—	—	—	—	—	—	—	—	—	—	—	—	—	P	—	0	0
1989	Mia★	16(0)	2	0	0.0(0)	0	—	—	—	—	—	—	—	—	—	—	—	—	—	—	P	—	0	0
1993	Was	15(0)	1	0	0.0(0)	0	—	—	—	—	—	—	—	—	—	—	—	—	—	—	P	—	0	0
1995	TB	16(0)	1	0	0.0(0)	0	—	—	—	—	1	1	100.0	48	48.0(48)	0	0	—	—	—	P	—	0	24
1997	Ten	16(0)	1	12	12.0(12)	0	—	—	—	—	—	—	—	—	—	—	—	—	—	—	P	—	0	12
1998	†SF	14(0)	1	0	0.0(0)	0	—	—	—	—	—	—	—	—	—	—	—	—	—	—	P	—	0	0
NFL	16	238(0)	9	4	0.4(12)	0	—	—	—	—	1	1	100.0	48	48.0(48)	0	0	—	—	—	P	—	0	28

ROCHE, ALDEN Alden Stephen, DE, 6´4˝/255 lbs; Southern (LA); 1970: Den, rnd 2; B4/9/1945 New Orleans, LA **1970** Den 14 **1971** GB 14 **1972**†GB 14 (RDE) **1973** GB 13 (RDE) **1974** GB 14 (RDE) **1975** GB 14 (RDE) **1976** GB 14 (RDE) **1977** Sea 13 (9, RDE) **1978** Sea 10 (3) **NFL** 120 (12) [9 yrs]

ROCHE, BRIAN Brian Matthew, TE, 6´4˝/255 lbs; Cal Poly-San Luis Obispo; San Jose State; 1996: SD, rnd 3; B5/5/1973 Downey, CA **1997** SD 5 (0) **1998** KC 4 (1)

YEAR	TEAM	G (GS, POS)	RUSH	YD	AVG (LG)	TD	REC	YD	AVG (LG)	TD	PASS	COMP	PCT	YD	AVG (LG)	TD	INT	SK	YD	QBR	KPR	OTD	PTS	TAY
1996	SD	13(0)	—	—	—	—	13	111	8.5(19)	0	—	—	—	—	—	—	—	—	—	—	—	—	0	56
NFL	3	22(1)	—	—	—	—	13	111	8.5(19)	0	—	—	—	—	—	—	—	—	—	—	—	—	0	56

ROCHESTER, PAUL Paul Gordon, DT, 6´2˝/255 lbs; Michigan State; B7/15/1938 Lansing, MI **1960** DalT-A 12 **1961** DalT-A✧14 (LDT) **1962**†DalT-A 13 (LDT) **1963** KC-A 9 (ldt) **1963** NYJ-A 4 **1964** NYJ-A 14 (LDT) **1965** NYJ-A 13 (LDT) **1966** NYJ-A 12 (LDT) **1967** NYJ-A 14 (LDT) **1968**†NYJ-A 14 (LDT) **1969**†NYJ-A 13 **NFL** 132 [10 yrs]

ROCK, WALT Walter Warfield, T-DT, 6´5˝/255 lbs; Maryland; 1963: SF, rnd 2/KC, rnd 2; B11/4/1941 Cleveland, OH **1963** SF 7 **1964** SF 14 (14, RT) **1965** SF✧14 (14, RT) **1966** SF☆14 (14, RT) **1967** SF 14 (14, RT) **1968** Was 14 (LT) **1969** Was 12 (RT) **1970** Was 13 (13, RT) **1971**†Was 14 (14, RT) **1972**†Was 14 (14, RT) **1973** Was 7 (6, rt) **NFL** 137 (103) [11 yrs]

ROCKENBACH, LYLE Lyle James, G, 5´9˝/192 lbs; Michigan State; B3/1/1915 Prairie View, IL **1943** Det 9 (1)

ROCKER, DAVID David Deaundra, DT, 6´4˝/267 lbs; Auburn; 1991: Hou, rnd 4; B3/12/1969 Atlanta, GA **1991** LARm 6 (3) **1992** LARm 3 (0) **1993** LARm 14 (0) **1994** LARm 11 (1) **NFL** 34 (4) [4 yrs]

ROCKER, TRACY Tracy Quinton, DT, 6´3˝/288 lbs; Auburn; 1989: Was, rnd 3; B4/9/1966 Atlanta, GA **1989** Was 16 (10, LDT) **1990** Was 8 (7, ldt) **NFL** 24 (17) [2 yrs]

ROCKFORD, JIM James Kyle, DB, 5´10˝/180 lbs; Oklahoma; 1985: TB, rnd 12; B9/5/1961 Bloomington, IN **1985** SD 1 (0)

ROCKINS, CHRIS Christopher Alexander, DB, 6´0˝/195 lbs; Oklahoma State; 1984: Cle, rnd 2; B5/18/1962 Sherman, TX **1984** Cle 16 (2) **1985**†Cle 16 (0) **1986**†Cle 16 (16, FS) **1987**†Cle 12 (1) **NFL** 60 (19) [4 yrs]

ROCKWELL, HANK Henry Albert, G, 6´4˝/231 lbs; Arizona State; B2/10/1917 Whittier, CA, D11/30/1997 Okaloosa County, FL **1941** Cle 10 (3) **1942** Cle 8 (1)

YEAR	TEAM	G (GS, POS)	RUSH	YD	AVG (LG)	TD	REC	YD	AVG (LG)	TD	PASS	COMP	PCT	YD	AVG (LG)	TD	INT	SK	YD	QBR	KPR	OTD	PTS	TAY
1940	Cle	11(2)	1	5	5.0(5)	0	1	5	5.0(5)	1	—	—	—	—	—	—	—	—	—	—	i	—	6	5
NFL	3	29(6)	1	5	5.0(5)	0	1	5	5.0(5)	1	—	—	—	—	—	—	—	—	—	—	i	—	6	62

1946 LAD-A 13 (1)

YEAR	TEAM	G (GS, POS)	RUSH	YD	AVG (LG)	TD	REC	YD	AVG (LG)	TD	PASS	COMP	PCT	YD	AVG (LG)	TD	INT	SK	YD	QBR	KPR	OTD	PTS	TAY
1948	LAD-A	13(4)	—	—	—	—	0	6	(6)	0	—	—	—	—	—	—	—	—	—	—	—	—	0	3
AAFC	2	26(5)	—	—	—	—	0	6	(6)	0	—	—	—	—	—	—	—	—	—	—	—	—	0	3

RODAK, MIKE Michael, BB-G, 5´10˝/194 lbs; Case Western Reserve; B2/11/1917 Orient, PA, D12/1980 Weirton, WV

YEAR	TEAM	G (GS, POS)	RUSH	YD	AVG (LG)	TD	REC	YD	AVG (LG)	TD	PASS	COMP	PCT	YD	AVG (LG)	TD	INT	SK	YD	QBR	KPR	OTD	PTS	TAY
1939	Cle	6(0)	1	-1	-1.0(-1)	0	4	54	13.5	0	1	0	0.0	0	0.0	0	1	—	—	—	—	—	0	-14
1940	Cle	1(0)	1	4	4.0(4)	0	—	—	—	—	—	—	—	—	—	—	—	—	—	—	—	—	0	4
1942	Pit	5(2)	—	—	—	—	—	—	—	—	—	—	—	—	—	—	—	—	—	—	—	—	—	—
NFL	3	12(2)	2	3	1.5(4)	0	4	54	13.5	0	1	0	0.0	0	0.0	0	1	—	—	—	—	—	0	-10

RODENBERGER, JEFF Jeffrey Lee, RB, 6´3˝/235 lbs; Maryland; B11/3/1959 Quakertown, PA

YEAR	TEAM	G (GS, POS)	RUSH	YD	AVG (LG)	TD	REC	YD	AVG (LG)	TD	PASS	COMP	PCT	YD	AVG (LG)	TD	INT	SK	YD	QBR	KPR	OTD	PTS	TAY
1987	NO	3(3)	17	35	2.1(5)	0	2	17	8.5(11)	0	—	—	—	—	—	—	—	—	—	—	—	—	0	44

RODENHAUSER, MARK Mark Todd, C, 6´5˝/270 lbs; Illinois State; B6/6/1961 Elmhurst, IL **1987**†ChiB 9 (3) **1989**†Min 16 (0) **1990** SD 16 (0) **1991** SD 10 (0) **1992** ChiB 13 (0) **1993**†Det 16 (0) **1994**†Det 16 (0) **1995** Car 16 (0) **1996**†Car 16 (0) **1997** Car 16 (0) **1998** Pit 16 (0) **1999**†Sea 8 (0) **NFL** 168 (3) [12 yrs]

RODER, MIRRO Mirro Victor, K, 6´1˝/218 lbs; none; B1/22/1944 Olomouc, Czech Republic [K] **1973** ChiB 13 **1974** ChiB 14 **1976** TB 2 **NFL** 29 [3 yrs]

RODERICK, BEN Benjamin Aaron, B, 5´9˝/175 lbs; Wooster; Boston College; Columbia; B5/11/1899 Navarre, OH, D11/30/1974 Canton, OH **1923** Can 4 (3) **1923** Buf 4 (4, FB) **1926** Can 11 (7, TB) **1927** Buf 3 (3, TB) **NFL** 22 (17) [3 yrs]

RODERICK, JOHN John William, WR, 6´0˝/180 lbs; SMU; 1966: Mia, rnd R1/GB, rnd 4; B8/21/1944 Fort Worth, TX **1967** Mia-A 1 **1968**†Oak-A 11

YEAR	TEAM	G (GS, POS)	RUSH	YD	AVG (LG)	TD	REC	YD	AVG (LG)	TD	PASS	COMP	PCT	YD	AVG (LG)	TD	INT	SK	YD	QBR	KPR	OTD	PTS	TAY
1966	Mia-A	6(4)	—	—	—	—	11	156	14.2(64)	1	—	—	—	—	—	—	—	—	—	—	k	—	6	85
NFL	3	18(4)	—	—	—	—	11	156	14.2(64)	1	—	—	—	—	—	—	—	—	—	—	k	—	6	88

RODGERS, AARON Aaron, QB, 6´2˝/223 lbs; California; 2005: GB, rnd 1; B12/2/1983 Chico, CA

YEAR	TEAM	G (GS, POS)	RUSH	YD	AVG (LG)	TD	REC	YD	AVG (LG)	TD	PASS	COMP	PCT	YD	AVG (LG)	TD	INT	SK	YD	QBR	KPR	OTD	PTS	TAY
2005	GB	3(0)	2	7	3.5(8)	0	—	—	—	—	16	9	56.3	65	4.1(16)	0	1	3	28	—	—	—	0	-1

RODGERS, DEL Roderick Del, RB, 5´10˝/210 lbs; Utah; 1982: GB, rnd 3; B6/22/1960 Tacoma, WA [R]

YEAR	TEAM	G (GS, POS)	RUSH	YD	AVG (LG)	TD	REC	YD	AVG (LG)	TD	PASS	COMP	PCT	YD	AVG (LG)	TD	INT	SK	YD	QBR	KPR	OTD	PTS	TAY
1982	†GB	9(0)	46	175	3.8(13)	1	3	23	7.7(16)	0	—	—	—	—	—	—	—	—	—	—	k	2	18	333
1984	GB	14(0)	25	94	3.8(15)	0	5	56	11.2(22)	0	—	—	—	—	—	—	—	—	—	—	k	1	6	390
1987	SF	7(0)	11	46	4.2(15)	1	2	45	22.5(24)	0	—	—	—	—	—	—	—	—	—	—	k	—	6	182
1988	†SF	1(0)	—	—	—	—	—	—	—	—	—	—	—	—	—	—	—	—	—	—	k	—	0	8
NFL	4	31(0)	82	315	3.8(15)	2	10	124	12.4(24)	0	—	—	—	—	—	—	—	—	—	—	k	3	30	912

RODGERS, DERRICK Derrick Andre, LB, 6´1˝/230 lbs; Arizona State; 1997: Mia, rnd 3; B10/14/1971 Memphis, TN **1997**†Mia 15 (14, RLB) **1998**†Mia 16 (16, LLB) **1999**†Mia 16 (15, LLB) **2000**†Mia 16 (14, LLB) **2001** Mia 14 (14, LLB) **2002** Mia 16 (15, LLB) **2003** NO 15 (15, RLB) **2004** NO 8 (8, RLB) **NFL** 116 (111) [8 yrs]

RODGERS, HOSEA Hosea Weaver, FB, 6´1˝/192 lbs; Alabama; North Carolina; 1949: LAD-A, rnd 3/1946: NYG, rnd 3; B12/25/1921 Brewton, AL

YEAR	TEAM	G (GS, POS)	RUSH	YD	AVG (LG)	TD	REC	YD	AVG (LG)	TD	PASS	COMP	PCT	YD	AVG (LG)	TD	INT	SK	YD	QBR	KPR	OTD	PTS	TAY
1949	LAD-A	12(9, FB)	131	494	3.8	5	7	97	13.9	0	1	0	0.0	0	0.0	0	0	—	—	—	—	—	30	593

RODGERS, JOHN John Darren, TE, 6´2˝/220 lbs; Louisiana Tech; B2/7/1960 Omaha, TX, D4/22/2003 Daingerfield, TX **1982**†Pit 7 (0) **1984** Pit 6 (0)

YEAR	TEAM	G (GS, POS)	RUSH	YD	AVG (LG)	TD	REC	YD	AVG (LG)	TD	PASS	COMP	PCT	YD	AVG (LG)	TD	INT	SK	YD	QBR	KPR	OTD	PTS	TAY
1983	Pit	15(1)	—	—	—	—	2	36	18.0(25)	0	—	—	—	—	—	—	—	—	—	—	—	—	0	18
NFL	3	28(1)	—	—	—	—	2	36	18.0(25)	0	—	—	—	—	—	—	—	—	—	—	—	1	6	18

RODGERS, JOHNNY John Steven, WR, 5´10˝/180 lbs; Nebraska; 1973: SD, rnd 1; B7/5/1951 Omaha, NE

YEAR	TEAM	G (GS, POS)	RUSH	YD	AVG (LG)	TD	REC	YD	AVG (LG)	TD	PASS	COMP	PCT	YD	AVG (LG)	TD	INT	SK	YD	QBR	KPR	OTD	PTS	TAY
1977	SD	11(7, WR)	3	44	14.7(33)	0	12	187	15.6(43)	0	—	—	—	—	—	—	—	—	—	—	kp	—	0	227
1978	SD	6	1	5	5.0(5)	0	5	47	9.4(12)	0	—	—	—	—	—	—	—	—	—	—	kp	—	0	184
NFL	2	17(7)	4	49	12.3(33)	0	17	234	13.8(43)	0	—	—	—	—	—	—	—	—	—	—	kp	—	0	410

RODGERS, TOM Thomas Edward, T, 6´0˝/248 lbs; Bucknell; 1947: Bos, rnd 29; B1/20/1923 New Kensington, PA, D9/9/1992 Las Vegas, NV **1947** Bos 9 (0)

RODGERS, TYRONE Tyrone Dworin, DT, 6´3˝/271 lbs; Oklahoma; Washington; B4/27/1969 Longview, TX **1992** Sea 16 (0) **1993** Sea 16 (0) **1994** Sea 5 (0) **NFL** 37 (0) [3 yrs]

RODGERS, WILLIE Willie Daniel, RB, 6´0˝/210 lbs; Kentucky State; 1972: Hou, rnd 12; B2/8/1949 Suffolk, VA, D9/27/1998 Houston, TX

YEAR	TEAM	G (GS, POS)	RUSH	YD	AVG (LG)	TD	REC	YD	AVG (LG)	TD	PASS	COMP	PCT	YD	AVG (LG)	TD	INT	SK	YD	QBR	KPR	OTD	PTS	TAY
1972	Hou	14	71	204	2.9(14)	2	6	61	10.2(15)	0	—	—	—	—	—	—	—	—	—	—	k	—	12	335
1974	Hou	14(FB)	122	413	3.4(20)	5	24	153	6.4(24)	0	—	—	—	—	—	—	—	—	—	—	—	—	30	540
1975	Hou	14	18	55	3.1(8)	1	—	—	—	—	—	—	—	—	—	—	—	—	—	—	k	—	8	63
NFL	3	42	211	672	3.2(20)	8	30	214	7.1(24)	0	—	—	—	—	—	—	—	—	—	—	k	—	50	937

RODRIGUEZ, JESS Jess, TB, 5´7˝/160 lbs; Salem (NC); B8/7/1901 Salem, WV, D10/12/1983 Clarksburg, WV **1929** Buf 5 (2)

RODRIGUEZ, KELLY Kelly, B, 5´10˝/180 lbs; West Virginia Wesleyan; B8/9/1907 Aviles, Spain **1930** Fra 13 (6, wb), 6 **1930** Min 2 (1) **NFL** 15 (7) [1 yr]

RODRIGUEZ, MIKE Miguel Eduardo, LB, 6´1˝/275 lbs; Alabama; B12/5/1961 Melbourne, FL **1987** LARd 1 (0)

RODRIGUEZ, RUBEN Ruben Angel, P, 6´2˝/210 lbs; Arizona; 1987: Sea, rnd 5; B3/3/1965 Visalia, CA

YEAR	TEAM	G (GS, POS)	RUSH	YD	AVG (LG)	TD	REC	YD	AVG (LG)	TD	PASS	COMP	PCT	YD	AVG (LG)	TD	INT	SK	YD	QBR	KPR	OTD	PTS	TAY
1987	†Sea	12(0)	1	0	0.0(0)	0	—	—	—	—	—	—	—	—	—	—	—	—	—	—	P	—	0	0
1988	†Sea	16(0)	1	0	0.0(0)	0	—	—	—	—	—	—	—	—	—	—	—	—	—	—	P	—	0	0
1989	Sea	16(0)	1	0	0.0(0)	0	—	—	—	—	1	1	100.0	4	4.0(4)	0	0	—	—	—	P	—	0	2
1992	Den	5(0)	—	—	—	—	—	—	—	—	—	—	—	—	—	—	—	—	—	—	P	—	0	0

YEAR	TEAM	G(GS, POS)	RUSH	YD	AVG(LG)	TD	REC	YD	AVG(LG)	TD	PASS	COMP	PCT	YD	AVG(LG)	TD	INT	SK	YD	QBR	KPR	OTD	PTS	TAY
1992	NYG	4(0)	—	—	—	—	—	—	—	—	—	—	—	—	—	—	—	—	—	—	P	—	0	0
NFL	4	53(0)	3	0	0.0	0	—	—	—	—	1	1	100.0	4	4.0(4)	0	0	—	—	—	P	—	0	2
Roe, Bill William Oliver, LB, 6´3˝/233 lbs; Colorado; 1980: Dal, rnd 3; B2/6/1958 South Bend, IN **1980**†Dal 16 (0) **1987** NO 3 (3) **NFL** 19 (3) [2 yrs]																								
Roe, James James Edward, WR, 6´1˝/187 lbs; Norfolk State; 1996: Bal, rnd 6; B8/23/1973 Richmond, VA																								
1996	Bal	1(0)	—	—	—	—	—	—	—	—	—	—	—	—	—	—	—	—	—	—	—	—	—	—
1997	Bal	12(4)	—	—	—	—	7	124	17.7(29)	0	—	—	—	—	—	—	—	—	—	—	kp	—	0	148
1998	Bal	10(3)	—	—	—	—	8	115	14.4(27)	1	—	—	—	—	—	—	—	—	—	—	kp	—	6	115
NFL	3	23(7)	—	—	—	—	15	239	15.9(29)	1	—	—	—	—	—	—	—	—	—	—	kp	—	6	263
Roedel, Herb Herbert Thomas, G, 6´3˝/230 lbs; Marquette; B3/30/1939 Appleton, WI **1961** Oak-A 14																								
Roehl, Jeff Jeffrey Alan, T, 6´4˝/300 lbs; Notre Dame; Northwestern; B5/18/1980 Evergreen Park, IL **2003** NYG 12 (2)																								
Roehlk, Jon Jon Michael, G, 6´2˝/257 lbs; Iowa; B6/25/1961 Davenport, IA **1987** ChiB 3 (3)																								
Roehnelt, Bill William Edward, LB, 6´1˝/227 lbs; Bradley; 1958: ChiB, rnd 19; B6/4/1936 Peoria, IL, D7/19/1968 **1958** ChiB 12 **1959** ChiB 12 **1960** Was 12 (RLB) **1961** Den-A 4 **1962** Den-A 14 (RLB) **NFL** 54 [5 yrs]																								
Roepke, Johnny John Peter, TB-WB, 5´11˝/175 lbs; Penn State; B12/28/1905, D2/26/1962 Passaic, NJ **[K]** **1928** Fra 10 (3), 10																								
Roeseler, Fritz Fred C., E, 6´1˝/189 lbs; North Central; Marquette; B10/1/1897 Milwaukee, WI, D7/18/1985 Milwaukee, WI **1922** Rac 11 (9, RE), 6 **1923** Rac 6 (3) **1924** Rac 3 (2) **1925** Mil 6 (3, RE) **NFL** 26 (17) [4 yrs]																								
Roethlisberger, Ben Ben, QB, 6´5˝/240 lbs; Miami (OH); 2004: Pit, rnd 1; B3/2/1982 Lima, OH																								
2004	†Pit	14(13, QB)	56	144	2.6(20)	1	—	—	—	—	295	196	66.4	2621	8.9(58)	17	11	30	213	98.1	—	—	6	1110
2005	†Pit	12(12, QB)	31	69	2.2(13)	3	—	—	—	—	268	168	62.7	2385	**8.9(85)**	17	9	23	129	98.6	P	—	18	1017
NFL	2	26(25)	87	213	2.4(20)	4	—	—	—	—	563	364	64.7	5006	8.9(85)	34	20	53	342	98.3	P	—	24	2126
Roffler, Bill William Hartman, DB, 6´1˝/200 lbs; Washington State; 1952: GB, rnd 10; B9/16/1930 Spokane, WA **1954** Phi 3																								
Rogalla, John John Francis, FB, 6´0˝/215 lbs; Scranton; 1940: NYG, rnd 17; B5/31/1917 Duryea, PA, D4/17/1999 Wyoming, PA **[K]**																								
1945	Phi	8(4)	2	2	1.0(6)	0	2	22	11.0(17)	0	—	—	—	—	—	—	—	—	—	—	K	—	1	13
Rogas, Dan Daniel William, G-DT-T, 6´1˝/230 lbs; Tulane; 1951: Cle, rnd 6; B8/9/1926 Port Arthur, TX **1951** Det 12 (RG) **1952** Phi 10 **NFL** 22 [2 yrs]																								
Rogel, Fran Francis Stephen, FB, 5´11˝/203 lbs; California (PA); Penn State; 1950: Pit, rnd 8; B12/12/1927 North Braddock, PA, D6/2/2002 Gibsonia, PA																								
1950	Pit	12(FB)	92	418	4.5(40)	3	24	304	12.7(64)	1	4	3	75.0	30	7.5(11)	0	0	—	—	—	k	—	24	625
1951	Pit	12(FB)	109	385	3.5(51)	3	10	59	5.9(24)	0	1	0	0.0	0	0.0	0	0	—	—	—	k	—	18	424
1952	Pit	12(FB)	84	230	2.7(14)	3	12	140	11.7(26)	0	—	—	—	—	—	—	—	—	—	—	—	—	18	330
1953	Pit	12(FB)	137	527	3.8(58)	2	19	95	5.0(19)	0	1	0	0.0	0	0.0	0	0	—	—	—	—	—	12	595
1954	Pit	12(FB)	111	415	3.7(16)	1	18	51	2.8(16)	1	—	—	—	—	—	—	—	—	—	—	—	—	12	456
1955	Pit	12(FB)	168	588	3.5(19)	2	24	222	9.3(28)	0	—	—	—	—	—	—	—	—	—	—	k	—	12	785
1956	Pit✧	12(FB)	131	476	3.6(40)	2	23	88	3.8(13)	0	—	—	—	—	—	—	—	—	—	—	—	—	12	540
1957	Pit	12(FB)	68	232	3.4(23)	1	20	128	6.4(18)	0	—	—	—	—	—	—	—	—	—	—	k	—	6	295
NFL	8	96	900	3271	3.6(58)	17	150	1087	7.2(64)	2	6	3	50.0	30	5.0(11)	0	0	—	—	—	k	—	114	4049
Rogers, Bill William Curtis, T, 5´11˝/243 lbs; Villanova; B6/24/1913 Westborough, MA, D4/30/1977 Northborough, MA **1938** Det 7 (3) **1939** Det 9 (0) **1940** Det 7 (0) **1944** Det 2 (0) **NFL** 25 (3) [4 yrs]																								
Rogers, Carlos Carlos Cornelius, DB, 6´0˝/199 lbs; Auburn; 2005: Was, rnd 1; B7/2/1981 Hephzibah, GA **2005**†Was 12 (5, lcb)																								
Rogers, Charles Charles, WR, 6´2˝/202 lbs; Michigan State; 2003: Det, rnd 1; B5/23/1981 Saginaw, MI																								
2003	Det	5(5, wr)	2	17	8.5(12)	0	22	243	11.0(33)	3	—	—	—	—	—	—	—	—	—	—	—	—	18	154
2004	Det	1(1)	—	—	—	—	—	—	—	—	—	—	—	—	—	—	—	—	—	—	—	—	—	—
2005	Det	9(3)	—	—	—	—	14	197	14.1(35)	1	—	—	—	—	—	—	—	—	—	—	—	—	6	104
NFL	3	15(9)	2	17	8.5(12)	0	36	440	12.2(35)	4	—	—	—	—	—	—	—	—	—	—	—	—	24	257
Rogers, Charley Charles Stagg, B, 5´10˝/167 lbs; Pennsylvania; B1903, D6/26/1986, **[C]** **1927** Fra 18 (11, WB), 18 **1928** Fra 13 (8, TB), 18 **1929** Fra 7 (2) **NFL** 38 (21), 36 [3 yrs]																								
Rogers, Charlie John Edward, RB, 5´9˝/180 lbs; Georgia Tech; 1999: Sea, rnd 5; B6/19/1976 Cliffwood, NJ **[R]** **1999**†Sea☆12 (0) **2000** Sea 15 (0) **2002** Buf 16 (0) **2003** Mia 11 (0)																								
2001	Sea	13(0)	—	—	—	—	1	7	7.0(7)	0	—	—	—	—	—	—	—	—	—	—	kp	—	0	493
NFL	5	67(0)	—	—	—	—	1	7	7.0(7)	0	—	—	—	—	—	—	—	—	—	—	kp	3	18	2304
Rogers, Chris Chris, DB, 5´10˝/192 lbs; Howard; B1/3/1977 Washington, DC **1999**†Min 10 (4)																								
Rogers, Cullen Cullen James, HB, 5´10˝/175 lbs; Texas A&M; 1943: Cle, rnd 16; B5/29/1921 Mart, TX, D11/1/1997 McLennan County, TX																								
1946	Pit	5(0)	6	-8	-1.3(4)	0	—	—	—	—	1	0	0.0	0	0.0	0	0	—	—	—	—	—	0	-8
Rogers, Don Donald Clinton, C-G, 6´2˝/240 lbs; South Carolina; 1959: SF, rnd 7; B12/4/1936 South Orange, NJ **1960**†LAC-A 14 (C) **1961**†SD-A☆14 (C) **1962** SD-A 12 (LG) **1963**†SD-A☆14 (C) **1964**†SD-A 14 (C) **NFL** 68 [5 yrs]																								
Rogers, Don Donald Lavert, DB, 6´1˝/206 lbs; UCLA; 1984: Cle, rnd 1; B9/17/1962 Texarkana, AR, D6/27/1986 Sacramento, CA **1984** Cle 15 (14, FS) **1985**†Cle 16 (16, FS) **NFL** 31 (30) [2 yrs]																								
Rogers, Doug Douglas Keith, DE, 6´5˝/266 lbs; Stanford; 1982: Atl, rnd 2; B6/23/1960 Chico, CA **1982**†Atl 9 (0) **1983** Atl 2 (0) **1983** NE 10 (0) **1984** NE 12 (0) **1986**†SF 8 (0) **NFL** 41 (0) [4 yrs]																								
Rogers, George George Washington, RB, 6´2˝/228 lbs; South Carolina; 1981: NO, rnd 1; B12/8/1958 Duluth, GA																								
1981	NO★	16(16, RB)	**378**	**1674**	4.4(79)	**13**	16	126	7.9(25)	0	—	—	—	—	—	—	—	—	—	—	—	—	78	**1867**
1982	NO★	6(5, RB)	122	535	4.4(38)	3	4	21	5.3(10)	0	—	—	—	—	—	—	—	—	—	—	—	—	18	576
1983	NO	13(12, RB)	256	1144	4.5(76)	5	12	69	5.8(22)	0	—	—	—	—	—	—	—	—	—	—	—	—	30	1229
1984	NO	16(16, RB)	239	914	3.8(28)	2	12	76	6.3(15)	0	—	—	—	—	—	—	—	—	—	—	—	—	12	972
1985	Was	15(5, rb)	231	1093	4.7(35)	7	4	29	7.3(23)	0	—	—	—	—	—	—	—	—	—	—	—	—	42	1178
1986	†Was	15(15, RB)	303	1203	4.0(42)	**18**	3	24	8.0(13)	0	—	—	—	—	—	—	—	—	—	—	—	—	108	1395
1987	†Was	11(9, RB)	163	613	3.8(29)	6	4	23	5.8(8)	0	—	—	—	—	—	—	—	—	—	—	—	—	36	685
NFL	7	92(78)	1692	7176	4.2(79)	54	55	368	6.7(25)	0	—	—	—	—	—	—	—	—	—	—	—	—	324	7900
Rogers, Glenn Glenn Edward, DB, 6´0˝/185 lbs; Memphis; B6/8/1969 Memphis, TN **1991** TB 5 (1)																								
Rogers, Glynn Glynn Odell, G, 5´10˝/220 lbs; TCU; B3/31/1914 Big Hill, TX, D1/6/1998 Hobbs, NM **1939** ChiC 1 (1)																								
Rogers, Jacob Jacob, T, 6´6˝/305 lbs; USC; 2004: Dal, rnd 2; B8/17/1981 Oxnard, CA **2004** Dal 2 (0)																								
Rogers, Jimmy James Lee, RB, 5´10˝/190 lbs; Oklahoma; B6/29/1955 Forrest City, AR **[R]**																								
1980	NO	16(9, RB)	80	366	4.6(24)	1	27	267	9.9(43)	2	—	—	—	—	—	—	—	—	—	—	k	—	18	835
1981	NO	15(0)	9	37	4.1(15)	0	2	12	6.0(9)	0	—	—	—	—	—	—	—	—	—	—	k	—	0	244
1982	NO	9(1)	60	178	3.0(32)	2	4	17	4.3(6)	0	—	—	—	—	—	—	—	—	—	—	k	—	12	216
1983	NO	16(0)	26	80	3.1(13)	0	—	—	—	—	—	—	—	—	—	—	—	—	—	—	k	—	0	78
1984	NO	16(0)	—	—	—	—	—	—	—	—	—	—	—	—	—	—	—	—	—	—	—	—	—	—
NFL	5	72(10)	175	661	3.8(32)	3	33	296	9.0(43)	2	—	—	—	—	—	—	—	—	—	—	k	—	30	1372
Rogers, John John Bert, C, 5´8˝/208 lbs; Notre Dame; B1/18/1910, D10/1968 **1933** Cin 9 (6, C) **1934** Cin 5 (5, C) **NFL** 14 (11) [2 yrs]																								
Rogers, Lamar Lamar, DE, 6´4˝/290 lbs; Auburn; 1991: Cin, rnd 2; B11/5/1967 Opp, AL **1991** Cin 11 (3) **1992** Cin 15 (12, LDE) **NFL** 26 (15) [2 yrs]																								
Rogers, Mel Melvin Nathaniel, LB, 6´2˝/231 lbs; Florida A&M; B4/23/1947 St. Petersburg, FL **1971** SD 13 **1973** SD 10 (5, llb) **1974** SD 3 **1976**†LARm 11 **1977**†ChiB 5 **NFL** 42 (5) [5 yrs]																								
Rogers, Nick Nicholas Quixote, LB, 6´2˝/250 lbs; Georgia Tech; 2002: Min, rnd 6; B5/31/1979 East Point, GA **2002** Min 16 (11, LLB) **2003** Min 16 (5, rlb) **2004** GB 10 (0) **2004**†Ind 1 (0) **2005** Mia 3 (0) **NFL** 46 (16) [4 yrs]																								

YEAR	TEAM	G (GS, POS)	RUSH	YD	AVG (LG)	TD	REC	YD	AVG (LG)	TD	PASS	COMP	PCT	YD	AVG (LG)	TD	INT	SK	YD	QBR	KPR	OTD	PTS	TAY

ROGERS, REGGIE Reginald O'Keith, DE, 6´6˝/278 lbs; Washington; 1987: Det, rnd 1; B1/21/1964 Sacramento, CA **1987** Det 6 (0) **1988** Det 5 (2) **1991** Buf 2 (0) **1992** TB 2 (0)
NFL 15 (2) [4 yrs]

ROGERS, SAM Sammy Lee, LB, 6´3˝/245 lbs; Colorado; 1994: Buf, rnd 2; B5/30/1970 Pontiac, MI **1994** Buf 14 (0) **1995**†Buf 16 (8, ROLB) **1996**†Buf 14 (14, ROLB)
1997 Buf 15 (15, ROLB) **1998**†Buf 15 (15, LOLB) **1999**†Buf 16 (16, LOLB) **2000** Buf 11 (11, ROLB) **2001** SD 15 (0) **2002**†Atl 15 (13, LOLB) **2003** Atl 2 (2) **NFL** 133 (94) [10 yrs]

ROGERS, SHAUN Shaun C., DT, 6´4˝/357 lbs; Texas; 2001: Det, rnd 2; B3/12/1979 Houston, TX **2001** Det 16 (16, LDT) **2002** Det 14 (12, LDT) **2003** Det 16 (16, RDT)
2004 Det★16 (16, RDT) **2005** Det◇14 (14, LDT) **NFL** 76 (74) [5 yrs]

ROGERS, STAN Stanley Gerald, T, 6´4˝/256 lbs; Maryland; 1975: Den, rnd 5; B3/10/1952 Peckville, PA **1975** Den 14 (2)

ROGERS, STEVE Steven Jerel, RB, 6´2˝/203 lbs; LSU; 1975: NO, rnd 7; B8/26/1953 Jonesboro, LA **1976** NYJ 1

| **1975** | NO | | 13 | 17 | 62 | 3.6(22) | 0 | 1 | 2 | 2.0(2) | 0 | — | — | — | — | — | — | — | — | — | k | — | 0 | 71 |
| **NFL** | 2 | | 14 | 17 | 62 | 3.6(22) | 0 | 1 | 2 | 2.0(2) | 0 | — | — | — | — | — | — | — | — | — | — | — | 0 | 63 |

ROGERS, STEVE Steven C., T, 6´4˝/260 lbs; Oregon State; Brigham Young; B1/9/1959 Escondido, CA **1987** KC 3 (3)

ROGERS, TRACY Tracy Darin, LB, 6´2˝/244 lbs; Fresno State; 1989: Hou, rnd 7; B8/13/1967 Taft, CA **1990** KC 10 (0) **1991**†KC 10 (1) **1992**†KC 8 (0) **1993**†KC 14 (14, LOLB)
1994†KC 14 (3) **1995**†KC 16 (0) **1996** KC 3 (1) **NFL** 75 (19) [7 yrs]

ROGERS, TYRONE Tyrone, DE, 6´5˝/280 lbs; Alabama State; B3/9/1974 Montgomery, AL **1999** Cle 3 (0) **2000** Cle 16 (0) **2001** Cle 16 (10, LDE) **2002**†Cle 14 (5, rde)
2003 Cle 8 (3) **2004** Cle 14 (0) **NFL** 71 (18) [6 yrs]

ROGERS, VICTOR Victor, T, 6´6˝/331 lbs; Colorado; 2002: Det, rnd 7; B11/10/1978 Seattle, WA **2004** Det 1 (0)

ROGERS, WALT Walter Charles, FB-LB, 5´9˝/215 lbs; Christian Brothers (MO); Ohio University; B4/18/1893 Shawnee, OK, D9/15/1964 Dallas, TX **1921** Col 1 (0) **1922** Col 3 (3)
NFL 4 (3) [2 yrs]

ROGGE, GEORGE George Ross, E, 6´0˝/186 lbs; Iowa; B9/3/1907 Odebolt, IA, D7/14/1997 Marion County, FL **1931** ChiC 6 (2), 6 **1933** ChiC 6 (1)

1932	ChiC	10(3)	—	—	—	—	6	96	16.0	0	—	—	—	—	—	—	—	—	—	—	—	—	0	48
1934	SL	2(1)	—	—	—	—	1	4	4.0(4)	0	—	—	—	—	—	—	—	—	—	—	—	—	0	2
NFL	4	24(7)	—	—	—	—	7	100	14.3(4)	0	—	—	—	—	—	—	—	—	—	—	—	6	55

ROGGEMAN, TOM Thomas John, G, 6´0˝/235 lbs; Purdue; B9/5/1931 Mishawaka, IN **1956**†ChiB 12 **1957** ChiB 12 **NFL** 24 [2 yrs]

ROHDE, LEN Leonard Emil, T, 6´4˝/247 lbs; Utah State; 1960: SF, rnd 5/Buf, rnd 1; B4/16/1938 Palatine, IL **1960** SF 12 **1961** SF 14 **1962** SF 14 (5, rt) **1963** SF 14 (14, LT)
1964 SF 14 (14, LT) **1965** SF 14 (14, LT) **1966** SF 14 (14, LT) **1967** SF 14 (14, LT) **1968** SF 14 (14, LT) **1969** SF☆14 (14, LT) **1970**†SF◇14 (LT) **1971**†SF 14 (14, LT)
1972†SF 14 (14, LT) **1973** SF 14 (14, LT) **1974** SF 14 (14, LT) **NFL** 208 (159) [15 yrs]

ROHLEDER, GEORGE George J., G-T-FB, 5´11˝/213 lbs; Wittenberg; B3/10/1898 Bryan, OH, D2/17/1958. [K] **1925** Col 9 (6, lg), 10 **1926** Akr 6 (2), 5 **NFL** 15 (8), 15 [2 yrs]

ROHRER, JEFF Jeffrey Charles, LB, 6´3˝/228 lbs; Yale; 1982: Dal, rnd 2; B12/25/1958 Inglewood, CA **1982**†Dal 8 (0) **1983**†Dal 16 (1) **1984** Dal 16 (0) **1985**†Dal 15 (13, RLB)
1986 Dal 16 (16, RLB) **1987** Dal 12 (12, RLB) **NFL** 83 (42) [6 yrs]

ROHRIG, HERM Herman Francis, WB-HB, 5´8˝/190 lbs; Nebraska; 1941: GB, rnd 6; B3/19/1918 Mason City, IA, D7/14/2002 Lincoln, NE [K]

1941	†GB	10(0)	21	2	0.1(18)	0	11	58	5.3(19)	0	1	1	100.0		3	3.0(3)	0	0	—	—	KPkpi	—	4	86
1946	GB	8(7, WB)	14	-23	-1.6(15)	0	2	36	18.0(21)	0	8	2	25.0	97	12.1(65)	1	1	—	—	kpi	—	0	207
1947	GB	7(3)	7	22	3.1(6)	0	—	—	—	—	—	—	—	—	—	—	—	—	—	pi	—	0	200
NFL	3	25(10)	42	1	0.0(18)	0	13	94	7.2(21)	0	9	3	33.3	100	11.1(65)	1	1	—	—	KPkpi	—	4	492

ROHSENBERGER, TUBBY Otto Lee, T, Wisconsin; B11/6/1896 Evansville, IN, D1/15/1954 **1921** Evv 2 (1)

ROKISKY, JOHN John Joseph, DE-E, 6´2˝/202 lbs; Duquesne; 1942: Pit, rnd 18; B7/24/1915 Mount Clare, WV, D11/28/1993 Wintersville, OH [K] **1948** NYY-A 6 (0)

1946	Cle-A	5(0)	—	—	—	—	1	13	13.0(13)	0	—	—	—	—	—	—	—	—	—	—	K	—	1	7
1947	ChiR-A	14(1)	—	—	—	—	1	8	8.0(8)	0	—	—	—	—	—	—	—	—	—	—	K	—	45	4
AAFC	3	25(1)	—	—	—	—	2	21	10.5(13)	0	—	—	—	—	—	—	—	—	—	—	K	—	46	11

ROLAND, BENJI Mitchell Benjamin, DE, 6´3˝/260 lbs; Auburn; 1989: Min, rnd 7; B4/4/1967 Eastman, GA **1990** TB 3 (1)

ROLAND, JOHNNY John Earl, RB, 6´2˝/220 lbs; Missouri; 1965: SL, rnd 4/NYJ, rnd R1; B5/21/1943 Corpus Christi, TX

1966	SL◇	14(HB)	192	695	3.6(50)	5	21	213	10.1(37)	0	8	5	62.5	130	16.3(45)	1	0	—	—	kp	1	36	1175
1967	SL★	13(FB)	234	876	3.7(70)	10	20	269	13.4(41)	1	4	0	0.0	0	0.0	0	1	—	—	kp	—	66	1081
1968	SL	14(HB)	121	455	3.8(45)	2	8	97	12.1(40)	0	1	0	0.0	0	0.0	0	1	—	—	p	—	12	480
1969	SL	14(HB)	138	498	3.6(21)	5	12	136	11.3(23)	1	—	—	—	—	—	—	—	—	—	p	—	36	624
1970	SL	14(rb)	94	392	4.2(20)	3	17	96	5.6(20)	1	—	—	—	—	—	—	—	—	—	kp	1	30	570
1971	SL	13(RB)	78	278	3.6(16)	0	15	108	7.2(15)	0	—	—	—	—	—	—	—	—	—	kp	—	0	321
1972	SL	14(rb)	105	414	3.9(18)	2	38	321	8.4(27)	2	—	—	—	—	—	—	—	—	—	—	—	24	605
1973	NYG	7(FB)	53	142	2.7(10)	1	22	190	8.6(30)	1	—	—	—	—	—	—	—	—	—	—	—	12	252
NFL	8	103	1015	3750	3.7(70)	28	153	1430	9.3(41)	6	13	5	38.5	130	10.0(45)	1	2	—	—	kp	2	216	5106

ROLLE, ANTREL Antrel, DB, 6´0˝/202 lbs; Miami (FL); 2005: Arz, rnd 1; B12/16/1982 Homestead, FL **2005** Arz 5 (4)

ROLLE, BUTCH Donald Demetrius, TE, 6´3˝/242 lbs; Michigan State; 1986: Buf, rnd 7; B8/19/1964 Miami, FL

1986	Buf	16(1)	—	—	—	—	4	56	14.0(20)	0	—	—	—	—	—	—	—	—	—	—	—	0	28
1987	Buf	12(0)	—	—	—	—	2	6	3.0(3)	2	—	—	—	—	—	—	—	—	—	k	—	12	4
1988	†Buf	16(0)	—	—	—	—	2	3	1.5(2)	2	—	—	—	—	—	—	—	—	—	k	—	12	9
1989	†Buf	16(1)	—	—	—	—	1	1	1.0(1)	1	—	—	—	—	—	—	—	—	—	k	—	6	-5
1990	†Buf	16(0)	—	—	—	—	3	6	2.0(3)	3	—	—	—	—	—	—	—	—	—	k	—	18	10
1991	†Buf	16(0)	—	—	—	—	3	10	3.3(5)	2	—	—	—	—	—	—	—	—	—	k	—	12	15
1992	Phx	16(14, TE)	—	—	—	—	13	64	4.9(12)	0	—	—	—	—	—	—	—	—	—	k	—	0	27
1993	Phx	16(5, te)	—	—	—	—	10	67	6.7(22)	1	—	—	—	—	—	—	—	—	—	—	—	6	39
NFL	8	124(21)	—	—	—	—	38	213	5.6(22)	11	—	—	—	—	—	—	—	—	—	k	—	66	127

ROLLE, DAVE David S., FB, 6´0˝/215 lbs; Oklahoma; B3/22/1937 Poteau, OK

| **1960** | Den-A | 14(FB) | 130 | 501 | 3.9(57) | 2 | 17 | 126 | 5.8(33) | 1 | — | — | — | — | — | — | — | — | — | — | — | 18 | 587 |

ROLLE, SAMARI Samari Toure, DB, 6´0˝/175 lbs; Florida State; 1998: Ten, rnd 2; B8/10/1976 Miami, FL [I] **1998** Ten 15 (1) **1999**†Ten 16 (16, RCB) **2000**†Ten★15 (15, RCB)
2001 Ten 14 (14, RCB) **2002**†Ten 16 (16, RCB) **2003**†Ten 13 (13, RCB) **2004** Ten 12 (11, RCB) **2005** Bal 16 (16, RCB) **NFL** 117 (102) [8 yrs]

ROLLER, DAVE David Euell, DT, 6´2˝/270 lbs; Kentucky; 1971: NYG, rnd 13; B10/28/1949 Dayton, TN **1971** NYG 14 **1975** GB 6 **1976** GB 13 (6, rdt) **1977** GB 13 (LDT)
1978 GB 16 (LDT) **1979** Min 15 (6, ldt) **1980**†Min 15 (2) **NFL** 92 (14) [7 yrs]

ROLLING, HENRY Henry Lee, LB, 6´2˝/232 lbs; Nevada-Reno; 1987: TB, rnd 5; B9/8/1965 Fort Eustis, VA **1988** TB 15 (0) **1989** TB 6 (0) **1990** SD 16 (8, lolb)
1991 SD 15 (13, LOLB) **1992**†SD 15 (15, LLB) **1993** LARm 12 (9, LLB) **1994** LARm 9 (2) **NFL** 88 (47) [7 yrs]

ROMAN, GEORGE George, T, 6´4˝/242 lbs; Case Western Reserve; 1948: Bos, rnd 11/Cle-A, rnd 29; B2/20/1925 Rankin, PA, D6/30/2002 Columbus, GA **1948** Bos 12 (0)
1949 NYB 8 (0) **1950**†NYG 6 **NFL** 26 [3 yrs]

ROMAN, JOHN John George, T-G, 6´4˝/255 lbs; Idaho State; 1975: Bal, rnd 13; B8/31/1952 Ventnor City, NJ **1976** NYJ 11 (2) **1977** NYJ 9 (2) **1979** NYJ 16 **1980** NYJ 16 (3)
1981†NYJ 16 (2) **1982**†NYJ 9 (1)

| **1978** | NYJ | 16(2) | — | — | — | — | 1 | -2 | -2.0(-2) | 0 | — | — | — | — | — | — | — | — | — | — | — | 0 | -1 |
| **NFL** | 7 | 93(12) | — | — | — | — | 1 | -2 | -2.0(-2) | 0 | — | — | — | — | — | — | — | — | — | — | — | 0 | -1 |

ROMAN, MARK Mark Emery, DB, 5´11˝/200 lbs; LSU; 2000: Cin, rnd 2; B3/26/1977 New Iberia, LA **2000** Cin 8 (2) **2001** Cin 13 (8, LCB) **2002** Cin 13 (1) **2003** Cin 16 (16, FS)
2004†GB 16 (15, SS) **2005** GB 16 (16, SS) **NFL** 82 (58) [6 yrs]

ROMAN, NICK Nicholas George, DE, 6´3˝/244 lbs; Ohio State; 1970: Cin, rnd 10; B9/23/1947 Canton, OH, D5/18/2003 Columbus, OH **1970**†Cin 4 **1971** Cin 12 **1972**†Cle 10 (lde/
rde) **1973** Cle 14 (RDE) **1974** Cle 12 (LDE/rde) **NFL** 52 [5 yrs]

ROMANIK, STEVE Stephen, QB, 6´1˝/190 lbs; Villanova; 1950: ChiB, rnd 3; B5/27/1924 Millville, NJ

1950	ChiB	1	—	—	—	—	—	—	—	—	2	0	0.0	0	0.0	0	0	—	—	—	—	0	0
1951	ChiB	12(qb)	12	23	1.9(10)	1	—	—	—	—	101	43	42.6	791	7.8(54)	3	9	—	—	43.0	—	6	84
1952	ChiB	10(qb)	6	9	1.5(7)	0	—	—	—	—	126	49	38.9	772	6.1(49)	4	11	—	—	34.2	—	0	-25

YEAR	TEAM	G (GS, POS)	RUSH	YD	AVG(LG)	TD	REC	YD	AVG(LG)	TD	PASS	COMP	PCT	YD	AVG(LG)	TD	INT	SK	YD	QBR	KPR	OTD	PTS	TAY
1953	ChiB	1	1	0	0.0(0)	0	—	—	—	—	8	1	12.5	9	1.1(9)	0	2	—	—	—	—	—	0	-76
1953	ChiC	6(qb)	1	1	1.0(1)	1	—	—	—	—	117	50	42.7	641	5.5(42)	4	9	—	—	39.9	—	—	6	-9
1954	ChiC	8	7	2	0.3(4)	1	—	—	—	—	79	36	45.6	343	4.3(38)	2	5	—	—	—	—	—	6	-7
NFL	5	38	27	35	1.3(10)	3	—	—	—	—	433	179	41.3	2556	5.9(54)	13	36	—	—	36.5	—	—	18	-32

ROMANISZYN, JIM James Christopher, LB, 6´2˝/224 lbs; Edinboro; 1973: Cle, rnd 13; B9/17/1951 Titusville, PA　**1973** Cle 14　**1974** Cle 14　**1976** NE 11 (2)　**NFL** 39 (2) [3 yrs]

ROMANO, JIM James John, C, 6´3˝/260 lbs; Penn State; 1982: LARd, rnd 2; B9/17/1959 Glen Cove, NY　**1982**†LARd 5 (0)　**1983** LARd 1 (0)　**1984** LARd 6 (2)　**1984** Hou 8 (7, c)　**1985** Hou 16 (16, C)　**1986** Hou 9 (9, c)　**NFL** 45 (34) [5 yrs]

ROMANOWSKI, BILL William Thomas, LB, 6´4˝/245 lbs; Boston College; 1988: SF, rnd 3; B4/2/1966 Vernon, CT　**1988**†SF 16 (8, rolb)　**1989**†SF 16 (4)　**1990**†SF 16 (16, ROLB)　**1991** SF 16 (16, ROLB)　**1992**†SF 16 (16, ROLB)　**1993**†SF 16 (16, RLB)　**1994** Phi 16 (15, LLB)　**1995**†Phi 16 (16, LLB)　**1996**†Den★16 (16, LLB)　**1997**†Den 16 (16, LLB)　**1998**†Den◇16 (16, LLB)　**1999** Den 16 (16, LLB)　**2000**†Den 16 (16, LLB)　**2001**†Oak 16 (16, LLB)　**2002**†Oak 16 (16, LLB)　**2003** Oak 3 (3)　**NFL** 243 (222) [16 yrs]

ROMASKO, DAVE David Sherman, RB, 6´3˝/241 lbs; Idaho; Carroll (MT); B11/3/1963 Pocatello, ID　**1987** Cin 3 (3)

ROMBOLI, RUDY Rudolph Louis, FB-LB, 5´10˝/213 lbs; none; B5/21/1923 Stoneham, MA, D1/3/1980 Boston, MA

1946	Bos	3(0)	1	-3	-3.0(3)	0	—	—	—	—	—	—	—	—	—	—	—	—	—	—	i	—	0	4
1947	Bos	12(9, FB)	23	50	2.2(15)	0	4	30	7.5(27)	0	—	—	—	—	—	—	—	—	—	—	ki	—	0	93
1948	Bos	12(3)	25	90	3.6(15)	1	8	77	9.6(33)	0	—	—	—	—	—	—	—	—	—	—	k	—	6	146
NFL	3	27(12)	49	137	2.8(15)	1	12	107	8.9(33)	0	—	—	—	—	—	—	—	—	—	—	ki	—	6	243

ROME, STAN Stanford Bernard, WR, 6´5˝/212 lbs; Clemson; 1979: KC, rnd 11; B6/4/1956 Valdosta, GA

1979	KC	9	1	-5	-5.0(-5)	0	—	—	—	—	—	—	—	—	—	—	—	—	—	—	—	—	0	-5
1980	KC	10(0)	—	—	—	—	3	58	19.3(33)	0	—	—	—	—	—	—	—	—	—	—	—	—	0	29
1981	KC	16(4)	—	—	—	—	17	203	11.9(23)	1	—	—	—	—	—	—	—	—	—	—	—	—	6	107
1982	KC	7(0)	—	—	—	—	2	25	12.5(16)	0	—	—	—	—	—	—	—	—	—	—	—	—	0	13
NFL	4	42(4)	1	-5	-5.0(-5)	0	22	286	13.0(33)	1	—	—	—	—	—	—	—	—	—	—	—	—	6	143

ROME, TAG Anthony Nicholas, WR, 5´9˝/175 lbs; Louisiana-Monroe; B8/13/1961 Donaldsonville, LA

| 1987 | SD | 3(1) | — | — | — | — | 6 | 49 | 8.2(13) | — | — | — | — | — | — | — | — | — | — | — | kp | — | 0 | 20 |

ROMEO, TONY Anthony Lamar, TE, 6´3˝/230 lbs; Florida State; 1961: Was, rnd 19; B3/7/1938 St. Petersburg, FL, D5/2/1996 Matthews, NC

1961	DalT-A	14	—	—	—	—	7	89	12.7(20)	0	—	—	—	—	—	—	—	—	—	—	—	—	0	45
1962	Bos-A	14(TE)	—	—	—	—	34	608	17.9(62)	1	—	—	—	—	—	—	—	—	—	—	—	—	6	309
1963	†Bos-A	14(TE)	—	—	—	—	32	418	13.1(31)	3	—	—	—	—	—	—	—	—	—	—	—	—	18	224
1964	Bos-A	14(TE)	—	—	—	—	26	445	17.1(38)	4	—	—	—	—	—	—	—	—	—	—	k	—	24	233
1965	Bos-A	14	—	—	—	—	15	203	13.5(36)	2	—	—	—	—	—	—	—	—	—	—	—	—	12	112
1966	Bos-A	14	—	—	—	—	2	46	23.0(29)	0	—	—	—	—	—	—	—	—	—	—	—	—	2	23
1967	Bos-A	5	—	—	—	—	1	4	4.0(4)	0	—	—	—	—	—	—	—	—	—	—	—	—	0	2
NFL	7	89	—	—	—	—	117	1813	15.5(62)	10	—	—	—	—	—	—	—	—	—	—	k	—	62	947

ROMER, RICH Richard H., LB, 6´3˝/222 lbs; Union (NY); 1988: Cin, rnd 7; B2/27/1966 East Greenbush, NY　**1988** Cin 4 (0)　**1989** Cin 5 (0)　**NFL** 9 (0) [2 yrs]

ROMERO, DARIO Dario, DT, 6´3˝/305 lbs; Eastern Washington; B4/13/1978 Spokane, WA　**2003** Mia 8 (1)　**2004** Mia 14 (1)　**NFL** 22 (2) [2 yrs]

ROMERO, RAY Ray Rene, G, 5´11˝/213 lbs; Kansas State; B12/31/1927 Wichita, KS　**1951** Phi 7

ROMES, CHARLES Charles Michael, DB, 6´1˝/191 lbs; North Carolina Central; 1977: Buf, rnd 12; B12/16/1954 Verdun, France [I]　**1977** Buf 14　**1978** Buf 16 (16, RCB)　**1979** Buf 16 (16, RCB)　**1980**†Buf 16 (16, RCB)　**1981**†Buf 16 (16, RCB)　**1982** Buf 9 (9, RCB)　**1983** Buf 16 (16, RCB)　**1984** Buf 16 (16, RCB)　**1985** Buf 16 (16, RCB)　**1986** Buf 16 (16, RCB)　**1987** SD 5 (0)　**1987**†Sea 0 (0)　**NFL** 156 (137) [11 yrs]

ROMINE, AL Alton Rollon, DB-HB, 6´2˝/191 lbs; Florida; North Alabama; B3/10/1932 Florence, AL　**1955** ChiB 1　**1955** GB 4　**1960** Den-A 14 (LS)　**1961** Bos-A 1

| 1958 | GB | 12 | 1 | 0 | 0.0(0) | 0 | — | — | — | — | — | — | — | — | — | — | — | — | — | pi | — | — | 0 | -8 |
| NFL | 4 | 32 | 1 | 0 | 0.0(0) | 0 | — | — | — | — | — | — | — | — | — | — | — | — | — | pi | — | — | 0 | 41 |

ROMNEY, MILT Milton Addas, B, 5´8˝/166 lbs; Utah; Chicago; B6/20/1899 Salt Lake City, UT, D11/10/1975 North Little Rock, AR [K]　**1923** Rac 8 (5, WB), 6　**1924** Rac 10 (8, BB), 6　**1925** ChiB 14 (3)　**1926** ChiB 16 (16, QB), 25　**1927** ChiB 14 (7, qb), 6　**1928** ChiB 11 (2), 13　**NFL** 73 (41), 56 [6 yrs]

ROMO, TONY Tony, QB, 6´2˝/219 lbs; Eastern Illinois; B4/21/1980 San Diego, CA　**2004** Dal 6 (0)

| 2005 | Dal | 16(0) | 2 | -2 | -1.0(-1) | 0 | — | — | — | — | — | — | — | — | — | — | — | — | — | — | — | — | 0 | -2 |
| NFL | 2 | 22(0) | 2 | -2 | -1.0(-1) | 0 | — | — | — | — | — | — | — | — | — | — | — | — | — | — | — | — | 0 | -2 |

RONZANI, GENE Eugene, B, 5´9˝/200 lbs; Marquette; B3/28/1909 Iron Mountain, MI, D9/12/1975 Lac du Flambeau, WI [KC]

1933	†ChiB	11(3)	26	91	3.5	0	3	62	20.7(42)	1	9	0	0.0	0	—	0	0	—	—	—	—	—	6	127
1934	†ChiB	12(11, RH)	84	485	5.8	0	5	114	22.8(37)	3	36	9	25.0	150	4.2	3	6	—	—	—	—	—	18	407
1935	ChiB☆	11(6, RH)	79	356	4.5	1	8	122	15.3(44)	1	41	16	39.0	230	5.6	2	5	—	—	K	—	—	15	357
1936	ChiB	10(2)	37	186	5.0	0	4	58	14.5(36)	2	12	8	66.7	170	14.2	1	2	—	—	—	—	—	12	235
1937	†ChiB	11(3)	12	17	1.4	0	2	40	20.0(21)	1	13	4	30.8	84	6.5	0	2	—	—	—	—	—	6	44
1938	ChiB	8(1)	7	12	1.7	0	—	—	—	—	1	0	0.0	0	—	0	0	—	—	—	—	—	0	12
1944	ChiB	8(5, qb)	12	26	2.2(14)	0	—	—	—	—	56	26	46.4	448	8.0(61)	9	5	—	—	—	i	—	0	99
1945	ChiB	7(3)	3	-20	-6.7(5)	0	—	—	—	—	24	10	41.7	119	5.0(29)	2	1	—	—	—	kp	—	0	-55
NFL	8	78(34)	260	1153	4.4(14)	1	22	396	18.0(44)	8	192	73	38.0	1201	6.3(61)	15	21	—	—	Kkpi	—	—	57	1227

ROONEY, BILL William, B-C, 6´2˝/194 lbs; none; B7/17/1896, Canada, D3/17/1966 Bronx, NY　**1923** Dul 5 (5, TB)　**1924** Dul 6 (5, FB), 12　**1925** Dul 2 (2, FB)　**1925** NYG 9 (1), 6　**1926** Bkn 7 (3)　**1927** Dul 9 (8, C)　**1929** ChiC 9 (3)　**NFL** 47 (27), 18 [6 yrs]

ROONEY, COBB Harry Cobb, B, 6´0˝/185 lbs; none; B3/23/1900 Virginia, MN, D5/14/1973 Bremerton, WA　**1924** Dul 6 (6, BB)　**1925** Dul 2 (2, BB)　**1926** Dul 14 (12, BB), 6　**1927** Dul 8 (8, BB), 6　**1928** NYY 3 (0)　**1929** ChiC 11 (4), 18　**1930** ChiC 10 (6, bb), 6　**NFL** 54 (38), 36 [7 yrs]

ROONEY, JOE Joseph P., E-T, 6´0˝/177 lbs; none; B8/28/1898, Canada, D3/1979 Franklin, MN　**1923** Dul 7 (7, RE), 6　**1924** Dul 6 (6, RE), 6　**1925** RI 10 (9, RE), 6　**1926** Dul 13 (9, RE), 6　**1927** Dul 9 (10, LE), 18　**1928** Pot 10 (10, RE), 6　**NFL** 55 (51), 48 [6 yrs]

ROOPENIAN, MARK Mark Christopher, NT, 6´5˝/254 lbs; Boston College; B7/10/1958 Medford, MA　**1982** Buf 9 (0)　**1983** Buf 3 (0)　**NFL** 12 (0) [2 yrs]

ROOS, MICHAEL Michael, T, 6´7˝/320 lbs; Eastern Washington; 2005: Ten, rnd 2; B10/5/1982 Tallin, Estonia

| 2005 | Ten | 16(16, RT) | — | — | — | — | 1 | -7 | -7.0(-7) | 0 | — | — | — | — | — | — | — | — | — | — | — | — | 0 | -4 |

ROOT, JIM James Frederic, QB, 6´1˝/185 lbs; Miami (OH); 1953: ChiC, rnd 23; B8/17/1931 Toledo, OH, D5/26/2003 Orange Park, FL

1953	ChiC	11(QB)	26	12	0.5(19)	1	—	—	—	—	192	80	41.7	1149	6.0(77)	8	11	—	—	51.8	—	—	6	197
1956	ChiC	9	17	45	2.6(18)	2	—	—	—	—	57	28	49.1	333	5.8(34)	3	5	—	—	—	—	—	12	47
NFL	2	20	43	57	1.3(19)	3	—	—	—	—	249	108	43.4	1482	6.0(77)	11	16	—	—	51.0	—	—	18	243

ROPER, DEDRICK Dedrick, LB, 6´2˝/245 lbs; Northwood (MI); B7/31/1981 Milpitas, CA　**2005** Phi 6 (0)

ROPER, JOHN John Alfred, LB, 6´1˝/232 lbs; Texas A&M; 1989: Chi, rnd 2; B10/4/1965 Houston, TX　**1989** ChiB 16 (10, RLB)　**1990**†ChiB 14 (0)　**1991** ChiB 16 (16, RLB)　**1992** ChiB 16 (13, RLB)　**1993** Dal 3 (0)　**1993** Phi 3 (0)　**NFL** 68 (39) [5 yrs]

ROQUE, JUAN Juan Armando, T, 6´8˝/333 lbs; Arizona State; 1997: Det, rnd 2; B2/6/1974 San Diego, CA　**1997** Det 13 (1)　**1999**†Det 4 (2)　**NFL** 17 (3) [2 yrs]

ROQUEMORE, DURWOOD Durwood Clinton, DB, 6´1˝/183 lbs; Texas A&M-Kingsville; 1982: KC, rnd 6; B1/19/1960 Dallas, TX　**1982** KC 9 (0)　**1983** KC 15 (3)　**1987** Buf 5 (2)　**NFL** 29 (5) [3 yrs]

RORISON, JIM James, T, 6´3˝/250 lbs; USC; B7/23/1916, D10/1980　**1938** Pit 6 (1)

RORK, SPENCER Joseph Spencer, B, 5´9˝/160 lbs; Kentucky; B8/18/1896 Paducah, KY, D4/1982 Key Largo, FL　**1922** Evv 2 (2, WB)

ROSADO, DAN Daniel Peter, C-G, 6´3˝/280 lbs; Northern Illinois; B7/6/1959 Lawton, OK　**1987** SD 4 (3)　**1988** SD 12 (11, C)　**NFL** 16 (14) [2 yrs]

ROSATO, SAL Salvatore, FB, 6´1˝/228 lbs; Villanova; B6/6/1918 Williamsport, PA, D1/12/1959 Alhambra, CA

| 1945 | †Was | 7(1) | 23 | 85 | 3.7(15) | 2 | 1 | 7 | 7.0(7) | 0 | — | — | — | — | — | — | — | — | — | — | k | — | 12 | 111 |
| 1946 | Was | 5(1) | 62 | 238 | 3.8(21) | 2 | 1 | 17 | 17.0(17) | 0 | — | — | — | — | — | — | — | — | — | — | p | — | 12 | 274 |

YEAR	TEAM	G(GS, POS)	RUSH	YD	AVG(LG)	TD	REC	YD	AVG(LG)	TD	PASS	COMP	PCT	YD	AVG(LG)	TD	INT	SK	YD	QBR	KPR	OTD	PTS	TAY
1947	Was	11(5, fb)	74	297	4.0(20)	0	7	107	15.3(26)	1	—	—	—	—	—	—	—	—	—	—	k	—	6	362
NFL	3	23(7)	159	620	3.9(21)	4	9	131	14.6(26)	1	—	—	—	—	—	—	—	—	—	—	kp	—	30	746

ROSATTI, RUDY Rudolph F., T, 6´0˝/211 lbs; Western Michigan; North Dakota State; Michigan; B9/12/1895 Norway, MI, D7/8/1975 Norway, MI   **1923** Cle 7 (7, LT) **1924** GB 11 (10, RT) **1926** GB 10 (9, RT) **1927** GB 6 (5, RT) **1928** NYG 11 (9, RT) **NFL** 45 (40) [5 yrs]

ROSDAHL, HATCH Harrison Lynn, DE-DT, 6´5˝/250 lbs; Penn State; 1963: SD, rnd 14/SF, rnd 4; B8/24/1941 Hackensack, NJ, D6/15/2004 Ridgefield Park, NJ   **1964** Buf-A 4 **1964** KC-A 7 **1965** KC-A 14 **1966** KC-A 7 **NFL** 32 [3 yrs]

ROSE, AL Alfred Grady, E, 6´3˝/205 lbs; Texas; B1/26/1907 Temple, TX, D1988

1930	Pro	11(11, LE)	—	—	—	—	—	—	—	—	—	—	—	—	—	—	—	—	—	—	—	—	—	—
1931	Pro	11(11, LE)	—	—	—	—	—	—	—	—	—	—	—	—	—	—	—	—	—	—	—	—	—	—
1932	GB	13(9, LE)	—	—	—	—	1	20	20.0(20)	0	—	—	—	—	—	—	—	—	—	—	—	2	12	20
1933	GB	12(7, LE)	—	—	—	—	6	89	14.8	1	—	—	—	—	—	—	—	—	—	—	—	—	6	50
1934	GB	9(5, le)	—	—	—	—	6	117	19.5(36)	2	—	—	—	—	—	—	—	—	—	—	—	—	12	69
1935	GB	12(7, le)	—	—	—	—	8	91	11.4	0	—	—	—	—	—	—	—	—	—	—	—	—	0	46
1936	GB	2(0)	—	—	—	—	—	—	—	—	—	—	—	—	—	—	—	—	—	—	—	—	—	—
NFL	7	70(50)	—	—	—	—	21	317	15.1(36)	5	—	—	—	—	—	—	—	—	—	—	—	3	48	199

ROSE, BARRY Barry Allan, WR, 6´0˝/185 lbs; Wisconsin-Stevens Point; 1992: Buf, rnd 10; B7/28/1968 Hudson, WI   **1993** Den 3 (0)

ROSE, CARLTON Carlton, LB, 6´2˝/220 lbs; Michigan; B2/8/1962 Pompano Beach, FL   **1987** Was 2 (2)

ROSE, DONOVAN Donovan James, DB, 6´1˝/187 lbs; Hampton; B3/9/1957 Norfolk, VA   **1980** KC 7 (0) **1986** Mia 12 (2) **1987** Mia 12 (1) **NFL** 31 (3) [3 yrs]

ROSE, GENE Roy Eugene, E, 6´1˝/185 lbs; Tennessee; 1936: NYG, rnd 4; B8/15/1913 Cincinnati, OH, D1/16/1986 Memphis, TN

| 1936 | NYG | 7(3) | — | 2 | 13 | 6.5(7) | 0 | 6 | 73 | 12.2 | 0 | — | — | — | — | — | — | — | — | — | — | — | 0 | 50 |

ROSE, GENE Eugene Harry, B, 5´8˝/172 lbs; Wisconsin; B7/11/1904 Racine, WI, D2/1/1979 Torrance, CA **[K]**   **1929** ChiC 13 (6, BB), 6 **1930** ChiC 12 (6, WB), 25 **1931** ChiC 8 (6, wb), 6

| 1932 | ChiC | 1(0) | 1 | 0 | 0.0 | 0 | — | — | — | — | 5 | 2 | 40.0 | 40 | 8.0 | 0 | 0 | — | — | — | — | — | 0 | 20 |
| NFL | 4 | 34(18) | 1 | 0 | 0.0 | 5 | — | — | — | — | 5 | 2 | 40.0 | 40 | 8.0 | 0 | 0 | — | — | — | K | — | 37 | 75 |

ROSE, GEORGE George Lee, DB, 5´11˝/200 lbs; Auburn; 1964: Min, rnd 3/Buf, rnd 3; B1/1/1942 Brunswick, GA   **1964** Min 14 (13, LCB) **1965** Min 10 (10, LCB) **1966** Min 10 **1967** NO 13 **NFL** 47 (23) [4 yrs]

ROSE, JOE Joseph Harold, TE, 6´3˝/228 lbs; California; 1980: Mia, rnd 7; B6/24/1957 Marysville, CA

1980	Mia	16(0)	—	—	—	—	13	149	11.5(50)	0	—	—	—	—	—	—	—	—	—	—	—	—	0	75
1981	†Mia	16(0)	—	—	—	—	23	316	13.7(50)	2	—	—	—	—	—	—	—	—	—	—	k	—	12	158
1982	†Mia	9(0)	—	—	—	—	16	182	11.4(44)	2	—	—	—	—	—	—	—	—	—	—	—	—	12	101
1983	†Mia	16(0)	—	—	—	—	29	345	11.9(37)	3	—	—	—	—	—	—	—	—	—	—	—	—	18	188
1984	†Mia	9(0)	—	—	—	—	12	195	16.3(34)	2	—	—	—	—	—	—	—	—	—	—	—	—	12	108
1985	†Mia	16(1)	—	—	—	—	19	306	16.1(42)	4	—	—	—	—	—	—	—	—	—	—	—	—	24	173
1987	LARm	1(0)	—	—	—	—	—	—	—	—	—	—	—	—	—	—	—	—	—	—	—	—	—	—
NFL	7	83(1)	—	—	—	—	112	1493	13.3(50)	13	—	—	—	—	—	—	—	—	—	—	k	—	78	802

ROSE, KEN Kenny Frank, LB, 6´1˝/215 lbs; UNLV; B6/9/1962 Sacramento, CA   **1987** NYJ 10 (3) **1988** NYJ 12 (0) **1989** NYJ 15 (1) **1990** Cle 7 (0) **1990**†Phi 8 (0) **1991** Phi 16 (0) **1992**†Phi 16 (0) **1993** Phi 5 (0) **1994** Phi 16 (0) **NFL** 105 (4) [8 yrs]

ROSE, TAM Walter Sumner, TB-HB, 5´11˝/170 lbs; Syracuse; B6/20/1889 Tonawanda, NY, D12/1965, NY **[C]**   **1921** Ton 1 (1, TB)

ROSECRANS, JIM James Edward, LB, 6´1˝/230 lbs; Penn State; B1/13/1953 Asheville, NC   **1976** NYJ 1

ROSEMA, ROCKY Roger William, LB, 6´2˝/230 lbs; Michigan; 1968: SL, rnd 5; B2/5/1946 Grand Rapids, MI   **1968** SL 12 **1969** SL 14 (RLB) **1970** SL 4 **1971** SL 2 **NFL** 32 [4 yrs]

ROSEN, STAN Stanley, BB-TB, 5´6˝/155 lbs; Rutgers; B3/28/1906 New York, NY, D7/23/1984 Claremont, NH   **1929** Buf 8 (2)

ROSENBACH, TIMM Timm Lane, QB, 6´2˝/210 lbs; Washington State; 1989: Phx, rnd S1; B10/27/1966 Everett, WA

1989	Phx	2(1)	6	26	4.3(8)	0	—	—	—	—	22	9	40.9	95	4.3(24)	0	1	2	19	—	—	—	0	34
1990	Phx	16(16, QB)	86	470	5.5(25)	3	—	—	—	—	437	237	54.2	3098	7.1(68)	16	17	43	285	72.8	—	—	18	1449
1992	Phx	8(3)	9	11	1.2(10)	0	—	—	—	—	92	49	53.3	483	5.3(45)	0	6	7	32	—	—	—	0	13
NFL	3	26(20)	101	507	5.0(25)	3	—	—	—	—	551	295	53.5	3676	6.7(68)	16	24	52	336	66.0	—	—	18	1495

ROSENFELS, SAGE Sage, QB, 6´4˝/222 lbs; Iowa State; 2001: Was, rnd 4; B3/6/1978 Maquoketa, IA

2002	Mia	4(0)	2	-9	-4.5(-2)	0	—	—	—	—	3	0	0.0	0	0.0	0	0	—	—	—	—	—	0	-9
2003	Mia	2(0)	1	-1	-1.0(-1)	0	—	—	—	—	6	4	66.7	50	8.3(21)	1	0	—	—	—	—	—	0	29
2004	Mia	3(1)	—	—	—	—	—	—	—	—	39	16	41.0	264	6.8(76)	1	3	3	16	—	—	—	0	17
2005	Mia	4(1)	6	15	2.5(12)	0	—	—	—	—	61	34	55.7	462	7.6(77)	4	3	—	—	—	—	—	0	146
NFL	4	13(2)	5	5	0.6(12)	0	—	—	—	—	109	54	49.5	776	7.1(77)	6	6	3	16	—	—	—	0	183

ROSENMEIER, ERIK Erik Michael, C, 6´4˝/240 lbs; Colgate; B5/26/1965 Plainfield, NJ   **1987** Buf 1 (0)

ROSENSTIEL, BOB Robert, TE, 6´3˝/240 lbs; Eastern Illinois; B2/7/1974 Prineville, OR   **1997** Oak 4 (0)

ROSENTHAL, MIKE Michael Paul, T-G, 6´7˝/310 lbs; Notre Dame; 1999: NYG, rnd 5; B6/10/1977 Pittsburgh, PA   **1999** NYG 9 (7, lg) **2000**†NYG 8 (2) **2001** NYG 7 (0) **2002**†NYG 16 (16, RT) **2003** Min 16 (16, RT) **2004** Min 2 (2) **2005** Min 16 (12, RT) **NFL** 74 (55) [7 yrs]

ROSEQUIST, TED Theodore Anthony, T, 6´4˝/222 lbs; John Carroll; Ohio State; B4/17/1908 Emlenton, PA, D11/29/1988 West Palm Beach, FL   **1935** ChiB 11 (0) **1937** Cle 7 (3)

1934	†ChiB	11(2)	—	—	—	—	2	20	10.0	0	—	—	—	—	—	—	—	—	—	—	—	—	0	10
1936	ChiB	4(1)	—	—	—	—	1	15	15.0(15)	0	—	—	—	—	—	—	—	—	—	—	—	—	0	8
NFL	4	33(6)	—	—	—	—	3	35	11.7(15)	0	—	—	—	—	—	—	—	—	—	—	—	—	0	18

ROSKIE, KEN Kenneth, FB, 6´1˝/220 lbs; South Carolina; 1943: GB, rnd 32; B11/29/1921 Rockford, IL, D8/1986 Redmond, WA

1946	SF-A	8(0)	9	16	1.8	0	0	7	(7)	0	—	—	—	—	—	—	—	—	—	—	—	—	0	20
1948	GB	5	28	5.6(9)	1	—	—	—	—	—	—	—	—	—	—	—	—	—	—	i	—	6	45
1948	Det	7(4)	1	1	1.0(1)	0	—	—	—	—	—	—	—	—	—	—	—	—	—	—	k	—	0	16
NFL	1	13(4)	6	29	4.8(9)	1	—	—	—	—	—	—	—	—	—	—	—	—	—	—	ki	—	6	61

ROSNAGLE, TED Theodore, DB, 6´3˝/205 lbs; Portland State; B9/29/1961 Pasadena, CA   **1985** Min 6 (0) **1987** Min 3 (3) **NFL** 9 (3) [2 yrs]

ROSS, ADRIAN Adrian Lamont, LB, 6´2˝/245 lbs; Colorado State; B2/19/1975 Santa Clara, CA   **1998** Cin 14 (1) **1999** Cin 16 (10, ROLB) **2000** Cin 13 (4) **2001** Cin 16 (1) **2002** Cin 16 (6, llb) **2003** Cin 15 (12, LLB) **NFL** 90 (34) [6 yrs]

ROSS, ALVIN Alvin, RB, 5´11˝/235 lbs; Oklahoma; Central Oklahoma; B5/3/1963 Chicago, IL

| 1987 | Phi | 2(0) | 14 | 54 | 3.9(12) | 1 | 5 | 41 | 8.2(17) | 0 | — | — | — | — | — | — | — | — | — | — | — | — | 6 | 85 |

ROSS, DAN Daniel Richard, TE, 6´4˝/238 lbs; Northeastern; 1979: Cin, rnd 2; B2/9/1957 Malden, MA, D5/16/2005 Haverill, MA

1979	Cin	16(TE)	—	—	—	—	41	516	12.6(41)	1	—	—	—	—	—	—	—	—	—	—	—	—	6	263
1980	Cin	16(16, TE)	—	—	—	—	56	724	12.9(37)	4	—	—	—	—	—	—	—	—	—	—	—	—	24	382
1981	†Cin☆	16(16, TE)	—	—	—	—	71	910	12.8(37)	5	—	—	—	—	—	—	—	—	—	—	—	—	30	480
1982	†Cin★	9(9, TE)	—	—	—	—	47	508	10.8(28)	3	—	—	—	—	—	—	—	—	—	—	—	—	18	269
1983	Cin	16(15, TE)	—	—	—	—	42	483	11.5(30)	3	—	—	—	—	—	—	—	—	—	—	—	—	18	257
1985	Cin	6(0)	—	—	—	—	6	63	10.5(20)	0	—	—	—	—	—	—	—	—	—	—	—	—	0	32
1985	Sea	10(5, te)	—	—	—	—	10	72	7.2(12)	2	—	—	—	—	—	—	—	—	—	—	—	—	12	46
1986	GB	15(10, TE)	—	—	—	—	17	143	8.4(16)	1	—	—	—	—	—	—	—	—	—	—	—	—	6	77
NFL	7	104(71)	—	—	—	—	290	3419	11.8(41)	19	—	—	—	—	—	—	—	—	—	—	—	—	114	1805

ROSS, DAVE David, E, 6´3˝/210 lbs; Los Angeles State; 1960: NYT, rnd 1/Det, rnd 12; B2/1/1938

| 1960 | NYT-A | 12 | — | — | — | — | 10 | 122 | 12.2(37) | 1 | — | — | — | — | — | — | — | — | — | — | — | — | 6 | 66 |

ROSS, DEREK Derek, DB, 5´10˝/197 lbs; Ohio State; 2002: Dal, rnd 3; B1/5/1980 Rock Hill, SC   **2002** Dal 14 (9, LCB) **2003** Dal 8 (0) **2003** Atl 2 (0) **2004** Min 9 (0) **NFL** 33 (9) [3 yrs]

YEAR	TEAM	G(GS, POS)	RUSH	YD	AVG(LG)	TD	REC	YD	AVG(LG)	TD	PASS	COMP	PCT	YD	AVG(LG)	TD	INT	SK	YD	QBR	KPR	OTD	PTS	TAY

ROSS, DOMINIQUE Dominique, RB, 6´0˝/203 lbs; Valdosta State; B1/12/1972 Jacksonville, FL **1995** Dal 1 (0) **1996**†Dal 2 (0) **NFL** 3 (0) [2 yrs]

ROSS, JERMAINE Jermaine Lewis, WR, 6´0˝/192 lbs; Purdue; B4/27/1971 Jeffersonville, IN

YEAR	TEAM	G(GS, POS)	RUSH	YD	AVG(LG)	TD	REC	YD	AVG(LG)	TD	...	KPR	OTD	PTS	TAY
1994	LARm	4 (0)	—	—	—	—	1	36	36.0 (36)	1		—	—	6	23
1996	SL	15 (0)	1	3	3.0 (3)	1	15	160	10.7 (28)	0		—	—	6	93
1997	SL	4 (0)	—	—	—	—	3	37	12.3 (14)	0		kp	—	0	61
NFL	3	23 (0)	1	3	3.0 (3)	1	19	233	12.3 (36)	1		kp	—	12	177

ROSS, KEVIN Kevin Lesley, DB, 5´9˝/185 lbs; Temple; 1984: KC, rnd 7; B1/16/1962 Camden, NJ [I] **1984** KC 16 (16, RCB) **1985** KC 16 (15, RCB) **1986**†KC 16 (16, RCB) **1987** KC 12 (11, RCB) **1988** KC 15 (14, RCB) **1989** KC★15 (13, RCB) **1990**†KC★16 (15, RCB) **1991** KC 14 (13, RCB) **1992**†KC 16 (16, LCB) **1993**†KC 15 (15, FS/rcb) **1994** Atl 16 (16, SS) **1995**†Atl 16 (15, SS) **1996** SD 16 (16, FS) **1997** KC 5 (0) **NFL** 204 (191) [14 yrs]

ROSS, LOUIS Louis Edward, DE, 6´6˝/248 lbs; South Carolina State; 1971: Buf, rnd 8; B8/31/1947 Orlando, FL **1971** Buf 5 **1972** Buf 14 **1975** KC 1 **NFL** 20 [3 yrs]

ROSS, MICAH Micah David, WR, 6´2˝/221 lbs; Jacksonville State; B1/13/1976 Jacksonville, FL **2001** Jax 5 (0) **2002** Jax 16 (0) **2003** Jax 1 (0) **2003** SD 6 (0) **2004** SD 7 (0) **2004** Car 10 (0) **NFL** 45 (0) [4 yrs]

ROSS, OLIVER Oliver Stevenson, RB, 6´0˝/210 lbs; Alabama A&M; 1973: Den, rnd 16; B9/18/1949 Gainesville, FL

YEAR	TEAM	G(GS, POS)	RUSH	YD	AVG(LG)	TD	REC	YD	AVG(LG)	TD	...	KPR	OTD	PTS	TAY
1973	Den	4	5	21	4.2 (8)	0	—	—	—	—		—	—	0	21
1974	Den	7	3	8	2.7 (7)	0	1	13	13.0 (13)	0		k	—	0	27
1975	Den	14	42	121	2.9 (21)	0	7	69	9.9 (30)	0		k	—	0	161
1976	Sea	10	13	23	1.8 (11)	0	2	22	11.0 (21)	0		k	—	0	239
NFL	4	35	63	173	2.7 (21)	0	10	104	10.4 (30)	0		k	—	0	447

ROSS, OLIVER Oliver Stevenson, T-G, 6´5˝/317 lbs; Iowa State; 1998: Dal, rnd 5; B9/27/1974 Culver City, CA **1998** Dal 2 (0) **2001**†Pit 16 (7, rg) **2002**†Pit 16 (1) **2003** Pit 16 (11, RT) **2004**†Pit 16 (16, RT) **2005** Arz 12 (11, RT) **NFL** 78 (46) [6 yrs]

ROSS, SCOTT Scott, LB, 6´1˝/235 lbs; USC; 1991: NO, rnd 11; B12/7/1968 El Toro, CA **1991** NO 4 (0)

ROSS, TIM Timothy Leon, LB, 6´5˝/225 lbs; Bowling Green State; B12/27/1958 Toledo, OH **1987** Det 3 (0)

ROSS, WILLIE William James, FB, 5´10˝/200 lbs; Nebraska; 1964: Buf, rnd 12/SL, rnd 9; B6/6/1941 Helena, AR

YEAR	TEAM	G(GS, POS)	RUSH	YD	AVG(LG)	TD	...	PTS	TAY
1964	†Buf-A	12	4	14	3.5 (12)	1		6	24

ROSSO, GEORGE George Anthony, DB, 5´11˝/177 lbs; Ohio State; 1954: Was, rnd 25; B1/15/1930 Pittsburgh, PA, D1/29/1994 Columbus, OH **1954** Was 12 (DB)

ROSSOVICH, TIM Timothy John, LB-DE, 6´4˝/240 lbs; USC; 1968: Phi, rnd 1; B3/14/1946 Palo Alto, CA **1968** Phi 14 (LDE) **1969** Phi✧14 (LDE) **1970** Phi 14 (8, MLB) **1971** Phi 13 (MLB) **1972** SD 6 (MLB) **1973** SD 13 (5, mlb) **1976** Hou 14 **NFL** 88 (13) [7 yrs]

ROSSUM, ALLEN Allen, DB, 5´8˝/178 lbs; Notre Dame; 1998: Phi, rnd 3; B10/22/1975 Dallas, TX [R] **1998** Phi 15 (2) **1999** Phi 16 (0) **2001**†GB 6 (0) **2002**†Atl 14 (0) **2003** Atl 16 (0) **2005** Atl 10 (0)

YEAR	TEAM	G(GS, POS)	RUSH	YD	AVG(LG)	TD	...	KPR	OTD	PTS	TAY
2000	GB	16 (0)	1	16	16.0 (16)	0		kp	1	6	667
2004	†Atl✧	16 (1)	1	0	0.0 (0)	0		kpiS	1	6	674
NFL	8	109 (3)	2	16	8.0 (16)	0		kpiS	6	36	4210

ROSTECK, ERNIE Ernest W., C, 6´1˝/218 lbs; none; B5/12/1922 Detroit, MI, D3/1986 Waterloo, IA **1943** Det 1 (0) **1944** Det 9 (0) **NFL** 10 (0) [2 yrs]

ROSTOSKY, PETE Peter Joseph, T, 6´4˝/259 lbs; Connecticut; B7/29/1961 Monongahela, PA **1984**†Pit 8 (2) **1985** Pit 16 (5, lt) **1986** Pit 11 (1) **NFL** 35 (8) [3 yrs]

ROTE, KYLE William Kyle, E-HB, 6´0˝/199 lbs; SMU; 1951: NYG, rnd B1; B10/27/1927 Bellevue, TX, D8/14/2002 Baltimore, MD

YEAR	TEAM	G(GS, POS)	RUSH	YD	AVG(LG)	TD	REC	YD	AVG(LG)	TD	PASS	COMP	PCT	YD	AVG(LG)	TD	INT	...	QBR	KPR	OTD	PTS	TAY
1951	NYG	5	21	114	5.4 (31)	1	8	62	7.8 (18)	0	—	—	—	—	—	—	—			k	—	6	250
1952	NYG	12 (LH)	103	421	4.1 (52)	2	21	240	11.4 (26)	2	4	2	50.0	113	28.3 (72)	1	0			k	—	24	653
1953	NYG✧	9 (RH)	63	213	3.4 (18)	1	26	440	16.9 (75)	5	8	2	25.0	45	5.6 (23)	0	1			—	—	36	451
1954	NYG✧	11 (RH)	30	59	2.0 (14)	0	29	551	19.0 (63)	2	6	2	33.3	36	6.0 (18)	1	1			—	—	12	328
1955	NYG★	12 (LE)	10	46	4.6 (14)	0	31	580	18.7 (71)	8	1	0	0.0	0	—	0	0			—	—	48	376
1956	†NYG★	12 (LE)	3	5	1.7 (3)	0	28	405	14.5 (31)	4	1	0	0.0	0	—	0	0			—	—	24	228
1957	NYG	12 (LE)	1	13	13.0 (13)	0	25	358	14.3 (33)	3	—	—	—	—	—	—	—			—	—	18	207
1958	†NYG	12 (LE)	—	—	—	—	12	244	20.3 (44)	3	—	—	—	—	—	—	—			—	—	18	137
1959	†NYG	10 (LE)	—	—	—	—	25	362	14.5 (34)	4	—	—	—	—	—	—	—			—	—	24	201
1960	NYG☆	12 (SE)	—	—	—	—	42	750	17.9 (71)	10	—	—	—	—	—	—	—			—	—	60	425
1961	†NYG	14 (LH)	—	—	—	—	53	805	15.2 (57)	7	—	—	—	—	—	—	—			—	—	42	438
NFL	11	121	231	871	3.8 (52)	4	300	4797	16.0 (75)	48	30	6	30.0	194	9.7 (72)	2	2			k	—	312	3692

ROTE, TOBIN Tobin Cornelius, QB, 6´3˝/211 lbs; Rice; 1950: GB, rnd 2; B1/18/1928 San Antonio, TX, D6/27/2000 Saginaw, MI

YEAR	TEAM	G(GS, POS)	RUSH	YD	AVG(LG)	TD	REC	YD	AVG(LG)	TD	PASS	COMP	PCT	YD	AVG(LG)	TD	INT	SK	YD	QBR	KPR	OTD	PTS	TAY
1950	GB	12 (QB)	27	158	5.9 (29)	0	—	—	—	—	224	83	37.1	1231	5.5 (96)	7	24	—	—	26.7	—	0	-152
1951	GB	12 (QB)	76	523	**6.9 (55)**	3	0	11	(11)	0	256	106	41.4	1540	6.0 (85)	15	20	—	—	48.6	P	18	604
1952	GB	12 (qb)	58	313	5.4 (30)	2	1	28	28.0 (28)	0	157	82	52.2	1268	8.1 (81)	13	8	—	—	**85.6**	—	18	731
1953	GB	12 (QB)	33	180	5.5 (21)	0	—	—	—	—	185	72	38.9	1005	5.4 (80)	5	15	—	—	32.4	P	0	108
1954	GB	12 (QB)	67	301	4.5 (30)	8	—	—	—	—	**382**	**180**	47.1	2311	6.0 (82)	14	18	—	—	59.1	—	48	887
1955	GB☆	12 (QB)	74	332	4.5 (49)	5	—	—	—	—	342	157	45.9	1977	5.8 (60)	17	19	—	—	57.8	—	30	696
1956	GB★	12 (QB)	84	398	4.7 (39)	11	—	—	—	—	**308**	**146**	47.4	**2203**	7.2 (66)	**18**	15	—	—	70.6	—	66	1100
1957	†Det	12 (qb)	70	366	5.2 (23)	1	—	—	—	—	177	76	42.9	1070	6.0 (48)	11	10	—	—	60.2	—	6	566
1958	Det	12 (QB)	77	351	4.6 (27)	3	—	—	—	—	257	118	45.9	1678	6.5 (65)	14	10	—	—	69.5	—	18	890
1959	Det	10 (QB)	35	156	4.5 (21)	2	—	—	—	—	162	62	38.3	861	5.3 (59)	5	19	—	—	26.8	—	12	-129
1963	†SD-A★	14 (14, QB)	24	62	2.6 (15)	2	—	—	—	—	286	170	**59.4**	2510	**8.8 (85)**	20	17	—	—	**86.7**	—	12	757
1964	†SD-A	14 (5, qb)	10	-12	-1.2 (9)	0	1	-11	-11.0 (-11)	0	163	74	45.4	1156	7.1 (82)	9	15	11	97	49.5	—	0	6
1966	Den-A	3	—	—	—	—	—	—	—	—	8	3	37.5	40	5.0 (20)	0	1	—	—	—	—	0	-20
NFL	13	149 (19)	635	3128	4.9 (55)	37	2	28	14.0 (28)	0	2907	1329	45.7	18850	6.5 (96)	148	191	11	97	56.8	P	—	228	6042

ROTH, MATT Matthew, DE, 6´3˝/272 lbs; Iowa; 2005: Mia, rnd 2; B10/14/1982 Villa Park, IL **2005** Mia 16 (0)

ROTH, PETE Peter William, RB, 5´11˝/200 lbs; Northern Illinois; B1/12/1962 Worthington, MN

YEAR	TEAM	G(GS, POS)	RUSH	YD	AVG(LG)	TD	...	KPR	OTD	PTS	TAY
1987	Mia	3 (0)	3	10	3.3 (9)	0		k	—	0	29

ROTHER, TIM Timothy Jay, DT, 6´7˝/285 lbs; Nebraska; 1988: LARd, rnd 4; B9/28/1965 St. Paul, NE **1989** LARd 16 (0) **1990** LARd 4 (0) **NFL** 20 (0) [2 yrs]

ROTHROCK, CLIFF Clifford Crossley, C, 5´10˝/190 lbs; North Dakota State; B1/10/1922 Fargo, ND, D10/5/2000 Anaheim, CA **1947** ChiR-A 2 (1)

ROTHSCHILD, DOUG Douglas Robert, LB, 6´2˝/231 lbs; Wheaton; B4/27/1965 Sunnyvale, CA **1987** ChiB 3 (0)

ROTHWELL, FRED Donald Fred, C, 6´3˝/240 lbs; Kansas State; 1974: Det, rnd 13; B10/8/1952 Lafayette, IN **1974** Det 14

ROTON, HERB Herbert Carl, E, 6´2˝/210 lbs; Auburn; B8/28/1913 Montgomery, AL, D8/3/2002 Montgomery, AL **1937** Phi 9 (1)

ROUDEBUSH, GEORGE George Milton, TB-FB, 5´11˝/180 lbs; Denison; B1/25/1894 Newtonville, OH, D3/1/1992 Chardon, OH **1920** Day 9 (0) **1921** Day 9 (3), 6 **NFL** 18 (3) [2 yrs]

ROUEN, TOM Thomas Francis, P, 6´3˝/225 lbs; Colorado State; Colorado; B6/9/1968 Hinsdale, IL [KP] **1994** Den☆16 (0) **1995** Den 16 (0) **1996**†Den 16 (0) **1997**†Den 16 (0) **2001** Den 16 (0) **2002**†Pit 2 (0) **2003**†Sea 16 (0) **2004** Sea 4 (0) **2005**†Sea 12 (0)

YEAR	TEAM	G(GS, POS)	RUSH	YD	AVG(LG)	TD	...	QBR	KPR	OTD	PTS	TAY
1993	†Den	16 (0)	1	0	0.0 (0)	0		—	P	—	0	0
1998	†Den	16 (0)	1	0	0.0 (0)	0		—	KP	—	0	0
1999	Den	16 (0)	1	0	0.0 (0)	0		—	P	—	0	0
2000	†Den	16 (0)	1	-11	-11.0 (-11)	0		—	P	—	0	-11
2002	Den	8 (0)	1	0	0.0 (0)	0		—	P	—	0	0
2002	NYG	2 (0)	1	0	0.0 (0)	0		—	P	—	0	0
NFL	13	188 (0)	6	-11	-1.8			—	P	—	0	-11

ROUNDTREE, RALEIGH Raleigh Cub, G-T, 6´4˝/295 lbs; South Carolina State; 1997: SD, rnd 4; B8/31/1975 Augusta, GA **1998** SD 15 (5, rg) **1999** SD 15 (5, rg) **2000** SD 16 (15, LG) **2001** SD 16 (16, LG) **2002** Arz 10 (6, lg) **NFL** 72 (47) [5 yrs]

ROUNDTREE, RAY Raymond Anthony, WR, 6´0˝/180 lbs; Penn State; 1988: Det, rnd 3; B4/19/1966 Aiken, SC **1988** Det 4 (0)

YEAR	TEAM	G(GS, POS)	RUSH	YD	AVG(LG)	TD	REC	YD	AVG(LG)	TD	PASS	COMP	PCT	YD	AVG(LG)	TD	INT	SK	YD	QBR	KPR	OTD	PTS	TAY

Rourke, Jim James Peter, T-G, 6´5˝/264 lbs; Boston College; 1979: Oak, rnd 9; B2/10/1957 Weymouth, MA **1980** KC 15 (9, RT) **1981** KC 12 (0) **1982** KC 9 (1) **1983** KC 11 (0) **1984** KC 13 (10, rt) **1985** NO 13 (5, lt) **1986** KC 4 (0) **1988**†Cin 0 (0) **NFL** 77 (25) [8 yrs]

Rousch, Tubby Frank, WB-G, 5´7˝/170 lbs; Toledo; B1898, deceased **1922** Tol 5 (0), 6

Rouse, Curtis Curtis Lamar, G-T, 6´3˝/316 lbs; Tennessee-Chattanooga; 1982: Min, rnd 11; B7/13/1960 Augusta, GA **1982**†Min 5 (0) **1983** Min 16 (1) **1984** Min 16 (15, LG) **1985** Min 16 (13, LT) **1986** Min 5 (0) **1987** SD 10 (3) **NFL** 68 (32) [6 yrs]

Rouse, James James David, RB, 6´0˝/220 lbs; Arkansas; 1990: Chi, rnd 8; B12/18/1966 Little Rock, AR

YEAR	TEAM	G(GS, POS)	RUSH	YD	AVG(LG)	TD	REC	YD	AVG(LG)	TD	PASS	COMP	PCT	YD	AVG(LG)	TD	INT	SK	YD	QBR	KPR	OTD	PTS	TAY
1990	†ChiB	16(0)	16	56	3.5(10)	0	—	—	—	—	—	—	—	—	—	—	—	—	—	—	k	—	0	28
1991	†ChiB	14(4)	27	74	2.7(10)	0	15	93	6.2(14)	0	—	—	—	—	—	—	—	—	—	—	k	—	0	101
NFL	2	30(4)	43	130	3.0(10)	0	15	93	6.2(14)	0	—	—	—	—	—	—	—	—	—	—	k	—	0	129

Rouse, Stillman Stillman Ivan, E, 6´2˝/205 lbs; Missouri; 1940: Det, rnd 15; B9/22/1917 St. Louis, MO, D12/22/1997

YEAR	TEAM	G(GS, POS)	RUSH	YD	AVG(LG)	TD	REC	YD	AVG(LG)	TD	PASS	COMP	PCT	YD	AVG(LG)	TD	INT	SK	YD	QBR	KPR	OTD	PTS	TAY
1940	Det	10(5, LE)	2	0	0.0	0	2	17	8.5	0	—	—	—	—	—	—	—	—	—	—	—	—	0	9

Rouse, Wardell Wardell, LB, 6´2˝/235 lbs; Clemson; 1995: TB, rnd 6; B6/9/1972 Clewiston, FL **1995** TB 16 (1)

Rouson, Lee Cecil Lee, RB, 6´1˝/220 lbs; Colorado; 1985: NYG, rnd 8; B10/18/1962 Elizabeth City, NC

YEAR	TEAM	G(GS, POS)	RUSH	YD	AVG(LG)	TD	REC	YD	AVG(LG)	TD	PASS	COMP	PCT	YD	AVG(LG)	TD	INT	SK	YD	QBR	KPR	OTD	PTS	TAY
1985	†NYG	2(0)	1	1	1.0(1)	0	—	—	—	—	—	—	—	—	—	—	—	—	—	—	k	—	0	6
1986	†NYG	14(1)	54	179	3.3(21)	2	8	121	15.1(37)	1	—	—	—	—	—	—	—	—	—	—	k	—	18	256
1987	NYG	12(2)	41	155	3.8(14)	0	11	129	11.7(26)	1	—	—	—	—	—	—	—	—	—	—	k	—	6	392
1988	NYG	16(0)	1	1	1.0(1)	0	4	61	15.3(31)	0	—	—	—	—	—	—	—	—	—	—	k	—	0	42
1989	†NYG	16(0)	11	51	4.6(9)	0	7	121	17.3(39)	0	—	—	—	—	—	—	—	—	—	—	k	—	0	114
1990	†NYG	16(0)	3	14	4.7(6)	0	1	12	12.0(12)	0	—	—	—	—	—	—	—	—	—	—	—	—	0	20
1991	Cle	16(3)	3	14	4.7(9)	0	2	9	4.5(6)	0	—	—	—	—	—	—	—	—	—	—	k	—	0	20
NFL	7	92(6)	114	415	3.6(21)	2	33	453	13.7(39)	2	—	—	—	—	—	—	—	—	—	—	k	—	24	848

Roussel, Tom Thomas James, LB, 6´3˝/235 lbs; Southern Mississippi; 1968: Was, rnd 2; B1/20/1945 Thibodeaux, LA **1968** Was 14 (LLB) **1969** Was 14 (LLB) **1970** Was 14 (1) **1971** NO 7 (LLB) **1972** NO 14 (LLB) **1973** Phi 3 **NFL** 66 (1) [6 yrs]

Roussos, Mike Michael Christ, T, 6´3˝/238 lbs; Pittsburgh; B2/8/1926 New Castle, PA, D4/6/1987 New Castle, PA **1948** Was 12 (3) **1949** Was 6 (3) **1949** Det 6 (0) **NFL** 24 (6) [2 yrs]

Routt, Stanford Stanford, DB, 6´0˝/191 lbs; Houston; 2005: Oak, rnd 2; B7/23/1983 Austin, TX **2005** Oak 14 (2)

Roveto, John John Charles, K, 6´0˝/180 lbs; Louisiana-Lafayette; B2/20/1958 Fort Lauderdale, FL **[K]** **1981** ChiB 11 (0) **1982** ChiB 7 (0) **NFL** 18 (0) [2 yrs]

Rovinski, Tony Anthony Charles, E-DE, 5´9˝/195 lbs; Holy Cross; B9/11/1908 Nanticoke, PA, D4/16/1973 Wilkes-Barre, PA **1933** NYG 1 (0)

Rowan, Ev Everett Lawrence, E-B, 6´1˝/187 lbs; Ohio State; B10/18/1902, OH, D11/9/1956 San Diego County, CA

YEAR	TEAM	G(GS, POS)	RUSH	YD	AVG(LG)	TD	REC	YD	AVG(LG)	TD	PASS	COMP	PCT	YD	AVG(LG)	TD	INT	SK	YD	QBR	KPR	OTD	PTS	TAY
1930	Bkn	2(0)	—	—	—	—	—	—	—	—	—	—	—	—	—	—	—	—	—	—	—	—	—	—
1932	Bkn	11(9, RE)	—	—	—	—	2	40	20.0	0	—	—	—	—	—	—	—	—	—	—	—	—	0	20
1933	Phi	2(1)	—	—	—	—	1	12	12.0	0	—	—	—	—	—	—	—	—	—	—	—	—	0	6
NFL	3	15(10)	—	—	—	—	3	52	17.3	0	—	—	—	—	—	—	—	—	—	—	—	—	0	26

Rowan, John John, TB-BB, 5´8˝/165 lbs; Tennessee; B6/3/1896 Decatur Township, OH, D4/1967 Belpre, OH **1923** Lou 3 (3, TB)

Rowden, Larry Larry David, LB, 6´2˝/220 lbs; Houston; 1971: Chi, rnd 10; B3/17/1949 Pampa, TX **1971** ChiB 14 **1972** ChiB 2 **NFL** 16 [2 yrs]

Rowe, Bob Robert Buell, HB, 6´0˝/198 lbs; Colgate; B5/28/1911 Jackson, MI, D12/23/1992 Slingerlands, NY

YEAR	TEAM	G(GS, POS)	RUSH	YD	AVG(LG)	TD	REC	YD	AVG(LG)	TD	PASS	COMP	PCT	YD	AVG(LG)	TD	INT	SK	YD	QBR	KPR	OTD	PTS	TAY
1934	Det	11(0)	16	44	2.8	0	1	4	4.0(4)	0	2	0	0.0	0	0.0	0	0	—	—	—	—	—	0	46
1935	Phi	4(0)	7	21	3.0	0	—	—	—	—	11	1	9.1	6	0.5(6)	0	2	—	—	—	—	—	0	-56
NFL	2	15(0)	23	65	2.8	0	1	4	4.0(4)	0	13	1	7.7	6	0.5(6)	0	2	—	—	—	—	—	0	-10

Rowe, Bob Robert Buell, DT-DE, 6´4˝/270 lbs; Western Michigan; 1967: SL, rnd 2; B5/23/1945 Flint, MI **1967** SL 11 **1968** SL✧14 (RDT) **1969** SL 13 (RDT) **1970** SL 14 (14, RDT) **1971** SL 14 (14, RDT) **1972** SL 14 (14, RDT) **1973** SL 14 (14, RDT) **1974**†SL 14 (14, RDT) **1975**†SL 14 (14, RDT) **NFL** 122 (84) [9 yrs]

Rowe, Dave David Homeyer, DT-NT, 6´7˝/280 lbs; Penn State; 1967: NO, rnd 2; B6/20/1945 Neptune, NJ **1967** NO 14 (14, RDT) **1968** NO 14 (RDT) **1969** NO 14 (RDT) **1970** NO 14 (RDT) **1971** NE 14 (9, LDT) **1972** NE 14 (9, LDT) **1973** NE 14 (14, LDT) **1974** SD 14 (14, LDT) **1975** SD 1 **1975**†Oak 10 (1) **1976**†Oak 14 (NT) **1977**†Oak 14 (14, NT) **1978** Oak 1 (1) **1978** Bal 13 (10, ldt/rdt) **NFL** 165 (86) [12 yrs]

Rowe, Harmon Harmon Beasley, DB-HB, 6´0˝/182 lbs; Baylor; San Francisco; 1946: Pit, rnd 3; B8/22/1923 Livingston, TX, D1/26/2002 Whitehouse, TX **1948** NYY-A 11 (0)

YEAR	TEAM	G(GS, POS)	RUSH	YD	AVG(LG)	TD	REC	YD	AVG(LG)	TD	PASS	COMP	PCT	YD	AVG(LG)	TD	INT	SK	YD	QBR	KPR	OTD	PTS	TAY
1947	†NYY-A	10(0)	2	-3	-1.5	0	—	—	—	—	—	—	—	—	—	—	—	—	—	—	ki	—	0	10
1949	NYY-A	9(0)	6	21	3.5	0	—	—	—	—	—	—	—	—	—	—	—	—	—	—	i	—	0	59
AAFC	3	30	8	18	2.3	0	—	—	—	—	—	—	—	—	—	—	—	—	—	—	kpi	—	0	76

1950 NYG 7 (DB) **1951** NYG 8 **1952** NYG 12 **NFL** 27 [3 yrs]

Rowe, Joe Joseph, DB, 6´0˝/195 lbs; Virginia; B12/8/1973 East Elmhurst, NY **1997** SL 2 (0)

Rowe, Patrick Patrick Donald Edward, WR, 6´1˝/195 lbs; San Diego State; 1992: Cle, rnd 2; B2/17/1969 San Diego, CA

YEAR	TEAM	G(GS, POS)	RUSH	YD	AVG(LG)	TD	REC	YD	AVG(LG)	TD	PASS	COMP	PCT	YD	AVG(LG)	TD	INT	SK	YD	QBR	KPR	OTD	PTS	TAY
1993	Cle	5(0)	—	—	—	—	3	37	12.3(16)	0	—	—	—	—	—	—	—	—	—	—	—	—	0	19

Rowe, Ray Raymond Henry, TE, 6´2˝/256 lbs; San Diego State; 1992: Was, rnd 6; B7/28/1969 Rota, Spain **1992**†Was 3 (0) **1993** Was 1 (0) **NFL** 4 (0) [2 yrs]

Rowell, Eugene Eugene Anthony, WR, 6´1˝/180 lbs; Southern Mississippi; 1990: Cle, rnd 9; B6/12/1968 Amityville, NY **1990** Cle 3 (0)

Rowell, Eugene Eugene Blair, DT, 6´3˝/265 lbs; Dubuque; B2/15/1958 San Diego, CA **1987** ChiB 1 (1)

Rowland, Brad Andrew Bradford, HB, 6´1˝/190 lbs; McMurry; 1951: ChiB, rnd 5; B7/14/1928 Hamlin, TX

YEAR	TEAM	G(GS, POS)	RUSH	YD	AVG(LG)	TD	REC	YD	AVG(LG)	TD	PASS	COMP	PCT	YD	AVG(LG)	TD	INT	SK	YD	QBR	KPR	OTD	PTS	TAY
1951	ChiB	12	10	50	5.0(20)	0	1	-2	-2.0(-2)	0	—	—	—	—	—	—	—	—	—	—	Pk	—	0	174

Rowland, Justin Justin David, DB, 6´2˝/188 lbs; TCU; 1959: ChiB, rnd 12; B5/10/1937 Hamlin, TX **1960** ChiB 6 **1961** Min 5 **1962** Den-A 10 **NFL** 21 [3 yrs]

Rowley, Bob Eldwood Robert, LB, 6´2˝/235 lbs; Virginia; B9/16/1941 Somerset, PA **1963** Pit 3 **1964** NYJ-A 6 **NFL** 9 [2 yrs]

Rowser, John John Felix, DB, 6´1˝/190 lbs; Michigan; 1967: GB, rnd 3; B4/24/1944 Birmingham, AL **[I]** **1967**†GB 14 **1968** GB 14 **1969** GB 14 **1970** Pit 7 (lcb) **1971** Pit 12 (LCB) **1972**†Pit 14 (LCB) **1973**†Pit 14 (LCB) **1974** Den 11 (10, LCB) **1975** Den 13 (13, FS) **1976** Den 14 (14, FS) **NFL** 127 (37) [10 yrs]

Roy, Spin Elmer T., E, 6´0˝/175 lbs; none; B10/19/1897, D8/1987 Loveland, OH **1921** Roc 2 (0) **1922** Roc 4 (4, LE), 6 **1923** Roc 4 (4, LE) **1924** Roc 7 (7, LE) **1925** Roc 2 (1) **1927** Buf 3 (0) **NFL** 22 (16) [6 yrs]

Roy, Frank Frank Edward, G, 6´2˝/230 lbs; Utah; 1965: SL, rnd 7; B6/19/1942 Montgomery, WV **1966** SL 11

Royal, Andre Andre Tierre, LB, 6´2˝/232 lbs; Alabama; B12/1/1972 Northport, AL **1995** Car 12 (0) **1996**†Car 16 (0) **1997** Car 16 (13, RILB) **1998** Ind 13 (9, rlb) **1999** Ind 3 (3) **NFL** 60 (25) [5 yrs]

Royal, Ricky Ricky Bernard, DB, 5´9˝/187 lbs; Sam Houston State; 1989: Phx, rnd 7; B7/26/1966 Gainesville, TX **1990** Atl 1 (0)

Royal, Robert Robert Shelton, TE, 6´4˝/257 lbs; LSU; 2002: Was, rnd 5; B5/15/1979 New Orleans, LA

YEAR	TEAM	G(GS, POS)	RUSH	YD	AVG(LG)	TD	REC	YD	AVG(LG)	TD	PASS	COMP	PCT	YD	AVG(LG)	TD	INT	SK	YD	QBR	KPR	OTD	PTS	TAY
2003	Was	6(6, te)	—	—	—	—	5	48	9.6(20)	0	—	—	—	—	—	—	—	—	—	—	—	—	0	24
2004	Was	14(9, TE)	—	—	—	—	8	70	8.8(23)	4	—	—	—	—	—	—	—	—	—	—	—	—	24	55
2005	†Was	15(14, TE)	—	—	—	—	18	131	7.3(29)	1	—	—	—	—	—	—	—	—	—	—	—	—	6	71
NFL	3	35(29)	—	—	—	—	31	249	8.0(29)	5	—	—	—	—	—	—	—	—	—	—	—	—	30	150

Royals, Mark Mark Alan, P, 6´5˝/225 lbs; Chowan Coll. (NC); Appalachian State; B6/22/1965 Hampton, VA **[P]** **1987** SL 1 (0) **1987** Phi 1 (0) **1990** TB 16 (0) **1991** TB 16 (0) **1993**†Pit 16 (0) **1997** NO 16 (0) **1998** NO 16 (0) **2002** Mia 16 (0) **2003** Mia 3 (0)

YEAR	TEAM	G(GS, POS)	RUSH	YD	AVG(LG)	TD	REC	YD	AVG(LG)	TD	PASS	COMP	PCT	YD	AVG(LG)	TD	INT	SK	YD	QBR	KPR	OTD	PTS	TAY
1992	†Pit	16(0)	—	—	—	—	—	—	—	—	1	1	100.0	44	44.0(44)	0	0	—	—	—	P	—	0	22
1994	†Pit	16(0)	1	-13	-13.0(-13)	0	—	—	—	—	—	—	—	—	—	—	—	—	—	—	P	—	0	-13
1995	†Det	16(0)	1	-7	-7.0(-7)	0	—	—	—	—	—	—	—	—	—	—	—	—	—	—	P	—	0	-7
1996	Det	16(0)	—	—	—	—	—	—	—	—	1	1	100.0	8	-8.0(-8)	0	0	—	—	—	P	—	0	-4
1999	†TB	16(0)	—	—	—	—	—	—	—	—	2	1	50.0	17	8.5(17)	0	0	—	—	—	P	—	0	9
2000	†TB	16(0)	—	—	—	—	—	—	—	—	1	1	100.0	36	36.0(36)	0	0	—	—	—	P	—	0	18
2001	†TB	16(0)	—	—	—	—	—	—	—	—	1	1	100.0	5	5.0(5)	0	0	—	—	—	P	—	0	3

YEAR	TEAM	G (GS, POS)	RUSH	YD	AVG (LG)	TD	REC	YD	AVG (LG)	TD	PASS	COMP	PCT	YD	AVG (LG)	TD	INT	SK	YD	QBR	KPR	OTD	PTS	TAY
2003	Jax	11(0)	—	—	—	—	—	—	—	—	1	0	0.0	0	0.0	0	1	—	—	—	P	—	0	-40
NFL	15	224(0)	2	-20	-10.0(-7)	0	—	—	—	—	7	5	71.4	94	13.4(44)	0	1	—	—	—	P	—	0	-13

Roye, Orpheus Orpheus Michael, DT-DE, 6´4˝/320 lbs; Florida State; 1996: Pit, rnd 6; B1/21/1973 Miami, FL **1996**†Pit 13 (1) **1997**†Pit 16 (0) **1998** Pit 16 (9, LDE) **1999** Pit 16 (16, LDE) **2000** Cle 16 (16, LDT) **2001** Cle 12 (10, lde/rdt) **2002**†Cle 16 (16, RDT) **2003** Cle 16 (15, RDT) **2004** Cle 15 (14, RDT) **2005** Cle 16 (16, LDE) **NFL** 152 (113) [10 yrs]

Royster, Mazio Mazio Denmar Vesey, RB, 6´1˝/205 lbs; USC; 1992: TB, rnd 11; B8/3/1970 Pomona, CA

YEAR	TEAM	G (GS, POS)	RUSH	YD	AVG (LG)	TD	REC	YD	AVG (LG)	TD	PASS	COMP	PCT	YD	AVG (LG)	TD	INT	SK	YD	QBR	KPR	OTD	PTS	TAY
1992	TB	5(0)	—	—	—	—	1	8	8.0(8)	0	—	—	—	—	—	—	—	—	—	—	—	—	0	4
1993	TB	14(0)	33	115	3.5(19)	1	5	18	3.6(10)	0	—	—	—	—	—	—	—	—	—	—	k	—	6	116
1994	TB	14(1)	9	7	0.8(6)	0	7	36	5.1(12)	0	—	—	—	—	—	—	—	—	—	—	—	—	0	25
NFL	3	33(1)	42	122	2.9(19)	1	13	62	4.8(12)	0	—	—	—	—	—	—	—	—	—	—	k	—	6	145

Royston, Ed Edwin F., G, 6´1˝/220 lbs; Wake Forest; 1948: NYG, rnd 9/1947: SF-A, rnd 19; B9/19/1923 Baltimore, MD **1948** NYG 10 (3) **1949** NYG 11 (9, RG) **NFL** 21 (12) [2 yrs]

Rozier, Bob Robert Earnest, DE, 6´3˝/240 lbs; California; 1979: SL, rnd 9; B7/28/1955 Anchorage, AK **1979** SL 6

Rozier, Mike Mike, RB, 5´10˝/209 lbs; Nebraska; 1984: Hou, rnd S1; B3/1/1961 Camden, NJ

YEAR	TEAM	G (GS, POS)	RUSH	YD	AVG (LG)	TD	REC	YD	AVG (LG)	TD	PASS	COMP	PCT	YD	AVG (LG)	TD	INT	SK	YD	QBR	KPR	OTD	PTS	TAY
1985	Hou	14(6, fb)	133	462	3.5(30)	8	9	96	10.7(52)	0	—	—	—	—	—	—	—	—	—	—	—	—	48	590
1986	Hou	13(13, RB)	199	662	3.3(19)	4	24	180	7.5(23)	0	1	1	100.0	13	13.0(13)	0	0	—	—	—	—	—	24	799
1987	†Hou★	11(11, RB)	229	957	4.2(41)	3	27	192	7.1(27)	0	—	—	—	—	—	—	—	—	—	—	—	—	18	1083
1988	†Hou✧	15(14, RB)	251	1002	4.0(28)	10	11	99	9.0(18)	1	—	—	—	—	—	—	—	—	—	—	—	—	66	1157
1989	†Hou	12(10, RB)	88	301	3.4(17)	2	4	28	7.0(8)	0	—	—	—	—	—	—	—	—	—	—	—	—	12	335
1990	Hou	3(0)	10	42	4.2(11)	0	5	46	9.2(24)	0	—	—	—	—	—	—	—	—	—	—	—	—	0	65
1990	Atl	13(5, rb)	153	675	4.4(67)	3	8	59	7.4(20)	0	—	—	—	—	—	—	—	—	—	—	—	—	18	735
1991	†Atl	11(0)	96	361	3.8(19)	0	2	15	7.5(9)	0	—	—	—	—	—	—	—	—	—	—	—	—	0	369
NFL	7	92(59)	1159	4462	3.8(67)	30	90	715	7.9(52)	1	1	1	100.0	13	13.0(13)	0	0	—	—	—	—	—	186	5131

Rozumek, Dave David John, LB, 6´1˝/215 lbs; New Hampshire; 1976: KC, rnd 15; B4/25/1954 Lawrence, MA **1976** KC 8 **1977** KC 14 **1978** KC 16 (16, LILB) **1979** KC 7 **NFL** 45 (16) [4 yrs]

Rozzell, Aubrey Aubrey Dale, LB, 6´2˝/215 lbs; Delta State; B11/2/1932 Rome, MS **1957** Pit 7

Rubbert, Ed Edward, QB, 6´5˝/225 lbs; Louisville; B5/28/1964 Suffern, NY

YEAR	TEAM	G (GS, POS)	RUSH	YD	AVG (LG)	TD	REC	YD	AVG (LG)	TD	PASS	COMP	PCT	YD	AVG (LG)	TD	INT	SK	YD	QBR	KPR	OTD	PTS	TAY
1987	Was	3(3)	9	31	3.4(14)	0	—	—	—	—	49	26	53.1	532	10.9(**88**)	4	1	1	9	—	—	—	0	277

Rubens, Larry Larry Dean, C, 6´1˝/253 lbs; Montana State; B1/25/1959 Spokane, WA **1982**†GB 9 (0) **1983** GB 16 (0) **1986**†ChiB 16 (0) **NFL** 41 (0) [3 yrs]

Rubick, Rob Robin James, TE, 6´3˝/232 lbs; Grand Valley State; 1982: Det, rnd 12; B9/27/1960 Newberry, MI

YEAR	TEAM	G (GS, POS)	RUSH	YD	AVG (LG)	TD	REC	YD	AVG (LG)	TD	PASS	COMP	PCT	YD	AVG (LG)	TD	INT	SK	YD	QBR	KPR	OTD	PTS	TAY
1982	†Det	7(0)	1	1	1.0(1)	1	—	—	—	—	—	—	—	—	—	—	—	—	—	—	—	—	6	11
1983	†Det	16(1)	—	—	—	—	10	81	8.1(15)	1	—	—	—	—	—	—	—	—	—	—	—	—	6	46
1984	Det	16(9, TE)	—	—	—	—	14	188	13.4(29)	1	—	—	—	—	—	—	—	—	—	—	—	—	6	99
1985	Det	9(4)	—	—	—	—	2	33	16.5(18)	0	—	—	—	—	—	—	—	—	—	—	—	—	0	17
1986	Det	16(2)	—	—	—	—	5	62	12.4(27)	0	—	—	—	—	—	—	—	—	—	—	—	—	0	31
1987	Det	9(8, TE)	—	—	—	—	13	147	11.3(22)	1	—	—	—	—	—	—	—	—	—	—	—	—	6	79
1988	Det	15(1)	—	—	—	—	—	—	—	—	—	—	—	—	—	—	—	—	—	—	—	—	—	—
NFL	7	88(25)	1	1	1.0(1)	1	44	511	11.6(29)	3	—	—	—	—	—	—	—	—	—	—	—	—	24	282

Rubino, Anthony Anthony Eugene, G, 5´10˝/208 lbs; Wake Forest; B6/20/1921 Elizabeth, PA, D11/30/1983 Elizabeth, PA **1943** Det 10 (5, RG) **1946** Det 11 (1) **NFL** 21 (6) [2 yrs]

Rubio, Angel Angel, DE, 6´2˝/300 lbs; Southeast Missouri State; 1998: Pit, rnd 7; B4/12/1975 Los Angeles, CA **1999** Arz 2 (0)

Rubke, Karl Karl John, LB-C-DT-DE, 6´4˝/240 lbs; USC; 1957: SF, rnd 5; B12/6/1935 Los Angeles, CA **1957**†SF 12 (mlb) **1958** SF 12 (MLB) **1959** SF 12 (LLB) **1960** SF 12 **1961** Min 13 (13, RLB) **1962** SF 14 (c) **1963** SF 14 (7, c) **1964** SF 14 **1965** SF 14 (10, LDE) **1966** Atl 14 (12, LDT) **1967** Atl 8 (LDT) **1968** Oak-A 4 **NFL** 143 (42) [12 yrs]

Rubley, T.J. Theron Joseph, QB, 6´3˝/212 lbs; Tulsa; 1992: LARm, rnd 9; B11/29/1968 Davenport, IA

YEAR	TEAM	G (GS, POS)	RUSH	YD	AVG (LG)	TD	REC	YD	AVG (LG)	TD	PASS	COMP	PCT	YD	AVG (LG)	TD	INT	SK	YD	QBR	KPR	OTD	PTS	TAY
1993	LARm	9(7, qb)	29	102	3.5(13)	0	—	—	—	—	189	108	57.1	1338	7.1(54)	8	6	13	106	80.1	—	—	0	571
1995	GB	1(0)	2	6	3.0(6)	0	—	—	—	—	6	4	66.7	39	6.5(17)	0	1	—	—	—	—	—	0	-15
NFL	2	10(7)	31	108	3.5(13)	0	—	—	—	—	195	112	57.4	1377	7.1(54)	8	7	13	106	78.1	—	—	0	557

Ruby, Martin Martin Owen, T, 6´4˝/249 lbs; Texas A&M; 1942: ChiB, rnd 5; B6/9/1922 Lubbock, TX, D1/3/2002 Salmon Arm, Canada **1947** Bkn-A☆14 (14, LT) **1948** Bkn-A☆14 (5, lt) **1949**†NYY-A☆11 (11, LT)

YEAR	TEAM	G (GS, POS)	RUSH	YD	AVG (LG)	TD	REC	YD	AVG (LG)	TD	PASS	COMP	PCT	YD	AVG (LG)	TD	INT	SK	YD	QBR	KPR	OTD	PTS	TAY
1946	Bkn-A☆	14(13, LT)	—	—	—	—	1	3	3.0(3)	0	—	—	—	—	—	—	—	—	—	—	—	—	0	2
AAFC	4	53(43)	—	—	—	—	1	3	3.0(3)	0	—	—	—	—	—	—	—	—	—	—	i	1	6	26

1950 NYY 12 (LT)

Rucci, Todd Todd Louis, G-T, 6´5˝/296 lbs; Penn State; 1993: NE, rnd 2; B7/14/1970 Upper Darby, PA **1993** NE 2 (1) **1994**†NE 13 (10, RG) **1995** NE 6 (5, rg) **1996**†NE 16 (12, RG) **1997**†NE 16 (16, RG) **1998**†NE 16 (16, RG) **1999** NE 16 (15, RG) **NFL** 85 (75) [7 yrs]

Rucinski, Ed Edward Anthony, E, 6´2˝/198 lbs; Indiana; 1941: Bkn, rnd 6; B7/12/1916 East Chicago, IN, D4/22/1995 Pinellas County, FL

YEAR	TEAM	G (GS, POS)	RUSH	YD	AVG (LG)	TD	REC	YD	AVG (LG)	TD	PASS	COMP	PCT	YD	AVG (LG)	TD	INT	SK	YD	QBR	KPR	OTD	PTS	TAY
1941	Bkn	11(8, RE)	2	13	6.5(7)	0	17	204	12.0(33)	1	—	—	—	—	—	—	—	—	—	—	—	—	6	120
1942	Bkn✧	11(9, RE)	—	—	—	—	9	99	11.0(24)	1	—	—	—	—	—	—	—	—	—	—	—	—	6	55
1943	ChiC☆	10(9, LE)	—	—	—	—	26	398	15.3(47)	3	—	—	—	—	—	—	—	—	—	—	—	—	18	214
1944	C-P	10(6, le)	16	72	4.5(22)	0	22	284	12.9(40)	1	—	—	—	—	—	—	—	—	—	—	ki	—	6	256
1945	ChiC☆	8(7, RE)	—	—	—	—	23	400	17.4(62)	2	—	—	—	—	—	—	—	—	—	—	—	—	12	210
1946	ChiC	10(2)	—	—	—	—	2	23	11.5(12)	0	—	—	—	—	—	—	—	—	—	—	—	—	0	12
NFL	6	60(41)	18	85	4.7(22)	0	99	1408	14.2(62)	8	—	—	—	—	—	—	—	—	—	—	ki	—	48	866

Rucka, Leo Leo Victor, LB, 6´3˝/212 lbs; Rice; 1954: SF, rnd 2; B8/18/1931 Baytown, TX **1956** SF 5

Rucker, Conrad Conrad Robert, TE, 6´3˝/255 lbs; Southern (LA); 1978: Hou, rnd 6; B11/15/1954 Cincinnati, OH **1980** TB 2 (0) **1980** LARm 2 (0)

YEAR	TEAM	G (GS, POS)	RUSH	YD	AVG (LG)	TD	REC	YD	AVG (LG)	TD	PASS	COMP	PCT	YD	AVG (LG)	TD	INT	SK	YD	QBR	KPR	OTD	PTS	TAY
1978	†Hou	13	—	—	—	—	2	38	19.0(22)	0	—	—	—	—	—	—	—	—	—	—	—	—	0	19
1979	†Hou	16	—	—	—	—	4	40	10.0(16)	0	—	—	—	—	—	—	—	—	—	—	—	—	0	20
NFL	3	33	—	—	—	—	6	78	13.0(22)	0	—	—	—	—	—	—	—	—	—	—	—	—	0	39

Rucker, Keith Keith, DT-NT, 6´4˝/332 lbs; Eastern Michigan; Ohio Wesleyan; B11/20/1968 Shaker Heights, OH **1992** Phx 14 (5, rdt) **1993** Phx 16 (15, RDT) **1994** Cin 16 (14, LDT) **1995** Cin 15 (15, RDT) **1997** Was 2 (0) **NFL** 63 (49) [5 yrs]

Rucker, Mike Michael Dean, DE, 6´5˝/275 lbs; Nebraska; 1999: Car, rnd 2; B2/28/1975 St. Joseph, MO **1999** Car 16 (0) **2000** Car 16 (1) **2001** Car 16 (16, RDE) **2002** Car 16 (16, RDE) **2003**†Car 14 (14, RDE) **2004** Car 16 (16, RDE) **2005**†Car 15 (14, RDE) **NFL** 109 (77) [7 yrs]

Rucker, Reggie Reginald Joseph, WR, 6´2˝/195 lbs; Boston University; B9/21/1947 Washington, DC

YEAR	TEAM	G (GS, POS)	RUSH	YD	AVG (LG)	TD	REC	YD	AVG (LG)	TD	PASS	COMP	PCT	YD	AVG (LG)	TD	INT	SK	YD	QBR	KPR	OTD	PTS	TAY
1970	†Dal	7	—	—	—	—	9	200	22.2(52)	1	—	—	—	—	—	—	—	—	—	—	—	—	6	105
1971	Dal	2	—	—	—	—	1	19	19.0(19)	1	—	—	—	—	—	—	—	—	—	—	—	—	6	15
1971	NYG	4	1	14	14.0(14)	0	1	9	9.0(9)	0	—	—	—	—	—	—	—	—	—	—	—	—	0	19
1971	NE	5	—	—	—	—	2	24	12.0(19)	0	—	—	—	—	—	—	—	—	—	—	k	—	0	27
1972	NE	14(14, WR)	3	5	1.7(8)	0	44	681	15.5(62)	3	—	—	—	—	—	—	—	—	—	—	k	—	18	468
1973	NE	14(14, WR)	2	-1	-0.5(0)	0	53	743	14.0(64)	3	—	—	—	—	—	—	—	—	—	—	k	—	18	414
1974	NE	10(10, WR)	—	—	—	—	27	436	16.1(69)	4	—	—	—	—	—	—	—	—	—	—	—	—	24	238
1975	Cle	14(WR)	—	—	—	—	**60**	770	12.8(40)	3	—	—	—	—	—	—	—	—	—	—	—	—	18	400
1976	Cle	14(WR)	2	30	15.0(27)	0	49	676	13.8(45)	8	—	—	—	—	—	—	—	—	—	—	—	—	48	408
1977	Cle	14(14, WR)	2	6	3.0(3)	0	36	565	15.7(40)	2	—	—	—	—	—	—	—	—	—	—	—	—	12	299
1978	Cle	15(15, WR)	2	14	7.0(9)	0	43	893	20.8(69)	8	—	—	—	—	—	—	—	—	—	—	k	—	48	487
1979	Cle	16(WR)	—	—	—	—	43	749	17.4(54)	6	—	—	—	—	—	—	—	—	—	—	—	—	36	405
1980	†Cle	16(16, WR)	—	—	—	—	52	768	14.8(45)	4	—	—	—	—	—	—	—	—	—	—	—	—	24	404

YEAR	TEAM	G (GS, POS)	RUSH	YD	AVG (LG)	TD	REC	YD	AVG (LG)	TD	PASS COMP	PCT	YD	AVG (LG)	TD	INT	SK	YD	QBR	KPR	OTD	PTS	TAY
1981	Cle	14 (11, WR)	—	—	—	—	27	532	19.7 (49)	1	—	—	—	—	—	—	—	—	—	—	—	6	271
NFL	12	159 (94)	—	12	68	5.7 (27)	0	447	7065	15.8 (69)	44	—	—	—	—	—	—	—	—	—	k	—	264	3957

RUDD, DWAYNE   Dwayne Dupree, LB, 6´2˝/235 lbs; Alabama; 1997: Min, rnd 1; B2/3/1976 Batesville, MS   **1997**†Min 16 (2) **1998**†Min☆15 (15, RLB) **1999**†Min 16 (16, RLB) **2000**†Min 14 (13, LLB) **2001** Cle 16 (16, RLB) **2002**†Cle 16 (15, RLB) **2003** TB 16 (2) **NFL** 109 (79) [7 yrs]

RUDDY, TIM   Timothy Daniel, C, 6´3˝/295 lbs; Notre Dame; 1994: Mia, rnd 2; B4/27/1972 Scranton, PA   **1994**†Mia 16 (0) **1995**†Mia 16 (16, C) **1996** Mia 16 (16, C) **1997**†Mia 15 (15, C) **1998** Mia 16 (16, C) **1999** Mia 16 (16, C) **2000**†Mia☆16 (16, C) **2001**†Mia 15 (15, C) **2002** Mia 16 (16, C) **2003** Mia 14 (14, C) **NFL** 156 (140) [10 yrs]

RUDNAY, JACK   John Carl, C, 6´3˝/240 lbs; Northwestern; 1969: KC, rnd 4; B11/20/1947 Cleveland, OH   **1970** KC 14 (C) **1971**†KC 13 (C) **1972** KC 14 (C) **1973** KC★14 (C) **1974** KC★14 (C) **1975** KC★14 (C) **1976** KC✧14 (13, C) **1977** KC 14 (C) **1978** KC 16 (16, C) **1979** KC☆16 (C) **1980** KC 12 (12, C) **1981** KC 16 (16, C) **1982** KC 7 (7, C) **NFL** 178 (64) [13 yrs]

RUDNICK, TIM   Timothy John, DB, 5´10˝/185 lbs; Notre Dame; 1974: Bal, rnd 11; B3/6/1952 Chicago, IL   **1974** Bal 14

RUDOLPH, BEN   Benjamin, DT-DE, 6´5˝/271 lbs; Long Beach State; 1981: NYJ, rnd 3; B8/29/1957 Evergreen, AL   **1981**†NYJ 15 (4) **1982** NYJ 9 (2) **1983** NYJ 16 (0) **1984** NYJ 16 (3) **1985**†NYJ 16 (1) **1986** NYJ 16 (3) **NFL** 88 (13) [6 yrs]

RUDOLPH, COLEMAN   Coleman Harris, DE-LB, 6´4˝/262 lbs; Georgia Tech; 1993: NYJ, rnd 2; B10/22/1970 Valdosta, GA   **1993** NYJ 4 (0) **1994** NYG 12 (2) **1995** NYG 16 (0) **1996** NYG 16 (2) **NFL** 48 (4) [4 yrs]

RUDOLPH, COUNCIL   Council, DE, 6´4˝/255 lbs; Kentucky State; 1972: SL, rnd 7; B1/18/1950 Anniston, AL   **1972** Hou 12 **1973** SL 5 **1974**†SL 14 (14, LDE) **1975**†SL 13 **1976** TB 14 (13, LDE) **1977** TB 14 (14, LDE) **NFL** 72 (41) [6 yrs]

RUDOLPH, JACK   John Lawrence, LB, 6´3˝/225 lbs; Georgia Tech; 1960: Bos, rnd 2; B3/21/1938 St. Louis, MO   **1960** Bos-A 8 (RLB) **1962** Bos-A 14 (RLB) **1963**†Bos-A 14 (RLB) **1964** Bos-A 14 (RLB) **1965** Bos-A 14 (RLB) **1966** Mia-A 11 (4) **NFL** 75 (4) [6 yrs]

RUDOLPH, JOE   Joseph D., G, 6´1˝/285 lbs; Wisconsin; B7/21/1972 Belle Vernon, PA   **1995**†Phi 4 (0) **1997** SF 6 (1) **NFL** 10 (1) [2 yrs]

RUDOLPH, MARTIN   Martin Jerome, DB, 5´10˝/183 lbs; Arizona; B10/19/1964 San Pedro, CA   **1987** Den 3 (1)

RUDZINSKI, PAUL   Paul Gerard, LB, 6´1˝/220 lbs; Michigan State; B7/28/1956 Detroit, MI   **1978** GB 16 **1979** GB 11 **1980** GB 6 (2) **NFL** 33 (2) [3 yrs]

RUEGAMER, GREY   Christopher Grey, C-G, 6´4˝/310 lbs; Arizona State; 1999: Mia, rnd 3; B6/11/1976 Las Vegas, NV   **2000** NE 6 (0) **2001**†NE 14 (1) **2002** NE 13 (2) **2003**†GB 15 (0) **2004** GB 15 (11, C) **2005** GB 13 (2) **NFL** 76 (16) [6 yrs]

RUETHER, MIKE   Mike Alan, G-C, 6´4˝/279 lbs; Texas; 1984: SL, rnd S1; B9/20/1962 Inglewood, CA   **1986** SL 10 (1) **1987** SL 12 (1) **1988** Den 14 (0) **1989** Den 3 (0) **1990** Atl 16 (0) **1992** Atl 16 (0) **1993** Atl 16 (0)

YEAR	TEAM	G (GS, POS)	RUSH	YD	AVG (LG)	TD	REC	YD	AVG (LG)	TD	PASS COMP	PCT	YD	AVG (LG)	TD	INT	SK	YD	QBR	KPR	OTD	PTS	TAY
1991	†Atl	16 (6, rg)	—	—	—	—	1	22	22.0 (22)	0	—	—	—	—	—	—	—	—	—	—	—	0	11
NFL	8	103 (8)	—	—	—	—	1	22	22.0 (22)	0	—	—	—	—	—	—	—	—	—	k	—	0	3

RUETTGERS, KEN   Kenneth Francis, T, 6´6˝/295 lbs; USC; 1985: GB, rnd 1; B8/20/1962 Bakersfield, CA   **1985** GB 15 (2) **1986** GB 16 (16, LT) **1987** GB 12 (12, LT) **1988** GB 15 (15, LT) **1989** GB 16 (16, LT) **1990** GB 11 (11, LT) **1991** GB 4 (4) **1992** GB 16 (16, LT) **1993**†GB 16 (16, LT) **1994**†GB 16 (16, LT) **1995**†GB 15 (15, LT) **1996** GB 4 (1) **NFL** 156 (140) [12 yrs]

RUETZ, HOWIE   Howard Peter, DT, 6´3˝/255 lbs; Loras; 1951: LA, rnd 26; B8/18/1927 Racine, WI   **1951** GB 12 (RDT) **1952** GB 3 **1953** GB 5 **NFL** 20 [3 yrs]

RUETZ, JOE   Joseph Hubert, G, 6´0˝/200 lbs; Notre Dame; B10/21/1916 Racine, WI, D1/2/2003 Palo Alto, CA   **1946** ChiR-A 13 (1) **1948** ChiR-A 13 (1) **AAFC** 26 (2) [2 yrs]

RUFF, GUY   Guy Moroney, LB, 6´1˝/215 lbs; Syracuse; B8/18/1960 Ravenna, OH   **1982**†Pit 2 (0)

RUFF, ORLANDO   Orlando Bernarda, LB, 6´3˝/250 lbs; Furman; B9/28/1976 Charleston, SC   **1999** SD 14 (0) **2000** SD 16 (14, MLB) **2001** SD 16 (15, MLB) **2002** SD 16 (0) **2003** NO 16 (9, mlb) **2004** NO 14 (8, mlb) **2005** Cle 16 (0) **NFL** 108 (46) [7 yrs]

RUH, EMMETT   Emmett E., WB-E, 5´8˝/168 lbs; Davis & Elkins; B8/29/1893 Columbus, OH, D9/23/1979 Fort Lauderdale, FL **[K]**   **1921** Col 7 (6, WB), 13 **1922** Col 7 (5, WB), 6 **NFL** 14 (11), 19 [2 yrs]

RUH, HOMER   Homer, E-B, 5´10˝/178 lbs; none; B9/19/1895 Columbus, OH, D10/4/1971 Madison, WI   **1920** Col 9 (5, LE) **1921** Col 7 (7, RE), 6 **1922** Col 7 (7, LE) **1923** Col 8 (0) **1924** Col 7 (7, LE) **1925** Col 8 (7, LE) **NFL** 46 (33) [6 yrs]

RUHMAN, CHRIS   Christopher Aamon, T, 6´5˝/321 lbs; Texas A&M; 1998: SF, rnd 3; B12/19/1974 Houston, TX   **1998** SF 6 (0) **1999** Cle 5 (2) **NFL** 11 (2) [2 yrs]

RUKAS, JUSTIN   Justin Matthew, G, 6´0˝/205 lbs; LSU; B2/24/1910 Gary, IN, D9/28/1973   **1936** Bkn 12 (7, RG)

RULE, GORDON   Gordon Alan, DB, 6´2˝/180 lbs; Dartmouth; 1968: GB, rnd 11; B3/1/1946 Columbus, OH   **1968** GB 1 **1969** GB 14 **NFL** 15 [2 yrs]

RUMPH, MIKE   Michael Jamaine, DB, 6´2˝/205 lbs; Miami (FL); 2002: SF, rnd 1; B11/8/1979 Boynton Beach, FL   **2002**†SF 16 (1) **2003** SF 15 (13, RCB) **2004** SF 2 (2) **2005** SF 3 (3) **NFL** 36 (19) [4 yrs]

RUNAGER, MAX   Max Culp, P, 6´1˝/189 lbs; South Carolina; 1979: Phi, rnd 8; B3/24/1956 Greenwood, SC **[P]**   **1979**†Phi 16 **1980**†Phi 16 (0) **1981**†Phi 15 (0) **1982** Phi 9 (0) **1985**†SF 16 (0) **1986**†SF 16 (0) **1987**†SF 12 (0) **1988** SF 1 (0)

YEAR	TEAM	G (GS, POS)	RUSH	YD	AVG (LG)	TD	REC	YD	AVG (LG)	TD	PASS COMP	PCT	YD	AVG (LG)	TD	INT	SK	YD	QBR	KPR	OTD	PTS	TAY
1983	Phi	12 (0)	1	6	6.0 (6)	0	—	—	—	—	—	—	—	—	—	—	—	—	P	—	0	6
1984	†SF	14 (0)	1	-5	-5.0 (-5)	0	—	—	—	—	—	—	—	—	—	—	—	—	P	—	0	-5
1988	†Cle	13 (0)	1	0	0.0 (0)	0	—	—	—	—	—	—	—	—	—	—	—	—	P	—	0	0
1989	Phi	4 (0)	2	5	2.5 (5)	0	—	—	—	—	—	—	—	—	—	—	—	—	P	—	0	5
NFL	11	144	5	6	1.2 (6)	0	—	—	—	—	—	—	—	—	—	—	—	—	P	—	0	6

RUNDQUIST, SWEDE   Elmer Theodore, T, 6´2˝/210 lbs; Illinois; B11/22/1894 Harvey, IL, D2/7/1958 Lackland AFB, TX   **1922** ChiC 10 (10, LT)

RUNDQUIST, PORKY   Henning, T-G-C, 5´10˝/220 lbs; Michigan Tech; B11/24/1893 Sweden, D12/1980 Ludington, MI   **1925** Dul 1 (1) **1926** Dul 4 (3) **NFL** 5 (4) [2 yrs]

RUNKEL, GIL   Gilbert A., C-G, /210 lbs; none; B6/2/1891, MI, D10/26/1976 Trenton, MI   **1920** Det 7 (3, C)

RUNNELS, TOMMY   Melvin Thomas, HB, 5´10˝/187 lbs; North Texas; 1956: LA, rnd 14; B1/28/1934 Fort Worth, TX

YEAR	TEAM	G (GS, POS)	RUSH	YD	AVG (LG)	TD	REC	YD	AVG (LG)	TD	PASS COMP	PCT	YD	AVG (LG)	TD	INT	SK	YD	QBR	KPR	OTD	PTS	TAY
1956	Was	11 (LH)	96	334	3.5 (17)	0	6	56	9.3 (22)	1	3	1	33.3	34	11.3 (34)	0	0	—	—	—	kp	—	6	555
1957	Was	10	20	52	2.6 (16)	0	1	4	4.0 (4)	0	1	1	100.0	35	35.0 (35)	0	0	—	—	—	kp	—	0	134
NFL	2	21	116	386	3.3 (17)	0	7	60	8.6 (22)	1	4	2	50.0	69	17.3 (35)	0	0	—	—	—	.kp	—	6	689

RUNYAN, JON   Jon Daniel, T, 6´7˝/330 lbs; Michigan; 1996: Hou, rnd 4; B11/27/1973 Flint, MI   **1996** Hou 10 (0) **1997** Ten 16 (16, RT) **1998** Ten 16 (16, RT) **1999**†Ten☆16 (16, RT) **2000**†Phi 16 (16, RT) **2001**†Phi 16 (16, RT) **2002**†Phi✧16 (16, RT) **2003** Phi 16 (16, RT) **2004** Phi 16 (16, RT) **2005** Phi 16 (16, RT) **NFL** 154 (144) [10 yrs]

RUPLE, ERNIE   Coy Ernest, DE, 6´4˝/256 lbs; Arkansas; 1968: Pit, rnd 2; B10/27/1945 Conway, AR   **1968** Pit 14

RUPP, JOHN   John, G, none; B12/1896, NY, deceased   **1920** Buf 1 (0)

RUPP, NELSON   Nelson Gadd, WB-FB, 5´10˝/180 lbs; Denison; B6/15/1891 Cincinnati, OH, D8/9/1948 South Norwalk, CT   **1921** Day 5 (2)

RUSH, BOB   Robert Jeffrey, C-T, 6´5˝/265 lbs; Memphis; 1977: SD, rnd 1; B2/27/1955 Santa Monica, CA   **1977** SD 14 **1979**†SD 16 (10, C) **1980**†SD 15 (1) **1981**†SD 16 (1) **1982**†SD 9 (0) **1983** KC 15 (15, C) **1984** KC 16 (16, C) **1985** KC 16 (16, C) **NFL** 117 (59) [8 yrs]

RUSH, CLIVE   Clive Harold, E, 6´2˝/197 lbs; Miami (OH); B2/14/1931 De Graff, OH, D8/22/1980 London, OH **[C]**

YEAR	TEAM	G (GS, POS)	RUSH	YD	AVG (LG)	TD	REC	YD	AVG (LG)	TD	PASS COMP	PCT	YD	AVG (LG)	TD	INT	SK	YD	QBR	KPR	OTD	PTS	TAY
1953	GB	11	1	-6	-6.0 (-6)	0	14	190	13.6 (24)	0	—	—	—	—	—	—	—	—	—	P	—	0	89

RUSH, JERRY   Gerald Mitchell, DT, 6´4˝/265 lbs; Michigan State; 1965: Det, rnd 2/Bos, rnd 1; B8/7/1942 Pontiac, MI   **1965** Det 11 **1966** Det 11 **1967** Det 14 (RDT) **1968** Det 14 (RDT) **1969** Det 11 (RDT) **1970** Det 14 (RDT) **1971** Det 14 (RDT) **NFL** 89 [7 yrs]

RUSH, TYRONE   Tyrone Antonio, RB, 5´11˝/196 lbs; North Alabama; B2/5/1971 Philadelphia, MS   **1994** Was 5 (0)

RUSHING, MARION   Marion Glen, LB, 6´2˝/223 lbs; Southern Illinois; B9/3/1936 Pinckneyville, IL   **1959** ChiC 12 **1962** SL 13 (LLB) **1963** SL 14 (llb) **1964** SL 12 **1965** SL 14 (llb) **1966** Atl 14 (LLB) **1967** Atl 14 (LLB) **1968** Atl 7 **1968** Hou-A 5 **NFL** 105 [8 yrs]

RUSINEK, MIKE   John Michael, NT, 6´3˝/250 lbs; California; B5/1/1963 Phoenix, AZ   **1987** Cle 3 (3)

RUSK, REGGIE   Reggie Leon, DB, 5´10˝/190 lbs; Kentucky; 1996: TB, rnd 7; B10/19/1972 Galveston, TX   **1996** TB 1 (0) **1997** TB 4 (0) **1997** Sea 2 (0) **1999** SD 9 (0) **2000** SD 7 (0) **NFL** 23 (0) [4 yrs]

RUSKUSKY, ROY   Roy J., E, 6´3˝/200 lbs; St. Mary's (CA); 1944: ChiB, rnd 25; B4/6/1921 Spring Valley, IL, D4/20/2001 Peoria, IL   **1947** NYY-A 11 (1)

RUSS, BERNARD   Bernard Dion, LB, 6´1˝/238 lbs; West Virginia; B11/4/1973 Utica, NY   **1997**†NE 2 (0) **1998** NE 1 (0) **1999** NE 6 (0) **NFL** 9 (0) [3 yrs]

Russ, Carl James Carlton, LB, 6´2˝/227 lbs; Michigan; 1975: Atl, rnd 13; B2/16/1953 Muskegon, MI **1975** Atl 14 **1976** NYJ 3 **1977** NYJ 2 **NFL** 19 [3 yrs]

Russ, Pat Patrick Joseph, DT, 6´3˝/255 lbs; Purdue; 1962: Min, rnd 14/Oak, rnd 16; B1/18/1940 Cincinnati, OH, D2/4/1984 Anderson Township, OH **1963** Min 14

Russ, Steve Steve, LB, 6´4˝/245 lbs; Air Force; 1995: Den, rnd 7; B9/16/1972 Stetsonville, WI **1997** Den 14 (0) **1999** Den 8 (0) **2000** Den 2 (0) **NFL** 24 (0) [3 yrs]

Russas, Al Alfred Victor, T-DE, 6´2˝/210 lbs; Tennessee; 1949: Det, rnd 13/Buf-A, rnd 10; B8/22/1923 Providence, RI, D2/14/1995 Dearborn, MI **1949** Det 9 (0)

Russell, Andy Charles Andrew, LB, 6´2˝/225 lbs; Missouri; 1963: Pit, rnd 16; B10/29/1941 Detroit, MI **[K]** **1963** Pit 14 (RLB) **1966** Pit 14 (RLB) **1967** Pit☆14 (RLB) **1968** Pit★14 (RLB) **1969** Pit 14 (RLB) **1970** Pit★14 (RLB) **1971** Pit✧14 (RLB) **1972**†Pit★14 (RLB) **1973**†Pit★14 (RLB) **1974**†Pit★14 (RLB) **1975**†Pit★14 (14, RLB) **1976**†Pit 14 (RLB) **NFL** 168 (14) [12 yrs]

Russell, Benny Bennett Coe, QB, 6´1˝/190 lbs; Louisville; 1966: Buf, rnd R11/SL, rnd 17; B5/12/1944 Brewton, AL, D12/15/1999

YEAR	TEAM	G (GS, POS)	RUSH	YD	AVG (LG)	TD	REC	YD	AVG (LG)	TD	PASS	COMP	PCT	YD	AVG (LG)	TD	INT	SK	YD	QBR	KPR	OTD	PTS	TAY
1968	Buf-A	1	—	—	—	—	—	—	—	—	2	1	50.0	3	1.5(3)	0	0	—	—	—	—	—	0	2

Russell, Bo Torance Albert, T, 6´1˝/223 lbs; Auburn; 1939: Was, rnd 8; B1/23/1916 Birmingham, AL **[K]** **1939** Was☆11 (3) **1940**†Was 11 (0) **NFL** 22 (3) [2 yrs]

Russell, Booker Booker Taylor, RB, 6´2˝/223 lbs; Southwest Texas State; B2/28/1956 Belton, TX, D3/9/2000 Belton, TX

YEAR	TEAM	G (GS, POS)	RUSH	YD	AVG (LG)	TD	REC	YD	AVG (LG)	TD	PASS	COMP	PCT	YD	AVG (LG)	TD	INT	SK	YD	QBR	KPR	OTD	PTS	TAY
1978	Oak	16	11	65	5.9(15)	0	—	—	—	—	—	—	—	—	—	—	—	—	—	—	k	—	0	32
1979	Oak	16	33	190	5.8(72)	4	6	79	13.2(26)	0	—	—	—	—	—	—	—	—	—	—	k	—	24	246
1980	SD	15(0)	8	41	5.1(10)	0	—	—	—	—	—	—	—	—	—	—	—	—	—	—	k	—	0	45
1981	†Phi	12(1)	38	123	3.2(17)	4	1	-5	-5.0(-5)	0	—	—	—	—	—	—	—	—	—	—	k	—	24	159
NFL	4	59(1)	90	419	4.7(72)	8	7	74	10.6(26)	0	—	—	—	—	—	—	—	—	—	—	k	—	48	481

Russell, Brian Brian William, DB, 6´2˝/204 lbs; San Diego State; B2/5/1978 West Covina, CA **2002** Min 16 (2) **2003** Min 16 (16, FS) **2005** Cle 16 (16, FS)

YEAR	TEAM	G (GS, POS)	RUSH	YD	AVG (LG)	TD	REC	YD	AVG (LG)	TD	PASS	COMP	PCT	YD	AVG (LG)	TD	INT	SK	YD	QBR	KPR	OTD	PTS	TAY
2004	†Min	16(16, FS)	1	4	4.0(4)	0	—	—	—	—	—	—	—	—	—	—	—	—	—	—	i	—	0	40
NFL	4	64(50)	1	4	4.0(4)	0	—	—	—	—	—	—	—	—	—	—	—	—	—	—	iS	—	0	228

Russell, Cliff Clifford, WR, 5´11˝/193 lbs; Utah; 2002: Was, rnd 3; B2/8/1979 Ewa Beach, HI

YEAR	TEAM	G (GS, POS)	RUSH	YD	AVG (LG)	TD	REC	YD	AVG (LG)	TD	PASS	COMP	PCT	YD	AVG (LG)	TD	INT	SK	YD	QBR	KPR	OTD	PTS	TAY
2003	Was	3(0)	—	—	—	—	2	10	5.0(7)	0	—	—	—	—	—	—	—	—	—	—	—	—	0	5
2004	Cin	13(1)	3	15	5.0(13)	0	1	21	21.0(21)	0	—	—	—	—	—	—	—	—	—	—	k	—	0	313
2005	Mia	2(0)	—	—	—	—	—	—	—	—	—	—	—	—	—	—	—	—	—	—	—	—	—	—
NFL	3	18(1)	3	15	5.0(13)	0	3	31	10.3(21)	0	—	—	—	—	—	—	—	—	—	—	k	—	0	318

Russell, Damien Damien Eduardo, DB, 6´1˝/204 lbs; Virginia Tech; 1992: SF, rnd 6; B8/20/1970 New York, NY **1993**†SF 16 (0)

Russell, Darrell Darrell A., DT-DE, 6´5˝/325 lbs; USC; 1997: Oak, rnd 1; B5/27/1976 Pensacola, FL, D12/15/2005 Los Angeles, CA **1997** Oak 16 (10, LDE) **1998** Oak★16 (16, LDT) **1999** Oak★16 (16, RDT) **2000**†Oak 16 (16, RDT) **2001** Oak 11 (7, LDT) **2003** Was 8 (0) **NFL** 83 (65) [6 yrs]

Russell, Darryl Darryl James, DB, 6´0˝/190 lbs; Appalachian State; B12/14/1964 Chicago Heights, IL **1987** Den 3 (0)

Russell, Derek Derek Dwayne, WR, 6´0˝/195 lbs; Arkansas; 1991: Den, rnd 4; B6/22/1969 Little Rock, AR

YEAR	TEAM	G (GS, POS)	RUSH	YD	AVG (LG)	TD	REC	YD	AVG (LG)	TD	PASS	COMP	PCT	YD	AVG (LG)	TD	INT	SK	YD	QBR	KPR	OTD	PTS	TAY
1991	†Den	13(5, wr)	—	—	—	—	21	317	15.1(40)	1	—	—	—	—	—	—	—	—	—	—	k	—	6	179
1992	Den	12(7, wr)	—	—	—	—	12	140	11.7(22)	0	—	—	—	—	—	—	—	—	—	—	k	—	0	119
1993	†Den	13(12, WR)	—	—	—	—	44	719	16.3(43)	3	—	—	—	—	—	—	—	—	—	—	k	1	24	479
1994	Den	12(12, WR)	1	6	6.0(6)	0	25	342	13.7(43)	1	—	—	—	—	—	—	—	—	—	—	k	—	6	212
1995	Hou	11(5, wr)	—	—	—	—	24	321	13.4(57)	0	—	—	—	—	—	—	—	—	—	—	—	—	0	161
1996	Hou	16(5, wr)	—	—	—	—	34	421	12.4(29)	2	—	—	—	—	—	—	—	—	—	—	—	—	12	221
1997	Ten	11(2)	—	—	—	—	12	141	11.8(23)	1	—	—	—	—	—	—	—	—	—	—	—	—	6	76
NFL	7	88(48)	1	6	6.0(6)	0	172	2401	14.0(57)	8	—	—	—	—	—	—	—	—	—	—	k	1	54	1445

Russell, Doug Douglas, TB-WB, 6´0˝/187 lbs; Muskingum; Kansas State; B6/11/1911 Bulger, PA, D10/10/1995 Lebanon, MO

YEAR	TEAM	G (GS, POS)	RUSH	YD	AVG (LG)	TD	REC	YD	AVG (LG)	TD	PASS	COMP	PCT	YD	AVG (LG)	TD	INT	SK	YD	QBR	KPR	OTD	PTS	TAY
1934	ChiC	11(5, tb)	75	407	5.4	1	1	2	2.0(2)	0	23	7	30.4	59	2.6	0	2	—	—	—	—	1	12	378
1935	ChiC	12(6, TB)	140	**499**	3.6	0	3	33	11.0	0	28	7	25.0	108	3.9	1	4	—	—	—	—	—	0	415
1936	ChiC	2(1)	3	11	3.7	0	—	—	—	—	1	0	0.0	0	0.0	0	0	—	—	—	—	—	0	11
1937	ChiC	11(10, WB)	23	76	3.3	0	12	263	21.9(37)	1	11	4	36.4	94	8.5	1	2	—	—	—	—	1	12	195
1938	ChiC	8(2)	31	60	1.9	1	6	36	6.0	0	7	1	14.3	98	14.0(**98**)	1	2	—	—	—	—	—	6	62
1939	ChiC	1(1)	4	-5	-1.3	0	—	—	—	—	—	—	—	—	—	—	—	—	—	—	—	—	0	-5
1939	Cle	7(2)	5	26	5.2	0	5	67	13.4(44)	1	1	0	0.0	0	0.0	0	0	—	—	—	P	—	6	65
NFL	6	52(27)	281	1074	3.8	2	27	401	14.9(44)	2	71	19	26.8	359	5.1(98)	3	10	—	—	—	P	2	36	1119

Russell, Jack James Monroe, E-DE, 6´1˝/215 lbs; Baylor; 1943: Pit, rnd 3; B8/29/1919 Nemo, TX, D1/16/2006 Cleburne, TX

YEAR	TEAM	G (GS, POS)	RUSH	YD	AVG (LG)	TD	REC	YD	AVG (LG)	TD	PASS	COMP	PCT	YD	AVG (LG)	TD	INT	SK	YD	QBR	KPR	OTD	PTS	TAY
1946	†NYY-A☆	14(6, le)	—	—	—	—	23	223	9.7	4	—	—	—	—	—	—	—	—	—	—	—	—	24	132
1947	†NYY-A☆	14(14, LE)	—	—	—	—	20	368	18.4	2	—	—	—	—	—	—	—	—	—	—	ki	1	18	228
1948	NYY-A	14(13, LE)	—	—	—	—	23	433	18.8(70)	6	—	—	—	—	—	—	—	—	—	—	i	—	36	242
1949	†NYY-A☆	12(12, LE)	—	—	—	—	7	130	18.6	1	—	—	—	—	—	—	—	—	—	—	i	1	12	70
AAFC	4	54(45)	—	—	—	—	73	1154	15.8(70)	13	—	—	—	—	—	—	—	—	—	—	ki	2	90	671
1950	NYY☆	11(LDE)	—	—	—	—	10	177	17.7(49)	2	—	—	—	—	—	—	—	—	—	—	k	1	18	77

Russell, Jim James L., G-T, 5´11˝/210 lbs; Temple; B8/18/1908 Sinnemahoning, PA, D1/21/1990 Evans City, PA **1936** Phi 11 (10, LG) **1937** Phi 3 (1) **NFL** 14 (11) [2 yrs]

Russell, Ken Kenneth E., T, 6´3˝/252 lbs; Bowling Green State; 1957: Det, rnd 6; B11/2/1935 Fostoria, OH **1957**†Det 10 (rt) **1958** Det 12 (rt) **1959** Det 4 **NFL** 26 [3 yrs]

Russell, Leonard Leonard James, RB, 6´2˝/240 lbs; Arizona State; 1991: NE, rnd 1; B11/17/1969 Long Beach, CA

YEAR	TEAM	G (GS, POS)	RUSH	YD	AVG (LG)	TD	REC	YD	AVG (LG)	TD	PASS	COMP	PCT	YD	AVG (LG)	TD	INT	SK	YD	QBR	KPR	OTD	PTS	TAY
1991	NE	16(15, RB)	266	959	3.6(24)	4	18	81	4.5(18)	0	—	—	—	—	—	—	—	—	—	—	—	—	24	1040
1992	NE	11(10, RB)	123	390	3.2(23)	2	11	24	2.2(12)	0	—	—	—	—	—	—	—	—	—	—	—	—	12	422
1993	NE	16(15, RB)	300	1088	3.6(21)	7	26	245	9.4(69)	0	—	—	—	—	—	—	—	—	—	—	—	—	42	1281
1994	Den	14(14, RB)	190	620	3.3(22)	9	38	227	6.0(19)	0	—	—	—	—	—	—	—	—	—	—	—	—	54	824
1995	SL	13(2)	66	203	3.1(18)	0	16	89	5.6(17)	0	—	—	—	—	—	—	—	—	—	—	—	—	0	248
1996	SD	15(15, RB)	219	713	3.3(21)	7	13	180	13.8(35)	0	—	—	—	—	—	—	—	—	—	—	k	—	42	868
NFL	6	85(71)	1164	3973	3.4(24)	29	122	846	6.9(69)	0	—	—	—	—	—	—	—	—	—	—	k	—	174	4681

Russell, Matt Matthew Jason, LB, 6´2˝/245 lbs; Colorado; 1997: Det, rnd 4; B7/5/1973 Tokyo, Japan **1997**†Det 14 (0)

Russell, Reb Lafayette H., B, 6´1˝/205 lbs; Nebraska; Northwestern; B5/31/1905 Osawatomie, KS, D3/16/1978 Coffeyville, KS

YEAR	TEAM	G (GS, POS)	RUSH	YD	AVG (LG)	TD	REC	YD	AVG (LG)	TD	PASS	COMP	PCT	YD	AVG (LG)	TD	INT	SK	YD	QBR	KPR	OTD	PTS	TAY
1933	NYG	3(1)	16	68	4.3	0	—	—	—	—	—	—	—	—	—	—	—	—	—	—	—	—	0	68
1933	Phi	7(4)	32	96	3.0	0	—	—	—	—	8	2	25.0	32	4.0	0	2	—	—	—	—	—	0	32
NFL	1	10(5)	48	164	3.4	0	—	—	—	—	8	2	25.0	32	4.0	0	2	—	—	—	—	—	0	100

Russell, Reggie Reginald, E, /190 lbs; none **1928** ChiB 1 (0)

Russell, Rusty William, T, 6´5˝/295 lbs; South Carolina; 1984: Phi, rnd 3; B8/16/1963 Orangeburg, SC **1984** Phi 1 (0)

Russell, Twan Twan Sanchez, LB, 6´1˝/230 lbs; Miami (FL); 1997: Was, rnd 5; B4/25/1974 Fort Lauderdale, FL **1997** Was 15 (0) **1998** Was 3 (0) **1999** Was 9 (0) **2000**†Mia 16 (2) **2001**†Mia 16 (2) **2002** Mia 3 (0) **2003** Atl 16 (0) **NFL** 78 (4) [7 yrs]

Russell, Wade Wade O'Brien, TE, 6´4˝/250 lbs; Taylor; B8/16/1963 Marion, IN

YEAR	TEAM	G (GS, POS)	RUSH	YD	AVG (LG)	TD	REC	YD	AVG (LG)	TD	PASS	COMP	PCT	YD	AVG (LG)	TD	INT	SK	YD	QBR	KPR	OTD	PTS	TAY
1987	Cin	3(0)	—	—	—	—	2	27	13.5(23)	1	—	—	—	—	—	—	—	—	—	—	—	—	6	19

Rust, Reggie Reginald Porter, TB-BB, 6´2˝/210 lbs; Oregon State; B5/23/1909 Santa Barbara, CA, D1/11/1984 Arroyo Grande, CA

YEAR	TEAM	G (GS, POS)	RUSH	YD	AVG (LG)	TD	REC	YD	AVG (LG)	TD	PASS	COMP	PCT	YD	AVG (LG)	TD	INT	SK	YD	QBR	KPR	OTD	PTS	TAY
1932	Bos	5(1)	17	57	3.4	0	1	12	12.0(12)	0	5	2	40.0	25	5.0	0	1	—	—	—	—	—	0	36

Rutgens, Joe Joseph Casimere, DT, 6´2˝/255 lbs; Illinois; 1961: Was, rnd 1/Oak, rnd 1; B1/26/1939 Cedar Point, IL **1961** Was 14 (13, RDT) **1962** Was 14 (14, RDT) **1963** Was✧14 (14, RDT) **1964** Was 13 (13, RDT) **1965** Was✧14 (14, RDT) **1966** Was 5 (rdt) **1967** Was 14 (RDT) **1968** Was 13 (RDT) **1969** Was 9 (RDT) **NFL** 110 (68) [9 yrs]

Ruth, Mike Michael Joseph, NT, 6´2˝/266 lbs; Boston College; 1986: NE, rnd 2; B6/25/1964 Norristown, PA **1986**†NE 6 (0) **1987** NE 1 (0) **NFL** 7 (0) [2 yrs]

Ruthstrom, Ralph Ralph David, B, 6´5˝/212 lbs; Sam Houston State; SMU; B7/12/1921 Schenectady, NY, D3/29/1962 Houston, TX

YEAR	TEAM	G (GS, POS)	RUSH	YD	AVG (LG)	TD	REC	YD	AVG (LG)	TD	PASS	COMP	PCT	YD	AVG (LG)	TD	INT	SK	YD	QBR	KPR	OTD	PTS	TAY
1945	Cle	6(1)	10	74	7.4(34)	0	—	—	—	—	—	—	—	—	—	—	—	—	—	—	pi	—	0	147
1946	LARm	6(4)	2	-4	-2.0(1)	0	1	9	9.0(9)	0	—	—	—	—	—	—	—	—	—	—	p	—	0	-3
1947	Was	2(1)	2	5	2.5(4)	0	—	—	—	—	—	—	—	—	—	—	—	—	—	—	k	—	0	-5
NFL	3	14(6)	14	75	5.4(34)	0	1	9	9.0(9)	0	—	—	—	—	—	—	—	—	—	—	kpi	—	0	140

YEAR	TEAM	G (GS, POS)	RUSH	YD	AVG (LG)	TD	REC	YD	AVG (LG)	TD	PASS	COMP	PCT	YD	AVG (LG)	TD	INT	SK	YD	QBR	KPR	OTD	PTS	TAY
1949	Bal-A	4(0)	—	—	—	—	—	—	—	—	—	—	—	—	—	—	—	—	—	—	i	—	0	10

RUTKOWSKI, CHARLIE Charles Robert, DE, 6´3˝/248 lbs; Ripon; B1/17/1938 Racine, WI **1960** Buf-A 2

RUTKOWSKI, ED Edward John Anthony, QB-HB-SE-WR, 6´1˝/198 lbs; Notre Dame; B3/21/1941 Kingston, PA

YEAR	TEAM	G (GS, POS)	RUSH	YD	AVG (LG)	TD	REC	YD	AVG (LG)	TD	PASS	COMP	PCT	YD	AVG (LG)	TD	INT	SK	YD	QBR	KPR	OTD	PTS	TAY
1963	†Buf-A	14(hb)	48	144	3.0(45)	0	19	264	13.9(58)	1	1	0	0.0	0	0.0	0	0	—	—	—	kp	—	6	509
1964	†Buf-A	14	—	—	—	—	13	234	18.0(46)	1	—	—	—	—	—	—	—	—	—	—	kp	—	6	310
1965	†Buf-A✧	14(SE)	—	—	—	—	18	247	13.7(47)	1	—	—	—	—	—	—	—	—	—	—	kp	—	6	223
1966	†Buf-A	14	1	10	10.0(10)	0	6	150	25.0(55)	1	—	—	—	—	—	—	—	—	—	—	kp	1	12	250
1967	Buf-A	14	—	—	—	—	6	59	9.8(17)	0	1	0	0.0	0	0.0	0	0	—	—	—	kp	—	0	24
1968	Buf-A	13(qb)	20	96	4.8(33)	1	1	27	27.0(27)	0	100	41	41.0	380	3.8(37)	0	6	—	—	—	kp	—	6	65
NFL	6	83	69	250	3.6(45)	1	63	981	15.6(58)	4	102	41	40.2	380	3.7(37)	0	6	—	—	—	kp	1	36	1380

RUTLAND, REGGIE see Najee Mustafaa

RUTLEDGE, CRAIG Craig Alan, DB, 6´0˝/190 lbs; UCLA; B1/30/1964 Upland, CA **1987** LARm 3 (0)

RUTLEDGE, JEFF Jeffrey Ronald, QB, 6´1˝/195 lbs; Alabama; 1979: LA, rnd 9; B1/22/1957 Birmingham, AL

YEAR	TEAM	G (GS, POS)	RUSH	YD	AVG (LG)	TD	REC	YD	AVG (LG)	TD	PASS	COMP	PCT	YD	AVG (LG)	TD	INT	SK	YD	QBR	KPR	OTD	PTS	TAY
1979	LARm	3(1)	5	27	5.4(14)	0	—	—	—	—	32	13	40.6	125	3.9(22)	1	4	3	27	—	—	—	0	-66
1980	LARm	1(0)	—	—	—	—	—	—	—	—	4	1	25.0	26	6.5(26)	0	0	1	8	—	—	—	0	13
1981	LARm	4(0)	5	-3	-0.6(4)	0	—	—	—	—	50	30	60.0	442	8.8(64)	3	4	6	62	—	—	—	0	73
1983	NYG	4(4, qb)	7	27	3.9(14)	0	—	—	—	—	174	87	50.0	1208	6.9(54)	3	8	15	110	—	—	—	0	326
1984	†NYG	16(0)	—	—	—	—	—	—	—	—	1	1	100.0	9	9.0(9)	0	0	—	—	—	—	—	0	5
1985	†NYG	16(0)	2	-6	-3.0(-2)	0	—	—	—	—	—	—	—	—	—	—	—	—	—	—	—	—	0	-6
1986	†NYG	16(0)	3	19	6.3(18)	0	—	—	—	—	3	1	33.3	13	4.3(13)	1	0	—	—	—	—	—	0	31
1987	NYG	13(4, qb)	15	31	2.1(20)	0	—	—	—	—	155	79	51.0	1048	6.8(50)	5	11	17	129	—	—	—	0	140
1988	NYG	1(0)	3	-1	-0.3(0)	0	—	—	—	—	17	11	64.7	113	6.6(33)	0	1	2	14	—	—	—	0	16
1989	†NYG	1(0)	—	—	—	—	—	—	—	—	—	—	—	—	—	—	—	—	—	—	—	—	—	—
1990	†Was	10(1)	4	12	3.0(12)	1	—	—	—	—	68	40	58.8	455	6.7(40)	2	1	6	34	—	—	—	6	220
1991	†Was	16(0)	8	-13	-1.6(-1)	0	—	—	—	—	22	11	50.0	189	8.6(40)	1	0	2	20	—	—	—	0	87
1992	†Was	16(0)	—	—	—	—	—	—	—	—	—	—	—	—	—	—	—	—	—	—	—	—	—	—
NFL	13	117(10)	52	93	1.8(20)	1	—	—	—	—	526	274	52.1	3628	6.9(64)	16	29	52	404	61.4	—	—	6	837

RUTLEDGE, JOHNNY Johnny Boykins, LB, 6´3˝/239 lbs; Florida; 1999: Arz, rnd 2; B1/4/1977 Belle Glade, FL **1999** Arz 6 (0) **2000** Arz 11 (4) **2001** Arz 14 (0) **2002** Arz 9 (0) **2003**†Den 6 (0) **NFL** 46 (4) [5 yrs]

RUTLEDGE, ROD Rodrick Almar, TE, 6´5˝/262 lbs; Alabama; 1998: NE, rnd 2; B8/12/1975 Birmingham, AL

YEAR	TEAM	G (GS, POS)	RUSH	YD	AVG (LG)	TD	REC	YD	AVG (LG)	TD	PASS	COMP	PCT	YD	AVG (LG)	TD	INT	SK	YD	QBR	KPR	OTD	PTS	TAY
1998	†NE	16(4)	—	—	—	—	—	—	—	—	—	—	—	—	—	—	—	—	—	—	—	—	—	—
1999	NE	16(2)	—	—	—	—	7	66	9.4(13)	0	—	—	—	—	—	—	—	—	—	—	—	—	0	33
2000	NE	16(11, TE)	—	—	—	—	15	103	6.9(16)	1	—	—	—	—	—	—	—	—	—	—	—	—	6	57
2001	†NE	15(14, TE)	—	—	—	—	5	35	7.0(9)	0	—	—	—	—	—	—	—	—	—	—	—	—	0	18
2002	Hou	7(5, te)	—	—	—	—	—	—	—	—	—	—	—	—	—	—	—	—	—	—	—	—	—	—
NFL	5	70(36)	—	—	—	—	27	204	7.6(16)	1	—	—	—	—	—	—	—	—	—	—	—	—	6	107

RUUD, BARRETT Barrett James, LB, 6´1˝/242 lbs; Nebraska; 2005: TB, rnd 2; B5/20/1983 Lincoln, NE **2005**†TB 16 (0)

RUUD, TOM Thomas Robert, LB, 6´3˝/223 lbs; Nebraska; 1975: Buf, rnd 1; B7/26/1953 Oliva, MN **1975** Buf 14 (3) **1976** Buf 14 **1977** Buf 8 **1978** Cin 7 **1979** Cin 16 **NFL** 59 (3) [5 yrs]

RUZEK, ROGER Roger Brian, K, 6´1˝/195 lbs; Weber State; B12/17/1960 San Francisco, CA **[K]** **1987** Dal☆12 (0) **1988** Dal 14 (0) **1990**†Phi 16 (0) **1991** Phi 16 (0) **1992**†Phi 16 (0) **1993** Phi 5 (0)

YEAR	TEAM	G (GS, POS)	RUSH	YD	AVG (LG)	TD	REC	YD	AVG (LG)	TD	PASS	COMP	PCT	YD	AVG (LG)	TD	INT	SK	YD	QBR	KPR	OTD	PTS	TAY
1989	Dal	9(0)	—	—	—	—	1	4	4.0(4)	0	—	—	—	—	—	—	—	—	—	—	KP	—	29	2
1989	†Phi	5(0)	—	—	—	—	—	—	—	—	1	1	100.0	22	22.0(22)	1	0	—	—	—	K	—	38	16
NFL	7	93(0)	—	—	—	—	1	4	4.0(4)	0	1	1	100.0	22	22.0(22)	1	0	—	—	—	KP	—	566	18

RUZICH, STEVE Stephen, G-LB-T-DT, 6´2˝/228 lbs; Ohio State; 1952: Cle, rnd 14; B12/24/1927 Cleveland, OH, D11/30/1991 Columbus, OH **1952** GB 12 (LG) **1953** GB 12 (LG) **1954** GB 12 **NFL** 36 [3 yrs]

RYAN, BILL William, T, 5´11˝/190 lbs; Fordham; B1901, deceased **1924** Roc 1 (0) **1924** ChiC 1 (0) **1925** Mil 1 (0) **NFL** 3 (0) [2 yrs]

RYAN, CASSY Clarence Daniel, BB-WB, 5´9˝/160 lbs; West Virginia; B5/10/1905 Mannington, WV, D1/6/1981 Fairmont, WV **1929** Buf 9 (6, BB), 12

RYAN, DAVE David Henry, TB-HB, 5´10˝/190 lbs; Hardin-Simmons; B2/3/1923 Kaufman, TX, D12/5/1988 Kaufman, TX **[K]**

YEAR	TEAM	G (GS, POS)	RUSH	YD	AVG (LG)	TD	REC	YD	AVG (LG)	TD	PASS	COMP	PCT	YD	AVG (LG)	TD	INT	SK	YD	QBR	KPR	OTD	PTS	TAY
1945	Det	10(5, tb)	36	93	2.6(8)	1	2	67	33.5(63)	1	44	13	29.5	331	7.5(61)	3	10	—	—	—	KPkpi	—	15	190
1946	Det	11(6, TB)	71	65	0.9(27)	1	1	-5	-5.0(-5)	0	154	73	47.4	965	6.3(**88**)	6	17	—	—	41.1	kpi	1	12	104
1947	Det	1(0)	—	—	—	—	—	—	—	—	—	—	—	—	—	—	—	—	—	—	—	—	—	—
1948	Bos	6(0)	3	1	0.3(3)	0	—	—	—	—	—	—	—	—	—	—	—	—	—	—	—	—	0	1
NFL	4	28(11)	110	159	1.4(27)	2	3	62	20.7(63)	1	198	86	43.4	1296	6.5(88)	9	27	—	—	41.1	KPkpi	1	27	295

RYAN, ED Edward Denis, E-DE, 6´2˝/215 lbs; British Columbia; St. Mary's (CA); 1948: Pit, rnd 9/ChiR-A, rnd 18; B12/29/1925 Banff, Canada, D10/21/2002 San Carlos, CA **1948** Pit 9 (2)

RYAN, FRANK Frank Bell, QB, 6´3˝/199 lbs; Rice; 1958: LA, rnd 5; B7/12/1936 Fort Worth, TX

YEAR	TEAM	G (GS, POS)	RUSH	YD	AVG (LG)	TD	REC	YD	AVG (LG)	TD	PASS	COMP	PCT	YD	AVG (LG)	TD	INT	SK	YD	QBR	KPR	OTD	PTS	TAY
1958	LARm	5	5	45	9.0(12)	0	—	—	—	—	14	5	35.7	34	2.4(14)	1	3	—	—	—	—	—	0	-53
1959	LARm	10(qb)	19	57	3.0(13)	1	—	—	—	—	89	42	47.2	709	8.0(67)	2	4	—	—	—	—	—	6	272
1960	LARm	11(5, qb)	19	85	4.5(24)	1	0	32	(32)	1	128	62	48.4	816	6.4(61)	7	9	—	—	—	—	—	12	199
1961	LARm	14	38	139	3.7(28)	0	—	—	—	—	142	72	50.7	1115	7.9(96)	5	7	—	—	68.3	—	—	0	442
1962	Cle	11(QB)	42	242	5.8(39)	1	—	—	—	—	194	112	57.7	1541	7.9(65)	10	7	—	—	85.4	—	—	6	793
1963	Cle	13(QB)	62	224	3.6(25)	2	0	-1	(-1)	0	256	135	52.7	2026	7.9(83)	25	13	20	179	90.4	—	—	12	862
1964	†Cle✧	14(QB)	37	217	5.9(19)	1	—	—	—	—	334	174	52.1	2404	7.2(62)	**25**	19	27	207	76.7	—	—	6	794
1965	†Cle★	12(QB)	19	72	3.8(18)	0	—	—	—	—	243	119	49.0	1751	7.2(80)	18	13	23	202	75.3	—	—	0	518
1966	Cle✧	14(QB)	36	156	4.3(17)	0	—	—	—	—	382	200	52.4	2974	7.8(54)	**29**	14	28	223	88.2	—	—	0	1228
1967	†Cle	13(13, QB)	22	57	2.6(12)	0	—	—	—	—	280	136	48.6	2026	7.2(49)	20	16	38	318	72.7	—	—	0	530
1968	†Cle	7(3)	11	64	5.8(19)	0	—	—	—	—	66	31	47.0	639	9.7(57)	7	6	10	79	—	—	—	0	179
1969	Was	1	—	—	—	—	—	—	—	—	1	1	100.0	4	4.0(4)	0	0	—	—	—	—	—	0	2
1970	Was	1	—	—	—	—	—	—	—	—	4	1	25.0	3	0.8(3)	0	0	4	35	—	—	—	0	2
NFL	13	126(21)	310	1358	4.4(39)	6	0	31	(32)	1	2133	1090	51.1	16042	7.5(96)	149	111	150	1243	77.6	—	—	42	5765

RYAN, JIM James Joseph, LB, 6´1˝/217 lbs; William & Mary; B5/18/1957 Camden, NJ **1979**†Den 16 **1980** Den 16 (0) **1981** Den 16 (0) **1982** Den 9 (9, LOLB) **1983**†Den 15 (12, LOLB) **1984**†Den 16 (14, LOLB) **1985** Den 16 (14, LOLB) **1986**†Den 16 (14, LOLB) **1987**†Den 14 (14, ROLB) **1988** Den 16 (14, ROLB) **NFL** 150 (91) [10 yrs]

RYAN, JOE Joseph James, DE, 6´2˝/235 lbs; Villanova; 1957: ChiB, rnd 25; B7/15/1934 Staten Island, NY, D1/20/2003 Staten Island, NY **1960** NYT-A 4

RYAN, KENT Orson Kent, HB, 6´2˝/193 lbs; Utah State; B2/2/1915 Midvale, UT

YEAR	TEAM	G (GS, POS)	RUSH	YD	AVG (LG)	TD	REC	YD	AVG (LG)	TD	PASS	COMP	PCT	YD	AVG (LG)	TD	INT	SK	YD	QBR	KPR	OTD	PTS	TAY
1938	Det	9(0)	24	180	7.5	0	7	78	11.1	0	9	2	22.2	27	3.0	0	0	—	—	—	—	—	0	233
1939	Det	6(2)	8	41	5.1	1	7	46	6.6	1	—	—	—	—	—	—	—	—	—	—	P	—	12	79
1940	Det	10(4)	22	42	1.9	0	9	96	10.7	0	2	0	0.0	0	0.0	0	0	—	—	—	Pi	—	0	125
NFL	3	25(6)	54	263	4.9	1	23	220	9.6	1	11	2	18.2	27	2.5	0	0	—	—	—	Pi	—	12	437

RYAN, PAT Patrick Lee, QB, 6´3˝/210 lbs; Tennessee; 1978: NYJ, rnd 11; B9/16/1955 Hutchinson, KS **[K]**

YEAR	TEAM	G (GS, POS)	RUSH	YD	AVG (LG)	TD	REC	YD	AVG (LG)	TD	PASS	COMP	PCT	YD	AVG (LG)	TD	INT	SK	YD	QBR	KPR	OTD	PTS	TAY
1978	NYJ	2	—	—	—	—	—	—	—	—	14	9	64.3	106	7.6(18)	0	2	—	—	—	—	—	0	-27
1979	NYJ	1	—	—	—	—	—	—	—	—	4	2	50.0	13	3.3(7)	0	1	2	14	—	—	—	0	-34
1980	NYJ	14(0)	—	—	—	—	—	—	—	—	—	—	—	—	—	—	—	—	—	—	—	—	—	—
1981	†NYJ	15(0)	3	-5	-1.7(-1)	0	—	—	—	—	10	4	40.0	48	4.8(18)	1	1	—	—	—	—	—	0	-16
1982	†NYJ	9(0)	1	-1	-1.0(-1)	0	—	—	—	—	18	12	66.7	146	8.1(20)	2	1	—	—	—	—	—	0	42
1983	NYJ	16(0)	4	23	5.8(25)	0	—	—	—	—	40	21	52.5	259	6.5(36)	2	2	1	3	—	K	—	1	83
1984	NYJ	16(11, QB)	23	92	4.0(16)	0	—	—	—	—	285	156	54.7	1939	6.8(44)	14	14	30	214	72.0	K	—	1	572

YEAR	TEAM	G (GS, POS)	RUSH	YD	AVG (LG)	TD	REC	YD	AVG (LG)	TD	PASS	COMP	PCT	YD	AVG (LG)	TD	INT	SK	YD	QBR	KPR	OTD	PTS	TAY
1985	†NYJ	16(0)	3	-5	-1.7(-1)	0	—	—	—	—	9	6	66.7	95	10.6(50)	0	0	—	—	—	—	—	0	43
1986	†NYJ	16(2)	8	28	3.5(18)	0	—	—	—	—	55	34	61.8	342	6.2(36)	2	1	5	33	—	—	—	0	169
1987	NYJ	13(1)	4	5	1.3(8)	1	—	—	—	—	53	32	60.4	314	5.9(35)	4	2	1	7	—	—	—	6	112
1988	NYJ	16(4)	5	22	4.4(15)	0	—	—	—	—	113	63	55.8	807	7.1(42)	5	4	5	24	—	—	—	0	291
1989	NYJ	7(1)	1	-1	-1.0(-1)	0	—	—	—	—	30	15	50.0	153	5.1(25)	1	3	2	26	—	—	—	0	-40
1991	Phi	4(0)	1	-2	-2.0(-2)	0	—	—	—	—	26	10	38.5	98	3.8(32)	0	4	4	21	—	—	—	0	-113
NFL	13	145(19)	53	156	2.9(25)	1	—	—	—	—	657	364	55.4	4320	6.6(50)	31	35	50	342	69.2	K	—	8	1081

RYAN, ROCKY John Raymond, DB-E, 6´1˝/202 lbs; Illinois; 1954: Phi, rnd 2; B7/5/1932 Tolono, IL

YEAR	TEAM	G (GS, POS)	RUSH	YD	AVG (LG)	TD	REC	YD	AVG (LG)	TD	PASS	COMP	PCT	YD	AVG (LG)	TD	INT	SK	YD	QBR	KPR	OTD	PTS	TAY
1956	Phi	12(DB)	—	—	—	—	1	31	31.0(31)	0	—	—	—	—	—	—	—	—	—	—	i	—	0	28
1957	Phi	9	—	—	—	—	4	91	22.8(46)	2	—	—	—	—	—	—	—	—	—	—	—	—	12	56
1958	Phi	3	—	—	—	—	—	—	—	—	—	—	—	—	—	—	—	—	—	—	pi	—	0	28
1958	ChiB	4	—	—	—	—	1	66	66.0(66)	0	—	—	—	—	—	—	—	—	—	—	—	—	0	33
NFL	3	28	—	—	—	—	6	188	31.3(66)	2	—	—	—	—	—	—	—	—	—	—	pi	—	12	144

RYAN, SEAN Sean O., TE, 6´5˝/254 lbs; Boston College; 2004: Dal, rnd 5; B3/27/1980 Buffalo, NY **2004** Dal 6 (1) **2005** Dal 3 (1) **NFL** 9 (2) [2 yrs]

RYAN, SOD John Joseph, T, 6´2˝/205 lbs; Detroit Mercy; B1906 Kewanee, IL **1929** ChiB 5 (1) **1930** Por 3 (1) **NFL** 8 (2) [2 yrs]

RYAN, TIM Timothy Edward, DE-DT, 6´4˝/268 lbs; USC; 1990: Chi, rnd 3; B9/8/1967 Memphis, TN **1990**†ChiB 15 (0) **1991** ChiB 16 (4) **1992** ChiB 16 (1) **1993** ChiB 11 (0) **NFL** 58 (5) [4 yrs]

RYAN, TIM Timothy Thomas, G, 6´2˝/280 lbs; Notre Dame; 1991: TB, rnd 5; B9/2/1968 Kansas City, MO **1991** TB 15 (0) **1992** TB 16 (1) **1993** TB 6 (0) **NFL** 37 (1) [3 yrs]

RYANS, LARRY Larry Bernard, WR, 5´11˝/182 lbs; Clemson; B7/28/1971 Greenwood, SC **1996** TB 3 (0)

RYCHLEC, TOM Thomas Richard, E, 6´3˝/220 lbs; American International; 1957: Det, rnd 10; B9/11/1934 Meriden, CT

YEAR	TEAM	G (GS, POS)	RUSH	YD	AVG (LG)	TD	REC	YD	AVG (LG)	TD	PASS	COMP	PCT	YD	AVG (LG)	TD	INT	SK	YD	QBR	KPR	OTD	PTS	TAY
1958	Det	12	—	—	—	—	2	21	10.5(33)	0	—	—	—	—	—	—	—	—	—	—	k	—	0	-5
1960	Buf-A	14(TE)	—	—	—	—	45	590	13.1(36)	0	—	—	—	—	—	—	—	—	—	—	k	—	0	283
1961	Buf-A	14(TE)	1	-18	-18.0(-18)	0	33	405	12.3(27)	2	—	—	—	—	—	—	—	—	—	—	—	—	12	195
1962	Buf-A	6	—	—	—	—	6	66	11.0(18)	1	—	—	—	—	—	—	—	—	—	—	p	—	6	57
1963	Den-A	3	—	—	—	—	1	7	7.0(7)	0	—	—	—	—	—	—	—	—	—	—	—	—	0	4
NFL	5	49	1	-18	-18.0(-18)	0	87	1089	12.5(36)	3	—	—	—	—	—	—	—	—	—	—	kp	—	18	534

RYCKMAN, BILLY William Thomas, WR, 5´11˝/172 lbs; Louisiana Tech; 1977: Atl, rnd 10; B2/28/1955 Lafayette, LA

YEAR	TEAM	G (GS, POS)	RUSH	YD	AVG (LG)	TD	REC	YD	AVG (LG)	TD	PASS	COMP	PCT	YD	AVG (LG)	TD	INT	SK	YD	QBR	KPR	OTD	PTS	TAY
1977	Atl	14	—	—	—	—	1	5	5.0(5)	1	—	—	—	—	—	—	—	—	—	—	kp	—	6	-3
1978	†Atl	16(15, WR)	—	—	—	—	45	679	15.1(59)	2	—	—	—	—	—	—	—	—	—	—	p	—	12	437
1979	Atl	14	—	—	—	—	4	59	14.8(20)	2	—	—	—	—	—	—	—	—	—	—	p	—	12	52
NFL	3	44(15)	—	—	—	—	50	743	14.9(59)	5	—	—	—	—	—	—	—	—	—	—	kp	—	30	486

RYCZEK, DAN Daniel Stanley, C, 6´3˝/249 lbs; Virginia; 1971: Was, rnd 13; B8/24/1949 Painesville, OH **1973**†Was 14 **1974**†Was 14 **1975** Was 14 **1977** TB 14 (13, C) **1978**†LARm 16 **1979**†LARm 16 (3)

YEAR	TEAM	G (GS, POS)	RUSH	YD	AVG (LG)	TD	REC	YD	AVG (LG)	TD	PASS	COMP	PCT	YD	AVG (LG)	TD	INT	SK	YD	QBR	KPR	OTD	PTS	TAY
1976	TB	14(14, C)	—	—	—	—	1	6	6.0(6)	0	—	—	—	—	—	—	—	—	—	—	—	—	0	3
NFL	7	102(30)	—	—	—	—	1	6	6.0(6)	0	—	—	—	—	—	—	—	—	—	—	k	—	0	-1

RYCZEK, PAUL Paul Andrew, C, 6´2˝/230 lbs; Virginia; 1974: Atl, rnd 10; B6/25/1952 Painesville, OH **1974** Atl 14 **1975** Atl 14 **1976** Atl 14 (4) **1977** Atl 14 **1978**†Atl 16 **1979** Atl 16 **1981** NO 8 (0) **1987** Phi 3 (0) **NFL** 99 (4) [8 yrs]

RYDALCH, RON Ronald James, DT, 6´4˝/260 lbs; Utah; 1974: NYJ, rnd 8; B1/1/1952 Tooele, UT **1975** ChiB 3 **1976** ChiB 13 (3) **1977**†ChiB 14 (RDT) **1978** ChiB 12 (5, rdt) **1979**†ChiB 16 **1980** ChiB 16 (0) **NFL** 74 (8) [6 yrs]

RYDER, NICK Nicholas F., FB, 5´11˝/210 lbs; Miami (FL); 1963: Det, rnd 10/NYJ, rnd 16; B10/31/1941 Nyack, NY

YEAR	TEAM	G (GS, POS)	RUSH	YD	AVG (LG)	TD	REC	YD	AVG (LG)	TD	PASS	COMP	PCT	YD	AVG (LG)	TD	INT	SK	YD	QBR	KPR	OTD	PTS	TAY
1963	Det	10	10	23	2.3(12)	1	—	—	—	—	—	—	—	—	—	—	—	—	—	—	k	—	6	21
1964	Det	14	11	11	1.0(7)	0	4	30	7.5(23)	1	—	—	—	—	—	—	—	—	—	—	k	—	6	38
NFL	2	24	21	34	1.6(12)	1	4	30	7.5(23)	1	—	—	—	—	—	—	—	—	—	—	k	—	12	59

RYDZEWSKI, FRANK Francis Xavier, C-T-G, 6´1˝/220 lbs; Notre Dame; B11/16/1892 Chicago, IL, D10/1979 Chicago, IL **1920** Cle 3 (3) **1920** ChiT 4 (3) **1920** Ham 2 (1) **1921** ChiC 8 (8, C) **1922** Ham 6 (6, C) **1923** ChiB 1 (0) **1923** Ham 5 (5, c) **1924** Ham 5 (4, C) **1925** Ham 1 (1) **1925** Mil 3 (1) **1926** Ham 4 (3, C) **NFL** 42 (35) [7 yrs]

RYKOVICH, JULIE Julius Alphonsus, HB-DB, 6´2˝/204 lbs; Notre Dame; Illinois; 1946: ChiB, rnd 2; B4/6/1923 Gary, IN, D12/22/1974 Merrillville, IN **[K]**

YEAR	TEAM	G (GS, POS)	RUSH	YD	AVG (LG)	TD	REC	YD	AVG (LG)	TD	PASS	COMP	PCT	YD	AVG (LG)	TD	INT	SK	YD	QBR	KPR	OTD	PTS	TAY
1947	Buf-A	12(9, RH)	92	414	4.5	4	4	44	11.0	0	—	—	—	—	—	—	—	—	—	—	kpi	—	24	662
1948	Buf-A	6(2)	43	249	5.8	5	2	-7	-3.5	0	—	—	—	—	—	—	—	—	—	—	k	—	30	299
1948	ChiR-A	6(4)	53	176	3.3	1	3	78	26.0	0	1	1	100.0	12	12.0(12)	0	0	—	—	—	Kkpi	—	6	320
AAFC	2	24(15)	188	839	4.5	10	9	115	12.8	0	1	1	100.0	12	12.0(12)	0	0	—	—	—	Kkpi	—	60	1281
1949	ChiB	11(3)	88	340	3.9(18)	6	16	210	13.1(45)	2	—	—	—	—	—	—	—	—	—	—	—	—	48	515
1950	†ChiB	12(RH)	122	394	3.2(18)	7	21	344	16.4(39)	0	—	—	—	—	—	—	—	—	—	—	P	—	42	636
1951	ChiB	12(RH)	83	399	4.8(56)	4	6	133	22.2(51)	0	3	0	0.0	0	0.0	0	1	—	—	—	—	—	24	466
1952	Was	11(RH)	94	361	3.8(21)	1	16	283	17.7(42)	1	—	—	—	—	—	—	—	—	—	—	K	—	13	518
1953	Was	12(RH)	73	251	3.4(19)	0	7	73	10.4(39)	1	—	—	—	—	—	—	—	—	—	—	k	—	6	302
NFL	5	58(3)	460	1745	3.8(56)	18	66	1043	15.8(51)	4	3	0	0.0	0	0.0	0	1	—	—	—	KPk	—	133	2436

RYMKUS, LOU Louis Joseph, T-DT, 6´4˝/231 lbs; Notre Dame; 1943: Was, rnd 7; B11/6/1919 Royalton, IL, D10/31/1998 Houston, TX **[C]** **1946**†Cle-A☆14 (13, RT) **1947**†Cle-A☆13 (9, RT) **1948**†Cle-A☆14 (14, RT) **1949**†Cle-A☆12 (11, RT) **AAFC** 53 (47) [4 yrs]

1943†Was☆10 (9, LT) **1950**†Cle☆12 (RT) **1951**†Cle☆11 (RT) **NFL** 33 (9) [3 yrs]

RYPIEN, MARK Mark Robert, QB, 6´4˝/231 lbs; Washington State; 1986: Was, rnd 6; B10/2/1962 Calgary, Canada

YEAR	TEAM	G (GS, POS)	RUSH	YD	AVG (LG)	TD	REC	YD	AVG (LG)	TD	PASS	COMP	PCT	YD	AVG (LG)	TD	INT	SK	YD	QBR	KPR	OTD	PTS	TAY
1988	Was	9(6, qb)	9	31	3.4(19)	1	—	—	—	—	208	114	54.8	1730	**8.3(60)**	18	13	14	115	—	—	—	6	476
1989	Was✧	14(14, QB)	26	56	2.2(15)	1	—	—	—	—	476	280	58.8	3768	7.9(80)	22	13	16	108	88.1	—	—	6	1540
1990	†Was	10(10, QB)	15	4	0.3(8)	0	—	—	—	—	304	166	54.6	2070	6.8(53)	16	11	6	33	78.4	—	—	0	679
1991	†Was★	16(16, QB)	15	6	0.4(11)	1	—	—	—	—	421	249	59.1	**3564**	8.5(82)	**28**	11	7	59	97.9	—	—	6	1498
1992	†Was	16(16, QB)	36	50	1.4(11)	2	—	—	—	—	**479**	269	56.2	3282	6.9(62)	13	17	23	176	71.7	—	—	12	1096
1993	Was	12(10, QB)	9	4	0.4(5)	3	—	—	—	—	319	166	52.0	1514	4.7(43)	4	10	16	87	56.3	—	—	18	411
1994	Cle	6(3)	7	4	0.6(2)	0	—	—	—	—	128	59	46.1	694	5.4(43)	4	3	2	11	—	—	—	0	251
1995	SL	11(3, qb)	9	10	1.1(5)	0	—	—	—	—	217	129	59.4	1448	6.7(50)	9	8	11	60	—	—	—	0	459
1996	†Phi	1(0)	—	—	—	—	—	—	—	—	13	10	76.9	76	5.8(16)	1	0	—	—	—	—	—	0	43
1997	SL	5(0)	1	1	1.0(1)	0	—	—	—	—	39	19	48.7	270	6.9(62)	0	2	1	9	—	—	—	0	56
2001	Ind	4(0)	—	—	—	—	—	—	—	—	9	5	55.6	57	6.3(21)	0	0	1	6	—	—	—	0	29
NFL	11	104(78)	127	166	1.3(19)	8	—	—	—	—	2613	1466	56.1	18473	7.1(82)	115	88	97	664	78.9	—	—	48	6538

RZEMPOLUCH, TED Theodore Charles, DB, 6´1˝/195 lbs; Virginia; B5/31/1941 Jersey City, NJ **1963** Was 6

SAALFELD, KELLY Kelly Dean, C, 6´3˝/246 lbs; Nebraska; 1980: GB, rnd 9; B2/15/1956 Columbus, NE **1980** NYG 7 (0)

SAAR, BRAD Bradford Louis, LB, 6´1˝/220 lbs; Penn State; Ball State; B2/24/1963 Buffalo, NY **1987** Ind 1 (0)

SABADOS, ANDY Andrew Alex, G, 5´11˝/209 lbs; The Citadel; 1939: ChiC, rnd 13; B11/24/1916 Aurora, IL, D7/5/2004 Mundelein, IL **1939** ChiC 8 (6, LG) **1940** ChiC 10 (6, LG) **NFL** 18 (12) [2 yrs]

SABAL, RON Ronald Joseph, T-G, 6´3˝/245 lbs; Purdue; 1958: Phi, rnd 19; B7/23/1936 Chicago, IL **1960** Oak-A 14 (LT) **1961** Oak-A 14 (LT) **NFL** 28 [2 yrs]

SABAN, LOU Louis Henry, C-B, 6´0˝/202 lbs; Indiana; 1944: ChiC, rnd 10; B10/13/1921 Brookfield, IL **[KC]** **1947**†Cle-A 14 (6, c) **1948**†Cle-A☆14 (0) **1949**†Cle-A☆12 (1)

YEAR	TEAM	G (GS, POS)	RUSH	YD	AVG (LG)	TD	REC	YD	AVG (LG)	TD	PASS	COMP	PCT	YD	AVG (LG)	TD	INT	SK	YD	QBR	KPR	OTD	PTS	TAY
1946	†Cle-A	14(2)	4	-4	-1.0	0	1	45	45.0(45)	0	3	0	0.0	0	0.0	0	1	—	—	—	i	—	0	-10
AAFC	4	54(9)	4	-4	-1.0	0	1	45	45.0(45)	0	3	0	0.0	0	0.0	0	1	—	—	—	Ki	1	27	34

SABASTEANSKI, JOE Joseph Edward, G-LB-C, 6´0˝/207 lbs; Fordham; 1943: Bkn, rnd 11; B2/24/1921 Portland, ME, D7/1/1972 **1947** Bos 10 (2) **1948** Bos 12 (5, rg) **1949** NYB 12 (5, rg) **NFL** 34 (12) [3 yrs]

SABATINO, BILL Louis William, DT, 6´3˝/245 lbs; Colorado; 1967: Cle, rnd 11; B8/9/1945 Alliance, OH **1968** Cle 7 **1969** Atl 6 **NFL** 13 [2 yrs]

YEAR	TEAM	G (GS, POS)	RUSH	YD	AVG (LG)	TD	REC	YD	AVG (LG)	TD	PASS	COMP	PCT	YD	AVG (LG)	TD	INT	SK	YD	QBR	KPR	OTD	PTS	TAY

SABB, DWAYNE Dwayne Irving, LB, 6´4˝/248 lbs; New Hampshire; 1992: NE, rnd 5; B10/9/1969 Union City, NJ   **1992** NE 16 (2) **1993** NE 14 (7, ROLB) **1994**†NE 16 (8, LOLB)
1995 NE 12 (0) **1996**†NE 16 (7, RLB) **NFL** 74 (24) [5 yrs]

SABUCO, TINO Valentino, C, 6´1˝/206 lbs; Wayne State (MI); San Francisco; B12/20/1926 Detroit, MI   **1949**†SF-A 10 (0)

SACCA, TONY Anthony John, QB, 6´5˝/230 lbs; Penn State; 1992: Phx, rnd 2; B4/17/1970 Delran, NJ

| 1992 | Phx | 2 (0) | — | — | — | — | — | — | — | — | 11 | 4 | 36.4 | 29 | 2.6 (16) | 0 | 2 | — | — | — | — | — | 0 | -66 |

SACCO, FRANK Frank J., LB, 6´4˝/240 lbs; Fordham; B4/8/1964   **1987** NE 2 (0)

SACHS, LENNY Leonard David, E, 5´8˝/176 lbs; American College of Physical Education; B8/7/1897 Chicago, IL, D10/27/1942 Chicago, IL   **1920** ChiC 8 (3) **1921** ChiC 8 (8, LE), 6
1922 ChiC 7 (4) **1923** Mil 12 (12, LE) **1924** Mil 2 (2) **1924** Ham 3 (1) **1925** ChiC 2 (0) **1925** Ham 4 (3, RE) **1926** Lou 4 (3, LE) **NFL** 50 (36) [7 yrs]

SACHSE, FRANK Francis Marion, B, 6´0˝/197 lbs; Texas Tech; B7/24/1917 Brice, TX, D10/1/1989 Dallas, TX

1943	Bkn	6 (0)	8	14	1.8 (7)	0	3	26	8.7 (14)	0	9	5	55.6	72	8.0 (57)	1	1	—	—	p	—	—	0	55
1944	Bkn	6 (0)	9	13	1.4 (5)	0	—	—	—	—	45	18	40.0	226	5.0 (50)	0	5	—	—	kp	—	—	0	-46
1945	Bos	8 (0)	5	9	1.8 (29)	0	—	—	—	—	21	9	42.9	203	9.7 (80)	2	0	—	—	i	—	—	0	136
NFL	3	20 (0)	22	36	1.6 (29)	0	3	26	8.7 (14)	0	75	32	42.7	501	6.7 (80)	3	6	—	—	kpi	—	—	0	145

SACHSE, JACK Jack Clarence, C-LB, 6´0˝/210 lbs; Southwestern (TX); Texas; 1944: Bkn, rnd 8; B1/14/1921 Wichita Falls, TX, D7/1958 Velpen, IN   **1945** Bos 4 (1)

SACK, JOHN Jacob Bernard, aka John Sacklowsky, G, 6´2˝/195 lbs; Pittsburgh; B2/22/1902 Pittsburgh, PA, D3/7/1980 Pittsburgh, PA   **1923** Col☆9 (9, LG) **1926** Can 3 (3)
NFL 12 (12) [2 yrs]

SACKSTEDER, NORB Norbert N., B, 5´9˝/173 lbs; Dayton; Christian Brothers (MO); B9/25/1895, D6/19/1986 St. Petersburg, FL   **1920** Day☆8 (8, WB) **1921** Det 7 (5, TB)
1922 Can 11 (9, WB), 24 **1925** Can 1 (0) **NFL** 27 (22) [4 yrs]

SACRINTY, NICK Nicholas William, QB, 6´0˝/185 lbs; Wake Forest; 1945: ChiB, rnd 17; B6/10/1924 Reidsville, NC

| 1947 | ChiB | 11 (0) | 4 | 4 | 1.0 (5) | 0 | — | — | — | — | 48 | 15 | 31.3 | 299 | 6.2 (44) | 5 | 3 | — | — | i | — | — | 0 | 61 |

SADDLER, ROD Roderick, DT-DE, 6´5˝/276 lbs; Texas A&M; 1987: SL, rnd 4; B9/26/1965 Atlanta, GA   **1987** SL 12 (3) **1988** Phx 16 (15, LDE/rdt) **1989** Phx 15 (15, LDT)
1990 Phx 16 (15, RDE) **1991** Phx 4 (0) **1991** Cin 2 (0) **NFL** 65 (48) [5 yrs]

SADER, STEVE Steven, FB, 5´11˝/180 lbs; none; B1921

| 1943 | P-P | 2 (0) | 3 | 5 | 1.7 (16) | 0 | — | — | — | — | — | — | — | — | — | — | — | — | — | — | — | — | 0 | 5 |

SADOWSKI, TROY Troy Robert, TE, 6´5˝/255 lbs; Georgia; 1989: Atl, rnd 6; B12/8/1965 Atlanta, GA

1990	Atl	13 (1)	—	—	—	—	—	—	—	—	—	—	—	—	—	—	—	—	—	—	—	—	—	—
1991	KC	14 (1)	—	—	—	—	—	—	—	—	—	—	—	—	—	—	—	—	—	—	—	—	—	—
1992	NYJ	6 (2)	—	—	—	—	1	20	20.0 (20)	0	—	—	—	—	—	—	—	—	—	—	—	—	0	10
1993	NYJ	13 (1)	—	—	—	—	2	14	7.0 (11)	0	—	—	—	—	—	—	—	—	—	k	—	—	0	-8
1994	Cin	15 (1)	—	—	—	—	11	54	4.9 (11)	0	—	—	—	—	—	—	—	—	—	—	—	—	0	27
1995	Cin	12 (1)	—	—	—	—	5	37	7.4 (10)	0	—	—	—	—	—	—	—	—	—	—	—	—	0	19
1996	Cin	16 (2)	—	—	—	—	3	15	5.0 (8)	0	—	—	—	—	—	—	—	—	—	k	—	—	0	-16
1997	†Pit	6 (0)	—	—	—	—	1	12	12.0 (12)	0	—	—	—	—	—	—	—	—	—	—	—	—	0	6
1998	†Jax	5 (0)	—	—	—	—	—	—	—	—	—	—	—	—	—	—	—	—	—	k	—	—	0	-15
NFL	9	100 (9)	—	—	—	—	23	152	6.6 (20)	0	—	—	—	—	—	—	—	—	—	k	—	—	0	23

SAENZ, EDDIE Edwin Matthew, HB-DB, 5´11˝/169 lbs; Loyola Marymount; USC; 1945: Was, rnd 15; B9/21/1922 Santa Monica, CA, D4/28/1971 Santa Monica, CA **[R]**

1946	Was	10 (3)	55	213	3.9 (12)	1	12	242	20.2 (66)	3	—	—	—	—	—	—	—	—	—	ki	—	24	453
1947	Was	12 (6, LH)	51	143	2.8 (18)	0	34	598	17.6 (74)	4	—	—	—	—	—	—	—	—	—	kp	2	36	1032
1948	Was	4 (2)	8	21	2.6 (5)	0	4	62	15.5 (28)	0	—	—	—	—	—	—	—	—	—	kp	—	0	121
1949	Was	12 (4)	53	170	3.2 (14)	0	23	251	10.9 (31)	0	—	—	—	—	—	—	—	—	—	kp	—	0	494
1950	Was	10 (DB)	20	64	3.2 (13)	1	10	165	16.5 (36)	1	—	—	—	—	—	—	—	—	—	kpi	—	12	379
1951	Was	2	3	8	2.7 (6)	0	1	9	9.0 (9)	0	—	—	—	—	—	—	—	—	—	kp	—	0	19
NFL	6	50 (15)	190	619	3.3 (18)	2	84	1327	15.8 (74)	8	—	—	—	—	—	—	—	—	—	kpi	2	72	2497

SAFFOLD, SAINT Samuel T., SE-WR, 6´4˝/202 lbs; San Jose State; 1966: SF, rnd 15/SD, rnd R7; B5/18/1944 Slater, MS

| 1968 | Cin-A | 14 (se) | 1 | 21 | 21.0 (21) | 0 | 16 | 172 | 10.8 (23) | 0 | — | — | — | — | — | — | — | — | — | k | — | 0 | 92 |

SAGAPOLUTELE, PIO Pio Ailka, DT-DE, 6´6˝/297 lbs; San Diego State; 1991: Cle, rnd 4; B11/28/1969 American Samoa   **1991** Cle 15 (8, lde) **1992** Cle 14 (0) **1993** Cle 8 (0)
1994 Cle 11 (0) **1995** Cle 15 (3) **1996**†NE 15 (10, RDT) **1997** NO 14 (13, RDT) **NFL** 92 (34) [7 yrs]

SAGELY, FLOYD Floyd Eugene, DB-E, 6´1˝/191 lbs; Arkansas; 1954: SF, rnd 6; B3/26/1932 Rudy, AR   **1954** SF 12 **1956** SF 3 **1957** ChiC 10 **NFL** 25 [3 yrs]

SAGER, KEN Kenneth A., TE, 6´4˝/228 lbs; Western Washington; B10/15/1963   **1987** Sea 3 (1)

SAGNELLA, TONY Anthony, DT, 6´5˝/260 lbs; Rutgers; B2/28/1964 New Haven, CT   **1987** Was 3 (2)

SAIDOCK, TOM Thomas, DT, 6´5˝/261 lbs; Michigan State; 1957: Phi, rnd 7; B2/26/1930 Detroit, MI   **1957** Phi 11 (5) **1960** NYT-A 14 (LDT) **1961** NYT-A 14 (LDT) **1962** Buf-A 2
NFL 41 (5) [4 yrs]

SAIMES, GEORGE George Thomas, DB, 5´11˝/186 lbs; Michigan State; 1963: KC, rnd 6/LA, rnd 6; B9/1/1941 Canton, OH **[I]**   **1964**†Buf-A★14 (RS) **1965**†Buf-A★14 (RS)
1966†Buf-A★14 (RS) **1967** Buf-A★14 (RS) **1968** Buf-A★13 (RS) **1969** Buf-A 8 (RS) **1970** Den 8 (2) **1971** Den 13 (13, FS) **1972** Den 9 (4)

| 1963 | †Buf-A | 14 (RS) | 12 | 41 | 3.4 (7) | 0 | 6 | 23 | 3.8 (9) | 0 | — | — | — | — | — | — | — | — | — | ki | — | 0 | 97 |
| NFL | 10 | 121 (19) | 12 | 41 | 3.4 (7) | 0 | 6 | 23 | 3.8 (9) | 0 | — | — | — | — | — | — | — | — | — | ki | 1 | 6 | 217 |

SAINDON, PAT Patrick Arthur, G, 6´3˝/273 lbs; Vanderbilt; B3/3/1961 Nice, France   **1986** NO 8 (1) **1987** Atl 3 (3) **NFL** 11 (4) [2 yrs]

SAIPAIA, BLAINE Blaine, T-G, 6´3˝/310 lbs; Colorado State; B8/25/1978 Oxnard, CA   **2004**†SL 8 (5, rt) **2005** SL 9 (3) **NFL** 17 (8) [2 yrs]

SALAAM, ABDUL Abdul, aka Larry J. Faulk, DT-NT-DE, 6´3˝/262 lbs; Kent State; 1976: NYJ, rnd 7; B2/12/1953 Brockton, AL   **1976** NYJ 14 (4) **1977** NYJ 14 (13, RDT)
1978 NYJ 15 (15, NT) **1979** NYJ 12 (12, LDT) **1980** NYJ 16 (16, LDT) **1981**†NYJ 16 (16, LDT) **1982**†NYJ 9 (9, LDT) **1983** NYJ 1 (0) **NFL** 97 (85) [8 yrs]

SALAAM, EPHRAIM Ephraim Mateen, T, 6´7˝/295 lbs; San Diego State; 1998: Atl, rnd 7; B6/19/1976 Chicago, IL   **1998**†Atl 16 (16, RT) **1999** Atl 16 (16, RT) **2000** Atl 14 (10, RT)
2001 Atl 14 (13, RT) **2002** Den 16 (16, LT) **2003**†Den 14 (14, LT) **2004** Jax 15 (12, LT) **2005** Jax 5 (2) **NFL** 110 (99) [8 yrs]

SALAAM, RASHAAN Rashaan Iman, RB, 6´1˝/224 lbs; Colorado; 1995: Chi, rnd 1; B10/8/1974 San Diego, CA

1995	ChiB	16 (12, RB)	296	1074	3.6 (42)	10	7	56	8.0 (18)	0	—	—	—	—	—	—	—	—	—	—	—	60	1202
1996	ChiB	12 (6, rb)	143	496	3.5 (32)	3	7	44	6.3 (11)	1	—	—	—	—	—	—	—	—	—	—	—	24	553
1997	ChiB	3 (3)	31	112	3.6 (17)	0	2	20	10.0 (18)	0	—	—	—	—	—	—	—	—	—	—	—	0	122
1999	Cle	2 (0)	1	2	2.0 (2)	0	—	—	—	—	—	—	—	—	—	—	—	—	—	—	—	0	2
NFL	4	33 (21)	471	1684	3.6 (42)	13	16	120	7.5 (18)	1	—	—	—	—	—	—	—	—	—	—	—	84	1879

SALATA, ANDY Andrew J., G, 5´10˝/188 lbs; Pittsburgh; B9/30/1905, D1/14/1978 Hancock, MI **[C]**   **1929** Ora 10 (10, RG) **1930** Nwk 10 (8, RG) **NFL** 20 (18) [2 yrs]

SALATA, PAUL Paul Thomas, E, 6´2˝/191 lbs; USC; B10/17/1926 Los Angeles, CA

1949	†SF-A	12 (1)	—	—	—	—	24	289	12.0	4	—	—	—	—	—	—	—	—	—	—	—	24	165
1950	SF	4	—	—	—	—	5	46	9.2 (17)	2	—	—	—	—	—	—	—	—	—	—	—	12	33
1950	Bal	7 (6, LE)	—	—	—	—	45	572	12.7 (57)	2	—	—	—	—	—	—	—	—	—	k	—	12	263
NFL	1	11 (6)	—	—	—	—	50	618	12.4 (57)	4	—	—	—	—	—	—	—	—	—	k	—	24	296

SALAVE'A, JOE Joe Fagaone, DT, 6´3˝/305 lbs; Arizona; 1998: Ten, rnd 4; B3/23/1975 Leone, American Samoa   **1998** Ten 13 (0) **1999**†Ten 10 (0) **2000**†Ten 15 (1)
2001 Ten 11 (0) **2003** SD 9 (1) **2004** Was 15 (9, LDT) **2005**†Was 14 (13, RDT) **NFL** 87 (24) [7 yrs]

SALDI, JAY John Jay, TE-WR, 6´3˝/225 lbs; South Carolina; B10/8/1954 White Plains, NY

1976	†Dal	13 (3)	1	19	19.0 (19)	0	1	6	6.0 (6)	0	—	—	—	—	—	—	—	—	—	k	—	0	-16
1977	†Dal	14	—	—	—	—	11	108	9.8 (23)	2	—	—	—	—	—	—	—	—	—	—	—	18	64
1978	Dal	4	—	—	—	—	3	8	2.7 (5)	2	—	—	—	—	—	—	—	—	—	k	—	12	-1
1979	†Dal	16	1	-1	-1.0 (-1)	0	14	181	12.9 (23)	1	—	—	—	—	—	—	—	—	—	—	—	6	95
1980	†Dal	16 (3)	—	—	—	—	25	311	12.4 (43)	1	—	—	—	—	—	—	—	—	—	k	—	6	169
1981	†Dal	16 (5, te)	—	—	—	—	8	82	10.3 (18)	1	—	—	—	—	—	—	—	—	—	—	—	6	46

YEAR	TEAM	G (GS, POS)	RUSH	YD	AVG (LG)	TD	REC	YD	AVG (LG)	TD	PASS	COMP	PCT	YD	AVG (LG)	TD	INT	SK	YD	QBR	KPR	OTD	PTS	TAY
1982	†Dal	5(0)	—	—	—	—	1	8	8.0(8)	0	—	—	—	—	—	—	—	—	—	—	—	—	0	4
1983	ChiB	13(6, te)	—	—	—	—	12	119	9.9(16)	0	—	—	—	—	—	—	—	—	—	—	—	—	0	60
1984	†ChiB	15(7, te)	—	—	—	—	9	90	10.0(20)	0	—	—	—	—	—	—	—	—	—	—	—	—	0	45
NFL	9	112(24)	2	18	9.0(19)	0	84	913	10.9(43)	7	—	—	—	—	—	—	—	—	—	—	k	1	48	497

SALEAUMUA, DAN Raymond Daniel, DT-NT-DE, 6´0˝/305 lbs; Arizona State; 1987: Det, rnd 7; B11/25/1964 San Diego, CA **1987** Det 9 (0) **1988** Det 16 (0) **1989** KC 16 (8, nt) **1990**†KC☆16 (16, NT) **1991**†KC 16 (16, NT) **1992**†KC 16 (16, RDT/nt) **1993**†KC 16 (16, RDE) **1994**†KC 14 (14, RDT) **1995**†KC★16 (16, RDT) **1996** KC 15 (14, RDT) **1997** Sea 16 (9, RDT) **1998** Sea 11 (6, ldt) **NFL** 177 (131) [12 yrs]

SALEH, TAREK Tarek Muhammad, LB, 6´1˝/240 lbs; Wisconsin; 1997: Car, rnd 4; B11/7/1974 Fairfield, CT **1997** Car 3 (0) **1998** Car 11 (1) **1999** Cle 16 (0) **2001** Cle 13 (0)

YEAR	TEAM	G (GS, POS)	RUSH	YD	AVG (LG)	TD	REC	YD	AVG (LG)	TD	PASS	COMP	PCT	YD	AVG (LG)	TD	INT	SK	YD	QBR	KPR	OTD	PTS	TAY
2000	Cle	16(0)	—	—	—	—	1	22	22.0(22)	0	—	—	—	—	—	—	—	—	—	—	k	—	0	-3
NFL	5	59(1)	—	—	—	—	1	22	22.0(22)	0	—	—	—	—	—	—	—	—	—	—	kS	—	0	-42

SALEM, ED Edward Joseph, DB-QB, 5´11˝/190 lbs; Alabama; 1951: Was, rnd 2; B8/28/1928 Tucson, AZ, D12/23/2001 Birmingham, AL

YEAR	TEAM	G (GS, POS)	RUSH	YD	AVG (LG)	TD	REC	YD	AVG (LG)	TD	PASS	COMP	PCT	YD	AVG (LG)	TD	INT	SK	YD	QBR	KPR	OTD	PTS	TAY
1951	Was	12(DB)	—	—	—	—	—	—	—	—	3	0	0.0	0	0.0	0	2	—	—	—	i	—	0	-79

SALEM, HARVEY Harvey Maynard, T-G, 6´6˝/283 lbs; California; 1983: Hou, rnd 2; B1/15/1961 Berkeley, CA **1983** Hou 16 (16, RT) **1984** Hou 16 (15, LT) **1985** Hou 14 (13, LT) **1986** Hou 1 (0) **1986** Det 13 (13, LG) **1987** Det 11 (11, RT) **1988** Det 16 (16, RT) **1989** Det 10 (8, RT) **1990** Det 15 (14, RT) **1991**†Den 10 (0) **1992** GB 4 (1) **NFL** 126 (107) [10 yrs]

SALEMI, SAM Sam, aka Smoke Salem, WB, 5´9˝/180 lbs; Columbia; St. John's (NY); Canisius; B6/4/1903 New York, NY, D7/7/1969 Brooklyn, NY **1928** NYY 5 (4), 6

SALISBURY, SEAN Richard Sean, QB, 6´5˝/225 lbs; USC; B3/9/1963 Long Beach, CA

YEAR	TEAM	G (GS, POS)	RUSH	YD	AVG (LG)	TD	REC	YD	AVG (LG)	TD	PASS	COMP	PCT	YD	AVG (LG)	TD	INT	SK	YD	QBR	KPR	OTD	PTS	TAY
1987	†Ind	2(0)	—	—	—	—	—	—	—	—	12	8	66.7	68	5.7(11)	0	2	2	18	—	—	—	0	-46
1992	†Min	10(4, qb)	11	0	0.0(4)	0	—	—	—	—	175	97	55.4	1203	6.9(51)	5	2	15	116	—	—	—	0	547
1993	†Min	11(4, qb)	10	-1	-0.1(6)	0	—	—	—	—	195	115	59.0	1413	7.2(55)	9	6	12	77	—	—	—	0	511
1994	†Min	1(1)	3	2	0.7(5)	0	—	—	—	—	34	16	47.1	156	4.6(38)	0	1	1	6	—	—	—	0	40
1996	SD	16(3, qb)	6	14	2.3(11)	0	—	—	—	—	161	82	50.9	984	6.1(56)	5	8	13	109	—	—	—	0	211
NFL	5	40(12)	30	15	0.5(11)	0	—	—	—	—	577	318	55.1	3824	6.6(56)	19	19	43	326	72.9	—	—	0	1262

SALLY, JEROME Jerome Eli, NT, 6´3˝/267 lbs; Missouri; B2/24/1959 Chicago, IL **1982** NYG 4 (1) **1983** NYG 16 (10, NT) **1984**†NYG 16 (1) **1985**†NYG 16 (1) **1986**†NYG 16 (1) **1987**†Ind 12 (8, NT) **1988** KC 3 (2) **NFL** 83 (24) [7 yrs]

SALMON, MIKE Michael William, DB, 6´1˝/210 lbs; USC; B12/27/1970 Long Beach, CA **1997** SF 1 (0)

SALONEN, BRIAN Brian Scott, LB-TE, 6´3˝/229 lbs; Montana; 1984: Dal, rnd 10; B7/29/1961 Glasgow, MT **1984** Dal 16 (0) **1985**†Dal 16 (0) **NFL** 32 (0) [2 yrs]

SALSBURY, JIM James Woodrow, G-T, 6´1˝/233 lbs; UCLA; 1955: Det, rnd 2; B8/8/1932 Los Angeles, CA, D3/29/2002 Paradise Valley, AZ **1955** Det 12 (RT) **1956** Det 11 (RG) **1957** GB 12 (RG)

YEAR	TEAM	G (GS, POS)	RUSH	YD	AVG (LG)	TD	REC	YD	AVG (LG)	TD	PASS	COMP	PCT	YD	AVG (LG)	TD	INT	SK	YD	QBR	KPR	OTD	PTS	TAY
1958	GB	12(LG)	0	3	(3)	0	—	—	—	—	—	—	—	—	—	—	—	—	—	—	—	—	0	3
NFL	4	47	0	3	(3)	0	—	—	—	—	—	—	—	—	—	—	—	—	—	—	k	—	0	1

SALSCHEIDER, JACK John Joseph, HB, 5´10˝/185 lbs; St. Thomas; 1949: NYG, rnd 8; B12/17/1924 St. Paul, MN, D5/14/1998 St. Croix Falls, MN

YEAR	TEAM	G (GS, POS)	RUSH	YD	AVG (LG)	TD	REC	YD	AVG (LG)	TD	PASS	COMP	PCT	YD	AVG (LG)	TD	INT	SK	YD	QBR	KPR	OTD	PTS	TAY
1949	NYG	11(1)	26	105	4.0(43)	0	4	9	2.3(13)	0	—	—	—	—	—	—	—	—	—	—	Pk	1	6	369

SALTER, BRYANT Bryant J., DB, 6´4˝/195 lbs; Pittsburgh; 1971: SD, rnd 5; B1/22/1950 Pittsburgh, PA **1971** SD 14 (SS) **1972** SD 14 (SS) **1973** SD 13 **1974**†Was 3 **1975** Was 14 (13, FS) **1976** Mia 12 (6, fs) **1976**†Bal 1 **NFL** 71 (19) [6 yrs]

SAM, P.K. P.K., WR, 6´3˝/195 lbs; Florida State; 2004: NE, rnd 5; B12/26/1983 Buford, GA **2004** NE 2 (0)

SAMPLE, CHUCK Charles E., FB, 5´9˝/205 lbs; Toledo; B1/5/1920 Green Bay, WI, D5/15/2001 Appleton, WI

YEAR	TEAM	G (GS, POS)	RUSH	YD	AVG (LG)	TD	REC	YD	AVG (LG)	TD	PASS	COMP	PCT	YD	AVG (LG)	TD	INT	SK	YD	QBR	KPR	OTD	PTS	TAY
1942	GB	9(1)	57	255	4.5(31)	4	6	35	5.8(10)	1	—	—	—	—	—	—	—	—	—	—	k	—	30	364
1945	GB	1(0)	2	2	1.0(3)	0	—	—	—	—	—	—	—	—	—	—	—	—	—	—	—	—	0	2
NFL	2	10(1)	59	257	4.4(31)	4	6	35	5.8(10)	1	—	—	—	—	—	—	—	—	—	—	k	—	30	366

SAMPLE, JOHNNY John B., DB, 6´1˝/203 lbs; Maryland-Eastern Shore; 1958: Bal, rnd 7; B6/15/1937 Cape Charles, VA, D4/26/2005 Philadelphia, PA **[I]** **1958**†Bal 12 **1959**†Bal 12 (5, db) **1961** Pit☆14 (LCB) **1962** Pit 6 **1963** Was 2 **1964** Was 14 (LCB) **1965** Was☆13 (LCB) **1966** NYJ-A☆13 (LCB) **1967** NYJ-A 14 (LCB) **1968**†NYJ-A☆14 (LCB)

YEAR	TEAM	G (GS, POS)	RUSH	YD	AVG (LG)	TD	REC	YD	AVG (LG)	TD	PASS	COMP	PCT	YD	AVG (LG)	TD	INT	SK	YD	QBR	KPR	OTD	PTS	TAY
1960	Bal☆	11(RS)	1	7	7.0(7)	0	—	—	—	—	—	—	—	—	—	—	—	—	—	—	kpi	1	6	304
NFL	11	125(5)	1	7	7.0(7)	0	—	—	—	—	—	—	—	—	—	—	—	—	—	—	kpi	6	36	1201

SAMPLETON, LAWRENCE Lawrence M., TE, 6´5˝/233 lbs; Texas; 1982: Phi, rnd 2; B9/25/1959 Waelder, TX

YEAR	TEAM	G (GS, POS)	RUSH	YD	AVG (LG)	TD	REC	YD	AVG (LG)	TD	PASS	COMP	PCT	YD	AVG (LG)	TD	INT	SK	YD	QBR	KPR	OTD	PTS	TAY
1982	Phi	9(0)	—	—	—	—	1	24	24.0(24)	0	—	—	—	—	—	—	—	—	—	—	—	—	0	12
1983	Phi	7(2)	—	—	—	—	2	28	14.0(19)	0	—	—	—	—	—	—	—	—	—	—	—	—	0	14
1984	Phi	16(0)	—	—	—	—	—	—	—	—	—	—	—	—	—	—	—	—	—	—	—	—	—	—
1987	Mia	3(3)	—	—	—	—	8	64	8.0(19)	0	—	—	—	—	—	—	—	—	—	—	—	—	0	32
NFL	4	35(5)	—	—	—	—	11	116	10.5(24)	0	—	—	—	—	—	—	—	—	—	—	—	—	0	58

SAMPSON, ARCHIE Archer M., G, 6´1˝/206 lbs; none; B10/29/1897 Muncie, IN, D10/1965 **1921** Day 9 (5, LG)

SAMPSON, CLINT Clinton Bernard, WR, 5´11˝/183 lbs; San Diego State; 1983: Den, rnd 3; B1/4/1961 Los Angeles, CA, D12/25/2005 Los Angeles, CA

YEAR	TEAM	G (GS, POS)	RUSH	YD	AVG (LG)	TD	REC	YD	AVG (LG)	TD	PASS	COMP	PCT	YD	AVG (LG)	TD	INT	SK	YD	QBR	KPR	OTD	PTS	TAY
1983	†Den	16(2)	—	—	—	—	10	200	20.0(49)	3	—	—	—	—	—	—	—	—	—	—	—	—	18	115
1984	†Den	12(3)	—	—	—	—	9	123	13.7(25)	1	—	—	—	—	—	—	—	—	—	—	—	—	6	67
1985	Den	16(0)	—	—	—	—	26	432	16.6(46)	4	—	—	—	—	—	—	—	—	—	—	—	—	24	236
1986	†Den	15(5, wr)	—	—	—	—	21	259	12.3(43)	0	—	—	—	—	—	—	—	—	—	—	—	—	0	130
NFL	4	59(10)	—	—	—	—	66	1014	15.4(49)	8	—	—	—	—	—	—	—	—	—	—	—	—	48	547

SAMPSON, EBER Eber, FB, 6´0˝/197 lbs; none; B1895, deceased **1921** Min 4 (4, FB), 12 **1922** Min 3 (3, FB) **1923** Min 7 (6, FB), 6 **NFL** 14 (13), 18 [3 yrs]

SAMPSON, GREG Ralph Gregory, T-DT-DE, 6´6˝/265 lbs; Stanford; 1972: Hou, rnd 1; B10/25/1950 Bellingham, WA **1972** Hou 14 **1973** Hou 13 **1974** Hou 14 (LT) **1975** Hou 14 (14, LT) **1976** Hou 8 (LT) **1977** Hou 14 (14, LT)

YEAR	TEAM	G (GS, POS)	RUSH	YD	AVG (LG)	TD	REC	YD	AVG (LG)	TD	PASS	COMP	PCT	YD	AVG (LG)	TD	INT	SK	YD	QBR	KPR	OTD	PTS	TAY
1978	†Hou☆	16(LT)	—	—	—	—	1	-4	-4.0(-4)	0	—	—	—	—	—	—	—	—	—	—	—	—	0	-2
NFL	7	93(28)	—	—	—	—	1	-4	-4.0(-4)	0	—	—	—	—	—	—	—	—	—	—	—	—	0	-2

SAMPSON, HOWARD Howard Earl, DB, 5´10˝/185 lbs; Arkansas; B7/7/1956 Baytown, TX **1978** GB 15 **1979** GB 16 **NFL** 31 [2 yrs]

SAMPSON, KEVIN Kevin M., T, 6´4˝/308 lbs; Syracuse; 2004: KC, rnd 7; B6/19/1981 Westwood, NJ **2004** KC 6 (0) **2005** KC 4 (1) **NFL** 10 (1) [2 yrs]

SAMS, B.J. Bradley Jamar, RB, 5´10˝/185 lbs; McNeese State; B10/29/1980 New Orleans, LA **[R]** **2005** Bal☆14 (0)

YEAR	TEAM	G (GS, POS)	RUSH	YD	AVG (LG)	TD	REC	YD	AVG (LG)	TD	PASS	COMP	PCT	YD	AVG (LG)	TD	INT	SK	YD	QBR	KPR	OTD	PTS	TAY
2004	Bal☆	16(1)	4	19	4.8(8)	1	1	2	2.0(2)	0	—	—	—	—	—	—	—	—	—	—	kp	2	18	716
NFL	2	30(1)	4	19	4.8(8)	1	1	2	2.0(2)	0	—	—	—	—	—	—	—	—	—	—	kp	2	18	1290

SAMS, RON Ronald F., C-G, 6´3˝/261 lbs; Pittsburgh; 1983: GB, rnd 6; B4/12/1961 Bridgeville, PA **1983** GB 3 (0) **1984** Min 12 (10, C) **NFL** 15 (10) [2 yrs]

SAMSON, MICHAEL Michael, DT, 6´3˝/294 lbs; Grambling State; B2/17/1973 Laurel, MS **1996**†Phi 2 (0)

SAMSON, SENECA Seneca Gadsden, HB, 5´8˝/160 lbs; Brown; B11/10/1899 New York, NY, D4/2/1930 Wakefield, RI **1926** Pro 2 (1)

SAMUEL, ASANTE Asante, DB, 5´10˝/185 lbs; Central Florida; 2003: NE, rnd 4; B1/6/1981 Fort Lauderdale, FL **2003**†NE 16 (1) **2004**†NE 13 (8, rcb) **2005**†NE 15 (15, LCB) **NFL** 44 (24) [3 yrs]

SAMUEL, DON Donald Allen, DB-HB, 5´11˝/190 lbs; Oregon State; 1946: LARm, rnd 3/1947: SF-A, rnd 4; B2/16/1924 Hood River, OR **1950** Pit 1

YEAR	TEAM	G (GS, POS)	RUSH	YD	AVG (LG)	TD	REC	YD	AVG (LG)	TD	PASS	COMP	PCT	YD	AVG (LG)	TD	INT	SK	YD	QBR	KPR	OTD	PTS	TAY
1949	Pit	5(1)	39	163	4.2(31)	1	1	2	2.0(2)	0	21	7	33.3	67	3.2(13)	0	1	—	—	—	pi	—	6	212
NFL	2	6(1)	39	163	4.2(31)	1	1	2	2.0(2)	0	21	7	33.3	67	3.2(13)	0	1	—	—	—	—	—	6	168

SAMUEL, KHARI Khari Iman Mitchell, LB, 6´3˝/240 lbs; Massachusetts; 1999: Chi, rnd 5; B10/14/1976 New York, NY **1999** ChiB 13 (1) **2000** ChiB 16 (0) **2001** ChiB 1 (0) **2001** Det 9 (0) **NFL** 39 (1) [3 yrs]

SAMUELS, CHRIS Christopher Auburn, RB, 5´10˝/202 lbs; Texas; 1991: SD, rnd 12; B5/16/1969 Montego Bay, Jamaica

YEAR	TEAM	G (GS, POS)	RUSH	YD	AVG (LG)	TD	REC	YD	AVG (LG)	TD	PASS	COMP	PCT	YD	AVG (LG)	TD	INT	SK	YD	QBR	KPR	OTD	PTS	TAY
1991	SD	3(0)	2	10	5.0(6)	0	2	33	16.5(29)	0	—	—	—	—	—	—	—	—	—	—	—	—	0	27

SAMUELS, CHRIS Chris, T, 6´5˝/310 lbs; Alabama; 2000: Was, rnd 1; B7/28/1977 Mobile, AL **2000** Was 16 (16, LT) **2001** Was★16 (16, LT) **2002** Was✧15 (15, LT) **2003** Was 13 (13, LT) **2004** Was 16 (16, LT) **2005**†Was✧16 (16, LT) **NFL** 92 (92) [6 yrs]

YEAR	TEAM	G(GS, POS)	RUSH	YD	AVG(LG)	TD	REC	YD	AVG(LG)	TD	PASS	COMP	PCT	YD	AVG(LG)	TD	INT	SK	YD	QBR	KPR	OTD	PTS	TAY
SAMUELS, TERRY Terrance Eugene, TE, 6´2˝/254 lbs; Kentucky; 1994: Arz, rnd 6; B9/27/1970 Louisville, KY																								
1994	Arz	16(5, te)	1	1	1.0(1)	0	8	57	7.1(17)	0	—	—	—	—	—	—	—	—	—	—	k	—	0	21
1995	Arz	4(1)	—	—	—	—	2	19	9.5(12)	0	—	—	—	—	—	—	—	—	—	—	—	—	0	10
NFL	2	20(6)	1	1	1.0(1)	0	10	76	7.6(17)	0	—	—	—	—	—	—	—	—	—	—	k	—	0	30
SAMUELS, TONY Andre Antonio, TE, 6´4˝/229 lbs; Florida A&M; Bethune-Cookman; 1977: KC, rnd 4; B12/30/1954 Tampa, FL, D9/12/2001 Tampa, FL																								
1977	KC	14(1)	—	—	—	—	5	65	13.0(32)	0	—	—	—	—	—	—	—	—	—	—	—	—	0	33
1978	KC	16	—	—	—	—	6	97	16.2(38)	0	—	—	—	—	—	—	—	—	—	—	—	—	0	49
1979	KC	16(13, TE)	—	—	—	—	14	147	10.5(30)	0	—	—	—	—	—	—	—	—	—	—	—	1	6	74
1980	KC	4(4)	—	—	—	—	8	110	13.8(34)	2	—	—	—	—	—	—	—	—	—	—	—	—	12	65
1980	TB	6(3)	—	—	—	—	—	—	—	—	—	—	—	—	—	—	—	—	—	—	k	—	0	-5
NFL	4	56(21)	—	—	—	—	33	419	12.7(38)	2	—	—	—	—	—	—	—	—	—	—	k	1	18	215
SAMUELSON, CARL Carl Clinton, DT-T, 6´4˝/250 lbs; Nebraska; 1947: LARm, rnd 10/1948: ChiR-A, rnd 2; B4/11/1923 Grand Island, NE, D8/17/1995 Lincoln, NE **1948** Pit 11 (0) **1949** Pit 12 (0) **1950** Pit☆8 (RDT) **1951** Pit 12 **NFL** 43 [4 yrs]																								
SANBORN, WILLIAM William, E, none; B1899, deceased **1921** Ton 1 (1, RE)																								
SANCHEZ, DAVIS Davis, DB, 5´10˝/190 lbs; Oregon; B8/7/1974 Vancouver, Canada **2001** SD 12 (2) **2002** SD 10 (0) **NFL** 22 (2) [2 yrs]																								
SANCHEZ, JOHN John Claude, T, 6´3˝/239 lbs; Redlands; San Francisco; 1944: NYG, rnd 9; B10/12/1920 Los Angeles, CA, D9/11/1992 Hayward, CA **1947** Det 3 (0) **1947** Was 4 (4) **1948** Was 12 (12, LT) **1949** Was 2 (1) **1949** NYG 8 (1) **1950**†NYG 12 (RT) **NFL** 41 (18) [4 yrs]																								
SANCHEZ, LUPE Guadalupe Ledezma, DB, 5´10˝/192 lbs; UCLA; 1984: KC, rnd S2; B10/28/1961 Tulare, CA **1986** Pit 11 (4) **1987** Pit 12 (3) **1988** Pit 16 (2) **NFL** 39 (9) [3 yrs]																								
SANDBERG, ARTIE Arthur W., BB-WB, /192 lbs; none; B9/13/1899, MN, D7/2/1983 Elbow Lake, MN **1926** LA 5 (2) **1929** Min 3 (2) **NFL** 8 (4) [2 yrs]																								
SANDBERG, SANDY Sigurd E., T, 6´2˝/228 lbs; Iowa Wesleyan; B6/14/1910 Eddyville, IA, D4/10/1989 St. Louis, MO **1934** SL 3 (3, LT) **1935** Pit 11 (9, LT) **1936** Pit 12 (10, LT) **1937** Pit 7 (6, LT) **1937** Bkn 3 (1) **NFL** 36 (29) [4 yrs]																								
SANDEFUR, DICK Wayne Thomas, FB, 5´10˝/195 lbs; Purdue; 1936: Pit, rnd 5; B8/1/1912 Evansville, IN, D5/15/1998 Metairie, LA **1937** Pit 1 (0)																								
1936	Pit	8(0)	7	13	1.9	0	—	—	—	—	—	—	—	—	—	—	—	—	—	—	—	—	0	13
NFL	2	9(0)	7	13	1.9	0	—	—	—	—	—	—	—	—	—	—	—	—	—	—	—	—	0	13
SANDEMAN, BILL William Stewart, T-DT, 6´6˝/252 lbs; Pacific; B11/30/1942 Providence, RI **1966** Dal 8 **1967** NO 2 **1967** Atl 11 **1968** Atl 4 **1969** Atl 13 (LT) **1970** Atl 6 **1971** Atl 14 (LT) **1972** Atl 14 (LT) **1973** Atl 12 (LT) **NFL** 84 [8 yrs]																								
SANDER, B.J. B.J., P, 6´3˝/212 lbs; Ohio State; 2004: GB, rnd 3; B7/29/1980 Cincinnati, OH																								
2005	GB	14(0)	1	-11	-11.0(-11)	0	—	—	—	—	1	1	100.0	4	4.0(4)	0	0	—	—	—	P	—	0	-9
SANDER, MARK Mark Leonard, LB, 6´2˝/232 lbs; Louisville; B3/21/1968 Louisville, KY **1992** Mia 12 (2)																								
SANDERS, BARRY Barry David, RB, 5´8˝/203 lbs; Oklahoma State; 1989: Det, rnd 1; B7/16/1968 Wichita, KS; HOF 2004																								
1989	Det★	15(13, RB)	280	**1470**	5.3(34)	14	24	282	11.8(46)	0	—	—	—	—	—	—	—	—	—	—	k	—	84	1794
1990	Det★	16(16, RB)	255	**1304**	5.1(45)	13	36	480	13.3(47)	3	—	—	—	—	—	—	—	—	—	—	—	—	96	1689
1991	†Det★	15(15, RB)	342	1548	4.5(69)	**16**	41	307	7.5(34)	1	—	—	—	—	—	—	—	—	—	—	—	—	102	**1867**
1992	Det★	16(16, RB)	312	1352	4.3(55)	9	29	225	7.8(48)	1	1	0	0.0	0	0.0	0	0	—	—	—	—	—	60	1560
1993	†Det★	11(11, RB)	243	1115	4.6(42)	3	36	205	5.7(17)	0	—	—	—	—	—	—	—	—	—	—	—	—	18	1248
1994	†Det★	16(16, RB)	331	**1883**	**5.7**(**85**)	7	44	283	6.4(22)	1	—	—	—	—	—	—	—	—	—	—	—	—	48	2100
1995	†Det★	16(16, RB)	314	1500	4.8(75)	11	48	398	8.3(40)	1	2	1	50.0	11	5.5(11)	0	0	—	—	—	—	—	72	1820
1996	Det★	16(16, RB)	307	**1553**	**5.1**(**54**)	11	24	147	6.1(28)	0	1	0	0.0	0	0.0	0	1	—	—	—	—	—	66	1697
1997	†Det★	16(16, RB)	**335**	**2053**	**6.1**(**82**)	**11**	33	305	9.2(66)	3	—	—	—	—	—	—	—	—	—	—	—	—	84	**2331**
1998	Det★	16(16, RB)	343	1491	4.3(73)	4	37	289	7.8(44)	0	—	—	—	—	—	—	—	—	—	—	—	—	24	1676
NFL	10	153(151)	3062	15269	5.0(85)	99	352	2921	8.3(66)	10	4	1	25.0	11	2.8(11)	0	1	—	—	—	k	—	654	17778
SANDERS, BOB Robert Joe, LB, 6´3˝/235 lbs; North Texas; 1966: Atl, rnd 9; B6/9/1943 Dallas, TX **1967** Atl 9																								
SANDERS, BOB Demond, DB, 5´8˝/200 lbs; Iowa; 2004: Ind, rnd 2; B2/24/1981 Erie, PA **2004**†Ind 6 (4) **2005**†Ind★14 (14, FS) **NFL** 20 (18) [2 yrs]																								
SANDERS, BRANDON Brandon Christopher, DB, 5´9˝/185 lbs; Arizona; B6/10/1973 San Diego, CA **1997**†NYG 12 (0) **1998** NYG 13 (0) **1999** NYG 9 (2) **NFL** 34 (2) [3 yrs]																								
SANDERS, CHARLIE Charles Alvin, TE, 6´4˝/225 lbs; Minnesota; 1968: Det, rnd 3; B8/25/1946 Richland, NC																								
1968	Det✧	14(TE)	2	3	1.5(2)	0	40	533	13.3(25)	1	—	—	—	—	—	—	—	—	—	—	—	—	6	275
1969	Det★	14(TE)	1	-8	-8.0(-8)	0	42	656	15.6(47)	3	—	—	—	—	—	—	—	—	—	—	—	—	18	335
1970	†Det★	14(TE)	—	—	—	—	40	544	13.6(34)	6	—	—	—	—	—	—	—	—	—	—	—	—	36	302
1971	Det★	13(TE)	—	—	—	—	31	502	16.2(49)	5	—	—	—	—	—	—	—	—	—	—	—	—	30	276
1972	Det	9(TE)	—	—	—	—	27	416	15.4(38)	2	—	—	—	—	—	—	—	—	—	—	—	—	12	218
1973	Det	14(TE)	1	-1	-1.0(-1)	0	28	433	15.5(54)	2	—	—	—	—	—	—	—	—	—	—	—	—	12	226
1974	Det★	14(14, TE)	—	—	—	—	42	532	12.7(47)	3	—	—	—	—	—	—	—	—	—	—	—	—	18	281
1975	Det★	13(12, TE)	—	—	—	—	37	486	13.1(32)	3	—	—	—	—	—	—	—	—	—	—	—	—	18	258
1976	Det★	13(13, TE)	—	—	—	—	35	545	15.6(36)	5	—	—	—	—	—	—	—	—	—	—	—	—	30	298
1977	Det	10	—	—	—	—	14	170	12.1(24)	1	—	—	—	—	—	—	—	—	—	—	—	—	6	90
NFL	10	128(39)	4	-6	-1.5(2)	0	336	4817	14.3(54)	31	—	—	—	—	—	—	—	—	—	—	—	—	186	2558
SANDERS, CHRIS Christopher Dwayne, WR, 6´1˝/188 lbs; Ohio State; 1995: Hou, rnd 3; B5/8/1972 Denver, CO																								
1995	Hou	16(10, WR)	2	-19	-9.5(-6)	0	35	823	**23.5**(**76**)	9	—	—	—	—	—	—	—	—	—	—	—	—	54	438
1996	Hou	16(15, WR)	—	—	—	—	48	882	**18.4**(**83**)	4	—	—	—	—	—	—	—	—	—	—	—	—	24	461
1997	Ten	15(14, WR)	1	-8	-8.0(-8)	0	31	498	16.1(55)	3	—	—	—	—	—	—	—	—	—	—	—	—	18	256
1998	Ten	14(1)	1	-9	-9.0(-9)	0	5	136	27.2(46)	0	—	—	—	—	—	—	—	—	—	—	—	—	0	59
1999	†Ten	16(0)	—	—	—	—	20	336	16.8(48)	1	—	—	—	—	—	—	—	—	—	—	—	—	6	173
2000	†Ten	16(14, WR)	—	—	—	—	33	536	16.2(54)	0	—	—	—	—	—	—	—	—	—	—	—	—	0	268
2001	Ten	4(0)	—	—	—	—	5	74	14.8(22)	0	—	—	—	—	—	—	—	—	—	—	—	—	0	37
NFL	7	97(54)	4	-36	-9.0(-6)	0	177	3285	18.6(83)	17	—	—	—	—	—	—	—	—	—	—	—	—	102	1692
SANDERS, CHRIS Christopher, WR, 6´2˝/217 lbs; Texas A&M; B4/22/1973 **1997** Was 1 (0)																								
SANDERS, CHUCK Charles Samuel, RB, 6´1˝/233 lbs; Slippery Rock; 1986: SD, rnd 11; B4/24/1964 Pittsburgh, PA																								
1986	Pit	14(2)	4	12	3.0(13)	0	2	19	9.5(10)	0	—	—	—	—	—	—	—	—	—	—	k	—	0	50
1987	Pit	5(0)	11	65	5.9(14)	1	1	11	11.0(11)	0	—	—	—	—	—	—	—	—	—	—	—	—	6	81
NFL	2	19(2)	15	77	5.1(14)	1	3	30	10.0(11)	0	—	—	—	—	—	—	—	—	—	—	k	—	6	130
SANDERS, CLARENCE Clarence, LB, 6´4˝/228 lbs; Cincinnati; 1976: SD, rnd 17; B12/28/1952 Montgomery, AL **1978** KC 16 **1980** KC 1 (0) **NFL** 17 [2 yrs]																								
SANDERS, DARNELL Darnell, TE, 6´6˝/270 lbs; Ohio State; 2002: Cle, rnd 4; B3/16/1979 Cleveland, OH																								
2002	†Cle	10(3)	—	—	—	—	3	23	7.7(14)	1	—	—	—	—	—	—	—	—	—	—	—	—	6	17
2003	Cle	16(12, TE)	—	—	—	—	15	95	6.3(12)	1	—	—	—	—	—	—	—	—	—	—	—	—	6	53
2004	Atl	2(0)	—	—	—	—	—	—	—	—	—	—	—	—	—	—	—	—	—	—	—	—	—	—
NFL	3	28(15)	—	—	—	—	18	118	6.6(14)	2	—	—	—	—	—	—	—	—	—	—	—	—	12	69
SANDERS, DARYL Daryl Theodore, T, 6´5˝/250 lbs; Ohio State; 1963: Det, rnd 1/KC, rnd 4; B4/24/1941 Canton, OH **1963** Det 14 (14, LT) **1964** Det 14 (14, LT) **1966** Det 14 (14, LT)																								
1965	Det	14(14, LT)	1	2	2.0(2)	0	—	—	—	—	—	—	—	—	—	—	—	—	—	—	—	—	0	2
NFL	4	56(56)	1	2	2.0(2)	0	—	—	—	—	—	—	—	—	—	—	—	—	—	—	—	—	0	2
SANDERS, DEION Deion Luwynn 'Prime Time', DB-WR, 6´1˝/195 lbs; Florida State; 1989: Atl, rnd 1; B8/9/1967 Fort Myers, FL **[RI]**																								
1989	Atl	15(10, RCB/lcb)	—	—	—	—	1	-8	-8.0(-8)	0	—	—	—	—	—	—	—	—	—	—	kpi	1	6	400
1990	Atl	16(16, RCB)	—	—	—	—	—	—	—	—	—	—	—	—	—	—	—	—	—	—	kpi	3	18	539
1991	†Atl★	15(15, RCB)	—	—	—	—	1	17	17.0(17)	0	—	—	—	—	—	—	—	—	—	—	kpiS	2	12	369
1992	Atl★	13(12, RCB)	1	-4	-4.0(-4)	0	3	45	15.0(37)	1	—	—	—	—	—	—	—	—	—	—	kpi	2	18	577

YEAR	TEAM	G (GS, POS)	RUSH	YD	AVG (LG)	TD	REC	YD	AVG (LG)	TD	PASS	COMP	PCT	YD	AVG (LG)	TD	INT	SK	YD	QBR	KPR	OTD	PTS	TAY
1993	Atl★	11 (10, RCB)	—	—	—	—	6	106	17.7 (70)	1	1	0	0.0	0	0.0	0	0	—	—	—	kpi	—	6	189
1994	†SF★	14 (12, RCB)	—	—	—	—	—	—	—	—	—	—	—	—	—	—	—	—	—	—	i	3	18	303
1995	†Dal☆	9 (9, LCB)	2	9	4.5 (8)	0	2	25	12.5 (19)	0	—	—	—	—	—	—	—	—	—	—	kpi	—	0	95
1996	†Dal★	16 (15, RCB/wr)	3	2	0.7 (3)	0	36	475	13.2 (41)	1	—	—	—	—	—	—	—	—	—	—	pi	1	12	237
1997	Dal★	13 (12, RCB)	1	-11	-11.0 (-11)	0	—	—	—	—	—	—	—	—	—	—	—	—	—	—	kpi	2	12	325
1998	†Dal★	11 (11, RCB)	—	—	—	—	7	100	14.3 (55)	0	—	—	—	—	—	—	—	—	—	—	kpi	3	18	464
1999	†Dal★	14 (14, RCB)	—	—	—	—	4	24	6.0 (9)	0	1	0	0.0	0	0.0	0	0	—	—	—	kpi	1	6	230
2000	Was	16 (15, RCB)	—	—	—	—	—	—	—	—	—	—	—	—	—	—	—	—	—	—	kpi	—	0	115
2004	Bal	9 (2)	1	-10	-10.0 (-10)	0	—	—	—	—	—	—	—	—	—	—	—	—	—	—	pi	1	6	88
2005	Bal	16 (4)	1	0	0.0 (0)	0	—	—	—	—	—	—	—	—	—	—	—	—	—	—	pi	—	0	47
NFL	14	188 (157)	9	-14	-1.6 (8)	0	60	784	13.1 (70)	3	2	0	0.0	0	0.0	0	0	—	—	—	kpiS	19	132	3976

SANDERS, ERIC Eric Downer, T-G-C, 6´6˝/277 lbs; Nevada-Reno; 1981: Atl, rnd 5; B10/22/1958 Reno, NV **1981** Atl 16 (6, rt) **1982**†Atl 9 (0) **1983** Atl 16 (0) **1984** Atl 10 (2) **1985** Atl 16 (7, lt) **1986** Atl 8 (3) **1986** Det 3 (0) **1987** Det 12 (0) **1988** Det 16 (0) **1989** Det 16 (7, rt) **1990** Det 16 (2) **1991** Det 14 (14, RT) **1992** Det 6 (1) **NFL** 158 (42) [12 yrs]

SANDERS, FRANK Frank Vondel, WR, 6´2˝/215 lbs; Auburn; 1995: Arz, rnd 2; B2/17/1973 Fort Lauderdale, FL

YEAR	TEAM	G (GS, POS)	RUSH	YD	AVG (LG)	TD	REC	YD	AVG (LG)	TD	PASS	COMP	PCT	YD	AVG (LG)	TD	INT	SK	YD	QBR	KPR	OTD	PTS	TAY
1995	Arz	16 (15, WR)	1	1	1.0 (1)	0	52	883	17.0 (48)	2	—	—	—	—	—	—	—	—	—	—	—	—	16	453
1996	Arz	16 (16, WR)	2	-4	-2.0 (1)	0	69	813	11.8 (34)	4	—	—	—	—	—	—	—	—	—	—	—	—	24	423
1997	Arz	16 (16, WR)	1	5	5.0 (5)	0	75	1017	13.6 (70)	4	1	1	100.0	26	26.0 (26)	0	0	—	—	—	—	—	26	547
1998	†Arz	16 (16, WR)	4	0	0.0 (7)	0	**89**	1145	12.9 (42)	3	—	—	—	—	—	—	—	—	—	—	—	—	18	588
1999	Arz	16 (16, WR)	—	—	—	—	79	954	12.1 (63)	1	1	0	0.0	0	0.0	0	0	—	—	—	—	—	6	482
2000	Arz	16 (16, WR)	—	—	—	—	54	749	13.9 (53)	6	—	—	—	—	—	—	—	—	—	—	—	—	36	405
2001	Arz	15 (13, WR)	—	—	—	—	41	618	15.1 (68)	2	1	0	0.0	0	0.0	0	0	—	—	—	—	—	12	319
2002	Arz	12 (12, WR)	3	2	0.7 (5)	0	34	400	11.8 (37)	2	—	—	—	—	—	—	—	—	—	—	—	—	14	212
2003	†Bal	13 (0)	—	—	—	—	14	170	12.1 (44)	0	—	—	—	—	—	—	—	—	—	—	—	—	0	85
NFL	9	136 (120)	11	4	0.4 (7)	0	507	6749	13.3 (70)	24	3	1	33.3	26	8.7 (26)	0	0	—	—	—	—	—	152	3512

SANDERS, GENE Eugene, T-G-DE-NT, 6´3˝/273 lbs; Washington; Texas A&M; 1979: TB, rnd 8; B11/10/1956 New Orleans, LA **1979**†TB 16 **1980** TB 11 (3) **1981**†TB 16 (14, LT) **1982** TB 4 (2) **1983** TB 12 (7, lt) **1984** TB 16 (14, LT) **1985** TB 2 (0) **NFL** 77 (40) [7 yrs]

SANDERS, GLENELL Glenell, LB, 6´1˝/240 lbs; Louisiana Tech; B11/4/1966 New Orleans, LA **1990**†ChiB 2 (0) **1991** LARm 16 (1) **1994** Den 1 (0) **1995** Ind 9 (0) **NFL** 28 (1) [4 yrs]

SANDERS, JACK Jack, G, 6´0˝/219 lbs; SMU; 1939: NYG, rnd 17; B3/11/1917 San Antonio, TX, D10/26/1991 Arnasas Pass, TX **[K]** **1940** Pit 10 (7, LG) **1941** Pit 11 (3) **1942** Pit 9 (9, LG) **1945** Phi 3 (0) **NFL** 33 (19) [4 yrs]

SANDERS, JAMES James, DB, 5´10˝/207 lbs; Fresno State; 2005: NE, rnd 4; B11/11/1983 Porterville, CA **2005**†NE 10 (2)

SANDERS, JOE Joseph, G-E, 5´10˝/250 lbs; none; B5/26/1901 Evansville, IN, D4/1979 Smithfield, NC **1922** Evv 2 (2, RG)

SANDERS, JOHN John Maurice, DB, 6´1˝/175 lbs; South Dakota; B1/11/1950 Chicago, IL **1974** NE 14 (10, LCB) **1975** NE 14 (14, FS) **1976** NE 2 **1977** Phi 14 (12, FS) **1978**†Phi 15 (15, FS) **1979** Phi 1 **NFL** 60 (51) [6 yrs]

SANDERS, KEN Kenneth Roy, DE, 6´5˝/240 lbs; Howard Payne; 1972: Det, rnd 3; B8/22/1950 Valley Mills, TX **1972** Det 6 **1973** Det 14 (14, LDE) **1974** Det 14 (14, LDE) **1975** Det 14 (14, LDE) **1976** Det 14 (14, LDE) **1977** Det 11 (11, LDE) **1978** Det 7 (7, lde) **1979** Det 5 **1980** Min 6 (0) **1981** Min 9 (0) **NFL** 100 (74) [10 yrs]

SANDERS, LEWIS Lewis Lindell, DB, 6´1˝/210 lbs; Maryland; 2000: Cle, rnd 4; B6/22/1978 Staten Island, NY **2000** Cle 11 (1) **2002**†Cle 16 (2) **2003** Cle 9 (1) **2004** Cle 16 (5, rcb) **2005** Hou 12 (3) **NFL** 64 (12) [5 yrs]

SANDERS, LONNIE Lonnie J., DB, 6´3˝/207 lbs; Michigan State; 1963: Was, rnd 2/Den, rnd 10; B11/6/1941 Detroit, MI **1963** Was 14 (RCB) **1964** Was 14 (RCB) **1965** Was 7 (RCB) **1966** Was 9 **1967** Was 13 **1968** SL 13 (RCB) **1969** SL 1 **NFL** 71 [7 yrs]

SANDERS, PAUL Paul E., HB, 5´11˝/192 lbs; Utah State; B12/15/1918 Otto, WY

YEAR	TEAM	G (GS, POS)	RUSH	YD	AVG (LG)	TD	REC	YD	AVG (LG)	TD	PASS	COMP	PCT	YD	AVG (LG)	TD	INT	SK	YD	QBR	KPR	OTD	PTS	TAY
1944	Bos	6 (1)	6	4	0.7 (8)	0	4	5	1.3 (5)	0	—	—	—	—	—	—	—	—	—	—	—	—	0	7

SANDERS, RICKY Ricky Wayne, WR, 5´11˝/182 lbs; Southwest Texas State; 1984: NE, rnd S1; B8/30/1962 Temple, TX

YEAR	TEAM	G (GS, POS)	RUSH	YD	AVG (LG)	TD	REC	YD	AVG (LG)	TD	PASS	COMP	PCT	YD	AVG (LG)	TD	INT	SK	YD	QBR	KPR	OTD	PTS	TAY
1986	†Was	10 (3)	—	—	—	—	14	286	20.4 (71)	2	—	—	—	—	—	—	—	—	—	—	—	—	12	153
1987	†Was	12 (5, wr)	1	-4	-4.0 (-4)	0	37	630	17.0 (57)	3	—	—	—	—	—	—	—	—	—	—	k	—	18	384
1988	Was	16 (4)	2	14	7.0 (7)	0	73	1148	15.7 (55)	**12**	—	—	—	—	—	—	—	—	—	—	k	—	72	725
1989	Was	16 (12, WR)	4	19	4.8 (13)	0	80	1138	14.2 (68)	4	1	1	100.0	32	32.0 (32)	0	0	—	—	—	kp	—	24	625
1990	†Was	16 (6, WR)	4	17	4.3 (12)	0	56	727	13.0 (38)	3	—	—	—	—	—	—	—	—	—	—	k	—	18	403
1991	†Was	16 (7, wr)	7	47	6.7 (17)	1	45	580	12.9 (45)	5	—	—	—	—	—	—	—	—	—	—	—	—	36	372
1992	†Was	15 (5, wr)	4	-6	-1.5 (3)	0	51	707	13.9 (62)	3	—	—	—	—	—	—	—	—	—	—	—	—	18	363
1993	Was	16 (11, WR)	1	7	7.0 (7)	0	58	638	11.0 (50)	4	—	—	—	—	—	—	—	—	—	—	—	—	24	346
1994	Atl	14 (12, WR)	—	—	—	—	67	599	8.9 (28)	1	—	—	—	—	—	—	—	—	—	—	—	—	6	305
1995	Atl	3 (1)	—	—	—	—	2	24	12.0 (21)	0	—	—	—	—	—	—	—	—	—	—	—	—	0	12
NFL	10	134 (66)	23	94	4.1 (17)	1	483	6477	13.4 (71)	37	1	1	100.0	32	32.0 (32)	0	0	—	—	—	kp	—	228	3687

SANDERS, SPEC Orban Eugene, TB-DB-HB, 6´1˝/196 lbs; Texas; 1942: Was, rnd 1; B1/26/1918 Temple, OK, D7/6/2003 Lawton, OK

YEAR	TEAM	G (GS, POS)	RUSH	YD	AVG (LG)	TD	REC	YD	AVG (LG)	TD	PASS	COMP	PCT	YD	AVG (LG)	TD	INT	SK	YD	QBR	KPR	OTD	PTS	TAY
1946	†NYY-A☆	13 (9, TB)	**140**	**709**	5.1	**6**	17	259	15.2	3	79	33	41.8	411	5.2 (47)	4	9	—	—	—	Pkpi	3	72	**1242**
1947	†NYY-A☆	14 (12, TB)	**231**	**1432**	6.2	**18**	1	13	13.0 (13)	0	171	93	54.4	1442	8.4 (55)	14	17	—	—	—	Pkpi	1	**114**	**2185**
1948	NYY-A☆	13 (9, TB)	**169**	759	4.5	9	—	—	—	—	168	78	46.4	918	5.5 (57)	5	11	—	—	—	Pkpi	—	54	1057
AAFC	3	40 (30)	540	2900	5.4	33	18	272	15.1 (13)	3	418	204	48.8	2771	6.6 (57)	23	37	—	—	—	Pkpi	4	240	4484
1950	NYY★	12 (DB)	—	—	—	—	—	—	—	—	3	2	66.7	58	19.3 (29)	0	0	—	—	—	Ppi	—	0	226

SANDERS, THOMAS Thomas Derrick, RB, 5´11˝/203 lbs; Texas A&M; 1985: Chi, rnd 9; B1/4/1962 Giddings, TX **[R]**

YEAR	TEAM	G (GS, POS)	RUSH	YD	AVG (LG)	TD	REC	YD	AVG (LG)	TD	PASS	COMP	PCT	YD	AVG (LG)	TD	INT	SK	YD	QBR	KPR	OTD	PTS	TAY
1985	†ChiB	15 (0)	25	104	4.2 (28)	1	1	9	9.0 (9)	0	—	—	—	—	—	—	—	—	—	—	k	—	6	114
1986	†ChiB	16 (1)	27	224	8.3 (75)	5	2	18	9.0 (18)	0	—	—	—	—	—	—	—	—	—	—	k	—	30	352
1987	†ChiB	12 (0)	23	122	5.3 (17)	1	3	53	17.7 (25)	0	—	—	—	—	—	—	—	—	—	—	k	—	6	208
1988	†ChiB	16 (0)	95	332	3.5 (20)	3	9	94	10.4 (39)	0	—	—	—	—	—	—	—	—	—	—	k	—	18	462
1989	ChiB	16 (0)	41	127	3.1 (19)	0	3	28	9.3 (16)	1	—	—	—	—	—	—	—	—	—	—	k	1	12	302
1990	†Phi	10 (0)	56	208	3.7 (39)	1	2	20	10.0 (12)	0	—	—	—	—	—	—	—	—	—	—	k	—	6	302
1991	Phi	5 (0)	54	122	2.3 (16)	1	8	62	7.8 (14)	0	—	—	—	—	—	—	—	—	—	—	k	—	6	173
NFL	7	90 (1)	321	1239	3.9 (75)	12	28	284	10.1 (39)	1	—	—	—	—	—	—	—	—	—	—	k	1	84	1912

SANDERSON, REGGIE Reginald John, RB, 5´10˝/206 lbs; Stanford; B11/4/1950 Galveston, TX

YEAR	TEAM	G (GS, POS)	RUSH	YD	AVG (LG)	TD	REC	YD	AVG (LG)	TD	PASS	COMP	PCT	YD	AVG (LG)	TD	INT	SK	YD	QBR	KPR	OTD	PTS	TAY
1973	ChiB	2	3	8	2.7 (6)	0	5	23	4.6 (9)	0	—	—	—	—	—	—	—	—	—	—	k	—	0	34

SANDERSON, SCOTT Scott Michael, T, 6´6˝/295 lbs; Washington State; 1997: Ten, rnd 3; B7/25/1974 Walnut Creek, CA **1997** Ten 10 (0) **1998** Ten 16 (3) **1999** Ten 3 (3) **2000** Ten 9 (0) **2002** NO 6 (0) **2003** ChiB 1 (0) **NFL** 45 (6) [6 yrs]

SANDHAM, TODD Todd, G, 6´3˝/255 lbs; Northeastern; B12/3/1963 **1987** NE 2 (0)

SANDIFER, BILL William Patrick, DT-DE, 6´6˝/278 lbs; UCLA; 1974: SF, rnd 1; B1/5/1952 Quantico, VA **1974** SF 4 **1975** SF 13 (12, LDT) **1976** SF 13 **1977** Sea 1 (1) **1978** Sea 15 (13, RDT/lde) **NFL** 46 (26) [5 yrs]

SANDIFER, DAN Daniel Padgett, DB-HB, 6´1˝/190 lbs; LSU; 1948: Was, rnd 5/Bal-A, rnd 4; B3/1/1927 Shreveport, LA, D8/15/1987 Shreveport, LA **[I]** **1950** SF 2 **1950** Phi 5 **1952** GB 12 (DB) **1953** ChiC 3 **1953** GB 1

YEAR	TEAM	G (GS, POS)	RUSH	YD	AVG (LG)	TD	REC	YD	AVG (LG)	TD	PASS	COMP	PCT	YD	AVG (LG)	TD	INT	SK	YD	QBR	KPR	OTD	PTS	TAY
1948	Was	12 (7, RH)	18	67	3.7 (13)	0	9	181	20.1 (**86**)	1	—	—	—	—	—	—	—	—	—	—	kpi	3	24	726
1949	Was	12 (0)	20	64	3.2 (21)	0	19	293	15.4 (35)	3	—	—	—	—	—	—	—	—	—	—	kpi	—	18	550
1950	Det	5	1	3	3.0 (3)	0	—	—	—	—	—	—	—	—	—	—	—	—	—	—	i	—	0	20
1951	Phi	12	35	113	3.2 (13)	1	2	36	18.0 (30)	1	—	—	—	—	—	—	—	—	—	—	kpi	—	12	263
NFL	6	64 (7)	74	247	3.3 (21)	1	30	510	17.0 (86)	5	—	—	—	—	—	—	—	—	—	—	kpi	3	54	1701

SANDIG, CURT Curtis Walter, HB, 5´10˝/170 lbs; St. Mary's (TX); 1942: Pit, rnd 5; B7/12/1918 Mart, TX

YEAR	TEAM	G (GS, POS)	RUSH	YD	AVG (LG)	TD	REC	YD	AVG (LG)	TD	PASS	COMP	PCT	YD	AVG (LG)	TD	INT	SK	YD	QBR	KPR	OTD	PTS	TAY
1942	Pit	11 (8, HB)	50	116	2.3 (39)	3	6	103	17.2 (38)	0	4	2	50.0	10	2.5 (8)	0	0	—	—	—	Pkpi	1	24	457
1946	Buf-A	9 (1)	22	52	2.4	1	2	15	7.5	0	—	—	—	—	—	—	—	—	—	—	Pkp	—	6	93

YEAR	TEAM	G(GS, POS)	RUSH	YD	AVG(LG)	TD	REC	YD	AVG(LG)	TD	PASS COMP	PCT	YD	AVG(LG)	TD	INT	SK	YD	QBR	KPR	OTD	PTS	TAY

SANDS, TERDELL Terdell Duane, DT, 6´7˝/337 lbs; Tennessee-Chattanooga; 2001: KC, rnd 7; B10/31/1979 Chattanooga, TN **2003** GB 1 (0) **2003** Oak 3 (1) **2004** Oak 15 (0) **2005** Oak 9 (0) **NFL** 28 (1) [3 yrs]

SANDUSKY, ALEX Alexander Vincent, G, 6´1˝/235 lbs; Clarion; 1954: Bal, rnd 16; B8/17/1932 McKees Rocks, PA **1954** Bal 12 (RG) **1955** Bal 12 (12, RG) **1956** Bal 11 (11, RG) **1957** Bal 12 (12, RG) **1958**†Bal 12 (12, RG) **1959**†Bal 12 (RG) **1960** Bal 12 (RG) **1961** Bal 14 (RG) **1962** Bal 13 (RG) **1963** Bal 14 (RG) **1964**†Bal☆14 (RG) **1965**†Bal 14 (RG) **1966** Bal 14 (RG) **NFL** 166 (47) [13 yrs]

SANDUSKY, JOHN John Thomas, T-DT, 6´1˝/251 lbs; Villanova; 1950: Cle, rnd 2; B12/28/1925 Philadelphia, PA, D3/5/2006 Coral Springs, FL [C] **1950**†Cle 12 **1951**†Cle 11 **1952**†Cle 11 (RT) **1953**†Cle 12 (RT) **1954**†Cle 12 (RT) **1955**†Cle 12 **1956** GB 12 (RT) **NFL** 82 [7 yrs]

SANDUSKY, MIKE Michael George, G, 6´0˝/231 lbs; Maryland; 1957: SF, rnd 4; B3/14/1935, NJ **1957** Pit 12 (LG) **1958** Pit 12 (LG) **1959** Pit 11 (LG) **1960** Pit◇12 (LG) **1961** Pit 12 (LG) **1962** Pit☆14 (LG) **1963** Pit 13 (LG) **1964** Pit 6 **1965** Pit 12 (LG) **NFL** 104 [9 yrs]

SANDY, JUSTIN Justin Michael, DB, 6´0˝/214 lbs; Northern Illinois; Northern Iowa; B2/22/1982 Wayne, NE **2004** Ten 1 (0) **2005** Ten 2 (1) **NFL** 3 (1) [2 yrs]

SANFORD, JIM James Leo, T, 5´8˝/195 lbs; Lehigh; B12/25/1898 Brooklyn, NY, D4/7/1938 New Brunswick, NJ **1924** Dul 1 (0)

SANFORD, LEO Ottis Leo, LB, 6´1˝/224 lbs; Louisiana Tech; 1951: ChiC, rnd 8; B10/4/1929 Dallas, TX **1951** ChiC 12 (12, RLB) **1952** ChiC 12 (12, RLB) **1953** ChiC 12 (12, RLB) **1954** ChiC 12 (12, MLB) **1955** ChiC 12 (12, RLB) **1956** ChiC◇12 (RLB) **1957** ChiC◇12 (RLB) **1958**†Bal 9 (LLB) **NFL** 93 (60) [8 yrs]

SANFORD, LUCIUS Lucius Martin, LB, 6´2˝/216 lbs; Georgia Tech; 1978: Buf, rnd 4; B2/14/1956 Milledgeville, GA **1978** Buf 16 (15, RLB) **1979** Buf 16 (16, ROLB) **1980**†Buf 16 (16, LOLB) **1981**†Buf 16 (16, LOLB) **1982** Buf 9 (0) **1983** Buf 16 (16, LOLB) **1984** Buf 8 (8, ROLB) **1985** Buf 11 (11, ROLB) **1986** Buf 10 (8, ROLB) **1987**†Cle 11 (8, LOLB) **NFL** 129 (114) [10 yrs]

SANFORD, RICK Richard Francis, DB, 6´1˝/192 lbs; South Carolina; 1979: NE, rnd 1; B1/9/1957 Rock Hill, SC **1979** NE 16 (4) **1980** NE 16 (10, ss) **1981** NE 16 (14, SS) **1982**†NE 9 (9, FS) **1983** NE 16 (16, FS) **1984** NE 16 (7, fs) **1985** Sea 5 (0) **NFL** 94 (60) [7 yrs]

SANFORD, SANDY Haywood Allen, E, 6´1˝/210 lbs; Alabama; 1940: Was, rnd 15; B6/15/1916 Plainview, AR, D3/25/2000 Lubbock, TX [K]

| 1940 | †Was | 7 (0) | — | — | — | — | 1 | 13 | 13.0(13) | 0 | — | — | — | — | — | — | — | — | — | K | — | 3 | 7 |

SANSEN, OLLIE Oliver Marsten, B, 6´1˝/193 lbs; Iowa; B3/6/1908 Alta, IA, D3/21/1987 San Lorenzo, CA

1932	Bkn	10 (7, WB)	44	148	3.4	1	2	45	22.5	0	—	—	—	—	—	—	—	—	—	—	—	6	181
1933	Bkn	10 (4)	12	29	2.4	1	—	—	—	—	—	—	—	—	—	—	—	—	—	—	—	6	39
1934	Bkn	11 (8, FB)	17	79	4.6	0	6	22	3.7	0	—	—	—	—	—	—	—	—	—	—	—	0	90
1935	Bkn	10 (3)	3	3	1.0	0	1	3	3.0(3)	0	—	—	—	—	—	—	—	—	—	—	—	0	5
NFL	4	41 (22)	76	259	3.4	2	9	70	7.8(3)	0	—	—	—	—	—	—	—	—	—	—	—	12	314

SANTIAGO, O.J. Otis Jason, TE, 6´7˝/265 lbs; Kent State; 1997: Atl, rnd 3; B4/4/1974 Whitby, Canada

1997	Atl	11 (11, TE)	—	—	—	—	17	217	12.8(30)	2	—	—	—	—	—	—	—	—	—	—	—	12	119
1998	†Atl	16 (16, TE)	—	—	—	—	27	428	15.9(62)	5	—	—	—	—	—	—	—	—	—	—	—	30	239
1999	Atl	14 (14, TE)	—	—	—	—	15	174	11.6(46)	0	—	—	—	—	—	—	—	—	—	—	—	0	87
2000	Dal	11 (0)	—	—	—	—	—	—	—	—	—	—	—	—	—	—	—	—	—	k	—	0	-2
2001	Cle	14 (12, TE)	—	—	—	—	17	153	9.0(27)	2	—	—	—	—	—	—	—	—	—	k	—	12	58
2003	Oak	12 (7, te)	—	—	—	—	5	69	13.8(36)	0	—	—	—	—	—	—	—	—	—	k	—	0	29
NFL	6	78 (60)	—	—	—	—	81	1041	12.9(62)	9	—	—	—	—	—	—	—	—	—	k	—	54	529

SANTONE, JOE Joseph, aka Joe Scanlon, G, /180 lbs; none; B10/1/1893 Campobasso, Italy, D10/27/1963 Hartford, CT **1926** Har 2 (0)

SANTORA, FRANK Frank, QB, 5´10˝/166 lbs; none; B5/22/1926 Garfield, NJ, D8/13/1997 **1944** Bos 1 (0)

SANYIKA, SEKOU Sekou, LB, 6´3˝/240 lbs; California; 2000: Arz, rnd 7; B3/17/1978 New Orleans, LA **2000** Arz 16 (0) **2001** Arz 16 (1) **NFL** 32 (1) [2 yrs]

SANZOTTA, MICKEY Dominic Franklin, B, 5´9˝/188 lbs; Case Western Reserve; 1942: Det, rnd 4; B4/28/1921 Geneva, OH, D1/21/1999 Geneva, OH

1942	Det	10 (5, FB)	71	268	3.8(18)	0	5	16	3.2(12)	0	15	4	26.7	45	3.0(17)	0	0	—	—	Ppi	—	0	326
1946	Det	10 (2)	6	72	12.0(51)	0	2	19	9.5(14)	0	1	0	0.0	0	—	—	—	—	—	kp	—	0	123
NFL	2	20 (7)	77	340	4.4(51)	0	7	35	5.0(14)	0	16	4	25.0	45	2.8(17)	0	0	—	—	Pkpi	—	0	448

SAPE, LAUVALE Lauvale, DT, 6´1˝/296 lbs; Utah; 2003: Buf, rnd 6; B8/29/1980 American Samoa **2003** Buf 2 (0) **2005** Buf 9 (0) **NFL** 11 (0) [2 yrs]

SAPIENZA, RICK Americo, DB-HB, 5´11˝/185 lbs; Villanova; B2/8/1936 Boston, MA

| 1960 | NYT-A | 2 | — | — | — | — | 1 | 4 | 4.0(4) | 0 | — | — | — | — | — | — | — | — | — | P | — | 0 | 2 |

SAPOLU, JESSE Manase Jesse, C-G, 6´4˝/271 lbs; Hawaii; 1983: SF, rnd 11; B3/10/1961 Laie, Western Samoa **1983**†SF 16 (1) **1984** SF 1 (0) **1987**†SF 12 (9, LG) **1988** SF 16 (16, LG) **1989** SF 16 (16, C) **1990**†SF 16 (16, C) **1991** SF 16 (16, C) **1992**†SF 16 (16, C) **1993**†SF◇16 (16, C) **1994**†SF★14 (13, LG) **1995**†SF☆16 (16, LG) **1996**†SF 16 (16, C) **1997**†SF 12 (3) **NFL** 183 (154) [13 yrs]

SAPP, BENNY Benjamin Lee, DB, 5´9˝/190 lbs; Northern Iowa; B1/20/1981 Fort Lauderdale, FL **2004** KC 15 (0) **2005** KC 16 (3) **NFL** 31 (3) [2 yrs]

SAPP, BOB Robert Malcolm, G, 6´4˝/319 lbs; Washington; 1997: Chi, rnd 3; B9/22/1973 Colorado Springs, CO **1997**†Min 1 (0)

SAPP, CECIL Cecil, RB, 5´11˝/229 lbs; Colorado State; B12/12/1978 Miami, FL

2003	Den	1 (0)	12	31	2.6(5)	0	—	—	—	—	—	—	—	—	—	—	—	—	—	—	—	0	31
2004	†Den	5 (0)	4	32	8.0(18)	0	—	—	—	—	—	—	—	—	—	—	—	—	—	k	—	0	51
2005	Den	16 (0)	5	21	4.2(10)	0	2	17	8.5(12)	0	—	—	—	—	—	—	—	—	—	k	—	0	28
NFL	3	22 (0)	21	84	4.0(18)	0	2	17	8.5(12)	0	—	—	—	—	—	—	—	—	—	k	—	0	110

SAPP, GEROME Gerome Darren, DB, 6´1˝/216 lbs; Notre Dame; 2003: Bal, rnd 6; B2/8/1981 Houston, TX **2003**†Bal 14 (0) **2004**†Ind 13 (0) **2005**†Ind 16 (2) **NFL** 43 (2) [3 yrs]

SAPP, PATRICK Patrick Zolley, LB, 6´4˝/258 lbs; Clemson; 1996: SD, rnd 2; B5/11/1973 Jacksonville, FL **1996** SD 16 (0) **1997** SD 16 (9, LLB) **1998**†Arz 16 (1) **1999** Arz 15 (5, rlb) **NFL** 63 (15) [4 yrs]

SAPP, THERON Theron Coleman, FB-HB, 6´1˝/203 lbs; Georgia; 1958: Phi, rnd 10; B6/15/1935 Macon, GA

1959	Phi	12	41	145	3.5(17)	1	6	47	7.8(13)	0	—	—	—	—	—	—	—	—	—	—	—	6	179
1960	†Phi	5	9	20	2.2(7)	0	2	20	10.0(14)	0	—	—	—	—	—	—	—	—	—	—	—	0	30
1961	Phi	14	7	24	3.4(8)	1	3	10	3.3(8)	0	—	—	—	—	—	—	—	—	—	—	—	6	39
1962	Phi	12	23	53	2.3(17)	2	6	80	13.3(34)	0	—	—	—	—	—	—	—	—	—	—	—	12	113
1963	Phi	4	8	21	2.6(9)	0	1	-5	-5.0(-5)	0	—	—	—	—	—	—	—	—	—	k	—	0	14
1963	Pit	10 (fb)	96	431	4.5(27)	1	3	41	13.7(22)	0	—	—	—	—	—	—	—	—	—	k	—	6	450
1964	Pit	11	4	15	3.8(5)	0	1	44	44.0(44)	0	—	—	—	—	—	—	—	—	—	k	—	0	20
1965	Pit	14	14	54	3.9(24)	0	1	10	10.0(10)	0	—	—	—	—	—	—	—	—	—	k	—	0	61
NFL	7	82	202	763	3.8(27)	5	23	247	10.7(44)	0	—	—	—	—	—	—	—	—	—	k	—	30	905

SAPP, WARREN Warren Carlos 'QB Killa', DT, 6´2˝/303 lbs; Miami (FL); 1995: TB, rnd 1; B12/19/1972 Orlando, FL [S] **1995** TB 16 (8, RDT) **1996** TB 15 (14, RDT) **1997**†TB★15 (15, RDT) **1998** TB☆16 (16, RDT) **1999**†TB★15 (15, RDT) **2000**†TB★16 (15, RDT) **2001**†TB☆16 (16, RDT) **2002**†TB★16 (16, RDT) **2004** Oak 16 (16, RDT) **2005** Oak 10 (10, RDT)

| 2003 | TB◇ | 15 (15, RDT) | — | — | — | — | 4 | 39 | 9.8(18) | 2 | — | — | — | — | — | — | — | — | — | S | — | 12 | 30 |
| NFL | 11 | 166 (156) | — | — | — | — | 4 | 39 | 9.8(18) | 2 | — | — | — | — | — | — | — | — | — | iS | 1 | 18 | 28 |

SARAFINY, AL Albert Joseph, C, 5´11˝/235 lbs; St. Edward's; B9/2/1906 Caspian, MI, D2/1981 Chicago, IL **1933** GB 7 (2)

SARAUSKY, TONY Anthony Olgird, B, 5´11˝/201 lbs; Fordham; B4/7/1913 Cambridge, MA, D6/21/1990 Littleton, NH [K]

1935	NYG	8 (1)	14	39	2.8	1	1	17	17.0(17)	0	9	3	33.3	21	2.3	0	2	—	—	K	—	7	-12
1936	NYG	11 (7, tb)	32	150	4.7	1	—	—	—	—	27	6	22.2	87	3.2	2	1	—	—	K	—	10	174
1937	NYG	4 (0)	4	18	4.5	0	—	—	—	—	10	3	30.0	31	3.1	0	0	—	—	—	—	0	34
1938	Bkn	4 (1)	8	42	5.3	0	—	—	—	—	8	2	25.0	10	1.3	0	0	—	—	—	—	0	47
NFL	4	27 (9)	58	249	4.3	2	1	17	17.0(17)	0	54	14	25.9	149	2.8	2	3	—	—	K	—	17	242

SARBOE, PHIL Phillip John, aka Phillip John Sorboe, BB-TB, 5´10˝/167 lbs; Washington State; B8/22/1911 Fairbanks, AK, D11/19/1985 Spokane, WA

1934	Bos	5 (0)	2	11	5.5	0	—	—	—	—	4	2	50.0	14	3.5	0	4	—	—	—	—	0	18
1934	ChiC	4 (2)	—	—	—	—	—	—	—	—	16	5	31.3	71	4.4	1	3	—	—	—	—	0	-80
1935	ChiC☆	12 (5, BB)	38	129	3.4	0	2	22	11.0	0	67	31	46.3	368	5.5	0	10	—	—	—	—	2	-66
1936	ChiC	6 (2)	45	21	0.5	0	—	—	—	—	62	25	40.3	398	6.4	1	8	—	—	—	—	0	-95

YEAR	TEAM	G(GS, POS)	RUSH	YD	AVG(LG)	TD	REC	YD	AVG(LG)	TD	PASS	COMP	PCT	YD	AVG(LG)	TD	INT	SK	YD	QBR	KPR	OTD	PTS	TAY
1936	Bkn	5(0)	38	82	2.2	0	1	18	18.0(18)	0	52	22	42.3	282	5.4	2	5	—	—	—	—	—	0	42
NFL	3	32(9)	123	243	2.0	0	3	40	13.3(18)	0	201	85	42.3	1133	5.6	4	26	—	—	—	—	2	12	-181
SARDISCO, TONY Anthony Guy, G-DE-LB, 6´2˝/226 lbs; Tulane; 1956: SF, rnd 6; B12/5/1932 Shreveport, LA **1956** SF 3 **1956** Was 7 **1960** Bos-A 13 (RDE) **1961** Bos-A☆13 (LG) **1962** Bos-A 14 (LG) **NFL** 50 [4 yrs]																								
SARGENT, BRODERICK Broderick Lawrence, RB, 5´10˝/215 lbs; Baylor; B9/16/1962 Waxahachie, TX																								
1986	SL	16(0)	—	—	—	—	1	8	8.0(8)	0	—	—	—	—	—	—	—	—	—	—	k	—	0	1
1987	SL	15(1)	18	90	5.0(16)	0	2	19	9.5(10)	0	—	—	—	—	—	—	—	—	—	—	k	—	0	92
1989	Dal	14(5, fb)	20	87	4.3(43)	1	6	50	8.3(21)	0	—	—	—	—	—	—	—	—	—	—	k	—	6	107
NFL	3	45(6)	38	177	4.7(43)	1	9	77	8.6(21)	0	—	—	—	—	—	—	—	—	—	—	k	—	6	200
SARGENT, KEVIN Kevin L., T, 6´6˝/289 lbs; Eastern Washington; B3/31/1969 Bremerton, WA **1992** Cin 16 (8, LT) **1993** Cin 1 (1) **1994** Cin 15 (15, LT) **1995** Cin 15 (15, LT) **1997** Cin 10 (8, LT) **1998** Cin 16 (16, LT) **NFL** 73 (63) [6 yrs]																								
SARK, HARVEY Harvey George, G, 5´10˝/210 lbs; Phillips; B1/30/1907 Lawrence, IN, deceased **1931** NYG 4 (2) **1934** Cin 1 (0) **NFL** 5 (2) [2 yrs]																								
SARRATT, CHARLEY Charles Franklin, QB, 6´1˝/185 lbs; Clemson; Oklahoma; 1947: ChiC, rnd 12; B10/22/1922 Greenville, SC																								
1948	Det	8(1)	3	3	1.0(3)	0	1	3	3.0(3)	0	1	1	100.0	48	48.0(48)	0	0	—	—	—	Pp	—	0	26
SARRINGHAUS, PAUL Paul Richard, HB, 6´0˝/185 lbs; Ohio State; 1944: Phi, rnd 9; B8/13/1920 Hamilton, OH, D4/7/1998 Middletown, OH																								
1946	ChiC	2(0)	2	1	0.5(1)	0	—	—	—	—	—	—	—	—	—	—	—	—	—	—	—	—	0	1
1948	Det	5(2)	19	38	2.0(7)	0	1	-1	-1.0(-1)	0	—	—	—	—	—	—	—	—	—	—	k	—	0	58
NFL	2	7(2)	21	39	1.9(7)	0	1	-1	-1.0(-1)	0	—	—	—	—	—	—	—	—	—	—	k	—	0	59
SARTIN, DAN Daniel Matthias, DT, 6´1˝/250 lbs; Mississippi; 1968: NO, rnd 4; B6/23/1946 Gulfport, MS **1969** SD-A 13																								
SARTIN, MARTIN Martin, RB, 5´10˝/202 lbs; Long Beach State; B3/9/1963 Philadelphia, PA																								
1987	SD	3(1)	19	52	2.7(10)	1	6	19	3.2(8)	0	—	—	—	—	—	—	—	—	—	—	k	—	6	114
SARTORI, LARRY Lawrence Matthews, G, 6´0˝/208 lbs; Fordham; B8/20/1917 Sheppton, PA, D11/6/1980 Paramus, NJ **1942** Det 10 (2) **1945** Det 1 (0) **NFL** 11 (2) [2 yrs]																								
SASA, DON Don, DT, 6´3˝/290 lbs; Washington State; 1995: SD, rnd 3; B9/16/1972 American Samoa **1995** SD 5 (0) **1996** SD 4 (1) **1997** Was 1 (0) **1998** Car 2 (0) **1998** Det 2 (0) **NFL** 14 (1) [4 yrs]																								
SATCHER, DOUG Douglas Kenneth, LB, 6´0˝/220 lbs; Southern Mississippi; 1966: Bos, rnd 9; B5/28/1945 Sandersville, MS **1966** Bos-A 14 **1967** Bos-A 14 (RLB) **1968** Bos-A 14 (13, RLB) **NFL** 42 (13) [3 yrs]																								
SATENSTEIN, OLLIE Bernard Oliver, G-E-T-C, 6´0˝/213 lbs; NYU; B1906, MA, D4/30/1959 Yonkers, NY **1929** SI 6 (3) **1930** SI 11 (9, LG) **1931** SI 11 (10, RG) **1932** SI 12 (2) **1933** NYG 9 (6, rg) **NFL** 49 (30) [5 yrs]																								
SATTERFIELD, AL Alfred Neal, T, 6´3˝/225 lbs; Vanderbilt; 1947: SF-A, rnd 5/Phi, rnd 8; B11/28/1921 Belleville, AR, D10/28/1989 Little Rock, AR **1947** SF-A 12 (0)																								
SATTERFIELD, BRIAN Brian Sydney, RB, 6´0˝/225 lbs; North Alabama; B12/22/1969 Ducktown, GA **1996** GB 1 (0)																								
SATTERWHITE, HOWARD Howard Eugene, WR, 5´11˝/185 lbs; Sam Houston State; B5/24/1953 Monthalia, TX **1977** Bal 1																								
1976	NYJ	12	—	—	—	—	7	110	15.7(31)	0	—	—	—	—	—	—	—	—	—	—	—	—	0	55
NFL	2	13	—	—	—	—	7	110	15.7(31)	0	—	—	—	—	—	—	—	—	—	—	—	—	0	55
SATURDAY, JEFF Jeffrey Bryant, C, 6´2˝/292 lbs; North Carolina; B6/8/1975 Atlanta, GA **1999**†Ind 11 (2) **2000**†Ind 16 (16, C) **2001** Ind 16 (16, C) **2002**†Ind 16 (16, C) **2003**†Ind 16 (16, C) **2005**†Ind★16 (16, C)																								
2004	†Ind	14(14, C)	—	—	—	—	—	—	—	—	1	0	0.0	0	0.0	0	0	—	—	—	—	—	0	0
NFL	7	105(96)	—	—	—	—	—	—	—	—	1	0	0.0	0	0.0	0	0	—	—	—	—	—	0	0
SAUER, CRAIG Craig Curtis, LB, 6´1˝/240 lbs; Minnesota; 1996: Atl, rnd 6; B12/13/1972 Sartell, MN **1996** Atl 16 (1) **1997** Atl 16 (1) **1998**†Atl 16 (6, rlb) **1999** Atl 16 (3) **2000** Min 9 (0) **NFL** 73 (11) [5 yrs]																								
SAUER, ED Edward Adam, T, 5´10˝/246 lbs; Miami (OH); B11/27/1898 Van Buren Township, OH, D2/15/1980 Dayton, OH **1920** Day 9 (8, RT) **1921** Can 1 (1) **1921** Day 9 (9, RT) **1922** Akr 2 (0) **1922** Day 8 (8, RT) **1923** Day☆8 (8, RT) **1924** Day 8 (8, RT) **1925** Pot 1 (1) **1925** Day 8 (8, RT) **1926** Day 5 (5, RT) **NFL** 59 (56) [7 yrs]																								
SAUER, GEORGE George Henry, TB-HB, 6´2˝/212 lbs; Nebraska; B12/11/1910 Stratton, NE, D2/5/1994 Waco, TX																								
1935	GB☆	9(6, tb)	89	334	3.8	3	3	32	10.7(14)	0	21	9	42.9	177	8.4	1	5	—	—	—	—	1	24	284
1936	†GB	9(4)	94	305	3.2	3	6	110	18.3	0	4	2	50.0	26	6.5	0	1	—	—	—	—	—	18	363
1937	GB	2(0)	7	17	2.4	0	—	—	—	—	—	—	—	—	—	—	—	—	—	—	—	—	0	17
NFL	3	20(10)	190	656	3.5	6	9	142	15.8(14)	0	25	11	44.0	203	8.1	1	6	—	—	—	—	1	42	664
SAUER, GEORGE George Henry, SE-WR, 6´2˝/195 lbs; Texas; 1965: NYJ, rnd R5; B11/10/1943 Sheboygan, WI																								
1965	NYJ-A	14(SE)	—	—	—	—	29	301	10.4(33)	2	—	—	—	—	—	—	—	—	—	—	k	—	12	166
1966	NYJ-A★	14(SE)	—	—	—	—	63	1079	17.1(77)	5	—	—	—	—	—	—	—	—	—	—	—	—	32	565
1967	NYJ-A★	14(SE)	1	-3	-3.0(-3)	0	**75**	1189	15.9(61)	6	—	—	—	—	—	—	—	—	—	—	—	—	38	622
1968	†NYJ-A★	14(SE)	2	21	10.5(15)	0	66	1141	17.3(43)	3	—	—	—	—	—	—	—	—	—	—	—	—	18	607
1969	†NYJ-A✧	14(SE)	1	5	5.0(5)	0	45	745	16.6(40)	8	—	—	—	—	—	—	—	—	—	—	k	—	48	403
1970	NYJ	14(WR)	—	—	—	—	31	510	16.5(67)	4	—	—	—	—	—	—	—	—	—	—	—	—	24	275
NFL	6	84	4	23	5.8(15)	0	309	4965	16.1(77)	28	—	—	—	—	—	—	—	—	—	—	k	—	172	2636
SAUERBRUN, TODD Todd Scott, P, 5´10˝/211 lbs; West Virginia; 1995: Chi, rnd 2; B1/4/1973 Setauket, NY **[KP]** **1995** ChiB 15 (0) **1998** ChiB 3 (0) **2000** KC 16 (0) **2002** Car★16 (0) **2004** Car 16 (0) **2005**†Den 16 (0)																								
1996	ChiB☆	16(0)	1	3	3.0(3)	0	—	—	—	—	2	2	100.0	63	31.5(47)	0	0	—	—	—	P	—	0	35
1997	ChiB	16(0)	2	8	4.0(8)	0	—	—	—	—	—	—	—	—	—	—	—	—	—	—	P	—	0	8
1999	ChiB	16(0)	1	-2	-2.0(-2)	0	—	—	—	—	—	—	—	—	—	—	—	—	—	—	P	—	0	-2
2001	Car★	16(0)	1	0	0.0(0)	0	—	—	—	—	—	—	—	—	—	—	—	—	—	—	P	—	0	0
2003	†Car★	16(0)	—	—	—	—	—	—	—	—	1	0	0.0	0	0.0	0	0	—	—	—	P	—	0	0
NFL	11	162(0)	5	9	1.8(8)	0	—	—	—	—	3	2	66.7	63	21.0(47)	0	0	—	—	—	KP	—	7	41
SAUL, BILL William Neal, LB, 6´4˝/224 lbs; Penn State; 1962: Bal, rnd 2/Buf, rnd 9; B11/19/1940 Unionville, PA **1962** Bal 14 **1963** Bal 14 **1964** Pit 13 (llb) **1966** Pit 14 (MLB) **1967** Pit 14 (MLB) **1968** Pit 3 **1969** NO 3 **1970** Det 13 **NFL** 88 [8 yrs]																								
SAUL, RICH Richard Robert, C-G-T, 6´3˝/241 lbs; Michigan State; 1970: LA, rnd 8; B2/5/1948 Butler, PA **1970** LARm 14 **1971** LARm 14 **1972** LARm 14 **1973**†LARm 14 **1974**†LARm 14 **1975**†LARm 14 (14, C) **1976**†LARm✧14 (14, C) **1977**†LARm✧14 (14, C) **1978**†LARm✧16 (15, C) **1979**†LARm★16 (16, C) **1980**†LARm★16 (16, C) **1981** LARm★16 (16, C) **NFL** 176 (105) [12 yrs]																								
SAUL, RON Ronald Reed, G, 6´2˝/255 lbs; Michigan State; 1970: Hou, rnd 5; B2/5/1948 Butler, PA **1970** Hou 14 **1971** Hou 3 **1972** Hou 13 (RG) **1973** Hou 3 **1974** Hou 14 (lg) **1975** Hou 14 (14, LG) **1976**†Was 11 (11, LG) **1977** Was 14 (14, LG) **1978** Was 15 (15, LG) **1979** Was 15 (15, LG) **1980** Was 16 (15, LG) **1981** Was 10 (7, rg) **NFL** 142 (91) [12 yrs]																								
SAULS, MACK Kirby McGee, DB, 6´0˝/185 lbs; Southwest Texas State; 1968: SL, rnd 13; B8/15/1945 Long Beach, CA **1968** SL 6 **1969** SL 4 **NFL** 10 [2 yrs]																								
SAUMER, PETE Sylvan Leon, B, 6´1˝/195 lbs; St. Olaf; B4/30/1910 St. Paul, MN, D1/1/1983 Reno, NV																								
1934	Cin	3(2)	48	183	3.8	1	1	6	6.0(6)	0	4	1	25.0	9	2.3(9)	0	0	—	—	—	—	—	6	201
1934	Pit	3(0)	7	21	3.0	0	—	—	—	—	3	0	0.0	0	0.0	0	1	—	—	—	—	—	0	-19
NFL	1	6(2)	55	204	3.7	1	1	6	6.0(6)	0	7	1	14.3	9	1.3(9)	0	1	—	—	—	—	—	6	182
SAUNDERS, BUCK Ward Bishop, BB, 6´1˝/190 lbs; California; B1892, deceased **1922** Tol 1 (0)																								
SAUNDERS, CEDRIC Cedric Randall, TE, 6´3˝/240 lbs; Ohio State; B9/30/1972 Tallahassee, FL **1995** TB 3 (0)																								
SAUNDERS, JOHN John Wesley, DB, 6´3˝/198 lbs; Toledo; 1972: LA, rnd 4; B4/29/1950 Toledo, OH, D2/11/2001 **1972** Buf 2 **1974** SF 4 **1975** SF 3 (1) **NFL** 9 (1) [3 yrs]																								
SAUNDERS, RUSS Russell S., FB, 5´9˝/190 lbs; USC; B1/26/1906, D4/28/1987 Burbank, CA **1931** GB 9 (1), 6																								
SAUNOOKE, STILLWELL Stillwell, E-WB, 5´8˝/175 lbs; Carlisle Indian; B9/1981 Whittier, NC, deceased **1922** Oor 9 (8, LE)																								
SAUTER, CORY Cory Justin, QB, 6´4˝/216 lbs; Minnesota; B11/21/1974 Hutchinson, MN																								
2002	ChiB	1(0)	2	8	4.0(7)	0	—	—	—	—	9	6	66.7	59	6.6(31)	0	0	4	20	—	—	—	0	38

YEAR	TEAM	G (GS, POS)	RUSH	YD	AVG (LG)	TD	REC	YD	AVG (LG)	TD	PASS	COMP	PCT	YD	AVG (LG)	TD	INT	SK	YD	QBR	KPR	OTD	PTS	TAY

SAVAGE, JOSH Josh, DE, 6´4˝/276 lbs; Utah; B9/28/1980 Ozark, AR   **2004** TB 6 (0) **2005** Atl 1 (0) **NFL** 7 (0) [2 yrs]

SAVAGE, SEBASTIAN Sebastian Eugene, DB, 5´10˝/187 lbs; North Carolina State; 1993: Buf, rnd 5; B12/12/1969 Carlisle, SC   **1994** Was 1 (0) **1995** Was 2 (0) **NFL** 3 (0) [2 yrs]

SAVAGE, TONY Anthony John, NT, 6´3˝/300 lbs; Washington State; 1990: NYJ, rnd 5; B7/7/1967 San Francisco, CA   **1990** SD 2 (0) **1992** SD 2 (0) **1992** Cin 1 (0) **NFL** 5 (0) [2 yrs]

SAVATSKY, OLLIE Oliver John, E, 6´2˝/215 lbs; Miami (OH); B5/13/1912 Cleveland, OH   **1937** Cle 1 (0)

SAVITSKY, GEORGE George Michael, T, 6´2˝/244 lbs; Pennsylvania; 1947: Phi, rnd 5/LAD-A, rnd 7; B7/30/1924 New York, NY   **1948**†Phi 12 (0) **1949**†Phi 12 (0) **NFL** 24 (0) [2 yrs]

SAVOIE, NICK Nicky John, TE, 6´5˝/253 lbs; LSU; 1997: NO, rnd 6; B9/21/1973 Cut Off, LA

| 1997 | NO | 1 (0) | — | — | — | — | 1 | 14 | 14.0 (14) | 0 | — | — | — | — | — | — | — | — | — | — | — | — | 0 | 7 |

SAVOLDI, JOE Joseph A., FB, 5´11˝/194 lbs; Notre Dame; B3/5/1908 Milan, Italy, D1/25/1974 Cadiz, KY   **1930** ChiB 3 (1), 6

SAWYER, BUZZ Robert Meade, P, 6´1˝/201 lbs; Texas A&M; Baylor; B11/18/1962 Waxahachie, TX   **1987** Dal 3 (0)

SAWYER, COREY Corey Franklyn, DB, 5´11˝/177 lbs; Florida State; 1994: Cin, rnd 4; B10/4/1971 Key West, FL   **1994** Cin 15 (0) **1995** Cin 12 (8, rcb) **1996** Cin 15 (2) **1997** Cin 15 (2) **1998** Cin 3 (0) **1999** NYJ 5 (0) **NFL** 65 (12) [6 yrs]

SAWYER, HERM Herman W., B, 5´8˝/170 lbs; Syracuse; B10/18/1898, D9/1968 New York, NY   **1922** Roc 3 (1)

SAWYER, JOHN John Wesley, TE, 6´2˝/230 lbs; Southern Mississippi; 1975: Hou, rnd 11; B7/26/1953 Brookhaven, MS

1975	Hou	8 (3)	—	—	—	—	7	144	20.6 (51)	1	—	—	—	—	—	—	—	—	—	—	—	—	6	77
1976	Hou	14 (4)	—	—	—	—	18	208	11.6 (53)	1	—	—	—	—	—	—	—	—	—	—	P	—	6	109
1977	Sea	14 (2)	—	—	—	—	10	105	10.5 (27)	0	—	—	—	—	—	—	—	—	—	—	—	—	0	53
1978	Sea	11 (5, te)	—	—	—	—	9	101	11.2 (20)	0	—	—	—	—	—	—	—	—	—	—	—	—	0	51
1980	Sea	16 (16, TE)	—	—	—	—	36	410	11.4 (32)	0	—	—	—	—	—	—	—	—	—	—	—	—	0	205
1981	Sea	16 (16, TE)	—	—	—	—	21	272	13.0 (30)	0	—	—	—	—	—	—	—	—	—	—	k	—	0	129
1982	Sea	7 (0)	—	—	—	—	8	92	11.5 (17)	0	—	—	—	—	—	—	—	—	—	—	—	—	0	46
1983	Was	7 (0)	—	—	—	—	—	—	—	—	—	—	—	—	—	—	—	—	—	—	k	—	0	0
1983	†Den	7 (4)	—	—	—	—	3	42	14.0 (17)	0	—	—	—	—	—	—	—	—	—	—	—	—	0	21
1984	Den	10 (8, te)	—	—	—	—	17	122	7.2 (25)	0	—	—	—	—	—	—	—	—	—	—	—	—	0	61
NFL	9	110 (58)	—	—	—	—	129	1496	11.6 (53)	2	—	—	—	—	—	—	—	—	—	—	Pk	—	12	751

SAWYER, JON Jonathan LaJuan, DB, 5´9˝/175 lbs; Cincinnati; B4/6/1964   **1987** NE 2 (0)

SAWYER, KEN Kenneth Lee, DB, 6´0˝/192 lbs; Syracuse; 1974: Cin, rnd 7; B7/22/1952 Clearfield, PA   **1974** Cin 12

SAWYER, TALANCE Talance, DE, 6´2˝/270 lbs; UNLV; 1999: Min, rnd 6; B6/14/1976 Bastrop, LA   **1999** Min 2 (0) **2000**†Min 16 (16, RDE) **2001** Min 16 (16, RDE/lde) **2002** Min 2 (0) **2003** Min 3 (0) **NFL** 39 (32) [5 yrs]

SAXON, JAMES James Elijah, FB, 5´11˝/237 lbs; San Jose State; 1988: KC, rnd 6; B3/23/1966 Buford, SC

1988	KC	16 (4)	60	236	3.9 (14)	2	19	177	9.3 (22)	0	—	—	—	—	—	—	—	—	—	—	k	—	12	355
1989	KC	16 (2)	58	233	4.0 (19)	3	11	86	7.8 (18)	0	1	0	0.0	0	0.0	0	1	—	—	—	k	—	18	237
1990	KC	6 (0)	3	15	5.0 (8)	0	1	5	5.0 (5)	0	—	—	—	—	—	—	—	—	—	—	k	—	0	24
1991	†KC	16 (0)	6	13	2.2 (8)	0	6	55	9.2 (22)	0	—	—	—	—	—	—	—	—	—	—	k	—	0	37
1992	†Mia	16 (0)	4	7	1.8 (4)	0	5	41	8.2 (14)	0	—	—	—	—	—	—	—	—	—	—	—	—	0	28
1993	Mia	16 (0)	5	13	2.6 (9)	0	—	—	—	—	—	—	—	—	—	—	—	—	—	—	k	—	0	5
1994	†Mia	16 (7, fb)	8	16	2.0 (7)	0	27	151	5.6 (25)	0	—	—	—	—	—	—	—	—	—	—	k	—	0	89
1995	†Phi	9 (3)	1	0	0.0 (0)	0	—	—	—	—	—	—	—	—	—	—	—	—	—	—	k	—	0	-12
NFL	8	111 (16)	145	533	3.7 (19)	5	69	515	7.5 (25)	0	1	0	0.0	0	0.0	0	1	—	—	—	k	—	30	761

SAXON, MIKE Michael Eric, P, 6´3˝/205 lbs; San Diego State; 1984: Det, rnd 11; B7/10/1962 Whittier, CA [P]   **1985**†Dal 16 (0) **1986** Dal 16 (0) **1987** Dal 12 (0) **1988** Dal 16 (0) **1991**†Dal 16 (0) **1992**†Dal 16 (0) **1995** Min 16 (0)

1989	Dal	16 (0)	1	1	1.0 (1)	0	—	—	—	—	1	1	100.0	4	4.0 (4)	0	0	—	—	P	—	—	0	3
1990	Dal	16 (0)	1	20	20.0 (20)	0	—	—	—	—	—	—	—	—	—	—	—	—	—	P	—	—	0	20
1993	NE	16 (0)	2	2	1.0 (2)	0	—	—	—	—	—	—	—	—	—	—	—	—	—	P	—	—	0	2
1994	†Min	16 (0)	1	0	0.0 (0)	0	—	—	—	—	1	0	0.0	0	0.0	0	0	—	—	P	—	—	0	0
NFL	11	172 (0)	5	23	4.6 (20)	0	—	—	—	—	2	1	50.0	4	2.0 (4)	0	0	—	—	P	—	—	0	25

SAXTON, BRIAN Paul Brian, TE, 6´6˝/256 lbs; Boston College; B3/13/1972 Whippany, NJ   **1997** Atl 3 (0)

| 1996 | NYG | 16 (2) | — | — | — | — | 4 | 31 | 7.8 (14) | 0 | — | — | — | — | — | — | — | — | — | — | k | — | 0 | 2 |
| NFL | 2 | 19 (2) | — | — | — | — | 4 | 31 | 7.8 (14) | 0 | — | — | — | — | — | — | — | — | — | — | — | — | 0 | 16 |

SAXTON, JIMMY James Everett, HB, 5´11˝/173 lbs; Texas; 1962: DalT, rnd 10/SL, rnd 11; B5/21/1940 Bryan, TX

| 1962 | †DalT-A | 13 | 3 | 1 | 0.3 (9) | 0 | 5 | 64 | 12.8 (33) | 0 | — | — | — | — | — | — | — | — | — | — | Pk | — | 0 | 50 |

SAYERS, GALE Gale Eugene 'The Kansas Comet', RB, 6´0˝/198 lbs; Kansas; 1965: Chi, rnd 1/KC, rnd 1; B5/30/1943 Wichita, KS; HOF 1977 [R]

1965	ChiB★	14 (HB)	166	867	5.2 (61)	14	29	507	17.5 (80)	6	3	2	66.7	53	17.7 (27)	1	1	—	—	—	kp	2	**132**	1805
1966	ChiB★	14 (HB)	229	**1231**	5.4 (58)	8	34	447	13.1 (80)	2	6	2	33.3	58	9.7 (39)	0	1	—	—	—	kp	2	72	**1941**
1967	ChiB★	13 (HB)	186	880	4.7 (70)	7	16	126	7.9 (32)	1	5	0	0.0	0	0.0	0	0	—	—	—	kp	4	72	1486
1968	ChiB☆	9 (HB)	138	856	**6.2** (63)	2	15	117	7.8 (21)	0	2	0	0.0	0	0.0	0	0	—	—	—	kp	—	12	1160
1969	ChiB★	14 (HB)	**236**	1032	4.4 (28)	8	17	116	6.8 (25)	0	2	0	0.0	0	0.0	0	0	1	3	—	kp	—	48	1299
1970	ChiB	2	23	52	2.3 (15)	0	1	-6	-6.0 (-6)	0	—	—	—	—	—	—	—	—	—	—	—	—	0	49
1971	ChiB	2	13	38	2.9 (9)	0	—	—	—	—	—	—	—	—	—	—	—	—	—	—	—	—	0	38
NFL	7	68	991	4956	5.0 (70)	39	112	1307	11.7 (80)	9	18	4	22.2	111	6.2 (39)	1	2	1	3	—	kp	8	336	7777

SAYERS, RON Ronald, RB, 6´1˝/209 lbs; Nebraska-Omaha; 1969: SD, rnd 2; B8/29/1947 Wichita, KS

| 1969 | SD-A | 8 | 14 | 53 | 3.8 (8) | 0 | — | — | — | — | — | — | — | — | — | — | — | — | — | — | k | — | 0 | 65 |

SAYLER, JACE James M., NT, 6´5˝/295 lbs; Michigan State; B2/27/1979 Rockford, IL   **2001**†NE 2 (1)

SAZIO, RALPH Ralph Joseph, T, 6´1˝/250 lbs; William & Mary; 1948: Buf-A, rnd 22/1947: Pit, rnd 28; B7/22/1922 Avellino, Italy

| 1948 | Bkn-A | 13 (8, RT) | 0 | 5 | 5.0 | 0 | — | — | — | — | — | — | — | — | — | — | — | — | — | — | — | — | 0 | 5 |

SBRANTI, RONALD Albert Raymond, LB, 6´2˝/230 lbs; Utah State; 1966: Den, rnd 9/SF, rnd 10; B10/24/1944 Antioch, CA   **1966** Den-A 14

SCAFIDE, JOHN John Andrew, T, 6´0˝/210 lbs; Tulane; B6/21/1911 Bay St. Louis, MS, D10/24/1979 Bay St. Louis, MS   **1933** Bos 2 (0)

SCAIFE, BO Oliver Edward, TE, 6´3˝/249 lbs; Texas; 2005: Ten, rnd 6; B1/6/1981 Denver, CO

| 2005 | Ten | 16 (5, te) | — | — | — | — | 37 | 273 | 7.4 (19) | 2 | — | — | — | — | — | — | — | — | — | — | — | — | 12 | 147 |

SCALES, CHARLIE Charles Anderson, HB-FB, 5´11˝/210 lbs; Indiana; B1/11/1938 Pittsburgh, PA

1960	Pit	12	26	81	3.1 (9)	0	1	-2	-2.0 (-2)	0	—	—	—	—	—	—	—	—	—	—	k	—	0	105
1961	Pit	14	50	184	3.7 (27)	0	7	43	6.1 (16)	0	—	—	—	—	—	—	—	—	—	—	k	—	0	202
1962	Cle	14 (hb)	56	239	4.3 (27)	3	8	67	8.4 (22)	0	1	0	0.0	0	0.0	0	1	—	—	—	k	—	18	282
1963	Cle	14	2	-3	-1.5 (2)	1	1	13	13.0 (13)	0	—	—	—	—	—	—	—	—	—	—	k	—	6	206
1964	†Cle	14	2	5	2.5 (3)	0	—	—	—	—	—	—	—	—	—	—	—	—	—	—	k	1	6	5
1965	†Cle	14	11	59	5.4 (20)	0	1	7	7.0 (7)	0	—	—	—	—	—	—	—	—	—	—	kp	—	0	86
1966	Atl	5	10	38	3.8 (10)	0	16	53	16.3 (15)	0	—	—	—	—	—	—	—	—	—	—	k	—	0	72
NFL	7	87	157	603	3.8 (27)	4	21	144	6.9 (22)	0	1	0	0.0	0	0.0	0	1	—	—	—	kp	1	30	956

SCALES, DWIGHT Dwight Austin, WR, 6´2˝/178 lbs; Grambling State; 1976: LA, rnd 5; B5/30/1953 Little Rock, AR

1976	†LARm	14	—	—	—	—	3	105	35.0 (80)	1	—	—	—	—	—	—	—	—	—	—	kp	—	6	115
1977	†LARm	12	—	—	—	—	5	104	20.8 (32)	1	—	—	—	—	—	—	—	—	—	—	—	—	6	57
1978	†LARm	13	—	—	—	—	5	105	21.0 (38)	0	—	—	—	—	—	—	—	—	—	—	—	1	6	53
1979	NYG	15 (4)	—	—	—	—	14	222	15.9 (55)	0	—	—	—	—	—	—	—	—	—	—	p	—	0	104
1981	†SD	16 (4)	—	—	—	—	19	429	22.6 (60)	1	—	—	—	—	—	—	—	—	—	—	—	—	6	220
1982	†SD	9 (2)	—	—	—	—	17	297	17.5 (29)	1	—	—	—	—	—	—	—	—	—	—	—	—	6	58
1983	SD	7 (1)	—	—	—	—	2	28	14.0 (14)	0	—	—	—	—	—	—	—	—	—	—	kp	—	0	39

YEAR	TEAM	G (GS, POS)	RUSH	YD	AVG (LG)	TD	REC	YD	AVG (LG)	TD	PASS	COMP	PCT	YD	AVG (LG)	TD	INT	SK	YD	QBR	KPR	OTD	PTS	TAY
1984	Sea	4(0)	—	—	—	—	2	22	11.0(11)	0	—	—	—	—	—	—	—	—	—	—	—	—	0	11
NFL	8	90(11)	—	—	—	—	56	1120	20.0(80)	4	—	—	—	—	—	—	—	—	—	—	kp	1	30	655
SCALES, GREG Gregory Denard, TE, 6´4˝/253 lbs; Wake Forest; 1988: NO, rnd 5; B5/9/1966 Winston-Salem, NC																								
1988	NO	12(0)	—	—	—	—	2	20	10.0(14)	1	—	—	—	—	—	—	—	—	—	—	—	—	6	15
1989	NO	14(4)	—	—	—	—	8	89	11.1(26)	0	—	—	—	—	—	—	—	—	—	—	k	—	0	30
1990	†NO	16(0)	—	—	—	—	8	64	8.0(20)	1	—	—	—	—	—	—	—	—	—	—	—	—	6	37
1991	NO	2(1)	—	—	—	—	3	23	7.7(14)	0	—	—	—	—	—	—	—	—	—	—	—	—	0	12
NFL	4	44(5)	—	—	—	—	21	196	9.3(26)	2	—	—	—	—	—	—	—	—	—	—	k	—	12	93
SCALES, HURLES Hurles Eulis, DB, 6´1˝/200 lbs; North Texas; 1973: Cin, rnd 14; B12/1/1950 Amarillo, TX **1974** ChiB 1 **1974**†SL 7 **1975** GB 7 **NFL** 15 [2 yrs]																								
SCALISSI, TED Theodore Glenn, HB, 5´8˝/173 lbs; Ripon; 1947: GB, rnd 17; B10/26/1921 Madison, WI, D1/6/1987 Janesville, WI																								
1947	ChiR-A	10(1)	35	37	1.1	0	5	67	13.4	2	—	—	—	—	—	—	—	—	—	—	kp	—	12	148
SCALZI, JOHNNY John Anthony, B, 5´7˝/168 lbs; Georgetown (DC); B3/22/1907 Stamford, CT, D9/27/1962 Port Chester, NY **1931** Bkn 7 (0)																								
SCANLAN, JERRY Jerry Lafaele, T-G, 6´5˝/270 lbs; Hawaii; B1/4/1957 Honolulu, HI **1980** Was 3 (0) **1981** Was 3 (0) **NFL** 6 (0) [2 yrs]																								
SCANLON, DEWEY Dewey D., WB, 5´9˝/192 lbs; Valparaiso; B8/16/1899 West Duluth, MN, D9/24/1944 St. Louis County, MN **[C]** **1926** Dul 1 (0)																								
SCANLON, JOHN John, TB-WB, /185 lbs; DePaul; B1900, IL, deceased **1921** ChiC 4 (1), 6 **1926** Lou 2 (1) **NFL** 6 (2) [2 yrs]																								
SCANLON, RICH Richard James, LB, 6´2˝/249 lbs; Syracuse; B12/23/1980 Oradell, NJ **2004** KC 6 (0) **2005** KC 16 (0) **NFL** 22 (0) [2 yrs]																								
SCARBATH, JACK John Carl, QB, 6´2˝/206 lbs; Maryland; 1953: Was, rnd 1; B8/12/1930 Baltimore, MD																								
1953	Was	12(qb)	22	98	4.5(40)	0	—	—	—	—	129	45	34.9	862	6.7(71)	9	12	—	—	43.5	—	—	0	94
1954	Was	10(qb)	17	36	2.1(6)	0	—	—	—	—	109	44	40.4	798	7.3(60)	7	13	—	—	48.1	—	—	0	-50
1956	Pit	7	4	19	4.8(21)	0	—	—	—	—	41	12	29.3	208	5.1(47)	2	5	—	—	—	—	—	0	-67
NFL	3	29	43	153	3.6(40)	0	—	—	—	—	279	101	36.2	1868	6.7(71)	18	30	—	—	42.1	—	—	0	-23
SCARBER, SAM Sam Willis, RB, 6´3˝/230 lbs; New Mexico; 1971: Dal, rnd 3; B6/24/1949 St. Louis, MO																								
1975	SD	11(1)	15	68	4.5(18)	1	12	68	5.7(12)	1	—	—	—	—	—	—	—	—	—	—	—	—	12	117
1976	SD	14(2)	61	236	3.9(14)	1	14	96	6.9(13)	1	—	—	—	—	—	—	—	—	—	—	—	—	12	299
NFL	2	25(3)	76	304	4.0(18)	2	26	164	6.3(13)	2	—	—	—	—	—	—	—	—	—	—	—	—	24	416
SCARDINA, JOHN John, T, 6´4˝/265 lbs; Concordia (WI); Lincoln (MO); B7/26/1958 Milwaukee, WI **1987** Min 3 (3)																								
SCARDINE, CARMEN Carmen, WB, none; B3/9/1911 Chicago, IL																								
1932	ChiC	1(0)	1	10	10.0(10)	0	1	3	3.0(3)	0	—	—	—	—	—	—	—	—	—	—	—	—	0	12
SCARLETT, NOEL Noel, DT, 6´3˝/320 lbs; Langston; 1999: Min, rnd 7; B1/21/1974 Atlanta, GA **2000** Dal 1 (0)																								
SCARPATI, JOE Joseph Henry, DB, 5´10˝/185 lbs; North Carolina State; 1964: Bos, rnd 13; B3/5/1943 Brooklyn, NY **[I]** **1964** Phi 12 (LS) **1966** Phi 14 (RS) **1967** Phi 14 (RS) **1969** Phi 14 (RS) **1970** NO 14 (FS)																								
1965	Phi	14(RS)	1	6	6.0(6)	0	—	—	—	—	—	—	—	—	—	—	—	—	—	—	i	—	0	-5
1968	Phi	14(RS)	—	—	—	—	—	—	—	—	2	1	50.0	3	1.5(3)	0	0	—	—	—	pi	—	0	6
NFL	7	96	1	6	6.0(6)	0	—	—	—	—	2	1	50.0	3	1.5(3)	0	0	—	—	—	pi	3	18	277
SCARPITTO, BOB Robert Frank, FL-WR-P, 5´11˝/192 lbs; Notre Dame; 1961: SD, rnd 9; B1/7/1939 Rahway, NY **[P]**																								
1961	†SD-A	7	—	—	—	—	9	163	18.1(69)	2	—	—	—	—	—	—	—	—	—	—	kp	—	12	124
1962	Den-A	14(FL)	—	—	—	—	35	667	19.1(67)	6	—	—	—	—	—	—	—	—	—	—	—	—	36	364
1963	Den-A	11(FL)	—	—	—	—	21	463	22.0(66)	5	—	—	—	—	—	—	—	—	—	—	k	—	30	250
1964	Den-A	14(FL)	1	5	5.0(5)	0	35	375	10.7(37)	4	—	—	—	—	—	—	—	—	—	—	—	—	24	213
1965	Den-A	14(FL)	4	94	23.5(44)	0	32	585	18.3(90)	5	—	—	—	—	—	—	—	—	—	—	P	—	30	412
1966	Den-A★	14(FL)	4	110	27.5(63)	1	21	335	16.0(62)	4	—	—	—	—	—	—	—	—	—	—	P	—	32	308
1967	Den-A☆	14	1	5	5.0(5)	0	1	14	14.0(14)	0	—	—	—	—	—	—	—	—	—	—	P	—	0	12
1968	Bos-A	14	—	—	—	—	2	49	24.5(33)	1	—	—	—	—	—	—	—	—	—	—	P	—	6	30
NFL	8	102	10	214	21.4(63)	1	156	2651	17.0(90)	27	—	—	—	—	—	—	—	—	—	—	Pkp	—	170	1710
SCARRY, MIKE Michael Joseph, C-T, 6´0˝/214 lbs; Waynesburg; B2/1/1920 Duquesne, PA **1944** Cle 10 (10, C) **1945**†Cle☆10 (10, C) **NFL** 20 (20) [2 yrs] **1946**†Cle-A☆14 (10, C) **1947**†Cle-A 11 (6, C) **AAFC** 25 (16) [2 yrs]																								
SCHAAKE, ELMER Elmer Earl, B, 5´11˝/207 lbs; Kansas; B2/7/1911 Lawrence, KS, D1/24/1996 San Mateo County, CA																								
1933	Por	10(7, fb)	125	412	3.3	0	4	23	5.8(22)	1	3	2	66.7	8	2.7	0	1	—	—	—	—	—	6	393
SCHABARUM, PETE Peter Frank, HB, 5´11˝/185 lbs; California; 1951: SF, rnd 2; B1/9/1929 Los Angeles, CA																								
1951	SF	12(rh)	76	311	4.1(67)	2	10	162	16.2(47)	0	—	—	—	—	—	—	—	—	—	—	—	—	12	412
1953	SF	10	18	104	5.8(23)	0	10	96	9.6(31)	0	—	—	—	—	—	—	—	—	—	—	kp	—	0	162
1954	SF	12	21	79	3.8(16)	1	4	70	17.5(42)	0	1	0	0.0	0	0.0	0	0	—	—	—	kpi	—	6	147
NFL	3	34	115	494	4.3(67)	3	24	328	13.7(47)	0	1	0	0.0	0	0.0	0	0	—	—	—	kpi	—	18	721
SCHAD, MIKE Michael, G, 6´5˝/290 lbs; Queens (Canada); 1986: LARm, rnd 1; B10/2/1963 Trenton, Canada **1987** LARm 1 (0) **1988** LARm 6 (0) **1989**†Phi 16 (16, LG) **1990**†Phi 12 (12, LG) **1992** Phi 14 (14, LG) **1993** Phi 13 (13, LG) **NFL** 62 (55) [6 yrs]																								
SCHAEFER, DON Donald Thomas, FB, 6´0˝/210 lbs; Notre Dame; 1956: Phi, rnd 3; B2/13/1934 Pittsburgh, PA																								
1956	Phi	12(FB)	102	320	3.1(11)	2	13	117	9.0(27)	0	3	1	33.3	11	3.7(11)	1	0	—	—	—	—	—	12	409
SCHAFFER, JOE Joseph Leonard, LB, 6´0˝/210 lbs; Tennessee; 1960: Buf, rnd 1; B10/14/1937 Cincinnati, OH **1960** Buf-A 14 (RLB)																								
SCHAFFNIT, PETE Peter Cornelius, B, 5´11˝/180 lbs; California; B1902 **1926** LA 9 (2)																								
SCHAFRATH, DICK Richard Phillip, T-G-DE, 6´3˝/253 lbs; Ohio State; 1959: Cle, rnd 2; B3/21/1937 Canton, OH **1959** Cle 12 **1960** Cle 12 (LT) **1961** Cle 13 (LT) **1962** Cle 14 (LT) **1963** Cle★14 (LT) **1964**†Cle★14 (LT) **1965** Cle★14 (LT) **1966** Cle✧13 (LT) **1967**†Cle✧14 (LT) **1968**†Cle✧14 (LT) **1969**†Cle☆14 (LT) **1970** Cle 14 (LT) **1971**†Cle 14 (LT) **NFL** 176 [13 yrs]																								
SCHAMEL, DUKE Duke Wayne, LB, 6´3˝/235 lbs; South Dakota; B11/3/1963 Glendale, CA **1987** Mia 3 (3)																								
SCHAMMEL, ZUD Francis William, G-DE, 6´2˝/235 lbs; Iowa; B8/26/1910 Waterloo, IA, D1/1973 **1937** GB 8 (3)																								
SCHANKWEILER, SCOTT Scott Brian, LB, 6´0˝/235 lbs; Maryland; B10/15/1963 Sunbury, PA **1987** Buf 3 (3)																								
SCHARER, EDDIE Edward, B, 5´6˝/165 lbs; Detroit Mercy; Notre Dame; B1/26/1902 Toledo, OH, D5/5/1989 Long Beach, CA **[K]** **1926** Det 12 (9, BB), 6 **1927** Pot 11 (3) **1928** Det 7 (0), 1 **NFL** 30 (12), 7 [3 yrs]																								
SCHAU, RYAN Ryan, T-G, 6´6˝/300 lbs; Illinois; B12/30/1975 Hammond, IN **1999** Phi 1 (0) **2000** Phi 10 (0) **2001** Phi 2 (1) **2002** Hou 4 (4) **NFL** 17 (5) [4 yrs]																								
SCHAUB, MATT Matthew Rutledge, QB, 6´5˝/235 lbs; Virginia; 2004: Atl, rnd 3; B6/25/1981 Pittsbugh, PA																								
2004	†Atl	6(1)	8	26	3.3(11)	0	—	—	—	—	70	33	47.1	330	4.7(59)	1	4	4	14	—	—	—	0	36
2005	Atl	16(1)	9	76	8.4(23)	0	—	—	—	—	64	33	51.6	495	7.7(53)	4	0	6	27	—	—	—	0	344
NFL	2	22(2)	17	102	6.0(23)	0	—	—	—	—	134	66	49.3	825	6.2(59)	5	4	10	41	—	—	—	0	380
SCHAUKOWITCH, CARL Carl, G, 6´3˝/235 lbs; Penn State; 1973: NYG, rnd 15; B2/14/1951 Pittsbugh, PA **1975** Den 11 (2)																								
SCHAUM, GREG Gregory James, DE, 6´4˝/246 lbs; Michigan State; 1976: Dal, rnd 7; B1/1/1954 Baltimore, MD **1976**†Dal 12 **1978**†NE 14 **NFL** 26 [2 yrs]																								
SCHEIB, SKIPPY Lee Raymond, C, 6´2˝/210 lbs; West Virginia Wesleyan; Washington-St. Louis; B7/28/1903 Saginaw, MI, D2/27/1989 Saginaw, MI **1930** Bkn 6 (6, c)																								
SCHEIN, JOE Joseph, T, 5´10˝/212 lbs; Brown; B11/11/1910 Brooklyn, NY, D5/27/1969 Providence, RI **1931** Pro 11 (11, RT)																								
SCHELL, HERB Herbert Phillip, B, 5´9˝/175 lbs; Ohio State; B1/5/1902 Boyertown, PA, D8/26/1985 Columbus, OH **[K]** **1924** Col 5 (1), 9																								
SCHENK, ED Edward, TE, 6´4˝/230 lbs; Baldwin-Wallace; Central Florida; B12/20/1960																								
1987	Min	3(0)	—	—	—	—	1	10	10.0(10)	0	—	—	—	—	—	—	—	—	—	—	—	—	0	5
SCHENKER, NATE Nathan, T, 6´2˝/220 lbs; Samford; B1/27/1918 Cleveland, OH **1939** Cle 4 (0)																								

YEAR	TEAM	G (GS, POS)	RUSH	YD	AVG(LG)	TD	REC	YD	AVG(LG)	TD	PASS	COMP	PCT	YD	AVG(LG)	TD	INT	SK	YD	QBR	KPR	OTD	PTS	TAY

SCHERER, BERNIE Bernard Joseph, E, 6'1"/190 lbs; Nebraska; 1936: GB, rnd 3; B1/28/1913 Spencer, NE, D3/17/2004 Sun City, AZ

YEAR	TEAM	G (GS, POS)	RUSH	YD	AVG(LG)	TD	REC	YD	AVG(LG)	TD	OTD	PTS	TAY
1936	†GB	8(1)	—	—	—	—	2	13	6.5(7)	0	1	6	17
1937	GB	9(2)	—	—	—	—	7	149	21.3(78)	2	—	12	85
1938	†GB	9(2)	—	—	—	—	2	31	15.5(16)	1	—	6	21
1939	Pit	9(3)	—	—	—	—	2	49	24.5	—	—	0	25
NFL 4		35(8)	—	—	—	—	13	242	18.6(78)	3	1	24	146

SCHEUER, BABE Abraham, T, 6'3"/240 lbs; NYU; B1912 **1934** NYG 1 (0)

SCHIBANOFF, ALEX Alexander, T, 6'1"/218 lbs; Franklin & Marshall; 1941: Det, rnd 14; B10/17/1919 Freehold, NJ, D11/27/1995 Wingdale, NY **1941** Det 2 (0) **1942** Det 6 (6, LT) **NFL** 8 (6) [2 yrs]

SCHICHTLE, HENRY Henry Ernest, QB, 6'2"/190 lbs; Hawaii; Wichita State; 1964: NYG, rnd 6; B10/13/1941 Tulsa, OK **1964** NYG 1

SCHICK, DOYLE Doyle Dean, DB, 6'1"/205 lbs; Kansas; 1961: Was, rnd 14; B2/23/1939 Lawrence, KS, D2/27/2001 Shawnee Mission, KS **1961** Was 5

SCHIEBEL, ART Arthur Charles, T, 6'0"/220 lbs; Colgate; B11/2/1907 New York, NY, D7/1/1985 Stroudsburg, PA **1932** SI 1 (0)

SCHIECHL, JOHN John George, C, 6'3"/244 lbs; Santa Clara; 1940: Phi, rnd 2; B8/22/1917 San Francisco, CA, D2/1964 Dade County, FL **1941** Pit 4 (2) **1942** Pit 2 (0) **1942** Det 9 (6, C) **1945** ChiB 9 (5, C) **1946**†ChiB 11 (3) **NFL** 35 (16) [4 yrs]

1947 SF-A 14 (11, C)

SCHIFINO, JAKE Vernon Martin, WR, 6'1"/201 lbs; Akron; 2002: Ten, rnd 5; B11/15/1979 Pittsburgh, PA **2003** Ten 13 (0) **2004** Ten 1 (0) **NFL** 14 (0) [2 yrs]

SCHILLING, RALPH Ralph Franklin, DE-E, 6'3"/218 lbs; Oklahoma City; B7/5/1921 Morris, OK, D5/9/1994 McAllen, TX **1946** Buf-A 2 (0)

YEAR	TEAM	G (GS, POS)	RUSH	YD	AVG(LG)	TD	REC	YD	AVG(LG)	TD	OTD	PTS	TAY
1946	Was	5(0)	—	—	—	—	1	14	14.0(14)	0	—	0	7

SCHILLINGER, ANDY Andrew Clemens, WR, 5'11"/179 lbs; Miami (OH); 1988: Phx, rnd 10; B11/22/1964 Lakewood, OH **1988** Phx 3 (0)

SCHINDLER, STEVE Steven Wayne, G, 6'3"/256 lbs; Boston College; 1977: Den, rnd 1; B7/24/1954 Caldwell, NJ **1977**†Den 14 (1) **1978** Den 14 (3) **NFL** 28 (4) [2 yrs]

SCHLECHT, JOHN John James, DT, 6'0"/290 lbs; Minnesota; B5/23/1978 St. Paul, MN **2001**†SF 8 (0)

SCHLEICH, VIC Victor, T, 6'3"/240 lbs; Nebraska; 1943: Bkn, rnd 10; B4/26/1920 Montrose, CO **1947**†NYY-A 11 (0)

SCHLEICHER, MAURY Maurice Gene, DE-LB, 6'3"/238 lbs; Penn State; 1959: ChiC, rnd 5; B7/17/1937 Walnutport, PA, D4/15/2004 San Jose, CA **1959** ChiC 10 **1960**†LAC-A 12 (LDE) **1961**†SD-A 14 **1962** SD-A 4 **NFL** 40 [4 yrs]

SCHLERETH, MARK Mark Frederick, G-C, 6'3"/282 lbs; Idaho; 1989: Was, rnd 10; B1/25/1968 Anchorage, AK **1989** Was 6 (6, rg) **1990**†Was 12 (7, rg) **1991**†Was◇16 (16, RG) **1992**†Was 16 (16, RG) **1993** Was 9 (8, rg) **1994** Was 16 (6, rg) **1995** Den 16 (16, LG) **1996**†Den 14 (14, LG) **1997**†Den 11 (11, LG) **1998**†Den◇16 (16, LG) **1999** Den 16 (16, LG) **2000** Den 8 (8, LG) **NFL** 156 (140) [12 yrs]

SCHLESINGER, CORY Cory Michael, FB, 6'0"/247 lbs; Nebraska; 1995: Det, rnd 6; B6/23/1972 Columbus, NE

YEAR	TEAM	G (GS, POS)	RUSH	YD	AVG(LG)	TD	REC	YD	AVG(LG)	TD	KPR	OTD	PTS	TAY
1995	†Det	16(1)	1	1	1.0(1)	0	1	2	2.0(2)	0		—	0	2
1996	Det	16(1)	—											
1997	†Det	16(2)	7	11	1.6(4)	0	5	69	13.8(33)	1		—	6	51
1998	Det	15(2)	5	17	3.4(5)	0	3	16	5.3(8)	1		—	6	30
1999	†Det	16(11, FB)	43	124	2.9(16)	0	21	151	7.2(25)	1	k	—	6	208
2000	Det	16(8, FB)	1	3	3.0(3)	0	12	73	6.1(13)	0	k	—	0	35
2001	Det	16(13, FB)	47	154	3.3(26)	3	60	466	7.8(38)	0	k	—	18	412
2002	Det	16(14, FB)	49	139	2.8(17)	2	35	263	7.5(43)	0	k	—	12	291
2003	Det	16(10, FB)	9	16	1.8(4)	0	34	247	7.3(33)	2	k	—	12	158
2004	Det	13(11, FB)	4	7	1.8(2)	0	10	91	9.1(30)	3	k	—	18	76
2005	Det	11(8, FB)	1	1	1.0(1)	0	8	31	3.9(8)	1		—	6	22
NFL 11		167(81)	167	473	2.8(26)	5	189	1409	7.5(43)	9	k	—	84	1282

SCHLEUSNER, VIN Vincent Louis, T, 6'3"/225 lbs; Iowa; B3/3/1908 Garner, IA, D6/5/1979 Rock Rapids, IA **1930** Por 14 (6, LT), 6 **1931** Por 11 (0) **NFL** 25 (6) [2 yrs]

SCHLICHTER, ART Arthur Ernest, QB, 6'3"/210 lbs; Ohio State; 1982: Bal, rnd 1; B4/25/1960 Washington Court House, OH

YEAR	TEAM	G (GS, POS)	RUSH	YD	AVG(LG)	TD	REC	PASS	COMP	PCT	YD	AVG(LG)	TD	INT	SK	YD	OTD	PTS	TAY
1982	Bal	3(0)	1	3	3.0(3)	0	—	37	17	45.9	197	5.3(24)	0	2	3	35	—	0	22
1984	Ind	9(5, qb)	19	145	7.6(22)	1	—	140	62	44.3	702	5.0(54)	3	7	23	170	—	6	241
1985	Ind	1(1)	2	13	6.5(9)	0	—	25	12	48.0	107	4.3(16)	0	2	2	6	—	0	-14
NFL 3		13(6)	22	161	7.3(22)	1	—	202	91	45.0	1006	5.0(54)	3	11	28	211	—	6	249

SCHLINKMAN, WALT Walter Gaye, FB, 5'9"/205 lbs; Texas Tech; 1945: GB, rnd 1; B5/2/1922 Channing, TX, D10/5/1994 Weimar, TX

YEAR	TEAM	G (GS, POS)	RUSH	YD	AVG(LG)	TD	REC	YD	AVG(LG)	TD	KPR	OTD	PTS	TAY
1946	GB	11(3)	97	379	3.9(44)	2	1	5	5.0(5)	0	k	—	12	415
1947	GB☆	12(0, fb)	115	439	3.8(20)	2	2	-6	-3.0(-1)	0	k	—	12	456
1948	GB	11(1, fb)	106	441	4.2(19)	4	—				k	—	24	510
1949	GB	12(2)	47	196	4.2(37)	0	—				k	—	0	204
NFL 4		46(6)	365	1455	4.0(44)	8	3	-1	-0.3(5)	0	k	—	48	1585

SCHLOPY, TODD Ross Todd, K, 5'10"/165 lbs; Michigan; B6/17/1961 Bradford, PA [K] **1987** Buf 3 (0)

SCHMAEHL, ART Arthur, FB, 5'8"/170 lbs; none; B2/5/1894 D12/1967 Chicago, IL **1921** GB 6 (6, FB), 12

SCHMARR, HERM Herman Raymond, DE, 6'2"/210 lbs; Catholic; 1937: Cle, rnd 8; B10/1/1912 New Britain, CT, D3/13/1989 Bradenton, FL **1943** Bkn 5 (2)

SCHMAUTZ, RAY Raymond Ludwig, LB, 6'1"/225 lbs; San Diego; 1966: Oak, rnd R8; B1/26/1943 Chula Vista, CA **1966** Oak-A 10

SCHMEDDING, JIM James Edward, G, 6'2"/250 lbs; Weber State; 1968: Chi, rnd 6; B2/10/1946 San Diego State, CA **1968** SD-A 1 **1969** SD-A 14 (lg) **1970** SD 9 **NFL** 24 [3 yrs]

SCHMIDT, BOB Robert Malcolm, C-T-G, 6'4"/248 lbs; Minnesota; 1958: ChiC, rnd 14; B7/9/1936 Rochester, MN **1959**†NYG 12 **1960** NYG 11 **1961**†Hou-A★12 (C) **1962**†Hou-A★14 (C) **1963** Hou-A★14 (C) **1964** Bos-A 14 (RT) **1966**†Buf-A 14 **1967** Buf-A 7 (c) **NFL** 98 [8 yrs]

SCHMIDT, GEORGE George, DE-C-LB, 6'2"/230 lbs; Illinois Tech; B10/28/1927 Chicago, IL, D8/29/1995 Schaumburg, IL **1952** GB 7 **1953** ChiC 6 **NFL** 13 [2 yrs]

SCHMIDT, HENRY Henry Joseph, DT-E, 6'4"/254 lbs; USC; Trinity (TX); 1958: SF, rnd 6; B9/28/1935 South Gate, CA **1959** SF 12 **1960** SF 12 **1961**†SD-A 14 **1962** SD-A 14 **1963**†SD-A 14 (LDT) **1964**†SD-A 14 **1965**†Buf-A◇8 **1966** NYJ-A 11 **NFL** 99 [8 yrs]

SCHMIDT, JOE Joseph Paul, LB, 6'1"/220 lbs; Pittsburgh; 1953: Det, rnd 7; B1/19/1932 Pittsburgh, PA; HOF 1973 [IC] **1953**†Det 12 (LLB) **1954**†Det★12 (LLB) **1955** Det★12 (LLB) **1956** Det★12 (MLB) **1957**†Det★12 (MLB) **1958** Det★12 (MLB) **1959**†Det★12 (MLB) **1960** Det★10 (MLB) **1961** Det★14 (MLB) **1962** Det★14 (MLB) **1963** Det☆10 **1964** Det 9 **1965** Det 14 (MLB) **NFL** 155 [13 yrs]

SCHMIDT, JOHN John Peter, C, 6'3"/210 lbs; Carnegie Mellon; B8/12/1918 Detroit, MI, D1/1979 **1940** Pit 1 (0)

SCHMIDT, KERMIT Kermit Roosevelt, E-HB, 6'0"/200 lbs; California-Davis; B7/3/1910, OK, D4/1980 Tulsa, OK **1932** Bos 1 (0)

YEAR	TEAM	G (GS, POS)	RUSH	YD	AVG(LG)	TD	REC	YD	AVG(LG)	TD	OTD	PTS	TAY
1933	Cin	5(1)	—	—	—	—	2	36	18.0	0	—	0	18
NFL 2		6(1)	—	—	—	—	2	36	18.0	0	—	0	18

SCHMIDT, ROY Roy Lee, G-T, 6'3"/248 lbs; Long Beach State; 1965: GB, rnd 13/Bos, rnd R11; B5/3/1942 Colorado Springs, CO **1967** NO 10 (LG) **1968** NO 9 **1969** Atl 9 **1970** Was 11 (6, rg) **1971**†Min 4 **NFL** 43 (6) [5 yrs]

SCHMIDT, TERRY Terry Richard, DB, 6'0"/177 lbs; Ball State; 1974: NO, rnd 5; B5/28/1952 Columbus, IN [I] **1974** NO 9 (9, RCB) **1975** NO 13 (9, RCB) **1976** ChiB 9 **1977**†ChiB 10 (1) **1978** ChiB 16 (16, LCB) **1979**†ChiB 16 (16, LCB) **1980** ChiB 16 (16, LCB) **1981** ChiB 16 (16, LCB) **1982** ChiB 9 (9, LCB) **1983** ChiB 13 (3) **1984**†ChiB 16 (0) **NFL** 143 (95) [11 yrs]

SCHMIESING, JOE Joseph Frank, DE-DT, 6'4"/245 lbs; Minnesota; New Mexico State; B4/1/1945 Melrose, MN **1968** SL 14 **1969** SL 11 **1970** SL 14 (rde) **1971** SL 9 (RDE) **1972** Det 14 (RDE) **1973** Bal 14 (RDE) **1974** NYJ 13 (RDT) **NFL** 80 [7 yrs]

SCHMIT, BOB Robert Steven, LB, 6'1"/220 lbs; Nebraska; B6/28/1950 Queens, NY **1975** NYG 13 **1976** NYG 2 **NFL** 15 [2 yrs]

SCHMITT, GEORGE George Paul, DB, 5'11"/193 lbs; Delaware; 1983: SL, rnd 6; B3/6/1961 Bryn Mawr, PA **1983** SL 16 (0)

SCHMITT, JOHN John Charles, C, 6'4"/250 lbs; Hofstra; B11/12/1942 Brooklyn, NY **1964** NYJ-A 2 **1965** NYJ-A 2 **1966** NYJ-A 14 (C) **1967** NYJ-A 14 (C) **1968**†NYJ-A☆14 (C) **1969**†NYJ-A☆14 (C) **1970** NYJ 14 (C) **1971** NYJ 14 (C) **1972** NYJ 14 (C) **1973** NYJ 14 (C) **1974** GB 14 **NFL** 130 [11 yrs]

YEAR	TEAM	G (GS, POS)	RUSH	YD	AVG(LG)	TD	REC	YD	AVG(LG)	TD	PASS	COMP	PCT	YD	AVG(LG)	TD	INT	SK	YD	QBR	KPR	OTD	PTS	TAY

SCHMITT, THEODORE Theodore Alfred, G, 5′11″/219 lbs; Pittsburgh; B10/2/1916 Pittsburgh, PA, D3/11/2001 Port Orange, FL **1938** Phi 11 (2) **1939** Phi 11 (8, LG)

YEAR	TEAM	G (GS, POS)	RUSH	YD	AVG(LG)	TD	REC	YD	AVG(LG)	TD	OTD	PTS	TAY
1940	Phi	11(2)	1	6	6.0(6)	0	1	8	8.0(8)	0		0	10
NFL	3	33(12)	1	6	6.0(6)	0	1	8	8.0(8)	0	1	6	10

SCHMITZ, BOB Robert Joseph, LB, 6′1″/235 lbs; Wisconsin; Montana State; 1961: Pit, rnd. 14; B9/10/1938 Marytown, WI, D6/8/2004 Glendale, AZ **1961** Pit 14 **1962** Pit 9 (MLB) **1963** Pit 11 (LLB) **1964** Pit 6 **1965** Pit 1 **1966** Pit 8 **1966** Min 2 **NFL** 51 [6 yrs]

SCHNARR, STEVEN Steven Donald, RB, 6′2″/216 lbs; Otterbein; B7/30/1952 Philadelphia, PA **1975** Buf 12

SCHNECK, MIKE Mike Louis, C, 6′0″/246 lbs; Wisconsin; B8/4/1977 Whitefish Bay, WI **1999** Pit 16 (0) **2000** Pit 16 (0) **2001**†Pit 16 (0) **2002**†Pit 12 (0) **2003** Pit 16 (0) **2004**†Pit 16 (0) **2005** Buf◇16 (0) **NFL** 108 (0) [7 yrs]

SCHNEIDER, DON Donald Paul, HB, 5′9″/170 lbs; Pennsylvania; 1947: Buf-A, rnd 23/1946: ChiB, rnd 5; B4/4/1924 Crafton, PA

YEAR	TEAM	G (GS, POS)	RUSH	YD	AVG(LG)	TD	REC	YD	AVG(LG)	TD	KPR	OTD	PTS	TAY
1948	†Buf-A	9(0)	15	70	4.7	0	1	14	14.0(14)	0	kp		0	93

SCHNEIDER, JOHN John J., WB, 5′10″/180 lbs; none; B2/15/1894 Columbus, OH, D7/19/1963 Cleveland, OH **1920** Col 8 (4, WB)

SCHNEIDER, LEROY Leroy, T, 5′11″/237 lbs; Tulane; B7/16/1923 Baltimore, MD, D7/14/1999 Pompano Beach, FL **1947** Bkn-A 1 (0)

SCHNEIDMAN, HERM Herman, BB-QB, 5′11″/200 lbs; Iowa; B11/22/1913 Rock Island, IL

YEAR	TEAM	G (GS, POS)	RUSH	YD	AVG(LG)	TD	REC	YD	AVG(LG)	TD		OTD	PTS	TAY
1935	GB	11(2)	4	12	3.0	0	2	16	8.0(8)	0			0	20
1936	†GB	7(2)	—	—	—	—	3	68	22.7(46)	1			6	39
1937	GB	11(3)	5	17	3.4	0	2	35	17.5(23)	0			6	40
1938	†GB	10(9, BB)	4	8	2.0	0	—	—	—	—			0	8
1939	GB	1(0)	—	—	—	—	—	—	—	—				
1940	ChiC	6(0)									i		0	43
NFL	6	46(16)	13	37	2.8	0	7	119	17.0(46)	2	i		12	150

SCHNELKER, BOB Robert Bernard, E, 6′3″/214 lbs; Bowling Green State; 1950: Cle, rnd 29; B10/17/1928 Galion, OH

YEAR	TEAM	G (GS, POS)	REC	YD	AVG(LG)	TD	OTD	PTS	TAY
1953	Phi	8	4	34	8.5(12)	—		0	17
1954	NYG	12(LE)	30	550	18.3(68)	8		48	315
1955	NYG	12(RE)	25	326	13.0(31)	2	1	18	173
1956	†NYG	12	9	122	13.6(19)	1		6	66
1957	NYG	12(RE)	20	450	22.5(70)	5		30	250
1958	†NYG◇	12(RE)	24	460	19.2(63)	5		30	255
1959	NYG★	11(RE)	37	714	19.3(66)	6		36	387
1960	NYG	12(TE)	38	610	16.1(70)	2		12	315
1961	Min	6	6	70	11.7(20)	1		6	40
1961	Pit	8	18	331	18.4(59)	3		18	181
NFL	9	105	211	3667	17.4(70)	33	1	204	1999

SCHNELLBACHER, OTTO Otto Ole, DB-E, 6′4″/188 lbs; Kansas; 1948: NYY-A, rnd 3/1947: ChiC, rnd 25; B4/15/1923 Sublette, KS [I] **1950**†NYG★12 (DB) **1951** NYG★12 (DB) **NFL** 24 [2 yrs]

YEAR	TEAM	G (GS, POS)	REC	YD	AVG(LG)	TD	KPR	OTD	PTS	TAY
1948	NYY-A	14(1)	5	72	14.4	0	pi	1	6	250
1949	†NYY-A	12(0)	1	11	11.0(11)	0	pi		0	23
AAFC	2	26(1)	6	83	13.8(11)	0	pi	1	6	273

SCHNELLER, JOHN John Benjamin, E, 6′2″/204 lbs; Wisconsin; B11/1/1911 Neenah, WI, D11/1978 Denver, CO

YEAR	TEAM	G (GS, POS)	RUSH	YD	AVG(LG)	TD	REC	YD	AVG(LG)	TD	OTD	PTS	TAY
1933	Por	9(6, le)	5	12	2.4	—	3	45	15.0	—		0	35
1934	Det	13(6, re)	—	—	—	—	4	58	14.5	—		0	29
1935	†Det	12(9, RE)	—	—	—	—	7	149	21.3(40)	2		12	85
1936	Det	12(8, RE)	—	—	—	—	7	124	17.7(30)	1		6	67
NFL	4	46(29)	5	12	2.4	0	21	376	17.9(40)	3		18	215

SCHNITKER, MIKE James Michael, G, 6′3″/245 lbs; Colorado; 1969: Den, rnd 4; B12/30/1946 Atcheson County, MO **1969** Den-A 7 **1970** Den 14 (2) **1972** Den 14 (5, rg) **1973** Den 14 (6, lg) **1974** Den 12

YEAR	TEAM	G (GS, POS)	REC	YD	AVG(LG)	TD	OTD	PTS	TAY
1971	Den	13(13, RG)	1	-11	-11.0(-11)	0		0	-6
NFL	6	74(26)	1	-11	-11.0(-11)	0		0	-6

SCHOBEL, AARON Aaron B., DE, 6′4″/262 lbs; TCU; 2001: Buf, rnd 2; B9/1/1977 Columbus, TX **2001** Buf 16 (11, RDE) **2002** Buf 16 (16, RDE) **2003** Buf 16 (16, RDE) **2004** Buf 16 (16, RDE) **2005** Buf 16 (16, RDE) **NFL** 80 (75) [5 yrs]

SCHOBEL, BO Robert Edward, DE, 6′5″/268 lbs; TCU; 2004: Ten, rnd 4; B3/24/1981 Columbus, TX **2004** Ten 5 (2) **2005** Ten 8 (0) **NFL** 13 (2) [2 yrs]

SCHOBEL, MATT Matthew Thomas, TE, 6′5″/257 lbs; Texas A&M; TCU; 2002: Cin, rnd 3; B11/4/1978 Columbus, TX

YEAR	TEAM	G (GS, POS)	REC	YD	AVG(LG)	TD	KPR	OTD	PTS	TAY
2002	Cin	16(10, TE)	27	212	7.9(20)	2			12	116
2003	Cin	15(1)	24	332	13.8(45)	2			12	176
2004	Cin	16(1)	21	201	9.6(76)	4			24	121
2005	†Cin	16(1)	18	193	10.7(28)	1	k		8	76
NFL	4	63(13)	90	938	10.4(76)	9	k		56	488

SCHOEMANN, LEROY Leroy Herbert, C, 6′1″/192 lbs; Marquette; B8/30/1914, D5/1972 **1938** GB 3 (1)

SCHOEN, TOM Thomas Ralph, DB, 5′11″/185 lbs; Notre Dame; 1968: Cle, rnd 8; B1/30/1946 Cleveland, OH **1970** Cle 4

SCHOENKE, RAY Raymond Francis, G-T, 6′4″/250 lbs; SMU; 1963: Dal, rnd 11/Oak, rnd 10; B9/10/1941 Wahiawa, HI **1963** Dal 9 **1964** Dal 14 (10, RT/rg) **1966** Was 11 (LG) **1967** Was 14 (14, LG) **1968** Was 11 (LG) **1969** Was 13 (LG) **1970** Was 14 (13, LG) **1971**†Was 14 (14, LG) **1972**†Was 12 **1973**†Was 7 (1) **1974**†Was 14 (13, LT) **1975** Was 12 (9, LG) **NFL** 145 (74) [12 yrs]

SCHOLL, ROY Roy Franklin, G, 5′8″/205 lbs; Lehigh; B9/15/1904, D10/8/1993 Topton, PA **1929** Bos 1 (0)

SCHOLTZ, BOB Robert Joseph, C-G-T, 6′4″/250 lbs; Notre Dame; 1960: Det, rnd 3/LAC, rnd 1; B12/25/1937 Watertown, SD **1960** Det 12 (C) **1961** Det 14 (C) **1962** Det 14 **1963** Det 9 **1964** Det 11 **1965** NYG 14 (C) **1966** NYG 7 **NFL** 81 [7 yrs]

SCHOLTZ, BRUCE Bruce Daniel, LB, 6′6″/240 lbs; Texas; 1982: Sea, rnd 2; B9/26/1958 La Grange, TX **1982** Sea 9 (9, LLB) **1983**†Sea 16 (16, LOLB) **1984**†Sea 16 (16, LOLB) **1985** Sea 16 (16, LOLB) **1986** Sea 16 (16, LOLB) **1987**†Sea 8 (7, LOLB) **1988** Sea 15 (15, LOLB) **1989** NE 8 (2) **NFL** 104 (97) [8 yrs]

SCHONERT, TURK Turk Leroy, QB, 6′1″/191 lbs; Stanford; 1980: Chi, rnd 9; B1/15/1957 Torrance, CA

YEAR	TEAM	G (GS, POS)	RUSH	YD	AVG(LG)	TD	PASS	COMP	PCT	YD	AVG(LG)	TD	INT	SK	YD	QBR	OTD	PTS	TAY
1981	Cin	4(0)	7	41	5.9(19)	0	19	10	52.6	166	8.7(36)	0	0	3	.4	—		0	124
1982	†Cin	2(0)	3	-8	-2.7(-3)	0	1	1	100.0	6	6.0(6)	0	0	1	8	—		0	-5
1983	Cin	9(3, qb)	29	117	4.0(15)	2	156	92	59.0	1159	7.4(54)	2	5	15	122	—		12	527
1984	Cin	8(3)	13	77	5.9(17)	1	117	78	66.7	945	8.1(57)	4	7	16	115	—		6	300
1985	Cin	7(0)	8	39	4.9(17)	0	51	33	64.7	460	9.0(71)	1	0	6	54	—		0	274
1986	Atl	8(5, qb)	11	12	1.1(7)	1	154	95	61.7	1032	6.7(41)	4	8	21	206	—		6	238
1987	Cin	11(0)	—	—	—	—													
1988	†Cin	16(0)	2	10	5.0(7)	—	4	2	50.0	20	5.0(17)	0	0	0	0	—		0	20
1989	Cin	7(1)	—	—	—	—	0	0	0.0	0	0.0	0	0	2	27	—		0	0
NFL	9	72(12)	73	288	3.9(19)	4	504	311	61.7	3788	7.5(71)	11	20	64	536	75.6		24	1477

SCHOTTEL, IVAN Ivan Estill, B-E, 6′2″/204 lbs; Northwest Missouri State; B10/11/1921 Cosby, MO, D8/21/2000 St. Joseph, MO **1948** Det 6 (4)

YEAR	TEAM	G (GS, POS)	RUSH	YD	AVG(LG)	TD	REC	YD	AVG(LG)	TD	KPR	OTD	PTS	TAY
1946	Det	10(3)	4	12	3.0(5)	0	4	147	36.8(70)	1	Pk		6	96
NFL	2	16(7)	4	12	3.0(5)	0	4	147	36.8(70)	1			6	91

SCHOTTENHEIMER, MARTY Martin Edward, LB, 6′3″/225 lbs; Pittsburgh; 1965: Buf, rnd 7/Bal, rnd 4; B9/23/1943 Canonsburg, PA [C] **1965**†Buf-A◇14 **1966**†Buf-A 14 **1967** Buf-A 14 (14, mlb) **1968** Bos-A 11 (1) **1970** Bos 12 (4) **NFL** 79 (10) [6 yrs]

SCHRADER, JIM James Lee, C-T, 6′2″/244 lbs; Notre Dame; 1954: Was, rnd 2; B6/27/1932 Weston, WV, D1/16/1972 Norristown, PA **1954** Was 10 **1956** Was 4 **1957** Was 12 (12, C) **1958** Was◇12 (12, C) **1959** Was◇12 (12, C) **1960** Was☆12 (12, C) **1961** Was☆14 (C) **1962** Phi☆13 (C) **1963** Phi 13 (C) **1964** Phi 14 **NFL** 116 (48) [10 yrs]

Schreiber, Adam Adam Blayne, G-C, 6´4˝/290 lbs; Texas; 1984: Sea, rnd 9; B2/20/1962 Galveston, TX **1984**†Sea 6 (0) **1985** NO 1 (0) **1986** Phi 9 (0) **1987** Phi 12 (12, LG) **1988** Phi 6 (0) **1988** NYJ 7 (0) **1989** NYJ 15 (0) **1990** Min 16 (0) **1991** Min 15 (0) **1992**†Min 16 (1) **1993**†Min 16 (16, C) **1994** NYG 16 (2) **1995** NYG 16 (0) **1996** NYG 15 (2) **1997** Atl 16 (0) **1998**†Atl 16 (0) **1999** Atl 3 (0) **NFL** 201 (33) [16 yrs]

Schreiber, Larry Lawrence Anthony, RB, 6´0˝/210 lbs; Tennessee Tech; 1970: SF, rnd 10; B8/11/1947 Covington, KY **[K]**

YEAR	TEAM	G (GS, POS)	RUSH	YD	AVG (LG)	TD	REC	YD	AVG (LG)	TD	PASS	COMP	PCT	YD	AVG (LG)	TD	INT	SK	YD	QBR	KPR	OTD	PTS	TAY
1971	†SF	14	34	180	5.3(23)	0	3	79	26.3(46)	1	—	—	—	—	—	—	—	—	—	—	K	—	7	225
1972	†SF	14	118	420	3.6(20)	2	31	283	9.1(64)	1	—	—	—	—	—	—	—	—	—	—	k	—	18	598
1973	SF	4(4)	42	163	3.9(13)	0	12	98	8.2(31)	0	—	—	—	—	—	—	—	—	—	—	—	—	0	212
1974	SF	14(14, FB)	174	634	3.6(21)	3	30	217	7.2(16)	1	—	—	—	—	—	—	—	—	—	—	—	—	24	778
1975	SF	14(14, FB)	134	337	2.5(15)	5	40	289	7.2(20)	1	—	—	—	—	—	—	—	—	—	—	—	—	36	537
1976	ChiB	14	4	15	3.8(11)	0	1	16	16.0(16)	0	—	—	—	—	—	—	—	—	—	—	—	—	0	23
NFL	6	74(32)	506	1749	3.5(23)	10	117	982	8.4(64)	4	—	—	—	—	—	—	—	—	—	—	Kk	—	85	2371

Schroeder, Bill William Henry, HB, 6´0˝/190 lbs; Wisconsin; B4/11/1923 Sheboygan, WI, D12/9/2003 Sheboygan, WI

YEAR	TEAM	G (GS, POS)	RUSH	YD	AVG (LG)	TD	REC	YD	AVG (LG)	TD	PASS	COMP	PCT	YD	AVG (LG)	TD	INT	SK	YD	QBR	KPR	OTD	PTS	TAY
1946	ChiR-A	14(3)	12	42	3.5	0	1	9	9.0(9)	0	2	1	50.0	10	5.0(10)	0	0	—	—	—	ki	—	0	62
1947	ChiR-A	12(3)	11	45	4.1	0	2	19	9.5	1	—	—	—	—	—	—	—	—	—	—	ki	2	18	225
AAFC	2	26(6)	23	87	3.8	0	3	28	9.3(9)	1	2	1	50.0	10	5.0(10)	0	0	—	—	—	ki	2	18	286

Schroeder, Bill William Fredrich, WR, 6´3˝/200 lbs; Wisconsin-LaCrosse; 1994: GB, rnd 6; B1/9/1971 Eau Claire, WI

YEAR	TEAM	G (GS, POS)	RUSH	YD	AVG (LG)	TD	REC	YD	AVG (LG)	TD	PASS	COMP	PCT	YD	AVG (LG)	TD	INT	SK	YD	QBR	KPR	OTD	PTS	TAY
1997	GB	15(1)	—	—	—	—	2	15	7.5(8)	1	—	—	—	—	—	—	—	—	—	—	kp	—	6	392
1998	GB	13(3)	—	—	—	—	31	452	14.6(46)	1	—	—	—	—	—	—	—	—	—	—	p	—	6	226
1999	GB	16(16, WR)	—	—	—	—	74	1051	14.2(51)	5	—	—	—	—	—	—	—	—	—	—	k	—	30	546
2000	GB	16(16, WR)	2	11	5.5(12)	0	65	999	15.4(55)	4	—	—	—	—	—	—	—	—	—	—	—	—	24	531
2001	†GB	14(14, WR)	1	6	6.0(6)	0	53	918	**17.3(67)**	9	—	—	—	—	—	—	—	—	—	—	—	—	54	510
2002	Det	14(13, WR)	—	—	—	—	36	595	16.5(46)	5	—	—	—	—	—	—	—	—	—	—	—	—	32	323
2003	Det	16(13, WR)	—	—	—	—	36	397	11.0(26)	2	1	0	0.0	0	0.0	0	0	—	—	—	—	—	12	209
2004	TB	7(2)	—	—	—	—	7	156	22.3(54)	1	—	—	—	—	—	—	—	—	—	—	kp	—	6	73
NFL	8	111(78)	3	17	5.7(12)	0	304	4583	15.1(67)	28	1	0	0.0	0	0.0	0	0	—	—	—	kp	—	170	2808

Schroeder, Gene Eugene Willard, E-DB, 6´3˝/192 lbs; Virginia; 1951: ChiB, rnd 1; B3/3/1929 Washington, DC

YEAR	TEAM	G (GS, POS)	RUSH	YD	AVG (LG)	TD	REC	YD	AVG (LG)	TD	PASS	COMP	PCT	YD	AVG (LG)	TD	INT	SK	YD	QBR	KPR	OTD	PTS	TAY
1951	ChiB	12(DB/re)	1	4	4.0(4)	0	24	461	19.2(75)	3	—	—	—	—	—	—	—	—	—	—	ki	—	18	290
1952	ChiB✧	12(RE)	—	—	—	—	39	660	16.9(56)	6	—	—	—	—	—	—	—	—	—	—	—	—	36	360
1954	ChiB	5	—	—	—	—	1	71	71.0(71)	1	—	—	—	—	—	—	—	—	—	—	—	—	6	41
1955	ChiB	12	—	—	—	—	17	315	18.5(51)	2	—	—	—	—	—	—	—	—	—	—	—	—	12	168
1956	†ChiB	11	—	—	—	—	20	315	15.8(32)	1	—	—	—	—	—	—	—	—	—	—	—	—	6	163
1957	ChiB	12	—	—	—	—	3	48	16.0(18)	0	—	—	—	—	—	—	—	—	—	—	—	—	0	24
NFL	6	64	1	4	4.0(4)	0	104	1870	18.0(75)	13	—	—	—	—	—	—	—	—	—	—	ki	—	78	1044

Schroeder, Jay Jay Brian, QB, 6´4˝/215 lbs; UCLA; 1984: Was, rnd 3; B6/28/1961 Milwaukee, WI

YEAR	TEAM	G (GS, POS)	RUSH	YD	AVG (LG)	TD	REC	YD	AVG (LG)	TD	PASS	COMP	PCT	YD	AVG (LG)	TD	INT	SK	YD	QBR	KPR	OTD	PTS	TAY
1985	Was	9(5, qb)	17	30	1.8(14)	0	—	—	—	—	209	112	53.6	1458	7.0(53)	5	5	15	114	—	P	—	0	584
1986	†Was★	16(16, QB)	36	47	1.3(20)	1	—	—	—	—	**541**	**276**	51.0	**4109**	7.6(71)	22	22	28	240	72.9	—	—	6	1342
1987	†Was	11(10, QB)	26	120	4.6(31)	3	—	—	—	—	267	129	48.3	1878	7.0(84)	12	10	17	149	71.0	—	—	18	749
1988	LARd	9(8, QB)	29	109	3.8(12)	1	—	—	—	—	256	113	44.1	1839	7.2(85)	13	13	19	178	64.6	—	—	6	584
1989	LARd	11(9, QB)	15	38	2.5(19)	0	—	—	—	—	194	91	46.9	1550	8.0(84)	8	13	20	132	—	—	—	0	333
1990	†LARd	16(16, QB)	37	81	2.2(17)	0	—	—	—	—	334	182	54.5	2849	**8.5(68)**	19	9	29	197	90.8	—	—	0	1241
1991	LARd	15(15, QB)	28	76	2.7(15)	0	—	—	—	—	357	189	52.9	2562	7.2(78)	15	16	31	238	71.4	—	—	0	792
1992	LARd	13(9, QB)	28	160	5.7(19)	0	—	—	—	—	253	123	48.6	1476	5.8(53)	11	11	25	180	63.3	—	—	0	513
1993	Cin	9(3, qb)	10	41	4.1(20)	0	—	—	—	—	159	78	49.1	832	5.2(37)	5	2	13	87	—	—	—	0	402
1994	Arz	9(8, QB)	16	59	3.7(16)	0	—	—	—	—	238	133	55.9	1510	6.3(48)	4	7	11	85	—	—	—	0	554
NFL	10	118(99)	242	761	3.1(31)	5	—	—	—	—	2808	1426	50.8	20063	7.1(85)	114	108	208	1600	71.7	P	—	30	7093

Schroll, Bill Charles William, LB-FB, 6´0˝/214 lbs; LSU; 1948: LA, rnd 14; B1/24/1926 Alexandria, LA **1949**†Buf-A 12 (0)

1951 GB 12 (LLB)

YEAR	TEAM	G (GS, POS)	RUSH	YD	AVG (LG)	TD	REC	YD	AVG (LG)	TD	PASS	COMP	PCT	YD	AVG (LG)	TD	INT	SK	YD	QBR	KPR	OTD	PTS	TAY
1950	Det	12(RLB)	1	1	1.0(1)	0	—	—	—	—	—	—	—	—	—	—	—	—	—	—	i	—	0	-1
NFL	2	24	1	1	1.0(1)	0	—	—	—	—	—	—	—	—	—	—	—	—	—	—	—	—	0	1

Schroy, Ken Kenneth Michael, DB, 6´2˝/198 lbs; Maryland; 1975: Phi, rnd 10; B9/22/1952 Valley Forge, PA **1977** NYJ 14 (2) **1978** NYJ 16 (2) **1979** NYJ 16 (1) **1980** NYJ 14 (10, SS) **1981**†NYJ 16 (16, SS) **1982**†NYJ 9 (9, SS) **1983** NYJ 16 (16, SS) **1984** NYJ 12 (7, ss) **NFL** 113 (63) [8 yrs]

Schuber, Jim James Buchanon, HB, 5´8˝/160 lbs; Navy; B6/23/1904 Ancon, Panama Canal Zone, D5/26/1982 Naples, FL **1930** Bkn 1 (0)

Schubert, Eric Eric Jon, K, 5´8˝/185 lbs; Pittsburgh; B5/28/1962 Abington, PA **[K]** **1985**†NYG 8 (0) **1986** SL 5 (0) **1987** NE 1 (0) **NFL** 14 (0) [3 yrs]

Schubert, Steve Steven William, WR, 5´10˝/185 lbs; Massachusetts; B3/15/1951 Brooklyn, NY **[R]**

YEAR	TEAM	G (GS, POS)	RUSH	YD	AVG (LG)	TD	REC	YD	AVG (LG)	TD	PASS	COMP	PCT	YD	AVG (LG)	TD	INT	SK	YD	QBR	KPR	OTD	PTS	TAY
1974	NE	8(3)	—	—	—	—	1	21	21.0(21)	1	—	—	—	—	—	—	—	—	—	—	kp	—	6	53
1975	ChiB	12	—	—	—	—	5	68	13.6(16)	0	—	—	—	—	—	—	—	—	—	—	kp	—	0	48
1976	ChiB	14(1)	—	—	—	—	4	74	18.5(25)	0	—	—	—	—	—	—	—	—	—	—	kp	—	0	30
1977	†ChiB	13	—	—	—	—	8	119	14.9(32)	0	—	—	—	—	—	—	—	—	—	—	p	1	6	206
1978	ChiB	13	—	—	—	—	4	51	12.8(19)	0	—	—	—	—	—	—	—	—	—	—	kp	1	6	150
1979	ChiB	14	—	—	—	—	2	29	14.5(15)	0	—	—	—	—	—	—	—	—	—	—	kp	1	6	153
NFL	6	74(4)	—	—	—	—	24	362	15.1(32)	1	—	—	—	—	—	—	—	—	—	—	kp	3	24	638

Schuehle, Jake Charles John, HB, 6´0˝/196 lbs; Rice; 1939: Phi, rnd 6; B9/28/1917 Hondo, TX, D1/8/2001 O'Hanis, TX **1939** Phi 2 (0)

Schuelke, Karl Karl Herman, FB, 5´10˝/200 lbs; Wisconsin; B9/5/1914 Marshfield, WI, D2/18/1992 Wausau, WI

YEAR	TEAM	G (GS, POS)	RUSH	YD	AVG (LG)	TD	REC	YD	AVG (LG)	TD	PASS	COMP	PCT	YD	AVG (LG)	TD	INT	SK	YD	QBR	KPR	OTD	PTS	TAY
1939	Pit	1(0)	2	2	1.0	0	—	—	—	—	—	—	—	—	—	—	—	—	—	—	—	—	0	2

Schuette, Carl Charles William, LB-C-DB, 6´1˝/206 lbs; Marquette; 1947: Det, rnd 22; B4/4/1922 Sheboygan, WI, D12/1975 **1948**†Buf-A 14 (0) **1949** Buf-A 10 (0) **AAFC** 24 [2 yrs]

1950 GB 12 (LLB) **1951** GB 12 **NFL** 24 [2 yrs]

Schuette, Paul Paul August, G, 6´0˝/220 lbs; Wisconsin; B3/10/1906 South Bend, IN, D10/20/1960 **1928** NYG 4 (2) **1930** ChiB 11 (6, lg) **1931** ChiB 11 (5, lg) **1932** ChiB 1 (0) **1932** Bos 4 (1) **NFL** 31 (14) [4 yrs]

Schuh, Harry Harry Frederick, T, 6´3˝/260 lbs; Memphis; 1965: Oak, rnd 1; B9/25/1942 Philadelphia, PA **1965** Oak-A 14 (RT) **1966** Oak-A 14 (14, RT) **1967**†Oak-A★14 (RT) **1968**†Oak-A☆14 (14, RT) **1969**†Oak-A★14 (14, RT) **1970**†Oak★14 (13, RT) **1971** LARm 14 (14, RT) **1972** LARm 14 (14, RT) **1973**†LARm 14 **1974** GB 14 (LT) **NFL** 140 (83) [10 yrs]

Schuh, Jeff Jeffrey John, LB, 6´2˝/228 lbs; Minnesota; 1981: Cin, rnd 7; B5/22/1958 Crystal, MN **1981**†Cin 16 (0) **1982**†Cin 9 (0) **1983** Cin 16 (0) **1984** Cin 16 (11, LOLB) **1985** Cin 16 (14, LOLB) **1986** GB 12 (2) **1986** Min 2 (0) **NFL** 87 (27) [6 yrs]

Schuhmacher, John John, G-T, 6´3˝/271 lbs; USC; 1978: Hou, rnd 12; B9/23/1955 Salem, OR **1978**†Hou 11 **1981** Hou 16 (15, LG) **1982** Hou 9 (9, LT) **1983** Hou 1 (1) **1984** Hou 16 (10, RG) **1985** Hou 16 (16, RG) **NFL** 69 (51) [6 yrs]

Schuler, Bill William Moughon, T, 6´0˝/215 lbs; Auburn; Yale; 1947: NYG, rnd 31; B10/18/1922 Birmingham, AL **1947** NYG 11 (8, LT) **1948** NYG 12 (11, RT) **NFL** 23 (19) [2 yrs]

Schulte, Rick Richard J., G-T, 6´2˝/270 lbs; Illinois; B11/24/1963 Chicago, IL **1987** Buf 3 (3)

Schulters, Lance Lance, DB, 6´2˝/202 lbs; Hofstra; 1998: SF, rnd 4; B5/27/1975 Guyana **1998**†SF 15 (0) **1999** SF✧13 (13, FS) **2000** SF 12 (12, SS) **2001**†SF 16 (16, SS) **2002**†Ten☆16 (16, FS) **2003**†Ten 16 (16, FS) **2004** Ten 3 (3) **2005** Mia 16 (16, FS) **NFL** 107 (92) [8 yrs]

Schultz, Charlie Charles William, T, 6´3˝/230 lbs; Minnesota; 1939: GB, rnd 20; B10/8/1916 St. Paul, MN, D3/15/1989 Pebble Beach, CA **1939**†GB✧9 (1) **1940** GB 2 (0) **1941**†GB 10 (7, RT) **NFL** 21 (8) [3 yrs]

Schultz, Chris Christopher, T, 6´8˝/277 lbs; Arizona; 1983: Dal, rnd 7; B2/16/1960 Hamilton, Canada **1983**†Dal 5 (0) **1985**†Dal 16 (8, lt) **NFL** 21 (8) [2 yrs]

SCHULTZ, ELBIE Eberle Hynson, T-G, 6´4˝/252 lbs; Oregon State; 1940: Phi, rnd 4; B12/23/1917 Eugene, OR, D5/20/2002 Arcata, CA **1940** Phi 11 (3) **1941** Pit 11 (9, LG) **1942** Pit 11 (11, LT) **1943** P-P☆10 (10, LG) **1944** C-P 10 (6, lg) **1945**†Cle☆10 (10, LT) **1946** LARm 11 (11, LT) **1947** LARm 12 (1) **NFL** 86 (61) [8 yrs]

SCHULTZ, HEINE Heinie, E, 5´10˝/182 lbs; none; deceased **1920** Det 1 (0)

SCHULTZ, JOHN John Andreas, WR, 5´10˝/182 lbs; Maryland; B6/10/1953 Binghamton, NY **1977**†Den 14 **1978** Den 4

YEAR	TEAM	G(GS, POS)	RUSH	YD	AVG(LG)	TD	REC	YD	AVG(LG)	TD	PASS	COMP	PCT	YD	AVG(LG)	TD	INT	SK	YD	QBR	KPR	OTD	PTS	TAY
1976	Den	14	—	—	—	—	2	29	14.5(16)	0	—	—	—	—	—	—	—	—	—	—	kp	—	0	49
NFL	3	32	—	—	—	—	2	29	14.5(16)	0	—	—	—	—	—	—	—	—	—	—	kp	—	0	105

SCHULTZ, PETE Peter, FB, /187 lbs; none **1920** ChiC 1 (0) **1922** Col 1 (1) **NFL** 2 (1) [2 yrs]

SCHULTZ, RANDY Randolph B., RB, 6´0˝/210 lbs; Northern Iowa; 1966: Cle, rnd 5/NYJ, rnd 20; B11/17/1943 Iowa Falls, IA, D10/4/1996 Cedar Falls, IA

YEAR	TEAM	G(GS, POS)	RUSH	YD	AVG(LG)	TD	REC	YD	AVG(LG)	TD	PASS	COMP	PCT	YD	AVG(LG)	TD	INT	SK	YD	QBR	KPR	OTD	PTS	TAY
1966	Cle	14	7	32	4.6(20)	0	—	—	—	—	—	—	—	—	—	—	—	—	—	—	k	—	0	39
1967	NO	8	32	117	3.7(22)	2	14	186	13.3(25)	0	—	—	—	—	—	—	—	—	—	—	—	—	12	230
1968	NO	9	43	152	3.5(15)	0	12	34	2.8(14)	0	—	—	—	—	—	—	—	—	—	—	—	—	0	169
NFL	3	31	82	301	3.7(22)	2	26	220	8.5(25)	0	—	—	—	—	—	—	—	—	—	—	k	—	12	438

SCHULTZ, WILLIAM William, G-T, 6´5˝/305 lbs; USC; 1990: Ind, rnd 4; B5/1/1967 Granada Hills, CA **1990** Ind 12 (0) **1991** Ind 10 (9, RG) **1993** Ind 14 (14, RG) **1995** Den 2 (0) **1997** ChiB 8 (3)

YEAR	TEAM	G(GS, POS)	RUSH	YD	AVG(LG)	TD	REC	YD	AVG(LG)	TD	PASS	COMP	PCT	YD	AVG(LG)	TD	INT	SK	YD	QBR	KPR	OTD	PTS	TAY
1992	Ind	10(2)	—	—	—	—	1	3	3.0(3)	1	—	—	—	—	—	—	—	—	—	—	—	—	6	7
NFL	6	56(28)	—	—	—	—	1	3	3.0(3)	1	—	—	—	—	—	—	—	—	—	—	—	—	6	7

SCHULZ, JODY Jody John, LB, 6´3˝/235 lbs; Chowan Coll. (NC); East Carolina; 1983: Phi, rnd 2; B8/17/1960 Easton, MD **1983** Phi 6 (4) **1984** Phi 15 (2) **1986** Phi 16 (0) **1987** Phi 7 (0) **NFL** 44 (6) [4 yrs]

SCHULZ, KURT Kurt Erich, DB, 6´1˝/208 lbs; Eastern Washington; 1992: Buf, rnd 7; B12/12/1968 Wenatchee, WA **[I]** **1992**†Buf 8 (1) **1993**†Buf 12 (0) **1994** Buf 16 (0) **1995**†Buf☆13 (13, FS) **1996**†Buf 15 (15, FS) **1997** Buf 15 (14, FS) **1998**†Buf 12 (12, FS) **1999**†Buf 16 (16, FS) **2000** Det 11 (11, FS) **2001** Det 11 (10, FS/ss) **NFL** 129 (92) [10 yrs]

SCHUMACHER, GREGG Gregg Harold, DE, 6´2˝/240 lbs; Illinois; 1965: SF, rnd 13; B6/30/1942 Chicago, IL **1967** LARm 11 **1968** LARm 14 (9, RDE) **NFL** 25 (9) [2 yrs]

SCHUMACHER, KURT Kurt, G-T, 6´3˝/252 lbs; Ohio State; 1975: NO, rnd 1; B12/26/1952 Cleveland, OH **1975** NO 13 **1976** NO 14 (9, LG) **1977** NO 14 **1978** TB 4 (4) **NFL** 45 (13) [4 yrs]

SCHUPP, WALT Walter Lee, T-G, 6´0˝/185 lbs; Miami (OH); B9/1895, deceased **1921** Cin 4 (4, RT)

SCHUSTER, DICK Richard Louis, G, 6´1˝/185 lbs; Dayton; Penn State; B3/2/1900, D2/8/1980 Binghamton, NY **1925** Can 4 (3)

SCHUTT, SCOTT Scott Joseph, LB, 6´4˝/218 lbs; North Dakota State; B8/31/1963 Prairie du Sac, WI **1987** Cin 3 (0)

SCHWAB, RAY Raymond, BB-E, /205 lbs; Oklahoma City; B2/28/1908, MO, D5/3/1988 Cheshire, CT **1931** NYG 1 (0) **1932** SI 1 (0) **NFL** 2 (0) [2 yrs]

SCHWALL, VIC Victor Henry, HB, 5´8˝/190 lbs; Northwestern; 1947: NYG, rnd 1/Mia-A, rnd 7; B1/21/1925 Oak Park, IL, D10/14/2000 Morton Grove, IL

YEAR	TEAM	G(GS, POS)	RUSH	YD	AVG(LG)	TD	REC	YD	AVG(LG)	TD	PASS	COMP	PCT	YD	AVG(LG)	TD	INT	SK	YD	QBR	KPR	OTD	PTS	TAY
1947	ChiC	11(0)	12	33	2.8(16)	0	—	—	—	—	—	—	—	—	—	—	—	—	—	—	k	—	0	38
1948	†ChiC	7(0)	15	107	7.1(23)	1	2	13	6.5(7)	0	1	0	0.0	0	0.0	0	0	—	—	—	—	—	6	124
1949	ChiC	11(0)	12	47	3.9(18)	0	3	8	2.7(18)	2	2	0	0.0	0	0.0	0	0	—	—	—	k	—	12	64
1950	ChiC	12	17	114	6.7(26)	0	1	7	7.0(7)	0	—	—	—	—	—	—	—	—	—	—	k	—	0	124
NFL	4	41	56	301	5.4(26)	1	6	28	4.7(18)	2	3	0	0.0	0	0.0	0	0	—	—	—	k	—	18	349

SCHWAMMEL, ADE Adolphe John, T, 6´2˝/225 lbs; Oregon State; B10/14/1908 Los Angeles, CA, D11/18/1979 Honolulu, HI **[K]** **1934** GB 13 (10, RT) **1935** GB☆11 (8, RT) **1936**†GB☆12 (7, RT) **1943** GB 2 (0) **1944** GB 8 (4) **NFL** 46 (29) [5 yrs]

SCHWANTZ, JIM James William, LB, 6´2˝/240 lbs; Purdue; B1/23/1970 Arlington Heights, IL **1992** ChiB 1 (0) **1994**†Dal 7 (0) **1995**†Dal 16 (0) **1996**†Dal★16 (0) **1997**†SF 16 (0) **1998** ChiB 16 (0) **NFL** 72 (0) [6 yrs]

SCHWARTZ, BRYAN Bryan Lee, LB, 6´4˝/253 lbs; Augustana (SD); 1995: Jax, rnd 2; B12/5/1971 St. Lawrence, SD **1995** Jax 14 (9, MLB) **1996** Jax 4 (3) **1997**†Jax 16 (16, MLB) **1998**†Jax 13 (12, MLB) **1999** Jax 8 (0) **NFL** 55 (40) [5 yrs]

SCHWARTZ, DON Donald Jeffret, DB, 6´1˝/191 lbs; Washington State; 1978: NO, rnd 4; B2/24/1956 Billings, MT **1978** NO 16 **1979** NO 14 (4) **1980** NO 16 (7, ss) **1981** SL 5 (1) **NFL** 51 (12) [4 yrs]

SCHWARTZ, ELMER Elmer George, B, 6´0˝/212 lbs; Washington State; B1907, deceased

YEAR	TEAM	G(GS, POS)	RUSH	YD	AVG(LG)	TD	REC	YD	AVG(LG)	TD	PASS	COMP	PCT	YD	AVG(LG)	TD	INT	SK	YD	QBR	KPR	OTD	PTS	TAY
1931	Por	12(5, FB)	—	—	—	—	—	—	—	—	—	—	—	—	—	—	—	—	—	—	—	—	—	—
1932	ChiC	3(1)	2	9	4.5	0	—	—	—	—	—	—	—	—	—	—	—	—	—	—	—	—	0	9
1933	Pit	10(5, hb)	38	94	2.5	0	2	20	10.0	0	22	5	22.7	103	4.7	0	3	—	—	—	—	—	0	36
NFL	3	25(11)	40	103	2.6	2	2	20	10.0	0	22	5	22.7	103	4.7	0	3	—	—	—	—	1	18	75

SCHWARTZ, PERRY Perry, E, 6´2˝/199 lbs; California; 1938: Bkn, rnd 6; B4/27/1915 Chicago, IL, D1/4/2001 Cloverdale, CA

YEAR	TEAM	G(GS, POS)	RUSH	YD	AVG(LG)	TD	REC	YD	AVG(LG)	TD	PASS	COMP	PCT	YD	AVG(LG)	TD	INT	SK	YD	QBR	KPR	OTD	PTS	TAY
1938	Bkn✧	10(9, LE)	2	-3	-1.5	0	8	132	16.5	1	—	—	—	—	—	—	—	—	—	—	—	—	6	68
1939	Bkn★	11(11, LE)	—	—	—	—	33	550	16.7(66)	3	—	—	—	—	—	—	—	—	—	—	—	—	18	290
1940	Bkn☆	11(11, LE)	—	—	—	—	21	370	17.6	3	—	—	—	—	—	—	—	—	—	—	—	—	18	200
1941	Bkn★	11(11, LE)	1	7	7.0(7)	0	25	362	**14.5(36)**	2	—	—	—	—	—	—	—	—	—	—	k	—	12	189
1942	Bkn★	11(10, LE)	2	20	10.0(17)	0	13	200	15.4(71)	1	—	—	—	—	—	—	—	—	—	—	k	—	6	120
NFL	5	54(52)	5	24	4.8(17)	0	100	1614	16.1(71)	10	—	—	—	—	—	—	—	—	—	—	k	—	60	867
1946	†NYY-A	14(1)	—	—	—	—	5	82	16.4	0	—	—	—	—	—	—	—	—	—	—	k	—	0	34

SCHWARZER, TED Edward, G-C, 5´11˝/190 lbs; Centenary; B2/13/1900 Austin, TX, D12/8/1980 Austin, TX **1926** Buf 6 (2)

SCHWEDA, BRIAN Brian Christopher, DE, 6´3˝/250 lbs; Kansas; 1965: Chi, rnd 8/Den, rnd 16; B4/30/1943 Kansas City, KS **1966** ChiB 14 **1967** NO 14 (RDE) **1968** NO 10 (RDE) **NFL** 38 [3 yrs]

SCHWEDER, JOHN John Anthony, G-MG-LB, 6´1˝/224 lbs; Pennsylvania; 1949: Phi, rnd 25; B12/23/1927 Bethlehem, PA, D6/9/2005 Muhlenburg, PA **1950** Bal 11 (3) **1951** Pit 12 (MG) **1952** Pit 12 (LG) **1953** Pit 12 (LG) **1954** Pit 12 (LG) **1955** Pit 12 (LG) **NFL** 71 (3) [6 yrs]

SCHWEDES, GERHARD Gerhard, HB, 6´1˝/205 lbs; Syracuse; 1960: Bos, rnd 1/Bal, rnd 4; B4/23/1938 Freiburg, Germany **1960** NYT-A 3 **1960** Bos-A 2

YEAR	TEAM	G(GS, POS)	RUSH	YD	AVG(LG)	TD	REC	YD	AVG(LG)	TD	PASS	COMP	PCT	YD	AVG(LG)	TD	INT	SK	YD	QBR	KPR	OTD	PTS	TAY
1961	Bos-A	5	10	14	1.4(5)	0	1	21	21.0(21)	0	—	—	—	—	—	—	—	—	—	—	k	—	0	10
NFL	2	10	10	14	1.4(5)	0	1	21	21.0(21)	0	—	—	—	—	—	—	—	—	—	—	—	—	0	25

SCHWEDES, SCOTT Scott Andrew, WR, 6´0˝/182 lbs; Syracuse; 1987: Mia, rnd 2; B6/30/1965 Syracuse, NY **[R]**

YEAR	TEAM	G(GS, POS)	RUSH	YD	AVG(LG)	TD	REC	YD	AVG(LG)	TD	PASS	COMP	PCT	YD	AVG(LG)	TD	INT	SK	YD	QBR	KPR	OTD	PTS	TAY
1987	Mia	12(0)	—	—	—	—	—	—	—	—	—	—	—	—	—	—	—	—	—	—	kp	—	0	125
1988	Mia	16(1)	—	—	—	—	6	130	21.7(42)	0	—	—	—	—	—	—	—	—	—	—	kp	—	0	179
1989	Mia	9(0)	—	—	—	—	7	174	24.9(65)	1	—	—	—	—	—	—	—	—	—	—	kp	1	12	201
1990	Mia	4(0)	—	—	—	—	6	66	11.0(19)	1	—	—	—	—	—	—	—	—	—	—	kp	—	6	104
1990	SD	5(0)	—	—	—	—	—	—	—	—	—	—	—	—	—	—	—	—	—	—	p	—	0	8
NFL	4	46(1)	—	—	—	—	19	370	19.5(65)	2	—	—	—	—	—	—	—	—	—	—	kp	1	18	617

SCHWEICKERT, BOB Robert Lynn, QB, 6´1˝/190 lbs; Virginia Tech; 1965: NYJ, rnd 4/SF, rnd 3; B9/17/1942 Richmond, VA **1965** NYJ-A 3

YEAR	TEAM	G(GS, POS)	RUSH	YD	AVG(LG)	TD	REC	YD	AVG(LG)	TD	PASS	COMP	PCT	YD	AVG(LG)	TD	INT	SK	YD	QBR	KPR	OTD	PTS	TAY
1967	NYJ-A	3	1	1	1.0(1)	0	—	—	—	—	—	—	—	—	—	—	—	—	—	—	—	—	0	1
NFL	2	6	1	1	1.0(1)	0	—	—	—	—	—	—	—	—	—	—	—	—	—	—	—	—	0	1

SCHWEIDLER, DICK Richard M., HB, 6´0˝/182 lbs; St. Louis; B8/18/1915 Culver, IN

YEAR	TEAM	G(GS, POS)	RUSH	YD	AVG(LG)	TD	REC	YD	AVG(LG)	TD	PASS	COMP	PCT	YD	AVG(LG)	TD	INT	SK	YD	QBR	KPR	OTD	PTS	TAY
1938	ChiB	10(0)	16	57	3.6	0	1	21	21.0(21)	0	1	0	0.0	0	0.0	0	0	—	—	—	—	—	0	68
1939	ChiB	4(0)	5	15	3.0	0	2	43	21.5	0	—	—	—	—	—	—	—	—	—	—	—	—	0	37
1946	†ChiB	5(2)	20	94	4.7(27)	3	1	11	11.0(11)	0	—	—	—	—	—	—	—	—	—	—	kpi	—	18	182
NFL	3	19(2)	41	166	4.0(27)	3	4	75	18.8(21)	0	1	0	0.0	0	0.0	0	0	—	—	—	kpi	—	18	286

SCHWEIGERT, STUART Stuart Eric, DB, 6´3˝/208 lbs; Purdue; 2004: Oak, rnd 3; B6/21/1981 Saginaw, MI **2004** Oak 16 (3) **2005** Oak 16 (13, FS) **NFL** 32 (16) [2 yrs]

SCHWENK, BUD Wilson Rutherford, QB-TB-HB, 6´2˝/201 lbs; Washington-St. Louis; 1942: ChiC, rnd 3; B8/26/1918 St. Louis, MO, D10/1/1980 St. Louis, MO

YEAR	TEAM	G(GS, POS)	RUSH	YD	AVG(LG)	TD	REC	YD	AVG(LG)	TD	PASS	COMP	PCT	YD	AVG(LG)	TD	INT	SK	YD	QBR	KPR	OTD	PTS	TAY
1942	ChiC	11(9, TB)	111	313	2.8(28)	2	—	—	—	—	**295**	126	42.7	1360	4.6(69)	6	**27**	—	—	25.5	Pki	—	12	-27
1946	Cle-A	4(0)	6	-1	-0.2	1	—	—	—	—	23	15	65.2	276	12.0(63)	4	0	—	—	—	—	—	6	167
1947	Bal-A	14(2, QB)	25	58	2.3	1	—	—	—	—	**327**	**168**	51.4	2236	6.8(72)	13	**20**	—	—	—	—	—	6	451

YEAR	TEAM	G (GS, POS)	RUSH	YD	AVG (LG)	TD	REC	YD	AVG (LG)	TD	PASS	COMP	PCT	YD	AVG (LG)	TD	INT	SK	YD	QBR	KPR	OTD	PTS	TAY
1948	NYY-A	8(0)	3	6	2.0	0	—	—	—	—	17	6	35.3	52	3.1	0	3	—	—	—	—	—	0	-88
AAFC	3	26(2)	34	63	1.9(28)	2	—	—	—	—	367	189	51.5	2564	7.0(72)	17	23	—	—	63.4	—	—	12	530

SCIARRA, JOHN John Michael, DB-QB, 5´11˝/185 lbs; UCLA; 1976: Chi, rnd 4; B3/2/1954 Los Angeles, CA **[R]** **1979**†Phi 16 (2) **1982** Phi 8 (1) **1983** Phi 10 (0)

YEAR	TEAM	G (GS, POS)	RUSH	YD	AVG (LG)	TD	REC	YD	AVG (LG)	TD	PASS	COMP	PCT	YD	AVG (LG)	TD	INT	SK	YD	QBR	KPR	OTD	PTS	TAY
1978	†Phi	16(2)	8	11	1.4(4)	2	—	—	—	—	1	0	0.0	0	0.0	0	0	—	—	—	pi	—	12	113
1980	†Phi	16(0)	3	11	3.7(9)	0	—	—	—	—	—	—	—	—	—	—	—	—	—	—	p	—	0	161
1981	†Phi	10(1)	1	0	0.0(0)	0	—	—	—	—	—	—	—	—	—	—	—	—	—	—	pi	—	0	1
NFL	6	76(6)	12	22	1.8(9)	2	—	—	—	—	1	0	0.0	0	0.0	0	0	—	—	—	pi	—	12	414

SCIBELLI, JOE Joseph Albert, G-T, 6´1˝/256 lbs; Notre Dame; American International; 1961: LA, rnd 10/NYT, rnd 10; B4/19/1939 Springfield, MA, D12/11/1991 Boston, MA **1962** LARm 14 **1963** LARm 14 **1964** LARm 14 **1965** LARm 14 (14, RG) **1966** LARm 14 (14, RG) **1967**†LARm 14 (RG) **1968** LARm✧14 (14, RG) **1969** LARm 7 (7, RG) **1970** LARm 14 (14, RG) **1971** LARm 14 (14, RG) **1972** LARm 13 (13, RG) **1973**†LARm☆14 (14, RG) **1974**†LARm 14 (14, RG) **1975**†LARm 14 (14, RG)

YEAR	TEAM	G (GS, POS)	RUSH	YD	AVG (LG)	TD	REC	YD	AVG (LG)	TD	PASS	COMP	PCT	YD	AVG (LG)	TD	INT	SK	YD	QBR	KPR	OTD	PTS	TAY
1961	LARm	14	—	—	—	—	1	1	1.0(1)	0	—	—	—	—	—	—	—	—	—	—	—	—	0	1
NFL	15	202(132)	—	—	—	—	1	1	1.0(1)	0	—	—	—	—	—	—	—	—	—	—	—	—	0	1

SCIFRES, MIKE Michael, P, 6´2˝/236 lbs; Western Illinois; 2003: SD, rnd 5; B10/8/1980 Metairie, LA **2003** SD 6 (0) **2005** SD 16 (0)

YEAR	TEAM	G (GS, POS)	RUSH	YD	AVG (LG)	TD	REC	YD	AVG (LG)	TD	PASS	COMP	PCT	YD	AVG (LG)	TD	INT	SK	YD	QBR	KPR	OTD	PTS	TAY
2004	†SD	16(0)	—	—	—	—	—	—	—	—	1	0	0.0	0	0.0	0	1	—	—	—	P	—	0	-40
NFL	3	38(0)	—	—	—	—	—	—	—	—	1	0	0.0	0	0.0	0	1	—	—	—	P	—	0	-40

SCIFRES, STEVE Steven William, G, 6´3˝/300 lbs; Wyoming; 1997: Dal, rnd 3; B1/22/1972 Colorado Springs, CO **1997** Dal 6 (0) **1998** Car 1 (0) **NFL** 7 (0) [2 yrs]

SCIOLI, BRAD Brad Elliott, DE-DT, 6´3˝/280 lbs; Penn State; 1999: Ind, rnd 5; B9/6/1976 Bridgeport, PA **1999**†Ind 10 (0) **2000**†Ind 16 (2) **2001** Ind 13 (12, LDE) **2002**†Ind 16 (13, LDT) **2003**†Ind 16 (0) **2004**†Ind 9 (0) **NFL** 80 (27) [6 yrs]

SCISSUM, WILLARD Willard Sebastian, T-G, 6´3˝/275 lbs; Alabama; B10/28/1962 Guntersville, AL **1987** Was 3 (3)

SCIULLO, STEVE Steven William, G, 6´5˝/330 lbs; Marshall; 2003: Ind, rnd 4; B8/27/1980 Pittsburgh, PA **2003**†Ind 13 (13, RG) **2004**†Phi 15 (5, lg) **NFL** 28 (18) [2 yrs]

SCOBEE, JOSH Josh, K, 6´1˝/191 lbs; Louisiana Tech; 2004: Jax, rnd 5; B6/23/1982 Longview, TX **[K]** **2004** Jax 16 (0) **2005**†Jax 16 (0) **NFL** 32 (0) [2 yrs]

SCOBEY, JOSH Josh, RB, 6´0˝/222 lbs; Kansas State; 2002: Arz, rnd 6; B12/11/1979 Oklahoma City, OK **[R]**

YEAR	TEAM	G (GS, POS)	RUSH	YD	AVG (LG)	TD	REC	YD	AVG (LG)	TD	PASS	COMP	PCT	YD	AVG (LG)	TD	INT	SK	YD	QBR	KPR	OTD	PTS	TAY
2003	Arz	15(0)	—	—	—	—	1	9	9.0(9)	0	—	—	—	—	—	—	—	—	—	—	k	1	6	604
2004	Arz	12(0)	27	89	3.3(10)	0	18	191	10.6(42)	0	—	—	—	—	—	—	—	—	—	—	k	—	0	428
2005	†Sea	16(0)	—	—	—	—	—	—	—	—	—	—	—	—	—	—	—	—	—	—	k	—	0	441
NFL	3	43(0)	27	89	3.3(10)	0	19	200	10.5(42)	0	—	—	—	—	—	—	—	—	—	—	k	1	6	1472

SCOGGINS, ERIC Eric Thomas, LB, 6´2˝/235 lbs; USC; 1981: Bal, rnd 12; B1/23/1959 Inglewood, CA **1982** SF 3 (0)

SCOGGINS, RON Ronald Alonzo, T, 6´6˝/305 lbs; UNLV; B8/3/1961 Inglewood, CA **1987** Sea 3 (0)

SCOLLARD, NICK Nicholas M., E-QB, 6´4˝/217 lbs; St. Joseph's (IN); 1946: Bos, rnd 2; B4/3/1920, D1/1985 Indianapolis, IN **[K]**

YEAR	TEAM	G (GS, POS)	RUSH	YD	AVG (LG)	TD	REC	YD	AVG (LG)	TD	PASS	COMP	PCT	YD	AVG (LG)	TD	INT	SK	YD	QBR	KPR	OTD	PTS	TAY
1946	Bos	11(4)	—	—	—	—	7	78	11.1(19)	1	—	—	—	—	—	—	—	—	—	—	Kk	1	33	41
1947	Bos	12(10, RE)	—	—	—	—	3	19	6.3(11)	0	—	—	—	—	—	—	—	—	—	—	K	—	5	10
1948	Bos	12(5, qb)	—	—	—	—	2	23	11.5(13)	0	—	—	—	—	—	—	—	—	—	—	K	—	14	12
1949	NYB	12(9, RE)	—	—	—	—	3	81	27.0(40)	2	—	—	—	—	—	—	—	—	—	—	Kkpi	—	39	38
NFL	4	47(28)	—	—	—	—	15	201	13.4(40)	3	—	—	—	—	—	—	—	—	—	—	Kkpi	1	91	100

SCOLNIK, GLENN Glenn, WR, 6´3˝/204 lbs; Indiana; 1973: Pit, rnd 6; B6/16/1951 Hammond, IN **1973** Pit 1

SCOTT, BART Bart Edward, LB, 6´2˝/235 lbs; Southern Illinois; B8/18/1980 Detroit, MI **2002** Bal 16 (0) **2003** Bal 16 (0) **2004** Bal 13 (0) **2005** Bal 16 (10, RLB) **NFL** 61 (10) [4 yrs]

SCOTT, BILL William James, DB, 6´0˝/188 lbs; Idaho; 1966: SD, rnd 16; B5/18/1944 Washington, DC **1968** Cin-A 14

SCOTT, BO Robert Marilla, RB, 6´3˝/215 lbs; Ohio State; 1965: Cle, rnd 3/Oak, rnd 20; B3/30/1943 Connellsville, PA

YEAR	TEAM	G (GS, POS)	RUSH	YD	AVG (LG)	TD	REC	YD	AVG (LG)	TD	PASS	COMP	PCT	YD	AVG (LG)	TD	INT	SK	YD	QBR	KPR	OTD	PTS	TAY
1969	†Cle	13(fb)	44	157	3.6(20)	0	6	25	4.2(14)	0	—	—	—	—	—	—	—	—	—	—	k	—	0	517
1970	Cle	13(FB)	151	625	4.1(63)	**7**	40	351	8.8(24)	4	—	—	—	—	—	—	—	—	—	—	—	—	66	891
1971	†Cle	14(FB)	179	606	3.4(35)	9	30	233	7.8(35)	1	—	—	—	—	—	—	—	—	—	—	—	—	60	818
1972	†Cle	12(FB)	123	571	4.6(27)	2	23	172	7.5(30)	0	—	—	—	—	—	—	—	—	—	—	—	—	12	677
1973	Cle	7	34	79	2.3(20)	0	6	23	3.8(9)	1	—	—	—	—	—	—	—	—	—	—	—	—	6	96
1974	Cle	14	23	86	3.7(20)	0	7	22	3.1(13)	0	—	—	—	—	—	—	—	—	—	—	—	—	0	97
NFL	6	73	554	2124	3.8(63)	18	112	826	7.4(35)	6	—	—	—	—	—	—	—	—	—	—	k	—	144	3094

SCOTT, BOB Robert, C-G-T, /195 lbs; none; B8/8/1895 Phil Campbell, AL, D8/1973 Phil Campbell, AL **1926** Pro 6 (1)

SCOTT, BOBBY Robert Benson, QB, 6´1˝/201 lbs; Tennessee; 1971: NO, rnd 14; B4/2/1949 Chattanooga, TN

YEAR	TEAM	G (GS, POS)	RUSH	YD	AVG (LG)	TD	REC	YD	AVG (LG)	TD	PASS	COMP	PCT	YD	AVG (LG)	TD	INT	SK	YD	QBR	KPR	OTD	PTS	TAY
1973	NO	6	9	18	2.0(4)	0	—	—	—	—	54	18	33.3	245	4.5(42)	1	3	4	29	—	—	—	0	26
1974	NO	5(1)	1	1	1.0(1)	0	—	—	—	—	71	31	43.7	366	5.2(36)	4	4	6	62	—	—	—	0	44
1975	NO	1	—	—	—	—	—	—	—	—	17	8	47.1	96	5.6(33)	0	1	1	12	—	—	—	0	8
1976	NO	11(8, QB)	12	48	4.0(13)	1	—	—	—	—	190	103	54.2	1065	5.6(60)	4	6	24	162	—	—	—	6	371
1977	NO	5(3)	4	11	2.8(9)	0	—	—	—	—	82	36	43.9	516	6.3(53)	3	8	5	43	—	P	—	0	-36
1978	NO	1	1	0	0.0(0)	0	—	—	—	—	5	3	60.0	36	7.2(23)	0	0	—	—	—	—	—	0	18
1979	NO	3	—	—	—	—	—	—	—	—	2	2	100.0	12	6.0(6)	0	0	—	—	—	—	—	0	6
1980	NO	5(0)	—	—	—	—	—	—	—	—	33	16	48.5	200	6.1(40)	2	1	4	41	—	—	—	0	70
1981	NO	4(1)	3	-4	-1.3(-1)	0	—	—	—	—	46	20	43.5	245	5.3(31)	1	5	7	72	—	—	—	0	-77
NFL	9	41(13)	30	74	2.5(13)	1	—	—	—	—	500	237	47.4	2781	5.6(60)	15	28	51	421	51.4	P	—	6	430

SCOTT, BRYAN Bryan Anderson, DB, 6´1˝/219 lbs; Penn State; 2003: Atl, rnd 2; B4/13/1981 Washington, DC **2003** Atl 15 (6, SS) **2004**†Atl 16 (16, SS) **2005** Atl 16 (13, FS) **NFL** 47 (35) [3 yrs]

SCOTT, CAREY Carey, DB, 5´11˝/214 lbs; Kentucky State; 2001: Min, rnd 6; B8/11/1979 Savannah, GA **2002** Oak 1 (0) **2002** Min 1 (0) **2003** Oak 5 (0) **NFL** 7 (0) [2 yrs]

SCOTT, CARLOS Carlos B., C-T, 6´4˝/295 lbs; Texas-El Paso; 1983: SL, rnd 7; B7/2/1960 Hempstead, TX **1983** SL 13 (1) **1984** SL 16 (0) **1985** SL 16 (0) **NFL** 45 (1) [3 yrs]

SCOTT, CEDRIC Cedric, DE, 6´5˝/274 lbs; Southern Mississippi; 2001: NYG, rnd 4; B10/19/1977 Gulfport, MS **2001** NYG 9 (0) **2002**†Cle 4 (0) **NFL** 13 (0) [2 yrs]

SCOTT, CHAD Chad Oliver, DB, 6´1˝/205 lbs; Towson State; Maryland; 1997: Pit, rnd 1; B9/6/1974 Capitol Heights, MD **1997**†Pit 13 (9, rcb) **1999** Pit 13 (12, LCB) **2000** Pit 16 (16, LCB) **2001**†Pit 15 (15, LCB) **2002**†Pit 15 (15, LCB) **2003** Pit 12 (12, LCB) **2004**†Pit 7 (7, lcb) **2005** NE 3 (0) **NFL** 94 (86) [8 yrs]

SCOTT, CHRIS Christopher Sterling, DE, 6´5˝/260 lbs; Purdue; 1984: Ind, rnd 3; B12/11/1961 Berea, OH **1984** Ind 14 (2) **1985** Ind 16 (12, RDE) **1987** Ind 3 (3) **NFL** 33 (17) [3 yrs]

SCOTT, CHUCK Charles John Miller, WR, 6´2˝/198 lbs; Vanderbilt; 1985: LARm, rnd 2; B5/24/1963 Jacksonville, FL

YEAR	TEAM	G (GS, POS)	RUSH	YD	AVG (LG)	TD	REC	YD	AVG (LG)	TD	PASS	COMP	PCT	YD	AVG (LG)	TD	INT	SK	YD	QBR	KPR	OTD	PTS	TAY
1986	LARm	9(0)	—	—	—	—	5	76	15.2(21)	0	—	—	—	—	—	—	—	—	—	—	—	—	0	38
1987	Dal	2(0)	—	—	—	—	1	11	11.0(11)	0	—	—	—	—	—	—	—	—	—	—	—	—	0	6
NFL	2	11(0)	—	—	—	—	6	87	14.5(21)	0	—	—	—	—	—	—	—	—	—	—	—	—	0	44

SCOTT, CLARENCE Clarence, DB, 6´1˝/186 lbs; Morgan State; B5/5/1944 Norristown, PA **1969** Bos-A 14 **1970** Bos 14 (14, SS) **1971** NE 5 (4) **1972** NE 10 (6, ss) **NFL** 43 (24) [4 yrs]

SCOTT, CLARENCE Clarence Raymond, DB, 6´0˝/190 lbs; Kansas State; 1971: Cle, rnd 1; B4/9/1949 Atlanta, GA **[I]** **1971**†Cle 13 (13, LCB) **1972**†Cle☆14 (LCB) **1973** Cle★14 (14, LCB) **1974** Cle 14 (14, LCB) **1975** Cle 14 (14, LCB) **1976** Cle 14 (14, LCB) **1977** Cle 14 (9, LCB) **1978** Cle 16 (12, LCB) **1979** Cle 16 (16, SS) **1980**†Cle 16 (16, SS) **1981** Cle 16 (16, SS) **1982**†Cle 9 (9, FS) **1983** Cle 16 (5, ss) **NFL** 186 (152) [13 yrs]

SCOTT, CLYDE Clyde Luther, HB-DB, 6´0˝/174 lbs; Navy; Arkansas; 1948: Phi, rnd 1/Buf-A, rnd 1; B8/29/1924 Dixie, LA

YEAR	TEAM	G (GS, POS)	RUSH	YD	AVG (LG)	TD	REC	YD	AVG (LG)	TD	PASS	COMP	PCT	YD	AVG (LG)	TD	INT	SK	YD	QBR	KPR	OTD	PTS	TAY
1949	†Phi	8(2)	40	195	4.9(39)	1	8	148	18.5(70)	1	—	—	—	—	—	—	—	—	—	—	kp	1	18	422
1950	Phi	1	13	46	3.5(22)	0	—	—	—	—	—	—	—	—	—	—	—	—	—	—	—	—	0	46
1951	Phi	12	45	161	3.6(40)	1	10	212	21.2(53)	3	—	—	—	—	—	—	—	—	—	—	kp	—	24	395
1952	Phi	2	—	—	—	—	—	—	—	—	—	—	—	—	—	—	—	—	—	—	i	—	0	-5
1952	Det	5	2	-2	-1.0(4)	0	1	21	21.0(21)	0	—	—	—	—	—	—	—	—	—	—	kp	—	0	31
NFL	4	28(2)	100	400	4.0(40)	2	19	381	20.1(70)	4	—	—	—	—	—	—	—	—	—	—	kpi	1	42	889

YEAR	TEAM	G (GS, POS)	RUSH	YD	AVG (LG)	TD	REC	YD	AVG (LG)	TD	PASS	COMP	PCT	YD	AVG (LG)	TD	INT	SK	YD	QBR	KPR	OTD	PTS	TAY

SCOTT, DARNAY   Darnay, WR, 6'1"/187 lbs; San Diego State; 1994: Cin, rnd 2; B7/7/1972 St. Louis, MO

1994	Cin	16 (12, WR)	10	106	10.6(23)	0	46	866	18.8(76)	5	1	1	100.0	53	53.0(53)	0	0	—	—		k	—	30	708
1995	Cin	16 (16, WR)	5	11	2.2(9)	0	52	821	15.8(88)	5	—	—	—	—	—	—	—	—	—			—	30	447
1996	Cin	16 (16, WR)	3	4	1.3(8)	0	58	833	14.4(50)	5	—	—	—	—	—	—	—	—	—			—	30	446
1997	Cin	16 (15, WR)	1	6	6.0(6)	0	54	797	14.8(77)	5	—	—	—	—	—	—	—	—	—			—	30	430
1998	Cin	13 (13, WR)	2	10	5.0(8)	0	51	817	16.0(70)	7	—	—	—	—	—	—	—	—	—			—	42	454
1999	Cin	16 (16, WR)	—	—	—		68	1022	15.0(76)	7	—	—	—	—	—	—	—	—	—			—	42	546
2001	Cin	16 (15, WR)	—	—	—		57	819	14.4(49)	2	—	—	—	—	—	—	—	—	—			—	12	420
2002	Dal	15 (1)	1	14	14.0(14)	0	22	218	9.9(17)	1	—	—	—	—	—	—	—	—	—			—	6	128
NFL	8	124 (104)	22	151	6.9(23)	0	408	6193	15.2(88)	37	1	1	100.0	53	53.0(53)	0	0	—	—		k	—	222	3576

SCOTT, DARRION   Darrion, DE, 6'3"/280 lbs; Ohio State; 2004: Min, rnd 3; B10/25/1981 Charleston, WV   **2004**†Min 12 (0)   **2005** Min 16 (15, LDE/rde)   **NFL** 28 (15) [2 yrs]

SCOTT, DAVE   Arthur David, G-T, 6'4"/276 lbs; Kansas; 1976: Atl, rnd 3; B12/26/1953 Hackensack, NJ   **1976** Atl 13   **1977** Atl 14 (14, LG)   **1978**†Atl 16 (16, LG)   **1979** Atl 16 (16, LG)   **1980**†Atl 16 (16, LG)   **1981** Atl 14 (14, LG)   **1982**†Atl 9 (0)   **NFL** 98 (76) [7 yrs]

SCOTT, DeQUINCY   DeQuincy, DT, 6'1"/280 lbs; Southern Mississippi; B3/5/1978 La Place, LA   **2002** SD 10 (0)   **2003** SD 16 (0)   **2004**†SD 14 (2)   **2005** SD 16 (0)   **NFL** 56 (2) [4 yrs]

SCOTT, ED   Edward, DB, 5'10"/182 lbs; Grambling State; B2/15/1961 New Orleans, LA   **1987** SL 3 (0)

SCOTT, FREDDIE   Fred Lee, WR, 6'2"/180 lbs; Amherst; 1974: Bal, rnd 7; B8/5/1952 Grady, AR

1974	Bal	14 (2)	2	12	6.0(9)	0	18	317	17.6(45)	0	—	—	—	—	—	—	—	—	—		kp	—	0	203
1975	Bal	8	—	—	—		—	—	—		—	—	—	—	—	—	—	—	—			—		
1976	†Bal	10	—	—	—		3	35	11.7(18)	0	—	—	—	—	—	—	—	—	—		k	—	0	23
1977	†Bal	14 (14, WR)	—	—	—		18	267	14.8(33)	2	—	—	—	—	—	—	—	—	—			—	12	144
1978	Det	16 (13, WR)	4	53	13.3(36)	0	37	564	15.2(47)	2	—	—	—	—	—	—	—	—	—		kp	—	12	387
1979	Det	14 (14, WR)	6	21	3.5(18)	0	62	929	15.0(50)	5	—	—	—	—	—	—	—	—	—			—	30	511
1980	Det	16 (16, WR)	5	86	17.2(48)	1	53	834	15.7(43)	4	—	—	—	—	—	—	—	—	—			—	30	533
1981	Det	16 (15, WR)	7	25	3.6(10)	0	53	1022	19.3(48)	5	1	0	0.0	0	0.0	0	—	—	—			—	30	561
1982	†Det	9 (7, WR)	1	-6	-6.0(-6)	0	13	231	17.8(36)	1	—	—	—	—	—	—	—	—	—			—	6	115
1983	†Det	15 (0)	—	—	—		5	71	14.2(25)	1	—	—	—	—	—	—	—	—	—			—	6	41
NFL	10	132 (81)	25	191	7.6(48)	1	262	4270	16.3(50)	20	1	0	0.0	0	0.0	0	—	—	—		kp	—	126	2515

SCOTT, FREDDIE   Freddie Lee, WR, 5'10"/188 lbs; Penn State; B8/26/1974 Miami Beach, FL   **1997** Atl 2 (0)   **1998** Ind 1 (0)

| 1996 | Atl | 10 (0) | — | — | — | | 7 | 80 | 11.4(27) | 0 | — | — | — | — | — | — | — | — | — | | | — | 0 | 40 |
| NFL | 3 | 13 (0) | — | — | — | | 7 | 80 | 11.4(27) | 0 | — | — | — | — | — | — | — | — | — | | | — | 0 | 40 |

SCOTT, GARI   Gari Jermaine, WR, 6'0"/191 lbs; Michigan State; 2000: Phi, rnd 4; B6/2/1978 West Palm Beach, FL

| 2001 | †Phi | 3 (0) | — | — | — | | 2 | 26 | 13.0(18) | 0 | — | — | — | — | — | — | — | — | — | | | — | 0 | 13 |

SCOTT, GEORGE   George Wendell, HB, 6'1"/180 lbs; Miami (OH); 1959: NYG, rnd 19; B7/14/1937 Bainbridge, OH, D3/4/1995 Buffalo, NY

| 1959 | NYG | 7 | 2 | 10 | 5.0(7) | 0 | 1 | 12 | 12.0(12) | 0 | — | — | — | — | — | — | — | — | — | | kp | — | 0 | 76 |

SCOTT, GREG   Gregory, DE, 6'4"/258 lbs; Hampton; 2002: Was, rnd 7; B10/2/1979 Franklin, VA   **2002** Was 3 (0)   **2004** Cin 1 (0)   **NFL** 4 (0) [2 yrs]

SCOTT, GUSS   Guss, DB, 5'10"/205 lbs; Florida; 2004: NE, rnd 3; B5/21/1982 Jacksonville, FL   **2005** NE 5 (2)

SCOTT, HERBERT   Herbert Carnell, G-T, 6'2"/254 lbs; Virginia Union; 1975: Dal, rnd 13; B1/18/1953 Virginia Beach, VA   **1975**†Dal 14 (4)   **1976**†Dal 14 (10, LG)   **1977**†Dal 11 (10, LG)   **1978**†Dal★16 (LG)   **1979**†Dal★16 (LG)   **1980**†Dal★16 (16, LG)   **1981**†Dal★16 (16, LG)   **1982**†Dal 6 (1)   **1983**†Dal☆16 (16, LG)   **1984** Dal 15 (9, lt)   **NFL** 140 (82) [10 yrs]

SCOTT, IAN   Josef Ian, DT, 6'2"/315 lbs; Florida; 2003: Chi, rnd 4; B11/8/1981 Greenville, SC   **2003** ChiB 6 (0)   **2004** ChiB 14 (13, RDT)   **2005**†ChiB 14 (13, LDT)   **NFL** 34 (26) [3 yrs]

SCOTT, JACK   John Edward, DT, 6'4"/260 lbs; Ohio State; 1959: Pit, rnd 26; B4/12/1936 Ashland, KY   **1960** Buf-A 14   **1961** Buf-A 7   **NFL** 21 [2 yrs]

SCOTT, JAKE   Jacob E., DB, 6'0"/188 lbs; Georgia; 1970: Mia, rnd 7; B7/20/1945 Greenwood, SC [RI]   **1970**†Mia 14 (13, FS)   **1971**†Mia★14 (14, FS)   **1972**†Mia★14 (13, SS)   **1973**†Mia★14 (13, SS)   **1974**†Mia★14 (14, FS)   **1975** Mia★14 (14, FS)   **1976**†Was 12 (12, FS)   **1977** Was 14 (14, FS)   **1978** Was 16 (16, FS)   **NFL** 126 (123) [9 yrs]

SCOTT, JAKE   Jake, G-T, 6'5"/283 lbs; Idaho; 2004: Ind, rnd 5; B4/16/1981 Lewiston, ID   **2004**†Ind 12 (9, RG)   **2005**†Ind 16 (16, RG)   **NFL** 28 (25) [2 yrs]

SCOTT, JAMES   James, WR, 6'1"/190 lbs; Trinity Valley CC (TX); 1975: NYJ, rnd 8; B3/28/1952 Longview, TX

1976	ChiB	11 (8, WR)	2	-4	-2.0(3)	0	26	512	19.7(63)	6	—	—	—	—	—	—	—	—	—			—	36	282
1977	†ChiB	14 (14, WR)	—	—	—		50	809	16.2(72)	3	—	—	—	—	—	—	—	—	—			—	18	420
1978	ChiB	15 (14, WR)	—	—	—		42	759	18.1(59)	5	—	—	—	—	—	—	—	—	—			—	30	405
1979	ChiB	10 (9, WR)	—	—	—		21	382	18.2(64)	3	—	—	—	—	—	—	—	—	—			—	18	206
1980	ChiB	15 (12, WR)	—	—	—		36	696	19.3(64)	3	—	—	—	—	—	—	—	—	—			—	18	363
1982	ChiB	5 (0)	—	—	—		2	44	22.0(27)	0	—	—	—	—	—	—	—	—	—			—	0	22
1983	ChiB	1 (0)	—	—	—		—	—	—		—	—	—	—	—	—	—	—	—			—		
NFL	7	71 (57)	2	-4	-2.0(3)	0	177	3202	18.1(72)	20	—	—	—	—	—	—	—	—	—			—	120	1697

SCOTT, JOE   Joseph Oscar, HB-DB-E, 6'1"/198 lbs; San Francisco; 1948: NYG, rnd 2/SF-A, rnd 1; B3/17/1926 Athens, TX

1948	NYG	10 (6, LH)	48	198	4.1(20)	2	17	235	13.8(43)	1	—	—	—	—	—	—	—	—	—		kpi	1	30	620
1949	NYG	8 (5, RH)	70	224	3.2(13)	6	15	111	7.4(24)	1	—	—	—	—	—	—	—	—	—		ki	—	42	454
1950	†NYG	10 (rh)	72	322	4.5(48)	0	9	240	26.7(61)	1	—	—	—	—	—	—	—	—	—		kp	—	18	626
1951	NYG	12 (RH)	94	367	3.9(37)	1	23	356	15.5(57)	2	—	—	—	—	—	—	—	—	—		k	—	18	629
1952	NYG	8 (RH)	38	107	2.8(30)	3	14	251	17.9(35)	1	—	—	—	—	—	—	—	—	—		k	—	24	353
1953	NYG	3	—	—	—		1	10	10.0(10)	0	—	—	—	—	—	—	—	—	—			—	0	5
NFL	6	51 (11)	322	1218	3.8(48)	14	79	1203	15.2(61)	7	—	—	—	—	—	—	—	—	—		kpi	1	132	2686

SCOTT, JOHNNY   Ian Grant, BB-TB-WB-FB, 5'10"/176 lbs; Lafayette; B5/3/1897 Trenton, NJ, D11/17/1964 Cape May, NJ   **1920** Buf 2 (1)   **1921** Buf 7 (3), 30   **1922** Buf 1 (1)   **1923** Buf 2 (2)   **NFL** 12 (7) [4 yrs]

SCOTT, KEVIN   Kevin Bernard, RB, 5'9"/181 lbs; Stanford; B10/24/1963 Fort Bragg, NC   **1988** SD 1 (0)

| 1989 | Dal | 3 (1) | 2 | -4 | -2.0(-1) | 0 | 9 | 63 | 7.0(12) | 0 | — | — | — | — | — | — | — | — | — | | | — | 0 | 28 |
| NFL | 2 | 4 (1) | 2 | -4 | -2.0(-1) | 0 | 9 | 63 | 7.0(12) | 0 | — | — | — | — | — | — | — | — | — | | | — | 0 | 28 |

SCOTT, KEVIN   Kevin Tommorse, DB, 5'9"/175 lbs; Stanford; 1991: Det, rnd 4; B5/19/1969 Phoenix, AZ   **1991**†Det 16 (0)   **1992** Det 16 (1)   **1993**†Det 12 (10, RCB)   **NFL** 44 (11) [3 yrs]

SCOTT, LANCE   Lance Robert, C, 6'3"/300 lbs; Utah; 1995: Arz, rnd 5; B2/15/1972 Salt Lake City, UT   **1997**†NYG 16 (11, C)   **1998** NYG 16 (16, C)   **NFL** 32 (27) [2 yrs]

SCOTT, LES   Leslie Henry, T-G-E, 5'10"/205 lbs; Hamline; B12/20/1899 Albert Lea, MN, D5/23/1993 Yuma, CO   **1923** Akr 6 (4, LT)   **1924** Min 6 (5, RT)   **NFL** 12 (9) [2 yrs]

SCOTT, LEW   Lewis Simon, DB, 5'11"/170 lbs; Oregon State; B6/6/1943 Bryn Mawr, PA   **1966** Den-A 13

SCOTT, LINDSAY   Lindsay Eugene, WR, 6'1"/195 lbs; Georgia; 1982: NO, rnd 1; B12/6/1960 Jessup, GA

1982	NO	8 (7, WR)	1	-4	-4.0(-4)	0	17	251	14.8(36)	0	—	—	—	—	—	—	—	—	—			—	0	122
1983	NO	16 (7, wr)	—	—	—		24	274	11.4(35)	1	—	—	—	—	—	—	—	—	—			—	6	137
1984	NO	16 (5, wr)	—	—	—		21	278	13.2(37)	0	—	—	—	—	—	—	—	—	—			—	0	144
1985	NO	9 (3)	—	—	—		7	61	8.7(15)	0	—	—	—	—	—	—	—	—	—			—	0	31
NFL	4	49 (22)	1	-4	-4.0(-4)	0	69	864	12.5(37)	1	—	—	—	—	—	—	—	—	—			—	6	433

SCOTT, LYNN   Lynn, DB, 6'0"/221 lbs; Northwestern Oklahoma State; B6/23/1977 Turpin, OK   **2001** Dal 14 (0)   **2002** Dal 14 (0)   **2003**†Dal 16 (0)   **2004** Dal 16 (9, SS)   **2005** Dal 6 (0)   **NFL** 66 (9) [5 yrs]

SCOTT, MALCOLM   Malcolm Matthew, TE, 6'4"/243 lbs; LSU; 1983: NYG, rnd 5; B7/10/1961 New Orleans, LA

1983	NYG	16 (1)	—	—	—		17	206	12.1(24)	0	—	—	—	—	—	—	—	—	—			—	0	103
1987	NO	3 (3)	—	—	—		6	35	5.8(11)	0	—	—	—	—	—	—	—	—	—			—	0	18
NFL	2	19 (4)	—	—	—		23	241	10.5(24)	0	—	—	—	—	—	—	—	—	—			—	0	121

YEAR	TEAM	G (GS, POS)	RUSH	YD	AVG (LG)	TD	REC	YD	AVG (LG)	TD	PASS	COMP	PCT	YD	AVG (LG)	TD	INT	SK	YD	QBR	KPR	OTD	PTS	TAY

SCOTT, NED Edward, T, 6´0˝/200 lbs; Monmouth (NJ); B6/8/1901, IL, D11/1987 Readlyn, IA **1924** RI 9 (9, LT)

SCOTT, PATRICK Patrick Sterling, WR, 5´10˝/170 lbs; Grambling State; 1987: GB, rnd 11; B9/13/1964 Shreveport, LA

1987	GB	8(3)	1	2	2.0(2)	0	8	79	9.9(16)	0	—	—	—	—	—	—	—	—	—	—	kp	—	0	85
1988	GB	16(0)	—	—	—	—	20	275	13.8(41)	1	—	—	—	—	—	—	—	—	—	—	k	—	6	170
NFL	2	24(3)	1	2	2.0(2)	0	28	354	12.6(41)	1	—	—	—	—	—	—	—	—	—	—	kp	—	6	254

SCOTT, PERRY Leonard Perry, E, 6´2˝/210 lbs; Muhlenberg; 1941: Det, rnd 15; B8/27/1917 East Orange, NJ, D4/4/1988 Allentown, PA

| 1942 | Det | 7(0) | — | — | — | — | 1 | 7 | 7.0(7) | 0 | — | — | — | — | — | — | — | — | — | — | — | — | 0 | 4 |

SCOTT, PHIL Phillip, E, none; B4/11/1906, D1/1/1975 Montclair, NJ **1929** Ora 8 (6, LE)

SCOTT, PRINCE Prince Arthur, E-DB, 6´1˝/190 lbs; Texas Tech; B6/30/1917 Grapevine, TX

| 1946 | Mia-A | 14(7, re) | — | — | — | — | 13 | 180 | 13.8 | 2 | — | — | — | — | — | — | — | — | — | — | kpi | — | 12 | 94 |

SCOTT, RALPH Ralph Vernon, T-G, 6´2˝/235 lbs; Wisconsin; B9/26/1894 Dewey Township, WI, D8/15/1936 Hardin, MT **[KC]** **1921** ChiS 11 (11, LT), 6 **1922** ChiB 12 (11, LT) **1923** ChiB☆11 (8, RT), 1 **1924** ChiB 10 (1) **1925** ChiB 13 (5, lg) **1927** NYY 10 (1) **NFL** 67 (37), 7 [6 yrs]

SCOTT, RANDY Randolph Charles, LB, 6´1˝/223 lbs; Alabama; B1/31/1959 Decatur, GA **1981** GB 16 (0) **1982**†GB 9 (4) **1983** GB 6 (5, lilb) **1984** GB 16 (16, LILB) **1985** GB 16 (16, LILB) **1986** GB 15 (15, LILB) **1987**†Min 2 (1) **NFL** 80 (57) [7 yrs]

SCOTT, RONALD Arthur Ronald, RB, 5´11˝/200 lbs; Southern (LA); B3/3/1963 Thibodeaux, LA

| 1987 | Mia | 3(2) | 47 | 199 | 4.2(24) | 3 | 2 | 7 | 3.5(5) | 0 | — | — | — | — | — | — | — | — | — | — | k | — | 18 | 240 |

SCOTT, SEAN Sean Vaughn, LB, 6´1˝/226 lbs; Maryland; B4/10/1966 Washington, DC **1988** Dal 5 (0)

SCOTT, STANLEY Stanley, DE, 6´3˝/255 lbs; Florida State; B1/30/1964 Tampa, FL **1987** Mia 3 (0)

SCOTT, TODD Todd Carlton, DB, 5´11˝/200 lbs; Louisiana-Lafayette; 1991: Min, rnd 6; B1/23/1968 Galveston, TX **1991** Min 16 (1) **1992**†Min★16 (16, SS) **1993**†Min 13 (12, SS) **1994**†Min 16 (15, SS) **1995** NYJ 10 (9, FS) **1996** TB 2 (2) **1997**†KC 10 (0) **NFL** 84 (55) [7 yrs]

SCOTT, TOM Thomas Coster, DE-LB, 6´2˝/218 lbs; Virginia; 1953: LA, rnd 5; B9/3/1930 Baltimore, MD **1953** Phi 12 (LDE) **1954** Phi 12 (LDE) **1955** Phi☆12 (LDE) **1956** Phi☆12 (LDE) **1957** Phi◇12 (LDE) **1958** Phi◇12 **1959**†NYG 11 **1960** NYG 12 **1961**†NYG 13 (RLB) **1962**†NYG 14 (RLB) **1963**†NYG 14 (RLB) **1964** NYG 14 (RLB) **NFL** 150 [12 yrs]

SCOTT, TOM Tom, T-G, 6´6˝/330 lbs; East Carolina; 1993: Cin, rnd 6; B6/25/1970 Burke County, NC **1993** Cin 13 (13, LT/lg)

SCOTT, TONY Tony M., DB, 5´10˝/193 lbs; North Carolina State; 2000: NYJ, rnd 6; B10/3/1976 Lawndale, NC **2000** NYJ 16 (0) **2001** NYJ 7 (0) **NFL** 23 (0) [2 yrs]

SCOTT, VICTOR Victor Ramone, DB, 6´0˝/200 lbs; Colorado; 1984: Dal, rnd 2; B6/1/1962 East St. Louis, IL **1984** Dal 16 (0) **1985**†Dal 16 (3) **1986** Dal 5 (0) **1987** Dal 6 (0) **1988** Dal 2 (0) **NFL** 45 (3) [5 yrs]

SCOTT, VIN Vincent Joseph, G, 5´8˝/215 lbs; Notre Dame; B7/10/1925 LeRoy, NY, D7/13/1992 Hamilton, Canada **1947** Buf-A 14 (0) **1948**†Buf-A 14 (0) **AAFC** 28 (0) [2 yrs]

SCOTT, WALTER Walter Bernard, DE, 6´3˝/285 lbs; East Carolina; B5/18/1973 Augusta, GA **1996** NE 1 (0)

SCOTT, WILBERT Wilbert James, LB, 6´0˝/215 lbs; Indiana; 1961: Pit, rnd 16; B3/13/1939 Connellsville, PA **1961** Pit 4

SCOTT, WILLIE Willie Louie, TE, 6´4˝/245 lbs; South Carolina; 1981: KC, rnd 1; B2/13/1959 Newberry, SC

1981	KC	16(2)	—	—	—	—	5	72	14.4(26)	1	—	—	—	—	—	—	—	—	—	—	—	—	6	41
1982	KC	9(4, TE)	—	—	—	—	8	49	6.1(13)	1	—	—	—	—	—	—	—	—	—	—	—	—	6	30
1983	KC	16(16, TE)	1	1	1.0(1)	0	29	247	8.5(22)	6	—	—	—	—	—	—	—	—	—	—	—	—	36	155
1984	KC	15(12, TE)	—	—	—	—	28	253	9.0(27)	3	—	—	—	—	—	—	—	—	—	—	k	—	18	136
1985	KC	16(5, te)	—	—	—	—	5	61	12.2(21)	0	—	—	—	—	—	—	—	—	—	—	—	—	0	31
1986	†NE	14(0)	—	—	—	—	8	41	5.1(8)	3	—	—	—	—	—	—	—	—	—	—	—	—	18	36
1987	NE	9(1)	—	—	—	—	5	35	7.0(15)	1	—	—	—	—	—	—	—	—	—	—	—	1	12	23
1988	NE	3(1)	—	—	—	—	1	8	8.0(8)	0	—	—	—	—	—	—	—	—	—	—	—	—	0	4
NFL	8	98(41)	1	1	1.0(1)	0	89	766	8.6(27)	15	—	—	—	—	—	—	—	—	—	—	k	1	96	453

SCOTT, YUSUF Ysuf Jamail, G, 6´3˝/348 lbs; Arizona; 1999: Arz, rnd 5; B11/30/1976 La Porte, TX **1999** Arz 10 (0) **2000** Arz 9 (0) **2001** Arz 5 (0) **NFL** 24 (0) [3 yrs]

SCOTTI, BEN Benjamin Joseph, DB, 6´1˝/185 lbs; Maryland; B6/9/1937 Newark, NJ **1959** Was 11 (8, DB) **1960** Was 11 (LCB) **1961** Was 14 **1962** Phi 14 (14, LCB) **1963** Phi 9 (LCB) **1964** SF 12 (rcb) **NFL** 71 (22) [6 yrs]

SCOTTS, COLIN Colin Roberts, DT, 6´5˝/263 lbs; Hawaii; 1987: SL, rnd 3; B4/26/1963 Sydney, Australia **1987** SL 7 (3)

SCRABIS, BOB Robert Dennis, QB, 6´3˝/225 lbs; Penn State; B3/26/1936 Pittsburgh, PA

1960	NYT-A	7	—	—	—	—	—	—	—	—	3	0	0.0	0	0.0	0	0	—	—	—	—	—	0	0
1961	NYT-A	11	1	1	1.0(1)	1	—	—	—	—	21	7	33.3	82	3.9(35)	1	2	—	—	—	—	—	6	-23*
1962	NYT-A	6	—	—	—	—	—	—	—	—	2	0	0.0	0	0.0	0	1	—	—	—	—	—	0	-40
NFL	3	24	1	1	1.0(1)	1	—	—	—	—	26	7	26.9	82	3.2(35)	1	3	—	—	—	—	—	6	-63

SCRAFFORD, KIRK Kirk Tippet, T-G, 6´6˝/270 lbs; Montana; B3/16/1967 Billings, MT **1990**†Cin 2 (0) **1991** Cin 9 (5, lt) **1992** Cin 8 (4) **1993**†Den 16 (0) **1994** Den 16 (8, RT) **1995**†SF 16 (11, rt/lt) **1996**†SF 7 (1) **1997**†SF 16 (16, RT) **1998**†SF 9 (8, RT) **NFL** 99 (53) [9 yrs]

SCRIBNER, BUCKY William Charles, P, 6´0˝/207 lbs; Kansas; 1983: GB, rnd 11; B7/11/1960 Lawrence, KS **[P]**

1983	GB	16(0)	—	—	—	—	—	—	—	—	—	—	—	—	—	—	—	—	—	—	P	—	0	0
1984	GB☆	16(0)	—	—	—	—	—	—	—	—	1	0	0.0	0	0.0	0	0	—	—	—	P	—	0	0
1987	†Min	4(0)	1	-7	-7.0(-7)	0	—	—	—	—	—	—	—	—	—	—	—	—	—	—	P	—	0	-7
1988	†Min	16(0)	1	0	0.0(0)	0	—	—	—	—	—	—	—	—	—	—	—	—	—	—	P	—	0	0
1989	†Min	15(0)	—	—	—	—	—	—	—	—	—	—	—	—	—	—	—	—	—	—	P	—	0	0
NFL	5	67(0)	2	-7	-3.5	0	—	—	—	—	1	0	0.0	0	0.0	0	0	—	—	—	P	—	0	-7

SCRIBNER, ROB Robert Bruce, RB, 6´0˝/200 lbs; UCLA; B4/9/1951 Dallas, TX

1973	†LARm	10	20	109	5.4(17)	0	2	19	9.5(13)	0	—	—	—	—	—	—	—	—	—	—	kp	—	0	285
1974	†LARm	11	9	24	2.7(5)	0	2	28	14.0(14)	1	—	—	—	—	—	—	—	—	—	—	kp	—	6	58
1975	†LARm	14	42	216	5.1(34)	2	2	28	14.0(25)	0	—	—	—	—	—	—	—	—	—	—	kp	—	12	334
1976	†LARm	14	2	12	6.0(11)	1	—	—	—	—	—	—	—	—	—	—	—	—	—	—	kp	—	6	45
NFL	4	49	73	361	4.9(34)	3	6	75	12.5(25)	1	—	—	—	—	—	—	—	—	—	—	kp	—	24	722

SCROGGINS, TRACY Tracy, DE-LB, 6´2˝/255 lbs; Tulsa; 1992: Det, rnd 2; B9/11/1969 Checotah, OK **[S]** **1992** Det 16 (7, rolb) **1993**†Det 16 (0) **1994**†Det 16 (9, ROLB) **1995**†Det 16 (16, RDE) **1996** Det 6 (6, rde) **1997**†Det 15 (6, rde) **1998** Det 11 (3) **1999**†Det 14 (11, RDE) **2000** Det 16 (15, RDE) **2001** Det 16 (16, RDE) **NFL** 142 (89) [10 yrs]

SCRUGGS, TED Edwin Theodore, E, 6´1˝/195 lbs; Rice; 1947: Bkn-A, rnd 13/1946: ChiB, rnd 6; B4/18/1923 Houston, TX, D11/30/2000 Houston, TX

1947	Bkn-A	12(0)	—	—	—	—	2	9	4.5	0	—	—	—	—	—	—	—	—	—	—	—	—	0	5
1948	Bkn-A	14(2)	—	—	—	—	1	8	8.0(8)	0	—	—	—	—	—	—	—	—	—	—	—	—	0	4
AAFC	2	26(2)	—	—	—	—	3	17	5.7(8)	0	—	—	—	—	—	—	—	—	—	—	—	—	0	9

SCRUTCHINS, ED Edward Sean, DE, 6´3˝/260 lbs; Toledo; 1963: SL, rnd 15; B7/28/1941 Americus, GA **1966** Hou-A 4

SCUDERO, JOE Joseph Andrew, DB-HB, 5´10˝/173 lbs; San Francisco; B7/2/1930 San Francisco, CA

1954	Was	12(DB)	21	19	0.9(12)	0	4	32	8.0(13)	1	—	—	—	—	—	—	—	—	—	—	kpi	—	6	69
1955	Was★	12(DB)	6	27	4.5(13)	0	—	—	—	—	—	—	—	—	—	—	—	—	—	—	kpi	2	12	522
1956	Was	11(DB)	2	3	1.5(2)	0	—	—	—	—	—	—	—	—	—	—	—	—	—	—	kpi	—	0	41
1957	Was	10	9	60	6.7(43)	0	2	30	15.0(18)	0	—	—	—	—	—	—	—	—	—	—	kp	—	0	164
1958	Was	8	5	30	6.0(9)	0	—	—	—	—	—	—	—	—	—	—	—	—	—	—	kp	—	0	94
1960	Pit	4(LCB)	—	—	—	—	—	—	—	—	—	—	—	—	—	—	—	—	—	—	p	—	0	-7
NFL	6	57	43	139	3.2(43)	0	6	62	10.3(18)	1	—	—	—	—	—	—	—	—	—	—	p	2	18	883

SCULLY, JOHN John Francis, G-C, 6´6˝/262 lbs; Notre Dame; 1981: Atl, rnd 4; B8/2/1958 Huntington, NY **1981** Atl 16 (0) **1982**†Atl 9 (0) **1983** Atl 16 (16, RG) **1984** Atl 16 (16, RG) **1985** Atl 8 (8, lg) **1986** Atl 14 (14, LG) **1987** Atl 12 (12, LG) **1988** Atl 11 (11, LG) **1990** Atl 10 (5, lg) **NFL** 112 (82) [9 yrs]

SCULLY, MIKE Michael John, C-G, 6´5˝/280 lbs; Illinois; B11/1/1965 Chicago, IL **1988** Was 1 (0)

YEAR	TEAM	G (GS, POS)	RUSH	YD	AVG(LG)	TD	REC	YD	AVG(LG)	TD	PASS	COMP	PCT	YD	AVG(LG)	TD	INT	SK	YD	QBR	KPR	OTD	PTS	TAY

SCURLOCK, MIKE Michael Lee, DB, 5'10"/200 lbs; Arizona; 1995: SL, rnd 5; B2/26/1972 Casa Grande, AZ **1995** SL 14 (1) **1996** SL 16 (0) **1997** SL 5 (0) **1998** SL 16 (0) **1999** Car 14 (0) **NFL** 65 (1) [5 yrs]

SCZUREK, STAN Stanley Rudolph, LB, 5'11"/230 lbs; Purdue; 1962: Cle, rnd 4/Buf, rnd 24; B3/7/1937 Cleveland, OH **1963** Cle 9 **1964**†Cle 14 **1965**†Cle 11 **1966** NYG 11 **NFL** 45 [4 yrs]

SEABAUGH, TODD Raymond Todd, LB, 6'4"/225 lbs; San Diego State; 1983: Pit, rnd 3; B3/16/1961 Encino, CA **1984**†Pit 16 (0)

SEABRIGHT, CHARLIE Charles Edward, BB-QB, 6'2"/204 lbs; West Virginia; B2/13/1918 McMechen, WV, D3/18/1981 Bridgeport, OH

YEAR	TEAM	G (GS, POS)	RUSH	YD	AVG(LG)	TD	REC	YD	AVG(LG)	TD	PASS	COMP	PCT	YD	AVG(LG)	TD	INT	SK	YD	QBR	KPR	OTD	PTS	TAY
1941	Cle	7(2)	—	—	—		5	44	8.8(14)	0	1	0	0.0	0	0.0	0	1				i		0	-18
1946	Pit	10(7, BB)	—	—	—		4	77	19.3(33)	1											i		6	42
1947	†Pit	12(12, BB)	1	4	4.0(4)	0	7	16	2.3(10)	0											ki	1	6	65
1948	Pit	12(11, BB)	—	—	—		8	63	7.9(16)	1	0	0	0.0	0	0.0	0	0				ki		6	37
1949	Pit	12(11, BB)	—	—	—		4	4	1.0(5)	0	1	1	100.0	17	17.0(17)	1	0				k		0	25
1950	Pit	10(BB)	—	—	—		3	37	12.3(13)	1	3	1	33.3	3	1.0(3)	0	0						6	25
NFL	6	63(43)	1	4	4.0(4)	0	31	241	7.8(33)	3	6	2	33.3	20	3.3(17)	1	1				ki	1	24	175

SEABRON, TOM Thomas Hall, LB, 6'3"/215 lbs; Michigan; 1979: SF, rnd 5; B5/24/1957 Baltimore, MD **1979** SF 10 **1980** SF 6 (0) **1980** SL 2 (0) **NFL** 18 [2 yrs]

SEAL, PAUL Paul Nathan, TE, 6'4"/222 lbs; Michigan; 1974: NO, rnd 2; B2/27/1952 Detroit, MI

YEAR	TEAM	G (GS, POS)	RUSH	YD	AVG(LG)	TD	REC	YD	AVG(LG)	TD	PTS	TAY
1974	NO	14(TE)	2	7	3.5(6)	1	32	466	14.6(42)	3	24	265
1975	NO	14(14, TE)	1	10	10.0(10)	0	28	414	14.8(38)	1	6	222
1976	NO	14(3)	2	-7	-3.5(-1)	0	9	72	8.0(15)	0	0	29
1977	SF	14	—	—	—		13	230	17.7(47)	1	6	120
1978	SF	14(5, te)	—	—	—		21	370	17.6(41)	2	12	195
1979	SF	15	—	—	—		3	34	11.3(14)	0	0	17
NFL	6	85(22)	5	10	2.0(10)	1	106	1586	15.0(47)	7	48	848

SEALBY, RANDY Randall Lee, LB, 6'2"/230 lbs; Missouri; B5/16/1960 Ann Arbor, MI **1987** NE 2 (1)

SEALE, EUGENE Eugene, LB, 5'10"/250 lbs; Lamar; B6/3/1964 Jasper, TX **1987**†Hou 9 (4) **1988**†Hou☆16 (0) **1989** Hou 15 (1) **1990**†Hou 15 (0) **1991**†Hou 15 (0) **1992**†Hou 9 (5) **NFL** 79 (5) [6 yrs]

SEALE, SAM Samuel Ricardo, DB, 5'9"/182 lbs; Western State (CO); 1984: LARd, rnd 8; B10/6/1962 Barbados **1984**†LARd 12 (0) **1985**†LARd 16 (0) **1986** LARd 16 (5, rcb) **1987** LARd 12 (5, rcb) **1988** SD 14 (8, LCB) **1989** SD 13 (12, RCB) **1990** SD 16 (13, RCB) **1991** SD 16 (16, RCB) **1992** LARd 5 (0) **1993** LARm 1 (0) **NFL** 121 (59) [10 yrs]

SEALS, GEORGE George Edward, G-DT-T, 6'3"/260 lbs; Missouri; 1964: NYG, rnd 4/SD, rnd 8; B10/2/1942 Higginsville, MO **1964** Was 12 (rt) **1965** ChiB 14 **1966** ChiB 14 **1967** ChiB 14 (LG) **1968** ChiB☆14 (LG) **1969** ChiB☆14 (LG) **1970** ChiB 14 (LDT) **1971** ChiB 14 (LDT) **1972** KC 11 **1973** KC 13 **NFL** 134 [10 yrs]

SEALS, LEON Leon, DE, 6'5"/265 lbs; Jackson State; 1987: Buf, rnd 4; B1/30/1964 New Orleans, LA **1987** Buf 13 (1) **1988**†Buf 16 (5, rde) **1989**†Buf 16 (0) **1990**†Buf 16 (16, LDE) **1991**†Buf 16 (16, LDE) **1992** Phi 5 (3) **NFL** 82 (41) [6 yrs]

SEALS, RAY Raymond Bernard, DE-NT, 6'3"/296 lbs; none; B6/17/1965 Syracuse, NY **1989** TB 2 (0) **1990** TB 8 (0) **1991** TB 10 (9, LDE) **1992** TB 11 (8, LDE) **1993** TB 16 (11, LDE) **1994**†Pit 13 (11, RDE) **1995**†Pit☆16 (16, RDE) **1997** Car 14 (7, RDE) **NFL** 90 (62) [8 yrs]

SEARCEY, BILL William Alexander, G, 6'1"/281 lbs; Alabama; B3/3/1958 Savannah, GA **1985** SD 1 (0)

SEARCY, LEON Leon, T, 6'4"/313 lbs; Miami (FL); 1992: Pit, rnd 1; B12/21/1969 Washington, DC **1992**†Pit 15 (0) **1993**†Pit 16 (16, RT) **1994**†Pit 16 (16, RT) **1995**†Pit☆16 (16, RT) **1996**†Jax 16 (16, RT) **1997**†Jax 16 (16, RT) **1998**†Jax 15 (15, RT) **1999**†Jax☆16 (16, RT) **NFL** 126 (111) [8 yrs]

SEARS, COREY Corey Alexander, DE, 6'3"/300 lbs; Mississippi State; B4/15/1973 San Antonio, TX **1998** SL 4 (0) **1999** Arz 9 (1) **2000** Arz 8 (2) **2002** Hou 16 (0) **2003** Hou 16 (12, LDE) **2004** Hou 15 (0) **NFL** 68 (15) [6 yrs]

SEARS, DICK Richard Maurice, T, 5'10"/185 lbs; Kansas State; B6/6/1899 Eureka, KS, D1/15/1972 Topeka, KS **1924** KC 1 (0)

SEARS, JIMMY James Herbert, DB-HB, 5'11"/183 lbs; USC; 1953: Bal, rnd 6; B3/20/1931 Los Angeles, CA, D1/4/2002 Woodland Hills, CA **1954** ChiC 1 **1960**†LAC-A 10
1961 Den-A 2

YEAR	TEAM	G (GS, POS)	RUSH	YD	AVG(LG)	TD	REC	YD	AVG(LG)	TD	PASS	COMP	PCT	YD	AVG(LG)	TD	INT	SK	YD	QBR	KPR	OTD	PTS	TAY
1957	ChiC	12	17	68	4.0(49)	1	5	66	13.2(27)	0	3	0	0.0	0	0.0	0	0				kp		6	206
1958	ChiC	12	17	51	3.0(13)	0	13	187	14.4(55)	2	1	0	0.0	0	0.0	0	0				kp		12	455
NFL	5	37	34	119	3.5(49)	1	18	253	14.1(55)	2	4	0	0.0	0	0.0	0	0				kpi		18	823

SEARS, VIC Victor Wilson, T-DT, 6'3"/223 lbs; Oregon State; 1941: Pit, rnd 5; B3/4/1918 Ashwood, OR **1941** Phi 11 (2) **1942** Phi 11 (11, LT) **1943** P-P☆10 (10, LT) **1945** Phi☆10 (9, LT) **1946** Phi 11 (11, LT) **1947**†Phi 7 (5, LT) **1948**†Phi 12 (12) **1949**†Phi☆11 (11, LT) **1950** Phi☆12 (LT) **1951** Phi 12 (LT) **1952** Phi☆12 (LDT) **1953** Phi 12 (LDT) **NFL** 131 (61) [12 yrs]

SEASHOLTZ, GEORGE George Donald, B, 5'8"/185 lbs; Lafayette; B11/14/1900 Pottstown, PA, D4/11/1945 Pottstown, PA **1922** Mil 4 (2) **1924** Ken 5 (4, FB), 12 **NFL** 9 (6) [2 yrs]

SEAU, JUNIOR Tiaina, LB, 6'3"/250 lbs; USC; 1990: SD, rnd 1; B1/19/1969 San Diego, CA [S] **1990** SD 16 (15, RILB) **1991** SD☆16 (16, RILB) **1992**†SD☆15 (15, RLB) **1993** SD☆16 (16, RLB) **1994**†SD☆16 (16, RLB) **1995**†SD☆16 (16, RLB) **1996** SD☆15 (15, RLB) **1997** SD☆15 (15, RLB) **1998** SD☆16 (16, RLB) **2000** SD☆16 (16, RLB) **2001** SD☆16 (16, RLB) **2002** SD◇13 (13, RLB) **2003** Mia 15 (15, RLB) **2004** Mia 8 (8, LLB) **2005** Mia 7 (5, llb)

YEAR	TEAM	G (GS, POS)	REC	YD	AVG(LG)	TD	KPR	OTD	PTS	TAY
1999	SD☆	14(14, RLB)	2	8	4.0(6)	0	iS		0	15
NFL	16	230(227)	2	8	4.0(6)	0	iS	1	6	139

SEAY, MARK Mark Edward, WR, 6'0"/175 lbs; Long Beach State; B4/11/1967 Los Angeles, CA

YEAR	TEAM	G (GS, POS)	REC	YD	AVG(LG)	TD	KPR	PTS	TAY
1993	SD	1(0)	—	—	—				
1994	†SD	16(14, WR)	58	645	11.1(49)	6		36	353
1995	†SD	16(0)	45	537	11.9(39)	3		20	284
1996	†Phi	16(0)	19	260	13.7(35)	0	kp	0	251
1997	Phi	12(2)	13	187	14.4(38)	1	p	6	191
NFL	5	61(16)	135	1629	12.1(49)	10	kp	62	1078

SEAY, VIRGIL Virgil LeVan, WR, 5'8"/175 lbs; Troy State; 1980: Den, rnd 10; B1/1/1958 Moultrie, GA

YEAR	TEAM	G (GS, POS)	REC	YD	AVG(LG)	TD	KPR	PTS	TAY
1981	Was	16(7, WR)	26	472	18.2(60)	3	kp	18	257
1982	†Was	8(0)	6	154	25.7(37)	0		0	77
1983	Was	14(1)	2	55	27.5(39)	1		6	148
1984	Was	11(2)	9	111	12.3(19)	1	kp	6	62
1984	Atl	3(0)	—	—	—		kp	0	2
NFL	4	52(10)	43	792	18.4(60)	5	kp	30	545

SEBASTIAN, MIKE Michael John, HB-WB, 5'11"/185 lbs; Pittsburgh; B6/7/1910 Greensburg, PA, D6/28/1989 Hemet, CA

YEAR	TEAM	G (GS, POS)	RUSH	YD	AVG(LG)	TD	REC	YD	AVG(LG)	TD	PASS	COMP	PCT	YD	AVG(LG)	TD	INT	PTS	TAY
1935	Bos	1(0)	1	0	0.0	0	—	—	—		1	1	100.0	12	12.0(12)	0	0	0	6
1935	Phi	4(0)	17	76	4.5	0	1	19	19.0(19)	0	4	0	0.0	0	0.0	0	1	0	46
1935	Pit	2(0)	4	3	0.8	0	—	—	—									0	3
1937	Cle	1(1)	6	4	0.7	0	—	—	—									0	4
NFL	2	8(1)	28	83	3.0	0	1	19	19.0(19)	0	6	1	16.7	12	2.0(12)	0	1	0	59

SEBEK, NICK Nicholas, QB, 6'1"/194 lbs; Indiana; 1949: Was, rnd 25; B10/11/1927 Niagara Falls, NY

YEAR	TEAM	G (GS, POS)	PASS	COMP	PCT	YD	AVG(LG)	TD	INT	PTS	TAY
1950	Was	2	0	0	0.0	0	0.0	0	2	0	-80

SEBO, SAM Samuel E., FB-WB, 5'7"/165 lbs; Syracuse; B1906, D9/10/1933 **1930** Nwk 2 (1)

SEBORG, HERMAN Herman W., G-B, 5'11"/195 lbs; Western Michigan; B1/9/1907 Grand Rapids, MI, D9/1985 Marcellus, NY **1930** Min 9 (5, rg) **1930** Fra 4 (2) **1931** Fra 7 (6, LG) **NFL** 20 (13) [2 yrs]

SECHRIST, WALT Walter F., G-T, 6'0"/258 lbs; none; B9/16/1896 Warsaw, IN, D12/19/1977 Bradenton, FL [K] **1920** Ham 1 (1) **1923** Ham 1 (1) **1924** Akr 1 (1), 1 **1925** Fra 9 (2) **1925** Cle 2 (2) **1926** Ham 4 (4, RG), 3 **1926** Lou 1 (0) **NFL** 19 (11), 4 [5 yrs]

SECORD, JOE Joseph L., C, /190 lbs; none; B8/22/1897 Green Bay, WI, D8/21/1970 Green Bay, WI **1922** GB 2 (2)

SECULES, SCOTT Thomas Wescott, QB, 6'3"/220 lbs; Virginia; 1988: Dal, rnd 6; B11/8/1964 Newport News, VA

YEAR	TEAM	G (GS, POS)	RUSH	YD	AVG(LG)	TD	PASS	COMP	PCT	YD	AVG(LG)	TD	INT	SK	YD	PTS	TAY
1989	Mia	15(0)	4	39	9.8(17)	0	50	22	44.0	286	5.7(44)	1	3			0	67
1990	†Mia	16(0)	8	34	4.3(17)	0	7	3	42.9	17	2.4(8)	0	1	1	9	0	3

YEAR	TEAM	G(GS, POS)	RUSH	YD	AVG(LG)	TD	REC	YD	AVG(LG)	TD	PASS	COMP	PCT	YD	AVG(LG)	TD	INT	SK	YD	QBR	KPR	OTD	PTS	TAY
1991	Mia	14(0)	4	30	7.5(12)	1	—	—	—	—	13	8	61.5	90	6.9(17)	1	1	1	6	—	—	—	6	50
1993	NE	12(4)	8	33	4.1(13)	0	—	—	—	—	134	75	56.0	918	6.9(**82**)	2	9	7	28	—	—	—	0	142
NFL	4	57(4)	24	136	5.7(17)	1	—	—	—	—	204	108	52.9	1311	6.4(82)	4	14	9	43	—	—	—	6	262

SEDBROOK, LEN Leonard Roy, B, 5´10˝/174 lbs; Phillips; B1/13/1905 Goltry, OK, D4/22/1986 Oklahoma City, OK **1928** Det 9 (5, WB), 24 **1929** NYG 15 (14, WB), 66 **1930** NYG 16 (9, WB), 48 **1931** NYG 11 (3), 12 **NFL** 51 (31), 150 [4 yrs]

SEDER, TIM Tim, K, 5´9˝/180 lbs; Ashland University; B9/17/1974 Ashland, OH **[K]**

YEAR	TEAM	G(GS, POS)	RUSH	YD	AVG(LG)	TD	REC	YD	AVG(LG)	TD	PASS	COMP	PCT	YD	AVG(LG)	TD	INT	SK	YD	QBR	KPR	OTD	PTS	TAY
2000	Dal	15(0)	1	1	1.0(1)	1	—	—	—	—	—	—	—	—	—	—	—	—	—	—	K	—	108	11
2001	Dal	8(0)	1	8	8.0(8)	1	—	—	—	—	—	—	—	—	—	—	—	—	—	—	K	—	51	18
2002	Jax	5(0)	—	—	—	—	—	—	—	—	—	—	—	—	—	—	—	—	—	—	K	—	35	0
NFL	3	28(0)	2	9	4.5(8)	2	—	—	—	—	—	—	—	—	—	—	—	—	—	—	K	—	194	29

SEDLOCK, ROBERT Robert John, T, 6´4˝/295 lbs; Georgia; B2/7/1937 Canton, OH **1960** Buf-A 14

SEDORIS, CHRIS Christopher Jude, C, 6´3˝/286 lbs; Purdue; B4/25/1973 Columbus, IN **1996** Was 9 (0)

SEEDBORG, JOHN John Sherwood, P, 6´0˝/227 lbs; Arizona State; 1964: Was, rnd 19; B1/23/1943 Paso Robles, CA **1965** Was 1

SEEDS, FRANK Frank, WB, /170 lbs; none; B3/26/1897, D10/1963, PA **1926** Can 1 (1)

SEEMAN, GEORGE George McHenry, E, 6´1˝/195 lbs; Nebraska; 1940: GB, rnd 8; B4/3/1916 Lincoln, NE, D8/31/1998 Glen, NH **1940** GB 1 (0)

SEGAL, MAURY Maurice, E, none; B1902, England, deceased **1925** Cle 5 (0)

SEGRETTA, ROCKY Rocco, aka Rocky Segrito, E, none; B1899, Italy, deceased **1926** Har 1 (0)

SEHORN, JASON Jason Heath, DB, 6´2˝/213 lbs; USC; 1994: NYG, rnd 2; B4/15/1971 Sacramento, CA **1994** NYG 8 (0) **1995** NYG 14 (0) **1996** NYG 16 (15, RCB) **1997**†NYG 16 (16, RCB) **1999** NYG 10 (10, RCB) **2000**†NYG 14 (14, RCB) **2001** NYG 13 (13, RCB) **2002**†NYG 16 (5, rcb) **2003**†SL 10 (3) **NFL** 117 (76) [9 yrs]

SEIBERT, ED Edward, G-E, 5´10˝/195 lbs; West Virginia; B10/24/1896, D7/1987 Indianapolis, IN **1923** Ham 2 (1)

SEIBERT, ED Edward White, T-G, 5´10˝/190 lbs; Otterbein; B1/7/1904 Fremont, OH, D2/8/1983 Dayton, OH **1927** Day 3 (0) **1928** Day 1 (1) **NFL** 4 (1) [2 yrs]

SEIBOLD, CHAMP Champ C., T, 6´4˝/240 lbs; Ripon; Wisconsin; B12/5/1912 Oshkosh, WI, D11/2/1971 Oshkosh, WI **1934** GB 1 (1) **1935** GB 6 (2) **1936**†GB 10 (3) **1937** GB 10 (4) **1938**†GB 11 (11, LT) **1940** GB 10 (1) **1942** ChiC 11 (0) **NFL** 59 (22) [7 yrs]

SEICK, RED Frederick Earl, G, 6´0˝/195 lbs; Manhattan; B4/28/1911 Lewiston, NY, D10/31/1989 Riverside County, CA **1942** NYG 6 (0)

SEIDELSON, RED Harry, G-T, 6´1˝/202 lbs; Pittsburgh; B8/13/1901 Romania, D7/6/1986 Pittsburgh, PA **1925** Fra 10 (7, rt) **1926** Akr 7 (7, LG) **NFL** 17 (14) [2 yrs]

SEIDMAN, MIKE Michael H., TE, 6´4˝/261 lbs; UCLA; 2003: Car, rnd 3; B2/11/1981 Westlake, CA

YEAR	TEAM	G(GS, POS)	RUSH	YD	AVG(LG)	TD	REC	YD	AVG(LG)	TD	PASS	COMP	PCT	YD	AVG(LG)	TD	INT	SK	YD	QBR	KPR	OTD	PTS	TAY
2003	Car	12(5, te)	—	—	—	—	5	35	7.0(14)	0	—	—	—	—	—	—	—	—	—	—	k	—	0	12
2004	Car	16(6, te)	—	—	—	—	13	123	9.5(27)	2	—	—	—	—	—	—	—	—	—	—	k	—	14	62
2005	†Car	12(1)	—	—	—	—	—	—	—	—	—	—	—	—	—	—	—	—	—	—	—	—	0	0
NFL	3	40(12)	—	—	—	—	18	158	8.8(27)	2	—	—	—	—	—	—	—	—	—	—	k	—	14	73

SEIFERT, MIKE Michael Patrick, DE, 6´3˝/245 lbs; Wisconsin; 1974: Cle, rnd 13; B3/30/1951 Port Washington, WI **1974** Cle 12 (RDE)

SEIGLER, DEXTER Dexter, DB, 5´9˝/178 lbs; Miami (FL); B1/11/1972 Miami, FL **1996** Sea 12 (0) **1997** Sea 2 (0) **NFL** 14 (0) [2 yrs]

SEIGLER, RICHARD Richard Joseph, LB, 6´3˝/239 lbs; Oregon State; 2004: SF, rnd 4; B10/19/1980 Las Vegas, NV **2004** SF 7 (0)

SEILER, PAUL Paul Herman, C-T, 6´4˝/258 lbs; Notre Dame; 1967: NYJ, rnd 1; B11/1/1945 Algona, IA, D9/25/2001 **1967** NYJ-A 2 **1969**†NYJ-A 11 **1971** Oak 8 **1972**†Oak 14 **1973**†Oak 4 (1) **NFL** 39 (1) [5 yrs]

SEIPLE, LARRY Lawrence Robert, TE-HB-P, 6´0˝/214 lbs; Kentucky; 1967: Mia, rnd 7; B2/14/1945 Allentown, PA **[P]**

YEAR	TEAM	G(GS, POS)	RUSH	YD	AVG(LG)	TD	REC	YD	AVG(LG)	TD	PASS	COMP	PCT	YD	AVG(LG)	TD	INT	SK	YD	QBR	KPR	OTD	PTS	TAY
1967	Mia-A	14	3	58	19.3(34)	0	1	21	21.0(21)	0	2	2	100.0	61	30.5(42)	0	0	—	—	—	P	—	0	99
1968	Mia-A	14	5	42	8.4(32)	0	7	69	9.9(20)	1	—	—	—	—	—	—	—	—	—	—	P	—	6	82
1969	Mia-A☆	14(8, TE)	1	6	6.0(6)	0	41	577	14.1(41)	5	1	1	100.0	8	8.0(8)	0	0	—	—	—	P	—	30	324
1970	†Mia	14	2	21	10.5(24)	0	2	14	7.0(7)	0	—	—	—	—	—	—	—	—	—	—	Pk	—	0	3
1971	†Mia	14	1	14	14.0(14)	0	1	32	32.0(32)	0	—	—	—	—	—	—	—	—	—	—	P	—	0	30
1972	†Mia	11	—	—	—	—	—	—	—	—	—	—	—	—	—	—	—	—	—	—	P	—	0	0
1973	†Mia	14	—	—	—	—	—	—	—	—	—	—	—	—	—	—	—	—	—	—	Pk	—	0	-15
1974	†Mia	14	—	—	—	—	—	—	—	—	—	—	—	—	—	—	—	—	—	—	P	—	0	0
1975	Mia	14	1	4	4.0(4)	0	10	84	8.4(15)	0	—	—	—	—	—	—	—	—	—	—	P	—	0	46
1976	Mia	14	3	14	4.7(7)	0	10	138	13.8(25)	1	—	—	—	—	—	—	—	—	—	—	P	—	6	88
1977	Mia	13	—	—	—	—	1	-1	-1.0(-1)	0	—	—	—	—	—	—	—	—	—	—	P	—	0	-1
NFL	11	150(8)	16	159	9.9(34)	0	73	934	12.8(41)	7	3	3	100.0	69	23.0(42)	0	0	—	—	—	Pk	—	42	656

SEITZ, WARREN Warren Troy, TE-WR, 6´4˝/217 lbs; Missouri; 1986: Pit, rnd 10; B9/29/1962 Kansas City, MO **1987** NYG 2 (0)

YEAR	TEAM	G(GS, POS)	RUSH	YD	AVG(LG)	TD	REC	YD	AVG(LG)	TD	PASS	COMP	PCT	YD	AVG(LG)	TD	INT	SK	YD	QBR	KPR	OTD	PTS	TAY
1986	Pit	16(0)	3	2	0.7(2)	0	—	—	—	—	—	—	—	—	—	—	—	—	—	—	k	—	0	-3
NFL	2	18(0)	3	2	0.7(2)	0	—	—	—	—	—	—	—	—	—	—	—	—	—	—	—	—	0	2

SELAWSKI, GENE Eugene Frank, T-G, 6´4˝/252 lbs; Purdue; 1958: LA, rnd 9; B11/28/1935 Cleveland, OH, D5/11/1993 Duluth, GA **1959** LARm 12 **1960** Cle 12 **1961**†SD-A 8 **NFL** 32 [3 yrs]

SELBY, ROB Robert Seth, G-T, 6´4˝/290 lbs; Auburn; 1991: Phi, rnd 3; B10/11/1967 Birmingham, AL **1991** Phi 13 (0) **1992**†Phi 16 (1) **1993** Phi 1 (0) **1994** Phi 2 (0) **1995** Arz 7 (4) **1996** Arz 13 (5, lg) **1997** Arz 10 (9, LG) **NFL** 62 (19) [7 yrs]

SELESKY, RON Ronald, C, 6´1˝/266 lbs; North Central; B9/4/1965 New Brunswick, NJ **1987** Min 2 (0)

SELF, CLARENCE Clarence Elbert, DB-HB, 5´8˝/181 lbs; Wisconsin; 1948: ChiC, rnd 12/1949: Cle-A, rnd 13; B10/10/1925 Birmingham, AL **1951** Det 12 (DB) **1954** GB 12 (DB) **1955** GB 2

YEAR	TEAM	G(GS, POS)	RUSH	YD	AVG(LG)	TD	REC	YD	AVG(LG)	TD	PASS	COMP	PCT	YD	AVG(LG)	TD	INT	SK	YD	QBR	KPR	OTD	PTS	TAY
1949	ChiC	12(0)	4	16	4.0(6)	0	—	—	—	—	—	—	—	—	—	—	—	—	—	—	pi	—	0	21
1950	Det	12(DB)	3	9	3.0(6)	0	1	12	12.0(12)	0	—	—	—	—	—	—	—	—	—	—	kpi	1	6	228
1952	GB	12(DB)	0	21	(21)	0	—	—	—	—	—	—	—	—	—	—	—	—	—	—	ki	—	0	56
NFL	6	62	7	46	6.6(21)	0	1	12	12.0(12)	0	—	—	—	—	—	—	—	—	—	—	kpi	1	6	318

SELFRIDGE, ANDY Andrew Paul, LB, 6´3˝/218 lbs; Virginia; 1972: SD, rnd 13; B1/12/1949 Cleveland, OH **1972** Buf 13 **1974** NYG 14 (7, rlb) **1975** NYG 14 (7, llb) **1976** Mia 1 **1977** NYG 11 **NFL** 53 (14) [5 yrs]

SELIGER, FRANK Frank H., T-G, /200 lbs; none; B8/31/1891 Chicago, IL, D8/28/1975 Hammond, IN **1920** Ham 4 (2, LT) **1921** Ham 1 (1) **NFL** 5 (3) [2 yrs]

SELLERS, GOLDIE Goldie, DB, 6´2˝/198 lbs; Grambling State; 1966: Den, rnd 8/Chi, rnd 20; B1/9/1942 Winnsboro, LA **1966** Den-A 14 (lcb) **1967** Den-A 13 (LCB) **1968**†KC-A 14 **1969**†KC-A 14 **NFL** 55 [4 yrs]

SELLERS, LANCE Lance Kevin, LB, 6´1˝/230 lbs; Boise State; 1987: Mia, rnd 6; B2/24/1963 Seattle, WA **1987** Cin 3 (3)

SELLERS, MIKE Mike, TE-WR, 6´3˝/260 lbs; Walla Walla CC (WA); B7/21/1975 Lacy, WA

YEAR	TEAM	G(GS, POS)	RUSH	YD	AVG(LG)	TD	REC	YD	AVG(LG)	TD	PASS	COMP	PCT	YD	AVG(LG)	TD	INT	SK	YD	QBR	KPR	OTD	PTS	TAY
1998	Was	14(1)	—	—	—	—	3	18	6.0(8)	0	—	—	—	—	—	—	—	—	—	—	k	—	0	12
1999	†Was	16(2)	—	—	—	—	7	105	15.0(33)	2	—	—	—	—	—	—	—	—	—	—	k	—	12	50
2000	Was	14(7, TE)	1	2	2.0(1)	0	8	78	9.8(24)	2	—	—	—	—	—	—	—	—	—	—	k	—	12	38
2001	Cle	9(7, TE)	—	—	—	—	7	73	10.4(28)	2	—	—	—	—	—	—	—	—	—	—	k	—	12	62
2004	Was	16(1)	—	—	—	—	1	14	14.0(14)	0	—	—	—	—	—	—	—	—	—	—	k	—	0	3
2005	†Was	15(6, wr)	1	1	1.0(2)	1	12	72	6.0(19)	7	—	—	—	—	—	—	—	—	—	—	k	—	48	87
NFL	6	84(24)	2	3	1.5(2)	1	38	360	9.5(33)	13	—	—	—	—	—	—	—	—	—	—	k	—	84	251

SELLERS, RON Ronald Franklin, WR, 6´4˝/205 lbs; Florida State; 1969: Bos, rnd 1; B2/5/1947 Jacksonville, FL

YEAR	TEAM	G(GS, POS)	RUSH	YD	AVG(LG)	TD	REC	YD	AVG(LG)	TD	PASS	COMP	PCT	YD	AVG(LG)	TD	INT	SK	YD	QBR	KPR	OTD	PTS	TAY
1969	Bos-A✧	12(9, WR)	—	—	—	—	27	705	26.1(77)	6	—	—	—	—	—	—	—	—	—	—	—	—	36	383
1970	Bos	13(13, WR)	—	—	—	—	38	550	14.5(48)	4	—	—	—	—	—	—	—	—	—	—	—	—	24	295
1971	NE	10(8, WR)	—	—	—	—	14	222	15.9(49)	3	—	—	—	—	—	—	—	—	—	—	—	—	18	126
1972	†Dal	14(8, WR)	—	—	—	—	31	653	21.1(55)	5	—	—	—	—	—	—	—	—	—	—	—	—	30	352

YEAR	TEAM	G (GS, POS)	RUSH	YD	AVG (LG)	TD	REC	YD	AVG (LG)	TD	PASS	COMP	PCT	YD	AVG (LG)	TD	INT	SK	YD	QBR	KPR	OTD	PTS	TAY
1973	†Mia	3	—	—	—	—	2	54	27.0 (42)	0	—	—	—	—	—	—	—	—	—	—	—	—	0	27
NFL	5	52 (38)	—	—	—	—	112	2184	19.5 (77)	18	—	—	—	—	—	—	—	—	—	—	—	—	108	1182

SELMON, DEWEY　Dewey Willis, LB-DT, 6′1″/246 lbs; Oklahoma; 1976: TB, rnd 2; B11/19/1953 Eufaula, OK　**1976** TB 12 (5, rdt)　**1977** TB 14 (14, LILB)　**1978** TB 16 (16, LILB)
1979†TB☆15 (15, LILB)　**1980** TB 15 (15, LILB)　**1982**†SD 8 (0)　**NFL** 80 (65) [6 yrs]

SELMON, LEE ROY　Lee Roy, DE-DT, 6′3″/256 lbs; Oklahoma; 1976: TB, rnd 1; B10/20/1954 Eufaula, OK; HOF 1995　**1976** TB 8 (6, RDT)　**1977** TB☆14 (14, RDE)
1978†TB☆14 (14, RDE)　**1979**†TB★16 (16, RDE)　**1980** TB★16 (16, RDE)　**1981**†TB✧14 (13, RDE)　**1982**†TB★9 (9, RDE)　**1983** TB★14 (13, RDE)　**1984**†TB★16 (16, RDE)
NFL 121 (117) [9 yrs]

SELTZER, HARRY　Harry, FB, 5′9″/195 lbs; Charleston (WV); B3/26/1919 Philadelphia, PA, D7/13/1990

| 1942 | Det | 6 (1) | 14 | 44 | 3.1 (24) | 0 | 2 | 23 | 11.5 (16) | 0 | — | — | — | — | — | — | — | — | — | — | — | — | 0 | 56 |

SEMES, BERNIE　Bernard Claude, HB, 5′7″/188 lbs; Duquesne; B1/29/1919 Braddock, PA, D1/30/2001 Beaver, PA

| 1944 | C-P | 8 (2) | 17 | 38 | 2.2 (3) | 0 | 3 | 22 | 7.3 (10) | 0 | — | — | — | — | — | — | — | — | — | i | — | — | 0 | 44 |

SEMPLE, TONY　Anthony Lee, G, 6′5″/286 lbs; Memphis; 1994: Det, rnd 5; B12/20/1970 Lincoln, IL　**1995**†Det 16 (0)　**1996** Det 15 (1)　**1997**†Det 16 (1)　**1998** Det 16 (3)
1999†Det 12 (12, LG)　**2000** Det 12 (8, LG)　**2001** Det 15 (12, LG)　**2002** Det 10 (10, LG)　**NFL** 112 (47) [8 yrs]

SENDLEIN, ROBIN　Robin Bruno, LB, 6′3″/225 lbs; Texas; 1981: Min, rnd 2; B12/1/1958 Las Vegas, NV　**1981** Min 16 (0)　**1982**†Min 9 (0)　**1983** Min 16 (1)　**1984** Min 15 (8, lolb)
1985†Mia 16 (3)　**NFL** 72 (12) [5 yrs]

SENN, BILL　William Franklin, B, 6′0″/177 lbs; Knox; B7/14/1905 Macomb, IL, D9/5/1973 Macomb, IL **[K]**　**1926** ChiB 15 (0), 45　**1927** ChiB☆13 (0), 36　**1928** ChiB 12 (4), 37
1929 ChiB 15 (7, rh), 24　**1930** ChiB 11 (1), 6　**1931** ChiB 1 (0), 7　**1931** Bkn 9 (6, WB))

1933	Cin	1 (0)	4	4	1.0	0	—	—	—	—	—	—	—	—	—	—	—	—	—	—	—	—	0	4
1934	SL	2 (0)	3	8	2.7	0	5	65	13.0	0	3	0	0.0	0	0.0	0	1	—	—	—	K	—	3	1
NFL	8	79 (18)	7	12	1.7	16	5	65	13.0	7	3	0	0.0	0	0.0	0	1	—	—	—	K	2	158	225

SENO, FRANK　Frank, HB, 6′0″/191 lbs; George Washington; B2/15/1921 Mendota, IL, D3/1974. **[R]**

1943	†Was	10 (1)	26	152	5.8 (52)	0	12	195	16.3 (36)	0	—	—	—	—	—	—	—	—	—	—	kpi	—	0	278
1944	Was	10 (3)	43	140	3.3 (14)	0	17	146	8.6 (47)	0	—	—	—	—	—	—	—	—	—	—	kpi	—	0	382
1945	ChiC	9 (8, RH)	93	355	3.8 (47)	2	7	129	18.4 (36)	0	1	0	0.0	0	0.0	0	—	—	—	—	kpi	—	12	611
1946	ChiC	11 (7, RH)	62	191	3.1 (27)	0	12	124	10.3 (27)	1	1	0	0.0	0	0.0	0	—	—	—	—	kpi	1	12	585
1947	Bos	11 (10, RH)	69	212	3.1 (22)	0	12	118	9.8 (30)	1	—	—	—	—	—	—	—	—	—	—	kpi	1	12	720
1948	Bos	12 (4)	71	242	3.4 (21)	0	13	322	24.8 (69)	3	—	—	—	—	—	—	—	—	—	—	kpi	—	18	498
1949	Was	4 (1)	—	—	—	—	—	—	—	—	—	—	—	—	—	—	—	—	—	—	k	—	0	9
NFL	7	67 (34)	364	1292	3.5 (52)	2	73	1034	14.2 (69)	5	2	0	0.0	0	0.0	0	—	—	—	—	kpi	2	54	3082

SENSABAUGH, GERALD　Gerald, DB, 6′1″/210 lbs; North Carolina; 2005: Jax, rnd 5; B6/13/1983 Kingsport, TN　**2005**†Jax 16 (2)

SENSANBAUGHER, DEAN　Dean Sparks, HB-DB, 5′9″/190 lbs; Army; Ohio State; B8/12/1925 Midvale, OH, D11/8/2005 Lakeland, FL

| 1948 | †Cle-A | 11 (0) | 18 | 59 | 3.3 | 1 | — | — | — | — | — | — | — | — | — | — | — | — | — | — | — | — | 6 | 69 |
| 1949 | NYB | 4 (2) | 20 | 36 | 1.8 (7) | 1 | — | — | — | — | — | — | — | — | — | — | — | — | — | — | kp | — | 6 | 86 |

SENSER, JOE　Joseph Spence, TE, 6′4″/235 lbs; West Chester; 1979: Min, rnd 6; B8/18/1956 Philadelphia, PA

1980	†Min	16 (0)	1	-1	-1.0 (-1)	0	42	447	10.6 (58)	7	1	0	0.0	0	0.0	0	—	—	—	—	—	—	42	258
1981	Min★	16 (16, TE)	1	2	2.0 (2)	0	79	1004	12.7 (53)	8	—	—	—	—	—	—	—	—	—	—	—	—	48	544
1982	†Min	9 (9, TE)	—	—	—	—	29	261	9.0 (22)	1	—	—	—	—	—	—	—	—	—	—	—	—	6	136
1984	Min	8 (1)	—	—	—	—	15	110	7.3 (26)	0	—	—	—	—	—	—	—	—	—	—	—	—	0	55
NFL	4	49 (26)	2	1	0.5 (2)	0	165	1822	11.0 (58)	16	1	0	0.0	0	0.0	0	—	—	—	—	—	—	96	992

SENSIBAUGH, MIKE　James Michael, DB, 5′11″/192 lbs; Ohio State; 1971: KC, rnd 8; B1/3/1949 Cincinnati, OH **[I]**　**1971** KC 7　**1972** KC 14 (FS)　**1973** KC 14 (FS)
1974 KC 14 (FS)　**1975** KC 14 (FS)　**1976** SL 14 (FS)　**1977** SL 10 (FS)　**1978** SL 5　**NFL** 92 [8 yrs]

SEPTIEN, RAFAEL　Jose Rafael, K, 5′10″/176 lbs; Louisiana-Lafayette; 1977: NO, rnd 10; B12/12/1953 Mexico City, Mexico **[K]**　**1977**†LARm 14　**1978**†Dal 16　**1979**†Dal 16
1980†Dal 16 (0)　**1981**†Dal★16 (0)　**1982**†Dal 9 (0)　**1983**†Dal 16 (0)　**1984** Dal 16 (0)　**1985**†Dal 16 (0)　**1986** Dal 16 (0)　**NFL** 151 [10 yrs]

SERGIENKO, GEORGE　George, T, 6′1″/248 lbs; American International; B5/22/1918 Chicopee Falls, MA, D12/4/1994 Chicopee, MA　**1943** Bkn 10 (8, RT)　**1944** Bkn 10 (3)
1945 Bos☆10 (10, LT)　**NFL** 30 (21) [3 yrs]

1946 Bkn-A 7 (3)

SERINI, WASH　William Washington, DG-G-T, 6′2″/236 lbs; Kentucky; B3/11/1922 Tuckahoe, NY, D6/21/1994 Highland, NY　**1948** ChiB☆12 (0)　**1949** ChiB☆12 (1)
1950†ChiB 12 (MG)　**1951** ChiB 12 (RG)　**1952** GB 11 (MG)　**NFL** 59 (1) [5 yrs]

SERWANGA, KATO　Kato, DB, 6′0″/205 lbs; Sacramento State; Pacific; California; B7/23/1976 Kampala, Uganda　**1999** NE 16 (3)　**2000** NE 15 (0)　**2001** Was 11 (0)
2002†NYG 3 (0)　**2003** NYG 13 (0)　**NFL** 58 (3) [5 yrs]

SERWANGA, WASSWA　Wasswa Kenneth, DB, 5′11″/203 lbs; Sacramento State; Pacific; UCLA; B7/23/1976 Kampala, Uganda　**1999** SF 9 (0)　**2000**†Min 7 (2)　**2001** Min 7 (0)
NFL 23 (2) [3 yrs]

SESTAK, TOM　Thomas Joseph, DT, 6′5″/267 lbs; Baylor; McNeese State; 1962: Buf, rnd 17/Det, rnd 16; B3/9/1936 Gonzales, TX, D4/3/1987 Buffalo, NY　**1962** Buf-A★14 (RDT)
1963†Buf-A★14 (RDT)　**1964** Buf-A★14 (RDT)　**1965**†Buf-A★14 (RDT)　**1966**†Buf-A☆14 (RDT)　**1967** Buf-A 14 (RDT)　**1968** Buf-A☆12 (RDT)　**NFL** 96 [7 yrs]

SETCAVAGE, JOE　Joseph W., BB, 5′11″/190 lbs; Duquesne; B11/12/1918 Mahonoy City, PA, D6/30/1996 North East, PA

| 1943 | Bkn | 10 (6, BB) | 1 | 3 | 3.0 (3) | 0 | 5 | 26 | 5.2 (17) | 0 | 1 | 0 | 0.0 | 0 | 0.0 | 0 | 0 | — | — | — | kpi | — | 0 | 8 |

SETRON, JOE　Joseph Louis, G, 5′9″/195 lbs; West Virginia; B8/10/1900 Buffalo, NY, D9/25/1958 Cleveland, OH　**1923** Cle 1 (0)

SETTLE, JOHN　John R., RB, 5′9″/207 lbs; Appalachian State; B6/2/1965 Reidsville, NC

1987	Atl	9 (1)	19	72	3.8 (12)	0	11	153	13.9 (36)	0	—	—	—	—	—	—	—	—	—	—	k	—	0	157
1988	Atl✧	16 (13, FB)	232	1024	4.4 (62)	7	68	570	8.4 (27)	1	—	—	—	—	—	—	—	—	—	—	—	—	48	1384
1989	Atl	15 (15, FB)	179	689	3.8 (20)	3	39	316	8.1 (33)	2	—	—	—	—	—	—	—	—	—	—	—	—	30	887
1990	Atl	6 (0)	9	16	1.8 (4)	0	—	—	—	—	—	—	—	—	—	—	—	—	—	—	—	—	0	16
NFL	4	46 (29)	439	1801	4.1 (62)	10	118	1039	8.8 (36)	3	—	—	—	—	—	—	—	—	—	—	k	—	78	2444

SETTLES, TONY　Anthony, LB, 6′3″/210 lbs; Elon; B8/29/1964　**1987** Was 3 (0)

SETTLES, TAWAMBI　Tawambi Jahmon, DB, 6′2″/194 lbs; Duke; B1/19/1976 Chattanooga, TN　**1998** Jax 7 (0)

SETZER, BOBBY　Robert Kelley, DE, 6′4″/280 lbs; Boise State; B6/16/1976 Walnut Creek, CA　**2001**†SF 14 (0)　**2002** ChiB 2 (0)　**NFL** 16 (0) [2 yrs]

SEUBERT, RICH　Rich, G, 6′5″/305 lbs; Western Illinois; B3/30/1979 Rozellville, WI　**2001** NYG 2 (0)　**2002**†NYG 16 (16, LG)　**2003** NYG 6 (6, lg)　**2005**†NYG 4 (1)
NFL 28 (23) [4 yrs]

SEURER, FRANK　Frank Anthony, QB, 6′1″/195 lbs; Kansas; 1984: Sea, rnd S3; B8/16/1962 Huntington Beach, CA　**1986** KC 1 (0)

| 1987 | KC | 8 (2) | 9 | 33 | 3.7 (11) | 0 | — | — | — | — | 55 | 26 | 47.3 | 340 | 6.2 (33) | 0 | 4 | 10 | 82 | — | — | — | 0 | 43 |
| NFL | 2 | 9 (2) | 9 | 33 | 3.7 (11) | 0 | — | — | — | — | 55 | 26 | 47.3 | 340 | 6.2 (33) | 0 | 4 | 10 | 82 | — | — | — | 0 | 43 |

SEVERSON, JEFF　Jeffrey Kent, DB, 6′1″/183 lbs; Long Beach State; 1971: Was, rnd 12; B9/16/1949 Fargo, ND　**1972**†Was 12　**1973** Hou 14 (SS)　**1974** Hou 14　**1975** Den 14 (3)
1976 SL 14　**1977** SL 14 (3)　**1979**†LARm 1　**NFL** 83 (6) [7 yrs]

SEVY, JEFF　Jeffrey Evan, T-G-DT-DE, 6′5″/260 lbs; California; 1974: Chi, rnd 12; B10/24/1951 Palo Alto, CA　**1976** ChiB 14 (14, RT/rg)　**1977**†ChiB 12 (2)　**1978** ChiB 14
1979 Sea 4 (1)　**1980** Sea 15 (4)

| 1975 | ChiB | 14 (12, RT) | — | — | — | — | 1 | 6 | 6.0 (6) | 0 | — | — | — | — | — | — | — | — | — | — | — | — | 0 | 3 |
| NFL | 6 | 73 (33) | — | — | — | — | 1 | 6 | 6.0 (6) | 0 | — | — | — | — | — | — | — | — | — | — | — | — | 0 | 3 |

SEWARD, ADAM　Adam Hartford, LB, 6′3″/253 lbs; Nevada-Las Vegas; 2005: Car, rnd 5; B6/15/1982 Champaign, IL　**2005** Car 4 (0)

SEWELL, HARLEY　Harley Edward, G-LB, 6′1″/230 lbs; Texas; 1953: Det, rnd 1; B4/18/1931 St. Jo, TX　**1953**†Det 12 (LG)　**1954**†Det 12 (LG)　**1955** Det☆12 (LG)
1956 Det☆12 (LG)　**1957**†Det★10 (LG)　**1958** Det★12 (LG)　**1959** Det✧11 (LG)　**1960** Det☆12 (LG)　**1961** Det 14 (LG)　**1962** Det★13 (LG)　**1963** LARm 2　**NFL** 122 [11 yrs]

Sewell, Steve Steven Edward, RB-WR, 6´3˝/210 lbs; Oklahoma; 1985: Den, rnd 1; B4/2/1963 San Francisco, CA

YEAR	TEAM	G (GS, POS)	RUSH	YD	AVG (LG)	TD	REC	YD	AVG (LG)	TD	PASS	COMP	PCT	YD	AVG (LG)	TD	INT	SK	YD	QBR	KPR	OTD	PTS	TAY
1985	Den	16(2)	81	275	3.4(16)	4	24	224	9.3(54)	1	1	0	0.0	0	0.0	0	0	—	—	—	k	—	30	446
1986	†Den	11(2)	23	123	5.3(15)	1	23	294	12.8(40)	1	1	1	100.0	23	23.0(23)	1	0	3	17	—	—	—	12	302
1987	†Den	7(0)	19	83	4.4(17)	2	13	209	16.1(72)	1	0	0	0.0	0	0.0	0	0	1	9	—	—	—	18	213
1988	Den	16(3)	32	135	4.2(26)	1	38	507	13.3(68)	5	1	0	0.0	0	0.0	0	0	—	—	—	—	—	36	424
1989	†Den	16(3)	7	44	6.3(10)	0	25	416	16.6(56)	3	—	—	—	—	—	—	—	—	—	—	—	—	18	267
1990	Den	12(1)	17	46	2.7(8)	3	26	268	10.3(36)	0	1	0	0.0	0	0.0	0	0	—	—	—	—	—	18	210
1991	†Den	16(1)	50	211	4.2(26)	2	38	436	11.5(60)	2	3	1	33.3	24	8.0(24)	0	0	—	—	—	k	—	24	470
NFL	7	94(12)	229	917	4.0(26)	13	187	2354	12.6(72)	13	7	2	28.6	47	6.7(24)	1	0	4	26	—	k	—	156	2331

Sexton, Brent Russell Brent, DB, 6´1˝/190 lbs; Elon; 1975: Pit, rnd 5; B7/23/1953 Fayetteville, NC **1977**†Pit 11

Sexton, Lin Linwood Bookard, HB-DB, 6´0˝/180 lbs; Wichita State; B4/16/1926 Wichita, KS

YEAR	TEAM	G (GS, POS)	RUSH	YD	AVG (LG)	TD	REC	YD	AVG (LG)	TD	PASS	COMP	PCT	YD	AVG (LG)	TD	INT	SK	YD	QBR	KPR	OTD	PTS	TAY
1948	LAD-A	11(1)	7	39	5.6	0	—	—	—	—	—	—	—	—	—	—	—	—	—	—	kpi	—	0	100

Seyboth, Frank Frank C., WB, 5´9˝/180 lbs; Vermont; B4/5/1904 Attleboro, MA, D4/30/1979 Attleboro, MA **1926** Pro 1 (0)

Seyfrit, Si Michael Franklin, E, 5´10˝/170 lbs; Notre Dame; B1/31/1898 Carlinville, IL, D9/1/1955 Bloomington, IL **1923** Tol 8 (8, RE), 6 **1924** Ham 5 (4, RE) **NFL** 13 (12) [2 yrs]

Seymour E, none

YEAR	TEAM	G (GS, POS)	RUSH	YD	AVG (LG)	TD	REC	YD	AVG (LG)	TD	PASS	COMP	PCT	YD	AVG (LG)	TD	INT	SK	YD	QBR	KPR	OTD	PTS	TAY
1941	ChiC	1(0)	—	—	—	—	1	3	3.0(3)	0	—	—	—	—	—	—	—	—	—	—	—	—	0	2

Seymour, Bob Robert Arnold, HB-FB, 6´2˝/205 lbs; Oklahoma; 1940: Was, rnd 10; B6/13/1916 Wyandotte, OK, D5/1977 Golden, CO

YEAR	TEAM	G (GS, POS)	RUSH	YD	AVG (LG)	TD	REC	YD	AVG (LG)	TD	PASS	COMP	PCT	YD	AVG (LG)	TD	INT	SK	YD	QBR	KPR	OTD	PTS	TAY
1940	†Was	9(0)	57	170	3.0	4	2	3	1.5	0	—	—	—	—	—	—	—	—	—	—	i	—	24	220
1941	Was	10(2)	62	137	2.2(17)	2	6	85	14.2(41)	2	—	—	—	—	—	—	—	—	—	—	kpi	—	24	365
1942	†Was✧	11(1)	54	190	3.5(18)	1	3	20	6.7(12)	0	—	—	—	—	—	—	—	—	—	—	pi	—	6	293
1943	†Was	10(2)	65	232	3.6(40)	0	17	167	9.8(32)	2	—	—	—	—	—	—	—	—	—	—	kpi	—	12	433
1944	Was	10(7, FB)	92	315	3.4(35)	3	19	263	13.8(71)	3	—	—	—	—	—	—	—	—	—	—	Ppi	—	36	503
1945	†Was	10(2)	30	102	3.4(23)	2	8	91	11.4(27)	1	—	—	—	—	—	—	—	—	—	—	i	—	18	181
NFL	6	60(14)	360	1146	3.2(40)	12	55	629	11.4(71)	8	—	—	—	—	—	—	—	—	—	—	Pkpi	—	120	1993
1946	LAD-A	13(8, LH)	37	165	4.5	0	17	188	11.1	3	—	—	—	—	—	—	—	—	—	—	kpi	—	18	436

Seymour, Jim James Patrick, WR, 6´4˝/210 lbs; Notre Dame; 1969: LA, rnd 1; B11/24/1946 Detroit, MI

YEAR	TEAM	G (GS, POS)	RUSH	YD	AVG (LG)	TD	REC	YD	AVG (LG)	TD	PASS	COMP	PCT	YD	AVG (LG)	TD	INT	SK	YD	QBR	KPR	OTD	PTS	TAY
1970	ChiB	7	—	—	—	—	6	145	24.2(53)	4	—	—	—	—	—	—	—	—	—	—	—	—	24	93
1971	ChiB	10	—	—	—	—	5	75	15.0(21)	0	—	—	—	—	—	—	—	—	—	—	—	—	0	38
1972	ChiB	14(WR)	1	-9	-9.0(-9)	0	10	165	16.5(35)	1	—	—	—	—	—	—	—	—	—	—	—	—	6	79
NFL	3	31	1	-9	-9.0(-9)	0	21	385	18.3(53)	5	—	—	—	—	—	—	—	—	—	—	—	—	30	209

Seymour, Paul Paul Christopher, TE, 6´5˝/252 lbs; Michigan; 1973: Buf, rnd 1; B2/6/1950 Detroit, MI

YEAR	TEAM	G (GS, POS)	RUSH	YD	AVG (LG)	TD	REC	YD	AVG (LG)	TD	PASS	COMP	PCT	YD	AVG (LG)	TD	INT	SK	YD	QBR	KPR	OTD	PTS	TAY
1973	Buf	14(14, TE)	—	—	—	—	10	114	11.4(22)	0	—	—	—	—	—	—	—	—	—	—	—	—	0	57
1974	Buf	14(14, TE)	—	—	—	—	15	246	16.4(40)	2	—	—	—	—	—	—	—	—	—	—	—	—	12	133
1975	Buf	14(14, TE)	—	—	—	—	19	268	14.1(32)	1	—	—	—	—	—	—	—	—	—	—	—	—	6	139
1976	Buf	13(13, TE)	—	—	—	—	16	169	10.6(22)	0	—	—	—	—	—	—	—	—	—	—	—	—	0	85
1977	Buf	14(13, TE)	—	—	—	—	2	21	10.5(11)	0	—	—	—	—	—	—	—	—	—	—	—	—	0	11
NFL	5	69(68)	—	—	—	—	62	818	13.2(40)	3	—	—	—	—	—	—	—	—	—	—	—	—	18	424

Seymour, Richard Richard Vershaun, DE-DT, 6´6˝/310 lbs; Georgia; 2001: NE, rnd 1; B10/6/1979 Gadsden, SC **2001**†NE 13 (10, RDE) **2002** NE★16 (16, RDE) **2003**†NE★15 (14, RDT) **2004**†NE★15 (15, RDE) **2005**†NE★12 (12, RDE) **NFL** 71 (67) [5 yrs]

Shabazz, Siddeeq Siddeeq Muneer, DB, 5´11˝/200 lbs; New Mexico State; 2003: Oak, rnd 7; B2/5/1981 Frankfurt, Germany **2003** Atl 7 (0) **2003** Oak 4 (0) **2004**†Atl 15 (0) **2005** NO 2 (0) **NFL** 28 (0) [3 yrs]

Shackelford, Don Donald Vernon, G, 6´4˝/255 lbs; Pacific; 1964: Den, rnd 6/Cle, rnd 4; B2/18/1943 Wichita Falls, TX **1964** Den-A 8

Shade, Sam Samuel Richard, DB, 6´1˝/196 lbs; Alabama; 1995: Cin, rnd 4; B6/14/1973 Birmingham, AL **1995** Cin 16 (2) **1996** Cin 12 (1) **1997** Cin 16 (12, SS) **1998** Cin 16 (14, SS) **1999**†Was 16 (16, SS) **2000** Was 16 (14, SS) **2001** Was 16 (15, SS) **2002** Was 9 (3) **NFL** 117 (77) [8 yrs]

Shaffer, Craig Craig Alan, LB, 6´0˝/230 lbs; Indiana State; 1982: SL, rnd 6; B3/31/1959 Terre Haute, IN **1982** SL 5 (0) **1983** SL 9 (0) **1984** SL 4 (0) **NFL** 18 (0) [3 yrs]

Shaffer, George George Adam, BB, 6´0˝/190 lbs; Washington & Jefferson; B6/20/1910, deceased

YEAR	TEAM	G (GS, POS)	RUSH	YD	AVG (LG)	TD	REC	YD	AVG (LG)	TD	PASS	COMP	PCT	YD	AVG (LG)	TD	INT	SK	YD	QBR	KPR	OTD	PTS	TAY
1933	Pit	5(5, BB)	5	6	1.2	0	1	11	11.0(11)	0	—	—	—	—	—	—	—	—	—	—	—	—	0	12

Shaffer, Kevin Kevin, T, 6´5˝/290 lbs; Tulsa; 2002: Atl, rnd 7; B3/2/1980 Salisbury, MD **2002**†Atl 6 (0) **2003** Atl 16 (8, lt) **2004**†Atl 15 (15, LT) **2005** Atl 16 (16, LT) **NFL** 53 (39) [4 yrs]

Shaffer, Lee Leland Knoy, B, 6´2˝/203 lbs; Kansas State; B5/9/1912 Minneola, KS, D1/24/1993 Hillsboro Beach, FL

YEAR	TEAM	G (GS, POS)	RUSH	YD	AVG (LG)	TD	REC	YD	AVG (LG)	TD	PASS	COMP	PCT	YD	AVG (LG)	TD	INT	SK	YD	QBR	KPR	OTD	PTS	TAY
1935	†NYG	12(5, wb)	—	—	—	—	7	123	17.6	0	—	—	—	—	—	—	—	—	—	—	—	—	0	62
1936	NYG	10(4)	3	10	3.3	0	2	30	15.0(17)	1	—	—	—	—	—	—	—	—	—	—	—	—	6	30
1937	NYG	9(1)	8	35	4.4	0	7	72	10.3	0	—	—	—	—	—	—	—	—	—	—	—	—	0	71
1938	†NYG✧	11(5, BB)	1	4	4.0(4)	0	12	86	7.2	2	—	—	—	—	—	—	—	—	—	—	—	—	12	57
1939	†NYG	9(2)	3	6	2.0(3)	0	2	8	4.0(5)	0	—	—	—	—	—	—	—	—	—	—	—	—	0	10
1940	NYG	11(5, wb)	7	20	2.9	1	15	121	8.1	2	—	—	—	—	—	—	—	—	—	—	i	—	18	95
1941	†NYG	10(0)	—	—	—	—	1	5	5.0(5)	0	—	—	—	—	—	—	—	—	—	—	i	—	0	2
1942	NYG	10(6, BB)	1	3	3.0(3)	0	3	20	6.7(10)	0	—	—	—	—	—	—	—	—	—	—	k	—	0	23
1943	†NYG	10(10, BB)	1	3	3.0(3)	0	3	66	22.0(40)	0	—	—	—	—	—	—	—	—	—	—	i	—	0	49
1945	NYG	6(1)	—	—	—	—	—	—	—	—	—	—	—	—	—	—	—	—	—	—	k	—	0	12
NFL	10	98(39)	24	81	3.4(4)	1	52	531	10.2(40)	5	—	—	—	—	—	—	—	—	—	—	ki	—	36	410

Shakespeare, Stanley Stanley C., WR, 6´0˝/190 lbs; Miami (FL); B2/5/1963 Auburn, NY, D4/26/2005 Jupiter, FL **1987** TB 1 (0)

Shank, Henry Henry A., HB, 5´8˝/160 lbs; Maryland; B5/29/1896 Sumner, IL, D11/1977 Mount Erie, IL **1920** Dec 5 (0)

Shanklin, Ron Ronnie Eugene, WR, 6´1˝/183 lbs; North Texas; 1970: Pit, rnd 2; B1/21/1948 Hubbard, TX, D4/18/2003 DeSoto, TX

YEAR	TEAM	G (GS, POS)	RUSH	YD	AVG (LG)	TD	REC	YD	AVG (LG)	TD	PASS	COMP	PCT	YD	AVG (LG)	TD	INT	SK	YD	QBR	KPR	OTD	PTS	TAY
1970	Pit	14(WR)	—	—	—	—	30	691	23.0(81)	4	—	—	—	—	—	—	—	—	—	—	—	—	24	366
1971	Pit	14(WR)	2	1	0.5(2)	0	49	652	13.3(42)	6	—	—	—	—	—	—	—	—	—	—	—	—	36	357
1972	†Pit	14(WR)	—	—	—	—	38	669	17.6(57)	3	—	—	—	—	—	—	—	—	—	—	—	—	18	350
1973	Pit★	13(WR)	3	1	0.3(10)	0	30	711	**23.7(67)**	10	—	—	—	—	—	—	—	—	—	—	—	—	60	407
1974	†Pit	12(WR)	—	—	—	—	19	324	17.1(35)	1	—	—	—	—	—	—	—	—	—	—	—	—	6	167
1976	ChiB	5(5, wr)	—	—	—	—	2	32	16.0(35)	0	—	—	—	—	—	—	—	—	—	—	—	—	0	16
NFL	6	72(5)	5	2	0.4(10)	0	168	3079	18.3(81)	24	—	—	—	—	—	—	—	—	—	—	—	—	144	1662

Shanks, Simon Simon, LB, 6´1˝/215 lbs; Tennessee State; B10/16/1971 Laurel, MS, D1/6/2006 Phoenix, AZ **1995** Arz 15 (0)

Shanle, Scott Scott, LB, 6´2˝/245 lbs; Nebraska; 2003: SL, rnd 7; B11/23/1979 Genoa, NE **2003** SL 5 (0) **2005** Dal 15 (8, RILB) **2004** Dal 16 (3) **NFL** 36 (11) [3 yrs]

Shanley T, /214 lbs; none **1927** Dul 1 (0)

Shanley, Jim James Donald, HB, 5´9˝/174 lbs; Oregon; B7/27/1936 Shelton, NE

YEAR	TEAM	G (GS, POS)	RUSH	YD	AVG (LG)	TD	REC	YD	AVG (LG)	TD	PASS	COMP	PCT	YD	AVG (LG)	TD	INT	SK	YD	QBR	KPR	OTD	PTS	TAY
1958	GB	12	23	30	1.3(5)	0	3	13	4.3(7)	0	—	—	—	—	—	—	—	—	—	—	p	—	0	72

Shann, Bob Robert Allen, DB, 6´1˝/189 lbs; Boston College; 1965: Phi, rnd 20; B3/27/1943 Andover, MA **1965** Phi 4 **1967** Phi 6 **NFL** 10 [2 yrs]

Shannon, Carver Carver Beauregard, DB-HB, 6´1˝/198 lbs; Southern Illinois; 1959: LA, rnd 19; B4/28/1938 Corinth, MS

YEAR	TEAM	G (GS, POS)	RUSH	YD	AVG (LG)	TD	REC	YD	AVG (LG)	TD	PASS	COMP	PCT	YD	AVG (LG)	TD	INT	SK	YD	QBR	KPR	OTD	PTS	TAY
1962	LARm	12(RCB)	—	—	—	—	—	—	—	—	—	—	—	—	—	—	—	—	—	—	i	—	0	13
1963	LARm	14(RS)	—	—	—	—	2	7	3.5(6)	0	—	—	—	—	—	—	—	—	—	—	kp	1	6	474
1964	LARm	12	17	35	2.1(8)	0	2	4	2.0(10)	0	—	—	—	—	—	—	—	—	—	—	kp	—	0	215
NFL	3	38	17	35	2.1(8)	0	4	11	2.8(10)	0	—	—	—	—	—	—	—	—	—	—	kpi	1	6	702

Shannon, John John Byron, DT-DE, 6´3˝/269 lbs; Kentucky; B1/18/1965 Lexington, KY **1988**†ChiB 13 (0) **1989** ChiB 12 (1) **NFL** 25 (1) [2 yrs]

Shannon, Larry Larry David, WR, 6´4˝/215 lbs; East Carolina; 1998: Mia, rnd 3; B2/2/1975 Gainesville, FL **1999** Mia 2 (0)

YEAR	TEAM	G(GS, POS)	RUSH	YD	AVG(LG)	TD	REC	YD	AVG(LG)	TD	PASS	COMP	PCT	YD	AVG(LG)	TD	INT	SK	YD	QBR	KPR	OTD	PTS	TAY

SHANNON, RANDY   Randy Leonard, LB, 6´0˝/221 lbs; Miami (FL); 1989: Dal, rnd 11; B2/24/1966 Miami, FL   **1989** Dal 16 (4)   **1990** Dal 1 (0)   **NFL** 17 (4) [2 yrs]

SHAPIRO, JACK   Jack Emanuel, B, 5´1˝/119 lbs; NYU; B3/22/1907 New York, NY, D2/5/2001 Carrollton, GA   **1929** SI 1 (0)

SHARE, NATE   Nathan Louis, G-T, 6´1˝/210 lbs; Tufts; B1901, NY, deceased   **1925** Pro 10 (10, LG)

SHARKEY, ED   Edward Joseph, LB-G-T-DG, 6´3˝/229 lbs; Duke; Nevada-Reno; B7/6/1927 Brooklyn, NY   **1947** NYY-A 9 (0)   **1948** NYY-A 10 (1)   **1949**†NYY-A 12 (0)
AAFC 31 (1) [3 yrs]
1950 NYY 12 (RLB)   **1952**†Cle 12   **1953** Bal 12   **1954** Phi 12   **1955** Phi 7   **1955** SF 5   **1956** SF 7 (llb)   **NFL** 67 [6 yrs]

SHAROCKMAN, ED   Edward Charles, DB, 6´0˝/200 lbs; Pittsburgh; 1961: Min, rnd 5/DalT, rnd 22; B11/4/1939 St. Clair, PA [I]   **1961** Min 1   **1962** Min 14 (14, RCB)
1963 Min 14 (14, RCB)   **1964** Min☆14 (14, RCB)   **1965** Min 14 (14, RCB)   **1966** Min 11 (10, RCB)   **1967** Min 14 (13, RCB)   **1968**†Min 14 (14, RCB)   **1969**†Min 11
1970†Min 14 (14, RCB)   **1971**†Min 14 (14, RCB)   **1972** Min 7   **NFL** 142 (121) [12 yrs]

SHARP, DAN   Daniel Ira, TE, 6´2˝/235 lbs; TCU; 1985: Mia, rnd 8; B2/5/1962 Dallas, TX

| **1987** | Atl | 9(0) | — | — | — | — | 2 | 6 | 3.0(5) | 0 | — | — | — | — | — | — | — | — | — | — | k | — | 0 | -1 |

SHARP, EV   Everett, T, 6´1˝/223 lbs; Cal Poly-Pomona; B6/25/1918 Corinth, MS, D2/1996 North Beach, MD   **1944** Was 5 (0)   **1945**†Was 9 (0)   **NFL** 14 (0) [2 yrs]

SHARP, RICK   Vaughan Richard, T, 6´3˝/265 lbs; Washington; 1970: Pit, rnd 12; B6/1/1948 London, England   **1970** Pit 14   **1971** Pit 3   **1972** Den 12   **NFL** 29 [3 yrs]

SHARPE, LUIS   Luis Ernesto, T, 6´5˝/275 lbs; UCLA; 1982: SL, rnd 1; B6/16/1960 Havana, Cuba   **1982**†SL 9 (9, LT)   **1984** SL☆16 (16, LT)   **1985** SL 16 (16, LT)
1986 SL 16 (16, LT)   **1987** SL★12 (12, LT)   **1988** Phx★16 (16, LT)   **1989** Phx◇14 (14, LT)   **1991** Phx 16 (16, LT)   **1992** Phx 15 (15, LT)   **1993** Phx 16 (16, LT)   **1994** Arz 11 (11, LT)

1983	SL	16(16, LT)	1	11	11.0(11)	0	—	—	—	—	—	—	—	—	—	—	—	—	—	—	—	—	0	11
1990	Phx☆	16(16, LT)	—	—	—	—	1	1	1.0(1)	1	—	—	—	—	—	—	—	—	—	—	—	—	6	6
NFL	13	189(189)	1	11	11.0(11)	0	1	1	1.0(1)	1	—	—	—	—	—	—	—	—	—	—	—	—	6	17

SHARPE, MONTIQUE   Monique, DT, 6´2˝/296 lbs; Wake Forest; 2003: KC, rnd 7; B3/10/1980 Washington, DC   **2003** KC 5 (0)

SHARPE, SHANNON   Shannon, TE, 6´2˝/228 lbs; Savannah State; 1990: Den, rnd 7; B6/26/1968 Chicago, IL

1990	Den	16(2)	—	—	—	—	7	99	14.1(33)	1	—	—	—	—	—	—	—	—	—	—	—	—	6	55
1991	†Den	16(9, TE)	1	15	15.0(15)	0	22	322	14.6(37)	1	—	—	—	—	—	—	—	—	—	—	—	—	6	181
1992	Den◇	16(11, TE)	2	-6	-3.0(-3)	0	53	640	12.1(55)	2	—	—	—	—	—	—	—	—	—	—	—	—	12	324
1993	†Den★	16(12, TE)	—	—	—	—	81	995	12.3(63)	9	—	—	—	—	—	—	—	—	—	—	k	—	54	528
1994	Den★	15(13, TE)	—	—	—	—	87	1010	11.6(44)	4	—	—	—	—	—	—	—	—	—	—	—	—	28	525
1995	Den★	13(12, TE)	—	—	—	—	63	756	12.0(49)	4	—	—	—	—	—	—	—	—	—	—	—	—	24	398
1996	†Den★	15(15, TE)	—	—	—	—	80	1062	13.3(51)	10	—	—	—	—	—	—	—	—	—	—	—	—	60	581
1997	†Den★	16(16, TE)	—	—	—	—	72	1107	15.4(68)	3	—	—	—	—	—	—	—	—	—	—	—	—	20	569
1998	†Den★	16(16, TE)	—	—	—	—	64	768	12.0(38)	10	—	—	—	—	—	—	—	—	—	—	—	—	60	434
1999	Den	5(5, te)	—	—	—	—	23	224	9.7(24)	0	—	—	—	—	—	—	—	—	—	—	—	—	0	112
2000	†Bal	16(15, TE)	—	—	—	—	67	810	12.1(59)	5	—	—	—	—	—	—	—	—	—	—	—	—	30	430
2001	†Bal◇	16(15, TE)	—	—	—	—	73	811	11.1(37)	2	—	—	—	—	—	—	—	—	—	—	—	—	12	416
2002	Den	13(13, TE)	—	—	—	—	61	686	11.2(82)	3	—	—	—	—	—	—	—	—	—	—	—	—	18	358
2003	†Den	15(15, TE)	—	—	—	—	62	770	12.4(28)	8	—	—	—	—	—	—	—	—	—	—	—	—	48	425
NFL	14	204(169)	3	9	3.0(15)	0	815	10060	12.3(82)	62	—	—	—	—	—	—	—	—	—	—	k	—	378	5334

SHARPE, STERLING   Sterling, WR, 6´0˝/207 lbs; South Carolina; 1988: GB, rnd 1; B4/6/1965 Chicago, IL

1988	GB	16(16, WR)	4	-2	-0.5(5)	0	55	791	14.4(51)	1	—	—	—	—	—	—	—	—	—	—	kp	—	6	404
1989	GB★	16(16, WR)	2	25	12.5(26)	0	90	1423	15.8(79)	12	—	—	—	—	—	—	—	—	—	—	—	1	78	797
1990	GB★	16(16, WR)	2	14	7.0(10)	0	67	1105	16.5(76)	6	—	—	—	—	—	—	—	—	—	—	—	—	36	597
1991	GB	16(16, WR)	4	4	1.0(12)	0	69	961	13.9(58)	4	—	—	—	—	—	—	—	—	—	—	—	—	24	505
1992	GB★	16(16, WR)	4	8	2.0(14)	0	108	1461	13.5(76)	13	—	—	—	—	—	—	—	—	—	—	—	—	78	804
1993	†GB★	16(16, WR)	4	8	2.0(5)	0	112	1274	11.4(54)	11	1	1	100.0	1	1.0(1)	1	—	—	—	—	—	—	66	701
1994	GB★	16(16, WR)	3	15	5.0(8)	0	94	1119	11.9(49)	18	—	—	—	—	—	—	—	—	—	—	—	—	108	665
NFL	7	112(112)	23	72	3.1(26)	0	595	8134	13.7(79)	65	1	1	100.0	1	1.0(1)	1	—	—	—	—	kp	—	396	4470

SHARPER, DARREN   Darren Mallory, DB, 6´2˝/210 lbs; William & Mary; 1997: GB, rnd 2; B11/3/1975 Richmond, VA [I]   **1997**†GB 14 (0)   **1998**†GB 16 (16, FS)   **1999** GB 16 (16, FS)
2000 GB★16 (16, FS)   **2001**†GB 16 (16, FS)   **2002** GB★13 (13, FS)   **2003**†GB 15 (15, FS)   **2004**†GB 15 (13, FS)   **2005** Min★14 (14, FS)   **NFL** 135 (119) [9 yrs]

SHARPER, JAMIE   Harry James, LB, 6´3˝/240 lbs; Virginia; 1997: Bal, rnd 2; B11/23/1974 Richmond, VA   **1997** Bal 16 (15, RLB)   **1998** Bal 16 (16, RLB)   **1999** Bal 16 (16, RLB)
2000†Bal 16 (16, RLB)   **2001**†Bal 16 (16, RLB)   **2002** Hou 16 (16, RILB)   **2003** Hou 16 (16, RILB)   **2004** Hou 16 (16, RILB)   **2005** Sea 8 (8, LOLB)   **NFL** 136 (135) [9 yrs]

SHAUB, HARRY   Harry, G, 5´7˝/215 lbs; Cornell; B7/15/1911, D4/22/1988 Fort Lauderdale, FL   **1935** Phi 1 (0)

SHAVERS, TYRONE   Tyrone Pernell, WR, 6´3˝/210 lbs; Lamar; 1990: Phx, rnd 6; B7/14/1967 Texarkana, TX   **1991** Cle 1 (0)

SHAW, BEN   Benjamin, G, 5´10˝/190 lbs; none; B1894, OH, deceased   **1923** Can 1 (0)

SHAW, BILLY   William Lewis, G, 6´2˝/258 lbs; Georgia Tech; 1961: Buf, rnd 2/Dal, rnd 14; B12/15/1938 Natchez, MS; HOF 1999   **1961** Buf-A 14 (LG)   **1962** Buf-A★14 (LG)
1963†Buf-A★14 (LG)   **1964**†Buf-A★14 (LG)   **1965**†Buf-A★14 (LG)   **1966**†Buf-A★14 (LG)   **1967** Buf-A★9 (LG)   **1968** Buf-A★13 (LG)   **1969** Buf-A★13 (LG)   **NFL** 119 [9 yrs]

SHAW, BOB   Robert, E, 6´4˝/226 lbs; Ohio State; 1944: Cle, rnd 10; B5/22/1921 Richwood, OH

1945	Cle	5(0)	—	—	—	—	—	—	—	—	—	—	—	—	—	—	—	—	—	—	k	—	0	-14
1946	LARm	10(7, LE)	—	—	—	—	4	63	15.8(28)	2	—	—	—	—	—	—	—	—	—	—	k	1	18	89
1949	†LARm	11(10, RE)	—	—	—	—	29	535	18.4(71)	6	—	—	—	—	—	—	—	—	—	—	—	—	36	298
1950	ChiC★	12(11, RE)	—	—	—	—	48	971	20.2(65)	12	—	—	—	—	—	—	—	—	—	—	—	—	72	546
NFL	4	38(28)	—	—	—	—	81	1569	19.4(71)	20	—	—	—	—	—	—	—	—	—	—	k	1	126	918

SHAW, BOB   Robert K., WR, 6´0˝/194 lbs; Winston-Salem State; B3/16/1947 Wilson, NC

| **1970** | NO | 4 | — | — | — | — | 1 | 49 | 49.0(49) | 0 | — | — | — | — | — | — | — | — | — | — | — | — | 0 | 25 |

SHAW, BOBBY   Bobby, WR, 6´1˝/185 lbs; California; 1998: Sea, rnd 6; B4/23/1975 San Francisco, CA

1999	Pit	15(1)	—	—	—	—	28	387	13.8(49)	3	—	—	—	—	—	—	—	—	—	—	p	—	18	242
2000	Pit	16(0)	—	—	—	—	40	672	16.8(45)	4	—	—	—	—	—	—	—	—	—	—	p	—	24	355
2001	†Pit	16(0)	—	—	—	—	24	409	17.0(90)	2	—	—	—	—	—	—	—	—	—	—	kp	—	12	227
2002	Jax	16(10, WR)	—	—	—	—	44	525	11.9(48)	1	—	—	—	—	—	—	—	—	—	—	kp	1	12	471
2003	Buf	16(7, wr)	—	—	—	—	56	732	13.1(54)	4	—	—	—	—	—	—	—	—	—	—	—	—	24	386
2004	Buf	4(0)	—	—	—	—	5	59	11.8(20)	0	—	—	—	—	—	—	—	—	—	—	—	—	0	30
2004	SD	7(0)	1	1	1.0(1)	0	—	—	—	—	—	—	—	—	—	—	—	—	—	—	—	—	0	1
NFL	6	90(18)	1	1	1.0(1)	0	197	2784	14.1(90)	14	—	—	—	—	—	—	—	—	—	—	kp	—	90	1710

SHAW, CHARLIE   Charles Edward, G, 6´2˝/220 lbs; Oklahoma State; 1950: SF, rnd 16; B3/6/1927 Durant, OK, D6/17/1994 Kingston, OK   **1950** SF 6

SHAW, DENNIS   Dennis Wendell, QB, 6´3˝/217 lbs; San Diego State; 1970: Buf, rnd 2; B3/3/1947 Los Angeles, CA

1970	Buf	14(QB)	39	210	5.4(20)	0	—	—	—	—	321	178	55.5	2507	7.8(48)	10	20	41	387	65.3	—	—	0	714
1971	Buf	13(QB)	14	82	5.9(12)	0	—	—	—	—	291	149	51.2	1813	6.2(75)	11	26	33	276	46.1	—	—	0	4
1972	Buf	14(QB)	35	138	3.9(16)	0	—	—	—	—	258	136	52.7	1666	6.5(58)	14	17	38	320	63.5	—	—	0	361
1973	Buf	4	4	2	0.5(1)	0	—	—	—	—	46	22	47.8	300	6.5(40)	0	4	11	75	—	—	—	0	-8
1974	SL	2	—	—	—	—	—	—	—	—	—	—	—	—	—	—	—	—	—	—	—	—	0	-22
1975	SL	3	3	-12	-4.0(-2)	0	—	—	—	—	8	4	50.0	61	7.6(21)	0	1	1	14	—	—	—	0	-22
NFL	6	50	95	420	4.4(20)	0	—	—	—	—	924	489	52.9	6347	6.9(75)	35	68	124	1072	56.8	—	—	0	1049

SHAW, ED   Edson Walter, T-FB-WB-G, 6´1˝/203 lbs; Nebraska; B8/7/1895 Tecumseh, NE, D10/30/1964 Omaha, NE [K]   **1920** RI☆7 (7, LT)   **1922** Can 12 (4), 38   **1923** Akr 2 (2)
NFL 21 (13) [3 yrs]

SHAW, ERIC   Eric Wendell, LB, 6´3˝/248 lbs; Florida State; Louisiana Tech; 1992: Cin, rnd 12; B9/17/1971 Pensacola, FL   **1992** Cin 11 (1)   **1993** Cin 14 (9, LILB)   **1994** Cin 3 (0)
NFL 28 (10) [3 yrs]

Shaw, George George Howard, QB, 6´1˝/183 lbs; Oregon; 1955: Bal, rnd B1; B7/25/1933 Portland, OR, D1/3/1998 Portland, OR **[K]**

YEAR	TEAM	G(GS, POS)	RUSH	YD	AVG(LG)	TD	REC	YD	AVG(LG)	TD	PASS	COMP	PCT	YD	AVG(LG)	TD	INT	SK	YD	QBR	KPR	OTD	PTS	TAY
1955	Bal	12(QB)	68	301	4.4(37)	3	—	—	—	—	237	119	50.2	1586	6.7(82)	10	19	—	—	52.5	—	—	18	414
1956	Bal	5	20	63	3.2(19)	0	—	—	—	—	75	45	60.0	645	8.6(49)	3	7	—	—	—	—	—	0	121
1957	Bal	7	5	30	6.0(11)	1	—	—	—	—	9	5	55.6	58	6.4(17)	1	1	—	—	—	—	—	6	34
1958	†Bal	12	5	-3	-0.6(3)	1	—	—	—	—	89	41	46.1	531	6.0(57)	7	4	—	—	—	K	—	6	148
1959	†NYG	5	3	3	1.0(1)	0	—	—	—	—	36	24	66.7	433	12.0(46)	1	1	—	—	—	—	—	0	185
1960	NYG	9(qb)	15	-12	-0.8(15)	0	—	—	—	—	155	76	49.0	1263	8.1(71)	11	13	—	—	65.6	—	—	0	155
1961	Min	8	10	39	3.9(19)	0	—	—	—	—	91	46	50.5	530	5.8(42)	4	4	14	122	—	—	—	0	164
1962	Den-A	13(qb)	4	10	2.5(9)	1	—	—	—	—	110	49	44.5	783	7.1(97)	4	14	—	—	41.4	—	—	6	-129
NFL	8	71	130	431	3.3(37)	6	—	—	—	—	802	405	50.5	5829	7.3(97)	41	63	14	122	58.8	K	—	36	1091

Shaw, Glenn Glenn Edd, FB, 6´2˝/220 lbs; Kentucky; 1960: Chi, rnd 11/DalT, rnd 1; B7/11/1938 Paducah, KY

YEAR	TEAM	G(GS, POS)	RUSH	YD	AVG(LG)	TD	REC	YD	AVG(LG)	TD	PASS	COMP	PCT	YD	AVG(LG)	TD	INT	SK	YD	QBR	KPR	OTD	PTS	TAY
1960	ChiB	12	—	—	—	—	—	—	—	—	—	—	—	—	—	—	—	—	—	—	—	—	—	—
1962	LARm	3	18	76	4.2(38)	0	3	51	17.0(30)	0	—	—	—	—	—	—	—	—	—	—	—	—	0	102
1963	Oak-A	12	20	46	2.3(15)	1	2	64	32.0(55)	1	—	—	—	—	—	—	—	—	—	—	k	—	12	82
1964	Oak-A	2	9	26	2.9(9)	2	3	31	10.3(15)	0	—	—	—	—	—	—	—	—	—	—	—	—	12	62
NFL	4	29	47	148	3.1(38)	3	8	146	18.3(55)	1	—	—	—	—	—	—	—	—	—	—	k	—	24	245

Shaw, Harold Harold Lamar, RB, 6´0˝/228 lbs; Southern Mississippi; 1998: NE, rnd 6; B9/3/1974 Magee, MS

YEAR	TEAM	G(GS, POS)	RUSH	YD	AVG(LG)	TD	REC	YD	AVG(LG)	TD	PASS	COMP	PCT	YD	AVG(LG)	TD	INT	SK	YD	QBR	KPR	OTD	PTS	TAY
1998	†NE	11(0)	—	—	—	—	—	—	—	—	—	—	—	—	—	—	—	—	—	—	—	—	—	—
1999	NE	8(0)	9	23	2.6(12)	0	2	31	15.5(29)	0	—	—	—	—	—	—	—	—	—	—	—	—	0	39
2000	NE	16(0)	9	12	1.3(5)	0	2	11	5.5(8)	0	—	—	—	—	—	—	—	—	—	—	—	—	0	18
NFL	3	35(0)	18	35	1.9(12)	0	4	42	10.5(29)	0	—	—	—	—	—	—	—	—	—	—	—	—	0	56

Shaw, Jesse Jesse M., G, 6´1˝/210 lbs; USC; B6/11/1907, D10/25/1965 Woodland Hills, CA **1931** ChiC 5 (0)

Shaw, Josh Josh, DT, 6´2˝/290 lbs; Michigan State; 2002: SF, rnd 5; B9/7/1979 Fort Lauderdale, FL **2002** SF 3 (0) **2004** Mia 5 (0) **NFL** 8 (0) [2 yrs]

Shaw, Nate Nathaniel, DB, 6´2˝/205 lbs; USC; 1967: LA, rnd 5; B5/20/1945 San Diego, CA **1969**†LARm 7 **1970** LARm 8 **NFL** 15 [2 yrs]

Shaw, Pete Kenneth Edward, DB, 5´10˝/183 lbs; Northwestern; 1977: SD, rnd 6; B8/25/1954 Newark, NJ **1977** SD 14 **1978** SD 16 (14, FS) **1979**†SD 16 (3) **1980** SD 12 (11, SS) **1981**†SD 16 (12, SS) **1982** NYG 9 (0) **1983** NYG 15 (1) **1984**†NYG 16 (2) **NFL** 114 (43) [8 yrs]

Shaw, Ricky Ricky Andrew, LB, 6´4˝/240 lbs; Oklahoma State; 1988: NYG, rnd 4; B7/28/1965 Mount Vernon, NY **1988** NYG 14 (0) **1989** NYG 7 (0) **1989**†Phi 8 (0) **1990** Phi 8 (0) **NFL** 37 (0) [3 yrs]

Shaw, Robert Robert Leslie, C-G, 6´4˝/245 lbs; Tennessee; 1979: Dal, rnd 1; B10/15/1956 Tuscaloosa, AL **1979**†Dal 16 (1) **1980**†Dal 14 (2) **1981** Dal 3 (3) **NFL** 33 (6) [3 yrs]

Shaw, Scott Scott Harold, G, 6´3˝/303 lbs; Michigan State; 1998: Mia, rnd 5; B6/2/1974 Detroit, MI **1998** Cin 2 (0)

Shaw, Sedrick Sedrick Anton, RB, 6´0˝/214 lbs; Iowa; 1997: NE, rnd 3; B11/16/1973 Austin, TX

YEAR	TEAM	G(GS, POS)	RUSH	YD	AVG(LG)	TD	REC	YD	AVG(LG)	TD	PASS	COMP	PCT	YD	AVG(LG)	TD	INT	SK	YD	QBR	KPR	OTD	PTS	TAY
1997	†NE	1(0)	—	—	—	—	—	—	—	—	—	—	—	—	—	—	—	—	—	—	—	—	—	—
1998	†NE	13(1)	48	236	4.9(71)	0	6	30	5.0(11)	0	—	—	—	—	—	—	—	—	—	—	k	—	0	252
1999	Cle	3(0)	3	2	0.7(3)	0	2	8	4.0(7)	0	—	—	—	—	—	—	—	—	—	—	—	—	0	6
1999	Cin	1(0)	4	20	5.0(10)	1	1	-4	-4.0(-4)	0	—	—	—	—	—	—	—	—	—	—	—	—	6	28
NFL	3	18(1)	55	258	4.7(71)	1	9	34	3.8(11)	0	—	—	—	—	—	—	—	—	—	—	k	—	6	286

Shaw, Terrance Terrance Bernard, DB, 6´0˝/200 lbs; Stephen F. Austin State; 1995: SD, rnd 2; B11/11/1973 Marshall, TX **1995**†SD 16 (14, RCB) **1996** SD 16 (16, RCB) **1997** SD 16 (16, RCB) **1998** SD 13 (13, RCB) **1999** SD 8 (8, RCB) **2000**†Mia 11 (3) **2001**†NE 13 (2) **2002**†Oak 16 (7, lcb) **2003** Oak 16 (8, rcb) **2004**†Min 15 (4) **NFL** 140 (91) [10 yrs]

Shay, Jerry Jerome Paul, aka Jerome Paul Dzedzeji, DT, 6´3˝/250 lbs; Purdue; 1966: Min, rnd 1/Den, rnd 1; B7/10/1944 Gary, IN **1966** Min 14 (2) **1967** Min 1 **1968** Atl 14 (LDT) **1969** Atl 14 (LDT) **1970** NYG 14 (LDT) **1971** NYG 6 **NFL** 63 (2) [6 yrs]

Shazor, Ernest Ernest, DB, 6´4˝/231 lbs; Michigan; B7/14/1983 Detroit, MI **2005** Arz 2 (0)

Shea, Aaron Aaron T., TE, 6´3˝/255 lbs; Michigan; 2000: Cle, rnd 4; B12/5/1976 Ottawa, IL

YEAR	TEAM	G(GS, POS)	RUSH	YD	AVG(LG)	TD	REC	YD	AVG(LG)	TD	PASS	COMP	PCT	YD	AVG(LG)	TD	INT	SK	YD	QBR	KPR	OTD	PTS	TAY
2000	Cle	15(8, te)	—	—	—	—	30	302	10.1(37)	2	—	—	—	—	—	—	—	—	—	—	—	—	12	161
2001	Cle	12(5, te)	—	—	—	—	14	86	6.1(12)	0	—	—	—	—	—	—	—	—	—	—	—	—	0	43
2002	Cle	7(3)	—	—	—	—	7	49	7.0(18)	0	—	—	—	—	—	—	—	—	—	—	—	—	0	25
2003	Cle	4(2)	—	—	—	—	2	9	4.5(7)	0	—	—	—	—	—	—	—	—	—	—	—	—	0	5
2004	Cle	15(8, te)	—	—	—	—	26	252	9.7(35)	4	—	—	—	—	—	—	—	—	—	—	k	—	24	135
2005	Cle	12(4)	—	—	—	—	18	153	8.5(27)	1	—	—	—	—	—	—	—	—	—	—	k	—	6	66
NFL	6	65(30)	—	—	—	—	97	851	8.8(37)	7	—	—	—	—	—	—	—	—	—	—	k	—	42	434

Shea, Pat Patrick Beardsley, G, 6´1˝/250 lbs; USC; B6/28/1939 La Jolla, CA **1962** SD-A 5 **1963**†SD-A 14 (RG) **1964**†SD-A 14 (LG)

YEAR	TEAM	G(GS, POS)	RUSH	YD	AVG(LG)	TD	REC	YD	AVG(LG)	TD	PASS	COMP	PCT	YD	AVG(LG)	TD	INT	SK	YD	QBR	KPR	OTD	PTS	TAY
1965	SD-A	8	1	-5	-5.0(-5)	0	—	—	—	—	—	—	—	—	—	—	—	—	—	—	—	—	0	-5
NFL	4	41	1	-5	-5.0(-5)	0	—	—	—	—	—	—	—	—	—	—	—	—	—	—	—	—	0	-5

Sheard, Shag Alfred Scotchard, BB-WB-TB, 5´11˝/177 lbs; St. Lawrence; B11/17/1898 Canton, NY, D11/11/1980 Canton, NY **[K]** **1923** Roc 4 (4, BB) **1924** Roc 7 (7, BB), 1 **1925** Roc 7 (7, WB), 12 **NFL** 18 (18), 13 [3 yrs]

Shearer, Brad Sterling Bradford, DT, 6´3˝/250 lbs; Texas; 1978: Chi, rnd 3; B8/10/1955 Houston, TX **1978** ChiB 15 (2) **1980** ChiB 13 (0) **1981** ChiB 6 (0) **NFL** 34 (2) [3 yrs]

Shearer, Ronald Ronald Elmer, T, 6´0˝/195 lbs; Drake; B9/12/1905 Creston, IA, D3/16/1998 Lee County, FL **1930** Por 1 (0)

Shearin, Joe Joseph Leslie, G-C, 6´4˝/254 lbs; Texas; 1982: LARm, rnd 7; B4/16/1960 Dallas, TX **1983**†LARm 16 (2) **1984**†LARm 15 (0) **1985** TB 10 (0) **1987** Dal 1 (0) **NFL** 42 (2) [4 yrs]

Shears, Larry Larry, DB, 5´10˝/185 lbs; Lincoln (MO); 1971: Atl, rnd 11; B8/1/1949 Mobile, AL **1971** Atl 9 **1972** Atl 1 **NFL** 10 [2 yrs]

Shedd, Kenny Kendrick Dwayne, WR, 5´10˝/168 lbs; Northern Iowa; 1993: NYJ, rnd 5; B2/14/1971 Davenport, IA

YEAR	TEAM	G(GS, POS)	RUSH	YD	AVG(LG)	TD	REC	YD	AVG(LG)	TD	PASS	COMP	PCT	YD	AVG(LG)	TD	INT	SK	YD	QBR	KPR	OTD	PTS	TAY
1996	Oak	16(1)	—	—	—	—	3	87	29.0(51)	1	—	—	—	—	—	—	—	—	—	—	k	—	8	55
1997	Oak	16(0)	—	—	—	—	10	115	11.5(19)	0	—	—	—	—	—	—	—	—	—	—	k	1	6	66
1998	Oak	15(0)	—	—	—	—	3	50	16.7(21)	0	—	—	—	—	—	—	—	—	—	—	k	—	0	27
1999	Oak	12(0)	—	—	—	—	—	—	—	—	—	—	—	—	—	—	—	—	—	—	—	1	6	0
2000	Was	1(0)	—	—	—	—	—	—	—	—	—	—	—	—	—	—	—	—	—	—	—	—	—	—
NFL	5	60(1)	—	—	—	—	16	252	15.8(51)	1	—	—	—	—	—	—	—	—	—	—	k	2	20	147

Shedlosky, Ed Edmond Francis, WB, 6´0˝/185 lbs; Tulsa; Fordham; B8/2/1920 Nanticoke, PA, deceased

YEAR	TEAM	G(GS, POS)	RUSH	YD	AVG(LG)	TD	REC	YD	AVG(LG)	TD	PASS	COMP	PCT	YD	AVG(LG)	TD	INT	SK	YD	QBR	KPR	OTD	PTS	TAY
1945	NYG	3(0)	9	11	1.2(4)	0	2	15	7.5(9)	0	—	—	—	—	—	—	—	—	—	—	kp	—	0	43

Sheehan, Fred Frederic William, G, 6´2˝/210 lbs; Georgetown (DC); B12/21/1902 Abington, MA, D9/2/1984 Boston, MA **1925** Pro 1 (1)

Sheeks, Paul Paul Preston, BB, 5´8˝/173 lbs; Dakota Wesleyan; South Dakota; B10/18/1889 Grand Rapids, ND, D9/17/1968 Akron, OH **[K]** **1921** Akr 12 (9, BB), 13 **1922** Akr 9 (7, BB), 17 **NFL** 21 (16), 30 [2 yrs]

Sheffield, Chris Christopher Jonathan, DB, 6´1˝/193 lbs; Albany State (GA); B1/9/1963 Cairo, GA **1986** Pit 10 (6, lcb) **1987** Pit 5 (0) **1987** Det 6 (0) **NFL** 21 (6) [2 yrs]

Shegog, Ron Ronald, DB, 5´11˝/190 lbs; Austin Peay State; B3/2/1963 Batesville, MS **1987** NE 3 (3)

Shehee, Rashaan Rashaan, RB, 5´10˝/205 lbs; Washington; 1998: KC, rnd 3; B6/20/1975 Los Angeles, CA

YEAR	TEAM	G(GS, POS)	RUSH	YD	AVG(LG)	TD	REC	YD	AVG(LG)	TD	PASS	COMP	PCT	YD	AVG(LG)	TD	INT	SK	YD	QBR	KPR	OTD	PTS	TAY
1998	KC	16(0)	22	57	2.6(10)	0	10	73	7.3(14)	0	—	—	—	—	—	—	—	—	—	—	k	—	0	106
1999	KC	9(5, rb)	65	238	3.7(18)	1	18	136	7.6(17)	0	—	—	—	—	—	—	—	—	—	—	—	—	6	316
NFL	2	25(5)	87	295	3.4(18)	1	28	209	7.5(17)	0	—	—	—	—	—	—	—	—	—	—	k	—	6	422

Shekleton, Vincent Vincent S., C, 5´8˝/165 lbs; Colgate; Marquette; B11/16/1896 Lawler, LA, D9/12/2000 Iowa City, IA **1922** Rac 3 (3)

Shelburne, John John Andrew, FB, 5´11˝/200 lbs; Dartmouth; B9/26/1894 Boston, MA, D1/29/1978 Boston, MA **1922** Ham 6 (6, FB)

Shelby, Willie Willie Earl, RB, 5´11˝/195 lbs; Alabama; 1976: Cin, rnd 5; B7/24/1953 Hattiesburg, MS

YEAR	TEAM	G(GS, POS)	RUSH	YD	AVG(LG)	TD	REC	YD	AVG(LG)	TD	PASS	COMP	PCT	YD	AVG(LG)	TD	INT	SK	YD	QBR	KPR	OTD	PTS	TAY
1976	Cin	13	5	9	1.8(3)	0	1	3	3.0(3)	0	—	—	—	—	—	—	—	—	—	—	kp	1	6	389
1977	Cin	14	—	—	—	—	—	—	—	—	—	—	—	—	—	—	—	—	—	—	kp	1	6	117

YEAR	TEAM	G (GS, POS)	RUSH	YD	AVG (LG)	TD	REC	YD	AVG (LG)	TD	PASS	COMP	PCT	YD	AVG (LG)	TD	INT	SK	YD	QBR	KPR	OTD	PTS	TAY
1978	SL	3	2	5	2.5(4)	0	1	11	11.0(11)	0	—	—	—	—	—	—	—	—	—	—	kp	—	0	125
NFL	3	30	7	14	2.0(4)	0	2	14	7.0(11)	0	—	—	—	—	—	—	—	—	—	—	kp	2	12	630

SHELDON, JAMES   James Hurton, E, 5´11˝/180 lbs; Brown; B1/9/1901 Oneonta, NY, D2/26/1980 Round Hill, VA   **1926** Bkn 1 (0)

SHELDON, MIKE   Michael Joseph, T, 6´4˝/305 lbs; Grand Valley State; B6/8/1973 Hinsdale, IL   **1997**†Mia 11 (0)   **1998**†Mia 9 (2)   **1999**†Mia 9 (0)   **NFL** 29 (2) [3 yrs]

SHELL, ART   Arthur, T, 6´5˝/265 lbs; Maryland-Eastern Shore; 1968: Oak, rnd 3; B11/26/1946 Charleston, SC; HOF 1989 **[C]**   **1968**†Oak-A 14   **1969**†Oak-A 14 (1)
1970†Oak 14 (14, LT)   **1971** Oak 14 (14, LT)   **1972**†Oak★14 (14, LT)   **1973**†Oak★14 (14, LT)   **1974**†Oak★14 (14, LT)   **1975**†Oak★14 (14, LT)   **1976**†Oak★14 (14, LT)
1977†Oak★14 (14, LT)   **1978** Oak★16 (16, LT)   **1979** Oak 11 (11, LT)   **1980**†Oak◇16 (16, LT)   **1981** Oak 16 (13, LT)   **1982**†LARd 8 (0)   **NFL** 207 (155) [15 yrs]

SHELL, DONNIE   Donnie, DB, 5´11˝/190 lbs; South Carolina State; B8/26/1952 Whitmire, SC **[I]**   **1974**†Pit 14   **1976**†Pit 14   **1977**†Pit 12 (12, SS)   **1978**†Pit★16 (16, SS)
1979†Pit★16 (16, SS)   **1980** Pit★16 (16, SS)   **1981** Pit★14 (14, SS)   **1982**†Pit★9 (9, SS)   **1983**†Pit 16 (16, SS)   **1984**†Pit 16 (16, SS)   **1985** Pit 16 (16, SS)   **1986** Pit 15 (15, SS)
1987 Pit 13 (13, SS)

| 1975 | †Pit | 14(2) | — | — | — | — | 2 | 39 | 19.5(20) | 0 | — | — | — | — | — | — | — | — | — | — | i | — | 0 | 44 |
| NFL | 14 | 201(161) | — | — | — | — | 2 | 39 | 19.5(20) | 0 | — | — | — | — | — | — | — | — | — | — | piS | 4 | 24 | 276 |

SHELL, TODD   Todd Andrew, LB, 6´4˝/225 lbs; Brigham Young; 1984: SF, rnd 1; B6/24/1962 Mesa, AZ   **1984**†SF 16 (0)   **1985**†SF 15 (13, LOLB)   **1986** SF 1 (0)   **1987**†SF 6 (2)
NFL 38 (15) [4 yrs]

SHELLEY, DECK   Dexter, aka Robert P. Shelley, B, 5´11˝/191 lbs; Texas; B6/4/1906 San Antonio, TX, D12/17/1968 Temple, TX **[K]**   **1931** Pro 8 (5, TB), 4   **1931** Por 2 (1)

1932	GB	5	3	0.6	0	—	—	—	—	—	—	—	—	—	—	—	—	—	—	—	—	—	0	3
1932	ChiC	2(1)	5	11	2.2	0	—	—	—	—	1	1	100.0	3	3.0(3)	0	0	—	—	—	—	—	0	13
NFL	2	14(7)	10	14	1.4	0	—	—	—	—	1	1	100.0	3	3.0(3)	0	0	—	—	—	K	—	4	31

SHELLEY, ELBERT   Elbert Vernell, DB, 5´11˝/190 lbs; Arkansas State; 1987: Atl, rnd 11; B12/24/1964 Tyronza, AR   **1987** Atl 4 (0)   **1988** Atl 12 (0)   **1989** Atl 10 (0)   **1990** Atl 12 (0)
1991†Atl 11 (0)   **1992** Atl★13 (0)   **1993** Atl★16 (0)   **1994** Atl◇16 (0)   **1995**†Atl★13 (0)   **1996** Atl 12 (0)   **NFL** 119 (0) [10 yrs]

SHELLEY, JONATHAN   Jonathan, DB, 6´0˝/176 lbs; Mississippi; 1987: SF, rnd 9; B8/6/1964 Vicksburg, MS   **1987** SF 1 (1)

SHELLING, CHRIS   Christopher A., DB, 5´10˝/180 lbs; Auburn; B11/3/1972 Columbus, GA   **1995** Cin 13 (0)   **1996** Cin 1 (0)   **1997** Atl 2 (0)   **NFL** 16 (0) [3 yrs]

SHELLO, KENDEL   Kendel Ray, DE, 6´3˝/301 lbs; Southern (LA); B11/24/1973 New Iberia, IA   **1996**†Ind 1 (0)   **1997** Ind 6 (0)   **1998** Ind 6 (1)   **NFL** 13 (1) [3 yrs]

SHELLOGG, ALEC   Alec Regis, T, 6´0˝/215 lbs; Notre Dame; B2/7/1914 New Castle, PA, D7/12/1968 Los Angeles County, CA   **1939** ChiB 1 (1)   **1939** Bkn 2 (0)   **NFL** 3 (1) [1 yr]

SHELTON, ANTHONY   Anthony Levala, DB, 6´1˝/195 lbs; Tennessee State; 1990: SF, rnd 11; B9/4/1967 Fayetteville, TN   **1990** SD 14 (0)   **1991** SD 11 (4)   **NFL** 25 (4) [2 yrs]

SHELTON, DAIMON   Daimon, FB, 6´0˝/262 lbs; Sacramento State; 1997: Jax, rnd 6; B9/15/1972 Duarte, CA

1997	Jax	13(0)	6	4	0.7(2)	0	—	—	—	—	—	—	—	—	—	—	—	—	—	—	—	—	0	4
1998	†Jax	14(8, FB)	30	95	3.2(16)	1	10	79	7.9(19)	0	—	—	—	—	—	—	—	—	—	—	—	—	6	145
1999	†Jax	16(9, FB)	1	2	2.0(2)	0	12	87	7.3(13)	0	—	—	—	—	—	—	—	—	—	—	k	—	0	31
2000	Jax	16(9, FB)	2	3	1.5(2)	0	4	48	12.0(16)	0	—	—	—	—	—	—	—	—	—	—	—	—	0	27
2001	ChiB	16(9, FB)	—	—	—	—	12	76	6.3(16)	1	—	—	—	—	—	—	—	—	—	—	—	—	6	43
2002	ChiB	12(8, FB)	—	—	—	—	7	34	4.9(8)	0	—	—	—	—	—	—	—	—	—	—	k	—	0	2
2004	Buf	16(12, FB)	—	—	—	—	17	114	6.7(24)	0	—	—	—	—	—	—	—	—	—	—	k	—	6	52
2005	Buf	16(11, FB)	1	0	0.0(0)	0	13	98	7.5(21)	1	—	—	—	—	—	—	—	—	—	—	k	—	6	50
NFL	8	119(66)	40	104	2.6(16)	1	75	536	7.1(24)	2	—	—	—	—	—	—	—	—	—	—	k	—	18	353

SHELTON, L.J.   Lonnie Jewel, T, 6´6˝/335 lbs; Eastern Michigan; 1999: Arz, rnd 1; B3/21/1976 Rochester Hills, MI   **1999** Arz 9 (7, lt)   **2000** Arz 14 (14, LT)   **2001** Arz 16 (16, LT)
2002 Arz 16 (16, LT)   **2003** Arz 15 (15, LT)   **2004** Arz 12 (9, RT)   **2005** Cle 16 (16, LT)   **NFL** 98 (93) [7 yrs]

SHELTON, MURRAY   Murray Norcross, E, 6´1˝/175 lbs; Cornell; B4/20/1893 Dunkirk, NY, D8/14/1985 Columbia, MO   **1920** Buf 11 (6, LE)

SHELTON, RICHARD   Richard Eddie, DB, 5´10˝/180 lbs; Liberty; 1989: Den, rnd 11; B1/2/1966 Marietta, GA   **1989** Den 3 (0)   **1990** Pit 2 (1)   **1991** Pit 14 (2)   **1992**†Pit 16 (3)
1993 Pit 9 (2)   **NFL** 44 (8) [5 yrs]

SHENEFELT, PAUL   Paul Jesse, T, 6´0˝/195 lbs; Manchester; B3/4/1911 Ames, IA, D10/30/1988 Palm Beach Gardens, FL   **1934** ChiC 2 (0)

SHEPARD, CHARLIE   Charles Lafayette, HB-DB, 6´2˝/215 lbs; North Texas; 1955: Bal, rnd 18; B7/11/1933 Dallas, TX

| 1956 | Pit | 12 | 30 | 91 | 3.0(14) | 0 | 1 | 31 | 31.0(31) | 0 | — | — | — | — | — | — | — | — | — | — | P | — | 0 | 107 |

SHEPARD, DERRICK   Derrick Lathell, WR, 5´10˝/186 lbs; Oklahoma; B1/22/1964 Odessa, TX, D8/4/1994 Laramie, WY **[R]**   **1987** Was 2 (1)   **1988** Was 5 (0)   **1990** Dal 8 (0)
1991 Dal 6 (0)

1989	NO	4(0)	—	—	—	—	2	36	18.0(23)	0	—	—	—	—	—	—	—	—	—	—	kp	1	6	99
1989	Dal	11(8, WR)	3	12	4.0(12)	0	18	268	14.9(37)	1	—	—	—	—	—	—	—	—	—	—	kp	—	6	300
NFL	5	36(9)	3	12	4.0(12)	0	20	304	15.2(37)	1	—	—	—	—	—	—	—	—	—	—	kp	1	12	725

SHEPHERD, BILL   William Leroy, B, 5´9˝/198 lbs; Western Maryland; B12/4/1911 Clearfield, PA, D3/8/1967 Detroit, MI **[K]**

1935	Bos	7(6, BB)	89	285	3.2	1	2	20	10.0(46)	0	55	21	38.2	318	5.8	1	14	—	—	—	K	—	7	-91
1935	†Det☆	5(3)	54	140	2.6	3	2	13	6.5	0	9	7	77.8	99	11.0	0	1	—	—	—	—	—	18	231
1936	Det	12(6, fb)	74	292	3.9	1	—	—	—	—	3	1	33.3	57	6.3	0	1	—	—	—	K	—	13	291
1937	Det☆	11(0)	93	325	3.5	2	—	—	—	—	46	19	41.3	297	6.5	2	7	—	—	—	K	—	31	234
1938	Det☆	9(3, fb)	100	455	4.6	3	—	—	—	—	32	8	25.0	167	5.2	0	6	—	—	—	K	—	23	329
1939	Det☆	11(10, FB)	105	420	4.0	2	14	143	10.2	1	1	0	0.0	0	0.0	0	0	—	—	—	P	—	18	517
1940	Det	3(2)	24	67	2.8	0	2	12	6.0	0	—	—	—	—	—	—	—	—	—	—	P	—	0	73
NFL	6	58(30)	539	1984	3.7	12	20	188	9.4(46)	1	152	58	38.2	938	6.2	4	28	—	—	—	KP	2	110	1582

SHEPHERD, EDELL   Edell Eugene, WR, 6´1˝/175 lbs; San Jose State; B5/18/1980 Los Angeles, CA

2003	TB	2(0)	—	—	—	—	4	38	9.5(14)	0	—	—	—	—	—	—	—	—	—	—	—	—	0	19
2005	†TB	16(0)	—	—	—	—	6	103	17.2(46)	1	—	—	—	—	—	—	—	—	—	—	k	—	6	171
NFL	2	18(0)	—	—	—	—	10	141	14.1(46)	1	—	—	—	—	—	—	—	—	—	—	k	—	6	190

SHEPHERD, GANNON   Gannon, T, 6´8˝/317 lbs; Duke; B1/3/1977 Flint, MI   **2001** Jax 1 (0)

SHEPHERD, JACOBY   Jacoby Lamar, DB, 6´2˝/204 lbs; Oklahoma State; 2000: SL, rnd 2; B8/31/1979 Lufkin, TX   **2000**†SL 15 (1)   **2001** SL 7 (0)   **2003** Det 4 (0)   **2003** NYJ 4 (0)
NFL 30 (1) [3 yrs]

SHEPHERD, JOHNNY   Johnny Ray, RB, 5´10˝/185 lbs; West Alabama; B4/24/1957 La Grange, NC

| 1987 | Buf | 2(1) | 12 | 42 | 3.5(19) | 0 | 1 | 2 | 2.0(2) | 0 | — | — | — | — | — | — | — | — | — | — | — | — | 0 | 43 |

SHEPHERD, LESLIE   Leslie Glenard, WR, 5´11˝/186 lbs; Temple; B11/3/1969 Washington, DC

1994	Was	3(0)	—	—	—	—	1	8	8.0(8)	0	—	—	—	—	—	—	—	—	—	—	—	—	0	4
1995	Was	14(4)	7	63	9.0(26)	1	29	486	16.8(73)	2	—	—	—	—	—	—	—	—	—	—	k	—	18	366
1996	Was	12(6, wr)	6	96	16.0(32)	2	23	344	15.0(52)	3	—	—	—	—	—	—	—	—	—	—	—	—	30	303
1997	Was	11(9, wr)	4	27	6.8(17)	0	29	562	19.4(68)	5	—	—	—	—	—	—	—	—	—	—	—	—	30	333
1998	Was	16(16, WR)	6	91	15.2(29)	1	43	712	16.6(43)	8	—	—	—	—	—	—	—	—	—	—	—	—	56	497
1999	Cle	9(8, wr)	1	5	5.0(5)	0	23	274	11.9(36)	0	—	—	—	—	—	—	—	—	—	—	—	—	0	142
2000	†Mia	13(11, WR)	4	3	0.8(14)	0	35	446	12.7(46)	4	—	—	—	—	—	—	—	—	—	—	kp	—	24	334
NFL	7	78(54)	28	285	10.2(32)	4	183	2832	15.5(73)	22	—	—	—	—	—	—	—	—	—	—	kp	—	158	1979

SHEPPARD, ASHLEY   Ashley Guy, LB, 6´3˝/240 lbs; Clemson; 1993: Min, rnd 4; B1/21/1969 Greenville, NC   **1993** Min 10 (0)   **1994**†Min 7 (0)   **1995** Jax 2 (0)   **1995** SL 2 (0)
NFL 21 (0) [3 yrs]

SHEPPARD, HENRY   Henry Fossett, G-T, 6´6˝/255 lbs; SMU; 1976: Cle, rnd 5; B11/12/1952 Cuero, TX   **1976** Cle 14 (1)   **1977** Cle 13 (13, LG)   **1978** Cle 14 (14, LG)
1979 Cle 16 (16, RT)   **1980**†Cle 16 (16, LG)   **1981** Cle 9 (3)   **NFL** 82 (62) [6 yrs]

SHEPPARD, LITO   Lito Decorian, DB, 5´10˝/194 lbs; Florida; 2002: Phi, rnd 1; B4/8/1981 Jacksonville, FL   **2002** Phi 12 (0)   **2003**†Phi 16 (9, RCB)   **2004**†Phi★15 (15, LCB)
2005 Phi 10 (10, LCB)   **NFL** 53 (34) [4 yrs]

YEAR	TEAM	G (GS, POS)	RUSH	YD	AVG (LG)	TD	REC	YD	AVG (LG)	TD	PASS	COMP	PCT	YD	AVG (LG)	TD	INT	SK	YD	QBR	KPR	OTD	PTS	TAY
SHERER, DAVE	David McDonald, E, 6´3˝/210 lbs; SMU; 1959: Bal, rnd 2; B2/14/1937 Galion, OH **1960** Dal 11																							
1959	†Bal	12	—	—	—	—	1	9	9.0(9)	0	—	—	—	—	—	—	—	—	—	—	P	—	0	5
NFL	2	23	—	—	—	—	1	9	9.0(9)	0	—	—	—	—	—	—	—	—	—	—	Pk	—	0	-11
SHERIFF, STAN	Bruce Stanley, LB-G-C, 6´1˝/224 lbs; Cal Poly-San Luis Obispo; 1954: LA, rnd 18; B4/24/1932 Honolulu, HI, D1/16/1993 Honolulu, HI **1954** Pit 12 (RLB)																							
1956 SF 7 (LLB) **1957** SF 2 **1957** Cle 3 **NFL** 24 [3 yrs]																							
SHERK, JERRY	Jerry Martin, DT-DE-NT, 6´4˝/258 lbs; Oklahoma State; 1970: Cle, rnd 2; B7/7/1948 Grants Pass, OR **1970** Cle 14 (RDT) **1971**†Cle 14 (RDT) **1972**†Cle 14 (RDT)																							
1973 Cle◇14 (RDT) **1974** Cle◇14 (RDT) **1975** Cle★14 (14, RDT) **1976** Cle★14 (RDT) **1977** Cle 7 (6, rdt) **1978** Cle 16 (16, RDT) **1979** Cle 10 (RDT) **1980** Cle 1 (1)																							
1981 Cle 15 (0) **NFL** 147 (37) [12 yrs]																							
SHERLAG, BOB	Robert Joseph, WR, 6´0˝/195 lbs; Memphis; 1966: Phi, rnd 6/Buf, rnd 5; B4/19/1943 Chicago, IL																							
1966	Atl	9	—	—	—	—	4	53	13.3(30)	1	—	—	—	—	—	—	—	—	—	—	kp	—	6	15
SHERMAN, ALLIE	Alexander, QB, 5´11˝/170 lbs; Brooklyn College; B2/10/1923 Brooklyn, NY [C]																							
1943	P-P	9(0)	17	-20	-1.2(5)	1	—	—	—	—	37	16	43.2	208	5.6(49)	2	1	—	—	—	—	—	6	64
1944	Phi	10(0)	22	-42	-1.9(17)	1	—	—	—	—	31	16	51.6	156	5.0(23)	1	2	—	—	—	Pi	—	6	-5
1945	Phi	10(1)	16	-7	-0.4(8)	1	—	—	—	—	29	15	51.7	172	5.9(26)	2	3	—	—	—	—	—	6	-21
1946	Phi	11(0)	21	8	0.4(12)	1	—	—	—	—	33	17	51.5	264	8.0(53)	4	3	—	—	—	—	—	0	40
1947	†Phi	11(0)	17	17	1.0(16)	1	—	—	—	—	5	2	40.0	23	4.6(13)	0	1	—	—	—	—	—	6	-2
NFL	5	51(1)	93	-44	-0.5(17)	4	—	—	—	—	135	66	48.9	823	6.1(53)	9	10	—	—	—	Pi	—	24	77
SHERMAN, BOB	Robert David, DB, 6´2˝/195 lbs; Iowa; 1964: Pit, rnd 12; B7/4/1942 Owosso, MI **1964** Pit 14 **1965** Pit 11 **NFL** 25 [2 yrs]																							
SHERMAN, HEATH	Heath, RB, 6´0˝/195 lbs; Texas A&M-Kingsville; 1989: Phi, rnd 6; B3/27/1967 Wharton, TX																							
1989	†Phi	15(1)	40	177	4.4(37)	2	8	85	10.6(17)	0	—	—	—	—	—	—	—	—	—	—	k	—	12	267
1990	†Phi	14(5, fb)	164	685	4.2(36)	1	23	167	7.3(26)	3	—	—	—	—	—	—	—	—	—	—	—	—	24	794
1991	Phi	16(5, RB)	106	279	2.6(12)	0	14	59	4.2(11)	0	—	—	—	—	—	—	—	—	—	—	k	—	0	310
1992	†Phi	16(7, FB)	112	583	5.2(34)	5	18	219	12.2(75)	1	—	—	—	—	—	—	—	—	—	—	—	—	36	748
1993	Phi	15(7, FB)	115	406	3.5(19)	2	12	78	6.5(21)	0	—	—	—	—	—	—	—	—	—	—	k	—	12	465
NFL	5	76(25)	537	2130	4.0(37)	10	75	608	8.1(75)	4	—	—	—	—	—	—	—	—	—	—	k	—	84	2582
SHERMAN, ROD	Rodney Jarvis, WR-FL, 6´0˝/190 lbs; USC; 1966: Oak, rnd R1/Bal, rnd 4; B12/25/1944 Pasadena, CA [K]																							
1967	†Oak-A	13(FL)	1	13	13.0(13)	1	5	61	12.2(22)	0	—	—	—	—	—	—	—	—	—	—	k	—	6	153
1968	Cin-A	13(FL)	1	3	3.0(3)	0	31	374	12.1(27)	1	—	—	—	—	—	—	—	—	—	—	K	—	10	195
1969	†Oak-A	14	—	—	—	—	—	—	—	—	—	—	—	—	—	—	—	—	—	—	kp	—	0	121
1970	†Oak	14(1)	1	2	2.0(2)	0	18	285	15.8(32)	2	—	—	—	—	—	—	—	—	—	—	kp	—	0	179
1971	Oak	12(5, WR)	—	—	—	—	12	187	15.6(32)	1	—	—	—	—	—	—	—	—	—	—	p	—	6	91
1972	Den	14(13, WR)	1	2	2.0(2)	0	38	661	17.4(35)	3	—	—	—	—	—	—	—	—	—	—	p	—	18	387
1973	†LARm	3	—	—	—	—	1	8	8.0(8)	0	—	—	—	—	—	—	—	—	—	—	—	—	0	4
NFL	7	83(19)	4	20	5.0(13)	1	105	1576	15.0(55)	5	—	—	—	—	—	—	—	—	—	—	Kkp	—	40	1128
SHERMAN, SOLLY	Saul S., QB, 6´1˝/190 lbs; Chicago; 1939: ChiB, rnd 18; B9/25/1917 Chicago, IL																							
1939	ChiB	7(1)	3	-5	-1.7	0	1	42	42.0(42)	0	4	2	50.0	43	10.8	0	0	—	—	—	i	1	6	48
1940	†ChiB◇	7(2)	8	10	1.3	—	—	—	—	—	4	1	25.0	15	3.8(15)	1	0	—	—	—	i	—	0	13
NFL	2	14(3)	11	5	0.5	0	1	42	42.0(42)	0	8	3	37.5	58	7.3(15)	1	0	—	—	—	i	1	6	60
SHERMAN, TOM	Thomas Joseph, QB, 6´0˝/190 lbs; Penn State; B12/5/1945 Bellevue, PA																							
1968	Bos-A	14(5, qb)	25	80	3.2(17)	0	—	—	—	—	226	90	39.8	1199	5.3(87)	12	16	19	190	45.6	—	—	0	100
1969	Bos-A	4	—	—	—	—	—	—	—	—	—	—	—	—	—	—	—	—	—	—	—	—	—	—
1969	Buf-A	1	2	14	7.0(10)	0	—	—	—	—	2	2	100.0	20	10.0(19)	1	0	—	—	—	—	—	0	29
NFL	2	19(5)	27	94	3.5(17)	0	—	—	—	—	228	92	40.4	1219	5.3(87)	13	16	19	190	47.8	—	—	0	129
SHERMAN, WILL	Willard Arthur, DB, 6´2˝/190 lbs; St. Mary's (CA); 1951: NYY, rnd 26; B10/20/1927 Weed, CA, D10/11/1997, [I] **1952** DalT 2 **1954** LARm 12 (DB)																							
1955†LARm✩12 (DB) **1956** LARm☆12 (DB) **1957** LARm★10 (DB) **1958** LARm★11 (DB) **1959** LARm 10 **1960** LARm 10 (LS)																							
1961	Min	8	—	—	—	—	2	40	20.0(32)	0	—	—	—	—	—	—	—	—	—	—	—	—	0	20
NFL	9	87	—	—	—	—	2	40	20.0(32)	0	—	—	—	—	—	—	—	—	—	—	kpi	4	24	578
SHERRARD, MIKE	Michael Watson, WR, 6´1˝/185 lbs; UCLA; 1986: Dal, rnd 1; B6/21/1963 Oakland, CA																							
1986	Dal	16(4)	2	11	5.5(8)	0	41	744	18.1(68)	5	—	—	—	—	—	—	—	—	—	—	—	—	30	408
1989	†SF	0(0)	—	—	—	—	—	—	—	—	—	—	—	—	—	—	—	—	—	—	—	—	0	0
1990	†SF	7(2)	—	—	—	—	17	264	15.5(43)	2	—	—	—	—	—	—	—	—	—	—	—	—	12	142
1991	SF	16(0)	—	—	—	—	24	296	12.3(31)	2	—	—	—	—	—	—	—	—	—	—	—	—	12	158
1992	†SF	16(8, wr)	—	—	—	—	38	607	16.0(56)	0	—	—	—	—	—	—	—	—	—	—	—	1	6	304
1993	NYG	6(5, wr)	—	—	—	—	24	433	18.0(55)	2	—	—	—	—	—	—	—	—	—	—	—	—	12	227
1994	NYG	16(14, WR)	1	-10	-10.0(-10)	0	53	825	15.6(55)	6	—	—	—	—	—	—	—	—	—	—	—	—	36	433
1995	NYG	13(13, WR)	—	—	—	—	44	577	13.1(50)	4	—	—	—	—	—	—	—	—	—	—	—	—	24	309
1996	†Den	15(0)	—	—	—	—	16	185	11.6(25)	1	—	—	—	—	—	—	—	—	—	—	—	—	6	98
NFL	9	105(46)	3	1	0.3(8)	0	257	3931	15.3(68)	22	—	—	—	—	—	—	—	—	—	—	—	1	138	2077
SHERROD, BUD	Horace Monroe, E-DE, 6´0˝/190 lbs; Tennessee; 1951: NYG, rnd 17; B12/2/1927 Knoxville, TN, D8/31/1980 Dallas, TX **1952** NYG 11																							
SHERRY, GERRY	Gerald, FB, none **1926** Lou 1 (1)																							
SHERWIN, TIM	Timothy Thomas, TE, 6´6˝/243 lbs; Boston College; 1981: Bal, rnd 4; B5/4/1958 Troy, NY																							
1981	Bal	16(2)	—	—	—	—	2	19	9.5(11)	0	—	—	—	—	—	—	—	—	—	—	—	—	0	10
1982	Bal	9(8, TE)	—	—	—	—	21	280	13.3(33)	0	—	—	—	—	—	—	—	—	—	—	—	1	6	140
1983	Bal	15(14, TE)	—	—	—	—	25	358	14.3(30)	0	—	—	—	—	—	—	—	—	—	—	—	—	0	179
1984	Ind	16(8, te)	—	—	—	—	11	169	15.4(31)	0	—	—	—	—	—	—	—	—	—	—	k	—	0	72
1985	Ind	8(0)	—	—	—	—	5	64	12.8(29)	0	—	—	—	—	—	—	—	—	—	—	—	—	0	32
1986	Ind	7(2)	—	—	—	—	3	26	8.7(15)	1	—	—	—	—	—	—	—	—	—	—	—	—	6	18
1987	Ind	8(5, te)	—	—	—	—	9	86	9.6(32)	1	—	—	—	—	—	—	—	—	—	—	—	—	6	48
1988	NYG	3(0)	—	—	—	—	—	—	—	—	—	—	—	—	—	—	—	—	—	—	—	—	—	—
NFL	8	82(39)	—	—	—	—	76	1002	13.2(33)	2	—	—	—	—	—	—	—	—	—	—	k	1	18	498
SHETLEY, RHOTEN	Rhoten Nathan, B, 5´11˝/208 lbs; Furman; 1940: Bkn, rnd 3; B2/7/1918 Wolf Creek, TN, D1/7/1993 Greenville, SC																							
1940	Bkn	11(8, BB)	7	30	4.3	0	8	126	15.8(22)	1	4	1	25.0	2	0.5(2)	0	1	—	—	—	i	—	6	91
1941	Bkn	11(10, BB)	1	7	7.0(7)	0	4	41	10.3(9)	0	0	0	0.0	0	0.0	0	0	—	—	—	ki	1	6	65
1942	Bkn	3(3)	—	—	—	—	3	19	6.3(10)	1	—	—	—	—	—	—	—	—	—	—	i	—	6	17
NFL	3	25(21)	8	37	4.6(7)	0	15	186	12.4(22)	2	5	1	20.0	2	0.4(2)	0	1	—	—	—	ki	1	18	172
1946	Bkn-A	13(5, fb)	9	21	2.3	0	1	10	10.0(10)	0	—	—	—	—	—	—	—	—	—	—	—	—	0	26
SHIANCOE, VISANTHE	Visanthe, TE, 6´4˝/250 lbs; Morgan State; 2003: NYG, rnd 3; B6/18/1980 Laurel, MD																							
2003	NYG	16(7, te)	—	—	—	—	10	56	5.6(10)	2	—	—	—	—	—	—	—	—	—	—	—	—	12	38
2004	NYG	16(7, te)	—	—	—	—	5	25	5.0(9)	1	—	—	—	—	—	—	—	—	—	—	k	—	6	11
2005	†NYG	16(4)	—	—	—	—	8	91	11.4(17)	0	—	—	—	—	—	—	—	—	—	—	k	—	0	36
NFL	3	48(18)	—	—	—	—	23	172	7.5(17)	3	—	—	—	—	—	—	—	—	—	—	k	—	18	84
SHIBEST, JAMES	James John, WR, 5´10˝/187 lbs; Arkansas; B10/31/1964 Fort Riley, KS **1987** Atl 1 (1)																							
SHIELD, JOE	Joseph Michael, QB, 6´1˝/185 lbs; Trinity (CT); 1985: GB, rnd 11; B6/26/1962 Brattleboro, VT **1986** GB 3 (0)																							
SHIELDS, BILLY	William Dean, T, 6´8˝/272 lbs; Georgia Tech; 1975: SD, rnd 6; B8/23/1953 Vicksburg, MS **1975** SD 11 **1976** SD 14 (14, LT) **1977** SD 13 (13, LT)																							
1978 SD 16 (16, LT) **1979**†SD 16 (16, LT) **1980**†SD 16 (16, LT) **1981**†SD 16 (16, LT) **1982**†SD 9 (9, LT) **1983** SD 16 (16, LT) **1984**†SF 10 (1) **1985** NYJ 3 (2) **1985** KC 2 (0)																							
NFL 142 (119) [11 yrs]																							

YEAR	TEAM	G (GS, POS)	RUSH	YD	AVG (LG)	TD	REC	YD	AVG (LG)	TD	PASS	COMP	PCT	YD	AVG (LG)	TD	INT	SK	YD	QBR	KPR	OTD	PTS	TAY

SHIELDS, BURRELL Burrell Alfredstein, HB, 6´2˝/203 lbs; John Carroll; 1952: Cle, rnd 6; B9/6/1929 Cleveland, OH, D6/23/1997

1954	Pit	6	7	28	4.0(13)	0	1	22	22.0(22)	0	—	—	—	—	—	—	—	—	—	—	kpi	—	0	75
1955	Bal	8	10	34	3.4(14)	0	3	27	9.0(19)	0	—	—	—	—	—	—	—	—	—	—	—	—	0	48
NFL	2	14	17	62	3.6(14)	0	4	49	12.3(22)	0	—	—	—	—	—	—	—	—	—	—	kpi	—	0	123

SHIELDS, JON Jon Rayborn, G, 6´5˝/293 lbs; Portland State; B4/30/1964 **1987** Dal 1 (0)

SHIELDS, LEBRON Lebron, DE-T, 6´4˝/250 lbs; Tennessee; 1960: Den, rnd 1; B7/23/1937 Walker County, GA **1960** Bal 12 **1961** Min 6 **NFL** 18 [2 yrs]

SHIELDS, PAUL Paul L., RB, 6´1˝/238 lbs; Arizona; B1/31/1976 Mesa, AZ **2000** Ind 8 (0)

| 1999 | †Ind | 13(3) | — | — | — | — | 4 | 37 | 9.3(21) | 0 | — | — | — | — | — | — | — | — | — | — | k | — | 0 | 7 |
| NFL | 2 | 21(3) | — | — | — | — | 4 | 37 | 9.3(21) | 0 | — | — | — | — | — | — | — | — | — | — | — | — | 0 | 19 |

SHIELDS, SCOTT Scott Paul, DB, 6´4˝/228 lbs; Weber State; 1999: Pit, rnd 2; B3/29/1976 San Diego, CA **1999** Pit 16 (1) **2000** Pit 10 (1) **NFL** 26 (2) [2 yrs]

SHIELDS, WILL Will Herthie, G, 6´3˝/315 lbs; Nebraska; 1993: KC, rnd 3; B9/15/1971 Fort Riley, KS **1993**†KC 16 (15, RG) **1994**†KC 16 (16, RG) **1995**†KC◇16 (16, RG) **1996** KC★16 (16, RG) **1997**†KC★16 (16, RG) **1999** KC★16 (16, RG) **2000** KC◇16 (16, RG) **2001** KC★16 (16, RG) **2002** KC★16 (16, RG) **2003**†KC★16 (16, RG) **2004** KC★16 (16, RG) **2005** KC★16 (16, RG)

| 1998 | KC◇ | 16(16, RG) | — | — | — | — | 1 | 4 | 4.0(4) | 0 | — | — | — | — | — | — | — | — | — | — | — | — | 0 | 2 |
| NFL | 13 | 208(207) | — | — | — | — | 1 | 4 | 4.0(4) | 0 | — | — | — | — | — | — | — | — | — | — | — | — | 0 | 2 |

SHINER, DICK Richard Earl, QB, 6´0˝/201 lbs; Maryland; 1964: Was, rnd 7/NYJ, rnd 20; B7/18/1942 Lebanon, PA

1964	Was	1	2	8	4.0(5)	0	—	—	—	—	1	0	0.0	0	0.0	0	0	—	—	—	—	—	0	8
1965	Was	14	12	35	2.9(29)	0	—	—	—	—	65	28	43.1	470	7.2(80)	3	4	—	—	—	—	—	0	125
1966	Was	14	1	10	10.0(10)	0	—	—	—	—	5	0	0.0	0	0.0	0	1	—	—	—	—	—	0	-30
1967	Cle	13	2	-7	-3.5(-3)	0	—	—	—	—	9	3	33.3	34	3.8(21)	0	1	2	24	—	—	—	0	-30
1968	Pit	13(QB)	14	53	3.8(12)	0	—	—	—	—	304	148	48.7	1856	6.1(61)	18	17	—	—	64.5	—	—	0	391
1969	Pit	12(QB)	14	55	3.9(18)	1	—	—	—	—	209	97	46.4	1422	6.8(63)	7	10	24	157	60.3	—	—	6	411
1970	NYG	14	—	—	—	—	—	—	—	—	12	9	75.0	87	7.3(26)	0	0	1	9	—	—	—	0	44
1971	Atl	10	10	9	0.9(4)	1	—	—	—	—	57	30	52.6	463	8.1(47)	5	5	10	89	—	—	—	6	76
1973	Atl	4	3	-2	-0.7(3)	0	—	—	—	—	64	34	53.1	401	6.3(34)	3	4	11	86	—	—	—	0	54
1973	NE	3	—	—	—	—	—	—	—	—	4	2	50.0	31	7.8(23)	0	1	—	—	—	—	—	0	16
1974	NE	1	—	—	—	—	—	—	—	—	6	3	50.0	37	6.2(18)	0	1	—	—	—	—	—	0	-22
NFL	10	99	58	161	2.8(29)	2	—	—	—	—	736	354	48.1	4801	6.5(80)	36	43	48	365	61.3	—	—	12	1042

SHINNERS, JOHN Joseph John T., G, 6´3˝/255 lbs; Xavier (OH); 1969: NO, rnd 1; B3/1/1947 Hartford, WI **1969** NO 2 **1970** NO 9 (rg) **1971** NO 14 **1972** Bal 6 **1973**†Cin 14 **1974** Cin 13 (RG) **1975**†Cin 14 **1976** Cin 13 (LG) **1977** Cin 12 (lg) **NFL** 97 [9 yrs]

SHINNICK, DON Donald Dee, LB, 6´0˝/232 lbs; UCLA; 1957: Bal, rnd 2; B5/15/1935 Kansas City, MO, D1/20/2004 Modesto, CA [I] **1957** Bal 12 (LLB) **1958**†Bal 12 (RLB) **1959**†Bal☆12 (RLB) **1960** Bal 12 (RLB) **1961** Bal 14 (RLB) **1962** Bal 14 (RLB) **1963** Bal 14 (RLB) **1964**†Bal 14 (RLB) **1965**†Bal 10 (RLB) **1966** Bal 14 (RLB) **1967** Bal 14 (RLB) **1968**†Bal 11 (RLB) **1969** Bal 6 **NFL** 159 [13 yrs]

SHIPKEY, JERRY Gerald Wade, LB-FB-DB, 6´1˝/213 lbs; USC; UCLA; 1947: Pit, rnd 8/LAD-A, rnd 2; B10/31/1925 Fullerton, CA

1948	Pit	12(4, FB)	64	199	3.1(16)	8	10	106	10.6(43)	0	—	—	—	—	—	—	—	—	—	—	k	—	48	336
1949	Pit	12(4)	26	93	3.6(14)	5	2	32	16.0(21)	0	—	—	—	—	—	—	—	—	—	—	i	—	30	220
1950	Pit◇	12(mlb)	18	17	0.9(11)	3	—	—	—	—	—	—	—	—	—	—	—	—	—	—	i	—	18	71
1951	Pit★	10(DB)	—	—	—	—	—	—	—	—	—	—	—	—	—	—	—	—	—	—	i	1	6	93
1952	Pit★	12(MLB)	1	1	1.0(1)	0	—	—	—	—	—	—	—	—	—	—	—	—	—	—	i	—	0	6
1953	ChiB	8	—	—	—	—	—	—	—	—	—	—	—	—	—	—	—	—	—	—	—	—	—	—
NFL	6	66(8)	109	310	2.8(16)	16	12	138	11.5(43)	0	—	—	—	—	—	—	—	—	—	—	ki	1	102	726

SHIPP, BILLY William Leonard, T, 6´5˝/275 lbs; Alabama; B10/16/1929 Mobile, AL **1954** NYG 11

SHIPP, JACKIE Jackie Renardo, LB, 6´2˝/235 lbs; Oklahoma; 1984: Mia, rnd 1; B3/17/1962 Muskogee, OK **1984**†Mia 16 (0) **1985**†Mia 16 (11, LILB) **1986** Mia 16 (14, LILB) **1987** Mia 12 (12, LILB) **1988** Mia 11 (4) **1989** LARd 3 (3) **NFL** 74 (44) [6 yrs]

SHIPP, JOE Joseph Delano, TE, 6´4˝/225 lbs; USC; B7/25/1955 Long Beach, CA

| 1979 | Buf | 16(2) | — | — | — | — | 3 | 43 | 14.3(27) | 1 | — | — | — | — | — | — | — | — | — | — | — | — | 6 | 27 |

SHIPP, MARCEL Marcel, RB, 5´11˝/230 lbs; Massachusetts; B8/8/1978 Paterson, NJ

2001	Arz	11(0)	—	—	—	—	—	—	—	—	—	—	—	—	—	—	—	—	—	—	k	—	0	28
2002	Arz	15(6, rb)	188	834	4.4(56)	6	38	413	10.9(80)	3	—	—	—	—	—	—	—	—	—	—	k	—	54	1146
2003	Arz	16(11, RB)	228	830	3.6(36)	0	30	184	6.1(34)	0	—	—	—	—	—	—	—	—	—	—	—	—	0	922
2005	Arz	15(11, RB)	157	451	2.9(19)	0	35	255	7.3(28)	0	—	—	—	—	—	—	—	—	—	—	—	—	0	579
NFL	4	57(28)	573	2115	3.7(56)	6	103	852	8.3(80)	3	—	—	—	—	—	—	—	—	—	—	k	—	54	2674

SHIRES, ABE Marshall Abraham, T, 6´2˝/220 lbs; Tennessee; 1941: Cle, rnd 2; B2/12/1917 Alderson, WV, D7/23/1993 Sacramento, CA **1945** Phi 7 (0)

SHIREY, FRED Charles Frederick, T, 6´2˝/223 lbs; Washington & Jefferson; Nebraska; 1938: Phi, rnd 5; B1/12/1916 Latrobe, PA, D11/1/1961 **1940** GB 3 (0) **1940** Cle 6 (0) **1941** Cle 3 (0) **NFL** 12 (0) [2 yrs]

SHIRK, GARY Gary Lee, TE, 6´1˝/220 lbs; Morehead State; B2/23/1950 Marysville, OH

1976	NYG	14	—	—	—	—	4	52	13.0(31)	1	—	—	—	—	—	—	—	—	—	—	k	—	6	50
1977	NYG	14(TE)	—	—	—	—	16	280	17.5(64)	2	—	—	—	—	—	—	—	—	—	—	k	—	12	143
1978	NYG	16(5, te)	—	—	—	—	10	127	12.7(45)	2	—	—	—	—	—	—	—	—	—	—	k	—	12	62
1979	NYG	16(TE)	—	—	—	—	31	471	15.2(61)	2	—	—	—	—	—	—	—	—	—	—	—	—	12	246
1980	NYG	16(14, TE)	—	—	—	—	21	211	10.0(21)	1	—	—	—	—	—	—	—	—	—	—	—	—	6	111
1981	†NYG	16(14, TE)	—	—	—	—	42	445	10.6(46)	3	—	—	—	—	—	—	—	—	—	—	—	—	18	238
1982	NYG	9(1)	—	—	—	—	6	54	9.0(19)	0	—	—	—	—	—	—	—	—	—	—	—	—	0	27
NFL	7	101(34)	—	—	—	—	130	1640	12.6(64)	11	—	—	—	—	—	—	—	—	—	—	k	—	66	875

SHIRK, JOHN John F., E-DE, 6´4˝/200 lbs; Oklahoma; 1940: ChiC, rnd 4; B6/24/1917 Oklahoma City, OK, D11/8/1993 Glendora, CA

| 1940 | ChiC◇ | 11(7, LE) | — | — | — | — | 11 | 91 | 8.3 | 0 | — | — | — | — | — | — | — | — | — | — | i | — | 0 | 49 |

SHIRKEY, GEORGE George Rogers, DT, 6´4˝/260 lbs; Stephen F. Austin State; 1958: SF, rnd 16; B8/20/1936 Fort Stockton, TX **1960**†Hou-A 14 (rdt) **1961**†Hou-A 7 **1962** Oak-A 14 (ldt) **NFL** 35 [3 yrs]

SHIRLEY, MARION Marion Vaughn, T, 6´4˝/260 lbs; Oklahoma State; Oklahoma City; 1948: NYY-A, rnd 18/1947: Bos, rnd 17; B4/17/1922 Denver, CO, D9/13/1996 Stafford, TX **1948** NYY-A 13 (1) **1949**†NYY-A 7 (0) **AAFC** 20 (1) [2 yrs]

SHIVER, CLAY Spencer Clay, C, 6´2˝/283 lbs; Florida State; 1996: Dal, rnd 3; B12/7/1972 Tifton, GA **1996** Dal 14 (0) **1997** Dal 16 (16, C) **1998** Dal 14 (9, C) **NFL** 44 (25) [3 yrs]

SHIVER, REX Raymond Orville, DB, 6´0˝/190 lbs; Miami (FL); B1/1/1932 Miami, FL **1956** LARm 8

SHIVER, SANDERS Sanders Thomas, LB, 6´2˝/227 lbs; Carson-Newman; 1976: Bal, rnd 5; B2/14/1954 Gadsden, SC **1976**†Bal 14 **1977**†Bal 14 **1978** Bal 16 (4) **1979** Bal 16 (16, LLB) **1980** Bal 14 (13, LLB) **1981** Bal 14 (11, LLB) **1982** Bal 8 (6, OLB) **1983** Bal 16 (0) **1984**†Mia 6 (0) **1985** Mia 14 (2) **NFL** 132 (52) [10 yrs]

SHIVERS, JASON Jason, DB, 6´1˝/193 lbs; Arizona State; 2004: SL, rnd 5; B11/4/1982 Phoenix, AZ **2004** ChiB 1 (0)

SHIVERS, ROY Roy Lee, RB, 5´11˝/200 lbs; Utah State; 1965: SL, rnd 19/SD, rnd R8; B7/5/1941 Halley, AR

1966	SL	13	1	5	5.0(5)	0	5	81	16.2(40)	0	—	—	—	—	—	—	—	—	—	—	kp	1	6	382
1967	SL	9	20	64	3.2(12)	1	3	15	5.0(14)	0	—	—	—	—	—	—	—	—	—	—	kp	—	6	98
1968	SL	14	44	184	4.2(42)	4	9	103	11.4(40)	3	—	—	—	—	—	—	—	—	—	—	k	—	42	309
1969	SL	12	27	115	4.3(17)	2	7	61	8.7(26)	1	—	—	—	—	—	—	—	—	—	—	kp	—	18	225
1970	SL	12	24	98	4.1(29)	2	3	44	14.7(22)	0	—	—	—	—	—	—	—	—	—	—	k	—	12	145
1971	SL	11	55	202	3.7(10)	1	10	76	7.6(19)	0	—	—	—	—	—	—	—	—	—	—	—	—	6	250
1972	SL	2	5	12	2.4(9)	0	1	20	20.0(20)	0	—	—	—	—	—	—	—	—	—	—	—	—	0	22
NFL	7	73	176	680	3.9(42)	10	38	400	10.5(40)	4	1	0	0.0	0	0.0	0	0	—	—	—	kp	1	90	1429

SHIVERS, WES Wesley Davis, T, 6´5˝/298 lbs; Mississippi State; 2000: Ten, rnd 7; B3/8/1977 Jackson, MS **2000** Atl 3 (0)

YEAR	TEAM	G(GS, POS)	RUSH	YD	AVG(LG)	TD	REC	YD	AVG(LG)	TD	PASS COMP	PCT	YD	AVG(LG)	TD	INT	SK	YD	QBR	KPR	OTD	PTS	TAY

SHLAPAK, BORIS   Boris Vladimir, K, 6´0˝/175 lbs; Drake; Michigan State; B5/18/1950 Chicago, IL **[K]**   **1972** Bal 8

SHOALS, ROGER   Roger Richard, T, 6´4˝/260 lbs; Maryland; 1961: Cle, rnd 16/1962: DalT, rnd 34; B12/13/1938 Baltimore, MD   **1963** Cle 2   **1964**†Cle 14   **1965** Det 14 (RT)
1966 Det 14   **1967** Det 4 (4)   **1968** Det 14 (LT)   **1969** Det 14 (LT)   **1970**†Det 14 (LT)   **1971** Den 14 (14, LT)   **NFL** 104 (18) [9 yrs]

SHOATE, JEFF   Jeff, DB, 5´11˝/175 lbs; Montana; San Diego State; 2004: Den, rnd 5; B3/23/1981 San Diego, CA   **2004**†Den 7 (0)

SHOATE, ROD   Roderick, LB, 6´1˝/214 lbs; Oklahoma; 1975: NE, rnd 2; B4/26/1953 Spiro, OK, D10/4/1999 Spiro, OK   **1975** NE 4   **1977** NE 14 (3)   **1978**†NE 15 (15, ROLB)
1979 NE 14 (14, ROLB)   **1980** NE 16 (16, ROLB)   **1981** NE 16 (16, ROLB)   **NFL** 79 (64) [6 yrs]

SHOCKEY, JEREMY   Jeremy Charles, TE, 6´5˝/253 lbs; Miami (FL); 2002: NYG, rnd 1; B8/18/1980 Ada, OK

2002	†NYG★	15(14, TE)	—	—	—	—	74	894	12.1(30)	2	—	—	—	—	—	—	—	—	—	—	—	12	457
2003	NYG◇	9(9, TE)	—	—	—	—	48	535	11.1(46)	2	—	—	—	—	—	—	—	—	—	—	—	12	278
2004	NYG	15(15, TE)	—	—	—	—	61	666	10.9(38)	6	—	—	—	—	—	—	—	—	—	—	—	36	363
2005	†NYG◇	15(15, TE)	—	—	—	—	65	891	13.7(59)	7	—	—	—	—	—	—	—	—	—	—	—	44	481
NFL	4	54(53)	—	—	—	—	248	2986	12.0(59)	17	—	—	—	—	—	—	—	—	—	—	—	104	1578

SHOCKLEY, ARNIE   Arnold, aka J. Parnel Jackson, T, 6´2˝/220 lbs; Southwestern Oklahoma State; B11/27/1904, TX, D8/1974 Melbourne, FL   **1929** Bos 6 (2)

SHOCKLEY, BILL   William Albert, HB-K, 6´0˝/185 lbs; West Chester; B3/13/1937 West Chester, PA, D12/7/1992 New York, NY **[K]**   **1961** Buf-A 2   **1962** NYT-A 14   **1968** Pit 1

1960	NYT-A	14	37	156	4.2(24)	0	8	69	8.6(42)	2	—	—	—	—	—	—	—	—	—	Kkp	—	86	354
1961	NYT-A	6	5	9	1.8(9)	0	3	27	9.0(13)	0	—	—	—	—	—	—	—	—	—	Kkp	—	22	92
NFL	4	37	42	165	3.9(24)	0	11	96	8.7(42)	2	—	—	—	—	—	—	—	—	—	Kkp	—	181	481

SHOEMAKE, HUB   Charles Hubbard, G, 6´0˝/186 lbs; Lake Forest; Illinois; Bethany (WV); B9/29/1899 Oskaloosa, IA, D3/10/1984 Washington, DC   **1920** Dec 6 (4)

SHOENER, HAL   Harold Phillip, E-DE, 6´3˝/200 lbs; Iowa; 1947: NYG, rnd 23; B1/2/1923 Reedsville, WV, D12/13/1983 Oakland, CA

1948	SF-A	14(1)	—	—	—	—	15	76	5.1	3	—	—	—	—	—	—	—	—	—	—	—	18	53
1949	†SF-A	12(10, LE)	—	—	—	—	7	84	12.0	0	—	—	—	—	—	—	—	—	—	kp	—	0	47
AAFC	2	26(11)	—	—	—	—	22	160	7.3	3	—	—	—	—	—	—	—	—	—	kp	—	18	100
1950	SF	12(LDE)	1	1	1.0(1)	0	—	—	—	—	—	—	—	—	—	—	—	—	—	ki	—	0	3

SHOENER, HERB   Herbert George, E-DE, 6´3˝/205 lbs; Lehigh; Iowa; 1947: Was, rnd 31; B1/2/1923 Reedsville, WV, D12/24/1985 Anaheim, CA   **1948** Was 7 (2)
1949 Was 11 (5, RE)   **NFL** 18 (7) [2 yrs]

SHOFNER, DEL   Delbert Martin, E-DB, 6´3˝/186 lbs; Baylor; 1957: LA, rnd 1; B12/11/1934 Center, TX

1957	LARm	12(DB)	—	—	—	—	—	—	—	—	—	—	—	—	—	—	—	—	—	Pi	—	0	17
1958	LARm★	12(FL)	—	—	—	—	51	1097	21.5(92)	8	1	0	0.0	0	0	0	0	0	—	P	—	48	589
1959	LARm★	12(LE)	1	6	6.0(6)	0	47	936	19.9(72)	7	—	—	—	—	—	—	—	—	—	P	—	42	509
1960	LARm	11	1	-15	-15.0(-15)	0	12	122	10.2(17)	1	—	—	—	—	—	—	—	—	—	Pi	—	6	65
1961	†NYG★	14(SE)	1	6	6.0(6)	0	68	1125	16.5(46)	11	—	—	—	—	—	—	—	—	—	—	—	66	624
1962	†NYG★	13(SE)	1	4	4.0(4)	0	53	1133	21.4(69)	12	—	—	—	—	—	—	—	—	—	—	—	72	631
1963	†NYG★	14(SE)	—	—	—	—	64	1181	18.5(70)	9	—	—	—	—	—	—	—	—	—	—	—	54	636
1964	NYG	6(SE)	—	—	—	—	22	323	14.7(54)	0	—	—	—	—	—	—	—	—	—	—	—	0	162
1965	NYG	12(SE)	—	—	—	—	22	388	17.6(49)	2	—	—	—	—	—	—	—	—	—	—	—	12	204
1966	NYG	9	—	—	—	—	3	19	6.3(9)	0	—	—	—	—	—	—	—	—	—	—	—	0	10
1967	NYG	10(FL)	—	—	—	—	7	146	20.9(33)	1	—	—	—	—	—	—	—	—	—	—	—	6	78
NFL	11	125	4	1	0.3(6)	0	349	6470	18.5(92)	51	1	0	0.0	0	0	0	0	0	—	Pi	—	306	3522

SHOFNER, JIM   James Bernard, DB, 6´2˝/191 lbs; TCU; 1958: Cle, rnd 1; B12/18/1935 Grapevine, TX **[IC]**   **1958**†Cle 12   **1959** Cle 12 (DB)   **1960** Cle 12 (RCB)   **1961** Cle 14 (RCB)
1962 Cle 14 (RCB)   **1963** Cle 12 (RCB)   **NFL** 76 [6 yrs]

SHONK, JOHN   John J., E, 6´1˝/190 lbs; West Virginia; 1941: Phi, rnd 19; B4/30/1918 Charleston, WV, D4/26/1984 Christianburg, VA

| 1941 | Phi | 10(0) | — | — | — | — | 5 | 52 | 10.4(14) | 0 | — | — | — | — | — | — | — | — | — | ki | — | 0 | 23 |

SHONTA, CHUCK   Charles Joseph, DB, 6´0˝/200 lbs; Eastern Michigan; B8/29/1937 Detroit, MI   **1960** Bos-A 14   **1962** Bos-A 14 (LCB)   **1963**†Bos-A 13 (lcb)   **1964** Bos-A 14
1965 Bos-A 14 (LCB)   **1966** Bos-A◇14 (LS)   **1967** Bos-A 14 (14, RS)

| 1961 | Bos-A | 8(RCB) | — | — | — | — | 1 | 9 | 9.0(9) | 0 | — | — | — | — | — | — | — | — | — | i | — | 0 | 12 |
| NFL | 8 | 105(14) | — | — | — | — | 1 | 9 | 9.0(9) | 0 | — | — | — | — | — | — | — | — | — | i | 1 | 6 | 191 |

SHOOK, AL   Albert, G, none; B1/15/1898 Pierce City, MO, D4/14/1984 Atchison, KS   **1921** Col 2 (1)

SHOOK, FREDERICK   Fredric Warden, C-LB, 6´0˝/218 lbs; TCU; B3/30/1919 Fort Worth, TX, D4/16/1992   **1941** ChiC 4 (0)

SHORT, BRANDON   Brandon Darrell, LB, 6´3˝/253 lbs; Penn State; 2000: NYG, rnd 4; B7/11/1977 McKeesport, PA   **2000**†NYG 11 (0)   **2001** NYG 16 (16, LLB)
2002†NYG 16 (15, LLB)   **2003** NYG 16 (12, LLB)   **2004** Car 16 (2)   **2005**†Car 16 (15, LLB)   **NFL** 91 (60) [6 yrs]

SHORT, JASON   Jason, LB, 6´4˝/254 lbs; Eastern Michigan; B7/15/1978 Painesville, OH   **2004** Phi 11 (0)   **2005** Phi 6 (0)   **NFL** 17 (0) [2 yrs]

SHORT, LAVAL   Laval Howard, NT, 6´3˝/250 lbs; Colorado; 1980: Den, rnd 5; B9/29/1958 Nashville, TN   **1980** Den 15 (0)   **1981** TB 4 (0)   **NFL** 19 (0) [2 yrs]

SHORTER, JIM   James, DB, 5´11˝/184 lbs; Detroit Mercy; 1962: Cle, rnd 14; B6/8/1939 Montgomery, AL, D6/1/2000 Los Angeles, CA   **1962** Cle 9   **1963** Cle 11   **1964** Was 14
1965 Was 13   **1966** Was 13 (RCB)   **1967** Was 13 (RCB)   **1969** Pit 14 (RCB)   **NFL** 87 [7 yrs]

SHORTHOSE, GEORGE   George Edward, WR, 6´0˝/198 lbs; Missouri; 1985: Mia, rnd 6; B12/22/1961 Stanton, CA   **1985** KC 3 (0)

SHORTS, PETER   John Peter, DT, 6´8˝/278 lbs; Illinois State; B7/12/1966 Janesville, WI   **1989** NE 1 (0)

SHOULDERS, DARIN   Darin, T, 6´3˝/288 lbs; Tulane; B5/23/1968 Jackson, MS   **1991** Ind 1 (0)

SHOULTS, PAUL   Paul Arthur, HB, 5´11˝/178 lbs; Miami (OH); 1948: ChiC, rnd 25/1949: SF-A, rnd 25; B10/9/1925 Washington Court House, OH

| 1949 | NYB | 12(6, LH) | 46 | 124 | 2.7(17) | 0 | 10 | 124 | 12.4(23) | 0 | — | — | — | — | — | — | — | — | — | kp | — | 0 | 234 |

SHROPSHIRE, DARRELL   Darrell, DT, 6´2˝/301 lbs; South Carolina; 2005: Atl, rnd 7; B3/18/1983 Kershaw, NC   **2005** Atl 10 (0)

SHUFELT, PETE   Peter Julian, LB, 6´3˝/241 lbs; Texas-El Paso; B10/28/1969 Chicago, IL   **1994** NYG 5 (0)

SHUGART, CLYDE   Clyde Earl, G-T, 6´1˝/221 lbs; Iowa State; 1939: Was, rnd 17; B12/7/1916 Elberon, IA   **1939** Was 11 (0)   **1940**†Was 9 (0)   **1941** Was◇11 (9, RG)
1942†Was◇11 (3)   **1943**†Was☆10 (5, lg)   **1944** Was 4 (3)   **NFL** 56 (20) [6 yrs]

SHUGARTS, BRET   J. Bret, DE, 6´2˝/250 lbs; Lock Haven; Clarion; Indiana (PA); B2/17/1960 Du Bois, PA   **1987** Pit 2 (1)

SHULA, DAVID   David Donald, WR, 5´11˝/182 lbs; Dartmouth; B5/28/1959 Lexington, KY **[C]**   **1981** Bal 16 (0)

SHULA, DON   Donald Francis, DB, 5´11˝/190 lbs; John Carroll; 1951: Cle, rnd 9; B1/4/1930 Grand River, OH; HOF 1997 **[IC]**   **1951**†Cle 12 (db)   **1952**†Cle 5   **1955** Bal 9 (DB)
1956 Bal 12 (DB)   **1957** Was 11 (DB)

1953	Bal	12(DB)	—	—	—	—	1	6	6.0(6)	0	—	—	—	—	—	—	—	—	—	i	—	0	34
1954	Bal	12(DB)	2	3	1.5(3)	0	—	—	—	—	—	—	—	—	—	—	—	—	—	i	—	0	62
NFL	7	73	2	3	1.5(3)	0	1	6	6.0(6)	0	—	—	—	—	—	—	—	—	—	ki	—	0	144

SHULER, HEATH   Joseph Heath, QB, 6´2˝/216 lbs; Tennessee; 1994: Was, rnd 1; B12/31/1971 Bryson City, NC

1994	Was	11(8, QB)	26	103	4.0(26)	0	—	—	—	—	265	120	45.3	1658	6.3(81)	10	12	12	83	59.6	—	—	0	502
1995	Was	7(5, qb)	18	57	3.2(13)	0	—	—	—	—	125	66	52.8	745	6.0(44)	3	7	13	76	—	—	—	0	165
1996	Was	1(0)	1	0	0.0(0)	0	—	—	—	—	—	—	—	—	—	—	—	—	—	—	—	—	0	0
1997	NO	10(9, QB)	22	38	1.7(8)	1	—	—	—	—	203	106	52.2	1288	6.3(89)	2	14	21	132	—	—	—	6	142
NFL	4	29(22)	67	198	3.0(26)	1	—	—	—	—	593	292	49.2	3691	6.2(89)	15	33	46	291	54.3	—	—	6	809

SHULER, MICKEY   Mickey Charles, TE, 6´3˝/232 lbs; Penn State; 1978: NYJ, rnd 3; B8/21/1956 Harrisburg, PA

1978	NYJ	16(1)	—	—	—	—	11	67	6.1(15)	3	—	—	—	—	—	—	—	—	—	k	—	18	46
1979	NYJ	16(6, te)	—	—	—	—	16	225	14.1(46)	3	—	—	—	—	—	—	—	—	—	k	—	18	128
1980	NYJ	16(9, TE)	—	—	—	—	22	226	10.3(26)	2	—	—	—	—	—	—	—	—	—	k	—	12	118
1981	†NYJ	6(0)	—	—	—	—	—	—	—	—	—	—	—	—	—	—	—	—	—	—	—	—	—
1982	†NYJ	9(2)	—	—	—	—	8	132	16.5(51)	3	—	—	—	—	—	—	—	—	—	—	—	18	81

YEAR	TEAM	G(GS, POS)	RUSH	YD	AVG(LG)	TD	REC	YD	AVG(LG)	TD	PASS	COMP	PCT	YD	AVG(LG)	TD	INT	SK	YD	QBR	KPR	OTD	PTS	TAY
1983	NYJ	16(7, te)	—	—	—	—	26	272	10.5(28)	1	—	—	—	—	—	—	—	—	—	—	k	—	6	129
1984	NYJ	16(16, TE)	—	—	—	—	68	782	11.5(49)	6	—	—	—	—	—	—	—	—	—	—	k	—	36	406
1985	†NYJ☆	16(13, TE)	—	—	—	—	76	879	11.6(35)	7	—	—	—	—	—	—	—	—	—	—	—	—	42	475
1986	†NYJ★	16(16, TE)	—	—	—	—	69	675	9.8(36)	4	—	—	—	—	—	—	—	—	—	—	k	—	24	325
1987	NYJ	11(10, TE)	—	—	—	—	43	434	10.1(32)	3	—	—	—	—	—	—	—	—	—	—	—	—	18	232
1988	NYJ★	15(15, TE)	—	—	—	—	70	805	11.5(42)	5	—	—	—	—	—	—	—	—	—	—	—	—	30	428
1989	NYJ	7(7, TE)	—	—	—	—	29	322	11.1(22)	0	—	—	—	—	—	—	—	—	—	—	—	—	0	161
1990	†Phi	16(6, te)	—	—	—	—	18	190	10.6(25)	0	—	—	—	—	—	—	—	—	—	—	—	—	0	95
1991	Phi	4(0)	—	—	—	—	6	91	15.2(21)	0	—	—	—	—	—	—	—	—	—	—	—	—	0	46
NFL	14	180(108)	—	—	—	—	462	5100	11.0(51)	37	—	—	—	—	—	—	—	—	—	—	k	—	222	2667

SHULL, STEVE Steven Mark, LB, 6´1˝/220 lbs; William & Mary; B3/27/1958 Philadelphia, PA **1980** Mia 16 (0) **1981**†Mia 16 (0) **1982**†Mia 9 (0) **NFL** 41 (0) [3 yrs]

SHULTZ, JOHNNY John H., WB-FB, 6´1˝/189 lbs; Temple; B9/8/1907, D11/26/1932 Ashland, PA **1930** Fra 6 (1)

SHUMANN, MIKE Michael William, WR, 6´1˝/178 lbs; Florida State; B10/13/1955 Louisville, KY

YEAR	TEAM	G(GS, POS)	RUSH	YD	AVG(LG)	TD	REC	YD	AVG(LG)	TD	PASS	COMP	PCT	YD	AVG(LG)	TD	INT	SK	YD	QBR	KPR	OTD	PTS	TAY
1978	SF	6(1)	—	—	—	—	—	—	—	—	—	—	—	—	—	—	—	—	—	—	p	—	0	0
1979	SF	16(14, WR)	1	19	19.0(19)	0	39	452	11.6(39)	4	—	—	—	—	—	—	—	—	—	—	—	—	24	265
1980	TB	6(0)	—	—	—	—	4	75	18.8(25)	1	—	—	—	—	—	—	—	—	—	—	—	—	6	43
1981	†SF	13(1)	—	—	—	—	3	21	7.0(8)	0	—	—	—	—	—	—	—	—	—	—	—	—	0	11
1982	†SL	6(0)	—	—	—	—	5	58	11.6(23)	0	—	—	—	—	—	—	—	—	—	—	—	—	0	29
1983	SL	16(0)	—	—	—	—	11	154	14.0(33)	0	—	—	—	—	—	—	—	—	—	—	—	—	0	77
NFL	6	63(16)	1	19	19.0(19)	0	62	760	12.3(39)	5	—	—	—	—	—	—	—	—	—	—	p	—	30	424

SHUMATE, MARK Mark Anthony, NT, 6´5˝/265 lbs; Wisconsin; 1983: KC, rnd 10; B3/30/1960 Poynette, WI **1985** NYJ 4 (0) **1985** GB 4 (0) **NFL** 8 (0) [1 yr]

SHUMON, RON Ronnie, LB, 6´1˝/230 lbs; Wichita State; 1978: Cin, rnd 9; B12/11/1955 Flint, MI **1978** Cin 13 **1979** SF 8 **NFL** 21 [2 yrs]

SHUPE, MARK Mark Andrew, C, 6´5˝/285 lbs; Arizona State; B4/24/1961 Lafayette, IN **1987** Buf 2 (1)

SHURNAS, MARSHALL Marshall Kenneth, E-DE, 6´1˝/205 lbs; Missouri; 1947: Cle-A, rnd 13/1944: Bos, rnd 17; B4/1/1922 St. Louis, MO

YEAR	TEAM	G(GS, POS)	RUSH	YD	AVG(LG)	TD	REC	YD	AVG(LG)	TD	PASS	COMP	PCT	YD	AVG(LG)	TD	INT	SK	YD	QBR	KPR	OTD	PTS	TAY
1947	Cle-A	11(1)	—	—	—	—	2	30	15.0	0	—	—	—	—	—	—	—	—	—	—	—	—	0	15

SHURTLEFF, BERT Bertrand Leslie, C-G, 5´11˝/190 lbs; Brown; B8/3/1897 Adamsville, RI, D2/15/1967 Anaheim, CA **1925** Pro 11 (3) **1929** Bos 4 (2) **NFL** 15 (5) [2 yrs]

SHURTLIFFE, RED Charles West, WB-TB, 5´9˝/160 lbs; Marietta; B4/12/1907, D9/1986 Lincolnville, SC **1929** Buf 4 (0)

SHURTZ, HUBERT Hubert D., T, 6´3˝/235 lbs; LSU; 1947: Phi, rnd 17; B7/1/1923 Pinckneyville, IL **1948** Pit 12 (1)

SHY, DON Donald Fredric, RB, 6´1˝/210 lbs; San Diego State; 1967: Pit, rnd 2; B11/15/1945 Cleveland, OH **[R]**

YEAR	TEAM	G(GS, POS)	RUSH	YD	AVG(LG)	TD	REC	YD	AVG(LG)	TD	PASS	COMP	PCT	YD	AVG(LG)	TD	INT	SK	YD	QBR	KPR	OTD	PTS	TAY
1967	Pit	14(HB)	99	341	3.4(33)	4	12	152	12.7(55)	1	—	—	—	—	—	—	—	—	—	—	kp	—	30	610
1968	Pit	13	35	106	3.0(39)	1	13	106	8.2(21)	0	—	—	—	—	—	—	—	—	—	—	k	—	6	431
1969	NO	14	21	75	3.6(22)	1	9	141	15.7(70)	1	—	—	—	—	—	—	—	—	—	—	k	—	12	368
1970	ChiB	8	79	227	2.9(45)	1	10	149	14.9(64)	0	—	—	—	—	—	—	—	—	—	—	—	—	6	312
1971	ChiB	11(RB)	116	420	3.6(21)	2	19	163	8.6(25)	0	1	1	100.0	23	23.0(23)	1	0	1	5	—	—	—	12	538
1972	ChiB	13(rb)	91	342	3.8(22)	1	10	109	10.9(28)	0	—	—	—	—	—	—	—	—	—	—	—	—	6	407
1973	SL	11	16	66	4.1(18)	0	3	15	5.0(6)	1	—	—	—	—	—	—	—	—	—	—	k	1	12	294
NFL	7	84	457	1577	3.5(45)	10	76	835	11.0(70)	3	1	1	100.0	23	23.0(23)	1	0	1	5	—	kp	1	84	2958

SHY, LES Leslie Freeman, RB, 6´1˝/206 lbs; Long Beach State; 1966: Dal, rnd 12; B4/5/1944 Cleveland, OH

YEAR	TEAM	G(GS, POS)	RUSH	YD	AVG(LG)	TD	REC	YD	AVG(LG)	TD	PASS	COMP	PCT	YD	AVG(LG)	TD	INT	SK	YD	QBR	KPR	OTD	PTS	TAY
1966	†Dal	11	17	118	6.9(68)	1	—	—	—	—	—	—	—	—	—	—	—	—	—	—	—	—	6	128
1967	†Dal	13	17	59	3.5(13)	0	3	36	12.0(19)	0	—	—	—	—	—	—	—	—	—	—	k	—	0	98
1968	†Dal	14	64	179	2.8(17)	1	10	105	10.5(41)	0	—	—	—	—	—	—	—	—	—	—	—	—	6	242
1969	†Dal	14	42	154	3.7(23)	1	8	124	15.5(49)	1	—	—	—	—	—	—	—	—	—	—	k	—	12	233
1970	NYG	13	4	13	3.3(6)	0	2	8	4.0(6)	0	—	—	—	—	—	—	—	—	—	—	k	—	0	246
NFL	5	65	144	523	3.6(68)	3	23	273	11.9(49)	1	—	—	—	—	—	—	—	—	—	—	k	—	24	947

SIANI, MIKE Michael Joseph, WR, 6´2˝/195 lbs; Villanova; 1972: Oak, rnd 1; B5/27/1950 Staten Island, NY

YEAR	TEAM	G(GS, POS)	RUSH	YD	AVG(LG)	TD	REC	YD	AVG(LG)	TD	PASS	COMP	PCT	YD	AVG(LG)	TD	INT	SK	YD	QBR	KPR	OTD	PTS	TAY
1972	†Oak	14(13, WR)	—	—	—	—	28	496	17.7(70)	5	—	—	—	—	—	—	—	—	—	—	—	—	30	273
1973	†Oak	14(14, WR)	—	—	—	—	45	742	16.5(**80**)	3	—	—	—	—	—	—	—	—	—	—	—	—	18	386
1974	Oak	6	—	—	—	—	3	30	10.0(13)	1	—	—	—	—	—	—	—	—	—	—	—	—	6	20
1975	†Oak	14(4)	—	—	—	—	17	294	17.3(44)	0	—	—	—	—	—	—	—	—	—	—	—	—	0	147
1976	†Oak	14	—	—	—	—	11	173	15.7(37)	2	—	—	—	—	—	—	—	—	—	—	—	—	12	97
1977	†Oak	12	—	—	—	—	24	344	14.3(39)	2	—	—	—	—	—	—	—	—	—	—	—	—	12	182
1978	Bal	7	—	—	—	—	6	151	25.2(49)	1	—	—	—	—	—	—	—	—	—	—	—	—	6	81
1979	Bal	10(5, wr)	—	—	—	—	15	214	14.3(31)	2	—	—	—	—	—	—	—	—	—	—	—	—	12	117
1980	Bal	10(1)	—	—	—	—	9	174	19.3(38)	1	—	—	—	—	—	—	—	—	—	—	—	—	6	92
NFL	9	101(37)	—	—	—	—	158	2618	16.6(80)	17	—	—	—	—	—	—	—	—	—	—	—	—	102	1394

SIANO, MIKE Michael P., WR, 6´4˝/220 lbs; Syracuse; B11/29/1963 Yeadon, PA

YEAR	TEAM	G(GS, POS)	RUSH	YD	AVG(LG)	TD	REC	YD	AVG(LG)	TD	PASS	COMP	PCT	YD	AVG(LG)	TD	INT	SK	YD	QBR	KPR	OTD	PTS	TAY
1987	Phi	3(0)	—	—	—	—	9	137	15.2(34)	1	—	—	—	—	—	—	—	—	—	—	k	—	6	72

SIANO, TONY Thomas Anthony, C, 5´8˝/172 lbs; Fordham; B1/10/1907, D4/1986 Rochelle Park, NJ **1932** Bos 9 (5, c) **1934** Bkn 11 (0) **NFL** 20 (5) [2 yrs]

SIAVII, JUNIOR Saousoalii Poe, DT, 6´4˝/323 lbs; Oregon; 2004: KC, rnd 2; B11/14/1978 Pago Pago, American Samoa **2004** KC 12 (0) **2005** KC 14 (0) **NFL** 26 (0) [2 yrs]

SIDLE, JIMMY James Corbin, RB, 6´2˝/215 lbs; Auburn; 1965: Dal, rnd 4/NYJ, rnd 9; B2/7/1943 Birmingham, AL, D11/14/1999 Montgomery, AL

YEAR	TEAM	G(GS, POS)	RUSH	YD	AVG(LG)	TD	REC	YD	AVG(LG)	TD	PASS	COMP	PCT	YD	AVG(LG)	TD	INT	SK	YD	QBR	KPR	OTD	PTS	TAY
1966	Atl	6	1	12	12.0(12)	0	1	16	16.0(16)	0	—	—	—	—	—	—	—	—	—	—	k	—	0	47

SIDNEY, DAINON Dainon Tarquinius, DB, 6´0˝/197 lbs; East Tennessee State; Alabama-Birmingham; 1998: Ten, rnd 3; B5/30/1975 Atlanta, GA **1998** Ten 16 (1) **1999**†Ten 16 (2) **2000**†Ten 11 (2) **2001** Ten 1 (1) **2002**†Ten 4 (0) **2003** Buf 2 (0) **NFL** 50 (6) [6 yrs]

SIDORIK, ALEX Alexander Theodore, T, 6´0˝/248 lbs; Mississippi State; 1947: Bos, rnd 11; B12/19/1919 Hartford, CT, D4/12/1980 Middletown, CT **1947** Bos 12 (0) **1948** Bal-A 9 (1) **1949** Bal-A 12 (0) **AAFC** 21 (1) [2 yrs]

SIEB, WALLY Walter John, aka Walter Lenz, HB, 5´10˝/165 lbs; Ripon; B5/6/1899 Butternut, WI, D1/18/1974 Racine, WI **[K]** **1922** Rac 2 (0), 13

SIEGAL, JOHN John Walter, E-DE, 6´1˝/203 lbs; Columbia; 1939: Bkn, rnd 17; B5/15/1918 Larksville, PA

YEAR	TEAM	G(GS, POS)	RUSH	YD	AVG(LG)	TD	REC	YD	AVG(LG)	TD	PASS	COMP	PCT	YD	AVG(LG)	TD	INT	SK	YD	QBR	KPR	OTD	PTS	TAY
1939	ChiB	10(1)	—	—	—	—	3	71	23.7(32)	1	—	—	—	—	—	—	—	—	—	—	—	—	6	41
1940	†ChiB✧	8(3)	—	—	—	—	4	53	13.3	0	—	—	—	—	—	—	—	—	—	—	i	1	6	42
1941	†ChiB✧	11(7, RE)	—	—	—	—	9	220	24.4(65)	3	—	—	—	—	—	—	—	—	—	—	—	—	18	125
1942	†ChiB✧	11(4)	—	—	—	—	13	264	20.3(32)	2	—	—	—	—	—	—	—	—	—	—	—	—	12	142
1943	ChiB	3(1)	—	—	—	—	2	29	14.5(18)	0	—	—	—	—	—	—	—	—	—	—	—	—	0	15
NFL	5	43(16)	—	—	—	—	31	637	20.5(65)	6	—	—	—	—	—	—	—	—	—	—	i	1	42	364

SIEGERT, HERB Herbert Frank, G-LB, 6´3˝/216 lbs; Illinois; 1949: Was, rnd 18/1948: SF-A, rnd 29; B1/10/1924 Pana, IL **1949** Was 12 (7, LG) **1950** Was 12 (RG) **1951** Was 12 (LG) **NFL** 36 (7) [3 yrs]

SIEGERT, WAYNE Wayne Ewald, T-LB-G, 6´3˝/225 lbs; Illinois; 1951: Det, rnd 13; B3/24/1929 Pana, IL **1951** NYY 4

SIEGFRIED, ORVILLE Orville Maynard, TB-HB, 5´10˝/160 lbs; Washington & Jefferson; B2/19/1903, D5/28/1965 **1923** SL 7 (6, TB)

SIEGLE, JULES Julius Joseph, FB-LB, 6´0˝/210 lbs; Northwestern; B2/16/1923 East Chicago, IN

YEAR	TEAM	G(GS, POS)	RUSH	YD	AVG(LG)	TD	REC	YD	AVG(LG)	TD	PASS	COMP	PCT	YD	AVG(LG)	TD	INT	SK	YD	QBR	KPR	OTD	PTS	TAY
1948	NYG	3(0)	2	6	3.0(8)	0	—	—	—	—	—	—	—	—	—	—	—	—	—	—	k	—	0	3

SIEMERING, LARRY Lawrence E., C, 6´3˝/206 lbs; San Francisco; B11/24/1910 Lodi, CA **1935** Bos 11 (2) **1936**†Bos 11 (1) **NFL** 22 (3) [2 yrs]

SIEMINSKI, CHUCK Charles Lee, DT, 6´5˝/270 lbs; Penn State; 1962: SF, rnd 4/Bos, rnd 14; B7/3/1940 Swoyersville, PA **1963** SF 14 **1964** SF 14 **1965** SF 14 **1966** Atl 14 (14, RDT) **1967** Atl 14 **1968** Det 8 **NFL** 78 (14) [6 yrs]

YEAR	TEAM	G (GS, POS)	RUSH	YD	AVG (LG)	TD	REC	YD	AVG (LG)	TD	PASS COMP	PCT	YD	AVG (LG)	TD	INT	SK	YD	QBR	KPR	OTD	PTS	TAY

SIEMON, JEFF Jeffrey Glenn, LB, 6'2"/235 lbs; Stanford; 1972: Min, rnd 1; B6/2/1950 Rochester, MN **1972** Min 13 (8, MLB) **1973**†Min★14 (14, MLB) **1974**†Min☆14 (14, MLB)
1975†Min★14 (14, MLB) **1976**†Min★14 (14, MLB) **1977**†Min★14 (13, MLB) **1978**†Min 16 (16, MLB) **1979** Min 16 (12, MLB) **1980**†Min 16 (2) **1982**†Min 9 (1)

| 1981 | Min | 16(15, LILB) | 1 | 0 | 0.0(0) | 0 | — | — | — | — | — | — | — | — | — | — | — | — | — | — | — | 0 | 0 |
| NFL | 11 | 156(123) | 1 | 0 | | 0 | — | — | — | — | — | — | — | — | — | — | — | i | | — | — | 0 | 49 |

SIENKIEWICZ, TROY Troy Allen, G-T, 6'5"/313 lbs; New Mexico State; 1995: SD, rnd 6; B5/27/1972 Charleston, SC **1996** SD 7 (0) **1997** SD 14 (6, lg) **1998** SD 7 (0)
NFL 28 (6) [3 yrs]

SIERACKI, STAN Stanley Joseph, T, 6'1"/192 lbs; Pennsylvania; B4/29/1904 Meriden, CT, D12/1986 McKeesport, PA **1926** Har 1 (0)

SIERADZKI, STEPHEN Stephen Henry, DB, 6'0"/194 lbs; Michigan State; B4/7/1924, D5/1968 **1948** NYY-A 2 (0)

SIEROCINSKI, STEVE Stephen Peter, T, 6'3"/245 lbs; none; B1922 **1946** Bos 3 (0)

SIES, HERB Dale Hubert, G-T, 6'1"/203 lbs; Pittsburgh; B1/2/1893 Ames, IA, deceased [KC] **1920** Cle 1 (1) **1921** Day 9 (9, RG) **1922** Day 8 (8, RG) **1923** RI☆8 (8, RG), 17
1924 Day 3 (2), 3 **NFL** 29 (28), 20 [5 yrs]

SIEVERS, ERIC Eric Scott, TE, 6'4"/236 lbs; Maryland; 1981: SD, rnd 4; B11/9/1957 Urbana, IL

1981	†SD	16(10, TE)	—	—	—	—	22	276	12.5(32)	3	—	—	—	—	—	—	—	—	k	—	—	18	127
1982	†SD	9(2)	—	—	—	—	12	173	14.4(26)	1	—	—	—	—	—	—	—	—	k	—	—	6	94
1983	SD	16(9, TE)	1	-7	-7.0(-7)	0	33	452	13.7(28)	3	—	—	—	—	—	—	—	—	k	—	—	18	225
1984	SD	14(13, TE)	—	—	—	—	41	438	10.7(32)	3	—	—	—	—	—	—	—	—	k	—	—	18	234
1985	SD	16(11, TE)	—	—	—	—	41	438	10.7(30)	6	—	—	—	—	—	—	—	—	k	—	—	36	237
1986	SD	9(1)	—	—	—	—	2	14	7.0(9)	0	—	—	—	—	—	—	—	—	—	—	—	0	7
1987	SD	12(1)	—	—	—	—	—	—	—	—	—	—	—	—	—	—	—	—	—	—	—		
1988	SD	5(0)	—	—	—	—	1	2	2.0(2)	0	—	—	—	—	—	—	—	—	—	—	—	0	1
1988	†LARm	1(0)	—	—	—	—	—	—	—	—	—	—	—	—	—	—	—	—	—	—	—		
1989	NE	16(5, te)	—	—	—	—	54	615	11.4(46)	0	—	—	—	—	—	—	—	—	—	—	—	0	308
1990	NE	8(1)	—	—	—	—	8	77	9.6(25)	0	—	—	—	—	—	—	—	—	—	—	—	0	39
NFL	10	122(53)	1	-7	-7.0(-7)	0	214	2485	11.6(46)	16	—	—	—	—	—	—	—	—	k	—	—	96	1271

SIGILLO, DOM Dominic Frederick, T-G, 6'0"/230 lbs; Xavier (OH); B3/7/1913 Storrs, CT, D7/1/1957 San Francisco, CA **1943**†ChiB 6 (0) **1944** ChiB 9 (3) **1945** Det 8 (2)
NFL 23 (5) [3 yrs]

SIGLAR, RICKY Ricky Allan, T-G, 6'7"/308 lbs; San Jose State; B6/14/1966 Albuquerque, NM **1990**†SF 16 (0) **1993**†KC 14 (14, RT) **1994** KC 16 (8, rt) **1995**†KC 16 (12, RT)
1996 KC 16 (16, RT) **1997** NO 16 (1) **1998** Car 1 (0) **1998** NO 1 (0) **1998** KC 4 (0) **NFL** 100 (51) [7 yrs]

SIGNAIGO, JOE Joseph Salvatore, G, 6'1"/220 lbs; Notre Dame; 1947: Cle-A, rnd 14/1946: LARm, rnd 10; B2/9/1923 Memphis, TN **1948** NYY-A 14 (9, RG)
1949†NYY-A☆12 (12, RG) **AAFC** 26 (21) [2 yrs]

1950 NYY☆12 (LG)

SIGURDSON, SIG Sigurd Frederick, E-DE, 6'2"/206 lbs; Pacific Lutheran; B11/27/1918 Seattle, WA

| 1947 | Bal-A | 8(3) | — | — | — | — | 8 | 104 | 13.0 | 0 | — | — | — | — | — | — | — | — | — | — | — | 0 | 52 |

SIKAHEMA, VAI Vai, RB, 5'9"/181 lbs; Brigham Young; 1986: SL, rnd 10; B8/29/1962 Nuku'Alofa, Tonga [R] **1987** SL★15 (0) **1988** Phx 12 (0) **1991** GB 11 (0) **1993** Phi 16 (0)

1986	SL★	16(0)	16	62	3.9(26)	0	19	99	9.9(27)	1	—	—	—	—	—	—	—	—	kp	2	18	736
1989	Phx	16(0)	38	145	3.8(27)	0	23	245	10.7(37)	0	1	0	0.0	0	0	0	—	—	kp	—	0	745
1990	Phx	16(0)	3	8	2.7(4)	0	7	51	7.3(13)	0	—	—	—	—	—	—	—	—	kp	—	0	299
1992	†Phi☆	16(0)	2	2	1.0(1)	0	13	142	10.9(22)	0	—	—	—	—	—	—	—	—	kp	1	6	524
NFL	8	118(2)	59	217	3.7(27)	0	53	537	10.1(37)	1	1	0	0.0	0	0	0	—	—	kp	4	30	3648

SIKICH, MIKE Michael P., G, 6'2"/243 lbs; Northwestern; 1971: Cle, rnd 11; B3/3/1949 Chicago, IL **1971** Cle 3

SIKICH, RUDY Rudolph H., T, 6'1"/220 lbs; Minnesota; 1944: Bkn, rnd 4; B2/12/1921 Hibbing, MN, D1/4/1998 **1945**†Cle 6 (2)

SIKORA, MIKE Michael Wasyl, G, 6'2"/230 lbs; Indiana; Oregon; B11/29/1926 Hammond, IN **1952** ChiC 12 (LG)

SILAS, SAM Samuel Louis, DT, 6'4"/255 lbs; Southern Illinois; 1963: Bos, rnd 6; B9/25/1940 Homeland, FL **1963** SL 14 **1964** SL 14 (LDT) **1965** SL★14 (LDT) **1966** SL 14 (LDT)
1967 SL 14 (LDT) **1968** NYG 14 **1969** SF 4 **1970** SF 12 **NFL** 100 [8 yrs]

SILEO, DAN Daniel William, DT, 6'2"/282 lbs; Maryland; Cincinnati; Miami (FL); 1987: TB, rnd S3; B1/3/1964 Stamford, CT **1987** TB 10 (0)

SILER, RICH Richard Anthony, TE, 6'4"/240 lbs; Illinois; Texas A&M; B11/1/1963 Miami, FL **1987** Mia 1 (0)

SILIPO, JOE Joseph Martin, TE, 6'3"/295 lbs; Tulane; B12/31/1957 Glen Cove, NY **1987** Buf 1 (1)

SILLIN, FRANK Franklin Paul, B, 5'11"/179 lbs; Western Maryland; B1904 Wapakoneta, OH, D12/30/1932 **1921** Day 1 (0) **1927** Day 7 (5, WB) **1928** Day 4 (2), 6
1929 Day 5 (5, WB) **NFL** 17 (12) [4 yrs]

SILVAN, NILO Nilo Kyle, WR, 5'9"/176 lbs; Tennessee; 1996: TB, rnd 6; B10/2/1973 Covington, LA **1996** TB 7 (0)

SILVESTRI, CARL Carl Anthony, DB, 5'11"/195 lbs; Wisconsin; 1965: SL, rnd 16; B3/27/1943 Milwaukee, WI, D11/25/2004 Mequon, WI **1965** SL 14 (rs) **1966** Atl 3 **NFL** 17 [2 yrs]

SILVESTRI, DON Donald Gerard, K, 6'4"/220 lbs; Pittsburgh; B12/25/1968 Perkasie, PA **1995** NYJ 16 (0) **1996** NYJ 12 (0) **NFL** 28 (0) [2 yrs]

SIMAS, BUTCH William T., BB-QB, 6'0"/185 lbs; St. Mary's (CA); B8/31/1908, D5/24/1989 Hermosa Beach, CA

1932	ChiC	7(5, BB)	2	0	0.0	0	1	23	23.0(23)	0	—	—	—	—	—	—	—	—	—	—	—	0	12
1933	ChiC	3(0)	—	—	—	—	1	9	9.0(9)	0	—	—	—	—	—	—	—	—	—	—	—	0	5
NFL	2	10(5)	2	0	0.0	0	2	32	16.0(23)	0	—	—	—	—	—	—	—	—	—	—	—	0	16

SIMENDINGER, KEN Kenneth Alphonse, HB, 5'10"/175 lbs; Lehigh; Holy Cross; B10/23/1899 Philadelphia, PA, D5/26/1972 Philadelphia, PA **1926** Har 2 (1)

SIMENSEN, DON Donald Roy, T, 6'2"/220 lbs; St. Thomas; B9/11/1926 Minot, ND, D4/22/1994 Fridley, MN **1951**†LARm 12 (LT) **1952**†LARm 12 (LT) **NFL** 24 [2 yrs]

SIMERSON, JOHN John Cooke, C-T, 6'3"/257 lbs; Purdue; 1957: Phi, rnd 22; B4/20/1935 Honolulu, HI, D8/2/1992 Los Angeles, CA **1957** Phi 12 (12, C) **1958** Phi 4 **1958** Pit 3
1960†Hou-A 14 **1961** Bos-A 10 **NFL** 43 (12) [4 yrs]

SIMIEN, TRACY Tracy Anthony, LB, 6'1"/252 lbs; TCU; B5/21/1967 Bay City, TX **1989**†Pit 0 (0) **1991**†KC 15 (12, LILB) **1992**†KC 15 (15, MLB/rilb) **1993**†KC 16 (14, LILB)
1994†KC 15 (15, MLB) **1995**†KC 16 (16, MLB) **1996** KC 16 (13, MLB) **1997**†KC 16 (0) **1999** SD 8 (4) **NFL** 117 (89) [9 yrs]

SIMINGTON, MILT Milton R., G, 6'2"/217 lbs; Arkansas; 1941: Cle, rnd 9; B8/26/1918 Wright City, OK, D1/17/1943 Shreveport, LA [K] **1941** Cle 7 (0) **1942** Pit★11 (11, RG)
NFL 18 (11) [2 yrs]

SIMKUS, ARNIE Arnold, DE-DT, 6'4"/240 lbs; Michigan; 1965: Cle, rnd 6; B3/25/1943 Schlava, Germany **1965** NYJ-A 1 **1967** Min 11 **NFL** 12 [2 yrs]

SIMMONDS, MIKE Michael Todd, G, 6'4"/285 lbs; Indiana State; 1987: TB, rnd 10; B8/12/1964 Bellville, IL **1989** TB 5 (5, lg)

SIMMONS, ANTHONY Anthony Lamont, LB, 6'0"/240 lbs; Clemson; 1998: Sea, rnd 1; B6/20/1976 Spartanburg, SC **1998** Sea 12 (4) **1999**†Sea 16 (16, MLB)
2000 Sea 16 (16, LLB) **2001** Sea 7 (7, llb) **2003**†Sea 13 (13, LLB) **2004** Sea 16 (16, llb) **NFL** 87 (79) [7 yrs]

SIMMONS, BOB Robert Gatling, G-T, 6'4"/260 lbs; Texas; 1976: NO, rnd 3; B7/7/1954 Temple, TX **1977** KC 14 (10, LG) **1978** KC 16 (15, LG) **1979** KC 16 (15, LG)
1980 KC 15 (15, LG) **1981** KC 4 (0) **1982** KC 8 (2) **1983** KC 15 (12, rg) **NFL** 88 (69) [7 yrs]

SIMMONS, BRIAN Brian Eugene, LB, 6'3"/244 lbs; North Carolina; 1998: Cin, rnd 1; B6/21/1975 New Bern, NC **1998** Cin 14 (12, LILB) **1999** Cin 16 (16, LILB/mlb) **2000** Cin 1 (1)
2001 Cin 16 (16, MLB) **2002** Cin 16 (15, MLB) **2003** Cin 16 (16, RLB) **2004** Cin 15 (15, RLB) **2005**†Cin 16 (16, RLB) **NFL** 110 (107) [8 yrs]

SIMMONS, CLEO Cleo, TE, 6'2"/225 lbs; Jackson State; B10/21/1960 Mobile, AL **1983**†Dal 11 (0)

SIMMONS, CLYDE Clyde, DE-DT, 6'5"/279 lbs; Western Carolina; 1986: Phi, rnd 9; B8/4/1964 Lanes, SC [S] **1986** Phi 16 (0) **1987** Phi 12 (12, RDE) **1988**†Phi 16 (16, RDE)
1989†Phi☆16 (16, RDE) **1990**†Phi 16 (16, RDE) **1991** Phi☆16 (16, RDE) **1992**†Phi★16 (16, RDE) **1993** Phi 16 (16, RDE) **1994** Arz 16 (16, RDE) **1995** Arz 16 (16, RDE)
1996†Jax 16 (14, RDE) **1997** Jax 16 (13, RDE) **1998** Cin 16 (16, RDE) **1999** ChiB 16 (0) **2000** ChiB 16 (2) **NFL** 236 (185) [15 yrs]

SIMMONS, DAVE David Alan, LB, 6'4"/245 lbs; Georgia Tech; 1965: SL, rnd 2/Buf, rnd 5; B8/3/1943 Elizabethtown, KY **1965** SL 14 **1966** SL 6 **1967** NO 11 **1968**†Dal 13
NFL 44 [4 yrs]

YEAR	TEAM	G (GS, POS)	RUSH	YD	AVG (LG)	TD	REC	YD	AVG (LG)	TD	PASS	COMP	PCT	YD	AVG (LG)	TD	INT	SK	YD	QBR	KPR	OTD	PTS	TAY

SIMMONS, DAVE — David Devone, LB, 6'4"/221 lbs; North Carolina; 1979: GB, rnd 6; B1/19/1957 Goldsboro, NC **1979** GB 16 **1980** Det 1 (0) **1982** Bal 6 (3) **1983** ChiB 13 (0)
NFL 36 (3) [4 yrs]

SIMMONS, ED — Edward Lamar, T-G, 6'5"/315 lbs; Eastern Washington; 1987: Was, rnd 6; B12/31/1963 Seattle, WA **1987** Was 5 (3) **1988** Was 16 (0) **1989** Was 16 (8, rt) **1990** Was 13 (11, RT) **1991**†Was 6 (2) **1992**†Was 16 (11, RT) **1993** Was 13 (13, RT) **1994** Was 16 (16, RT) **1995** Was 16 (16, RT) **1996** Was 11 (11, RT) **1997** Was 14 (13, RT)
NFL 142 (104) [11 yrs]

SIMMONS, FLOYD — Floyd Weston, B, 6'1"/200 lbs; Notre Dame; 1948: Pit, rnd 24; B2/19/1925 Portland, OH, D8/6/1996 Portland, OR

YEAR	TEAM	G (GS, POS)	RUSH	YD	AVG (LG)	TD	REC	YD	AVG (LG)	TD	KPR	PTS	TAY
1948	ChiR-A	11(2)	36	121	3.4	1	2	60	30.0		k	12	198

SIMMONS, JACK — John Charles, C-G-T, 6'4"/236 lbs; Maryland; Detroit Mercy; 1946: Det, rnd 22; B10/8/1924 Grosse Pointe, MI, D9/17/1978 Royal Oak, MI **1948**†Bal-A 10 (0)
1949 Det 12 (11, C) **1950** Det 12 (12, C) **1951** ChiC 12 (12, C) **1952** ChiC 12 (12, C) **1953** ChiC 12 (12, C) **1954** ChiC 12 (12, C) **1955** ChiC 12 (12, C) **1956** ChiC◇12 (C)
NFL 96 (71) [8 yrs]

SIMMONS, JASON — Jason Lawrence, DB, 5'9"/198 lbs; Arizona State; 1998: Pit, rnd 5; B3/30/1976 Inglewood, CA **1998** Pit 6 (0) **1999** Pit 16 (0) **2000** Pit 15 (0) **2001**†Pit 12 (0) **2002** Hou 15 (0) **2005** Hou 14 (1)

YEAR	TEAM	G (GS, POS)	RUSH	YD	AVG (LG)	TD	KPR	PTS	TAY
2003	Hou	16(2)	1	7	7.0(7)	0		0	7
2004	Hou	10(6, fs)	1	1	1.0(1)	0	i	0	-4
NFL	8	104(9)	2	8	4.0(7)	0	iS	0	3

SIMMONS, JEFF — Jeffrey Thomas, WR, 6'3"/195 lbs; USC; 1983: LARm, rnd 7; B7/6/1960 Stockton, CA **1983** LARm 3 (0)

SIMMONS, JERRY — Jerry Bernard, WR-SE, 6'0"/190 lbs; Bethune-Cookman; B11/14/1942 Nichols, FL

YEAR	TEAM	G (GS, POS)	RUSH	YD	AVG (LG)	TD	REC	YD	AVG (LG)	TD	KPR	PTS	TAY
1965	Pit	4					2	16	8.0(9)	0	k	0	21
1966	Pit	13					6	68	11.3(21)	1	kp	6	75
1967	NO	2					2	25	12.5(16)	0		0	13
1967	Atl	12(SE)					21	287	13.7(30)	2	kp	12	147
1968	Atl	14(SE)	1	-6	-6.0(-6)	0	28	479	17.1(61)	2		0	234
1969	Atl	2					1	4	4.0(4)	0		0	2
1969	ChiB	8					13	178	13.7(48)	0		0	89
1971	Den	14(12, WR)	1	7	7.0(7)	0	25	403	16.1(47)	1		6	214
1972	Den	9(8, WR)					17	235	13.8(35)	2		12	128
1973	Den	14(13, WR)	1	-4	-4.0(-4)	0	13	249	19.2(53)	1		6	126
1974	Den	14(2)					10	161	16.1(36)	2		12	91
NFL	9	106(35)	3	-1	-1.0(7)	0	138	2105	15.3(61)	9	kp	54	1137

SIMMONS, JIM — James A., B, 6'0"/186 lbs; Southwestern Oklahoma State; B4/17/1902, TX, D2/1984 Elmore City, OK **1927** Cle 12 (6, FB), 30 **1928** Pro 8 (4) **NFL** 20 (10) [2 yrs]

SIMMONS, JOHN — John Christopher, DB, 5'11"/192 lbs; SMU; 1981: Cin, rnd 3; B12/1/1958 Little Rock, AR **1981**†Cin 11 (0) **1982**†Cin 2 (0) **1983** Cin 16 (0) **1984** Cin 16 (2) **1985** Cin 9 (0) **1986** Cin 10 (0) **1986** GB 6 (0) **1987** Ind 2 (0) **NFL** 72 (2) [7 yrs]

SIMMONS, KENDALL — Henry Alexander Kendall, G, 6'3"/313 lbs; Auburn; 2002: Pit, rnd 1; B3/11/1979 Ripley, MA **2002**†Pit 14 (14, RG) **2003** Pit 16 (16, RG) **2005**†Pit 16 (16, RG)
NFL 46 (46) [3 yrs]

SIMMONS, KING — King David, DB, 6'2"/200 lbs; Texas Tech; 1986: Cle, rnd 12; B2/12/1963 Atlanta, GA **1987** SD 3 (1)

SIMMONS, LEON — Leon, LB, 6'0"/225 lbs; Grambling State; B9/27/1938 Dallas, TX **1963** Den-A 2

SIMMONS, MARCELLO — Marcello Muhammad, DB, 6'1"/180 lbs; SMU; 1993: Cin, rnd 4; B8/8/1971 Tomball, TX **1993** Cin 16 (2)

SIMMONS, MICHAEL — Michael Glenn, DE, 6'4"/269 lbs; Mississippi State; B11/14/1965 Eupora, MS **1989** NO 1 (0) **1990**†NO 16 (3) **NFL** 17 (3) [2 yrs]

SIMMONS, ROY — Roy Franklin, G, 6'3"/264 lbs; Georgia Tech; 1979: NYG, rnd 8; B11/8/1956 Savannah, GA **1979** NYG 16 **1980** NYG 16 (16, LG) **1981**†NYG 16 (10, LG) **1983**†Was 10 (0) **NFL** 58 (26) [4 yrs]

SIMMONS, SAM — Samuel Leeland, WR, 5'9"/200 lbs; Northwestern; 2002: Mia, rnd 5; B11/25/1979 Kansas City, KS **2003** Mia 11 (0)

SIMMONS, STACEY — Stacey Andrew, WR, 5'9"/183 lbs; Florida; 1990: Ind, rnd 4; B8/5/1968 Clearwater, FL

YEAR	TEAM	G (GS, POS)	REC	YD	AVG (LG)	TD	KPR	PTS	TAY
1990	Ind	14(1)	4	33	8.3(12)	0	k	0	80

SIMMONS, TERRANCE — Terrance Demon, DT, 6'6"/296 lbs; Alabama State; B5/3/1976 Moss Point, MS **2002** Car 2 (0)

SIMMONS, TONY — Anthony Earl, DE, 6'4"/270 lbs; Tennessee; 1985: SD, rnd 12; B12/18/1962 Oakland, CA **1985** SD 13 (0) **1987** SD 3 (3) **NFL** 16 (3) [2 yrs]

SIMMONS, TONY — Tony De'Angelo, WR, 6'1"/205 lbs; Wisconsin; 1998: NE, rnd 2; B12/8/1974 Chicago, IL

YEAR	TEAM	G (GS, POS)	REC	YD	AVG (LG)	TD	KPR	PTS	TAY
1998	†NE	11(6, wr)	23	474	20.6(63)	3		18	252
1999	NE	15(1)	19	276	14.5(58)	2	k	12	190
2000	NE	12(2)	14	231	16.5(46)	1	k	6	143
2001	Cle	1(0)							
2001	Ind	6(0)	2	17	8.5(12)	0	k	0	6
2002	NYG	3(0)							
NFL	5	48(9)	58	998	17.2(63)	6	k	36	590

SIMMONS, VICTOR — Victor T., LB, 6'2"/230 lbs; Central State (OH); B5/9/1964 Chicago, IL **1987** Dal 3 (0)

SIMMONS, WAYNE — Wayne General, LB, 6'2"/245 lbs; Clemson; 1993: GB, rnd 1; B12/15/1969 Beaufort, SC, D8/23/2002 Independence, MO **1993**†GB 14 (8, LOLB) **1994**†GB 12 (1) **1995**†GB 16 (16, LLB) **1996**†GB 16 (16, LLB) **1997** GB 6 (6, llb) **1997**†KC 10 (8, lilb) **1998** KC 10 (10, LILB) **1998**†Buf 6 (0) **NFL** 90 (65) [6 yrs]

SIMMS, BOB — Robert Alderson, LB-E, 6'1"/230 lbs; Rutgers; 1960: NYG, rnd 10/Hou, rnd 1; B9/3/1938 Clendenin, WV **1961**†NYG 14 **1962** Pit 3 **1962** NYG 5

YEAR	TEAM	G (GS, POS)	REC	YD	AVG (LG)	TD	KPR	PTS	TAY
1960	NYG	9	1	58	58.0(58)	0		0	29
NFL	3	31	1	58	58.0(58)	0	k	0	28

SIMMS, CHRIS — Chris, QB, 6'4"/220 lbs; Texas; 2003: TB, rnd 3; B8/29/1980 Franklin Lakes, NJ

YEAR	TEAM	G (GS, POS)	RUSH	YD	AVG (LG)	TD	REC	YD	AVG (LG)	TD	PASS	COMP	PCT	YD	AVG (LG)	TD	INT	SK	YD	QBR	PTS	TAY
2004	TB	5(2)	7	14	2.0(12)	0					73	42	57.5	467	6.4(75)	1	3	10	75	—	0	133
2005	†TB	11(10, QB)	19	31	1.6(10)	0	1	-3	-3.0(-3)	0	313	191	61.0	2035	6.5(78)	10	7	29	205	81.4	0	817
NFL	2	16(12)	26	45	1.7(12)	0	1	-3	-3.0(-3)	0	386	233	60.4	2502	6.5(78)	11	10	39	280	78.1	0	950

SIMMS, PHIL — Phillip Martin, QB, 6'3"/216 lbs; Morehead State; 1979: NYG, rnd 1; B11/3/1954 Lebanon, KY

YEAR	TEAM	G (GS, POS)	RUSH	YD	AVG (LG)	TD	REC	YD	AVG (LG)	TD	PASS	COMP	PCT	YD	AVG (LG)	TD	INT	SK	YD	QBR	PTS	TAY
1979	NYG	12(QB)	29	166	5.7(27)	1					265	134	50.6	1743	6.6(61)	13	14	39	319	66.0	6	553
1980	NYG	13(13, QB)	36	190	5.3(20)	1					402	193	48.0	2321	5.8(58)	15	19	36	233	58.9	6	676
1981	NYG	10(10, QB)	19	42	2.2(24)	0					316	172	54.4	2031	6.4(80)	11	9	38	301	74.0	0	753
1983	NYG	2(0)									13	7	53.8	130	10.0(36)	0	1	3	35	—	0	25
1984	†NYG	16(16, QB)	42	162	3.9(21)	0	1	13	13.0(13)	0	533	286	53.7	4044	7.6(65)	22	18	55	434	78.1	0	1581
1985	†NYG◇	16(16, QB)	37	132	3.6(28)	0					495	275	55.6	**3829**	**7.7(70)**	22	20	52	396	78.6	0	1357
1986	†NYG☆	16(16, QB)	43	72	1.7(18)	1					468	259	55.3	3487	7.5(49)	21	22	45	359	74.6	6	1051
1987	NYG	9(9, QB)	14	44	3.1(20)	0					282	163	57.8	2230	7.9(50)	17	9	35	225	90.0	0	884
1988	NYG	15(15, QB)	33	152	4.6(17)	1					479	263	54.9	3359	7.0(62)	21	11	50	405	82.1	6	1497
1989	†NYG	15(15, QB)	32	141	4.4(15)	1					405	228	56.3	3061	7.6(62)	14	14	40	244	77.6	6	1192
1990	†NYG	14(14, QB)	21	61	2.9(20)	1					311	184	59.2	2284	7.3(80)	15	4	20	104	**92.7**	6	1128
1991	NYG	6(4)	9	42	4.7(19)	1					141	82	58.2	993	7.0(38)	8	4	14	79	—	6	429
1992	NYG	4(4)	6	17	2.8(7)	0					137	83	60.6	912	6.7(38)	5	3	10	67	—	0	378
1993	†NYG◇	16(16, QB)	28	31	1.1(9)	0	1	-6	-6.0(-6)	0	400	247	61.8	3038	7.6(62)	15	9	37	217	88.3	6	1262
NFL	14	164(148)	349	1252	3.6(28)	6	2	7	3.5(13)	0	4647	2576	55.4	33462	7.2(80)	199	157	477	3418	78.5	36	12762

SIMON, COREY — Corey, DT, 6'2"/293 lbs; Florida State; 2000: Phi, rnd 1; B3/2/1977 Boynton Beach, FL **2000**†Phi 16 (16, LDT) **2001**†Phi 16 (16, LDT) **2002**†Phi 14 (14, LDT) **2003**†Phi◇16 (16, LDT) **2004** Phi 16 (16, LDT) **2005** Ind 13 (13, LDT) **NFL** 91 (91) [6 yrs]

SIMON, JIM — James E., G-T, 6'4"/240 lbs; Miami (FL); 1963: Det, rnd 15/Bos, rnd 9; B3/22/1940 Pittsburgh, PA **1963** Det 13 **1964** Det 14 **1965** Det 14 **1966** Atl 14 (2) **1967** Atl 14 (RG) **1968** Atl 13 (LG) **NFL** 82 (2) [6 yrs]

YEAR	TEAM	G (GS, POS)	RUSH	YD	AVG (LG)	TD	REC	YD	AVG (LG)	TD	PASS	COMP	PCT	YD	AVG (LG)	TD	INT	SK	YD	QBR	KPR	OTD	PTS	TAY

SIMON, JOHN   John Ray, RB, 5′11″/202 lbs; Louisiana Tech; B12/11/1978 Baton Rouge, LA

YEAR	TEAM	G (GS, POS)	RUSH	YD	AVG (LG)	TD	REC	YD	AVG (LG)	TD											KPR	OTD	PTS	TAY
2002	†Ten	12(0)	9	18	2.0(13)	1	16	167	10.4(42)	3	—	—	—	—	—	—	—	—	—	—	kpi	—	24	329
2003	Was	4(0)	3	9	3.0(6)	0	3	21	7.0(12)	0	—	—	—	—	—	—	—	—	—	—	k	—	0	26
NFL	2	16(0)	12	27	2.3(13)	1	19	188	9.9(42)	3	—	—	—	—	—	—	—	—	—	—	kpi	—	24	354

SIMONE, MIKE   Michael Anthony, LB, 6′0″/210 lbs; Stanford; B5/20/1950 Ravenna, OH   **1972** Den 14   **1973** Den 14 (3)   **1974** Den 14   **NFL** 42 (3) [3 yrs]

SIMONEAU, MARK   Mark, LB, 6′0″/234 lbs; Kansas State; 2000: Atl, rnd 3; B1/16/1977 Phillipsburg, KS [K]   **2000** Atl 14 (4)   **2001** Atl 16 (5, llb)   **2002**†Atl 15 (0)   **2003**†Phi 16 (16, MLB)   **2004** Phi 14 (13, LLB/mlb)   **2005** Phi 16 (0)   **NFL** 91 (38) [6 yrs]

SIMONETTI, LENNY   Leonard Patrick, T, 5′11″/225 lbs; Tennessee; B11/20/1919 Roswell, OH, D8/14/1973 Dennison, OH   **1946**†Cle-A 0 (0)   **1947**†Cle-A 14 (0)   **1948**†Cle-A 14 (0)   **AAFC** 28 (1) [3 yrs]

SIMONINI, ED   Edward Charles, LB, 6′0″/210 lbs; Texas A&M; 1976: Bal, rnd 3; B2/2/1954 Portsmouth, VA   **1976**†Bal 14   **1977**†Bal 14 (14, MLB)   **1978** Bal 16 (16, MLB)   **1979** Bal 13 (10, MLB)   **1980** Bal 16 (16, MLB)   **1981** Bal 1 (1)   **1982** NO 9 (0)   **NFL** 83 (57) [7 yrs]

SIMONS, JOHN   John Brimhall, FB-E, 5′11″/200 lbs; Hamline; B1/22/1901 St. Paul, MN, D1/22/1978 Las Vegas, NV [K]   **1924** Min 6 (6, FB), 1

SIMONS, KEITH   Keith Michael, DT-NT, 6′3″/254 lbs; Minnesota; 1976: KC, rnd 3; B4/26/1954 Ypsilanti, MI   **1976** KC 6 (6, rdt)   **1977** KC 14 (6, RDT)   **1978** SL 13   **1979** SL 16   **NFL** 49 (12) [4 yrs]

SIMONS, KEVIN   Kevin Bradley, T, 6′3″/315 lbs; Tennessee; B4/25/1967 Miami, FL   **1989** Cle 1 (0)

SIMONSON, DAVE   David Arnold, T, 6′6″/246 lbs; Minnesota; 1974: Bal, rnd 12; B5/2/1952 Austin, MN   **1974** Bal 13   **1975** NYG 2   **1976** Hou 2   **1976** Sea 5   **1977** Det 7   **NFL** 29 [4 yrs]

SIMONTON, KEN   Ken, RB, 5′8″/191 lbs; Oregon State; B6/7/1979 Pittsburg, CA

2003	Buf	2(0)	2	4	2.0(2)	0	—	—	—	—	—	—	—	—	—	—	—	—	—	—	—	—	0	4

SIMPKINS, RON   Ronald Bernard, LB, 6′1″/235 lbs; Michigan; 1980: Cin, rnd 7; B4/2/1958 Detroit, MI   **1980** Cin 16 (2)   **1982**†Cin 5 (0)   **1983** Cin 15 (0)   **1984** Cin 16 (11, LILB)   **1985** Cin 16 (9, LILB)   **1986** Cin 16 (0)   **1988** GB 7 (0)   **NFL** 91 (22) [7 yrs]

SIMPSON, AL   Allen Ralph, G-T, 6′5″/255 lbs; Colorado State; 1975: NYG, rnd 2; B7/27/1951 Pittsburgh, PA   **1975** NYG 13   **1976** NYG 10 (8, LG)   **NFL** 23 (8) [2 yrs]

SIMPSON, ANTOINE   Antoine Lagree, DT, 6′2″/310 lbs; Houston; B12/7/1976 Gary, IN   **1999** Mia 4 (0)   **2000** SD 7 (0)   **NFL** 11 (0) [2 yrs]

SIMPSON, BILL   William Thomas, DB, 6′1″/184 lbs; Michigan State; 1974: LA, rnd 2; B12/5/1951 Detroit, MI [I]   **1974**†LARm 14 (4)   **1975**†LARm 14 (14, FS)   **1976**†LARm 14 (14, FS)   **1977** LARm☆ 14 (14, FS)   **1978**†LARm☆ 16 (16, FS)   **1980**†Buf 11 (11, FS)   **1981** Buf 16 (16, FS)   **1982** Buf 9 (9, FS)   **NFL** 108 (98) [8 yrs]

SIMPSON, BOB   Robert Morris, DE, 6′5″/235 lbs; Colorado; 1976: Mia, rnd 8; B3/29/1954 Bloomington, IL   **1978** Mia 5

SIMPSON, CARL   Carl Wilhelm, DT, 6′2″/292 lbs; Florida State; 1993: Chi, rnd 2; B4/18/1970 Baxley, GA   **1993** ChiB 11 (0)   **1994**†ChiB 15 (8, ldt)   **1995** ChiB 16 (8, ldt)   **1996** ChiB 16 (16, RDT)   **1997** ChiB 16 (16, RDT)   **1998**†Arz 13 (1)   **NFL** 87 (49) [6 yrs]

SIMPSON, EBER   Eber Edward, BB-QB, 5′8″/170 lbs; Wisconsin-Oshkosh; Wisconsin; B7/24/1895 Oshkosh, WI, deceased   **1923** SL 7 (7, BB)

SIMPSON, HOWARD   Howard Jesse, DE, 6′5″/230 lbs; Auburn; 1964: Buf, rnd 10; B12/14/1942 Lancaster, SC   **1964** Min 3

SIMPSON, JACKIE   Jack Maylon, LB-K, 6′0″/225 lbs; Mississippi; 1958: Was, rnd 21; B8/20/1936 Corinth, MS [K]   **1961** Den-A 6   **1962** Oak-A 14 (MLB)   **1963** Oak-A 14 (LLB)   **1964** Oak-A 2   **NFL** 36 [4 yrs]

SIMPSON, JACKIE   John Maylen, DB, 5′10″/183 lbs; Florida; B4/2/1934 Miami, FL, D6/2/1983 Pontiac, MI   **1958**†Bal 2   **1959**†Bal 10   **1960** Bal 12   **1961** Pit 8   **1962** Pit 13   **NFL** 45 [5 yrs]

SIMPSON, JIMMY   James Felix, BB-TB, 5′10″/160 lbs; Detroit Mercy; B10/6/1897, D8/1979 Toledo, OH   **1922** Tol 3 (3)   **1924** Ken 4 (4, BB)   **NFL** 7 (7) [2 yrs]

SIMPSON, KEITH   Keith Edward, DB, 6′1″/195 lbs; Memphis; 1978: Sea, rnd 1; B3/9/1956 Memphis, TN   **1978** Sea 13 (2)   **1979** Sea 15 (11, SS)   **1980** Sea 16 (16, SS)   **1981** Sea 12 (12, LCB)   **1982** Sea 8 (8, LCB)   **1983**†Sea 14 (6, lcb)   **1984**†Sea 15 (15, LCB)   **1985** Sea 15 (0)   **NFL** 108 (70) [8 yrs]

SIMPSON, MIKE   Michael Harry, DB, 5′9″/170 lbs; Houston; 1969: SD, rnd 13; B3/13/1947 Mena, AR   **1970** SF 7   **1971**†SF 8   **1972**†SF 13 (9, FS)   **1973** SF 13 (7, FS)   **NFL** 41 (16) [4 yrs]

SIMPSON, NATE   Nathan Joseph, RB, 5′11″/189 lbs; Tennessee State; 1977: GB, rnd 5; B11/30/1954 Nashville, TN

1977	GB	12	60	204	3.4(40)	0	5	19	3.8(14)	0	—	—	—	—	—	—	—	—	—	—	k	—	0	199
1978	GB	16	27	58	2.1(11)	0	1	4	4.0(4)	0	—	—	—	—	—	—	—	—	—	—	—	—	0	60
1979	GB	15	66	235	3.6(22)	1	11	46	4.2(10)	0	—	—	—	—	—	—	—	—	—	—	—	—	6	268
NFL	3	43	153	497	3.2(40)	1	17	69	4.1(14)	0	—	—	—	—	—	—	—	—	—	—	k	—	6	527

SIMPSON, O.J.   Orenthal James 'The Juice', RB, 6′2″/212 lbs; USC; 1969: Buf, rnd 1; B7/9/1947 San Francisco, CA; HOF 1985

1969	Buf-A◇	13(HB)	181	697	3.9(32)	2	30	343	11.4(55)	3	—	—	—	—	—	—	—	—	—	—	k	—	30	1118
1970	Buf	8(0)	120	488	4.1(56)	5	10	139	13.9(36)	0	2	0	0.0	0	0.0	0	0	—	—	—	k	—	36	846
1971	Buf	14(RB)	183	742	4.1(46)	5	21	162	7.7(38)	0	2	0	0.0	0	0.0	0	0	—	—	—	k	—	30	920
1972	Buf★	14(RB)	292	1251	4.3(94)	6	27	198	7.3(25)	0	8	5	62.5	113	14.1(34)	1	0	1	11	—	k	—	36	**1478**
1973	Buf★	14(RB)	332	2003	6.0(80)	12	6	70	11.7(24)	0	2	1	50.0	3	-1.5(-3)	0	0	—	—	—	—	—	72	2157
1974	†Buf★	14(RB)	270	1125	4.2(41)	3	15	189	12.6(29)	1	1	0	0.0	0	0.0	0	0	—	—	—	—	—	24	1255
1975	Buf★	14(RB)	329	1817	5.5(88)	16	28	426	15.2(54)	7	—	—	—	—	—	—	—	—	—	—	—	—	138	2225
1976	Buf★	14(RB)	290	1503	5.2(75)	8	22	259	11.8(43)	1	—	—	—	—	—	—	—	—	—	—	—	—	54	1718
1977	Buf	7(RB)	126	557	4.4(39)	0	16	138	8.6(18)	0	1	0	0.0	0	0.0	0	0	—	—	—	—	—	0	626
1978	SF	10(10, RB)	161	593	3.7(34)	1	21	172	8.2(19)	2	—	—	—	—	—	—	—	—	—	—	—	—	18	699
1979	SF	13(8, RB)	120	460	3.8(22)	3	7	46	6.6(14)	0	—	—	—	—	—	—	—	—	—	—	—	—	18	513
NFL	11	135(18)	2404	11236	4.7(94)	61	203	2142	10.6(64)	14	16	6	37.5	110	6.9(34)	1	0	1	11	—	k	1	456	13552

SIMPSON, TIM   Timothy James, G-C, 6′2″/284 lbs; Illinois; 1992: Cle, rnd 12; B3/5/1969 Peoria, IL   **1994**☆Pit 4 (0)

SIMPSON, TRAVIS   Travis Theron, C, 6′3″/272 lbs; Oklahoma; B11/19/1963 Norman, OK   **1987** GB 3 (0)

SIMPSON, WILLIE   William, FB, 6′0″/218 lbs; San Francisco State; B3/11/1938

1962	Oak-A	10	10	32	3.2(11)	0	—	—	—	—	—	—	—	—	—	—	—	—	—	—	k	—	0	24

SIMS, BARRY   Barry, T-G, 6′5″/300 lbs; Utah State; Utah; B12/1/1974 Park City, UT   **1999** Oak 16 (10, lt/rg)   **2000**†Oak 16 (8, lt)   **2001**†Oak 15 (15, LT)   **2002**†Oak 15 (15, LT)   **2003** Oak 16 (16, LT)   **2004** Oak 16 (16, LT)   **2005** Oak 16 (16, LT)   **NFL** 110 (96) [7 yrs]

SIMS, BILLY   Billy Ray, RB, 6′0″/212 lbs; Oklahoma; 1980: Det, rnd 1; B9/18/1955 St. Louis, MO

1980	Det★	16(16, RB)	·313	1303	4.2(52)	**13**	51	621	12.2(87)	3	—	—	—	—	—	—	—	—	—	—	—	—	96	**1759**
1981	Det★	14(14, RB)	296	1437	4.9(51)	**13**	28	451	16.1(81)	2	—	—	—	—	—	—	—	—	—	—	—	—	90	1803
1982	†Det★	9(8, RB)	172	639	3.7(29)	4	34	342	10.1(52)	0	—	—	—	—	—	—	—	—	—	—	—	—	24	850
1983	†Det	13(12, RB)	220	1040	4.7(41)	7	42	419	10.0(54)	3	—	—	—	—	—	—	—	—	—	—	—	—	42	1320
1984	Det	8(8, RB)	130	687	5.3(81)	5	31	239	7.7(20)	0	—	—	—	—	—	—	—	—	—	—	—	—	30	857
NFL	5	60(58)	1131	5106	4.5(81)	42	186	2072	11.1(87)	5	—	—	—	—	—	—	—	—	—	—	—	—	282	6587

SIMS, DARRYL   Darryl Leon, DE-NT, 6′3″/278 lbs; Wisconsin; 1985: Pit, rnd 1; B7/23/1961 Winston-Salem, NC   **1985** Pit 16 (0)   **1986** Pit 16 (0)   **1987**†Cle 10 (4)   **1988**†Cle 16 (6, lde)   **NFL** 58 (10) [4 yrs]

SIMS, DAVID   David Bernard, RB, 6′3″/216 lbs; Georgia Tech; 1977: Sea, rnd 7; B10/26/1955 Atlanta, GA

1977	Sea	14(3)	99	369	3.7(17)	5	12	174	14.7(82)	1	3	4	1	25.0	43	10.8(43)	1	1	—	—	—	k	—	48	501
1978	Sea	12(9, FB)	174	752	4.3(44)	**14**	30	195	6.5(25)	1	1	1	100.0	15	15.0(15)	0	0	—	—	—	—	—	90	1002
1979	Sea	3(3)	20	53	2.7(8)	0	4	28	7.0(13)	0	2	1	50.0	18	9.0(18)	0	0	—	—	—	—	—	0	76
NFL	3	29(15)	293	1174	4.0(44)	19	46	399	8.7(82)	4	7	3	42.9	76	10.9(43)	1	1	—	—	—	k	—	138	1579

SIMS, GEORGE   George P., DB, 5′11″/170 lbs; Baylor; 1949: LARm, rnd 2/Bal-A, rnd 1; B10/23/1927 Afton, TX   **1949**†LARm 12 (0)   **1950** LARm 9   **NFL** 21 [2 yrs]

SIMS, JACK   Jack Willard, G, 6′3″/260 lbs; Hawaii; B4/21/1962 San Mateo, CA   **1987** Sea 3 (2)

SIMS, JIM   James, LB, 6′0″/195 lbs; USC; 1974: NYG, rnd 12; B12/28/1953 Galveston, TX   **1976** TB 2 (1)

YEAR	TEAM	G (GS, POS)	RUSH	YD	AVG (LG)	TD	REC	YD	AVG (LG)	TD	PASS	COMP	PCT	YD	AVG (LG)	TD	INT	SK	YD	QBR	KPR	OTD	PTS	TAY

Sims, Joe Joseph Anthony, T, 6´3˝/310 lbs; Nebraska; 1991: Atl, rnd 11; B3/1/1969 Sudbury, MA **1991**†Atl 6 (0) **1992** GB 15 (0) **1993**†GB 13 (5, rt) **1994**†GB 15 (15, RT) **1995** GB 4 (1) **NFL** 53 (21) [5 yrs]

Sims, Keith Keith Alexander, G, 6´3˝/309 lbs; Iowa State; 1990: Mia, rnd 2; B6/17/1967 Baltimore, MD **1990**†Mia 14 (13, LG) **1992**†Mia 16 (16, LG) **1993** Mia✧16 (16, LG) **1994**†Mia★16 (16, LG) **1995**†Mia★16 (16, LG) **1996** Mia 15 (15, LG) **1997**†Mia 8 (4) **1998** Was 4 (0) **1999**†Was 12 (12, LG) **2000** Was 13 (13, LG)

YEAR	TEAM	G (GS, POS)	RUSH	YD	AVG (LG)	TD	REC	YD	AVG (LG)	TD	PASS	COMP	PCT	YD	AVG (LG)	TD	INT	SK	YD	QBR	KPR	OTD	PTS	TAY
1991	Mia	12 (12, LG)	—	—	—	—	1	9	9.0 (9)	0	—	—	—	—	—	—	—	—	—	—	—	—	0	5
NFL	11	142 (133)	—	—	—	—	1	9	9.0 (9)	0	—	—	—	—	—	—	—	—	—	—	k	—	0	-2

Sims, Ken Kenneth L., DB, 5´9˝/177 lbs; Iowa; B11/9/1963 East St. Louis, IL **1987** SL 3 (2)

Sims, Kenneth Kenneth Wayne, DE, 6´5˝/272 lbs; Texas; 1982: NE, rnd 1; B10/31/1959 Kosse, TX **1982**†NE 9 (9, LDE) **1983** NE 5 (2) **1984** NE 16 (16, LDE) **1985** NE 13 (13, LDE) **1986** NE 3 (0) **1987** NE 12 (8, LDE) **1988** NE 1 (1) **1989** NE 15 (15, LDE) **NFL** 74 (64) [8 yrs]

Sims, Marvin Marvin, FB, 6´4˝/234 lbs; Clemson; 1980: Bal, rnd 12; B6/8/1957 Columbus, GA **1981** Bal 16 (0)

YEAR	TEAM	G (GS, POS)	RUSH	YD	AVG (LG)	TD	REC	YD	AVG (LG)	TD	PASS	COMP	PCT	YD	AVG (LG)	TD	INT	SK	YD	QBR	KPR	OTD	PTS	TAY
1980	Bal	16 (3)	54	186	3.4 (13)	2	9	64	7.1 (13)	0	—	—	—	—	—	—	—	—	—	—	k	—	12	233
NFL	2	32 (3)	54	186	3.4 (13)	2	9	64	7.1 (13)	0	—	—	—	—	—	—	—	—	—	—	k	—	12	240

Sims, Mickey Robert Anderson, DT-NT, 6´5˝/278 lbs; South Carolina State; 1977: Cle, rnd 4; B3/5/1955 Union, SC **1977** Cle 12 (7, RDT) **1978** Cle 15 **1979** Cle 16 (LDT/nt) **NFL** 43 (7) [3 yrs]

Sims, Reggie Reginald Kenneth, TE, 6´4˝/253 lbs; Northern Illinois; B7/30/1962 Waynesboro, GA **1987** Cin 1 (0)

Sims, Ryan Ryan O'Neal, DT, 6´4˝/315 lbs; North Carolina; 2002: KC, rnd 1; B5/4/1980 Spartanburg, SC **2002** KC 6 (2) **2003**†KC 16 (16, RDT) **2004** KC 15 (13, LDT) **2005** KC 6 (5, ldt) **NFL** 43 (36) [4 yrs]

Sims, Tom Thomas Sidney, DT-NT, 6´2˝/291 lbs; Western Michigan; Pittsburgh; 1990: KC, rnd 6; B4/18/1967 Detroit, MI **1991**†KC 14 (0) **1992**†KC 12 (0) **1993** Ind 5 (3) **1994** Ind 16 (1) **NFL** 47 (4) [4 yrs]

Sims, Tommy Thomas Edward, DB, 6´0˝/190 lbs; Tennessee; 1986: Ind, rnd 7; B9/29/1964 Americus, GA **1986** Ind 1 (0)

Sims, Wes Wesley O., G, 6´4˝/317 lbs; Oklahoma; 2005: SD, rnd 6; B4/8/1981 Weatherford, OK **2005** SD 2 (0)

Sims, William William Alfred, LB, 6´3˝/258 lbs; Louisiana-Lafayette; B12/30/1970 Frankfurt, Germany **1994** Min 8 (0)

Sinceno, Kaseem Kaseem T., TE, 6´4˝/259 lbs; Syracuse; B3/26/1976 Bronx, NY

YEAR	TEAM	G (GS, POS)	RUSH	YD	AVG (LG)	TD	REC	YD	AVG (LG)	TD	PASS	COMP	PCT	YD	AVG (LG)	TD	INT	SK	YD	QBR	KPR	OTD	PTS	TAY
1998	Phi	10 (0)	—	—	—	—	3	42	14.0 (22)	1	—	—	—	—	—	—	—	—	—	—	—	—	6	26
2000	ChiB	11 (11, TE)	—	—	—	—	23	206	9.0 (28)	0	—	—	—	—	—	—	—	—	—	—	k	—	0	100
NFL	2	21 (11)	—	—	—	—	26	248	9.5 (28)	1	—	—	—	—	—	—	—	—	—	—	k	—	6	126

Sinclair, Michael Michael Glenn, DE, 6´4˝/267 lbs; Eastern New Mexico; 1991: Sea, rnd 6; B1/31/1968 Galveston, TX **[S]** **1992** Sea 12 (1) **1993** Sea 9 (1) **1994** Sea 12 (2) **1995** Sea 16 (15, LDE) **1996** Sea★16 (16, LDE) **1997** Sea★16 (16, LDE) **1998** Sea★16 (16, LDE) **1999**†Sea 15 (15, LDE) **2000** Sea 16 (16, LDE) **2001** Sea 16 (16, LDE) **2002** Phi 4 (0) **NFL** 148 (114) [11 yrs]

Singer, Curt Curt Edward, T, 6´5˝/278 lbs; Tennessee; 1984: Was, rnd 6; B11/4/1961 Aliquippa, PA **1986** Sea 11 (0) **1988** Det 3 (0) **1989** NYJ 6 (1) **1991** Sea 13 (0) **NFL** 33 (1) [4 yrs]

Singer, Karl Karl Kenneth, T, 6´3˝/250 lbs; Purdue; 1966: Bos, rnd 1/Cle, rnd 19; B10/12/1943 Warren, OH **1966** Bos-A 14 **1967** Bos-A 14 **1968** Bos-A 11 (1) **NFL** 39 (1) [3 yrs]

Singer, Walt Walter Wallace, E-DE, 6´0˝/198 lbs; Syracuse; B12/6/1911 Jersey City, NJ, D2/5/1992 New York, NY

YEAR	TEAM	G (GS, POS)	RUSH	YD	AVG (LG)	TD	REC	YD	AVG (LG)	TD	PASS	COMP	PCT	YD	AVG (LG)	TD	INT	SK	YD	QBR	KPR	OTD	PTS	TAY
1935	†NYG	10 (5, LE)	—	—	—	—	2	22	11.0	1	—	—	—	—	—	—	—	—	—	—	—	—	6	16
1936	NYG	12 (10, LE)	—	—	—	—	6	38	6.3	0	—	—	—	—	—	—	—	—	—	—	—	1	6	19
NFL	2	22 (15)	—	—	—	—	8	60	7.5	1	—	—	—	—	—	—	—	—	—	—	—	1	12	35

Singletary, Bill Williams James, LB, 6´2˝/233 lbs; Temple; 1973: SD, rnd 4; B3/18/1951 Camden, NJ **1974** NYG 3

Singletary, Mike Michael, LB, 6´0˝/230 lbs; Baylor; 1981: Chi, rnd 2; B10/9/1958 Houston, TX; HOF 1998 **1981** ChiB 16 (9, MLB) **1982** ChiB 9 (9, MLB) **1983** ChiB★16 (16, MLB) **1984**†ChiB★16 (16, MLB) **1985**†ChiB★16 (16, MLB) **1986**†ChiB★14 (14, MLB) **1987**†ChiB★12 (12, MLB) **1988**†ChiB★16 (16, MLB) **1989** ChiB★16 (16, MLB) **1990**†ChiB★16 (16, MLB) **1991**†ChiB★16 (16, MLB) **1992** ChiB✧16 (16, MLB) **NFL** 179 (172) [12 yrs]

Singletary, Reggie Reggie Leslie, G-T-DT, 6´3˝/279 lbs; North Carolina State; 1986: Phi, rnd 12; B1/17/1964 Whiteville, NC **1986** Phi 16 (6, rdt) **1988**†Phi 16 (9, RG) **1989**†Phi 1 (0) **1990**†Phi 16 (16, RT)

YEAR	TEAM	G (GS, POS)	RUSH	YD	AVG (LG)	TD	REC	YD	AVG (LG)	TD	PASS	COMP	PCT	YD	AVG (LG)	TD	INT	SK	YD	QBR	KPR	OTD	PTS	TAY
1987	Phi	12 (0)	—	—	—	—	1	-11	-11.0 (-11)	0	—	—	—	—	—	—	—	—	—	—	—	—	0	-6
NFL	5	61 (31)	—	—	—	—	1	-11	-11.0 (-11)	0	—	—	—	—	—	—	—	—	—	—	S	—	0	-6

Singleton, Alshermond Alshermond Glendale, LB, 6´2˝/228 lbs; Temple; 1997: TB, rnd 4; B8/7/1975 Newark, NJ **1997** TB 12 (0) **1998** TB 15 (0) **1999**†TB 15 (0) **2000**†TB 13 (1) **2001**†TB 16 (0) **2002**†TB 16 (14, LLB) **2003**†Dal 16 (15, LLB) **2004** Dal 13 (12, LLB) **2005** Dal 8 (7, llb) **NFL** 124 (49) [9 yrs]

Singleton, Bill William, G, 5´9˝/190 lbs; Washington-St. Louis; B2/7/1897, D10/1971 Sycamore, IL **1922** Ham 1 (0)

Singleton, Chris Chris, LB, 6´2˝/246 lbs; Arizona; 1990: NE, rnd 1; B2/20/1967 Parsippany, NJ **1990** NE 13 (4) **1991** NE 12 (11, ROLB) **1992** NE 8 (7, rolb) **1993** NE 8 (4) **1993** Mia 9 (0) **1994** Mia 11 (11, LLB) **1995**†Mia 16 (15, LLB) **1996** Mia 14 (13, RLB) **NFL** 91 (65) [7 yrs]

Singleton, John John Edward, TB-WB, 5´11˝/175 lbs; none; B11/27/1896 Gallipolis, OH, D10/23/1937 Dayton, OH **1929** Day 5 (2)

Singleton, Nate Nathaniel, WR, 5´11˝/190 lbs; Grambling State; 1992: NYG, rnd 11; B7/5/1968 New Orleans, LA

YEAR	TEAM	G (GS, POS)	RUSH	YD	AVG (LG)	TD	REC	YD	AVG (LG)	TD	PASS	COMP	PCT	YD	AVG (LG)	TD	INT	SK	YD	QBR	KPR	OTD	PTS	TAY
1993	SF	16 (0)	—	—	—	—	8	126	15.8 (33)	1	—	—	—	—	—	—	—	—	—	—	—	—	6	68
1994	†SF	16 (1)	—	—	—	—	21	294	14.0 (43)	2	—	—	—	—	—	—	—	—	—	—	kp	—	12	153
1995	†SF	6 (2)	—	—	—	—	8	108	13.5 (23)	1	—	—	—	—	—	—	—	—	—	—	p	—	6	61
1996	SF	2 (0)	—	—	—	—	1	11	11.0 (11)	0	—	—	—	—	—	—	—	—	—	—	kp	—	0	23
1997	Bal	4 (0)	—	—	—	—	—	—	—	—	—	—	—	—	—	—	—	—	—	—	k	—	0	4
NFL	5	44 (3)	—	—	—	—	38	539	14.2 (43)	4	—	—	—	—	—	—	—	—	—	—	kp	—	24	309

Singleton, Ron Ronald Lee, T, 6´7˝/260 lbs; Grambling State; 1976: SD, rnd 4; B4/15/1952 New Orleans, LA **1976** SD 13 **1977** SF 1 **1978** SF 14 (9, lt) **1979** SF 16 (15, LT) **1980** SF 15 (15, LT) **NFL** 59 (39) [5 yrs]

Sinko, Steve Stephen Patrick, T-G, 6´3˝/232 lbs; Duquesne; B9/15/1910 Chisholm, MN, D3/1/1999 Barnstable, MA **1934** Bos 10 (2) **1935** Bos 9 (0) **1936**†Bos 11 (1) **NFL** 30 (3) [3 yrs]

Sinkovitz, Frank Frank Bernard, LB-C, 6´1˝/218 lbs; Duke; B5/20/1923 Steelton, PA, D8/6/1989 Baltimore, MD **1947**†Pit 9 (0) **1948** Pit 9 (3) **1949** Pit 12 (3) **1950** Pit 11 (LLB) **1951** Pit 12 (LLB) **1952** Pit 11 (RLB) **NFL** 64 (6) [6 yrs]

Sinkwich, Frankie Francis Frank, B, 5´11˝/190 lbs; Georgia; 1943: Det, rnd 1; B10/10/1920 McKees Rocks, PA, D10/22/1990 Athens, GA **[K]**

YEAR	TEAM	G (GS, POS)	RUSH	YD	AVG (LG)	TD	REC	YD	AVG (LG)	TD	PASS	COMP	PCT	YD	AVG (LG)	TD	INT	SK	YD	QBR	KPR	OTD	PTS	TAY
1943	Det☆	10 (4, TB)	93	266	2.9 (17)	1	1	8	8.0 (8)	0	126	50	39.7	699	5.5 (67)	7	20	—	—	37.2	KPkpi	1	12	135
1944	Det☆	10 (9, TB)	150	563	3.8 (72)	6	—	—	—	—	148	58	39.2	1060	7.2 (57)	12	20	—	—	52.0	KPkpi	—	66	573
NFL	2	20 (13)	243	829	3.4 (72)	7	1	8	8.0 (8)	0	274	108	39.4	1759	6.4 (67)	19	40	—	—	45.2	KPkpi	1	78	708
1946	NYY-A	4 (0)	7	20	2.9	0	—	—	—	—	12	5	41.7	61	5.1	0	2	—	—	—	—	—	0	-30
1947	NYY-A	3 (1)	16	33	2.1	0	—	—	—	—	15	8	53.3	93	6.2	0	0	—	—	—	P	—	0	80
1947	Bal-A	8 (2)	55	208	3.8	0	1	3	3.0 (3)	0	—	—	—	—	—	—	—	—	—	—	Pkp	—	0	263
AAFC	2	15 (3)	78	261	3.3 (72)	0	1	3	3.0 (8)	0	27	13	48.1	154	5.7 (67)	0	2	—	—	35.1	Pkp	—	0	313

Sinnott, Greg Edward Greg, T, 6´7˝/280 lbs; Utah State; B8/29/1964 Santa Cruz, CA **1987** LARm 1 (0)

Sinnott, John John Desmond, T, 6´4˝/275 lbs; Brown; 1980: SL, rnd 3; B4/18/1958 Wexford, Ireland **1982** Bal 9 (7, LT)

Sipe, Brian Brian Winfield, QB, 6´1˝/195 lbs; San Diego State; 1972: Cle, rnd 13; B8/8/1949 San Diego, CA **[K]**

YEAR	TEAM	G (GS, POS)	RUSH	YD	AVG (LG)	TD	REC	YD	AVG (LG)	TD	PASS	COMP	PCT	YD	AVG (LG)	TD	INT	SK	YD	QBR	KPR	OTD	PTS	TAY
1974	Cle	10 (5, qb)	16	44	2.8 (17)	4	—	—	—	—	108	59	54.6	603	5.6 (37)	1	7	15	122	—	—	—	24	111
1975	Cle	7 (2)	9	60	6.7 (21)	0	—	—	—	—	88	45	51.1	427	4.9 (22)	1	3	8	58	—	—	—	0	159
1976	Cle	14 (12, QB)	18	71	3.9 (17)	0	—	—	—	—	312	178	57.1	2113	6.8 (52)	17	14	16	142	77.3	K	—	1	653
1977	Cle	9 (9, QB)	10	14	1.4 (9)	0	—	—	—	—	195	112	57.4	1233	6.3 (52)	9	14	16	114	—	—	—	0	116
1978	Cle	16 (16, QB)	28	87	3.1 (35)	3	—	—	—	—	399	222	55.6	2906	7.3 (69)	21	15	29	229	80.7	—	—	18	1075
1979	Cle☆	16 (16, QB)	45	178	4.0 (34)	2	—	—	—	—	**535**	286	53.5	3793	7.1 (74)	**28**	**26**	43	347	73.4	—	—	12	1195
1980	†Cle★	16 (16, QB)	20	55	2.8 (24)	1	—	—	—	—	554	337	60.8	4132	7.5 (65)	**30**	14	23	217	**91.4**	—	—	6	1721

YEAR	TEAM	G (GS, POS)	RUSH	YD	AVG (LG)	TD	REC	YD	AVG (LG)	TD	PASS	COMP	PCT	YD	AVG (LG)	TD	INT	SK	YD	QBR	KPR	OTD	PTS	TAY
1981	Cle	16 (16, QB)	38	153	4.0 (22)	1	—	—	—	—	567	313	55.2	3876	6.8 (62)	17	**25**	34	310	68.2	—	—	6	1186
1982	Cle	6 (6, QB)	13	44	3.4 (12)	0	—	—	—	—	185	101	54.6	1064	5.8 (40)	4	8	13	117	60.7	—	—	0	276
1983	Cle	15 (14, QB)	26	56	2.2 (9)	0	—	—	—	—	496	291	58.7	3566	7.2 (66)	**26**	23	27	233	79.1	—	—	0	1049
NFL	10	125 (112)	223	762	3.4 (35)	11	—	—	—	—	3439	1944	56.5	23713	6.9 (74)	154	149	224	1889	74.8	K	—	67	7539

SIRAGUSA, TONY Anthony 'The Goose', DT-NT, 6´3˝/330 lbs; Pittsburgh; B5/14/1967 Kenilworth, NJ **1990** Ind 13 (6, nt) **1991** Ind 13 (6, nt) **1992** Ind 16 (12, NT) **1993** Ind 14 (14, RDT) **1994** Ind 16 (16, RDT) **1995**†Ind 14 (14, RDT) **1996** Ind 10 (10, RDT) **1997** Bal 14 (13, RDT) **1998** Bal 15 (15, RDT) **1999** Bal 14 (14, RDT) **2000**†Bal 15 (15, RDT) **2001**†Bal 15 (13, RDT) **NFL** 169 (148) [12 yrs]

SIRMON, PETER Peter Anton, LB, 6´2˝/237 lbs; Oregon; 2000: Ten, rnd 4; B2/18/1977 Walla Walla, WA **2000** Ten 5 (0) **2001** Ten 16 (0) **2002**†Ten 16 (11, LLB) **2003**†Ten 14 (14, LLB) **2005** Ten 14 (13, LLB) **NFL** 65 (38) [5 yrs]

SIROCHMAN, GEORGE George, G, 6´2˝/215 lbs; Duquesne; B3/23/1918 Maxwell, PA, D1/2/1996 Washington, PA **1942** Pit 2 (0) **1944** Det 9 (1) **NFL** 11 (1) [2 yrs]

SISEMORE, JERRY Jerald Grant, T-G, 6´4˝/265 lbs; Texas; 1973: Phi, rnd 1; B7/16/1951 Olton, TX **1973** Phi 13 (13, RT) **1974** Phi 14 (14, RT) **1975** Phi 14 (14, RT) **1976** Phi 14 (14, RG) **1977** Phi 14 (14, RG) **1978**†Phi 16 (16, RT) **1979**†Phi★16 (16, RT) **1980**†Phi 16 (16, RT) **1981**†Phi★16 (16, RT) **1982** Phi 7 (7, RT) **1983** Phi 14 (13, RT) **1984** Phi 2 (2) **NFL** 156 (155) [12 yrs]

SISK, JOHN John Martin, DB, 6´3˝/195 lbs; Marquette; Miami (FL); 1963: Chi, rnd 17/KC, rnd 29; B7/15/1941 Milwaukee, WI **1964** ChiB 3

SISK, JOHNNY John Martin, HB, 6´2˝/197 lbs; Marquette; B12/11/1905 New Haven, CT, D5/27/1986 Wauwatosa, WI

YEAR	TEAM	G (GS, POS)	RUSH	YD	AVG (LG)	TD	REC	YD	AVG (LG)	TD	PASS	COMP	PCT	YD	AVG (LG)	TD	INT	SK	YD	QBR	KPR	OTD	PTS	TAY
1932	ChiB	13 (1)	28	124	4.4	0	3	32	10.7	0	3	1	33.3	8	2.7 (8)	0	0	—	—	—	—	—	0	144
1933	†ChiB	13 (10, RH)	52	219	4.2	1	5	93	18.6	0	1	0	0.0	0	0.0	0	0	—	—	—	—	—	6	276
1934	†ChiB	8 (1)	41	166	4.0	1	2	44	22.0	0	9	2	22.2	13	1.4	0	2	—	—	—	—	—	6	125
1935	ChiB	12 (3)	38	222	5.8	1	1	44	44.0 (44)	0	1	1	100.0	1	-1.0 (-1)	0	0	—	—	—	—	—	6	254
1936	ChiB	10 (4)	41	163	4.0	0	1	39	39.0 (39)	0	—	—	—	—	—	—	—	—	—	—	—	—	0	183
NFL	5	56 (19)	200	894	4.5	3	12	252	21.0 (44)	0	14	4	28.6	20	1.4 (8)	0	2	—	—	—	—	—	18	980

SISLEY, BRIAN Brian, DE, 6´4˝/235 lbs; South Dakota State; B1/18/1964 Hot Springs, AR **1987** NYG 3 (0)

SISSON, SCOTT Scott O'Neal, K, 6´0˝/197 lbs; Georgia Tech; 1993: NE, rnd 5; B7/21/1971 Marietta, GA **[K]** **1993** NE 13 (0) **1996**†Min 16 (0) **NFL** 29 (0) [2 yrs]

SISTRUNK, MANNY Manuel, DT-DE, 6´5˝/269 lbs; Arkansas-Pine Bluff; 1970: Was, rnd 5; B6/16/1947 Montgomery, AL **1970** Was 10 (3) **1971**†Was 14 (14, LDT) **1972**†Was 12 (4) **1973**†Was 12 (2) **1974** Was 2 (1) **1975** Was 13 (1) **1976** Phi 14 (13, LDT) **1977** Phi 14 (14, LDE) **1978**†Phi 16 (10, LDE) **1979**†Phi 16 **NFL** 123 (62) [10 yrs]

SISTRUNK, OTIS Otis, DT-DE-NT, 6´4˝/265 lbs; none; B9/18/1946 Columbus, GA **1972**†Oak 14 (14, LDT) **1973**†Oak 14 (14, LDT) **1974**†Oak★14 (14, LDT) **1975**†Oak☆14 (14, LDT) **1976**†Oak 14 (RDE) **1977**†Oak 12 (12, RDE) **1978** Oak 16 (16, NT) **NFL** 98 (84) [7 yrs]

SITES, VINNIE Vincent J., E, 6´2˝/215 lbs; Pittsburgh; B7/9/1912 Pittston, PA, D9/12/1983 San Diego, CA

YEAR	TEAM	G (GS, POS)	RUSH	YD	AVG (LG)	TD	REC	YD	AVG (LG)	TD	PASS	COMP	PCT	YD	AVG (LG)	TD	INT	SK	YD	QBR	KPR	OTD	PTS	TAY
1936	Pit	12 (7, RE)	—	—	—	—	2	22	11.0	0	—	—	—	—	—	—	—	—	—	—	—	—	0	11
1937	Pit	7 (1)	—	—	—	—	2	10	5.0	0	—	—	—	—	—	—	—	—	—	—	—	—	0	5
NFL	2	19 (8)	—	—	—	—	4	32	8.0	0	—	—	—	—	—	—	—	—	—	—	—	—	0	16

SITKO, EMIL Emil Martin, HB, 5´8˝/183 lbs; Notre Dame; 1946: LA, rnd 1; B9/7/1923 Fort Wayne, IN, D12/15/1973 Fort Wayne, IN

YEAR	TEAM	G (GS, POS)	RUSH	YD	AVG (LG)	TD	REC	YD	AVG (LG)	TD	PASS	COMP	PCT	YD	AVG (LG)	TD	INT	SK	YD	QBR	KPR	OTD	PTS	TAY
1950	SF	8	23	105	4.6 (15)	1	3	43	14.3 (28)	1	—	—	—	—	—	—	—	—	—	—	—	—	12	142
1951	ChiC	11	52	183	3.5 (61)	0	4	28	7.0 (15)	0	—	—	—	—	—	—	—	—	—	—	k	—	0	371
1952	ChiC	11 (RH)	88	348	4.0 (46)	1	2	16	8.0 (10)	0	—	—	—	—	—	—	—	—	—	—	k	—	6	370
NFL	3	30	163	636	3.9 (61)	2	9	87	9.7 (28)	1	—	—	—	—	—	—	—	—	—	—	k	—	18	883

SIVELL, JIM Ralph James, G, 5´9˝/205 lbs; Auburn; 1938: Bkn, rnd 10; B3/12/1914 Chipley, GA, D3/16/1997 Troup County, GA **1938** Bkn 11 (5, lg) **1939** Bkn 10 (2) **1940** Bkn 11 (11, RG) **1941** Bkn✧11 (11, RG) **1942** Bkn 8 (8, RG) **1944** Bkn 5 (0) **1944**†NYG 5 (5, RG) **1945** NYG 9 (6, RG) **NFL** 70 (48) [7 yrs]

1946 Mia-A 10 (1)

SIWEK, MIKE Michael Joseph, DT, 6´3˝/265 lbs; Western Michigan; 1970: SL, rnd 11; B4/12/1948 Mishawaka, IN **1970** SL 2

SKAGGS, JIM James Lee, G-T, 6´3˝/250 lbs; Washington; 1962: Phi, rnd 10/Oak, rnd 12; B1/3/1940 Wetumka, OK **1963** Phi 3 **1964** Phi 14 (6, lt) **1965** Phi 14 (14, RG) **1966** Phi 14 (14, RG) **1967** Phi 14 (RG) **1969** Phi 7 (RG) **1970** Phi 14 (RG) **1971** Phi 10 **1972** Phi 10 (6, lg) **NFL** 100 (40) [9 yrs]

SKAGGS, JUSTIN Justin, WR, 6´2˝/200 lbs; Evangel (MO); B4/22/1979 Wentzville, MO **2002** Was 1 (0)

SKANSI, PAUL Paul Anthony, WR, 5´11˝/186 lbs; Washington; 1983: Pit, rnd 5; B1/11/1960 Tacoma, WA **[R]**

YEAR	TEAM	G (GS, POS)	RUSH	YD	AVG (LG)	TD	REC	YD	AVG (LG)	TD	PASS	COMP	PCT	YD	AVG (LG)	TD	INT	SK	YD	QBR	KPR	OTD	PTS	TAY
1983	Pit	15 (0)	—	—	—	—	3	39	13.0 (21)	0	—	—	—	—	—	—	—	—	—	—	p	—	0	168
1984	†Sea	7 (0)	—	—	—	—	7	85	12.1 (27)	0	—	—	—	—	—	—	—	—	—	—	p	—	0	108
1985	Sea	12 (0)	—	—	—	—	21	269	12.8 (32)	1	—	—	—	—	—	—	—	—	—	—	kp	—	6	370
1986	Sea	16 (0)	—	—	—	—	22	271	12.3 (30)	0	—	—	—	—	—	—	—	—	—	—	kp	—	0	155
1987	†Sea	12 (0)	—	—	—	—	19	207	10.9 (25)	1	—	—	—	—	—	—	—	—	—	—	—	—	6	109
1988	†Sea	16 (1)	—	—	—	—	24	238	9.9 (21)	1	—	—	—	—	—	—	—	—	—	—	—	—	6	124
1989	Sea	16 (1)	—	—	—	—	39	488	12.5 (26)	5	—	—	—	—	—	—	—	—	—	—	—	—	30	269
1990	Sea	16 (0)	—	—	—	—	22	257	11.7 (25)	2	—	—	—	—	—	—	—	—	—	—	—	—	12	139
1991	Sea	5 (0)	—	—	—	—	9	96	10.7 (21)	0	—	—	—	—	—	—	—	—	—	—	p	—	0	48
NFL	9	115 (2)	—	—	—	—	166	1950	11.7 (32)	10	—	—	—	—	—	—	—	—	—	—	kp	—	60	1487

SKAUGSTAD, DARYLE Daryle Eugene, NT, 6´5˝/254 lbs; California; 1980: Hou, rnd 2; B4/8/1957 Seattle, WA **1981** Hou 16 (0) **1982** Hou 9 (0) **1983** SF 3 (0) **1983** GB 9 (2) **NFL** 37 (2) [3 yrs]

SKEATE, GIL Gilbert, FB, 5´10˝/190 lbs; Gonzaga; B5/19/1901, D1/1952 **1927** GB 2 (1)

SKENE, DOUG Douglas C., G, 6´6˝/295 lbs; Michigan; 1993: Phi, rnd 8; B6/17/1970 Fairview, TX **1994** NE 6 (6, rg)

SKIBINSKI, JOE Joseph John, G, 5´11˝/245 lbs; Purdue; 1951: Cle, rnd 15; B12/23/1928 Chicago, IL **1952**†Cle 12 (rg) **1955** GB 12 (LG) **1956** GB 12 (LG) **NFL** 36 [3 yrs]

SKIBINSKI, JOHN John Joseph, RB, 6´0˝/222 lbs; Purdue; 1978: Chi, rnd 6; B4/27/1955 Chicago, IL **1978** ChiB 16 **1981** ChiB 11 (0)

YEAR	TEAM	G (GS, POS)	RUSH	YD	AVG (LG)	TD	REC	YD	AVG (LG)	TD	PASS	COMP	PCT	YD	AVG (LG)	TD	INT	SK	YD	QBR	KPR	OTD	PTS	TAY
1979	ChiB	1 (1)	3	10	3.3 (4)	0	1	4	4.0 (4)	0	—	—	—	—	—	—	—	—	—	—	—	—	0	12
1980	ChiB	16 (0)	13	54	4.2 (8)	0	5	18	3.6 (8)	0	—	—	—	—	—	—	—	—	—	—	—	—	0	63
NFL	4	44 (1)	16	64	4.0 (8)	0	6	22	3.7 (8)	0	—	—	—	—	—	—	—	—	—	—	k	—	0	66

SKINNER, GERALD Gerald Lynn, T, 6´4˝/260 lbs; Arkansas; 1977: NE, rnd 4; B9/12/1954 Malvern, AR **1978** GB 15

SKINNER, LEW Lewis B., G-C, Purdue; B11/1898 Indianapolis, IN, deceased **1920** Ham 1 (1) **1922** Evv 1 (1) **NFL** 2 (2) [2 yrs]

SKLADANY, JOE Joseph Peter, E, 5´10˝/210 lbs; Pittsburgh; B5/25/1911 Larksville, PA, D8/9/1972 Pittsburgh, PA

YEAR	TEAM	G (GS, POS)	RUSH	YD	AVG (LG)	TD	REC	YD	AVG (LG)	TD	PASS	COMP	PCT	YD	AVG (LG)	TD	INT	SK	YD	QBR	KPR	OTD	PTS	TAY
1934	Pit	12 (12, RE)	—	—	—	—	9	222	24.7 (62)	2	—	—	—	—	—	—	—	—	—	—	—	—	12	121

SKLADANY, LEO Leo Bernard, E, 6´1˝/210 lbs; Pittsburgh; 1949: Phi, rnd 17/Bkn-A, rnd 6; B8/9/1927 Larksville, PA, D3/18/2003 Pittsburgh, PA **1949**†Phi 3 (1) **1950**†NYG 4 **NFL** 7 (1) [2 yrs]

SKLADANY, TOM Thomas Edward, P, 6´0˝/192 lbs; Ohio State; 1977: Cle, rnd 2; B6/29/1955 Bethel Park, PA **[P]**

YEAR	TEAM	G (GS, POS)	RUSH	YD	AVG (LG)	TD	REC	YD	AVG (LG)	TD	PASS	COMP	PCT	YD	AVG (LG)	TD	INT	SK	YD	QBR	KPR	OTD	PTS	TAY
1978	Det☆	16	—	—	—	—	—	—	—	—	1	0	0.0	0	0.0	0	0	—	—	—	P	—	0	0
1979	Det	2	—	—	—	—	—	—	—	—	1	0	0.0	0	0.0	0	0	—	—	—	P	—	0	0
1980	Det	16 (0)	—	—	—	—	—	—	—	—	2	2	100.0	38	19.0 (19)	0	0	—	—	—	P	—	0	19
1981	Det★	16 (0)	—	—	—	—	—	—	—	—	3	3	100.0	43	14.3 (19)	0	0	—	—	—	P	—	0	22
1982	†Det	7 (0)	—	—	—	—	—	—	—	—	1	0	0.0	0	0.0	0	0	—	—	—	P	—	0	0
1983	Phi	4 (0)	—	—	—	—	—	—	—	—	—	—	—	—	—	—	—	—	—	—	P	—	0	0
NFL	6	61	—	—	—	—	—	—	—	—	8	5	62.5	81	10.1 (19)	0	0	—	—	—	P	—	0	41

SKLOPAN, JOHN John Joseph, DB, 5´10˝/200 lbs; Southern Mississippi; 1963: KC, rnd 8/Min, rnd 12; B9/12/1940 Pittsburgh, PA **1963** Den-A 3

SKOCZEN, STAN Stanley Edward, HB, 5´11˝/187 lbs; Case Western Reserve; B10/12/1920 Independence, OH

YEAR	TEAM	G (GS, POS)	RUSH	YD	AVG (LG)	TD	REC	YD	AVG (LG)	TD	PASS	COMP	PCT	YD	AVG (LG)	TD	INT	SK	YD	QBR	KPR	OTD	PTS	TAY
1944	Cle	1 (0)	1	0	0.0 (0)	0	—	—	—	—	—	—	—	—	—	—	—	—	—	—	—	—	0	0

SKOGLUND, BOB Robert Walter, DE, 6´1˝/198 lbs; Notre Dame; 1947: GB, rnd 13; B7/29/1925 Chicago, IL, D1/1/1949 Chicago, IL **1947** GB 9 (1)

Skorich, Nick Nicholas Leonard, G, 5´9˝/197 lbs; Cincinnati; 1943: Pit, rnd 17; B6/26/1921 Bellaire, OH, D10/2/2004 Princeton, NJ **[C]** **1946** Pit 8 (0) **1947**†Pit 12 (6, RG) **1948** Pit 12 (1) **NFL** 32 (7) [3 yrs]

Skoronski, Bob Robert Francis, T-C, 6´3˝/249 lbs; Indiana; 1956: GB, rnd 5; B3/5/1934 Ansonia, CT **1956** GB 12 (LT) **1959** GB 12 (LT) **1960**†GB 12 (LT) **1961**†GB 13 (LT) **1962**†GB 13 (LT) **1963** GB 14 (LT) **1964** GB 14 (C) **1965**†GB 14 (LT) **1966**†GB✧14 (LT) **1967**†GB 14 (LT) **1968** GB 14 (LT) **NFL** 146 [11 yrs]

Skoronski, Ed Edmund John, E-C-LB, 6´2˝/213 lbs; Georgetown (DC); Purdue; B10/15/1910 Chicago, IL, D12/22/1996 **1935** Pit 3 (0) **1937** Cle 3 (0) **1937** Bkn 5 (4)

YEAR	TEAM	G(GS, POS)	RUSH	YD	AVG(LG)	TD	REC	YD	AVG(LG)	TD	PASS	COMP	PCT	YD	AVG(LG)	TD	INT	SK	YD	QBR	KPR	OTD	PTS	TAY
1936	Pit	12(6, LE)	—	—	—	—	8	95	11.9(19)	1	—	—	—	—	—	—	—	—	—	—	—	—	6	53
NFL	3	23(10)	—	—	—	—	8	95	11.9(19)	1	—	—	—	—	—	—	—	—	—	—	—	—	6	53

Skorupan, John John Paul, LB, 6´2˝/222 lbs; Penn State; 1973: Buf, rnd 6; B5/17/1951 Beaver, PA **1973** Buf 14 (LLB) **1974** Buf 6 (lilb) **1975** Buf 14 (14, LOLB) **1976** Buf 14 (14, LLB) **1977** Buf 2 **1978** NYG 16 **1979** NYG 14 **1980** NYG 12 (10, ROLB) **NFL** 92 (38) [8 yrs]

Skow, Jim James Jeffrey, DE, 6´3˝/253 lbs; Nebraska; 1986: Cin, rnd 3; B6/29/1963 Omaha, NE **1986** Cin 16 (1) **1987** Cin 12 (12, RDE) **1988**†Cin 16 (16, RDE) **1989** Cin 11 (11, LDE) **1990** TB 12 (10, RDE) **1991** Sea 11 (1) **1992** SD 1 (0) **1992** LARm 4 (2) **NFL** 83 (53) [7 yrs]

Skrepenak, Greg Gregory Andrew, T-G, 6´7˝/316 lbs; Michigan; 1992: LARd, rnd 2; B1/31/1970 Wilkes-Barre, PA **1992** LARd 10 (0) **1994** LARd 12 (10, RT) **1995** Oak 14 (14, RT) **1996**†Car 16 (16, RG) **1997** Car 16 (16, RG) **NFL** 68 (56) [5 yrs]

Skudin, Dave Harry David, G-E, 5´11˝/195 lbs; NYU; B1/21/1905 Brooklyn, NY, D4/13/1972 **1929** SI 6 (6, LG)

Slaby, Lou Louis Richard, LB, 6´3˝/235 lbs; Pittsburgh; 1963: NYG, rnd 5/Den, rnd 4; B12/13/1941 Cleveland, OH **1964** NYG 14 (MLB) **1965** NYG 12 **1966** Det 13 **NFL** 39 [3 yrs]

Slackford, Fritz Frederick William, WB-FB-E, 6´0˝/180 lbs; Denison; Notre Dame; B3/1894 Sandusky, OH, deceased **1920** Day 6 (0) **1921** Can 10 (8, WB), 12 **NFL** 16 (8) [2 yrs]

Slade, Chris Christopher Carroll, LB, 6´5˝/245 lbs; Virginia; 1993: NE, rnd 2; B1/30/1971 Newport News, VA **[S]** **1993** NE 16 (5, rolb) **1994**†NE 16 (16, ROLB) **1995** NE 16 (16, ROLB) **1996**†NE 16 (9, llb) **1997**†NE★16 (16, LLB) **1998**†NE 15 (15, LLB) **1999** NE 16 (16, LLB) **2000** NE 16 (15, LILB) **2001** Car 15 (0) **NFL** 142 (108) [9 yrs]

Slagle, George George, G, none; B8/9/1898, SD, D4/1983 Hollister, ID **1926** Lou 1 (0)

Slater, Duke Frederick Wayman, T, 6´1˝/215 lbs; Iowa; B12/9/1898 Normal, IL, D8/14/1966 Chicago, IL **1922** RI 7 (7, RT) **1922** Mil 2 (2) **1923** RI☆8 (8, RT) **1924** RI☆8 (8, RT) **1925** RI☆11 (11, RT) **1926** ChiC 2 (0) **1927** ChiC☆11 (11, RT) **1928** ChiC 6 (6, RT) **1929** ChiC☆13 (13, RT), 6 **1930** ChiC☆13 (12, RT) **1931** ChiC 9 (9, RT) **NFL** 90 (87) [10 yrs]

Slater, Howie Howard Whitman, FB, 5´10˝/186 lbs; Washington State; B3/9/1903 Deer Park, WA, deceased **1926** Mil 9 (8, FB), 6

Slater, Jackie Jackie Ray, T-G, 6´4˝/277 lbs; Jackson State; 1976: LA, rnd 3; B5/27/1954 Jackson, MS; HOF 2001 **1976**†LARm 14 **1977**†LARm 14 (1) **1978**†LARm 16 **1979**†LARm 16 (16, RT) **1980**†LARm 15 (15, RT) **1981** LARm 11 (11, rt/lt) **1982** LARm 9 (9, RT) **1983**†LARm★16 (16, RT) **1984** LARm 7 (7, rt) **1985**†LARm★16 (16, RT) **1986**†LARm★16 (16, RT) **1987** LARm★12 (12, RT) **1988**†LARm★16 (16, RT) **1989**†LARm★16 (16, RT) **1990** LARm★15 (15, RT) **1991** LARm 13 (13, RT) **1992** LARm 16 (16, RT) **1993** LARm 8 (8, RT) **1994** LARm 12 (7, rt) **1995** SL 1 (1) **NFL** 259 (211) [20 yrs]

Slater, Mark Mark William, C, 6´2˝/257 lbs; Minnesota; 1978: Phi, rnd 12; B2/1/1955 Crosby, ND **1978** SD 9 **1979**†Phi 16 **1980**†Phi 16 (0) **1981**†Phi 16 (0) **1982** Phi 9 (0) **1983** Phi 16 (0) **NFL** 82 [6 yrs]

Slater, Walt Walter Edward, TB, 5´11˝/187 lbs; Tennessee; 1946: Phi, rnd 5/1947: SF-A, rnd 13; B1/31/1920 Providence, RI

YEAR	TEAM	G(GS, POS)	RUSH	YD	AVG(LG)	TD	REC	YD	AVG(LG)	TD	PASS	COMP	PCT	YD	AVG(LG)	TD	INT	SK	YD	QBR	KPR	OTD	PTS	TAY
1947	†Pit	11(8, tb)	46	167	3.6(19)	0	—	—	—	—	39	18	46.2	215	5.5(37)	1	5	—	—	—	kpi	—	0	543

Slaton, Mike Michael Lee, DB, 6´2˝/194 lbs; South Dakota; 1986: Min, rnd 9; B9/25/1964 Sacramento, CA **1987** Min 1 (0)

Slaton, Tony Tony Tyrone, C-G, 6´3˝/265 lbs; USC; 1984: Buf, rnd 6; B4/12/1961 Merced, CA **1985**†LARm 13 (5, c) **1986**†LARm 14 (0) **1987** LARm 11 (0) **1988**†LARm 15 (1) **1989**†LARm 15 (15, RG) **1990** Dal 6 (4) **NFL** 74 (25) [6 yrs]

Slaughter, Chad Chad, T, 6´8˝/340 lbs; Alcorn State; B6/4/1978 Dallas, TX **2003** Oak 6 (1) **2004** Oak 10 (0) **2005** Oak 11 (0) **NFL** 27 (1) [3 yrs]

Slaughter, Chuck Charles Gary, T, 6´5˝/260 lbs; South Carolina; 1982: NO, rnd 8; B11/21/1958 Conway, SC **1982** NO 1 (0)

Slaughter, Mickey Milton Eugene, QB, 6´2˝/204 lbs; Louisiana Tech; 1963: Den, rnd 7; B8/22/1941 Monroe, LA

YEAR	TEAM	G(GS, POS)	RUSH	YD	AVG(LG)	TD	REC	YD	AVG(LG)	TD	PASS	COMP	PCT	YD	AVG(LG)	TD	INT	SK	YD	QBR	KPR	OTD	PTS	TAY
1963	Den-A	13(QB)	29	127	4.4(19)	1	—	—	—	—	223	112	50.2	1689	7.6(74)	12	15	—	—	65.4	—	—	6	442
1964	Den-A	14(qb)	20	54	2.7(18)	0	—	—	—	—	189	97	51.3	930	4.9(39)	3	11	—	—	46.4	—	—	2	94
1965	Den-A	10(QB)	20	75	3.8(13)	0	—	—	—	—	147	75	51.0	864	5.9(51)	6	12	—	—	48.7	—	—	0	57
1966	Den-A	3	1	10	10.0(10)	0	—	—	—	—	25	7	28.0	124	5.0(67)	1	0	—	—	—	—	—	0	77
NFL	4	40	70	266	3.8(19)	1	—	—	—	—	584	291	49.8	3607	6.2(74)	22	38	—	—	54.8	—	—	8	670

Slaughter, T.J. Tavaris Jermell, LB, 6´0˝/234 lbs; Southern Mississippi; 2000: Jax, rnd 3; B2/20/1977 Birmingham, AL **2000** Jax 16 (7, MLB) **2001** Jax 9 (8, RLB) **2002** Jax 11 (11, RLB) **2003** Bal 1 (0) **2003** GB 1 (0) **2003** Jax 6 (3) **2004** Bal 14 (1) **2005** NO 10 (1) **NFL** 68 (31) [6 yrs]

Slaughter, Webster Webster Melvin, WR, 6´1˝/175 lbs; San Diego State; 1986: Cle, rnd 2; B10/19/1964 Stockton, CA

YEAR	TEAM	G(GS, POS)	RUSH	YD	AVG(LG)	TD	REC	YD	AVG(LG)	TD	PASS	COMP	PCT	YD	AVG(LG)	TD	INT	SK	YD	QBR	KPR	OTD	PTS	TAY
1986	†Cle	16(16, WR)	1	1	1.0(1)	0	40	577	14.4(47)	4	—	—	—	—	—	—	—	—	—	—	p	1	30	307
1987	†Cle	12(12, WR)	—	—	—	—	47	806	17.1(54)	7	—	—	—	—	—	—	—	—	—	—	—	—	42	438
1988	†Cle	8(8, WR)	—	—	—	—	30	462	15.4(41)	3	—	—	—	—	—	—	—	—	—	—	—	—	18	246
1989	†Cle★	16(16, WR)	—	—	—	—	65	1236	**19.0**(**97**)	6	—	—	—	—	—	—	—	—	—	—	—	—	36	648
1990	Cle	16(16, WR)	5	29	5.8(17)	0	59	847	14.4(50)	4	—	—	—	—	—	—	—	—	—	—	—	—	24	473
1991	Cle	16(16, WR)	—	—	—	—	64	906	14.2(62)	3	—	—	—	—	—	—	—	—	—	—	p	—	18	495
1992	†Hou	12(9, WR)	3	20	6.7(10)	0	39	486	12.5(36)	4	—	—	—	—	—	—	—	—	—	—	kp	—	24	331
1993	Hou✧	14(14, WR)	—	—	—	—	77	904	11.7(41)	5	—	—	—	—	—	—	—	—	—	—	—	—	30	477
1994	Hou	16(12, WR)	—	—	—	—	68	846	12.4(57)	2	—	—	—	—	—	—	—	—	—	—	—	—	12	433
1995	†KC	16(7, wr)	—	—	—	—	34	514	15.1(38)	4	—	—	—	—	—	—	—	—	—	—	—	—	24	277
1996	NYJ	10(1)	—	—	—	—	32	434	13.6(53)	2	—	—	—	—	—	—	—	—	—	—	—	—	12	227
1998	SD	10(0)	—	—	—	—	8	93	11.6(31)	0	—	—	—	—	—	—	—	—	—	—	—	—	0	47
NFL	12	162(127)	9	50	5.6(17)	0	563	8111	14.4(97)	44	—	—	—	—	—	—	—	—	—	—	kp	1	270	4398

Slay, Henry Henry, DT, 6´2˝/290 lbs; West Virginia; 1998: Atl, rnd 7; B4/28/1975 Elyria, OH **1998** Phi 3 (0)

Slechta, Jeremy Jeremy, DT, 6´6˝/265 lbs; Nebraska; B5/12/1980 LaVista, NE **2002**†Phi 13 (0) **2003** Hou 2 (0) **NFL** 15 (0) [2 yrs]

Sledge, Leroy Leroy James, RB, 6´2˝/230 lbs; Bakersfield College (J.C.); B10/11/1946 Richmond, VA

YEAR	TEAM	G(GS, POS)	RUSH	YD	AVG(LG)	TD	REC	YD	AVG(LG)	TD	PASS	COMP	PCT	YD	AVG(LG)	TD	INT	SK	YD	QBR	KPR	OTD	PTS	TAY
1971	Hou	6	24	74	3.1(19)	0	6	32	5.3(10)	1	—	—	—	—	—	—	—	—	—	—	—	—	6	95

Sleight, Red Elmer Noble, T, 6´2˝/226 lbs; Purdue; B7/8/1907 Morris, IL, D8/9/1978 Naples, FL **1930** GB 13 (10, RT) **1931** GB 13 (9, RT) **NFL** 26 (19) [2 yrs]

Sligh, Richard Richard Ellis, DT, 7´0˝/300 lbs; North Carolina Central; 1967: Oak, rnd 10; B8/18/1944 Newberry, SC, D12/23/1998 Roxboro, NC **1967**†Oak-A 8

Slivinski, Steve Stephen Paul, G-LB, 5´10˝/214 lbs; Washington; 1939: Was, rnd 13; B8/23/1917 Cicero, IL **1939** Was 11 (2) **1940**†Was☆10 (10, RG) **1941** Was 11 (1) **1942**†Was★11 (8, RG) **1943**†Was☆10 (9, RG) **NFL** 53 (30) [5 yrs]

Sloan, Bonnie Bonnie Ryan, DT, 6´5˝/260 lbs; Austin Peay State; 1973: SL, rnd 10; B6/1/1948 Lebanon, TN **1973** SL 4

Sloan, David David Lyle, TE, 6´6˝/260 lbs; New Mexico; 1995: Det, rnd 3; B6/8/1972 Fresno, CA

YEAR	TEAM	G(GS, POS)	RUSH	YD	AVG(LG)	TD	REC	YD	AVG(LG)	TD	PASS	COMP	PCT	YD	AVG(LG)	TD	INT	SK	YD	QBR	KPR	OTD	PTS	TAY
1995	†Det	16(7, TE)	—	—	—	—	17	184	10.8(24)	1	—	—	—	—	—	—	—	—	—	—	k	—	6	96
1996	Det	4(4)	—	—	—	—	7	51	7.3(18)	0	—	—	—	—	—	—	—	—	—	—	—	—	0	26
1997	†Det	14(12, TE)	—	—	—	—	29	264	9.1(25)	0	—	—	—	—	—	—	—	—	—	—	—	—	0	132
1998	Det	10(2)	—	—	—	—	11	146	13.3(33)	1	—	—	—	—	—	—	—	—	—	—	—	—	6	78
1999	†Det✧	16(15, TE)	—	—	—	—	47	591	12.6(74)	4	—	—	—	—	—	—	—	—	—	—	—	—	24	316
2000	Det	15(10, TE)	—	—	—	—	32	379	11.8(59)	2	—	—	—	—	—	—	—	—	—	—	—	—	12	200
2001	Det	15(15, TE)	—	—	—	—	37	409	11.1(27)	7	—	—	—	—	—	—	—	—	—	—	—	—	42	240
2002	NO	16(14, TE)	—	—	—	—	12	127	10.6(29)	0	—	—	—	—	—	—	—	—	—	—	—	—	0	64
2003	NO	4(0)	—	—	—	—	—	—	—	—	—	—	—	—	—	—	—	—	—	—	—	—	—	—
NFL	9	110(79)	—	—	—	—	192	2151	11.2(74)	15	—	—	—	—	—	—	—	—	—	—	k	—	90	1150

Sloan, Dwight Dwight Henry 'Paddlefoot', B, 5´10˝/180 lbs; Arkansas; 1938: ChiC, rnd 10; B4/7/1914 Rudy, AR, D3/18/1998 San Antonio, TX

YEAR	TEAM	G(GS, POS)	RUSH	YD	AVG(LG)	TD	REC	YD	AVG(LG)	TD	PASS	COMP	PCT	YD	AVG(LG)	TD	INT	SK	YD	QBR	KPR	OTD	PTS	TAY
1938	ChiC	10(7, TB)	56	126	2.3	0	1	10	10.0(10)	0	79	37	46.8	333	4.2	1	7	—	—	—	—	—	0	23
1939	Det	10(1, TB)	79	225	2.8	4	—	—	—	—	102	45	44.1	658	6.5	2	3	—	—	60.0	P	—	24	484

YEAR	TEAM	G (GS, POS)	RUSH	YD	AVG (LG)	TD	REC	YD	AVG (LG)	TD	PASS	COMP	PCT	YD	AVG (LG)	TD	INT	SK	YD	QBR	KPR	OTD	PTS	TAY
1940	Det	11 (5, tb)	58	225	3.9	0	—	—	—	—	46	18	39.1	260	5.7	0	8	—	—	—	Pi	—	0	34
NFL	3	31 (13)	193	576	3.0	4	1	10	10.0 (10)	0	227	100	44.1	1251	5.5	3	18	—	—	33.1	Pi	—	24	541

SLOAN, STEVE Stephen Charles, QB, 6´0˝/185 lbs; Alabama; 1966: Atl, rnd 11; B8/19/1944 Austin, TN

YEAR	TEAM	G (GS, POS)	RUSH	YD	AVG (LG)	TD	REC	YD	AVG (LG)	TD	PASS	COMP	PCT	YD	AVG (LG)	TD	INT	SK	YD	QBR	KPR	OTD	PTS	TAY
1966	Atl	3	—	—	—	—	—	—	—	—	13	6	46.2	96	7.4 (32)	0	2	3	32	—	—	—	0	-32
1967	Atl	5	1	2	2.0 (2)	0	—	—	—	—	18	4	22.2	38	2.1 (15)	0	2	10	78	—	—	—	0	-59
NFL	2	8	1	2	2.0 (2)	0	—	—	—	—	31	10	32.3	134	4.3 (32)	0	4	13	110	—	—	—	0	-91

SLONE, PETE Peter J., E, 5´8˝/160 lbs; none; B12/23/1896 Braddock, PA, D8/1962 **1921** Mun 1 (0)

SLOSBURG, PHIL Phillip Jay, B, 5´10˝/170 lbs; Temple; 1948: Bos, rnd 6/ChiR-A, rnd 10; B10/30/1926 Philadelphia, PA

YEAR	TEAM	G (GS, POS)	RUSH	YD	AVG (LG)	TD	REC	YD	AVG (LG)	TD	PASS	COMP	PCT	YD	AVG (LG)	TD	INT	SK	YD	QBR	KPR	OTD	PTS	TAY
1948	Bos	12 (2)	32	89	2.8 (16)	0	2	29	14.5 (16)	0	20	8	40.0	119	5.9 (68)	1	3	—	—	—	kp	—	0	161
1949	NYB	3 (2)	37	121	3.3 (23)	1	4	11	2.8 (9)	0	—	—	—	—	—	—	—	—	—	—	kpi	—	6	182
NFL	2	15 (4)	69	210	3.0 (23)	1	6	40	6.7 (16)	0	20	8	40.0	119	5.9 (68)	1	3	—	—	—	kpi	—	6	343

SLOUGH, ELMER Elmer Cumming, TB-BB-WB, 5´8˝/160 lbs; Oklahoma; B7/19/1903 Madill, OK, deceased **1926** Buf 8 (7, TB), 12

SLOUGH, GREG Gregory C., LB, 6´3˝/230 lbs; USC; 1971: Oak, rnd 6; B2/26/1948 Detroit, MI **1971** Oak 13 **1972**†Oak 9 **NFL** 22 [2 yrs]

SLOVACEK, EMIL Emil Raymond, T, 6´3˝/300 lbs; Stephen F. Austin State; B2/26/1963 Dallas, TX **1987** SD 2 (0)

SLOVAK, MARTY Martin, TB-DB, 5´9˝/179 lbs; Toledo; B12/25/1916 Newport, MI, D3/22/1950 Toledo, OH

YEAR	TEAM	G (GS, POS)	RUSH	YD	AVG (LG)	TD	REC	YD	AVG (LG)	TD	PASS	COMP	PCT	YD	AVG (LG)	TD	INT	SK	YD	QBR	KPR	OTD	PTS	TAY
1939	Cle	10 (0)	42	135	3.2	0	—	—	—	—	27	13	48.1	97	3.6	2	5	—	—	—	P	—	0	-7
1940	Cle	9 (4)	53	129	2.4	1	—	—	—	—	28	17	60.7	234	8.4	0	4	—	—	—	i	—	6	106
1941	Cle	8 (2)	46	132	2.9 (14)	0	—	—	—	—	54	27	50.0	307	5.7 (48)	2	9	—	—	—	kp	—	0	-19
NFL	3	27 (6)	141	396	2.8 (14)	1	—	—	—	—	109	57	52.3	638	5.9 (48)	4	18	—	—	—	Pkpi	—	6	81

SLUTZKER, SCOTT Scott Lawrence, TE, 6´4˝/250 lbs; Iowa; 1996: Ind, rnd 3; B12/20/1972 Hasbrouck Heights, NJ

YEAR	TEAM	G (GS, POS)	RUSH	YD	AVG (LG)	TD	REC	YD	AVG (LG)	TD	PASS	COMP	PCT	YD	AVG (LG)	TD	INT	SK	YD	QBR	KPR	OTD	PTS	TAY
1996	†Ind	15 (0)	—	—	—	—	—	—	—	—	—	—	—	—	—	—	—	—	—	—	—	—	—	—
1997	Ind	12 (2)	—	—	—	—	3	22	7.3 (11)	0	—	—	—	—	—	—	—	—	—	—	—	—	0	11
1998	NO	3 (0)	—	—	—	—	1	10	10.0 (10)	0	—	—	—	—	—	—	—	—	—	—	—	—	0	5
1999	NO	11 (2)	—	—	—	—	11	164	14.9 (42)	1	—	—	—	—	—	—	—	—	—	—	—	—	6	87
NFL	4	41 (4)	—	—	—	—	15	196	13.1 (42)	1	—	—	—	—	—	—	—	—	—	—	—	—	6	103

SLYKER, BILL William Valentine, E, 6´1˝/180 lbs; Ohio State; B2/14/1899 Huron, OH, D9/1/1949 Evansville, IN **1922** Evv 1 (1), 6

SMAGALA, STAN Stanley Adam, DB, 5´10˝/184 lbs; Notre Dame; 1990: Dal, rnd 5; B4/6/1968 Chicago, IL **1990** Dal 3 (0) **1991**†Dal 8 (0) **NFL** 11 (0) [2 yrs]

SMAIL, ALEX Alex, LB, 5´8˝/235 lbs; Detroit Mercy; B5/31/1926 Dearborn, MI, D6/21/2004 Dearborn, MI **1952** Pit 1

SMALL, DONOVAN Donovan Oliver, DB, 5´11˝/190 lbs; Minnesota; B7/10/1964 Kingston, Jamaica **1987** Hou 1 (0)

SMALL, ELDRIDGE Eldridge, DB, 6´1˝/190 lbs; Texas A&M-Kingsville; 1972: NYG, rnd 1; B8/2/1949 Houston, TX **1972** NYG 14 **1973** NYG 8 **1974** NYG 12 (RCB) **NFL** 34 [3 yrs]

SMALL, GEORGE George Michael, NT, 6´2˝/260 lbs; North Carolina A&T; B11/18/1956 Shreveport, LA **1980** NYG 7 (0)

SMALL, GERALD Gerald David, DB, 5´11˝/192 lbs; San Jose State; 1978: Mia, rnd 4; B8/10/1956 Washington, DC **[I]** **1978**†Mia 16 (4) **1979**†Mia 16 (16, RCB) **1980** Mia 16 (16, RCB) **1981**†Mia 16 (16, RCB) **1982**†Mia 9 (9, RCB) **1983** Mia 15 (15, RCB) **1984** Atl 16 (1) **NFL** 104 (77) [7 yrs]

SMALL, JESSIE Jessie Lee, LB, 6´3˝/239 lbs; Eastern Kentucky; 1989: Phi, rnd 2; B11/30/1966 Boston, GA **1989**†Phi 16 (1) **1990**†Phi 15 (14, RLB) **1991** Phi 16 (8, RLB) **1992** Phx 6 (0) **NFL** 53 (23) [4 yrs]

SMALL, FRED John Frederick, LB, 5´11˝/227 lbs; Washington; 1985: Pit, rnd 9; B7/15/1963 Los Angeles, CA, D6/24/2003 Inglewood, CA **1985** Pit 16 (0)

SMALL, JOHN John Kenneth, DT-LB, 6´4˝/269 lbs; The Citadel; 1970: Atl, rnd 1; B11/20/1946 Lumberton, NC **1970** Atl 10 **1971** Atl 14 (LDT) **1972** Atl 9 **1973** Det 1 **1974** Det 13 **NFL** 47 [5 yrs]

SMALL, O.J. O.J., WR, 6´1˝/223 lbs; Florida; B8/18/1982 Jacksonville, FL

YEAR	TEAM	G (GS, POS)	RUSH	YD	AVG (LG)	TD	REC	YD	AVG (LG)	TD	PASS	COMP	PCT	YD	AVG (LG)	TD	INT	SK	YD	QBR	KPR	OTD	PTS	TAY
2005	Ten	2 (0)	—	—	—	—	1	6	6.0 (6)	0	—	—	—	—	—	—	—	—	—	—	—	—	0	3

SMALL, TORRANCE Torrance Ramon, WR, 6´3˝/209 lbs; Alcorn State; 1992: NO, rnd 5; B9/4/1970 Tampa, FL

YEAR	TEAM	G (GS, POS)	RUSH	YD	AVG (LG)	TD	REC	YD	AVG (LG)	TD	PASS	COMP	PCT	YD	AVG (LG)	TD	INT	SK	YD	QBR	KPR	OTD	PTS	TAY
1992	†NO	13 (2)	—	—	—	—	23	278	12.1 (33)	3	—	—	—	—	—	—	—	—	—	—	—	—	18	154
1993	NO	11 (0)	—	—	—	—	16	164	10.3 (17)	1	—	—	—	—	—	—	—	—	—	—	—	—	6	87
1994	NO	16 (0)	—	—	—	—	49	719	14.7 (75)	5	—	—	—	—	—	—	—	—	—	—	—	—	32	385
1995	NO	16 (1)	6	75	12.5 (44)	1	38	461	12.1 (32)	5	0	0	0.0	0	0.0	0	0	1	4	—	—	—	36	341
1996	NO	16 (13, WR)	4	51	12.8 (22)	1	50	558	11.2 (41)	2	—	—	—	—	—	—	—	—	—	—	—	—	18	350
1997	SL	13 (7, wr)	—	—	—	—	32	488	15.3 (46)	1	—	—	—	—	—	—	—	—	—	—	—	—	6	249
1998	Ind	16 (4)	1	2	2.0 (2)	0	45	681	15.1 (53)	7	1	0	0.0	0	0.0	0	0	—	—	—	—	—	42	378
1999	Phi	15 (15, WR)	—	—	—	—	49	655	13.4 (84)	4	2	0	0.0	0	0.0	0	0	—	—	—	—	—	24	348
2000	†Phi	14 (14, WR)	1	1	1.0 (1)	0	40	569	14.2 (70)	3	1	0	0.0	0	0.0	0	1	—	—	—	—	—	20	261
2001	NE	3 (0)	—	—	—	—	4	29	7.3 (11)	0	—	—	—	—	—	—	—	—	—	—	—	—	0	15
NFL	10	133 (56)	12	129	10.8 (44)	2	346	4602	13.3 (84)	31	4	0	0.0	0	0.0	0	1	1	4	—	—	—	202	2565

SMALLS, FRED Frederick, LB, 6´3˝/225 lbs; West Virginia; 1986: SD, rnd 7; B1/7/1963 Beaufort, SC **1987** Phi 3 (3)

SMART, IAN Ian, RB, 5´8˝/192 lbs; C.W. Post; B10/28/1980 Jamaica, NY

YEAR	TEAM	G (GS, POS)	RUSH	YD	AVG (LG)	TD	REC	YD	AVG (LG)	TD	PASS	COMP	PCT	YD	AVG (LG)	TD	INT	SK	YD	QBR	KPR	OTD	PTS	TAY
2004	TB	4 (0)	2	26	13.0 (25)	0	2	10	5.0 (5)	0	—	—	—	—	—	—	—	—	—	—	k	—	0	78

SMART, ROD Rod 'He Hate Me', RB, 5´11˝/201 lbs; Western Kentucky; B1/9/1977 Lakeland, FL **[R]**

YEAR	TEAM	G (GS, POS)	RUSH	YD	AVG (LG)	TD	REC	YD	AVG (LG)	TD	PASS	COMP	PCT	YD	AVG (LG)	TD	INT	SK	YD	QBR	KPR	OTD	PTS	TAY
2001	Phi	6 (0)	2	6	3.0 (6)	0	—	—	—	—	—	—	—	—	—	—	—	—	—	—	—	—	0	6
2002	Car	16 (0)	1	2	2.0 (2)	0	—	—	—	—	—	—	—	—	—	—	—	—	—	—	—	—	0	2
2003	†Car	16 (0)	20	49	2.5 (6)	0	3	11	3.7 (5)	0	—	—	—	—	—	—	—	—	—	—	k	1	6	397
2004	Car	3 (0)	3	4	1.3 (3)	0	1	5	5.0 (5)	0	—	—	—	—	—	—	—	—	—	—	k	—	0	56
2005	†Car	12 (0)	3	6	2.0 (6)	0	—	—	—	—	—	—	—	—	—	—	—	—	—	—	k	—	0	186
NFL	5	53 (0)	29	67	2.3 (6)	0	4	16	4.0 (5)	0	—	—	—	—	—	—	—	—	—	—	k	1	6	646

SMEACH, METZ Metzger Franklin, T, 6´3˝/195 lbs; Georgetown (DC); B6/1/1895 Connellsville, PA, D5/26/1985 Garrettsville, OH **1921** Was 3 (2, LT)

SMEDLEY, ERIC Eric Alan, DB, 5´11˝/199 lbs; Indiana; 1996: Buf, rnd 7; B7/23/1973 Charleston, WV **1996**†Buf 6 (0) **1997** Buf 13 (1) **1998**†Buf 16 (0) **1999**†Ind 7 (0) **NFL** 42 (1) [4 yrs]

SMEENGE, JOEL Joel Andrew, DE-LB, 6´6˝/262 lbs; Western Michigan; 1990: NO, rnd 3; B4/1/1968 Holland, MI **1990** NO 15 (0) **1991**†NO 14 (0) **1992**†NO 11 (0) **1993** NO 16 (2) **1994** NO 16 (2) **1995** Jax 15 (15, LDE) **1996** Jax 10 (10, LDE) **1997**†Jax 16 (0) **1998**†Jax 16 (14, LDE) **1999**†Jax 15 (7, lde) **2000** Jax 12 (1) **NFL** 156 (51) [11 yrs]

SMEJA, RUDY Rudolph M., E, 6´2˝/195 lbs; Michigan; 1944: ChiB, rnd 3; B12/1/1920 Chicago, IL, D10/1982

YEAR	TEAM	G (GS, POS)	RUSH	YD	AVG (LG)	TD	REC	YD	AVG (LG)	TD	PASS	COMP	PCT	YD	AVG (LG)	TD	INT	SK	YD	QBR	KPR	OTD	PTS	TAY
1944	ChiB	10 (3)	—	—	—	—	7	110	15.7 (19)	1	—	—	—	—	—	—	—	—	—	—	k	—	6	52
1945	ChiB	8 (8, LE)	—	—	—	—	1	11	11.0 (11)	0	—	—	—	—	—	—	—	—	—	—	—	—	0	6
1946	Phi	11 (1)	—	—	—	—	3	45	15.0 (17)	0	—	—	—	—	—	—	—	—	—	—	k	—	0	20
NFL	3	29 (12)	—	—	—	—	11	166	15.1 (19)	1	—	—	—	—	—	—	—	—	—	—	k	—	6	77

SMEREK, DON Donald Frederick, DT-DE, 6´7˝/255 lbs; Nevada-Reno; B12/20/1957 Waterford, MI **1981** Dal 2 (0) **1982**†Dal 7 (0) **1983**†Dal 15 (0) **1984** Dal 16 (0) **1985**†Dal 10 (1) **1986** Dal 11 (0) **1987** Dal 8 (3) **NFL** 69 (4) [7 yrs]

SMERLAS, FRED Frederic Charles, NT-DT, 6´3˝/277 lbs; Boston College; 1979: Buf, rnd 2; B4/8/1957 Waltham, MA **1979** Buf 13 (3) **1980**†Buf★16 (16, NT) **1981**†Buf★16 (16, NT) **1982** Buf★9 (9, NT) **1983** Buf★16 (16, NT) **1984** Buf 16 (16, NT) **1985** Buf 16 (16, NT) **1986** Buf 16 (16, NT) **1987** Buf 12 (12, NT) **1988**†Buf★16 (16, NT) **1989**†Buf☆16 (16, NT) **1990** SF 6 (0) **1991** NE 16 (1) **1992** NE 16 (0) **NFL** 200 (153) [14 yrs]

SMIGELSKY, DAVE David William, P, 5´11˝/180 lbs; Virginia Tech; B7/3/1959 Perth Amboy, NJ **1982** Atl 6 (0)

SMILANICH, BRANKO Branko Michael, HB, 5´11˝/180 lbs; Arizona; B10/17/1915 Chisholm, MN, D4/11/2001 Pasadena, CA

YEAR	TEAM	G (GS, POS)	RUSH	YD	AVG (LG)	TD	REC	YD	AVG (LG)	TD	PASS	COMP	PCT	YD	AVG (LG)	TD	INT	SK	YD	QBR	KPR	OTD	PTS	TAY
1939	Cle	2 (0)	1	-3	-3.0 (-3)	0	—	—	—	—	2	1	50.0	11	5.5 (11)	0	0	—	—	—	—	—	0	3

SMILEY, JUSTIN Justin, G, 6´4˝/296 lbs; Alabama; 2004: SF, rnd 2; B11/11/1981 Eliabell, GA **2004** SF 16 (9, RG) **2005** SF 16 (16, LG) **NFL** 32 (25) [2 yrs]

Smiley, Tommie Tommie Belton, RB, 6´1˝/235 lbs; Arizona; Lamar; 1968: Cin, rnd 2; B2/18/1944 Port Arthur, TX

YEAR	TEAM	G (GS, POS)	RUSH	YD	AVG (LG)	TD	REC	YD	AVG (LG)	TD	PASS	COMP	PCT	YD	AVG (LG)	TD	INT	SK	YD	QBR	KPR	OTD	PTS	TAY
1968	Cin-A	8(FB)	63	146	2.3(11)	1	19	86	4.5(17)	0	—	—	—	—	—	—	—	—	—	—	—	—	6	199
1969	Den-A	14(9, FB)	56	166	3.0(26)	3	5	23	4.6(17)	1	—	—	—	—	—	—	—	—	—	—	—	—	24	213
1970	Hou	7	1	0	0.0(0)	0	—	—	—	—	—	—	—	—	—	—	—	—	—	—	—	—	0	0
NFL	3	29(9)	120	312	2.6(26)	4	24	109	4.5(17)	1	—	—	—	—	—	—	—	—	—	—	—	—	30	412

Smith, Aaron Aaron Clayton, LB, 6´2˝/223 lbs; Utah State; 1984: Den, rnd 6; B8/10/1962 Los Angeles, CA **1984** Den 10 (0)

Smith, Aaron Aaron Douglas, DE, 6´5˝/300 lbs; Northern Colorado; 1999: Pit, rnd 4; B4/9/1976 Colorado Springs, CO **1999** Pit 6 (0) **2000** Pit 16 (15, LDE) **2001**†Pit 16 (16, LDE) **2002**†Pit 16 (16, LDE) **2003** Pit 16 (16, LDE) **2004**†Pit✧16 (15, LDE) **2005**†Pit 16 (16, LDE) **NFL** 102 (94) [7 yrs]

Smith, Akili Kabisa Akili Maradu, QB, 6´3˝/220 lbs; Oregon; 1999: Cin, rnd 1; B8/21/1975 San Diego, CA

YEAR	TEAM	G (GS, POS)	RUSH	YD	AVG (LG)	TD	REC	YD	AVG (LG)	TD	PASS	COMP	PCT	YD	AVG (LG)	TD	INT	SK	YD	QBR	KPR	OTD	PTS	TAY
1999	Cin	7(4, qb)	19	114	6.0(24)	1	1	6	6.0(6)	0	153	80	52.3	805	5.3(39)	2	6	19	110	—	—	—	6	300
2000	Cin	12(11, QB)	41	232	5.7(21)	0	—	—	—	—	267	118	44.2	1253	4.7(46)	3	6	36	191	52.8	—	—	0	634
2001	Cin	2(1)	6	20	3.3(6)	0	—	—	—	—	8	5	62.5	37	4.6(14)	0	0	1	3	—	—	—	0	39
2002	Cin	1(1)	4	5	1.3(3)	0	—	—	—	—	33	12	36.4	117	3.5(24)	0	1	3	23	—	—	—	0	24
NFL	4	22(17)	70	371	5.3(24)	1	1	6	6.0(6)	0	461	215	46.6	2212	4.8(46)	5	13	59	327	52.8	—	—	6	995

Smith, Al Al Fredrick, LB, 6´1˝/244 lbs; Cal Poly-Pomona; Utah State; 1987: Hou, rnd 6; B11/26/1964 Los Angeles, CA **1987**†Hou 12 (11, RILB) **1988**†Hou 16 (16, RILB) **1989**†Hou 15 (15, RILB) **1990**†Hou 15 (15, MLB) **1991**†Hou★16 (16, MLB) **1992**†Hou★16 (16, MLB) **1993**†Hou 16 (16, MLB) **1994** Hou 16 (16, MLB) **1995** Hou 2 (2) **1996** Hou 1 (1) **NFL** 125 (124) [10 yrs]

Smith, Alex Alex, TE, 6´4˝/258 lbs; Stanford; 2005: TB, rnd 3; B5/22/1982 Denver, CO

YEAR	TEAM	G (GS, POS)	RUSH	YD	AVG (LG)	TD	REC	YD	AVG (LG)	TD	PASS	COMP	PCT	YD	AVG (LG)	TD	INT	SK	YD	QBR	KPR	OTD	PTS	TAY
2005	†TB	16(10, TE)	—	—	—	—	41	367	9.0(24)	2	—	—	—	—	—	—	—	—	—	—	k	—	12	191

Smith, Alex Alexander D., QB, 6´4˝/212 lbs; Utah; 2005: SF, rnd 1; B5/7/1984 Seattle, WA

YEAR	TEAM	G (GS, POS)	RUSH	YD	AVG (LG)	TD	REC	YD	AVG (LG)	TD	PASS	COMP	PCT	YD	AVG (LG)	TD	INT	SK	YD	QBR	KPR	OTD	PTS	TAY
2005	SF	9(7, QB)	30	103	3.4(19)	0	—	—	—	—	165	84	50.9	875	5.3(47)	1	11	29	185	40.8	—	—	0	106

Smith, Allen Houston Allen, E-DE, 6´2˝/218 lbs; Mississippi; 1947: ChiB, rnd 8; B3/29/1922 Hazlehurst, MS, D10/18/1970 Hattiesburg, MS **1947** ChiB 12 (5, le)

YEAR	TEAM	G (GS, POS)	RUSH	YD	AVG (LG)	TD	REC	YD	AVG (LG)	TD	PASS	COMP	PCT	YD	AVG (LG)	TD	INT	SK	YD	QBR	KPR	OTD	PTS	TAY
1948	ChiB	10(4)	—	—	—	—	3	29	9.7(18)	0	—	—	—	—	—	—	—	—	—	—	—	—	0	15
NFL	2	22(9)	—	—	—	—	3	29	9.7(18)	0	—	—	—	—	—	—	—	—	—	—	k	—	0	3

Smith, Allen Allen Duncan, RB, 5´11˝/202 lbs; Fort Valley State; 1966: Buf, rnd 15; B11/20/1942 Fort Valley, GA **1967** Buf-A 5

YEAR	TEAM	G (GS, POS)	RUSH	YD	AVG (LG)	TD	REC	YD	AVG (LG)	TD	PASS	COMP	PCT	YD	AVG (LG)	TD	INT	SK	YD	QBR	KPR	OTD	PTS	TAY
1966	†Buf-A	14	31	148	4.8(20)	0	1	1	1.0(1)	0	—	—	—	—	—	—	—	—	—	—	—	—	0	149
NFL	2	19	31	148	4.8(20)	0	1	1	1.0(1)	0	—	—	—	—	—	—	—	—	—	—	k	—	0	255

Smith, Allen Allen Tyrone, HB, 5´11˝/195 lbs; Findlay; 1966: NYJ, rnd R6/Det, rnd 20; B10/7/1942 Chattanooga, TN **1966** NYJ-A 1

Smith, Anthony Anthony Wayne, DE, 6´3˝/265 lbs; Alabama; Arizona; 1990: LARd, rnd 1; B6/28/1967 Elizabeth City, NC **[S]** **1991**†LARd 16 (2) **1992** LARd 15 (1) **1993**†LARd 16 (2) **1994** LARd 16 (16, RDE) **1995** Oak 16 (11, LDE) **1996** Oak 6 (4) **1997** Oak 13 (13, RDE) **NFL** 98 (49) [7 yrs]

Smith, Antonio Antonio, DE, 6´3˝/274 lbs; Oklahoma State; 2004: Arz, rnd 5; B10/21/1981 Oklahoma City, OK **2004** Arz 2 (0) **2005** Arz 11 (8, rde) **NFL** 13 (8) [2 yrs]

Smith, Antowain Antowain Drurell, RB, 6´2˝/232 lbs; Houston; 1997: Buf, rnd 1; B3/14/1972 Millbrook, AL

YEAR	TEAM	G (GS, POS)	RUSH	YD	AVG (LG)	TD	REC	YD	AVG (LG)	TD	PASS	COMP	PCT	YD	AVG (LG)	TD	INT	SK	YD	QBR	KPR	OTD	PTS	TAY
1997	Buf	16(0, rb)	194	840	4.3(56)	8	28	177	6.3(19)	0	—	—	—	—	—	—	—	—	—	—	—	—	48	1009
1998	†Buf	16(14, RB)	300	1124	3.7(30)	8	5	11	2.2(9)	0	—	—	—	—	—	—	—	—	—	—	—	—	48	1210
1999	†Buf	14(11, rb)	165	614	3.7(52)	6	2	32	16.0(23)	0	—	—	—	—	—	—	—	—	—	—	—	—	36	690
2000	Buf	11(3)	101	354	3.5(59)	4	3	20	6.7(9)	0	—	—	—	—	—	—	—	—	—	—	k	—	24	389
2001	†NE	16(15, RB)	287	1157	4.0(44)	12	19	192	10.1(41)	1	—	—	—	—	—	—	—	—	—	—	—	—	78	1378
2002	NE	16(15, RB)	252	982	3.9(42)	6	31	243	7.8(35)	2	—	—	—	—	—	—	—	—	—	—	—	—	50	1174
2003	†NE	13(6, rb)	182	642	3.5(30)	3	14	92	6.6(16)	0	—	—	—	—	—	—	—	—	—	—	—	—	18	718
2004	Ten	13(4)	137	509	3.7(43)	4	22	169	7.7(31)	0	—	—	—	—	—	—	—	—	—	—	—	—	24	634
2005	NO	16(7, RB)	166	659	4.0(42)	3	12	46	3.8(8)	0	—	—	—	—	—	—	—	—	—	—	k	—	18	727
NFL	9	131(75)	1784	6881	3.9(59)	54	136	982	7.2(41)	3	—	—	—	—	—	—	—	—	—	—	k	—	344	7927

Smith, Art Arthur Henry Thompson, LB, 6´1˝/222 lbs; Hawaii; B4/20/1956 Honolulu, HI **1980** Den 2 (0)

Smith, Artie Artie Enlow, DE, 6´5˝/296 lbs; Louisiana Tech; 1993: SF, rnd 5; B5/15/1970 Stillwater, OK **1993**†SF 16 (6, rde) **1994** SF 2 (0) **1994** Cin 7 (0) **1995** Cin 16 (16, RDE) **1996** Cin 16 (12, RDE) **1998**†Dal 16 (0) **NFL** 73 (34) [5 yrs]

Smith, Barry Barrett Benjamin, WR, 6´1˝/190 lbs; Florida State; 1973: GB, rnd 1; B1/15/1951 West Palm Beach, FL

YEAR	TEAM	G (GS, POS)	RUSH	YD	AVG (LG)	TD	REC	YD	AVG (LG)	TD	PASS	COMP	PCT	YD	AVG (LG)	TD	INT	SK	YD	QBR	KPR	OTD	PTS	TAY
1973	GB	14(WR)	1	5	5.0(5)	0	15	233	15.5(24)	2	—	—	—	—	—	—	—	—	—	—	—	—	12	132
1974	GB	14(WR)	—	—	—	—	20	294	14.7(27)	1	—	—	—	—	—	—	—	—	—	—	—	—	6	152
1975	GB	13(WR)	—	—	—	—	6	77	12.8(20)	1	—	—	—	—	—	—	—	—	—	—	—	—	6	44
1976	TB	13	—	—	—	—	4	88	22.0(39)	0	—	—	—	—	—	—	—	—	—	—	—	—	0	44
NFL	4	54	1	5	5.0(5)	0	45	692	15.4(39)	4	—	—	—	—	—	—	—	—	—	—	—	—	24	371

Smith, Barty Barton Elliott, RB, 6´3˝/240 lbs; Richmond; 1974: GB, rnd 1; B4/23/1952 Richmond, VA

YEAR	TEAM	G (GS, POS)	RUSH	YD	AVG (LG)	TD	REC	YD	AVG (LG)	TD	PASS	COMP	PCT	YD	AVG (LG)	TD	INT	SK	YD	QBR	KPR	OTD	PTS	TAY
1974	GB	8	9	19	2.1(4)	0	—	—	—	—	—	—	—	—	—	—	—	—	—	—	—	—	0	19
1975	GB	14	60	243	4.1(17)	4	16	140	8.8(33)	1	—	—	—	—	—	—	—	—	—	—	k	—	30	351
1976	GB	8(5, rb)	97	355	3.7(16)	5	11	88	8.0(35)	0	—	—	—	—	—	—	—	—	—	—	—	—	30	449
1977	GB	14(FB)	166	554	3.3(11)	2	37	340	9.2(42)	1	—	—	—	—	—	—	—	—	—	—	—	—	18	749
1978	GB	16(FB)	154	567	3.7(33)	4	37	256	6.9(24)	0	—	—	—	—	—	—	—	—	—	—	k	—	24	720
1979	GB	6(fb)	57	201	3.5(23)	3	19	155	8.2(22)	1	—	—	—	—	—	—	—	—	—	—	—	—	24	314
1980	GB	1(0)	1	3	3.0(3)	0	—	—	—	—	—	—	—	—	—	—	—	—	—	—	—	—	0	3
NFL	7	67(5)	544	1942	3.6(33)	18	120	979	8.2(42)	3	—	—	—	—	—	—	—	—	—	—	k	—	126	2605

Smith, Ben Ben H., E-BB-DE, 6´3˝/208 lbs; Alabama; B6/16/1911 Haleyville, AL, deceased

YEAR	TEAM	G (GS, POS)	RUSH	YD	AVG (LG)	TD	REC	YD	AVG (LG)	TD	PASS	COMP	PCT	YD	AVG (LG)	TD	INT	SK	YD	QBR	KPR	OTD	PTS	TAY
1933	GB	9(3)	—	—	—	—	2	23	11.5(13)	0	—	—	—	—	—	—	—	—	—	—	—	—	0	12
1934	Pit	11(10, LE)	—	—	—	—	14	218	**15.6**	0	—	—	—	—	—	—	—	—	—	—	—	—	0	109
1935	Pit	11(6, re)	—	—	—	—	9	166	18.4	0	—	—	—	—	—	—	—	—	—	—	—	—	0	83
1937	Was	11(0, BB)	—	—	—	—	2	37	18.5	0	—	—	—	—	—	—	—	—	—	—	—	—	0	19
NFL	4	42(19)	—	—	—	—	27	444	16.4(13)	0	—	—	—	—	—	—	—	—	—	—	—	—	0	222

Smith, Ben Benjamin Joseph, DB, 5´11˝/185 lbs; Georgia; 1990: Phi, rnd 1; B5/14/1967 Warner Robins, GA **1990**†Phi 16 (13, LCB) **1991** Phi 10 (10, LCB) **1993** Phi 13 (3) **1994** Den 14 (14, LCB) **1995** Arz 2 (0) **1996** Arz 2 (0) **NFL** 57 (40) [6 yrs]

Smith, Bill William Arley, E-DE, 6´1˝/198 lbs; Washington; B1/13/1912 Seattle, WA, D6/20/1999 Carmel, CA **[K]**

YEAR	TEAM	G (GS, POS)	RUSH	YD	AVG (LG)	TD	REC	YD	AVG (LG)	TD	PASS	COMP	PCT	YD	AVG (LG)	TD	INT	SK	YD	QBR	KPR	OTD	PTS	TAY
1934	ChiC☆	11(3)	13	56	4.3	2	6	103	17.2(21)	1	1	1	100.0	9	9.0(9)	0	0	—	—	—	K	—	25	137
1935	ChiC☆	11(10, LE)	8	33	4.1	0	24	318	13.3(46)	2	—	—	—	—	—	—	—	—	—	—	K	—	35	202
1936	ChiC☆	11(6, le)	2	13	6.5	0	20	414	20.7(38)	1	1	0	0.0	0	0.0	0	1	—	—	—	K	—	11	185
1937	ChiC	9(2)	—	—	—	—	3	52	17.3	0	—	—	—	—	—	—	—	—	—	—	K	1	9	26
1938	ChiC☆	11(11, RE)	—	—	—	—	18	338	18.8	1	—	—	—	—	—	—	—	—	—	—	K	—	16	174
1939	ChiC★	11(9, RE)	1	3	3.0(3)	0	21	387	18.4(60)	4	—	—	—	—	—	—	—	—	—	—	KP	—	36	217
NFL	6	64(41)	24	105	4.4(3)	2	92	1612	17.5(60)	9	2	1	50.0	9	4.5(9)	0	1	—	—	—	KP	1	132	941

Smith, Bill William Gerald, T, 6´2˝/250 lbs; North Carolina; 1948: Cle-A, rnd 9/ChiC, rnd 3; B10/23/1926 Lexington, NC **1948** ChiR-A 2 (0) **1948** LAD-A 10 (0) **AAFC** 12 (0) [1 yr]

Smith, Billy Ray Billy Ray, LB, 6´3˝/235 lbs; Arkansas; 1983: SD, rnd 1; B8/10/1961 Fayetteville, AR **1983** SD 16 (16, RILB) **1984** SD 16 (16, RILB) **1985** SD 15 (15, RILB) **1986** SD☆16 (15, LOLB) **1988** SD 9 (8, rolb) **1989** SD☆16 (16, LOLB) **1990** SD 11 (10, LOLB) **1991** SD 14 (3) **1992** SD 1 (0)

YEAR	TEAM	G (GS, POS)	RUSH	YD	AVG (LG)	TD	REC	YD	AVG (LG)	TD	PASS	COMP	PCT	YD	AVG (LG)	TD	INT	SK	YD	QBR	KPR	OTD	PTS	TAY
1987	SD☆	12(12, LOLB)	—	—	—	—	—	—	—	—	1	0	0.0	0	0.0	0	1	—	—	—	iS	—	0	-37
NFL	10	126(111)	—	—	—	—	—	—	—	—	1	0	0.0	0	0.0	0	1	—	—	—	kiS	1	6	-21

Smith, Billy Ray Sr. Billy Ray, DT-DE, 6´4˝/240 lbs; Auburn; Arkansas; 1957: LA, rnd 3; B1/27/1935 Augusta, AR, D3/21/2001 Little Rock, AR **1957** LARm 12 (12, RDE) **1958** Pit 12 (LDE) **1959** Pit 6 (rde) **1960** Pit 12 (RDE) **1961** Bal 14 (RDT) **1962** Bal 13 (RDT) **1964**†Bal 13 (RDT) **1965**†Bal 14 (RDT) **1966** Bal 14 (13, LDT) **1967** Bal 14 (RDT) **1968**†Bal☆14 (LDT) **1969** Bal 14 (LDT) **1970**†Bal 14 (LDT) **NFL** 166 (25) [13 yrs]

Smith, Blane Blane, LB, 6´3˝/238 lbs; Purdue; 1977: Cle, rnd 7; B7/13/1954 Gary, IN **1977** GB 1

YEAR	TEAM	G(GS, POS)	RUSH	YD	AVG(LG)	TD	REC	YD	AVG(LG)	TD	PASS	COMP	PCT	YD	AVG(LG)	TD	INT	SK	YD	QBR	KPR	OTD	PTS	TAY

SMITH, BOB James Robert, DB-HB-WB, 6´1˝/191 lbs; Tulsa; Iowa; 1947: Bkn-A, rnd 11/Was, rnd 24; B8/20/1925 Ranger, TX, D3/1/2002 Flower Mound, TX [I]   **1948** Bkn-A 10 (2)

1948	Buf-A	3(0)	1	7	7.0(7)	0	—	—	—	—	—	—	—	—	—	—	—	—	—	—	Ppi	—	0	16
1949	ChiH-A	3(0)	—	—	—	—	1	31	31.0(31)	0	—	—	—	—	—	—	—	—	—	—	Ppi	—	0	16
AAFC	2	16(2)	1	7	7.0(7)	0	1	31	31.0(31)	0	—	—	—	—	—	—	—	—	—	—	Ppi	—	0	28

1950 Det 12 (DB)   **1951** Det 12 (DB)   **1953**†Det 12 (DB)   **1954** Det 2

1949	Det	12(2)	33	162	4.9(20)	0	2	16	8.0(12)	0	—	—	—	—	—	—	—	—	—	—	kpi	1	6	435
1952	†Det★	12(DB)	3	12	4.0(10)	0	1	18	18.0(18)	0	—	—	—	—	—	—	—	—	—	—	Pi	1	6	170
NFL	5	62(2)	36	174	4.8(20)	0	3	34	11.3(31)	0	—	—	—	—	—	—	—	—	—	—	Pkpi	3	18	877

SMITH, BOB Robert Bert, DB, 6´0˝/181 lbs; Miami (OH); 1968: Hou, rnd 16; B12/28/1945 Williamson, WV   **1968** Hou-A 6

SMITH, BOB Robert Gerald, HB, 5´10˝/195 lbs; Nebraska; 1955: Cle, rnd 15; B2/23/1933 Council Bluffs, IA

1955	†Cle	10	37	142	3.8(31)	1	2	12	6.0(10)	0	—	—	—	—	—	—	—	—	—	—	kp	—	6	283
1956	Cle	2	2	10	5.0(7)	0	—	—	—	—	—	—	—	—	—	—	—	—	—	—	k	—	0	9
1956	Phi	4	9	8	0.9(5)	0	—	—	—	—	—	—	—	—	—	—	—	—	—	—	—	—	0	8
NFL	2	16	48	160	3.3(31)	1	2	12	6.0(10)	0	—	—	—	—	—	—	—	—	—	—	kp	—	6	300

SMITH, BOB Robert Lee, FB, 6´0˝/205 lbs; Texas A&M; 1951: Cle, rnd 4; B2/28/1929 Houston, TX, D1/5/2005 Dallas, TX

1953	Det	3	6	51	8.5(30)	0	1	11	11.0(11)	0	—	—	—	—	—	—	—	—	—	—	—	—	0	57
1954	†Det	12	3	1	0.3(1)	0	—	—	—	—	—	—	—	—	—	—	—	—	—	—	—	—	0	1
NFL	2	15	9	52	5.8(30)	0	1	11	11.0(11)	0	—	—	—	—	—	—	—	—	—	—	—	—	0	58

SMITH, BOBBY Robert Lee, DB, 5´11˝/197 lbs; UCLA; 1961: LA, rnd 7/NYT, rnd 26; B7/5/1938 Plain Dealing, LA   **1962** LARm 14   **1963** LARm 14 (RCB)   **1964** LARm 14 (LS)
1965 LARm 7   **1965** Det 6   **1966** Det 14 (RCB)   **NFL** 69 [5 yrs]

SMITH, BOBBY Robert Lee, HB, 6´0˝/203 lbs; North Texas; 1964: Buf, rnd 11/Pit, rnd 7; B5/18/1942 Corpus Christi, TX

1964	†Buf-A	14(HB)	62	306	4.9(37)	4	6	72	12.0(25)	0	—	—	—	—	—	—	—	—	—	—	k	—	24	405
1965	†Buf-A◇	14	43	137	3.2(13)	1	12	116	9.7(21)	0	—	—	—	—	—	—	—	—	—	—	—	—	6	205
1966	Pit	8	24	93	3.9(21)	0	3	26	8.7(21)	0	—	—	—	—	—	—	—	—	—	—	—	—	0	106
NFL	3	36	129	536	4.2(37)	5	21	214	10.2(25)	0	—	—	—	—	—	—	—	—	—	—	k	—	30	716

SMITH, BRAD Bradley James, LB, 6´2˝/228 lbs; TCU; B9/5/1969 Houston, TX   **1993** Cin 7 (0)

SMITH, BRADY Brady McKay, DE, 6´5˝/274 lbs; Colorado State; 1996: NO, rnd 3; B6/5/1973 Royal Oak, MI   **1996** NO 16 (4)   **1997** NO 16 (2)   **1998** NO 14 (5, lde)
1999 NO 16 (16, RDE)   **2000** Atl 15 (14, RDE)   **2001** Atl 15 (15, RDE)   **2002**†Atl 14 (14, RDE)   **2003** Atl 16 (14, RDE)   **2004**†Atl 16 (16, RDE)   **2005** Atl 5 (5, rde)
NFL 143 (105) [10 yrs]

SMITH, BRENT Gary Brent, G-T, 6´5˝/305 lbs; Mississippi State; 1997: Mia, rnd 3; B11/21/1973 Dallas, TX   **1998**†Mia 8 (7, lt)   **1999** Mia 13 (4)   **2000**†Mia 16 (2)
2003 NYJ 16 (16, RG)   **2004** NYJ 4 (1)   **NFL** 57 (30) [5 yrs]

SMITH, BRIAN Brian Mark, LB-DT, 6´6˝/242 lbs; Auburn; 1989: LARm, rnd 2; B4/23/1966 Brooklyn, NY   **1989** LARm 3 (0)   **1990** LARm 16 (4)   **NFL** 19 (4) [2 yrs]

SMITH, BRUCE Bruce Phillip, HB-DB-TB, 6´0˝/197 lbs; Minnesota; 1942: GB, rnd 13; B2/8/1920 Faribault, MN, D8/28/1967 Alexandria, MN

1945	GB	3(2)	21	94	4.5(27)	0	—	—	—	—	—	—	—	—	—	—	—	—	—	—	kp	—	0	147
1946	GB	6(2)	22	119	5.4(36)	0	—	—	—	—	—	—	—	—	—	—	—	—	—	—	kp	—	0	127
1947	GB	10(6, lh)	47	288	6.1(37)	1	4	50	12.5(36)	1	—	—	—	—	—	—	—	—	—	—	kp	—	14	361
1948	GB	4(1)	6	21	3.5(20)	0	—	—	—	—	1	0	0.0	0	0.0	0	0	—	—	—	—	—	0	21
1948	LARm	8(0)	12	38	3.2(0)	0	4	29	7.3(10)	0	—	—	—	—	—	—	—	—	—	—	p	—	0	58
NFL	4	31(11)	108	560	5.2(37)	1	8	79	9.9(36)	1	1	0	0.0	0	0.0	0	0	—	—	—	kp	—	14	714

SMITH, BRUCE Bruce Bernard, DE, 6´4˝/262 lbs; Virginia Tech; 1985: Buf, rnd 1; B6/18/1963 Norfolk, VA [S]   **1986** Buf☆16 (15, RDE)   **1987** Buf★12 (12, RDE)
1988†Buf★12 (12, RDE)   **1989**†Buf★16 (16, RDE)   **1990**†Buf★16 (16, RDE)   **1991**†Buf 5 (5, rde)   **1992**†Buf★15 (15, RDE)   **1993**†Buf★16 (16, RDE)   **1994** Buf★15 (15, RDE)
1995†Buf★15 (15, RDE)   **1996**†Buf★16 (16, RDE)   **1997** Buf★16 (16, RDE)   **1998**†Buf★15 (15, RDE)   **1999**†Buf 16 (16, RDE)   **2000** Was 16 (16, RDE)   **2001** Was 14 (14, RDE)
2002 Was 16 (16, RDE)   **2003** Was 16 (8, LDE)

| 1985 | Buf | 16(13, RDE) | 1 | 0 | 0.0(0) | 0 | — | — | — | — | — | — | — | — | — | — | — | — | — | — | S | — | 0 | 0 |
| NFL | 19 | 279(267) | 1 | 0 | 0.0 | 0 | — | — | — | — | — | — | — | — | — | — | — | — | — | — | iS | 1 | 10 | -10 |

SMITH, BUBBA Charles Aaron, DE-DT, 6´7˝/265 lbs; Michigan State; 1967: Bal, rnd 1; B2/28/1945 Beaumont, TX   **1967** Bal 13   **1968**†Bal★14 (LDE)   **1969** Bal 14 (LDE)
1970†Bal★14 (LDE)   **1971**†Bal★14 (LDE)   **1973** Oak 12 (12, LDE)   **1974**†Oak 14 (13, LDE)   **1975** Hou 12   **1976** Hou 4   **NFL** 111 (25) [9 yrs]

SMITH, BYRON Byron Keith, DE-DT, 6´5˝/278 lbs; California; 1984: Ind, rnd S3; B12/21/1962 Los Angeles, CA   **1984** Ind 3 (0)   **1985** Ind 16 (7, rde)   **NFL** 19 (7) [2 yrs]

SMITH, CARL Carl Eddie, FB, 6´0˝/200 lbs; Tennessee; 1959: Det, rnd 9; B11/22/1932 Washington Court House, OH, D5/29/2003 Washington Court House, OH

| 1960 | Buf-A | 14 | 19 | 61 | 3.2(13) | 0 | 7 | 127 | 18.1(58) | 1 | — | — | — | — | — | — | — | — | — | — | k | — | 6 | 172 |

SMITH, CEDRIC Cedric Delon, FB, 5´11˝/238 lbs; Florida; 1990: Min, rnd 5; B5/27/1968 Enterprise, AL

1990	Min	15(1)	9	19	2.1(7)	0	—	—	—	—	—	—	—	—	—	—	—	—	—	—	k	—	0	20
1991	†NO	6(0)	—	—	—	—	—	—	—	—	—	—	—	—	—	—	—	—	—	—	—	—	0	0
1994	Was	14(8, FB)	10	48	4.8(13)	0	15	118	7.9(28)	1	—	—	—	—	—	—	—	—	—	—	—	—	6	112
1995	Was	6(0)	3	13	4.3(5)	0	—	—	—	—	—	—	—	—	—	—	—	—	—	—	—	—	0	13
1996	Arz	15(2)	14	15	1.1(3)	1	3	3	1.0(2)	1	—	—	—	—	—	—	—	—	—	—	k	—	12	31
1997	Arz	16(3)	4	5	1.3(2)	1	2	20	10.0(18)	0	—	—	—	—	—	—	—	—	—	—	k	—	6	30
NFL	6	72(14)	40	100	2.5(13)	2	20	141	7.1(28)	2	—	—	—	—	—	—	—	—	—	—	k	—	24	206

SMITH, CHARLES Charles Harlin, HB-DB, 5´11˝/170 lbs; Georgia; 1947: ChiC, rnd 16; B3/13/1924 Aldrich, MO

| 1947 | ChiC | 7(0) | 9 | 23 | 2.6(12) | 0 | 1 | -6 | -6.0(-6) | 0 | — | — | — | — | — | — | — | — | — | — | ki | — | 0 | 19 |

SMITH, CHARLIE Charles W., DE, 6´2˝/205 lbs; Abilene Christian; 1956: SF, rnd 8; B4/6/1933 Sweetwater, TX

| 1956 | SF | 12 | — | — | — | — | 1 | 13 | 13.0(13) | 0 | — | — | — | — | — | — | — | — | — | — | k | — | 0 | 6 |

SMITH, CHARLIE Charles Albert, WR, 6´1˝/185 lbs; Grambling State; B7/26/1950 Monroe, LA

1974	Phi	14	—	—	—	—	1	28	28.0(28)	0	—	—	—	—	—	—	—	—	—	—	p	—	0	1
1975	Phi	14(12, WR)	9	85	9.4(36)	0	37	515	13.9(46)	6	—	—	—	—	—	—	—	—	—	—	—	—	36	373
1976	Phi	14(14, WR)	9	25	2.8(14)	1	27	412	15.3(48)	4	—	—	—	—	—	—	—	—	—	—	k	—	30	243
1977	Phi	14(14, WR)	2	13	6.5(8)	0	33	464	14.1(32)	4	—	—	—	—	—	—	—	—	—	—	—	—	24	265
1978	†Phi	14(5, wr)	—	—	—	—	11	142	12.9(27)	2	—	—	—	—	—	—	—	—	—	—	—	—	12	81
1979	†Phi	16(12, WR)	—	—	—	—	24	399	16.6(39)	1	—	—	—	—	—	—	—	—	—	—	—	—	6	191
1980	†Phi	16(16, WR)	5	33	6.6(16)	0	47	825	17.6(46)	3	—	—	—	—	—	—	—	—	—	—	k	—	18	461
1981	†Phi	16(14, WR)	2	5	2.5(5)	0	38	564	14.8(45)	4	—	—	—	—	—	—	—	—	—	—	—	—	24	307
NFL	8	118(87)	27	161	6.0(36)	1	218	3349	15.4(48)	24	—	—	—	—	—	—	—	—	—	—	kp	—	150	1921

SMITH, CHARLIE Charles Henry, RB, 6´0˝/205 lbs; Utah; 1968: Oak, rnd 4; B1/18/1946 Natchez, MS

1968	†Oak-A	14(3)	95	504	**5.3(65)**	5	22	321	14.6(43)	2	—	—	—	—	—	—	—	—	—	—	kp	—	42	772
1969	†Oak-A	14(14, HB)	177	600	3.4(26)	2	30	322	10.7(32)	2	—	—	—	—	—	—	—	—	—	—	k	—	24	888
1970	†Oak	14(14, RB)	168	681	4.1(24)	3	23	173	7.5(27)	2	—	—	—	—	—	—	—	—	—	—	—	—	30	808
1971	Oak	8	11	4	0.4(8)	1	2	67	33.5(44)	0	—	—	—	—	—	—	—	—	—	—	k	—	6	33
1972	†Oak	14(13, RB)	170	686	4.0(28)	3	28	353	12.6(43)	2	—	—	—	—	—	—	—	—	—	—	k	—	60	938
1973	†Oak	14(14, RB)	173	682	3.9(19)	4	28	260	9.3(20)	1	—	—	—	—	—	—	—	—	—	—	—	—	30	850
1974	†Oak	13(7, rb)	64	194	3.0(22)	1	8	100	12.5(30)	1	—	—	—	—	—	—	—	—	—	—	k	—	12	259
1975	SD	4	—	—	—	—	—	—	—	—	—	—	—	—	—	—	—	—	—	—	k	—	0	102
NFL	8	95(65)	858	3351	3.9(65)	24	141	1596	11.3(44)	10	—	—	—	—	—	—	—	—	—	—	kp	—	204	4648

SMITH, CHRIS Christopher Montane, RB, 6´1˝/232 lbs; Notre Dame; B6/1/1963 Cincinnati, OH   **1986** KC 1 (0)

| 1987 | KC | 3(3) | 26 | 114 | 4.4(11) | 0 | 2 | 21 | 10.5(16) | 0 | — | — | — | — | — | — | — | — | — | — | — | — | 0 | 125 |
| NFL | 2 | 4(3) | 26 | 114 | 4.4(11) | 0 | 2 | 21 | 10.5(16) | 0 | — | — | — | — | — | — | — | — | — | — | — | — | 0 | 125 |

YEAR	TEAM	G (GS, POS)	RUSH	YD	AVG (LG)	TD	REC	YD	AVG (LG)	TD	PASS	COMP	PCT	YD	AVG (LG)	TD	INT	SK	YD	QBR	KPR	OTD	PTS	TAY

SMITH, CHUCK Charles Henry, DE-LB, 6´2˝/257 lbs; Tennessee; 1992: Atl, rnd 2; B12/21/1969 Athens, GA [S] **1992** Atl 16 (0) **1993** Atl 15 (1) **1994** Atl 15 (10, LDE) **1995**†Atl 14 (13, LDE) **1996** Atl 15 (15, RDE) **1997** Atl☆16 (15, RDE) **1998**†Atl 16 (16, RDE) **1999** Atl 16 (16, RDE) **2000** Car 2 (2) **NFL** 125 (88) [9 yrs]

SMITH, CLIFTON Clifton M., LB, 6´3˝/255 lbs; Syracuse; B7/21/1980 Freeport, NY **2003** Was 1 (0)

SMITH, CLYDE Clyde Wise, C, 5´10˝/184 lbs; Missouri; B7/17/1904 Steelville, MO, D12/30/1982 Lawrenceville, IL **1925** KC 1 (1) **1926** KC☆9 (7, C) **1927** Cle☆12 (12, C) **1928** Pro☆11 (11, C) **NFL** 33 (31) [4 yrs]

SMITH, COREY Corey Dominique, DE, 6´2˝/250 lbs; North Carolina State; B11/2/1978 Richmond, VA **2002** TB 6 (0) **2003** TB 1 (0) **2004** SF 1 (0) **2004** TB 4 (0) **2005** SF 14 (0) **NFL** 26 (0) [4 yrs]

SMITH, DALLIS Dallis Kevin, DB, 5´11˝/170 lbs; Valdosta State; B7/31/1965 **1987** Sea 3 (3)

SMITH, DAN Daniel Eugene, DB, 5´10˝/180 lbs; Northeastern State (OK); B1/29/1935 Matoy, OK **1961** Den-A 4

SMITH, DARRIN Darrin Andrew, LB, 6´1˝/236 lbs; Miami (FL); 1993: Dal, rnd 2; B4/15/1970 Miami, FL **1993**†Dal 16 (13, RLB) **1994**†Dal 16 (16, RLB) **1995**†Dal 9 (9, rlb) **1996**†Dal 16 (16, RLB) **1997** Phi 7 (7, LLB) **1998** Sea 13 (12, LLB) **1999**†Sea 15 (15, LLB) **2000**†NO 16 (11, MLB) **2001** NO 16 (16, RLB) **2002** NO 15 (15, LLB) **2003** NO 14 (10, MLB) **2004** NO 3 (0) **NFL** 156 (140) [12 yrs]

SMITH, DARYL Daryl Dimitri, DB, 5´9˝/185 lbs; North Alabama; 1985: Den, rnd 9; B5/8/1963 Opelika, AL **1987** Cin 3 (3) **1988**†Cin 7 (0) **1989** Min 5 (1) **NFL** 15 (4) [3 yrs]

SMITH, DARYL Daryl Lamont, LB, 6´2˝/235 lbs; Georgia Tech; 2004: Jax, rnd 2; B4/14/1982 Albany, GA **2004** Jax 15 (13, LLB) **2005**†Jax 16 (16, RLB) **NFL** 31 (29) [2 yrs]

SMITH, DARYLE Daryle Ray, T, 6´5˝/277 lbs; Tennessee; B1/18/1964 Knoxville, TN **1987** Dal 9 (7, lt) **1988** Dal 14 (4) **1989** Cle 4 (0) **1990** Phi 3 (0) **1991** Phi 14 (1) **1992**†Phi 16 (4) **NFL** 60 (16) [6 yrs]

SMITH, DAVE David William, FB, 6´1˝/210 lbs; Ripon; 1959: GB, rnd 21; B3/23/1937 Milwaukee, WI

YEAR	TEAM	G (GS, POS)	RUSH	YD	AVG (LG)	TD	REC	YD	AVG (LG)	TD	PASS	COMP	PCT	YD	AVG (LG)	TD	INT	SK	YD	QBR	KPR	OTD	PTS	TAY
1960	†Hou-A☆	14 (14, FB)	154	643	4.2(65)	5	22	216	9.8(40)	1	2	5	60.0	70	14.0(31)	1	0	—	—	—	—	—	42	851
1961	†Hou-A	14	60	258	4.3(21)	2	10	131	13.1(37)	1	2	1	50.0	33	16.5(33)	0	0	—	—	—	kp	—	18	365
1962	†Hou-A	14	56	249	4.4(41)	1	17	117	6.9(20)	2	3	2	66.7	34	11.3(19)	0	0	—	—	—	k	—	18	352
1963	Hou-A	14	50	202	4.0(16)	3	24	270	11.3(36)	2	2	0	0.0	0	0.0	0	0	—	—	—	—	—	30	377
1964	Hou-A	9	8	16	2.0(8)	0	7	38	5.4(15)	0	—	—	—	—	—	—	—	—	—	—	—	—	0	35
NFL		5	65(14)	328	1368	4.2(65)	11	80	772	9.6(40)	7	12	6	50.0	137	11.4(33)	1	0	—	—	—	kp	—	108	1980

SMITH, DAVE David, RB, 6´1˝/210 lbs; Utah; 1970: GB, rnd 13; B12/9/1947 Salt Lake City, UT

YEAR	TEAM	G (GS, POS)	RUSH	YD	AVG (LG)	TD	REC	YD	AVG (LG)	TD	...	PTS	TAY
1970	SD	7	14	42	3.0(15)	0	4	65	16.3(42)	0		0	75

SMITH, DAVE David Allan, T, 6´6˝/290 lbs; Southern Illinois; B12/12/1964 Hammond, IN **1988**†Cin 4 (0)

SMITH, DAVE David Lewis, WR, 6´2˝/205 lbs; Waynesburg; Indiana State; 1970: Pit, rnd 8; B5/18/1947 New York, NY

YEAR	TEAM	G (GS, POS)	RUSH	YD	AVG (LG)	TD	REC	YD	AVG (LG)	TD	...	PTS	TAY
1970	Pit	14 (WR)	1	6	6.0(6)	0	30	458	15.3(87)	2		12	245
1971	Pit	14 (WR)	1	-10	-10.0(-10)	0	47	663	14.1(49)	5		30	347
1972	Pit	6 (wr)	—	—	—	—	10	98	9.8(25)	0		0	49
1972	Hou	8 (wr)	—	—	—	—	20	218	10.9(24)	0		0	109
1973	KC	2	—	—	—	—	2	20	10.0(17)	0		0	10
NFL		4	44	2	-4	-2.0(6)	0	109	1457	13.4(87)	7		42	760

SMITH, DENNIS Dennis, DB, 6´3˝/200 lbs; USC; 1981: Den, rnd 1; B2/3/1959 Santa Monica, CA [I] **1981** Den 16 (4) **1982** Den 8 (8, SS) **1983**†Den 14 (13, SS) **1984**†Den☆15 (15, SS) **1985** Den★13 (12, SS) **1986**†Den★14 (14, SS) **1987**†Den 6 (6, SS) **1988** Den 11 (11, SS) **1989**†Den★14 (14, SS) **1990** Den◇15 (15, SS) **1991**†Den◇16 (16, SS) **1992** Den 16 (16, SS) **1993**†Den◇14 (14, SS) **1994** Den 12 (12, FS) **NFL** 184 (170) [14 yrs]

SMITH, DENNIS Dennis Preston, RB, 6´0˝/230 lbs; Utah; B2/14/1967 Hemet, CA **1990** Phx 4 (0)

SMITH, DEREK Derek Mecham, LB, 6´2˝/245 lbs; Arizona State; 1997: Was, rnd 3; B1/18/1975 American Fork, UT **1997** Was 16 (16, RLB) **1998** Was 16 (15, RLB) **1999**†Was 16 (16, MLB) **2000** Was 16 (14, MLB) **2001**†SF 14 (14, MLB) **2002**†SF 16 (16, MLB) **2003** SF 16 (16, MLB) **2004** SF 14 (14, MLB) **2005** SF 16 (16, RILB/lilb) **NFL** 140 (137) [9 yrs]

SMITH, DETRON Detron Nigel, RB, 5´10˝/229 lbs; Texas A&M; 1996: Den, rnd 3; B2/25/1974 Dallas, TX

YEAR	TEAM	G (GS, POS)	RUSH	YD	AVG (LG)	TD	REC	YD	AVG (LG)	TD	...	KPR	OTD	PTS	TAY
1996	Den	13 (0)	—	—	—	—	—	—	—	—					
1997	†Den	16 (0)	4	10	2.5(11)	0	4	41	10.3(17)	1		k	—	6	21
1998	†Den	15 (2)	—	—	—	—	3	24	8.0(16)	0		k	—	0	18
1999	Den★	16 (0)	1	7	7.0(7)	0	4	23	5.8(11)	0		k	—	0	16
2000	†Den	16 (0)	—	—	—	—	1	1	1.0(1)	0		k	—	6	4
2001	Den	15 (0)	—	—	—	—	—	—	—	—		k	—	0	-11
2002	†Ind	11 (2)	—	—	—	—	1	14	14.0(14)	0		k	—	0	8
2003	Ind	11 (0)	—	—	—	—	—	—	—	—		k	—	0	0
NFL		8	113 (4)	5	17	3.4(11)	0	13	103	7.9(17)	2		k	—	12	55

SMITH, DICK Richard Scott, C, 6´2˝/225 lbs; Ohio State; B1/24/1912 East Chicago, IN, D4/15/1980 New Canaan, CT **1933** Bos 1 (0) **1933** ChiB 1 (0) **1933** Phi 3 (2) **NFL** 5 (2) [1 yr]

SMITH, DICK Richard Henry, DB-HB, 6´0˝/205 lbs; Northwestern; 1966: KC, rnd 9; B6/19/1944 Hamilton, OH **1967** Was 10

YEAR	TEAM	G (GS, POS)	RUSH	YD	AVG (LG)	TD	REC	YD	AVG (LG)	TD	...	KPR	OTD	PTS	TAY
1968	Was	10	3	5	1.7(3)	0	1	15	15.0(15)	0		ki	—	0	86
NFL		2	20	3	5	1.7(3)	0	1	15	15.0(15)	0		ki	—	0	131

SMITH, DON Donald, G, none **1930** Nwk 2 (1)

SMITH, DON Donald L., G, 6´4˝/240 lbs; Florida A&M; 1967: Den, rnd 15; B2/8/1943 **1967** Den-A 2

SMITH, DON Donald Michael, RB-WR, 5´11˝/200 lbs; Mississippi State; 1987: TB, rnd 2; B10/30/1963 Hamilton, MS

YEAR	TEAM	G (GS, POS)	RUSH	YD	AVG (LG)	TD	REC	YD	AVG (LG)	TD	PASS	COMP	PCT	YD	AVG(LG)	TD	...	KPR	OTD	PTS	TAY
1988	TB	10 (3)	13	46	3.5(15)	1	12	138	11.5(25)	0	—	—	—	—	—	—		k	—	6	178
1989	TB	11 (0)	7	37	5.3(17)	0	7	110	15.7(44)	0	—	—	—	—	—	—		k	—	0	92
1990	†Buf	16 (2)	20	82	4.1(13)	2	21	225	10.7(39)	0	1	0	0.0	0	0.0	0		k	—	12	378
NFL		3	37 (5)	40	165	4.1(17)	3	40	473	11.8(44)	0	1	0	0.0	0	0.0	0		k	—	18	648

SMITH, DON Donald Loren, NT-DE-DT, 6´5˝/256 lbs; Miami (FL); 1979: Atl, rnd 1; B5/9/1957 Oakland, CA **1979** Atl 16 (16, RDE) **1980**†Atl 16 (9, NT) **1981** Atl☆16 (16, NT) **1982**†Atl 9 (9, NT) **1983** Atl 14 (13, RDT) **1984** Atl 16 (16, RDE) **1985** Buf 16 (3) **1986** Buf 5 (0) **1987** NYJ 3 (0) **NFL** 111 (82) [9 yrs]

SMITH, DONALD Donald Ray, DB, 5´11˝/189 lbs; Liberty; 1990: Min, rnd 10; B2/21/1968 Danville, VA **1991** Dal 3 (0)

SMITH, DONNELL Donnell, DE, 6´4˝/245 lbs; Southern (LA); 1971: GB, rnd 5; B5/25/1949 Lakeland, FL **1971** GB 4 **1973** NE 12 **1974** NE 9 **NFL** 25 [3 yrs]

SMITH, DOUG Arthur Douglas, NT-DT, 6´4˝/294 lbs; Auburn; 1984: Hou, rnd 2; B6/13/1959 Mesic, NC **1985** Hou 11 (1) **1986** Hou 13 (7, nt) **1987**†Hou 15 (13, NT) **1988**†Hou 12 (10, NT) **1989**†Hou 15 (12, NT) **1990** Hou 14 (13, RDT) **1991** Hou 15 (15, RDT) **1992** Hou 6 (6, rdt) **NFL** 101 (77) [8 yrs]

SMITH, DOUG Douglas Batrone, DB, 6´0˝/192 lbs; Ohio State; B2/4/1963 Atlanta, GA **1987** NYG 3 (3)

SMITH, DOUG Carl Douglas, C-G-T, 6´3˝/259 lbs; Bowling Green State; B11/25/1956 Columbus, OH **1978**†LARm 16 (2) **1979** LARm 4 (1) **1980** LARm 8 (8, RG) **1981** LARm 16 (13, RT/rg) **1982** LARm 9 (9, C) **1983**†LARm 14 (14, C) **1984**†LARm◇16 (16, C) **1985** LARm◇13 (13, C) **1986**†LARm★16 (16, C) **1987** LARm◇12 (12, C) **1988**†LARm◇16 (16, C) **1989**†LARm 16 (16, C) **1990** LARm 16 (16, C) **1991** LARm 15 (8, c) **NFL** 187 (160) [14 yrs]

SMITH, DWIGHT Dwight, DB, 5´10˝/201 lbs; Akron; 2001: TB, rnd 3; B8/13/1978 Detroit, MI **2001**†TB 15 (0) **2002**†TB 16 (2) **2003** TB 16 (16, RCB/fs) **2004** TB 16 (16, SS) **2005** NO 15 (15, SS) **NFL** 78 (49) [5 yrs]

SMITH, ED Edward, BB-FB-TB-DB, 6´2˝/207 lbs; NYU; 1936: Bos, rnd 3; B6/17/1913 New York, NY [K]

YEAR	TEAM	G (GS, POS)	RUSH	YD	AVG (LG)	TD	REC	YD	AVG (LG)	TD	PASS	COMP	PCT	YD	AVG(LG)	TD	INT	...	KPR	OTD	PTS	TAY
1936	†Bos	8 (4, BB)	7	39	5.6	0	—	—	—	—	40	11	27.5	120	3.0	1	2		K	—	3	24
1937	GB	2 (0)	—	—	—	—	—	—	—	—	2	0	0.0	0	0.0	0	1		—	—	0	-40
NFL		2	10 (4)	7	39	5.6	0	—	—	—	—	42	11	26.2	120	2.9	1	3		K	—	3	-16

SMITH, ED Oscar Edwin, HB-DB, 6´3˝/185 lbs; Texas-El Paso; 1948: GB, rnd 3/LAD-A, rnd 21; B7/20/1923 Fort Monroe, VA

YEAR	TEAM	G (GS, POS)	RUSH	YD	AVG (LG)	TD	REC	YD	AVG (LG)	TD	...	KPR	OTD	PTS	TAY
1948	GB	12 (1)	27	85	3.1(10)	0	12	121	10.1(49)	0		kp	—	0	284
1949	GB	3 (0)	9	15	1.7(11)	0	—	—	—	—		kp	—	0	20

YEAR	TEAM	G(GS, POS)	RUSH	YD	AVG(LG)	TD	REC	YD	AVG(LG)	TD	PASS	COMP	PCT	YD	AVG(LG)	TD	INT	SK	YD	QBR	KPR	OTD	PTS	TAY
1949	NYB	8(1)	7	9	1.3(0)	0	—	—	—	—	—	—	—	—	—	—	—	—	—	—	pi	—	0	27
NFL	2	23(2)	43	109	2.5(11)	0	12	121	10.1(49)	0	—	—	—	—	—	—	—	—	—	—	kpi	—	0	331

SMITH, ED — Edwin Alexander, DE, 6'5"/241 lbs; Colorado College; 1973: Den, rnd 13; B10/23/1950 Nassau, Bahamas **1973** Den 5 **1974** Den 11 (3) **NFL** 16 (3) [2 yrs]

SMITH, ED — Henry Edward, LB, 6'2"/216 lbs; Vanderbilt; 1979: Pit, rnd 12; B5/18/1957 Knoxville, TN **1980** Bal 16 (0) **1981** Bal 16 (8, mlb) **NFL** 32 (8) [2 yrs]

SMITH, ED — Edward Martin, TE, 6'4"/253 lbs; none; B6/5/1969 Trenton, NJ **1998**†Atl 15 (0) **1999** Det 3 (0) **1999** Phi 7 (1)

YEAR	TEAM	G(GS, POS)	RUSH	YD	AVG(LG)	TD	REC	YD	AVG(LG)	TD	KPR	OTD	PTS	TAY
1997	Atl	5(1)	—	—	—	—	1	2	2.0(2)	0	—	—	0	1
NFL	3	30(2)	—	—	—	—	1	2	2.0(2)	0	k	—	0	-13

SMITH, ELLIOT — Elliott, DB, 6'2"/192 lbs; Alcorn State; 1989: SD, rnd 5; B8/14/1967 Jackson, MS **1989** SD 2 (0) **1990** Den 9 (3) **NFL** 11 (3) [2 yrs]

SMITH, EMANUEL — Emanuel, WR, 6'1"/210 lbs; Arkansas; 2000: Jax, rnd 6; B2/3/1976 Jackson, MS **2000** Jax 1 (0)

SMITH, EMMITT — Emmitt J., RB, 5'10"/221 lbs; Florida; 1990: Dal, rnd 1; B5/15/1969 Pensacola, FL

YEAR	TEAM	G(GS, POS)	RUSH	YD	AVG(LG)	TD	REC	YD	AVG(LG)	TD	PASS	COMP	PCT	YD	AVG(LG)	TD	INT	KPR	OTD	PTS	TAY
1990	Dal◇	16(15, RB)	241	937	3.9(48)	11	24	228	9.5(57)	0	—	—	—	—	—	—	—	—	—	66	1161
1991	†Dal★	16(16, RB)	365	1563	4.3(75)	12	49	258	5.3(14)	1	—	—	—	—	—	—	—	—	—	78	1817
1992	†Dal★	16(16, RB)	373	1713	4.6(68)	18	59	335	5.7(26)	1	—	—	—	—	—	—	—	—	—	114	2066
1993	†Dal★	14(13, RB)	283	1486	5.3(62)	9	57	414	7.3(86)	1	—	—	—	—	—	—	—	—	—	60	1788
1994	†Dal★	15(15, RB)	368	1484	4.0(46)	21	50	341	6.8(68)	1	—	—	—	—	—	—	—	—	—	132	1870
1995	†Dal★	16(16, RB)	377	1773	4.7(60)	25	62	375	6.0(40)	0	—	—	—	—	—	—	—	—	—	150	2211
1996	†Dal☆	15(15, RB)	327	1204	3.7(42)	12	47	249	5.3(22)	3	—	—	—	—	—	—	—	—	—	90	1464
1997	Dal	16(16, RB)	261	1074	4.1(44)	4	40	234	5.8(24)	0	—	—	—	—	—	—	—	—	—	26	1231
1998	†Dal	16(16, RB)	319	1332	4.2(32)	13	27	175	6.5(24)	2	—	—	—	—	—	—	—	—	—	90	1560
1999	†Dal◇	15(15, RB)	329	1397	4.2(63)	11	27	119	4.4(14)	2	—	—	—	—	—	—	—	—	—	78	1577
2000	Dal	16(16, RB)	294	1203	4.1(52)	9	11	79	7.2(19)	0	—	—	—	—	—	—	—	—	—	54	1333
2001	Dal	14(14, RB)	261	1021	3.9(44)	3	17	116	6.8(22)	0	—	—	—	—	—	—	—	—	—	18	1109
2002	Dal	16(16, RB)	254	975	3.8(30)	5	16	89	5.6(17)	0	—	—	—	—	—	—	—	—	—	30	1070
2003	Arz	10(5, rb)	90	256	2.8(22)	2	14	107	7.6(36)	0	—	—	—	—	—	—	—	—	—	12	330
2004	Arz	15(15, RB)	267	937	3.5(29)	9	10	105	7.0(18)	0	1	1	100.0	21	21.0(21)	1	0	—	—	54	1095
NFL	15	226(219)	4409	18355	4.2(75)	164	515	3224	6.3(86)	11	1	1	100.0	21	21.0(21)	1	0	—	—	1052	21678

SMITH, ERIC — Blane Eric, DB, 5'10"/190 lbs; SMU; B12/22/1959 Houston, TX **1987** KC 3 (1)

SMITH, ERIC — Eric Lamonte, WR, 5'11"/183 lbs; LSU; B1/5/1971 Vero Beach, FL

YEAR	TEAM	G(GS, POS)	RUSH	YD	AVG(LG)	TD	REC	YD	AVG(LG)	TD	KPR	OTD	PTS	TAY
1997	ChiB	7(0)	1	12	12.0(12)	0	2	22	11.0(12)	0	k	—	0	69

SMITH, ERNIE — Ernest Frederick, T, 6'2"/224 lbs; USC; B11/26/1909 Spearfish, SD, D4/25/1985 Altadena, CA **[K]** **1935** GB 12 (7, LT) **1936**†GB☆12 (9, LT) **1937** GB☆10 (7, LT) **1939**†GB◇6 (2) **NFL** 40 (25) [4 yrs]

SMITH, ERNIE — Ernest W., DB-HB, 6'3"/190 lbs; Compton CC (CA); San Diego City Coll; B7/6/1930 **1955** SF 1 **1956** SF 3 **NFL** 4 [2 yrs]

SMITH, FERNANDO — Fernando Dewitt, DE, 6'6"/277 lbs; Jackson State; 1994: Min, rnd 2; B8/2/1971 Flint, MI **1994** Min 7 (0) **1995** Min 12 (1) **1996**†Min 16 (16, LDE) **1997**†Min 12 (11, LDE) **1998** Jax 14 (0) **1999** Bal 15 (0) **2000**†Min 1 (0) **2000** SL 2 (0) **NFL** 79 (28) [7 yrs]

SMITH, FLETCHER — Fletcher Leon, DB-K, 6'0"/178 lbs; Tennessee State; 1966: KC, rnd 8; B10/13/1943 Hearne, TX **[K]** **1966**†KC-A 11 **1967** KC-A 13 (rcb) **1968** Cin-A 14 (LCB) **1969** Cin-A 14 (LCB) **1970**†Cin 14 (SS) **1971** Cin 14 (SS) **NFL** 80 [6 yrs]

SMITH, FRANKIE — Frankie Lee, DB, 5'9"/186 lbs; Baylor; 1992: Atl, rnd 4; B10/8/1968 Fort Worth, TX **1993** Mia 5 (1) **1994**†Mia 13 (2) **1995** Mia 11 (1) **1996**†SF 14 (0) **1997**†SF 16 (0) **1998** ChiB 15 (0) **1999** ChiB 15 (0) **2000** ChiB 14 (0) **NFL** 103 (4) [8 yrs]

SMITH, FRANKY — Frank Lee, T, 6'6"/279 lbs; Alabama A&M; B1/16/1956 Birmingham, AL **1980** KC 4 (2)

SMITH, GARY — Gary Lovell, G, 6'2"/265 lbs; Virginia Tech; B1/27/1960 Bitburg AFB, Germany **1984** Cin 8 (2)

SMITH, GAYLON — Gaylon Wesley, FB-WB-BB-DB-LB, 5'11"/202 lbs; Rhodes; 1939: Cle, rnd 2; B7/15/1916 Lonoke, AR

YEAR	TEAM	G(GS, POS)	RUSH	YD	AVG(LG)	TD	REC	YD	AVG(LG)	TD	PASS	COMP	PCT	YD	AVG(LG)	TD	INT	KPR	OTD	PTS	TAY
1939	Cle	11(4, WB)	58	98	1.7	2	3	57	19.0	0	5	4	80.0	3	0.6	0	0	Pi	—	12	148
1940	Cle	11(8, BB)	19	18	0.9	—	2	65	32.5	0	18	10	55.6	150	8.3(38)	2	2	Pi	—	0	89
1941	Cle	4(0)	11	22	2.0(12)	0	—	—	—	—	2	0	0.0	0	0.0	0	1	Ppi	—	0	21
1942	Cle	11(6, FB)	83	332	4.0(50)	2	3	61	20.3(33)	0	12	2	16.7	49	4.1(19)	0	0	kpi	—	12	418
NFL	4	37(18)	171	470	2.7(50)	4	8	183	22.9(33)	0	37	16	43.2	202	5.5(38)	2	4	Pkpi	—	24	676
1946	Cle-A	14(1)	62	240	3.9	5	7	73	10.4	0	—	—	—	—	—	—	—	i	—	30	322

SMITH, GENE — Henry Eugene, G, 5'9"/190 lbs; Georgia; B9/25/1905 Montgomery, AL, D12/10/1979 Atlanta, GA **1930** Fra 1 (0) **1930** Por 4 (3) **NFL** 5 (3) [1 yr]

SMITH, GEORGE — George James, FB-DB, 6'1"/200 lbs; Villanova; 1943: ChiC, rnd 21; B3/26/1921, D6/27/1994 McKeesport, PA

YEAR	TEAM	G(GS, POS)	RUSH	YD	AVG(LG)	TD	KPR	OTD	PTS	TAY
1943	ChiC	3(0)	4	12	3.0(10)	0	—	—	0	21

SMITH, GEORGE — George William, C, 6'2"/220 lbs; California; B6/3/1914 Los Angeles, CA, D3/5/1986 Walnut Creek, CA **[K]** **1937**†Was 7 (2) **1941** Was 9 (6, C) **1942** Was◇4 (0) **1943**†Was☆9 (8, C) **1944** Bkn 10 (8, C) **1945** Bos 10 (8, C) **NFL** 49 (32) [6 yrs]

1947 SF-A 10 (2)

SMITH, GORDIE — Gordon Chilton, TE, 6'2"/220 lbs; Arizona State; Missouri; B4/9/1939 Douglas, AZ

YEAR	TEAM	G(GS, POS)	RUSH	YD	AVG(LG)	TD	REC	YD	AVG(LG)	TD	KPR	OTD	PTS	TAY
1961	Min	9(8, TE)	—	—	—	—	12	320	26.7(71)	4	—	—	24	180
1962	Min	5	—	—	—	—	7	138	19.7(40)	0	—	—	6	74
1963	Min	14(6, te)	—	—	—	—	6	177	29.5(54)	2	k	—	12	93
1964	Min	12	1	2	2.0(2)	0	10	211	21.1(44)	1	—	—	6	113
1965	Min	14(9, TE)	—	—	—	—	22	431	19.6(49)	5	—	—	30	241
NFL	5	54(23)	1	2	2.0(2)	0	57	1277	22.4(71)	13	k	—	78	700

SMITH, GREG — Gregory, DE-NT, 6'3"/270 lbs; Kansas; 1982: KC, rnd 7; B10/22/1959 Chicago, IL **1984** Min 16 (6, rde)

SMITH, HAL — Harold Wallace, DT, 6'5"/250 lbs; UCLA; 1957: ChiC, rnd 18; B10/3/1935 Santa Monica, CA **1960** Bos-A 10 (RDT) **1960** Den-A 3 **1961** Oak-A 8 (RDT) **NFL** 21 [2 yrs]

SMITH, HANK — Henry A., C-G-T, 6'1"/189 lbs; none; B7/23/1893 Lancaster, NY, D2/3/1985 Buffalo, NY **1920** Roc 10 (1, LG) **1921** Roc 5 (3, LG) **1922** Roc 5 (5, RT) **1923** Roc 2 (2, c) **1923** RI 4 (3) **1924** Roc 7 (6, C) **1925** Roc 5 (5, C) **NFL** 38 (25) [6 yrs]

SMITH, HARRY — Harry Elliott, T, 5'11"/215 lbs; USC; 1940: Det, rnd 5; B8/26/1918 Russellville, MO **1940** Det◇10 (8, RT)

SMITH, HERMAN — Herman, DE, 6'5"/261 lbs; Portland State; B1/25/1971 Mound Bayou, MS **1995** TB 3 (0) **1996** TB 5 (0) **NFL** 8 (0) [2 yrs]

SMITH, HOLDEN — Holden Eugene, WR, 6'1"/191 lbs; California; 1981: Bal, rnd 11; B11/5/1958 San Jose, CA

YEAR	TEAM	G(GS, POS)	RUSH	YD	AVG(LG)	TD	REC	YD	AVG(LG)	TD	OTD	PTS	TAY
1982	Bal	3(0)	—	—	—	—	2	36	18.0(23)	0	—	0	18

SMITH, HUGH — Hugh Ben, WR, 6'4"/217 lbs; Kansas; B8/27/1936 Henryetta, OK **1962** Was 2

SMITH, HUNTER — Hunter Dwight, P, 6'2"/209 lbs; Notre Dame; 1999: Ind, rnd 7; B8/9/1977 Sherman, TX **[P]**

YEAR	TEAM	G(GS, POS)	RUSH	YD	AVG(LG)	TD	PASS	COMP	PCT	YD	AVG(LG)	TD	INT	QBR	OTD	PTS	TAY
1999	†Ind	16(0)	—	—	—	—	—	—	—	—	—	—	—	P	—	0	0
2000	†Ind	16(0)	1	11	11.0(11)	0	—	—	—	—	—	—	—	P	—	0	11
2001	Ind	16(0)	—	—	—	—	—	—	—	—	—	—	—	P	—	0	0
2002	†Ind	16(0)	—	—	—	—	—	—	—	—	—	—	—	P	—	0	0
2003	†Ind	16(0)	1	21	21.0(21)	1	—	—	—	—	—	—	—	P	—	6	31
2004	†Ind	16(0)	1	2	2.0(2)	0	—	—	—	—	—	—	—	P	—	0	2
2005	†Ind	16(0)	—	—	—	—	1	0	0.0	0	0.0	0	0	P	—	0	0
NFL	7	112(0)	3	34	11.3(21)	1	1	0	0.0	0	0.0	0	0	P	—	6	44

SMITH, IRV — Irvin Martin, TE, 6'3"/249 lbs; Notre Dame; 1993: NO, rnd 1; B10/13/1971 Trenton, NJ

YEAR	TEAM	G(GS, POS)	RUSH	YD	AVG(LG)	TD	REC	YD	AVG(LG)	TD	KPR	OTD	PTS	TAY
1993	NO	16(te)	—	—	—	—	16	180	11.3(23)	2	—	—	12	100
1994	NO	16(16, TE)	—	—	—	—	41	330	8.0(19)	3	k	—	18	160
1995	NO	16(16, TE)	—	—	—	—	45	466	10.4(43)	3	k	—	20	239

YEAR	TEAM	G(GS, POS)	RUSH	YD	AVG(LG)	TD	REC	YD	AVG(LG)	TD	PASS	COMP	PCT	YD	AVG(LG)	TD	INT	SK	YD	QBR	KPR	OTD	PTS	TAY
1996	NO	7(7, TE)	—	—	—	—	15	144	9.6(37)	0	—	—	—	—	—	—	—	—	—	—	—	—	0	72
1997	NO	11(8, TE)	—	—	—	—	17	180	10.6(25)	1	—	—	—	—	—	—	—	—	—	—	—	—	6	95
1998	†SF	16(8, te)	—	—	—	—	25	266	10.6(25)	5	—	—	—	—	—	—	—	—	—	—	k	—	30	163
1999	Cle	13(13, TE)	—	—	—	—	24	222	9.3(22)	1	—	—	—	—	—	—	—	—	—	—	k	—	6	86
NFL	7	95(76)	—	—	—	—	183	1788	9.8(43)	15	—	—	—	—	—	—	—	—	—	—	k	—	92	915
SMITH, J.D.	J.D., FB-HB-DB, 6´1˝/205 lbs; North Carolina A&T; 1955: ChiB, rnd 15; B7/19/1932 Plainville, SC																							
1956	ChiB	6	—	—	—	—	—	—	—	—	—	—	—	—	—	—	—	—	—	—	—	—	—	—
1956	SF	5	—	—	—	—	—	—	—	—	—	—	—	—	—	—	—	—	—	—	—	—	—	—
1957	†SF	12(DB)	—	—	—	—	—	—	—	—	—	—	—	—	—	—	—	—	—	—	ki	—	0	165
1958	SF	12	26	209	8.0(80)	3	6	59	9.8(23)	0	—	—	—	—	—	—	—	—	—	—	k	—	18	400
1959	SF★	12(LH)	207	1036	5.0(73)	10	13	133	10.2(21)	1	—	—	—	—	—	—	—	—	—	—	—	—	66	1208
1960	SF	12(12, FB/lh)	174	780	4.5(41)	5	36	181	5.0(21)	1	—	—	—	—	—	—	—	—	—	—	—	—	36	926
1961	SF	14(12, LH)	167	823	4.9(33)	8	28	343	12.3(57)	1	1	0	0.0	0	0.0	0	1	—	—	—	k	—	54	1093
1962	SF✧	14(14, FB)	258	907	3.5(28)	6	21	197	9.4(47)	1	—	—	—	—	—	—	—	—	—	—	—	—	42	1071
1963	SF	14(13, FB)	162	560	3.5(52)	5	17	196	11.5(40)	1	—	—	—	—	—	—	—	—	—	—	—	—	36	713
1964	SF	2	13	55	4.2(16)	0	—	—	—	—	—	—	—	—	—	—	—	—	—	—	—	—	0	55
1965	Dal	14(3)	86	295	3.4(24)	2	5	10	2.0(5)	1	—	—	—	—	—	—	—	—	—	—	—	—	18	325
1966	Dal	14	7	7	1.0(2)	1	1	3	3.0(3)	0	—	—	—	—	—	—	—	—	—	—	—	—	6	19
NFL	11	131(54)	1100	4672	4.2(80)	40	127	1122	8.8(57)	6	1	0	0.0	0	0.0	0	1	—	—	—	ki	—	276	5972
SMITH, J.D.	James D., FB-HB, 6´1˝/210 lbs; Compton CC (CA); B1936																							
1960	Oak-A	14	63	214	3.4(41)	6	17	194	11.4(31)	1	—	—	—	—	—	—	—	—	—	—	k	1	50	549
1961	ChiB	3	3	6	2.0(5)	0	—	—	—	—	—	—	—	—	—	—	—	—	—	—	k	—	0	9
NFL	2	17	66	220	3.3(41)	6	17	194	11.4(31)	1	—	—	—	—	—	—	—	—	—	—	k	1	50	558
SMITH, J.D.	Jesse Daley, T, 6´2˝/250 lbs; Rice; 1959: Phi, rnd 2; B5/27/1936 Richland Springs, TX **1959** Phi 11 (11, RT) **1960**†Phi 12 (12, RT) **1961** Phi✧14 (14, RT) **1962** Phi 14 (14, RT) **1963** Phi 14 (14, RT) **1964** Det 7 (RT) **1966** Det 14 (RT) **NFL** 86 (65) [7 yrs]																							
SMITH, J.T.	John Thomas, WR, 6´2˝/185 lbs; North Texas; B10/29/1955 Leonard, TX **[R]**																							
1978	Was	3	—	—	—	—	—	—	—	—	—	—	—	—	—	—	—	—	—	—	kp	—	0	16
1978	KC	6	—	—	—	—	—	—	—	—	—	—	—	—	—	—	—	—	—	—	—	—	—	—
1979	KC	16(13, WR)	—	—	—	—	33	444	13.5(34)	3	—	—	—	—	—	—	—	—	—	—	p	2	30	579
1980	KC★	16(16, WR)	—	—	—	—	46	655	14.2(77)	2	—	—	—	—	—	—	—	—	—	—	p	2	24	739
1981	KC☆	16(15, WR)	—	—	—	—	63	852	13.5(42)	2	—	—	—	—	—	—	—	—	—	—	p	—	12	714
1982	KC	5(3)	—	—	—	—	10	168	16.8(51)	1	—	—	—	—	—	—	—	—	—	—	p	—	6	100
1983	KC	9(1)	—	—	—	—	7	85	12.1(18)	0	—	—	—	—	—	—	—	—	—	—	kp	—	0	113
1984	KC	15(0)	—	—	—	—	8	69	8.6(16)	0	—	—	—	—	—	—	—	—	—	—	kp	—	0	278
1985	SL	14(4)	3	36	12.0(30)	0	43	581	13.5(34)	1	—	—	—	—	—	—	—	—	—	—	kp	—	6	484
1986	SL	16(16, WR)	—	—	—	—	80	1014	12.7(45)	6	—	—	—	—	—	—	—	—	—	—	p	—	36	538
1987	SL☆	15(14, WR)	—	—	—	—	**91**	**1117**	12.3(38)	8	—	—	—	—	—	—	—	—	—	—	—	—	48	599
1988	Phx✧	16(16, WR)	1	15	15.0(15)	0	83	986	11.9(29)	5	—	—	—	—	—	—	—	—	—	—	p	—	30	567
1989	Phx	9(8, wr)	2	21	10.5(11)	0	62	778	12.5(31)	5	—	—	—	—	—	—	—	—	—	—	—	—	30	435
1990	Phx	13(8, wr)	1	4	4.0(4)	0	18	225	12.5(45)	2	—	—	—	—	—	—	—	—	—	—	p	—	12	146
NFL	13	169(114)	7	76	10.9(30)	0	544	6974	12.8(77)	35	—	—	—	—	—	—	—	—	—	—	kp	4	234	5305
SMITH, JACK	Jack Bullas, DE-E, 6´1˝/200 lbs; Stanford; B8/11/1917 Los Angeles, CA **1942** Phi 6 (0) **1943** Was 3 (0) **NFL** 9 (0) [2 yrs]																							
SMITH, JACK	Jack, DB, 6´4˝/204 lbs; Memphis; Troy State; 1971: Phi, rnd 6; B12/4/1947 Ocilla, GA **1971** Phi 5																							
SMITH, JACKIE	Jackie Larue, TE, 6´4˝/235 lbs; Northwestern State (LA); 1963: SL, rnd 10; B2/23/1940 Columbia, MS; HOF 1994																							
1963	SL	14(TE)	—	—	—	—	28	445	15.9(55)	2	—	—	—	—	—	—	—	—	—	—	—	—	12	233
1964	SL	14(te)	—	—	—	—	47	657	14.0(78)	4	—	—	—	—	—	—	—	—	—	—	P	—	24	349
1965	SL	14(TE)	—	—	—	—	41	648	15.8(70)	2	—	—	—	—	—	—	—	—	—	—	P	—	12	334
1966	SL★	14(TE)	1	8	8.0(8)	0	45	810	18.0(69)	3	—	—	—	—	—	—	—	—	—	—	P	—	18	428
1967	SL★	14(TE)	9	86	9.6(18)	0	56	1205	21.5(76)	9	1	0	0.0	0	0.0	0	1	—	—	—	—	—	54	694
1968	SL★	14(TE)	12	163	13.6(37)	3	49	789	16.1(65)	2	—	—	—	—	—	—	—	—	—	—	—	—	30	598
1969	SL★	14(TE)	4	0	0.0(9)	0	43	561	13.0(34)	1	—	—	—	—	—	—	—	—	—	—	—	—	6	286
1970	SL★	14(TE)	5	43	8.6(26)	0	37	687	18.6(59)	4	—	—	—	—	—	—	—	—	—	—	—	—	24	407
1971	SL	9(TE)	1	10	10.0(10)	0	21	379	18.0(61)	4	—	—	—	—	—	—	—	—	—	—	—	—	24	220
1972	SL	14(TE)	5	31	6.2(17)	0	26	407	15.7(71)	2	2	0	0.0	0	0.0	0	0	—	—	—	—	—	12	245
1973	SL	14(TE)	1	-14	-14.0(-14)	0	41	600	14.6(42)	1	—	—	—	—	—	—	—	—	—	—	—	—	6	291
1974	†SL	14(14, TE)	—	—	—	—	25	413	16.5(**81**)	3	—	—	—	—	—	—	—	—	—	—	—	—	18	222
1975	†SL	9(7, TE)	—	—	—	—	13	246	18.9(45)	2	—	—	—	—	—	—	—	—	—	—	k	—	12	143
1976	SL	12	—	—	—	—	3	22	7.3(16)	0	—	—	—	—	—	—	—	—	—	—	k	—	0	29
1977	SL	14	—	—	—	—	5	49	9.8(13)	1	—	—	—	—	—	—	—	—	—	—	k	—	6	30
1978	†Dal	12	—	—	—	—	—	—	—	—	—	—	—	—	—	—	—	—	—	—	—	—	—	—
NFL	16	210(21)	38	327	8.6(37)	3	480	7918	16.5(81)	40	3	0	0.0	0	0.0	0	1	—	—	—	Pk	—	258	4504
SMITH, JEFF	Jeffrey, LB, 6´0˝/237 lbs; USC; 1966: NYG, rnd 10; B11/12/1943 Freeport, LA **1966** NYG 14																							
SMITH, JEFF	Jeff Keith, RB, 5´9˝/201 lbs; Nebraska; 1985: KC, rnd 10; B3/22/1962 Wichita, KS **[R]**																							
1985	KC	13(1)	30	118	3.9(27)	0	18	157	8.7(45)	2	—	—	—	—	—	—	—	—	—	—	k	—	12	366
1986	†KC	15(0)	54	238	4.4(32)	3	33	230	7.0(18)	3	—	—	—	—	—	—	—	—	—	—	kp	—	36	620
1987	TB	12(8, RB)	100	309	3.1(46)	2	20	197	9.9(34)	2	—	—	—	—	—	—	—	—	—	—	k	—	24	447
1988	TB	16(3)	20	87	4.3(23)	0	16	134	8.4(22)	0	—	—	—	—	—	—	—	—	—	—	kp	—	0	189
NFL	4	56(12)	204	752	3.7(46)	5	87	718	8.3(45)	7	—	—	—	—	—	—	—	—	—	—	kp	—	72	1621
SMITH, JEFF	Jeffery Lee, C, 6´3˝/322 lbs; Tennessee; 1996: KC, rnd 7; B5/25/1973 Decatur, TN **1997** KC 3 (0) **1998** KC 11 (3) **1999** KC 15 (2) **2000** Jax 14 (12, C) **2001** Jax 16 (16, C) **NFL** 59 (33) [5 yrs]																							
SMITH, JEFF	Jeffrey Allen, TE, 6´3˝/240 lbs; Tennessee; B12/28/1962 Milan, TN																							
1987	NYG	3(3)	—	—	—	—	6	72	12.0(19)	0	—	—	—	—	—	—	—	—	—	—	—	—	0	36
SMITH, JEFF	Jeffrey A., DE, 6´4˝/248 lbs; Air Force; B5/4/1962 Earlham, TN **1987** Cin 3 (2)																							
SMITH, JERMAINE	Matt Jermaine, DT, 6´2˝/289 lbs; Georgia; 1997: GB, rnd 4; B2/3/1972 Augusta, GA **1997** GB 9 (0) **1999** GB 10 (0) **NFL** 19 (0) [2 yrs]																							
SMITH, JERRY	Jerome Anthony, G-LB, 6´1˝/230 lbs; Wisconsin; 1952: SF, rnd 8; B9/9/1930 Dayton, OH **[C]** **1952** SF 12 (LG) **1953** SF 12 (LG) **1956** SF 2 **1956** GB 3 **NFL** 29 [3 yrs]																							
SMITH, JERRY	Gerald Thomas, TE-SE-FL, 6´3˝/208 lbs; Arizona State; 1965: Was, rnd 9/KC, rnd 18; B7/19/1943 Eugene, OR, D10/15/1986 Silver Spring, MD																							
1965	Was	14(5, te)	—	—	—	—	19	257	13.5(54)	2	—	—	—	—	—	—	—	—	—	—	—	—	12	139
1966	Was	14(14, TE/se)	—	—	—	—	54	686	12.7(35)	6	—	—	—	—	—	—	—	—	—	—	—	—	36	373
1967	Was★	14(TE)	—	—	—	—	67	849	12.7(43)	12	—	—	—	—	—	—	—	—	—	—	—	—	72	485
1968	Was	13(FL)	—	—	—	—	45	626	13.9(56)	6	—	—	—	—	—	—	—	—	—	—	—	—	36	343
1969	Was★	14(TE)	3	8	2.7(6)	0	54	682	12.6(28)	9	—	—	—	—	—	—	—	—	—	—	—	—	54	394
1970	Was	14(14, TE)	2	29	14.5(20)	0	43	575	13.4(41)	9	—	—	—	—	—	—	—	—	—	—	—	—	54	362
1971	†Was	8(7, TE)	1	5	5.0(5)	0	16	227	14.2(31)	1	—	—	—	—	—	—	—	—	—	—	—	—	6	124
1972	†Was	14(14, TE)	1	9	9.0(9)	0	21	353	16.8(34)	7	—	—	—	—	—	—	—	—	—	—	—	—	42	221
1973	†Was	13(9, TE)	—	—	—	—	19	215	11.3(25)	0	—	—	—	—	—	—	—	—	—	—	p	—	0	103
1974	†Was	14(14, TE)	1	5	5.0(5)	0	44	554	12.6(30)	3	—	—	—	—	—	—	—	—	—	—	—	—	18	297
1975	Was	14(14, TE)	—	—	—	—	31	391	12.6(27)	3	—	—	—	—	—	—	—	—	—	—	—	—	18	211
1976	†Was	13(2)	—	—	—	—	7	75	10.7(20)	2	—	—	—	—	—	—	—	—	—	—	—	—	12	48

YEAR	TEAM	G (GS, POS)	RUSH	YD	AVG (LG)	TD	REC	YD	AVG (LG)	TD	PASS	COMP	PCT	YD	AVG (LG)	TD	INT	SK	YD	QBR	KPR	OTD	PTS	TAY
1977	Was	9	—	—	—	—	1	6	6.0(6)	0	—	—	—	—	—	—	—	—	—	—	—	—	0	3
NFL	13	168(93)	8	56	7.0(20)	0	421	5496	13.1(56)	60	—	—	—	—	—	—	—	—	—	—	p	—	360	3099

Smith, Jim James Dale, T, 6´4˝/270 lbs; Colorado; 1944: Cle, rnd 27; B9/9/1922 Alto, TX **1947** LAD-A 7 (1)

Smith, Jim James McCoy, DB, 6´3˝/195 lbs; Oregon; 1968: Was, rnd 1; B11/4/1946 Yazoo City, MS **1968** Was 14

Smith, Jim James Arthur, WR, 6´2˝/205 lbs; Michigan; 1977: Pit, rnd 3; B7/20/1955 Harvey, IL **[R]**

YEAR	TEAM	G (GS, POS)	RUSH	YD	AVG (LG)	TD	REC	YD	AVG (LG)	TD	PASS	COMP	PCT	YD	AVG (LG)	TD	INT	SK	YD	QBR	KPR	OTD	PTS	TAY
1977	†Pit	14	—	—	—	—	4	80	20.0(26)	0	—	—	—	—	—	—	—	—	—	—	kp	—	0	295
1978	†Pit	9	—	—	—	—	6	83	13.8(29)	2	—	—	—	—	—	—	—	—	—	—	kp	—	12	73
1979	†Pit	15(4)	1	12	12.0(12)	0	17	243	14.3(25)	2	—	—	—	—	—	—	—	—	—	—	p	—	12	210
1980	Pit	12(10, WR)	1	-1	-1.0(-1)	0	37	711	19.2(45)	9	—	—	—	—	—	—	—	—	—	—	p	—	54	393
1981	Pit	15(3)	1	15	15.0(15)	0	29	571	19.7(46)	7	—	—	—	—	—	—	—	—	—	—	p	—	42	390
1982	†Pit	8(0)	—	—	—	—	17	387	22.8(51)	4	—	—	—	—	—	—	—	—	—	—	—	—	24	214
1985	LARd	6(0)	—	—	—	—	3	28	9.3(14)	1	—	—	—	—	—	—	—	—	—	—	—	—	6	19
NFL	7	79(17)	3	26	8.7(15)	0	113	2103	18.6(51)	25	—	—	—	—	—	—	—	—	—	—	kp	—	150	1592

Smith, Jim Ray James Ray, G-T-DE, 6´3˝/241 lbs; Baylor; 1954: Cle, rnd 6; B2/27/1932 West Columbia, TX **1956** Cle 6 **1957**†Cle☆12 (LG) **1958**†Cle★12 (LG) **1959** Cle★12 (LG) **1960** Cle★12 (LG) **1961** Cle★14 (LG) **1962** Cle★13 (LG) **1963** Dal 8 (7, LG) **1964** Dal 4 **NFL** 93 (7) [9 yrs]

Smith, Jimmy James Earl, DB, 6´3˝/190 lbs; Utah State; 1969: Den, rnd 10; B7/12/1945 Stockton, CA **1969** Den-A 2

Smith, Jimmy Jimmy Lee, WR, 6´1˝/213 lbs; Jackson State; 1992: Dal, rnd 2; B2/9/1969 Detroit, MI

YEAR	TEAM	G (GS, POS)	RUSH	YD	AVG (LG)	TD	REC	YD	AVG (LG)	TD	PASS	COMP	PCT	YD	AVG (LG)	TD	INT	SK	YD	QBR	KPR	OTD	PTS	TAY
1992	†Dal	7(0)	—	—	—	—	—	—	—	—	—	—	—	—	—	—	—	—	—	—	—	—	—	—
1995	Jax	16(4)	—	—	—	—	22	288	13.1(33)	3	—	—	—	—	—	—	—	—	—	—	k	2	30	349
1996	†Jax	16(9, WR)	—	—	—	—	83	**1244**	15.0(62)	7	—	—	—	—	—	—	—	—	—	—	k	—	42	676
1997	†Jax✧	16(16, WR)	—	—	—	—	82	1324	16.1(75)	4	—	—	—	—	—	—	—	—	—	—	—	—	24	682
1998	†Jax★	16(15, WR)	—	—	—	—	78	1182	15.2(72)	8	—	—	—	—	—	—	—	—	—	—	—	—	48	631
1999	†Jax★	16(16, WR)	—	—	—	—	**116**	1636	14.1(62)	6	—	—	—	—	—	—	—	—	—	—	—	—	38	848
2000	Jax✧	15(14, WR)	—	—	—	—	91	1213	13.3(65)	8	—	—	—	—	—	—	—	—	—	—	—	—	48	647
2001	Jax✧	16(16, WR)	1	-3	-3.0(-3)	0	112	1373	12.3(35)	8	—	—	—	—	—	—	—	—	—	—	—	—	48	724
2002	Jax	16(16, WR)	1	2	2.0(2)	0	80	1027	12.8(47)	7	—	—	—	—	—	—	—	—	—	—	—	—	44	551
2003	Jax	12(12, WR)	—	—	—	—	54	805	14.9(67)	4	—	—	—	—	—	—	—	—	—	—	—	—	24	423
2004	Jax	16(16, WR)	—	—	—	—	74	1172	15.8(65)	6	—	—	—	—	—	—	—	—	—	—	—	—	36	616
2005	†Jax	16(16, WR)	—	—	—	—	70	1023	14.6(45)	6	—	—	—	—	—	—	—	—	—	—	—	—	36	542
NFL	12	178(150)	2	-1	-0.5(2)	0	862	12287	14.3(75)	67	—	—	—	—	—	—	—	—	—	—	k	2	418	6687

Smith, Jimmy James Kevin, RB, 6´0˝/205 lbs; Purdue; Elon; 1984: Was, rnd 4; B9/25/1960 Kankakee, IL **1984** Was 1 (0) **1984** LARd 7 (0)

YEAR	TEAM	G (GS, POS)	RUSH	YD	AVG (LG)	TD	REC	YD	AVG (LG)	TD	PASS	COMP	PCT	YD	AVG (LG)	TD	INT	SK	YD	QBR	KPR	OTD	PTS	TAY
1987	Min	1(1)	7	13	1.9(5)	0	—	—	—	—	—	—	—	—	—	—	—	—	—	—	k	—	0	25
NFL	2	9(1)	7	13	1.9(5)	0	—	—	—	—	—	—	—	—	—	—	—	—	—	—	k	—	0	33

Smith, Joe Joe H., E-DB, 6´1˝/183 lbs; Schreiner College; Texas Tech; 1948: Bal-A, rnd 5/1947: ChiC, rnd 28; B7/23/1922 Electra, TX, D4/8/1978 Odessa, TX

YEAR	TEAM	G (GS, POS)	RUSH	YD	AVG (LG)	TD	REC	YD	AVG (LG)	TD	PASS	COMP	PCT	YD	AVG (LG)	TD	INT	SK	YD	QBR	KPR	OTD	PTS	TAY
1948	Bal-A	12(0)	1	1	1.0(1)	0	8	131	16.4	1	—	—	—	—	—	—	—	—	—	—	i	—	6	67

Smith, Joey Joey Leon, WR, 5´10˝/177 lbs; Louisville; B5/30/1969 Knoxville, TN **1991** NYG 1 (0)

YEAR	TEAM	G (GS, POS)	RUSH	YD	AVG (LG)	TD	REC	YD	AVG (LG)	TD	PASS	COMP	PCT	YD	AVG (LG)	TD	INT	SK	YD	QBR	KPR	OTD	PTS	TAY
1992	NYG	16(1)	—	—	—	—	3	45	15.0(22)	0	—	—	—	—	—	—	—	—	—	—	k	—	0	137
NFL	2	17(1)	—	—	—	—	3	45	15.0(22)	0	—	—	—	—	—	—	—	—	—	—	k	—	0	126

Smith, John John Michael, K, 6´0˝/186 lbs; King Alfred's (England); Southampton (England); B12/30/1949 Leafield, England **[K]** **1974** NE 14 **1975** NE 14 **1976**†NE 14 **1977** NE 14 **1978** NE 3 **1979** NE 16 **1980** NE★16 (0) **1981** NE 16 (0) **1982**†NE 4 (0) **1983** NE 5 (0) **NFL** 116 [10 yrs]

Smith, John John G., T, 6´2˝/200 lbs; Florida; B1919 **1945** Phi 1 (0)

Smith, John John Henry, WR, 6´0˝/175 lbs; Tennessee State; 1979: Cle, rnd 10; B1/27/1956 Tuskegee, AL **1979** Cle 6

Smith, Johnny Ray Johnny Ray, DB, 5´9˝/183 lbs; Lamar; 1981: TB, rnd 11; B9/7/1957 Crockett, TX **1982** TB 9 (1) **1983** TB 16 (1) **1984** SD 1 (0) **NFL** 26 (2) [3 yrs]

Smith, Jonathan Jonathan Dewayne, WR, 5´10˝/194 lbs; Georgia Tech; 2004: Buf, rnd 7; B11/28/1981 Argyle, GA

YEAR	TEAM	G (GS, POS)	RUSH	YD	AVG (LG)	TD	REC	YD	AVG (LG)	TD	PASS	COMP	PCT	YD	AVG (LG)	TD	INT	SK	YD	QBR	KPR	OTD	PTS	TAY
2004	Buf	9(0)	2	11	5.5(8)	0	3	21	7.0(11)	0	—	—	—	—	—	—	—	—	—	—	kp	1	6	157
2005	Buf	7(1)	1	1	1.0(1)	0	5	56	11.2(19)	1	—	—	—	—	—	—	—	—	—	—	kp	—	6	94
NFL	2	16(1)	3	12	4.0(8)	0	8	77	9.6(19)	1	—	—	—	—	—	—	—	—	—	—	kp	1	12	251

Smith, Justin Justin, DE, 6´4˝/270 lbs; Missouri; 2001: Cin, rnd 1; B9/30/1979 Jefferson City, MO **2001** Cin 15 (11, RDE) **2002** Cin 16 (16, RDE) **2003** Cin 16 (16, RDE) **2004** Cin 16 (16, RDE) **2005**†Cin 16 (16, LDE) **NFL** 79 (75) [5 yrs]

Smith, Justin Justin Curtis, LB, 6´0˝/218 lbs; Indiana; B6/5/1979 Indianapolis, IN **2003** TB 2 (0) **2003** SL 3 (0) **NFL** 5 (0) [1 yr]

Smith, Keith Keith, DB, 5´11˝/192 lbs; McNeese State; 2004: Det, rnd 3; B3/20/1980 Leesville, LA **2004** Det 15 (2) **2005** Det 15 (2) **NFL** 30 (4) [2 yrs]

Smith, Kendal Kendal Carson, WR, 5´10˝/189 lbs; Utah State; 1989: Cin, rnd 7; B11/23/1965 San Mateo, CA

YEAR	TEAM	G (GS, POS)	RUSH	YD	AVG (LG)	TD	REC	YD	AVG (LG)	TD	PASS	COMP	PCT	YD	AVG (LG)	TD	INT	SK	YD	QBR	KPR	OTD	PTS	TAY
1989	Cin	11(0)	—	—	—	—	10	140	14.0(41)	1	—	—	—	—	—	—	—	—	—	—	kp	—	6	59
1990	Cin	9(2)	—	—	—	—	7	45	6.4(11)	0	—	—	—	—	—	—	—	—	—	—	kp	—	0	27
NFL	2	20(2)	—	—	—	—	17	185	10.9(41)	1	—	—	—	—	—	—	—	—	—	—	kp	—	6	86

Smith, Ken Kenneth Leslie, TE, 6´4˝/225 lbs; New Mexico; B7/27/1951 Houston, TX **1973** Cle 13

Smith, Ken Kenneth James, G, 6´2˝/285 lbs; Evansville; Miami (OH); B10/16/1960 Indianapolis, IN **1987** Cin 3 (0)

Smith, Kenny Kenny, DT-DE, 6´4˝/295 lbs; Alabama; 2001: NO, rnd 3; B9/8/1977 Meridian, MS **2001** NO 6 (0) **2002** NO 9 (1) **2003** NO 15 (9, RDT) **NFL** 30 (10) [3 yrs]

Smith, Kevin Kevin Linn, TE, 6´4˝/255 lbs; UCLA; 1992: LARd, rnd 7; B7/25/1969 Bakersfield, CA **1992** LARd 1 (0) **1993**†LARd 10 (1) **1996** GB 1 (0)

YEAR	TEAM	G (GS, POS)	RUSH	YD	AVG (LG)	TD	REC	YD	AVG (LG)	TD	PASS	COMP	PCT	YD	AVG (LG)	TD	INT	SK	YD	QBR	KPR	OTD	PTS	TAY
1994	LARd	3(0)	1	2	2.0(2)	0	1	8	8.0(8)	0	—	—	—	—	—	—	—	—	—	—	—	—	0	6
NFL	4	15(1)	1	2	2.0(2)	0	1	8	8.0(8)	0	—	—	—	—	—	—	—	—	—	—	k	—	0	-9

Smith, Kevin Kevin Anthony, DB, 5´11˝/204 lbs; Rhode Island; B4/2/1967 Newport, RI **1991** Pit 16 (1)

Smith, Kevin Kevin Ray, DB, 5´11˝/183 lbs; Texas A&M; 1992: Dal, rnd 1; B4/7/1970 Orange, TX **1992**†Dal 16 (6, lcb) **1993**†Dal 16 (16, LCB) **1994**†Dal 16 (16, LCB) **1995** Dal 1 (1) **1996**†Dal☆16 (16, LCB) **1997** Dal 16 (16, LCB) **1998**†Dal 14 (14, LCB) **1999** Dal 8 (8, LCB) **NFL** 103 (93) [8 yrs]

Smith, L.J. John, TE, 6´3˝/258 lbs; Rutgers; 2003: Phi, rnd 2; B5/13/1980 Highland Park, NJ

YEAR	TEAM	G (GS, POS)	RUSH	YD	AVG (LG)	TD	REC	YD	AVG (LG)	TD	PASS	COMP	PCT	YD	AVG (LG)	TD	INT	SK	YD	QBR	KPR	OTD	PTS	TAY
2003	†Phi	15(5, te)	—	—	—	—	27	321	11.9(36)	1	—	—	—	—	—	—	—	—	—	—	—	—	6	166
2004	†Phi	16(8, te)	—	—	—	—	34	377	11.1(31)	5	—	—	—	—	—	—	—	—	—	—	—	—	30	214
2005	Phi	16(16, TE)	—	—	—	—	61	682	11.2(48)	3	—	—	—	—	—	—	—	—	—	—	—	—	18	356
NFL	3	47(29)	—	—	—	—	122	1380	11.3(48)	9	—	—	—	—	—	—	—	—	—	—	—	—	54	735

Smith, Lamar Lamar Huter, RB, 5´11˝/230 lbs; Houston; 1994: Sea, rnd 3; B11/29/1970 Fort Wayne, IN

YEAR	TEAM	G (GS, POS)	RUSH	YD	AVG (LG)	TD	REC	YD	AVG (LG)	TD	PASS	COMP	PCT	YD	AVG (LG)	TD	INT	SK	YD	QBR	KPR	OTD	PTS	TAY
1994	Sea	2(0)	2	-1	-0.5(0)	0	—	—	—	—	—	—	—	—	—	—	—	—	—	—	—	—	0	-1
1995	Sea	13(0)	36	215	6.0(68)	0	1	10	10.0(10)	0	—	—	—	—	—	—	—	—	—	—	k	—	0	225
1996	Sea	16(2, rb)	153	680	4.4(29)	8	9	58	6.4(22)	0	—	—	—	—	—	—	—	—	—	—	—	—	54	789
1997	Sea	12(2)	91	392	4.3(35)	2	23	183	8.0(22)	0	—	—	—	—	—	—	—	—	—	—	k	—	14	503
1998	NO	14(9, RB)	138	457	3.3(33)	1	24	249	10.4(35)	2	2	1	50.0	20	10.0(20)	1	0	—	—	—	—	—	18	617
1999	NO	13(2)	60	205	3.4(24)	0	20	151	7.6(26)	1	1	0	0.0	0	0.0	0	0	—	—	—	—	—	6	286
2000	†Mia	15(15, RB)	309	1139	3.7(68)	14	31	201	6.5(28)	2	1	0	0.0	0	0.0	0	0	—	—	—	—	—	96	1390
2001	†Mia	16(16, RB)	313	968	3.1(25)	6	30	234	7.8(65)	2	—	—	—	—	—	—	—	—	—	—	—	—	48	1155
2002	Car	11(11, RB)	209	737	3.5(59)	7	20	167	8.4(58)	0	—	—	—	—	—	—	—	—	—	—	—	—	42	891
2003	NO	4(0)	11	61	5.5(17)	0	1	2	2.0(2)	0	—	—	—	—	—	—	—	—	—	—	—	—	0	62
NFL	10	116(57)	1322	4853	3.7(68)	38	159	1255	7.9(65)	7	4	1	25.0	20	5.0(20)	1	0	—	—	—	k	—	278	5915

Smith, Lance Lance, G-T, 6´3˝/283 lbs; LSU; 1985: SL, rnd 3; B1/1/1963 New York, NY **1985** SL 14 (5, rt) **1986** SL 15 (13, RT) **1987** SL 15 (15, RG) **1988** Phx 16 (16, RG) **1989** Phx 16 (16, RG) **1990** Phx 16 (16, RG) **1991** Phx 16 (16, RG) **1992** Phx 16 (16, RG) **1993** Phx 16 (16, RG) **1994** NYG☆13 (13, RG) **1995** NYG 13 (13, RG) **1996** NYG 16 (10, LG) **NFL** 182 (165) [12 yrs]

YEAR	TEAM	G (GS, POS)	RUSH	YD	AVG (LG)	TD	REC	YD	AVG (LG)	TD	PASS COMP	PCT	YD	AVG (LG)	TD	INT	SK	YD	QBR	KPR	OTD	PTS	TAY

SMITH, LARRY William Lawrence, RB, 6´3˝/220 lbs; Florida; 1969: LA, rnd 1; B9/2/1947 Tampa, FL

1969	†LARm	14 (14, HB)	166	599	3.6 (46)	1	46	300	6.5 (38)	2	1	0	0.0	0	0.0	0	0	2	13	—	—	—	18	769
1970	LARm	11 (9, RB)	77	338	4.4 (19)	1	24	164	6.8 (17)	1	2	0	0.0	0	0.0	0	0	—	—	—	—	—	12	435
1971	LARm	14 (6, rb)	91	404	4.4 (64)	5	31	324	10.5 (34)	0	—	—	—	—	—	—	—	—	—	—	—	—	30	616
1972	LARm	12	60	276	4.6 (68)	2	15	186	12.4 (47)	1	—	—	—	—	—	—	—	—	—	—	—	—	18	394
1973	†LARm	14	79	291	3.7 (16)	2	10	65	6.5 (11)	0	2	2	100.0	31	15.5 (21)	0	0	—	—	k	—	—	12	360
1974	Was	7 (6, rb)	55	149	2.7 (13)	0	23	137	6.0 (14)	1	—	—	—	—	—	—	—	—	—	k	—	—	6	250
NFL	6	72 (35)	528	2057	3.9 (68)	11	149	1176	7.9 (47)	5	5	2	40.0	31	6.2 (21)	0	0	2	13	—	k	—	96	2824

SMITH, LARRY Lawrence Abell, LB, 6´1˝/210 lbs; Kentucky; B2/7/1965　**1987** Hou 3 (0)

SMITH, LARRY Larry, DT, 6´5˝/310 lbs; Florida State; 1999: Jax, rnd 2; B12/4/1974 Kingsland, GA　**1999**†Jax 15 (0)　**2000** Jax 14 (4)　**2001** Jax 7 (0)　**2002** Jax 15 (3)
2003†GB 10 (0)　**2004** GB 3 (0)　**NFL** 64 (7) [6 yrs]

SMITH, LAVERNE Laverne, RB, 5´10˝/193 lbs; Kansas; 1977: Pit, rnd 4; B9/12/1954 Greenwood, MS

| 1977 | Pit | 7 | 14 | 55 | 3.9 (16) | 0 | — | — | — | — | — | — | — | — | — | — | — | — | — | k | — | 0 | 180 |

SMITH, LAWRENCE Lawrence Anthony, G-T, 6´3˝/295 lbs; Tennessee State; B8/16/1979 Atlanta, GA　**2004** Buf 16 (8, lg)

SMITH, LEN Leonard Marshall, T, 5´11˝/195 lbs; Wisconsin-Oshkosh; Wisconsin; B12/14/1896, deceased　**1923** Rac 10 (10, RT)　**1924** Rac 10 (9, RT)　**NFL** 20 (19) [2 yrs]

SMITH, LEONARD Leonard Phillip, DB, 5´11˝/200 lbs; McNeese State; 1983: SL, rnd 1; B9/2/1960 New Orleans, LA　**1983** SL 16 (0)　**1984** SL 12 (11, SS)　**1985** SL 16 (16, SS)
1986 SL☆16 (16, SS)　**1987** SL 15 (15, SS)　**1988** Phx 3 (3)　**1988**†Buf 13 (12, SS)　**1989** Buf 15 (15, SS)　**1990**†Buf 16 (16, SS)　**1991**†Buf 16 (16, SS)　**NFL** 138 (120) [9 yrs]

SMITH, LUCIOUS Lucious Irvin, DB, 5´10˝/190 lbs; San Diego State; Cal State-Fullerton; B1/17/1957 Columbus, GA　**1980**†LARm 16 (0)　**1981** LARm 16 (0)　**1982** LARm 8 (0)
1983 KC 16 (13, RCB)　**1984** Buf 4 (3)　**1985** SD 5 (0)　**NFL** 74 (19) [6 yrs]

SMITH, LYMAN Lyman Scott-William, DT, 6´5˝/250 lbs; Duke; 1978: Mia, rnd 3; B9/24/1956 Portland, OR　**1978**†Min 11

SMITH, MARK Mark Anthony, DT-DE, 6´4˝/290 lbs; Auburn; 1997: Arz, rnd 7; B8/28/1974 Vicksburg, MS　**1997** Arz 16 (4)　**1998**†Arz 14 (13, RDT)　**1999** Arz 2 (0)
2000 Arz 14 (7, rdt)　**2001** Cle 16 (11, RDT)　**2002** Cle 5 (0)　**NFL** 67 (35) [6 yrs]

SMITH, MARQUIS Marquis, DB, 6´2˝/213 lbs; California; 1999: Cle, rnd 3; B1/13/1975 San Diego, CA　**1999** Cle 16 (2)　**2000** Cle 16 (16, SS)　**2001** Cle 14 (2)　**NFL** 46 (20) [3 yrs]

SMITH, MARTY Martin Joseph, DT-DE, 6´3˝/250 lbs; Louisville; 1975: Pit, rnd 15; B10/20/1953 Pattison, MS　**1976** Buf 14 (12, RDT)

SMITH, MARV Marvin McCammon, TB, 5´11˝/185 lbs; Purdue; B4/15/1898 Canton, OH, D4/24/1986 Muncie, IN　**1921** Can 1 (0)

SMITH, MARVEL Marvel Amos, T, 6´5˝/310 lbs; Arizona State; 2000: Pit, rnd 2; B8/6/1978 Oakland, CA　**2000** Pit 12 (9, RT)　**2001**†Pit 16 (16, RT)　**2002**†Pit 16 (16, RT)
2003 Pit 6 (6, lt)　**2004**†Pit 16 (16, LT)　**2005**†Pit 13 (12, LT)　**NFL** 79 (75) [6 yrs]

SMITH, MATT Matthew Morgan, LB, 6´2˝/234 lbs; West Virginia; B9/1/1965 Columbus, OH　**1987** Den 3 (0)

SMITH, MAURICE Maurice, RB, 6´0˝/235 lbs; North Carolina A&T; B9/7/1976 Palmyra, NC

2000	Atl	10 (0)	19	69	3.6 (16)	0	1	5	5.0 (5)	0	—	—	—	—	—	—	—	—	—	—	—	0	72
2001	Atl	16 (12, RB)	237	760	3.2 (58)	5	19	230	12.1 (79)	1	—	—	—	—	—	—	—	—	—	—	—	36	930
2002	Atl	2 (0)									—	—	—	—	—	—	—	—	—	—	—		
NFL	3	28 (12)	256	829	3.2 (58)	5	20	235	11.8 (79)	1	—	—	—	—	—	—	—	—	—	—	—	36	1002

SMITH, MICHAEL Michael Chandler, WR, 5´8˝/160 lbs; Kansas State; B11/21/1970 New Orleans, LA　**1992**†KC 2 (0)

SMITH, MIKE Michael Wayne, DB, 6´0˝/171 lbs; Texas-El Paso; 1985: Mia, rnd 4; B10/24/1962 Houston, TX　**1985**†Mia 7 (0)　**1986** Mia 14 (0)　**1987** Mia 8 (0)　**NFL** 29 (0) [3 yrs]

SMITH, MIKE Mike, LB, 6´2˝/238 lbs; Texas Tech; 2005: Bal, rnd 7; B9/2/1981 Lubbock, TX　**2005** Bal 6 (0)

SMITH, MIKE Michael T., WR, 5´10˝/194 lbs; Grambling State; 1980: Atl, rnd 7; B4/28/1958 Bastrop, LA　**1980**†Atl 5 (0)

SMITH, MILT Milton Bradley, DB-QB, 6´3˝/185 lbs; UCLA; 1944: Phi, rnd 23; B7/7/1919, D10/1/1988 Landrum, SC　**1945** Phi 5 (0)

SMITH, MONTE Monte Gene, G, 6´5˝/270 lbs; North Dakota; 1989: Den, rnd 9; B4/24/1967 Madison, WI　**1989**†Den 14 (0)

SMITH, MUSA Musa, RB, 6´0˝/232 lbs; Georgia; 2003: Bal, rnd 3; B5/31/1982 Elliottsburg, PA

2003	†Bal	11 (0)	9	31	3.4 (11)	2	—	—	—	—	—	—	—	—	—	—	—	—	—	k	—	12	38
2004	Bal	9 (0)	12	48	4.0 (13)	0	2	31	15.5 (25)	0	—	—	—	—	—	—	—	—	—	—	—	0	64
2005	Bal	1 (0)	—	—	—	—	3	5	1.7 (4)	0	—	—	—	—	—	—	—	—	—	—	—	0	3
NFL	3	21 (0)	21	79	3.8 (13)	2	5	36	7.2 (25)	0	—	—	—	—	—	—	—	—	—	k	—	12	104

SMITH, NEIL Neil, DE, 6´4˝/270 lbs; Nebraska; 1988: KC, rnd 1; B4/10/1966 New Orleans, LA **[S]**　**1988** KC 13 (7, lde)　**1989** KC 15 (15, LDE)　**1990**†KC 16 (15, LDE)
1991†KC✫16 (16, LDE)　**1992**†KC✫16 (16, LDE)　**1993**†KC★16 (15, LDE)　**1994**†KC★14 (13, LDE)　**1995**†KC★16 (14, RDE)　**1996** KC☆16 (16, LDE)　**1997**†Den★14 (13, LDE)
1998†Den 14 (14, LDE)　**1999** Den 15 (8, LDE)　**2000** SD 10 (0)　**NFL** 191 (162) [13 yrs]

SMITH, NOLAND Noland, WR, 5´5˝/154 lbs; Tennessee State; 1967: KC, rnd 6; B10/20/1943 Jackson, MS **[R]**　**1969** KC-A 6　**1969** SF 7

1967	KC-A	14	1	8	8.0 (8)	0	1	42	42.0 (42)	0	—	—	—	—	—	—	—	—	—	kp	1	6	654
1968	†KC-A	12	2	-2	-1.0 (1)	0	1	15	15.0 (15)	0	—	—	—	—	—	—	—	—	—	kp	1	6	400
NFL	3	39	3	6	2.0 (8)	0	2	57	28.5 (42)	0	—	—	—	—	—	—	—	—	—	kp	2	12	1282

SMITH, OAK Okla Eugene, E-FB-WB, 6´2˝/185 lbs; Drake; B2/27/1894 Downing, MO, D5/2/1974 Long Beach, CA　**1920** RI☆9 (4, LE)　**1921** RI 7 (5, LE)　**NFL** 16 (9) [2 yrs]

SMITH, OLIN Olin Bashford, T-G, 6´1˝/230 lbs; Ohio Wesleyan; B3/25/1900 Holgate, OH, D5/4/1966 Columbus, OH **[K]**　**1924** Cle☆8 (5, RT), 8

SMITH, OLLIE Ollie P., WR, 6´3˝/203 lbs; Tennessee State; 1973: Bal, rnd 4; B3/8/1949 Jackson, MS

1973	Bal	7	1	-3	-3.0 (-3)	0	1	37	37.0 (37)	0	—	—	—	—	—	—	—	—	—	—	—	0	16
1974	Bal	1	—	—	—	—	1	14	14.0 (14)	0	—	—	—	—	—	—	—	—	—	—	—	0	7
1976	GB	13	—	—	—	—	20	364	18.2 (47)	1	—	—	—	—	—	—	—	—	—	k	—	6	184
1977	GB	12 (WR)	—	—	—	—	22	357	16.2 (41)	0	—	—	—	—	—	—	—	—	—	k	—	0	179
NFL	4	33	1	-3	-3.0 (-3)	0	44	772	17.5 (47)	1	—	—	—	—	—	—	—	—	—	k	—	6	385

SMITH, OMAR Omar Dave, C, 6´2˝/295 lbs; Kentucky; B9/8/1977 Spanish Town, Jamaica　**2002**†NYG 7 (0)　**2003** NYG 4 (0)　**NFL** 11 (0) [2 yrs]

SMITH, ONTERRIO Onterrio Raymond Lloyd, RB, 5´10˝/214 lbs; Tennessee; Oregon; 2003: Min, rnd 4; B12/8/1980 Sacramento, CA

2003	Min	15 (3)	107	579	5.4 (47)	5	15	129	8.6 (20)	0	—	—	—	—	—	—	—	—	—	k	—	32	877
2004	†Min	11 (6, rb)	124	544	4.4 (38)	2	36	394	10.9 (63)	2	—	—	—	—	—	—	—	—	—	k	—	26	791
NFL	2	26 (9)	231	1123	4.9 (47)	7	51	523	10.3 (63)	2	—	—	—	—	—	—	—	—	—	k	—	58	1668

SMITH, ORLAND Orland Francis, T-G, 5´11˝/215 lbs; Brown; B11/5/1905 Gorham, ME, D8/14/1977 Providence, RI　**1927** Pro 13 (9, RT)　**1928** Pro 9 (2)　**1929** Pro 10 (4)
NFL 32 (15) [3 yrs]

SMITH, OSCAR Oscar E., RB, 5´9˝/203 lbs; Nicholls State; 1986: Det, rnd 5; B4/5/1963 Tampa, FL　**1986** Det 2 (0)

SMITH, OTIS Otis, DB, 5´11˝/198 lbs; Southern (LA); Missouri; B10/22/1965 New Orleans, LA **[I]**　**1991** Phi 15 (1)　**1992**†Phi 16 (1)　**1993** Phi 15 (0)　**1994** Phi 16 (2)
1995 NYJ 11 (10, RCB)　**1996** NYJ 2 (0)　**1996**†NE 11 (6, rcb)　**1997** NYJ 16 (16, RCB)　**1998**†NYJ 16 (16, RCB)　**1999** NYJ 1 (1)　**2000** NE 16 (14, RCB)　**2001**†NE 15 (15, RCB)
2002 NE 14 (13, RCB)　**2003** Det 16 (13, LCB)　**NFL** 180 (108) [13 yrs]

SMITH, PAT Cedric Crawford, FB, 6´0˝/198 lbs; Michigan; B3/12/1895 Minneapolis, MN, D4/23/1969 Detroit, MI　**1920** Buf 7 (6, FB)　**1921** Buf 11 (11, FB), 18　**1923** Buf 1 (1)
NFL 19 (18) [3 yrs]

SMITH, PAUL Paul Edward, DT-DE, 6´3˝/256 lbs; New Mexico; 1968: Den, rnd 9; B8/13/1945 Ada, OK, D3/14/2000 Aurora, CO　**1968** Den-A 12 (lde)　**1969** Den-A 14 (1)
1970 Den 14 (14, LDT)　**1971** Den 14 (14, RDT)　**1972** Den★14 (14, RDT)　**1973** Den★14 (14, LDT)　**1974** Den 4 (2)　**1975** Den 13 (12, RDT)　**1976** Den 11 (10, RDE)
1977†Den 12 (2)　**1978** Den 11　**1979** Was 15 (2)　**1980** Was 16 (5, rdt)　**NFL** 164 (90) [13 yrs]

SMITH, PAUL Paul, RB, 5´11˝/234 lbs; Texas-El Paso; 2000: SF, rnd 5; B1/1/1978 El Paso, TX

2000	SF	10 (0)	18	72	4.0 (14)	0	2	55	27.5 (47)	0	—	—	—	—	—	—	—	—	—	k	—	0	132
2001	†SF	15 (0)	4	27	6.8 (13)	1	—	—	—	—	—	—	—	—	—	—	—	—	—	k	—	6	29
2002	†SF	11 (0)	18	90	5.0 (16)	0	5	33	6.6 (11)	0	—	—	—	—	—	—	—	—	—	k	—	0	109
2003	Det	7 (0)	2	5	2.5 (3)	0	5	45	9.0 (21)	0	—	—	—	—	—	—	—	—	—		—	0	28

YEAR	TEAM	G (GS, POS)	RUSH	YD	AVG (LG)	TD	REC	YD	AVG (LG)	TD	PASS	COMP	PCT	YD	AVG (LG)	TD	INT	SK	YD	QBR	KPR	OTD	PTS	TAY
2005	Det	12 (5, fb)	4	16	4.0 (6)	0	6	49	8.2 (11)	0	—	—	—	—	—	—	—	—	—	—	—	—	0	41
NFL	5	55 (5)	46	210	4.6 (16)	1	18	182	10.1 (47)	0	—	—	—	—	—	—	—	—	—	—	k	—	6	337

SMITH, PERRY Eathlon Perry, DB, 6´1˝/195 lbs; Mesa; Colorado State; 1973: Oak, rnd 4; B3/29/1951 Spartanburg, SC **1973** GB 8 (7, LCB) **1974** GB 12 **1975** GB 14 (12, LCB) **1976** GB 13 (13, RCB) **1977** SL 3 (3) **1978** SL 16 (3) **1979** SL 16 (4) **1980** Den 14 (1) **1981** Den 12 (4) **NFL** 108 (47) [9 yrs]

SMITH, PHIL Phillip Keith, WR, 6´3˝/190 lbs; San Diego State; 1983: Bal, rnd 4; B4/28/1960 Los Angeles, CA

YEAR	TEAM	G (GS, POS)	RUSH	YD	AVG (LG)	TD	REC	YD	AVG (LG)	TD	PASS	COMP	PCT	YD	AVG (LG)	TD	INT	SK	YD	QBR	KPR	OTD	PTS	TAY
1983	Bal	1 (0)	—	—	—	—	—	—	—	—	—	—	—	—	—	—	—	—	—	—	—	—	—	—
1984	Ind	16 (0)	2	-10	-5.0 (-3)	0	—	—	—	—	—	—	—	—	—	—	—	—	—	—	k	1	6	171
1986	Phi	3 (2)	—	—	—	—	6	94	15.7 (36)	0	—	—	—	—	—	—	—	—	—	—	p	—	0	45
1987	LARm	2 (2)	—	—	—	—	3	95	31.7 (51)	0	—	—	—	—	—	—	—	—	—	—	p	—	0	43
NFL	4	22 (4)	2	-10	-5.0 (-3)	0	9	189	21.0 (51)	0	—	—	—	—	—	—	—	—	—	—	kp	1	6	259

SMITH, QUINTIN Quintin Anton, WR, 5´10˝/172 lbs; Kansas; B8/17/1968 Houston, TX

YEAR	TEAM	G (GS, POS)	RUSH	YD	AVG (LG)	TD	REC	YD	AVG (LG)	TD	PASS	COMP	PCT	YD	AVG (LG)	TD	INT	SK	YD	QBR	KPR	OTD	PTS	TAY
1990	ChiB	4 (0)	—	—	—	—	2	20	10.0 (12)	0	—	—	—	—	—	—	—	—	—	—	—	—	0	10

SMITH, RALPH Ralph Allon, TE, 6´2˝/215 lbs; Mississippi; 1962: Phi, rnd 8/SD, rnd 12; B12/1/1938 Brookhaven, MS

YEAR	TEAM	G (GS, POS)	RUSH	YD	AVG (LG)	TD	REC	YD	AVG (LG)	TD	PASS	COMP	PCT	YD	AVG (LG)	TD	INT	SK	YD	QBR	KPR	OTD	PTS	TAY
1962	Phi	13	1	13	13.0 (13)	0	1	29	29.0 (29)	0	—	—	—	—	—	—	—	—	—	—	p	—	0	25
1963	Phi	14	—	—	—	—	5	63	12.6 (16)	1	—	—	—	—	—	—	—	—	—	—	k	—	6	25
1964	Phi	11 (2)	—	—	—	—	4	35	8.8 (12)	0	—	—	—	—	—	—	—	—	—	—	—	—	0	18
1965	†Cle	14	—	—	—	—	—	—	—	—	—	—	—	—	—	—	—	—	—	—	—	—	—	—
1966	Cle	14 (te)	—	—	—	—	13	183	14.1 (28)	3	—	—	—	—	—	—	—	—	—	—	k	—	18	92
1967	†Cle	14 (TE)	—	—	—	—	14	211	15.1 (49)	1	—	—	—	—	—	—	—	—	—	—	—	1	12	111
1968	†Cle	14	1	13	13.0 (13)	0	2	11	5.5 (7)	0	—	—	—	—	—	—	—	—	—	—	k	—	0	7
1969	Atl	14	—	—	—	—	2	17	8.5 (10)	0	—	—	—	—	—	—	—	—	—	—	—	—	0	9
NFL	8	108 (2)	2	26	13.0 (13)	0	41	549	13.4 (49)	5	—	—	—	—	—	—	—	—	—	—	kp	1	36	284

SMITH, RAONALL Raonall Aarrig, LB, 6´2˝/241 lbs; Washington State; 2002: Min, rnd 2; B10/22/1978 Mesa, AZ **2003** Min 7 (0) **2004** Min 7 (3) **2005** Min 16 (6, llb) **NFL** 30 (9) [3 yrs]

SMITH, RAY Raymond Henry, C, 5´10˝/195 lbs; Tulsa; Missouri; B1908 **1930** Pro 10 (7, C) **1931** Pro 10 (10, C) **1933** Phi 1 (0) **NFL** 21 (17) [3 yrs]

SMITH, RAY GENE Ray Gene, DB-HB, 5´10˝/187 lbs; Midwestern State; B11/27/1928 Andarko, OK, D8/15/2005 Garland, TX **1954** ChiB 7 **1956**†ChiB☆12 (DB)

YEAR	TEAM	G (GS, POS)	RUSH	YD	AVG (LG)	TD	REC	YD	AVG (LG)	TD	PASS	COMP	PCT	YD	AVG (LG)	TD	INT	SK	YD	QBR	KPR	OTD	PTS	TAY
1955	ChiB	12 (DB)	—	—	—	—	1	13	13.0 (13)	0	—	—	—	—	—	—	—	—	—	—	kpi	—	0	5
1957	ChiB	5	1	8	8.0 (8)	0	3	37	12.3 (21)	0	—	—	—	—	—	—	—	—	—	—	pi	—	0	35
NFL	4	36	1	8	8.0 (8)	0	4	50	12.5 (21)	0	—	—	—	—	—	—	—	—	—	—	kpi	—	0	151

SMITH, RED Richard Paul, TB-WB-BB-G-FB, 5´10˝/192 lbs; Lawrence; Notre Dame; B5/18/1904 Combined Locks, WI, D3/8/1978 Toledo, OH **[K]** **1927** GB 5 (1) **1928** NYG 1 (0) **1928** NYY 10 (8, WB), 20 **1929** GB 5 (2) **1930** Nwk 7 (2), 1 **1931** NYG 9 (5, tb), 2 **NFL** 37 (18), 23 [5 yrs]

SMITH, REGGIE Reginald R., WR, 5´4˝/168 lbs; North Carolina Central; B7/15/1956 Kinston, NC **[R]** **1980**†Atl 8 (0) **1981** Atl 15 (0) **1987** NYJ 1 (0) **NFL** 24 (0) [3 yrs]

SMITH, REGGIE Reginald Lernard, T, 6´5˝/295 lbs; Kansas; 1984: Den, rnd S3; B8/29/1961 Chicago, IL **1987** TB 3 (3)

SMITH, REX Matthew Everett, E, 6´0˝/195 lbs; Wisconsin-LaCrosse; Beloit; B3/8/1896 Rushford, MN **1922** GB 2 (0)

SMITH, RICHARD Richard, WR, 5´10˝/191 lbs; Arkansas; B7/16/1980 Shreveport, LA **2004** KC 4 (0)

SMITH, RICKY Ricky DeCarlo, DB-WR, 6´0˝/182 lbs; Alabama State; 1982: NE, rnd 6; B7/20/1960 Quincy, FL **1982**†NE 9 (0) **1983** NE 16 (0) **1984** NE 1 (0) **1984** Was 11 (0) **1987** Det 12 (0) **NFL** 49 (0) [4 yrs]

SMITH, RICO Rico Louis, WR, 6´0˝/185 lbs; Colorado; 1992: Cle, rnd 6; B1/14/1969 Compton, CA

YEAR	TEAM	G (GS, POS)	RUSH	YD	AVG (LG)	TD	REC	YD	AVG (LG)	TD	PASS	COMP	PCT	YD	AVG (LG)	TD	INT	SK	YD	QBR	KPR	OTD	PTS	TAY
1992	Cle	10 (1)	—	—	—	—	5	64	12.8 (21)	0	—	—	—	—	—	—	—	—	—	—	—	—	0	32
1993	Cle	10 (1)	—	—	—	—	4	55	13.8 (17)	0	—	—	—	—	—	—	—	—	—	—	k	—	0	26
1994	Cle	5 (4)	—	—	—	—	2	61	30.5 (50)	0	—	—	—	—	—	—	—	—	—	—	—	—	0	31
1995	Cle	4 (2)	—	—	—	—	13	173	13.3 (29)	1	—	—	—	—	—	—	—	—	—	—	—	—	6	92
NFL	4	29 (8)	—	—	—	—	24	353	14.7 (50)	1	—	—	—	—	—	—	—	—	—	—	k	—	6	180

SMITH, RILEY Riley Henry, BB-LB, 6´2˝/200 lbs; Alabama; 1936: Bos, rnd 1; B7/14/1911 Carrollton, MS, D8/9/1999 Mobile, AL **[K]**

YEAR	TEAM	G (GS, POS)	RUSH	YD	AVG (LG)	TD	REC	YD	AVG (LG)	TD	PASS	COMP	PCT	YD	AVG (LG)	TD	INT	SK	YD	QBR	KPR	OTD	PTS	TAY
1936	†Bos☆	12 (10)	30	26	0.9	0	3	76	25.3 (30)	2	33	14	42.4	239	7.2	0	3	—	—	—	K	—	38	74
1937	†Was☆	11 (11)	12	39	3.3	2	11	93	8.5	0	9	4	44.4	33	3.7 (39)	3	0	—	—	—	K	1	55	147
1938	Was☆	7 (6, BB)	3	-7	-2.3	0	4	131	32.8 (39)	1	4	1	25.0	18	4.5 (18)	0	0	—	—	—	K	—	15	73
NFL	3	30 (27)	45	58	1.3	2	18	300	16.7 (39)	3	46	19	41.3	290	6.3 (39)	3	3	—	—	—	K	1	108	293

SMITH, ROBAIRE Robaire Frederick, DE-DT, 6´4˝/310 lbs; Michigan State; 2000: Ten, rnd 6; B11/15/1977 Flint, MI **2000** Ten 8 (0) **2001** Ten 10 (0) **2002**†Ten 16 (2) **2003**†Ten 16 (15, LDT) **2004** Hou 16 (16, RDE) **2005** Hou 16 (16, RDE) **NFL** 82 (49) [6 yrs]

SMITH, ROBERT Robert Benjamin, DE, 6´6˝/255 lbs; Grambling State; 1984: Min, rnd S2; B12/3/1962 Bogalusa, LA **1985** Min 16 (0)

SMITH, ROBERT Robert Scott, RB, 6´2˝/212 lbs; Ohio State; 1993: Min, rnd 1; B3/4/1972 Euclid, OH

YEAR	TEAM	G (GS, POS)	RUSH	YD	AVG (LG)	TD	REC	YD	AVG (LG)	TD	PASS	COMP	PCT	YD	AVG (LG)	TD	INT	SK	YD	QBR	KPR	OTD	PTS	TAY
1993	Min	10 (2)	82	399	4.9 (26)	2	24	111	4.6 (12)	0	—	—	—	—	—	—	—	—	—	—	kp	—	12	470
1994	†Min	14 (0)	31	106	3.4 (14)	1	15	105	7.0 (15)	0	—	—	—	—	—	—	—	—	—	—	k	—	6	348
1995	Min	9 (7, RB)	139	632	4.5 (58)	5	7	35	5.0 (11)	0	—	—	—	—	—	—	—	—	—	—	—	—	32	700
1996	Min	8 (7, RB)	162	692	4.3 (57)	3	7	39	5.6 (16)	0	—	—	—	—	—	—	—	—	—	—	—	—	18	742
1997	†Min	14 (14, RB)	232	1266	5.5 (78)	6	37	197	5.3 (20)	1	—	—	—	—	—	—	—	—	—	—	—	—	42	1430
1998	†Min✧	14 (14, RB)	249	1187	4.8 (74)	6	28	291	10.4 (67)	2	—	—	—	—	—	—	—	—	—	—	—	—	48	1403
1999	†Min	13 (12, RB)	221	1015	4.6 (70)	2	24	166	6.9 (34)	0	—	—	—	—	—	—	—	—	—	—	—	—	12	1118
2000	†Min★	16 (16, RB)	295	**1521**	5.2 (72)	7	36	348	9.7 (53)	3	—	—	—	—	—	—	—	—	—	—	—	—	60	1780
NFL	8	98 (72)	1411	6818	4.8 (78)	32	178	1292	7.3 (67)	6	—	—	—	—	—	—	—	—	—	—	kp	—	230	7988

SMITH, ROD Rod, WR, 6´0˝/200 lbs; Missouri Southern State; B5/15/1970 Texarkana, AR

YEAR	TEAM	G (GS, POS)	RUSH	YD	AVG (LG)	TD	REC	YD	AVG (LG)	TD	PASS	COMP	PCT	YD	AVG (LG)	TD	INT	SK	YD	QBR	KPR	OTD	PTS	TAY
1995	Den	16 (1)	—	—	—	—	6	152	25.3 (43)	1	—	—	—	—	—	—	—	—	—	—	kp	—	6	75
1996	†Den	10 (1)	1	1	1.0 (1)	0	16	237	14.8 (49)	2	—	—	—	—	—	—	—	—	—	—	kp	—	12	312
1997	†Den	16 (16, WR)	5	16	3.2 (21)	0	70	1180	16.9 (78)	**12**	—	—	—	—	—	—	—	—	—	—	p	—	72	673
1998	†Den	16 (16, WR)	6	63	10.5 (37)	0	86	1222	14.2 (58)	6	1	1	100.0	14	14.0 (14)	0	0	—	—	—	—	1	42	711
1999	Den	15 (15, WR)	—	—	—	—	79	1020	12.9 (71)	4	1	0	0.0	0	0.0	0	0	—	—	—	k	—	24	525
2000	†Den★	16 (16, WR)	6	99	16.5 (50)	1	100	**1602**	16.0 (49)	8	—	—	—	—	—	—	—	—	—	—	—	—	54	950
2001	Den★	15 (14, WR)	3	27	9.0 (17)	0	**113**	1343	11.9 (65)	11	—	—	—	—	—	—	—	—	—	—	—	—	68	754
2002	Den	16 (16, WR)	6	9	1.5 (9)	0	89	1027	11.5 (46)	5	1	0	0.0	0	0.0	0	0	—	—	—	—	—	30	548
2003	†Den	15 (15, WR)	10	98	9.8 (26)	0	74	845	11.4 (38)	3	1	1	100.0	72	72.0 (72)	0	0	—	—	—	p	1	24	679
2004	†Den	16 (16, WR)	5	33	6.6 (14)	0	79	1144	14.5 (85)	7	—	—	—	—	—	—	—	—	—	—	p	—	42	753
2005	†Den✧	16 (16, WR)	1	7	7.0 (7)	0	85	1105	13.0 (72)	6	1	0	0.0	0	0.0	0	0	1	11	—	—	—	36	590
NFL	11	167 (142)	43	353	8.2 (50)	1	797	10877	13.6 (85)	65	5	2	40.0	86	17.2 (72)	0	0	1	11	—	kp	2	410	6568

SMITH, ROD Rodney Marc, DB, 5´11˝/187 lbs; Notre Dame; 1992: NE, rnd 2; B3/12/1970 St. Paul, MN **1992** NE 16 (1) **1993** NE 16 (9, LCB) **1994**†NE 16 (7, lcb) **1995** Car 16 (5, rcb) **1996**†Car 8 (1) **1997** Car 16 (2) **1998** Car 6 (2) **1998** GB 8 (0) **NFL** 102 (27) [7 yrs]

SMITH, RON Ronald, DB-WR, 6´1˝/195 lbs; Wisconsin; B5/3/1943 Chicago, IL **[R]** **1965** ChiB 14 **1966** Atl 14 (14, LCB) **1968** LARm 14 (14, LS) **1969**†LARm 14 (11, RCB) **1970** ChiB 14 **1971** ChiB 14 (SS) **1972** ChiB✧14 (SS) **1973** SD 14 (9, SS) **1974**†Oak 14

YEAR	TEAM	G (GS, POS)	RUSH	YD	AVG (LG)	TD	REC	YD	AVG (LG)	TD	PASS	COMP	PCT	YD	AVG (LG)	TD	INT	SK	YD	QBR	KPR	OTD	PTS	TAY
1967	Atl	13	8	42	5.3 (12)	0	11	227	20.6 (60)	0	—	—	—	—	—	—	—	—	—	—	kp	1	6	549
NFL	10	139 (48)	8	42	5.3 (12)	0	11	227	20.6 (60)	0	—	—	—	—	—	—	—	—	—	—	kpi	6	36	3719

SMITH, RON Ronald, DT, 6´3˝/308 lbs; Baylor; Lane; B8/18/1978 St. Louis, MO **2002** Cin 5 (0)

SMITH, RON Ronnie Bernard, WR, 6´0˝/185 lbs; San Diego State; 1978: LA, rnd 2; B11/20/1956 Lakeland, FL

YEAR	TEAM	G (GS, POS)	RUSH	YD	AVG (LG)	TD	REC	YD	AVG (LG)	TD	PASS	COMP	PCT	YD	AVG (LG)	TD	INT	SK	YD	QBR	KPR	OTD	PTS	TAY
1978	†LARm	16	—	—	—	—	1	15	15.0 (15)	0	—	—	—	—	—	—	—	—	—	—	—	—	0	8
1979	†LARm	12 (2)	—	—	—	—	16	300	18.8 (38)	1	—	—	—	—	—	—	—	—	—	—	—	—	6	155
1980	†SD	15 (0)	—	—	—	—	4	48	12.0 (24)	0	—	—	—	—	—	—	—	—	—	—	k	—	0	60
1981	†SD	9 (1)	—	—	—	—	3	84	28.0 (39)	2	—	—	—	—	—	—	—	—	—	—	k	—	12	54

YEAR	TEAM	G (GS, POS)	RUSH	YD	AVG(LG)	TD	REC	YD	AVG(LG)	TD	PASS COMP	PCT	YD	AVG(LG)	TD	INT	SK	YD	QBR	KPR	OTD	PTS	TAY
1981	Phi	3(0)	1	7	7.0(7)	0	4	84	21.0(42)	0	—	—	—	—	—	—	—	—	—	—	—	—	0	49
1982	Phi	9(9, WR)	—	—	—	—	34	475	14.0(41)	1	—	—	—	—	—	—	—	—	—	—	—	—	6	243
1983	Phi	2(0)	—	—	—	—	1	8	8.0(8)	0	—	—	—	—	—	—	—	—	—	—	—	—	0	4
NFL	6	66(12)	1	7	7.0(7)	0	63	1014	16.1(42)	4	—	—	—	—	—	—	—	—	—	—	k	—	24	572

SMITH, RON   Ronald Christopher, QB, 6′5″/220 lbs; Wake Forest; Richmond; 1964: LA, rnd 10/SD, rnd 23; B6/27/1942 Richmond, VA   **1965** LARm 1

| 1966 | Pit | 9(QB) | 4 | -9 | -2.3(2) | 0 | — | — | — | — | 181 | 79 | 43.6 | 1249 | 6.9(84) | 8 | 12 | — | — | 54.3 | — | — | 0 | 176 |
| NFL | 2 | 10 | 4 | -9 | -2.3(2) | 0 | — | — | — | — | 181 | 79 | 43.6 | 1249 | 6.9(84) | 8 | 12 | — | — | 54.3 | — | — | 0 | 176 |

SMITH, ROYCE   Royce Lionel, G, 6′3″/250 lbs; Georgia; 1972: NO, rnd 1; B6/17/1949 Savannah, GA, D1/22/2004 Claxton, GA   **1972** NO 10 (RG)   **1973** NO 14   **1974** Atl 14   **1975** Atl 14   **1976** Atl 10   **NFL** 62 [5 yrs]

SMITH, RUSS   Eugene Russell, G-C, 5′10″/220 lbs; Navy; Southern Illinois; Illinois; B11/11/1895 Carbondale, IL, D7/7/1958 Johnson City, IL   **1921** ChiS 11 (11, RG)   **1922** ChiB 10 (10, RG)   **1923** Can 1 (0)   **1923** Mil 7 (7, LG)   **1924** Mil 1 (0)   **1924** Cle 6 (1)   **1925** Det 9 (6, RG)   **1925** ChiB 1 (0)   **1926** Ham 3 (2)   **NFL** 49 (37) [6 yrs]

SMITH, RUSS   Russell Conway, RB, 6′0″/212 lbs; Miami (FL); 1966: SD, rnd 5; B8/4/1944 Bronxville, NY, D4/1/2001 Long Beach, CA

1967	SD-A	12	22	115	5.2(16)	1	1	6	6.0(6)	0	—	—	—	—	—	—	—	—	—	—	kp	—	6	134
1968	SD-A	14(fb)	88	426	4.8(37)	4	7	71	10.1(24)	0	3	0	0.0	0	0.0	0	0	—	—	—	kp	—	24	492
1969	SD-A	14	51	211	4.1(16)	2	10	144	14.4(55)	0	—	—	—	—	—	—	—	—	—	—	kp	—	12	351
1970	SD	12	52	163	3.1(21)	3	5	44	8.8(11)	0	—	—	—	—	—	—	—	—	—	—	kp	—	18	195
NFL	4	52	213	915	4.3(37)	10	23	265	11.5(55)	0	3	0	0.0	0	0.0	0	0	—	—	—	kp	—	60	1172

SMITH, SAMMIE   Sammie Lee, RB, 6′2″/226 lbs; Florida State; 1989: Mia, rnd 1; B5/16/1967 Orlando, FL

1989	Mia	13(12, RB)	200	659	3.3(25)	6	7	81	11.6(34)	0	—	—	—	—	—	—	—	—	—	—	—	—	36	760
1990	†Mia	16(16, RB)	226	831	3.7(33)	8	11	134	12.2(53)	1	—	—	—	—	—	—	—	—	—	—	—	—	54	983
1991	Mia	12(6, rb)	83	297	3.6(18)	1	14	95	6.8(12)	0	—	—	—	—	—	—	—	—	—	—	—	—	6	355
1992	Den	3(1)	23	94	4.1(15)	0	—	—	—	—	—	—	—	—	—	—	—	—	—	—	k	—	0	95
NFL	4	44(35)	532	1881	3.5(33)	15	32	310	9.7(53)	1	—	—	—	—	—	—	—	—	—	—	k	—	96	2192

SMITH, SEAN   Sean Lamar, DE-DT, 6′4″/280 lbs; Grambling State; 1987: Chi, rnd 4; B3/27/1965 Bogalusa, LA   **1987** †ChiB 10 (0)   **1988** †ChiB 9 (3)   **1989** Dal 2 (0)   **1989** TB 3 (1)   **1989** †LARm 2 (1)   **NFL** 26 (5) [3 yrs]

SMITH, SEAN   Sean Warfield, DE, 6′7″/280 lbs; Georgia Tech; 1990: NE, rnd 11; B5/29/1967 Cincinnati, OH   **1990** NE 15 (0)   **1991** NE 2 (0)   **NFL** 17 (0) [2 yrs]

SMITH, SHAUN   Shaun, DT, 6′2″/320 lbs; South Carolina; B8/19/1981 Brooklyn, NY   **2004** NO 5 (1)   **2004** Cin 3 (1)   **2005** †Cin 13 (5, ldt)   **NFL** 21 (7) [2 yrs]

SMITH, SHERMAN   Sherman Lennell, RB, 6′4″/225 lbs; Miami (OH); 1976: Sea, rnd 2; B11/1/1954 Youngstown, OH

1976	Sea	12(9, RB)	119	537	4.5(53)	4	36	384	10.7(34)	1	2	0	0.0	0	0.0	0	0	—	—	—	k	—	30	777
1977	Sea	14(14, RB)	163	763	4.7(39)	4	30	419	14.0(44)	2	1	0	0.0	0	0.0	0	0	—	—	—	k	—	36	1034
1978	Sea	12(12, RB)	165	805	4.9(67)	6	28	366	13.1(64)	1	—	—	—	—	—	—	—	—	—	—	—	—	42	1053
1979	Sea☆	16(15, RB)	194	775	4.0(31)	11	48	499	10.4(35)	4	1	1	100.0	11	11.0(11)	0	0	—	—	—	—	—	90	1160
1980	Sea	3(2)	23	94	4.1(23)	0	6	72	12.0(19)	1	—	—	—	—	—	—	—	—	—	—	—	—	6	135
1981	Sea	16(8, RB)	83	253	3.0(21)	3	44	406	9.2(28)	1	—	—	—	—	—	—	—	—	—	—	—	—	24	491
1982	Sea	9(8, RB)	63	202	3.2(19)	0	19	196	10.3(39)	0	1	0	0.0	0	0.0	0	0	—	—	—	—	—	0	300
1983	SD	13(2)	24	91	3.8(20)	0	6	51	8.5(21)	0	1	0	0.0	0	0.0	0	0	—	—	—	k	—	0	119
NFL	8	95(70)	834	3520	4.2(67)	28	217	2393	11.0(64)	10	6	1	16.7	11	1.8(11)	0	0	—	—	—	k	—	228	5068

SMITH, SHEVIN   Shevin Jamar, DB, 5′11″/191 lbs; Florida State; 1998: TB, rnd 6; B6/17/1975 Miami, FL   **1998** TB 3 (0)   **1999** †TB 16 (0)   **NFL** 19 (0) [2 yrs]

SMITH, SID   Sidney Ercil, C-T, 6′4″/260 lbs; USC; 1970: KC, rnd 1; B7/6/1948 Wichita, KS   **1970** KC 14   **1972** KC 14   **1974** Hou 11 (C)

| 1971 | †KC | 14 | — | — | — | 1 | 1 | 12 | 12.0(12) | 0 | — | — | — | — | — | — | — | — | — | — | — | — | 0 | 6 |
| NFL | 4 | 53 | — | — | — | 1 | 1 | 12 | 12.0(12) | 0 | — | — | — | — | — | — | — | — | — | — | k | — | 0 | 3 |

SMITH, STEVE   Stephen Conant, T-DE, 6′2″/250 lbs; Michigan; 1966: SF, rnd 5/Hou, rnd 16; B5/29/1944 St. Louis, MO   **1966** Pit 3   **1968** †Min 14   **1969** †Min 14   **1970** †Min 14   **1971** Phi 14 (RT)   **1972** Phi 14 (RT)   **1973** Phi 14 (LT)   **1974** Phi 13 (LT)   **NFL** 100 [8 yrs]

SMITH, STEVE   Steven Anthony, RB, 6′1″/236 lbs; Penn State; 1987: LARd, rnd 3; B8/30/1964 Washington, DC

1987	LARd	7(3)	5	18	3.6(15)	0	3	46	15.3(32)	0	—	—	—	—	—	—	—	—	—	—	—	—	0	41
1988	LARd	16(6, fb)	38	162	4.3(21)	3	26	299	11.5(45)	6	—	—	—	—	—	—	—	—	—	—	k	—	54	373
1989	LARd	16(16, FB)	117	471	4.0(21)	1	19	140	7.4(14)	0	—	—	—	—	—	—	—	—	—	—	k	—	6	540
1990	†LARd	16(15, FB)	81	327	4.0(17)	2	4	30	7.5(17)	3	—	—	—	—	—	—	—	—	—	—	—	—	30	377
1991	†LARd	16(16, FB)	62	265	4.3(19)	1	15	130	8.7(37)	1	—	—	—	—	—	—	—	—	—	—	k	—	12	330
1992	LARd	16(15, FB)	44	129	2.9(15)	0	28	217	7.8(19)	1	—	—	—	—	—	—	—	—	—	—	—	—	6	243
1993	†LARd	16(13, FB)	47	156	3.3(13)	0	18	187	10.4(22)	0	—	—	—	—	—	—	—	—	—	—	—	—	0	250
1994	Sea	16(0)	26	80	3.1(12)	2	11	142	12.9(25)	1	—	—	—	—	—	—	—	—	—	—	—	—	18	176
1995	Sea	9(8, FB)	9	19	2.1(4)	0	7	59	8.4(17)	1	—	—	—	—	—	—	—	—	—	—	—	—	6	50
NFL	9	128(92)	429	1627	3.8(21)	9	131	1250	9.5(45)	13	—	—	—	—	—	—	—	—	—	—	k	—	132	2378

SMITH, STEVE   Stevonne, WR, 5′9″/179 lbs; Utah; 2001: Car, rnd 3; B5/12/1979 Los Angeles, CA [R]

2001	Car★	15(1)	4	43	10.8(39)	0	10	154	15.4(33)	0	—	—	—	—	—	—	—	—	—	—	kp	3	18	935
2002	Car	15(13, WR)	1	-4	-4.0(-4)	0	54	872	16.1(69)	3	—	—	—	—	—	—	—	—	—	—	kp	2	30	843
2003	Car	16(11, WR)	11	42	3.8(14)	0	88	1110	12.6(67)	7	—	—	—	—	—	—	—	—	—	—	kp	1	48	1005
2004	Car	1(1)	—	—	—	—	6	60	10.0(15)	0	1	0	0.0	0	0.0	0	0	—	—	—	p	—	0	30
2005	†Car★	16(16, WR)	4	25	6.3(20)	1	103	1563	15.2(80)	12	—	—	—	—	—	—	—	—	—	—	kp	6	78	1044
NFL	5	63(42)	20	106	5.3(39)	1	261	3759	14.4(80)	22	1	0	0.0	0	0.0	0	0	—	—	—	kp	6	174	3857

SMITH, STEVE   Steven Michael, DB, 6′1″/190 lbs; Oregon; 2002: Jax, rnd 7; B6/28/1979 Torrance, CA   **2002** Jax 4 (0)

SMITH, STRUGGY   Henri F., DB, 6′2″/190 lbs; Appalachian State; B2/13/1964 Charlotte, NC   **1987** Atl 2 (0)

SMITH, STU   Stuart Moore, FB-LB-TB-DB, 6′0″/195 lbs; Bucknell; B2/3/1915 Montour Falls, NY, D11/7/1969 Baltimore, MD

1937	Pit	10(6, FB)	66	211	3.2	0	—	—	—	—	2	0	0.0	0	0.0	0	1	—	—	—	—	—	0	171
1938	Pit◇	11(11, FB)	80	241	3.0	0	3	30	10.0	0	—	—	—	—	—	—	—	—	—	—	—	—	0	256
NFL	2	21(17)	146	452	3.1	0	3	30	10.0	0	2	0	0.0	0	0.0	0	1	—	—	—	—	—	0	427

SMITH, TERRELLE   Terrelle Vernon, FB, 6′0″/246 lbs; Arizona State; 2000: NO, rnd 4; B3/12/1978 West Covina, CA

2000	NO	14(9, FB)	29	131	4.5(16)	0	12	65	5.4(10)	0	—	—	—	—	—	—	—	—	—	—	—	—	0	164
2001	NO	14(9, FB)	5	8	1.6(6)	0	4	30	7.5(12)	2	—	—	—	—	—	—	—	—	—	—	—	—	12	33
2002	NO	16(8, FB)	5	11	2.2(5)	0	9	30	3.3(10)	0	—	—	—	—	—	—	—	—	—	—	—	—	0	26
2003	NO	15(10, FB)	—	—	—	0	6	28	4.7(8)	0	—	—	—	—	—	—	—	—	—	—	—	—	0	14
2004	Cle	16(9, FB)	4	9	2.3(4)	0	7	39	5.6(9)	0	—	—	—	—	—	—	—	—	—	—	—	—	0	29
2005	Cle	16(15, FB)	6	9	1.5(4)	0	12	58	4.8(9)	1	—	—	—	—	—	—	—	—	—	—	k	—	6	37
NFL	6	91(60)	49	168	3.4(16)	0	50	250	5.0(16)	3	—	—	—	—	—	—	—	—	—	—	k	—	18	302

SMITH, THOMAS   Thomas Eric, RB, 6′1″/216 lbs; Iowa; Miami (FL); 1973: Mia, rnd 7; B10/4/1949 Waterloo, IN   **1973** Mia 2

SMITH, THOMAS   Thomas Lee, DB, 5′11″/188 lbs; North Carolina; 1993: Buf, rnd 1; B12/5/1970 Gates, NC   **1993** †Buf 16 (1)   **1994** Buf 16 (16, RCB)   **1995** †Buf 16 (16, RCB)   **1996** †Buf 16 (16, RCB)   **1997** Buf 16 (16, RCB)   **1998** Buf 14 (14, RCB)   **1999** †Buf 16 (16, RCB)   **2000** ChiB 16 (16, RCB)   **2001** Ind 11 (0)   **NFL** 137 (111) [9 yrs]

SMITH, TIM   Timothy Francis, WR, 6′2″/201 lbs; Nebraska; 1980: Hou, rnd 3; B3/20/1957 Tucson, AZ

1980	†Hou	16(0)	—	—	—	2	21	10.5(13)	0	—	—	—	—	—	—	—	—	—	—	—	k	—	0	-5
1981	Hou	4(1)	—	—	—	2	37	18.5(25)	0	—	—	—	—	—	—	—	—	—	—	—	—	—	0	19
1982	Hou	9(0)	—	—	—	—	—	—	—	—	—	—	—	—	—	—	—	—	—	—	—	—	0	7
1983	Hou☆	16(16, WR)	2	16	8.0(9)	0	83	1176	14.2(47)	6	—	—	—	—	—	—	—	—	—	—	—	—	36	634
1984	Hou	16(14, WR)	—	—	—	—	69	1141	16.5(75)	4	—	—	—	—	—	—	—	—	—	—	—	—	24	591
1985	Hou	16(16, WR)	—	—	—	—	46	660	14.3(37)	2	—	—	—	—	—	—	—	—	—	—	P	—	12	340
1986	Hou	13(0)	—	—	—	—	4	72	18.0(25)	0	—	—	—	—	—	—	—	—	—	—	—	—	0	36
NFL	7	90(47)	2	16	8.0(9)	0	206	3107	15.1(75)	12	—	—	—	—	—	—	—	—	—	—	Pk	—	72	1622

YEAR	TEAM	G (GS, POS)	RUSH	YD	AVG(LG)	TD	REC	YD	AVG(LG)	TD	PASS	COMP	PCT	YD	AVG(LG)	TD	INT	SK	YD	QBR	KPR	OTD	PTS	TAY

SMITH, TIMMY   Timothy LaRay, RB, 5´11˝/216 lbs; Texas Tech; 1987: Was, rnd 5; B1/24/1964 Hobbs, NM

1987	†Was	7 (0)	29	126	4.3(15)	0	1	-2	-2.0(-2)	0	—	—	—	—	—	—	—	—	—	—	—	—	0	125
1988	Was	14 (8, FB)	155	470	3.0(29)	3	8	53	6.6(16)	0	—	—	—	—	—	—	—	—	—	—	—	—	18	527
1990	Dal	1 (1)	6	6	1.0(3)	0	—	—	—	—	—	—	—	—	—	—	—	—	—	—	—	—	0	6
NFL	3	22 (9)	190	602	3.2(29)	3	9	51	5.7(16)	0	—	—	—	—	—	—	—	—	—	—	—	—	18	658

SMITH, TODY   Lawrence Edward, DE, 6´5˝/250 lbs; Michigan State; USC; 1971: Dal, rnd 1; B12/24/1948 Orange, TX, D7/18/1999 Los Angeles, CA   **1971**†Dal 7   **1972**†Dal 10 (6, lde)   **1973** Hou 14 (LDE)   **1974** Hou 14 (LDE)   **1975** Hou 13 (LDE)   **1976** Hou 9 (LDE)   **1976** Buf 2   **NFL** 69 (6) [6 yrs]

SMITH, TOMMIE   Tommie, WR, 6´3˝/190 lbs; San Jose State; 1967: LA, rnd 9; B6/6/1944 Clarksville, TN

| 1969 | Cin-A | 2 | — | — | — | — | 1 | 41 | 41.0(41) | 0 | — | — | — | — | — | — | — | — | — | — | — | — | 0 | 21 |

SMITH, TONY   Tony Derrell, RB, 6´1˝/212 lbs; Southern Mississippi; 1992: Atl, rnd 1; B6/29/1970 Chicago, IL   **1993** Atl 15 (0)   **1994** Atl 4 (0)

| 1992 | Atl | 14 (6, rb) | 87 | 329 | 3.8(32) | 2 | 2 | 14 | 7.0(8) | 0 | — | — | — | — | — | — | — | — | — | — | kp | — | 12 | 498 |
| NFL | 3 | 33 (6) | 87 | 329 | 3.8(32) | 2 | 2 | 14 | 7.0(8) | 0 | — | — | — | — | — | — | — | — | — | — | kp | 1 | 18 | 1109 |

SMITH, TORIN   Tony Nathaniel, DE, 6´4˝/320 lbs; Hampton; B9/30/1961   **1987** NYG 1 (0)

SMITH, TRAVIAN   Travian, LB, 6´4˝/240 lbs; Oklahoma; 1998: Oak, rnd 5; B8/26/1975 Shepherd, TX   **1998** Oak 2 (0)   **1999** Oak 16 (1)   **2000**†Oak 16 (0)   **2001**†Oak 16 (2)   **2002**†Oak 16 (2)   **2003** Oak 10 (7, LLB)   **2004** Oak 8 (4)   **NFL** 84 (16) [7 yrs]

SMITH, TRENT   Trent, TE, 6´5˝/245 lbs; Oklahoma; 2003: Bal, rnd 7; B9/15/1979 Norman, OK

| 2005 | SF | 5 (2) | — | — | — | — | 3 | 7 | 2.3(6) | 0 | — | — | — | — | — | — | — | — | — | — | — | — | 0 | 4 |

SMITH, TROY   Troy, WR, 6´2˝/193 lbs; East Carolina; 1999: Phi, rnd 6; B6/30/1977 Greenville, NC

| 1999 | Phi | 1 (0) | — | — | — | — | 1 | 14 | 14.0(14) | 0 | — | — | — | — | — | — | — | — | — | — | — | — | 0 | 7 |

SMITH, TRUETT   Truett Henry, BB, 6´2˝/208 lbs; Wyoming; Mississippi State; 1950: Pit, rnd 7; B3/17/1924 New Orleans, LA, D12/29/2000 Jackson, MS   **1950** Pit 9

| 1951 | Pit | 11 (BB) | 1 | 1 | 1.0(1) | 0 | 4 | 71 | 17.8(24) | 0 | — | — | — | — | — | — | — | — | — | — | — | — | 0 | 37 |
| NFL | 2 | 20 | 1 | 1 | 1.0(1) | 0 | 4 | 71 | 17.8(24) | 0 | — | — | — | — | — | — | — | — | — | — | — | — | 0 | 37 |

SMITH, VERNICE   Vernice Carlton, G-T, 6´3˝/300 lbs; Florida A&M; B10/24/1965 Orlando, FL   **1990** Phx 11 (0)   **1991** Phx 14 (7, LG)   **1992** Phx 12 (2)   **1993** ChiB 6 (5, rg)   **1993** Was 8 (3)   **1994** Was 4 (0)   **1995** Was 9 (5, rg)   **1997** SL 10 (2)   **NFL** 74 (24) [7 yrs]

SMITH, VINSON   Vinson Robert, LB, 6´2˝/243 lbs; East Carolina; B7/3/1965 Statesville, NC   **1988** Atl 3 (0)   **1990** Dal 16 (1)   **1991**†Dal 13 (12, RLB)   **1992**†Dal 16 (13, LLB)   **1993** ChiB 16 (13, RLB)   **1994**†ChiB 12 (10, RLB)   **1995** ChiB 16 (13, LLB)   **1996** ChiB 15 (12, RLB)   **1997** Dal 14 (3)   **1998** NO 15 (0)   **1999** NO 12 (0)   **NFL** 148 (77) [11 yrs]

SMITH, VITAMIN   Verda Thomas, HB, 5´8˝/179 lbs; Abilene Christian; B10/30/1923 Sweetwater, TX, D2/14/2000 Lake Dallas, TX **[R]**

1949	†LARm	12 (4)	40	117	2.9(26)	2	5	63	12.6(24)	1	—	—	—	—	—	—	—	—	—	—	kp	1	24	516
1950	†LARm	12 (RH)	51	250	4.9(25)	1	16	279	17.4(67)	4	1	1	100.0	11	11.0(11)	0	0	—	—	—	kp	3	48	975
1951	†LARm	12 (RH)	52	143	2.8(31)	1	16	278	17.4(67)	1	—	—	—	—	—	—	—	—	—	—	kp	—	12	425
1952	†LARm	12 (RH)	57	133	2.3(20)	3	16	254	15.9(56)	3	1	0	0.0	0	0.0	0	0	—	—	—	kp	—	36	378
1953	LARm	11	8	26	3.3(21)	0	6	151	25.2(54)	3	2	1	50.0	50	25.0(50)	0	0	—	—	—	kp	—	18	126
NFL	5	59 (4)	208	669	3.2(31)	7	59	1025	17.4(67)	12	4	2	50.0	61	15.3(50)	0	0	—	—	—	kp	4	138	2419

SMITH, WADDELL   James Waddell, WR, 6´2˝/180 lbs; Kansas; 1977: KC, rnd 8; B8/24/1955 New Orleans, LA

| 1984 | Dal | 2 (0) | 1 | -5 | -5.0(-5) | 0 | 1 | 7 | 7.0(7) | 0 | — | — | — | — | — | — | — | — | — | — | — | — | 0 | -2 |

SMITH, WADE   Wade L., T, 6´4˝/300 lbs; Memphis; 2003: Mia, rnd 3; B4/26/1981 Dallas, TX   **2003** Mia 16 (16, LT)   **2004** Mia 6 (2)   **NFL** 22 (18) [2 yrs]

SMITH, WARREN   Warren, G, /175 lbs; Western Michigan; B1895, MN, deceased   **1921** GB 2 (2)

SMITH, WAYNE   Wayne Lester, DB, 6´0˝/171 lbs; Wisconsin-LaCrosse; Purdue; 1980: Det, rnd 11; B5/9/1957 Chicago, IL   **1980** Det 16 (8, LCB)   **1981** Det 16 (16, LCB)   **1982** Det 5 (5, LCB)   **1982** SL 1 (0)   **1983** SL 16 (16, RCB)   **1984** SL 16 (15, RCB)   **1985** SL 16 (16, RCB)   **1986** SL 16 (7, rcb)   **1987** Min 6 (1)   **NFL** 108 (84) [8 yrs]

SMITH, WEE WILLIE   Willie Merton, DB-TB-FB, 5´6˝/148 lbs; Idaho; B7/2/1910 Lexington, NE, D9/4/1996 Albuquerque, NM

| 1934 | NYG | 9 (1) | 80 | 323 | 4.0 | 2 | 2 | 32 | 16.0 | 0 | 5 | 2 | 40.0 | 37 | 7.4(27) | 1 | 1 | — | — | — | — | 1 | 12 | 343 |

SMITH, WES   Wes, WR, 5´11˝/194 lbs; Texas A&M-Commerce; 1986: SL, rnd 10; B6/24/1963   **1987** GB 1 (0)

SMITH, WILFRED   Wilfrid Russell, T-G-E-C, 6´4˝/204 lbs; DePauw; B4/7/1899 Milroy, IN, D8/3/1976 Chicago, IL   **1920** Mun 1 (0)   **1921** Mun 2 (2, RT)   **1922** Lou 1 (1)   **1923** ChiC 3 (1)   **1923** Ham 5 (4, RG)   **1924** ChiC 6 (3)   **1925** ChiC 13 (5, LE)   **NFL** 31 (16) [6 yrs]

SMITH, WILL   Will, DE, 6´4˝/265 lbs; Ohio State; 2004: NO, rnd 1; B7/4/1981 Queens, NY   **2004** NO 16 (4)   **2005** NO 16 (9, lde)   **NFL** 32 (13) [2 yrs]

SMITH, WILLIE   Willie, G-T, 6´3˝/255 lbs; Michigan; 1959: ChiB, rnd 8; B11/1/1937 Little Rock, AR   **1960** Den-A 14 (RG)   **1961** Oak-A 14 (LG)   **NFL** 28 [2 yrs]

*SMITH, WILLIE   Willie, TE, 6´2˝/235 lbs; Miami (FL); 1986: Cle, rnd 10; B8/6/1964 Jacksonville, FL

| 1987 | Mia | 3 (0) | — | — | — | — | 2 | 13 | 6.5(8) | 1 | — | — | — | — | — | — | — | — | — | — | — | — | 6 | 12 |

SMITH, ZEKE   Roger Zeke, LB-G-DE, 6´2˝/235 lbs; Auburn; 1960: NYT, rnd 1; B9/29/1936 Walker Springs, AL   **1960** Bal 12   **1961**†NYG 12   **NFL** 24 [2 yrs]

SMITH, ZURIEL   Zuriel, WR, 5´11˝/166 lbs; Hampton; 2003: Dal, rnd 6; B1/15/1980 Richmond, VA

| 2003 | Dal | 9 (0) | — | — | — | — | 3 | 46 | 15.3(32) | 0 | — | — | — | — | — | — | — | — | — | — | kp | — | 0 | 235 |

SMOLINSKI, MARK   Mark Wayne, FB-TE, 6´1˝/215 lbs; Wyoming; B5/9/1939 Alpena, MI

1961	Bal	14	31	98	3.2(14)	0	9	100	11.1(25)	1	—	—	—	—	—	—	—	—	—	—	kp	—	6	132
1962	Bal	14	85	265	3.1(11)	1	13	128	9.8(33)	1	—	—	—	—	—	—	—	—	—	—	k	—	12	334
1963	NYJ-A	14 (FB)	150	561	3.7(56)	4	34	278	8.2(49)	1	—	—	—	—	—	—	—	—	—	—	k	—	30	740
1964	NYJ-A	14	34	117	3.4(19)	1	3	19	6.3(12)	0	—	—	—	—	—	—	—	—	—	—	k	—	6	126
1965	NYJ-A	12	24	59	2.5(14)	0	6	25	4.2(12)	0	—	—	—	—	—	—	—	—	—	—	k	—	0	80
1966	NYJ-A	14	21	69	3.3(21)	2	11	74	6.7(24)	1	—	—	—	—	—	—	—	—	—	—	k	—	18	100
1967	NYJ-A	13	64	139	2.2(10)	1	21	177	8.4(22)	3	—	—	—	—	—	—	—	—	—	—	k	—	24	241
1968	†NYJ-A	14	12	15	1.3(5)	0	6	40	6.7(19)	0	—	—	—	—	—	—	—	—	—	—	k	1	6	37
NFL	8	109	421	1323	3.1(56)	9	103	841	8.2(49)	7	—	—	—	—	—	—	—	—	—	—	kp	1	102	1789

SMOOT, FRED   Frederick D., DB, 5´11˝/174 lbs; Mississippi State; 2001: Was, rnd 2; B4/17/1979 Jackson, MS   **2001** Was 14 (13, RCB)   **2002** Was 16 (16, RCB)   **2003** Was 15 (15, RCB)   **2004** Was 15 (15, RCB)   **2005** Min 11 (8, rcb)   **NFL** 71 (67) [5 yrs]

SMOOT, RAYMOND   Raymond Eugene, G-T, 6´4˝/305 lbs; LSU; B7/24/1970 Leesville, LA   **1993** SD 2 (0)

SMUKLER, DAVE   David, FB-LB, 6´1˝/226 lbs; Missouri; Temple; B5/28/1914 Newark, NJ, D2/22/1971 Los Angeles, CA **[K]**

1936	Phi	10 (8, FB)	99	321	3.2	0	—	—	—	—	68	21	30.9	345	5.1	3	6	—	—	—	K	—	5	269
1937	Phi	11 (11, FB)	92	247	2.7	1	1	-4	-4.0(-4)	0	118	42	35.6	432	3.7	5	14	—	21.5	K	—	17	-64
1938	Phi	11 (10, FB)	96	313	3.3	1	—	—	—	—	102	42	41.2	524	5.1	7	8	—	48.0	K	—	18	310
1939	Phi	4 (4)	45	218	4.8	0	—	—	—	—	20	7	35.0	56	2.8	0	4	—	P	—	0	86
1944	Bos	2 (1)	2	7	3.5(6)	0	—	—	—	—	—	—	—	—	—	—	—	—	—	P	—	0	7
NFL	5	38 (34)	334	1106	3.3(6)	2	1	-4	-4.0(-4)	0	308	112	36.4	1357	4.4	15	32	—	27.4	KP	1	40	608

SMYTH, BILL   William Krantz, DE-E-T, 6´3˝/243 lbs; Notre Dame; Cincinnati; Penn State; 1947: LA, rnd 7; B4/8/1922 Batavia, OH, D11/6/1966 Ottawa, Canada

1947	LARm	12 (3)	—	—	—	—	3	26	8.7(11)	0	—	—	—	—	—	—	—	—	—	—	—	—	0	13
1948	LARm	11 (4)	—	—	—	—	6	66	11.0(21)	1	—	—	—	—	—	—	—	—	—	—	—	—	6	38
1949	†LARm	12 (0)	—	—	—	—	2	21	10.5(14)	0	—	—	—	—	—	—	—	—	—	—	—	—	0	11
1950	†LARm	11	—	—	—	—	2	10	5.0(6)	0	—	—	—	—	—	—	—	—	—	—	—	—	0	5
NFL	4	46 (7)	—	—	—	—	13	123	9.5(21)	1	—	—	—	—	—	—	—	—	—	—	—	—	6	67

SMYTH, LOU   Louis Lehman, B, 6´1˝/200 lbs; Texas; Centre; B3/19/1898 Cleburne, TX, D9/11/1964 Long Beach, CA   **1920** Can 9 (3)   **1921** Can 6 (4), 12   **1922** Can 5 (4), 6   **1923** Can☆12 (9, TB), 42   **1924** Roc 1 (1)   **1925** Roc 7 (7, TB)   **1925** Fra 3 (2), 12   **1926** Fra 4 (2)   **1926** Har 5 (5, FB), 6   **1926** Pro 3 (3)   **NFL** 55 (40), 78 [7 yrs]

SNEAD, NORM   Norman Bailey, QB, 6´4˝/215 lbs; Wake Forest; 1961: Was, rnd 1/Buf, rnd 5; B7/31/1939 Halifax County, VA

1961	Was	14 (14, QB)	34	47	1.4(9)	3	—	—	—	—	375	172	45.9	2337	6.2(80)	11	22	—	51.6	—	—	18	421
1962	Was	14 (QB)	20	10	0.5(9)	0	—	—	—	—	354	184	52.0	2926	8.3(85)	22	22	—	74.7	—	—	18	733
1963	Was◇	14 (QB)	23	100	4.3(16)	2	—	—	—	—	363	175	48.2	3043	8.4(77)	13	27	—	58.1	—	—	12	627

YEAR	TEAM	G (GS, POS)	RUSH	YD	AVG (LG)	TD	REC	YD	AVG (LG)	TD	PASS	COMP	PCT	YD	AVG (LG)	TD	INT	SK	YD	QBR	KPR	OTD	PTS	TAY
1964	Phi	12(12, QB)	16	59	3.7(19)	2	—	—	—	—	283	138	48.8	1906	6.7(87)	14	12	20	160	69.6	—	—	12	622
1965	Phi✧	11(11, QB)	24	81	3.4(20)	3	—	—	—	—	288	150	52.1	2346	8.1(78)	15	13	26	191	78.0	—	—	18	839
1966	Phi	10(10, QB)	15	32	2.1(17)	1	—	—	—	—	226	103	45.6	1275	5.6(48)	8	11	25	190	55.1	—	—	6	280
1967	Phi	14(QB)	9	30	3.3(21)	2	—	—	—	—	434	240	55.3	3399	7.8(87)	29	24	48	351	80.0	—	—	12	935
1968	Phi	11(QB)	9	27	3.0(9)	0	—	—	—	—	291	152	52.2	1655	5.7(55)	11	**21**	20	154	51.8	—	—	0	70
1969	Phi	13(QB)	8	2	0.3(5)	2	—	—	—	—	379	190	50.1	2768	7.3(80)	19	**23**	21	170	65.7	—	—	12	581
1970	Phi	14(QB)	18	35	1.9(16)	3	—	—	—	—	335	181	54.0	2323	6.9(79)	15	**20**	21	181	66.1	—	—	18	502
1971	Min	7	6	6	1.0(5)	1	—	—	—	—	75	37	49.3	470	6.3(55)	1	6	7	67	—	—	—	6	16
1972	NYG✧	14(QB)	10	21	2.1(15)	0	—	—	—	—	325	196	**60.3**	2307	7.1(94)	17	12	8	66	84.0	—	—	0	780
1973	NYG	10(QB)	4	13	3.3(14)	0	—	—	—	—	235	131	55.7	1483	6.3(46)	7	**22**	9	67	45.8	—	—	0	-91
1974	NYG	5	3	4	1.3(3)	0	—	—	—	—	111	67	60.4	615	5.5(53)	3	7	5	42	—	—	—	0	47
1974	SF	3	1	25	25.0(25)	0	—	—	—	—	48	30	62.5	368	7.7(39)	2	1	2	15	—	—	—	0	179
1975	SF	9(qb)	9	30	3.3(10)	1	—	—	—	—	189	108	57.1	1337	7.1(60)	9	10	16	109	73.0	—	—	6	354
1976	NYG	3	3	-1	-0.3(0)	0	—	—	—	—	42	22	52.4	239	5.7(31)	0	4	5	27	—	—	—	0	-42
NFL	16	178(47)	212	521	2.5(25)	23	—	—	—	—	4353	2276	52.3	30797	7.1(94)	196	257	233	1790	65.5	—	—	138	6850

SNEDDON, BOB Robert Lee, DB-HB-WB, 5´10˝/180 lbs; Weber State; St. Mary's (CA); 1944: Was, rnd 10; B7/9/1921 Ogden, UT

YEAR	TEAM	G (GS, POS)	RUSH	YD	AVG (LG)	TD	REC	YD	AVG (LG)	TD	PASS	COMP	PCT	YD	AVG (LG)	TD	INT	SK	YD	QBR	KPR	OTD	PTS	TAY
1944	Was	10(0)	14	30	2.1(19)	0	3	42	14.0(30)	0	—	—	—	—	—	—	—	—	—	—	i	—	0	66
1945	Det	1(0)	—	—	—	—	—	—	—	—	—	—	—	—	—	—	—	—	—	—	—	—	—	—
NFL	2	11(0)	14	30	2.1(19)	0	3	42	14.0(30)	0	—	—	—	—	—	—	—	—	—	—	—	—	0	51
1946	LAD-A	11(0)	3	6	2.0	0	2	11	5.5	0	—	—	—	—	—	—	—	—	—	—	i	—	0	22

SNEE, CHRIS Christopher, G, 6´3˝/331 lbs; Boston College; 2004: NYG, rnd 2; B1/8/1982 Edison, NJ **2004** NYG 11 (11, RG) **2005**†NYG 16 (16, RG) **NFL** 27 (27) [2 yrs]

SNELL, DONALD Donald Wayne, WR, 6´2˝/177 lbs; Virginia Tech; B3/13/1965 **1987** Sea 1 (0)

SNELL, GEORGE George Albert, B, 5´10˝/185 lbs; Penn State; B7/9/1897, deceased **1926** Bkn 11 (11, FB), 6 **1927** Buf 3 (1) **NFL** 14 (12) [2 yrs]

SNELL, MATT Matthews, RB, 6´2˝/219 lbs; Ohio State; 1964: NYJ, rnd 1/NYG, rnd 4; B8/18/1941 Garfield, GA

YEAR	TEAM	G (GS, POS)	RUSH	YD	AVG (LG)	TD	REC	YD	AVG (LG)	TD	PASS	COMP	PCT	YD	AVG (LG)	TD	INT	SK	YD	QBR	KPR	OTD	PTS	TAY
1964	NYJ-A★	14(FB)	215	948	4.4(42)	5	56	393	7.0(41)	1	1	0	0.0	0	0.0	0	1	—	—	—	k	—	36	1213
1965	NYJ-A☆	14(FB)	169	763	4.5(44)	4	38	264	6.9(35)	0	—	—	—	—	—	—	—	—	—	—	—	—	24	935
1966	NYJ-A✧	12(FB)	178	644	3.6(25)	4	48	346	7.2(25)	4	1	0	0.0	0	0.0	0	0	—	—	—	—	—	48	877
1967	NYJ-A	7(FB)	61	207	3.4(13)	0	11	54	4.9(21)	0	—	—	—	—	—	—	—	—	—	—	—	—	0	234
1968	†NYJ-A☆	14(FB)	179	747	4.2(60)	6	16	105	6.6(39)	1	1	1	100.0	26	26.0(26)	0	0	—	—	—	k	—	42	861
1969	†NYJ-A★	14(FB)	191	695	3.6(34)	4	22	187	8.5(54)	1	—	—	—	—	—	—	—	—	—	—	—	—	30	834
1970	NYJ	3	64	281	4.4(19)	1	2	26	13.0(27)	0	—	—	—	—	—	—	—	—	—	—	—	—	6	304
1971	NYJ	5	—	—	—	—	—	—	—	—	—	—	—	—	—	—	—	—	—	—	—	—	—	—
1972	NYJ	4	—	—	—	—	—	—	—	—	—	—	—	—	—	—	—	—	—	—	k	—	0	-1
NFL	9	87	1057	4285	4.1(60)	24	193	1375	7.1(54)	7	3	1	33.3	26	8.7(26)	0	1	—	—	—	k	—	186	5256

SNELL, RAY Ray Michael, G-T, 6´4˝/262 lbs; Wisconsin; 1980: TB, rnd 1; B2/24/1958 Baltimore, MD **1980** TB 13 (11, RG) **1981**†TB 16 (12, LG) **1982**†TB 7 (6, LG) **1983** TB 9 (6, lg) **1984**†Pit 13 (6, lt) **1985** Pit 5 (0) **1985** Det 2 (1) **NFL** 65 (42) [6 yrs]

SNELLING, KEN Kenneth Edward, FB-LB, 6´0˝/210 lbs; UCLA; 1943: GB, rnd 7; B12/11/1918 Musselshell, MT, D9/17/1944 Ruch, OR

YEAR	TEAM	G (GS, POS)	RUSH	YD	AVG (LG)	TD	REC	YD	AVG (LG)	TD	PASS	COMP	PCT	YD	AVG (LG)	TD	INT	SK	YD	QBR	KPR	OTD	PTS	TAY
1945	GB	2(0)	3	10	3.3(8)	0	—	—	—	—	—	—	—	—	—	—	—	—	—	—	—	—	0	10

SNIADECKI, JIM James Bert, LB, 6´2˝/230 lbs; Indiana; 1969: SF, rnd 4; B3/23/1947 South Bend, IN **1969** SF 14 **1970**†SF 14 **1971**†SF 14 **1972** SF 2 **1973** SF 14 (11, MLB) **NFL** 58 (11) [5 yrs]

SNIDER, MAL Malcolm Pratt, G-T, 6´4˝/251 lbs; Stanford; 1969: Atl, rnd 3; B4/5/1947 Battle Creek, MI **1969** Atl 14 (RG) **1970** Atl 14 (LT) **1971** Atl 13 (RG) **1972**†GB 14 (RG) **1973** GB 14 (LT) **1974** GB 14 **NFL** 83 [6 yrs]

SNIDER, MATT Matthew Kale, FB, 6´2˝/240 lbs; Richmond; B1/26/1976 Des Moines, IA **1999** GB 8 (0) **2000** GB 16 (0) **2001** Min 4 (0) **NFL** 28 (0) [3 yrs]

SNIDOW, RON Ronald Wayne, DE-DT, 6´3˝/250 lbs; Oregon; 1963: Was, rnd 3/Buf, rnd 10; B12/30/1941 Newport News, VA **1963** Was 13 **1964** Was 14 (RDE) **1965** Was 14 (LDE) **1966** Was 14 (LDE) **1967** Was 14 (LDE) **1968**†Cle 13 (13, LDE) **1969**†Cle☆14 (LDE) **1970** Cle 14 (LDE) **1971**†Cle 13 (lde) **1972** Cle 3 **NFL** 126 (13) [10 yrs]

SNIPES, ANGELO Angelo Bernard, LB, 6´0˝/222 lbs; West Georgia; B1/11/1963 Atlanta, GA **1986** Was 10 (0) **1986** SD 6 (0) **1987** SD 2 (0) **1987** KC 4 (0) **1988** KC 15 (8, lolb) **1989** KC 2 (0) **NFL** 39 (8) [4 yrs]

SNOOTS, LEE John Lee, B, 5´9˝/185 lbs; none; B8/12/1892, D11/29/1968 Columbus, OH **1920** Col 7 (3, TB) **1922** Col 7 (7, TB), 6 **1923** Col 10 (10, FB), 6 **1925** Col 1 (1) **NFL** 25 (21), 12 [4 yrs]

SNORTON, MATT Hickman Matthew, TE, 6´5˝/250 lbs; Michigan State; 1964: Den, rnd 3/Det, rnd 2; B9/26/1942 Crofton, KY **1964** Den-A 5

SNOW, JACK Jack Thomas, WR-SE, 6´2˝/190 lbs; Notre Dame; 1965: Min, rnd 1/SD, rnd 7; B1/25/1943 Rock Springs, WY, D1/9/2006 St. Louis, MO

YEAR	TEAM	G (GS, POS)	RUSH	YD	AVG (LG)	TD	REC	YD	AVG (LG)	TD	PASS	COMP	PCT	YD	AVG (LG)	TD	INT	SK	YD	QBR	KPR	OTD	PTS	TAY
1965	LARm	14(SE)	—	—	—	—	38	559	14.7(60)	3	—	—	—	—	—	—	—	—	—	—	—	—	18	295
1966	LARm	14(14, SE)	—	—	—	—	34	634	18.6(84)	3	—	—	—	—	—	—	—	—	—	—	—	—	18	332
1967	†LARm✧	14(SE)	—	—	—	—	28	735	**26.3**(**80**)	8	—	—	—	—	—	—	—	—	—	—	—	—	48	408
1968	LARm	14(13, SE)	—	—	—	—	29	500	17.2(54)	3	—	—	—	—	—	—	—	—	—	—	—	—	18	265
1969	†LARm	14(14, SE)	—	—	—	—	49	734	15.0(74)	6	—	—	—	—	—	—	—	—	—	—	—	—	36	397
1970	LARm	14(14, WR)	—	—	—	—	51	859	16.8(71)	7	—	—	—	—	—	—	—	—	—	—	—	—	42	465
1971	LARm	14(14, WR)	1	-10	-10.0(-10)	0	37	666	18.0(68)	5	—	—	—	—	—	—	—	—	—	—	—	—	30	348
1972	LARm	14(14, WR)	—	—	—	—	30	590	19.7(57)	4	—	—	—	—	—	—	—	—	—	—	—	—	24	315
1973	†LARm	14(14, WR)	—	—	—	—	16	252	15.8(38)	2	—	—	—	—	—	—	—	—	—	—	—	—	12	136
1974	†LARm	14(14, WR)	1	13	13.0(13)	0	24	397	16.5(44)	3	—	—	—	—	—	—	—	—	—	—	—	—	18	227
1975	LARm	10	—	—	—	—	4	86	21.5(42)	1	—	—	—	—	—	—	—	—	—	—	—	—	6	48
NFL	11	150(111)	2	3	1.5(13)	0	340	6012	17.7(84)	45	—	—	—	—	—	—	—	—	—	—	—	—	270	3234

SNOW, JUSTIN Justin, TE, 6´3˝/240 lbs; Baylor; B12/21/1976 Fort Worth, TX **2000**†Ind 16 (0) **2001** Ind 16 (0) **2002**†Ind 16 (0) **2003**†Ind 16 (0) **2004**†Ind 16 (0) **2005**†Ind 16 (0) **NFL** 96 (0) [6 yrs]

SNOW, PERCY Percy Lee, LB, 6´2˝/248 lbs; Michigan State; 1990: KC, rnd 1; B11/5/1967 Canton, OH **1990**†KC 15 (14, LILB) **1992**†KC 15 (1) **1993** ChiB 10 (0) **NFL** 40 (15) [3 yrs]

SNOWDEN, CAL Calvin Reginald, DE, 6´4˝/253 lbs; Indiana; 1969: SL, rnd 9; B11/29/1946 Washington, DC **1969** SL 7 **1970** SL 14 **1971** Buf 14 (RDE) **1972** SD 8 **1973** SD 4 **NFL** 47 [5 yrs]

SNOWDEN, JIM James John, T-DE, 6´3˝/255 lbs; Notre Dame; 1964: Was, rnd 5/KC, rnd 15; B1/12/1942 Youngstown, OH **1965** Was 14 (LT) **1966** Was 14 (RT) **1967** Was 14 (14, RT) **1968** Was 14 (14, RT) **1969** Was 14 (LT) **1970** Was 14 (14, LT) **1971**†Was 14 (14, LT) **NFL** 98 (56) [7 yrs]

SNYDER, ADAM Adam Richard, T-G, 6´5˝/316 lbs; Oregon; 2005: SF, rnd 3; B1/30/1982 Fullerton, CA **2005** SF 16 (8, LT)

SNYDER, AL Albert Russell, WR, 6´1˝/196 lbs; Holy Cross; 1963: Bos, rnd 23; B6/20/1941 Baltimore, MD **1966** Bal 5

YEAR	TEAM	G (GS, POS)	RUSH	YD	AVG (LG)	TD	REC	YD	AVG (LG)	TD	PASS	COMP	PCT	YD	AVG (LG)	TD	INT	SK	YD	QBR	KPR	OTD	PTS	TAY
1964	Bos-A	2	—	—	—	—	1	12	12.0(12)	0	—	—	—	—	—	—	—	—	—	—	—	—	0	6
NFL	2	7	—	—	—	—	1	12	12.0(12)	0	—	—	—	—	—	—	—	—	—	—	—	—	0	6

SNYDER, BOB Robert A., TB-QB, 6´0˝/200 lbs; Ohio University; B2/6/1913 Fremont, OH, D1/4/2001 Sylvania, OH **[KC]**

YEAR	TEAM	G (GS, POS)	RUSH	YD	AVG (LG)	TD	REC	YD	AVG (LG)	TD	PASS	COMP	PCT	YD	AVG (LG)	TD	INT	SK	YD	QBR	KPR	OTD	PTS	TAY
1937	Cle	10(6, TB)	82	232	2.8	1	3	20	6.7(16)	0	66	25	37.9	378	5.7	2	6	—	—	—	K	—	16	211
1938	Cle	10(6, TB)	44	78	1.8	0	1	16	16.0(16)	0	87	36	41.4	631	7.3	7	9	—	—	—	K	—	10	77
1939	ChiB	8(0)	15	56	3.7	0	—	—	—	—	12	5	41.7	135	11.3	0	2	—	—	—	KP	—	4	44
1940	†ChiB✧	11(0)	7	12	1.7	0	—	—	—	—	22	5	22.7	145	6.6(39)	1	1	—	—	—	KP	—	7	50
1941	†ChiB✧	11(0)	7	-10	-1.4(13)	0	—	—	—	—	28	13	46.4	353	12.6(59)	3	2	—	—	—	KPi	—	26	121
1943	†ChiB	10(7, qb)	6	-20	-3.3(3)	0	—	—	—	—	26	7	26.9	116	4.5(55)	0	4	—	—	—	KPi	—	45	-119
NFL	6	60(19)	161	348	2.2(13)	1	4	36	9.0(16)	0	241	91	37.8	1758	7.3(59)	13	24	—	—	—	KPi	—	108	382

SNYDER, BULL William Howard, G, 6´2˝/230 lbs; Ohio University; B10/29/1911 London, OH, D10/29/1973 Dayton, OH **1934** Pit 5 (0) **1935** Pit 7 (3) **NFL** 12 (3) [2 yrs]

YEAR	TEAM	G(GS, POS)	RUSH	YD	AVG(LG)	TD	REC	YD	AVG(LG)	TD	PASS	COMP	PCT	YD	AVG(LG)	TD	INT	SK	YD	QBR	KPR	OTD	PTS	TAY
SNYDER, JIM James, TB, /162 lbs; none; B1/1909, deceased **1925** Mil 1 (0)																								
SNYDER, LOREN Loren Howard, QB, 6´4˝/207 lbs; Northern Colorado; B11/28/1963																								
1987	Dal	2(0)	2	0	0.0(0)	0	—	—	—	—	9	4	44.4	44	4.9(22)	0	0	—	—	—	—	—	0	22
SNYDER, LUM Kenneth David, T, 6´5˝/228 lbs; Georgia Tech; 1952: Phi, rnd 3; B8/12/1930 Cleveland, TN, D10/11/1985 Winter Haven, FL **1952** Phi☆11 (RT) **1953** Phi★12 (RT) **1954** Phi★12 (RT) **1955** Phi☆12 (RT) **1958** Phi 12 (RT) **NFL** 59 [5 yrs]																								
SNYDER, PAT Patrick A., LB, 6´1˝/225 lbs; Purdue; B11/23/1963 **1987** Ind 2 (0) **1991** Ind 1 (0) **NFL** 3 (0) [2 yrs]																								
SNYDER, SNITZ Gerald Theodore, B, 5´8˝/190 lbs; Maryland; B8/6/1905 Windber, PA, D6/1983 Brooklyn Heights, OH **1929** NYG 12 (2), 18 **1930** SI 11 (7, FB) **NFL** 23 (9) [2 yrs]																								
SNYDER, TODD James Todd, WR, 6´1˝/187 lbs; Ohio University; 1970: Atl, rnd 3; B10/22/1948 Athens, OH																								
1970	Atl	12(WR)	—	—	—	—	23	311	13.5(43)	2	—	—	—	—	—	—	—	—	—	—	—	—	12	166
1971	Atl	4	—	—	—	—	—	—	—	—	—	—	—	—	—	—	—	—	—	—	—	—	—	—
1972	Atl	14	—	—	—	—	1	19	19.0(19)	0	—	—	—	—	—	—	—	—	—	—	—	—	0	10
NFL	3	30	—	—	—	—	24	330	13.8(43)	2	—	—	—	—	—	—	—	—	—	—	—	—	12	175
SOAR, HANK Albert Henry, B, 6´2˝/205 lbs; Providence; B8/17/1914 Alton, RI, D12/24/2001 Pawtucket, RI **[K]**																								
1937	NYG	9(3, fb)	120	442	3.7	0	6	77	12.8	1	21	5	23.8	83	4.0(38)	1	2	—	—	—	K	1	17	462
1938	†NYG✧	11(6, fb)	122	401	3.3	2	13	164	12.6	0	7	1	14.3	0	0.0	0	3	—	—	—	K	—	13	383
1939	†NYG	11(6, fb)	66	158	2.4	2	12	134	11.2	0	—	—	—	—	—	—	—	—	—	—	K	1	20	255
1940	NYG	11(3)	80	246	3.1	1	4	36	9.0(12)	1	—	—	—	—	—	—	—	—	—	—	Ki	—	12	296
1941	†NYG	11(0)	29	90	3.1(19)	0	—	—	—	—	5	3	60.0	75	15.0(38)	1	0	—	—	—	Kpi	—	3	188
1942	NYG	11(1)	49	187	3.8(49)	1	—	—	—	—	10	3	30.0	34	3.4(20)	0	1	—	—	—	KPkpi	—	8	263
1943	†NYG	4(4)	2	8	4.0(5)	0	—	—	—	—	—	—	—	—	—	—	—	—	—	—	pi	—	0	41
1944	NYG	3(1)	9	10	1.1(10)	0	—	—	—	—	10	4	40.0	113	11.3(35)	2	1	—	—	—	pi	—	0	72
1946	†NYG	11(1)	1	3	3.0(3)	0	—	—	—	—	—	—	—	—	—	—	—	—	—	—	pi	—	0	86
NFL	9	82(25)	478	1545	3.2(49)	6	35	411	11.7(12)	2	53	16	30.2	305	5.8(38)	4	7	—	—	—	KPkpi	2	73	2045
SOBIESKI, BEN Ben, T, 6´5˝/315 lbs; Iowa; 2003: Buf, rnd 5; B5/3/1979 Mahtomedi, MN **2003** Buf 1 (0)																								
SOBOCINSKI, PHIL Phillip Lee, C, 6´3˝/235 lbs; Wisconsin; B12/6/1940 South Milwaukee, WI **1968** Atl 7 (C)																								
SOBOLESKI, JOE Joseph Robert, G-T-DT, 6´0˝/213 lbs; Michigan; 1949: Cle-A, rnd 29/NYG, rnd 9; B8/22/1926 **1949** ChiH-A 5 (0) **1949** Was 7 (1) **1950** Det 12 (RG) **1951** NYY 2 **1952** DalT 1 **NFL** 22 (1) [3 yrs]																								
SOCHIA, BRIAN Brian John, NT-DE, 6´3˝/270 lbs; Northwestern Oklahoma State; B7/2/1961 Massena, NY **1983** Hou 12 (10, NT) **1984** Hou 16 (3) **1985** Hou 16 (0) **1986** Mia 6 (0) **1987** Mia 12 (12, NT) **1988** Mia✧16 (16, NT) **1989** Mia 16 (16, NT) **1990**†Mia 5 (2) **1991** Mia 3 (2) **1991**†Den 10 (3) **1992** Den 16 (13, LDE) **NFL** 128 (77) [10 yrs]																								
SODASKI, JOHN John Joseph, LB-DB, 6´2˝/222 lbs; Villanova; 1969: Pit, rnd 9; B1/14/1948 Phoenixville, PA **1970** Pit 3 **1972** Phi 4 **1973** Phi 14 (9, RLB) **NFL** 21 (9) [3 yrs]																								
SOFISH, ALEC Alexander N., G, 6´2˝/200 lbs; Grove City; B1908, D3/1959 **1931** Pro 11 (8, RG)																								
SOHN, BENNY Benjamin Foster, B, 5´8˝/170 lbs; Washington; B11/18/1911, D11/1969																								
1934	Cin	2(0)	1	7	7.0(7)	0	—	—	—	—	—	—	—	—	—	—	—	—	—	—	—	—	0	7
SOHN, BEN Benjamin Forester, G-T, 6´3˝/230 lbs; USC; 1941: NYG, rnd 9; B9/16/1918 San Diego, CA, D7/15/1999 San Diego, CA **1941**†NYG 11 (3)																								
SOHN, KURT Kurt Frederick, WR, 5´11˝/180 lbs; North Carolina State; Fordham; B6/26/1957 Ithaca, NY																								
1981	†NYJ	16(0)	—	—	—	—	—	—	—	—	—	—	—	—	—	—	—	—	—	—	kp	—	0	139
1982	†NYJ	9(0)	—	—	—	—	—	—	—	—	—	—	—	—	—	—	—	—	—	—	k	—	0	74
1984	NYJ	5(0)	—	—	—	—	2	28	14.0(16)	0	—	—	—	—	—	—	—	—	—	—	—	—	0	14
1985	†NYJ	15(6, wr)	1	12	12.0(12)	0	39	534	13.7(39)	4	—	—	—	—	—	—	—	—	—	—	kp	—	24	330
1986	†NYJ	15(1)	2	-11	-5.5(-3)	0	8	129	16.1(24)	2	—	—	—	—	—	—	—	—	—	—	kp	—	12	197
1987	NYJ	12(4)	—	—	—	—	23	261	11.3(31)	2	—	—	—	—	—	—	—	—	—	—	kp	—	12	144
1988	NYJ	15(0)	—	—	—	—	7	66	9.4(17)	2	—	—	—	—	—	—	—	—	—	—	kp	—	12	61
NFL	7	87(11)	3	1	0.3(12)	0	79	1018	12.9(39)	10	—	—	—	—	—	—	—	—	—	—	kp	—	60	958
SOKOLOSKY, JOHN John Joseph, C, 6´2˝/240 lbs; Wayne State (MI); B4/2/1956 Detroit, MI **1978** Det 11																								
SOLEAU, ROBERT Robert Heyde, LB, 6´2˝/230 lbs; William & Mary; 1964: Pit, rnd 11; B4/2/1941 Amherst, MA **1964** Pit 14																								
SOLIDAY, JAKE Jake, WR, 6´1˝/195 lbs; Northern Iowa; B11/16/1978 Mansfield, OH																								
2002	Arz	4(0)	—	—	—	—	4	39	9.8(16)	0	—	—	—	—	—	—	—	—	—	—	—	—	0	20
SOLOMON, ARIEL Ariel Mace, C, 6´5˝/290 lbs; Colorado; 1991: Pit, rnd 10; B7/16/1968 Brooklyn, NY **1991** Pit 5 (2) **1992** Pit 4 (0) **1993**†Pit 16 (0) **1994**†Pit 16 (0) **1995** Pit 4 (0) **1996**†Min 16 (0) **NFL** 61 (2) [6 yrs]																								
SOLOMON, FREDDIE Fred, WR-QB-RB, 5´11˝/185 lbs; Tampa; 1975: Mia, rnd 2; B1/11/1953 Sumter, SC **[R]**																								
1975	Mia	14(5, wr)	4	87	21.8(35)	0	22	339	15.4(58)	2	—	—	—	—	—	—	—	—	—	—	kp	1	18	560
1976	Mia	10(8, WR)	4	60	15.0(59)	1	27	453	16.8(53)	2	1	0	0.0	0	0.0	0	0	—	—	—	kp	1	24	454
1977	Mia	13(6, WR)	6	43	7.2(14)	0	12	181	15.1(54)	1	—	—	—	—	—	—	—	—	—	—	kp	1	12	397
1978	SF	16(15, WR)	14	70	5.0(17)	1	31	458	14.8(58)	2	10	5	50.0	85	8.5(30)	0	1	3	34	—	p	—	18	312
1979	SF	15(12, WR)	6	85	14.2(56)	1	57	807	14.2(44)	7	1	1	100.0	12	12.0(12)	0	0	—	—	—	p	—	48	567
1980	SF☆	16(13, WR)	8	56	7.0(11)	0	48	658	13.7(**93**)	8	1	0	0.0	0	0.0	0	0	—	—	—	kp	2	60	609
1981	†SF	15(15, WR)	9	43	4.8(16)	0	59	969	16.4(60)	8	1	1	100.0	25	25.0(25)	0	0	—	—	—	p	—	48	608
1982	SF	9(7, WR)	1	-4	-4.0(-4)	0	19	323	17.0(46)	3	—	—	—	—	—	—	—	—	—	—	p	—	18	230
1983	†SF	13(11, WR)	1	3	3.0(3)	0	31	662	21.4(77)	4	—	—	—	—	—	—	—	—	—	—	p	—	24	363
1984	†SF	14(13, WR)	6	72	12.0(47)	1	40	737	18.4(64)	10	—	—	—	—	—	—	—	—	—	—	—	—	66	501
1985	†SF	16(12, WR)	2	4	2.0(6)	0	25	259	10.4(39)	1	1	0	0.0	0	0.0	0	0	—	—	—	—	—	6	139
NFL	11	151(117)	61	519	8.5(59)	4	371	5846	15.8(93)	48	15	7	46.7	122	8.1(30)	0	1	3	34	—	kp	5	342	4736
SOLOMON, FREDDIE Freddie Lee, WR, 5´10˝/180 lbs; South Carolina State; B8/15/1972 Gainesville, FL																								
1996	Phi	12(0)	—	—	—	—	8	125	15.6(23)	0	—	—	—	—	—	—	—	—	—	—	p	—	0	65
1997	Phi	15(5, wr)	—	—	—	—	29	455	15.7(56)	3	—	—	—	—	—	—	—	—	—	—	p	—	20	248
1998	Phi	16(1)	—	—	—	—	21	193	9.2(20)	1	—	—	—	—	—	—	—	—	—	—	p	—	6	147
NFL	3	43(6)	—	—	—	—	58	773	13.3(56)	4	—	—	—	—	—	—	—	—	—	—	p	—	26	459
SOLOMON, JESSE Jesse William, LB, 6´0˝/240 lbs; Florida State; 1986: Min, rnd 12; B11/4/1963 Madison, FL **1986** Min 13 (4) **1987**†Min 12 (12, LLB) **1988** Min 16 (16, LLB) **1989** Min 4 (1) **1989** Dal 11 (1) **1990** Dal 9 (0) **1991** TB 13 (12, MLB) **1993** Atl 16 (16, LLB) **1994**†Mia 6 (0)																								
1992	Atl	16(14, LILB)	2	12	6.0(12)	0	—	—	—	—	—	—	—	—	—	—	—	—	—	—	iS	—	0	20
NFL	9	116(76)	2	12	6.0(12)	0	—	—	—	—	—	—	—	—	—	—	—	—	—	—	iS	1	6	143
SOLOMON, ROLAND Roland Howard, DB, 6´0˝/193 lbs; Utah; B2/6/1956 Fort Worth, TX **1980** Dal 10 (0) **1980**†Buf 1 (0) **1981** Den 4 (0) **NFL** 15 (0) [2 yrs]																								
SOLT, RON Ronald Matthew, G, 6´3˝/279 lbs; Maryland; 1984: Ind, rnd 1; B5/19/1962 Bainbridge, MD **1984** Ind 16 (16, RG) **1985** Ind 15 (15, RG) **1986** Ind 16 (16, RG) **1987** Ind★12 (12, RG) **1988** Ind 1 (0) **1988** Phi 1 (0) **1989**†Phi 13 (12, RG) **1990**†Phi 15 (15, RG) **1991** Phi 15 (15, RG) **1992** Ind 12 (12, RG) **NFL** 116 (113) [9 yrs]																								
SOLTAU, GORDIE Gordon Leroy, E, 6´2˝/195 lbs; Minnesota; 1950: GB, rnd 3; B1/25/1925 Duluth, MN **[K]**																								
1950	SF	12(le)	—	—	—	—	14	170	12.1(28)	1	—	—	—	—	—	—	—	—	—	—	K	—	44	90
1951	SF★	12(LE)	1	-4	-4.0(-4)	0	59	826	14.0(48)	7	—	—	—	—	—	—	—	—	—	—	K	—	90	444
1952	SF★	12(LE)	—	—	—	—	55	774	14.1(49)	7	—	—	—	—	—	—	—	—	—	—	K	—	**94**	422
1953	SF★	12(LE)	—	—	—	—	43	620	14.4(54)	6	—	—	—	—	—	—	—	—	—	—	K	—	**114**	340
1954	SF	11(LE)	—	—	—	—	22	316	14.4(42)	2	—	—	—	—	—	—	—	—	—	—	K	—	76	168
1955	SF	12(LE)	—	—	—	—	26	358	13.8(36)	1	—	—	—	—	—	—	—	—	—	—	K	—	42	184
1956	SF	12(LE)	—	—	—	—	18	299	16.6(33)	1	—	—	—	—	—	—	—	—	—	—	K	—	71	155
1957	†SF	12	—	—	—	—	5	47	9.4(18)	0	—	—	—	—	—	—	—	—	—	—	K	—	60	24

YEAR	TEAM	G(GS, POS)	RUSH	YD	AVG(LG)	TD	REC	YD	AVG(LG)	TD	PASS	COMP	PCT	YD	AVG(LG)	TD	INT	SK	YD	QBR	KPR	OTD	PTS	TAY
1958	SF	12	—	—	—	—	7	77	11.0(22)	0	—	—	—	—	—	—	—	—	—	—	K	—	53	39
NFL	9	107	1	-4	-4.0(-4)	0	249	3487	14.0(54)	25	—	—	—	—	—	—	—	—	—	—	K	—	644	1865

SOLTIS, BOB Robert Lawrence, DB, 6´2˝/205 lbs; Minnesota; 1959: NYG, rnd 16; B4/1/1936 **1960** Bos-A 14 **1961** Bos-A 3 **NFL** 17 [2 yrs]

SOLWOLD, MIKE Michael Stuart, C, 6´6˝/244 lbs; Wisconsin; B9/30/1977 Menomonee Falls, WI **2001** Dal 8 (0) **2002** TB 4 (0) **2004** Bal 1 (0) **NFL** 13 (0) [3 yrs]

SOMERS, GEORGE George Anthony, T, 6´2˝/253 lbs; La Salle; 1939: Phi, rnd 8; B10/5/1915 Fountain Springs, PA **[K]** **1939** Phi 9 (3) **1940** Phi 10 (7, RT) **1941** Pit 10 (5, lt) **1942** Pit 11 (0) **NFL** 40 (15) [4 yrs]

SOMMER, DON Donald Martin, T, 6´4˝/290 lbs; Texas-El Paso; 1986: Hou, rnd 10; B2/1/1964 Corsicana, TX **1987** Buf 3 (3)

SOMMER, MIKE Michael Sandor, HB-DB, 5´11˝/190 lbs; George Washington; 1958: Was, rnd 2; B10/9/1934 Washington, DC

YEAR	TEAM	G(GS, POS)	RUSH	YD	AVG(LG)	TD	REC	YD	AVG(LG)	TD	PASS	COMP	PCT	YD	AVG(LG)	TD	INT	SK	YD	QBR	KPR	OTD	PTS	TAY
1958	Was	2	—	—	—	—	—	—	—	—	—	—	—	—	—	—	—	—	—	—	kp	—	0	5
1959	Was	1	1	4	4.0(4)	0	—	—	—	—	—	—	—	—	—	—	—	—	—	—	k	—	0	8
1959	†Bal	8(LH)	61	227	3.7(53)	2	7	111	15.9(56)	0	—	—	—	—	—	—	—	—	—	—	k	—	12	349
1960	Bal	1	—	—	—	—	—	—	—	—	—	—	—	—	—	—	—	—	—	—	k	—	0	-5
1961	Bal	4	6	10	1.7(9)	0	1	31	31.0(31)	0	—	—	—	—	—	—	—	—	—	—	—	—	0	26
1961	Was	2	5	-9	-1.8(1)	0	—	—	—	—	—	—	—	—	—	—	—	—	—	—	kp	—	0	45
1963	Oak-A	4	5	21	4.2(13)	0	1	24	24.0(24)	0	—	—	—	—	—	—	—	—	—	—	kp	—	0	84
NFL	5	22	78	253	3.2(53)	2	9	166	18.4(56)	0	—	—	—	—	—	—	—	—	—	—	kp	—	12	511

SOMMERS, JACK Jack William, C, 6´3˝/222 lbs; UCLA; 1941: ChiC, rnd 11; B2/9/1919, **[K]** **1947** Was 8 (0)

SONGIN, BUTCH Edward Frank, QB, 6´2˝/190 lbs; Boston College; 1950: Cle, rnd 19/1949: Buf-A, rnd 13; B5/11/1924 Walpole, MA, D5/26/1976 Wrentham, MA

YEAR	TEAM	G(GS, POS)	RUSH	YD	AVG(LG)	TD	REC	YD	AVG(LG)	TD	PASS	COMP	PCT	YD	AVG(LG)	TD	INT	SK	YD	QBR	KPR	OTD	PTS	TAY
1960	Bos-A	14(QB)	11	40	3.6(20)	2	—	—	—	—	392	187	47.7	2476	6.3(78)	22	15	—	—	70.9	—	—	12	808
1961	Bos-A	14(qb)	8	39	4.9(11)	0	—	—	—	—	212	98	46.2	1429	6.7(58)	14	9	—	—	73.0	—	—	0	464
1962	NYT-A	7	4	11	2.8(10)	0	—	—	—	—	90	42	46.7	442	4.9(64)	2	7	—	—	—	—	—	0	-38
NFL	3	35	23	90	3.9(20)	2	—	—	—	—	694	327	47.1	4347	6.3(78)	38	31	—	—	67.1	—	—	12	1234

SONGY, TREG Treg Joseph, DB, 6´2˝/200 lbs; Tulane; 1985: NO, rnd 12; B6/15/1962 New Orleans, LA **1987** NYJ 2 (0)

SONNENBERG, GUS Gustave Adolph, T-FB-TB, 5´6˝/196 lbs; Dartmouth; Detroit Mercy; B3/6/1898 Ewen, MI, D9/13/1944 Bethesda, MD **[K]** **1923** Buf 1 (1) **1923** Col☆10 (10, LT), 6 **1925** Det☆12 (12, LT), 27 **1926** Det☆12 (12, LT), 34 **1927** Pro☆14 (11, LT), 16 **1928** Pro☆11 (10, LT), 10 **1930** Pro 1 (0) **NFL** 61 (56), 93 [6 yrs]

SOPOAGA, ISAAC Isaac, DT, 6´2˝/321 lbs; Hawaii; 2004: SF, rnd 4; B9/4/1981 Pago Pago, American Samoa **2005** SF 16 (1)

SORCE, ROSS Ross Paul, T, 6´4˝/255 lbs; Georgetown (DC); B1920 Pittsburgh, PA, D12/28/1959 Bethel, PA **1945** Pit 1 (0)

SORENSEN, NICK Nicholas Carl, DB, 6´3˝/210 lbs; Virginia Tech; B7/31/1978 Winter Haven, FL **2001**†SL 7 (0) **2002** SL 16 (0) **2003** Jax 14 (0) **2004** Jax 16 (0) **2005** Jax 10 (0) **NFL** 63 (0) [5 yrs]

SORENSON, GLEN Glen G., G, 6´0˝/217 lbs; Utah State; B2/29/1920 Salt Lake City, UT, D2/26/1972 Salt Lake City, UT **[K]** **1943** GB 7 (2) **1944**†GB 10 (6, LG) **1945** GB 10 (5, lg) **NFL** 27 (13) [3 yrs]

SOREY, JIM James, DT, 6´4˝/285 lbs; Texas Southern; 1960: Buf, rnd 2/Chi, rnd 14; B9/5/1936 Marianna, FL **1960** Buf-A 14 (RDT) **1961** Buf-A 14 (RDT) **1962** Buf-A 14 **NFL** 42 [3 yrs]

SOREY, REVIE Revie Cee, G, 6´2˝/260 lbs; Illinois; 1975: Chi, rnd 5; B9/10/1953 Brooklyn, NY **1975** ChiB 14 **1976** ChiB 14 (9, RG) **1977**†ChiB☆14 (14, RG) **1978** ChiB☆16 (16, RG) **1979**†ChiB☆16 (16, RG) **1980** ChiB 16 (16, RG) **1981** ChiB 16 (4) **1983** ChiB 3 (2) **NFL** 109 (77) [8 yrs]

SORGI, JIM Jim, QB, 6´3˝/194 lbs; Wisconsin; 2004: Ind, rnd 6; B12/3/1980 Fraser, MI

YEAR	TEAM	G(GS, POS)	RUSH	YD	AVG(LG)	TD	REC	YD	AVG(LG)	TD	PASS	COMP	PCT	YD	AVG(LG)	TD	INT	SK	YD	QBR	KPR	OTD	PTS	TAY
2004	Ind	4(0)	8	-5	-0.6(2)	0	—	—	—	—	29	17	58.6	175	6.0(71)	2	0	1	8	—	—	—	0	93
2005	Ind	5(0)	12	1	0.1(6)	0	—	—	—	—	61	42	68.9	444	7.3(45)	3	1	3	14	—	—	—	0	198
NFL	2	9(0)	20	-4	-0.2(6)	0	—	—	—	—	90	59	65.6	619	6.9(71)	5	1	4	22	—	—	—	0	291

SORRELL, HENRY Henry Thomas, LB, 6´2˝/225 lbs; Tennessee-Chattanooga; 1966: Den, rnd R8; B6/10/1943 Talladega, AL **1967** Den-A 10

SORTET, BILL Wilbur John, E, 6´1˝/187 lbs; West Virginia; B6/25/1912 Vincennes, IN, D1/22/1998 Charleston, WV

YEAR	TEAM	G(GS, POS)	RUSH	YD	AVG(LG)	TD	REC	YD	AVG(LG)	TD	PASS	COMP	PCT	YD	AVG(LG)	TD	INT	SK	YD	QBR	KPR	OTD	PTS	TAY
1933	Pit	9(1)	—	—	—	—	1	28	28.0(28)	0	—	—	—	—	—	—	—	—	—	—	—	—	0	14
1934	Pit	12(1)	—	—	—	—	7	93	13.3(21)	1	—	—	—	—	—	—	—	—	—	—	—	—	6	52
1935	Pit	12(8, RE)	—	—	—	—	7	178	25.4	0	—	—	—	—	—	—	—	—	—	—	—	—	0	89
1936	Pit	12(5, re)	1	47	47.0(47)	0	14	197	14.1(55)	1	—	—	—	—	—	—	—	—	—	—	—	—	6	151
1937	Pit	9(6, RE)	—	—	—	—	9	121	13.4(26)	1	—	—	—	—	—	—	—	—	—	—	—	—	6	66
1938	Pit	8(3)	1	-5	-5.0(-5)	0	11	166	15.1(50)	4	—	—	—	—	—	—	—	—	—	—	—	—	24	98
1939	Pit	11(8, RE)	—	—	—	—	16	196	12.3	1	—	—	—	—	—	—	—	—	—	—	—	—	6	103
1940	Pit	11(8, RE)	—	—	—	—	7	112	16.0	0	—	—	—	—	—	—	—	—	—	—	—	—	0	56
NFL	8	84(40)	2	42	21.0(47)	0	72	1091	15.2(55)	8	—	—	—	—	—	—	—	—	—	—	—	—	48	628

SORTUN, RICK Henrik Martin, G, 6´2˝/235 lbs; Washington; 1964: SL, rnd 12; B9/26/1942 Tacoma, WA **1964** SL 14 **1965** SL 13 **1967** SL 13 **1968** SL 14 **1969** SL 14

YEAR	TEAM	G(GS, POS)	RUSH	YD	AVG(LG)	TD	REC	YD	AVG(LG)	TD	PASS	COMP	PCT	YD	AVG(LG)	TD	INT	SK	YD	QBR	KPR	OTD	PTS	TAY
1966	SL	14(rg/lg)	—	—	—	—	1	7	7.0(7)	0	—	—	—	—	—	—	—	—	—	—	—	—	0	4
NFL	6	82	—	—	—	—	1	7	7.0(7)	0	—	—	—	—	—	—	—	—	—	—	k	—	0	-12

SOSSAMON, LOU Louis Cody, C-LB, 6´1˝/207 lbs; South Carolina; 1943: Pit, rnd 6; B6/2/1921 Gaffney, SC **1946** NYY-A 14 (1) **1947**†NYY-A☆14 (14, C) **1948** NYY-A 14 (11, C) **AAFC** 42 (26) [3 yrs]

SOUCHAK, FRANK Frank S., E, 6´0˝/205 lbs; Pittsburgh; 1938: NYG, rnd 6; B1916 Berwick, PA

YEAR	TEAM	G(GS, POS)	RUSH	YD	AVG(LG)	TD	REC	YD	AVG(LG)	TD	PASS	COMP	PCT	YD	AVG(LG)	TD	INT	SK	YD	QBR	KPR	OTD	PTS	TAY
1939	Pit	4(0)	—	—	—	—	1	12	12.0(12)	0	—	—	—	—	—	—	—	—	—	—	—	—	0	6

SOUDERS, CECIL Cecil B., E-T, 6´1˝/210 lbs; Ohio State; 1945: Was, rnd 25; B1/3/1921 Bucyrus, OH

YEAR	TEAM	G(GS, POS)	RUSH	YD	AVG(LG)	TD	REC	YD	AVG(LG)	TD	PASS	COMP	PCT	YD	AVG(LG)	TD	INT	SK	YD	QBR	KPR	OTD	PTS	TAY
1947	Det	11(4)	—	—	—	—	15	184	12.3(34)	1	—	—	—	—	—	—	—	—	—	—	—	—	6	97
1948	Det	12(6, RE)	—	—	—	—	2	19	9.5(11)	0	—	—	—	—	—	—	—	—	—	—	—	—	0	10
1949	Det	12(5, lt)	—	—	—	—	—	—	—	—	—	—	—	—	—	—	—	—	—	—	k	—	0	-8
NFL	3	35(15)	—	—	—	—	17	203	11.9(34)	1	—	—	—	—	—	—	—	—	—	—	k	—	6	99

SOUTH, RONNIE LEE Ronnie Lee, QB-P, 6´1˝/195 lbs; Arkansas; 1968: NO, rnd 5; B5/8/1945 Wynne, AR

YEAR	TEAM	G(GS, POS)	RUSH	YD	AVG(LG)	TD	REC	YD	AVG(LG)	TD	PASS	COMP	PCT	YD	AVG(LG)	TD	INT	SK	YD	QBR	KPR	OTD	PTS	TAY
1968	NO	4	4	5	1.3(2)	0	—	—	—	—	38	14	36.8	129	3.4(19)	1	3	2	14	—	P	—	0	-46

SOUTHARD, TOM Tommy, WR, 6´0˝/185 lbs; Furman; B6/29/1955 **1978** SL 2

SOWARD, R. JAY Rodney Jay, WR, 5´11˝/178 lbs; USC; 2000: Jax, rnd 1; B1/16/1978 Pomona, CA

YEAR	TEAM	G(GS, POS)	RUSH	YD	AVG(LG)	TD	REC	YD	AVG(LG)	TD	PASS	COMP	PCT	YD	AVG(LG)	TD	INT	SK	YD	QBR	KPR	OTD	PTS	TAY
2000	Jax	13(2)	3	28	9.3(20)	0	14	154	11.0(45)	1	—	—	—	—	—	—	—	—	—	—	kp	—	6	181

SOWELL, JERALD Jerald Monye, FB, 6´0˝/237 lbs; Tulane; 1997: GB, rnd 7; B1/21/1974 Elyria, OH

YEAR	TEAM	G(GS, POS)	RUSH	YD	AVG(LG)	TD	REC	YD	AVG(LG)	TD	PASS	COMP	PCT	YD	AVG(LG)	TD	INT	SK	YD	QBR	KPR	OTD	PTS	TAY
1997	NYJ	9(0)	7	35	5.0(10)	0	1	8	8.0(8)	0	—	—	—	—	—	—	—	—	—	—	—	—	0	39
1998	†NYJ	16(2)	40	164	4.1(33)	0	10	59	5.9(13)	0	—	—	—	—	—	—	—	—	—	—	—	—	0	194
1999	NYJ	16(0)	3	5	1.7(3)	0	—	—	—	—	1	0	0.0	0	0.0	0	0	—	—	—	—	—	0	5
2000	NYJ	16(0)	2	0	0.0(1)	0	6	84	14.0(62)	0	—	—	—	—	—	—	—	—	—	—	k	—	0	36
2001	†NYJ	16(0)	4	9	2.3(4)	0	1	19	19.0(19)	0	—	—	—	—	—	—	—	—	—	—	k	—	0	10
2002	†NYJ	16(0)	1	0	0.0(0)	0	9	85	9.4(31)	1	—	—	—	—	—	—	—	—	—	—	k	—	6	53
2003	NYJ	16(16, FB)	1	2	2.0(2)	0	47	436	9.3(44)	1	—	—	—	—	—	—	—	—	—	—	—	—	6	225
2004	†NYJ	16(16, FB)	2	28	14.0(19)	0	45	342	7.6(34)	1	—	—	—	—	—	—	—	—	—	—	—	—	6	204
2005	NYJ	16(14, FB)	1	1	1.0(1)	1	28	155	5.5(28)	2	—	—	—	—	—	—	—	—	—	—	—	—	18	99
NFL	9	137(48)	61	244	4.0(33)	1	147	1188	8.1(62)	5	1	0	0.0	0	0.0	0	0	—	—	—	k	—	36	863

SOWELL, ROBERT Robert Donnell, DB, 5´11˝/175 lbs; Howard; B6/23/1961 Columbus, OH **1983**†Mia 16 (0) **1984**†Mia 16 (0) **1985** Mia 10 (1) **1987** Mia 3 (3) **NFL** 45 (4) [4 yrs]

SOWELLS, RICH Richard Allen, DB, 6´0˝/179 lbs; Alcorn State; 1971: NYJ, rnd 12; B10/27/1948 Prairie View, TX **1971** NYJ 8 (lcb) **1972** NYJ 11 **1973** NYJ 12 **1974** NYJ 14 (LCB) **1975** NYJ 14 (13, LCB) **1976** NYJ 10 **1977** Hou 9 **NFL** 78 (13) [7 yrs]

SPACH, STEPHEN Stephen, TE, 6´4˝/250 lbs; Fresno State; B7/18/1982 Clovis, CA

YEAR	TEAM	G(GS, POS)	RUSH	YD	AVG(LG)	TD	REC	YD	AVG(LG)	TD	PASS	COMP	PCT	YD	AVG(LG)	TD	INT	SK	YD	QBR	KPR	OTD	PTS	TAY
2005	Phi	13(1)	—	—	—	—	7	42	6.0(8)	0	—	—	—	—	—	—	—	—	—	—	—	—	0	21

YEAR	TEAM	G(GS, POS)	RUSH	YD	AVG(LG)	TD	REC	YD	AVG(LG)	TD	PASS COMP	PCT	YD	AVG(LG)	TD	INT	SK	YD	QBR	KPR	OTD	PTS	TAY

SPADACCINI, VIC Victor Michael, B, 6´0˝/222 lbs; Minnesota; 1938: Cle, rnd 12; B3/2/1916 Keewatin, MN, D4/28/1981 West St. Paul, MN **[K]**

1938	Cle	10(3)	9	46	5.1	0	8	101	12.6	0	—	—	—	—	—	—	—	—	—	—	—	0	97
1939	Cle	11(11, BB)	—	—	—	—	32	292	9.1	1	—	—	—	—	—	—	—	—	—	K	—	18	151
1940	Cle◇	9(3)	—	—	—	—	22	276	12.5	2	1	0	0.0	0	0.0	0	0	—	—	Ki	1	23	226
NFL	3	30(17)	9	46	5.1	0	62	669	10.8	3	1	0	0.0	0	0.0	0	0	—	—	Ki	1	41	474

SPAGNA, BUTCH Joseph, G-T, 6´0˝/215 lbs; Brown; Lehigh; B5/15/1897 New York, NY, D12/11/1948 Philadelphia, PA   **1920** Cle 4 (3)   **1920** Buf 3 (3, LT)   **1921** Buf 4 (2) **1924** Fra 14 (14, LG), 6   **1925** Fra 7 (6, RG)   **NFL** 32 (28) [4 yrs]

SPAGNOLA, JOHN John Stephen, TE, 6´4˝/240 lbs; Yale; 1979: NE, rnd 9; B8/1/1957 Bethlehem, PA

1979	Phi	16(3)	—	—	—	—	2	24	12.0(14)	0	—	—	—	—	—	—	—	—	—	—	—	0	12
1980	†Phi	16(5, te)	—	—	—	—	18	193	10.7(20)	3	—	—	—	—	—	—	—	—	—	k	—	18	97
1981	†Phi	11(3)	—	—	—	—	6	83	13.8(28)	0	—	—	—	—	—	—	—	—	—	—	—	0	42
1982	Phi	9(9, TE)	—	—	—	—	26	313	12.0(57)	2	—	—	—	—	—	—	—	—	—	—	—	12	167
1984	Phi	16(16, TE)	—	—	—	—	65	701	10.8(34)	1	—	—	—	—	—	—	—	—	—	—	—	6	356
1985	Phi	16(16, TE)	—	—	—	—	64	772	12.1(35)	5	—	—	—	—	—	—	—	—	—	—	—	30	411
1986	Phi	15(12, TE)	—	—	—	—	39	397	10.2(38)	1	—	—	—	—	—	—	—	—	—	—	—	6	204
1987	Phi	12(12, TE)	—	—	—	—	36	350	9.7(22)	2	—	—	—	—	—	—	—	—	—	—	—	12	185
1988	†Sea	16(4)	—	—	—	—	5	40	8.0(16)	1	—	—	—	—	—	—	—	—	—	—	—	6	25
1989	GB	6(0)	—	—	—	—	2	13	6.5(14)	0	—	—	—	—	—	—	—	—	—	—	—	0	7
NFL	10	133(80)	—	—	—	—	263	2886	11.0(57)	15	—	—	—	—	—	—	—	—	—	k	—	90	1503

SPAIN, DICK Richard Raymond, C-T, 5´8˝/180 lbs; none; B5/20/1893 Evansville, IN, D10/3/1948 Los Angeles County, CA   **1921** Evv 1 (0)   **1922** Evv 3 (3, C)   **NFL** 4 (3) [2 yrs]

SPANGLER, GENE Eugene Douglas, WB-DB, 5´10˝/196 lbs; Tulsa; B12/17/1922 Huntington, AR

| 1946 | Det | 6(0) | 1 | 1 | 1.0(1) | 0 | — | — | — | — | — | — | — | — | — | — | — | — | — | k | — | 0 | 4 |

SPANI, GARY Gary Leland, LB, 6´2˝/229 lbs; Kansas State; 1978: KC, rnd 3; B1/9/1956 Satanta, KS   **1978** KC 14 (13, RILB)   **1979** KC 16 (16, RILB)   **1980** KC 16 (16, RILB) **1981** KC 16 (16, RILB)   **1982** KC 8 (8, RILB)   **1983** KC 10 (9, RILB)   **1984** KC 14 (14, RILB)   **1985** KC 14 (13, RILB)   **1986**†KC 16 (3)   **NFL** 124 (108) [9 yrs]

SPANIEL, FRANK Francis James, HB, 5´10˝/185 lbs; Notre Dame; 1950: Was, rnd 5; B5/21/1928 Vandergrift, PA, D10/27/1994 North Fort Myers, FL

1950	Was	6	1	1	1.0(1)	0	—	—	—	—	—	—	—	—	—	—	—	—	—	kp	—	0	42
1950	Bal	6(1)	14	21	1.5(15)	1	5	84	16.8(35)	0	—	—	—	—	—	—	—	—	—	ki	1	12	173
NFL	1	12(1)	15	22	1.5(15)	1	5	84	16.8(35)	0	—	—	—	—	—	—	—	—	—	kpi	1	12	215

SPANN, GARY Gary Lynn, LB, 6´1˝/218 lbs; TCU; 1986: GB, rnd 10; B2/3/1963 Dallas, TX   **1987** KC 2 (1)

SPARENBERG, DAVE David, G, 6´3˝/257 lbs; Western Ontario; B5/28/1959 Chatham, Canada   **1987** Cle 1 (0)

SPARKMAN, AL Temple Alan, T, 6´6˝/253 lbs; Texas A&M; B2/17/1926 Baltimore, MD   **1948** LARm 12 (2)   **1949**†LARm 4 (0)   **NFL** 16 (2) [2 yrs]

SPARKS, DAVE David Walter, G-T, 6´1˝/229 lbs; South Carolina; 1951: SF, rnd 15; B4/28/1928 Arlington, VA, D12/5/1954 Arlington, VA   **1951** SF 8   **1954** Was 10   **NFL** 18 [2 yrs]

SPARKS, PHILLIPPI Phillipi Dwaine, DB, 5´11˝/195 lbs; Arizona State; 1992: NYG, rnd 2; B4/15/1969 Oklahoma City, OK **[I]**   **1992** NYG 16 (2)   **1993**†NYG 5 (3) **1994** NYG 11 (11, LCB)   **1995** NYG 16 (16, LCB)   **1996** NYG 14 (14, LCB)   **1997**†NYG 13 (13, LCB)   **1998** NYG 13 (13, LCB)   **1999** NYG 11 (11, LCB)   **2000** Dal 16 (12, LCB) **NFL** 115 (95) [9 yrs]

SPARLIS, AL Albert Alexander, G, 5´11˝/185 lbs; UCLA; 1946: GB, rnd 30; B5/20/1920 Los Angeles, CA, D7/9/2005 Porterville, CA   **1946** GB 3 (1)

SPARR, ED Edwin Andrew, T, 5´11˝/210 lbs; Carroll (WI); B7/29/1898 Hazelhurst, WI, D5/19/1974 Detroit, MI   **1926** Rac 2 (1)

SPAVITAL, JIM James J., FB-LB, 6´1˝/210 lbs; Oklahoma State; 1948: LAD-A, rnd 8/ChiC, rnd 1; B9/15/1926 Oklahoma City, OK, D3/7/1993 Stillwater, OK

| 1949 | LAD-A | 12(3) | 15 | 44 | 2.9 | 0 | 1 | -1 | -1.0(-1) | 0 | — | — | — | — | — | — | — | — | — | kpi | — | 0 | 127 |
| 1950 | Bal | 11(7, FB) | 58 | 246 | 4.2(96) | 2 | 21 | 238 | 11.3(45) | 1 | — | — | — | — | — | — | — | — | — | — | — | 18 | 390 |

SPEAR, GLEN Glen Owen, FB-WB-E, 5´10˝/185 lbs; Drake; B1/18/1900 Fairfield, NE, D12/19/1971 Sutton, NE   **1926** KC 10 (8, FB), 6

SPEARMAN, ARMEGIS Armegis DeWayne, LB, 6´2˝/251 lbs; Mississippi; B4/5/1978 Oxford, MS   **2000** Cin 15 (11, MLB)   **2002** Cin 7 (0)   **2003** Hou 1 (0)   **NFL** 23 (11) [3 yrs]

SPEARS, ANTHONY William Anthony, DE, 6´5˝/260 lbs; Portland State; B11/4/1965 Martinez, CA   **1989**†Hou 0 (0)

SPEARS, ERNEST Ernest Phillip, DB, 5´11˝/192 lbs; USC; 1990: NO, rnd 10; B11/6/1967 Oceanside, CA   **1990**†NO 16 (0)

SPEARS, MARCUS Marcus DeWayne, T, 6´4˝/320 lbs; Northwestern State (LA); 1994: Chi, rnd 2; B9/28/1971 Baton Rouge, LA   **1997** KC 3 (0)   **1998** KC 12 (0)   **1999** KC 10 (2) **2000** KC 13 (0)   **2001** KC 16 (16, RT)   **2002** KC 9 (0)   **2003**†KC 15 (0)   **2004** Hou 16 (3)

| 1996 | ChiB | 9(0) | — | — | — | — | 1 | 1 | 1.0(1) | 1 | — | — | — | — | — | — | — | — | — | — | — | 6 | 6 |
| NFL | 9 | 103(21) | — | — | — | — | 1 | 1 | 1.0(1) | 1 | — | — | — | — | — | — | — | — | — | k | — | 6 | 2 |

SPEARS, MARCUS Marcus Raishon, DE, 6´4˝/298 lbs; LSU; 2005: Dal, rnd 1; B3/8/1983 Baton Rouge, LA   **2005** Dal 16 (10, LDE)

SPEARS, RON Ronald Darnell, DE, 6´6˝/255 lbs; San Diego State; B11/23/1959 Los Angeles, CA   **1982**†NE 7 (0)   **1983** NE 1 (1)   **1983** GB 13 (1)   **NFL** 21 (2) [2 yrs]

SPECHT, ROBERT Robert, WB-TB, 5´9˝/170 lbs; none; deceased   **1920** Ham 7 (3, WB)

SPECK, DUTCH Norman John, G-C-T, 5´10˝/220 lbs; none; B7/30/1886 Canton, OH, D11/18/1952 Canton, OH   **1920** Can 9 (2)   **1921** Can 7 (6, LG)   **1922** Can 11 (5, c) **1923** Can 6 (1)   **1924** Akr 1 (1)   **1925** Can 5 (1)   **1926** Can 7 (3)   **NFL** 46 (19) [7 yrs]

SPEEDIE, MAC Mac Curtis, E, 6´3˝/203 lbs; Utah; 1942: Det, rnd 15; B1/12/1920 Odell, IL, D3/12/1993 Laguna Hills, CA **[KC]**

1946	†Cle-A☆	14(10, LE)	—	—	—	—	24	564	23.5(79)	7	—	—	—	—	—	—	—	—	—	KPk	—	43	303
1947	†Cle-A☆	14(9, LE)	1	-7	-7.0(-7)	0	67	1146	17.1(99)	6	—	—	—	—	—	—	—	—	—	—	1	42	596
1948	†Cle-A☆	12(11, LE)	1	7	7.0(7)	0	58	816	14.1(56)	4	—	—	—	—	—	—	—	—	—	k	—	24	433
1949	†Cle-A☆	12(11, LE)	—	—	—	—	62	1028	16.6	7	—	—	—	—	—	—	—	—	—	—	—	42	549
AAFC	4	52(41)	2	0	0.0(7)	0	211	3554	16.8(99)	24	—	—	—	—	—	—	—	—	—	KPk	1	151	1881
1950	†Cle★	12(LE)	—	—	—	—	42	548	13.0(45)	1	—	—	—	—	—	—	—	—	—	—	—	6	279
1951	†Cle	10(LE)	—	—	—	—	34	589	17.3(51)	3	—	—	—	—	—	—	—	—	—	—	—	18	310
1952	†Cle☆	12(LE)	—	—	—	—	62	911	14.7(50)	5	—	—	—	—	—	—	—	—	—	—	—	30	481
NFL	3	34	—	—	—	—	138	2048	14.8(99)	9	—	—	—	—	—	—	—	—	—	—	—	54	1069

SPEEGLE, CLIFF Clifton M., C, 6´1˝/195 lbs; Oklahoma; B11/5/1917 Roosevelt, OK, D9/5/1994 Dallas, TX   **1945** ChiC 8 (6, C)

SPEEGLE, NICK Nicholas David, LB, 6´6˝/250 lbs; New Mexico; 2005: Cle, rnd 6; B11/29/1981 Albuquerque, NM   **2005** Cle 14 (0)

SPEELMAN, HARRY Harry E., G, 5´11˝/220 lbs; Michigan State; B10/4/1916, D4/1/1983 Pigeon, MI   **1940** Det 4 (0)

SPEER, DEL Delfonico Arnese, DB, 6´0˝/196 lbs; Florida; B2/1/1970 Miami, FL   **1993** Cle 16 (2)   **1994** Cle 8 (0)   **1994** Sea 1 (0)   **NFL** 25 (2) [2 yrs]

SPEIGHTS, DICK Richard Blan, DB, 5´11˝/176 lbs; Wyoming; B6/30/1946 Battle Creek, MI   **1968** SD-A 2

SPEK, JEFF Jeffrey Martin, TE, 6´3˝/240 lbs; UNLV; San Diego State; 1984: Dal, rnd S3; B10/1/1960 Calgary, Canada   **1986** TB 2 (0)

SPELLACY, FRANK William Francis, E, none; B4/6/1901 Corning, NY, deceased   **1922** Buf 1 (1)

SPELLMAN, ALONZO Alonzo Robert, DE-DT, 6´4˝/287 lbs; Ohio State; 1992: Chi, rnd 1; B9/27/1971 Mount Holly, NJ   **1992** ChiB 15 (0)   **1993** ChiB 16 (0)   **1994**†ChiB 16 (16, RDE) **1995** ChiB 16 (16, LDE)   **1996** ChiB 16 (15, RDE)   **1997** ChiB 7 (5, rde)   **1999**†Dal 16 (16, LDT)   **2000** Dal 16 (15, RDE)   **2001** Det 5 (0)   **NFL** 123 (83) [9 yrs]

SPELLMAN, JACK John Franklin, E-T-B, 5´10˝/201 lbs; Brown; B6/14/1899 Middletown, CT, D8/1/1966 Mangula, Zimbabwe   **1925** Pro 10 (7, lt), 6   **1926** Pro 11 (2, WB) **1927** Pro 14 (10, RE)   **1928** Pro 11 (10, RE)   **1929** Pro☆12 (11, RE)   **1930** Pro 11 (10, RE)   **1931** Pro 11 (10, RE)   **1932** Bos 7 (4)   **NFL** 88 (70) [8 yrs]

SPENCE, BLAKE Blake Andrew, TE, 6´4˝/249 lbs; Oregon; 1998: NYJ, rnd 5; B6/20/1975 Garden Grove, CA

1998	†NYJ	5(0)	—	—	—	—	1	5	5.0(5)	0	—	—	—	—	—	—	—	—	—	—	—	0	3
1999	NYJ	10(0)	—	—	—	—	3	15	5.0(9)	1	—	—	—	—	—	—	—	—	—	—	—	6	13
2000	TB	3(0)	—	—	—	—	—	—	—	—	—	—	—	—	—	—	—	—	—	—	—	—	—
NFL	3	18(0)	—	—	—	—	4	20	5.0(9)	1	—	—	—	—	—	—	—	—	—	—	—	6	15

SPENCE, JULIAN Julian Carroll, DB-FL, 5´11˝/170 lbs; Sam Houston State; B5/5/1929 Austin, TX, D3/6/1990 Houston, TX **1956** ChiC 8 (db) **1957** SF 3 **1960**†Hou-A☆14 (RS)

YEAR	TEAM	G(GS, POS)	RUSH	YD	AVG(LG)	TD	REC	YD	AVG(LG)	TD	PASS	COMP	PCT	YD	AVG(LG)	TD	INT	SK	YD	QBR	KPR	OTD	PTS	TAY
1961	†Hou-A	10	—	—	—	—	1	14	14.0(14)	0	—	—	—	—	—	—	—	—	—	—	i	—	0	25
NFL	4	35	—	—	—	—	1	14	14.0(14)	0	—	—	—	—	—	—	—	—	—	—	i	—	0	12

SPENCER, CHRIS Christopher Clarks, C, 6´3˝/309 lbs; Mississippi; 2005: Sea, rnd 1; B3/28/1982 Madison, MS **2005** Sea 8 (0)

SPENCER, CODY Cody, LB, 6´3˝/235 lbs; North Texas; 2004: Oak, rnd 6; B6/1/1981 Port Lavaca, TX **2004** Ten 7 (0) **2005** Ten 16 (0) **NFL** 23 (0) [2 yrs]

SPENCER, DARRYL Darryl Eugene, WR, 5´8˝/172 lbs; Miami (FL); B3/21/1970 Merritt Island, FL

YEAR	TEAM	G(GS, POS)	RUSH	YD	AVG(LG)	TD	REC	YD	AVG(LG)	TD	PASS	COMP	PCT	YD	AVG(LG)	TD	INT	SK	YD	QBR	KPR	OTD	PTS	TAY
1994	Atl	8(0)	—	—	—	—	2	51	25.5(40)	0	—	—	—	—	—	—	—	—	—	—	—	—	0	26
1995	Atl	5(1)	—	—	—	—	5	60	12.0(22)	0	—	—	—	—	—	—	—	—	—	—	—	—	0	30
NFL	2	13(1)	—	—	—	—	7	111	15.9(40)	0	—	—	—	—	—	—	—	—	—	—	—	—	0	56

SPENCER, HERB Herbert Seabrook, LB, 6´3˝/230 lbs; Newberry; B9/23/1959 Charleston, SC **1987** Atl 3 (2)

SPENCER, JIM James M., G, 6´0˝/205 lbs; Dayton; B11/1/1901, D2/28/1972 Cleveland, OH **1928** Day 5 (4, RG) **1929** Day 6 (5, RG) **NFL** 11 (9) [2 yrs]

SPENCER, JIMMY James Arthur, DB, 5´9˝/188 lbs; Florida; 1991: Was, rnd 8; B3/29/1969 Manning, SC **[I]** **1992**†NO 16 (4) **1993** NO 16 (3) **1994** NO 16 (16, LCB) **1995** NO 16 (15, LCB) **1996** Cin 15 (14, RCB) **1997** Cin 16 (9, RCB) **1998** SD 15 (4) **1999** SD 14 (7, lcb) **2000**†Den 16 (6, lcb) **2001** Den 16 (1) **2002** Den 5 (0) **2003**†Den 16 (2) **NFL** 177 (81) [12 yrs]

SPENCER, JOE Joseph Emerson, T-DT, 6´3˝/239 lbs; Oklahoma State; 1948: Bkn-A, rnd 4/1945: Phi, rnd 19; B8/15/1923 Elk City, OK, D10/24/1996 Houston, TX **1948** Bkn-A 13 (1) **1949**†Cle-A 11 (0) **AAFC** 24 (1) [2 yrs]

1950 GB 12 (RT) **1951** GB 12 (RT) **NFL** 24 [2 yrs]

SPENCER, MO Thurmon Maurice, DB, 6´0˝/175 lbs; North Carolina Central; 1974: Atl, rnd 3; B6/15/1952 Winston-Salem, NC **1974** SL 7 **1974** NO 5 **1975** NO 14 (rcb) **1976** NO 14 (14, RCB) **1978** NO 16 (16, RCB) **NFL** 56 (30) [4 yrs]

SPENCER, OLLIE Oliver Lee, T-G-C, 6-2˝/245 lbs; Kansas; 1953: Det, rnd 6; B4/17/1931 Hopewell, KS, D4/28/1991 Ukiah, CA **1953**†Det 12 (RT) **1956** Det 12 (RT) **1957** GB 12 (RT) **1958** GB 12 (RT) **1959** Det 12 (RT) **1960** Det 12 (LT) **1961** Det 13 **1963** Oak-A 14 (rg) **NFL** 99 [8 yrs]

SPENCER, SHAWNTAE Shawntae, DB, 6´1˝/181 lbs; Pittsburgh; 2004: SF, rnd 2; B2/22/1982 Rankin, PA **2004** SF 16 (12, RCB) **2005** SF 15 (14, RCB) **NFL** 31 (26) [2 yrs]

SPENCER, TIM Timothy Arnold, RB, 6´1˝/224 lbs; Ohio State; 1983: SD, rnd 11; B12/10/1960 Martins Ferry, OH

YEAR	TEAM	G(GS, POS)	RUSH	YD	AVG(LG)	TD	REC	YD	AVG(LG)	TD	PASS	COMP	PCT	YD	AVG(LG)	TD	INT	SK	YD	QBR	KPR	OTD	PTS	TAY
1985	SD	16(15, FB)	124	478	3.9(24)	10	11	135	12.3(43)	0	—	—	—	—	—	—	—	—	—	—	—	—	60	646
1986	SD	14(12, FB)	99	350	3.5(23)	6	6	48	8.0(15)	0	—	—	—	—	—	—	—	—	—	—	k	—	36	440
1987	SD	12(7, FB)	73	228	3.1(16)	0	17	123	7.2(18)	0	—	—	—	—	—	—	—	—	—	—	—	—	0	290
1988	SD	16(1)	44	215	4.9(24)	0	1	14	14.0(14)	0	—	—	—	—	—	—	—	—	—	—	k	—	0	223
1989	SD	16(11, RB)	134	521	3.9(15)	3	18	112	6.2(23)	0	—	—	—	—	—	—	—	—	—	—	—	—	18	607
1990	SD	4(0)	—	—	—	—	—	—	—	—	—	—	—	—	—	—	—	—	—	—	—	—	—	—
NFL	6	78(46)	474	1792	3.8(24)	19	53	432	8.2(43)	0	—	—	—	—	—	—	—	—	—	—	k	—	114	2205

SPENCER, TODD Todd Lamont, RB, 6´0˝/203 lbs; USC; B7/26/1962 Portland, OR

YEAR	TEAM	G(GS, POS)	RUSH	YD	AVG(LG)	TD	REC	YD	AVG(LG)	TD	PASS	COMP	PCT	YD	AVG(LG)	TD	INT	SK	YD	QBR	KPR	OTD	PTS	TAY
1984	Pit	7(0)	1	0	0.0(0)	0	—	—	—	—	—	—	—	—	—	—	—	—	—	—	k	—	0	103
1985	Pit	16(0)	13	56	4.3(11)	0	3	25	8.3(13)	0	—	—	—	—	—	—	—	—	—	—	k	—	0	281
1987	SD	3(2)	14	24	1.7(5)	0	2	47	23.5(45)	0	—	—	—	—	—	—	—	—	—	—	—	—	0	48
NFL	3	26(2)	28	80	2.9(11)	0	5	72	14.4(45)	0	—	—	—	—	—	—	—	—	—	—	k	—	0	431

SPENCER, WILLIE Willie Thomas, RB, 6´3˝/235 lbs; none; B1/28/1953 Massillon, OH

YEAR	TEAM	G(GS, POS)	RUSH	YD	AVG(LG)	TD	REC	YD	AVG(LG)	TD	PASS	COMP	PCT	YD	AVG(LG)	TD	INT	SK	YD	QBR	KPR	OTD	PTS	TAY
1976	Min	3	4	2	0.5(2)	0	—	—	—	—	—	—	—	—	—	—	—	—	—	—	—	—	0	2
1977	NYG	13	62	184	3.0(9)	3	4	20	5.0(15)	0	—	—	—	—	—	—	—	—	—	—	k	—	18	223
1978	NYG	15	38	61	1.6(9)	2	2	25	12.5(22)	0	—	—	—	—	—	—	—	—	—	—	k	—	12	93
NFL	3	31	104	247	2.4(9)	5	6	45	7.5(22)	0	—	—	—	—	—	—	—	—	—	—	k	—	30	318

SPETH, GEORGE George Carl, T, 6´2˝/220 lbs; Murray State; 1942: Det, rnd 18; B7/25/1918 Buffalo, NY **1942** Det 10 (5, lt)

SPEYRER, COTTON Charles Wayne, WR, 6´0˝/175 lbs; Texas; 1971: Was, rnd 2; B4/29/1949 Port Arthur, TX

YEAR	TEAM	G(GS, POS)	RUSH	YD	AVG(LG)	TD	REC	YD	AVG(LG)	TD	PASS	COMP	PCT	YD	AVG(LG)	TD	INT	SK	YD	QBR	KPR	OTD	PTS	TAY
1972	Bal	5	—	—	—	—	8	114	14.3(21)	0	—	—	—	—	—	—	—	—	—	—	—	—	0	57
1973	Bal	14(WR)	1	1	1.0(1)	0	17	311	18.3(47)	4	1	1	100.0	54	54.0(54)	1	0	—	—	—	k	1	30	460
1974	Bal	13	—	—	—	—	9	110	12.2(27)	1	—	—	—	—	—	—	—	—	—	—	kp	—	6	283
1975	Mia	4	—	—	—	—	—	—	—	—	—	—	—	—	—	—	—	—	—	—	—	—	—	—
NFL	4	36	1	1	1.0(1)	0	34	535	15.7(47)	5	1	1	100.0	54	54.0(54)	1	0	—	—	—	kp	1	36	800

SPICER, PAUL Paul, DE, 6´4˝/287 lbs; DuPage (IL); Saginaw Valley State (MI); B8/18/1975 Indianapolis, IN **1999** Det 2 (0) **2000** Jax 3 (0) **2001** Jax 16 (4) **2002** Jax 16 (4) **2003** Jax 16 (1) **2004** Jax 2 (2) **2005**†Jax 15 (14, RDE) **NFL** 70 (25) [7 yrs]

SPICER, ROB Robin Edward, LB, 6´4˝/238 lbs; Indiana; 1973: NYJ, rnd 9; B7/20/1951 Detroit, MI **1973** NYJ 13

SPIEGEL, ADOLPH Clarence Adolph, T-G, 5´11˝/190 lbs; Campion; B7/12/1898 Evansville, IN, D5/28/1970 Evansville, IN **1921** Evv 5 (5, RT) **1922** Evv 1 (1) **NFL** 6 (6) [2 yrs]

SPIELMAN, CHRIS Charles Christopher, LB, 6´0˝/247 lbs; Ohio State; 1988: Det, rnd 2; B10/11/1965 Canton, OH **1988** Det 16 (16, LILB) **1989** Det★16 (16, LILB) **1990** Det✧12 (12, LILB) **1991**†Det★16 (16, LILB) **1992** Det☆16 (16, LILB) **1993**†Det 16 (16, LILB) **1994** Det★16 (16, LILB) **1995**†Det☆16 (16, MLB) **1996**†Buf 16 (16, LILB) **1997** Buf 8 (8, LILB) **NFL** 148 (148) [10 yrs]

SPIERS, BOB Robert Hugh, T-G, 5´11˝/193 lbs; Hiram; Ohio State; B1/4/1895, OH, D7/8/1984 Naples, FL **1922** Akr 10 (8, RT) **1925** Cle 3 (2) **NFL** 13 (10) [2 yrs]

SPIKES, CAMERON Cameron Wade, G, 6´4˝/325 lbs; Texas A&M; 1999: SL, rnd 5; B11/6/1976 Madisonville, TX **1999** SL 5 (0) **2000** SL 9 (0) **2001**†SL 5 (0) **2002** Hou 12 (5, lg) **2003** Arz 16 (16, LG) **2004** Arz 16 (9, RG) **NFL** 63 (30) [6 yrs]

SPIKES, IRVING Irving E., RB, 5´8˝/212 lbs; Alabama; Louisiana-Monroe; B12/21/1970 Ocean Springs, MS **[R]**

YEAR	TEAM	G(GS, POS)	RUSH	YD	AVG(LG)	TD	REC	YD	AVG(LG)	TD	PASS	COMP	PCT	YD	AVG(LG)	TD	INT	SK	YD	QBR	KPR	OTD	PTS	TAY
1994	†Mia	12(1)	70	312	4.5(40)	2	4	16	4.0(9)	0	—	—	—	—	—	—	—	—	—	—	k	—	12	489
1995	†Mia	9(0)	32	126	3.9(17)	1	5	18	3.6(13)	1	—	—	—	—	—	—	—	—	—	—	k	—	12	258
1996	Mia	15(1)	87	316	3.6(49)	3	8	81	10.1(19)	1	—	—	—	—	—	—	—	—	—	—	k	—	24	653
1997	Mia	12(1)	63	180	2.9(14)	2	7	70	10.0(24)	0	—	—	—	—	—	—	—	—	—	—	k	—	12	440
NFL	4	48(3)	252	934	3.7(49)	8	24	185	7.7(24)	2	—	—	—	—	—	—	—	—	—	—	k	—	60	1840

SPIKES, JACK Jack Erwin, FB-HB-K, 6´2˝/210 lbs; TCU; 1960: Den, rnd 1/Pit, rnd 1; B2/5/1937 Big Spring, TX **[K]**

YEAR	TEAM	G(GS, POS)	RUSH	YD	AVG(LG)	TD	REC	YD	AVG(LG)	TD	PASS	COMP	PCT	YD	AVG(LG)	TD	INT	SK	YD	QBR	KPR	OTD	PTS	TAY
1960	DalT-A	14(FB)	115	457	4.0(36)	5	11	158	14.4(25)	0	—	—	—	—	—	—	—	—	—	—	K	—	104	586
1961	DalT-A	6(fb)	39	334	8.6(74)	5	8	136	17.0(46)	0	—	—	—	—	—	—	—	—	—	—	K	—	54	452
1962	†DalT-A	10	57	232	4.1(17)	0	10	132	13.2(35)	1	—	—	—	—	—	—	—	—	—	—	Kk	—	7	303
1963	KC-A	14	84	257	3.1(15)	2	11	125	11.4(30)	1	1	0	0.0	0	0.0	0	1	—	—	—	Kk	—	47	287
1964	KC-A	7(hb)	34	112	3.3(13)	0	5	17	3.4(12)	0	1	0	0.0	0	0.0	0	0	—	—	—	—	—	0	121
1965	Hou-A	14	47	173	3.7(20)	3	8	57	7.1(17)	0	—	—	—	—	—	—	—	—	—	—	Kk	—	27	213
1966	†Buf-A	14	28	119	4.3(36)	3	2	45	22.5(27)	1	—	—	—	—	—	—	—	—	—	—	—	—	24	177
1967	Buf-A	7	4	9	2.3(6)	0	1	9	9.0(9)	0	—	—	—	—	—	—	—	—	—	—	—	—	0	14
NFL	8	86	408	1693	4.1(74)	18	56	679	12.1(46)	3	2	0	0.0	0	0.0	0	1	—	—	—	Kk	—	263	2151

SPIKES, TAKEO Takeo Gerard, LB, 6´2˝/242 lbs; Auburn; 1998: Cin, rnd 1; B12/17/1976 Sandersville, GA **1998** Cin 16 (16, RILB) **1999** Cin 16 (16, RILB/rlb) **2000** Cin 16 (16, RLB) **2001** Cin 15 (15, RLB) **2002** Cin 16 (16, RLB) **2003** Buf★16 (16, RLB) **2004** Buf★16 (16, RLB) **2005** Buf 3 (3) **NFL** 114 (114) [8 yrs]

SPILIS, JOHN John Arthur, WR, 6´3˝/205 lbs; Northern Illinois; 1969: GB, rnd 3; B10/14/1947 Chicago, IL

YEAR	TEAM	G(GS, POS)	RUSH	YD	AVG(LG)	TD	REC	YD	AVG(LG)	TD	PASS	COMP	PCT	YD	AVG(LG)	TD	INT	SK	YD	QBR	KPR	OTD	PTS	TAY
1969	GB	12	—	—	—	—	7	89	12.7(16)	0	—	—	—	—	—	—	—	—	—	—	—	—	0	45
1970	GB	14	—	—	—	—	6	76	12.7(18)	0	—	—	—	—	—	—	—	—	—	—	—	—	0	38
1971	GB	14(WR)	—	—	—	—	14	281	20.1(39)	1	—	—	—	—	—	—	—	—	—	—	—	—	6	146
NFL	3	40	—	—	—	—	27	446	16.5(39)	1	—	—	—	—	—	—	—	—	—	—	—	—	6	228

SPILLER, PHILIP Philip A., DB, 6´0˝/195 lbs; Los Angeles State; 1967: SL, rnd 16; B4/2/1945 Santa Monica, CA **1967** SL 14 **1968** Atl 7 **1968** Cin-A 4 **NFL** 25 [2 yrs]

SPILLERS, RAY Raymond Carl, T, 6´3˝/218 lbs; Arkansas; B10/23/1912 North Little Rock, AR, D1/26/2001 Little Rock, AR **1937** Phi 10 (3)

YEAR	TEAM	G (GS, POS)	RUSH	YD	AVG (LG)	TD	REC	YD	AVG (LG)	TD	PASS COMP	PCT	YD	AVG (LG)	TD	INT	SK	YD	QBR	KPR	OTD	PTS	TAY

SPINDLER, MARC   Marc Rudolph, DE-NT-DT, 6´5˝/290 lbs; Pittsburgh; 1990: Det, rnd 3; B11/28/1969 Scranton, PA   **1990** Det 3 (2)   **1991** Det 16 (16, LDE)   **1992** Det 13 (13, LDE) **1993**†Det 16 (16, LDE)   **1994** Det 9 (4, NT)   **1995** NYJ 10 (4)   **1996** NYJ 15 (5, ldt)   **1997**†Det 10 (0)   **1998** Det 15 (1)   **NFL** 107 (65) [9 yrs]

SPINKS, JACK   John Robert, T-G-FB-DT, 6´0˝/236 lbs; Alcorn State; 1952: Pit, rnd 11; B8/15/1930 Tooomsuba, MS, D9/29/1994 Jackson, MS   **1955** GB 6   **1956** GB 1   **1956** NYG 3 **1957** NYG 7 (RT)

YEAR	TEAM	G	RUSH	YD	AVG (LG)	TD	REC	YD	AVG (LG)	TD										KPR	OTD	PTS	TAY
1952	Pit	10	22	94	4.3 (42)	0	2	22	11.0 (23)	0	—	—	—	—	—	—	—	—	—	—	—	0	105
1953	ChiC	3	6	0	0.0 (7)	0	1	6	6.0 (6)	0	—	—	—	—	—	—	—	—	—	—	—	0	3
NFL	5	30	28	94	3.4 (42)	0	3	28	9.3 (23)	0	—	—	—	—	—	—	—	—	—	—	—	0	108

SPINNEY, ART   Arthur F., G-DE, 6´0˝/230 lbs; Boston College; 1950: Bal, rnd 15; B11/8/1927 Saugus, MA, D5/27/1994 Lynn, MA   **1953** Bal 12   **1954** Bal 12 (LG)   **1955** Bal 12 (LG) **1956** Bal 11 (LG)   **1957** Bal☆11 (LG)   **1958**†Bal☆12 (LG)   **1959**†Bal★12 (LG)   **1960** Bal★10 (LG)

| 1950 | Bal | 2 (1) | — | — | — | — | 2 | 19 | 9.5 (12) | 0 | — | — | — | — | — | — | — | — | — | — | — | 0 | 10 |
| NFL | 9 | 94 (1) | — | — | — | — | 2 | 19 | 9.5 (12) | 0 | — | — | — | — | — | — | — | — | k | — | — | 0 | 5 |

SPIRES, GREG   Gregory Tyrone, DE, 6´1˝/265 lbs; Florida State; 1998: NE, rnd 3; B8/12/1974 Marianna, FL   **1998**†NE 15 (1)   **1999** NE 11 (1)   **2000** NE 16 (2)   **2001** Cle 16 (4) **2002**†TB 16 (16, LDE)   **2003** TB 15 (15, LDE)   **2004** TB 16 (16, LDE)   **2005**†TB 16 (16, LDE)   **NFL** 121 (71) [8 yrs]

SPIRIDA, JOHNNY   John Martin, BB-E, 6´0˝/195 lbs; St. Anselm; B11/4/1914, D4/1966

| 1939 | Was | 9 (1) | 2 | 5 | 2.5 | 0 | 2 | 95 | 47.5 | 0 | — | — | — | — | — | — | — | — | — | P | — | 0 | 53 |

SPITULSKI, BOB   Bob, LB, 6´3˝/240 lbs; Central Florida; 1992: Sea, rnd 3; B9/10/1969 Toledo, OH   **1992** Sea 4 (0)   **1993** Sea 6 (0)   **1994** Sea 16 (1)   **NFL** 26 (1) [3 yrs]

SPIVA, ANDY   Howard Anthony, LB, 6´2˝/220 lbs; Tennessee; 1977: SL, rnd 5; B2/6/1955 Chattanooga, TN, D4/3/1979 Atlanta, GA   **1977** Atl 13

SPIVEY, MIKE   Michael James, DB, 6´0˝/197 lbs; Colorado; 1977: Chi, rnd 2; B3/10/1954 Houston, TX   **1977**†ChiB 14   **1978** ChiB 16 (3)   **1979**†ChiB 16   **1980** Oak 9 (0) **1980** NO 2 (1)   **1981** NO 12 (0)   **1982**†Atl 8 (0)   **NFL** 77 (3) [6 yrs]

SPIVEY, SEBRON   Sebron Ervin, WR, 5´11˝/180 lbs; Southern Illinois; B8/2/1964

| 1987 | Dal | 2 (1) | — | — | — | — | 2 | 34 | 17.0 (25) | 0 | — | — | — | — | — | — | — | — | k | — | — | 0 | 36 |

SPONAUGLE, BOB   Robert Ralph, E, 6´1˝/203 lbs; Pennsylvania; B1/31/1928 Harrisburg, PA, D11/19/1986 Hershey, PA

| 1949 | NYB | 4 (1) | — | — | — | — | 2 | 26 | 13.0 (14) | 0 | — | — | — | — | — | — | — | — | — | — | — | 0 | 13 |

SPOON, BRANDON   Thomas Brandon, LB, 6´2˝/242 lbs; North Carolina; 2001: Buf, rnd 4; B7/5/1978 Burlington, NC   **2001** Buf 14 (14, MLB)

SPRADLIN, DANNY   Daniel Ray, LB, 6´1˝/235 lbs; Tennessee; 1981: Dal, rnd 5; B3/3/1959 Detroit, MI   **1981**†Dal 16 (0)   **1982**†Dal 9 (0)   **1983** TB 16 (2)   **1984** TB 15 (0) **1985** SL 7 (0)   **NFL** 63 (2) [5 yrs]

SPRAGAN, DONNIE   Donald, LB, 6´3˝/239 lbs; Pacific; Stanford; B7/12/1976 Oakland, CA   **2002** Den 16 (0)   **2003**†Den 16 (8, RLB)   **2004**†Den 16 (14, LLB)   **2005** Mia 16 (9, LLB) **NFL** 64 (31) [4 yrs]

SPRIGGS, MARCUS   Thomas Marcus, T-G, 6´3˝/310 lbs; Houston; 1997: Buf, rnd 6; B5/30/1974 Hattiesburg, MS   **1997** Buf 2 (0)   **1998** Buf 1 (0)   **1999**†Buf 11 (2) **2000** Buf 16 (11, RT)   **2001** Mia 1 (1)   **2002** Mia 16 (4)   **2003** GB 2 (0)   **NFL** 49 (18) [7 yrs]

SPRIGGS, MARCUS   Marcus, DT, 6´4˝/314 lbs; Ohio State; Troy State; 1999: Cle, rnd 6; B7/26/1976 Washington, DC   **1999** Cle 10 (0)   **2000** Cle 8 (0)   **NFL** 18 (0) [2 yrs]

SPRINGER, HAL   Harold Clayton, E, 6´4˝/212 lbs; Central Oklahoma; B5/10/1922 Albuquerque, NM, D5/17/1981 Staten Island, NY

| 1945 | NYG | 7 (2) | — | — | — | — | 4 | 63 | 15.8 (36) | 0 | — | — | — | — | — | — | — | — | — | — | — | 0 | 32 |

SPRINGS, KIRK   Kirk Edward, DB, 6´0˝/192 lbs; Miami (OH); B8/16/1958 Cincinnati, OH   **1981**†NYJ 10 (0)   **1982**†NYJ 9 (0)   **1983** NYJ 16 (0)   **1984** NYJ 16 (11, SS) **1985**†NYJ 16 (14, SS)   **NFL** 67 (25) [5 yrs]

SPRINGS, RON   Ronald Edward, RB, 6´0˝/213 lbs; Ohio State; 1979: Dal, rnd 5; B11/4/1956 Williamsburg, VA

1979	†Dal	16	67	248	3.7 (15)	2	25	251	10.0 (27)	1	3	1	33.3	30	10.0 (30)	1	0	1	4	—	k	—	18	629
1980	†Dal	15 (6, fb)	89	326	3.7 (20)	6	15	212	14.1 (58)	1	—	—	—	—	—	—	—	—	—	—	—	—	42	497
1981	†Dal	16 (13, FB)	172	625	3.6 (16)	10	46	359	7.8 (32)	2	1	0	0.0	0	0	0	1	—	—	—	—	—	72	875
1982	†Dal	9 (9, FB)	59	243	4.1 (46)	2	17	163	9.6 (34)	2	—	—	—	—	—	—	—	—	—	—	—	—	24	355
1983	†Dal	16 (14, FB)	149	541	3.6 (19)	7	73	589	8.1 (80)	1	2	1	50.0	15	7.5 (15)	1	0	—	—	—	k	—	48	921
1984	Dal	16 (12, FB)	68	197	2.9 (16)	1	46	454	9.9 (57)	3	1	0	0.0	0	0	0	0	—	—	—	—	—	24	449
1985	TB	12 (0)	16	54	3.4 (11)	0	3	44	14.7 (22)	0	—	—	—	—	—	—	—	—	—	—	k	—	0	113
1986	TB	12 (8, FB)	74	285	3.9 (40)	0	24	187	7.8 (46)	0	—	—	—	—	—	—	—	—	—	—	P	—	0	379
NFL	8	112 (62)	694	2519	3.6 (46)	28	249	2259	9.1 (80)	10	7	2	28.6	45	6.4 (30)	2	1	1	4	—	Pk	—	228	4216

SPRINGS, SHAWN   Shawn, DB, 6´0˝/204 lbs; Ohio State; 1997: Sea, rnd 1; B3/11/1975 Williamsburg, MD [I]   **1997** Sea 10 (10, LCB)   **1998** Sea◇16 (16, LCB) **1999**†Sea 16 (16, LCB)   **2000** Sea 16 (16, LCB)   **2001** Sea 8 (7, lcb)   **2002** Sea 15 (15, LCB)   **2003**†Sea 12 (8, LCB)   **2004** Was☆15 (15, LCB)   **2005**†Was 15 (15, RCB) **NFL** 123 (118) [9 yrs]

SPRINGSTEEN, BILL   William Watson, C-E, 6´0˝/200 lbs; Lehigh; B10/27/1899 New York, NY, D10/1/1985 Lakeville, CT   **1925** Fra 18 (17, C)   **1926** Fra 17 (14, LE) **1927** ChiC 11 (10, C)   **1928** ChiC 4 (2)   **NFL** 50 (43) [4 yrs]

SPRINKLE, ED   Edward Alexander, DE-E-G-LB, 6´1˝/206 lbs; Hardin-Simmons; Navy; B9/3/1923 Bradshaw, TX

1944	ChiB	9 (3)	—	—	—	—	—	—	—	—	—	—	—	—	—	—	—	—	—	i	—	0	10
1945	ChiB	6 (4)	—	—	—	—	—	—	—	—	—	—	—	—	—	—	—	—	—	—	—	0	—
1946	†ChiB	11 (9, RE)	—	—	—	—	7	124	17.7 (34)	2	—	—	—	—	—	—	—	—	—	ki	1	18	82
1947	ChiB	12 (5, RE)	—	—	—	—	4	43	10.8 (15)	0	—	—	—	—	—	—	—	—	—	—	—	0	22
1948	ChiB	10 (2)	1	-2	-2.0 (-2)	0	10	132	13.2 (34)	3	—	—	—	—	—	—	—	—	—	—	—	18	79
1949	ChiB☆	12 (6, re)	1	5	5.0 (5)	0	4	69	17.3 (47)	1	0	1	0.0	0	0	0	0	—	—	—	—	2	40
1950	†ChiB★	12 (RDE)	1	-1	-1.0 (-1)	0	4	70	17.5 (27)	0	—	—	—	—	—	—	—	—	—	k	—	0	24
1951	ChiB★	12 (RDE)	—	—	—	—	2	11	5.5 (7)	1	—	—	—	—	—	—	—	—	—	i	1	12	6
1952	ChiB★	12 (RDE)	—	—	—	—	1	2	2.0 (2)	1	—	—	—	—	—	—	—	—	—	k	—	6	-15
1953	ChiB	12 (RDE)	—	—	—	—	—	—	—	—	—	—	—	—	—	—	—	—	—	k	1	6	-15
1954	ChiB★	12 (RDE)	—	—	—	—	—	—	—	—	—	—	—	—	—	—	—	—	—	ki	—	0	-36
1955	ChiB	12	—	—	—	—	—	—	—	—	—	—	—	—	—	—	—	—	—	—	—	0	0
NFL	12	132 (29)	3	2	0.7 (5)	0	42	451	14.1 (47)	7	0	1	0.0	0	0	0	0	—	—	ki	3	62	196

SPRINKLE, HUGH   Hubert Owen, T-G, 6´2˝/220 lbs; Missouri; Carnegie Mellon; B1897, D12/11/1961   **1923** Akr 2 (0)   **1924** Akr 5 (5, RT)   **1925** Cle 7 (6, RT)   **NFL** 14 (11) [3 yrs]

SPROLES, DARREN   Darren, RB, 5´6˝/181 lbs; Kansas State; 2005; SD, rnd 4; B6/20/1983 Waterloo, IA

| 2005 | SD | 15 (0) | 8 | 50 | 6.3 (21) | 0 | 3 | 10 | 3.3 (6) | 0 | — | — | — | — | — | — | — | — | — | kp | — | 0 | 656 |

SPROTTE, JIMMY   John Wild, LB, 6´3˝/237 lbs; Arizona; 1998: Ten, rnd 7; B10/2/1974 Olathe, KS   **1998** Cin 5 (0)   **1999** Cin 4 (0)   **NFL** 9 (0) [2 yrs]

SPROUL, DENNIS   Dennis Eugene, QB, 6´2˝/210 lbs; Arizona State; 1978: GB, rnd 8; B7/7/1956 Downey, CA

| 1978 | GB | 6 | 2 | 0 | 0.0 (0) | 0 | — | — | — | — | 13 | 5 | 38.5 | 87 | 6.7 (25) | 0 | 0 | 1 | 7 | — | — | — | 0 | 44 |

SPRUILL, JIM   James Winfred, T, 6´3˝/225 lbs; Rice; 1948: Det, rnd 18; B2/26/1923 Dublin, TX   **1948** Bal-A 14 (6, rt)   **1949** Bal-A 14 (9, RT)   **AAFC** 28 (15) [2 yrs]

SPURRIER, STEVE   Steven Orr, QB-P, 6´2˝/204 lbs; Florida; 1967: SF, rnd 1; B4/20/1945 Miami Beach, FL [C]

1967	SF	14 (2)	5	18	3.6 (9)	0	—	—	—	—	50	23	46.0	211	4.2 (21)	0	7	—	—	—	P	—	0	-157
1968	SF	14	1	-15	-15.0 (-15)	0	—	—	—	—	—	—	—	—	—	—	—	—	—	—	P	—	0	-15
1969	SF	6 (6, QB)	5	49	9.8 (29)	0	—	—	—	—	146	81	55.5	926	6.3 (75)	5	11	11	87	54.8	P	—	0	97
1970	†SF	14	2	-18	-9.0 (-5)	0	—	—	—	—	4	3	75.0	49	12.3 (26)	1	0	—	—	—	P	—	0	12
1971	†SF	6	1	2	2.0 (2)	0	—	—	—	—	4	1	25.0	46	11.5 (46)	0	0	—	—	—	P	—	0	25
1972	SF	13 (9, QB)	11	51	4.6 (15)	0	—	—	—	—	269	147	54.6	1983	7.4 (81)	18	16	14	114	75.9	—	—	0	493
1973	SF	11 (5, qb)	9	32	3.6 (12)	0	—	—	—	—	157	83	52.9	882	5.6 (58)	4	7	13	79	59.5	—	—	12	233
1974	SF	3	—	—	—	—	—	—	—	—	3	1	33.3	2	0.7 (2)	0	0	1	7	—	—	—	0	1
1975	SF	11 (6, QB)	15	91	6.1 (14)	0	—	—	—	—	207	102	49.3	1151	5.6 (68)	5	7	11	80	60.3	—	—	0	412
1976	TB	14 (12, QB)	12	48	4.0 (10)	0	—	—	—	—	311	156	50.2	1628	5.2 (38)	7	12	32	267	57.1	—	—	0	417
NFL	10	106 (40)	61	258	4.2 (29)	2	—	—	—	—	1151	597	51.9	6878	6.0 (81)	40	60	82	634	60.1	P	—	12	1517

YEAR	TEAM	G (GS, POS)	RUSH	YD	AVG (LG)	TD	REC	YD	AVG (LG)	TD	PASS COMP	PCT	YD	AVG (LG)	TD	INT	SK	YD	QBR	KPR	OTD	PTS	TAY

SQUIREK, JACK   Jack Steven, LB, 6´4˝/230 lbs; Illinois; 1982: LARd, rnd 2; B2/16/1959 Cleveland, OH   **1982**†LARd 9 (0)   **1983**†LARd 16 (1)   **1984**†LARd 12 (7, rilb)
1985†LARd 16 (0)   **1986** Mia 2 (0)   **NFL** 55 (8) [5 yrs]

SQUYRES, SEAMAN   Charles Seaman, HB, 6´2˝/205 lbs; Rice; B3/2/1910, D11/30/1979 Houston, TX

| **1933** | Cin | 4 (2) | 11 | 22 | 2.0 | 0 | — | — | — | — | 9 | 2 | 22.2 | 15 | 1.7 | 0 | 1 | — | — | — | — | 0 | -11 |

ST. CLAIR, BOB   Robert Bruce 'The Geek', T, 6´9˝/263 lbs; San Francisco; Tulsa; 1953: SF, rnd 3; B2/18/1931 San Francisco, CA; HOF 1990   **1953** SF☆10 (RT)
1954 SF☆12 (RT)   **1955** SF☆12 (RT)   **1956** SF★12 (RT)   **1957**†SF 5 (rt)   **1958** SF★12 (RT)   **1959** SF☆12 (RT)   **1960** SF★10 (10, RT)   **1961** SF★12 (11, RT)   **1962** SF☆8 (7, RT)
1963 SF☆14 (14, RT)   **NFL** 119 (42) [11 yrs]

ST. CLAIR, JOHN   John Bradley, T, 6´4˝/320 lbs; Virginia; 2000: SL, rnd 3; B7/15/1977 Roanoke, VA   **2002** SL 16 (16, RT)   **2004** Mia 14 (14, RT)   **2005**†ChiB 13 (2)

| **2003** | †SL | 16 (0) | — | — | — | — | 1 | 18 | 18.0 (18) | 0 | — | — | — | — | — | — | — | — | k | — | 0 | -3 |
| **NFL** | 4 | 59 (32) | — | — | — | — | 1 | 18 | 18.0 (18) | 0 | — | — | — | — | — | — | — | — | k | — | 0 | -3 |

ST. CLAIR, MIKE   Richard Michael, DE, 6´5˝/248 lbs; Iowa Central; Grambling State; 1976: Cle, rnd 4; B9/2/1953 Cleveland, OH   **1976** Cle 14 (rde)   **1977** Cle 11 (10, RDE)
1978 Cle 16 (12, LDE)   **1979** Cle 16   **1980** Cin 10 (0)   **1981**†Cin 16 (0)   **1982**†Cin 8 (0)   **NFL** 91 (22) [7 yrs]

ST. GERMAINE, TED   Thomas Leo, T-C-G, 6´2˝/250 lbs; Carlisle Indian; Howard; B1885 Lac du Flambeau, WI, D10/4/1947 Lac du Flambeau, WI   **1922** Oor 5 (5, LT)

ST. JEAN, LEN   Leonard Wayne, G, 5´11˝/250 lbs; Northern Michigan; 1964: Bos, rnd 9/GB, rnd 17; B10/27/1941 Newberry, MI   **1964** Bos-A 14   **1965** Bos-A 14
1966 Bos-A❖14 (RG)   **1967** Bos-A 14 (RG)   **1968** Bos-A 14 (13, RG)   **1969** Bos-A 14 (14, RG)   **1970** Bos 14 (14, RG)   **1971** NE 14 (13, RG)   **1972** NE 14 (14, RG)
1973 NE 14 (14, RG)   **NFL** 140 (82) [10 yrs]

ST. JOHN, HERB   Herbert LaGrande, G, 5´10˝/215 lbs; Georgia; 1948: Bkn-A, rnd 10/GB, rnd 21; B1/17/1926 Perry, FL   **1948** Bkn-A 10 (3)   **1949** ChiH-A 11 (11, LG)
AAFC 21 (14) [2 yrs]

ST. LOUIS, BRAD   Brad Allen, TE, 6´3˝/247 lbs; Southwest Missouri State; 2000: Cin, rnd 7; B8/19/1976 Waverly, MO   **2000** Cin 16 (0)   **2001** Cin 11 (0)   **2002** Cin 16 (0)
2003 Cin 16 (0)   **2004** Cin 16 (0)   **2005**†Cin 16 (0)   **NFL** 91 (0) [6 yrs]

ST. PIERRE, BRIAN   Brian, QB, 6´3˝/230 lbs; Boston College; 2003: Pit, rnd 5; B11/28/1979 Salem, MA

| **2004** | Pit | 1 (0) | 4 | -3 | -0.8 (2) | 0 | — | — | — | — | 1 | 0 | 0.0 | 0 | 0.0 | 0 | 0 | — | — | — | — | 0 | -3 |

STAAT, JEREMY   Jeremy Ray, DE, 6´5˝/300 lbs; Arizona State; 1998: Pit, rnd 2; B10/10/1976 Bakersfield, CA   **1998** Pit 5 (0)   **1999** Pit 16 (2)   **2000** Pit 7 (0)   **2003** SL 2 (0)
NFL 30 (2) [4 yrs]

STABLEIN, BRIAN   Brian Patrick, WR, 6´1˝/193 lbs; Ohio State; 1993: Den, rnd 8; B4/14/1970 Erie, PA

1995	†Ind	15 (0)	—	—	—	—	8	95	11.9 (16)	0	—	—	—	—	—	—	—	—	p	—	0	48
1996	†Ind	16 (0)	—	—	—	—	18	192	10.7 (30)	1	—	—	—	—	—	—	—	—	p	—	6	127
1997	Ind	16 (0)	—	—	—	—	25	253	10.1 (30)	1	—	—	—	—	—	—	—	—	p	—	8	180
1998	Det	10 (0)	—	—	—	—	7	80	11.4 (15)	0	—	—	—	—	—	—	—	—	p	—	0	40
1999	†Det	16 (2)	—	—	—	—	11	119	10.8 (42)	1	—	—	—	—	—	—	—	—	p	—	8	69
2000	Det	14 (5, wr)	—	—	—	—	8	53	6.6 (11)	0	—	—	—	—	—	—	—	—	—	—	0	27
NFL	6	87 (7)	—	—	—	—	77	792	10.3 (42)	3	—	—	—	—	—	—	—	—	—	—	22	489

STABLER, KEN   Kenneth Michael 'The Snake', QB, 6´3˝/215 lbs; Alabama; 1968: Oak, rnd 2; B12/25/1945 Foley, AL

1970	Oak	3	1	-4	-4.0 (-4)	0	—	—	—	—	7	2	28.6	52	7.4 (33)	0	1	—	—	—	—	0	-18
1971	Oak	14 (1)	4	29	7.3 (18)	2	—	—	—	—	48	24	50.0	268	5.6 (23)	1	4	4	37	—	—	12	28
1972	†Oak	14 (1)	6	27	4.5 (15)	0	—	—	—	—	74	44	59.5	524	7.1 (22)	4	3	9	72	—	—	0	189
1973	†Oak★	14 (11, QB)	21	101	4.8 (13)	0	—	—	—	—	260	163	**62.7**	1997	**7.7 (80)**	14	10	34	261	**88.3**	—	0	770
1974	†Oak★	14 (13, QB)	12	-2	-0.2 (6)	1	—	—	—	—	310	178	57.4	2469	8.0 (67)	**26**	12	18	141	94.9	—	6	893
1975	Oak	14 (13, QB)	6	-5	-0.8 (0)	0	—	—	—	—	293	171	58.4	2296	7.8 (53)	16	24	19	202	67.4	—	0	263
1976	†Oak★	12 (12, QB)	7	-2	-0.3 (5)	1	—	—	—	—	291	194	**66.7**	2737	**9.4 (88)**	**27**	17	19	141	**103.4**	—	6	832
1977	†Oak❖	13 (13, QB)	3	-3	-1.0 (0)	0	—	—	—	—	294	169	57.5	2176	7.4 (44)	20	20	16	141	75.2	—	0	385
1978	Oak	16 (16, QB)	4	0	0.0 (0)	0	—	—	—	—	406	237	58.4	2944	7.3 (49)	16	**30**	37	347	63.3	—	0	352
1979	Oak	16 (16, QB)	16	-4	-0.3 (13)	0	—	—	—	—	498	304	61.0	3615	7.3 (66)	26	22	34	284	82.2	—	0	1054
1980	†Hou	16 (16, QB)	15	-22	-1.5 (0)	0	—	—	—	—	457	293	**64.1**	3202	7.0 (79)	13	28	27	264	68.7	—	0	524
1981	Hou	13 (12, QB)	10	-3	-0.3 (4)	0	—	—	—	—	285	165	57.9	1988	7.0 (71)	14	18	29	254	69.5	—	0	341
1982	NO	8 (8, QB)	3	-4	-1.3 (0)	0	—	—	—	—	189	117	61.9	1343	7.1 (48)	6	10	13	106	71.8	—	0	298
1983	NO	14 (14, QB)	9	-14	-1.6 (0)	0	—	—	—	—	311	176	56.6	1988	6.4 (48)	9	18	18	159	61.4	—	0	305
1984	NO	3 (0)	1	-1	-1.0 (-1)	0	—	—	—	—	70	33	47.1	339	4.8 (29)	2	5	5	40	—	—	0	-22
NFL	15	184 (146)	118	93	0.8 (18)	4	—	—	—	—	3793	2270	59.8	27938	7.4 (88)	194	222	281	2514	75.3	—	24	6192

STACCO, ED   Edward Adam, T, 6´2˝/261 lbs; Colgate; 1946: Det, rnd 25; B4/16/1925 Carbondale, PA   **1947** Det 10 (0)   **1948** Was 4 (0)   **NFL** 14 (0) [2 yrs]

STACHELSKI, DAVE   Dave, TE, 6´3˝/250 lbs; Boise State; 2000: NE, rnd 5; B3/1/1977 Chicago, IL   **2000**†NO 4 (0)

| **2001** | NO | 5 (0) | — | — | — | — | 1 | 5 | 5.0 (5) | 0 | — | — | — | — | — | — | — | — | — | — | 0 | 3 |
| **NFL** | 2 | 9 (0) | — | — | — | — | 1 | 5 | 5.0 (5) | 0 | — | — | — | — | — | — | — | — | — | — | 0 | 3 |

STACHOWICZ, RAY   Raymond Mark, P, 5´11˝/185 lbs; Michigan State; 1981: GB, rnd 3; B3/6/1959 Cleveland, OH   **1981** GB 16 (0)   **1983** ChiB 2 (0)

| **1982** | †GB | 9 (0) | 2 | 0 | 0.0 (0) | 0 | — | — | — | — | — | — | — | — | — | — | — | — | P | — | 0 | 0 |
| **NFL** | 3 | 27 (0) | 2 | 0 | 0.0 (0) | 0 | — | — | — | — | — | — | — | — | — | — | — | — | P | — | 0 | 0 |

STACHOWSKI, RICH   Richard Charles, NT, 6´4˝/245 lbs; California; B3/29/1961 Los Angeles, CA   **1983**†Den 14 (0)

STACKHOUSE, CHARLES   Charles, FB, 6´2˝/250 lbs; Mississippi; B4/11/1980 West Memphis, AR

2002	†NYG	16 (2)	—	—	—	—	13	88	6.8 (18)	3	—	—	—	—	—	—	—	—	—	—	18	59
2003	Min	14 (2)	1	0	0.0 (0)	0	6	30	5.0 (10)	0	—	—	—	—	—	—	—	—	—	—	0	15
NFL	2	30 (4)	1	0	0.0	0	19	118	6.2 (18)	3	—	—	—	—	—	—	—	—	—	—	18	74

STACKPOOL, JACK   John Lawrence, FB, 6´1˝/207 lbs; Washington; 1942: Phi, rnd 10; B9/6/1917 Chicago, IL, D8/20/1976 Lincoln City, OR

| **1942** | Phi | 8 (4) | 15 | 47 | 3.1 (9) | 0 | 2 | 59 | 29.5 (39) | 0 | — | — | — | — | — | — | — | — | k | — | 0 | 75 |

STACY, BILLY   Billy McGovern, DB-FL, 6´1˝/191 lbs; Mississippi State; 1959: ChiC, rnd 1; B7/30/1936 Drew, MS [I]   **1959** ChiC 12 (DB)   **1960** SL 11 (lcb)   **1962** SL 13 (LCB)
1963 SL 9 (ls)

| **1961** | SL❖ | 13 (LCB/fl) | — | — | — | — | 12 | 241 | 20.1 (80) | 1 | — | — | — | — | — | — | — | — | kpi | — | 3 | 24 | 220 |
| **NFL** | 5 | 58 | — | — | — | — | 12 | 241 | 20.1 (80) | 1 | — | — | — | — | — | — | — | — | kpi | — | 6 | 42 | 729 |

STACY, RED   James William, T-G, 6´2˝/210 lbs; Oklahoma; B3/4/1912 Hollis, OK, D4/23/1998 Loomis, CA   **1935**†Det 12 (3)   **1936** Det 10 (5, rt)   **1937** Det 9 (0)   **NFL** 31 (8) [3 yrs]

STACY, SIRAN   Siran, RB, 5´11˝/203 lbs; Alabama; 1992: Phi, rnd 2; B8/6/1968 Geneva, AL   **1992**†Phi 16 (0)

STADNIK, JOHN   John Steven, C, 6´4˝/273 lbs; Western Illinois; B2/18/1959 Chicago, IL   **1987** SD 3 (3)

STAFF, SPIKE   Edgar Jonathan, G, 6´0˝/210 lbs; Brown; B3/13/1892 Brockton, MA, D2/14/1970 Providence, RI   **1925** Pro 1 (0)

STAFFORD, DICK   Richard Wade, DE, 6´4˝/255 lbs; Texas Tech; B8/21/1940 Matador, TX   **1962** Phi 7   **1963** Phi 4   **NFL** 11 [2 yrs]

STAFFORD, HARRY   Albert Harrison, HB, 5´11˝/205 lbs; Texas; B6/18/1912 Austin, TX, D11/23/2004 Edna, TX

| **1934** | NYG | 6 (3) | 4 | 4 | 1.0 | 0 | 4 | 70 | 17.5 | 0 | — | — | — | — | — | — | — | — | — | — | 0 | 39 |

STAGGERS, JON   Jonathan Leroy, WR, 5´10˝/185 lbs; Missouri; 1970: Pit, rnd 5; B12/14/1948 Richmond, VA [R]

1970	Pit	12	—	—	—	—	6	118	19.7 (31)	0	—	—	—	—	—	—	—	—	kp	—	6	192
1971	Pit	14	1	5	5.0 (5)	0	8	103	12.9 (20)	0	—	—	—	—	—	—	—	—	kp	—	6	285
1972	GB	11	1	-8	-8.0 (-8)	0	8	123	15.4 (48)	1	1	0	—	—	—	0	—	—	kp	1	12	267
1973	GB	14 (WR)	4	33	8.3 (20)	1	25	412	16.5 (50)	3	—	—	—	—	—	—	—	—	p	—	24	259
1974	GB	14 (WR)	—	—	—	—	32	450	14.1 (63)	0	—	—	—	—	—	—	—	—	p	—	0	347
1975	Det	5 (4)	2	26	13.0 (14)	0	14	174	12.4 (23)	2	—	—	—	—	—	—	—	—	—	—	12	123
NFL	6	70 (4)	8	56	7.0 (20)	1	93	1380	14.8 (63)	7	1	0	0.0	0	0.0	0	—	—	kp	3	66	1472

STAGGS, JEFF   Jeffrey Hugh, LB-DE, 6´1˝/240 lbs; Brigham Young; San Diego State; 1966: SD, rnd R3; B5/14/1944 Elgin, IL   **1967** SD-A 14 (LLB)   **1968** SD-A 12 (LLB)
1969 SD-A 13 (LLB)   **1970** SD 14 (LLB)   **1971** SD 5   **1972** SL 8 (rlb)   **1973** SL 13   **1974** SD 3 (1)   **NFL** 82 (1) [8 yrs]

STAHL, JAKE Edward Adam, G-T, 5´11˝/185 lbs; Pittsburgh; B1/16/1891 Scranton, PA, D10/8/1966 Pittsburgh, PA **1920** Cle 3 (0) **1921** Day 1 (1) **1921** Cle 1 (1) **NFL** 5 (2) [2 yrs]

STAHLMAN, DICK Richard Frederick, T-G, 6´2˝/219 lbs; DePaul; Northwestern; B10/20/1902 Chicago, IL, D5/11/1970 Chicago, IL **1924** KC 1 (1) **1924** Ham 1 (1) **1924** Ken 5 (5, RG) **1924** Akr 2 (1) **1925** Akr☆8 (8, RT) **1927** NYG 10 (10, lt) **1930** NYG 7 (2) **1931** GB☆14 (10, LT) **1932** GB 13 (10, RT) **1933**†ChiB 8 (2) **NFL** 69 (50) [7 yrs]

STAI, BRENDAN Brenden Michael, G, 6´4˝/305 lbs; Nebraska; 1995: Pit, rnd 3; B3/30/1972 Phoenix, AZ **1995**†Pit 16 (9, rg) **1996**†Pit 9 (9, RG) **1997**†Pit 11 (9, RG) **1998** Pit 16 (16, RG) **1999** Pit 16 (16, RG) **2000** Jax 16 (16, RG) **2001** Det 16 (16, RG) **2002** Was 5 (5, rg) **NFL** 105 (96) [8 yrs]

STALCUP, JERRY Gerald Newell, LB, 6´1˝/240 lbs; Wisconsin; 1960: LA, rnd 6/Oak, rnd 1; B11/19/1938 Rockford, IL **1960** LARm 12 **1961** Den-A 8 (RLB) **1962** Den-A 14 (llb) NFL 34 [3 yrs]

STALEY, BILL William Patrick, DT, 6´3˝/250 lbs; Utah State; 1968: Cin, rnd 2; B9/9/1946 Walnut Creek, CA **1968** Cin-A 12 (RDT) **1969** Cin-A 11 (RDT) **1970** ChiB 11 (RDT) **1971** ChiB 11 (RDT) **1972** ChiB 4 **NFL** 49 [5 yrs]

STALEY, DUCE Duce, RB, 5´11˝/220 lbs; South Carolina; 1997: Phi, rnd 3; B2/27/1975 Tampa, FL

YEAR	TEAM	G(GS, POS)	RUSH	YD	AVG(LG)	TD	REC	YD	AVG(LG)	TD	PASS	COMP	PCT	YD	AVG(LG)	TD	INT	SK	YD	QBR	KPR	OTD	PTS	TAY
1997	Phi	16(0)	7	29	4.1(12)	0	2	22	11.0(22)	0	—	—	—	—	—	—	—	—	—	—	k	—	0	474
1998	Phi	16(13, RB)	258	1065	4.1(64)	5	57	432	7.6(33)	1	—	—	—	—	—	—	—	—	—	—	k	—	36	1340
1999	Phi	16(16, RB)	325	1273	3.9(29)	4	41	294	7.2(19)	2	0	0	0.0	0	0.0	0	0	1	8	—	—	—	36	1470
2000	Phi	5(5, rb)	79	344	4.4(60)	1	25	201	8.0(26)	0	—	—	—	—	—	—	—	—	—	—	—	—	6	455
2001	†Phi	13(10, RB)	166	604	3.6(44)	2	63	626	9.9(46)	2	—	—	—	—	—	—	—	—	—	—	—	—	24	947
2002	†Phi	16(16, RB)	269	1029	3.8(57)	5	51	541	10.6(45)	3	—	—	—	—	—	—	—	—	—	—	—	—	50	1365
2003	†Phi	16(4)	96	463	4.8(22)	5	36	382	10.6(52)	2	—	—	—	—	—	—	—	—	—	—	—	—	42	714
2004	†Pit	10(10, rb)	192	830	4.3(38)	1	6	55	9.2(21)	0	—	—	—	—	—	—	—	—	—	—	—	—	6	868
2005	†Pit	5(1)	38	148	3.9(17)	1	6	34	5.7(9)	0	—	—	—	—	—	—	—	—	—	—	—	—	6	175
NFL	9	113(75)	1430	5785	4.0(64)	24	287	2587	9.0(52)	10	0	0	0.0	0	0.0	0	0	1	8	—	k	—	206	7807

STALLINGS, DENNIS Dennis Dawon, LB, 6´0˝/240 lbs; Illinois; 1997: Ten, rnd 6; B5/25/1974 East St. Louis, IL **1997** Ten 13 (0) **1998** Ten 15 (0) **NFL** 28 (0) [2 yrs]

STALLINGS, DON Alva Donald, DT-DE-T, 6´4˝/250 lbs; North Carolina; 1960: Was, rnd 5/NYT, rnd 1; B11/18/1938 Rocky Mount, NC **1960** Was 9

STALLINGS, LARRY Larry Joseph, LB, 6´1˝/230 lbs; Georgia Tech; 1963: SL, rnd 18/Buf, rnd 9; B12/11/1941 Evansville, TN **1963** SL 14 (LLB) **1964** SL 8 (LLB) **1965** SL 7 (LLB) **1966** SL 14 (LLB) **1967** SL 14 (LLB) **1968** SL 14 (LLB) **1969** SL 14 (LLB) **1970** SL★14 (LLB) **1971** SL 14 (LLB) **1972** SL 13 (LLB) **1973** SL 14 (LLB) **1974**†SL 14 (14, LLB) **1975**†SL 13 (13, LLB) **1976** SL 14 (LLB) **NFL** 181 (27) [14 yrs]

STALLINGS, RAMONDO Ramondo Antonio, DE, 6´7˝/286 lbs; San Diego State; 1994: Cin, rnd 7; B11/21/1971 Winston-Salem, NC **1994** Cin 6 (0) **1995** Cin 13 (2) **1996** Cin 12 (3) **1997** Cin 6 (0) **NFL** 37 (5) [4 yrs]

STALLINGS, ROBERT Robert Raymond, TE, 6´6˝/250 lbs; Southern Mississippi; B1/23/1964 McComb, MS **1986** SL 3 (0)

STALLS, DAVE David Milton, DE-DT-NT, 6´5˝/250 lbs; Northern Colorado; 1977: Dal, rnd 7; B9/19/1955 Madison, WI **1977**†Dal 11 **1978**†Dal 16 **1979**†Dal 16 (12, LDT) **1980** TB 15 (3) **1981**†TB 16 (7, lde) **1982**†TB 9 (9, LDE) **1983** TB 6 (0) **1983**†LARd 6 (0) **1985** LARd 4 (0) **NFL** 99 (31) [8 yrs]

STALLWORTH, DONTE Donte Lamar, WR, 6´0˝/197 lbs; Tennessee; 2002: NO, rnd 1; B11/10/1980 Sacramento, CA

YEAR	TEAM	G(GS, POS)	RUSH	YD	AVG(LG)	TD	REC	YD	AVG(LG)	TD	PASS	COMP	PCT	YD	AVG(LG)	TD	INT	SK	YD	QBR	KPR	OTD	PTS	TAY
2002	NO	13(7, wr)	2	2	1.0(4)	0	42	594	14.1(57)	8	—	—	—	—	—	—	—	—	—	—	—	—	48	339
2003	NO	11(3)	1	3	3.0(3)	0	25	485	19.4(76)	3	—	—	—	—	—	—	—	—	—	—	kp	—	18	331
2004	NO	16(10, WR)	6	37	6.2(26)	0	58	767	13.2(45)	5	—	—	—	—	—	—	—	—	—	—	p	—	30	422
2005	NO	16(13, WR)	2	2	1.0(3)	0	70	945	13.5(43)	7	—	—	—	—	—	—	—	—	—	—	p	—	42	527
NFL	4	56(33)	11	44	4.0(26)	0	195	2791	14.3(76)	23	—	—	—	—	—	—	—	—	—	—	kp	—	138	1618

STALLWORTH, JOHN Johnny Lee, WR, 6´2˝/191 lbs; Alabama A&M; 1974: Pit, rnd 4; B7/15/1952 Tuscaloosa, AL; HOF 2002

YEAR	TEAM	G(GS, POS)	RUSH	YD	AVG(LG)	TD	REC	YD	AVG(LG)	TD	PASS	COMP	PCT	YD	AVG(LG)	TD	INT	SK	YD	QBR	KPR	OTD	PTS	TAY
1974	†Pit	13(2)	1	-9	-9.0(-9)	0	16	269	16.8(56)	1	—	—	—	—	—	—	—	—	—	—	—	—	6	131
1975	†Pit	11(9, wr)	—	—	—	—	20	423	21.1(59)	4	—	—	—	—	—	—	—	—	—	—	—	—	24	232
1976	†Pit	8(3)	0	47	(47)	1	9	111	12.3(25)	2	—	—	—	—	—	—	—	—	—	—	—	—	18	123
1977	†Pit	14(14, WR)	6	47	7.8(15)	0	44	784	17.8(49)	7	—	—	—	—	—	—	—	—	—	—	—	—	42	474
1978	†Pit	16(16, WR)	—	—	—	—	41	798	19.5(70)	9	—	—	—	—	—	—	—	—	—	—	—	—	54	444
1979	†Pit★	16(16, WR)	—	—	—	—	70	1183	16.9(65)	8	—	—	—	—	—	—	—	—	—	—	—	—	48	632
1980	Pit	3(2)	—	—	—	—	9	197	21.9(50)	1	—	—	—	—	—	—	—	—	—	—	—	—	6	104
1981	Pit	16(16, WR)	1	17	17.0(17)	0	63	1098	17.4(55)	5	—	—	—	—	—	—	—	—	—	—	—	—	30	591
1982	†Pit✧	9(9, WR)	1	9	9.0(9)	0	27	441	16.3(74)	7	—	—	—	—	—	—	—	—	—	—	—	—	42	265
1983	†Pit✧	4(4, WR)	—	—	—	—	8	100	12.5(20)	0	—	—	—	—	—	—	—	—	—	—	—	—	0	50
1984	†Pit★	16(16, WR)	—	—	—	—	80	**1395**	17.4(51)	11	—	—	—	—	—	—	—	—	—	—	—	—	66	753
1985	Pit	16(16, WR)	—	—	—	—	75	937	12.5(41)	5	—	—	—	—	—	—	—	—	—	—	—	—	30	494
1986	Pit	11(9, WR)	—	—	—	—	34	466	13.7(40)	1	—	—	—	—	—	—	—	—	—	—	—	—	6	238
1987	Pit	12(11, WR)	—	—	—	—	41	521	12.7(45)	2	—	—	—	—	—	—	—	—	—	—	—	—	12	271
NFL	14	165(143)	9	111	12.3(47)	1	537	8723	16.2(74)	63	—	—	—	—	—	—	—	—	—	—	—	—	384	4798

STALLWORTH, RON Ronald Tobias, DE, 6´5˝/262 lbs; Auburn; 1989: NYJ, rnd 4; B2/25/1966 Pensacola, FL **1989** NYJ 16 (9, rde) **1990** NYJ 16 (16, LDE) **NFL** 32 (25) [2 yrs]

STALLWORTH, TIM Timothy James, WR, 5´10˝/185 lbs; Washington State; 1990: LARm, rnd 6; B8/26/1966 Pacoima, CA **1990** Den 1 (0)

STAMER, JOSH Josh, LB, 6´2˝/238 lbs; South Dakota; B10/11/1977 Sutherland, IA **2003** Buf 16 (0) **2004** Buf 16 (0) **2005** Buf 16 (0) **NFL** 48 (0) [3 yrs]

STAMPER, JOHN John, DE, 6´4˝/265 lbs; South Carolina; 2002: TB, rnd 6; B8/30/1978 Andrews, SC **2002** ChiB 4 (0)

STAMPS, SYLVESTER Sylvester, RB-WR, 5´7˝/172 lbs; Jackson State; B2/24/1961 Vicksburg, MS **[R]**

YEAR	TEAM	G(GS, POS)	RUSH	YD	AVG(LG)	TD	REC	YD	AVG(LG)	TD	PASS	COMP	PCT	YD	AVG(LG)	TD	INT	SK	YD	QBR	KPR	OTD	PTS	TAY
1984	Atl	10(0)	3	15	5.0(8)	0	4	48	12.0(31)	0	—	—	—	—	—	—	—	—	—	—	k	—	0	206
1985	Atl	2(0)	—	—	—	—	—	—	—	—	—	—	—	—	—	—	—	—	—	—	k	—	0	29
1986	Atl	14(0)	30	220	7.3(48)	0	20	221	11.1(39)	1	—	—	—	—	—	—	—	—	—	—	kp	—	6	493
1987	Atl☆	7(0)	1	6	6.0(6)	0	4	40	10.0(19)	0	—	—	—	—	—	—	—	—	—	—	k	1	6	336
1988	Atl	4(1)	3	0	0.0(3)	0	5	22	4.4(7)	0	—	—	—	—	—	—	—	—	—	—	k	—	0	50
1989	TB	10(0)	29	141	4.9(21)	1	15	82	5.5(21)	0	—	—	—	—	—	—	—	—	—	—	k	—	6	202
NFL	6	47(1)	66	382	5.8(48)	1	48	413	8.6(39)	1	—	—	—	—	—	—	—	—	—	—	kp	1	18	1316

STAMS, FRANK Frank Michael, LB, 6´2˝/240 lbs; Notre Dame; 1989: LARm, rnd 2; B7/17/1965 Akron, OH **1989**†LARm 16 (3) **1990** LARm 14 (13, RILB) **1991** LARm 5 (0) **1992** Cle 12 (0) **1993** Cle 14 (0) **1994**†Cle 16 (15, RLB) **1995** KC 1 (0) **1995** Cle 4 (0) **NFL** 82 (31) [7 yrs]

STANBACK, HARRY Harry David, DE, 6´5˝/255 lbs; North Carolina; 1981: Atl, rnd 6; B8/17/1958 Rockingham, NC **1982** Bal 2 (1)

STANBACK, HASKEL Haskel LaVon, RB, 6´0˝/210 lbs; Tennessee; 1974: Cin, rnd 5; B3/19/1952 Kannapolis, NC

YEAR	TEAM	G(GS, POS)	RUSH	YD	AVG(LG)	TD	REC	YD	AVG(LG)	TD	PASS	COMP	PCT	YD	AVG(LG)	TD	INT	SK	YD	QBR	KPR	OTD	PTS	TAY
1974	Atl	13	57	235	4.1(23)	1	8	39	4.9(18)	0	—	—	—	—	—	—	—	—	—	—	—	—	6	265
1975	Atl	14(RB)	105	440	4.2(26)	5	14	115	8.2(14)	0	1	1	100.0	41	41.0(41)	1	0	—	—	—	—	—	30	573
1976	Atl	14	95	324	3.4(30)	3	21	174	8.3(28)	1	—	—	—	—	—	—	—	—	—	—	k	—	24	449
1977	Atl	14(RB)	247	873	3.5(35)	6	30	261	8.7(36)	0	—	—	—	—	—	—	—	—	—	—	—	—	36	1064
1978	†Atl	15(RB)	188	588	3.1(26)	5	12	108	9.0(20)	0	—	—	—	—	—	—	—	—	—	—	—	—	30	692
1979	Atl	13	36	202	5.6(55)	5	13	89	6.8(22)	0	—	—	—	—	—	—	—	—	—	—	k	—	30	316
NFL	6	83	728	2662	3.7(55)	25	98	786	8.0(36)	1	1	1	100.0	41	41.0(41)	1	0	—	—	—	k	—	156	3358

STANCIEL, JEFF Jeffrey Richard, RB, 6´0˝/192 lbs; Mississippi Valley State; 1969: Atl, rnd 10; B5/4/1947 Moorhead, MS

YEAR	TEAM	G(GS, POS)	RUSH	YD	AVG(LG)	TD	REC	YD	AVG(LG)	TD	PASS	COMP	PCT	YD	AVG(LG)	TD	INT	SK	YD	QBR	KPR	OTD	PTS	TAY
1969	Atl	2	4	-1	-0.3(4)	0	—	—	—	—	—	—	—	—	—	—	—	—	—	—	k	—	0	-6

STANDLEE, NORM Norman S., FB-LB, 6´2˝/238 lbs; Stanford; 1941: ChiB, rnd 1; B7/19/1919 Downey, CA, D1/4/1981 Mountain View, CA

YEAR	TEAM	G(GS, POS)	RUSH	YD	AVG(LG)	TD	REC	YD	AVG(LG)	TD	PASS	COMP	PCT	YD	AVG(LG)	TD	INT	SK	YD	QBR	KPR	OTD	PTS	TAY
1946	SF-A☆	13(10, FB)	134	651	4.9	2	2	-5	-2.5	0	—	—	—	—	—	—	—	—	—	—	Pk	—	12	687
1947	SF-A☆	14(12, FB)	145	585	4.0	8	2	22	11.0	0	—	—	—	—	—	—	—	—	—	—	k	—	48	655
1948	SF-A	14(13, FB)	52	261	5.0(57)	3	1	1	1.0(1)	0	—	—	—	—	—	—	—	—	—	—	k	—	18	308
1949	†SF-A	12(8, FB)	44	237	5.4	4	—	—	—	—	—	—	—	—	—	—	—	—	—	—	P	—	24	277
AAFC	4	53(43)	375	1734	4.6(57)	17	5	18	3.6(1)	0	—	—	—	—	—	—	—	—	—	—	Pk	—	102	1926
1941	†ChiB★	10(3, fb)	81	414	5.1(46)	5	2	-3	-1.5(3)	0	—	—	—	—	—	—	—	—	—	—	Pki	—	30	486
1950	SF✧	11(RLB)	12	23	1.9(8)	1	—	—	—	—	—	—	—	—	—	—	—	—	—	—	k	—	6	35
1951	SF	11(LLB)	16	65	4.1(13)	0	—	—	—	—	—	—	—	—	—	—	—	—	—	—	—	—	0	65

YEAR	TEAM	G(GS, POS)	RUSH	YD	AVG(LG)	TD	REC	YD	AVG(LG)	TD	PASS	COMP	PCT	YD	AVG(LG)	TD	INT	SK	YD	QBR	KPR	OTD	PTS	TAY
1952	SF	1	2	8	4.0(9)	0	—	—	—	—	—	—	—	—	—	—	—	—	—	—	—	—	0	8
NFL	4	33(3)	111	510	4.6(57)	6	2	-3	-1.5(3)	0	—	—	—	—	—	—	—	—	—	—	Pki	—	36	594

Stanfel, Dick Richard Anthony, G, 6´3˝/236 lbs; San Francisco; 1951: Det, rnd 2; B7/20/1927 San Francisco, CA **[C]** **1952**†Det 12 (RG) **1953**†Det★12 (RG) **1954**†Det☆6 **1955** Det✧9 (RG) **1956** Was★11 (RG) **1957** Was★12 (RG) **1958** Was★11 (RG) **NFL** 73 [7 yrs]

Stanfill, Bill William Thomas, DE, 6´5˝/250 lbs; Georgia; 1969: Mia, rnd 1; B1/13/1947 Cairo, GA **1969** Mia-A✧13 (13, RDE) **1970**†Mia 14 (14, RDE) **1971**†Mia★13 (13, RDE) **1972**†Mia★14 (14, RDE) **1973**†Mia★14 (13, RDE) **1974**†Mia★14 (13, RDE) **1975** Mia 13 (8, RDE) **1976** Mia 14 (3) **NFL** 109 (91) [8 yrs]

Stankavage, Scott Leo Scott, QB, 6´1˝/194 lbs; North Carolina; B7/5/1962 Philadelphia, PA

YEAR	TEAM	G(GS, POS)	RUSH	YD	AVG(LG)	TD	REC	YD	AVG(LG)	TD	PASS	COMP	PCT	YD	AVG(LG)	TD	INT	SK	YD	QBR	KPR	OTD	PTS	TAY
1984	Den	1(0)	—	—	—	—	—	—	—	—	18	4	22.2	58	3.2(16)	0	1	1	13	—	—	—	0	-11
1987	Mia	3(0)	—	—	—	—	—	—	—	—	7	4	57.1	8	1.1(8)	0	1	—	—	—	—	—	0	-36
NFL	2	4(0)	—	—	—	—	—	—	—	—	25	8	32.0	66	2.6(16)	0	2	1	13	—	—	—	0	-47

Stanley, Basil Basil Laron, G, 5´9˝/195 lbs; Wabash; Notre Dame; Illinois; St. Mary's (CA); B2/8/1896 Montpelier, OH, D7/17/1975 San Francisco, CA **1924** RI 1 (0)

Stanley, C.B. Clair B., T, 6´4˝/225 lbs; Tulsa; 1944: ChiB, rnd 6; B1/25/1919 Holdenville, OK, D4/1977 Tulsa, OK **1946** Buf-A 13 (11, LT)

Stanley, Chad Benjamin Chadwick, P, 6´3˝/205 lbs; Stephen F. Austin State; B1/29/1976 Ore City, TX **[P]**

YEAR	TEAM	G(GS, POS)	RUSH	YD	AVG(LG)	TD	REC	YD	AVG(LG)	TD	PASS	COMP	PCT	YD	AVG(LG)	TD	INT	SK	YD	QBR	KPR	OTD	PTS	TAY
1999	SF	16(0)	1	0	0.0(0)	0	—	—	—	—	—	—	—	—	—	—	—	—	—	—	P	—	0	0
2000	SF	16(0)	—	—	—	—	—	—	—	—	—	—	—	—	—	—	—	—	—	—	P	—	0	0
2001	Arz	4(0)	—	—	—	—	—	—	—	—	—	—	—	—	—	—	—	—	—	—	P	—	0	0
2002	Hou	16(0)	1	6	6.0(6)	0	—	—	—	—	—	—	—	—	—	—	—	—	—	—	P	—	0	6
2003	Hou	16(0)	1	12	12.0(12)	0	—	—	—	—	—	—	—	—	—	—	—	—	—	—	P	—	0	12
2004	Hou	16(0)	1	5	5.0(5)	0	—	—	—	—	—	—	—	—	—	—	—	—	—	—	P	—	0	5
2005	Hou	16(0)	1	0	0.0(0)	0	—	—	—	—	—	—	—	—	—	—	—	—	—	—	P	—	0	0
NFL	7	100(0)	5	23	4.6(12)	0	—	—	—	—	—	—	—	—	—	—	—	—	—	—	P	—	0	23

Stanley, Israel Israel Damon, DT, 6´3˝/260 lbs; Arizona State; B4/21/1970 San Diego, CA **1995** NO 14 (0)

Stanley, Matt Matthew Charles, FB, 6´3˝/245 lbs; UCLA; B4/27/1979 Pasadena, CA **2004** SF 1 (0)

Stanley, Sylvester Sylvester Walter, NT, 6´2˝/286 lbs; Michigan; B5/14/1970 Youngstown, OH **1994** NE 7 (0)

Stanley, Walter Walter, WR, 5´9˝/180 lbs; Colorado; Mesa; 1985: GB, rnd 4; B11/5/1962 Chicago, IL **[R]**

YEAR	TEAM	G(GS, POS)	RUSH	YD	AVG(LG)	TD	REC	YD	AVG(LG)	TD	PASS	COMP	PCT	YD	AVG(LG)	TD	INT	SK	YD	QBR	KPR	OTD	PTS	TAY
1985	GB	13(0)	—	—	—	—	—	—	—	—	—	—	—	—	—	—	—	—	—	—	kp	—	0	186
1986	GB	16(4)	1	19	19.0(19)	0	35	723	**20.7**(**62**)	2	—	—	—	—	—	—	—	—	—	—	kp	1	18	691
1987	GB	12(12, WR)	4	38	9.5(24)	0	38	672	17.7(70)	3	—	—	—	—	—	—	—	—	—	—	kp	—	18	424
1988	GB	7(7, WR)	1	1	1.0(1)	0	28	436	15.6(56)	0	—	—	—	—	—	—	—	—	—	—	kp	—	0	220
1989	Det☆	14(12, WR)	—	—	—	—	24	304	12.7(37)	0	—	—	—	—	—	—	—	—	—	—	kp	—	0	428
1990	Was	9(1)	—	—	—	—	2	15	7.5(12)	0	—	—	—	—	—	—	—	—	—	—	kp	—	0	106
1992	SD	1(0)	—	—	—	—	—	—	—	—	—	—	—	—	—	—	—	—	—	—	—	—	—	—
1992	NE	13(0)	—	—	—	—	3	63	21.0(36)	0	—	—	—	—	—	—	—	—	—	—	kp	—	0	213
NFL	7	85(36)	6	58	9.7(24)	0	130	2213	17.0(70)	5	—	—	—	—	—	—	—	—	—	—	kp	1	36	2267

Stansauk, Don Donald J., DT-T, 6´1˝/255 lbs; Denver; 1950: Det, rnd 18; B4/2/1925 Los Angeles, CA, D1/27/2004 Malibu, CA **1950** GB 11 (LDT) **1951** GB 4 **NFL** 15 [2 yrs]

Stansbury, Ed Edmund Elisala, aka Ed Ieremia-Stansbury, RB, 6´0˝/257 lbs; UCLA; B5/3/1979 El Paso, TX **2002** Hou 1 (0)

Stanton, Bill William McKimmon, DE, 6´2˝/210 lbs; North Carolina State; 1948: Phi, rnd 27; B4/21/1924 Dillon, SC **1949** Buf-A 10 (0)

Stanton, Henry Henry R., E, 6´2˝/200 lbs; Arizona; 1942: Bkn, rnd 6; B8/24/1920, D3/11/1975 Phoenix, AZ **1947** NYY-A 9 (0)

YEAR	TEAM	G(GS, POS)	RUSH	YD	AVG(LG)	TD	REC	YD	AVG(LG)	TD	PASS	COMP	PCT	YD	AVG(LG)	TD	INT	SK	YD	QBR	KPR	OTD	PTS	TAY
1946	NYY-A	6(0)	—	—	—	—	2	25	12.5	0	—	—	—	—	—	—	—	—	—	—	—	—	0	13
AAFC	2	15(0)	—	—	—	—	2	25	12.5	0	—	—	—	—	—	—	—	—	—	—	—	—	0	13

Stanton, Jack John Edward, HB, 6´1˝/190 lbs; North Carolina State; B6/7/1938 Bridgeville, PA **1961** Pit 2

Starch, Ken Kenneth Earl, RB, 5´11˝/219 lbs; Wisconsin; B3/5/1954 Madison, WI **1976** GB 6

Stargell, Tony Tony L., DB, 5´11˝/190 lbs; Tennessee State; 1990: NYJ, rnd 3; B8/7/1966 La Grange, GA **1990** NYJ 16 (16, LCB) **1991**†NYJ 16 (7, lcb) **1992** Ind 13 (3) **1993** Ind 16 (1) **1994** TB 10 (2) **1995** TB 14 (6, cb) **1996** KC 8 (4) **1997** ChiB 1 (0) **NFL** 94 (39) [8 yrs]

Stark, Chad Chad William, RB, 6´1˝/220 lbs; North Dakota State; 1987: NYG, rnd 12; B4/4/1965 Decorah, IA **1987** Sea 2 (0)

Stark, Howard Howard Bailey, T, 6´0˝/210 lbs; Wisconsin; B12/20/1896, D3/13/1981 Nashotah, WI **1923** Rac 3 (3)

Stark, Rohn Rohn Taylor, P, 6´3˝/203 lbs; Florida State; 1982: Bal, rnd 2; B5/4/1959 Minneapolis, MN **[P]**

YEAR	TEAM	G(GS, POS)	RUSH	YD	AVG(LG)	TD	REC	YD	AVG(LG)	TD	PASS	COMP	PCT	YD	AVG(LG)	TD	INT	SK	YD	QBR	KPR	OTD	PTS	TAY
1982	Bal☆	9(0)	1	8	8.0(8)	0	—	—	—	—	1	0	0.0	0	0.0	0	0	—	—	—	P	—	0	8
1983	Bal☆	16(0)	1	8	8.0(8)	0	—	—	—	—	1	0	0.0	0	0.0	0	0	—	—	—	P	—	0	8
1984	Ind☆	16(0)	2	0	0.0(0)	0	—	—	—	—	1	0	0.0	0	0.0	0	1	—	—	—	P	—	0	-40
1985	Ind★	16(0)	—	—	—	—	—	—	—	—	1	0	0.0	0	0.0	0	0	—	—	—	P	—	0	0
1986	Ind★	16(0)	—	—	—	—	—	—	—	—	—	—	—	—	—	—	—	—	—	—	P	—	0	0
1987	†Ind	12(0)	—	—	—	—	—	—	—	—	—	—	—	—	—	—	—	—	—	—	P	—	0	0
1988	Ind	16(0)	—	—	—	—	—	—	—	—	—	—	—	—	—	—	—	—	—	—	P	—	0	0
1989	Ind	16(0)	1	-11	-11.0(-11)	0	—	—	—	—	—	—	—	—	—	—	—	—	—	—	P	—	0	-11
1990	Ind★	16(0)	—	—	—	—	—	—	—	—	1	1	100.0	40	40.0(40)	0	0	—	—	—	P	—	0	20
1991	Ind	16(0)	1	-13	-13.0(-13)	0	—	—	—	—	—	—	—	—	—	—	—	—	—	—	P	—	0	-13
1992	Ind★	16(0)	—	—	—	—	—	—	—	—	1	1	100.0	17	17.0(17)	0	0	—	—	—	P	—	0	9
1993	Ind	16(0)	1	11	11.0(11)	0	—	—	—	—	—	—	—	—	—	—	—	—	—	—	P	—	0	11
1994	Ind	16(0)	—	—	—	—	—	—	—	—	—	—	—	—	—	—	—	—	—	—	P	—	0	0
1995	†Pit	16(0)	—	—	—	—	—	—	—	—	—	—	—	—	—	—	—	—	—	—	P	—	0	0
1996	†Car	16(0)	—	—	—	—	—	—	—	—	—	—	—	—	—	—	—	—	—	—	P	—	0	0
1997	Sea	4(0)	—	—	—	—	—	—	—	—	—	—	—	—	—	—	—	—	—	—	P	—	0	0
NFL	16	233(0)	7	3	0.4(11)	0	—	—	—	—	6	2	33.3	57	9.5(40)	0	1	—	—	—	P	—	0	-9

Starke, George George Lawrence, T, 6´5˝/260 lbs; Columbia; 1971: Was, rnd 11; B7/18/1948 New York, NY **1973**†Was 14 (8, RT) **1974**†Was 14 (14, RT) **1975** Was 14 (14, RT) **1976**†Was 14 (14, RT) **1977** Was 14 (14, RT) **1978** Was 9 (9, RT) **1979** Was 16 (16, RT) **1980** Was 13 (13, RT) **1981** Was 14 (13, RT) **1982**†Was 9 (9, RT) **1983**†Was 16 (16, RT) **1984** Was 9 (7, rt) **NFL** 156 (147) [12 yrs]

Starkey, Jason Jason, C, 6´4˝/290 lbs; Marshall; B7/15/1977 Barboursville, WV **2000** Arz 2 (0) **2001** Arz 14 (1) **2003** Arz 4 (0)

YEAR	TEAM	G(GS, POS)	RUSH	YD	AVG(LG)	TD	REC	YD	AVG(LG)	TD	PASS	COMP	PCT	YD	AVG(LG)	TD	INT	SK	YD	QBR	KPR	OTD	PTS	TAY
2002	Arz	16(8, C)	—	—	—	—	1	7	7.0(7)	0	—	—	—	—	—	—	—	—	—	—	—	—	0	4
NFL	4	36(9)	—	—	—	—	1	7	7.0(7)	0	—	—	—	—	—	—	—	—	—	—	—	—	0	4

Starks, Duane Duane Lonell, DB, 5´10˝/170 lbs; Miami (FL); 1998: Bal, rnd 1; B5/23/1974 Miami, FL **[I]** **1998** Bal 16 (8, RCB) **1999** Bal 16 (6, rcb) **2000**†Bal 15 (15, LCB) **2001**†Bal 15 (15, LCB) **2002** Arz 10 (10, LCB) **2004** Arz 15 (8, lcb) **2005** NE 7 (6, rcb) **NFL** 94 (68) [7 yrs]

Starks, Marshall Marshall L., DB, 6´0˝/195 lbs; Illinois; 1961: SL, rnd 8; B3/6/1939 **1963** NYJ-A 14 (rcb) **1964** NYJ-A 4 **NFL** 18 [2 yrs]

Starks, Max Max W., T, 6´7˝/349 lbs; Florida; 2004: Pit, rnd 3; B1/10/1982 Orlando, FL **2004** Pit 10 (0) **2005**†Pit 16 (16, RT) **NFL** 26 (16) [2 yrs]

Starks, Randy Randolph, DT, 6´4˝/302 lbs; Maryland; 2004: Ten, rnd 3; B12/14/1983 Petersburg, VA **2004** Ten 14 (8, rdt) **2005** Ten 16 (16, LDT) **NFL** 30 (24) [2 yrs]

Starks, Scott Scott, DB, 5´8˝/172 lbs; Wisconsin; 2005: Jax, rnd 3; B6/27/1983 St. Louis, MO **2005**†Jax 16 (0)

Starks, Timothy Timothy Jerome, DB, 5´9˝/175 lbs; Kent State; B12/30/1963 Mobile, AL **1987** Min 1 (0)

Starling, Kendrick Kendrick, WR, 6´0˝/193 lbs; San Jose State; B12/27/1979 Marshall, TX **2004** Hou 8 (0)

Starnes, John John Greg, P, 6´3˝/185 lbs; North Texas; B12/25/1962 Corpus Christi, TX **1987** Atl 1 (0)

Staroba, Paul Paul Louis, WR, 6´3˝/204 lbs; Michigan; 1971: Cle, rnd 3; B1/20/1949 Flint, MI

YEAR	TEAM	G(GS, POS)	RUSH	YD	AVG(LG)	TD	REC	YD	AVG(LG)	TD	PASS	COMP	PCT	YD	AVG(LG)	TD	INT	SK	YD	QBR	KPR	OTD	PTS	TAY
1972	Cle	8	—	—	—	—	1	19	19.0(19)	1	—	—	—	—	—	—	—	—	—	—	—	—	6	15
1973	GB	2	1	11	11.0(11)	0	1	23	23.0(23)	0	—	—	—	—	—	—	—	—	—	—	P	—	0	23
NFL	2	10	1	11	11.0(11)	0	2	42	21.0(23)	1	—	—	—	—	—	—	—	—	—	—	P	—	6	37

STARR, BART Bryan Bartlett, QB, 6´1˝/197 lbs; Alabama; 1956: GB, rnd 17; B1/9/1934 Montgomery, AL; HOF 1977 **[C]**

YEAR	TEAM	G(GS, POS)	RUSH	YD	AVG(LG)	TD	REC	YD	AVG(LG)	TD	PASS	COMP	PCT	YD	AVG(LG)	TD	INT	SK	YD	QBR	KPR	OTD	PTS	TAY
1956	GB	9	5	35	7.0(14)	0	—	—	—	—	44	24	54.5	325	7.4(39)	2	3	—	—	—	—	—	0	88
1957	GB	12(QB)	31	98	3.2(16)	3	—	—	—	—	215	117	54.4	1489	6.9(77)	8	10	—	—	69.3	—	—	18	513
1958	GB	12(QB)	25	113	4.5(20)	1	—	—	—	—	157	78	49.7	875	5.6(55)	3	12	—	—	41.2	—	—	6	96
1959	GB	12(4, qb)	16	83	5.2(39)	0	—	—	—	—	134	70	52.2	972	7.3(44)	6	7	—	—	69.0	—	—	0	319
1960	†GB✧	12(QB)	7	12	1.7(13)	0	—	—	—	—	172	98	57.0	1358	7.9(**91**)	4	8	—	—	70.8	—	—	0	391
1961	†GB★	14(QB)	12	56	4.7(21)	1	—	—	—	—	295	172	58.3	2418	8.2(78)	16	16	—	—	80.3	—	—	6	715
1962	†GB★	14(QB)	21	72	3.4(18)	1	—	—	—	—	285	178	**62.5**	2438	8.6(83)	12	9	—	—	90.7	—	—	6	1001
1963	GB	13(QB)	13	116	8.9(20)	0	—	—	—	—	244	132	54.1	1855	7.6(53)	15	10	11	109	82.3	—	—	0	719
1964	GB☆	14(QB)	24	165	6.9(28)	3	—	—	—	—	272	163	59.9	2144	7.9(73)	15	4	42	323	**97.1**	—	—	18	1182
1965	†GB	14(QB)	18	169	9.4(38)	1	—	—	—	—	251	140	55.8	2055	8.2(77)	16	9	34	303	89.0	—	—	6	927
1966	†GB★	14(QB)	21	104	5.0(21)	2	—	—	—	—	251	156	**62.2**	2257	**9.0(83)**	14	3	26	183	**105.0**	—	—	12	1203
1967	†GB	14(QB)	21	90	4.3(23)	0	—	—	—	—	210	115	54.8	1823	**8.7(84)**	9	17	34	322	64.4	—	—	0	367
1968	GB	12(QB)	11	62	5.6(15)	1	—	—	—	—	171	109	**63.7**	1617	**9.5(63)**	15	8	29	261	**104.3**	—	—	6	636
1969	GB	12(QB)	7	60	8.6(18)	0	—	—	—	—	148	92	**62.2**	1161	7.8(51)	9	6	24	217	89.9	—	—	0	446
1970	GB	14(QB)	12	62	5.2(15)	1	—	—	—	—	255	140	54.9	1645	6.5(65)	8	13	29	252	63.9	—	—	6	415
1971	GB	4	3	11	3.7(9)	1	—	—	—	—	45	24	53.3	286	6.4(31)	0	3	6	64	—	—	—	6	44
NFL	16	196(4)	247	1308	5.3(39)	15	—	—	—	—	3149	1808	57.4	24718	7.8(91)	152	138	235	2034	80.5	—	—	90	9057

STARRET, BEN Benjamin L., BB-TB, 5´11˝/213 lbs; St. Mary's (CA); B11/19/1917 Santa Rosa, CA, D1/1982 Burnt Ranch, CA

YEAR	TEAM	G(GS, POS)	RUSH	YD	AVG(LG)	TD	REC	YD	AVG(LG)	TD	PASS	COMP	PCT	YD	AVG(LG)	TD	INT	SK	YD	QBR	KPR	OTD	PTS	TAY
1941	Pit	4(0)	7	9	1.3(15)	0	—	—	—	—	2	0	0.0	0	0.0	0	1	—	—	—	k	—	0	-19
1942	GB	5(2)	—	—	—	—	—	—	—	—	—	—	—	—	—	—	—	—	—	—	P	—	0	0
1943	GB	7(0)	1	1	1.0(1)	0	—	—	—	—	—	—	—	—	—	—	—	—	—	—	i	—	0	0
1944	GB	7(3)	10	21	2.1(8)	2	1	6	6.0(6)	0	—	—	—	—	—	—	—	—	—	—	Pk	—	12	42
1945	GB	8(0)	5	26	5.2(13)	0	—	—	—	—	—	—	—	—	—	—	—	—	—	—	ki	—	0	36
NFL	5	31(5)	23	57	2.5(15)	2	1	6	6.0(6)	0	2	0	0.0	0	0.0	0	1	—	—	—	Pki	—	12	59

STARRING, STEPHEN Stephen Dale, WR, 5´10˝/172 lbs; McNeese State; 1983: NE, rnd 3; B7/30/1961 Baton Rouge, LA **[R]**

YEAR	TEAM	G(GS, POS)	RUSH	YD	AVG(LG)	TD	REC	YD	AVG(LG)	TD	PASS	COMP	PCT	YD	AVG(LG)	TD	INT	SK	YD	QBR	KPR	OTD	PTS	TAY
1983	NE	15(3)	—	—	—	—	17	389	22.9(76)	2	—	—	—	—	—	—	—	—	—	—	—	—	12	205
1984	NE	16(16, WR)	2	-16	-8.0(0)	0	46	657	14.3(65)	4	—	—	—	—	—	—	—	—	—	—	p	—	24	356
1985	†NE	16(1)	—	—	—	—	16	235	14.7(40)	0	—	—	—	—	—	—	—	—	—	—	kp	—	0	400
1986	†NE	14(2)	1	0	0.0(0)	0	16	295	18.4(47)	2	—	—	—	—	—	—	—	—	—	—	kp	—	12	408
1987	NE	11(1)	2	13	6.5(10)	0	17	289	17.0(34)	3	—	—	—	—	—	—	—	—	—	—	kp	—	18	285
1988	Det	6(0)	—	—	—	—	5	89	17.8(40)	0	—	—	—	—	—	—	—	—	—	—	k	—	0	55
1988	TB	6(0)	—	—	—	—	3	75	25.0(53)	0	—	—	—	—	—	—	—	—	—	—	—	—	0	38
NFL	6	84(23)	5	-3	-0.6(10)	0	120	2029	16.9(76)	11	—	—	—	—	—	—	—	—	—	—	kp	—	66	1744

STASICA, LEO Leo Walter, B, 5´11˝/185 lbs; Illinois; Colorado; 1941: Bkn, rnd 3; B6/15/1916 Rockford, IL, D9/1982 Denver, CO

YEAR	TEAM	G(GS, POS)	RUSH	YD	AVG(LG)	TD	REC	YD	AVG(LG)	TD	PASS	COMP	PCT	YD	AVG(LG)	TD	INT	SK	YD	QBR	KPR	OTD	PTS	TAY
1941	Bkn	5(0)	3	17	5.7(5)	0	—	—	—	—	2	1	50.0	14	7.0(14)	0	0	—	—	—	kp	—	0	56
1943	†Was	6(0)	9	-10	-1.1(4)	0	—	—	—	—	6	1	16.7	34	5.7(34)	0	1	—	—	—	Ppi	—	0	-32
1944	Bos	7(0)	22	-16	-0.7(10)	0	—	—	—	—	47	21	44.7	225	4.8(42)	1	7	—	—	—	Pkpi	—	0	-124
NFL	3	18(0)	34	-9	-0.3(10)	0	—	—	—	—	55	23	41.8	273	5.0(42)	1	8	—	—	—	Pkpi	—	0	-100

STASICA, STAN Stanley Joseph, HB-DB, 5´10˝/175 lbs; South Carolina; Illinois; 1944: Cle, rnd 8; B6/24/1919 Rockford, IL **1946** Mia-A 1 (0)

STATEN, RALPH Ralph Lahquan, DB, 6´3˝/205 lbs; Alabama; 1997: Bal, rnd 7; B12/3/1974 Mobile, AL **1997** Bal 10 (3) **1998** Bal 15 (3) **NFL** 25 (6) [2 yrs]

STATEN, RANDY Randolph Wilbert, DE, 6´1˝/225 lbs; Minnesota; B1/24/1944 Charlotte, NC **1967** NYG 14

STATEN, ROBERT Robert, RB, 5´11˝/240 lbs; Jackson State; B11/23/1969 Shubata, MS **1996** TB 6 (0)

STATION, LARRY Larry Wilson, LB, 5´11˝/227 lbs; Iowa; 1986: Pit, rnd 11; B12/5/1963 Omaha, NE **1986** Pit 6 (0)

STATON, JIM James Brooks, DT, 6´4˝/246 lbs; Wake Forest; 1951: Was, rnd 2; B5/23/1927 Ansonville, NC, D9/16/1993 Greensboro, NC **1951** Was 8

STATUTO, ART Arthur John, C, 6´2˝/221 lbs; Notre Dame; 1948: Phi, rnd 31; B7/17/1925 Saugus, MA **1949**†Buf-A 12 (12, C)

YEAR	TEAM	G(GS, POS)	RUSH	YD	AVG(LG)	TD	REC	YD	AVG(LG)	TD	PASS	COMP	PCT	YD	AVG(LG)	TD	INT	SK	YD	QBR	KPR	OTD	PTS	TAY
1948	†Buf-A	14(8, C)	—	—	—	—	0	2	(2)	0	—	—	—	—	—	—	—	—	—	—	—	—	0	1
AAFC	2	26(20)	—	—	—	—	0	2	(2)	0	—	—	—	—	—	—	—	—	—	—	—	—	0	1

1950†LARm 12

STAUBACH, ROGER Roger Thomas 'Roger the Dodger', QB, 6´3˝/197 lbs; Navy; 1964: Dal, rnd 10/KC, rnd 16; B2/5/1942 Cincinnati, OH; HOF 1985

YEAR	TEAM	G(GS, POS)	RUSH	YD	AVG(LG)	TD	REC	YD	AVG(LG)	TD	PASS	COMP	PCT	YD	AVG(LG)	TD	INT	SK	YD	QBR	KPR	OTD	PTS	TAY
1969	†Dal	6	15	60	4.0(19)	1	—	—	—	—	47	23	48.9	421	9.0(75)	1	2	12	106	—	—	—	6	206
1970	†Dal	8(3)	27	221	8.2(25)	0	—	—	—	—	82	44	53.7	542	6.6(43)	2	8	19	130	—	—	—	0	182
1971	†Dal★	13(10, QB)	41	343	8.4(31)	2	—	—	—	—	211	126	59.7	1882	**8.9(85)**	15	4	23	175	**104.8**	—	—	12	1219
1972	†Dal	4	6	45	7.5(20)	0	—	—	—	—	20	9	45.0	98	4.9(21)	0	2	8	59	—	—	—	0	14
1973	†Dal	14(QB)	46	250	5.4(18)	3	—	—	—	—	286	179	**62.6**	2428	**8.5(53)**	**23**	15	43	269	**94.6**	—	—	18	1009
1974	Dal	14(QB)	47	320	6.8(29)	3	1	-13	-13.0(-13)	0	360	190	52.8	2552	7.1(58)	11	15	45	309	68.4	—	—	18	1075
1975	†Dal✧	13(QB)	55	316	5.7(17)	4	—	—	—	—	348	198	56.9	2666	**7.7(62)**	17	16	36	213	78.5	—	—	24	1134
1976	†Dal★	14(14, QB)	43	184	4.3(18)	3	—	—	—	—	369	208	56.4	2715	7.4(53)	14	11	29	215	79.9	—	—	18	1202
1977	†Dal★	14(QB)	51	171	3.4(33)	3	—	—	—	—	**361**	**210**	58.2	**2620**	**7.3(67)**	**18**	9	30	219	**87.0**	—	—	18	1241
1978	†Dal★	15(QB)	42	182	4.3(23)	1	—	—	—	—	413	231	55.9	3190	**7.7(91)**	**25**	16	32	219	**84.9**	—	—	6	1272
1979	†Dal★	16(16, QB)	37	172	4.6(20)	0	—	—	—	—	461	267	57.9	3586	**7.8(75)**	**27**	11	36	240	**92.3**	—	—	0	1660
NFL	11	131(43)	410	2264	5.5(33)	20	1	-13	-13.0(-13)	0	2958	1685	57.0	22700	7.7(91)	153	109	313	2154	83.4	—	—	120	10213

STAUCH, SCOTT Scott Roy, RB, 5´11˝/204 lbs; UCLA; B1/3/1959 Seattle, WA

YEAR	TEAM	G(GS, POS)	RUSH	YD	AVG(LG)	TD	REC	YD	AVG(LG)	TD	PASS	COMP	PCT	YD	AVG(LG)	TD	INT	SK	YD	QBR	KPR	OTD	PTS	TAY
1981	NO	10(0)	2	6	3.0(5)	0	1	7	7.0(7)	0	—	—	—	—	—	—	—	—	—	—	k	—	0	30

STAUROVSKY, JASON Jason Charles, K, 5´9˝/167 lbs; Tulsa; B3/23/1963 Tulsa, OK **[K]** **1987** SL 2 (0) **1988** NE 8 (0) **1989** NE 7 (0) **1990** NE 16 (0) **1991** NE 9 (0) **1992** NYJ 4 (0) **NFL** 46 (0) [6 yrs]

STAUTBERG, JERRY Gerald James, G-LB, 6´2˝/228 lbs; Cincinnati; B4/6/1929 Cincinnati, OH **1951** ChiB 3

STAUTNER, ERNIE Ernest Alfred, DT-DE-G, 6´1˝/230 lbs; Boston College; 1950: Pit, rnd 2/1949: SF-A, rnd S1; B4/20/1925 Prinzing-by-Cham, Germany, D2/16/2006 Carbondale, CO; HOF 1969 **1950** Pit 12 (LDT) **1951** Pit 12 (RDT) **1952** Pit★12 (RDT) **1953** Pit★11 (RDT) **1954** Pit☆12 (RDT) **1955** Pit★12 (RG) **1956** Pit★12 (RDT) **1957** Pit★12 (RDT) **1958** Pit★12 (RDE) **1959** Pit★12 (RDE/rdt) **1960** Pit★12 (LDT) **1961** Pit★14 (RDE) **1962** Pit 14 (RDE) **1963** Pit 14 **NFL** 173 [14 yrs]

STAUTZENBERGER, ODELL Weldon Odell, G, 6´0˝/218 lbs; Texas A&M; 1947: Bos, rnd 27; B10/23/1924 San Antonio, TX, D5/5/2002 Alexandria, LA **1949**†Buf-A 9 (6, lg)

STAYSNIAK, JOE Joseph Andrew, G, 6´4˝/292 lbs; Ohio State; 1990: SD, rnd 7; B12/8/1966 Elyria, OH **1991**†Buf 2 (0) **1992** KC 6 (0) **1993** Ind 14 (1) **1994** Ind 16 (16, RG) **1995**†Ind 16 (16, RG/lg) **1996** Arz 9 (0) **NFL** 63 (33) [6 yrs]

STEBER, JOHN John Warren, G-DG, 6´0˝/225 lbs; Georgia Tech; Vanderbilt; 1945: Was, rnd 7; B9/12/1923 Mobile, AL, D10/1975 **1946** Was 10 (8, RG) **1947** Was 12 (9, LG) **1948** Was 12 (8, LG) **1949** Was 9 (3) **1950** Was 12 (LG) **NFL** 55 (28) [5 yrs]

STECKER, AARON Aaron, RB, 5´10˝/205 lbs; Wisconsin; Western Illinois; B11/13/1975 Green Bay, WI **[R]**

YEAR	TEAM	G(GS, POS)	RUSH	YD	AVG(LG)	TD	REC	YD	AVG(LG)	TD	PASS	COMP	PCT	YD	AVG(LG)	TD	INT	SK	YD	QBR	KPR	OTD	PTS	TAY
2000	TB	10(0)	12	31	2.6(14)	0	1	15	15.0(15)	0	—	—	—	—	—	—	—	—	—	—	k	—	0	267
2001	†TB	13(0)	24	72	3.0(17)	1	10	101	10.1(35)	1	—	—	—	—	—	—	—	—	—	—	k	—	12	262
2002	†TB	16(1)	28	174	6.2(59)	0	13	69	5.3(12)	0	—	—	—	—	—	—	—	—	—	—	k	—	0	588
2003	TB	16(1)	37	125	3.4(15)	0	9	48	5.3(14)	1	—	—	—	—	—	—	—	—	—	—	k	—	6	299
2004	NO	16(3)	58	244	4.2(42)	2	29	174	6.0(26)	0	—	—	—	—	—	—	—	—	—	—	k	1	18	560
2005	NO	15(4)	95	363	3.8(32)	0	35	281	8.0(41)	0	—	—	—	—	—	—	—	—	—	—	k	—	0	711
NFL	6	86(9)	254	1009	4.0(59)	3	97	688	7.1(41)	2	—	—	—	—	—	—	—	—	—	—	k	1	36	2685

STEDMAN, TROY Troy M., LB, 6´3˝/243 lbs; Iowa Central; Washburn; 1988: KC, rnd 7; B4/19/1965 Cedar Falls, IA **1988** KC 5 (0)

STEED, JOEL Joel Edward, NT, 6´2˝/300 lbs; Colorado; 1992: Pit, rnd 3; B2/17/1969 Frankfurt, Germany **1992** Pit 11 (4) **1993**†Pit 14 (12, NT) **1994**†Pit 16 (16, NT) **1995**†Pit 12 (11, NT) **1996**†Pit 16 (14, NT) **1997**†Pit★16 (16, NT) **1998** Pit 16 (16, NT) **1999** Pit 14 (14, NT) **NFL** 115 (103) [8 yrs]

Steele, Ben Benjamin Joseph, TE, 6´5˝/250 lbs; Mesa; B5/27/1978 Denver, CO **2005** GB 2 (0)

YEAR	TEAM	G (GS, POS)	RUSH	YD	AVG (LG)	TD	REC	YD	AVG (LG)	TD	PASS	COMP	PCT	YD	AVG (LG)	TD	INT	SK	YD	QBR	KPR	OTD	PTS	TAY
2004	†GB	15(0)	—	—	—	—	4	42	10.5(27)	0	—	—	—	—	—	—	—	—	—	—	—	—	0	21
NFL	2	17(0)	—	—	—	—	4	42	10.5(27)	0	—	—	—	—	—	—	—	—	—	—	—	—	0	21

Steele, Chuck Charles Anson, C, 6´1˝/255 lbs; California; B6/22/1964 Los Angeles, CA **1987** Det 3 (1)

Steele, Cliff Clifford, BB-WB, 5´8˝/150 lbs; Syracuse; Fordham; B1898, deceased **[K]** **1921** Roc 1 (1) **1922** Roc 1 (1), 1 **1922** Akr 4 (2) **NFL** 6 (4) [2 yrs]

Steele, Ernie Ernest Raymond, HB-DB, 6´0˝/187 lbs; Washington; 1942: Pit, rnd 10; B11/2/1917 Bothell, WA **[KI]**

YEAR	TEAM	G (GS, POS)	RUSH	YD	AVG (LG)	TD	REC	YD	AVG (LG)	TD	PASS	COMP	PCT	YD	AVG (LG)	TD	INT	SK	YD	QBR	KPR	OTD	PTS	TAY
1942	Phi	10(1)	24	124	5.2(55)	0	7	114	16.3(36)	1	—	—	—	—	—	—	—	—	—	—	KPkpi	1	13	414
1943	P-P☆	10(1, lh)	85	409	4.8(47)	4	9	168	18.7(60)	2	1	0	0.0	0	0.0	0	1	—	—	—	kp	—	36	666
1944	Phi	9(2)	59	247	4.2(56)	5	1	22	22.0(22)	0	—	—	—	—	—	—	—	—	—	—	kpi	—	30	570
1945	Phi	7(1)	20	212	10.6(46)	2	3	42	14.0(31)	0	2	1	50.0	12	6.0(12)	0	1	—	—	—	kpi	—	12	268
1946	Phi	9(4)	31	108	3.5(43)	1	5	69	13.8(24)	0	—	—	—	—	—	—	—	—	—	—	kpi	—	6	244
1947	†Phi	12(5, lh)	26	138	5.3(49)	1	4	62	15.5(44)	0	—	—	—	—	—	—	—	—	—	—	kpi	—	6	367
1948	†Phi	12(2)	13	99	7.6(56)	1	2	43	21.5(32)	1	1	0	0.0	0	0.0	0	1	—	—	—	kpi	—	12	121
NFL	7	69(16)	258	1337	5.2(56)	14	31	520	16.8(60)	4	4	1	25.0	12	3.0(12)	0	3	—	—	—	KPkpi	1	115	2649

Steele, Glen James Lendale, DT, 6´4˝/300 lbs; Michigan; 1998: Cin, rnd 4; B10/4/1974 Ligonier, IN **1998** Cin 10 (0) **1999** Cin 16 (1) **2000** Cin 16 (1) **2001** Cin 16 (1) **2002** Cin 16 (7, ldt) **2003** Cin 16 (0) **NFL** 90 (10) [6 yrs]

Steele, Larry Lawrence Clinton, P, 5´10˝/182 lbs; Santa Rosa J.C.; B1/5/1950 Santa Rosa, CA **1974** Den 1

Steele, Markus Markus, LB, 6´3˝/240 lbs; USC; 2001: Dal, rnd 4; B7/24/1979 Cleveland, OH **2001** Dal 15 (10, LLB) **2002** Dal 13 (2) **2003**†Dal 14 (0) **NFL** 42 (12) [3 yrs]

Steele, Robert Robert Hugh, WR, 6´4˝/196 lbs; North Alabama; B8/2/1956 Columbus, GA **1978**†Dal 14

YEAR	TEAM	G (GS, POS)	RUSH	YD	AVG (LG)	TD	REC	YD	AVG (LG)	TD	PASS	COMP	PCT	YD	AVG (LG)	TD	INT	SK	YD	QBR	KPR	OTD	PTS	TAY
1979	Min	16	—	—	—	—	1	10	10.0(10)	0	—	—	—	—	—	—	—	—	—	—	k	—	0	-10
NFL	2	30	—	—	—	—	1	10	10.0(10)	0	—	—	—	—	—	—	—	—	—	—	—	—	0	5

Steele, Red Percy Davis, E, 6´0˝/176 lbs; Miami (OH); Harvard; B8/9/1897 McArthur, OH, D3/28/1974 Ojai, CA **1921** Can 8 (5, LE)

Steels, Anthony William Anthony, RB, 5´9˝/200 lbs; Nebraska; B1/8/1959 Sacramento, CA

YEAR	TEAM	G (GS, POS)	RUSH	YD	AVG (LG)	TD	REC	YD	AVG (LG)	TD	PASS	COMP	PCT	YD	AVG (LG)	TD	INT	SK	YD	QBR	KPR	OTD	PTS	TAY
1985	SD	6(0)	6	12	2.0(3)	0	—	—	—	—	—	—	—	—	—	—	—	—	—	—	kp	—	0	85
1985	Buf	9(0)	4	26	6.5(22)	0	2	9	4.5(6)	0	—	—	—	—	—	—	—	—	—	—	k	—	0	69
1987	SD	2(0)	1	3	3.0(3)	0	1	4	4.0(4)	0	—	—	—	—	—	—	—	—	—	—	—	—	0	5
NFL	2	17(0)	11	41	3.7(22)	0	3	13	4.3(6)	0	—	—	—	—	—	—	—	—	—	—	kp	—	0	159

Steen, Frank Frank William, E, 6´1˝/190 lbs; Rice; B10/5/1913 Longview, TX, D4/2/1998 Houston, TX **1939** GB 3 (1)

Steen, Jim James, T, 6´2˝/205 lbs; Syracuse; B3/28/1913 Brooklyn, NY, D11/23/1983 Detroit, MI **1935**†Det 9 (1) **1936** Det 11 (4) **NFL** 20 (5) [2 yrs]

Steere, Dick Edward Richard, G, 6´4˝/240 lbs; Drake; 1951: SF, rnd 5; B3/2/1927 Chicago, IL **1951** Phi 5

Steffen, Jim James William, DB, 6´0˝/195 lbs; Occidental; UCLA; 1959: Det, rnd 13; B5/1/1936 Orange, CA **1959** Det 8 **1960** Det 12 **1961** Det 8 **1961** Was 6 (RCB) **1962** Was 14 (RCB) **1963** Was 13 (LCB) **1964** Was 13 (LS) **1965** Was 14 (LS) **NFL** 88 [7 yrs]

Stefik, Bob Robert Mathias, E, 5´11˝/180 lbs; Niagara; B10/8/1923 Madison, WI **[K]** **1948**†Buf-A 1 (0)

Stegall, Milt Milt Eugene, WR, 6´0˝/184 lbs; Miami (OH); B1/25/1970 Cincinnati, OH

YEAR	TEAM	G (GS, POS)	RUSH	YD	AVG (LG)	TD	REC	YD	AVG (LG)	TD	PASS	COMP	PCT	YD	AVG (LG)	TD	INT	SK	YD	QBR	KPR	OTD	PTS	TAY
1992	Cin	16(0)	—	—	—	—	3	35	11.7(13)	1	—	—	—	—	—	—	—	—	—	—	k	—	6	78
1993	Cin	4(0)	—	—	—	—	1	8	8.0(8)	0	—	—	—	—	—	—	—	—	—	—	—	—	0	4
1994	Cin	1(0)	—	—	—	—	—	—	—	—	—	—	—	—	—	—	—	—	—	—	k	—	0	1
NFL	3	21(0)	—	—	—	—	4	43	10.8(13)	1	—	—	—	—	—	—	—	—	—	—	k	—	6	83

Stegent, Larry Larry Raymond, RB, 6´1˝/200 lbs; Texas A&M; 1970: SL, rnd 1; B12/1/1947 Houston, TX

YEAR	TEAM	G (GS, POS)	RUSH	YD	AVG (LG)	TD	REC	YD	AVG (LG)	TD	PASS	COMP	PCT	YD	AVG (LG)	TD	INT	SK	YD	QBR	KPR	OTD	PTS	TAY
1971	SL	7	—	—	—	—	1	12	12.0(12)	0	—	—	—	—	—	—	—	—	—	—	k	—	0	-9

Steger, Pete Peter, HB-WB-BB, none; B11/1896 Chicago, IL, deceased **1921** ChiC 6 (4, RH)

Stehouwer, Ron Ronald Dwayne, G, 6´2˝/230 lbs; Colorado State; 1960: LAC, rnd 1; B2/4/1937 Hopkins, MI **1960** Pit 12 **1961** Pit 14 **1962** Pit 14 **1963** Pit 14 **1964** Pit 14 (LG) **NFL** 68 [5 yrs]

Stein, Bill William Earl, C-G-T, 6´0˝/190 lbs; Macalester; Fordham; B5/28/1899 Two Harbors, MN, D8/27/1983 Two Harbors, MN **1923** Dul 6 (6, LG) **1924** Dul 6 (6, LT) **1925** Dul 3 (3, C) **1926** Dul 14 (11, C) **1927** Dul 3 (1) **1928** ChiC 2 (2) **1929** ChiC 5 (2) **NFL** 39 (31) [7 yrs]

Stein, Bob Robert Allen, LB, 6´3˝/235 lbs; Minnesota; 1969: KC, rnd 5; B1/22/1948 Minneapolis, MN **[K]** **1969**†KC-A 14 **1970** KC 14 **1971**†KC 14 **1972** KC 8 **1973**†LARm 13 **1974**†LARm 14 **1975** SD 3 **1975**†Min 9 **NFL** 89 [7 yrs]

Stein, Herb Herbert Alfred, C-G, 6´1˝/186 lbs; Pittsburgh; B3/27/1898 Warren, OH, D10/25/1980 Rocky River, OH **1921** Buf 1 (0) **1922** Tol☆8 (7, RG) **1924** Fra☆13 (13, C) **1925** Pot 12 (6, C) **1926** Pot☆10 (10, C) **1928** Pot 10 (10, C) **NFL** 54 (46) [6 yrs]

Stein, Russ Russell Frederick, T-E-C, 6´1˝/210 lbs; Washington & Jefferson; B4/21/1896 Warren, OH, D6/1/1970 Niles, OH **[K]** **1922** Tol 7 (6, LT), 5 **1924** Fra 12 (12, LT), 15 **1925** Pot☆10 (8, RT) **1926** Can 8 (7, RE) **NFL** 37 (33), 20 [4 yrs]

Stein, Sammy Samuel, E-T, 6´0˝/195 lbs; none; B4/1/1905 New York, NY, D3/30/1966 Las Vegas, NV **1929** SI 9 (7, LE), 6 **1930** SI 12 (11, LE), 6 **1931** NYG 8 (3) **1932** Bkn 2 (0) **NFL** 31 (21), 12 [4 yrs]

Steinbach, Eric Eric, G, 6´6˝/297 lbs; Iowa; 2003: Cin, rnd 2; B4/4/1980 New Lenox, IL **2003** Cin 15 (15, LG) **2004** Cin 16 (15, LG) **2005**†Cin 16 (16, LG) **NFL** 47 (46) [3 yrs]

Steinbach, Larry Lawrence Joseph, T-G, 6´0˝/214 lbs; St. Thomas; B12/23/1900 New Rockford, ND, D1/29/1967 Carrington, ND **1930** ChiB 11 (9, RT) **1931** ChiB 4 (3) **1931** ChiC 3 (2) **1932** ChiC 7 (1) **1933** ChiC 1 (0)

YEAR	TEAM	G (GS, POS)	RUSH	YD	AVG (LG)	TD	REC	YD	AVG (LG)	TD	PASS	COMP	PCT	YD	AVG (LG)	TD	INT	SK	YD	QBR	KPR	OTD	PTS	TAY
1933	Phi	3(0)	—	—	—	—	1	5	5.0(5)	0	—	—	—	—	—	—	—	—	—	—	—	—	0	3
NFL	4	29(15)	—	—	—	—	1	5	5.0(5)	0	—	—	—	—	—	—	—	—	—	—	—	—	0	3

Steinbrunner, Don Donald Thomas, T, 6´3˝/220 lbs; Washington State; 1953: Cle, rnd 6; B4/5/1932 Bellingham, WA, D7/20/1967 Kontum, Vietnam **1953**†Cle 8

Steiner, Rebel Rebel Roy, DB, 6´0˝/185 lbs; Alabama; 1949: GB, rnd 12; B8/27/1927 Birmingham, AL **1950** GB 12 (DB) **1951** GB 12 (DB) **NFL** 24 [2 yrs]

Steinfeld, Al Alan A., G-C-T, 6´5˝/256 lbs; C.W. Post; B10/28/1958 Brooklyn, NY **1982** KC 7 (0) **1983** Hou 8 (0) **1983** NYG 5 (0) **NFL** 20 (0) [2 yrs]

Steinfort, Fred Frederick W., K, 5´11˝/180 lbs; Boston College; 1976: Oak, rnd 5; B11/3/1952 Wetter, Germany **[K]** **1976** Oak 7 **1977** Atl 7 **1978** Atl 6 **1979**†Den 1 **1980** Den☆16 (0) **1981** Den 16 (0) **1983** Buf 2 (0) **1983** NE 9 (0) **NFL** 64 [7 yrs]

Steinke, Gil Gilbert Ervin, HB, 6´0˝/175 lbs; Texas A&M-Kingsville; B5/3/1919 Brenham, TX, D5/10/1995 San Antonio, TX

YEAR	TEAM	G (GS, POS)	RUSH	YD	AVG (LG)	TD	REC	YD	AVG (LG)	TD	PASS	COMP	PCT	YD	AVG (LG)	TD	INT	SK	YD	QBR	KPR	OTD	PTS	TAY
1945	Phi	7(1)	7	46	6.6(18)	1	2	12	6.0(9)	0	—	—	—	—	—	—	—	—	—	—	kp	—	6	82
1946	Phi	10(0)	38	154	4.1(40)	1	5	107	21.4(32)	2	—	—	—	—	—	—	—	—	—	—	kpi	1	24	403
1947	Phi	6(3)	16	50	3.1(15)	0	4	90	22.5(60)	1	—	—	—	—	—	—	—	—	—	—	kpi	—	6	138
1948	Phi	2(1)	5	17	3.4(8)	0	—	—	—	—	—	—	—	—	—	—	—	—	—	—	k	—	0	19
NFL	4	25(5)	66	267	4.0(40)	2	11	209	19.0(60)	3	—	—	—	—	—	—	—	—	—	—	kpi	1	36	642

Steinkemper, Bill William Jacob, T, 6´2˝/220 lbs; Notre Dame; B12/27/1913 Anna, OH, D11/26/1973 Franklin Park, IL **1943**†ChiB 10 (9, LT)

Steinkuhler, Dean Dean Elmer, T, 6´3˝/283 lbs; Nebraska; 1984: Hou, rnd 1; B1/27/1961 Burr, NE **1984** Hou 10 (10, RT) **1986** Hou 16 (16, RT) **1987**†Hou 11 (11, RT) **1988**†Hou 16 (16, RT) **1989**†Hou 16 (16, RT) **1990**†Hou 15 (7, rt) **1991**†Hou 16 (1) **NFL** 100 (77) [7 yrs]

Steinmetz, Ken Kenneth Clifton, FB-LB, 6´0˝/188 lbs; none; B8/7/1924 Providence, RI, D10/13/1995 Las Vegas, NV

YEAR	TEAM	G (GS, POS)	RUSH	YD	AVG (LG)	TD	REC	YD	AVG (LG)	TD	PASS	COMP	PCT	YD	AVG (LG)	TD	INT	SK	YD	QBR	KPR	OTD	PTS	TAY
1944	Bos	8(2)	11	24	2.2(8)	0	—	—	—	—	1	0	0.0	0	0.0	0	0	—	—	—	P	—	0	24
1945	Bos	10(0)	4	12	3.0(9)	0	—	—	—	—	—	—	—	—	—	—	—	—	—	—	Pi	—	0	7
NFL	2	18(2)	15	36	2.4(9)	0	—	—	—	—	1	0	0.0	0	0.0	0	0	—	—	—	Pi	—	0	31

Stemke, Kevin Kevin, LB, 6´3˝/240 lbs; Wisconsin; B11/23/1978 Green Bay, WI **2002** Oak 2 (0) **2004**†SL 6 (0) **NFL** 8 (0) [2 yrs]

Stemrick, Greg Gregory Earl, DB, 5´11˝/185 lbs; Colorado State; B10/25/1951 Cincinnati, OH **1975** Hou 11 **1977** Hou 9 **1978**†Hou 16 (16, RCB) **1979**†Hou 16 (16, RCB) **1980**†Hou★16 (16, RCB) **1981** Hou 16 (15, RCB) **1982** Hou 8 (8, RCB) **1983** NO 11 (0)

YEAR	TEAM	G (GS, POS)	RUSH	YD	AVG (LG)	TD	REC	YD	AVG (LG)	TD	PASS	COMP	PCT	YD	AVG (LG)	TD	INT	SK	YD	QBR	KPR	OTD	PTS	TAY
1976	Hou	14	—	—	—	—	1	10	10.0(10)	0	—	—	—	—	—	—	—	—	—	—	i	—	0	0
NFL	9	117(71)	—	—	—	—	1	10	10.0(10)	0	—	—	—	—	—	—	—	—	—	—	kpi	1	6	188

YEAR	TEAM	G(GS, POS)	RUSH	YD	AVG(LG)	TD	REC	YD	AVG(LG)	TD	PASS COMP	PCT	YD	AVG(LG)	TD	INT	SK	YD	QBR	KPR	OTD	PTS	TAY

STENERUD, JAN Jan, K, 6´2˝/187 lbs; Montana State; 1966: KC, rnd R3; B11/26/1942 Fetsund, Norway; HOF 1991 **[K]** **1967** KC-A☆14 **1968**†KC-A★14 **1969**†KC-A★14 **1970** KC★14 **1971**†KC★14 **1972** KC 14 **1973** KC★14 **1974** KC☆14 **1975** KC★14 **1977** KC 14 **1978** KC 16 **1979** KC 16 **1980** GB 4 (0) **1981** GB☆16 (0) **1982**†GB 9 (0) **1983** GB 16 (0) **1984** Min★16 (0) **1985** Min 16 (0)

| 1976 | KC☆ | 14 | 1 | 0 | 0.0(0) | 0 | — | — | — | — | — | — | — | — | — | — | — | — | — | KP | — | 90 | 0 |
| NFL | | 19 | 263 | 1 | 0 | 0 | — | — | — | — | — | — | — | — | — | — | — | — | — | KP | — | 1699 | 0 |

STENGER, BRIAN Brian Francis, LB, 6´4˝/241 lbs; Notre Dame; B1/16/1947 Euclid, OH **1969** Pit 14 **1970** Pit 7 **1971** Pit 14 **1972**†Pit 14 **1973** NE 10 (2) **NFL** 59 (2) [5 yrs]

STENN, PAUL Paul James, aka Paul Stenko Jr., T, 6´2˝/242 lbs; Villanova; B7/12/1918 Berwick, PA, D8/2/2003 Berwick, PA **1942** NYG 11 (0) **1946** Was 11 (9, RT) **1947**†Pit 11 (5, rt) **1948** ChiB 12 (3) **1950**†ChiB 12 (RT) **1951** ChiB 12 (RT)

| 1949 | ChiB | 11(5) | — | — | — | — | 2 | 11 | 5.5(11) | 0 | — | — | — | — | — | — | — | — | — | — | — | 0 | 6 |
| NFL | | 7 | 80(22) | — | — | — | 2 | 11 | 5.5(11) | 0 | — | — | — | — | — | — | — | — | — | k | — | 0 | 7 |

STENNETT, STUD Frederick F., B, 6´0˝/194 lbs; St. Mary's (CA); B2/8/1907 LeRoy, KS, D8/23/1989 Ventura, CA **1931** Por 10 (2)

| 1932 | ChiC | 2(1) | 7 | -3 | -0.4 | 0 | — | — | — | — | 3 | 1 | 33.3 | 11 | 3.7(11) | 0 | 0 | — | — | — | — | 0 | 3 |
| NFL | | 2 | 12(3) | 7 | -3 | -0.4 | 0 | — | — | — | — | 3 | 1 | 33.3 | 11 | 3.7(11) | 0 | 0 | — | — | — | — | 0 | 3 |

STENSRUD, MIKE Michael Iver, NT-DE-DT, 6´5˝/280 lbs; Iowa State; 1979: Hou, rnd 2; B2/19/1956 Forest City, IA **1979**†Hou 6 **1980**†Hou 16 (0) **1981** Hou 16 (1) **1982** Hou 9 (9, NT) **1983** Hou 16 (6, nt) **1984** Hou 16 (14, NT) **1985** Hou 16 (16, NT) **1986** Min 11 (4) **1987** TB 12 (12, NT) **1988** KC 13 (5, lde) **1989** Was 8 (0) **NFL** 139 (67) [11 yrs]

STENSTROM, STEVE Stephen Ryan, QB, 6´2˝/206 lbs; Stanford; 1995: KC, rnd 4; B12/23/1971 El Toro, CA

1996	ChiB	1(0)	—	—	—	—	—	—	—	—	4	3	75.0	37	9.3(28)	0	0	1	5	—	—	0	19
1997	ChiB	3(0)	1	6	6.0(6)	0	—	—	—	—	14	8	57.1	70	5.0(18)	0	2	2	19	—	—	0	-39
1998	ChiB	7(7, qb)	18	79	4.4(14)	2	—	—	—	—	196	112	57.1	1252	6.4(48)	4	6	19	137	70.4	—	—	12	505
1999	SF	6(3)	3	15	5.0(8)	0	1	9	9.0(9)	0	100	54	54.0	536	5.4(32)	0	4	10	66	52.8	—	—	0	128
NFL		17	7(10)	22	100	4.5(14)	2	1	9	9.0(9)	0	314	177	56.4	1895	6.0(48)	4	12	32	227	62.5	—	—	12	612

STEPANEK, JOE Joseph Paul, DT, 6´5˝/268 lbs; Minnesota; B11/6/1963 Tama, IA **1987** Min 1 (1)

STEPANOVICH, ALEX Alex, C, 6´4˝/300 lbs; Ohio State; 2004: Arz, rnd 4; B9/25/1981 Berea, OH **2004** Arz 16 (16, C) **2005** Arz 9 (9, c) **NFL** 25 (25) [2 yrs]

STEPHEN, SCOTT Scott Dewitt, LB, 6´2˝/237 lbs; Arizona State; 1987: GB, rnd 3; B6/18/1964 Los Angeles, CA **1987** GB 8 (0) **1988** GB 16 (0) **1989** GB 16 (2) **1990** GB 16 (16, LOLB) **1991** GB 16 (16, LOLB) **1992** LARm 16 (0) **NFL** 88 (34) [6 yrs]

STEPHENS, BILL William Alexander, C, 5´8˝/185 lbs; Brown; B7/28/1904 New York, NY, D7/25/1993 Claremont, CA **1926** Bkn 5 (4)

STEPHENS, BRUCE Bruce Anthony, WR, 5´9˝/170 lbs; Columbia; B10/31/1956 Columbus, GA **1978** NYJ 6

STEPHENS, CALVIN Calvin Herbert, G, 6´2˝/285 lbs; South Carolina; 1991: NE, rnd 3; B10/25/1967 Kings Mountain, NC **1992** NE 13 (1)

STEPHENS, DARNELL Darnell Jermain, LB, 6´0˝/248 lbs; Clemson; B12/9/1973 San Antonio, TX **1995** TB 12 (0) **1996** TB 1 (0) **NFL** 13 (0) [2 yrs]

STEPHENS, HAL Hal Franklin, DE, 6´4˝/252 lbs; East Carolina; 1984: LARm, rnd 5; B4/14/1961 Whiteville, NC **1985** Det 1 (0) **1985** KC 1 (0) **NFL** 2 (0) [1 yr]

STEPHENS, HAROLD Ernest Harold, QB, 5´11˝/175 lbs; Hardin-Simmons; B10/30/1938 Caps, TX

| 1962 | NYT-A | 6 | 6 | 33 | 5.5(14) | 0 | — | — | — | — | 22 | 15 | 68.2 | 123 | 5.6(26) | 0 | 0 | — | — | — | — | 0 | 95 |

STEPHENS, JAMAIN Jamain, T, 6´6˝/336 lbs; North Carolina A&T; 1996: Pit, rnd 1; B1/9/1974 Lumberton, NC **1997** Pit 7 (1) **1998** Pit 11 (10, RT) **1999** Cin 7 (2) **2000** Cin 5 (2) **2001** Cin 9 (2) **NFL** 39 (15) [5 yrs]

STEPHENS, JOHN John Milton, RB, 6´1˝/220 lbs; Northwestern State (LA); 1988: NE, rnd 1; B2/23/1966 Shreveport, LA

1988	NE★	16(14, RB)	297	1168	3.9(52)	4	14	98	7.0(17)	0	—	—	—	—	—	—	—	—	—	—	1	30	1257
1989	NE	14(12, RB)	244	833	3.4(35)	7	21	207	9.9(37)	0	—	—	—	—	—	—	—	—	—	—	42	1007
1990	NE	16(14, RB)	212	808	3.8(26)	2	28	196	7.0(43)	1	1	0	0.0	0	0.0	0	1	—	—	—	—	18	891
1991	NE	14(3)	63	163	2.6(13)	2	16	119	7.4(24)	0	—	—	—	—	—	—	—	—	—	—	12	243
1992	NE	16(16, FB)	75	277	3.7(19)	2	21	161	7.7(32)	0	—	—	—	—	—	—	—	—	—	—	12	378
1993	GB	5(5, rb)	48	173	3.6(22)	1	5	31	6.2(10)	0	—	—	—	—	—	—	—	—	—	—	6	199
1993	†KC	7(0)	6	18	3.0(7)	0	—	—	—	—	—	—	—	—	—	—	—	—	—	k	0	31
NFL		6	88(64)	945	3440	3.6(52)	18	105	812	7.7(43)	1	1	0	0.0	0	0.0	0	1	—	—	k	1	120	4004

STEPHENS, JOHNNY John Bailey, E, 6´1˝/190 lbs; Marshall; B1/15/1914 Parkersburg, WV, D9/10/1996 Bellaire, TX

| 1938 | Cle | 11(6, re) | — | — | — | — | 6 | 75 | 12.5 | — | — | — | — | — | — | — | — | — | — | — | — | 0 | 38 |

STEPHENS, LARRY Lawrence Clifton, DE-DT, 6´3˝/250 lbs; Texas; 1960: Cle, rnd 2/NYT, rnd 1; B9/24/1938 Buda, TX **1960** Cle 12 **1961** Cle 14 (rdt) **1962** LARm 14 **1963** Dal 14 (10, lde/rde) **1964** Dal 13 (RDE) **1965** Dal 13 **1966**†Dal 14 (6, lde) **1967**†Dal 9 **NFL** 103 (16) [8 yrs]

STEPHENS, LEONARD Leonard, TE, 6´3˝/249 lbs; Howard; B7/9/1978 Miami, FL

| 2002 | Was | 5(0) | — | — | — | — | 1 | 13 | 13.0(13) | 0 | — | — | — | — | — | — | — | — | — | — | — | 0 | 7 |

STEPHENS, MAC MacArthur, LB, 6´3˝/220 lbs; Minnesota; B1/21/1968 Akron, OH **1990** NYJ 4 (0) **1991** Min 3 (0) **NFL** 7 (0) [2 yrs]

STEPHENS, RAY Leslie Ray, C-G, 5´11˝/190 lbs; Idaho; B12/16/1902, D1944 **1927** NYY 10 (8, C)

STEPHENS, RED Louis Edward, G, 6´0˝/230 lbs; San Francisco; 1952: ChiC, rnd 23; B5/10/1930 Denver, CO, D3/13/2003 Placitas, NM **1955** Was☆11 (11, RG) **1956** Was☆11 (LG) **1957** Was 12 (LG) **1958** Was 12 (12, LG) **1959** Was 12 (12, RG) **1960** Was 12 (LG) **NFL** 70 (35) [6 yrs]

STEPHENS, REGGIE Reginald Dewayne, DB, 5´9˝/200 lbs; Rutgers; B2/21/1975 Dallas, TX **1999** NYG 1 (0) **2000**†NYG 15 (0) **2002** NYG 8 (0) **NFL** 24 (0) [3 yrs]

STEPHENS, RICHARD Michard Scott, G, 6´7˝/310 lbs; Tulsa; 1989: Cin, rnd 9; B1/1/1965 St. Louis, MO **1993**†LARd 16 (1) **1995** Oak 13 (1) **NFL** 29 (2) [2 yrs]

STEPHENS, ROD Rodrequis La'Vant, LB, 6´1˝/231 lbs; Georgia Tech; B6/14/1966 Atlanta, GA **1989** Sea 10 (0) **1990** Sea 4 (0) **1991** Sea 16 (0) **1992** Sea 16 (5, mlb) **1993** Sea 13 (13, MLB) **1994** Sea 16 (16, MLB) **1995** Was 16 (16, MLB) **1996** Was 16 (15, MLB) **NFL** 107 (65) [8 yrs]

STEPHENS, SANTO Santo Sean, LB, 6´4˝/244 lbs; Temple; B6/16/1969 Washington, DC **1993**†KC 16 (0) **1994** Cin 14 (3) **1995** Jax 13 (0) **NFL** 43 (3) [3 yrs]

STEPHENS, STEVE Stephen B., TE, 6´3˝/227 lbs; Oklahoma State; 1979: Bal, rnd 10; B3/4/1957 Tampa, FL **1981**†NYJ 16 (0)

STEPHENS, THOMAS Thomas Glenn, TE-DB, 6´2˝/215 lbs; Syracuse; 1959: Bal, rnd 11; B8/29/1935 Galveston, TX **1962** Bos-A 3 **1963** Bos-A 14 **1964** Bos-A 14

1960	Bos-A	9(TE)	—	—	—	—	22	320	14.5(53)	3	—	—	—	—	—	—	—	—	—	—	18	175
1961	Bos-A	9(TE)	—	—	—	—	19	186	9.8(31)	2	—	—	—	—	—	—	—	—	k	1	18	94
NFL		5	49	—	—	—	—	41	506	12.3(53)	5	—	—	—	—	—	—	—	—	kpi	1	36	333

STEPHENS, TRAVIS Travis Tremaine, RB, 5´8˝/194 lbs; Tennessee; 2002: TB, rnd 4; B6/26/1978 Clarksville, TN

| 2002 | TB | 1(0) | — | — | — | — | 1 | 6 | 6.0(6) | 0 | — | — | — | — | — | — | — | — | — | — | — | 0 | 3 |

STEPHENS, TREMAYNE Tremayne Raphael, RB, 5´11˝/206 lbs; North Carolina State; B4/16/1976 Greenville, SC

1998	SD	13(1)	35	122	3.5(12)	1	9	45(5)	0	—	—	—	—	—	—	—	—	—	k	—	6	246
1999	SD	11(2)	24	61	2.5(9)	3	18	133	7.4(22)	—	—	—	—	—	—	—	—	—	k	—	24	228
NFL		2	24(3)	59	183	3.1(12)	4	20	142	7.1(22)	1	—	—	—	—	—	—	—	—	k	—	30	473

STEPHENSON, DAVE James David, G-C-DG, 6´2˝/232 lbs; Tennessee; West Virginia; 1950: LA, rnd 15; B10/22/1925 Clendenin, WV, D7/19/1975 Charleston, WV **1950**†LARm 12 (rg) **1951** GB 12 **1952** GB 11 (RG) **1953** GB 12 (C/rg) **1954** GB 12 **1955** GB 2 **NFL** 61 [6 yrs]

STEPHENSON, DWIGHT Dwight Eugene, C-T, 6´2˝/255 lbs; Alabama; 1980: Mia, rnd 2; B11/20/1957 Murfreesboro, NC; HOF 1998 **1980** Mia 16 (0) **1981**†Mia 16 (5, c) **1982**†Mia 9 (9, C) **1983**†Mia★16 (16, C) **1984**†Mia★16 (16, C) **1985**†Mia★16 (16, C) **1986** Mia★16 (16, C) **1987** Mia★9 (9, C) **NFL** 114 (87) [8 yrs]

STEPHENSON, KAY George Kay, QB, 6´1˝/210 lbs; Florida; B12/17/1944 DeFuniak Springs, FL **[C]**

1967	SD-A	7	2	11	5.5(7)	0	—	—	—	—	26	11	42.3	117	4.5(21)	2	2	1	7	—	—	0	-1
1968	Buf-A	10	4	30	7.5(12)	0	—	—	—	—	79	29	36.7	364	4.6(55)	4	7	—	—	—	—	0	-48
NFL		2	17	6	41	6.8(12)	0	—	—	—	—	105	40	38.1	481	4.6(55)	6	9	1	7	—	—	0	-49

YEAR	TEAM	G(GS, POS)	RUSH	YD	AVG(LG)	TD	REC	YD	AVG(LG)	TD	PASS COMP	PCT	YD	AVG(LG)	TD	INT	SK	YD	QBR	KPR	OTD	PTS	TAY

STEPNOSKI, MARK Mark Matthew, C-G, 6′2″/269 lbs; Pittsburgh; 1989: Dal, rnd 3; B1/20/1967 Erie, PA **1989** Dal 16 (4) **1990** Dal 16 (16, C) **1991**†Dal 16 (16, C) **1992**†Dal★14 (14, C) **1993** Dal★13 (13, C) **1994**†Dal★16 (16, C) **1995** Hou✧16 (16, C) **1996** Hou★16 (16, C) **1997** Ten 16 (16, C) **1999**†Dal 15 (15, C) **2000** Dal 11 (11, C) **2001** Dal 16 (16, C)

YEAR	TEAM	G(GS, POS)	RUSH	YD	AVG(LG)	TD	REC	YD	AVG	TD							SK			KPR	OTD	PTS	TAY
1998	Ten	13(13, C)	1	0	0.0(0)	0	—	—	—	—											—	0	0
NFL		13	194(182)	1	0	0.0(0)	0													k	—	0	0

STEPONOVICH, MIKE Michael M., G, 5′9″/205 lbs; St. Mary's (CA); B11/22/1908 Lead, SD, D5/24/1974 Inglewood, CA **1933** Bos 1 (0)

STEPONOVICH, TONY Anthony Andrew, G-E, 5′11″/185 lbs; USC; B1/15/1907 Globe, AZ, D1/5/2000 Riverside, CA **1930** Min 9 (6, LG) **1930** Fra 3 (3) **NFL** 12 (9) [1 yr]

STEPTOE, JACK Jack Eugene, WR, 6′1″/173 lbs; Utah; B1/21/1956 Los Angeles, CA

| 1978 | SF | 6 | — | — | — | — | 2 | 46 | 23.0(35) | 1 | — | — | — | — | — | — | — | — | — | p | — | 6 | 102 |

STERLING, JOHN John Fitzgerald, RB, 6′2″/203 lbs; Central Oklahoma; B9/15/1964 Altus, OK

| 1987 | GB | 2(0) | 5 | 20 | 4.0(9) | 0 | — | — | — | — | — | — | — | — | — | — | — | — | — | k | — | 0 | 5 |

STERNAMAN, DUTCH Edward Carl, HB-QB-FB, 5′8″/176 lbs; Illinois; B2/9/1895 Chicago, IL, D2/1/1973 Chicago, IL **[K]** **1920** Dec 13 (8, LH) **1921** ChiS 11 (11, LH), 36 **1922** ChiB★11 (11, LH), 51 **1923** ChiB★11 (10, LH), 41 **1924** ChiB 11 (11, LH), 23 **1925** ChiB 17 (11, LH), 6 **1926** ChiB 14 (1), 11 **1927** ChiB 5 (4, QB) **NFL** 93 (67), 168 [8 yrs]

STERNAMAN, JOEY Joseph Theodore, QB-BB, 5′6″/152 lbs; Illinois; B2/1/1900 Springfield, IL, D3/10/1988 Oak Park, IL **[KC]** **1922** ChiB 12 (11, QB), 32 **1923** Dul 7 (7, BB), 17 **1923** ChiB★3 (3), 17 **1924** ChiB★11 (9, QB), 75 **1925** ChiB★17 (17, QB), 62 **1927** ChiB 14 (7), 16 **1928** ChiB 13 (11, QB), 30 **1929** ChiB 15 (12, QB), 8 **1930** ChiB 9 (2), 11 **NFL** 101 (79), 268 [8 yrs]

STERR, GIL Gilbert N., BB, 5′6″/150 lbs; Carroll (WI); B7/3/1900 Beaver Dam, WI, D3/12/1974 Beaver Dam, WI **1926** Rac 3 (2, BB)

STETZ, BILL William Alan, G, 6′3″/250 lbs; Boston College; 1967: NO, rnd 13; B9/28/1945 Milwaukee, WI **1967** Phi 2

STEUBER, BOB Robert James, HB, 6′2″/200 lbs; Missouri; Depauw; 1943: ChiB, rnd 1; B10/25/1921 Wenonah, NJ, D11/29/1996 St. Louis, MO **[K]**

1943	ChiB	1(0)	1	3	3.0(3)	0	—	—	—	—	—	—	—	—	—	—	—	—	—	—	—	0	3
1946	Cle-A	6(1)	8	19	2.4	0	1	9	9.0(9)	0	—	—	—	—	—	—	—	—	—	ki	—	0	94
1947	LAD-A	3(0)	1	2	2.0(2)	0	—	—	—	—	—	—	—	—	—	—	—	—	—	—	—	0	2
1948	Buf-A	9(7, RH)	69	437	6.3	3	2	14	7.0	0	2	1	50.0	4	-2.0(-4)	0	0	—	—	KPk	—	41	505
AAFC	3	18(8)	78	458	5.9(3)	3	3	23	7.7(9)	0	2	1	50.0	4	-2.0(-4)	0	0	—	—	KPki	—	41	601

STEUSSIE, TODD Todd Edward, T, 6′6″/308 lbs; California; 1994: Min, rnd 1; B12/1/1970 Canoga Park, CA **1994**†Min 16 (16, LT) **1995** Min 16 (16, LT) **1996**†Min 16 (16, LT) **1997**†Min★16 (16, LT) **1998**†Min★15 (15, LT) **1999** Min 16 (16, LT) **2000**†Min 16 (16, LT) **2001** Car 16 (16, LT) **2002** Car 16 (16, LT) **2003**†Car 16 (16, LT) **2004** TB 16 (5, rt) **2005**†TB 15 (0) **NFL** 190 (164) [12 yrs]

STEVENS, BILLY William S., QB, 6′2″/195 lbs; Texas-El Paso; 1968: GB, rnd 3; B8/27/1945 Galveston, TX

1968	GB	2	—	—	—	—	—	—	—	—	2	0	0.0	0	0.0	0	0	—	—	—	—	0	0
1969	GB	1	—	—	—	—	—	—	—	—	3	1	33.3	12	4.0(12)	0	0	—	—	—	—	0	6
NFL	2	3	—	—	—	—	—	—	—	—	5	1	20.0	12	2.4(12)	0	0	—	—	—	—	0	6

STEVENS, DICK Richard Glenn, T, 6′4″/240 lbs; Baylor; 1970: Phi, rnd 13; B2/23/1948 Dublin, TX **1970** Phi 14 **1971** Phi 14 **1972** Phi 7 **1973** Phi 11 **1974** Phi 14 **NFL** 60 [5 yrs]

STEVENS, DON Donald James, HB, 5′9″/176 lbs; Illinois; 1952: Phi, rnd 30; B5/25/1928 Massillon, OH, D9/10/2000 Philadelphia, PA **1954** Phi 4

| 1952 | Phi | 11 | 33 | 95 | 2.9(36) | 0 | 13 | 174 | 13.4(39) | 0 | — | — | — | — | — | — | — | — | — | kp | 1 | 6 | 477 |
| NFL | 2 | 15 | 33 | 95 | 2.9(36) | 0 | 13 | 174 | 13.4(39) | 0 | — | — | — | — | — | — | — | — | — | kp | 1 | 6 | 468 |

STEVENS, HOWARD Howard Melvin, RB, 5′5″/165 lbs; Randolph-Macon; Louisville; 1973: NO, rnd 16; B2/9/1950 Harrisonburg, WV **[R]**

1973	NO	14	45	183	4.1(15)	2	4	39	9.8(14)	0	—	—	—	—	—	—	—	—	—	kp	—	12	509
1974	NO	14	43	190	4.4(25)	1	13	81	6.2(20)	0	—	—	—	—	—	—	—	—	—	kp	—	6	686
1975	†Bal	12	—	—	—	—	—	—	—	—	—	—	—	—	—	—	—	—	—	kp	—	0	242
1976	†Bal	14	1	3	3.0(3)	1	—	—	—	—	—	—	—	—	—	—	—	—	—	kp	—	6	393
1977	Bal	12	—	—	—	—	—	—	—	—	—	—	—	—	—	—	—	—	—	kp	—	0	182
NFL	5	66	89	376	4.2(25)	4	17	120	7.1(20)	0	—	—	—	—	—	—	—	—	—	kp	—	24	2011

STEVENS, JERRAMY Jerramy, TE, 6′7″/260 lbs; Washington; 2002: Sea, rnd 1; B11/13/1979 Boise, ID

2002	Sea	12(1)	—	—	—	—	26	252	9.7(29)	3	—	—	—	—	—	—	—	—	—	—	—	18	141
2003	†Sea	16(2)	—	—	—	—	6	72	12.0(20)	0	—	—	—	—	—	—	—	—	—	—	—	0	36
2004	†Sea	16(5, te)	—	—	—	—	31	349	11.3(32)	3	—	—	—	—	—	—	—	—	—	k	—	20	187
2005	†Sea	16(12, TE)	—	—	—	—	45	554	12.3(35)	5	—	—	—	—	—	—	—	—	—	—	—	30	302
NFL	4	60(20)	—	—	—	—	108	1227	11.4(35)	11	—	—	—	—	—	—	—	—	—	k	—	68	666

STEVENS, LARRY Larry Ernest, LB, 6′2″/241 lbs; Michigan; B1/22/1982 Tacoma, WA **2004** Cin 9 (0) **2005** Cin 7 (0) **NFL** 16 (0) [2 yrs]

STEVENS, MARK Mark, QB, 6′1″/190 lbs; Purdue; Utah; B2/19/1962 Passaic, NJ

| 1987 | SF | 2(0) | 10 | 45 | 4.5(16) | 1 | — | — | — | — | 4 | 2 | 50.0 | 52 | 13.0(39) | 1 | 0 | — | — | — | — | 6 | 86 |

STEVENS, MATT Matthew Anthony, QB, 6′0″/190 lbs; UCLA; B7/30/1964 Sulphur, LA

| 1987 | KC | 3(2) | 3 | 7 | 2.3(6) | 0 | — | — | — | — | 57 | 32 | 56.1 | 315 | 5.5(23) | 1 | 1 | 6 | 53 | — | — | 0 | 130 |

STEVENS, MATT Matthew Brian, DB, 6′0″/205 lbs; Appalachian State; 1996: Buf, rnd 3; B6/14/1973 Chapel Hill, NC **1996**†Buf 13 (11, SS) **1997** Phi 11 (0) **1998** Phi 7 (1) **1998** Was 3 (0) **1999**†Was 15 (1) **2000** Was 15 (4) **2001** NE 15 (4) **2002** Hou 16 (FS) **2003** Hou 12 (5, fs) **NFL** 108 (42) [8 yrs]

STEVENS, PETE Peter Paul, C, 6′0″/215 lbs; Temple; B6/18/1909 Wilkes-Barre, PA, D5/5/1989 Melbourne, FL **1936** Phi 4 (2)

STEVENSON, ART Arthur, C, 6′0″/190 lbs; Fordham; B12/27/1897, D6/1986 Brooklyn, NY **1926** NYG 2 (1) **1928** Bkn 2 (0) **1928** NYY 1 (0) **NFL** 5 (1) [2 yrs]

STEVENSON, DOMINIQUE Antone Dominique, LB, 6′0″/235 lbs; Tennessee; 2002: Buf, rnd 7; B12/28/1977 Gaffney, SC **2002** Buf 4 (0) **2003** Buf 16 (0) **2004** Was 1 (0) **NFL** 21 (0) [3 yrs]

STEVENSON, MARK Martin Lindsey, G-C, /196 lbs; Notre Dame; B3/1893, D3/30/1961 Columbus, OH **1922** Col 8 (6, LG)

STEVENSON, MARK Mark Oliver, G-C, 6′3″/285 lbs; Missouri; Western Illinois; B2/24/1956 Waukegan, IL **1985** Det 2 (0)

STEVENSON, RALPH Ralph Lee, G-LB, 5′10″/196 lbs; Oklahoma; 1940: Cle, rnd 18; B4/11/1917 Ponca City, OK, D7/7/1987 Norman, OK **1940** Cle 3 (0)

STEVENSON, RICKY Ricky Anthony, DB, 5′11″/198 lbs; Arizona; 1970: Cle, rnd 4; B6/27/1948 St. Louis, MO **1970** Cle 1

STEVERSON, NORRIS Norris Joseph, TB, 5′10″/185 lbs; Arizona State; B7/20/1910 Mesa, AZ, D3/23/2004 Mesa, AZ

| 1934 | Cin | 5(3) | 8 | 22 | 2.8 | 0 | — | — | — | — | 3 | 1 | 33.3 | 14 | 4.7(14) | 0 | 0 | — | — | — | — | 0 | 29 |

STEWARD, DEAN Harold Dean, HB, 6′0″/210 lbs; Ursinus; B7/12/1923 Elizabeth, NJ, D8/9/1979 Budd Lake, NJ

| 1943 | P-P | 6(0) | 1 | -6 | -6.0(-6) | 0 | — | — | — | — | — | — | — | — | — | — | — | — | — | P | — | 0 | -6 |

STEWART, ANDREW Andrew, DE, 6′5″/265 lbs; Cincinnati; 1989: Cle, rnd 4; B11/20/1965 Queens, NY **1989**†Cle 16 (0)

STEWART, CHARLIE Charlie, G, 5′9″/160 lbs; Cornell; Colgate; B7/8/1890 Pittsfield, MA, D12/18/1965 North Grafton, MA **1920** Roc 2 (0) **1923** Akr 2 (1) **NFL** 4 (1) [2 yrs]

STEWART, CURTIS Curtis James, RB, 5′11″/208 lbs; Auburn; B6/4/1963 Montgomery, AL **1989** Dal 2 (0)

STEWART, DALEROY Daleroy Andrew, DT, 6′4″/327 lbs; Southern Mississippi; 2001: Dal, rnd 6; B11/2/1978 Vero Beach, FL **2003**†Dal 15 (1) **2004** Dal 1 (0) **2004** NYJ 1 (0) **2004** SF 9 (0) **NFL** 26 (1) [2 yrs]

STEWART, JAMES James Ottis, RB, 6′1″/224 lbs; Tennessee; 1995: Jax, rnd 1; B12/27/1971 Morristown, TN

1995	Jax	14(8, RB)	137	525	3.8(22)	2	21	190	9.0(38)	1	—	—	—	—	—	—	—	—	—	—	—	18	645
1996	†Jax	13(11, RB)	190	723	3.8(34)	8	30	177	5.9(21)	2	—	—	—	—	—	—	—	—	—	—	—	60	902
1997	Jax	16(5, rb)	136	555	4.1(33)	8	41	336	8.2(40)	1	—	—	—	—	—	—	—	—	—	—	—	54	808
1998	Jax	3(3)	53	217	4.1(44)	2	6	42	7.0(19)	1	—	—	—	—	—	—	—	—	—	—	—	18	263
1999	†Jax	14(7, RB)	249	931	3.7(34)	13	21	108	5.1(19)	0	—	—	—	—	—	—	—	—	—	—	—	78	1115
2000	Det	16(16, RB)	339	1184	3.5(38)	10	32	287	9.0(32)	1	—	—	—	—	—	—	—	—	—	—	—	72	1433
2001	Det	11(10, RB)	143	685	4.8(56)	1	23	242	10.5(56)	1	—	—	—	—	—	—	—	—	—	—	—	12	821

YEAR	TEAM	G (GS, POS)	RUSH	YD	AVG (LG)	TD	REC	YD	AVG (LG)	TD	PASS	COMP	PCT	YD	AVG (LG)	TD	INT	SK	YD	QBR	KPR	OTD	PTS	TAY
2002	Det	14 (9, RB)	231	1021	4.4 (30)	4	46	333	7.2 (52)	2	1	0	0.0	0	0.0	0	0	—	—	—	—	—	36	1238
NFL	8	101 (69)	1478	5841	4.0 (56)	48	220	1715	7.8 (56)	9	1	0	0.0	0	0.0	0	0	—	—	—	—	—	348	7224

STEWART, JAMES James, RB, 6´2˝/238 lbs; Miami (FL); 1995: Min, rnd 5; B12/8/1971 Vero Beach, FL

YEAR	TEAM	G (GS, POS)	RUSH	YD	AVG (LG)	TD	REC	YD	AVG (LG)	TD	PASS	COMP	PCT	YD	AVG (LG)	TD	INT	SK	YD	QBR	KPR	OTD	PTS	TAY
1995	Min	4 (0)	31	144	4.6 (51)	0	1	3	3.0 (3)	0	—	—	—	—	—	—	—	—	—	—	—	—	0	146

STEWART, JASON Jason, DT, 6´1˝/285 lbs; Fresno State; B11/14/1980 **2004**†Ind 0 (0)

STEWART, JIMMY James, DB, 5´11˝/190 lbs; Tulsa; 1977: NO, rnd 8; B10/15/1954 St. Louis, MO **1977** NO 9 (1) **1979** Det 5 **NFL** 14 (1) [2 yrs]

STEWART, JOE Joseph Lawrence, WR, 5´11˝/180 lbs; Missouri; 1978: Oak, rnd 4; B11/18/1955 Evanston, IL **1978** Oak 16

YEAR	TEAM	G (GS, POS)	RUSH	YD	AVG (LG)	TD	REC	YD	AVG (LG)	TD	PASS	COMP	PCT	YD	AVG (LG)	TD	INT	SK	YD	QBR	KPR	OTD	PTS	TAY
1979	Oak	3	—	—	—	—	1	3	3.0 (3)	0	—	—	—	—	—	—	—	—	—	—	k	—	0	35
NFL	2	19	—	—	—	—	1	3	3.0 (3)	0	—	—	—	—	—	—	—	—	—	—	k	—	0	95

STEWART, KORDELL Kordell 'Slash', QB, 6´1˝/218 lbs; Colorado; 1995: Pit, rnd 2; B10/16/1972 New Orleans, LA

YEAR	TEAM	G (GS, POS)	RUSH	YD	AVG (LG)	TD	REC	YD	AVG (LG)	TD	PASS	COMP	PCT	YD	AVG (LG)	TD	INT	SK	YD	QBR	KPR	OTD	PTS	TAY
1995	†Pit	10 (2)	15	86	5.7 (22)	1	14	235	16.8 (71)	1	7	5	71.4	60	8.6 (32)	1	0	1	0	—	—	—	12	254
1996	†Pit	16 (2)	39	171	4.4 (80)	5	17	293	17.2 (48)	3	30	11	36.7	100	3.3 (15)	0	2	3	37	—	—	—	48	353
1997	†Pit	16 (16, QB)	88	476	5.4 (74)	11	—	—	—	—	440	236	53.6	3020	6.9 (69)	21	**17**	20	152	75.2	—	—	66	1521
1998	Pit	16 (16, QB)	81	406	5.0 (56)	2	1	17	17.0 (17)	0	458	252	55.0	2560	5.6 (55)	11	18	33	211	62.9	P	—	12	1050
1999	Pit	16 (12, QB)	56	258	4.6 (21)	2	9	113	12.6 (28)	1	275	160	58.2	1464	5.3 (42)	6	10	22	131	64.9	—	—	18	702
2000	Pit	16 (11, QB)	78	436	5.6 (45)	7	—	—	—	—	289	151	52.2	1860	6.4 (45)	11	8	30	150	73.6	—	—	42	1171
2001	†Pit✧	16 (16, QB)	96	537	**5.6** (**48**)	5	—	—	—	—	442	266	60.2	3109	7.0 (90)	14	11	29	175	81.7	—	—	30	1772
2002	Pit	8 (5, qb)	43	191	4.4 (25)	2	—	—	—	—	166	109	65.7	1155	7.0 (64)	6	6	7	46	82.8	—	—	12	579
2003	ChiB	9 (7, QB)	59	290	4.9 (25)	3	—	—	—	—	251	126	50.2	1418	5.6 (61)	7	12	25	146	56.8	—	—	20	584
2004	Bal	2 (0)	1	-1	-1.0 (-1)	0	—	—	—	—	—	—	—	—	—	—	—	—	—	—	P	—	0	-1
2005	Bal	1 (0)	4	24	6.0 (13)	0	—	—	—	—	—	—	—	—	—	—	—	—	—	—	—	—	0	24
NFL	11	126 (87)	560	2874	5.1 (80)	38	41	658	16.0 (71)	5	2358	1316	55.8	14746	6.3 (90)	77	84	170	1048	70.7	P	—	260	8006

STEWART, MARK Mark Anthony, LB, 6´2˝/230 lbs; Washington; 1983: Min, rnd 5; B10/13/1959 Palo Alto, CA **1984** Min 4 (0)

STEWART, MATT Matt, LB, 6´3˝/232 lbs; Vanderbilt; 2001: Atl, rnd 4; B8/31/1979 Columbus, OH **2001** Atl 15 (0) **2002**†Atl 16 (13, ROLB) **2003** Atl 16 (16, ROLB) **2004**†Atl 16 (15, RLB) **2005** Cle 14 (12, LOLB) **NFL** 77 (56) [5 yrs]

STEWART, MICHAEL Michael Anthony, DB, 5´11˝/202 lbs; Fresno State; 1987: LARm, rnd 8; B7/12/1965 Atascadero, CA **1987** LARm 12 (4) **1988**†LARm 16 (10, SS) **1989**†LARm 16 (15, SS) **1990** LARm 16 (11, FS) **1991** LARm 16 (16, SS) **1992** LARm 11 (6, ss) **1993** LARm 16 (14, SS) **1994**†Mia 16 (16, SS) **1995**†Mia 16 (16, SS) **1996** Mia 9 (0) **NFL** 144 (108) [10 yrs]

STEWART, QUINCY Quincy Jermaine, LB, 6´1˝/234 lbs; Louisiana Tech; B3/27/1978 Tyler, TX **2001**†SF 16 (0) **2002**†SF 15 (0) **2003** NYJ 12 (0) **NFL** 43 (0) [3 yrs]

STEWART, RALPH Ralph Edward, C-LB, 6´0˝/205 lbs; Notre Dame; Missouri; 1947: NYG, rnd 26; B12/10/1925 St. Louis, MO **1947** NYY-A 9 (0) **1948** NYY-A 1 (0) **1948** Bal-A 14 (1) **AAFC** 24 (1) [2 yrs]

STEWART, RAYNA Rayna Cottrell, DB, 5´10˝/198 lbs; Northern Arizona; 1996: Hou, rnd 5; B6/18/1973 Oklahoma City, OK **1996** Hou 15 (0) **1997** Ten 16 (5, ss) **1998**†Mia 14 (0) **1999**†Jax 14 (0) **2000** Jax 12 (10, fs) **NFL** 71 (15) [5 yrs]

STEWART, RYAN Ryan Evan, DB, 6´1˝/207 lbs; Georgia Tech; 1996: Det, rnd 3; B9/30/1973 Moncks Corner, SC **1996** Det 14 (2) **1997**†Det 8 (0) **1998** Det 16 (0) **1999** Det 2 (0) **2000** Det 1 (0) **NFL** 41 (2) [5 yrs]

STEWART, STEVE Steven Andrew, LB, 6´2˝/217 lbs; Minnesota; 1978: Atl, rnd 2; B5/1/1956 Minneapolis, MN **1978**†Atl 12 **1979** GB 3 **NFL** 15 [2 yrs]

STEWART, TONY Tony Alexander, TE, 6´5˝/260 lbs; Penn State; 2001: Phi, rnd 5; B8/9/1979 Lohne, Germany

YEAR	TEAM	G (GS, POS)	RUSH	YD	AVG (LG)	TD	REC	YD	AVG (LG)	TD	PASS	COMP	PCT	YD	AVG (LG)	TD	INT	SK	YD	QBR	KPR	OTD	PTS	TAY
2001	Phi	3 (1)	—	—	—	—	5	52	10.4 (15)	1	—	—	—	—	—	—	—	—	—	—	—	—	6	31
2002	Cin	3 (0)	—	—	—	—	1	6	6.0 (6)	0	—	—	—	—	—	—	—	—	—	—	—	—	0	3
2003	Cin	16 (7, te)	—	—	—	—	21	212	10.1 (21)	0	—	—	—	—	—	—	—	—	—	—	k	—	0	104
2004	Cin	16 (9, TE)	—	—	—	—	10	48	4.8 (9)	1	—	—	—	—	—	—	—	—	—	—	k	—	6	4
2005	†Cin	14 (3)	—	—	—	—	4	26	6.5 (10)	0	—	—	—	—	—	—	—	—	—	—	—	—	0	13
NFL	5	52 (20)	—	—	—	—	41	344	8.4 (21)	2	—	—	—	—	—	—	—	—	—	—	k	—	12	155

STEWART, VAUGHN Vaughn Morton, C, 6´1˝/190 lbs; Alabama; B1/16/1919 Anniston, AL, D12/18/1992 Huntsville, AL **1943** Bkn 1 (0) **1943** ChiC 9 (8, C) **1944** Bkn 9 (2) **NFL** 19 (10) [2 yrs]

STEWART, WAYNE Wayne Murray, TE, 6´7˝/219 lbs; California; 1969: NYJ, rnd 15; B8/18/1947 Cochrane, Canada

YEAR	TEAM	G (GS, POS)	RUSH	YD	AVG (LG)	TD	REC	YD	AVG (LG)	TD	PASS	COMP	PCT	YD	AVG (LG)	TD	INT	SK	YD	QBR	KPR	OTD	PTS	TAY
1969	†NYJ-A	14	—	—	—	—	5	39	7.8 (9)	0	—	—	—	—	—	—	—	—	—	—	—	—	0	20
1970	NYJ	7	—	—	—	—	1	7	7.0 (7)	0	—	—	—	—	—	—	—	—	—	—	—	—	0	4
1971	NYJ	3	—	—	—	—	—	—	—	—	—	—	—	—	—	—	—	—	—	—	—	—	—	—
1972	NYJ	14	—	—	—	—	2	26	13.0 (22)	1	—	—	—	—	—	—	—	—	—	—	—	—	6	18
1974	SD	14 (13, TE)	—	—	—	—	19	283	14.9 (29)	1	—	—	—	—	—	—	—	—	—	—	k	—	6	133
NFL	5	52 (13)	—	—	—	—	27	355	13.1 (29)	2	—	—	—	—	—	—	—	—	—	—	k	—	12	174

STICKEL, WALT Walter Eugene, T-DT, 6´3˝/247 lbs; Tulsa; Pennsylvania; 1945: ChiB, rnd 21; B3/31/1922 Philadelphia, PA, D12/6/1987 Tequesta, FL **1946**†ChiB 11 (3) **1947** ChiB 12 (12, RT) **1948** ChiB 10 (9, RT) **1949** ChiB 12 (6, RT) **1950** Phi 12 (LDT) **1951** Phi 11 (LDT) **NFL** 68 (30) [6 yrs]

STICKLES, MONTY Montford Anthony, TE-SE, 6´4˝/235 lbs; Notre Dame; 1960: SF, rnd 1/LAC, rnd 1; B8/16/1938 Kingston, NY

YEAR	TEAM	G (GS, POS)	RUSH	YD	AVG (LG)	TD	REC	YD	AVG (LG)	TD	PASS	COMP	PCT	YD	AVG (LG)	TD	INT	SK	YD	QBR	KPR	OTD	PTS	TAY
1960	SF	12 (6, TE)	—	—	—	—	22	252	11.5 (28)	0	—	—	—	—	—	—	—	—	—	—	—	—	0	126
1961	SF	14 (12, TE)	—	—	—	—	43	794	18.5 (54)	5	—	—	—	—	—	—	—	—	—	—	—	—	30	422
1962	SF	14 (14, TE/se)	—	—	—	—	22	366	16.6 (48)	3	—	—	—	—	—	—	—	—	—	—	—	—	18	198
1963	SF	12 (8, TE)	—	—	—	—	11	152	13.8 (31)	0	—	—	—	—	—	—	—	—	—	—	k	—	0	61
1964	SF	14 (14, TE)	—	—	—	—	40	685	17.1 (53)	3	—	—	—	—	—	—	—	—	—	—	—	—	18	358
1965	SF	14 (14, TE)	—	—	—	—	35	343	9.8 (22)	1	—	—	—	—	—	—	—	—	—	—	—	—	6	177
1966	SF	14 (14, TE)	—	—	—	—	27	315	11.7 (38)	2	—	—	—	—	—	—	—	—	—	—	—	—	12	168
1967	SF	8 (8, TE)	—	—	—	—	7	86	12.3 (19)	0	—	—	—	—	—	—	—	—	—	—	—	—	0	43
1968	NO	13 (TE)	—	—	—	—	15	206	13.7 (35)	2	—	—	—	—	—	—	—	—	—	—	—	—	12	113
NFL	9	115 (90)	—	—	—	—	222	3199	14.4 (54)	16	—	—	—	—	—	—	—	—	—	—	k	—	96	1665

STIDHAM, HOWARD Howard, LB, 6´2˝/215 lbs; Tennessee Tech; 1976: SF, rnd 15; B12/17/1954 Radcliff, KY **1977** SF 4

STIEF, DAVE David P., WR-DB, 6´3˝/195 lbs; Portland State; 1978: SL, rnd 7; B1/29/1956 Portland, OR, D5/28/2000 Corbett, OR

YEAR	TEAM	G (GS, POS)	RUSH	YD	AVG (LG)	TD	REC	YD	AVG (LG)	TD	PASS	COMP	PCT	YD	AVG (LG)	TD	INT	SK	YD	QBR	KPR	OTD	PTS	TAY
1978	SL	15 (3)	1	-8	-8.0 (-8)	0	24	477	19.9 (55)	4	1	1	100.0	43	43.0 (43)	0	0	—	—	—	—	—	24	272
1979	SL	16 (4)	—	—	—	—	22	324	14.7 (32)	0	—	—	—	—	—	—	—	—	—	—	—	—	0	162
1980	SL	16 (2)	—	—	—	—	16	165	10.3 (23)	0	—	—	—	—	—	—	—	—	—	—	—	—	0	83
1981	SL	12 (0)	1	8	8.0 (8)	0	5	77	15.4 (29)	1	—	—	—	—	—	—	—	—	—	—	—	—	6	52
1982	†SL	9 (0)	—	—	—	—	—	—	—	—	—	—	—	—	—	—	—	—	—	—	—	—	—	—
1983	Was	3 (0)	—	—	—	—	—	—	—	—	—	—	—	—	—	—	—	—	—	—	—	—	—	—
NFL	6	71 (9)	2	0	0.0 (8)	0	67	1043	15.6 (55)	5	1	1	100.0	43	43.0 (43)	0	0	—	—	—	—	—	30	568

STIENKE, JIM James Lee, DB, 5´11˝/182 lbs; Southwest Texas State; 1973: Cle, rnd 2; B11/7/1950 Houston, TX **1973** Cle 7 **1974** NYG 13 **1975** NYG 14 (14, RCB) **1976** NYG 13 (RCB) **1977** NYG 14 (14, FS) **1978** Atl 5 **NFL** 66 (28) [6 yrs]

STIEVE, TERRY Terrence Allen, G, 6´2˝/256 lbs; Wisconsin; 1976: NO, rnd 6; B3/10/1954 Baraboo, WI **1976** NO 14 (6, lg) **1977** NO 14 (10, LG) **1978** SL 16 (13, RG) **1979** SL 14 (14, RG) **1981** SL 16 (16, LG) **1982** SL 9 (9, LG) **1983** SL 16 (16, LG) **1984** SL 14 (14, LG) **NFL** 113 (98) [8 yrs]

STIFLER, JIM James Madison, E-WB, 5´10˝/175 lbs; Brown; B8/25/1901 Swarthmore, PA, D7/17/1954 Boston, MA **1926** Pro 7 (3) **1927** Pro 2 (1) **NFL** 9 (4) [2 yrs]

STIGER, JIM James Edward, HB, 5´11˝/204 lbs; Washington; 1963: Dal, rnd 19; B1/7/1941 Carthio, TX, D12/14/1981 Lompoc, CA

YEAR	TEAM	G (GS, POS)	RUSH	YD	AVG (LG)	TD	REC	YD	AVG (LG)	TD	PASS	COMP	PCT	YD	AVG (LG)	TD	INT	SK	YD	QBR	KPR	OTD	PTS	TAY
1963	Dal	14 (hb)	31	140	4.5 (14)	1	13	131	10.1 (42)	0	—	—	—	—	—	—	—	—	—	—	kp	—	6	449
1964	Dal	14 (HB)	68	280	4.1 (64)	1	9	85	9.4 (31)	1	1	0	0.0	0	0.0	0	0	—	—	—	p	—	12	333
1965	Dal	5	11	50	4.5 (16)	0	1	9	9.0 (9)	0	—	—	—	—	—	—	—	—	—	—	kp	—	0	52
1965	LARm	6	3	12	4.0 (4)	0	—	—	—	—	—	—	—	—	—	—	—	—	—	—	p	—	0	53
1966	LARm	14	24	95	4.0 (19)	0	8	72	9.0 (18)	1	—	—	—	—	—	—	—	—	—	—	kp	—	6	275

YEAR	TEAM	G (GS, POS)	RUSH	YD	AVG (LG)	TD	REC	YD	AVG (LG)	TD	PASS	COMP	PCT	YD	AVG (LG)	TD	INT	SK	YD	QBR	KPR	OTD	PTS	TAY
1967	LARm	5	3	6	2.0(3)	0	—	—	—	—	—	—	—	—	—	—	—	—	—	—	p	—	0	-5
NFL	5	58	140	583	4.2(64)	2	31	297	9.6(42)	2	1	0	0.0	0	0.0	0	0	—	—	—	kp	—	24	1156

STILL, ART Arthur Barry, DE, 6´7˝/253 lbs; Kentucky; 1978: KC, rnd 1; B12/5/1955 Camden, NJ **1978** KC 16 (16, LDE) **1979** KC☆16 (16, LDE) **1980** KC★16 (16, LDE) **1981** KC✧11 (11, LDE) **1982** KC★9 (9, LDE) **1983** KC 15 (12, LDE) **1984** KC★16 (16, LDE) **1985** KC 9 (8, LDE) **1986**†KC☆16 (16, LDE) **1987** KC 12 (12, LDE) **1988**†Buf 15 (15, LDE) **1989**†Buf 16 (16, LDE) **NFL** 167 (163) [12 yrs]

STILL, BRYAN Bryan Andrei, WR, 5´11˝/174 lbs; Virginia Tech; 1996: SD, rnd 2; B6/3/1974 Newport News, VA

YEAR	TEAM	G (GS, POS)	RUSH	YD	AVG (LG)	TD	REC	YD	AVG (LG)	TD	PASS	COMP	PCT	YD	AVG (LG)	TD	INT	SK	YD	QBR	KPR	OTD	PTS	TAY
1996	SD	16(0)	—	—	—	—	6	142	23.7(56)	0	—	—	—	—	—	—	—	—	—	—	kp	—	0	120
1997	SD	15(4)	—	—	—	—	24	324	13.5(39)	0	—	—	—	—	—	—	—	—	—	—	—	—	0	162
1998	SD	14(9, WR)	—	—	—	—	43	605	14.1(67)	2	—	—	—	—	—	—	—	—	—	—	—	—	12	313
1999	SD	4(0)	—	—	—	—	8	96	12.0(28)	0	—	—	—	—	—	—	—	—	—	—	k	—	0	41
1999	Atl	3(1)	—	—	—	—	2	14	7.0(10)	0	—	—	—	—	—	—	—	—	—	—	—	—	0	7
NFL	4	52(14)	—	—	—	—	83	1181	14.2(67)	2	—	—	—	—	—	—	—	—	—	—	kp	—	12	643

STILL, JIM James Edward, B, 6´3˝/193 lbs; Georgia Tech; 1948: LAD-A, rnd 26/ChiC, rnd 16; B3/5/1924 Columbia, SC, D1/3/1999 Green Cove Springs, FL

YEAR	TEAM	G (GS, POS)	RUSH	YD	AVG (LG)	TD	REC	YD	AVG (LG)	TD	PASS	COMP	PCT	YD	AVG (LG)	TD	INT	SK	YD	QBR	KPR	OTD	PTS	TAY
1948	†Buf-A	12(1)	5	-26	-5.2	0	—	—	—	—	14	5	35.7	89	6.4	1	3	—	—	—	Pi	—	0	-65
1949	†Buf-A	9(1)	2	6	3.0	0	—	—	—	—	12	6	50.0	86	7.2	1	1	—	—	—	P	—	0	14
AAFC	2	21(2)	7	-20	-2.9	0	—	—	—	—	26	11	42.3	175	6.7	2	4	—	—	—	Pi	—	0	-51

STILLS, GARY Gary, DE, 6´2˝/244 lbs; West Virginia; 1999: KC, rnd 3; B7/11/1974 Trenton, NJ **1999** KC 2 (0) **2000** KC 12 (0) **2001** KC 10 (0) **2002** KC 16 (1) **2003**†KC 16 (0) **2004** KC 16 (0) **2005** KC 16 (0) **NFL** 88 (1) [7 yrs]

STILLS, KEN Kenneth Lee, DB, 5´10˝/185 lbs; Wisconsin; 1985: GB, rnd 8; B9/6/1963 Oceanside, CA **1985** GB 8 (1) **1986** GB 16 (10, FS) **1987** GB 11 (11, FS) **1988** GB 14 (13, FS) **1989** GB 16 (16, FS) **1990** Min 12 (3) **NFL** 77 (54) [6 yrs]

STILLWELL, ROGER Roger Howard, DT-DE, 6´5˝/260 lbs; Stanford; 1975: Chi, rnd 9; B11/17/1951 Santa Monica, CA **1975** ChiB 13 (11, LDT) **1976** ChiB 13 (10, RDE) **1977** ChiB 5 **NFL** 31 (21) [3 yrs]

STINCHCOMB, JON Jonathan, T, 6´5˝/302 lbs; Georgia; 2003: NO, rnd 2; B8/27/1979 Lilburn, GA **2003** NO 6 (0) **2004** NO 4 (0) **NFL** 10 (0) [2 yrs]

STINCHCOMB, MATT Matthew Douglass, G-T, 6´6˝/310 lbs; Georgia; 1999: Oak, rnd 1; B6/3/1977 Lilburn, GA **2000**†Oak 13 (9, LT) **2001**†Oak 15 (1) **2002**†Oak 16 (6, lg) **2003** Oak 6 (4) **2004** TB 16 (16, LG) **NFL** 66 (36) [5 yrs]

STINCHCOMB, PETE Gaylord Roscoe, B, 5´8˝/157 lbs; Ohio State; B6/24/1895 Sycamore, OH, D8/24/1973 Findlay, OH **[C]** **1921** ChiS☆11 (8, RH), 24 **1922** ChiB☆12 (6, RH), 18 **1923** Col 7 (3) **1923** Cle☆1 (0) **1926** Lou 3 (1, TB) **NFL** 34 (18), 42 [4 yrs]

STINCIC, THOMAS Thomas Dorn, LB, 6´4˝/230 lbs; Michigan; 1969: Dal, rnd 3; B11/24/1946 Cleveland, OH **1969**†Dal 14 **1970**†Dal 14 **1971**†Dal 7 **1972** NO 7 **NFL** 42 [4 yrs]

STINGLEY, DARRYL Darryl Floyd, WR, 6´0˝/194 lbs; Purdue; 1973: NE, rnd 1; B9/18/1951 Chicago, IL

YEAR	TEAM	G (GS, POS)	RUSH	YD	AVG (LG)	TD	REC	YD	AVG (LG)	TD	PASS	COMP	PCT	YD	AVG (LG)	TD	INT	SK	YD	QBR	KPR	OTD	PTS	TAY
1973	NE	14(10, WR)	6	64	10.7(19)	0	23	339	14.7(25)	2	—	—	—	—	—	—	—	—	—	—	kp	—	12	303
1974	NE	5(2)	5	63	12.6(23)	1	10	139	13.9(20)	1	—	—	—	—	—	—	—	—	—	—	—	—	12	148
1975	NE	14(14, WR)	6	39	6.5(21)	0	21	378	18.0(45)	2	—	—	—	—	—	—	—	—	—	—	kp	—	12	290
1976	†NE	13(13, WR)	8	45	5.6(27)	0	17	370	21.8(58)	4	—	—	—	—	—	—	—	—	—	—	p	—	24	247
1977	NE	14(14, WR)	3	33	11.0(34)	1	39	657	16.8(68)	5	—	—	—	—	—	—	—	—	—	—	—	—	36	397
NFL	5	60(53)	28	244	8.7(34)	2	110	1883	17.1(68)	14	—	—	—	—	—	—	—	—	—	—	kp	—	96	1384

STINNETTE, JAMES James Edward, FB-LB, 6´1˝/230 lbs; Oregon State; 1960: NYT, rnd 1; B12/3/1938 Corvallis, OR

YEAR	TEAM	G (GS, POS)	RUSH	YD	AVG (LG)	TD	REC	YD	AVG (LG)	TD	PASS	COMP	PCT	YD	AVG (LG)	TD	INT	SK	YD	QBR	KPR	OTD	PTS	TAY
1961	Den-A	14	18	8	0.4(9)	0	11	58	5.3(15)	1	—	—	—	—	—	—	—	—	—	—	ki	—	6	68
1962	Den-A	10	21	87	4.1(14)	1	13	109	8.4(32)	0	—	—	—	—	—	—	—	—	—	—	k	—	6	149
NFL	2	24	39	95	2.4(14)	1	24	167	7.0(32)	1	—	—	—	—	—	—	—	—	—	—	ki	—	12	217

STINSON, LEMUEL Lemuel Dale, DB, 5´9˝/166 lbs; Texas Tech; 1988: Chi, rnd 6; B5/10/1966 Houston, TX **1988**†ChiB 15 (1) **1989** ChiB 12 (4) **1990** ChiB 10 (10, RCB) **1991**†ChiB 16 (16, RCB) **1992** ChiB 16 (11, RCB) **NFL** 69 (42) [5 yrs]

STITH, CAREL Carel Lewis, DT-DE, 6´5˝/270 lbs; Nebraska; 1967: Hou, rnd 4; B5/24/1945 Lincoln, NE **1967**†Hou-A 14 **1968** Hou-A 3 **1969**†Hou-A 14 (LDT) **NFL** 31 [3 yrs]

STITH, HOWARD Howard Seymore, G, none; B1/1896, D4/6/1951 Louisville, KY **1921** Lou 1 (0)

STITH, SHYRONE Shyrone Orenthal, RB, 5´7˝/206 lbs; Virginia Tech; 2000: Jax, rnd 7; B4/2/1978 Portsmouth, VA **2002** Ind 1 (0)

YEAR	TEAM	G (GS, POS)	RUSH	YD	AVG (LG)	TD	REC	YD	AVG (LG)	TD	PASS	COMP	PCT	YD	AVG (LG)	TD	INT	SK	YD	QBR	KPR	OTD	PTS	TAY
2000	Jax	14(0)	20	55	2.8(12)	1	—	—	—	—	—	—	—	—	—	—	—	—	—	—	k	—	6	355
NFL	2	15(0)	20	55	2.8(12)	1	—	—	—	—	—	—	—	—	—	—	—	—	—	—		—	6	65

STITS, BILL William David, DB-HB, 6´4˝/194 lbs; UCLA; 1954: Det, rnd 4; B7/26/1931 Lomita, CA **1954**†Det✧12 (DB) **1957**†SF 12 (DB) **1958** SF 12 (DB) **1959** Was 5 **1959**†NYG 5 **1960** NYG 12 **1961** NYG 10

YEAR	TEAM	G (GS, POS)	RUSH	YD	AVG (LG)	TD	REC	YD	AVG (LG)	TD	PASS	COMP	PCT	YD	AVG (LG)	TD	INT	SK	YD	QBR	KPR	OTD	PTS	TAY
1955	Det	12(DB/rh)	46	165	3.6(15)	0	5	17	3.4(14)	0	2	2	100.0	62	31.0(41)	1	0	—	—	—	pi	1	6	207
1956	Det	12(db)	3	0	0.0(6)	0	3	52	17.3(27)	0	1	0	0.0	0	0.0	0	1	—	—	—	ki	—	0	-5
NFL	8	92	49	165	3.4(15)	0	8	69	8.6(27)	0	3	2	66.7	62	20.7(41)	1	1	—	—	—	kpi	1	6	574

STOBBS, BILL Thomas William, BB, 5´7˝/165 lbs; Washington & Jefferson; B5/28/1896 Wheeling, WV, D11/14/1968 Richmond, VA **1921** Det 7 (7, BB)

STOCK, HERB Herbert Louis, TB-HB, 6´0˝/182 lbs; Kenyon; B9/3/1899 Columbus, OH, D12/21/1987 Columbus, OH **1924** Col 7 (5, TB)

STOCK, JOHN John H., E, 6´2˝/210 lbs; Pittsburgh; B1934 **1956** Pit 2

STOCK, MARK Mark Anthony, WR, 5´11˝/177 lbs; VMI; 1989: Pit, rnd 6; B4/27/1966 Canton, OH

YEAR	TEAM	G (GS, POS)	RUSH	YD	AVG (LG)	TD	REC	YD	AVG (LG)	TD	PASS	COMP	PCT	YD	AVG (LG)	TD	INT	SK	YD	QBR	KPR	OTD	PTS	TAY
1989	†Pit	8(0)	—	—	—	—	4	74	18.5(27)	0	—	—	—	—	—	—	—	—	—	—	—	—	0	37
1993	Was	3(0)	—	—	—	—	—	—	—	—	—	—	—	—	—	—	—	—	—	—	—	—	—	—
1996	†Ind	14(0)	—	—	—	—	2	24	12.0(13)	0	—	—	—	—	—	—	—	—	—	—	kp	—	0	74
NFL	3	25(0)	—	—	—	—	6	98	16.3(27)	0	—	—	—	—	—	—	—	—	—	—	kp	—	0	111

STOCKEMER, RALPH Ralph William, RB, 6´1˝/212 lbs; Baylor; B12/20/1962 Shreveport, LA

YEAR	TEAM	G (GS, POS)	RUSH	YD	AVG (LG)	TD	REC	YD	AVG (LG)	TD	PASS	COMP	PCT	YD	AVG (LG)	TD	INT	SK	YD	QBR	KPR	OTD	PTS	TAY
1987	KC	2(0)	1	2	2.0(2)	0	1	4	4.0(4)	0	—	—	—	—	—	—	—	—	—	—	—	—	0	4

STOCKTON, MULE Willis Herschel, G, 6´1˝/214 lbs; McMurry; B12/29/1913 Abilene, TX, D11/12/1965 Odessa, TX **1937** Phi 11 (11, LG) **1938** Phi 11 (8, LG) **NFL** 22 (19) [2 yrs]

STOCKTON, HUST John Houston, FB-TB-HB, 5´11˝/193 lbs; Gonzaga; B9/23/1901, D4/27/1967 Bremerton, WA **1925** Fra 14 (13, FB) **1926** Fra☆17 (14, FB), 12 **1928** Fra 13 (6, fb), 24 **1929** Pro 1 (0) **1929** Bos 8 (7, TB), 6 **NFL** 53 (40), 42 [4 yrs]

STOCZ, ERIC Eric Richard, TE, 6´4˝/258 lbs; Westminster (PA); B5/25/1974 Warren, OH **1996** Det 1 (0) **1997**†Det 6 (0) **NFL** 7 (0) [2 yrs]

STOECKLEIN, EARL Earl E., G, 6´2˝/205 lbs; none; B10/1/1896 Dayton, OH, D1/6/1975 Bridgeport, CT **1920** Day 2 (0)

STOEPEL, TERRY Terry K., TE, 6´4˝/235 lbs; Tulsa; B2/8/1945 Cincinnati, OH **1970** Hou 14

YEAR	TEAM	G (GS, POS)	RUSH	YD	AVG (LG)	TD	REC	YD	AVG (LG)	TD	PASS	COMP	PCT	YD	AVG (LG)	TD	INT	SK	YD	QBR	KPR	OTD	PTS	TAY
1967	ChiB	6	—	—	—	—	1	6	6.0(6)	0	—	—	—	—	—	—	—	—	—	—	k	—	0	-12
NFL	2	20	—	—	—	—	1	6	6.0(6)	0	—	—	—	—	—	—	—	—	—	—	—	—	0	3

STOERNER, CLINT Clint, WB, 6´2˝/210 lbs; Arkansas; B12/29/1977 Baytown, TX

YEAR	TEAM	G (GS, POS)	RUSH	YD	AVG (LG)	TD	REC	YD	AVG (LG)	TD	PASS	COMP	PCT	YD	AVG (LG)	TD	INT	SK	YD	QBR	KPR	OTD	PTS	TAY
2000	Dal	2(0)	—	—	—	—	—	—	—	—	5	3	60.0	53	10.6(29)	1	0	2	21	—	—	—	0	32
2001	Dal	4(2)	9	27	3.0(13)	1	—	—	—	—	49	26	53.1	314	6.4(28)	3	5	5	22	—	—	—	6	9
NFL	2	6(2)	9	27	3.0(13)	1	—	—	—	—	54	29	53.7	367	6.8(29)	4	5	7	43	—	—	—	6	41

STOFA, JOHN John Carl, QB, 6´3˝/210 lbs; Buffalo; B6/29/1942 Johnstown, PA

YEAR	TEAM	G (GS, POS)	RUSH	YD	AVG (LG)	TD	REC	YD	AVG (LG)	TD	PASS	COMP	PCT	YD	AVG (LG)	TD	INT	SK	YD	QBR	KPR	OTD	PTS	TAY
1966	Mia-A	7	3	17	5.7(14)	0	—	—	—	—	57	29	50.9	425	7.5(48)	4	2	3	29	—	—	—	0	170
1967	Mia-A	1	2	2	1.0(8)	1	—	—	—	—	2	2	100.0	51	25.5(45)	0	0	—	—	—	—	—	6	38
1968	Cin-A	10(QB)	10	1	0.1(13)	0	—	—	—	—	177	85	48.0	896	5.1(60)	5	5	17	140	—	—	—	0	274
1969	Mia-A	1	—	—	—	—	—	—	—	—	23	14	60.9	146	6.3(42)	0	2	2	17	—	—	—	0	-7
1970	Mia	8	2	5	2.5(4)	0	—	—	—	—	53	16	30.2	240	4.5(52)	3	2	5	45	—	—	—	0	60
NFL	5	27	17	25	1.5(14)	1	—	—	—	—	312	146	46.8	1758	5.6(60)	12	11	27	231	—	—	—	6	534

STOFER, KEN Kenneth Lamont, QB-DB, 5´9˝/188 lbs; Cornell; B8/10/1919 Lakewood, OH

YEAR	TEAM	G (GS, POS)	RUSH	YD	AVG (LG)	TD	REC	YD	AVG (LG)	TD	PASS	COMP	PCT	YD	AVG (LG)	TD	INT	SK	YD	QBR	KPR	OTD	PTS	TAY
1946	Buf-A	11(1)	16	36	2.3	0	1	14	14.0(14)	0	26	9	34.6	86	3.3	1	1	—	—	—	Pkp	—	0	130

YEAR	TEAM	G (GS, POS)	RUSH	YD	AVG (LG)	TD	REC	YD	AVG (LG)	TD	PASS	COMP	PCT	YD	AVG (LG)	TD	INT	SK	YD	QBR	KPR		OTD	PTS	TAY

STOFKO, ED Albert Edward, TB-DB, 6´1˝/192 lbs; St. Francis (PA); 1944: Pit, rnd 9; B5/17/1920 Johnstown, PA, D12/19/1988 Johnstown, PA

| 1945 | Pit | 2(1) | 13 | -16 | -1.2(6) | 0 | — | — | — | — | 17 | 7 | 41.2 | 94 | 5.5(26) | 0 | 4 | — | — | P | — | | — | 0 | -129 |

STOJACK, FRANK Frank Nicholas, G, 5´10˝/194 lbs; Washington State; B2/11/1912 Wycliff, Canada, D8/30/1987 Tacoma, WA **1935** Bkn 12 (3) **1936** Bkn 11 (4) **NFL 23 (7) [2 yrs]**

STOKES, BARRY Barry Wade, T-G, 6´4˝/310 lbs; Eastern Michigan; B12/20/1973 Flint, MI **1998** Mia 3 (0) **2000** GB 8 (0) **2001**†GB 16 (3) **2002**†Cle 16 (16, LG) **2003** Cle 13 (13, LT) **2005** Atl 16 (1) **NFL 72 (33) [6 yrs]**

STOKES, DIXIE Lee James, C, 6´0˝/205 lbs; Centenary; B8/24/1913 Shreveport, LA, D12/1967, **[K]** **1937** Det 11 (7, C) **1938** Det 10 (6, C) **1939** Det 1 (0) **1943** ChiC 6 (2) **NFL 28 (15) [4 yrs]**

STOKES, ERIC Eric R., C-G, 6´4˝/255 lbs; Northeastern; 1985: Cin, rnd 6; B1/13/1962 Derby, CT **1987** NE 1 (1)

STOKES, ERIC Eric, DB, 5´11˝/200 lbs; Nebraska; 1997: Sea, rnd 5; B12/18/1973 Hebron, NE **1997** Sea 7 (0) **1998** Sea 4 (0) **NFL 11 (0) [2 yrs]**

STOKES, FRED Louis Fred, DE, 6´3˝/274 lbs; Georgia Southern; 1987: LARm, rnd 12; B3/14/1964 Vidalia, GA **1987** LARm 8 (0) **1988** LARm 5 (0) **1989** Was 16 (5, rde) **1990**†Was 16 (3) **1991**†Was 16 (10, RDE) **1992**†Was 16 (11, RDE) **1993** LARm 15 (15, RDE) **1994** LARm 16 (15, RDE) **1995** SL 16 (2) **1996** NO 9 (0) **NFL 133 (61) [10 yrs]**

STOKES, J.J. Jerel Jamal, WR, 6´4˝/218 lbs; UCLA; 1995: SF, rnd 1; B10/6/1972 San Diego, CA

1995	†SF	12(2)	—	—	—	—	38	517	13.6(41)	4	—	—	—	—	—	—	—	—	—	—	—		—	24	279
1996	†SF	6(6, wr)	—	—	—	—	18	249	13.8(40)	0	—	—	—	—	—	—	—	—	—	—	—		—	0	125
1997	†SF	16(16, WR)	—	—	—	—	58	733	12.6(36)	4	—	—	—	—	—	—	—	—	—	—	—		—	24	387
1998	†SF	16(11, WR)	—	—	—	—	63	770	12.2(33)	8	—	—	—	—	—	—	—	—	—	—	—		—	48	425
1999	SF	16(4)	—	—	—	—	34	429	12.6(47)	3	—	—	—	—	—	—	—	—	—	—	—		—	20	230
2000	SF	16(3)	1	6	6.0(6)	0	30	524	17.5(53)	3	—	—	—	—	—	—	—	—	—	—	—		—	20	283
2001	†SF	16(16, WR)	—	—	—	—	54	585	10.8(47)	7	—	—	—	—	—	—	—	—	—	—	—		—	42	328
2002	†SF	13(8, wr)	—	—	—	—	32	332	10.4(51)	1	—	—	—	—	—	—	—	—	—	—	—		—	6	171
2003	Jax	5(3)	—	—	—	—	13	116	8.9(22)	0	—	—	—	—	—	—	—	—	—	—	—		—	0	58
2003	NE	2(0)	—	—	—	—	2	38	19.0(31)	0	—	—	—	—	—	—	—	—	—	—	—		—	0	19
NFL	9	118(69)	1	6	6.0(6)	0	342	4293	12.6(53)	30	—	—	—	—	—	—	—	—	—	—	—		—	184	2303

STOKES, JESSE Jesse Van, DB, 6´0˝/190 lbs; Corpus Christi; 1966: Min, rnd 19; B8/27/1944 Kerrville, TX **1968** Den-A 2

STOKES, SIMS Sims Edward, WR, 6´1˝/197 lbs; Kansas; Northern Arizona; 1967: Dal, rnd 6; B4/18/1944 Mobile, AL **1967**†Dal 3

STOKES, TIM Timothy Paul, T, 6´5˝/252 lbs; Oregon; 1973: LA, rnd 3; B3/16/1950 Oakland, CA **1974** LARm 6 **1975** Was 5 (5, lt) **1976**†Was 14 (14, LT) **1977** Was 14 (14, LT) **1978** GB 16 (16, LT) **1979** GB 16 (4) **1980** GB 15 (15, LT) **1981** NYG 3 (1) **1981** GB 8 (4) **1982**†GB 8 (1) **NFL 105 (74) [9 yrs]**

STOKLEY, BRANDON Brandon, WR, 5´11˝/197 lbs; Louisiana-Lafayette; 1999: Bal, rnd 4; B6/23/1976 Blacksburg, VA

1999	Bal	2(0)	—	—	—	—	1	28	28.0(28)	1	—	—	—	—	—	—	—	—	—	—	—		—	6	19
2000	†Bal	7(1)	1	6	6.0(6)	0	11	184	16.7(32)	2	—	—	—	—	—	—	—	—	—	—	—		—	12	108
2001	†Bal	16(5, wr)	1	1	1.0(1)	0	24	344	14.3(46)	2	—	—	—	—	—	—	—	—	—	—	—		—	12	183
2002	Bal	8(5, wr)	6	31	5.2(14)	0	24	357	14.9(35)	2	—	—	—	—	—	—	—	—	—	—	—		—	12	220
2003	†Ind	6(3)	—	—	—	—	22	211	9.6(37)	3	—	—	—	—	—	—	—	—	—	—	—		—	18	121
2004	†Ind	16(3)	—	—	—	—	68	1077	15.8(69)	10	—	—	—	—	—	—	—	—	—	—	—		—	60	589
2005	†Ind	15(4)	—	—	—	—	41	543	13.2(45)	1	—	—	—	—	—	—	—	—	—	—	—		—	6	277
NFL	7	70(21)	8	38	4.8(14)	0	191	2744	14.4(69)	21	—	—	—	—	—	—	—	—	—	—	—		—	126	1515

STOLFA, ANTON Anton James, QB-DB, 6´0˝/195 lbs; Luther; 1939: ChiB, rnd 14; B9/6/1917 Cicero, IL, D5/8/1976 Iowa City, IA **1939** ChiB 1 (0)

STOLHANDSKE, TOM Carl Thomas, LB-DE, 6´2˝/210 lbs; Texas; 1953: SF, rnd 1; B6/28/1931 Baytown, TX **1955** SF 12

STOLTENBERG, BRYAN Bryan Douglas, C-G, 6´1˝/300 lbs; Colorado; 1996: SD, rnd 6; B8/25/1972 Kearney, NE **1996** SD 9 (0) **1997** NYG 3 (0) **1998** Car 14 (10, C) **1999** Car 16 (7, lg) **2000** Car 8 (1) **NFL 50 (18) [5 yrs]**

STONE, AVATUS Avatus Harry, HB, 6´1˝/195 lbs; Syracuse; 1953: ChiC, rnd 9; B4/21/1931 Washington, DC **1958** Bal 1

STONE, BILLY William John, HB-DB, 6´0˝/191 lbs; Bradley; 1949: ChiC, rnd 12; B10/25/1925 Peoria, IL, D5/16/2004 Peoria, IL

1949	Bal-A	12(1, lh)	51	205	4.0	2	31	621	20.0(66)	6	—	—	—	—	—	—	—	—	—	k	—		—	48	576
1950	Bal	8(2, DB)	14	113	8.1(72)	1	12	324	27.0(69)	4	—	—	—	—	—	—	—	—	—	kpi	—		—	30	333
1951	ChiB	12(DB)	30	123	4.1(42)	1	18	320	17.8(62)	1	—	—	—	—	—	—	—	—	—	kpi	—		—	12	381
1952	ChiB	10(RH)	50	196	3.9(48)	2	13	283	21.8(59)	2	—	—	—	—	—	—	—	—	—	ki	—		—	24	386
1953	ChiB	12(LH)	72	169	2.3(28)	2	34	376	11.1(51)	4	—	—	—	—	—	—	—	—	—	p	—		—	36	389
1954	ChiB	12(LH)	79	306	3.9(23)	3	35	395	11.3(42)	3	—	—	—	—	—	—	—	—	—	kp	—		—	36	614
NFL	6	54(2)	245	907	3.7(72)	9	112	1698	15.2(69)	14	—	—	—	—	—	—	—	—	—	kpi	—		—	138	2102

STONE, DONNIE Edward Donald, HB-FB, 6´1˝/205 lbs; Arkansas; 1959: ChiB, rnd 21; B1/5/1937 Sioux City, IA

1961	Den-A★	14(HB)	127	505	4.0(34)	4	38	344	9.1(37)	4	2	1	50.0	18	9.0(18)	1	0	—	—	—	k		—	48	831
1962	Den-A	11(HB)	94	360	3.8(27)	3	20	223	11.1(56)	2	3	1	33.3	13	4.3(13)	0	0	—	—	—	—		—	30	518
1963	Den-A	14(HB)	96	382	4.0(39)	3	22	208	9.5(55)	1	3	0	0.0	0	0	0	0	—	—	—	—		—	24	521
1964	Den-A	9	12	26	2.2(5)	0	4	38	9.5(16)	0	—	—	—	—	—	—	—	—	—	—	—		—	0	45
1965	†Buf-A	14	19	61	3.2(14)	0	6	29	4.8(9)	0	—	—	—	—	—	—	—	—	—	—	—		—	0	76
1966	Hou-A	5	6	18	3.0(12)	0	1	17	17.0(17)	0	—	—	—	—	—	—	—	—	—	—	—		—	0	27
NFL	6	67	354	1352	3.8(39)	10	91	859	9.4(56)	7	8	2	25.0	31	3.9(18)	1	0	—	—	—	k		—	102	2017

STONE, DWIGHT Dwight, WR-RB, 6´0˝/191 lbs; Middle Tennessee State; B1/28/1964 Florala, AL **[R]**

1987	Pit	14(0)	17	135	7.9(51)	0	1	22	22.0(22)	0	—	—	—	—	—	—	—	—	—	—	k		—	0	294
1988	Pit	16(6, rb)	40	127	3.2(11)	0	11	196	17.8(72)	1	—	—	—	—	—	—	—	—	—	—	k		1	12	415
1989	†Pit	16(8, wr)	10	53	5.3(32)	0	7	92	13.1(16)	0	—	—	—	—	—	—	—	—	—	—	k		—	0	167
1990	Pit	16(2)	2	-6	-3.0(10)	0	19	332	17.5(90)	1	—	—	—	—	—	—	—	—	—	—	k		—	6	181
1991	Pit	16(8, WR)	1	2	2.0(2)	0	32	649	20.3(89)	5	—	—	—	—	—	—	—	—	—	—	k		—	30	337
1992	†Pit	15(12, WR)	12	118	9.8(30)	0	34	501	14.7(49)	3	—	—	—	—	—	—	—	—	—	—	k		—	18	423
1993	†Pit	16(15, WR)	12	121	10.1(38)	1	41	587	14.3(49)	2	—	—	—	—	—	—	—	—	—	—	k		—	18	438
1994	†Pit	15(1)	2	7	3.5(4)	0	7	81	11.6(25)	0	—	—	—	—	—	—	—	—	—	—	k		—	2	65
1995	Car	16(0)	1	3	3.0(3)	0	—	—	—	—	—	—	—	—	—	—	—	—	—	—	k		—	0	92
1996	†Car	16(0)	1	6	6.0(6)	0	1	11	11.0(11)	0	—	—	—	—	—	—	—	—	—	—	k		—	0	12
1997	Car	16(0)	—	—	—	—	—	—	—	—	—	—	—	—	—	—	—	—	—	—	k		—	2	31
1998	Car	16(0)	—	—	—	—	1	7	7.0(7)	0	—	—	—	—	—	—	—	—	—	—	k		1	6	121
1999	NYJ	16(0)	2	27	13.5(36)	0	—	—	—	—	—	—	—	—	—	—	—	—	—	—	k		—	0	296
2000	NYJ	12(0)	3	3	1.0(0)	0	—	—	—	—	—	—	—	—	—	—	—	—	—	—	k		—	0	183
NFL	14	216(52)	103	596	5.8(51)	1	154	2478	16.1(90)	12	—	—	—	—	—	—	—	—	—	—	k		2	94	3052

STONE, JACK Jack Richard, T, 6´2˝/245 lbs; Oregon; 1960: DalT, rnd 1; B7/28/1936 Ellensburg, WA **1960** DalT-A 14 **1961** Oak-A 14 (RT) **1962** Oak-A 14 (RT) **NFL 42 [3 yrs]**

STONE, JOHN John, WR, 5´11˝/180 lbs; Wake Forest; B7/7/1979 **2003** Oak 1 (0)

| 2004 | Oak | 4(0) | — | — | — | — | 3 | 80 | 26.7(55) | 0 | — | — | — | — | — | — | — | — | — | — | k | | — | 0 | 45 |
| NFL | 2 | 5(0) | — | — | — | — | 3 | 80 | 26.7(55) | 0 | — | — | — | — | — | — | — | — | — | — | — | | — | 0 | 40 |

STONE, KEN Kenneth Bernard, DB-WR, 6´1˝/179 lbs; Vanderbilt; 1973: Was, rnd 10; B9/14/1950 Cincinnati, OH **[I]** **1973** Buf 6 **1973**†Was 4 **1974**†Was 14 **1975** Was 3 **1976** TB 14 (14, FS) **1978** SL 14 (FS) **1979** SL 16 (FS) **1980** SL 16 (9, FS)

| 1977 | SL | 14 | — | — | — | — | 1 | 40 | 40.0(40) | 0 | — | — | — | — | — | — | — | — | — | — | — | | — | 0 | 20 |
| NFL | 8 | 101(23) | — | — | — | — | 1 | 40 | 40.0(40) | 0 | — | — | — | — | — | — | — | — | — | kpi | — | | 1 | 6 | 310 |

STONE, MICHAEL Michael, DB, 6´0˝/201 lbs; Memphis; 2001: Arz, rnd 2; B2/13/1978 Southfield, MI **2001** Arz 7 (0) **2002** Arz 16 (0) **2004** Arz 14 (0) **2005**†NE 13 (3) **NFL 50 (3) [4 yrs]**

STONE, RON Ronald Christopher, G, 6´5˝/325 lbs; Boston College; 1993: Dal, rnd 4; B7/20/1971 Boston, MA **1994**†Dal 16 (0) **1995**†Dal 16 (1) **1996** NYG 16 (16, RG) **1997**†NYG 16 (16, RG) **1998** NYG 14 (14, RG) **1999** NYG 16 (16, RG) **2000**†NYG★15 (15, RG) **2001** NYG◇15 (15, RG) **2002**†SF★15 (15, RG) **2003** SF 13 (13, RG) **2004** Oak 5 (5, rg) **2005** Oak 16 (16, RG) **NFL 173 (142) [12 yrs]**

YEAR	TEAM	G (GS, POS)	RUSH	YD	AVG (LG)	TD	REC	YD	AVG (LG)	TD	PASS COMP	PCT	YD	AVG (LG)	TD	INT	SK	YD	QBR	KPR	OTD	PTS	TAY

STONEBRAKER, JOHN John S., E, 6´3˝/200 lbs; USC; B4/25/1918 Frankfort, IN, D1/25/2000 Claremont, CA **1942** GB 8 (2)

STONEBREAKER, MIKE Michael David, LB, 6´0˝/226 lbs; Notre Dame; 1991: Chi, rnd 9; B1/14/1967 Baltimore, MD **1991**†ChiB 16 (0) **1994** NO 2 (0) **NFL** 18 (0) [2 yrs]

STONEBREAKER, STEVE Thornton Steven, LB-TE, 6´3˝/223 lbs; Detroit Mercy; 1961: Min, rnd 12/1962: Den, rnd 34; B10/28/1938 Moline, IL, D3/29/1995 River Ridge, LA
1963 Min 14 (10, RLB) **1964**†Bal☆14 (13, LLB) **1965**†Bal☆14 (14, LLB) **1966** Bal 4 **1967** NO 10 (10, LLB) **1968** NO 14

| 1962 | Min | 14 (9, TE) | — | — | — | — | 12 | 227 | 18.9 (56) | 1 | — | — | — | — | — | — | — | — | — | — | k | — | 6 | 116 |
| NFL | 7 | | 84 (56) | — | — | — | — | 12 | 227 | 18.9 (56) | 1 | — | — | — | — | — | — | — | — | — | ki | 1 | 12 | 121 |

STONESIFER, DON Donald Humphrey, E, 6´0˝/200 lbs; Northwestern; 1951: ChiC, rnd 3; B1/29/1927 Chicago, IL

1951	ChiC	12 (RE)	—	—	—	—	27	343	12.7 (48)	2	—	—	—	—	—	—	—	—	—	—		—	12	182
1952	ChiC	12 (RE)	—	—	—	—	54	617	11.4 (26)	0	—	—	—	—	—	—	—	—	—	k		—	0	306
1953	ChiC	12 (RE)	—	—	—	—	56	684	12.2 (46)	2	—	—	—	—	—	—	—	—	—	—		—	12	352
1954	ChiC	12 (LE)	—	—	—	—	44	607	13.8 (39)	3	—	—	—	—	—	—	—	—	—	—		—	18	319
1955	ChiC	12 (LE)	—	—	—	—	28	330	11.8 (28)	5	—	—	—	—	—	—	—	—	—	—		—	30	190
1956	ChiC	12 (LE)	—	—	—	—	22	320	14.5 (58)	2	—	—	—	—	—	—	—	—	—	k		—	12	170
NFL	6		72	—	—	—	—	231	2901	12.6 (58)	14	—	—	—	—	—	—	—	—	—		—	84	1518

STOOPS, MIKE Michael J., DB, 6´1˝/182 lbs; Iowa; B12/13/1961 Youngstown, OH **1987** ChiB 3 (1)

STORER, JACK John Waddell, TB, 5´10˝/180 lbs; Lehigh; B11/11/1900 Wheeling, WV, D1/16/1927 Wheeling, WV **1924** Fra 14 (13, TB), 48

STORM, ED Edward Charles, B, 6´1˝/195 lbs; Santa Clara; B10/2/1907 Salinas, CA, D1980 Castroville, CA

1934	Phi	10 (5, fb)	81	281	3.5	2	5	34	6.8	0	30	8	26.7	97	3.2	0	6	—	—	—	—	—	12	127
1935	Phi	11 (3)	84	164	2.0	0	3	44	14.7	0	44	15	34.1	372	8.5	3	10	—	—	—	—	—	0	-13
NFL	2		21 (8)	165	445	2.7	2	8	78	9.8	0	74	23	31.1	469	6.3	3	16	—	—	—	—	—	12	114

STORR, GREG Gregory Scott, LB, 6´2˝/225 lbs; Boston College; 1982: Min, rnd 6; B10/16/1960 Reading, PA **1987** Mia 3 (0)

STORY, BILL William Frank, T, 6´3˝/245 lbs; Southern Illinois; 1973: KC, rnd 9; B11/21/1951 Memphis, TN **1975** KC 14

STORZ, ERIK Erik Erwin, LB, 6´2˝/234 lbs; Boston College; B6/24/1975 Rockaway, NJ **1998**†Jax 1 (0) **1999** Jax 7 (0) **2000** Jax 10 (2) **NFL** 18 (2) [3 yrs]

STOTSBERY, HAL Herald, T, 5´11˝/235 lbs; Xavier (OH); B1907 Belmont County, OH, deceased **1930** Bkn 2 (0)

STOTTER, RICHARD Richard Lee, LB, 6´0˝/225 lbs; Houston; 1968: Hou, rnd 14; B4/5/1945 Cleveland, OH **1968** Hou-A 3

STOUDT, CLIFF Clifford Lewis, QB, 6´4˝/215 lbs; Youngstown State; 1977: Pit, rnd 5; B3/27/1955 Oberlin, OH

1980	Pit	6 (1)	9	35	3.9 (13)	0	—	—	—	—	60	32	53.3	493	8.2 (72)	2	2	4	19	—	—	—	0	212
1981	Pit	2 (0)	3	11	3.7 (10)	0	—	—	—	—	3	1	33.3	17	5.7 (17)	0	0	—	—	—	—	—	0	20
1982	†Pit	6 (0)	11	28	2.5 (8)	0	—	—	—	—	35	14	40.0	154	4.4 (24)	0	5	1	8	—	—	—	0	-95
1983	†Pit	16 (16, QB)	77	479	6.2 (23)	4	—	—	—	—	381	197	51.7	2553	6.7 (52)	12	21	51	339	60.6	—	—	24	1016
1986	SL	5 (2)	7	53	7.6 (17)	0	—	—	—	—	91	52	57.1	542	6.0 (24)	3	7	7	43	—	—	—	0	59
1987	SL	12 (0)	1	-2	-2.0 (-2)	0	—	—	—	—	1	0	0.0	0	—	0	0	—	—	—	—	—	0	-2
1988	Phx	16 (2)	14	57	4.1 (14)	0	—	—	—	—	113	63	55.8	747	6.6 (52)	6	8	13	85	64.3	—	—	0	141
1989	Mia	3 (0)																						
NFL	8		66 (21)	122	661	5.4 (23)	4	—	—	—	—	684	359	52.5	4506	6.6 (72)	23	43	76	494	58.3	—	—	24	1349

STOUFFER, KELLY Kelly Wayne, QB, 6´3˝/210 lbs; Colorado State; 1987: SL, rnd 1; B7/6/1964 Scottsbluff, NC

1988	Sea	8 (6, qb)	19	27	1.4 (17)	0	—	—	—	—	173	98	56.6	1106	6.4 (53)	4	6	13	110	69.2	—	—	0	360
1989	Sea	3 (2)	2	11	5.5 (9)	0	—	—	—	—	59	29	49.2	270	4.6 (29)	0	3	9	90	—	—	—	0	26
1991	Sea	2 (1)	—	—	—	—	—	—	—	—	15	6	40.0	57	3.8 (19)	0	1	2	9	—	—	—	0	-12
1992	Sea	9 (7, qb)	9	37	4.1 (11)	0	—	—	—	—	190	92	48.4	900	4.7 (33)	3	9	26	222	47.7	—	—	0	142
NFL	4		22 (16)	30	75	2.5 (17)	0	—	—	—	—	437	225	51.5	2333	5.3 (53)	7	19	50	431	54.5	—	—	0	517

STOUGH, GLEN Glen Kintigh, T, 6´5˝/240 lbs; Duke; 1945: Pit, rnd 27; B9/7/1921 Irwin, PA **1945** Pit 10 (5, LT)

STOUT, PETE J. Peter, FB-LB, 6´0˝/201 lbs; Texas-Arlington; TCU; 1946: NYG, rnd 5/1948: NYY-A, rnd 7; B6/1/1924 Throckmorton, TX

1949	Was	6 (3)	62	245	4.0 (74)	4	8	102	12.8 (39)	2	—	—	—	—	—	—	—	—	—	—	i	—	36	349
1950	Was	8	9	53	5.9 (19)	0	2	15	7.5 (8)	0	—	—	—	—	—	—	—	—	—	—	i	—	0	65
NFL	2		14 (3)	71	298	4.2 (74)	4	10	117	11.7 (39)	2	—	—	—	—	—	—	—	—	—	—	i	—	36	414

STOUTMIRE, OMAR Omar Array, DB, 5´11˝/205 lbs; Fresno State; 1997: Dal, rnd 7; B7/9/1974 Pensacola, FL **1997** Dal 16 (2) **1998**†Dal 16 (12, FS) **1999** NYJ 12 (5, fs)
2000†NYG 16 (0) **2001** NYG 16 (0) **2002**†NYG 16 (16, FS) **2003** NYG 16 (16, FS) **2004** NYG 1 (0) **2005**†Was 10 (0) **NFL** 119 (51) [9 yrs]

STOVALL, DICK Richard Southerton, LB-G-C, 6´0˝/202 lbs; Abilene Christian; B5/4/1922 Albany, TX **1947** Det 11 (0) **1948** Det 10 (0) **1949** Was 10 (1) **NFL** 31 (1) [3 yrs]

STOVALL, JERRY Jerry Lane, DB-P, 6´2˝/205 lbs; LSU; 1963: SL, rnd 1/NYJ, rnd 1; B4/30/1941 West Monroe, LA **1964** SL 14 (LS) **1965** SL 10 (LS) **1967** SL◇14 (LS)
1968 SL 4 (ls) **1969** SL◇10 (LS) **1970** SL 11 (SS) **1971** SL 6 (SS)

1963	SL	14 (14, LS)	1	32	32.0 (32)	0	—	—	—	—	—	—	—	—	—	—	—	—	—	Pki	—	0	221
1966	SL★	14 (LS)	1	17	17.0 (17)	0	—	—	—	—	—	—	—	—	—	—	—	—	—	Pi	1	6	55
NFL	9		97 (14)	2	49	24.5 (32)	0	—	—	—	—	—	—	—	—	—	—	—	—	—	Pki	2	12	715

STOVER, JEFF Jeffrey Owen, DE-DT, 6´5˝/275 lbs; Oregon; B5/22/1958 Corning, CA **1982** SF 9 (1) **1983**†SF 16 (0) **1984**†SF 6 (2) **1985**†SF 16 (12, LDE)
1986†SF 15 (6, LDE) **1987**†SF 12 (5, lde) **1988**†SF 7 (0) **NFL** 81 (26) [7 yrs]

STOVER, MATT John Matthew, K, 5´11˝/178 lbs; Louisiana Tech; 1990: NYG, rnd 12; B1/27/1968 Dallas, TX [K] **1991** Cle 16 (0) **1993** Cle 16 (0) **1994**†Cle☆16 (0)
1995 Cle 16 (0) **1996** Bal 16 (0) **1997** Bal 16 (0) **1998** Bal 16 (0) **1999** Bal 16 (0) **2000**†Bal☆16 (0) **2001**†Bal 16 (0) **2002** Bal 15 (0) **2003**†Bal 16 (0) **2004** Bal 16 (0)
2005 Bal 16 (0)

| 1992 | Cle | 16 (0) | — | — | — | — | — | — | — | — | 1 | 0 | 0.0 | 0 | 0.0 | 0 | 1 | — | — | — | K | — | 92 | -40 |
| NFL | 15 | | 239 (0) | — | — | — | — | — | — | — | — | 1 | 0 | 0.0 | 0 | 0.0 | 0 | 1 | — | — | — | KP | — | 1594 | -40 |

STOVER, SMOKEY Stewart Lynn, LB, 6´0˝/227 lbs; Louisiana-Monroe; B8/24/1938 McPherson, KS **1960** DalT-A 14 (RLB) **1961** DalT-A 14 (RLB) **1962**†DalT-A 14 **1963** KC-A 14
1964 KC-A 14 **1965** KC-A 14 **1966**†KC-A 14 **NFL** 98 [7 yrs]

STOWE, OTTO Otto William, WR, 6´2˝/188 lbs; Iowa State; 1971: Mia, rnd 2; B2/25/1949 Chicago, IL

1971	†Mia	12	—	—	—	—	5	68	13.6 (21)	1	—	—	—	—	—	—	—	—	—	—	—	—	6	39
1972	†Mia	9	—	—	—	—	13	276	21.2 (49)	2	—	—	—	—	—	—	—	—	—	—	—	—	12	148
1973	Dal	7 (7, WR)	3	28	9.3 (14)	0	23	389	16.9 (45)	6	—	—	—	—	—	—	—	—	—	—	—	—	36	253
1974	Den	8	1	1	1.0 (1)	0	2	9	4.5 (5)	1	—	—	—	—	—	—	—	—	—	—	—	—	6	11
NFL	4		36 (7)	4	29	7.3 (14)	0	43	742	17.3 (49)	10	—	—	—	—	—	—	—	—	—	—	—	—	60	450

STOWE, TYRONNE Tyronne Kevin, LB, 6´2˝/250 lbs; Rutgers; B5/30/1965 Passaic, NJ **1987** Pit 13 (3) **1988** Pit 10 (4) **1989**†Pit 16 (0) **1990** Pit 16 (0) **1991** Phx 13 (3)
1992 Phx 15 (15, LILB/llb) **1993** Phx 15 (15, RLB/llb) **1994** Sea 16 (16, MLB) **1995** Sea 6 (6, mlb) **NFL** 120 (61) [9 yrs]

STOWERS, TOMMIE Tommie D., TE, 6´3˝/240 lbs; Missouri; 1990: SD, rnd 11; B11/18/1966 Kansas City, MO **1993** NO 4 (0) **1994**†KC 1 (0)

| 1992 | †NO | 12 (0) | — | — | — | — | 4 | 23 | 5.8 (8) | 0 | — | — | — | — | — | — | — | — | — | — | — | — | 0 | 12 |
| NFL | 3 | | 17 (0) | — | — | — | — | 4 | 23 | 5.8 (8) | 0 | — | — | — | — | — | — | — | — | — | — | — | — | 2 | 12 |

STOYANOVICH, PETE Peter, K, 5´11˝/187 lbs; Indiana; 1989: Mia, rnd 8; B4/28/1967 Dearborn, MI [K] **1989** Mia 16 (0) **1990**†Mia☆16 (0) **1991** Mia☆14 (0) **1992**†Mia☆16 (0)
1993 Mia 16 (0) **1994**†Mia 16 (0) **1995**†Mia 16 (0) **1996** KC 16 (0) **1997**†KC☆16 (0) **1998** KC 16 (0) **1999** KC 16 (0) **2000** KC 5 (0) **2000** SL 3 (0) **NFL** 182 (0) [12 yrs]

STRACHAN, MIKE Michael David, RB, 6´0˝/199 lbs; Iowa State; 1975: NO, rnd 9; B5/24/1953 Miami, FL

1975	NO	11 (11, RB)	161	668	4.1 (21)	2	30	224	7.5 (27)	0	—	—	—	—	—	—	—	—	—	—	k	—	12	816
1976	NO	10 (3)	66	258	3.9 (31)	2	6	22	3.7 (14)	0	—	—	—	—	—	—	—	—	—	—		—	12	289
1977	NO	13 (3)	55	271	4.9 (18)	0	3	26	8.7 (10)	0	—	—	—	—	—	—	—	—	—	—		—	0	284
1978	NO	15 (rb)	108	388	3.6 (21)	4	10	51	5.1 (15)	0	1	0	0.0	0	0.0	0	—	—	—	—		—	24	454
1979	NO	10	62	276	4.5 (23)	6	3	9	3.0 (5)	0	—	—	—	—	—	—	—	—	—	—		—	36	341
1980	NO	3 (2)	20	41	2.1 (10)	0	5	60	12.0 (23)	0	—	—	—	—	—	—	—	—	—	—		—	0	71
NFL	6		62 (19)	472	1902	4.0 (31)	14	57	392	6.9 (27)	0	1	0	0.0	0	0.0	0	—	—	—	—	k	—	84	2254

YEAR	TEAM	G (GS, POS)	RUSH	YD	AVG(LG)	TD	REC	YD	AVG(LG)	TD	PASS	COMP	PCT	YD	AVG(LG)	TD	INT	SK	YD	QBR	KPR	OTD	PTS	TAY

STRACHAN, STEVE Stephen Michael, RB, 6´1˝/221 lbs; Boston College; 1985: LARd, rnd 11; B3/22/1963 Everett, MA

1985	LARd	4(0)	2	1	0.5(1)	0	—	—	—	—	—	—	—	—	—	—	—	—	—	—	—	—	0	1
1986	LARd	16(1)	18	53	2.9(10)	0	—	—	—	—	—	—	—	—	—	—	—	—	—	—	—	—	0	53
1987	LARd	11(3)	28	108	3.9(20)	0	4	42	10.5(14)	0	—	—	—	—	—	—	—	—	—	—	—	—	0	129
1988	LARd	16(0)	4	12	3.0(5)	0	3	19	6.3(13)	1	—	—	—	—	—	—	—	—	—	—	—	—	6	27
1989	LARd	16(0)	—	—	—	—	—	—	—	—	—	—	—	—	—	—	—	—	—	—	—	—	—	—
NFL	**5**	63(4)	52	174	3.3(20)	0	7	61	8.7(14)	1	—	—	—	—	—	—	—	—	—	—	—	—	6	210

STRACK, CHARLIE Charles William, G, 6´0˝/215 lbs; Colgate; Oklahoma State; B7/15/1899 Nyack, NY, D5/1967 Spring Valley, NY **1928** ChiC 3 (3, LG)

STRACKA, TIM Timothy Terrill, TE, 6´3˝/225 lbs; Wisconsin; 1983: Cle, rnd 6; B9/27/1959 Madison, WI

1983	Cle	13(0)	—	—	—	—	1	12	12.0(12)	0	—	—	—	—	—	—	—	—	—	—	—	—	0	6
1984	Cle	6(1)	—	—	—	—	1	15	15.0(15)	0	—	—	—	—	—	—	—	—	—	—	—	—	0	8
NFL	**2**	19(1)	—	—	—	—	2	27	13.5(15)	0	—	—	—	—	—	—	—	—	—	—	—	—	0	14

STRADA, JOHN John Frank, TE, 6´3˝/230 lbs; William Jewell; B11/13/1952 Kansas City, MO **1974** NYG 1

| 1974 | KC | 11 | — | — | — | — | 1 | 16 | 16.0(16) | 0 | — | — | — | — | — | — | — | — | — | — | — | — | 0 | 8 |
| **NFL** | **1** | 12 | — | — | — | — | 1 | 16 | 16.0(16) | 0 | — | — | — | — | — | — | — | — | — | — | — | — | 0 | 8 |

STRADER, RED Norman Parker, B, 5´9˝/200 lbs; St. Mary's (CA); B12/21/1902 Newton, NJ, D5/26/1956 Berkeley, CA **1927** ChiC 6 (4), 6

STRADFORD, TROY Troy Edwin, RB-WR, 5´9˝/191 lbs; Boston College; 1987: Mia, rnd 4; B9/11/1964 Elizabeth, NJ

1987	Mia	12(5, rb)	145	619	4.3(51)	6	48	457	9.5(34)	1	1	1	100.0	6	6.0(6)	0	0	—	—	—	kp	—	42	964
1988	Mia	15(6, rb)	95	335	3.5(18)	2	56	424	7.6(36)	1	1	0	0.0	0	0.0(0)	0	0	—	—	—	kp	—	18	573
1989	Mia	7(4)	66	240	3.6(13)	1	25	233	9.3(32)	0	—	—	—	—	—	—	—	—	—	—	p	—	6	426
1990	Mia	14(0)	37	138	3.7(15)	1	30	257	8.6(23)	0	—	—	—	—	—	—	—	—	—	—	kp	—	6	277
1991	†KC	10(0)	1	7	7.0(7)	0	9	91	10.1(17)	0	—	—	—	—	—	—	—	—	—	—	kp	—	0	175
1992	LARm	2(0)	3	12	4.0(5)	0	—	—	—	—	—	—	—	—	—	—	—	—	—	—	kp	—	0	22
1992	Det	6(0)	9	29	3.2(11)	0	2	15	7.5(12)	0	—	—	—	—	—	—	—	—	—	—	k	—	0	12
NFL	**6**	66(15)	356	1380	3.9(51)	10	170	1479	8.7(36)	2	2	1	50.0	6	3.0(6)	0	0	—	—	—	kp	—	72	2447

STRAHAN, ART Arthur Ray, DT-DE, 6´5˝/250 lbs; Texas Southern; B7/17/1943 Newton, TX **1965** Hou-A 4 **1968** Atl 5 **NFL** 9 [2 yrs]

STRAHAN, MICHAEL Michael Anthony, DE, 6´5˝/275 lbs; Texas Southern; 1993: NYG, rnd 2; B11/21/1971 Houston, TX [S] **1993** NYG 9 (0) **1994** NYG 15 (15, RDE) **1995** NYG 15 (15, LDE) **1996** NYG 16 (16, LDE) **1997**†NYG★16 (16, LDE) **1998** NYG★16 (15, LDE) **1999** NYG◇16 (16, LDE) **2000**†NYG 16 (16, LDE) **2001** NYG★16 (16, LDE) **2002**†NYG★16 (16, LDE) **2003** NYG★16 (16, LDE) **2004** NYG 8 (8, LDE) **2005**†NYG★16 (16, LDE) **NFL** 191 (181) [13 yrs]

STRAIT, DERRICK Derrick, DB, 5´11˝/195 lbs; Oklahoma; 2004: NYJ, rnd 3; B8/27/1980 Austin, TX **2004**†NYJ 5 (1) **2005** NYJ 16 (2) **NFL** 21 (3) [2 yrs]

STRALKA, CLEM Clement Frank, G-T, 5´10˝/215 lbs; Georgetown (DC); B5/19/1913 Glen Lyon, PA, D1/10/1994 Denver, CO **1938** Was 9 (1) **1939** Was 10 (9, LG) **1940**†Was 10 (0) **1941** Was 11 (10, LG) **1942**†Was 11 (3) **1945**†Was 8 (0) **NFL** 62 (24) [7 yrs]

STRAMIELLO, MIKE Michael, E, 6´1˝/198 lbs; Colgate; B2/2/1907 New York, NY, D2/6/2000 Naples, FL [K] **1930** Bkn 12 (12, LE), 12 **1931** Bkn 13 (11, LE), 6 **1932** Bkn 3 (1) **1932** SI 5 (3) **1934** Bkn 2 (0) **NFL** 35 (27), 18 [4 yrs]

STRAND, ELI Eli S., G, 6´2˝/250 lbs; Iowa State; B2/11/1943 Mount Vernon, NY **1966** Pit 8 **1967** NO 14 **NFL** 22 [2 yrs]

STRAND, LEIF Leif Richard, C, 6´0˝/210 lbs; Fordham; Minnesota; B1/6/1899 Two Harbors, MN, D4/26/1968 Orlando, FL **1924** Dul 6 (6, C)

STRANSKY, BOB Robert Joseph, HB, 6´1˝/180 lbs; Colorado; 1958: Bal, rnd 2; B6/30/1936 Yankton, SD

| 1960 | Den-A | 14 | 28 | 78 | 2.8(16) | 0 | 3 | 11 | 3.7(11) | 0 | — | — | — | — | — | — | — | — | — | — | k | — | 0 | 132 |

STRASSNER, DUTCH Clarence, E, Findlay; B3/31/1904 Canton, OH, D6/1978 Burghill, OH **1925** Can 3 (2)

STRATTON, MIKE David Michael, LB, 6´3˝/224 lbs; Tennessee; 1962: Buf, rnd 13; B4/10/1941 Vonore, TN [I] **1962** Buf-A 12 (RLB) **1964**†Buf-A★14 (RLB) **1965**†Buf-A★14 (RLB) **1966**†Buf-A★14 (RLB) **1967** Buf-A★14 (RLB) **1968** Buf-A★14 (RLB) **1969** Buf-A☆14 (RLB) **1970** Buf 9 (RLB) **1971** Buf 13 (RLB) **1972** Buf 10 (RLB) **1973** SD 14 (10, LLB)

| 1963 | †Buf-A◇ | 14(RLB) | — | — | — | — | 1 | 19 | 19.0(19) | 0 | — | — | — | — | — | — | i | — | — | — | — | 1 | 6 | 36 |
| **NFL** | **12** | 156(10) | — | — | — | — | 1 | 19 | 19.0(19) | 0 | — | — | — | — | — | — | i | — | — | — | — | 2 | 14 | 169 |

STRAUSBAUGH, JIMMY James Edwin, HB, 5´9˝/190 lbs; Ohio State; 1941: GB, rnd 20; B2/25/1918 Chillicothe, OH, D11/25/1991 Chillicothe, OH

| 1946 | ChiC | 11(1) | 37 | 183 | 4.9(29) | 3 | 5 | 56 | 11.2(21) | 0 | 1 | 1 | 100.0 | 35 | 35.0(35) | 0 | 0 | — | — | — | kp | — | 18 | 297 |

STRAUSS, DUTCH J. Arthur, FB-WB, 5´10˝/205 lbs; Phillips; B1/7/1897 Hennessey, OK, D8/10/1969 Enid, OK **1923** Tol 6 (4, FB) **1924** KC 7 (6, FB), 6 **NFL** 13 (10) [2 yrs]

STRAUTHERS, THOMAS Thomas Bryan, DE-DT, 6´4˝/262 lbs; Jackson State; 1983: Phi, rnd 10; B4/6/1961 Wesson, MS **1983** Phi 4 (0) **1984** Phi 16 (0) **1985** Phi 16 (3) **1986** Phi 11 (1) **1988** Det 10 (0) **1989**†Min 12 (0) **1990** Min 13 (2) **1991** Min 15 (1) **NFL** 97 (7) [8 yrs]

STRAW, DON Donald McAlpine, G-T, 5´11˝/210 lbs; Washington & Jefferson; B11/22/1896, D7/31/1961 **1920** Det 1 (1) **1921** Det 1 (1) **NFL** 2 (2) [2 yrs]

STRAYHORN, LES Leslie Dewey, RB, 5´10˝/205 lbs; East Carolina; 1973: Dal, rnd 17; B9/1/1951 Trenton, NC

1973	†Dal	11	11	62	5.6(24)	1	—	—	—	—	—	—	—	—	—	—	—	—	—	—	k	—	6	86
1974	Dal	13	11	66	6.0(24)	0	2	12	6.0(10)	0	—	—	—	—	—	—	—	—	—	—	k	—	0	61
NFL	**2**	24	22	128	5.8(24)	1	2	12	6.0(10)	0	—	—	—	—	—	—	—	—	—	—	k	—	6	147

STREATER, ERIC Eric Maurice, WR, 5´11˝/165 lbs; North Carolina; B3/21/1964 Sylva, NC

| 1987 | TB | 3(3) | 1 | 5 | 5.0(5) | 0 | 5 | 117 | 23.4(61) | 2 | — | — | — | — | — | — | — | — | — | — | — | — | 12 | 74 |

STREETER, GEORGE George Leon, DB, 6´2˝/212 lbs; Notre Dame; 1989: Chi, rnd 11; B8/28/1967 Chicago, IL **1989** ChiB 4 (0) **1990** Ind 4 (0) **NFL** 8 (0) [2 yrs]

STREETS, TAI Tai, WR, 6´3˝/207 lbs; Michigan; 1999: SF, rnd 6; B4/20/1977 Matteson, IL

1999	SF	2(0)	—	—	—	—	2	25	12.5(14)	0	—	—	—	—	—	—	—	—	—	—	—	—	0	13
2000	SF	15(1)	1	0	0.0(0)	0	19	287	15.1(39)	0	—	—	—	—	—	—	—	—	—	—	k	—	0	204
2001	†SF	16(3)	—	—	—	—	28	345	12.3(52)	1	—	—	—	—	—	—	—	—	—	—	—	—	6	178
2002	†SF	16(14, WR)	—	—	—	—	72	756	10.5(47)	5	—	—	—	—	—	—	—	—	—	—	—	—	30	403
2003	SF	16(16, WR)	—	—	—	—	47	595	12.7(41)	7	—	—	—	—	—	—	—	—	—	—	—	—	42	333
2004	Det	13(12, WR)	—	—	—	—	28	260	9.3(22)	1	—	—	—	—	—	—	—	—	—	—	—	—	8	135
NFL	**6**	78(46)	1	0	0.0	0	196	2268	11.6(52)	14	—	—	—	—	—	—	—	—	—	—	k	—	86	1264

STRENGER, RICH Richard Gene, T, 6´7˝/280 lbs; Michigan; 1983: Det, rnd 2; B3/10/1960 Port Washington, WI **1983**†Det 16 (4) **1984** Det 1 (1) **1985** Det 13 (6, rt) **1986** Det 16 (16, RT) **1987** Det 3 (3) **NFL** 49 (30) [5 yrs]

STRIBLING, BILL Majure Blanks, E, 6´1˝/206 lbs; Mississippi; 1950: NYG, rnd 21; B11/5/1927 Edinburg, MS

1951	NYG	6(RE)	—	—	—	—	18	226	12.6(42)	2	—	—	—	—	—	—	—	—	—	—	—	—	12	123
1952	NYG	12(RE)	—	—	—	—	26	399	15.3(55)	5	—	—	—	—	—	—	—	—	—	—	k	—	30	221
1953	NYG	12(RE)	—	—	—	—	16	175	10.9(19)	0	—	—	—	—	—	—	—	—	—	—	—	—	0	88
1955	Phi	12(LE)	—	—	—	—	38	568	14.9(56)	6	—	—	—	—	—	—	—	—	—	—	—	—	36	314
1956	Phi	2	—	—	—	—	1	5	5.5(7)	0	—	—	—	—	—	—	—	—	—	—	—	—	0	6
1957	Phi	12(RE)	—	—	—	—	14	194	13.9(58)	1	—	—	—	—	—	—	—	—	—	—	—	—	6	102
NFL	**6**	56	—	—	—	—	114	1573	13.8(58)	14	—	—	—	—	—	—	—	—	—	—	k	—	84	853

STRICKER, TONY Antony Elling, DB, 6´0˝/185 lbs; Cameron; Colorado; B9/2/1940 Lawton, OK **1963** NYJ-A 12 (LCB)

STRICKLAND, BILL William, G, 5´9˝/220 lbs; Western Illinois; Lombard; B9/14/1898 Youngstown, OH, D1/31/1976 Quincy, IL **1923** Mil 3 (1)

STRICKLAND, BISHOP Frank Bishop, FB, 5´10˝/195 lbs; South Carolina; 1951: SF, rnd 6; B1/4/1927 Mullins, SC

| 1951 | SF | 9 | 34 | 165 | 4.9(15) | 0 | — | — | — | — | — | — | — | — | — | — | — | — | — | — | k | — | 0 | 164 |

STRICKLAND, DAVE David G., G, 6´0˝/220 lbs; Memphis; B6/13/1931 Holly Springs, MS **1960** Den-A 14

STRICKLAND, DONALD Donald Darell, DB, 5´10˝/187 lbs; Colorado; 2003: Ind, rnd 3; B11/24/1980 Redwood City, CA **2003**†Ind 11 (8, fs) **2004** Ind 4 (4) **2005** Ind 1 (0) **2005** Phi 3 (0) **NFL** 19 (12) [3 yrs]

STRICKLAND, FRED Fredrick William, LB, 6´2˝/246 lbs; Purdue; 1988: LARm, rnd 2; B8/15/1966 Buffalo, NY **1988**†LARm 16 (0) **1989**†LARm 12 (12, RILB) **1990** LARm 5 (5, lilb) **1991** LARm 14 (10, RLB) **1992** LARm 16 (0) **1993**†Min 16 (15, RLB) **1994**†GB 16 (14, MLB) **1995**†GB 14 (10, MLB) **1996**†Dal 16 (16, MLB) **1997** Dal 15 (14, MLB) **1998**†Dal 16 (15, MLB) **1999** Was 5 (0) **NFL** 161 (111) [12 yrs]

STRICKLAND, LARRY Lawrence Wayne, C, 6´4˝/248 lbs; North Texas; 1953: ChiB, rnd 13; B9/3/1931 Tyler, TX, D8/29/1979 Tyler, TX **1954** ChiB 12 (C) **1955** ChiB 12 (C) **1956**†ChiB★12 (C) **1957** ChiB☆11 (C) **1958** ChiB 12 (C) **1959** ChiB 3 **NFL** 62 [6 yrs]

STRIEGEL, BILL William Joseph, G-T-LB, 6´2˝/235 lbs; Pacific; 1958: Phi, rnd 8; B5/28/1936 Easton, KS, D7/23/1992 San Joaquin County, CA **1959** Phi 12 **1960** Oak-A 1 **1960** Bos-A 5 **NFL** 18 [2 yrs]

STRINGER, ART Arthur, LB, 6´1˝/223 lbs; Ball State; 1976: Hou, rnd 9; B1/30/1954 Troy, AL **1977** Hou 13 **1978** Hou 7 **1979**†Hou 8 (8, RILB) **1980** Hou 8 (8, LILB) **1981** Hou 5 (1) **NFL** 41 (17) [5 yrs]

STRINGER, BOB Robert Jean, LB-FB, 6´1˝/197 lbs; Tulsa; 1952: Phi, rnd 14; B10/8/1929 Shawnee, OK

YEAR	TEAM	G(GS, POS)	RUSH	YD	AVG(LG)	TD	REC	YD	AVG(LG)	TD	PASS	COMP	PCT	YD	AVG(LG)	TD	INT	SK	YD	QBR	KPR	OTD	PTS	TAY
1952	Phi	12	2	5	2.5(3)	0	1	4	4.0(4)	0	—	—	—	—	—	—	—	—	—	—	ki	—	0	18
1953	Phi	12	1	5	5.0(5)	0	—	—	—	—	—	—	—	—	—	—	—	—	—	—	ki	—	0	3
NFL	2	24	3	10	3.3(5)	0	1	4	4.0(4)	0	—	—	—	—	—	—	—	—	—	—	ki	—	0	21

STRINGER, GENE Eugene Charles, B, 6´0˝/200 lbs; John Carroll; B5/29/1903 Cleveland, OH, D6/1/1985 Pueblo, CO **1925** Cle 10 (3)

STRINGER, KOREY Korey Damont, T, 6´4˝/350 lbs; Ohio State; 1995: Min, rnd 1; B5/8/1974 Warren, OH, D8/1/2001 Mankato, MN **1996**†Min 16 (15, RT) **1997**†Min 15 (15, RT) **1998**†Min 14 (14, RT) **1999**†Min 16 (16, RT) **2000**†Min✧16 (16, RT)

YEAR	TEAM	G(GS, POS)	RUSH	YD	AVG(LG)	TD	REC	YD	AVG(LG)	TD	PASS	COMP	PCT	YD	AVG(LG)	TD	INT	SK	YD	QBR	KPR	OTD	PTS	TAY
1995	Min	16(15, RT)	—	—	—	—	1	-1	-1.0(-1)	0	—	—	—	—	—	—	—	—	—	—	—	—	0	-1
NFL	6	93(91)	—	—	—	—	1	-1	-1.0(-1)	0	—	—	—	—	—	—	—	—	—	—	—	—	0	-1

STRINGER, SCOTT Scott Lee, DB, 5´11˝/180 lbs; California; B8/5/1951 Tracy, CA **1974** SL 5

STRINGERT, HAL Harold Lloyd, DB, 5´11˝/185 lbs; Hawaii; Willamette; B1/2/1952 Honolulu, HI **1975** SD 6 **1976** SD 11 (2) **1977** SD 14 (14, LCB) **1978** SD 13 (10, LCB) **1979**†SD 15 (1) **1980**†SD 10 (0) **NFL** 69 (27) [6 yrs]

STRINGFELLOW, JOE Joseph Elbert, TB, 6´0˝/185 lbs; Southern Mississippi; 1942: Det, rnd 12; B3/10/1918 Meridian, MS, D9/16/1992 Savannah, GA

YEAR	TEAM	G(GS, POS)	RUSH	YD	AVG(LG)	TD	REC	YD	AVG(LG)	TD	PASS	COMP	PCT	YD	AVG(LG)	TD	INT	SK	YD	QBR	KPR	OTD	PTS	TAY
1942	Det	9(2)	16	41	2.6(11)	0	8	89	11.1(20)	0	13	5	38.5	67	5.2(21)	0	2	—	—	—	Pk	—	0	63

STROCK, DON Donald Joseph, QB, 6´5˝/220 lbs; Virginia Tech; 1973: Mia, rnd 5; B11/27/1950 Pottstown, PA

YEAR	TEAM	G(GS, POS)	RUSH	YD	AVG(LG)	TD	REC	YD	AVG(LG)	TD	PASS	COMP	PCT	YD	AVG(LG)	TD	INT	SK	YD	QBR	KPR	OTD	PTS	TAY
1974	Mia	1	1	-7	-7.0(-7)	0	—	—	—	—	—	—	—	—	—	—	—	—	—	—	—	—	0	-7
1975	Mia	6(3)	6	38	6.3(18)	1	—	—	—	—	45	26	57.8	230	5.1(25)	2	2	3	29	—	—	—	6	93
1976	Mia	4(1)	2	13	6.5(11)	1	—	—	—	—	47	21	44.7	359	7.6(53)	3	2	4	41	—	—	—	6	138
1977	Mia	4	—	—	—	—	—	—	—	—	4	2	50.0	12	3.0(9)	0	1	—	—	—	—	—	0	-34
1978	†Mia	16(7, qb)	10	23	2.3(12)	0	—	—	—	—	135	72	53.3	825	6.1(57)	12	6	9	73	83.1	—	—	0	256
1979	†Mia	16(4)	3	18	6.0(11)	0	—	—	—	—	100	56	56.0	830	8.3(53)	6	6	2	22	78.3	—	—	0	223
1980	Mia	16(2)	1	-3	-3.0(-3)	0	—	—	—	—	62	30	48.4	313	5.0(33)	1	5	5	49	—	—	—	0	-42
1981	†Mia	16(1)	14	-26	-1.9(9)	0	—	—	—	—	130	79	60.8	901	6.9(52)	6	8	6	45	71.3	—	—	0	135
1982	†Mia	9(0)	3	-9	-3.0(0)	0	—	—	—	—	55	30	54.5	306	5.6(43)	2	5	1	5	—	—	—	0	-46
1983	†Mia	15(2)	6	-16	-2.7(0)	0	—	—	—	—	52	34	65.4	403	7.8(47)	4	1	3	30	—	—	—	0	166
1984	†Mia	16(0)	2	-5	-2.5(0)	0	—	—	—	—	6	4	66.7	27	4.5(12)	0	0	—	—	—	—	—	0	9
1985	†Mia	16(0)	2	-6	-3.0(-3)	0	—	—	—	—	9	7	77.8	141	15.7(67)	1	0	—	—	—	—	—	0	70
1986	Mia	16(0)	1	0	0.0(0)	0	—	—	—	—	20	14	70.0	152	7.6(21)	2	0	—	—	—	—	—	0	86
1987	Mia	12(0)	—	—	—	—	—	—	—	—	23	13	56.5	114	5.0(26)	0	1	—	—	—	P	—	0	17
1988	†Cle	4(2)	6	-2	-0.3(5)	0	—	—	—	—	91	55	60.4	736	8.1(41)	6	5	4	26	—	—	—	0	196
NFL	15	167(22)	57	18	0.3(18)	2	—	—	—	—	779	443	56.9	5349	6.9(67)	45	42	37	320	74.9	P	—	12	1258

STRODE, WOODY Woodrow Wilson Woodwine, E, 6´3˝/205 lbs; UCLA; B7/25/1914 Los Angeles, CA, D12/31/1994 Glendora, CA

YEAR	TEAM	G(GS, POS)	RUSH	YD	AVG(LG)	TD	REC	YD	AVG(LG)	TD	PASS	COMP	PCT	YD	AVG(LG)	TD	INT	SK	YD	QBR	KPR	OTD	PTS	TAY
1946	LARm	10(0)	—	—	—	—	4	37	9.3(19)	0	—	—	—	—	—	—	—	—	—	—	k	—	0	10

STROFOLINO, MIKE Michael James, LB, 6´2˝/230 lbs; Villanova; 1965: LA, rnd 4/Den, rnd 13; B2/6/1944 Brooklyn, NY **1965** LARm 9 **1965**†Bal 3 **1966** SL 8 **1967** SL 1 **1968** SL 14 (mlb) **NFL** 35 [4 yrs]

STROHMEYER, GEORGE George Ferdinand, C-LB, 5´10˝/205 lbs; Texas A&M; Notre Dame; 1947: NYY-A, rnd 8/1946: LARm, rnd 13; B1/27/1924 Kansas City, MO, D1/12/1992 Murphys, CA **1948** Bkn-A☆14 (7, c) **1949** ChiH-A 12 (1) **AAFC** 26 (8) [2 yrs]

STROM, FRANK Frank E., T, 6´2˝/252 lbs; Tulsa; B8/29/1916 Ballinger, TX, D6/8/1992 Clinton, OK **1944** Bkn 7 (0)

STROM, RICK Richard James, QB, 6´2˝/210 lbs; Georgia Tech; B3/11/1965 Pittsburgh, PA

YEAR	TEAM	G(GS, POS)	RUSH	YD	AVG(LG)	TD	REC	YD	AVG(LG)	TD	PASS	COMP	PCT	YD	AVG(LG)	TD	INT	SK	YD	QBR	KPR	OTD	PTS	TAY
1989	Pit	3(0)	4	-3	-0.8(0)	0	—	—	—	—	1	0	0.0	0	0.0	0	0	—	—	—	—	—	0	-3
1990	Pit	6(0)	4	10	2.5(10)	0	—	—	—	—	21	14	66.7	162	7.7(22)	0	1	5	29	—	—	—	0	51
1991	Pit	1(0)	—	—	—	—	—	—	—	—	—	—	—	—	—	—	—	—	—	—	—	—	—	—
NFL	3	10(0)	8	7	0.9(10)	0	—	—	—	—	22	14	63.6	162	7.4(22)	0	1	5	29	—	—	—	0	48

STROMBERG, MICHAEL Michael David, LB, 6´2˝/235 lbs; Temple; 1967: NYJ, rnd 14; B5/25/1945 Brooklyn, NY **1968** NYJ-A 2 (2)

STRONG, FRANK Frank, LB, 6´1˝/232 lbs; USC; B1/14/1980 Stockton, CA **2002** SF 6 (0)

STRONG, JIM James Harold, RB, 6´1˝/215 lbs; Houston; 1970: SF, rnd 7; B12/12/1946 San Antonio, TX

YEAR	TEAM	G(GS, POS)	RUSH	YD	AVG(LG)	TD	REC	YD	AVG(LG)	TD	PASS	COMP	PCT	YD	AVG(LG)	TD	INT	SK	YD	QBR	KPR	OTD	PTS	TAY
1970	SF	3	2	3	1.5(3)	0	—	—	—	—	—	—	—	—	—	—	—	—	—	—	—	—	0	3
1971	NO	14(FB)	95	404	4.3(39)	3	16	78	4.9(14)	0	—	—	—	—	—	—	—	—	—	—	k	—	18	472
1972	NO	14	37	120	3.2(9)	0	14	123	8.8(16)	0	—	—	—	—	—	—	—	—	—	—	k	—	0	175
NFL	3	31	134	527	3.9(39)	3	30	201	6.7(16)	0	—	—	—	—	—	—	—	—	—	—	k	—	18	650

STRONG, KEN Elmer Kenneth, FB-TB-HB-WB-DB-K, 6´0˝/206 lbs; NYU; B3/21/1906 West Haven, CT, D10/5/1979 New York, NY; HOF 1967 **[K]** **1929** SI☆10 (10, HB), 39 **1930** SI☆12 (11, WB), 53 **1931** SI☆11 (9, TB), 53 **1945** NYG 9 (9, fb), 41 **1946**†NYG 11 (11, fb), 44 **1947** NYG 10 (9, FB), 30

YEAR	TEAM	G(GS, POS)	RUSH	YD	AVG(LG)	TD	REC	YD	AVG(LG)	TD	PASS	COMP	PCT	YD	AVG(LG)	TD	INT	SK	YD	QBR	KPR	OTD	PTS	TAY
1932	SI	11(7, FB)	96	375	3.9	2	5	56	11.2	0	23	4	17.4	94	4.1	1	3	—	—	—	K	—	15	355
1933	†NYG☆	14(11, FB)	96	272	2.8	3	10	146	14.6	2	11	8	72.7	194	17.6	2	0	—	—	—	K	1	**64**	502
1934	†NYG☆	13(11, FB)	138	431	3.1	6	7	52	7.4	0	15	8	53.3	92	6.1	0	1	—	—	—	K	—	56	523
1935	†NYG	11(7, FB)	46	151	3.3	1	—	—	—	—	3	0	0.0	0	0.0	0	1	—	—	—	K	—	29	121
1939	NYG	9(3)	1	1	1.0(1)	0	—	—	—	—	—	—	—	—	—	—	—	—	—	—	KP	—	19	1
1944	†NYG	10(6, fb)	2	-2	-1.0(2)	0	—	—	—	—	—	—	—	—	—	—	—	—	—	—	KP	—	41	-2
NFL	12	131(104)	379	1228	3.2(2)	24	22	254	11.5	7	52	20	38.5	380	7.3	6	5	—	—	—	KP	3	484	1680

STRONG, MACK Mack Carlington, FB, 6´0˝/245 lbs; Georgia; B9/11/1971 Columbus, GA

YEAR	TEAM	G(GS, POS)	RUSH	YD	AVG(LG)	TD	REC	YD	AVG(LG)	TD	PASS	COMP	PCT	YD	AVG(LG)	TD	INT	SK	YD	QBR	KPR	OTD	PTS	TAY
1994	Sea	8(1)	27	114	4.2(14)	2	3	3	1.0(5)	0	—	—	—	—	—	—	—	—	—	—	—	—	12	136
1995	Sea	16(2)	8	23	2.9(9)	1	12	117	9.8(25)	3	—	—	—	—	—	—	—	—	—	—	k	—	24	112
1996	Sea	14(8, FB)	5	8	1.6(4)	0	9	78	8.7(20)	0	—	—	—	—	—	—	—	—	—	—	—	—	0	47
1997	Sea	16(9, FB)	4	8	2.0(6)	0	13	91	7.0(20)	2	—	—	—	—	—	—	—	—	—	—	k	—	12	65
1998	Sea	16(5, fb)	15	47	3.1(9)	0	8	48	6.0(11)	2	—	—	—	—	—	—	—	—	—	—	—	—	12	81
1999	†Sea	14(1)	1	0	0.0(0)	0	1	5	5.0(5)	0	—	—	—	—	—	—	—	—	—	—	—	—	0	3
2000	Sea	16(12, FB)	3	9	3.0(4)	0	23	141	6.1(24)	1	—	—	—	—	—	—	—	—	—	—	k	—	6	96
2001	Sea	16(13, FB)	17	55	3.2(12)	0	17	141	8.3(35)	0	—	—	—	—	—	—	—	—	—	—	k	—	0	127
2002	Sea	16(12, FB)	23	94	4.1(9)	0	22	120	5.5(12)	2	—	—	—	—	—	—	—	—	—	—	k	—	12	173
2003	†Sea	16(10, FB)	37	174	4.7(21)	1	29	216	7.4(32)	0	—	—	—	—	—	—	—	—	—	—	k	—	6	307
2004	†Sea	16(13, FB)	36	131	3.6(11)	0	21	99	4.7(13)	0	—	—	—	—	—	—	—	—	—	—	—	—	0	181
2005	†Sea★	16(7, FB)	17	78	4.6(16)	0	22	166	7.5(27)	0	—	—	—	—	—	—	—	—	—	—	—	—	0	161
NFL	12	180(93)	193	741	3.8(21)	4	180	1225	6.8(35)	10	—	—	—	—	—	—	—	—	—	—	k	—	84	1486

STRONG, RAY Raymond, RB, 5´9˝/184 lbs; UNLV; 1978: Atl, rnd 10; B5/7/1956 Berkeley, CA

YEAR	TEAM	G(GS, POS)	RUSH	YD	AVG(LG)	TD	REC	YD	AVG(LG)	TD	PASS	COMP	PCT	YD	AVG(LG)	TD	INT	SK	YD	QBR	KPR	OTD	PTS	TAY
1978	†Atl	14(1)	30	99	3.3(14)	2	7	56	8.0(21)	0	—	—	—	—	—	—	—	—	—	—	k	—	12	152
1979	Atl	6	2	7	3.5(4)	0	1	6	6.0(6)	0	—	—	—	—	—	—	—	—	—	—	k	—	0	128
1980	†Atl	16(0)	6	42	7.0(21)	1	—	—	—	—	—	—	—	—	—	—	—	—	—	—	k	—	6	70
1981	Atl	16(0)	3	6	2.0(3)	0	1	9	9.0(9)	0	—	—	—	—	—	—	—	—	—	—	—	—	0	11

YEAR	TEAM	G (GS, POS)	RUSH	YD	AVG (LG)	TD	REC	YD	AVG (LG)	TD	PASS	COMP	PCT	YD	AVG (LG)	TD	INT	SK	YD	QBR	KPR	OTD	PTS	TAY
1982	†Atl	9(0)	4	9	2.3(4)	0	—	—	—	—	—	—	—	—	—	—	—	—	—	—	—	—	0	9
NFL	5	61(1)	45	163	3.6(21)	3	9	71	7.9(21)	0	—	—	—	—	—	—	—	—	—	—	k	—	18	370

Strong, William William Blake, DB, 5´10˝/191 lbs; North Carolina State; 1995: NO, rnd 5; B11/3/1971 Chester, SC **1996** NO 9 (0)

Stroschein, James James Breckenridge, DE, 6´1˝/205 lbs; UCLA; 1951: NYY, rnd 24; B4/3/1929 Santa Ana, CA, D8/7/1983 Covina, CA **1951** NYY 11

Strosnider, Aubrey Aubrey J., T, 6´1˝/205 lbs; Dayton; B5/9/1904, D10/27/1964 Cleveland, OH **1928** Day 1 (0)

Stroth, Vince Vincent Martin, T-G-TE, 6´4˝/267 lbs; Brigham Young; B11/25/1960 San Jose, CA **1985** SF 1 (0) **1987** Hou 9 (3) **1988** Hou 6 (0) **NFL** 16 (3) [3 yrs]

Strother, Billy William Gregory, LB, 6´0˝/230 lbs; New Mexico; B1/8/1982 Evansville, IN **2004** Was 2 (0) **2004** Mia 1 (0) **NFL** 3 (0) [1 yr]

Strother, Deon Deon, RB, 5´11˝/213 lbs; USC; B4/12/1972 Saginaw, MI **1994** Den 2 (0)

Stroud, Jack Jack Chester, G-T, 6´1˝/235 lbs; Tennessee; 1951: NYG, rnd 5; B1/29/1928 Fresno, CA, D6/1/1994 Flemington, NJ **1953** NYG 12 (lg) **1954** NYG 6 (rg) **1955** NYG✧12 (RG) **1956**†NYG☆11 (RG) **1957** NYG★11 (RG) **1958**†NYG 7 (RG) **1959**†NYG☆12 (RG) **1960** NYG★12 (RG) **1961**†NYG☆12 (RG) **1962**†NYG☆14 (RT) **1963**†NYG 14 (RT) **1964** NYG 9 **NFL** 132 [12 yrs]

Stroud, Marcus Marcus Lavar, DT, 6´6˝/312 lbs; Georgia; 2001: Jax, rnd 1; B6/25/1978 Thomasville, GA **2001** Jax 16 (0) **2002** Jax 16 (16, LDT) **2003** Jax★16 (16, LDT) **2004** Jax★16 (16, LDT) **2005**†Jax★16 (16, LDT/rdt) **NFL** 80 (64) [5 yrs]

Stroud, Morris Morris, TE, 6´10˝/255 lbs; Clark Atlanta; 1969: KC, rnd 3; B5/17/1946 Miami, FL

YEAR	TEAM	G (GS, POS)	RUSH	YD	AVG (LG)	TD	REC	YD	AVG (LG)	TD	PASS	COMP	PCT	YD	AVG (LG)	TD	INT	SK	YD	QBR	KPR	OTD	PTS	TAY
1969	†KC-A	0	—	—	—	—	—	—	—	—	—	—	—	—	—	—	—	—	—	—	—	—	0	0
1970	KC	13(te)	—	—	—	—	4	86	21.5(50)	1	—	—	—	—	—	—	—	—	—	—	—	—	6	48
1971	†KC	14(TE)	—	—	—	—	22	454	20.6(54)	1	—	—	—	—	—	—	—	—	—	—	—	—	6	232
1972	KC	14(TE)	—	—	—	—	4	80	20.0(44)	1	—	—	—	—	—	—	—	—	—	—	—	—	6	45
1973	KC	14(TE)	—	—	—	—	12	216	18.0(48)	2	—	—	—	—	—	—	—	—	—	—	—	—	12	118
1974	KC	14(TE)	—	—	—	—	12	141	11.8(25)	2	—	—	—	—	—	—	—	—	—	—	—	—	12	81
NFL	6	69	—	—	—	—	54	977	18.1(54)	7	—	—	—	—	—	—	—	—	—	—	—	—	42	524

Strozier, Art Arthur A., TE, 6´2˝/220 lbs; Kansas State; B5/23/1946 Kansas City, MO

YEAR	TEAM	G (GS, POS)	RUSH	YD	AVG (LG)	TD	REC	YD	AVG (LG)	TD	PASS	COMP	PCT	YD	AVG (LG)	TD	INT	SK	YD	QBR	KPR	OTD	PTS	TAY
1970	SD	14	—	—	—	—	2	40	20.0(28)	0	—	—	—	—	—	—	—	—	—	—	—	—	0	20
1971	SD	6	—	—	—	—	1	6	6.0(6)	0	—	—	—	—	—	—	—	—	—	—	—	—	0	3
NFL	2	20	—	—	—	—	3	46	15.3(28)	0	—	—	—	—	—	—	—	—	—	—	—	—	0	23

Strozier, Wilbur Wilbur Lamar, TE, 6´4˝/255 lbs; Georgia; 1987: Den, rnd 7; B11/12/1964 La Grange, GA **1987**†Sea 12 (3) **1988** SD 6 (0) **NFL** 18 (3) [2 yrs]

Strugar, George George Ralph, DT, 6´5˝/239 lbs; Washington; 1957: LA, rnd 3; B4/2/1934 Cle Elum, WA, D6/13/1997 Anza, CA **1957** LARm 9 (ldt) **1958** LARm 12 (LDT) **1959** LARm 11 (LDT) **1960** LARm 11 (LDT) **1961** LARm 14 **1962** Pit 1 **1962** NYT-A 12 (LDT) **1963** NYJ-A 8 **NFL** 78 [7 yrs]

Strutt, Art Arthur Eugene, HB, 6´0˝/202 lbs; Duquesne; B12/4/1912 Mingo Junction, OH

YEAR	TEAM	G (GS, POS)	RUSH	YD	AVG (LG)	TD	REC	YD	AVG (LG)	TD	PASS	COMP	PCT	YD	AVG (LG)	TD	INT	SK	YD	QBR	KPR	OTD	PTS	TAY
1935	Pit	9(5, HB)	46	111	2.4	0	7	112	16.0	0	2	0	0.0	0	0.0	0	0	—	—	—	—	1	6	177
1936	Pit	10(5, hb)	84	180	2.1	1	11	166	15.1	0	1	1	100.0	15	15.0(15)	0	0	—	—	—	—	—	6	281
NFL	2	19(10)	130	291	2.2	1	18	278	15.4	0	3	1	33.3	15	5.0(15)	0	0	—	—	—	—	1	12	458

Stryzinski, Dan Daniel Thomas, P, 6´0˝/237 lbs; Indiana; B5/15/1965 Indianapolis, IN **[P]** **1993** TB 16 (0) **1996** Atl 16 (0) **1997** Atl 16 (0) **1998**†Atl 16 (0) **1999** Atl 16 (0) **2000** Atl 16 (0) **2002** KC 16 (0)

YEAR	TEAM	G (GS, POS)	RUSH	YD	AVG (LG)	TD	REC	YD	AVG (LG)	TD	PASS	COMP	PCT	YD	AVG (LG)	TD	INT	SK	YD	QBR	KPR	OTD	PTS	TAY
1990	Pit	16(0)	3	17	5.7(9)	0	—	—	—	—	—	—	—	—	—	—	—	—	—	—	P	—	0	17
1991	Pit	16(0)	4	-11	-2.8(0)	0	—	—	—	—	—	—	—	—	—	—	—	—	—	—	P	—	0	-11
1992	TB	16(0)	1	7	7.0(7)	0	—	—	—	—	2	2	100.0	14	7.0(12)	0	0	—	—	—	P	—	0	14
1994	TB	16(0)	—	—	—	—	—	—	—	—	1	1	100.0	21	21.0(21)	0	0	—	—	—	P	—	0	11
1995	†Atl	16(0)	1	0	0.0(0)	0	—	—	—	—	—	—	—	—	—	—	—	—	—	—	P	—	0	0
2001	KC	16(0)	1	-10	-10.0(-10)	0	—	—	—	—	—	—	—	—	—	—	—	—	—	—	P	—	0	-10
2003	NYJ	16(0)	—	—	—	—	—	—	—	—	1	0	0.0	0	0.0	0	0	—	—	—	P	—	0	0
NFL	14	224(0)	10	3	0.3(9)	0	—	—	—	—	4	3	75.0	35	8.8(21)	0	0	—	—	—	P	—	0	21

Strzelczyk, Justin Justin Conrad, T-G, 6´6˝/301 lbs; Maine; 1990: Pit, rnd 11; B8/18/1968 Seneca, NY, D9/30/2004 Herkimer, NY **1990** Pit 16 (0) **1991** Pit 16 (0) **1992**†Pit 16 (7, rt) **1993**†Pit 16 (12, RG) **1994**†Pit 16 (5, rg) **1995**†Pit 16 (14, RG) **1996**†Pit 16 (16, RT) **1997**†Pit 14 (14, RT) **1998** Pit 7 (7, rt) **NFL** 133 (75) [9 yrs]

Strzykalski, Johnny John Raymond, HB, 5´9˝/190 lbs; Marquette; 1946: GB, rnd 1; B12/14/1921 Milwaukee, WI, D6/19/2002 Hendersonville, NC

YEAR	TEAM	G (GS, POS)	RUSH	YD	AVG (LG)	TD	REC	YD	AVG (LG)	TD	PASS	COMP	PCT	YD	AVG (LG)	TD	INT	SK	YD	QBR	KPR	OTD	PTS	TAY
1946	SF-A	13(11, RH)	79	346	4.4(50)	2	9	80	8.9	0	—	—	—	—	—	—	—	—	—	—	kpi	—	12	494
1947	SF-A☆	14(13, RH)	143	906	**6.3**(**50**)	5	15	258	17.2	3	4	1	25.0	38	9.5(38)	0	0	—	—	—	kpi	—	48	1198
1948	SF-A☆	14(13, RH)	141	915	6.5(48)	4	26	485	18.7(59)	7	1	0	0.0	0	0.0	0	0	—	—	—	kpi	—	66	1425
1949	SF-A	7(4)	66	287	4.3(44)	3	6	99	16.5	1	—	—	—	—	—	—	—	—	—	—	kp	—	24	408
AAFC	4	48(41)	429	2454	5.7(50)	14	56	922	16.5(59)	11	5	1	20.0	38	7.6(38)	0	0	—	—	—	kpi	—	150	3524
1950	SF★	12(RH)	136	612	4.5(38)	2	24	187	7.8(28)	1	—	—	—	—	—	—	—	—	—	—	—	—	18	731
1951	SF	11(RH)	81	296	3.7(13)	3	12	105	8.8(13)	0	—	—	—	—	—	—	—	—	—	—	—	—	18	379
1952	SF	10	16	53	3.3(11)	0	1	4	4.0(4)	0	—	—	—	—	—	—	—	—	—	—	—	—	0	55
NFL	3	33	233	961	4.1(50)	5	37	296	8.0(59)	1	—	—	—	—	—	—	—	—	—	—	—	—	36	1164

Stuart, Jim James Robert, T, 6´0˝/212 lbs; Oregon; 1941: Was, rnd 5; B7/2/1919 Enterprise, OR, D12/15/1985 Hermiston, OR **1941** Was 5 (1)

Stuart, Roy Roy J., G-LB, 5´8˝/188 lbs; Tulsa; B7/25/1920 Shawnee, OK **1942** Cle 10 (6, RG) **1943** Det 6 (0) **NFL** 16 (6) [2 yrs]

1946 Buf-A 9 (0)

Stubblefield, Dana Dana William, DT, 6´2˝/300 lbs; Kansas; 1993: SF, rnd 1; B11/14/1970 Cleves, OH **[S]** **1993**†SF 16 (14, LDT) **1994**†SF★14 (14, RDT) **1995**†SF★16 (16, RDT) **1996**†SF☆15 (15, RDT) **1997**†SF★16 (16, RDT) **1998** Was 7 (7, rdt) **1999**†Was 16 (16, RDT) **2000** Was 15 (14, RDT) **2001**†SF 16 (16, RDT) **2002**†SF 15 (15, RDT) **2003** Oak 8 (6, ldt) **NFL** 154 (149) [11 yrs]

Stubbs, Danny Daniel, DE-LB, 6´4˝/265 lbs; Miami (FL); 1988: SF, rnd 2; B1/3/1965 Long Branch, NJ **[S]** **1988**†SF 16 (1) **1989**†SF 16 (0) **1990** Dal 16 (15, LDE) **1991** Dal 9 (0) **1991** Cin 7 (0) **1992** Cin 16 (12, ROLB) **1993** Cin 16 (0) **1995**†Phi 16 (5, lde) **1996** Mia 16 (15, RDE) **1997** Mia 1 (0) **1998**†Mia 5 (1) **NFL** 134 (49) [10 yrs]

Stuckey, Henry Henry L., DB, 6´1˝/180 lbs; Missouri; 1972: Det, rnd 8; B8/24/1950 Oakland, CA **1972**†Mia 0 **1973**†Mia 6 **1974**†Mia 14 **1975** NYG 4 (4, rcb) **1976** NYG 3 **NFL** 27 (4) [5 yrs]

Stuckey, Jim James Davis, DE, 6´4˝/251 lbs; Clemson; 1980: SF, rnd 1; B6/21/1958 Cayce, SC **1980** SF 16 (9, lde) **1981**†SF 15 (15, LDE) **1982** SF 9 (9, LDE) **1983**†SF 16 (3) **1984**†SF 16 (7, LDE) **1985**†SF 15 (1) **1986** SF 1 (0) **1986** NYJ 5 (1) **NFL** 93 (45) [7 yrs]

Stuckey, Shawn Shawn, LB, 6´0˝/230 lbs; Vanderbilt; Troy State; B10/22/1975 Daleville, AL **1998**†NE 6 (0)

Studaway, Mark Mark Wayne, DE, 6´3˝/273 lbs; Tennessee; 1984: Hou, rnd 4; B9/20/1960 Memphis, TN **1984** Hou 6 (0) **1985** TB 6 (0) **1987** Atl 2 (2) **NFL** 14 (2) [3 yrs]

Studdard, Dave David Derald, T-G-TE, 6´4˝/260 lbs; Texas; 1978: Bal, rnd 9; B11/22/1955 San Antonio, TX **1980** Den 16 (12, RT) **1982** Den 9 (9, RG) **1983**†Den 16 (16, LT) **1985** Den 16 (15, LT) **1987**†Den 14 (14, LT) **1988** Den 11 (4)

YEAR	TEAM	G (GS, POS)	RUSH	YD	AVG (LG)	TD	REC	YD	AVG (LG)	TD	PASS	COMP	PCT	YD	AVG (LG)	TD	INT	SK	YD	QBR	KPR	OTD	PTS	TAY
1979	†Den	16(16, RT)	—	—	—	—	1	2	2.0(2)	1	—	—	—	—	—	—	—	—	—	—	—	—	6	6
1981	Den	16(16, RT)	—	—	—	—	1	10	10.0(10)	0	—	—	—	—	—	—	—	—	—	—	—	—	0	5
1984	†Den	16(16, LT)	—	—	—	—	1	-4	-4.0(-4)	0	—	—	—	—	—	—	—	—	—	—	—	—	0	-2
1986	†Den	15(15, LT)	—	—	—	—	1	2	2.0(2)	1	—	—	—	—	—	—	—	—	—	—	—	—	6	6
NFL	10	145(133)	—	—	—	—	4	10	2.5(10)	2	—	—	—	—	—	—	—	—	—	—	k	—	12	-7

Studdard, Les Leslie Elvin, C, 6´4˝/260 lbs; Texas; 1981: KC, rnd 10; B12/14/1958 El Paso, TX **1983** Hou 6 (0)

YEAR	TEAM	G (GS, POS)	RUSH	YD	AVG (LG)	TD	REC	YD	AVG (LG)	TD	PASS	COMP	PCT	YD	AVG (LG)	TD	INT	SK	YD	QBR	KPR	OTD	PTS	TAY
1982	KC	9(2)	1	0	0.0(0)	0	—	—	—	—	—	—	—	—	—	—	—	—	—	—	—	—	0	0
NFL	2	15(2)	1	0	0.0	0	—	—	—	—	—	—	—	—	—	—	—	—	—	—	—	—	0	0

Studdard, Vern Vernon Aaron, WR, 5´11˝/175 lbs; Mississippi; 1971: NYJ, rnd 11; B4/30/1948 Columbus, MS **1971** NYJ 8

Studstill, Darren Darren Henry, DB, 6´1˝/186 lbs; West Virginia; 1994: Dal, rnd 6; B8/9/1970 Palm Beach Gardens, FL **1994** Dal 1 (0) **1995** Jax 8 (0) **1996**†Jax 7 (0) **NFL** 16 (0) [3 yrs]

YEAR	TEAM	G (GS, POS)	RUSH	YD	AVG(LG)	TD	REC	YD	AVG(LG)	TD	PASS	COMP	PCT	YD	AVG(LG)	TD	INT	SK	YD	QBR	KPR	OTD	PTS	TAY

STUDSTILL, PAT   Patrick Lewis, FL-HB-WR-P, 6′0″/180 lbs; Houston; B6/4/1938 Shreveport, LA [PR]

1961	Det	14	—	—	—	—	5	54	10.8(25)	0	—	—	—	—	—	—	—	—	—	—	Pkp	1	6	280
1962	Det	14(RH)	1	-11	-11.0(-11)	0	36	479	13.3(51)	4	—	—	—	—	—	—	—	—	—	—	kp	—	24	772
1964	Det	14	—	—	—	—	7	102	14.6(27)	1	—	—	—	—	—	—	—	—	—	—	kp	—	6	381
1965	Det◇	14(fl)	1	-4	-4.0(-4)	0	28	389	13.9(55)	3	—	—	—	—	—	—	—	—	—	—	Pkp	—	18	335
1966	Det★	14(FL)	2	20	10.0(15)	0	67	**1266**	18.9(**99**)	5	—	—	—	—	—	—	—	—	—	—	P	—	30	678
1967	Det☆	7(FL)	—	—	—	—	10	162	16.2(37)	2	—	—	—	—	—	—	—	—	—	—	P	—	12	91
1968	LARm	14	—	—	—	—	7	108	15.4(25)	1	1	0	0.0	0	0.0	0	0	0	—	—	P	—	6	59
1969	†LARm	14	—	—	—	—	3	28	9.3(11)	0	—	—	—	—	—	—	—	—	—	—	P	—	0	14
1970	LARm	14	1	23	23.0(23)	0	18	252	14.0(40)	2	—	—	—	—	—	—	—	—	—	—	P	—	12	159
1971	LARm	14	—	—	—	—	—	—	—	—	—	—	—	—	—	—	—	—	—	—	P	—	0	0
1972	NE	14	1	11	11.0(11)	0	—	—	—	—	0	0	0	0	0.0	0	0	0	—	—	P	—	0	11
NFL	11	147	6	39	6.5(23)	0	181	2840	15.7(99)	18	3	0	0.0	0	0.0	0	0	0	—	—	Pkp	1	114	2779

STUDWELL, SCOTT   John Scott, LB, 6′2″/228 lbs; Illinois; 1977: Min, rnd 9; B8/27/1954 Evansville, IN   **1977**†Min 14 (3)   **1978**†Min 13   **1979** Min 14 (4)   **1980**†Min 16 (14, MLB)   **1981** Min 16 (16, RILB)   **1982**†Min 8 (8, RILB)   **1983** Min 16 (16, LILB)   **1984** Min☆16 (15, LILB)   **1985** Min 14 (12, LILB)   **1986** Min 15 (15, MLB)   **1987**†Min◇12 (11, MLB)   **1988**†Min★16 (16, MLB)   **1989**†Min☆16 (16, MLB)   **1990** Min 15 (15, MLB)   **NFL** 201 (161) [14 yrs]

STUESSY, MEL   Melvin Matthias, T, 5′9″/180 lbs; St. Edward's; B8/8/1901, D10/1980 Woodstock, IL   **1926** ChiC 1 (0)

STUHLDREHER, HARRY   Harry Augustus, TB, 5′7″/185 lbs; Notre Dame; B10/14/1901 Massillon, OH, D1/25/1965 Pittsburgh, PA   **1926** Bkn 1 (0)

STUKES, CHARLIE   Charles, DB, 6′3″/212 lbs; Maryland-Eastern Shore; 1967: Bal, rnd 4; B9/13/1943 Chesapeake, VA [I]   **1967** Bal 14 (1)   **1968**†Bal 14 (1)   **1969** Bal 14 (LCB)   **1970**†Bal 11 (LCB)   **1971**†Bal 14 (LCB)   **1972** Bal 12 (LCB)   **1973**†LARm 14 (14, RCB)   **1974**†LARm 14 (13, RCB)   **NFL** 107 (29) [8 yrs]

STURGEON, CECIL   Cecil Owen, T, 6′2″/254 lbs; North Dakota State; B6/27/1919 Carenduff, Canada, D2/1972   **1941** Phi 6 (0)

STURGEON, LYLE   Lyle Robert, T, 6′3″/250 lbs; North Dakota State; B1/18/1914 Carenduff, Canada, D11/30/1958 Green Bay, WI   **1937** GB 7 (1)

STURGIS, OSCAR   Oscar L., DE, 6′5″/280 lbs; North Carolina; 1995: Dal, rnd 7; B1/12/1971 Hamlet, NC   **1995** Dal 1 (0)

STURM, JERRY   Jerry Gordon, C-T-G, 6′3″/260 lbs; Illinois; B12/31/1936 English, IN   **1962** Den-A 14 (LT)   **1963** Den-A 14 (C)   **1964** Den-A◇14 (C)   **1965** Den-A 14 (LG)   **1966** Den-A◇14 (LG)   **1967** NO 7 (rt)   **1968** NO 14 (LT)   **1969** NO 14 (C)   **1970** NO 10 (C)   **1971** Hou 14 (c)   **1972** Phi 1

| 1961 | Den-A | 14 | 8 | 31 | 3.9(9) | 0 | 2 | -1 | -0.5(0) | 0 | — | — | — | — | — | — | — | — | — | — | — | — | 0 | 31 |
| NFL | 12 | 144 | 8 | 31 | 3.9(9) | 0 | 2 | -1 | -0.5 | 0 | — | — | — | — | — | — | — | — | — | — | k | — | 0 | -13 |

STURT, FRED   Frederick Neil, G, 6′4″/255 lbs; Bowling Green State; 1973: SL, rnd 3; B1/6/1951 Toledo, OH   **1974** Was 7   **1976**†NE 14   **1977** NE 14   **1978** NE 1   **1978** NO 12 (11, LG)   **1979** NO 16   **1980** NO 15 (13, RG)   **1981** NO 16 (16, LG)   **NFL** 95 (40) [7 yrs]

STURTRIDGE, DICK   Richard Nelson, HB, 6′1″/171 lbs; DePauw; B3/8/1904 Vandergrift, PA, D12/4/1978 Los Angeles, CA [K]   **1928** ChiB 10 (0), 19   **1929** ChiB 2 (1)   **NFL** 12 (1) [2 yrs]

STUVAINTS, RUSSELL   Russell, DB, 6′0″/195 lbs; Youngstown State; B8/28/1980 Pittsburgh, PA   **2003** Pit 4 (0)   **2004**†Pit 15 (0)   **2005** Pit 4 (0)   **NFL** 23 (0) [3 yrs]

STYDAHAR, JOE   Joseph Lee, T, 6′4″/233 lbs; Pittsburgh; West Virginia; 1936: ChiB, rnd 1; B3/16/1912 Kaylor, WV, D3/23/1977 Beckley, WV; HOF 1967 [KC]   **1936** ChiB☆12 (12, LT)   **1937**†ChiB☆10 (9, LT)   **1938** ChiB★11 (10, LT)   **1940**†ChiB★10 (7, LT)   **1941**†ChiB☆8 (2)   **1942**†ChiB☆9 (2)   **1945** ChiB 3 (0)   **1946** ChiB 10 (1)

| 1939 | ChiB★ | 11(10, LT) | — | — | — | — | 1 | 9 | 9.0(9) | 0 | — | — | — | — | — | — | — | — | — | — | K | — | 4 | 5 |
| NFL | 9 | 84(53) | — | — | — | — | 1 | 9 | 9.0(9) | 0 | — | — | — | — | — | — | — | — | — | — | Ki | — | 28 | 55 |

STYLES, LORENZO   Lorenzo Cavelle, LB, 6′1″/245 lbs; Ohio State; 1995: Atl, rnd 3; B1/31/1974 Columbus, OH   **1995**†Atl 12 (0)   **1996** Atl 16 (0)   **1997** SL 3 (0)   **1998** SL 7 (3)   **1999**†SL 16 (0)   **2000**†SL 16 (5, rlb)   **NFL** 70 (8) [6 yrs]

STYNCHULA, ANDY   Andrew Ralph, DE-DT, 6′3″/252 lbs; Penn State; 1960: Was, rnd 3/NYT, rnd 2; B1/7/1939 Greenwald, PA, D8/1/1985 Great Harbour Cay, Bahamas [K]   **1960** Was 12 (12, RDE)   **1961** Was 14 (14, RDE)   **1962** Was 13 (13, RDE)   **1963** Was 14 (RDE)   **1964** NYG 14 (LDT)   **1965** NYG 11 (RDE)   **1966** Bal 8   **1967** Bal 13   **1968**†Dal 5   **NFL** 104 (39) [9 yrs]

SUALUA, NICKY   Nicky, RB, 5′11″/260 lbs; Ohio State; 1997: Dal, rnd 4; B4/16/1975 Santa Ana, CA   **1997** Dal 10 (1)   **1998**†Dal 16 (0)   **NFL** 26 (1) [2 yrs]

SUBIS, NICK   Nicholas Alexander, T-C, 6′4″/278 lbs; San Diego State; 1991: Den, rnd 6; B12/24/1967 Inglewood, CA   **1991**†Den 16 (0)

SUCHY, LARRY   Larry Wayne, DB, 5′10″/180 lbs; Mississippi College; B7/12/1946 Heidelberg, MS, D4/30/1972 Leland, MS   **1968** Atl 1

SUCHY, PAUL   Paul, E, /188 lbs; none; B3/28/1904, D11/1986 Inverness, IL   **1925** Cle 2 (1)

SUCI, BOB   Robert Leslie, DB, 5′10″/185 lbs; Michigan State; B4/7/1939 Flint, MI   **1962**†Hou-A 6   **1963**†Bos-A 14 (LCB)   **NFL** 20 [2 yrs]

SUCIC, STEVE   Stephen, HB-FB, 6′0″/210 lbs; Illinois; B4/21/1921 Chicago, IL, D6/29/2001 University Park, IL

1946	LARm	4(0)	7	18	2.6(9)	0	1	1	1.0(1)	0	—	—	—	—	—	—	—	—	—	—	k	—	0	24
1947	Bos	3(1)	3	3	1.0(2)	0	—	—	—	—	—	—	—	—	—	—	—	—	—	—	—	—	0	3
1947	Det	5(0)	—	—	—	—	1	20	20.0(20)	0	—	—	—	—	—	—	—	—	—	—	k	—	0	13
1948	Det	3(2)	6	20	3.3(8)	0	—	—	—	—	—	—	—	—	—	—	—	—	—	—	—	—	0	20
NFL	3	15(3)	16	41	2.6(9)	0	2	21	10.5(20)	0	—	—	—	—	—	—	—	—	—	—	k	—	0	60

SUESS, RAY   Raymond R., G-T-E, /204 lbs; none; B8/8/1903, D8/11/1970 Santa Ana, CA   **1926** Dul 7 (4)   **1927** Dul 9 (9, RG)   **NFL** 16 (13) [2 yrs]

SUFFRIDGE, BOB   Robert Lee, G, 6′0″/205 lbs; Tennessee; 1941: Pit, rnd 6; B3/17/1916 Fountain City, TN, D2/3/1974 Knoxville, TN   **1941** Phi☆10 (9, RG)   **1945** Phi 10 (1)   **NFL** 20 (10) [2 yrs]

SUGAR, LEO   Leo Tateusz, DE, 6′1″/214 lbs; Purdue; 1952: ChiC, rnd 11; B4/6/1929 Flint, MI   **1954** ChiC 12 (LDE)   **1955** ChiC 12 (LDE)   **1956** ChiC 12 (LDE)   **1958** ChiC◇12 (LDE)   **1959** ChiC 12 (LDE)   **1960** SL◇12 (LDE)   **1961** Phi☆14 (LDE)   **1962** Det 6

| 1957 | ChiC | 12(LDE) | — | — | — | — | 1 | 14 | 14.0(14) | 0 | — | — | — | — | — | — | — | — | — | — | — | 2 | 12 | 7 |
| NFL | 9 | 104 | — | — | — | — | 1 | 14 | 14.0(14) | 0 | — | — | — | — | — | — | — | — | — | — | kpi | 3 | 18 | 18 |

SUGGS, LEE   Lee Ernest, RB, 6′0″/205 lbs; Virginia Tech; 2003: Cle, rnd 4; B8/11/1980 Roanoke, VA

2003	Cle	7(0)	56	289	5.2(78)	2	2	0	0.0(1)	0	—	—	—	—	—	—	—	—	—	—	k	—	12	417
2004	Cle	10(4, rb)	199	744	3.7(39)	2	20	178	8.9(59)	1	—	—	—	—	—	—	—	—	—	—	—	—	18	858
2005	Cle	8(0)	8	15	1.9(7)	0	6	26	4.3(8)	0	—	—	—	—	—	—	—	—	—	—	—	—	0	28
NFL	3	25(4)	263	1048	4.0(78)	4	28	204	7.3(59)	1	—	—	—	—	—	—	—	—	—	—	k	—	30	1303

SUGGS, SHAFER   Shafer L., DB, 6′1″/200 lbs; Ball State; 1976: NYJ, rnd 2; B4/28/1953 Elkhart, IN   **1976** NYJ 11 (10, LCB)   **1977** NYJ 9 (8, SS)   **1978** NYJ 16 (16, SS)   **1979** NYJ 16 (15, SS)   **1980** NYJ 4 (4)   **1980** Cin 4 (0)   **NFL** 60 (53) [5 yrs]

SUGGS, TERRELL   Terrell Raymonn, LB-DE, 6′3″/260 lbs; Arizona State; 2003: Bal, rnd 1; B10/11/1982 Minneapolis, MN   **2003**†Bal 16 (1)   **2004** Bal◇16 (16, LOLB)   **2005** Bal 16 (16, RDE)   **NFL** 48 (33) [3 yrs]

SUGGS, WALT   William Walter, T-C, 6′5″/260 lbs; Mississippi State; 1961: Hou, rnd 3; B5/15/1939 Hattiesburg, MS   **1962**†Hou-A 14   **1963** Hou-A 14 (LT)   **1964** Hou-A 14 (LT)   **1965** Hou-A 14 (LT)   **1966** Hou-A☆14 (LT)   **1967**†Hou-A★14 (LT)   **1968** Hou-A★14 (LT)   **1969**†Hou-A☆14 (LT)   **1970** Hou 14 (LT)   **1971** Hou 11 (C)   **NFL** 137 [10 yrs]

SUHEY, MATT   Matthew Jerome, RB, 5′11″/217 lbs; Penn State; 1980: Chi, rnd 2; B7/7/1958 Bellefonte, PA

1980	ChiB	16(1)	22	45	2.0(10)	0	7	60	8.6(21)	0	—	—	—	—	—	—	—	—	—	—	kp	—	0	195
1981	ChiB	15(14, FB)	150	521	3.5(26)	3	33	168	5.1(15)	0	—	—	—	—	—	—	—	—	—	—	—	—	18	635
1982	ChiB	9(8, FB)	70	206	2.9(15)	3	36	333	9.3(45)	0	—	—	—	—	—	—	—	—	—	—	—	—	18	403
1983	ChiB	16(13, FB)	149	681	4.6(39)	4	49	429	8.8(52)	1	1	1	100.0	74	74.0(74)	1	0	—	—	—	—	—	30	983
1984	ChiB	16(16, FB)	124	424	3.4(21)	4	42	312	7.4(23)	2	1	0	0.0	0	0.0	0	0	1	9	—	—	—	36	630
1985	†ChiB	16(16, FB)	115	471	4.1(17)	1	33	295	8.9(35)	1	—	—	—	—	—	—	—	—	—	—	—	—	12	634
1986	†ChiB	16(14, FB)	84	270	3.2(17)	2	24	235	9.8(58)	0	—	—	—	—	—	—	—	—	—	—	—	—	12	408
1987	ChiB	12(2)	7	24	3.4(6)	0	7	54	7.7(12)	0	—	—	—	—	—	—	—	—	—	—	k	—	0	45
1988	†ChiB	16(16, FB)	87	253	2.9(19)	2	20	154	7.7(29)	0	—	—	—	—	—	—	—	—	—	—	—	—	12	350
1989	ChiB	16(0)	20	51	2.6(8)	1	9	73	8.1(22)	1	—	—	—	—	—	—	—	—	—	—	k	—	12	106
NFL	10	148(100)	828	2946	3.6(39)	20	260	2113	8.1(58)	5	2	1	50.0	74	37.0(74)	1	0	1	9	—	kp	—	150	4387

SUHEY, STEVE   Steven Joseph, G, 5′11″/215 lbs; Penn State; B1/8/1922 Janesville, NY, D1/8/1977 State College, PA   **1948** Pit 12 (4)   **1949** Pit 12 (10, RG)   **NFL** 24 (14) [2 yrs]

SUISHAM, SHAUN Shaun, K, 6´0˝/199 lbs; Bowling Green State; B12/29/1981 Wallaceburg, Canada **[K]** **2005** Dal 3 (0)

SULAITIS, JOE Joseph, B-G-DE-E, 6´2˝/212 lbs; none; B6/20/1921 Hoboken, NJ, D2/8/1980 Point Pleasant, NJ

YEAR	TEAM	G (GS, POS)	RUSH	YD	AVG (LG)	TD	REC	YD	AVG (LG)	TD	PASS	COMP	PCT	YD	AVG (LG)	TD	INT	SK	YD	QBR	KPR	OTD	PTS	TAY
1943	NYG	7(0)	1	6	6.0(6)	0	1	12	12.0(12)	0	—	—	—	—	—	—	—	—	—	—	—	—	0	12
1944	NYG	6(2)	9	38	4.2(16)	0	—	—	—	—	17	4	23.5	53	3.1(22)	1	4	—	—	—	—	—	0	-91
1945	NYG	8(4, BB)	10	37	3.7(10)	0	2	12	6.0(6)	0	13	7	53.8	126	9.7(38)	0	0	—	—	—	k	—	0	111
1946	Bos	3(0)	—	—	—	—	—	—	—	—	—	—	—	—	—	—	—	—	—	—	—	—	—	—
1947	NYG	11(10, BB)	—	—	—	—	7	53	7.6(16)	0	—	—	—	—	—	—	—	—	—	—	ki	—	0	33
1948	NYG	12(4)	5	18	3.6(10)	1	26	298	11.5(26)	1	1	0	0.0	0	0.0	0	0	—	—	—	k	—	12	188
1949	NYG	12(6, fb)	14	42	3.0(12)	0	3	35	11.7(18)	0	—	—	—	—	—	—	—	—	—	—	k	—	0	72
1950	†NYG	12(LG)	—	—	—	—	1	3	3.0(3)	0	—	—	—	—	—	—	—	—	—	—	k	—	0	54
1951	NYG	12(LG)	—	—	—	—	4	25	6.3(10)	0	—	—	—	—	—	—	—	—	—	—	k	—	0	35
1952	NYG	12(LLB)	—	—	—	—	4	31	7.8(16)	0	—	—	—	—	—	—	—	—	—	—	k	—	0	47
1953	NYG	12(RDE)	—	—	—	—	—	—	—	—	—	—	—	—	—	—	—	—	—	—	ki	—	0	1
NFL	11	107(26)	39	141	3.6(16)	1	48	469	9.8(26)	1	31	11	35.5	179	5.8(38)	1	4	—	—	—	ki	—	12	460

SULFSTED, ALEX Alex, T, 6´3˝/320 lbs; Miami (OH); 2001: KC, rnd 6; B12/21/1977 Loveland, OH **2002** Was 14 (3) **2004** Cin 3 (0) **NFL** 17 (3) [2 yrs]

SULIMA, GEORGE George E., E-DE, 6´2˝/200 lbs; Boston University; 1951: Pit, rnd 3; B2/27/1928 New Britain, CT, D10/31/1987 Colchester, VT

YEAR	TEAM	G (GS, POS)	RUSH	YD	AVG (LG)	TD	REC	YD	AVG (LG)	TD	PASS	COMP	PCT	YD	AVG (LG)	TD	INT	SK	YD	QBR	KPR	OTD	PTS	TAY
1952	Pit	9	—	—	—	—	9	176	19.6(69)	1	—	—	—	—	—	—	—	—	—	—	—	—	6	93
1953	Pit	10(le)	—	—	—	—	10	131	13.1(17)	0	—	—	—	—	—	—	—	—	—	—	—	—	0	66
1954	Pit	12(LE)	—	—	—	—	30	439	14.6(37)	1	—	—	—	—	—	—	—	—	—	—	—	—	6	225
NFL	3	31	—	—	—	—	49	746	15.2(69)	2	—	—	—	—	—	—	—	—	—	—	—	—	12	383

SULLINS, JOHN John Robertson, LB, 6´1˝/225 lbs; Alabama; B9/7/1969 Oxford, MS **1992** Den 6 (0)

SULLIVAN FB, none; deceased **1920** RI 1 (0)

SULLIVAN, BOB Robert Joseph, HB-DB, 5´10˝/190 lbs; Holy Cross; B8/15/1923 Lowell, MA, D6/19/1981 North Andover, MA

YEAR	TEAM	G (GS, POS)	RUSH	YD	AVG (LG)	TD	REC	YD	AVG (LG)	TD	PASS	COMP	PCT	YD	AVG (LG)	TD	INT	SK	YD	QBR	KPR	OTD	PTS	TAY
1948	SF-A	13(0)	33	121	3.7	0	4	58	14.5	1	—	—	—	—	—	—	—	—	—	—	ki	—	6	166

SULLIVAN, BOB Robert Gerard, HB, 5´9˝/191 lbs; Iowa; 1947: LAD-A, rnd 17/Bos, rnd 13; B12/24/1924 Attleboro, MA, D11/12/1992 Carmichael, CA

YEAR	TEAM	G (GS, POS)	RUSH	YD	AVG (LG)	TD	REC	YD	AVG (LG)	TD	PASS	COMP	PCT	YD	AVG (LG)	TD	INT	SK	YD	QBR	KPR	OTD	PTS	TAY
1947	Pit	3(1)	21	61	2.9(14)	0	4	72	18.0(50)	1	9	3	33.3	52	5.8(24)	0	1	—	—	—	kp	—	6	119
1948	Bkn-A	2(1)	2	-1	-0.5	0	—	—	—	—	—	—	—	—	—	—	—	—	—	—	k	—	0	6

SULLIVAN, CARL Carl Jeffery, DE, 6´4˝/248 lbs; San Jose State; B4/30/1962 San Jose, CA **1987** GB 3 (3)

SULLIVAN, CHRIS Christopher Patrick, DE, 6´4˝/279 lbs; Boston College; 1996: NE, rnd 4; B3/14/1973 North Attleboro, MA **1996**†NE 16 (0) **1997**†NE 16 (10, LDE) **1998**†NE 15 (10, rde) **1999** NE 16 (0) **2000** Pit 15 (2) **NFL** 78 (22) [5 yrs]

SULLIVAN, DAN Daniel Joseph, G-T, 6´3˝/250 lbs; Boston College; 1962: Bal, rnd 3/SD, rnd 10; B9/1/1939 Boston, MA **1962** Bal 14 **1963** Bal 7 **1964**†Bal 14 **1965**†Bal 14 **1966** Bal 13 (LG) **1967** Bal 14 (RG) **1968**†Bal☆14 (RG) **1969** Bal 10 (RG) **1970**†Bal 14 (RT) **1971**†Bal 12 **1972** Bal 14 (RG) **NFL** 140 [11 yrs]

SULLIVAN, DAVE David Allan, WR, 5´11˝/185 lbs; Virginia; 1973: Cle, rnd 15; B1/31/1951 Steelton, PA **1973** Cle 1

YEAR	TEAM	G (GS, POS)	RUSH	YD	AVG (LG)	TD	REC	YD	AVG (LG)	TD	PASS	COMP	PCT	YD	AVG (LG)	TD	INT	SK	YD	QBR	KPR	OTD	PTS	TAY
1974	Cle	6	—	—	—	—	5	92	18.4(37)	0	—	—	—	—	—	—	—	—	—	—	—	—	0	46
NFL	2	7	—	—	—	—	5	92	18.4(37)	0	—	—	—	—	—	—	—	—	—	—	—	—	0	46

SULLIVAN, FRANK Frank Joseph, C-LB, 6´3˝/206 lbs; Loyola (LA); B8/16/1912 Nashville, TN, D6/1956 **1935** ChiB 11 (6, c) **1936** ChiB 3 (0) **1937** ChiB 7 (3) **1938** ChiB 10 (1) **1939** ChiB 9 (2) **1940** Pit 9 (2) **NFL** 49 (14) [6 yrs]

SULLIVAN, GEORGE George Henry, B, 5´9˝/170 lbs; Pennsylvania; B3/15/1897, D7/5/1989 Woodbury, NJ **1924** Fra 6 (4), 30 **1925** Fra 16 (8, TB), 18 **NFL** 22 (12), 48 [2 yrs]

SULLIVAN, GEORGE George Albert, E, 6´2˝/205 lbs; Notre Dame; 1947: Bos, rnd 6/ChiR-A, rnd 1; B3/3/1926 Norwood, MA **1948** Bos 1 (0)

SULLIVAN, GERRY Gerald B., T-C-G, 6´4˝/250 lbs; Illinois; 1974: Cle, rnd 7; B1/15/1952 Oak Park, IL **1974** Cle 13 (8, RT) **1975** Cle 14 (7, RT) **1976** Cle 14 **1977** Cle 14 **1978** Cle 16 (3) **1979** Cle 16 **1980**†Cle 16 (0) **1981** Cle 16 (8, c) **NFL** 119 (26) [8 yrs]

SULLIVAN, HEW Harold C., G, /195 lbs; none; B3/2/1898, MN, D10/3/1975 Minneapolis, MN **1926** Dul 1 (0)

SULLIVAN, JACK John Henry, FB, /170 lbs; none; deceased **1921** Buf 3 (0)

SULLIVAN, JACK John Henry, FB, /170 lbs; North Carolina State; B11/12/1891 Holyoke, MA, deceased **1921** Was 1 (1, FB)

SULLIVAN, JIM James Edmund, DT-DE, 6´4˝/240 lbs; Lincoln (MO); B8/20/1944 Detroit, MI **1970** Atl 7

SULLIVAN, JOHN John Patrick, LB, 6´1˝/221 lbs; Illinois; 1979: Chi, rnd 6; B10/1/1956 Massapequa Park, NY **1979** NYJ 12 **1980** NYJ 16 (0) **NFL** 28 [2 yrs]

SULLIVAN, JOHN John Lloyd, DB, 6´1˝/196 lbs; California; 1984: GB, rnd S3; B11/15/1961 Hartford, CT **1986** GB 6 (3) **1986** SD 9 (0) **1987** SF 1 (1) **NFL** 16 (4) [2 yrs]

SULLIVAN, JOHNATHAN Johnathan Lamar, DT, 6´3˝/313 lbs; Georgia; 2003: NO, rnd 1; B1/21/1981 Griffin, GA **2003** NO 14 (13, LDT) **2004** NO 7 (4) **2005** NO 15 (0) **NFL** 36 (17) [3 yrs]

SULLIVAN, KENT Kent Allen, P, 5´11˝/197 lbs; California Lutheran; B5/15/1964 Plymouth, IN **1991** Hou 1 (0) **1992** KC 1 (0) **1993** Hou 1 (0) **1993** SD 2 (0) **NFL** 5 (0) [3 yrs]

SULLIVAN, MARQUES Marques D., G-T, 6´5˝/325 lbs; Illinois; 2001: Buf, rnd 5; B2/2/1978 Oak Park, IL **2001** Buf 10 (2) **2002** Buf 16 (16, RG) **2003** Buf 6 (4) **NFL** 32 (22) [3 yrs]

SULLIVAN, MIKE Michael Gerard, G-C, 6´3˝/292 lbs; Miami (FL); 1991: Dal, rnd 6; B12/22/1967 Chicago, IL **1992** TB 9 (0) **1993** TB 11 (3) **1994** TB 16 (1) **1995** TB 12 (0) **NFL** 48 (4) [4 yrs]

SULLIVAN, PAT Patrick Joseph, QB, 6´0˝/198 lbs; Auburn; 1972: Atl, rnd 2; B1/18/1950 Birmingham, AL

YEAR	TEAM	G (GS, POS)	RUSH	YD	AVG (LG)	TD	REC	YD	AVG (LG)	TD	PASS	COMP	PCT	YD	AVG (LG)	TD	INT	SK	YD	QBR	KPR	OTD	PTS	TAY
1972	Atl	14	2	8	4.0(10)	0	—	—	—	—	19	3	15.8	44	2.3(18)	0	3	2	28	—	—	—	0	-90
1973	Atl	4	3	19	6.3(9)	0	—	—	—	—	26	14	53.8	175	6.7(21)	1	0	2	19	—	—	—	0	112
1974	Atl	6	3	19	6.3(12)	0	—	—	—	—	105	48	45.7	556	5.3(48)	1	8	10	92	33.7	—	—	0	-18
1975	Atl	6	6	9	1.5(4)	0	—	—	—	—	70	28	40.0	380	5.4(49)	3	5	8	52	—	—	—	0	14
NFL	4	30	14	55	3.9(12)	0	—	—	—	—	220	93	42.3	1155	5.3(49)	5	16	22	191	36.5	—	—	0	18

SULLIVAN, STEVE Stephen Patrick, B, 5´11˝/180 lbs; Montana; B7/1/1898 Butte, MT, D8/17/1969 Concord, CA **1922** Mil 2 (1) **1922** Evv 1 (1, TB) **1922** Ham 2 (1) **1923** Ham 4 (0) **1924** KC 1 (1) **1924** Ham 1 (0) **NFL** 11 (4) [3 yrs]

SULLIVAN, TOM Thomas Ashley, RB, 6´0˝/190 lbs; Miami (FL); 1972: Phi, rnd 15; B3/5/1950 Jacksonville, FL, D10/10/2002 Summerville, SC

YEAR	TEAM	G (GS, POS)	RUSH	YD	AVG (LG)	TD	REC	YD	AVG (LG)	TD	PASS	COMP	PCT	YD	AVG (LG)	TD	INT	SK	YD	QBR	KPR	OTD	PTS	TAY
1972	Phi	12	13	13	1.0(5)	0	4	17	4.3(7)	0	—	—	—	—	—	—	—	—	—	—	kp	—	0	49
1973	Phi	13(RB)	217	968	4.5(37)	4	50	322	6.4(29)	1	—	—	—	—	—	—	—	—	—	—	k	—	30	1274
1974	Phi	14(RB)	244	760	3.1(28)	**11**	39	312	8.0(23)	1	—	—	—	—	—	—	—	—	—	—	—	—	72	1031
1975	Phi	14(RB)	173	632	3.7(28)	0	28	276	9.9(35)	0	—	—	—	—	—	—	—	—	—	—	k	—	0	767
1976	Phi	13(RB)	99	399	4.0(26)	2	14	116	8.3(20)	1	—	—	—	—	—	—	—	—	—	—	k	—	18	515
1977	Phi	14(13, RB)	125	363	2.9(14)	0	26	223	8.6(30)	2	—	—	—	—	—	—	—	—	—	—	—	—	12	485
1978	Cle	4	5	7	1.4(5)	0	1	20	20.0(20)	0	—	—	—	—	—	—	—	—	—	—	k	—	0	47
NFL	7	84(13)	876	3142	3.6(37)	17	162	1286	7.9(35)	5	—	—	—	—	—	—	—	—	—	—	kp	—	132	4167

SULLY, IVORY Ivory Ulysses, DB, 6´0˝/198 lbs; Delaware; B6/20/1957 Salisbury, MD **1979**†LARm 8 **1980**†LARm 16 (0) **1981** LARm 16 (0) **1982** LARm 9 (0) **1983**†LARm 16 (0) **1984**†LARm 16 (0) **1985** TB 16 (16, FS) **1986** TB 16 (9, fs) **1987** Det 11 (1) **NFL** 124 (26) [9 yrs]

SUMINSKI, DAVE David Mitchell, G, 5´11˝/230 lbs; Wisconsin; 1953: Was, rnd 15; B6/18/1931 Ashland, WI, D9/22/2005 Ashland, WI **1953** Was 2 **1953** ChiC 6 (LG) **NFL** 8 [1 yr]

SUMLER, TONY Tony Bernard, DB, 5´10˝/185 lbs; Wichita State; B4/10/1956 Detroit, MI **1978** Det 1

SUMMERALL, PAT George Allen, DE-E-K, 6´4˝/228 lbs; Arkansas; 1952: Det, rnd 4; B5/10/1930 Lake City, FL **[K]** **1952** Det 2 **1953** ChiC 12 (LDE) **1954** ChiC 12 **1955** ChiC 11 **1956** ChiC 12 (RDE) **1957** ChiC 12 (RDE) **1958**†NYG 10 **1961**†NYG 14

YEAR	TEAM	G (GS, POS)	RUSH	YD	AVG (LG)	TD	REC	YD	AVG (LG)	TD	PASS	COMP	PCT	YD	AVG (LG)	TD	INT	SK	YD	QBR	KPR	OTD	PTS	TAY
1959	†NYG	12	—	—	—	—	2	32	16.0(21)	0	—	—	—	—	—	—	—	—	—	—	Kk	—	90	4
1960	NYG	12	—	—	—	—	1	15	15.0(15)	0	1	0	0.0	0	0.0	0	0	—	—	—	K	—	71	8
NFL	10	109	—	—	—	—	3	47	15.7(21)	0	1	0	0.0	0	0.0	0	0	—	—	—	Kki	1	563	31

YEAR	TEAM	G(GS, POS)	RUSH	YD	AVG(LG)	TD	REC	YD	AVG(LG)	TD	PASS COMP	PCT	YD	AVG(LG)	TD	INT	SK	YD	QBR	KPR	OTD	PTS	TAY

SUMMERELL, CARL Carl Leigh, QB, 6´4˝/208 lbs; East Carolina; 1974: NYG, rnd 4; B12/6/1951 Virginia Beach, VA

1974	NYG	7	2	8	4.0(6)	0	—	—	—	—	13	6	46.2	59	4.5(26)	0	3	1	6	—	—	—	0	-83
1975	NYG	3	3	4	1.3(4)	0	—	—	—	—	16	7	43.8	98	6.1(41)	0	2	2	24	—	—	—	0	-27
NFL	2	10	5	12	2.4(6)	0	—	—	—	—	29	13	44.8	157	5.4(41)	0	5	3	30	—	—	—	0	-110

SUMMERHAYS, BOB Robert William, LB-FB, 6´1˝/210 lbs; Army; Utah; 1949: GB, rnd 4; B3/19/1927 Salt Lake City, UT **1950** GB 11 (RLB) **1951** GB 12 (RLB)

| 1949 | GB | 12(2) | 29 | 101 | 3.5(14) | 0 | 1 | 34 | 34.0(34) | 0 | — | — | — | — | — | | | | | | | | 0 | 118 |
| NFL | 3 | 35(4) | 29 | 101 | 3.5(14) | 0 | 1 | 34 | 34.0(34) | 0 | — | — | — | — | — | | | | | ki | | 1 | 6 | 231 |

SUMMERS, DON Donald O., TE, 6´4˝/230 lbs; Oregon Tech; Boise State; B2/22/1961 Grants Pass, OR **1983**†Den 0 (0) **1985** Den 2 (0)

1984	†Den	16(4)	—	—	—	—	3	32	10.7(16)	0	—	—	—	—	—								0	16
1987	GB	3(1)	—	—	—	—	7	83	11.9(17)	1	—	—	—	—	—								6	47
NFL	4	21(3)	—	—	—	—	10	115	11.5(17)	1	—	—	—	—	—								6	63

SUMMERS, FREDDIE Freddie S., DB, 6´1˝/180 lbs; Washington (MD); 1969: Cle, rnd 4; B2/16/1947 Columbia, SC **1969** Cle 8 **1970** Cle 12 **1971** Cle 3 **NFL** 23 [3 yrs]

SUMMERS, JIM James, DB, 5´10˝/180 lbs; Michigan State; 1967: Den, rnd 9; B12/23/1945 Orangeburg, SC **1967** Den-A 11

SUMMERS, WILBUR Wilbur Thomas, P, 6´4˝/220 lbs; Louisville; 1976: Den, rnd 15; B8/6/1954 Irvington, NJ

| 1977 | Det | 13 | 1 | 0 | 0.0(0) | 0 | — | — | — | — | 1 | 1 | 100.0 | 5 | 5.0(5) | 0 | 0 | — | — | P | — | — | 0 | 3 |

SUMNER, CHARLIE Charles Edward, DB, 6´1˝/194 lbs; William & Mary; 1954: ChiB, rnd 22; B10/19/1930 Radford, VA [I] **1955** ChiB 10 (DB) **1958** ChiB 12 (DB) **1959** ChiB 12 (DB) **1960** ChiB 12 (RS) **1961** Min 13 (12, RS) **1962** Min 14 **NFL** 73 (12) [6 yrs]

SUMNER, WALT Walter Herman, DB, 6´1˝/195 lbs; Florida State; 1969: Cle, rnd 7; B2/2/1947 Ocilla, GA **1969**†Cle 14 (RCB) **1970** Cle 12 (RCB) **1971**†Cle 14 (SS/lcb) **1972**†Cle 13 (FS) **1973** Cle 13 (SS) **1974** Cle 10 (SS) **NFL** 76 [6 yrs]

SUMPTER, TONY Anthony B., G, 6´1˝/215 lbs; Cameron; B9/12/1923 Fletcher, OK **1946** ChiR-A 12 (6, RG) **1947** ChiR-A 1 (0) **AAFC** 13 (6) [2 yrs]

SUNDE, MILT Milton John, G, 6´2˝/250 lbs; Minnesota; 1964: Min, rnd 20; B2/1/1942 Minneapolis, MN **1964** Min 14 **1965** Min 14 (14, LG) **1966** Min◇14 (14, LG) **1967** Min 10 (8, LG) **1968**†Min 14 (6, rg) **1969**†Min 14 (14, RG) **1970**†Min 14 (14, RG) **1971**†Min 14 (14, RG) **1972** Min 14 (14, RG) **1973**†Min 14 (8, RG) **1974**†Min 11 **NFL** 147 (106) [11 yrs]

SUNTER, IAN Ian James, K, 6´1˝/215 lbs; none; B12/21/1952 Dundee, Scotland [K] **1976** Det 3 **1980** Cin 10 (0) **NFL** 13 [2 yrs]

SUPERICK, STEVE Stephen Wayne, P, 5´11˝/204 lbs; West Virginia; B8/9/1963 Memphis, TN **1987** Hou 2 (0)

SUPERNAW, KYWIN Kywin, DB, 6´1˝/206 lbs; Northeastern Oklahoma A&M; Indiana; B6/2/1975 Claremore, OK **1998** Det 2 (0) **1999** Det 2 (0) **2000** Det 13 (3) **NFL** 17 (3) [3 yrs]

SUPULSKI, LEN Leonard Peter, E, 6´0˝/175 lbs; Dickinson; B12/15/1920 Kingston, PA, D8/31/1943 near Kearney, NE

| 1942 | Phi | 9(0) | 1 | 1 | 1.0(1) | 0 | 8 | 149 | 18.6(41) | 1 | — | — | — | — | — | — | — | — | i | — | 6 | 81 |

SURTAIN, PATRICK Patrick Frank, DB, 5´11˝/192 lbs; Southern Mississippi; 1998: Mia, rnd 2; B6/19/1976 New Orleans, LA [I] **1998**†Mia 16 (0) **1999**†Mia 16 (6, lcb) **2000**†Mia 16 (16, LCB) **2001** Mia 16 (16, LCB) **2002** Mia★14 (14, LCB) **2003** Mia★15 (15, LCB) **2004** Mia 15 (15, LCB) **2005** KC 15 (15, LCB) **NFL** 123 (97) [8 yrs]

SUSOEFF, NICK Nicholas Peter, E, 6´1˝/215 lbs; Washington State; 1943: Cle, rnd 6; B4/15/1921 Umapine, OR, D1/31/1967 Santa Clara County, CA

1946	SF-A	6(2)	—	—	—	—	5	98	19.6	0	—	—	—	—	—				k	—	0	44
1947	SF-A	14(13, LE)	—	—	—	—	24	223	9.3	2	—	—	—	—	—					—	12	122
1948	SF-A	13(13, LE)	—	—	—	—	27	237	8.8	1	—	—	—	—	—				k	—	6	121
1949	SF-A	11(1)	—	—	—	—	5	52	10.4	1	—	—	—	—	—					—	6	31
AAFC	4	44(29)	—	—	—	—	61	610	10.0	4	—	—	—	—	—				k	—	24	317

SUSTERIC, ED Edward J., FB-LB, 6´0˝/205 lbs; Findlay; B1/7/1922 Cleveland, OH, D1/18/1967 Brecksville, OH

| 1949 | †Cle-A | 11(1) | 23 | 114 | 5.0 | 1 | 1 | 7 | 7.0(7) | 0 | — | — | — | — | — | | | | k | — | 6 | 137 |

SUTCH, GEORGE George Russell, B, 6´1˝/205 lbs; Rochester; Temple; 1943: ChiC, rnd 22; B8/28/1921 Jeffersonville, PA, D12/4/1987 Island, WA

| 1946 | ChiC | 3(0) | 5 | 4 | 0.8(4) | 0 | — | — | — | — | — | — | — | — | — | | | | k | — | 0 | -7 |

SUTHERIN, DON Donald Paul, DB, 5´10˝/193 lbs; Ohio State; 1958: NYG, rnd 8; B2/29/1936 Empire, OH [K] **1959** NYG 2 **1959** Pit 6 **1960** Pit 4 **NFL** 12 [2 yrs]

SUTHERLAND, DOUG Douglas A., DT-G-DE, 6´3˝/250 lbs; Wisconsin-Superior; 1970: NO, rnd 14; B8/1/1948 Superior, WI **1970** NO 10 **1971** Min 11 **1972** Min 14 **1973**†Min 9 **1974**†Min 14 (8, LDT) **1975**†Min 14 (14, LDT) **1976**†Min 14 (14, LDT) **1977**†Min 14 (14, LDT) **1978**†Min 16 (16, LDT) **1979** Min 16 (10, LDT) **1980**†Min 16 (14, LDT) **1981** Sea 16 (6, rdt) **NFL** 164 (96) [12 yrs]

SUTHERLAND, VINNY Vincent Joseph, WR, 5´8˝/188 lbs; Purdue; 2001: Atl, rnd 5; B4/22/1978 West Palm Beach, FL **2002** ChiB 1 (0) **2002**†SF 0 (0)

| 2001 | †SF | 15(0) | 1 | 16 | 16.0(16) | 0 | 1 | 5 | 5.0(5) | 0 | — | — | — | — | — | | | | kp | — | 0 | 451 |
| NFL | 2 | 16(0) | 1 | 16 | 16.0(16) | 0 | 1 | 5 | 5.0(5) | 0 | — | — | — | — | — | | | | kp | — | 0 | 455 |

SUTRO, JOHN John Robert, T, 6´4˝/245 lbs; San Jose State; 1962: GB, rnd 6/Oak, rnd 20; B5/8/1940 **1962** SF 5

SUTTER, EDDIE Edward Lee, LB, 6´3˝/240 lbs; Northwestern; B10/3/1969 Peoria, IL **1993** Cle 15 (0) **1994**†Cle 16 (0) **1995** Cle 16 (0) **1996** Bal 16 (4) **1997** Atl 16 (0) **NFL** 79 (4) [5 yrs]

SUTTER, RYAN Ryan Allen, DB, 6´1˝/203 lbs; Colorado; 1998: Bal, rnd 5; B9/14/1974 Fort Collins, CO **1998** Car 1 (0)

SUTTLE, JASON Jason John, DB, 5´10˝/182 lbs; Wisconsin; B12/2/1974 Minneapolis, MN **1999** Den 5 (0) **2000**†Den 5 (0) **2001** SF 1 (0) **NFL** 11 (0) [3 yrs]

SUTTON, ARCHIE Archie Michael, T, 6´4˝/262 lbs; Illinois; 1965: Min, rnd 2; B11/2/1941 New Orleans, LA **1965** Min 14 **1966** Min 3 **1967** Min 2 **NFL** 19 [3 yrs]

SUTTON, ED Edward Wike, HB-DB, 6´1˝/205 lbs; North Carolina; 1957: Was, rnd 3; B3/16/1935 Sylva, NC

1957	Was	12(LH)	108	407	3.8(31)	5	2	32	16.0(17)	1	5	3	60.0	95	19.0(51)	0	0	—	—	ki	—	36	536
1958	Was	10(LH)	93	335	3.6(18)	3	6	112	18.7(26)	0	3	0	0.0	0	0.0(0)	0	0	—	—	—	—	18	421
1959	Was	11(lh)	61	232	3.8(30)	1	4	63	15.8(26)	0	7	2	28.6	51	7.3(29)	1	0	—	—	k	—	6	304
1960	NYG	12	20	135	6.8(44)	0	2	30	15.0(16)	0	—	—	—	—	—				k	—	0	193
NFL	4	45	282	1109	3.9(44)	9	14	237	16.9(26)	1	15	5	33.3	146	9.7(51)	1	0	—	—	ki	—	60	1454

SUTTON, ERIC Eric Dontay, DB, 5´10˝/169 lbs; San Diego State; B10/24/1972 Los Angeles, CA **1996** Was 4 (0)

SUTTON, FRANK Frank LaRose, T, 6´3˝/280 lbs; Jackson State; B3/29/1963 **1987** NYG 2 (2)

SUTTON, JOE Joseph Boyle, DB-HB, 5´11˝/180 lbs; Temple; B4/26/1924 Philadelphia, PA

| 1949 | Buf-A | 9(1) | 9 | 63 | 7.0 | 0 | 5 | 63 | 12.6 | 1 | — | — | — | — | — | | | | kp | — | 6 | 154 |

1951 Phi 11 (DB) **1952** Phi 10 (DB)

| 1950 | Phi | 9(DB) | 1 | 1 | 1.0(1) | 0 | — | — | — | — | — | — | — | — | — | | | | kpi | — | 0 | 64 |
| NFL | 3 | 30 | 1 | 1 | 1.0(1) | 0 | — | — | — | — | — | — | — | — | — | | | | kpi | — | 0 | 101 |

SUTTON, JON Jonathan E., DB, 6´1˝/195 lbs; New Mexico; B7/2/1957 New Orleans, LA **1987** NO 2 (0)

SUTTON, MICKEY Michael Thomas, DB, 6´0˝/190 lbs; Auburn; 1965: KC, rnd 6/Chi, rnd 7; B7/17/1943 Mobile, AL **1966** Hou-A 5

SUTTON, MICKEY William Earl, DB, 5´8˝/165 lbs; Montana; B8/28/1960 Greenville, MS [R] **1986**†LARm 16 (0) **1987** LARm 12 (3) **1988**†LARm 15 (0) **1989** GB 3 (0) **1989** Buf 12 (0) **1990** LARm 7 (4) **NFL** 65 (7) [5 yrs]

SUTTON, MIKE Mike, DE, 6´4˝/272 lbs; LSU; B4/21/1975 Jacksonville, NC **1998** Ten 1 (0)

SUTTON, MITCH Mitchell Andrew, DE, 6´4˝/260 lbs; Kansas; 1974: Phi, rnd 3; B5/10/1951 Stone Mountain, GA **1974** Phi 14 **1975** Phi 4 **NFL** 18 [2 yrs]

SUTTON, REGGIE Reginald Eugene, DB, 5´10˝/190 lbs; Miami (FL); 1986: NO, rnd 5; B2/15/1965 Miami, FL **1987**†NO 11 (3) **1988** NO 15 (7, lcb) **NFL** 26 (10) [2 yrs]

SUTTON, RICKY Frederick DeWayne, DE-DT, 6´2˝/281 lbs; Auburn; B4/27/1971 Atlanta, GA **1993**†Pit 7 (0)

SVARE, HARLAND Harland James, LB-TB, 6´0˝/214 lbs; Washington State; 1953: LA, rnd 17; B11/15/1930 Clarkfield, MN [C] **1953** LARm 10 **1954** LARm 10 **1955** NYG 12 (RLB) **1956**†NYG 11 (RLB) **1957** NYG 12 (RLB) **1958**†NYG☆10 (RLB) **1959**†NYG 12 (RLB) **1960** NYG 12 (RLB) **NFL** 89 [8 yrs]

SVENDSEN, BUD Earl Gilbert, C-LB-G, 6´1˝/190 lbs; Minnesota; 1937: GB, rnd 4; B2/7/1915 Minneapolis, MN, D8/6/1996 Edina, MN **1937** GB 10 (2) **1939**†GB◇11 (10, C) **1940** Bkn 11 (10, C) **1941** Bkn 11 (11, C) **1942** Bkn 4 (3) **1943** Bkn 10 (6, C) **NFL** 57 (42) [6 yrs]

YEAR	TEAM	G (GS, POS)	RUSH°	YD	AVG(LG)	TD	REC	YD	AVG(LG)	TD	PASS	COMP	PCT	YD	AVG(LG)	TD	INT	SK	YD	QBR	KPR	OTD	PTS	TAY

SVENDSEN, GEORGE George Peter, C, 6'4"/230 lbs; Oregon State; Minnesota; B3/22/1913 Minneapolis, MN, D8/6/1995 Minneapolis, MN **1935** GB 9 (3) **1936**†GB 11 (7, C) **1940** GB 10 (4) **1941**†GB☆11 (8, C)

YEAR	TEAM	G (GS, POS)	RUSH	YD	AVG(LG)	TD	REC	YD	AVG(LG)	TD	KPR	OTD	PTS	TAY
1937	GB	11(9, C)	—	—	—	—	1	11	11.0(11)	0			0	6
NFL	5	52(31)	—	—	—	—	1	11	11.0(11)	0	i	—	0	44

SVERCHEK, PAUL Paul Anthony, NT, 6'3"/252 lbs; Cal Poly-San Luis Obispo; 1984: Min, rnd 8; B5/9/1961 San Luis Obispo, CA **1984** Min 3 (0)

SVIHUS, BOB Robert Craig, T, 6'4"/245 lbs; USC; 1965: Oak, rnd 3/Dal, rnd 4; B6/21/1943 Los Angeles, CA **1965** Oak-A 14 (14, LT) **1966** Oak-A 14 (14, LT) **1967**†Oak-A 14 (14, LT) **1968**†Oak-A 14 (14, LT) **1969**†Oak-A 13 (13, LT) **1970**†Oak 13 (1) **1971** NYJ 14 (LT) **1972** NYJ 14 (LT) **1973** NYJ 12 **NFL** 122 (70) [9 yrs]

SVITEK, WILL Will, T, 6'6"/301 lbs; Stanford; 2005: KC, rnd 6; B6/8/1982 Prague, Czech Republic **2005** KC 1 (0)

SVOBODA, BILL William Ray, LB-FB, 6'0"/210 lbs; Tulane; 1950: ChiC, rnd 3; B7/12/1928 Wichita Falls, TX, D6/20/1980 Houma, LA **1950** ChiC 12 (RLB) **1952** ChiC 9 **1953** ChiC◇12 **1954** NYG 11 (LLB) **1955** NYG 12 (LLB) **1956**†NYG☆11 (LLB) **1957** NYG 11 (LLB) **1958**†NYG 10 (LLB)

YEAR	TEAM	G (GS, POS)	RUSH	YD	AVG(LG)	TD	REC	YD	AVG(LG)	TD	KPR	OTD	PTS	TAY
1951	ChiC	12	5	15	3.0(6)	0	6	-9	-1.5(3)	0	k	—	0	25
NFL	9	100	5	15	3.0(6)	0	6	-9	-1.5(3)	0	ki	—	0	88

SWAIN, AL Arthur Alton, E, 6'1"/190 lbs; Trinity (TX); B9/5/1904 Alvord, TX, D9/24/1993 Farmersville, GA **1926** Buf 3 (0), 6

SWAIN, BILL William Steven, LB, 6'2"/230 lbs; Oregon; B2/22/1941 Dickinson, ND **1963** LARm 14 **1964** Min 14 **1965** NYG 14 **1967** NYG 14 (LLB) **1968** Det 12 **1969** Det 14 **NFL** 82 [6 yrs]

SWAIN, JOHN John Wesley, DB, 6'1"/195 lbs; Miami (FL); 1981: Min, rnd 4; B9/4/1959 Miami, FL **1981** Min 12 (1) **1982**†Min 9 (5, LCB) **1983** Min 14 (7, LCB) **1984** Min 15 (10, LCB) **1985** Mia 6 (0) **1985** Pit 9 (1) **1986** Pit 11 (10, LCB) **1987** Mia 1 (1) **NFL** 77 (35) [7 yrs]

SWAN, RUSS Russell Scott, LB, 6'4"/223 lbs; Virginia; B3/30/1963 Fairview Park, OH **1987** Dal 5 (3)

SWANCUTT, BILL Bill, DE, 6'4"/264 lbs; Oregon State; 2005: Det, rnd 6; B9/4/1982 Salem, OR **2005** Det 8 (2)

SWANKE, KARL Karl Vance, T-C-G, 6'6"/257 lbs; Boston College; 1980: GB, rnd 6; B12/29/1957 Elmhurst, IL **1980** GB 16 (0) **1982** GB 8 (8, LT) **1983** GB 16 (16, LT) **1984** GB 15 (14, LT) **1985** GB 15 (15, LT)

YEAR	TEAM	G (GS, POS)	RUSH	YD	AVG(LG)	TD	REC	YD	AVG(LG)	TD	KPR	OTD	PTS	TAY
1981	GB	4(0)	—	—	—	—	1	2	2.0(2)	1		—	6	6
1986	GB	10(8, C)	1	0	0.0(0)	0	—					—	0	0
NFL	7	84(61)	1	0	0.0	0	1	2	2.0(2)	1		—	6	6

SWANN, CHARLES Charles Derek, WR, 6'1"/188 lbs; Indiana State; 1992: NYG, rnd 12; B10/29/1970 Memphis, TN **1994** Den 13 (0)

SWANN, ERIC Eric Jerrod, DT-DE, 6'5"/307 lbs; none; 1991: Phx, rnd 1; B8/16/1970 Swann Station, NC **1991** Phx 12 (3) **1992** Phx 16 (11, LDE/ldt) **1993** Phx 9 (9, LDT) **1994** Arz 16 (16, LDT) **1995** Arz★13 (12, LDT) **1996** Arz☆16 (15, LDT) **1998** Arz 7 (5, ldt) **1999** Arz 9 (0) **2000** Car 16 (3)

YEAR	TEAM	G (GS, POS)	RUSH	YD	AVG(LG)	TD	KPR	OTD	PTS	TAY
1997	Arz	13(13, LDT)	1	0	0.0(0)	0	S	—	0	0
NFL	10	127(87)	1	0	0.0	0	iS	1	12	42

SWANN, LYNN Lynn Curtis, WR, 5'11"/180 lbs; USC; 1974: Pit, rnd 1; B3/7/1952 Alcoa, TN; HOF 2001

YEAR	TEAM	G (GS, POS)	RUSH	YD	AVG(LG)	TD	REC	YD	AVG(LG)	TD	KPR	OTD	PTS	TAY
1974	†Pit	11(2)	1	14	14.0(14)	0	11	208	18.9(54)	2	kp	1	18	491
1975	†Pit★	14(12, WR)	3	13	4.3(11)	0	49	781	15.9(43)	11	p	—	66	488
1976	†Pit☆	12(10, WR)	1	2	2.0(2)	0	28	516	18.4(47)	3	p	—	18	271
1977	†Pit☆	14(14, WR)	2	6	3.0(14)	0	50	789	15.8(46)	7	p	—	42	479
1978	†Pit★	16(16, WR)	1	7	7.0(7)	0	61	880	14.4(62)	11	p	—	66	502
1979	†Pit	13(11, WR)	1	9	9.0(9)	0	41	808	19.7(65)	5	p	—	36	442
1980	Pit	13(11, WR)	1	-4	-4.0(-4)	0	44	710	16.1(68)	7		—	42	386
1981	Pit	13(12, WR)	—	—	—	—	34	505	14.9(44)	5		—	30	278
1982	†Pit	9(8, WR)	1	25	25.0(25)	0	18	265	14.7(60)	0	k	—	0	143
NFL	9	115(96)	11	72	6.5(25)	0	336	5462	16.3(68)	51	kp	1	318	3478

SWANSON, ERIC Eric Charles, WR, 5'11"/186 lbs; Tennessee; 1986: SL, rnd 7; B8/25/1963 San Bernardino, CA **1986** SL 9 (0)

SWANSON, EVAR Ernest Evar, E-WB-BB, 5'9"/171 lbs; Lombard; B10/15/1902 DeKalb, IL, D7/17/1973 Galesburg, IL [K] **1924** Mil 9 (9, RE), 18 **1925** RI 2 (1) **1925** ChiC 2 (2) **1926** ChiC 7 (6, le), 1 **1927** ChiC 7 (7, LE), 5 **NFL** 27 (25), 24 [4 yrs]

SWANSON, PETE Peter C., G, 6'5"/315 lbs; Stanford; B3/26/1974 Hollister, CA **2000** SL 3 (0)

SWANSON, SHANE Shane Dru, WR, 5'9"/200 lbs; Nebraska; 1985: Cle, rnd 12; B10/4/1962 Tracy, CA

YEAR	TEAM	G (GS, POS)	RUSH	YD	AVG(LG)	TD	REC	YD	AVG(LG)	TD	KPR	OTD	PTS	TAY
1987	Den	3(2)	—	—	—	—	6	87	14.5(35)	1	kp	—	6	235

SWANSON, TERRY Terry G., P, 6'0"/210 lbs; Massachusetts; B1/8/1944 Cambridge, MA **1967** Bos-A 14 **1968** Bos-A 10 **1969** Cin-A 2 **NFL** 26 [3 yrs]

SWARN, GEORGE George W., RB, 5'10"/205 lbs; Miami (OH); 1987: SL, rnd 5; B2/15/1964 Cincinnati, OH **1987** Cle 1 (0)

SWARTWOUDT, GREGG Gregg Henry, T, 6'3"/275 lbs; North Dakota; B3/21/1964 **1987** NYG 1 (0)

SWATLAND, RICHARD Richard Thomas, G, 6'3"/245 lbs; Notre Dame; 1968: NO, rnd 8; B10/8/1945 Stamford, CT **1968** Hou-A 4

SWAYDA, SHAWN Shawn Gerald, DE, 6'5"/290 lbs; Arizona State; 1997: Chi, rnd 6; B9/4/1974 Phoenix, AZ **1998** Atl 5 (0) **1999** Atl 4 (0) **2000** Atl 16 (0) **2001** Atl 10 (0) **NFL** 35 (0) [4 yrs]

SWAYNE, HARRY Harry Vonray, T-DE, 6'5"/290 lbs; Rutgers; 1987: TB, rnd 7; B2/2/1965 Philadelphia, PA **1987** TB 8 (2) **1988** TB 10 (1) **1989** TB 16 (0) **1990** TB 10 (0) **1991** SD 12 (12, LT) **1992**†SD 16 (16, LT) **1993** SD 11 (11, LT) **1994**†SD 16 (16, LT) **1995**†SD 16 (16, LT) **1996** SD 16 (3) **1997**†Den 7 (0) **1998**†Den 16 (16, RT) **1999** Bal 6 (6, rt) **2000**†Bal 13 (13, RT) **2001**†Mia 13 (1) **NFL** 186 (113) [15 yrs]

SWAYNE, KEVIN Kevin, WR, 6'1"/191 lbs; Wayne State (NE); B1/17/1975 Riverside, CA

YEAR	TEAM	G (GS, POS)	RUSH	YD	AVG(LG)	TD	REC	YD	AVG(LG)	TD	KPR	OTD	PTS	TAY
2001	†NYJ	15(1)	—	—	—	—	13	203	15.6(27)	0		—	0	102
2002	†NYJ	15(0)	—	—	—	—	5	78	15.6(24)	0	k	—	0	37
2003	NYJ	15(0)	—	—	—	—	2	29	14.5(27)	1	k	—	6	23
NFL	3	45(1)	—	—	—	—	20	310	15.5(27)	1	k	—	6	161

SWEENEY, CALVIN Calvin Eugene, WR, 6'2"/190 lbs; California-Riverside; USC; 1979: Pit, rnd 4; B1/12/1955 Riverside, CA

YEAR	TEAM	G (GS, POS)	RUSH	YD	AVG(LG)	TD	REC	YD	AVG(LG)	TD	KPR	OTD	PTS	TAY
1980	Pit	15(0)	—	—	—	—	12	282	23.5(34)	1	k	—	6	143
1981	Pit	14(0)	—	—	—	—	2	53	26.5(32)	0		—	0	27
1982	†Pit	7(1)	—	—	—	—	5	50	10.0(17)	0		—	0	25
1983	Pit	16(16, WR)	1	-2	-2.0(-2)	0	39	577	14.8(42)	5		—	30	312
1984	†Pit	7(1)	—	—	—	—	2	25	12.5(16)	0		—	0	13
1985	Pit	16(0)	—	—	—	—	16	234	14.6(69)	0		—	0	117
1986	Pit	16(7, wr)	—	—	—	—	21	337	16.0(58)	1		—	6	159
1987	Pit	9(6, WR)	—	—	—	—	16	217	13.6(34)	0		—	0	109
NFL	8	102(31)	1	-2	-2.0(-2)	0	113	1775	15.7(69)	7	k	—	42	903

SWEENEY, JAKE Jacob Baum, T, 6'3"/240 lbs; Cincinnati; B5/25/1922 Cincinnati, OH, D7/28/1996 Glendale, OH **1944** ChiB 8 (3)

SWEENEY, JIM James Joseph, C-T-G, 6'4"/287 lbs; Pittsburgh; 1984: NYJ, rnd 2; B8/8/1962 Pittsburgh, PA **1984** NYJ 10 (2) **1985**†NYJ 16 (16, LG) **1986**†NYJ 16 (16, LT) **1987** NYJ 12 (12, LT) **1988** NYJ 16 (16, LG) **1989** NYJ 16 (16, C) **1990** NYJ 16 (16, C) **1991**†NYJ 16 (16, C) **1992** NYJ 16 (16, C) **1993** NYJ 16 (16, C) **1994** NYJ 16 (16, C) **1995** Sea 16 (16, C) **1996**†Pit 16 (0) **1997**†Pit 16 (1) **1998** Pit 8 (1) **1999** Pit 6 (5) **NFL** 228 (176) [16 yrs]

SWEENEY, KEVIN Kevin Joseph, QB, 6'0"/191 lbs; Fresno State; 1987: Dal, rnd 7; B11/16/1963 Bozeman, MT

YEAR	TEAM	G (GS, POS)	RUSH	YD	AVG(LG)	TD	PASS	COMP	PCT	YD	AVG(LG)	TD	INT	SK	YD	QBR	OTD	PTS	TAY
1987	Dal	3(2)	5	8	1.6(5)	0	28	14	50.0	291	10.4(77)	4	1	3	15	—	—	0	134
1988	Dal	3(2)	6	34	5.7(10)	0	78	33	42.3	314	4.0(28)	3	5	9	80	—	—	0	6
NFL	2	6(4)	11	42	3.8(10)	0	106	47	44.3	605	5.7(77)	7	6	12	95	—	—	0	140

SWEENEY, NEAL Neal, WR, 6'2"/170 lbs; Tulsa; 1967: Den, rnd 6; B6/13/1945 Van Nuys, CA

YEAR	TEAM	G (GS, POS)	RUSH	YD	AVG(LG)	TD	REC	YD	AVG(LG)	TD	KPR	OTD	PTS	TAY
1967	Den-A	10	—	—	—	—	6	136	22.7(48)	0		—	0	68

SWEENEY, STEVE Steven Hollis, WR, 6'3"/205 lbs; California; 1973: Oak, rnd 9; B9/6/1950 Bozeman, MT

YEAR	TEAM	G (GS, POS)	RUSH	YD	AVG(LG)	TD	REC	YD	AVG(LG)	TD	KPR	OTD	PTS	TAY
1973	†Oak	14	—	—	—	—	2	52	26.0(34)	1		—	6	31

Sweeney, Walt Walter Francis, G, 6´4˝/256 lbs; Syracuse; 1963: SD, rnd 1/Cle, rnd 8; B4/18/1941 Cohasset, MA **1963**†SD-A 14 **1964**†SD-A✧14 (RG) **1966** SD-A✧14 (RG) **1967** SD-A★14 (RG) **1968** SD-A★14 (RG) **1969** SD-A★14 (RG) **1970** SD★14 (RG) **1971** SD★14 (RG) **1972** SD✧14 (RG) **1973** SD 14 (RG) **1974**†Was 14 (14, RG) **1975** Was 13 (13, RG)

YEAR	TEAM	G(GS, POS)	RUSH	YD	AVG(LG)	TD	REC	YD	AVG(LG)	TD	PASS	COMP	PCT	YD	AVG(LG)	TD	INT	SK	YD	QBR	KPR	OTD	PTS	TAY
1965	†SD-A★	14(RG)	0	8	(8)	0	—	—	—	—	—	—	—	—	—	—	—	—	—	—	—	—	0	8
NFL	13	181(27)	0	8	(8)	0	—	—	—	—	—	—	—	—	—	—	—	—	—	—	k	—	0	9

Sweet, Fred Frederick, B, 5´10˝/165 lbs; Brown; B8/17/1901 Philadelphia, PA, D10/31/1976 Cape May, NJ **[K]** **1925** Pro 8 (1), 7 **1926** Pro 9 (4) **NFL** 17 (5) [2 yrs]

Sweet, Joe Joseph Lamar, WR, 6´2˝/196 lbs; Tennessee State; 1971: LA, rnd 17; B7/5/1948 Lakeland, FL **1973** LARm 8 **1974** NE 4

YEAR	TEAM	G(GS, POS)	RUSH	YD	AVG(LG)	TD	REC	YD	AVG(LG)	TD	PASS	COMP	PCT	YD	AVG(LG)	TD	INT	SK	YD	QBR	KPR	OTD	PTS	TAY
1972	LARm	11	1	1	1.0(1)	0	2	26	13.0(17)	1	—	—	—	—	—	—	—	—	—	—	—	—	8	19
1975	SD	11	—	—	—	—	8	147	18.4(52)	0	—	—	—	—	—	—	—	—	—	—	—	—	0	74
NFL	4	34	1	1	1.0(1)	0	10	173	17.3(52)	1	—	—	—	—	—	—	—	—	—	—	—	—	8	93

Sweet, Tony Anthony, TE, 6´4˝/230 lbs; Montclair State; B12/13/1963

YEAR	TEAM	G(GS, POS)	RUSH	YD	AVG(LG)	TD	REC	YD	AVG(LG)	TD	PASS	COMP	PCT	YD	AVG(LG)	TD	INT	SK	YD	QBR	KPR	OTD	PTS	TAY
1987	NYJ	3(2)	—	—	—	—	3	45	15.0(22)	0	—	—	—	—	—	—	—	—	—	—	—	—	0	23

Sweetan, Karl Karl Robert, QB, 6´1˝/203 lbs; Texas A&M; Wake Forest; 1965: Det, rnd 18; B10/2/1942 Dallas, TX, D7/2/2000 Las Vegas, TX

YEAR	TEAM	G(GS, POS)	RUSH	YD	AVG(LG)	TD	REC	YD	AVG(LG)	TD	PASS	COMP	PCT	YD	AVG(LG)	TD	INT	SK	YD	QBR	KPR	OTD	PTS	TAY
1966	Det	10(8, QB)	34	219	6.4(34)	1	—	—	—	—	309	157	50.8	1809	5.9(**99**)	4	14	—	—	54.3	—	—	6	594
1967	Det	10(QB)	17	93	5.5(18)	1	—	—	—	—	177	74	41.8	901	5.1(52)	10	11	—	—	51.1	—	—	6	164
1968	NO	5	4	-5	-1.3(2)	0	—	—	—	—	78	27	34.6	318	4.1(42)	1	9	5	29	—	—	—	0	-201
1969	LARm	5	1	-1	-1.0(-1)	0	—	—	—	—	13	5	38.5	101	7.8(67)	1	0	1	4	—	—	—	0	55
1970	LARm	6	—	—	—	—	—	—	—	—	13	6	46.2	81	6.2(22)	1	0	2	15	—	—	—	0	46
NFL	5	36(8)	56	306	5.5(34)	2	—	—	—	—	590	269	45.6	3210	5.4(99)	17	34	8	48	48.3	—	—	12	656

Sweetland, Fred Frederick Greenhalge, WB-FB, 5´10˝/175 lbs; Washington & Lee; Fordham; B11/1893 Everett, MA, deceased **1920** Akr 4 (0) **1921** NYG 1 (0) **NFL** 5 (0) [2 yrs]

Sweiger, Bob Robert Michael, WB-BB-HB, 6´0˝/209 lbs; Minnesota; 1942: NYG, rnd 3; B9/20/1919 Minneapolis, MN, D11/1/1975 Hennepin County, MN

YEAR	TEAM	G(GS, POS)	RUSH	YD	AVG(LG)	TD	REC	YD	AVG(LG)	TD	PASS	COMP	PCT	YD	AVG(LG)	TD	INT	SK	YD	QBR	KPR	OTD	PTS	TAY
1946	†NYY-A	13(5, wb)	7	22	3.1	0	8	55	6.9	1	—	—	—	—	—	—	—	—	—	—	Pkpi	—	6	154
1947	†NYY-A	14(11, WB)	9	44	4.9	0	11	108	9.8	1	—	—	—	—	—	—	—	—	—	—	ki	1	12	151
1948	NYY-A	14(14, WB)	3	4	1.3	0	12	129	10.8	0	—	—	—	—	—	—	—	—	—	—	k	—	0	57
1949	ChiH-A	12(12, BB)	3	17	5.7	0	11	126	11.5	0	—	—	—	—	—	—	—	—	—	—	ki	—	0	110
AAFC	4	53(42)	22	87	4.0	0	42	418	10.0	2	—	—	—	—	—	—	—	—	—	—	Pkpi	1	18	471

Swenson, Bob Robert Charles, LB, 6´3˝/225 lbs; California; B7/1/1953 Stockton, CA **1975** Den 14 **1976** Den 14 (6, LOLB) **1977**†Den 14 (14, LOLB) **1978**†Den 16 (15, LOLB) **1979**†Den☆16 (16, LOLB) **1981** Den★16 (16, LOLB) **1982** Den 4 (0) **1983** Den 2 (2) **NFL** 96 (69) [8 yrs]

Swiacki, Bill William Adam, E, 6´2˝/195 lbs; Holy Cross; Columbia; 1946: Bos, rnd 16/1947: Buf-A, rnd 20; B10/2/1922 Southbridge, MA, D7/7/1976 Sturbridge, MA

YEAR	TEAM	G(GS, POS)	RUSH	YD	AVG(LG)	TD	REC	YD	AVG(LG)	TD	PASS	COMP	PCT	YD	AVG(LG)	TD	INT	SK	YD	QBR	KPR	OTD	PTS	TAY
1948	NYG☆	12(1, le)	—	—	—	—	39	550	14.1(65)	10	—	—	—	—	—	—	—	—	—	—	k	—	60	310
1949	NYG	12(9, LE)	—	—	—	—	47	652	13.9(42)	4	—	—	—	—	—	—	—	—	—	—	—	—	24	346
1950	†NYG	12(LE)	—	—	—	—	20	280	14.0(38)	3	—	—	—	—	—	—	—	—	—	—	k	—	18	151
1951	Det	12	—	—	—	—	16	188	11.8(24)	0	—	—	—	—	—	—	—	—	—	—	—	—	0	94
1952	†Det	11	—	—	—	—	17	213	12.5(26)	1	—	—	—	—	—	—	—	—	—	—	—	—	6	112
NFL	5	59(10)	—	—	—	—	139	1883	13.5(65)	18	—	—	—	—	—	—	—	—	—	—	k	—	108	1013

Swiadon, Phil Phillip Edward, G, 6´0˝/220 lbs; NYU; B12/5/1914 Brooklyn, NY **1943** Bkn 3 (0)

Swider, Larry Lawrence John, P, 6´2˝/195 lbs; Pittsburgh; 1977: Den, rnd 7; B2/1/1955 Limestone, ME **[P]** **1980** SL 16 (0) **1982**†TB 9 (0)

YEAR	TEAM	G(GS, POS)	RUSH	YD	AVG(LG)	TD	REC	YD	AVG(LG)	TD	PASS	COMP	PCT	YD	AVG(LG)	TD	INT	SK	YD	QBR	KPR	OTD	PTS	TAY
1979	Det	14	1	0	0.0(0)	0	—	—	—	—	1	1	100.0	36	36.0(36)	0	0	—	—	—	P	—	0	18
1981	†TB	13(0)	1	-9	-9.0(-9)	0	—	—	—	—	—	—	—	—	—	—	—	—	—	—	P	—	0	-9
NFL	4	52	2	-9	-4.5	0	—	—	—	—	1	1	100.0	36	36.0(36)	0	0	—	—	—	P	—	0	9

Swift, Doug Douglas A., LB, 6´3˝/226 lbs; Amherst; B10/24/1948 Syracuse, NY **1970**†Mia 14 (8, LLB) **1971**†Mia 14 (14, LLB) **1972**†Mia 14 (14, LLB) **1973**†Mia 14 (14, LLB) **1974** Mia 8 (7, llb) **1975** Mia 14 (13, LLB) **NFL** 78 (70) [6 yrs]

Swift, Justin Justin Charles, TE, 6´3˝/265 lbs; Kansas State; 1999: Den, rnd 7; B8/14/1975 Kansas City, KS

YEAR	TEAM	G(GS, POS)	RUSH	YD	AVG(LG)	TD	REC	YD	AVG(LG)	TD	PASS	COMP	PCT	YD	AVG(LG)	TD	INT	SK	YD	QBR	KPR	OTD	PTS	TAY
1999	Phi	1(0)	—	—	—	—	—	—	—	—	—	—	—	—	—	—	—	—	—	—	—	—	—	—
2000	SF	16(1)	—	—	—	—	1	8	8.0(8)	0	—	—	—	—	—	—	—	—	—	—	—	—	0	4
2001	†SF	16(2)	—	—	—	—	11	66	6.0(13)	1	—	—	—	—	—	—	—	—	—	—	—	—	6	38
2002	†SF	16(4)	—	—	—	—	10	63	6.3(11)	0	—	—	—	—	—	—	—	—	—	—	—	—	0	32
NFL	4	49(7)	—	—	—	—	22	137	6.2(13)	1	—	—	—	—	—	—	—	—	—	—	—	—	6	74

Swift, Michael Michael Aaron, DB, 5´10˝/165 lbs; Austin Peay State; B2/28/1974 Dyersburg, TN **1997** SD 12 (1) **1999** Car 15 (0) **2000** Jax 1 (0) **NFL** 28 (1) [3 yrs]

Swilley, Dennis Dennis Neal, C-G-T, 6´3˝/253 lbs; Texas A&M; North Texas; 1977: Min, rnd 2; B6/28/1955 Bossier City, LA **1977**†Min 14 **1978**†Min 14 **1979** Min 16 (16, C) **1980**†Min 16 (16, C) **1981** Min 16 (15, C) **1982**†Min 9 (9, C) **1983** Min 16 (16, C) **1985** Min 16 (13, C) **1986** Min 16 (16, C) **1987** Min 6 (0) **NFL** 139 (101) [10 yrs]

Swilling, Pat Patrick Travis, LB-DE, 6´3˝/245 lbs; Georgia Tech; 1986: NO, rnd 3; B10/25/1964 Toccoa, GA **[S]** **1986** NO 16 (0) **1987**†NO☆12 (12, ROLB) **1988** NO 15 (14, ROLB) **1989** NO★16 (15, ROLB) **1990**†NO★16 (16, ROLB) **1991**†NO★16 (16, ROLB) **1992**†NO☆16 (16, ROLB) **1993**†Det✧14 (14, ROLB) **1994**†Det 16 (7, rolb) **1995** Oak☆16 (16, RDE) **1996** Oak 16 (16, RDE) **1998** Oak 16 (0) **NFL** 185 (142) [12 yrs]

Swiney, Erwin Erwin Bernard, DB, 6´0˝/192 lbs; Nebraska; B10/8/1978 Dallas, TX **2002**†GB 3 (0) **2003** GB 6 (0) **NFL** 9 (0) [2 yrs]

Swinford, Wayne Lenis Wayne, DB-WR, 6´0˝/192 lbs; Georgia; 1965: SF, rnd 9; B5/3/1943 Anniston, AL **1965** SF 14 **1966** SF 7 **1967** SF 5 **NFL** 26 [3 yrs]

Swinger, Rashod Rashod Alexander, DT-DE, 6´2˝/286 lbs; Rutgers; B11/27/1974 Paterson, NJ **1997** Arz 1 (0) **1998**†Arz 16 (11, LDT) **1999** Arz 15 (14, LDT) **NFL** 32 (25) [3 yrs]

Swink, Jim James Edward, HB, 6´1˝/185 lbs; TCU; 1957: ChiB, rnd 2; B3/14/1936 Sacul, TX

YEAR	TEAM	G(GS, POS)	RUSH	YD	AVG(LG)	TD	REC	YD	AVG(LG)	TD	PASS	COMP	PCT	YD	AVG(LG)	TD	INT	SK	YD	QBR	KPR	OTD	PTS	TAY
1960	DalT-A	5	10	15	1.5(5)	0	4	37	9.3(32)	0	—	—	—	—	—	—	—	—	—	—	k	—	0	55

Swinney, Clovis Clovis G., DT, 6´3˝/249 lbs; Arkansas; Arkansas State; 1970: NO, rnd 3; B8/17/1945 Mexico, MO **1970** NO 14 **1971** NYJ 4 **NFL** 18 [2 yrs]

Swinton, Reggie Reginald Terrell, WR, 6´0˝/186 lbs; Murray State; B7/24/1975 Little Rock, AR **[R]**

YEAR	TEAM	G(GS, POS)	RUSH	YD	AVG(LG)	TD	REC	YD	AVG(LG)	TD	PASS	COMP	PCT	YD	AVG(LG)	TD	INT	SK	YD	QBR	KPR	OTD	PTS	TAY
2001	Dal	15(1)	1	-4	-4.0(-4)	0	7	117	16.7(45)	0	—	—	—	—	—	—	—	—	—	—	kp	1	12	816
2002	Dal	14(0)	1	23	23.0(23)	0	7	63	9.0(16)	0	—	—	—	—	—	—	—	—	—	—	kp	1	6	388
2003	Dal	1(0)	—	—	—	—	—	—	—	—	—	—	—	—	—	—	—	—	—	—	kp	—	0	15
2003	Det	11(1)	3	11	3.7(9)	0	9	100	11.1(25)	0	—	—	—	—	—	—	—	—	—	—	kp	2	12	648
2004	Det	13(1)	1	3	3.0(3)	0	18	213	11.8(28)	1	—	—	—	—	—	—	—	—	—	—	kp	—	6	279
2005	Arz	15(0)	—	—	—	—	—	—	—	—	—	—	—	—	—	—	—	—	—	—	kp	—	0	635
NFL	5	69(3)	6	33	5.5(23)	0	41	493	12.0(45)	2	—	—	—	—	—	—	—	—	—	—	kp	4	36	2780

Swisher, Bob Robert Emerson, HB, 5´11˝/163 lbs; Northwestern; B7/14/1914 Victoria, IL, D9/27/1979 Memphis, TN

YEAR	TEAM	G(GS, POS)	RUSH	YD	AVG(LG)	TD	REC	YD	AVG(LG)	TD	PASS	COMP	PCT	YD	AVG(LG)	TD	INT	SK	YD	QBR	KPR	OTD	PTS	TAY
1938	ChiB	9(0)	22	133	6.0	0	5	65	13.0	0	4	1	25.0	8	2.0(8)	1	1	—	—	—	—	—	0	135
1939	ChiB	9(5, lh)	30	192	6.4	2	7	228	32.6(85)	1	—	—	—	—	—	—	—	—	—	—	P	—	18	331
1940	†ChiB✧	9(0)	15	70	4.7	0	2	106	53.0	0	1	0	0.0	0	0.0	0	0	—	—	—	—	—	0	123
1941	†ChiB✧	11(3)	37	149	4.0(20)	0	6	179	29.8(53)	2	—	—	—	—	—	—	—	—	—	—	kpi	1	18	420
1945	ChiB	3(0)	—	—	—	—	2	4	2.0(4)	0	—	—	—	—	—	—	—	—	—	—	i	—	0	-3
NFL	5	41(8)	104	544	5.2(20)	2	22	582	26.5(85)	3	5	1	20.0	8	1.6(8)	1	1	—	—	—	Pkpi	1	36	1005

Swistowicz, Mike Michael Paul, HB-DB, 5´10˝/185 lbs; Notre Dame; 1950: NYY, rnd 5; B4/22/1927 Chicago, IL, deceased **1950** NYY 1 **1950** ChiC 8 **NFL** 9 [1 yr]

Switzer, Marvin Marvin Duane, DB, 6´0˝/192 lbs; Kansas State; B10/28/1954 Bogue, KS **1978** Buf 10 (1)

Switzer, Veryl Veryl Allen, HB-DB, 5´11˝/190 lbs; Kansas State; 1954: GB, rnd 1; B8/6/1932 Nicodemus, KS

YEAR	TEAM	G(GS, POS)	RUSH	YD	AVG(LG)	TD	REC	YD	AVG(LG)	TD	PASS	COMP	PCT	YD	AVG(LG)	TD	INT	SK	YD	QBR	KPR	OTD	PTS	TAY
1954	GB	12	15	59	3.9(33)	0	17	166	9.8(28)	2	—	—	—	—	—	—	—	—	—	—	kp	2	24	548
1955	GB	12	16	101	6.3(38)	0	14	103	7.4(22)	1	—	—	—	—	—	—	—	—	—	—	kp	—	6	386
NFL	2	24	31	160	5.2(38)	0	31	269	8.7(28)	3	—	—	—	—	—	—	—	—	—	—	kp	2	30	934

Swoope, Craig Craig Avery, DB, 6´1˝/205 lbs; Illinois; 1986: TB, rnd 4; B2/3/1964 Fort Pierce, FL **1986** TB 15 (13, SS) **1987** TB 1 (0) **1987**†Ind 3 (0) **1988** Ind 11 (4) **NFL** 30 (17) [3 yrs]

YEAR	TEAM	G (GS, POS)	RUSH	YD	AVG (LG)	TD	REC	YD	AVG (LG)	TD	PASS	COMP	PCT	YD	AVG (LG)	TD	INT	SK	YD	QBR	KPR	OTD	PTS	TAY

SWOOPES, PAT Patrick Roaman, NT, 6´4˝/280 lbs; Mississippi State; 1986: NO, rnd 11; B3/4/1964 Florence, AL **1987** NO 9 (3) **1989** NO 15 (0) **1991** KC 4 (0) **1991** Mia 3 (0) **NFL** 31 (3) [3 yrs]

SWORD, SAM Sam Lee-Arthur, LB, 6´1˝/245 lbs; Michigan; B12/9/1974 Saginaw, MI **1999** Oak 10 (5, llb) **2000†**Ind 3 (0) **2001** Ind 16 (2) **2002†**Ind 16 (1) **NFL** 45 (8) [4 yrs]

SYDNER, JEFF Jeffrey Lynn, WR, 5´6˝/177 lbs; Hawaii; 1992: Phi, rnd 6; B11/11/1969 Columbus, OH **1992†**Phi 15 (0) **1995** NYJ 6 (0)

YEAR	TEAM	G (GS, POS)	RUSH	YD	AVG (LG)	TD	REC	YD	AVG (LG)	TD	PASS	COMP	PCT	YD	AVG (LG)	TD	INT	SK	YD	QBR	KPR	OTD	PTS	TAY
1993	Phi	4(0)	—	—	—	—	2	42	21.0(31)	0	—	—	—	—	—	—	—	—	—	—	k	—	0	44
1994	Phi	16(0)	—	—	—	—	1	10	10.0(10)	0	—	—	—	—	—	—	—	—	—	—	kp	—	0	278
NFL	4	41(0)	—	—	—	—	3	52	17.3(31)	0	—	—	—	—	—	—	—	—	—	—	kp	—	0	565

SYDNEY, HARRY Harry Flanroy, RB, 6´0˝/217 lbs; Kansas; B6/26/1959 Petersburg, VA

YEAR	TEAM	G (GS, POS)	RUSH	YD	AVG (LG)	TD	REC	YD	AVG (LG)	TD	PASS	COMP	PCT	YD	AVG (LG)	TD	INT	SK	YD	QBR	KPR	OTD	PTS	TAY
1987	†SF	14(0)	29	125	4.3(15)	0	1	3	3.0(3)	0	1	1	100.0	50	50.0(50)	1	0	—	—	—	k	—	0	220
1988	†SF	16(0)	9	50	5.6(13)	0	2	18	9.0(9)	0	1	0	0.0	0	0.0	0	0	—	—	—	k	—	0	52
1989	†SF	7(0)	9	56	6.2(18)	0	9	71	7.9(13)	0	—	—	—	—	—	—	—	—	—	—	k	—	0	63
1990	†SF	16(0)	35	166	4.7(19)	2	10	116	11.6(23)	1	—	—	—	—	—	—	—	—	—	—	k	—	18	252
1991	SF	16(0)	57	245	4.3(32)	5	13	90	6.9(19)	2	1	0	0.0	0	0.0	0	0	—	—	—	k	—	42	348
1992	GB	16(10, FB)	51	163	3.2(19)	2	49	384	7.8(20)	1	—	—	—	—	—	—	—	—	—	—	—	—	18	380
NFL	6	85(10)	190	805	4.2(32)	9	84	682	8.1(23)	4	3	1	33.3	50	16.7(50)	1	0	—	—	—	k	—	78	1314

SYDNOR, WILLIE George Ross, WR, 5´11˝/170 lbs; Northwestern; Villanova; Syracuse; B3/21/1959 Bryn Mawr, PA **1982** Pit 8 (0)

SYKES, ALFRED Alfred J., WR, 6´2˝/170 lbs; Florida A&M; 1971: NE, rnd 14; B12/20/1947 Tallahassee, FL

YEAR	TEAM	G (GS, POS)	RUSH	YD	AVG (LG)	TD	REC	YD	AVG (LG)	TD	PASS	COMP	PCT	YD	AVG (LG)	TD	INT	SK	YD	QBR	KPR	OTD	PTS	TAY
1971	NE	4(1)	—	—	—	—	1	15	15.0(15)	0	—	—	—	—	—	—	—	—	—	—	—	—	0	8

SYKES, BOB Robert Eugene, FB, 6´1˝/218 lbs; San Jose State; B3/15/1927 Oakland, CA

YEAR	TEAM	G (GS, POS)	RUSH	YD	AVG (LG)	TD	REC	YD	AVG (LG)	TD	PASS	COMP	PCT	YD	AVG (LG)	TD	INT	SK	YD	QBR	KPR	OTD	PTS	TAY
1952	Was	4	4	10	2.5(4)	0	1	5	5.0(5)	0	—	—	—	—	—	—	—	—	—	—	—	—	0	13

SYKES, EUGENE Eugene Charles, DB, 6´1˝/201 lbs; LSU; 1963: Buf, rnd 19/Phi, rnd 8; B9/26/1941 New Orleans, LA **1963†**Buf-A 9 **1964†**Buf-A 10 (LS) **1965** Buf-A 4 **1967** Den-A 4 **NFL** 27 [4 yrs]

SYKES, JASHON Jashon, LB, 6´2˝/236 lbs; Colorado; B9/25/1979 Los Angeles, CA **2003†**Den 16 (8, LLB) **2004** Den 3 (0) **NFL** 19 (8) [2 yrs]

SYKES, JOHN John, WR, 5´11˝/195 lbs; Morgan State; 1972: Bal, rnd 7; B5/13/1949 Baltimore, MD **1972** SD 2

SYLVESTER, JOHN John J., DB-HB, 6´0˝/183 lbs; Temple; B1/14/1923 Norristown, PA **1948†**Bal-A 12 (0)

YEAR	TEAM	G (GS, POS)	RUSH	YD	AVG (LG)	TD	REC	YD	AVG (LG)	TD	PASS	COMP	PCT	YD	AVG (LG)	TD	INT	SK	YD	QBR	KPR	OTD	PTS	TAY
1947	NYY-A	7(0)	17	101	5.9	0	1	5	5.0(5)	0	1	0	0.0	0	0.0	0	0	—	—	—	Pkp	—	0	136
AAFC	2	19(0)	17	101	5.9	0	1	5	5.0(5)	0	1	0	0.0	0	0.0	0	0	—	—	—	Pkpi	—	0	137

SYLVESTER, STEVE Steven Phillip, C-G-T, 6´4˝/260 lbs; Notre Dame; 1975: Oak, rnd 10; B3/4/1953 Cincinnati, OH **1975** Oak 11 **1976†**Oak 14 **1977†**Oak 14 **1978** Oak 16 (2) **1979** Oak 16 (16, RG) **1980†**Oak 7 (2) **1981** Oak 15 (9, C) **1982** LARd 4 (0) **1983†**LARd 9 (2) **NFL** 106 (31) [9 yrs]

SYMANK, JOHN John Richard, DB, 5´11˝/180 lbs; Florida; 1957: GB, rnd 23; B8/31/1935 La Grange, TX, D1/23/2002 Dauphin Island, AL **1957** GB 12 (DB) **1958** GB 12 **1959** GB 12 **1960†**GB 12 (LCB) **1961†**GB 14 **1962†**GB 14 **1963** SL 13 **NFL** 89 [7 yrs]

SYMONETTE, JOSH Joshua, DB, 5´10˝/180 lbs; Tennessee Tech; B5/8/1978 Miami, FL **2000** Was 3 (0)

SYNHORST, JOHN John Benjamin, T, Iowa; B11/13/1895 Leighton, IA, D3/19/1982 Des Moines, IA **1920** RI 2 (0)

SYTSMA, STAN Stanley Allan, LB, 6´2˝/220 lbs; Minnesota; 1979: NO, rnd 7; B5/3/1956 Glendale, AZ **1980** Atl 2 (0)

SYVRUD, J.J. J.J., LB, 6´3˝/265 lbs; Jamestown; 1999: NYJ, rnd 7; B5/10/1977 Rock Springs, ND **1999** NYJ 1 (0)

SZAFARYN, LEN Leonard Adolph, T-G-LB-DT, 6´2˝/226 lbs; North Carolina; 1949: Was, rnd 3/Bkn-A, rnd 2; B1/19/1928 Ambridge, PA, D9/23/1990 Baden, PA **1949** Was 12 (6, LT) **1950** GB 12 **1953** GB 7 **1954** GB 12 (12, LT) **1955** GB 12 (12, LT) **1956** GB 12 **1957** Phi 1 (1) **1958** Phi 7 **NFL** 75 (31) [8 yrs]

SZAKASH, PAUL Paul Michael, E-BB-FB, 6´0˝/213 lbs; Montana; 1938: Det, rnd 7; B5/5/1913 Chicago, IL, D10/24/1984 Missoula, MT **[K]**

YEAR	TEAM	G (GS, POS)	RUSH	YD	AVG (LG)	TD	REC	YD	AVG (LG)	TD	PASS	COMP	PCT	YD	AVG (LG)	TD	INT	SK	YD	QBR	KPR	OTD	PTS	TAY
1938	Det	7(2)	20	55	2.8	0	1	0	0.0	0	—	—	—	—	—	—	—	—	—	—	—	—	0	55
1939	Det	11(1)	3	11	3.7	0	—	—	—	—	—	—	—	—	—	—	—	—	—	—	K	—	0	11
1941	Det	10(7, RE)	—	—	—	—	3	77	25.7(47)	0	—	—	—	—	—	—	—	—	—	—	k	—	0	41
1942	Det	10(3)	—	—	—	—	5	53	10.6(21)	0	—	—	—	—	—	—	—	—	—	—	—	—	0	27
NFL	4	38(13)	23	66	2.9	0	9	130	14.4(47)	0	—	—	—	—	—	—	—	—	—	—	Kk	—	0	133

SZALAY, THATCHER Thatcher, G, 6´4˝/303 lbs; Montana; B1/18/1979 Kalispell, MT **2005** Bal 3 (0)

SZARO, RICH Richard Julian, K, 5´11˝/205 lbs; Harvard; B3/7/1948 Rzeszow, Poland **[K]** **1975** NO 11 **1976** NO 14 **1977** NO 14 **1978** NO 4 **1979** NYJ 1 **NFL** 44 [5 yrs]

SZCZECKO, JOE Joseph, DT, 6´0˝/245 lbs; Northwestern; B8/25/1942 Lahr, Germany **1966** Atl 12 **1967** Atl 12 (7, RDT) **1968** Atl 10 **1969** NYG 14 (LDT) **NFL** 48 (7) [4 yrs]

SZOT, WALT Walter Stanley, DT-T, 6´1˝/222 lbs; Bucknell; 1944: ChiC, rnd 18; B3/30/1920 Clifton, NJ, D11/3/1981 Passaic, NJ **1946** ChiC 9 (1) **1947** ChiC 12 (0) **1948** ChiC 12 (0) **1949** Pit 12 (2) **1950** Pit 11 **NFL** 56 (3) [5 yrs]

SZOTT, DAVE David Andrew, G, 6´4˝/289 lbs; Penn State; 1990: KC, rnd 7; B12/12/1967 Passaic, NJ **1990†**KC 16 (11, LG) **1991†**KC 16 (16, LG) **1992†**KC 16 (16, LG) **1993†**KC 14 (13, LG) **1994†**KC 16 (16, LG) **1995†**KC☆16 (16, LG) **1996** KC 16 (16, LG) **1997†**KC☆16 (16, LG) **1998** KC 1 (1) **1999** KC 14 (14, LG) **2000** KC 1 (1) **2001** Was 16 (16, LG) **2002†**NYJ 4 (4) **2003** NYJ 15 (15, LG) **NFL** 177 (171) [14 yrs]

SZYMAKOWSKI, DAVE David John, WR, 6´2˝/198 lbs; West Texas A&M; 1968: NO, rnd 3; B3/15/1946 Bethlehem, PA **1968** NO 3

SZYMANSKI, DICK Richard Frank, C-LB, 6´3˝/233 lbs; Notre Dame; 1955: Bal, rnd 2; B10/7/1932 Toledo, OH **1955** Bal★12 (C) **1957** Bal 5 **1958** Bal 8 **1959†**Bal 12 (12, MLB) **1960** Bal 12 (MLB) **1962** Bal✧14 (C) **1963** Bal 14 (C) **1964†**Bal✧14 (C) **1965†**Bal 10 (10, C) **1966** Bal 14 (C) **1967** Bal 14 (C) **1968†**Bal 14

YEAR	TEAM	G (GS, POS)	RUSH	YD	AVG (LG)	TD	REC	YD	AVG (LG)	TD	PASS	COMP	PCT	YD	AVG (LG)	TD	INT	SK	YD	QBR	KPR	OTD	PTS	TAY
1961	Bal	14(C)	—	—	—	—	1	5	5.0(5)	0	—	—	—	—	—	—	—	—	—	—	—	—	0	3
NFL	13	157(22)	—	—	—	—	1	5	5.0(5)	0	—	—	—	—	—	—	—	—	—	—	i	1	6	22

SZYMANSKI, FRANK Francis Stanislaus, C, 5´11˝/225 lbs; Notre Dame; 1945: Det, rnd 1; B7/6/1923 Detroit, MI, D4/26/1987 Detroit, MI **1945** Det 4 (0) **1946** Det 11 (6, C) **1947** Det 12 (3) **1948** Phi 9 (0) **1949** ChiB 11 (0) **NFL** 47 (9) [5 yrs]

SZYMANSKI, JIM James Paul, DE, 6´5˝/268 lbs; Michigan State; 1990: Den, rnd 10; B9/7/1967 Sterling Heights, MI **1990** Den 6 (6, rde) **1991** Den 1 (0) **NFL** 7 (6) [2 yrs]

TABOR, PAUL Paul Carol, C-G, 6´4˝/241 lbs; Oklahoma; 1980: Chi, rnd 5; B11/30/1956 Little Rock, AR **1980** ChiB 16 (0)

TABOR, PHIL Philip Martin, DE-NT-DT, 6´4˝/255 lbs; Oklahoma; 1979: NYG, rnd 4; B11/30/1956 Little Rock, AR **1979** NYG 15 **1980** NYG 16 (6, nt) **1981†**NYG 16 (1) **1982** NYG 9 (7, RDE) **NFL** 56 (14) [4 yrs]

TACKETT, DOYLE Doyle Lee, B, 6´0˝/205 lbs; none; B8/22/1923 Hector, AR, D9/7/2002 Atkins, AR **1948** Bkn-A 1 (0)

YEAR	TEAM	G (GS, POS)	RUSH	YD	AVG (LG)	TD	REC	YD	AVG (LG)	TD	PASS	COMP	PCT	YD	AVG (LG)	TD	INT	SK	YD	QBR	KPR	OTD	PTS	TAY
1946	Bkn-A	14(3)	11	-6	-0.5	0	10	191	19.1	2	—	—	—	—	—	—	—	—	—	—	kpi	—	12	110
1947	Bkn-A	12(2)	—	—	—	—	0	25	(25)	0	—	—	—	—	—	—	—	—	—	—	i	—	0	25
AAFC	3	27(5)	11	-6	-0.5	0	10	216	21.6(25)	2	—	—	—	—	—	—	—	—	—	—	kpi	—	12	139

TACKWELL, COOKIE Charles O., E-T, 6´2˝/215 lbs; Kansas State; B3/27/1906, D8/1984, **[K]** **1930** Fra 17 (11, RE), 7 **1930** Min 1 (1) **1931** Fra 8 (3), 1 **1931** ChiB 4 (4, lt), 2 **1932** ChiB 11 (1), 3 **1933** Cin 5 (5, RE)

YEAR	TEAM	G (GS, POS)	RUSH	YD	AVG (LG)	TD	REC	YD	AVG (LG)	TD	PASS	COMP	PCT	YD	AVG (LG)	TD	INT	SK	YD	QBR	KPR	OTD	PTS	TAY
1933	ChiB	3(0)	—	—	—	—	1	20	20.0(20)	0	—	—	—	—	—	—	—	—	—	—	—	—	0	10
1934	Cin	8(7, RE)	1	6	6.0(6)	0	5	58	11.6	0	—	—	—	—	—	—	—	—	—	—	—	—	0	35
NFL	5	57(32)	1	6	6.0(6)	0	6	78	13.0(20)	1	—	—	—	—	—	—	—	—	—	—	K	—	13	50

TAFFONI, JOE Joseph Albert, T-G, 6´3˝/255 lbs; West Virginia; Tennessee-Martin; 1967: Cle, rnd 4; B3/27/1945 Brownsville, PA **1967†**Cle 14 **1968†**Cle 13 **1969†**Cle 14 (rt) **1970** Cle 14 (RT) **1972** NYG 14 (RT) **1973** NYG 9 (RT) **NFL** 78 [6 yrs]

TAFOYA, JOE Joseph Peter, DE, 6´4˝/278 lbs; Arizona; 2001: TB, rnd 7; B9/6/1978 Pittsburg, CA **2001†**ChiB 5 (0) **2002** ChiB 14 (1) **2003** ChiB 16 (0) **2005†**Sea 15 (1) **NFL** 50 (2) [4 yrs]

TAGGE, JERRY Jerry Lee, QB, 6´2˝/220 lbs; Nebraska; 1972: GB, rnd 1; B4/12/1950 Omaha, NE

YEAR	TEAM	G (GS, POS)	RUSH	YD	AVG (LG)	TD	REC	YD	AVG (LG)	TD	PASS	COMP	PCT	YD	AVG (LG)	TD	INT	SK	YD	QBR	KPR	OTD	PTS	TAY
1972	GB	4	8	-3	-0.4(2)	1	—	—	—	—	29	10	34.5	154	5.3(31)	0	0	3	27	—	—	—	6	84
1973	GB	7(qb)	15	62	4.1(41)	2	—	—	—	—	106	56	52.8	720	6.8(50)	2	7	9	54	53.2	—	—	12	172
1974	GB	7(QB)	18	58	3.2(12)	0	—	—	—	—	146	70	47.9	709	4.9(30)	1	10	5	35	36.0	—	—	0	18
NFL	3	18	41	117	2.9(41)	3	—	—	—	—	281	136	48.4	1583	5.6(50)	3	17	17	116	44.2	—	—	18	274

YEAR	TEAM	G (GS, POS)	RUSH	YD	AVG(LG)	TD	REC	YD	AVG(LG)	TD	PASS	COMP	PCT	YD	AVG(LG)	TD	INT	SK	YD	QBR	KPR	OTD	PTS	TAY

TAGLIAFERRI, JOHN   John Stanton, RB, 5´11˝/195 lbs; Cornell; B4/14/1964 Orange, NJ
| 1987 | Mia | 3(1) | 13 | 45 | 3.5(7) | 1 | 12 | 117 | 9.8(27) | 0 | — | — | — | — | — | — | — | — | — | — | — | — | 6 | 114 |

TAIBI, JOE   Joseph Paul, DE, 6´5˝/265 lbs; Southern Colorado; Idaho; B2/22/1963   **1987** NYG 3 (0)

TAIT, ART   Arthur William, DE, 5´11˝/205 lbs; Mississippi State; B2/8/1929 Memphis, TN   **1951** NYY 12 (LDE)   **1952** DalT 8   **NFL** 20 [2 yrs]

TAIT, JOHN   John, T, 6´6˝/323 lbs; Brigham Young; 1999: KC, rnd 1; B1/26/1975 Phoenix, AZ   **1999** KC 12 (3)   **2000** KC 15 (15, LT)   **2001** KC 16 (16, LT)   **2003**†KC 16 (16, RT) **2004** ChiB 13 (13, RT)   **2005**†ChiB 15 (15, LT)
| 2002 | KC | 16(16, RT) | 1 | 28 | 28.0(28) | 0 | — | — | — | — | — | — | — | — | — | — | — | — | — | — | — | — | 0 | 28 |
| NFL | 7 | 103(94) | 1 | 28 | 28.0(28) | 0 | — | — | — | — | — | — | — | — | — | — | — | — | — | — | — | — | 0 | 28 |

TALAMINI, BOB   Robert Guy, G, 6´1˝/255 lbs; Kentucky; 1960: Hou, rnd 2; B1/8/1939 Louisville, KY   **1961**†Hou-A☆14 (LG)   **1962**†Hou-A★14 (LG)   **1963** Hou-A★14 (LG) **1964** Hou-A★14 (LG)   **1965** Hou-A★14 (LG)   **1966** Hou-A★14 (LG)   **1967**†Hou-A★14 (LG)   **1968**†NYJ-A 14 (LG)
| 1960 | †Hou-A | 14(LG) | — | — | — | — | — | — | — | — | — | — | — | 0 | 14 (14) | 0 | — | — | — | — | — | — | 0 | 14 |
| NFL | 9 | 126 | — | — | — | — | — | — | — | — | — | — | — | 0 | 14 (14) | 0 | — | — | — | — | — | — | 0 | 14 |

TALBERT, DIRON   Diron Vester, DT-DE, 6´5˝/255 lbs; Texas; 1966: LA, rnd 5/SD, rnd R2; B7/1/1944 Pascagoula, MS   **1967**†LARm 2   **1968** LARm 14   **1969**†LARm 14 (13, RDE) **1970** LARm 14 (14, RDT)   **1971**†Was 14 (14, RDT)   **1972** Was 14 (14, RDT)   **1973**†Was☆14 (14, RDT)   **1974**†Was◇14 (14, RDT)   **1975** Was 14 (13, RDT)   **1976**†Was 14 (14, RDT) **1977** Was 14 (14, RDT)   **1978** Was 12 (12, RDT)   **1979** Was 16 (16, RDT)   **1980** Was 16 (5, rdt)   **NFL** 186 (157) [14 yrs]

TALBERT, DON   Don Larry, T-LB, 6´5˝/255 lbs; Texas; 1961: Dal, rnd 8/1962: Hou, rnd 34; B3/1/1939 Louisville, MS   **1962** Dal 14 (4)   **1965** Dal 14   **1966** Atl 12 (12, LT) **1967** Atl 12 (LT)   **1968** Atl 14 (LT)   **1969** NO 14 (LT)   **1970** NO 14 (LT)   **1971** Dal 9   **NFL** 103 (16) [8 yrs]

TALBOT, JOHN   John Orechia, E, 6´2˝/182 lbs; Brown; B4/27/1900 South Weymouth, MA, D12/5/1981 Keene, NH   **1926** Pro 2 (0)

TALBOTT, JIM   James Stropes, BB, North Dakota; B7/26/1893 Marco, IN, D11/9/1972 Hollywood, FL   **1920** Ham 1 (0)

TALCOTT, DAN   Daniel, T, 6´3˝/235 lbs; UNLV; 1945: Phi, rnd 26; B5/21/1921 Grass Valley, CA, D4/22/1955 Reno, NV   **1947**†Phi 8 (0)

TALIAFERRO, GEORGE   George, HB-TB-QB-DB, 5´11˝/196 lbs; Indiana; 1949: LAD-A, rnd 1/ChiB, rnd 13; B1/8/1927 Gates, TN **[R]**
1949	LAD-A☆	11(4, tb)	95	472	5.0	5	0	42	(42)	1	124	45	36.3	790	6.4	4	14	—	—	—	Pkp	1	42	574
1950	NYY	12(LH)	88	411	4.7(44)	4	21	299	14.2(43)	5	7	3	42.9	83	11.9(50)	1	0	—	—	—	Pkp	—	54	854
1951	NYY◇	12(lh)	62	330	5.3(65)	3	16	230	14.4(47)	2	33	13	39.4	251	7.6(51)	1	3	—	—	—	Pkpi	—	30	790
1952	DalT★	12(12, LH)	100	419	4.2(38)	1	21	244	11.6(78)	1	63	16	25.4	298	4.7(48)	2	6	—	—	—	kp	—	12	530
1953	Bal◇	11(LH)	102	479	4.7(50)	2	20	346	17.3(54)	2	55	15	27.3	211	3.8(45)	2	5	—	—	—	Pkp	—	24	670
1954	Bal	11	48	157	3.3(29)	0	14	122	8.7(29)	1	2	0	0.0	0	0.0	0	1	—	—	—	kp	—	6	221
1955	Phi	3	3	-2	-0.7(0)	0	3	17	5.7(14)	0	—	—	—	—	—	—	—	—	—	—	k	—	0	8
NFL	6	61(12)	403	1794	4.5(65)	10	95	1258	13.2(78)	11	160	47	29.4	843	5.3(51)	6	15	—	—	—	Pkpi	—	126	3072

TALIAFERRO, MIKE   Myron Eugene, QB, 6´2˝/202 lbs; Illinois; 1963: NYJ, rnd 28/NYG, rnd 10; B7/26/1941 Houston, TX
1964	NYJ-A	14	9	45	5.0(14)	0	—	—	—	—	73	23	31.5	341	4.7(66)	2	5	9	123	—	—	—	0	26
1965	NYJ-A	14	7	4	0.6(10)	0	—	—	—	—	119	45	37.8	531	4.5(37)	3	7	—	—	36.1	—	—	0	5
1966	NYJ-A	14	—	—	—	—	—	—	—	—	41	19	46.3	177	4.3(21)	2	2	—	—	—	—	—	2	19
1967	NYJ-A	14	2	20	10.0(12)	0	—	—	—	—	20	11	55.0	96	4.8(20)	1	1	2	22	—	—	—	0	33
1968	Bos-A	7(7, QB)	8	51	6.4(21)	0	—	—	—	—	176	67	38.1	889	5.1(70)	4	15	18	156	26.9	—	—	0	-85
1969	Bos-A◇	14(14, QB)	12	-16	-1.3(4)	0	—	—	—	—	331	160	48.3	2160	6.5(77)	19	18	24	261	66.0	—	—	0	439
1970	Bos	11(4, qb)	3	11	3.7(6)	0	—	—	—	—	173	78	45.1	871	5.0(45)	4	11	15	158	41.8	—	—	0	27
1972	Buf	5	5	19	3.8(14)	0	—	—	—	—	33	16	48.5	176	5.3(24)	1	4	6	48	—	—	—	0	-48
NFL	8	82(25)	46	134	2.9(21)	0	—	—	—	—	966	419	43.4	5241	5.4(77)	36	63	74	768	46.1	—	—	2	415

TALLANT, DAVE   David, T, 6´1˝/205 lbs; Muskingum; Grove City; B8/1896 Murrysville, PA, deceased   **1921** Ham 4 (4, RT)   **1922** Ham 5 (3, LT)   **1923** Ham 7 (6, LT)   **1924** Ham 1 (1) **1925** Ham 3 (3, RT)   **NFL** 20 (17) [5 yrs]

TALLEY, BEN   Benjamin Jermaine, LB, 6´3˝/248 lbs; Tennessee; 1995: NYG, rnd 4; B7/14/1972 Griffin, GA   **1995** NYG 4 (0)   **1998**†Atl 8 (0)   **NFL** 12 (0) [2 yrs]

TALLEY, DARRYL   Darryl Victor, LB, 6´4˝/235 lbs; West Virginia; 1983: Buf, rnd 2; B7/10/1960 Cleveland, OH   **1983** Buf 16 (0)   **1984** Buf 16 (16, LOLB)   **1985** Buf 16 (5, lolb) **1986** Buf 16 (16, LOLB/rolb)   **1987** Buf 12 (12, ROLB)   **1988**†Buf 16 (15, ROLB)   **1989**†Buf 16 (16, ROLB)   **1990**†Buf★16 (16, ROLB)   **1991**†Buf◇16 (16, ROLB) **1992**†Buf 16 (16, ROLB)   **1993**†Buf☆16 (16, ROLB)   **1994** Buf 16 (16, ROLB)   **1995**†Atl 16 (15, RLB)   **1996**†Min 12 (12, LLB)   **NFL** 216 (187) [14 yrs]

TALLEY, JOHN   John Thomas Eugene, WR, 6´5˝/245 lbs; West Virginia; B12/19/1964 Cleveland, OH
1990	Cle	14(2)	—	—	—	—	2	28	14.0(19)	0	—	—	—	—	—	—	—	—	—	—	k	—	0	5
1991	Cle	3(1)	—	—	—	—	1	13	13.0(13)	0	—	—	—	—	—	—	—	—	—	—	—	—	0	7
NFL	2	17(3)	—	—	—	—	3	41	13.7(19)	0	—	—	—	—	—	—	—	—	—	—	k	—	0	12

TALLEY, STAN   Robert Stanley, P, 6´5˝/220 lbs; TCU; B9/5/1958 Dallas, TX   **1987** LARd 12 (0)

TALLMAN, CHARLES   Charles W., T, none; B1/9/1896, NY, D4/1970 Franklin, NJ   **1921** Ton 1 (1, RT)

TALTON, KEN   Kenneth B., RB, 6´0˝/208 lbs; Cornell; B6/25/1956 Mansfield, OH   **1980** Det 2 (0)

TALTON, TYREE   Tyree, DB, 5´11˝/201 lbs; Northern Iowa; 1999: Det, rnd 5; B5/10/1976 Beloit, WI   **1999**†Det 12 (0)

TAMBURELLO, BEN   Ben Allen, G-C, 6´3˝/278 lbs; Auburn; 1987: Phi, rnd 3; B9/9/1964 Birmingham, AL   **1987** Phi 2 (1)   **1988**†Phi 16 (4)   **1989**†Phi 16 (4)   **1990**†Phi 16 (2) **NFL** 50 (11) [4 yrs]

TAMBURO, SAM   Samuel Joseph, DE, 6´2˝/200 lbs; Penn State; 1949: NYB, rnd 6/ChiH-A, rnd 6; B7/1/1926 New Kensington, PA, D12/18/1998 New Kensington, PA **1949** NYB 12 (2)

TAMM, RALPH   Ralph Earl, G-C, 6´4˝/280 lbs; West Chester; 1988: NYJ, rnd 9; B3/11/1966 Philadelphia, PA   **1990** Cle 16 (12, LG)   **1991** Cle 1 (0)   **1991** Was 2 (0)   **1991** Cin 1 (0) **1992**†SF 14 (1)   **1993**†SF 16 (16, RG)   **1994** SF 1 (1)   **1995** Den 13 (1)   **1996** Den 9 (0)   **1997**†KC 16 (0)   **1998** KC 16 (0)   **1999** KC 16 (0)   **NFL** 121 (31) [10 yrs]

TANDY, GEORGE   George Wendell, C-E, 6´1˝/210 lbs; North Carolina; B11/27/1893 Jacksonville, IL, D5/11/1969 Springfield, IL   **1920** Roc 1 (0)   **1921** Cle 5 (2)   **NFL** 6 (2) [2 yrs]

TANGUAY, BILL   James Peter, TB, 6´0˝/190 lbs; NYU; B5/24/1909, D3/23/1971 Broward County, FL
| 1933 | Pit | 3(0) | — | — | — | — | — | — | — | — | 17 | 5 | 29.4 | 101 | 5.9 | 1 | 5 | — | — | — | — | — | 0 | -145 |

TANNEN, STEVE   Steven Olson, DB, 6´1˝/194 lbs; Florida; 1970: NYJ, rnd 1; B7/23/1948 Miami, FL   **1970** NYJ 14 (LCB)   **1971** NYJ 11   **1972** NYJ 13 (LCB)   **1973** NYJ 9 **1974** NYJ 14 (8, FS)   **NFL** 61 (8) [5 yrs]

TANNER, BARRON   Barron Keith, DT, 6´3˝/360 lbs; Oklahoma; 1997: Mia, rnd 5; B9/14/1973 Athens, TX   **1997**†Mia 16 (0)   **1998**†Mia 13 (0)   **2000** Arz 4 (0)   **2001** Arz 16 (16, RDT) **2002** Arz 15 (8, RDT)   **2003** Arz 14 (2)   **NFL** 78 (26) [6 yrs]

TANNER, BOB   Robert Erwin, E-T, 6´0˝/190 lbs; Minnesota; B9/27/1907 Fairmont, MN, D12/8/1997 Homasassa, FL   **1930** Fra 12 (8, re), 12

TANNER, HAMP   Elijah Hampton, T, 6´2˝/280 lbs; Georgia; 1950: NYG, rnd 30; B10/31/1927 Nichols, GA, D12/6/2004 Winterville, GA   **1951** SF 12   **1952** DalT 10   **NFL** 22 [2 yrs]

TANNER, JOHN   John Porter, B, 5´5˝/165 lbs; Centre; B12/3/1897 Owensboro, KY, D12/23/1976 Owensboro, KY **[K]**   **1922** Tol 2 (0)   **1923** Cle 6 (5, WB), 8   **1924** Cle 2 (0), 12 **NFL** 10 (5), 20 [3 yrs]

TANNER, JOHN   John Vance, LB, 6´4˝/241 lbs; Tennessee Tech; 1971: SD, rnd 9; B3/8/1945 Orlando, FL
1971	SD	14	—	—	—	—	1	6	6.0(6)	0	—	—	—	—	—	—	—	—	—	—	—	—	0	3
1973	NE	13	—	—	—	—	—	—	—	—	—	—	—	—	—	—	—	—	—	—	—	—	0	—
1974	NE	13(2)	—	—	—	—	2	23	11.5(21)	1	—	—	—	—	—	—	—	—	—	—	k	—	6	4
NFL	3	40(2)	—	—	—	—	3	29	9.7(21)	1	—	—	—	—	—	—	—	—	—	—	k	—	6	7

TANT, JAY   Jay William, TE, 6´3˝/254 lbs; Northwestern; 2000: Arz, rnd 5; B12/4/1977 Kettering, OH
| 2000 | Arz | 5(0) | — | — | — | — | 1 | 4 | 4.0(4) | 0 | — | — | — | — | — | — | — | — | — | — | — | — | 0 | 2 |

TANUVASA, MAA   Maa Junior, DE-DT, 6´2˝/270 lbs; Hawaii; 1993: LARm, rnd 8; B11/6/1970 Nu'uli, American Samoa   **1995** Den 1 (0)   **1996** Den 16 (1)   **1997**†Den 15 (5, rdt) **1998**†Den 16 (16, RDE)   **1999** Den 16 (16, RDE/lde)   **2000**†Den 16 (16, LDE)   **2001** SD 2 (0)   **NFL** 82 (54) [7 yrs]

TAPEH, THOMAS   Thomas Teah, FB, 6´1˝/233 lbs; Minnesota; 2004: Phi, rnd 5; B3/28/1980 St. Paul, MN
| 2004 | Phi | 7(0) | 12 | 42 | 3.5(10) | 0 | 2 | 15 | 7.5(13) | 0 | — | — | — | — | — | — | — | — | — | — | — | — | 0 | 50 |

YEAR	TEAM	G(GS, POS)	RUSH	YD	AVG(LG)	TD	REC	YD	AVG(LG)	TD	PASS	COMP	PCT	YD	AVG(LG)	TD	INT	SK	YD	QBR	KPR	OTD	PTS	TAY

Tarasovic, George George Kenneth, DE-LB-C, 6´4˝/245 lbs; Boston College; LSU; 1952: Pit, rnd 2; B5/6/1930 Granville, NY **1952** Pit 12 (LDE) **1953** Pit 12 (LDE) **1956** Pit 12 **1957** Pit 12 (LLB) **1958** Pit 12 **1959** Pit☆12 (LDE) **1960** Pit 12 (LDE) **1961** Pit 12 (LLB) **1962** Pit 14 (LLB) **1963** Pit 8 **1963** Phi 6 (6, LDE) **1964** Phi 11 (11, LDE) **1965** Phi 14 **1966** Den-A 6 **NFL** 155 (17) [13 yrs]

Tarbox, Bruce Bruce P., G, 6´2˝/230 lbs; Syracuse; 1961: NYG, rnd 2; B5/10/1939 Nyack, NY, D3/6/1979 Pittsburgh, PA **1961** LARm 7

Tardits, Richard Richard, LB, 6´2˝/228 lbs; Georgia; 1989: Phx, rnd 5; B7/30/1965 Biarritz, France **1990** NE 2 (1) **1991** NE 16 (0) **1992** NE 9 (0) **NFL** 27 (1) [3 yrs]

Tarkenton, Fran Francis Abury, QB, 6´0˝/190 lbs; Georgia; 1961: Min, rnd 3/Bos, rnd 5; B2/3/1940 Richmond, VA; HOF 1986

YEAR	TEAM	G(GS, POS)	RUSH	YD	AVG(LG)	TD	REC	YD	AVG(LG)	TD	PASS	COMP	PCT	YD	AVG(LG)	TD	INT	SK	YD	QBR	KPR	OTD	PTS	TAY
1961	Min	14(10, QB)	56	308	5.5(52)	5	—	—	—	—	280	157	56.1	1997	7.1(71)	18	17	44	416	74.7	—	—	30	767
1962	Min	14(14, QB)	41	361	8.8(31)	2	0	-12	(-12)	0	329	163	49.5	2595	7.9(**89**)	22	25	45	450	66.9	—	—	12	783
1963	Min	14(14, QB)	28	162	5.8(24)	1	—	—	—	—	297	170	57.2	2311	7.8(67)	15	15	42	448	78.0	—	—	6	803
1964	Min✧	14(14, QB)	50	330	6.6(31)	2	—	—	—	—	306	171	55.9	2506	8.2(64)	22	11	46	446	91.8	—	—	12	1273
1965	Min✧	14(14, QB)	56	356	6.4(36)	1	—	—	—	—	329	171	52.0	2609	7.9(72)	19	11	28	250	83.8	—	—	6	1326
1966	Min	14(12, QB)	62	376	6.1(28)	4	—	—	—	—	358	192	53.6	2561	7.2(68)	17	16	37	322	73.8	—	—	24	1142
1967	NYG✧	14(QB)	44	306	7.0(22)	2	—	—	—	—	377	204	54.1	3088	8.2(70)	29	19	29	283	85.9	—	—	12	1255
1968	NYG✧	14(QB)	57	301	5.3(22)	3	—	—	—	—	337	182	54.0	2555	7.6(84)	21	12	27	255	84.6	—	—	18	1234
1969	NYG✧	14(QB)	37	172	4.6(21)	0	—	—	—	—	409	220	53.8	2918	7.1(65)	23	8	36	289	87.2	—	—	0	**1426**
1970	NYG★	14(QB)	43	236	5.5(20)	2	—	—	—	—	389	219	56.3	2777	7.1(59)	19	12	36	249	82.2	—	—	12	1260
1971	NYG	13(QB)	30	111	3.7(16)	3	—	—	—	—	386	**226**	58.5	2567	6.7(81)	11	21	27	232	65.4	—	—	18	640
1972	Min☆	14(14, QB)	27	180	6.7(21)	0	—	—	—	—	378	215	56.9	2651	7.0(76)	18	13	26	203	80.2	—	—	0	1076
1973	†Min☆	14(14, QB)	41	202	4.9(16)	1	—	—	—	—	274	169	61.7	2113	7.7(54)	15	7	31	270	93.2	—	—	6	1064
1974	†Min★	13(13, QB)	21	120	5.7(15)	2	—	—	—	—	351	199	56.7	**2598**	7.4(80)	17	12	17	142	82.1	—	—	12	1044
1975	†Min★	14(14, QB)	16	108	6.8(21)	2	—	—	—	—	**425**	**273**	**64.2**	**2994**	7.0(46)	**25**	13	27	245	**91.8**	—	—	12	1230
1976	†Min★	13(13, QB)	27	45	1.7(20)	1	—	—	—	—	412	**255**	**61.9**	**2961**	7.2(56)	17	8	25	221	89.3	—	—	6	1301
1977	Min	9(9, QB)	15	6	0.4(8)	0	—	—	—	—	258	155	**60.1**	1734	6.7(59)	9	14	22	232	69.2	—	—	0	358
1978	†Min	16(16, QB)	24	-6	-0.3(15)	1	—	—	—	—	**572**	**345**	60.3	**3468**	6.1(58)	**25**	**32**	27	254	68.9	—	—	6	583
NFL	18	246(171)	675	3674	5.4(52)	32	0	-12	(-12)	0	6467	3686	57.0	47003	7.3(89)	342	266	572	5207	80.4	—	—	192	18560

Tarle, Jim Jim, K, 6´0˝/221 lbs; South Carolina; Arkansas State; B12/27/1972 Jacksonville, FL **2000** Jax 6 (0) **2001** Jax 9 (0) **NFL** 15 (0) [2 yrs]

Tarr, Jerry Gerald LaVern, WR, 6´0˝/190 lbs; Oregon; 1962: Den, rnd 17; B8/27/1939 Bakersfield, CA

YEAR	TEAM	G(GS, POS)	RUSH	YD	AVG(LG)	TD	REC	YD	AVG(LG)	TD	PASS	COMP	PCT	YD	AVG(LG)	TD	INT	SK	YD	QBR	KPR	OTD	PTS	TAY
1962	Den-A	14	—	—	—	—	8	211	26.4(97)	2	—	—	—	—	—	—	—	—	—	—	k	—	12	213

Tarr, Jim James Lloyd, E, 6´2˝/190 lbs; Missouri; B9/26/1906 Nevada, MO, D5/6/1995 Eugene, OR **1931** Cle 1 (1)

Tarrant, Bob Robert Everett, E, 6´0˝/180 lbs; Pittsburg State; B4/4/1914 Hamilton, KS, D12/16/1991 Danbury, CT **1936** NYG 1 (0)

Tarrant, Jimmy James Robert, QB, 5´9˝/160 lbs; Samford; Tennessee; B2/18/1921 Birmingham, AL

YEAR	TEAM	G(GS, POS)	RUSH	YD	AVG(LG)	TD	REC	YD	AVG(LG)	TD	PASS	COMP	PCT	YD	AVG(LG)	TD	INT	SK	YD	QBR	KPR	OTD	PTS	TAY
1946	Mia-A	4(1)	5	-46	-9.2	0	—	—	—	—	12	5	41.7	95	7.9	1	0	—	—	—	—	—	0	7

Tarver, John John William, RB, 6´3˝/227 lbs; Colorado; 1972: NE, rnd 7; B1/1/1949 Bakersfield, CA

YEAR	TEAM	G(GS, POS)	RUSH	YD	AVG(LG)	TD	REC	YD	AVG(LG)	TD	PASS	COMP	PCT	YD	AVG(LG)	TD	INT	SK	YD	QBR	KPR	OTD	PTS	TAY
1972	NE	8(3)	42	132	3.1(21)	1	11	112	10.2(22)	1	—	—	—	—	—	—	—	—	—	—	—	—	12	203
1973	NE	9(7, fb)	72	321	4.5(28)	4	9	51	5.7(13)	0	—	—	—	—	—	—	—	—	—	—	k	—	24	389
1974	NE	14	41	101	2.5(18)	2	9	37	4.1(12)	0	—	—	—	—	—	—	—	—	—	—	—	—	12	140
1975	Phi	8	7	20	2.9(9)	0	5	14	2.8(8)	0	—	—	—	—	—	—	—	—	—	—	—	—	0	27
NFL	4	39(10)	162	574	3.5(28)	7	34	214	6.3(22)	1	—	—	—	—	—	—	—	—	—	—	k	—	48	758

Taseff, Carl Carl N., DB-HB, 5´11˝/192 lbs; John Carroll; 1951: Cle, rnd 22; B9/28/1928 Parma, OH, D2/27/2005 Weston, FL **[RI]**

YEAR	TEAM	G(GS, POS)	RUSH	YD	AVG(LG)	TD	REC	YD	AVG(LG)	TD	PASS	COMP	PCT	YD	AVG(LG)	TD	INT	SK	YD	QBR	KPR	OTD	PTS	TAY
1951	Cle	9	13	49	3.8(15)	2	1	18	18.0(18)	0	—	—	—	—	—	—	—	—	—	—	kp	—	12	90
1953	Bal	9(DB)	1	1	1.0(1)	1	—	—	—	—	—	—	—	—	—	—	—	—	—	—	kpi	1	12	135
1954	Bal	12(DB)	41	228	5.6(32)	0	16	159	9.9(30)	1	—	—	—	—	—	—	—	—	—	—	kpi	—	6	392
1955	Bal	11(DB)	—	—	—	—	1	3	3.0(3)	0	—	—	—	—	—	—	—	—	—	—	kpi	—	0	30
1956	Bal	12(DB)	1	2	2.0(2)	0	—	—	—	—	—	—	—	—	—	—	—	—	—	—	kpi	2	12	184
1957	Bal	4(db)	—	—	—	—	—	—	—	—	—	—	—	—	—	—	—	—	—	—	pi	—	0	27
1958	†Bal☆	12(DB)	—	—	—	—	—	—	—	—	—	—	—	—	—	—	—	—	—	—	kpi	—	0	103
1959	†Bal	12(DB)	—	—	—	—	—	—	—	—	—	—	—	—	—	—	—	—	—	—	pi	1	6	79
1960	Bal	12	4	3	0.8(4)	0	1	13	13.0(13)	0	—	—	—	—	—	—	—	—	—	—	kp	—	0	86
1961	Bal	7	—	—	—	—	—	—	—	—	—	—	—	—	—	—	—	—	—	—	pi	—	0	24
1961	Phi	5	—	—	—	—	—	—	—	—	—	—	—	—	—	—	—	—	—	—	—	—	—	—
1962	Buf-A	11(LS)	—	—	—	—	—	—	—	—	1	0	0.0	0	0.0	0	0	—	—	—	pi	—	0	9
NFL	11	116	60	283	4.7(32)	3	19	193	10.2(30)	1	1	0	0.0	0	0.0	0	0	—	—	—	kpi	4	48	1158

Tasker, Steve Steven Jay, WR, 5´9˝/185 lbs; Northwestern; 1985: Hou, rnd 9; B4/10/1962 Smith Center, KS **1986** Hou 2 (0) **1986** Buf 7 (0) **1987** Buf★12 (0) **1988**†Buf 14 (0) **1989**†Buf 16 (0) **1994** Buf★14 (3) **1997** Buf 14 (0)

YEAR	TEAM	G(GS, POS)	RUSH	YD	AVG(LG)	TD	REC	YD	AVG(LG)	TD	PASS	COMP	PCT	YD	AVG(LG)	TD	INT	SK	YD	QBR	KPR	OTD	PTS	TAY
1985	Hou	7(0)	2	16	8.0(13)	0	2	19	9.5(14)	0	—	—	—	—	—	—	—	—	—	—	k	—	0	218
1990	†Buf★	16(0)	—	—	—	—	2	44	22.0(24)	2	—	—	—	—	—	—	—	—	—	—	—	—	12	32
1991	†Buf★	16(0)	—	—	—	—	2	39	19.5(20)	1	—	—	—	—	—	—	—	—	—	—	—	—	6	25
1992	†Buf★	15(2)	1	9	9.0(9)	0	2	24	12.0(17)	0	—	—	—	—	—	—	—	—	—	—	—	—	0	21
1993	†Buf★	15(0)	—	—	—	—	2	26	13.0(22)	0	—	—	—	—	—	—	—	—	—	—	p	—	0	8
1995	†Buf★	13(5, wr)	8	74	9.3(17)	0	20	255	12.8(43)	3	—	—	—	—	—	—	—	—	—	—	p	—	18	336
1996	†Buf	8(5, wr)	9	31	3.4(11)	0	21	372	17.7(62)	3	—	—	—	—	—	—	—	—	—	—	p	—	18	240
NFL	13	169(15)	20	130	6.5(17)	0	51	779	15.3(62)	9	—	—	—	—	—	—	—	—	—	—	kp	—	56	990

Tassos, Damon Damon Gus, G, 6´1˝/225 lbs; Texas A&M; 1945: Bos, rnd 3; B12/5/1923 San Antonio, TX, D2/28/2001 San Antonio, TX **[K]** **1945** Det 9 (3) **1946** Det 11 (10, RG) **1947** GB 12 (10, RG) **1948** GB 11 (9, RG) **1949** GB 12 (10, RG) **NFL** 55 (42) [5 yrs]

Tatarek, Bob Robert Francis, DT, 6´4˝/270 lbs; Miami (FL); 1968: Buf, rnd 2; B7/3/1946 Greensburg, PA **1968** Buf-A 14 **1969** Buf-A 14 (RDT) **1970** Buf 4 **1971** Buf 14 (RDT) **1972** Buf 1 **1972** Det 2 **NFL** 49 [5 yrs]

Tate, David David Fitzgerald, DB, 6´1˝/197 lbs; Colorado; 1988: Chi, rnd 8; B11/22/1964 Denver, CO **1988**†ChiB 16 (4) **1989** ChiB 14 (4) **1990** ChiB 16 (1) **1991**†ChiB 16 (0) **1992** ChiB 16 (3) **1993**†NYG 14 (1) **1994** Ind 16 (8, ss) **1995**†Ind 16 (16, SS) **1996** Ind 10 (10, SS) **1997** Ind 8 (2) **NFL** 142 (49) [10 yrs]

Tate, Franklin Franklin Eugene, LB, 6´2˝/225 lbs; North Carolina Central; B11/14/1952 Gastonia, NC **1975** SD 4

Tate, John John, LB, 6´2˝/230 lbs; Jackson State; 1975: NYG, rnd 8; B5/1/1953 Mobile, AL **1976** NYG 2

Tate, Lars Lars Jamel, RB, 6´2˝/215 lbs; Georgia; 1988: TB, rnd 2; B2/2/1966 Indianapolis, IN

YEAR	TEAM	G(GS, POS)	RUSH	YD	AVG(LG)	TD	REC	YD	AVG(LG)	TD	PASS	COMP	PCT	YD	AVG(LG)	TD	INT	SK	YD	QBR	KPR	OTD	PTS	TAY
1988	TB	15(5, RB)	122	467	3.8(47)	7	5	23	4.6(9)	1	—	—	—	—	—	—	—	—	—	—	—	—	48	554
1989	TB	15(14, RB)	167	589	3.5(48)	8	11	75	6.8(19)	1	—	—	—	—	—	—	—	—	—	—	—	—	54	712
1990	ChiB	3(0)	3	5	1.7(4)	0	—	—	—	—	—	—	—	—	—	—	—	—	—	—	k	—	0	-10
NFL	3	33(19)	292	1061	3.6(48)	15	16	98	6.1(19)	2	—	—	—	—	—	—	—	—	—	—	k	—	102	1255

Tate, Robert Robert, DB-WR, 5´10˝/188 lbs; Cincinnati; 1997: Min, rnd 6; B10/19/1973 Crowley, IA **1997** Min 4 (0) **2000**†Min 16 (16, RCB) **2001** Min 16 (5, rcb) **2002** Bal 13 (1) **2004** Arz 14 (0) **2005** Arz 13 (5, LCB)

YEAR	TEAM	G(GS, POS)	RUSH	YD	AVG(LG)	TD	REC	YD	AVG(LG)	TD	PASS	COMP	PCT	YD	AVG(LG)	TD	INT	SK	YD	QBR	KPR	OTD	PTS	TAY
1998	†Min	15(1)	—	—	—	—	1	17	17.0(17)	0	—	—	—	—	—	—	—	—	—	—	k	—	0	22
1999	†Min	16(1)	1	4	4.0(4)	0	1	3	3.0(3)	0	—	—	—	—	—	—	—	—	—	—	kpi	1	6	281
NFL	8	107(29)	1	4	4.0(4)	0	2	20	10.0(17)	0	—	—	—	—	—	—	—	—	—	—	kpi	1	6	488

Tate, Rodney Rodney Dane, RB, 5´11˝/190 lbs; Texas; 1982: Cin, rnd 4; B2/14/1959 Okmulgee, OK

YEAR	TEAM	G(GS, POS)	RUSH	YD	AVG(LG)	TD	REC	YD	AVG(LG)	TD	PASS	COMP	PCT	YD	AVG(LG)	TD	INT	SK	YD	QBR	KPR	OTD	PTS	TAY
1982	†Cin	9(0)	2	2	1.0(2)	0	—	—	—	—	—	—	—	—	—	—	—	—	—	—	k	—	0	106
1983	Cin	12(8, rb)	25	77	3.1(13)	0	18	142	7.9(25)	0	—	—	—	—	—	—	—	—	—	—	k	—	0	171
1984	Atl	7(0)	—	—	—	—	—	—	—	—	—	—	—	—	—	—	—	—	—	—	k	—	0	13
NFL	3	28(8)	27	79	2.9(13)	0	18	142	7.9(25)	0	—	—	—	—	—	—	—	—	—	—	k	—	0	290

Tate, Willy William Russell, TE, 6´3˝/251 lbs; Oregon; B9/7/1972 Fontana, CA **1996** TB 13 (0) **1998** KC 1 (0) **NFL** 14 (0) [2 yrs]

Tatman, Pete Allen Kent, RB, 6´1˝/220 lbs; Nebraska; 1967: Min, rnd 10; B4/27/1945 Sutherland, NE **1967** Min 5

YEAR	TEAM	G (GS, POS)	RUSH	YD	AVG (LG)	TD	REC	YD	AVG (LG)	TD	PASS	COMP	PCT	YD	AVG (LG)	TD	INT	SK	YD	QBR	KPR	OTD	PTS	TAY

TATUM, JACK John David 'The Assassin', DB, 5´10˝/200 lbs; Ohio State; 1971: Oak, rnd 1; B11/18/1948 Cherryville, NC **[I]** **1971** Oak 14 (14, FS) **1972**†Oak 14 (14, FS) **1973**†Oak★13 (13, FS) **1974**†Oak★10 (10, FS) **1975**†Oak★13 (13, FS) **1976**†Oak☆14 (FS) **1977**†Oak☆11 (11, FS) **1978** Oak 15 (15, FS) **1979** Oak 16 (16, FS) **1980**†Hou 16 (0) **NFL** 136 (106) [10 yrs]

TATUM, JESS Jess Bolt, E-DE, 6´1˝/215 lbs; North Carolina State; B10/8/1914 Mitchell, SC, D2/4/1992 Lancaster, NC

YEAR	TEAM	G (GS, POS)	RUSH	YD	AVG (LG)	TD	REC	YD	AVG (LG)	TD	PASS	COMP	PCT	YD	AVG (LG)	TD	INT	SK	YD	QBR	KPR	OTD	PTS	TAY
1938	Pit	5(4, RE)	—	—	—	—	1	16	16.0(16)	0	—	—	—	—	—	—	—	—	—	—	—	—	0	8

TATUM, KINNON Kinnon Ray, LB, 6´0˝/222 lbs; Notre Dame; 1997: Car, rnd 3; B7/19/1975 Fayetteville, NC **1997** Car 16 (0) **1998** Car 15 (0) **NFL** 31 (0) [2 yrs]

TATUPU, LOFA Lofa, LB, 5´11˝/226 lbs; USC; 2005: Sea, rnd 2; B11/15/1982 Wrentham, MA **2005**†Sea✧16 (16, MLB)

TATUPU, MOSI Mosiula Faasuka, RB, 6´0˝/227 lbs; USC; 1978: NE, rnd 8; B4/26/1955 Pago Pago, American Samoa

YEAR	TEAM	G (GS, POS)	RUSH	YD	AVG (LG)	TD	REC	YD	AVG (LG)	TD	PASS	COMP	PCT	YD	AVG (LG)	TD	INT	SK	YD	QBR	KPR	OTD	PTS	TAY
1978	†NE	16	3	6	2.0(3)	0	—	—	—	—	—	—	—	—	—	—	—	—	—	—	k	—	0	8
1979	NE	16	23	71	3.1(12)	0	2	9	4.5(5)	0	—	—	—	—	—	—	—	—	—	—	k	—	0	46
1980	NE	16(0)	33	97	2.9(11)	3	4	27	6.8(11)	0	—	—	—	—	—	—	—	—	—	—	—	—	18	141
1981	NE	16(1)	38	201	5.3(43)	2	12	132	11.0(41)	1	—	—	—	—	—	—	—	—	—	—	—	—	18	292
1982	†NE	9(0)	30	168	5.6(26)	0	—	—	—	—	—	—	—	—	—	—	—	—	—	—	—	—	0	168
1983	NE	16(1)	106	578	**5.5(55)**	4	10	97	9.7(17)	1	—	—	—	—	—	—	—	—	—	—	—	—	30	672
1984	NE	16(4)	133	553	4.2(20)	4	16	159	9.9(24)	0	—	—	—	—	—	—	—	—	—	—	k	—	24	667
1985	†NE	16(2)	47	152	3.2(11)	2	2	16	8.0(15)	0	—	—	—	—	—	—	—	—	—	—	—	—	12	180
1986	†NE★	16(5, fb)	71	172	2.4(13)	1	15	145	9.7(25)	0	—	—	—	—	—	—	—	—	—	—	—	1	12	255
1987	NE	12(9, FB)	79	248	3.1(19)	0	15	136	9.1(23)	0	1	1	100.0	15	15.0(15)	1	0	—	—	—	—	—	0	329
1988	NE	16(0)	22	75	3.4(22)	2	8	58	7.3(17)	0	—	—	—	—	—	—	—	—	—	—	k	—	12	122
1989	NE	14(0)	11	38	3.5(20)	0	10	54	5.4(11)	0	1	1	100.0	15	15.0(15)	0	0	—	—	—	k	—	0	60
1990	NE	15(0)	16	56	3.5(15)	0	2	10	5.0(6)	0	—	—	—	—	—	—	—	—	—	—	—	—	0	61
1991	LARm	5(0)	—	—	—	—	—	—	—	—	—	—	—	—	—	—	—	—	—	—	—	—	—	—
NFL	14	199(22)	612	2415	3.9(55)	18	96	843	8.8(41)	2	2	2	100.0	30	15.0(15)	1	0	—	—	—	k	1	126	2998

TAUGHER, BIFF Claude B., FB, 5´10˝/185 lbs; Carroll (WI); Marquette; B3/2/1895 Marathon, WI, deceased **1922** GB 2 (1), 6

TAUSCH, TERRY Terry Wayne, G-T, 6´5˝/275 lbs; Texas; 1982: Min, rnd 2; B2/5/1959 New Braunfels, TX **1982** Min 2 (0) **1983** Min 10 (0) **1984** Min 16 (16, RG) **1985** Min 16 (15, RG) **1986** Min 16 (16, RG) **1987** Min 5 (5, rg) **1988**†Min 16 (16, RG) **1989**†SF 9 (0) **NFL** 90 (68) [8 yrs]

TAUSCHER, MARK Mark Gerald, T-G, 6´4˝/320 lbs; Wisconsin; 2000: GB, rnd 7; B6/17/1977 Marshfield, WI **2000** GB 16 (14, RT) **2001**†GB 16 (16, RT) **2002** GB 2 (2) **2003**†GB 16 (16, RT) **2004**†GB 16 (16, RT) **2005** GB 16 (16, RT) **NFL** 82 (80) [6 yrs]

TAUTALATASI, JUNIOR Taivale, RB, 5´10˝/207 lbs; Washington State; 1986: Phi, rnd 10; B3/24/1963 Oakland, CA

YEAR	TEAM	G (GS, POS)	RUSH	YD	AVG (LG)	TD	REC	YD	AVG (LG)	TD	PASS	COMP	PCT	YD	AVG (LG)	TD	INT	SK	YD	QBR	KPR	OTD	PTS	TAY
1986	Phi	16(2)	51	163	3.2(50)	0	41	325	7.9(56)	2	—	—	—	—	—	—	—	—	—	—	k	—	12	410
1987	Phi	12(1)	26	69	2.7(17)	0	25	176	7.0(22)	0	—	—	—	—	—	—	—	—	—	—	k	—	0	165
1988	Phi	10(0)	14	28	2.0(9)	0	5	48	9.6(21)	0	—	—	—	—	—	—	—	—	—	—	—	—	0	52
1989	Dal	13(0)	6	15	2.5(6)	0	17	157	9.2(23)	0	—	—	—	—	—	—	—	—	—	—	k	—	0	88
NFL	4	51(3)	97	275	2.8(50)	0	88	706	8.0(56)	2	—	—	—	—	—	—	—	—	—	—	k	—	12	714

TAUTOLO, JOHN John William, G, 6´3˝/267 lbs; UCLA; B5/29/1959 Long Beach, CA **1982** NYG 1 (0) **1983** NYG 6 (2) **1987** LARd 3 (3) **NFL** 10 (5) [3 yrs]

TAUTOLO, TERRY Terry Lynn, LB, 6´2˝/232 lbs; UCLA; 1976: Phi, rnd 13; B8/30/1954 Corona, CA **1976** Phi 13 **1977** Phi 14 (2) **1978**†Phi 16 (2) **1979**†Phi 16 (8, LILB) **1980** SF 14 (4) **1981** SF 5 (0) **1981** Det 11 (0) **1982**†Det 2 (0) **1983** Mia 9 (0) **1984** Det 4 (0) **NFL** 104 (16) [9 yrs]

TAVENER, JOHN John Harold, C-LB, 6´0˝/225 lbs; Indiana; 1944: ChiC, rnd 4; B1/10/1921 Newark, OH, D9/19/1993 Johnstown, OH **1946** Mia-A 3 (1)

TAVES, JOSH Josh Heinrich, DE, 6´7˝/280 lbs; Northeastern; B5/13/1972 Truro, MA **2000**†Oak 16 (0) **2001**†Oak 8 (3) **2002** Car 5 (0) **NFL** 29 (3) [3 yrs]

TAYLOR, AARON Aaron Matthew, G, 6´4˝/305 lbs; Notre Dame; 1994: GB, rnd 1; B11/14/1972 San Francisco, CA **1995**†GB 16 (16, LG) **1996**†GB 16 (16, LG) **1997**†GB 14 (14, LG) **1998** SD 15 (15, LG) **1999** SD 14 (14, LG) **NFL** 75 (75) [5 yrs]

TAYLOR, ALPHONSO Aphonso, DT, 6´3˝/350 lbs; Temple; B9/7/1969 Trenton, NJ **1993** Den 3 (0)

TAYLOR, ALTIE Altie, RB, 5´10˝/200 lbs; Utah State; 1969: Det, rnd 2; B9/29/1947 Pittsburg, CA

YEAR	TEAM	G (GS, POS)	RUSH	YD	AVG (LG)	TD	REC	YD	AVG (LG)	TD	PASS	COMP	PCT	YD	AVG (LG)	TD	INT	SK	YD	QBR	KPR	OTD	PTS	TAY
1969	Det	10	118	348	2.9(26)	0	13	86	6.6(20)	0	—	—	—	—	—	—	—	—	—	—	—	—	0	391
1970	†Det	14(RB)	198	666	3.4(34)	2	27	261	9.7(42)	2	—	—	—	—	—	—	—	—	—	—	—	—	24	827
1971	Det	14(RB)	174	736	4.2(36)	4	26	270	10.4(64)	1	—	—	—	—	—	—	—	—	—	—	—	—	30	916
1972	Det	13(RB)	154	658	4.3(38)	4	29	250	8.6(40)	2	—	—	—	—	—	—	—	—	—	—	—	—	36	833
1973	Det	13(RB)	176	719	4.1(34)	5	27	252	9.3(35)	0	—	—	—	—	—	—	—	—	—	—	k	—	30	1010
1974	Det	13(12, RB)	150	532	3.5(27)	5	30	293	9.8(34)	1	—	—	—	—	—	—	—	—	—	—	—	—	36	734
1975	Det	14(14, RB)	195	638	3.3(24)	4	21	111	5.3(17)	0	—	—	—	—	—	—	—	—	—	—	—	—	24	734
1976	Hou	11	5	11	2.2(8)	0	2	15	7.5(8)	0	—	—	—	—	—	—	—	—	—	—	k	—	0	96
NFL	8	102(26)	1170	4308	3.7(38)	24	175	1538	8.8(64)	6	—	—	—	—	—	—	—	—	—	—	k	—	180	5539

TAYLOR, BEN Benjamin Frazier, LB, 6´2˝/245 lbs; Virginia Tech; 2002: Cle, rnd 4; B8/31/1978 Bellaire, OH **2002** Cle 7 (0) **2003** Cle 13 (8, RLB) **2004** Cle 3 (2) **2005** Cle 16 (16, RILB) **NFL** 39 (26) [4 yrs]

TAYLOR, BILLY William Turner, RB, 6´0˝/215 lbs; Texas Tech; 1978: NYG, rnd 4; B7/6/1956 San Antonio, TX

YEAR	TEAM	G (GS, POS)	RUSH	YD	AVG (LG)	TD	REC	YD	AVG (LG)	TD	PASS	COMP	PCT	YD	AVG (LG)	TD	INT	SK	YD	QBR	KPR	OTD	PTS	TAY
1978	NYG	13	73	250	3.4(19)	0	9	70	7.8(18)	0	—	—	—	—	—	—	—	—	—	—	k	—	0	312
1979	NYG	16(FB)	198	700	3.5(31)	7	28	253	9.0(43)	4	—	—	—	—	—	—	—	—	—	—	k	—	66	958
1980	NYG	11(10, RB)	147	580	3.9(35)	4	33	253	7.7(42)	0	—	—	—	—	—	—	—	—	—	—	—	—	24	747
1981	NYG	5(3)	36	110	3.1(14)	2	8	71	8.9(39)	0	—	—	—	—	—	—	—	—	—	—	—	—	12	166
1981	NYJ	3(0)	2	1	0.5(2)	0	—	—	—	—	—	—	—	—	—	—	—	—	—	—	—	—	0	1
1982	LARd	1(0)	4	3	0.8(2)	0	—	—	—	—	—	—	—	—	—	—	—	—	—	—	—	—	0	3
NFL	5	49(13)	460	1644	3.6(35)	13	78	647	8.3(43)	4	—	—	—	—	—	—	—	—	—	—	k	—	102	2186

TAYLOR, BOB Robert F., DE-DT, 6´3˝/240 lbs; Maryland-Eastern Shore; 1963: NYG, rnd 9; B2/5/1940 Columbia, SC **1963**†NYG 14 **1964** NYG 14 **NFL** 28 [2 yrs]

TAYLOR, BOBBY Robert, DB, 6´3˝/216 lbs; Notre Dame; 1995: Phi, rnd 2; B12/28/1973 Houston, TX **1995**†Phi 16 (12, RCB) **1996**†Phi 16 (16, RCB) **1997** Phi 6 (5, rcb) **1998** Phi 11 (10, RCB) **1999** Phi 15 (14, RCB) **2000**†Phi 16 (15, RCB) **2001**†Phi 16 (14, RCB) **2002**†Phi★16 (16, RCB) **2003**†Phi 7 (7, rcb) **2004** Sea 10 (0) **NFL** 129 (109) [10 yrs]

TAYLOR, BRIAN Brian, DB-RB, 5´10˝/185 lbs; Oregon State; B10/1/1967 New Orleans, LA **1991**†Buf 3 (0)

YEAR	TEAM	G (GS, POS)	RUSH	YD	AVG (LG)	TD	REC	YD	AVG (LG)	TD	PASS	COMP	PCT	YD	AVG (LG)	TD	INT	SK	YD	QBR	KPR	OTD	PTS	TAY
1989	ChiB	5(0)	2	7	3.5(7)	0	—	—	—	—	—	—	—	—	—	—	—	—	—	—	—	—	0	7
NFL	2	8(0)	2	7	3.5(7)	0	—	—	—	—	—	—	—	—	—	—	—	—	—	—	k	—	0	10

TAYLOR, BRUCE Bruce Lawrence, DB, 6´0˝/193 lbs; Boston University; 1970: SF, rnd 1; B5/28/1948 Perth Amboy, NJ **[R]** **1970**†SF☆14 (RCB) **1971**†SF✧14 (14, RCB) **1972**†SF 14 (14, RCB) **1973** SF 14 (12, RCB) **1974** SF 14 (8, RCB) **1975** SF 12 (11, RCB) **1976** SF 13 (13, RCB) **1977** SF 14 (14, RCB) **NFL** 109 (86) [8 yrs]

TAYLOR, CHARLEY Charles Robert, WR-SE-RB, 6´3˝/210 lbs; Arizona State; 1964: Was, rnd 1/Hou, rnd 2; B9/28/1941 Grand Prairie, TX; HOF 1984

YEAR	TEAM	G (GS, POS)	RUSH	YD	AVG (LG)	TD	REC	YD	AVG (LG)	TD	PASS	COMP	PCT	YD	AVG (LG)	TD	INT	SK	YD	QBR	KPR	OTD	PTS	TAY
1964	Was★	14(HB)	199	755	3.8(50)	5	53	814	15.4(80)	5	10	2	20.0	54	5.4(41)	0	1	—	—	—	k	—	60	1229
1965	Was✧	13(HB)	145	402	2.8(39)	3	40	577	14.4(69)	3	4	1	25.0	45	11.3(45)	1	0	—	—	—	k	—	36	763
1966	Was★	14(14, SE/hb)	87	262	3.0(24)	3	**72**	1119	15.5(86)	12	—	—	—	—	—	—	—	—	—	—	kp	—	90	1003
1967	Was★	12(SE)	—	—	—	—	**70**	990	14.1(86)	9	—	—	—	—	—	—	—	—	—	—	p	—	54	540
1968	Was☆	14(SE)	2	-3	-1.5(4)	0	48	650	13.5(47)	5	—	—	—	—	—	—	—	—	—	—	—	—	30	347
1969	Was☆	14(SE)	3	24	8.0(18)	0	71	883	12.4(88)	8	—	—	—	—	—	—	—	—	—	—	—	—	48	506
1970	Was☆	10(10, WR)	1	17	17.0(17)	0	42	593	14.1(41)	8	—	—	—	—	—	—	—	—	—	—	—	—	48	354
1971	Was	6(WR)	—	—	—	—	24	370	15.4(71)	4	—	—	—	—	—	—	—	—	—	—	—	—	24	205
1972	†Was★	14(14, WR)	3	39	13.0(17)	0	49	673	13.7(70)	7	—	—	—	—	—	—	—	—	—	—	—	—	42	411
1973	†Was★	14(14, WR)	1	-7	-7.0(-7)	0	59	801	13.6(53)	7	—	—	—	—	—	—	—	—	—	—	—	—	42	429
1974	†Was★	14(14, WR)	1	-1	-1.0(-1)	0	54	738	13.7(51)	5	—	—	—	—	—	—	—	—	—	—	—	—	30	393
1975	Was★	14(14, WR)	—	—	—	—	53	744	14.0(64)	6	—	—	—	—	—	—	—	—	—	—	—	—	36	402
1977	Was	12(7, WR)	—	—	—	—	14	158	11.3(19)	0	—	—	—	—	—	—	—	—	—	—	—	—	0	79
NFL	13	165(87)	442	1488	3.4(50)	11	649	9110	14.0(88)	79	14	3	21.4	99	7.1(45)	1	1	—	—	—	kp	—	540	6659

TAYLOR, CHESTER — Chester Lamar, RB, 5'11"/213 lbs; Toledo; 2002: Bal, rnd 6; B9/22/1979 River Rouge, MI

YEAR	TEAM	G (GS, POS)	RUSH	YD	AVG(LG)	TD	REC	YD	AVG(LG)	TD	PASS	COMP	PCT	YD	AVG(LG)	TD	INT	SK	YD	QBR	KPR	OTD	PTS	TAY
2002	Bal	15(2)	33	122	3.7(17)	0	14	129	9.2(20)	2	—	—	—	—	—	—	—	—	—	—	k	—	14	283
2003	†Bal	16(1)	63	276	4.4(32)	2	20	132	6.6(23)	0	—	—	—	—	—	—	—	—	—	—	k	—	12	465
2004	Bal	16(4, rb)	160	714	4.5(47)	2	30	184	6.1(23)	0	—	—	—	—	—	—	—	—	—	—	k	—	12	826
2005	Bal	15(1)	117	487	4.2(52)	0	41	292	7.1(20)	1	—	—	—	—	—	—	—	—	—	—	k	—	6	711
NFL	4	62(8)	373	1599	4.3(52)	4	105	737	7.0(23)	3	—	—	—	—	—	—	—	—	—	—	k	—	44	2285

TAYLOR, CHUCK — Charles G., BB-LB, 5'10"/190 lbs; Arkansas Tech; Ouachita Baptist; B1/12/1920 Tupelo, AR, D6/3/1977, CO

YEAR	TEAM	G (GS, POS)	RUSH	YD	AVG(LG)	TD	REC	YD	AVG(LG)	TD	KPR	OTD	PTS	TAY
1944	Bkn	10(3)	7	19	2.7(8)	0	2	22	11.0(18)	0	kp	—	0	42

TAYLOR, CHUCK — Charles Albert, G, 5'11"/205 lbs; Stanford; 1943: Cle, rnd 4; B1/24/1920 Portland, OR, D5/7/1994 Stanford, CA   **1946** Mia-A 14 (13, RG)

TAYLOR, CLIFF — Clifton Durett, RB, 5'11"/198 lbs; Memphis; 1974: Chi, rnd 3; B5/10/1952 Memphis, TN

YEAR	TEAM	G (GS, POS)	RUSH	YD	AVG(LG)	TD	REC	YD	AVG(LG)	TD	KPR	OTD	PTS	TAY
1974	ChiB	14	9	18	2.0(9)	1	3	23	7.7(8)	0	k	—	6	202
1976	GB	7	14	47	3.4(17)	1	2	21	10.5(18)	0	k	—	6	82
NFL	2	21	23	65	2.8(17)	2	5	44	8.8(18)	0	k	—	12	283

TAYLOR, CORDELL — Cordell Jerome, DB, 5'11"/190 lbs; Hampton; 1998: Jax, rnd 2; B12/22/1973 Norfolk, VA   **1998** Jax 11 (0)   **1999** Sea 2 (0)   **NFL** 13 (0) [2 yrs]

TAYLOR, CORKY — Cecil Reign, DB-HB, 5'10"/189 lbs; Kansas State; 1955: LA, rnd 2; B10/31/1933 Kansas City, MO   **1957** LARm 2

YEAR	TEAM	G (GS, POS)	RUSH	YD	AVG(LG)	TD	REC	YD	AVG(LG)	TD	KPR	OTD	PTS	TAY
1955	LARm	10	26	95	3.7(13)	0	7	47	6.7(17)	1	i	1	12	179
NFL	2	12	26	95	3.7(13)	0	7	47	6.7(17)	1	kpi	1	12	225

TAYLOR, CRAIG — Craig Garrett, RB, 5'11"/224 lbs; West Virginia; 1989: Cin, rnd 6; B1/3/1966 Elizabeth, NJ

YEAR	TEAM	G (GS, POS)	RUSH	YD	AVG(LG)	TD	REC	YD	AVG(LG)	TD	KPR	OTD	PTS	TAY
1989	Cin	12(0)	30	111	3.7(16)	3	4	44	11.0(18)	2	k	—	30	163
1990	Cin	12(1)	51	216	4.2(24)	2	3	22	7.3(20)	1	k	—	18	253
1991	Cin	12(3)	33	153	4.6(34)	2	21	122	5.8(16)	0	—	—	12	234
NFL	3	36(4)	114	480	4.2(34)	7	28	188	6.7(20)	3	k	—	60	650

TAYLOR, DAVE — David Merritt, T, 6'4"/260 lbs; Catawba; 1973: Bal, rnd 5; B10/17/1949 Statesville, NC   **1973** Bal 13   **1974** Bal 14 (LT)   **1975**†Bal 14 (14, LT)   **1976**†Bal 14 (LT)   **1977**†Bal 14 (LT)   **1979** Bal 3   **NFL** 72 (14) [6 yrs]

TAYLOR, DERRICK — Derrick Howard, DB, 5'11"/186 lbs; Davidson; North Carolina State; B3/15/1964 St. Louis, MO   **1987** NO 3 (3)

TAYLOR, ED — Everett Earl, DB, 6'0"/174 lbs; Memphis; B5/13/1953 Memphis, TN   **1975** NYJ 14 (9, FS)   **1976** NYJ 11 (11, RCB)   **1977** NYJ 14 (14, RCB)   **1978** NYJ 16 (16, RCB)   **1979** NYJ 4   **1979**†Mia 5   **1980** Mia 16 (3)   **1981** Mia 6 (2)   **NFL** 86 (55) [7 yrs]

TAYLOR, ERIC — Eric, DT, 6'2"/305 lbs; Memphis; 2004: Pit, rnd 7; B12/14/1981 Winchester, TN   **2005** Min 1 (0)

TAYLOR, ERK — Erquiet, G-T, 6'2"/210 lbs; Auburn; B10/7/1907, D11/2/1959 Jefferson County, AL   **1931** SI 11 (2)

TAYLOR, FRED — Frederick Antwon, RB, 6'1"/234 lbs; Florida; 1998: Jax, rnd 1; B1/27/1976 Pahokee, FL

YEAR	TEAM	G (GS, POS)	RUSH	YD	AVG(LG)	TD	REC	YD	AVG(LG)	TD	OTD	PTS	TAY
1998	†Jax	15(12, RB)	264	1223	4.6(77)	14	44	421	9.6(78)	3	—	102	1589
1999	†Jax	10(9, rb)	159	732	4.6(52)	6	10	83	8.3(41)	0	—	36	834
2000	Jax	13(13, RB)	292	1399	4.8(71)	12	36	240	6.7(19)	2	—	84	1649
2001	Jax	2(2)	30	116	3.9(24)	0	2	13	6.5(11)	0	—	0	123
2002	Jax	16(16, RB)	287	1314	4.6(62)	6	49	408	8.3(72)	0	—	52	1598
2003	Jax	16(16, RB)	345	1572	4.6(62)	6	48	370	7.7(60)	1	—	42	1822
2004	Jax	14(14, RB)	260	1224	4.7(46)	2	36	345	9.6(64)	1	—	18	1422
2005	†Jax	11(11, RB)	194	787	4.1(71)	3	13	83	6.4(13)	0	—	18	859
NFL	8	97(93)	1831	8367	4.6(77)	51	238	1963	8.2(78)	7	—	352	9894

TAYLOR, GENE — Eugene Yarman, WR, 6'2"/189 lbs; Fresno State; 1987: NE, rnd 6; B11/12/1962 Oakland, OH

YEAR	TEAM	G (GS, POS)	RUSH	YD	AVG(LG)	TD	REC	YD	AVG(LG)	TD	PTS	TAY
1987	TB	8(0)	—	—	—	—	2	21	10.5(11)	0	0	11
1988	TB	4(0)	—	—	—	—	5	53	10.6(14)	0	0	27
1991	NE	1(0)	—	—	—	—	—	—	—	—		
NFL	3	13(0)	—	—	—	—	7	74	10.6(14)	0	0	37

TAYLOR, GREG — Gregory O'Neil, RB, 5'8"/175 lbs; Virginia; 1982: NE, rnd 12; B10/23/1958 Richmond, VA   **1982** NE 1 (0)

TAYLOR, HENRY — Henry, DT, 6'2"/295 lbs; South Carolina; B11/29/1975 Broward County, FL   **1998** Det 1 (0)   **2000** Atl 5 (0)   **2001** ChiB 1 (0)   **2001** Mia 2 (0)   **NFL** 9 (0) [3 yrs]

TAYLOR, HOSEA — Hosea, DE, 6'5"/255 lbs; Houston; 1981: Bal, rnd 8; B12/3/1958 Jefferson, TX   **1981** Bal 16 (6, rde)   **1983** Bal 4 (1)   **NFL** 20 (7) [2 yrs]

TAYLOR, HUGH — Hugh Wilson 'Bones', E, 6'4"/194 lbs; Louisiana-Monroe; Tulane; Oklahoma City; B7/6/1923 Wynne, AR, D11/1/1992 Wynne, AR [C]

YEAR	TEAM	G (GS, POS)	RUSH	YD	AVG(LG)	TD	REC	YD	AVG(LG)	TD	PASS	COMP	PCT	YD	AVG(LG)	TD	INT	OTD	PTS	TAY
1947	Was	10(0)	1	7	7.0(7)	0	26	511	19.7(62)	6	—	—	—	—	—	—	—	—	36	293
1948	Was	12(0)	—	—	—	—	20	341	17.0(66)	3	1	0	0.0	0	0.0	0	0	—	18	186
1949	Was	12(4)	—	—	—	—	45	781	17.4(76)	9	—	—	—	—	—	—	—	—	54	436
1950	Was	12(LE)	—	—	—	—	39	833	21.4(70)	9	—	—	—	—	—	—	—	—	54	462
1951	Was	12(LE)	—	—	—	—	29	444	15.3(47)	3	—	—	—	—	—	—	—	—	18	237
1952	Was◇	12(LE)	—	—	—	—	41	961	23.4(70)	12	—	—	—	—	—	—	—	—	72	541
1953	Was☆	12(LE)	—	—	—	—	35	703	20.1(71)	8	—	—	—	—	—	—	—	—	48	392
1954	Was◇	12(RE)	—	—	—	—	37	659	17.8(60)	8	—	—	—	—	—	—	—	—	48	370
NFL	8	94(4)	1	7	7.0(7)	0	272	5233	19.2(76)	58	1	0	0.0	0	0.0	0	0	—	348	2914

TAYLOR, IKE — Ivan, DB, 6'0"/195 lbs; Louisiana-Lafayette; 2003: Pit, rnd 4; B5/5/1980 New Orleans, LA   **2003** Pit 16 (1)   **2004**†Pit 13 (1)   **2005**†Pit 16 (15, LCB)   **NFL** 45 (17) [3 yrs]

TAYLOR, J.T. — James Michael, T, 6'4"/265 lbs; Missouri; 1978: NO, rnd 2; B8/12/1956 Peoria, IL   **1978** NO 16 (16, LT)   **1979** NO 16 (16, LT)   **1980** NO 13 (13, LT)   **1981** NO 12 (12, LT)   **NFL** 57 (57) [4 yrs]

TAYLOR, JAMAAR — Henry Jamaar, WR, 6'1"/194 lbs; Notre Dame; Texas A&M; 2004: NYG, rnd 6; B2/25/1981 Giessen, West Germany   **2005** NYG 5 (0)

YEAR	TEAM	G (GS, POS)	RUSH	YD	AVG(LG)	TD	REC	YD	AVG(LG)	TD	OTD	PTS	TAY
2004	NYG	8(0)	1	-8	-8.0(-8)	0	6	146	24.3(52)	0	—	0	65
NFL	2	13(0)	1	-8	-8.0(-8)	0	6	146	24.3(52)	0	—	0	65

TAYLOR, JASON — Jason Paul, DE, 6'6"/255 lbs; Akron; 1997: Mia, rnd 3; B9/1/1974 Pittsburgh, PA [S]   **1997**†Mia 13 (11, RDE)   **1998** Mia 16 (15, RDE)   **1999**†Mia 15 (15, RDE)   **2000**†Mia★16 (16, RDE)   **2001**†Mia★16 (16, RDE)   **2002** Mia★16 (16, RDE)   **2003** Mia 16 (16, RDE)   **2004** Mia★16 (16, RDE)   **2005** Mia◇16 (16, RDE)   **NFL** 140 (137) [9 yrs]

TAYLOR, JAY — Emanuel Jay, DB, 5'10"/170 lbs; San Jose State; 1989: Phx, rnd 6; B11/8/1967 San Diego, CA   **1989** Phx 16 (2)   **1990** Phx 16 (16, LCB)   **1991** Phx 16 (1)   **1993**†KC 15 (1)   **1994**†KC 16 (4)   **NFL** 79 (24) [5 yrs]

TAYLOR, JAY — Jay, K, 6'1"/191 lbs; West Virginia; B10/23/1976 Hershey, PA [K]   **2004** TB 5 (0)

TAYLOR, JESSE — Jesse C., RB, 6'0"/200 lbs; Cincinnati; 1971: Was, rnd 10; B5/26/1948 Pittsburgh, PA

YEAR	TEAM	G (GS, POS)	RUSH	YD	AVG(LG)	TD	KPR	OTD	PTS	TAY
1972	SD	14	13	58	4.5(17)	0	kp	1	6	264

TAYLOR, JIM — James Charles, FB, 6'0"/214 lbs; LSU; 1958: GB, rnd 2; B9/20/1935 Baton Rouge, LA; HOF 1976

YEAR	TEAM	G (GS, POS)	RUSH	YD	AVG(LG)	TD	REC	YD	AVG(LG)	TD	PASS	COMP	PCT	YD	AVG(LG)	TD	INT	SK	YD	KPR	OTD	PTS	TAY
1958	GB	12(FB)	52	247	4.8(25)	1	4	72	18.0(31)	1	—	—	—	—	—	—	—	—	—	k	—	12	378
1959	GB	12(FB)	120	452	3.8(21)	6	9	71	7.9(20)	2	—	—	—	—	—	—	—	—	—	—	—	48	558
1960	†GB★	12(FB)	230	1101	4.8(32)	11	15	121	8.1(27)	0	—	—	—	—	—	—	—	—	—	—	—	66	1272
1961	†GB★	14(FB)	243	1307	5.4(53)	15	25	175	7.0(18)	1	—	—	—	—	—	—	—	—	—	—	—	96	1550
1962	†GB★	14(FB)	272	1474	5.4(51)	19	22	106	4.8(25)	0	—	—	—	—	—	—	—	—	—	—	—	114	1717
1963	GB★	13(FB)	248	1018	4.1(40)	6	13	68	5.2(27)	1	0	0	0.0	0	0.0	0	0	1	10	—	—	60	1147
1964	GB★	13(FB)	235	1169	5.0(84)	12	38	354	9.3(35)	3	—	—	—	—	—	—	—	—	—	—	—	90	1481
1965	GB	14(FB)	207	734	3.5(35)	4	20	207	10.4(41)	0	—	—	—	—	—	—	—	—	—	—	—	24	878
1966	†GB☆	14(FB)	204	705	3.5(19)	4	41	331	8.1(21)	0	—	—	—	—	—	—	—	—	—	—	—	36	921
1967	NO	14(FB)	130	390	3.0(16)	2	38	251	6.6(27)	0	—	—	—	—	—	—	—	—	—	—	—	12	536
NFL	10	132	1941	8597	4.4(84)	83	225	1756	7.8(41)	7	0	0	0.0	0	0.0	0	0	1	10	k	—	558	10435

TAYLOR, JIM BOB — James Robert, QB, 6'2"/205 lbs; SMU; Georgia Tech; 1983: Bal, rnd 11; B9/9/1959 San Antonio, TX

YEAR	TEAM	G (GS, POS)	PASS	COMP	PCT	YD	AVG(LG)	TD	INT	PTS	TAY
1983	Bal	8(0)	—	2	50.0	20	10.0(20)	0	1	0	-30

TAYLOR, JIM James Glen, C-LB, 6´2˝/232 lbs; Baylor; 1956: Pit, rnd 3; B6/27/1934 Rowden, TX **1956** Pit 12 (C) **1957** ChiC 5 **1958** ChiC 12 **NFL** 29 [3 yrs]

TAYLOR, JOE Joseph Lee, DB, 6´1˝/200 lbs; North Carolina A&T; B8/27/1939 Miami, FL **1967** ChiB 14 **1968** ChiB 14 (RCB) **1969** ChiB 14 (RCB) **1970** ChiB 11 (RCB) **1971** ChiB 13 (RCB) **1972** ChiB 14 (RCB) **1973** ChiB 14 (RCB) **1974** ChiB 14 (RCB) **NFL** 108 [8 yrs]

TAYLOR, JOHN John Gregory, WR, 6´1˝/185 lbs; Delaware State; 1986: SF, rnd 3; B3/31/1962 Pennsauken, NJ **[R]**

YEAR	TEAM	G(GS, POS)	RUSH	YD	AVG(LG)	TD	REC	YD	AVG(LG)	TD	PASS	COMP	PCT	YD	AVG(LG)	TD	INT	SK	YD	QBR	KPR	OTD	PTS	TAY
1987	†SF	12(2)	—	—	—	—	9	151	16.8(34)	0	—	—	—	—	—	—	—	—	—	—	p	1	6	80
1988	†SF★	12(4)	—	—	—	—	14	325	23.2(73)	2	—	—	—	—	—	—	—	—	—	—	kp	2	24	574
1989	†SF★	15(15, WR)	1	6	6.0(6)	0	60	1077	18.0(**95**)	10	—	—	—	—	—	—	—	—	—	—	kp	—	60	853
1990	†SF	14(14, WR)	—	—	—	—	49	748	15.3(78)	7	—	—	—	—	—	—	—	—	—	—	p	—	42	491
1991	SF	16(16, WR)	—	—	—	—	64	1011	15.8(**97**)	9	—	—	—	—	—	—	—	—	—	—	p	—	54	663
1992	†SF	9(8, WR)	1	10	10.0(10)	0	25	428	17.1(54)	3	—	—	—	—	—	—	—	—	—	—	—	—	18	239
1993	†SF	16(16, WR)	2	17	8.5(12)	0	56	940	16.8(76)	5	1	1	100.0	41	41.0(41)	0	0	—	—	—	—	—	30	533
1994	†SF	15(15, WR)	2	-2	-1.0(1)	0	41	531	13.0(35)	5	—	—	—	—	—	—	—	—	—	—	—	—	30	289
1995	†SF	12(12, WR)	—	—	—	—	29	387	13.3(40)	2	1	1	100.0	21	21.0(21)	0	0	—	—	—	p	—	12	215
NFL	9	121(102)	6	31	5.2(12)	0	347	5598	16.1(97)	43	2	2	100.0	62	31.0(41)	0	0	—	—	—	kp	3	276	3934

TAYLOR, JOHNNY John Herbert, LB, 6´4˝/237 lbs; Hawaii; B6/21/1961 Seattle, WA **1984** Atl 2 (0) **1985** Atl 15 (5, llb) **1986** Atl 5 (2) **1986** Mia 1 (0) **1987** SD 7 (3) **NFL** 30 (10) [4 yrs]

TAYLOR, KEITH Keith Gerard, DB, 5´11˝/200 lbs; Illinois; 1988: NO, rnd 5; B12/21/1964 Pennsauken, NJ **1988** Ind 3 (0) **1989** Ind 16 (0) **1990** Ind 16 (16, SS) **1991** Ind 16 (10, FS) **1992**†NO 16 (4) **1993** NO 16 (14, SS) **1994** Was 1 (1) **1995** Was 16 (4) **1996** Was 3 (0) **NFL** 103 (49) [9 yrs]

TAYLOR, KEN Kenneth Daniel, DB, 6´1˝/185 lbs; Oregon State; B9/2/1963 San Jose, CA **1985**†ChiB 16 (1) **1986** SD 14 (11, LCB) **NFL** 30 (12) [2 yrs]

TAYLOR, KITRICK Kittrick Lavell, WR, 5´11˝/194 lbs; Washington State; 1987: KC, rnd 5; B7/22/1964 Los Angeles, CA

YEAR	TEAM	G(GS, POS)	RUSH	YD	AVG(LG)	TD	REC	YD	AVG(LG)	TD	PASS	COMP	PCT	YD	AVG(LG)	TD	INT	SK	YD	QBR	KPR	OTD	PTS	TAY
1988	KC	16(0)	1	2	2.0(2)	0	9	105	11.7(36)	0	—	—	—	—	—	—	—	—	—	—	kp	—	0	102
1989	NE	4(0)	—	—	—	—	—	—	—	—	—	—	—	—	—	—	—	—	—	—	kp	—	0	7
1990	SD	3(0)	—	—	—	—	—	—	—	—	—	—	—	—	—	—	—	—	—	—	p	1	6	92
1991	SD	12(0)	—	—	—	—	24	218	9.1(27)	0	—	—	—	—	—	—	—	—	—	—	p	—	0	238
1992	GB	10(0)	—	—	—	—	2	63	31.5(35)	1	—	—	—	—	—	—	—	—	—	—	—	—	6	37
1993	†Den	2(0)	—	—	—	—	1	28	28.0(28)	0	—	—	—	—	—	—	—	—	—	—	—	—	0	14
NFL	6	47(0)	1	2	2.0(2)	0	36	414	11.5(36)	1	—	—	—	—	—	—	—	—	—	—	kp	1	12	489

TAYLOR, LAWRENCE Lawrence Julius 'LT', LB, 6´3˝/237 lbs; North Carolina; 1981: NYG, rnd 1; B2/4/1959 Williamsburg, VA; HOF 1999 **[S]** **1981**†NYG★16 (16, ROLB) **1982** NYG★9 (8, ROLB) **1983** NYG★16 (16, ROLB/rilb) **1984**†NYG★16 (16, ROLB) **1985**†NYG★16 (16, ROLB) **1986**†NYG★16 (16, ROLB) **1987** NYG★12 (11, ROLB) **1988** NYG★12 (12, ROLB) **1989**†NYG★16 (15, ROLB) **1990**†NYG★16 (16, ROLB) **1991** NYG 14 (14, ROLB) **1992** NYG 9 (9, ROLB) **1993**†NYG 16 (15, ROLB) **NFL** 184 (180) [13 yrs]

TAYLOR, LELAND Leland Morrisclay, DT, 6´3˝/305 lbs; Louisville; 1997: Bal, rnd 7; B10/25/1972 Louisville, KY **1997** Bal 1 (0)

TAYLOR, LENNY Leonard Moore, WR, 5´10˝/173 lbs; Tennessee; 1984: GB, rnd 12; B2/15/1961 Miami, FL

YEAR	TEAM	G(GS, POS)	RUSH	YD	AVG(LG)	TD	REC	YD	AVG(LG)	TD	PASS	COMP	PCT	YD	AVG(LG)	TD	INT	SK	YD	QBR	KPR	OTD	PTS	TAY
1984	GB	2(0)	—	—	—	—	1	8	8.0(8)	0	—	—	—	—	—	—	—	—	—	—	—	—	0	4
1987	Atl	3(2)	1	-13	-13.0(-13)	0	12	171	14.3(28)	1	—	—	—	—	—	—	—	—	—	—	—	—	6	78
NFL	2	5(2)	1	-13	-13.0(-13)	0	13	179	13.8(28)	1	—	—	—	—	—	—	—	—	—	—	—	—	6	82

TAYLOR, LIONEL Lionel Thomas, E-WR-FL, 6´2˝/215 lbs; New Mexico Highlands; B8/15/1935 Kansas City, MO

YEAR	TEAM	G(GS, POS)	RUSH	YD	AVG(LG)	TD	REC	YD	AVG(LG)	TD	PASS	COMP	PCT	YD	AVG(LG)	TD	INT	SK	YD	QBR	KPR	OTD	PTS	TAY
1959	ChiB	8	—	—	—	—	—	—	—	—	—	—	—	—	—	—	—	—	—	—	—	—	—	—
1960	Den-A☆	12(SE)	2	-6	-3.0(-2)	0	**92**	1235	13.4(80)	12	—	—	—	—	—	—	—	—	—	—	—	—	72	672
1961	Den-A★	14(SE)	—	—	—	—	**100**	1176	11.8(52)	4	2	0	0.0	0	0.0	0	1	—	—	—	—	—	24	568
1962	Den-A★	14(SE)	2	26	13.0(18)	0	**77**	908	11.8(45)	4	2	0	0.0	0	0.0	0	0	—	—	—	—	—	24	500
1963	Den-A☆	14(SE)	—	—	—	—	**78**	1101	14.1(72)	10	1	0	0.0	0	0.0	0	0	—	—	—	—	—	60	601
1964	Den-A	14(SE)	—	—	—	—	76	873	11.5(57)	7	1	0	0.0	0	0.0	0	1	—	—	—	—	—	42	432
1965	Den-A★	14(SE)	—	—	—	—	**85**	1131	13.3(63)	6	—	—	—	—	—	—	—	—	—	—	—	—	36	596
1966	Den-A	14(SE)	—	—	—	—	35	448	12.8(29)	1	—	—	—	—	—	—	—	—	—	—	—	—	6	229
1967	†Hou-A	8	—	—	—	—	18	233	12.9(23)	1	—	—	—	—	—	—	—	—	—	—	—	—	6	122
1968	Hou-A	9	—	—	—	—	6	90	15.0(35)	0	—	—	—	—	—	—	—	—	—	—	—	—	0	45
NFL	10	121	4	20	5.0(18)	0	567	7195	12.7(80)	45	6	0	0.0	0	0.0	0	2	—	—	—	—	—	270	3763

TAYLOR, MALCOLM Malcolm, DE, 6´6˝/288 lbs; Tennessee State; 1982: Hou, rnd 5; B6/20/1960 Crystal Springs, MS **1982** Hou 9 (0) **1983** Hou 16 (3) **1986** Hou 3 (0) **1987** LARd 12 (3) **1988** LARd 15 (3) **1989** Atl 13 (0) **NFL** 68 (9) [6 yrs]

TAYLOR, MICHAEL Michael, LB, 6´1˝/230 lbs; Michigan; 1972: NYJ, rnd 1; B9/21/1949 Detroit, MI **1972** NYJ 14 **1973** NYJ 8 **NFL** 22 [2 yrs]

TAYLOR, MIKE Michael Ray, T, 6´4˝/255 lbs; USC; 1968: Pit, rnd 1; B5/5/1945 San Francisco, CA **1968** Pit 14 **1969** Pit 9 (LT) **1969** NO 1 **1970** NO 11 **1971**†Was 5 **1973** SL 6 **NFL** 46 [5 yrs]

TAYLOR, OTIS Otis, WR-FL, 6´3˝/215 lbs; Prairie View A&M; 1965: KC, rnd 4/Phi, rnd 15; B8/11/1942 Houston, TX

YEAR	TEAM	G(GS, POS)	RUSH	YD	AVG(LG)	TD	REC	YD	AVG(LG)	TD	PASS	COMP	PCT	YD	AVG(LG)	TD	INT	SK	YD	QBR	KPR	OTD	PTS	TAY
1965	KC-A	14	2	17	8.5(15)	0	26	446	17.2(48)	5	—	—	—	—	—	—	—	—	—	—	—	—	30	265
1966	†KC-A★	14(FL)	2	33	16.5(19)	0	58	1297	**22.4**(**89**)	8	1	0	0.0	0	0.0	0	1	—	—	—	k	—	48	652
1967	KC-A☆	14(FL)	5	29	5.8(24)	1	59	958	16.2(71)	**11**	—	—	—	—	—	—	—	—	—	—	—	—	72	573
1968	†KC-A	11(FL)	5	41	8.2(30)	1	20	420	21.0(67)	4	—	—	—	—	—	—	—	—	—	—	—	—	30	281
1969	†KC-A	11(FL)	2	-2	-1.0(10)	0	41	696	17.0(79)	7	—	—	—	—	—	—	—	—	—	—	—	—	42	381
1970	KC	13(WR)	3	13	4.3(7)	0	34	618	18.2(59)	3	—	—	—	—	—	—	—	—	—	—	—	—	18	337
1971	†KC★	14(WR)	1	25	25.0(25)	1	57	**1110**	19.5(82)	7	—	—	—	—	—	—	—	—	—	—	—	—	48	625
1972	KC★	14(WR)	5	13	2.6(11)	0	57	821	14.4(44)	6	—	—	—	—	—	—	—	—	—	—	—	—	36	454
1973	KC	14(WR)	4	-14	-3.5(5)	0	34	565	16.6(46)	4	—	—	—	—	—	—	—	—	—	—	—	—	24	289
1974	KC	10(WR)	1	6	6.0(6)	0	24	375	15.6(64)	2	—	—	—	—	—	—	—	—	—	—	—	—	12	204
1975	KC	1	—	—	—	—	—	—	—	—	—	—	—	—	—	—	—	—	—	—	—	—	—	—
NFL	11	130	30	161	5.4(30)	3	410	7306	17.8(89)	57	1	0	0.0	0	0.0	0	1	—	—	—	k	—	360	4059

TAYLOR, ROB Robert Earl, T, 6´6˝/293 lbs; Northwestern; 1982: Phi, rnd 12; B11/14/1960 St. Charles, IL **1986** TB 16 (13, LT) **1987** TB 5 (5, LT) **1988** TB 16 (16, RT) **1989** TB 16 (16, RT) **1990** TB 16 (16, RT) **1991** TB 16 (12, RT) **1992** TB 9 (6, rt) **1993** TB 16 (7, rt) **NFL** 110 (91) [8 yrs]

TAYLOR, ROGER Roger Wayne, T, 6´6˝/271 lbs; Oklahoma State; 1981: KC, rnd 3; B1/5/1958 Shawnee, OK **1981** KC 13 (0)

TAYLOR, ROSEY Roosevelt, DB, 5´11˝/186 lbs; Grambling State; B7/4/1937 New Orleans, LA **[I]** **1961** ChiB 14 (RS) **1962** ChiB 14 (RS) **1963**†ChiB★14 (RS) **1964** ChiB☆14 (RS) **1965** ChiB☆14 (RS) **1966** ChiB 14 (RS) **1967** ChiB 14 (RS) **1968** ChiB✧14 (RS) **1969** ChiB 6 **1969** SF 8 (rs) **1970**†SF 14 (14, FS) **1971**†SF 12 (FS) **1972**†Was 14 (14, FS) **NFL** 166 (28) [12 yrs]

TAYLOR, RYAN Ryan, LB, 6´2˝/230 lbs; Auburn; B12/11/1976 Dublin, GA **2000** Cle 4 (0)

TAYLOR, SAMMIE Samuel, WR, 6´0˝/194 lbs; Grambling State; B4/23/1940 Houston, TX

YEAR	TEAM	G(GS, POS)	RUSH	YD	AVG(LG)	TD	REC	YD	AVG(LG)	TD	PASS	COMP	PCT	YD	AVG(LG)	TD	INT	SK	YD	QBR	KPR	OTD	PTS	TAY
1965	SD-A	12	—	—	—	—	1	13	13.0(13)	0	—	—	—	—	—	—	—	—	—	—	—	—	0	7

TAYLOR, SEAN Sean Michael, DB, 6´3˝/220 lbs; Miami (FL); 2004: Was, rnd 1; B4/1/1983 Miami, FL **2004** Was 15 (13, FS) **2005**†Was 15 (15, FS) **NFL** 30 (28) [2 yrs]

TAYLOR, SHANNON Shannon Andre, LB, 6´3˝/247 lbs; Virginia; 2000: SD, rnd 6; B2/16/1975 Roanoke, VA **2000** SD 11 (0) **2001** Bal 11 (0) **2002** Bal 16 (2) **2003** Jax 2 (0) **NFL** 40 (2) [4 yrs]

TAYLOR, STEVE Steven Lawrence, DB, 6´3˝/204 lbs; Kansas; 1976: KC, rnd 6; B12/27/1953 Fort Worth, TX **1976** KC 14

TAYLOR, TARZAN John Lachlan, G-T, 5´11˝/178 lbs; Ohio State; B1/10/1895 Superior, WI, D5/1/1971 Green Bay, WI **1921** ChiS 11 (11, LG) **1922** Can 11 (11, LG) **1926** Bkn 2 (1) **NFL** 24 (23) [3 yrs]

TAYLOR, TERRY Terry Lee, DB, 5´10˝/188 lbs; Southern Illinois; 1984: Sea, rnd 1; B7/18/1961 Warren, OH **[I]** **1984**†Sea 16 (1) **1985** Sea 16 (16, LCB) **1986** Sea 16 (15, LCB) **1987** Sea 12 (12, LCB) **1988**†Sea 14 (8, LCB) **1989** Det 15 (15, LCB) **1990** Det 2 (2) **1991**†Det 11 (0) **1992** Cle 16 (16, RCB) **1993** Cle 10 (7, LCB) **1994** Sea 5 (3) **1995**†Atl 16 (5, lcb) **NFL** 149 (100) [12 yrs]

TAYLOR, TOM Thomas Joseph, G, 6´3˝/267 lbs; Georgia Tech; B9/14/1962 Lancaster, CA **1987** LARm 3 (3)

YEAR	TEAM	G(GS, POS)	RUSH	YD	AVG(LG)	TD	REC	YD	AVG(LG)	TD	PASS	COMP	PCT	YD	AVG(LG)	TD	INT	SK	YD	QBR	KPR	OTD	PTS	TAY

TAYLOR, TONY Tony, RB, 5´9˝/191 lbs; Northwestern State (LA); B3/9/1978 Pineville, LA

| 2001 | Dal | 1(0) | 1 | 0 | 0.0(0) | 0 | — | — | — | — | — | — | — | — | — | — | — | — | — | — | — | — | 0 | 0 |

TAYLOR, TRAVIS Travis Lamont, WR, 6´1˝/200 lbs; Florida; 2000: Bal, rnd 1; B3/30/1978 Fernandina Beach, FL

2000	Bal	9(8, WR)	2	11	5.5(12)	0	28	276	9.9(40)	3	—	—	—	—	—	—	—	—	—	—	+	—	18	164
2001	†Bal	16(13, WR)	5	46	9.2(16)	0	42	560	13.3(63)	3	—	—	—	—	—	—	—	—	—	—	—	—	18	341
2002	Bal	16(15, WR)	11	105	9.5(39)	0	61	869	14.2(64)	6	—	—	—	—	—	—	—	—	—	—	—	—	36	570
2003	†Bal	16(16, WR)	11	62	5.6(16)	0	39	632	16.2(73)	3	—	—	—	—	—	—	—	—	—	—	—	—	18	393
2004	Bal	10(9, WR)	—	—	—	—	34	421	12.4(47)	0	—	—	—	—	—	—	—	—	—	—	—	—	0	211
2005	Min	16(13, WR)	2	3	1.5(5)	0	50	604	12.1(31)	4	—	—	—	—	—	—	—	—	—	—	p	—	24	320
NFL	6	83(74)	31	227	7.3(39)	0	254	3362	13.2(73)	19	—	—	—	—	—	—	—	—	—	—	p	—	114	1998

TAYLOR, TROY Troy Scott, QB, 6´4˝/200 lbs; California; 1990: NYJ, rnd 4; B4/5/1968 Downey, CA

1990	NYJ	2(0)	2	20	10.0(15)	1	—	—	—	—	10	7	70.0	49	4.9(15)	1	0	2	3	—	—	—	6	60
1991	†NYJ	5(0)	7	23	3.3(13)	0	—	—	—	—	10	5	50.0	76	7.6(51)	1	1	—	—	—	—	—	0	26
NFL	2	7(0)	9	43	4.8(15)	1	—	—	—	—	20	12	60.0	125	6.3(51)	2	1	2	3	—	—	—	6	86

TAYLOR, WILLIE Willis T., WR, 6´1˝/179 lbs; Pittsburgh; 1978: TB, rnd 9; B12/9/1955 Montclair, NJ   **1978** GB 1

TAYS, JIMMY James Elmer, B, 5´8˝/174 lbs; Penn State; Chicago; B3/10/1899 Chicago, IL, D6/21/1986 Champaign, IL   **1925** ChiC 9 (2), 6   **1927** Day 7 (7, BB)   **1930** Nwk 1 (0)   **1930** SI 3 (1)   **NFL** 20 (10) [3 yrs]

TEAFATILLER, GUY Guy Robert, DT, 6´2˝/260 lbs; Illinois; 1986: Buf, rnd 10; B5/10/1964 Concord, CA   **1987** ChiB 3 (2)

TEAGUE, GEORGE George Theo, DB, 6´1˝/198 lbs; Alabama; 1993: GB, rnd 1; B2/18/1971 Lansing, MI   **1993**†GB 16 (12, FS)   **1994**†GB 16 (16, FS)   **1995**†GB 15 (15, FS)   **1996**†Dal 16 (8, fs)   **1997**†Mia 15 (6, fs)   **1998**†Dal 16 (5, fs)   **1999**†Dal 14 (14, FS)   **2000** Dal 9 (9, FS)   **2001** Dal 16 (16, FS)   **NFL** 133 (101) [9 yrs]

TEAGUE, MATTHEW Matthew Nathaniel, LB, 6´5˝/240 lbs; Prairie View A&M; 1980: Atl, rnd S7; B10/22/1958 Cincinnati, OH   **1981** Atl 11 (0)

TEAGUE, PAT Patrick Ethan, LB, 6´1˝/225 lbs; North Carolina State; B10/22/1963 Asheville, NC   **1987** TB 1 (1)

TEAGUE, TREY Fred Everette, C-T, 6´5˝/300 lbs; Tennessee; 1998: Den, rnd 7; B12/27/1974 Jackson, TN   **1999** Den 16 (4)   **2000** Den 2 (0)   **2001** Den 16 (16, LT)   **2002** Buf 16 (16, C)   **2003** Buf 16 (16, C)   **2004** Buf 12 (12, C)   **2005** Buf 16 (16, C)   **NFL** 94 (80) [7 yrs]

TEAL, JIM James Franklin, LB, 6´3˝/225 lbs; Purdue; 1972: Det, rnd 10; B5/14/1950 Baltimore, MD   **1973** Det 14

TEAL, JIMMY Jimmy Dewayne, WR, 5´10˝/170 lbs; Texas A&M; 1985: Buf, rnd 5; B8/18/1962 Lufkin, TX

1985	Buf	3(0)	—	—	—	—	1	24	24.0(24)	0	—	—	—	—	—	—	—	—	—	—	k	—	0	17
1986	Buf	5(1)	—	—	—	—	6	60	10.0(20)	1	—	—	—	—	—	—	—	—	—	—	—	—	6	35
1987	Sea	4(2)	—	—	—	—	14	198	14.1(47)	0	—	—	—	—	—	—	—	—	—	—	kp	—	12	122
1988	Sea	2(0)	—	—	—	—	—	—	—	—	—	—	—	—	—	—	—	—	—	—	—	—	—	—
NFL	4	14(3)	—	—	—	—	21	282	13.4(47)	3	—	—	—	—	—	—	—	—	—	—	kp	—	18	174

TEAL, WILLIE Willie, DB, 5´10˝/195 lbs; LSU; 1980: Min, rnd 2; B12/20/1957 Texarkana, TX   **1980**†Min 0 (0)   **1981** Min 16 (16, RCB)   **1982**†Min 9 (9, RCB)   **1983** Min 16 (16, RCB)   **1984** Min 11 (4)   **1985** Min 16 (16, LCB)   **1986** Min 11 (0)   **1987** LARd 1 (0)   **NFL** 80 (61) [8 yrs]

TEARRY, LARRY Larry Wayne, C, 6´3˝/260 lbs; Wake Forest; 1978: Det, rnd 4; B4/24/1956 Erwin, NC   **1978** Det 14 (12, C)   **1979** Det 11 (C)   **NFL** 25 (12) [2 yrs]

TEBELL, GUS Gustave Kenneth, E, 5´10˝/178 lbs; Wisconsin; B9/6/1897 St. Charles, IL, D5/28/1969 Richmond, VA **[KC]**   **1923** Col☆10 (10, LE), 37   **1924** Col 1 (1), 6   **NFL** 11 (11), 43 [2 yrs]

TEERLINCK, JOHN John Edward, DT, 6´5˝/248 lbs; Western Illinois; 1974: SD, rnd 5; B4/9/1951 Rochester, NY   **1974** SD 14 (2)   **1975** SD 6 (5, rdt)   **NFL** 20 (7) [2 yrs]

TEETER, AL Allen M., E, 6´1˝/202 lbs; Minnesota; B6/24/1908 Austin, MN, D4/14/1994 Holiday, FL

| 1932 | SI | 5(2) | — | — | — | — | 1 | 11 | 11.0(11) | 0 | — | — | — | — | — | — | — | — | — | — | — | — | 0 | 6 |

TEETER, MIKE Michael Lee, DE-DT, 6´2˝/267 lbs; Michigan; B10/4/1967 Grand Haven, MI   **1991** Min 1 (0)   **1993**†Hou 14 (0)   **1994** Hou 14 (0)   **NFL** 29 (0) [3 yrs]

TEEUWS, LEN Leonard, DT-T, 6´5˝/242 lbs; Tulane; 1952: LA, rnd 25; B4/19/1927 Oak Park, IL   **1952** LARm 12   **1953** LARm 12 (RDT)   **1954** ChiC 12 (LT)   **1955** ChiC 12 (LT)   **1956** ChiC 12 (RDT)   **1957** ChiC 12 (RDT)   **NFL** 72 [6 yrs]

TEICHELMAN, LANCE Lance Theodore, DE-DT, 6´4˝/274 lbs; Texas A&M; 1994: Ind, rnd 7; B10/21/1970 San Antonio, TX   **1994** Ind 1 (0)

TEIFKE, MIKE Michael Edward, C, 6´4˝/255 lbs; Akron; B12/29/1963   **1987** Cle 3 (0)

TELTSCHIK, JOHN John Robert, P, 6´2˝/212 lbs; Texas; 1986: Chi, rnd 9; B3/8/1964 Floresville, TX **[P]**

1986	Phi	16(0)	1	0	0.0(0)	0	—	—	—	—	—	—	—	—	—	—	—	—	—	—	P	—	0	0
1987	Phi	12(0)	3	32	10.7(23)	0	—	—	—	0	0	0.0	0	0.0	0	0	1	7	—	P	—	0	32
1988	†Phi	16(0)	2	36	18.0(23)	0	—	—	—	3	1	33.3	18	6.0(18)	0	0	—	—	—	P	—	0	45
1989	Phi	10(0)	1	23	23.0(23)	0	—	—	—	—	—	—	—	—	—	—	—	—	—	P	—	0	23
NFL	4	54(0)	7	91	13.0(23)	0	—	—	—	3	1	33.3	18	6.0(18)	0	0	1	7	—	P	—	0	100

TEMP, JIM James Arhur, DE, 6´4˝/245 lbs; Wisconsin; 1955: GB, rnd 2; B10/10/1933 La Crosse, WI   **1957** GB 12   **1958** GB 12 (RDE)   **1959** GB 12 (LDE)   **1960** GB 7   **NFL** 43 [4 yrs]

TEMPLE, MARK Mark Vernon, TB, 5´10˝/175 lbs; Oregon; B3/28/1911 Pendleton, OR   **1936**†Bos 2 (0)

| 1936 | Bkn | 7(0) | 5 | 4 | 0.8 | 1 | 1 | 10 | 10.0(10) | 0 | 7 | 0 | 0.0 | 0 | 0.0 | 0 | 5 | — | — | — | — | — | 6 | -181 |
| NFL | 1 | 9(0) | 5 | 4 | 0.8 | 1 | 1 | 10 | 10.0(10) | 0 | 7 | 0 | 0.0 | 0 | 0.0 | 0 | 5 | — | — | — | — | — | 6 | -181 |

TEN NAPEL, GARTH Garth, LB, 6´1˝/213 lbs; Texas A&M; 1976: Det, rnd 7; B3/27/1954 Los Angeles, CA   **1976** Det 14   **1977** Det 14 (2)   **1978** Atl 1   **NFL** 29 (2) [3 yrs]

TENNELL, DEREK Derek Wayne, TE, 6´5˝/245 lbs; UCLA; 1987: Sea, rnd 7; B2/12/1964 Los Angeles, CA

1987	†Cle	11(2)	—	—	—	—	9	102	11.3(24)	3	—	—	—	—	—	—	—	—	—	—	—	—	18	66
1988	†Cle	16(3)	—	—	—	—	9	88	9.8(26)	1	—	—	—	—	—	—	—	—	—	—	k	—	6	45
1989	Cle	14(3)	—	—	—	—	1	4	4.0(4)	1	—	—	—	—	—	—	—	—	—	—	—	—	6	7
1991	†Det	15(2)	—	—	—	—	4	43	10.8(18)	0	—	—	—	—	—	—	—	—	—	—	—	—	0	22
1992	Min	3(2)	—	—	—	—	2	12	6.0(8)	0	—	—	—	—	—	—	—	—	—	—	—	—	0	6
1992	†Dal	0(0)	—	—	—	—	—	—	—	—	—	—	—	—	—	—	—	—	—	—	—	—	0	0
1993	†Min	16(6, te)	—	—	—	—	15	122	8.1(17)	0	—	—	—	—	—	—	—	—	—	—	—	—	0	61
NFL	6	75(18)	—	—	—	—	40	371	9.3(26)	5	—	—	—	—	—	—	—	—	—	—	k	—	30	207

TENNER, BOB Robert Johnson, E, 6´0˝/212 lbs; Minnesota; B6/1/1913 Minneapolis, MN, D11/17/1984 Minneapolis, MN

| 1935 | GB | 11(2) | — | — | — | — | 3 | 38 | 12.7(29) | 0 | — | — | — | — | — | — | — | — | — | — | — | — | 0 | 19 |

TENSI, STEVE Stephen Michael, QB, 6´5˝/215 lbs; Florida State; 1965: SD, rnd 4/Bal, rnd 16; B12/8/1942 Cincinnati, OH

1965	SD-A	1																						
1966	SD-A	14(2)	1	-1	-1.0(-1)	0	—	—	—	—	52	21	40.4	405	7.8(63)	5	1	—	—	—	—	—	0	187
1967	Den-A	14(QB)	24	4	0.2(13)	0	—	—	—	—	325	131	40.3	1915	5.9(76)	16	17	—	—	54.8	—	—	0	362
1968	Den-A	7(qb)	6	2	0.3(2)	0	—	—	—	—	119	48	40.3	709	6.0(72)	5	8	—	—	46.5	—	—	0	62
1969	Den-A	13(12, QB)	12	63	5.3(17)	0	—	—	—	—	286	131	45.8	1990	7.0(79)	14	12	29	208	68.1	—	—	0	648
1970	Den	7(2)	4	14	3.5(15)	0	—	—	—	—	80	38	47.5	539	6.7(42)	3	8	6	35	—	—	—	0	-22
NFL	6	56(16)	47	82	1.7(17)	0	—	—	—	—	862	369	42.8	5558	6.4(79)	43	46	35	243	59.0	—	—	0	1236

TEPE, LOU Louis Charles, C-LB, 6´2˝/208 lbs; Duke; 1953: Pit, rnd 30; B6/18/1930 North Bergen, NJ   **1953** Pit 10   **1954** Pit 12 (LLB)   **1955** Pit 12 (C)   **NFL** 34 [3 yrs]

TERCERO, SCOTT Scott, G, 6´4˝/303 lbs; California; 2003: SL, rnd 6; B10/28/1981 Whittier, CA   **2004** SL 8 (4)

TERESA, TONY Anthony Michael, HB, 5´9˝/188 lbs; San Jose State; B12/8/1933 Pittsburg, CA, D10/16/1984 Salinas, CA   **1958** SF 1

| 1960 | Oak-A | 14(HB) | 139 | 608 | 4.4(83) | 6 | 35 | 393 | 11.2(38) | 4 | 18 | 9 | 50.0 | 111 | 6.2(25) | 1 | 3 | — | — | — | kp | — | 60 | 813 |
| NFL | 2 | 15 | 139 | 608 | 4.4(83) | 6 | 35 | 393 | 11.2(38) | 4 | 18 | 9 | 50.0 | 111 | 6.2(25) | 1 | 3 | — | — | — | — | — | 60 | 825 |

TERESHINSKI, JOE Joseph Peter, DE-E-LB, 6´2˝/215 lbs; Georgia; 1946: Was, rnd 13/1947: NYY-A, rnd 4; B12/7/1923 Glen Lyon, PA

YEAR	TEAM	G (GS, POS)	RUSH	YD	AVG (LG)	TD	REC	YD	AVG (LG)	TD	PASS	COMP	PCT	YD	AVG (LG)	TD	INT	SK	YD	QBR	KPR	OTD	PTS	TAY
1947	Was	11 (9, RE)	—	—	—	—	10	76	7.6 (20)	1	—	—	—	—	—	—	—	—	—	—	—	—	6	43
1948	Was	11 (7, RE)	—	—	—	—	4	98	24.5 (76)	1	—	—	—	—	—	—	—	—	—	—	—	—	6	54
1949	Was	9 (2)	—	—	—	—	4	36	9.0 (12)	0	—	—	—	—	—	—	—	—	—	—	—	—	0	18
1950	Was	12 (RE)	—	—	—	—	17	148	8.7 (17)	0	—	—	—	—	—	—	—	—	—	—	—	—	0	74
1951	Was	12 (RDE)	—	—	—	—	6	74	12.3 (21)	2	—	—	—	—	—	—	—	—	—	—	—	—	12	47
1952	Was	12 (RDE)	—	—	—	—	2	19	9.5 (11)	0	—	—	—	—	—	—	—	—	—	—	i	—	0	36
1953	Was	12 (RDE)	—	—	—	—	—	—	—	—	—	—	—	—	—	—	—	—	—	—	—	—	—	—
1954	Was	7	—	—	—	—	—	—	—	—	—	—	—	—	—	—	—	—	—	—	—	—	—	—
NFL	8	86 (18)	—	—	—	—	43	451	10.5 (76)	4	—	—	—	—	—	—	—	—	—	—	i	—	24	272

TERLEP, GEORGE George Rudolph, QB-DB, 5´10˝/180 lbs; Notre Dame; B4/12/1923 Elkhart, IN

YEAR	TEAM	G (GS, POS)	RUSH	YD	AVG (LG)	TD	REC	YD	AVG (LG)	TD	PASS	COMP	PCT	YD	AVG (LG)	TD	INT	SK	YD	QBR	KPR	OTD	PTS	TAY
1946	Buf-A	12 (4, qb)	36	29	0.8	1	—	—	—	—	123	48	39.0	574	4.7	7	14	—	—	—	Pk	—	6	-191
1947	Buf-A	11 (1)	4	11	2.8	0	—	—	—	—	23	5	21.7	51	2.2	2	3	—	—	—	pi	—	0	-67
1948	Buf-A	3 (0)	—	—	—	—	—	—	—	—	2	0	0.0	0	0.0	0	1	—	—	—	—	—	0	-40
1948	†Cle-A	9 (0)	1	4	4.0	0	—	—	—	—	2	1	50.0	27	13.5 (27)	0	1	—	—	—	—	—	0	-23
AAFC	3	35 (5)	41	44	1.1	1	—	—	—	—	150	54	36.0	652	4.3 (27)	9	19	—	—	—	Pkpi	—	6	-320

TERRELL, CLAUDE Claude Edward, G, 6´2˝/343 lbs; New Mexico; 2005: SL, rnd 4; B4/20/1982 Texas City, TX **2005** SL 14 (10, LG)

TERRELL, DARYL Daryl, T-G, 6´4˝/317 lbs; Southern Mississippi; B1/25/1975 Vossburg, MS **1999** NO 12 (1) **2000**†NO 16 (0) **2001** NO 16 (10, LT) **2002** Jax 9 (0) **2003** Was 3 (0) **NFL** 56 (11) [5 yrs]

TERRELL, DAVID David, WR, 6´3˝/215 lbs; Michigan; 2001: Chi, rnd 1; B3/13/1979 Richmond, VA

YEAR	TEAM	G (GS, POS)	RUSH	YD	AVG (LG)	TD	REC	YD	AVG (LG)	TD	PASS	COMP	PCT	YD	AVG (LG)	TD	INT	SK	YD	QBR	KPR	OTD	PTS	TAY
2001	†ChiB	16 (6, wr)	—	—	—	—	34	415	12.2 (62)	4	—	—	—	—	—	—	—	—	—	—	k	—	24	221
2002	ChiB	5 (1)	—	—	—	—	9	127	14.1 (52)	3	—	—	—	—	—	—	—	—	—	—	—	—	18	79
2003	ChiB	16 (7, wr)	1	4	4.0 (4)	0	43	361	8.4 (35)	1	—	—	—	—	—	—	—	—	—	—	—	—	6	190
2004	ChiB	16 (15, WR)	3	10	3.3 (20)	0	42	699	16.6 (63)	1	—	—	—	—	—	—	—	—	—	—	—	—	6	365
2005	Den	1 (0)	—	—	—	—	—	—	—	—	—	—	—	—	—	—	—	—	—	—	—	—	—	—
NFL	5	54 (29)	4	14	3.5 (20)	0	128	1602	12.5 (63)	9	—	—	—	—	—	—	—	—	—	—	k	—	54	853

TERRELL, DAVID David, DB, 6´0˝/190 lbs; Texas-El Paso; 1998: Was, rnd 7; B7/8/1975 Floydada, TX **2000** Was 16 (0) **2001** Was 16 (16, FS) **2002** Was 16 (16, FS) **2003** Was 13 (1) **2004** Oak 16 (0) **NFL** 77 (33) [5 yrs]

TERRELL, MARVIN Marvin, G, 6´1˝/235 lbs; Mississippi; 1960: DalT, rnd 1/Bal, rnd 2; B6/10/1938 West Memphis, AR **1960** DalT-A 9 **1961** DalT-A 3 **1962**†DalT-A✧12 (LG) **1963** KC-A 14 (LG) **NFL** 38 [4 yrs]

TERRELL, PAT Patrick Christopher, DB, 6´1˝/204 lbs; Notre Dame; 1990: LARm, rnd 2; B3/18/1968 Memphis, TN **1990** LARm 15 (1) **1991** LARm 16 (16, FS) **1992** LARm 15 (11, FS) **1993** LARm 13 (3) **1994** NYJ 16 (2) **1995** Car 16 (13, FS) **1996**†Car 16 (16, FS) **1997** Car 16 (5, fs) **1998**†GB 16 (3) **NFL** 139 (70) [9 yrs]

TERRELL, RAY Raymond Willard, HB-DB, 6´0˝/185 lbs; Mississippi; B6/29/1919 Water Valley, AR, D2/11/1997 Gulfport, MS

YEAR	TEAM	G (GS, POS)	RUSH	YD	AVG (LG)	TD	REC	YD	AVG (LG)	TD	PASS	COMP	PCT	YD	AVG (LG)	TD	INT	SK	YD	QBR	KPR	OTD	PTS	TAY
1946	†Cle-A	9 (4)	39	117	3.0	0	4	21	5.3	0	2	0	0.0	0	0.0	0	0	—	—	—	ki	1	6	259
1947	Bal-A	10 (5, rh)	21	20	1.0	0	6	21	3.5	0	—	—	—	—	—	—	—	—	—	—	kpi	—	0	120
1947	†Cle-A	3 (1)	5	28	5.6	0	—	—	—	—	—	—	—	—	—	—	—	—	—	—	—	—	0	28
AAFC	2	22 (10)	65	165	2.5	0	10	42	4.2	0	2	0	0.0	0	0.0	0	0	—	—	—	kpi	1	6	406

TERRILL, CRAIG Craig Adam, DT, 6´3˝/284 lbs; Purdue; 2004: Sea, rnd 6; B6/26/1980 Lebanon, IN **2004**†Sea 4 (0) **2005**†Sea 16 (0) **NFL** 20 (0) [2 yrs]

TERRY, ADAM Adam, T, 6´8˝/330 lbs; Syracuse; 2005: Bal, rnd 2; B9/1/1982 Glen Falls, NY **2005** Bal 7 (0)

TERRY, CHRIS Christopher Alexander, T, 6´5˝/295 lbs; Georgia; 1999: Car, rnd 2; B8/8/1975 Jacksonville, FL **1999** Car 16 (16, RT) **2000** Car 16 (16, RT) **2001** Car 15 (15, RT) **2002** Car 10 (10, RT) **2002** Sea 5 (5, rt) **2003**†Sea 12 (10, RT) **2004** Sea 8 (8, RT) **NFL** 82 (80) [6 yrs]

TERRY, COREY Corey TeWana, LB, 6´3˝/246 lbs; Tennessee; 1999: Ind, rnd 7; B3/6/1976 Warrenton, NC **1999**†Jax 8 (0) **2000** NO 7 (0) **NFL** 15 (0) [2 yrs]

TERRY, DOUG Douglas Maurice, DB, 5´11˝/204 lbs; Kansas; B12/12/1969 Dumas, AR **1992**†KC 16 (1) **1993** KC 15 (8, ss) **1994**†KC 10 (1) **1995**†KC 16 (0) **NFL** 57 (10) [4 yrs]

TERRY, JEB Jeb, G, 6´6˝/308 lbs; North Carolina; 2004: TB, rnd 5; B4/10/1981 Dallas, TX **2004** TB 4 (0) **2005**†TB 16 (0) **NFL** 20 (0) [2 yrs]

TERRY, JOE Joseph Thomas, LB, 6´2˝/230 lbs; Cal State-Hayward; B5/7/1965 **1987** Sea 2 (0)

TERRY, NAT Nathaniel, DB, 5´11˝/167 lbs; Florida State; 1978: Pit, rnd 11; B7/20/1956 Tampa, FL **1978** Pit 6 **1978** Det 4 **NFL** 10 [1 yr]

TERRY, RICK Richard Ross, DT, 6´4˝/302 lbs; North Carolina; 1997: NYJ, rnd 2; B4/5/1974 Lexington, NC **1997** NYJ 14 (0) **1998** Car 7 (3) **1999** Car 8 (0) **NFL** 29 (3) [3 yrs]

TERRY, RYAN Ryan L., RB, 5´11˝/203 lbs; Iowa; B9/20/1971 Fort Bragg, NC **1995** Arz 15 (0)

YEAR	TEAM	G (GS, POS)	RUSH	YD	AVG (LG)	TD	REC	YD	AVG (LG)	TD	PASS	COMP	PCT	YD	AVG (LG)	TD	INT	SK	YD	QBR	KPR	OTD	PTS	TAY
1996	Arz	5 (0)	—	—	—	—	1	0	0.0 (0)	0	—	—	—	—	—	—	—	—	—	—	k	—	0	24
NFL	2	20 (0)	—	—	—	—	1	0	0.0	0	—	—	—	—	—	—	—	—	—	—	k	—	0	277

TERRY, TIM Tim, LB, 6´3˝/235 lbs; Temple; B7/26/1974 Hempstead, NY **1997** Cin 5 (0) **2000** Sea 6 (0) **2001** Sea 16 (0) **2002** Sea 16 (8, rlb) **NFL** 43 (8) [4 yrs]

TERSCH, RUDY Fred, T-G, /195 lbs; none; B4/1/1895, D10/1964, MN **1921** Min 3 (3, RG) **1922** Min 4 (4, LT) **1923** Min 8 (8, LT), 6 **NFL** 15 (15) [3 yrs]

TESSER, RAY Raymond Charles, E-DE, 6´2˝/204 lbs; Carnegie Mellon; B6/2/1912 Titusville, PA, D11/2/1982 Corry, PA

YEAR	TEAM	G (GS, POS)	RUSH	YD	AVG (LG)	TD	REC	YD	AVG (LG)	TD	PASS	COMP	PCT	YD	AVG (LG)	TD	INT	SK	YD	QBR	KPR	OTD	PTS	TAY
1933	Pit	11 (10, RE)	—	—	—	—	14	282	20.1	0	1	0	0.0	0	0.0	0	0	—	—	—	—	—	0	141
1934	Pit	12 (1)	—	—	—	—	5	67	13.4	0	1	0	0.0	0	0.0	0	0	—	—	—	—	—	0	34
NFL	2	23 (11)	—	—	—	—	19	349	18.4	0	2	0	0.0	0	0.0	0	0	—	—	—	—	—	0	175

TESTAVERDE, VINNY Vincent Frank, QB, 6´5˝/235 lbs; Miami (FL); 1987: TB, rnd 1; B11/13/1963 Brooklyn, NY

YEAR	TEAM	G (GS, POS)	RUSH	YD	AVG (LG)	TD	REC	YD	AVG (LG)	TD	PASS	COMP	PCT	YD	AVG (LG)	TD	INT	SK	YD	QBR	KPR	OTD	PTS	TAY
1987	TB	6 (4, qb)	13	50	3.8 (17)	1	—	—	—	—	165	71	43.0	1081	6.6 (40)	5	6	18	140	60.2	—	—	6	386
1988	TB	15 (15, QB)	28	138	4.9 (24)	1	—	—	—	—	466	222	47.6	3240	7.0 (59)	13	**35**	33	292	48.8	—	—	6	433
1989	TB	14 (14, QB)	25	139	5.6 (16)	0	—	—	—	—	480	258	53.8	3133	6.5 (78)	20	**22**	38	294	68.9	—	—	0	926
1990	TB	14 (13, QB)	38	280	7.4 (48)	1	1	3	3.0 (3)	0	365	203	55.6	2818	**7.7** (**89**)	17	**18**	38	330	75.6	—	—	6	1066
1991	TB	13 (12, QB)	32	101	3.2 (19)	0	—	—	—	—	326	166	50.9	1994	6.1 (87)	8	15	35	234	59.0	—	—	0	538
1992	TB	14 (14, QB)	36	197	5.5 (18)	2	—	—	—	—	358	206	57.5	2554	7.1 (81)	14	16	35	259	74.2	—	—	12	924
1993	Cle	10 (6, QB)	18	74	4.1 (14)	0	—	—	—	—	230	130	56.5	1797	7.8 (62)	14	9	17	101	85.7	—	—	0	683
1994	†Cle	14 (13, QB)	21	37	1.8 (12)	2	—	—	—	—	376	207	55.1	2575	6.8 (81)	16	18	12	83	70.7	—	—	12	705
1995	Cle	13 (12, QB)	18	62	3.4 (14)	2	1	7	7.0 (7)	0	392	241	61.5	2883	7.4 (70)	17	10	17	87	87.8	—	—	12	1212
1996	Bal✧	16 (16, QB)	34	188	5.5 (22)	2	—	—	—	—	549	325	59.2	4177	7.6 (86)	**33**	19	34	270	88.7	—	—	14	1702
1997	Bal	13 (13, QB)	34	138	4.1 (16)	0	1	-4	-4.0 (-4)	0	470	271	57.7	2971	6.3 (54)	18	15	20	129	75.9	—	—	0	1112
1998	†NYJ★	14 (13, QB)	24	104	4.3 (25)	1	—	—	—	—	421	259	61.5	3256	7.7 (82)	**29**	7	19	140	**101.6**	—	—	6	1607
1999	NYJ	1 (1)	—	—	—	—	—	—	—	—	15	10	66.7	96	6.4 (27)	1	1	—	—	—	—	—	0	13
2000	NYJ	16 (16, QB)	25	32	1.3 (15)	0	—	—	—	—	**590**	328	55.6	3732	6.3 (63)	21	**25**	13	71	69.0	—	—	0	1003
2001	†NYJ	16 (16, QB)	31	25	0.8 (12)	0	—	—	—	—	441	260	59.0	2752	6.2 (40)	15	14	18	122	75.3	—	—	0	916
2002	†NYJ	5 (4)	2	23	11.5 (24)	0	—	—	—	—	83	54	65.1	499	6.0 (35)	3	3	9	62	—	—	—	0	168
2003	NYJ	7 (7, qb)	6	17	2.8 (13)	0	—	—	—	—	198	123	62.1	1385	7.0 (61)	7	2	6	48	90.6	—	—	0	665
2004	Dal	16 (15, QB)	21	38	1.8 (10)	1	—	—	—	—	495	297	60.0	3532	7.1 (53)	17	**20**	34	182	76.4	—	—	6	1099
2005	NYJ	6 (4)	7	4	0.6 (2)	2	—	—	—	—	106	60	56.6	777	7.3 (47)	1	6	12	102	59.4	—	—	12	178
NFL	19	223 (208)	413	1647	4.0 (48)	15	3	6	2.0 (7)	0	6526	3691	56.6	45252	6.9 (89)	269	261	408	2946	75.2	—	—	92	15331

TESTERMAN, DON Donald Ray, RB, 6´2˝/230 lbs; Ferrum; Virginia Tech; Lenoir-Rhyne; Clemson; 1976: Mia, rnd 10; B11/7/1952 Danville, VA

YEAR	TEAM	G (GS, POS)	RUSH	YD	AVG (LG)	TD	REC	YD	AVG (LG)	TD	PASS	COMP	PCT	YD	AVG (LG)	TD	INT	SK	YD	QBR	KPR	OTD	PTS	TAY
1976	Sea	14 (8, FB)	67	246	3.7 (16)	1	25	232	9.3 (25)	1	—	—	—	—	—	—	—	—	—	—	k	—	12	376
1977	Sea	14 (13, FB)	119	459	3.9 (20)	1	31	219	7.1 (25)	4	—	—	—	—	—	—	—	—	—	—	k	—	30	598
1978	Sea	16 (5, fb)	43	155	3.6 (16)	0	17	143	8.4 (21)	0	—	—	—	—	—	—	—	—	—	—	k	—	0	231
1980	Mia	5 (0)	1	5	5.0 (5)	0	—	—	—	—	—	—	—	—	—	—	—	—	—	—	—	—	0	5
NFL	4	49 (26)	230	865	3.8 (20)	2	73	594	8.1 (25)	5	—	—	—	—	—	—	—	—	—	—	k	—	42	1209

TETEAK, DERAL Deral Dean, LB-G, 5´10˝/210 lbs; Wisconsin; 1952: GB, rnd 9; B12/11/1929 Oconto, WI **1952** GB✧12 (LLB) **1953** GB 7 **1954** GB 6 **1955** GB 12 **1956** GB 12 (RLB) **NFL** 49 [5 yrs]

TEVIS, LEE Lee Kessler, FB-LB, 5´11˝/190 lbs; George Washington; Miami (OH); B9/29/1921. **[K]**

YEAR	TEAM	G (GS, POS)	RUSH	YD	AVG (LG)	TD	REC	YD	AVG (LG)	TD	PASS	COMP	PCT	YD	AVG (LG)	TD	INT	SK	YD	QBR	KPR	OTD	PTS	TAY
1947	Bkn-A	8(0)	4	44	11.0	0	—	—	—	—	3	0	0.0	0	0.0	0	0	—	—	—	Pi	—	0	43
1948	Bkn-A	14(4, fb)	—	—	—	—	1	-8	-8.0(-8)	0	1	0	0.0	0	0.0	0	0	—	—	—	KPkp	—	10	35
AAFC	2	22(4)	4	44	11.0	0	1	-8	-8.0(-8)	0	4	0	0.0	0	0.0	0	0	—	—	—	KPkpi	—	10	78

TEW, LOWELL Lowell William, FB, 5´11˝/195 lbs; Alabama; 1948: NYY-A, rnd 1/Was, rnd 1; B1/2/1927 Waynesboro, MS, D3/16/1981 Laurel, MS

YEAR	TEAM	G (GS, POS)	RUSH	YD	AVG (LG)	TD	REC	YD	AVG (LG)	TD	PASS	COMP	PCT	YD	AVG (LG)	TD	INT	SK	YD	QBR	KPR	OTD	PTS	TAY
1948	NYY-A	14(2)	24	95	4.0	5	7	97	13.9	0	—	—	—	—	—	—	—	—	—	—	k	—	30	224
1949	NYY-A	1(1)	14	65	4.6	1	—	—	—	—	—	—	—	—	—	—	—	—	—	—	k	—	6	77
AAFC	2	15(3)	38	160	4.2	6	7	97	13.9	0	—	—	—	—	—	—	—	—	—	—	k	—	36	301

THACKER, AL Alvin Monroe, G, 5´10˝/200 lbs; Charleston (WV); B3/1/1919 Kayford, WV, D6/16/2001 Okeechobee, FL **1942** Phi 3 (0)

THARP, CORKY Thomas Allen, DB, 5´10˝/180 lbs; Alabama; 1955: LA, rnd 6; B4/19/1931 Birmingham, AL **1960** NYT-A 9 (RS)

THARPE, LARRY Larry James, T, 6´4˝/300 lbs; Tennessee State; 1992: Det, rnd 6; B11/19/1970 Macon, GA **1992** Det 11 (0) **1993** Det 5 (3) **1995** Arz 16 (16, RT/lt) **1997**†Det 16 (15, RT) **1998** Det 16 (9, RT) **2000** Pit 12 (5, rt) **NFL** 76 (48) [6 yrs]

THARP, RICHARD Richard Thomas, DE-NT, 6´3˝/255 lbs; Louisville; 1983: Buf, rnd 10; B10/31/1960 New York, NY **1987** Buf 3 (3)

THAXTON, GALAND Galand Walter, LB, 6´1˝/242 lbs; Wyoming; B10/23/1964 Mildinhall, England **1989** Atl 16 (0) **1991** SD 14 (0) **NFL** 30 (0) [2 yrs]

THAXTON, JIM James Ivory, TE-WR, 6´2˝/240 lbs; Tennessee State; 1973: SD, rnd 4; B1/11/1949 Brownsville, TX

YEAR	TEAM	G (GS, POS)	RUSH	YD	AVG (LG)	TD	REC	YD	AVG (LG)	TD	PASS	COMP	PCT	YD	AVG (LG)	TD	INT	SK	YD	QBR	KPR	OTD	PTS	TAY
1973	SD	10(3)	—	—	—	—	7	119	17.0(31)	2	—	—	—	—	—	—	—	—	—	—	—	—	12	70
1974	SD	2	—	—	—	—	—	—	—	—	—	—	—	—	—	—	—	—	—	—	—	—	—	—
1974	Cle	12(te)	1	-10	-10.0(-10)	0	4	71	17.8(34)	0	—	—	—	—	—	—	—	—	—	—	i	—	0	21
1976	NO	11(1)	—	—	—	—	7	112	16.0(25)	1	—	—	—	—	—	—	—	—	—	—	k	—	6	126
1977	NO	14(6, te)	1	-3	-3.0(-3)	0	14	211	15.1(41)	1	—	—	—	—	—	—	—	—	—	—	—	—	6	116
1978	SL	5	—	—	—	—	3	31	10.3(16)	1	—	—	—	—	—	—	—	—	—	—	—	—	8	21
NFL	5	54(10)	2	-13	-6.5(-3)	0	35	544	15.5(41)	5	—	—	—	—	—	—	—	—	—	—	ki	—	32	352

THAYER, HARRY Harry James, T-G, 6´1˝/215 lbs; Tennessee; B3/21/1907 Charleston, WV, D5/8/1961 Knoxville, TN **1933** Por 9 (4)

THAYER, TOM Thomas Allen, G-C, 6´4˝/271 lbs; Notre Dame; 1983: Chi, rnd 4; B8/16/1961 Joliet, IL **1985**†ChiB 16 (13, RG) **1986**†ChiB 16 (16, RG) **1987**†ChiB 11 (11, RG) **1988**†ChiB 16 (16, RG) **1989** ChiB 16 (16, RG) **1990**†ChiB 16 (16, RG) **1991**†ChiB 16 (16, RG) **1992** ChiB 16 (16, RG) **1993** Mia 3 (0) **NFL** 126 (120) [9 yrs]

THEISMANN, JOE Joseph Robert, QB, 6´0˝/192 lbs; Notre Dame; 1971: Mia, rnd 4; B9/9/1949 New Brunswick, NJ

YEAR	TEAM	G (GS, POS)	RUSH	YD	AVG (LG)	TD	REC	YD	AVG (LG)	TD	PASS	COMP	PCT	YD	AVG (LG)	TD	INT	SK	YD	QBR	KPR	OTD	PTS	TAY
1974	†Was	9	3	12	4.0(12)	1	—	—	—	—	11	9	81.8	145	13.2(69)	1	0	2	11	—	p	—	6	182
1975	Was	14	3	34	11.3(21)	0	—	—	—	—	22	10	45.5	96	4.4(30)	1	3	2	18	—	p	—	0	-38
1976	†Was	14(5, qb)	17	97	5.7(22)	1	—	—	—	—	163	79	48.5	1036	6.4(44)	8	10	22	172	59.8	—	—	6	265
1977	Was	14(6, qb)	29	149	5.1(14)	1	—	—	—	—	182	84	46.2	1097	6.0(52)	7	9	30	241	57.9	—	—	6	383
1978	Was	16(14, QB)	37	177	4.8(20)	1	—	—	—	—	390	187	47.9	2593	6.6(63)	13	18	42	391	61.6	—	—	6	829
1979	Was☆	16(16, QB)	46	181	3.9(22)	4	—	—	—	—	395	233	59.0	2797	7.1(62)	20	13	34	263	83.9	—	—	24	1200
1980	Was	16(15, QB)	29	175	6.0(37)	3	—	—	—	—	454	262	57.7	2962	6.5(54)	17	16	31	282	75.2	—	—	18	1131
1981	Was	16(16, QB)	36	177	4.9(24)	2	—	—	—	—	496	293	59.1	3568	7.2(79)	19	20	28	259	77.3	—	—	12	1276
1982	†Was★	9(9, QB)	31	150	4.8(16)	0	—	—	—	—	252	161	**63.9**	2033	8.1(78)	13	9	30	223	**91.3**	—	—	0	872
1983	†Was★	16(16, QB)	37	234	6.3(22)	1	—	—	—	—	459	276	60.1	3714	8.1(84)	29	11	34	242	97.0	—	—	6	1806
1984	†Was	16(16, QB)	62	314	5.1(27)	1	—	—	—	—	477	283	59.3	3391	7.1(80)	24	13	48	341	86.6	—	—	6	1620
1985	Was	11(11, QB)	25	115	4.6(25)	2	—	—	—	—	301	167	55.5	1774	5.9(55)	8	16	37	314	59.6	P	—	12	422
NFL	12	167(124)	355	1815	5.1(37)	17	—	—	—	—	3602	2044	56.7	25206	7.0(84)	160	138	340	2757	77.4	Pp	—	102	9945

THELWELL, RYAN Ryan, WR, 6´2˝/192 lbs; Minnesota; 1998: SF, rnd 7; B4/6/1973 London, Canada

YEAR	TEAM	G (GS, POS)	RUSH	YD	AVG (LG)	TD	REC	YD	AVG (LG)	TD	PASS	COMP	PCT	YD	AVG (LG)	TD	INT	SK	YD	QBR	KPR	OTD	PTS	TAY
1998	SD	6(3)	—	—	—	—	16	268	16.8(55)	1	—	—	—	—	—	—	—	—	—	—	—	—	6	139

THEOFILEDES, HARRY Aris Harry, QB, 5´10˝/180 lbs; Waynesburg; B4/19/1944 Homestead, PA

YEAR	TEAM	G (GS, POS)	RUSH	YD	AVG (LG)	TD	REC	YD	AVG (LG)	TD	PASS	COMP	PCT	YD	AVG (LG)	TD	INT	SK	YD	QBR	KPR	OTD	PTS	TAY
1968	Was	5	3	0	0.0(7)	0	—	—	—	—	20	11	55.0	211	10.6(39)	2	1	—	—	—	—	—	0	76

THIBAUT, JIM James Pierre, FB-LB, 5´11˝/205 lbs; Tulane; 1942: Bkn, rnd 12; B8/31/1919 New Orleans, LA

YEAR	TEAM	G (GS, POS)	RUSH	YD	AVG (LG)	TD	REC	YD	AVG (LG)	TD	PASS	COMP	PCT	YD	AVG (LG)	TD	INT	SK	YD	QBR	KPR	OTD	PTS	TAY
1946	Buf-A	3(0)	10	48	4.8	1	—	—	—	—	—	—	—	—	—	—	—	—	—	—	—	—	6	58

THIBERT, JIM James Gerald, LB, 6´3˝/230 lbs; Toledo; 1962: SD, rnd 22; B6/14/1940 Toledo, OH **1965** Den-A 13

THIBODEAUX, KEITH Keith Trevis, DB, 5´11˝/189 lbs; Northwestern State (LA); 1997: Was, rnd 5; B5/16/1974 Opelousas, LA **1997** Was 15 (0) **1999** Atl 8 (0) **1999** Min 3 (0) **2000**†Min 16 (0) **2001** Min 5 (1) **2001** GB 7 (0) **NFL** 54 (1) [4 yrs]

THIELE, DUTCH Carl Louis, E, 6´1˝/195 lbs; Denison; B11/14/1892 Dayton, OH, D7/11/1986 Dayton, OH **1920** Day 9 (8, LE) **1921** Day 7 (5, LE), 6 **1922** Day 7 (7, LE), 6 **1923** Day 8 (8, LE) **NFL** 31 (28), 12 [4 yrs]

THIELEMANN, R.C. Ray Charles, G-C, 6´4˝/255 lbs; Arkansas; 1977: Atl, rnd 2; B8/12/1955 Houston, TX **1977** Atl 14 (14, RG) **1978**†Atl 16 (16, RG) **1979** Atl 11 (11, RG) **1980**†Atl 16 (16, RG) **1981** Atl✧16 (16, RG) **1982**†Atl★9 (9, RG) **1983** Atl★16 (16, LG) **1984** Atl 16 (16, LG) **1985** Was 3 (1) **1986**†Was 14 (13, RG) **1987**†Was 12 (12, RG) **1988** Was 14 (8, rg) **NFL** 157 (148) [12 yrs]

THIELSCHER, KARL Karl Leavitt, FB, 5´11˝/180 lbs; Dartmouth; B4/24/1894 Brookline, MA, D5/5/1990 Palm Beach, FL **1920** Buf 1 (0)

THIERRY, JOHN John Fitzgerald, DE, 6´4˝/265 lbs; Alcorn State; 1994: Chi, rnd 1; B9/4/1971 Opelousas, LA **1994**†ChiB 16 (1) **1995** ChiB 16 (7, RDE) **1996** ChiB 16 (2) **1997** ChiB 9 (9, LDE) **1998** ChiB 16 (9, LDE) **1999** Cle 16 (10, LDE) **2000** GB 16 (16, RDE) **2001** GB 12 (12, RDE) **2002**†Atl 14 (4) **NFL** 131 (70) [9 yrs]

THIGPEN, YANCEY Yancey Dirk, WR, 6´1˝/208 lbs; Winston-Salem State; 1991: SD, rnd 4; B8/15/1969 Tarboro, NC

YEAR	TEAM	G (GS, POS)	RUSH	YD	AVG (LG)	TD	REC	YD	AVG (LG)	TD	PASS	COMP	PCT	YD	AVG (LG)	TD	INT	SK	YD	QBR	KPR	OTD	PTS	TAY
1991	SD	4(1)	—	—	—	—	—	—	—	—	—	—	—	—	—	—	—	—	—	—	—	—	—	—
1992	†Pit	12(0)	—	—	—	—	1	2	2.0(2)	0	—	—	—	—	—	—	—	—	—	—	k	—	0	15
1993	Pit	12(0)	—	—	—	—	9	154	17.1(39)	3	—	—	—	—	—	—	—	—	—	—	k	—	18	100
1994	†Pit	15(6, wr)	—	—	—	—	36	546	15.2(60)	4	—	—	—	—	—	—	—	—	—	—	k	—	24	339
1995	†Pit★	16(15, WR)	1	1	1.0(1)	0	85	1307	15.4(43)	5	—	—	—	—	—	—	—	—	—	—	—	—	30	680
1996	Pit	6(2)	—	—	—	—	12	244	20.3(39)	2	—	—	—	—	—	—	—	—	—	—	—	—	12	132
1997	†Pit★	16(15, WR)	1	3	3.0(3)	0	79	1398	17.7(69)	7	—	—	—	—	—	—	—	—	—	—	—	—	44	737
1998	Ten	9(8, WR)	—	—	—	—	38	493	13.0(55)	3	—	—	—	—	—	—	—	—	—	—	—	—	18	262
1999	†Ten	10(10, WR)	—	—	—	—	38	648	17.1(35)	4	—	—	—	—	—	—	—	—	—	—	p	—	24	360
2000	†Ten	12(0)	—	—	—	—	15	289	19.3(56)	2	—	—	—	—	—	—	—	—	—	—	p	—	12	159
NFL	10	112(57)	2	4	2.0(3)	0	313	5081	16.2(69)	30	—	—	—	—	—	—	—	—	—	—	kp	—	182	2783

THOMAS, AARON Aaron Norman, TE-SE, 6´3˝/210 lbs; Oregon State; 1961: SF, rnd 4/DalT, rnd 16; B11/7/1937 Dierks, AR

YEAR	TEAM	G (GS, POS)	RUSH	YD	AVG (LG)	TD	REC	YD	AVG (LG)	TD	PASS	COMP	PCT	YD	AVG (LG)	TD	INT	SK	YD	QBR	KPR	OTD	PTS	TAY
1961	SF	14(7, SE)	1	-15	-15.0(-15)	0	15	301	20.1(70)	2	—	—	—	—	—	—	—	—	—	—	—	—	12	146
1962	SF	2	1	-9	-9.0(-9)	0	—	—	—	—	—	—	—	—	—	—	—	—	—	—	—	—	0	-9
1962	†NYG	12	—	—	—	—	4	80	20.0(37)	0	—	—	—	—	—	—	—	—	—	—	—	—	0	40
1963	†NYG	14	—	—	—	—	22	469	21.3(55)	3	—	—	—	—	—	—	—	—	—	—	—	—	18	250
1964	NYG✧	14(TE)	—	—	—	—	43	624	14.5(42)	6	—	—	—	—	—	—	—	—	—	—	—	—	36	342
1965	NYG	13(TE)	—	—	—	—	27	631	23.4(71)	5	—	—	—	—	—	—	—	—	—	—	—	—	30	341
1966	NYG	14(TE)	—	—	—	—	43	683	15.9(50)	4	—	—	—	—	—	—	—	—	—	—	—	—	24	362
1967	NYG	14(TE)	—	—	—	—	51	877	17.2(48)	9	—	—	—	—	—	—	—	—	—	—	—	—	54	484
1968	NYG	12(TE)	2	14	7.0(23)	0	29	449	15.5(49)	4	—	—	—	—	—	—	—	—	—	—	—	—	24	259
1969	NYG	10	—	—	—	—	22	348	15.8(37)	3	—	—	—	—	—	—	—	—	—	—	—	—	18	189
1970	NYG	14	—	—	—	—	6	92	15.3(29)	1	—	—	—	—	—	—	—	—	—	—	—	—	6	51
NFL	10	133(7)	4	-10	-2.5(23)	0	262	4554	17.4(71)	37	—	—	—	—	—	—	—	—	—	—	—	—	222	2452

THOMAS, ADALIUS Adalius Donquail, LB-DE, 6´2˝/270 lbs; Southern Mississippi; 2000: Bal, rnd 6; B8/17/1977 Equality, AL **2000**†Bal 3 (0) **2001**†Bal 16 (2) **2002** Bal 16 (12, RDE) **2003** Bal★13 (11, LOLB) **2004** Bal 16 (16, ROLB) **2005** Bal 16 (16, LLB) **NFL** 80 (57) [6 yrs]

THOMAS, ANDRE Andre, RB, 6´0˝/205 lbs; Mississippi; B11/28/1960 Tupelo, MS

YEAR	TEAM	G (GS, POS)	RUSH	YD	AVG (LG)	TD	REC	YD	AVG (LG)	TD	PASS	COMP	PCT	YD	AVG (LG)	TD	INT	SK	YD	QBR	KPR	OTD	PTS	TAY
1987	Min	1(0)	6	4	0.7(5)	0	2	13	6.5(10)	0	—	—	—	—	—	—	—	—	—	—	—	—	0	11

Thomas, Anthony Anthony Jermaine, RB, 6´2˝/228 lbs; Michigan; 2001: Chi, rnd 2; B11/7/1977 Winnfield, LA

YEAR	TEAM	G(GS, POS)	RUSH	YD	AVG(LG)	TD	REC	YD	AVG(LG)	TD	PASS	COMP	PCT	YD	AVG(LG)	TD	INT	SK	YD	QBR	KPR	OTD	PTS	TAY
2001	†ChiB	14(10, RB)	278	1183	4.3(46)	7	22	178	8.1(23)	0	—	—	—	—	—	—	—	—	—	—	—	—	44	1342
2002	ChiB	12(12, RB)	214	721	3.4(34)	6	24	163	6.8(19)	0	—	—	—	—	—	—	—	—	—	—	—	—	36	863
2003	ChiB	13(13, RB)	244	1024	4.2(67)	6	9	36	4.0(9)	0	—	—	—	—	—	—	—	—	—	—	—	—	36	1102
2004	ChiB	12(2)	122	404	3.3(41)	2	17	132	7.8(30)	0	—	—	—	—	—	—	—	—	—	—	—	—	12	490
2005	Dal	6(2)	36	80	2.2(12)	0	2	5	2.5(5)	0	—	—	—	—	—	—	—	—	—	—	—	—	0	83
2005	NO	4(0)	7	12	1.7(4)	0	2	8	4.0(6)	0	—	—	—	—	—	—	—	—	—	—	—	—	0	16
NFL	5	61(39)	901	3424	3.8(67)	21	76	522	6.9(30)	0	—	—	—	—	—	—	—	—	—	—	—	—	128	3895

Thomas, Ben Benjamin, DE-NT, 6´4˝/280 lbs; Auburn; 1985: NE, rnd 2; B7/2/1961 Ashburn, GA **1985**†NE 15 (0) **1986** NE 4 (1) **1986** GB 9 (0) **1988** Pit 8 (5, lde) **1989** Atl 16 (13, RDE) **1991** LARm 2 (0) **NFL** 54 (19) [5 yrs]

Thomas, Bill William Jeffrey, RB, 6´2˝/225 lbs; Boston College; 1972: Dal, rnd 1; B8/7/1949 Ossining, NY

YEAR	TEAM	G(GS, POS)	RUSH	YD	AVG(LG)	TD	REC	YD	AVG(LG)	TD	PASS	COMP	PCT	YD	AVG(LG)	TD	INT	SK	YD	QBR	KPR	OTD	PTS	TAY
1972	Dal	7	—	—	—	—	—	—	—	—	—	—	—	—	—	—	—	—	—	—	k	—	0	20
1973	Hou	6	10	39	3.9(17)	0	1	4	4.0(4)	0	—	—	—	—	—	—	—	—	—	—	—	—	0	41
1974	KC	14	3	-3	-1.0(2)	0	—	—	—	—	—	—	—	—	—	—	—	—	—	—	k	—	0	193
NFL	3	27	13	36	2.8(17)	0	1	4	4.0(4)	0	—	—	—	—	—	—	—	—	—	—	k	—	0	254

Thomas, Blair Blair Lamar, RB, 5´10˝/198 lbs; Penn State; 1990: NYJ, rnd 1; B10/7/1967 Philadelphia, PA

YEAR	TEAM	G(GS, POS)	RUSH	YD	AVG(LG)	TD	REC	YD	AVG(LG)	TD	PASS	COMP	PCT	YD	AVG(LG)	TD	INT	SK	YD	QBR	KPR	OTD	PTS	TAY
1990	NYJ	15(11, RB)	123	620	5.0(41)	1	20	204	10.2(55)	1	—	—	—	—	—	—	—	—	—	—	—	—	12	737
1991	NYJ	16(12, RB)	189	728	3.9(25)	3	30	195	6.5(18)	1	1	1	100.0	16	16.0(16)	1	0	—	—	—	—	—	24	874
1992	NYJ	9(7, RB)	97	440	4.5(19)	0	7	49	7.0(10)	0	—	—	—	—	—	—	—	—	—	—	—	—	0	465
1993	NYJ	11(5, rb)	59	221	3.7(24)	1	7	25	3.6(7)	0	—	—	—	—	—	—	—	—	—	—	k	—	6	253
1994	NE	4(0)	19	67	3.5(13)	1	2	15	7.5(9)	0	—	—	—	—	—	—	—	—	—	—	k	—	6	80
1994	†Dal	2(1)	24	70	2.9(11)	1	2	1	0.5(5)	0	—	—	—	—	—	—	—	—	—	—	—	—	6	81
1995	Car	7(0)	22	90	4.1(13)	0	3	24	8.0(14)	0	—	—	—	—	—	—	—	—	—	—	—	—	0	102
NFL	6	64(36)	533	2236	4.2(41)	7	71	513	7.2(55)	2	1	1	100.0	16	16.0(16)	1	0	—	—	—	k	—	54	2590

Thomas, Bob Robert Randall, K, 5´10˝/178 lbs; Notre Dame; 1974: LA, rnd 15; B8/7/1952 Rochester, NY **[K]** **1975** ChiB 14 **1976** ChiB 14 **1977**†ChiB 14 **1978** ChiB 16 **1979**†ChiB 16 **1980** ChiB 16 (0) **1981** ChiB 2 (0) **1982** Det 2 (0) **1982** ChiB 2 (0) **1983** ChiB 16 (0) **1984**†ChiB 16 (0) **1985** SD 15 (0) **1986** NYG 1 (0) **NFL** 144 [12 yrs]

Thomas, Bob Robert Lee, RB, 5´10˝/201 lbs; Arizona State; 1971: Cin, rnd 15; B8/23/1948 Pittsburgh, PA

YEAR	TEAM	G(GS, POS)	RUSH	YD	AVG(LG)	TD	REC	YD	AVG(LG)	TD	PASS	COMP	PCT	YD	AVG(LG)	TD	INT	SK	YD	QBR	KPR	OTD	PTS	TAY
1971	LARm	6	—	—	—	—	—	—	—	—	—	—	—	—	—	—	—	—	—	—	k	—	0	-3
1972	LARm	14	77	433	5.6(49)	3	11	95	8.6(19)	0	—	—	—	—	—	—	—	—	—	—	k	—	18	603
1973	SD	14	22	48	2.2(12)	0	7	51	7.3(37)	1	—	—	—	—	—	—	—	—	—	—	—	—	6	79
1974	SD	14(2)	21	56	2.7(12)	0	1	9	9.0(9)	0	—	—	—	—	—	—	—	—	—	—	k	—	0	63
NFL	4	48(2)	120	537	4.5(49)	3	19	155	8.2(37)	1	—	—	—	—	—	—	—	—	—	—	k	—	24	741

Thomas, Broderick Broderick, LB-DE, 6´4˝/250 lbs; Nebraska; 1989: TB, rnd 1; B2/20/1967 Houston, TX **1989** TB 16 (0) **1990** TB 16 (15, LOLB) **1991** TB 16 (16, RLB) **1992** TB 16 (16, RLB) **1993** TB 16 (8, llb) **1994** Det 16 (16, LOLB) **1995** Min 16 (16, LLB) **1996**†Dal 16 (9, LLB) **1997** Dal 16 (0) **NFL** 144 (96) [9 yrs]

Thomas, Bryan Bryan, DE, 6´4˝/266 lbs; Alabama-Birmingham; 2002: NYJ, rnd 1; B6/7/1979 Birmingham, AL **2002**†NYJ 15 (0) **2003** NYJ 16 (10, RDE) **2004**†NYJ 14 (6, rde) **2005** NYJ 16 (4) **NFL** 61 (20) [4 yrs]

Thomas, Cal Calvin O., G, 6´2˝/210 lbs; Tulsa; B7/1/1915, D4/14/1982 Harper Woods, MI **1939** Det 5 (0) **1940** Det 8 (1) **NFL** 13 (1) [2 yrs]

Thomas, Calvin Calvin Lewis, RB, 5´11˝/239 lbs; Illinois; B1/7/1960 St. Louis, MO

YEAR	TEAM	G(GS, POS)	RUSH	YD	AVG(LG)	TD	REC	YD	AVG(LG)	TD	PASS	COMP	PCT	YD	AVG(LG)	TD	INT	SK	YD	QBR	KPR	OTD	PTS	TAY
1982	ChiB	6(0)	5	4	0.8(3)	0	—	—	—	—	—	—	—	—	—	—	—	—	—	—	—	—	0	4
1983	ChiB	13(0)	8	25	3.1(9)	0	2	13	6.5(7)	0	—	—	—	—	—	—	—	—	—	—	—	—	0	32
1984	†ChiB	16(0)	40	186	4.7(37)	1	9	39	4.3(9)	0	—	—	—	—	—	—	—	—	—	—	—	—	6	216
1985	†ChiB	14(0)	31	125	4.0(17)	4	5	45	9.0(15)	0	—	—	—	—	—	—	—	—	—	—	—	—	24	188
1986	†ChiB	16(0)	56	224	4.0(23)	0	4	18	4.5(18)	0	—	—	—	—	—	—	—	—	—	—	—	—	0	233
1987	†ChiB	12(0)	25	88	3.5(18)	0	—	—	—	—	—	—	—	—	—	—	—	—	—	—	—	—	0	88
1988	ChiB	1(0)	5	20	4.0(8)	0	—	—	—	—	—	—	—	—	—	—	—	—	—	—	—	—	0	20
1988	Den	2(0)	1	0	0.0(0)	0	—	—	—	—	—	—	—	—	—	—	—	—	—	—	—	—	0	0
NFL	7	80(0)	171	672	3.9(37)	5	20	115	5.8(18)	0	—	—	—	—	—	—	—	—	—	—	—	—	30	780

Thomas, Carl Carl Herbert, T-E-BB-FB, 5´10˝/195 lbs; Pennsylvania; B3/2/1897 Philadelphia, PA, D10/30/1961 **1920** Roc 1 (0) **1921** Roc 5 (5, RT) **1922** Buf 9 (9, LT), 6 **1923** Buf 10 (5) **NFL** 25 (19) [4 yrs]

Thomas, Carlton Carlton Fitzgerald, DB, 6´0˝/200 lbs; Elizabeth City State; B11/25/1963 Portsmouth, VA **1987** KC 4 (2)

Thomas, Charlie Charles Ray, RB, 5´9˝/180 lbs; Tennessee State; B11/27/1948 Houston, TX **1975** KC 7

Thomas, Chris Chris Eric, WR, 6´2˝/185 lbs; Cal Poly-San Luis Obispo; B7/16/1971 Ventura, CA

YEAR	TEAM	G(GS, POS)	RUSH	YD	AVG(LG)	TD	REC	YD	AVG(LG)	TD	PASS	COMP	PCT	YD	AVG(LG)	TD	INT	SK	YD	QBR	KPR	OTD	PTS	TAY
1995	SF	15(0)	—	—	—	—	6	73	12.2(23)	0	—	—	—	—	—	—	—	—	—	—	kp	—	0	61
1997	Was	13(0)	—	—	—	—	11	93	8.5(17)	0	—	—	—	—	—	—	—	—	—	—	—	—	0	47
1998	Was	14(0)	—	—	—	—	14	173	12.4(25)	0	—	—	—	—	—	—	—	—	—	—	—	—	0	87
1999	Was	2(0)	—	—	—	—	—	—	—	—	—	—	—	—	—	—	—	—	—	—	—	—	—	—
1999	SL	6(0)	—	—	—	—	1	6	6.0(6)	0	—	—	—	—	—	—	—	—	—	—	—	—	0	3
2000	†SL	16(0)	—	—	—	—	—	—	—	—	—	—	—	—	—	—	—	—	—	—	—	—	0	0
2001	KC	10(5, wr)	—	—	—	—	19	247	13.0(28)	1	—	—	—	—	—	—	—	—	—	—	—	—	6	129
NFL	6	76(5)	—	—	—	—	51	592	11.6(28)	1	—	—	—	—	—	—	—	—	—	—	kp	—	6	325

Thomas, Chuck Charles Gene, C, 6´3˝/277 lbs; Oklahoma; 1985: Hou, rnd 8; B12/24/1960 Houston, TX **1985** Atl 4 (0) **1987**†SF 7 (3) **1988**†SF 16 (0) **1989**†SF 16 (0) **1990**†SF 16 (0) **1991** SF 12 (0) **1992**†SF 2 (0) **NFL** 73 (3) [7 yrs]

Thomas, Clendon Bobby Clendon, DB-E-FL-HB, 6´2˝/196 lbs; Oklahoma; 1958: LA, rnd 2; B12/28/1935 Oklahoma City, OK **[I]** **1958** LARm 6 **1961** LARm 13 (RS) **1962** Pit☆14 (LS) **1963** Pit★13 (LS) **1966** Pit☆14 (LS) **1967** Pit 13 (LS) **1968** Pit 14 (LS)

YEAR	TEAM	G(GS, POS)	RUSH	YD	AVG(LG)	TD	REC	YD	AVG(LG)	TD	PASS	COMP	PCT	YD	AVG(LG)	TD	INT	SK	YD	QBR	KPR	OTD	PTS	TAY
1959	LARm	10	—	—	—	—	1	6	6.0(6)	0	—	—	—	—	—	—	—	—	—	—	kp	—	0	44
1960	LARm	12(RS)	16	63	3.9(33)	0	17	275	16.2(58)	2	—	—	—	—	—	—	—	—	—	—	i	—	12	206
1964	Pit	14(SE/ls)	2	7	3.5(4)	0	17	334	19.6(49)	1	—	—	—	—	—	—	—	—	—	—	ki	—	6	240
1965	Pit	14(SE)	—	—	—	—	25	431	17.2(80)	1	—	—	—	—	—	—	—	—	—	—	p	—	6	205
NFL	11	137	18	70	3.9(33)	0	60	1046	17.4(80)	4	—	—	—	—	—	—	—	—	—	—	Pkpi	1	30	902

Thomas, Corey Corey, WR, 6´0˝/174 lbs; Duke; B6/6/1975 Wilson, NC **1998** Det 1 (0)

Thomas, Cornell Cornell, DE, 6´3˝/250 lbs; West Georgia; B11/11/1972 Livingston, NJ **1994**†SD 0 (0)

Thomas, Curtland Curtland Parrish, WR, 6´0˝/185 lbs; Missouri; 1984: Was, rnd 12; B2/19/1962 St. Louis, MO

YEAR	TEAM	G(GS, POS)	RUSH	YD	AVG(LG)	TD	REC	YD	AVG(LG)	TD	PASS	COMP	PCT	YD	AVG(LG)	TD	INT	SK	YD	QBR	KPR	OTD	PTS	TAY
1987	NO	2(0)	—	—	—	—	1	14	14.0(14)	0	—	—	—	—	—	—	—	—	—	—	k	—	0	3

Thomas, Damon Damon Andrew, WR, 6´2˝/215 lbs; Wayne State (NE); B12/15/1970 Clovis, CA

YEAR	TEAM	G(GS, POS)	RUSH	YD	AVG(LG)	TD	REC	YD	AVG(LG)	TD	PASS	COMP	PCT	YD	AVG(LG)	TD	INT	SK	YD	QBR	KPR	OTD	PTS	TAY
1994	Buf	3(0)	—	—	—	—	2	31	15.5(17)	0	—	—	—	—	—	—	—	—	—	—	—	—	0	16
1995	Buf	14(0)	—	—	—	—	1	18	18.0(18)	0	—	—	—	—	—	—	—	—	—	—	p	—	0	4
NFL	2	17(0)	—	—	—	—	3	49	16.3(18)	0	—	—	—	—	—	—	—	—	—	—	p	—	0	20

Thomas, Dave Dave Garfield, DB, 6´3˝/213 lbs; Tennessee; 1993: Dal, rnd 8; B8/25/1968 Miami, FL **1993**†Dal 12 (0) **1994**†Dal 16 (0) **1995** Jax 16 (2) **1996** Jax 9 (5, lcb) **1997**†Jax 16 (15, LCB/rcb) **1998**†Jax 14 (13, RCB) **1999**†Jax 15 (0) **2000**†NYG 16 (16, LCB) **2001** NYG 16 (2) **NFL** 130 (53) [9 yrs]

Thomas, Dee Derward Heith, DB, 5´10˝/176 lbs; Nicholls State; 1990: Hou, rnd 10; B11/7/1967 Morgan City, LA **1990** Hou 6 (0)

Thomas, Derrick Derrick Vincent, LB, 6´3˝/243 lbs; Alabama; 1989: KC, rnd 1; B1/1/1967 Miami, FL, D2/8/2000 Kansas City, MO **[S]** **1989** KC★16 (16, ROLB) **1990**†KC★15 (15, ROLB) **1991**†KC★16 (15, ROLB) **1992**†KC★16 (16, RLB/rolb) **1993**†KC★16 (15, ROLB) **1994**†KC★16 (15, RLB) **1995**†KC★15 (15, ROLB) **1996** KC★16 (14, LOLB) **1997**†KC✧12 (10, LOLB) **1998** KC 15 (10, LOLB) **1999** KC 16 (16, LLB) **NFL** 169 (157) [11 yrs]

Thomas, Derrick Derrick LeRoy, RB, 6´0˝/232 lbs; Arkansas; B3/8/1965 Paducah, KY

YEAR	TEAM	G(GS, POS)	RUSH	YD	AVG(LG)	TD	REC	YD	AVG(LG)	TD	PASS	COMP	PCT	YD	AVG(LG)	TD	INT	SK	YD	QBR	KPR	OTD	PTS	TAY
1987	TB	1(0)	1	2	2.0(2)	0	—	—	—	—	—	—	—	—	—	—	—	—	—	—	—	—	0	2

YEAR	TEAM	G (GS, POS)	RUSH	YD	AVG(LG)	TD	REC	YD	AVG(LG)	TD	PASS	COMP	PCT	YD	AVG(LG)	TD	INT	SK	YD	QBR	KPR	OTD	PTS	TAY

THOMAS, DONNIE Donnie Murrice, LB, 6´2˝/245 lbs; Indiana; 1976: NE, rnd 11; B3/12/1953 Michigan City, IN **1976**†NE 3 (1)

THOMAS, DONTARRIOUS Dontarrious Donta, LB, 6´2˝/241 lbs; Auburn; 2004: Min, rnd 2; B9/2/1980 Perry, AL **2004**†Min 16 (5, rlb) **2005** Min 14 (2) **NFL** 30 (7) [2 yrs]

THOMAS, DOUG Douglas Sandy, WR, 5´10˝/178 lbs; Clemson; 1991: Sea, rnd 2; B9/18/1969 Rockingham, NC

1991	Sea	11(0)	—	—	—	—	3	27	9.0(11)	0	—	—	—	—	—	—	—	—	—	—	—	—	0	14
1992	Sea	12(4)	3	7	2.3(8)	0	8	85	10.6(19)	0	—	—	—	—	—	—	—	—	—	—	k	—	0	54
1993	Sea	16(0)	1	4	4.0(4)	0	11	95	8.6(20)	0	—	—	—	—	—	—	—	—	—	—	—	—	0	52
NFL	3	39(4)	4	11	2.8(8)	0	22	207	9.4(20)	0	—	—	—	—	—	—	—	—	—	—	k	—	0	119

THOMAS, DUANE Duane Julius, RB, 6´1˝/220 lbs; West Texas A&M; 1970: Dal, rnd 1; B6/21/1947 Dallas, TX

1970	†Dal	14(8, rb/fb)	151	803	**5.3(47)**	5	10	73	7.3(17)	0	—	—	—	—	—	—	—	—	—	—	k	—	30	1021
1971	†Dal	11(9, RB)	175	793	4.5(56)	11	13	153	11.8(34)	2	1	0	0	0	0.0	0	—	0	0	0	k	—	78	1024
1973	Was	13	32	95	3.0(13)	0	5	40	8.0(13)	0	—	—	—	—	—	—	—	—	—	—	—	—	0	115
1974	Was	11(3)	95	347	3.7(66)	5	10	31	3.1(9)	1	—	—	—	—	—	—	—	—	—	—	—	—	36	418
NFL	4	49(20)	453	2038	4.5(66)	21	38	297	7.8(34)	3	1	0	0	0	0.0	0	—	0	0	0	k	—	144	2577

THOMAS, EARL Earl Lewis, WR-TE, 6´3˝/224 lbs; Houston; 1971: Chi, rnd 6; B10/4/1948 Greenville, TX

1971	ChiB	11	—	—	—	—	3	40	13.3(28)	0	—	—	—	—	—	—	—	—	—	—	—	—	0	20
1972	ChiB	14(TE)	5	13	2.6(8)	0	20	365	18.3(44)	3	—	—	—	—	—	—	—	—	—	—	—	1	24	303
1973	ChiB	14(WR)	1	5	5.0(5)	0	24	343	14.3(38)	4	1	0	0	0.0		0	—	0	1	—	—	—	24	169
1974	†SL	14(11, WR)	—	—	—	—	34	513	15.1(52)	5	—	—	—	—	—	—	—	—	—	—	—	—	30	282
1975	SL	11(WR)	—	—	—	—	21	375	17.9(80)	2	—	—	—	—	—	—	—	—	—	—	—	—	12	198
1976	Hou	7	—	—	—	—	4	15	3.8(14)	0	—	—	—	—	—	—	—	—	—	—	—	—	0	8
NFL	6	71(11)	6	18	3.0(8)	0	106	1651	15.6(80)	14	1	0	0	0.0		0	—	0	1	—	—	1	90	978

THOMAS, EARLIE Early Bee, DB, 6´1˝/190 lbs; Colorado State; 1970: NYJ, rnd 11; B12/11/1945 Denton, TX **1970** NYJ 14 (RCB) **1971** NYJ☆13 (RCB) **1972** NYJ 14 (RCB) **1973** NYJ 12 (RCB) **1974** NYJ 8 **1975** Den 10 (6, rcb) **NFL** 71 (6) [6 yrs]

THOMAS, ED Edward Lee, TE, 6´3˝/240 lbs; Houston; B5/4/1966 New Orleans, LA **1990** TB 7 (0)

| 1991 | TB | 6(0) | — | — | — | — | 4 | 55 | 13.8(19) | 0 | — | — | — | — | — | — | — | — | — | — | — | — | 0 | 28 |
| NFL | 2 | 13(0) | — | — | — | — | 4 | 55 | 13.8(19) | 0 | — | — | — | — | — | — | — | — | — | — | — | — | 0 | 28 |

THOMAS, EDWARD Edward Tervin, LB, 6´0˝/235 lbs; Georgia Southern; B9/27/1974 Thomasville, GA **2000** SF 4 (0) **2000** Jax 4 (0) **2001** Jax 16 (4) **2002** Jax 4 (0) **NFL** 28 (4) [3 yrs]

THOMAS, EMMITT Emmitt Earl, DB, 6´2˝/192 lbs; Bishop; B6/3/1943 Angleton, TX **[I]** **1966**†KC-A 14 (3) **1967** KC-A 11 (6, lcb) **1968**†KC-A☆14 (LCB) **1969** KC-A☆14 (RCB) **1970** KC☆14 (RCB) **1971**†KC★14 (RCB) **1972** KC★14 (RCB) **1973** KC 14 (RCB) **1974** KC★14 (RCB) **1975** KC★14 (RCB) **1976** KC 14 (14, RCB) **1977** KC 14 (RCB) **1978** KC 16 (RCB) **NFL** 181 (23) [13 yrs]

THOMAS, ENID Enid Anthony, WB-BB-TB, 5´8˝/170 lbs; Slippery Rock; Pennsylvania; B1/28/1897 Clairton, PA, D10/2/1968 **1926** Har 7 (5)

THOMAS, ERIC Eric Jason, DB, 5´11˝/184 lbs; Tulane; 1987: Cin, rnd 2; B9/11/1964 Tucson, AZ **1987** Cin 12 (3) **1988**†Cin★16 (16, RCB) **1989** Cin 16 (15, RCB) **1990**†Cin 4 (2) **1991** Cin 16 (16, RCB) **1992** Cin 16 (16, RCB) **1993** NYJ 16 (16, LCB) **1994** NYJ 1 (0) **1995** Den 14 (0) **NFL** 111 (84) [9 yrs]

THOMAS, FRED Frederick L., DB, 5´9˝/184 lbs; Mississippi Valley State; Mississippi; Tennessee-Martin; 1996: Sea, rnd 2; B9/11/1973 Bruce, MS **1996** Sea 15 (0) **1997** Sea 16 (3) **1998** Sea 15 (2) **1999** Sea 1 (0) **2000**†NO 11 (0) **2001** NO 16 (16, RCB) **2002** NO 15 (14, RCB) **2003** NO 16 (14, RCB) **2004** NO 15 (7, rcb) **2005** NO 16 (11, RCB) **NFL** 136 (67) [10 yrs]

THOMAS, GARTH Garth C., G, 6´3˝/260 lbs; Washington; B11/26/1963 Bellevue, WA **1987** Sea 1 (1)

THOMAS, GENE Eugene Warren, RB, 6´1˝/210 lbs; Florida A&M; B9/1/1942 Barberton, OH

1966	†KC-A	14	7	53	7.6(28)	1	—	—	—	—	—	—	—	—	—	—	—	—	—	—	k	—	6	80
1967	KC-A	14	35	133	3.8(19)	1	13	99	7.6(27)	2	—	—	—	—	—	—	—	—	—	—	k	—	18	169
1968	Bos-A	9	88	215	2.4(25)	2	10	85	8.5(32)	0	—	—	—	—	—	—	—	—	—	—	k	—	12	285
NFL	3	37	130	401	3.1(28)	4	23	184	8.0(32)	2	—	—	—	—	—	—	—	—	—	—	k	—	36	533

THOMAS, GEORGE George Carroll, HB-DB, 6´1˝/183 lbs; Oklahoma; 1950: Was, rnd 1; B3/4/1928 Fairland, OK, D5/23/1989 Scottsdale, AL

1950	Was	12	20	41	2.1(18)	0	2	7	3.5(4)	0	—	—	—	—	—	—	—	—	—	—	kp	—	0	94
1951	Was	12	42	130	3.1(17)	0	7	193	27.6(53)	2	—	—	—	—	—	—	—	—	—	—	k	—	12	237
1952	NYG	7	6	18	3.0(11)	0	1	8	8.0(8)	0	—	—	—	—	—	—	—	—	—	—	—	—	0	22
NFL	3	31	68	189	2.8(18)	0	10	208	20.8(53)	2	—	—	—	—	—	—	—	—	—	—	kp	—	12	352

THOMAS, GEORGE George Ray, WR, 5´9˝/169 lbs; UNLV; 1988: Atl, rnd 6; B7/11/1964 Riverside, CA

1989	Atl	16(0)	—	—	—	—	4	46	11.5(16)	0	—	—	—	—	—	—	—	—	—	—	k	—	0	60
1990	Atl	13(2)	—	—	—	—	18	383	21.3(72)	1	—	—	—	—	—	—	—	—	—	—	—	—	6	197
1991	†Atl	12(6, WR)	—	—	—	—	28	365	13.0(37)	2	—	—	—	—	—	—	—	—	—	—	—	—	12	193
1992	Atl	5(1)	—	—	—	—	6	54	9.0(18)	0	—	—	—	—	—	—	—	—	—	—	—	—	0	27
1992	TB	5(1)	—	—	—	—	—	—	—	—	—	—	—	—	—	—	—	—	—	—	k	—	0	27
NFL	4	51(10)	—	—	—	—	56	848	15.1(72)	3	—	—	—	—	—	—	—	—	—	—	k	—	18	503

THOMAS, HENRY Henry Lee, DT-NT, 6´2˝/277 lbs; LSU; 1987: Min, rnd 3; B1/12/1965 Houston, TX **[S]** **1987**†Min 12 (12, LDT) **1988**†Min 15 (15, LDT) **1989**†Min 14 (14, LDT) **1990** Min 16 (16, LDT) **1991** Min✩16 (15, RDT) **1992**†Min★16 (16, LDT) **1993**†Min☆13 (13, LDT) **1994**†Min☆16 (16, LDT) **1995**†Det 16 (16, LDT) **1996** Det 15 (15, LDT) **1997**†NE 16 (16, RDT) **1998**†NE 16 (15, RDT) **1999** NE 16 (16, RDT) **2000** NE 16 (5, nt) **NFL** 213 (200) [14 yrs]

THOMAS, HENRY Henry Louis, G, 6´2˝/275 lbs; Southwest Texas State; B2/12/1964 Richmond, TX **1987** NO 3 (2)

THOMAS, HOLLIS Hollis, DT, 6´0˝/306 lbs; Northern Illinois; B1/10/1974 Abilene, TX **1996**†Phi 16 (5, ldt) **1997** Phi 16 (16, LDT) **1998** Phi 12 (12, LDT) **1999** Phi 16 (16, LDT) **2000**†Phi 16 (16, LDT) **2001** Phi 14 (14, RDT) **2003** Phi 7 (2) **2005** Phi 16 (16, LDT) **NFL** 126 (95) [9 yrs]

THOMAS, IKE Isaac, DB-WR, 6´2˝/193 lbs; Bishop; 1971: Dal, rnd 2; B11/4/1947 Newton, LA **1971**†Dal 7 **1972**†GB 12 **1973** GB 13 **1975** Buf 5 **NFL** 37 [4 yrs]

THOMAS, J.T. James, DB, 6´2˝/196 lbs; Florida State; 1973: Pit, rnd 1; B4/22/1951 Macon, GA **[I]** **1973**†Pit 14 **1974**†Pit 14 (14, LCB) **1975**†Pit 14 (14, LCB) **1976**†Pit☆14 (14, LCB) **1977** Pit 14 (14, LCB) **1979**†Pit 14 (13, FS) **1980** Pit 16 (3) **1981** Pit 16 (16, FS) **1982** Den 9 (0) **NFL** 125 (88) [9 yrs]

THOMAS, J.T. Johnny le'Mon, WR, 5´10˝/180 lbs; Arizona State; 1995: SL, rnd 7; B7/11/1971 San Bernardino, CA

1995	SL	15(1)	—	—	—	—	5	42	8.4(12)	0	—	—	—	—	—	—	—	—	—	—	k	—	0	354
1996	SL	16(1)	1	-1	-1.0(-1)	0	7	46	6.6(11)	0	—	—	—	—	—	—	—	—	—	—	k	—	0	215
1997	SL	4(0)	—	—	—	—	2	25	12.5(16)	0	—	—	—	—	—	—	—	—	—	—	k	—	0	35
1998	SL	16(1)	—	—	—	—	20	287	14.4(42)	0	—	—	—	—	—	—	—	—	—	—	k	—	0	163
NFL	4	51(3)	1	-1	-1.0(-1)	0	34	400	11.8(42)	0	—	—	—	—	—	—	—	—	—	—	k	—	0	766

THOMAS, JASON Jason, G, 6´3˝/300 lbs; South Carolina; Hampton; 2000: SD, rnd 7; B7/10/1977 Savannah, GA **2002** Bal 13 (0) **2003** Bal 1 (0) **NFL** 14 (0) [2 yrs]

THOMAS, JESSE Jesse LeRoy, DB, 5´10˝/180 lbs; Michigan State; 1951: NYY, rnd 10; B5/23/1928 Guthrie, OK **1955** Bal 12 (DB) **1956** Bal 11 (DB) **1957** Bal 10 **1960** LAC-A 3 **NFL** 36 [4 yrs]

THOMAS, JEWERL Jewerl, RB, 5´10˝/230 lbs; UCLA; San Jose State; 1980: LA, rnd 3; B9/10/1957 Hanford, CA

1980	†LARm	16(2)	65	427	6.6(61)	2	5	30	6.0(11)	0	—	—	—	—	—	—	—	—	—	—	k	1	18	453
1981	LARm	15(1)	34	118	3.5(40)	0	5	37	7.4(13)	0	—	—	—	—	—	—	—	—	—	—	k	—	0	137
1982	LARm	8(0)	16	80	5.0(11)	0	8	49	6.1(11)	0	—	—	—	—	—	—	—	—	—	—	—	—	0	105
1983	KC	10(1)	44	115	2.6(11)	0	10	51	5.1(9)	0	2	1	50.0	18	9.0(18)	1	1	—	—	—	—	—	0	115
1984	SD	7(0)	14	43	3.1(9)	2	—	—	—	—	—	—	—	—	—	—	—	—	—	—	—	—	12	63
NFL	5	56(4)	173	783	4.5(61)	4	28	167	6.0(13)	0	2	1	50.0	18	9.0(18)	1	1	—	—	—	k	1	30	872

THOMAS, JIM James F., G, 5´11˝/200 lbs; Oklahoma; 1939: ChiC, rnd 12; B5/6/1917, D6/1981 Florence, SC **1939** ChiC 5 (1) **1940** ChiC 8 (0) **NFL** 13 (1) [2 yrs]

THOMAS, JIMMY James, RB-WR, 6´2˝/214 lbs; Texas-Arlington; 1969: SF, rnd 6; B8/17/1947 Greenville, TX

1969	SF	14	23	190	8.3(75)	1	18	364	20.2(75)	5	—	—	—	—	—	—	—	—	—	—	—	—	36	407
1970	†SF	14	31	89	2.9(14)	0	12	221	18.4(61)	3	—	—	—	—	—	—	—	—	—	—	k	—	18	302
1971	†SF	10	3	36	12.0(25)	1	3	33	11.0(14)	0	—	—	—	—	—	—	—	—	—	—	—	—	6	63

YEAR	TEAM	G (GS, POS)	RUSH	YD	AVG (LG)	TD	REC	YD	AVG (LG)	TD	PASS	COMP	PCT	YD	AVG (LG)	TD	INT	SK	YD	QBR	KPR	OTD	PTS	TAY
1972	†SF	14	52	250	4.8(22)	1	15	148	9.9(29)	0	—	—	—	—	—	—	—	—	—	—	—	—	6	334
1973	SF	11	56	259	4.6(16)	1	19	157	8.3(66)	0	—	—	—	—	—	—	—	—	—	—	k	—	6	354
NFL	5	63	165	824	5.0(75)	4	67	923	13.8(75)	8	—	—	—	—	—	—	—	—	—	—	k	—	72	1459

THOMAS, JOE Joseph Earl, WR, 5´11˝/175 lbs; Mississippi Valley State; 1986: Den, rnd 9; B3/25/1963 Lafayette, LA **1987** NO 1 (0)

THOMAS, JOEY Joseph, DB, 6´0˝/195 lbs; Washington; Montana State; 2004: GB, rnd 3; B8/29/1980 Seattle, WA **2004**†GB 14 (0) **2005** GB 6 (1) **2005** NO 5 (0) **NFL** 25 (1) [2 yrs]

THOMAS, JOHN John Webster, aka John Webster, FB, 6´1˝/188 lbs; Jamestown; Chicago; B2/13/1900 Ochyeyedan, IA, D8/19/1977 Woodstock, IL **1924** Rac 2 (1) **1925** Pro 1 (0) **NFL** 3 (1) [2 yrs]

THOMAS, JOHN John Louis, G-T-LB, 6´4˝/246 lbs; Pacific; 1957: SF, rnd 23; B1/25/1935 Tyler, TX **1958** SF 12 (lt) **1959** SF 12 (LT) **1960** SF 9 (LT) **1961** SF 14 (12, LT) **1962** SF 14 (13, MLB/lt) **1963** SF 14 (12, LG) **1964** SF 14 (14, LG) **1965** SF 14 (14, LG) **1966** SF★14 (14, LG) **1967** SF 5 (5, lg) **NFL** 122 (84) [10 yrs]

THOMAS, JOHN John Henry, T, 6´4˝/280 lbs; Toledo; B3/6/1964 Cincinnati, OH **1987** NYJ 3 (3)

THOMAS, JOHNNY Johnny, DB, 5´9˝/188 lbs; Baylor; 1987: Was, rnd 7; B8/3/1964 Houston, TX **1988** Was 4 (0) **1989** SD 13 (0) **1990** Was 4 (0) **1992**†Was 16 (0) **1993** Was 16 (0) **1994** Was 16 (0) **1995** Cle 16 (0) **1996**†Phi 9 (0) **NFL** 94 (0) [8 yrs]

THOMAS, JOSH Josh Lloyd, DE, 6´5˝/271 lbs; Syracuse; B6/26/1981 Plymouth, MA **2004** Ind 11 (0) **2005**†Ind 12 (2) **NFL** 23 (2) [2 yrs]

THOMAS, JUQUA Juqua Demail, DE, 6´2˝/250 lbs; Oklahoma State; B5/15/1978 Houston, TX **2001** Ten 7 (0) **2002** Ten 9 (0) **2003**†Ten 15 (0) **2004** Ten 10 (0) **2005** Phi 16 (1) **NFL** 57 (1) [5 yrs]

THOMAS, KELLY Kelly Scott, T, 6´6˝/270 lbs; USC; 1983: TB, rnd 4; B9/9/1960 Lynwood, CA **1983** TB 14 (12, RT) **1984** TB 10 (2) **1987** LARm 3 (3) **NFL** 27 (17) [3 yrs]

THOMAS, KEN Kenneth Ray, RB, 5´9˝/211 lbs; San Jose State; 1983: KC, rnd 7; B2/11/1960 Hanford, CA, D11/13/2002 Independence, MO

YEAR	TEAM	G (GS, POS)	RUSH	YD	AVG (LG)	TD	REC	YD	AVG (LG)	TD	PASS	COMP	PCT	YD	AVG (LG)	TD	INT	SK	YD	QBR	KPR	OTD	PTS	TAY
1983	KC	14(0)	15	55	3.7(28)	0	28	236	8.4(25)	1	—	—	—	—	—	—	—	—	—	—	k	—	6	169

THOMAS, KEVIN Kevin Alan, C, 6´2˝/268 lbs; Arizona State; B7/27/1964 Tucson, AZ **1988** TB 10 (0)

THOMAS, KEVIN Marvin Kevin, DB, 6´0˝/182 lbs; UNLV; 2002: Buf, rnd 6; B7/28/1978 Phoenix, AZ **2002** Buf 6 (1) **2003** Buf 16 (1)

YEAR	TEAM	G (GS, POS)	RUSH	YD	AVG (LG)	TD	REC	YD	AVG (LG)	TD	PASS	COMP	PCT	YD	AVG (LG)	TD	INT	SK	YD	QBR	KPR	OTD	PTS	TAY
2004	Buf	16(1)	—	—	—	—	1	24	24.0(24)	0	—	—	—	—	—	—	—	—	—	—	S	—	0	12
NFL	3	38(3)	—	—	—	—	1	24	24.0(24)	0	—	—	—	—	—	—	—	—	—	—	iS	—	0	38

THOMAS, KIWAUKEE Kiwaukee Sanchez, DB, 5´11˝/192 lbs; Georgia Southern; 2000: Jax, rnd 5; B6/19/1977 Warner Robins, GA **2000** Jax 16 (3) **2001** Jax 16 (5, lcb) **2002** Jax 16 (0) **2003** Jax 11 (1) **2004** Jax 16 (2) **2005** Mia 10 (0) **NFL** 85 (11) [6 yrs]

THOMAS, LAMAR Lamar Nathaniel, WR, 6´1˝/175 lbs; Miami (FL); 1993: TB, rnd 3; B2/12/1970 Ocala, FL

YEAR	TEAM	G (GS, POS)	RUSH	YD	AVG (LG)	TD	REC	YD	AVG (LG)	TD	PASS	COMP	PCT	YD	AVG (LG)	TD	INT	SK	YD	QBR	KPR	OTD	PTS	TAY
1993	TB	14(2)	—	—	—	—	8	186	23.3(62)	2	—	—	—	—	—	—	—	—	—	—	—	—	12	103
1994	TB	11(0)	—	—	—	—	7	94	13.4(27)	0	—	—	—	—	—	—	—	—	—	—	—	—	0	47
1995	TB	11(0)	1	5	5.0(5)	0	10	107	10.7(24)	0	—	—	—	—	—	—	—	—	—	—	—	—	0	59
1996	Mia	9(3)	—	—	—	—	10	166	16.6(34)	1	—	—	—	—	—	—	—	—	—	—	—	—	6	88
1997	†Mia	12(6, WR)	—	—	—	—	28	402	14.4(26)	2	—	—	—	—	—	—	—	—	—	—	—	—	12	211
1998	†Mia	16(2)	—	—	—	—	43	603	14.0(56)	5	—	—	—	—	—	—	—	—	—	—	—	—	30	327
NFL	6	73(13)	1	5	5.0(5)	0	106	1558	14.7(62)	10	—	—	—	—	—	—	—	—	—	—	—	—	60	834

THOMAS, LAVALE Lavale Alvin, RB, 6´0˝/205 lbs; Fresno State; B12/12/1963 Los Angeles, CA **1988** GB 1 (0)

YEAR	TEAM	G (GS, POS)	RUSH	YD	AVG (LG)	TD	REC	YD	AVG (LG)	TD	PASS	COMP	PCT	YD	AVG (LG)	TD	INT	SK	YD	QBR	KPR	OTD	PTS	TAY
1987	GB	1(1)	5	19	3.8(5)	0	2	52	26.0(30)	1	—	—	—	—	—	—	—	—	—	—	—	—	6	50
NFL	2	2(1)	5	19	3.8(5)	0	2	52	26.0(30)	1	—	—	—	—	—	—	—	—	—	—	—	—	6	50

THOMAS, LEE Lee Edward, DE, 6´5˝/246 lbs; Wiley; Jackson State; B3/12/1946 Karnack, TX **1971** SD 9 **1972** SD 14 **1973** Cin 9 **NFL** 32 [3 yrs]

THOMAS, LYNN Ronald Lynn, DB, 5´11˝/181 lbs; Pittsburgh; 1981: SF, rnd 5; B7/9/1959 Pascagoula, MS **1981**†SF 15 (0) **1982** SF 9 (1) **NFL** 24 (1) [2 yrs]

THOMAS, MARK Mark Andrew, DE, 6´5˝/272 lbs; North Carolina State; 1992: SF, rnd 4; B5/6/1969 Lilburn, GA **1993** SF 11 (1) **1994** SF 9 (0) **1995** Car 10 (0) **1996**†Car 12 (0) **1997** ChiB 16 (7, lde) **1998** ChiB 10 (4) **1998** Ind 4 (1) **1999**†Ind 15 (2) **2000**†Ind 14 (1) **2001** Ind 12 (0) **NFL** 113 (16) [9 yrs]

THOMAS, MARK Mark David, TE, 6´4˝/252 lbs; North Carolina State; B4/26/1976 Kinston, NC **1999** NYG 2 (0)

THOMAS, MARVIN Marvin, DE, 6´5˝/264 lbs; Memphis; 1997: Chi, rnd 7; B10/19/1973 Bay Minette, AL **1998** Det 4 (0)

THOMAS, MIKE Malcolm, RB, 5´11˝/190 lbs; Oklahoma; UNLV; 1975: Was, rnd 5; B7/17/1953 Greenville, TX

YEAR	TEAM	G (GS, POS)	RUSH	YD	AVG (LG)	TD	REC	YD	AVG (LG)	TD	PASS	COMP	PCT	YD	AVG (LG)	TD	INT	SK	YD	QBR	KPR	OTD	PTS	TAY
1975	Was	14(10, RB)	235	919	3.9(34)	4	40	483	12.1(33)	3	—	—	—	—	—	—	—	—	—	—	—	—	42	1216
1976	†Was★	13(12, RB)	254	1101	4.3(28)	5	28	290	10.4(34)	4	0	0	0.0	0	0.0	0	0	1	6	—	—	—	54	1316
1977	Was	13(13, RB)	228	806	3.5(31)	3	28	245	8.8(25)	2	—	—	—	—	—	—	—	—	—	—	—	—	30	969
1978	Was	13(13, RB)	161	533	3.3(26)	3	35	387	11.1(35)	2	—	—	—	—	—	—	—	—	—	—	—	—	30	767
1979	†SD	14(9, RB)	91	353	3.9(21)	1	32	388	12.1(32)	0	1	1	100.0	18	18.0(18)	0	0	—	—	—	—	—	6	566
1980	†SD	10(5, rb)	118	484	4.1(18)	3	29	218	7.5(27)	0	2	0	0.0	0	0.0	0	1	—	—	—	—	—	18	583
NFL	6	77(62)	1087	4196	3.9(34)	19	192	2011	10.5(35)	11	3	1	33.3	18	6.0(18)	0	1	1	6	—	—	—	180	5416

THOMAS, NORRIS Norris Lee, DB, 6´0˝/180 lbs; Southern Mississippi; 1976: Mia, rnd 9; B5/3/1954 Inverness, MS **1977** Mia 14 (14, LCB) **1978**†Mia 16 (16, LCB) **1979**†Mia 16 (16, LCB) **1980** TB 16 (1) **1981**†TB 16 (15, LCB) **1982**†TB 9 (9, LCB) **1983** TB 10 (0) **1984** TB 15 (0) **NFL** 112 (71) [8 yrs]

THOMAS, ORLANDO Orlando Paul, DB, 6´1˝/215 lbs; Louisiana-Lafayette; 1995: Min, rnd 2; B10/21/1972 Crowley, LA **[I]** **1995** Min☆16 (11, FS) **1996**†Min 16 (16, FS) **1997**†Min 15 (13, FS) **1998**†Min 16 (16, FS) **1999** Min 13 (12, FS) **2000**†Min 9 (9, FS) **2001** Min 13 (10, FS) **NFL** 98 (87) [7 yrs]

THOMAS, PAT Patrick Shane, DB, 5´9˝/183 lbs; Texas A&M; 1976: LA, rnd 2; B9/1/1954 Plano, TX **[I]** **1976**†LARm 14 **1977**†LARm 14 (12, LCB) **1978**†LARm★16 (16, LCB) **1979**†LARm 8 (7, rcb) **1980** LARm★14 (14, LCB) **1981** LARm 12 (9, LCB) **1982** LARm 9 (9, LCB) **NFL** 87 (67) [7 yrs]

THOMAS, PAT Pat, LB, 6´2˝/230 lbs; North Carolina State; 2005: Jax, rnd 6; B1/26/1983 Miami, FL **2005**†Jax 9 (0)

THOMAS, RALPH Ralph Werner, E-DE, 5´11˝/190 lbs; San Francisco; B12/6/1927 Kenosha, WI **1952** ChiC 11 **1956** Was 12

YEAR	TEAM	G (GS, POS)	RUSH	YD	AVG (LG)	TD	REC	YD	AVG (LG)	TD	PASS	COMP	PCT	YD	AVG (LG)	TD	INT	SK	YD	QBR	KPR	OTD	PTS	TAY
1955	Was	12(RE)	—	—	—	—	9	105	11.7(25)	2	—	—	—	—	—	—	—	—	—	—	—	1	18	63
NFL	3	35	—	—	—	—	9	105	11.7(25)	2	—	—	—	—	—	—	—	—	—	—	k	1	18	48

THOMAS, RANDY Randy, G, 6´5˝/306 lbs; Mississippi State; 1999: NYJ, rnd 2; B1/19/1976 East Point, GA **1999** NYJ 16 (16, RG) **2000** NYJ 16 (16, RG) **2001**†NYJ 13 (13, RG) **2002**†NYJ 16 (16, RG) **2003** Was 16 (16, RG) **2004** Was 15 (15, RG) **2005** Was 14 (14, RG) **NFL** 106 (106) [7 yrs]

THOMAS, RATCLIFF Ratcliff, LB, 6´1˝/238 lbs; Maryland; B1/2/1974 Alexandria, VA **1998** Ind 5 (0) **1999**†Ind 16 (0) **2000**†Ind 12 (0) **NFL** 33 (0) [3 yrs]

THOMAS, REX Rolla, WB-FB-TB-HB, 5´9˝/174 lbs; Tulsa; St. John's (NY); B1/14/1901 Weatherford, OK, deceased **[K]** **1926** Bkn 10 (10, WB), 25 **1927** Cle 13 (9, WB), 18 **1928** Det 10 (5, wb), 12 **1930** Bkn 6 (3), 31 **1931** Bkn 8 (1), 6 **NFL** 47 (28), 92 [5 yrs]

THOMAS, RICKY Ricky L., DB, 6´0˝/185 lbs; Alabama; B3/29/1965 Eglin AFB, FL **1987** Sea 1 (1)

THOMAS, ROBB Robb Douglass, WR, 5´11˝/175 lbs; Oregon State; 1989: KC, rnd 6; B3/29/1966 Portland, OR

YEAR	TEAM	G (GS, POS)	RUSH	YD	AVG (LG)	TD	REC	YD	AVG (LG)	TD	PASS	COMP	PCT	YD	AVG (LG)	TD	INT	SK	YD	QBR	KPR	OTD	PTS	TAY
1989	KC	8(1)	—	—	—	—	8	58	7.3(12)	2	—	—	—	—	—	—	—	—	—	—	—	—	12	39
1990	†KC	16(12, WR)	—	—	—	—	41	545	13.3(47)	4	—	—	—	—	—	—	—	—	—	—	—	—	24	293
1991	†KC	15(12, WR)	—	—	—	—	43	495	11.5(39)	1	—	—	—	—	—	—	—	—	—	—	—	—	6	253
1992	Sea	15(0)	1	-1	-1.0(-1)	0	11	136	12.4(31)	0	—	—	—	—	—	—	—	—	—	—	—	—	0	67
1993	Sea	16(0)	—	—	—	—	7	67	9.6(16)	0	—	—	—	—	—	—	—	—	—	—	—	—	0	34
1994	Sea	16(1)	—	—	—	—	4	70	17.5(35)	0	—	—	—	—	—	—	—	—	—	—	—	—	0	35
1995	Sea	15(2)	—	—	—	—	12	239	19.9(50)	1	—	—	—	—	—	—	—	—	—	—	—	—	6	125
1996	TB	12(8, WR)	—	—	—	—	33	427	12.9(31)	2	—	—	—	—	—	—	—	—	—	—	—	—	12	224
1997	†TB	16(1)	—	—	—	—	13	129	9.9(21)	0	—	—	—	—	—	—	—	—	—	—	—	—	0	65
1998	TB	7(0)	—	—	—	—	2	63	31.5(50)	1	—	—	—	—	—	—	—	—	—	—	—	—	6	37
NFL	10	136(37)	1	-1	-1.0(-1)	0	174	2229	12.8(50)	11	—	—	—	—	—	—	—	—	—	—	—	—	66	1169

THOMAS, ROBERT Robert Lee, FB-LB, 6´1˝/260 lbs; Henderson State; B12/1/1974 Little Rock, AR

YEAR	TEAM	G (GS, POS)	RUSH	YD	AVG (LG)	TD	REC	YD	AVG (LG)	TD	PASS	COMP	PCT	YD	AVG (LG)	TD	INT	SK	YD	QBR	KPR	OTD	PTS	TAY
1998	†Dal	16(0)	—	—	—	—	—	—	—	—	—	—	—	—	—	—	—	—	—	—	—	—	—	—
1999	†Dal	16(7, FB)	8	35	4.4(10)	0	10	64	6.4(13)	0	—	—	—	—	—	—	—	—	—	—	—	—	0	67
2000	Dal	16(15, FB)	15	51	3.4(9)	0	23	117	5.1(14)	2	—	—	—	—	—	—	—	—	—	—	—	—	12	120

YEAR	TEAM	G (GS, POS)	RUSH	YD	AVG (LG)	TD	REC	YD	AVG (LG)	TD	PASS	COMP	PCT	YD	AVG (LG)	TD	INT	SK	YD	QBR	KPR	OTD	PTS	TAY
2001	Dal	5(5, fb)	6	40	6.7(24)	0	5	19	3.8(6)	1	—	—	—	—	—	—	—	—	—	—	—	—	6	55
2002	Dal	15(9, FB)	10	31	3.1(14)	0	12	80	6.7(23)	0	—	—	—	—	—	—	—	—	—	—	—	—	0	71
NFL	5	68(36)	39	157	4.0(24)	0	50	280	5.6(23)	3	—	—	—	—	—	—	—	—	—	—	—	—	18	312

THOMAS, ROBERT Robert W., LB, 6´1˝/237 lbs; UCLA; 2002: SL, rnd 1; B7/17/1980 El Centro, CA **2002** SL 16 (10, LLB) **2003** SL 12 (9, MLB) **2004**†SL 14 (11, MLB) **2005** GB 10 (9, RLB) **NFL** 52 (39) [4 yrs]

THOMAS, RODELL Rodell, LB, 6´2˝/225 lbs; Alabama State; B8/2/1958 Quincy, FL **1981** Mia 3 (0) **1981** Sea 11 (1) **1982** Sea 8 (0) **1983**†Mia 16 (2) **1984** Mia 14 (1) **NFL** 52 (4) [4 yrs]

THOMAS, RODNEY Rodney Dejuane, RB, 5´10˝/210 lbs; Texas A&M; 1995: Hou, rnd 3; B3/30/1973 Trinity, TX

YEAR	TEAM	G (GS, POS)	RUSH	YD	AVG (LG)	TD	REC	YD	AVG (LG)	TD	PASS	COMP	PCT	YD	AVG (LG)	TD	INT	SK	YD	QBR	KPR	OTD	PTS	TAY
1995	Hou	16(10, RB)	251	947	3.8(74)	5	39	204	5.2(19)	2	—	—	—	—	—	—	—	—	—	—	k	—	44	1112
1996	Hou	16(0)	49	151	3.1(24)	1	13	128	9.8(33)	0	—	—	—	—	—	—	—	—	—	—	k	—	6	230
1997	Ten	16(1)	67	310	4.6(25)	3	14	111	7.9(22)	0	—	—	—	—	—	—	—	—	—	—	k	—	18	487
1998	Ten	11(0)	24	100	4.2(21)	2	6	55	9.2(20)	0	—	—	—	—	—	—	—	—	—	—	k	—	12	167
1999	†Ten	16(0)	43	164	3.8(22)	1	9	72	8.0(26)	0	—	—	—	—	—	—	—	—	—	—	—	—	6	210
2000	†Ten	16(0)	61	175	2.9(20)	0	8	35	4.4(9)	1	—	—	—	—	—	—	—	—	—	—	—	—	6	198
2001	Atl	12(0)	37	126	3.4(21)	0	2	26	13.0(15)	0	—	—	—	—	—	—	—	—	—	—	—	—	0	139
NFL	7	103(11)	532	1973	3.7(74)	12	91	631	6.9(33)	3	—	—	—	—	—	—	—	—	—	—	k	—	92	2542

THOMAS, RODNEY Rodney Lamar, DB, 5´10˝/190 lbs; Brigham Young; 1988: Mia, rnd 5; B12/21/1965 Los Angeles, CA **1988** Mia 12 (1) **1989** Mia 16 (2) **1990**†Mia 15 (0) **1991** LARm 3 (0) **NFL** 46 (3) [4 yrs]

THOMAS, RUSS John Russell, T, 6´3˝/237 lbs; Ohio State; 1946: Det, rnd 3; B7/24/1924 Griffithsville, WV, D3/19/1991 Naples, FL **1946** Det 11 (9, LT) **1947** Det☆12 (12, LT) **1948** Det 12 (5, LT) **1949** Det 9 (1) **NFL** 44 (27) [4 yrs]

THOMAS, SEAN Sean, DB, 5´11˝/190 lbs; TCU; 1985: Cin, rnd 3; B4/12/1962 Sacramento, CA **1985** Cin 5 (0) **1985** Atl 6 (0) **NFL** 11 (0) [1 yr]

THOMAS, SKIP Alonzo, DB, 6´1˝/205 lbs; USC; 1972: Oak, rnd 7; B2/7/1950 Higginsville, MO **1972**†Oak 14 **1973**†Oak 14 (3) **1974**†Oak 14 (14, LCB) **1975**†Oak 14 (14, LCB) **1976**†Oak 14 (LCB) **1977**†Oak 12 (12, LCB) **NFL** 82 (43) [6 yrs]

THOMAS, SLOAN Sloan Edward, WR, 6´2˝/200 lbs; Texas; 2004: Ten, rnd 7; B12/22/1981 Clarksville, TN **2005** Ten 1 (0)

THOMAS, SPEEDY Louis Timothy, WR-FL, 6´1˝/170 lbs; Utah; 1969: Cin, rnd 3; B4/13/1947 Houston, TX, D7/29/2003 Houston, TX

YEAR	TEAM	G (GS, POS)	RUSH	YD	AVG (LG)	TD	REC	YD	AVG (LG)	TD	PASS	COMP	PCT	YD	AVG (LG)	TD	INT	SK	YD	QBR	KPR	OTD	PTS	TAY
1969	Cin-A	14(FL)	4	16	4.0(16)	1	33	481	14.6(62)	3	—	—	—	—	—	—	—	—	—	—	p	—	24	277
1970	†Cin	14(WR)	2	7	3.5(13)	0	21	257	12.2(27)	2	—	—	—	—	—	—	—	—	—	—	p	—	12	146
1971	Cin	12(WR)	2	-1	-0.5(0)	0	22	327	14.9(**90**)	2	—	—	—	—	—	—	—	—	—	—	p	—	12	163
1972	Cin	11(WR)	—	—	—	—	17	171	10.1(18)	1	—	—	—	—	—	—	—	—	—	—	—	—	6	91
1973	NO	6	—	—	—	—	—	—	—	—	—	—	—	—	—	—	—	—	—	—	—	—	—	—
1974	NO	1	—	—	—	—	1	3	3.0(3)	0	—	—	—	—	—	—	—	—	—	—	—	—	0	2
NFL	6	58	8	22	2.8(16)	1	94	1239	13.2(90)	8	—	—	—	—	—	—	—	—	—	—	p	—	54	677

THOMAS, SPENCER Spencer Lee, DB, 6´2˝/185 lbs; Washburn; B3/9/1951 Kansas City, KS **1975** Was 14 (1) **1976** Bal 2 **NFL** 16 (1) [2 yrs]

THOMAS, STAN Stanley, T, 6´5˝/295 lbs; Texas; 1991: Chi, rnd 1; B10/28/1968 El Centro, CA **1991** ChiB 15 (7, lt) **1992** ChiB 11 (0) **1993**†Hou 14 (0) **1994** Hou 16 (0) **NFL** 56 (7) [4 yrs]

THOMAS, THURMAN Thurman Lee, RB, 5´10˝/198 lbs; Oklahoma State; 1988: Buf, rnd 2; B5/16/1966 Houston, TX

YEAR	TEAM	G (GS, POS)	RUSH	YD	AVG (LG)	TD	REC	YD	AVG (LG)	TD	PASS	COMP	PCT	YD	AVG (LG)	TD	INT	SK	YD	QBR	KPR	OTD	PTS	TAY
1988	†Buf	15(15, RB)	207	881	4.3(37)	2	18	208	11.6(34)	0	—	—	—	—	—	—	—	—	—	—	—	—	12	1005
1989	†Buf★	16(16, RB)	298	1244	4.2(38)	6	60	669	11.1(74)	6	—	—	—	—	—	—	—	—	—	—	—	—	72	1669
1990	†Buf★	16(16, RB)	271	**1297**	4.8(80)	11	49	532	10.9(63)	2	—	—	—	—	—	—	—	—	—	—	—	—	78	1683
1991	†Buf★	15(15, RB)	**288**	**1407**	4.9(33)	7	62	631	10.2(50)	5	—	—	—	—	—	—	—	—	—	—	—	—	72	**1818**
1992	†Buf★	16(16, RB)	312	1487	**4.8**(**44**)	9	58	626	10.8(43)	3	—	—	—	—	—	—	—	—	—	—	—	—	72	1905
1993	†Buf★	16(16, RB)	**355**	**1315**	3.7(27)	6	48	387	8.1(37)	0	1	0	0.0	0	0.0	0	0	—	—	—	—	—	36	1569
1994	Buf☆	15(15, RB)	287	1093	3.8(29)	7	50	349	7.0(28)	2	—	—	—	—	—	—	—	—	—	—	—	—	54	1348
1995	†Buf	14(14, RB)	267	1005	3.8(49)	6	26	220	8.5(60)	2	—	—	—	—	—	—	—	—	—	—	—	—	48	1185
1996	†Buf	15(15, RB)	281	1033	3.7(36)	8	26	254	9.8(69)	0	—	—	—	—	—	—	—	—	—	—	—	—	48	1240
1997	Buf	16(16, RB)	154	643	4.2(24)	1	30	208	6.9(30)	0	—	—	—	—	—	—	—	—	—	—	—	—	6	757
1998	†Buf	14(3)	93	381	4.1(17)	2	26	220	8.5(26)	1	—	—	—	—	—	—	—	—	—	—	—	—	18	516
1999	†Buf	5(3)	36	152	4.2(31)	0	3	37	12.3(23)	1	—	—	—	—	—	—	—	—	—	—	—	—	6	176
2000	Mia	9(0)	28	136	4.9(25)	0	16	117	7.3(15)	1	0	0	0.0	0	0.0	0	0	1	2	—	—	—	6	200
NFL	13	182(160)	2877	12074	4.2(80)	65	472	4458	9.4(74)	23	1	0	0.0	0	0.0	0	0	1	2	—	—	—	528	15068

THOMAS, TODD Todd Robin, C, 6´5˝/261 lbs; North Dakota; 1981: KC, rnd 5; B12/2/1959 Mankato, MN, D3/5/2000 Houston, TX **1981** KC 15 (0)

THOMAS, TRA William, T, 6´7˝/349 lbs; Florida State; 1998: Phi, rnd 1; B11/20/1974 DeLand, FL **1998** Phi 16 (16, LT) **1999** Phi 16 (15, LT) **2000**†Phi 16 (16, LT) **2001**†Phi✧15 (15, LT) **2002**†Phi★16 (16, LT) **2003**†Phi 15 (15, LT) **2004**†Phi★15 (15, LT) **2005** Phi 10 (10, LT) **NFL** 119 (118) [8 yrs]

THOMAS, TRE Carl Grady, DB, 6´2˝/216 lbs; Texas; B7/12/1975 Houston, TX **1999** NYG 2 (0)

THOMAS, VERN Vernon P., E, /155 lbs; none; B2/2/1898, IL, D4/1973 Richland, NY **1920** Roc 10 (0)

THOMAS, WHITEY William C., E, 5´10˝/180 lbs; Penn State; B8/17/1895, D8/1978 Lavallette, NJ **1924** Fra 14 (14, LE)

THOMAS, WILLIAM William Harrison, LB, 6´2˝/223 lbs; Texas A&M; 1991: Phi, rnd 4; B8/13/1968 Amarillo, TX **[I]** **1991** Phi 16 (7, rlb) **1992**†Phi 16 (15, RLB) **1993** Phi 16 (16, RLB) **1994** Phi 16 (16, RLB) **1995**†Phi★16 (16, RLB) **1996**†Phi✧16 (16, RLB) **1997** Phi 14 (14, RLB) **1998** Phi 16 (16, RLB) **1999** Phi 14 (13, RLB) **2000**†Oak 16 (16, LLB) **2001**†Oak 16 (15, LLB) **NFL** 172 (160) [11 yrs]

THOMAS, ZACH Zachary Dwayne, WR, 6´0˝/182 lbs; South Carolina State; B9/8/1960 Cocoa, FL **1984** Den 12 (0) **1984** TB 2 (0)

YEAR	TEAM	G (GS, POS)	RUSH	YD	AVG (LG)	TD	REC	YD	AVG (LG)	TD	PASS	COMP	PCT	YD	AVG (LG)	TD	INT	SK	YD	QBR	KPR	OTD	PTS	TAY
1983	†Den	16(0)	—	—	—	—	12	182	15.2(44)	0	—	—	—	—	—	—	—	—	—	—	kp	1	6	457
NFL	2	30(0)	—	—	—	—	12	182	15.2(44)	0	—	—	—	—	—	—	—	—	—	—	kp	1	6	558

THOMAS, ZACH Zachary Michael, LB, 5´11˝/230 lbs; Texas Tech; 1996: Mia, rnd 5; B9/1/1973 Pampa, TX **1996** Mia 16 (16, MLB) **1997**†Mia 15 (15, MLB) **1998**†Mia☆16 (16, MLB) **1999**†Mia★16 (16, MLB) **2000**†Mia✧11 (11, MLB) **2001**†Mia★15 (15, MLB) **2002** Mia★16 (16, MLB) **2003** Mia★15 (15, MLB) **2004** Mia 13 (13, MLB) **2005** Mia★14 (14, MLB) **NFL** 147 (147) [10 yrs]

THOMASELLI, RICH Richard J., RB, 6´1˝/199 lbs; West Virginia Wesleyan; B2/26/1957 Follansbee, WV **1981** Hou 12 (0)

YEAR	TEAM	G (GS, POS)	RUSH	YD	AVG (LG)	TD	REC	YD	AVG (LG)	TD	PASS	COMP	PCT	YD	AVG (LG)	TD	INT	SK	YD	QBR	KPR	OTD	PTS	TAY
1982	Hou	9(0)	—	—	—	—	1	8	8.0(8)	0	—	—	—	—	—	—	—	—	—	—	k	—	0	-4
NFL	2	21(0)	—	—	—	—	1	8	8.0(8)	0	—	—	—	—	—	—	—	—	—	—	—	—	0	4

THOMASON, BOBBY Robert Lee, QB, 6´1˝/196 lbs; VMI; 1949: LARm, rnd 1/NYY-A, rnd 1; B3/26/1928 Birmingham, AL

YEAR	TEAM	G (GS, POS)	RUSH	YD	AVG (LG)	TD	REC	YD	AVG (LG)	TD	PASS	COMP	PCT	YD	AVG (LG)	TD	INT	SK	YD	QBR	KPR	OTD	PTS	TAY
1949	LARm	6(0)	—	—	—	—	—	—	—	—	12	6	50.0	50	4.2(15)	0	1	—	—	—	—	—	0	-15
1951	GB	11(qb)	5	-5	-1.0(10)	0	—	—	—	—	221	125	**56.6**	1306	5.9(75)	11	9	—	—	73.5	—	—	0	343
1952	Phi	12(QB)	17	88	5.2(23)	0	—	—	—	—	212	95	44.8	1334	6.3(44)	8	9	—	—	60.5	—	—	0	435
1953	Phi★	12(QB)	9	23	2.6(20)	1	—	—	—	—	304	162	53.3	2462	8.1(62)	**21**	20	—	—	75.8	—	—	6	569
1954	Phi	10(qb)	10	45	4.5(19)	0	—	—	—	—	170	83	48.8	1242	7.3(63)	10	13	—	—	61.0	—	—	0	196
1955	Phi✧	10(qb)	17	29	1.7(20)	0	—	—	—	—	171	88	51.5	1337	7.8(63)	10	7	—	—	80.0	—	—	0	468
1956	Phi✧	12(QB)	21	48	2.3(19)	2	—	—	—	—	164	82	50.0	1119	6.8(52)	4	**21**	—	—	40.7	—	—	12	-193
1957	Phi	12(QB)	15	62	4.1(19)	3	—	—	—	—	92	46	50.0	630	6.8(67)	4	10	—	—	—	—	—	18	27
NFL	8	85	94	290	3.1(23)	6	—	—	—	—	1346	687	51.0	9480	7.0(75)	68	90	—	—	62.9	—	—	36	1830

THOMASON, JEFF Jeffery David, TE, 6´5˝/243 lbs; Oregon; B12/30/1969 San Diego, CA

YEAR	TEAM	G (GS, POS)	RUSH	YD	AVG (LG)	TD	REC	YD	AVG (LG)	TD	PASS	COMP	PCT	YD	AVG (LG)	TD	INT	SK	YD	QBR	KPR	OTD	PTS	TAY
1992	Cin	4(1)	—	—	—	—	2	14	7.0(10)	0	—	—	—	—	—	—	—	—	—	—	—	—	0	7
1993	Cin	3(0)	—	—	—	—	2	8	4.0(5)	0	—	—	—	—	—	—	—	—	—	—	—	—	0	4
1995	†GB	16(1)	—	—	—	—	3	32	10.7(15)	0	—	—	—	—	—	—	—	—	—	—	k	—	0	17
1996	†GB	16(1)	—	—	—	—	3	45	15.0(24)	0	—	—	—	—	—	—	—	—	—	—	k	—	0	28
1997	†GB	13(1)	—	—	—	—	9	115	12.8(27)	1	—	—	—	—	—	—	—	—	—	—	—	—	6	63
1998	GB	16(2)	—	—	—	—	9	89	9.9(22)	0	—	—	—	—	—	—	—	—	—	—	—	—	0	45
1999	GB	14(2)	—	—	—	—	14	140	10.0(22)	2	—	—	—	—	—	—	—	—	—	—	—	—	12	80

YEAR	TEAM	G (GS, POS)	RUSH	YD	AVG (LG)	TD	REC	YD	AVG (LG)	TD	PASS	COMP	PCT	YD	AVG (LG)	TD	INT	SK	YD	QBR	KPR	OTD	PTS	TAY
2000	†Phi	16(5, te)	—	—	—	—	10	46	4.6(11)	5	—	—	—	—	—	—	—	—	—	—	k	—	30	43
2001	†Phi	14(0)	—	—	—	—	5	33	6.6(11)	0	—	—	—	—	—	—	—	—	—	—	—	—	0	17
2002	†Phi	16(3)	—	—	—	—	10	128	12.8(24)	2	—	—	—	—	—	—	—	—	—	—	k	—	12	71
2004	†Phi	0(0)	—	—	—	—	—	—	—	—	—	—	—	—	—	—	—	—	—	—	—	—	0	0
NFL	11	128(16)	—	—	—	—	67	650	9.7(27)	10	—	—	—	—	—	—	—	—	—	—	k	—	60	373

Thomason, Jim James N., WB, 6´0˝/200 lbs; Texas A&M; 1941: Det, rnd 1; B10/4/1919, D6/2/1989 Lyons, TX

YEAR	TEAM	G (GS, POS)	RUSH	YD	AVG (LG)	TD	REC	YD	AVG (LG)	TD	PASS	COMP	PCT	YD	AVG (LG)	TD	INT	SK	YD	QBR	KPR	OTD	PTS	TAY
1945	Det	5(0)	9	9	1.0(10)	0	1	6	6.0(6)	0	—	—	—	—	—	—	—	—	—	—	—	—	0	12

Thomason, Stumpy John Griffin, B, 5´7˝/189 lbs; Georgia Tech; B2/24/1906 Atlanta, GA, D4/20/1989 Thomasville, NC **[K]**

YEAR	TEAM	G (GS, POS)	RUSH	YD	AVG (LG)	TD	REC	YD	AVG (LG)	TD	PASS	COMP	PCT	YD	AVG (LG)	TD	INT	SK	YD	QBR	KPR	OTD	PTS	TAY
1930	Bkn☆	6(6, WB)	—	—	—	—	—	—	—	—	—	—	—	—	—	—	—	—	—	—	—	—	—	—
1931	Bkn	13(13, TB)	—	—	—	—	—	—	—	—	—	—	—	—	—	—	—	—	—	—	—	—	—	—
1932	Bkn	10(4)	64	197	3.1	0	1	25	25.0(25)	1	10	1	10.0	4	-0.4(-4)	0	2	—	—	—	—	—	6	133
1933	Bkn	9(4)	45	158	3.5	0	—	—	—	—	—	—	—	—	—	—	—	—	—	—	—	—	0	158
1934	Bkn	8(3)	40	131	3.3	0	—	—	—	—	—	—	—	—	—	—	—	—	—	—	—	—	0	131
1935	Bkn	1(0)	—	—	—	—	—	—	—	—	—	—	—	—	—	—	—	—	—	—	—	—	—	—
1935	Phi	7(7, BB)	3	14	4.7	0	1	16	16.0(16)	0	—	—	—	—	—	—	—	—	—	—	—	—	0	22
1936	Phi	12(9, HB)	109	333	3.1	0	—	—	—	—	10	1	10.0	11	1.1(11)	0	3	—	—	—	K	1	7	219
NFL	7	66(46)	261	833	3.2	3	2	41	20.5(25)	3	20	2	10.0	7	0.3(11)	0	5	—	—	—	K	1	43	702

Thomasson, Leon Leon S., DB, 5´11˝/190 lbs; Texas Southern; B6/20/1963 Dayton, OH **1987** Atl 3 (2)

Thome, Chris Christopher John, C, 6´4˝/278 lbs; Minnesota; 1991: Min, rnd 5; B1/15/1969 St. Cloud, MN **1991** Cle 8 (0) **1992** Cle 3 (0) **NFL** 11 (0) [2 yrs]

Thompson, Alvie Alvie Gunder, T-G, 6´3˝/210 lbs; Lombard; Nebraska; B1/27/1901 Cambridge, NE **1925** KC 8 (7, RT) **1926** KC 2 (1) **NFL** 10 (8) [2 yrs]

Thompson, Anthony Anthony Q., RB, 5´11˝/207 lbs; Indiana; 1990: Phx, rnd 2; B4/8/1967 Terre Haute, IN

YEAR	TEAM	G (GS, POS)	RUSH	YD	AVG (LG)	TD	REC	YD	AVG (LG)	TD	PASS	COMP	PCT	YD	AVG (LG)	TD	INT	SK	YD	QBR	KPR	OTD	PTS	TAY
1990	Phx	13(3)	106	390	3.7(40)	4	2	11	5.5(6)	0	—	—	—	—	—	—	—	—	—	—	—	—	24	436
1991	Phx	16(3)	126	376	3.0(22)	1	7	52	7.4(14)	0	1	0	0.0	0	0.0	0	0	—	—	—	—	—	6	412
1992	Phx	1(0)	8	8	1.0(6)	1	—	—	—	—	—	—	—	—	—	—	—	—	—	—	—	—	6	18
1992	LARm	7(0)	11	57	5.2(12)	0	5	11	2.2(7)	0	—	—	—	—	—	—	—	—	—	—	k	—	0	37
NFL	3	37(6)	251	831	3.3(40)	6	14	74	5.3(14)	0	1	0	0.0	0	0.0	0	0	—	—	—	k	—	36	902

Thompson, Anthony Anthony, LB, 6´1˝/227 lbs; East Carolina; 1990: Den, rnd 10; B6/19/1967 Stantonsburg, NC **1990** Den 10 (0)

Thompson, Arland Arland Baron, G, 6´4˝/265 lbs; Baylor; 1980: Chi, rnd 4; B9/19/1957 Lockney, TX **1980** Den 2 (0) **1981** GB 9 (1) **1982** Bal 3 (1) **1987** KC 3 (3) **NFL** 17 (5) [4 yrs]

Thompson, Aundra Aundra, WR-RB, 6´1˝/186 lbs; Texas A&M-Commerce; 1976: GB, rnd 5; B1/2/1953 Dallas, TX

YEAR	TEAM	G (GS, POS)	RUSH	YD	AVG (LG)	TD	REC	YD	AVG (LG)	TD	PASS	COMP	PCT	YD	AVG (LG)	TD	INT	SK	YD	QBR	KPR	OTD	PTS	TAY
1977	GB	14	—	—	—	—	2	12	6.0(14)	0	—	—	—	—	—	—	—	—	—	—	k	—	0	28
1978	GB	16(16, WR)	4	25	6.3(13)	0	26	527	20.3(57)	2	—	—	—	—	—	—	—	—	—	—	k	—	12	333
1979	GB	15(15, WR)	2	-18	-9.0(-7)	0	25	395	15.8(50)	3	—	—	—	—	—	—	—	—	—	—	k	1	24	326
1980	GB	15(15, WR)	5	5	1.0(16)	0	40	609	15.2(55)	2	—	—	—	—	—	—	—	—	—	—	k	—	12	378
1981	GB	3(2)	1	2	2.0(2)	0	2	30	15.0(25)	0	—	—	—	—	—	—	—	—	—	—	—	—	0	17
1981	SD	1(0)	—	—	—	—	—	—	—	—	—	—	—	—	—	—	—	—	—	—	k	—	0	14
1981	NO	10(0)	—	—	—	—	6	81	13.5(25)	0	—	—	—	—	—	—	—	—	—	—	—	—	0	41
1982	NO	9(2)	1	2	2.0(2)	0	8	138	17.3(48)	1	—	—	—	—	—	—	—	—	—	—	k	—	6	137
NFL	6	83(50)	13	16	1.2(16)	0	109	1792	16.4(57)	8	—	—	—	—	—	—	—	—	—	—	k	1	54	1272

Thompson, Bennie Bennie, DB, 6´0˝/210 lbs; Grambling State; B2/10/1963 New Orleans, LA **1989** NO 2 (0) **1990**†NO 16 (2) **1991**†NO★16 (0) **1992**†KC 16 (0) **1993**†KC 16 (0) **1994**†Cle 16 (0) **1995** Cle 13 (0) **1996** Bal 16 (0) **1997** Bal 16 (0) **1998** Bal★16 (0) **1999** Bal 16 (0) **NFL** 159 (2) [11 yrs]

Thompson, Bill William, C, /182 lbs; none; B1907, deceased **1925** Mil 1 (0)

Thompson, Bill William Allen, DB, 6´1˝/201 lbs; Maryland-Eastern Shore; 1969: Den, rnd 3; B10/10/1946 Greenville, SC **[RI]** **1969** Den-A☆14 (14, RCB) **1970** Den 9 (9, RCB) **1971** Den 14 (14, RCB) **1972** Den 8 (8, rcb) **1973** Den 14 (14, SS) **1974** Den 14 (14, SS) **1975** Den 14 (14, SS) **1976** Den 14 (14, SS) **1977**†Den★14 (14, SS) **1978**†Den★16 (16, SS) **1979**†Den☆16 (16, SS) **1980** Den 16 (16, SS) **1981** Den★16 (16, SS) **NFL** 179 (179) [13 yrs]

Thompson, Bob Robert Lee, WR, 5´9˝/170 lbs; Youngstown State; 1986: NO, rnd 6; B9/9/1962 Hollywood, FL **1987** Den 2 (0)

Thompson, Bobby Robert Lee, DB, 5´11˝/188 lbs; Arizona; 1962: Det, rnd 3/DalT, rnd 12; B3/30/1939 Minden, LA **1964** Det 14 (RCB) **1965** Det 11 (RCB) **1966** Det 14 (RS) **1967** Det 12 **1968** Det 14 **1969** NO 7 (LS) **NFL** 72 [6 yrs]

Thompson, Bobby Bobby, RB, 5´11˝/195 lbs; Oklahoma; B1/16/1947 Raleigh, NC

YEAR	TEAM	G (GS, POS)	RUSH	YD	AVG (LG)	TD	REC	YD	AVG (LG)	TD	PASS	COMP	PCT	YD	AVG (LG)	TD	INT	SK	YD	QBR	KPR	OTD	PTS	TAY
1975	Det	14(1)	51	268	5.3(46)	1	19	122	6.4(22)	0	—	—	—	—	—	—	—	—	—	—	k	—	6	574
1976	Det	14	13	42	3.2(9)	0	10	108	10.8(38)	0	—	—	—	—	—	—	—	—	—	—	k	—	0	197
NFL	2	28(1)	64	310	4.8(46)	1	29	230	7.9(38)	0	—	—	—	—	—	—	—	—	—	—	k	—	6	771

Thompson, Broderick Broderick, T-G, 6´5˝/295 lbs; Kansas; B8/14/1960 Birmingham, AL, D2/4/2002 Boulder City, NV **1985**†Dal 11 (1) **1987** SD 9 (4) **1988** SD 16 (16, LG) **1989** SD 16 (16, LG) **1990** SD 16 (16, RT) **1991** SD 16 (16, RT) **1992**†SD 12 (12, RT) **1993** Phi 10 (10, LT) **1994** Phi 14 (14, RT) **1995** Den 16 (16, RT) **1996**†Den 16 (16, RT) **NFL** 152 (137) [11 yrs]

Thompson, Chaun Chaun, LB, 6´2˝/250 lbs; West Texas A&M; 2003: Cle, rnd 2; B5/22/1980 Mount Pleasant, TX **2003** Cle 16 (0) **2004** Cle 16 (13, LLB) **2005** Cle 16 (15, ROLB) **NFL** 48 (28) [3 yrs]

Thompson, Chris Chris, DB, 6´0˝/187 lbs; Nicholls State; 2004: Jax, rnd 5; B5/19/1982 New Orleans, LA **2005**†ChiB 12 (1)

Thompson, Craig Craig Antonio, TE, 6´2˝/244 lbs; North Carolina A&T; 1992: Cin, rnd 5; B1/13/1969 Hartsville, SC

YEAR	TEAM	G (GS, POS)	RUSH	YD	AVG (LG)	TD	REC	YD	AVG (LG)	TD	PASS	COMP	PCT	YD	AVG (LG)	TD	INT	SK	YD	QBR	KPR	OTD	PTS	TAY
1992	Cin	16(3)	—	—	—	—	19	194	10.2(32)	2	—	—	—	—	—	—	—	—	—	—	—	—	12	107
1993	Cin	13(0)	—	—	—	—	17	87	5.1(10)	1	—	—	—	—	—	—	—	—	—	—	—	—	6	49
NFL	2	29(3)	—	—	—	—	36	281	7.8(32)	3	—	—	—	—	—	—	—	—	—	—	—	—	18	156

Thompson, Darrell Darrell Alexander, RB, 6´0˝/215 lbs; Minnesota; 1990: GB, rnd 1; B11/23/1967 Rochester, MN

YEAR	TEAM	G (GS, POS)	RUSH	YD	AVG (LG)	TD	REC	YD	AVG (LG)	TD	PASS	COMP	PCT	YD	AVG (LG)	TD	INT	SK	YD	QBR	KPR	OTD	PTS	TAY
1990	GB	16(0)	76	264	3.5(37)	1	3	1	0.3(1)	0	—	—	—	—	—	—	—	—	—	—	k	1	12	343
1991	GB	13(13, FB)	141	471	3.3(40)	1	7	71	10.1(18)	0	—	—	—	—	—	—	—	—	—	—	k	—	6	539
1992	GB	7(4)	76	254	3.3(33)	2	13	129	9.9(43)	1	—	—	—	—	—	—	—	—	—	—	—	—	18	344
1993	†GB	16(11, RB)	169	654	3.9(60)	3	18	129	7.2(34)	0	—	—	—	—	—	—	—	—	—	—	k	—	18	785
1994	†GB	8(0)	2	-2	-1.0(2)	0	—	—	—	—	—	—	—	—	—	—	—	—	—	—	k	—	0	5
NFL	5	60(28)	464	1641	3.5(60)	7	41	330	8.0(43)	1	—	—	—	—	—	—	—	—	—	—	k	1	54	2014

Thompson, Dave David Dean, WB, 5´10˝/215 lbs; Denison; B11/17/1897, deceased **1921** Cin 1 (0)

Thompson, Dave David Wayne, T-C-G, 6´4˝/270 lbs; Clemson; 1971: Det, rnd 2; B2/1/1949 Langdale, AL **1971** Det 14 **1972** Det 7 **1973** Det 14 **1974** NO 14 (LT) **1975** NO 7 (LT/c) **NFL** 56 [5 yrs]

Thompson, David David Farod, RB, 5´8˝/196 lbs; Oklahoma State; B1/13/1975 Okmulgee, OK **1998** SL 1 (0)

YEAR	TEAM	G (GS, POS)	RUSH	YD	AVG (LG)	TD	REC	YD	AVG (LG)	TD	PASS	COMP	PCT	YD	AVG (LG)	TD	INT	SK	YD	QBR	KPR	OTD	PTS	TAY
1997	SL	11(0)	16	30	1.9(9)	1	—	—	—	—	—	—	—	—	—	—	—	—	—	—	k	—	6	415
NFL	2	12(0)	16	30	1.9(9)	1	—	—	—	—	—	—	—	—	—	—	—	—	—	—	—	—	6	40

Thompson, Del Delbert Ray, RB, 6´0˝/203 lbs; Texas; Texas-El Paso; 1982: KC, rnd 5; B2/21/1958 Kermit, TX

YEAR	TEAM	G (GS, POS)	RUSH	YD	AVG (LG)	TD	REC	YD	AVG (LG)	TD	PASS	COMP	PCT	YD	AVG (LG)	TD	INT	SK	YD	QBR	KPR	OTD	PTS	TAY
1982	KC	6(0)	4	7	1.8(4)	0	—	—	—	—	—	—	—	—	—	—	—	—	—	—	k	—	0	18

Thompson, Derrius Derrius Damon, WR, 6´2˝/220 lbs; Baylor; B7/5/1977 Dallas, TX

YEAR	TEAM	G (GS, POS)	RUSH	YD	AVG (LG)	TD	REC	YD	AVG (LG)	TD	PASS	COMP	PCT	YD	AVG (LG)	TD	INT	SK	YD	QBR	KPR	OTD	PTS	TAY
1999	Was	1(0)	—	—	—	—	—	—	—	—	—	—	—	—	—	—	—	—	—	—	—	—	—	—
2000	Was	4(0)	—	—	—	—	—	—	—	—	—	—	—	—	—	—	—	—	—	—	—	—	—	—
2001	Was	16(0)	—	—	—	—	3	52	17.3(31)	1	—	—	—	—	—	—	—	—	—	—	k	—	6	3
2002	Was	16(14, WR)	10	77	7.7(26)	0	53	773	14.6(47)	4	—	—	—	—	—	—	—	—	—	—	k	—	24	485
2003	Mia	16(12, WR)	—	—	—	—	26	359	13.8(31)	0	—	—	—	—	—	—	—	—	—	—	—	—	0	180
2004	Mia	16(3)	—	—	—	—	23	359	15.6(36)	4	—	—	—	—	—	—	—	—	—	—	—	—	24	200
NFL	6	69(29)	10	77	7.7(26)	0	105	1543	14.7(47)	9	—	—	—	—	—	—	—	—	—	—	k	—	54	867

YEAR	TEAM	G(GS, POS)	RUSH	YD	AVG(LG)	TD	REC	YD	AVG(LG)	TD	PASS	COMP	PCT	YD	AVG(LG)	TD	INT	SK	YD	QBR	KPR	OTD	PTS	TAY

THOMPSON, DOMINIQUE Dominique, WR, 6'1"/190 lbs; William & Mary; B12/28/1982 Durham, NC

YEAR	TEAM	G(GS,POS)	RUSH	YD	AVG(LG)	TD	REC	YD	AVG(LG)	TD	OTD	PTS	TAY
2005	SL	2(0)	—	—	—		1	13	13.0(13)	0	—	0	7

THOMPSON, DON Robert Donald, G, 6'2"/205 lbs; Redlands; B12/29/1903, D8/1973 Los Angeles, CA **1926** LA 10 (9, LG), 12

THOMPSON, DON Donald Wayne, DE, 6'4"/240 lbs; Ferrum; Richmond; B10/7/1939 Danville, VA **1962** Bal 10 **1963** Bal 14 **1964** Phi 3 **NFL** 27 [3 yrs]

THOMPSON, DONNEL Donnel, LB, 5'11"/234 lbs; Wisconsin; B2/17/1978 Madison, WI **2000** Pit 8 (0) **2001** Ind 4 (0) **2002**†Ind 16 (0) **NFL** 28 (0) [3 yrs]

THOMPSON, DONNELL Lawrence Donnell, DE, 6'4"/270 lbs; North Carolina; 1981: Bal, rnd 1; B10/27/1958 Lumberton, NC **1981** Bal 13 (12, LDE) **1982** Bal 9 (9, LDE) **1983** Bal 14 (13, LDE) **1984** Ind 10 (10, LDE) **1985** Ind 15 (13, LDE) **1986** Ind 16 (16, LDE) **1987**†Ind 12 (12, LDE) **1988** Ind 16 (16, LDE) **1989** Ind 16 (16, LDE) **1990** Ind 12 (12, LDE) **1991** Ind 14 (14, LDE) **NFL** 147 (143) [11 yrs]

THOMPSON, EMMUEL Emmuel Lee, DB, 5'11"/180 lbs; Texas A&M-Kingsville; B11/15/1959 Houston, TX **1987** Hou 3 (0)

THOMPSON, ERNIE Ernie, RB, 5'11"/244 lbs; Indiana; 1991: LARm, rnd 12; B10/25/1969 Terre Haute, IN

YEAR	TEAM	G(GS,POS)	RUSH	YD	AVG(LG)	TD	REC	YD	AVG(LG)	TD	OTD	PTS	TAY
1991	LARm	4(0)	2	9	4.5(9)	0	2	35	17.5(22)	1	—	6	32
1993	†KC	16(2)	11	28	2.5(14)	0	4	33	8.3(13)	0	—	0	45
NFL	2	20(2)	13	37	2.8(14)	0	6	68	11.3(22)	1	—	6	76

THOMPSON, GARY Gary, DB, 6'0"/180 lbs; San Jose State; B2/23/1959 Castro Valley, CA **1983** Buf 16 (0) **1984** Buf 8 (1) **NFL** 24 (1) [2 yrs]

THOMPSON, GEORGE George Delmar, G-T, 6'1"/210 lbs; Iowa; B8/31/1899 Lehigh, IA, D8/1965, IL **1923** RI 7 (5, LG) **1924** RI 9 (9, LG) **1925** RI 11 (11, LG) **NFL** 27 (25) [3 yrs]

THOMPSON, HAL Harold Charles, E-DE, 6'1"/205 lbs; Delaware; B10/18/1922 Manasquan, NJ

YEAR	TEAM	G(GS,POS)	RUSH	YD	AVG(LG)	TD	REC	YD	AVG(LG)	TD	OTD	PTS	TAY
1947	Bkn-A	12(1)	1	4	4.0(4)	0	15	148	9.9	0	—	0	78
1948	Bkn-A	9(0)	—	—	—		4	37	9.3	1	—	6	24
AAFC	2	21(1)	1	4	4.0(4)	0	19	185	9.7	1	—	6	102

THOMPSON, HARRY Harry Julius, G, 6'2"/225 lbs; UCLA; B1/8/1926 Memphis, TN, D11/26/2003 Los Angeles, CA **1950**†LARm 12 (RG) **1951**†LARm 12 **1952**†LARm 12 (RG) **1953** LARm 8 (RG) **1954** LARm 12 (RG) **1955** ChiC 12 (LG) **NFL** 68 [6 yrs]

THOMPSON, JACK Jack Byron, QB, 6'3"/217 lbs; Washington State; 1979: Cin, rnd 1; B5/19/1956 Tutuwila, American Samoa

YEAR	TEAM	G(GS,POS)	RUSH	YD	AVG(LG)	TD	REC	YD	AVG(LG)	TD	PASS	COMP	PCT	YD	AVG(LG)	TD	INT	SK	YD	QBR	KPR	OTD	PTS	TAY
1979	Cin	9(1)	21	116	5.5(21)	5	—	—	—		87	39	44.8	481	5.5(50)	1	5	16	178	—	—		30	212
1980	Cin	14(4, qb)	18	84	4.7(15)	1	—	—	—		234	115	49.1	1324	5.7(59)	11	12	13	113	60.9	—		6	331
1981	†Cin	8(0)	—	—	—		—				49	21	42.9	267	5.4(21)	1	2	7	61	—	—		0	59
1982	Cin	1(0)																						
1983	TB	14(13, QB)	26	27	1.0(10)	0	—	—	—		423	249	58.9	2906	6.9(80)	18	21	39	289	73.3	—		0	730
1984	TB	5(3)	5	35	7.0(13)	0	—	—	—		52	25	48.1	337	6.5(74)	2	5	10	54	—	—		0	14
NFL	6	51(21)	70	262	3.7(21)	6	—	—	—		845	449	53.1		6.3(80)	33	45	85	695	63.4	—		36	1345

THOMPSON, JAMES James, WR, 6'0"/178 lbs; Memphis; B1/9/1953 Memphis, TN

YEAR	TEAM	G(GS,POS)	RUSH	YD	AVG(LG)	TD	REC	YD	AVG(LG)	TD	KPR	OTD	PTS	TAY
1978	NYG	13	—	—	—		7	113	16.1(46)	0	p	—	0	51

THOMPSON, JESSE Jesse, WR, 6'1"/185 lbs; California; 1978: Det, rnd 6; B3/12/1956 Merced, CA

YEAR	TEAM	G(GS,POS)	RUSH	YD	AVG(LG)	TD	REC	YD	AVG(LG)	TD	KPR	OTD	PTS	TAY
1978	Det	11(1)	2	7	3.5(10)	0	18	175	9.7(21)	4	kp	—	24	332
1980	Det	11(2)	1	-4	-4.0(-4)	0	11	137	12.5(19)	0	kp	—	0	65
NFL	2	22(3)	3	3	1.0(10)	0	29	312	10.8(21)	4	kp	—	24	396

THOMPSON, JIM James L., DT, 6'3"/255 lbs; Southern Illinois; B12/4/1940 Peoria, IL **1965** Den-A 4

THOMPSON, JOHN John Washington, TE, 6'3"/228 lbs; Weber State; Utah State; 1979: GB, rnd 9; B1/18/1957 Jackson, MS **1979** GB 16 **1980** GB 7 (0) **1981** GB 2 (0)

YEAR	TEAM	G(GS,POS)	RUSH	YD	AVG(LG)	TD	REC	YD	AVG(LG)	TD	OTD	PTS	TAY
1982	†GB	9(0)	—	—	—		2	24	12.0(23)	2	—	12	22
NFL	4	34	—	—	—		2	24	12.0(23)	2	—	12	22

THOMPSON, JOHNNY John Henry, G, 5'10"/215 lbs; Lafayette; B10/24/1905 Lykens, PA **1929** Fra 4 (0)

THOMPSON, KEN Kenneth Wayne, WR, 6'1"/178 lbs; West Texas A&M; Utah State; B12/6/1958 Snyder, TX

YEAR	TEAM	G(GS,POS)	RUSH	YD	AVG(LG)	TD	REC	YD	AVG(LG)	TD	OTD	PTS	TAY
1982	†SL	1(0)	—	—	—		1	5	5.0(5)	0	—	0	3
1983	SL	5(0)	—	—	—		2	31	15.5(22)	0	—	0	16
NFL	2	6(0)	—	—	—		3	36	12.0(22)	0	—	0	18

THOMPSON, KEVIN Kevin James, QB, 6'5"/236 lbs; Penn State; B7/27/1977 Gaithersburg, MD

YEAR	TEAM	G(GS,POS)	RUSH	YD	AVG(LG)	TD	PASS	COMP	PCT	YD	AVG(LG)	TD	INT	SK	OTD	PTS	TAY
2000	Cle	1(0)	1	0	0.0(0)	0	1	1	100.0	8	8.0(8)	0	0	0	—	0	4

THOMPSON, LAMONT Lamont Darnell, DB, 6'1"/220 lbs; Washington State; 2002: Cin, rnd 2; B7/30/1978 Richmond, CA **2002** Cin 13 (0) **2003**†Ten 16 (0) **2004** Ten 16 (13, FS) **2005** Ten 16 (16, FS) **NFL** 61 (29) [4 yrs]

THOMPSON, LEONARD Leonard Irwin, WR-HB, 5'11"/192 lbs; Oklahoma State; 1975: Det, rnd 8; B7/28/1952 Oklahoma City, OK

YEAR	TEAM	G(GS,POS)	RUSH	YD	AVG(LG)	TD	REC	YD	AVG(LG)	TD	PASS	COMP	PCT	YD	AVG(LG)	TD	INT	SK	KPR	OTD	PTS	TAY
1975	Det	14(1)	1	-12	-12.0(-12)	0	—												k	—	0	79
1976	Det	14(1)	1	0	0.0(0)	0	3	52	17.3(21)	0									k	—	0	37
1977	Det	14(3)	31	91	2.9(16)	1	7	42	6.0(18)	0	1	0	0.0	0	0.0	0	0		k	1	12	131
1978	Det	16(1)	1	7	7.0(7)	0	10	167	16.7(45)	4									kp	—	24	202
1979	Det	15(1)	5	24	4.8(16)	0	24	451	18.8(82)	2									kp	—	12	393
1980	Det	16(12, WR)	6	61	10.2(30)	0	19	511	26.9(79)	3										—	18	332
1981	Det	16(16, WR)	10	75	7.5(21)	1	30	550	18.3(**94**)	3										—	24	375
1982	†Det	9(7, WR)	2	16	8.0(13)	0	17	328	19.3(70)	4										—	24	200
1983	†Det	13(12, WR)	4	72	18.0(40)	1	41	752	18.3(80)	3										—	24	473
1984	Det	16(15, WR)	3	-7	-2.3(4)	0	50	773	15.5(66)	6										—	36	410
1985	Det	16(13, WR)	—	—	—		51	736	14.4(48)	5										—	30	393
1986	Det	16(1)	—	—	—		25	320	12.8(36)	5										—	30	185
NFL	12	175(83)	64	327	5.1(40)	3	277	4682	16.9(94)	35	1	0	0.0	0	0.0	0	0		kp	1	234	3208

THOMPSON, LEROY Ulys Leroy, RB, 5'11"/216 lbs; Penn State; 1991: Pit, rnd 6; B2/3/1969 Knoxville, TN

YEAR	TEAM	G(GS,POS)	RUSH	YD	AVG(LG)	TD	REC	YD	AVG(LG)	TD	KPR	OTD	PTS	TAY
1991	Pit	13(0)	20	60	3.0(14)	0	14	118	8.4(32)	0	k	—	0	112
1992	†Pit	15(2)	35	157	4.5(25)	1	22	278	12.6(29)	0	k	—	6	327
1993	†Pit	15(6, rb)	205	763	3.7(36)	3	38	259	6.8(28)	0	k	—	18	940
1994	†NE	16(1)	102	312	3.1(13)	2	65	465	7.2(27)	5	k	—	42	696
1995	†KC	16(0)	28	73	2.6(10)	0	9	37	4.1(7)	0	k	—	0	154
1996	TB	5(0)	14	25	1.8(10)	0	5	36	7.2(12)	0	k	—	0	43
NFL	6	80(9)	404	1390	3.4(36)	6	153	1193	7.8(32)	5	k	—	66	2271

THOMPSON, MARTY Glenn Martin, TE, 6'3"/243 lbs; Fresno State; B12/9/1969 Whittier, CA

YEAR	TEAM	G(GS,POS)	RUSH	YD	AVG(LG)	TD	REC	YD	AVG(LG)	TD	OTD	PTS	TAY
1993	Det	6(2)	—	—	—		1	15	15.0(15)	0	—	0	8

THOMPSON, MICHAEL Michael Anthony, T, 6'4"/295 lbs; Tennessee State; 2000: Atl, rnd 4; B2/11/1977 Savannah, GA **2000** Atl 2 (2) **2001** Atl 2 (1) **2002** Atl 8 (1) **NFL** 12 (4) [3 yrs]

THOMPSON, MIKE Michael John, DT, 6'4"/279 lbs; Wisconsin; 1995: Jax, rnd 4; B12/22/1971 Portage, WI **1995** Jax 2 (0) **1998** Cin 9 (0) **1999** Cle 10 (0) **2000** Cle 12 (0) **NFL** 33 (0) [4 yrs]

THOMPSON, NORM Norman Jack, DB, 6'1"/180 lbs; Utah; 1971: SL, rnd 1; B3/5/1945 San Francisco, CA [I] **1971** SL 14 (rcb) **1972** SL 12 (LCB) **1973** SL 11 (lcb) **1974**†SL 12 (12, LCB) **1975** SL 14 (LCB) **1976** SL 13 (LCB) **1977**†Bal 14 (LCB) **1978** Bal 13 (9, LCB) **1979** Bal 12 **NFL** 115 (21) [9 yrs]

THOMPSON, PINKY Lloyd V., HB, Bucknell; B2/16/1906 Tonawanda, NY, D9/9/1975 Tonawanda, NY **1927** Buf 2 (0)

THOMPSON, RAYNOCH Raynoch Joseph, LB, 6'3"/224 lbs; Tennessee; 2000: Arz, rnd 2; B11/21/1977 Los Angeles, CA **2000** Arz 11 (9, LLB) **2001** Arz 14 (14, LLB) **2002** Arz 16 (16, LLB) **2003** Arz 12 (12, LLB) **2004** Arz 11 (11, LLB) **NFL** 64 (54) [5 yrs]

THOMPSON, REYNA Reyna Onald, DB, 6'0"/194 lbs; Baylor; 1986: Mia, rnd 9; B8/28/1963 Dallas, TX **1986** Mia 16 (4) **1987** Mia 9 (1) **1988** Mia 16 (2) **1989**†NYG 16 (0) **1990**†NYG★16 (4) **1991** NYG 12 (1) **1992** NYG 16 (0) **1993** NE 15 (6, lcb) **NFL** 116 (18) [8 yrs]

Thompson, Ricky Ricky Don, WR, 6´0˝/176 lbs; Baylor; 1976: Bal, rnd 8; B5/15/1954 El Paso, TX

YEAR	TEAM	G (GS, POS)	RUSH	YD	AVG (LG)	TD	REC	YD	AVG (LG)	TD	PASS	COMP	PCT	YD	AVG (LG)	TD	INT	SK	YD	QBR	KPR	OTD	PTS	TAY
1976	†Bal	9	—	—	—	—	1	11	11.0(11)	0	—	—	—	—	—	—	—	—	—	—	—	—	0	6
1977	Bal	5	—	—	—	—	1	15	15.0(15)	0	—	—	—	—	—	—	—	—	—	—	—	—	0	8
1978	Was	16(4)	—	—	—	—	23	350	15.2(49)	1	—	—	—	—	—	—	—	—	—	—	—	—	6	180
1979	Was	15(15, WR)	—	—	—	—	22	368	16.7(35)	4	—	—	—	—	—	—	—	—	—	—	—	—	24	204
1980	Was	16(15, WR)	—	—	—	—	22	313	14.2(54)	5	—	—	—	—	—	—	—	—	—	—	k	—	30	167
1981	Was	16(5, wr)	—	—	—	—	28	423	15.1(57)	4	—	—	—	—	—	—	—	—	—	—	—	—	24	232
1982	SL	3(0)	—	—	—	—	—	—	—	—	—	—	—	—	—	—	—	—	—	—	—	—	—	—
NFL	7	80(39)	—	—	—	—	97	1480	15.3(57)	14	—	—	—	—	—	—	—	—	—	—	k	—	84	795

Thompson, Robert Robert Charles, LB, 6´3˝/227 lbs; Michigan; 1983: Hou, rnd 8; B2/4/1960 Chicago, IL **1983** TB 10 (1) **1984** TB 9 (1) **1987** Det 3 (2) **NFL** 22 (4) [3 yrs]

Thompson, Rocky Ralph Gary, aka Ralph Gary Symonds-Thompson, RB, 5´11˝/200 lbs; West Texas A&M; 1971: NYG, rnd 1; B11/8/1947 Paget, Bermuda

YEAR	TEAM	G (GS, POS)	RUSH	YD	AVG (LG)	TD	REC	YD	AVG (LG)	TD	PASS	COMP	PCT	YD	AVG (LG)	TD	INT	SK	YD	QBR	KPR	OTD	PTS	TAY
1971	NYG	14	54	177	3.3(23)	1	16	85	5.3(12)	0	—	—	—	—	—	—	—	—	—	—	k	1	12	647
1972	NYG	14	9	35	3.9(13)	0	—	—	—	—	—	—	—	—	—	—	—	—	—	—	k	1	6	431
1973	NYG	1	5	5	1.0(4)	0	—	—	—	—	—	—	—	—	—	—	—	—	—	—	—	—	0	5
NFL	3	29	68	217	3.2(23)	1	16	85	5.3(12)	0	—	—	—	—	—	—	—	—	—	—	k	2	18	1083

Thompson, Russ John Russell, T, 6´5˝/249 lbs; Nebraska; B5/10/1912 Edgar, NE, D2/12/2001 Lusk, WY **1936** ChiB 9 (3) **1937**†ChiB 11 (7, RT) **1938** ChiB 11 (5, RT) **1939** ChiB 11 (8, RT) **1940** Phi 11 (5, LT) **NFL** 53 (28) [5 yrs]

Thompson, Steve Stephen Merall, DT-DE, 6´2˝/250 lbs; Washington; 1968: NYJ, rnd 2; B2/12/1945 Seattle, WA **1968**†NYJ-A 4 **1969**†NYJ-A 14 (LDT) **1970** NYJ 12 **1972** NYJ 5 **1973** NYJ 8 **NFL** 43 [5 yrs]

Thompson, Steve Steven Kenneth, DT, 6´2˝/275 lbs; Minnesota; B6/24/1965 Aurora, IL **1987** Was 1 (0)

Thompson, Ted Ted Clarence, LB, 6´1˝/220 lbs; SMU; B1/17/1953 Atlanta, TX **[K]** **1975** Hou 14 **1976** Hou 14 **1977** Hou 14 **1978**†Hou 16 **1979**†Hou 16 (2) **1980**†Hou 15 (3) **1981** Hou 16 (1) **1982** Hou 9 (2) **1983** Hou 16 (0) **1984** Hou 16 (0) **NFL** 146 (8) [10 yrs]

Thompson, Tiny George Bryant, G, 5´10˝/233 lbs; Syracuse; B1899, deceased **1922** Roc 5 (5, RG)

Thompson, Tom Thomas Lee, RB, 6´1˝/205 lbs; Southern Illinois; B9/22/1951 Oxford, MS

YEAR	TEAM	G (GS, POS)	RUSH	YD	AVG (LG)	TD	REC	YD	AVG (LG)	TD	PASS	COMP	PCT	YD	AVG (LG)	TD	INT	SK	YD	QBR	KPR	OTD	PTS	TAY
1974	SD	12	6	8	1.3(8)	0	—	—	—	—	—	—	—	—	—	—	—	—	—	—	k	—	0	70

Thompson, Tommy Thomas Pryor, QB, 6´1˝/192 lbs; Tulsa; B8/15/1916 Hutchinson, KS, D4/21/1989 Calico Rock, AR

YEAR	TEAM	G (GS, POS)	RUSH	YD	AVG (LG)	TD	REC	YD	AVG (LG)	TD	PASS	COMP	PCT	YD	AVG (LG)	TD	INT	SK	YD	QBR	KPR	OTD	PTS	TAY
1940	Pit	11(2)	40	39	1.0	0	4	55	13.8	0	28	9	32.1	145	5.2(31)	1	3	—	—	—	i	—	0	32
1941	Phi	11(5, qb)	54	-2	-0.0(14)	0	4	30	7.5(0)	1	162	86	53.1	959	5.9(50)	8	14	—	—	51.4	Pkpi	—	6	-4
1942	Phi★	11(10, QB)	92	-32	-0.3(22)	1	—	—	—	—	203	95	46.8	1410	6.9(65)	8	16	—	—	50.3	kpi	—	6	112
1945	Phi	8(0)	8	-13	-1.6(7)	0	—	—	—	—	28	15	53.6	146	5.2(27)	0	2	—	—	—	i	—	0	3
1946	Phi	10(3, qb)	34	-116	-3.4(6)	0	—	—	—	—	103	57	55.3	745	7.2(45)	6	9	—	—	61.3	—	—	0	-74
1947	†Phi	12(1, QB)	23	52	2.3(16)	2	—	—	—	—	201	106	52.7	1680	8.4(69)	16	15	—	—	76.3	—	—	12	392
1948	†Phi☆	12(4, QB)	12	46	3.8(13)	1	—	—	—	—	246	141	57.3	1965	8.0(70)	**25**	11	—	—	**98.4**	—	—	6	724
1949	†Phi☆	12(9, QB)	15	17	1.1(5)	2	—	—	—	—	214	116	54.2	1727	8.1(75)	16	11	—	—	**84.4**	—	—	12	541
1950	Phi	12(QB)	15	34	2.3(7)	0	—	—	—	—	239	107	44.8	1608	6.7(75)	11	22	—	—	44.4	—	—	0	13
NFL	9	99(34)	293	25	0.1(22)	6	8	85	10.6	1	1424	732	51.4	10385	7.3(75)	91	103	—	—	66.5	Pkpi	—	42	1739

Thompson, Tommy Tommy Ralph, P, 5´10˝/192 lbs; Oregon; B4/27/1972 Lompoc, CA **1995**†SF 16 (0) **1996**†SF 16 (0) **1997**†SF 16 (0) **NFL** 48 (0) [3 yrs]

Thompson, Tommy Thomas Wright, LB-C, 6´1˝/221 lbs; William & Mary; 1948: Cle-A, rnd 7/Was, rnd 3; B1/6/1927 Jersey City, NJ, D10/1/1990 Baltimore, MD **1949**†Cle-A 9 (0) **1950**†Cle 12 **1951**†Cle☆12 (mlb) **1952**†Cle☆12 (MLB) **1953** Cle☆9 (RLB) **NFL** 45 [4 yrs]

Thompson, Tuffy Clarence Leonard, HB, 5´11˝/172 lbs; Minnesota; B9/28/1914 Montevideo, MN, D2/5/2000 Jacksonville, FL

YEAR	TEAM	G (GS, POS)	RUSH	YD	AVG (LG)	TD	REC	YD	AVG (LG)	TD	PASS	COMP	PCT	YD	AVG (LG)	TD	INT	SK	YD	QBR	KPR	OTD	PTS	TAY
1937	Pit	7(4)	43	80	1.9	0	6	126	21.0(55)	1	14	6	42.9	100	7.1(39)	1	4	—	—	—	—	—	6	43
1938	Pit	10(3, HB)	39	139	3.6	1	9	55	6.1	0	7	0	0.0	0	0.0	0	3	—	—	—	—	—	6	57
1939	GB	1(1)	6	9	1.5	0	1	1	1.0(1)	0	—	—	—	—	—	—	—	—	—	—	—	—	0	10
NFL	3	18(8)	88	228	2.6	1	16	182	11.4(55)	1	21	6	28.6	100	4.8(39)	1	7	—	—	—	—	—	12	109

Thompson, Tyson Tyson, RB, 6´1˝/215 lbs; San Jose State; B5/21/1981 Irving, TX

YEAR	TEAM	G (GS, POS)	RUSH	YD	AVG (LG)	TD	REC	YD	AVG (LG)	TD	PASS	COMP	PCT	YD	AVG (LG)	TD	INT	SK	YD	QBR	KPR	OTD	PTS	TAY
2005	Dal	15(0)	46	182	4.0(16)	0	3	16	5.3(8)	0	—	—	—	—	—	—	—	—	—	—	k	—	0	734

Thompson, Vince Vincent, RB, 6´0˝/230 lbs; Villanova; B2/21/1957 Trenton, NJ

YEAR	TEAM	G (GS, POS)	RUSH	YD	AVG (LG)	TD	REC	YD	AVG (LG)	TD	PASS	COMP	PCT	YD	AVG (LG)	TD	INT	SK	YD	QBR	KPR	OTD	PTS	TAY
1981	Det	13(1)	35	211	6.0(30)	1	4	40	10.0(17)	0	—	—	—	—	—	—	—	—	—	—	—	—	6	241
1983	Det	10(2)	40	138	3.5(10)	1	4	16	4.0(8)	0	—	—	—	—	—	—	—	—	—	—	—	—	6	156
NFL	2	23(3)	75	349	4.7(30)	2	8	56	7.0(17)	0	—	—	—	—	—	—	—	—	—	—	—	—	12	397

Thompson, Warren Warren Keith, LB, 6´3˝/241 lbs; Oklahoma State; B4/13/1963 Birmingham, AL **1987** NYG 3 (3)

Thompson, Weegie Willis Hope, WR, 6´6˝/212 lbs; Florida State; 1984: Pit, rnd 4; B3/21/1961 Pensacola, FL

YEAR	TEAM	G (GS, POS)	RUSH	YD	AVG (LG)	TD	REC	YD	AVG (LG)	TD	PASS	COMP	PCT	YD	AVG (LG)	TD	INT	SK	YD	QBR	KPR	OTD	PTS	TAY
1984	†Pit	16(7, wr)	—	—	—	—	17	291	17.1(59)	3	—	—	—	—	—	—	—	—	—	—	—	—	18	161
1985	Pit	16(0)	—	—	—	—	8	138	17.3(42)	1	—	—	—	—	—	—	—	—	—	—	—	—	6	74
1986	Pit	16(4)	—	—	—	—	17	191	11.2(20)	5	—	—	—	—	—	—	—	—	—	—	—	—	30	121
1987	Pit	12(3)	—	—	—	—	17	313	18.4(63)	1	—	—	—	—	—	—	—	—	—	—	—	—	6	162
1988	Pit	16(11, WR)	—	—	—	—	16	370	23.1(50)	1	—	—	—	—	—	—	—	—	—	—	—	—	6	190
1989	†Pit	16(0)	—	—	—	—	4	74	18.5(28)	0	—	—	—	—	—	—	—	—	—	—	k	—	0	18
NFL	6	92(25)	—	—	—	—	79	1377	17.4(63)	11	—	—	—	—	—	—	—	—	—	—	k	—	66	725

Thompson, Woody Alexander Woodrow, RB, 6´1˝/228 lbs; Miami (FL); 1975: Atl, rnd 3; B8/20/1952 Erie, PA

YEAR	TEAM	G (GS, POS)	RUSH	YD	AVG (LG)	TD	REC	YD	AVG (LG)	TD	PASS	COMP	PCT	YD	AVG (LG)	TD	INT	SK	YD	QBR	KPR	OTD	PTS	TAY
1975	Atl	14	68	247	3.6(18)	0	14	92	6.6(14)	0	—	—	—	—	—	—	—	—	—	—	k	—	0	295
1976	Atl	7	42	152	3.6(10)	0	16	111	6.9(26)	0	—	—	—	—	—	—	—	—	—	—	—	—	0	208
1977	Atl	14(FB)	132	478	3.6(22)	1	12	56	4.7(9)	0	—	—	—	—	—	—	—	—	—	—	—	—	6	516
NFL	3	35	242	877	3.6(22)	1	42	259	6.2(26)	0	—	—	—	—	—	—	—	—	—	—	k	—	6	1019

Thoms, Art Arthur William, DT, 6´5˝/260 lbs; Syracuse; 1969: Oak, rnd 1; B10/20/1946 Teaneck, NJ **1969**†Oak-A 12 (1) **1970**†Oak 6 (3) **1971** Oak 14 (11, LDT) **1972**†Oak 14 (14, RDT) **1973**†Oak 13 (13, RDT) **1974**†Oak☆14 (14, RDT) **1975**†Oak 13 (11, RDT) **1977** Phi 12 **NFL** 98 (67) [8 yrs]

Thomsen, Fred Frederick Charles, E, 5´11˝/180 lbs; Nebraska; B4/25/1897 Minden, AR, D1/7/1986 Springfield, MO **1924** RI 9 (7, LE)

Thornbladh, Bob Robert N.M., LB, 6´1˝/220 lbs; Michigan; 1974: KC, rnd 11; B9/19/1952 Cleveland, OH **1974** KC 14

Thornburg, Jeremy Jeremy, DB, 6´0˝/190 lbs; Northern Arizona; B5/7/1982 San Diego, CA **2005** SF 2 (0) **2005** GB 4 (0) **NFL** 6 (0) [1 yr]

Thornhill, Tiny Claudis Earl, T, 5´11˝/185 lbs; Pittsburgh; B4/14/1893 Richmond, VA, D6/28/1956 Berkeley, CA **1920** Cle 8 (7, LT) **1920** Buf 2 (2) **NFL** 10 (9) [1 yr]

Thornhill, Josh Josh, LB, 6´2˝/243 lbs; Michigan State; B1/19/1980 Lansing, MI **2002** Det 7 (0)

Thornton, Bill William Albert, FB, 6´1˝/215 lbs; Nebraska; 1963: SL, rnd 5/NYJ, rnd 22; B9/20/1939 Toledo, OH

YEAR	TEAM	G (GS, POS)	RUSH	YD	AVG (LG)	TD	REC	YD	AVG (LG)	TD	PASS	COMP	PCT	YD	AVG (LG)	TD	INT	SK	YD	QBR	KPR	OTD	PTS	TAY
1963	SL	14	19	111	5.8(55)	1	4	10	2.5(8)	0	—	—	—	—	—	—	—	—	—	—	k	—	6	136
1964	SL	13	39	236	6.1(62)	1	7	43	6.1(19)	0	—	—	—	—	—	—	—	—	—	—	k	—	6	258
1965	SL	14	31	188	6.1(38)	0	1	6	6.0(6)	0	—	—	—	—	—	—	—	—	—	—	—	—	0	191
1967	SL	6	4	9	2.3(7)	0	1	9	9.0(9)	0	—	—	—	—	—	—	—	—	—	—	—	—	0	14
NFL	4	47	93	544	5.8(62)	2	13	68	5.2(19)	0	—	—	—	—	—	—	—	—	—	—	k	—	12	598

Thornton, Bruce Bruce Edward, DE-DT, 6´5˝/263 lbs; Illinois; 1979: Dal, rnd 8; B2/14/1958 Detroit, MI **1979**†Dal 16 **1980**†Dal 13 (0) **1981**†Dal 12 (0) **1982** SL 6 (0) **NFL** 47 [4 yrs]

Thornton, Bruce Bruce, DB, 5´11˝/195 lbs; Georgia; 2004: Dal, rnd 4; B1/31/1980 La Grange, GA **2004** Dal 1 (0) **2005** SF 12 (11, LCB) **NFL** 13 (11) [2 yrs]

Thornton, Bubba Charles Garland, WR, 6´0˝/174 lbs; TCU; 1969: Buf, rnd 14; B3/9/1947 Fort Worth, TX

YEAR	TEAM	G (GS, POS)	RUSH	YD	AVG (LG)	TD	REC	YD	AVG (LG)	TD	PASS	COMP	PCT	YD	AVG (LG)	TD	INT	SK	YD	QBR	KPR	OTD	PTS	TAY
1969	Buf-A	14	—	—	—	—	14	134	9.6(21)	0	—	—	—	—	—	—	—	—	—	—	k	—	0	366

YEAR	TEAM	G (GS, POS)	RUSH	YD	AVG(LG)	TD	REC	YD	AVG(LG)	TD	PASS COMP	PCT	YD	AVG(LG)	TD	INT	SK	YD	QBR	KPR	OTD	PTS	TAY

THORNTON, DAVID David Dontay, LB, 6'2"/230 lbs; North Carolina; 2002: Ind, rnd 4; B11/1/1978 Goldsboro, NC   **2002**†Ind 15 (0) **2003**†Ind 16 (16, RLB) **2004**†Ind 16 (15, LLB) **2005**†Ind 16 (16, LLB) **NFL** 63 (47) [4 yrs]

THORNTON, DICK Harry Richard, BB, 5'6"/165 lbs; Michigan; Missouri-Rolla; B2/4/1908 Chicago, IL, D1/15/1973 Chicago, IL

| 1933 | Phi | 4(1) | 5 | 14 | 2.8 | 0 | 2 | 14 | 7.0 | 0 | 13 | 2 | 15.4 | 52 | 4.0 | 0 | 4 | — | — | — | — | 0 | -113 |

THORNTON, GEORGE George Renardo, DT-DE-NT, 6'3"/300 lbs; Alabama; 1991: SD, rnd 2; B4/27/1968 Montgomery, AL   **1991** SD 16 (3) **1992**†SD 16 (13, RDT) **1993** NYG 5 (0) **NFL** 37 (16) [3 yrs]

THORNTON, JACK Lawrence Jackson, LB, 6'1"/230 lbs; Auburn; B4/23/1944 Washington, GA, D3/2/2002 Lexington, GA   **1966** Mia-A 6 (6, rlb)

THORNTON, JAMES James Michael, TE, 6'2"/242 lbs; Cal State-Fullerton; 1988: Chi, rnd 4; B2/8/1965 Santa Rosa, CA

1988	†ChiB	16(12, TE)	—	—	—	—	15	135	9.0(19)	0	—	—	—	—	—	—	—	—	—	—	—	—	0	68
1989	ChiB	16(16, TE)	1	4	4.0(4)	0	24	392	16.3(39)	3	—	—	—	—	—	—	—	—	—	—	—	—	18	215
1990	†ChiB	16(16, TE)	—	—	—	—	19	254	13.4(32)	1	—	—	—	—	—	—	—	—	—	—	—	—	6	132
1991	†ChiB	16(13, TE)	—	—	—	—	17	278	16.4(33)	1	—	—	—	—	—	—	—	—	—	—	—	—	6	144
1993	NYJ	13(6, te)	—	—	—	—	12	108	9.0(22)	2	—	—	—	—	—	—	—	—	—	—	—	—	12	64
1994	NYJ	15(5, te)	—	—	—	—	20	171	8.6(25)	0	—	—	—	—	—	—	—	—	—	—	k	—	0	71
1995	Hou	4(2)	—	—	—	—	—	—	—	—	—	—	—	—	—	—	—	—	—	—	—	—	—	—
NFL	7	96(70)	1	4	4.0(4)	0	107	1338	12.5(36)	7	—	—	—	—	—	—	—	—	—	—	k	—	42	693

THORNTON, JOHN John Jason, DT, 6'3"/297 lbs; West Virginia; 1999: Ten, rnd 2; B10/2/1976 Philadelphia, PA   **1999**†Ten 16 (3) **2000**†Ten 16 (16, LDT) **2001** Ten 3 (0) **2002**†Ten 16 (16, LDT) **2003** Cin 16 (16, LDT) **2004** Cin 16 (16, LDT) **2005**†Cin 16 (16, RDT) **NFL** 99 (83) [7 yrs]

THORNTON, JOHN John Earvin, DT, 6'3"/303 lbs; Cincinnati; B6/28/1969 Flint, MI   **1991** Cle 5 (0)

THORNTON, KALEN Kalen Bruce, LB, 6'3"/245 lbs; Texas; B5/12/1982 Dallas, TX   **2004** Dal 16 (0)

THORNTON, REGGIE Reginald Orlando, WR, 5'10"/170 lbs; Bowling Green State; 1990: Min, rnd 5; B9/26/1967 Detroit, MI   **1993** Cin 1 (0)

| 1991 | Ind | 5(0) | — | — | — | — | 1 | 38 | 38.0(38) | 0 | — | — | — | — | — | — | — | — | — | — | — | — | 0 | 19 |
| NFL | 2 | 6(0) | — | — | — | — | 1 | 38 | 38.0(38) | 0 | — | — | — | — | — | — | — | — | — | — | — | — | 0 | 19 |

THORNTON, RUPE Rupert Vance, G-T, 5'10"/205 lbs; Santa Clara; 1942: ChiC, rnd 7; B1/5/1920 Denver, CO   **1946** SF-A 11 (0) **1947** SF-A 14 (0) **AAFC** 25 (0) [2 yrs]

THORNTON, SIDNEY Sidney, RB, 5'11"/230 lbs; Northwestern State (LA); 1977: Pit, rnd 2; B9/2/1954 New Orleans, LA

1977	†Pit	13	27	103	3.8(18)	2	1	5	5.0(5)	0	—	—	—	—	—	—	—	—	—	—	—	—	12	126
1978	Pit	16	71	264	3.7(27)	2	5	66	13.2(24)	1	—	—	—	—	—	—	—	—	—	—	k	—	18	344
1979	†Pit	13(10, RB)	118	585	5.0(75)	6	16	231	14.4(32)	4	—	—	—	—	—	—	—	—	—	—	—	—	60	781
1980	Pit	12(5, rb)	78	325	4.2(28)	3	15	131	8.7(29)	1	—	—	—	—	—	—	—	—	—	—	k	—	24	426
1981	Pit	16(6, rb)	56	202	3.6(17)	4	8	78	9.8(30)	0	—	—	—	—	—	—	—	—	—	—	k	—	24	267
1982	Pit	4(2)	6	33	5.5(13)	1	1	4	4.0(4)	0	—	—	—	—	—	—	—	—	—	—	—	—	6	45
NFL	6	74(21)	356	1512	4.2(75)	18	46	515	11.2(32)	6	—	—	—	—	—	—	—	—	—	—	k	—	144	1988

THORP, DON Donald Kevin, NT-DE, 6'4"/260 lbs; Illinois; 1984: NO, rnd 6; B7/10/1962 Chicago, IL   **1984** NO 5 (0) **1987** Ind 5 (3) **1988** Ind 1 (0) **1988** KC 3 (0) **NFL** 14 (3) [3 yrs]

THORPE, JACK Jack, aka Deadeye, G-C-T-WB, 6'0"/210 lbs; none; B1899, deceased   **1923** Oor 8 (6, RG)

THORPE, JIM James Francis, aka Bright Path, TB-E-FB, 6'1"/202 lbs; Carlisle Indian; B5/28/1888 Prague, OK, D3/28/1953 Lomita, CA; HOF 1963 [KC]   **1920** Can 9 (2, TB) **1921** Cle 5 (3), 11 **1922** Oor 5 (2), 18 **1923** Oor☆9 (9, TB), 3 **1924** RI 9 (9, TB), 7 **1925** NYG 3 (3) **1925** RI 2 (2) **1926** Can 9 (7, tb), 12 **1928** ChiC 1 (0) **NFL** 52 (37), 51 [8 yrs]

THORPE, WILFRED Wilfred Egner, G-LB-DE, 6'3"/205 lbs; Arkansas; 1940: Cle, rnd 9; B1/8/1917 Little Rock, AR, D7/17/1998 Little Rock, AR   **1941** Cle 5 (2) **1942** Cle 11 (5, rg) **NFL** 16 (7) [2 yrs]

THRASH, JAMES James, WR, 6'0"/200 lbs; Missouri Southern State; B4/28/1975 Denver, CO [R]

1997	Was	4(0)	—	—	—	—	2	24	12.0(17)	0	—	—	—	—	—	—	—	—	—	—	—	—	0	12
1998	Was	10(1)	—	—	—	—	10	163	16.3(28)	1	—	—	—	—	—	—	—	—	—	—	k	—	6	126
1999	†Was	16(0)	1	37	37.0(37)	0	3	44	14.7(25)	0	—	—	—	—	—	—	—	—	—	—	k	1	6	214
2000	Was	16(8, WR)	10	82	8.2(34)	0	50	653	13.1(50)	2	—	—	—	—	—	—	—	—	—	—	kp	—	12	800
2001	†Phi	15(15, WR)	6	57	9.5(24)	0	63	833	13.2(64)	8	—	—	—	—	—	—	—	—	—	—	k	—	48	540
2002	†Phi	16(16, WR)	18	126	7.0(32)	2	52	635	12.2(39)	6	—	—	—	—	—	—	—	—	—	—	—	—	48	494
2003	†Phi	16(16, WR)	5	52	10.4(47)	0	49	558	11.4(51)	1	—	—	—	—	—	—	—	—	—	—	kp	—	6	638
2004	Was	16(4)	—	—	—	—	17	203	11.9(31)	0	—	—	—	—	—	—	—	—	—	—	kp	—	0	220
2005	†Was	12(2)	1	8	8.0(8)	0	14	194	13.9(41)	0	—	—	—	—	—	—	—	—	—	—	kp	—	0	197
NFL	9	121(62)	41	362	8.8(47)	2	260	3307	12.7(64)	18	—	—	—	—	—	—	—	—	—	—	kp	1	126	3239

THREADGILL, BRUCE Bruce Craig, DB-QB, 6'0"/190 lbs; Mississippi State; 1978: SF, rnd 5; B5/7/1956 Nocona, TX

| 1978 | SF | 14 | — | — | — | — | — | — | — | — | 2 | 0 | 0.0 | 0 | 0.0 | 0 | 2 | — | — | — | — | — | 0 | -80 |

THREATS, JABBAR Anaphayus Jabbar, DE, 6'5"/268 lbs; Michigan State; B4/26/1975 Springfield, OH   **1997** Jax 2 (0) **1998** Jax 2 (0) **NFL** 4 (0) [2 yrs]

THRIFT, CLIFF Clifford Ray, LB, 6'1"/232 lbs; East Central (OK); 1979: SD, rnd 3; B5/3/1956 Dallas, TX   **1979**†SD 16 **1980** SD 15 (0) **1981**†SD 7 (5, mlb) **1982**†SD 9 (9, MLB) **1983** SD 6 (0) **1984** SD 16 (0) **1985**†ChiB 16 (2) **1986**†LARm 12 (0) **NFL** 97 (16) [8 yrs]

THROWER, JIM James Fredrick, DB, 6'2"/195 lbs; Texas A&M-Commerce; B11/6/1947 Camden, AR   **1970** Phi 5 **1971** Phi 14 **1972** Phi 5 **1973** Det 10 **1974** Det 12 (1) **NFL** 46 (1) [5 yrs]

THROWER, WILLIE Willie Lee, QB, 5'11"/182 lbs; Michigan State; B3/22/1930 New Kensington, PA, D2/20/2002 New Kensington, PA

| 1953 | ChiB | 1 | — | — | — | — | — | — | — | — | 8 | 3 | 37.5 | 27 | 3.4(12) | 0 | 1 | — | — | — | — | — | 0 | -27 |

THUERK, OWEN Owen, E, 6'2"/193 lbs; none; B2/5/1918   **1941** Det 3 (0)

THUNDER, BAPTISTE Baptiste, T, 5'10"/215 lbs; none; B1890, MN, D12/17/1935 Beltrami County, MN   **1922** Oor 1 (1)

THURBON, BOB Robert William, HB, 5'10"/176 lbs; Pittsburgh; B2/22/1918 Erie, PA, D9/20/2000 Charlotte, NC

1943	P-P	10(1)	71	291	4.1(25)	5	6	100	16.7(43)	1	—	—	—	—	—	—	—	—	—	—	kpi	—	36	463
1944	C-P	10(7, RH)	69	185	2.7(25)	4	7	134	19.1(37)	1	—	—	—	—	—	—	—	—	—	—	Pkpi	—	30	409
NFL	2	20(8)	140	476	3.4(25)	9	13	234	18.0(43)	2	—	—	—	—	—	—	—	—	—	—	Pkpi	—	66	872
1946	Buf-A	2(0)	3	2	0.7	0	1	-3	-3.0(-3)	0	—	—	—	—	—	—	—	—	—	—	k	—	0	1

THURE, BRIAN Brian Douglas, T, 6'5"/300 lbs; California; 1995: Was, rnd 6; B9/3/1973 Downey, CA   **1995** Was 4 (0)

THURLOW, STEVE Stephen Charles, RB, 6'3"/222 lbs; Stanford; 1964: NYG, rnd 2; B4/25/1942 Long Beach, CA

1964	NYG	11	64	210	3.3(13)	0	7	74	10.6(17)	1	5	3	60.0	65	13.0(33)	0	0	1	5	—	—	—	6	285
1965	NYG	14(HB)	106	440	4.2(43)	4	9	54	6.0(30)	1	1	1	100.0	49	49.0(49)	0	0	—	—	—	k	—	30	541
1966	NYG	1	1	7	7.0(7)	0	—	—	—	—	—	—	—	—	—	—	—	—	—	—	—	—	0	7
1966	Was	12(FB)	79	253	3.2(20)	0	23	165	7.2(22)	0	—	—	—	—	—	—	—	—	—	—	—	—	0	336
1967	Was	6	13	33	2.5(5)	0	10	95	9.5(21)	0	—	—	—	—	—	—	—	—	—	—	—	—	0	81
1968	Was	6(FB)	51	184	3.6(11)	0	12	151	12.6(56)	0	—	—	—	—	—	—	—	—	—	—	—	—	0	260
NFL	5	50	314	1127	3.6(43)	4	61	539	8.8(56)	2	6	4	66.7	114	19.0(49)	0	0	1	5	—	k	—	36	1508

THURMAN, ANDRAE Andrae Carnell, WR, 5'11"/192 lbs; Arizona; Southern Oregon; B10/25/1980 Houston, TX

2004	†GB	2(0)	—	—	—	—	2	12	6.0(9)	0	—	—	—	—	—	—	—	—	—	—	k	—	0	20
2005	Ten	5(0)	—	—	—	—	—	—	—	—	—	—	—	—	—	—	—	—	—	—	kp	—	0	-2
2005	GB	10(1)	—	—	—	—	7	92	13.1(33)	0	—	—	—	—	—	—	—	—	—	—	k	—	0	62
NFL	2	17(1)	—	—	—	—	9	104	11.6(33)	0	—	—	—	—	—	—	—	—	—	—	k	—	0	80

THURMAN, DENNIS Dennis Lee, DB, 5'11"/176 lbs; USC; 1978: Dal, rnd 11; B4/13/1956 Los Angeles, CA [I]   **1978**†Dal 16 **1979**†Dal 16 **1980**†Dal 16 (16, FS) **1981**†Dal☆16 (16, RCB) **1982**†Dal 9 (9, RCB) **1983** Dal 16 (15, RCB) **1984** Dal 16 (0) **1985**†Dal 16 (3) **1986** SL 16 (3) **NFL** 137 (62) [9 yrs]

THURMAN, JOHN John Cochran, T, 6'1"/225 lbs; Pennsylvania; B2/9/1900, D3/5/1976 Pasadena, CA   **1926** LA☆10 (10, LT)

Thurman, Junior Ulysses, DB, 6´0˝/180 lbs; USC; B9/8/1964 Los Angeles, CA **1987** NO 3 (0)

Thurman, Odell Odell Lamar, LB, 6´1˝/237 lbs; Georgia; 2005: Cin, rnd 2; B7/9/1983 Monticello, GA **2005**†Cin 16 (15, MLB)

Thurston, Fuzzy Frederick Charles, G, 6´1˝/247 lbs; Valparaiso; 1956: Phi, rnd 5; B12/29/1933 Altoona, WI **1958**†Bal 4 **1959** GB 12 (LG) **1960**†GB 12 (LG) **1961**†GB☆14 (LG) **1962**†GB☆14 (LG) **1963** GB☆14 (LG) **1964** GB☆11 (LG) **1965**†GB 14 **1966**†GB☆12 (LG) **1967**†GB 9 **NFL** 116 [10 yrs]

Thweatt, Byron Byron Douglas, LB, 6´2˝/233 lbs; Virginia; B3/21/1977 Petersburg, VA **2001** Ten 5 (0)

Tice, John John, TE, 6´5˝/242 lbs; Maryland; 1983: NO, rnd 3; B6/22/1960 Bay Shore, NY

YEAR	TEAM	G(GS, POS)	RUSH	YD	AVG(LG)	TD	REC	YD	AVG(LG)	TD	PASS	COMP	PCT	YD	AVG(LG)	TD	INT	SK	YD	QBR	KPR	OTD	PTS	TAY
1983	NO	16(1)	—	—	—	—	7	33	4.7(12)	1	—	—	—	—	—	—	—	—	—	—	—	—	6	22
1984	NO	10(0)	—	—	—	—	6	55	9.2(17)	1	—	—	—	—	—	—	—	—	—	—	—	—	6	33
1985	NO	16(8, te)	—	—	—	—	24	266	11.1(39)	2	—	—	—	—	—	—	—	—	—	—	—	—	12	143
1986	NO	16(13, TE)	—	—	—	—	37	330	8.9(29)	3	—	—	—	—	—	—	—	—	—	—	—	—	18	180
1987	†NO	12(8, TE)	—	—	—	—	16	181	11.3(27)	6	—	—	—	—	—	—	—	—	—	—	—	—	36	121
1988	NO	15(12, TE)	—	—	—	—	26	297	11.4(40)	1	—	—	—	—	—	—	—	—	—	—	—	—	6	154
1989	NO	15(2)	—	—	—	—	9	98	10.9(23)	1	—	—	—	—	—	—	—	—	—	—	—	—	6	54
1990	†NO	16(4)	—	—	—	—	11	113	10.3(19)	0	—	—	—	—	—	—	—	—	—	—	—	—	0	57
1991	†NO	15(7, TE)	—	—	—	—	22	230	10.5(22)	0	—	—	—	—	—	—	—	—	—	—	—	—	0	115
1992	NO	3(1)	—	—	—	—	—	—	—	—	—	—	—	—	—	—	—	—	—	—	—	—	—	—
NFL	10	134(56)	—	—	—	—	158	1603	10.1(40)	15	—	—	—	—	—	—	—	—	—	—	—	—	90	877

Tice, Mike Michael Peter, TE, 6´7˝/253 lbs; Maryland; B2/2/1959 Bay Shore, NY **[C]**

YEAR	TEAM	G(GS, POS)	RUSH	YD	AVG(LG)	TD	REC	YD	AVG(LG)	TD	PASS	COMP	PCT	YD	AVG(LG)	TD	INT	SK	YD	QBR	KPR	OTD	PTS	TAY
1981	Sea	16(3)	—	—	—	—	5	47	9.4(14)	0	—	—	—	—	—	—	—	—	—	—	—	—	0	24
1982	Sea	9(9, TE)	—	—	—	—	9	46	5.1(12)	0	—	—	—	—	—	—	—	—	—	—	—	—	0	23
1983	†Sea	15(1)	—	—	—	—	—	—	—	—	—	—	—	—	—	—	—	—	—	—	k	—	0	-2
1984	†Sea	16(8, TE)	—	—	—	—	8	90	11.3(30)	3	—	—	—	—	—	—	—	—	—	—	—	—	18	60
1985	Sea	9(2)	—	—	—	—	2	13	6.5(7)	0	—	—	—	—	—	—	—	—	—	—	k	—	0	9
1986	Sea	16(15, TE)	—	—	—	—	15	150	10.0(25)	0	—	—	—	—	—	—	—	—	—	—	k	—	0	77
1987	†Sea	12(12, TE)	—	—	—	—	14	106	7.6(27)	2	—	—	—	—	—	—	—	—	—	—	—	—	12	63
1988	†Sea	16(16, TE)	—	—	—	—	29	244	8.4(26)	0	—	—	—	—	—	—	—	—	—	—	k	—	0	124
1989	Was	16(5, te)	—	—	—	—	1	2	2.0(2)	0	—	—	—	—	—	—	—	—	—	—	—	—	0	1
1990	Sea	5(2)	—	—	—	—	—	—	—	—	—	—	—	—	—	—	—	—	—	—	—	—	—	—
1991	Sea	16(15, TE)	—	—	—	—	10	70	7.0(16)	4	—	—	—	—	—	—	—	—	—	—	k	—	24	56
1992	†Min	12(9, TE)	—	—	—	—	5	65	13.0(34)	1	—	—	—	—	—	—	—	—	—	—	—	—	6	38
1993	†Min	16(12, TE)	—	—	—	—	6	39	6.5(21)	1	—	—	—	—	—	—	—	—	—	—	—	—	6	25
1995	Min	3(1)	—	—	—	—	3	22	7.3(9)	0	—	—	—	—	—	—	—	—	—	—	—	—	0	11
NFL	14	177(110)	—	—	—	—	107	894	8.4(34)	11	—	—	—	—	—	—	—	—	—	—	k	—	66	507

Tidd, Glenn Glenn E., C-G-T-WB, 5´11˝/202 lbs; none; B4/23/1894 Silvercreek Township, OH, D10/3/1970 Dayton, OH **1920** Day 8 (3) **1921** Day 5 (1) **1922** Day 4 (0), 6 **1923** Day 6 (0) **1924** Day 8 (1), 6 **NFL** 31 (5), 12 [5 yrs]

Tidmore, Sam Samuel Edward, LB, 6´1˝/230 lbs; Ohio State; 1962: Cle, rnd 6/Buf, rnd 20; B10/28/1938 Decatur, IL **1962** Cle 13 **1963** Cle 5 **NFL** 18 [2 yrs]

Tidwell, Billy Billy Reyhne, HB-DB, 5´9˝/178 lbs; Texas A&M; 1952: SF, rnd 3; B8/3/1930 Hearne, TX, D12/19/1990 Trinity, TX

YEAR	TEAM	G(GS, POS)	RUSH	YD	AVG(LG)	TD	REC	YD	AVG(LG)	TD	PASS	COMP	PCT	YD	AVG(LG)	TD	INT	SK	YD	QBR	KPR	OTD	PTS	TAY
1954	SF	10	1	1	1.0(1)	0	—	—	—	—	1	0	0.0	0	0.0	0	0	—	—	—	kp	—	0	123

Tidwell, Travis Travis Vaughn, QB, 5´10˝/185 lbs; Auburn; 1950: NYG, rnd 1; B2/5/1925 Florence, AL, D7/1/2004 Trussville, AL

YEAR	TEAM	G(GS, POS)	RUSH	YD	AVG(LG)	TD	REC	YD	AVG(LG)	TD	PASS	COMP	PCT	YD	AVG(LG)	TD	INT	SK	YD	QBR	KPR	OTD	PTS	TAY
1950	†NYG	8	29	133	4.6(54)	2	—	—	—	—	55	25	45.5	338	6.1(47)	4	3	—	—	—	—	—	12	222
1951	NYG	6	11	14	1.3(13)	0	—	—	—	—	21	8	38.1	155	7.4(56)	1	4	—	—	—	—	—	0	-64
NFL	2	14	40	147	3.7(54)	2	—	—	—	—	76	33	43.4	493	6.5(56)	5	7	—	—	—	—	—	12	159

Tierney, Festus Festus Patrick, G-T, 6´1˝/198 lbs; Minnesota; B7/1/1899 St. Paul, MN, D8/14/1973 Minneapolis, MN **1922** Ham 6 (6, RG) **1922** Tol 2 (0) **1923** Min 8 (8, LG) **1924** Min 6 (6, RG) **1925** Mil 3 (3, RG) **NFL** 25 (23) [4 yrs]

Tierney, Leo Clarence Leo, C, 6´3˝/248 lbs; Georgia Tech; 1977: Cle, rnd 12; B1/28/1954 San Antonio, TX **1978** Cle 2 **1978** NYG 5 **NFL** 7 [1 yr]

Tiffin, Van Van Leigh, K, 5´9˝/155 lbs; Alabama; B9/6/1965 Tupelo, MS **[K]** **1987** TB 3 (0) **1987** Mia 1 (0) **NFL** 4 (0) [1 yr]

Tigges, Mark Mark John, T, 6´3˝/290 lbs; Western Illinois; B2/5/1964 Algona, IA **1987** Cin 3 (3)

Tiggle, Calvin Calvin Bernard, LB, 6´1˝/235 lbs; Georgia Tech; 1991: TB, rnd 7; B11/10/1968 Fort Washington, MD **1991** TB 16 (0) **1992** TB 8 (4) **NFL** 24 (4) [2 yrs]

Tilleman, Mike Michael John, DT, 6´7˝/272 lbs; Montana; 1965: Min, rnd 12; B3/30/1944 Chinook, MT **1966** Min 12 **1967** NO 14 (LDT) **1968** NO 14 (LDT) **1969** NO 14 (LDT) **1970** NO 14 (LDT) **1971** Hou 14 (LDT) **1972** Hou 14 (LDT) **1973** Atl 13 **1974** Atl 12 (LDT) **1975** Atl 14 (LDT) **1976** Atl 14 (14, LDT) **NFL** 149 (14) [11 yrs]

Tiller, Jim James Thomas, HB, 5´9˝/165 lbs; Purdue; B12/21/1935 Fremont, OH

YEAR	TEAM	G(GS, POS)	RUSH	YD	AVG(LG)	TD	REC	YD	AVG(LG)	TD	PASS	COMP	PCT	YD	AVG(LG)	TD	INT	SK	YD	QBR	KPR	OTD	PTS	TAY
1962	NYT-A	11	31	43	1.4(25)	0	13	108	8.3(19)	0	—	—	—	—	—	—	—	—	—	—	kp	—	0	231

Tiller, Morgan Morgan John, E, 6´1˝/195 lbs; Denver; B10/13/1918 Trinidad, CO, D12/6/1983 Oakton, VA **1944** Bos 4 (0)

YEAR	TEAM	G(GS, POS)	RUSH	YD	AVG(LG)	TD	REC	YD	AVG(LG)	TD	PASS	COMP	PCT	YD	AVG(LG)	TD	INT	SK	YD	QBR	KPR	OTD	PTS	TAY
1945	Pit	10(0)	—	—	—	—	10	146	14.6(35)	0	—	—	—	—	—	—	—	—	—	—	k	—	0	75
NFL	2	14(0)	—	—	—	—	10	146	14.6(35)	0	—	—	—	—	—	—	—	—	—	—	k	—	0	72

Tilley, Emmett Emmett, LB, 5´11˝/240 lbs; Duke; B2/13/1961 Durham, NC **1983** Mia 6 (0)

Tilley, Pat Patrick Lee, WR, 5´10˝/178 lbs; Louisiana Tech; 1976: SL, rnd 4; B2/15/1953 Shreveport, LA

YEAR	TEAM	G(GS, POS)	RUSH	YD	AVG(LG)	TD	REC	YD	AVG(LG)	TD	PASS	COMP	PCT	YD	AVG(LG)	TD	INT	SK	YD	QBR	KPR	OTD	PTS	TAY
1976	SL	13(5, wr)	—	—	—	—	26	407	15.7(45)	1	—	—	—	—	—	—	—	—	—	—	p	—	6	280
1977	SL	14	—	—	—	—	5	64	12.8(31)	0	—	—	—	—	—	—	—	—	—	—	p	—	0	78
1978	SL	16(16, WR)	1	32	32.0(32)	0	62	900	14.5(43)	3	—	—	—	—	—	—	—	—	—	—	p	—	18	495
1979	SL	16(16, WR)	—	—	—	—	57	938	16.5(51)	6	—	—	—	—	—	—	—	—	—	—	—	—	36	499
1980	SL★	14(14, WR)	—	—	—	—	68	966	14.2(60)	6	—	—	—	—	—	—	—	—	—	—	—	—	36	513
1981	SL	16(16, WR)	—	—	—	—	66	1040	15.8(75)	3	—	—	—	—	—	—	—	—	—	—	—	—	18	535
1982	†SL	9(8, WR)	—	—	—	—	36	465	12.9(34)	2	—	—	—	—	—	—	—	—	—	—	—	—	12	243
1983	SL	16(16, WR)	—	—	—	—	44	690	15.7(71)	5	—	—	—	—	—	—	—	—	—	—	—	—	30	370
1984	SL	16(16, WR)	—	—	—	—	52	758	14.6(42)	5	—	—	—	—	—	—	—	—	—	—	—	—	30	404
1985	SL	16(16, WR)	—	—	—	—	49	726	14.8(46)	6	—	—	—	—	—	—	—	—	—	—	p	—	36	387
1986	SL	1(1)	—	—	—	—	3	51	17.0(18)	0	—	—	—	—	—	—	—	—	—	—	—	—	0	26
NFL	11	147(124)	1	32	32.0(32)	0	468	7005	15.0(75)	37	—	—	—	—	—	—	—	—	—	—	p	—	222	3829

Tillison, Ed Edward L., FB, 6´0˝/225 lbs; Northwest Missouri State; 1992: Det, rnd 11; B2/12/1969 Pearl River, LA

YEAR	TEAM	G(GS, POS)	RUSH	YD	AVG(LG)	TD	REC	YD	AVG(LG)	TD	PASS	COMP	PCT	YD	AVG(LG)	TD	INT	SK	YD	QBR	KPR	OTD	PTS	TAY
1992	Det	6(0)	4	22	5.5(10)	0	—	—	—	—	—	—	—	—	—	—	—	—	—	—	k	—	0	34

Tillman, Andre Andre, TE, 6´4˝/230 lbs; Texas Tech; 1974: Mia, rnd 2; B11/1/1952 Dallas, TX

YEAR	TEAM	G(GS, POS)	RUSH	YD	AVG(LG)	TD	REC	YD	AVG(LG)	TD	PASS	COMP	PCT	YD	AVG(LG)	TD	INT	SK	YD	QBR	KPR	OTD	PTS	TAY
1975	Mia	14(8, TE)	—	—	—	—	5	60	12.0(16)	0	—	—	—	—	—	—	—	—	—	—	—	—	0	30
1976	Mia	14(14, TE)	—	—	—	—	13	130	10.0(16)	1	—	—	—	—	—	—	—	—	—	—	k	—	6	55
1977	Mia	14(14, TE)	—	—	—	—	17	169	9.9(37)	2	—	—	—	—	—	—	—	—	—	—	—	—	12	95
1978	†Mia	16(16, TE)	—	—	—	—	31	398	12.8(33)	3	—	—	—	—	—	—	—	—	—	—	—	—	18	214
NFL	4	58(52)	—	—	—	—	66	757	11.5(37)	6	—	—	—	—	—	—	—	—	—	—	k	—	36	394

Tillman, Cedric Cedric Cornell, WR, 6´2˝/204 lbs; Alcorn State; 1992: Den, rnd 11; B7/22/1970 Natchez, MS

YEAR	TEAM	G(GS, POS)	RUSH	YD	AVG(LG)	TD	REC	YD	AVG(LG)	TD	PASS	COMP	PCT	YD	AVG(LG)	TD	INT	SK	YD	QBR	KPR	OTD	PTS	TAY
1992	Den	9(1)	—	—	—	—	12	211	17.6(81)	1	—	—	—	—	—	—	—	—	—	—	—	—	6	111
1993	†Den	14(3)	—	—	—	—	17	193	11.4(30)	2	—	—	—	—	—	—	—	—	—	—	—	—	12	107
1994	Den	16(3)	—	—	—	—	28	455	16.3(63)	1	—	—	—	—	—	—	—	—	—	—	—	—	6	233
1995	Jax	13(2)	—	—	—	—	30	368	12.3(28)	3	—	—	—	—	—	—	—	—	—	—	p	—	18	195
NFL	4	52(9)	—	—	—	—	87	1227	14.1(81)	7	—	—	—	—	—	—	—	—	—	—	p	—	42	645

Tillman, Charles Charles, DB, 6´1˝/196 lbs; Louisiana-Lafayette; 2003: Chi, rnd 2; B2/23/1981 Chicago, IL **2003** ChiB 16 (13, LCB) **2004** ChiB 8 (7, lcb) **2005**†ChiB 15 (15, LCB) **NFL** 39 (35) [3 yrs]

YEAR	TEAM	G (GS, POS)	RUSH	YD	AVG (LG)	TD	REC	YD	AVG (LG)	TD	PASS	COMP	PCT	YD	AVG (LG)	TD	INT	SK	YD	QBR	KPR	OTD	PTS	TAY

TILLMAN, FADDIE Faddie Charles, DT-DE, 6´5˝/235 lbs; Boise State; 1971: Atl, rnd 10; B10/7/1948 Dallas, TX **1972** NO 1

TILLMAN, LAWYER Lawyer James, WR-TE, 6´5˝/230 lbs; Auburn; 1989: Cle, rnd 2; B5/20/1966 Mobile, AL

YEAR	TEAM	G (GS, POS)	RUSH	YD	AVG (LG)	TD	REC	YD	AVG (LG)	TD	PASS	COMP	PCT	YD	AVG (LG)	TD	INT	SK	YD	QBR	KPR	OTD	PTS	TAY
1989	†Cle	14(1)	—	—	—	—	6	70	11.7(19)	2	—	—	—	—	—	—	—	—	—	—	—	1	18	45
1992	Cle	11(9, WR)	2	15	7.5(15)	0	25	498	19.9(52)	0	—	—	—	—	—	—	—	—	—	—	—	—	0	264
1993	Cle	7(0)	—	—	—	—	5	68	13.6(18)	1	—	—	—	—	—	—	—	—	—	—	—	—	6	39
1995	Car	5(0)	—	—	—	—	2	22	11.0(12)	0	—	—	—	—	—	—	—	—	—	—	—	—	0	11
NFL	4	37(10)	2	15	7.5(15)	0	38	658	17.3(52)	3	—	—	—	—	—	—	—	—	—	—	—	1	24	359

TILLMAN, LEWIS Lewis Daniel, RB, 6´0˝/204 lbs; Jackson State; 1989: NYG, rnd 4; B4/16/1966 Oklahoma City, OK

YEAR	TEAM	G (GS, POS)	RUSH	YD	AVG (LG)	TD	REC	YD	AVG (LG)	TD	PASS	COMP	PCT	YD	AVG (LG)	TD	INT	SK	YD	QBR	KPR	OTD	PTS	TAY
1989	†NYG	16(0)	79	290	3.7(19)	0	1	9	9.0(9)	0	—	—	—	—	—	—	—	—	—	—	—	—	0	295
1990	†NYG	16(3)	84	231	2.8(17)	1	8	18	2.3(16)	0	—	—	—	—	—	—	—	—	—	—	—	—	6	250
1991	NYG	16(1)	65	287	4.4(17)	1	5	30	6.0(12)	0	—	—	—	—	—	—	—	—	—	—	k	—	6	311
1992	NYG	16(0)	6	13	2.2(6)	0	1	15	15.0(15)	0	—	—	—	—	—	—	—	—	—	—	—	—	0	21
1993	†NYG	16(7, rb)	121	585	4.8(58)	3	1	21	21.0(21)	0	—	—	—	—	—	—	—	—	—	—	—	—	18	626
1994	†ChiB	16(15, RB)	275	899	3.3(25)	7	27	222	8.2(39)	0	—	—	—	—	—	—	—	—	—	—	—	—	42	1080
1995	ChiB	13(1)	29	78	2.7(9)	0	—	—	—	—	—	—	—	—	—	—	—	—	—	—	k	—	0	83
NFL	7	109(27)	659	2383	3.6(58)	12	43	315	7.3(39)	0	—	—	—	—	—	—	—	—	—	—	k	—	72	2665

TILLMAN, PAT Patrick Daniel, DB, 5´11˝/204 lbs; Arizona State; 1998: Arz, rnd 7; B11/6/1976 Fremont, CA, D4/22/2004, Afghanistan **1998**†Arz 16 (10, FS) **2000** Arz 16 (16, SS) **2001** Arz 12 (12, SS)

YEAR	TEAM	G (GS, POS)	RUSH	YD	AVG (LG)	TD	REC	YD	AVG (LG)	TD	PASS	COMP	PCT	YD	AVG (LG)	TD	INT	SK	YD	QBR	KPR	OTD	PTS	TAY
1999	Arz	16(1)	1	4	4.0(4)	0	—	—	—	—	—	—	—	—	—	—	—	—	—	—	ki	—	0	-11
NFL	4	60(39)	1	4	4.0(4)	0	—	—	—	—	—	—	—	—	—	—	—	—	—	—	kiS	—	0	14

TILLMAN, PETE Alonzo Monroe, C-LB, 6´0˝/210 lbs; Southwestern Oklahoma State; Oklahoma; B5/9/1922 Mangum, OK, D3/31/1998 Farmington, NM **1949** Bal-A 11 (5, c)

TILLMAN, RUSTY Russell Arthur, LB, 6´2˝/230 lbs; Arizona; Northern Arizona; B2/27/1946 Beloit, MI **1970** Was 14 (2) **1971**†Was 9 **1972**†Was 14 **1973**†Was 14 **1974**†Was 14 (1) **1975** Was 14 **1976**†Was 14 **1977** Was 14 **NFL** 107 (3) [8 yrs]

TILLMAN, SPENCER Spencer Allen, RB, 5´11˝/206 lbs; Oklahoma; 1987: Hou, rnd 5; B4/21/1964 Tulsa, OK

YEAR	TEAM	G (GS, POS)	RUSH	YD	AVG (LG)	TD	REC	YD	AVG (LG)	TD	PASS	COMP	PCT	YD	AVG (LG)	TD	INT	SK	YD	QBR	KPR	OTD	PTS	TAY
1987	Hou	5(1)	12	29	2.4(13)	1	—	—	—	—	—	—	—	—	—	—	—	—	—	—	k	—	6	24
1988	†Hou	16(0)	3	5	1.7(2)	0	—	—	—	—	—	—	—	—	—	—	—	—	—	—	k	—	0	3
1989	†SF	15(0)	—	—	—	—	—	—	—	—	—	—	—	—	—	—	—	—	—	—	k	—	0	56
1990	†SF	16(0)	—	—	—	—	—	—	—	—	—	—	—	—	—	—	—	—	—	—	k	—	0	21
1991	SF	16(0)	13	40	3.1(8)	0	2	3	1.5(3)	0	—	—	—	—	—	—	—	—	—	—	k	—	0	39
1992	†Hou	16(0)	1	1	1.0(1)	0	—	—	—	—	—	—	—	—	—	—	—	—	—	—	k	—	0	8
1993	†Hou	15(0)	9	94	10.4(34)	0	1	4	4.0(4)	1	—	—	—	—	—	—	—	—	—	—	—	—	6	101
1994	Hou	16(0)	2	12	6.0(9)	0	—	—	—	—	—	—	—	—	—	—	—	—	—	—	k	—	0	3
NFL	8	115(1)	40	181	4.5(34)	1	3	7	2.3(4)	1	—	—	—	—	—	—	—	—	—	—	k	—	12	255

TILLMAN, TRAVARES Travares Arastius, DB, 6´1˝/190 lbs; Georgia Tech; 2000: Buf, rnd 2; B10/8/1977 Lyons, GA **2000** Buf 15 (4) **2001** Buf 13 (6, fs) **2003** Car 7 (0) **2004** Car 6 (1) **2005** Mia 15 (10, SS) **NFL** 56 (21) [5 yrs]

TILLMON, TONY Anthony Vinzell, DB, 5´10˝/170 lbs; Texas; B9/12/1963 Borger, TX **1987** LARd 3 (1)

TILTON, RON Ronald John, G, 6´4˝/250 lbs; Florida; Tulane; B8/9/1963 Homestead, FL **1986**†Was 7 (0)

TIMBERLAKE, BOB Robert W., K, 6´4˝/220 lbs; Michigan; 1965: NYG, rnd 3/Buf, rnd 13; B10/18/1943 Middletown, OH **[K]** **1965** NYG 12

TIMBERLAKE, GEORGE George Robert, LB-G, 6´1˝/220 lbs; USC; 1954: GB, rnd 3; B11/3/1932 Long Beach, CA **1955** GB 6

TIMES, KEN Kenneth, NT-DT, 6´2˝/246 lbs; Southern (LA); 1980: SF, rnd 5; B1/1/1956 Deerfield Beach, FL **1980** SF 3 (0) **1981** SL 2 (0) **NFL** 5 (0) [2 yrs]

TIMMER, KIRK Kirk Richard, LB, 6´3˝/242 lbs; Montana State; 1987: NYJ, rnd 11; B12/18/1963 Butte, MT **1987** Dal 1 (0)

TIMMERMAN, ADAM Adam Larry, G, 6´4˝/310 lbs; South Dakota State; 1995: GB, rnd 7; B8/14/1971 Cherokee, IA **1995**†GB 13 (0) **1996**†GB 16 (16, RG) **1997**†GB 16 (16, RG) **1998**†GB 16 (16, RG) **1999**†SL 16 (16, RG) **2000**†SL 16 (15, RG) **2001**†SL★16 (16, RG) **2004**†SL 16 (16, RG) **2005** SL 16 (16, RG)

YEAR	TEAM	G (GS, POS)	RUSH	YD	AVG (LG)	TD	REC	YD	AVG (LG)	TD	PASS	COMP	PCT	YD	AVG (LG)	TD	INT	SK	YD	QBR	KPR	OTD	PTS	TAY
2002	SL	16(16, RG)	—	—	—	—	0	3	(3)	0	—	—	—	—	—	—	—	—	—	—	—	—	0	2
2003	†SL	16(16, RG)	—	—	—	—	1	-7	-7.0(-7)	0	—	—	—	—	—	—	—	—	—	—	—	—	0	-4
NFL	11	173(159)	—	—	—	—	1	-4	-4.0(3)	0	—	—	—	—	—	—	—	—	—	—	—	—	0	-2

TIMMONS, CHARLIE Charles Truman, FB-LB, 5´10˝/210 lbs; Clemson; Georgia; 1942: Was, rnd 19; B2/8/1917 Piedmont, SC, D3/27/1996 Greenville, SC

YEAR	TEAM	G (GS, POS)	RUSH	YD	AVG (LG)	TD	REC	YD	AVG (LG)	TD	PASS	COMP	PCT	YD	AVG (LG)	TD	INT	SK	YD	QBR	KPR	OTD	PTS	TAY
1946	Bkn-A	13(1)	23	65	2.8	0	1	4	4.0(4)	0	—	—	—	—	—	—	—	—	—	—	—	—	0	67

TIMPSON, MICHAEL Michael Dwain, WR, 5´10˝/178 lbs; Penn State; 1989: NE, rnd 4; B6/6/1967 Baxley, GA

YEAR	TEAM	G (GS, POS)	RUSH	YD	AVG (LG)	TD	REC	YD	AVG (LG)	TD	PASS	COMP	PCT	YD	AVG (LG)	TD	INT	SK	YD	QBR	KPR	OTD	PTS	TAY
1989	NE	2(0)	—	—	—	—	—	—	—	—	—	—	—	—	—	—	—	—	—	—	k	—	0	-17
1990	NE	5(0)	—	—	—	—	5	91	18.2(42)	0	—	—	—	—	—	—	—	—	—	—	k	—	0	63
1991	NE	16(2)	1	-4	-4.0(-4)	0	25	471	18.8(60)	2	—	—	—	—	—	—	—	—	—	—	k	—	12	249
1992	NE	16(2)	—	—	—	—	26	315	12.1(25)	1	—	—	—	—	—	—	—	—	—	—	kp	—	6	168
1993	NE	16(7, wr)	—	—	—	—	42	654	15.6(48)	2	—	—	—	—	—	—	—	—	—	—	—	—	12	337
1994	†NE	15(14, WR)	2	14	7.0(10)	0	74	941	12.7(37)	3	—	—	—	—	—	—	—	—	—	—	k	—	18	513
1995	ChiB	16(0)	3	28	9.3(16)	1	24	289	12.0(36)	2	—	—	—	—	—	—	—	—	—	—	k	—	18	343
1996	ChiB	15(15, WR)	3	21	7.0(13)	0	62	802	12.9(49)	0	—	—	—	—	—	—	—	—	—	—	—	—	0	422
1997	Phi	15(10, WR)	—	—	—	—	42	484	11.5(26)	2	—	—	—	—	—	—	—	—	—	—	—	—	12	252
NFL	9	116(50)	9	59	6.6(16)	1	300	4047	13.5(60)	12	—	—	—	—	—	—	—	—	—	—	kp	—	78	2328

TINDALE, TIM Timothy Scott, FB, 5´10˝/220 lbs; Western Ontario (Canada); B4/15/1971 London, Canada

YEAR	TEAM	G (GS, POS)	RUSH	YD	AVG (LG)	TD	REC	YD	AVG (LG)	TD	PASS	COMP	PCT	YD	AVG (LG)	TD	INT	SK	YD	QBR	KPR	OTD	PTS	TAY
1995	†Buf	16(0)	5	16	3.2(6)	0	—	—	—	—	—	—	—	—	—	—	—	—	—	—	k	—	0	-12
1996	†Buf	14(3)	14	49	3.5(15)	0	1	-1	-1.0(-1)	0	—	—	—	—	—	—	—	—	—	—	—	—	0	49
1997	Buf	7(0)	—	—	—	—	4	105	26.3(45)	0	—	—	—	—	—	—	—	—	—	—	—	—	0	53
NFL	3	37(3)	19	65	3.4(15)	0	5	104	20.8(45)	0	—	—	—	—	—	—	—	—	—	—	k	—	0	89

TINGELHOFF, MICK Henry Michael, C, 6´2˝/237 lbs; Nebraska; B5/22/1940 Lexington, NC **1962** Min 14 (14, C) **1963** Min 14 (14, C) **1964** Min★14 (14, C) **1965** Min★14 (14, C) **1966** Min★14 (14, C) **1967** Min★14 (14, C) **1968**†Min★14 (14, C) **1969**†Min★14 (14, C) **1970**†Min☆14 (14, C) **1971**†Min 14 (14, C) **1972** Min 14 (14, C) **1973**†Min 14 (14, C) **1974**†Min 14 (14, C) **1975**†Min 14 (14, C) **1976**†Min 14 (14, C) **1977**†Min 14 (14, C) **1978**†Min 16 (16, C) **NFL** 240 (240) [17 yrs]

TINKER, GERALD Gerald Alexander, WR, 5´9˝/173 lbs; Memphis; Kent State; 1974: Atl, rnd 2; B1/19/1951 Miami, FL

YEAR	TEAM	G (GS, POS)	RUSH	YD	AVG (LG)	TD	REC	YD	AVG (LG)	TD	PASS	COMP	PCT	YD	AVG (LG)	TD	INT	SK	YD	QBR	KPR	OTD	PTS	TAY
1974	Atl	12	2	5	2.5(9)	0	1	12	12.0(12)	0	—	—	—	—	—	—	—	—	—	—	kp	1	6	415
1975	Atl	8	—	—	—	—	3	37	12.3(35)	1	—	—	—	—	—	—	—	—	—	—	kp	—	6	129
1975	GB	6	1	5	5.0(5)	0	4	84	21.0(35)	1	—	—	—	—	—	—	—	—	—	—	—	—	6	52
NFL	2	26	3	10	3.3(9)	0	8	133	16.6(35)	2	—	—	—	—	—	—	—	—	—	—	kp	1	18	596

TINOISAMOA, PISA Pisa, LB, 6´1˝/235 lbs; Hawaii; 2003: SL, rnd 2; B7/15/1981 San Diego, CA **2003**†SL 16 (15, LLB) **2004**†SL 16 (16, RLB) **2005** SL 16 (16, LLB) **NFL** 48 (47) [3 yrs]

TINSLEY, BUDDY Robert Porter, T, 6´4˝/245 lbs; Baylor; 1948: Phi, rnd 7; B8/16/1924 Damon, TX **1949** LAD-A 10 (10, RT)

TINSLEY, GAYNELL Gaynell Charles, E, 6´1˝/198 lbs; LSU; 1937: ChiC, rnd 2; B2/1/1915 Ruple, LA, D7/24/2002 Baton Rouge, LA

YEAR	TEAM	G (GS, POS)	RUSH	YD	AVG (LG)	TD	REC	YD	AVG (LG)	TD	PASS	COMP	PCT	YD	AVG (LG)	TD	INT	SK	YD	QBR	KPR	OTD	PTS	TAY
1937	ChiC☆	11(11, LE)	1	2	2.0(2)	0	36	**675**	18.8(**97**)	5	—	—	—	—	—	—	—	—	—	—	—	1	36	365
1938	ChiC★	11(10, LE)	4	26	6.5	0	**41**	516	12.6(**98**)	1	—	—	—	—	—	—	—	—	—	—	—	—	6	289
1940	ChiC	7(4)	1	17	17.0(17)	0	16	165	10.3	1	—	—	—	—	—	—	—	—	—	—	i	—	6	105
NFL	3	29(25)	6	45	7.5(17)	0	93	1356	14.6(98)	7	—	—	—	—	—	—	—	—	—	—	i	1	48	758

TINSLEY, JESS Jess D., T-E, 6´0˝/201 lbs; LSU; B10/18/1908, D4/1977 Blevins, AR **1929** ChiC 12 (6, LT) **1930** ChiC 10 (6, LT) **1931** ChiC 6 (2) **1932** ChiC 10 (4) **1933** ChiC 11 (1) **NFL** 49 (19) [5 yrs]

TINSLEY, KEITH Keith Anthony, WR, 5´9˝/184 lbs; Pittsburgh; B3/31/1965 Detroit, MI

YEAR	TEAM	G (GS, POS)	RUSH	YD	AVG (LG)	TD	REC	YD	AVG (LG)	TD	PASS	COMP	PCT	YD	AVG (LG)	TD	INT	SK	YD	QBR	KPR	OTD	PTS	TAY
1987	Cle	3(1)	—	—	—	—	1	17	17.0(17)	0	—	—	—	—	—	—	—	—	—	—	k	—	0	10

YEAR	TEAM	G(GS, POS)	RUSH	YD	AVG(LG)	TD	REC	YD	AVG(LG)	TD	PASS	COMP	PCT	YD	AVG(LG)	TD	INT	SK	YD	QBR	KPR	OTD	PTS	TAY

TINSLEY, PETE   Elijah Pope, G, 5'8"/205 lbs; Georgia; 1938: GB, rnd 11; B3/16/1913 Spartanburg, SC, D5/11/1995, MI   **1938**†GB 9 (0)   **1939**†GB✧10 (1)   **1940** GB 7 (2) **1941**†GB☆9 (7, RG)   **1942** GB 11 (1)   **1943** GB 10 (4)   **1944**†GB 10 (7, RG)   **1945** GB 10 (9, RG)   **NFL** 76 (31) [8 yrs]

TINSLEY, SCOTT   Scott, QB, 6'2"/195 lbs; USC; B11/14/1959 Oklahoma City, OK

| 1987 | Phi | 3(3) | 4 | 2 | 0.5(2) | 0 | — | — | — | — | 86 | 48 | 55.8 | 637 | 7.4(62) | 3 | 4 | 6 | 55 | — | — | — | 0 | 176 |

TINSLEY, SID   Sidney Wallace, HB, 5'9"/168 lbs; Clemson; B1/14/1920 Spartanburg, SC, deceased

| 1945 | Pit | 9(0) | 5 | 3 | 0.6(4) | 0 | — | — | — | — | — | — | — | — | — | — | — | — | — | Pi | — | — | 0 | -4 |

TIPPETT, ANDRE   Andre Bernard, LB, 6'3"/240 lbs; Iowa; 1982: NE, rnd 2; B12/27/1959 Birmingham, AL [S]   **1982**†NE 9 (1)   **1983** NE 15 (13, LOLB)   **1984** NE★16 (16, LOLB) **1985**†NE★16 (16, LOLB)   **1986**†NE★11 (11, LOLB)   **1987** NE★13 (13, LOLB)   **1988** NE★12 (11, LOLB)   **1990** NE 13 (13, ROLB/lolb)   **1991** NE 16 (16, LOLB) **1992** NE 14 (13, LOLB)   **1993** NE 16 (16, LOLB)   **NFL** 151 (139) [11 yrs]

TIPPINS, KEN   Kenneth, LB, 6'1"/235 lbs; Middle Tennessee State; B7/22/1966 Adel, GA   **1989** Dal 6 (0)   **1990** Atl 16 (2)   **1991**†Atl 16 (7, lilb)   **1992** Atl 16 (15, LOLB) **1993** Atl 14 (1)   **1994** Atl 16 (7, rlb)   **1995**†Atl 16 (0)   **NFL** 100 (32) [7 yrs]

TIPTON, DAVE   David Lance, DE-DT, 6'6"/245 lbs; Stanford; 1971: NYG, rnd 4; B4/23/1949 Hollister, CA   **1971** NYG 5   **1972** NYG 14   **1973** NYG 6   **1974** SD 11 (6, lde) **1975** SD 14   **1976** Sea 12 (12, LDE)   **NFL** 62 (18) [6 yrs]

TIPTON, DAVID   David Joseph, NT-DT, 6'1"/255 lbs; Western Illinois; B12/10/1953 Superior, WI   **1975** NE 4   **1976**†NE 8   **NFL** 12 [2 yrs]

TIPTON, HOWIE   Howard Durward, G-WB-BB-E, 5'11"/186 lbs; USC; B4/19/1911 Los Angeles, CA, D3/19/1966 San Bernardino County, CA

1933	ChiC	11(6, wb)	16	46	2.9	0	5	106	21.2(47)	1	—	—	—	—	—	—	—	—	—	—	—	—	6	104
1934	ChiC	10(4)	1	10	10.0(10)	0	—	—	—	—	—	—	—	—	—	—	—	—	—	—	—	—	0	10
1935	ChiC	7(5, rg)	—	—	—	—	—	—	—	—	—	—	—	—	—	—	—	—	—	—	—	—		
1936	ChiC	12(9, RG)	—	—	—	—	1	15	15.0(15)	0	—	—	—	—	—	—	—	—	—	—	—	—	0	8
1937	ChiC	11(7, BB)	9	23	2.6	0	1	2	2.0(2)	0	—	—	—	—	—	—	—	—	—	—	—	—	0	24
NFL	5	51(31)	26	79	3.0(10)	0	7	123	17.6(47)	1	—	—	—	—	—	—	—	—	—	—	—	—	6	146

TIPTON, RICO   Enrico A., LB, 6'2"/240 lbs; Washington State; B7/31/1961 Pittsburg, CA   **1987** Sea 3 (2)

TITCHENAL, BOB   Robert Alden, E-C-LB-DE, 6'2"/194 lbs; San Jose State; B10/17/1917 Ventura, CA   **1940**†Was 11 (7, C)   **1941** Was 11 (4)

1942	Was✧	10(1)	—	—	—	—	1	7	7.0(7)	0	—	—	—	—	—	—	—	—	—	i	—	—	0	18
NFL	3	32(12)	—	—	—	—	1	7	7.0(7)	0	—	—	—	—	—	—	—	—	—	i	—	—	0	11
1946	SF-A	14(13, RE)	1	2	2.0(2)	0	7	160	22.9	2	—	—	—	—	—	—	—	—	—	—	—	—	12	92
1947	LAD-A	14(2)	1	0	0.0	0	7	97	13.9	0	—	—	—	—	—	—	—	—	—	—	—	—	0	49
AAFC	2	28(15)	2	2	1.0(2)	0	14	257	18.4(7)	2	—	—	—	—	—	—	—	—	—	—	—	—	12	141

TITENSOR, GLEN   Glen Weston, G-C, 6'4"/263 lbs; UCLA; Brigham Young; 1981: Dal, rnd 3; B2/21/1958 Bellflower, GA   **1981**†Dal 16 (0)   **1982** Dal 4 (0)   **1983**†Dal 15 (1) **1984** Dal 15 (12, LG)   **1985**†Dal 16 (16, LG)   **1986** Dal 10 (1)   **1988** Dal 16 (16, LG)   **NFL** 92 (46) [7 yrs]

TITMAS, HERB   Herbert James, BB, 5'8"/185 lbs; Syracuse; B12/14/1905, D8/16/1976 Cleveland, OH   **1931** Pro 11 (5, BB), 6

TITTLE, Y.A.   Yelberton Abraham 'The Bald Eagle', QB, 6'0"/192 lbs; LSU; 1948: Det, rnd 1; B10/24/1926 Marshall, TX; HOF 1971

1948	†Bal-A	14(12, QB)	52	157	3.0	4	—	—	—	—	289	161	55.7	2522	**8.7(80)**	16	9	—	—	—	—	—	24	1178
1949	Bal-A	11(7, QB)	29	89	3.1	2	—	—	—	—	**289**	148	51.2	2209	7.6(80)	14	**18**	—	—	—	—	—	12	564
AAFC	2	25(19)	81	246	3.0	6	—	—	—	—	578	309	53.5	4731	8.2(80)	30	27	—	—	78.6	—	—	36	1742
1950	Bal	12(9, QB)	20	77	3.8(33)	2	—	—	—	—	315	**161**	51.1	1884	6.0(62)	8	19	—	—	52.9	—	—	12	319
1951	SF	12(qb)	13	18	1.4(5)	1	—	—	—	—	114	63	55.3	808	7.1(48)	8	9	—	—	68.2	—	—	6	112
1952	SF	12(QB)	11	-11	-1.0(4)	0	—	—	—	—	208	106	51.0	1407	6.8(77)	11	12	—	—	66.3	—	—	0	268
1953	SF✧	11(QB)	14	41	2.9(14)	6	—	—	—	—	259	149	57.5	2121	8.2(71)	20	16	—	—	84.1	—	—	36	622
1954	SF✧	12(QB)	28	68	2.4(10)	4	—	—	—	—	295	170	57.6	2205	7.5(70)	9	9	—	—	78.7	—	—	24	896
1955	SF	12(QB)	23	114	5.0(35)	0	—	—	—	—	287	147	51.2	2185	7.6(78)	**17**	**28**	—	—	56.6	—	—	0	172
1956	SF	10(QB)	24	67	2.8(13)	4	—	—	—	—	218	124	56.9	1641	7.5(77)	7	12	—	—	68.6	—	—	24	483
1957	†SF★	12(QB)	40	220	5.5(45)	6	—	—	—	—	279	**176**	**63.1**	2157	7.7(46)	13	15	—	—	80.0	—	—	36	824
1958	SF	11(QB)	22	35	1.6(12)	2	—	—	—	—	208	120	57.7	1467	7.1(64)	9	15	—	—	63.9	—	—	12	234
1959	SF✧	11(QB)	11	24	2.2(22)	0	1	4	4.0(4)	0	199	102	51.3	1331	6.7(75)	10	15	—	—	58.0	—	—	0	142
1960	SF	9(qb)	10	61	6.1(28)	0	—	—	—	—	127	69	54.3	694	5.5(45)	4	3	—	—	70.8	—	—	0	308
1961	†NYG★	13(QB)	25	85	3.4(17)	3	—	—	—	—	285	163	57.2	2272	8.0(62)	17	12	—	—	85.3	—	—	18	856
1962	†NYG★	14(QB)	17	108	6.4(23)	2	—	—	—	—	375	200	53.3	3224	8.6(69)	**33**	20	—	—	89.5	—	—	12	1105
1963	†NYG☆	13(QB)	18	99	5.5(18)	2	—	—	—	—	367	221	**60.2**	3145	**8.6(70)**	36	14	24	205	**104.8**	—	—	12	1312
1964	NYG	14(QB)	15	-7	-0.5(7)	1	—	—	—	—	281	147	52.3	1798	6.4(54)	10	22	30	243	51.6	—	—	6	72
NFL	1 5	178(9)	291	999	3.4(45)	33	1	4	4.0(4)	0	3817	2118	55.5	28339	7.4(80)	212	221	54	448	73.6	—	—	198	7721

TITUS, GEORGE   George Timms, C-LB, 5'10"/185 lbs; Holy Cross; 1944: Pit, rnd 8; B1/7/1922 Brooklyn, NY   **1946** Pit 11 (0)

TITUS, SI   Silas John, C, 6'0"/195 lbs; Holy Cross; B9/23/1918 Brooklyn, NY, D2/17/1989 Pittsburgh, PA   **1940** Bkn 4 (0)   **1941** Bkn 6 (0)   **1942** Bkn 9 (0)   **1945** Pit 9 (3) **NFL** 28 (3) [4 yrs]

TIUMALU, CASEY   Casey James, RB, 5'8"/206 lbs; Brigham Young; B6/19/1961 San Diego, CA   **1987** LARm 3 (0)

TOBECK, ROBBIE   Robert Lee, C-G, 6'4"/297 lbs; Washington State; B3/6/1970 Tarpon Springs, FL   **1994** Atl 5 (0)   **1995**†Atl 16 (16, LG)   **1997** Atl 16 (15, LG)   **1998**†Atl 16 (16, C) **1999** Atl 15 (15, G)   **2000** Sea 4 (0)   **2001** Sea 16 (16, C)   **2002** Sea 16 (16, C)   **2003**†Sea 16 (16, C)   **2004**†Sea 16 (16, C)   **2005**†Sea✧16 (16, C)

| 1996 | Atl | 16(16, LG) | — | — | — | — | 2 | 15 | 7.5(14) | 1 | — | — | — | — | — | — | — | — | — | — | — | — | 6 | 13 |
| NFL | 12 | 168(158) | — | — | — | — | 2 | 15 | 7.5(14) | 1 | — | — | — | — | — | — | — | — | — | — | — | — | 6 | 13 |

TOBEY, DAVE   David Morgan, LB, 6'3"/231 lbs; Oregon; 1965: Pit, rnd 10; B3/17/1943 Portland, OR   **1966** Min 14 (1)   **1967** Min 2   **1968** Den-A 7   **NFL** 23 (1) [3 yrs]

TOBIN, BILL   William Hugh, HB, 5'11"/210 lbs; Missouri; 1963: SF, rnd 14; B2/16/1941 Burlington Junction, MO

| 1963 | Hou-A | 10(HB) | 75 | 271 | 3.6(32) | 4 | 13 | 173 | 13.3(33) | 1 | — | — | — | — | — | — | — | — | — | — | k | — | 30 | 398 |

TOBIN, ELGIE   Elza Williams, G-BB, 5'9"/180 lbs; West Virginia; Penn State; B5/1885, deceased [C]   **1920** Akr 1 (0)   **1921** Akr 8 (2, LG)   **NFL** 9 (2) [2 yrs]

TOBIN, GEORGE   George Edward, G-LB, 5'10"/205 lbs; Notre Dame; B7/9/1921 Belmont, PA, D1/2/1999 Farmington Hills, MI   **1947** NYG 11 (0)

TOBIN, LEO   Leaman, G-LB, 5'9"/220 lbs; Grove City; B3/1890, deceased [K]   **1921** Akr 12 (6), 1

TOBIN, REX   Ernest V., E, none; B2/1900 Duluth, MN, deceased   **1925** Dul 1 (0)

TOBIN, STEVE   Steven Arthur, C, 6'4"/258 lbs; Minnesota; B3/29/1957 Breckenridge, MN   **1980** NYG 4 (0)

TOBUREN, NELSON   Nelson Edward, LB, 6'3"/235 lbs; Wichita State; 1961: GB, rnd 14; B11/24/1938 Boulder, CO   **1961**†GB 14   **1962** GB 10   **NFL** 24 [2 yrs]

TODD, DICK   Richard S., B, 5'11"/172 lbs; Texas A&M; 1939: Was, rnd 5; B10/2/1914 Thrall, TX, D11/9/1999 Bryan, TX [KC]

1939	Was	10(1)	57	266	4.7(60)	2	19	230	12.1(59)	3	4	3	75.0	86	21.5	0	0	—	—	—	KP	—	1	38	469
1940	†Was★	11(1)	76	408	**5.4(51)**	4	20	402	20.1(81)	4	1	1	100.0	7	7.0(7)	0	0	—	—	—	Pi	—	1	54	676
1941	Was	7(6, FB)	55	138	2.5(11)	0	8	125	15.6(35)	1	—	—	—	—	—	—	—	—	—	—	Pkp	—	1	18	407
1942	†Was✧	11(1)	65	195	3.0(22)	0	23	328	14.3(53)	4	6	1	16.7	11	1.8(11)	0	1	—	—	—	KPkpi	—	1	26	514
1945	†Was	6(1)	7	54	7.7(31)	0	—	—	—	—	—	—	—	—	—	—	—	—	—	—	pi	—	—	0	111
1946	Was	11(8, LH)	41	266	6.5(29)	3	8	107	13.4(23)	2	—	—	—	—	—	—	—	—	—	—	kpi	—	1	30	407
1947	Was	11(7, qb)	10	45	4.5(12)	0	4	84	21.0(38)	0	—	—	—	—	—	—	—	—	—	—	kpi	—	—	0	208
1948	Was	12(1, lh)	57	201	3.5(21)	1	37	550	14.9(78)	6	—	—	—	—	—	—	—	—	—	—	kp	—	1	42	527
NFL	8	79(25)	368	1573	4.3(60)	11	119	1826	15.3(81)	20	11	5	45.5	104	9.5(11)	0	2	—	—	—	KPkpi	—	3	208	3317

TODD, JIM   James Ulysses, HB, 5'11"/195 lbs; Ball State; 1966: Phi, rnd 9; B3/2/1943 Greenville, MS

| 1966 | Det | 10 | 2 | 6 | 3.0(3) | 0 | — | — | — | — | — | — | — | — | — | — | — | — | — | — | kp | — | 0 | 53 |

TODD, JOE   Joseph Robert, LB, 6'0"/218 lbs; Hofstra; B4/17/1979 Mansfield, MA   **2001** NYJ 1 (0)

TODD, LARRY Lawrence, RB, 6´1˝/185 lbs; Arizona State; 1965: Oak, rnd R1/SF, rnd 4; B10/7/1942 Memphis, AZ, D1/17/1990 Oakland, CA

YEAR	TEAM	G(GS, POS)	RUSH	YD	AVG(LG)	TD	REC	YD	AVG(LG)	TD	PASS	COMP	PCT	YD	AVG(LG)	TD	INT	SK	YD	QBR	KPR	OTD	PTS	TAY
1965	Oak-A	14	32	183	5.7(57)	0	8	106	13.3(43)	0	1	0	0.0	0	0.0	0	0	—	—	—	k	—	0	397
1966	Oak-A	14	—	—	—	—	14	134	9.6(17)	1	—	—	—	—	—	—	—	—	—	—	—	—	6	72
1967	†Oak-A	5	29	116	4.0(16)	2	4	42	10.5(17)	0	—	—	—	—	—	—	—	—	—	—	k	—	12	205
1968	Oak-A	3	13	89	6.8(31)	2	4	40	10.0(18)	0	—	—	—	—	—	—	—	—	—	—	—	—	12	129
1969	†Oak-A	11	47	198	4.2(51)	1	16	149	9.3(48)	1	—	—	—	—	—	—	—	—	—	—	—	—	12	288
1970	†Oak	10	17	39	2.3(13)	0	5	51	10.2(23)	0	—	—	—	—	—	—	—	—	—	—	—	—	0	65
NFL	6	57	138	625	4.5(57)	5	51	522	10.2(48)	2	1	0	0.0	0	0.0	0	0	—	—	—	k	—	42	1155

TODD, RICHARD Carl Richard, QB, 6´2˝/207 lbs; Alabama; 1976: NYJ, rnd 1; B11/19/1953 Birmingham, AL

YEAR	TEAM	G(GS, POS)	RUSH	YD	AVG(LG)	TD	REC	YD	AVG(LG)	TD	PASS	COMP	PCT	YD	AVG(LG)	TD	INT	SK	YD	QBR	KPR	OTD	PTS	TAY
1976	NYJ	13(6, qb)	28	107	3.8(22)	1	—	—	—	—	162	65	40.1	870	5.4(44)	3	12	29	233	33.2	—	—	6	87
1977	NYJ	12(11, QB)	24	46	1.9(13)	2	—	—	—	—	265	133	50.2	1863	7.0(87)	11	17	24	203	60.3	—	—	12	373
1978	NYJ	5(5, qb)	14	18	1.3(10)	0	—	—	—	—	107	60	56.1	849	7.9(49)	6	10	15	122	61.6	—	—	0	73
1979	NYJ	15(15, QB)	36	93	2.6(21)	5	—	—	—	—	334	171	51.2	2660	**8.0(72)**	16	22	25	222	66.5	—	—	30	673
1980	NYJ	16(16, QB)	49	330	6.7(31)	5	—	—	—	—	479	264	55.1	3329	6.9(55)	17	**30**	42	326	62.7	—	—	30	930
1981	†NYJ	16(16, QB)	32	131	4.1(19)	0	1	1	1.0(1)	0	497	279	56.1	3231	6.5(49)	25	13	30	224	81.8	—	—	0	1352
1982	†NYJ	9(9, QB)	13	-5	-0.4(7)	1	—	—	—	—	261	153	58.6	1961	7.5(56)	14	8	23	206	87.3	—	—	6	736
1983	NYJ	16(16, QB)	35	101	2.9(17)	0	—	—	—	—	518	308	59.5	3478	6.7(64)	18	**26**	42	314	70.3	—	—	0	890
1984	NO	15(14, QB)	28	111	4.0(15)	0	—	—	—	—	312	161	51.6	2178	7.0(74)	11	**19**	33	267	60.6	—	—	0	495
1985	NO	2(0)	—	—	—	—	—	—	—	—	32	16	50.0	191	6.0(56)	3	4	1	10	—	—	—	0	-50
NFL	10	119(108)	259	932	3.6(31)	14	1	1	1.0(1)	0	2967	1610	54.3	20610	6.9(87)	124	161	264	2127	67.6	—	—	84	5558

TOEFIELD, LABRANDON LaBrandon Cordell, RB, 5´11˝/232 lbs; LSU; 2003: Jax, rnd 4; B9/24/1980 Independence, LA

YEAR	TEAM	G(GS, POS)	RUSH	YD	AVG(LG)	TD	REC	YD	AVG(LG)	TD	PASS	COMP	PCT	YD	AVG(LG)	TD	INT	SK	YD	QBR	KPR	OTD	PTS	TAY
2003	Jax	16(0)	53	212	4.0(30)	2	14	105	7.5(16)	1	2	1	50.0	32	16.0(32)	0	0	—	—	—	k	—	18	368
2004	Jax	14(0)	51	169	3.3(16)	0	28	151	5.4(16)	1	0	0	0.0	0	0.0	0	0	1	7	—	k	—	6	248
2005	Jax	9(2)	36	142	3.9(32)	4	3	17	5.7(11)	0	—	—	—	—	—	—	—	—	—	—	—	—	24	191
NFL	3	39(2)	140	523	3.7(32)	6	45	273	6.1(16)	2	2	1	50.0	32	16.0(32)	0	0	1	7	—	k	—	48	806

TOEWS, JEFF Jeffrey Mark, G-T, 6´3˝/255 lbs; Washington; 1979: Mia, rnd 2; B11/4/1957 San Jose, CA **1979** Mia 11 **1980** Mia 7 (0) **1981** Mia 9 (7, lg) **1982**†Mia 9 (1) **1983** Mia 8 (1) **1984**†Mia 16 (0) **1985** Mia 11 (5, rt) **NFL** 71 (14) [7 yrs]

TOEWS, LOREN Loren James, LB, 6´3˝/220 lbs; California; 1973: Pit, rnd 8; B11/3/1951 Dinuba, CA **1973**†Pit 14 **1974**†Pit 14 **1975**†Pit 14 **1976**†Pit 14 (2) **1977**†Pit 14 (14, RLB) **1978**†Pit 11 (10, RLB) **1979**†Pit 11 **1980** Pit 16 (4) **1981** Pit 16 (4) **1982**†Pit 9 (9, LILB) **1983**†Pit 16 (16, LILB) **NFL** 149 (59) [11 yrs]

TOFFLEMIRE, JOE Joseph Salvatore, C, 6´3˝/275 lbs; Arizona; 1989: Sea, rnd 2; B7/7/1965 Los Angeles, CA **1990** Sea 16 (0) **1992** Sea 16 (16, C) **1994** Sea 1 (0) **NFL** 33 (16) [3 yrs]

TOFIL, JOE Joe John, E, 6´1˝/205 lbs; Indiana; B3/15/1918 Campbell, OH, D5/1973

YEAR	TEAM	G(GS, POS)	RUSH	YD	AVG(LG)	TD	REC	YD	AVG(LG)	TD	PASS	COMP	PCT	YD	AVG(LG)	TD	INT	SK	YD	QBR	KPR	OTD	PTS	TAY
1942	Bkn	11(0)	—	—	—	—	3	33	11.0(17)	0	—	—	—	—	—	—	—	—	—	—	—	—	0	17

TOIBIN, BRENDAN Brendan Patrick, K, 6´0˝/205 lbs; Richmond; B2/2/1964 Columbia, SC **[K]** **1987** Was 1 (0)

TOLAR, CHARLEY Charles Guy, FB, 5´6˝/199 lbs; Northwestern State (LA); 1959: Pit, rnd 27; B9/5/1937 Natchitoches, LA, D4/29/2003 League City, TX

YEAR	TEAM	G(GS, POS)	RUSH	YD	AVG(LG)	TD	REC	YD	AVG(LG)	TD	PASS	COMP	PCT	YD	AVG(LG)	TD	INT	SK	YD	QBR	KPR	OTD	PTS	TAY
1960	†Hou-A	14	54	179	3.3(40)	3	7	71	10.1(21)	0	—	—	—	—	—	—	—	—	—	—	kp	—	18	314
1961	†Hou-A★	14(FB)	157	577	3.7(28)	4	24	219	9.1(32)	1	1	0	0.0	0	0.0	0	0	—	—	—	k	—	30	744
1962	†Hou-A★	14(FB)	**244**	1012	4.1(25)	7	30	251	8.4(35)	1	1	0	0.0	0	0.0	0	1	—	—	—	k	—	48	1161
1963	Hou-A	14(FB)	194	659	3.4(33)	3	41	275	6.7(33)	0	—	—	—	—	—	—	—	—	—	—	k	—	18	816
1964	Hou-A	14(FB)	139	515	3.7(40)	4	35	244	7.0(52)	0	—	—	—	—	—	—	—	—	—	—	—	—	24	677
1965	Hou-A	11(FB)	73	230	3.2(18)	0	25	138	5.5(21)	0	1	0	0.0	0	0.0	0	0	—	—	—	—	—	0	299
1966	Hou-A	14(FB)	46	105	2.3(17)	0	13	68	5.2(14)	0	1	0	0.0	0	0.0	0	0	—	—	—	—	—	0	139
NFL	7	95	907	3277	3.6(40)	21	175	1266	7.2(52)	2	4	0	0.0	0	0.0	0	1	—	—	—	kp	—	138	4148

TOLBERT, JIM Love James, DB, 6´4˝/200 lbs; Lincoln (MO); 1966: SD, rnd 7; B3/12/1944 Fairfield, AL **1966** SD-A 1 **1967** SD-A 14 (3) **1968** SD-A 12 **1969** SD-A 4 **1970** SD 14 (FS) **1971** SD 12 **1972** Hou 3 **1973** SL 13 (SS) **1974**†SL 14 (10, SS) **1975**†SL 14 (2) **1976** SD 4 **NFL** 105 (15) [11 yrs]

TOLBERT, TONY Tony Lewis, DE, 6´6˝/268 lbs; Texas-El Paso; 1989: Dal, rnd 4; B12/29/1967 Tuskegee, AL **[S]** **1989** Dal 16 (5, lde) **1990** Dal 16 (4) **1991**†Dal 16 (16, LDE) **1992**†Dal 16 (16, LDE) **1993**†Dal 16 (16, LDE) **1994**†Dal 16 (15, LDE) **1995**†Dal 16 (16, LDE) **1996**†Dal★16 (16, LDE) **1997** Dal 16 (16, LDE) **NFL** 144 (120) [9 yrs]

TOLER, KEN Kenneth Pack, WR, 6´2˝/195 lbs; Mississippi; 1981: NE, rnd 7; B4/9/1959 Greenville, MS

YEAR	TEAM	G(GS, POS)	RUSH	YD	AVG(LG)	TD	REC	YD	AVG(LG)	TD	PASS	COMP	PCT	YD	AVG(LG)	TD	INT	SK	YD	QBR	KPR	OTD	PTS	TAY
1981	NE	16(0)	—	—	—	—	5	70	14.0(23)	0	—	—	—	—	—	—	—	—	—	—	k	—	0	48
1982	†NE	9(0)	1	4	4.0(4)	0	2	63	31.5(33)	2	—	—	—	—	—	—	—	—	—	—	—	—	12	46
NFL	2	25(0)	1	4	4.0(4)	0	7	133	19.0(33)	2	—	—	—	—	—	—	—	—	—	—	k	—	12	94

TOLES, ALVIN Alvin, LB, 6´1˝/211 lbs; Tennessee; 1985: NO, rnd 1; B3/23/1963 Barnesville, GA **1985** NO 16 (2) **1986** NO 16 (15, RILB) **1987** NO 12 (0) **1988** NO 11 (0) **NFL** 55 (17) [4 yrs]

TOLLE, STUART Stuart Alexander, NT, 6´3˝/265 lbs; Bowling Green State; B2/7/1962 Columbus, OH **1987** Det 1 (0)

TOLLEFSON, CHUCK Charles William, G, 6´0˝/215 lbs; Iowa; B2/28/1917 Elk Point, SD, D8/20/1989 Green Bay, WI **1944** GB 7 (1) **1945** GB 9 (5, LG) **1946** GB 2 (0) **NFL** 18 (6) [3 yrs]

TOLLESON, TOMMY Thomas Anthony, WR, 6´1˝/195 lbs; Alabama; 1966: Atl, rnd 15/NYJ, rnd 17; B1/30/1943 Birmingham, AL **1966** Atl 8

TOLLEY, ED Edgar A., G, 5´8˝/175 lbs; none; B1900, OH, deceased **1929** Day 1 (0)

TOLLIVER, BILLY JOE Billy Joe, QB, 6´1˝/217 lbs; Texas Tech; 1989: SD, rnd 2; B2/7/1966 Dallas, TX

YEAR	TEAM	G(GS, POS)	RUSH	YD	AVG(LG)	TD	REC	YD	AVG(LG)	TD	PASS	COMP	PCT	YD	AVG(LG)	TD	INT	SK	YD	QBR	KPR	OTD	PTS	TAY
1989	SD	5(5, qb)	7	0	0.0(3)	0	—	—	—	—	185	89	48.1	1097	5.9(49)	5	8	9	75	57.9	—	—	0	254
1990	SD	15(14, QB)	14	22	1.6(14)	0	—	—	—	—	410	216	52.7	2574	6.3(45)	16	16	19	150	68.9	—	—	0	749
1991	Atl	7(2)	9	6	0.7(7)	0	—	—	—	—	82	40	48.8	531	6.5(75)	4	2	7	29	—	—	—	0	212
1992	Atl	9(5, qb)	4	15	3.8(15)	0	—	—	—	—	131	73	55.7	787	6.0(30)	5	5	16	98	70.4	—	—	0	234
1993	Atl	7(2)	7	48	6.9(24)	0	—	—	—	—	76	39	51.3	464	6.1(42)	3	5	3	15	—	—	—	0	95
1994	Hou	10(7, QB)	12	37	3.1(10)	2	—	—	—	—	240	121	50.4	1287	5.4(44)	6	7	27	166	62.6	—	—	12	451
1997	Atl	6(1)	7	8	1.1(12)	0	—	—	—	—	115	63	54.8	685	6.0(47)	5	1	14	104	83.4	—	—	0	336
1997	KC	3(0)	2	-1	-0.5(0)	0	—	—	—	—	1	1	100.0	8	-8.0(-8)	0	0	—	—	—	—	—	0	-5
1998	NO	7(4, qb)	11	43	3.9(16)	0	—	—	—	—	199	110	55.3	1427	7.2(82)	8	4	11	88	83.1	—	—	0	637
1999	NO	10(7, QB)	26	142	5.5(33)	3	—	—	—	—	268	139	51.9	1916	7.1(57)	7	16	19	152	58.9	—	—	18	525
NFL	9	79(47)	99	320	3.2(33)	5	—	—	—	—	1707	891	52.2	10760	6.3(82)	59	64	125	877	67.7	—	—	30	3485

TOM, MEL Melvyn Maile, DE, 6´4˝/249 lbs; Hawaii; San Jose State; 1966: Phi, rnd 6/Oak, rnd R9; B8/4/1941 Honolulu, HI **1967** Phi 14 (rde) **1968** Phi 14 (RDE) **1969** Phi 14 (RDE) **1970** Phi 14 (RDE) **1971** Phi 14 (RDE) **1972** Phi 14 (RDE) **1973** Phi 4 **1973** ChiB 9 (RDE) **1974** ChiB 14 (rde) **1975** ChiB 6 **NFL** 117 [9 yrs]

TOMAINI, ARMY Amadeo Frederick, T, 6´0˝/245 lbs; Catawba; B2/5/1918 Long Branch, NJ, D5/25/2005 Tallahassee, FL **1945** NYG 8 (1)

TOMAINI, JOHNNY John P., E-T, 6´0˝/192 lbs; Georgetown (DC); B7/19/1902 Long Branch, NJ, D7/21/1985 Spring Lake Heights, NJ **[K]** **1929** Ora 11 (7, re), 1 **1930** Nwk 12 (10, RE), 6 **1930** Bkn 2 (1) **1931** Bkn 10 (3) **NFL** 35 (21), 7 [3 yrs]

TOMASELLO, CARL Carl Antonio, E, 6´0˝/210 lbs; Scranton; 1940: NYG, rnd 5; B1/26/1917 Dunmore, PA, D10/29/1991 Rutherford, NJ **1940** NYG 1 (0)

TOMASETTI, LOU Louis Vincent, FB-HB, 6´0˝/198 lbs; Bucknell; 1939: Pit, rnd 11; B1/8/1916 Old Forge, PA, D3/23/2004 Doylestown, PA

YEAR	TEAM	G(GS, POS)	RUSH	YD	AVG(LG)	TD	REC	YD	AVG(LG)	TD	PASS	COMP	PCT	YD	AVG(LG)	TD	INT	SK	YD	QBR	KPR	OTD	PTS	TAY
1939	Pit	11(6, HB)	49	86	1.8	1	4	22	5.5	0	47	13	27.7	140	3.0	1	7	—	—	—	P	—	6	-98
1940	Pit	10(9, HB)	68	246	3.6	1	6	129	21.5(26)	1	6	3	50.0	30	5.0	0	2	—	—	—	—	—	12	261
1941	Phi	6(3)	10	37	3.7(11)	0	5	54	10.8(40)	1	—	—	—	—	—	—	—	—	—	—	p	—	6	89
1941	Det	4(2)	6	4	0.7(0)	0	—	—	—	—	—	—	—	—	—	—	—	—	—	—	kpi	—	0	28
1942	Phi	10(5, FB)	45	102	2.3(14)	0	4	22	5.5(8)	0	—	—	—	—	—	—	—	—	—	—	kpi	—	0	183
NFL	4	41(25)	178	475	2.7(14)	2	19	227	11.9(40)	2	53	16	30.2	170	3.2	1	9	—	—	—	Pkpi	—	24	463
1946	Buf-A	14(2)	43	139	3.2	1	6	81	13.5	1	—	—	—	—	—	—	—	—	—	—	kpi	—	12	348
1947	Buf-A	13(6, fb)	92	326	3.5	2	13	125	9.6	0	—	—	—	—	—	—	—	—	—	—	ki	1	18	472
1948	†Buf-A	14(9, FB)	134	716	5.3	7	22	213	9.7	1	—	—	—	—	—	—	—	—	—	—	k	—	48	882

YEAR	TEAM	G(GS, POS)	RUSH	YD	AVG(LG)	TD	REC	YD	AVG(LG)	TD	PASS	COMP	PCT	YD	AVG(LG)	TD	INT	SK	YD	QBR	KPR	OTD	PTS	TAY
1949	†Buf-A	12(4)	54	249	4.6	2	9	56	6.2	1	—	—	—	—	—	—	—	—	—	—	kp	—	18	309
AAFC	4	53(21)	323	1430	4.4(14)	12	50	475	9.5(40)	3	—	—	—	—	—	—	—	—	—	—	kpi	1	96	2010

Tomasic, Andy andrew John, TB-DB, 6´0˝/175 lbs; Temple; 1942: Pit, rnd 16; B12/10/1919 Hokendauqua, PA **[K]**

YEAR	TEAM	G(GS, POS)	RUSH	YD	AVG(LG)	TD	REC	YD	AVG(LG)	TD	PASS	COMP	PCT	YD	AVG(LG)	TD	INT	SK	YD	QBR	KPR	OTD	PTS	TAY
1942	Pit	11(0)	60	214	3.6(34)	0	1	27	27.0(27)	0	54	11	20.4	174	3.2(41)	0	5	—	—	—	KPkpi	1	6	353
1946	Pit	4(0)	—	—	—	—	—	—	—	—	12	4	33.3	53	4.4(20)	0	1	—	—	—	Pp	—	0	2
NFL	2	15(0)	60	214	3.6(34)	0	1	27	27.0(27)	0	66	15	22.7	227	3.4(41)	0	6	—	—	—	KPkpi	1	6	354

Tomberlin, Pat Howard Patrick, G-T, 6´2˝/312 lbs; Florida State; 1989: Ind, rnd 4; B1/29/1966 Jacksonville, FL **1990** Ind 16 (10, RG) **1993** TB 2 (0) **NFL** 18 (10) [2 yrs]

Tomczak, Mike Michael John, QB, 6´1˝/202 lbs; Ohio State; B10/23/1962 Chicago, IL

YEAR	TEAM	G(GS, POS)	RUSH	YD	AVG(LG)	TD	REC	YD	AVG(LG)	TD	PASS	COMP	PCT	YD	AVG(LG)	TD	INT	SK	YD	QBR	KPR	OTD	PTS	TAY
1985	†ChiB	6(0)	2	3	1.5(3)	0	—	—	—	—	6	2	33.3	33	5.5(24)	0	0	—	—	—	—	—	0	20
1986	ChiB	13(7, QB)	23	117	5.1(16)	3	—	—	—	—	151	74	49.0	1105	7.3(**85**)	2	10	4	30	50.2	—	—	18	310
1987	†ChiB	12(6, qb)	18	54	3.0(10)	1	—	—	—	—	178	97	54.5	1220	6.9(56)	5	10	9	59	62.0	—	—	6	299
1988	†ChiB	14(5, qb)	13	40	3.1(17)	1	—	—	—	—	170	86	50.6	1310	7.7(76)	7	6	5	47	75.4	—	—	6	500
1989	ChiB	16(11, QB)	24	71	3.0(18)	1	—	—	—	—	306	156	51.0	2058	6.7(79)	16	16	10	68	68.2	—	—	6	550
1990	†ChiB	16(2)	12	41	3.4(14)	2	1	5	5.0(5)	0	104	39	37.5	521	5.0(48)	3	5	11	70	43.8	—	—	12	139
1991	GB	12(7, qb)	17	93	5.5(48)	1	—	—	—	—	238	128	53.8	1490	6.3(75)	11	9	13	105	72.6	—	—	6	543
1992	Cle	12(8, QB)	24	39	1.6(16)	0	—	—	—	—	211	120	56.9	1693	**8.0**(**52**)	7	7	12	85	80.1	—	—	0	641
1993	†Pit	7(1)	5	-4	-0.8(2)	0	—	—	—	—	54	29	53.7	398	7.4(39)	2	5	7	43	—	—	—	0	5
1994	†Pit	6(2)	4	22	5.5(13)	0	—	—	—	—	93	54	58.1	804	8.6(84)	4	0	4	33	—	—	—	0	444
1995	Pit	7(4)	11	25	2.3(11)	0	—	—	—	—	113	65	57.5	666	5.9(29)	1	9	6	42	44.3	—	—	0	3
1996	†Pit	16(15, QB)	22	-7	-0.3(6)	0	—	—	—	—	401	222	55.4	2767	6.9(70)	15	17	16	105	71.8	—	—	0	772
1997	†Pit	16(0)	7	13	1.9(17)	0	—	—	—	—	24	16	66.7	185	7.7(28)	1	2	—	—	—	—	—	0	31
1998	Pit	16(0)	—	—	—	—	—	—	—	—	30	21	70.0	204	6.8(42)	2	2	2	18	—	—	—	0	32
1999	Pit	16(5, qb)	16	19	1.2(17)	0	—	—	—	—	258	139	53.9	1625	6.3(49)	12	8	15	104	75.8	—	—	0	572
NFL	15	185(73)	198	526	2.7(48)	9	1	5	5.0(5)	0	2337	1248	53.4	16079	6.9(85)	88	106	114	809	68.9	—	—	54	4858

Tomich, Jared Jared James, DE, 6´2˝/258 lbs; Nebraska; 1997: NO, rnd 2; B4/24/1974 St. John, IN **1997** NO 16 (1) **1998** NO 16 (11, LDE) **1999** NO 8 (6, LDE) **2000** NO 14 (0) **2002** GB 2 (0) **NFL** 56 (18) [5 yrs]

Tomlin, Tommy John Thomas, G-T, 5´10˝/197 lbs; Syracuse; B9/1893 South Miller District, VA, D5/11/1953 Woodstock, NY **1920** Akr 11 (9, LG) **1921** Ham 2 (2) **1921** Akr 5 (5, lg) **1922** Mil 4 (4, LG) **1925** NYG 9 (6, lg) **1926** NYG 4 (4) **NFL** 35 (30) [5 yrs]

Tomlinson, LaDainian LaDainian, RB, 5´10˝/221 lbs; TCU; 2001: SD, rnd 1; B6/23/1979 Rosebud, TX

YEAR	TEAM	G(GS, POS)	RUSH	YD	AVG(LG)	TD	REC	YD	AVG(LG)	TD	PASS	COMP	PCT	YD	AVG(LG)	TD	INT	SK	YD	QBR	KPR	OTD	PTS	TAY
2001	SD	16(16, RB)	339	1236	3.6(54)	10	59	367	6.2(27)	0	—	—	—	—	—	—	—	—	—	—	—	—	60	1520
2002	SD★	16(16, RB)	372	1683	4.5(76)	14	79	489	6.2(30)	1	—	—	—	—	—	—	—	—	—	—	—	—	90	2073
2003	SD☆	16(16, RB)	313	1645	5.3(73)	13	**100**	725	7.3(73)	4	1	1	100.0	21	21.0(21)	1	0	—	—	—	—	—	102	2173
2004	†SD★	15(15, RB)	339	1335	3.9(42)	**17**	53	441	8.3(74)	1	2	1	50.0	38	19.0(38)	0	0	1	1	—	—	—	108	1750
2005	SD★	16(16, RB)	339	1462	4.3(62)	18	51	370	7.3(41)	2	4	3	75.0	47	11.8(26)	3	0	—	—	—	—	—	120	1876
NFL	5	79(79)	1702	7361	4.3(76)	72	342	2392	7.0(74)	8	7	5	71.4	106	15.1(38)	4	0	1	1	—	—	—	480	9390

Tomlinson, Dick Richard Kent, G, 6´1˝/205 lbs; Kansas; 1950: Pit, rnd 21; B8/5/1928 Chicago, IL **1950** Pit 11 (LG) **1951** Pit 12 (LG) **NFL** 23 [2 yrs]

Tommerson, Clarence Clarence Leonard, HB, 6´2˝/196 lbs; Wisconsin; B4/8/1915 La Crosse, WI, D1/6/2000 Fort Lauderdale, FL **1938** Pit 3 (0) **1939** Pit 1 (0) **NFL** 4 (0) [2 yrs]

Toneff, Bob Robert, DT-DE-T-LB-G, 6´2˝/260 lbs; Notre Dame; 1952: SF, rnd 2; B6/23/1930 Detroit, MI **1952** SF☆12 (LT) **1954** SF 10 (RLB) **1955** SF★11 (LDT) **1956** SF 12 (LG) **1957**†SF 12 (RDE) **1958** SF 12 (RDE) **1959** Was★12 (12, LDT) **1960** Was★12 (12, LDT) **1961** Was★14 (14, LDT) **1962** Was☆14 (LDT) **1963** Was 14 (LDT) **1964** Was 14 (LDT) **NFL** 149 (38) [12 yrs]

Tonelli, Mario Mario George, FB, 5´11˝/200 lbs; Notre Dame; 1939: NYG, rnd 21; B3/28/1916 Lemont, IL, D1/7/2003 Chicago, IL

YEAR	TEAM	G(GS, POS)	RUSH	YD	AVG(LG)	TD	REC	YD	AVG(LG)	TD	PASS	COMP	PCT	YD	AVG(LG)	TD	INT	SK	YD	QBR	KPR	OTD	PTS	TAY
1940	ChiC	9(3)	51	148	2.9	1	5	53	10.6	0	—	—	—	—	—	—	—	—	—	—	P	—	6	185

Tonelli, Tony Amerigo S., C-G, 6´0˝/210 lbs; USC; 1939: Det, rnd 19; B9/1/1917 Wheeling, WV, D1/30/1987 Newport Beach, CA **1939** Det 9 (0)

Toner, Ed Edward William, DT, 6´2˝/250 lbs; Massachusetts; 1966: Bos, rnd R3/Bal, rnd 18; B9/11/1944 Reading, MA **1967** Bos-A 14 **1968** Bos-A 5 **1969** Bos-A 7 **NFL** 26 [3 yrs]

Toner, Ed Edward William, RB, 6´0˝/240 lbs; Boston College; B3/22/1968 Lynn, MA

YEAR	TEAM	G(GS, POS)	RUSH	YD	AVG(LG)	TD	REC	YD	AVG(LG)	TD	PASS	COMP	PCT	YD	AVG(LG)	TD	INT	SK	YD	QBR	KPR	OTD	PTS	TAY
1992	Ind	8(0)	—	—	—	—	—	—	—	—	—	—	—	—	—	—	—	—	—	—	—	—	—	—
1993	Ind	16(1)	2	6	3.0(6)	0	1	5	5.0(5)	0	—	—	—	—	—	—	—	—	—	—	—	—	0	9
1994	Ind	9(0)	1	11	11.0(11)	0	—	—	—	—	—	—	—	—	—	—	—	—	—	—	k	—	0	4
NFL	3	33(1)	3	17	5.7(11)	0	1	5	5.0(5)	0	—	—	—	—	—	—	—	—	—	—	k	—	0	13

Toner, Tom Thomas Edward, LB, 6´3˝/235 lbs; Idaho State; 1973: GB, rnd 6; B1/25/1950 Woburn, MA, D8/26/1990 Solana Beach, CA **1973** GB 14 (llb) **1975** GB 14 (9, LLB) **1976** GB 11 **1977** GB 14 (LLB) **NFL** 53 (9) [4 yrs]

Toney, Anthony Anthony, RB, 6´0˝/227 lbs; Texas A&M; 1986: Phi, rnd 2; B9/23/1962 Salinas, CA

YEAR	TEAM	G(GS, POS)	RUSH	YD	AVG(LG)	TD	REC	YD	AVG(LG)	TD	PASS	COMP	PCT	YD	AVG(LG)	TD	INT	SK	YD	QBR	KPR	OTD	PTS	TAY
1986	Phi	12(5, fb)	69	285	4.1(43)	1	13	177	13.6(47)	0	—	—	—	—	—	—	—	—	—	—	—	—	6	384
1987	Phi	11(11, FB)	127	473	3.7(36)	5	39	341	8.7(33)	1	1	0	0.0	0	0.0	0	0	—	—	—	—	—	36	699
1988	†Phi	15(13, FB)	139	502	3.6(20)	4	34	256	7.5(24)	1	—	—	—	—	—	—	—	—	—	—	—	—	30	675
1989	†Phi	14(14, FB)	172	582	3.4(44)	3	19	124	6.5(15)	0	—	—	—	—	—	—	—	—	—	—	—	—	18	674
1990	†Phi	15(11, FB)	132	452	3.4(20)	1	17	133	7.8(32)	3	—	—	—	—	—	—	—	—	—	—	—	—	24	544
NFL	5	67(54)	639	2294	3.6(44)	14	122	1031	8.5(47)	5	1	0	0.0	0	0.0	0	0	—	—	—	—	—	114	2975

Tongue, Marco Marco Charles, DB, 5´9˝/177 lbs; Bowie State; B4/6/1960 Annapolis, MD **1983** Bal 7 (0) **1984** Buf 1 (0) **NFL** 8 (0) [2 yrs]

Tongue, Reggie Reginald Clinton, DB, 6´0˝/204 lbs; Oregon State; 1996: KC, rnd 2; B4/11/1973 Baltimore, MD **1996** KC 16 (0) **1997**†KC 16 (16, SS) **1998** KC 15 (15, SS) **1999** KC 16 (16, SS) **2000** Sea 16 (6, ss) **2001** Sea 16 (16, SS) **2002** Sea 16 (16, SS) **2003**†Sea 14 (14, SS) **2004**†NYJ 16 (16, SS) **2005** Oak 4 (1) **NFL** 145 (116) [10 yrs]

Tonnemaker, Clayton Frank Clayton, LB-C, 6´2˝/237 lbs; Minnesota; 1950: GB, rnd 1/1949: Buf-A, rnd 15; B6/8/1928 Ogilvie, MN, D12/25/1996 St. Paul, MN **[K]** **1950** GB☆12 (C) **1953** GB★12 (LLB) **1954** GB☆12 (LLB) **NFL** 36 [3 yrs]

Toogood, Charlie Charles Wayne, DT-T-G, 6´0˝/232 lbs; Nebraska; 1951: LA, rnd 3; B7/16/1927 North Platte, NE, D2/24/1997 Auburn, CA **1951**†LARm 8 (RDT) **1952**†LARm 10 (LDT) **1953** LARm 12 (LDT) **1954** LARm 12 (RT) **1955**†LARm 12 (RT) **1956** LARm 7 **1957** ChiC 6 **NFL** 67 [7 yrs]

Toomay, Pat Patrick Jay, DE, 6´5˝/247 lbs; Vanderbilt; 1970: Dal, rnd 6; B5/17/1945 Pomona, CA **1970**†Dal 14 (3) **1971**†Dal 14 **1972**†Dal 14 (RDE) **1973**†Dal 14 (RDE) **1974** Dal 14 (RDE) **1975** Buf 14 **1976** TB 14 (14, RDE) **1977**†Oak 14 (2) **1978** Oak 16 (2) **1979** Oak 14 (13, LDE) **NFL** 142 (34) [10 yrs]

Toomer, Amani Amani, WR, 6´3˝/208 lbs; Michigan; 1996: NYG, rnd 2; B9/8/1974 Berkeley, CA **[R]**

YEAR	TEAM	G(GS, POS)	RUSH	YD	AVG(LG)	TD	REC	YD	AVG(LG)	TD	PASS	COMP	PCT	YD	AVG(LG)	TD	INT	SK	YD	QBR	KPR	OTD	PTS	TAY
1996	NYG	7(1)	—	—	—	—	1	12	12.0(12)	0	—	—	—	—	—	—	—	—	—	—	kp	2	12	260
1997	†NYG	16(0)	—	—	—	—	16	263	16.4(56)	1	—	—	—	—	—	—	—	—	—	—	p	1	12	367
1998	NYG	16(0)	—	—	—	—	27	360	13.3(37)	5	1	0	0.0	0	0.0	0	0	—	—	—	kp	—	30	288
1999	NYG	16(16, WR)	1	4	4.0(4)	0	79	1183	15.0(80)	6	—	—	—	—	—	—	—	—	—	—	p	—	36	635
2000	†NYG	16(15, WR)	5	91	18.2(28)	1	78	1094	14.0(54)	7	—	—	—	—	—	—	—	—	—	—	—	—	48	683
2001	NYG	16(14, WR)	3	8	2.7(9)	0	72	1054	14.6(60)	5	—	—	—	—	—	—	—	—	—	—	p	—	30	561
2002	†NYG	16(16, WR)	1	2	2.0(2)	0	82	1343	16.4(82)	8	—	—	—	—	—	—	—	—	—	—	—	—	48	714
2003	NYG	16(16, WR)	1	5	5.0(5)	0	63	1057	16.8(77)	5	—	—	—	—	—	—	—	—	—	—	—	—	30	559
2004	NYG	15(14, WR)	—	—	—	—	51	747	14.6(48)	0	—	—	—	—	—	—	—	—	—	—	—	—	0	374
2005	†NYG	16(16, WR)	—	—	—	—	60	684	11.4(37)	7	—	—	—	—	—	—	—	—	—	—	—	—	42	377
NFL	10	150(108)	11	110	10.0(28)	1	529	7797	14.7(82)	44	1	0	0.0	0	0.0	0	0	—	—	—	kp	3	288	4816

Toon, Al Albert Lee, WR, 6´4˝/205 lbs; Wisconsin; 1985: NYJ, rnd 1; B4/30/1963 Newport News, VA

YEAR	TEAM	G(GS, POS)	RUSH	YD	AVG(LG)	TD	REC	YD	AVG(LG)	TD	PASS	COMP	PCT	YD	AVG(LG)	TD	INT	SK	YD	QBR	KPR	OTD	PTS	TAY
1985	†NYJ	15(8, WR)	1	5	5.0(5)	0	46	662	14.4(78)	3	—	—	—	—	—	—	—	—	—	—	—	—	18	351
1986	†NYJ★	16(16, WR)	2	-3	-1.5(2)	0	85	1176	13.8(62)	8	—	—	—	—	—	—	—	—	—	—	—	—	48	625
1987	NYJ★	12(11, WR)	—	—	—	—	**68**	976	14.4(58)	5	—	—	—	—	—	—	—	—	—	—	—	—	30	513
1988	NYJ★	15(15, WR)	1	5	5.0(5)	0	**93**	1067	11.5(42)	5	—	—	—	—	—	—	—	—	—	—	—	—	30	564
1989	NYJ	11(10, WR)	—	—	—	—	63	693	11.0(37)	2	—	—	—	—	—	—	—	—	—	—	—	—	12	357

YEAR	TEAM	G (GS, POS)	RUSH	YD	AVG(LG)	TD	REC	YD	AVG(LG)	TD	PASS	COMP	PCT	YD	AVG(LG)	TD	INT	SK	YD	QBR	KPR	OTD	PTS	TAY
1990	NYJ	14 (12, WR)	—	—	—	—	57	757	13.3(46)	6	2	0	0.0	0	0.0	0	0	—	—	—	—	—	36	409
1991	†NYJ	15 (15, WR)	—	—	—	—	74	963	13.0(32)	0	1	1	100.0	27	27.0(27)	0	0	—	—	—	—	—	0	495
1992	NYJ	9 (8, WR)	—	—	—	—	31	311	10.0(32)	2	—	—	—	—	—	—	—	—	—	—	—	—	12	166
NFL	8	107 (95)	4	7	1.8(5)	0	517	6605	12.8(78)	31	3	1	33.3	27	9.0(27)	0	0	—	—	—	—	—	186	3478

TOOROCK, CHIEF Meyer, WB, 5´9˝/180 lbs; NYU; B1902, deceased **1926** Bkn 2 (0)

TOOTLE, JEFF Jeffrey Edward, LB, 6´2˝/240 lbs; Mesa; B8/29/1962 Salina, KS **1987** NYG 3 (1)

TOPOR, TED Ted Peter, LB, 6´1˝/210 lbs; Michigan; 1953: Det, rnd 15; B5/1/1930 East Chicago, IL **1955** Det 6

TOPP, BOB Eugene Robert, E, 6´2˝/180 lbs; Michigan; 1954: NYG, rnd 13; B4/22/1932 Kalamazoo, MI

| 1954 | NYG | 6 | | | | | 6 | 90 | 15.0(31) | 3 | | | | | | | | | | | k | | 18 | 55 |

TORAN, STACEY Stacey Jeffrey, DB, 6´2˝/200 lbs; Notre Dame; 1984: LARd, rnd 6; B11/10/1961 Indianapolis, IN, D8/5/1989 Marina del Rey, CA **1984**†LARd 16 (0)
1985LARd 16 (9, ss) **1986** LARd 16 (16, SS) **1987** LARd 12 (12, SS) **1988** LARd 12 (4) **NFL** 72 (41) [5 yrs]

TORBOR, REGGIE Reggie, LB, 6´3˝/242 lbs; Auburn; 2004: NYG, rnd 4; B1/25/1981 Baton Rouge, LA **2004** NYG 16 (1) **2005** NYG 14 (9, LLB) **NFL** 30 (10) [2 yrs]

TORCZON, LaVERNE LaVern Joseph, DE, 6´3˝/250 lbs; Nebraska; 1957: Cle, rnd 18; B1/1/1936 Columbus, NE **1960** Buf-A☆14 (RDE) **1961** Buf-A★14 (RDE) **1962** Buf-A 4
1962 NYT-A 10 (RDE) **1963** NYJ-A 14 (RDE) **1964** NYJ-A 14 (RDE) **1965** NYJ-A 14 **1966** Mia-A 14 (13, RDE) **NFL** 98 (13) [7 yrs]

TORGESON, LaVERN LaVern Earl, LB-C, 6´0˝/215 lbs; Washington State; 1951: Det, rnd 5; B2/28/1929 La Crosse, WA **1951** Det 12 (C/RLB) **1952**†Det 12 (RLB)
1953†Det 11 **1954**†Det★12 (RLB) **1955** Was★11 (LLB) **1956** Was◇12 (LLB) **1957** Was☆12 (LLB) **NFL** 82 [7 yrs]

TORKELSON, ERIC Eric Grove, RB, 6´2˝/194 lbs; Connecticut; 1974: GB, rnd 11; B3/23/1952 Troy, NY

1974	GB	14	13	60	4.6(21)	0	2	10	5.0(8)	0											kp	1	6	65
1975	GB	14	42	226	5.4(29)	2	6	37	6.2(12)	0											k	—	12	279
1976	GB	14 (6, rb)	88	289	3.3(15)	2	19	140	7.4(31)	0											k	—	12	412
1977	GB	14 (7, RB)	103	309	3.0(29)	1	11	107	9.7(14)	0											k	—	6	379
1978	GB	14	6	18	3.0(6)	0	2	36	18.0(31)	0												—	0	36
1979	GB	14 (8, FB)	98	401	4.1(15)	3	19	139	7.3(14)	0												—	18	501
1981	GB	9 (0)	1	4	4.0(4)	0	—	—	—	—												—	0	4
NFL	7	93 (21)	351	1307	3.7(29)	8	59	469	7.9(31)	0											kp	1	54	1675

TORRANCE, JACK Jack, T, 6´5˝/285 lbs; LSU; B6/20/1912 Oak Grove, LA, D11/10/1969 Baton Rouge, LA **1939** ChiB 8 (2) **1940**†ChiB◇7 (1) **NFL** 15 (3) [2 yrs]

TORRENCE, LEIGH Leigh, DB, 6´0˝/183 lbs; Stanford; B1/4/1982 Atlanta, GA **2005** Atl 10 (0)

TORRETTA, GINO Gino Louis, QB, 6´2˝/215 lbs; Miami (FL); 1993: Min, rnd 7; B8/10/1970 Pinole Valley, CA **1993** Min 1 (0)

| 1996 | Sea | 1 (0) | 2 | 12 | 6.0(13) | 0 | — | — | — | — | 16 | 5 | 31.3 | 41 | 2.6(32) | 1 | 1 | 3 | 17 | | | — | 0 | -3 |
| NFL | 2 | 2 (0) | 2 | 12 | 6.0(13) | 0 | — | — | — | — | 16 | 5 | 31.3 | 41 | 2.6(32) | 1 | 1 | 3 | 17 | | | — | 0 | -3 |

TORREY, BOB Robert Douglas, RB, 6´4˝/231 lbs; Penn State; 1979: NYG, rnd 6; B1/30/1957 Ceres, NY **1979** NYG 6 **1980** Phi 1 (0)

| 1979 | †Mia | 7 | 13 | 61 | 4.7(17) | 1 | 2 | 3 | 1.5(8) | 0 | — | — | — | — | — | — | — | | | | | — | 6 | 73 |
| NFL | 2 | 14 | 13 | 61 | 4.7(17) | 1 | 2 | 3 | 1.5(8) | 0 | — | — | — | — | — | — | — | | | | | — | 6 | 73 |

TOSCANI, BUD Francis, WB-HB, 5´8˝/168 lbs; St. Mary's (CA); B4/19/1909, D6/1966

1932	Bkn	5 (1)	9	37	4.1																	—	0	37
1932	ChiC	3 (1)	15	43	2.9	0	1	12	12.0(12)	0												—	0	49
NFL	1	8 (2)	24	80	3.3	0	1	12	12.0(12)	0												—	0	86

TOSI, FLAVIO Flavio Joseph, E, 6´1˝/191 lbs; Boston College; B4/30/1912 Beverly, MA, D12/18/1994 Beverly, MA

1934	Bos	9 (2)	—	—	—	—	3	26	8.7	0												—	0	13
1935	Bos	11 (5, le)	—	—	—	—	10	169	16.9	1												—	6	90
1936	†Bos	7 (0)	—	—	—	—	4	70	17.5	0												1	6	35
NFL	3	27 (7)	—	—	—	—	17	265	15.6	1												1	12	138

TOSI, JOHN John Joseph, C-G-T, 5´10˝/225 lbs; Niagara; 1939: Pit, rnd 15; B12/3/1913 Wilmington, DE, D11/24/2002 Wilmington, DE **1939** Pit 3 (1) **1939** Bkn 1 (1)
NFL 4 (2) [1 yr]

TOSI, MAO Falemao, DT-DE, 6´6˝/305 lbs; Idaho; 2000: Arz, rnd 5; B12/12/1976 Anchorage, AK **2000** Arz 15 (10, RDT) **2001** Arz 11 (1) **NFL** 26 (11) [2 yrs]

TOTH, TOM Thomas Jeffrey, G-T, 6´5˝/279 lbs; Western Michigan; 1985: NE, rnd 4; B5/23/1962 Chicago, IL **1986** Mia 13 (0) **1987** Mia 12 (12, RG) **1988** Mia 9 (4)
1989 Mia 16 (2) **1990** SD 1 (0) **NFL** 51 (18) [5 yrs]

TOTH, ZOLLIE Zollie Anthony, FB, 6´2˝/219 lbs; LSU; 1950: NYY, rnd 4; B1/26/1924 McKeesport, PA

1950	NYY◇	11 (FB)	131	636	4.9(51)	5	15	189	12.6(60)	3											—	—	48	796
1951	NYY	10 (FB)	119	384	3.2(16)	4	10	100	10.0(23)	0											—	—	24	474
1952	DalT	12 (6, FB)	82	266	3.2(18)	4	13	54	4.2(20)	0											k	—	24	336
1954	Bal	12 (FB)	86	303	3.5(15)	1	11	51	4.6(13)	0	1	0	0.0	0	0.0	0	1	—	—		k	—	6	297
NFL	4	45 (6)	418	1589	3.8(51)	14	49	394	8.0(60)	3	1	0	0.0	0	0.0	0	1	—	—		k	—	102	1902

TOTTEN, ERIK Erik Terry, DB, 5´9˝/194 lbs; Western Washington; B1/21/1980 Renton, WA **2002** Pit 1 (0)

TOTTEN, WILLIE Willie Horace, QB, 6´2˝/195 lbs; Mississippi Valley State; B7/4/1962 Leflore, MS

| 1987 | Buf | 2 (1) | 12 | 11 | 0.9(7) | 0 | — | — | — | — | 33 | 13 | 39.4 | 155 | 4.7(37) | 2 | 2 | 5 | 62 | | | — | 0 | 19 |

TOUSSAINT, DARREL Darrel Lee, DB, 6´0˝/175 lbs; Northwestern State (LA); B10/3/1958 Chicago, IL **1987** NO 2 (0)

TOVAR, STEVE Steven Eric, LB, 6´3˝/246 lbs; Ohio State; 1993: Cin, rnd 3; B4/25/1970 Elyria, OH **1993** Cin 16 (9, lilb) **1994** Cin 16 (16, MLB) **1995** Cin 14 (13, MLB)
1996 Cin 13 (13, MLB) **1997** Cin 14 (5, lilb) **1998** SD 16 (2) **1999** Car 16 (6, mlb) **2000** SD 16 (2) **NFL** 121 (64) [8 yrs]

TOWLE, STEVE Stephen Richards, LB, 6´2˝/233 lbs; Kansas; 1975: Mia, rnd 6; B10/23/1953 Kansas City, KS **1975** Mia 14 (5, mlb) **1976** Mia 14 (14, MLB) **1977** Mia 12 (12, LILB/
rilb) **1978**†Mia 13 (13, LILB) **1979**†Mia 16 (16, LILB) **1980** Mia 9 (0) **NFL** 78 (60) [6 yrs]

TOWLE, THURSTON Edward Thurston, E, 5´10˝/172 lbs; Brown; B1/1/1905 Pawtucket, RI, D10/19/1960 Providence, RI **1929** Bos 1 (0)

TOWLER, DAN Daniel Lee, FB, 6´2˝/225 lbs; Washington & Jefferson; 1950: LA, rnd 25; B3/6/1928 Donora, PA, D8/1/2001 Pasadena, CA

1950	†LARm	12	46	130	2.8(34)	4	8	63	7.9(17)	0	—	—	—	—	—	—	—				k	—	36	194
1951	†LARm	12 (FB)	126	854	6.8(79)	6	16	257	16.1(46)	3	—	—	—	—	—	—	—				k	—	36	1038
1952	†LARm★	12 (FB)	156	894	5.7(44)	10	11	68	6.2(13)	0	—	—	—	—	—	—	—				kp	—	60	1017
1953	LARm★	12 (FB)	152	879	5.8(73)	7	11	125	11.4(49)	1	—	—	—	—	—	—	—					—	48	1017
1954	LARm★	12 (FB)	149	599	4.0(24)	11	10	127	12.7(36)	0	—	—	—	—	—	—	—					—	66	773
1955	†LARm	7	43	137	3.2(14)	3	6	25	4.2(11)	0	—	—	—	—	—	—	—					—	18	180
NFL	6	67	672	3493	5.2(79)	43	62	665	10.7(49)	1	—	—	—	—	—	—	—				kp	—	264	4217

TOWNES, WILLIE Willie Carroll, DE-DT, 6´4˝/260 lbs; Tulsa; 1966: Dal, rnd 2/Bos, rnd R1; B7/21/1943 Hattiesburg, MS **1966**†Dal 13 (8, LDE) **1967**†Dal 14 (13, LDE)
1968 Dal 5 (4) **1970** NO 6 **NFL** 38 (25) [4 yrs]

TOWNS, BOBBY Robert Forrest, DB, 6´1˝/180 lbs; Georgia; 1960: SL, rnd 11/Hou, rnd 2; B3/17/1938 Elberton, GA **1960** SL 4 **1961** Bos-A 2 **NFL** 6 [2 yrs]

TOWNS, LESTER Lester, LB, 6´1˝/252 lbs; Washington; 2000: Car, rnd 7; B8/28/1977 Los Angeles, CA **2000** Car 16 (14, MLB) **2001** Car 16 (15, MLB) **2002** Car 8 (0)
2003†Car 15 (1) **2005** Arz 2 (1) **2005** Mia 4 (0) **NFL** 61 (31) [5 yrs]

TOWNS, MORRIS Morris M., T, 6´4˝/270 lbs; Missouri; 1977: Hou, rnd 1; B1/10/1954 St. Louis, MO **1977** Hou 1 **1978**†Hou 16 (12, rt) **1979**†Hou 16 (14, RT)
1980†Hou 16 (12, RT) **1981** Hou 16 (16, RT) **1982** Hou 9 (9, RT) **1983** Hou 14 (3) **1984** Was 4 (0) **NFL** 92 (66) [8 yrs]

TOWNSELL, JO-JO Joseph Ray, WR, 5´9˝/180 lbs; UCLA; 1983: NYJ, rnd 3; B11/4/1960 Reno, NV [R]

1985	†NYJ	16 (6, wr)					12	187	15.6(36)	0											kp	—	0	141
1986	†NYJ	14 (1)	1	2	2.0(2)	0	1	11	11.0(11)	0											kp	1	6	177
1987	NYJ	9	1	-2	-2.0(-2)	0	4	37	9.3(11)	0											kp	1	6	355
1988	NYJ☆	16 (0)					4	40	10.0(19)	0											kp	1	6	400
1989	NYJ	16 (16, WR)	—	—	—	—	45	787	17.5(63)	0											kp	—	30	696

YEAR	TEAM	G (GS, POS)	RUSH	YD	AVG (LG)	TD	REC	YD	AVG (LG)	TD	PASS	COMP	PCT	YD	AVG (LG)	TD	INT	SK	YD	QBR	KPR	OTD	PTS	TAY
1990	NYJ	9(0)	—	—	—	—	4	57	14.3(18)	0	—	—	—	—	—	—	—	—	—	—	kp	—	0	151
NFL	6	83(23)	2	0	0.0(2)	0	70	1119	16.0(63)	5	—	—	—	—	—	—	—	—	—	—	kp	3	48	1918

TOWNSEND, ANDRE Andre, DE-NT, 6´3˝/265 lbs; Mississippi; 1984: Den, rnd 2; B10/8/1962 Chicago, IL **1984**†Den 16 (0) **1985** Den 16 (1) **1986**†Den 16 (16, LDE) **1987**†Den 12 (11, LDE) **1988** Den 16 (16, RDE) **1989**†Den 13 (10, RDE) **1990** Den 15 (0) **NFL** 104 (54) [7 yrs]

TOWNSEND, BRIAN Brian Lewis, LB, 6´3˝/242 lbs; Michigan; 1992: LARm, rnd 11; B11/7/1968 Cincinnati, OH **1992** Cin 3 (0)

TOWNSEND, CURTIS Curtis, LB, 6´1˝/229 lbs; Arkansas; 1977: SD, rnd 10; B1/20/1955 Birmingham, AL **1978** SL 9

TOWNSEND, DESHEA Trevor Deshea, DB, 5´9˝/191 lbs; Alabama; 1998: Pit, rnd 4; B9/8/1975 Batesville, MS **1998** Pit 12 (0) **1999** Pit 16 (4) **2000** Pit 16 (0) **2001**†Pit 16 (1) **2002**†Pit 16 (3) **2003** Pit 16 (8, lcb) **2004**†Pit 15 (15, RCB) **2005**†Pit 16 (15, RCB) **NFL** 123 (46) [8 yrs]

TOWNSEND, GREG Gregory, DE-LB-DT-NT, 6´3˝/264 lbs; TCU; 1983: LARd, rnd 4; B11/3/1961 Los Angeles, CA **[S]** **1983**†LARd 16 (0) **1984**†LARd 16 (0) **1985**†LARd 16 (0) **1986** LARd 15 (4) **1987** LARd 13 (1) **1988** LARd☆16 (11, LDE) **1989** LARd☆16 (12, ROLB) **1990**†LARd★16 (16, RDE) **1991**†LARd★16 (16, RDE) **1992** LARd 14 (14, RDE) **1993**†LARd 16 (16, RDE/rdt) **1994** Phi 16 (12, RDE) **1997** Oak 4 (0) **NFL** 190 (102) [13 yrs]

TOWNSEND, OTTO Otto, G-T, /190 lbs; none; deceased **1922** Min 2 (2)

TRACEY, JOHN John Joseph, LB-E-DE, 6´3˝/225 lbs; Texas A&M; 1959: LA, rnd 4; B6/27/1933 Philadelphia, PA, D9/18/1978 Medford Lakes, NJ **1960** SL 12 (LLB) **1961** Phi 9 **1963**†Buf-A 14 (LLB) **1964**†Buf-A 14 (LLB) **1966**†Buf-A✧14 (LLB)

YEAR	TEAM	G (GS, POS)	RUSH	YD	AVG (LG)	TD	REC	YD	AVG (LG)	TD	PASS	COMP	PCT	YD	AVG (LG)	TD	INT	SK	YD	QBR	KPR	OTD	PTS	TAY
1959	ChiC	8(RE)	—	—	—	—	17	258	15.2(51)	0	—	—	—	—	—	—	—	—	—	—	k	—	0	128
1962	Buf-A	12(2)	—	—	—	—	1	28	28.0(28)	0	—	—	—	—	—	—	—	—	—	—	—	—	0	14
1965	†Buf-A★	14(LLB)	—	—	—	—	1	2	2.0(2)	0	—	—	—	—	—	—	—	—	—	—	i	—	0	4
1967	Buf-A	13(LLB)	—	—	—	—	1	15	15.0(15)	0	—	—	—	—	—	—	—	—	—	—	i	—	0	6
NFL	9	110(2)	—	—	—	—	20	303	15.1(51)	0	—	—	—	—	—	—	—	—	—	—	ki	—	4	156

TRACY, TOM John Thomas, HB-FB, 5´9˝/205 lbs; Tennessee; 1956: Det, rnd 5; B9/7/1934 Birmingham, AL, D1/24/1996 Madison Heights, MI **[K]**

YEAR	TEAM	G (GS, POS)	RUSH	YD	AVG (LG)	TD	REC	YD	AVG (LG)	TD	PASS	COMP	PCT	YD	AVG (LG)	TD	INT	SK	YD	QBR	KPR	OTD	PTS	TAY
1956	Det	4	12	32	2.7(9)	0	3	6	2.0(5)	0	—	—	—	—	—	—	—	—	—	—	—	—	0	35
1957	†Det	9	16	46	2.9(17)	0	6	24	4.0(7)	0	—	—	—	—	—	—	—	—	—	—	—	—	0	58
1958	Pit✧	12(LH)	169	714	4.2(64)	5	32	535	16.7(56)	4	16	6	37.5	270	16.9(72)	2	2	—	—	—	—	—	54	1117
1959	Pit	12(LH)	199	794	4.0(51)	3	23	273	11.9(45)	5	12	3	25.0	159	13.3(68)	0	2	—	—	—	kp	—	48	1010
1960	Pit★	12(HB)	192	680	3.5(28)	5	24	349	14.5(65)	4	22	9	40.9	322	14.6(70)	4	1	—	—	—	Kk	—	63	1081
1961	Pit	14(HB)	147	402	2.7(26)	2	14	133	9.5(38)	1	12	4	33.3	73	6.1(38)	0	0	—	—	—	K	—	20	530
1962	Pit	4	20	116	5.8(35)	0	2	11	5.5(6)	0	1	1	100.0	7	7.0(7)	0	0	—	—	—	—	—	0	125
1963	Pit	6	10	11	1.1(5)	0	1	21	21.0(21)	0	1	0	0.0	0	0.0	0	0	—	—	—	K	—	2	22
1963	Was	2	19	50	2.6(9)	1	6	91	15.2(34)	0	3	1	33.3	23	7.7(23)	0	0	—	—	—	—	—	6	117
1964	Was	14	24	67	2.8(16)	1	2	25	12.5(24)	0	—	—	—	—	—	—	—	—	—	—	—	—	6	90
NFL	9	89	808	2912	3.6(64)	17	113	1468	13.0(65)	14	67	24	35.8	854	12.7(72)	6	5	—	—	—	Kkp	—	199	4183

TRAFFORD, ROD Rodney, TE, 6´3˝/250 lbs; South Carolina; B11/28/1978 Morristown, NJ

YEAR	TEAM	G (GS, POS)	RUSH	YD	AVG (LG)	TD	REC	YD	AVG (LG)	TD	PASS	COMP	PCT	YD	AVG (LG)	TD	INT	SK	YD	QBR	KPR	OTD	PTS	TAY
2004	Buf	4(0)	—	—	—	—	3	25	8.3(10)	0	—	—	—	—	—	—	—	—	—	—	—	—	0	13

TRAFTON, GEORGE George Edward, C, 6´2˝/230 lbs; Notre Dame; B12/6/1896 Chicago, IL, D9/5/1971 Los Angeles, CA; HOF 1964 **1920** Dec☆13 (8, C) **1921** ChiS 10 (10, C) **1923** ChiB☆12 (12, C) **1924** ChiB☆11 (11, C) **1925** ChiB☆17 (15, C) **1926** ChiB☆14 (14, C) **1927** ChiB☆14 (7, C) **1928** ChiB 9 (9, C) **1929** ChiB 12 (8, C) **1930** ChiB 14 (4) **1931** ChiB 11 (1) **1932** ChiB 11 (1) **NFL** 148 (100) [12 yrs]

TRAHAN, JOHN John, WR, 5´9˝/160 lbs; Southern Colorado; B4/19/1961 Grand Forks, ND

YEAR	TEAM	G (GS, POS)	RUSH	YD	AVG (LG)	TD	REC	YD	AVG (LG)	TD	PASS	COMP	PCT	YD	AVG (LG)	TD	INT	SK	YD	QBR	KPR	OTD	PTS	TAY
1987	KC	3(3)	—	—	—	—	4	40	10.0(14)	0	—	—	—	—	—	—	—	—	—	—	—	—	0	20

TRAINOR, MIKE Michael Joseph, WB-HB, 5´9˝/165 lbs; Canisius; B12/18/1899 New York, NY, D4/23/1980 Lake Success, NY **1923** Buf 12 (9, WB), 12 **1924** Buf 11 (4), 6 **NFL** 23 (13), 18 [2 yrs]

TRAMMEL, ALLEN Allen Raymond, DB, 6´0˝/190 lbs; Florida; B7/19/1942 Montgomery, AL **1966** Hou-A 3

TRAPILO, STEVE Stephen Paul, G, 6´5˝/290 lbs; Boston College; 1987: NO, rnd 4; B9/20/1964 Boston, MA **1987**†NO 11 (11, RG) **1988** NO 9 (9, rg) **1989** NO 16 (16, RG) **1990**†NO 16 (16, RG) **1992** NO 5 (0) **NFL** 57 (52) [5 yrs]

TRAPP, JAMES James Harold, DB-WR, 6´0˝/195 lbs; Clemson; 1993: LARd, rnd 3; B12/28/1969 Greenville, SC **1993** LARd 14 (2) **1994** LARd 16 (2) **1995** Oak 14 (2) **1996** Oak 12 (4) **1997** Oak 16 (16, SS) **1998** Oak 16 (0) **1999** Bal 16 (0) **2000**†Bal 16 (1) **2001** Bal 10 (4) **2002** Bal 14 (1) **2003** Jax 5 (0) **NFL** 149 (32) [11 yrs]

TRAPP, RICHARD Richard Earl, FL-WR, 6´1˝/175 lbs; Florida; 1968: Buf, rnd 3; B9/21/1946 Lynwood, CA

YEAR	TEAM	G (GS, POS)	RUSH	YD	AVG (LG)	TD	REC	YD	AVG (LG)	TD	PASS	COMP	PCT	YD	AVG (LG)	TD	INT	SK	YD	QBR	KPR	OTD	PTS	TAY
1968	Buf-A	14(FL)	—	—	—	—	24	235	9.8(27)	0	—	—	—	—	—	—	—	—	—	—	p	—	0	119
1969	SD-A	8	—	—	—	—	2	39	19.5(24)	0	—	—	—	—	—	—	—	—	—	—	p	—	0	20
NFL	2	22	—	—	—	—	26	274	10.5(27)	0	—	—	—	—	—	—	—	—	—	—	p	—	0	138

TRASK, ORVILLE Orville Luther, DT, 6´4˝/260 lbs; Rice; 1956: ChiC, rnd 24; B12/3/1934 Pueblo, CO **1960**†Hou-A☆14 (LDT) **1961**†Hou-A 14 (LDT) **1962** Oak-A 7 (LDT) **NFL** 35 [3 yrs]

TRAVENIO, HERB Herbert Charles, LB-K, 6´0˝/218 lbs; none; B2/28/1933, **[K]** **1964** SD-A 3 **1965**†SD-A 14 (LLB) **NFL** 17 [2 yrs]

TRAVIS, BRICK James Edward, T, 6´1˝/205 lbs; Tarkio; Missouri; B9/17/1897 Tarkio, MO, D9/18/1982 Chesterfield, MO **1921** RI 5 (4) **1923** SL 7 (7, RT) **NFL** 12 (11) [2 yrs]

TRAVIS, JOHN John Reginald, FB, 6´1˝/216 lbs; San Jose State; 1966: SD, rnd 18; B8/23/1943 San Jose, CA **1966** SD-A 6

TRAVIS, MACK Mack Henry, NT, 6´1˝/280 lbs; California; B7/3/1970 Las Vegas, NV **1993** Det 4 (0)

TRAYLOR, KEITH Byron Keith, DT-NT, 6´2˝/340 lbs; Oklahoma; Central Oklahoma; 1991: Den, rnd 3; B9/3/1969 Little Rock, AR **1991**†Den 16 (2) **1992** Den 16 (3) **1993** GB 5 (0) **1995**†KC 16 (0) **1996** KC 15 (1) **1997**†Den 16 (16, LDT) **1998**†Den 15 (14, LDT) **1999** Den 15 (15, LDT) **2000**†Den 16 (16, LDT) **2001**†ChiB 16 (15, RDT) **2002** ChiB 15 (15, RDT) **2003** ChiB 10 (10, LDT) **2004**†NE 16 (10, NT) **2005** Mia 13 (13, LDT) **NFL** 200 (130) [14 yrs]

TRAYNHAM, JERRY Gerald Francis, K, 5´10˝/190 lbs; USC; B1/23/1939 Sacramento, CA

YEAR	TEAM	G (GS, POS)	RUSH	YD	AVG (LG)	TD	REC	YD	AVG (LG)	TD	PASS	COMP	PCT	YD	AVG (LG)	TD	INT	SK	YD	QBR	KPR	OTD	PTS	TAY
1961	Den-A	2	6	12	2.0(8)	0	1	-1	-1.0(-1)	0	—	—	—	—	—	—	—	—	—	—	—	—	0	12

TRAYNHAM, WADE Wade Lamar, K, 6´2˝/218 lbs; Frederick CC (MD); B2/3/1942 Hampton, VA **[K]** **1966** Atl 2 **1967** Atl 14 **NFL** 16 [2 yrs]

TRAYNOR, BARNEY Bernard Philip, C, 6´1˝/190 lbs; Colgate; B11/24/1896 Beaver Dam, WI, D8/26/1980 Austin, TX **1925** Mil 5 (5, C)

TRAYNOWICZ, MARK Mark Joseph, G-C, 6´5˝/277 lbs; Nebraska; 1985: Buf, rnd 2; B11/20/1962 Omaha, NE **1985** Buf 16 (0) **1986** Buf 14 (0) **1987** Buf 11 (0) **1988** Buf 4 (0) **1988** Phx 5 (0) **1989** Phx 2 (0) **NFL** 52 (0) [5 yrs]

TREADAWAY, JOHN John Charles, T, 6´5˝/258 lbs; Hardin-Simmons; B8/21/1917 Moscow, TN **1948** NYG 12 (0) **1949** Det 7 (0) **NFL** 19 (0) [2 yrs]

°**TREADWELL, DAVID** David Mark, K, 6´1˝/180 lbs; Clemson; B2/27/1965 Columbia, SC **[K]** **1989**†Den★16 (0) **1990** Den 16 (0) **1991**†Den 16 (0) **1992** Den 16 (0) **1993**†NYG 16 (0) **1994** NYG 13 (0) **NFL** 93 (0) [6 yrs]

TREAUDO, AHMAD Ahmad, DB, 5´10˝/181 lbs; Southern (LA); B4/15/1982 **2005** Atl 1 (0)

TREBOTICH, BUZZ Ivan Peter, B, 5´10˝/208 lbs; St. Mary's (CA); B12/30/1920 Oakland, CA, D8/4/1992 Napa, CA

YEAR	TEAM	G (GS, POS)	RUSH	YD	AVG (LG)	TD	REC	YD	AVG (LG)	TD	PASS	COMP	PCT	YD	AVG (LG)	TD	INT	SK	YD	QBR	KPR	OTD	PTS	TAY
1944	Det	10(0)	1	2	2.0(2)	0	—	—	—	—	—	—	—	—	—	—	—	—	—	—	—	—	0	2
1945	Det	9(5, BB)	3	3	1.0(4)	0	—	—	—	—	1	1	100.0	8	8.0(8)	0	0	—	—	—	i	—	0	38
NFL	2	19(5)	4	5	1.3(4)	0	—	—	—	—	1	1	100.0	8	8.0(8)	0	0	—	—	—	i	—	0	40
1947	Bal-A	2(0)	3	-4	-1.3	0	—	—	—	—	—	—	—	—	—	—	—	—	—	—	k	—	0	-2

TREGGS, BRIAN Brian Allen, WR, 5´9˝/161 lbs; California; B6/11/1970 Los Angeles, CA **1992** Sea 2 (0)

TREJO, STEPHEN Stephen Nicolas, FB, 6´2˝/254 lbs; Arizona State; B11/20/1977 Mesa, AZ

YEAR	TEAM	G (GS, POS)	RUSH	YD	AVG (LG)	TD	REC	YD	AVG (LG)	TD	PASS	COMP	PCT	YD	AVG (LG)	TD	INT	SK	YD	QBR	KPR	OTD	PTS	TAY
2001	Det	14(0)	—	—	—	—	5	61	12.2(20)	0	—	—	—	—	—	—	—	—	—	—	—	—	0	31
2002	Det	16(0)	1	0	0.0(0)	0	2	13	6.5(8)	0	—	—	—	—	—	—	—	—	—	—	—	—	0	7
2003	Det	16(0)	—	—	—	—	1	2	2.0(2)	0	—	—	—	—	—	—	—	—	—	—	—	—	0	1
2004	Det	11(2)	—	—	—	—	4	37	9.3(18)	0	—	—	—	—	—	—	—	—	—	—	k	—	0	1
2004	SL	2(0)	—	—	—	—	—	—	—	—	—	—	—	—	—	—	—	—	—	—	—	—	—	—
NFL	4	59(2)	1	0	0.0	0	12	113	9.4(20)	0	—	—	—	—	—	—	—	—	—	—	k	—	0	39

TREMBLE, GREG Gregory Deshawn, DB, 5´11˝/188 lbs; Georgia; B4/16/1972 Warner Robins, GA **1995** Dal 7 (0) **1995** Phi 4 (0) **NFL** 11 (0) [1 yr]

TREU, ADAM Adam, C, 6´5˝/300 lbs; Nebraska; 1997: Oak, rnd 3; B6/24/1974 Lincoln, NE **1997** Oak 16 (0) **1998** Oak 16 (0) **1999** Oak 16 (0) **2000**†Oak 16 (0) **2001**†Oak 16 (14, C) **2002**†Oak 16 (0) **2003** Oak 16 (4) **2004** Oak 16 (16, C) **2005** Oak 16 (10, C) **NFL** 144 (44) [9 yrs]

TRIGGS, JACK John Stephen, FB, 6´0˝/200 lbs; Providence; B1/11/1903 Brockton, MA, D2/16/1951 Brockton, MA **1926** Pro 3 (0)

TRIGILIO, FRANK Frank J., FB, 5´11˝/200 lbs; Vermont; Alfred; B1/19/1919, NY

YEAR	TEAM	G(GS, POS)	RUSH	YD	AVG(LG)	TD	REC	YD	AVG(LG)	TD	PASS	COMP	PCT	YD	AVG(LG)	TD	INT	SK	YD	QBR	KPR	OTD	PTS	TAY
1946	LAD-A	1(0)	3	2	0.7	0	—	—	—	—	—	—	—	—	—	—	—	—	—	—	—	—	0	2
1946	Mia-A	7(1)	38	124	3.3	1	—	—	—	—	—	—	—	—	—	—	—	—	—	—	—	—	6	134
AAFC	1	8(1)	41	126	3.1	1	—	—	—	—	—	—	—	—	—	—	—	—	—	—	—	—	6	136

TRIMBLE, STEVE Steven Garfield, DB, 5´10˝/181 lbs; Maryland; B5/11/1958 Cumberland, MD **1981** Den 3 (0) **1982** Den 6 (1) **1983**†Den 5 (1) **1987** ChiB 3 (3) **NFL** 17 (5) [4 yrs]

TRIMBLE, WAYNE Wayne Allen, DB, 6´3˝/203 lbs; Alabama; 1967: SF, rnd 4; B12/10/1944 Cullman, AL **1967** SF 1

TRIPLETT, BILL William Clarence, RB-DB, 6´2˝/215 lbs; Miami (OH); 1962: NYG, rnd 6/Bos, rnd 9; B5/9/1940 Indianola, MS

YEAR	TEAM	G(GS, POS)	RUSH	YD	AVG(LG)	TD	REC	YD	AVG(LG)	TD	PASS	COMP	PCT	YD	AVG(LG)	TD	INT	SK	YD	QBR	KPR	OTD	PTS	TAY
1962	SL	14	2	12	6.0(10)	0	—	—	—	—	—	—	—	—	—	—	—	—	—	—	ki	—	0	279
1963	SL	13(HB)	134	652	4.9(63)	5	31	396	12.8(38)	3	—	—	—	—	—	—	—	—	—	—	k	—	48	934
1965	SL	14(HB)	174	617	3.5(59)	6	26	256	9.8(37)	1	—	—	—	—	—	—	—	—	—	—	—	—	42	810
1966	SL	8	13	25	1.9(5)	0	2	6	3.0(11)	0	—	—	—	—	—	—	—	—	—	—	—	—	0	28
1967	NYG	11	58	171	2.9(14)	2	7	69	9.9(16)	0	—	—	—	—	—	—	—	—	—	—	k	—	12	260
1968	Det	12(FB)	120	384	3.2(17)	0	28	135	4.8(25)	0	—	—	—	—	—	—	—	—	—	—	—	—	0	452
1969	Det	14(FB)	111	377	3.4(33)	3	13	141	10.8(62)	1	—	—	—	—	—	—	—	—	—	—	—	—	24	483
1970	†Det	14	48	156	3.3(11)	1	6	52	8.7(15)	0	—	—	—	—	—	—	—	—	—	—	—	—	6	192
1971	Det	14	4	4	1.0(6)	0	—	—	—	—	—	—	—	—	—	—	—	—	—	—	k	—	0	29
1972	Det	14	17	48	2.8(9)	0	—	—	—	—	—	—	—	—	—	—	—	—	—	—	k	—	0	45
NFL	10	128	681	2446	3.6(63)	17	113	1055	9.3(62)	5	—	—	—	—	—	—	—	—	—	—	ki	—	132	3511

TRIPLETT, MEL Melvin C., FB, 6´1˝/215 lbs; Toledo; 1955: NYG, rnd 5; B12/24/1931 Indianola, MS, D7/25/2002 Toledo, OH

YEAR	TEAM	G(GS, POS)	RUSH	YD	AVG(LG)	TD	REC	YD	AVG(LG)	TD	PASS	COMP	PCT	YD	AVG(LG)	TD	INT	SK	YD	QBR	KPR	OTD	PTS	TAY
1955	NYG	12(fb)	34	138	4.1(19)	0	3	9	3.0(12)	0	—	—	—	—	—	—	—	—	—	—	k	—	0	145
1956	†NYG	12(FB)	125	515	4.1(25)	5	6	48	8.0(35)	1	—	—	—	—	—	—	—	—	—	—	k	—	36	581
1957	NYG	10(FB)	61	216	3.5(16)	0	4	75	18.8(33)	0	—	—	—	—	—	—	—	—	—	—	—	—	0	254
1958	†NYG	12(FB)	118	466	3.9(24)	1	7	110	15.7(32)	0	—	—	—	—	—	—	—	—	—	—	k	—	6	530
1959	†NYG	11(FB)	91	381	4.2(20)	1	6	78	13.0(25)	0	—	—	—	—	—	—	—	—	—	—	—	—	6	430
1960	NYG	12(FB)	124	573	4.6(40)	4	5	48	9.6(24)	2	—	—	—	—	—	—	—	—	—	—	k	—	36	655
1961	Min	14(8, FB)	80	407	5.1(37)	1	10	41	4.1(15)	0	—	—	—	—	—	—	—	—	—	—	k	—	6	434
1962	Min	14	52	160	3.1(18)	2	2	30	15.0(27)	1	—	—	—	—	—	—	—	—	—	—	—	—	18	200
NFL	8	97(8)	685	2856	4.2(40)	14	43	439	10.2(35)	4	—	—	—	—	—	—	—	—	—	—	k	—	108	3228

TRIPLETT, WALLY Wallace, HB-DB, 5´10˝/170 lbs; Penn State; 1949: Det, rnd 19/Bkn-A, rnd 3; B4/18/1926 La Mott, PA

YEAR	TEAM	G(GS, POS)	RUSH	YD	AVG(LG)	TD	REC	YD	AVG(LG)	TD	PASS	COMP	PCT	YD	AVG(LG)	TD	INT	SK	YD	QBR	KPR	OTD	PTS	TAY
1949	Det	11(5, RH)	53	221	4.2(80)	1	8	90	11.3(32)	0	—	—	—	—	—	—	—	—	—	—	p	1	12	462
1950	Det	7	14	92	6.6(14)	0	6	70	11.7(18)	0	—	—	—	—	—	—	—	—	—	—	kp	2	12	467
1952	ChiC	2	—	—	—	—	—	—	—	—	—	—	—	—	—	—	—	—	—	—	p	—	0	16
1953	ChiC	4	3	8	2.7(16)	0	3	15	5.0(6)	0	—	—	—	—	—	—	—	—	—	—	k	—	0	119
NFL	4	24(5)	70	321	4.6(80)	1	17	175	10.3(32)	0	—	—	—	—	—	—	—	—	—	—	kp	3	24	1064

TRIPOLI, PAUL Paul Randall, DB, 6´0˝/197 lbs; Alabama; B12/14/1961 Utica, NY **1987** TB 13 (4)

TRIPPI, CHARLIE Charles Louis, HB-QB-DB, 6´0˝/186 lbs; Georgia; 1945: ChiC, rnd 1/1947: NYY-A, rnd S; B12/14/1922 Pittston, PA; HOF 1968

YEAR	TEAM	G(GS, POS)	RUSH	YD	AVG(LG)	TD	REC	YD	AVG(LG)	TD	PASS	COMP	PCT	YD	AVG(LG)	TD	INT	SK	YD	QBR	KPR	OTD	PTS	TAY
1947	†ChiC☆	11(9, LH)	83	401	4.8(41)	2	23	240	10.4(62)	0	2	1	50.0	49	24.5(49)	0	1	—	—	—	kpi	1	18	787
1948	†ChiC☆	12(11, LH)	128	690	5.4(50)	6	22	228	10.4(33)	2	8	4	50.0	118	14.8(64)	1	0	—	—	—	Pkp	2	60	**1230**
1949	ChiC	12(12, LH)	112	553	4.9(55)	3	34	412	12.1(44)	6	2	0	0.0	0	0.0	0	0	—	—	—	Pkp	—	54	1086
1950	ChiC	12(11, LH)	99	426	4.3(22)	3	32	270	8.4(28)	1	3	1	33.3	19	6.3(19)	0	0	—	—	—	Pkp	—	24	644
1951	ChiC	12(QB)	78	501	6.4(32)	4	—	—	—	—	191	88	46.1	1191	6.2(80)	8	13	—	—	52.1	P	—	24	657
1952	ChiC★	11(QB)	72	350	4.9(59)	4	5	66	13.2(21)	0	181	84	46.4	890	4.9(56)	5	13	—	—	40.5	P	—	24	373
1953	ChiC✧	12(LH)	97	433	4.5(21)	0	11	87	7.9(21)	2	34	20	58.8	195	5.7(21)	2	1	—	—	—	Pkp	—	12	767
1954	ChiC	12(DB)	18	152	8.4(57)	1	3	18	6.0(7)	0	13	7	53.8	85	6.5(22)	0	3	—	—	—	Pkpi	—	6	142
1955	ChiC	5	—	—	—	—	—	—	—	—	—	—	—	—	—	—	—	—	—	—	P	—	0	0
NFL	9	99(43)	687	3506	5.1(59)	23	130	1321	10.2(62)	11	434	205	47.2	2547	5.9(80)	16	31	—	—	48.4	Pkpi	3	222	5684

TRIPPLETT, LARRY Larry, DT, 6´2˝/300 lbs; Washington; 2002: Ind, rnd 2; B1/18/1979 Los Angeles, CA **2002**†Ind 13 (10, RDT) **2003**†Ind 16 (16, LDT) **2004**†Ind 16 (0) **2005**†Ind 15 (4) **NFL** 60 (30) [4 yrs]

TRIPSON, JOHN John Robert, T, 6´3˝/220 lbs; Mississippi State; 1941: Det, rnd 6; B9/17/1919 Madero, TX, D7/6/1997 Vero Beach, FL **1941** Det✧11 (9, LT)

TRIPUCKA, FRANK Francis Joseph, QB, 6´2˝/192 lbs; Notre Dame; 1949: Phi, rnd 1/Buf-A, rnd S2; B12/8/1927 Bloomfield, NJ

YEAR	TEAM	G(GS, POS)	RUSH	YD	AVG(LG)	TD	REC	YD	AVG(LG)	TD	PASS	COMP	PCT	YD	AVG(LG)	TD	INT	SK	YD	QBR	KPR	OTD	PTS	TAY
1949	Det	6(4, qb)	12	36	3.0(18)	1	—	—	—	—	145	62	42.8	833	5.7(64)	9	14	—	—	42.8	P	—	6	-53
1950	ChiC	10(1, qb)	4	35	8.8(21)	1	—	—	—	—	108	47	43.5	720	6.7(81)	4	7	—	—	51.5	P	—	6	145
1951	ChiC	3	1	14	14.0(14)	0	—	—	—	—	29	17	58.6	244	8.4(48)	2	1	—	—	—	P	—	0	106
1952	ChiC	6	1	-3	-3.0(-3)	0	—	—	—	—	12	5	41.7	40	3.3(13)	0	0	—	—	—	P	—	0	17
1952	DalT	6(6, QB)	9	28	3.1(15)	3	—	—	—	—	174	86	49.4	769	4.4(42)	3	17	—	—	27.8	P	—	18	-223
1960	Den-A☆	14(QB)	10	0	0.0(8)	0	—	—	—	—	**478**	**248**	51.9	**3038**	6.4(80)	24	**34**	—	—	58.9	—	—	0	279
1961	Den-A	14(QB)	4	-8	-2.0(0)	0	—	—	—	—	344	167	48.5	1690	4.9(87)	10	21	—	—	47.3	—	—	0	47
1962	Den-A✧	14(QB)	2	-1	-0.5(1)	1	—	—	—	—	**440**	**240**	54.5	**2917**	6.6(96)	17	25	—	—	64.4	—	—	6	553
1963	Den-A	2	—	—	—	—	—	—	—	—	15	7	46.7	31	2.1(14)	0	5	—	—	—	—	—	0	-185
NFL	8	75(11)	43	101	2.3(21)	6	—	—	—	—	1745	879	50.4	10282	5.9(96)	69	124	—	—	52.2	P	—	36	687

TROCANO, RICK Richard Charles, QB-DB, 6´0˝/188 lbs; Pittsburgh; 1981: Pit, rnd 11; B4/4/1959 Cleveland, OH **1981** Cle 6 (0) **1982** Cle 2 (0) **NFL** 8 (0) [2 yrs]

TROCOLOR, BOB Robert G., QB-HB, 6´2˝/207 lbs; Long Island; Alabama; B3/31/1917 Oak Hill, TX, D7/27/1984 Franklin Lakes, NJ

YEAR	TEAM	G(GS, POS)	RUSH	YD	AVG(LG)	TD	REC	YD	AVG(LG)	TD	PASS	COMP	PCT	YD	AVG(LG)	TD	INT	SK	YD	QBR	KPR	OTD	PTS	TAY
1942	NYG	7(0)	26	0	0.0(19)	0	—	—	—	—	5	3	60.0	52	10.4(29)	1	1	—	—	—	Pkp	—	0	25
1943	NYG	5(0)	6	-4	-0.7(11)	0	—	—	—	—	7	2	28.6	4	0.6(3)	0	1	—	—	—	Pkp	—	0	4
1944	Bkn	2(0)	3	8	2.7(5)	0	—	—	—	—	—	—	—	—	—	—	—	—	—	—	P	—	0	8
NFL	3	14(0)	35	4	0.1(19)	0	—	—	—	—	12	5	41.7	56	4.7(29)	1	2	—	—	—	Pkp	—	0	37

TROSCH, GENE Eugene Lloyd, DE, 6´7˝/277 lbs; Miami (FL); 1967: KC, rnd 1; B6/7/1945 Steubenville, OH **1967** KC-A 14 **1969**†KC-A 13 **NFL** 27 [2 yrs]

TROST, MILT Milton Frank, T-E, 6´1˝/206 lbs; Marquette; B3/4/1913 Detroit, MI, D4/2/1986 Zephyrhills, FL **1935** ChiB 5 (0) **1936** ChiB 11 (0) **1937**†ChiB 10 (2) **1938** ChiB 10 (1) **1939** ChiB 10 (1) **1940** Phi 7 (2) **NFL** 53 (6) [6 yrs]

TROTTER, JEREMIAH Jeremiah, LB, 6´1˝/262 lbs; Stephen F. Austin State; 1998: Phi, rnd 3; B1/20/1977 Texarkana, TX **1998** Phi 8 (0) **1999** Phi 16 (16, MLB) **2000**†Phi★16 (16, MLB) **2001**†Phi★16 (16, MLB) **2002** Was 12 (12, MLB) **2003** Was 16 (16, MLB) **2004**†Phi✧16 (9, MLB) **2005** Phi✧15 (15, MLB) **NFL** 115 (100) [8 yrs]

TROUP, BILL Paul William, QB, 6´5˝/220 lbs; Virginia; South Carolina; B4/2/1951 Pittsburgh, PA

YEAR	TEAM	G(GS, POS)	RUSH	YD	AVG(LG)	TD	REC	YD	AVG(LG)	TD	PASS	COMP	PCT	YD	AVG(LG)	TD	INT	SK	YD	QBR	KPR	OTD	PTS	TAY
1974	Bal	1	—	—	—	—	—	—	—	—	—	—	—	—	—	—	—	—	—	—	—	—	—	—
1976	†Bal	14	5	-1	-0.2(6)	1	—	—	—	—	18	8	44.4	117	6.5(32)	0	1	1	4	—	—	—	6	28
1977	†Bal	14	7	-8	-1.1(7)	0	—	—	—	—	2	0	0.0	0	0.0	0	1	—	—	—	—	—	0	-48
1978	Bal	12(QB)	18	25	1.4(10)	1	—	—	—	—	296	154	52.0	1882	6.4(67)	10	21	32	340	53.6	—	—	6	186
1980	GB	2(0)	—	—	—	—	—	—	—	—	12	4	33.3	48	4.0(24)	0	3	2	20	—	—	—	0	-96
NFL	5	43	30	16	0.5(10)	2	—	—	—	—	328	166	50.6	2047	6.2(67)	10	26	35	364	47.4	—	—	12	70

TROUPE, BEN Benjamin LaShaun, TE, 6´4˝/262 lbs; Florida; 2004: Ten, rnd 2; B9/1/1982 Swainsboro, GA

YEAR	TEAM	G(GS, POS)	RUSH	YD	AVG(LG)	TD	REC	YD	AVG(LG)	TD	PASS	COMP	PCT	YD	AVG(LG)	TD	INT	SK	YD	QBR	KPR	OTD	PTS	TAY
2004	Ten	14(6, te)	—	—	—	—	33	329	10.0(33)	1	—	—	—	—	—	—	—	—	—	—	—	—	6	170
2005	Ten	15(11, TE)	—	—	—	—	55	530	9.6(35)	4	—	—	—	—	—	—	—	—	—	—	—	—	24	285
NFL	2	29(17)	—	—	—	—	88	859	9.8(35)	5	—	—	—	—	—	—	—	—	—	—	—	—	30	455

TROUT, DAVID David Marshall, K, 5´6˝/165 lbs; Pittsburgh; B11/12/1957 Mount Pleasant, PA [K] **1981** Pit 16 (0) **1987** Pit 3 (0) **NFL** 19 (0) [2 yrs]

YEAR	TEAM	G (GS, POS)	RUSH	YD	AVG(LG)	TD	REC	YD	AVG(LG)	TD	PASS COMP	PCT	YD	AVG(LG)	TD	INT	SK	YD	QBR	KPR	OTD	PTS	TAY

TROWBRIDGE, RAY　Raymond Newton, E, 6'0"/170 lbs; Boston College; Purdue; B7/19/1898 South Bend, IN, D1/17/1975 Atlanta, GA　**1920** Cle 3 (0)　**1921** NYG 2 (1)　**NFL** 5 (1) [2 yrs]

TRUAX, BILLY　William Frederick, TE, 6'5"/240 lbs; LSU; 1964: Cle, rnd 2/Hou, rnd 2; B7/15/1943 Gulfport, MS

YEAR	TEAM	G (GS, POS)	RUSH	YD	AVG(LG)	TD	REC	YD	AVG(LG)	TD	OTD	PTS	TAY
1964	LARm	10	—	—	—	—	—	—	—	—	—	—	—
1965	LARm	14	—	—	—	—	6	108	18.0(59)	1	—	6	59
1966	LARm	14(TE)	—	—	—	—	29	314	10.8(21)	0	1	6	157
1967	†LARm	14(TE)	—	—	—	—	37	487	13.2(41)	4	—	24	264
1968	LARm	14(13, TE)	—	—	—	—	35	417	11.9(22)	5	—	18	224
1969	†LARm	14(13, TE)	—	—	—	—	37	431	11.6(49)	5	—	30	241
1970	LARm	14(14, TE)	—	—	—	—	36	420	11.7(34)	3	—	18	225
1971	†Dal	12(10, TE)	—	—	—	—	15	232	15.5(25)	1	—	6	121
1972	†Dal	6	—	—	—	—	4	49	12.3(18)	0	—	0	25
1973	Dal	2	—	—	—	—	—	—	—	—	—	—	—
NFL	10	114(50)	—	—	—	—	199	2458	12.4(59)	17	1	108	1314

TRUAX, DALTON　Dalton Lloyd, T, 6'2"/236 lbs; Tulane; 1957: GB, rnd 3; B1/17/1935 New Orleans, LA　**1960** Oak-A 14

TRUDEAU, JACK　Jack Francis, QB, 6'3"/227 lbs; Illinois; 1986: Ind, rnd 2; B9/9/1962 Forest Lake, MN

YEAR	TEAM	G (GS, POS)	RUSH	YD	AVG(LG)	TD	PASS COMP	PCT	YD	AVG(LG)	TD	INT	SK	YD	QBR	OTD	PTS	TAY
1986	Ind	12(11, QB)	13	21	1.6(8)	1	417 204	48.9	2225	5.3(84)	8	18	29	213	53.5	—	6	464
1987	†Ind	10(8, QB)	15	7	0.5(9)	0	229 128	55.9	1587	6.9(55)	6	6	13	100	75.4	—	0	591
1988	Ind	2(2)	—	—	—	—	34 14	41.2	158	4.6(48)	0	3	2	13	—	—	0	-41
1989	Ind	13(12, QB)	35	91	2.6(17)	2	362 190	52.5	2317	6.4(71)	15	13	20	125	71.3	—	12	825
1990	Ind	6(4)	10	28	2.8(9)	0	144 84	58.3	1078	7.5(73)	6	6	14	104	78.4	—	0	357
1991	Ind	2(0)	—	—	—	—	7 2	28.6	19	2.7(11)	0	1	1	6	—	—	0	-31
1992	Ind	11(5, qb)	13	6	0.5(5)	0	181 105	58.0	1271	7.0(81)	4	8	11	85	68.6	—	0	342
1993	Ind	5(5, qb)	5	3	0.6(2)	0	162 85	52.5	992	6.1(68)	2	7	2	11	57.4	—	0	229
1994	NYJ	5(2)	6	30	5.0(15)	0	91 50	54.9	496	5.5(24)	1	4	9	52	—	—	0	123
1995	Car	1(0)	—	—	—	—	17 11	64.7	100	5.9(19)	0	3	2	8	—	—	0	-70
NFL	10	67(49)	97	186	1.9(17)	3	1644 873	53.1	10243	6.2(84)	42	69	103	717	63.3	—	18	2788

TRUESDELL, HAL　Harold Palmer, T, 6'0"/200 lbs; Hamline; B1907, D1932　**1930** Min 1 (0)

TRUFANT, MARCUS　Marcus Lavon, DB, 5'11"/199 lbs; Washington State; 2003: Sea, rnd 1; B12/25/1980 Tacoma, WA　**2003**†Sea 16 (16, RCB/lcb)　**2004**†Sea 16 (16, LCB)　**2005**†Sea 15 (15, RCB)　**NFL** 47 (47) [3 yrs]

TRUITT, DAVE　David Moreland, TE, 6'4"/232 lbs; North Carolina; B2/18/1964　**1987** Was 1 (0)

TRUITT, GREG　Gregory Hoyt, C, 6'0"/235 lbs; Penn State; B12/8/1965 Sarasota, FL　**1994** Cin 16 (0)　**1995** Cin 16 (0)　**1996** Cin 16 (0)　**1997** Cin 16 (0)　**1998** Cin 11 (0)　**NFL** 75 (0) [5 yrs]

TRUITT, OLANDA　Olanda Raynard, WR, 6'0"/187 lbs; Pittsburgh; Mississipi State; 1993: LARd, rnd 5; B1/4/1971 Bessemer, AL

YEAR	TEAM	G (GS, POS)	RUSH	YD	AVG(LG)	TD	REC	YD	AVG(LG)	TD	KPR	OTD	PTS	TAY
1993	Min	8(0)	—	—	—	—	4	40	10.0(13)	0		—	0	20
1994	Was	9(0)	—	—	—	—	2	89	44.5(77)	1		—	6	50
1995	Was	5(2)	—	—	—	—	9	154	17.1(47)	1		—	6	82
1996	Oak	10(0)	—	—	—	—	—	—	—	—		—	—	—
1997	Oak	14(0)	—	—	—	—	7	91	13.0(19)	1	k	—	6	72
NFL	5	46(2)	—	—	—	—	22	374	17.0(77)	3	k	—	18	223

TRULL, DON　Donald Dean, QB, 6'1"/195 lbs; Baylor; 1963: Hou, rnd 14/Bal, rnd 9; B10/20/1941 Oklahoma City, OK

YEAR	TEAM	G (GS, POS)	RUSH	YD	AVG(LG)	TD	PASS COMP	PCT	YD	AVG(LG)	TD	INT	SK	YD	QBR	OTD	PTS	TAY
1964	Hou-A	14	12	42	3.5(15)	0	86 36	41.9	439	5.1(36)	1	2	—	—	—	—	0	187
1965	Hou-A	14	29	145	5.0(18)	2	107 38	35.5	528	4.9(57)	5	5	—	—	48.3	—	12	254
1966	Hou-A	14(qb)	38	139	3.7(23)	7	172 84	48.8	1200	7.0(62)	10	5	—	—	79.1	—	42	659
1967	Hou-A	3	3	-5	-1.7(7)	0	11 4	36.4	38	3.5(16)	0	2	0	18	—	—	0	14
1967	Bos-A	7(3)	19	35	1.8(10)	3	81 27	33.3	442	5.5(52)	1	7	11	75	—	—	18	11
1968	Hou-A	11(4)	14	47	3.4(15)	2	105 53	50.5	864	8.2(60)	10	3	9	94	98.3	—	0	409
1969	†Hou-A	14	8	25	3.1(7)	2	75 34	45.3	469	6.3(57)	3	3	11	85	—	—	12	55
NFL	6	77(7)	123	428	3.5(23)	14	637 276	43.3	3980	6.2(62)	30	28	33	272	61.6	—	84	1588

TRULUCK, R-KAL　R-Kal K-Quan, DE, 6'4"/255 lbs; Cortland State; B9/30/1974 Brooklyn, NY　**2002** KC 6 (0)　**2003**†KC 14 (0)　**2004**†GB 14 (1)　**2005** Arz 7 (0)　**NFL** 41 (1) [4 yrs]

TRUMPY, BOB　Robert Theodore, TE-WR, 6'6"/228 lbs; Illinois; Utah; 1968: Cin, rnd 12; B3/6/1945 Springfield, IL

YEAR	TEAM	G (GS, POS)	RUSH	YD	AVG(LG)	TD	REC	YD	AVG(LG)	TD	OTD	PTS	TAY
1968	Cin-A◇	14(TE)	1	-1	-1.0(-1)	0	37	639	17.3(80)	3	—	18	334
1969	Cin-A★	14(TE)	—	—	—	—	37	835	22.6(80)	9	—	54	463
1970	†Cin★	11(TE)	—	—	—	—	29	480	16.6(53)	2	—	12	250
1971	Cin	14(TE/wr)	—	—	—	—	40	531	13.3(44)	3	—	18	281
1972	Cin	12(TE)	—	—	—	—	44	500	11.4(38)	2	—	12	260
1973	†Cin◇	14(TE)	—	—	—	—	29	435	15.0(53)	5	—	30	243
1974	Cin	13(TE)	—	—	—	—	21	330	15.7(41)	2	—	12	175
1975	†Cin	11(TE)	—	—	—	—	22	276	12.5(35)	1	—	6	143
1976	Cin	13(TE)	—	—	—	—	21	323	15.4(48)	7	—	42	197
1977	Cin	12(TE)	—	—	—	—	18	251	13.9(32)	1	—	6	131
NFL	10	128	1	-1	-1.0(-1)	0	298	4600	15.4(80)	35	—	210	2474

TRUVILLION, ERIC　Eric Brian, WR, 6'4"/205 lbs; Florida A&M; B6/18/1959 New York, NY

YEAR	TEAM	G (GS, POS)	RUSH	YD	AVG(LG)	TD	REC	YD	AVG(LG)	TD	OTD	PTS	TAY
1987	Det	3(3)	—	—	—	—	12	207	17.3(53)	1	—	6	109

TRYON, EDDIE　Joseph Edward, TB-WB, 5'8"/180 lbs; Colgate; B7/25/1900 Medford, MA, D5/1/1982 St. Petersburg, FL [K]　**1927** NYY☆14 (11, TB), 44

TSCHAPPAT, CHALMERS　John Chalmers, T, 5'11"/180 lbs; West Virginia Wesleyan; B6/1896 Bellaire, OH, deceased　**1921** Day 2 (1)

TSOUTSOUVAS, LOU　Louis Samuel, C, 5'11"/210 lbs; Stanford; B7/4/1915 Fresno, CA, D7/17/2001 Santa Paula, CA　**1938** Pit 5 (4)

TSOUTSOUVAS, SAM　John Samuel, C-LB, 6'0"/205 lbs; Oregon State; B10/8/1917 Madera, CA, D3/27/1989 Santa Barbara, CA　**1940** Det 3 (0)

TUAOLO, ESERA　Esera Tavai, NT-DT, 6'2"/277 lbs; Oregon State; 1991: GB, rnd 2; B7/11/1968 Honolulu, HI　**1991** GB 16 (16, NT)　**1992** GB 4 (0)　**1992**†Min 3 (0)　**1993**†Min 11 (3)　**1994** Min 16 (0)　**1995** Min 15 (0, LDT)　**1996** Min 14 (9, LDT)　**1997**†Jax 6 (1)　**1998**†Atl 13 (1)　**1999** Car 12 (0)　**NFL** 111 (46) [9 yrs]

TUATAGALOA, NATU　Gerardus Mauritius, DE, 6'4"/273 lbs; California; 1989: Cin, rnd 5; B5/25/1966 San Francisco, CA　**1989** Cin 14 (0)　**1990**†Cin 16 (7, lde)　**1991** Cin 16 (4)　**1992** Sea 13 (0)　**1993** Sea 16 (15, RDE)　**1995** Hou 1 (0)　**NFL** 76 (26) [6 yrs]

TUBBS, JERRY　Gerald J., LB-C, 6'2"/221 lbs; Oklahoma; 1957: ChiC, rnd 1; B1/23/1935 Throckmorton, TX　**1957** ChiC 11 (MLB)　**1958** ChiC 7　**1958** SF 4 (llb)　**1959** SF 12 (MLB)　**1960** Dal 12 (MLB)　**1961** Dal 14 (MLB)　**1962** Dal★14 (MLB)　**1963** Dal 14 (MLB)　**1964** Dal 13 (MLB)　**1965** Dal 14 (MLB)　**1966** Dal 4　**NFL** 119 [10 yrs]

TUBBS, MARCUS　Marcus Dwayne, DT, 6'4"/310 lbs; Texas; 2004: Sea, rnd 1; B5/16/1981 Dallas, TX　**2004** Sea 11 (3)　**2005**†Sea 13 (12, RDT)　**NFL** 24 (15) [2 yrs]

TUBBS, WINFRED　Winfred O'Neal, LB, 6'4"/250 lbs; Texas; 1994: NO, rnd 3; B9/24/1970 Hollywood, FL　**1994** NO 13 (7, RILB)　**1995** NO 7 (6, mlb)　**1996** NO 16 (13, MLB)　**1997** NO☆16 (16, MLB)　**1998**†SF☆16 (16, MLB)　**1999** SF 16 (15, MLB)　**2000** SF 14 (14, RLB)　**NFL** 98 (87) [7 yrs]

TUCK, JUSTIN　Justin Lee, DE, 6'5"/256 lbs; Notre Dame; 2005: NYG, rnd 3; B3/29/1983 Kellton, AL　**2005**†NYG 14 (1)

TUCKER, B.J.　B.J., DB, 5'11"/188 lbs; Wisconsin; 2003: Dal, rnd 6; B10/12/1980 Sierra Leone, West Africa　**2005** SF 6 (0)

TUCKER, BILL　William, RB, 6'2"/219 lbs; Tennessee State; 1967: SF, rnd 3; B9/14/1943 Union, SC

YEAR	TEAM	G (GS, POS)	RUSH	YD	AVG(LG)	TD	REC	YD	AVG(LG)	TD	KPR	OTD	PTS	TAY
1967	SF	14	3	5	1.7(3)	0	2	22	11.0(12)	0	kp	—	0	76
1968	SF	14	30	135	4.5(18)	3	15	197	13.1(43)	4	k	—	42	312
1969	SF	13	20	72	3.6(24)	2	14	104	7.4(18)	2	k	—	24	139
1970	†SF	14	42	137	3.3(11)	1	17	108	6.4(28)	1	k	—	12	408

YEAR	TEAM	G (GS, POS)	RUSH	YD	AVG (LG)	TD	REC	YD	AVG (LG)	TD	PASS	COMP	PCT	YD	AVG (LG)	TD	INT	SK	YD	QBR	KPR	OTD	PTS	TAY
1971	ChiB	14	32	82	2.6(11)	0	11	65	5.9(21)	0	—	—	—	—	—	—	—	—	—	—	—	—	0	115
NFL	5	69	127	431	3.4(24)	6	59	496	8.4(43)	7	—	—	—	—	—	—	—	—	—	—	kp	—	78	1049

Tucker, Bob Robert Louis, TE, 6´3˝/230 lbs; Bloomsburg; B6/8/1945 Hazleton, PA

YEAR	TEAM	G (GS, POS)	RUSH	YD	AVG (LG)	TD	REC	YD	AVG (LG)	TD	PASS	COMP	PCT	YD	AVG (LG)	TD	INT	SK	YD	QBR	KPR	OTD	PTS	TAY
1970	NYG	14(TE)	—	—	—	—	40	571	14.3(41)	5	—	—	—	—	—	—	—	—	—	—	—	—	30	311
1971	NYG	12(TE)	1	1	1.0(1)	0	**59**	791	13.4(63)	4	—	—	—	—	—	—	—	—	—	—	—	—	24	417
1972	NYG☆	14(TE)	3	6	2.0(13)	1	55	764	13.9(39)	4	—	—	—	—	—	—	—	—	—	—	—	—	30	418
1973	NYG	14(TE)	1	4	4.0(4)	0	50	681	13.6(33)	5	—	—	—	—	—	—	—	—	—	—	—	—	30	370
1974	NYG	13(TE)	—	—	—	—	41	496	12.1(29)	2	—	—	—	—	—	—	—	—	—	—	—	—	12	258
1975	NYG	14(TE)	1	-5	-5.0(-5)	0	34	484	14.2(47)	1	—	—	—	—	—	—	—	—	—	—	—	—	6	242
1976	NYG	14(TE)	—	—	—	—	42	498	11.9(39)	1	—	—	—	—	—	—	—	—	—	—	—	—	6	254
1977	NYG	5	—	—	—	—	6	91	15.2(22)	0	—	—	—	—	—	—	—	—	—	—	—	—	0	46
1977	†Min	8	—	—	—	—	9	109	12.1(29)	2	—	—	—	—	—	—	—	—	—	—	—	—	12	65
1978	†Min	16(16, TE)	—	—	—	—	47	540	11.5(35)	0	—	—	—	—	—	—	—	—	—	—	—	—	0	270
1979	Min	16(15, TE)	—	—	—	—	24	223	9.3(21)	2	—	—	—	—	—	—	—	—	—	—	—	—	12	122
1980	†Min	16(13, TE)	—	—	—	—	15	173	11.5(25)	1	—	—	—	—	—	—	—	—	—	—	—	—	6	92
NFL	11	156(44)	6	6	1.0(13)	1	422	5421	12.8(63)	27	—	—	—	—	—	—	—	—	—	—	—	—	168	2862

Tucker, Erroll Erroll R., DB, 5´8˝/169 lbs; Utah; 1986: Pit, rnd 5; B7/6/1964 Pittsburgh, PA **1988**†Buf 9 (0) **1989** Buf 4 (0) **1989** NE 5 (0) **NFL** 18 (0) [2 yrs]

Tucker, Gary Gary, RB, 5´11˝/205 lbs; Vanderbilt; Tennessee Chattanooga; 1967: Mia, rnd 5; B2/19/1945 Shelbyville, TN

YEAR	TEAM	G (GS, POS)	RUSH	YD	AVG (LG)	TD	REC	YD	AVG (LG)	TD	PASS	COMP	PCT	YD	AVG (LG)	TD	INT	SK	YD	QBR	KPR	OTD	PTS	TAY
1968	Mia-A	14	4	13	3.3(7)	0	—	—	—	—	—	—	—	—	—	—	—	—	—	—	kp	—	0	37

Tucker, Jason Jason, WR, 6´1˝/182 lbs; TCU; 1998: Cin, rnd 6; B6/24/1976 Waco, TX

YEAR	TEAM	G (GS, POS)	RUSH	YD	AVG (LG)	TD	REC	YD	AVG (LG)	TD	PASS	COMP	PCT	YD	AVG (LG)	TD	INT	SK	YD	QBR	KPR	OTD	PTS	TAY
1999	†Dal	15(4)	1	8	8.0(8)	0	23	439	19.1(**90**)	2	—	—	—	—	—	—	—	—	—	—	kp	—	12	553
2000	Dal	16(7, wr)	4	42	10.5(17)	1	13	126	9.7(18)	0	—	—	—	—	—	—	—	—	—	—	kp	—	6	438
NFL	2	31(11)	5	50	10.0(17)	1	36	565	15.7(90)	2	—	—	—	—	—	—	—	—	—	—	kp	—	18	991

Tucker, Mark Mark Frederick, G, 6´3˝/290 lbs; USC; 1991: Atl, rnd 7; B4/29/1968 Spokane, WA **1994** Arz 16 (3)

Tucker, Rex Rex Truman, G, 6´5˝/315 lbs; Texas A&M; 1999: Chi, rnd 3; B12/20/1976 Midland, TX **1999** ChiB 2 (1) **2000** ChiB 6 (0) **2001**†ChiB 16 (16, LG) **2002** ChiB 5 (5, lg) **2004** ChiB 6 (5, rg) **2005** SL 8 (3) **NFL** 43 (30) [6 yrs]

Tucker, Ross Ross, G, 6´4˝/316 lbs; Princeton; B3/2/1979 Wyomissing, PA **2001** Was 3 (0) **2002** Was 3 (0) **2002** Dal 7 (7, LG) **2003** Buf 12 (5, rg) **2004** Buf 16 (12, LG) **2005**†NE 1 (0) **NFL** 42 (24) [5 yrs]

Tucker, Ryan Ryan Huey, T, 6´6˝/325 lbs; TCU; 1997: SL, rnd 4; B6/12/1975 Midland, TX **1997** SL 7 (0) **1998** SL 5 (0) **2000**†SL 16 (16, RT) **2001**†SL 15 (15, RT) **2002**†Cle 14 (14, RT) **2003** Cle 16 (16, RT) **2004** Cle 7 (7, rt) **2005** Cle 16 (16, RT)

YEAR	TEAM	G (GS, POS)	RUSH	YD	AVG (LG)	TD	REC	YD	AVG (LG)	TD	PASS	COMP	PCT	YD	AVG (LG)	TD	INT	SK	YD	QBR	KPR	OTD	PTS	TAY
1999	†SL	16(0)	—	—	—	—	1	2	2.0(2)	1	—	—	—	—	—	—	—	—	—	—	—	—	6	6
NFL	9	112(84)	—	—	—	—	1	2	2.0(2)	1	—	—	—	—	—	—	—	—	—	—	—	—	6	6

Tucker, Torrin Torrin, T-G, 6´6˝/329 lbs; Southern Mississippi; B12/25/1979 Meridian, MS **2003**†Dal 7 (1) **2004** Dal 13 (13, RT) **2005** Dal 16 (10, LT) **NFL** 36 (24) [3 yrs]

Tucker, Travis Travis Tyrone, TE, 6´3˝/234 lbs; Southern Connecticut State; 1985: Cle, rnd 11; B9/19/1963 Brooklyn, NY

YEAR	TEAM	G (GS, POS)	RUSH	YD	AVG (LG)	TD	REC	YD	AVG (LG)	TD	PASS	COMP	PCT	YD	AVG (LG)	TD	INT	SK	YD	QBR	KPR	OTD	PTS	TAY
1985	†Cle	16(2)	—	—	—	—	2	20	10.0(10)	0	—	—	—	—	—	—	—	—	—	—	—	—	0	10
1986	†Cle	16(0)	—	—	—	—	2	29	14.5(16)	0	—	—	—	—	—	—	—	—	—	—	—	—	0	15
1987	Cle	4(0)	—	—	—	—	—	—	—	—	—	—	—	—	—	—	—	—	—	—	—	—	—	—
NFL	3	36(2)	—	—	—	—	4	49	12.3(16)	0	—	—	—	—	—	—	—	—	—	—	—	—	0	25

Tucker, Wendell Wendell Edward, WR-FL, 5´10˝/185 lbs; South Carolina State; B9/4/1943 Philadelphia, PA

YEAR	TEAM	G (GS, POS)	RUSH	YD	AVG (LG)	TD	REC	YD	AVG (LG)	TD	PASS	COMP	PCT	YD	AVG (LG)	TD	INT	SK	YD	QBR	KPR	OTD	PTS	TAY
1967	LARm	7	—	—	—	—	—	—	—	—	—	—	—	—	—	—	—	—	—	—	kp	—	0	87
1968	LARm	10	—	—	—	—	7	124	17.7(60)	4	—	—	—	—	—	—	—	—	—	—	—	—	24	82
1969	†LARm	14(14, FL)	—	—	—	—	38	629	16.6(**93**)	7	—	—	—	—	—	—	—	—	—	—	—	—	42	350
1970	LARm	12(12, WR)	—	—	—	—	12	230	19.2(51)	0	—	—	—	—	—	—	—	—	—	—	—	—	0	115
NFL	4	43(26)	—	—	—	—	57	983	17.2(93)	11	—	—	—	—	—	—	—	—	—	—	kp	—	66	634

Tuckett, Phil Phillip Evans, WR, 6´0˝/185 lbs; Weber State; B4/27/1946 Eugene, OR **1968** SD-A 1

Tuckey, Dick Richard James Kenneth, TB, 6´2˝/205 lbs; Manhattan; B9/29/1913 Naugetuck, CT, D12/25/1974 West Haven, CT **[K]**

YEAR	TEAM	G (GS, POS)	RUSH	YD	AVG (LG)	TD	REC	YD	AVG (LG)	TD	PASS	COMP	PCT	YD	AVG (LG)	TD	INT	SK	YD	QBR	KPR	OTD	PTS	TAY
1938	Was	3(0)	9	39	4.3	0	—	—	—	—	6	1	16.7	30	5.0(30)	0	1	—	—	—	K	—	0	14
1938	Cle	4(0)	14	37	2.6	0	1	10	10.0(10)	0	26	7	26.9	110	4.2	1	2	—	—	—	K	—	2	22
NFL	1	7(0)	23	76	3.3	0	1	10	10.0(10)	0	32	8	25.0	140	4.4(30)	1	3	—	—	—	K	—	2	36

Tufts, Sean Sean, LB, 6´4˝/245 lbs; Colorado; 2004: Car, rnd 6; B3/26/1982 Englewood, CO **2004** Car 3 (0) **2005**†Car 12 (0) **NFL** 15 (0) [2 yrs]

Tuggle, Anthony Anthony Ivan, DB, 6´1˝/211 lbs; Southern (LA); Nicholls State; 1985: Cin, rnd 4; B9/13/1963 Baton Rouge, LA **1985** Pit 2 (0) **1987** Pit 2 (0) **NFL** 4 (0) [2 yrs]

Tuggle, Jessie Jessie Floyd, LB, 5´11˝/230 lbs; Valdosta State; B4/4/1965 Spalding County, GA **1987** Atl 12 (4) **1988** Atl 16 (8, RILB) **1989** Atl 16 (16, RILB) **1990** Atl 16 (14, LILB) **1991**†Atl☆16 (16, RILB) **1992** Atl✧15 (15, RILB) **1993** Atl 16 (16, MLB) **1994** Atl★16 (16, MLB) **1995**†Atl✧16 (16, MLB) **1996** Atl 16 (16, MLB) **1997** Atl✧16 (15, MLB) **1998**†Atl★16 (16, MLB) **1999** Atl 14 (14, MLB) **2000** Atl 8 (7, MLB) **NFL** 209 (189) [14 yrs]

Tuggle, John John Davis, RB, 6´1˝/210 lbs; California; 1983: NYG, rnd 12; B1/13/1961 Honolulu, HI

YEAR	TEAM	G (GS, POS)	RUSH	YD	AVG (LG)	TD	REC	YD	AVG (LG)	TD	PASS	COMP	PCT	YD	AVG (LG)	TD	INT	SK	YD	QBR	KPR	OTD	PTS	TAY
1983	NYG	16(5, fb)	17	49	2.9(7)	1	3	50	16.7(27)	0	—	—	—	—	—	—	—	—	—	—	k	—	6	105

Tuiasosopo, Manu Manu'ula Asovalu, DT-NT-DE, 6´3˝/255 lbs; UCLA; 1979: Sea, rnd 1; B8/30/1957 Los Angeles, CA **1979** Sea 16 (16, RDT) **1980** Sea 16 (16, RDT) **1981** Sea 16 (16, RDE/rdt) **1982** Sea 9 (8, RDT) **1983**†Sea 16 (8, nt) **1984**†SF 16 (16, NT) **1985**†SF 15 (7, nt) **1986**†SF 15 (7, nt) **NFL** 119 (94) [8 yrs]

Tuiasosopo, Marques Marques, QB, 6´1˝/220 lbs; Washington; 2001: Oak, rnd 2; B3/22/1979 Seattle, WA

YEAR	TEAM	G (GS, POS)	RUSH	YD	AVG (LG)	TD	REC	YD	AVG (LG)	TD	PASS	COMP	PCT	YD	AVG (LG)	TD	INT	SK	YD	QBR	KPR	OTD	PTS	TAY
2001	Oak	1(0)	1	1	1.0(1)	0	—	—	—	—	4	3	75.0	34	8.5(15)	0	0	—	—	—	—	—	0	18
2002	†Oak	3(0)	2	-3	-1.5(-1)	0	—	—	—	—	—	—	—	—	—	—	—	—	—	—	—	—	0	-3
2003	Oak	4(1)	6	22	3.7(8)	0	—	—	—	—	45	25	55.6	324	7.2(35)	0	3	2	14	—	—	—	0	64
2005	Oak	1(1)	2	19	9.5(10)	0	—	—	—	—	26	14	53.8	124	4.8(20)	1	2	6	40	—	—	—	0	6
NFL	4	9(2)	11	39	3.5(10)	0	—	—	—	—	75	42	56.0	482	6.4(35)	1	5	8	54	—	—	—	0	85

Tuiasosopo, Navy Navy Asoaoga, C, 6´2˝/285 lbs; Utah State; B5/24/1965 American Samoa **1987** LARm 3 (3)

Tuinei, Mark Mark Pulemau, T-C-DT, 6´5˝/302 lbs; UCLA; Hawaii; B3/31/1960 Nanakuli, HI, D5/6/1999 Plano, TX **1983**†Dal 10 (0) **1984** Dal 16 (0) **1985**†Dal 16 (0) **1986** Dal 16 (11, LT) **1987** Dal 8 (8, LT) **1988** Dal 5 (4) **1989** Dal 16 (16, LT) **1990** Dal 13 (13, LT) **1991**†Dal 12 (12, LT) **1992**†Dal 15 (15, LT) **1993**†Dal 16 (16, LT) **1994**†Dal★15 (15, LT) **1995**†Dal★16 (16, LT) **1996**†Dal 15 (15, LT) **1997** Dal 6 (6, lt) **NFL** 195 (147) [15 yrs]

Tuinei, Tom Tumua, DT, 6´4˝/250 lbs; Hawaii; 1980: Det, rnd 9; B2/21/1958 Oceanside, CA **1980** Det 12 (2)

Tuinei, Van Vaega Van, DE, 6´3˝/266 lbs; Arizona; B2/16/1971 Garden Grove, CA **1997** SD 3 (0) **1998** Ind 12 (0) **1999** ChiB 16 (8, RDE) **2000** ChiB 14 (2) **NFL** 45 (10) [4 yrs]

Tuipala, Joe Joseph Lafaele, LB, 6´1˝/244 lbs; San Diego State; B9/13/1976 Honolulu, HI **2001** Jax 12 (0) **2002** Jax 15 (0) **NFL** 27 (0) [2 yrs]

Tuipulotu, Peter Peter Henry, RB, 5´11˝/210 lbs; Brigham Young; B2/20/1969 Nu'ukalofa, Tonga **1992** SD 6 (0)

Tuitele, Maugaula Maugaula Norman, LB, 6´2˝/255 lbs; Colorado State; B5/26/1978 Torrance, CA **2000** NE 1 (0) **2001** NE 1 (0) **2002** Buf 9 (0) **2002** NE 3 (0) **2004** Oak 1 (0) **NFL** 15 (0) [4 yrs]

Tullis, Walter Walter Henry, WR, 6´0˝/170 lbs; Delaware State; 1976: Was, rnd 12; B4/12/1953 Americus, GA **1978** GB 16

YEAR	TEAM	G (GS, POS)	RUSH	YD	AVG (LG)	TD	REC	YD	AVG (LG)	TD	PASS	COMP	PCT	YD	AVG (LG)	TD	INT	SK	YD	QBR	KPR	OTD	PTS	TAY
1979	GB	16	—	—	—	—	10	173	17.3(52)	1	—	—	—	—	—	—	—	—	—	—	—	—	6	92
NFL	2	32	—	—	—	—	10	173	17.3(52)	1	—	—	—	—	—	—	—	—	—	—	p	—	6	87

Tullis, Willie Willie James, DB, 6´0˝/193 lbs; Southern Mississippi; Troy State; 1981: Hou, rnd 8; B4/5/1958 Newville, AL **1981** Hou 16 (0) **1982** Hou 9 (3) **1983** Hou 16 (16, RCB) **1984** Hou 16 (15, RCB) **1985** NO 14 (1) **1986** NO 7 (1) **1987**†Ind 12 (12, LCB) **1988** Ind 16 (9, LCB) **NFL** 106 (57) [8 yrs]

Tully, Darrell Darrell Dean, TB-DB, 6´1˝/200 lbs; Texas A&M-Commerce; 1939: Det, rnd 7; B12/14/1917 Henryetta, OK, D2/4/1997 Harris County, TX

YEAR	TEAM	G (GS, POS)	RUSH	YD	AVG (LG)	TD	REC	YD	AVG (LG)	TD	PASS	COMP	PCT	YD	AVG (LG)	TD	INT	SK	YD	QBR	KPR	OTD	PTS	TAY
1939	Det	9(2)	31	50	1.6	1	—	—	—	—	75	20	26.7	356	4.7	2	13	—	—	—	—	—	6	-272

Tully, George George Chandler, E, 5´10˝/180 lbs; Dartmouth; B3/12/1904 Orange, NJ, D5/1/1980 Worcester, MA **1927** Fra 1 (0)

YEAR	TEAM	G (GS, POS)	RUSH	YD	AVG(LG)	TD	REC	YD	AVG(LG)	TD	PASS COMP	PCT	YD	AVG(LG)	TD	INT	SK	YD	QBR	KPR	OTD	PTS	TAY

TUMAN, JERAME Jerame Dean, TE, 6´4˝/255 lbs; Michigan; 1999: Pit, rnd 5; B3/24/1976 Liberal, KS

1999	Pit	7(0)	—	—	—	—	—	—	—	—	—	—	—	—	—	—	—	—	—	—	—			
2000	Pit	16(1)	—	—	—	—	—	—	—	—	—	—	—	—	—	—	—	—	—	—	k	—	0	-16
2001	†Pit	16(7, te)	—	—	—	—	7	96	13.7(32)	1	—	—	—	—	—	—	—	—	—	—	—	—	6	53
2002	†Pit	13(7, te)	—	—	—	—	4	63	15.8(27)	1	—	—	—	—	—	—	—	—	—	—	—	—	6	37
2003	Pit	16(12, TE)	—	—	—	—	12	113	9.4(23)	0	—	—	—	—	—	—	—	—	—	—	—	—	0	57
2004	†Pit	16(16, TE)	—	—	—	—	9	89	9.9(26)	3	—	—	—	—	—	—	—	—	—	—	—	—	18	60
2005	†Pit	15(9, te)	—	—	—	—	3	57	19.0(27)	0	—	—	—	—	—	—	—	—	—	—	—	—	0	29
NFL	7	99(52)	—	—	—	—	35	418	11.9(32)	5	—	—	—	—	—	—	—	—	—	—	k	—	30	218

TUMULTY, TOM Thomas Patrick, LB, 6´3˝/247 lbs; Pittsburgh; 1996: Cin, rnd 6; B2/11/1973 Penn Hills, PA   **1996** Cin 16 (3)   **1997** Cin 11 (11, LILB)   **1998** Cin 4 (4)   **NFL** 31 (18) [3 yrs]

TUNNELL, EMLEN Emlen Lewis, DB, 6´1˝/187 lbs; Toledo; Iowa; B3/29/1922 Bryn Mawr, PA; D7/23/1975 Pleasantville, NY; HOF 1967 [RI]   **1950**†NYG★12 (DB)
1951 NYG★12 (DB)   **1952** NYG★12 (DB)   **1953** NYG◇12 (DB)   **1954** NYG★12 (DB)   **1955** NYG★12 (DB)   **1956**†NYG★12 (DB)   **1957** NYG★12 (DB)   **1958**†NYG 12 (DB)
1959 GB◇12 (DB)   **1960**†GB 13 (LS)   **1961**†GB 12

1948	NYG	10(3)	17	43	2.5(15)	0	4	32	8.0(14)	0	2	1	50.0	23	11.5(23)	0	0	—	—	—	kpi	1	6	223
1949	NYG☆	12(3)	—	—	—	—	1	7	7.0(7)	0	—	—	—	—	—	—	—	—	—	—	kpi	3	18	416
NFL	14	167(6)	17	43	2.5(15)	0	5	39	7.8(14)	0	2	1	50.0	23	11.5(23)	0	0	—	—	—	kpi	10	60	2505

TUPA, TOM Thomas Joseph, QB-P, 6´4˝/225 lbs; Ohio State; 1988: Phx, rnd 3; B2/6/1966 Cleveland, OH [P]

1988	Phx	2(0)	—	—	—	—	—	—	—	—	6	4	66.7	49	8.2(22)	0	0	1	11	—	—	—	0	25
1989	Phx	14(3)	15	75	5.0(13)	0	—	—	—	—	134	65	48.5	973	7.3(77)	3	9	14	94	52.2	P	—	0	217
1990	Phx	15(0)	1	0	0.0(0)	0	—	—	—	—	—	—	—	—	—	—	—	—	—	—	—	—	0	0
1991	Phx	11(11, QB)	28	97	3.5(17)	1	—	—	—	—	315	165	52.4	2053	6.5(62)	6	13	24	197	62.0	—	—	6	644
1992	Ind	3(0)	3	9	3.0(0)	0	—	—	—	—	33	17	51.5	156	4.7(19)	1	2	5	40	—	—	—	0	12
1994	†Cle	16(0)	—	—	—	—	—	—	—	—	—	—	—	—	—	—	—	—	—	—	P	—	6	0
1995	Cle	16(0)	1	9	9.0(9)	0	—	—	—	—	1	1	100.0	25	25.0(25)	0	0	—	—	—	P	—	0	22
1996	†NE	16(0)	—	—	—	—	—	—	—	—	2	0	0.0	0	0.0	0	0	—	—	—	P	—	0	0
1997	†NE	16(0)	—	—	—	—	—	—	—	—	—	—	—	—	—	—	—	—	—	—	P	—	0	0
1998	†NE	16(0)	2	-2	-1.0(-1)	0	—	—	—	—	—	—	—	—	—	—	—	—	—	—	P	—	0	-2
1999	NYJ★	16(0)	2	8	4.0(4)	0	—	—	—	—	11	6	54.5	165	15.0(65)	2	0	3	30	—	P	—	0	101
2000	NYJ	16(0)	—	—	—	—	—	—	—	—	—	—	—	—	—	—	—	—	—	—	P	—	0	0
2001	†NYJ	15(0)	—	—	—	—	—	—	—	—	1	1	100.0	9	9.0(9)	0	0	—	—	—	P	—	0	5
2002	†TB	16(0)	1	-9	-9.0(-9)	0	—	—	—	—	1	0	0.0	0	0.0	0	1	—	—	—	P	—	0	-49
2003	TB	16(0)	—	—	—	—	—	—	—	—	—	—	—	—	—	—	—	—	—	—	P	—	0	0
2004	Was	16(0)	—	—	—	—	—	—	—	—	—	—	—	—	—	—	—	—	—	—	P	—	0	0
NFL	16	220(14)	53	187	3.5(17)	1	—	—	—	—	504	259	51.4	3430	6.8(77)	12	25	47	372	60.5	P	—	12	972

TUPPER, JEFF Jeffrey Culver, DE, 6´5˝/269 lbs; Oklahoma; 1986: SL, rnd 5; B12/26/1962 Joplin, MO   **1986** Phi 3 (0)   **1987** Den 4 (3)   **NFL** 7 (3) [2 yrs]

TURBERT, FRANK Francis J., HB, 5´11˝/200 lbs; Duke; Charleston; B9/7/1918 New Haven, CT, D8/1/1987 Pembroke Pines, FL

| 1944 | Bos | 5(1) | 14 | -16 | -1.1(9) | 0 | 1 | 16 | 16.0(16) | 0 | 15 | 5 | 33.3 | 37 | 2.5(21) | 0 | 0 | — | — | — | p | — | 0 | 13 |

TURK, DAN Daniel Anthony, C-G, 6´4˝/290 lbs; Drake; Wisconsin; 1985: Pit, rnd 4; B6/25/1962 Milwaukee, WI, D12/23/2000 Ashburn, VA   **1985** Pit 1 (0)   **1986** Pit 16 (4)
1987 TB 13 (3)   **1988** TB 12 (10, RG)   **1989** LARd 16 (4)   **1990**†LARd 16 (0)   **1991**†LARd 16 (0)   **1992** LARd 16 (0)   **1993**†LARd 16 (0)   **1994** LARd 16 (0)   **1995** Oak 16 (16, C)
1996 Oak 16 (2)   **1997** Was 16 (0)   **1998** Was 16 (0)   **1999**†Was 16 (0)   **NFL** 218 (39) [15 yrs]

TURK, GODWIN Godwin Lee, LB, 6´3˝/230 lbs; California; Southern (LA); 1974: NYJ, rnd 3; B10/15/1950 Houston, TX   **1975** NYJ 14 (14, LLB)   **1976** Den 13 (2)   **1977**†Den 13 (3)
1978†Den 16 (1)   **NFL** 56 (20) [4 yrs]

TURK, MATT Matt Edward, P, 6´5˝/250 lbs; Wisconsin-Whitewater; B6/16/1968 Greenfield, WI [P]

1995	Was	16(0)	—	—	—	—	—	—	—	—	—	—	—	—	—	—	—	—	—	—	P	—	0	0
1996	Was★	16(0)	1	0	0.0(0)	0	—	—	—	—	—	—	—	—	—	—	—	—	—	—	P	—	0	0
1997	Was★	16(0)	1	0	0.0(0)	0	—	—	—	—	—	—	—	—	—	—	—	—	—	—	P	—	0	0
1998	Was★	16(0)	2	-12	-6.0(0)	0	—	—	—	—	—	—	—	—	—	—	—	—	—	—	P	—	0	-12
1999	†Was	14(0)	—	—	—	—	—	—	—	—	—	—	—	—	—	—	—	—	—	—	P	—	0	0
2000	†Mia	16(0)	—	—	—	—	—	—	—	—	—	—	—	—	—	—	—	—	—	—	P	—	0	0
2001	†Mia	16(0)	—	—	—	—	—	—	—	—	—	—	—	—	—	—	—	—	—	—	P	—	0	0
2002	†NYJ	16(0)	1	14	14.0(14)	0	—	—	—	—	1	0	0.0	0	0.0	0	1	—	—	—	P	—	0	-26
2003	Mia	13(0)	3	30	10.0(0)	0	—	—	—	—	—	—	—	—	—	—	—	—	—	—	P	—	0	30
2004	Mia	16(0)	1	3	3.0(3)	0	—	—	—	—	—	—	—	—	—	—	—	—	—	—	P	—	0	3
NFL	10	155(0)	9	35	3.9(23)	0	—	—	—	—	1	0	0.0	0	0.0	0	1	—	—	—	P	—	0	-5

TURLEY, DOUG Douglas Pershing, E-DE, 6´2˝/215 lbs; Scranton; B11/25/1918 Nanticoke, PA, D11/1/1992 Oak Hill, DE

1944	Was	7(0)	—	—	—	—	8	112	14.0(35)	1	—	—	—	—	—	—	—	—	—	—	k	—	6	58
1945	†Was	10(8, RE)	—	—	—	—	17	185	10.9(29)	1	—	—	—	—	—	—	—	—	—	—	—	—	6	98
1946	Was	9(4)	—	—	—	—	6	105	17.5(25)	0	—	—	—	—	—	—	—	—	—	—	—	—	0	53
1947	Was	12(3)	—	—	—	—	6	95	15.8(24)	1	—	—	—	—	—	—	—	—	—	—	k	—	6	48
1948	Was	12(4)	—	—	—	—	8	111	13.9(33)	0	—	—	—	—	—	—	—	—	—	—	—	1	6	56
NFL	5	50(19)	—	—	—	—	45	608	13.5(35)	3	—	—	—	—	—	—	—	—	—	—	k	1	24	311

TURLEY, JOHN John O., BB, 5´10˝/183 lbs; Ohio Wesleyan; B11/20/1912 Delaware, OH, D7/21/1977 Dayton, OH   **1936** Pit 4 (4)

| 1935 | Pit | 10(9, BB) | 4 | -3 | -0.8 | 0 | — | — | — | — | 27 | 12 | 44.4 | 144 | 5.3 | 1 | 6 | — | — | — | — | — | 0 | -166 |
| NFL | 2 | 14(13) | 4 | -3 | -0.8 | 0 | — | — | — | — | 27 | 12 | 44.4 | 144 | 5.3 | 1 | 6 | — | — | — | — | — | 0 | -166 |

TURLEY, KYLE Kyle John, T-G, 6´5˝/309 lbs; San Diego State; 1998: NO, rnd 1; B9/24/1975 Moreno Valley, CA   **1998** NO 15 (15, LG)   **1999** NO 16 (16, RT)   **2001** NO 16 (16, RT)
2002 NO 16 (16, LT)   **2003**†SL 16 (16, RT)

| 2000 | †NO☆ | 16(16, RT) | — | — | — | — | 1 | 16 | 16.0(16) | 0 | — | — | — | — | — | — | — | — | — | — | — | — | 0 | 8 |
| NFL | 6 | 95(95) | — | — | — | — | 1 | 16 | 16.0(16) | 0 | — | — | — | — | — | — | — | — | — | — | — | — | 0 | 8 |

TURNBOW, GUY Guy Nicholson, T-E-DB, 6´2˝/217 lbs; Mississippi; B3/28/1908 Brookhaven, MS, D10/4/1975 Oxford, MS [K]   **1933** Phi 9 (7, RT)   **1934** Phi 2 (0)   **NFL** 11 (7) [2 yrs]

TURNBOW, JESSE Jesse James, DT, 6´7˝/272 lbs; Tennessee; 1978: Cle, rnd 8; B10/8/1956 Cincinnati, OH   **1978** Cle 16

TURNBULL, RENALDO Renaldo Antonio, DE-LB, 6´4˝/250 lbs; West Virginia; 1990: NO, rnd 1; B1/5/1966 St. Thomas, Virgin Islands   **1990**†NO★16 (6, rde)   **1991** NO 16 (0)
1992†NO 14 (0)   **1993** NO★15 (14, ROLB)   **1994** NO 16 (16, ROLB)   **1995** NO 15 (15, RDE)   **1996** NO 12 (7, rde)   **1997** Car 16 (2)   **NFL** 120 (60) [8 yrs]

TURNER, BAKE Robert Hardy, WR-SE, 6´1˝/179 lbs; Texas Tech; 1962: Bal, rnd 12; B7/22/1940 Alpine, TX [R]

1962	Bal	14	1	17	17.0(17)	0	1	11	11.0(74)	0	—	—	—	—	—	—	—	—	—	—	kp	—	6	327
1963	NYJ-A◇	14(WR)	—	—	—	—	71	1009	14.2(53)	6	—	—	—	—	—	—	—	—	—	—	k	—	36	624
1964	NYJ-A	14(SE)	—	—	—	—	58	974	16.8(71)	9	—	—	—	—	—	—	—	—	—	—	—	—	54	532
1965	NYJ-A	13(4)	—	—	—	—	31	402	13.0(62)	0	—	—	—	—	—	—	—	—	—	—	—	—	12	339
1966	NYJ-A	14	—	—	—	—	7	115	16.4(42)	0	—	—	—	—	—	—	—	—	—	—	kp	—	0	88
1967	NYJ-A	8	—	—	—	—	3	40	13.3(20)	2	—	—	—	—	—	—	—	—	—	—	k	—	0	0
1968	†NYJ-A	13	—	—	—	—	10	241	24.1(71)	3	—	—	—	—	—	—	—	—	—	—	k	—	12	240
1969	†NYJ-A	14	1	-4	-4.0(-4)	0	11	221	20.1(54)	3	—	—	—	—	—	—	—	—	—	—	Pk	—	18	151
1970	Bos	13(13, WR)	—	—	—	—	28	428	15.3(43)	2	—	—	—	—	—	—	—	—	—	—	—	—	12	224
NFL	9	118(17)	2	13	6.5(17)	0	220	3541	16.1(74)	25	—	—	—	—	—	—	—	—	—	—	Pkp	—	150	2523

TURNER, BILL William James, G, 6´4˝/245 lbs; Boston College; B3/5/1960   **1987** NE 2 (0)

TURNER, BUFF Milton, T-G, /188 lbs; none; B1/1891, MD, deceased   **1921** Was 3 (0)

YEAR	TEAM	G(GS, POS)	RUSH	YD	AVG(LG)	TD	REC	YD	AVG(LG)	TD	PASS	COMP	PCT	YD	AVG(LG)	TD	INT	SK	YD	QBR	KPR	OTD	PTS	TAY

TURNER, Bulldog   Clyde Douglas, C-T-LB-G, 6´1˝/237 lbs; Hardin-Simmons; 1940: ChiB, rnd 1; B3/10/1919 Plains, TX, D10/30/1998 Gatesville, TX; HOF 1966 [C]
1940†ChiB★11 (10, C) **1941**†ChiB★11 (10, C) **1942**†ChiB☆11 (11, C) **1943**†ChiB☆10 (10, C) **1945** ChiB 2 (2) **1946**†ChiB☆11 (8, C) **1947** ChiB☆11 (9, C) **1948** ChiB☆12 (11, C)
1949 ChiB 12 (12, C) **1950**†ChiB◇12 (C) **1951** ChiB◇12 (C)

YEAR	TEAM	G(GS, POS)	RUSH	YD	AVG(LG)	TD	REC	YD	AVG(LG)	TD	KPR	OTD	PTS	TAY
1944	ChiB☆	10(9, C)	1	48	48.0(48)	1	—	—	—	—	pi	—	6	96
1952	ChiB	12(RT)	—	—	—	—	1	2	2.0(2)	0	k	—	0	15
NFL 13		138(91)	1	48	48.0(48)	1	1	2	2.0(2)	0	kpi	3	24	277

TURNER, Calvin   Calvin Eugene, DE, 6´4˝/270 lbs; West Virginia; B4/10/1960 Fairmont, WV   **1987** TB 3 (0)

TURNER, Cecil   Cecil Angelo, FL-WR, 5´10˝/176 lbs; Cal Poly-San Luis Obispo; 1968: Chi, rnd 5; B4/2/1944 Washington, DC [R]

YEAR	TEAM	G(GS, POS)	RUSH	YD	AVG(LG)	TD	REC	YD	AVG(LG)	TD	KPR	OTD	PTS	TAY
1968	ChiB	14(FL)	2	16	8.0(14)	0	14	208	14.9(80)	2	kp	—	12	167
1969	ChiB	9	—	—	—	—	1	19	19.0(19)	0	kp	—	0	178
1970	ChiB◇	14	3	-3	-1.0(1)	0	2	53	26.5(34)	0	kp	4	24	466
1971	ChiB	14	—	—	—	—	1	13	13.0(13)	0	kp	—	0	199
1972	ChiB	14	3	0	0.0(11)	0	3	71	23.7(36)	0	k	—	0	205
1973	ChiB	11	—	—	—	—	—	—	—	—	k	—	0	7
NFL 6		76	8	13	1.6(14)	0	21	364	17.3(80)	2	kp	4	36	1220

TURNER, Clem   Clement, RB, 6´1˝/236 lbs; Cincinnati; 1969: Cin, rnd 4; B5/28/1945 Cincinnati, OH

YEAR	TEAM	G(GS, POS)	RUSH	YD	AVG(LG)	TD	REC	YD	AVG(LG)	TD	KPR	OTD	PTS	TAY
1969	Cin-A	14	23	105	4.6(34)	0	5	14	2.8(8)	0	k	—	0	82
1970	Den	11	29	106	3.7(14)	2	8	23	2.9(11)	0	k	—	12	154
1971	Den	14	17	43	2.5(9)	0	7	65	9.3(17)	1	k	—	6	106
1972	Den	12	5	16	3.2(13)	0	1	10	10.0(10)	0	k	—	0	31
NFL 4		51	74	270	3.6(34)	2	21	112	5.3(17)	1	k	—	18	372

TURNER, Daryl   Daryl, WR, 6´3˝/194 lbs; Michigan State; 1984: Sea, rnd 2; B12/15/1961 Wadley, GA

YEAR	TEAM	G(GS, POS)	REC	YD	AVG(LG)	TD	KPR	OTD	PTS	TAY
1984	†Sea	16(8, WR)	35	715	20.4(80)	10	—		60	408
1985	Sea	16(12, WR)	34	670	19.7(54)	13	—		78	400
1986	Sea	15(12, WR)	18	334	18.6(72)	7	—		42	202
1987	†Sea	12(8, WR)	14	153	10.9(20)	6	—		36	107
NFL 4		59(40)	101	1872	18.5(80)	36	—		216	1116

TURNER, Deacon   David L., RB, 5´11˝/212 lbs; San Diego State; 1978: Cin, rnd 2; B1/2/1955 Jackson, MS

YEAR	TEAM	G(GS, POS)	RUSH	YD	AVG(LG)	TD	REC	YD	AVG(LG)	TD	KPR	OTD	PTS	TAY
1978	Cin	16(5, rb)	84	333	4.0(65)	0	11	50	4.5(8)	0	k	—	0	367
1979	Cin	16(1)	28	86	3.1(10)	1	2	18	9.0(10)	0	k	—	6	429
1980	Cin	12(1)	30	130	4.3(24)	0	12	73	6.1(15)	1	k	—	6	210
NFL 3		44(7)	142	549	3.9(65)	1	25	141	5.6(15)	1	k	—	12	1006

TURNER, Dwaine   Dwain Fitzgerald, NT, 6´0˝/290 lbs; Rice; B10/7/1964 Houston, TX   **1987** Hou 1 (0)

TURNER, Eric   Eric Ray, DB, 6´1˝/208 lbs; UCLA; 1991: Cle, rnd 1; B9/20/1968 Ventura, CA, D5/28/2000 Thousand Oaks, CA [I]   **1991** Cle 8 (7, ss) **1992** Cle 15 (13, SS)
1993 Cle 16 (16, FS) **1994**†Cle★16 (16, FS) **1995** Cle 8 (8, FS) **1996** Bal◇14 (14, FS) **1997** Oak 16 (15, FS) **1998** Oak 6 (6, ss) **1999** Oak 10 (10, FS) **NFL** 109 (105) [9 yrs]

TURNER, Floyd   Floyd, WR, 5´11˝/192 lbs; Northwestern State (LA); 1989: NO, rnd 6; B5/29/1966 Shreveport, LA

YEAR	TEAM	G(GS, POS)	RUSH	YD	AVG(LG)	TD	REC	YD	AVG(LG)	TD	KPR	OTD	PTS	TAY
1989	NO	13(1)	2	8	4.0(6)	0	22	279	12.7(54)	1	p	—	6	155
1990	†NO	16(0)	—	—	—	—	21	396	18.9(68)	4		—	24	218
1991	†NO	16(4)	—	—	—	—	64	927	14.5(65)	8		—	48	504
1992	NO	2(2)	—	—	—	—	5	43	8.6(18)	0	p	—	0	17
1993	NO	10(2)	—	—	—	—	12	163	13.6(52)	1		—	6	87
1994	Ind	16(16, WR)	3	-3	-1.0(5)	0	52	593	11.4(28)	6		—	36	324
1995	†Ind	14(12, WR)	—	—	—	—	35	431	12.3(47)	4		—	28	236
1996	Bal	11(6, WR)	2	12	6.0(6)	0	38	461	12.1(27)	2		—	12	253
1998	Bal	16(3)	—	—	—	—	32	512	16.0(66)	5		—	34	281
NFL 9		114(46)	7	17	2.4(6)	0	281	3805	13.5(68)	31	p	—	194	2072

TURNER, Hal   Harold, DE, 6´2˝/235 lbs; Tennessee State; 1952: Det, rnd 28; B12/5/1929, D6/1981 Doddsville, MS   **1954**†Det 3

TURNER, Herschel   Herschel, T-G, 6´3˝/230 lbs; Kentucky; 1964: SL, rnd 2/Oak, rnd 9; B6/17/1942 Houston, TX   **1964** SL 14 (5, lt) **1965** SL 13 **NFL** 27 (5) [2 yrs]

TURNER, J.T.   James Denis, G, 6´3˝/253 lbs; Duke; B4/17/1953 Moultrie, GA   **1977** NYG 13 **1978** NYG 16 (16, RG) **1979** NYG 16 (16, RG) **1980** NYG 16 (15, RG)
1981†NYG 16 (16, RG) **1982** NYG 9 (8, RG) **1983** NYG 16 (16, RG) **1984** Was 1 (0) **NFL** 103 (87) [8 yrs]

TURNER, Jay   Jay Lewis, BB-LB, 5´10˝/202 lbs; George Washington; B7/11/1914 Springfield, MO, D11/1960

YEAR	TEAM	G(GS, POS)	RUSH	YD	AVG(LG)	TD	REC	YD	AVG(LG)	TD	KPR	OTD	PTS	TAY
1938	Was	8(4)	5	25	5.0	0	2	10	5.0	0	—		0	30
1939	Was	8(1)	2	1	0.5	0	2	15	7.5	0	P	—	0	9
NFL 2		16(5)	7	26	3.7	0	4	25	6.3	0	P	—	0	39

TURNER, Jim   James Alfonso, WB, 5´8˝/165 lbs; Northwestern; B4/18/1899 Abbeville, SC, D3/28/1932 Chicago, IL   **1923** Mil 3 (2), 6

TURNER, Jim   James Kay, C, 6´2˝/210 lbs; Oklahoma State; B1/14/1912 Roff, OK   **1937** Cle 7 (2)

TURNER, Jim   James Bayard, K, 6´2˝/205 lbs; Utah State; 1963: Was, rnd 19; B3/28/1941 Martinez, CA [K]   **1965** NYJ-A 14 **1966** NYJ-A 14 **1968**†NYJ-A★14 **1969**†NYJ-A★14
1971 Den 14 **1972** Den 14 **1974** Den 14 **1975** Den 14 **1976** Den☆14

YEAR	TEAM	G(GS, POS)	RUSH	YD	AVG(LG)	TD	REC	YD	AVG(LG)	TD	PASS	COMP	PCT	YD	AVG(LG)	TD	INT	KPR	OTD	PTS	TAY
1964	NYJ-A	14	1	3	3.0(3)	0	—	—	—	—	—	—	—	—	—	—	—	K	—	72	3
1967	NYJ-A	14	—	—	—	—	—	—	—	—	4	2	50.0	25	6.3(13)	0	0	K	—	87	13
1970	NYJ	14	1	1	1.0(1)	0	—	—	—	—	—	—	—	—	—	—	—	K	—	85	1
1973	Den	14	—	—	—	—	—	—	—	—	1	0	0.0	0	0.0(0)	0	—	K	—	106	-40
1977	†Den	14	—	—	—	—	1	25	25.0(25)	1	—	—	—	—	—	—	—	K	—	76	18
1978	†Den	16	—	—	—	—	1	-4	-4.0(-4)	0	—	—	—	—	—	—	—	K	—	64	-2
1979	†Den	16	—	—	—	—	1	6	6.0(6)	0	—	—	—	—	—	—	—	K	—	71	3
NFL 16		228	2	4	2.0(3)	0	3	27	9.0(25)	1	5	2	40.0	25	5.0(13)	0	1	K	—	1439	-5

TURNER, Jimmie   James, LB, 6´2˝/220 lbs; Presbyterian; B2/16/1962 Vienna, GA   **1984** Dal 5 (0)

TURNER, Jimmy   James Lee, DB, 6´0˝/187 lbs; UCLA; 1983: Cin, rnd 3; B6/15/1959 Sherman, TX   **1983** Cin 16 (0) **1984** Cin 16 (8, ss) **1985** Cin 16 (0) **1986** Cin 8 (0)
1986 Atl 6 (0) **1987** Atl 2 (0) **NFL** 64 (8) [5 yrs]

TURNER, John   John, DB, 6´0˝/197 lbs; Miami (FL); 1978: Min, rnd 2; B2/22/1956 Miami, FL [I]   **1978**†Min 14 **1979** Min 16 (16, LCB) **1980**†Min 16 (16, LCB)
1981 Min 13 (10, LCB) **1982**†Min 9 (9, FS) **1983** Min 16 (15, FS) **1984** Min 15 (6, rcb) **1985** Min 2 (0) **NFL** 116 (76) [9 yrs]

TURNER, Keena   Keena, LB, 6´2˝/222 lbs; Purdue; 1980: SF, rnd 2; B10/22/1958 Chicago, IL   **1980** SF 16 (4) **1981**†SF 16 (14, ROLB) **1982** SF☆9 (9, ROLB)
1983†SF 15 (14, ROLB) **1984**†SF 16 (16, ROLB) **1985**†SF☆15 (15, ROLB) **1986**†SF 16 (16, ROLB) **1987** SF 10 (10, ROLB) **1988**†SF 11 (8, ROLB) **1989**†SF 13 (12, ROLB)
1990†SF 16 (0) **NFL** 153 (118) [11 yrs]

TURNER, Kevin   Kevin Ray, LB, 6´2˝/223 lbs; Pacific; B2/5/1958 Fremont, CA   **1980** NYG 3 (1) **1981** Was 4 (0) **1981** Sea 8 (0) **1982**†Cle 8 (0) **NFL** 23 (1) [3 yrs]

TURNER, Kevin   Paul Kevin, FB, 6´1˝/231 lbs; Alabama; 1992: NE, rnd 3; B6/12/1969 Prattville, AL

YEAR	TEAM	G(GS, POS)	RUSH	YD	AVG(LG)	TD	REC	YD	AVG(LG)	TD	PASS	COMP	PCT	YD	AVG(LG)	TD	INT	KPR	OTD	PTS	TAY
1992	NE	16(1)	10	40	4.0(11)	0	7	52	7.4(19)	2	—	—	—	—	—	—	—	k	—	12	72
1993	NE	16(9, FB)	50	231	4.6(49)	0	39	333	8.5(26)	2	1	0	0.0	0	0.0	0	0		—	12	408
1994	†NE	16(9, FB)	36	111	3.1(13)	1	52	471	9.1(32)	2	—	—	—	—	—	—	—		—	18	367
1995	Phi	2(2)	2	9	4.5(12)	0	4	29	7.3(11)	0	—	—	—	—	—	—	—		—	6	24
1996	†Phi	16(13, FB)	18	39	2.2(7)	0	43	409	9.5(41)	1	—	—	—	—	—	—	—		—	6	249
1997	Phi	16(10, FB)	18	96	5.3(29)	0	48	443	9.2(36)	3	—	—	—	—	—	—	—	k	—	18	336
1998	Phi	16(15, FB)	20	94	4.7(19)	0	34	232	6.8(18)	0	—	—	—	—	—	—	—	k	—	0	210
1999	Phi	8(7, FB)	6	15	2.5(5)	0	9	46	5.1(14)	0	—	—	—	—	—	—	—	k	—	0	38
NFL 8		106(66)	160	635	4.0(49)	1	236	2015	8.5(41)	10	1	0	0.0	0	0.0	0	0		—	66	1702

TURNER, Larry   Lawrence Edward, C, 6´2˝/280 lbs; Eastern Kentucky; 2004: SL, rnd 7; B3/8/1982 Huber Heights, OH   **2004**†SL 14 (1) **2005** SL 6 (0) **NFL** 20 (1) [2 yrs]

YEAR	TEAM	G (GS, POS)	RUSH	YD	AVG(LG)	TD	REC	YD	AVG(LG)	TD	PASS	COMP	PCT	YD	AVG(LG)	TD	INT	SK	YD	QBR	KPR	OTD	PTS	TAY

TURNER, MARCUS   Marcus Jared, DB, 6´0˝/190 lbs; UCLA; 1989: KC, rnd 11; B1/13/1966 Harbor City, CA   **1989** Phx 13 (0)   **1990** Phx 16 (1)   **1991** Phx 3 (0)   **1992** NYJ 16 (0)   **1993** NYJ 16 (0)   **1994** NYJ 16 (1)   **1995** NYJ 6 (1)   **NFL** 86 (3) [7 yrs]

TURNER, MAURICE   Maurice Antoine, RB, 5´11˝/200 lbs; Utah State; 1983: Min, rnd 12; B9/10/1960 Salt Lake City, UT   **1984** Min 13 (0)   **1985** Min 10 (0)   **1985** GB 3 (0)   **1987** NYJ 1 (0)   **NFL** 27 (0) [3 yrs]

TURNER, MICHAEL   Michael, RB, 5´10˝/223 lbs; Northern Illinois; 2004: SD, rnd 5; B2/13/1982 North Chicago, IL

2004	SD	14 (1)	20	104	5.2(30)	0	4	8	2.0(7)	0	—	—	—	—	—	—	—	—	—	k	—	0	111
2005	SD	16 (0)	57	335	5.9(83)	3	—	—	—	—	—	—	—	—	—	—	—	—	—	k	—	18	350
NFL	2	30 (1)	77	439	5.7(83)	3	4	8	2.0(7)	0	—	—	—	—	—	—	—	—	—	k	—	18	461

TURNER, MIKE   Jerry Michael, G, 6´3˝/255 lbs; LSU; B9/10/1960 Oceanside, CA   **1987** Min 1 (0)

TURNER, NATE   Nathaniel Adam, TE, 6´1˝/255 lbs; Nebraska; 1992: Buf, rnd 6; B5/28/1969 Chicago, IL

1993	†Buf	13 (0)	11	36	3.3(10)	0	—	—	—	—	—	—	—	—	—	—	—	—	—	k	—	0	31
1994	Buf	13 (0)	2	4	2.0(4)	0	1	26	26.0(26)	1	—	—	—	—	—	—	—	—	—	k	—	6	34
1995	Car	2 (0)	—	—	—	—	—	—	—	—	—	—	—	—	—	—	—	—	—	—	—	—	—
NFL	3	28 (0)	13	40	3.1(10)	0	1	26	26.0(26)	1	—	—	—	—	—	—	—	—	—	k	—	6	65

TURNER, NATE   Nathaniel J., WR, 6´3˝/210 lbs; UNLV; B5/26/1978 Compton, CA   **2001** SD 1 (0)

TURNER, ODESSA   Odessa, WR, 6´3˝/205 lbs; Northwestern State (LA); 1987: NYG, rnd 4; B10/12/1964 Monroe, LA

1987	NYG	7 (2)	—	—	—	—	10	195	19.5(36)	1	—	—	—	—	—	—	—	—	—	—	—	6	103
1988	NYG	4 (1)	—	—	—	—	10	128	12.8(28)	1	—	—	—	—	—	—	—	—	—	—	—	6	69
1989	†NYG	13 (10, WR)	2	11	5.5(14)	0	38	467	12.3(44)	4	—	—	—	—	—	—	—	—	—	—	—	24	265
1990	NYG	4 (3)	—	—	—	—	6	69	11.5(18)	0	—	—	—	—	—	—	—	—	—	—	—	0	35
1991	NYG	16 (3)	—	—	—	—	21	356	17.0(55)	0	—	—	—	—	—	—	—	—	—	—	—	0	178
1992	†SF	16 (0)	—	—	—	—	9	200	22.2(57)	2	—	—	—	—	—	—	—	—	—	k	—	12	95
1993	†SF	7 (0)	—	—	—	—	3	64	21.3(32)	0	—	—	—	—	—	—	—	—	—	—	—	0	32
NFL	7	67 (19)	2	11	5.5(14)	0	97	1479	15.2(57)	8	—	—	—	—	—	—	—	—	—	—	—	48	776

TURNER, RICHARD   Richard Junior, NT, 6´2˝/260 lbs; Oklahoma; 1981: GB, rnd 4; B2/14/1959 Hugo, OK   **1981** GB 15 (0)   **1982** †GB 9 (0)   **1983** GB 6 (5, nt)   **NFL** 30 (5) [3 yrs]

TURNER, RICKY   Ricky, QB, 6´0˝/190 lbs; Washington State; B5/14/1962 Los Angeles, CA

| 1988 | Ind | 4 (0) | 16 | 42 | 2.6(14) | 2 | — | — | — | — | 4 | 3 | 75.0 | 92 | 23.0(37) | 0 | 0 | 2 | 15 | — | — | — | 12 | 108 |

TURNER, ROBERT   Robert Dean, RB, 5´11˝/200 lbs; Oklahoma State; 1977: Mia, rnd 9; B3/6/1954 Wynnewood, OK   **1978** Hou 4

TURNER, ROCKY   Harley, DB-WR, 6´0˝/190 lbs; Tennessee-Chattanooga; 1972: NYJ, rnd 10; B8/6/1950 Augusta, GA   **1972** NYJ 8   **1973** NYJ 14   **NFL** 22 [2 yrs]

TURNER, SAM   Samuel Washington, G, /195 lbs; none; B4/16/1902 Richardson, TX, D8/5/1976 Windsor, VA   **1921** Was 2 (0)

TURNER, SCOTT   Eric Scott, DB, 5´10˝/190 lbs; Illinois; 1995: Was, rnd 7; B2/26/1972 Richardson, TX   **1995** Was 16 (0)   **1996** Was 16 (0)   **1997** Was 9 (0)   **1998** SD 16 (1)   **1999** SD 15 (0)   **2000** SD 16 (2)   **2001** SD 4 (1)   **2003** †Den 9 (0)   **NFL** 101 (4) [8 yrs]

TURNER, T.J.   Thomas James, DE-NT, 6´4˝/276 lbs; Houston; 1986: Mia, rnd 3; B5/16/1963 Lufkin, TX   **1986** Mia 16 (15, LDE)   **1987** Mia 12 (12, LDE)   **1988** Mia 16 (16, LDE)   **1989** Mia 14 (11, LDE)   **1990** †Mia 14 (12, LDE)   **1991** Mia 13 (12, LDE/nt)   **1992** †Mia 16 (5, lde)   **NFL** 101 (83) [7 yrs]

TURNER, T.J.   Thomas S., LB, 6´3˝/255 lbs; Michigan State; 2001: NE, rnd 7; B10/1/1978 Dayton, OH   **2001** NE 2 (0)

TURNER, TINY   Irwin L., G, 6´0˝/195 lbs; Ohio State; B1895, deceased   **1920** Day 1 (1)

TURNER, VERNON   Vernon Maurice, WR-RB, 5´8˝/185 lbs; Carson-Newman; B1/6/1967 Brooklyn, NY [R]

1990	Buf	1 (0)	—	—	—	—	—	—	—	—	—	—	—	—	—	—	—	—	—	—	—	—	—
1991	LARm	15 (0)	7	44	6.3(11)	0	3	41	13.7(19)	1	—	—	—	—	—	—	—	—	—	kp	—	6	253
1992	LARm	12 (0)	2	14	7.0(9)	0	5	42	8.4(16)	0	—	—	—	—	—	—	—	—	—	kp	—	0	236
1993	Det	7 (0)	—	—	—	—	1	7	7.0(7)	0	—	—	—	—	—	—	—	—	—	kp	—	0	176
1993	TB	1 (0)	—	—	—	—	—	—	—	—	—	—	—	—	—	—	—	—	—	k	—	0	-29
1994	TB	12 (1)	4	13	3.3(9)	0	—	—	—	—	—	—	—	—	—	—	—	—	—	kp	1	6	377
1995	Det	6 (0)	—	—	—	—	—	—	—	—	—	—	—	—	—	—	—	—	—	kp	—	0	77
NFL	6	54 (1)	13	71	5.5(11)	0	9	90	10.0(19)	1	—	—	—	—	—	—	—	—	—	kp	1	12	1089

TURNER, VINCE   Vincent Kerby, DB, 5´11˝/190 lbs; Missouri; 1964: Bal, rnd 9; B12/31/1942   **1964** NYJ-A 6

TURNER, WYLIE   Wylie Dewayen, DB, 5´10˝/182 lbs; Angelo State (TX); B4/19/1957 Dallas, TX   **1979** GB 12   **1980** GB 16 (0)   **NFL** 28 [2 yrs]

TURNURE, TOM   Thomas William, C-G, 6´4˝/250 lbs; Washington; 1980: Det, rnd 3; B7/9/1957 Seattle, WA   **1980** Det 3 (0)   **1981** Det 16 (0)   **1982** †Det 9 (0)   **1983** †Det 16 (0)   **1985** Det 6 (0)   **1986** Det 13 (0)   **NFL** 63 (0) [6 yrs]

TURPIN, MILES   Miles John, LB, 6´4˝/230 lbs; California; B5/15/1964 Minneapolis, MN   **1986** GB 1 (0)   **1987** TB 4 (2)   **NFL** 5 (2) [2 yrs]

TURRAL, WILLIE   Willie James, RB, 5´10˝/190 lbs; New Mexico; B2/1/1964 Tallahassee, FL   **1987** Phi 1 (0)

TUTEN, MELVIN   Melvin Eugene, T, 6´6˝/305 lbs; Syracuse; 1995: Cin, rnd 3; B11/11/1971 Washington, DC   **1996** Cin 16 (7, lt)   **1999** Den 2 (0)   **2000** Car 3 (0)   **2001** Car 15 (1)   **2002** Car 14 (7, rt)

TUTEN, RICK   Richard Lamar, P, 6´2˝/221 lbs; Miami (FL); Florida State; B1/5/1965 Perry, FL [P]   **1989** †Phi 2 (0)   **1990** †Buf 14 (0)   **1991** Sea 10 (0)   **1995** Sea 16 (0)   **1996** Sea 16 (0)   **1997** Sea 11 (0)   **1999** SL 8 (0)

| 1995 | Cin | 16 (2) | — | — | — | — | 2 | 12 | 6.0(9) | 1 | — | — | — | — | — | — | — | — | — | — | — | 6 | 11 |
| NFL | 6 | 66 (17) | — | — | — | — | 2 | 12 | 6.0(9) | 1 | — | — | — | — | — | — | — | — | — | — | — | 6 | 11 |

1992	Sea	16 (0)	1	0	0.0(0)	0	—	—	—	—	1	0	0.0	0	0.0	0	0	—	—	P	—	0	0
1993	Sea	16 (0)	—	—	—	—	—	—	—	—	1	0	0.0	0	0.0	0	0	—	—	P	—	0	0
1994	Sea★	16 (0)	—	—	—	—	—	—	—	—	1	0	0.0	0	0.0	0	0	—	—	P	—	2	0
1998	SL	16 (0)	—	—	—	—	—	—	—	—	1	0	0.0	0	0.0	0	0	—	—	P	—	0	0
NFL	11	141 (0)	1	0	0.0	—	—	—	—	—	4	0	0.0	0	0.0	0	0	—	—	P	—	2	0

TUTHILL, JAMES   James Joseph, K, 6´2˝/250 lbs; Cal Poly-San Luis Obispo; B3/25/1976 Upland, CA [K]   **2002** Was 11 (0)   **2002** SD 1 (0)   **NFL** 12 (0) [1 yr]

TUTSON, TOM   Thomas, DB, 6´1˝/180 lbs; South Carolina State; 1982: Mia, rnd 6; B5/20/1958 Jacksonville, FL   **1983** Atl 10 (0)

TUTTLE, GEORGE   George Karl, E, 5´11˝/180 lbs; Minnesota; B1/14/1905 Minneapolis, MN, D10/20/1986 Minneapolis, MN   **1927** GB 1 (0)

TUTTLE, ORVILLE   James Orville, G, 5´9˝/210 lbs; Phillips; Oklahoma City; B9/18/1912 Licking, MO   **1937** NYG☆11 (10, RG)   **1939** †NYG★11 (11, RG)   **1940** NYG☆11 (11, LG)   **1941** †NYG 11 (2)   **1946** NYG 5 (0)

| 1938 | †NYG★ | 11 (8, RG) | — | — | — | — | 1 | -2 | -2.0(-2) | 0 | — | — | — | — | — | — | — | — | — | — | — | 0 | -1 |
| NFL | 6 | 60 (42) | — | — | — | — | 1 | -2 | -2.0(-2) | 0 | — | — | — | — | — | — | — | — | — | — | — | 0 | -1 |

TUTTLE, PERRY   Perry Warren, WR, 6´0˝/178 lbs; Clemson; 1982: Buf, rnd 1; B8/2/1959 Lexington, NC

1982	Buf	7 (1)	—	—	—	—	7	107	15.3(26)	0	—	—	—	—	—	—	—	—	—	p	—	0	54
1983	Buf	9 (3)	—	—	—	—	17	261	15.4(38)	3	—	—	—	—	—	—	—	—	—	—	—	18	146
1984	TB	3 (0)	—	—	—	—	—	—	—	—	—	—	—	—	—	—	—	—	—	—	—	0	4
1984	Atl	5 (0)	—	—	—	—	1	7	7.0(7)	0	—	—	—	—	—	—	—	—	—	—	—	0	4
NFL	3	24 (4)	—	—	—	—	25	375	15.0(38)	3	—	—	—	—	—	—	—	—	—	p	—	18	203

TWEDELL, FRANK   Francis A., G, 5´11˝/220 lbs; Minnesota; 1939: GB, rnd 7; B5/29/1917 Austin, MN, D5/1969   **1939** GB 4 (0)

TWEET, RODNEY   Rodney Lee, WR, 6´1˝/195 lbs; South Dakota; B2/20/1964 Madison, SD   **1987** Cin 2 (0)

TWILLEY, HOWARD   Howard James, WR-FL, 5´10˝/185 lbs; Tulsa; 1966: Mia, rnd 12/Min, rnd 14; B12/25/1943 Houston, TX

1966	Mia-A	6	—	—	—	—	10	128	12.8(20)	0	—	—	—	—	—	—	—	—	—	—	—	0	64
1967	Mia-A	14 (5, fl)	—	—	—	—	24	314	13.1(42)	2	—	—	—	—	—	—	—	—	—	—	—	12	167
1968	Mia-A	14 (14, FL)	—	—	—	—	39	604	15.5(40)	1	—	—	—	—	—	—	—	—	—	—	—	6	307
1969	Mia-A	4	—	—	—	—	10	158	15.8(33)	1	—	—	—	—	—	—	—	—	—	p	—	6	79

YEAR	TEAM	G(GS, POS)	RUSH	YD	AVG(LG)	TD	REC	YD	AVG(LG)	TD	PASS	COMP	PCT	YD	AVG(LG)	TD	INT	SK	YD	QBR	KPR	OTD	PTS	TAY
1970	†Mia	14(13, WR)	—	—	—	—	22	281	12.8(23)	5	—	—	—	—	—	—	—	—	—	—	—	—	30	166
1971	†Mia	14(12, WR)	—	—	—	—	23	349	15.2(41)	4	—	—	—	—	—	—	—	—	—	—	—	—	24	195
1972	†Mia	13(11, WR)	—	—	—	—	20	364	18.2(44)	3	—	—	—	—	—	—	—	—	—	—	—	—	18	197
1973	†Mia	6	—	—	—	—	2	30	15.0(29)	0	—	—	—	—	—	—	—	—	—	—	—	—	0	15
1974	†Mia	13(4)	—	—	—	—	24	256	10.7(21)	2	—	—	—	—	—	—	—	—	—	—	—	—	12	138
1975	Mia	14(8, WR)	—	—	—	—	24	366	15.3(32)	4	—	—	—	—	—	—	—	—	—	—	—	—	24	203
1976	Mia	8(6, wr)	—	—	—	—	14	214	15.3(39)	1	—	—	—	—	—	—	—	—	—	—	—	—	6	112
NFL	11	120(73)	—	—	—	—	212	3064	14.5(44)	23	—	—	—	—	—	—	—	—	—	—	p	—	138	1642

Twombly, Darren Darren William, C, 6´4˝/270 lbs; Boston College; B5/14/1965 **1987** NE 1 (1)

Twyner, Gunnard Gunnard, WR, 5´10˝/165 lbs; Western Illinois; B7/14/1973 Bettendorf, IA **1997** NO 2 (0)

YEAR	TEAM	G(GS, POS)	RUSH	YD	AVG(LG)	TD	REC	YD	AVG(LG)	TD	PASS	COMP	PCT	YD	AVG(LG)	TD	INT	SK	YD	QBR	KPR	OTD	PTS	TAY
1997	Cin	2(0)	—	—	—	—	4	45	11.3(16)	0	—	—	—	—	—	—	—	—	—	—	k	—	0	35
NFL	1	4(0)	—	—	—	—	4	45	11.3(16)	0	—	—	—	—	—	—	—	—	—	—	—	—	0	23

Tyler, Andre Andre Miguel, WR, 6´0˝/180 lbs; Stanford; 1982: TB, rnd 6; B7/17/1959 Tucson, AZ

YEAR	TEAM	G(GS, POS)	RUSH	YD	AVG(LG)	TD	REC	YD	AVG(LG)	TD	PASS	COMP	PCT	YD	AVG(LG)	TD	INT	SK	YD	QBR	KPR	OTD	PTS	TAY
1983	TB	14(0)	—	—	—	—	6	77	12.8(21)	0	—	—	—	—	—	—	—	—	—	—	p	—	0	112

Tyler, Maurice Maurice Michael, DB, 6´0˝/188 lbs; Morgan State; 1972: Buf, rnd 10; B7/19/1950 Karnack, TX **1972** Buf 14 (SS) **1973** Den 14 (2) **1974** Den 14 **1975** SD 13 **1976** Det 9 **1977** NYJ 14 (4) **1978** NYG 8 **NFL** 86 (6) [7 yrs]

Tyler, Pete Glenn Pete, BB, 5´11˝/190 lbs; Hardin-Simmons; B6/18/1914, D6/8/1986 San Angelo, TX

YEAR	TEAM	G(GS, POS)	RUSH	YD	AVG(LG)	TD	REC	YD	AVG(LG)	TD	PASS	COMP	PCT	YD	AVG(LG)	TD	INT	SK	YD	QBR	KPR	OTD	PTS	TAY
1937	ChiC	6(1)	5	-5	-1.0	0	7	60	8.6	1	1	0	0.0	0	0.0	0	0	—	—	—	—	—	6	30
1938	ChiC	10(5, bb)	1	1	1.0(1)	0	2	24	12.0(26)	1	—	—	—	—	—	—	—	—	—	—	—	—	6	18
NFL	2	16(6)	6	-4	-0.7(1)	0	9	84	9.3(26)	2	1	0	0.0	0	0.0	0	0	—	—	—	—	—	12	48

Tyler, Robert Robert, TE, 6´5˝/259 lbs; South Carolina State; 1988: Sea, rnd 8; B10/12/1965 Savannah, GA

YEAR	TEAM	G(GS, POS)	RUSH	YD	AVG(LG)	TD	REC	YD	AVG(LG)	TD	PASS	COMP	PCT	YD	AVG(LG)	TD	INT	SK	YD	QBR	KPR	OTD	PTS	TAY
1989	Sea	9(9, TE)	—	—	—	—	14	148	10.6(27)	0	—	—	—	—	—	—	—	—	—	—	—	—	0	74

Tyler, Toussaint Toussaint L'Overture, RB, 6´2˝/220 lbs; Washington; 1981: NO, rnd 9; B3/19/1959 Los Angeles, CA

YEAR	TEAM	G(GS, POS)	RUSH	YD	AVG(LG)	TD	REC	YD	AVG(LG)	TD	PASS	COMP	PCT	YD	AVG(LG)	TD	INT	SK	YD	QBR	KPR	OTD	PTS	TAY
1981	NO	16(0)	36	183	5.1(42)	0	23	135	5.9(18)	0	—	—	—	—	—	—	—	—	—	—	—	—	0	251
1982	NO	2(0)	10	21	2.1(11)	0	4	31	7.8(12)	0	—	—	—	—	—	—	—	—	—	—	—	—	0	37
NFL	2	18(0)	46	204	4.4(42)	0	27	166	6.1(18)	0	—	—	—	—	—	—	—	—	—	—	—	—	0	287

Tyler, Wendell Wendell Avery, RB, 5´10˝/198 lbs; UCLA; 1977: LA, rnd 3; B5/20/1955 Shreveport, LA

YEAR	TEAM	G(GS, POS)	RUSH	YD	AVG(LG)	TD	REC	YD	AVG(LG)	TD	PASS	COMP	PCT	YD	AVG(LG)	TD	INT	SK	YD	QBR	KPR	OTD	PTS	TAY
1977	†LARm	14	61	317	5.2(44)	3	1	3	3.0(3)	0	—	—	—	—	—	—	—	—	—	—	k	—	18	512
1978	LARm	2	14	45	3.2(18)	0	2	17	8.5(16)	0	—	—	—	—	—	—	—	—	—	—	k	—	0	55
1979	†LARm	16(12, RB)	218	1109	**5.1**(**63**)	9	32	308	9.6(71)	1	—	—	—	—	—	—	—	—	—	—	k	—	60	1359
1980	LARm	4(4)	30	157	5.2(17)	0	2	8	4.0(5)	0	—	—	—	—	—	—	—	—	—	—	—	—	0	161
1981	LARm	15(15, RB)	260	1074	4.1(69)	12	45	436	9.7(67)	5	—	—	—	—	—	—	—	—	—	—	—	—	102	1437
1982	LARm	9(9, RB)	137	564	4.1(54)	**9**	38	375	9.9(40)	4	—	—	—	—	—	—	—	—	—	—	—	—	**78**	862
1983	†SF	14(14, RB)	176	856	4.9(39)	4	34	285	8.4(26)	2	—	—	—	—	—	—	—	—	—	—	—	—	36	1049
1984	†SF✧	16(15, RB)	246	1262	5.1(40)	7	28	230	8.2(26)	2	—	—	—	—	—	—	—	—	—	—	—	—	54	1457
1985	†SF	13(12, RB)	171	867	5.1(30)	6	20	154	7.7(16)	2	—	—	—	—	—	—	—	—	—	—	—	—	48	1014
1986	SF	5(2)	31	127	4.1(14)	0	—	—	—	—	—	—	—	—	—	—	—	—	—	—	—	—	0	127
NFL	10	108(83)	1344	6378	4.7(69)	50	202	1816	9.0(71)	16	—	—	—	—	—	—	—	—	—	—	k	—	396	8031

Tylski, Rich Richard Lee, G, 6´5˝/309 lbs; Utah State; B2/27/1971 San Diego, CA **1996**†Jax 16 (7, rg) **1997**†Jax 13 (13, RG) **1998** Jax 11 (8, rg) **1999**†Jax 10 (8, rg) **2000** Pit 16 (16, RG) **2001**†Pit 12 (10, RG) **2004** Car 16 (1) **NFL** 94 (63) [7 yrs]

Tyner, Scott Scott Dalton, P, 6´1˝/189 lbs; Oklahoma State; B4/11/1972 Houston, TX **1994** Atl 6 (0)

Tynes, Buddy David Lane, B, 6´0˝/185 lbs; Texas; B2/26/1902 Cooper, TX, D11/28/1994 Anchorage, KY **1924** Col 8 (6, FB), 12 **1925** Col 9 (7, TB), 6 **NFL** 17 (13), 18 [2 yrs]

Tynes, Lawrence Lawrence James, K, 6´0˝/188 lbs; Troy State; B5/3/1978 Greenock, Scotland **[K]** **2004** KC 16 (0) **2005** KC 16 (0) **NFL** 32 (0) [2 yrs]

Tyree, David David Mikel, WR, 6´0˝/205 lbs; Syracuse; 2003: NYG, rnd 6; B1/3/1980 Livingston, NJ

YEAR	TEAM	G(GS, POS)	RUSH	YD	AVG(LG)	TD	REC	YD	AVG(LG)	TD	PASS	COMP	PCT	YD	AVG(LG)	TD	INT	SK	YD	QBR	KPR	OTD	PTS	TAY
2003	NYG	16(3)	1	-9	-9.0(-9)	0	16	211	13.2(48)	0	—	—	—	—	—	—	—	—	—	—	—	—	0	97
2004	NYG	16(1)	—	—	—	—	10	155	15.5(49)	1	—	—	—	—	—	—	—	—	—	—	—	—	6	83
2005	†NYG★	13(0)	—	—	—	—	5	52	10.4(18)	1	—	—	—	—	—	—	—	—	—	—	—	—	6	31
NFL	3	45(4)	1	-9	-9.0(-9)	0	31	418	13.5(49)	2	—	—	—	—	—	—	—	—	—	—	—	—	12	210

Tyree, Jim James Edward, E-DE, 6´3˝/204 lbs; Oklahoma; 1944: Bkn, rnd 12/1947: SF-A, rnd 11; B5/30/1922 Sperry, OK

YEAR	TEAM	G(GS, POS)	RUSH	YD	AVG(LG)	TD	REC	YD	AVG(LG)	TD	PASS	COMP	PCT	YD	AVG(LG)	TD	INT	SK	YD	QBR	KPR	OTD	PTS	TAY
1948	Bos	12(10, LE)	—	—	—	—	13	106	8.2(32)	0	—	—	—	—	—	—	—	—	—	—	k	1	6	55

Tyrer, Jim James Efflo, T, 6´6˝/280 lbs; Ohio State; 1961: DalT, rnd 3/Chi, rnd 14; B2/25/1939 Newark, OH, D9/15/1980 Kansas City, MO **1961** DalT-A 14 **1962**†DalT-A★14 (LT) **1963** KC-A★14 (LT) **1964** KC-A★14 (LT) **1965** KC-A★14 (LT) **1966**†KC-A★14 (LT) **1967** KC-A☆14 (LT) **1968**†KC-A★14 (LT) **1969**†KC-A★14 (LT) **1970** KC★14 (LT) **1971**†KC★14 (LT) **1972** KC 14 (LT) **1973** KC 12 (LT) **1974**†Was 14 (1) **NFL** 194 (1) [14 yrs]

Tyrrell, Joe Joseph Paul, G, 5´11˝/215 lbs; Temple; 1952: Phi, rnd 24; B4/6/1929 Philadelphia, PA, D6/10/1994 Philadelphia, PA **1952** Phi 2

Tyrrell, Tim Timothy Gordan, RB, 6´1˝/204 lbs; Northern Illinois; B2/19/1961 Chicago, IL **1984** Atl 11 (0) **1985** Atl 16 (0) **1986** Atl 3 (0) **1988**†LARm 12 (0)

YEAR	TEAM	G(GS, POS)	RUSH	YD	AVG(LG)	TD	REC	YD	AVG(LG)	TD	PASS	COMP	PCT	YD	AVG(LG)	TD	INT	SK	YD	QBR	KPR	OTD	PTS	TAY
1986	†LARm	6(1)	—	—	—	—	1	9	9.0(9)	0	—	—	—	—	—	—	—	—	—	—	—	—	0	5
1987	LARm	11(0)	11	44	4.0(13)	0	6	59	9.8(16)	0	—	—	—	—	—	—	—	—	—	—	k	—	0	100
1989	†Pit	7(0)	1	3	3.0(3)	0	—	—	—	—	—	—	—	—	—	—	—	—	—	—	—	—	0	3
NFL	6	66(1)	12	47	3.9(13)	0	7	68	9.7(16)	0	—	—	—	—	—	—	—	—	—	—	k	—	0	90

Tyson, Dick Richard Hal, G, 6´2˝/245 lbs; Tulsa; 1966: Oak, rnd 4/LA, rnd 3; B1/5/1943 Kansas City, MO **1966** Oak-A 3 **1967** Den-A 7 **NFL** 10 [2 yrs]

Ucovich, Mitch Michael A., T, 5´11˝/208 lbs; San Jose State; B9/27/1915 San Jose, CA, D12/1/1989 San Jose, CA **1944** Was 8 (1) **1945** ChiC 1 (1) **NFL** 9 (2) [2 yrs]

Udeze, Kenechi Kenechi, DE, 6´4˝/285 lbs; USC; 2004: Min, rnd 1; B3/5/1983 Los Angeles, CA **2004**†Min 16 (15, RDE) **2005** Min 3 (2) **NFL** 19 (17) [2 yrs]

Uecker, Keith Richard Keith, T-G, 6´5˝/278 lbs; Auburn; 1982: Den, rnd 9; B6/20/1960 Hollywood, FL **1982** Den 5 (2) **1983**†Den 16 (0) **1984** GB 6 (2) **1985** GB 7 (7, lg) **1987** GB 8 (8, RT) **1988** GB 16 (16, RT) **1990** GB 13 (13, RG) **1991** GB 14 (1) **NFL** 85 (49) [8 yrs]

Uguccioni, Rocky Enrico R., E, 6´0˝/195 lbs; Murray State; B4/19/1918 New London, CT

YEAR	TEAM	G(GS, POS)	RUSH	YD	AVG(LG)	TD	REC	YD	AVG(LG)	TD	PASS	COMP	PCT	YD	AVG(LG)	TD	INT	SK	YD	QBR	KPR	OTD	PTS	TAY
1944	Bkn	10(1)	—	—	—	—	7	94	13.4(26)	0	—	—	—	—	—	—	—	—	—	—	p	1	6	64

Uhlenhake, Jeff Jeffrey Alan, C, 6´3˝/285 lbs; Ohio State; 1989: Mia, rnd 5; B1/28/1966 Indianapolis, IN **1989** Mia 16 (15, C) **1990**†Mia 16 (16, C) **1991** Mia 13 (10, C) **1992** Mia 13 (13, C) **1993** Mia 5 (5, c) **1994** NO 16 (15, C) **1995** NO 14 (14, C) **1996** Was 12 (11, C) **1997** Was 14 (13, C) **NFL** 119 (112) [9 yrs]

Uhrinyak, Steven Steven James, G, 6´2˝/218 lbs; Franklin & Marshall; B11/23/1914 **1939** Was 1 (0)

Ulbrich, Jeff Jeff, LB, 6´0˝/249 lbs; San Jose State; Hawaii; 2000: SF, rnd 3; B2/17/1977 San Jose, CA **2000** SF 4 (0) **2001**†SF 14 (14, RLB) **2002**†SF 14 (13, RLB) **2003** SF 15 (15, RLB) **2004** SF 16 (14, LLB/rlb) **2005** SF 5 (5, rilb) **NFL** 68 (61) [6 yrs]

Ulinski, Ed Edward Franklin, G, 5´11˝/203 lbs; Marshall; B12/7/1919 Pittsburgh, PA **1947**†Cle-A 14 (4, lg) **1948**†Cle-A☆14 (13, LG) **1949**†Cle-A 12 (10, LG)

YEAR	TEAM	G(GS, POS)	RUSH	YD	AVG(LG)	TD	REC	YD	AVG(LG)	TD	PASS	COMP	PCT	YD	AVG(LG)	TD	INT	SK	YD	QBR	KPR	OTD	PTS	TAY
1946	†Cle-A☆	14(11, LG)	1	2	2.0	0	—	—	—	—	—	—	—	—	—	—	—	—	—	—	—	—	0	2
AAFC	4	54(38)	1	2	2.0	0	—	—	—	—	—	—	—	—	—	—	—	—	—	—	—	—	0	2

Ulinski, Harry Harry John, C, 6´4˝/229 lbs; Kentucky; 1950: Was, rnd 4; B4/4/1925 Pittsburgh, PA **1950** Was 12 **1951** Was 12 **1953** Was 12 (C) **1954** Was 12 (C) **1955** Was✧12 (C) **1956** Was 12 **NFL** 72 [6 yrs]

Ullery, Jiggs William Warner, TB-WB-FB, 6´0˝/200 lbs; Penn State; B5/2/1897, D12/23/1989 Centerville, PA **1922** Day 7 (5, tb)

Ulmer, Artie Charles Artie, LB, 6´3˝/247 lbs; Georgia Southern; Valdosta State; 1997: Min, rnd 7; B7/30/1973 Rincon, GA **1999** Den 7 (0) **2000** SF 12 (2) **2001** Atl 15 (0) **2002**†Atl 15 (0) **2003** Atl 16 (0) **2004**†Atl 16 (0) **2005** Atl 9 (0) **NFL** 90 (2) [7 yrs]

Ulmer, Mike Michael Walter, DB, 6´0˝/196 lbs; Doane; B12/28/1954 York, NE **1980** ChiB 3 (0) **1987** Phi 1 (0) **NFL** 4 (0) [2 yrs]

Ulrich, Chuck Charles, DT, 6´4˝/250 lbs; Illinois; 1952: Phi, rnd 4; B12/14/1929 Chicago, IL **1954** ChiC 11 (LDT) **1955** ChiC 12 (LDT) **1956** ChiC 5 (ldt) **1957** ChiC 11 (LDT) **1958** ChiC 12 (LDT) **NFL** 51 [5 yrs]

Ulrich, Hub Hubert Jr., E-DE, 6´0˝/205 lbs; Kansas; 1942: Cle, rnd 9; B12/12/1920 Jennings, OK, D3/10/1974 Topeka, KS

YEAR	TEAM	G (GS, POS)	RUSH	YD	AVG (LG)	TD	REC	YD	AVG (LG)	TD	PASS	COMP	PCT	YD	AVG (LG)	TD	INT	SK	YD	QBR	KPR	OTD	PTS	TAY
1946	Mia-A	14 (6, LE)	—	—	—	—	4	75	18.8	1	—	—	—	—	—	—	—	—	—	—	—	—	6	43

Ulrich, Matt Matt, G, 6´2˝/309 lbs; Northwestern; B12/30/1981 Streamwood, IL **2005**†Ind 5 (0)

Ulufale, Mike Mike Fuimaono, DT-DE, 6´4˝/277 lbs; Brigham Young; 1996: Dal, rnd 3; B2/1/1972 Honolulu, HI **1996** Dal 3 (0)

Umenyiora, Osi Osi, DE, 6´3˝/280 lbs; Troy State; 2003: NYG, rnd 2; B11/16/1980 London, England **2003** NYG 13 (1) **2004** NYG 16 (7, rde) **2005**†NYG★16 (16, RDE) **NFL** 45 (24) [3 yrs]

Umont, Frank Frank William, G-T, 5´11˝/218 lbs; none; B11/21/1917 Staten Island, NY, D6/20/1991 Fort Lauderdale, FL **1944**†NYG 8 (0) **1945** NYG 8 (0) **NFL** 16 (0) [2 yrs]

Umphrey, Rich Richard Vernon, C-G, 6´3˝/263 lbs; Utah; Colorado; 1982: NYG, rnd 5; B12/13/1958 Garden Grove, CA **1982** NYG 9 (7, C) **1983** NYG 10 (10, C) **1984**†NYG 15 (0) **1985** SD 11 (1) **NFL** 45 (18) [4 yrs]

Unck, Mason Mason Douglas, LB, 6´3˝/235 lbs; Arizona State; B9/7/1980 Ogden, UT **2003** Cle 1 (0) **2004** Cle 11 (0) **2005** Cle 16 (0) **NFL** 28 (0) [3 yrs]

Underwood, Dimitrius Demetrius Paul, DT, 6´6˝/276 lbs; Michigan State; 1999: Min, rnd 1; B3/29/1977 Philadelphia, PA **2000** Dal 15 (0) **2001** Dal 4 (0) **NFL** 19 (0) [2 yrs]

Underwood, Jack John, E-G-C, 6´0˝/196 lbs; none; B8/1897 Duluth, MN, D1938 Duluth, MN **1924** Dul 6 (6, LE), 12 **1925** Dul 2 (2, RE) **1926** Dul 12 (11, LE), 6 **1927** Pot 1 (0) **1927** Buf 3 (2, LE) **1929** ChiC 9 (2) **NFL** 33 (23), 18 [5 yrs]

Underwood, John John Arthur, G, 6´3˝/265 lbs; Rice; B1900, D12/15/1932 Bonham, TX **1923** Mil 12 (12, RG)

Underwood, Marviel Marviel, DB, 5´10˝/205 lbs; San Diego State; 2005: GB, rnd 4; B2/17/1982 Oakland, CA **2005** GB 16 (0)

Underwood, Olen Olen Olesus, LB, 6´1˝/220 lbs; Texas; 1965: NYG, rnd 14; B5/25/1942 Holly Grove, TX **1965** NYG 10 (RLB) **1966** Hou-A 11 **1967**†Hou-A 14 (RLB) **1968** Hou-A 14 (RLB) **1969**†Hou-A 14 (RLB) **1970** Hou 12 (LLB) **1971** Den 14 (4) **NFL** 89 (4) [7 yrs]

Underwood, Wayne Forrest Wayne, T, 6´1˝/190 lbs; Davis & Elkins; Marshall; B12/8/1913 West Union, WV, D10/26/1967 Grantsville, WV **1937** Cle 3 (2)

Ungerer, Joe Joseph C., T, 6´0˝/243 lbs; Fordham; 1941: Bkn, rnd 20; B12/10/1916 Bethlehem, PA, D7/15/1990 Absecon, NJ **1944** Was 5 (2) **1945**†Was 10 (5, RT) **NFL** 15 (7) [2 yrs]

Unitas, Johnny John Constantine, QB, 6´1˝/194 lbs; Louisville; 1955: Pit, rnd 9; B5/7/1933 Pittsburgh, PA, D9/11/2002 Timonuim, MD; HOF 1979

YEAR	TEAM	G (GS, POS)	RUSH	YD	AVG (LG)	TD	REC	YD	AVG (LG)	TD	PASS	COMP	PCT	YD	AVG (LG)	TD	INT	SK	YD	QBR	KPR	OTD	PTS	TAY
1956	Bal	12 (QB)	28	155	5.5 (34)	1	1	1	1.0 (1)	0	198	110	55.6	1498	7.6 (54)	9	10	—	—	74.0	—	—	6	560
1957	Bal★	12 (QB)	42	171	4.1 (24)	1	—	—	—	—	**301**	172	57.1	**2550**	8.5 (82)	**24**	17	—	—	**88.0**	—	—	6	896
1958	†Bal★	10 (QB)	33	139	4.2 (28)	3	—	—	—	—	263	136	51.7	2007	7.6 (77)	**19**	7	—	—	**90.0**	—	—	18	988
1959	†Bal★	12 (QB)	29	145	5.0 (21)	2	—	—	—	—	**367**	**193**	52.6	**2899**	7.9 (71)	**32**	14	—	—	92.0	—	—	12	1215
1960	Bal★	12 (QB)	36	195	5.4 (27)	0	—	—	—	—	**378**	**190**	50.3	**3099**	8.2 (80)	**25**	24	—	—	73.7	—	—	0	910
1961	Bal✧	14 (QB)	54	190	3.5 (18)	2	—	—	—	—	**420**	229	54.5	2990	7.1 (72)	16	**24**	—	—	66.1	—	—	12	825
1962	Bal✧	14 (QB)	50	137	2.7 (25)	0	—	—	—	—	389	222	57.1	2967	7.6 (80)	23	23	—	—	76.5	—	—	0	816
1963	Bal★	14 (QB)	47	224	4.8 (26)	0	—	—	—	—	410	**237**	57.8	**3481**	8.5 (64)	20	12	42	290	89.7	—	—	0	1585
1964	†Bal★	14 (QB)	37	162	4.4 (20)	2	—	—	—	—	305	158	51.8	2824	**9.3** (**74**)	19	6	37	254	96.4	—	—	12	1449
1965	Bal☆	11 (11, QB)	17	68	4.0 (18)	1	—	—	—	—	282	164	58.2	2530	**9.0** (**61**)	23	12	29	221	**97.4**	—	—	6	978
1966	Bal✧	14 (QB)	20	44	2.2 (16)	1	—	—	—	—	348	195	56.0	2748	7.9 (89)	22	**24**	21	146	74.0	—	—	6	578
1967	Bal★	14 (QB)	22	89	4.0 (13)	0	—	—	—	—	436	255	**58.5**	3428	7.9 (88)	20	16	25	198	83.6	—	—	0	1263
1968	†Bal	5	3	-1	-0.3 (5)	0	—	—	—	—	32	11	34.4	139	4.3 (37)	2	4	2	15	—	—	—	0	-82
1969	Bal	13 (QB)	11	23	2.1 (13)	0	—	—	—	—	327	178	54.4	2342	7.2 (52)	12	20	12	93	64.0	—	—	0	454
1970	†Bal☆	14 (QB)	9	16	1.8 (9)	0	—	—	—	—	321	166	51.7	2213	6.9 (55)	14	18	19	158	65.1	—	—	0	473
1971	†Bal	13 (qb)	9	5	0.6 (3)	0	—	—	—	—	176	92	52.3	942	5.4 (35)	3	9	15	129	52.3	—	—	0	131
1972	Bal	8 (qb)	3	15	5.0 (8)	0	—	—	—	—	157	88	56.1	1111	7.1 (63)	4	6	14	114	70.8	—	—	0	351
1973	SD	5 (4)	—	—	—	—	—	—	—	—	76	34	44.7	471	6.2 (51)	3	7	14	96	—	—	—	0	-30
NFL	18	211 (15)	450	1777	3.9 (34)	13	1	1	1.0 (1)	0	5186	2830	54.6	40239	7.8 (89)	290	253	230	1714	78.2	—	—	78	13357

Unitas, Pong Matthew J., G, /180 lbs; none; B9/13/1895, D10/28/1972 Baltimore, MD **1921** Was 2 (0)

Unrein, Terry Terrance Lynn, NT-DE, 6´5˝/281 lbs; Colorado State; 1986: SD, rnd 3; B10/24/1962 Brighton, CO **1986** SD 12 (7, nt) **1987** SD 9 (2) **NFL** 21 (9) [2 yrs]

Unutoa, Morris Morris Taua, C, 6´1˝/284 lbs; Brigham Young; B3/10/1971 Torrance, CA **1996**†Phi 16 (0) **1997** Phi 16 (0) **1998** Phi 16 (0) **1999**†TB 12 (0) **2000**†TB 16 (0) **2001** Buf 8 (0) **2002** TB 2 (0) **NFL** 86 (0) [7 yrs]

Unverzagt, Eric Eric James, LB, 6´1˝/241 lbs; Wisconsin; 1996: Sea, rnd 4; B12/18/1972 Central Islip, NY **1996** Sea 8 (0) **1997** Sea 1 (0) **NFL** 9 (0) [2 yrs]

Upchurch, Rick Richard, WR, 5´10˝/175 lbs; Minnesota; 1975: Den, rnd 4; B5/20/1952 Toledo, OH **[R]**

YEAR	TEAM	G (GS, POS)	RUSH	YD	AVG (LG)	TD	REC	YD	AVG (LG)	TD	PASS	COMP	PCT	YD	AVG (LG)	TD	INT	SK	YD	QBR	KPR	OTD	PTS	TAY
1975	Den	14	16	97	6.1 (15)	1	18	436	24.2 (90)	2	0	0	0.0	0	0.0	0	0	1	9	—	kp	—	18	996
1976	Den☆	13 (9, WR)	6	71	11.8 (25)	1	12	340	28.3 (59)	1	—	—	—	—	—	—	—	—	—	—	kp	4	36	821
1977	†Den☆	14 (1)	1	19	19.0 (19)	1	12	245	20.4 (45)	2	—	—	—	—	—	—	—	—	—	—	kp	1	24	726
1978	†Den★	12	5	31	6.2 (11)	0	17	210	12.4 (29)	1	—	—	—	—	—	—	—	—	—	—	kp	1	12	566
1979	†Den★	16 (16, WR)	3	17	5.7 (18)	0	64	937	14.6 (47)	7	1	0	0.0	0	0.0	0	0	—	—	—	kp	—	42	679
1980	Den✧	16 (14, WR)	5	49	9.8 (21)	0	46	605	13.2 (35)	3	—	—	—	—	—	—	—	—	—	—	p	—	18	535
1981	Den	13 (10, WR)	5	56	11.2 (37)	0	32	550	17.2 (63)	3	—	—	—	—	—	—	—	—	—	—	p	—	18	364
1982	Den★	9 (8, WR)	2	-10	-5.0 (-3)	0	26	407	15.7 (51)	3	0	0	0.0	0	0.0	0	0	1	3	—	p	2	30	396
1983	Den	12 (11, WR)	6	19	3.2 (9)	0	40	639	16.0 (40)	2	2	0	0.0	0	0.0	0	0	—	—	—	p	—	12	381
NFL	9	119 (69)	49	349	7.1 (37)	3	267	4369	16.4 (90)	24	3	0	0.0	0	0.0	0	0	2	12	—	kp	8	210	5462

Uperesa, Tuufuli Tuufuli, G, 6´3˝/254 lbs; Montana; 1970: Phi, rnd 16; B1/20/1948 American Samoa **1971** Phi 2

Upshaw, Gene Eugene Thurman, G, 6´5˝/255 lbs; Texas A&M-Kingsville; 1967: Oak, rnd 1; B8/15/1945 Robstown, TX; HOF 1987 **1967**†Oak-A☆14 (14, LG) **1968**†Oak-A★14 (14, LG) **1969**†Oak-A☆14 (14, LG) **1970**†Oak☆14 (14, LG) **1971** Oak☆14 (14, LG) **1972**†Oak★14 (14, LG) **1973**†Oak★14 (14, LG) **1974**†Oak★14 (14, LG) **1975**†Oak★14 (14, LG) **1976**†Oak★14 (14, LG) **1977**†Oak★14 (14, LG) **1978** Oak 16 (16, LG) **1979** Oak 16 (16, LG) **1980**†Oak 16 (16, LG) **1981** Oak 15 (5, lg) **NFL** 217 (207) [15 yrs]

Upshaw, Marvin Marvin Allen, DE-DT, 6´4˝/260 lbs; Trinity (TX); 1968: Cle, rnd 1; B11/22/1946 Robstown, TX **1968**†Cle 14 (rdt) **1969**†Cle 14 (RDT) **1970** KC 7 **1971**†KC 14 (LDE) **1972** KC 14 (LDE) **1973** KC 14 (LDE) **1974** KC 14 (LDE) **1975** KC 4 **1976** SL 4 **NFL** 99 [9 yrs]

Upshaw, Regan Regan Charles, DE, 6´4˝/265 lbs; California; 1996: TB, rnd 1; B8/12/1975 Berrien Springs, MI **1996** TB 16 (16, RDE) **1997**†TB 15 (15, RDE) **1998** TB 16 (16, RDE) **1999** TB 1 (0) **1999**†Jax 6 (0) **2000**†Oak 16 (7, rde) **2001**†Oak 16 (15, LDE) **2002**†Oak 5 (1) **2003** Was 16 (8, lde) **2004** NYG 3 (0) **NFL** 110 (78) [9 yrs]

Uram, Andy Andrew, RB, 5´10˝/188 lbs; Minnesota; 1938: GB, rnd 6; B3/22/1915 Minneapolis, MN, D12/9/1984 Green Bay, WI **[K]**

YEAR	TEAM	G (GS, POS)	RUSH	YD	AVG (LG)	TD	REC	YD	AVG (LG)	TD	PASS	COMP	PCT	YD	AVG (LG)	TD	INT	SK	YD	QBR	KPR	OTD	PTS	TAY
1938	†GB	11 (2)	28	145	5.2 (70)	2	4	46	11.5	0	—	—	—	—	—	—	—	—	—	—	—	—	12	188
1939	†GB✧	10 (5, HB)	52	272	5.2 (97)	1	7	93	13.3 (21)	2	1	0	0.0	0	0.0	0	0	—	—	—	—	—	18	339
1940	GB	11 (4)	71	270	3.8	1	10	188	18.8 (44)	2	—	—	—	—	—	—	—	—	—	—	Ki	—	19	396
1941	†GB	11 (3)	49	258	5.3 (61)	0	6	124	20.7 (44)	0	—	—	—	—	—	—	—	—	—	—	kpi	1	6	440
1942	GB	11 (3)	24	75	3.1 (8)	0	21	420	20.0 (64)	4	—	—	—	—	—	—	—	—	—	—	Kkpi	1	31	426
1943	GB	8 (0)	15	53	3.5 (9)	0	10	212	21.2 (51)	2	6	2	33.3	60	10.0 (48)	1	1	—	—	—	pi	—	12	217
NFL	6	62 (17)	239	1073	4.5 (97)	4	58	1083	18.7 (64)	10	7	2	28.6	60	8.6 (48)	1	1	—	—	—	Kkpi	2	98	2006

Urban, Alex Alexander William, DE-E, 6´3˝/207 lbs; South Carolina; B7/16/1917 Bessemer, PA

YEAR	TEAM	G (GS, POS)	RUSH	YD	AVG (LG)	TD	REC	YD	AVG (LG)	TD	PASS	COMP	PCT	YD	AVG (LG)	TD	INT	SK	YD	QBR	KPR	OTD	PTS	TAY
1941	†GB	7 (0)	—	—	—	—	2	26	13.0 (14)	1	—	—	—	—	—	—	—	—	—	—	—	—	6	18
1944	GB	3 (1)	1	2	2.0 (2)	0	1	10	10.0 (10)	0	—	—	—	—	—	—	—	—	—	—	k	—	0	12
1945	GB	1 (0)	—	—	—	—	1	55	55.0 (55)	0	—	—	—	—	—	—	—	—	—	—	—	—	0	28
NFL	3	11 (1)	1	2	2.0 (2)	0	4	91	22.8 (55)	1	—	—	—	—	—	—	—	—	—	—	k	—	6	58

Urban, Gasper Gasper George, G-LB, 6´1˝/215 lbs; Notre Dame; 1946: LA, rnd 17; B3/18/1923 Lynn, MA, D5/17/1998 St. Augustine, FL **1948** ChiR-A 14 (1)

Urban, Jerheme Jerheme, WR, 6´3˝/212 lbs; Trinity (TX); B11/26/1980 Victoria, TX

YEAR	TEAM	G (GS, POS)	RUSH	YD	AVG (LG)	TD	REC	YD	AVG (LG)	TD	PASS	COMP	PCT	YD	AVG (LG)	TD	INT	SK	YD	QBR	KPR	OTD	PTS	TAY
2004	Sea	7 (1)	—	—	—	—	6	117	19.5 (33)	1	—	—	—	—	—	—	—	—	—	—	—	—	6	64
2005	Sea	4 (1)	—	—	—	—	7	151	21.6 (46)	0	—	—	—	—	—	—	—	—	—	—	—	—	0	76
NFL	2	11 (2)	—	—	—	—	13	268	20.6 (46)	1	—	—	—	—	—	—	—	—	—	—	—	—	6	139

URBAN, LUKE Louis John, E-BB, 5´8˝/165 lbs; Boston College; B3/22/1897 Fall River, MA, D12/7/1980 Somerset, MA **1921** Buf☆12 (12, LE), 6 **1922** Buf☆9 (8, RE) **1923** Buf☆11 (11, RE), 6 **NFL** 32 (31), 12 [3 yrs]

URBANEK, JIM James Eugene, DT, 6´4˝/270 lbs; Mississippi; 1968: Mia, rnd 3; B4/8/1945 Oxford, MS **1968** Mia-A 8

URCH, SCOTT Scott Eric, T, 6´2˝/270 lbs; Virginia; B7/25/1965 Niagara Falls, NY **1987** NYG 3 (1)

UREMOVICH, EMIL Emil, T-DE-E, 6´2˝/233 lbs; Indiana; 1941: Pit, rnd 11; B9/29/1916 Gary, IN, D4/22/1994 Knox, IN **1941** Det 10 (1) **1942** Det 11 (10, RT) **1945** Det☆8 (8, RT) **1946** Det 11 (6, RT) **NFL** 40 (25) [4 yrs]

1948 ChiR-A 8 (0)

URENDA, HERMAN Herman Joseph, E-DB, 6´0˝/182 lbs; Pacific; B4/24/1938 Brentwood, CA **1963** Oak-A 2

URLACHER, BRIAN Brian Keith, LB, 6´4˝/258 lbs; New Mexico; 2000: Chi, rnd 1; B5/25/1978 Pasco, WA **2000** ChiB✧16 (14, MLB) **2003** ChiB✧16 (16, MLB) **2004** ChiB 9 (9, MLB) **2005**†ChiB★16 (16, MLB)

YEAR	TEAM	G (GS, POS)	RUSH	YD	AVG (LG)	TD	REC	YD	AVG (LG)	TD	PASS	COMP	PCT	YD	AVG (LG)	TD	INT	SK	YD	QBR	KPR	OTD	PTS	TAY
2001	†ChiB★	16 (16, MLB)	—	—	—	—	1	27	27.0 (27)	1	—	—	—	—	—	—	—	—	—	—	iS	1	12	64
2002	ChiB★	16 (16, MLB)	—	—	—	—	—	—	—	—	1	0	0.0	0	0.0	0	0	—	—	—	iS	—	0	-5
NFL	6	89 (87)	—	—	—	—	1	27	27.0 (27)	1	1	0	0.0	0	0.0	0	0	—	—	—	iS	1	12	105

URSELLA, RUBE Reuben J., B, 5´9˝/172 lbs; none; B1/11/1890 Minneapolis, MN, D2/1/1980 Minneapolis, MN **[KC]** **1920** RI 7 (4, BB) **1921** Min 4 (4, BB), 7 **1924** RI 7 (7, WB), 13 **1925** RI 11 (9, WB), 11 **1926** Akr 8 (5, bb) **1926** Ham 1 (1) **1929** Min 8 (3) **NFL** 46 (33), 31 [6 yrs]

USHER, DARRYL Darryl Craig, WR, 5´8˝/170 lbs; Illinois; 1988: NE, rnd 7; B1/3/1965 Los Angeles, CA, D2/24/1990 Phoenix, AZ **1989** SD 6 (0)

YEAR	TEAM	G (GS, POS)	RUSH	YD	AVG (LG)	TD	REC	YD	AVG (LG)	TD	PASS	COMP	PCT	YD	AVG (LG)	TD	INT	SK	YD	QBR	KPR	OTD	PTS	TAY
1989	Phx	7 (0)	—	—	—	—	1	8	8.0 (8)	0	—	—	—	—	—	—	—	—	—	—	kp	—	0	101
NFL	1	13 (0)	—	—	—	—	1	8	8.0 (8)	0	—	—	—	—	—	—	—	—	—	—	kp	—	0	110

USHER, EDDIE Edward T., B, 5´11˝/192 lbs; Michigan; B6/19/1898 Toledo, OH, D4/1973 Bradenton, FL **1921** Buf 1 (0) **1922** RI 5 (3), 6 **1922** GB 5 (5, WB), 6 **1924** GB 1 (0) **1924** KC 6 (2) **NFL** 18 (10), 12 [3 yrs]

USHER, LOU Louis C., T-G-C, 6´2˝/240 lbs; Detroit Mercy; Syracuse; B1898 Chicago, IL **1920** Roc 4 (1, RT) **1921** Roc 1 (1) **1921** Ham 1 (0) **1921** ChiS 3 (0) **1923** Ham 3 (3, RT) **1923** ChiB 8 (4) **1924** Ham 1 (1) **1924** Ken 5 (5, RT) **1924** Mil 5 (4) **1926** Ham 4 (4, RT) **NFL** 35 (23) [5 yrs]

UTECHT, BEN Ben, TE, 6´6˝/251 lbs; Minnesota; B6/30/1981 Hastings, NE

YEAR	TEAM	G (GS, POS)	RUSH	YD	AVG (LG)	TD	REC	YD	AVG (LG)	TD	PASS	COMP	PCT	YD	AVG (LG)	TD	INT	SK	YD	QBR	KPR	OTD	PTS	TAY
2005	†Ind	12 (2)	—	—	—	—	3	59	19.7 (26)	2	—	—	—	—	—	—	—	—	—	—	k	—	12	32

UTLEY, MIKE Michael Gerald, G-T, 6´6˝/288 lbs; Washington State; 1989: Det, rnd 3; B12/20/1965 Seattle, WA **1989** Det 5 (5, rg) **1990** Det 16 (1) **1991** Det 11 (11, RG) **NFL** 32 (17) [3 yrs]

UTT, BEN Benjamin Michael, G-T, 6´5˝/275 lbs; Georgia Tech; B6/13/1959 Richmond, CA **1982** Bal 9 (3) **1983** Bal 16 (8, rg) **1984** Ind 16 (15, LG) **1985** Ind 16 (16, LG) **1986** Ind 9 (9, LG) **1988** Ind 16 (16, RG) **1989** Ind 16 (16, RG)

YEAR	TEAM	G (GS, POS)	RUSH	YD	AVG (LG)	TD	REC	YD	AVG (LG)	TD	PASS	COMP	PCT	YD	AVG (LG)	TD	INT	SK	YD	QBR	KPR	OTD	PTS	TAY
1987	Ind	12 (12, LG)	—	—	—	—	1	-4	-4.0 (-4)	0	—	—	—	—	—	—	—	—	—	—	—	—	0	-2
NFL	8	110 (95)	—	—	—	—	1	-4	-4.0 (-4)	0	—	—	—	—	—	—	—	—	—	—	—	—	0	-2

UWAEZUOKE, IHEANYI Iheanyi, WR, 6´2˝/198 lbs; California; 1996: SF, rnd 5; B7/24/1973 Lagos, Nigeria

YEAR	TEAM	G (GS, POS)	RUSH	YD	AVG (LG)	TD	REC	YD	AVG (LG)	TD	PASS	COMP	PCT	YD	AVG (LG)	TD	INT	SK	YD	QBR	KPR	OTD	PTS	TAY
1996	†SF	14 (0)	—	—	—	—	7	91	13.0 (29)	1	—	—	—	—	—	—	—	—	—	—	k	—	6	57
1997	†SF	14 (0)	—	—	—	—	14	165	11.8 (25)	0	—	—	—	—	—	—	—	—	—	—	kp	—	0	327
1998	SF	7 (0)	—	—	—	—	3	67	22.3 (35)	0	—	—	—	—	—	—	—	—	—	—	—	—	0	34
1998	†Mia	4 (0)	—	—	—	—	—	—	—	—	—	—	—	—	—	—	—	—	—	—	—	—	—	—
1999	†Det	10 (0)	—	—	—	—	1	5	5.0 (5)	0	—	—	—	—	—	—	—	—	—	—	p	—	0	63
2000	Car	11 (2)	—	—	—	—	4	46	11.5 (21)	0	—	—	—	—	—	—	—	—	—	—	p	1	6	156
NFL	5	60 (2)	—	—	—	—	29	374	12.9 (35)	1	—	—	—	—	—	—	—	—	—	—	kp	1	12	635

UZDAVINIS, WALT Walter Alfred, DE-E-T, 6´2˝/210 lbs; Fordham; B6/19/1911 Middleboro, MA, D12/23/1988 Glastonbury, CT

YEAR	TEAM	G (GS, POS)	RUSH	YD	AVG (LG)	TD	REC	YD	AVG (LG)	TD	PASS	COMP	PCT	YD	AVG (LG)	TD	INT	SK	YD	QBR	KPR	OTD	PTS	TAY
1937	Cle	7 (3)	—	—	—	—	1	15	15.0 (15)	0	—	—	—	—	—	—	—	—	—	—	—	—	0	8

VACANTI, SAM Samuel Filadelfo, QB, 5´11˝/203 lbs; Iowa; Purdue; Nebraska; 1947: ChiR-A, rnd 22/1945: NYG, rnd 21; B3/20/1922 Omaha, NE, D12/17/1981 Omaha, NE **[K]**

YEAR	TEAM	G (GS, POS)	RUSH	YD	AVG (LG)	TD	REC	YD	AVG (LG)	TD	PASS	COMP	PCT	YD	AVG (LG)	TD	INT	SK	YD	QBR	KPR	OTD	PTS	TAY
1947	ChiR-A	13 (8, QB)	11	-9	-0.8	1	—	—	—	—	225	96	42.7	1571	7.0	16	16	—	—	—	—	—	6	227
1948	ChiR-A	9 (3)	7	7	1.0	2	—	—	—	—	116	47	40.5	633	5.5	2	15	—	—	—	—	—	12	-247
1948	†Bal-A	5 (0)	—	—	—	—	—	—	—	—	—	—	—	—	—	—	—	—	—	—	—	—	—	—
1949	Bal-A	12 (5, qb)	7	10	1.4	0	—	—	—	—	27	11	40.7	134	5.0	0	1	—	—	—	Kk	—	3	32
AAFC	3	39 (16)	25	8	0.3	3	—	—	—	—	368	154	41.8	2338	6.4	18	32	—	—	—	Kk	—	21	12

VACTOR, TED Theodore Francis, DB, 6´0˝/185 lbs; Nebraska; B5/27/1944 Washington, PA **1969** Was 14 **1970** Was 14 **1971**†Was 14 **1972**†Was 14 **1973** Was 9 **1975** ChiB 4 **NFL** 69 [6 yrs]

VAINOWSKI, PETE Peter S., G, none; B9/7/1902, D7/16/1957 Chicago, IL **1926** Lou 1 (1)

VAIRO, DOM Dominic Martin, E, 6´2˝/203 lbs; Notre Dame; B11/2/1912 Calumet, MI, D7/31/2002 Calumet, MI **1935** GB 1 (0)

VALDEZ, VERN Vernon, DB, 6´0˝/190 lbs; Cal Poly-Pomona; San Diego; B8/12/1935 **1960** LARm 9 **1961** Buf-A 13 (RCB) **1962** Oak-A 10 (LS) **NFL** 32 [3 yrs]

VALENTINE, IRA Ira Lynn, RB, 6´0˝/212 lbs; Texas A&M; 1987: Hou, rnd 12; B6/4/1963 Marshall, TX

YEAR	TEAM	G (GS, POS)	RUSH	YD	AVG (LG)	TD	REC	YD	AVG (LG)	TD	PASS	COMP	PCT	YD	AVG (LG)	TD	INT	SK	YD	QBR	KPR	OTD	PTS	TAY
1987	†Hou	7 (0)	5	10	2.0 (4)	0	2	10	5.0 (7)	0	—	—	—	—	—	—	—	—	—	—	k	—	0	13

VALENTINE, ZACK Zachary Bernard, LB, 6´2˝/220 lbs; East Carolina; 1979: Pit, rnd 2; B5/29/1957 Edenton, NC **1979**†Pit 16 **1980** Pit 16 (0) **1981** Pit 16 (0) **1982** Phi 8 (0) **NFL** 56 [4 yrs]

VALERIO, JOE Joseph William, C, 6´5˝/295 lbs; Pennsylvania; 1991: KC, rnd 2; B2/11/1969 Swarthmore, PA

YEAR	TEAM	G (GS, POS)	RUSH	YD	AVG (LG)	TD	REC	YD	AVG (LG)	TD	PASS	COMP	PCT	YD	AVG (LG)	TD	INT	SK	YD	QBR	KPR	OTD	PTS	TAY
1992	†KC	16 (3)	—	—	—	—	—	—	—	—	—	—	—	—	—	—	—	—	—	—	—	—	—	—
1993	†KC	13 (0)	—	—	—	—	1	1	1.0 (1)	1	—	—	—	—	—	—	—	—	—	—	—	—	6	6
1994	†KC	16 (1)	—	—	—	—	2	5	2.5 (4)	2	—	—	—	—	—	—	—	—	—	—	—	—	12	13
1995	KC	16 (0)	—	—	—	—	1	1	1.0 (1)	1	—	—	—	—	—	—	—	—	—	—	k	—	6	-10
1996	SL	1 (0)	—	—	—	—	—	—	—	—	—	—	—	—	—	—	—	—	—	—	—	—	0	0
NFL	5	62 (4)	—	—	—	—	4	7	1.8 (4)	4	—	—	—	—	—	—	—	—	—	—	k	—	24	9

VALLEZ, EMILIO Emilio Fidel, TE, 6´2˝/210 lbs; New Mexico; 1968: Chi, rnd 12; B4/30/1946 Vegvita, NM **1968** ChiB 6 **1969** ChiB 3 **NFL** 9 [2 yrs]

VAN BROCKLIN, NORM Norman Mack 'The Dutchman', QB, 6´1˝/190 lbs; Oregon; 1949: LARm, rnd 4/ChiH-A, rnd 11; B3/15/1926 Eagle Butte, SD, D5/2/1983 Social Circle, GA; HOF 1971 **[PC]**

YEAR	TEAM	G (GS, POS)	RUSH	YD	AVG (LG)	TD	REC	YD	AVG (LG)	TD	PASS	COMP	PCT	YD	AVG (LG)	TD	INT	SK	YD	QBR	KPR	OTD	PTS	TAY
1949	†LARm	8 (0)	4	-1	-0.3 (2)	0	—	—	—	—	58	32	55.2	601	10.4 (51)	6	2	—	—	—	P	—	0	250
1950	†LARm✧	12 (QB)	15	22	1.5 (16)	1	—	—	—	—	233	127	54.5	2061	**8.8** (**58**)	18	14	—	—	**85.1**	P	—	6	593
1951	LARm✧	12 (QB)	7	2	0.3 (4)	2	—	—	—	—	194	100	51.5	1725	8.9 (81)	13	11	—	—	80.8	P	—	12	510
1952	†LARm★	12 (QB)	7	-10	-1.4 (9)	0	—	—	—	—	205	113	**55.1**	1736	**8.5** (**84**)	14	17	—	—	71.5	P	—	0	248
1953	LARm✧	12 (QB)	8	11	1.4 (6)	0	—	—	—	—	286	156	54.5	2393	8.4 (70)	19	14	—	—	84.1	P	—	0	743
1954	LARm★	12 (QB)	6	-10	-1.7 (5)	0	—	—	—	—	260	139	53.5	**2637**	**10.1** (**80**)	13	21	—	—	71.9	P	—	0	534
1955	†LARm★	12 (QB)	11	24	2.2 (9)	0	—	—	—	—	272	144	52.9	1890	6.9 (74)	8	15	—	—	62.0	P	—	0	409
1956	LARm	12 (qb)	4	1	0.3 (1)	1	—	—	—	—	124	68	54.8	966	7.8 (58)	7	12	—	—	59.5	P	—	6	49
1957	LARm	12 (QB)	10	-4	-0.4 (3)	4	—	—	—	—	265	132	49.8	2105	7.9 (70)	20	**21**	—	—	68.8	P	—	24	349
1958	Phi✧	12 (QB)	8	5	0.6 (2)	1	—	—	—	—	**374**	**198**	52.9	2409	6.4 (91)	15	20	—	—	64.1	P	—	6	495
1959	Phi✧	12 (QB)	11	13	1.2 (12)	2	—	—	—	—	340	191	56.2	2617	7.7 (71)	16	14	—	—	79.5	P	—	12	862
1960	†Phi★	12 (QB)	11	-13	-1.2 (1)	0	—	—	—	—	284	153	53.9	2471	8.7 (64)	24	17	—	—	86.5	P	—	0	663
NFL	12	140	102	40	0.4 (16)	11	—	—	—	—	2895	1553	53.6	23611	8.2 (91)	173	178	—	—	75.1	P	—	66	5701

VAN BUREN, COURTNEY Courtney, T, 6´5˝/350 lbs; Arkansas-Pine Bluff; 2003: SD, rnd 3; B2/22/1980 St. Louis, MO **2003** SD 8 (7, RT) **2004** SD 1 (0) **NFL** 9 (7) [2 yrs]

VAN BUREN, EBERT Harry Ebert, DB-LB-FB-HB, 6´2˝/210 lbs; LSU; 1951: Phi, rnd 1; B12/6/1924 Tela, Honduras

YEAR	TEAM	G (GS, POS)	RUSH	YD	AVG (LG)	TD	REC	YD	AVG (LG)	TD	PASS	COMP	PCT	YD	AVG (LG)	TD	INT	SK	YD	QBR	KPR	OTD	PTS	TAY
1951	Phi	12	16	60	3.8 (11)	0	—	—	—	—	—	—	—	—	—	—	—	—	—	—	i	—	0	78
1952	Phi	12	7	1	0.1 (6)	0	4	73	18.3 (38)	0	—	—	—	—	—	—	—	—	—	—	kp	1	8	30
1953	Phi	12 (DB)	—	—	—	—	—	—	—	—	—	—	—	—	—	—	—	—	—	—	i	—	0	8
NFL	3	36	23	61	2.7 (11)	0	4	73	18.3 (38)	0	—	—	—	—	—	—	—	—	—	—	kpi	1	8	116

Van Buren, Steve Stephen W., HB, 6´0˝/200 lbs; LSU; 1944: Phi, rnd 1; B12/28/1920 La Ceiba, Honduras; HOF 1965 **[KR]**

YEAR	TEAM	G(GS, POS)	RUSH	YD	AVG(LG)	TD	REC	YD	AVG(LG)	TD	PASS	COMP	PCT	YD	AVG(LG)	TD	INT	SK	YD	QBR	KPR	OTD	PTS	TAY
1944	Phi☆	9(6, LH)	80	444	5.6(70)	5	—	—	—	—	—	—	—	—	—	—	—	—	—	—	Pkpi	2	42	837
1945	Phi☆	10(9, LH)	143	**832**	5.8(69)	**15**	10	123	12.3(44)	2	1	0	0.0	0	0.0	0	0	—	—	—	Kkpi	1	**110**	**1323**
1946	Phi☆	9(8, LH)	116	529	4.6(58)	5	6	75	12.5(33)	0	1	1	100.0	35	35.0(35)	0	0	—	—	—	Pkp	1	36	862
1947	†Phi☆	12(7, LH)	**217**	**1008**	4.6(45)	**13**	9	79	8.8(35)	0	—	—	—	—	—	—	—	—	—	—	ki	1	84	**1370**
1948	†Phi☆	11(8, LH)	**201**	**945**	4.7(29)	**10**	10	96	9.6(34)	0	1	0	0.0	0	0.0	0	0	—	—	—	ki	—	60	1197
1949	†Phi☆	12(10, LH)	**263**	**1146**	4.4(41)	**11**	4	88	22.0(50)	1	—	—	—	—	—	—	—	—	—	—	k	—	72	**1413**
1950	Phi☆	10(LH)	**188**	629	3.3(41)	4	2	34	17.0(29)	0	—	—	—	—	—	—	—	—	—	—	k	—	24	721
1951	Phi	10(LH)	112	327	2.9(17)	6	4	28	7.0(18)	0	—	—	—	—	—	—	—	—	—	—	—	—	36	401
NFL	8	83(48)	1320	5860	4.4(70)	69	45	523	11.6(50)	3	3	1	33.3	35	11.7(35)	0	0	—	—	—	KPkpi	5	464	8123

Van Divier, Randy Randall Lee, T-G, 6´5˝/274 lbs; Washington; 1981: Bal, rnd 3; B6/5/1958 Anaheim, CA **1981** Bal 16 (1)

Van Doren, Bob Robert S., DE, 6´3˝/215 lbs; USC; 1953: Cle, rnd 5; B1929 Baltimore, MD **1953** SF 10

Van Duyne, Bob Robert Scott, G-T, 6´5˝/243 lbs; Idaho; 1974: Bal, rnd 10; B5/15/1952 San Bernardino, CA **1974** Bal 14 **1975**†Bal 14 (5, lg) **1976**†Bal 14 **1977**†Bal 9 **1978** Bal 14 (12, RT) **1979** Bal 16 **1980** Bal 7 (0) **NFL** 88 (17) [7 yrs]

Van Dyke, Alex Franklin Alexander, WR, 6´0˝/205 lbs; Nevada-Reno; 1996: NYJ, rnd 2; B7/24/1974 Sacramento, CA

YEAR	TEAM	G(GS, POS)	RUSH	YD	AVG(LG)	TD	REC	YD	AVG(LG)	TD	PASS	COMP	PCT	YD	AVG(LG)	TD	INT	SK	YD	QBR	KPR	OTD	PTS	TAY
1996	NYJ	15(1)	—	—	—	—	17	118	6.9(12)	1	—	—	—	—	—	—	—	—	—	—	k	—	6	128
1997	NYJ	5(0)	—	—	—	—	3	53	17.7(18)	2	—	—	—	—	—	—	—	—	—	—	k	—	12	85
1998	†NYJ	16(0)	—	—	—	—	5	40	8.0(15)	0	—	—	—	—	—	—	—	—	—	—	—	—	0	20
1999	Phi	2(0)	—	—	—	—	—	—	—	—	—	—	—	—	—	—	—	—	—	—	—	—	—	—
2000	Phi	4(0)	—	—	—	—	1	8	8.0(8)	0	—	—	—	—	—	—	—	—	—	—	—	—	0	4
NFL	5	42(1)	—	—	—	—	26	219	8.4(18)	3	—	—	—	—	—	—	—	—	—	—	k	—	18	237

Van Dyke, Bruce Bruce Robert, G, 6´2˝/255 lbs; Missouri; 1966: Phi, rnd 12/KC, rnd 15; B8/6/1944 Lancaster, CA **1966** Phi 4 **1967** Pit 14 (14, RG) **1968** Pit 14 (RG) **1969** Pit 14 (RG) **1970** Pit 14 (RG) **1971** Pit 12 (RG) **1972**†Pit☆13 (RG) **1973**†Pit★14 (RG) **1974** GB 1 **1975** GB 14 (LG) **1976** GB 14 (LG) **NFL** 128 (14) [11 yrs]

Van Dyke, Jimmy James B., WB-TB-BB, 5´7˝/140 lbs; none; B10/2/1898 Louisville, KY, D8/30/1980 Louisville, KY **[K]** **1921** Lou 1 (1) **1922** Lou 3 (2, WB), 7 **1923** Lou 1 (1) **NFL** 5 (4) [3 yrs]

Van Dyke, Ralph Ralph Waldo, T, 6´6˝/273 lbs; Southern Illinois; 1987: Atl, rnd 4; B1/19/1964 Chicago Heights, IL **1987** Cle 2 (2)

Van Dyne, Chase Charles M., T, 6´1˝/194 lbs; Missouri; B2/12/1901, D9/1962 **1925** Buf 8 (6, RT)

van Eeghen, Mark Mark, RB, 6´2˝/223 lbs; Colgate; 1974: Oak, rnd 3; B4/19/1952 Cambridge, MA

YEAR	TEAM	G(GS, POS)	RUSH	YD	AVG(LG)	TD	REC	YD	AVG(LG)	TD	PASS	COMP	PCT	YD	AVG(LG)	TD	INT	SK	YD	QBR	KPR	OTD	PTS	TAY
1974	†Oak	14	28	139	5.0(17)	0	4	33	8.3(12)	0	—	—	—	—	—	—	—	—	—	—	—	—	0	156
1975	†Oak	14(8, FB)	136	597	4.4(22)	2	12	42	3.5(18)	1	—	—	—	—	—	—	—	—	—	—	k	—	18	650
1976	†Oak	14(14, FB)	233	1012	4.3(21)	3	17	173	10.2(21)	0	—	—	—	—	—	—	—	—	—	—	—	—	18	1129
1977	†Oak	14(14, FB)	324	1273	3.9(27)	7	15	135	9.0(30)	0	—	—	—	—	—	—	—	—	—	—	—	—	42	1411
1978	Oak	16(16, FB)	270	1080	4.0(34)	9	27	291	10.8(33)	0	—	—	—	—	—	—	—	—	—	—	—	1	60	1316
1979	Oak	16(16, FB)	223	818	3.7(19)	7	51	474	9.3(36)	2	—	—	—	—	—	—	—	—	—	—	—	—	54	1135
1980	†Oak	16(16, FB)	222	838	3.8(34)	5	29	259	8.9(37)	0	—	—	—	—	—	—	—	—	—	—	—	—	30	1018
1981	Oak	8(3)	39	150	3.8(11)	2	7	60	8.6(13)	0	—	—	—	—	—	—	—	—	—	—	—	—	12	200
1982	†NE	9(5, FB)	82	386	4.7(17)	0	2	14	7.0(9)	1	—	—	—	—	—	—	—	—	—	—	—	—	6	398
1983	NE	15(11, FB)	95	358	3.8(11)	2	10	102	10.2(23)	0	—	—	—	—	—	—	—	—	—	—	—	—	12	429
NFL	10	136(103)	1652	6651	4.0(34)	37	174	1583	9.1(37)	4	—	—	—	—	—	—	—	—	—	—	k	1	252	7840

Van Every, Hal Harold, TB-HB, 6´0˝/195 lbs; Minnesota; 1940: GB, rnd 1; B2/10/1918 Minnetonka Beach, MN

YEAR	TEAM	G(GS, POS)	RUSH	YD	AVG(LG)	TD	REC	YD	AVG(LG)	TD	PASS	COMP	PCT	YD	AVG(LG)	TD	INT	SK	YD	QBR	KPR	OTD	PTS	TAY
1940	GB	9(2)	38	154	4.1	0	4	41	10.3(23)	0	41	12	29.3	199	4.9	4	6	—	—	—	Pi	—	0	69
1941	†GB	11(3)	25	127	5.1(31)	2	1	3	3.0(3)	0	30	11	36.7	195	6.5(44)	0	2	—	—	—	Pkpi	1	18	342
NFL	2	20(5)	63	281	4.5(31)	2	5	44	8.8(23)	0	71	23	32.4	394	5.5(44)	4	8	—	—	—	Pkpi	1	18	411

Van Galder, Tim Thomas Scott, QB, 6´2˝/200 lbs; Iowa State; 1966: SL, rnd 6/Hou, rnd R2; B5/26/1944 Racine, WI

YEAR	TEAM	G(GS, POS)	RUSH	YD	AVG(LG)	TD	REC	YD	AVG(LG)	TD	PASS	COMP	PCT	YD	AVG(LG)	TD	INT	SK	YD	QBR	KPR	OTD	PTS	TAY
1972	SL	5(qb)	9	28	3.1(16)	0	—	—	—	—	79	40	50.6	434	5.5(71)	1	7	10	76	—	—	—	0	-30

Van Heusen, Billy William Proctor, WR-SE-P, 6´1˝/200 lbs; Maryland; B8/27/1946 New Rochelle, NY **[P]**

YEAR	TEAM	G(GS, POS)	RUSH	YD	AVG(LG)	TD	REC	YD	AVG(LG)	TD	PASS	COMP	PCT	YD	AVG(LG)	TD	INT	SK	YD	QBR	KPR	OTD	PTS	TAY
1968	Den-A	13(se)	1	6	6.0(6)	0	19	353	18.6(50)	3	—	—	—	—	—	—	—	—	—	—	Pp	—	18	198
1969	Den-A	5	—	—	—	—	3	64	21.3(36)	0	—	—	—	—	—	—	—	—	—	—	P	—	0	32
1970	Den	14(5, wr)	—	—	—	—	16	382	23.9(74)	2	1	0	0.0	0	0.0	0	0	—	—	—	P	—	12	201
1971	Den	14	1	10	10.0(10)	0	1	10	10.0(10)	0	1	0	0.0	0	0.0	0	0	—	—	—	P	—	0	15
1972	Den	14	3	76	25.3(66)	1	4	59	14.8(25)	0	—	—	—	—	—	—	—	—	—	—	P	—	6	116
1973	Den	14(1)	4	34	8.5(32)	0	8	149	18.6(62)	1	1	0	0.0	0	0.0	0	0	1	10	—	P	—	6	114
1974	Den☆	14(12, WR)	1	-1	-1.0(-1)	0	16	421	26.3(73)	4	1	1	100.0	41	41.0(41)	0	0	—	—	—	P	—	24	250
1975	Den	14(13, WR)	2	26	13.0(24)	0	15	246	16.4(28)	1	1	1	100.0	30	30.0(30)	0	0	—	—	—	P	—	6	169
1976	Den	7	1	20	20.0(20)	0	—	—	—	—	—	—	—	—	—	—	—	—	—	—	P	—	0	20
NFL	9	109(31)	13	171	13.2(66)	1	82	1684	20.5(74)	11	5	2	40.0	71	14.2(41)	0	0	1	10	—	Pp	—	72	1114

Van Horn, Charlie Charles Edgar, B, 6´2˝/185 lbs; Washington & Lee; B11/23/1901, D1/5/1994 Arlington, VA **1927** Buf 4 (2) **1929** Ora 4 (2) **NFL** 8 (4) [2 yrs]

Van Horn, Doug Douglas Claydon, G-T, 6´3˝/245 lbs; Ohio State; 1966: Det, rnd 4/KC, rnd 5; B6/24/1944 Sedalia, MO **1966** Det 14 **1968** NYG 3 **1969** NYG 14 (RG) **1970** NYG 14 (RG) **1971** NYG 12 (RG) **1972** NYG 14 (RG) **1973** NYG 14 (RG) **1974** NYG 14 (RT) **1975** NYG 14 (14, RT) **1976** NYG 14 (14, RT) **1977** NYG 14 (LG) **1978** NYG 16 (16, LG) **1979** NYG 15 (LG) **NFL** 172 (44) [13 yrs]

Van Horne, Keith Keith, T, 6´6˝/281 lbs; USC; 1981: Chi, rnd 1; B11/6/1957 Mount Lebanon, PA **1981** ChiB 14 (12, RT) **1982** ChiB 9 (9, RT) **1983** ChiB 14 (10, RT) **1984**†ChiB 14 (14, RT) **1985**†ChiB 16 (16, RT) **1986**†ChiB 16 (16, RT) **1987**†ChiB 12 (12, RT) **1988**†ChiB 15 (14, RT) **1989** ChiB 15 (15, RT) **1990**†ChiB 16 (16, RT) **1991**†ChiB 16 (16, RT) **1992** ChiB 16 (16, RT) **1993** ChiB 13 (3) **NFL** 186 (169) [13 yrs]

Van Meter, Ed Edward, G, 6´1˝/212 lbs; none; B1899, deceased **1921** Was 2 (1)

Van Note, Jeff Jeffrey Aloysius, C-G-LB, 6´2˝/247 lbs; Kentucky; 1969: Atl, rnd 11; B2/7/1946 South Orange, NJ **1969** Atl 1 **1970** Atl 14 (14, C) **1971** Atl 14 (14, C) **1972** Atl 14 (14, C) **1973** Atl 14 (14, C) **1974** Atl✧14 (14, C) **1975** Atl★14 (14, C) **1976** Atl 10 (10, C) **1977** Atl 14 (14, C) **1978** Atl 16 (16, C) **1979** Atl☆16 (16, C) **1980**†Atl★16 (16, C) **1981** Atl★16 (16, C) **1982**†Atl★9 (9, C) **1983** Atl 16 (16, C) **1984** Atl 16 (13, C) **1985** Atl 16 (16, C) **1986** Atl 16 (0) **NFL** 246 (226) [18 yrs]

Van Pelt, Alex Gregory Alexander, QB, 6´1˝/220 lbs; Pittsburgh; 1993: Pit, rnd 8; B5/1/1970 Pittsburgh, PA

YEAR	TEAM	G(GS, POS)	RUSH	YD	AVG(LG)	TD	REC	YD	AVG(LG)	TD	PASS	COMP	PCT	YD	AVG(LG)	TD	INT	SK	YD	QBR	KPR	OTD	PTS	TAY
1995	†Buf	1(0)	—	—	—	—	—	—	—	—	18	10	55.6	106	5.9(19)	2	0	—	—	—	—	—	0	63
1996	Buf	1(0)	3	-5	-1.7(-1)	0	—	—	—	—	5	2	40.0	9	1.8(5)	0	0	—	—	—	—	—	0	-1
1997	Buf	6(3)	11	33	3.0(9)	1	—	—	—	—	124	60	48.4	684	5.5(39)	2	10	4	33	37.2	—	—	6	-5
1998	Buf	1(0)	1	-1	-1.0(-1)	0	—	—	—	—	—	—	—	—	—	—	—	—	—	—	—	—	0	-1
1999	Buf	1(0)	1	-1	-1.0(-1)	0	—	—	—	—	1	1	100.0	9	9.0(9)	0	0	—	—	—	—	—	0	4
2000	Buf	1(0)	—	—	—	—	—	—	—	—	8	4	50.0	67	8.4(36)	0	0	—	—	—	—	—	0	34
2001	Buf	12(8, qb)	12	33	2.8(15)	0	—	—	—	—	307	178	58.0	2056	6.7(80)	12	11	14	73	76.4	—	—	0	681
2002	Buf	2(0)	—	—	—	—	—	—	—	—	2	2	100.0	5	2.5(4)	0	0	—	—	—	—	—	0	3
2003	Buf	6(0)	4	-6	-1.5(-1)	0	—	—	—	—	12	5	41.7	49	4.1(14)	0	3	1	7	—	—	—	0	-102
NFL	9	31(11)	32	53	1.7(15)	1	—	—	—	—	477	262	54.9	2985	6.3(80)	16	24	19	113	64.1	—	—	6	676

Van Pelt, Brad Bradley Alan, LB, 6´5˝/235 lbs; Michigan State; 1973: NYG, rnd 2; B4/5/1951 Owosso, MI **[I]** **1973** NYG 5 **1974** NYG 12 (LLB) **1975** NYG 14 (14, RLB) **1976** NYG★14 (LLB) **1977** NYG★14 (LLB) **1978** NYG★14 (14, LLB) **1980** NYG★15 (14, LOLB) **1981**†NYG 14 (13, LOLB) **1982** NYG 9 (9, LOLB) **1983** NYG 16 (16, LOLB) **1984**†LARd 9 (8, LOLB) **1985**†LARd 16 (15, LOLB) **1986**†Cle 16 (0)

YEAR	TEAM	G(GS, POS)	RUSH	YD	AVG(LG)	TD	REC	YD	AVG(LG)	TD	PASS	COMP	PCT	YD	AVG(LG)	TD	INT	SK	YD	QBR	KPR	OTD	PTS	TAY
1979	NYG★	16(LOLB)	—	—	—	—	1	20	20.0(20)	0	—	—	—	—	—	—	—	—	—	—	—	—	0	10
NFL	14	184(103)	—	—	—	—	1	20	20.0(20)	0	—	—	—	—	—	—	—	—	—	—	iS	—	0	45

Van Pelt, Bradlee Bradlee, QB, 6´2˝/220 lbs; Colorado; 2004: Den, rnd 7; B7/3/1980 Owosso, MI

YEAR	TEAM	G(GS, POS)	RUSH	YD	AVG(LG)	TD	REC	YD	AVG(LG)	TD	PASS	COMP	PCT	YD	AVG(LG)	TD	INT	SK	YD	QBR	KPR	OTD	PTS	TAY
2005	Den	3(0)	11	48	4.4(11)	1	—	—	—	—	8	2	25.0	7	0.9(5)	0	0	—	—	—	—	—	6	62

Van Raaphorst, Dick Richard William, K, 6´0˝/218 lbs; Ohio State; 1964: Cle, rnd 10; B12/10/1942 Port Huron, MI **[K]** **1964** Dal 14 **1966** SD-A✧14 **1967** SD-A 14 **NFL** 42 [3 yrs]

YEAR	TEAM	G (GS, POS)	RUSH	YD	AVG (LG)	TD	REC	YD	AVG (LG)	TD	PASS	COMP	PCT	YD	AVG (LG)	TD	INT	SK	YD	QBR	KPR	OTD	PTS	TAY

VAN RAAPHORST, JEFF   Jeffrey Richard, QB, 6′1″/210 lbs; Arizona State; B12/7/1963 Columbus, OH

| 1987 | Atl | 2 (1) | 1 | 6 | 6.0 (6) | 0 | — | — | — | — | 34 | 18 | 52.9 | 174 | 5.1 (24) | 1 | 2 | 3 | 19 | — | — | — | 0 | 18 |

VAN SICKLE, CLYDE   Clyde Huntus, G, 6′1″/220 lbs; Arkansas; B5/26/1907 Pryor, OK, D2/15/1995 Dallas, TX   **1930** Fra 11 (7, rg)   **1932** GB 1 (1)   **1933** GB 8 (2)
NFL 20 (10) [3 yrs]

VAN TONE, ART   Arthur, WB-DB, 5′10″/185 lbs; Southern Mississippi; B9/30/1918 Ottawa, OH, D8/9/1990 Conyers, GA

1943	Det	10 (2)	2	1	0.5 (2)	0	6	112	18.7 (72)	1	3	1	33.3	7	2.3 (7)	0	1	—	—	—	pi	—	6	77
1944	Det	10 (8, WB)	25	30	1.2 (26)	1	9	237	26.3 (43)	4	1	0	0.0	0	0.0	0	0	—	—	—	Pkpi	1	36	322
1945	Det	2 (2)	3	14	4.7 (7)	0	3	67	22.3 (41)	0	—	—	—	—	—	—	—	—	—	—	—	—	18	48
NFL	3	22 (12)	30	45	1.5 (26)	1	18	416	23.1 (72)	5	4	1	25.0	7	1.8 (7)	0	1	—	—	—	Pkpi	1	42	446
1946	Bkn-A	9 (3)	4	10	2.5	0	7	152	21.7 (51)	3	—	—	—	—	—	—	—	—	—	—	kpi	—	18	96

VAN VALKENBERG, PETE   Peter, RB, 6′2″/192 lbs; Brigham Young; 1973: NO, rnd 3; B5/19/1950 Salt Lake City, UT   **1974** GB 5   **1974** ChiB 6

| 1973 | Buf | 13 | 2 | 20 | 10.0 (12) | 0 | 1 | 7 | 7.0 (7) | 0 | — | — | — | — | — | — | — | — | — | — | k | — | 0 | 9 |
| NFL | 2 | 24 | 2 | 20 | 10.0 (12) | 0 | 1 | 7 | 7.0 (7) | 0 | — | — | — | — | — | — | — | — | — | — | kp | — | 0 | 23 |

VAN WAGNER, JIM   James Parker, RB, 6′2″/202 lbs; Michigan Tech; 1977: SF, rnd 7; B5/3/1955 Ann Arbor, MI

| 1978 | NO | 5 | — | — | — | — | 1 | -1 | -1.0 (-1) | 0 | — | — | — | — | — | — | — | — | — | — | — | — | 0 | -1 |

VANCE, ERIC   Eric Devon, DB, 6′2″/215 lbs; Vanderbilt; B7/14/1975 Tampa, FL   **1998** TB 3 (1)   **1999** TB 6 (0)   **2000**†TB 14 (0)   **2001** TB 10 (0)   **2002** Ind 2 (0)   **NFL** 35 (1) [5 yrs]

VANCE, JOE   Joseph Albert, WB-FB, 6′1″/180 lbs; Southwest Texas State; Texas; B9/16/1905 Devine, TX, D7/4/1978 San Antonio, TX   **1931** Bkn 11 (4), 12

VANDEN BOSCH, KYLE   Kyle, DE, 6′4″/263 lbs; Nebraska; 2001: Arz, rnd 2; B11/17/1978 Larchwood, IA   **2001** Arz 3 (3)   **2002** Arz 16 (16, RDE)   **2004** Arz 16 (1)
2005 Ten◇16 (16, LDE)   **NFL** 51 (36) [4 yrs]

VANDER KELEN, RON   Ronald, QB, 6′1″/185 lbs; Wisconsin; 1963: NYJ, rnd 21; B11/6/1939 Green Bay, WI

1963	Min	6	8	65	8.1 (20)	0	—	—	—	—	58	27	46.6	376	6.5 (53)	1	2	9	70	—	—	—	0	178
1964	Min	5	1	10	10.0 (10)	0	—	—	—	—	19	7	36.8	78	4.1 (18)	0	1	2	45	—	—	—	0	9
1965	Min	4	4	13	3.3 (20)	0	—	—	—	—	40	18	45.0	252	6.3 (38)	2	0	7	65	—	—	—	0	149
1966	Min	3 (1)	4	19	4.8 (15)	0	—	—	—	—	20	10	50.0	147	7.3 (43)	0	1	1	9	—	—	—	0	53
1967	Min	11	9	9	1.0 (16)	1	—	—	—	—	115	45	39.1	522	4.5 (42)	3	7	6	35	36.9	—	—	6	15
NFL	5	29 (1)	26	116	4.5 (20)	1	—	—	—	—	252	107	42.5	1375	5.5 (53)	6	11	25	224	50.0	—	—	6	404

VANDER POEL, MARK   John Mark, T, 6′7″/303 lbs; Colorado; 1991: Ind, rnd 4; B3/5/1968 Upland, CA   **1991** Ind 10 (1)   **1992** Ind 13 (0)   **NFL** 23 (1) [2 yrs]

VANDERBEEK, MATT   Matthew James, LB, 6′3″/257 lbs; Michigan State; B8/16/1967 Sagautuck, MI   **1990** Ind 16 (7, rilb)   **1991** Ind 5 (1)   **1992** Ind 15 (0)   **1993**†Dal 16 (0)
1994†Dal 12 (0)   **1995** Was 16 (0)   **1996** Was 1 (0)   **NFL** 81 (8) [7 yrs] .

VANDERBUNDT, SKIP   William Gerard, LB, 6′3″/225 lbs; Oregon State; 1968: SF, rnd 3; B12/4/1946 Martinez, CA   **1969** SF 14 (12, RLB)   **1970**†SF 12 (RLB)
1971†SF 14 (14, RLB)   **1972**†SF 14 (14, RLB)   **1973** SF 9   **1974** SF 14   **1975** SF 14 (14, LLB)   **1976** SF 14 (14, LLB)   **1977** SF 14 (14, LLB/mlb)   **1978** NO 15   **NFL** 134 (82) [10 yrs]

VANDERJAGT, MIKE   Michael John, K, 6′5″/211 lbs; West Virginia; B3/24/1970 Oakville, Canada **[K]**   **1998** Ind 14 (0)   **1999**†Ind☆16 (0)   **2000**†Ind 16 (0)   **2001** Ind 16 (0)
2002†Ind 16 (0)   **2003**†Ind★16 (0)   **2004**†Ind 15 (0)   **2005**†Ind 16 (0)   **NFL** 125 (0) [8 yrs]

VANDERLOO, VIV   Vivian Bernard, FB, 5′10″/190 lbs; Iowa State; B4/11/1897 Coon Rapids, IA, D6/18/1972 Mesa, AZ   **1921** RI 3 (3, FB)

VANDERSEA, PHIL   Phillip John, LB-DE, 6′3″/245 lbs; Massachusetts; 1965: GB, rnd 16/Den, rnd R9; B2/25/1943 Whitinsville, MA   **1966**†GB 14   **1967** NO 8   **1968** GB 10
1969 GB 14   **NFL** 46 [4 yrs]

VANDEWEGHE, AL   Alfred Bernard, E-DE, 5′11″/200 lbs; William & Mary; 1946: Phi, rnd 10; B10/25/1920 Wyckoff, NJ

| 1946 | Buf-A | 5 (3) | — | — | — | — | 6 | 67 | 11.2 | 1 | — | — | — | — | — | — | — | — | — | — | k | 1 | 12 | 39 |

VANHORSE, SEAN   Sean Joseph, DB, 5′10″/180 lbs; Howard; 1990: Mia, rnd 6; B7/22/1968 Baltimore, MD   **1992**†SD 16 (9, rcb)   **1993** SD 15 (10, RCB)   **1994**†SD 16 (1)
1995†Det 14 (0)   **1996** Min 9 (0)   **NFL** 70 (20) [5 yrs]

VANN, NORWOOD   Norwood Jacob, LB, 6′1″/228 lbs; East Carolina; 1984: LARm, rnd 10; B2/18/1962 Philadelphia, PA   **1984**†LARm 16 (0)   **1985**†LARm 8 (0)   **1986**†LARm 16 (0)
1987 LARm 11 (0)   **1988** LARd 1 (0)   **NFL** 52 (0) [5 yrs]

VANOVER, TAMARICK   Tamarick, WR, 5′11″/210 lbs; Florida State; 1995: KC, rnd 3; B2/15/1970 Tallahassee, FL **[R]**

1995	†KC	15 (0)	6	31	5.2 (13)	0	11	231	21.0 (57)	2	—	—	—	—	—	—	—	—	—	—	kp	3	30	922
1996	KC☆	13 (6, wr)	4	6	1.5 (6)	0	21	241	11.5 (24)	1	—	—	—	—	—	—	—	—	—	—	kp	1	12	532
1997	†KC☆	16 (0)	5	50	10.0 (17)	0	7	92	13.1 (42)	0	—	—	—	—	—	—	—	—	—	—	kp	2	14	867
1998	KC	12 (0)	2	1	0.5 (2)	0	—	—	—	—	—	—	—	—	—	—	—	—	—	—	kp	—	0	471
1999	KC	14 (0)	—	—	—	—	—	—	—	—	—	—	—	—	—	—	—	—	—	—	kp	2	12	618
2002	SD	7 (0)	—	—	—	—	—	—	—	—	—	—	—	—	—	—	—	—	—	—	kp	—	0	119
NFL	6	77 (6)	17	88	5.2 (17)	0	39	564	14.5 (57)	3	—	—	—	—	—	—	—	—	—	—	kp	8	68	3528

VANOY, VERN   Vernon Eugene, DT, 6′8″/275 lbs; Kansas; 1969: NYG, rnd 3; B12/31/1946 Kansas City, MO   **1971** NYG 6   **1972**†GB 13   **1973** Hou 1   **NFL** 20 [3 yrs]

VANT HULL, FRED   Frederick Nels, G-LB, 6′0″/214 lbs; Minnesota; B8/21/1920 Winnepeg, Canada, D4/10/1975 Minneapolis, MN   **1942** GB 8 (0)

VANZO, FRED   Fred Ferdinand, BB-LB, 6′2″/230 lbs; Northwestern; 1938: NYG, rnd 3; B1/8/1916 Universal, IN, D2/7/1976 Plymouth, MN

1938	Det	10 (7, BB)	—	—	—	—	4	52	13.0	0	—	—	—	—	—	—	—	—	—	—	—	—	0	26
1939	Det★	10 (10, BB)	5	46	9.2	0	4	110	27.5	0	—	—	—	—	—	—	—	—	—	—	—	—	0	101
1940	Det☆	10 (10, BB)	1	-1	-1.0 (-1)	0	7	75	10.7	0	—	—	—	—	—	—	—	—	—	—	—	—	0	37
1941	Det	6 (5, bb)	—	—	—	—	2	20	10.0 (12)	0	—	—	—	—	—	—	—	—	—	—	—	—	0	10
1941	ChiC	3 (1)	—	—	—	—	—	—	—	—	—	—	—	—	—	—	—	—	—	—	—	—	0	—
NFL	4	39 (33)	6	45	7.5	0	17	257	15.1 (12)	0	—	—	—	—	—	—	—	—	—	—	—	—	0	174

VARAJON, MIKE   Michael Joseph, RB, 6′1″/232 lbs; Toledo; B7/12/1964 Detroit, MI

| 1987 | SF | 3 (1) | 18 | 82 | 4.6 (11) | 0 | 3 | 25 | 8.3 (12) | 0 | — | — | — | — | — | — | — | — | — | — | k | — | 0 | 93 |

VARDELL, TOMMY   Thomas Arthur, RB, 6′2″/234 lbs; Stanford; 1992: Cle, rnd 1; B2/20/1969 El Cajon, CA

1992	Cle	14 (10, FB)	99	369	3.7 (35)	4	13	128	9.8 (23)	0	—	—	—	—	—	—	—	—	—	—	k	—	24	417
1993	Cle	16 (12, FB)	171	644	3.8 (54)	3	19	151	7.9 (28)	1	—	—	—	—	—	—	—	—	—	—	k	—	24	753
1994	Cle	5 (5, fb)	15	48	3.2 (9)	0	16	137	8.6 (19)	1	—	—	—	—	—	—	—	—	—	—	—	—	6	122
1995	Cle	4	9	2	2.3 (6)	0	6	18	3.0 (7)	0	—	—	—	—	—	—	—	—	—	—	—	—	0	18
1996	†SF	11 (7, fb)	58	192	3.3 (17)	2	28	179	6.4 (22)	0	—	—	—	—	—	—	—	—	—	—	—	—	12	302
1997	†Det	16 (10, FB)	32	122	3.8 (41)	6	16	218	13.6 (37)	0	—	—	—	—	—	—	—	—	—	—	k	—	36	291
1998	Det	14 (9, FB)	18	37	2.1 (17)	6	14	143	10.2 (31)	1	—	—	—	—	—	—	—	—	—	—	k	—	42	182
1999	SF	6 (4)	6	6	1.0 (5)	1	7	36	5.1 (11)	0	—	—	—	—	—	—	—	—	—	—	—	—	6	34
NFL	8	87 (57)	403	1427	3.5 (54)	18	119	1010	8.5 (37)	3	—	—	—	—	—	—	—	—	—	—	k	—	126	2117

VARDIAN, JOHNNY   John Joseph, HB-DB, 5′8″/167 lbs; none; B9/25/1921 Johnstown, PA, D8/8/1989 Tampa, FL

1946	Mia-A	6 (1)	5	-1	-1.6	0	7	108	15.4	0	1	1	100.0	4	-4.0 (-4)	0	0	—	—	—	k	—	0	52
1947	Bal-A	14 (5, RH)	35	57	1.6	0	16	280	17.5	1	—	—	—	—	—	—	—	—	—	—	kpi	—	6	314
1948	Bal-A	12 (0)	6	13	2.2	0	3	26	8.7	0	—	—	—	—	—	—	—	—	—	—	kp	—	6	66
AAFC	3	32 (6)	46	62	1.3	0	26	414	15.9	1	1	1	100.0	4	-4.0 (-4)	0	0	—	—	—	kpi	—	6	432

VARGO, LARRY   Lawrence F., DB-LB, 6′3″/215 lbs; Detroit Mercy; 1961: Det, rnd 11/Buf, rnd 21; B4/5/1939 Iron Mountain, MI   **1962** Det 9 (1)   **1963** Det 14   **1965** Min 13 (11, RS)
1966 NYG 7 (RLB)

| 1964 | Min | 14 (12, RS) | — | — | — | — | 1 | 13 | 13.0 (13) | 0 | — | — | — | — | — | — | — | — | — | — | i | — | 0 | 2 |
| NFL | 5 | 57 (24) | — | — | — | — | 1 | 13 | 13.0 (13) | 0 | — | — | — | — | — | — | — | — | — | — | ki | 1 | 6 | 41 |

YEAR	TEAM	G (GS, POS)	RUSH	YD	AVG(LG)	TD	REC	YD	AVG(LG)	TD	PASS COMP	PCT	YD	AVG(LG)	TD	INT	SK	YD	QBR	KPR	OTD	PTS	TAY

VARRICHIONE, FRANK Frank Joseph, T, 6´1˝/234 lbs; Notre Dame; 1955: Pit, rnd 1; B1/14/1932 Natick, MA   **1955** Pit◇12 (RT) **1957** Pit☆12 (RT) **1958** Pit☆12 (RT)
1959 Pit☆12 (RT) **1961** LARm 14 (RT) **1962** LARm◇12 (RT) **1963** LARm 14 (RT) **1964** LARm☆10 (RT) **1965** LARm 11

1956	Pit	12(RT)	0	-2	(-2)	0	—	—	—	—	—	—	—	—	—	—	—	—	k	—	0	-9
1960	Pit◇	12(RT)	—	—	—	0	0	-7	(-7)	0	—	—	—	—	—	—	—	—	k	—	0	-19
NFL	11	133	0	-2	(-2)	0	0	-7	(-7)	0	—	—	—	—	—	—	—	—	k	—	0	-57

VARTY, MIKE Michael Scott Matthew, LB, 6´1˝/223 lbs; Northwestern; 1974: Was, rnd 7; B2/10/1952 Detroit, MI   **1974**†Was 2 **1975**†Bal 6 **NFL** 8 [2 yrs]

VASHER, NATHAN Nathaniel DeWayne, DB, 5´11˝/180 lbs; Texas; 2004: Chi, rnd 4; B11/17/1981 Wichita Falls, TX   **2004** ChiB 16 (7, cb) **2005**†ChiB★16 (15, RCB)
NFL 32 (22) [2 yrs]

VASICEK, VIC Victor Frederick, LB-G-DG, 5´11˝/223 lbs; USC; Texas; 1949: Buf-A, rnd 8/Was, rnd 10; B5/5/1926 El Campo, TX, D6/20/2003 Midland, TX   **1950**†LARm 12 (LLB)

| 1949 | †Buf-A | 12(3) | — | — | — | 0 | 5 | — | 0 | — | — | — | — | — | — | — | — | — | — | — | 0 | 3 |

VASSAU, ROY Roy E., T, 6´0˝/220 lbs; St. Thomas; B12/1893 St. Paul, MN, deceased   **1923** Mil 1 (1)

VASYS, ARUNAS Arunas Bruno, LB, 6´2˝/235 lbs; Notre Dame; 1966: Phi, rnd 16; B8/18/1943 Lithuania   **1966** Phi 10 **1967** Phi 9 **1968** Phi 3 **NFL** 22 [3 yrs]

VATAHA, RANDY Randel Edward, WR, 5´10˝/176 lbs; Stanford; 1971: LA, rnd 17; B12/4/1948 Santa Maria, CA

1971	NE	14(13, WR)	—	—	—	—	51	872	17.1(88)	9	—	—	—	—	—	—	—	—	—	—	54	481
1972	NE	14(14, WR)	—	—	—	—	25	369	14.8(44)	2	—	—	—	—	—	—	—	—	—	—	12	195
1973	NE	14(4)	2	-15	-7.5(-4)	0	20	341	17.0(48)	2	—	—	—	—	—	—	—	—	—	1	18	166
1974	NE	12(9, WR)	3	21	7.0(24)	0	25	561	22.4(59)	3	—	—	—	—	—	—	—	—	—	—	18	317
1975	NE	14(14, WR)	1	4	4.0(4)	0	46	720	15.7(47)	6	—	—	—	—	—	—	—	—	—	—	36	394
1976	†NE	12(8, WR)	—	—	—	—	11	192	17.5(44)	1	—	—	—	—	—	—	—	—	—	—	6	101
1977	GB	6	—	—	—	—	10	109	10.9(20)	0	—	—	—	—	—	—	—	—	—	—	0	55
NFL	7	86(62)	6	10	1.7(24)	0	188	3164	16.8(88)	23	—	—	—	—	—	—	—	—	—	1	144	1707

VATTEROTT, CHARLES Charles Francis, G-T, 6´4˝/263 lbs; Southwest Texas State; B1/31/1964 St. Louis, MO   **1987** SL 2 (1)

VAUGHAN, HARP John J., B, 5´7˝/150 lbs; none; B11/19/1903, PA, D12/26/1976 Macclenny, FL

1933	Pit	8(1)	26	74	2.8	1	6	101	16.8	0	8	2	25.0	2	0.3	0	3	—	—	—	6	16
1934	Pit	11(7, bb)	58	196	3.4	0	2	56	28.0	0	42	19	45.2	262	6.2(62)	2	5	—	—	—	0	165
NFL	2	19(8)	84	270	3.2	1	8	157	19.6	0	50	21	42.0	264	5.3(62)	2	8	—	—	—	6	181

VAUGHAN, PUG Charles Wesley, TB, 5´11˝/181 lbs; Tennessee; B3/18/1911 Knoxville, TN, D3/30/1964 Knoxville, TN

1935	†Det	7(1)	13	51	3.9	0	9	9.0(9)	0	15	7	46.7	104	6.9	2	2	—	—	—	0	38
1936	ChiC	12(1)	67	79	1.2	0	—	—	—	79	30	38.0	546	6.9	2	10	—	—	—	0	-38
NFL	2	19(2)	80	130	1.6	0	9	9.0(9)	0	94	37	39.4	650	6.9	4	12	—	—	—	0	-1

VAUGHAN, RUBEN Ruben Charles, DT-NT-DE, 6´2˝/261 lbs; Colorado; 1979: SF, rnd 6; B8/5/1956 Los Angeles, CA   **1979** SF 13 (1) **1982**†LARd 9 (0) **1984** Min 5 (0)
NFL 27 (1) [3 yrs]

VAUGHN, CLARENCE Clarence, DB, 6´0˝/202 lbs; Northern Illinois; 1987: Was, rnd 8; B7/17/1964 Chicago, IL   **1987**†Was 5 (0) **1988** Was 14 (0) **1989** Was 16 (4) **1990** Was 1 (0)
1991 Was 12 (0) **NFL** 48 (4) [5 yrs]

VAUGHN, DARRICK Darrick, DB, 5´11˝/193 lbs; Southwest Texas State; 2000: Atl, rnd 7; B10/2/1978 Houston, TX [R]   **2000** Atl☆16 (0) **2001** Atl 16 (0) **2003** Hou 16 (0)
NFL 48 (0) [3 yrs]

VAUGHN, JON Jonathan Stewart, RB, 5´9˝/203 lbs; Michigan; 1991: NE, rnd 5; B3/12/1970 Florissant, MO [R]

1991	NE	16(2)	31	146	4.7(23)	2	9	89	9.9(32)	0	2	1	50.0	13	6.5(13)	1	0	—	—	—	k	1	18	439
1992	NE☆	16(5, rb)	113	451	4.0(36)	1	13	84	6.5(28)	0	—	—	—	—	—	—	—	—	—	k	1	12	777
1993	Sea	16(2)	36	153	4.3(37)	0	—	—	—	—	—	—	—	—	—	—	—	—	k	0	193
1994	Sea	9(0)	27	96	3.6(16)	1	1	5	5.0(5)	1	—	—	—	—	—	—	—	—	—	k	1	20	297
1994	†KC	3(0)	—	—	—	—	—	—	—	—	—	—	—	—	—	—	—	—	—	k	1	6	171
NFL	4	60(9)	207	846	4.1(37)	4	23	178	7.7(32)	1	2	1	50.0	13	6.5(13)	1	0	—	—	—	k	4	56	1877

VAUGHN, KHALEED Khaleed, DE, 6´4˝/276 lbs; Clemson; B5/20/1981 Atlanta, GA   **2004**†Atl 3 (0)

VAUGHN, BOB Robert Curtis, G, 6´4˝/230 lbs; Mississippi; 1968: Den, rnd 3; B6/8/1945 Memphis, TN   **1968** Den-A 1

VAUGHN, TOM Thomas Robert, DB, 5´11˝/190 lbs; Iowa State; 1965: Det, rnd 5/Den, rnd 11; B2/28/1943 Troy, OH   **1965** Det 14 **1966** Det 13 **1967** Det 14 (RS)
1968 Det 13 (RS) **1969** Det 14 (RS) **1970**†Det 11 (fs) **1971** Det 9 (FS) **NFL** 88 [7 yrs]

VAUGHN, BILL William Lee, B, 5´10˝/192 lbs; SMU; B1/10/1902 Van Zandt County, TX, D4/21/1971 Mesquite, TX   **1926** Buf 10 (2)

VAUGHT, TED Teddy Gene, DE-E, 6´0˝/208 lbs; TCU; B7/19/1932 Littlefield, TX   **1955** SF 2

VEACH, WALT William Walter, HB, 5´11˝/180 lbs; none; B9/29/1892, D2/1976 Vienna, IL   **1920** Dec 2 (0)

VEAL, DEMETRIN Demetrin Leeotis, DE, 6´2˝/288 lbs; Tennessee; 2003: Atl, rnd 7; B8/11/1981 Paramount, CA   **2003** Atl 3 (0) **2005**†Den 15 (0) **NFL** 18 (0) [2 yrs]

VEALS, ELTON Elton Alvin, RB, 5´11˝/230 lbs; Tulane; 1984: Pit, rnd 11; B3/26/1961 Baton Rouge, LA

| 1984 | †Pit | 15(1) | 31 | 87 | 2.8(9) | 0 | — | — | — | — | — | — | — | — | — | — | — | — | k | — | 0 | 67 |

VEASEY, CRAIG Anthony Craig, DT, 6´2˝/285 lbs; Houston; 1990: Pit, rnd 3; B12/25/1966 Clear Lake, TX   **1990** Pit 10 (0) **1991** Pit 13 (2) **1992** Hou 4 (0) **1993** Hou 1 (0)
1993 Mia 14 (0) **1994**†Mia 12 (1) **1995** Hou 15 (2) **NFL** 69 (5) [6 yrs]

VEDDER, LOU Louis D., FB, 5´7˝/165 lbs; none; B4/20/1897 Ypsilanti, MI, D3/1990 Avon Park, FL   **1927** Buf 2 (0)

VEINGARD, ALAN Alan Stuart, T-G, 6´5˝/277 lbs; Texas A&M-Commerce; B7/24/1963 Brooklyn, NY   **1986** GB 16 (16, RT) **1987** GB 11 (2) **1989** GB 16 (16, RT) **1990** GB 16 (4)
1991†Dal 16 (4) **1992** Dal 11 (1) **NFL** 86 (43) [6 yrs]

VELAND, TONY Tony Marceles, DB, 6´1˝/209 lbs; Nebraska; 1996: Den, rnd 6; B3/11/1973 Omaha, NE   **1997**†Den 12 (0) **1998** Car 15 (5, fs) **NFL** 27 (5) [2 yrs]

VELLA, JOHN John, T, 6´4˝/258 lbs; USC; 1972: Oak, rnd 2; B4/21/1950 Cleveland, OH   **1972** Oak 14 **1973**†Oak 14 (4) **1974**†Oak 13 (13, RT) **1975**†Oak 13 (13, RT)
1976†Oak 14 (RT) **1977**†Oak 5 (3) **1979** Oak 11 **1980** Min 8 (0) **NFL** 92 (33) [8 yrs]

VELLONE, JIM James Carl, G, 6´3˝/255 lbs; USC; B8/20/1944 Camp Lejeune, NC, D8/21/1977 Huntington Beach, CA   **1966** Min 14 (9, RG) **1967** Min 14 (8, lg)
1968†Min 14 (14, LG) **1969**†Min 13 (13, LG) **1970**†Min 11 (8, LG) **NFL** 66 (52) [5 yrs]

VENTURELLI, FRED Fred, K, 5´11˝/235 lbs; none; B8/22/1917 Farmington, IL, D1/20/1990 Racine, WI [K]   **1948** ChiB 1 (0)

VENUTO, SAM Samuel Joseph, HB, 6´1˝/195 lbs; Guilford; B11/2/1927 Havertown, PA

| 1952 | Was | 3 | 4 | 16 | 4.0(6) | 1 | — | — | — | — | — | — | — | — | — | — | — | — | k | — | 6 | 24 |

VERBA, ROSS Ross Robert, T-G, 6´4˝/308 lbs; Iowa; 1997: GB, rnd 1; B10/31/1973 Des Moines, IA   **1997**†GB 16 (11, LT) **1998**†GB 16 (16, LT) **1999** GB 11 (10, LT)
2000 GB 16 (16, LG) **2001** Cle 15 (15, LG) **2002** Cle 16 (16, LT) **2004** Cle 16 (16, LT) **NFL** 106 (100) [7 yrs]

VERDIN, CLARENCE Clarence, WR, 5´8˝/160 lbs; Louisiana-Lafayette; 1984: Was, rnd S3; B6/14/1963 New Orleans, LA [R]

1986	Was	8(0)	—	—	—	—	—	—	—	—	—	—	—	—	—	—	—	—	k	—	0	60
1987	Was	3(1)	1	14	14.0(14)	0	2	62	31.0(55)	0	—	—	—	—	—	—	—	—	—	k	—	0	109
1988	Ind	16(11, WR)	8	77	9.6(44)	0	20	437	21.9(54)	4	—	—	—	—	—	—	—	—	—	kp	1	30	495
1989	Ind☆	16(7, wr)	4	39	9.8(26)	0	20	381	19.0(82)	2	—	—	—	—	—	—	—	—	—	kp	1	12	512
1990	Ind★	15(5, wr)	—	—	—	—	14	178	12.7(45)	0	—	—	—	—	—	—	—	—	—	kp	0	415
1991	Ind	16(0)	1	4	4.0(4)	0	21	214	10.2(28)	2	—	—	—	—	—	—	—	—	—	kp	1	6	310
1992	Ind★	16(1)	—	—	—	—	3	37	12.3(21)	0	—	—	—	—	—	—	—	—	—	kp	2	12	417
1993	Ind	16(0)	3	33	11.0(29)	0	20	10.0(19)	1	—	—	—	—	—	—	—	—	—	kp	2	12	417
1994	Atl	12(0)	—	—	—	—	—	—	—	—	—	—	—	—	—	—	—	—	kp	—	0	364
NFL	9	118(25)	17	167	9.8(44)	0	82	1329	16.2(82)	7	—	—	—	—	—	—	—	—	—	kp	5	72	3052

VERDON, JIMMY Jimmy, DT, 6´3˝/280 lbs; Arizona State; 2005: NO, rnd 7; B11/4/1981 Pomona, CA   **2005** NO 4 (0)

YEAR	TEAM	G (GS, POS)	RUSH	YD	AVG(LG)	TD	REC	YD	AVG(LG)	TD	PASS COMP	PCT	YD	AVG(LG)	TD	INT	SK	YD	QBR	KPR	OTD	PTS	TAY

VEREB, ED Edward John, HB, 6´0˝/190 lbs; Maryland; 1956: Was, rnd 1; B5/21/1934 Pittsburgh, PA

| 1960 | Was | 9 | 19 | 38 | 2.0(15) | 0 | 9 | 119 | 13.2(26) | 0 | 1 | 0 | 0.0 | 0 | 0.0 | 0 | 0 | — | — | kp | — | 0 | 137 |

VEREEN, CARL Carl Harry, T, 6´2˝/247 lbs; Georgia Tech; 1957: GB, rnd 4; B1/27/1936 Miami, FL   **1957** GB 12

VERGARA, GEORGE George Aloysius, E, 6´1˝/190 lbs; Fordham; Notre Dame; B3/18/1901 New York, NY, D8/13/1982 Montrose, NY   **1925** GB 12 (10, RE)

VERHULST, CHRIS Christopher Sean, TE, 6´3˝/249 lbs; Cal State-Chico; 1988: Hou, rnd 5; B5/16/1966 Sacramento, CA

1988	Hou	1(0)	—	—	—	—	—	—	—	—	—	—	—	—	—	—	—	—	—	k	—	0	9
1989	†Hou	16(0)	—	—	—	—	4	48	12.0(21)	0	—	—	—	—	—	—	—	—	—	k	—	0	7
1990	Den	11(1)	—	—	—	—	3	13	4.3(6)	0	—	—	—	—	—	—	—	—	—	k	—	0	7
NFL	3	28(1)	—	—	—	—	7	61	8.7(21)	0	—	—	—	—	—	—	—	—	—	k	—	0	16

VERIS, GARIN Garin Lee, DE, 6´4˝/255 lbs; Stanford; 1985: NE, rnd 2; B2/27/1963 Chillicothe, OH   **1985**†NE 16 (4) **1986**†NE 16 (15, RDE) **1987** NE 12 (12, RDE) **1988** NE 11 (9, RDE) **1990** NE 7 (2) **1991** NE 16 (4) **1992** SF 10 (0) **NFL** 88 (46) [7 yrs]

VERRY, NORM David Norman, T, 6´1˝/240 lbs; USC; 1943: GB, rnd 9; B9/18/1922 Hanford, CA   **1946** ChiR-A 10 (3) **1947** ChiR-A 1 (1) **AAFC** 11 (4) [2 yrs]

VERSER, DAVID David, WR, 6´1˝/200 lbs; Kansas; 1981: Cin, rnd 1; B3/1/1958 Kansas City, KS

1981	†Cin	16(0)	2	11	5.5(9)	0	6	161	26.8(73)	2	—	—	—	—	—	—	—	—	—	k	—	12	358
1982	†Cin	9(0)	1	1	1.0(1)	0	4	98	24.5(56)	1	—	—	—	—	—	—	—	—	—	k	—	6	135
1983	Cin	13(0)	2	31	15.5(29)	0	7	82	11.7(22)	0	—	—	—	—	—	—	—	—	—	k	—	0	130
1984	Cin	11(0)	2	5	2.5(3)	0	6	113	18.8(28)	0	—	—	—	—	—	—	—	—	—	k	—	0	63
1985	TB	1(0)	—	—	—	—	—	—	—	—	—	—	—	—	—	—	—	—	—	k	—	0	1
1987	Cle	2(1)	1	9	9.0(9)	0	—	—	—	—	—	—	—	—	—	—	—	—	—	—	—	0	9
NFL	6	52(1)	8	57	7.1(29)	0	23	454	19.7(73)	3	—	—	—	—	—	—	—	—	—	k	—	18	695

VERSTEGEN, MIKE Michael Robert, G-T, 6´6˝/311 lbs; Wisconsin; 1995: NO, rnd 3; B10/24/1971 Appleton, WI   **1996** NO 8 (4) **1997** NO 14 (8, RG) **NFL** 22 (12) [2 yrs]

VERTEFEUILLE, BRIAN Brian Lionel, T, 6´3˝/252 lbs; Idaho State; 1974: SD, rnd 13; B4/4/1951 Willimantic, CT   **1974** SD 14 (1)

VESSELS, BILLY Billy Dale, HB, 6´0˝/190 lbs; Oklahoma; 1953: Bal, rnd 1; B3/22/1931 Cleveland, OK, D11/17/2001 Coral Gables, FL

| 1956 | Bal | 12 | 44 | 215 | 4.9(31) | 2 | 11 | 177 | 16.1(30) | 1 | — | — | — | — | — | — | — | — | — | k | — | 18 | 468 |

VESSER, JOHN John Martin, E, 6´0˝/186 lbs; Idaho; B10/1/1900 Coeur d'Alene, ID, D3/20/1996 Pocatello, ID   **1927** ChiC 11 (7, RE), 6 **1930** ChiC 9 (6, le) **1931** ChiC 1 (1) **NFL** 21 (14) [3 yrs]

VETRANO, JOE Joseph George, HB-DB, 5´9˝/170 lbs; Southern Mississippi; B10/15/1918 Neptune, NJ, D5/10/1995 Berkeley, CA **[K]**

1946	SF-A	13(2)	23	69	3.0	1	4	37	9.3	0	—	—	—	—	—	—	—	—	—	KPkpi	—	49	168
1947	SF-A	14(2)	10	11	1.1	0	—	—	—	—	—	—	—	—	—	—	—	—	—	Kkp	—	50	130
1948	SF-A	14(1)	12	71	5.9	1	1	34	34.0(34)	0	—	—	—	—	—	—	—	—	—	KPk	—	83	121
1949	†SF-A	12(0)	11	50	4.5	0	—	—	—	—	—	—	—	—	—	—	—	—	—	Kp	—	65	61
AAFC	4	53(5)	56	201	3.6	2	5	71	14.2(34)	0	—	—	—	—	—	—	—	—	—	KPkpi	—	247	480

VETTER, JACK Jack Robbins, HB-DB, 6´2˝/198 lbs; McPherson; B10/30/1920 Kansas City, MO

| 1942 | Bkn | 4(0) | 1 | 4 | 4.0(4) | 0 | — | — | — | — | — | — | — | — | — | — | — | — | — | — | — | 0 | 4 |

VEXALL, ROY Roy, FB, /190 lbs; none; B6/6/1902, D5/82 Blaine, MN   **1924** Dul 2 (1) **1925** Dul 1 (0) **NFL** 3 (1) [2 yrs]

VEZMAR, WALT Walter, G, 5´11˝/235 lbs; Michigan State; 1947: Det, rnd 13; B1/1/1925 Detroit, MI, D5/28/1981 Pollock, LA   **1946** Det 11 (0) **1947** Det 2 (0) **NFL** 13 (0) [2 yrs]

VIAENE, DAVID David Ronald, C-T-G, 6´5˝/300 lbs; Wisconsin-Platteville; Minnesota-Duluth; 1988: Hou, rnd 8; B7/14/1965 Appleton, WI   **1989** NE 16 (4) **1990** NE 4 (4) **1992** GB 1 (0) **NFL** 21 (8) [3 yrs]

VICK, DICK Richard D., WB-BB-TB, 5´9˝/167 lbs; Washington & Jefferson; B4/16/1892 Edwards Township, MN, D9/1980 Bozeman, MT   **1924** Ken 5 (4, WB) **1925** Det 11 (8, BB) **1926** Det 6 (4) **1926** Can 7 (7, WB) **NFL** 29 (23) [3 yrs]

VICK, ERNIE Henry Arthur, C-G-T, 5´10˝/190 lbs; Michigan; B7/2/1900 Toledo, OH, D7/16/1980 Ann Arbor, MI   **1925** Det 10 (8, C) **1927** ChiB 10 (7, c) **1928** ChiB 1 (0) **1928** Det 6 (2) **NFL** 27 (17) [3 yrs]

VICK, MICHAEL Michael Dwayne 'Superman', QB, 6´0˝/215 lbs; Virginia Tech; 2001: Atl, rnd 1; B6/26/1980 Newport News, VA

2001	Atl	8(2)	31	289	9.3(35)	1	—	—	—	—	113	50	44.2	785	6.9(52)	2	3	21	113	62.7	—	—	6	582
2002	†Atl◇	15(15, QB)	113	777	6.9(46)	8	0	16	(16)	0	421	231	54.9	2936	7.0(74)	16	8	33	206	81.6	—	—	48	2093
2003	Atl	5(4)	40	255	6.4(43)	1	—	—	—	—	100	50	50.0	585	5.8(49)	4	3	9	64	69.0	—	—	6	458
2004	†Atl◇	15(15, QB)	120	902	7.5(58)	3	—	—	—	—	321	181	56.4	2313	7.2(62)	14	12	46	266	78.1	—	—	18	1679
2005	Atl◇	15(15, QB)	102	597	5.9(32)	6	1	-14	-14.0(-14)	0	387	214	55.3	2412	6.2(58)	15	13	33	201	73.1	—	—	36	1411
NFL	5	58(51)	406	2820	6.9(58)	19	1	2	2.0(16)	0	1342	726	54.1	9031	6.7(74)	51	39	142	850	75.8	—	—	114	6222

VICK, ROGER Roger Hamilton, RB, 6´3˝/239 lbs; Texas A&M; 1987: NYJ, rnd 1; B8/11/1964 Conroe, TX

1987	NYJ	12(10, FB)	77	257	3.3(14)	1	13	108	8.3(32)	0	—	—	—	—	—	—	—	—	—	—	—	6	321
1988	NYJ	16(12, FB)	128	540	4.2(17)	3	19	120	6.3(17)	0	—	—	—	—	—	—	—	—	—	—	—	18	630
1989	NYJ	16(10, FB)	112	434	3.9(39)	5	34	241	7.1(21)	2	—	—	—	—	—	—	—	—	—	k	—	42	615
1990	†Phi	14(0)	16	58	3.6(17)	1	—	—	—	—	—	—	—	—	—	—	—	—	—	k	—	6	60
NFL	4	58(32)	333	1289	3.9(39)	10	66	469	7.1(23)	2	—	—	—	—	—	—	—	—	—	k	—	72	1626

VICKERS, KIPP Kipp, T-G, 6´2˝/300 lbs; Miami (FL); B8/27/1969 Holiday, FL   **1995**†Ind 9 (0) **1996** Ind 10 (6, LT) **1997** Ind 9 (0) **1999**†Was 11 (0) **2000**†Bal 12 (2) **2001**†Bal 16 (14, RT/rg) **2002** Was 5 (2) **NFL** 72 (24) [7 yrs]

VIDAL, GENE Eugene Luther, FB, 5´10˝/170 lbs; Nebraska; South Dakota; Army; B4/13/1895 Madison, SD, D2/20/1969 Palos Verdes, CA   **1921** Was 1 (1)

VIDONI, VIC Victor Joseph, E-DE, 6´1˝/210 lbs; Duquesne; B12/8/1912 Fostoria, OH, D10/17/1994 Black Horse, OH

1935	Pit	11(8, LE)	—	—	—	—	11	111	10.1	0	—	—	—	—	—	—	—	—	—	—	—	0	56
1936	Pit	2(2)	—	—	—	—	2	35	17.5	0	—	—	—	—	—	—	—	—	—	—	—	0	18
NFL	2	13(10)	—	—	—	—	13	146	11.2	0	—	—	—	—	—	—	—	—	—	—	—	0	73

VIGORITO, TOMMY Thomas J., RB-WR, 5´10˝/193 lbs; Virginia; 1981: Mia, rnd 5; B10/23/1959 Passaic, NJ **[R]**

1981	†Mia	16(1)	35	116	3.3(30)	1	33	237	7.2(31)	2	—	—	—	—	—	—	—	—	—	kp	1	24	488
1982	†Mia	9(1)	19	99	5.2(33)	1	24	186	7.8(26)	0	—	—	—	—	—	—	—	—	—	p	1	12	304
1983	Mia	1(0)	—	—	—	—	1	7	7.0(7)	0	—	—	—	—	—	—	—	—	—	p	—	0	61
1985	†Mia	9(0)	—	—	—	—	1	9	9.0(9)	0	—	—	—	—	—	—	—	—	—	p	—	0	92
NFL	4	35(2)	54	215	4.0(33)	2	59	439	7.4(31)	2	—	—	—	—	—	—	—	—	—	kp	2	36	944

VILLA, DANNY Daniel, T-C-G, 6´5˝/304 lbs; Arizona State; 1987: NE, rnd 5; B9/21/1964 Nogales, AZ   **1987** NE 11 (7, LT) **1988** NE 16 (14, LT) **1989** NE 15 (15, LT) **1990** NE 16 (16, RT/c) **1991** NE 10 (10, RG) **1992** Phx 16 (12, RT/c) **1993**†KC 13 (3) **1994**†KC 14 (0) **1995**†KC 16 (0) **1996** KC 16 (0) **1997**†NE 7 (0) **1998** Car 7 (0) **NFL** 157 (77) [12 yrs]

VILLANUCCI, VINCE Vincent Anthony, NT, 6´2˝/265 lbs; Bowling Green State; B5/30/1964 Lorain, OH   **1987** GB 2 (0)

VILLANUEVA, DANNY Daniel Dario, K, 5´11˝/200 lbs; New Mexico State; B11/5/1937 Tucumcari, NM **[KP]**   **1960** LARm 12 **1962** LARm 14 **1963** LARm 14 **1964** LARm 14 **1965** Dal 14

1961	LARm	14	—	—	—	—	—	—	—	—	1	0	0.0	0	0.0	0	0	0	0	—	KP	—	71	0
1966	†Dal	14	1	23	23.0(23)	0	—	—	—	—	—	—	—	—	—	—	—	—	—	KP	—	107	23
1967	†Dal	14	1	-15	-15.0(-15)	0	—	—	—	—	—	—	—	—	—	—	—	—	—	KP	—	56	-15
NFL	8	110	2	8	—	—	—	—	—	—	1	0	0.0	0	0.0	0	0	0	0	—	KP	—	491	8

VILLAPIANO, PHIL Philip James, LB, 6´2˝/225 lbs; Bowling Green State; 1971: Oak, rnd 2; B2/26/1949 Long Branch, NJ   **1971** Oak 14 (14, LLB) **1972** Oak☆14 (14, LLB) **1973**†Oak★14 (14, LLB) **1974**†Oak★14 (14, LLB) **1975**†Oak★14 (13, LLB) **1976**†Oak★14 (14, LOLB) **1977** Oak 2 (2) **1978** Oak 16 (16, ROLB) **1979** Oak 16 (16, RILB) **1980**†Buf 16 (0) **1981**†Buf 16 (4) **1982** Buf 9 (0) **1983** Buf 4 (0) **NFL** 163 (121) [13 yrs]

VILLARRIAL, CHRIS Chris, G-C, 6´3˝/318 lbs; Indiana (PA); 1996: Chi, rnd 5; B6/9/1973 Hummelstown, PA   **1996** ChiB 14 (8, rg) **1997** ChiB 11 (11, C) **1998** ChiB 16 (16, RG) **1999** ChiB 15 (15, RG) **2000** ChiB 16 (16, RG) **2001**†ChiB 16 (16, RG) **2002** ChiB 15 (15, RG) **2003** ChiB 13 (13, RG) **2004** Buf 16 (16, RG) **2005** Buf 15 (15, RG) **NFL** 147 (140) [10 yrs]

YEAR	TEAM	G (GS, POS)	RUSH	YD	AVG (LG)	TD	REC	YD	AVG (LG)	TD	PASS	COMP	PCT	YD	AVG (LG)	TD	INT	SK	YD	QBR	KPR	OTD	PTS	TAY

VILMA, JONATHAN Jonathan Polynice, LB, 6´2˝/220 lbs; Miami (FL); 2004: NYJ, rnd 1; B4/16/1982 Coral Gables, FL **2004**†NYJ 16 (14, MLB) **2005** NYJ✧16 (16, MLB) **NFL** 32 (30) [2 yrs]

VILTZ, THEOPHILE Theophile Anthony, DB, 6´2˝/190 lbs; USC; 1964: Dal, rnd 18; B4/20/1943 Lafayette, LA **1966** Hou-A 14 (LCB)

VINATIERI, ADAM Adam Matthew, K, 6´0˝/202 lbs; South Dakota State; B12/28/1972 Yankton, SD **[K]** **1996**†NE 16 (0) **1997**†NE 16 (0) **1998**†NE 16 (0) **1999** NE 16 (0) **2000** NE 16 (0) **2001**†NE 16 (0) **2002** NE★16 (0) **2003**†NE 16 (0) **2005**†NE 16 (0)

YEAR	TEAM	G (GS, POS)	RUSH	YD	AVG (LG)	TD	REC	YD	AVG (LG)	TD	PASS	COMP	PCT	YD	AVG (LG)	TD	INT	SK	YD	QBR	KPR	OTD	PTS	TAY
2004	†NE★	16(0)	—	—	—	—	—	—	—	—	1	1	100.0	4	4.0(4)	1	0	—	—	—	K	—	**141**	7
NFL	10	160(0)	—	—	—	—	—	—	—	—	1	1	100.0	4	4.0(4)	1	0	—	—	—	KP	—	1158	7

VINCE, RALPH Ralph D., G, 5´8˝/175 lbs; Washington & Jefferson; B3/18/1900 Vinci, Italy, D10/29/1996 Shaker Heights, OH **1923** Cle 7 (7, RG) **1925** Cle 6 (4) **NFL** 13 (11) [2 yrs]

VINCENT, KEYDRICK Keydrick Trepell, G, 6´5˝/330 lbs; Mississippi; B4/13/1978 Bartow, FL **2001**†Pit 5 (1) **2002**†Pit 7 (1) **2003** Pit 10 (9, LG) **2004**†Pit 16 (16, RG) **2005** Bal 9 (9, RG) **NFL** 47 (36) [5 yrs]

VINCENT, SHAWN Shawn David, DB, 5´10˝/180 lbs; Akron; B6/2/1968 Bellaire, OH **1991** Pit 10 (1)

VINCENT, TED Theodore Michael, DT, 6´4˝/262 lbs; Wichita State; 1978: Cin, rnd 3; B8/10/1956 O'Fallon, MO **1978** Cin 16 **1979** SF 16 (15, LDT) **1980** SF 12 (10, RDT) **NFL** 44 (25) [3 yrs]

VINCENT, TROY Troy Darnell, DB, 6´1˝/200 lbs; Wisconsin; 1992: Mia, rnd 1; B6/8/1971 Trenton, NJ **[I]** **1992**†Mia 15 (14, LCB) **1993** Mia 13 (13, LCB) **1994**†Mia 13 (12, LCB) **1995**†Mia 16 (16, LCB) **1996**†Phi 16 (16, LCB) **1997** Phi 16 (16, LCB) **1998** Phi 13 (13, LCB) **1999** Phi✧14 (14, LCB) **2000**†Phi★16 (16, LCB) **2001**†Phi★15 (15, LCB) **2002**†Phi★15 (15, LCB) **2003**†Phi✧13 (13, LCB) **2004** Buf 7 (7, fs) **2005** Buf 16 (16, FS) **NFL** 198 (196) [14 yrs]

VINES, SCOTTIE Scott Blaine, WR, 6´2˝/220 lbs; Wyoming; B4/17/1979 Alexander City, AL

YEAR	TEAM	G (GS, POS)	RUSH	YD	AVG (LG)	TD	REC	YD	AVG (LG)	TD	PASS	COMP	PCT	YD	AVG (LG)	TD	INT	SK	YD	QBR	KPR	OTD	PTS	TAY
2004	Det	6(1)	—	—	—	—	3	51	17.0(26)	0	—	—	—	—	—	—	—	—	—	—	—	—	0	26
2005	Det	13(11, WR)	1	7	7.0(7)	0	40	417	10.4(40)	0	—	—	—	—	—	—	—	—	—	—	—	—	0	216
NFL	2	19(12)	1	7	7.0(7)	0	43	468	10.9(40)	0	—	—	—	—	—	—	—	—	—	—	—	—	0	241

VINNOLA, PAUL Paul Peter, HB-DB, 5´10˝/180 lbs; Santa Clara; B8/24/1922 Denver, CO, D10/23/1994 Denver, CO

YEAR	TEAM	G (GS, POS)	RUSH	YD	AVG (LG)	TD	REC	YD	AVG (LG)	TD	PASS	COMP	PCT	YD	AVG (LG)	TD	INT	SK	YD	QBR	KPR	OTD	PTS	TAY
1946	LAD-A	13(0)	23	36	1.6	0	4	39	9.8	0	—	—	—	—	—	—	—	—	—	—	kpi	—	0	77

VINSON, FERNANDUS Fernandus Lamar, DB, 5´10˝/197 lbs; North Carolina State; 1991: Cin, rnd 7; B11/3/1968 Montgomery, AL **1991** Cin 13 (0) **1992** Cin 13 (4) **1993** Cin 16 (7, ss) **1994** Cin 16 (4) **NFL** 58 (15) [4 yrs]

VINSON, FRED Fred, DB, 5´11˝/180 lbs; Vanderbilt; 1999: GB, rnd 2; B4/2/1977 Aiken, SC **1999** GB 16 (1)

VINSON, TONY Anthony Cho, RB, 6´1˝/229 lbs; Purdue; Towson State; 1994: SD, rnd 5; B3/13/1971 Frankfurt, Germany **1997** Bal 13 (0) **1999** Bal 3 (0) **NFL** 16 (0) [2 yrs]

VINYARD, KEN Kenneth Raymond, K, 5´10˝/190 lbs; Texas Tech; 1969: GB, rnd 6; B6/18/1947 Amarillo, TX **[K]** **1970** Atl 14

VIRKUS, SCOTT Scott, DE, 6´5˝/260 lbs; Purdue; B9/7/1959 Rochester, MN **1983** Buf 15 (0) **1984** Buf 2 (0) **1984** NE 5 (0) **1984** Ind 1 (0) **1985** Ind 15 (0) **NFL** 38 (0) [3 yrs]

VISGER, GEORGE George Anthony, DT, 6´4˝/250 lbs; Colorado; 1980: NYJ, rnd 6; B9/26/1958 Stockton, CA **1980** SF 3 (0)

VISNIC, LARRY Lawrence, G-LB-BB, 5´11˝/190 lbs; Benedictine; 1943: NYG, rnd 8; B4/7/1919 Jacobsburg, OH **1943**†NYG 7 (0) **1944** NYG 7 (0) **1945** NYG 8 (4, LG) **NFL** 22 (4) [3 yrs]

VITAL, LIONEL Lionel, RB, 5´9˝/195 lbs; Nicholls State; 1985: Was, rnd 7; B7/15/1963 New Iberia, LA

YEAR	TEAM	G (GS, POS)	RUSH	YD	AVG (LG)	TD	REC	YD	AVG (LG)	TD	PASS	COMP	PCT	YD	AVG (LG)	TD	INT	SK	YD	QBR	KPR	OTD	PTS	TAY
1987	Was	3(3)	80	346	4.3(22)	2	1	13	13.0(13)	0	—	—	—	—	—	—	—	—	—	—	k	—	12	374

VITIELLO, SANDRO Sandro, K, 6´2˝/197 lbs; Massachusetts; 1980: Cin, rnd 10; B2/21/1958 Broccastella, Italy **[K]** **1980** Cin 2 (0)

VLASIC, MARK Mark Richard, QB, 6´3˝/205 lbs; Iowa; 1987: SD, rnd 4; B10/25/1963 Rochester, PA

YEAR	TEAM	G (GS, POS)	RUSH	YD	AVG (LG)	TD	REC	YD	AVG (LG)	TD	PASS	COMP	PCT	YD	AVG (LG)	TD	INT	SK	YD	QBR	KPR	OTD	PTS	TAY
1987	SD	1(0)	—	—	—	—	—	—	—	—	6	3	50.0	8	1.3(7)	0	1	1	13	—	—	—	0	-36
1988	SD	2(2)	2	0	0.0(0)	0	—	—	—	—	52	25	48.1	270	5.2(57)	1	2	3	32	—	—	—	0	60
1990	SD	6(1)	1	0	0.0(0)	0	—	—	—	—	40	19	47.5	168	4.2(27)	1	2	—	—	—	—	—	0	9
1991	†KC	6(0)	1	-1	-1.0(-1)	0	—	—	—	—	44	28	63.6	316	7.2(30)	2	0	2	16	—	—	—	0	167
NFL	4	15(3)	4	-1	-0.3	0	—	—	—	—	142	75	52.8	762	5.4(57)	4	5	6	61	—	—	—	0	200

VODICKA, JOE Joseph J., HB, 5´10˝/189 lbs; Illinois State; B3/4/1921 Chicago, IL, D2/1985 Chicago, IL **1943**†ChiB 3 (0) **1945** ChiB 4 (2)

YEAR	TEAM	G (GS, POS)	RUSH	YD	AVG (LG)	TD	REC	YD	AVG (LG)	TD	PASS	COMP	PCT	YD	AVG (LG)	TD	INT	SK	YD	QBR	KPR	OTD	PTS	TAY
1945	ChiC	4(1)	3	-1	-0.3(3)	0	1	3	3.0(3)	0	—	—	—	—	—	—	—	—	—	—	kp	—	0	-6
NFL	2	11(3)	3	-1	-0.3(3)	0	1	3	3.0(3)	0	—	—	—	—	—	—	—	—	—	—	—	—	0	1

VOGDS, EVAN Evan Edward, G, 5´10˝/210 lbs; Wisconsin; B2/10/1923 Johnsburg, WI, D8/6/1994 Fond du Lac, WI **1946** ChiR-A 14 (11, LG) **1947** ChiR-A 13 (0) **AAFC** 27 (11) [2 yrs]

1948 GB 12 (12, LG) **1949** GB 12 (10, LG) **NFL** 24 (22) [2 yrs]

VOGEL, BOB Robert Louis, T, 6´5˝/250 lbs; Ohio State; 1963: Bal, rnd 1/Bos, rnd 3; B9/23/1941 Columbus, OH **1963** Bal 13 (13, LT) **1964**†Bal★14 (14, LT) **1965**†Bal★14 (LT) **1966** Bal☆14 (LT) **1967** Bal★14 (LT) **1968**†Bal★14 (LT) **1969** Bal☆14 (LT) **1970**†Bal☆14 (LT) **1971**†Bal★14 (LT) **1972** Bal 14 (LT) **NFL** 139 (27) [10 yrs]

VOGEL, PAUL Paul Richard, LB, 6´1˝/220 lbs; South Carolina; B2/2/1961 New York, NY **1987** Hou 1 (0)

VOGELAAR, CARROLL Carroll Robert, T-DT, 6´3˝/253 lbs; Loyola Marymount; San Francisco; 1947: Bos, rnd 5; B4/8/1920 Idyllwild, CA, D12/7/1967 Palm Springs, CA **1947** Bos 12 (10, RT) **1948** Bos 12 (12, RT) **1949** NYB 12 (12, RT) **1950** NYY 10 (LDT) **NFL** 46 (34) [4 yrs]

VOGLER, TIM Timothy Gene, G-C, 6´3˝/259 lbs; Ohio State; B10/2/1956 Troy, OH **1979** Buf 10 **1980** Buf 10 (0) **1981**†Buf 14 (0) **1982** Buf 6 (0) **1983** Buf 16 (0) **1984** Buf 16 (2) **1985** Buf 14 (14, RG) **1986** Buf 9 (3) **1987** Buf 12 (12, RG) **1988** Buf 10 (10, RG) **NFL** 117 (41) [10 yrs]

VOIGHT, MIKE Michael Ray, RB, 6´0˝/214 lbs; North Carolina; 1977: Cin, rnd 3; B2/28/1954 Norfolk, VA

YEAR	TEAM	G (GS, POS)	RUSH	YD	AVG (LG)	TD	REC	YD	AVG (LG)	TD	PASS	COMP	PCT	YD	AVG (LG)	TD	INT	SK	YD	QBR	KPR	OTD	PTS	TAY
1977	Hou	14	7	20	2.9(6)	0	—	—	—	—	—	—	—	—	—	—	—	—	—	—	k	—	0	56

VOIGHT, BOB Robert, DT, 6´5˝/265 lbs; Los Angeles State; 1961: Min, rnd 18; B1938 **1961** Oak-A 14 (LDT)

VOIGHT, WALTER Walter, G-C-BB, 5´8˝/200 lbs; none; B4/15/1895, D5/1972 **1920** ChiT 7 (1) **1921** Ham 3 (1) **1921** ChiC 1 (1) **NFL** 11 (3) [2 yrs]

VOIGT, STU Stuart Alan, TE, 6´1˝/223 lbs; Wisconsin; 1970: Min, rnd 10; B8/12/1948 Madison, WI

YEAR	TEAM	G (GS, POS)	RUSH	YD	AVG (LG)	TD	REC	YD	AVG (LG)	TD	PASS	COMP	PCT	YD	AVG (LG)	TD	INT	SK	YD	QBR	KPR	OTD	PTS	TAY
1970	Min	3	—	—	—	—	—	—	—	—	—	—	—	—	—	—	—	—	—	—	—	—	—	—
1971	†Min	12(9, TE)	—	—	—	—	15	214	14.3(25)	1	—	—	—	—	—	—	—	—	—	—	k	—	6	97
1972	Min	14	1	1	1.0(1)	1	6	50	8.3(14)	1	—	—	—	—	—	—	—	—	—	—	k	—	12	28
1973	†Min	13(13, TE)	1	2	2.0(2)	0	23	318	13.8(43)	2	—	—	—	—	—	—	—	—	—	—	—	—	12	171
1974	†Min	14(13, TE)	—	—	—	—	32	268	8.4(22)	5	—	—	—	—	—	—	—	—	—	—	—	—	30	159
1975	†Min	13(13, TE)	—	—	—	—	34	363	10.7(22)	4	—	—	—	—	—	—	—	—	—	—	—	—	24	202
1976	†Min	14(14, TE)	—	—	—	—	28	303	10.8(44)	1	—	—	—	—	—	—	—	—	—	—	—	—	6	157
1977	†Min	14(14, TE)	—	—	—	—	20	212	10.6(24)	1	—	—	—	—	—	—	—	—	—	—	—	—	6	111
1978	†Min	15	—	—	—	—	4	52	13.0(27)	0	—	—	—	—	—	—	—	—	—	—	—	—	0	26
1979	Min	16	—	—	—	—	15	139	9.3(18)	2	—	—	—	—	—	—	—	—	—	—	k	—	12	65
1980	Min	3(3)	—	—	—	—	—	—	—	—	—	—	—	—	—	—	—	—	—	—	—	—	—	—
NFL	11	131(79)	2	3	1.5(2)	1	177	1919	10.8(44)	17	—	—	—	—	—	—	—	—	—	—	k	—	108	1015

VOKATY, OTTO Otto, B, 6´1˝/191 lbs; Heidelberg; B1/17/1909 **1931** Cle 8 (4, FB), 24 **1933** ChiC 1 (0)

YEAR	TEAM	G (GS, POS)	RUSH	YD	AVG (LG)	TD	REC	YD	AVG (LG)	TD	PASS	COMP	PCT	YD	AVG (LG)	TD	INT	SK	YD	QBR	KPR	OTD	PTS	TAY
1932	NYG	6(1)	22	61	2.8	0	1	20	20.0(20)	0	—	—	—	—	—	—	—	—	—	—	—	—	0	71
1934	Cin	3(0)	8	39	4.9	0	1	22	22.0(22)	0	—	—	—	—	—	—	—	—	—	—	—	—	0	50
NFL	4	18(5)	30	100	3.3	4	2	42	21.0(22)	0	—	—	—	—	—	—	—	—	—	—	—	—	24	161

VOLEK, BILLY John William, QB, 6´2˝/214 lbs; Fresno State; B4/28/1976 Hemet, CA

YEAR	TEAM	G (GS, POS)	RUSH	YD	AVG (LG)	TD	REC	YD	AVG (LG)	TD	PASS	COMP	PCT	YD	AVG (LG)	TD	INT	SK	YD	QBR	KPR	OTD	PTS	TAY
2001	Ten	1(0)	—	—	—	—	—	—	—	—	3	0	0.0	0	0.0	0	0	—	—	—	—	—	0	0
2003	Ten	7(1)	11	4	0.4(5)	1	—	—	—	—	69	44	63.8	545	7.9(50)	4	1	6	45	—	—	—	6	267
2004	Ten	10(8, qb)	11	50	4.5(14)	1	1	0	0.0(0)	0	357	218	61.1	2486	7.0(48)	18	10	30	216	87.1	—	—	6	993
2005	Ten	6(1)	1	3	3.0(3)	0	—	—	—	—	88	50	56.8	474	5.4(55)	4	2	9	45	—	—	—	0	180
NFL	4	24(10)	23	57	2.5(14)	2	1	0	0.0	0	517	312	60.3	3505	6.8(55)	26	13	45	306	86.9	—	—	12	1440

VOLGENAU, ELMER Elmer Porter, G, 6´2˝/190 lbs; Colgate; B8/2/1900 New Haven, CT, D12/6/1965 Clarence Compact, NY **1924** Roc 1 (1)

YEAR	TEAM	G(GS, POS)	RUSH	YD	AVG(LG)	TD	REC	YD	AVG(LG)	TD	PASS	COMP	PCT	YD	AVG(LG)	TD	INT	SK	YD	QBR	KPR	OTD	PTS	TAY

VOLK, RICK Richard Robert, DB, 6´3˝/195 lbs; Michigan; 1967: Bal, rnd 2; B3/15/1945 Toledo, OH **[RI]** **1967** Bal✧14 (RS) **1968**†Bal☆14 (RS) **1969** Bal★14 (RS) **1970**†Bal☆12 (FS) **1971**†Bal★14 (FS) **1972** Bal 14 (FS) **1973** Bal 14 (FS) **1974** Bal 14 (FS) **1975**†Bal 13 (4) **1976** NYG 8 (8, FS) **1977** Mia 3 **1978**†Mia 16 (13, FS) **NFL** 150 (25) [12 yrs]

VOLLENWEIDER, JIM James Stephen, HB, 6´1˝/205 lbs; Miami (FL); 1962: SF, rnd 8/Oak, rnd 18; B9/2/1939, WI, D6/1/1998 Ewa Beach, HI

YEAR	TEAM	G(GS, POS)	RUSH	YD	AVG(LG)	TD	REC	YD	AVG(LG)	TD	PASS	COMP	PCT	YD	AVG(LG)	TD	INT	SK	YD	QBR	KPR	OTD	PTS	TAY
1962	SF	14	11	37	3.4(10)	0	4	21	5.3(10)	0	—	—	—	—	—	—	—	—	—	—	k	—	0	71
1963	SF	13	47	124	2.6(12)	2	1	26	26.0(26)	0	1	0	0.0	0	0.0	0	1	—	—	—	k	—	12	132
NFL	2	27	58	161	2.8(12)	2	5	47	9.4(26)	0	1	0	0.0	0	0.0	0	1	—	—	—	k	—	12	203

VOLLERS, KURT Kurt, T, 6´7˝/317 lbs; Notre Dame; B4/4/1979 San Gabriel, CA **2002** Dal 1 (0) **2003**†Dal 13 (8, RT) **2004** Dal 13 (3) **2005** Ind 2 (0) **NFL** 29 (11) [4 yrs]

VOLOK, BILLY William James, G-T, 6´2˝/215 lbs; Tulsa; B3/23/1910 Lucas, KS, D8/6/1991 Drumright, OK **1934** ChiC 9 (6, LG) **1935** ChiC 12 (1) **1936** ChiC 12 (3) **1938** ChiC 11 (3) **1939** ChiC 1 (0)

YEAR	TEAM	G(GS, POS)	RUSH	YD	AVG(LG)	TD	REC	YD	AVG(LG)	TD	PASS	COMP	PCT	YD	AVG(LG)	TD	INT	SK	YD	QBR	KPR	OTD	PTS	TAY
1937	ChiC	11(4)	—	—	—	—	1	9	9.0(9)	0	—	—	—	—	—	—	—	—	—	—	—	—	0	5
NFL	6	56(17)	—	—	—	—	1	9	9.0(9)	0	—	—	—	—	—	—	—	—	—	—	—	1	6	5

VOLZ, PETE Peter, E-G, /190 lbs; Northwestern; B1/13/1897, D11/1957 **1920** ChiT 1 (1) **1921** Cin 4 (3, RE) **NFL** 5 (4) [2 yrs]

VOLZ, WILBUR Wilbur Edward, HB-DB, 6´0˝/192 lbs; Missouri; B1/1/1924 Rdwardsville, IL

YEAR	TEAM	G(GS, POS)	RUSH	YD	AVG(LG)	TD	REC	YD	AVG(LG)	TD	PASS	COMP	PCT	YD	AVG(LG)	TD	INT	SK	YD	QBR	KPR	OTD	PTS	TAY
1949	†Buf-A	8(0)	4	7	1.8	1	1	6	6.0(6)	0	—	—	—	—	—	—	—	—	—	—	k	—	6	18

VON DER AHE, SCOTT Scott Fraser, LB, 5´11˝/242 lbs; Arizona State; 1997: Ind, rnd 6; B10/12/1975 Lancaster, CA **1997** Ind 9 (2)

VON OELHOFFEN, KIMO Kimo Kukuiokalani, DE-NT-DT, 6´4˝/300 lbs; Hawaii; Boise State; 1994: Cin, rnd 6; B1/30/1971 Kaunakakai, HI **1994** Cin 7 (0) **1995** Cin 16 (1) **1996** Cin 11 (1) **1997** Cin 13 (13, NT) **1998** Cin 16 (16, NT) **1999** Cin 16 (5, ldt) **2000** Pit 16 (16, NT) **2001**†Pit 15 (15, RDE) **2002**†Pit 16 (16, RDE) **2003** Pit 16 (16, RDE) **2004**†Pit 16 (15, RDE) **2005**†Pit 16 (16, RDE) **NFL** 174 (130) [12 yrs]

VON SCHAMANN, UWE Uwe Detief Walter, K, 6´0˝/190 lbs; Oklahoma; 1979: Mia, rnd 7; B4/23/1956 Berlin, Germany **[K]** **1979**†Mia 16 **1980** Mia 16 (0) **1981**†Mia 16 (0) **1982**†Mia 9 (0) **1983**†Mia 16 (0) **1984**†Mia 16 (0) **NFL** 89 [6 yrs]

VON SONN, ANDY Andrew Vsevold, LB, 6´2˝/229 lbs; UCLA; 1962: Chi, rnd 14/Den, rnd 27; B11/5/1940 Los Angeles, CA **1964** LARm 14 (7, llb)

VOSBERG, DON Donald Theodore, E-DE, 6´3˝/196 lbs; Marquette; 1941: NYG, rnd 7; B10/3/1919 Dubuque, IA, D6/21/1997 Tucson, AZ **1941** NYG 7 (0)

VOSS, DOC George, G-T, none; B9/27/1891 Buffalo, NY, D5/5/1977 Buffalo, NY **1920** Buf 4 (0)

VOSS, LLOYD Lloyd John, DE-DT, 6´4˝/256 lbs; Nebraska; 1964: GB, rnd 1/NYJ, rnd 2; B2/13/1942 Adrian, NM **1964** GB 14 (1) **1965**†GB 14 **1966** Pit 14 (RDE) **1967** Pit 13 (RDE) **1968** Pit 14 (LDE) **1969** Pit 14 (LDE) **1970** Pit 14 (LDE) **1971** Pit 13 (RDT) **1972** Den 13 (7, LDE) **NFL** 123 (8) [9 yrs]

VOSS, TILLIE Walter Clarence, E-T, 6´3˝/207 lbs; Detroit Mercy; B3/28/1897 Detroit, MI, D12/14/1975 Stuart, FL **[K]** **1921** Det 7 (7, RE), 8 **1921** Buf 4 (4) **1922** RI 7 (7, LE), 18 **1922** Akr☆3 (2) **1923** Tol☆8 (8, LT), 7 **1924** GB☆11 (11, RE), 30 **1925** Det 10 (10, RE) **1926** NYG 12 (11, LE) **1927** ChiB 11 (8, LE) **1928** ChiB 13 (13, LE), 6 **1929** Day 1 (0) **1929** Buf 8 (7, LE) **NFL** 95 (88), 69 [9 yrs]

VOYTEK, ED Edward Louis, G, 6´2˝/235 lbs; Purdue; 1957: Was, rnd 22; B4/4/1935 Cleveland, OH **1957** Was 12 **1958** Was 12 **NFL** 24 [2 yrs]

VRABEL, MIKE Michael George, LB, 6´4˝/261 lbs; Ohio State; 1997: Pit, rnd 3; B8/14/1975 Akron, OH **1997**†Pit 15 (0) **1998** Pit 11 (0) **1999** Pit 10 (0) **2000** Pit 15 (0) **2001**†NE 16 (12, LLB) **2003**†NE 13 (9, RLB)

YEAR	TEAM	G(GS, POS)	RUSH	YD	AVG(LG)	TD	REC	YD	AVG(LG)	TD	PASS	COMP	PCT	YD	AVG(LG)	TD	INT	SK	YD	QBR	KPR	OTD	PTS	TAY
2002	NE	16(13, LLB)	—	—	—	—	1	1	1.0(1)	1	—	—	—	—	—	—	—	—	—	—	iS	—	6	1
2004	†NE	16(15, ROLB)	—	—	—	—	2	3	1.5(2)	2	—	—	—	—	—	—	—	—	—	—	S	—	12	12
2005	†NE	16(16, RILB)	—	—	—	—	3	4	1.3(2)	3	—	—	—	—	—	—	—	—	—	—	iS	1	24	40
NFL	9	128(65)	—	—	—	—	6	8	1.3(2)	6	—	—	—	—	—	—	—	—	—	—	kiS	1	42	45

VUCINICH, MILT Milton Christopher, C, 6´0˝/215 lbs; Stanford; 1943: ChiB, rnd 7; B11/1/1920 San Francisco, CA **1945** ChiB 3 (0)

WADDELL, MICHAEL Michael, DB, 5´11˝/183 lbs; North Carolina; 2004: Ten, rnd 4; B1/9/1981 Ellerbe, NC **2004** Ten 16 (4) **2005** Ten 16 (1) **NFL** 32 (5) [2 yrs]

WADDELL, REGGIE Reggie Duane, DB, 6´0˝/185 lbs; Texas A&M; Western Illinois; B11/14/1977 Houston, TX **2001** Bal 1 (0)

WADDLE, TOM Gregory Thomas, WR, 6´0˝/185 lbs; Boston College; B2/20/1967 Cincinnati, OH

YEAR	TEAM	G(GS, POS)	RUSH	YD	AVG(LG)	TD	REC	YD	AVG(LG)	TD	PASS	COMP	PCT	YD	AVG(LG)	TD	INT	SK	YD	QBR	KPR	OTD	PTS	TAY
1989	ChiB	3(0)	—	—	—	—	1	8	8.0(8)	0	—	—	—	—	—	—	—	—	—	—	p	—	0	1
1990	ChiB	5(0)	—	—	—	—	2	32	16.0(23)	0	—	—	—	—	—	—	—	—	—	—	—	—	0	16
1991	†ChiB	16(13, WR)	—	—	—	—	55	599	10.9(37)	3	—	—	—	—	—	—	—	—	—	—	p	—	18	321
1992	ChiB	12(12, WR)	—	—	—	—	46	674	14.7(68)	4	—	—	—	—	—	—	—	—	—	—	p	—	24	345
1993	ChiB	15(15, WR)	—	—	—	—	44	552	12.5(38)	1	—	—	—	—	—	—	—	—	—	—	—	—	6	281
1994	†ChiB	9(1)	—	—	—	—	25	244	9.8(22)	1	—	—	—	—	—	—	—	—	—	—	p	—	6	120
NFL	6	60(41)	—	—	—	—	173	2109	12.2(68)	9	—	—	—	—	—	—	—	—	—	—	p	—	54	1084

WADDY, BILLY Wiliam Dean, WR, 5´11˝/187 lbs; Colorado; 1977: LA, rnd 2; B2/19/1954 Wharton, TX

YEAR	TEAM	G(GS, POS)	RUSH	YD	AVG(LG)	TD	REC	YD	AVG(LG)	TD	PASS	COMP	PCT	YD	AVG(LG)	TD	INT	SK	YD	QBR	KPR	OTD	PTS	TAY
1977	†LARm	14(11, WR)	2	34	17.0(30)	0	23	355	15.4(42)	1	—	—	—	—	—	—	—	—	—	—	p	—	6	281
1978	†LARm	11(2)	5	31	6.2(11)	0	14	258	18.4(68)	1	—	—	—	—	—	—	—	—	—	—	p	—	6	160
1979	†LARm	13(6, WR)	—	—	—	—	14	220	15.7(40)	3	—	—	—	—	—	—	—	—	—	—	—	—	18	125
1980	†LARm	15(15, WR)	1	-1	-1.0(-1)	0	38	670	17.6(44)	5	—	—	—	—	—	—	—	—	—	—	p	—	30	359
1981	LARm	15(14, WR)	—	—	—	—	31	460	14.8(46)	0	—	—	—	—	—	—	—	—	—	—	—	—	0	230
1982	LARm	3(1)	2	-11	-5.5(5)	0	—	—	—	—	—	—	—	—	—	—	—	—	—	—	—	—	0	-11
1984	Min	4(0)	3	24	8.0(11)	0	—	—	—	—	—	—	—	—	—	—	—	—	—	—	kp	—	0	35
NFL	7	75(49)	13	77	5.9(30)	0	120	1963	16.4(68)	10	—	—	—	—	—	—	—	—	—	—	kp	—	60	1179

WADDY, JUDE Jude Michael, LB, 6´2˝/220 lbs; William & Mary; B9/12/1975 Washington, DC **1998** GB 13 (0) **1999** GB 14 (8, RLB) **NFL** 27 (8) [2 yrs]

WADDY, RAY Raymond, DB, 5´11˝/175 lbs; Texas A&M-Kingsville; B8/21/1956 Freeport, TX **1979** Was 16 **1980** Was 7 (0) **NFL** 23 [2 yrs]

WADE, BILLY William James, QB, 6´2˝/202 lbs; Vanderbilt; 1952: LA, rnd B1; B10/4/1930 Nashville, TN

YEAR	TEAM	G(GS, POS)	RUSH	YD	AVG(LG)	TD	REC	YD	AVG(LG)	TD	PASS	COMP	PCT	YD	AVG(LG)	TD	INT	SK	YD	QBR	KPR	OTD	PTS	TAY
1954	LARm	10	28	190	6.8(35)	1	—	—	—	—	59	31	52.5	509	8.6(48)	2	1	—	—	—	—	—	6	425
1955	†LARm	7	11	43	3.9(14)	0	—	—	—	—	71	31	43.7	316	4.5(25)	1	3	—	—	—	—	—	0	86
1956	LARm	12(QB)	26	93	3.6(33)	3	—	—	—	—	178	91	51.1	1461	8.2(76)	10	13	—	—	67.2	—	—	18	384
1957	LARm	5	1	5	5.0(5)	0	—	—	—	—	24	10	41.7	116	4.8(35)	1	1	—	—	—	—	—	0	28
1958	LARm✧	12(QB)	42	90	2.1(22)	2	—	—	—	—	341	181	53.1	**2875**	8.4(**93**)	18	**22**	—	—	72.2	—	—	12	758
1959	LARm	12(QB)	25	95	3.8(17)	2	—	—	—	—	261	153	58.6	2001	7.7(72)	12	17	—	—	71.1	—	—	12	496
1960	LARm	11(QB)	26	171	6.6(66)	2	0	10	(10)	0	182	106	58.2	1294	7.1(63)	12	11	—	—	77.0	—	—	12	463
1961	ChiB	13(QB)	45	255	5.7(29)	2	—	—	—	—	250	139	55.6	2258	9.0(**98**)	22	13	—	—	**93.7**	—	—	12	994
1962	ChiB☆	14(QB)	40	146	3.7(21)	5	—	—	—	—	**412**	**225**	54.6	3172	7.7(73)	18	24	—	—	70.0	—	—	30	912
1963	†ChiB★	14(QB)	45	132	2.9(17)	6	—	—	—	—	356	192	53.9	2301	6.5(63)	15	12	—	—	74.0	—	—	36	938
1964	ChiB	11(QB)	24	96	4.0(31)	1	—	—	—	—	327	182	55.7	1944	5.9(68)	13	14	—	—	68.6	—	—	6	583
1965	ChiB	5	5	18	3.6(16)	0	—	—	—	—	41	20	48.8	204	5.0(29)	0	2	5	40	—	—	—	0	40
1966	ChiB	2	—	—	—	—	—	—	—	—	21	9	42.9	79	3.8(14)	0	1	—	—	—	—	—	0	-1
NFL	13	128	318	1334	4.2(66)	24	0	10	(10)	0	2523	1370	54.3	18530	7.3(98)	124	134	5	40	72.2	—	—	144	6104

WADE, BOB Robert Pernell, DB, 6´2˝/200 lbs; Morgan State; 1967: Bal, rnd 15; B12/9/1944 Baltimore, MD **1968** Pit 14 (RCB) **1969** Was 13 **1970** Den 3 (2) **NFL** 30 (2) [3 yrs]

WADE, BOBBY Robert Louis, WR, 5´10˝/193 lbs; Arizona; 2003: Chi, rnd 5; B2/25/1981 Orange County, CA

YEAR	TEAM	G(GS, POS)	RUSH	YD	AVG(LG)	TD	REC	YD	AVG(LG)	TD	PASS	COMP	PCT	YD	AVG(LG)	TD	INT	SK	YD	QBR	KPR	OTD	PTS	TAY
2003	ChiB	12(1)	5	14	2.8(6)	0	12	137	11.4(24)	0	—	—	—	—	—	—	—	—	—	—	p	—	0	82
2004	ChiB	16(14, WR)	12	76	6.3(14)	0	42	481	11.5(40)	0	—	—	—	—	—	—	—	—	—	—	—	—	0	317
2005	ChiB	12(0)	—	—	—	—	10	80	8.0(17)	0	—	—	—	—	—	—	—	—	—	—	p	1	6	202
2005	Ten	2(1)	1	1	1.0(1)	0	4	40	10.0(15)	0	—	—	—	—	—	—	—	—	—	—	—	—	0	21
NFL	3	42(16)	18	91	5.1(14)	0	68	738	10.9(40)	0	—	—	—	—	—	—	—	—	—	—	p	1	6	621

WADE, CHARLIE Charles Garnell, WR, 5´10˝/164 lbs; Tennessee State; 1973: Mia, rnd 17; B2/23/1950 Nashville, TN **1975** GB 2 **1977** KC 6

YEAR	TEAM	G(GS, POS)	RUSH	YD	AVG(LG)	TD	REC	YD	AVG(LG)	TD	PASS	COMP	PCT	YD	AVG(LG)	TD	INT	SK	YD	QBR	KPR	OTD	PTS	TAY
1974	ChiB	14(WR)	1	-15	-15.0(-15)	0	39	683	17.5(73)	1	—	—	—	—	—	—	—	—	—	—	—	—	6	332
NFL	3	22	1	-15	-15.0(-15)	0	39	683	17.5(73)	1	—	—	—	—	—	—	—	—	—	—	—	—	6	332

YEAR	TEAM	G (GS, POS)	RUSH	YD	AVG (LG)	TD	REC	YD	AVG (LG)	TD PASS	COMP	PCT	YD	AVG (LG)	TD	INT	SK	YD	QBR	KPR	OTD	PTS	TAY

WADE, JIM — James, HB-DB, 5´11˝/175 lbs; Oklahoma City; 1948: LA, rnd 27; B2/14/1926 Talihina, OK

| 1949 | NYB | 10 (1) | 9 | 23 | 2.6 (6) | 0 | 4 | 58 | 14.5 (33) | 0 | — | — | — | — | — | — | — | — | — | kpi | — | 0 | 69 |

WADE, JOHN — John Robert, C, 6´5˝/299 lbs; Marshall; 1998: Jax, rnd 5; B1/25/1975 Harrisonburg, VA **1998**†Jax 5 (0) **1999**†Jax 16 (16, C) **2000** Jax 2 (2) **2001** Jax 15 (0) **2002** Jax 16 (16, C) **2003** TB 16 (16, C) **2004** TB 8 (8, C) **2005**†TB 16 (16, C) **NFL** 94 (74) [8 yrs]

WADE, TODD — Todd McLaurin, T, 6´8˝/315 lbs; Mississippi; 2000: Mia, rnd 2; B10/30/1976 Greenwood, MS **2000**†Mia 16 (16, RT) **2001**†Mia 15 (15, RT) **2002** Mia 16 (16, RT) **2003** Mia 16 (16, RT) **2004** Hou 14 (13, RT) **2005** Hou 9 (9, RT) **NFL** 86 (85) [6 yrs]

WADE, TOMMY — Thomas Virgil, QB, 6´2˝/195 lbs; Texas; B3/23/1942 Henderson, TX

1964	Pit	1									3	1	33.3	7	2.3 (7)	0	0	—	—	—	—	0	4
1965	Pit	4	8	43	5.4 (41)	0	—	—	—		66	33	50.0	463	7.0 (49)	2	13	—	—	—	—	0	-236
NFL	2	5	8	43	5.4 (41)	0	—	—	—		69	34	49.3	470	6.8 (49)	2	13	—	—	—	—	0	-232

WADSWORTH, ANDRE — Andre, DE, 6´4˝/278 lbs; Florida State; 1998: Arz, rnd 1; B10/19/1974 St. Croix, Virgin Islands **1998**†Arz 16 (15, LDE) **1999** Arz 11 (7, LDE) **2000** Arz 9 (8, lde) **NFL** 36 (30) [3 yrs]

WAECHTER, HENRY° — Henry Carl, DE-DT, 6´5˝/270 lbs; Nebraska; 1982: Chi, rnd 7; B2/13/1959 Epworth, IA **1982** ChiB 9 (2) **1983** Bal 11 (0) **1984** Ind 1 (0) **1984**†ChiB 2 (2) **1985**†ChiB 13 (0) **1986**†ChiB 16 (0) **1987** Was 1 (0) **NFL** 53 (4) [6 yrs]

WAERIG, JOHN — John, TE, 6´2˝/264 lbs; Wisconsin; Maryland; B4/8/1976 Philadelphia, PA

| 2001 | Det | 1 (0) | — | — | — | | 1 | 6 | 6.0 (6) | 0 | | | | | | | | | | | — | 0 | 3 |

WAFER, CARL — Carl, DE, 6´4˝/250 lbs; Tennessee State; 1974: Den, rnd 2; B1/17/1951 Magnolia, AR **1974** GB 2 **1974** NYG 1 **NFL** 3 [1 yr]

WAGER, CLINT — Clinton B., E, 6´6˝/218 lbs; St. Mary's (MN); B1/20/1920 Winona, MN, D2/29/1996 Excelsior, MN

1942	ChiB	7 (0)	—	—	—		—	—	—												—	0	
1943	ChiC	5 (1)	—	—	—		1	11	11.0 (11)	0											—	0	6
1944	C-P	8 (0)	—	—	—		5	73	14.6 (38)	0											—	0	37
1945	ChiC	3 (0)	-	-	-		1	32	32.0 (32)	0											—	0	16
NFL	4	23 (1)	—	—	—		7	116	16.6 (38)	0											—	0	58

WAGER, JOHN — John Byron, C-G-T, 5´11˝/203 lbs; Carthage; B4/28/1905 Massillon, OH, D6/22/1982 Portsmouth, OH **1931** Por 11 (5) **1932** Por 9 (1) **1933** Por 10 (3) **NFL** 30 (9) [3 yrs]

WAGES, HARMON — Harmon Leon, RB, 6´1˝/215 lbs; Florida; B5/18/1946 Jacksonville, FL

1968	Atl	13	59	211	3.6 (31)	0	16	121	7.6 (55)	1	2	1	50.0	21	10.5 (21)	0	0	—	—	k	—	6	295
1969	Atl	14 (HB)	72	375	5.2 (66)	0	22	228	10.4 (88)	1	1	1	100.0	16	16.0 (16)	1	0	—	—	k	—	18	513
1970	Atl	13 (RB)	119	422	3.5 (40)	1	26	153	5.9 (24)	2	1	1	100.0	13	13.0 (13)	0	0	1	9	—	k	—	18	532
1971	Atl	14	64	266	4.2 (27)	1	19	249	13.1 (47)	1	—	—	—	—	—	—	—	—	—	k	—	12	412
1973	Atl	6	18	47	2.6 (13)	1	2	14	7.0 (14)	0	—	—	—	—	—	—	—	—	—	k	—	6	49
NFL	5	60	332	1321	4.0 (66)	5	85	765	9.0 (88)	5	4	3	75.0	50	12.5 (21)	1	0	1	9	—	k	—	60	1801

WAGNER, BARRY — Barry, WR, 6´3˝/213 lbs; Alabama A&M; B11/24/1967 Greensboro, AL

| 1992 | ChiB | 1 (0) | — | — | — | | 1 | 16 | 16.0 (16) | 0 | | | | | | | | | | | — | 0 | 8 |

WAGNER, BRYAN — Bryan Jeffrey, P, 6´2˝/200 lbs; California Lutheran; Cal State-Northridge; B3/28/1962 Escondido, CA [P] **1987** ChiB 10 (0) **1989**†Cle 16 (0) **1990** Cle 16 (0) **1991** NE 3 (0) **1992** GB 7 (0) **1993**†GB 16 (0) **1994**†SD 14 (0) **1995** NE 8 (0)

| 1988 | †ChiB | 16 (0) | 2 | 0 | 0.0 (0) | 0 | — | — | — | | 1 | 1 | 100.0 | 3 | 3.0 (3) | 0 | 0 | — | — | P | — | 0 | 2 |
| NFL | 9 | 106 (0) | 2 | 0 | 0.0 (0) | 0 | — | — | — | | 1 | 1 | 100.0 | 3 | 3.0 (3) | 0 | 0 | — | — | P | — | 0 | 2 |

WAGNER, BUFF — Almore C., B, 5´9˝/165 lbs; Carroll (WI); B2/21/1897 Marinette, WI, D12/12/1962 Olmsted County, MN **1921** GB 4 (1)

WAGNER, LOWELL — Lowell R., B, 6´0˝/194 lbs; USC; B8/21/1923 Santa Monica, CA, D9/26/2005 Kirkland, WA [I]

1946	†NYY-A	13 (7, WB)	15	29	1.9	0	9	126	14.0	1	—	—	—	—	—	—	—	—	—	kp	1	12	211
1947	NYY-A	7 (3)	—	—	—		4	50	12.5	1	—	—	—	—	—	—	—	—	—	—	—	6	30
1948	NYY-A	14 (3, wb)	—	—	—		6	99	16.5	1	—	—	—	—	—	—	—	—	—	i	—	6	81
1949	†SF-A	10 (3)	3	17	5.7	0	—	—	—		—	—	—	—	—	—	—	—	—	pi	1	6	115
AAFC	4	44 (16)	18	46	2.6	0	19	275	14.5	3	—	—	—	—	—	—	—	—	—	kpi	2	30	437
1950	SF	12 (DB)	2	5	2.5 (3)	0	—	—	—		—	—	—	—	—	—	—	—	—	pi	—	0	-4
1951	SF	12 (DB)	—	—	—		—	—	—		—	—	—	—	—	—	—	—	—	i	—	0	70
1952	SF☆	12 (DB)	—	—	—		1	6	6.0 (6)	0	—	—	—	—	—	—	—	—	—	i	—	0	42
1953	SF	10 (DB)	1	4	4.0 (4)	0	—	—	—		—	—	—	—	—	—	—	—	—	i	—	0	109
1955	SF	1	—	—	—		—	—	—		—	—	—	—	—	—	—	—	—	—	—	0	
NFL	5	47	3	9	3.0 (4)	0	1	6	6.0 (6)	0	—	—	—	—	—	—	—	—	—	pi	—	0	217

WAGNER, MIKE — Michael Robert, DB, 6´1˝/210 lbs; Western Illinois; 1971: Pit, rnd 11; B6/22/1949 Waukegan, IL [I] **1971** Pit 12 (SS) **1972**†Pit 14 (SS) **1973**†Pit☆14 (SS) **1974**†Pit 13 (SS) **1975**†Pit★12 (SS) **1976**†Pit★14 (SS) **1977** Pit 3 (3) **1978**†Pit☆14 (FS) **1979** Pit 8 **1980** Pit 15 (13, FS) **NFL** 119 (16) [10 yrs]

WAGNER, RAY — Raymond John, E, 5´10˝/173 lbs; Columbia; B2/25/1902 Buffalo, NY, D12/3/1990 St. Petersburg, FL **1929** Ora 1 (1) **1930** Nwk 5 (1) **1931** Bkn 6 (0) **NFL** 12 (2) [3 yrs]

WAGNER, RAY — Raymond L., T, 6´4˝/290 lbs; Kent State; B11/15/1957 Altoona, PA **1982** Cin 4 (0)

WAGNER, SID — Sidney P., G, 5´11˝/192 lbs; Michigan State; 1936: Det, rnd 1; B10/29/1912 Lansing, MI, D11/17/1972 Forest, MI **1936** Det 5 (4) **1937** Det 11 (6, RG) **1938** Det 11 (9, LG) **NFL** 27 (19) [3 yrs]

WAGNER, STEVE — Steven John, DB, 6´2˝/208 lbs; Wisconsin; 1976: Min, rnd 5; B4/18/1954 Milwaukee, WI **1976** GB 11 **1977** GB 14 **1978** GB 16 **1980** Phi 4 (0)

| 1979 | GB | 16 | 1 | 16 | 16.0 (16) | 0 | — | — | — | | — | — | — | — | — | — | — | — | — | k | — | 0 | 9 |
| NFL | 5 | 61 | 1 | 16 | 16.0 (16) | 0 | — | — | — | | — | — | — | — | — | — | — | — | — | k | — | 0 | -13 |

WAGONER, DANNY — Daniel Wright, DB, 5´10˝/180 lbs; Kansas; 1982: Det, rnd 9; B12/12/1959 High Point, NC **1982**†Det 1 (0) **1983**†Det 14 (0) **1984** Det 1 (0) **1984** Min 4 (0) **1985** Atl 14 (0) **NFL** 34 (0) [4 yrs]

WAGSTAFF, JIM — James Burke, DB, 6´2˝/192 lbs; Idaho State; 1958: Det, rnd 21; B6/12/1936 American Falls, ID **1959** ChiC 3 **1960** Buf-A☆14 (LS) **1961** Buf-A 14 (LS) **NFL** 31 [3 yrs]

WAHLE, MIKE — Michael James, G-T, 6´6˝/307 lbs; Navy; 1998: GB, rnd S2; B3/29/1977 Portland, OR **1998** GB 1 (0) **1999** GB 16 (13, LG/lt) **2000** GB 16 (6, lt) **2001**†GB 16 (16, LG) **2003**†GB 16 (16, LG) **2004**†GB 16 (16, LG) **2005**†Car★16 (16, LG)

| 2002 | †GB | 16 (16, LG) | — | — | — | | 1 | 7 | 7.0 (7) | 0 | — | — | — | — | — | — | — | — | — | — | — | 0 | 4 |
| NFL | 8 | 113 (99) | — | — | — | | 1 | 7 | 7.0 (7) | 0 | — | — | — | — | — | — | — | — | — | — | — | 0 | 4 |

WAHLER, JIM — James Joseph, NT-DT, 6´4˝/275 lbs; UCLA; 1989: Phx, rnd 4; B7/29/1966 San Jose, CA **1989** Phx 13 (11, RDT) **1990** Phx 16 (16, NT) **1991** Phx 15 (13, NT) **1992** Phx 5 (5, nt) **1992**†Was 5 (0) **1993** Was 8 (0) **NFL** 62 (45) [5 yrs]

WAHLROOS, DREW — Drew, LB, 6´3˝/230 lbs; Colorado; B6/7/1980 Poway, CA **2004**†SL 6 (0) **2005** SL 15 (0) **NFL** 21 (0) [2 yrs]

WAINRIGHT, FRANK — Frank Wesley, TE, 6´3˝/243 lbs; Northern Colorado; 1991: NO, rnd 8; B10/10/1967 Peoria, IL **1993** NO 16 (2) **1995** Phi 7 (0) **1995** Mia 6 (0) **1997** Mia 9 (0) **1998**†Mia 16 (1) **1999** Bal 16 (0) **2000** Bal 8 (0)

1991	†NO	14 (2)	—	—	—		1	3	3.0 (3)	0	—	—	—	—	—	—	—	—	—	—	—	0	2
1992	†NO	13 (4)	—	—	—		9	143	15.9 (29)	0	—	—	—	—	—	—	—	—	—	—	—	0	72
1996	Mia	16 (0)	—	—	—		1	2	2.0 (2)	1	—	—	—	—	—	—	—	—	—	k	—	6	1
NFL	9	121 (9)	—	—	—		11	148	13.5 (29)	1	—	—	—	—	—	—	—	—	—	k	—	6	74

WAINSCOTT, LOYD — Loyd Dale, LB, 6´2˝/235 lbs; Texas; 1969: Hou, rnd 16; B10/26/1946 Texas City, TX **1969**†Hou-A 14 **1970** Hou 11 **NFL** 25 [2 yrs]

WAITE, CARL — Carl Ebenezer, B-E, 5´9˝/205 lbs; Rutgers; Georgetown (DC); B2/27/1902 White Plains, NY, D10/14/1961 Monticello, NY **1928** Fra 8 (3), 6 **1929** Ora 12 (10, FB), 6 **1930** Nwk 7 (2), 6 **NFL** 27 (15), 18 [3 yrs]

WAITE, WILL — Willard H., C-G-T-B, 6´2˝/200 lbs; none; B1/4/1893 Columbus, OH, D1/1964 Cleveland, OH **1920** Col 10 (5, C) **1921** Col 7 (2) **NFL** 17 (7) [2 yrs]

YEAR	TEAM	G (GS, POS)	RUSH	YD	AVG(LG)	TD	REC	YD	AVG(LG)	TD	PASS	COMP	PCT	YD	AVG(LG)	TD	INT	SK	YD	QBR	KPR	OTD	PTS	TAY

WAITERS, VAN Van Allen, LB, 6´4˝/240 lbs; Indiana; 1988: Cle, rnd 3; B2/27/1965 Coral Gables, FL **1988**†Cle 16 (0) **1990** Cle 16 (6, rlb) **1991** Cle 16 (9, LLB) **1992**†Min 16 (1)

YEAR	TEAM	G (GS, POS)	REC	YD	AVG(LG)	TD	KPR	PTS	TAY
1989	†Cle	16(5, rolb)	1	14	14.0(14)	1	—	6	12
NFL	5	80(21)	1	14	14.0(14)	1	piS	6	17

WAITS, ALEX Alexander John, P, 6´2˝/208 lbs; Texas; B6/21/1968 Glasgow, Scotland **1991** Sea 3 (0)

WAKEFIELD, FRED Fred, DE-T, 6´7˝/288 lbs; Illinois; B9/17/1978 Tuscola, IL **2001** Arz 16 (12, LDE) **2002** Arz 16 (15, LDE) **2003** Arz 10 (5, lde) **2005** Arz 15 (9, rt) **NFL** 57 (41) [4 yrs]

WALBRIDGE, LARRY Lyman Norman, C, 5´7˝/200 lbs; Lafayette; Fordham; B9/11/1897 Wellsboro, PA, D1/11/1982 Woodland Hills, CA **1925** NYG 2 (0)

WALCZAK, MARK Mark Charles, TE, 6´6˝/246 lbs; Arizona; B4/26/1962 Rochester, NY **1987** Buf 2 (0) **1987** Ind 8 (0) **1988** Phx 16 (0) **1989** SD 6 (0) **1991** SD 1 (0) **NFL** 33 (0) [4 yrs]

WALDEMORE, STAN Stanley A., G-C-T, 6´4˝/263 lbs; Nebraska; 1978: Atl, rnd 3; B2/20/1955 Newark, NJ **1978** NYJ 4 **1979** NYJ 16 (1) **1980** NYJ 16 (8, lg) **1981**†NYJ 16 (2) **1982**†NYJ 9 (9, LG) **1983** NYJ 4 (4) **1984** NYJ 14 (14, LG) **NFL** 79 (38) [7 yrs]

WALDEN, BOBBY Robert Earl, P, 6´0˝/190 lbs; Georgia; 1961: Hou, rnd 4; B3/9/1938 Boston, GA [P]

YEAR	TEAM	G	RUSH	YD	AVG(LG)	TD	PASS	COMP	PCT	YD	AVG(LG)	TD	INT	SK	KPR	PTS	TAY
1964	Min	14	1	18	18.0(18)	0	—	—	—	—	—	—	—	—	P	0	18
1965	Min	14	—	—	—	—	—	—	—	—	—	—	—	—	P	0	0
1966	Min	14	5	82	16.4(45)	0	—	—	—	—	—	—	—	—	P	0	82
1967	Min	14	—	—	—	—	—	—	—	—	—	—	—	—	P	0	0
1968	Pit	14	2	5	2.5(5)	0	1	0	0.0	0	0.0	0	0	0	P	0	5
1969	Pit◇	14	—	—	—	—	—	—	—	—	—	—	—	—	P	0	0
1970	Pit	13	—	—	—	—	1	1	100.0	20	20.0(20)	0	0	0	P	0	10
1971	†Pit	14	1	14	14.0(14)	0	1	1	100.0	10	10.0(10)	0	0	0	P	0	19
1972	†Pit	14	—	—	—	—	1	0	0.0	0	0.0	0	0	—	P	0	0
1973	†Pit	14	1	0	0.0(0)	0	—	—	—	—	—	—	—	—	P	0	0
1974	†Pit	14	—	—	—	—	—	—	—	—	—	—	—	—	P	0	0
1975	†Pit☆	14	—	—	—	—	3	2	66.7	39	13.0(20)	0	0	—	P	0	20
1976	†Pit	14	3	7	2.3(7)	0	—	—	—	—	—	—	—	—	P	0	7
1977	Pit	13	1	0	0.0(0)	0	—	—	—	—	—	—	—	—	P	0	0
NFL	14	194	14	126	9.0(45)	0	7	4	57.1	69	9.9(20)	0	0	0	P	0	161

WALDRON, TIM Austin, G-C, /195 lbs; Gonzaga; B1903 **1927** ChiC 4 (4, LG)

WALDROP, ROB Robert F., DT, 6´1˝/276 lbs; Arizona; 1994: KC, rnd 5; B12/1/1971 Atlanta, GA **1994** KC 3 (0)

WALDROUP, KERWIN Kerwin, DE, 6´3˝/260 lbs; Michigan; Central State (OH); 1996: Det, rnd 5; B8/1/1974 Chicago, IL **1996** Det 16 (10, RDE) **1997** Det 11 (11, RDE) **1998** Det 13 (13, RDE) **NFL** 40 (34) [3 yrs]

WALDSMITH, RALPH Ralph George, C-G, 5´9˝/225 lbs; Akron; B8/7/1892 Akron, OH, D6/7/1925 Wilkes-Barre, PA **1921** Cle 4 (4, C) **1922** Can 5 (2) **NFL** 9 (6) [2 yrs]

WALEN, MARK Mark Hartley, DT-DE, 6´5˝/265 lbs; UCLA; 1986: Dal, rnd 3; B3/10/1963 San Francisco, CA **1987** Dal 9 (0) **1988** Dal 15 (2) **NFL** 24 (2) [2 yrs]

WALENDY, CRAIG Craig H., RB, 6´2˝/228 lbs; UCLA; B7/11/1977 Westlake, OH **2000**†NYG 12 (0)

WALIK, BILLY William S., WR-DB, 5´11˝/180 lbs; Villanova; 1970: Phi, rnd 11; B11/8/1947 New Haven, CT

YEAR	TEAM	G	REC	YD	AVG(LG)	TD	KPR	PTS	TAY
1970	Phi	14	1	0	0.0(0)	0	kp	0	303
1971	Phi	8	—	—	—	—	kp	0	182
1972	Phi	10	1	15	15.0(15)	1	kp	6	153
NFL	3	32	2	15	7.5(15)	1	kp	6	638

WALKER, AARON Aaron Scott, TE, 6´6˝/252 lbs; Florida; 2003: SF, rnd 5; B3/14/1980 Titusville, FL

YEAR	TEAM	G (GS)	REC	YD	AVG(LG)	TD	PTS	TAY
2003	SF	16(2)	8	116	14.5(26)	1	6	63
2004	SF	16(4)	10	115	11.5(30)	0	0	58
NFL	2	32(6)	18	231	12.8(30)	1	6	121

WALKER, ADAM Adam, RB, 5´11˝/220 lbs; Carthage; B4/9/1963 New York, NY

YEAR	TEAM	G (GS)	RUSH	YD	AVG(LG)	TD	REC	YD	AVG(LG)	TD	PTS	TAY
1987	Min	2(0)	5	24	4.8(11)	0	2	3	1.5(2)	0	0	26

WALKER, ADAM Adam Clayton, RB, 6´1˝/210 lbs; Pittsburgh; B6/7/1968 Pittsburgh, PA

YEAR	TEAM	G (GS, POS)	RUSH	YD	AVG(LG)	TD	REC	YD	AVG(LG)	TD	KPR	PTS	TAY
1992	SF	1(0)	—	—	—	—	—	—	—	—	—	—	—
1993	SF	10(0)	5	17	3.4(1)	0	1	4	4.0(4)	0	k	0	25
1994	†SF	8(0)	13	54	4.2(14)	1	—	—	—	—	k	6	56
1995	†SF	13(7, fb)	14	44	3.1(16)	1	11	78	7.1(15)	0	k	6	95
1996	†Phi	13(0)	—	—	—	—	—	—	—	—	—	—	—
NFL	5	45(7)	32	115	3.6(16)	2	12	82	6.8(15)	0	k	12	176

WALKER, BILL William Bradley, G, 6´0˝/220 lbs; VMI; B9/16/1920 Richmond, VA, D5/28/2002 Pompano Beach, FL **1944** Bos 10 (6, RG) **1945** Bos 4 (0) **NFL** 14 (6) [2 yrs]

WALKER, BRACY Bracy Wardell, DB, 6´0˝/210 lbs; North Carolina; 1994: KC, rnd 4; B10/28/1970 Portsmouth, VA **1994** KC 2 (0) **1994** Cin 7 (0) **1995** Cin 14 (14, SS) **1996** Cin 16 (16, SS) **1997** Mia 12 (0) **1998** KC 8 (0) **1999** KC 16 (1) **2000** KC 15 (0) **2001** KC 15 (0) **2002** Det 14 (1) **2003** Det 16 (1) **2004** Det 16 (16, SS) **2005** Det 16 (4) **NFL** 167 (53) [12 yrs]

WALKER, BRIAN Brian, DB, 6´1˝/205 lbs; Washington State; B5/31/1972 Colorado Springs, CO **1996** Was 16 (4) **1997** Was 5 (0) **1998**†Mia 16 (0) **1999** Sea 5 (0) **2000**†Mia 16 (16, SS) **2001**†Mia 13 (13, SS) **2002** Det 10 (9, FS) **2003** Det 16 (16, FS) **NFL** 97 (58) [8 yrs]

WALKER, BRUCE Bruce Romell, NT, 6´4˝/310 lbs; UCLA; 1994: Phi, rnd 2; B7/18/1972 Compton, CA **1995** NE 11 (5, nt)

WALKER, BYRON Byron Burneil, WR, 6´4˝/190 lbs; The Citadel; B7/28/1960 Scott AFB, IL

YEAR	TEAM	G (GS)	REC	YD	AVG(LG)	TD	OTD	PTS	TAY
1982	Sea	9(1)	10	156	15.6(40)	2	—	12	88
1983	†Sea	16(0)	12	248	20.7(50)	2	—	12	134
1984	†Sea	16(0)	13	236	18.2(41)	1	—	6	123
1985	Sea	16(0)	19	285	15.0(28)	2	1	18	153
1986	Sea	1(0)	—	—	—	—	—	—	—
NFL	5	58(3)	54	925	17.1(50)	7	1	48	498

WALKER, CHUCK Charles David, DT-DE, 6´3˝/250 lbs; Duke; 1963: SL, rnd 12/Buf, rnd 22; B8/10/1941 Uniontown, PA **1964** SL 3 **1965** SL 14 **1966** SL◇14 (RDT) **1967** SL☆13 (RDT) **1968** SL 14 (RDE) **1969** SL☆14 (RDE) **1970** SL 11 (RDE) **1971** SL 11 (rde) **1972** SL 2 **1972** Atl 9 (LDT) **1973** Atl 14 (LDT) **1974** Atl 14 **1975** Atl 10 **NFL** 143 [12 yrs]

WALKER, CLARENCE Clarence, HB, 6´1˝/205 lbs; Southern Illinois; B9/23/1938 DeQuincy, LA

YEAR	TEAM	G	RUSH	YD	AVG(LG)	TD	PTS	TAY
1963	Den-A	1	2	14	7.0(9)	0	0	14

WALKER, CLEO Cleo Franklin, LB-C, 6´3˝/219 lbs; Louisville; 1970: GB, rnd 7; B2/7/1948 Columbus, GA **1970** GB 11 **1971** Atl 11 **NFL** 22 [2 yrs]

WALKER, COREY Corey, RB, 5´10˝/188 lbs; Arkansas State; B6/4/1973 Memphis, TN

YEAR	TEAM	G (GS)	RUSH	YD	AVG(LG)	TD	REC	YD	AVG(LG)	TD	KPR	PTS	TAY
1998	Phi	14(0)	12	55	4.6(20)	0	2	35	17.5(33)	0	k	0	103

WALKER, DARNELL Darnell Robert, DB, 5´8˝/168 lbs; Oklahoma; 1993: Atl, rnd 7; B1/17/1970 St. Louis, MO **1993** Atl 15 (8, LCB) **1994** Atl 16 (5, lcb) **1995**†Atl 15 (7, LCB) **1996** Atl 16 (9, RCB) **1997**†SF 16 (11, RCB) **1998**†SF 16 (16, LCB/rcb) **1999** SF 15 (8, LCB) **2000** Det 10 (2) **NFL** 119 (66) [8 yrs]

WALKER, DARWIN Darwin Jamar, DT, 6´3˝/294 lbs; North Carolina State; Tennessee; 2000: Arz, rnd 3; B6/15/1977 Walterboro, SC **2000** Arz 1 (0) **2001**†Phi 10 (0) **2002**†Phi 16 (16, RDT) **2003**†Phi 16 (16, RDT) **2004**†Phi 16 (16, RDT) **2005** Phi 13 (12, RDT) **NFL** 72 (60) [6 yrs]

WALKER, DENARD Denard Antuan, DB, 6´1˝/198 lbs; LSU; 1997: Ten, rnd 3; B8/9/1973 Dallas, TX **1997** Ten 15 (11, LCB) **1998** Ten 16 (16, LCB) **1999**†Ten 15 (14, LCB) **2000**†Ten 15 (15, LCB) **2001** Den 16 (15, RCB) **2002** Den 16 (16, RCB) **2003** Min 16 (8, lcb) **2004** Oak 16 (4) **2005** Oak 9 (0) **NFL** 134 (99) [9 yrs]

WALKER, DERRICK Derrick Norval, TE, 6´0˝/246 lbs; Michigan; 1990: SD, rnd 6; B6/23/1967 Glenwood, IL

YEAR	TEAM	G (GS, POS)	REC	YD	AVG(LG)	TD	PTS	TAY
1990	SD	16(13, TE)	23	240	10.4(23)	1	6	125
1991	SD	16(16, TE)	20	134	6.7(14)	0	0	67

YEAR	TEAM	G(GS, POS)	RUSH	YD	AVG(LG)	TD	REC	YD	AVG(LG)	TD	PASS	COMP	PCT	YD	AVG(LG)	TD	INT	SK	YD	QBR	KPR	OTD	PTS	TAY
1992	†SD	16(16, TE)	—	—	—	—	34	393	11.6(59)	2	—	—	—	—	—	—	—	—	—	—	—	—	12	207
1993	SD	12(11, TE)	—	—	—	—	21	212	10.1(25)	1	—	—	—	—	—	—	—	—	—	—	—	—	6	111
1994	†KC	15(11, TE)	—	—	—	—	36	382	10.6(57)	2	—	—	—	—	—	—	—	—	—	—	—	—	12	201
1995	†KC	16(3)	—	—	—	—	25	205	8.2(18)	1	—	—	—	—	—	—	—	—	—	—	—	—	6	108
1996	KC	11(9, TE)	—	—	—	—	9	73	8.1(24)	1	—	—	—	—	—	—	—	—	—	—	—	—	6	42
1997	†KC	16(5, te)	—	—	—	—	5	60	12.0(22)	0	—	—	—	—	—	—	—	—	—	—	—	—	0	30
1999	Oak	11(3)	—	—	—	—	7	71	10.1(21)	1	—	—	—	—	—	—	—	—	—	—	—	—	6	41
NFL	9	129(87)	—	—	—	—	180	1770	9.8(59)	9	—	—	—	—	—	—	—	—	—	—	—	—	54	930

Walker, Doak Ewell Doak, HB-DB, 5´11˝/173 lbs; SMU; 1949: NYB, rnd 1/Cle-A, rnd 9; B1/1/1927 Dallas, TX, D9/27/1998 Steamboat Springs, CO; HOF 1986 **[K]**

YEAR	TEAM	G(GS, POS)	RUSH	YD	AVG(LG)	TD	REC	YD	AVG(LG)	TD	PASS	COMP	PCT	YD	AVG(LG)	TD	INT	SK	YD	QBR	KPR	OTD	PTS	TAY
1950	Det★	12(LH)	83	386	4.7(30)	5	35	534	15.3(43)	6	7	1	14.3	6	0.9(6)	0	0	—	—	—	KPkpi	—	**128**	898
1951	Det★	12(LH)	79	356	4.5(34)	2	22	421	19.1(63)	4	5	2	40.0	29	5.8(22)	1	0	—	—	—	KPkp	—	97	859
1952	†Det	7(lh)	26	106	4.1(20)	0	11	90	8.2(18)	0	2	1	50.0	9	4.5(9)	0	1	—	—	—	K	—	14	116
1953	†Det★	12(LH)	66	337	5.1(50)	2	30	502	16.7(83)	3	7	3	42.9	31	4.4(23)	1	0	—	—	—	Kk	—	93	723
1954	†Det★	12(lh)	32	240	7.5(38)	1	32	564	17.6(66)	3	4	0	0.0	0	0.0	0	1	—	—	—	Kkp	1	106	666
1955	Det★	12(lh)	23	95	4.1(51)	2	22	428	19.5(70)	5	3	0	0.0	0	0.0	0	0	—	—	—	KPkpi	—	**96**	373
NFL	6	67	309	1520	4.9(51)	12	152	2539	16.7(83)	21	28	7	25.0	75	2.7(23)	2	2	—	—	—	KPkpi	1	534	3634

Walker, Donnie Donnie Mack, DB, 6´2˝/180 lbs; Central State (OH); 1973: Buf, rnd 4; B12/26/1950 Bronx, NY **1973** Buf 11 **1974**†Buf 14 **1975** NYJ 2 **NFL** 27 [3 yrs]

Walker, Dwight Dwight Gerard, RB-WR, 5´10˝/185 lbs; Nicholls State; 1982: Cle, rnd 4; B1/10/1959 Metairie, LA

YEAR	TEAM	G(GS, POS)	RUSH	YD	AVG(LG)	TD	REC	YD	AVG(LG)	TD	PASS	COMP	PCT	YD	AVG(LG)	TD	INT	SK	YD	QBR	KPR	OTD	PTS	TAY
1982	†Cle	9(0)	—	—	—	—	8	136	17.0(46)	0	—	—	—	—	—	—	—	—	—	—	kp	—	0	174
1983	Cle	16(0)	19	100	5.3(15)	0	29	273	9.4(35)	1	3	1	33.3	25	8.3(25)	0	1	—	—	—	kp	—	6	417
1984	Cle	11(1)	1	-8	-8.0(-8)	0	10	122	12.2(25)	0	—	—	—	—	—	—	—	—	—	—	p	—	0	73
1987	NO	2(0)	—	—	—	—	2	15	7.5(8)	0	—	—	—	—	—	—	—	—	—	—	—	—	0	8
NFL	4	38(1)	20	92	4.6(15)	0	49	546	11.1(46)	1	3	1	33.3	25	8.3(25)	0	1	—	—	—	kp	—	6	672

Walker, Elliott Elliot, RB, 5´11˝/193 lbs; Pittsburgh; 1978: SF, rnd 6; B9/10/1956 Indianola, MS **1978** SF 9

Walker, Frank Frank Bernard, DB, 5´10˝/198 lbs; Tuskegee; 2003: NYG, rnd 6; B8/6/1981 Tuskegee, AL **2003** NYG 10 (7, RCB) **2004** NYG 13 (1) **2005** NYG 7 (0) **NFL** 30 (8) [3 yrs]

Walker, Fulton Fulton Luther, DB, 5´10˝/193 lbs; West Virginia; 1981: Mia, rnd 6; B4/30/1958 Martinsburg, WV **[R]** **1981**†Mia 16 (2) **1982**†Mia 9 (0) **1983**†Mia☆15 (0) **1984**†Mia 12 (0) **1985** Mia 2 (0) **1985**†LARd 13 (0) **1986** LARd 14 (0) **NFL** 81 (2) [6 yrs]

Walker, Gary Gary Lamar, DT-DE, 6´3˝/305 lbs; Auburn; 1995: Hou, rnd 5; B2/28/1973 Royston, GA **1995** Hou 15 (9, LDT) **1996** Hou 16 (16, LDT) **1997** Ten 15 (15, LDT) **1998** Ten 16 (16, LDT) **1999**†Jax 16 (16, LDT) **2000** Jax 15 (14, LDT) **2001** Jax✧16 (16, LDT) **2002** Hou★16 (16, LDE) **2003** Hou 4 (4) **2004** Hou 15 (15, LDE) **2005** Hou 11 (11, LDE) **NFL** 155 (148) [11 yrs]

Walker, Gary Gary Wayne, C, 6´3˝/283 lbs; Boston University; 1986: Ind, rnd 5; B12/15/1963 Hassfurt, Germany **1987** Dal 1 (0)

Walker, Glen Glen Joe, P, 6´1˝/210 lbs; USC; B1/16/1952 Torrance, CA

YEAR	TEAM	G(GS, POS)	RUSH	YD	AVG(LG)	TD	REC	YD	AVG(LG)	TD	PASS	COMP	PCT	YD	AVG(LG)	TD	INT	SK	YD	QBR	KPR	OTD	PTS	TAY
1977	†LARm	14	—	—	—	—	—	—	—	—	1	1	100.0	13	13.0(13)	0	0	—	—	—	P	—	0	7
1978	†LARm	16	—	—	—	—	—	—	—	—	1	0	0.0	0	0.0	0	1	—	—	—	P	—	0	-40
NFL	2	30	—	—	—	—	—	—	—	—	2	1	50.0	13	6.5(13)	0	1	—	—	—	P	—	0	-34

Walker, Greg Gregory, T, 6´5˝/341 lbs; Clemson; B10/1/1981 Wichita, KS **2004** NYG 7 (0)

Walker, Herschel Herschel Junior, RB, 6´1˝/225 lbs; Georgia; 1985: Dal, rnd 5; B3/3/1962 Wrightsville, GA **[R]**

YEAR	TEAM	G(GS, POS)	RUSH	YD	AVG(LG)	TD	REC	YD	AVG(LG)	TD	PASS	COMP	PCT	YD	AVG(LG)	TD	INT	SK	YD	QBR	KPR	OTD	PTS	TAY
1986	Dal	16(9, rb)	151	737	**4.9**(**84**)	12	76	837	11.0(84)	2	—	—	—	—	—	—	—	—	—	—	—	—	84	1286
1987	Dal★	12(11, RB)	209	891	4.3(60)	7	60	715	11.9(44)	1	—	—	—	—	—	—	—	—	—	—	—	—	48	1324
1988	Dal★	16(16, RB)	**361**	**1514**	4.2(38)	5	53	505	9.5(50)	2	—	—	—	—	—	—	—	—	—	—	—	—	42	1827
1989	Dal	5(5, rb)	81	246	3.0(20)	2	22	261	11.9(52)	1	—	—	—	—	—	—	—	—	—	—	—	—	18	402
1989	†Min	11(10, RB)	169	669	4.0(47)	5	18	162	9.0(24)	1	—	—	—	—	—	—	—	—	—	—	k	1	42	994
1990	Min	16(16, RB)	184	770	4.2(58)	5	35	315	9.0(32)	4	2	1	50.0	12	6.0(12)	0	0	—	—	—	k	—	54	1310
1991	Min	15(15, RB)	198	825	4.2(71)	10	33	204	6.2(19)	0	—	—	—	—	—	—	—	—	—	—	k	—	60	1035
1992	†Phi	16(16, RB)	267	1070	4.0(38)	8	38	278	7.3(41)	2	1	0	0.0	0	0.0	0	0	—	—	—	k	—	60	1323
1993	Phi	16(16, RB)	174	746	4.3(35)	1	75	610	8.1(55)	3	0	0	0.0	0	0.0	0	0	1	5	—	k	—	24	1095
1994	Phi	16(14, RB)	113	528	4.7(91)	5	50	500	10.0(**93**)	2	—	—	—	—	—	—	—	—	—	—	k	1	48	1114
1995	NYG	16(3)	31	126	4.1(36)	0	31	234	7.5(34)	1	—	—	—	—	—	—	—	—	—	—	k	—	6	514
1996	†Dal	16(1)	10	83	8.3(39)	1	7	89	12.7(24)	0	—	—	—	—	—	—	—	—	—	—	k	—	6	512
1997	Dal	16(6, fb)	6	20	3.3(11)	0	14	149	10.6(64)	2	—	—	—	—	—	—	—	—	—	—	k	—	12	522
NFL	12	187(138)	1954	8225	4.2(91)	61	512	4859	9.5(93)	21	3	1	33.3	12	4.0(12)	0	0	1	5	—	k	2	504	13255

Walker, Jackie Jackie A., LB-TE, 6´5˝/245 lbs; Jackson State; 1986: TB, rnd 2; B11/3/1962 Monroe, LA **1986** TB 15 (3) **1987** TB 12 (6, LOLB) **1988** TB 16 (0) **1989** TB 14 (0) **NFL** 57 (9) [4 yrs]

Walker, James James Charles, LB, 6´1˝/250 lbs; Kansas State; B12/9/1958 Muskogee, OK **1983** KC 3 (2)

Walker, Javon Javon Lataff, WR, 6´3˝/220 lbs; Florida State; 2002: GB, rnd 1; B10/14/1978 Galveston, TX

YEAR	TEAM	G(GS, POS)	RUSH	YD	AVG(LG)	TD	REC	YD	AVG(LG)	TD	PASS	COMP	PCT	YD	AVG(LG)	TD	INT	SK	YD	QBR	KPR	OTD	PTS	TAY
2002	†GB	15(2)	1	11	11.0(11)	0	23	319	13.9(30)	1	—	—	—	—	—	—	—	—	—	—	k	—	6	420
2003	†GB	16(3)	2	1	0.5(1)	0	41	716	17.5(66)	9	—	—	—	—	—	—	—	—	—	—	—	—	54	404
2004	†GB✧	16(12, WR)	—	—	—	—	89	1382	15.5(79)	12	—	—	—	—	—	—	—	—	—	—	—	—	72	751
2005	GB	1(1)	—	—	—	—	4	27	6.8(9)	0	—	—	—	—	—	—	—	—	—	—	—	—	0	14
NFL	4	48(18)	3	12	4.0(11)	0	157	2444	15.6(79)	22	—	—	—	—	—	—	—	—	—	—	k	—	132	1588

Walker, Jay Jewell Jay, QB, 6´3˝/229 lbs; Long Beach State; Howard; 1994: NE, rnd 7; B1/24/1972 Los Angeles, CA **1997**†Min 0 (0)

YEAR	TEAM	G(GS, POS)	RUSH	YD	AVG(LG)	TD	REC	YD	AVG(LG)	TD	PASS	COMP	PCT	YD	AVG(LG)	TD	INT	SK	YD	QBR	KPR	OTD	PTS	TAY
1996	Min	1(0)	—	—	—	—	—	—	—	—	2	2	100.0	31	15.5(19)	0	0	—	—	—	—	—	0	16
NFL	2	1(0)	—	—	—	—	—	—	—	—	2	2	100.0	31	15.5(19)	0	0	—	—	—	—	—	0	16

Walker, Jeff Jeffrey Lynn, T-G, 6´4˝/295 lbs; Memphis; 1986: SD, rnd 3; B1/22/1963 Jonesboro, AR **1986** SD 16 (0) **1988** NO 1 (0) **1989** NO 13 (0) **NFL** 30 (0) [3 yrs]

Walker, Jimmy James Charles, DT, 6´2˝/265 lbs; Arkansas; B12/30/1957 Camden, AR **1987** Min 2 (2)

Walker, Joe Joe, DB, 5´10˝/204 lbs; Nebraska; B3/19/1977 Memphis, TN **2001** Ten 16 (3) **2002**†Ind 5 (0) **NFL** 21 (3) [2 yrs]

Walker, John John Wayne, NT-DT, 6´6˝/270 lbs; Nebraska-Omaha; 1983: NYJ, rnd 5; B9/12/1961 Omaha, NE **1987** KC 3 (2)

Walker, Kenny Kenny Wayne, DE, 6´3˝/260 lbs; Nebraska; 1991: Den, rnd 8; B4/6/1967 Crane, TX **1991**†Den 16 (1) **1992** Den 15 (15, RDE) **NFL** 31 (16) [2 yrs]

Walker, Kenyatta Idrees Kenyatta, T, 6´5˝/302 lbs; Florida; 2001: TB, rnd 1; B2/1/1979 Meridian, MS **2001**†TB 16 (16, LT) **2002**†TB 13 (13, RT) **2003** TB 14 (14, RT) **2004** TB 13 (11, RT) **2005**†TB 16 (16, RT) **NFL** 72 (70) [5 yrs]

Walker, Kevin Kevin Cornelius, DB, 5´11˝/180 lbs; East Carolina; 1986: TB, rnd 6; B10/20/1963 Greensboro, NC **1986** TB 4 (0) **1987** TB 3 (3) **NFL** 7 (3) [2 yrs]

Walker, Kevin Kevin P., LB, 6´2˝/238 lbs; Maryland; 1988: Cin, rnd 3; B12/24/1965 Denville, NJ **1988** Cin 3 (0) **1989** Cin 16 (0) **1990**†Cin 16 (15, RILB) **1991** Cin 5 (4) **1992** Cin 4 (4) **NFL** 44 (23) [5 yrs]

Walker, Langston Langston, T-G, 6´8˝/345 lbs; California; 2002: Oak, rnd 2; B9/3/1979 Oakland, CA **2002**†Oak 12 (2) **2003** Oak 16 (8, rt) **2004** Oak 16 (1) **2005** Oak 6 (6, lg) **NFL** 50 (17) [4 yrs]

Walker, Louie Louis, LB, 6´1˝/216 lbs; Colorado State; B7/23/1952 Los Angeles, CA **1974** Dal 8

Walker, Malcolm Malcolm Ernest, C-T, 6´4˝/250 lbs; Rice; 1965: Dal, rnd 2/Hou, rnd 2; B5/24/1943 Dallas, TX **1966**†Dal 5 **1967**†Dal 14 **1968**†Dal 14 (C) **1969**†Dal 14 (C) **1970** GB 11 **NFL** 58 [5 yrs]

Walker, Marquis Marquis Roche, DB, 5´10˝/175 lbs; Southeast Missouri State; B7/6/1972 St. Louis, MO **1996** Was 1 (0) **1996** SL 8 (4) **1997** SL 10 (0) **1998** Oak 16 (7, rcb) **1999** Oak 16 (0) **2000** Det 12 (2) **NFL** 63 (13) [5 yrs]

Walker, Mickey George Mickey, G-LB-C, 6´0˝/235 lbs; Michigan State; 1961: NYT, rnd 23; B10/14/1939 Petoskey, MI **1961**†NYG 14 **1962**†NYG 14 **1963**†NYG 13 **1964** NYG 7 **1965** NYG 4 **NFL** 52 [5 yrs]

YEAR	TEAM	G (GS, POS)	RUSH	YD	AVG(LG)	TD	REC	YD	AVG(LG)	TD	PASS COMP	PCT	YD	AVG(LG)	TD	INT	SK	YD	QBR	KPR	OTD	PTS	TAY

WALKER, MIKE Michael R., K, 6´0˝/190 lbs; none; B10/18/1949 Lancaster, England [K]   **1972** NE 8

WALKER, MIKE Joseph Michael, DE, 6´4˝/235 lbs; Tulane; 1971: Min, rnd 11; B11/7/1949 Texarkana, AR   **1971** NO 5

WALKER, PAUL Paul Frederick, E-DB, 6´3˝/210 lbs; Yale; 1945: Det, rnd 10; B7/9/1925 Springfield, MO, D10/20/1972 West Hartford, CT

| 1948 | NYG | 12(11, LE) | — | — | — | — | 1 | 11 | 11.0(11) | 0 | — | — | — | — | — | — | — | — | — | — | i | — | 0 | 6 |

WALKER, QUENTIN LaQuentin Antonio, RB, 6´1˝/205 lbs; Virginia; 1984: SL, rnd 7; B8/27/1961 Teaneck, NJ   **1984** SL 3 (0)

WALKER, RAMON Ramon D., DB, 6´0˝/197 lbs; Pittsburgh; 2002: Hou, rnd 5; B11/8/1979 Akron, OH   **2002** Hou 8 (1) **2003** Hou 11 (0) **2005** Hou 16 (0) **NFL** 35 (1) [3 yrs]

WALKER, RANDY Randell Paul, P, 5´10˝/177 lbs; Northwestern State (LA); 1974: GB, rnd 12; B8/29/1951 Shreveport, LA

| 1974 | GB | 14 | 1 | 18 | 18.0(18) | 0 | — | — | — | — | — | — | — | — | — | — | — | — | — | P | — | — | 0 | 18 |

WALKER, RICK Richard, TE, 6´4˝/235 lbs; UCLA; 1977: Cin, rnd 4; B5/28/1955 Santa Ana, CA

1977	Cin	6(3)	—	—	—	—	1	13	13.0(13)	0	—	—	—	—	—	—	—	—	—	—	—	—	0	7
1978	Cin	15	—	—	—	—	12	126	10.5(28)	2	—	—	—	—	—	—	—	—	—	—	—	—	12	73
1979	Cin	10	—	—	—	—	1	14	14.0(14)	1	—	—	—	—	—	—	—	—	—	—	—	—	6	12
1980	Was	15(3)	1	-8	-8.0(-8)	0	10	88	8.8(15)	1	—	—	—	—	—	—	—	—	—	—	—	—	6	41
1981	Was	16(14, TE)	1	5	5.0(5)	0	11	112	10.2(24)	1	—	—	—	—	—	—	—	—	—	—	—	—	6	66
1982	†Was	9(8, TE)	2	11	5.5(6)	0	12	92	7.7(25)	1	—	—	—	—	—	—	—	—	—	—	—	—	6	62
1983	†Was	16(16, TE)	2	10	5.0(11)	0	17	168	9.9(29)	2	—	—	—	—	—	—	—	—	—	—	—	—	12	104
1984	†Was	16(14, TE)	1	2	2.0(2)	0	5	52	10.4(19)	1	—	—	—	—	—	—	—	—	—	—	—	—	6	33
1985	Was	16(0)	3	16	5.3(9)	0	1	8	8.0(8)	0	—	—	—	—	—	—	—	—	—	—	—	—	0	20
NFL	9	119(58)	10	36	3.6(11)	0	70	673	9.6(29)	9	—	—	—	—	—	—	—	—	—	—	—	—	54	418

WALKER, ROBERT Robert, RB, 5´10˝/208 lbs; West Virginia; B6/26/1972 Huntington, WV   **1996** NYG 1 (0)

WALKER, ROD Roderick Dion, DT, 6´3˝/320 lbs; Troy State; B2/4/1976 Milton, FL   **2001** GB 11 (0) **2002** †GB 13 (5, ldt) **2003** GB 7 (1) **NFL** 31 (6) [3 yrs]

WALKER, SAMMY Sammy William, DB, 5´11˝/203 lbs; Texas Tech; 1991: Pit, rnd 4; B1/20/1969 McKinney, TX   **1991** Pit 2 (0) **1992** †Pit 16 (4) **1993** †GB 6 (1) **NFL** 24 (5) [3 yrs]

WALKER, TIM Timothy Alan, LB, 6´1˝/230 lbs; Savannah State; B5/12/1958 Hartford, CT   **1980** Sea 16 (0)

WALKER, TONY Tony Maurice, LB, 6´3˝/235 lbs; Southeast Missouri State; 1990: Ind, rnd 6; B4/2/1968 Birmingham, AL   **1990** Ind 14 (0) **1991** Ind 16 (0) **1992** Ind 13 (1) **NFL** 43 (1) [3 yrs]

WALKER, VAL JOE Val Joe, DB, 6´1˝/179 lbs; SMU; 1952: NYG, rnd 7; B1/7/1930 Tahoka, TX   **1953** GB 12 (DB) **1954** GB 10 (DB) **1955** GB 12 (DB) **1956** GB 12 (DB) **1957** †SF 12 (db) **NFL** 58 [5 yrs]

WALKER, WAYNE Wayne, P, 6´3˝/230 lbs; Northwestern State (LA); 1966: KC, rnd 13; B10/14/1944 Shreveport, LA [K]   **1967** KC-A 4 **1968** Hou-A 8 **NFL** 12 [2 yrs]

WALKER, WAYNE Ronald Wayne, WR, 5´8˝/162 lbs; Texas Tech; B12/27/1966 Waco, TX

| 1989 | SD | 13(4) | 1 | 9 | 9.0(9) | 0 | 24 | 395 | 16.5(49) | 1 | — | — | — | — | — | — | — | — | — | p | — | 6 | 213 |

WALKER, WAYNE Wayne Harrison, LB, 6´2˝/225 lbs; Idaho; 1958: Det, rnd 4; B9/30/1936 Boise, ID [K]   **1958** Det 12 (RLB) **1959** Det 9 (RLB) **1960** Det☆12 (RLB) **1961** Det 14 (RLB) **1962** Det 14 (RLB) **1963** Det★14 (RLB) **1964** Det★14 (RLB) **1965** Det★14 (RLB) **1966** Det☆13 (rlb) **1967** Det 14 (RLB) **1968** Det 14 (RLB) **1969** Det 14 (RLB) **1970** †Det 14 (RLB) **1971** Det 14 (RLB) **1972** Det 14 (RLB) **NFL** 200 [15 yrs]

WALKER, WESLEY Wesley Darcel, WR, 6´0˝/179 lbs; California; 1977: NYJ, rnd 2; B5/26/1955 San Bernardino, CA

1977	NYJ	14(14, WR)	3	25	8.3(11)	0	35	740	21.1(87)	3	—	—	—	—	—	—	—	—	—	—	—	18	410
1978	NYJ★	16(16, WR)	1	-3	-3.0(-3)	0	48	1169	24.4(77)	8	—	—	—	—	—	—	—	—	—	—	—	48	622
1979	NYJ	9(9, WR)	—	—	—	—	23	569	24.7(71)	5	—	—	—	—	—	—	—	—	—	—	—	30	310
1980	NYJ	10(7, WR)	—	—	—	—	18	376	20.9(47)	1	—	—	—	—	—	—	—	—	—	—	—	6	193
1981	†NYJ	13(13, WR)	—	—	—	—	47	770	16.4(49)	9	—	—	—	—	—	—	—	—	—	—	—	54	430
1982	†NYJ★	9(9, WR)	—	—	—	—	39	620	15.9(56)	6	—	—	—	—	—	—	—	—	—	—	—	36	340
1983	NYJ	16(16, WR)	—	—	—	—	61	868	14.2(64)	7	—	—	—	—	—	—	—	—	—	—	—	42	469
1984	NYJ	12(10, WR)	1	1	1.0(1)	0	41	623	15.2(44)	7	—	—	—	—	—	—	—	—	—	—	—	42	348
1985	†NYJ	12(10, WR)	—	—	—	—	34	725	21.3(96)	5	—	—	—	—	—	—	—	—	—	—	—	32	388
1986	†NYJ☆	16(8, WR)	—	—	—	—	49	1016	20.7(83)	12	—	—	—	—	—	—	—	—	—	—	—	72	568
1987	NYJ	5(4)	—	—	—	—	9	190	21.1(59)	1	—	—	—	—	—	—	—	—	—	—	—	6	100
1988	NYJ	16(10, WR)	1	12	12.0(12)	0	26	551	21.2(50)	7	—	—	—	—	—	—	—	—	—	—	—	42	323
1989	NYJ	6(3)	—	—	—	—	8	89	11.1(31)	0	—	—	—	—	—	—	—	—	—	—	—	0	45
NFL	13	154(129)	6	35	5.8(12)	0	438	8306	19.0(96)	71	—	—	—	—	—	—	—	—	—	—	—	428	4543

WALKER, WILLIE Willie, WR, 6´3˝/200 lbs; Tennessee State; 1966: Det, rnd 4; B9/15/1942 Anguilla, MS

| 1966 | Det | 9 | 1 | 4 | 4.0(4) | 0 | 1 | 21 | 21.0(21) | 0 | — | — | — | — | — | — | — | — | — | — | — | 0 | 15 |

WALL, EDDIE Edmund A., aka Eddie Waleski, BB, 5´9˝/170 lbs; Allegheny; Grove City; B4/21/1907 Braddock, PA, D9/9/1986 York, PA   **1930** Fra 1 (0)

WALLACE, AARON Aaron Jon, LB, 6´3˝/240 lbs; Texas A&M; 1990: LARd, rnd 2; B4/17/1967 Paris, TX   **1990** †LARd 16 (0) **1991** †LARd 16 (0) **1992** LARd 16 (16, LLB) **1993** †LARd 16 (14, LLB) **1994** LARd 16 (6, llb) **1995** Oak 13 (0) **1997** Oak 5 (0) **1998** Oak 4 (0) **NFL** 102 (36) [8 yrs]

WALLACE, AL Alonzo Dwight, DE, 6´5˝/258 lbs; Maryland; B3/25/1974 Delray Beach, FL   **1997** Phi 1 (0) **1998** Phi 15 (0) **2002** Car 16 (4) **2003** †Car 16 (2) **2004** Car 16 (0) **2005** †Car 16 (2) **NFL** 80 (8) [6 yrs]

WALLACE, BEV Beverly William, QB, 6´2˝/180 lbs; Compton CC (CA); B3/7/1923, D6/17/1992 Newport Beach, CA

1947	SF-A	4(0)	—	—	—	—	—	—	—	—	16	5	31.3	48	3.0	0	2	—	—	—	P	—	0	-56
1948	SF-A	10(0)	3	2	0.7	0	—	—	—	—	22	8	36.4	114	5.2	1	3	—	—	—	P	—	0	-56
1949	SF-A	9(1)	2	2	1.0	1	—	—	—	—	23	9	39.1	95	4.1	0	4	—	—	—	P	—	6	-101
AAFC	3	23(1)	5	4	0.8	1	—	—	—	—	61	22	36.1	257	4.2	1	9	—	—	—	P	—	6	-213
1951	NYY	1	1	-8	-8.0(-8)	0	—	—	—	—	8	1	12.5	9	1.1(9)	0	0	—	—	—	—	—	0	-4

WALLACE, BOB Robert Charles, WR-TE, 6´3˝/211 lbs; Texas-El Paso; 1968: Chi, rnd 2; B10/7/1945 Texarkana, AR

1968	ChiB	12	3	29	9.7(18)	0	19	281	14.8(27)	2	—	—	—	—	—	—	—	—	—	—	kp	—	12	212
1969	ChiB	14(WR)	4	16	4.0(15)	0	47	553	11.8(45)	3	—	—	—	—	—	—	—	—	—	—	—	—	30	318
1970	ChiB	5	—	—	—	—	15	160	10.7(33)	0	—	—	—	—	—	—	—	—	—	—	—	—	0	80
1971	ChiB	14(TE)	1	0	0.0(0)	0	27	400	14.8(58)	2	1	0	0.0	0	0.0	0	0	—	—	—	—	—	12	210
1972	ChiB	14	—	—	—	—	1	9	9.0(9)	0	1	0	0.0	0	0.0	0	0	—	—	—	—	—	0	5
NFL	5	59	8	45	5.6(18)	0	109	1403	12.9(58)	9	2	0	0.0	0	0.0	0	0	—	—	—	kp	—	54	824

WALLACE, CAL Calvin Kerr, DE, 6´3˝/230 lbs; West Virginia Tech; B4/17/1965 Montgomery, WV   **1987** GB 1 (0)

WALLACE, DUTCH Clarence, G-C-T, 6´0˝/203 lbs; none; B4/18/1900 Akron, OH, D2/1977 Akron, OH [K]   **1923** Akr 5 (4, RG) **1924** Akr 7 (6, lg), 2 **1925** Cle 10 (10, RG) **1926** Can 7 (5, lg) **1926** Akr 1 (1) **NFL** 30 (26) [4 yrs]

WALLACE, GORDON Gordon Lewis, TB-FB-C, 5´10˝/170 lbs; Rochester; B8/6/1899, D12/29/1992 Ticonderoga, NY   **1923** Roc 2 (2, TB) **1924** Roc 1 (0) **NFL** 3 (2) [2 yrs]

WALLACE, HENRY Henry Marshall, DB, 6´0˝/195 lbs; Pacific; B9/26/1938 Bakersfield, CA   **1960** LAC-A 2

WALLACE, JACKIE Jackie, DB, 6´3˝/197 lbs; Arizona; 1973: Min, rnd 2; B3/13/1951 New Orleans, LA [R]   **1974** †Min 14 (14, RCB) **1975** †Bal 14 (10, FS) **1976** †Bal 14 (14, FS) **1978** †LARm☆14 **1979** †LARm 4

| 1977 | †LARm | 10 | — | — | — | — | 1 | 13 | 13.0(13) | 0 | — | — | — | — | — | — | — | — | — | i | — | 0 | 25 |
| **NFL** | 6 | 70(38) | — | — | — | — | 1 | 13 | 13.0(13) | 0 | — | — | — | — | — | — | — | — | — | kpi | 2 | 12 | 668 |

WALLACE, JOHN John James, E, 6´0˝/180 lbs; Notre Dame; B9/2/1904 Coal City, IL, D7/3/1981 Mission Viejo, CA   **1928** ChiB 12 (3), 6 **1929** Day 4 (2) **NFL** 16 (5) [2 yrs]

WALLACE, RAY Raymond Duryea, RB, 6´0˝/224 lbs; Purdue; 1986: Hou, rnd 6; B12/3/1963 Indianapolis, IN

1986	Hou	8(4)	52	218	4.2(19)	3	17	177	10.4(35)	2	—	—	—	—	—	—	—	—	—	—	—	30	347
1987	†Hou	12(9, FB)	19	102	5.4(19)	0	7	34	4.9(7)	0	—	—	—	—	—	—	—	—	—	—	—	0	119
1989	Pit	9(0)	5	10	2.0(5)	1	—	—	—	—	—	—	—	—	—	—	—	—	—	—	—	6	20
NFL	3	29(13)	76	330	4.3(19)	4	24	211	8.8(35)	2	—	—	—	—	—	—	—	—	—	—	—	36	486

YEAR	TEAM	G(GS, POS)	RUSH	YD	AVG(LG)	TD	REC	YD	AVG(LG)	TD	PASS	COMP	PCT	YD	AVG(LG)	TD	INT	SK	YD	QBR	KPR	OTD	PTS	TAY

WALLACE, RIAN Rian, LB, 6′4″/243 lbs; Temple; 2005: Pit, rnd 5; B5/24/1982 Pottstown, PA   **2005**†Pit 4 (0)

WALLACE, RODNEY Rodney Allan, T-G, 6′5″/255 lbs; New Mexico; 1971: Dal, rnd 10; B2/10/1949 Pueblo, CO   **1971**†Dal 11 **1972**†Dal 14 **1973**†Dal 12 **NFL** 37 [3 yrs]

WALLACE, ROGER Roger Lee, WR, 5′11″/180 lbs; Bowling Green State; 1974: SL, rnd 12; B7/22/1952 Urabana, OH   **1976** NYG 3

WALLACE, SENECA Seneca, QB, 5′11″/196 lbs; Iowa State; 2003: Sea, rnd 4; B8/6/1980 Sacramento, CA

| 2005 | †Sea | 7(0) | 6 | -5 | -0.8(0) | 0 | — | — | — | — | 25 | 13 | 52.0 | 173 | 6.9(42) | 1 | 1 | 3 | 20 | — | — | — | 0 | 47 |

WALLACE, STAN Stanley Howard, DB-HB, 6′3″/208 lbs; Illinois; 1954: ChiB, rnd 1; B11/15/1931 Hillsboro, IL, D12/6/1999 Urbana, IL   **1954** ChiB 7 **1956**†ChiB 6 (DB) **1957** ChiB 12 (DB) **1958** ChiB☆12 **NFL** 37 [4 yrs]

WALLACE, STEVE Barron Steven, T-G, 6′4″/285 lbs; Auburn; 1986: SF, rnd 4; B12/27/1964 Atlanta, GA   **1986**†SF 16 (0) **1987**†SF 11 (4) **1988**†SF 16 (16, LT) **1989**†SF 16 (1) **1990**†SF 16 (16, RT) **1991** SF 16 (16, LT) **1992**†SF★16 (16, LT) **1993**†SF 15 (15, LT) **1994**†SF☆15 (15, LT) **1995**†SF 13 (12, LT) **1996**†SF 16 (16, LT) **1997**†KC 10 (0) **NFL** 176 (127) [12 yrs]

WALLACE, TACO Taco, WR, 6′1″/190 lbs; Kansas State; 2003: Sea, rnd 7; B4/14/1981 Harbor City, CA   **2003**†Sea 1 (0) **2005** GB 1 (0) **2004** Sea 2 (0) **NFL** 4 (0) [3 yrs]

WALLER, BILL William Howell, E, 6′1″/190 lbs; Illinois; B12/16/1911 Thompsonville, IL, D11/79

| 1938 | Bkn | 10(1) | — | — | — | — | 3 | 15 | 5.0 | 0 | — | — | — | — | — | — | — | — | — | — | — | — | 0 | 8 |

WALLER, RON Ronald Bowles, HB, 5′11″/180 lbs; Maryland; 1955: LA, rnd 2; B2/14/1933 Hastings, FL [C]

1955	†LARm★	12(LH)	151	716	4.7(55)	7	24	228	9.5(30)	1	1	0	0.0	0	0.0	0	0	—	—	kp	—	48	1101
1956	LARm☆	9(LH)	83	543	6.5(46)	1	9	76	8.4(16)	0	3	1	33.3	44	14.7(44)	0	0	—	—	kp	—	6	719
1957	LARm	11	48	292	6.1(76)	0	5	40	8.0(17)	0	6	2	33.3	35	5.8(30)	0	0	—	—	kp	—	0	377
1958	LARm	10	3	13	4.3(2)	0	3	75	25.0(63)	0	—	—	—	—	—	—	—	—	—	kp	—	0	8
1960	LAC-A	2	9	5	0.6(3)	0	3	24	8.0(23)	0	1	0	0.0	0	0.0	0	1	—	—	—	—	0	-23
NFL		44	294	1569	5.3(76)	8	44	443	10.1(63)	1	11	3	27.3	79	7.2(44)	0	1	—	—	kp	—	54	2181

WALLERSTEDT, BRETT Brett Robert, LB, 6′1″/240 lbs; Arizona State; 1993: Phx, rnd 6; B11/24/1970 Tacoma, WA   **1993** Phx 7 (0) **1994** Cin 10 (0) **1995** Cin 11 (2) **1997** SL 2 (0) **NFL** 30 (2) [4 yrs]

WALLNER, FRED Frederick William, LB-G, 6′2″/231 lbs; Notre Dame; 1951: ChiC, rnd 20; B4/28/1928 Greenfield, MA, D11/4/1999 Wethersford, CT   **1951** ChiC 12 (rg) **1952** ChiC 9 **1954** ChiC 12 (LLB) **1955** ChiC☆12 (LLB) **1960** Hou-A 7 **NFL** 52 [5 yrs]

WALLS, CRAIG Craig Stevens, LB, 6′1″/215 lbs; Indiana; B12/24/1958 Pittsburgh, PA   **1987** Buf 3 (0)

WALLS, EVERSON Everson Collins, DB, 6′1″/194 lbs; Grambling State; B12/28/1959 Dallas, TX [I]   **1981**†Dal☆16 (12, LCB) **1982**†Dal★9 (9, LCB) **1983**†Dal★16 (16, LCB) **1984** Dal☆16 (16, LCB) **1985**†Dal★16 (16, LCB) **1986** Dal 16 (16, LCB) **1987** Dal 12 (12, LCB) **1988** Dal 16 (16, LCB) **1989** Dal 16 (14, LCB) **1990**†NYG 16 (16, RCB) **1991** NYG 14 (14, RCB) **1992** NYG 6 (2) **1992** Cle 10 (5, lcb) **1993** Cle 7 (7, lcb) **NFL** 186 (171) [13 yrs]

WALLS, HENRY Henry Jerod, LB, 6′2″/220 lbs; Clemson; B2/13/1964 Lexington, NC   **1987** NYJ 3 (0)

WALLS, HERKIE McCurey Hercules, WR, 5′8″/159 lbs; Texas; 1983: Hou, rnd 7; B7/18/1961 Garland, TX

1983	Hou	16(3)	5	44	8.8(14)	0	12	276	23.0(48)	1	—	—	—	—	—	—	—	—	—	k	—	6	162
1984	Hou	14(10, WR)	4	20	5.0(20)	0	18	291	16.2(76)	1	—	—	—	—	—	—	—	—	—	k	—	6	235
1985	Hou	6(0)	—	—	—	—	1	7	7.0(7)	0	—	—	—	—	—	—	—	—	—	—	—	0	58
1987	TB	2(2)	—	—	—	—	1	13	13.0(13)	0	—	—	—	—	—	—	—	—	—	kp	—	0	45
NFL		4	38(15)	9	64	7.1(20)	0	32	587	18.3(76)	2	—	—	—	—	—	—	—	—	kp	—	12	499

WALLS, LENNY Lenny, DB, 6′4″/192 lbs; Boston College; B9/26/1979 San Francisco, CA   **2002** Den 13 (0) **2003**†Den 16 (16, LCB) **2004** Den 7 (1) **2005** Den 7 (3) **NFL** 43 (20) [4 yrs]

WALLS, RAYMOND Raymond Omonical Tyshone, DB, 5′10″/188 lbs; Southern Mississippi; 2001: Ind, rnd 5; B7/24/1979 Kentwood, LA   **2001** Ind 4 (0) **2002** Cle 4 (0) **2003** Bal 10 (0) **2004** Bal 16 (1) **2005** Arz 7 (2) **NFL** 41 (3) [5 yrs]

WALLS, WESLEY Charles Wesley, TE, 6′5″/240 lbs; Mississippi; 1989: SF, rnd 2; B3/26/1966 Batesville, MS

1989	†SF	16(0)	—	—	—	—	4	16	4.0(9)	1	—	—	—	—	—	—	—	—	—	—	—	6	13
1990	†SF	16(0)	—	—	—	—	5	27	5.4(11)	0	—	—	—	—	—	—	—	—	—	k	—	0	15
1991	SF	15(0)	—	—	—	—	2	24	12.0(21)	0	—	—	—	—	—	—	—	—	—	—	—	0	12
1993	SF	6(0)	—	—	—	—	—	—	—	—	—	—	—	—	—	—	—	—	—	—	—	0	0
1994	NO	15(7, TE)	—	—	—	—	38	406	10.7(31)	4	—	—	—	—	—	—	—	—	—	—	—	26	223
1995	NO	16(11, TE)	—	—	—	—	57	694	12.2(29)	4	—	—	—	—	—	—	—	—	—	k	—	26	358
1996	†Car★	16(15, TE)	—	—	—	—	61	713	11.7(40)	10	—	—	—	—	—	—	—	—	—	—	—	60	407
1997	Car★	15(15, TE)	—	—	—	—	58	746	12.9(52)	6	—	—	—	—	—	—	—	—	—	—	—	36	403
1998	Car◇	14(14, TE)	—	—	—	—	49	506	10.3(30)	5	—	—	—	—	—	—	—	—	—	—	—	30	278
1999	Car★	16(16, TE)	—	—	—	—	63	822	13.0(37)	12	—	—	—	—	—	—	—	—	—	—	—	72	471
2000	Car	8(8, TE)	—	—	—	—	31	422	13.6(54)	2	—	—	—	—	—	—	—	—	—	—	—	12	221
2001	Car★	14(14, TE)	—	—	—	—	43	452	10.5(25)	5	—	—	—	—	—	—	—	—	—	—	—	30	251
2002	Car	15(14, TE)	—	—	—	—	19	241	12.7(27)	4	—	—	—	—	—	—	—	—	—	—	—	24	141
2003	†GB	14(1)	—	—	—	—	20	222	11.1(36)	1	—	—	—	—	—	—	—	—	—	—	—	6	116
NFL		14	196(115)	—	—	—	—	450	5291	11.8(54)	54	—	—	—	—	—	—	—	—	k	—	328	2908

WALLS, WILL William Thomas, E, 6′4″/214 lbs; TCU; B12/8/1912 Lonoke, AR, D1/2/1993 Dallas, TX

1937	NYG	11(4)	—	—	—	—	7	55	7.9	0	—	—	—	—	—	—	—	—	—	—	—	0	28
1938	NYG	4(1)	—	—	—	—	1	23	23.0(23)	0	—	—	—	—	—	—	—	—	—	—	—	0	12
1939	†NYG	10(6, RE)	—	—	—	—	2	19	9.5(11)	0	—	—	—	—	—	—	—	—	—	—	—	0	10
1941	†NYG	11(0)	—	—	—	—	4	76	19.0(36)	0	—	—	—	—	—	—	—	—	—	k	—	0	36
1942	NYG	11(10, RE)	—	—	—	—	7	192	27.4(60)	2	—	—	—	—	—	—	—	—	—	k	—	12	102
1943	†NYG	8(6, RE)	—	—	—	—	14	231	16.5(39)	2	—	—	—	—	—	—	—	—	—	k	—	12	114
NFL		6	55(27)	—	—	—	—	35	596	17.0(60)	4	—	—	—	—	—	—	—	—	k	—	24	300

WALQUIST, LAURIE Lawrence Wilfred, B, 5′8″/167 lbs; Illinois; B3/9/1898 Rockford, IL, D9/28/1985 Deerfield Lake, IL [K]   **1922** ChiB 12 (6, rh) **1924** ChiB 9 (7, RH), 6 **1925** ChiB 16 (13, RH), 18 **1926** ChiB 15 (15, RH), 12 **1927** ChiB 14 (14, RH), 6 **1928** ChiB 12 (10, RH), 12 **1929** ChiB 13 (7, RH), 18 **1930** ChiB 10 (1), 7 **1931** ChiB 10 (4) **NFL** 111 (77), 79 [9 yrs]

WALSH, BILL William Henry, C, 6′2″/230 lbs; Notre Dame; 1949: Pit, rnd 3/Bkn-A, rnd 2; B9/8/1927 Phillipsburg, NJ; HOF 1993   **1949** Pit☆12 (9, C) **1950** Pit◇12 (C) **1951** Pit◇12 (C) **1952** Pit☆12 (C) **1953** Pit 12 (C) **1954** Pit☆12 (C) **NFL** 72 (9) [6 yrs]

WALSH, CHRIS Christopher Lee, WR, 6′1″/194 lbs; Stanford; 1992: Buf, rnd 9; B12/12/1968 Cleveland, OH

1992	Buf	2(0)	—	—	—	—	—	—	—	—	—	—	—	—	—	—	—	—	—	—	—	—	—
1993	Buf	3(0)	—	—	—	—	—	—	—	—	—	—	—	—	—	—	—	—	—	—	—	—	—
1994	†Min	10(0)	—	—	—	—	—	—	—	—	—	—	—	—	—	—	—	—	—	k	—	0	-9
1995	Min	16(0)	—	—	—	—	7	66	9.4(16)	0	—	—	—	—	—	—	—	—	—	—	—	0	30
1996	Min	15(0)	—	—	—	—	4	39	9.8(17)	1	1	0	0.0	0	0.0	0	0	—	—	—	—	8	25
1997	†Min	14(0)	—	—	—	—	11	114	10.4(19)	1	—	—	—	—	—	—	—	—	—	k	—	6	57
1998	Min	15(0)	—	—	—	—	2	46	23.0(25)	0	—	—	—	—	—	—	—	—	—	—	—	0	23
1999	†Min	16(1)	—	—	—	—	2	24	12.0(18)	1	—	—	—	—	—	—	—	—	—	—	—	6	17
2000	†Min	16(0)	—	—	—	—	18	191	10.6(21)	0	—	—	—	—	—	—	—	—	—	kp	—	0	81
2001	Min	16(0)	—	—	—	—	9	67	7.4(19)	0	—	—	—	—	—	—	—	—	—	kp	—	0	26
2002	Min	16(3)	—	—	—	—	14	172	12.3(28)	1	—	—	—	—	—	—	—	—	—	—	—	6	91
NFL		11	139(4)	—	—	—	—	67	719	10.7(28)	4	1	0	0.0	0	0.0	0	0	—	—	kp	—	26	340

WALSH, ED Edward Henry, T, 6′4″/243 lbs; Widener; B7/11/1935 Fort Meade, MD   **1961** NYT-A 6

WALSH, JIM James Kevin, RB, 5′11″/220 lbs; San Jose State; B12/17/1956 Burlingame, CA

| 1980 | Sea | 4(0) | 2 | 4 | 2.0(2) | 0 | — | — | — | — | — | — | — | — | — | — | — | — | — | — | — | 0 | 4 |

YEAR	TEAM	G (GS, POS)	RUSH	YD	AVG(LG)	TD	REC	YD	AVG(LG)	TD	PASS COMP	PCT	YD	AVG(LG)	TD	INT	SK	YD	QBR	KPR	OTD	PTS	TAY

WALSH, STEVE Steven John, QB, 6´3˝/207 lbs; Miami (FL); 1989: Dal, rnd S1; B12/1/1966 St. Paul, MN

1989	Dal	8(5, qb)	6	16	2.7(14)	0	—	—	—	—	219	110	50.2	1371	6.3(46)	5	9	11	84	60.5	—	—	0	367
1990	Dal	1(0)	1	0	0.0(0)	0	—	—	—	—	9	4	44.4	40	4.4(20)	0	0	—	—	—	—	—	0	20
1990	†NO	12(11, QB)	19	25	1.3(18)	0	—	—	—	—	327	175	53.5	1970	6.0(58)	12	13	10	76	67.5	—	—	0	550
1991	NO	8(7, qb)	8	0	0.0(3)	0	—	—	—	—	255	141	55.3	1638	6.4(41)	11	6	16	134	79.5	—	—	0	634
1993	NO	2(1)	4	-4	-1.0(-1)	0	—	—	—	—	38	20	52.6	271	7.1(54)	2	3	—	—	—	—	—	0	22
1994	†ChiB	12(11, QB)	30	4	0.1(12)	1	—	—	—	—	343	208	60.6	2078	6.1(50)	10	8	11	52	77.9	—	—	6	783
1995	ChiB	1(0)	—	—	—	—	—	—	—	—	—	—	—	—	—	—	—	—	—	—	—	—	—	—
1996	SL	3(3)	6	10	1.7(13)	0	—	—	—	—	77	33	42.9	344	4.5(32)	0	5	4	27	—	—	—	0	-18
1997	†TB	12(0)	6	-4	-0.7(0)	0	—	—	—	—	17	6	35.3	58	3.4(38)	0	1	—	—	—	—	—	0	-15
1998	TB	5(0)	—	—	—	—	—	—	—	—	19	9	47.4	58	3.1(12)	0	3	1	9	—	—	—	0	-91
1999	†Ind	16(0)	—	—	—	—	—	—	—	—	13	7	53.8	47	3.6(11)	0	2	—	—	—	—	—	0	-57
NFL	10	80(38)	80	47	0.6(18)	1	—	—	—	—	1317	713	54.1	7875	6.0(58)	40	50	53	382	66.4	—	—	6	2195

WALSH, WARD William Ward, RB, 6´0˝/213 lbs; Colorado; B11/21/1947 Paradise, CA

1971	Hou	13	38	129	3.4(19)	0	6	36	6.0(16)	1	—	—	—	—	—	—	—	—	—	—	k	—	6	161
1972	Hou	6	8	36	4.5(14)	0	4	22	5.5(16)	0	—	—	—	—	—	—	—	—	—	—	—	1	6	47
1972	GB	2	—	—	—	—	—	—	—	—	—	—	—	—	—	—	—	—	—	—	—	—	—	—
NFL	2	21	46	165	3.6(19)	0	10	58	5.8(16)	1	—	—	—	—	—	—	—	—	—	—	k	1	12	208

WALSON, BULLETS Charles, BB, /174 lbs; none; B1/6/1893, D12/1963, NJ **1921** Was 2 (1, BB), 6

WALSTON, BOBBY Robert Harold, E-HB-K, 6´0˝/190 lbs; Georgia; 1951: Phi, rnd 14; B10/17/1928 Columbus, OH, D10/7/1987 Roselle, IL **[K]**

1951	Phi☆	12(LE)	—	—	—	—	31	512	16.5(43)	8	—	—	—	—	—	—	—	—	—	—	Kk	—	94	278
1952	Phi	12(LE)	—	—	—	—	26	469	18.0(65)	3	—	—	—	—	—	—	—	—	—	—	Kp	—	82	253
1953	Phi	12(LE)	—	—	—	—	41	750	18.3(62)	5	—	—	—	—	—	—	—	—	—	—	K	—	87	400
1954	Phi	12(LE)	—	—	—	—	31	581	18.7(75)	11	—	—	—	—	—	—	—	—	—	—	K	—	114	346
1955	Phi	12(RH)	1	-3	-3.0(-3)	0	27	443	16.4(63)	3	—	—	—	—	—	—	—	—	—	—	K	—	30	234
1956	Phi	12(LE)	—	—	—	—	39	590	15.1(51)	3	—	—	—	—	—	—	—	—	—	—	K	—	53	310
1957	Phi	12(LE)	1	7	7.0(7)	0	11	266	24.2(49)	1	—	—	—	—	—	—	—	—	—	—	K	—	53	145
1958	Phi	12(LE)	—	—	—	—	21	298	14.2(71)	3	—	—	—	—	—	—	—	—	—	—	K	—	67	164
1959	Phi	12(LE)	2	8	4.0(7)	0	16	279	17.4(40)	3	—	—	—	—	—	—	—	—	—	—	K	—	51	163
1960	†Phi◇	12(TE)	—	—	—	—	30	563	18.8(49)	4	—	—	—	—	—	—	—	—	—	—	K	—	105	302
1961	Phi◇	14(TE)	—	—	—	—	34	569	16.7(68)	2	—	—	—	—	—	—	—	—	—	—	K	—	97	295
1962	Phi	14	—	—	—	—	4	43	10.8(16)	0	—	—	—	—	—	—	—	—	—	—	K	—	48	22
NFL	12	148	4	12	3.0(7)	0	311	5363	17.2(75)	46	—	—	—	—	—	—	—	—	—	—	Kkp	—	881	2909

WALTER, DAVE David Lee Russell, QB, 6´3˝/230 lbs; Michigan Tech; 1987: NYG, rnd 11; B12/9/1964 West Branch, MI

| 1987 | Cin | 3(2) | 16 | 70 | 4.4(16) | 0 | — | — | — | — | 21 | 10 | 47.6 | 113 | 5.4(35) | 0 | 0 | 2 | 15 | — | — | — | 0 | 127 |

WALTER, JOE Joseph Follmann, T-G, 6´7˝/292 lbs; Texas Tech; 1985: Cin, rnd 7; B6/18/1963 Dallas, TX   **1985** Cin 14 (0) **1986** Cin 15 (8, rt) **1987** Cin 12 (12, RT) **1988** Cin 16 (16, RT) **1989** Cin 10 (7, rt) **1990**†Cin 16 (16, RT) **1991** Cin 15 (14, RT) **1992** Cin 16 (16, RT) **1993** Cin 16 (16, RT/lt) **1995** Cin 16 (16, RT) **1996** Cin 15 (15, RT) **1997** Cin 5 (0) **NFL** 166 (136) [12 yrs]

WALTER, KEN Kenneth Matthew, P, 6´1˝/207 lbs; Kent State; B8/15/1972 Cleveland, OH **[P]**   **1999** Car 16 (0) **2001**†NE 11 (0) **2002** NE 16 (0) **2004**†Sea 6 (0)

1997	Car	16(0)	1	-5	-5.0(-5)	0	—	—	—	—	—	—	—	—	—	—	—	—	—	—	P	—	0	-5
1998	Car	16(0)	3	0	0.0(0)	0	—	—	—	—	1	0	0.0	0	0.0	0	0	—	—	—	P	—	0	0
2000	Car	16(0)	1	0	0.0(0)	0	—	—	—	—	1	0	0.0	0	0.0	0	0	—	—	—	P	—	0	0
2003	†NE	15(0)	2	0	0.0(0)	0	—	—	—	—	—	—	—	—	—	—	—	—	—	—	P	—	0	0
NFL	8	112(0)	7	-5	-0.7	0	—	—	—	—	2	0	0.0	0	0.0	0	0	—	—	—	P	—	0	-5

WALTER, KEVIN Kevin Patrick, WR, 6´3˝/221 lbs; Eastern Michigan; 2003: NYG, rnd 7; B8/4/1981 Lake Forest, IL

2003	Cin	11(0)	—	—	—	—	3	18	6.0(9)	0	—	—	—	—	—	—	—	—	—	—	—	—	0	9
2004	Cin	16(0)	—	—	—	—	8	67	8.4(18)	0	—	—	—	—	—	—	—	—	—	—	—	—	0	34
2005	†Cin	16(2)	—	—	—	—	19	211	11.1(33)	1	—	—	—	—	—	—	—	—	—	—	—	—	6	111
NFL	3	43(2)	—	—	—	—	30	296	9.9(33)	1	—	—	—	—	—	—	—	—	—	—	—	—	6	153

WALTER, MIKE Michael David, LB, 6´3˝/240 lbs; Oregon; 1983: Dal, rnd 2; B11/30/1960 Salem, OR   **1983** Dal 15 (0) **1984**†SF 16 (0) **1985**†SF 14 (14, RILB) **1986**†SF 16 (2) **1987**†SF 12 (12, RILB) **1988**†SF 16 (16, RILB) **1989**†SF☆16 (16, RILB) **1990**†SF 3 (3) **1991** SF 11 (11, RILB) **1992**†SF 15 (13, RILB) **1993**†SF 15 (9, MLB) **NFL** 149 (96) [11 yrs]

WALTER, TYSON Tyson, C-T, 6´4˝/310 lbs; Ohio State; 2002: Dal, rnd 6; B3/17/1978 Bainbridge, OH   **2002** Dal 10 (8, C) **2003**†Dal 16 (0) **2004** Dal 13 (1) **NFL** 39 (9) [3 yrs]

WALTERS, DALE Dale James, P, 6´0˝/200 lbs; Rice; B6/21/1961 Dighton, KS   **1987** Cle 2 (0)

WALTERS, DANNY Daniel Eugene, DB, 6´1˝/189 lbs; Arkansas; 1983: SD, rnd 4; B11/4/1960 Prescott, AR   **1983** SD 16 (16, RCB) **1984** SD 8 (7, RCB) **1985** SD 16 (16, RCB) **1986** SD 2 (2) **1987** SD 12 (5, rcb) **NFL** 54 (46) [5 yrs]

WALTERS, JOEY Joseph Laverne, WR, 6´0˝/175 lbs; Clemson; B10/29/1954 Florence, SC

| 1987 | Hou | 5(0) | — | — | — | — | 5 | 99 | 19.8(51) | 0 | — | — | — | — | — | — | — | — | — | — | kp | — | 0 | 62 |

WALTERS, LES Lester Kenneth, DB, 6´0˝/185 lbs; Penn State; 1958: Bal, rnd 4; B2/13/1937 Palmyra, PA   **1958** Was 8 (6, DB)

WALTERS, MATT Matthew Jeremy, DE, 6´5˝/272 lbs; Miami (FL); 2003: NYJ, rnd 5; B8/22/1979 Melbourne, FL   **2003** NYJ 11 (0)

WALTERS, PETE Peter Hudson, G, 6´2˝/265 lbs; Western Kentucky; B3/17/1959 Compton, CA   **1987** Phi 3 (3)

WALTERS, ROD Wayne Roderick, G-T, 6´3˝/258 lbs; Iowa; 1976: KC, rnd 1; B2/27/1954 Lansing, MI   **1976** KC 14 **1978** KC 16 (4) **1979** KC 16 (2) **1980** KC 6 (1) **1980** Mia 1 (0) **1980** Det 2 (0) **NFL** 55 (7) [4 yrs]

WALTERS, STAN Stanley Peter, T, 6´6˝/275 lbs; Syracuse; 1972: Cin, rnd 9; B5/27/1948 Rutherford, NJ   **1972** Cin 8 (LT) **1973** Cin 4 **1974** Cin 14 (RT) **1975** Phi 14 (14, LT) **1976** Phi 14 (14, LT) **1977** Phi☆14 (14, LT) **1978**†Phi★16 (16, LT) **1979**†Phi★16 (16, LT) **1980**†Phi 16 (16, LT) **1981**†Phi 16 (16, LT) **1982** Phi 9 (9, LT) **1983** Phi 12 (10, LT) **NFL** 153 (125) [12 yrs]

WALTERS, TOM Thomas Herrin, DB, 6´2˝/195 lbs; Southern Mississippi; 1964: Was, rnd 16; B6/11/1942 Petal, MS   **1964** Was 13 **1965** Was 14 **1966** Was 12 **1967** Was 10 **NFL** 49 [4 yrs]

WALTERS, TROY Troy M., WR, 5´7˝/172 lbs; Stanford; 2000: Min, rnd 5; B12/15/1976 Bloomington, IN **[R]**

2000	†Min	12(0)	1	3	3.0(3)	0	1	5	5.0(5)	0	—	—	—	—	—	—	—	—	—	—	kp	—	0	390
2001	Min	6(0)	—	—	—	—	—	—	—	—	—	—	—	—	—	—	—	—	—	—	kp	—	0	169
2002	†Ind	16(1)	2	33	16.5(17)	0	18	207	11.5(27)	0	—	—	—	—	—	—	—	—	—	—	kp	—	0	587
2003	†Ind	15(4)	1	6	6.0(6)	0	36	456	12.7(46)	3	—	—	—	—	—	—	—	—	—	—	kp	—	18	335
2004	†Ind	5(0)	—	—	—	—	1	5	5.0(5)	0	—	—	—	—	—	—	—	—	—	—	kp	—	0	9
2005	†Ind	16(1)	—	—	—	—	14	152	10.9(39)	3	—	—	—	—	—	—	—	—	—	—	kp	—	18	156
NFL	6	70(6)	4	42	10.5(17)	0	70	825	11.8(46)	6	—	—	—	—	—	—	—	—	—	—	kp	—	36	1645

WALTERSCHEID, LEN Leonard Raymond, DB, 5´11˝/190 lbs; Southern Utah; B9/13/1954 Gainesville, TX   **1977**†ChiB 14 **1978** ChiB 14 (3) **1979**†ChiB 15 (2) **1980** ChiB 15 (2) **1981** ChiB 6 (4) **1982** ChiB 9 (8, FS) **1983** Buf 3 (0) **1984** Buf 3 (0) **NFL** 79 (19) [8 yrs]

WALTON, ALVIN Alvin Earl, DB, 6´0˝/180 lbs; Kansas; 1986: Was, rnd 3; B3/14/1964 Riverside, CA   **1986**†Was 16 (4) **1987**†Was☆12 (12, SS) **1988** Was 16 (16, SS) **1989** Was 13 (12, SS) **1990**†Was 16 (16, SS) **1991**†Was 4 (2) **NFL** 77 (62) [6 yrs]

WALTON, BRUCE Bruce Edward, T-G-C, 6´6˝/251 lbs; UCLA; 1973: Dal, rnd 5; B6/14/1951 San Diego, CA   **1973** Dal 7 **1974** Dal 13 **1975**†Dal 13 **NFL** 33 [3 yrs]

WALTON, CHUCK Charles Richard, G, 6´3˝/253 lbs; Iowa State; 1963: Det, rnd 4/SD, rnd 13; B7/7/1941 Shattuck, OK, D10/4/1998 Shattuck, OK   **1968** Det 14 (LG) **1969** Det 14 (LG) **1970**†Det 14 (LG) **1971** Det 14 (LG) **1972** Det 10 (LG) **1973** Det 4 **1974** Det 14 (10, LG)

| 1967 | Det | 14(LG) | — | — | — | — | 1 | -4 | -4.0(-4) | 0 | — | — | — | — | — | — | — | — | — | — | — | — | 0 | -2 |
| NFL | 8 | 98(10) | — | — | — | — | 1 | -4 | -4.0(-4) | 0 | — | — | — | — | — | — | — | — | — | — | — | — | 0 | -2 |

YEAR | TEAM | G (GS, POS) | RUSH | YD | AVG (LG) | TD | REC | YD | AVG (LG) | TD | PASS | COMP | PCT | YD | AVG (LG) | TD | INT | SK | YD | QBR | KPR | OTD | PTS | TAY

WALTON, FRANK Frank Joseph, G, 5´11˝/230 lbs; Pittsburgh; B12/25/1911 Beaver Falls, PA, D9/22/1953 Beaver Falls, PA **1934** Bos 12 (11, LG) **1944** Was 10 (1) **1945** Was 3 (0) **NFL** 25 (12) [3 yrs]

WALTON, JOE Joseph Frank, E-DE, 5´11˝/202 lbs; Pittsburgh; 1957: Was, rnd 2; B12/15/1935 Beaver Falls, PA **[C]**

YEAR	TEAM	G (GS, POS)	RUSH	YD	AVG (LG)	TD	REC	YD	AVG (LG)	TD	PASS	COMP	PCT	YD	AVG (LG)	TD	INT	SK	YD	QBR	KPR	OTD	PTS	TAY
1957	Was	12	—	—	—	—	3	57	19.0 (24)	0	—	—	—	—	—	—	—	—	—	—	i	—	0	79
1958	Was	12 (RE)	—	—	—	—	32	532	16.6 (41)	5	—	—	—	—	—	—	—	—	—	—	—	—	30	291
1959	Was	9 (RE)	—	—	—	—	21	317	15.1 (41)	3	—	—	—	—	—	—	—	—	—	—	—	—	18	174
1960	Was	12 (TE)	—	—	—	—	27	401	14.9 (35)	3	—	—	—	—	—	—	—	—	—	—	—	—	18	216
1961	†NYG	12 (TE)	—	—	—	—	36	544	15.1 (37)	2	—	—	—	—	—	—	—	—	—	—	—	—	12	282
1962	†NYG	13 (TE)	—	—	—	—	33	406	12.3 (37)	9	—	—	—	—	—	—	—	—	—	—	—	—	54	248
1963	†NYG	12 (TE)	—	—	—	—	26	371	14.3 (43)	6	—	—	—	—	—	—	—	—	—	—	—	—	36	216
NFL	7	82	—	—	—	—	178	2628	14.8 (43)	28	—	—	—	—	—	—	—	—	—	—	i	—	168	1504

WALTON, JOHN John B., QB, 6´2˝/210 lbs; Elizabeth City State; B10/4/1947 Elizabeth City, NC

YEAR	TEAM	G (GS, POS)	RUSH	YD	AVG (LG)	TD	REC	YD	AVG (LG)	TD	PASS	COMP	PCT	YD	AVG (LG)	TD	INT	SK	YD	QBR	KPR	OTD	PTS	TAY
1976	Phi	3	2	1	0.5 (1)	0	—	—	—	—	28	12	42.9	125	4.5 (33)	0	2	1	6	—	—	—	0	-17
1978	Phi	4	2	0	0.0 (0)	0	—	—	—	—	1	0	0.0	0	0.0	0	0	—	—	—	—	—	0	0
1979	†Phi	8	6	-5	-0.8 (2)	0	—	—	—	—	36	19	52.8	213	5.9 (31)	3	1	—	—	—	—	—	0	77
NFL	3	15	10	-4	-0.4 (2)	0	—	—	—	—	65	31	47.7	338	5.2 (33)	3	3	1	6	—	—	—	0	60

WALTON, LARRY Lawrence James, WR-FL, 6´0˝/180 lbs; Arizona State; 1969: Det, rnd 3; B2/8/1947 Johnstown, PA

YEAR	TEAM	G (GS, POS)	RUSH	YD	AVG (LG)	TD	REC	YD	AVG (LG)	TD	PASS	COMP	PCT	YD	AVG (LG)	TD	INT	SK	YD	QBR	KPR	OTD	PTS	TAY
1969	Det	14 (FL)	2	6	3.0 (17)	0	12	109	9.1 (16)	0	1	1	100.0	43	43.0 (43)	1	0	—	—	—	kp	—	0	116
1970	†Det	13 (WR)	2	20	10.0 (16)	0	30	532	17.7 (56)	5	—	—	—	—	—	—	—	—	—	—	kp	—	30	307
1971	Det	14 (WR)	1	-7	-7.0 (-7)	0	30	491	16.4 (60)	5	0	0	0.0	0	0.0	0	0	1	15	—	p	—	30	272
1972	Det	14 (WR)	—	—	—	—	24	485	20.2 (48)	6	—	—	—	—	—	—	—	—	—	—	p	—	36	346
1973	Det	13 (WR)	5	100	20.0 (57)	1	22	309	14.0 (49)	4	—	—	—	—	—	—	—	—	—	—	p	—	30	289
1974	Det	13 (13, WR)	2	3	1.5 (10)	0	31	404	13.0 (48)	3	2	1	50.0	29	14.5 (29)	0	0	—	—	—	k	—	18	242
1976	Det	14 (14, WR)	1	5	5.0 (5)	0	20	293	14.6 (28)	3	—	—	—	—	—	—	—	—	—	—	—	—	18	167
1978	Buf	12 (2)	—	—	—	—	4	66	16.5 (32)	1	—	—	—	—	—	—	—	—	—	—	—	—	6	38
NFL	8	107 (29)	13	127	9.8 (57)	1	173	2689	15.5 (60)	27	3	2	66.7	72	24.0 (43)	1	0	1	15	—	kp	—	168	1775

WALTON, RILEY Riley Henry, TE, 6´4˝/245 lbs; Tennessee State; B8/6/1962 Nashville, TN **1987** KC 2 (0)

WALTON, SAM Samuel Thaw, T, 6´5˝/270 lbs; Texas A&M-Commerce; 1968: NYJ, rnd 3; B1/3/1943 Memphis, TN, D5/9/2002 Memphis, TN **1968**†NYJ-A 14 (14, RT) **1969** NYJ-A 6 **1971** Hou 14 (RT) **NFL** 34 (14) [3 yrs]

WALTON, SHANE Shane Scott, DB, 5´11˝/195 lbs; Notre Dame; 2003: SL, rnd 5; B10/9/1979 San Diego, CA **2003** SL 4 (0)

WALTON, WAYNE Gerald Wayne, T-G, 6´5˝/255 lbs; Abilene Christian; 1971: NYG, rnd 2; B10/15/1948 Waco, TX **1971** NYG 14 **1973** KC 14 **1974** KC 9 **NFL** 37 [3 yrs]

WALTON, WHIP Whip, LB, 6´2˝/225 lbs; San Diego State; 1978: Min, rnd 3; B7/16/1955 Westminister, CA **1980** NYG 2 (0)

WALZ, ZACK Zachary Christian, LB, 6´4˝/228 lbs; Dartmouth; 1998: Arz, rnd 6; B2/13/1976 Mountain View, CA **1998**†Arz 16 (0) **1999** Arz 9 (9, RLB) **2000** Arz 6 (5, llb) **2001** Arz 15 (2) **NFL** 46 (16) [4 yrs]

WAND, SETH Seth Phillip, T, 6´7˝/327 lbs; Northwest Missouri State; 2003: Hou, rnd 3; B8/6/1979 Springfield, MO **2003** Hou 16 (2) **2004** Hou 16 (16, LT) **2005** Hou 13 (0) **NFL** 45 (18) [3 yrs]

WANLESS, GEORGE George S., WB-E-G, 5´8˝/160 lbs; none; B7/1898 Louisville, KY, deceased **1922** Lou 1 (0) **1923** Lou 2 (1, WB) **NFL** 3 (1) [2 yrs]

WANSLEY, TIM Tim, DB, 5´8˝/186 lbs; Georgia; 2002: TB, rnd 7; B11/7/1979 Buford, GA **2002** TB 1 (0) **2003** TB 12 (6, rcb) **NFL** 13 (6) [2 yrs]

WANTLAND, HAL Howell Smith, DB, 6´0˝/195 lbs; Tennessee; 1966: Was, rnd 16; B7/9/1944 Columbia, TN **1966** Mia-A 2

WAR EAGLE T-G, 5´9˝/195 lbs; none; deceased **1922** Oor 5 (3)

WARD TB-WB, none **1920** Ham 3 (2, TB)

WARD, B.J. B.J., DB, 6´3˝/208 lbs; Florida State; B11/4/1981 Dallas, TX **2005** Bal 15 (0)

WARD, BILL William Hogan, G-T, 6´0˝/212 lbs; Pennsylvania; B7/23/1895 Cambridge, MA, D5/21/1973 Garden City, NY **1921** Buf 9 (3), 6

WARD, BILL William Clark, G, 6´0˝/230 lbs; Washington State; Washington; B2/19/1921 Sequim, WA, D12/3/1992 Bellingham, WA **1946** Was 10 (10, LG) **1947** Was 6 (3) **1947** Det 4 (2) **1948** Det 12 (12, RG) **1949** Det 12 (11, RG) **NFL** 44 (38) [4 yrs]

WARD, CARL Carl Davis, DB, 5´9˝/180 lbs; Michigan; 1967: Cle, rnd 4; B7/26/1944 Hartsond, AL **1967**†Cle 14 **1968**†Cle 14 **1969** NO 2 **NFL** 30 [3 yrs]

WARD, CHRIS Christopher Lamar, T, 6´3˝/267 lbs; Ohio State; 1978: NYJ, rnd 1; B12/16/1955 Cleveland, OH **1978** NYJ 16 (16, LT) **1979** NYJ 16 (16, LT) **1980** NYJ 14 (14, LT) **1981**†NYJ☆16 (16, LT) **1982**†NYJ 9 (9, LT) **1983** NYJ 16 (16, LT) **1984** NO 13 (8, lt) **NFL** 100 (95) [7 yrs]

WARD, CHRIS Christopher Jamal, DE, 6´3˝/271 lbs; Kentucky; 1997: Bal, rnd 7; B2/4/1974 Atlanta, GA **1997** Bal 5 (0)

WARD, DAVID David, E-DE, 5´10˝/195 lbs; Haskell Indian; New Mexico; B3/10/1907, D3/1982 Clovis, NM **1933** Bos 1 (0)

WARD, DAVID David Fontaine, LB, 6´2˝/230 lbs; Southern Arkansas; B3/10/1964 Helena, AR **1987** Cin 3 (0) **1989** NE 16 (0) **NFL** 19 (0) [2 yrs]

WARD, DEDRIC Dedric Lamar, WR, 5´9˝/187 lbs; Northern Iowa; 1997: NYJ, rnd 3; B9/29/1974 Cedar Rapids, IA **[R]**

YEAR	TEAM	G (GS, POS)	RUSH	YD	AVG (LG)	TD	REC	YD	AVG (LG)	TD	PASS	COMP	PCT	YD	AVG (LG)	TD	INT	SK	YD	QBR	KPR	OTD	PTS	TAY
1997	NYJ	11 (0)	2	25	12.5 (21)	0	18	212	11.8 (33)	1	—	—	—	—	—	—	—	—	—	—	kp	—	6	131
1998	†NYJ	16 (2)	2	7	3.5 (4)	0	25	477	19.1 (71)	4	—	—	—	—	—	—	—	—	—	—	kp	—	24	313
1999	NYJ	16 (10, wr)	1	-1	-1.0 (-1)	0	22	325	14.8 (56)	3	—	—	—	—	—	—	—	—	—	—	p	—	18	275
2000	NYJ	16 (16, WR)	4	23	5.8 (12)	0	54	801	14.8 (61)	3	—	—	—	—	—	—	—	—	—	—	p	—	18	518
2001	†Mia	13 (1)	2	21	10.5 (16)	0	21	209	10.0 (20)	0	—	—	—	—	—	—	—	—	—	—	p	—	0	169
2002	Mia	16 (1)	—	—	—	—	19	172	9.1 (22)	0	—	—	—	—	—	—	—	—	—	—	p	—	0	175
2003	Bal	3 (0)	—	—	—	—	—	—	—	—	—	—	—	—	—	—	—	—	—	—	kp	—	0	16
2003	†NE	4 (0)	—	—	—	—	7	106	15.1 (31)	1	—	—	—	—	—	—	—	—	—	—	p	—	6	58
2004	Dal	8 (0)	1	11	11.0 (11)	0	1	5	5.0 (5)	0	—	—	—	—	—	—	—	—	—	—	p	—	0	58
NFL	8	103 (30)	12	86	7.2 (21)	0	167	2307	13.8 (71)	12	—	—	—	—	—	—	—	—	—	—	kp	—	72	1711

WARD, DERRICK Derrick, RB, 5´11˝/233 lbs; Fresno State; Ottawa (KS); 2004: NYJ, rnd 7; B8/30/1980 Los Angeles, CA **2004** NYG 5 (0)

YEAR	TEAM	G (GS, POS)	RUSH	YD	AVG (LG)	TD	REC	YD	AVG (LG)	TD	PASS	COMP	PCT	YD	AVG (LG)	TD	INT	SK	YD	QBR	KPR	OTD	PTS	TAY
2005	NYG	14 (0)	35	123	3.5 (12)	0	2	13	6.5 (8)	0	—	—	—	—	—	—	—	—	—	—	—	—	0	130
NFL	2	19 (0)	35	123	3.5 (12)	0	2	13	6.5 (8)	0	—	—	—	—	—	—	—	—	—	—	k	1	6	336

WARD, ELMER Elmer Henry, C, 6´2˝/215 lbs; Utah State; B10/13/1912 Willard, UT, D3/26/1996 Ogden, UT **1935**†Det 11 (2)

WARD, HINES Hines, WR, 6´0˝/205 lbs; Georgia; 1998: Pit, rnd 3; B3/8/1976 Seoul, South Korea

YEAR	TEAM	G (GS, POS)	RUSH	YD	AVG (LG)	TD	REC	YD	AVG (LG)	TD	PASS	COMP	PCT	YD	AVG (LG)	TD	INT	SK	YD	QBR	KPR	OTD	PTS	TAY
1998	Pit	16 (0)	1	13	13.0 (13)	0	15	246	16.4 (45)	0	1	1	100.0	17	17.0 (17)	0	0	—	—	—	—	—	0	145
1999	Pit	16 (14, WR)	2	-2	-1.0 (3)	0	61	638	10.5 (42)	7	—	—	—	—	—	—	—	—	—	—	kp	—	44	358
2000	Pit	16 (15, WR)	4	53	13.3 (23)	0	48	672	14.0 (77)	4	—	—	—	—	—	—	—	—	—	—	k	—	24	490
2001	†Pit✧	16 (16, WR)	10	83	8.3 (36)	0	94	1003	10.7 (34)	4	1	0	0.0	0	0.0	0	0	1	3	—	—	—	24	605
2002	†Pit★	16 (16, WR)	12	142	11.8 (39)	0	112	1329	11.9 (72)	**12**	—	—	—	—	—	—	—	—	—	—	—	—	78	867
2003	Pit★	16 (16, WR)	11	61	5.5 (25)	0	95	1163	12.2 (50)	10	—	—	—	—	—	—	—	—	—	—	—	—	60	693
2004	†Pit★	16 (16, WR)	7	25	3.6 (16)	1	80	1004	12.6 (58)	4	—	—	—	—	—	—	—	—	—	—	—	—	30	557
2005	†Pit	15 (15, WR)	3	10	3.3 (7)	0	69	975	14.1 (**85**)	11	—	—	—	—	—	—	—	—	—	—	—	—	66	553
NFL	8	127 (108)	50	385	7.7 (39)	1	574	7030	12.2 (85)	52	2	1	50.0	17	8.5 (17)	0	0	1	3	—	kp	—	326	4266

WARD, JIM James Edgar Harold, QB, 6´2˝/196 lbs; Gettysburg; 1966: Bal, rnd 14; B7/16/1944 Frederick, MD

YEAR	TEAM	G (GS, POS)	RUSH	YD	AVG (LG)	TD	REC	YD	AVG (LG)	TD	PASS	COMP	PCT	YD	AVG (LG)	TD	INT	SK	YD	QBR	KPR	OTD	PTS	TAY
1967	Bal	6	5	23	4.6 (8)	0	—	—	—	—	16	9	56.3	115	7.2 (21)	2	1	—	—	—	—	—	0	51
1968	†Bal	5	—	—	—	—	—	—	—	—	9	3	33.3	46	5.1 (22)	0	1	3	27	—	—	—	0	-17
1971	Phi	2	—	—	—	—	—	—	—	—	1	1	100.0	4	4.0 (4)	0	0	—	—	—	—	—	0	2
NFL	3	13	5	23	4.6 (8)	0	—	—	—	—	26	13	50.0	165	6.3 (22)	2	2	3	27	—	—	—	0	36

YEAR	TEAM	G(GS, POS)	RUSH	YD	AVG(LG)	TD	REC	YD	AVG(LG)	TD	PASS	COMP	PCT	YD	AVG(LG)	TD	INT	SK	YD	QBR	KPR	OTD	PTS	TAY
WARD, JOHN John Henry, G-DE-C, 6´4˝/258 lbs; Oklahoma State; 1970: Min, rnd 1; B5/27/1948 Enid, OK **1970**†Min 14 **1971**†Min 14 **1972** Min 14 **1975**†Min 14 **1976** TB 4 (3) **1976** ChiB 10																								
1973	Min	8	—	—	—	—	1	1	1.0(1)	0	—	—	—	—	—	—	—	—	—	—	—	—	0	1
NFL	6	78(3)	—	—	—	—	1	1	1.0(1)	0	—	—	—	—	—	—	—	—	—	—	—	—	0	1
WARD, JOHNNY John, T, 6´2˝/215 lbs; USC; B1907 **1930** Fra 4 (4) **1930** Min 9 (9, LT) **NFL** 13 (13) [1 yr]																								
WARD, LASHAUN LaShaun Brandon, WR, 5´11˝/198 lbs; California; B9/22/1980 Pasadena, CA **2003** KC 1 (0)																								
WARD, PAUL Paul Earl, DT-G, 6´3˝/247 lbs; Whitworth; B1/30/1937 Santa Fe, NM **1961** Det 8 **1962** Det 6 **NFL** 14 [2 yrs]																								
WARD, PHILLIP Phillip Eugene, LB, 6´2˝/235 lbs; UCLA; B11/11/1974 Gardena, CA **1998** SL 2 (0) **2000** NO 2 (0) **NFL** 4 (0) [2 yrs]																								
WARD, RONNIE Rodney Glen, LB, 6´0˝/232 lbs; Kansas; 1997: Mia, rnd 3; B2/11/1974 St. Louis, MO **1997** Mia 4 (0)																								
WARDLOW, DUANE Clyde Duane, DE, 6´4˝/215 lbs; Washington; 1954: LA, rnd 11; B7/2/1932 **1954** LARm 12 (LDE) **1956** LARm 9 (RDE) **NFL** 21 [2 yrs]																								
WARE, ANDRE Andre Trevor, QB, 6´2˝/205 lbs; Houston; 1990: Det, rnd 1; B7/31/1968 Galveston, TX																								
1990	Det	4(1)	7	64	9.1(30)	0	—	—	—	—	30	13	43.3	164	5.5(33)	1	2	4	22	—	—	—	0	71
1991	†Det	1(0)	4	6	1.5(10)	0	—	—	—	—	—	—	—	—	—	—	—	—	—	—	—	—	0	6
1992	Det	4(3)	20	124	6.2(32)	0	—	—	—	—	86	50	58.1	677	7.9(59)	3	4	16	104	—	—	—	0	318
1993	Det	5(2)	7	23	3.3(8)	0	—	—	—	—	45	20	44.4	271	6.0(47)	1	2	7	20	—	—	—	0	84
NFL	4	14(6)	38	217	5.7(32)	0	—	—	—	—	161	83	51.6	1112	6.9(59)	5	8	27	146	—	—	—	0	478
WARE, CHARLIE Charles, T, 6´3˝/245 lbs; Birmingham-Southern; B3/2/1918 Atlanta, GA **1944** Bkn 7 (0)																								
WARE, DEMARCUS Demarcus, LB, 6´4˝/247 lbs; Troy; 2005: Dal, rnd 1; B7/31/1982 Auburn, AL **2005** Dal 16 (16, ROLB)																								
WARE, DEREK Derek Gene, TE, 6´2˝/255 lbs; Texas A&M; Central Oklahoma; 1992: Phx, rnd 7; B9/17/1967 Sacramento, CA																								
1992	Phx	15(0)	—	—	—	—	1	13	13.0(13)	0	—	—	—	—	—	—	—	—	—	—	—	—	0	7
1993	Phx	16(1)	—	—	—	—	3	45	15.0(27)	0	—	—	—	—	—	—	—	—	—	—	—	—	0	23
1994	Arz	15(12, TE)	—	—	—	—	17	171	10.1(33)	1	—	—	—	—	—	—	—	—	—	—	—	—	6	91
1995	Cin	7(0)	—	—	—	—	2	36	18.0(21)	0	—	—	—	—	—	—	—	—	—	—	—	—	0	18
1996	Dal	5(1)	—	—	—	—	1	5	5.0(5)	0	—	—	—	—	—	—	—	—	—	—	—	—	0	3
NFL	5	58(14)	—	—	—	—	24	270	11.3(33)	1	—	—	—	—	—	—	—	—	—	—	—	—	6	140
WARE, KEVIN Kevin, TE, 6´3˝/259 lbs; Washington; B9/30/1980 San Diego, CA																								
2003	Was	11(2)	—	—	—	—	3	17	5.7(7)	0	—	—	—	—	—	—	—	—	—	—	—	—	0	9
2004	SF	5(0)	—	—	—	—	1	9	9.0(9)	0	—	—	—	—	—	—	—	—	—	—	—	—	0	5
NFL	2	16(2)	—	—	—	—	4	26	6.5(9)	0	—	—	—	—	—	—	—	—	—	—	—	—	0	13
WARE, MATT Matthew Jesse, DB, 6´3˝/213 lbs; UCLA; 2004: Phi, rnd 3; B12/2/1982 Santa Monica, CA **2004**†Phi 12 (0) **2005** Phi 16 (0) **NFL** 28 (0) [2 yrs]																								
WARE, TIMMIE Timothy Eugene, WR, 5´10˝/171 lbs; USC; B4/2/1962 Los Angeles, CA																								
1986	SD	9(0)	—	—	—	—	1	11	11.0(11)	0	—	—	—	—	—	—	—	—	—	—	—	—	0	6
1987	SD	12(1)	—	—	—	—	2	38	19.0(23)	0	—	—	—	—	—	—	—	—	—	—	—	—	0	19
1989	LARd	13(0)	—	—	—	—	—	—	—	—	—	—	—	—	—	—	—	—	—	—	k	—	0	26
NFL	3	34(1)	—	—	—	—	3	49	16.3(23)	0	—	—	—	—	—	—	—	—	—	—	k	—	0	51
WARFIELD, ERIC Eric Andrew, DB, 6´0˝/200 lbs; Nebraska; 1998: KC, rnd 7; B3/3/1976 Vicksburg, MS **[I]** **1998** KC 12 (0) **1999** KC 16 (1) **2000** KC 13 (3) **2001** KC 16 (16, RCB) **2002** KC 16 (16, LCB) **2003**†KC 15 (15, LCB) **2004** KC 16 (16, LCB) **2005** KC 11 (10, RCB) **NFL** 115 (77) [8 yrs]																								
WARFIELD, PAUL Paul Dryden, WR-SE, 6´0˝/188 lbs; Ohio State; 1964: Cle, rnd 1/Buf, rnd 4; B11/28/1942 Warren, OH; HOF 1983																								
1964	†Cle★	14(SE)	—	—	—	—	52	920	17.7(62)	9	—	—	—	—	—	—	—	—	—	—	k	—	54	494
1965	†Cle	1	—	—	—	—	3	30	10.0(13)	0	—	—	—	—	—	—	—	—	—	—	—	—	0	15
1966	Cle	14(SE)	—	—	—	—	36	741	20.6(51)	5	—	—	—	—	—	—	—	—	—	—	—	1	36	396
1967	†Cle	14(SE)	2	10	5.0(18)	0	32	702	21.9(49)	8	—	—	—	—	—	—	—	—	—	—	—	—	48	401
1968	†Cle★	14(SE)	—	—	—	—	50	1067	21.3(65)	**12**	—	—	—	—	—	—	—	—	—	—	—	—	72	594
1969	†Cle★	14(SE)	2	23	11.5(16)	0	42	886	21.1(82)	10	—	—	—	—	—	—	—	—	—	—	—	—	60	516
1970	†Mia★	11(11, WR)	2	13	6.5(16)	0	28	703	**25.1**(**54**)	6	—	—	—	—	—	—	—	—	—	—	—	—	36	395
1971	†Mia★	14(14, WR)	9	115	12.8(39)	0	43	996	**23.2**(**86**)	**11**	—	—	—	—	—	—	—	—	—	—	—	—	66	668
1972	†Mia★	12(11, WR)	4	23	5.8(21)	0	29	606	20.9(47)	3	—	—	—	—	—	—	—	—	—	—	—	—	18	341
1973	†Mia★	14(14, WR)	1	15	15.0(15)	0	29	514	17.7(45)	**11**	—	—	—	—	—	—	—	—	—	—	—	—	66	327
1974	†Mia★	9(9, WR)	—	—	—	—	27	536	19.9(54)	2	—	—	—	—	—	—	—	—	—	—	—	—	12	278
1976	Cle	14(WR)	1	3	3.0(3)	0	38	613	16.1(37)	6	—	—	—	—	—	—	—	—	—	—	—	—	36	340
1977	Cle	12(9, wr)	1	2	2.0(2)	0	18	251	13.9(52)	2	—	—	—	—	—	—	—	—	—	—	—	—	12	138
NFL	13	157(68)	22	204	9.3(39)	0	427	8565	20.1(86)	85	—	—	—	—	—	—	—	—	—	—	k	1	516	4901
WARLICK, ERNIE Ernest, TE, 6´3˝/235 lbs; North Carolina Central; B7/21/1932 Washington, DC																								
1962	Buf-A✧	14(TE)	—	—	—	—	35	482	13.8(25)	2	—	—	—	—	—	—	—	—	—	—	—	—	12	251
1963	†Buf-A✧	14(TE)	—	—	—	—	24	479	20.0(55)	1	—	—	—	—	—	—	—	—	—	—	—	—	6	245
1964	†Buf-A✧	14(TE)	—	—	—	—	23	478	20.8(45)	0	—	—	—	—	—	—	—	—	—	—	—	—	0	239
1965	†Buf-A✧	14	—	—	—	—	8	112	14.0(27)	1	—	—	—	—	—	—	—	—	—	—	—	—	6	61
NFL	4	56	—	—	—	—	90	1551	17.2(55)	4	—	—	—	—	—	—	—	—	—	—	—	—	24	796
WARNE, JIM James E., T, 6´7˝/315 lbs; Arizona State; 1987: Cin, rnd 11; B11/27/1964 Phoenix, AZ **1987** Det 3 (3)																								
WARNER, CHARLEY Charles Allen, DB-HB, 6´0˝/176 lbs; Prairie View A&M; B4/14/1940 Granger, TX **[R]** **1963** KC-A 14 **1964** KC-A 5 **1964**†Buf-A 4 **1966**†Buf-A 14																								
1965	†Buf-A✧	14	1	2	2.0(2)	0	1	11	11.0(11)	1	—	—	—	—	—	—	—	—	—	—	kpi	3	24	458
NFL	4	51	1	2	2.0(2)	0	1	11	11.0(11)	1	—	—	—	—	—	—	—	—	—	—	kpi	4	30	1162
WARNER, CURT Curtis Edward, RB, 5´11˝/205 lbs; Penn State; 1983: Sea, rnd 1; B3/18/1961 Wyoming, WV																								
1983	†Sea★	16(16, RB)	**335**	**1449**	4.3(60)	13	42	325	7.7(28)	1	—	—	—	—	—	—	—	—	—	—	—	—	84	**1747**
1984	Sea	1(1)	10	40	4.0(9)	0	1	19	19.0(19)	0	—	—	—	—	—	—	—	—	—	—	—	—	0	50
1985	Sea☆	16(16, RB)	291	1094	3.8(38)	8	47	307	6.5(27)	1	—	—	—	—	—	—	—	—	—	—	—	—	54	1333
1986	Sea★	16(16, RB)	**319**	**1481**	4.6(60)	**13**	41	342	8.3(26)	0	—	—	—	—	—	—	—	—	—	—	—	—	78	**1782**
1987	†Sea★	12(12, RB)	**234**	985	4.2(57)	8	17	167	9.8(30)	2	—	—	—	—	—	—	—	—	—	—	—	—	60	1159
1988	†Sea	16(16, RB)	266	1025	3.9(29)	10	22	154	7.0(17)	2	—	—	—	—	—	—	—	—	—	—	—	—	72	1212
1989	Sea	16(15, RB)	194	631	3.3(34)	3	23	153	6.7(24)	1	—	—	—	—	—	—	—	—	—	—	—	—	24	743
1990	LARm	7(2)	49	139	2.8(9)	1	—	—	—	—	—	—	—	—	—	—	—	—	—	—	—	—	6	149
NFL	8	100(94)	1698	6844	4.0(60)	56	193	1467	7.6(30)	7	—	—	—	—	—	—	—	—	—	—	—	—	378	8173
WARNER, JOSH Joshua, C-G, 6´5˝/320 lbs; Brockport State; B5/15/1979 Cato, NY **2003** ChiB 10 (0)																								
WARNER, KURT Kurtis Eugene, QB, 6´2˝/220 lbs; Northern Iowa; B6/22/1971 Burlington, IA																								
1998	SL	1(0)	—	—	—	—	—	—	—	—	11	4	36.4	39	3.5(21)	0	0	—	—	—	—	—	0	20
1999	†SL★	16(16, QB)	23	92	4.0(22)	1	—	—	—	—	499	325	**65.1**	4353	**8.7**(**75**)	**41**	13	29	201	**109.2**	—	—	6	1964
2000	†SL✧	11(11, QB)	18	17	0.9(11)	0	—	—	—	—	347	235	**67.7**	3429	**9.9**(**85**)	21	18	20	115	**98.3**	—	—	0	1117
2001	†SL★	16(16, QB)	28	60	2.1(23)	0	—	—	—	—	546	**375**	**68.7**	**4830**	**8.8**(**65**)	**36**	**22**	38	233	**101.4**	—	—	0	1775
2002	SL	7(6, qb)	8	33	4.1(9)	0	—	—	—	—	220	144	**65.5**	1431	6.5(43)	3	11	21	130	67.4	—	—	0	324
2003	SL	2(1)	1	0	0.0(0)	0	—	—	—	—	65	38	58.5	365	5.6(37)	1	1	6	38	—	—	—	0	148
2004	NYG	10(9, QB)	13	30	2.3(13)	1	—	—	—	—	277	174	62.8	2054	7.4(62)	6	4	39	196	86.5	—	—	6	937
2005	Arz	10(10, QB)	13	28	2.2(13)	0	1	0	0.0(0)	0	375	242	64.5	2713	7.2(63)	11	9	23	158	85.8	—	—	0	1080
NFL	8	73(69)	104	260	2.5(23)	2	1	0	0.0	0	2340	1537	65.7	19214	8.2(85)	119	78	176	1071	94.1	—	—	12	7362
WARNER, RON Ron, DE, 6´2˝/270 lbs; Kansas; 1998: NO, rnd 7; B9/26/1975 Independence, KS **1998** NO 1 (0) **2002**†TB 4 (0) **2003** TB 4 (0) **2003** Was 1 (0) **2004** Was 14 (2) **NFL** 24 (2) [4 yrs]																								
WARNKE, DAVID David, K, 5´11˝/185 lbs; Augsburg; B12/30/1960, **[K]** **1983** TB 1 (0)																								

YEAR	TEAM	G (GS, POS)	°RUSH	YD	AVG(LG)	TD	REC	YD	AVG(LG)	TD	PASS	COMP	PCT	YD	AVG(LG)	TD	INT	SK	YD	QBR	KPR	°OTD	PTS	TAY

WARREN   WB, none; deceased   **1920** Ham 2 (0)

WARREN, BUSS   Buist Lamb, TB-HB, 5′11″/175 lbs; Tennessee; B8/13/1916 Provo, UT, D5/1986 Newhall, CA

1945	Phi	1 (0)	1	-7	-7.0 (-7)	0	—	—	—	—	—	—	—	—	—	—	—	—	—	—	—	—	0	-7
1945	Pit	8 (4, tb)	95	292	3.1 (75)	2	1	-1	-1.0 (-1)	0	92	36	39.1	368	4.0 (47)	0	10	—	—	—	kpi	—	12	273
NFL	1	9 (4)	96	285	3.0 (75)	2	1	-1	-1.0 (-1)	0	92	36	39.1	368	4.0 (47)	0	10	—	—	—	kpi	—	12	266

WARREN, CHRIS   Christopher Collins, RB, 6′2″/228 lbs; Virginia; Ferrum; 1990: Sea, rnd 4; B1/24/1968 Silver Spring, MD **[R]**

1990	Sea	16 (0)	6	11	1.8 (4)	1	—	—	—	—	—	—	—	—	—	—	—	—	—	—	kp	—	6	283
1991	Sea	16 (1)	11	13	1.2 (7)	0	2	9	4.5 (12)	0	—	—	—	—	—	—	—	—	—	—	kp	1	6	433
1992	Sea	16 (16, RB)	223	1017	4.6 (52)	3	16	134	8.4 (33)	0	—	—	—	—	—	—	—	—	—	—	kp	—	18	1300
1993	Sea◇	14 (14, RB)	273	1072	3.9 (45)	7	15	99	6.6 (21)	0	—	—	—	—	—	—	—	—	—	—	—	—	42	1192
1994	Sea★	16 (15, RB)	333	**1545**	**4.6 (41)**	9	41	323	7.9 (51)	2	—	—	—	—	—	—	—	—	—	—	—	—	68	**1807**
1995	Sea★	16 (16, RB)	310	1346	4.3 (52)	**15**	35	247	7.1 (20)	1	—	—	—	—	—	—	—	—	—	—	—	—	96	1625
1996	Sea	14 (14, RB)	203	855	4.2 (51)	5	40	273	6.8 (33)	0	—	—	—	—	—	—	—	—	—	—	—	—	32	1042
1997	Sea	15 (13, RB)	200	847	4.2 (36)	4	45	257	5.7 (20)	0	—	—	—	—	—	—	—	—	—	—	—	—	24	1016
1998	Dal	9 (0)	59	291	4.9 (49)	4	13	66	5.1 (15)	1	—	—	—	—	—	—	—	—	—	—	kp	—	30	385
1999	†Dal	16 (1)	99	403	4.1 (25)	2	34	224	6.6 (24)	0	—	—	—	—	—	—	—	—	—	—	—	—	12	535
2000	Dal	13 (0)	59	254	4.3 (32)	2	31	302	9.7 (76)	1	—	—	—	—	—	—	—	—	—	—	—	—	18	430
2000	†Phi	1 (1)	15	42	2.8 (11)	0	1	1	1.0 (1)	0	—	—	—	—	—	—	—	—	—	—	—	—	0	43
NFL	11	162 (91)	1791	7696	4.3 (52)	52	273	1935	7.1 (76)	5	—	—	—	—	—	—	—	—	—	—	kp	1	352	10088

WARREN, DEWEY   Madison Dewey, QB, 6′0″/205 lbs; Tennessee; 1968: Cin, rnd 6; B5/7/1945 Savannah, GA

| 1968 | Cin-A | 7 | 4 | 17 | 4.3 (12) | 0 | — | — | — | — | 80 | 47 | 58.7 | 506 | 6.3 (45) | 1 | 4 | 10 | 69 | — | — | — | 0 | 115 |

WARREN, DON   Donald James, TE, 6′4″/242 lbs; San Diego State; 1979: Was, rnd 4; B5/5/1956 Bellingham, WA

1979	Was	16 (10, TE)	—	—	—	—	26	303	11.7 (23)	0	—	—	—	—	—	—	—	—	—	—	—	—	0	152
1980	Was	13 (12, TE)	—	—	—	—	31	323	10.4 (35)	0	—	—	—	—	—	—	—	—	—	—	—	—	0	162
1981	Was	16 (16, TE)	—	—	—	—	29	335	11.6 (32)	1	—	—	—	—	—	—	—	—	—	—	—	—	6	173
1982	†Was	9 (9, TE)	—	—	—	—	27	310	11.5 (29)	0	—	—	—	—	—	—	—	—	—	—	—	—	0	155
1983	†Was	13 (13, TE)	—	—	—	—	20	225	11.3 (33)	2	—	—	—	—	—	—	—	—	—	—	—	—	12	123
1984	†Was	16 (16, TE)	—	—	—	—	18	192	10.7 (26)	0	—	—	—	—	—	—	—	—	—	—	—	—	0	96
1985	Was	16 (16, TE)	1	5	5.0 (5)	0	15	163	10.9 (19)	1	—	—	—	—	—	—	—	—	—	—	—	—	6	92
1986	†Was	16 (16, TE)	—	—	—	—	20	164	8.2 (20)	1	—	—	—	—	—	—	—	—	—	—	—	—	6	87
1987	†Was	12 (12, TE)	—	—	—	—	7	43	6.1 (9)	0	—	—	—	—	—	—	—	—	—	—	—	—	0	22
1988	Was	14 (14, TE)	—	—	—	—	12	112	9.3 (32)	0	—	—	—	—	—	—	—	—	—	—	—	—	0	56
1989	Was	15 (15, TE)	—	—	—	—	15	167	11.1 (25)	1	—	—	—	—	—	—	—	—	—	—	—	—	6	89
1990	†Was	16 (15, TE)	—	—	—	—	15	123	8.2 (18)	1	—	—	—	—	—	—	—	—	—	—	—	—	6	67
1991	†Was	10 (7, TE)	—	—	—	—	5	51	10.2 (17)	0	—	—	—	—	—	—	—	—	—	—	—	—	0	26
1992	Was	11 (10, TE)	—	—	—	—	4	25	6.3 (11)	0	—	—	—	—	—	—	—	—	—	—	—	—	0	13
NFL	14	193 (181)	1	5	5.0 (5)	0	244	2536	10.4 (35)	7	—	—	—	—	—	—	—	—	—	—	—	—	42	1308

WARREN, FRANK   Frank William, DE-NT, 6′4″/285 lbs; Auburn; 1981: NO, rnd 3; B9/14/1959 Birmingham, AL, D12/14/2002 Birmingham, AL **[S]**   **1981** NO 16 (0)   **1982** NO 9 (1)   **1983** NO 16 (1)   **1984** NO 16 (3)   **1985** NO 16 (0)   **1986** NO 16 (0)   **1987** †NO 12 (0)   **1988** NO 16 (12, LDE)   **1989** NO 16 (16, LDE)   **1991** †NO 16 (16, RDE)   **1992** †NO 16 (16, RDE)   **1993** NO 8 (7, rde)   **1994** NO 16 (11, NT)   **NFL** 189 (83) [13 yrs]

WARREN, GERARD   Gerard T., DT, 6′4″/325 lbs; Florida; 2001: Cle, rnd 1; B7/25/1978 Lake City, FL   **2001** Cle 15 (15, LDT)   **2002** †Cle 16 (16, LDT)   **2003** Cle 15 (15, LDT)   **2004** Cle 13 (13, LDT)   **2005** †Den 16 (16, RDT)   **NFL** 76 (75) [5 yrs]

WARREN, GREG   Greg, C, 6′3″/252 lbs; North Carolina; B10/18/1981 Goldsboro, NC   **2005** †Pit 16 (0)

WARREN, JIMMY   James David, DB, 5′11″/175 lbs; Illinois; B7/20/1939 Ferriday, LA **[I]**   **1964** †SD-A 14 (RCB)   **1965** †SD-A 14 (LCB)   **1966** Mia-A◇14 (14, LCB)   **1967** Mia-A☆14 (14, LCB)   **1968** Mia-A☆ 14 (14, LCB)   **1969** Mia-A 13 (13, LCB)   **1970** †Oak 10   **1971** Oak 14 (1)   **1972** †Oak 7   **1973** Oak 10 (1)   **1974** †Oak 14 (4)   **1977** †Oak 2   **NFL** 140 (61) [12 yrs]

WARREN, JOHN   John Sheppard, P, 6′0″/207 lbs; Tennessee; B11/8/1960 Jessup, GA   **1983** Dal 9 (0)   **1984** Dal 3 (0)   **NFL** 12 (0) [2 yrs]

WARREN, LAMONT   Lamont Allen, RB, 5′11″/202 lbs; Colorado; 1994: Ind, rnd 6; B1/4/1973 Indianapolis, IN

1994	Ind	11 (0)	18	80	4.4 (34)	0	3	14	15.7 (29)	0	1	0	0.0	0	0.0	0	0	—	—	—	k	—	0	130
1995	†Ind	12 (1)	47	152	3.2 (42)	1	17	159	9.4 (18)	0	—	—	—	—	—	—	—	—	—	—	k	—	6	332
1996	†Ind	13 (3)	67	230	3.4 (53)	1	22	174	7.9 (17)	0	—	—	—	—	—	—	—	—	—	—	k	—	6	336
1997	Ind	13 (0)	28	80	2.9 (11)	2	20	192	9.6 (31)	0	1	0	0.0	0	0.0	0	0	—	—	—	k	—	12	200
1998	Ind	12 (2)	25	61	2.4 (14)	1	11	44	4.0 (12)	1	—	—	—	—	—	—	—	—	—	—	k	—	12	130
1999	NE	16 (2)	35	120	3.4 (34)	0	29	262	9.0 (21)	1	—	—	—	—	—	—	0	0	1	7	k	—	6	251
2001	Det	16 (3)	61	191	3.1 (8)	3	40	334	8.4 (36)	1	2	0	0.0	0	0.0	0	0	—	—	—	k	—	26	350
2002	Det	3 (1)	6	8	1.3 (18)	0	4	56	14.0 (39)	2	—	—	—	—	—	—	—	—	—	—	k	—	12	46
NFL	8	96 (12)	287	922	3.2 (53)	8	146	1270	8.7 (39)	5	4	0	0.0	0	0.0	0	0	1	7	—	k	—	80	1774

WARREN, MORRIE   Morrison Fulbright, FB-LB, 5′11″/208 lbs; Arizona State; B12/6/1923 Marlin, TX, D4/9/2002 Tempe, AZ

| 1948 | Bkn-A | 2 (0) | 1 | 1 | 1.0 | 0 | — | — | — | — | — | — | — | — | — | — | — | — | — | — | — | — | 0 | -22 |

WARREN, STEVE   Steven Jerome, DT, 6′1″/298 lbs; Nebraska; 2000: GB, rnd 3; B1/22/1978 Lawton, OK   **2000** GB 13 (0)   **2002** †GB 12 (0)   **NFL** 25 (0) [2 yrs]

WARREN, TERRENCE   Terrence Lamonte, WR, 6′1″/205 lbs; Hampton; 1993: Sea, rnd 5; B8/2/1969 Suffolk, VA   **1993** Sea 2 (0)   **1995** SF 1 (0)

| 1994 | Sea | 14 (0) | 3 | 15 | 5.0 (11) | 0 | — | — | — | — | — | — | — | — | — | — | — | — | — | — | k | — | 0 | 155 |
| NFL | 3 | 17 (0) | 3 | 15 | 5.0 (11) | 0 | — | — | — | — | — | — | — | — | — | — | — | — | — | — | k | — | 0 | 162 |

WARREN, TY   Ty'ron Markeith, DE-DT, 6′5″/300 lbs; Texas A&M; 2003: NE, rnd 1; B2/6/1981 Bryan, TX   **2003** †NE 16 (4)   **2004** NE 16 (16, LDE)   **2005** NE 16 (16, LDE)   **NFL** 48 (36) [3 yrs]

WARREN, VINCE   Vincent Leo, WR, 6′0″/180 lbs; San Diego State; 1986: NYG, rnd 5; B2/18/1963 Little Rock, AR   **1986** NYG 4 (0)

WARREN, XAVIER   Xavier Rogerlyn, DE, 6′1″/250 lbs; Tulsa; B8/12/1964 Cleburne, TX   **1987** Pit 2 (0)

WARRICK, PETER   Peter, WR, 5′11″/192 lbs; Florida State; 2000: Cin, rnd 1; B6/19/1977 Bradenton, FL

2000	Cin	16 (16, WR)	16	148	9.3 (77)	2	51	592	11.6 (46)	4	—	—	—	—	—	—	—	—	—	—	p	1	42	582
2001	Cin	16 (14, WR)	8	14	1.8 (13)	0	70	667	9.5 (33)	1	—	—	—	—	—	—	—	—	—	—	p	—	6	379
2002	Cin	15 (10, WR)	8	22	2.8 (12)	0	53	606	11.4 (37)	6	—	—	—	—	—	—	—	—	—	—	p	—	36	349
2003	Cin	15 (14, WR)	18	157	8.7 (50)	0	79	819	10.4 (77)	7	—	—	—	—	—	—	—	—	—	—	p	1	48	760
2004	Cin	4 (1)	2	14	7.0 (8)	0	11	127	11.5 (30)	0	—	—	—	—	—	—	—	—	—	—	—	—	0	78
2005	†Sea	13 (5, wr)	1	5	5.0 (5)	0	11	180	16.4 (42)	0	—	—	—	—	—	—	—	—	—	—	p	—	0	94
NFL	6	79 (60)	53	360	6.8 (77)	2	275	2991	10.9 (77)	18	—	—	—	—	—	—	—	—	—	—	p	2	132	2241

WARRINGTON, TEX   Caleb Van, G-C-LB, 6′2″/210 lbs; William & Mary; Auburn; 1944: Bos, rnd 9; B3/21/1921 Dover, DE, D9/20/1983 Gifford, FL   **1946** Bkn-A 12 (6, C)   **1948** Bkn-A 14 (11, LG)

| 1947 | Bkn-A | 13 (9, LG) | — | — | — | — | 0 | 2 | (2) | 0 | — | — | — | — | — | — | — | — | — | — | — | — | 0 | 1 |
| AAFC | 3 | 39 (26) | — | — | — | — | 0 | 2 | (2) | 0 | — | — | — | — | — | — | — | — | — | — | — | — | 0 | 1 |

WARWEG, EARL   Earl O., WB, 5′6″/145 lbs; none; B1/11/1892 Indianapolis, IN, D12/7/1979 Newburgh, IN   **1921** Evv 1 (0)

WARWICK, LONNIE   Lonnie Preston, LB, 6′3″/238 lbs; Tennessee; Tennessee Tech; B2/26/1942 Raleigh, WV   **1965** Min 14 (7, llb)   **1966** Min 12 (12, MLB)   **1967** Min 14 (14, MLB)   **1968** †Min 14 (14, MLB)   **1969** †Min 14 (14, MLB)   **1970** †Min 14 (14, MLB)   **1971** †Min 4   **1972** Min 6   **1973** Atl 14   **1974** Atl 14   **NFL** 120 (75) [10 yrs]

WARZEKA, RON   Ronald Dwain, DT, 6′4″/250 lbs; Montana State; 1957: SF, rnd 14; B12/24/1935 Great Falls, MT   **1960** Oak-A 14

WASHINGTON, AL   Alvin Kent, LB, 6′3″/235 lbs; Ohio State; 1981: NYJ, rnd 4; B9/25/1958 Erie, PA   **1981** †NYJ 16 (0)

WASHINGTON, ANTHONY   Anthony Wayne, DB, 6′1″/204 lbs; California; Fresno State; 1981: Pit, rnd 2; B2/4/1958 San Francisco, CA   **1981** Pit 16 (1)   **1982** †Pit 9 (0)   **1983** †Was 16 (3)   **1984** †Was 16 (2)   **NFL** 57 (6) [4 yrs]

YEAR	TEAM	G(GS, POS)	RUSH	YD	AVG(LG)	TD	REC	YD	AVG(LG)	TD	PASS COMP	PCT	YD	AVG(LG)	TD	INT	SK	YD	QBR	KPR	OTD	PTS	TAY

WASHINGTON, BRIAN   Brian Wayne, DB, 6´1˝/210 lbs; Nebraska; 1988: Cle, rnd 10; B9/10/1965 Richmond, VA [I]   **1988**†Cle 16 (14, SS)   **1990** NYJ 14 (13, SS)
1991†NYJ 16 (16, SS)   **1992** NYJ 16 (16, SS)   **1993** NYJ 16 (16, SS)   **1994** NYJ 15 (15, SS)   **1995**†KC 15 (14, SS)   **1996** KC 16 (16, SS)   **NFL** 124 (120) [8 yrs]

WASHINGTON, CHARLES   Charles Edwin, DB, 6´1˝/212 lbs; Texas; Cameron; 1989: Ind, rnd 7; B10/8/1966 Shreveport, LA   **1989** Ind 16 (0)   **1990**†KC 6 (0)   **1991** KC 16 (1)
1992 Atl 14 (0)   **1993** Atl 6 (0)   **1994** Atl 16 (1)   **NFL** 74 (2) [6 yrs]

WASHINGTON, CHRIS   Christopher, LB, 6´4˝/231 lbs; Iowa State; 1984: TB, rnd 6; B3/6/1962 Jackson, MS   **1984** TB 16 (7, rolb)   **1985** TB 16 (16, ROLB/lolb)
1986 TB 16 (16, ROLB)   **1987** TB 12 (12, ROLB/lolb)   **1988** TB 16 (1)   **1990** Phx 8 (0)   **NFL** 84 (52) [6 yrs]

WASHINGTON, CHUCK   Charles Edward, DB, 5´11˝/186 lbs; Arkansas; B1/9/1964 Topeka, KS   **1987** GB 3 (3)

WASHINGTON, CLARENCE   Clarence Cornelius, DT, 6´3˝/264 lbs; Arkansas-Pine Bluff; 1969: Pit, rnd 11; B12/23/1946 Little Rock, AR   **1969** Pit 13   **1970** Pit 14   **NFL** 27 [2 yrs]

WASHINGTON, CLYDE   Clyde George, DB-P, 6´1˝/197 lbs; Purdue; 1960: Cle, rnd 10; B3/21/1938 Carlisle, PA, D12/29/1974 Carlisle, PA   **1963** NYJ-A 14 (RCB)
1964 NYJ-A 8 (RCB)   **1965** NYJ-A 14 (RCB)

1960	Bos-A	13(LCB)	2	10	5.0(7)	0	—	—	—	—	—	—	—	—	—	—	—	—	—	Pi	—	0	8
1961	Bos-A	14	1	3	3.0(3)	0	—	—	—	—	—	—	—	—	—	—	—	—	—	i	—	0	28
NFL		5	63	3	13	4.3(7)	0	—	—	—	—	—	—	—	—	—	—	—	—	—	Pi	—	0	28

WASHINGTON, DAMON   Damon Keane, RB, 5´11˝/193 lbs; Colorado State; B2/20/1977 Lockney, TX   **2000**†NYG 3 (0)   **2002** NYG 12 (0)

| 2001 | NYG | 10(0) | 28 | 89 | 3.2(22) | 0 | 4 | 25 | 6.3(16) | 0 | — | — | — | — | — | — | — | — | — | k | — | 0 | 111 |
| NFL | | 3 | 25(0) | 28 | 89 | 3.2(22) | 0 | 4 | 25 | 6.3(16) | 0 | — | — | — | — | — | — | — | k | — | 0 | 128 |

WASHINGTON, DAVE   David, LB-TE, 6´5˝/223 lbs; Alcorn State; 1970: Den, rnd 9; B9/12/1948 Tuscaloosa, AL   **1970** Den 13 (11, RLB)   **1973** Buf 7   **1974**†Buf☆14 (ROLB)
1975 SF 14 (14, RLB)   **1976** SF✧14 (14, RLB)   **1977** SF 9 (9, RLB)   **1978** Det 16 (3)   **1979** Det 7   **1980** NO 16 (0)

1971	Den	14(10, LLB)	—	—	—	—	1	0	0.0(0)	0	—	—	—	—	—	—	—	—	—	i	—	0	3
1972	Buf	14	—	—	—	—	1	4	4.0(4)	0	—	—	—	—	—	—	—	—	—	i	—	0	1
NFL		11	138(61)	—	—	—	—	2	4	2.0(4)	0	—	—	—	—	—	—	—	ki	3	20	139

WASHINGTON, DAVE   David Eugene, TE, 6´4˝/228 lbs; USC; B12/28/1940 Oroville, CA

| 1968 | Den-A | 2 | — | — | — | — | 1 | 12 | 12.0(12) | 0 | — | — | — | — | — | — | — | — | — | — | — | 0 | 6 |

WASHINGTON, DEWAYNE   Dewayne Neron, DB, 5´11˝/195 lbs; North Carolina State; 1994: Min, rnd 1; B12/27/1972 Durham, NC [I]   **1994**†Min 16 (16, RCB)
1995 Min 15 (14, RCB)   **1996**†Min 16 (16, RCB)   **1997** Min 16 (16, RCB)   **1998** Pit 16 (16, RCB)   **1999** Pit 16 (16, RCB)   **2000** Pit 16 (16, RCB)   **2001**†Pit 16 (16, RCB)
2002†Pit 16 (16, RCB)   **2003** Pit 16 (12, RCB)   **2004** Jax 16 (16, RCB)   **2005** KC 16 (1)   **NFL** 191 (171) [12 yrs]

WASHINGTON, DICK   Richard, DB, 6´1˝/205 lbs; Bethune-Cookman; B2/15/1945 Savannah, GA   **1968** Mia-A 4

WASHINGTON, ERIC   Eric Christopher, DB, 6´2˝/190 lbs; Texas-El Paso; 1972: SL, rnd 10; B4/22/1950 Washington, DC   **1972** SL 6 (rcb)   **1973** SL 9   **NFL** 15 [2 yrs]

WASHINGTON, FABIEN   Fabien, DB, 5´10˝/183 lbs; Washington; 2005: Oak, rnd 1; B6/9/1983 Bradenton, FL   **2005** Oak 16 (11, RCB)

WASHINGTON, FRED   Fred Earl, T, 6´5˝/268 lbs; North Texas; B6/14/1944 Marlin, TX, D8/1985 Beaumont, TX   **1968** Was 1

WASHINGTON, FRED   Fred Earl, DT, 6´2˝/277 lbs; TCU; 1990: Chi, rnd 2; B7/11/1967 Denison, TX, D12/21/1990 Lake Forest, IL   **1990** ChiB 11 (0)

WASHINGTON, GENE   Eugene, WR, 6´3˝/208 lbs; Michigan State; 1967: Min, rnd 1; B1/25/1944 La Porte, TX

1967	Min	14	—	—	—	—	13	384	29.5(85)	2	—	—	—	—	—	—	—	—	—	—	12	202
1968	†Min	14(14, WR)	—	—	—	—	46	756	16.4(61)	6	—	—	—	—	—	—	—	—	—	—	36	408
1969	†Min★	14(14, WR)	—	—	—	—	39	821	21.1(83)	9	—	—	—	—	—	—	—	—	—	—	54	456
1970	†Min✧	14(14, WR)	—	—	—	—	44	702	16.0(49)	4	—	—	—	—	—	—	—	—	—	—	24	371
1971	†Min	13(8, WR)	—	—	—	—	12	165	13.8(51)	0	—	—	—	—	—	—	—	—	—	—	0	83
1972	Min	12(11, WR)	—	—	—	—	18	259	14.4(39)	˙2	—	—	—	—	—	—	—	—	—	—	12	140
1973	Den	14	—	—	—	—	10	150	15.0(28)	3	—	—	—	—	—	—	—	—	—	—	18	90
NFL		7	95(61)	—	—	—	—	182	3237	17.8(85)	26	—	—	—	—	—	—	—	—	—	156	1749

WASHINGTON, GENE   Gene Alden, WR-SE, 6´2˝/185 lbs; Stanford; 1969: SF, rnd 1; B1/14/1947 Tuscaloosa, AL

1969	SF★	14(14, SE)	1	-4	-4.0(-4)	.0	51	711	13.9(52)	3	—	—	—	—	—	—	—	—	—	—	18	367
1970	†SF★	13(WR)	—	—	—	—	53	**1100**	20.8(79)	12	—	—	—	—	—	—	—	—	—	—	72	610
1971	†SF★	14(14, WR)	—	—	—	—	46	**884**	19.2(71)	4	—	—	—	—	—	—	—	—	—	—	24	462
1972	†SF★	14(14, WR)	—	—	—	—	46	918	20.0(62)	**12**	—	—	—	—	—	—	—	—	—	—	72	519
1973	SF	13(13, WR)	—	—	—	—	37	606	16.4(58)	2	—	—	—	—	—	—	—	—	—	—	12	313
1974	SF	14(14, WR)	2	4	2.0(7)	0	29	615	**21.2(58)**	6	—	—	—	—	—	—	—	—	—	—	36	342
1975	SF	14(14, WR)	1	-4	-4.0(-4)	0	44	735	16.7(68)	9	1	0	0.0	0	0	—	—	—	—	—	54	409
1976	SF	14(14, WR)	1	3	3.0(3)	0	33	457	13.8(55)	6	—	—	—	—	—	—	—	—	—	—	36	262
1977	SF	14(14, WR)	—	—	—	—	32	638	19.9(47)	5	—	—	—	—	—	—	—	—	—	—	30	344
1979	Det	16(WR)	1	24	24.0(24)	0	14	192	13.7(32)	1	—	—	—	—	—	—	—	—	—	—	6	125
NFL		10	140(111)	6	23	3.8(24)	0	385	6856	17.8(79)	60	1	0	0.0	0	0	—	—	—	—	—	360	3751

WASHINGTON, GENE   Eugene Henry, WR, 5´9˝/172 lbs; Georgia; 1977: SD, rnd 9; B6/6/1953 Gadsden, SC   **1979** NYG 2

WASHINGTON, HARRY   Harry, WR, 6´0˝/180 lbs; Colorado State; B7/30/1956 Tacoma, WA   **1979**†ChiB 6

| 1978 | †Min | 10 | — | — | — | — | 1 | 24 | 24.0(24) | 0 | — | — | — | — | — | — | — | — | — | k | — | 0 | 23 |
| NFL | | 2 | 16 | — | — | — | — | 1 | 24 | 24.0(24) | 0 | — | — | — | — | — | — | — | — | — | — | 0 | 12 |

WASHINGTON, JAMES   James McArthur, DB, 6´1˝/209 lbs; UCLA; 1988: LARm, rnd 5; B1/10/1965 Los Angeles, CA   **1988**†LARm 16 (0)   **1989**†LARm 9 (0)   **1990** Dal 15 (10, SS)
1991†Dal 16 (16, SS)   **1992**†Dal 16 (15, FS/ss)   **1993** Dal 14 (1)   **1994**†Dal 16 (16, FS)   **1995** Was 12 (12, SS)   **NFL** 114 (70) [8 yrs]

WASHINGTON, JOE   Joe Dan, RB, 5´10˝/179 lbs; Oklahoma; 1976: SD, rnd 1; B9/24/1953 Crockett, TX

1977	SD	13	62	217	3.5(19)	0	31	244	7.9(29)	0	1	1	100.0	32	32.0(32)	1	0	—	—	—	—	0	360
1978	Bal	16(12, RB)	240	956	4.0(29)	0	45	377	8.4(33)	1	4	2	50.0	80	20.0(54)	2	0	—	—	kp	1	12	1426
1979	Bal✧	15(15, RB)	242	884	3.7(26)	4	**82**	750	9.1(43)	3	1	0	0.0	0	0	1	—	—	—	k	—	42	1260
1980	Bal	16(11, RB)	144	502	3.5(17)	1	51	494	9.7(33)	3	—	—	—	—	—	—	—	—	—	—	24	774
1981	Was	14(13, RB)	210	916	4.4(32)	4	70	558	8.0(32)	3	2	1	50.0	32	16.0(32)	0	0	—	—	—	—	42	1266
1982	†Was	7(1)	44	190	4.3(40)	1	19	134	7.1(17)	1	1	1	100.0	35	35.0(35)	2	0	—	—	—	—	12	290
1983	†Was	15(1)	145	772	**5.3(41)**	0	47	454	9.7(67)	6	—	—	—	—	—	—	—	—	—	k	—	36	1030
1984	†Was	7(0)	56	192	3.4(12)	1	14	74	5.7(12)	0	1	0	0.0	0	0	0	0	—	—	—	—	6	239
1985	Atl	16(0)	52	210	4.0(14)	1	37	328	8.9(34)	1	—	—	—	—	—	—	—	—	—	—	12	389
NFL		9	119(53)	1195	4839	4.0(41)	12	395	3413	8.6(67)	18	11	5	45.5	179	16.3(54)	3	1	—	—	kp	1	186	7033

WASHINGTON, JOE   Joseph Willie, RB, 5´9˝/180 lbs; Illinois State; B7/10/1951 Baton Rouge, LA

| 1973 | Atl | 9 | 4 | 36 | 9.0(16) | 0 | — | — | — | — | — | — | — | — | — | — | — | — | — | k | — | 0 | 168 |

WASHINGTON, JOHN   John Earl, DE-NT, 6´4˝/280 lbs; Oklahoma State; 1986: NYG, rnd 3; B2/20/1963 Houston, TX   **1986** NYG 16 (0)   **1987** NYG 12 (2)   **1988** NYG 16 (2)
1989†NYG 16 (14, LDE)   **1990**†NYG 16 (13, RDE/lde)   **1991** NYG 12 (8, NT)   **1992** NYG 12 (2)   **1992** Atl 3 (0)   **1993** NE 16 (13, RDE)   **NFL** 119 (53) [8 yrs]

WASHINGTON, KEITH   Keith LeMon, DE, 6´4˝/285 lbs; UNLV; B12/18/1972 Dallas, TX   **1996** Det 12 (0)   **1997** Bal 10 (1)   **1998** Bal 16 (0)   **1999** Bal 16 (0)   **2000**†Bal 16 (0)
2001 Den 16 (16, LDE)   **2002** Den 10 (0)   **2003** NYG 14 (6, rde)   **2004** NYG 8 (8, RDE)   **NFL** 118 (31) [9 yrs]

WASHINGTON, KELLEY   James Kelley, WR, 6´3˝/218 lbs; Tennessee; 2003: Cin, rnd 3; B8/21/1979 Stephens City, VA

2003	Cin	16(3)	1	5	5.0(5)	0	22	299	13.6(51)	4	—	—	—	—	—	—	—	—	—	—	24	175
2004	Cin	16(2)	1	-1	-1.0(-1)	0	31	378	12.2(28)	3	—	—	—	—	—	—	—	—	—	—	18	203
2005	Cin	7(0)	—	—	—	—	10	101	10.1(18)	1	—	—	—	—	—	—	—	—	—	—	6	56
NFL		3	39(5)	2	4	2.0(5)	0	63	778	12.3(51)	8	—	—	—	—	—	—	—	—	—	—	48	433

WASHINGTON, KENNY   Kenneth Stanley, HB-DB, 6´1˝/212 lbs; UCLA; B8/31/1918 Los Angeles, CA, D6/24/1971 Los Angeles, CA

1946	LARm	6(0)	23	114	5.0(19)	1	6	83	13.8(20)	0	8	1	12.5	19	2.4(19)	0	0	—	—	k	—	6	184
1947	LARm	11(2)	60	444	**7.4(92)**	5	3	40	13.3(21)	0	5	2	40.0	14	2.8(18)	0	1	—	—	kp	—	30	532
1948	LARm	10(3)	57	301	5.3(31)	2	6	104	17.3(43)	1	1	0	0.0	0	0	0	0	—	—	kpi	—	18	444
NFL		3	27(5)	140	859	6.1(92)	8	15	227	15.1(43)	1	14	3	21.4	33	2.4(19)	0	1	—	—	kpi	—	54	1160

YEAR	TEAM	G(GS, POS)	RUSH	YD	AVG(LG)	TD	REC	YD	AVG(LG)	TD	PASS	COMP	PCT	YD	AVG(LG)	TD	INT	SK	YD	QBR	KPR	OTD	PTS	TAY

Washington, Lionel Lionel, DB, 6´0˝/185 lbs; Tulane; 1983: SL, rnd 4; B10/21/1960 New Orleans, LA **[I]** **1983** SL 16 (8, LCB) **1984** SL 15 (15, LCB) **1985** SL 5 (2) **1986** SL 16 (12, LCB) **1987** LARd 11 (10, LCB) **1988** LARd 12 (0) **1989** LARd 16 (16, RCB) **1990**†LARd 15 (15, RCB) **1991**†LARd 16 (16, RCB) **1992** LARd 16 (16, RCB) **1993**†LARd 16 (16, RCB) **1994** LARd 11 (7, rcb) **1995** Den 16 (16, RCB) **1996**†Den 14 (12, RCB) **1997** Oak 9 (3) **NFL** 204 (164) [15 yrs]

Washington, Marcus° Marcus Cornelius, LB, 6´3˝/247 lbs; Auburn; 2000: Ind, rnd 2; B10/17/1977 Auburn, AL **2000**†Ind 16 (0) **2001** Ind 16 (16, LLB) **2002** Ind 15 (15, RLB) **2003**†Ind 16 (16, LLB) **2004** Was✧16 (16, LLB) **2005**†Was 16 (16, LLB) **NFL** 95 (79) [6 yrs]

Washington, Mark Mark Henry, DB, 5´10˝/188 lbs; Morgan State; 1970: Dal, rnd 13; B12/28/1947 Chicago, IL **1970**†Dal 14 **1971** Dal 2 **1972**†Dal 10 **1973**†Dal 14 **1974** Dal 13 (6, lcb) **1975**†Dal 14 (LCB) **1976**†Dal 13 (5, rcb) **1977**†Dal 13 (4) **1978**†Dal 13 **1979** NE 12 **NFL** 118 (15) [10 yrs]

Washington, Marvin Marvin Andrew, DE-DT, 6´6˝/275 lbs; Texas-El Paso; Idaho; 1989: NYJ, rnd 6; B10/22/1965 Denver, CO **1989** NYJ 16 (0) **1990** NYJ 16 (0) **1991**†NYJ 15 (15, LDE) **1992** NYJ 16 (14, RDE) **1993** NYJ 16 (16, LDE) **1994** NYJ 15 (15, LDE) **1995** NYJ 16 (16, RDE) **1996** NYJ 14 (14, LDT/lde) **1997** SF 10 (1) **1998**†Den 16 (0) **1999** SF 5 (5, lde) **NFL** 155 (96) [11 yrs]

Washington, Mickey Mickey Lin, DB, 5´9˝/195 lbs; Texas A&M; 1990: Phx, rnd 8; B7/8/1968 Galveston, TX **1990** NE 9 (0) **1991** NE 16 (4) **1992** Was 3 (0) **1993**†Buf 16 (6, lcb) **1994** Buf 16 (16, LCB) **1995** Jax 16 (16, RCB) **1996**†Jax 16 (16, RCB) **1997** NO 16 (2) **NFL** 108 (60) [8 yrs]

Washington, Mike Michael Lee, DB, 6´2˝/197 lbs; Alabama; 1975: Bal, rnd 3; B7/1/1953 Montgomery, AL **[I]** **1976** TB 6 (5, lcb) **1977** TB 14 (14, RCB) **1978** TB 16 (16, RCB) **1979**†TB 15 (15, RCB) **1980** TB 16 (16, RCB) **1981**†TB 14 (12, RCB) **1982** TB 8 (8, RCB) **1983** TB 10 (10, RCB) **1984** TB 1 (0) **NFL** 100 (96) [9 yrs]

Washington, Nate Nate, WR, 6´3˝/256 lbs; Kansas State; B8/28/1983 Toledo, OH **2005**†Pit 1 (0)

Washington, Patrick Patrick Orlando, FB, 6´2˝/240 lbs; Virginia; B3/4/1978 Washington, DC

YEAR	TEAM	G(GS, POS)	RUSH	YD	AVG(LG)	TD	REC	YD	AVG(LG)	TD	PASS	COMP	PCT	YD	AVG(LG)	TD	INT	SK	YD	QBR	KPR	OTD	PTS	TAY
2001	Jax	16(6, FB)	—	—	—	—	5	36	7.2(12)	0	—	—	—	—	—	—	—	—	—	—	—	—	0	18
2002	Jax	14(3)	—	—	—	—	1	5	5.0(5)	0	—	—	—	—	—	—	—	—	—	—	k	—	0	-38
NFL	2	30(9)	—	—	—	—	6	41	6.8(12)	0	—	—	—	—	—	—	—	—	—	—	k	—	0	-20

Washington, Rashad Rashad, DB, 6´3˝/210 lbs; Kansas State; 2004: NYJ, rnd 7; B3/15/1980 Wichita, KS **2004** NYJ 6 (0) **2005** NYJ 16 (0) **NFL** 22 (0) [2 yrs]

Washington, Robert Robert James, T, 6´4˝/251 lbs; Alcorn State; B4/2/1963 **1987** Pit 3 (0)

Washington, Ronnie Ronald Carroll, LB, 6´1˝/245 lbs; Louisiana-Monroe; 1985: Atl, rnd 8; B7/29/1963 Monroe, LA **1985** Atl 16 (1) **1987** LARd 2 (1) **1989** Ind 2 (0) **NFL** 20 (2) [3 yrs]

Washington, Russ Russell Eugene, T-DT, 6´6˝/289 lbs; Missouri; 1968: SD, rnd 1; B12/17/1946 Kansas City, MO **1968** SD-A 14 (12, LDT) **1969** SD-A 14 (13, LDT) **1970** SD 14 (13, RT) **1971** SD 14 (14, RT) **1972** SD 14 (14, RT) **1973** SD☆14 (14, RT) **1974** SD★14 (14, RT) **1975** SD✧14 (14, RT) **1976** SD 14 (14, RT) **1977** SD★14 (14, RT) **1978** SD★16 (16, RT) **1979**†SD★16 (16, RT) **1980** SD 6 (6, rt) **1981**†SD 13 (13, RT) **1982**†SD☆9 (9, RT) **NFL** 200 (196) [15 yrs]

Washington, Sam Samuel Lee, DB, 5´8˝/180 lbs; Mississippi Valley State; B3/7/1960 Tampa, FL **1982**†Pit 4 (0) **1983**†Pit 16 (0) **1984**†Pit 14 (14, RCB) **1985** Pit 7 (0) **1985** Cin 8 (0) **NFL** 49 (14) [4 yrs]

Washington, Ted Theodore Bernard, LB, 6´1˝/244 lbs; Mississippi Valley State; 1972: KC, rnd 17; B2/16/1948 Tampa, FL **1973** Hou 1 **1974** Hou 14 (ROLB) **1975** Hou 14 (LOLB) **1976** Hou 13 (LOLB) **1977** Hou 14 (LOLB) **1978**†Hou 16 (LOLB) **1979**†Hou 15 (LOLB) **1980**†Hou 16 (15, LOLB) **1981** Hou 16 (16, LOLB) **1982** Hou 9 (1) **NFL** 128 (32) [10 yrs]

Washington, Ted Theodore, NT-DT, 6´5˝/365 lbs; Louisville; 1991: SF, rnd 1; B4/13/1968 Tampa, FL **1991** SF 16 (0) **1992**†SF 16 (6, nt) **1993**†SF 12 (12, RDT) **1994** Den 15 (15, LDT) **1995**†Buf 16 (15, NT) **1996**†Buf 16 (16, NT) **1997** Buf★16 (16, NT) **1998**†Buf★16 (16, NT) **1999**†Buf 16 (16, NT) **2000** Buf✧16 (16, NT) **2001**†ChiB★16 (15, LDT) **2002** ChiB 2 (2) **2003**†NE 10 (10, LDT) **2004** Oak 16 (16, LDT) **2005** Oak 16 (16, LDT) **NFL** 215 (187) [15 yrs]

Washington, Teddy Harold L., RB, 5´11˝/210 lbs; Colorado; San Diego State; 1968: Cin, rnd 13; B11/20/1945

YEAR	TEAM	G(GS, POS)	RUSH	YD	AVG(LG)	TD	REC	YD	AVG(LG)	TD	PASS	COMP	PCT	YD	AVG(LG)	TD	INT	SK	YD	QBR	KPR	OTD	PTS	TAY
1968	Cin-A	1	1	4	4.0(4)	0	—	—	—	—	—	—	—	—	—	—	—	—	—	—	—	—	0	4

Washington, Tim Timothy Bernard, DB, 5´9˝/184 lbs; California; Fresno State; 1982: SF, rnd 12; B11/7/1959 Fresno, CA, D1/4/1992 Fremont, CA **1982** SF 1 (0) **1982** KC 1 (0) **NFL** 2 (0) [1 yr]

Washington, Todd Todd Page, G-C, 6´3˝/310 lbs; Virginia Tech; 1998: TB, rnd 4; B9/19/1976 Nassawadox, VA **1998** TB 4 (0) **1999**†TB 6 (0) **2000**†TB 10 (0) **2001**†TB 15 (1) **2002**†TB 16 (2) **2003** Hou 16 (14, LG) **2004** Hou 15 (0) **2005** Hou 15 (0) **NFL** 97 (17) [8 yrs]

Washington, Vic Victor Arnold, RB-DB-WR, 5´11˝/197 lbs; Wyoming; 1970: SF, rnd 4; B3/23/1946 Plainfield, NJ **[R]**

YEAR	TEAM	G(GS, POS)	RUSH	YD	AVG(LG)	TD	REC	YD	AVG(LG)	TD	PASS	COMP	PCT	YD	AVG(LG)	TD	INT	SK	YD	QBR	KPR	OTD	PTS	TAY
1971	†SF✧	14(RB)	191	811	4.2(42)	3	36	317	8.8(40)	4	—	—	—	—	—	—	—	—	—	—	k	—	42	**1383**
1972	†SF	13(13, RB)	141	468	3.3(33)	3	43	393	9.1(33)	1	—	—	—	—	—	—	—	—	—	—	k	1	30	1076
1973	SF	13(13, RB)	151	534	3.5(25)	8	33	238	7.2(20)	0	—	—	—	—	—	—	—	—	—	—	k	—	48	922
1974	Hou	12(RB)	74	281	3.8(23)	2	13	92	7.1(15)	0	—	—	—	—	—	—	—	—	—	—	k	—	12	419
1975	Buf	13	9	49	5.4(9)	0	2	21	10.5(15)	0	—	—	—	—	—	—	—	—	—	—	k	—	0	458
1976	Buf	2	22	65	3.0(10)	0	3	29	9.7(11)	0	—	—	—	—	—	—	—	—	—	—	k	—	0	98
NFL	6	67(26)	588	2208	3.8(42)	16	130	1090	8.4(40)	5	—	—	—	—	—	—	—	—	—	—	k	1	132	4354

Waskiewicz, Jim James Allan, C-LB-T, 6´4˝/240 lbs; Wichita State; 1966: NYJ, rnd 4; B2/10/1944 Milwaukee, WI **1966** NYJ-A 14 **1967** NYJ-A 13 **1969** Atl 12 **NFL** 39 [3 yrs]

Wasserbach, Lloyd Lloyd George, T, 5´11˝/205 lbs; Wisconsin; 1943: GB, rnd 21; B1/30/1921 Baileys Harbor, WI **1946** ChiR-A 12 (3) **1947** ChiR-A 5 (0) **AAFC** 17 (3) [2 yrs]

Waterfield, Bob Robert Stanton, QB, 6´1˝/200 lbs; UCLA; 1944: Cle, rnd 5; B7/26/1920 Elmira, NY, D3/25/1983 Burbank, CA; HOF 1965 **[KPIC]**

YEAR	TEAM	G(GS, POS)	RUSH	YD	AVG(LG)	TD	REC	YD	AVG(LG)	TD	PASS	COMP	PCT	YD	AVG(LG)	TD	INT	SK	YD	QBR	KPR	OTD	PTS	TAY
1945	†Cle☆	10(4, QB)	18	18	1.0(16)	5	—	—	—	—	171	89	52.0	1609	**9.4**(**84**)	**14**	**17**	—	—	72.4	KPpi	—	64	349
1946	LARm☆	11(4, QB)	16	-60	-3.8(6)	1	—	—	—	—	**251**	**127**	50.6	1747	7.0(57)	**17**	17	—	—	67.6	KPpi	—	61	283
1947	LARm	12(8, QB)	3	6	2.0(4)	1	2	14	7.0(18)	0	221	96	43.4	1210	5.5(45)	8	18	—	—	39.2	KPpi	—	54	-24
1948	LARm	11(8, QB)	7	12	1.7(10)	0	—	—	—	—	180	87	48.3	1354	7.5(80)	14	18	—	—	60.0	KPi	—	56	27
1949	†LARm☆	12(11, QB)	5	-4	-0.8(5)	1	—	—	—	—	296	154	52.0	2168	7.3(71)	17	**24**	—	—	61.3	KP	—	76	215
1950	†LARm★	12(qb)	8	14	1.8(13)	1	—	—	—	—	213	122	**57.3**	1540	7.2(72)	11	13	—	—	71.7	KP	—	81	329
1951	†LARm★	11(qb)	9	49	5.4(25)	3	—	—	—	—	176	88	50.0	1566	**8.9**(**91**)	13	10	—	—	**81.8**	KP	—	98	527
1952	†LARm	12(qb)	9	-14	-1.6(19)	1	1	5	5.0(5)	0	109	51	46.8	655	6.0(63)	3	11	—	—	35.7	KP	—	83	-99
NFL	8	91(35)	75	21	0.3(25)	13	3	19	6.3(18)	0	1617	814	50.3	11849	7.3(91)	97	128	—	—	61.6	KPpi	—	573	1606

Waters, Andre Andre, DB, 5´11˝/200 lbs; Cheyney (PA); B3/10/1962 Belle Glade, FL **1984** Phi 16 (0) **1985** Phi 16 (0) **1986** Phi 16 (16, SS) **1987** Phi 12 (12, SS) **1988**†Phi 16 (16, SS) **1989**†Phi 16 (13, SS) **1990**†Phi 14 (13, SS) **1991** Phi☆16 (16, SS) **1992**†Phi 6 (6, ss) **1993** Phi 9 (8, SS) **1994** Arz 12 (4) **1995** Arz 7 (0) **NFL** 156 (104) [12 yrs]

Waters, Bob Robert Lee, QB, 6´2˝/184 lbs; Presbyterian; 1960: SF, rnd 7/LAC, rnd 2; B6/22/1938 Millen, GA

YEAR	TEAM	G(GS, POS)	RUSH	YD	AVG(LG)	TD	REC	YD	AVG(LG)	TD	PASS	COMP	PCT	YD	AVG(LG)	TD	INT	SK	YD	QBR	KPR	OTD	PTS	TAY
1960	SF	8	1	8	8.0(8)	0	—	—	—	—	2	2	100.0	61	30.5(41)	1	0	—	—	—	—	—	0	44
1961	SF	8	47	233	5.0(35)	3	—	—	—	—	28	13	46.4	183	6.5(26)	1	2	—	—	—	—	—	18	280
1962	SF	7	12	42	3.5(14)	0	—	—	—	—	6	2	33.3	28	4.7(15)	0	0	—	—	—	—	—	0	56
1963	SF	7	5	-2	-0.4(8)	0	—	—	—	—	88	42	47.7	435	4.9(42)	1	6	—	—	—	—	—	0	-20
NFL	4	30	65	281	4.3(35)	3	—	—	—	—	124	59	47.6	707	5.7(42)	3	8	—	—	—	—	—	18	360

Waters, Brian Brian Demond, G, 6´3˝/318 lbs; North Texas; B2/18/1977 Waxahachie, TX **2000** KC 6 (0) **2001** KC 16 (8, LG) **2002** KC 16 (16, LG) **2003** KC 16 (16, LG) **2004** KC★16 (16, LG) **2005** KC★16 (16, LG) **NFL** 86 (72) [6 yrs]

Waters, Charlie Charlie Tutan, DB, 6´1˝/193 lbs; Clemson; 1970: Dal, rnd 3; B9/10/1948 Miami, FL **[I]** **1970**†Dal 14 (6, FS) **1971**†Dal 14 (3) **1972**†Dal 14 **1973**†Dal 14 (LCB) **1975**†Dal 14 (SS) **1976**†Dal✧14 (14, SS) **1978**†Dal★16 (SS) **1980**†Dal 16 (16, SS) **1981**†Dal 16 (16, SS)

YEAR	TEAM	G(GS, POS)	RUSH	YD	AVG(LG)	TD	REC	YD	AVG(LG)	TD	PASS	COMP	PCT	YD	AVG(LG)	TD	INT	SK	YD	QBR	KPR	OTD	PTS	TAY
1974	Dal	14(7, LCB)	1	6	6.0(6)	0	—	—	—	—	—	—	—	—	—	—	—	—	—	—	pi	—	0	25
1977	†Dal★	14(SS)	—	—	—	—	—	—	—	—	0	0	0.0	0	0.0	0	0	1	12	—	i	1	6	-4
NFL	11	160(62)	1	6	6.0(6)	0	—	—	—	—	0	0	0.0	0	0.0	0	0	1	12	—	kpi	3	20	435

Waters, Dale Dale Bernard, T-E-G, 6´2˝/212 lbs; Florida; B5/27/1909 Henry County, IN, D12/19/2001 Prescott, AZ **1931** Por 1 (0) **1931** Cle 6 (4) **1933** Bos 11 (2)

YEAR	TEAM	G(GS, POS)	RUSH	YD	AVG(LG)	TD	REC	YD	AVG(LG)	TD	PASS	COMP	PCT	YD	AVG(LG)	TD	INT	SK	YD	QBR	KPR	OTD	PTS	TAY
1932	Bos	9(6, RT)	1	15	15.0(15)	0	—	—	—	—	1	0	0.0	0	0.0	0	1	—	—	—	—	—	0	-25
NFL	3	27(12)	1	15	15.0(15)	0	—	—	—	—	1	0	0.0	0	0.0	0	1	—	—	—	—	—	0	-25

Waters, Mike Robert Michael, TE-RB, 6´2˝/228 lbs; San Diego State; 1985: NYJ, rnd 9; B3/15/1962 San Diego, CA

YEAR	TEAM	G(GS, POS)	RUSH	YD	AVG(LG)	TD	REC	YD	AVG(LG)	TD	PASS	COMP	PCT	YD	AVG(LG)	TD	INT	SK	YD	QBR	KPR	OTD	PTS	TAY
1986	Phi	5(2)	5	8	1.6(5)	0	2	27	13.5(19)	0	—	—	—	—	—	—	—	—	—	—	p	—	0	17
1987	NO	5(0)	—	—	—	—	5	140	28.0(82)	1	—	—	—	—	—	—	—	—	—	—	—	—	6	75
NFL	2	10(2)	5	8	1.6(5)	0	7	167	23.9(82)	1	—	—	—	—	—	—	—	—	—	—	p	—	6	92

YEAR	TEAM	G (GS, POS)	RUSH	YD	AVG(LG)	TD	REC	YD	AVG(LG)	TD	PASS	COMP	PCT	YD	AVG(LG)	TD	INT	SK	YD	QBR	KPR	OTD	PTS	TAY

WATFORD, JERRY Jerry Ray, G-E-DE, 6´3˝/205 lbs; Alabama; 1953: ChiC, rnd 8; B12/19/1930 Gadsden, AL, D3/10/1993 Blountville, TN **1953** ChiC 12 (RG) **1954** ChiC 12
NFL 24 [2 yrs]

WATHEN, PETE Chapeze, E-BB, 5´10˝/175 lbs; Kentucky; B5/15/1903 Owensboro, KY, D7/5/1949 Owensboro, KY **1922** Evv 2 (2, RE)

WATKINS, BOBBY Robert Archibald, HB, 5´10˝/198 lbs; Ohio State; 1955: ChiB, rnd 2; B3/30/1932 New Bedford, MA

YEAR	TEAM	G (GS, POS)	RUSH	YD	AVG(LG)	TD	REC	YD	AVG(LG)	TD	KPR	OTD	PTS	TAY
1955	ChiB	12(RH)	110	553	5.0(33)	8	6	79	13.2(34)	0	k	—	48	743
1956	†ChiB	9(LH)	68	276	4.1(25)	2	2	3	1.5(6)	1	—	—	18	303
1957	ChiB	12(rh)	57	212	3.7(19)	1	3	90	30.0(74)	1	—	—	12	272
1958	ChiC	5	3	17	5.7(9)	0	4	62	15.5(48)	1	k	—	6	62
NFL	4	38	238	1058	4.4(33)	11	15	234	15.6(74)	3	k	—	84	1379

WATKINS, BOBBY Bobby Lawrence, DB, 5´10˝/184 lbs; Southwest Texas State; 1982: Det, rnd 2; B5/31/1960 Cottonwood, ID [I] **1982**†Det 9 (4) **1983**†Det 16 (16, LCB) **1984** Det 16 (16, LCB) **1985** Det 16 (16, LCB) **1986** Det 5 (4) **1987** Det 5 (5, lcb) **1988** Det 16 (0) NFL 83 (61) [7 yrs]

WATKINS, FOSTER Foster Forrest, QB-HB, 5´9˝/163 lbs; West Texas A&M; 1939: Phi, rnd 15; B11/17/1916 Memphis, TN, D12/29/2002 Wichita Falls, TX [K]

YEAR	TEAM	G (GS, POS)	RUSH	YD	AVG(LG)	TD	REC	YD	AVG(LG)	TD	PASS	COMP	PCT	YD	AVG(LG)	TD	INT	KPR	OTD	PTS	TAY
1940	Phi	9(0, qb)	14	-76	-5.4	0	—	—	—	—	85	28	32.9	565	6.6	1	3	KP	—	2	92
1941	Phi	11(1)	15	11	0.7(8)	0	4	36	9.0(16)	0	10	6	60.0	62	6.2(15)	1	0	kp	—	0	69
NFL	2	20(1)	29	-65	-2.2(8)	0	4	36	9.0(16)	0	95	34	35.8	627	6.6(15)	2	3	KPkp	—	2	161

WATKINS, GORDON Gordon Campbell, T-G, 6´1˝/220 lbs; Georgia Tech; B5/19/1907 Atlanta, GA, D4/8/1974 Atlanta, GA **1930** Min 2 (2) **1930** Fra 8 (7, RT) **1931** Bkn 7 (3) NFL 17 (12) [2 yrs]

WATKINS, KENDELL Kendell Mairo, TE, 6´1˝/305 lbs; Mississippi State; 1995: Dal, rnd 2; B3/8/1973 Jackson, MS

YEAR	TEAM	G (GS, POS)	RUSH	YD	AVG(LG)	TD	REC	YD	AVG(LG)	TD	KPR	OTD	PTS	TAY
1995	†Dal	16(0)	—	—	—	—	1	8	8.0(8)	0	k	—	0	-17

WATKINS, LARRY Lawrence, RB, 6´2˝/230 lbs; Alcorn State; B10/5/1946 Bessemer, AL

YEAR	TEAM	G (GS, POS)	RUSH	YD	AVG(LG)	TD	REC	YD	AVG(LG)	TD	KPR	OTD	PTS	TAY
1969	Det	14	62	201	3.2(12)	1	13	87	6.7(20)	0	—	—	6	255
1970	Phi	11	32	96	3.0(11)	1	3	6	2.0(5)	0	—	—	6	109
1971	Phi	12	35	98	2.8(11)	1	6	40	6.7(9)	0	—	—	6	128
1972	Phi	14(FB)	67	262	3.9(28)	1	6	-2	-0.3(4)	0	—	—	6	271
1973	Buf	14(FB)	98	414	4.2(17)	2	12	86	7.2(28)	0	k	—	18	485
1974	†Buf	10	41	170	4.1(13)	2	1	7	7.0(7)	0	—	—	12	194
1975	NYG	14	68	303	4.5(12)	3	7	43	6.1(12)	0	—	—	18	355
1976	NYG	13	26	96	3.7(13)	1	2	8	4.0(12)	0	k	—	6	104
1977	NYG	9	19	71	3.7(9)	0	1	9	9.0(9)	0	—	—	0	76
NFL	9	111	448	1711	3.8(28)	12	51	284	5.6(28)	1	k	—	78	1975

WATKINS, TOM Thomas, HB, 6´0˝/195 lbs; Iowa State; 1960: Cle, rnd 15/1961: Oak, rnd 8; B10/23/1937 West Memphis, AR [R]

YEAR	TEAM	G (GS, POS)	RUSH	YD	AVG(LG)	TD	REC	YD	AVG(LG)	TD	PASS	COMP	PCT	YD	AVG(LG)	TD	INT	KPR	OTD	PTS	TAY
1961	Cle	10(hb)	43	209	4.9(21)	0	4	66	16.5(35)	1	—	—	—	—	—	—	—	k	—	6	338
1962	Det	13	113	485	4.3(60)	3	12	85	7.1(29)	0	—	—	—	—	—	—	—	kp	—	18	757
1963	Det	13(LH)	97	423	4.4(32)	2	16	168	10.5(32)	1	—	—	—	—	—	—	—	kp	1	24	913
1964	Det	14(LH)	80	218	2.7(15)	1	10	125	12.5(37)	1	1	1	100.0	58	58.0(58)	1	0	kp	2	24	636
1965	Det	11	29	95	3.3(12)	0	5	53	10.6(28)	0	—	—	—	—	—	—	—	kp	—	0	570
1967	Det	13(hb)	106	361	3.4(28)	4	8	93	11.6(27)	1	—	—	—	—	—	—	—	kp	—	30	546
1968	Pit	1																kp	—	0	-3
NFL	7	75	468	1791	3.8(60)	10	55	590	10.7(37)	4	1	1	100.0	58	58.0(58)	1	0	kp	3	102	3755

WATSON, ALLAN Allan, K, 5´9˝/162 lbs; Newport (Wales); B11/5/1944 Blockwood, Wales [K] **1970** Pit 4

WATSON, BEN Benjamin, TE, 6´3˝/255 lbs; Duke; Georgia; 2004: NE, rnd 1; B12/18/1980 Norfolk, VA

YEAR	TEAM	G (GS, POS)	RUSH	YD	AVG(LG)	TD	REC	YD	AVG(LG)	TD	KPR	OTD	PTS	TAY
2004	NE	1(1)	—	—	—	—	2	16	8.0(14)	0	—	—	0	8
2005	†NE	15(9, TE)	—	—	—	—	29	441	15.2(35)	4	k	—	24	227
NFL	2	16(10)	—	—	—	—	31	457	14.7(35)	4	k	—	24	235

WATSON, CHRIS Chris, DB, 6´1˝/192 lbs; Eastern Illinois; 1999: Den, rnd 3; B6/30/1977 Chicago, IL [R] **1999** Den 14 (1) **2000** Buf 16 (5, lcb) **2001** Buf 14 (0) **2002** Buf 14 (8, lcb) NFL 58 (14) [4 yrs]

WATSON, COURTNEY Courtney, LB, 6´1˝/234 lbs; Notre Dame; 2004: NO, rnd 2; B9/18/1980 Sarasota, FL **2004** NO 12 (8, MLB) **2005** NO 9 (6, mlb) NFL 21 (14) [2 yrs]

WATSON, DAVE Carl David, G, 6´1˝/245 lbs; Georgia Tech; 1963: Bos, rnd 11/Chi, rnd 9; B1941 **1963**†Bos-A 14 **1964** Bos-A 14 NFL 28 [2 yrs]

WATSON, ED Edward Louis, LB, 6´4˝/220 lbs; Grambling State; 1969: Hou, rnd 9; B5/8/1945 Coushatta, LA **1969** Hou-A 3

WATSON, EDDIE Edwin David, RB, 6´0˝/229 lbs; Purdue; 1998: GB, rnd 7; B9/29/1976 New Orleans, LA

YEAR	TEAM	G (GS, POS)	RUSH	YD	AVG(LG)	TD	OTD	PTS	TAY
1999	Phi	6(0)	4	17	4.3(6)	0	—	0	17

WATSON, ERNEST Ernest J., BB, Olivet; B12/13/1895, D3/10/1995 Newberry, MI **1920** Det 2 (0)

WATSON, JIM James Robert, C, 6´0˝/205 lbs; Pacific; B3/26/1921 Stockton, CA, D5/11/2004 Marysville, CA **1945** Was 4 (1)

WATSON, JOE Joseph LaVerne, C-LB, 6´3˝/235 lbs; Rice; 1950: Det, rnd 1; B8/19/1925 Sherman, TX **1950** Det 8

WATSON, JOHN John Ace, G-T-C, 6´4˝/249 lbs; Oklahoma; 1971: SF, rnd 7; B1/11/1949 Palo Alto, CA **1971**†SF 14 **1972**†SF 14 **1973** SF 14 (12, LG) **1974** SF 13 (12, LG) **1975** SF 14 (12, LT) **1976** SF 11 (5, rg/c) **1977** NO 5 **1978** NO 5 **1979** NO 5 NFL 95 (41) [9 yrs]

WATSON, JUSTIN Justin Sean, RB, 6´0˝/220 lbs; San Diego State; B1/7/1975 Bronx, NY

YEAR	TEAM	G (GS, POS)	RUSH	YD	AVG(LG)	TD	REC	YD	AVG(LG)	TD	OTD	PTS	TAY
1999	SL	8(0)	47	179	3.8(21)	0	—	—	—	—	—	0	179
2000	†SL	14(2)	54	249	4.6(49)	4	10	56	5.6(15)	0	—	24	317
2001	†SL	11(0)	1	0	0.0(0)	0	—	—	—	—	—	0	0
NFL	3	33(2)	102	428	4.2(49)	4	10	56	5.6(15)	0	—	24	496

WATSON, KENNY Kenny, RB, 5´11˝/214 lbs; Penn State; B3/13/1978 Harrisburg, PA **2003** Cin 8 (0) **2005** Cin 1 (0)

YEAR	TEAM	G (GS, POS)	RUSH	YD	AVG(LG)	TD	REC	YD	AVG(LG)	TD	KPR	OTD	PTS	TAY
2002	Was	16(4)	116	534	4.6(24)	1	32	253	7.9(62)	0	k	—	12	827
2004	Cin	16(0)	26	161	6.2(25)	0	25	171	6.8(21)	1	k	—	6	297
NFL	4	41(4)	142	695	4.9(25)	1	57	424	7.4(62)	1	k	—	18	1131

WATSON, LOUIS Louis Teddy, WR, 5´11˝/175 lbs; Mississippi Valley State; B1/11/1963 Mobile, AL

YEAR	TEAM	G (GS, POS)	RUSH	YD	AVG(LG)	TD	REC	YD	AVG(LG)	TD	OTD	PTS	TAY
1987	Cle	2(0)	—	—	—	—	1	9	9.0(9)	0	—	0	5

WATSON, PETE Rodney Peter, TE, 6´1˝/210 lbs; Tufts; B9/19/1950 New York, NY **1972** Cin 2

WATSON, RAT Grady, B, 5´10˝/181 lbs; Southwestern (TX); Texas; B5/12/1899 Orange, TX, D4/1985 Edmond, OK [K] **1922** Tol 7 (7, BB), 9 **1923** Tol 5 (3), 1 **1924** Ham 3 (1) **1924** KC 1 (1) **1925** Ham 2 (0) **1927** Buf 2 (0) NFL 20 (12), 10 [5 yrs]

WATSON, REMI Remi Fitzgerald, WR, 6´0˝/174 lbs; South Carolina State; Bethune-Cookman; B8/8/1964

YEAR	TEAM	G (GS, POS)	RUSH	YD	AVG(LG)	TD	REC	YD	AVG(LG)	TD	OTD	PTS	TAY
1987	Cle	1(0)	—	—	—	—	1	13	13.0(13)	0	—	0	7

WATSON, SID Sidney John, HB, 5´11˝/187 lbs; Northeastern; B5/4/1932 Andover, MA, D4/25/2004 Naples, FL [K]

YEAR	TEAM	G (GS, POS)	RUSH	YD	AVG(LG)	TD	REC	YD	AVG(LG)	TD	KPR	OTD	PTS	TAY
1955	Pit	12	29	31	1.1(15)	0	19	223	11.7(62)	1	kp	—	6	359
1956	Pit	12(LH)	112	298	2.7(18)	4	12	138	11.5(37)	0	Kkp	—	37	454
1957	Pit	11	12	21	1.8(12)	0	3	24	8.0(11)	0	—	—	0	33
1958	Was	10	46	166	3.6(23)	0	5	38	7.6(24)	1	kp	—	6	349
NFL	4	45	199	516	2.6(23)	4	39	423	10.8(62)	2	Kkp	—	49	1195

WATSON, STEVE Stephen Ross, WR, 6´4˝/195 lbs; Temple; B5/28/1957 Baltimore, MD

YEAR	TEAM	G (GS, POS)	RUSH	YD	AVG(LG)	TD	REC	YD	AVG(LG)	TD	KPR	OTD	PTS	TAY
1979	†Den	16	—	—	—	—	6	83	13.8(22)	0	—	—	0	42
1980	Den	16(1)	—	—	—	—	6	146	24.3(52)	0	k	—	0	63
1981	Den★	16(13, WR)	2	6	3.0(6)	0	60	1244	20.7(95)	13	—	—	78	693
1982	Den	9(9, WR)	1	-4	-4.0(-4)	0	36	555	15.4(41)	2	—	—	12	284
1983	†Den	16(16, WR)	3	17	5.7(10)	0	59	1133	19.2(78)	5	—	—	30	609

YEAR	TEAM	G (GS, POS)	RUSH	YD	AVG (LG)	TD	REC	YD	AVG (LG)	TD	PASS	COMP	PCT	YD	AVG (LG)	TD	INT	SK	YD	QBR	KPR	OTD	PTS	TAY
1984	†Den	16(16, WR)	—	—	—	—	69	1170	17.0(73)	7	—	—	—	—	—	—	—	—	—	—	—	—	42	620
1985	Den	16(15, WR)	—	—	—	—	61	915	15.0(60)	5	—	—	—	—	—	—	—	—	—	—	—	—	30	483
1986	†Den	16(16, WR)	—	—	—	—	45	699	15.5(46)	3	—	—	—	—	—	—	—	—	—	—	—	—	18	365
1987	†Den	5(1)	—	—	—	—	11	167	15.2(49)	1	—	—	—	—	—	—	—	—	—	—	—	—	6	89
NFL	9	126(87)	6	19	3.2(10)	—	353	6112	17.3(95)	36	—	—	—	—	—	—	—	—	—	—	k	—	216	3245

WATSON, TIM   James Timothy, DB, 6´2˝/214 lbs; Howard; 1993: GB, rnd 6; B8/13/1970 Fort Valley, GA   **1993**†KC 4 (0)   **1994** KC 1 (0)   **1995** KC 4 (0)   **1995** NYG 1 (0)
1997 Phi 3 (0)   **NFL** 13 (0) [4 yrs]

WATT, JOE   Joseph Chester, HB-DB, 5´11˝/184 lbs; Syracuse; 1947: Bos, rnd 7/Buf-A, rnd 8; B6/18/1919 Montreal, Canada, D6/27/1983 Ithaca, NY   **1947** Bos 1 (0)
1949 NYB 5 (1)

1947	Det	8(4)	11	7	0.6(7)	0	4	104	26.0(75)	2	—	—	—	—	—	—	—	—	—	—	kpi	—	12	174
1948	Det	12(5, rh)	20	54	2.7(10)	0	2	29	14.5(24)	0	—	—	—	—	—	—	—	—	—	—	kpi	—	0	135
NFL	3	26(10)	31	61	2.0(10)	0	6	133	22.2(75)	2	—	—	—	—	—	—	—	—	—	—	kpi	—	12	327

WATT, WALT   Walter Wilson, HB-DB, 6´0˝/187 lbs; Miami (FL); 1945: ChiC, rnd 3; B6/16/1922 Dennison, OH

| 1945 | ChiC | 4(0) | 6 | 9 | 1.5(4) | 0 | 1 | 22 | 22.0(22) | 0 | — | — | — | — | — | — | — | — | — | — | k | — | 0 | 23 |

WATTELET, FRANK   Frank Lee, DB, 6´0˝/185 lbs; Kansas; B10/25/1958 Paola, KS   **1981** NO 16 (3)   **1982** NO 9 (9, FS)   **1983** NO 16 (16, FS)   **1984** NO 16 (16, FS)   **1987** NO 2 (2)
1987 LARm 5 (0)   **1988** LARm 2 (0)

1985	NO	16(16, FS)	2	42	21.0(23)	0	—	—	—	—	—	—	—	—	—	—	—	—	—	—	iS	—	0	32
1986	NO	16(16, FS)	—	—	—	—	—	—	—	—	1	1	100.0	13	13.0(13)	0	0	—	—	—	i	—	0	26
NFL	8	98(78)	2	42	21.0(23)	0	—	—	—	—	1	1	100.0	13	13.0(13)	0	0	—	—	—	kiS	2	12	123

WATTERS, BOB   Robert Lee, DE, 6´4˝/247 lbs; Lincoln (MO); 1958: NYG, rnd 28; B9/25/1935 Fort Worth, TX, D1/9/1996 Fort Worth, TX   **1962** NYT-A 12 (LDE)
1963 NYJ-A 12 (LDE)   **1964** NYJ-A 5   **NFL** 29 [3 yrs]

WATTERS, LEN   Leonard Alvyn, E, 5´10˝/185 lbs; Springfield; B6/4/1898 Dubuque, IA, D12/10/1986 Venice, FL   **1924** Buf 8 (8, LE), 6

WATTERS, ORLANDO   Orlando L., DB, 5´11˝/173 lbs; Arkansas; B10/26/1971 Anniston, AL   **1994** Sea 16 (8, RCB)

WATTERS, RICKY   Richard James, RB, 6´1˝/217 lbs; Notre Dame; 1991: SF, rnd 2; B4/7/1969 Harrisburg, PA

1992	†SF◇	14(13, RB)	206	1013	4.9(43)	9	43	405	9.4(35)	2	1	1	0.0	0	0.0	0	0	—	—	—	—	66	1316
1993	†SF◇	13(13, RB)	208	950	4.6(39)	10	31	326	10.5(48)	1	—	—	—	—	—	—	—	—	—	—	—	66	1218
1994	†SF★	16(16, RB)	239	877	3.7(23)	6	66	719	10.9(65)	5	—	—	—	—	—	—	—	—	—	—	—	66	1322
1995	†Phi★	16(16, RB)	337	1273	3.8(57)	11	62	434	7.0(24)	1	—	—	—	—	—	—	—	—	—	—	—	72	1605
1996	†Phi★	16(16, RB)	353	1411	4.0(56)	13	51	444	8.7(36)	0	—	—	—	—	—	—	—	—	—	—	—	78	1763
1997	Phi	16(16, RB)	285	1110	3.9(28)	7	48	440	9.2(37)	0	—	—	—	—	—	—	—	—	—	—	—	42	1400
1998	Sea	16(16, RB)	319	1239	3.9(39)	9	52	373	7.2(24)	0	1	1	100.0	1	1.0(1)	1	0	—	—	—	—	56	1521
1999	†Sea	16(16, RB)	325	1210	3.7(45)	5	40	387	9.7(25)	2	—	—	—	—	—	—	—	—	—	—	—	42	1464
2000	Sea	16(16, RB)	278	1242	4.5(55)	7	63	613	9.7(59)	2	—	—	—	—	—	—	—	—	—	—	—	54	1629
2001	Sea	5(4)	72	318	4.4(40)	1	11	107	9.7(34)	0	—	—	—	—	—	—	—	—	—	—	—	6	382
NFL	10	144(142)	2622	10643	4.1(57)	78	467	4248	9.1(65)	13	2	1	50.0	1	0.5(1)	1	0	—	—	—	—	548	13618

WATTERS, SCOTT   Scott Henry, LB, 6´2˝/230 lbs; Wittenberg; B1/1/1965 Columbus, OH   **1987** Buf 3 (3)

WATTS, DAMON   Damon Shanel, DB, 5´10˝/180 lbs; Indiana; B4/8/1972 Indianapolis, IN   **1994** Ind 16 (8, LCB)   **1995**†Ind 13 (0)   **1996** Ind 10 (0)   **1997** Ind 8 (6, RCB)
NFL 47 (14) [4 yrs]

WATTS, DARIUS   Darius Orlando, WR, 6´2˝/181 lbs; Marshall; 2004: Den, rnd 2; B12/19/1981 Atlanta, GA

2004	†Den	16(2)	5	33	6.6(10)	0	31	385	12.4(28)	1	—	—	—	—	—	—	—	—	—	—	—	6	231
2005	Den	6(0)	—	—	—	—	2	22	11.0(12)	0	—	—	—	—	—	—	—	—	—	—	—	0	11
NFL	2	22(2)	5	33	6.6(10)	0	33	407	12.3(28)	1	—	—	—	—	—	—	—	—	—	—	—	6	242

WATTS, ELBERT   Elbert T., DB, 6´1˝/205 lbs; Oklahoma; USC; 1986: LARm, rnd 9; B3/20/1963 Carson, CA   **1986** GB 9 (0)

WATTS, GEORGE   George, T, 6´1˝/225 lbs; Appalachian State; 1942: Was, rnd 17; B7/12/1918 McAdenville, NC, D1991   **1942** Was◇8 (0)

WATTS, RANDY   Randy, DE-DT, 6´6˝/275 lbs; East Carolina; Catwaba; 1987: KC, rnd 9; B6/22/1963 Sandersville, GA   **1987** Dal 5 (0)

WATTS, RICKEY   Rickey Ricardo, WR, 6´1˝/203 lbs; Tulsa; 1979: Chi, rnd 2; B5/16/1957 Longview, TX

1979	†ChiB	16(6, wr)	1	-6	-6.0(-6)	0	24	421	17.5(63)	3	—	—	—	—	—	—	—	—	—	—	k	1	24	309
1980	ChiB	15(1)	1	-16	-16.0(-16)	0	22	444	20.2(89)	1	—	—	—	—	—	—	—	—	—	—	kp	—	12	223
1981	ChiB	12(9, WR)	—	—	—	—	27	465	17.2(42)	3	—	—	—	—	—	—	—	—	—	—	—	—	18	248
1982	ChiB	9(0)	1	-1	-1.0(-1)	0	8	217	27.1(40)	0	—	—	—	—	—	—	—	—	—	—	k	—	0	228
1983	ChiB	4(0)	—	—	—	—	—	—	—	—	—	—	—	—	—	—	—	—	—	—	k	—	0	4
NFL	5	56(16)	3	-23	-7.7(-1)	0	81	1547	19.1(89)	8	—	—	—	—	—	—	—	—	—	—	kp	1	54	1011

WATTS, ROBERT   Robert, LB, 6´3˝/218 lbs; Boston College; 1977: NO, rnd 3; B6/16/1954 New York, NY   **1978** Oak 2

WATTS, TED   Ted W., DB, 6´0˝/195 lbs; Texas Tech; 1981: Oak, rnd 1; B5/29/1952 Tarpon Springs, FL   **1981** Oak 16 (0)   **1982**†LARd 9 (9, RCB)   **1983**†LARd 16 (13, RCB)
1984†LARd 16 (0)   **1985**†NYG 16 (3)   **1987** SD 1 (0)   **NFL** 74 (25) [6 yrs]

WAY, CHARLES   Charles Christopher, RB, 6´0˝/245 lbs; Virginia; 1995: NYG, rnd 6; B12/27/1972 Philadelphia, PA

1995	NYG	16(4)	2	6	3.0(6)	0	7	76	10.9(34)	1	—	—	—	—	—	—	—	—	—	—	k	—	6	42
1996	NYG	16(12, FB)	22	79	3.6(18)	1	32	328	10.3(37)	1	—	—	—	—	—	—	—	—	—	—	k	—	12	247
1997	†NYG☆	16(16, FB)	151	698	4.6(42)	4	37	304	8.2(62)	1	—	—	—	—	—	—	—	—	—	—	k	—	30	911
1998	NYG	16(15, FB)	113	432	3.8(21)	3	31	131	4.2(16)	1	—	—	—	—	—	—	—	—	—	—	—	—	24	533
1999	NYG	11(8, FB)	49	141	2.9(17)	2	11	59	5.4(16)	0	—	—	—	—	—	—	—	—	—	—	—	—	12	191
NFL	5	75(55)	337	1356	4.0(42)	10	118	898	7.6(62)	4	—	—	—	—	—	—	—	—	—	—	—	—	84	1923

WAY, CHARLIE   Charles Ash, WB, 5´8˝/144 lbs; Penn State; B12/29/1897 Embreeville, PA, D1/31/1988 Honeybrook, PA   **1921** Can 6 (0), 6   **1924** Fra☆13 (8, WB), 24
NFL 19 (8), 30 [2 yrs]

WAYMER, DAVE   David Benjamin, DB, 6´1˝/195 lbs; Notre Dame; 1980: NO, rnd 2; B7/1/1958 Brooklyn, NY, D4/28/1993 Mooresville, NC [I]   **1980** NO 16 (10, RCB)
1981 NO 16 (13, LCB)   **1982** NO 9 (9, LCB)   **1983** NO 16 (16, LCB)   **1984** NO 16 (16, LCB)   **1985** NO 16 (15, LCB)   **1987**†NO★12 (12, LCB)   **1988** NO 16 (9, LCB)
1989 NO 16 (16, FS)   **1990**†SF 16 (9, fs/ss)   **1991** SF 16 (15, SS)   **1992** LARd 16 (0)

| 1986 | NO | 16(15, LCB) | — | — | — | — | — | — | — | — | 1 | 13 | 13.0(13) | 0 | — | — | — | — | — | — | i | — | 0 | 10 |
| NFL | 13 | 197(155) | — | — | — | — | — | — | — | — | 1 | 13 | 13.0(13) | 0 | — | — | — | — | — | — | kpiS | 1 | 6 | 326 |

WAYNE, NATE   Nathaniel, LB, 6´0˝/237 lbs; Mississippi; 1998: Den, rnd 7; B1/12/1975 Chicago, IL   **1998** Den 1 (0)   **1999** Den 15 (0)   **2000** GB 16 (13, RLB)
2001†GB 12 (12, RLB)   **2002**†GB 16 (15, RLB)   **2003** Phi 16 (16, LLB)   **2004**†Phi 9 (7, llb)   **2005** Det 5 (0)   **NFL** 90 (63) [8 yrs]

WAYNE, REGGIE   Reggie, WR, 6´0˝/203 lbs; Miami (FL); 2001: Ind, rnd 1; B11/17/1978 New Orleans, LA

2001	Ind	13(9, WR)	—	—	—	—	27	345	12.8(43)	0	—	—	—	—	—	—	—	—	—	—	—	—	0	173
2002	†Ind	16(7, WR)	—	—	—	—	49	716	14.6(49)	4	—	—	—	—	—	—	—	—	—	—	—	—	24	378
2003	†Ind	16(16, WR)	—	—	—	—	68	838	12.3(57)	7	—	—	—	—	—	—	—	—	—	—	—	—	42	454
2004	†Ind	16(16, WR)	1	-4	-4.0(-4)	0	77	1210	15.7(71)	12	—	—	—	—	—	—	—	—	—	—	—	—	72	661
2005	†Ind	16(16, WR)	—	—	—	—	83	1055	12.7(66)	5	—	—	—	—	—	—	—	—	—	—	—	—	30	553
NFL	5	77(64)	1	-4	-4.0(-4)	0	304	4164	13.7(71)	28	—	—	—	—	—	—	—	—	—	—	—	—	168	2218

WAYT, RUSSELL   Russell Gene, LB, 6´4˝/235 lbs; Rice; 1965: Dal, rnd 8/Hou, rnd 6; B10/6/1942 Oklahoma City, OK   **1965** Dal 9

WEAR, BOB   Robert Foster, C-LB, 5´11˝/205 lbs; Sacramento State; Penn State; B1/5/1919 Yeagertown, PA, D4/22/1992 Martinsburg, PA   **1942** Phi 3 (0)

WEARY, FRED   Joseph Frederick, DB, 5´10˝/181 lbs; Florida; 1998: NO, rnd 4; B4/12/1974 Jacksonville, FL   **1998** NO 14 (1)   **1999** NO 16 (11, RCB)   **2000** NO 12 (12, RCB)
2001 NO 14 (1)   **2002**†Atl 16 (0)   **2003** SL 11 (0)   **2005** Hou 4 (4)   **NFL** 87 (29) [7 yrs]

WEARY, FRED   Fred Edward, G, 6´4˝/308 lbs; Tennessee; 2002: Hou, rnd 3; B9/30/1977 Montgomery, AL   **2002** Hou 16 (12, RG)   **2003** Hou 14 (2)   **2004** Hou 2 (1)
NFL 32 (15) [3 yrs]

YEAR	TEAM	G(GS, POS)	RUSH	YD	AVG(LG)	TD	REC	YD	AVG(LG)	TD	PASS	COMP	PCT	YD	AVG(LG)	TD	INT	SK	YD	QBR	KPR	OTD	PTS	TAY

WEATHERALL, JIM James Preston, DT-T, 6´4˝/245 lbs; Oklahoma; 1952: Phi, rnd 2; B10/26/1929 Graham, OK, D8/2/1992 Oklahoma City, OK **1955** Phi✧12 **1956** Phi✧12 (12, RDT) **1957** Phi 12 (LDT) **1958** Was 9 (LDT) **1959** Det 8 **1960** Det 12 **NFL** 65 (12) [6 yrs]

WEATHERFORD, JIM James Earl, DB, 5´11˝/186 lbs; Tennessee; 1969: Atl, rnd 15; B8/16/1946 Athens, GA **1969** Atl 14 (LS)

WEATHERINGTON, COLSTON Colston, DE, 6´5˝/289 lbs; Central Missouri State; 2001: Dal, rnd 7; B10/29/1977 Graceville, FL **2002** Dal 3 (0)

WEATHERLY, BONES Gerald Craft, LB, 6´5˝/218 lbs; Rice; 1949: ChiB, rnd 8; B12/26/1928 Houston, TX, D12/28/2004 **1950** ChiB 6 **1952** ChiB 5 **1953** ChiB 12 (RLB) **1954** ChiB 12 (LLB) **NFL** 35 [4 yrs]

WEATHERLY, JIM James E., C, 6´3˝/245 lbs; Mount San Antonio College (J.C.); B4/13/1952 Hazen, AR **1976** Atl 3

WEATHERS, ANDRE Andre Le'Melle, DB, 6´0˝/190 lbs; Michigan; 1999: NYG, rnd 6; B8/6/1976 Flint, MI **1999** NYG 9 (0) **2000** NYG 1 (0) **NFL** 10 (0) [2 yrs]

WEATHERS, CARL Carl, LB, 6´2˝/220 lbs; San Diego State; B1/14/1948 New Orleans, LA **1970**†Oak 7 **1971** Oak 1 **NFL** 8 [2 yrs]

WEATHERS, CLARENCE Clarence, WR, 5´9˝/170 lbs; Delaware State; B1/10/1962 Green Pond, SC

YEAR	TEAM	G(GS, POS)	RUSH	YD	AVG(LG)	TD	REC	YD	AVG(LG)	TD	PASS	COMP	PCT	YD	AVG(LG)	TD	INT	SK	YD	QBR	KPR	OTD	PTS	TAY
1983	NE	16(0)	1	28	28.0(28)	0	19	379	19.9(58)	3	—	—	—	—	—	—	—	—	—	—	kp	—	18	227
1984	NE	9(0)	—	—	—	—	8	115	14.4(29)	2	—	—	—	—	—	—	—	—	—	—	p	—	12	70
1985	†Cle	13(7, WR)	1	18	18.0(18)	0	16	449	28.1(72)	3	—	—	—	—	—	—	—	—	—	—	kp	—	18	338
1986	†Cle	16(0)	—	—	—	—	9	100	11.1(16)	0	—	—	—	—	—	—	—	—	—	—	—	—	0	50
1987	†Cle	12(0)	—	—	—	—	11	153	13.9(37)	2	—	—	—	—	—	—	—	—	—	—	—	—	12	87
1988	†Cle	16(6, wr)	—	—	—	—	29	436	15.0(49)	1	—	—	—	—	—	—	—	—	—	—	p	—	6	223
1989	Ind	4(0)	—	—	—	—	6	62	10.3(19)	0	—	—	—	—	—	—	—	—	—	—	—	—	0	31
1989	KC	11(0)	—	—	—	—	17	192	11.3(27)	0	—	—	—	—	—	—	—	—	—	—	—	—	0	96
1990	GB	14(0)	—	—	—	—	33	390	11.8(29)	1	—	—	—	—	—	—	—	—	—	—	—	—	6	200
1991	GB	14(0)	—	—	—	—	12	150	12.5(22)	0	—	—	—	—	—	—	—	—	—	—	—	—	0	75
NFL	9	125(13)	2	46	23.0(28)	0	160	2426	15.2(72)	12	—	—	—	—	—	—	—	—	—	—	kp	—	72	1395

WEATHERS, COP Guy Barton, G, 5´9˝/230 lbs; Baylor; B6/9/1898 Gatesville, TX, D9/27/1964 Marlin, TX **1926** Buf 5 (2)

WEATHERS, CURTIS Curtis Lenard, LB-TE, 6´5˝/224 lbs; Mississippi; 1979: Cle, rnd 9; B9/16/1956 Memphis, TN **1980**†Cle 10 (0) **1981** Cle 13 (0) **1982**†Cle 7 (5, ROLB) **1983** Cle 16 (0) **1984** Cle 16 (1) **1985**†Cle 16 (2)

YEAR	TEAM	G(GS, POS)	RUSH	YD	AVG(LG)	TD	REC	YD	AVG(LG)	TD	PASS	COMP	PCT	YD	AVG(LG)	TD	INT	SK	YD	QBR	KPR	OTD	PTS	TAY
1979	Cle	16	—	—	—	—	1	14	14.0(14)	0	—	—	—	—	—	—	—	—	—	—	k	—	0	-8
NFL	7	94(8)	—	—	—	—	1	14	14.0(14)	0	—	—	—	—	—	—	—	—	—	—	kiS	—	0	-4

WEATHERS, ROBERT Robert James, RB, 6´2˝/220 lbs; Arizona State; 1982: NE, rnd 2; B9/13/1960 Westfield, NY

YEAR	TEAM	G(GS, POS)	RUSH	YD	AVG(LG)	TD	REC	YD	AVG(LG)	TD	PASS	COMP	PCT	YD	AVG(LG)	TD	INT	SK	YD	QBR	KPR	OTD	PTS	TAY
1982	NE	6(2)	24	83	3.5(18)	1	3	24	8.0(22)	0	—	—	—	—	—	—	—	—	—	—	—	—	6	105
1983	NE	15(4)	73	418	5.7(77)	1	23	212	9.2(19)	0	—	—	—	—	—	—	—	—	—	—	k	—	6	557
1984	NE	2(0)	—	—	—	—	—	—	—	—	—	—	—	—	—	—	—	—	—	—	—	—	—	—
1985	†NE	16(0)	41	174	4.2(42)	1	2	18	9.0(13)	0	—	—	—	—	—	—	—	—	—	—	k	—	6	196
1986	NE	5(0)	21	58	2.8(16)	1	1	14	14.0(14)	0	—	—	—	—	—	—	—	—	—	—	—	—	6	75
NFL	5	44(6)	159	733	4.6(77)	4	29	268	9.2(22)	0	—	—	—	—	—	—	—	—	—	—	k	—	24	933

WEATHERSBY, DENNIS Dennis, DB, 6´1˝/204 lbs; Oregon State; 2003: Cin, rnd 4; B6/16/1980 Glendora, CA **2003** Cin 4 (0)

WEATHERSPOON, CEPHUS Cephous, WR, 6´1˝/182 lbs; Fort Lewis; 1972: NO, rnd 13; B6/14/1948 Meridian, MS **1972** NO 1

WEATHERSPOON, CHUCK Johnny, RB, 5´7˝/229 lbs; Houston; 1991: Phi, rnd 9; B7/31/1968 Hinesville, GA **1991** TB 4 (0)

WEATHERWAX, JIM James Michael, DT, 6´7˝/260 lbs; West Texas A&M; Los Angeles State; 1965: GB, rnd 11/SD, rnd R5; B1/9/1943 Porterville, CA **1966**†GB 14 **1967**†GB 14 (3) **1969** GB 6 **NFL** 34 (3) [3 yrs]

WEAVER, ANTHONY Anthony Lee, DE, 6´3˝/290 lbs; Notre Dame; 2002: Bal, rnd 2; B7/28/1980 Abilene, TX **2002** Bal 16 (16, LDE) **2003**†Bal 15 (15, LDE) **2004** Bal 16 (15, LDE) **2005** Bal 10 (8, lde) **NFL** 57 (54) [4 yrs]

WEAVER, BUCK Charles A., G, 6´4˝/235 lbs; Chicago; B11/1/1905 Cushman, AR, D9/1967 **1930** ChiC 6 (1) **1930** Por 4 (3) **NFL** 10 (4) [1 yr]

WEAVER, CHARLIE Charles Earl, LB, 6´2˝/220 lbs; USC; 1971: Det, rnd 2; B7/12/1949 Greenwood, MS **1971** Det 14 **1972** Det 14 **1973** Det 13 (RLB) **1974** Det 14 (14, RLB) **1975** Det 12 (9, RLB) **1976** Det☆14 (14, RLB) **1977** Det 14 (13, RLB) **1978** Det 16 (16, RLB) **1979** Det 8 (MLB) **1980** Det 16 (16, LLB) **1981** Det 7 (0) **1981** Was 5 (0) **NFL** 147 (82) [11 yrs]

WEAVER, EMANUEL Emanuel, NT, 6´4˝/260 lbs; South Carolina State; 1982: Cin, rnd 2; B6/28/1960 New Orleans, LA **1982**†Cin 5 (0) **1987** Atl 2 (2) **NFL** 7 (2) [2 yrs]

WEAVER, GARY Gary Lynn, LB, 6´1˝/224 lbs; Fresno State; 1973: Oak, rnd 7; B3/13/1949 Florence, AL **1973**†Oak 10 **1974**†Oak 14 **1975** GB 14 (5, llb) **1976** GB 14 (14, LLB) **1977** GB 5 (llb) **1978** GB 16 (LLB) **1979** GB 14 (LLB) **NFL** 87 (19) [7 yrs]

WEAVER, HERMAN William Herman 'Thunder Foot', P, 6´4˝/210 lbs; Tennessee; 1970: Det, rnd 9; B11/17/1948 Villa Rica, GA **[P]**

YEAR	TEAM	G(GS, POS)	RUSH	YD	AVG(LG)	TD	REC	YD	AVG(LG)	TD	PASS	COMP	PCT	YD	AVG(LG)	TD	INT	SK	YD	QBR	KPR	OTD	PTS	TAY
1970	†Det	14	—	—	—	—	—	—	—	—	—	—	—	—	—	—	—	—	—	—	P	—	0	0
1971	Det	13	—	—	—	—	—	—	—	—	—	—	—	—	—	—	—	—	—	—	P	—	0	0
1972	Det	14	—	—	—	—	—	—	—	—	—	—	—	—	—	—	—	—	—	—	P	—	0	0
1973	Det	14	1	18	18.0(18)	0	—	—	—	—	—	—	—	—	—	—	—	—	—	—	P	—	0	18
1974	Det	14	—	—	—	—	—	—	—	—	—	—	—	—	—	—	—	—	—	—	P	—	0	0
1975	Det☆	14	—	—	—	—	—	—	—	—	1	0	0.0	0	0.0	0	0	—	—	—	P	—	0	0
1976	Det	14	1	0	0.0(0)	0	—	—	—	—	2	1	50.0	14	7.0(14)	0	0	—	—	—	P	—	0	7
1977	Sea	13	1	-2	-2.0(-2)	0	—	—	—	—	—	—	—	—	—	—	—	—	—	—	P	—	0	-2
1978	Sea	16	2	-5	-2.5(0)	0	—	—	—	—	1	1	100.0	9	9.0(9)	0	0	—	—	—	P	—	0	-1
1979	Sea	16	2	-6	-3.0(0)	0	—	—	—	—	4	3	75.0	73	18.3(39)	0	0	—	—	—	P	—	0	31
1980	Sea	16(0)	—	—	—	—	—	—	—	—	2	0	0.0	0	0.0	0	0	—	—	—	P	—	0	0
NFL	11	158	7	5	0.7(18)	0	—	—	—	—	10	5	50.0	96	9.6(39)	0	0	—	—	—	P	—	0	53

WEAVER, JED Timothy Jed, TE, 6´4˝/258 lbs; Oregon; 1999: Phi, rnd 7; B8/11/1976 Bend, OR

YEAR	TEAM	G(GS, POS)	RUSH	YD	AVG(LG)	TD	REC	YD	AVG(LG)	TD	PASS	COMP	PCT	YD	AVG(LG)	TD	INT	SK	YD	QBR	KPR	OTD	PTS	TAY
1999	Phi	16(10, TE)	—	—	—	—	11	91	8.3(14)	0	—	—	—	—	—	—	—	—	—	—	—	—	2	46
2000	†Mia	16(0)	—	—	—	—	10	179	17.9(41)	0	—	—	—	—	—	—	—	—	—	—	k	—	0	90
2001	†Mia	16(7, te)	—	—	—	—	18	215	11.9(27)	2	—	—	—	—	—	—	—	—	—	—	—	—	12	118
2002	Mia	16(4)	—	—	—	—	6	75	12.5(25)	3	—	—	—	—	—	—	—	—	—	—	k	—	18	46
2003	SF	16(16, TE)	—	—	—	—	35	437	12.5(30)	1	—	—	—	—	—	—	—	—	—	—	—	—	6	224
2004	NE	10(1)	—	—	—	—	8	93	11.6(25)	0	—	—	—	—	—	—	—	—	—	—	—	—	0	47
NFL	6	90(38)	—	—	—	—	88	1090	12.4(41)	6	—	—	—	—	—	—	—	—	—	—	k	—	38	568

WEAVER, JOHN John Dean, G, 6´2˝/215 lbs; Miami (OH); B3/31/1926 Dayton, OH **1949** NYB 12 (6, RG)

WEAVER, LARRYE Lawrence Bernard, HB-DB, 5´11˝/190 lbs; Antelope Valley (J.C.); Fullerton (J.C.); B11/17/1931 Monte Vista, CO

YEAR	TEAM	G(GS, POS)	RUSH	YD	AVG(LG)	TD	REC	YD	AVG(LG)	TD	PASS	COMP	PCT	YD	AVG(LG)	TD	INT	SK	YD	QBR	KPR	OTD	PTS	TAY
1955	NYG	6	3	0	0.0(2)	0	—	—	—	—	—	—	—	—	—	—	—	—	—	—	—	—	0	0

WEAVER, LEONARD Leonard, RB, 6´0˝/251 lbs; Carson-Newman; B9/23/1982 Melbourne, FL

YEAR	TEAM	G(GS, POS)	RUSH	YD	AVG(LG)	TD	REC	YD	AVG(LG)	TD	PASS	COMP	PCT	YD	AVG(LG)	TD	INT	SK	YD	QBR	KPR	OTD	PTS	TAY
2005	Sea	16(0)	17	80	4.7(24)	0	1	12	12.0(12)	0	—	—	—	—	—	—	—	—	—	—	—	—	0	86

WEAVER, RED James Redwick, C, 5´10˝/185 lbs; Centre; B7/19/1897 Garland, TX, D11/23/1968 Mayfield, KY **[KC]** **1923** Col 10 (9, C), 2

WEBB, ALLAN Allan, DB-HB, 5´11˝/180 lbs; Arnold; B1/22/1933 Washington, DC **1962**†NYG 14 (LS) **1963**†NYG 7 (LS) **1964** NYG 14 **1965** NYG 3

YEAR	TEAM	G(GS, POS)	RUSH	YD	AVG(LG)	TD	REC	YD	AVG(LG)	TD	PASS	COMP	PCT	YD	AVG(LG)	TD	INT	SK	YD	QBR	KPR	OTD	PTS	TAY
1961	†NYG	10	6	51	8.5(21)	0	—	—	—	—	—	—	—	—	—	—	—	—	—	—	kp	—	0	123
NFL	5	48	6	51	8.5(21)	0	—	—	—	—	—	—	—	—	—	—	—	—	—	—	kpi	—	0	211

WEBB, ART Arthur E., T-G, 5´10˝/210 lbs; none; B2/17/1893 Cleveland, OH, D4/9/1973 Cleveland, OH **1920** Roc 8 (1, RG) **1922** Mil 8 (8, LT) **NFL** 16 (9) [2 yrs]

WEBB, CHUCK Charles Eugene, FB, 5´9˝/201 lbs; Tennessee; 1991: GB, rnd 3; B11/17/1969 Toledo, OH **1991** GB 2 (0)

WEBB, DON Donald Wayne, DB, 5´10˝/182 lbs; Iowa State; 1961: Bos, rnd 24; B5/22/1939 Jefferson City, MO **[I]** **1961** Bos-A 14 (LCB) **1964** Bos-A 14 (LCB) **1965** Bos-A 14 (rcb) **1966** Bos-A 14 (LCB) **1967** Bos-A☆14 (LS) **1968** Bos-A 10 (9, RS) **1969** Bos-A✧14 (14, RS) **1970** Bos 14 (14, FS) **1971** NE 12 (12, FS)

YEAR	TEAM	G(GS, POS)	RUSH	YD	AVG(LG)	TD	REC	YD	AVG(LG)	TD	PASS	COMP	PCT	YD	AVG(LG)	TD	INT	SK	YD	QBR	KPR	OTD	PTS	TAY
1962	Bos-A	14	—	—	—	—	1	11	11.0(11)	0	—	—	—	—	—	—	—	—	—	—	—	—	0	6
NFL	10	134(49)	—	—	—	—	1	11	11.0(11)	0	—	—	—	—	—	—	—	—	—	—	ki	4	24	278

YEAR	TEAM	G(GS, POS)	RUSH	YD	AVG(LG)	TD	REC	YD	AVG(LG)	TD	PASS COMP	PCT	YD	AVG(LG)	TD	INT	SK	YD	QBR	KPR	OTD	PTS	TAY

WEBB, GEORGE   George Louis, E, 6´1˝/180 lbs; Texas Tech; B4/2/1916 Itasca, TX, D9/9/1993 Amarillo, TX

| 1943 | Bkn | 9(2) | — | — | — | — | 7 | 60 | 8.6(15) | 0 | — | — | — | — | — | — | — | — | — | — | — | 0 | 30 |

WEBB, JIMMY   James Roger, DT-DE, 6´5˝/247 lbs; Mississippi State; 1975: SF, rnd 1; B4/13/1952 Jackson, MS   **1975** SF 14 (1) **1976** SF 14 (14, LDT) **1977** SF 14 (LDT)
1978 SF 16 (16, LDT) **1979** SF 16 (15, RDT) **1980** SF 16 (12, LDE/rde) **1981**†SD 16 (1) **NFL** 106 (59) [7 yrs]

WEBB, KEN   Kenneth Lee, HB-FB, 5´11˝/207 lbs; Presbyterian; 1958: Det, rnd 14; B8/15/1935 Albany, GA, D9/20/2003 Carthage, TX

1958	Det	12(fb)	56	172	3.1(22)	2	11	85	7.7(34)	1	—	—	—	—	—	—	—	—	—	k	—	18	289
1959	Det	12(LH)	60	222	3.7(29)	2	12	201	16.8(67)	0	—	—	—	—	—	—	—	—	—	k	—	12	455
1960	Det	12	59	166	2.8(17)	2	10	68	6.8(25)	0	—	—	—	—	—	—	—	—	—	k	—	12	213
1961	Det	11	7	6	0.9(3)	1	1	7	7.0(7)	0	—	—	—	—	—	—	—	—	—	—	—	6	25
1962	Det	14	70	267	3.8(25)	1	10	120	12.0(53)	0	—	—	—	—	—	—	—	—	—	—	—	6	337
1963	Cle	12(2)	12	58	4.8(19)	0	2	2	1.0(5)	0	—	—	—	—	—	—	—	—	—	k	—	0	56
NFL	6	73(2)	264	891	3.4(29)	8	46	483	10.5(67)	1	—	—	—	—	—	—	—	—	—	k	—	54	1374

WEBB, RICHMOND   Richmond Jewel, T, 6´6˝/310 lbs; Texas A&M; 1990: Mia, rnd 1; B1/11/1967 Dallas, TX   **1990**†Mia★16 (16, LT) **1991** Mia◇14 (14, LT) **1992**†Mia★16 (16, LT)
1993 Mia★16 (16, LT) **1994**†Mia★16 (16, LT) **1995**†Mia★16 (16, LT) **1996** Mia◇16 (16, LT) **1997**†Mia 16 (16, LT) **1998**†Mia 9 (9, LT) **1999** Mia 15 (14, LT) **2000**†Mia 14 (14, LT)
2001 Cin 16 (16, LT) **2002** Cin 4 (4) **NFL** 184 (183) [13 yrs]

WEBBER, HARRY   Harry S., E, /173 lbs; Morningside; B10/18/1892, SD, D10/6/1970 Santa Clara County, CA   **1920** RI 3 (2) **1923** RI 1 (0) **NFL** 4 (2) [2 yrs]

WEBBER, DUTCH   Howard Gilbert, E-B, 6´2˝/190 lbs; Kansas State; B12/15/1901 Oxford, NE, D6/1985 Ulysses, KS   **1924** KC 9 (9, LE) **1925** KC 8 (8, LE) **1925** Cle 4 (4)
1926 Har 8 (8, LE) **1926** NYG 2 (1) **1926** KC 1 (0) **1927** Cle 3 (3) **1928** GB 3 (1) **1930** Pro 1 (1) **1930** Nwk 3 (0) **NFL** 42 (35) [6 yrs]

WEBER, CHARLIE   Charles Louis, G, 6´1˝/203 lbs; Colgate; B9/3/1892 New York, NY, D10/1964   **1926** Bkn 8 (4, RG)

WEBER, CHUCK   Charles Frederick, LB-DE-G, 6´1˝/229 lbs; West Chester; B3/25/1930 Philadelphia, PA   **1955**†Cle 11 **1956** Cle 4 **1956** ChiC 5 **1957** ChiC 12
1958 ChiC 10 (RLB) **1959** Phi 12 (MLB) **1960**†Phi 12 (MLB) **1961** Phi 14 (MLB) **NFL** 80 [7 yrs]

WEBER, DICK   Richard Wilfred, TB, 5´11˝/195 lbs; St. Louis; B4/10/1919 Lawrence, MA, D11/19/1991 Salem, NH

| 1945 | Det | 3(0) | 7 | 10 | 1.4(7) | 0 | — | — | — | — | 22 | 6 | 27.3 | 70 | 3.2(27) | 0 | 5 | — | — | Pk | — | 0 | -146 |

WEBSTER, ALEX   Alexander 'Big Red', HB-FB, 6´3˝/225 lbs; North Carolina State; 1953: Was, rnd 11; B4/19/1931 Kearny, NJ [C]

1955	NYG☆	12(RH)	128	634	5.0(71)	5	22	269	12.2(48)	1	—	—	—	—	—	—	—	—	—	—	—	36	824
1956	†NYG☆	12(RH)	178	694	3.9(34)	7	21	197	9.4(43)	3	—	—	—	—	—	—	—	—	—	—	—	60	878
1957	NYG	11(RH)	135	478	3.5(34)	5	30	330	11.0(41)	1	—	—	—	—	—	—	—	—	—	—	—	36	698
1958	†NYG◇	9(RH)	100	398	4.0(54)	3	25	279	11.2(37)	3	—	—	—	—	—	—	—	—	—	—	—	36	-583
1959	†NYG	10(RH)	79	250	3.2(16)	5	27	381	14.1(41)	2	1	0	0.0	0	0.0	0	0	—	—	—	—	42	501
1960	NYG	8	22	48	2.2(10)	0	8	106	13.3(27)	0	—	—	—	—	—	—	—	—	—	—	—	0	101
1961	†NYG◇	14(FB)	196	928	4.7(59)	2	26	313	12.0(58)	3	—	—	—	—	—	—	—	—	—	—	—	30	1120
1962	†NYG	14(FB)	207	743	3.6(55)	5	47	477	10.1(58)	4	—	—	—	—	—	—	—	—	—	—	—	54	1052
1963	†NYG	7(FB)	75	255	3.4(12)	4	15	128	8.5(19)	0	—	—	—	—	—	—	—	—	—	—	—	24	359
1964	NYG	12	76	210	2.8(14)	3	19	199	10.5(40)	0	—	—	—	—	—	—	—	—	—	—	—	18	340
NFL	10	109	1196	4638	3.9(71)	39	240	2679	11.2(59)	17	1	0	0.0	0	0.0	0	0	—	—	—	—	336	6453

WEBSTER, COREY   Corey James, DB, 6´0˝/204 lbs; LSU; 2005: NYG, rnd 2; B3/2/1982 Vacherie, LA   **2005**†NYG 15 (2)

WEBSTER, CORNELL   Cornell Preston, DB, 6´0˝/180 lbs; UCLA; Tulsa; B11/2/1954 Greeneville, TN   **1977** Sea 14 **1978** Sea 15 (14, LCB) **1980** Sea 8 (6, lcb)

| 1979 | Sea | 15(14, LCB) | — | — | — | 1 | 39 | 39.0(39) | 0 | — | — | — | — | — | — | — | — | — | — | i | 1 | 6 | 15 |
| NFL | 4 | 52(34) | — | — | — | 1 | 39 | 39.0(39) | 0 | — | — | — | — | — | — | — | — | — | — | ki | 1 | 6 | 76 |

WEBSTER, DAVE   David, DB, 6´4˝/220 lbs; Prairie View A&M; B7/23/1937   **1960** DalT-A☆14 (RCB) **1961** DalT-A★14 (RS) **NFL** 28 [2 yrs]

WEBSTER, ELNARDO   Elnardo Julian, LB, 6´2˝/243 lbs; Rutgers; 1992: Pit, rnd 9; B12/23/1969 Goritza, Italy   **1992**†Pit 3 (0)

WEBSTER, GEORGE   George Delano, LB, 6´4˝/220 lbs; Michigan State; 1967: Hou, rnd 1; B11/25/1945 Anderson, SC   **1967**†Hou-A★14 (14, LLB) **1968** Hou-A★14 (LLB)
1969†Hou-A★14 (LLB) **1970** Hou 7 (llb) **1971** Hou 10 (LLB) **1972** Hou 5 (rlb) **1972**†Pit 6 **1973**†Pit 12 **1974** NE 14 (12, LOLB) **1975** NE 10 (10, LOLB) **1976**†NE 13 (3)
NFL 119 (39) [10 yrs]

WEBSTER, JASON   Jason Richmond, DB, 5´10˝/187 lbs; Texas A&M; 2000: SF, rnd 2; B9/8/1977 Houston, TX   **2000** SF 16 (10, RCB) **2001**†SF 16 (16, RCB)
2002 SF 16 (16, RCB) **2003** SF 5 (2) **2004**†Atl 10 (9, rcb) **2005** Atl 15 (13, RCB) **NFL** 78 (66) [6 yrs]

WEBSTER, KEVIN   Kevin, G, 6´2˝/260 lbs; Northern Iowa; B3/6/1962 Berwyn, IL   **1987** Min 3 (3)

WEBSTER, LARRY   Larry Melvin, DT-DE, 6´5˝/290 lbs; Maryland; 1992: Mia, rnd 3; B1/18/1969 Elkton, MD   **1992**†Mia 16 (0) **1993** Mia 13 (9, LDT) **1994**†Mia 16 (7, lde)
1995 Cle 10 (0) **1997** Bal 15 (0) **1998** Bal 16 (16, LDT) **2000**†Bal 15 (0) **2001**†Bal 15 (0) **2002**†NYJ 15 (0) **NFL** 137 (35) [10 yrs]

WEBSTER, MIKE   Michael Lewis, C-G, 6´1˝/255 lbs; Wisconsin; 1974: Pit, rnd 5; B3/18/1952 Tomahawk, WI, D9/24/2002 Pittsburgh, PA; HOF 1997   **1974**†Pit 14 (1) **1975**†Pit 14 (14, C)
1976†Pit 14 (14, C) **1977**†Pit☆14 (14, C) **1978**†Pit★16 (16, C) **1979**†Pit★16 (16, C) **1980** Pit★16 (16, C) **1981** Pit★16 (16, C) **1982**†Pit★9 (9, C) **1983**†Pit★16 (16, C)
1984†Pit★16 (16, C) **1985** Pit★16 (16, C) **1986** Pit 12 (12, C) **1987** Pit★15 (15, C) **1988** Pit 16 (16, C) **1989** KC 16 (16, C) **1990** KC 9 (7, c) **NFL** 245 (217) [17 yrs]

WEBSTER, NATE   Nathaniel, LB, 6´0˝/230 lbs; Miami (FL); 2000: TB, rnd 3; B11/29/1977 Miami, FL   **2000** TB 16 (0) **2001**†TB 16 (1) **2002**†TB 16 (0) **2003** TB 15 (5, mlb)
2004 Cin 3 (3) **2005** Cin 1 (0) **NFL** 67 (9) [6 yrs]

WEBSTER, TIM   Timothy Duane, K, 6´0˝/195 lbs; Arkansas; B9/11/1949 Henryetta, OK [K]   **1971** GB 4

WEDDERBURN, FLOYD   Floyd E., G, 5´11˝/325 lbs; Penn State; 1999: Sea, rnd 5; B5/5/1976 Kingston, Jamaica   **2000** Sea 16 (16, RG) **2001** Sea 16 (0) **2002** Sea 14 (10, RG)
NFL 46 (26) [3 yrs]

WEDDINGTON, MIKE   Michael Wayne, LB, 6´4˝/245 lbs; Oklahoma; B10/9/1960 Belton, TX   **1986** GB 3 (0) **1987** GB 12 (0) **1988** GB 16 (2) **1989** GB 15 (0) **1990** GB 6 (0)
NFL 52 (2) [5 yrs]

WEDEL, DICK   Richard Wesley, G, 5´11˝/205 lbs; Wake Forest; 1948: ChiC, rnd 24/ChiR-A, rnd 29; B5/29/1923 Toledo, OH, D6/8/2002 Charlotte, NC   **1948** ChiC 1 (0)

WEDEMEYER, HERM   Herman John, B, 5´10˝/178 lbs; St. Mary's (CA); 1947: LAD-A, rnd S/LARm, rnd 1; B5/20/1924 Honolulu, HI, D1/25/1999 Honolulu, HI

1948	LAD-A	14(10, WB)	79	249	3.2	0	36	330	9.2	2	30	9	30.0	79	2.6	0	3	—	—	—	Pkp	—	12	672
1949	Bal-A☆	11(5, lh)	64	291	4.5	0	10	112	11.2	2	1	0	0.0	0	0.0	0	1	—	—	—	Pkp	—	0	600
AAFC	2	25(15)	143	540	3.8	0	46	442	9.6	2	31	9	29.0	79	2.5	0	4	—	—	—	Pkp	—	12	1272

WEED, TAD   Thurlow, K, 5´5˝/140 lbs; Ohio State; B1/18/1933 Columbus, OH [K]   **1955** Pit 6

WEEDON, DON   John Donald, G, 5´11˝/220 lbs; Texas; B1/13/1919 Bryan, TX, D11/19/1981 Austin, TX   **1947**†Phi 12 (0)

WEEKS, GEORGE   George Ellison, DE, 6´2˝/195 lbs; Alabama; 1943: Phi, rnd 14; B12/16/1918 Dothan, AL, D3/1980 Florence, AL   **1944** Bkn 3 (0)

WEESE, NORRIS   Norris Lee, QB-P, 6´1˝/195 lbs; Mississippi; 1974: LA, rnd 4; B8/12/1951 Baton Rouge, LA, D1/19/1995 Denver, CO

1976	Den	14	23	142	6.2(20)	0	—	—	—	—	47	24	51.1	314	6.7(43)	1	6	9	45	—	P	—	0	64
1977	†Den	14	11	56	5.1(21)	1	—	—	—	—	20	11	55.0	119	5.9(31)	1	0	2	15	—	P	—	6	131
1978	†Den	13(1)	17	48	2.8(8)	1	—	—	—	—	87	55	63.2	723	8.3(31)	4	5	12	94	—	—	—	6	240
1979	†Den	16(6, qb)	18	116	6.4(20)	3	—	—	—	—	97	53	54.6	731	7.5(50)	1	3	13	86	—	—	—	18	397
NFL	4	57(7)	69	362	5.2(21)	5	—	—	—	—	251	143	57.0	1887	7.5(50)	7	14	36	240	—	P	—	30	831

WEGENER, BUCKY   William Leslie, G, 6´0˝/245 lbs; Missouri; 1962: SL, rnd 16; B10/31/1939   **1962**†Hou-A 4 **1963** Hou-A 14 **NFL** 18 [2 yrs]

WEGER, MIKE   Michael Roy, DB, 6´2˝/200 lbs; Bowling Green State; 1967: Det, rnd 9; B10/2/1945 Dallas, TX   **1967** Det 14 **1968** Det 14 (LS) **1969** Det 13 (LS) **1970**†Det 14 (SS)
1971 Det 14 (SS) **1972** Det 14 (SS) **1973** Det 12 (SS) **1975** Det 13 (4) **1976** Hou 4 **1977** Hou 11 **NFL** 123 (4) [10 yrs]

WEGERT, TED   Theodore Addison, HB, 5´11˝/202 lbs; none; B4/17/1932 Riverhead, NY, D2/18/1986 Port Charlotte, FL

1955	Phi	7	26	120	4.6(38)	2	3	17	5.7(12)	0	—	—	—	—	—	—	—	—	—	k	—	12	176
1956	Phi	7	47	127	2.7(19)	1	6	46	7.7(19)	0	—	—	—	—	—	—	—	—	—	—	—	6	160
1960	NYT-A	6	31	124	4.0(11)	1	5	68	13.6(32)	1	—	—	—	—	—	—	—	—	—	—	—	12	173
1960	Den-A	4	5	37	7.4(32)	0	—	—	—	—	—	—	—	—	—	—	—	—	—	k	—	0	90

YEAR	TEAM	G (GS, POS)	RUSH	YD	AVG (LG)	TD	REC	YD	AVG (LG)	TD	PASS	COMP	PCT	YD	AVG (LG)	TD	INT	SK	YD	QBR	KPR	OTD	PTS	TAY
1960	Buf-A	2	—	—	—	—	—	—	—	—	—	—	—	—	—	—	—	—	—	—	kp	—	0	54
NFL	3	26	109	408	3.7(38)	4	14	131	9.4(32)	1	—	—	—	—	—	—	—	—	—	—	kp	—	30	653

WEHBA, RAY Raymond E., E, 6´0˝/215 lbs; USC; B8/16/1916 Sherman, TX, D6/2/2003 Miami, FL

YEAR	TEAM	G (GS, POS)	RUSH	YD	AVG (LG)	TD	REC	YD	AVG (LG)	TD	PASS	COMP	PCT	YD	AVG (LG)	TD	INT	SK	YD	QBR	KPR	OTD	PTS	TAY
1943	Bkn	10(9, LE)	—	—	—	—	4	43	10.8(19)	0	—	—	—	—	—	—	—	—	—	—	k	—	0	22
1944	†GB	10(1)	—	—	—	—	6	67	11.2(17)	0	—	—	—	—	—	—	—	—	—	—	i	—	0	36
NFL	2	20(10)	—	—	—	—	10	110	11.0(19)	0	—	—	—	—	—	—	—	—	—	—	ki	—	0	57

WEHRLI, ROGER Roger Russell, DB, 6´0˝/190 lbs; Missouri; 1969: SL, rnd 1; B11/26/1947 New Point, MO **[K]** **1969** SL 13 (LCB) **1970** SL★14 (RCB) **1971** SL★13 (RCB/fs) **1972** SL 14 (SS) **1973** SL 11 (RCB) **1974**†SL★14 (14, RCB) **1975**†SL★14 (13, RCB) **1979** SL★16 (RCB) **1981** SL 16 (9, RCB)

YEAR	TEAM	G (GS, POS)	RUSH	YD	AVG (LG)	TD	REC	YD	AVG (LG)	TD	PASS	COMP	PCT	YD	AVG (LG)	TD	INT	SK	YD	QBR	KPR	OTD	PTS	TAY
1976	SL★	14(13, RCB)	2	8	4.0(8)	0	—	—	—	—	1	0	0.0	0	0.0	0	0	—	—	—	i	—	0	19
1977	SL★	14(RCB)	1	19	19.0(19)	0	—	—	—	—	—	—	—	—	—	—	—	—	—	—	i	—	0	38
1978	SL	16(RCB)	1	0	0.0(0)	0	—	—	—	—	—	—	—	—	—	—	—	—	—	—	i	—	0	-17
1980	SL	16(16, RCB)	—	—	—	—	—	—	—	—	0	0	0.0	0	0.0	0	0	1	11	—	i	—	0	20
1982	SL	8(1)	1	18	18.0(18)	1	—	—	—	—	—	—	—	—	—	—	—	—	—	—	—	—	6	28
NFL	14	193(66)	5	45	9.0(19)	1	—	—	—	—	1	0	0.0	0	0.0	0	0	1	11	—	Kkpi	2	19	247

WEIDNER, BERT Bert James, G-C, 6´2˝/295 lbs; Kent State; 1989: Mia, rnd 11; B1/20/1966 Eden, NY **1990**†Mia 8 (0) **1991** Mia 15 (10, c/lg) **1992**†Mia 16 (3) **1993** Mia 16 (11, RG) **1994**†Mia 14 (14, RG) **1995**†Mia 12 (1) **NFL** 81 (39) [6 yrs]

WEIGEL, LEE Lee Elmer, RB, 5´11˝/220 lbs; Wisconsin-Eau Claire; B11/15/1963

YEAR	TEAM	G (GS, POS)	RUSH	YD	AVG (LG)	TD	REC	YD	AVG (LG)	TD	PASS	COMP	PCT	YD	AVG (LG)	TD	INT	SK	YD	QBR	KPR	OTD	PTS	TAY
1987	GB	2(0)	10	26	2.6(7)	0	1	17	17.0(17)	0	—	—	—	—	—	—	—	—	—	—	—	—	0	35

WEIL, JACK Jack Lee, P, 5´11˝/175 lbs; Wyoming; B3/16/1962 Denver, CO **1986** Den 6 (0) **1987** Was 3 (0) **NFL** 9 (0) [2 yrs]

WEIMER, CHUCK Howard Lee, B, 5´9˝/178 lbs; Wilmington (DE); B9/5/1904 London, OH, D4/27/1990 Grove City, OH **[K]** **1929** Buf 9 (8, TB), 18 **1930** Bkn 11 (7, TB), 13 **1931** Cle 7 (1) **NFL** 27 (16), 31 [3 yrs]

WEINBERG, HENRY Henry K., G-T, 5´7˝/190 lbs; Duquesne; B3/4/1910 Mount Pleasant, PA, D10/31/1992 Baton Rouge, LA **1934** Pit 8 (1)

WEINBERG, SOL Sol Edward, aka Sol Weinberger, TB, 5´9˝/165 lbs; Case Western Reserve; B6/2/1894, D7/1962, NJ **1923** Cle 2 (0)

WEINER, ART Arthur Edward, E-DE, 6´3˝/212 lbs; North Carolina; 1950: NYY, rnd 2; B8/16/1924 Newark, NJ

YEAR	TEAM	G (GS, POS)	RUSH	YD	AVG (LG)	TD	REC	YD	AVG (LG)	TD	PASS	COMP	PCT	YD	AVG (LG)	TD	INT	SK	YD	QBR	KPR	OTD	PTS	TAY
1950	NYY	12(LE)	—	—	—	—	35	722	20.6(58)	6	—	—	—	—	—	—	—	—	—	—	—	—	36	391

WEINER, BERNIE Bernard Morris, G-T, 5´11˝/222 lbs; Kansas State; 1941: Bkn, rnd 11; B1/24/1918 Newark, NJ, D10/25/2004 West Orange, NJ **1942** Bkn 10 (3)

WEINER, REDS Albert, B, 5´9˝/180 lbs; Muhlenberg; B1/24/1911 Woodbine, NJ, D9/17/1988 Sea Isle City, NJ **[K]**

YEAR	TEAM	G (GS, POS)	RUSH	YD	AVG (LG)	TD	REC	YD	AVG (LG)	TD	PASS	COMP	PCT	YD	AVG (LG)	TD	INT	SK	YD	QBR	KPR	OTD	PTS	TAY
1934	Phi	5(0)	9	37	4.1	0	—	—	—	—	6	3	50.0	40	6.7	2	0	—	—	—	K	—	6	67

WEINER, TODD Todd Michael, T, 6´4˝/297 lbs; Kansas State; 1998: Sea, rnd 2; B9/16/1975 Bristol, PA **1998** Sea 6 (0) **1999**†Sea 11 (1) **2000** Sea 16 (6, rt) **2001** Sea 16 (13, RT) **2003** Atl 16 (16, RT) **2004**†Atl 16 (16, RT) **2005** Atl 15 (15, RT)

YEAR	TEAM	G (GS, POS)	RUSH	YD	AVG (LG)	TD	REC	YD	AVG (LG)	TD	PASS	COMP	PCT	YD	AVG (LG)	TD	INT	SK	YD	QBR	KPR	OTD	PTS	TAY
2002	†Atl	16(15, RT)	—	—	—	—	1	0	0.0(0)	0	—	—	—	—	—	—	—	—	—	—	—	—	0	0
NFL	8	112(82)	—	—	—	—	1	0	0.0	0	—	—	—	—	—	—	—	—	—	—	—	—	0	0

WEINKE, CHRIS Christopher Jon, QB, 6´4˝/232 lbs; Florida State; 2001: Car, rnd 4; B7/31/1972 St. Paul, MN

YEAR	TEAM	G (GS, POS)	RUSH	YD	AVG (LG)	TD	REC	YD	AVG (LG)	TD	PASS	COMP	PCT	YD	AVG (LG)	TD	INT	SK	YD	QBR	KPR	OTD	PTS	TAY
2001	Car	15(15, QB)	37	128	3.5(23)	6	—	—	—	—	540	293	54.3	2931	5.4(48)	11	19	26	177	62.0	—	—	36	949
2002	Car	6(1)	5	9	1.8(13)	0	—	—	—	—	38	17	44.7	180	4.7(24)	0	3	6	35	—	—	—	0	-21
2005	†Car	3(0)	8	-5	-0.6(1)	0	—	—	—	—	13	7	53.8	64	4.9(18)	1	0	—	—	—	—	—	0	32
NFL	3	24(16)	50	132	2.6(23)	6	—	—	—	—	591	317	53.6	3175	5.4(48)	12	22	32	212	60.4	—	—	36	960

WEINMEISTER, ARNIE Arnold George, DT-T, 6´4˝/235 lbs; Washington; 1945: Bkn, rnd 17; B3/23/1923 Rhein, Canada, D6/28/2000 Seattle, WA; HOF 1984 **1948** NYY-A☆14 (8, LT) **1949**†NYY-A☆11 (11, RT) **AAFC** 25 (19) [2 yrs]

1951 NYG★12 (LDT) **1952** NYG★12 (LDT) **1953** NYG★12 (LDT)

YEAR	TEAM	G (GS, POS)	RUSH	YD	AVG (LG)	TD	REC	YD	AVG (LG)	TD	PASS	COMP	PCT	YD	AVG (LG)	TD	INT	SK	YD	QBR	KPR	OTD	PTS	TAY
1950	†NYG★	10(LDT)	—	—	—	—	1	16	16.0(16)	0	—	—	—	—	—	—	—	—	—	—	—	—	0	8
NFL	4	46	—	—	—	—	1	16	16.0(16)	0	—	—	—	—	—	—	—	—	—	—	—	—	2	8

WEINSTOCK, IZZY Isadore, FB-BB, 5´11˝/190 lbs; Pittsburgh; B6/27/1913 Wilkes-Barre, PA, D9/26/1997 Fort Lauderdale, FL **[K]**

YEAR	TEAM	G (GS, POS)	RUSH	YD	AVG (LG)	TD	REC	YD	AVG (LG)	TD	PASS	COMP	PCT	YD	AVG (LG)	TD	INT	SK	YD	QBR	KPR	OTD	PTS	TAY
1935	Phi	11(2)	58	176	3.0	0	8	107	13.4	0	5	1	20.0	12	2.4(12)	0	1	—	—	—	—	—	0	196
1937	Pit	11(6, fb)	30	88	2.9	0	—	—	—	—	—	—	—	—	—	—	—	—	—	—	K	—	4	88
1938	Pit	2(2)	1	0	0.0	0	—	—	—	—	—	—	—	—	—	—	—	—	—	—	—	—	0	0
NFL	3	24(10)	89	264	3.0	0	8	107	13.4	0	5	1	20.0	12	2.4(12)	0	1	—	—	—	K	—	4	284

WEIR, ED Samuel Edwin, T-E, 5´10˝/192 lbs; Nebraska; B3/14/1903 Superior, NE, D5/15/1991 Lincoln, NE **[KC]** **1926** Fra 4 (4), 5 **1927** Fra☆18 (18, LT), 1 **1928** Fra 14 (3), 7 **NFL** 36 (25), 13 [3 yrs]

WEIR, JOE Joseph Erwin, E, 5´11˝/185 lbs; Nebraska; B8/26/1905 Superior, NE, D2/6/1986 Sioux City, NE **1927** Fra 12 (8, RE)

WEIR, SAMMY Samuel Orville, WR, 5´9˝/170 lbs; Arkansas State; B3/18/1941 Moxie, AR

YEAR	TEAM	G (GS, POS)	RUSH	YD	AVG (LG)	TD	REC	YD	AVG (LG)	TD	PASS	COMP	PCT	YD	AVG (LG)	TD	INT	SK	YD	QBR	KPR	OTD	PTS	TAY
1965	Hou-A	9	—	—	—	—	1	12	12.0(12)	0	—	—	—	—	—	—	—	—	—	—	kp	—	0	66
1966	NYJ-A	11	—	—	—	—	1	4	4.0(4)	0	—	—	—	—	—	—	—	—	—	—	kp	—	0	41
NFL	2	20	—	—	—	—	2	16	8.0(12)	0	—	—	—	—	—	—	—	—	—	—	kp	—	0	107

WEISACOSKY, ED Edward L., LB, 6´1˝/230 lbs; Miami (FL); 1966: Mia, rnd 6; B5/4/1944 Pottsville, PA **1967** NYG 14 **1968** Mia-A 8 **1969** Mia-A 14 (14, RLB) **1970** Mia 3 **1971** NE 14 (10, LLB) **1972** NE 14 (13, LLB) **NFL** 67 (37) [6 yrs]

WEISENBAUGH, HEINIE Henry A., B, 5´11˝/190 lbs; Pittsburgh; B3/12/1914 Tarentum, PA, D1965

YEAR	TEAM	G (GS, POS)	RUSH	YD	AVG (LG)	TD	REC	YD	AVG (LG)	TD	PASS	COMP	PCT	YD	AVG (LG)	TD	INT	SK	YD	QBR	KPR	OTD	PTS	TAY
1935	Bos	4(1)	15	39	2.6	0	1	6	6.0(6)	0	—	—	—	—	—	—	—	—	—	—	—	—	0	42
1935	Pit	5(5, hb)	21	11	0.5	0	6	67	11.2	2	11	1	9.1	14	1.3(14)	0	1	—	—	—	—	—	12	22
1936	†Bos	9(1)	3	9	3.0	0	3	37	12.3	0	—	—	—	—	—	—	—	—	—	—	—	—	0	28
NFL	2	18(7)	39	59	1.5	0	10	110	11.0(6)	2	11	1	9.1	14	1.3(14)	0	1	—	—	—	—	—	12	91

WEISGERBER, DICK Richard Arthur, B, 5´10˝/205 lbs; Willamette; B2/19/1915 Kearny, NJ, D6/1/1984 Sturgeon Bay, WI **[K]**

YEAR	TEAM	G (GS, POS)	RUSH	YD	AVG (LG)	TD	REC	YD	AVG (LG)	TD	PASS	COMP	PCT	YD	AVG (LG)	TD	INT	SK	YD	QBR	KPR	OTD	PTS	TAY
1938	GB	4(1)	6	13	2.2	0	—	—	—	—	—	—	—	—	—	—	—	—	—	—	—	—	0	13
1939	†GB✧	4(1)	—	—	—	—	—	—	—	—	—	—	—	—	—	—	—	—	—	—	—	—	—	—
1940	GB	10(1)	—	—	—	—	1	37	37.0(37)	0	—	—	—	—	—	—	—	—	—	—	i	—	0	50
1942	GB	9(4)	5	21	4.2(6)	0	—	—	—	—	—	—	—	—	—	—	—	—	—	—	K	—	2	21
NFL	4	27(7)	11	34	3.1(6)	0	1	37	37.0(37)	0	—	—	—	—	—	—	—	—	—	—	Ki	—	2	84

WEISHUHN, CLAYTON Clayton Charles, LB, 6´2˝/220 lbs; Angelo State (TX); 1982: NE, rnd 3; B10/9/1959 San Angelo, TX **1982**†NE 9 (9, RILB) **1983** NE 16 (16, RILB) **1984** NE 1 (1) **1986** NE 4 (0) **1987** GB 9 (0) **NFL** 39 (26) [5 yrs]

WEISS, HOWIE Howard William, FB, 6´0˝/210 lbs; Wisconsin; 1939: Det, rnd 3; B10/12/1917 Fort Atkinson, WI, D11/23/1997 Milwaukee, WI

YEAR	TEAM	G (GS, POS)	RUSH	YD	AVG (LG)	TD	REC	YD	AVG (LG)	TD	PASS	COMP	PCT	YD	AVG (LG)	TD	INT	SK	YD	QBR	KPR	OTD	PTS	TAY
1939	Det	9(1)	37	150	4.1	0	4	25	6.3	0	—	—	—	—	—	—	—	—	—	—	—	—	0	163
1940	Det	11(4, FB)	79	298	3.8	3	4	56	14.0	0	—	—	—	—	—	—	—	—	—	—	i	1	24	360
NFL	2	20(5)	116	448	3.9	3	8	81	10.1	0	—	—	—	—	—	—	—	—	—	—	i	1	24	523

WEISS, JOHN John, E-DB, 6´3˝/198 lbs; none; B2/7/1922 Jersey City, NJ, D8/1976

YEAR	TEAM	G (GS, POS)	RUSH	YD	AVG (LG)	TD	REC	YD	AVG (LG)	TD	PASS	COMP	PCT	YD	AVG (LG)	TD	INT	SK	YD	QBR	KPR	OTD	PTS	TAY
1944	†NYG	10(0)	—	—	—	—	1	10	10.0(10)	0	—	—	—	—	—	—	—	—	—	—	—	—	0	5
1945	NYG	10(10, RE)	—	—	—	—	4	82	20.5(39)	1	—	—	—	—	—	—	—	—	—	—	k	—	6	52
1946	NYG	7(0)	—	—	—	—	4	70	17.5(35)	1	—	—	—	—	—	—	—	—	—	—	—	—	6	40
1947	NYG	1(0)	—	—	—	—	—	—	—	—	—	—	—	—	—	—	—	—	—	—	—	—	—	—
NFL	4	28(10)	—	—	—	—	9	162	18.0(39)	2	—	—	—	—	—	—	—	—	—	—	k	—	12	97

WEISSENHOFER, RON Ronald Allen, LB, 6´3˝/235 lbs; Notre Dame; B2/3/1964 Chicago, IL **1987** NO 1 (0)

WELBORNE, TRIPP Sullivan Anthony, DB, 6´0˝/205 lbs; Michigan; 1991: Min, rnd 7; B11/20/1968 Reidsville, NC **1992** Min 2 (0)

WELBOURN, JOHN John R., G-T, 6´5˝/318 lbs; California; 1999: Phi, rnd 4; B3/30/1976 Torrance, CA **1999** Phi 1 (1) **2000**†Phi 16 (16, LG) **2001**†Phi 15 (15, LG) **2002**†Phi 11 (11, LG) **2003**†Phi 13 (13, LG) **2004** KC 10 (10, RT) **2005** KC 12 (9, RT) **NFL** 78 (75) [7 yrs]

WELCH, CLAXTON Claxton Nathaniel, RB, 5´11˝/203 lbs; Oregon; 1969: Dal, rnd 9; B7/3/1947 Portland, OR

YEAR	TEAM	G (GS, POS)	RUSH	YD	AVG (LG)	TD	REC	YD	AVG (LG)	TD	PASS	COMP	PCT	YD	AVG (LG)	TD	INT	SK	YD	QBR	KPR	OTD	PTS	TAY
1969	†Dal	6	6	21	3.5(6)	0	—	—	—	—	—	—	—	—	—	—	—	—	—	—	k	—	0	58
1970	NO	1	—	—	—	—	—	—	—	—	—	—	—	—	—	—	—	—	—	—	—	—	—	—
1970	†Dal	8	5	13	2.6(5)	1	—	—	—	—	—	—	—	—	—	—	—	—	—	—	—	—	6	23
1971	†Dal	14	14	51	3.6(14)	1	1	-1	-1.0(-1)	0	—	—	—	—	—	—	—	—	—	—	k	—	8	106
1973	NE	2(1)	1	-2	-2.0(-2)	0	6	22	3.7(8)	0	—	—	—	—	—	—	—	—	—	—	—	—	0	9
NFL	4	31(1)	26	83	3.2(14)	2	7	21	3.0(8)	0	—	—	—	—	—	—	—	—	—	—	k	—	14	196

WELCH, GIBBY Gilbert Lawrence, B, 5´11˝/178 lbs; Pittsburgh; B12/24/1904 Parkersburg, WV, D2/10/1984 Pittsburgh, PA **1928** NYY 13 (12, BB), 48 **1929** Pro 12 (10, BB), 36 **NFL** 25 (22), 84 [2 yrs]

WELCH, HERB Herbert Doyan, DB, 5´11˝/180 lbs; UCLA; 1985: NYG, rnd 12; B1/12/1961 Los Angeles, CA **1985**†NYG 16 (0) **1986**†NYG 16 (2) **1987** NYG 12 (2) **1989** Was 9 (0) **1990** Det 16 (4) **1991** Det 10 (0) **NFL** 79 (8) [6 yrs]

WELCH, JIM James Evan, DB, 6´0˝/196 lbs; SMU; 1960: Bal, rnd 3/Hou, rnd 2; B3/17/1938 Anson, TX **1962** Bal 13 (RS) **1963** Bal 14 (RS) **1964**†Bal 13 (RS) **1965**†Bal 14 **1966** Bal 11

YEAR	TEAM	G (GS, POS)	RUSH	YD	AVG (LG)	TD	REC	YD	AVG (LG)	TD	PASS	COMP	PCT	YD	AVG (LG)	TD	INT	SK	YD	QBR	KPR	OTD	PTS	TAY
1960	Bal	11	5	23	4.6(7)	0	—	—	—	—	—	—	—	—	—	—	—	—	—	—	k	—	0	43
1961	Bal	14	1	60	60.0(60)	1	—	—	—	—	—	—	—	—	—	—	—	—	—	—	k	—	6	141
1967	Bal	10	2	6	3.0(4)	0	—	—	—	—	—	—	—	—	—	—	—	—	—	—	—	—	0	6
1968	Det	14	3	14	4.7(11)	0	—	—	—	—	—	—	—	—	—	—	—	—	—	—	—	—	0	14
NFL	9	114	11	103	9.4(60)	1	—	—	—	—	—	—	—	—	—	—	—	—	—	—	ki	—	6	258

WELDIN, HAROLD Harold George, C, 6´1˝/198 lbs; Northwestern; B5/25/1909, D12/15/1988 Hilton Head, SC **1934** SL 1 (0)

WELDON, BODIE John Ambrose, WB-TB, 5´7˝/165 lbs; Lafayette; B11/7/1895 Watertown, NY, D5/24/1928 Columbus, OH **1920** Buf 9 (5, WB)

WELDON, CASEY William Casey, QB, 6´1˝/206 lbs; Florida State; 1992: Phi, rnd 4; B2/3/1969 Americus, GA

YEAR	TEAM	G (GS, POS)	RUSH	YD	AVG (LG)	TD	REC	YD	AVG (LG)	TD	PASS	COMP	PCT	YD	AVG (LG)	TD	INT	SK	YD	QBR	KPR	OTD	PTS	TAY
1993	TB	3(0)	—	—	—	—	—	—	—	—	11	6	54.5	55	5.0(20)	0	1	1	11	—	—	—	0	-13
1994	TB	2(0)	—	—	—	—	—	—	—	—	9	7	77.8	63	7.0(27)	0	0	—	—	—	—	—	0	32
1995	TB	16(0)	5	5	1.0(6)	1	—	—	—	—	91	42	46.2	519	5.7(40)	1	2	9	55	—	—	—	6	200
1996	TB	3(0)	2	-1	-0.5(0)	0	—	—	—	—	9	5	55.6	76	8.4(42)	0	1	2	10	—	—	—	0	-3
1999	Was	2(0)	5	-4	-0.8(0)	0	—	—	—	—	—	—	—	—	—	—	—	—	—	—	—	—	0	-4
NFL	5	26(0)	12	0	0.0(6)	1	—	—	—	—	120	60	50.0	713	5.9(42)	1	4	12	76	—	—	—	6	212

WELDON, LARRY Lawrence Davis, QB, 6´0˝/198 lbs; Presbyterian; B6/24/1915 Sumter, SC, D8/17/1990 Virginia Beach, VA **[K]** **1945** Was 4 (0)

YEAR	TEAM	G (GS, POS)	RUSH	YD	AVG (LG)	TD	REC	YD	AVG (LG)	TD	PASS	COMP	PCT	YD	AVG (LG)	TD	INT	SK	YD	QBR	KPR	OTD	PTS	TAY
1944	Was	8(0)	8	8	1.0(24)	0	—	—	—	—	6	4	66.7	33	5.5(14)	0	0	—	—	—	Kk	—	4	8
NFL	2	12(0)	8	8	1.0(24)	0	—	—	—	—	6	4	66.7	33	5.5(14)	0	0	—	—	—	Kk	—	5	8

WELKER, WES Wes, WR, 5´9˝/190 lbs; Texas Tech; B5/1/1981 Oklahoma City, OK **[KR]** **2004** SD 1 (0) **2004** Mia 14 (0)

YEAR	TEAM	G (GS, POS)	RUSH	YD	AVG (LG)	TD	REC	YD	AVG (LG)	TD	PASS	COMP	PCT	YD	AVG (LG)	TD	INT	SK	YD	QBR	KPR	OTD	PTS	TAY
2005	Mia	16(1)	1	5	5.0(5)	0	29	434	15.0(47)	0	—	—	—	—	—	—	—	—	—	—	kp	—	0	861
NFL	2	31(1)	1	5	5.0(5)	0	29	434	15.0(47)	0	—	—	—	—	—	—	—	—	—	—	Kkp	1	10	1620

WELLBORN, JOE Joseph Holler, C, 6´2˝/230 lbs; Texas A&M; B6/3/1944 Wellborn, MS **1966** NYG 7

WELLER, BUB Raymond Fred, T-E, 6´4˝/224 lbs; Nebraska; B8/7/1902 Seward, NE, D2/21/1986 Citrus Heights, CA **[K]** **1923** SL☆7 (7, LT) **1924** Mil☆13 (13, RT) **1925** ChiC 3 (2) **1926** ChiC☆12 (10, LT) **1927** ChiC 11 (11, LT), 8 **1928** Fra 15 (14, RT) **NFL** 61 (57) [6 yrs]

WELLER, RABBIT Louis, WB, 5´5˝/150 lbs; Haskell Indian; B3/2/1904 Anadarko, OK, D4/17/1979 Albuquerque, NM

YEAR	TEAM	G (GS, POS)	RUSH	YD	AVG (LG)	TD	REC	YD	AVG (LG)	TD	PASS	COMP	PCT	YD	AVG (LG)	TD	INT	SK	YD	QBR	KPR	OTD	PTS	TAY
1933	Bos	7(0)	12	112	9.3(50)	2	1	1	1.0(1)	0	2	0	0.0	0	0.0	0	0	—	—	—	—	—	12	133

WELLMAN, GARY Gary James, WR, 5´9˝/170 lbs; USC; 1991: Hou, rnd 5; B8/9/1967 Syracuse, NY

YEAR	TEAM	G (GS, POS)	RUSH	YD	AVG (LG)	TD	REC	YD	AVG (LG)	TD	PASS	COMP	PCT	YD	AVG (LG)	TD	INT	SK	YD	QBR	KPR	OTD	PTS	TAY
1992	Hou	9(0)	—	—	—	—	—	—	—	—	—	—	—	—	—	—	—	—	—	—	—	—	—	—
1993	†Hou	11(3)	2	6	3.0(4)	0	31	430	13.9(44)	1	—	—	—	—	—	—	—	—	—	—	—	—	6	226
1994	Hou	8(0)	1	-3	-3.0(-3)	0	10	112	11.2(25)	0	—	—	—	—	—	—	—	—	—	—	—	—	0	53
NFL	3	28(3)	3	3	1.0(4)	0	41	542	13.2(44)	1	—	—	—	—	—	—	—	—	—	—	—	—	6	279

WELLMAN, MIKE Michael Jay, C, 6´3˝/253 lbs; Kansas; 1979: LA, rnd 3; B7/15/1956 Newton, KS **1979** GB 16 **1980** GB 4 (0) **NFL** 20 [2 yrs]

WELLS, ARTHUR Arthur Lee, TE, 6´4˝/236 lbs; Grambling State; 1987: NO, rnd 11; B2/1/1963 Shreveport, LA **1987** TB 2 (0)

WELLS, BILLY William Prescott, HB, 5´9˝/180 lbs; Michigan State; 1954: Was, rnd 5; B12/7/1931 Menomonie, MI, D12/25/2001 Altadena, CA

YEAR	TEAM	G (GS, POS)	RUSH	YD	AVG (LG)	TD	REC	YD	AVG (LG)	TD	PASS	COMP	PCT	YD	AVG (LG)	TD	INT	SK	YD	QBR	KPR	OTD	PTS	TAY
1954	Was★	12(RH)	100	516	5.2(88)	3	19	295	15.5(48)	1	—	—	—	—	—	—	—	—	—	—	kp	—	24	772
1956	Was	7(rh)	69	185	2.7(17)	1	6	86	14.3(34)	0	—	—	—	—	—	—	—	—	—	—	kp	1	12	261
1957	Was	1	—	—	—	—	—	—	—	—	—	—	—	—	—	—	—	—	—	—	k	—	0	4
1957	Pit	10(LH)	154	532	3.5(51)	0	14	89	6.4(17)	0	—	—	—	—	—	—	—	—	—	—	kp	1	6	766
1958	Phi	12	24	92	3.8(12)	1	4	49	12.3(21)	0	—	—	—	—	—	—	—	—	—	—	kp	—	6	316
1960	Bos-A	12	14	59	4.2(13)	0	14	206	14.7(78)	1	—	—	—	—	—	—	—	—	—	—	kp	—	6	283
NFL	5	54	361	1384	3.8(88)	5	57	725	12.7(78)	2	—	—	—	—	—	—	—	—	—	—	kp	2	54	2401

WELLS, BOB Robert Leroy, T, 6´4˝/280 lbs; Johnson C. Smith; 1968: SD, rnd 15; B8/4/1945 New York, NY, D8/7/1994 Decatur, GA **1968** SD-A 2 **1969** SD-A 14 **1970** SD 4 **NFL** 20 [3 yrs]

WELLS, DANA Dana Clemmer, NT, 6´0˝/272 lbs; Arizona; 1989: Cin, rnd 11; B8/5/1966 Phoenix, AZ **1989** Cin 1 (0)

WELLS, DEAN Donald Dean, LB, 6´3˝/248 lbs; Kentucky; 1993: Sea, rnd 4; B7/20/1970 Louisville, KY **1993** Sea 14 (1) **1994** Sea 15 (0) **1995** Sea 14 (10, MLB) **1996** Sea 16 (15, MLB) **1997** Sea 16 (16, MLB) **1998** Sea 9 (8, MLB) **1999** Car 16 (10, MLB) **2000** Car 16 (14, LLB) **2001** Car 13 (3) **NFL** 129 (77) [9 yrs]

WELLS, DON Donald Ray, DE-E, 6´2˝/200 lbs; Georgia; 1945: GB, rnd 6; B7/12/1922 Waycross, GA, D2/14/1989 Stuart, FL **1947** GB 12 (0) **1948** GB 12 (1) **1949** GB 3 (0)

YEAR	TEAM	G (GS, POS)	RUSH	YD	AVG (LG)	TD	REC	YD	AVG (LG)	TD	PASS	COMP	PCT	YD	AVG (LG)	TD	INT	SK	YD	QBR	KPR	OTD	PTS	TAY
1946	GB	11(3)	—	—	—	—	2	74	37.0(65)	0	—	—	—	—	—	—	—	—	—	—	—	—	0	37
NFL	4	38(4)	—	—	—	—	2	74	37.0(65)	0	—	—	—	—	—	—	—	—	—	—	—	—	0	37

WELLS, HAROLD Harold, LB, 6´2˝/220 lbs; Purdue; B11/26/1938 St. Louis, MO **1965** Phi 14 **1966** Phi 14 (14, RLB) **1967** Phi 14 (RLB) **1968** Phi 14 (RLB) **NFL** 56 (14) [4 yrs]

WELLS, JOEL Joel Whitlock, HB, 6´1˝/200 lbs; Clemson; 1957: GB, rnd 2; B11/26/1935 Columbia, SC

YEAR	TEAM	G (GS, POS)	RUSH	YD	AVG (LG)	TD	REC	YD	AVG (LG)	TD	PASS	COMP	PCT	YD	AVG (LG)	TD	INT	SK	YD	QBR	KPR	OTD	PTS	TAY
1961	NYG	14	65	216	3.3(17)	1	6	31	5.2(19)	1	—	—	—	—	—	—	—	—	—	—	kp	—	12	345

WELLS, JONATHAN Jonathan, RB, 6´1˝/243 lbs; Ohio State; 2002: Hou, rnd 4; B7/21/1979 River Ridge, LA

YEAR	TEAM	G (GS, POS)	RUSH	YD	AVG (LG)	TD	REC	YD	AVG (LG)	TD	PASS	COMP	PCT	YD	AVG (LG)	TD	INT	SK	YD	QBR	KPR	OTD	PTS	TAY
2002	Hou	16(11, RB)	197	529	2.7(37)	3	9	48	5.3(9)	0	—	—	—	—	—	—	—	—	—	—	—	—	18	583
2003	Hou	13(0)	5	14	2.8(10)	0	2	17	8.5(12)	0	—	—	—	—	—	—	—	—	—	—	k	—	0	17
2004	Hou	16(1)	82	299	3.6(14)	3	11	79	7.2(28)	2	—	—	—	—	—	—	—	—	—	—	k	—	32	376
2005	Hou	15(6, rb)	90	325	3.6(14)	4	22	179	8.1(20)	0	—	—	—	—	—	—	—	—	—	—	k	—	24	486
NFL	4	60(18)	374	1167	3.1(37)	10	44	323	7.3(28)	2	—	—	—	—	—	—	—	—	—	—	k	—	74	1461

WELLS, KENT Kent Eugene, DT, 6´4˝/295 lbs; Nebraska; 1990: Was, rnd 6; B7/25/1967 Lincoln, NE **1990** NYG 6 (0)

WELLS, MIKE Michael Eugene, QB, 6´5˝/225 lbs; Illinois; 1973: Min, rnd 4; B6/18/1951 Normal, IL **1977** Cin 7

WELLS, MIKE Michael, TE, 6´3˝/233 lbs; San Diego State; B1/22/1962 Quincy, CA **1987** SF 1 (1)

WELLS, MIKE Michael Allan, DT, 6´3˝/292 lbs; Iowa; 1994: Min, rnd 4; B1/16/1971 Arnold, MO **1994** Det 4 (0) **1995**†Det 15 (0) **1996** Det 16 (1) **1997**†Det 16 (16, LDT) **1998** ChiB 16 (16, RDT) **1999** ChiB 16 (16, RDT) **2001** Ind 16 (0)

YEAR	TEAM	G (GS, POS)	RUSH	YD	AVG (LG)	TD	REC	YD	AVG (LG)	TD	PASS	COMP	PCT	YD	AVG (LG)	TD	INT	SK	YD	QBR	KPR	OTD	PTS	TAY
2000	ChiB	16(14, RDT)	—	—	—	—	1	13	13.0(13)	0	—	—	—	—	—	—	—	—	—	—	iS	—	0	23
NFL	8	115(63)	—	—	—	—	1	13	13.0(13)	0	—	—	—	—	—	—	—	—	—	—	iS	1	6	23

WELLS, NORM Norman Edward, DT, 6´5˝/261 lbs; Northwestern; 1980: Dal, rnd 12; B9/8/1957 Detroit, MI **1980**†Dal 3 (0)

WELLS, RAY Ray, LB, 6´1˝/234 lbs; Arizona; B8/20/1980 Oakland, CA **2003**†Ten 16 (0) **2004** SF 6 (0) **NFL** 22 (0) [2 yrs]

WELLS, REGGIE Reggie, G-T, 6´4˝/298 lbs; Clarion; 2003: Arz, rnd 6; B11/3/1980 Liberty, PA **2003** Arz 15 (1) **2004** Arz 16 (16, LG) **2005** Arz 9 (9, LG) **NFL** 40 (26) [3 yrs]

WELLS, SCOTT Scott Darvin, G-C, 6´2˝/300 lbs; Tennessee; 2004: GB, rnd 7; B1/7/1981 Spring Hill, TN **2004**†GB 5 (2) **2005** GB 16 (10, LG) **NFL** 21 (12) [2 yrs]

YEAR	TEAM	G (GS, POS)	RUSH	YD	AVG(LG)	TD	REC	YD	AVG(LG)	TD	PASS COMP	PCT	YD	AVG(LG)	TD	INT	SK	YD	QBR	KPR	OTD	PTS	TAY

WELLS, TERRY Terrence Lorenzo, RB, 5´11˝/195 lbs; Southern Mississippi; B4/20/1951 Wade, MS

1974	Hou	6	—	—	—	—	1	9	9.0(9)	0	—	—	—	—	—	—	—	—	—	—	—	0	5
1975	GB	13	33	139	4.2(25)	0	6	11	1.8(4)	0	—	—	—	—	—	—	—	—	—	k	—	0	156
NFL	2	19	33	139	4.2(25)	0	7	20	2.9(9)	0	—	—	—	—	—	—	—	—	—	k	—	0	160

WELLS, WARREN Warren, SE-WR, 6´1˝/190 lbs; Texas Southern; 1964: Det, rnd 12; B11/14/1942 Franklin, LA

1964	Det	9	—	—	—	—	2	21	10.5(13)	0	—	—	—	—	—	—	—	—	—	—	—	0	11
1967	†Oak-A	14	1	7	7.0(7)	0	13	302	23.2(50)	6	—	—	—	—	—	—	—	—	—	—	—	36	188
1968	†Oak-A◇	14(12, SE)	2	38	19.0(41)	1	53	1137	21.5(**94**)	**11**	—	—	—	—	—	—	—	—	—	—	—	72	672
1969	†Oak-A☆	14(14, SE)	3	24	8.0(17)	0	47	1260	26.8(80)	**14**	—	—	—	—	—	—	—	—	—	—	—	84	724
1970	†Oak★	14(13, WR)	3	34	11.3(14)	0	43	935	21.7(60)	11	—	—	—	—	—	—	—	—	—	—	—	66	557
NFL	5	65(39)	9	103	11.4(41)	1	158	3655	23.1(94)	42	—	—	—	—	—	—	—	—	—	—	—	258	2151

WELLSANDT, DOUG Douglas D., TE, 6´3˝/248 lbs; Washington State; 1990: Cin, rnd 8; B2/9/1967 Moses Lake, WA

| 1990 | NYJ | 16(2) | 1 | -3.0(-3) | | 0 | 5 | 57 | 11.4(20) | 0 | — | — | — | — | — | — | — | — | — | — | — | 0 | 26 |

WELMAS, WOODCHUCK Philip J., E, 5´7˝/170 lbs; Carlisle Indian; B1893, deceased **1923** Oor 4 (3)

WELSH, JIM James Edward, G-T, 5´11˝/250 lbs; Colgate; B9/17/1902, D2/12/1958 Lake County, FL **[K] 1923** Roc 2 (2, RG) **1924** Fra☆10 (8, rg), 38 **1925** Fra 8 (6, rg) **1926** Pot☆13 (13, LG), 30 **NFL** 33 (29), 68 [4 yrs]

WELSH, JONATHAN Jonathan, DE, 6´3˝/233 lbs; Wisconsin; 2005: Ind, rnd 5; B6/9/1982 Houston, TX **2005** Ind 6 (0)

WELTER, TOM Thomas Lawrence, T-G, 6´5˝/280 lbs; Nebraska; B2/24/1964 Yankton, SD **1987** SL 3 (3)

WELTMAN, LARRY Lawrence Abraham, B, 5´10˝/150 lbs; Syracuse; B6/1898 Pittsfield, MA, D9/12/1959 Troy, NY **1922** Roc 4 (3, BB)

WEMPLE, DON Donald Lester, E, 6´2˝/195 lbs; Colgate; B10/14/1917 Gloversville, NY, D6/23/1943, India

| 1941 | Bkn | 11(0) | — | — | — | — | 2 | 37 | 18.5(29) | 1 | — | — | — | — | — | — | — | — | — | — | — | 6 | 24 |

WENDELL, MARTIN Martin Peter, G, 5´10˝/215 lbs; Notre Dame; 1948: Buf-A, rnd 6/Phi, rnd 8; B11/22/1926 Chicago, IL **1949** ChiH-A 10 (8, RG)

WENDER, JACK Jack, RB, 6´0˝/210 lbs; Fresno State; B5/31/1954 San Francisco, CA **1977** TB 2

WENDLER, HAL Harold William, BB, 5´10˝/175 lbs; Ohio State; B1/20/1902 Gibsonburg, OH, D8/23/1984 Baton Rouge, LA **1926** Ham 1 (1) **1926** Akr 7 (3) **NFL** 8 (4) [1 yr]

WENDLICK, JOE Joseph Peter, E, 6´0˝/213 lbs; Oregon State; 1939: Det, rnd 6; B12/14/1915 Portland, OR, D1/6/2003 Gearhart, OR

1940	Phi	9(2)	—	—	—	—	8	67	8.4	0	—	—	—	—	—	—	—	—	—	—	—	0	34
1941	Pit	10(6, RE)	—	—	—	—	7	84	12.0(19)	0	—	—	—	—	—	—	—	—	—	—	—	0	42
NFL	2	19(8)	—	—	—	—	15	151	10.1(19)	0	—	—	—	—	—	—	—	—	—	—	—	0	76

WENDRYHOSKI, JOE Joseph Stanley, C, 6´2˝/245 lbs; Illinois; 1961: NYT, rnd 13; B3/1/1938 West Frankfort, IL **1964** LARm 13 **1965** LARm 4 **1966** LARm 14 **1967** NO 14 (14, C) **1968** NO 14 (14, C) **NFL** 59 (28) [5 yrs]

WENDT, KEN Kenneth Robert, G, 6´0˝/195 lbs; Marquette; B1/29/1910 Chicago, IL, D1/19/1982 Chicago, IL **1932** ChiC 1 (0)

WENGLIKOWSKI, AL Alan Lee, LB, 6´1˝/215 lbs; Pittsburgh; 1984: KC, rnd 10; B8/3/1960 Burlington, IA **1984** Buf 5 (0) **1987** Buf 1 (0) **NFL** 6 (0) [2 yrs]

WENIG, OBE Ervine C., E, 5´10˝/185 lbs; Morningside; B12/23/1895, D9/25/1959 Springfield, MO **[K] 1920** RI☆1 (0) **1921** RI 7 (6, RE), 26 **1922** RI 6 (1) **NFL** 14 (7) [3 yrs]

WENKE, AD Adolph Eilert, T, 6´4˝/220 lbs; Nebraska; B1/22/1898 Pender, NE, D3/3/1961 Lincoln, NE **1923** Mil 11 (11, RT)

WENTWORTH, CY Shirley P., B, 5´8˝/160 lbs; New Hampshire; B1/2/1904 Salem, MA, D1/19/1986 Salem, MA **[K] 1925** Pro☆12 (12, TB), 18 **1926** Pro 8 (7, TB), 6 **1929** Bos 6 (3), 24 **NFL** 26 (22), 48 [3 yrs]

WENTZ, BARNEY Byron W., FB, 5´11˝/204 lbs; Penn State; B4/21/1901 Shenandoah, PA, D5/1963, PA **[K] 1925** Pot☆12 (12, FB), 31 **1926** Pot 14 (13, FB), 60 **1927** Pot 12 (8, FB), 17 **1928** Pot 2 (0) **NFL** 40 (33), 108 [4 yrs]

WENZEL, JEFF Jeffrey Gustave, T, 6´7˝/270 lbs; Tulane; B10/21/1963 New Orleans, LA **1987** Phi 3 (3)

WENZEL, RALPH Ralph Milton, E, 6´0˝/205 lbs; Tulane; 1940: Pit, rnd 2; B7/22/1918 Ferda, AR, D11/6/2001 Lexington, KY **1942** Pit 6 (0)

WENZEL, RALPH Ralph Richard, G, 6´2˝/250 lbs; San Jose State; San Diego State; 1966: GB, rnd 11; B3/13/1943 San Mateo, CA **1966** Pit 6 **1967** Pit 13 **1968** Pit 2 **1969** Pit 8 **1970** Pit 14 **1972** SD 14 **1973** SD 14 **NFL** 71 [7 yrs]

WERDER, RED Gerard Joseph, C-T, 5´11˝/185 lbs; Dayton; B8/1/1894 Pittsburgh, PA, D4/11/1942 Los Angeles, CA **1920** Buf 4 (0) **1921** Ton 1 (1, C) **NFL** 5 (1) [2 yrs]

WERDER, DICK Richard Irving, G, 5´9˝/210 lbs; Georgetown (DC); B7/31/1922 Buffalo, NY, D2/14/2002 Buffalo, NY **1948** NYY-A 3 (1)

WERL, BOB Robert George, DE-G, 6´3˝/240 lbs; Miami (FL); 1965: NYJ, rnd R4/LA, rnd 12; B1/7/1943 Pittsburgh, PA, D3/27/1988 Pittsburgh, PA **1966** NYJ-A 8

WERNER, CLYDE Clyde Leroy, LB, 6´4˝/225 lbs; Washington; 1970: KC, rnd 2; B12/10/1947 Munising, MI **1970** KC 7 **1972** KC 14 **1973** KC 14 **1974** KC 14 **1976** KC 14 **NFL** 63 [5 yrs]

WERNER, GREG Gregory Alan, TE, 6´4˝/236 lbs; DePauw; B10/21/1966 Batesville, IN

| 1989 | NYJ | 10(4) | — | — | — | — | 8 | 115 | 14.4(36) | 0 | — | — | — | — | — | — | — | — | — | — | — | 0 | 58 |

WERSCHING, RAY Raimund, K, 5´11˝/213 lbs; California; B8/21/1950 Mondsee, Austria **[K] 1973** SD 14 **1974** SD 14 **1975** SD 14 **1976** SD 9 **1977** SF 10 **1978** SF 16 **1979** SF 16 **1980** SF 16 (0) **1981**†SF 12 (0) **1982** SF 9 (0) **1983**†SF 16 (0) **1984**†SF 16 (0) **1985**†SF 16 (0) **1986**†SF☆16 (0) **1987**†SF 12 (0) **NFL** 206 [15 yrs]

WERWAISS, MULE Elbert L., T-G, /235 lbs; none; B2/15/1905, CT, D3/23/1965 Los Angeles County, CA **1926** Har 9 (7, LT)

WESBECHER, AL Aloysius Augustus, C-T, 5´10˝/190 lbs; Washington & Jefferson; B11/3/1892 Greensburg, PA, D3/27/1966 Greensburg, PA **1920** Cle 5 (2)

WESLEY, DANTE Dante, DB, 6´1˝/211 lbs; Arkansas-Pine Bluff; 2002: Car, rnd 4; B4/5/1979 St. Louis, MO **2002** Car 13 (1) **2003**†Car 16 (1) **2004** Car 13 (0) **2005**†Car 16 (0) **NFL** 58 (2) [4 yrs]

WESLEY, GREG Gregory Lashon, DB, 6´2˝/208 lbs; Arkansas-Pine Bluff; 2000: KC, rnd 3; B3/19/1978 Little Rock, AR **[I] 2000** KC 16 (16, SS) **2001** KC 16 (16, SS) **2002** KC 13 (13, SS) **2003**†KC 16 (16, SS) **2004** KC 12 (11, SS) **2005** KC 16 (16, FS) **NFL** 89 (88) [6 yrs]

WESLEY, JOE Joseph, LB, 6´1˝/229 lbs; LSU; B11/10/1976 Jackson, MS **1999** SF 8 (0) **2001** Jax 6 (0) **NFL** 14 (0) [2 yrs]

WESLEY, BULL Lecil Olen, C-G-T-FB, 6´1˝/190 lbs; Alabama; B9/26/1901 Guin, AL, D1/1980 Tuscaloosa, AL **1926** Pro 7 (7, rg) **1927** Pro 10 (4) **1928** NYG 5 (3) **1930** Por 13 (5, c) **NFL** 35 (19) [4 yrs]

WESSON, RICKY Ricky Charles, DB, 5´9˝/163 lbs; SMU; B6/29/1955 Dallas, TX **1977** KC 14

WEST, BELF David Belford, T, 6´2˝/200 lbs; Colgate; B5/7/1896 Hamilton, NY, D9/11/1973 Cooperstown, NY **[K] 1921** Can☆10 (9, LT), 7

WEST, BILL William Henry, DB, 5´10˝/185 lbs; Tennessee State; 1971: Oak, rnd 10; B3/3/1947 Weirton, WV **1972** Den 8

WEST, BURR William Hodges, T, 6´1˝/220 lbs; Tennessee; B9/30/1918 Knoxville, KY **1941** Phi 10 (1)

WEST, CHARLIE Charles, DB, 6´1˝/197 lbs; Angelo State; Texas-El Paso; 1968: Min, rnd 2; B8/31/1946 Terrell, TX **[R] 1968**†Min 14 **1969**†Min 14 **1970**†Min 14 **1971**†Min 14 (14, LCB) **1972** Min 14 (13, LCB) **1973**†Min 5 **1974** Det 13 (9, SS) **1975** Det 14 (14, SS) **1976** Det☆14 (14, SS) **1977** Det 13 (13, SS) **1978**†Den 16 **1979**†Den 16 (7, fs) **NFL** 161 (84) [12 yrs]

WEST, DAVE David Norman, DB, 6´3˝/190 lbs; Central State (OH); B6/5/1938 Selma, OH **1963** NYJ-A 2

WEST, DEREK Derek Steven, T, 6´8˝/309 lbs; Colorado; 1995: Ind, rnd 5; B3/28/1972 Denver, CO **1995**†Ind 3 (0) **1996** Ind 1 (0) **1997** Ind 1 (0) **NFL** 5 (0) [3 yrs]

WEST, ED Edward Lee, TE, 6´1˝/250 lbs; Auburn; B8/2/1961 Colbert County, AL

1984	GB	16(0)	1	2	2.0(2)	1	6	54	9.0(29)	4	—	—	—	—	—	—	—	—	—	—	—	30	59
1985	GB	16(0)	1	0	0.0(0)	0	8	95	11.9(30)	1	—	—	—	—	—	—	—	—	—	—	—	6	53
1986	GB	16(6, te)	—	—	—	—	15	199	13.3(46)	1	—	—	—	—	—	—	—	—	—	—	—	6	105
1987	GB	12(11, TE)	—	—	—	—	19	261	13.7(40)	1	—	—	—	—	—	—	—	—	—	—	—	6	136
1988	GB	16(16, TE)	—	—	—	—	30	276	9.2(35)	3	—	—	—	—	—	—	—	—	—	—	—	18	153
1989	GB	13(12, TE)	—	—	—	—	22	269	12.2(31)	5	—	—	—	—	—	—	—	—	—	—	—	30	160
1990	GB	16(16, TE)	—	—	—	—	27	356	13.2(50)	5	—	—	—	—	—	—	—	—	—	k	—	30	188
1991	GB	16(16, TE)	—	—	—	—	15	151	10.1(21)	3	—	—	—	—	—	—	—	—	—	—	—	18	91

YEAR	TEAM	G (GS, POS)	RUSH	YD	AVG (LG)	TD	REC	YD	AVG (LG)	TD	PASS	COMP	PCT	YD	AVG (LG)	TD	INT	SK	YD	QBR	KPR	OTD	PTS	TAY
1992	GB	16(8, te)	—	—	—	—	4	30	7.5(10)	0	—	—	—	—	—	—	—	—	—	—	k	—	0	0
1993	†GB	16(7, te)	—	—	—	—	25	253	10.1(24)	0	—	—	—	—	—	—	—	—	—	—	—	—	0	127
1994	†GB	14(12, TE)	—	—	—	—	31	377	12.2(26)	2	—	—	—	—	—	—	—	—	—	—	—	—	14	199
1995	†Phi	16(14, TE)	—	—	—	—	20	190	9.5(26)	1	—	—	—	—	—	—	—	—	—	—	—	—	6	100
1996	†Phi	16(4)	—	—	—	—	8	91	11.4(29)	0	—	—	—	—	—	—	—	—	—	—	—	—	0	46
1997	Atl	12(3)	—	—	—	—	7	63	9.0(23)	1	—	—	—	—	—	—	—	—	—	—	—	—	6	37
NFL	14	211(125)	2	2	1.0(2)	1	237	2665	11.2(50)	27	—	—	—	—	—	—	—	—	—	—	k	—	170	1450

WEST, JEFF Jeffrey Harold, P-TE, 6´3˝/212 lbs; Cincinnati; 1975: Cin, rnd 5; B4/6/1953 Wheeling, WV **[P]** **1975**†SL 14 **1982** Sea 9 (0) **1983**†Sea 16 (0) **1984**†Sea 16 (0) **1985** Sea 2 (0)

YEAR	TEAM	G (GS, POS)	RUSH	YD	AVG (LG)	TD	REC	YD	AVG (LG)	TD	PASS	COMP	PCT	YD	AVG (LG)	TD	INT	SK	YD	QBR	KPR	OTD	PTS	TAY
1976	SD	6	1	0	0.0(0)	0	—	—	—	—	—	—	—	—	—	—	—	—	—	—	P	—	0	0
1977	SD	13	—	—	—	—	1	3	3.0(3)	0	—	—	—	—	—	—	—	—	—	—	P	—	0	2
1978	SD	16	1	0	0.0(0)	0	—	—	—	—	—	—	—	—	—	—	—	—	—	—	P	—	0	0
1979	†SD	16	1	-2	-2.0(-2)	0	—	—	—	—	—	—	—	—	—	—	—	—	—	—	P	—	0	-2
1981	Sea	15(0)	3	25	8.3(27)	0	—	—	—	—	1	0	0.0	0	0.0	0	0	—	—	—	P	—	0	25
NFL	10	123	6	23	3.8(27)	0	1	3	3.0(3)	0	1	0	0.0	0	0.0	0	0	—	—	—	P	—	0	25

WEST, LYLE Lyle, DB, 6´0˝/210 lbs; San Jose State; 1999: NYG, rnd 6; B12/20/1976 Columbus, GA **1999** NYG 6 (0) **2000**†NYG 16 (2) **2002** KC 16 (0) **2003** KC 13 (0) **NFL** 51 (2) [4 yrs]

WEST, MEL Melvin Gerald, HB, 5´9˝/190 lbs; Missouri; 1961: Bos, rnd 11/SL, rnd 15; B1/14/1939 Columbia, MO

YEAR	TEAM	G (GS, POS)	RUSH	YD	AVG (LG)	TD	REC	YD	AVG (LG)	TD	PASS	COMP	PCT	YD	AVG (LG)	TD	INT	SK	YD	QBR	KPR	OTD	PTS	TAY
1961	Bos-A	4	26	90	3.5(31)	0	5	42	8.4(18)	0	—	—	—	—	—	—	—	—	—	—	k	—	0	197
1961	NYT-A	9	46	232	5.0(35)	3	8	104	13.0(37)	0	—	—	—	—	—	—	—	—	—	—	kp	—	18	380
1962	NYT-A	3	9	16	1.8(7)	0	1	1	1.0(1)	0	—	—	—	—	—	—	—	—	—	—	kp	—	0	98
NFL	2	16	81	338	4.2(35)	3	14	147	10.5(37)	0	—	—	—	—	—	—	—	—	—	—	kp	—	18	675

WEST, PAT Patrick Michael, FB, 6´0˝/201 lbs; Pittsburgh; USC; 1945: Cle, rnd 28; B2/21/1923 Florence, PA, D2/7/1996 Winston-Salem, NC

YEAR	TEAM	G (GS, POS)	RUSH	YD	AVG (LG)	TD	REC	YD	AVG (LG)	TD	PASS	COMP	PCT	YD	AVG (LG)	TD	INT	SK	YD	QBR	KPR	OTD	PTS	TAY
1945	†Cle	10(6, fb)	19	45	2.4(9)	0	1	-2	-2.0(-2)	0	—	—	—	—	—	—	—	—	—	—	—	—	0	44
1946	LARm	10(7, FB)	40	226	5.7(72)	1	—	—	—	—	—	—	—	—	—	—	—	—	—	—	k	—	6	225
1947	LARm	12(5, FB)	42	162	3.9(21)	2	—	—	—	—	—	—	—	—	—	—	—	—	—	—	ki	—	12	207
1948	LARm	4(0)	4	24	6.0(16)	0	3	37	12.3(17)	0	—	—	—	—	—	—	—	—	—	—	—	—	0	43
1948	GB	3(0)	—	—	—	—	—	—	—	—	—	—	—	—	—	—	—	—	—	—	—	—	—	—
NFL	4	39(18)	105	457	4.4(72)	3	4	35	8.8(17)	0	—	—	—	—	—	—	—	—	—	—	ki	—	18	519

WEST, ROBERT Robert Harold, WR, 6´4˝/218 lbs; San Diego State; 1972: Dal, rnd 4; B10/3/1950 San Diego, CA

YEAR	TEAM	G (GS, POS)	RUSH	YD	AVG (LG)	TD	REC	YD	AVG (LG)	TD	PASS	COMP	PCT	YD	AVG (LG)	TD	INT	SK	YD	QBR	KPR	OTD	PTS	TAY
1972	KC	11(wr)	2	2	1.0(10)	0	9	165	18.3(42)	2	—	—	—	—	—	—	—	—	—	—	—	1	18	95
1973	KC	8	—	—	—	—	4	65	16.3(23)	0	—	—	—	—	—	—	—	—	—	—	k	—	0	18
1974	SF	10	—	—	—	—	—	—	—	—	—	—	—	—	—	—	—	—	—	—	k	—	0	-15
NFL	3	29	2	2	1.0(10)	0	13	230	17.7(42)	2	—	—	—	—	—	—	—	—	—	—	k	1	18	97

WEST, RONNIE Ronnie Lee, WR, 6´1˝/215 lbs; Valdosta State; Pittsburg State; 1992: Min, rnd 9; B6/23/1968 Pineview, GA **1992**†Min 12 (0)

WEST, STAN Stanley Byron, DG-G-C, 6´2˝/235 lbs; Oklahoma; 1950: LA, rnd 1; B9/22/1926 Weatherford, OK, D1/19/2005 Norman, OK **1950**†LARm 12 (MG) **1951**†LARm★12 (MG) **1952**†LARm★12 (MG) **1953** LARm 12 (MG) **1954** LARm 9 **1955** NYG 11 **1956** ChiC 11 (MG) **1957** ChiC 5 **NFL** 84 [8 yrs]

WEST, TROY Troy H., DB, 6´1˝/205 lbs; USC; 1983: LARm, rnd 8; B8/26/1961 Los Angeles, CA **1987** Phi 3 (3)

WEST, WALTER Walter James, FB-DB, 6´0˝/197 lbs; Pittsburgh; B10/26/1917 Florence, PA, D9/13/1984 Carlsbad, CA **[K]**

YEAR	TEAM	G (GS, POS)	RUSH	YD	AVG (LG)	TD	REC	YD	AVG (LG)	TD	PASS	COMP	PCT	YD	AVG (LG)	TD	INT	SK	YD	QBR	KPR	OTD	PTS	TAY
1944	Cle	9(3)	66	220	3.3(31)	1	9	64	7.1(18)	0	—	—	—	—	—	—	—	—	—	—	Kkpi	—	12	252

WEST, WILLIE Willie Tennyson, DB, 5´10˝/190 lbs; Oregon; 1960: SL, rnd 4/Den, rnd 1; B5/1/1938 Lexington, MS **[I]** **1961** SL 14 (lcb) **1962** Buf-A 12 (LCB) **1963**†Buf-A✧14 (LCB) **1964** Den-A 7 (RCB) **1964** NYJ-A 3 **1965** NYJ-A 14 **1966** Mia-A★14 (14, RS) **1967** Mia-A 7 (6, LS) **1968** Mia-A 13 (9, rs/ls)

YEAR	TEAM	G (GS, POS)	RUSH	YD	AVG (LG)	TD	REC	YD	AVG (LG)	TD	PASS	COMP	PCT	YD	AVG (LG)	TD	INT	SK	YD	QBR	KPR	OTD	PTS	TAY
1960	SL	7	7	45	6.4(14)	0	—	—	—	—	—	—	—	—	—	—	—	—	—	—	kp	—	0	253
NFL	9	105(29)	7	45	6.4(14)	0	—	—	—	—	—	—	—	—	—	—	—	—	—	—	kpi	2	12	765

WESTBROOK, BRIAN Brian, RB, 5´8˝/200 lbs; Villanova; 2002: Phi, rnd 3; B9/2/1979 Washington, DC

YEAR	TEAM	G (GS, POS)	RUSH	YD	AVG (LG)	TD	REC	YD	AVG (LG)	TD	PASS	COMP	PCT	YD	AVG (LG)	TD	INT	SK	YD	QBR	KPR	OTD	PTS	TAY
2002	†Phi	15(3)	46	193	4.2(18)	0	9	86	9.6(20)	0	1	1	100.0	25	25.0(25)	1	0	—	—	—	—	—	0	254
2003	Phi☆	15(8, RB)	117	613	5.2(62)	7	37	332	9.0(38)	4	—	—	—	—	—	—	—	—	—	—	kp	2	78	1237
2004	†Phi✧	13(12, RB)	177	812	4.6(50)	3	73	703	9.6(50)	6	0	0	0.0	0	0.0	0	0	1	4	—	p	—	54	1228
2005	Phi	12(12, RB)	156	617	4.0(31)	3	61	616	10.1(62)	4	0	0	0.0	0	0.0	0	0	1	3	—	p	—	44	995
NFL	4	55(35)	496	2235	4.5(62)	13	180	1737	9.6(62)	14	1	1	100.0	25	25.0(25)	1	0	2	7	—	kp	2	176	3713

WESTBROOK, BRYANT Bryant Antoine, DB, 6´0˝/199 lbs; Texas; 1997: Det, rnd 1; B12/19/1974 Charlotte, NC **1997**†Det 15 (14, LCB) **1998** Det 16 (16, LCB) **1999**†Det 10 (8, rcb) **2000** Det 13 (13, LCB) **2001** Det 10 (3) **2002** Dal 1 (1) **2002**†GB 6 (0) **NFL** 71 (55) [6 yrs]

WESTBROOK, DON Donald Joseph, WR, 5´10˝/185 lbs; Nebraska; 1975: Bal, rnd 6; B11/1/1952 Cheyenne, WY

YEAR	TEAM	G (GS, POS)	RUSH	YD	AVG (LG)	TD	REC	YD	AVG (LG)	TD	PASS	COMP	PCT	YD	AVG (LG)	TD	INT	SK	YD	QBR	KPR	OTD	PTS	TAY
1977	NE	13	—	—	—	—	—	—	—	—	—	—	—	—	—	—	—	—	—	—	p	—	0	0
1978	†NE	16	1	-2	-2.0(-2)	0	3	38	12.7(19)	0	—	—	—	—	—	—	—	—	—	—	k	—	0	37
1979	NE	16	2	8	4.0(4)	0	9	173	19.2(38)	1	2	2	100.0	52	26.0(28)	0	0	—	—	—	kp	—	6	107
1980	NE	14(0)	—	—	—	—	4	60	15.0(21)	0	—	—	—	—	—	—	—	—	—	—	k	—	0	29
1981	NE	12(1)	—	—	—	—	7	122	17.4(32)	2	—	—	—	—	—	—	—	—	—	—	—	—	12	71
NFL	5	71(1)	3	6	2.0(4)	0	23	393	17.1(38)	3	2	2	100.0	52	26.0(28)	0	0	—	—	—	kp	—	18	244

WESTBROOK, MICHAEL Michael Deanailo, WR, 6´3˝/220 lbs; Colorado; 1995: Was, rnd 1; B7/7/1972 Detroit, MI

YEAR	TEAM	G (GS, POS)	RUSH	YD	AVG (LG)	TD	REC	YD	AVG (LG)	TD	PASS	COMP	PCT	YD	AVG (LG)	TD	INT	SK	YD	QBR	KPR	OTD	PTS	TAY
1995	Was	11(9, WR)	6	114	19.0(58)	1	34	522	15.4(45)	1	—	—	—	—	—	—	—	—	—	—	—	—	12	390
1996	Was	11(6, WR)	2	2	1.0(2)	0	34	505	14.9(45)	1	—	—	—	—	—	—	—	—	—	—	—	—	6	260
1997	Was	13(9, WR)	3	-11	-3.7(7)	0	34	559	16.4(40)	3	—	—	—	—	—	—	—	—	—	—	—	—	18	284
1998	Was	11(10, WR)	1	11	11.0(11)	0	44	736	16.7(75)	6	—	—	—	—	—	—	—	—	—	—	—	—	36	409
1999	†Was	16(16, WR)	7	35	5.0(12)	0	65	1191	18.3(65)	9	—	—	—	—	—	—	—	—	—	—	—	—	56	676
2000	Was	2(2)	—	—	—	—	9	103	11.4(21)	0	—	—	—	—	—	—	—	—	—	—	—	—	0	52
2001	Was	16(16, WR)	2	8	4.0(8)	0	57	664	11.6(76)	4	—	—	—	—	—	—	—	—	—	—	—	—	24	360
2002	Cin	9(4)	1	1	1.0(1)	0	8	94	11.8(26)	2	—	—	—	—	—	—	—	—	—	—	—	—	12	58
NFL	8	89(72)	22	160	7.3(58)	1	285	4374	15.3(76)	26	—	—	—	—	—	—	—	—	—	—	—	—	164	2487

WESTBROOKS, GREG Gregory Melvin, LB, 6´2˝/215 lbs; Mesa; Colorado; 1975: NO, rnd 17; B2/24/1953 Chicago, IL **1975** NO 14 (2) **1976** NO 14 (14, RLB) **1977** NO 7 (6, rlb) **1978** SL 10 **1978** Oak 1 **1979** Oak 4 **1979**†LARm 5 **1980** Oak 1 (0) **1980**†LARm 6 (0) **1981** Oak 4 (0) **NFL** 66 (22) [7 yrs]

WESTER, CLEVE Cleveland F., RB, 5´8˝/188 lbs; Concordia (MN); B6/14/1964

YEAR	TEAM	G (GS, POS)	RUSH	YD	AVG (LG)	TD	REC	YD	AVG (LG)	TD	PASS	COMP	PCT	YD	AVG (LG)	TD	INT	SK	YD	QBR	KPR	OTD	PTS	TAY
1987	Det	3(1)	33	113	3.4(14)	0	—	—	—	—	—	—	—	—	—	—	—	—	—	—	—	—	0	113

WESTFALL, BOB Robert Barton, FB-LB-TB, 5´8˝/190 lbs; Michigan; 1942: Det, rnd 1; B5/5/1919 Detroit, MI, D10/23/1980 Adrian, MI

YEAR	TEAM	G (GS, POS)	RUSH	YD	AVG (LG)	TD	REC	YD	AVG (LG)	TD	PASS	COMP	PCT	YD	AVG (LG)	TD	INT	SK	YD	QBR	KPR	OTD	PTS	TAY
1944	Det	10(10, FB)	65	277	4.3(75)	3	16	218	13.6(45)	2	47	23	48.9	342	7.3(46)	4	6	—	—	—	Pkpi	—	30	459
1945	Det☆	9(4, FB)	82	234	2.9(19)	6	12	209	17.4(43)	3	4	3	75.0	91	22.8(63)	1	0	—	—	—	kp	—	54	471
1946	Det	10(3)	28	54	1.9(9)	1	17	142	8.4(24)	0	2	1	50.0	5	-2.5(-5)	0	1	—	—	—	k	—	6	91
1947	Det	12(3)	34	132	3.9(18)	1	2	19	9.5(14)	0	—	—	—	—	—	—	—	—	—	—	k	—	6	149
NFL	4	41(20)	209	697	3.3(75)	11	47	588	12.5(45)	5	53	27	50.9	428	8.1(63)	5	7	—	—	—	Pkpi	—	96	1169

WESTFALL, ED Edgar Ralph, B, 5´9˝/170 lbs; Ohio Wesleyan; B11/8/1909, D3/1968, OH **[K]**

YEAR	TEAM	G (GS, POS)	RUSH	YD	AVG (LG)	TD	REC	YD	AVG (LG)	TD	PASS	COMP	PCT	YD	AVG (LG)	TD	INT	SK	YD	QBR	KPR	OTD	PTS	TAY
1932	Bos	2(0)	5	16	3.2	0	—	—	—	—	5	0	0.0	0	0.0	0	0	—	—	—	—	—	0	16
1933	Bos	3(0)	3	26	8.7	0	—	—	—	—	4	1	25.0	33	8.3(33)	1	1	—	—	—	—	—	0	8
1933	Pit	6(4)	44	61	1.4	1	4	79	19.8(60)	1	26	8	30.8	100	3.8	0	5	—	—	—	K	—	16	-35
NFL	2	11(4)	52	103	2.0	1	4	79	19.8(60)	1	35	9	25.7	133	3.8(33)	1	6	—	—	—	K	—	16	-11

WESTMORELAND, DICK Richard Carl, DB, 6´1˝/190 lbs; North Carolina A&T; B2/17/1941 Charlotte, NC **[I]** **1963**†SD-A☆14 **1964**†SD-A☆14 (LCB) **1965**†SD-A 4 **1966** Mia-A 14 (14, RCB) **1967** Mia-A★14 (14, RCB) **1968** Mia-A 11 (9, RCB) **1969** Mia-A 10 (6, rcb) **NFL** 81 (43) [7 yrs]

YEAR	TEAM	G (GS, POS)	RUSH	YD	AVG (LG)	TD	REC	YD	AVG (LG)	TD	PASS	COMP	PCT	YD	AVG (LG)	TD	INT	SK	YD	QBR	KPR	OTD	PTS	TAY

WESTMORELAND, ERIC Eric Lebron, LB, 6´0˝/230 lbs; Tennessee; 2001: Jax, rnd 3; B3/11/1977 Jasper, TN **2001** Jax 11 (2) **2002** Jax 15 (2) **2003** Jax 2 (0) **2004** Cle 16 (0) **NFL** 44 (4) [4 yrs]

WESTON, JEFF Jeffrey Graham, T-DT, 6´5˝/259 lbs; Notre Dame; 1979: Mia, rnd 9; B4/10/1956 Jersey City, NJ **1979** NYG 16 **1980** NYG 6 (3) **1981**†NYG 14 (5, lt) **1982** NYG 1 (1) **NFL** 37 (9) [4 yrs]

WESTON, RHONDY Rhondy, DE, 6´5˝/274 lbs; Florida; 1989: Dal, rnd 3; B6/7/1966 Belle Glade, FL **1989** TB 12 (2)

WETNIGHT, RYAN Ryan Scott, TE, 6´2˝/235 lbs; Stanford; B11/5/1970 Fresno, CA

YEAR	TEAM	G (GS, POS)	RUSH	YD	AVG (LG)	TD	REC	YD	AVG (LG)	TD	PASS	COMP	PCT	YD	AVG (LG)	TD	INT	SK	YD	QBR	KPR	OTD	PTS	TAY
1993	ChiB	10(1)	—	—	—	—	9	93	10.3(25)	1	—	—	—	—	—	—	—	—	—	—	—	—	6	52
1994	†ChiB	11(0)	—	—	—	—	11	104	9.5(19)	1	—	—	—	—	—	—	—	—	—	—	—	—	6	57
1995	ChiB	12(2)	—	—	—	—	24	193	8.0(22)	2	—	—	—	—	—	—	—	—	—	—	—	—	12	107
1996	ChiB	11(5, te)	—	—	—	—	21	223	10.6(38)	1	—	—	—	—	—	—	—	—	—	—	—	—	6	117
1997	ChiB	16(3)	—	—	—	—	46	464	10.1(34)	1	—	—	—	—	—	—	—	—	—	—	k	—	6	231
1998	ChiB	15(3)	—	—	—	—	23	168	7.3(30)	2	—	—	—	—	—	—	—	—	—	—	—	—	12	94
1999	ChiB	16(4)	—	—	—	—	38	277	7.3(22)	1	—	—	—	—	—	—	—	—	—	—	—	—	6	144
2000	GB	10(0)	—	—	—	—	3	20	6.7(9)	0	—	—	—	—	—	—	—	—	—	—	k	—	0	-5
NFL	8	101(18)	—	—	—	—	175	1542	8.8(38)	9	—	—	—	—	—	—	—	—	—	—	k	—	54	795

WETOSKA, BOB Robert Stephen, T-G-C, 6´3˝/240 lbs; Notre Dame; 1959: Was, rnd 5; B8/22/1937 Minneapolis, MN **1960** ChiB 12 (rt) **1961** ChiB 14 **1962** ChiB 14 **1963**†ChiB☆14 (RT) **1964** ChiB☆14 (RT) **1965** ChiB☆14 (14, RT) **1966** ChiB 14 (14, RT) **1967** ChiB 12 (11, RT) **1968** ChiB 14 (RT) **1969** ChiB 6 **NFL** 128 (39) [10 yrs]

WETTERLUND, CHET Chester Jerome, TB-DB, 6´2˝/185 lbs; Illinois Wesleyan; 1942: ChiC, rnd 9; B3/19/1918 Chicago, IL, D9/5/1944 offshore, NJ

YEAR	TEAM	G (GS, POS)	RUSH	YD	AVG (LG)	TD	REC	YD	AVG (LG)	TD	PASS	COMP	PCT	YD	AVG (LG)	TD	INT	SK	YD	QBR	KPR	OTD	PTS	TAY
1942	Det	6(3)	23	6	0.3(12)	0	—	—	—	—	44	13	29.5	230	5.2(51)	0	10	—	—	—	Pkpi	—	0	-259

WETTSTEIN, MAX Max Elbert, TE, 6´3˝/225 lbs; Florida State; B7/3/1944 Leesburg, FL **1966** Den-A 2

WETZ, HARLAN Harlan Henry, T, 6´5˝/265 lbs; Texas; 1947: Bkn-A, rnd 5/ChiB, rnd 6; B9/15/1925 New Braunfels, TX, D11/14/1983 San Antonio, TX **1947** Bkn-A 11 (0)

WETZEL, BUZZ Damon Henry, FB-LB, 5´10˝/190 lbs; Ohio State; B11/7/1910 Roseville, OH, D10/15/1985 El Paso, TX

YEAR	TEAM	G (GS, POS)	RUSH	YD	AVG (LG)	TD	REC	YD	AVG (LG)	TD	PASS	COMP	PCT	YD	AVG (LG)	TD	INT	SK	YD	QBR	KPR	OTD	PTS	TAY
1935	ChiB	1(0)	3	0	0.0	0	—	—	—	—	—	—	—	—	—	—	—	—	—	—	—	—	0	0
1935	Pit	9(5, fb)	19	41	2.2	1	4	18	4.5	0	8	2	25.0	21	2.6	0	1	—	—	—	—	—	6	31
NFL	1	10(5)	22	41	1.9	1	4	18	4.5	0	8	2	25.0	21	2.6	0	1	—	—	—	—	—	6	31

WETZEL, MARTY William Martin, LB, 6´3˝/235 lbs; Tulane; 1981: NYJ, rnd 10; B1/29/1958 New Orleans, LA **1981** NYJ 5 (0)

WETZEL, RON Ronald Joseph, TE, 6´5˝/242 lbs; Arizona State; 1983: KC, rnd 4; B11/10/1960 Pittsburgh, PA **1983** KC 16 (0)

WEXLER, BILL William W., C, 5´9˝/170 lbs; NYU; B12/25/1904, D12/1983 Loch Sheldrake, NY **1930** SI 1 (0)

WHALEN, BILL William, C-T-G, 5´7˝/165 lbs; none; B9/11/1900, D1/1975 Chicago, IL **1920** ChiC 6 (2) **1922** ChiC 3 (1) **1923** ChiC 1 (1) **1924** ChiC 1 (1) **NFL** 11 (5) [4 yrs]

WHALEN, JAMES James Patrick, TE, 6´2˝/244 lbs; Kentucky; 2000: TB, rnd 5; B9/11/1977 Portland, OR **2000** Dal 3 (0) **2003** Dal 7 (0)

YEAR	TEAM	G (GS, POS)	RUSH	YD	AVG (LG)	TD	REC	YD	AVG (LG)	TD	PASS	COMP	PCT	YD	AVG (LG)	TD	INT	SK	YD	QBR	KPR	OTD	PTS	TAY
2002	Dal	16(6, te)	—	—	—	—	17	152	8.9(33)	0	—	—	—	—	—	—	—	—	—	—	—	—	0	76
NFL	3	26(6)	—	—	—	—	17	152	8.9(33)	0	—	—	—	—	—	—	—	—	—	—	—	—	0	76

WHALEN, JERRY Gerald Cornelius, C-G, 6´1˝/235 lbs; Canisius; B4/23/1928 Buffalo, NY, D11/1973 Buffalo, NY **1948**†Buf-A 7 (0)

WHALEN, JIM James Francis, TE, 6´2˝/210 lbs; Boston College; 1965: Bos, rnd 3/Min, rnd 4; B5/20/1943 Cambridge, MA

YEAR	TEAM	G (GS, POS)	RUSH	YD	AVG (LG)	TD	REC	YD	AVG (LG)	TD	PASS	COMP	PCT	YD	AVG (LG)	TD	INT	SK	YD	QBR	KPR	OTD	PTS	TAY
1965	Bos-A	14(TE)	—	—	—	—	22	381	17.3(67)	0	—	—	—	—	—	—	—	—	—	—	—	—	0	191
1966	Bos-A	14(TE)	—	—	—	—	29	502	17.3(45)	4	—	—	—	—	—	—	—	—	—	—	—	—	24	271
1967	Bos-A	14(TE)	—	—	—	—	39	651	16.7(41)	5	—	—	—	—	—	—	—	—	—	—	—	—	30	351
1968	Bos-A☆	14(13, TE)	1	0	0.0(0)	0	47	718	15.3(87)	7	—	—	—	—	—	—	—	—	—	—	—	—	42	394
1969	Bos-A	14(11, TE)	—	—	—	—	16	235	14.7(47)	1	—	—	—	—	—	—	—	—	—	—	—	—	6	123
1970	Den	14(13, TE)	—	—	—	—	36	503	14.0(34)	3	—	—	—	—	—	—	—	—	—	—	—	—	18	267
1971	Den	3(2)	—	—	—	—	7	124	17.7(41)	0	—	—	—	—	—	—	—	—	—	—	—	—	0	62
1971	Phi	2	—	—	—	—	1	41	41.0(41)	0	—	—	—	—	—	—	—	—	—	—	—	—	0	21
NFL	7	89(39)	1	0	0.0	0	197	3155	16.0(87)	20	—	—	—	—	—	—	—	—	—	—	—	—	120	1678

WHALEY, BEN Benjamin Franklyn, G, 5´11˝/210 lbs; Virginia State; B10/14/1926 Richmond, VA **1949** LAD-A 3 (0)

WHAM, TOM Thomas Arthur, DE-E, 6´2˝/217 lbs; Furman; 1949: ChiC, rnd 5/ChiH-A, rnd 13; B11/22/1923 Greenville, SC **1950** ChiC☆11 (RDE) **1951** ChiC✧12

YEAR	TEAM	G (GS, POS)	RUSH	YD	AVG (LG)	TD	REC	YD	AVG (LG)	TD	PASS	COMP	PCT	YD	AVG (LG)	TD	INT	SK	YD	QBR	KPR	OTD	PTS	TAY
1949	ChiC	12(1)	—	—	—	—	1	11	11.0(11)	0	—	—	—	—	—	—	—	—	—	—	i	1	6	57
NFL	3	35(1)	—	—	—	—	1	11	11.0(11)	0	—	—	—	—	—	—	—	—	—	—	ki	2	12	37

WHARTON, HOGAN Robert Glen, G, 6´2˝/250 lbs; Houston; 1958: SF, rnd 11; B12/13/1935 Hood County, TX **1960**†Hou-A 14 (RG) **1961**†Hou-A 14 (RG) **1962**†Hou-A 14 (RG) **1963** Hou-A 14 (RG) **NFL** 56 [4 yrs]

WHARTON, TRAVELLE Travelle, T-G, 6´4˝/300 lbs; South Carolina; 2004: Car, rnd 3; B5/19/1981 Greenville, SC **2004** Car 11 (11, LG) **2005**†Car 16 (16, LT) **NFL** 27 (27) [2 yrs]

WHATLEY, JIM James William, T-DE-E, 6´5˝/223 lbs; Alabama; B3/11/1913 Tuscaloosa, AL, D5/31/2001 Athens, GA **1936** Bkn 11 (2) **1937** Bkn 11 (7, LT) **1938** Bkn 11 (1) **NFL** 33 (10) [3 yrs]

WHEAT, WARREN Warren, G, 6´6˝/274 lbs; Brigham Young; 1989: LARm, rnd 8; B5/13/1967 Phoenix, AZ **1989** Sea 2 (0) **1991** Sea 14 (7, LG) **NFL** 16 (7) [2 yrs]

WHEATLEY, AUSTIN Austin, TE, 6´5˝/254 lbs; Iowa; 2000: NO, rnd 5; B11/16/1977 Milan, IL **2000** NO 4 (0)

WHEATLEY, TYRONE Tyrone Anthony, RB, 6´0˝/235 lbs; Michigan; 1995: NYG, rnd 1; B1/19/1972 Inkster, MI

YEAR	TEAM	G (GS, POS)	RUSH	YD	AVG (LG)	TD	REC	YD	AVG (LG)	TD	PASS	COMP	PCT	YD	AVG (LG)	TD	INT	SK	YD	QBR	KPR	OTD	PTS	TAY
1995	NYG	13(1)	78	245	3.1(19)	3	5	27	5.4(16)	0	—	—	—	—	—	—	—	—	—	—	k	—	18	325
1996	NYG	14(0)	112	400	3.6(37)	1	12	51	4.3(13)	2	1	1	100.0	24	24.0(24)	1	0	—	—	—	k	—	18	621
1997	NYG	14(7, RB)	152	583	3.8(38)	4	16	140	8.8(27)	0	—	—	—	—	—	—	—	—	—	—	—	—	24	693
1998	NYG	5(0)	14	52	3.7(15)	0	—	—	—	—	—	—	—	—	—	—	—	—	—	—	k	—	0	53
1999	Oak	16(9, RB)	242	936	3.9(30)	8	21	196	9.3(28)	3	—	—	—	—	—	—	—	—	—	—	—	—	66	1129
2000	†Oak	14(13, RB)	232	1046	4.5(80)	9	20	156	7.8(17)	1	—	—	—	—	—	—	—	—	—	—	—	—	60	1219
2001	†Oak	11(3)	88	276	3.1(22)	5	12	61	5.1(11)	1	—	—	—	—	—	—	—	—	—	—	—	—	36	362
2002	†Oak	14(0)	108	419	3.9(36)	2	12	71	5.9(17)	0	—	—	—	—	—	—	—	—	—	—	—	—	12	475
2003	Oak	15(5, rb)	159	678	4.3(41)	4	12	120	10.0(25)	0	—	—	—	—	—	—	—	—	—	—	—	—	24	778
2004	Oak	8(7, RB)	85	327	3.8(60)	4	15	78	5.2(20)	0	—	—	—	—	—	—	—	—	—	—	—	—	24	406
NFL	10	124(45)	1270	4962	3.9(80)	40	125	900	7.2(28)	7	1	1	100.0	24	24.0(24)	1	0	—	—	—	k	—	282	6059

WHEATON, KENNY Kenneth Tyron, DB, 5´10˝/195 lbs; Oregon; 1997: Dal, rnd 3; B3/8/1975 Phoenix, AZ **1997** Dal 2 (0) **1998** Dal 15 (1) **1999** Dal 5 (0) **NFL** 22 (1) [3 yrs]

WHEELER, COWBOY Kyle, E, 5´9˝/180 lbs; Ripon; B4/1898 Stiles Township, WI, deceased **1921** GB 3 (0) **1922** GB 9 (5, le) **1923** GB 10 (5, LE), 6 **NFL** 22 (10) [3 yrs]

WHEELER, DAMEN Damen Keoki, DB, 5´9˝/170 lbs; Colorado; 2000: SD, rnd 6; B9/3/1977 Sacramento, CA **2001** Jax 5 (0)

WHEELER, DWIGHT Dwight, T-C-G, 6´3˝/269 lbs; Tennessee State; 1978: NE, rnd 4; B1/13/1955 Memphis, TN **1978** NE 2 **1979** NE 13 (10, LT) **1980** NE 16 (16, LT) **1981** NE 16 (11, LT) **1982**†NE 9 (0) **1983** NE 16 (3) **1984** LARd 4 (0) **1987** SD 3 (3) **1987** LARd 4 (1) **1988** LARd 8 (0) **NFL** 91 (44) [9 yrs]

WHEELER, ERNIE Ernest Martin, DB-TB, 6´1˝/190 lbs; North Dakota State; 1939: Pit, rnd 5; B1/28/1915 Fargo, ND, D6/18/1982 Detroit Lakes, MN

YEAR	TEAM	G (GS, POS)	RUSH	YD	AVG (LG)	TD	REC	YD	AVG (LG)	TD	PASS	COMP	PCT	YD	AVG (LG)	TD	INT	SK	YD	QBR	KPR	OTD	PTS	TAY
1939	Pit	5(3)	15	8	0.5	0	—	—	—	—	13	3	23.1	59	4.5(30)	1	6	—	—	—	P	—	0	-198
1939	ChiC	2(0)	2	-8	-4.0	0	—	—	—	—	4	2	50.0	35	8.8	0	1	—	—	—	—	—	0	-31
1942	ChiC	3(0)	—	—	—	—	—	—	—	—	—	—	—	—	—	—	—	—	—	—	P	—	0	0
NFL	2	10(3)	17	0	0.0	0	—	—	—	—	17	5	29.4	94	5.5(30)	1	7	—	—	—	P	—	0	-228

WHEELER, LEONARD Leonard Tyrone, DB, 6´0˝/192 lbs; Mississippi; Troy State; 1992: Cin, rnd 3; B1/15/1969 Toccoa, GA **1992** Cin 16 (2) **1993** Cin 16 (3) **1995** Cin 16 (1) **1996** Cin 13 (0) **1997**†Min 15 (0) **1998** Car 16 (0) **NFL** 92 (6) [6 yrs]

WHEELER, MANCH Machester Haynes, QB, 6´1˝/190 lbs; Maine; B3/2/1939 Augusta, ME

YEAR	TEAM	G (GS, POS)	RUSH	YD	AVG (LG)	TD	REC	YD	AVG (LG)	TD	PASS	COMP	PCT	YD	AVG (LG)	TD	INT	SK	YD	QBR	KPR	OTD	PTS	TAY
1962	Buf-A	4	3	7	2.3(7)	0	—	—	—	—	—	—	—	—	—	—	—	—	—	—	—	—	0	7

WHEELER, MARK Mark Anthony, DT-NT, 6´3˝/285 lbs; Texas A&M; 1992: TB, rnd 3; B4/1/1970 San Marcos, TX **1992** TB 16 (16, LDT) **1993** TB 10 (10, LDT) **1994** TB 15 (8, ldt) **1995** TB 14 (12, LDT) **1996**†NE 16 (15, LDT) **1997**†NE 14 (14, LDT) **1998**†NE 10 (2) **1999** Phi 13 (0) **NFL** 108 (77) [8 yrs]

YEAR	TEAM	G(GS, POS)	RUSH	YD	AVG(LG)	TD	REC	YD	AVG(LG)	TD	PASS	COMP	PCT	YD	AVG(LG)	TD	INT	SK	YD	QBR	KPR	OTD	PTS	TAY

WHEELER, MARK   Mark William, TE, 6´2˝/232 lbs; Kentucky; B6/15/1964 Indianapolis, IN
| 1987 | Det | 3(0) | — | — | — | — | 2 | 17 | 8.5(9) | 0 | — | — | — | — | — | — | — | — | — | — | — | — | 0 | 9 |

WHEELER, RON   Ronald Wayne, TE, 6´5˝/235 lbs; Washington; B9/5/1958 Oakland, CA
| 1987 | LARd | 3(1) | — | — | — | — | 3 | 61 | 20.3(29) | 0 | — | — | — | — | — | — | — | — | — | — | — | — | 0 | 31 |

WHEELER, TED   Theodore I., G-TE, 6´3˝/245 lbs; West Texas A&M; 1967: SL, rnd 9; B9/16/1945 Detroit, MI   **1967** SL 4 **1968** SL 5 **1970** ChiB 6 **NFL** 15 [3 yrs]

WHEELER, WAYNE   Wayne B., WR, 6´2˝/185 lbs; Alabama; 1974: Chi, rnd 3; B3/28/1950 Orlando, FL
| 1974 | ChiB | 12 | — | — | — | — | 5 | 59 | 11.8(19) | 1 | — | — | — | — | — | — | — | — | — | — | — | — | 6 | 35 |

WHEELWRIGHT, ERNIE   Ernest, RB, 6´3˝/235 lbs; Southern Illinois; B11/28/1939 Columbus, OH, D5/1/2001 Las Vegas, NV
1964	NYG	11(FB)	100	402	4.0(26)	0	14	204	14.6(33)	3	—	—	—	—	—	—	—	—	—	—	—	—	18	519
1965	NYG	13	24	96	4.0(16)	0	2	17	8.5(12)	0	—	—	—	—	—	—	—	—	—	—	—	—	0	105
1966	Atl	14(FB)	121	458	3.8(65)	3	15	137	9.1(35)	3	—	—	—	—	—	—	—	—	—	—	—	—	36	572
1967	Atl	3	21	43	2.0(6)	1	4	46	11.5(30)	0	—	—	—	—	—	—	—	—	—	—	—	—	6	76
1967	NO	9(HB)	59	198	3.4(13)	0	9	61	6.8(18)	0	—	—	—	—	—	—	—	—	—	—	—	—	0	229
1968	NO	12	21	99	4.7(15)	1	1	-9	-9.0(-9)	0	—	—	—	—	—	—	—	—	—	—	—	—	6	105
1969	NO	13	25	85	3.4(17)	4	9	68	8.5(20)	1	—	—	—	—	—	—	—	—	—	—	—	—	30	164
1970	NO	4	16	45	2.8(9)	0	1	7	7.0(7)	0	—	—	—	—	—	—	—	—	—	—	—	—	0	49
NFL	7	79	387	1426	3.7(65)	9	54	531	9.8(35)	7	—	—	—	—	—	—	—	—	—	—	—	—	96	1817

WHELAN, TOM   Thomas Joseph, E-C-G, 5´10˝/180 lbs; Notre Dame; Dartmouth; Georgetown (DC); B1/3/1894 Lynn, MA, D6/26/1957 Boston, MA   **1920** Can 12 (5, re)   **1921** Cle 8 (7, RE), 6 **NFL** 20 (12) [2 yrs]

WHELAN, TOMMY   Thomas Joseph, TB-DB, 5´8˝/165 lbs; Catholic; B3/4/1911 New York, NY, D6/1974 Olney, MD   **1933** Pit 1 (0)

WHELIHAN, CRAIG   Craig Dominic, QB, 6´5˝/220 lbs; Oregon State; Pacific; 1995: SD, rnd 6; B4/15/1971 Santa Clara, CA
1997	SD	9(7, qb)	13	29	2.2(7)	0	—	—	—	—	237	118	49.8	1357	5.7(61)	6	10	21	168	58.3	—	—	0	338
1998	SD	10(7, QB)	18	38	2.1(13)	0	—	—	—	—	320	149	46.6	1803	5.6(55)	8	19	15	111	48.0	—	—	2	220
NFL	2	19(14)	31	67	2.2(13)	0	—	—	—	—	557	267	47.9	3160	5.7(61)	14	29	36	279	52.4	—	—	2	557

WHIGHAM, LARRY   Larry Jerome, DB, 6´2˝/205 lbs; Louisiana-Monroe; 1994: Sea, rnd 4; B6/23/1972 Hattiesburg, MS   **1994**†NE★16 (0) **1995** NE 16 (0) **1996**†NE 16 (1) **1997**†NE★16 (0) **1998**†NE 16 (0) **1999** NE 16 (0) **2000** NE 14 (4) **2001**†ChiB★14 (0) **2002** ChiB 16 (1) **NFL** 136 (6) [9 yrs]

WHIPPLE, RAY   Raymond Christopher, E, 5´9˝/170 lbs; Notre Dame; B11/14/1893, D12/1973 Crest Hill, IL   **1920** Det 5 (3, RE)

WHIRE, JODIE   John Joseph, FB-LB, 6´1˝/185 lbs; Georgia; B6/11/1910 Albany, GA, D2/1983 Albany, GA
| 1933 | Phi | 2(1) | 8 | 14 | 1.8 | 0 | 1 | 15 | 15.0(15) | 0 | 5 | 1 | 20.0 | 10 | 2.0(10) | 0 | 2 | — | — | — | — | — | 0 | -54 |

WHISENHUNT, KEN   Kenneth Moore, TE, 6´3˝/237 lbs; Georgia Tech; 1985: Atl, rnd 12; B2/28/1962 Atlanta, GA
1985	Atl	16(0)	1	3	3.0(3)	0	3	48	16.0(29)	0	—	—	—	—	—	—	—	—	—	—	k	—	0	0
1986	Atl	16(14, TE)	1	20	20.0(20)	0	20	184	9.2(23)	3	—	—	—	—	—	—	—	—	—	—	—	—	18	127
1987	Atl	7(7, TE)	—	—	—	—	17	145	8.5(26)	1	—	—	—	—	—	—	—	—	—	—	—	—	6	78
1988	Atl	16(15, TE)	—	—	—	—	16	174	10.9(25)	1	—	—	—	—	—	—	—	—	—	—	—	—	6	92
1990	Was	2(0)	—	—	—	—	—	—	—	—	—	—	—	—	—	—	—	—	—	—	—	—	—	—
1991	NYJ	7(2)	—	—	—	—	4	34	8.5(16)	0	—	—	—	—	—	—	—	—	—	—	—	—	0	17
1992	NYJ	10(5, te)	—	—	—	—	2	11	5.5(10)	0	—	—	—	—	—	—	—	—	—	—	—	—	0	6
NFL	7	74(43)	2	23	11.5(20)	0	62	596	9.6(29)	5	—	—	—	—	—	—	—	—	—	—	k	—	30	319

WHITAKER, BILL   William Andrew, DB, 6´0˝/182 lbs; Missouri; 1981: GB, rnd 7; B11/18/1959 Kansas City, MO   **1981** GB 16 (0) **1982**†GB 9 (0) **1983** SL 7 (0) **1984** SL 7 (0) **NFL** 39 (0) [4 yrs]

WHITAKER, CRESTON   Creston B., WR, 6´2˝/187 lbs; North Texas; B8/12/1947 Quincy, IL
| 1972 | NO | 2 | — | — | — | — | 1 | 6 | 6.0(6) | 0 | — | — | — | — | — | — | — | — | — | — | — | — | 0 | 3 |

WHITAKER, DANTA   Danta Antonio, TE, 6´4˝/252 lbs; Mississippi Valley State; 1988: NYG, rnd 7; B3/14/1964 Atlanta, GA
1990	†KC	16(3)	—	—	—	—	2	17	8.5(16)	1	—	—	—	—	—	—	—	—	—	—	p	—	6	9
1992	Min	6(2)	—	—	—	—	1	4	4.0(4)	0	—	—	—	—	—	—	—	—	—	—	—	—	0	2
1993	ChiB	5(4)	—	—	—	—	6	53	8.8(18)	0	—	—	—	—	—	—	—	—	—	—	—	—	0	27
NFL	3	27(9)	—	—	—	—	9	74	8.2(18)	1	—	—	—	—	—	—	—	—	—	—	p	—	6	37

WHITAKER, RONYELL   Ronyell Deshawn, DB, 5´9˝/196 lbs; Virginia Tech; B3/19/1979 Norfolk, VA   **2003** TB 4 (1)

WHITCOMB, FRANK   Frank E., G-T-C, 6´3˝/217 lbs; Syracuse; B12/7/1896, D8/23/1977 Fulton, NY   **1920** Roc 5 (0) **1921** Roc 3 (2) **NFL** 8 (2) [2 yrs]

WHITE, ADRIAN   Adrian Darnell, DB, 6´0˝/200 lbs; Southern Illinois; Florida; 1987: NYG, rnd 2; B4/6/1964 Orange Park, FL   **1987** NYG 6 (1) **1988** NYG 16 (0) **1989**†NYG 15 (0) **1991** NYG 13 (0) **1992** GB 15 (0) **1993** NE 5 (4) **NFL** 70 (5) [6 yrs]

WHITE, ALBERTO   Alberto Eduardo, DE, 6´3˝/260 lbs; Texas Southern; 1992: LARd, rnd 10; B4/8/1971 Miami, FL   **1994** LARd 8 (0) **1995** SL 2 (0) **1996** SL 3 (0) **NFL** 13 (0) [3 yrs]

WHITE, ALLIE   Thomas Allison, G-T, 5´11˝/212 lbs; TCU; 1939: Phi, rnd 13; B3/23/1915 Crosby, TX, D10/21/1996 Fort Worth, TX   **1939** Phi 7 (0)

WHITE, ANDRE   Andre Moses, TE, 6´3˝/225 lbs; Florida A&M; 1966: Den, rnd R10/Was, rnd 19; B10/7/1944 Winter Park, FL
1967	Den-A	14	—	—	—	—	5	87	17.4(40)	0	—	—	—	—	—	—	—	—	—	—	—	—	2	44
1968	Cin-A	3	—	—	—	—	2	18	9.0(11)	0	—	—	—	—	—	—	—	—	—	—	—	—	0	9
1968	SD-A	5	—	—	—	—	—	—	—	—	—	—	—	—	—	—	—	—	—	—	—	—	—	—
NFL	2	22	—	—	—	—	7	105	15.0(40)	0	—	—	—	—	—	—	—	—	—	—	—	—	2	53

WHITE, BOB   Robert William, HB, 5´11˝/176 lbs; Stanford; 1951: SF, rnd 16; B5/25/1929 Los Angeles, CA   **1955** Cle 8 **1955** Bal 3
1951	SF	12	8	33	4.1(9)	0	3	36	12.0(22)	0	—	—	—	—	—	—	—	—	—	—	i	—	0	57
1952	SF	12	24	33	1.4(17)	1	12	173	14.4(60)	2	—	—	—	—	—	—	—	—	—	—	—	—	18	140
NFL	3	35	32	66	2.1(17)	1	15	209	13.9(60)	2	—	—	—	—	—	—	—	—	—	—	kpi	—	18	405

WHITE, BOB   Robert Arlen, C-G, 6´5˝/272 lbs; Rhode Island; 1986: NYJ, rnd 7; B4/9/1963 Fitchburg, MA   **1987** Dal 4 (3) **1988** Dal 12 (3) **1989** Dal 8 (4) **NFL** 24 (10) [3 yrs]

WHITE, BOB   Loren Robert, FB, 6´2˝/220 lbs; Ohio State; 1960: Hou, rnd 1/Cle, rnd 8; B8/22/1938 Portsmouth, OH   **1960** Hou-A 6

WHITE, BRAD   Bradley Dee, NT-DT, 6´2˝/256 lbs; Tennessee; 1981: TB, rnd 12; B8/18/1958 Rexburg, ID   **1981**†TB 16 (0) **1982**†TB 9 (0) **1983** TB 16 (0) **1984** Ind 15 (2) **1985** Ind 16 (15, NT) **1987** Min 1 (1) **NFL** 73 (18) [6 yrs]

WHITE, BUCK   Roy Eldon, FB, 6´0˝/195 lbs; Howard Payne; Valparaiso; B2/28/1900 Brownwood, TX, D5/15/1993 San Antonio, TX   **1925** ChiB 10 (1), 18 **1927** ChiB 13 (6, fb), 12 **1928** ChiB 13 (11, FB), 18 **1929** ChiB 10 (7, fb), 12 **NFL** 46 (25), 60 [4 yrs]

WHITE, BUCKY   Robert, DB, 6´2˝/180 lbs; Lamar; B11/24/1962   **1987** Hou 3 (3)

WHITE, CHARLES   Charles Raymond, RB, 5´10˝/190 lbs; USC; 1980: Cle, rnd 1; B1/22/1958 Los Angeles, CA
1980	†Cle	14(7, rb)	86	279	3.2(16)	5	17	153	9.0(31)	1	—	—	—	—	—	—	—	—	—	—	k	—	36	416
1981	Cle	16(9, RB)	97	342	3.5(26)	1	27	219	8.1(21)	0	—	—	—	—	—	—	—	—	—	—	k	—	6	525
1982	†Cle	9(9, RB)	69	259	3.8(18)	3	34	283	8.3(36)	0	—	—	—	—	—	—	—	—	—	—	—	—	18	431
1984	Cle	10(1)	24	62	2.6(8)	0	5	29	5.8(17)	0	—	—	—	—	—	—	—	—	—	—	k	—	0	82
1985	†LARm	16(0)	70	310	4.4(32)	3	1	12	12.0(12)	0	—	—	—	—	—	—	—	—	—	—	kp	—	18	386
1986	†LARm	16(0)	22	126	5.7(19)	0	1	7	7.0(7)	0	—	—	—	—	—	—	—	—	—	—	k	—	0	166
1987	LARm★	15(12, RB)	**324**	**1374**	4.2(58)	11	23	121	5.3(20)	0	—	—	—	—	—	—	—	—	—	—	k	—	66	**1573**
1988	†LARm	12(3)	88	323	3.7(13)	0	6	36	6.0(18)	0	—	—	—	—	—	—	—	—	—	—	k	—	0	348
NFL	8	108(41)	780	3075	3.9(58)	23	114	860	7.5(36)	1	—	—	—	—	—	—	—	—	—	—	kp	—	144	3924

WHITE, CHARLIE   Charles Frankie, RB, 6´0˝/222 lbs; Bethune-Cookman; 1977: NYJ, rnd 7; B8/31/1953 Suffern, NY
1977	NYJ	13(3)	50	151	3.0(27)	1	2	5	2.5(3)	1	—	—	—	—	—	—	—	—	—	—	—	—	12	169
1978	TB	7(1)	11	42	3.8(8)	0	2	31	15.5(18)	0	—	—	—	—	—	—	—	—	—	—	—	—	0	58
NFL	2	20(4)	61	193	3.2(27)	1	4	36	9.0(18)	1	—	—	—	—	—	—	—	—	—	—	—	—	12	226

YEAR	TEAM	G (GS, POS)	RUSH	YD	AVG(LG)	TD	REC	YD	AVG(LG)	TD	PASS	COMP	PCT	YD	AVG(LG)	TD	INT	SK	YD	QBR	KPR	OTD	PTS	TAY

WHITE, CHRIS Robert Christopher, DB, 6´3˝/200 lbs; Tennessee; B3/1/1962 Cleveland, OH **1987** Sea 1 (0)

WHITE, CHRIS Christopher James, DE, 6´3˝/285 lbs; Southern (LA); 1999: Jax, rnd 7; B9/28/1976 Shreveport, LA **2000** Atl 5 (0)

WHITE, CHRIS Chris LaBryant, C, 6´2˝/285 lbs; Southern Mississippi; B2/8/1983 Winona, MS **2005** GB 1 (0)

WHITE, CLAYTON Clayton, LB, 5´11˝/225 lbs; North Carolina State; B12/2/1977 Dunn, NC **2001** NYG 16 (0)

WHITE, CRAIG Craig C., WR, 6´1˝/194 lbs; Missouri; 1984: Buf, rnd 11; B10/8/1961 St. Joseph, MO

YEAR	TEAM	G (GS, POS)	RUSH	YD	AVG(LG)	TD	REC	YD	AVG(LG)	TD	KPR	OTD	PTS	TAY
1984	Buf	14(0)	—	—	—		4	28	7.0(11)	—	k	—	0	4

WHITE, DANNY Wilford Daniel, QB-P, 6´2˝/193 lbs; Arizona State; 1974: Dal, rnd 3; B2/9/1952 Mesa, AZ [P]

YEAR	TEAM	G (GS, POS)	RUSH	YD	AVG(LG)	TD	REC	YD	AVG(LG)	TD	PASS	COMP	PCT	YD	AVG(LG)	TD	INT	SK	YD	QBR	KPR	OTD	PTS	TAY
1976	†Dal	14	6	17	2.8(14)	0	—	—	—		20	13	65.0	213	10.6(56)	2	2	1	15	—	P	—	0	54
1977	†Dal	14	1	-2	-2.0(-2)	0	—	—	—		10	4	40.0	35	3.5(12)	0	1	2	15	—	P	—	0	-25
1978	†Dal	16	5	7	1.4(4)	0	—	—	—		34	20	58.8	215	6.3(35)	0	1	1	10	—	P	—	0	75
1979	†Dal☆	16	1	25	25.0(25)	0	—	—	—		39	19	48.7	267	6.8(45)	1	2	4	46	—	P	—	0	84
1980	†Dal	16(16, QB)	27	114	4.2(48)	1	1	-9	-9.0(-9)	0	436	260	59.6	3287	7.5(58)	28	25	30	252	80.7	P	—	6	903
1981	†Dal☆	16(15, QB)	38	104	2.7(17)	0	—	—	—		391	223	57.0	3098	7.9(73)	22	13	30	234	87.5	P	—	0	1243
1982	†Dal★	9(9, QB)	17	91	5.4(21)	0	—	—	—		247	156	63.2	2079	**8.4**(49)	16	12	25	264	91.1	P	—	0	731
1983	†Dal	16(16, QB)	18	31	1.7(22)	4	1	15	15.0(15)	0	**533**	**334**	62.7	3980	7.5(80)	29	23	37	314	85.6	P	—	30	1299
1984	†Dal	14(6, qb)	6	21	3.5(8)	0	—	—	—		233	126	54.1	1580	6.8(66)	11	11	26	211	71.5	P	—	0	426
1985	†Dal	14(14, QB)	22	44	2.0(21)	1	1	12	12.0(12)	1	450	267	59.3	3157	7.0(56)	21	17	30	257	80.6	P	—	12	1069
1986	Dal	7(6, qb)	8	16	2.0(10)	1	—	—	—		153	95	62.1	1157	7.6(63)	12	5	10	98	**97.9**	—	—	6	465
1987	Dal	11(9, QB)	10	14	1.4(8)	1	—	—	—		362	215	59.4	2617	7.2(43)	12	17	44	353	73.2	—	—	0	713
1988	Dal	3(0)	—	—	—		—	—	—		42	29	69.0	274	6.5(24)	1	3	5	47	—	—	—	0	22
NFL	13	166(91)	159	482	3.0(48)	8				2	2950	1761	59.7	21959	7.4(80)	155	132	245	2116	81.7	P	—	60	7056

WHITE, DARYL Robert Daryl, G, 6´3˝/250 lbs; Nebraska; 1974: Cin, rnd 4; B10/12/1951 Newark, NJ **1974** Det 10

WHITE, DAVID David Maurice, LB, 6´2˝/235 lbs; Nebraska; B2/27/1970 Oak Ridge, TN **1993** NE 6 (0) **1995**†Buf 15 (1) **1996**†Buf 16 (5, lolb) **NFL** 37 (6) [3 yrs]

WHITE, DEWAYNE Dewayne, DE, 6´2˝/273 lbs; Louisville; 2003: TB, rnd 2; B10/19/1979 Marbury, AL **2003** TB 12 (1) **2004** TB 16 (3) **2005**†TB 16 (1) **NFL** 44 (5) [3 yrs]

WHITE, DEZ Edward Dezmon, WR, 6´1˝/215 lbs; Georgia Tech; 2000: Chi, rnd 3; B8/23/1979 Orange Park, PA

YEAR	TEAM	G (GS, POS)	RUSH	YD	AVG(LG)	TD	REC	YD	AVG(LG)	TD	KPR	OTD	PTS	TAY
2000	ChiB	15(0)	—	—	—		10	87	8.7(25)	1		—	6	49
2001	†ChiB	14(6, WR)	—	—	—		45	428	9.5(32)	0		—	0	214
2002	ChiB	16(14, WR)	3	11	3.7(21)	0	51	656	12.9(76)	4	k	—	24	376
2003	ChiB	15(11, WR)	2	13	6.5(12)	0	49	583	11.9(49)	3		—	18	320
2004	†Atl	16(15, WR)	3	14	4.7(26)	0	30	370	12.3(54)	2		—	12	209
2005	Atl	6(4)	—	—	—		2	25	12.5(14)	1		—	6	18
NFL	6	82(50)	8	38	4.8(26)	0	187	2149	11.5(76)	11	k	—	66	1185

WHITE, DWAYNE Dwayne Allen, G-C, 6´2˝/315 lbs; Alcorn State; 1990: NYJ, rnd 7; B2/10/1967 Philadelphia, PA **1990** NYJ 11 (5, c) **1991**†NYJ 16 (16, RG)
1992 NYJ 16 (16, RG) **1993** NYJ 15 (15, RG) **1994** NYJ 16 (16, RG) **1995** SL 15 (15, RG) **1996** SL 16 (16, RG) **NFL** 105 (99) [7 yrs]

WHITE, DWIGHT Dwight Lynn, DE, 6´4˝/255 lbs; Texas A&M-Commerce; 1971: Pit, rnd 4; B7/30/1949 Hampton, VA **1971** Pit 14 (RDE) **1972**†Pit★14 (RDE) **1973**†Pit★14 (RDE)
1974†Pit★14 (RDE) **1975**†Pit 9 (RDE) **1976**†Pit★14 (RDE) **1977**†Pit 14 (14, RDE) **1978**†Pit 15 (11, RDE) **1979** Pit 11 **1980** Pit 7 (1) **NFL** 126 (40) [10 yrs]

WHITE, ED Edward Alvin, G-T, 6´1˝/269 lbs; California; 1969: Min, rnd 2; B4/4/1947 San Diego, CA **1969** Min 14 **1970**†Min 14 (7, lg) **1971**†Min 14 (14, LG)
1973†Min 14 (14, LG) **1974**†Min☆13 (13, LG) **1975**†Min★13 (11, RG) **1976**†Min☆13 (13, RG) **1977**†Min★13 (8, RG) **1978** SD 15 (15, RG) **1979**†SD★16 (16, RG)
1980†SD 16 (16, RG) **1981** SD 16 (16, RG) **1982**†SD 9 9, RG) **1983** SD 16 (16, RG) **1984** SD 15 (13, RT) **1985** SD 16 (16, LG)

YEAR	TEAM	G (GS, POS)	RUSH	YD	AVG(LG)	TD	REC	YD	AVG(LG)	TD	OTD	PTS	TAY
1972	Min	14(14, LG)	—	—	—		0	3	(3)	0	—	0	2
NFL	17	241(211)	—	—	—		0	3	(3)	0	—	0	2

WHITE, ELLERY Ellery, WB-FB, /175 lbs; none **1926** LA 8 (6, WB)

WHITE, FREEMAN Freeman, TE-LB-DB, 6´5˝/225 lbs; Nebraska; 1966: NYG, rnd 9/Den, rnd 2; B12/17/1943 Montgomery, AL **1966** NYG 14 **1967** NYG 14 **1968** NYG 14

YEAR	TEAM	G (GS, POS)	RUSH	YD	AVG(LG)	TD	REC	YD	AVG(LG)	TD	KPR	OTD	PTS	TAY
1969	NYG	13(TE)	—	—	—		29	315	10.9(23)	1		—	6	163
NFL	4	55	—	—	—		29	315	10.9(23)	1	ki	—	6	190

WHITE, GENE Eugene George, G, 6´2˝/205 lbs; Indiana; B8/3/1919 South Bend, IN, D4/24/1989 South Bend, IN **1946** Buf-A 1 (0)

WHITE, GENE Gene Carlton, DB, 6´2˝/205 lbs; Georgia; B6/21/1932 Greensboro, NC **1954** GB 9

WHITE, GENE Eugene, HB, 6´1˝/197 lbs; Florida A&M; 1962: Oak, rnd 33/1961: NYG, rnd 14; B1940

YEAR	TEAM	G (GS, POS)	RUSH	YD	AVG(LG)	TD	REC	YD	AVG(LG)	TD	OTD	PTS	TAY
1962	Oak-A	7	—	—	—		6	101	16.8(47)	1	—	8	56

WHITE, GERALD Gerald Eugene, RB, 5´11˝/223 lbs; Michigan; B12/9/1964

YEAR	TEAM	G (GS, POS)	RUSH	YD	AVG(LG)	TD	REC	YD	AVG(LG)	TD	OTD	PTS	TAY
1987	Dal	3(3)	1	-4	-4.0(-4)	0	5	46	9.2(14)	0	—	0	19

WHITE, HARVEY Harvey Talbert, QB-E, 6´1˝/191 lbs; Clemson; 1960: Bos, rnd 1; B3/3/1938

YEAR	TEAM	G (GS, POS)	RUSH	YD	AVG(LG)	TD	REC	YD	AVG(LG)	TD	PASS	COMP	PCT	YD	AVG(LG)	TD	INT	OTD	PTS	TAY
1960	Bos-A	9	5	7	1.4(5)	0	2	24	12.0(13)	0	7	3	42.9	44	6.3(23)	0	0	—	0	41

WHITE, JAMEL Jamel, RB, 5´9˝/222 lbs; South Dakota; B2/11/1978 Los Angeles, CA

YEAR	TEAM	G (GS, POS)	RUSH	YD	AVG(LG)	TD	REC	YD	AVG(LG)	TD	KPR	OTD	PTS	TAY
2000	Cle	13(0)	47	145	3.1(14)	0	13	100	7.7(25)	0	k	—	0	485
2001	Cle	16(7, rb)	126	443	3.5(51)	5	44	418	9.5(45)	1	k	—	38	761
2002	†Cle	14(6, rb)	106	470	4.4(54)	3	63	452	7.2(33)	0	k	—	18	717
2003	Cle	16(3)	70	266	3.8(23)	1	46	303	6.6(22)	1	k	—	12	405
2004	TB	7(0)	13	20	1.5(10)	0	4	17	4.3(12)	0		—	0	68
2004	Bal	6(0)	14	62	4.4(16)	0	2	4	2.0(6)	0		—	0	5
2005	Bal	5(0)	6	17	2.8(5)	0	—	—	—			—	0	5
NFL	6	77(16)	382	1423	3.7(54)	9	172	1294	7.5(45)	2	k	—	68	2504

WHITE, JAMES James Curtis, DT-NT, 6´3˝/265 lbs; Oklahoma State; 1976: Min, rnd 1; B10/26/1953 Hot Springs, AR **1976**†Min 14 **1977**†Min 14 **1978**†Min 16 (10, RDT)
1979 Min 16 (16, RDT) **1980**†Min 16 (16, RDT) **1981** Min 16 (16, NT) **1982**†Min 9 (3) **1983** Min 16 (0) **NFL** 117 (61) [8 yrs]

WHITE, JAN Jan Andre, TE, 6´2˝/216 lbs; Ohio State; 1971: Buf, rnd 2; B10/6/1948 Harrisburg, PA

YEAR	TEAM	G (GS, POS)	RUSH	YD	AVG(LG)	TD	REC	YD	AVG(LG)	TD	OTD	PTS	TAY
1971	Buf	13(TE)	—	—	—		13	130	10.0(21)	0	—	0	65
1972	Buf	14(TE)	—	—	—		12	148	12.3(18)	2	—	12	84
NFL	2	27	—	—	—		25	278	11.1(21)	2	—	12	149

WHITE, JEFF Jeffrey Charles, K-P, 5´10˝/170 lbs; Texas-El Paso; B6/10/1948 Bronxville, NY [K] **1973** NE 11

WHITE, JERIS Jeris Jerome, DB, 5´9˝/188 lbs; Hawaii; 1974: Mia, rnd 2; B9/3/1952 Fort Worth, TX **1974**†Mia 14 (5, lcb) **1976** Mia 14 (14, LCB)
1977 TB 14 (14, LCB) **1978** TB 16 (16, LCB) **1979**†TB 16 (16, LCB) **1980** Was 16 (1) **1981** Was 16 (8, lcb) **1982**†Was 9 (9, LCB) **NFL** 129 (83) [9 yrs]

WHITE, JIM James Joseph William, T-DT, 6´2˝/227 lbs; Notre Dame; B2/8/1920 Edgewater, NJ, D4/1987 Dumont, NJ **1946**†NYG☆11 (10, RT) **1947** NYG☆11 (9, RT)
1948 NYG 11 (6, LT) **1949** NYG 11 (10, LT) **1950**†NYG 11 (LT) **NFL** 55 (35) [5 yrs]

WHITE, JIM James Charles, DE, 6´4˝/256 lbs; Colorado State; 1972: NE, rnd 3; B9/5/1948 Chicago, IL **1972** NE 13 (6, lde) **1974** Hou 12 **1975** Hou 14 **1976** Sea 2
1976 Den 7 (1) **NFL** 48 (7) [4 yrs]

WHITE, JOHN John L., TE, 6´3˝/230 lbs; Texas Southern; B10/9/1935

YEAR	TEAM	G (GS, POS)	RUSH	YD	AVG(LG)	TD	REC	YD	AVG(LG)	TD	OTD	PTS	TAY
1960	Hou-A	4	—	—	—		1	18	18.0(18)	0	—	0	20
1961	†Hou-A	14(TE)	—	—	—		13	238	18.3(49)	1	—	6	124
NFL	2	18	—	—	—		14	256	18.3(49)	1	—	6	144

WHITE, JOSE Jose Cornelius, DT, 6´3˝/290 lbs; Howard; 1995: Min, rnd 7; B3/2/1973 Washington, SC **1997**†Jax 3 (0) **1998**†Jax 15 (0) **NFL** 18 (0) [2 yrs]

WHITE, LAWRENCE Lawrence, WR, 6´2˝/187 lbs; Dana; B6/3/1963 Tuscaloosa, AL **1987** ChiB 2 (0)

YEAR	TEAM	G (GS, POS)	RUSH	YD	AVG(LG)	TD	REC	YD	AVG(LG)	TD	PASS	COMP	PCT	YD	AVG(LG)	TD	INT	SK	YD	QBR	KPR	OTD	PTS	TAY

WHITE, LEE   Lee Andrew, RB, 6´2″/232 lbs; Weber State; 1968: NYJ, rnd 1; B5/9/1946 Las Vegas, NV

1968	NYJ-A	1																						
1969	NYJ-A	14	28	88	3.1(10)	0	1	-2	-2.0(-2)	0	—	—	—	—	—	—	—	—	—	—	k	—	0	77
1970	NYJ	14	70	215	3.1(16)	0	12	125	10.4(19)	1	—	—	—	—	—	—	—	—	—	—	—	—	6	283
1971	LARm	7	2	11	5.5(6)	0	—				—	—	—	—	—	—	—	—	—	—	—	—	0	11
1972	SD	8	23	75	3.3(12)	0	3	20	6.7(8)	0	—	—	—	—	—	—	—	—	—	—	—	—	0	85
NFL	5	44	123	389	3.2(16)	0	16	143	8.9(19)	1	—	—	—	—	—	—	—	—	—	—	k	—	6	456

WHITE, LEON   Thomas Leon, LB, 6´3″/240 lbs; Brigham Young; 1986: Cin, rnd 5; B10/4/1963 San Diego, CA   **1986** Cin 16 (0)   **1987** Cin 12 (0)   **1988**†Cin 16 (16, LOLB)   **1989** Cin 16 (16, LOLB)   **1990**†Cin 16 (13, LOLB)   **1991** Cin 16 (0)   **1992** LARm 13 (1)   **1993** LARm 14 (0)   **NFL** 119 (46) [8 yrs]

WHITE, LORENZO   Lorenzo Maurice, RB, 5´11″/222 lbs; Michigan State; 1988: Hou, rnd 1; B4/12/1966 Hollywood, FL

1988	†Hou	11(0)	31	115	3.7(16)	0	—				—	—	—	—	—	—	—	—	—	—	k	1	6	201
1989	†Hou	16(0)	104	349	3.4(33)	5	6	37	6.2(11)	0	—	—	—	—	—	—	—	—	—	—	k	—	30	466
1990	†Hou	16(16, RB)	168	702	4.2(22)	8	39	368	9.4(29)	4	—	—	—	—	—	—	—	—	—	—	—	—	72	986
1991	†Hou	13(0)	110	465	4.2(20)	4	27	211	7.8(20)	0	—	—	—	—	—	—	—	—	—	—	—	—	24	611
1992	†Hou✧	16(16, RB)	265	1226	4.6(44)	7	57	641	11.2(69)	1	—	—	—	—	—	—	—	—	—	—	—	—	48	1622
1993	Hou	8(8, rb)	131	465	3.5(14)	2	34	229	6.7(20)	0	—	—	—	—	—	—	—	—	—	—	—	—	12	600
1994	Hou	15(8, RB)	191	757	4.0(33)	3	21	188	9.0(41)	1	—	—	—	—	—	—	—	—	—	—	—	—	24	933
1995	Cle	12(2)	62	163	2.6(11)	1	8	64	8.0(28)	0	—	—	—	—	—	—	—	—	—	—	k	—	6	205
NFL	8	107(50)	1062	4242	4.0(44)	30	192	1738	9.1(69)	6	—	—	—	—	—	—	—	—	—	—	k	1	222	5622

WHITE, LYMAN   Lyman Dan, LB, 6´0″/217 lbs; LSU; 1981: Atl, rnd 2; B1/3/1959 Lafayette, LA   **1981** Atl 16 (1)   **1982** Atl 2 (0)   **NFL** 18 (1) [2 yrs]

WHITE, MAC   Wilbur McKee, E-WB, 6´0″/178 lbs; Marietta; B2/22/1890 Hillsboro, OH, D12/1973 Hillsboro, OH   **1922** Tol 7 (2)   **1923** Tol 8 (6, LE)   **NFL** 15 (8) [2 yrs]

WHITE, MARSH   Marshall Reginald, RB, 6´2″/220 lbs; Arkansas; 1975: NYG, rnd 12; B4/1/1953 Bonham, TX

1975	NYG	14	17	90	5.3(14)	1	3	15	5.0(15)	0	—	—	—	—	—	—	—	—	—	—	—	—	6	108
1976	NYG	14	69	223	3.2(29)	1	2	7	3.5(4)	0	—	—	—	—	—	—	—	—	—	—	—	—	6	237
NFL	2	28	86	313	3.6(29)	2	5	22	4.4(15)	0	—	—	—	—	—	—	—	—	—	—	—	12	344

WHITE, MIKE   James Michael, DT-DE-NT, 6´5″/266 lbs; Albany State (GA); 1979: Cin, rnd 4; B8/11/1957 Augusta, GA   **1979** Cin 16   **1980** Cin 15 (1)   **1981** Sea 15 (7, RDT)   **1982** Sea 5 (0)   **NFL** 51 (8) [4 yrs]

WHITE, PAUL   Paul Grover, HB-DB, 6´1″/183 lbs; Michigan; 1944: Det, rnd 11; B11/13/1921, D6/3/1974 Duluth, GA

| 1947 | †Pit | 11(1) | 22 | 85 | 3.9(52) | 1 | 2 | 55 | 27.5(55) | 0 | 1 | 1 | 33.3 | 21 | 7.0(21) | 0 | 0 | — | — | — | kpi | — | 6 | 175 |

WHITE, PAUL   Paul Nathaniel, RB, 6´0″/200 lbs; Texas-El Paso; 1970: SL, rnd 9; B9/17/1948 San Antonio, TX, D6/23/2001 San Antonio, TX   **1970** SL 5

| 1971 | SL | 6 | 1 | 3 | 3.0(3) | 0 | — | | | | — | — | — | — | — | — | — | — | — | — | — | — | 0 | 3 |
| NFL | 2 | 11 | 1 | 3 | 3.0(3) | 0 | — | | | | — | — | — | — | — | — | — | — | — | — | k | — | 0 | 23 |

WHITE, PHIL   Phillip Elmer, B, 6´2″/210 lbs; Oklahoma; B5/17/1900 Enid, OK, D5/29/1982 Oklahoma State, OK **[K]**   **1925** KC 8 (8, FB), 16   **1925** NYG 3 (1), 18   **1927** NYG 12 (3), 19   **NFL** 23 (12), 53 [2 yrs]

WHITE, RALPH   Ralph S., E, 5´9″/175 lbs; NYU; B11/18/1902, D3/1982 Riverhead, NY   **1927** Buf 3 (1)

WHITE, RANDY   Randy Lee 'The Manster', DT-LB-DE, 6´4″/257 lbs; Maryland; 1975: Dal, rnd 1; B1/15/1953 Wilmington, DE; HOF 1994 **[S]**   **1975**†Dal 14   **1976**†Dal 14   **1977**†Dal★14 (RDT)   **1978**†Dal★16 (RDT)   **1979**†Dal★15 (RDT)   **1980**†Dal★16 (16, RDT)   **1981**†Dal★16 (16, RDT)   **1982**†Dal★9 (9, RDT)   **1983**†Dal★16 (16, RDT)   **1984** Dal★16 (16, RDT)   **1985**†Dal★16 (16, RDT)   **1986** Dal 16 (16, RDT)   **1987** Dal 15 (14, RDT)   **1988** Dal 16 (1)   **NFL** 209 (120) [14 yrs]

WHITE, RAY   Raymond C., LB, 6´1″/227 lbs; Syracuse; 1971: SD, rnd 5; B5/18/1949 Weymouth, MA   **1971** SD 14   **1972** SD 4   **1975**†SL 14 (1)   **1976** SL 6 (5, mlb)   **NFL** 38 (6) [4 yrs]

WHITE, REGGIE   Reginald Howard 'The Minister of Defense', DE-DT, 6´5″/291 lbs; Tennessee; 1984: Phi, rnd S1; B12/19/1961 Chattanooga, TN, D12/26/2004 Huntersville, NC; HOF 2006 **[S]**   **1985** Phi 13 (12, LDE)   **1986**†Phi★16 (16, RDT/lde)   **1987** Phi★12 (12, LDE)   **1988**†Phi★16 (16, LDE)   **1989**†Phi★16 (16, LDE)   **1990**†Phi★16 (16, LDE)   **1991** Phi★16 (16, LDE)   **1992**†Phi★16 (16, LDE)   **1993**†GB★16 (16, LDE)   **1994**†GB★16 (15, LDE)   **1995**†GB★15 (13, LDE)   **1996**†GB★16 (16, LDE)   **1997**†GB★16 (16, LDE)   **1998**†GB★16 (16, LDE)   **2000** Car 16 (16, LDE)   **NFL** 232 (228) [15 yrs]

WHITE, REGGIE   Reggie, RB, 6´0″/223 lbs; Oklahoma State; B7/11/1979 Liberty, TX   **2001** Jax 5 (0)

WHITE, REGGIE   Reginald Eugene, NT-DT, 6´4″/296 lbs; Oklahoma State; North Carolina A&T; 1992: SD, rnd 6; B3/22/1970 Baltimore, MD   **1992** SD 3 (0)   **1993** SD 8 (0)   **1994**†SD 11 (0)   **1995** NE 16 (6, NT)   **NFL** 38 (6) [4 yrs]

WHITE, ROBB   Robb Steven, DE-NT, 6´4″/270 lbs; South Dakota; B5/26/1965 Aberdeen, SD   **1988** NYG 1 (0)   **1989**†NYG 15 (0)   **1990** TB 7 (1)   **NFL** 23 (1) [3 yrs]

WHITE, ROBERT   Robert, E, /150 lbs; none; B9/28/1903, D7/1982 Louisville, KY   **1923** Lou 2 (1)

WHITE, RODDY   Sharod L., WR, 6´1″/201 lbs; Alabama-Birmingham; 2005: Atl, rnd 1; B11/2/1981 James Island, SC

| 2005 | Atl | 16(8, WR) | 4 | 12 | 3.0(16) | 0 | 29 | 446 | 15.4(54) | 3 | — | — | — | — | — | — | — | — | — | — | — | — | 18 | 250 |

WHITE, RUSSELL   Russell Lamar, RB, 5´11″/216 lbs; California; 1993: LARm, rnd 3; B12/15/1970 Pacoima, CA

| 1993 | LARm | 5(0) | 2 | 10 | 5.0(5) | 0 | — | | | | — | — | — | — | — | — | — | — | — | — | k | — | 0 | 12 |

WHITE, SAMMY   Samuel, WR, 5´11″/190 lbs; Grambling State; 1976: Min, rnd 2; B3/16/1954 Winnsboro, LA

1976	†Min★	14(14, WR)	5	-10	-2.0(6)	0	51	906	17.8(56)	10	—	—	—	—	—	—	—	—	—	—	kp	—	60	561
1977	†Min★	14(14, WR)	—	—	—		41	760	18.5(69)	9	—	—	—	—	—	—	—	—	—	—	k	—	54	433
1978	†Min☆	16(16, WR)	5	30	6.0(16)	0	53	741	14.0(33)	9	—	—	—	—	—	—	—	—	—	—	kp	—	54	446
1979	Min	15(15, WR)	1	6	6.0(6)	0	42	715	17.0(55)	4	—	—	—	—	—	—	—	—	—	—	—	—	24	384
1980	†Min	16(16, WR)	4	65	16.3(45)	0	53	887	16.7(50)	5	—	—	—	—	—	—	—	—	—	—	—	—	30	534
1981	Min	16(16, WR)	2	-1	-0.5(1)	0	66	1001	15.2(53)	3	—	—	—	—	—	—	—	—	—	—	—	—	18	510
1982	†Min	7(6, WR)	—	—	—		29	503	17.3(65)	5	—	—	—	—	—	—	—	—	—	—	p	—	30	277
1983	Min	11(10, WR)	1	7	7.0(7)	0	29	412	14.2(43)	4	—	—	—	—	—	—	—	—	—	—	—	—	24	233
1984	Min	13(11, WR)	—	—	—		21	399	19.0(47)	1	—	—	—	—	—	—	—	—	—	—	—	—	6	205
1985	Min	6(0)	—	—	—		8	76	9.5(15)	0	—	—	—	—	—	—	—	—	—	—	—	—	0	38
NFL	10	128(118)	18	97	5.4(45)	0	393	6400	16.3(69)	50	—	—	—	—	—	—	—	—	—	—	kp	—	300	3618

WHITE, SHELDON   Sheldon Darnell, DB, 5´11″/188 lbs; Miami (OH); 1988: NYG, rnd 3; B3/1/1965 Dayton, OH   **1988** NYG 16 (5, lcb)   **1989**†NYG 16 (1)   **1990** Det 3 (0)   **1991**†Det 16 (0)   **1992** Det 13 (0)   **1993** Cin 8 (1)   **NFL** 72 (7) [6 yrs]

WHITE, SHERMAN   Sherman Eugene, DE, 6´5″/250 lbs; California; 1972: Cin, rnd 1; B10/6/1948 Mamchester, NH   **1972** Cin 13 (13, RDE)   **1973**†Cin 13 (13, RDE)   **1974** Cin 12 (12, RDE)   **1975**†Cin 14 (14, RDE)   **1976** Buf 13 (13, RDE)   **1977** Buf 14 (14, RDE)   **1978** Buf 16 (16, RDE)   **1979** Buf 15 (9, RDE)   **1980**†Buf 15 (13, RDE)   **1981** Buf 16 (16, RDE)   **1982** Buf 9 (9, RDE)   **1983** Buf 8 (8, RDE)   **NFL** 158 (150) [12 yrs]

WHITE, STAN   Stanley Ray, LB, 6´1″/225 lbs; Ohio State; 1972: Bal, rnd 17; B10/24/1949 Dover, OH **[I]**   **1972** Bal 14   **1973** Bal 14 (14, RLB)   **1974** Bal 14 (14, RLB)   **1975**†Bal 14 (14, RLB)   **1976**†Bal 14 (14, RLB)   **1977**†Bal★14 (14, RLB)   **1978** Bal 12 (12, RLB)   **1980** Det 16 (16, RLB)   **1981** Det 16 (16, RLB)   **1982**†Det 9 (9, RLB)

| 1979 | Bal | 16(16, RLB) | 1 | 3 | 3.0(3) | 0 | — | | | | — | — | — | — | — | — | — | — | — | — | i | — | 0 | 9 |
| NFL | 11 | 153(139) | 1 | 3 | 3.0(3) | 0 | — | | | | — | — | — | — | — | — | — | — | — | — | ki | — | 2 | 12 | 283 |

WHITE, STEVE   Stephen Gregory, DE, 6´2″/256 lbs; Tennessee; 1996: Phi, rnd 6; B10/25/1973 Memphis, TN   **1996** TB 4 (0)   **1997**†TB 15 (1)   **1998** TB 16 (0)   **1999**†TB 13 (13, RDE)   **2000**†TB 15 (0)   **2001**†TB 16 (1)   **2002**†NYJ 15 (0)   **NFL** 94 (15) [7 yrs]

WHITE, TARZAN   Arthur Pershing, G, 5´9″/217 lbs; Alabama; 1937: NYG, rnd 2; B12/6/1915 Lockhart, AL, D1/23/1996 Gaylesville, AL   **1937** NYG 11 (2)   **1938**†NYG✧10 (2)   **1939** NYG 6 (3)   **1940** ChiC 10 (4)   **1941** ChiC 8 (8, LG)   **1945** NYG 5 (3)   **NFL** 50 (19) [6 yrs]

WHITE, TRACY   Tracy, LB, 6´0″/230 lbs; Howard; B4/14/1981 Charleston, SC   **2003** Sea 11 (0)   **2004** Sea 10 (2)   **2005** Jax 15 (0)   **NFL** 36 (2) [3 yrs]

WHITE, WALTER   Walter Lee, TE, 6´3″/216 lbs; Maryland; 1975: Pit, rnd 3; B7/19/1951 Charlottesville, VA

1975	KC	14	3	-10	-3.3(0)	0	23	559	24.3(69)	3	1	1	0.0	0	0.0	0	1	—	—	—	—	—	18	245
1976	KC	14(5, te)	2	15	7.5(8)	0	47	808	17.2(41)	7	—	—	—	—	—	—	—	—	—	—	—	—	42	454
1977	KC	13(12, TE)	2	-3	-1.5(3)	0	48	674	14.0(48)	5	—	—	—	—	—	—	—	—	—	—	—	—	30	359
1978	KC	16(16, TE)	—	—	—		42	340	8.1(24)	1	1	1	100.0	44	44.0(44)	0	0	—	—	—	—	—	6	197

YEAR	TEAM	G (GS, POS)	RUSH	YD	AVG (LG)	TD	REC	YD	AVG (LG)	TD	PASS	COMP	PCT	YD	AVG (LG)	TD	INT	SK	YD	QBR	KPR	OTD	PTS	TAY
1979	KC	6(3)	—	—	—	—	3	15	5.0(12)	0	—	—	—	—	—	—	—	—	—	—	—	—	0	8
NFL	5	63(36)	7	2	0.3(8)	0	163	2396	14.7(69)	16	2	1	50.0	44	22.0(44)	0	1	—	—	—	—	—	96	1262

WHITE, WHIZZER Byron Raymond, TB-HB, 6´1˝/187 lbs; Colorado; 1938: Pit, rnd 1; B6/8/1917 Fort Collins, CO, D4/15/2002 Denver, CO **[K]**

YEAR	TEAM	G (GS, POS)	RUSH	YD	AVG (LG)	TD	REC	YD	AVG (LG)	TD	PASS	COMP	PCT	YD	AVG (LG)	TD	INT	SK	YD	QBR	KPR	OTD	PTS	TAY
1938	Pit☆	11(11, TB)	**152**	**567**	3.7(79)	4	7	88	12.6	0	73	29	39.7	393	5.4	2	**18**	—	—	—	—	—	24	138
1940	Det☆	11(9, TB)	**146**	**514**	3.5	5	4	55	13.8	0	80	35	43.8	461	5.8	0	12	—	—	—	KPi	—	32	359
1941	Det☆	11(8, TB)	89	240	2.7(20)	2	5	158	31.6(71)	1	62	22	35.5	338	5.5(47)	2	5	—	—	—	Pkpi	1	24	697
NFL	3	33(28)	387	1321	3.4(79)	11	16	301	18.8(71)	1	215	86	40.0	1192	5.5(47)	4	35	—	—	—	KPkpi	1	80	1194

WHITE, WILBUR Wilbur Walter, B, 6´0˝/167 lbs; Colorado State; B4/30/1912 Seibert, CO, D4/1968

YEAR	TEAM	G (GS, POS)	RUSH	YD	AVG (LG)	TD	REC	YD	AVG (LG)	TD	PASS	COMP	PCT	YD	AVG (LG)	TD	INT	SK	YD	QBR	KPR	OTD	PTS	TAY
1935	Bkn	8(0)	16	41	2.6	0	—	—	—	—	32	10	31.3	73	2.3	2	5	—	—	—	—	—	0	-113
1936	Det	3(0)	8	21	2.6	0	2	21	10.5	0	1	0	0.0	0	0.0	0	1	—	—	—	—	—	0	-9
NFL	2	11(0)	24	62	2.6	0	2	21	10.5	0	33	10	30.3	73	2.2	2	6	—	—	—	—	—	0	-121

WHITE, WILFORD Wilford Parley, HB, 5´9˝/172 lbs; Arizona State; 1951: ChiB, rnd 3; B9/26/1928 Mesa, AZ **[K]**

YEAR	TEAM	G (GS, POS)	RUSH	YD	AVG (LG)	TD	REC	YD	AVG (LG)	TD	PASS	COMP	PCT	YD	AVG (LG)	TD	INT	SK	YD	QBR	KPR	OTD	PTS	TAY
1951	ChiB	6	9	86	9.6(38)	1	4	45	11.3(22)	1	1	0	0.0	0	0.0	0	0	—	—	—	Kp	—	16	185
1952	ChiB	11	19	-19	-1.0(18)	0	8	152	19.0(49)	0	2	0	0.0	0	0.0	0	0	—	—	—	Kkp	—	7	118
NFL	2	17	28	67	2.4(38)	1	12	197	16.4(49)	1	3	0	0.0	0	0.0	0	0	—	—	—	Kkp	—	23	303

WHITE, WILLIAM William Eugene, DB, 5´10˝/199 lbs; Ohio State; 1988: Det, rnd 4; B2/19/1966 Lima, OH **[I]** **1988** Det 16 (0) **1989** Det 15 (15, FS) **1990** Det 16 (16, SS) **1991**†Det 16 (16, SS) **1992** Det 16 (16, SS) **1993**†Det 16 (16, SS) **1994**†KC 15 (13, FS) **1995**†KC 16 (5, fs) **1996** KC 12 (2) **1997** Atl 16 (16, SS) **1998**†Atl 16 (16, SS) **NFL** 170 (131) [11 yrs]

WHITED, MARV Marvin Eugene, G-BB, 5´10˝/208 lbs; Oklahoma; 1942: Was, rnd 15; B7/26/1918 Crowell, TX, deceased **1945**†Was 10 (6, lg)

YEAR	TEAM	G (GS, POS)	RUSH	YD	AVG (LG)	TD	REC	YD	AVG (LG)	TD	PASS	COMP	PCT	YD	AVG (LG)	TD	INT	SK	YD	QBR	KPR	OTD	PTS	TAY
1942	Was✧	5(0)	1	3	3.0(3)	0	—	—	—	—	—	—	—	—	—	—	—	—	—	—	—	—	0	3
NFL	2	15(6)	1	3	3.0(3)	0	—	—	—	—	—	—	—	—	—	—	—	—	—	—	i	—	0	10

WHITED, MIKE Michael Dougals, T, 6´4˝/250 lbs; Pacific; B3/30/1958 Chico, CA **1980** Det 16 (2)

WHITEHEAD, BUD Ruben Angus, DB, 6´0˝/185 lbs; Florida State; 1961: SD, rnd 16; B1/1/1939 Marianna, FL **1961**†SD-A 9 **1962** SD-A 14 (LS) **1963**†SD-A 14 (LCB) **1965**†SD-A 14 (RS) **1966** SD-A 14 (RS) **1968** SD-A 3

YEAR	TEAM	G (GS, POS)	RUSH	YD	AVG (LG)	TD	REC	YD	AVG (LG)	TD	PASS	COMP	PCT	YD	AVG (LG)	TD	INT	SK	YD	QBR	KPR	OTD	PTS	TAY
1964	†SD-A	12(RS)	—	—	—	—	1	-4	-4.0(-4)	0	—	—	—	—	—	—	—	—	—	—	Pi	—	0	26
1967	SD-A	14(RS)	—	—	—	—	—	—	—	—	1	0	0.0	0	0.0	0	0	—	—	—	—	—	0	0
NFL	8	94	—	—	—	—	1	-4	-4.0(-4)	0	1	0	0.0	0	0.0	0	0	—	—	—	Pki	1	6	261

WHITEHEAD, WALKER B. Walker, TB, 6´0˝/180 lbs; none; B6/22/1902, IN, D1/3/1969 Evansville, IN **1922** Evv 1 (1)

WHITEHEAD, WILLIE William, DE-DT, 6´3˝/285 lbs; Auburn; B1/26/1973 Tuskegee, AL **1999** NO 16 (3) **2000**†NO 16 (2) **2001** NO 14 (0) **2002** NO 12 (10, LDE) **2003** NO 11 (10, RDE/lde) **2004** NO 8 (0) **2005** NO 16 (15, RDT) **NFL** 93 (40) [7 yrs]

WHITEHURST, DAVID Charles David, QB, 6´2˝/204 lbs; Furman; 1977: GB, rnd 8; B4/27/1955 Baumhaulder, Germany

YEAR	TEAM	G (GS, POS)	RUSH	YD	AVG (LG)	TD	REC	YD	AVG (LG)	TD	PASS	COMP	PCT	YD	AVG (LG)	TD	INT	SK	YD	QBR	KPR	OTD	PTS	TAY
1977	GB	7(5, qb)	14	55	3.9(19)	1	—	—	—	—	105	50	47.6	634	6.0(48)	1	7	10	68	42.3	—	—	6	107
1978	GB	16(16, QB)	28	67	2.4(18)	1	—	—	—	—	328	168	51.2	2093	6.4(58)	10	17	35	258	59.9	—	—	6	494
1979	GB	13(13, QB)	18	73	4.1(17)	4	—	—	—	—	322	179	55.6	2247	7.0(78)	10	18	32	256	64.5	—	—	24	567
1980	GB	2(0)	—	—	—	—	—	—	—	—	15	5	33.3	55	3.7(24)	0	1	3	19	—	—	—	0	-13
1981	GB	9(3)	15	51	3.4(15)	1	—	—	—	—	128	66	51.6	792	6.2(46)	7	5	10	78	72.8	—	—	6	292
1982	†GB	3(0)	—	—	—	—	—	—	—	—	47	18	38.3	235	5.0(22)	0	1	7	43	—	—	—	0	78
1983	GB	4(0)	2	-4	-2.0(0)	0	—	—	—	—	35	18	51.4	149	4.3(19)	0	2	2	16	—	—	—	0	-10
NFL	7	54(37)	77	242	3.1(19)	7	—	—	—	—	980	504	51.4	6205	6.3(78)	28	51	99	738	59.2	—	—	42	1515

WHITESIDE, KEYON Keyon Shontel, LB, 6´0˝/229 lbs; Tennessee; 2003: Ind, rnd 5; B1/31/1980 Forest City, NC **2003**†Ind 5 (0) **2004** Ind 7 (0) **NFL** 12 (0) [2 yrs]

WHITFIELD, A.D. A.D., RB, 5´10˝/200 lbs; North Texas; B9/2/1943 Rosebud, TX

YEAR	TEAM	G (GS, POS)	RUSH	YD	AVG (LG)	TD	REC	YD	AVG (LG)	TD	PASS	COMP	PCT	YD	AVG (LG)	TD	INT	SK	YD	QBR	KPR	OTD	PTS	TAY
1965	Dal	2	1	0	0.0(0)	0	—	—	—	—	—	—	—	—	—	—	—	—	—	—	—	—	0	0
1966	Was	14(HB)	93	472	5.1(63)	2	18	101	5.6(29)	1	—	—	—	—	—	—	—	—	—	—	—	—	18	548
1967	Was	13(HB)	91	384	4.2(44)	1	36	494	13.7(53)	2	—	—	—	—	—	—	—	—	—	—	—	—	18	651
1968	Was	10	37	125	3.4(17)	0	13	107	8.2(18)	0	—	—	—	—	—	—	—	—	—	—	—	—	0	179
NFL	4	39	222	981	4.4(63)	3	67	702	10.5(53)	3	—	—	—	—	—	—	—	—	—	—	—	—	36	1377

WHITFIELD, BOB Robert Lectress, T, 6´5˝/310 lbs; Stanford; 1992: Atl, rnd 1; B10/18/1971 Carson, CA **1992** Atl 11 (0) **1993** Atl 16 (16, RT) **1994** Atl 16 (16, RT) **1995**†Atl 16 (16, LT) **1996** Atl☆16 (16, LT) **1997** Atl 16 (16, LT) **1998**†Atl✧16 (16, LT) **1999** Atl 16 (16, LT) **2000** Atl 15 (15, LT) **2001** Atl 16 (16, LT) **2002**†Atl 16 (16, LT) **2003** Atl 8 (8, LT) **2004** Jax 10 (0) **2005** NYG 16 (2) **NFL** 204 (169) [14 yrs]

WHITING, BRANDON Brandon Renee, DE-DT, 6´3˝/285 lbs; California; 1998: Phi, rnd 4; B7/30/1976 Santa Rosa, CA **1998** Phi 16 (5, ldt) **1999** Phi 13 (2) **2000**†Phi 16 (11, LDE) **2001**†Phi 13 (12, LDE) **2002**†Phi 16 (15, LDE) **2003**†Phi 14 (14, LDE) **2004** SF 5 (5, rde) **NFL** 93 (64) [7 yrs]

WHITING, TEAG Teag, T, 6´3˝/310 lbs; Brigham Young; B4/16/1979 Burley, ID **2002** Arz 1 (0)

WHITLATCH, BLAKE Blake, LB, 6´1˝/233 lbs; LSU; 1978: SD, rnd 9; B10/13/1955 Baton Rouge, LA **1978** NYJ 4

WHITLEY, CURTIS Curtis Wayne, C, 6´1˝/295 lbs; Chowan Coll. (NC); Clemson; 1992: SD, rnd 5; B5/10/1969 Lowgrounds, NC **1992** SD 3 (0) **1993** SD 15 (0) **1994**†SD 12 (2) **1995** Car 16 (16, C) **1996**†Car 11 (8, C) **1997** Oak 15 (1) **NFL** 72 (27) [6 yrs]

WHITLEY, HALL Hall Wood, LB, 6´2˝/225 lbs; Texas A&M-Kingsville; 1957: Bal, rnd 15; B7/18/1935 **1960** NYT-A 4

WHITLEY, JAMES James Lavell, DB, 5´11˝/190 lbs; Michigan; B5/13/1979 Decatur, IL **2002** SL 13 (1) **2003** SL 3 (0) **2003**†GB 3 (0) **2004** GB 6 (0) **NFL** 25 (1) [3 yrs]

WHITLEY, TAYLOR Taylor, G, 6´4˝/315 lbs; Texas A&M; 2003: Mia, rnd 3; B2/21/1980 Baytown, TX **2004** Mia 16 (11, RG) **2005** Den 2 (0) **NFL** 18 (11) [2 yrs]

WHITLEY, WILSON Wilson Carl, DT-NT, 6´3˝/265 lbs; Houston; 1977: Cin, rnd 1; B4/28/1955 Brenham, TX, D10/25/1992 Marietta, GA **1977** Cin 13 (13, RDT) **1978** Cin 16 (16, LDT) **1979** Cin 14 (13, RDT) **1980** Cin 16 (16, NT) **1981**†Cin 14 (12, NT) **1982**†Cin 9 (9, NT) **NFL** 82 (79) [6 yrs]

WHITLOW, BOB Robert Edward, C, 6´2˝/236 lbs; Indiana; Arizona; B2/15/1936 Shelbyville, IN **1960** Was 12 **1961** Was 8 **1961** Det 6 **1962** Det 14 (14, C) **1963** Det 14 (14, C) **1964** Det 12 (C) **1965** Det 9 **1966** Atl 11 **1968**†Cle 14 **NFL** 100 (28) [8 yrs]

WHITLOW, KEN Kenneth Moody, C-LB, 6´1˝/190 lbs; Rice; 1941: Bkn, rnd 22; B11/30/1917 Wichita Falls, TX, D11/12/1969 Houston, TX **1946** Mia-A 13 (7, C)

WHITMAN, JOSH Joshua Harmon, TE, 6´4˝/245 lbs; Illinois; B8/5/1978 West Lafayette, IN **2001** SD 4 (1)

WHITMAN, S.J. Laverne Scott, DB, 5´11˝/185 lbs; Tulsa; 1951: ChiC, rnd 22; B8/17/1926 Hollis, OK **1951** ChiC 12 (DB) **1952** ChiC 7 (DB) **1953** ChiC 3 **1953** ChiB 9 (DB) **1954** ChiB 8 (DB) **NFL** 39 [4 yrs]

WHITMARSH, VIC Victor L., E, 5´11˝/190 lbs; Syracuse; B3/1896 Detroit, MI, deceased **1921** Det 3 (1)

WHITMORE, DAVE David Lawrence, DB, 6´0˝/232 lbs; Stephen F. Austin State; 1990: NYG, rnd 4; B7/6/1967 Daingerfield, TX **1990**†NYG 16 (0) **1991** SF 11 (0) **1992**†SF 16 (12, SS) **1993** KC 6 (6, fs) **1994**†KC 12 (10, SS) **1995**†Phi 3 (0) **NFL** 64 (28) [6 yrs]

WHITMYER, NAT Nathaniel, DB, 5´11˝/180 lbs; Washington; B8/31/1940 Washington, DC **1963** LARm 7 **1966** SD-A 14 (2) **NFL** 21 (2) [2 yrs]

WHITSELL, DAVE David Andrew, DB, 6´0˝/189 lbs; Indiana; 1958: Det, rnd 24; B6/14/1936 Shelby, MI, D10/7/1999 Kenner, LA **[I]** **1958** Det 12 **1959** Det 12 **1960** Det 11 **1961** ChiB 14 (RCB) **1962** ChiB 14 (RCB) **1965** ChiB 14 (RCB) **1966** ChiB 14 (RCB) **1967** NO★14 (LCB) **1969** NO 14 (RS)

YEAR	TEAM	G (GS, POS)	RUSH	YD	AVG (LG)	TD	REC	YD	AVG (LG)	TD	PASS	COMP	PCT	YD	AVG (LG)	TD	INT	SK	YD	QBR	KPR	OTD	PTS	TAY
1963	†ChiB	14(RCB)	1	-8	-8.0(-8)	0	—	—	—	—	—	—	—	—	—	—	—	—	—	—	i	1	6	33
1964	ChiB	14(RCB)	1	14	14.0(14)	0	—	—	—	—	—	—	—	—	—	—	—	—	—	—	i	—	0	61
1968	NO	14(RS)	1	-1	-1.0(-1)	0	—	—	—	—	—	—	—	—	—	—	—	—	—	—	ki	1	6	-2
NFL	12	161	3	5	1.7(14)	0	—	—	—	—	—	—	—	—	—	—	—	—	—	—	ki	5	30	480

WHITTED, ALVIS Alvis James, WR, 6´0˝/185 lbs; North Carolina State; 1998: Jax, rnd 7; B9/4/1974 Durham, NC

YEAR	TEAM	G (GS, POS)	RUSH	YD	AVG (LG)	TD	REC	YD	AVG (LG)	TD	PASS	COMP	PCT	YD	AVG (LG)	TD	INT	SK	YD	QBR	KPR	OTD	PTS	TAY
1998	†Jax	16(0)	3	13	4.3(16)	0	2	61	30.5(55)	0	—	—	—	—	—	—	—	—	—	—	—	1	6	44
1999	†Jax	14(1)	1	9	9.0(9)	0	—	—	—	—	—	—	—	—	—	—	—	—	—	—	k	1	6	86
2000	Jax	16(3)	—	—	—	—	13	137	10.5(37)	3	—	—	—	—	—	—	—	—	—	—	k	—	18	91
2001	Jax	11(0)	1	4	4.0(4)	0	2	17	8.5(10)	0	—	—	—	—	—	—	—	—	—	—	—	—	0	13
2002	†Oak	9(0)	—	—	—	—	—	—	—	—	—	—	—	—	—	—	—	—	—	—	k	—	0	-10
2003	Oak	16(2)	6	37	6.2(16)	0	7	106	15.1(36)	1	—	—	—	—	—	—	—	—	—	—	k	—	6	83

YEAR	TEAM	G (GS, POS)	RUSH	YD	AVG (LG)	TD	REC	YD	AVG (LG)	TD	PASS COMP	PCT	YD	AVG (LG)	TD	INT	SK	YD	QBR	KPR	OTD	PTS	TAY
2004	Oak	11 (5, wr)	—	—	—		9	227	25.2 (57)	2	—	—	—	—	—	—	—	—	—	k	—	14	145
2005	Oak	15 (0)	2	51	25.5 (27)	0	14	183	13.1 (26)	0	—	—	—	—	—	—	—	—	—	k	—	0	143
NFL	8	108 (11)	13	114	8.8 (27)	0	47	731	15.6 (57)	6	—	—	—	—	—	—	—	—	—	k	2	50	593

WHITTEN, BOBBY   Bobby Gene, G, 6´3˝/265 lbs; Kansas; B5/7/1959 Junction City, KS   **1981** Cin 1 (0)

WHITTEN, TODD   Phillip Todd, QB, 6´0˝/185 lbs; Stephen F. Austin State; B2/16/1965 Dallas, TX

| 1987 | NE | 1 (0) | 2 | -6 | -3.0 (-2) | 0 | — | — | — | — | — | — | — | — | — | — | — | — | — | — | — | 0 | -6 |

WHITTENTON, JESSE   Urshell Jesse, DB, 6´0˝/193 lbs; Texas-El Paso; 1956: LA, rnd 5; B5/9/1934 Big Spring, TX [I]   **1956** LARm 12 (12, DB)   **1957** LARm 12 (DB)
1958 GB 8 (DB)   **1959** GB☆12 (DB)   **1960**†GB☆12 (RCB)   **1961**†GB★14 (RCB)   **1962**†GB 14 (RCB)   **1963** GB✧14 (RCB)   **1964** GB 14   **NFL** 112 (12) [9 yrs]

WHITTICKER, WILL   William, G, 6´5˝/329 lbs; Michigan State; 2005: GB, rnd 7; B8/2/1982 Evansville, IN   **2005** GB 15 (14, RG)

WHITTINGHAM, CARY   Cary L., LB, 6´2˝/230 lbs; Brigham Young; 1986: Cin, rnd 9; B5/30/1963 San Luis Obispo, CA   **1987** LARm 3 (0)

WHITTINGHAM, FRED   Fred George, LB-G, 6´1˝/240 lbs; Brigham Young; Cal Poly-San Luis Obispo; B2/4/1939 Boston, MA, D10/27/2003 Provo, UT   **1964** LARm 5   **1966** Phi 14
1967 NO 7 (MLB)   **1968** NO 13 (MLB)   **1969**†Dal 7   **1970** Bos 13   **1971** Phi 4   **NFL** 63 [7 yrs]

WHITTINGHAM, KYLE   Kyle David, LB, 6´0˝/232 lbs; Brigham Young; B11/21/1959 San Luis Obispo, CA   **1987** LARm 3 (3)

WHITTINGTON, ARTHUR   Arthur Lee, RB, 5´11˝/185 lbs; SMU; 1978: Oak, rnd 7; B9/4/1955 Cuero, TX [R]

1978	Oak	16 (9, RB)	172	661	3.8 (26)	7	23	106	4.6 (20)	0	—	—	—	—	—	—	—	—	—	k	—	42	912
1979	Oak	9 (7, RB)	109	397	3.6 (22)	2	19	240	12.6 (39)	0	—	—	—	—	—	—	—	—	—	k	—	12	508
1980	†Oak	15 (3)	91	299	3.3 (42)	3	19	205	10.8 (55)	0	—	—	—	—	—	—	—	—	—	k	—	24	519
1981	Oak	16 (2)	69	220	3.2 (13)	1	23	213	9.3 (22)	0	—	—	—	—	—	—	—	—	—	k	1	24	519
1982	Buf	2 (0)	7	15	2.1 (4)	0	—	—	—	—	—	—	—	—	—	—	—	—	—	kp	—	18	529
NFL	5	58 (21)	448	1592	3.6 (42)	13	84	764	9.1 (55)	0	—	—	—	—	—	—	—	—	—	kp	1	96	2491

WHITTINGTON, BERNARD   Bernard Maurice, DE-DT, 6´6˝/280 lbs; Indiana; B8/20/1971 St. Louis, MO   **1994** Ind 13 (8, LDE)   **1995**†Ind 16 (13, LDE)   **1996** Ind 16 (14, LDE)
1997 Ind 15 (6, ldt)   **1998** Ind 15 (11, LDE)   **1999**†Ind 15 (15, LDT/lde)   **2000**†Ind 15 (12, LDT)   **2001** Cin 16 (5, lde)   **2002** Cin 16 (11, LDE)   **NFL** 137 (95) [9 yrs]

WHITTINGTON, C.L.   Columbus Lorenzo, DB, 6´1˝/200 lbs; Prairie View A&M; B8/1/1952 Beaumont, TX   **1974** Hou 14   **1975** Hou 14 (fs)   **1976** Hou 14 (FS)   **1978**†Hou 12
NFL 54 [4 yrs]

WHITTINGTON, MIKE   Michael Scott, LB, 6´2˝/220 lbs; Notre Dame; B8/9/1958 Miami, FL   **1980** NYG 16 (6, rolb)   **1981**†NYG 6 (0)   **1982** NYG 9 (0)   **1983** NYG 8 (0)
NFL 39 (6) [4 yrs]

WHITTLE, JASON   Jason, G, 6´4˝/305 lbs; Southwest Missouri State; B3/7/1975 Springfield, MO   **1998** NYG 1 (0)   **1999** NYG 16 (1)   **2000**†NYG 16 (2)   **2001** NYG 16 (2)
2002†NYG 14 (14, RG)   **2003** TB 16 (5, lg)   **2004** NYG 16 (16, LG)   **2005**†NYG 14 (0)   **NFL** 109 (40) [8 yrs]

WHITTLE, RICKY   Ricky Jerome, RB, 5´9˝/200 lbs; Oregon; 1996: NO, rnd 4; B12/3/1971 Fresno, CA

| 1996 | NO | 10 (0) | 20 | 52 | 2.6 (15) | 0 | 26 | 162 | 6.2 (28) | 0 | — | — | — | — | — | — | — | — | — | — | — | 0 | 133 |

WHITWELL, MIKE   Michael Carroll, DB-WR, 6´0˝/175 lbs; Texas A&M; 1982: Cle, rnd 6; B11/14/1958 Kenedy, TX   **1982**†Cle 9 (0)   **1983** Cle 16 (16, FS)   **NFL** 25 (16) [2 yrs]

WIATRAK, JOHN   John Philip, C, 6´0˝/220 lbs; Washington; 1937: Cle, rnd 4; B3/30/1913 Chicago, IL, D10/21/2000 Olympia, WA   **1939** Det 1 (0)

WIBERG, OSSIE   Oscar Malker Hilding, B, 5´11˝/207 lbs; Nebraska Wesleyan; B10/11/1904 Edgar, NE, D8/14/1989 Gering, NE [K]   **1927** Cle 10 (8, bb), 25
1928 Det 10 (10, BB), 13   **1930** NYG 17 (14, FB), 30   **1933** Cin 1 (0)

| 1932 | Bkn | 6 (3) | 17 | 59 | 3.5 | 0 | 1 | 29 | 29.0 (29) | 0 | 3 | 1 | 33.3 | 20 | 6.7 (20) | 0 | 0 | — | — | K | — | 1 | 84 |
| NFL | 5 | 44 (35) | 17 | 59 | 3.5 | 0 | 1 | 29 | 29.0 (29) | 0 | 3 | 1 | 33.3 | 20 | 6.7 (20) | 0 | 0 | — | — | K | 1 | 69 | 94 |

WICHARD, MURRAY   Murray, NT-DE, 6´2˝/260 lbs; Frostburg State; B11/16/1963   **1987** NE 3 (0)

WICKERT, TOM   Thomas Kirk, T-G, 6´4˝/246 lbs; Washington State; 1974: Mia, rnd 9; B4/5/1952 Astoria, OR   **1974**†Mia 13   **1975** NO 1   **1976** NO 7 (7, LT)   **1977** Det 1   **1977** KC 5
NFL 27 (7) [4 yrs]

WICKETT, LLOYD   Lloyd Meldrum, T, 6´1˝/208 lbs; Oregon State; 1943: Det, rnd 5; B4/3/1920 Ontario, Canada, D4/9/2001 Jefferson, OR   **1943** Det 4 (0)   **1946** Det 10 (2)
NFL 14 (2) [2 yrs]

WICKS, BOB   Robert Blaine, WR, 6´3˝/200 lbs; Utah State; 1972: SL, rnd 8; B7/24/1950 Pasadena, CA   **1974** GB 1   **1974** NO 5

| 1972 | SL | 9 | — | — | — | | 1 | 8 | 8.0 (8) | 0 | — | — | — | — | — | — | — | — | — | — | — | 0 | 4 |
| NFL | 2 | 15 | — | — | — | | 1 | 8 | 8.0 (8) | 0 | — | — | — | — | — | — | — | — | — | — | — | 0 | 4 |

WIDBY, RON   George Ronald, P, 6´4˝/210 lbs; Tennessee; 1967: NO, rnd 4; B3/9/1945 Knoxville, TN [P]   **1968**†Dal☆13   **1969**†Dal☆14   **1970**†Dal 14   **1971**†Dal★14   **1973** GB 12

| 1972 | †GB | 14 | — | — | — | | 2 | 2 | 100.0 | 102 | 51.0 (68) | 1 | 0 | — | — | — | — | — | — | P | — | 0 | 56 |
| NFL | 6 | 81 | — | — | — | | 2 | 2 | 100.0 | 102 | 51.0 (68) | 1 | 0 | — | — | — | — | — | — | P | — | 0 | 56 |

WIDELL, DAVE   David Harold, C-T-G, 6´7˝/303 lbs; Boston College; 1988: Dal, rnd 4; B5/14/1965 Hartford, CT   **1988** Dal 14 (9, LT)   **1989** Dal 15 (2)   **1990** Den 16 (5, lt)
1991 Den 16 (2)   **1992** Den 16 (1)   **1993**†Den 15 (15, LG/c)   **1994** Den 16 (16, C)   **1995** Jax 16 (16, C)   **1996**†Jax 15 (14, C)   **1997**†Jax 16 (12, C)   **1998** Atl 1 (0)
NFL 156 (92) [11 yrs]

WIDELL, DOUG   Douglas Joseph, G-T, 6´4˝/289 lbs; Boston College; 1989: Den, rnd 2; B9/23/1966 Hartford, CT   **1989**†Den 16 (10, LG)   **1990** Den 16 (16, LG)
1991†Den 16 (16, LG)   **1993** GB 16 (9, LG)   **1994** Det 16 (16, RG)   **1995** Det 11 (10, LG)   **1996** Ind 16 (16, LG)   **1997** Ind 16 (16, LG)

| 1992 | Den | 16 (16, RG) | — | — | — | | 1 | -7 | -7.0 (-7) | 0 | — | — | — | — | — | — | — | — | — | — | — | 0 | -4 |
| NFL | 9 | 139 (125) | — | — | — | | 1 | -7 | -7.0 (-7) | 0 | — | — | — | — | — | — | — | — | — | — | — | 0 | -4 |

WIDERQUIST, CHET   Chester Carl, T-G, 6´1˝/219 lbs; Northwestern; Washington & Jefferson; B9/23/1895 Moline, IL, D7/14/1976 Knoxville, IA   **1923** Mil 1 (0)   **1924** Mil 13 (13, LT)
1925 RI☆11 (11, LT)   **1926** ChiC 1 (0)   **1928** ChiC 6 (6, LT)   **1928** Det 4 (3)   **1929** Min 9 (8, LT)   **NFL** 45 (41) [6 yrs]

WIDICK, BUD   Ralph Hayden, C-T, 6´1˝/205 lbs; Emporia State; B11/7/1900 Belle Plaine, KS, D2/3/1968 Atchison, KS   **1924** KC 2 (0)

WIDMER, COREY   Corey Edward, LB-DT, 6´3˝/256 lbs; Montana State; 1992: NYG, rnd 7; B12/25/1968 Alexandria, VA   **1992** NYG 8 (0)   **1993**†NYG 11 (0)   **1994** NYG 16 (5, mlb)
1995 NYG 16 (0)   **1996** NYG 16 (16, MLB)   **1997**†NYG 16 (16, MLB)   **1998** NYG 15 (13, MLB)   **1999** NYG 16 (16, MLB)   **NFL** 114 (64) [8 yrs]

WIDSETH, ED   Edwin Clarence, T, 6´1˝/223 lbs; Minnesota-Crookston; Minnesota; 1937: NYG, rnd 1; B1/5/1910 Gonvick, MN, D12/3/1998 Minneapolis, MN   **1937** NYG☆11 (5, lt)
1938†NYG★11 (11, LT)   **1939**†NYG☆11 (3)   **1940** NYG 11 (3)   **NFL** 44 (22) [4 yrs]

WIEGAND, ERIC   Eric, C, 6´2˝/260 lbs; Missouri-Rolla; B3/13/1964   **1987** Atl 2 (0)

WIEGERT, ZACH   Zachary Allen, G-T, 6´5˝/309 lbs; Nebraska; 1995: SL, rnd 2; B8/16/1972 Fremont, NE   **1995** SL 5 (2)   **1996** SL 16 (16, RT)   **1998** SL 13 (13, RG)
2000 Jax 8 (8, RT)   **2001** Jax 16 (16, RG)   **2002** Jax 7 (7, lt)   **2003** Hou 15 (14, RG)   **2004** Hou 13 (13, RG)   **2005** Hou 12 (12, RG/rt)

1997	SL	15 (15, RG)	—	—	—		1	1	1.0 (1)	0	—	—	—	—	—	—	—	—	—	—	1	6	1
1999	†Jax	16 (12, RG)	—	—	—		1	-3	-3.0 (-3)	0	—	—	—	—	—	—	—	—	—	—	—	0	-2
NFL	11	136 (128)	—	—	—		2	-2	-1.0 (1)	0	—	—	—	—	—	—	—	—	—	—	1	6	-1

WIEGMANN, CASEY   Casey Peter, C, 6´2˝/285 lbs; Iowa; B7/20/1973 Parkerburg, IA   **1997** NYJ 3 (0)   **1997** ChiB 1 (0)   **1998** ChiB 15 (15, C)   **1999** ChiB 16 (0)
2000 ChiB 16 (10, C)   **2001** KC 15 (15, C)   **2002** KC 16 (16, C)   **2003**†KC 16 (16, C)   **2004** KC 16 (16, C)   **2005** KC 16 (16, C)   **NFL** 131 (104) [9 yrs]

WIEHL, JOE   Joseph John, T, 5´11˝/254 lbs; Washington & Jefferson; Duquesne; B1/30/1910 Coal Center, PA, D1/22/1996 Charleroi, PA   **1935** Pit 3 (0)

WIESE, BOB   Robert Lee, B, 6´3˝/198 lbs; Michigan; 1945: Det, rnd 5/1947: SF-A, rnd 2; B1/25/1923 Jamestown, ND, D11/1971   **1948** Det 4 (1)

| 1947 | Det | 12 (2) | 20 | 61 | 3.1 (21) | 0 | 5 | 53 | 10.6 (24) | 0 | — | — | — | — | — | — | — | — | — | Pi | — | 0 | 117 |
| NFL | 2 | 16 (3) | 20 | 61 | 3.1 (21) | 0 | 5 | 53 | 10.6 (24) | 0 | — | — | — | — | — | — | — | — | — | Pi | — | 0 | 117 |

WIETECHA, RAY   Raymond Walter, C, 6´1˝/225 lbs; Michigan State; Northwestern; 1950: NYG, rnd 12; B11/4/1928 East Chicago, IN, D12/14/2002 Phoenix, AZ   **1953** NYG 12
1954 NYG 12 (12, C)   **1955** NYG 12 (12, C)   **1956**†NYG☆12 (12, C)   **1957** NYG★12 (12, C)   **1958**†NYG☆12 (12, C)   **1959**†NYG☆12 (12, C)   **1960** NYG✧12 (12, C)
1961†NYG☆14 (14, C)   **1962**†NYG★14 (14, C)   **NFL** 124 (98) [10 yrs]

WIETHE, SOCKO   John Albert, G-LB, 6´0˝/198 lbs; Xavier (OH); B10/17/1912 Cincinnati, OH, D5/3/1989 Cincinnati, OH   **1940** Det☆10 (9, LG)   **1941** Det 8 (5, RG)   **1942** Det 6 (0)

| 1939 | Det☆ | 11 (11, LG) | — | — | — | | 2 | 5 | 2.5 | 0 | — | — | — | — | — | — | — | — | — | — | — | 0 | 3 |
| NFL | 4 | 35 (25) | — | — | — | | 2 | 5 | 2.5 | 0 | — | — | — | — | — | — | — | — | — | i | — | 0 | 4 |

WIGGIN, PAUL Paul David, DE, 6´3˝/242 lbs; Stanford; 1956: Cle, rnd 6; B11/18/1934 Modesto, CA [C] **1957**†Cle 12 (lde) **1958**†Cle 12 (LDE) **1959** Cle 12 (RDE) **1960** Cle 12 (LDE/rde) **1961** Cle 14 (RDE) **1962** Cle 14 (LDE) **1963** Cle 14 (LDE) **1964**†Cle 14 (LDE) **1965**†Cle✧14 (LDE) **1966** Cle 14 (LDE) **1967**†Cle✧14 (LDE/rde) **NFL** 146 [11 yrs]

WIGGINS, JERMAINE Jermain, TE, 6´2˝/255 lbs; Marshall; Georgia; B1/18/1975 East Boston, MA

YEAR	TEAM	G(GS, POS)	RUSH	YD	AVG(LG)	TD	REC	YD	AVG(LG)	TD	PASS	COMP	PCT	YD	AVG(LG)	TD	INT	SK	YD	QBR	KPR	OTD	PTS	TAY
2000	NYJ	11(0)	—	—	—	—	2	4	2.0(3)	1	—	—	—	—	—	—	—	—	—	—	k	—	6	4
2000	NE	4(2)	—	—	—	—	16	203	12.7(59)	1	—	—	—	—	—	—	—	—	—	—	—	—	6	107
2001	†NE	16(6, te)	—	—	—	—	14	133	9.5(31)	4	—	—	—	—	—	—	—	—	—	—	—	—	24	87
2002	Ind	3(0)	—	—	—	—	2	17	8.5(9)	0	—	—	—	—	—	—	—	—	—	—	—	—	0	9
2002	Car	11(1)	—	—	—	—	8	45	5.6(17)	1	—	—	—	—	—	—	—	—	—	—	k	—	6	31
2003	†Car	16(11, TE)	—	—	—	—	8	80	10.0(23)	1	—	—	—	—	—	—	—	—	—	—	—	—	6	45
2004	†Min	14(13, TE)	—	—	—	—	71	705	9.9(39)	4	—	—	—	—	—	—	—	—	—	—	—	—	24	373
2005	Min	16(9, TE)	—	—	—	—	69	568	8.2(24)	1	—	—	—	—	—	—	—	—	—	—	—	—	6	289
NFL	6	91(42)	—	—	—	—	190	1755	9.2(59)	13	—	—	—	—	—	—	—	—	—	—	k	—	78	943

WIGGINS, PAUL Paul Anthony, T, 6´3˝/305 lbs; Oregon; 1997: Pit, rnd 3; B8/17/1973 Portland, OR **1997** Pit 1 (0) **1998** Was 1 (0) **NFL** 2 (0) [2 yrs]

WIGGS, GENE Eugene O., G, none; B1900, IN, deceased **1921** Lou 2 (2, LG)

WIGGS, HUBERT Hubert Thomas, FB-T, 5´8˝/180 lbs; Vanderbilt; B9/29/1893 Tullahoma, TN, D10/18/1977, [C] **1921** Lou 1 (0) **1922** Lou 3 (3, FB) **1923** Lou 3 (3, FB) **NFL** 7 (6) [3 yrs]

WIGHTKIN, BILL William John, T-DE-E, 6´3˝/235 lbs; Notre Dame; 1949: ChiB, rnd 8; B7/28/1927 Detroit, MI, D1/25/1997 Westchester, IL **1954** ChiB 12 (LT) **1955** ChiB★12 (LT) **1956**†ChiB☆12 (LT) **1957** ChiB 11 (LT)

YEAR	TEAM	G(GS, POS)	RUSH	YD	AVG(LG)	TD	REC	YD	AVG(LG)	TD	PASS	COMP	PCT	YD	AVG(LG)	TD	INT	SK	YD	QBR	KPR	OTD	PTS	TAY
1950	†ChiB	12(LDE)	—	—	—	—	3	24	8.0(17)	0	—	—	—	—	—	—	—	—	—	—	—	—	0	12
1951	ChiB	10(LDE)	—	—	—	—	1	47	47.0(47)	0	—	—	—	—	—	—	—	—	—	—	p	1	6	32
1952	ChiB	11(LDE)	—	—	—	—	7	120	17.1(29)	2	—	—	—	—	—	—	—	—	—	—	—	—	12	79
1953	ChiB	12(LDE)	—	—	—	—	2	22	11.0(13)	0	—	—	—	—	—	—	—	—	—	—	k	1	6	-4
NFL	8	92	—	—	—	—	13	213	16.4(47)	2	—	—	—	—	—	—	—	—	—	—	kp	2	24	119

WILBUR, JOHN John Leonard, G-DE, 6´3˝/251 lbs; Stanford; B5/21/1943 San Diego, CA **1966** Dal 8 **1967**†Dal 14 **1968**†Dal 14 (RG) **1969**†Dal 14 (RG) **1970** LARm 8 **1971**†Was 14 (14, RG) **1972**†Was☆14 (14, RG) **1973**†Was 14 (14, RG) **1974** Was 1 **NFL** 101 (42) [9 yrs]

WILBURN, BARRY Barry Todd, DB, 6´2˝/196 lbs; Mississippi; 1985: Was, rnd 8; B12/9/1963 Memphis, TN [I] **1985** Was 16 (1) **1986**†Was 16 (5, rcb) **1987**†Was☆12 (12, RCB) **1988** Was 10 (10, LCB) **1989** Was 8 (1) **1992** Cle 6 (3) **1995**†Phi 16 (0) **1996** Phi 7 (2) **NFL** 91 (34) [8 yrs]

WILBURN, J.R. Johnnie Richard, FL-WR, 6´2˝/190 lbs; South Carolina; 1965: Pit, rnd 13/Buf, rnd R7; B4/27/1943 Portsmouth, VA

YEAR	TEAM	G(GS, POS)	RUSH	YD	AVG(LG)	TD	REC	YD	AVG(LG)	TD	PASS	COMP	PCT	YD	AVG(LG)	TD	INT	SK	YD	QBR	KPR	OTD	PTS	TAY
1966	Pit	14	—	—	—	—	7	103	14.7(42)	0	—	—	—	—	—	—	—	—	—	—	—	—	0	52
1967	Pit	14(FL)	—	—	—	—	51	767	15.0(66)	5	—	—	—	—	—	—	—	—	—	—	—	—	30	409
1968	Pit	14(FL)	—	—	—	—	39	514	13.2(41)	3	—	—	—	—	—	—	—	—	—	—	—	—	18	272
1969	Pit	10(FL)	2	29	14.5(35)	0	20	373	18.6(53)	0	—	—	—	—	—	—	—	—	—	—	—	—	0	216
1970	Pit	6	5	25	5.0(10)	0	6	77	12.8(15)	0	—	—	—	—	—	—	—	—	—	—	—	—	0	64
NFL	5	58	7	54	7.7(35)	0	123	1834	14.9(66)	8	—	—	—	—	—	—	—	—	—	—	—	—	48	1011

WILBURN, STEVE Steven T., DE, 6´4˝/266 lbs; Illinois State; B2/25/1961 Chicago, IL, D6/8/2005 Schaumburg, IL **1987** NE 3 (3)

WILCHER, MIKE Michael D., LB, 6´3˝/238 lbs; North Carolina; 1983: LARm, rnd 2; B3/20/1960 Washington, DC **1983**†LARm 15 (0) **1984**†LARm 15 (5, rolb) **1985**†LARm 16 (15, ROLB) **1986**†LARm 16 (16, ROLB) **1987** LARm 12 (12, ROLB) **1988**†LARm 16 (15, ROLB) **1989**†LARm 16 (16, ROLB) **1990** LARm 16 (15, ROLB) **1991** SD 2 (0) **NFL** 124 (94) [9 yrs]

WILCOTS, SOLOMON Solomon, DB, 5´11˝/189 lbs; Colorado; 1987: Cin, rnd 8; B10/3/1964 Los Angeles, CA **1987** Cin 12 (0) **1988**†Cin 16 (16, FS) **1989** Cin 16 (0) **1990**†Cin 16 (10, FS) **1991** Min 16 (1) **1992**†Pit 16 (0) **NFL** 92 (27) [6 yrs]

WILCOX, DANIEL Daniel, TE, 6´1˝/229 lbs; Appalachian State; B3/23/1977 Atlanta, GA **2001**†NYJ 1 (0) **2003** TB 2 (0)

YEAR	TEAM	G(GS, POS)	RUSH	YD	AVG(LG)	TD	REC	YD	AVG(LG)	TD	PASS	COMP	PCT	YD	AVG(LG)	TD	INT	SK	YD	QBR	KPR	OTD	PTS	TAY
2004	Bal	16(5, te)	—	—	—	—	25	219	8.8(20)	1	—	—	—	—	—	—	—	—	—	—	—	—	6	115
2005	Bal	13(3)	—	—	—	—	20	154	7.7(17)	1	—	—	—	—	—	—	—	—	—	—	—	—	6	82
NFL	4	32(8)	—	—	—	—	45	373	8.3(20)	2	—	—	—	—	—	—	—	—	—	—	—	—	12	197

WILCOX, DAVE David, LB, 6´3˝/241 lbs; Boise State; Oregon; 1964: SF, rnd 3/Hou, rnd 6; B9/29/1942 Ontario, OR; HOF 2000 **1964** SF 14 (9, LLB) **1965** SF 14 (14, LLB) **1966** SF★14 (14, LLB) **1967** SF☆14 (14, LLB) **1968** SF★14 (14, LLB) **1969** SF★14 (14, LLB) **1970**†SF★13 (LLB) **1971**†SF★14 (14, LLB) **1972**†SF★14 (14, LLB) **1973** SF★14 (14, LLB) **1974** SF 14 (11, LLB) **NFL** 153 (132) [11 yrs]

WILCOX, FIRPO John Harrison, T, 6´0˝/205 lbs; Oklahoma; B4/23/1903 Bixby, OK **1926** Buf 10 (10, RT) **1930** SI 2 (1) **NFL** 12 (11) [2 yrs]

WILCOX, JOHN John Dale, DT, 6´5˝/230 lbs; Boise State; Oregon; 1960: Phi, rnd 15/Bos, rnd 2; B3/15/1938 Vale, OR **1960**†Phi 12

WILCOX, JOSH Joshua David, TE, 6´2˝/253 lbs; Oregon; B6/5/1974 Eugene, OR

YEAR	TEAM	G(GS, POS)	RUSH	YD	AVG(LG)	TD	REC	YD	AVG(LG)	TD	PASS	COMP	PCT	YD	AVG(LG)	TD	INT	SK	YD	QBR	KPR	OTD	PTS	TAY
1998	NO	3(1)	—	—	—	—	1	10	10.0(10)	0	—	—	—	—	—	—	—	—	—	—	—	—	0	5
1999	NO	8(4)	—	—	—	—	6	61	10.2(19)	0	—	—	—	—	—	—	—	—	—	—	—	—	0	31
NFL	2	11(5)	—	—	—	—	7	71	10.1(19)	0	—	—	—	—	—	—	—	—	—	—	—	—	0	36

WILCOX, NED Edmund Quincy, B, 5´11˝/185 lbs; Swarthmore; B2/7/1904, D9/1968, NJ **1926** Fra 12 (4), 18 **1927** Fra 14 (13, FB), 12 **NFL** 26 (17), 30 [2 yrs]

WILDE, GEORGE George Hall, HB-DB, 6´1˝/193 lbs; Texas A&M; TCU; B3/26/1923 Olney, TX, D5/26/1975 Marshall, TX

YEAR	TEAM	G(GS, POS)	RUSH	YD	AVG(LG)	TD	REC	YD	AVG(LG)	TD	PASS	COMP	PCT	YD	AVG(LG)	TD	INT	SK	YD	QBR	KPR	OTD	PTS	TAY
1947	Was	9(2)	4	-1	-0.3(2)	0	6	45	7.5(18)	1	—	—	—	—	—	—	—	—	—	—	k	—	6	31

WILDER, BERT Albert Green, DE-DT, 6´3˝/245 lbs; North Carolina State; 1962: NYT, rnd 14/LA, rnd 11; B4/14/1939 Greensboro, NC **1964** NYJ-A 14 (LDE) **1965** NYJ-A 14 **1966** NYJ-A 14 (2) **1967** NYJ-A 13 **NFL** 55 (2) [4 yrs]

WILDER, HAL Harold Fremont, G, 5´10˝/190 lbs; Nebraska Wesleyan; Nebraska; B2/8/1893 Merrick, NE, D2/5/1989 Lincoln, NE **1923** SL 1 (1)

WILDER, JAMES James Curtis, RB, 6´3˝/225 lbs; Missouri; 1981: TB, rnd 2; B5/12/1958 Sikeston, MO

YEAR	TEAM	G(GS, POS)	RUSH	YD	AVG(LG)	TD	REC	YD	AVG(LG)	TD	PASS	COMP	PCT	YD	AVG(LG)	TD	INT	SK	YD	QBR	KPR	OTD	PTS	TAY
1981	†TB	16(16, FB)	107	370	3.5(23)	4	48	507	10.6(38)	1	—	—	—	—	—	—	—	—	—	—	k	—	30	673
1982	†TB	9(9, FB)	83	324	3.9(47)	3	53	466	8.8(32)	1	—	—	—	—	—	—	—	—	—	—	—	—	24	592
1983	TB	10(10, FB)	161	640	4.0(75)	4	57	380	6.7(31)	2	—	—	—	—	—	—	—	—	—	—	—	—	36	880
1984	TB★	16(16, RB)	**407**	1544	3.8(37)	13	85	685	8.1(50)	0	1	1	100.0	16	16.0(16)	1	0	—	—	—	—	—	78	2030
1985	TB	16(16, RB)	365	1300	3.6(28)	10	53	341	6.4(20)	0	—	—	—	—	—	—	—	—	—	—	—	—	60	1571
1986	TB	12(12, RB)	190	704	3.7(45)	2	43	326	7.6(25)	1	—	—	—	—	—	—	—	—	—	—	—	—	18	892
1987	TB	12(12, FB)	106	488	4.6(21)	0	40	328	8.2(32)	1	—	—	—	—	—	—	—	—	—	—	—	—	6	657
1988	TB	7(7, fb)	86	343	4.0(19)	1	15	124	8.3(24)	0	—	—	—	—	—	—	—	—	—	—	—	—	6	415
1989	TB	15(4)	70	244	3.5(14)	0	36	335	9.3(27)	3	—	—	—	—	—	—	—	—	—	—	k	—	18	439
1990	Was	1(0)	—	—	—	—	—	—	—	—	—	—	—	—	—	—	—	—	—	—	—	—	—	—
1990	Det	15(0)	11	51	4.6(13)	0	1	8	8.0(8)	1	—	—	—	—	—	—	—	—	—	—	—	—	6	60
NFL	10	129(102)	1586	6008	3.8(75)	37	431	3500	8.1(50)	10	1	1	100.0	16	16.0(16)	1	0	—	—	—	k	—	282	8207

WILDS, GARNELL Garnell Wayman, DB, 5´11˝/196 lbs; Virginia Tech; B6/8/1981 Tampa, FL **2004** Was 2 (0) **2005** Car 3 (0) **NFL** 5 (0) [2 yrs]

WILDUNG, DICK Richard Kay, T-DT-G, 6´0˝/221 lbs; Minnesota; 1943: GB, rnd 1; B8/16/1921 Anoka, MN **1946** GB 11 (7, LG) **1947** GB☆12 (10, LG) **1948** GB☆12 (11, LT) **1949** GB☆12 (9, LT) **1950** GB 12 (LT) **1951** GB✧12 (LDT) **1953** GB 12 (LDT) **NFL** 83 (37) [7 yrs]

WILEY, CHARLES Charles Kennedy, NT, 6´2˝/268 lbs; UNLV; B12/9/1964 **1987** Sea 1 (1)

WILEY, CHUCK Samuel Charles, DE, 6´5˝/275 lbs; LSU; 1998: Car, rnd 3; B3/6/1975 Baton Rouge, LA **1999** Car 16 (16, RDE) **2000** Atl 16 (0) **2001** Atl 16 (1) **2002** Min 16 (0) **2003** Min 7 (4) **2004** Min 5 (2) **2004** NYG 3 (0) **NFL** 79 (23) [6 yrs]

WILEY, JACK John Franklin, T-DT, 5´11˝/208 lbs; Waynesburg; B4/18/1920 Wind Ridge, PA **1946** Pit 11 (8, LT) **1947**†Pit 11 (11, LT) **1948** Pit 12 (7, lt) **1950** Pit 11

YEAR	TEAM	G(GS, POS)	RUSH	YD	AVG(LG)	TD	REC	YD	AVG(LG)	TD	PASS	COMP	PCT	YD	AVG(LG)	TD	INT	SK	YD	QBR	KPR	OTD	PTS	TAY
1949	Pit	12(10, LT)	—	—	—	—	1	10	10.0(10)	0	—	—	—	—	—	—	—	—	—	—	—	—	0	5
NFL	5	57(36)	—	—	—	—	1	10	10.0(10)	0	—	—	—	—	—	—	—	—	—	—	—	—	0	5

WILEY, MARCELLUS Marcellus Vernon, DE, 6´4˝/275 lbs; Columbia; 1997: Buf, rnd 2; B11/30/1974 Compton, CA **1997** Buf 16 (0) **1998**†Buf 16 (3) **1999**†Buf 16 (1) **2000** Buf 16 (15, RDE) **2001** SD★14 (14, LDE) **2002** SD 14 (14, LDE) **2003** SD 16 (16, LDE) **2004** Dal 16 (15, RDE) **2005**†Jax 11 (1) **NFL** 135 (79) [9 yrs]

YEAR	TEAM	G(GS, POS)	RUSH	YD	AVG(LG)	TD	REC	YD	AVG(LG)	TD	PASS COMP	PCT	YD	AVG(LG)	TD	INT	SK	YD	QBR	KPR	OTD	PTS	TAY

WILEY, MICHAEL   Michael Deshawn, RB, 5'11"/189 lbs; Ohio State; 2000: Dal, rnd 5; B1/5/1978 Spring Valley, CA

2000	Dal	10(0)	24	88	3.7(11)	0	14	72	5.1(15)	1	—	—	—	—	—	—	—	—	—	k	—	6	237
2001	Dal	16(0)	34	247	7.3(58)	1	16	99	6.2(17)	1	—	—	—	—	—	—	—	—	—	k	—	6	332
2002	Dal	16(1)	22	168	7.6(46)	1	13	144	11.1(31)	0	0	0	0.0	0	0.0	0	0	1	4	—	k	—	6	252
NFL	3	42(1)	80	503	6.3(58)	1	43	315	7.3(31)	2	0	0	0.0	0	0.0	0	0	1	4	—	k	—	18	821

WILFORD, ERNEST   Ernest Lee, WR, 6'4"/216 lbs; Virginia Tech; 2004: Jax, rnd 4; B1/14/1979 Richmond, VA

2004	Jax	15(3)	—	—	—	—	19	271	14.3(46)	2	—	—	—	—	—	—	—	—	—	—	—	14	146
2005	†Jax	16(8, WR)	—	—	—	—	41	681	16.6(39)	7	—	—	—	—	—	—	—	—	—	—	—	42	376
NFL	2	31(11)	—	—	—	—	60	952	15.9(46)	9	—	—	—	—	—	—	—	—	—	—	—	56	521

WILFORK, VINCE   Vince Lamar, NT-DT, 6'2"/350 lbs; Miami (FL); 2004: NE, rnd 1; B11/14/1981 Boynton Beach, FL   **2004**†NE 16 (6, nt)   **2005**†NE 16 (16, NT)   **NFL** 32 (22) [2 yrs]

WILHELM, ERIK   Erik Bradley, QB, 6'3"/217 lbs; Oregon State; 1989: Cin, rnd 3; B11/19/1965 Dayton, OH

1989	Cin	6(0)	6	30	5.0(14)	0	—	—	—	—	56	30	53.6	425	7.6(46)	4	2	3	17	—	—	0	183
1990	†Cin	7(0)	6	6	1.0(4)	0	—	—	—	—	19	12	63.2	117	6.2(19)	0	0	1	2	—	—	0	65
1991	Cin	4(1)	1	9	9.0(9)	0	—	—	—	—	42	24	57.1	217	5.2(29)	0	2	1	8	—	—	0	38
1993	Cin	1(0)	—	—	—	—	—	—	—	—	6	4	66.7	63	10.5(27)	0	0	—	—	—	—	0	32
1994	Cin	1(0)	—	—	—	—	—	—	—	—	—	—	—	—	—	—	—	—	—	—	—	0	—
1996	Cin	3(0)	6	24	4.0(18)	0	—	—	—	—	13	7	53.8	90	6.9(38)	1	2	3	16	—	—	0	-6
NFL	6	22(1)	19	69	3.6(18)	0	—	—	—	—	136	77	56.6	912	6.7(46)	5	6	8	43	—	—	0	310

WILHELM, MATT   Matt, LB, 6'4"/245 lbs; Ohio State; 2003: SD, rnd 4; B2/2/1981 Oberlin, OH   **2003** SD 2 (0)   **2004**†SD 7 (0)   **2005** SD 16 (0)   **NFL** 25 (0) [3 yrs]

WILKENS, ELMER   Elmer Sutter, E, 5'9"/175 lbs; Indiana; B6/25/1901 Fort Wayne, IN, D3/18/1967 Fort Wayne, IN   **1925** GB 6 (4)

WILKERSON, BASIL   Basil, E-T, /215 lbs; Oklahoma City; B1/22/1907 Duncan, OK, D9/2/1967 Odessa, TX   **1932** Bos 6 (1)   **1932** SI 3 (0)   **1934** Cin 1 (0)   **NFL** 10 (1) [2 yrs]

WILKERSON, BRUCE   Bruce Alan, T-G, 6'5"/295 lbs; Tennessee; 1987: LARd, rnd 2; B7/28/1964 Loudon, TN   **1987** LARd 11 (5, rg)   **1988** LARd 16 (16, RG)   **1989** LARd 16 (16, RT)   **1990**†LARd 8 (1)   **1991**†LARd 16 (16, LT)   **1992** LARd 15 (15, LT)   **1993**†LARd 14 (14, RT)   **1994** LARd 11 (6, rt)   **1995** Jax 10 (0)   **1996**†GB 14 (2)   **1997**†GB 16 (3)   **NFL** 147 (94) [11 yrs]

WILKERSON, DARYL   Daryl Wayne, DE, 6'4"/255 lbs; Houston; B9/25/1958 Houston, TX   **1981** Bal 5 (0)

WILKERSON, DOUG   Douglas, G, 6'3"/253 lbs; North Carolina Central; 1970: Hou, rnd 1; B3/27/1947 Fayetteville, NC   **1970** Hou 9   **1971** SD 14 (14, LG)   **1972** SD 14 (14, LG)   **1973** SD 14 (14, LG)   **1974** SD 14 (14, LG)   **1975** SD 14 (14, LG)   **1976** SD 14 (14, LG)   **1977** SD 14 (14, LG)   **1978** SD 16 (16, LG)   **1979**†SD☆12 (12, LG)   **1980**†SD★16 (16, LG)   **1981**†SD★16 (16, LG)   **1982**†SD★9 (9, LG)   **1983** SD 12 (12, LG)   **1984** SD 16 (16, LG)   **NFL** 204 (195) [15 yrs]

WILKERSON, ERIC   Eric LaShawn, RB-WR, 5'9"/185 lbs; Kent State; B12/19/1966 Cleveland, OH   **1989**†Pit 1 (0)

WILKERSON, JIMMY   Jimmy, DE, 6'2"/272 lbs; Oklahoma; 2003: KC, rnd 6; B1/4/1981 Omaha, TX   **2003**†KC 12 (0)   **2004** KC 15 (0)   **2005** KC 16 (2)   **NFL** 43 (2) [3 yrs]

WILKES, REGGIE   Reginald Wayman, LB, 6'4"/235 lbs; Georgia Tech; 1978: Phi, rnd 3; B5/27/1956 Pine Bluff, AR [K]   **1978** Phi 16 (13, LOLB)   **1979**†Phi 16 (16, RLB)   **1980**†Phi 16 (0)   **1981**†Phi 14 (8, lolb)   **1982** Phi 9 (7, ROLB)   **1983** Phi 14 (12, LOLB)   **1984** Phi 14 (14, LOLB)   **1985** Phi 16 (16, LOLB)   **1986** Atl 16 (16, LOLB)   **1987** Atl 6 (5, lolb)   **NFL** 137 (107) [10 yrs]

WILKIN, WILLIE   Wilbur B. 'Wee Willie', T, 6'4"/261 lbs; St. Mary's (CA); B4/21/1916 Bingham Canyon, UT, D5/16/1973 Palo Alto, CA [KC]   **1938** Was 11 (3)   **1939** Was 11 (4)   **1940**†Was◇11 (9, LT)   **1941** Was★11 (10, LT)   **1942**†Was★11 (8, LT)   **1943**†Was 9 (3)   **NFL** 64 (37) [6 yrs]

| 1946 | ChiR-A | 10(8, LT) | — | — | — | — | 3 | (3) | — | 0 | — | — | — | — | — | — | — | — | — | — | — | 0 | 20 |

WILKINS, DAVID   David, DE-LB, 6'4"/240 lbs; Eastern Kentucky; B2/24/1969 Cincinnati, OH   **1992**†SF 13 (0)

WILKINS, DICK   Richard Maurice, E, 6'2"/194 lbs; Oregon; 1948: NYG, rnd 25; B9/28/1925 Portland, OR

1949	LAD-A	11(3, le)	8	28	3.5	0	32	589	18.4	3	1	0	0.0	0	0.0	0	0	—	—	—	—	18	338
1952	DalT	12(11, LE)	—	—	—	—	32	416	13.0(42)	3	—	—	—	—	—	—	—	—	—	—	—	18	223
1954	NYG	6	—	—	—	—	4	45	11.3(18)	1	—	—	—	—	—	—	—	—	—	—	—	6	28
NFL	2	18(11)	—	—	—	—	36	461	12.8(42)	4	—	—	—	—	—	—	—	—	—	—	—	24	251

WILKINS, GABE   Gabriel Nicholas, DE-DT, 6'5"/304 lbs; Gardner-Webb; 1994: GB, rnd 4; B9/1/1971 Cowpens, SC   **1994**†GB 15 (0)   **1995**†GB 13 (8, RDT)   **1996**†GB 16 (1)   **1997**†GB 16 (16, RDE)   **1998**†SF 8 (4)   **1999** SF 16 (16, RDE)   **NFL** 84 (45) [6 yrs]

WILKINS, GARY   Gary Clifton, TE-RB, 6'1"/235 lbs; Georgia Tech; B11/23/1963 West Palm Beach, FL

1986	Buf	16(2)	3	18	6.0(11)	0	8	74	9.3(26)	0	—	—	—	—	—	—	—	—	—	—	—	0	55
1987	Buf	1(0)	—	—	—	—	—	—	—	—	—	—	—	—	—	—	—	—	—	—	—	0	—
1988	Atl	14(1)	—	—	—	—	11	134	12.2(33)	0	—	—	—	—	—	—	—	—	—	—	—	0	67
1989	Atl	13(1)	—	—	—	—	8	179	22.4(36)	3	—	—	—	—	—	—	—	—	—	—	—	18	105
1990	Atl	16(13, TE)	—	—	—	—	12	175	14.6(37)	2	—	—	—	—	—	—	—	—	—	k	—	12	90
1991	Atl	5(0)	—	—	—	—	3	22	7.3(12)	1	—	—	—	—	—	—	—	—	—	k	—	6	16
NFL	6	65(17)	3	18	6.0(11)	0	42	584	13.9(37)	6	—	—	—	—	—	—	—	—	—	k	—	36	332

WILKINS, JEFF   Jeffrey Allen, K, 6'2"/205 lbs; Youngstown State; B4/19/1972 Youngstown, OH [K]   **1994** Phi 6 (0)   **1995**†SF 7 (0)   **1996**†SF 16 (0)   **1997** SL 16 (0)   **1998** SL 16 (0)   **1999**†SL 16 (0)   **2000**†SL 11 (0)   **2001**†SL 16 (0)   **2002** SL 16 (0)

2003	†SL★	16(0)	1	7	7.0(7)	0	—	—	—	—	—	—	—	—	—	—	—	—	—	K	—	**163**	7
2004	†SL	16(0)	1	-5	-5.0(-5)	0	—	—	—	—	1	0	0.0	0	0.0	0	0	—	—	K	—	89	-5
2005	SL	16(0)	1	-4	-4.0(-4)	0	—	—	—	—	—	—	—	—	—	—	—	—	—	KP	—	117	-4
NFL	12	168(0)	3	-2	-0.7(7)	0	—	—	—	—	1	0	0.0	0	0.0	0	0	—	—	KP	—	1188	-2

WILKINS, MARCUS   Marcus Wesley, LB, 6'2"/235 lbs; Texas; B1/2/1980 Austin, TX   **2002** GB 5 (0)   **2003** GB 7 (0)   **2004** Cin 16 (0)   **2005**†Cin 15 (0)   **NFL** 43 (0) [4 yrs]

WILKINS, ROY   Roy Lee, LB-DE, 6'3"/224 lbs; Georgia; 1957: LA, rnd 6; B12/26/1934 Murray County, GA, D10/✦/2002 Norwalk, GA   **1958** LARm 12   **1959** LARm 12   **1960** Was 12   **1961** Was 14 (6, LLB)   **NFL** 50 (6) [4 yrs]

WILKINS, TERRENCE   Terrence Olondo, WR, 5'10"/180 lbs; Virginia; B7/29/1975 Washington, DC [R]

1999	†Ind	16(11, WR)	1	2	2.0(2)	0	42	565	13.5(80)	4	—	—	—	—	—	—	—	—	—	kp	3	42	877
2000	†Ind	14(7, wr)	3	8	2.7(6)	0	43	569	13.2(43)	3	—	—	—	—	—	—	—	—	—	kp	—	18	457
2001	Ind	11(4)	—	—	—	—	34	332	9.8(28)	0	—	—	—	—	—	—	—	—	—	kp	1	6	637
2002	SL	13(0)	6	56	9.3(18)	0	5	31	6.2(14)	0	—	—	—	—	—	—	—	—	—	kp	—	0	558
2003	Ind	3(0)	—	—	—	—	—	—	—	—	—	—	—	—	—	—	—	—	—	kp	—	0	105
NFL	5	57(22)	10	66	6.6(18)	0	124	1497	12.1(80)	7	—	—	—	—	—	—	—	—	—	kp	4	66	2633

WILKINSON, BOB   Robert Raymond, E-DB-HB, 6'3"/215 lbs; Loyola Marymount; UCLA; 1950: NYG, rnd 10; B10/8/1926

1951	NYG	12	—	—	—	—	11	182	16.5(69)	1	—	—	—	—	—	—	—	—	—	—	i	—	6	103
1952	NYG	7	26	26	1.0(7)	0	6	148	24.7(70)	2	—	—	—	—	—	—	—	—	—	—	—	—	12	110
NFL	2	19	26	26	1.0(7)	0	17	330	19.4(70)	3	—	—	—	—	—	—	—	—	—	—	i	—	18	213

WILKINSON, DAN   Daniel Raymon, DT-DE, 6'4"/335 lbs; Ohio State; 1994: Cin, rnd 1; B3/13/1973 Dayton, OH [S]   **1994** Cin 16 (14, RDT)   **1995** Cin 14 (14, LDT)   **1996** Cin 16 (16, LDT)   **1997** Cin 15 (15, RDE)   **1998** Was 16 (16, LDT)   **1999**†Was 16 (16, LDT)   **2000** Was 16 (16, LDT)   **2001** Was 16 (16, LDT)   **2002** Was 12 (11, LDT)   **2003** Det 16 (16, LDT)   **2004** Det 16 (16, LDT)   **2005** Det 16 (16, RDT)   **NFL** 185 (182) [12 yrs]

WILKINSON, JERRY   Gerald Edward, DE, 6'9"/248 lbs; Oregon State; 1979: LA, rnd 4; B2/27/1956 San Francisco, CA   **1979**†LARm 16   **1980** Cle 7 (0)   **1980** SF 6 (0)   **NFL** 29 [2 yrs]

WILKS, JIM   Jimmy Ray, DE-NT, 6'5"/266 lbs; California; San Diego State; 1981: NO, rnd 12; B3/12/1958 Los Angeles, CA   **1981** NO 16 (0)   **1982** NO 8 (8, RDE)   **1983** NO 16 (16, nt)   **1984** NO 16 (16, RDE)   **1985** NO 16 (16, RDE)   **1986** NO 16 (16, RDE)   **1987**†NO 12 (12, RDE)   **1988** NO 16 (16, NT)   **1989** NO 16 (15, NT)   **1990**†NO 15 (15, RDE)   **1991**†NO 16 (15, NT)   **1992**†NO 12 (9, NT)   **1993** NO 8 (1)   **NFL** 183 (154) [13 yrs]

WILL, ERWIN   Erwin Arthur, DT, 6'5"/275 lbs; Dayton; 1965: Phi, rnd 7; B1/14/1943 Cleveland, OH   **1965** Phi 5

WILLARD, JERROTT   Jerrott Michael, LB, 6'1"/233 lbs; California; 1995: KC, rnd 5; B7/11/1972 Fullerton, CA   **1998** KC 1 (0)

YEAR	TEAM	G (GS, POS)	RUSH	YD	AVG (LG)	TD	REC	YD	AVG (LG)	TD	PASS	COMP	PCT	YD	AVG (LG)	TD	INT	SK	YD	QBR	KPR	OTD	PTS	TAY

WILLARD, KEN Kenneth Henderson, RB, 6´1˝/219 lbs; North Carolina; 1965: SF, rnd 1; B7/14/1943 Richmond, VA

YEAR	TEAM	G (GS, POS)	RUSH	YD	AVG (LG)	TD	REC	YD	AVG (LG)	TD	PASS	COMP	PCT	YD	AVG (LG)	TD	INT	SK	YD	QBR	KPR	OTD	PTS	TAY
1965	SF★	14 (14, FB)	189	778	4.1 (32)	5	32	253	7.9 (29)	4	1	0	0.0	0	0.0	0	1	—	—	—	—	—	54	935
1966	SF✧	14 (14, FB)	191	763	4.0 (49)	5	42	351	8.4 (52)	2	—	—	—	—	—	—	—	—	—	—	—	—	42	999
1967	SF	13 (13, FB)	169	510	3.0 (20)	5	23	242	10.5 (25)	1	—	—	—	—	—	—	—	—	—	—	—	—	36	686
1968	SF★	14 (14, FB)	227	967	4.3 (69)	7	36	232	6.4 (20)	0	—	—	—	—	—	—	—	—	—	—	—	—	42	1153
1969	SF✧	14 (14, FB)	171	557	3.3 (18)	7	36	326	9.1 (36)	3	—	—	—	—	—	—	—	—	—	—	—	—	60	805
1970	†SF	14 (14, FB)	236	789	3.3 (20)	7	31	259	8.4 (32)	3	—	—	—	—	—	—	—	—	—	—	—	—	60	1004
1971	†SF	14 (14, FB)	216	855	4.0 (49)	4	27	202	7.5 (33)	1	—	—	—	—	—	—	—	—	—	—	—	—	30	1001
1972	SF	14 (11, FB)	100	345	3.5 (23)	4	24	131	5.5 (15)	1	—	—	—	—	—	—	—	—	—	—	—	—	30	456
1973	SF	14 (10, FB)	83	366	4.4 (33)	1	22	160	7.3 (26)	1	—	—	—	—	—	—	—	—	—	—	k	—	12	446
1974	†SL	7 (3)	40	175	4.4 (12)	0	4	28	7.0 (17)	1	—	—	—	—	—	—	—	—	—	—	—	—	6	194
NFL	10	132 (121)	1622	6105	3.8 (69)	45	277	2184	7.9 (52)	17	1	0	0.0	0	0.0	0	1	—	—	—	k	—	372	7677

WILLEGALE, HENRY Henry Minard, B, 5´11˝/190 lbs; Carleton; B6/9/1901 Madison, WI, D6/26/1964 Minneapolis, MN **1929** Min 9 (6, WB)

WILLERT C, none; deceased **1922** Ham 1 (0)

WILLEY, NORM Norman Earle, DE-G-E, 6´2˝/224 lbs; Marshall; 1950: Phi, rnd 13; B8/22/1927 Hastings, WV **1950** Phi 12 (RDE) **1951** Phi 11 (RDE) **1952** Phi 12 (RDE/lg) **1953** Phi☆12 (RDE) **1955** Phi★12 (RDE) **1956** Phi 9 (RDE) **1957** Phi 12 (RDE)

YEAR	TEAM	G (GS, POS)	RUSH	YD	AVG (LG)	TD	REC	YD	AVG (LG)	TD	PASS	COMP	PCT	YD	AVG (LG)	TD	INT	SK	YD	QBR	KPR	OTD	PTS	TAY
1954	Phi★	12 (RDE)	—	—	—	—	2	50	25.0 (37)	0	—	—	—	—	—	—	—	—	—	—	—	1	6	25
NFL	8	92	—	—	—	—	2	50	25.0 (37)	0	—	—	—	—	—	—	—	—	—	—	ki	2	12	68

WILLGING, COLE Coleman G., E-DE, 6´3˝/205 lbs; Xavier (OH); B1911, D3/10/1973 Cincinnati, OH

YEAR	TEAM	G (GS, POS)	RUSH	YD	AVG (LG)	TD	REC	YD	AVG (LG)	TD	PASS	COMP	PCT	YD	AVG (LG)	TD	INT	SK	YD	QBR	KPR	OTD	PTS	TAY
1934	Cin	4 (0)	—	—	—	—	2	14	7.0	0	—	—	—	—	—	—	—	—	—	—	—	—	0	7

WILLHITE, GERALD Gerald William, RB, 5´10˝/200 lbs; San Jose State; 1982: Den, rnd 1; B5/30/1959 Sacramento, CA **[R]**

YEAR	TEAM	G (GS, POS)	RUSH	YD	AVG (LG)	TD	REC	YD	AVG (LG)	TD	PASS	COMP	PCT	YD	AVG (LG)	TD	INT	SK	YD	QBR	KPR	OTD	PTS	TAY
1982	Den	9 (2)	70	347	5.0 (23)	2	26	227	8.7 (27)	0	2	0	0.0	0	0.0	0	1	—	—	—	kp	—	12	556
1983	†Den	8 (0)	43	188	4.4 (24)	3	14	153	10.9 (26)	1	1	0	0.0	0	0.0	0	0	—	—	—	—	—	24	300
1984	†Den	16 (1)	77	371	4.8 (52)	2	27	298	11.0 (63)	0	2	1	50.0	20	10.0 (20)	0	0	—	—	—	kp	—	12	699
1985	Den	15 (4)	66	237	3.6 (14)	3	35	297	8.5 (21)	1	3	0	0.0	0	0.0	0	0	—	—	—	kp	—	24	520
1986	†Den☆	16 (12, FB)	85	365	4.3 (42)	5	64	529	8.3 (31)	3	4	1	25.0	11	2.8 (11)	0	0	—	—	—	kp	1	54	958
1987	Den	3 (1)	26	141	5.4 (29)	0	9	25	2.8 (6)	0	1	0	0.0	0	0.0	0	0	—	—	—	p	—	0	156
1988	Den	11 (1)	13	39	3.0 (7)	2	32	238	7.4 (15)	0	—	—	—	—	—	—	—	—	—	—	p	—	12	203
NFL	7	78 (21)	380	1688	4.4 (52)	17	207	1767	8.5 (63)	5	13	2	15.4	31	2.4 (20)	0	1	—	—	—	kp	1	138	3390

WILLHITE, KEVIN Kevin Alfred, RB, 5´11˝/208 lbs; Oregon; B5/11/1963 Sacramento, CA

YEAR	TEAM	G (GS, POS)	RUSH	YD	AVG (LG)	TD	REC	YD	AVG (LG)	TD	PASS	COMP	PCT	YD	AVG (LG)	TD	INT	SK	YD	QBR	KPR	OTD	PTS	TAY
1987	GB	3 (3)	53	251	4.7 (61)	0	6	37	6.2 (12)	0	—	—	—	—	—	—	—	—	—	—	—	—	0	307

WILLIAMS, A.D. A.D., E-FL, 6´2˝/210 lbs; Pacific; 1956: LA, rnd 3; B11/21/1933 Little Rock, AR

YEAR	TEAM	G (GS, POS)	RUSH	YD	AVG (LG)	TD	REC	YD	AVG (LG)	TD	PASS	COMP	PCT	YD	AVG (LG)	TD	INT	SK	YD	QBR	KPR	OTD	PTS	TAY
1959	GB	12	—	—	—	—	1	11	11.0 (11)	0	—	—	—	—	—	—	—	—	—	—	—	—	0	6
1960	Cle	12	—	—	—	—	1	5	5.0 (5)	0	—	—	—	—	—	—	—	—	—	—	—	—	0	3
1961	Min	13	—	—	—	—	13	174	13.4 (49)	1	—	—	—	—	—	—	—	—	—	—	—	—	6	92
NFL	3	37	—	—	—	—	15	190	12.7 (49)	1	—	—	—	—	—	—	—	—	—	—	—	—	6	100

WILLIAMS, AENEAS Aeneas Demetrius, DB, 5´11˝/200 lbs; Southern (LA); 1991: Phx, rnd 3; B1/29/1968 New Orleans, LA **[I]** **1991** Phx 16 (15, RCB/lcb) **1992** Phx 16 (16, RCB) **1993** Phx 16 (16, LCB) **1994** Arz★16 (16, LCB) **1995** Arz★16 (16, LCB) **1996** Arz★16 (16, LCB) **1997** Arz★16 (16, LCB) **1998**†Arz✧16 (16, LCB) **1999** Arz✧16 (16, LCB) **2000** Arz 16 (16, LCB) **2001**†SL★16 (16, LCB) **2002** SL 6 (6, lcb) **2003**†SL✧16 (16, FS) **2004** SL 13 (10, FS) **NFL** 211 (207) [14 yrs]

WILLIAMS, AL Alphonso, WR, 5´10˝/180 lbs; Nevada-Reno; 1984: Det, rnd S1; B10/5/1961 Vidalia, GA

YEAR	TEAM	G (GS, POS)	RUSH	YD	AVG (LG)	TD	REC	YD	AVG (LG)	TD	PASS	COMP	PCT	YD	AVG (LG)	TD	INT	SK	YD	QBR	KPR	OTD	PTS	TAY
1987	SD	3 (3)	1	11	11.0 (11)	0	12	247	20.6 (57)	1	—	—	—	—	—	—	—	—	—	—	p	—	6	186

WILLIAMS, ALFRED Alfred Hamilton, DE-LB, 6´6˝/260 lbs; Colorado; 1991: Cin, rnd 1; B11/6/1968 Houston, TX **[S]** **1991** Cin 16 (15, ROLB) **1992** Cin 15 (6, rolb) **1993** Cin 16 (16, ROLB) **1994** Cin 16 (16, RDE) **1995**†SF 16 (0) **1996**†Den☆16 (16, RDE) **1997**†Den 16 (16, RDE) **1998**†Den 10 (0) **1999** Den 7 (6, rde) **NFL** 128 (91) [9 yrs]

WILLIAMS, ALLEN Allen, RB, 5´11˝/205 lbs; Georgia; B9/17/1972 Thomasville, GA **1995**†Det 5 (0)

WILLIAMS, ALONZO Alonzo Fitzgerald, RB, 5´9˝/192 lbs; Mesa; 1987: LARm, rnd 12; B8/9/1963 Los Angeles, CA

YEAR	TEAM	G (GS, POS)	RUSH	YD	AVG (LG)	TD	REC	YD	AVG (LG)	TD	PASS	COMP	PCT	YD	AVG (LG)	TD	INT	SK	YD	QBR	KPR	OTD	PTS	TAY
1987	LARm	3 (0)	2	9	4.5 (7)	0	—	—	—	—	—	—	—	—	—	—	—	—	—	—	k	—	0	48

WILLIAMS, ANDREW Andrew B., DE, 6´2˝/263 lbs; Miami (FL); 2003: SF, rnd 3; B4/18/1979 Tampa, FL **2003** SF 2 (0) **2004** SF 7 (3) **NFL** 9 (3) [2 yrs]

WILLIAMS, ARMON Armon Abdule, DB, 6´1˝/221 lbs; Arizona; 1997: Ten, rnd 7; B8/13/1973 Chandler, AZ **1997** Ten 6 (0)

WILLIAMS, BEN Robert Jerry, DE-NT, 6´3˝/251 lbs; Mississippi; 1976: Buf, rnd 3; B9/1/1954 Yazoo City, MS **1976** Buf 13 (7, lde) **1977** Buf 14 (14, LDE) **1978** Buf 16 (16, LDE) **1979** Buf 16 (15, LDE) **1980**†Buf☆16 (16, LDE) **1981**†Buf☆16 (16, LDE) **1982** Buf★9 (9, LDE) **1983** Buf 16 (16, LDE) **1984** Buf 15 (15, LDE) **1985** Buf 16 (16, LDE) **NFL** 147 (140) [10 yrs]

WILLIAMS, BEN Lewis Ben, DT, 6´2˝/265 lbs; Minnesota; B5/28/1970 Belzoni, MS **1998** Min 1 (0) **1999** Phi 3 (0) **NFL** 4 (0) [2 yrs]

WILLIAMS, BERNARD Bennie Bernard, T, 6´8˝/317 lbs; Georgia; 1994: Phi, rnd 1; B7/18/1972 Memphis, TN **1994** Phi 16 (16, LT)

WILLIAMS, BERT Albert Donnell, LB, 6´3˝/229 lbs; Texas-El Paso; B9/7/1964 San Antonio, TX **1987** Pit 3 (3)

WILLIAMS, BILLY Billy Louis, WR, 5´11˝/175 lbs; Tennessee; 1995: Arz, rnd 7; B6/7/1971 Alcoa, TN **1996** SL 1 (0)

WILLIAMS, BOB Robert Allen, QB, 6´1˝/197 lbs; Notre Dame; 1951: ChiB, rnd 1; B1/2/1930 Cumberland, MD

YEAR	TEAM	G (GS, POS)	RUSH	YD	AVG (LG)	TD	REC	YD	AVG (LG)	TD	PASS	COMP	PCT	YD	AVG (LG)	TD	INT	SK	YD	QBR	KPR	OTD	PTS	TAY
1951	ChiB	8	5	0	0.0 (3)	0	—	—	—	—	33	14	42.4	146	4.4 (19)	1	2	—	—	—	P	—	0	-2
1952	ChiB	11	11	33	3.0 (12)	0	—	—	—	—	87	45	51.7	579	6.7 (56)	6	5	—	—	—	P	—	0	153
1955	ChiB	10	13	79	6.1 (19)	0	—	—	—	—	40	15	37.5	256	6.4 (37)	3	5	—	—	—	P	—	0	22
NFL	3	29	29	112	3.9 (19)	0	—	—	—	—	160	74	46.3	981	6.1 (56)	10	12	—	—	—	P	—	0	173

WILLIAMS, BOBBIE Bobbie, G, 6´3˝/320 lbs; Arkansas; 2000: Phi, rnd 2; B9/25/1976 Jefferson, TX **2001** Phi 1 (1) **2002**†Phi 16 (0) **2003**†Phi 16 (11, RG) **2004** Cin 16 (16, RG) **2005**†Cin 16 (16, RG) **NFL** 65 (44) [5 yrs]

WILLIAMS, BOBBY Bobby Ray, DB, 6´0˝/205 lbs; Central Oklahoma; 1966: SL, rnd 11; B2/28/1942 Geiger, AL **[R]** **1966** SL 14 **1967** SL 14 **1969** Det 13 **1970**†Det 14 **1971** Det 14 **NFL** 69 [5 yrs]

WILLIAMS, BOO Eddie Lee, TE, 6´4˝/270 lbs; Arkansas; B6/22/1979 Tallahassee, FL

YEAR	TEAM	G (GS, POS)	RUSH	YD	AVG (LG)	TD	REC	YD	AVG (LG)	TD	PASS	COMP	PCT	YD	AVG (LG)	TD	INT	SK	YD	QBR	KPR	OTD	PTS	TAY
2001	NO	11 (4)	—	—	—	—	20	202	10.1 (26)	3	—	—	—	—	—	—	—	—	—	—	—	—	18	116
2002	NO	16 (3)	—	—	—	—	13	143	11.0 (32)	2	—	—	—	—	—	—	—	—	—	—	—	—	14	82
2003	NO	16 (6, te)	—	—	—	—	41	436	10.6 (31)	5	—	—	—	—	—	—	—	—	—	—	—	—	30	243
2004	NO	16 (8, te)	—	—	—	—	33	362	11.0 (22)	2	—	—	—	—	—	—	—	—	—	—	—	—	12	191
NFL	4	59 (21)	—	—	—	—	107	1143	10.7 (32)	12	—	—	—	—	—	—	—	—	—	—	—	—	74	632

WILLIAMS, BOYD Boyd Horace, C, 6´3˝/218 lbs; Syracuse; B5/4/1922 Patton, PA, D8/26/1997 **1947**†Phi 6 (0)

WILLIAMS, BRENT Brent Dione, DE, 6´4˝/283 lbs; Toledo; 1986: NE, rnd 7; B10/23/1964 Flint, MI **1986**†NE 16 (16, LDE) **1987** NE 12 (5, lde) **1988** NE 16 (16, LDE) **1989** NE 16 (16, RDE) **1990** NE 16 (16, LDE) **1991** NE 16 (16, RDE) **1992** NE 16 (15, RDE) **1993** NE 13 (2) **1994** Sea 10 (9, RDE) **1995** Sea 11 (9, RDE) **1996** NYJ 5 (0) **NFL** 147 (120) [11 yrs]

WILLIAMS, BRETT Brett, T, 6´5˝/321 lbs; Florida State; 2003: KC, rnd 4; B5/2/1980 Kissimmee, FL **2004** KC 5 (0)

WILLIAMS, BRIAN Brian, DB, 5´11˝/198 lbs; North Carolina State; 2002: Min, rnd 4; B7/2/1979 High Point, NC **2002** Min 16 (7, LCB) **2003** Min 16 (16, LCB/rcb) **2004**†Min 16 (16, RCB) **2005** Min 14 (9, RCB) **NFL** 62 (48) [4 yrs]

WILLIAMS, BRIAN Brian Keith, TE, 6´5˝/240 lbs; Southern (LA); 1981: Min, rnd 12; B10/14/1957 New Orleans, LA **1982** NE 1 (0)

WILLIAMS, BRIAN Brian Marcee, LB, 6´1˝/240 lbs; USC; 1995: GB, rnd 3; B12/17/1972 Dallas, TX **1995**†GB 13 (0) **1996**†GB 16 (16, RLB) **1997**†GB 16 (16, RLB) **1998**†GB 16 (15, RLB) **1999** GB 7 (7, rlb) **2000** GB 4 (3) **2001** NO 4 (0) **2001** Det 2 (1) **2002** Det 3 (3) **NFL** 81 (61) [8 yrs]

WILLIAMS, BRIAN Brian Scott, C, 6´1˝/235 lbs; Minnesota; 1989: NYG, rnd 1; B6/8/1966 Mount Lebanon, PA **1989** NYG 14 (4) **1990**†NYG 16 (1) **1991** NYG 14 (1) **1992** NYG 13 (1) **1993**†NYG 16 (1) **1994** NYG 14 (14, C) **1995** NYG 16 (16, C) **1996** NYG 14 (14, C) **1999** NYG 12 (12, C) **NFL** 129 (64) [9 yrs]

YEAR	TEAM	G (GS, POS)	RUSH	YD	AVG(LG)	TD	REC	YD	AVG(LG)	TD	PASS	COMP	PCT	YD	AVG(LG)	TD	INT	SK	YD	QBR	KPR	OTD	PTS	TAY

WILLIAMS, BROCK   Brock, DB, 5´10˝/195 lbs; Notre Dame; 2001: NE, rnd 3; B8/11/1979 Hammond, LA   **2003** ChiB 10 (0)   **2004** Oak 2 (0)   **NFL** 12 (0) [2 yrs]

WILLIAMS, BROOKS   Kim Brooks, TE, 6´4˝/226 lbs; North Carolina; 1978: NO, rnd 8; B12/7/1954 Baltimore, MD

1978	NO	16	—	—	—	—	—	—	—	—	—	—	—	—	—	—	—	—	—	—	—	—	—	—
1979	NO	16	—	—	—	—	2	22	11.0(14)	0	—	—	—	—	—	—	—	—	—	—	k	—	0	-7
1980	NO	12(7, TE)	—	—	—	—	26	351	13.5(56)	2	—	—	—	—	—	—	—	—	—	—	—	—	12	186
1981	NO	7(0)	—	—	—	—	5	50	10.0(13)	0	—	—	—	—	—	—	—	—	—	—	—	—	0	25
1981	ChiB	5(0)	—	—	—	—	3	32	10.7(16)	0	—	—	—	—	—	—	—	—	—	—	k	—	0	36
1982	ChiB	9(0)	—	—	—	—	—	—	—	—	—	—	—	—	—	—	—	—	—	—	—	—	—	—
1983	NE	13(1)	—	—	—	—	1	0	0.0(0)	0	—	—	—	—	—	—	—	—	—	—	—	—	0	0
NFL	6	78(8)	—	—	—	—	37	455	12.3(56)	2	—	—	—	—	—	—	—	—	—	—	k	—	12	240

WILLIAMS, BYRON   Byron Keith, WR, 6´2˝/182 lbs; Texas-Arlington; 1983: GB, rnd 10; B10/31/1960 Texarkana, TX

1983	NYG	5(0)	—	—	—	—	20	346	17.3(43)	1	—	—	—	—	—	—	—	—	—	—	—	—	6	178
1984	†NYG	16(0)	—	—	—	—	24	471	19.6(65)	2	—	—	—	—	—	—	—	—	—	—	—	—	12	246
1985	†NYG	16(5, wr)	2	18	9.0(17)	0	15	280	18.7(45)	0	—	—	—	—	—	—	—	—	—	—	—	—	0	158
NFL	3	37(5)	2	18	9.0(17)	0	59	1097	18.6(65)	3	—	—	—	—	—	—	—	—	—	—	—	—	18	582

WILLIAMS, CADILLAC   Carnell, RB, 5´11˝/217 lbs; Auburn; 2005: TB, rnd 1; B4/21/1982 Attalla, AL

| 2005 | †TB | 14(14, RB) | 290 | 1178 | 4.1(71) | 6 | 20 | 81 | 4.1(15) | 0 | — | — | — | — | — | — | — | — | — | — | — | — | 36 | 1279 |

WILLIAMS, CALVIN   Calvin John, WR, 5´11˝/187 lbs; Purdue; 1990: Phi, rnd 5; B3/3/1967 Baltimore, MD

1990	†Phi	16(14, WR)	2	20	10.0(18)	0	37	602	16.3(45)	9	—	—	—	—	—	—	—	—	—	—	p	—	54	355
1991	Phi	12(11, WR)	—	—	—	—	33	326	9.9(30)	3	—	—	—	—	—	—	—	—	—	—	—	—	18	178
1992	†Phi	16(15, WR)	—	—	—	—	42	598	14.2(49)	7	—	—	—	—	—	—	—	—	—	—	—	—	42	334
1993	Phi	16(14, WR)	—	—	—	—	60	725	12.1(80)	10	—	—	—	—	—	—	—	—	—	—	—	—	60	413
1994	Phi	16(14, WR)	2	11	5.5(6)	0	58	813	14.0(53)	3	—	—	—	—	—	—	—	—	—	—	—	—	18	433
1995	†Phi	16(15, WR)	1	-2	-2.0(-2)	0	63	768	12.2(37)	2	—	—	—	—	—	—	—	—	—	—	—	—	14	392
1996	Bal	7(2)	—	—	—	—	13	85	6.5(19)	1	—	—	—	—	—	—	—	—	—	—	—	—	6	48
1996	†Phi	1(0)	—	—	—	—	2	8	4.0(4)	0	—	—	—	—	—	—	—	—	—	—	—	—	0	4
NFL	7	100(85)	5	29	5.8(18)	0	308	3925	12.7(80)	35	—	—	—	—	—	—	—	—	—	—	p	—	212	2156

WILLIAMS, CHAD   Chad Kelton, DB, 5´9˝/207 lbs; Southern Mississippi; 2002: Bal, rnd 6; B1/22/1979 Birmingham, AL   **2002** Bal 16 (0)   **2003**†Bal 16 (1)   **2004** Bal 16 (1)   **2005** Bal 16 (3)   **NFL** 64 (5) [4 yrs]

WILLIAMS, CHARLES   Charles, DB, 6´1˝/180 lbs; Jackson State; 1978: Phi, rnd 9; B9/14/1953 Magee, MS   **1978** Phi 7 (1)

WILLIAMS, CHARLIE   Charlie U., DB, 6´0˝/193 lbs; Bowling Green State; 1995: Dal, rnd 3; B2/2/1972 Detroit, MI   **1995**†Dal 16 (0)   **1996**†Dal 7 (0)   **1997** Dal 16 (0)   **1998**†Dal 15 (3)   **1999**†Dal 16 (8, lcb)   **2000** Dal 11 (0)   **NFL** 81 (11) [6 yrs]

WILLIAMS, CHRIS   Chris Albany, DB, 6´0˝/197 lbs; LSU; 1981: Buf, rnd 2; B1/2/1959 Alexandria, LA   **1981**†Buf 0 (0)   **1982** Buf 5 (0)   **1983** Buf 16 (5, fs)   **NFL** 21 (5) [3 yrs]

WILLIAMS, CHRIS   Chris, NT, 6´3˝/304 lbs; American International; B11/23/1968 Chelsea, MA   **1991** Phx 15 (0)

WILLIAMS, CLANCY   Clarence, DB, 6´3˝/194 lbs; Washington State; 1965: LA, rnd 1/SD, rnd 8; B9/24/1942 Deweyville, TX, D9/21/1986 Seattle, WA [I]   **1966** LARm 14 (LCB)   **1967**†LARm 14 (LCB)   **1968** LARm 14 (14, LCB)   **1969**†LARm 14 (14, LCB)   **1970** LARm 14 (12, LCB)   **1971** LARm 6   **1972** LARm 9 (6, lcb)

| 1965 | LARm | 12(LCB) | 3 | 3 | 1.0(2) | 0 | — | — | — | — | — | — | — | — | — | — | — | — | — | — | k | — | 0 | 81 |
| **NFL** | 8 | 97(46) | 3 | 3 | 1.0(2) | 0 | — | — | — | — | — | — | — | — | — | — | — | — | — | — | ki | 2 | 12 | 641 |

WILLIAMS, CLARENCE   Clarence, RB, 5´9˝/194 lbs; South Carolina; 1977: SD, rnd 5; B1/25/1955 Oakley, SC, D9/17/1994 Columbia, SC

1977	SD	14	50	215	4.3(46)	2	3	20	6.7(9)	0	—	—	—	—	—	—	—	—	—	—	kp	—	12	361
1978	SD	10(1)	27	76	2.8(12)	0	1	17	17.0(17)	0	—	—	—	—	—	—	—	—	—	—	k	—	0	138
1979	†SD	16(16, FB)	200	752	3.8(55)	12	51	352	6.9(14)	0	—	—	—	—	—	—	—	—	—	—	k	—	72	1052
1980	†SD	13(9, RB)	97	258	2.7(13)	3	26	230	8.8(26)	1	—	—	—	—	—	—	—	—	—	—	—	—	24	408
1981	†SD	14(1)	20	26	1.3(6)	0	12	108	9.0(15)	1	—	—	—	—	—	—	—	—	—	—	k	—	6	72
NFL	5	67(27)	394	1327	3.4(55)	17	93	727	7.8(26)	2	—	—	—	—	—	—	—	—	—	—	kp	—	114	2031

WILLIAMS, CLARENCE   Clarence, TE-RB, 6´2˝/240 lbs; Washington State; 1993: Den, rnd 7; B8/7/1969 Los Angeles, CA

| 1993 | Cle | 7(1) | — | — | — | — | 1 | 14 | 14.0(14) | 0 | — | — | — | — | — | — | — | — | — | — | — | — | 0 | 7 |

WILLIAMS, CLARENCE   Clarence, RB, 5´9˝/193 lbs; Michigan; B5/16/1977 Detroit, MI

| 2000 | Arz | 3(0) | — | — | — | — | 1 | 5 | 5.0(5) | 0 | — | — | — | — | — | — | — | — | — | — | — | — | 0 | 3 |

WILLIAMS, CLYDE   Clyde Walter, T, 6´2˝/210 lbs; Georgia Tech; B9/17/1910   **1935** Phi 3 (0)

WILLIAMS, CLYDE   Clyde A., G-T, 6´3˝/250 lbs; Southern (LA); B7/27/1940 Shreveport, LA   **1967** SL 9   **1968** SL 10   **1969** SL 13   **1970** SL 14 (RG)   **1971** SL 14 (RG)   **NFL** 60 [5 yrs]

WILLIAMS, COREY   Corey, DT, 6´4˝/292 lbs; Arkansas State; 2004: GB, rnd 6; B8/17/1980 Harmony Grove, AR   **2004**†GB 12 (0)   **2005** GB 12 (0)   **NFL** 24 (0) [2 yrs]

WILLIAMS, CY   Burton Caswell, T, 6´0˝/200 lbs; Florida; B10/10/1903, FL, deceased   **1929** SI 10 (9, LT)   **1930** SI 12 (12, LT)   **1932** Bkn 1 (0)   **NFL** 23 (21) [3 yrs]

WILLIAMS, D.J.   Genos Derwin, LB, 6´2˝/247 lbs; Miami (FL); 2004: Den, rnd 1; B7/20/1982 Pittsburg, CA   **2004**†Den 16 (14, RLB)   **2005**†Den 16 (14, LLB)   **NFL** 32 (28) [2 yrs]

WILLIAMS, DAN   Daniel, DE-DT, 6´4˝/290 lbs; Tennessee State; Toledo; 1993: Den, rnd 1; B12/15/1969 Ypsilanti, MI   **1993** Den 13 (11, LDE)   **1994** Den 12 (8, rdt)   **1995** Den 6 (1, lde)   **1996** Den 15 (15, LDE)   **1997**†KC 15 (6, rde)   **1999** KC 14 (9, rde)   **2000** KC 12 (10, rdt)   **NFL** 87 (65) [7 yrs]

WILLIAMS, DARRENT   Darrent, DB, 5´8˝/188 lbs; Oklahoma State; 2005: Den, rnd 2; B9/27/1982 Fort Worth, TX   **2005**†Den 12 (9, RCB)

WILLIAMS, DARRYL   Darryl Edwin, DB, 6´0˝/198 lbs; Miami (FL); 1992: Cin, rnd 1; B1/7/1970 Miami, FL [I]   **1992** Cin 16 (12, FS)   **1993** Cin 16 (16, FS)   **1994** Cin 16 (16, FS)   **1995** Cin 16 (16, FS)   **1996** Sea 16 (16, FS)   **1997** Sea★16 (16, FS)   **1998** Sea 16 (16, FS)   **1999**†Sea 13 (12, SS)   **2000** Cin 16 (16, FS)   **2001** Cin 15 (1)   **NFL** 156 (137) [10 yrs]

WILLIAMS, DAVE   David Ray, RB, 6´2˝/210 lbs; Colorado; 1976: Dal, rnd 7; B3/10/1954 Minden, LA [R]

1977	SF	12	2	6	3.0(6)	0	—	—	—	—	—	—	—	—	—	—	—	—	—	—	kp	1	6	133
1978	SF	16	15	18	1.2(6)	0	10	63	6.3(13)	0	—	—	—	—	—	—	—	—	—	—	k	1	6	295
1979	†ChiB	14(12, FB)	127	401	3.2(16)	1	42	354	8.4(54)	5	—	—	—	—	—	—	—	—	—	—	—	—	36	613
1980	ChiB	16(3)	26	57	2.2(14)	0	22	132	6.0(18)	0	—	—	—	—	—	—	—	—	—	—	k	1	6	394
1981	ChiB	8(0)	2	19	9.5(15)	0	18	126	7.0(18)	2	—	—	—	—	—	—	—	—	—	—	k	—	12	233
NFL	5	66(15)	172	501	2.9(16)	1	92	675	7.3(54)	7	—	—	—	—	—	—	—	—	—	—	kp	3	66	1668

WILLIAMS, DAVE   David Laverne, WR-SE, 6´2˝/207 lbs; Washington; 1967: SL, rnd 1; B8/10/1945 Cedar Rapids, IA

1967	SL	14	1	7	7.0(7)	0	28	404	14.5(49)	5	—	—	—	—	—	—	—	—	—	—	—	—	30	235
1968	SL	12(SE)	3	47	15.7(43)	0	43	682	15.9(71)	6	—	—	—	—	—	—	—	—	—	—	—	—	36	418
1969	SL	14(SE)	1	1	1.0(1)	0	56	702	12.5(61)	7	—	—	—	—	—	—	—	—	—	—	—	—	42	387
1970	SL	14(WR)	—	—	—	—	23	364	15.8(58)	3	—	—	—	—	—	—	—	—	—	—	—	—	18	197
1971	SL	13(WR)	—	—	—	—	12	182	15.2(37)	1	—	—	—	—	—	—	—	—	—	—	—	—	6	96
1972	SD	12	1	14	14.0(14)	0	14	315	22.5(62)	3	—	—	—	—	—	—	—	—	—	—	—	—	18	196
1973	SD	6	—	—	—	—	7	118	16.9(30)	0	—	—	—	—	—	—	—	—	—	—	—	—	0	59
1973	†Pit	1	—	—	—	—	—	—	—	—	—	—	—	—	—	—	—	—	—	—	—	—	—	—
NFL	7	86	6	69	11.5(43)	0	183	2768	15.1(71)	25	—	—	—	—	—	—	—	—	—	—	—	—	150	1587

WILLIAMS, DAVERN   Davern, DT, 6´3˝/300 lbs; Auburn; Troy State; 2003: Mia, rnd 7; B2/13/1980 Brewton, AL   **2004** NYG 3 (1)

WILLIAMS, DAVID   David Lamar, WR, 6´3˝/190 lbs; Illinois; 1986: Chi, rnd 3; B6/10/1963 Los Angeles, CA

1986	TB	15(0)	—	—	—	—	6	91	15.2(25)	0	—	—	—	—	—	—	—	—	—	—	k	—	0	45
1987	LARd	3(2)	—	—	—	—	4	104	26.0(44)	0	—	—	—	—	—	—	—	—	—	—	—	—	0	52
NFL	2	18(2)	—	—	—	—	10	195	19.5(44)	0	—	—	—	—	—	—	—	—	—	—	k	—	0	97

WILLIAMS, DAVID   David Wayne, T, 6´5˝/294 lbs; Florida; 1989: Hou, rnd 1; B6/21/1966 Mulberry, FL   **1989** Hou 14 (0)   **1990**†Hou 15 (9, RT)   **1991**†Hou 16 (16, RT)   **1992**†Hou 16 (16, RT)   **1993**†Hou 15 (15, RT)   **1994** Hou 16 (16, RT)   **1995** Hou 10 (9, RT)   **1996** NYJ 14 (14, RT)   **1997** NYJ 12 (11, RT)   **NFL** 128 (106) [9 yrs]

WILLIAMS, DEL Delano Roger, G-C, 6´2˝/240 lbs; Florida State; 1967: NO, rnd 3; B11/9/1945 Live Oak, FL, D11/28/1984 New Orleans, LA **1967** NO 14 (RG) **1968** NO 14 (RG) **1969** NO 14 (RG) **1970** NO 14 (RG/c) **1971** NO 14 (RG) **1972** NO 8 (rg) **1973** NO 14 (RG) **NFL** 92 [7 yrs]

WILLIAMS, DELVIN Delvin, RB, 6´0˝/195 lbs; Kansas; 1974: SF, rnd 2; B4/17/1951 Houston, TX

YEAR	TEAM	G(GS, POS)	RUSH	YD	AVG(LG)	TD	REC	YD	AVG(LG)	TD	PASS	COMP	PCT	YD	AVG(LG)	TD	INT	SK	YD	QBR	KPR	OTD	PTS	TAY
1974	SF	13(2)	36	201	5.6(71)	3	1	9	9.0(9)	0	—	—	—	—	—	—	—	—	—	—	—	—	18	236
1975	SF	14(10, RB)	117	631	**5.4(52)**	3	34	370	10.9(30)	1	—	—	—	—	—	—	—	—	—	—	k	—	24	860
1976	SF✧	13(13, RB)	248	1203	**4.9(80)**	7	27	283	10.5(**85**)	2	1	1	100.0	18	18.0(18)	0	0	—	—	—	—	—	54	1434
1977	SF	14(14, RB)	268	931	3.5(40)	7	20	179	8.9(17)	2	1	0	0.0	0	0.0	0	1	—	—	—	k	—	54	1055
1978	†Mia★	16(15, RB)	272	1258	4.6(58)	8	18	192	10.7(42)	0	1	0	0.0	0	0.0	0	0	—	—	—	—	—	48	1434
1979	†Mia	14(13, RB)	184	703	3.8(39)	3	21	175	8.3(38)	1	1	0	0.0	0	0.0	0	0	—	—	—	—	—	24	826
1980	Mia	15(10, RB)	187	671	3.6(65)	2	31	207	6.7(19)	0	1	0	0.0	0	0.0	0	0	—	—	—	—	—	12	795
1981	GB	1(0)	—	—	—	—	—	—	—	—	—	—	—	—	—	—	—	—	—	—	—	—	—	—
NFL	8	100(77)	1312	5598	4.3(80)	33	152	1415	9.3(85)	6	5	1	20.0	18	3.6(18)	0	1	—	—	—	k	—	234	6638

WILLIAMS, DEMISE Demise Lamar, DB, 6´1˝/225 lbs; Oklahoma State; B7/9/1964 Greenville, SC **1987** LARd 1 (0)

WILLIAMS, DEMORRIO Demorrio, LB, 6´1˝/210 lbs; Nebraska; 2004: Atl, rnd 4; B7/6/1980 Beckville, TX **2004**†Atl 16 (1) **2005** Atl 16 (16, RLB) **NFL** 32 (17) [2 yrs]

WILLIAMS, DERWIN Derwin Dewayne, WR, 6´0˝/180 lbs; New Mexico; 1984: NE, rnd 7; B5/6/1961 Brownwood, TX

YEAR	TEAM	G(GS, POS)	RUSH	YD	AVG(LG)	TD	REC	YD	AVG(LG)	TD	PASS	COMP	PCT	YD	AVG(LG)	TD	INT	SK	YD	QBR	KPR	OTD	PTS	TAY
1985	†NE	16(0)	—	—	—	—	9	163	18.1(30)	0	—	—	—	—	—	—	—	—	—	—	—	—	0	82
1986	†NE	16(0)	—	—	—	—	2	35	17.5(26)	0	—	—	—	—	—	—	—	—	—	—	—	—	0	18
1987	NE	10(0)	—	—	—	—	3	30	10.0(12)	0	—	—	—	—	—	—	—	—	—	—	—	—	0	15
NFL	3	42(0)	—	—	—	—	14	228	16.3(30)	0	—	—	—	—	—	—	—	—	—	—	—	—	0	114

WILLIAMS, DOC Dan Adauf, G, 6´7˝/218 lbs; St. Cloud State; B4/3/1899 St. Cloud, MN, D4/11/1992 Arden Hills, MN **1923** Dul 6 (6, RG) **1924** Dul☆6 (6, RG) **1925** Dul 3 (2, LG) **1926** Dul 13 (10, RG) **NFL** 28 (24) [4 yrs]

WILLIAMS, DOKIE Darryl Eugene, WR, 5´11˝/180 lbs; UCLA; 1983: LARd, rnd 5; B8/25/1960 Oceanside, CA

YEAR	TEAM	G(GS, POS)	RUSH	YD	AVG(LG)	TD	REC	YD	AVG(LG)	TD	PASS	COMP	PCT	YD	AVG(LG)	TD	INT	SK	YD	QBR	KPR	OTD	PTS	TAY
1983	†LARd	16(0)	—	—	—	—	14	259	18.5(50)	3	—	—	—	—	—	—	—	—	—	—	k	—	18	158
1984	†LARd	16(3)	—	—	—	—	22	509	23.1(75)	4	—	—	—	—	—	—	—	—	—	—	k	—	24	536
1985	†LARd	16(16, WR)	—	—	—	—	48	925	19.3(55)	5	—	—	—	—	—	—	—	—	—	—	k	—	30	492
1986	LARd	15(15, WR)	3	27	9.0(19)	0	43	843	19.6(53)	8	—	—	—	—	—	—	—	—	—	—	—	—	48	489
1987	LARd	11(5, wr)	—	—	—	—	21	330	15.7(33)	5	—	—	—	—	—	—	—	—	—	—	k	—	30	201
NFL	5	74(39)	3	27	9.0(19)	0	148	2866	19.4(75)	25	—	—	—	—	—	—	—	—	—	—	k	—	150	1874

WILLIAMS, DON Don Donaho, G, 5´8˝/210 lbs; Texas; 1941: Phi, rnd 10; B5/23/1919 Claude, TX, D8/11/2001 Waco, TX **1941** Pit 6 (0)

WILLIAMS, DONNIE Charles Donell, WR, 6´3˝/210 lbs; Prairie View A&M; 1970: LA, rnd 2; B3/12/1948 Dallas, TX

YEAR	TEAM	G(GS, POS)	RUSH	YD	AVG(LG)	TD	REC	YD	AVG(LG)	TD	PASS	COMP	PCT	YD	AVG(LG)	TD	INT	SK	YD	QBR	KPR	OTD	PTS	TAY
1970	LARm	5	—	—	—	—	1	9	9.0(9)	0	—	—	—	—	—	—	—	—	—	—	—	—	0	5

WILLIAMS, DOUG Douglas Lee, QB, 6´4˝/220 lbs; Grambling State; 1978: TB, rnd 1; B8/9/1955 Zachary, LA

YEAR	TEAM	G(GS, POS)	RUSH	YD	AVG(LG)	TD	REC	YD	AVG(LG)	TD	PASS	COMP	PCT	YD	AVG(LG)	TD	INT	SK	YD	QBR	KPR	OTD	PTS	TAY
1978	TB	10(10, QB)	27	23	0.9(7)	1	—	—	—	—	194	73	37.6	1170	6.0(56)	7	8	6	69	53.4	—	—	6	333
1979	†TB	16(16, QB)	35	119	3.4(16)	2	—	—	—	—	397	166	41.8	2448	6.2(66)	18	**24**	7	57	52.5	—	—	12	493
1980	TB	16(16, QB)	58	370	6.4(27)	4	—	—	—	—	521	254	48.8	3396	6.5(61)	20	16	23	194	69.9	—	—	24	1568
1981	†TB	16(16, QB)	48	209	4.4(29)	4	—	—	—	—	471	238	50.5	3563	7.6(84)	19	14	18	135	76.8	—	—	24	1566
1982	†TB	9(9, QB)	35	158	4.5(14)	2	—	—	—	—	307	164	53.4	2071	6.7(62)	9	11	11	128	69.6	—	—	12	819
1986	†Was	1(0)	—	—	—	—	—	—	—	—	1	0	0.0	0	0.0	0	0	—	—	—	—	—	0	0
1987	†Was	5(2)	7	9	1.3(7)	1	—	—	—	—	143	81	56.6	1156	8.1(62)	11	5	7	53	94.0	—	—	6	452
1988	Was	11(10, QB)	9	0	0.0(4)	1	—	—	—	—	380	213	56.1	2609	6.9(58)	15	12	10	88	77.4	—	—	6	910
1989	Was	4(2)	1	-4	-4.0(-4)	0	—	—	—	—	93	51	54.8	585	6.3(46)	1	3	2	10	—	—	—	0	174
NFL	9	88(81)	220	884	4.0(29)	15	—	—	—	—	2507	1240	49.5	16998	6.8(84)	100	93	84	734	69.4	—	—	90	6313

WILLIAMS, DOUG Douglas, T-G, 6´5˝/286 lbs; Texas A&M; 1986: NYJ, rnd 2; B10/1/1962 Cincinnati, OH **1986** Hou 15 (2) **1987** Hou 8 (7, lt) **NFL** 23 (9) [2 yrs]

WILLIAMS, ED Edward Lee, RB, 6´2˝/245 lbs; Langston; B6/19/1950 Oklahoma City, OK

YEAR	TEAM	G(GS, POS)	RUSH	YD	AVG(LG)	TD	REC	YD	AVG(LG)	TD	PASS	COMP	PCT	YD	AVG(LG)	TD	INT	SK	YD	QBR	KPR	OTD	PTS	TAY
1974	Cin	14	58	238	4.1(18)	3	13	98	7.5(19)	1	—	—	—	—	—	—	—	—	—	—	k	—	24	325
1975	†Cin	14	35	136	3.9(19)	2	10	96	9.6(20)	1	—	—	—	—	—	—	—	—	—	—	—	—	18	209
1976	TB	12(10, FB)	87	324	3.7(19)	2	23	166	7.2(18)	0	—	—	—	—	—	—	—	—	—	—	—	—	12	427
1977	TB	14(5, fb)	63	198	3.1(14)	0	10	67	6.7(15)	0	—	—	—	—	—	—	—	—	—	—	—	—	0	232
NFL	4	54(15)	243	896	3.7(19)	7	56	427	7.6(20)	2	—	—	—	—	—	—	—	—	—	—	k	—	54	1193

WILLIAMS, ED Edwin Eugene, LB, 6´4˝/244 lbs; Texas; 1984: NE, rnd 2; B9/8/1961 Odessa, TX **1984** NE 14 (0) **1985**†NE 13 (0) **1986** NE 8 (0) **1987** NE 12 (7, ROLB) **1990** NE 15 (3) **NFL** 62 (10) [5 yrs]

WILLIAMS, ELIJAH Elijah Elgebra, E, 5´10˝/181 lbs; Florida; 1998: Atl, rnd 6; B8/20/1975 Milton, FL **1999** Atl 15 (2) **2000** Atl 15 (3) **2001** Atl 5 (1)

YEAR	TEAM	G(GS, POS)	RUSH	YD	AVG(LG)	TD	REC	YD	AVG(LG)	TD	PASS	COMP	PCT	YD	AVG(LG)	TD	INT	SK	YD	QBR	KPR	OTD	PTS	TAY
1998	†Atl	15(0)	2	-2	-1.0(2)	0	—	—	—	—	—	—	—	—	—	—	—	—	—	—	k	—	0	25
NFL	4	50(6)	2	-2	-1.0(2)	0	—	—	—	—	—	—	—	—	—	—	—	—	—	—	ki	—	0	17

WILLIAMS, ELLERY Ellery Frederick, E, 6´0˝/185 lbs; Santa Clara; 1950: SF, rnd 8; B3/20/1926 St. Louis, MO

YEAR	TEAM	G(GS, POS)	RUSH	YD	AVG(LG)	TD	REC	YD	AVG(LG)	TD	PASS	COMP	PCT	YD	AVG(LG)	TD	INT	SK	YD	QBR	KPR	OTD	PTS	TAY
1950	†NYG	12	—	—	—	—	4	78	19.5(34)	0	—	—	—	—	—	—	—	—	—	—	—	—	0	39

WILLIAMS, ERIC Eric Michael, DE-DT-NT, 6´4˝/282 lbs; Washington State; 1984: Det, rnd 3; B2/24/1962 Stockton, CA **1984** Det 12 (1) **1985** Det 12 (12, LDE) **1986** Det 16 (16, NT) **1987** Det 11 (11, LDE) **1988** Det 16 (16, LDE) **1989** Det 16 (16, LDE) **1990** Was 13 (8, LDT) **1991**†Was 15 (15, LDT) **1992** Was 6 (6, LDT) **1993** Was 4 (4) **NFL** 121 (105) [10 yrs]

WILLIAMS, ERIC Eric D., LB, 6´2˝/227 lbs; USC; 1977: SL, rnd 8; B6/17/1955 Los Angeles, CA **1977** SL 14 (8, LLB) **1978** SL 13 (11, rilb) **1979** SL 16 (16, LOLB) **1980** SL 12 (12, LILB) **1981** SL 15 (11, LLB/lilb) **1982** LARm 3 (0) **1983**†LARm 11 (0) **1984** SD 13 (0) **NFL** 97 (58) [8 yrs]

WILLIAMS, ERIC Eric Thomas, DB, 6´1˝/188 lbs; North Carolina State; 1983: Pit, rnd 6; B2/21/1960 Raleigh, NC **1983** Pit 3 (1) **1984**†Pit 16 (12, FS) **1985** Pit 14 (14, FS) **1986** Pit 16 (16, FS) **1987** Det 1 (0) **NFL** 50 (43) [5 yrs]

WILLIAMS, ERIK Erik George, T, 6´6˝/324 lbs; Central State (OH); 1991: Dal, rnd 3; B9/7/1968 Philadelphia, PA **1991**†Dal 11 (3) **1992**†Dal 16 (16, RT) **1993**†Dal★16 (16, RT) **1994** Dal 7 (7, rt) **1995**†Dal☆15 (15, RT) **1996**†Dal★16 (16, RT) **1997** Dal✧15 (15, RT) **1998**†Dal 15 (15, RT) **1999**†Dal✧14 (14, RT) **2000** Dal 16 (16, RT) **2001** Bal 5 (0) **NFL** 146 (133) [11 yrs]

WILLIAMS, ERWIN Erwin B., WR, 6´5˝/214 lbs; Maryland-Eastern Shore; B6/21/1947 Portsmouth, VA

YEAR	TEAM	G(GS, POS)	RUSH	YD	AVG(LG)	TD	REC	YD	AVG(LG)	TD	PASS	COMP	PCT	YD	AVG(LG)	TD	INT	SK	YD	QBR	KPR	OTD	PTS	TAY
1969	Pit	9	—	—	—	—	3	14	4.7(6)	1	—	—	—	—	—	—	—	—	—	—	—	—	6	12

WILLIAMS, EUGENE Eugene, LB, 6´1˝/220 lbs; Tulsa; 1982: Sea, rnd 7; B6/15/1960 Longview, TX **1982** Sea 9 (1) **1983** Sea 4 (0) **NFL** 13 (1) [2 yrs]

WILLIAMS, FRANK Frank Ralph, FB-LB, 6´0˝/212 lbs; Utah State; 1948: NYG, rnd 20/SF-A, rnd 30; B2/27/1922 Bountiful, UT **[K]**

YEAR	TEAM	G(GS, POS)	RUSH	YD	AVG(LG)	TD	REC	YD	AVG(LG)	TD	PASS	COMP	PCT	YD	AVG(LG)	TD	INT	SK	YD	QBR	KPR	OTD	PTS	TAY
1948	NYG	9(7, fb)	—	—	—	—	1	5	5.0(5)	0	—	—	—	—	—	—	—	—	—	—	K	—	4	3

WILLIAMS, FRANK Frank Gordon, FB, 6´2˝/215 lbs; Pepperdine; B5/9/1932 Bowie County, TX **1961** LARm 2

WILLIAMS, FRED Fred, DT-G, 6´4˝/249 lbs; Arkansas; 1952: ChiB, rnd 5; B2/8/1929 Little Rock, AR, D10/11/2000 Heber Springs, AR **1952** ChiB✧12 (LDT) **1953** ChiB✧12 (LDT) **1954** ChiB 12 (LG) **1955** ChiB 12 (LDT) **1956**†ChiB 12 (LDT) **1957** ChiB 12 (LDT) **1958** ChiB★12 (LDT) **1959** ChiB✧11 (LDT) **1960** ChiB 12 (RDT) **1961** ChiB 14 (RDT) **1962** ChiB 14 **1963**†ChiB 5 (rdt) **1964** Was 14 **1965** Was 14 (LDT) **NFL** 168 [14 yrs]

WILLIAMS, GARDNER Gardner, DB, 6´2˝/199 lbs; St. Mary's (CA); 1984: LARd, rnd 11; B12/11/1961 Washington, DC **1984** Det 3 (0)

WILLIAMS, GARLAND Garland Hare, T, 6´3˝/220 lbs; Duke; Georgia; 1947: Bkn-A, rnd 7/1945: ChiC, rnd 28; B8/21/1921 Parkin, AR, D4/7/1989 Alpharetta, GA **1947** Bkn-A 14 (13, RT) **1948** Bkn-A 12 (4) **AAFC** 26 (17) [2 yrs]

WILLIAMS, GARY Gary Leon, WR, 6´2˝/215 lbs; Ohio State; 1983: Cin, rnd 11; B9/4/1959 Wilmington, OH **1984** Cin 8 (1)

WILLIAMS, GENE Eugene, G-T, 6´2˝/310 lbs; Iowa State; 1991: Mia, rnd 5; B10/14/1968 Blair, NE **1991** Mia 10 (0) **1992** Mia 5 (0) **1993** Cle 16 (14, RT) **1994**†Cle 15 (9, RT) **1995**†Atl 12 (3) **1996** Atl 10 (0) **1997** Atl 15 (15, RG) **1998**†Atl 16 (16, RG) **1999** Atl 15 (8, rg) **NFL** 114 (65) [9 yrs]

WILLIAMS, GEORGE George Roger, DT, 6´3˝/294 lbs; North Carolina State; B12/8/1975 Roseboro, NC **1998** NYG 2 (0) **1999** NYG 16 (0) **2000**†NYG 13 (0) **NFL** 31 (0) [3 yrs]

YEAR	TEAM	G (GS, POS)	RUSH	YD	AVG (LG)	TD	REC	YD	AVG (LG)	TD	PASS	COMP	PCT	YD	AVG (LG)	TD	INT	SK	YD	QBR	KPR	OTD	PTS	TAY

WILLIAMS, GERALD Gerald, NT-DE-DT, 6´3˝/290 lbs; Auburn; 1986: Pit, rnd 2; B9/8/1963 Waycross, GA **1986** Pit 16 (0) **1987** Pit 9 (1) **1988** Pit 16 (16, NT) **1989**†Pit 16 (16, NT) **1990** Pit 16 (15, NT) **1991** Pit 16 (15, NT) **1992**†Pit 10 (10, NT) **1993**†Pit 10 (8, lde) **1994** Pit 11 (11, LDE) **1995** Car 16 (16, RDE) **1996**†Car 16 (15, RDE) **1997** Car 5 (5, rde) **1997** GB 4 (0) **NFL** 161 (128) [12 yrs]

WILLIAMS, GERARD Gerard Anthony, DB, 6´1˝/184 lbs; Langston; B5/25/1952 Oklahoma City, OK **1976**†Was 14 **1977** Was 14 (11, LCB) **1978** Was 16 (5, lcb) **1979** SF 15 (14, RCB) **1980** SF 5 (1) **1980** SL 4 (0) **NFL** 68 (31) [5 yrs]

WILLIAMS, GEROME Meltrix Gerome, DB, 6´2˝/210 lbs; Houston; B7/9/1973 Houston, TX **1997** SD 6 (0) **1998** SD 16 (0) **NFL** 22 (0) [2 yrs]

WILLIAMS, GRANT Grant James, T, 6´7˝/320 lbs; Louisiana Tech; B5/10/1974 Hattiesburg, MS **1996** Sea 8 (0) **1997** Sea 16 (8, rt/lt) **1998** Sea 16 (0) **1999**†Sea 16 (15, RT) **2000** NE 15 (8, RT) **2001**†NE 14 (4) **2002** SL 5 (3) **2003**†SL 16 (0) **2004**†SL 16 (11, RT) **NFL** 122 (49) [9 yrs]

WILLIAMS, GREG Gregory, DB, 5´11˝/185 lbs; Mississippi State; B8/1/1959 Greenville, MS **1982**†Was 9 (0) **1983**†Was 16 (0) **1984**†Was 16 (0) **1985** Was 16 (0) **NFL** 57 (0) [4 yrs]

WILLIAMS, HARRY Harry, WR, 6´3˝/180 lbs; Tuskegee; 2005: NYJ, rnd 7; B8/10/1982 Augusta, GA **2005** NYJ 1 (0)

WILLIAMS, HARVEY Harvey Lavance, RB, 6´2˝/226 lbs; LSU; 1991: KC, rnd 1; B4/22/1967 Hempstead, TX

YEAR	TEAM	G (GS, POS)	RUSH	YD	AVG (LG)	TD	REC	YD	AVG (LG)	TD	PASS	COMP	PCT	YD	AVG (LG)	TD	INT	SK	YD	QBR	KPR	OTD	PTS	TAY
1991	†KC	14(1)	97	447	4.6(21)	1	16	147	9.2(17)	2	1	0	0.0	0	0.0	0	0	—	—	—	k	—	18	705
1992	†KC	14(0)	78	262	3.4(11)	1	5	24	4.8(12)	0	—	—	—	—	—	—	—	—	—	—	k	—	6	374
1993	KC	7(6, rb)	42	149	3.5(19)	0	7	42	6.0(14)	0	—	—	—	—	—	—	—	—	—	—	k	—	0	178
1994	LARd	16(10, RB)	282	983	3.5(28)	4	47	391	8.3(27)	3	—	—	—	—	—	—	—	—	—	—	k	—	44	1267
1995	Oak	16(16, RB)	255	1114	4.4(60)	9	54	375	6.9(28)	0	1	1	100.0	13	13.0(13)	1	0	—	—	—	—	—	54	1403
1996	Oak	13(5, rb)	121	431	3.6(44)	0	22	143	6.5(20)	0	2	1	50.0	18	9.0(18)	1	0	—	—	—	—	—	0	517
1997	Oak	14(6, fb)	18	70	3.9(13)	3	16	147	9.2(32)	2	—	—	—	—	—	—	—	—	—	—	—	—	32	184
1998	Oak	16(3)	128	496	3.9(25)	2	26	173	6.7(15)	0	1	1	100.0	27	27.0(27)	0	0	—	—	—	—	—	12	616
NFL	8	110(47)	1021	3952	3.9(60)	20	193	1442	7.5(32)	7	5	3	60.0	58	11.6(27)	2	0	—	—	—	k	—	166	5242

WILLIAMS, HENRY Henry James, DB, 5´10˝/180 lbs; San Diego State; 1979: Oak, rnd 6; B12/2/1956 Greensboro, AL **1979** Oak 16 (13, RCB) **1983**†LARm 5 (0) **1983** SD 1 (0) **NFL** 22 (13) [2 yrs]

WILLIAMS, HENRY Henry Lee, WR, 5´6˝/185 lbs; East Carolina; B5/31/1962 Memphis, TN

YEAR	TEAM	G (GS, POS)	RUSH	YD	AVG (LG)	TD	REC	YD	AVG (LG)	TD	PASS	COMP	PCT	YD	AVG (LG)	TD	INT	SK	YD	QBR	KPR	OTD	PTS	TAY
1989	Phi	13(0)	—	—	—	—	4	32	8.0(11)	0	—	—	—	—	—	—	—	—	—	—	kp	—	0	172

WILLIAMS, HERB Herbert Earl, DB, 6´1˝/190 lbs; Southern (LA); 1980: SF, rnd 6; B8/30/1958 Lafayette, LA **1980** SF 9 (0) **1981** SL 3 (0) **1982** SL 7 (2) **NFL** 19 (2) [3 yrs]

WILLIAMS, HOWIE Howard Lee, DB, 6´1˝/190 lbs; Howard; B12/4/1936 Spartanburg, SC **1962**†GB 1 **1963** GB 7 **1963** SF 7 **1964** Oak-A 12 (RCB) **1965** Oak-A 14 (14, RS) **1966** Oak-A 14 (RS) **1967**†Oak-A 13 (LS) **1968**†Oak-A 13 (2) **1969**†Oak-A 14 (4) **NFL** 95 (20) [8 yrs]

WILLIAMS, IKE Ivan Andy, TB-HB, 5´10˝/180 lbs; Georgia Tech; B1/3/1903, D5/1977 Flint, TX **1929** SI 6 (5, TB)

WILLIAMS, INKY Jay Mayo, E, 5´11˝/174 lbs; Brown; B7/25/1894, D1/2/1980 Chicago, IL **1921** Can 1 (0) **1921** Ham 5 (5, LE) **1922** Ham 6 (6, LE) **1923** Ham☆6 (6, LE), 6 **1924** Ham 3 (3, LE) **1924** Day 1 (1) **1925** Ham 3 (3, LE) **1925** Cle 9 (7, LE) **1926** Ham 3 (3, LE) **NFL** 37 (34) [6 yrs]

WILLIAMS, JAKE Jacob Crawford, T-E-G-C, 6´0˝/205 lbs; TCU; B1904 **1929** ChiC 8 (5, lt) **1930** ChiC 9 (5, lt) **1931** ChiC 8 (4, LT) **1933** ChiC 11 (9, LT)

YEAR	TEAM	G (GS, POS)	RUSH	YD	AVG (LG)	TD	REC	YD	AVG (LG)	TD	PASS	COMP	PCT	YD	AVG (LG)	TD	INT	SK	YD	QBR	KPR	OTD	PTS	TAY
1932	ChiC☆	8(5, LT)	—	—	—	—	1	15	15.0(15)	0	—	—	—	—	—	—	—	—	—	—	—	—	0	8
NFL	5	44(28)	—	—	—	—	1	15	15.0(15)	0	—	—	—	—	—	—	—	—	—	—	—	—	0	8

WILLIAMS, JAMAL Jamal, DT-NT, 6´3˝/305 lbs; Oklahoma State; 1998: SD, rnd S2; B4/28/1976 Washington, DC **1998** SD 9 (0) **1999** SD 16 (2) **2000** SD 16 (16, LDT) **2001** SD 3 (3) **2002** SD 12 (10, LDT) **2003** SD 15 (15, LDT) **2004**†SD☆15 (15, NT) **2005** SD★16 (16, NT) **NFL** 102 (77) [8 yrs]

WILLIAMS, JAMEL Jamel Ishmael, DB, 5´11˝/205 lbs; Nebraska; 1997: Was, rnd 5; B12/22/1973 Merrillville, IN **1997** Was 16 (0) **1998** Was 16 (0) **1999** Was 3 (0) **NFL** 35 (0) [3 yrs]

WILLIAMS, JAMES James L., WR, 5´10˝/186 lbs; Marshall; 2000: Sea, rnd 6; B3/6/1978 Vicksburg, MS

YEAR	TEAM	G (GS, POS)	RUSH	YD	AVG (LG)	TD	REC	YD	AVG (LG)	TD	PASS	COMP	PCT	YD	AVG (LG)	TD	INT	SK	YD	QBR	KPR	OTD	PTS	TAY
2000	Sea	10(0)	1	-5	-5.0(-5)	0	8	99	12.4(18)	0	—	—	—	—	—	—	—	—	—	—	k	—	2	76
2001	Sea	6(2)	—	—	—	—	12	212	17.7(49)	1	—	—	—	—	—	—	—	—	—	—	k	—	6	151
2002	Sea	13(2)	—	—	—	—	9	99	11.0(18)	0	—	—	—	—	—	—	—	—	—	—	k	—	0	89
2003	Det	1(0)	—	—	—	—	—	—	—	—	—	—	—	—	—	—	—	—	—	—	—	—	—	—
NFL	4	30(4)	1	-5	-5.0(-5)	0	29	410	14.1(49)	1	—	—	—	—	—	—	—	—	—	—	k	—	8	315

WILLIAMS, JAMES James Earl, DB, 5´10˝/190 lbs; Fresno State; 1990: Buf, rnd 1; B3/30/1967 Osceola, AR **1990**†Buf 16 (5, lcb) **1991**†Buf 8 (4) **1992**†Buf 15 (8, lcb) **1993**†Buf 15 (11, LCB) **1994** Arz 15 (7, RCB) **1996** SF 1 (0) **NFL** 70 (35) [6 yrs]

WILLIAMS, JAMES E. James Edward, LB, 6´0˝/236 lbs; Mississippi State; 1990: NO, rnd 6; B10/10/1968 Natchez, MS **1990**†NO 14 (0) **1991**†NO 16 (4) **1992**†NO 16 (0) **1993** NO 16 (9, LILB) **1994** NO 16 (7, rilb) **1995** Jax 12 (6, llb) **1997**†SF 16 (0) **1998**†SF 15 (0) **1999** Cle 16 (0) **NFL** 137 (26) [9 yrs]

WILLIAMS, JAMES James Otis, T-DE-DT, 6´7˝/329 lbs; Cheyney (PA); B3/29/1968 Pittsburgh, PA **1991**†ChiB 14 (0) **1992** ChiB 5 (0) **1993** ChiB 3 (0) **1994**†ChiB 16 (15, RT) **1995** ChiB 16 (16, RT) **1996** ChiB 16 (16, RT) **1997** ChiB 16 (16, RT) **1998** ChiB 16 (16, RT) **1999** ChiB 16 (16, RT) **2000** ChiB 16 (16, RT) **2001**†ChiB★16 (16, RT) **2002** ChiB 16 (16, RT) **NFL** 166 (143) [12 yrs]

WILLIAMS, JAMIE Jamie Earl, TE, 6´4˝/240 lbs; Nebraska; 1983: NYG, rnd 3; B2/25/1960 Vero Beach, FL

YEAR	TEAM	G (GS, POS)	RUSH	YD	AVG (LG)	TD	REC	YD	AVG (LG)	TD	PASS	COMP	PCT	YD	AVG (LG)	TD	INT	SK	YD	QBR	KPR	OTD	PTS	TAY
1983	SL	1(0)	—	—	—	—	—	—	—	—	—	—	—	—	—	—	—	—	—	—	—	—	—	—
1984	Hou	16(16, TE)	—	—	—	—	41	545	13.3(32)	3	—	—	—	—	—	—	—	—	—	—	k	—	18	273
1985	Hou	16(16, TE)	—	—	—	—	39	444	11.4(29)	1	—	—	—	—	—	—	—	—	—	—	k	—	6	218
1986	Hou	16(16, TE)	—	—	—	—	22	227	10.3(33)	1	—	—	—	—	—	—	—	—	—	—	—	—	6	119
1987	†Hou	12(12, TE)	—	—	—	—	13	158	12.2(25)	3	—	—	—	—	—	—	—	—	—	—	—	—	18	94
1988	†Hou	16(16, TE)	—	—	—	—	6	46	7.7(10)	0	—	—	—	—	—	—	—	—	—	—	—	—	0	23
1989	†SF	3(0)	—	—	—	—	3	38	12.7(17)	0	—	—	—	—	—	—	—	—	—	—	—	—	0	19
1990	†SF	16(0)	—	—	—	—	9	54	6.0(9)	0	—	—	—	—	—	—	—	—	—	—	k	—	0	4
1991	SF	16(7, te)	—	—	—	—	22	235	10.7(21)	1	—	—	—	—	—	—	—	—	—	—	—	—	6	123
1992	†SF	16(1)	—	—	—	—	7	76	10.9(21)	1	—	—	—	—	—	—	—	—	—	—	—	—	6	43
1993	†SF	16(0)	—	—	—	—	16	132	8.3(15)	1	—	—	—	—	—	—	—	—	—	—	—	—	6	71
1994	LARd	16(0)	—	—	—	—	3	25	8.3(16)	0	—	—	—	—	—	—	—	—	—	—	k	—	0	-3
NFL	12	160(84)	—	—	—	—	181	1980	10.9(33)	11	—	—	—	—	—	—	—	—	—	—	k	—	66	983

WILLIAMS, JARVIS Jarvis Eric, DB, 5´11˝/200 lbs; Florida; 1988: Mia, rnd 2; B5/16/1965 Palatka, FL **1988** Mia 16 (16, FS) **1989** Mia 16 (16, SS) **1990**†Mia 16 (16, SS) **1991** Mia 11 (11, SS) **1992**†Mia 16 (10, SS) **1993** Mia 16 (14, SS) **1994** NYG 13 (12, SS) **NFL** 104 (95) [7 yrs]

WILLIAMS, JAY Jay Omar, DE, 6´3˝/275 lbs; Wake Forest; B10/13/1971 Washington, DC **1995** SL 7 (0) **1996** SL 2 (0) **1997** SL 16 (2) **1998** SL 16 (1) **1999**†SL 16 (0) **2000** Car 16 (14, RDE) **2001** Car 16 (13, LDE) **2002** Mia 16 (0) **2003** Mia 16 (0) **2004** Mia 16 (1) **NFL** 137 (31) [10 yrs]

WILLIAMS, JEFF Franklin Jeffrey, HB, 6´1˝/210 lbs; Oklahoma State; B5/7/1943 High Springs, FL

YEAR	TEAM	G (GS, POS)	RUSH	YD	AVG (LG)	TD	REC	YD	AVG (LG)	TD	PASS	COMP	PCT	YD	AVG (LG)	TD	INT	SK	YD	QBR	KPR	OTD	PTS	TAY
1966	Min	3	1	2	2.0(2)	0	—	—	—	—	—	—	—	—	—	—	—	—	—	—	kp	—	0	-4

WILLIAMS, JEFF Jeffrey Scott, G-T, 6´4˝/256 lbs; Rhode Island; 1977: LA, rnd 5; B4/15/1955 Gloucester, MA **1977** LARm 1 **1978** Was 7 (6, rt) **1979** Was 16 (16, RG) **1980** Was 15 (15, RG) **1981**†SD 12 (0) **1982** ChiB 5 (5, RG) **NFL** 56 (42) [6 yrs]

WILLIAMS, JERMAINE Jermaine Mequell, RB, 6´0˝/228 lbs; Houston; B7/3/1972 Greenville, NC

YEAR	TEAM	G (GS, POS)	RUSH	YD	AVG (LG)	TD	REC	YD	AVG (LG)	TD	PASS	COMP	PCT	YD	AVG (LG)	TD	INT	SK	YD	QBR	KPR	OTD	PTS	TAY
1998	Oak	10(0)	—	—	—	—	—	—	—	—	—	—	—	—	—	—	—	—	—	—	—	—	—	—
1999	Oak	15(0)	—	—	—	—	1	20	20.0(20)	0	—	—	—	—	—	—	—	—	—	—	—	—	0	10
2000	Jax	7(0)	2	8	4.0(4)	0	—	—	—	—	—	—	—	—	—	—	—	—	—	—	k	—	0	28
2001	KC	11(2)	—	—	—	—	2	11	5.5(9)	0	—	—	—	—	—	—	—	—	—	—	—	—	0	6
2001	Oak	1(0)	—	—	—	—	—	—	—	—	—	—	—	—	—	—	—	—	—	—	—	—	—	—
NFL	4	44(2)	2	8	4.0(4)	0	3	31	10.3(20)	0	—	—	—	—	—	—	—	—	—	—	k	—	0	44

WILLIAMS, JERROL Jerrol Lynn, LB, 6´4˝/245 lbs; Purdue; 1989: Pit, rnd 4; B7/5/1967 Las Vegas, NV **1989**†Pit 16 (3) **1990** Pit 16 (1) **1991** Pit 16 (4) **1992**†Pit 16 (16, LOLB) **1993** SD 6 (5, llb) **1994** KC 6 (0) **1996** Bal 9 (6, rolb) **NFL** 85 (35) [7 yrs]

WILLIAMS, JERRY Jerome Ralph, DB-HB, 5´10˝/175 lbs; Idaho; Washington State; 1949: LA, rnd 7; B11/1/1923 Spokane, WA, D12/31/1998 Chandler, AZ **[C]**

YEAR	TEAM	G(GS, POS)	RUSH	YD	AVG(LG)	TD	REC	YD	AVG(LG)	TD	PASS	COMP	PCT	YD	AVG(LG)	TD	INT	SK	YD	QBR	KPR	OTD	PTS	TAY
1949	†LARm	12(0)	19	103	5.4(18)	3	7	102	14.6(42)	0	—	—	—	—	—	—	—	—	—	—	pi	1	24	234
1950	†LARm	12(DB)	13	108	8.3(38)	1	4	21	5.3(11)	1	—	—	—	—	—	—	—	—	—	—	pi	—	12	163
1951	†LARm	10(DB)	21	106	5.0(32)	2	5	49	9.8(13)	0	—	—	—	—	—	—	—	—	—	—	kpi	2	24	244
1952	†LARm	12(DB)	11	65	5.9(26)	0	—	—	—	—	—	—	—	—	—	—	—	—	—	—	pi	—	0	90
1953	Phi	12(LH)	61	345	5.7(48)	3	31	438	14.1(40)	1	—	—	—	—	—	—	—	—	—	—	kp	—	24	682
1954	Phi	11(RH)	47	183	3.9(33)	1	44	668	15.2(**84**)	3	—	—	—	—	—	—	—	—	—	—	p	—	24	580
NFL	6	69	172	910	5.3(48)	10	91	1278	14.0(84)	5	—	—	—	—	—	—	—	—	—	—	kpi	3	108	1992

WILLIAMS, JIM James Edward, RB, 5´10˝/210 lbs; Fresno State; B11/22/1963 Brunswick, GA **1987** Sea 1 (0)

WILLIAMS, JIMMY James Henry, LB, 6´3˝/228 lbs; Nebraska; 1982: Det, rnd 1; B11/15/1960 Washington, DC **1982** Det 6 (0) **1983**†Det 16 (16, RLB) **1984** Det 16 (16, RLB) **1985** Det 16 (16, LOLB) **1986** Det 10 (10, LOLB) **1987** Det 12 (12, LOLB) **1988** Det 5 (5, lolb) **1989** Det 16 (16, LOLB) **1990** Det 10 (9, LOLB) **1990** Min 4 (0) **1991** Min 14 (12, LLB) **1992** TB 16 (16, LLB) **1993** TB 11 (8, LLB) **NFL** 152 (136) [12 yrs]

WILLIAMS, JIMMY Jimmy Ray, DB, 5´11˝/190 lbs; Vanderbilt; 2001: Buf, rnd 6; B3/10/1979 Baton Rouge, LA **[R]** **2001** SF 10 (0) **2002** SF 13 (0) **2003** SF 15 (0) **2004** SF 12 (6, lcb) **2005**†Sea 14 (1) **NFL** 64 (7) [5 yrs]

WILLIAMS, JOE Joseph John, B, 5´9˝/178 lbs; Ohio State; B3/19/1915, D5/5/1997 **1937** Cle 1 (0) **1939** Pit 1 (0) **NFL** 2 (0) [2 yrs]

WILLIAMS, JOE Joseph Alford, G-E-FB, 6´0˝/238 lbs; Lafayette; B3/3/1896 New York, NY, D1/18/1949 **1923** Can 8 (5, rg) **1925** NYG 10 (9, RG), 6 **1926** NYG☆12 (8, RG) **NFL** 30 (22) [3 yrs]

WILLIAMS, JOE Joseph Harold, RB, 6´0˝/193 lbs; Wyoming; 1970: Dal, rnd 12; B3/30/1947 Center, TX

YEAR	TEAM	G(GS, POS)	RUSH	YD	AVG(LG)	TD	REC	YD	AVG(LG)	TD	PASS	COMP	PCT	YD	AVG(LG)	TD	INT	SK	YD	QBR	KPR	OTD	PTS	TAY
1971	†Dal	12	21	67	3.2(16)	1	3	59	19.7(35)	0	—	—	—	—	—	—	—	—	—	—	k	—	6	104
1972	NO	14	31	72	2.3(11)	0	16	116	7.3(32)	0	—	—	—	—	—	—	—	—	—	—	k	—	0	123
NFL	2	26	52	139	2.7(16)	1	19	175	9.2(35)	0	—	—	—	—	—	—	—	—	—	—	k	—	6	227

WILLIAMS, JOE Joseph Dennis, LB, 6´4˝/237 lbs; Grambling State; B3/5/1965 Baton Rouge, LA **1987** Pit 3 (0)

WILLIAMS, JOEL Joel Herschel, C, 6´1˝/220 lbs; Louisiana-Lafayette; Texas; 1948: Was, rnd 22; B3/18/1926 San Angelo, TX, D3/10/1997 Ector County, TX **1948** SF-A 14 (14, C)

YEAR	TEAM	G(GS, POS)	RUSH	YD	AVG(LG)	TD	REC	YD	AVG(LG)	TD	PASS	COMP	PCT	YD	AVG(LG)	TD	INT	SK	YD	QBR	KPR	OTD	PTS	TAY
1950	Bal	12(12, C)	0	50	(50)	1	—	—	—	—	—	—	—	—	—	—	—	—	—	—	—	—	6	60

WILLIAMS, JOEL Joel, LB, 6´1˝/222 lbs; Peru State; Wisconsin-LaCrosse; B12/13/1956 Miami, FL **1979** Atl 16 **1980**†Atl 16 (16, ROLB) **1981** Atl 10 (8, ROLB) **1982**†Atl☆9 (9, ROLB) **1983** Phi 16 (16, ROLB) **1984** Phi 16 (16, ROLB) **1985** Phi 7 (0) **1986** Atl 15 (14, ROLB) **1987** Atl 8 (8, ROLB) **1988** Atl 14 (12, ROLB/lilb) **1989** Atl 10 (3) **NFL** 137 (102) [11 yrs]

WILLIAMS, JOEL Joel David, TE, 6´3˝/242 lbs; Notre Dame; 1987: Mia, rnd 8; B3/16/1965 Pittsburgh, PA **1987** Mia 3 (0)

WILLIAMS, JOHN John McKay, T-G-DE, 6´3˝/256 lbs; Minnesota; 1968: Bal, rnd 1; B10/27/1945 Jackson, MS **1968**†Bal 14 **1969** Bal 13 **1970**†Bal 14 (RG) **1971**†Bal 14 (RG) **1972** LARm 14 **1973**†LARm 14 (14, RT) **1974**†LARm 14 (14, RT) **1975**†LARm 14 (14, RT) **1976**†LARm 14 (14, RT) **1977**†LARm 14 (14, RT) **1978**†LARm 16 (16, RT) **1979** LARm 11 **NFL** 166 (86) [12 yrs]

WILLIAMS, JOHN John Alan, RB, 5´11˝/213 lbs; Wisconsin; B10/26/1960 Muskegon, MI

YEAR	TEAM	G(GS, POS)	RUSH	YD	AVG(LG)	TD	REC	YD	AVG(LG)	TD	PASS	COMP	PCT	YD	AVG(LG)	TD	INT	SK	YD	QBR	KPR	OTD	PTS	TAY
1985	Dal	8(0)	13	40	3.1(9)	0	—	—	—	—	—	—	—	—	—	—	—	—	—	—	k	—	0	79
1985	Sea	2(0)	1	2	2.0(2)	0	—	—	—	—	—	—	—	—	—	—	—	—	—	—	—	—	0	2
1986	NO	7(0)	—	—	—	—	1	5	5.0(5)	0	—	—	—	—	—	—	—	—	—	—	—	—	0	3
1987	Ind	2(0)	—	—	—	—	—	—	—	—	—	—	—	—	—	—	—	—	—	—	—	—	—	—
NFL	3	19(0)	14	42	3.0(9)	0	1	5	5.0(5)	0	—	—	—	—	—	—	—	—	—	—	k	—	0	84

WILLIAMS, JOHN John Wesley, DB, 5´7˝/180 lbs; Southern (LA); B7/26/1974 Hammond, LA **1997** Bal 4 (0) **1998** Bal 16 (0) **NFL** 20 (0) [2 yrs]

WILLIAMS, JOHN L. John L., FB, 5´11˝/231 lbs; Florida; 1986: Sea, rnd 1; B11/23/1964 Palatka, FL

YEAR	TEAM	G(GS, POS)	RUSH	YD	AVG(LG)	TD	REC	YD	AVG(LG)	TD	PASS	COMP	PCT	YD	AVG(LG)	TD	INT	SK	YD	QBR	KPR	OTD	PTS	TAY
1986	Sea	16(16, FB)	129	538	4.2(36)	0	33	219	6.6(23)	0	—	—	—	—	—	—	—	—	—	—	—	—	0	648
1987	†Sea	12(10, FB)	113	500	4.4(48)	1	38	420	11.1(75)	3	—	—	—	—	—	—	—	—	—	—	—	—	24	735
1988	†Sea	16(16, FB)	189	877	4.6(44)	4	58	651	11.2(75)	3	—	—	—	—	—	—	—	—	—	—	—	—	42	1258
1989	Sea	15(15, FB)	146	499	3.4(21)	1	76	657	8.6(51)	6	—	—	—	—	—	—	—	—	—	—	—	—	42	868
1990	Sea✧	16(16, FB)	187	714	3.8(25)	3	73	699	9.6(60)	0	—	—	—	—	—	—	—	—	—	—	—	—	18	1094
1991	Sea✧	16(16, FB)	188	741	3.9(42)	4	61	499	8.2(35)	1	—	—	—	—	—	—	—	—	—	—	—	—	30	1036
1992	Sea	16(16, FB)	114	339	3.0(14)	1	74	556	7.5(27)	2	—	—	—	—	—	—	—	—	—	—	—	—	18	637
1993	Sea	16(9, FB)	82	371	4.5(38)	3	58	450	7.8(25)	1	1	0	0.0	0	0.0	0	0	—	—	—	—	—	24	631
1994	†Pit	15(12, FB)	68	317	4.7(23)	1	51	378	7.4(23)	2	—	—	—	—	—	—	—	—	—	—	—	—	18	526
1995	†Pit	11(9, FB)	29	110	3.8(31)	0	24	127	5.3(20)	1	—	—	—	—	—	—	—	—	—	—	—	—	6	179
NFL	10	149(135)	1245	5006	4.0(48)	18	546	4656	8.5(75)	19	1	0	0.0	0	0.0	0	0	—	—	—	—	—	222	7609

WILLIAMS, JOHNNY John Elliott, DB-HB, 5´11˝/177 lbs; USC; 1951: Was, rnd 26; B6/30/1927 Los Angeles, CA, D2/26/2005 Dana Point, CA **1953** Was 12 (DB) **1954** SF 11 (DB)

YEAR	TEAM	G(GS, POS)	RUSH	YD	AVG(LG)	TD	REC	YD	AVG(LG)	TD	PASS	COMP	PCT	YD	AVG(LG)	TD	INT	SK	YD	QBR	KPR	OTD	PTS	TAY
1952	Was★	12(DB)	2	3	1.5(2)	0	1	13	13.0(13)	0	—	—	—	—	—	—	—	—	—	—	kpi	3	18	544
NFL	3	35	2	3	1.5(2)	0	1	13	13.0(13)	0	—	—	—	—	—	—	—	—	—	—	kpi	3	18	724

WILLIAMS, JON Jonathan, RB, 5´9˝/205 lbs; Penn State; 1984: NE, rnd 3; B6/1/1961 Somerville, NJ **1984** NE 9 (0)

WILLIAMS, JOSH Josh Sinclair, DT, 6´3˝/290 lbs; Michigan; 2000: Ind, rnd 4; B8/9/1976 Denver, CO **2000**†Ind 14 (7, ldt) **2001** Ind 16 (16, LDT) **2002**†Ind 7 (3) **2003**†Ind 16 (4) **2004**†Ind 16 (15, RDT) **2005** Ind 4 (3) **NFL** 73 (48) [6 yrs]

WILLIAMS, K.D. Kevin Dewayne, LB, 6´0˝/240 lbs; Henderson State; B4/22/1973 Tampa, FL **1999** Oak 9 (8, LLB) **2000** GB 16 (3) **2001**†GB 12 (0) **NFL** 37 (11) [3 yrs]

WILLIAMS, KARL Karl Danell, WR, 5´10˝/177 lbs; Texas A&M-Kingsville; B4/10/1971 Albion, MI **[R]**

YEAR	TEAM	G(GS, POS)	RUSH	YD	AVG(LG)	TD	REC	YD	AVG(LG)	TD	PASS	COMP	PCT	YD	AVG(LG)	TD	INT	SK	YD	QBR	KPR	OTD	PTS	TAY
1996	TB	16(0)	1	-3	-3.0(-3)	0	22	246	11.2(25)	0	—	—	—	—	—	—	—	—	—	—	kp	1	6	512
1997	†TB	16(7, wr)	1	5	5.0(5)	0	33	486	14.7(55)	4	—	—	—	—	—	—	—	—	—	—	kp	1	30	697
1998	TB	13(6, wr)	—	—	—	—	21	252	12.0(29)	1	—	—	—	—	—	—	—	—	—	—	p	—	6	164
1999	†TB	13(4)	—	—	—	—	21	176	8.4(14)	0	—	—	—	—	—	—	—	—	—	—	kp	—	0	141
2000	†TB	13(0)	—	—	—	—	2	35	17.5(27)	0	—	—	—	—	—	—	—	—	—	—	kp	1	6	327
2001	†TB	15(3)	—	—	—	—	24	314	13.1(42)	1	—	—	—	—	—	—	—	—	—	—	kp	1	12	368
2002	†TB	16(2)	3	-5	-1.7(0)	0	7	77	11.0(17)	1	—	—	—	—	—	—	—	—	—	—	kp	1	12	248
2003	TB	13(0)	1	2	2.0(2)	0	7	114	16.3(43)	0	—	—	—	—	—	—	—	—	—	—	kp	—	2	94
2004	Arz	15(2)	2	6	3.0(3)	0	18	197	10.9(33)	0	—	—	—	—	—	—	—	—	—	—	kp	—	0	184
NFL	9	130(24)	8	5	0.6(5)	0	155	1897	12.2(55)	7	—	—	—	—	—	—	—	—	—	—	kp	5	74	2734

WILLIAMS, KEITH Keith, WR-RB, 5´10˝/173 lbs; Southwest Missouri State; 1986: Atl, rnd 6; B9/30/1964 St. Louis, MO

YEAR	TEAM	G(GS, POS)	RUSH	YD	AVG(LG)	TD	REC	YD	AVG(LG)	TD	PASS	COMP	PCT	YD	AVG(LG)	TD	INT	SK	YD	QBR	KPR	OTD	PTS	TAY
1986	Atl	12(0)	3	18	6.0(8)	0	12	164	13.7(32)	1	—	—	—	—	—	—	—	—	—	—	k	—	6	150

WILLIAMS, KENDALL Kendall Edwin, DB, 5´9˝/180 lbs; Arizona State; B2/7/1959 Long Beach, CA **1983** Bal 16 (4)

WILLIAMS, KEVIN Kevin Lewis, WR, 5´8˝/164 lbs; USC; 1981: NO, rnd 7; B1/7/1958 Los Angeles, CA, D2/1/1996 Cajon Junction, CA **1981** Bal 11 (0)

WILLIAMS, KEVIN Kevin Ray, WR, 5´9˝/195 lbs; Miami (FL); 1993: Dal, rnd 2; B1/25/1971 Dallas, TX **[R]**

YEAR	TEAM	G(GS, POS)	RUSH	YD	AVG(LG)	TD	REC	YD	AVG(LG)	TD	PASS	COMP	PCT	YD	AVG(LG)	TD	INT	SK	YD	QBR	KPR	OTD	PTS	TAY
1993	†Dal	16(1)	7	26	3.7(12)	2	20	151	7.6(33)	2	—	—	—	—	—	—	—	—	—	—	kp	2	36	577
1994	†Dal	15(2)	6	20	3.3(8)	0	13	181	13.9(29)	0	—	—	—	—	—	—	—	—	—	—	kp	2	12	788
1995	†Dal	16(16, WR)	10	53	5.3(14)	0	38	613	16.1(48)	2	—	—	—	—	—	—	—	—	—	—	kp	—	12	819
1996	†Dal	10(9, WR)	4	11	2.8(9)	0	27	323	12.0(31)	1	—	—	—	—	—	—	—	—	—	—	kp	—	6	341
1997	Arz	16(0)	1	-2	-2.0(-2)	0	20	273	13.6(31)	1	—	—	—	—	—	—	—	—	—	—	kp	—	6	975
1998	†Buf	16(0)	5	46	9.2(28)	0	29	392	13.5(55)	1	—	—	—	—	—	—	—	—	—	—	kp	—	6	785
1999	†Buf	16(0)	1	13	13.0(13)	0	31	381	12.3(35)	0	—	—	—	—	—	—	—	—	—	—	kp	—	0	580
2000	SF	16(0)	—	—	—	—	—	—	—	—	—	—	—	—	—	—	—	—	—	—	kp	—	0	176
NFL	8	121(28)	34	167	4.9(28)	2	178	2314	13.0(55)	7	—	—	—	—	—	—	—	—	—	—	kp	4	78	5038

WILLIAMS, KEVIN Kevin, DT-DE, 6´5˝/311 lbs; Oklahoma State; 2003: Min, rnd 1; B8/16/1980 Arkadelphia, AR **2003** Min 16 (16, LDE) **2004**†Min★16 (16, RDT) **2005** Min 14 (14, RDT) **NFL** 46 (46) [3 yrs]

WILLIAMS, KEVIN Kevin Deleon, RB, 6´0˝/208 lbs; UCLA; 1993: Den, rnd 5; B2/17/1970 Marshall, TX **1993** GB 3 (0)

YEAR	TEAM	G(GS, POS)	RUSH	YD	AVG(LG)	TD	REC	YD	AVG(LG)	TD	PASS COMP	PCT	YD	AVG(LG)	TD	INT	SK	YD	QBR	KPR	OTD	PTS	TAY

WILLIAMS, KEVIN   Kevin J., DB, 5´9˝/169 lbs; Iowa State; B11/28/1961 San Diego, CA   **1985** Was 12 (0)   **1986** Buf 1 (0)   **1988** Was 5 (0)   **NFL** 18 (0) [3 yrs]

WILLIAMS, KEVIN   Kevin L., DB, 6´0˝/190 lbs; Oklahoma State; 1998: NYJ, rnd 3; B8/4/1975 Pine Bluff, AR   **1998**†NYJ 15 (6, fs)   **1999** NYJ 4 (0)   **2000** NYJ 9 (7, fs) **2000**†Mia 2 (0)   **2002** Hou 13 (0)   **NFL** 43 (13) [4 yrs]

WILLIAMS, LAMANZER   Lamanzer Deshan, DE, 6´4˝/276 lbs; Minnesota; 1998: Jax, rnd 6; B11/17/1974 Greensboro, AR   **1998**†Jax 2 (0)

WILLIAMS, LARRY   Lawrence Richard, G-C, 6´5˝/292 lbs; Notre Dame; 1985: Cle, rnd 10; B7/3/1963 Orange, CA   **1986**†Cle 16 (11, LG)   **1987**†Cle 12 (8, LG)   **1988** Cle 14 (14, LG) **1991**†NO 6 (2)   **1992** NE 13 (9, rg)   **NFL** 61 (44) [5 yrs]

WILLIAMS, LAWRENCE   Douglas Lawrence, WR, 5´10˝/173 lbs; Texas Tech; 1975: NE, rnd 7; B9/3/1953 Wichita Falls, TX

YEAR	TEAM	G(GS, POS)	RUSH	YD	AVG(LG)	TD	REC	YD	AVG(LG)	TD										KPR	OTD	PTS	TAY
1976	KC	12					1	9	9.0(9)	0										k	—	0	318
1977	KC	6 (wr)	2	30	15.0(17)	1	7	94	13.4(24)	0										k	—	6	151
1977	Cle	3																		k	—	0	79
NFL	2	21	2	30	15.0(17)	1	8	103	12.9(24)	0										k	—	6	548

WILLIAMS, LEE   Lee Eric, DE-DT, 6´6˝/269 lbs; Bethune-Cookman; 1984: SD, rnd S1; B10/15/1962 Fort Lauderdale, FL [S]   **1984** SD 8 (0)   **1985** SD 16 (16, LDE) **1986** SD☆16 (16, LDE)   **1987** SD 12 (12, LDE)   **1988** SD★16 (16, LDE)   **1989** SD☆16 (16, LDE)   **1990** SD 16 (16, LDE)   **1991** Hou 10 (5, rde)   **1992**†Hou 16 (5, rdt) **1993** Hou 14 (5, rdt)   **NFL** 140 (107) [10 yrs]

WILLIAMS, LEONARD   Leonard, RB, 6´0˝/205 lbs; Western Carolina; B6/27/1960 Man, WV

YEAR	TEAM	G(GS, POS)	RUSH	YD	AVG(LG)	TD	REC	YD	AVG(LG)	TD											OTD	PTS	TAY
1987	Buf	2 (0)	9	25	2.8(9)	0	1	5	5.0(5)	0											—	0	28

WILLIAMS, LESTER   Lester, NT-DE, 6´3˝/275 lbs; Miami (FL); 1982: NE, rnd 1; B1/19/1959 Miami, FL   **1982**†NE 9 (9, NT)   **1983** NE 15 (1)   **1984** NE 7 (0)   **1985**†NE 9 (3) **1986** SD 4 (0)   **1987** Sea 2 (0)   **NFL** 46 (13) [6 yrs]

WILLIAMS, LOUIS   Louis Randall, C, 6´4˝/291 lbs; LSU; 2001: Car, rnd 7; B4/11/1979 Fort Walton Beach, FL   **2002** Car 2 (0)

WILLIAMS, MADIEU   Madieu, DB, 6´1˝/193 lbs; Towson State; Maryland; 2004: Cin, rnd 2; B10/18/1981 Sierra Leone, West Africa   **2004** Cin 16 (13, FS)   **2005** Cin 4 (3) **NFL** 20 (16) [2 yrs]

WILLIAMS, MARCUS   Marcus, TE-WR, 6´5˝/230 lbs; Washington State; B12/12/1977 Oakland, CA   **2002** Oak 14 (0)

WILLIAMS, MARK   Mark Anthony, LB, 6´3˝/242 lbs; Ohio State; B5/17/1971 Camp Springs, MD   **1994**†GB 16 (0)   **1995** Jax 11 (10, RLB)   **1996** SL 2 (0)   **NFL** 29 (10) [3 yrs]

WILLIAMS, MARV   Marvin Lee, TE, 6´3˝/233 lbs; Cal State-Fullerton; B10/11/1963   **1987** Was 2 (0)

WILLIAMS, MAURICE   Maurice Carlos, T, 6´5˝/310 lbs; Michigan; 2001: Jax, rnd 2; B1/26/1979 Detroit, MI   **2001** Jax 16 (16, RT)   **2002** Jax 5 (5, rt)   **2003** Jax 16 (16, RT) **2004** Jax 16 (16, RT)   **2005**†Jax 16 (16, RT)   **NFL** 69 (69) [5 yrs]

WILLIAMS, MAXIE   Maxie Foy, G-T, 6´4˝/250 lbs; Southeastern Louisiana; 1965: Hou, rnd 10; B6/28/1940 Granite Falls, NC   **1965** Hou-A 14   **1966** Mia-A 14 (14, LT) **1967** Mia-A 14 (14, LT)   **1968** Mia-A 14 (13, lt/lg)   **1969** Mia-A 14 (13, LG)   **1970**†Mia 13 (9, LG)   **NFL** 83 (63) [6 yrs]

WILLIAMS, MELVIN   Melvin, DE, 6´2˝/269 lbs; Kansas State; 2003: NO, rnd 5; B2/2/1979 St. Louis, MO   **2003** NO 14 (2)   **2004** SF 3 (0)   **NFL** 17 (2) [2 yrs]

WILLIAMS, MICHAEL   Michael, RB, 6´2˝/220 lbs; Mississippi College; 1983: Phi, rnd 4; B7/16/1961 Altmore, AL

YEAR	TEAM	G(GS, POS)	RUSH	YD	AVG(LG)	TD	REC	YD	AVG(LG)	TD										KPR	OTD	PTS	TAY
1983	Phi	15 (9, RB)	103	385	3.7(32)	0	17	142	8.4(29)	0										k	—	0	470
1984	Phi	16 (1)	33	83	2.5(8)	0	7	47	6.7(15)	0											—	0	107
1987	Atl	3 (1)	14	49	3.5(9)	0	9	70	7.8(15)	0										k	—	0	69
NFL	3	34 (11)	150	517	3.4(32)	0	33	259	7.8(29)	0										k	—	0	646

WILLIAMS, MICHAEL   Michael Dean, DB, 5´10˝/185 lbs; UCLA; B5/28/1970 Los Angeles, CA   **1995** SF 4 (0)

WILLIAMS, MIKE   Michael J., WR, 5´11˝/190 lbs; Northeastern; 1989: LARm, rnd 10; B10/9/1966 Mount Kisco, NY

YEAR	TEAM	G(GS, POS)	RUSH	YD	AVG(LG)	TD	REC	YD	AVG(LG)	TD										KPR	OTD	PTS	TAY
1989	Det	1 (0)	—	—	—		—	—	—											—	—	—	—
1991	Mia	3 (0)	—	—	—		—	—	—												—	—	—
1992	†Mia	15 (0)	—	—	—		3	43	14.3(18)	0										k	—	0	65
1993	Mia	13 (0)	—	—	—		1	11	11.0(11)	0										k	—	0	66
1994	†Mia	15 (0)	—	—	—		15	221	14.7(29)	0										k	—	0	90
1995	Mia	12 (0)	—	—	—		2	17	8.5(15)	0											—	0	9
NFL	6	59 (0)	—	—	—		21	292	13.9(29)	0										k	—	0	228

WILLIAMS, MIKE   Michael, WR, 6´5˝/229 lbs; USC; 2005: Det, rnd 1; B1/4/1984 Tampa, FL

YEAR	TEAM	G(GS, POS)	RUSH	YD	AVG(LG)	TD	REC	YD	AVG(LG)	TD											OTD	PTS	TAY
2005	Det	14 (4)	—	—	—		29	350	12.1(49)	1											—	6	180

WILLIAMS, MIKE   Michael D., T, 6´6˝/370 lbs; Texas; 2002: Buf, rnd 1; B1/11/1980 Dallas, TX   **2002** Buf 14 (14, RT)   **2003** Buf 13 (13, RT)   **2004** Buf 15 (15, RT)   **2005** Buf 9 (5, rt) **NFL** 51 (47) [4 yrs]

WILLIAMS, MIKE   Michael, TE, 6´4˝/249 lbs; Alabama A&M; 1982: Was, rnd 5; B8/27/1959 Lafayette, AL   **1983**†Was 7 (0)   **1984** Was 1 (0)

YEAR	TEAM	G(GS, POS)	RUSH	YD	AVG(LG)	TD	REC	YD	AVG(LG)	TD											OTD	PTS	TAY
1982	Was	6 (1)	—	—	—		3	14	4.7(6)	0											—	0	7
NFL	3	14 (1)	—	—	—		3	14	4.7(6)	0											—	0	7

WILLIAMS, MIKE   Michael Anthony, TE-FB, 6´3˝/222 lbs; New Mexico; 1979: KC, rnd 8; B10/14/1957 New Kingston, PA

YEAR	TEAM	G(GS, POS)	RUSH	YD	AVG(LG)	TD	REC	YD	AVG(LG)	TD										KPR	OTD	PTS	TAY
1979	KC	14	69	261	3.8(22)	1	16	129	8.1(25)	2											—	18	346
1980	KC	16 (11, TE)	—	—	—		2	9	4.5(6)	1										k	—	6	29
1981	KC	3 (0)	2	0	0.0(3)	0	1	3	3.0(3)	0										k	—	0	-7
NFL	3	33 (11)	71	261	3.7(22)	1	19	141	7.4(25)	3										k	—	24	368

WILLIAMS, MIKE   Mikell Herman, DB, 5´10˝/181 lbs; LSU; 1975: SD, rnd 1; B11/22/1953 New Orleans, LA [I]   **1975** SD 14 (14, RCB)   **1976** SD 14 (11, RCB) **1977** SD 10 (10, RCB)   **1978** SD 16 (15, RCB)   **1979**†SD 16 (16, RCB)   **1980**†SD 14 (14, RCB)   **1981**†SD 14 (12, RCB)   **1982**†SD 9 (8, RCB)   **1983**†LARm 2 (0) **NFL** 109 (100) [9 yrs]

WILLIAMS, MOE   Maurice Jabari, RB, 6´1˝/205 lbs; Kentucky; 1996: Min, rnd 3; B7/26/1974 Columbus, GA

YEAR	TEAM	G(GS, POS)	RUSH	YD	AVG(LG)	TD	REC	YD	AVG(LG)	TD										KPR	OTD	PTS	TAY
1996	Min	9 (0)																					
1997	†Min	14 (0)	22	59	2.7(8)	1	4	14	3.5(7)	0										k	—	6	224
1998	Min	12 (1)	—	—	—		1	64	64.0(64)	0										k	—	0	21
1999	†Min	14 (0)	24	69	2.9(10)	1	1	12	12.0(12)	0										k	1	12	185
2000	†Min	16 (0)	23	67	2.9(10)	0	4	31	7.8(12)	0										k	2	147
2001	†Bal	15 (2)	65	291	4.5(55)	0	23	210	9.1(46)	0											—	0	396
2002	Min	16 (0)	84	414	4.9(44)	11	27	251	9.3(36)	0										k	—	66	806
2003	Min	16 (7, RB)	174	745	4.3(61)	5	65	644	9.9(42)	3											—	48	1132
2004	†Min	14 (1)	30	161	5.4(49)	3	21	233	11.1(28)	1											—	24	313
2005	Min	13 (0)	13	20	1.5(9)	0	4	25	6.5(25)	0										k	—	0	47
NFL	10	132 (12)	435	1826	4.2(61)	21	154	1511	9.8(64)	4										k	1	158	3270

WILLIAMS, MONK   Charles Lee, FL, 5´7˝/155 lbs; Arkansas-Pine Bluff; 1968: Cin, rnd 6; B2/15/1945 Shreveport, LA, D3/18/2003 Durham, NC   **1968** Cin-A 2

WILLIAMS, NEWTON   Newton Dennis, RB, 5´10˝/204 lbs; Arizona State; 1982: SF, rnd 5; B5/10/1959 Charlotte, NC   **1982** SF 6 (0)

YEAR	TEAM	G(GS, POS)	RUSH	YD	AVG(LG)	TD	REC	YD	AVG(LG)	TD											OTD	PTS	TAY
1983	Bal	16 (0)	28	77	2.8(13)	0	4	46	11.5(19)	0											—	0	100
NFL	2	22 (0)	28	77	2.8(13)	0	4	46	11.5(19)	0											—	0	100

WILLIAMS, OLIVER   Oliver Lavell, WR, 6´3˝/194 lbs; Illinois; 1983: Chi, rnd 12; B10/17/1960 Chicago, IL

YEAR	TEAM	G(GS, POS)	RUSH	YD	AVG(LG)	TD	REC	YD	AVG(LG)	TD										KPR	OTD	PTS	TAY
1985	Ind	8 (1)	—	—	—		9	175	19.4(36)	1										k	—	6	92
1986	Ind	3 (0)	—	—	—		—	—	—											k	—	0	0
1987	Hou	3 (2)	—	—	—		11	165	15.0(36)	1											—	6	88
NFL	3	14 (3)	—	—	—		20	340	17.0(36)	2										k	—	12	179

WILLIAMS, PAT   Patrick, DT, 6´3˝/315 lbs; Northeastern State (OK); Texas A&M; B10/24/1972 Monroe, LA   **1997** Buf 1 (0)   **1998**†Buf 13 (0)   **1999**†Buf 16 (0)   **2000** Buf 16 (4) **2001** Buf 13 (13, RDT)   **2002** Buf 16 (16, RDT)   **2003** Buf 16 (16, RDT)   **2004** Buf 16 (15, RDT)   **2005** Min 16 (16, LDT)   **NFL** 123 (80) [9 yrs]

WILLIAMS, PAYTON   Payton Mychal, DB, 5´7˝/170 lbs; Fresno State; B11/19/1978 Riverside, CA   **2000** Ind 7 (0)

WILLIAMS, PERRY Perry Andrew, RB, 6´2˝/219 lbs; Purdue; 1969: GB, rnd 4; B12/11/1946 Cincinnati, OH

YEAR	TEAM	G(GS, POS)	RUSH	YD	AVG(LG)	TD	REC	YD	AVG(LG)	TD	PASS	COMP	PCT	YD	AVG(LG)	TD	INT	SK	YD	QBR	KPR	OTD	PTS	TAY
1969	GB	14	18	55	3.1(13)	0	4	63	15.8(24)	0	—	—	—	—	—	—	—	—	—	—	k	—	0	72
1970	GB	13	17	44	2.6(4)	0	3	11	3.7(6)	0	—	—	—	—	—	—	—	—	—	—	k	—	0	55
1971	GB	14	3	4	1.3(3)	0	—	—	—	—	—	—	—	—	—	—	—	—	—	—	k	—	0	15
1972	†GB	14	33	139	4.2(14)	0	—	—	—	—	—	—	—	—	—	—	—	—	—	—	k	—	0	133
1973	GB	14	32	87	2.7(9)	1	5	44	8.8(14)	0	—	—	—	—	—	—	—	—	—	—	k	—	6	128
1974	ChiB	14(FB)	74	218	2.9(12)	1	25	167	6.7(13)	0	—	—	—	—	—	—	—	—	—	—	—	—	6	312
NFL	6	83	177	547	3.1(14)	2	37	285	7.7(24)	0	—	—	—	—	—	—	—	—	—	—	k	—	12	714

WILLIAMS, PERRY Perry Lamar, DB, 6´2˝/203 lbs; North Carolina State; 1983: NYG, rnd 7; B5/12/1961 Hamlet, NC **1984**†NYG 16 (16, RCB) **1985**†NYG 16 (16, RCB) **1986**†NYG 16 (16, RCB) **1987** NYG 10 (10, RCB) **1988** NYG 16 (16, RCB) **1989**†NYG 16 (16, RCB) **1990**†NYG 16 (2) **1991** NYG 16 (7, ss) **1992** NYG 16 (16, RCB) **1993** NYG 8 (6, rcb) **NFL** 146 (121) [10 yrs]

WILLIAMS, PERRY Perry Michael, DB, 6´1˝/200 lbs; Clemson; B4/12/1964 Cartersville, GA **1987** NE 3 (0)

WILLIAMS, POOH BEAR Clarence, RB, 6´1˝/265 lbs; Florida State; B1/20/1975 Crescent City, FL

YEAR	TEAM	G(GS, POS)	RUSH	YD	AVG(LG)	TD	REC	YD	AVG(LG)	TD	PASS	COMP	PCT	YD	AVG(LG)	TD	INT	SK	YD	QBR	KPR	OTD	PTS	TAY
1998	Buf	3(0)	2	5	2.5(3)	0	—	—	—	—	—	—	—	—	—	—	—	—	—	—	—	—	0	5

WILLIAMS, POP Arthur Vincent, B, 6´0˝/207 lbs; Connecticut; B5/4/1906 Jewett City, CT, D2/5/1979 Brooklyn, CT **1928** Pro 7 (5, fb), 24 **1929** Pro 12 (8, WB), 42 **1930** Pro 11 (8, WB), 12 **1931** Pro 8 (2) **1932** Bkn 1 (0) **NFL** 39 (23), 78 [5 yrs]

WILLIAMS, PRYOR Pryor Allen, G-C, 6´1˝/226 lbs; Auburn; Vanderbilt; B12/26/1893 Athens, AL, D1/1/1948 Birmingham, AL **1921** Det 3 (1)

WILLIAMS, QUENTIN Quentin, DB, 5´11˝/204 lbs; Wake Forest; B9/24/1982 Goldsboro, NC **2004** Mia 6 (0)

WILLIAMS, RALPH Ralph, G-T, 6´3˝/280 lbs; Southern (LA); B3/27/1958 Monroe, LA **1982** Hou 7 (5, LG) **1983** Hou 1 (0) **1985** NO 16 (14, RG) **1986** NO 6 (6, rg) **NFL** 30 (25) [4 yrs]

WILLIAMS, RANDAL Randal Ellison, WR, 6´3˝/220 lbs; New Hampshire; B5/21/1978 Bronx, NY **2001** Dal 7 (0) **2002** Dal 11 (0) **2003**†Dal 15 (0)

YEAR	TEAM	G(GS, POS)	RUSH	YD	AVG(LG)	TD	REC	YD	AVG(LG)	TD	PASS	COMP	PCT	YD	AVG(LG)	TD	INT	SK	YD	QBR	KPR	OTD	PTS	TAY
2004	Dal	2(2)	1	13	13.0(13)	0	1	14	14.0(14)	0	—	—	—	—	—	—	—	—	—	—	—	—	0	20
2005	Oak	16(4)	—	—	—	—	13	164	12.6(34)	0	—	—	—	—	—	—	—	—	—	—	—	—	0	82
NFL	5	51(6)	1	13	13.0(13)	0	14	178	12.7(34)	0	—	—	—	—	—	—	—	—	—	—	k	1	6	142

WILLIAMS, RAY Raymond Darrell, RB, 5´9˝/170 lbs; Washington State; 1980: Det, rnd 12; B9/22/1958 Welch, WV

YEAR	TEAM	G(GS, POS)	RUSH	YD	AVG(LG)	TD	REC	YD	AVG(LG)	TD	PASS	COMP	PCT	YD	AVG(LG)	TD	INT	SK	YD	QBR	KPR	OTD	PTS	TAY
1980	Det	6(1)	2	17	8.5(11)	1	10	146	14.6(22)	1	0	0	0.0	0	0.0	0	0	1	8	—	kp	1	18	332

WILLIAMS, RAY Raymond Michael, DB, 5´11˝/180 lbs; Rhode Island; B11/9/1965 Providence, RI **1987** Pit 1 (0)

WILLIAMS, REGGIE Reginald, LB, 6´1˝/228 lbs; Dartmouth; 1976: Cin, rnd 3; B9/19/1954 Flint, MI **1976** Cin 14 (RLB) **1977** Cin 14 (RLB) **1978** Cin 16 (RLB) **1979** Cin 12 (RLB) **1980** Cin 14 (13, ROLB) **1981**†Cin 16 (16, ROLB) **1982**†Cin 9 (9, ROLB) **1983** Cin 16 (16, ROLB) **1984** Cin 16 (16, ROLB) **1985** Cin 16 (15, ROLB) **1986** Cin 16 (16, ROLB) **1987** Cin 15 (15, ROLB) **1988**†Cin 16 (16, ROLB) **1989** Cin 16 (16, ROLB) **NFL** 206 (148) [14 yrs]

WILLIAMS, REGGIE Reggie, WR, 6´4˝/225 lbs; Washington; 2004: Jax, rnd 1; B5/17/1983 Landstuhl, Germany

YEAR	TEAM	G(GS, POS)	RUSH	YD	AVG(LG)	TD	REC	YD	AVG(LG)	TD	PASS	COMP	PCT	YD	AVG(LG)	TD	INT	SK	YD	QBR	KPR	OTD	PTS	TAY
2004	Jax	16(15, WR)	—	—	—	—	27	268	9.9(26)	1	—	—	—	—	—	—	—	—	—	—	—	—	10	139
2005	†Jax	16(7, wr)	2	3	1.5(10)	0	35	445	12.7(41)	0	—	—	—	—	—	—	—	—	—	—	—	—	0	226
NFL	2	32(22)	2	3	1.5(10)	0	62	713	11.5(41)	1	—	—	—	—	—	—	—	—	—	—	—	—	10	365

WILLIAMS, RENAUD Renaud, LB, 6´0˝/211 lbs; Hofstra; B2/23/1981 Westbury, NY **2004** Mia 2 (0) **2005** SF 2 (0) **NFL** 4 (0) [2 yrs]

WILLIAMS, REX Rex B., C, 6´2˝/203 lbs; Texas Tech; 1940: NYG, rnd 7; B7/16/1916 Bonham, TX, D11/1980 Rogers, AR **1940** ChiC 2 (0) **1945** Det 1 (0) **NFL** 3 (0) [2 yrs]

WILLIAMS, RICHARD Richard, WR, 5´11˝/170 lbs; Abilene Christian; 1974: Cin, rnd 4; B1/30/1952 Campville, FL **1974** NO 2

WILLIAMS, RICHARD Richard Keith, RB, 6´0˝/205 lbs; Memphis; 1983: Was, rnd 2; B8/13/1960 Eustis, FL **1984** Atl 1 (0) **1984** Hou 7 (0)

YEAR	TEAM	G(GS, POS)	RUSH	YD	AVG(LG)	TD	REC	YD	AVG(LG)	TD	PASS	COMP	PCT	YD	AVG(LG)	TD	INT	SK	YD	QBR	KPR	OTD	PTS	TAY
1983	Atl	14(0)	1	5	5.0(5)	0	—	—	—	—	—	—	—	—	—	—	—	—	—	—	k	—	0	121
NFL	2	22(0)	1	5	5.0(5)	0	—	—	—	—	—	—	—	—	—	—	—	—	—	—	k	—	0	130

WILLIAMS, RICKY Ricky C., RB, 6´1˝/195 lbs; Langston; 1983: NE, rnd 9; B4/27/1960 Santa Monica, CA **1985** LARd 2 (0) **1987** LARd 1 (0) **NFL** 3 (0) [2 yrs]

WILLIAMS, RICKY Errick Lynne, RB, 5´10˝/226 lbs; Texas; 1999: NO, rnd 1; B5/21/1977 San Diego, CA

YEAR	TEAM	G(GS, POS)	RUSH	YD	AVG(LG)	TD	REC	YD	AVG(LG)	TD	PASS	COMP	PCT	YD	AVG(LG)	TD	INT	SK	YD	QBR	KPR	OTD	PTS	TAY
1999	NO	12(12, RB)	253	884	3.5(25)	2	28	172	6.1(29)	0	1	0	0.0	0	0.0	0	0	—	—	—	—	—	12	990
2000	†NO	10(10, RB)	248	1000	4.0(26)	8	44	409	9.3(24)	1	1	1	100.0	34	34.0(34)	0	0	—	—	—	—	—	54	1307
2001	NO	16(16, RB)	313	1245	4.0(46)	6	60	511	8.5(42)	1	—	—	—	—	—	—	—	—	—	—	—	—	42	1566
2002	Mia★	16(16, RB)	**383**	**1853**	4.8(63)	16	47	363	7.7(52)	1	—	—	—	—	—	—	—	—	—	—	—	—	102	2200
2003	Mia	16(16, RB)	**392**	1372	3.5(45)	9	50	351	7.0(59)	1	—	—	—	—	—	—	—	—	—	—	—	—	60	1643
2005	Mia	12(4, rb)	168	743	4.4(35)	6	17	93	5.5(19)	0	—	—	—	—	—	—	—	—	—	—	—	—	36	850
NFL	6	82(74)	1757	7097	4.0(63)	47	246	1899	7.7(59)	4	2	1	50.0	34	17.0(34)	0	0	—	—	—	—	—	306	8554

WILLIAMS, RICKY Ricky Antwan, RB, 5´7˝/195 lbs; Texas Tech; B8/29/1978 Dallas, TX

YEAR	TEAM	G(GS, POS)	RUSH	YD	AVG(LG)	TD	REC	YD	AVG(LG)	TD	PASS	COMP	PCT	YD	AVG(LG)	TD	INT	SK	YD	QBR	KPR	OTD	PTS	TAY
2002	Ind	10(0)	11	35	3.2(10)	0	1	20	20.0(20)	1	—	—	—	—	—	—	—	—	—	—	k	—	6	55
2003	†Ind	13(4)	48	155	3.2(19)	2	22	157	7.1(17)	1	—	—	—	—	—	—	—	—	—	—	k	—	18	266
NFL	2	23(4)	59	190	3.2(19)	2	23	177	7.7(20)	2	—	—	—	—	—	—	—	—	—	—	k	—	24	321

WILLIAMS, ROBERT Robert Cole, DB, 5´10˝/190 lbs; Baylor; B10/2/1962 Galveston, TX **1987** Dal 11 (3) **1988** Dal 16 (14, RCB) **1989** Dal 13 (11, RCB) **1990** Dal 16 (6, rcb) **1991**†Dal 16 (2) **1992** Dal 9 (0) **1993** Dal 4 (0) **1993**†KC 0 (0) **NFL** 85 (36) [7 yrs]

WILLIAMS, ROBERT Robert M., DB, 5´10˝/177 lbs; North Carolina; 1998: KC, rnd 5; B5/29/1977 Shelby, NC **1998** KC 16 (1) **1999** KC 1 (0) **1999** Sea 1 (0) **NFL** 18 (1) [2 yrs]

WILLIAMS, ROBERT Robert Anthony, DB, 5´11˝/202 lbs; Eastern Illinois; B9/26/1962 Chicago, IL **1984**†Pit 2 (0)

WILLIAMS, RODNEY Rodney Allen, WR, 6´0˝/185 lbs; Arizona; B8/15/1973 Santa Monica, CA **1998** Oak 1 (0) **1999** Oak 5 (0) **NFL** 6 (0) [2 yrs]

WILLIAMS, RODNEY Rodney Colin, P, 6´0˝/178 lbs; Georgia Tech; 1999: SL, rnd 7; B4/25/1977 Decatur, GA

YEAR	TEAM	G(GS, POS)	RUSH	YD	AVG(LG)	TD	REC	YD	AVG(LG)	TD	PASS	COMP	PCT	YD	AVG(LG)	TD	INT	SK	YD	QBR	KPR	OTD	PTS	TAY
2001	NYG	15(0)	2	16	8.0(11)	0	—	—	—	—	—	—	—	—	—	—	—	—	—	—	P	—	0	16

WILLIAMS, ROGER Roger J., DB-WR, 5´10˝/180 lbs; Grambling State; 1969: LA, rnd 13; B7/1/1945 Jeanerette, LA **1971** LARm 4 **1972** LARm 14 **NFL** 18 [2 yrs]

WILLIAMS, ROLAND Roland Lamar, TE, 6´5˝/265 lbs; Syracuse; 1998: SL, rnd 4; B4/27/1975 Rochester, NY

YEAR	TEAM	G(GS, POS)	RUSH	YD	AVG(LG)	TD	REC	YD	AVG(LG)	TD	PASS	COMP	PCT	YD	AVG(LG)	TD	INT	SK	YD	QBR	KPR	OTD	PTS	TAY
1998	SL	13(9, TE)	—	—	—	—	15	144	9.6(33)	1	—	—	—	—	—	—	—	—	—	—	—	—	6	77
1999	†SL	16(15, TE)	—	—	—	—	25	226	9.0(24)	6	—	—	—	—	—	—	—	—	—	—	—	—	36	143
2000	†SL	16(11, TE)	—	—	—	—	11	102	9.3(31)	3	—	—	—	—	—	—	—	—	—	—	—	—	20	66
2001	†Oak	16(15, TE)	—	—	—	—	33	298	9.0(49)	3	—	—	—	—	—	—	—	—	—	—	—	—	18	164
2002	Oak	16(12, TE)	—	—	—	—	27	213	7.9(19)	0	—	—	—	—	—	—	—	—	—	—	—	—	0	107
2003	TB	1(0)	—	—	—	—	—	—	—	—	—	—	—	—	—	—	—	—	—	—	—	—	—	—
2004	Oak	12(3)	—	—	—	—	—	—	—	—	—	—	—	—	—	—	—	—	—	—	—	—	—	—
2005	SL	4(3)	—	—	—	—	3	21	7.0(12)	0	—	—	—	—	—	—	—	—	—	—	—	—	0	11
NFL	8	94(68)	—	—	—	—	114	1004	8.8(49)	13	—	—	—	—	—	—	—	—	—	—	—	—	80	567

WILLIAMS, ROLLIE Rolland Franklin, WB-BB, 5´8˝/170 lbs; Wisconsin; B10/11/1897 Edgerton, WI, D4/5/1968 North Liberty, IA **1923** Rac 2 (2), 6

WILLIAMS, RONNIE Ronald, TE, 6´3˝/258 lbs; Oklahoma State; B1/19/1966 Wichita Falls, TX

YEAR	TEAM	G(GS, POS)	RUSH	YD	AVG(LG)	TD	REC	YD	AVG(LG)	TD	PASS	COMP	PCT	YD	AVG(LG)	TD	INT	SK	YD	QBR	KPR	OTD	PTS	TAY
1993	Mia	11(0)	—	—	—	—	—	—	—	—	—	—	—	—	—	—	—	—	—	—	—	—	0	0
1994	†Mia	14(0)	—	—	—	—	2	26	13.0(17)	0	—	—	—	—	—	—	—	—	—	—	k	—	0	8
1995	†Mia	16(2)	—	—	—	—	3	28	9.3(13)	0	—	—	—	—	—	—	—	—	—	—	k	—	0	4
1996	Sea	14(3)	—	—	—	—	5	25	5.0(11)	1	—	—	—	—	—	—	—	—	—	—	—	—	6	18
NFL	4	55(5)	—	—	—	—	10	79	7.9(17)	1	—	—	—	—	—	—	—	—	—	—	k	—	6	30

WILLIAMS, ROOSEVELT Roosevelt, DB, 6´0˝/196 lbs; Tuskegee; 2002: Chi, rnd 3; B9/10/1978 Jacksonville, FL **2002** ChiB 13 (2) **2003** Cle 7 (3) **NFL** 20 (5) [2 yrs]

WILLIAMS, ROY Roy Orville, DT, 6´7˝/265 lbs; Pacific; 1963: Det, rnd 2/SD, rnd 4; B4/30/1937 Moorhead, MN **1963** SF 7

WILLIAMS, ROY Roy, DB, 6´0˝/235 lbs; Oklahoma; 2002: Dal, rnd 1; B8/14/1980 Redwood City, CA **2002** Dal 16 (16, FS) **2003**†Dal★16 (16, FS) **2004** Dal✧16 (16, FS) **2005** Dal✧16 (16, SS) **NFL** 64 (64) [4 yrs]

YEAR	TEAM	G(GS, POS)	RUSH	YD	AVG(LG)	TD	REC	YD	AVG(LG)	TD	PASS	COMP	PCT	YD	AVG(LG)	TD	INT	SK	YD	QBR	KPR	OTD	PTS	TAY

WILLIAMS, ROY   Roy Eugene, WR, 6´4˝/210 lbs; Texas; 2004: Det, rnd 1; B12/20/1981 Odessa, TX

2004	Det	14 (12, WR)	1	1	1.0(1)	0	54	817	15.1(46)	8	1	0	0.0	0	0.0	0	0	—	—	—	—	—	48	450
2005	Det	13 (12, WR)	—	—	—	—	45	687	15.3(51)	8	—	—	—	—	—	—	—	—	—	—	—	—	48	384
NFL	2	27 (24)	1	1	1.0(1)	0	99	1504	15.2(51)	16	1	0	0.0	0	0.0	0	0	—	—	—	—	—	96	833

WILLIAMS, ROYDELL   Roydell, WR, 6´1˝/192 lbs; Tulane; 2005: Ten, rnd 4; B3/14/1981 New Orleans, LA

| 2005 | Ten | 11 (2) | — | — | — | — | 21 | 299 | 14.2(50) | 2 | — | — | — | — | — | — | — | — | — | — | — | — | 12 | 160 |

WILLIAMS, SAM   Samuel F., DE-E-LB, 6´5˝/235 lbs; Michigan State; 1956: LA, rnd 24; B3/9/1931 Dansville, MI   **1959** LARm 12 (RE)   **1960** Det 12   **1962** Det 13 (RDE)   **1963** Det 14 (RDE)   **1964** Det 14 (RDE)   **1965** Det 14 (RDE)   **1966** Atl 14 (14, RDE)   **1967** Atl 14 (RDE)

| 1961 | Det | 12 | — | — | — | — | 1 | 10 | 10.0(10) | 0 | — | — | — | — | — | — | — | — | — | — | k | — | 0 | -6 |
| NFL | 9 | 119 (14) | — | — | — | — | 1 | 10 | 10.0(10) | 0 | — | — | — | — | — | — | — | — | — | — | ki | 3 | 20 | 21 |

WILLIAMS, SAM   Samuel Charles, aka Samaji Adi Akili, DB, 6´2˝/192 lbs; New Mexico Highlands; California; 1974: SD, rnd 12; B7/22/1952 Cameron, TX   **1974** SD 13 (12, RCB)   **1975** SD 11 (SS)   **1976** Hou 4   **NFL** 28 (12) [3 yrs]

WILLIAMS, SAM   Sam, DE, 6´5˝/265 lbs; Fresno State; 2003: Oak, rnd 3; B7/28/1980 Clayton, CA   **2003** Oak 1 (0)   **2004** Oak 9 (4)   **NFL** 10 (4) [2 yrs]

WILLIAMS, SAMMY   Sammy, T, 6´5˝/318 lbs; Oklahoma; 1998: Bal, rnd 6; B12/14/1974 Magnolia, MS   **1999** KC 1 (0)   **2000**†Bal 1 (0)   **2001**†Bal 15 (7, rt)   **2002** SD 12 (7, rt)   **NFL** 29 (14) [4 yrs]

WILLIAMS, SCOTT   Edmund Scott, RB, 6´2˝/234 lbs; Georgia; 1985: SL, rnd 9; B7/21/1962 Charlotte, NC

1986	Det	16 (0)	13	22	1.7(5)	2	2	9	4.5(6)	0	—	—	—	—	—	—	—	—	—	—	—	—	12	47
1987	Det	5 (2)	8	29	3.6(8)	0	4	16	4.0(7)	1	—	—	—	—	—	—	—	—	—	—	—	—	6	42
1988	Det	11 (0)	9	22	2.4(5)	1	3	46	15.3(32)	0	—	—	—	—	—	—	—	—	—	—	—	—	6	55
NFL	3	32 (2)	30	73	2.4(8)	3	9	71	7.9(32)	1	—	—	—	—	—	—	—	—	—	—	—	—	24	144

WILLIAMS, SHAUD   Shaud, RB, 5´7˝/193 lbs; Texas Tech; Alabama; B10/2/1980 Andrews, TX

2004	Buf	4 (0)	42	167	4.0(27)	2	3	19	6.3(10)	0	—	—	—	—	—	—	—	—	—	—	p	—	12	192
2005	Buf	16 (0)	45	161	3.6(28)	0	17	118	6.9(23)	0	—	—	—	—	—	—	—	—	—	—	—	—	0	220
NFL	2	20 (0)	87	328	3.8(28)	2	20	137	6.8(23)	0	—	—	—	—	—	—	—	—	—	—	p	—	12	412

WILLIAMS, SHAUN   Shaun LeJon, DB, 6´2˝/218 lbs; UCLA; 1998: NYG, rnd 1; B10/10/1976 Los Angeles, CA   **1998** NYG 13 (0)   **1999** NYG 11 (0)   **2000**†NYG 16 (16, FS)   **2001** NYG 16 (16, FS)   **2002**†NYG 16 (16, SS)   **2003** NYG 10 (10, SS)   **2004** NYG 2 (2)   **2005** NYG 8 (0)   **NFL** 92 (60) [8 yrs]

WILLIAMS, SHERMAN   Sherman Cedric, RB, 5´8˝/198 lbs; Alabama; 1995: Dal, rnd 2; B8/13/1973 Mobile, AL

1995	†Dal	11 (0)	48	205	4.3(44)	1	3	28	9.3(24)	0	—	—	—	—	—	—	—	—	—	—	—	—	6	229
1996	†Dal	16 (1)	69	269	3.9(27)	0	5	41	8.2(13)	0	1	0	0.0	0	0.0	0	0	—	—	—	—	—	0	290
1997	Dal	16 (0)	121	468	3.9(18)	2	21	159	7.6(18)	0	—	—	—	—	—	—	—	—	—	—	—	—	12	568
1998	Dal	16 (2)	64	220	3.4(24)	1	11	104	9.5(30)	0	—	—	—	—	—	—	—	—	—	—	k	—	6	325
1999	Dal	1 (0)	—	—	—	—	—	—	—	—	—	—	—	—	—	—	—	—	—	—	—	—	—	—
NFL	5	60 (3)	302	1162	3.8(44)	4	40	332	8.3(30)	0	1	0	0.0	0	0.0	0	0	—	—	—	k	—	24	1411

WILLIAMS, SID   Sidney, LB, 6´2˝/235 lbs; Southern (LA); 1964: Cle, rnd 16; B3/24/1942 Shreveport, LA   **1964**†Cle 14   **1965**†Cle 14 (RLB)   **1966** Cle 13   **1967** Was 10 (llb)   **1968**†Bal 12   **1969** Pit 7   **NFL** 70 [6 yrs]

WILLIAMS, STAN   Stanley Neil, DB-E, 6´2˝/195 lbs; Baylor; 1952: Cle, rnd 8; B12/5/1929 Callahan County, TX

| 1952 | DalT | 12 (6, DB) | — | — | — | — | 9 | 123 | 13.7(32) | 0 | — | — | — | — | — | — | — | — | — | — | i | 1 | 6 | 121 |

WILLIAMS, STEPFRET   Stepfret, WR, 6´0˝/170 lbs; Louisiana-Monroe; 1996: Dal, rnd 3; B6/14/1973 Minden, LA

1996	Dal	5 (1)	—	—	—	—	1	32	32.0(32)	0	—	—	—	—	—	—	—	—	—	—	—	—	0	16
1997	Dal	16 (0)	—	—	—	—	30	308	10.3(20)	1	—	—	—	—	—	—	—	—	—	—	p	—	6	163
1998	Cin	5 (0)	—	—	—	—	6	81	13.5(19)	1	—	—	—	—	—	—	—	—	—	—	kp	—	6	57
NFL	3	26 (1)	—	—	—	—	37	421	11.4(32)	2	—	—	—	—	—	—	—	—	—	—	kp	—	12	236

WILLIAMS, STEVE   Steven Ford, DE, 6´6˝/260 lbs; Western Carolina; 1972: SF, rnd 10; B1/12/1951 Columbia, SC   **1974** Bal 12

WILLIAMS, SWEENY   Clarence, DE, 6´5˝/255 lbs; Prairie View A&M; 1969: Dal, rnd 11; B9/3/1946 Brazoria, TX   **1970** GB 14 (8, LDE)   **1971** GB 14 (14, LDE)   **1972**†GB 14 (14, LDE)   **1973** GB 14 (14, LDE)   **1974** GB 14 (14, LDE)   **1975** GB 14 (14, LDE)   **1976** GB 14 (14, LDE)   **1977** GB 13   **NFL** 111 (92) [8 yrs]

WILLIAMS, TANK   Clevan, DB, 6´3˝/223 lbs; Stanford; 2002: Ten, rnd 2; B6/30/1980 Gulfport, MS   **2002**†Ten 16 (16, SS)   **2003**†Ten 16 (16, SS)   **2004** Ten 9 (9, SS)   **2005** Ten 16 (16, SS)   **NFL** 57 (57) [4 yrs]

WILLIAMS, TED   Theodore Patrick, B, 5´11˝/183 lbs; Notre Dame; Boston College; 1942: Phi, rnd 3; B6/3/1916 Bay Bulls, Canada, D10/30/1993 Gloucester, MA

1942	Phi	11 (2)	50	183	3.7(33)	2	9	58	6.4(15)	0	—	—	—	—	—	—	—	—	—	—	k	—	12	245
1944	Bos	10 (6, LH)	52	13	0.3(25)	1	6	28	4.7(16)	0	6	0	0.0	0	0.0	0	2	—	—	—	kpi	—	6	6
NFL	2	21 (8)	102	196	1.9(33)	3	15	86	5.7(16)	0	6	0	0.0	0	0.0	0	2	—	—	—	kpi	—	18	251

WILLIAMS, TERRY   Terrance, DB, 5´11˝/197 lbs; Bethune-Cookman; 1988: NYJ, rnd 2; B10/14/1965 Homestead, FL   **1988** NYJ 8 (0)   **1989** NYJ 3 (0)   **NFL** 11 (0) [2 yrs]

WILLIAMS, TEX   Jack Gressert, C-LB, 5´11˝/193 lbs; Auburn; B8/21/1919 Lancaster, PA   **1942** Phi 5 (0)

1946 Mia-A 6 (0)

WILLIAMS, TOBY   Tobias, NT-DE-DT, 6´3˝/264 lbs; Nebraska; 1983: NE, rnd 10; B11/19/1959 Washington, DC   **1983** NE 16 (10, LDE)   **1984** NE 16 (15, RDE)   **1985** NE 5 (3)   **1986**†NE 16 (16, NT)   **1987** NE 12 (12, NT)   **1988** NE 15 (0)   **NFL** 80 (56) [6 yrs]

WILLIAMS, TODD   Todd Lamonte, G, 6´5˝/330 lbs; Florida State; 2003: Ten, rnd 7; B9/4/1978 Bradenton, FL   **2004** Ten 6 (0)   **2005** Ten 1 (0)   **NFL** 7 (0) [2 yrs]

WILLIAMS, TOM   William Thomas, DT-DE, 6´4˝/250 lbs; California-Davis; 1970: SD, rnd 2; B7/21/1948 Hempstead, NY   **1970** SD 14 (ldt)   **1971** SD 13 (LDE)   **NFL** 27 [2 yrs]

WILLIAMS, TONY   Anthony Demetric, DT, 6´2˝/296 lbs; Memphis; 1997: Min, rnd 5; B7/9/1975 Germantown, TN   **1997**†Min 6 (2)   **1998**†Min 14 (9, RDT)   **1999**†Min 16 (12, RDT)   **2000**†Min 16 (15, RDT)   **2001** Cin 13 (13, RDT)   **2002** Cin 16 (16, RDT)   **2003** Cin 16 (16, RDT)   **2004** Cin 6 (6, rdt)   **NFL** 103 (89) [8 yrs]

WILLIAMS, TRAVIS   Travis Bill, TB-HB, 6´0˝/200 lbs; Indiana; B1/5/1892 Boonville, IN, D11/1986 Evansville, IN   **1921** Evv 3 (3, TB), 6   **1922** Evv 1 (0)   **NFL** 4 (3) [2 yrs]

WILLIAMS, TRAVIS   Travis, RB, 6´1˝/210 lbs; Arizona State; 1967: GB, rnd 4; B1/14/1946 El Dorado, AR, D2/17/1991 Martinez, CA **[R]**

1967	†GB	14	35	188	5.4(37)	1	5	80	16.0(29)	1	—	—	—	—	—	—	—	—	—	—	k	4	36	752
1968	GB	14	33	63	1.9(9)	0	5	48	9.6(17)	0	—	—	—	—	—	—	—	—	—	—	k	—	0	266
1969	GB	13 (HB)	129	536	4.2(39)	4	27	275	10.2(60)	3	—	—	—	—	—	—	—	—	—	—	kp	2	54	1100
1970	GB	7 (rb)	74	276	3.7(37)	1	12	127	10.6(55)	1	—	—	—	—	—	—	—	—	—	—	kp	—	12	408
1971	LARm	14	18	103	5.7(36)	0	3	68	22.7(43)	0	—	—	—	—	—	—	—	—	—	—	kp	1	6	514
NFL	5	62	289	1166	4.0(39)	6	52	598	11.5(60)	5	—	—	—	—	—	—	—	—	—	—	kp	7	108	3039

WILLIAMS, TYRONE   Upton Tyrone, DB, 5´11˝/193 lbs; Nebraska; 1996: GB, rnd 3; B5/31/1973 Bradenton, FL   **1996**†GB 16 (0)   **1997**†GB 16 (15, LCB)   **1998**†GB 16 (16, RCB)   **1999** GB 16 (16, RCB)   **2000** GB 16 (16, RCB)   **2001**†GB 16 (16, RCB)   **2002** GB 15 (15, RCB)   **2003** Atl 6 (6, rcb)   **2004** Dal 3 (2)   **NFL** 120 (102) [9 yrs]

WILLIAMS, TYRONE   Tyrone M., DE, 6´4˝/292 lbs; Wyoming; B10/22/1972 Philadelphia, PA   **1997** ChiB 3 (0)   **1999** Phi 4 (0)   **2000** Phi 3 (0)   **2000** KC 10 (0)   **2001** KC 7 (0)   **2001** Was 4 (0)   **NFL** 31 (0) [4 yrs]

WILLIAMS, TYRONE   Tyrone Robert, WR, 6´5˝/220 lbs; Western Ontario (Canada); 1992: Phx, rnd 9; B3/26/1970 Halifax, Canada

| 1993 | Dal | 5 (0) | — | — | — | — | 1 | 25 | 25.0(25) | 0 | — | — | — | — | — | — | — | — | — | — | — | — | 0 | 13 |

WILLIAMS, VAN   George Van, RB, 6´0˝/208 lbs; East Tennessee State; Carson-Newman; 1982: Buf, rnd 4; B3/15/1959 Johnson City, TN

1983	Buf	16 (1)	3	11	3.7(5)	0	—	—	—	—	—	—	—	—	—	—	—	—	—	—	kp	—	0	181
1984	Buf	16 (0)	18	51	2.8(7)	0	5	46	9.2(32)	1	—	—	—	—	—	—	—	—	—	—	k	—	6	314
1985	Buf	2 (0)	—	—	—	—	1	7	7.0(7)	0	—	—	—	—	—	—	—	—	—	—	k	—	0	9
1987	NYG	3 (3)	29	108	3.7(17)	0	5	36	7.2(12)	0	—	—	—	—	—	—	—	—	—	—	—	—	0	126
NFL	4	37 (4)	50	170	3.4(17)	0	11	89	8.1(32)	1	—	—	—	—	—	—	—	—	—	—	kp	—	6	630

WILLIAMS, VAUGHN   Vaughn Aaron, DB, 6´2˝/193 lbs; Stanford; B12/14/1961 Denver, CO   **1984** Ind 10 (1)

WILLIAMS, VINCE Vincent Bernard, RB, 6´0˝/231 lbs; Oregon; 1982: SF, rnd 6; B10/24/1959 Tacoma, WA, D8/10/1999 Tacoma, WA **1983** SF 1 (0)

YEAR	TEAM	G (GS, POS)	RUSH	YD	AVG (LG)	TD	REC	YD	AVG (LG)	TD	PASS	COMP	PCT	YD	AVG (LG)	TD	INT	SK	YD	QBR	KPR	OTD	PTS	TAY
1982	SF	2(0)	20	68	3.4(12)	0	4	33	8.3(13)	0	—	—	—	—	—	—	—	—	—	—	—	—	0	85
NFL	2	3(0)	20	68	3.4(12)	0	4	33	8.3(13)	0	—	—	—	—	—	—	—	—	—	—	—	—	0	85

WILLIAMS, WALLY Wally James, G-C, 6´2˝/305 lbs; Florida A&M; B2/19/1971 Tallahassee, FL **1993** Cle 2 (0) **1994**†Cle 11 (7, lg) **1995** Cle 16 (16, LG) **1996** Bal 15 (13, C/rg) **1997** Bal 10 (10, C) **1998** Bal 13 (13, LG/c) **1999** NO 6 (6, lg) **2000**†NO 16 (16, LG) **2001** NO 15 (15, LG) **2002** NO 4 (0) **NFL** 108 (96) [10 yrs]

WILLIAMS, WALT Walter L., DB-TB-HB, 6´2˝/195 lbs; Boston University; B2/12/1919, D8/8/1990

YEAR	TEAM	G (GS, POS)	RUSH	YD	AVG (LG)	TD	REC	YD	AVG (LG)	TD	PASS	COMP	PCT	YD	AVG (LG)	TD	INT	SK	YD	QBR	KPR	OTD	PTS	TAY
1946	ChiR-A	14(0)	21	19	0.9	1	1	3	3.0(3)	0	30	13	43.3	226	7.5	1	5	—	—	—	Pkpi	1	12	101
1947	Bos	10(3)	—	—	—	—	1	2	2.0(2)	0	1	0	0.0	0	0.0	0	1	—	—	—	p	—	0	-30

WILLIAMS, WALT Walter, DB, 6´1˝/185 lbs; Ashland University; New Mexico State; 1977: Det, rnd 2; B7/10/1954 Bedford Hills, NY **1977** Det 14 (6, rcb) **1978** Det 15 (11, LCB) **1979** Det 12 (7, LCB) **1980** Det 16 (8, lcb) **1981** Min 16 (5, lcb) **1982** Min 1 (0) **1982** ChiB 4 (0) **1983** ChiB 15 (0) **NFL** 93 (37) [7 yrs]

WILLIAMS, WALTER Walter Charles, RB, 6´1˝/206 lbs; Grambling State; B9/8/1977 Baton Rouge, LA

YEAR	TEAM	G (GS, POS)	RUSH	YD	AVG (LG)	TD	REC	YD	AVG (LG)	TD	PASS	COMP	PCT	YD	AVG (LG)	TD	INT	SK	YD	QBR	KPR	OTD	PTS	TAY
2004	GB	1(0)	6	42	7.0(28)	0	—	—	—	—	—	—	—	—	—	—	—	—	—	—	—	—	0	42
2005	GB	2(0)	—	—	—	—	1	19	19.0(19)	0	—	—	—	—	—	—	—	—	—	—	—	—	0	10
NFL	2	3(0)	6	42	7.0(28)	0	1	19	19.0(19)	0	—	—	—	—	—	—	—	—	—	—	—	—	0	52

WILLIAMS, WANDY Wanqalin Jacob, RB, 6´1˝/189 lbs; Kansas; Hofstra; 1969: Den, rnd 6; B1/3/1946 Brooklyn, NY **1970** Den 1

YEAR	TEAM	G (GS, POS)	RUSH	YD	AVG (LG)	TD	REC	YD	AVG (LG)	TD	PASS	COMP	PCT	YD	AVG (LG)	TD	INT	SK	YD	QBR	KPR	OTD	PTS	TAY
1969	Den-A	11(2)	10	18	1.8(8)	1	5	56	11.2(14)	0	—	—	—	—	—	—	—	—	—	—	k	—	6	285
NFL	2	12(2)	10	18	1.8(8)	1	5	56	11.2(14)	0	—	—	—	—	—	—	—	—	—	—	—	—	6	56

WILLIAMS, WARREN Warren, RB, 6´0˝/209 lbs; Miami (FL); 1988: Pit, rnd 6; B7/29/1965 Fort Myers, FL

YEAR	TEAM	G (GS, POS)	RUSH	YD	AVG (LG)	TD	REC	YD	AVG (LG)	TD	PASS	COMP	PCT	YD	AVG (LG)	TD	INT	SK	YD	QBR	KPR	OTD	PTS	TAY
1988	Pit	15(8, RB)	87	409	4.7(33)	0	11	66	6.0(21)	1	—	—	—	—	—	—	—	—	—	—	k	—	6	442
1989	Pit	5(2)	37	131	3.5(13)	1	6	48	8.0(16)	0	—	—	—	—	—	—	—	—	—	—	—	—	6	165
1990	Pit	14(4)	68	389	5.7(70)	3	5	42	8.4(13)	1	—	—	—	—	—	—	—	—	—	—	—	—	24	445
1991	Pit	16(3)	57	262	4.6(21)	4	15	139	9.3(29)	0	—	—	—	—	—	—	—	—	—	—	—	—	24	372
1992	†Pit	16(0)	2	0	0.0(2)	0	1	44	44.0(44)	0	—	—	—	—	—	—	—	—	—	—	k	—	0	7
1993	Ind	5(0)	—	—	—	—	—	—	—	—	—	—	—	—	—	—	—	—	—	—	—	—	—	—
NFL	6	71(17)	251	1191	4.7(70)	8	38	339	8.9(44)	2	—	—	—	—	—	—	—	—	—	—	k	—	60	1431

WILLIAMS, WILLIE Willie Albert, DB, 6´0˝/190 lbs; Grambling State; 1965: NYG, rnd 8; B12/29/1942 Atlanta, GA **[I]** **1965** NYG 14 **1966** Oak-A 6 **1967** NYG 6 **1968** NYG 14 (RCB) **1969** NYG✧14 (RCB) **1970** NYG 14 (RCB) **1971** NYG 10 (RCB) **1972** NYG 14 (RCB) **1973** NYG 14 (RCB) **NFL** 106 [9 yrs]

WILLIAMS, WILLIE Willie, T, 6´6˝/300 lbs; LSU; 1990: Phx, rnd S9; B8/6/1967 Houston, TX

YEAR	TEAM	G (GS, POS)	RUSH	YD	AVG (LG)	TD	REC	YD	AVG (LG)	TD	PASS	COMP	PCT	YD	AVG (LG)	TD	INT	SK	YD	QBR	KPR	OTD	PTS	TAY
1991	Phx	16(3)	—	—	—	—	1	3	3.0(3)	1	—	—	—	—	—	—	—	—	—	—	—	—	6	7
1994	NO	16(5, rt)	—	—	—	—	1	7	7.0(7)	0	—	—	—	—	—	—	—	—	—	—	—	—	0	4
NFL	2	32(8)	—	—	—	—	2	10	5.0(7)	1	—	—	—	—	—	—	—	—	—	—	—	—	6	10

WILLIAMS, WILLIE Willie James, DB, 5´9˝/182 lbs; Western Carolina; 1993: Pit, rnd 6; B12/26/1970 Columbia, SC **[I]** **1993**†Pit 16 (0) **1994**†Pit 16 (1) **1995**†Pit 16 (15, LCB) **1996**†Pit 15 (14, RCB) **1997** Sea 16 (16, RCB) **1998** Sea 14 (14, RCB) **1999**†Sea 15 (14, RCB) **2000** Sea 16 (15, RCB) **2001** Sea 14 (14, RCB) **2002** Sea 15 (1) **2003**†Sea 15 (0) **2004**†Pit 16 (10, LCB) **2005** Pit 4 (1) **NFL** 188 (115) [13 yrs]

WILLIAMS, WINDELL Dale Windell, E, 6´2˝/185 lbs; Rice; Louisiana-Lafayette; 1945: Det, rnd 15; B3/10/1923 Fort Towson, OK, D5/12/1992 Houston, TX

YEAR	TEAM	G (GS, POS)	RUSH	YD	AVG (LG)	TD	REC	YD	AVG (LG)	TD	PASS	COMP	PCT	YD	AVG (LG)	TD	INT	SK	YD	QBR	KPR	OTD	PTS	TAY
1948	†Bal-A	14(1, re)	—	—	—	—	32	360	11.3	2	—	—	—	—	—	—	—	—	—	—	k	—	12	195
1949	Bal-A	12(4)	—	—	—	—	20	266	13.3	1	—	—	—	—	—	—	—	—	—	—	—	—	6	138
AAFC	2	26(5)	—	—	—	—	52	626	12.0	3	—	—	—	—	—	—	—	—	—	—	k	—	18	333

WILLIAMSON, CARLTON Carlton, DB, 6´0˝/204 lbs; Pittsburgh; 1981: SF, rnd 3; B6/12/1958 Atlanta, GA **1981**†SF 16 (16, SS) **1982** SF 8 (8, SS) **1983**†SF 9 (8, SS) **1984**†SF✧15 (15, SS) **1985**†SF✧16 (16, SS) **1986**†SF 16 (16, SS) **1987**†SF 8 (1) **NFL** 88 (80) [7 yrs]

WILLIAMSON, ERNIE Ernest Warriner, T, 6´4˝/245 lbs; Apprentice; North Carolina; 1947: Was, rnd 10; B9/9/1922 Crewe, VA, D3/6/2002 Chapel Hill, NC **1947** Was 9 (3, LT) **1948** NYG 2 (0) **NFL** 11 (3) [2 yrs]

1949 LAD-A 12 (0)

WILLIAMSON, FRED Frederick Robert 'The Hammer', DB, 6´3˝/219 lbs; Northwestern; B3/5/1937 Gary, IN **[I]** **1960** Pit 11 **1961** Oak-A★14 (LCB) **1962** Oak-A★14 (LCB) **1963** Oak-A★14 (LCB) **1964** Oak-A☆14 (LCB) **1965** KC-A☆14 (LCB) **1966**†KC-A 12 (LCB) **1967** KC-A 11 (LCB) **NFL** 104 [8 yrs]

WILLIAMSON, GREG Gregory Scott, DB, 5´11˝/185 lbs; Fresno State; B5/11/1964 Long Beach, CA **1987** LARm 3 (3)

WILLIAMSON, J.R. John Robert, LB-C, 6´2˝/220 lbs; Louisiana Tech; 1964: Oak, rnd 9/Bal, rnd 8; B10/9/1941 El Dorado, AR **1964** Oak-A 14 (llb) **1965** Oak-A 14 (14, LLB) **1966** Oak-A 13 (13, LLB) **1967**†Oak-A 13 **1968** Bos-A 14 **1969** Bos-A 14 (1) **1970** Bos 11 **NFL** 93 (28) [7 yrs]

WILLIAMSON, TROY Troy, WR, 6´1˝/203 lbs; South Carolina; 2005: Min, rnd 1; B4/30/1983 Aiken, SC

YEAR	TEAM	G (GS, POS)	RUSH	YD	AVG (LG)	TD	REC	YD	AVG (LG)	TD	PASS	COMP	PCT	YD	AVG (LG)	TD	INT	SK	YD	QBR	KPR	OTD	PTS	TAY
2005	Min	14(3)	3	28	9.3(11)	0	24	372	15.5(56)	2	—	—	—	—	—	—	—	—	—	—	k	—	12	236

WILLIG, MATT Matthew Joseph, T, 6´8˝/315 lbs; USC; B1/21/1969 Santa Fe Springs, CA **1993** NYJ 3 (0) **1994** NYJ 16 (3) **1995** NYJ 15 (12, LT) **1996** Atl 12 (0) **1997** Atl 16 (13, RT) **1998**†GB 16 (0) **2000** SF 16 (3) **2001**†SF 15 (0) **2002**†SF 11 (3) **2003**†Car 13 (0) **2004** Car 16 (9, RT) **2005** SL 4 (0) **NFL** 153 (43) [12 yrs]

WILLINGHAM, LARRY Larry Levi, DB, 6´0˝/190 lbs; Auburn; 1971: SL, rnd 4; B12/22/1948 Cullman, AL **1971** SL 9 **1972** SL 11 **NFL** 20 [2 yrs]

WILLIS, BILL William Karnet, DG-G, 6´2˝/213 lbs; Ohio State; B10/5/1921 Columbus, OH; HOF 1977 **1946**†Cle-A☆13 (9, RG) **1947**†Cle-A☆13 (12, RG) **1948**†Cle-A☆14 (0) **1949**†Cle-A☆12 (1) **AAFC** 52 (22) [4 yrs]

1950†Cle★12 (MG) **1951**†Cle★12 (MG) **1952**†Cle★12 (MG) **1953**†Cle☆11 (MG) **NFL** 47 [4 yrs]

WILLIS, CHESTER Chester O'Neal, RB, 5´11˝/195 lbs; Auburn; 1981: Oak, rnd 11; B5/2/1958 Elberton, GA

YEAR	TEAM	G (GS, POS)	RUSH	YD	AVG (LG)	TD	REC	YD	AVG (LG)	TD	PASS	COMP	PCT	YD	AVG (LG)	TD	INT	SK	YD	QBR	KPR	OTD	PTS	TAY
1981	Oak	15(0)	16	54	3.4(15)	1	1	24	24.0(24)	0	—	—	—	—	—	—	—	—	—	—	k	—	6	160
1982	†LARd	8(0)	6	15	2.5(5)	0	—	—	—	—	—	—	—	—	—	—	—	—	—	—	k	—	0	11
1983	†LARd	13(0)	5	0	0.0(4)	0	—	—	—	—	—	—	—	—	—	—	—	—	—	—	—	—	0	0
1984	†LARd	16(0)	5	4	0.8(2)	0	—	—	—	—	—	—	—	—	—	—	—	—	—	—	k	—	0	2
NFL	4	52(0)	32	73	2.3(15)	1	1	24	24.0(24)	0	—	—	—	—	—	—	—	—	—	—	k	—	6	173

WILLIS, DONALD Donald Kirk, G, 6´3˝/325 lbs; Washington; North Carolina A&T; B7/15/1973 Goleta, CA **1996** NO 4 (0) **2000** KC 16 (2) **2001** KC 14 (4) **2002** KC 13 (0) **2003**†KC 16 (0) **NFL** 63 (6) [5 yrs]

WILLIS, FRED Frederick Francis, RB, 6´0˝/212 lbs; Boston College; 1971: Cin, rnd 4; B12/9/1947 Natick, MA

YEAR	TEAM	G (GS, POS)	RUSH	YD	AVG (LG)	TD	REC	YD	AVG (LG)	TD	PASS	COMP	PCT	YD	AVG (LG)	TD	INT	SK	YD	QBR	KPR	OTD	PTS	TAY
1971	Cin	14(FB)	135	590	4.4(36)	7	24	223	9.3(29)	0	2	1	50.0	8	4.0(8)	0	0	—	—	—	k	—	42	797
1972	Cin	5	42	127	3.0(12)	0	9	46	5.1(10)	0	1	1	100.0	16	16.0(16)	0	0	—	—	—	—	—	0	158
1972	Hou	8(FB)	92	334	3.6(43)	0	36	251	7.0(27)	2	3	0	0.0	0	0.0	0	1	—	—	—	—	—	12	430
1973	Hou	14(FB)	171	579	3.4(25)	4	**57**	371	6.5(50)	1	1	0	0.0	0	0.0	0	0	—	—	—	—	—	30	810
1974	Hou	10	74	239	3.2(18)	3	25	130	5.2(21)	1	—	—	—	—	—	—	—	—	—	—	—	—	24	339
1975	Hou	13	118	420	3.6(23)	2	20	104	5.2(20)	0	—	—	—	—	—	—	—	—	—	—	—	—	12	492
1976	Hou	13(FB)	148	542	3.7(44)	2	32	255	8.0(42)	1	—	—	—	—	—	—	—	—	—	—	—	—	18	695
NFL	6	77	780	2831	3.6(44)	18	203	1380	6.8(50)	5	7	2	28.6	24	3.4(16)	0	1	—	—	—	k	—	138	3719

WILLIS, JAMAL Jamalsikou Leirus, RB, 6´2˝/218 lbs; Brigham Young; B12/12/1972 Lawton, OK

YEAR	TEAM	G (GS, POS)	RUSH	YD	AVG (LG)	TD	REC	YD	AVG (LG)	TD	PASS	COMP	PCT	YD	AVG (LG)	TD	INT	SK	YD	QBR	KPR	OTD	PTS	TAY
1995	SF	11(1)	12	35	2.9(15)	0	3	8	2.7(5)	0	—	—	—	—	—	—	—	—	—	—	k	—	0	211

WILLIS, JAMES James Edward, LB, 6´2˝/237 lbs; Auburn; 1993: GB, rnd 5; B9/2/1972 Huntsville, AL **1993** GB 13 (0) **1994** GB 12 (0) **1995**†Phi 5 (0) **1996**†Phi 16 (13, MLB) **1997** Phi 15 (15, MLB) **1998** Phi 16 (16, MLB) **1999**†Sea 16 (0) **NFL** 93 (44) [7 yrs]

WILLIS, JASON Jason Patrick, WR, 6´1˝/196 lbs; Oregon; B7/26/1980 Los Angeles, CA **2004**†Sea 1 (0)

WILLIS, KEITH Keith, DE-NT, 6´1˝/260 lbs; Northeastern; B7/29/1959 Newark, NJ **[S]** **1982**†Pit 9 (0) **1983**†Pit 14 (4) **1984**†Pit 12 (2) **1985** Pit 16 (16, LDE) **1986** Pit 16 (16, LDE) **1987** Pit 11 (10, LDE) **1989**†Pit 16 (16, LDE) **1990** Pit 16 (16, LDE) **1991** Pit 16 (7, lde) **1992**†Buf 12 (1) **1993** Was 1 (0) **NFL** 139 (88) [11 yrs]

WILLIS, KEN Robert Kenneth, K, 5´11˝/190 lbs; Kentucky; B10/6/1966 Owensboro, KY **[K]** **1990** Dal 16 (0) **1991**†Dal 16 (0) **1992** TB 9 (0) **1992** NYG 6 (0) **NFL** 47 (0) [3 yrs]

WILLIS, LARRY Larry Lee, DB, 5´11˝/171 lbs; Texas-El Paso; B7/18/1948 Phoenix, AZ **1973** Was 1

Willis, Leonard Leonard Leroy, WR, 5´11˝/183 lbs; Ohio State; 1976: Min, rnd 4; B3/4/1953 Washington, DC **1976**†Min 14 **1977** NO 7 **1977** Buf 4 **1979** Buf 7

YEAR	TEAM	G(GS, POS)	RUSH	YD	AVG(LG)	TD	REC	YD	AVG(LG)	TD	PASS	COMP	PCT	YD	AVG(LG)	TD	INT	SK	YD	QBR	KPR	OTD	PTS	TAY
1978	Buf	4	—	—	—	—	2	41	20.5(23)	0	—	—	—	—	—	—	—	—	—	—	k	—	0	6
NFL	4	36	—	—	—	—	2	41	20.5(23)	0	—	—	—	—	—	—	—	—	—	—	kp	—	0	310

Willis, Mitch Otis Mitchell, NT-DT, 6´8˝/278 lbs; SMU; 1984: LARd, rnd 7; B3/16/1962 Dallas, TX **1985**†LARd 11 (0) **1986** LARd 16 (1) **1987** LARd 10 (0) **1988** LARd 1 (0) **1988** Atl 9 (0) **1990** Dal 4 (0) **NFL** 51 (1) [5 yrs]

Willis, Peter Tom Peter Tom, QB, 6´2˝/188 lbs; Florida State; 1990: Chi, rnd 3; B1/4/1967 Morris, AL

YEAR	TEAM	G(GS, POS)	RUSH	YD	AVG(LG)	TD	REC	YD	AVG(LG)	TD	PASS	COMP	PCT	YD	AVG(LG)	TD	INT	SK	YD	QBR	KPR	OTD	PTS	TAY
1990	ChiB	3(0)	—	—	—	—	—	—	—	—	13	9	69.2	106	8.2(18)	1	1	1	7	—	—	—	0	18
1991	ChiB	4(0)	2	6	3.0(8)	0	—	—	—	—	18	11	61.1	171	9.5(42)	1	1	2	9	—	—	—	0	57
1992	ChiB	9(2)	1	2	2.0(2)	0	—	—	—	—	92	54	58.7	716	7.8(68)	4	8	10	58	—	—	—	0	60
1993	ChiB	5(1)	2	6	3.0(6)	0	—	—	—	—	60	30	50.0	268	4.5(29)	0	5	5	20	—	—	—	0	-60
NFL	4	21(3)	5	14	2.8(8)	0	—	—	—	—	183	104	56.8	1261	6.9(68)	6	15	18	94	—	—	—	0	75

Willis, Ray Ray, T, 6´2˝/327 lbs; Florida State; 2005: Sea, rnd 4; B8/13/1982 Angleton, TX **2005** Sea 6 (0)

Wills, Ladell Ladell P., LB, 6´3˝/240 lbs; Jackson State; B5/30/1962 Flint, MI **1987** NYJ 3 (1)

Willson, Joe Joseph Putnam, G, 5´11˝/185 lbs; Pennsylvania; B1/7/1902 Bath, NY, D8/3/1998 Smethport, PA **1926** Buf 6 (6, LG) **1927** Buf 1 (0) **NFL** 7 (6) [2 yrs]

Willson, Diddie Osborne Putnam, G-E-DE, 5´10˝/196 lbs; Pennsylvania; B1/17/1911 Crosby, PA, D1/19/1961 Phelps, NY **1933** Phi 7 (1) **1934** Phi 11 (11, LG) **1935** Phi 10 (10, RG) **NFL** 28 (22) [3 yrs]

Wilmer, Ray Bonnie Raymond, DB, 6´2˝/190 lbs; Louisiana Tech; B6/27/1962 Pineville, LA **1984** Sea 3 (0)

Wilmot, Trevor Trevor Richard, LB, 6´2˝/215 lbs; Indiana; B10/30/1972 Evanston, IL **1995**†Ind 7 (0)

Wilmsmeyer, Klaus Klaus, P, 6´2˝/210 lbs; Louisville; 1992: TB, rnd 12; B12/4/1967 Mississauga, Canada **[P]** **1994**†SF 16 (0) **1996** NO 16 (0) **1998**†Mia 16 (0)

YEAR	TEAM	G(GS, POS)	RUSH	YD	AVG(LG)	TD	REC	YD	AVG(LG)	TD	PASS	COMP	PCT	YD	AVG(LG)	TD	INT	SK	YD	QBR	KPR	OTD	PTS	TAY
1992	†SF	15(0)	2	0	0.0(10)	0	—	—	—	—	—	—	—	—	—	—	—	—	—	—	P	—	0	0
1993	†SF	15(0)	2	0	0.0(0)	0	—	—	—	—	—	—	—	—	—	—	—	—	—	—	P	—	0	0
1995	NO	16(0)	—	—	—	—	—	—	—	—	1	1	100.0	18	18.0(18)	0	0	—	—	—	P	—	0	9
NFL	6	94(0)	4	0	0.0(10)	0	—	—	—	—	1	1	100.0	18	18.0(18)	0	0	—	—	—	P	—	2	9

Wilner, Jeff Jeffrey Scott, TE, 6´4˝/245 lbs; Wesleyan; Connecticut; B12/31/1971 East Meadowbrook, NY **1995** GB 2 (0)

YEAR	TEAM	G(GS, POS)	RUSH	YD	AVG(LG)	TD	REC	YD	AVG(LG)	TD	PASS	COMP	PCT	YD	AVG(LG)	TD	INT	SK	YD	QBR	KPR	OTD	PTS	TAY
1994	†GB	11(1)	—	—	—	—	5	31	6.2(9)	0	—	—	—	—	—	—	—	—	—	—	—	—	0	16
NFL	2	13(1)	—	—	—	—	5	31	6.2(9)	0	—	—	—	—	—	—	—	—	—	—	—	—	0	16

Wilsbach, Frank Frank Ferdinand, G, 6´0˝/215 lbs; Bucknell; B4/23/1904 Harrisburg, PA **1925** Fra 4 (2)

Wilson, Abe Abraham Y., TB-G, 5´10˝/192 lbs; Washington; B10/6/1899, D5/1981 Everett, WA **1927** Pro 14 (12, TB) **1928** Pro 9 (5, rg) **1929** Pro 10 (3, TB) **NFL** 33 (20) [3 yrs]

Wilson, Adrian Adrian, DB, 6´3˝/222 lbs; North Carolina State; 2001: Arz, rnd 3; B10/12/1979 High Point, NC **2001** Arz 16 (0) **2002** Arz 14 (14, SS) **2003** Arz 16 (15, SS) **2004** Arz 16 (16, SS) **2005** Arz 16 (16, SS) **NFL** 78 (61) [5 yrs]

Wilson, Al Alda Kauwa, LB, 6´0˝/240 lbs; Tennessee; 1999: Den, rnd 1; B6/21/1977 Jackson, TN **1999** Den 16 (12, MLB) **2000**†Den 15 (14, MLB) **2001** Den✧16 (16, MLB) **2002** Den✧16 (15, MLB) **2003**†Den 16 (16, MLB) **2004**†Den 16 (16, MLB) **2005**†Den★15 (15, MLB) **NFL** 110 (104) [7 yrs]

Wilson, Antonio Antonio, LB, 6´2˝/247 lbs; Texas A&M-Commerce; 2000: Min, rnd 4; B12/29/1977 Seagoville, TX **2000** Min 1 (0) **2001** Min 10 (0) **2002** Min 5 (1) **NFL** 16 (1) [3 yrs]

Wilson, Ben Benjamin Ivery, FB-HB, 6´0˝/225 lbs; USC; 1962: LA, rnd 5/SD, rnd 28; B3/9/1939 Houston, TX

YEAR	TEAM	G(GS, POS)	RUSH	YD	AVG(LG)	TD	REC	YD	AVG(LG)	TD	PASS	COMP	PCT	YD	AVG(LG)	TD	INT	SK	YD	QBR	KPR	OTD	PTS	TAY
1963	LARm	13(FB)	109	394	3.6(39)	1	9	173	19.2(77)	1	—	—	—	—	—	—	—	—	—	—	k	—	12	498
1964	LARm	14(HB)	159	553	3.5(27)	5	15	116	7.7(30)	1	—	—	—	—	—	—	—	—	—	—	—	—	36	666
1965	LARm	14	60	189	3.2(20)	1	9	110	12.2(38)	0	1	1	100.0	8	8.0(8)	0	0	—	—	—	k	—	6	279
1967	†GB	14(fb)	103	453	4.4(40)	2	14	88	6.3(21)	0	—	—	—	—	—	—	—	—	—	—	—	—	12	517
NFL	4	55	431	1589	3.7(40)	9	47	487	10.4(77)	2	1	1	100.0	8	8.0(8)	0	0	—	—	—	k	—	66	1960

Wilson, Bernard Raphael Bernard, DT-NT, 6´3˝/303 lbs; Tennessee State; B8/17/1970 Nashville, TN **1993** TB 13 (2) **1994** TB 1 (0) **1994** Arz 13 (12, RDT) **1995** Arz 16 (14, RDT) **1996** Arz 16 (16, RDT) **1997** Arz 16 (14, RDT) **1998**†Arz 16 (3) **NFL** 91 (61) [6 yrs]

Wilson, Billy William Stanton, E, 5´10˝/184 lbs; Gonzaga; B5/8/1911 Union, OR, D12/1972 Renton, WA **1935** ChiC 11 (7, RE) **1938** Pit 4 (1) **1938** Phi 1 (0)

YEAR	TEAM	G(GS, POS)	RUSH	YD	AVG(LG)	TD	REC	YD	AVG(LG)	TD	PASS	COMP	PCT	YD	AVG(LG)	TD	INT	SK	YD	QBR	KPR	OTD	PTS	TAY
1936	ChiC	12(10, RE)	—	—	—	—	1	12	12.0(12)	0	—	—	—	—	—	—	—	—	—	—	—	—	0	6
1937	ChiC	11(1)	—	—	—	—	1	2	2.0(2)	0	—	—	—	—	—	—	—	—	—	—	—	—	0	1
NFL	4	39(19)	—	—	—	—	2	14	7.0(12)	0	—	—	—	—	—	—	—	—	—	—	—	—	0	7

Wilson, Billy William Gene, E-FL, 6´3˝/190 lbs; San Jose State; 1950: SF, rnd 22; B2/3/1927 Sayre, OK

YEAR	TEAM	G(GS, POS)	RUSH	YD	AVG(LG)	TD	REC	YD	AVG(LG)	TD	PASS	COMP	PCT	YD	AVG(LG)	TD	INT	SK	YD	QBR	KPR	OTD	PTS	TAY
1951	SF	9(RE)	—	—	—	—	18	268	14.9(38)	3	—	—	—	—	—	—	—	—	—	—	k	—	18	134
1952	SF	9(RE)	—	—	—	—	23	304	13.2(40)	3	—	—	—	—	—	—	—	—	—	—	—	—	18	167
1953	SF	12(RE)	—	—	—	—	51	840	16.5(61)	**10**	—	—	—	—	—	—	—	—	—	—	—	—	60	470
1954	SF★	12(RE)	—	—	—	—	**60**	830	13.8(43)	5	—	—	—	—	—	—	—	—	—	—	—	—	30	440
1955	SF★	12(RE)	—	—	—	—	53	831	15.7(72)	7	—	—	—	—	—	—	—	—	—	—	—	—	42	451
1956	SF★	12(RE)	—	—	—	—	**60**	889	14.8(77)	5	—	—	—	—	—	—	—	—	—	—	—	—	30	470
1957	†SF★	11(RE)	—	—	—	—	**52**	757	14.6(40)	6	—	—	—	—	—	—	—	—	—	—	—	—	36	409
1958	SF★	9(RE)	—	—	—	—	43	592	13.8(44)	5	—	—	—	—	—	—	—	—	—	—	—	—	30	321
1959	SF✧	10(RE)	—	—	—	—	44	540	12.3(57)	4	—	—	—	—	—	—	—	—	—	—	—	—	24	290
1960	SF	4	—	—	—	—	3	51	17.0(19)	1	—	—	—	—	—	—	—	—	—	—	—	—	6	31
NFL	10	100	—	—	—	—	407	5902	14.5(77)	49	—	—	—	—	—	—	—	—	—	—	k	—	294	3181

Wilson, Bobby Robert Edward, TB-HB, 5´9˝/147 lbs; SMU; 1936: Bkn, rnd 5; B8/16/1913 Nacogdoches, TX, D5/15/1999 Brenham, TX

YEAR	TEAM	G(GS, POS)	RUSH	YD	AVG(LG)	TD	REC	YD	AVG(LG)	TD	PASS	COMP	PCT	YD	AVG(LG)	TD	INT	SK	YD	QBR	KPR	OTD	PTS	TAY
1936	Bkn	12(5, TB)	104	505	4.9(51)	3	1	12	12.0(12)	1	40	11	27.5	148	3.7	0	9	—	—	—	—	—	24	260

Wilson, Bobby Bobby, DT, 6´2˝/297 lbs; Michigan State; 1991: Was, rnd 1; B3/4/1968 Chicago, IL **1991**†Was 16 (1) **1992** Was 5 (5, ldt) **1993** Was 12 (9, LDT) **1994** Was 9 (9, LDT) **NFL** 42 (24) [4 yrs]

Wilson, Brenard Brenard Kenric, DB, 6´0˝/178 lbs; Vanderbilt; B8/15/1955 Daytona Beach, FL **1979** Phi 14 (14, FS) **1980**†Phi 16 (16, FS) **1981**†Phi 15 (15, FS) **1982** Phi 8 (8, FS) **1983** Phi 16 (2) **1984** Phi 16 (5, lcb) **1985** Phi 16 (1) **1986** Phi 16 (0) **1987** Phi 1 (0) **1987** Atl 8 (1) **NFL** 126 (62) [9 yrs]

Wilson, Brett Brett Allan, RB, 6´0˝/220 lbs; Illinois; B12/29/1960 La Grange, IL

YEAR	TEAM	G(GS, POS)	RUSH	YD	AVG(LG)	TD	REC	YD	AVG(LG)	TD	PASS	COMP	PCT	YD	AVG(LG)	TD	INT	SK	YD	QBR	KPR	OTD	PTS	TAY
1987	Min	3(1)	5	16	3.2(6)	0	2	14	7.0(9)	0	—	—	—	—	—	—	—	—	—	—	—	—	0	23

Wilson, Butch George Marvin, TE, 6´2˝/228 lbs; Alabama; 1963: Bal, rnd 2/Oak, rnd 6; B9/18/1941 Birmingham, AL

YEAR	TEAM	G(GS, POS)	RUSH	YD	AVG(LG)	TD	REC	YD	AVG(LG)	TD	PASS	COMP	PCT	YD	AVG(LG)	TD	INT	SK	YD	QBR	KPR	OTD	PTS	TAY
1963	Bal	2	—	—	—	—	—	—	—	—	—	—	—	—	—	—	—	—	—	—	—	—	—	—
1964	†Bal	11	—	—	—	—	7	86	12.3(20)	1	—	—	—	—	—	—	—	—	—	—	—	—	6	48
1965	†Bal	14	—	—	—	—	1	38	38.0(38)	0	—	—	—	—	—	—	—	—	—	—	—	—	0	19
1966	Bal	14	—	—	—	—	3	27	9.0(11)	2	—	—	—	—	—	—	—	—	—	—	—	—	12	24
1967	Bal	13	—	—	—	—	—	—	—	—	—	—	—	—	—	—	—	—	—	—	—	—	—	—
1968	NYG	14	—	—	—	—	4	34	8.5(13)	0	—	—	—	—	—	—	—	—	—	—	—	—	0	17
1969	NYG	14	—	—	—	—	10	132	13.2(33)	0	—	—	—	—	—	—	—	—	—	—	—	—	0	66
NFL	7	82	—	—	—	—	25	317	12.7(38)	3	—	—	—	—	—	—	—	—	—	—	—	—	18	174

Wilson, Camp Warren Camp, FB, 6´1˝/200 lbs; Tarleton State; Hardin-Simmons; Tulsa; B3/29/1922 Pecos, TX, D3/22/2001 Sierra Vista, AZ

YEAR	TEAM	G(GS, POS)	RUSH	YD	AVG(LG)	TD	REC	YD	AVG(LG)	TD	PASS	COMP	PCT	YD	AVG(LG)	TD	INT	SK	YD	QBR	KPR	OTD	PTS	TAY
1946	Det	10(5, FB)	64	207	3.2(15)	3	7	62	8.9(26)	0	—	—	—	—	—	—	—	—	—	—	Pk	—	18	265
1947	Det	12(7, FB)	89	412	4.6(48)	0	5	96	19.2(38)	0	—	—	—	—	—	—	—	—	—	—	k	—	0	461
1948	Det	11(6, FB)	157	612	3.9(38)	2	2	9	4.5(6)	0	—	—	—	—	—	—	—	—	—	—	k	—	12	735
1949	Det	12(6, FB)	68	222	3.3(24)	1	6	31	5.2(19)	0	—	—	—	—	—	—	—	—	—	—	—	—	6	248
NFL	4	45(24)	378	1453	3.8(48)	6	20	198	9.9(38)	0	—	—	—	—	—	—	—	—	—	—	Pk	—	36	1708

Wilson, Cedrick Cedrick, WR, 5´10˝/183 lbs; Tennessee; 2001: SF, rnd 6; B12/17/1978 Memphis, TN

YEAR	TEAM	G(GS, POS)	RUSH	YD	AVG(LG)	TD	REC	YD	AVG(LG)	TD	PASS	COMP	PCT	YD	AVG(LG)	TD	INT	SK	YD	QBR	KPR	OTD	PTS	TAY
2001	SF	6(0)	—	—	—	—	—	—	—	—	—	—	—	—	—	—	—	—	—	—	kp	—	0	31
2002	†SF	16(0)	—	—	—	—	15	166	11.1(22)	1	—	—	—	—	—	—	—	—	—	—	kp	—	6	152
2003	SF	16(3)	1	-4	-4.0(-4)	0	35	396	11.3(29)	2	1	1	100.0	6	6.0(6)	0	0	—	—	—	kp	1	18	505

YEAR	TEAM	G(GS, POS)	RUSH	YD	AVG(LG)	TD	REC	YD	AVG(LG)	TD	PASS	COMP	PCT	YD	AVG(LG)	TD	INT	SK	YD	QBR	KPR	OTD	PTS	TAY
2004	SF	15(15, WR)	1	6	6.0(6)	0	47	641	13.6(39)	3	—	—	—	—	—	—	—	—	—	—	kp	—	18	399
2005	†Pit	16(1)	1	0	0.0(0)	0	26	451	17.3(46)	0	—	—	—	—	—	—	—	—	—	—	k	—	0	234
NFL	5	69(19)	3	2	0.7(6)	0	123	1654	13.4(46)	6	1	1	100.0	6	6.0(6)	0	0	—	—	—	kp	1	42	1320

Wilson, Charles Charles Joseph, WR, 5´10˝/185 lbs; Memphis; 1990: GB, rnd 5; B7/1/1968 Tallahassee, FL **[R]**

1990	GB	15(0)	—	—	—	—	7	84	12.0(18)	0	—	—	—	—	—	—	—	—	—	—	k	—	0	315
1991	GB	15(2)	3	3	1.0(5)	0	19	305	16.1(75)	1	—	—	—	—	—	—	—	—	—	—	k	1	12	348
1992	TB	2(0)	—	—	—	—	—	—	—	—	—	—	—	—	—	—	—	—	—	—	k	—	0	8
1993	TB	15(1)	2	7	3.5(4)	0	15	225	15.0(24)	0	—	—	—	—	—	—	—	—	—	—	k	—	0	229
1994	TB	14(8, WR)	2	15	7.5(11)	0	31	652	21.0(71)	6	—	—	—	—	—	—	—	—	—	—	k	—	36	472
1995	NYJ	15(11, WR)	—	—	—	—	41	484	11.8(24)	4	—	—	—	—	—	—	—	—	—	—	—	—	24	262
NFL	6	76(22)	7	25	3.6(11)	0	113	1750	15.5(75)	11	—	—	—	—	—	—	—	—	—	—	k	1	72	1633

Wilson, Darrell Darrell Kenton, DB, 5´11˝/180 lbs; Connecticut; B7/28/1958 Camden, NJ **1981** NE 1 (0)

Wilson, Darryal Darryal Edgar, WR, 6´0˝/182 lbs; Tennessee; 1983: NE, rnd 2; B9/19/1960 Florence, AL **1983** NE 9 (0)

Wilson, Dave David Carlton, QB, 6´3˝/206 lbs; Illinois; 1981: NO, rnd S1; B4/27/1959 Anaheim, CA

1981	NO	11(4, qb)	5	1	0.2(9)	0	—	—	—	—	159	82	51.6	1058	6.7(50)	1	11	12	121	46.1	—	—	0	95
1983	NO	8(2)	5	3	0.6(5)	1	—	—	—	—	112	66	58.9	770	6.9(42)	5	7	17	146	68.7	—	—	6	143
1984	NO	5(2)	3	-7	-2.3(-2)	0	—	—	—	—	93	51	54.8	647	7.0(54)	7	4	7	54	—	—	—	0	192
1985	NO	10(10, QB)	18	7	0.4(17)	0	—	—	—	—	293	145	49.5	1843	6.3(50)	11	15	39	291	60.7	—	—	0	384
1986	NO	14(13, QB)	14	19	1.4(14)	1	—	—	—	—	342	189	55.3	2353	6.9(63)	10	17	22	191	65.8	—	—	6	576
1987	†NO	4(0)	—	—	—	—	—	—	—	—	24	13	54.2	243	10.1(38)	2	0	2	21	—	—	—	0	132
1988	NO	1(0)	—	—	—	—	—	—	—	—	16	5	31.3	73	4.6(25)	0	1	—	—	—	—	—	0	-4
NFL	7	53(31)	45	23	0.5(17)	2	—	—	—	—	1039	551	53.0	6987	6.7(63)	36	55	99	824	63.8	—	—	12	1517

Wilson, David David Alan, DB, 5´10˝/192 lbs; California; 1992: Min, rnd 7; B6/10/1970 Los Angeles, CA **1992** NE 1 (0) **1992**†Min 3 (0) **NFL** 4 (0) [1 yr]

Wilson, Don Donald Allen, DB, 6´2˝/190 lbs; North Carolina State; B7/28/1961 Washington, DC **1984** Buf 16 (11, FS) **1985** Buf 16 (5, fs) **NFL** 32 (16) [2 yrs]

Wilson, Drip Drip, C, none; B1903 **1931** Cle 1 (0)

Wilson, Earl Earl, DE, 6´4˝/276 lbs; Kentucky; B9/13/1958 Long Branch, NJ **1985** SD 16 (9, RDE) **1986** SD 16 (6, rde) **1987** SD 1 (1) **NFL** 33 (16) [3 yrs]

Wilson, Eddie Edward Adair, QB-P, 6´0˝/190 lbs; Arizona; 1962: DalT, rnd 3/Det, rnd 2; B8/14/1940 Redding, CA

1962	†DalT-A	14	1	5	5.0(5)	0	—	—	—	—	11	6	54.5	65	5.9(22)	0	0	—	—	—	P	—	0	38
1963	KC-A	14(1)	8	45	5.6(21)	0	—	—	—	—	82	39	47.6	537	6.5(48)	3	2	—	—	—	P	—	0	249
1964	KC-A	14	6	5	0.8(8)	1	—	—	—	—	47	25	53.2	392	8.3(55)	1	1	—	—	—	P	—	6	176
1965	Bos-A	14	8	4	0.5(17)	0	—	—	—	—	46	20	43.5	257	5.6(30)	1	3	—	—	—	P	—	0	18
NFL	4	56(1)	23	59	2.6(21)	1	—	—	—	—	186	90	48.4	1251	6.7(55)	5	6	—	—	—	P	—	6	480

Wilson, Eric Eric Wendell, LB, 6´1˝/247 lbs; Maryland; 1985: GB, rnd 7; B10/17/1962 Charlottesville, VA **1985** Buf 14 (0) **1987** Was 3 (3) **NFL** 17 (3) [2 yrs]

Wilson, Eugene Eugene W., DB, 5´10˝/195 lbs; Illinois; 2003: NE, rnd 2; B8/17/1980 Merrillville, IN **2003**†NE 16 (15, FS) **2004**†NE 15 (14, FS) **2005**†NE 16 (16, FS) **NFL** 47 (45) [3 yrs]

Wilson, Frank Frank Henry, TE-FB, 6´2˝/233 lbs; Rice; 1981: Pit, rnd 8; B10/11/1958 Austin, TX **1982** Pit 1 (0)

Wilson, Gene Ollie Eugene, E, 5´10˝/177 lbs; SMU; 1947: GB, rnd 6/LAD-A, rnd 14; B6/24/1926 Arp, TX, D7/4/2002 Houston, TX

1947	GB	9(0)	1	-2	-2.0(-2)	0	3	34	11.3(15)	0	—	—	—	—	—	—	—	—	—	—	—	—	0	15
1948	GB	12(3)	—	—	—	—	2	23	11.5(14)	0	—	—	—	—	—	—	—	—	—	—	i	—	0	15
NFL	2	21(3)	1	-2	-2.0(-2)	0	5	57	11.4(15)	0	—	—	—	—	—	—	—	—	—	—	i	—	0	30

Wilson, George George Bownan, B, 5´11˝/185 lbs; Lafayette; B7/18/1905 Glenside, PA, D5/3/1990 Bryn Mawr, PA **1929** Fra 18 (4)

Wilson, George George William, E-DE, 6´1˝/199 lbs; Northwestern; B2/3/1914 Chicago, IL, D11/23/1978 Detroit, MI **[C]**

1937	†ChiB	11(2)	—	—	—	—	1	20	20.0(20)	0	—	—	—	—	—	—	—	—	—	—	—	1	6	10
1938	ChiB	11(5, le)	—	—	—	—	4	81	20.3	1	—	—	—	—	—	—	—	—	—	—	—	—	6	46
1939	ChiB	11(9, RE)	—	—	—	—	5	66	13.2	0	—	—	—	—	—	—	—	—	—	—	—	—	0	33
1940	†ChiB✧	11(5, RE)	—	—	—	—	4	90	22.5	1	—	—	—	—	—	—	—	—	—	—	—	—	6	50
1941	†ChiB★	11(5, re)	—	—	—	—	4	75	18.8(21)	0	—	—	—	—	—	—	—	—	—	—	—	—	0	38
1942	†ChiB★	11(11, RE)	—	—	—	—	9	89	9.9(16)	0	—	—	—	—	—	—	—	—	—	—	i	2	12	52
1943	†ChiB☆	10(10, RE)	—	—	—	—	21	293	14.0(28)	5	—	—	—	—	—	—	—	—	—	—	i	—	30	177
1944	ChiB☆	10(10, RE)	—	—	—	—	24	265	11.0(24)	4	—	—	—	—	—	—	—	—	—	—	—	—	24	153
1945	ChiB	9(5, RE)	—	—	—	—	28	259	9.3(18)	3	—	—	—	—	—	—	—	—	—	—	p	—	18	142
1946	†ChiB	11(4)	—	—	—	—	11	104	9.5(17)	1	—	—	—	—	—	—	—	—	—	—	—	—	6	57
NFL	10	106(66)	—	—	—	—	111	1342	12.1(28)	15	—	—	—	—	—	—	—	—	—	—	pi	3	108	755

Wilson, George George William, QB, 6´2˝/185 lbs; Notre Dame; Xavier (OH); 1965: Det, rnd 20/Buf, rnd R12; B5/29/1943 Oak Park, IL

1966	Mia-A	14(7, qb)	27	137	5.1(37)	0	—	—	—	—	112	46	41.1	764	6.8(80)	5	10	11	77	42.4	P	—	2	144

Wilson, George George, WR, 6´0˝/210 lbs; Arkansas; B3/14/1981 Paducah, KY **2005** Buf 3 (0)

Wilson, Gibril Gibril Donald, DB, 6´1˝/190 lbs; Tennessee; 2004: NYG, rnd 5; B11/12/1981 San Jose, CA **2004** NYG 8 (7, SS) **2005**†NYG 16 (16, SS) **NFL** 24 (23) [2 yrs]

Wilson, Gillis Gillis R., DE, 6´2˝/282 lbs; Southern (LA); 2000: Car, rnd 5; B10/15/1977 Morgan City, LA **2001** Car 5 (0)

Wilson, Gordon Gordon K., G-T, 6´0˝/228 lbs; Texas-El Paso; 1941: Cle, rnd 16; B11/23/1915 Fort Towson, OK, D6/8/1997 **1941** Cle 1 (0) **1942** ChiC 11 (7, RG) **1943** ChiC 10 (10, RG) **1944** Bos 1 (0) **1944** Bkn 7 (2) **1945** ChiC 9 (1) **NFL** 39 (20) [5 yrs]

Wilson, Harry Harry Edward, RB, 5´11˝/204 lbs; Nebraska; 1967: Phi, rnd 3; B9/28/1944 Steubenville, OH

1967	Phi	3	—	—	—	—	2	20	10.0(12)	0	—	—	—	—	—	—	—	—	—	—	k	—	0	55
1969	Phi	2	4	7	1.8(4)	0	1	6	6.0(6)	0	—	—	—	—	—	—	—	—	—	—	—	—	0	10
1970	Phi	1	—	—	—	—	—	—	—	—	—	—	—	—	—	—	—	—	—	—	—	—	—	—
NFL	3	6	4	7	1.8(4)	0	3	26	8.7(12)	0	—	—	—	—	—	—	—	—	—	—	k	—	0	65

Wilson, J.C. James C., DB, 6´0˝/178 lbs; Tampa; Pittsburgh; 1978: Hou, rnd 8; B3/11/1956 Cleveland, OH **1978**†Hou 16 (2) **1979**†Hou 16 (16, LCB) **1980**†Hou 16 (16, LCB) **1981** Hou 16 (14, LCB) **1982** Hou 7 (6, LCB) **1983** Hou 13 (0) **NFL** 84 (54) [6 yrs]

Wilson, Jack Jack William, HB, 6´0˝/200 lbs; Baylor; 1942: Cle, rnd 1; B11/20/1917 Paris, TX, D4/11/2001 Waco, TX

1946	LARm	9(3)	19	120	6.3(35)	0	3	30	10.0(15)	1	—	—	—	—	—	—	—	—	—	—	kpi	—	6	296
1947	LARm	1(0)	3	3	1.0(4)	0	1	-5	-5.0(-5)	0	—	—	—	—	—	—	—	—	—	—	—	—	0	1
NFL	2	10(3)	22	123	5.6(35)	0	4	25	6.3(15)	1	—	—	—	—	—	—	—	—	—	—	kpi	—	6	297

Wilson, Jamie James Wesley, T, 6´6˝/300 lbs; Marshall; B6/6/1973 Newport News, VA **1999**†Ind 5 (0)

Wilson, Jerrel Jerrel Douglas, RB-P, 6´2˝/222 lbs; Southern Mississippi; 1963: KC, rnd 11/LA, rnd 17; B10/4/1941 New Orleans, LA, D4/9/2005 Bronson, TX **[KP]**

1963	KC-A	14	9	41	4.6(12)	0	2	21	10.5(15)	0	—	—	—	—	—	—	—	—	—	—	Pk	—	0	57
1964	KC-A	14	1	-10	-10.0(-10)	0	1	11	11.0(11)	0	—	—	—	—	—	—	—	—	—	—	P	—	0	-5
1965	KC-A	14	2	4	2.0(3)	0	—	—	—	—	—	—	—	—	—	—	—	—	—	—	P	—	2	4
1966	†KC-A☆	14	3	7	2.3(5)	0	1	7	7.0(7)	0	—	—	—	—	—	—	—	—	—	—	P	—	2	11
1967	KC-A	10	1	10	10.0(10)	0	—	—	—	—	—	—	—	—	—	—	—	—	—	—	P	—	0	10
1968	†KC-A☆	14	5	1	0.2(3)	0	1	14	14.0(14)	0	—	—	—	—	—	—	—	—	—	—	P	—	0	8
1969	†KC-A	14	—	—	—	—	—	—	—	—	—	—	—	—	—	—	—	—	—	—	P	—	0	0
1970	KC✧	14	—	—	—	—	—	—	—	—	—	—	—	—	—	—	—	—	—	—	P	—	0	0
1971	†KC★	14	—	—	—	—	—	—	—	—	—	—	—	—	—	—	—	—	—	—	P	—	0	0
1972	KC★	14	—	—	—	—	—	—	—	—	1	1	100.0	20	20.0(20)	0	0	—	—	—	P	—	0	10
1973	KC☆	14	—	—	—	—	—	—	—	—	1	1	100.0	9	9.0(9)	0	0	—	—	—	P	—	0	5
1974	KC☆	14	—	—	—	—	—	—	—	—	2	0	0.0	0	0.0	0	0	—	—	—	P	—	0	0

YEAR	TEAM	G (GS, POS)	RUSH	YD	AVG (LG)	TD	REC	YD	AVG (LG)	TD	PASS	COMP	PCT	YD	AVG (LG)	TD	INT	SK	YD	QBR	KPR	OTD	PTS	TAY
1975	KC☆	11	—	—	—	—	—	—	—	—	—	—	—	—	—	—	—	—	—	—	P	—	0	0
1976	KC	14	—	—	—	—	—	—	—	—	—	—	—	—	—	—	—	—	—	—	P	—	0	0
1977	KC	14	—	—	—	—	—	—	—	—	—	—	—	—	—	—	—	—	—	—	P	—	0	0
1978	†NE	14	1	0	0.0(0)	0	—	—	—	—	—	—	—	—	—	—	—	—	—	—	KP	—	0	0
NFL	16	217	22	53	2.4(12)	0	5	53	10.6(15)	0	4	2	50.0	29	7.3(20)	0	0	—	—	—	KPk	—	4	99

Wilson, Jerry Gerald Roscoe, DE, 6´3˝/238 lbs; Auburn; 1959: ChiC, rnd 2; B12/9/1936 Birmingham, AL **1959** Phi 12 **1960** Phi 4 **1960** SF 6 **NFL** 22 [2 yrs]

Wilson, Jerry Jerry Lee, DB, 5´10˝/190 lbs; Southern (LA); 1995: TB, rnd 4; B7/17/1973 Alexandria, LA **1996** Mia 2 (0) **1997**†Mia 16 (0) **1998**†Mia 16 (0) **1999**†Mia 16 (1) **2000**†Mia 16 (1) **2001** NO 1 (0) **2002** NO 7 (0) **2002** SD 5 (0) **2003** SD 16 (16, FS) **2004**†SD 16 (16, FS) **2005** SD 9 (1) **NFL** 120 (35) [10 yrs]

Wilson, Jim James Bentley, E, 5´7˝/155 lbs; Cornell; B7/8/1896 Buffalo, NY, D9/25/1986 Clarence, NY **1922** Buf 4 (3)

Wilson, Jim James Milligan, G-T, 6´3˝/258 lbs; Georgia; 1964: SF, rnd 4/Bos, rnd 14; B6/12/1942 Pittsburgh, PA **1965** SF 11 **1966** SF 14 **1967** Atl 7 **1968** LARm 14 **NFL** 46 [4 yrs]

Wilson, Joe Joseph, RB, 5´10˝/210 lbs; Holy Cross; 1973: Cin, rnd 8; B8/11/1950 Raeford, BC

1973	†Cin	13	10	39	3.9(11)	0	—	—	—	—	—	—	—	—	—	—	—	—	—	—	k	—	0	92
1974	NE	12	15	57	3.8(12)	0	3	38	12.7(23)	0	—	—	—	—	—	—	—	—	—	—	k	—	0	79
NFL	2	25	25	96	3.8(12)	0	3	38	12.7(23)	0	—	—	—	—	—	—	—	—	—	—	k	—	0	171

Wilson, Johnny John Samuel, E, 6´3˝/203 lbs; Case Western Reserve; B11/2/1915 Dover, OH, D8/24/2002 Rawlings, MD

1939	Cle	11(11, RE)	—	—	—	—	8	108	13.5	1	—	—	—	—	—	—	—	—	—	—	—	—	6	59
1940	Cle	10(4)	—	—	—	—	7	93	13.3	1	—	—	—	—	—	—	—	—	—	—	—	—	6	52
1941	Cle	11(3)	—	—	—	—	5	115	23.0(57)	1	—	—	—	—	—	—	—	—	—	—	—	—	6	63
1942	Cle	3(3)	—	—	—	—	6	113	18.8(45)	1	—	—	—	—	—	—	—	—	—	—	—	1	12	62
NFL	4	35(21)	—	—	—	—	26	429	16.5(57)	4	—	—	—	—	—	—	—	—	—	—	—	1	30	235

Wilson, Karl Karl Wendell, DE-DT, 6´5˝/274 lbs; LSU; 1987: SD, rnd 3; B9/10/1964 Amite, LA **1987** SD 7 (0) **1988** SD 13 (2) **1989** Phx 15 (6, rde) **1990**†Mia 16 (2) **1991** LARm 13 (10, LDE) **1992** NYJ 2 (0) **1993** NYJ 5 (0) **1993** Mia 2 (0) **1993**†SF 5 (0) **1994** TB 14 (2) **1995**†Buf 11 (1) **NFL** 103 (23) [9 yrs]

Wilson, Kris Kristopher, TE, 6´3˝/250 lbs; Pittsburgh; 2004: KC, rnd 2; B8/22/1981 Lancaster, PA **2004** KC 3 (0)

2005	KC	14(1)	1	6	6.0(6)	0	3	33	11.0(16)	0	—	—	—	—	—	—	—	—	—	—	—	—	0	23
NFL	2	17(1)	1	6	6.0(6)	0	3	33	11.0(16)	0	—	—	—	—	—	—	—	—	—	—	—	—	0	23

Wilson, Larry Lawrence Frank, DB, 6´0˝/190 lbs; Utah; 1960: SL, rnd 7/Buf, rnd 1; B3/24/1938 Rigby, ID; HOF 1978 **[IC]** **1960** SL 11 (11, RS) **1961** SL 11 (11, RS) **1962** SL✧14 (14, RS) **1965** SL★10 (RS) **1966** SL★14 (14, RS) **1967** SL★14 (14, RS) **1969** SL★14 (RS) **1970** SL★13 (FS) **1971** SL☆14 (FS/ss)

1963	SL★	14(RS)	2	38	19.0(35)	1	—	—	—	—	—	—	—	—	—	—	—	—	—	—	i	1	12	95
1964	SL	14(RS)	2	-14	-7.0(4)	0	—	—	—	—	—	—	—	—	—	—	—	—	—	—	i	1	6	25
1968	SL★	14(RS)	1	12	12.0(12)	0	—	—	—	—	—	—	—	—	—	—	—	—	—	—	pi	—	0	6
1972	SL	12(FS)	—	—	—	—	—	—	—	—	2	0	0.0	0	0.0	0	0	—	—	—	i	—	0	20
NFL	13	169(64)	5	36	7.2(35)	1	—	—	—	—	2	0	0.0	0	0.0	0	0	—	—	—	kpi	7	50	680

Wilson, Lee Leland Moore, E-WB, 5´11˝/184 lbs; Cornell College; B7/24/1905, D1/17/1970 Clarion, IA **1929** Min 9 (3) **1930** Min 8 (6, RE) **1930** Fra 4 (4) **1931** Fra 5 (5, LE) **NFL** 26 (18) [3 yrs]

Wilson, Marc Marc Douglas, QB, 6´6˝/205 lbs; Brigham Young; 1980: Oak, rnd 1; B2/15/1957 Bremerton, WA

1980	Oak	2(0)	1	3	3.0(3)	0	—	—	—	—	5	3	60.0	31	6.2(12)	0	0	—	—	—	—	—	0	19
1981	Oak	13(9, QB)	30	147	4.9(18)	2	—	—	—	—	366	173	47.3	2311	6.3(66)	14	19	30	241	58.9	—	—	12	633
1982	†LARd	8(0)	—	—	—	—	—	—	—	—	2	1	50.0	4	2.0(4)	0	0	—	—	—	—	—	0	2
1983	†LARd	10(3)	13	122	9.4(23)	0	—	—	—	—	117	67	57.3	864	7.4(50)	8	6	10	75	82.0	—	—	0	354
1984	†LARd	16(10, QB)	30	56	1.9(14)	1	—	—	—	—	282	153	54.3	2151	7.6(**92**)	15	17	37	228	71.7	—	—	6	537
1985	†LARd	16(13, QB)	24	98	4.1(17)	2	—	—	—	—	388	193	49.7	2608	6.7(59)	16	21	27	202	62.7	—	—	12	662
1986	LARd	16(8, qb)	14	45	3.2(13)	0	—	—	—	—	240	129	53.8	1721	7.2(57)	12	15	34	227	67.4	—	—	0	366
1987	LARd	15(7, QB)	17	91	5.4(16)	0	—	—	—	—	266	152	57.1	2070	7.8(47)	12	8	33	238	84.6	—	—	0	866
1989	NE	14(4, qb)	7	42	6.0(11)	0	—	—	—	—	150	75	50.0	1006	6.7(65)	3	5	10	71	64.5	—	—	0	360
1990	NE	16(6, QB)	5	7	1.4(6)	0	—	—	—	—	265	139	52.5	1625	6.1(36)	6	11	29	228	61.6	—	—	0	410
NFL	10	126(60)	141	611	4.3(23)	5	—	—	—	—	2081	1085	52.1	14391	6.9(92)	86	102	210	1510	67.7	—	—	30	4207

Wilson, Marcus Edmond Marcus, RB, 6´1˝/215 lbs; Virginia; 1990: LARd, rnd 6; B4/16/1968 Rochester, NY **1992** GB 6 (0) **1994** GB 12 (0) **1995**†GB 14 (0)

1991	LARd	1(0)	6	21	3.5(8)	0	—	—	—	—	—	—	—	—	—	—	—	—	—	—	—	—	0	21
1993	†GB	16(0)	6	3	0.5(5)	0	2	18	9.0(11)	0	—	—	—	—	—	—	—	—	—	—	k	—	0	74
NFL	5	49(0)	12	24	2.0(8)	0	2	18	9.0(11)	0	—	—	—	—	—	—	—	—	—	—	k	—	0	79

Wilson, Mark Mark, TE, 6´6˝/295 lbs; California; 2004: Was, rnd 5; B11/11/1980 San Jose, CA **2004** Was 2 (1)

Wilson, Mike Samuel Marshall, E-BB, 5´10˝/167 lbs; Lehigh; B12/2/1896 Edge Hill, PA, D5/16/1978 Boynton Beach, FL **1922** Roc 1 (1) **1923** RI 8 (8, RE), 6 **1924** RI☆8 (7, RE), 6 **NFL** 17 (16), 12 [3 yrs]

Wilson, Mike Michael Ruben, WR, 6´3˝/213 lbs; Washington State; 1981: Dal, rnd 9; B12/19/1958 Los Angeles, CA

1981	†SF	16(0)	—	—	—	—	9	125	13.9(27)	1	—	—	—	—	—	—	—	—	—	—	k	—	6	75
1982	SF	6(1)	—	—	—	—	6	80	13.3(27)	1	—	—	—	—	—	—	—	—	—	—	—	—	6	45
1983	†SF	15(3)	—	—	—	—	30	433	14.4(49)	0	—	—	—	—	—	—	—	—	—	—	—	—	0	217
1984	†SF	13(3)	—	—	—	—	17	245	14.4(44)	1	—	—	—	—	—	—	—	—	—	—	k	—	6	127
1985	†SF	16(0)	—	—	—	—	10	165	16.5(52)	2	—	—	—	—	—	—	—	—	—	—	—	—	12	93
1986	SF	11(1)	—	—	—	—	9	104	11.6(18)	1	—	—	—	—	—	—	—	—	—	—	k	—	6	52
1987	†SF	11(8, WR)	—	—	—	—	29	450	15.5(46)	5	—	—	—	—	—	—	—	—	—	—	—	—	30	250
1988	†SF	16(11, WR)	—	—	—	—	33	405	12.3(31)	3	—	—	—	—	—	—	—	—	—	—	k	—	18	205
1989	†SF	16(1)	—	—	—	—	9	103	11.4(19)	1	—	—	—	—	—	—	—	—	—	—	—	—	6	57
1990	†SF	16(0)	—	—	—	—	7	89	12.7(34)	0	—	—	—	—	—	—	—	—	—	—	p	—	0	41
NFL	10	136(28)	—	—	—	—	159	2199	13.8(52)	15	—	—	—	—	—	—	—	—	—	—	kp	—	90	1159

Wilson, Mike Michael DeForest, T-G, 6´3˝/245 lbs; Dayton; 1969: Cin, rnd 14; B10/20/1947 Wilmington, OH **1969** Cin-A 3 **1970**†Cin 14 (RT) **1971** Buf 5 **1975** KC 4 (3) **NFL** 26 (3) [4 yrs]

Wilson, Mike Michael S., DB, 5´11˝/200 lbs; Western Illinois; B11/19/1946 Washington, DC **1969** SL 3

Wilson, Mike William Michael, T, 6´5˝/275 lbs; Georgia; 1977: Cin, rnd 4; B5/28/1955 Norfolk, VA **1978** Cin 9 (LT) **1979** Cin 16 (LT) **1980** Cin 16 (15, RT) **1981**†Cin 16 (16, RT) **1982**†Cin 9 (9, RT) **1983** Cin 16 (16, RT) **1984** Cin 16 (16, RT) **1985** Cin 16 (16, RT) **1986** Sea 16 (16, RT) **1987**†Sea 12 (12, RT) **1988**†Sea 16 (16, RT) **1989** Sea 16 (16, RT) **NFL** 174 (148) [12 yrs]

Wilson, Milt Milt, T-G-TB, /215 lbs; Carnegie Mellon **1923** Akr 5 (4) **1924** Akr 2 (0) **NFL** 7 (4) [2 yrs]

Wilson, Milton Richard Milton, G, 5´10˝/200 lbs; Wisconsin-Oshkosh; B5/29/1897, WI, D12/1967 **1921** GB 6 (4, RG)

Wilson, Mule Faye, WB-HB, 5´11˝/192 lbs; Texas A&M; B8/10/1903 Red Oak, TX, D2/12/1991 Fort Worth, TX **[K]** **1926** Buf 9 (8, WB) **1927** NYG 13 (8, WB), 36 **1928** NYG 13 (12, WB), 7 **1929** NYG 9 (4), 6 **1930** NYG 10 (1), 24 **1930** SI 3 (2) **1930** GB 1 (0) **1931** GB 12 (5), 12

1932	Por	10(3)	5	9	1.8	0	—	—	—	—	—	—	—	—	—	—	—	—	—	—	—	—	0	9
1933	Por	5(0)	3	10	3.3	0	1	8	8.0(8)	0	—	—	—	—	—	—	—	—	—	—	—	—	0	14
NFL	8	85(43)	8	19	2.4	8	1	8	8.0(8)	5	—	—	—	—	—	—	—	—	—	—	K	1	85	143

Wilson, Nemiah Nemiah, DB, 6´0˝/165 lbs; Grambling State; B4/6/1943 Baton Rouge, LA **[I]** **1965** Den-A 14 **1966** Den-A 14 (RCB) **1967** Den-A✧14 (RCB) **1968**†Oak-A 1 **1969**†Oak-A 14 (12, LCB) **1970**†Oak 14 (11, RCB) **1971** Oak 13 (13, LCB) **1972**†Oak 14 (14, LCB) **1973**†Oak 13 (12, LCB) **1974**†Oak 12 (5, rcb) **1975** ChiB 7 (rcb) **NFL** 130 (67) [11 yrs]

Wilson, Otis Otis Ray, LB, 6´2˝/227 lbs; Syracuse; Louisville; 1980: Chi, rnd 1; B9/15/1957 New York, NY **1980** ChiB 16 (1) **1981** ChiB 15 (12, LLB) **1982** ChiB 9 (9, LLB) **1983** ChiB 16 (16, LLB) **1984**†ChiB☆15 (15, LLB) **1985**†ChiB★16 (16, LLB) **1986**†ChiB 15 (14, LLB) **1987**†ChiB 7 (7, LLB) **1989** LARd 1 (1) **NFL** 110 (91) [9 yrs]

Wilson, Perce Percy, BB, /150 lbs; none; B1890, D9/20/1936 **1920** Det 7 (3, BB)

YEAR	TEAM	G (GS, POS)	RUSH	YD	AVG (LG)	TD	REC	YD	AVG (LG)	TD	PASS COMP	PCT	YD	AVG (LG)	TD	INT	SK	YD	QBR	KPR	OTD	PTS	TAY

WILSON, RAY Wiltha Ray, DB, 6´1˝/202 lbs; New Mexico; B8/26/1971 Panama City, FL   **1994** NO 3 (0)   **1994**†GB 3 (0)   **NFL** 6 (0) [1 yr]

WILSON, REINARD James Reinard, LB-DE, 6´2˝/261 lbs; Florida State; 1997: Cin, rnd 1; B12/17/1973 Gainesville, FL   **1997** Cin 16 (3)   **1998** Cin 16 (15, ROLB)   **1999** Cin 15 (0)   **2000** Cin 14 (0)   **2001** Cin 16 (5, rde)   **2002** Cin 16 (0)   **NFL** 93 (23) [6 yrs]

WILSON, ROBERT Robert, WR, 5´11˝/176 lbs; Florida A&M; B6/23/1974 Tallahassee, FL   **1998** Sea 16 (0)   **1999** Sea 2 (0)

2000	†NO	15(0)	—	—	—	—	11	154	14.0(30)	0	—	—	—	—	—	—	—	—	—	—	—	0	88
2001	NO	15(1)	—	—	—	—	21	277	13.2(44)	0	—	—	—	—	—	—	—	—	—	—	—	0	139
NFL	4	48(1)	—	—	—	—	32	431	13.5(44)	0	—	—	—	—	—	—	—	—	—	k	—	0	228

WILSON, ROBERT Robert Eugene, RB, 6´0˝/255 lbs; Texas A&M; 1991: TB, rnd 3; B1/13/1969 South Park, TX

1991	TB	16(15, FB)	42	179	4.3(20)	0	20	121	6.1(15)	2	—	—	—	—	—	—	—	—	—	k	—	12	239
1994	†Dal	2(0)	1	-1	-1.0(-1)	0	—	—	—	—	—	—	—	—	—	—	—	—	—	—	—	0	-1
1994	†Mia	2(0)	—	—	—	—	—	—	—	—	—	—	—	—	—	—	—	—	—	—	—	—	—
1995	Mia	16(0)	1	5	5.0(5)	0	1	3	3.0(3)	0	—	—	—	—	—	—	—	—	—	—	—	0	7
1996	Mia	15(0)	1	0	0.0(0)	0	2	5	2.5(3)	1	—	—	—	—	—	—	—	—	—	k	—	6	5
NFL	4	51(15)	45	183	4.1(20)	0	23	129	5.6(15)	3	—	—	—	—	—	—	—	—	—	k	—	18	249

WILSON, SHEDDRICK Sheddrick Roderica, WR, 6´2˝/210 lbs; LSU; B11/23/1973 Thomasville, GA

| 1996 | Hou | 11(0) | — | — | — | — | 2 | 24 | 12.0(14) | 0 | — | — | — | — | — | — | — | — | — | — | — | 0 | 12 |

WILSON, STANLEY Stanley T., RB, 5´10˝/209 lbs; Oklahoma; 1983: Cin, rnd 9; B8/23/1961 Los Angeles, CA

1983	Cin	10(2)	56	267	4.8(18)	1	12	107	8.9(19)	1	—	—	—	—	—	—	—	—	—	k	—	12	392
1984	Cin	1(0)	17	74	4.4(9)	0	2	15	7.5(11)	0	—	—	—	—	—	—	—	—	—	—	—	0	82
1986	Cin	10(3)	68	379	5.6(58)	8	4	45	11.3(34)	0	—	—	—	—	—	—	—	—	—	—	—	48	482
1988	†Cin	15(6, fb)	112	398	3.6(19)	2	9	110	12.2(28)	1	—	—	—	—	—	—	—	—	—	—	—	18	478
NFL	4	36(11)	253	1118	4.4(58)	11	27	277	10.3(34)	2	—	—	—	—	—	—	—	—	—	k	—	78	1433

WILSON, STANLEY Stanley, DB, 5´11˝/189 lbs; Stanford; 2005: Det, rnd 3; B11/5/1982 Carson, CA   **2005** Det 9 (0)

WILSON, STEVE see Mustafah Muhammad

WILSON, STEVE Steven Anthony, DB-WR, 5´10˝/195 lbs; Howard; B8/24/1957 Los Angeles, CA [I]   **1980**†Dal 16 (11, LCB)   **1981**†Dal 16 (4)   **1982** Den 8 (2)   **1983**†Den 16 (3)   **1984**†Den 15 (1)   **1985** Den 14 (4)   **1987**†Den 11 (5, rcb)   **1988** Den 12 (2)

1979	†Dal	16	—	—	—	—	3	76	25.3(45)	0	—	—	—	—	—	—	—	—	—	kp	—	0	142
1986	†Den	16(0)	—	—	—	—	1	43	43.0(43)	1	—	—	—	—	—	—	—	—	—	i	—	6	17
NFL	10	140(32)	—	—	—	—	4	119	29.8(45)	1	—	—	—	—	—	—	—	—	—	kpiS	—	6	512

WILSON, STEVE Steven Alan, C-G-T, 6´4˝/265 lbs; Georgia; 1976: TB, rnd 5; B5/19/1954 Fort Sill, OK   **1976** TB 10 (5, rg)   **1977** TB 14 (8, c)   **1978** TB 16 (16, C)   **1979**†TB 16 (16, C)   **1980** TB 15 (14, C)   **1981**†TB 15 (15, C)   **1982**†TB 8 (6, C)   **1983** TB 10 (10, C)   **1984** TB 16 (13, C)   **1985** TB 5 (1)   **NFL** 125 (104) [10 yrs]

WILSON, STU William Stuart, E-WB-TB, 6´2˝/209 lbs; Washington & Jefferson; B7/1/1907, D9/15/1957 Elizabeth, NJ [K]

| 1932 | SI | 11(7, RE) | 7 | -9 | -1.3 | 0 | 1 | 11 | 11.0(11) | 1 | 7 | 1 | 14.3 | 18 | 2.6(18) | 0 | 1 | — | — | — | K | — | 12 | -30 |

WILSON, TED Ted, WR, 5´9˝/170 lbs; Central Florida; 1987: Was, rnd 10; B7/14/1964 Zephyrhills

| 1987 | Was | 3(2) | 2 | 28 | 14.0(16) | 1 | 5 | 112 | 22.4(64) | 1 | — | — | — | — | — | — | — | — | — | kp | — | 12 | 207 |

WILSON, TIM Timothy, FB, 6´3˝/226 lbs; Maryland; 1977: Hou, rnd 3; B1/14/1954 New Castle, DE, deceased

1977	Hou	10(5, fb)	99	343	3.5(16)	3	20	107	5.3(17)	0	—	—	—	—	—	—	—	—	—	k	—	18	430
1978	†Hou	16(13, FB)	126	431	3.4(24)	0	15	91	6.1(14)	1	—	—	—	—	—	—	—	—	—	k	—	6	481
1979	†Hou	16(16, FB)	84	319	3.8(19)	2	29	208	7.2(24)	1	—	—	—	—	—	—	—	—	—	k	—	18	448
1980	†Hou	16(16, FB)	66	257	3.9(15)	1	30	170	5.7(13)	1	—	—	—	—	—	—	—	—	—	—	—	12	357
1981	Hou	16(9, FB)	13	35	2.7(7)	0	5	33	6.6(11)	0	—	—	—	—	—	—	—	—	—	k	—	0	48
1982	Hou	9(1)	—	—	—	—	—	—	—	—	—	—	—	—	—	—	—	—	—	k	—	0	10
1983	NO	6(0)	8	21	2.6(7)	0	—	—	—	—	—	—	—	—	—	—	—	—	—	—	—	0	21
1984	NO	12(0)	2	8	4.0(5)	0	—	—	—	—	—	—	—	—	—	—	—	—	—	k	—	0	9
NFL	8	101(60)	398	1414	3.6(24)	6	99	609	6.2(24)	3	—	—	—	—	—	—	—	—	—	k	—	54	1803

WILSON, TOMMY Thomas Lee, HB-FB, 6´0˝/203 lbs; none; B9/1/1932 Stamford, CT

1956	LARm	12(lh)	64	470	7.3(46)	0	6	86	14.3(34)	0	1	0	0.0	0	0.0	0	0	—	—	kp	1	6	765
1957	LARm★	11(LH)	127	616	4.9(46)	3	7	95	13.6(19)	0	—	—	—	—	—	—	—	—	—	kp	—	24	847
1958	LARm	12(lh)	73	475	6.5(82)	9	9	101	11.2(38)	1	1	0	0.0	0	0.0	0	0	1	—	k	—	60	665
1959	LARm	12(lh)	40	210	5.3(60)	0	12	83	6.9(20)	1	—	—	—	—	—	—	—	—	—	k	—	6	395
1960	LARm	11	41	139	3.4(35)	0	11	82	7.5(40)	2	—	—	—	—	—	—	—	—	—	k	—	12	208
1961	LARm	11	44	220	5.0(34)	1	1	12	12.0(12)	0	—	—	—	—	—	—	—	—	—	—	—	6	236
1962	Cle	14(HB)	46	141	3.1(17)	1	8	110	13.8(42)	0	—	—	—	—	—	—	—	—	—	k	—	6	348
1963	Min	8	73	282	3.9(30)	4	7	48	6.9(21)	0	—	—	—	—	—	—	—	—	—	—	—	24	346
NFL	8	91	508	2553	5.0(82)	18	61	617	10.1(42)	5	2	0	0.0	0	0.0	0	0	1	—	kp	1	144	3809

WILSON, TROY Troy Anthony, DB, 5´10˝/170 lbs; Notre Dame; B9/19/1965 San Antonio, TX   **1987** Cle 3 (3)

WILSON, TROY Troy Ethan, DE, 6´4˝/257 lbs; Pittsburg State; 1993: SF, rnd 7; B11/22/1970 Topeka, KS   **1993**†SF 10 (0)   **1994**†SF 11 (0)   **1995** Den 3 (0)   **1998** NO 15 (0)   **1999** NO 16 (4)   **2000** ChiB 6 (0)   **2001**†SF 0 (0)   **NFL** 61 (4) [7 yrs]

WILSON, WADE Charles Wade, QB, 6´3˝/210 lbs; Texas A&M-Commerce; 1981: Min, rnd 8; B2/1/1959 Greenville, TX

1981	Min	3(0)	—	—	—	—	—	—	—	—	13	6	46.2	48	3.7(22)	0	2	2	19	—	—	—	0	-56
1983	Min	1(1)	3	-3	-1.0(2)	0	—	—	—	—	28	16	57.1	124	4.4(36)	1	2	3	22	—	—	—	0	-16
1984	Min	8(5, qb)	9	30	3.3(12)	0	—	—	—	—	195	102	52.3	1019	5.2(38)	5	11	20	159	52.5	—	—	0	125
1985	Min	4(1)	—	—	—	—	—	—	—	—	60	33	55.0	404	6.7(42)	3	3	4	28	—	—	—	0	97
1986	Min	9(3)	13	9	0.7(13)	1	—	—	—	—	143	80	55.9	1165	8.1(39)	7	5	13	94	84.4	P	—	6	437
1987	†Min	12(7, QB)	41	263	6.4(38)	5	—	—	—	—	264	140	53.0	2106	8.0(73)	14	13	26	194	76.7	—	—	30	916
1988	†Min◇	14(10, QB)	36	136	3.8(15)	2	—	—	—	—	332	204	61.4	2746	8.3(68)	15	9	33	227	91.5	—	—	12	1244
1989	†Min	14(12, QB)	32	132	4.1(23)	1	—	—	—	—	362	194	53.6	2543	7.0(50)	9	12	27	194	70.5	—	—	6	979
1990	Min	6(4)	12	79	6.6(24)	0	—	—	—	—	146	82	56.2	1155	7.9(75)	9	8	15	90	79.6	—	—	0	382
1991	Min	5(5, qb)	13	33	2.5(15)	0	—	—	—	—	122	72	59.0	825	6.8(46)	3	10	8	42	53.5	—	—	0	61
1992	Atl	9(3, qb)	15	62	4.1(12)	0	—	—	—	—	163	111	68.1	1366	8.4(60)	13	4	8	58	110.1	—	—	0	650
1993	NO	14(14, QB)	31	230	7.4(44)	0	—	—	—	—	388	221	57.0	2457	6.3(42)	12	15	37	225	70.1	—	—	0	919
1994	NO	4(0)	7	15	2.1(9)	0	—	—	—	—	28	20	71.4	172	6.1(16)	2	0	3	17	—	—	—	0	101
1995	†Dal	7(0)	10	12	1.2(11)	0	—	—	—	—	57	38	66.7	391	6.9(38)	1	3	4	29	—	—	—	0	93
1996	Dal	3(1)	4	5	1.3(8)	0	—	—	—	—	18	8	44.4	79	4.4(20)	0	1	1	7	—	—	—	0	5
1997	Dal	7(0)	6	-2	-0.3(3)	0	—	—	—	—	21	12	57.1	115	5.5(32)	0	1	4	26	—	—	—	0	56
1998	Oak	5(3)	7	24	3.4(12)	0	—	—	—	—	88	52	59.1	568	6.5(68)	7	4	9	77	—	—	—	0	183
NFL	17	125(69)	239	1025	4.3(44)	9	—	—	—	—	2428	1391	57.3	17283	7.1(75)	99	102	217	1508	75.6	P	—	54	6172

WILSON, WALTER Walter James, TE-WR, 5´10˝/185 lbs; East Carolina; 1990: SD, rnd 3; B10/6/1966 Baltimore, MD

| 1990 | SD | 14(5, te) | 1 | 0 | 0.0(0) | 0 | 10 | 87 | 8.7(20) | 0 | — | — | — | — | — | — | — | — | — | — | — | 0 | 44 |

WILSON, WAYNE Wayne MacArthur, RB, 6´3˝/215 lbs; Shepherd; 1979: Hou, rnd 12; B9/4/1957 Montgomery County, MD

1979	NO	14	5	26	5.2(16)	0	—	—	—	—	—	—	—	—	—	—	—	—	—	k	—	0	91
1980	NO	15(7, FB)	63	188	3.0(15)	1	31	241	7.8(42)	1	—	—	—	—	—	—	—	—	—	k	—	12	348
1981	NO	16(0)	44	137	3.1(13)	1	31	384	12.4(55)	4	—	—	—	—	—	—	—	—	—	k	—	30	616
1982	NO	8(7, FB)	103	413	4.0(20)	2	25	175	7.0(34)	2	—	—	—	—	—	—	—	—	—	k	—	30	628
1983	NO	14(8, fb)	199	787	4.0(29)	9	20	178	8.9(24)	2	—	—	—	—	—	—	—	—	—	k	—	66	1080
1984	NO	14(2)	74	261	3.5(36)	3	33	314	9.5(34)	3	—	—	—	—	—	—	—	—	—	k	—	24	451
1985	NO	16(10, FB)	168	645	3.8(41)	1	38	228	6.0(21)	2	—	—	—	—	—	—	—	—	—	—	—	18	779
1986	Min	7(0)	8	14	1.8(6)	0	—	—	—	—	—	—	—	—	—	—	—	—	—	k	—	0	17

YEAR	TEAM	G(GS, POS)	RUSH	YD	AVG(LG)	TD	REC	YD	AVG(LG)	TD	PASS	COMP	PCT	YD	AVG(LG)	TD	INT	SK	YD	QBR	KPR	OTD	PTS	TAY
1986	NO	5(0)	2	5	2.5(3)	0	1	-3	-3.0(-3)	0	—	—	—	—	—	—	—	—	—	—	—	—	0	4
1987	Was	2(0)	18	55	3.1(11)	2	2	16	8.0(9)	0	—	—	—	—	—	—	—	—	—	—	k	—	12	85
NFL	9	111(34)	684	2531	3.7(41)	18	181	1533	8.5(55)	14	—	—	—	—	—	—	—	—	—	—	k	—	192	4098

Wilson, Wildcat George Schly, TB, 5´11˝/200 lbs; Washington; B9/6/1901 Everett, WA, D12/27/1963 San Francisco, CA **1927** Pro 14 (12), 24 **1928** Pro☆11 (11, TB), 30 **1929** Pro 12 (12), 6 **NFL** 37 (35), 60 [3 yrs]

Wiltz, Jason Jason, DT-DE, 6´4˝/300 lbs; Nebraska; 1999: NYJ, rnd 4; B11/23/1976 New Orleans, LA **1999** NYJ 12 (1) **2000** NYJ 15 (1) **NFL** 27 (2) [2 yrs]

Wimberly, Ab Abner Perry, DE-E, 6´1˝/213 lbs; LSU; 1948: LAD-A, rnd 19/Bos, rnd 12; B5/4/1926 Oak Ridge, LA, D9/19/1976 Oak Ridge, LA

YEAR	TEAM	G(GS, POS)	RUSH	YD	AVG(LG)	TD	REC	YD	AVG(LG)	TD	PASS	COMP	PCT	YD	AVG(LG)	TD	INT	SK	YD	QBR	KPR	OTD	PTS	TAY
1949	LAD-A	12(4)	—	—	—	—	3	22	7.3	0	—	—	—	—	—	—	—	—	—	—	i	2	12	32
1950	GB	11	—	—	—	—	2	18	9.0(10)	0	—	—	—	—	—	—	—	—	—	—	i	—	0	4
1951	GB	12(RDE)	—	—	—	—	1	10	10.0(10)	0	—	—	—	—	—	—	—	—	—	—	k	—	0	-21
1952	GB✧	12	—	—	—	—	—	—	—	—	—	—	—	—	—	—	—	—	—	—	i	—	0	0
NFL	3	35	—	—	—	—	3	28	9.3(10)	0	—	—	—	—	—	—	—	—	—	—	ki	—	0	-17

Wimberly, By Adlai Byron, T-G, 6´2˝/200 lbs; Washington & Jefferson; B9/3/1892 Stevenson, AL, D5/10/1956 Detroit, MI **1925** Det 11 (5, rt)

Wimberly, Derek Derek Nathaniel, DE, 6´4˝/270 lbs; Purdue; B1/4/1964 Miami, FL **1987** Mia 3 (3)

Wimberly, Marcus Marcus Juanald, DB, 5´11˝/192 lbs; Miami (FL); 1997: Atl, rnd 5; B7/8/1974 Memphis, TN **1997** Atl 6 (0)

Wimbush, Derrick Derrick, RB, 6´1˝/211 lbs; Fort Valley State; B8/26/1980 Mauck, GA

YEAR	TEAM	G(GS, POS)	RUSH	YD	AVG(LG)	TD	REC	YD	AVG(LG)	TD	PASS	COMP	PCT	YD	AVG(LG)	TD	INT	SK	YD	QBR	KPR	OTD	PTS	TAY
2005	†Jax	14(1)	3	12	4.0(7)	1	5	26	5.2(6)	0	—	—	—	—	—	—	—	—	—	—	k	1	12	415

Wimmer, Gary Gary Edwin, LB, 6´2˝/225 lbs; Stanford; B3/9/1961 Pocatello, ID **1983** Sea 3 (0)

Winans, Jeff Jeff Dow, G-DE-T-DT, 6´5˝/265 lbs; USC; 1973: Buf, rnd 2; B10/12/1951 Turlock, CA **1973** Buf 9 **1975** Buf 11 (3) **1976** NO 3 **1977** TB 11 (11, LG) **1978** TB 1 (1) **NFL** 35 (15) [5 yrs]

Winans, Tydus Tydus Oran, WR, 5´11˝/180 lbs; Fresno State; 1994: Was, rnd 3; B7/26/1972 Los Angeles, CA

YEAR	TEAM	G(GS, POS)	RUSH	YD	AVG(LG)	TD	REC	YD	AVG(LG)	TD	PASS	COMP	PCT	YD	AVG(LG)	TD	INT	SK	YD	QBR	KPR	OTD	PTS	TAY
1994	Was	15(0)	1	5	5.0(5)	0	19	344	18.1(51)	2	—	—	—	—	—	—	—	—	—	—	—	—	14	187
1995	Was	8(1)	—	—	—	—	4	77	19.3(32)	0	—	—	—	—	—	—	—	—	—	—	—	—	0	39
1996	Cin	2(0)	—	—	—	—	—	—	—	—	—	—	—	—	—	—	—	—	—	—	—	—	—	—
NFL	3	25(1)	1	5	5.0(5)	0	23	421	18.3(51)	2	—	—	—	—	—	—	—	—	—	—	—	—	14	226

Winborn, Jamie Jamie, LB, 5´11˝/242 lbs; Vanderbilt; 2001: SF, rnd 2; B5/14/1979 Wetumpka, AL **2001**†SF 14 (4) **2002** SF 3 (3) **2003** SF 9 (0) **2004** SF 14 (10, RLB) **2005** SF 3 (2) **2005** Jax 5 (0) **NFL** 48 (19) [5 yrs]

Winburn, Ernie Earnest, E, 5´11˝/175 lbs; Central Missouri State; B4/1897 Lees Summitt, MO, deceased **1923** SL 1 (0)

Windauer, Bill William Joseph, DT-DT, 6´4˝/250 lbs; Iowa; 1973: Bal, rnd 8; B11/22/1949 Chicago, IL **1973** Bal 2 **1974** Bal 9 (5, rdt) **1975** NYG 4 **1976** Atl 3 **NFL** 18 (5) [4 yrs]

Windbiel, Joe Joseph C., C, 6´1˝/220 lbs; Dayton; B3/6/1897, IL, D6/25/1971 Fort Lauderdale, FL **1921** Evv 5 (5, C)

Winder, Sammy Sammy, RB, 5´11˝/203 lbs; Southern Mississippi; 1982: Den, rnd 5; B7/15/1959 Madison, MS

YEAR	TEAM	G(GS, POS)	RUSH	YD	AVG(LG)	TD	REC	YD	AVG(LG)	TD	PASS	COMP	PCT	YD	AVG(LG)	TD	INT	SK	YD	QBR	KPR	OTD	PTS	TAY
1982	Den	8(2)	67	259	3.9(18)	1	11	83	7.5(22)	0	—	—	—	—	—	—	—	—	—	—	—	—	6	311
1983	†Den	14(13, RB)	196	757	3.9(52)	3	23	150	6.5(17)	0	—	—	—	—	—	—	—	—	—	—	—	—	18	862
1984	†Den★	16(15, RB)	**296**	1153	3.9(24)	4	44	288	6.5(21)	2	—	—	—	—	—	—	—	—	—	—	—	—	36	1347
1985	Den	14(12, RB)	199	714	3.6(42)	8	31	197	6.4(24)	0	1	0	0.0	0	0.0	0	0	—	—	—	—	—	48	893
1986	†Den✧	16(15, RB)	240	789	3.3(31)	9	26	171	6.6(20)	5	—	—	—	—	—	—	—	—	—	—	—	—	84	990
1987	†Den	12(10, RB)	196	741	3.8(19)	6	14	74	5.3(13)	1	—	—	—	—	—	—	—	—	—	—	—	—	42	843
1988	Den	16(12, FB)	149	543	3.6(35)	4	17	103	6.1(14)	1	—	—	—	—	—	—	—	—	—	—	k	—	30	636
1989	†Den	16(2)	110	351	3.2(16)	2	14	91	6.5(19)	0	—	—	—	—	—	—	—	—	—	—	—	—	12	417
1990	Den	15(2)	42	120	2.9(19)	2	17	145	8.5(17)	0	—	—	—	—	—	—	—	—	—	—	k	—	12	208
NFL	9	127(83)	1495	5427	3.6(52)	39	197	1302	6.6(24)	9	1	0	0.0	0	0.0	0	0	—	—	—	k	—	288	6504

Windham, Dave David Rogers, LB, 6´2˝/240 lbs; Jackson State; 1984: NE, rnd 9; B3/14/1961 Mobile, AL **1987** Was 3 (0)

Windsor, Bob Robert Edward, TE, 6´4˝/220 lbs; Kentucky; 1966: SF, rnd 2/SD, rnd R1; B12/19/1942 Washington, DC

YEAR	TEAM	G(GS, POS)	RUSH	YD	AVG(LG)	TD	REC	YD	AVG(LG)	TD	PASS	COMP	PCT	YD	AVG(LG)	TD	INT	SK	YD	QBR	KPR	OTD	PTS	TAY
1967	SF	14(6, te)	1	7	7.0(7)	0	21	254	12.1(55)	2	—	—	—	—	—	—	—	—	—	—	k	1	18	150
1968	SF	14	—	—	—	—	8	146	18.3(62)	2	—	—	—	—	—	—	—	—	—	—	—	—	12	83
1969	SF	14(14, TE)	5	39	7.8(13)	0	49	597	12.2(32)	2	—	—	—	—	—	—	—	—	—	—	—	—	12	348
1970	†SF	14(14, TE)	—	—	—	—	31	363	11.7(35)	2	—	—	—	—	—	—	—	—	—	—	k	—	12	177
1971	†SF	13	1	21	21.0(21)	0	2	32	16.0(30)	0	—	—	—	—	—	—	—	—	—	—	k	—	0	43
1972	NE	14(14, TE)	1	-4	-4.0(-4)	0	33	383	11.6(24)	1	—	—	—	—	—	—	—	—	—	—	—	—	6	193
1973	NE	13(9, TE)	1	-6	-6.0(-6)	0	23	348	15.1(36)	4	—	—	—	—	—	—	—	—	—	—	k	—	24	173
1974	NE	7(7, TE)	—	—	—	—	12	127	10.6(20)	1	—	—	—	—	—	—	—	—	—	—	—	—	6	69
1975	NE	14(3)	—	—	—	—	6	57	9.5(12)	0	—	—	—	—	—	—	—	—	—	—	—	—	0	29
NFL	9	117(67)	9	57	6.3(21)	0	185	2307	12.5(62)	14	—	—	—	—	—	—	—	—	—	—	k	1	90	1263

Winey, Brandon Brandon Joseph, T, 6´7˝/315 lbs; LSU; 2001: Mia, rnd 6; B1/27/1978 Lake Charles, LA **2003** Was 11 (3) **2004** NYG 13 (0) **NFL** 24 (3) [2 yrs]

Winfield, Antoine Antoine D., DB, 5´9˝/190 lbs; Ohio State; 1999: Buf, rnd 1; B6/24/1977 Akron, OH **1999**†Buf 16 (2) **2000** Buf 11 (11, LCB) **2001** Buf 16 (16, LCB) **2002** Buf 13 (13, LCB) **2003** Buf 16 (16, LCB) **2004**†Min 14 (12, LCB) **2005** Min 16 (16, LCB) **NFL** 102 (86) [7 yrs]

Winfield, Vernon Vernon Hall, G, 6´2˝/248 lbs; Minnesota; 1972: Phi, rnd 6; B8/27/1949 Norfolk, VA **1972** Phi 9 **1973** Phi 5 (5, lg) **NFL** 14 (5) [2 yrs]

Winfrey, Chuck Carl LeNell, LB, 6´0˝/230 lbs; Wisconsin; B3/27/1949 Chicago, IL **1971**†Min 14 **1972** Pit 1 **NFL** 15 [2 yrs]

Winfrey, Stan Stanley, RB, 5´11˝/223 lbs; Arkansas State; 1975: Mia, rnd 2; B2/20/1953 Forrest City, AR **1977** TB 2 **1977** Mia 3

YEAR	TEAM	G(GS, POS)	RUSH	YD	AVG(LG)	TD	REC	YD	AVG(LG)	TD	PASS	COMP	PCT	YD	AVG(LG)	TD	INT	SK	YD	QBR	KPR	OTD	PTS	TAY
1975	Mia	11	3	10	3.3(5)	0	—	—	—	—	—	—	—	—	—	—	—	—	—	—	k	—	0	20
1976	Mia	14	52	205	3.9(13)	1	6	55	9.2(16)	1	—	—	—	—	—	—	—	—	—	—	k	—	12	242
NFL	3	30	55	215	3.9(13)	1	6	55	9.2(16)	1	—	—	—	—	—	—	—	—	—	—	k	—	12	262

Wing, Chris Christopher R., LB, 6´2˝/235 lbs; Boise State; B5/28/1971 Redmond, WA **1997** NYJ 2 (0)

Wingate, Elmer Elmer Horsey, DE, 6´3˝/230 lbs; Maryland; 1951: NYY, rnd 4; B10/26/1928 Baltimore, MD **1953** Bal 12

Wingate, Heath Heath L., C, 6´2˝/240 lbs; Bowling Green State; 1966: Was, rnd 13/Bos, rnd R4; B12/5/1944 Toledo, OH **1967** Was 3

Wingate, Leonard Leonard Junior, DT, 6´3˝/265 lbs; South Carolina State; 1985: LARd, rnd 8; B11/3/1961 Charleston, SC **1987** Atl 1 (1)

Wingle, Blake Blake Leo, G, 6´2˝/267 lbs; Cal Poly-San Luis Obispo; UCLA; 1983: Pit, rnd 9; B4/17/1960 Pottsville, CA **1983**†Pit 16 (0) **1984** Pit 15 (10, RG) **1985** Pit 3 (0) **1985** GB 2 (0) **1987** Cle 3 (2) **NFL** 39 (12) [4 yrs]

Wingo, Rich Richard Allen, LB, 6´1˝/230 lbs; Alabama; 1979: GB, rnd 7; B7/16/1956 Elkhart, IN **[K]** **1979** GB 16 (14, MLB) **1981** GB 16 (16, LILB) **1982**†GB 5 (5, LILB) **1983** GB 16 (11, LILB) **1984** GB 16 (0) **NFL** 69 (46) [5 yrs]

Wink, Dean Dean Albert, DE-DT, 6´4˝/246 lbs; Yankton; B9/25/1944 Moville, IA **1967** Phi 5 **1968** Phi 7 **NFL** 12 [2 yrs]

Winkel, Bob Robert Alexander, DT-DE, 6´4˝/253 lbs; Kentucky; 1979: Min, rnd 7; B10/23/1955 Paducah, KY **1979** NYJ 15 **1980** NYJ 16 (0) **NFL** 31 [2 yrs]

Winkelman, Ben Ben Hartwell, B-E, 6´1˝/190 lbs; Arkansas; B2/28/1899 Fayetteville, AR, D12/18/1981 Citrus Heights, CA **[K]** **1922** Mil 1 (1) **1923** Mil 12 (12, TB/re), 44 **1924** Mil 13 (13, WB), 15 **NFL** 26 (26), 59 [3 yrs]

Winkler, Bernie Bernard Arthur, T, 6´1˝/232 lbs; Millsaps; Texas Tech; 1948: LAD-A, rnd 14/1947: Phi, rnd 30; B12/5/1925 The Grove, TX, D6/28/1990 New Braunfels, TX **1948** LAD-A 4 (0)

Winkler, Francis Francis Michael, DE, 6´3˝/230 lbs; Memphis; 1968: GB, rnd 5; B10/20/1946 Memphis, TN **1968** GB 7 **1969** GB 14 **NFL** 21 [2 yrs]

Winkler, Jim James Carl, DT-G, 6´2˝/250 lbs; Texas A&M; 1949: LARm, rnd 3/SF-A, rnd S2; B7/21/1927 Moody, TX, D2/14/2001 Ventura, CA **1951**†LARm 12 (LDT) **1952**†LARm✧11 (RDT) **1953** Bal 9 **NFL** 32 [3 yrs]

Winkler, Joe Joseph C., C, 6´1˝/200 lbs; Purdue; 1945: Cle, rnd 12; B3/9/1922 Hammond, IN, D3/21/2001 Lansing, IL **1945** Cle 8 (0)

YEAR	TEAM	G(GS, POS)	RUSH	YD	AVG(LG)	TD	REC	YD	AVG(LG)	TD	PASS COMP	PCT	YD	AVG(LG)	TD	INT	SK	YD	QBR	KPR	OTD	PTS	TAY

WINKLER, RANDY Randolph Stanley, T-G, 6´5˝/255 lbs; Tarleton State; 1966: Det, rnd 12/Mia, rnd R10; B7/18/1943 Temple, TX **1967** Det 8 **1968** Atl 12 **1971** GB 7
NFL 27 [3 yrs]

WINN, BRYANT Bryant M., LB, 6´4˝/231 lbs; Houston; 1985: Was, rnd 12; B11/7/1961 Memphis, TN **1987** Den 3 (3)

WINNESHICK, BILL William, C, 5´8˝/180 lbs; Carlisle Indian; B1894, NC, deceased **1922** Oor 5 (4, C)

WINSLOW, BOB Robert E., DE, 6´2˝/205 lbs; USC; 1940: Det, rnd 7; B9/18/1916 Rifle, CO, D1/11/1994 Fallbrook, CA **1940** Bkn 2 (0) **1940** Det 8 (4) **NFL** 10 (4) [1 yr]

WINSLOW, DOUG Charles Douglas, WR, 5´11˝/181 lbs; Drake; 1973: NO, rnd 8; B7/19/1951 Des Moines, IA **1976** Was 5

| 1973 | NO | 12 | — | — | — | — | 4 | 45 | 11.3(14) | 0 | — | — | — | — | — | — | — | — | — | p | — | 0 | 45 |
| NFL | | 2 | 17 | — | — | — | — | 4 | 45 | 11.3(14) | 0 | — | — | — | — | — | — | — | — | kp | — | 0 | 47 |

WINSLOW, GEORGE George Arthur, P, 6´4˝/205 lbs; Wisconsin; Villanova; B7/28/1963 Philadelphia, PA **1987** Cle 5 (0)

| 1989 | NO | 5(0) | 1 | 0 | 0.0(0) | 0 | — | — | — | — | — | — | — | — | — | — | — | — | P | — | 0 | 0 |
| NFL | | 2 | 10(0) | 1 | 0 | 0.0(0) | 0 | — | — | — | — | — | — | — | — | — | — | — | P | — | 0 | 0 |

WINSLOW, KELLEN Kellen Boswell, TE, 6´5˝/251 lbs; Missouri; 1979: SD, rnd 1; B11/5/1957 St. Louis, MO; HOF 1995

1979	SD	7(1)	—	—	—	—	25	255	10.2(30)	2	—	—	—	—	—	—	—	—	—	—	—	12	138
1980	†SD★	16(11, TE)	—	—	—	—	89	1290	14.5(65)	9	—	—	—	—	—	—	—	—	—	—	—	54	690
1981	†SD★	16(16, TE)	—	—	—	—	88	1075	12.2(67)	10	2	0	0.0	0	0.0	0	—	—	—	—	—	60	588
1982	†SD★	9(9, TE)	—	—	—	—	54	721	13.4(40)	6	1	0	0.0	0	0.0	0	0	—	—	—	—	36	391
1983	SD◇	16(16, TE)	—	—	—	—	88	1172	13.3(46)	8	—	—	—	—	—	—	—	—	—	—	—	48	626
1984	SD	7(7, TE)	—	—	—	—	55	663	12.1(33)	2	—	—	—	—	—	—	—	—	—	—	—	12	342
1985	SD	10(6, te)	—	—	—	—	25	318	12.7(26)	0	—	—	—	—	—	—	—	—	—	—	—	0	159
1986	SD	16(16, TE)	—	—	—	—	64	728	11.4(28)	5	—	—	—	—	—	—	—	—	—	k	—	30	370
1987	SD★	12(12, TE)	—	—	—	—	53	519	9.8(30)	3	—	—	—	—	—	—	—	—	—	—	—	18	275
NFL		9	109(94)	—	—	—	—	541	6741	12.5(67)	45	3	0	0.0	0	0.0	0	0	—	—	k	—	270	3577

WINSLOW, KELLEN Kellen Boswell, TE, 6´5˝/233 lbs; Miami (FL); 2004: Cle, rnd 1; B7/21/1983 San Diego, CA

| 2004 | Cle | 2(2) | — | — | — | — | 5 | 50 | 10.0(21) | 0 | — | — | — | — | — | — | — | — | — | — | — | 0 | 25 |

WINSLOW, PAUL Paul Lawrence, DB, 5´11˝/200 lbs; North Carolina Central; 1960: GB, rnd 13/DalT, rnd 2; B2/28/1938 Elizabeth City, NC

| 1960 | †GB | 12 | 2 | -3 | -1.5(3) | 0 | — | — | — | — | — | — | — | — | — | — | — | — | — | — | 1 | 6 | -3 |

WINSTON, CHARLIE Charles Soudder, G, 6´1˝/185 lbs; Purdue; B6/1890 Washington, IN, D11/11/1944 Chicago, IL **1920** Day 5 (5, RG)

WINSTON, DEMOND Edward DeMond, LB, 6´2˝/239 lbs; Vanderbilt; 1990: NO, rnd 4; B9/14/1968 Birmingham, AL **1990** †NO 16 (0) **1992** †NO 16 (0) **1993** NO 16 (0)
1994 NO 3 (0) **NFL** 51 (0) [4 yrs]

WINSTON, DIRT Dennis Edward, LB, 6´0˝/228 lbs; Arkansas; 1977: Pit, rnd 5; B10/25/1955 Forrest City, PA **1977** †Pit 13 (4) **1978** †Pit 16 **1979** †Pit 16 (11, RLB) **1980** Pit 14 (3)
1981 Pit 14 (4) **1982** NO 9 (9, RILB) **1983** NO 16 (16, RILB) **1984** NO 16 (16, LILB) **1985** NO 2 (1) **1985** Pit 10 (0) **1986** Pit 16 (0) **NFL** 142 (64) [10 yrs]

WINSTON, KELTON Kelton Earl, DB, 6´0˝/195 lbs; Wiley; 1962: Chi, rnd 9; B10/22/1940 Corsicana, TX, D11/30/1980 Los Angeles, CA **1967** †LARm 9 **1968** LARm 11
NFL 20 [2 yrs]

WINSTON, LLOYD Lloyd Leonard, FB, 6´2˝/215 lbs; USC; B9/22/1939

1962	SF	2	1	-15	-15.0(-15)	0	1	2	2.0(2)	0	—	—	—	—	—	—	—	—	—	k	—	0	8
1963	SF	4	27	127	4.7(38)	1	2	13	6.5(10)	0	—	—	—	—	—	—	—	—	—	—	—	6	144
NFL		2	6	28	112	4.0(38)	1	3	15	5.0(10)	0	—	—	—	—	—	—	—	—	k	—	6	152

WINSTON, ROY Roy Charles, LB, 5´11˝/222 lbs; LSU; 1962: Min, rnd 4/SD, rnd 6; B9/15/1940 Baton Rouge, LA **1962** Min 13 **1963** Min 14 (14, LLB) **1964** Min 14 (14, LLB)
1965 Min 14 (7, LLB) **1966** Min 12 (12, LLB) **1967** Min 14 (12, LLB) **1969** Min 14 (14, LLB) **1970** Min 14 (14, LLB) **1971** †Min 14 (14, LLB)
1972 Min 13 (13, LLB) **1973** †Min 13 (13, LLB) **1974** †Min 12 (8, LLB) **1975** Min 9 (9, LLB) **1976** †Min 7 **NFL** 191 (158) [15 yrs]

WINTER, BILL William Ross, LB, 6´3˝/220 lbs; St. Olaf; 1962: NYG, rnd 18; B1/28/1940 Milbank, SD, D5/29/1995 **1962** †NYG 11 (LLB) **1963** NYG 10 (LLB) **1964** NYG 12 (LLB)
NFL 33 [3 yrs]

WINTER, BLAISE Blaise, DE-DT-NT, 6´3˝/278 lbs; Syracuse; 1984: Ind, rnd 2; B1/31/1962 Blauvelt, NY **1984** Ind 16 (15, RDE) **1986** SD 4 (0) **1987** SD 3 (3) **1988** GB 16 (8, NT)
1989 GB 16 (10, LDE) **1990** GB 13 (0) **1992** †SD 16 (15, LDT) **1993** SD 16 (16, RDT) **1994** SD 2 (0) **NFL** 102 (67) [9 yrs]

WINTERNHEIMER, LEON Leon, G-T, 6´1˝/240 lbs; none; deceased **1921** Evv 1 (0) **1922** Evv 2 (1) **NFL** 3 (1) [2 yrs]

WINTERS, CHET Chester, RB, 5´11˝/205 lbs; Oklahoma; B10/22/1960 Chicago, IL **1983** GB 4 (0)

WINTERS, FRANK Frank Mitchell, C-G, 6´3˝/291 lbs; Western Illinois; 1987: Cle, rnd 10; B1/23/1964 Hoboken, NJ **1987** †Cle 12 (0) **1988** †Cle 16 (0) **1989** †NYG 15 (0)
1990 †KC 16 (, lg) **1991** †KC 16 (0) **1992** GB 16 (11, LG) **1993** †GB 16 (16, C/lg) **1994** †GB 16 (16, C/lg) **1995** †GB 16 (16, C) **1996** †GB◇16 (16, C) **1997** †GB 13 (13, C)
1998 GB 13 (13, C) **1999** GB 16 (16, C) **2000** GB 14 (14, C) **2001** GB 4 (0) **2002** †GB 16 (10, C) **NFL** 231 (147) [16 yrs]

WINTERS, SONNY Lindell A., BB-QB, 5´7˝/155 lbs; Ohio Wesleyan; B1/2/1900 Napoleon, OH, D10/5/1945 Ashland, KY **[K]** **1923** Col 10 (10, BB), 18 **1924** Col 8 (8, BB), 14
NFL 18 (18), 32 [2 yrs]

WINTHER, RICHARD Richard Lew, C, 6´4˝/261 lbs; Mississippi; 1971: NO, rnd 4; B10/22/1947 Charles City, IA **1971** GB 11 **1972** NO 5 **NFL** 16 [2 yrs]

WIPER, DON Donald William, BB, 5´10˝/150 lbs; Ohio State; B7/8/1900 Columbus, OH, D11/8/1961 Columbus, OH **1922** Col 2 (1)

WIRE, COY Coy, DB, 6´0˝/205 lbs; Stanford; 2002: Buf, rnd 3; B11/7/1978 Camp Hill, PA **2002** Buf 16 (15, SS) **2003** Buf 16 (1) **2004** Buf 12 (3) **2005** Buf 14 (0)
NFL 58 (19) [4 yrs]

WIRGOWSKI, DENNIS Dennis, DE-DT, 6´5˝/257 lbs; Purdue; 1970: Bos, rnd 9; B9/20/1947 Bay City, MI **1970** Bos 14 (4) **1971** NE 9 (8, RDE) **1972** NE 14 (14, RDE)
1973 Phi 13 (8, LDE) **NFL** 50 (34) [4 yrs]

WISDOM, TERRENCE Terrence Bancroft, G, 6´4˝/300 lbs; Syracuse; B12/4/1971 Brooklyn, NY **1995** NYJ 5 (0)

WISE, MIKE Michael Allen, DE, 6´7˝/271 lbs; California-Davis; 1986: LARd, rnd 4; B6/5/1964 Greenbrae, CA, D8/21/1992 Yolo County, CA **1986** LARd 6 (0)
1988 LARd 16 (14, RDE) **1989** LARd 16 (9, rde) **1990** †LARd 12 (2) **1991** Cle 3 (2) **NFL** 53 (27) [5 yrs]

WISE, PHIL Phillip Vaughn, DB, 6´0˝/190 lbs; South Dakota; Nebraska-Omaha; 1971: NYJ, rnd 6; B4/25/1949 Omaha, NE **1971** NYJ 14 (SS) **1972** NYJ 9 **1973** NYJ 8
1974 NYJ 14 (6, fs) **1975** NYJ 5 (4) **1976** NYJ 12 (SS) **1977** †Min 13 **1978** †Min 16 (16, SS) **1979** Min 1 **NFL** 92 (26) [9 yrs]

WISENER, GARY Gary Gayle, DB, 6´1˝/206 lbs; Baylor; 1960: Bos, rnd 1; B8/24/1938 Warren, AR **1960** Dal 10 **1961** Hou-A 5 **NFL** 15 [2 yrs]

WISHOM, JERRON Jerron, DB, 6´0˝/195 lbs; Louisiana Tech; B3/1/1982 Lutcher, LA **2005** GB 5 (0)

WISKA, JEFF Jeffrey Rolland, G, 6´3˝/265 lbs; Michigan State; 1982: NYG, rnd 7; B10/17/1959 Detroit, MI **1986** Cle 1 (0) **1987** Mia 3 (3) **NFL** 4 (3) [2 yrs]

WISNE, JERRY Gerald Edward, T, 6´6˝/308 lbs; Notre Dame; 1999: Chi, rnd 5; B7/28/1976 Rochester, MN **1999** ChiB 7 (1) **2002** GB 2 (0) **NFL** 9 (1) [2 yrs]

WISNIEWSKI, LEO Leo Joseph, NT, 6´1˝/263 lbs; Penn State; 1982: LARd, rnd 2; B11/6/1959 Hancock, MI **1982** Bal 7 (7, NT) **1983** Bal 15 (14, NT) **1984** Ind 14 (14, NT)
NFL 36 (35) [3 yrs]

WISNIEWSKI, STEVE Stephen Adam, G, 6´4˝/294 lbs; Penn State; 1989: Dal, rnd 2; B4/7/1967 Rutland, VT **1989** LARd 15 (15, RG) **1990** †LARd★16 (16, LG)
1991 †LARd★15 (15, LG) **1992** LARd★16 (16, LG) **1993** †LARd★16 (16, LG) **1994** LARd★16 (16, LG) **1995** Oak★16 (16, LG) **1996** Oak◇16 (16, LG) **1997** Oak◇16 (16, LG)
1998 Oak 16 (16, LG) **1999** Oak 16 (16, LG) **2000** †Oak★16 (16, LG) **2001** †Oak 16 (16, LG) **NFL** 206 (206) [13 yrs]

WISSINGER, ZEKE Zonar Albert, T, 6´0˝/195 lbs; Pittsburgh; B10/30/1902 Johnstown, PA, D11/1963, PA **1926** Pot 5 (4)

WISSMAN, PETE Lawrence Peter, LB-C, 6´0˝/215 lbs; Miami (OH); Washington-St. Louis; St. Louis; 1949: SF-A, rnd 15/NYB, rnd 7; B10/9/1923 St. Louis, MO **1949** †SF-A 12 (2)
1950 SF 12 (MLB) **1951** SF 9 (RLB) **1952** SF 12 **1954** SF 3 **NFL** 36 [4 yrs]

WISTERT, AL Albert Alexander, T-G-DT, 6´1˝/214 lbs; Michigan; 1943: Phi, rnd 5; B12/28/1920 Chicago, IL **1943** P-P 9 (1) **1944** Phi☆8 (7, RT) **1945** Phi☆10 (10, RT)
1946 Phi☆9 (9, RT) **1947** †Phi☆12 (12, RT) **1948** †Phi☆12 (12, RT) **1949** †Phi☆12 (11, RT) **1950** Phi★11 (RT) **1951** Phi☆12 (LG) **NFL** 95 (62) [9 yrs]

WISTROM, GRANT Grant Alden, DE, 6´4˝/272 lbs; Nebraska; 1998: SL, rnd 1; B7/3/1976 Webb City, MO **1998** SL 13 (0) **1999** †SL 16 (16, RDE) **2000** †SL 16 (16, RDE)
2001 †SL 15 (15, RDE) **2002** SL 15 (14, RDE) **2003** †SL 16 (16, RDE) **2004** Sea 9 (9, RDE) **2005** †Sea 16 (16, RDE) **NFL** 116 (102) [8 yrs]

YEAR	TEAM	G (GS, POS)	RUSH	YD	AVG (LG)	TD	REC	YD	AVG (LG)	TD	PASS	COMP	PCT	YD	AVG (LG)	TD	INT	SK	YD	QBR	KPR	OTD	PTS	TAY

WITCHER, AL   Thomas Albert, E, 6´1˝/200 lbs; Baylor; 1960: Oak, rnd 1/1959: LA, rnd 13; B9/28/1936

| 1960 | †Hou-A | 14 | — | — | — | — | 4 | 34 | 8.5 (13) | 1 | — | — | — | — | — | — | — | — | — | — | i | — | 6 | 17 |

WITCHER, DICK   Richard Vernon, WR-FL-SE-TE, 6´3˝/204 lbs; UCLA; 1966: SF, rnd 8; B10/10/1944 Salinas, CA

1966	SF	14	—	—	—	—	10	115	11.5 (24)	1	—	—	—	—	—	—	—	—	—	—	—	—	6	63
1967	SF	14 (9, FL)	—	—	—	—	46	705	15.3 (63)	3	—	—	—	—	—	—	—	—	—	—	—	—	18	368
1968	SF	14 (13, SE)	—	—	—	—	39	531	13.6 (59)	1	—	—	—	—	—	—	—	—	—	—	—	1	12	271
1969	SF	14 (7, FL)	—	—	—	—	33	435	13.2 (49)	3	—	—	—	—	—	—	—	—	—	—	—	—	18	233
1970	†SF	11 (WR)	—	—	—	—	22	288	13.1 (28)	2	—	—	—	—	—	—	—	—	—	—	—	—	12	154
1971	†SF	14 (14, WR)	—	—	—	—	18	250	13.9 (50)	3	—	—	—	—	—	—	—	—	—	—	—	—	18	140
1972	†SF	14 (6, wr)	—	—	—	—	3	22	7.3 (17)	1	—	—	—	—	—	—	—	—	—	—	—	—	6	16
1973	SF	14	—	—	—	—	1	13	13.0 (13)	0	—	—	—	—	—	—	—	—	—	—	—	—	0	7
NFL	8	109 (49)	—	—	—	—	172	2359	13.7 (63)	14	—	—	—	—	—	—	—	—	—	—	—	1	90	1250

WITHERSPOON, DERRICK   Derrick Leon, RB, 5´10˝/196 lbs; Clemson; B2/14/1971 Sumter, SC [R]   **1996**†Phi 16 (0)   **1997** Phi 3 (0)

| 1995 | †Phi | 15 (0) | 2 | 7 | 3.5 (5) | 0 | — | — | — | — | — | — | — | — | — | — | — | — | — | — | k | 1 | 6 | 206 |
| NFL | 3 | 34 (0) | 2 | 7 | 3.5 (5) | 0 | — | — | — | — | — | — | — | — | — | — | — | — | — | — | k | 3 | 18 | 738 |

WITHERSPOON, TERRY   Terry, FB, 5´11˝/250 lbs; Clemson; B8/22/1977 Monroe, NC

| 2001 | Dal | 3 (0) | — | — | — | — | 1 | 9 | 9.0 (9) | 0 | — | — | — | — | — | — | — | — | — | — | — | — | 0 | 5 |

WITHERSPOON, WILL   William Cordell, LB, 6´1˝/234 lbs; Georgia; 2002: Car, rnd 3; B8/19/1980 San Antonio, TX   **2002** Car 15 (8, mlb)   **2003**†Car 16 (16, RLB)
2004 Car 16 (16, RLB)   **2005**†Car 15 (15, RLB)   **NFL** 62 (55) [4 yrs]

WITHROW, CAL   James Calvin, C, 6´0˝/240 lbs; Kentucky; B7/4/1945 Portsmouth, OH   **1970** SD 4   **1971** GB 14   **1972**†GB 14   **1973** GB 14   **1974**†SL 12   **NFL** 58 [5 yrs]

WITHROW, CORY   Cory, C, 6´2˝/287 lbs; Washington State; B4/5/1975 Spokane, WA   **2000**†Min 12 (0)   **2001** Min 16 (1)   **2002** Min 16 (0)   **2003** Min 8 (0)   **2004**†Min 12 (5, c)
2005 Min 16 (7, c)   **NFL** 80 (13) [6 yrs]

WITHYCOMBE, MIKE   William Michael, G-T-C, 6´5˝/300 lbs; Fresno State; 1988: NYJ, rnd 5; B11/18/1964 Meridian, MS   **1988** NYJ 6 (1)   **1989** NYJ 5 (1)   **1991** Pit 2 (0)
1991 Cin 3 (0)   **1992** Cin 14 (3)   **NFL** 30 (5) [4 yrs]

WITKOWSKI, JOHN   John Joseph, QB, 6´1˝/200 lbs; Columbia; 1984: Det, rnd 6; B6/18/1962 Queens, NY

1984	Det	3 (1)	7	33	4.7 (10)	0	—	—	—	34	13	38.2	210	6.2 (39)	0	0	11	74	—	—	—	0	138
1988	Det	2 (0)	1	0	0.0 (0)	0	—	—	—	1	0	0.0	0	0.0	0	0	0	0	—	—	—	0	0
NFL	2	5 (1)	8	33	4.1 (10)	0	—	—	—	35	13	37.1	210	6.0 (39)	0	0	11	74	—	—	—	0	138

WITMAN, JON   Jon Doyle, RB, 6´2˝/240 lbs; Penn State; 1996: Pit, rnd 3; B6/1/1972 Wrightsville, PA

1996	†Pit	16 (4)	17	69	4.1 (15)	0	2	15	7.5 (11)	0	—	—	—	—	—	—	—	—	—	—	k	—	0	82
1997	†Pit	16 (2)	5	11	2.2 (4)	0	1	3	3.0 (3)	0	—	—	—	—	—	—	—	—	—	—	—	—	0	13
1998	Pit	16 (8, FB)	1	2	2.0 (2)	0	13	74	5.7 (15)	0	—	—	—	—	—	—	—	—	—	—	—	—	0	39
1999	Pit	16 (11, FB)	6	18	3.0 (7)	0	12	106	8.8 (38)	0	—	—	—	—	—	—	—	—	—	—	—	—	0	71
2000	Pit	6 (5, fb)	3	5	1.7 (2)	0	5	33	6.6 (11)	0	—	—	—	—	—	—	—	—	—	—	—	—	0	22
2001	†Pit	15 (12, FB)	5	24	4.8 (14)	0	6	32	5.3 (12)	0	—	—	—	—	—	—	—	—	—	—	—	—	0	40
NFL	6	85 (42)	37	129	3.5 (15)	0	39	263	6.7 (38)	0	—	—	—	—	—	—	—	—	—	—	k	—	0	266

WITT, BILLY   Billy, DE, 6´5˝/258 lbs; North Alabama; 1986: Buf, rnd 11; B4/25/1964   **1987** Buf 2 (2)

WITT, MEL   Hillery Melvin, DE-DT, 6´3˝/250 lbs; Texas-Arlington; 1967: Bos, rnd 5; B11/23/1945 Fort Worth, TX   **1967** Bos-A 1   **1968** Bos-A 14 (6, rde)   **1969** Bos-A 6 (1)
1970 Bos 14 (6, LDE)   **NFL** 35 (13) [4 yrs]

WITTE, EARL   Earl John, BB-DB, 6´0˝/188 lbs; Gustavus-Adolphus; B12/12/1906 St. Peter, MN, D11/1/1991

| 1934 | GB | 5 (2) | 8 | 22 | 2.8 | 0 | — | — | — | — | — | — | — | — | — | — | — | — | — | — | — | — | 0 | 22 |

WITTE, MARK   Mark Steven, TE, 6´3˝/236 lbs; North Texas; 1983: TB, rnd 11; B12/3/1959 Corpus Christi, TX

1983	TB	16 (2)	—	—	—	—	2	15	7.5 (10)	0	—	—	—	—	—	—	—	—	—	—	—	—	0	8
1984	TB	16 (0)	—	—	—	—	—	—	—	—	—	—	—	—	—	—	—	—	—	—	—	—	0	0
1985	TB	16 (0)	—	—	—	—	3	28	9.3 (13)	0	—	—	—	—	—	—	—	—	—	—	—	—	0	14
1987	Det	3 (3)	—	—	—	—	1	19	19.0 (19)	0	—	—	—	—	—	—	—	—	—	—	—	—	0	10
NFL	4	51 (5)	—	—	—	—	6	62	10.3 (19)	0	—	—	—	—	—	—	—	—	—	—	—	—	0	31

WITTECK, MIKE   Michael Robert, LB, 6´2˝/225 lbs; Northwestern; B2/21/1964 Queens, NY, D3/15/1990 Floral Park, NY   **1987** NYJ 3 (0)

WITTEN, JASON   Christopher Jason, TE, 6´5˝/257 lbs; Tennessee; 2003: Dal, rnd 3; B5/6/1982 Elizabethton, TN

2003	†Dal	15 (7, te)	—	—	—	—	35	347	9.9 (36)	1	—	—	—	—	—	—	—	—	—	—	—	—	6	179
2004	Dal★	16 (15, TE)	—	—	—	—	87	980	11.3 (42)	6	—	—	—	—	—	—	—	—	—	—	—	—	38	520
2005	Dal◇	16 (16, TE)	—	—	—	—	66	757	11.5 (34)	6	—	—	—	—	—	—	—	—	—	—	—	—	36	409
NFL	3	47 (38)	—	—	—	—	188	2084	11.1 (42)	13	—	—	—	—	—	—	—	—	—	—	—	—	80	1107

WITTENBORN, JOHN   John Otis, G-K, 6´2˝/238 lbs; Southeast Missouri State; 1958: SF, rnd 17; B3/1/1936 Sparta, IL [K]   **1958** SF 12   **1959** SF 12   **1960** SF 4   **1960**†Phi 8 (LG)
1961 Phi 13 (LG)   **1962** Phi 14 (LG)   **1964** Hou-A 5 (RG)   **1965** Hou-A 14   **1966** Hou-A 14   **1967**†Hou-A 14

| 1968 | Hou-A | 6 | — | — | — | — | 1 | -8 | -8.0 (-8) | 0 | — | — | — | — | — | — | — | — | — | — | K | — | 23 | -4 |
| NFL | 10 | 116 | — | — | — | — | 1 | -8 | -8.0 (-8) | 0 | — | — | — | — | — | — | — | — | — | — | K | — | 101 | -4 |

WITTER, RAY   Ray Charles, E-TB-BB-G, 5´10˝/183 lbs; Syracuse; Alfred; B2/19/1896 Perry, NY, D8/4/1983 Batavia, NY   **1920** Roc 1 (0)   **1921** Roc 5 (5, RE)   **1922** Roc 1 (1)
1923 Roc 3 (1)   **NFL** 10 (7) [4 yrs]

WITTUM, TOM   Thomas Howard, P, 6´1˝/190 lbs; Northern Illinois; 1972: SF, rnd 8; B1/11/1950 Berwyn, IL [KP]

1973	SF★	14	1	63	63.0 (63)	0	—	—	—	—	—	—	—	—	—	—	—	—	—	P	—	0	63
1974	SF★	14	1	13	13.0 (13)	0	—	—	—	—	—	—	—	—	—	—	—	—	—	P	—	0	13
1975	SF	14	1	-10	-10.0 (-10)	0	2	29	14.5 (18)	0	—	—	—	—	—	—	—	—	—	P	—	0	5
1976	SF	14	—	—	—	—	—	—	—	—	—	—	—	—	—	—	—	—	—	P	—	0	0
1977	SF	14	—	—	—	—	—	—	—	3	1	33.3	15	5.0 (15)	0	0	—	—	—	KP	—	5	8
NFL	5	70	3	66	22.0 (63)	0	2	29	14.5 (18)	0	3	1	33.3	15	5.0 (15)	0	0	—	—	—	KP	—	5	88

WITUCKI, CAS   Casimir Leo, G, 5´11˝/245 lbs; Indiana; 1950: Was, rnd 21; B5/26/1928 South Bend, IN   **1950** Was 12 (rg)   **1951** Was 12 (RG)   **1953** Was 11 (RG)
1954 Was 12 (RG)   **1955** Was 2   **1956** Was 5   **NFL** 54 [6 yrs]

WIZBICKI, ALEX   Alexander John, DB-HB, 5´11˝/188 lbs; Dartmouth; Holy Cross; 1945: Pit, rnd 18; B10/6/1921 Brooklyn, NY   **1948**†Buf-A 9 (1)

1947	Buf-A	13 (2)	9	44	4.9	0	—	—	—	—	—	—	—	—	—	—	—	—	—	kp	1	6	203
1949	†Buf-A	12 (1)	5	-10	-2.0	0	—	—	—	—	—	—	—	—	—	—	—	—	—	ki	—	0	-7
AAFC	3	34 (4)	14	34	2.4	0	—	—	—	—	—	—	—	—	—	—	—	—	—	kpi	1	6	248

1950 GB 11

WOERNER, ERNIE   Erwin, T, 5´8˝/200 lbs; Bucknell; B5/26/1906, NJ, D12/26/1972 Atlantic Highlands, NJ   **1930** Nwk 8 (4)

WOERNER, SCOTT   Scott Allison, DB, 6´0˝/190 lbs; Georgia; 1981: Atl, rnd 3; B12/18/1958 Baytown, TX   **1981** Atl 16 (0)   **1987** NO 1 (0)   **NFL** 17 (0) [2 yrs]

WOFFORD, JAMES   James, RB, 6´0˝/186 lbs; UNLV; B6/6/1978 Bakersfield, CA   **2002** Min 9 (0)

WOHLABAUGH, DAVE   David Vincent, C, 6´3˝/296 lbs; Syracuse; 1995: NE, rnd 4; B4/13/1972 Hamburg, NY   **1995** NE 11 (11, C)   **1996**†NE 16 (16, C)   **1997**†NE 14 (14, C)
1998†NE 16 (16, C)   **1999** Cle 15 (15, C)   **2000** Cle 12 (12, C)   **2001** Cle 16 (16, C)   **2002**†Cle 12 (12, C)   **2003**†SL 16 (16, C)   **NFL** 128 (128) [9 yrs]

WOIT, RICHIE   Richard Edward, DB, 5´8˝/175 lbs; Arkansas State; 1954: Det, rnd 25; B7/5/1931 Chicago, IL   **1955** Det 1

WOITT, JOHN   John Merit, DB, 5´11˝/171 lbs; Mississippi State; B6/29/1946 Yakima, WA   **1968** SF 14   **1969** SF 14   **NFL** 28 [2 yrs]

YEAR	TEAM	G (GS, POS)	RUSH	YD	AVG (LG)	TD	REC	YD	AVG (LG)	TD	PASS	COMP	PCT	YD	AVG (LG)	TD	INT	SK	YD	QBR	KPR	OTD	PTS	TAY

WOJCIECHOWICZ, ALEX Alexander Francis 'Wojey', C-LB-E, 5´11˝/217 lbs; Fordham; 1938: Det, rnd 1; B8/12/1915 South River, NJ, D7/13/1992 Forked River, NJ; HOF 1968 **1938** Det 11 (5, c) **1939** Det☆11 (11, C) **1940** Det 11 (5, c) **1941** Det 10 (9, C) **1943** Det 9 (8, C) **1944** Det☆10 (10, C) **1945** Det 10 (4) **1946** Det 3 (3) **1946** Phi 7 (1) **1947**†Phi 12 (11, C) **1948**†Phi 10 (1) **1949**†Phi 12 (1) **1950** Phi 7 (llb)

YEAR	TEAM	G (GS, POS)	RUSH	YD	AVG (LG)	TD	REC	YD	AVG (LG)	TD	PASS	COMP	PCT	YD	AVG (LG)	TD	INT	SK	YD	QBR	KPR	OTD	PTS	TAY
1942	Det	11 (6, RE)	—	—	—	—	4	44	11.0 (13)	0	—	—	—	—	—	—	—	—	—	—	ki	—	0	2
NFL	13	134 (75)	—	—	—	—	4	44	11.0 (13)	0	—	—	—	—	—	—	—	—	—	—	ki	1	6	86

WOJCIECHOWSKI, JOHN John Stanley, T-G, 6´4˝/272 lbs; Michigan State; B7/30/1963 Detroit, IL **1987**†ChiB 4 (4) **1988**†ChiB 16 (10, LT) **1989** ChiB 13 (1) **1990**†ChiB 13 (1) **1991**†ChiB 16 (9, LT) **1992** ChiB 16 (4) **1993** ChiB 14 (10, RG) **NFL** 92 (39) [7 yrs]

WOJCIK, GREGORY Gregory Steven, DT, 6´6˝/268 lbs; USC; B1/27/1946 Jamestown, ND **1971** LARm 10 **1972** SD 7 **1973** SD 10 **1975** SD 6 **NFL** 33 [4 yrs]

WOLDEN, AL Alan M., RB, 6´3˝/232 lbs; Bemidji State; B4/11/1965 Gonvick, MN

YEAR	TEAM	G (GS, POS)	RUSH	YD	AVG (LG)	TD	REC	YD	AVG (LG)	TD	PASS	COMP	PCT	YD	AVG (LG)	TD	INT	SK	YD	QBR	KPR	OTD	PTS	TAY
1987	ChiB	3 (0)	2	8	4.0 (7)	0	1	26	26.0 (26)	0	—	—	—	—	—	—	—	—	—	—	—	—	0	21

WOLF, DICK Richard D., B, 5´9˝/160 lbs; Miami (OH); B8/29/1900 Versailles, OH, D6/28/1967 Marion, IN **1923** Cle 5 (0), 6 **1924** Cle 6 (0), 12 **1925** Cle 14 (13, BB), 6 **1927** Cle 1 (0) **NFL** 26 (13), 24 [4 yrs]

WOLF, JIM James Arthur, DT-DE, 6´2˝/240 lbs; Prairie View A&M; 1974: Pit, rnd 6; B4/4/1952 San Antonio, TX **1974**†Pit 11 **1976** KC 14 (7, ldt) **NFL** 25 (7) [2 yrs]

WOLF, JOE Joseph Francis, T-G, 6´6˝/293 lbs; Boston College; 1989: Phx, rnd 1; B12/28/1966 Allentown, PA **1989** Phx 16 (15, LG/rt) **1990** Phx 15 (0) **1991** Phx 8 (6, lg) **1992** Phx 3 (2) **1993** Phx 8 (5, lg) **1994** Arz 7 (6, rt) **1995** Arz 6 (1) **1996** Arz 16 (15, RT) **1997** Arz 15 (9, rt) **NFL** 94 (59) [9 yrs]

WOLFE, RED Hugh Othello, FB, 6´0˝/205 lbs; Texas; 1938: Pit, rnd 3; B6/13/1912 Mason, TX **[K]**

YEAR	TEAM	G (GS, POS)	RUSH	YD	AVG (LG)	TD	REC	YD	AVG (LG)	TD	PASS	COMP	PCT	YD	AVG (LG)	TD	INT	SK	YD	QBR	KPR	OTD	PTS	TAY
1938	NYG✧	8 (1)	15	19	1.3	0	2	23	11.5 (15)	0	—	—	—	—	—	—	—	—	—	—	K	—	0	31

WOLFF, WAYNE Wayne William, G, 6´2˝/243 lbs; Wake Forest; 1961: Buf, rnd 17/Cle, rnd 10; B1/28/1938 Greensburg, PA **1961** Buf-A 2

WOLFLEY, CRAIG Craig Alan, G-T, 6´1˝/265 lbs; Syracuse; 1980: Pit, rnd 5; B5/19/1958 Buffalo, NY **1980** Pit 16 (0) **1981** Pit 16 (16, LG) **1982**†Pit 9 (9, LG) **1983**†Pit 14 (14, LG) **1984**†Pit 9 (9, LG) **1985** Pit 13 (13, LG) **1986** Pit 9 (9, LG) **1987** Pit 12 (12, LG) **1988** Pit 16 (16, LT) **1989**†Pit 15 (4) **1990** Min 8 (2) **1991** Min 16 (0) **NFL** 153 (104) [12 yrs]

WOLFLEY, RON Ronald Paul, RB, 6´0˝/225 lbs; West Virginia; 1985: SL, rnd 4; B10/14/1962 Blasdell, NY

YEAR	TEAM	G (GS, POS)	RUSH	YD	AVG (LG)	TD	REC	YD	AVG (LG)	TD	PASS	COMP	PCT	YD	AVG (LG)	TD	INT	SK	YD	QBR	KPR	OTD	PTS	TAY
1985	SL	16 (2)	24	64	2.7 (11)	0	2	18	9.0 (17)	0	—	—	—	—	—	—	—	—	—	—	k	—	0	112
1986	SL✧	16 (1)	8	19	2.4 (8)	0	2	32	16.0 (28)	0	—	—	—	—	—	—	—	—	—	—	—	—	0	29
1987	SL★	12 (4)	26	87	3.3 (8)	1	8	68	8.5 (16)	0	—	—	—	—	—	—	—	—	—	—	—	—	6	131
1988	Phx✧	16 (0)	9	43	4.8 (20)	0	2	11	5.5 (8)	0	—	—	—	—	—	—	—	—	—	—	—	—	0	49
1989	Phx★	16 (1)	13	36	2.8 (5)	1	5	38	7.6 (22)	0	—	—	—	—	—	—	—	—	—	—	—	—	6	65
1990	Phx	13 (2)	2	3	1.5 (2)	0	—	—	—	—	—	—	—	—	—	—	—	—	—	—	—	—	0	3
1991	Phx	16 (0)	—	—	—	—	—	—	—	—	—	—	—	—	—	—	—	—	—	—	—	—	—	—
1992	Cle	15 (0)	1	2	2.0 (2)	0	2	8	4.0 (6)	1	—	—	—	—	—	—	—	—	—	—	—	—	6	11
1993	Cle	16 (5, rb)	—	—	—	—	5	25	5.0 (9)	1	—	—	—	—	—	—	—	—	—	—	—	—	6	18
1995	SL	9 (0)	3	9	3.0 (4)	0	—	—	—	—	—	—	—	—	—	—	—	—	—	—	—	—	0	9
NFL	10	145 (15)	86	263	3.1 (20)	2	26	200	7.7 (28)	2	—	—	—	—	—	—	—	—	—	—	k	—	24	426

WOLFORD, OSCAR Oscar, G-C-E, 6´0˝/188 lbs; none; B3/14/1897 St. Clairsville, OH, D2/3/1977 Walnut Creek, OH **1920** Col 7 (4, RG) **1921** Col 8 (7, RG), 12 **1922** Col 8 (8, C) **1924** Col 4 (0) **NFL** 27 (19) [4 yrs]

WOLFORD, WILL William Charles, T-G, 6´5˝/294 lbs; Vanderbilt; 1986: Buf, rnd 1; B5/18/1964 Louisville, KY **1986** Buf 16 (16, RG) **1987** Buf 9 (9, LT) **1988**†Buf 16 (16, LT) **1989**†Buf 16 (16, LT) **1990**†Buf✧14 (14, LT) **1991**†Buf 15 (15, LT) **1992**†Buf★16 (16, LT) **1993** Ind 12 (12, LT) **1994** Ind 16 (16, LT) **1995**†Ind✧16 (16, LT) **1996**†Pit☆16 (16, LG) **1997**†Pit 16 (16, LG) **1998** Pit 13 (13, LT) **NFL** 191 (191) [13 yrs]

WOLSKI, BILL William Frank, FB, 5´11˝/203 lbs; Notre Dame; 1966: Atl, rnd 5/NYJ, rnd 10; B5/23/1944 Muskegon, MI **1966** Atl 2

WOLTER, WHITEY Herbert Max, TB-WB-BB, 5´10˝/170 lbs; Wisconsin-Milwaukee; B8/22/1899 Milwaukee, WI, D4/1966 Los Angeles, CA **1924** Ken 3 (2, TB)

WOLTMAN, CLEM Clement J., T, 6´1˝/214 lbs; Purdue; 1938: Phi, rnd 8; B12/4/1914 South Bend, IN, D1/16/1988 Seminole County, FL **1938** Phi 10 (8, RT) **1939** Phi 11 (8, RT) **1940** Phi 10 (3) **NFL** 31 (19) [3 yrs]

WOMACK, BRUCE Bruce Larimore, G, 6´3˝/210 lbs; West Texas A&M; 1951: Det, rnd 29; B5/12/1929 Floydada, TX **1951** Det 3

WOMACK, FLOYD Floyd Seneca, T, 6´4˝/333 lbs; Mississippi State; 2001: Sea, rnd 4; B11/15/1978 Cleveland, MS **2001** Sea 5 (0) **2002** Sea 11 (10, RT) **2003**†Sea 11 (4) **2004**†Sea 15 (8, rt) **2005**†Sea 11 (1) **NFL** 53 (23) [5 yrs]

WOMACK, JEFF Jeffrey Allen, RB, 5´9˝/188 lbs; Memphis; B6/26/1963 McMinnville, TN

YEAR	TEAM	G (GS, POS)	RUSH	YD	AVG (LG)	TD	REC	YD	AVG (LG)	TD	PASS	COMP	PCT	YD	AVG (LG)	TD	INT	SK	YD	QBR	KPR	OTD	PTS	TAY
1987	Min	2 (1)	9	20	2.2 (13)	0	5	46	9.2 (23)	1	—	—	—	—	—	—	—	—	—	—	k	—	6	50

WOMACK, JOE Joe Neil, HB, 5´9˝/210 lbs; Los Angeles State; 1960: Pit, rnd 13; B12/10/1936 Fort Worth, TX

YEAR	TEAM	G (GS, POS)	RUSH	YD	AVG (LG)	TD	REC	YD	AVG (LG)	TD	PASS	COMP	PCT	YD	AVG (LG)	TD	INT	SK	YD	QBR	KPR	OTD	PTS	TAY
1962	Pit	11 (HB)	128	468	3.7 (28)	5	6	57	9.5 (33)	0	—	—	—	—	—	—	—	—	—	—	k	—	30	548

WOMBLE, ROYCE Royce Cullen, HB-FL, 6´0˝/185 lbs; North Texas; B8/12/1931 Webb, TX

YEAR	TEAM	G (GS, POS)	RUSH	YD	AVG (LG)	TD	REC	YD	AVG (LG)	TD	PASS	COMP	PCT	YD	AVG (LG)	TD	INT	SK	YD	QBR	KPR	OTD	PTS	TAY
1954	Bal	12 (LH)	60	174	2.9 (24)	0	30	338	11.3 (78)	3	—	—	—	—	—	—	—	—	—	—	k	—	18	393
1955	Bal	3	4	2	0.5 (4)	0	1	14	14.0 (14)	0	—	—	—	—	—	—	—	—	—	—	—	—	0	9
1956	Bal	12	20	72	3.6 (12)	0	9	180	20.0 (43)	2	—	—	—	—	—	—	—	—	—	—	—	—	12	172
1957	Bal	10	7	18	2.6 (7)	0	7	69	9.9 (37)	0	—	—	—	—	—	—	—	—	—	—	—	—	0	53
1960	†LAC-A	14	—	—	—	—	32	316	9.9 (34)	4	—	—	—	—	—	—	—	—	—	—	—	—	24	178
NFL	5	51	91	266	2.9 (24)	0	79	917	11.6 (78)	9	—	—	—	—	—	—	—	—	—	—	k	—	54	805

WONDOLOWSKI, BILL William Walter, WR, 5´10˝/168 lbs; Eastern Montana; B11/29/1946 Jersey City, NJ **1969** SF 1

WONG, JOE Joseph Hauoli L., G, 6´6˝/315 lbs; Hawaii; Brigham Young; 1999: Mia, rnd 7; B2/24/1976 Waimanalo, HI **2003** Oak 2 (0)

WONG, KAILEE Kailee Warner, LB, 6´2˝/250 lbs; Stanford; 1998: Min, rnd 2; B5/23/1976 Eugene, OR **1998** Min 15 (0) **1999**†Min 13 (8, LLB) **2000**†Min 16 (16, MLB) **2001** Min 16 (16, MLB) **2002** Hou 16 (16, LOLB) **2003** Hou 16 (16, LOLB) **2004** Hou 16 (16, ROLB) **2005** Hou 5 (5, lilb) **NFL** 113 (93) [8 yrs]

WONSLEY, GEORGE George Ivory, RB, 5´10˝/218 lbs; Mississippi State; 1984: Ind, rnd 4; B11/23/1960 Moss Point, MS

YEAR	TEAM	G (GS, POS)	RUSH	YD	AVG (LG)	TD	REC	YD	AVG (LG)	TD	PASS	COMP	PCT	YD	AVG (LG)	TD	INT	SK	YD	QBR	KPR	OTD	PTS	TAY
1984	Ind	14 (0)	37	111	3.0 (13)	0	9	47	5.2 (17)	0	—	—	—	—	—	—	—	—	—	—	k	—	0	127
1985	Ind	16 (10, RB)	138	716	**5.2 (36)**	6	30	257	8.6 (26)	0	—	—	—	—	—	—	—	—	—	—	—	—	36	905
1986	Ind	16 (6, rb)	60	214	3.6 (46)	1	16	175	10.9 (60)	0	—	—	—	—	—	—	—	—	—	—	k	—	6	313
1987	†Ind	11 (0)	18	71	3.9 (12)	1	5	48	9.6 (16)	0	—	—	—	—	—	—	—	—	—	—	k	—	6	109
1988	Ind	16 (0)	26	48	1.8 (4)	1	—	—	—	—	—	—	—	—	—	—	—	—	—	—	—	—	6	58
1989	NE	5 (0)	2	-2	-1.0 (0)	0	—	—	—	—	—	—	—	—	—	—	—	—	—	—	k	—	0	22
NFL	6	78 (16)	281	1158	4.1 (46)	9	60	527	8.8 (60)	0	—	—	—	—	—	—	—	—	—	—	k	—	54	1533

WONSLEY, NATHAN Nathan, RB, 5´10˝/190 lbs; Mississippi; B12/7/1963 Moss Point, MS

YEAR	TEAM	G (GS, POS)	RUSH	YD	AVG (LG)	TD	REC	YD	AVG (LG)	TD	PASS	COMP	PCT	YD	AVG (LG)	TD	INT	SK	YD	QBR	KPR	OTD	PTS	TAY
1986	TB	10 (2)	73	339	4.6 (59)	3	8	57	7.1 (11)	0	—	—	—	—	—	—	—	—	—	—	k	—	18	456

WONSLEY, OTIS Otis, RB, 5´10˝/214 lbs; Alcorn State; 1980: NYG, rnd 9; B8/13/1957 Pascagoula, MS

YEAR	TEAM	G (GS, POS)	RUSH	YD	AVG (LG)	TD	REC	YD	AVG (LG)	TD	PASS	COMP	PCT	YD	AVG (LG)	TD	INT	SK	YD	QBR	KPR	OTD	PTS	TAY
1981	Was	15 (0)	3	11	3.7 (7)	0	1	5	5.0 (5)	0	—	—	—	—	—	—	—	—	—	—	k	—	0	48
1982	†Was	9 (0)	11	36	3.3 (7)	0	1	1	1.0 (1)	1	—	—	—	—	—	—	—	—	—	—	k	—	6	41
1983	†Was	16 (0)	25	88	3.5 (9)	0	—	—	—	—	—	—	—	—	—	—	—	—	—	—	k	—	0	94
1984	†Was	16 (0)	18	38	2.1 (7)	4	—	—	—	—	—	—	—	—	—	—	—	—	—	—	—	—	24	78
1985	Was	16 (1)	4	8	2.0 (5)	0	—	—	—	—	—	—	—	—	—	—	—	—	—	—	k	—	0	4
NFL	5	72 (1)	61	181	3.0 (9)	4	2	6	3.0 (5)	1	—	—	—	—	—	—	—	—	—	—	k	—	30	264

WOOD FB, none; deceased **1920** Det 2 (1)

WOOD, BILL William Rodgers, DB, 5´11˝/190 lbs; West Virginia Wesleyan; B4/17/1939 Allentown, PA **1963** NYJ-A 1

WOOD, BO Charles Henry, DE, 6´3˝/235 lbs; North Carolina; 1967: NO, rnd 6; B1/24/1945 Camden, NJ **1967** Atl 14

WOOD, BOBBY Robert Harry, T, 6´2˝/230 lbs; Alabama; 1940: Cle, rnd 4; B1/14/1916 McComb, MS, D10/22/1973 McComb, MS **1940** ChiC 1 (0) **1940** GB 2 (0) **NFL** 3 (0) [1 yr]

YEAR	TEAM	G (GS, POS)	RUSH	YD	AVG(LG)	TD	REC	YD	AVG(LG)	TD	PASS COMP	PCT	YD	AVG(LG)	TD	INT	SK	YD	QBR	KPR	OTD	PTS	TAY

WOOD, DICK   Malcolm Richard, QB, 6'5"/205 lbs; Auburn; 1959: Bal, rnd 12; B2/29/1936 Lanett, AL

1962	SD-A	6(2)	1	0	0.0(0)	0	—	—	—	—	97	41	42.3	655	6.8(47)	4	7	—	—	—	—	—	0	68
1962	Den-A	1	—	—	—	—	—	—	—	—	—	—	—	—	—	—	—	—	—	—	—	—		
1963	NYJ-A	12(QB)	7	17	2.4(11)	1	—	—	—	—	352	160	45.5	2204	6.3(60)	18	19	—	—	60.6	—	—	6	459
1964	NYJ-A	13(QB)	9	6	0.7(6)	1	—	—	—	—	358	169	47.2	2298	6.4(71)	17	25	18	139	54.9	—	—	6	250
1965	Oak-A	14(qb)	4	16	4.0(21)	1	—	—	—	—	157	69	43.9	1003	6.4(57)	8	6	—	—	66.4	—	—	6	328
1966	Mia-A	14(4, QB)	5	6	1.2(7)	1	—	—	—	—	230	83	36.1	993	4.3(71)	4	14	20	207	30.6	—	—	6	-28
NFL	5	60(6)	26	45	1.7(21)	4	—	—	—	—	1194	522	43.7	7153	6.0(71)	51	71	38	346	52.9	—	—	24	1077

WOOD, DUANE   Duane Scott, DB, 6'1"/200 lbs; Oklahoma State; B9/20/1937 Wilburton, OK [I]   **1960** DalT-A 9 (LCB)   **1961** DalT-A 14 (LCB)   **1962**†DalT-A 14 (LCB)   **1963** KC-A◊14 (LCB)   **1964** KC-A 14 (LCB)   **NFL** 65 [5 yrs]

WOOD, GARY   Gary Fay, QB, 5'11"/192 lbs; Cornell; 1964: NYG, rnd 8/Bos, rnd 17; B2/5/1942 Taylor, NY, D3/2/1994 Dix Hills, NY [K]

1964	NYG	12	39	158	4.1(14)	3	—	—	—	—	143	66	46.2	952	6.7(70)	6	3	14	125	73.5	—	—	18	574
1965	NYG	9	5	68	13.6(25)	0	—	—	—	—	36	15	41.7	190	5.3(28)	1	2	4	41	—	K	—	1	88
1966	NYG	14(qb)	28	196	7.0(28)	3	—	—	—	—	170	81	47.6	1142	6.7(58)	6	13	24	222	49.7	—	—	18	307
1967	NO	2	—	—	—	—	—	—	—	—	11	5	45.5	62	5.6(27)	0	1	0	8	—	—	—	0	31
1968	NYG	14	2	0	0.0(2)	0	—	—	—	—	24	9	37.5	123	5.1(43)	0	5	3	18	—	—	—	0	-139
1969	NYG	12	1	3	3.0(3)	0	—	—	—	—	16	10	62.5	106	6.6(25)	1	0	—	—	—	—	—	0	61
NFL	6	63	75	425	5.7(28)	6	—	—	—	—	400	186	46.5	2575	6.4(70)	14	23	46	414	55.4	K	—	37	923

WOOD, JOHN   John Curtis, DT, 6'3"/249 lbs; LSU; 1973: Den, rnd 3; B1/20/1951 Lake Charles, LA   **1973** NO 2

WOOD, MARV   Marvin, WB-FB-E, 6'1"/195 lbs; California; B11/28/1900 Borden, IN, D12/18/1973 Bloomington, IN   **1924** Ken 4 (2)

WOOD, MIKE   Michael Stephen, K, 5'11"/199 lbs; Southeast Missouri State; 1978: Min, rnd 8; B9/3/1954 Kirkwood, MO [K]   **1978** Min 7   **1979** SL 3   **1979**†SD 9   **1980** SD 1 (0)   **1981** Bal 16 (0)

1978	SL	8	—	—	—	—	—	—	—	—	1	1	100.0	29	29.0(29)	0	0	—	—	—	P	—	0	15
1982	Bal	6(0)	—	—	—	—	—	—	—	—	1	1	100.0	5	5.0(5)	1	0	—	—	—	K	—	24	8
NFL	5	50	—	—	—	—	—	—	—	—	2	2	100.0	34	17.0(29)	1	0	—	—	—	KP	—	156	22

WOOD, RICHARD   Richard Marion, LB, 6'2"/224 lbs; USC; 1975: NYJ, rnd 3; B5/31/1953 Elizabeth, NJ   **1975** NYJ 14 (5, rlb)   **1976** TB 13 (10, RLB)   **1977** TB 14 (14, RILB)   **1978** TB 16 (16, RILB)   **1979**†TB 16 (16, RILB)   **1980** TB 16 (16, RILB)   **1981**†TB 16 (16, RILB)   **1982**†TB 9 (0)   **1983** TB 16 (1)   **1984** TB 16 (0)   **NFL** 146 (94) [10 yrs]

WOOD, WILLIE   William Vernell, DB, 5'10"/190 lbs; USC; B12/23/1936 Washington, DC; HOF 1989 [KRI]   **1960**†GB 12   **1961**†GB 14 (RS)   **1962**†GB★14 (RS)   **1963** GB☆14 (RS)   **1964** GB★14 (RS)   **1965**†GB★14 (LS)   **1966**†GB★14 (LS)   **1967**†GB★14 (RS)   **1968** GB★14 (RS)   **1969** GB★14 (RS)   **1970** GB★14 (FS)   **1971** GB☆14 (FS)   **NFL** 166 [12 yrs]

WOODALL, AL   Frank Alley, QB, 6'5"/205 lbs; Duke; 1969: NYJ, rnd 2; B12/7/1945 Erwin, NC

1969	NYJ-A	4	4	13	3.3(11)	0	—	—	—	—	9	4	44.4	67	7.4(35)	0	2	3	21	—	—	—	0	-34
1970	NYJ	10(QB)	28	110	3.9(27)	0	—	—	—	—	188	96	51.1	1265	6.7(67)	9	9	29	222	68.7	—	—	0	428
1971	NYJ	5	13	26	2.0(7)	0	—	—	—	—	97	42	43.3	395	4.1(26)	0	2	9	85	—	—	—	0	144
1973	NYJ	9(QB)	13	68	5.2(17)	0	—	—	—	—	201	101	50.2	1228	6.1(56)	9	8	19	127	67.8	—	—	0	407
1974	NYJ	3	2	-3	-1.5(-1)	0	—	—	—	—	8	3	37.5	15	1.9(8)	0	2	—	—	—	—	—	0	-76
NFL	5	31	60	214	3.6(27)	0	—	—	—	—	503	246	48.9	2970	5.9(67)	18	23	60	455	60.3	—	—	0	869

WOODALL, LEE   Lee Artis, LB, 6'1"/224 lbs; West Chester; 1994: SF, rnd 6; B10/31/1969 Carlisle, PA   **1994**†SF 15 (13, LLB)   **1995**†SF★16 (16, LLB)   **1996** SF 16 (13, LLB)   **1997**†SF◊16 (16, LLB)   **1998**†SF 15 (15, LLB)   **1999** SF 16 (16, LLB)   **2000** Car 16 (16, RLB)   **2001** Den 14 (0)   **NFL** 124 (105) [8 yrs]

WOODARD, CEDRIC   Cedric Darnell, DT, 6'2"/310 lbs; Texas; 2000: Bal, rnd 6; B9/5/1977 Bay City, TX   **2001** Sea 16 (0)   **2002** Sea 12 (0)   **2003**†Sea 16 (13, LDT)   **2004**†Sea 16 (16, LDT)   **NFL** 60 (29) [4 yrs]

WOODARD, DICK   Richard Ernest, LB-C, 6'2"/224 lbs; Iowa; 1948: NYG, rnd 21; B7/26/1926 Britt, IA   **1949** LAD-A 12 (0)   **1950**†NYG 12 (LLB)   **1951** NYG 11 (LLB)   **1952** Was 12   **1953** NYG 12 (RLB)   **NFL** 47 [4 yrs]

WOODARD, KEN   Kenneth Emil, LB, 6'1"/218 lbs; Tuskegee; 1982: Den, rnd 10; B1/22/1960 Detroit, MI   **1982** Den 9 (0)   **1983**†Den 16 (0)   **1984**†Den 16 (2)   **1985** Den 16 (9, ROLB)   **1986**†Den 16 (1)   **1987** Pit 7 (0)   **1988** SD 8 (0)   **1989** SD 16 (0)   **NFL** 104 (13) [8 yrs]

WOODARD, MARC   Marc Sionn, LB, 6'0"/238 lbs; Mississippi State; 1993: Pit, rnd 5; B2/21/1970 Kosciusko, MS   **1994** Phi 16 (0)   **1995**†Phi 16 (0)   **1996**†Phi 16 (2)   **NFL** 48 (2) [3 yrs]

WOODARD, RAY   Raymond Lee, DE, 6'6"/290 lbs; Texas; 1984: SD, rnd 8; B8/20/1961 Corrigan, TX   **1987** Den 3 (1)   **1987** KC 6 (0)   **NFL** 9 (1) [1 yr]

WOODBERRY, DENNIS   Dennis Earl, DB, 5'10"/183 lbs; Southern Arkansas; 1984: Atl, rnd S3; B4/22/1961 Texarkana, AR   **1986** Atl 7 (0)   **1987**†Was 12 (3)   **1988** Was 12 (0)   **NFL** 31 (3) [3 yrs]

WOODBURY, TORY   Tory, QB, 6'2"/208 lbs; Winston-Salem State; B7/12/1978 Winston-Salem, NC   **2001** NYJ 10 (0)

| 2002 | NYJ | 2(0) | — | — | — | — | 1 | 13 | 13.0(13) | 0 | — | — | — | — | — | — | — | — | — | — | — | — | 0 | 7 |
| NFL | 2 | 12(0) | — | — | — | — | 1 | 13 | 13.0(13) | 0 | — | — | — | — | — | — | — | — | — | — | — | — | 0 | 7 |

WOODCOCK, JOHN   John Maurer, DT-DE, 6'3"/246 lbs; New Mexico; Hawaii; 1976: Det, rnd 3; B3/19/1954 Eureka, CA   **1976** Det 14 (4)   **1977** Det 14 (4)   **1978** Det 16 (14, LDT)   **1980** Det 8 (8, ldt)   **1981**†SD 12 (12, RDE)   **1982**†SD 6 (1)   **NFL** 70 (43) [6 yrs]

WOODEN, SHAWN   Shawn Anthony, DB, 5'11"/205 lbs; Notre Dame; 1996: Mia, rnd 6; B10/23/1975 Philadelphia, PA   **1996** Mia 16 (11, FS/ss)   **1997**†Mia 16 (15, SS)   **1998** Mia 2 (1)   **1999**†Mia 15 (6, ss)   **2000** ChiB 11 (0)   **2001**†Mia 13 (0)   **2002** Mia 16 (16, ss)   **2003** Mia 15 (0)   **NFL** 104 (35) [8 yrs]

WOODEN, TERRY   Terrence Tylon, LB, 6'3"/239 lbs; Syracuse; 1990: Sea, rnd 2; B1/14/1967 Hartford, CT   **1990** Sea 8 (8, LLB)   **1991** Sea 16 (15, LLB)   **1992** Sea 8 (8, LLB)   **1993** Sea 16 (16, LLB)   **1994** Sea 15 (15, LLB)   **1995** Sea 16 (16, LLB)   **1996** Sea 9 (9, LLB)   **1997**†KC 15 (8, LILB)   **1998** Oak 16 (10, LLB)   **NFL** 120 (105) [9 yrs]

WOODESHICK, TOM   Thomas, RB, 6'0"/225 lbs; West Virginia; 1963: Phi, rnd 8/Buf, rnd 4; B12/3/1941 Wilkes-Barre, PA

1963	Phi	14	5	18	3.6(11)	0	1	-3	-3.0(-3)	0	—	—	—	—	—	—	—	—	—	—	k	—	0	44
1964	Phi	13	37	180	4.9(13)	2	4	12	3.0(8)	0	—	—	—	—	—	—	—	—	—	—	—	—	12	206
1965	Phi	13	28	145	5.2(14)	0	6	86	14.3(60)	0	—	—	—	—	—	—	—	—	—	—	—	—	0	188
1966	Phi	14(4)	85	330	3.9(21)	4	10	118	11.8(40)	1	—	—	—	—	—	—	—	—	—	—	—	—	30	434
1967	Phi	14(FB)	155	670	4.3(41)	6	34	391	11.5(43)	4	—	—	—	—	—	—	—	—	—	—	—	—	60	946
1968	Phi★	14(FB)	217	947	4.4(54)	3	36	328	9.1(55)	0	—	—	—	—	—	—	—	—	—	—	—	—	18	1141
1969	Phi☆	12(FB)	186	831	4.5(21)	4	22	177	8.0(15)	0	—	—	—	—	—	—	—	—	—	—	—	—	24	960
1970	Phi	6(fb)	52	254	4.9(57)	2	6	28	4.7(10)	0	—	—	—	—	—	—	—	—	—	—	—	—	12	288
1971	Phi	11(fb)	66	188	2.8(19)	0	6	36	6.0(11)	1	—	—	—	—	—	—	—	—	—	—	—	—	6	211
1972	SL	4	5	14	2.8(6)	0	1	2	2.0(2)	0	—	—	—	—	—	—	—	—	—	—	—	—	0	15
NFL	10	115(4)	836	3577	4.3(57)	21	126	1175	9.3(60)	6	—	—	—	—	—	—	—	—	—	—	k	—	162	4432

WOODFIN, ZAC   Zac, LB, 6'1"/235 lbs; Alabama-Birmingham; B3/19/1983 Montgomery, AL   **2005** Bal 1 (0)

WOODIN, WHITEY   Howard Lee, G-T, 5'10"/208 lbs; Marquette; B11/29/1894 Fort Atkinson, WI, D2/9/1974 Green Bay, WI [K]   **1922** Rac 4 (2)   **1922** GB 6 (5, LG)   **1923** GB 10 (10, LG)   **1924** GB 11 (10, LG)   **1925** GB 11 (9, LG)   **1926** GB 13 (8, LG), 1   **1927** GB 7 (3)   **1928** GB 10 (2)   **1929** GB 6 (3)   **1930** GB 10 (1)   **1931** GB 2 (2), 9   **NFL** 90 (55) [10 yrs]

WOODLEY, DAVID   David Eugene, QB, 6'2"/210 lbs; LSU; 1980: Mia, rnd 8; B10/25/1958 Shreveport, LA, D5/4/2003 Shreveport, LA

1980	Mia	13(11, QB)	55	214	3.9(17)	3	—	—	—	—	327	176	53.8	1850	5.7(61)	14	17	17	127	63.1	—	—	18	559
1981	†Mia	15(15, QB)	63	272	4.3(26)	4	—	—	—	—	366	191	52.2	2470	6.7(69)	12	13	24	191	69.8	—	—	24	1087
1982	†Mia	9 (9, QB)	36	207	5.8(29)	2	1	15	15.0(15)	1	179	98	54.7	1080	6.0(46)	5	8	10	82	63.5	—	—	18	485
1983	Mia	5 (5, qb)	19	78	4.1(15)	0	1	6	6.0(6)	0	89	43	48.3	528	5.9(64)	3	4	10	80	—	—	—	0	200
1984	Pit	7 (7, qb)	11	14	1.3(7)	0	—	—	—	—	156	85	54.5	1273	8.2(80)	8	7	10	67	79.9	—	—	0	411
1985	Pit	9 (6, qb)	17	71	4.2(13)	2	—	—	—	—	183	94	51.4	1357	7.4(69)	6	14	13	84	54.8	—	—	12	240
NFL	6	58(53)	201	856	4.3(29)	11	2	21	10.5(15)	1	1300	687	52.8	8558	6.6(80)	48	63	84	631	65.7	—	—	72	2981

WOODLEY, RICHARD   Richard L., DB, 5'9"/180 lbs; TCU; B1/13/1972 Texas City, TX   **1996** Det 11 (0)

WOODLIEF, DOUG   Douglas Eugene, LB, 6'3"/225 lbs; Memphis; 1965: LA, rnd 5/SD, rnd R4; B9/4/1943 Marianna, FL   **1965** LARm 14 (MLB)   **1966** LARm 14   **1967**†LARm 13   **1968** LARm 14   **1969**†LARm 14 (11, MLB)   **NFL** 69 (11) [5 yrs]

YEAR	TEAM	G(GS, POS)	RUSH	YD	AVG(LG)	TD	REC	YD	AVG(LG)	TD	PASS	COMP	PCT	YD	AVG(LG)	TD	INT	SK	YD	QBR	KPR	OTD	PTS	TAY

WOODRING, JOHN John, LB, 6´2˝/232 lbs; Brown; 1981: NYJ, rnd 6; B4/4/1959 Philadelphia, PA **1981**†NYJ 12 (0) **1982**†NYJ 9 (1) **1983** NYJ 14 (10, llb) **1984** NYJ 15 (5, mlb) **1985**†NYJ 2 (0) **NFL** 52 (16) [5 yrs]

WOODRUFF, DWAYNE Dwayne Donzell, DB, 5´11˝/198 lbs; Louisville; 1979: Pit, rnd 6; B2/18/1957 Bowling Green, KY **[I]** **1979**†Pit 16 (1) **1980** Pit 16 (0) **1981** Pit 16 (14, LCB) **1982**†Pit 9 (9, LCB) **1983**†Pit 15 (15, LCB) **1984**†Pit 16 (14, LCB) **1985** Pit 12 (10, LCB) **1987** Pit 12 (12, LCB) **1988** Pit 14 (13, LCB) **1989**†Pit 16 (16, LCB) **1990** Pit 15 (1) **NFL** 157 (105) [11 yrs]

WOODRUFF, JIM James L., E, 6´3˝/210 lbs; Pittsburgh; B8/3/1903, NE, D12/1971 Atlanta, GA **1926** ChiC 1 (0) **1929** Buf 6 (5, le) **NFL** 7 (5) [2 yrs]

WOODRUFF, LEE Lee Thornton, B, 6´0˝/202 lbs; Mississippi; B1909 Batesville, MS, deceased **[K]**

YEAR	TEAM	G(GS, POS)	RUSH	YD	AVG(LG)	TD	REC	YD	AVG(LG)	TD	PASS	COMP	PCT	YD	AVG(LG)	TD	INT	SK	YD	QBR	KPR	OTD	PTS	TAY
1931	Pro	11(7, FB)	—	—	—	—	—	—	—	—	—	—	—	—	—	—	—	—	—	—	—	—	—	—
1932	Bos	7(4)	—	—	—	—	2	35	17.5	0	—	—	—	—	—	—	—	—	—	—	—	—	0	18
1933	Phi	9(2)	22	74	3.4	1	3	57	19.0	0	1	0	0.0	0	0.0	0	1	—	—	—	—	1	12	83
NFL	3	27(13)	22	74	3.4	5	5	92	18.4	0	1	0	0.0	0	0.0	0	1	—	—	—	K	1	37	140

WOODRUFF, TONY Anthony DeWayne, WR, 6´0˝/178 lbs; Fresno State; 1982: Phi, rnd 9; B11/12/1958 Hazen, AR

YEAR	TEAM	G(GS, POS)	RUSH	YD	AVG(LG)	TD	REC	YD	AVG(LG)	TD	PASS	COMP	PCT	YD	AVG(LG)	TD	INT	SK	YD	QBR	KPR	OTD	PTS	TAY
1982	Phi	1(0)	—	—	—	—	—	—	—	—	—	—	—	—	—	—	—	—	—	—	—	—	—	—
1983	Phi	6(1)	—	—	—	—	6	70	11.7(29)	2	—	—	—	—	—	—	—	—	—	—	—	—	12	45
1984	Phi	16(6, wr)	—	—	—	—	30	484	16.1(38)	3	—	—	—	—	—	—	—	—	—	—	—	—	18	257
NFL	3	23(7)	—	—	—	—	36	554	15.4(38)	5	—	—	—	—	—	—	—	—	—	—	—	—	30	302

WOODS, CARL Carl Frank, RB, 5´11˝/200 lbs; Vanderbilt; B10/22/1964 Gallatin, TN

YEAR	TEAM	G(GS, POS)	RUSH	YD	AVG(LG)	TD	REC	YD	AVG(LG)	TD	PASS	COMP	PCT	YD	AVG(LG)	TD	INT	SK	YD	QBR	KPR	OTD	PTS	TAY
1987	NE	2(0)	4	20	5.0(13)	1	—	—	—	—	—	—	—	—	—	—	—	—	—	—	—	—	6	30

WOODS, CHRIS Christopher Wyatt, WR, 5´11˝/190 lbs; Auburn; 1984: LARd, rnd S1; B7/19/1962 Birmingham, AL **1988** LARd 2 (0) **1989** Den 1 (0)

YEAR	TEAM	G(GS, POS)	RUSH	YD	AVG(LG)	TD	REC	YD	AVG(LG)	TD	PASS	COMP	PCT	YD	AVG(LG)	TD	INT	SK	YD	QBR	KPR	OTD	PTS	TAY
1987	LARd	9(1)	—	—	—	—	1	14	14.0(14)	0	—	—	—	—	—	—	—	—	—	—	kp	—	0	76
NFL	3	12(1)	—	—	—	—	1	14	14.0(14)	0	—	—	—	—	—	—	—	—	—	—	kp	—	0	79

WOODS, DON Donald Ray, RB, 6´1˝/210 lbs; New Mexico Highlands; New Mexico; 1974: GB, rnd 6; B2/17/1951 Denton, TX

YEAR	TEAM	G(GS, POS)	RUSH	YD	AVG(LG)	TD	REC	YD	AVG(LG)	TD	PASS	COMP	PCT	YD	AVG(LG)	TD	INT	SK	YD	QBR	KPR	OTD	PTS	TAY
1974	SD	12(9, RB)	227	1162	5.1(56)	7	26	349	13.4(75)	3	3	1	33.3	28	9.3(28)	1	1	—	—	—	k	—	60	1417
1975	SD	5(5, rb)	87	317	3.6(17)	2	13	101	7.8(22)	0	—	—	—	—	—	—	—	—	—	—	—	—	12	388
1976	SD	11(10, RB)	126	450	3.6(24)	3	34	224	6.6(34)	1	2	1	50.0	11	5.5(11)	1	0	—	—	—	—	—	24	608
1977	SD	14(14, RB)	118	405	3.4(29)	1	18	218	12.1(78)	1	1	0	0.0	0	0.0	0	0	—	—	—	k	—	12	541
1978	SD	16(7, FB)	151	514	3.4(27)	3	34	295	8.7(29)	0	—	—	—	—	—	—	—	—	—	—	k	—	18	699
1979	†SD	15	—	—	—	—	—	—	—	—	—	—	—	—	—	—	—	—	—	—	—	—	0	10
1980	SD	2(0)	4	10	2.5(5)	0	—	—	—	—	—	—	—	—	—	—	—	—	—	—	—	—	0	10
1980	SF	10(5, rb)	50	229	4.6(23)	0	20	171	8.6(23)	0	2	1	50.0	6	3.0(6)	0	0	1	8	—	—	—	0	318
NFL	7	85(50)	763	3087	4.0(56)	16	145	1358	9.4(78)	5	8	3	37.5	45	5.6(28)	2	1	1	8	—	k	—	126	3989

WOODS, FLASH Gerald E., HB, 6´0˝/180 lbs; Butler; B4/26/1902, D10/20/1989 Fulton County, GA **1926** Col 2 (2)

WOODS, GLENN Clarence Glenn, DE, 6´4˝/250 lbs; Prairie View A&M; 1969: Hou, rnd 8; B1/7/1946 Kilgore, TX **1969** Hou-A 7

WOODS, ICKEY Elbert L., RB, 6´2˝/231 lbs; UNLV; 1988: Cin, rnd 2; B2/28/1966 Fresno, CA

YEAR	TEAM	G(GS, POS)	RUSH	YD	AVG(LG)	TD	REC	YD	AVG(LG)	TD	PASS	COMP	PCT	YD	AVG(LG)	TD	INT	SK	YD	QBR	KPR	OTD	PTS	TAY
1988	†Cin☆	16(10, FB)	203	1066	**5.3(56)**	**15**	21	199	9.5(25)	0	—	—	—	—	—	—	—	—	—	—	—	—	90	1316
1989	Cin	2(2)	29	94	3.2(12)	2	—	—	—	—	—	—	—	—	—	—	—	—	—	—	—	—	12	114
1990	†Cin	10(6, fb)	64	268	4.2(32)	6	20	162	8.1(22)	0	—	—	—	—	—	—	—	—	—	—	—	—	36	409
1991	Cin	9(2)	36	97	2.7(12)	4	6	36	6.0(16)	0	—	—	—	—	—	—	—	—	—	—	—	—	24	155
NFL	4	37(20)	332	1525	4.6(56)	27	47	397	8.4(25)	0	—	—	—	—	—	—	—	—	—	—	—	—	162	1994

WOODS, JEROME Jerome Harlan, DB, 6´2˝/210 lbs; Memphis; 1996: KC, rnd 1; B3/17/1973 Memphis, TN **1996** KC 16 (0) **1997**†KC 16 (16, FS) **1998** KC 16 (16, FS) **1999** KC 15 (15, FS) **2000** KC 16 (16, FS) **2001** KC 16 (16, FS) **2003**†KC✧16 (16, FS) **2004** KC 10 (10, FS) **2005** KC 7 (0) **NFL** 128 (105) [9 yrs]

WOODS, JERRY Jerry Lee, DB, 5´10˝/187 lbs; Northern Michigan; 1989: Det, rnd 7; B2/13/1966 Dyersburg, TN **1989** Det 2 (0) **1990** GB 16 (0) **NFL** 18 (0) [2 yrs]

WOODS, JIMMY James John, C-T-G, 5´9˝/196 lbs; none; B5/5/1894 Jamestown, NY, D12/1966 Salmanca, NY **1920** Roc 9 (0) **1921** Roc 3 (0) **1922** Roc 1 (0) **1923** Roc 4 (3, C) **1924** Roc 5 (0) **NFL** 22 (3) [5 yrs]

WOODS, LARRY Larry Dobie, DT, 6´6˝/260 lbs; Tennessee State; 1971: Det, rnd 4; B5/11/1948 Florence, AL **1971** Det 1 **1972** Det 12 (LDT) **1973** Mia 3 **1974** NYJ 13 **1975** NYJ 12 **1976** Sea 6 **NFL** 47 [6 yrs]

WOODS, LEVAR LeVar, LB, 6´3˝/244 lbs; Iowa; B3/15/1978 Cleveland, OH **2001** Arz 15 (0) **2002** Arz 15 (2) **2003** Arz 16 (3) **2004** Arz 14 (3) **2005** Det 6 (3) **NFL** 66 (11) [5 yrs]

WOODS, MIKE Michael Jay, LB, 6´2˝/233 lbs; Tampa; Cincinnati; 1978: Bal, rnd 2; B11/1/1954 Cleveland, OH **1979** Bal 16 **1980** Bal 13 (12, RLB) **1981** Bal 7 (7, rlb) **NFL** 36 (19) [3 yrs]

WOODS, RASHAUN Rashaun Dorrell, WR, 6´2˝/185 lbs; Oklahoma State; 2004: SF, rnd 1; B10/17/1980 Oklahoma City, OK

YEAR	TEAM	G(GS, POS)	RUSH	YD	AVG(LG)	TD	REC	YD	AVG(LG)	TD	PASS	COMP	PCT	YD	AVG(LG)	TD	INT	SK	YD	QBR	KPR	OTD	PTS	TAY
2004	SF	14(0)	—	—	—	—	7	160	22.9(59)	1	—	—	—	—	—	—	—	—	—	—	—	—	6	85

WOODS, RICK Rick L., DB, 6´0˝/196 lbs; Boise State; 1982: Pit, rnd 4; B11/16/1959 Boise, ID **1982**†Pit 5 (0) **1983**†Pit 15 (9, FS) **1984**†Pit 15 (4) **1985** Pit 16 (9, lcb) **1986** Pit 15 (0) **1987** TB 5 (5, fs) **NFL** 71 (27) [6 yrs]

WOODS, ROB Alex Robert, T, 6´5˝/295 lbs; Eastern Washington; California-Santa Barbara; Arizona; 1989: Cin, rnd 4; B10/3/1965 Fayetteville, NC **1991** Cle 2 (1)

WOODS, ROBERT Robert Christopher, WR, 5´7˝/170 lbs; Grambling State; 1978: KC, rnd 5; B7/3/1955 New Orleans, LA **1979** Det 1

YEAR	TEAM	G(GS, POS)	RUSH	YD	AVG(LG)	TD	REC	YD	AVG(LG)	TD	PASS	COMP	PCT	YD	AVG(LG)	TD	INT	SK	YD	QBR	KPR	OTD	PTS	TAY
1978	†Hou	3	2	4	2.0(5)	0	6	96	16.0(80)	2	—	—	—	—	—	—	—	—	—	—	kp	—	12	113
NFL	2	4	2	4	2.0(5)	0	6	96	16.0(80)	2	—	—	—	—	—	—	—	—	—	—	kp	—	12	119

WOODS, ROBERT Robert Earl, T-G, 6´3˝/255 lbs; Tennessee State; 1973: NYJ, rnd 2; B7/26/1950 Florence, AL **1973** NYJ 14 (LT) **1974** NYJ 14 (LT) **1975** NYJ 14 (14, LT) **1976** NYJ 10 (LT) **1977** NYJ 2 **1977** NO 4 **1978** NO 16 (13, RT) **1979** NO 15 (15, RT) **1980** NO 10 (6, rt) **NFL** 99 (48) [8 yrs]

WOODS, TONY Stanley Anthony, DE-LB, 6´4˝/282 lbs; Pittsburgh; 1987: Sea, rnd 1; B10/11/1965 Newark, NJ **1987**†Sea 12 (7, lolb) **1988**†Sea 16 (16, ROLB) **1989** Sea 16 (12, LOLB) **1990** Sea 16 (15, RDE) **1991** Sea 14 (14, RDE) **1992** Sea 15 (15, RDE) **1993** LARm 14 (8, LDE) **1994** Was 15 (15, LDE) **1995** Was 16 (16, LDE) **1996** Was 13 (7, LDE) **NFL** 147 (125) [10 yrs]

WOODS, TONY Clinton Anthony, DT, 6´5˝/265 lbs; Oklahoma; 1989: Chi, rnd 8; B3/14/1966 Fort Lee, VA **1989** ChiB 15 (2)

WOODSIDE, KEITH Keith A., RB, 5´11˝/203 lbs; Texas A&M; 1988: GB, rnd 3; B7/29/1964 Natchez, MS

YEAR	TEAM	G(GS, POS)	RUSH	YD	AVG(LG)	TD	REC	YD	AVG(LG)	TD	PASS	COMP	PCT	YD	AVG(LG)	TD	INT	SK	YD	QBR	KPR	OTD	PTS	TAY
1988	GB	16(9, RB)	83	195	2.3(10)	3	39	352	9.0(49)	2	—	—	—	—	—	—	—	—	—	—	k	—	30	469
1989	GB	16(16, RB)	46	273	5.9(68)	1	59	527	8.9(33)	0	—	—	—	—	—	—	—	—	—	—	k	—	6	555
1990	GB	16(13, RB)	46	182	4.0(21)	1	24	184	7.7(25)	0	—	—	—	—	—	—	—	—	—	—	—	—	6	284
1991	GB	16(12, RB)	84	326	3.9(29)	1	22	185	8.4(28)	0	—	—	—	—	—	—	—	—	—	—	—	—	6	429
NFL	4	64(50)	259	976	3.8(68)	6	144	1248	8.7(49)	2	—	—	—	—	—	—	—	—	—	—	k	—	48	1736

WOODSON, ABE Abraham Benjamin, DB-HB, 5´11˝/188 lbs; Illinois; 1957: SF, rnd 2; B2/15/1934 Jackson, MS **[R]** **1959** SF★12 (DB) **1962** SF★14 (14, RCB) **1963** SF★14 (14, RCB) **1964** SF 14 (12, RCB) **1965** SL 13 **1966** SL 14 (RCB)

YEAR	TEAM	G(GS, POS)	RUSH	YD	AVG(LG)	TD	REC	YD	AVG(LG)	TD	PASS	COMP	PCT	YD	AVG(LG)	TD	INT	SK	YD	QBR	KPR	OTD	PTS	TAY
1958	SF	9	2	12	6.0(9)	0	—	—	—	—	—	—	—	—	—	—	—	—	—	—	kpi	—	0	143
1960	SF★	12(12, RCB)	4	4	1.0(4)	0	—	—	—	—	—	—	—	—	—	—	—	—	—	—	kpi	—	0	346
1961	SF★	14(11, RCB/lcb)	14	23	1.6(14)	0	8	74	9.3(28)	0	—	—	—	—	—	—	—	—	—	—	kpi	2	12	546
NFL	9	116(63)	20	39	2.0(14)	0	8	74	9.3(28)	0	—	—	—	—	—	—	—	—	—	—	kpi	8	48	3241

WOODSON, CHARLES Charles, DB, 6´1˝/200 lbs; Michigan; 1998: Oak, rnd 1; B10/7/1976 Fremont, OH **1998** Oak✧16 (16, LCB) **2001**†Oak★16 (15, LCB) **2002**†Oak 8 (7, LCB) **2003** Oak 15 (15, LCB) **2004** Oak 13 (12, RCB) **2005** Oak 6 (6, rcb)

YEAR	TEAM	G(GS, POS)	RUSH	YD	AVG(LG)	TD	REC	YD	AVG(LG)	TD	PASS	COMP	PCT	YD	AVG(LG)	TD	INT	SK	YD	QBR	KPR	OTD	PTS	TAY
1999	Oak★	16(16, LCB)	—	—	—	—	1	19	19.0(19)	0	—	—	—	—	—	—	—	—	—	—	i	1	6	30
2000	†Oak★	16(16, LCB)	—	—	—	—	1	8	8.0(8)	0	—	—	—	—	—	—	—	—	—	—	i	—	0	20
NFL	8	106(103)	—	—	—	—	2	27	13.5(19)	0	—	—	—	—	—	—	—	—	—	—	piS	2	12	294

WOODSON, DARREN Darren Ray, DB, 6´1˝/219 lbs; Arizona State; 1992: Dal, rnd 2; B4/25/1969 Phoenix, AZ **[I]** **1992**†Dal 16 (2) **1993**†Dal 16 (15, SS) **1994**†Dal★16 (16, SS) **1995**†Dal★16 (16, SS) **1996**†Dal★16 (16, SS) **1997** Dal✧14 (14, SS) **1998**†Dal★16 (15, SS) **1999**†Dal 15 (15, SS) **2000** Dal 11 (11, SS) **2001** Dal 16 (16, SS) **2002** Dal 10 (10, SS) **2003**†Dal 16 (16, SS) **NFL** 178 (162) [12 yrs]

WOODSON, FREDDIE Frederick, G-DT-DE, 6´2˝/255 lbs; Florida A&M; B6/9/1944 Savannah, GA **1967** Mia-A 12 (7, LG) **1968** Mia-A 14 (1) **1969** Mia-A 1 **NFL** 27 (8) [3 yrs]

YEAR	TEAM	G (GS, POS)	RUSH	YD	AVG (LG)	TD	REC	YD	AVG (LG)	TD	PASS	COMP	PCT	YD	AVG (LG)	TD	INT	SK	YD	QBR	KPR	OTD	PTS	TAY

WOODSON, MARV Marvin Lewis, DB-HB, 6´1˝/190 lbs; Indiana; 1964: Bal, rnd 1/Den, rnd 3; B9/19/1941 Hattiesburg, MS **1964** Pit 4 **1965** Pit 13 (LCB) **1966** Pit 14 (LCB)
1967 Pit◊14 (LCB) **1968** Pit 14 (LCB) **1969** Pit 8 **1969** NO 5 **NFL** 72 [6 yrs]

WOODSON, ROD Roderick Kevin, DB, 5´11˝/205 lbs; Purdue; 1987: Pit, rnd 1; B3/10/1965 Fort Wayne, IN **[RI]** **1987** Pit 8 (0) **1988** Pit 16 (16, RCB) **1989**†Pit★15 (14, RCB)
1990 Pit★16 (16, RCB) **1991** Pit★15 (15, RCB) **1992**†Pit★16 (16, LCB) **1994**†Pit★16 (16, LCB) **1995**†Pit☆1 (1) **1996**†Pit☆16 (16, FS) **1997**†SF 14 (14, LCB)
1998 Bal 16 (16, LCB) **1999** Bal◊16 (16, FS) **2000**†Bal◊16 (16, FS) **2001**†Bal◊16 (16, FS) **2002**†Oak★16 (16, FS) **2003** Oak 10 (10, FS)

| 1993 | †Pit★ | 16 (16, LCB) | 1 | 0 | 0.0 (0) | 0 | — | — | — | — | — | — | — | — | — | — | — | — | — | — | kpiS | 1 | 6 | 305 |
| NFL | 17 | 238 (229) | 1 | 0 | 0.0 (0) | 0 | — | — | — | — | — | — | — | — | — | — | — | — | — | — | kpiS | 17 | 102 | 3944 |

WOODY, DAMIEN Damien Michael, C-G, 6´3˝/320 lbs; Boston College; 1999: NE, rnd 1; B11/3/1977 Beaverdam, VA **1999** NE 16 (16, C) **2000** NE 16 (16, C) **2001**†NE 16 (15, C)
2002 NE◊16 (15, C) **2003**†NE 14 (14, LG) **2004** Det 16 (16, RG) **2005** Det 16 (16, RG) **NFL** 110 (108) [7 yrs]

WOOLF, SCOTT Rodney Scott, QB, 6´1˝/190 lbs; Ohio State; Mount Union; B12/26/1961 Salem, OR **1987** LARd 1 (0)

WOOLFOLK, ANDRE Andre Maurice, DB, 6´1˝/197 lbs; Oklahoma; 2003: Ten, rnd 1; B1/26/1980 Denver, CO **2003** Ten 6 (1) **2004** Ten 10 (2) **2005** Ten 13 (7, lcb)
NFL 29 (10) [3 yrs]

WOOLFOLK, BUTCH Harold E., RB, 6´1˝/210 lbs; Michigan; 1982: NYG, rnd 1; B3/1/1960 Milwaukee, WI

1982	NYG	9 (8, RB)	112	439	3.9 (18)	2	23	224	9.7 (40)	2	—	—	—	—	—	—	—	—	—	—	k	—	24	709
1983	NYG	16 (16, RB)	246	857	3.5 (22)	4	28	368	13.1 (44)	0	—	—	—	—	—	—	—	—	—	—	k	—	24	1064
1984	†NYG	15 (8, rb)	40	92	2.3 (17)	1	9	53	5.9 (13)	0	—	—	—	—	—	—	—	—	—	—	k	—	6	151
1985	Hou	16 (14, RB)	103	392	3.8 (43)	1	80	814	10.2 (80)	4	—	—	—	—	—	—	—	—	—	—	k	—	30	829
1986	Hou	10 (5, FB)	23	57	2.5 (15)	0	28	314	11.2 (30)	2	—	—	—	—	—	—	—	—	—	—	k	—	12	232
1987	Det	12 (0)	12	82	6.8 (31)	0	19	166	8.7 (13)	0	—	—	—	—	—	—	—	—	—	—	k	—	0	219
1988	Det	3 (0)	1	4	4.0 (4)	0	—	—	—	—	—	—	—	—	—	—	—	—	—	—	k	—	0	43
NFL	7	81 (51)	537	1923	3.6 (43)	8	187	1939	10.4 (80)	8	—	—	—	—	—	—	—	—	—	—	k	—	96	3247

WOOLFORD, DONNELL Donnell, DB, 5´9˝/192 lbs; Clemson; 1989: Chi, rnd 1; B1/6/1966 Baltimore, MD **[I]** **1989** ChiB 11 (11, LCB) **1990**†ChiB 13 (13, LCB)
1991†ChiB 15 (15, LCB) **1992** ChiB 16 (16, LCB) **1993** ChiB◊16 (16, LCB) **1994**†ChiB☆16 (16, LCB) **1995** ChiB 9 (9, LCB) **1996** ChiB 15 (15, LCB) **1997**†Pit 15 (12, LCB)
NFL 126 (123) [9 yrs]

WOOLFORD, GARY Gary Steven, DB, 6´0˝/180 lbs; Western Illinois; Florida State; 1977: Hou, rnd 6; B5/4/1954 Cairo, IL **1980** NYG 12 (8, FS)

WOOLSEY, ROLLY Roland Bert, DB, 6´1˝/182 lbs; Boise State; 1975: Dal, rnd 6; B8/11/1953 Provo, UT **1975**†Dal 14 **1976** Sea 14 (11, RCB) **1977** Cle 14 **1978** SL 2
NFL 44 (11) [4 yrs]

WOOTEN, JOHN John B., G, 6´2˝/235 lbs; Colorado; 1959: Cle, rnd 5; B12/5/1936 Clarksville, TX **1959** Cle 12 **1960** Cle 12 **1961** Cle 14 (RG) **1962** Cle 14 (RG)
1963 Cle 14 (LG) **1964**†Cle 14 (LG) **1965**†Cle★14 (LG) **1966** Cle 14 (LG) **1967**†Cle★14 (LG) **1968** Was 14 (RG) **NFL** 136 [10 yrs]

WOOTEN, MIKE Michael Carroll, C, 6´3˝/260 lbs; VMI; B10/23/1962 Roanoke, VA **1987** Was 3 (0)

WOOTEN, RON Ronald John, G, 6´4˝/274 lbs; North Carolina; 1981: NE, rnd 6; B6/28/1959 Bourne, MA **1982**†NE 9 (7, RG) **1983** NE 16 (16, RG) **1984** NE 16 (16, RG)
1985†NE 14 (14, RG) **1986**†NE 16 (16, RG) **1987** NE 13 (13, RG) **1988** NE 14 (14, RG) **NFL** 98 (96) [7 yrs]

WOOTEN, TITO Tito J., DB, 6´0˝/191 lbs; North Carolina; Louisiana-Monroe; 1994: NYG, rnd S4; B12/12/1971 Goldsboro, NC **1994** NYG 16 (2) **1995** NYG 16 (3)
1996 NYG 13 (12, FS) **1997**†NYG 16 (16, FS) **1998** NYG 14 (13, FS) **1999** Ind 8 (1) **NFL** 83 (47) [6 yrs]

WORD, BARRY Barry Quentin, RB, 6´2˝/242 lbs; Virginia; 1986: NO, rnd 3; B1/17/1963 Long Island, VA

1987	†NO	12 (1)	36	133	3.7 (20)	2	6	54	9.0 (17)	0	—	—	—	—	—	—	—	—	—	—	k	—	12	235
1988	NO	2 (0)									—	—	—	—	—	—	—	—	—	—		—		
1990	†KC	16 (3, RB)	204	1015	5.0 (53)	4	4	28	7.0 (10)	0	—	—	—	—	—	—	—	—	—	—	k	—	24	1064
1991	†KC	16 (3, RB)	160	684	4.3 (37)	4	2	13	6.5 (8)	0	—	—	—	—	—	—	—	—	—	—		—	24	731
1992	†KC	12 (11, RB)	163	607	3.7 (44)	4	9	80	8.9 (22)	0	—	—	—	—	—	—	—	—	—	—		—	24	687
1993	Min	13 (8, RB)	142	458	3.2 (14)	2	9	105	11.7 (27)	0	—	—	—	—	—	—	—	—	—	—		—	12	531
1994	Arz	1 (0)									—	—	—	—	—	—	—	—	—	—		—		
NFL	7	72 (26)	705	2897	4.1 (53)	16	30	280	9.3 (27)	0	—	—	—	—	—	—	—	—	—	—	k	—	96	3247

WORD, MARK Mark Bernard, DE, 6´5˝/305 lbs; Jacksonville State; B11/23/1975 Miami, FL **1999** KC 5 (0) **2002** Cle 16 (2) **2003** Cle 16 (2) **NFL** 37 (4) [3 yrs]

WORD, ROSCOE Roscoe, DB, 5´11˝/170 lbs; Jackson State; 1974: NYJ, rnd 3; B7/24/1952 Pine Bluff, AR **1974** NYJ 14 (RCB) **1975** NYJ 14 (10, RCB) **1976** NYJ 2 **1976** Buf 1
1976 NYG 4 **1976** TB 2 (2) **NFL** 37 (12) [3 yrs]

WORDEN, JIM James Crawford, HB, 5´10˝/180 lbs; Waynesburg; B6/21/1915 Lorain, OH, D6/7/1983 Lorain, OH

| 1945 | Cle | 5 (0) | 4 | 3 | 0.8 (7) | 0 | — | — | — | — | — | — | — | — | — | — | — | — | — | — | — | — | 0 | 3 |

WORDEN, NEIL Neil James, FB, 5´10˝/198 lbs; Notre Dame; 1954: Phi, rnd 1; B7/1/1931 Milwaukee, WI

1954	Phi	12 (fb)	58	128	2.2 (12)	1	7	63	9.0 (23)	0	—	—	—	—	—	—	—	—	—	—	—	—	6	170
1957	Phi	12	42	133	3.2 (17)	0	1	3	3.0 (3)	0	—	—	—	—	—	—	—	—	—	—	k	—	6	138
NFL	2	24	100	261	2.6 (17)	1	8	66	8.3 (23)	0	—	—	—	—	—	—	—	—	—	—	k	—	6	307

WORDEN, STU Stuart Barrett, G-T-C-LB, 6´0˝/210 lbs; Hampden-Sydney; B5/6/1907 Abingdon, VA, D3/17/1978 Elkton, VA **1930** Bkn 11 (8, LT) **1932** Bkn 12 (8, lg)
1933 Bkn 10 (9, LG) **1934** Bkn 11 (10, LG) **NFL** 44 (35) [4 yrs]

WORK, JOE Joseph Ranisa, E-WB, 5´10˝/177 lbs; Miami (OH); B1/25/1900, D10/1979 Adena, OH **1923** Cle 7 (4, LE) **1924** Cle 8 (5, RE), 6 **1925** Cle 4 (4, RE)
NFL 19 (13) [3 yrs]

WORKMAN, BLAKE Blake, BB-TB, 5´11˝/185 lbs; Tulsa; B8/12/1908, D6/1983 Opelousas, LA **1934** SL 3 (3, BB)

| 1933 | Cin | 4 (1) | 7 | 11 | 1.6 | 0 | 2 | 19 | 9.5 | 0 | 6 | 0 | 0.0 | 0 | 0 | — | — | — | — | — | — | — | 0 | 21 |
| NFL | 2 | 7 (4) | 7 | 11 | 1.6 | 0 | 2 | 19 | 9.5 | 0 | 6 | 0 | 0.0 | 0 | 0 | — | — | — | — | — | — | — | 0 | 21 |

WORKMAN, HOGE Harry Hall, B, 5´11˝/173 lbs; Ohio State; B9/25/1899 Huntington, WV, D5/20/1972 Fort Myers, FL **[KC]** **1924** Cle☆9 (8, TB), 25 **1931** Cle 9 (5, TB), 2

| 1932 | NYG | 1 (0) | 1 | 1 | 1.0 (1) | 0 | — | — | — | — | — | — | — | — | — | — | — | — | — | — | — | — | 0 | 1 |
| NFL | 3 | 19 (13) | 1 | 1 | 1.0 (1) | 0 | — | — | — | — | — | — | — | — | — | — | — | — | — | — | K | — | 27 | 46 |

WORKMAN, VINCE Vincent Innocent, RB, 5´10˝/215 lbs; Ohio State; 1989: GB, rnd 5; B5/9/1968 Buffalo, NY

1989	GB	15 (0)	4	8	2.0 (3)	1	—	—	—	—	—	—	—	—	—	—	—	—	—	—	k	—	6	70
1990	GB	15 (0)	8	51	6.4 (31)	0	4	30	7.5 (9)	1	—	—	—	—	—	—	—	—	—	—	k	—	6	71
1991	GB	16 (0)	71	237	3.3 (30)	7	46	371	8.1 (25)	4	—	—	—	—	—	—	—	—	—	—	kp	—	66	527
1992	GB	10 (10, RB)	159	631	4.0 (44)	2	47	290	6.2 (21)	0	—	—	—	—	—	—	—	—	—	—	k	—	12	798
1993	TB	16 (11, FB)	78	284	3.6 (21)	2	54	411	7.6 (42)	0	—	—	—	—	—	—	—	—	—	—	k	—	24	512
1994	TB	15 (8, rb)	79	291	3.7 (18)	0	11	82	7.5 (23)	0	—	—	—	—	—	—	—	—	—	—	k	—	0	332
1995	Car	9 (0)	35	139	4.0 (14)	1	13	74	5.7 (14)	0	1	0	0.0								k	—	6	186
1995	Ind	1 (0)	9	26	2.9 (13)	0	—	—	—	—	—	—	—	—	—	—	—	—	—	—		—	0	26
1996	Ind	9 (0)	24	70	2.9 (11)	0	4	36	9.0 (18)	0	—	—	—	—	—	—	—	—	—	—		—	0	88
NFL	8	106 (29)	467	1737	3.7 (44)	13	179	1264	7.1	1	1	0	0.0	0	0	—	—	—	—	—	kp	—	120	2609

WORLEY, TIM Timothy Ashley, RB, 6´2˝/228 lbs; Georgia; 1989: Pit, rnd 1; B9/24/1966 Lumberton, NC

1989	†Pit	15 (14, RB)	195	770	3.9 (38)	5	15	113	7.5 (19)	0	—	—	—	—	—	—	—	—	—	—	—	—	30	877
1990	Pit	11 (8, RB)	109	418	3.8 (38)	0	8	70	8.8 (27)	0	—	—	—	—	—	—	—	—	—	—	—	—	0	453
1991	Pit	2 (0)	22	117	5.3 (16)	0	—	—	—	—	—	—	—	—	—	—	—	—	—	—	—	—	0	117
1993	Pit	5 (0)	10	33	3.3 (8)	0	3	13	4.3 (9)	0	—	—	—	—	—	—	—	—	—	—	k	—	0	65
1993	ChiB	10 (3)	110	437	4.0 (28)	2	8	49	6.1 (15)	0	—	—	—	—	—	—	—	—	—	—	k	—	12	488
1994	ChiB	5 (0)	9	17	1.9 (4)	1	1	8	8.0 (8)	0	—	—	—	—	—	—	—	—	—	—	k	—	6	23
NFL	5	48 (25)	455	1792	3.9 (38)	8	35	253	7.2 (27)	0	—	—	—	—	—	—	—	—	—	—	k	—	48	2022

WORRELL, CAMERON Cameron, DB, 5´11˝/199 lbs; Fresno State; B12/14/1979 Merced County, CA **2003** ChiB 14 (0) **2004** ChiB 13 (0) **NFL** 27 (0) [2 yrs]

WORTHAM, BARRON Barron Winfred, LB, 5´11˝/244 lbs; Texas-El Paso; 1994: Hou, rnd 6; B11/1/1969 Fort Worth, TX **1994** Hou 16 (1) **1995** Hou 16 (5, mlb)
1996 Hou 15 (14, MLB) **1997** Ten 16 (16, MLB) **1998** Ten 13 (0) **1999**†Ten 16 (15, MLB) **2000** Dal 16 (11, MLB) **NFL** 108 (62) [7 yrs]

WORTHAM, CORNELIUS James, LB, 6´1˝/234 lbs; Alabama; 2005: Sea, rnd 7; B1/25/1982 Calhoun City, MS **2005**†Sea 8 (0)

WORTHEN, NAZ Nasrallah Onea, WR, 5´8˝/177 lbs; North Carolina State; 1989: KC, rnd 3; B3/27/1966 Jacksonville, FL **1990** KC 9 (0)

YEAR	TEAM	G(GS, POS)	RUSH	YD	AVG(LG)	TD	REC	YD	AVG(LG)	TD	PASS	COMP	PCT	YD	AVG(LG)	TD	INT	SK	YD	QBR	KPR	OTD	PTS	TAY
1989	KC	10(1)	—	—	—	—	5	69	13.8(21)	0	—	—	—	—	—	—	—	—	—	—	kp	—	0	111
NFL	2	19(1)	—	—	—	—	5	69	13.8(21)	0	—	—	—	—	—	—	—	—	—	—	kp	—	0	227

WORTHEN, SHAWN Shawn, DT, 6´0˝/316 lbs; TCU; 2001: Min, rnd 4; B12/2/1975 San Antonio, TX **2001** Min 4 (0)

WORTMAN, KEITH Keith Delane, T-G-C, 6´2˝/260 lbs; Nebraska; 1972: GB, rnd 10; B7/20/1950 Billings, MT **1972**†GB 13 **1973** GB 8 **1974** GB 12 (12, lt) **1975** GB 13 (13, RG) **1976** SL 3 **1977** SL 14 (3) **1978** SL 14 (LT/rg) **1979** SL 13 (LT) **1980** SL 2 (2) **1981** SL 4 (3) **NFL** 96 (33) [10 yrs]

WOSTOUPAL, JOE Joseph, C, 6´3˝/208 lbs; Nebraska; B8/10/1903 West Point, NE, deceased **1926** KC 5 (4) **1928** Det☆8 (8, C) **1929** NYG☆15 (15, C) **1930** NYG☆15 (11, C) **NFL** 43 (38) [4 yrs]

WOUDENBERG, JOHN John William, T, 6´3˝/226 lbs; Denver; St. Mary's (CA); 1940: ChiB, rnd 6; B5/25/1918 Denver, CO, D5/3/2005 Denver, CO **1940** Pit 7 (0) **1941** Pit 11 (8, RT)

YEAR	TEAM	G(GS, POS)	RUSH	YD	AVG(LG)	TD	REC	YD	AVG(LG)	TD	PASS	COMP	PCT	YD	AVG(LG)	TD	INT	SK	YD	QBR	KPR	OTD	PTS	TAY
1942	Pit✧	11(11, RT)	—	—	—	—	1	-1	-1.0(-1)	0	—	—	—	—	—	—	—	—	—	—	—	—	0	-1
NFL	3	29(19)	—	—	—	—	1	-1	-1.0(-1)	0	—	—	—	—	—	—	—	—	—	—	—	—	0	-1

1946 SF-A 14 (14, RT) **1947** SF-A☆14 (14, RT) **1948** SF-A☆14 (14, RT) **1949**†SF-A 12 (10, RT) **AAFC** 29 (19) [3 yrs]

WOULFE, MIKE Michael Jerome, LB, 6´2˝/225 lbs; Colorado; 1962: Phi, rnd 15/SD, rnd 26; B8/14/1939 Chicago, IL **1962** Phi 13

WOZNIAK, JOHN John Edward, G-LB, 6´0˝/218 lbs; Alabama; 1948: Bkn-A, rnd 16/Pit, rnd 5; B8/2/1921 Arnold City, PA, D8/1982 Tuscaloosa, AL **1949**†NYY-A 12 (12, LG)

YEAR	TEAM	G(GS, POS)	RUSH	YD	AVG(LG)	TD	REC	YD	AVG(LG)	TD	PASS	COMP	PCT	YD	AVG(LG)	TD	INT	SK	YD	QBR	KPR	OTD	PTS	TAY
1948	Bkn-A	14(9, RG)	0	13	(13)	0	—	—	—	—	—	—	—	—	—	—	—	—	—	—	i	—	0	15
AAFC	2	26(21)	0	13	(13)	0	—	—	—	—	—	—	—	—	—	—	—	—	—	—	—	—	0	13

1950 NYY 12 (RG)

YEAR	TEAM	G(GS, POS)	RUSH	YD	AVG(LG)	TD	REC	YD	AVG(LG)	TD	PASS	COMP	PCT	YD	AVG(LG)	TD	INT	SK	YD	QBR	KPR	OTD	PTS	TAY
1951	NYY	12(RG)	—	—	—	—	1	4	4.0(4)	0	—	—	—	—	—	—	—	—	—	—	—	—	0	2
1952	DalT★	12(11, RG)	—	—	—	—	1	-1	-1.0(-1)	0	—	—	—	—	—	—	—	—	—	—	k	—	0	-12
NFL	3	36(11)	—	—	—	—	2	3	1.5(4)	0	—	—	—	—	—	—	—	—	—	—	k	—	0	-10

WRAGGE, TONY Tony James, G, 6´4˝/311 lbs; New Mexico State; B8/14/1979 Creighton, NE **2002** Arz 2 (1)

WRAY, LUD James R. Ludlow, C, 6´0˝/180 lbs; Pennsylvania; B2/7/1894 Philadelphia, PA, D7/24/1967 Philadelphia, PA **[C]** **1920** Buf 11 (6, C) **1921** Buf 7 (7, C) **NFL** 18 (13) [2 yrs]

WREN, DARRYL Daryl Tyrone, DB, 6´1˝/188 lbs; Pittsburg State; 1991: Buf, rnd 3; B1/25/1967 Tulsa, OK **1993** NE 12 (5, lcb) **1994** NE 8 (0) **NFL** 20 (5) [2 yrs]

WREN, JUNIOR Lowe, DB, 6´0˝/192 lbs; Missouri; 1952: Cle, rnd 24; B12/10/1929 Kansas City, MO, D10/28/2003 Miami, FL **1956** Cle 12 (db) **1957**†Cle 12 (DB) **1958**†Cle 12 (DB) **1959** Cle 12 (DB) **1960** Pit 12 (RCB) **1961** NYT-A 2 **NFL** 62 [6 yrs]

WRIGHSTER, GEORGE George Frederick, TE, 6´3˝/260 lbs; Oregon; 2003: Jax, rnd 4; B4/1/1981 Memphis, TN

YEAR	TEAM	G(GS, POS)	RUSH	YD	AVG(LG)	TD	REC	YD	AVG(LG)	TD	PASS	COMP	PCT	YD	AVG(LG)	TD	INT	SK	YD	QBR	KPR	OTD	PTS	TAY
2003	Jax	15(2)	—	—	—	—	13	150	11.5(30)	2	—	—	—	—	—	—	—	—	—	—	—	—	12	85
2004	Jax	4(3)	—	—	—	—	10	69	6.9(12)	1	—	—	—	—	—	—	—	—	—	—	—	—	6	40
2005	†Jax	16(6, te)	—	—	—	—	13	120	9.2(27)	2	—	—	—	—	—	—	—	—	—	—	—	—	12	70
NFL	3	35(11)	—	—	—	—	36	339	9.4(30)	5	—	—	—	—	—	—	—	—	—	—	—	—	30	195

WRIGHT, AB Albert Owen, TB, 6´1˝/190 lbs; Oklahoma State; B11/16/1905 Terlton, OK, D5/23/1995 Muskogee, OK **1930** Fra 4 (2)

WRIGHT, ADRIAN Adrian Douglas, RB, 6´1˝/230 lbs; Virginia Union; B10/13/1961 Charleston, WV

YEAR	TEAM	G(GS, POS)	RUSH	YD	AVG(LG)	TD	REC	YD	AVG(LG)	TD	PASS	COMP	PCT	YD	AVG(LG)	TD	INT	SK	YD	QBR	KPR	OTD	PTS	TAY
1987	TB	3(3)	37	112	3.0(11)	0	13	98	7.5(15)	1	—	—	—	—	—	—	—	—	—	—	k	—	6	168

WRIGHT, ALEXANDER Alexander, WR, 6´0˝/195 lbs; Auburn; 1990: Dal, rnd 2; B7/19/1967 Albany, GA **[R]**

YEAR	TEAM	G(GS, POS)	RUSH	YD	AVG(LG)	TD	REC	YD	AVG(LG)	TD	PASS	COMP	PCT	YD	AVG(LG)	TD	INT	SK	YD	QBR	KPR	OTD	PTS	TAY
1990	Dal	15(1)	3	26	8.7(14)	0	11	104	9.5(20)	0	—	—	—	—	—	—	—	—	—	—	k	1	6	184
1991	†Dal	16(5, wr)	2	-1	-0.5(3)	0	10	170	17.0(53)	0	—	—	—	—	—	—	—	—	—	—	kp	1	6	293
1992	Dal	3(0)	—	—	—	—	—	—	—	—	—	—	—	—	—	—	—	—	—	—	k	—	0	-3
1992	LARd	10(1)	—	—	—	—	12	175	14.6(41)	2	—	—	—	—	—	—	—	—	—	—	k	—	12	153
1993	†LARd	15(15, WR)	—	—	—	—	27	462	17.1(68)	4	—	—	—	—	—	—	—	—	—	—	k	—	24	268
1994	LARd	16(15, WR)	—	—	—	—	16	294	18.4(76)	2	—	—	—	—	—	—	—	—	—	—	k	—	12	289
1995	SL	8(7, wr)	1	17	17.0(17)	0	23	368	16.0(50)	2	—	—	—	—	—	—	—	—	—	—	—	—	12	211
1996	SL	3(0)	—	—	—	—	2	24	12.0(13)	0	—	—	—	—	—	—	—	—	—	—	—	—	0	12
NFL	7	86(44)	6	42	7.0(17)	0	101	1597	15.8(76)	10	—	—	—	—	—	—	—	—	—	—	kp	2	72	1407

WRIGHT, ALVIN Alvin, NT-DT-DE, 6´2˝/274 lbs; Jacksonville State; B2/5/1961 Wedowee, AL **1986** LARm 4 (0) **1987** LARm 15 (3) **1988**†LARm 16 (15, NT) **1989**†LARm 16 (16, NT) **1990** LARm☆16 (16, NT) **1991** LARm 13 (11, LDT) **1992** LARm 1 (1) **1992** Cle 3 (0) **NFL** 84 (62) [7 yrs]

WRIGHT, ANTHONY Anthony Lavron, QB, 6´1˝/211 lbs; South Carolina; B2/14/1976 Vanceboro, NC

YEAR	TEAM	G(GS, POS)	RUSH	YD	AVG(LG)	TD	REC	YD	AVG(LG)	TD	PASS	COMP	PCT	YD	AVG(LG)	TD	INT	SK	YD	QBR	KPR	OTD	PTS	TAY
2000	Dal	4(2)	12	36	3.0(19)	0	—	—	—	—	53	22	41.5	237	4.5(46)	0	3	12	92	—	—	—	0	35
2001	Dal	4(3)	17	57	3.4(12)	0	—	—	—	—	98	48	49.0	529	5.4(80)	5	5	5	30	—	—	—	0	147
2003	†Bal	7(7, qb)	28	73	2.6(17)	0	—	—	—	—	178	94	52.8	1199	6.7(64)	9	8	19	125	72.3	—	—	0	398
2005	Bal	9(7, qb)	18	68	3.8(22)	0	—	—	—	—	266	164	61.7	1582	5.9(48)	6	9	19	147	71.7	—	—	0	529
NFL	4	24(19)	75	234	3.1(22)	0	—	—	—	—	595	328	55.1	3547	6.0(80)	20	25	55	394	66.6	—	—	0	1108

WRIGHT, CHARLES Charles James, DB, 5´9˝/178 lbs; Tulsa; 1987: SL, rnd 10; B4/5/1964 Carthage, MO **1987** SL 3 (0) **1988** Dal 3 (0) **1988** TB 2 (0) **NFL** 8 (0) [2 yrs]

WRIGHT, DANA Dana Jerome, RB, 6´1˝/219 lbs; Kent State; Findlay; 1987: NYG, rnd 9; B6/2/1963 Ravenna, OH

YEAR	TEAM	G(GS, POS)	RUSH	YD	AVG(LG)	TD	REC	YD	AVG(LG)	TD	PASS	COMP	PCT	YD	AVG(LG)	TD	INT	SK	YD	QBR	KPR	OTD	PTS	TAY
1987	Cin	5(0)	24	74	3.1(10)	0	4	28	7.0(11)	0	—	—	—	—	—	—	—	—	—	—	k	—	0	159

WRIGHT, ELMO Elmo, WR, 6´0˝/190 lbs; Houston; 1971: KC, rnd 1; B7/3/1949 Brazoria, TX

YEAR	TEAM	G(GS, POS)	RUSH	YD	AVG(LG)	TD	REC	YD	AVG(LG)	TD	PASS	COMP	PCT	YD	AVG(LG)	TD	INT	SK	YD	QBR	KPR	OTD	PTS	TAY
1971	†KC	14(WR)	1	-10	-10.0(-10)	0	26	528	20.3(69)	3	—	—	—	—	—	—	—	—	—	—	—	—	18	269
1972	KC	7	1	24	24.0(24)	0	11	81	7.4(14)	0	—	—	—	—	—	—	—	—	—	—	—	—	0	65
1973	KC	11(WR)	5	29	5.8(13)	0	16	252	15.8(44)	2	—	—	—	—	—	—	—	—	—	—	—	—	12	165
1974	KC	13(WR)	3	26	8.7(17)	1	13	209	16.1(51)	1	—	—	—	—	—	—	—	—	—	—	—	—	12	146
1975	Hou	2	—	—	—	—	—	—	—	—	—	—	—	—	—	—	—	—	—	—	—	—	—	—
1975	NE	4(4)	—	—	—	—	4	46	11.5(20)	0	—	—	—	—	—	—	—	—	—	—	—	—	0	23
NFL	5	51(4)	10	69	6.9(24)	1	70	1116	15.9(69)	6	—	—	—	—	—	—	—	—	—	—	—	—	42	667

WRIGHT, ERIC Eric Cortez, DB, 6´1˝/183 lbs; Missouri; 1981: SF, rnd 2; B4/18/1959 St. Louis, MO **1981**†SF 16 (16, RCB) **1982** SF 7 (7, RCB) **1983**†SF☆16 (15, RCB) **1984**†SF★16 (14, RCB) **1985** SF★16 (16, RCB) **1986** SF 2 (1) **1987** SF 2 (2) **1988**†SF 15 (10, RCB) **1989**†SF 11 (1) **1990** SF 9 (0) **NFL** 110 (82) [10 yrs]

WRIGHT, ERIC Eric LaMon, WR, 6´0˝/196 lbs; Stephen F. Austin State; B8/4/1969 Pittsburg, TX **1991**†ChiB 0 (0)

YEAR	TEAM	G(GS, POS)	RUSH	YD	AVG(LG)	TD	REC	YD	AVG(LG)	TD	PASS	COMP	PCT	YD	AVG(LG)	TD	INT	SK	YD	QBR	KPR	OTD	PTS	TAY
1992	ChiB	13(0)	—	—	—	—	5	56	11.2(24)	0	—	—	—	—	—	—	—	—	—	—	—	—	0	28
NFL	2	13(0)	—	—	—	—	5	56	11.2(24)	0	—	—	—	—	—	—	—	—	—	—	—	—	0	28

WRIGHT, ERNIE Ernest Henry, T, 6´4˝/270 lbs; Ohio State; 1961: LA, rnd 15; B11/6/1939 Toledo, OH **1960**†LAC-A☆14 (LT) **1961**†SD-A★14 (LT) **1962** SD-A 14 (LT) **1963**†SD-A✧14 (LT) **1964**†SD-A 14 (LT) **1965**†SD-A✧14 (LT) **1966** SD-A 13 (LT) **1967** SD-A 14 (LT) **1968** Cin-A 14 (14, LT) **1969** Cin-A 14 (LT) **1970**†Cin 14 (LT) **1971** Cin 7 (LT) **1972** SD 14 **NFL** 174 (14) [13 yrs]

WRIGHT, FEARON Fearon, LB, 6´2˝/235 lbs; Rhode Island; B9/30/1978 Jamaica **2001** Min 7 (0)

WRIGHT, FELIX Felix Carl, DB, 6´2˝/190 lbs; Drake; B6/22/1959 Carthage, MO **[I]** **1985**†Cle 16 (0) **1986**†Cle 16 (0) **1987**†Cle 12 (7, FS) **1988**†Cle 16 (16, FS) **1989**†Cle 16 (16, SS) **1990** Cle 16 (16, SS) **1991** Min 16 (16, FS) **1992** Min 13 (13, FS) **1993**†KC 0 (0) **NFL** 121 (84) [9 yrs]

WRIGHT, GEORGE George Wayne, DT, 6´3˝/265 lbs; Sam Houston State; 1969: Bal, rnd 9; B3/3/1947 Houston, TX **1970**†Bal 2 **1971**†Bal 10 **1972** Cle 4 **NFL** 16 [3 yrs]

WRIGHT, GORDON Gordon Arnold, G, 6´3˝/248 lbs; Delaware State; B12/15/1943 East Meadow, NY **1967** Phi 3 **1969** NYJ-A 2 **NFL** 5 [2 yrs]

WRIGHT, JAMES James Willie, TE, 6´3˝/240 lbs; TCU; 1978: Atl, rnd 7; B9/1/1956 Fort Hood, TX

YEAR	TEAM	G(GS, POS)	RUSH	YD	AVG(LG)	TD	REC	YD	AVG(LG)	TD	PASS	COMP	PCT	YD	AVG(LG)	TD	INT	SK	YD	QBR	KPR	OTD	PTS	TAY
1978	†Atl	15	—	—	—	—	2	26	13.0(18)	0	—	—	—	—	—	—	—	—	—	—	k	—	0	14
1980	Den	1(0)	—	—	—	—	—	—	—	—	—	—	—	—	—	—	—	—	—	—	—	—	—	—
1981	Den	16(0)	1	11	11.0(11)	0	3	22	7.3(14)	1	—	—	—	—	—	—	—	—	—	—	—	—	6	27
1982	Den	9(3)	1	-4	-4.0(-4)	0	9	120	13.3(39)	1	—	—	—	—	—	—	—	—	—	—	—	—	6	61
1983	Den	6(6, te)	1	-11	-11.0(-11)	0	13	134	10.3(23)	0	—	—	—	—	—	—	—	—	—	—	—	—	0	56
1984	†Den	16(10, TE)	—	—	—	—	11	118	10.7(21)	1	—	—	—	—	—	—	—	—	—	—	—	—	6	64

YEAR	TEAM	G(GS, POS)	RUSH	YD	AVG(LG)	TD	REC	YD	AVG(LG)	TD	PASS	COMP	PCT	YD	AVG(LG)	TD	INT	SK	YD	QBR	KPR	OTD	PTS	TAY
1985	Den	16(12, TE)	—	—	—	—	28	246	8.8(30)	1	—	—	—	—	—	—	—	—	—	—	—	—	6	128
NFL	7	79(31)	3	-4	-1.3(11)	0	66	666	10.1(39)	4	—	—	—	—	—	—	—	—	—	—	k	—	24	350

WRIGHT, JASON Jason Gomillion, RB, 5´10˝/210 lbs; Northwestern; B7/12/1982 Upland, CA

YEAR	TEAM	G(GS, POS)	RUSH	YD	AVG(LG)	TD	REC	YD	AVG(LG)	TD	PASS	COMP	PCT	YD	AVG(LG)	TD	INT	SK	YD	QBR	KPR	OTD	PTS	TAY
2004	Atl	2(0)	3	10	3.3(8)	0	—	—	—	—	—	—	—	—	—	—	—	—	—	—	—	—	0	10
2005	Cle	3(0)	11	27	2.5(6)	1	3	15	5.0(15)	0	—	—	—	—	—	—	—	—	—	—	k	—	6	47
NFL	2	5(0)	14	37	2.6(8)	1	3	15	5.0(15)	0	—	—	—	—	—	—	—	—	—	—	k	—	6	57

WRIGHT, JEFF Jeffrey Ralph, DB, 5´11˝/190 lbs; Minnesota; 1971: Min, rnd 15; B6/13/1949 Edina, MN **1971**†Min 14 **1972** Min 13 **1973**†Min 14 (14, SS) **1974**†Min 11 (10, SS) **1975** Min 3 (2) **1976**†Min 14 (14, SS) **1977**†Min 14 (14, SS) **NFL** 83 (54) [7 yrs]

WRIGHT, JEFF Jeff Dee, NT, 6´2˝/274 lbs; Tulsa; Central Missouri State; 1988: Buf, rnd 8; B6/13/1963 San Bernardino, CA **1988**†Buf 15 (0) **1989**†Buf 15 (0) **1990**†Buf 16 (16, NT) **1991**†Buf 9 (9, NT) **1992**†Buf 16 (16, NT) **1993**†Buf 15 (15, NT) **1994** Buf 12 (11, NT) **NFL** 98 (67) [7 yrs]

WRIGHT, JIM Jim Sid, G, 6´1˝/222 lbs; Texas-Arlington; SMU; 1944: Bkn, rnd 13/1947: Bkn-A, rnd 4; B9/12/1921 Sulphur Springs, TX **1947** Bos 12 (2)

WRIGHT, JIM James Earl, DB, 5´11˝/190 lbs; Memphis; 1961: Bos, rnd 14/Phi, rnd 3; B3/27/1939 Columbus, MS **1964** Den-A 10

WRIGHT, JOHN John Oliver, B, 5´11˝/225 lbs; Maryland; Georgia; 1947: NYG, rnd 30; B7/13/1921 Baltimore, MD, D5/30/2000 Salisbury, MD

YEAR	TEAM	G(GS, POS)	RUSH	YD	AVG(LG)	TD	REC	YD	AVG(LG)	TD	PASS	COMP	PCT	YD	AVG(LG)	TD	INT	SK	YD	QBR	KPR	OTD	PTS	TAY
1947	Bal-A	13(0)	38	113	3.0	0	—	—	—	—	—	—	—	—	—	—	—	—	—	—	i	—	0	113

WRIGHT, JOHN John William, WR, 6´0˝/197 lbs; Illinois; 1968: Atl, rnd 2; B1/11/1946 Oak Park, IL **1968** Atl 5

YEAR	TEAM	G(GS, POS)	RUSH	YD	AVG(LG)	TD	REC	YD	AVG(LG)	TD	PASS	COMP	PCT	YD	AVG(LG)	TD	INT	SK	YD	QBR	KPR	OTD	PTS	TAY
1969	Det	14	—	—	—	—	12	130	10.8(26)	2	—	—	—	—	—	—	—	—	—	—	—	1	18	75
NFL	2	19	—	—	—	—	12	130	10.8(26)	2	—	—	—	—	—	—	—	—	—	—	—	1	18	75

WRIGHT, JOHNNIE John Lee, RB, 6´2˝/210 lbs; South Carolina; 1982: Bal, rnd 12; B9/13/1958 Fort Myers, FL

YEAR	TEAM	G(GS, POS)	RUSH	YD	AVG(LG)	TD	REC	YD	AVG(LG)	TD	PASS	COMP	PCT	YD	AVG(LG)	TD	INT	SK	YD	QBR	KPR	OTD	PTS	TAY
1982	Bal	7(0)	1	3	3.0(3)	0	1	12	12.0(12)	0	—	—	—	—	—	—	—	—	—	—	—	—	0	9

WRIGHT, KEITH William Keith, WR, 5´10˝/172 lbs; Memphis; 1978: Cle, rnd 5; B1/30/1956 Mercedes, TX **[R]**

YEAR	TEAM	G(GS, POS)	RUSH	YD	AVG(LG)	TD	REC	YD	AVG(LG)	TD	PASS	COMP	PCT	YD	AVG(LG)	TD	INT	SK	YD	QBR	KPR	OTD	PTS	TAY
1978	Cle☆	16	—	—	—	—	8	76	9.5(20)	0	—	—	—	—	—	—	—	—	—	—	kp	—	0	480
1979	Cle	5	—	—	—	—	1	13	13.0(13)	0	—	—	—	—	—	—	—	—	—	—	kp	—	0	174
1980	†Cle	12(0)	—	—	—	—	3	62	20.7(39)	3	—	—	—	—	—	—	—	—	—	—	kp	—	18	231
NFL	3	33	—	—	—	—	12	151	12.6(39)	3	—	—	—	—	—	—	—	—	—	—	kp	—	18	885

WRIGHT, KENNY Kenneth D., DB, 6´1˝/205 lbs; Arkansas; Northwestern State (LA); 1999: Min, rnd 4; B9/14/1977 Ruston, LA **1999**†Min 16 (12, LCB) **2000**†Min 16 (6, lcb) **2001** Min 15 (8, lcb) **2002** Hou 16 (0) **2003** Hou 15 (5, lcb) **2004** Hou 16 (0) **2005**†Jax 16 (16, RCB) **NFL** 110 (47) [7 yrs]

WRIGHT, KENYATTA Kenyatta Terrell, LB, 6´0˝/240 lbs; Oklahoma State; B2/19/1978 Vian, OK **2000** Buf 16 (1) **2001** Buf 11 (1) **2003** NYJ 16 (0) **2004**†NYJ 16 (0) **2005** NYJ 15 (0) **NFL** 74 (2) [5 yrs]

WRIGHT, LAWRENCE Lawrence D., DB, 6´2˝/209 lbs; Florida; B9/6/1973 Miami, FL **1997** Cin 4 (0) **1999** Cin 14 (0) **NFL** 18 (0) [2 yrs]

WRIGHT, LONNIE Lawrence, DB, 6´2˝/205 lbs; Colorado State; B1/23/1945 Newark, NJ **1967** Den-A 12

YEAR	TEAM	G(GS, POS)	RUSH	YD	AVG(LG)	TD	REC	YD	AVG(LG)	TD	PASS	COMP	PCT	YD	AVG(LG)	TD	INT	SK	YD	QBR	KPR	OTD	PTS	TAY
1966	Den-A	14(LS)	—	—	—	—	1	-2	-2.0(-2)	0	—	—	—	—	—	—	—	—	—	—	i	—	0	9
NFL	2	26	—	—	—	—	1	-2	-2.0(-2)	0	—	—	—	—	—	—	—	—	—	—	i	—	0	11

WRIGHT, LOUIS Louis Donnel, DB, 6´2˝/200 lbs; Arizona State; San Jose State; 1975: Den, rnd 1; B1/31/1953 Gilmer, TX **[I]** **1975** Den 11 (11, LCB) **1976** Den 14 (14, LCB) **1977**†Den★14 (14, LCB) **1978**†Den★16 (16, LCB) **1979**†Den★16 (16, LCB) **1980** Den☆15 (15, LCB) **1981** Den☆8 (8, LCB) **1982** Den 9 (9, LCB) **1983**†Den★16 (16, LCB) **1984**†Den☆16 (15, LCB) **1985** Den★15 (15, LCB) **1986**†Den 16 (16, LCB) **NFL** 166 (165) [12 yrs]

WRIGHT, MANUEL Manuel, DT, 6´6˝/329 lbs; USC; B4/13/1984 Compton, CA **2005** Mia 3 (0)

WRIGHT, MIKE Mike, DT-DE, 6´4˝/295 lbs; Cincinnati; B3/1/1982 Cincinnati, OH **2005** NE 13 (0)

WRIGHT, NATE Nathaniel, DB, 5´11˝/180 lbs; San Diego State; B12/21/1946 Madison, FL **[I]** **1969** Atl 3 **1969** SL 10 (RCB) **1970** SL 14 **1971** Min 3 **1972** Min 14 **1973**†Min 14 (14, LCB) **1975**†Min 14 (14, LCB) **1976**†Min☆14 (13, LCB) **1977**†Min 14 (14, LCB) **1978** Min 16 (16, LCB) **1979** Min 10 **1980** Min 16 (4)

YEAR	TEAM	G(GS, POS)	RUSH	YD	AVG(LG)	TD	REC	YD	AVG(LG)	TD	PASS	COMP	PCT	YD	AVG(LG)	TD	INT	SK	YD	QBR	KPR	OTD	PTS	TAY
1974	†Min☆	14(14, LCB)	—	—	—	—	1	6	6.0(6)	0	—	—	—	—	—	—	—	—	—	—	i	—	0	64
NFL	12	156(89)	—	—	—	—	1	6	6.0(6)	0	—	—	—	—	—	—	—	—	—	—	kpi	1	6	183

WRIGHT, RALPH Ralph, T, 6´0˝/230 lbs; Kentucky; B1/16/1908 Sturgis, KY, deceased **1933** Bkn 6 (0)

WRIGHT, RANDY Randall Steven, QB, 6´2˝/200 lbs; Wisconsin; 1984: GB, rnd 6; B1/12/1961 St. Charles, IL

YEAR	TEAM	G(GS, POS)	RUSH	YD	AVG(LG)	TD	REC	YD	AVG(LG)	TD	PASS	COMP	PCT	YD	AVG(LG)	TD	INT	SK	YD	QBR	KPR	OTD	PTS	TAY
1984	GB	8(1)	8	11	1.4(5)	0	—	—	—	—	62	27	43.5	310	5.0(56)	2	6	4	17	—	—	—	0	-64
1985	GB	5(1)	8	8	1.0(8)	0	—	—	—	—	74	39	52.7	552	7.5(38)	2	4	8	67	—	—	—	0	134
1986	GB	16(16, QB)	18	41	2.3(18)	1	—	—	—	—	492	263	53.5	3247	6.6(62)	17	**23**	33	243	66.2	—	—	6	840
1987	GB	9(7, QB)	13	70	5.4(27)	0	—	—	—	—	247	132	53.4	1507	6.1(66)	6	11	20	128	61.6	—	—	0	414
1988	GB	8(7, qb)	8	43	5.4(19)	2	—	—	—	—	244	141	57.8	1490	6.1(51)	4	13	31	176	58.9	—	—	12	308
NFL	5	46(32)	55	173	3.1(27)	3	—	—	—	—	1119	602	53.8	7106	6.4(66)	31	57	96	631	61.4	—	—	18	1631

WRIGHT, RAYFIELD Larry Rayfield, T-TE, 6´6˝/255 lbs; Fort Valley State; 1967: Dal, rnd 7; B8/23/1945 Griffin, GA; HOF 2006 **1967** Dal 10 **1970**†Dal 14 (RT) **1971**†Dal★14 (RT) **1972**†Dal★14 (RT) **1973**†Dal★12 (RT) **1974** Dal★14 (RT) **1975**†Dal★13 (RT) **1976**†Dal★14 (14, RT) **1977**†Dal 2 **1978**†Dal 15 (11, RT) **1979**†Dal 16 (5, rt)

YEAR	TEAM	G(GS, POS)	RUSH	YD	AVG(LG)	TD	REC	YD	AVG(LG)	TD	PASS	COMP	PCT	YD	AVG(LG)	TD	INT	SK	YD	QBR	KPR	OTD	PTS	TAY
1968	†Dal	14	1	-10	-10.0(-10)	0	1	15	15.0(15)	1	—	—	—	—	—	—	—	—	—	—	—	—	6	3
1969	†Dal	14(3)	—	—	—	—	1	12	12.0(12)	0	—	—	—	—	—	—	—	—	—	—	—	—	0	6
NFL	13	166(33)	1	-10	-10.0(-10)	0	2	27	13.5(15)	1	—	—	—	—	—	—	—	—	—	—	—	—	6	9

WRIGHT, STEVE Stephen Thomas, T, 6´6˝/250 lbs; Alabama; 1964: GB, rnd 5/NYJ, rnd 8; B7/17/1942 Birmingham, AL **1964** GB 14 **1965**†GB 14 (RT) **1966**†GB 14 **1967**†GB 14 **1968** NYG 10 (RT) **1969** NYG 2 **1970** Was 14 (1) **1971** ChiB 14 (RT) **1972** SL 5 **NFL** 101 (1) [9 yrs]

WRIGHT, STEVE Stephen Hough, T-G-TE, 6´6˝/271 lbs; Northern Iowa; B4/8/1959 St. Louis, MO **1981**†Dal 16 (0) **1982**†Dal 9 (0) **1983** Bal 13 (10, RG) **1984** Ind 12 (9, LT) **1987** LARd 9 (6, rt) **1988** LARd 15 (3) **1989** LARd 16 (3) **1990**†LARd 16 (16, RT) **1991**†LARd 16 (16, RT) **1992** LARd 7 (4) **NFL** 129 (67) [10 yrs]

WRIGHT, SYLVESTER Sylvester L., DE-LB, 6´2˝/258 lbs; Kansas; B12/30/1971 Detroit, MI **1995** Phi 6 (0) **1996**†Phi 16 (0) **NFL** 22 (0) [2 yrs]

WRIGHT, TED Weldon H., HB-QB, 6´0˝/185 lbs; North Texas; B11/15/1913 Savoy, TX **[K]**

YEAR	TEAM	G(GS, POS)	RUSH	YD	AVG(LG)	TD	REC	YD	AVG(LG)	TD	PASS	COMP	PCT	YD	AVG(LG)	TD	INT	SK	YD	QBR	KPR	OTD	PTS	TAY
1934	Bos	10(2)	19	123	6.5(59)	1	1	25	25.0(25)	0	4	1	25.0	25	6.3(25)	0	1	—	—	—	K	—	8	118
1935	Bos	6(1)	15	43	2.9	0	—	—	—	—	18	4	22.2	51	2.8	0	1	—	—	—	—	—	0	29
1935	Bkn	3(0)	—	—	—	—	—	—	—	—	—	—	—	—	—	—	—	—	—	—	—	—	—	—
NFL	2	19(3)	34	166	4.9(59)	1	1	25	25.0(25)	0	22	5	22.7	76	3.5(25)	0	2	—	—	—	K	—	8	147

WRIGHT, TERRY Terry Leon, DB, 6´0˝/195 lbs; Temple; B7/17/1964 Phoenix, AZ **1987**†Ind 13 (2) **1988** Ind 8 (0) **NFL** 21 (2) [2 yrs]

WRIGHT, TOBY Toby Lin, DB, 5´11˝/212 lbs; Nebraska; 1994: LARm, rnd 2; B11/19/1970 Phoenix, AZ **1994** LARm 16 (2) **1996** SL 12 (12, SS) **1997** SL 11 (11, SS) **1998** SL 3 (3) **1999** Was 1 (0)

YEAR	TEAM	G(GS, POS)	RUSH	YD	AVG(LG)	TD	REC	YD	AVG(LG)	TD	PASS	COMP	PCT	YD	AVG(LG)	TD	INT	SK	YD	QBR	KPR	OTD	PTS	TAY
1995	SL	16(16, SS)	1	9	9.0(9)	0	—	—	—	—	—	—	—	—	—	—	—	—	—	—	iS	1	6	58
NFL	6	59(44)	1	9	9.0(9)	0	—	—	—	—	—	—	—	—	—	—	—	—	—	—	iS	3	18	82

WRIGHT, WILLIE Willie Don, TE, 6´4˝/239 lbs; Wyoming; B3/9/1968 Riverton, WY **1992** Phx 9 (0)

WRIGHTMAN, TIM Timothy John, TE, 6´3˝/237 lbs; UCLA; 1982: Chi, rnd 3; B3/27/1960 Los Angeles, CA

YEAR	TEAM	G(GS, POS)	RUSH	YD	AVG(LG)	TD	REC	YD	AVG(LG)	TD	PASS	COMP	PCT	YD	AVG(LG)	TD	INT	SK	YD	QBR	KPR	OTD	PTS	TAY
1985	†ChiB	16(3)	—	—	—	—	24	407	17.0(49)	1	—	—	—	—	—	—	—	—	—	—	—	—	6	209
1986	†ChiB	16(0)	—	—	—	—	22	241	11.0(29)	0	—	—	—	—	—	—	—	—	—	—	—	—	0	121
NFL	2	32(3)	—	—	—	—	46	648	14.1(49)	1	—	—	—	—	—	—	—	—	—	—	—	—	6	329

WUERFFEL, DANNY Daniel Carl, QB, 6´1˝/212 lbs; Florida; 1997: NO, rnd 4; B5/27/1974 Fort Walton Beach, FL

YEAR	TEAM	G(GS, POS)	RUSH	YD	AVG(LG)	TD	REC	YD	AVG(LG)	TD	PASS	COMP	PCT	YD	AVG(LG)	TD	INT	SK	YD	QBR	KPR	OTD	PTS	TAY
1997	NO	7(2)	6	26	4.3(10)	0	—	—	—	—	91	42	46.2	518	5.7(47)	4	8	18	116	—	—	—	0	-15
1998	NO	5(4)	11	60	5.5(18)	0	—	—	—	—	119	62	52.1	695	5.8(64)	5	5	23	131	66.3	—	—	0	233
1999	NO	4(0)	2	29	14.5(29)	1	—	—	—	—	48	22	45.8	191	4.0(22)	0	3	5	32	—	—	—	6	15
2000	GB	1(0)	2	-2	-1.0(-1)	0	—	—	—	—	—	—	—	—	—	—	—	—	—	—	—	—	0	-2
2001	ChiB	1(0)	—	—	—	—	—	—	—	—	—	—	—	—	—	—	—	—	—	—	—	—	—	—
2002	Was	7(4)	10	76	7.6(26)	0	—	—	—	—	92	58	63.0	719	7.8(40)	3	6	11	83	—	—	—	0	211
NFL	6	25(10)	31	189	6.1(29)	1	—	—	—	—	350	184	52.6	2123	6.1(64)	12	22	57	362	56.4	—	—	6	441

YEAR	TEAM	G (GS, POS)	RUSH	YD	AVG(LG)	TD	REC	YD	AVG(LG)	TD	PASS COMP	PCT	YD	AVG(LG)	TD	INT	SK	YD	QBR	KPR	OTD	PTS	TAY

WUKITS, AL Albert Robert, C-LB-G, 6´3˝/218 lbs; Duquesne; 1943: Pit, rnd 11; B12/16/1917 Millvale, PA, D10/15/1978 Pittsburgh, PA **1943** P-P 10 (1) **1944** C-P 10 (3)
1945 Pit 3 (1) **NFL** 23 (5) [3 yrs]

1946 Buf-A 8 (5, c) **1946** Mia-A 7 (2) **AAFC** 15 (7) [1 yr]

WULFF, JIM James Francis, DB-HB, 5´10˝/184 lbs; Michigan State; 1958: Cle, rnd 6; B3/22/1936 Chicago, IL, D2/19/2000 Williamsburg, MI **1960** Was 9

| 1961 | Was | 8 (lcb) | — | — | — | — | 1 | 6 | 6.0(6) | 0 | — | — | — | — | — | — | — | — | — | i | — | 0 | -1 |
| NFL | | 2 | 17 | | — | — | — | 1 | 6 | 6.0(6) | 0 | — | — | — | — | — | — | — | — | — | — | 0 | 3 |

WUNSCH, HARRY Harry Frederick, G, 5´11˝/212 lbs; Notre Dame; B11/20/1910 Chicago, IL, D4/1954 **1934** GB 2 (0)

WUNSCH, JERRY Gerald, T-G, 6´6˝/339 lbs; Wisconsin; 1997: TB, rnd 2; B1/21/1974 Eau Claire, WI **1997**†TB 16 (0) **1998** TB 16 (1) **1999**†TB 16 (13, RT) **2000**†TB 16 (16, RT)
2001†TB 16 (16, RT) **2002** Sea 15 (5, rt) **2003** Sea 12 (0) **2004**†Sea 5 (0) **NFL** 112 (51) [8 yrs]

WYANT, FRED Frederick Mount, QB, 6´0˝/200 lbs; West Virginia; 1956: Was, rnd 3; B4/26/1934 Weston, WV

| 1956 | Was | 10 | — | — | — | — | — | — | — | — | 2 | 1 | 50.0 | 17 | 8.5(17) | 0 | 0 | — | — | — | — | 0 | 9 |

WYATT, ALVIN Alvin B., DB, 5´10˝/184 lbs; Bethune-Cookman; 1970: Oak, rnd 6; B12/13/1947 Jacksonville, FL **1970** Oak 11 **1971** Buf 14 (RCB) **1972** Buf 14 (fs) **1973** Hou 4
NFL 43 [4 yrs]

WYATT, ANTWUAN Antwaun Bernard, WR, 5´10˝/193 lbs; Bethune-Cookman; 1997: Phi, rnd 6; B7/18/1975 Daytona Beach, FL **1997** Phi 1 (0)

WYATT, DOUG John Douglas, DB, 6´1˝/195 lbs; Tulsa; 1970: NO, rnd 17; B10/18/1946 Tyler, TX **1970** NO 14 (LCB) **1971** NO 12 (FS) **1972** NO 14 (FS) **1973** Det 6
1974 Det 12 (5, ss) **NFL** 58 (5) [5 yrs]

WYATT, KERVIN Kervin Doran, LB, 6´1˝/235 lbs; Maryland; B10/17/1957 Washington, DC **1980** NYG 4 (3)

WYATT, KEVIN Kevin Michael, DB, 5´10˝/199 lbs; Arkansas; 1986: Mia, rnd 5; B3/14/1964 Norfolk, VA **1986** SD 16 (0) **1987** KC 2 (0) **NFL** 18 (0) [2 yrs]

WYATT, WILLIE Willie Porter, NT, 5´11˝/275 lbs; Alabama; B9/27/1967 Birmingham, AL **1990** TB 7 (3)

WYCHE, SAM Samuel David, QB, 6´4˝/218 lbs; Furman; B1/5/1945 Atlanta, GA [C]

1968	Cin-A	3	12	74	6.2(21)	0	1	5	5.0(5)	0	55	35	63.6	494	9.0(80)	2	2	11	68	—	—	—	0	254
1969	Cin-A	7	12	107	8.9(22)	1	—	—	—	—	108	54	50.0	838	7.8(80)	7	4	28	180	82.3	—	—	6	411
1970	†Cin	14	19	118	6.2(23)	2	—	—	—	—	57	26	45.6	411	7.2(51)	3	2	10	73	—	—	—	12	279
1971	Was	1	1	4	4.0(4)	0	—	—	—	—	—	—	—	—	—	—	—	—	—	—	—	—	0	4
1972	†Was	7	—	—	—	—	—	—	—	—	—	—	—	—	—	—	—	—	—	—	—	—		
1974	Det	14	1	0	0.0(0)	0	—	—	—	—	1	0	0.0	0	0	0	1	—	—	—	—	—	0	-40
1976	SL	1	—	—	—	—	—	—	—	—	1	1	100.0	5	5.0(5)	0	0	—	—	—	—	—	0	3
NFL		7	47	45	303	6.7(23)	3	1	5	5.0(5)	0	222	116	52.3	1748	7.9(80)	12	9	49	321	79.6	—	—	18	910

WYCHECK, FRANK Frank John, TE, 6´3˝/253 lbs; Maryland; 1993: Was, rnd 6; B10/14/1971 Philadelphia, PA

1993	Was	9 (7, TE)	—	—	—	—	16	113	7.1(20)	0	—	—	—	—	—	—	—	—	—	—	—	0	57
1994	Was	9 (1)	—	—	—	—	7	55	7.9(20)	1	—	—	—	—	—	—	—	—	—	k	—	6	57
1995	Hou	16 (10, TE)	1	1	1.0(1)	1	40	471	11.8(36)	1	—	—	—	—	—	—	—	—	—	k	—	12	252
1996	Hou	16 (16, TE)	2	3	1.5(3)	0	53	511	9.6(29)	6	—	—	—	—	—	—	—	—	—	k	—	36	264
1997	Ten	16 (16, TE)	—	—	—	—	63	748	11.9(42)	4	—	—	—	—	—	—	—	—	—	k	—	26	382
1998	Ten◇	16 (16, TE)	—	—	—	—	70	768	11.0(38)	2	—	—	—	—	—	—	—	—	—	k	—	12	389
1999	†Ten◇	16 (16, TE)	—	—	—	—	69	641	9.3(35)	2	1	1	100.0	61	61.0(61)	1	0	—	—	—	—	—	12	366
2000	†Ten★	16 (16, TE)	—	—	—	—	70	636	9.1(26)	4	2	2	100.0	53	26.5(30)	1	0	—	—	—	—	—	24	370
2001	Ten	16 (16, TE)	1	1	1.0(1)	0	60	672	11.2(30)	4	1	1	100.0	21	21.0(21)	0	0	—	—	—	—	—	24	368
2002	†Ten	15 (15, TE)	—	—	—	—	40	346	8.6(19)	2	2	1	50.0	13	6.5(13)	0	0	—	—	—	—	—	12	190
2003	†Ten	10 (6, te)	—	—	—	—	17	165	9.7(25)	2	—	—	—	—	—	—	—	—	—	—	—	12	93
NFL		11	155 (135)	4	5	1.3(3)	1	505	5126	10.2(42)	28	6	5	83.3	148	24.7(61)	2	0	—	—	k	—	176	2784

WYCINSKI, CRAIG Craig Peter, G, 6´3˝/243 lbs; Michigan State; 1970: Cle, rnd 7; B1/4/1948 Detroit, MI **1972** Cle 6

WYCOFF, DOUG Stephen Douglas, B, 6´0˝/206 lbs; Georgia Tech; B9/16/1903 St. Louis, MO, D10/27/1981 Atlanta, GA [KC] **1927** NYG 11 (9, BB), 19 **1929** SI☆9 (7, BB), 12
1930 SI 12 (7, fb), 24 **1931** NYG 12 (11, BB), 12

1932	SI	12 (11, BB)	135	454	3.4	1	—	—	—	—	31	10	32.3	140	4.5	0	2	—	—	—	—	—	6	454
1934	Bos	12 (5, fb)	106	326	3.1	—	—	—	—	—	30	6	20.0	93	3.1	1	7	—	—	—	—	—	6	108
NFL		6	68 (50)	241	780	3.2	11	—	—	—	—	61	16	26.2	233	3.8	8	9	—	—	K	—	2	79	707

WYDO, FRANK Frank, T-DT, 6´4˝/225 lbs; Duquesne; Cornell; 1947: Pit, rnd 5/Buf-A, rnd 25; B6/15/1924 Footedale, PA, D2/17/1979 Uniontown, PA **1947**†Pit 12 (7, RT)
1948 Pit 12 (9, RT) **1950** Pit 12 (RT) **1951** Pit 12 (RT) **1952** Phi 12 (12, LT) **1953** Phi☆12 (12, LT) **1954** Phi 12 (12, LT) **1955** Phi 12 (LT) **1956** Phi 12 (RT) **1957** Phi 12

| 1949 | Pit | 12 (11, RT) | — | — | — | — | 2 | 21 | 10.5(12) | 0 | — | — | — | — | — | — | — | — | — | — | — | 0 | 11 |
| NFL | | 11 | 68 (63) | — | — | — | — | 2 | 21 | 10.5(12) | 0 | — | — | — | — | — | — | — | — | — | ki | — | 0 | -6 |

WYHONIC, JOHN John N., aka John Wyhowanec, G, 6´0˝/213 lbs; Alabama; 1942: Phi, rnd 14; B12/23/1919 Tiltonville, OH, D7/19/1989 Arcadia, FL **1946** Phi 11 (2)
1947†Phi 12 (2) **NFL** 23 (4) [2 yrs]

1948†Buf-A 13 (1) **1949** Buf-A 3 (0) **AAFC** 16 (1) [2 yrs]

WYKOFF, LEE Lee Arlo, FB-HB, 6´1˝/195 lbs; Washburn; B3/10/1898 Marietta, KS, D4/30/1974 Kansas City, MO **1923** SL 4 (0)

WYLAND, PUDGE Guido B., G, 5´10˝/180 lbs; Iowa; B6/5/1891 Minden, IA, D12/8/1974 Moline, IL **1920** RI 9 (5, LG)

WYMAN, ARNIE Arnold Douglas, FB-HB, 5´11˝/172 lbs; Minnesota; B8/20/1895 Minneapolis, MN, D3/4/1961 Hennepin County, MN **1920** RI 6 (6, FB)

WYMAN, DAVID David Matthew, LB, 6´2˝/248 lbs; Stanford; 1987: Sea, rnd 2; B3/31/1964 San Diego, CA **1987**†Sea 4 (0) **1988**†Sea 16 (16, RILB) **1989** Sea 16 (16, RILB)
1990 Sea 8 (8, mlb) **1991** Sea 6 (5, mlb) **1992** Sea 11 (11, MLB) **1994** Den 4 (0) **1995** Den 11 (11, MLB)

| 1993 | †Den | 16 (16, RILB) | — | — | — | — | 1 | 1 | 1.0(1) | 1 | — | — | — | — | — | — | — | — | — | iS | — | 6 | 10 |
| NFL | | 9 | 92 (83) | — | — | — | — | 1 | 1 | 1.0(1) | 1 | — | — | — | — | — | — | — | — | — | iS | — | 6 | 24 |

WYMAN, DEVIN Devin Edward, DT, 6´7˝/290 lbs; Kentucky State; 1996: NE, rnd 6; B8/29/1973 East Palo Alto, CA **1996** NE 9 (4) **1997** NE 6 (0) **NFL** 15 (4) [2 yrs]

WYMS, ELLIS Ellis Rashad, DE, 6´3˝/279 lbs; Mississippi State; 2001: TB, rnd 6; B4/12/1979 Indianola, MS **2001**†TB 4 (0) **2002**†TB 14 (0) **2003** TB 13 (0) **2004** TB 6 (0)
2005†TB 16 (1) **NFL** 53 (1) [5 yrs]

WYNN, DEXTER Dexter, DB, 5´9˝/165 lbs; Colorado State; 2004: Phi, rnd 6; B2/25/1981 Sumter, SC **2004**†Phi 12 (0) **2005** Phi 10 (0) **NFL** 22 (0) [2 yrs]

WYNN, MILTON Milton Thomas, WR, 6´2˝/207 lbs; Washington State; 2001: SL, rnd 4; B9/21/1978 Mission Hills, CA **2002** Bal 3 (0)

| 2001 | TB | 1 (0) | — | — | — | — | 4 | 69 | 17.3(36) | 0 | — | — | — | — | — | — | — | — | — | — | — | 0 | 35 |
| NFL | | 2 | 4 (0) | — | — | — | — | 4 | 69 | 17.3(36) | 0 | — | — | — | — | — | — | — | — | — | — | — | 0 | 35 |

WYNN, RENALDO Renaldo Lavalle, DE-DT, 6´3˝/292 lbs; Notre Dame; 1997: Jax, rnd 1; B9/3/1974 Chicago, IL **1997**†Jax 16 (8, LDT) **1998** Jax 15 (15, RDE/rdt)
1999†Jax 12 (10, LDE) **2000** Jax 14 (14, LDE) **2001** Jax 16 (16, LDE) **2002** Was 16 (16, LDE) **2003** Was 16 (16, RDE) **2004** Was 16 (16, LDE) **2005**†Was 16 (15, LDE)
NFL 137 (126) [9 yrs]

WYNN, SPERGON Spergon, QB, 6´3˝/226 lbs; Minnesota; Southwest Texas State; 2000: Cle, rnd 6; B8/10/1978 Houston, TX

2000	Cle	7 (1)	3	15	5.0(11)	0	—	—	—	—	54	22	40.7	167	3.1(32)	0	1	13	89	—	—	—	0	59
2001	Min	3 (2)	8	61	7.6(14)	0	—	—	—	—	98	48	49.0	418	4.3(47)	1	6	10	65	—	—	—	0	35
NFL		2	10 (3)	11	76	6.9(14)	0	—	—	—	—	152	70	46.1	585	3.8(47)	1	7	23	154	—	—	—	0	94

WYNN, WILL William, DE, 6´4˝/245 lbs; Tennessee State; 1973: Phi, rnd 7; B1/15/1949 Apex, NC **1973** Phi 12 (RDE) **1974** Phi 14 (LDE) **1975** Phi 14 (13, LDE)
1976 Phi 14 (14, RDE) **1977** Was 1 **NFL** 55 (27) [5 yrs]

WYNNE, CHET Chester Allen, FB-TB, 6´0˝/180 lbs; Notre Dame; B11/23/1898, D7/17/1967 Chicago, IL **1922** Roc 2 (2, FB)

WYNNE, ELMER Elmer Burton, FB, 6´1˝/193 lbs; Nebraska; Notre Dame; B1/20/1901 Long Island, KS, D11/9/1989 Brush, CO **1928** ChiB 10 (2) **1929** Day 5 (5, FB)
NFL 15 (7) [2 yrs]

YEAR	TEAM	G (GS, POS)	RUSH	YD	AVG(LG)	TD	REC	YD	AVG(LG)	TD	PASS COMP	PCT	YD	AVG(LG)	TD	INT	SK	YD	QBR	KPR	OTD	PTS	TAY

WYNNE, HARRY — Harry Clayton, E, 6´4˝/203 lbs; Arkansas; 1943: Pit, rnd 24; B7/10/1920 Senatobia, MS, D11/28/1989

1944	Bos	10(0)	—	—	—	—	10	205	20.5(42)	0	—	—	—	—	—	—	—	—	—	k	—	0	99
1945	NYG	5(1)	—	—	—	—	2	25	12.5(20)	0	—	—	—	—	—	—	—	—	—	—	—	0	13
NFL	2	15(1)	—	—	—	—	12	230	19.2(42)	0	—	—	—	—	—	—	—	—	—	—	—	0	111

WYRICK, JIMMY — Jimmy, DB, 5´9˝/176 lbs; Minnesota; B12/31/1976 DeSoto, TX   **2000** Det 6 (0)   **2001** Det 16 (0)   **2002** Det 15 (0)   **2003** Det 7 (1)   **2003** Mia 4 (0)   **2004** Mia 14 (0)   **NFL** 62 (1) [5 yrs]

WYSOCKI, PETE — Peter Joseph, LB, 6´2˝/225 lbs; Western Michigan; B10/3/1948 Detroit, MI, D6/14/2003 Vienna, CA   **1975** Was 13   **1976**†Was 14   **1977** Was 13   **1978** Was 16   **1979** Was 16 (9, RLB)   **1980** Was 16 (8, rlb)   **NFL** 88 (17) [6 yrs]

YABLOCK, IZZY — Julius, BB-TB, 5´10˝/172 lbs; Colgate; B7/28/1907 Brooklyn, NY, D8/15/1983 Encino, CA   **1930** Bkn 7 (6, bb)   **1931** Bkn 6 (4)   **1931** SI 7 (5, BB)   **NFL** 20 (15) [2 yrs]

YABLONSKI, VINNIE — Ventan Constantine, FB-LB, 5´8˝/195 lbs; Fordham; Columbia; 1946: ChiC, rnd 12/1947: Buf-A, rnd 18; B3/4/1923 Worcester, MA **[K]**

1948	†ChiC	12(2)	48	233	4.9(47)	0	1	13	13.0(13)	0	—	—	—	—	—	—	—	—	—	K	—	3	240
1949	ChiC	12(2)	32	97	3.0(22)	0	6	35	5.8(15)	0	—	—	—	—	—	—	—	—	—	K	—	16	115
1950	ChiC	12	30	110	3.7(39)	1	7	71	10.1(31)	0	—	—	—	—	—	—	—	—	—	K	—	19	156
1951	ChiC	4	14	20	1.4(6)	0	1	8	8.0(8)	0	—	—	—	—	—	—	—	—	—	K	—	14	24
NFL	4	40(4)	124	460	3.7(47)	1	15	127	8.5(31)	0	—	—	—	—	—	—	—	—	—	K	—	52	534

YACCINO, JOHN — John Nino, DB, 6´0˝/190 lbs; Pittsburgh; B6/27/1940 Hazleton, PA   **1962** Buf-A 3

YACKANICH, JOE — Joseph Peter, G, 5´10˝/205 lbs; Fordham; 1944: Cle, rnd 20; B3/31/1922, D8/1969 Lansing, IL   **1946**†NYY-A 11 (0)   **1947**†NYY-A 14 (0)   **1948** NYY-A 1 (0)   **AAFC** 26 (0) [3 yrs]

YAGIELLO, RAY — Raymond Walter, G-LB, 6´0˝/220 lbs; Franklin & Marshall; Catawba; 1948: LA, rnd 22; B9/23/1923 Orange, NJ   **1948** LARm 12 (0)   **1949**†LARm 12 (7, RG)   **NFL** 24 (7) [2 yrs]

YAKAVONIS, RAY — Raymond, NT, 6´4˝/250 lbs; East Stroudsburg; 1980: Min, rnd 6; B1/20/1957 Wilkes-Barre, PA   **1981** Min 15 (0)   **1982**†Min 2 (0)   **1983** Min 2 (0)   **1983** KC 2 (0)   **NFL** 21 (0) [3 yrs]

YAMINI, BASHIR — Bashir Jihad, WR, 6´3˝/190 lbs; Iowa; B9/10/1977 Dolton, IL   **2000** Ten 5 (0)

YANCHAR, WILLIAM — William J., DT, 6´3˝/251 lbs; Purdue; 1970: Cle, rnd 10; B3/25/1948 Euclid, OH   **1970** Cle 5

YANCY, CARLOS — Carlos Delanio, DB, 6´0˝/185 lbs; Georgia; 1995: NE, rnd 7; B6/24/1970 Sarasota, FL   **1995** NE 4 (0)

YANKOWSKI, RON — Ronald William, DE, 6´5˝/244 lbs; Kansas State; 1971: SL, rnd 8; B10/23/1946 Arlington, MA   **1971** SL 12 (LDE)   **1972** SL 10 (RDE)   **1973** SL 14 (RDE)   **1974**†SL 14 (14, RDE)   **1975**†SL 13 (13, RDE)   **1976** SL 5 (rde)   **1977** SL 14 (13, RDE)   **1978** SL 16   **1979** SL 16   **1980** SL 14 (13, RDE)   **NFL** 128 (53) [10 yrs]

YARBER, ERIC — Eric Lamone, WR, 5´8˝/156 lbs; Idaho; 1986: Was, rnd 12; B9/22/1963 Chicago, IL   **1986**†Was 2 (0)

| 1987 | †Was | 12(0) | — | — | — | — | 1 | 5 | 5.0(5) | 0 | — | — | — | — | — | — | — | — | — | p | — | 0 | 91 |
| NFL | 2 | 14(0) | — | — | — | — | 1 | 5 | 5.0(5) | 0 | — | — | — | — | — | — | — | — | — | p | — | 0 | 189 |

YARBOROUGH, RYAN — Ryan Kenneth, WR, 6´2˝/195 lbs; Wyoming; 1994: NYJ, rnd 2; B4/26/1971 Baltimore, MD

1994	NYJ	13(0)	—	—	—	—	6	42	7.0(12)	1	—	—	—	—	—	—	—	—	—	—	—	6	26
1995	NYJ	16(2)	—	—	—	—	18	230	12.8(38)	2	—	—	—	—	—	—	—	—	—	—	—	12	125
1997	Bal	16(3)	—	—	—	—	16	183	11.4(26)	0	—	—	—	—	—	—	—	—	—	—	—	0	92
1998	Bal	6(1)	—	—	—	—	4	39	9.8(18)	0	—	—	—	—	—	—	—	—	—	—	—	0	20
NFL	4	51(6)	—	—	—	—	44	494	11.2(38)	3	—	—	—	—	—	—	—	—	—	—	—	18	262

YARBROUGH, JIM — James Edward, DB, 6´0˝/195 lbs; Murray State; B11/20/1963   **1987** NYG 3 (0)

YARBROUGH, JIM — James Kelley, T, 6´5˝/265 lbs; Florida; 1969: Det, rnd 2; B10/28/1946 Charlotte, NC   **1969** Det 14   **1970** Det 12   **1971** Det 14 (LT)   **1972** Det 13 (LT)   **1973** Det 10 (LT)   **1974** Det 12 (12, LT)   **1975** Det 13 (13, LT)   **1976** Det 11 (5, lt)   **1977** Det 13 (11, LT)   **NFL** 112 (41) [9 yrs]

YARNO, GEORGE — George Anthony, G-C-T, 6´2˝/260 lbs; Washington State; B8/12/1957 Spokane, WA **[K]**   **1979**†TB 15   **1980** TB 16 (10, LG)   **1981**†TB 16 (5, lg)   **1982**†TB 9 (3)   **1983** TB 14 (11, rg/lg)   **1985** TB 12 (12, LT)   **1986** TB 16 (16, LG)   **1987** TB 11 (8, LG)   **1988** Atl 16 (5, c)   **1989** Hou 11 (3)   **NFL** 136 (73) [10 yrs]

YARNO, JOHN — John Richard, C, 6´5˝/251 lbs; Idaho; 1977: Sea, rnd 4; B12/17/1954 Spokane, WA   **1977** Sea 10   **1978** Sea 13 (13, C)   **1979** Sea 16 (16, C)   **1980** Sea 15 (15, C)   **1981** Sea 11 (9, C)   **1982** Sea 9 (9, C)   **NFL** 74 (62) [6 yrs]

YARR, TOMMY — Thomas Cornelius, C, 5´10˝/205 lbs; Notre Dame; B12/4/1908 Dabob, WA, D12/24/1941 Chicago, IL   **1933** ChiC 8 (3)

YARY, RON — Anthony Ronald, T, 6´5˝/255 lbs; USC; 1968: Min, rnd 1; B8/16/1946 Chicago, IL; HOF 2001   **1968**†Min 14   **1969**†Min 11 (6, rt)   **1970**†Min☆14 (14, RT)   **1971**†Min★14 (14, RT)   **1972** Min★14 (14, RT)   **1973**†Min★14 (14, RT)   **1974**†Min★14 (14, RT)   **1975**†Min★14 (14, RT)   **1976**†Min★14 (14, RT)   **1977**†Min★14 (14, RT)   **1978**†Min 16 (16, RT)   **1979** Min 16 (16, RT)   **1981** Min 16 (16, RT)   **1982** LARm 8 (0)

| 1980 | †Min | 14(14, RT) | — | — | — | — | 1 | 5 | 5.0(5) | 0 | — | — | — | — | — | — | — | — | — | k | — | 0 | -10 |
| NFL | 15 | 207(180) | — | — | — | — | 1 | 5 | 5.0(5) | 0 | — | — | — | — | — | — | — | — | — | k | — | 0 | -10 |

YATES, BILLY — Billy L., G, 6´2˝/305 lbs; Texas A&M; B4/15/1980 Fort Worth, TX   **2003** Mia 3 (0)   **2005**†NE 4 (0)   **NFL** 7 (0) [2 yrs]

YATES, BOB — Robert E., T-C, 6´1˝/240 lbs; Syracuse; 1960: Den, rnd 1/NYG, rnd 7; B11/20/1938   **1961** Bos-A 14   **1962** Bos-A 14   **1963**†Bos-A 14   **1964** Bos-A 12   **1965** Bos-A 14   **NFL** 68 [5 yrs]

YATES, MAX — Max, LB, 6´2˝/228 lbs; Marshall; B10/30/1979 Newport News, VA   **2004** Min 1 (0)

YEAGER, HOWIE — Howard Leon, WB, 5´11˝/173 lbs; California-Santa Barbara; B2/19/1915 Orosi, CA, D7/22/2000 Purcellville, VA

| 1941 | NYG | 10(1) | 22 | 67 | 3.0(39) | 1 | 11 | 220 | 20.0(65) | 3 | — | — | — | — | — | — | — | — | — | kp | — | 24 | 276 |

YEAGER, JIM — James Roland, T-G, 6´1˝/230 lbs; Lehigh; B9/21/1903 Reading, PA, D1/13/1972 Reading, PA   **1926** Bkn 11 (9, LT)

YEARBY, WILLIAM — William M., DE, 6´3˝/235 lbs; Michigan; 1966: NYJ, rnd 1; B7/24/1944 Birmingham, AL   **1966** NYJ-A 9

YEAST, CRAIG — Craig Nelson, WR, 5´7˝/165 lbs; Kentucky; 1999: Cin, rnd 4; B11/20/1976 Danville, KY

1999	Cin	9(0)	2	-16	-8.0(-3)	0	3	20	6.7(8)	0	—	—	—	—	—	—	—	—	—	kp	2	12	178
2000	Cin	15(7, WR)	1	15	15.0(15)	0	24	301	12.5(27)	0	—	—	—	—	—	—	—	—	—	kp	—	0	222
2001	NYJ	11(0)	—	—	—	—	—	—	—	—	—	—	—	—	—	—	—	—	—	kp	—	0	285
NFL	3	35(7)	3	-1	-0.3(15)	0	27	321	11.9(27)	0	—	—	—	—	—	—	—	—	—	kp	2	12	685

YEATES, JEFF — Jeffrey Lee, DE-DT-G, 6´3˝/248 lbs; Boston College; 1973: Buf, rnd 4; B8/3/1951 Buffalo, NY   **1974** Buf 10   **1975** Buf 13   **1976** Buf 3   **1976** Atl 2   **1977** Atl 13   **1978**†Atl 16 (12, LDE)   **1979** Atl 16 (16, LDE)   **1980**†Atl 16 (14, LDE)   **1981** Atl 16 (16, LDE)   **1982**†Atl 9 (9, LDE)   **1983** Atl 16 (16, LDE)   **1984** Atl 8 (0)   **NFL** 138 (83) [11 yrs]

YEATS, JAMES — James Melvin, TE, 6´4˝/245 lbs; Florida; B1936   **1960** Hou-A 1

YEBOAH-KODIE, PHIL — Phillip Anthony, LB, 6´2˝/225 lbs; Penn State; 1995: Den, rnd 5; B1/22/1971, Ghana   **1996** Ind 2 (0)

YEISLEY, DON — Donald Lee, E, 6´1˝/185 lbs; Chicago; B1/21/1904 Chelsea, IA, D10/1971 Victor, IA   **1928** ChiC 3 (0)

YELVERTON, BILL — William Grover, DE, 6´4˝/220 lbs; Mississippi; 1956: SF, rnd 18; B5/19/1933 Taylorsville, MS   **1960** Den-A 10 (rde)

YELVINGTON, DICK — Richard Joseph, T-G, 6´2˝/232 lbs; Georgia; 1951: NYG, rnd 23; B7/27/1928 Titusville, FL   **1952** NYG 7 (RT)   **1953** NYG 12 (RT)   **1954** NYG 12 (RT)   **1955** NYG 11 (RT)   **1956**†NYG 12 (RT)   **1957** NYG 8 (LG)   **NFL** 62 [6 yrs]

YEPREMIAN, GARO — Garabed Sarko, K, 5´8˝/175 lbs; none; B6/2/1944 Larnaca, Cyprus **[K]**   **1966** Det 9   **1967** Det 8   **1970**†Mia 13   **1971**†Mia☆14   **1972**†Mia 14   **1973**†Mia★14   **1974**†Mia 14   **1975** Mia 14   **1976** Mia 14   **1977** Mia 14   **1978**†Mia◇16   **1979** NO 14   **1980** TB 16 (0)   **1981** TB 3 (0)   **NFL** 177 [14 yrs]

YERGES, HOWARD — Howard E., TB, 5´9˝/155 lbs; Ohio State; B1896, deceased   **1920** Col 1 (1)

YEWCIC, TOM — Thomas, QB-P-HB, 5´11˝/185 lbs; Michigan State; 1954: Pit, rnd 27; B5/9/1932 Conemaugh, PA **[P]**

1961	Bos-A	14	11	51	4.6(13)	1	6	56	9.3(46)	0	8	3	37.5	25	3.1(18)	1	2	—	—	—	P	—	6	27
1962	Bos-A	14(qb)	33	215	6.5(27)	2	—	—	—	—	126	54	42.9	903	7.2(78)	7	5	—	—	69.6	P	—	12	522
1963	†Bos-A	14	22	161	7.3(46)	1	—	—	—	—	70	29	41.4	444	6.3(57)	2	6	—	—	—	P	—	6	213
1964	Bos-A	5	2	0.4(2)		0	—	—	—	—	1	1	100.0	2	2.0(2)	0	0	—	—	—	P	—	0	3
1965	Bos-A	14					1	13	13.0(13)	0	1	0	0.0	0	0.0	0	0	—	—	—	P	—	0	7

YEAR	TEAM	G(GS, POS)	RUSH	YD	AVG(LG)	TD	REC	YD	AVG(LG)	TD	PASS	COMP	PCT	YD	AVG(LG)	TD	INT	SK	YD	QBR	KPR	OTD	PTS	TAY
1966	Bos-A	7	1	-5	-5.0(-5)	0	—	—	—	—	—	—	—	—	—	—	—	—	—	—	P	—	0	-5
NFL	6	77	72	424	5.9(46)	4	7	69	9.9(46)	0	206	87	42.2	1374	6.7(78)	12	12	—	—	60.2	P	—	24	766

YEZERSKI, JOHN John G., T, 6´4˝/240 lbs; St. Mary's (CA); B9/22/1914, D1/1979 Boring, OR **1936** Bkn 9 (1)

YODER, TODD Todd, TE, 6´4˝/250 lbs; Vanderbilt; B3/18/1978 New Palestine, IN

YEAR	TEAM	G(GS, POS)	RUSH	YD	AVG(LG)	TD	REC	YD	AVG(LG)	TD	PASS	COMP	PCT	YD	AVG(LG)	TD	INT	SK	YD	QBR	KPR	OTD	PTS	TAY
2000	†TB	9(0)	—	—	—	—	1	1	1.0(1)	0	—	—	—	—	—	—	—	—	—	—	p	—	0	-5
2001	†TB	16(1)	—	—	—	—	4	48	12.0(24)	0	—	—	—	—	—	—	—	—	—	—	—	1	6	24
2002	†TB	16(0)	—	—	—	—	2	26	13.0(16)	0	—	—	—	—	—	—	—	—	—	—	k	—	0	7
2003	TB	16(1)	—	—	—	—	7	68	9.7(20)	2	—	—	—	—	—	—	—	—	—	—	k	—	12	37
2004	Jax	16(8, te)	—	—	—	—	14	157	11.2(56)	0	—	—	—	—	—	—	—	—	—	—	—	—	0	79
NFL	5	73(10)	—	—	—	—	28	300	10.7(56)	2	—	—	—	—	—	—	—	—	—	—	kp	1	18	142

YOHN, DAVE John David, LB, 6´0˝/220 lbs; Gettysburg; B10/10/1937 **1962** Bal 4 **1963** NYJ-A 14 (MLB) **NFL** 18 [2 yrs]

YOHO, MACK Mack, DE-K, 6´2˝/230 lbs; Miami (OH); B6/14/1936 Reader, WV **[K]** **1960** Buf-A 14 (LDE) **1961** Buf-A 14 (LDE) **1962** Buf-A 14 (RDE) **1963**†Buf-A 14 (RDE) **NFL** 56 [4 yrs]

YOKAS, FRANK Frank P., G, 5´11˝/210 lbs; none; B2/27/1924 Rock Island, IL, D5/12/1994 Los Angeles, CA **1946** LAD-A 12 (0) **1947** Bal-A 13 (2) **AAFC** 25 (2) [2 yrs]

YONAKOR, JOHN John Joseph, E-DE-DT, 6´5˝/222 lbs; Notre Dame; 1945: Phi, rnd 1; B8/4/1921 Boston, MA, D4/18/2001 Euclid, OH **1949**†Cle-A 12 (1)

YEAR	TEAM	G(GS, POS)	RUSH	YD	AVG(LG)	TD	REC	YD	AVG(LG)	TD	PASS	COMP	PCT	YD	AVG(LG)	TD	INT	SK	YD	QBR	KPR	OTD	PTS	TAY
1946	†Cle-A	14(5, re)	—	—	—	—	7	98	14.0	2	—	—	—	—	—	—	—	—	—	—	—	—	12	59
1947	†Cle-A	14(7, re)	—	—	—	—	6	95	15.8	2	—	—	—	—	—	—	—	—	—	—	k	—	12	43
1948	†Cle-A	14(2)	—	—	—	—	5	27	5.4	0	—	—	—	—	—	—	—	—	—	—	i	—	0	10
AAFC	4	54(15)	—	—	—	—	18	220	12.2	4	—	—	—	—	—	—	—	—	—	—	kpi	—	24	107

1950 NYY 8 **1952** Was 12 **NFL** 54 (15) [4 yrs]

YONAMINE, WALLY Wallace, HB-DB, 5´9˝/180 lbs; none; B6/1925 Maui, HI

YEAR	TEAM	G(GS, POS)	RUSH	YD	AVG(LG)	TD	REC	YD	AVG(LG)	TD	PASS	COMP	PCT	YD	AVG(LG)	TD	INT	SK	YD	QBR	KPR	OTD	PTS	TAY
1947	SF-A	12(3)	19	74	3.9	0	3	40	13.3	0	—	—	—	—	—	—	—	—	—	—	kpi	—	0	150

YOUEL, JIM James Stewart, QB-DB, 6´0˝/175 lbs; Iowa; B2/13/1922 Vinton, IA

YEAR	TEAM	G(GS, POS)	RUSH	YD	AVG(LG)	TD	REC	YD	AVG(LG)	TD	PASS	COMP	PCT	YD	AVG(LG)	TD	INT	SK	YD	QBR	KPR	OTD	PTS	TAY
1946	Was	9(4)	16	60	3.8(36)	1	—	—	—	—	48	20	41.7	352	7.3(66)	2	3	—	—	—	Pkpi	—	6	210
1947	Was	6(1)	10	44	4.4(19)	1	—	—	—	—	62	21	33.9	398	6.4(55)	3	3	—	—	—	P	—	6	148
1948	Bos	6(1)	15	63	4.2(20)	0	—	—	—	—	25	6	24.0	63	2.5(16)	2	3	—	—	—	P	—	0	-16
1948	Was	2(0)	4	16	4.0(0)	1	1	20	20.0(20)	0	11	3	27.3	36	3.3(14)	0	1	—	—	—	—	—	6	14
NFL	3	23(6)	45	183	4.1(36)	3	1	20	20.0(20)	0	146	50	34.2	849	5.8(66)	7	10	—	—	—	Pkpi	—	18	357

YOUMANS, MAURY Maurice Edward, DE, 6´4˝/251 lbs; Syracuse; 1959: ChiB, rnd 9/1960: Hou, rnd 1; B10/18/1936 Eagle Bay, NY **1960** ChiB 8 (LDE) **1961** ChiB 14 (LDE) **1962** ChiB 6 **1964** Dal 14 (3) **1965** Dal 14 (LDE) **NFL** 56 (3) [5 yrs]

YOUNCE, LEN Leonard Alonzo, G-LB, 6´1˝/208 lbs; Oregon State; 1941: NYG, rnd 8; B1/8/1917 Dayton, OR, D3/28/2000 Enterprise, OR **[K]** **1941** NYG☆11 (5, rg) **1943**†NYG☆10 (10, LG) **1944**†NYG☆10 (10, LG) **1946**†NYG☆11 (11, RG) **1947** NYG☆12 (12, RG) **1948** NYG☆11 (9, RG) **NFL** 65 (57) [6 yrs]

YOUNG, ADRIAN Matthew Adrian, LB, 6´1˝/232 lbs; USC; 1968: Phi, rnd 3; B1/31/1946 Dublin, Ireland **1968** Phi 10 **1969** Phi 13 **1970** Phi 14 (LLB) **1971** Phi 2 **1972** Phi 1 **1972** Det 10 **1973** ChiB 2 **NFL** 52 [6 yrs]

YOUNG, AL John Allen, B, 5´10˝/180 lbs; California; B4/28/1902, D3/14/1980 Corning, CA **1926** LA 7 (4)

YOUNG, AL Alfred L., WR, 6´1˝/195 lbs; South Carolina State; 1971: Pit, rnd 13; B8/24/1949 Norway, SC **1971** Pit 1

YEAR	TEAM	G(GS, POS)	RUSH	YD	AVG(LG)	TD	REC	YD	AVG(LG)	TD	PASS	COMP	PCT	YD	AVG(LG)	TD	INT	SK	YD	QBR	KPR	OTD	PTS	TAY
1972	†Pit	14	—	—	—	—	6	86	14.3(33)	0	—	—	—	—	—	—	—	—	—	—	—	—	0	43
NFL	2	15	—	—	—	—	6	86	14.3(33)	0	—	—	—	—	—	—	—	—	—	—	—	—	0	43

YOUNG, ALMON Almon, G, 6´3˝/290 lbs; Bethune-Cookman; B7/3/1962 Eustis, FL **1987** Hou 3 (3)

YOUNG, ANDRE Andre Benoise, DB, 6´0˝/199 lbs; Louisiana Tech; 1982: SD, rnd 10; B11/22/1960 West Monroe, LA **1982**†SD 8 (2) **1983** SD 15 (10, SS) **1984** SD 13 (3) **NFL** 36 (15) [3 yrs]

YOUNG, ANTHONY Anthony Ricardo, DB, 5´11˝/187 lbs; Temple; 1985: Ind, rnd 3; B10/8/1963 Columbia, SC **1985** Ind 14 (12, FS)

YOUNG, BEN Benjamin, TE, 6´2˝/225 lbs; Texas-Arlington; B1/13/1960 Toledo, OH

YEAR	TEAM	G(GS, POS)	RUSH	YD	AVG(LG)	TD	REC	YD	AVG(LG)	TD	PASS	COMP	PCT	YD	AVG(LG)	TD	INT	SK	YD	QBR	KPR	OTD	PTS	TAY
1983	Atl	11(6, te)	—	—	—	—	6	74	12.3(19)	1	—	—	—	—	—	—	—	—	—	—	—	—	6	42

YOUNG, BILL William A., T, 6´1˝/247 lbs; Alabama; B5/20/1914 Argenta, AL, D1/21/1994 Jacksonville, FL **1937**†Was 6 (0) **1939** Was 8 (0) **1940** Was 10 (1) **1941** Was 6 (1) **1942**†Was✧10 (7, RT) **1946** Was 8 (1)

YEAR	TEAM	G(GS, POS)	RUSH	YD	AVG(LG)	TD	REC	YD	AVG(LG)	TD	PASS	COMP	PCT	YD	AVG(LG)	TD	INT	SK	YD	QBR	KPR	OTD	PTS	TAY
1938	Was	11(1)	—	—	—	—	1	62	62.0(62)	1	—	—	—	—	—	—	—	—	—	—	—	—	6	36
NFL	7	59(11)	—	—	—	—	1	62	62.0(62)	1	—	—	—	—	—	—	—	—	—	—	—	—	6	36

YOUNG, BILLY William George, G, 5´10˝/210 lbs; Ohio State; B12/17/1901, D7/29/1971 Kenton, OH **1929** GB 2 (0)

YOUNG, BOB Robert Allen, G-DE-DT, 6´1˝/270 lbs; Texas; Southwest Texas State; Howard Payne; 1964: SL, rnd 19; B9/3/1942 Marshall, TX, D6/17/1995 Missouri City, TX **1966** Den-A 11 (RDE) **1967** Den-A 5 **1968** Den-A 14 (RG) **1969** Den-A 14 (14, RG) **1970** Den 14 (12, RG) **1971** Hou 14 (LG) **1972** SL 14 (RG) **1973** SL 13 **1974**†SL 9 (8, LG) **1975**†SL 12 (LG) **1976** SL 14 (14, LG) **1977** SL☆14 (14, LG) **1978** SL★16 (LG) **1979** SL★13 (LG) **1980**†Hou 15 (12, LG) **1981** NO 2 (0) **NFL** 194 (74) [16 yrs]

YOUNG, BRIAN James Brian, DT, 6´2˝/290 lbs; Texas-El Paso; 2000: SL, rnd 5; B7/8/1977 Lawton, OK **2000** SL 11 (0) **2001**†SL 16 (16, LDT) **2002** SL 16 (3) **2003**†SL 16 (12, RDT) **2004** NO 15 (15, RDT) **2005** NO 16 (16, LDT) **NFL** 90 (62) [6 yrs]

YOUNG, BRYANT Bryant Colby, DT-DE, 6´3˝/291 lbs; Notre Dame; 1994: SF, rnd 1; B1/27/1972 Chicago Heights, IL **[S]** **1994**†SF 16 (16, LDT) **1995**†SF 12 (12, LDT) **1996**†SF★16 (16, LDT) **1997**†SF 12 (12, LDT) **1998** SF☆12 (12, LDT) **1999** SF★16 (16, LDT) **2000** SF 15 (15, LDT) **2001**†SF★16 (16, LDT) **2002**†SF✧16 (16, LDT) **2003** SF 16 (16, LDT) **2004** SF 16 (16, RDT) **2005** SF 13 (13, LDE) **NFL** 176 (176) [12 yrs]

YOUNG, BUDDY Claude Henry, HB-FB-DB, 5´4˝/175 lbs; Illinois; B1/5/1926 Chicago, IL, D9/4/1983 Terrell, TX **[R]**

YEAR	TEAM	G(GS, POS)	RUSH	YD	AVG(LG)	TD	REC	YD	AVG(LG)	TD	PASS	COMP	PCT	YD	AVG(LG)	TD	INT	SK	YD	QBR	KPR	OTD	PTS	TAY
1947	†NYY-A☆	14(8, FB)	116	712	6.1	3	27	303	11.2(50)	2	2	1	50.0	13	6.5(13)	0	0	—	—	—	kp	2	42	1169
1948	NYY-A	12(11, FB)	70	245	3.5	1	21	259	12.3	4	—	—	—	—	—	—	—	—	—	—	kp	—	30	529
1949	†NYY-A☆	12(11, LH)	76	495	6.5(71)	5	12	171	14.3	2	—	—	—	—	—	—	—	—	—	—	kp	1	48	928
AAFC	3	38(30)	262	1452	5.5(71)	9	60	733	12.2(50)	8	2	1	50.0	13	6.5(13)	0	0	—	—	—	kp	3	120	2625
1950	NYY☆	12(RH)	76	334	4.4(20)	1	20	302	15.1(69)	1	—	—	—	—	—	—	—	—	—	—	kp	—	12	745
1951	NYY	12(LH)	46	165	3.6(17)	1	31	508	16.4(48)	3	—	—	—	—	—	—	—	—	—	—	kp	2	36	852
1952	DalT	12(11, RH)	71	243	3.4(30)	3	22	269	12.2(45)	2	3	0	0.0	0	0.0	0	1	—	—	—	kp	—	30	681
1953	Bal	10(RH)	40	135	3.4(24)	0	12	201	16.8(49)	3	—	—	—	—	—	—	—	—	—	—	kp	1	24	453
1954	Bal✧	10(RH)	70	311	4.4(57)	2	15	272	18.1(78)	3	—	—	—	—	—	—	—	—	—	—	kp	—	30	585
1955	Bal	11(RH)	32	87	2.7(25)	1	19	426	22.4(82)	1	—	—	—	—	—	—	—	—	—	—	kp	—	12	397
NFL	6	67(11)	335	1275	3.8(71)	8	119	1978	16.6(82)	13	3	0	0.0	0	0.0	0	1	—	—	—	kp	3	144	3712

YOUNG, CHARLE Charle Edward, TE, 6´4˝/234 lbs; USC; 1973: Phi, rnd 1; B2/5/1951 Fresno, CA

YEAR	TEAM	G(GS, POS)	RUSH	YD	AVG(LG)	TD	REC	YD	AVG(LG)	TD	PASS	COMP	PCT	YD	AVG(LG)	TD	INT	SK	YD	QBR	KPR	OTD	PTS	TAY
1973	Phi★	14(14, TE)	4	24	6.0(17)	1	55	854	15.5(80)	6	—	—	—	—	—	—	—	—	—	—	—	—	42	491
1974	Phi★	14(14, TE)	6	38	6.3(14)	0	**63**	696	11.0(29)	3	—	—	—	—	—	—	—	—	—	—	—	—	18	401
1975	Phi★	14(14, TE)	2	1	0.5(3)	0	49	659	13.4(47)	3	—	—	—	—	—	—	—	—	—	—	—	—	18	346
1976	Phi	14(14, TE)	1	6	6.0(6)	0	30	374	12.5(29)	0	—	—	—	—	—	—	—	—	—	—	—	—	0	193
1977	†LARm	14	—	—	—	—	5	35	7.0(17)	1	—	—	—	—	—	—	—	—	—	—	—	—	6	23
1978	†LARm	16	2	6	3.0(5)	0	18	213	11.8(19)	0	—	—	—	—	—	—	—	—	—	—	—	—	0	113
1979	†LARm	15	—	—	—	—	13	144	11.1(23)	2	—	—	—	—	—	—	—	—	—	—	—	—	12	82
1980	SF	16(16, TE)	—	—	—	—	29	325	11.2(41)	2	—	—	—	—	—	—	—	—	—	—	k	—	12	172
1981	†SF	16(16, TE)	—	—	—	—	37	400	10.8(29)	5	—	—	—	—	—	—	—	—	—	—	—	—	30	225
1982	SF	9(9, TE)	—	—	—	—	22	189	8.6(30)	0	—	—	—	—	—	—	—	—	—	—	—	—	0	95
1983	†Sea	16(16, TE)	—	—	—	—	36	529	14.7(47)	2	—	—	—	—	—	—	—	—	—	—	—	—	12	275
1984	†Sea	15(15, TE)	1	5	5.0(5)	0	33	337	10.2(31)	1	—	—	—	—	—	—	—	—	—	—	—	—	6	179
1985	Sea	14(14, TE)	—	—	—	—	28	351	12.5(32)	2	—	—	—	—	—	—	—	—	—	—	—	—	12	186
NFL	13	187(142)	16	80	5.0(17)	1	418	5106	12.2(80)	27	—	—	—	—	—	—	—	—	—	—	k	—	168	2777

YEAR	TEAM	G (GS, POS)	RUSH	YD	AVG(LG)	TD	REC	YD	AVG(LG)	TD	PASS	COMP	PCT	YD	AVG(LG)	TD	INT	SK	YD	QBR	KPR	OTD	PTS	TAY

YOUNG, CHARLEY   Charles Lee, RB, 6´1˝/213 lbs; North Carolina State; 1974: Dal, rnd 1; B10/13/1952 Raleigh, NC

YEAR	TEAM	G (GS, POS)	RUSH	YD	AVG(LG)	TD	REC	YD	AVG(LG)	TD	KPR	PTS	TAY
1974	Dal	14	33	205	6.2(53)	0	11	73	6.6(14)	0	k	0	283
1975	†Dal	12	50	225	4.5(29)	2	18	184	10.2(42)	1	k	18	351
1976	Dal	11(2)	48	208	4.3(24)	0	11	134	12.2(25)	1	—	6	280
NFL	3	37(2)	131	638	4.9(53)	2	40	391	9.8(42)	2	k	24	914

YOUNG, CHRIS   Christopher Lamont, DB, 6´0˝/210 lbs; Georgia Tech; 2002: Den, rnd 7; B1/23/1980 Senoia, GA   **2003**†Den 11 (0)   **2004**†Den 10 (0)   **NFL** 21 (0) [2 yrs]

YOUNG, DAVE   David Joseph, TE, 6´5˝/242 lbs; Purdue; 1981: NYG, rnd 2; B2/9/1959 Akron, OH

YEAR	TEAM	G (GS, POS)	REC	YD	AVG(LG)	TD	PTS	TAY
1981	†NYG	11(0)	5	49	9.8(15)	1	6	30
1983	Bal	1(0)	—	—	—	—	—	—
1984	Ind	13(9, TE)	14	164	11.7(28)	2	12	92
NFL	3	25(9)	19	213	11.2(28)	3	18	122

YOUNG, DAVID   David F., DB, 6´1˝/209 lbs; Georgia Southern; 2003: Jax, rnd 6; B5/17/1979 Columbia, SC   **2003** NYJ 5 (0)

YOUNG, DICK   Richard, FB-HB, 5´11˝/210 lbs; Tennessee-Chattanooga; 1954: ChiC, rnd 18; B8/25/1930 Trumbull, CT

YEAR	TEAM	G (GS, POS)	RUSH	YD	AVG(LG)	TD	REC	YD	AVG(LG)	TD	KPR	PTS	TAY
1955	Bal	11	17	39	2.3(10)	0	2	15	7.5(11)	0	kp	0	52
1956	Bal	12	5	7	1.4(3)	0	—	—	—	—	k	0	2
1957	Pit	11	56	153	2.7(14)	2	4	38	9.5(12)	0	—	12	192
NFL	3	34	78	199	2.6(14)	2	6	53	8.8(12)	0	kp	12	246

YOUNG, DUANE   Curtis Duane, TE, 6´3˝/270 lbs; Michigan State; 1991: SD, rnd 5; B5/29/1968 Kalamazoo, MI

YEAR	TEAM	G (GS, POS)	REC	YD	AVG(LG)	TD	PTS	TAY
1991	SD	7(5, te)	2	12	6.0(6)	0	0	6
1992	†SD	16(12, TE)	4	45	11.3(14)	0	0	23
1993	SD	16(15, TE)	6	41	6.8(12)	2	12	31
1994	†SD	14(14, TE)	17	217	12.8(31)	1	6	114
1995	†SD	16(16, TE)	9	90	10.0(22)	0	0	45
1998	Buf	4(0)	—	—	—	—	—	—
NFL	6	73(62)	38	405	10.7(31)	3	18	218

YOUNG, FLOYD   Floyd Alexander, DB, 6´0˝/170 lbs; Texas A&M-Kingsville; B11/23/1975 New Orleans, LA   **1997**†TB 12 (1)   **1998** TB 11 (0)   **1999**†TB 6 (0)   **2000**†TB 7 (0)
NFL 36 (1) [4 yrs]

YOUNG, FREDD   Frederick Kimball, LB, 6´1˝/233 lbs; New Mexico State; 1984: Sea, rnd 3; B11/14/1961 Dallas, TX   **1984**†Sea★16 (0)   **1985** Sea◇16 (13, LILB)
1986 Sea★15 (15, LILB)   **1987**†Sea★13 (13, LILB)   **1988** Ind 15 (12, LILB)   **1989** Ind 15 (15, RILB)   **1990** Ind 11 (11, RILB)   **NFL** 101 (79) [7 yrs]

YOUNG, GEORGE   George Donald, DE-E, 6´3˝/214 lbs; Baldwin-Wallace; Georgia; B5/10/1924 Wilkes-Barre, PA, D9/21/1969 Chicago, IL   **1947**†Cle-A 13 (2)   **1949**†Cle-A 9 (0)

YEAR	TEAM	G (GS, POS)	REC	YD	AVG(LG)	TD	OTD	PTS	TAY
1946	†Cle-A	13(2)	3	37	12.3	0	—	0	19
1948	†Cle-A	14(0)	2	20	10.0	0	1	6	10
AAFC	4	49(4)	5	57	11.4	0	1	6	29

1950†Cle 12 (LDE)   **1951**†Cle 12 (LDE)   **1952**†Cle 12 (LDE)   **1953**†Cle 12 (LDE)   **NFL** 48 [4 yrs]

YOUNG, GLEN   Glen Edward, WR, 6´2˝/205 lbs; Mississippi State; 1983: Phi, rnd 3; B10/11/1960 Greenwood, MS [R]

YEAR	TEAM	G (GS, POS)	REC	YD	AVG(LG)	TD	KPR	PTS	TAY
1983	Phi	16(0)	3	125	41.7(71)	1	kp	6	248
1984	Cle	2(1)	1	47	47.0(47)	0	k	0	83
1985	†Cle	15(2)	5	111	22.2(45)	1	k	6	434
1987	†Cle	10(0)	—	—	—	—	k	0	142
1988	Cle	15(0)	2	34	17.0(25)	0	k	0	217
NFL	5	58(3)	11	317	28.8(71)	2	kp	12	1123

YOUNG, GLEN   Glen H., LB, 6´3˝/250 lbs; Syracuse; B5/2/1969 Scarborough, Canada   **1995** SD 16 (0)   **1996** SD 6 (1)   **NFL** 22 (1) [2 yrs]

YOUNG, GLENN   Glenn Charles, DB, 6´2˝/205 lbs; Purdue; B12/22/1929 Woodstock, IL   **1956** GB 4

YOUNG, HERM   Herman DeVerne, E, 5´11˝/178 lbs; Detroit Mercy; B3/21/1906 Flint, MI, D5/16/1985 Bradenton, FL   **1930** Pro 3 (0), 6

YOUNG, JIM   James Norman, HB, 6´0˝/205 lbs; Queens (Canada); B6/6/1943 Hamilton, Canada   **1966** Min 4

YEAR	TEAM	G (GS, POS)	RUSH	YD	AVG(LG)	TD	KPR	PTS	TAY
1965	Min	2	3	4	1.3(4)	0	kp	0	9
NFL	2	6	3	4	1.3(4)	0	kp	0	36

YOUNG, JIM   James Alexander, DE, 6´2˝/260 lbs; Texas Southern; B7/8/1950 Houston, TX   **1977** Hou 13 (LDE)   **1978**†Hou 16 (16, LDE)   **1979** Hou 5   **NFL** 34 (16) [3 yrs]

YOUNG, JOE   Joseph Albert, DE, 6´3˝/245 lbs; Marquette; Arizona; 1955: ChiB, rnd 24; B8/3/1933 Chicago, IL   **1960** Den-A 14 (LDE)   **1961** Den-A 6   **NFL** 20 [2 yrs]

YOUNG, KEVIN   Kevin, DE, 6´5˝/265 lbs; Tulane; Utah State; B11/8/1964 New Orleans, LA   **1987** NO 1 (0)

YOUNG, LLOYD   Lloyd, G-C-T-E, 6´2˝/192 lbs; Macalester; North Dakota; B5/27/1903 Austin, MN, D6/10/1978 Austin, MN   **1925** Pro 11 (4)   **1926** Pro 13 (10, RG)   **1927** Pro 1 (1)
1929 Min 8 (8, C)   **1930** Min 2 (1)   **NFL** 35 (24) [5 yrs]

YOUNG, LONNIE   Lonnie R., DB, 6´1˝/205 lbs; Michigan State; 1985: SL, rnd 12; B7/18/1963 Flint, MI   **1985** SL 16 (10, FS)   **1986** SL 13 (13, FS)   **1987** SL 12 (12, FS)
1988 Phx 12 (12, FS)   **1989** Phx 10 (9, FS)   **1990** Phx 16 (16, FS)   **1991**†NYJ 12 (11, FS)   **1992** NYJ 13 (13, FS)   **1993** NYJ 9 (2)   **1994** SD 12 (0)   **1995** NYJ 7 (0)   **1996** NYJ 15 (0)
NFL 147 (98) [12 yrs]

YOUNG, MICHAEL   Michael, LB, 6´2˝/245 lbs; Illinois; B6/1/1978 St. Louis, MO   **2002** Arz 16 (2)   **2003** Arz 6 (0)   **NFL** 22 (2) [2 yrs]

YOUNG, MIKE   Michael David, WR, 6´1˝/187 lbs; UCLA; 1985: LARm, rnd 6; B2/21/1962 Hanford, CA

YEAR	TEAM	G (GS, POS)	REC	YD	AVG(LG)	TD	PTS	TAY
1985	†LARm	15(1)	14	157	11.2(23)	0	0	79
1986	†LARm	16(1)	15	181	12.1(21)	3	18	106
1987	LARm	12(0)	4	56	14.0(26)	1	6	33
1988	LARm	8(0)	2	27	13.5(18)	0	0	14
1989	†Den	16(0)	22	402	18.3(47)	2	12	211
1990	Den	16(1)	28	385	13.8(42)	4	24	213
1991	†Den	16(13, WR)	44	629	14.3(52)	2	12	325
1992	Den	3(0)	1	11	11.0(11)	0	0	6
1993	Phi	10(0)	14	186	13.3(49)	2	12	103
1994	KC	2(0)	—	—	—	—	—	—
NFL	10	114(16)	144	2034	14.1(52)	14	84	1087

YOUNG, MITCHELL   Mitchell, DE, 6´4˝/260 lbs; Arkansas State; B7/18/1961 Coldwater, MS   **1987** Atl 1 (0)

YOUNG, PAUL   Paul Wesly, C, 6´4˝/195 lbs; Oklahoma; B12/7/1908 Melrose, NM, D10/19/1978 Cambridge, NE   **1933** GB 2 (1)

YOUNG, RANDY   Randolph, E, 6´0˝/175 lbs; Millikin; B1898, D11/1/1975   **1920** Dec 1 (0)

YOUNG, RANDY   Randall Louis, T, 6´5˝/250 lbs; Iowa State; 1976: Mia, rnd 12; B7/4/1954 Montgomery, AL   **1976** TB 9

YOUNG, RENARD   Renard F., DB, 5´10˝/184 lbs; San Diego State; UNLV; B7/31/1961 Los Angeles, CA   **1987** Sea 3 (3)

YOUNG, RICKEY   Rickey Dornial, RB, 6´2˝/196 lbs; Jackson State; 1975: SD, rnd 7; B12/7/1953 Mobile, AL

YEAR	TEAM	G (GS, POS)	RUSH	YD	AVG(LG)	TD	REC	YD	AVG(LG)	TD	KPR	PTS	TAY
1975	SD	14(8, RB)	138	577	4.2(48)	5	21	166	7.9(16)	1	k	36	813
1976	SD	14(14, FB)	162	802	5.0(46)	4	47	441	9.4(33)	1	—	30	1068
1977	SD	14(14, FB)	157	543	3.5(15)	4	48	423	8.8(28)	0	—	24	795
1978	†Min	16(16, RB)	134	417	3.1(16)	1	88	704	8.0(48)	5	k	36	797
1979	Min	16(16, RB)	188	708	3.8(26)	3	72	519	7.2(18)	4	—	42	1018
1980	†Min	16(16, RB)	130	351	2.7(14)	3	64	499	7.8(22)	2	—	30	641
1981	Min	16(13, RB)	47	129	2.7(13)	0	43	296	6.9(22)	2	k	12	287
1982	†Min	9(1)	16	49	3.1(11)	1	4	44	11.0(25)	1	—	12	86
1983	Min	16(4)	39	90	2.3(9)	2	21	193	9.2(48)	0	k	12	189
NFL	9	131(102)	1011	3666	3.6(48)	23	408	3285	8.1(48)	16	k	234	5692

YOUNG, ROBERT Robert E., DE-DT, 6´6˝/273 lbs; Mississippi State; 1991: LARm, rnd 5; B1/29/1969 Jackson, MS **1991** LARm 16 (13, RDT) **1992** LARm 11 (1) **1993** LARm 6 (6, lde) **1994** LARm 16 (16, LDE) **1995** SL 14 (0) **1996** Hou 15 (13, RDE) **NFL** 78 (49) [6 yrs]

YOUNG, RODNEY Rodney Menard, DB, 6´0˝/210 lbs; LSU; 1995: NYG, rnd 3; B1/25/1973 Grambling, LA **1995** NYG 10 (0) **1996** NYG 12 (0) **1997**†NYG 9 (0) **1998** NYG 2 (0) **NFL** 33 (0) [4 yrs]

YOUNG, ROY Roy O., T, 6´2˝/215 lbs; Texas A&M; 1938: Was, rnd 7; B9/1/1917 Abbeville, LA, D5/5/1987 Scottsdale, AZ **1938** Was 9 (1)

YOUNG, ROYNELL Roynell, DB, 6´1˝/181 lbs; Alcorn State; 1980: Phi, rnd 1; B12/1/1957 New Orleans, LA **[I]** **1980**†Phi 16 (16, LCB) **1981**†Phi★13 (13, LCB) **1982** Phi 9 (9, LCB) **1983** Phi 16 (16, LCB) **1984** Phi 7 (0) **1985** Phi 14 (13, LCB) **1986** Phi 16 (16, LCB) **1987** Phi 11 (11, LCB) **1988**†Phi 15 (15, LCB) **NFL** 117 (109) [9 yrs]

YOUNG, RUSS Russell Charles, FB, 6´0˝/190 lbs; none; B9/15/1899 Bryan, OH, D5/13/1984 Roseville, CA **1925** Day 4 (1)

YOUNG, RYAN Ryan, T, 6´5˝/320 lbs; Kansas State; 1999: NYJ, rnd 7; B6/28/1976 St. Louis, MO **1999** NYJ 15 (7, rt) **2000** NYJ 16 (16, RT) **2001**†NYJ 16 (16, RT) **2002** Hou 10 (8, RT) **2003** Dal 11 (8, rt) **NFL** 68 (55) [5 yrs]

YOUNG, SAM Samuel Leslie, HB, 6´1˝/190 lbs; Manchester; North Dakota; B2/11/1905 Austin, MN, D12/1/1991 Glendale, AZ **1927** Pro 2 (1)

YOUNG, STEVE Steven Russell, T, 6´8˝/272 lbs; Colorado; 1976: TB, rnd 3; B7/18/1953 Spokane, WA **1976** TB 13 (11, LT) **1977** Mia 14 **NFL** 27 (11) [2 yrs]

YOUNG, STEVE John Steven, QB, 6´2˝/205 lbs; Brigham Young; 1984: TB, rnd S1; B10/11/1961 Salt Lake City, UT; HOF 2005

YEAR	TEAM	G(GS, POS)	RUSH	YD	AVG(LG)	TD	REC	YD	AVG(LG)	TD	PASS	COMP	PCT	YD	AVG(LG)	TD	INT	SK	YD	QBR	KPR	OTD	PTS	TAY
1985	TB	5(5, qb)	40	233	5.8(20)	1	—	—	—	—	138	72	52.2	935	6.8(59)	3	8	21	158	56.9	—	—	6	406
1986	TB	14(14, QB)	74	425	5.7(31)	5	—	—	—	—	363	195	53.7	2282	6.3(46)	8	13	47	326	65.5	—	—	30	1136
1987	†SF	8(3)	26	190	7.3(29)	1	—	—	—	—	69	37	53.6	570	8.3(50)	10	0	3	25	—	—	—	6	535
1988	†SF	11(3)	27	184	6.8(49)	1	—	—	—	—	101	54	53.5	680	6.7(73)	3	3	13	75	72.2	—	—	6	429
1989	†SF	10(3)	38	126	3.3(22)	2	—	—	—	—	92	64	69.6	1001	10.9(50)	8	3	12	84	—	—	—	12	567
1990	†SF	6(1)	15	159	10.6(31)	0	—	—	—	—	62	38	61.3	427	6.9(34)	2	0	8	41	—	—	—	0	383
1991	SF	11(10, QB)	66	415	6.3(21)	4	—	—	—	—	279	180	64.5	2517	**9.0**(**97**)	17	8	13	79	**101.8**	—	—	24	1479
1992	†SF★	16(16, QB)	76	537	7.1(39)	4	—	—	—	—	402	268	66.7	**3465**	**8.6**(**80**)	**25**	7	29	152	107.0	—	—	24	**2155**
1993	†SF★	16(16, QB)	69	407	5.9(35)	2	2	2	1.0(6)	0	462	314	68.0	**4023**	**8.7**(**80**)	**29**	16	31	160	**101.5**	—	—	12	**1945**
1994	†SF★	16(16, QB)	58	293	5.1(27)	7	—	—	—	—	461	324	**70.3**	3969	**8.6**(**69**)	**35**	10	31	163	**112.8**	—	—	42	**2123**
1995	†SF★	11(11, QB)	50	250	5.0(29)	3	—	—	—	—	447	299	66.9	3200	7.2(57)	20	11	25	115	92.3	—	—	18	1540
1996	†SF★	12(12, QB)	52	310	6.0(33)	4	—	—	—	—	316	214	**67.7**	2410	**7.6**(**52**)	14	6	34	160	**97.2**	—	—	26	1385
1997	†SF★	15(15, QB)	50	199	4.0(13)	3	—	—	—	—	356	241	**67.7**	3029	**8.5**(**82**)	19	6	35	220	**104.7**	—	—	18	1599
1998	†SF★	15(15, QB)	70	454	6.5(24)	6	—	—	—	—	517	322	62.3	4170	8.1(81)	**36**	12	48	234	101.1	—	—	36	**2299**
1999	SF	3(3)	11	57	5.2(14)	0	—	—	—	—	84	45	53.6	446	5.3(53)	3	4	8	63	—	—	—	0	135
NFL	15	169(143)	722	4239	5.9(49)	43	2	2	1.0(6)	0	4149	2667	64.3	33124	8.0(97)	232	107	358	2055	96.8	—	—	260	18112

YOUNG, THEO Theo Thomas, TE, 6´2˝/237 lbs; Arkansas; 1987: Pit, rnd 12; B4/25/1965 Newport, AR

YEAR	TEAM	G(GS, POS)	RUSH	YD	AVG(LG)	TD	REC	YD	AVG(LG)	TD	PASS	COMP	PCT	YD	AVG(LG)	TD	INT	SK	YD	QBR	KPR	OTD	PTS	TAY
1987	Pit	12(1)	—	—	—	—	2	10	5.0(6)	0	—	—	—	—	—	—	—	—	—	—	—	—	0	5

YOUNG, TYRONE Tyrone Donnive, WR, 6´6˝/190 lbs; Florida; B4/29/1960 Ocala, FL

YEAR	TEAM	G(GS, POS)	RUSH	YD	AVG(LG)	TD	REC	YD	AVG(LG)	TD	PASS	COMP	PCT	YD	AVG(LG)	TD	INT	SK	YD	QBR	KPR	OTD	PTS	TAY
1983	NO	16(0)	—	—	—	—	7	85	12.1(32)	3	—	—	—	—	—	—	—	—	—	—	—	—	18	58
1984	NO	16(8, WR)	—	—	—	—	29	597	20.6(74)	3	—	—	—	—	—	—	—	—	—	—	—	—	18	314
NFL	2	32(8)	—	—	—	—	36	682	18.9(74)	6	—	—	—	—	—	—	—	—	—	—	—	—	36	371

YOUNG, WADDY Walter Roland, E, 6´3˝/205 lbs; Oklahoma; 1939: Bkn, rnd 3; B9/4/1916 Ponca City, OK, D1/9/1945 Tokyo, Japan

YEAR	TEAM	G(GS, POS)	RUSH	YD	AVG(LG)	TD	REC	YD	AVG(LG)	TD	PASS	COMP	PCT	YD	AVG(LG)	TD	INT	SK	YD	QBR	KPR	OTD	PTS	TAY
1939	Bkn	11(5, RE)	—	—	—	—	8	100	12.5	0	—	—	—	—	—	—	—	—	—	—	—	—	0	50
1940	Bkn	11(10, RE)	1	1	1.0(1)	0	7	85	12.1	0	—	—	—	—	—	—	—	—	—	—	—	—	0	44
NFL	2	22(15)	1	1	1.0(1)	0	15	185	12.3	0	—	—	—	—	—	—	—	—	—	—	—	—	0	94

YOUNG, WALTER Walter, WR, 6´5˝/214 lbs; Illinois; 2003: Car, rnd 7; B12/7/1979 Chicago Heights, IL **2003** Car 7 (0)

YOUNG, WILBUR Wilbur Eugene, DE-DT, 6´6˝/285 lbs; William Penn; 1971: KC, rnd 2; B4/20/1949 New York, NY **1971**†KC 13 (1) **1972** KC 14 (13, RDE) **1973** KC 13 (11, RDE) **1974** KC 14 (14, RDE) **1975** KC 13 (11, RDE) **1976** KC 14 (12, RDE) **1977** KC 13 (11, RDE) **1978** SD 10 (2) **1979**†SD☆16 (16, LDT) **1980**†SD 12 (4) **1981** Was 7 (3) **1981**†SD 5 (2) **1982**†SD 9 (2) **NFL** 153 (102) [12 yrs]

YOUNG, WILLIE William Joseph Lull, T, 6´0˝/265 lbs; Grambling State; B6/27/1943 Ruston, LA **1966** NYG 14 (LT) **1970** NYG 13 (LT) **1971** NYG 14 (LT) **1972** NYG 14 (LT) **1974** NYG 12 (LT) **1975** NYG 12 (LT)

YEAR	TEAM	G(GS, POS)	RUSH	YD	AVG(LG)	TD	REC	YD	AVG(LG)	TD	PASS	COMP	PCT	YD	AVG(LG)	TD	INT	SK	YD	QBR	KPR	OTD	PTS	TAY
1967	NYG	14(LT)	0	2	(2)	0	—	—	—	—	—	—	—	—	—	—	—	—	—	—	—	—	0	2
1968	NYG	14(LT)	2	-2	-1.0(5)	0	—	—	—	—	—	—	—	—	—	—	—	—	—	—	—	—	0	-2
1969	NYG	14(LT)	—	—	—	—	1	8	8.0(8)	0	—	—	—	—	—	—	—	—	—	—	—	—	0	4
1973	NYG	14(LT)	—	—	—	—	1	-5	-5.0(-5)	0	—	—	—	—	—	—	—	—	—	—	—	—	0	-3
NFL	10	135	2	0	0.0(5)	0	2	3	1.5(8)	0	—	—	—	—	—	—	—	—	—	—	k	—	0	-23

YOUNG, WILLIE Willie, T, 6´4˝/270 lbs; Alcorn State; B11/12/1947 Jefferson, MS **1971** Buf 14 (LT) **1972** Buf 1 **1973** Mia 1 **NFL** 16 [3 yrs]

YOUNGBLOOD, GEORGE George Alton, DB, 6´3˝/205 lbs; Los Angeles State; 1966: LA, rnd 7/KC, rnd R1; B1/4/1945 Los Angeles, CA **1966** LARm 14 **1967** Cle 11 **1967** NO 1 **1968** NO 4 **1969** ChiB 14 (LS) **NFL** 44 [4 yrs]

YOUNGBLOOD, JACK Herbert Jackson, DE, 6´4˝/247 lbs; Florida; 1971: LA, rnd 1; B1/26/1950 Jacksonville, FL; HOF 2001 **1971** LARm 14 (3) **1972** LARm 14 (7, LDE) **1973**†LARm★14 (14, LDE) **1974**†LARm★14 (14, LDE) **1975**†LARm★14 (14, LDE) **1976**†LARm★14 (14, LDE) **1977**†LARm★14 (14, LDE) **1978**†LARm★16 (16, LDE) **1979**†LARm★16 (16, LDE) **1980**†LARm☆16 (16, LDE) **1981** LARm 16 (16, LDE) **1982** LARm 9 (9, LDE) **1983**†LARm 16 (16, LDE) **1984**†LARm☆15 (15, LDE) **NFL** 202 (184) [14 yrs]

YOUNGBLOOD, JIM James Lee, LB, 6´3˝/235 lbs; Tennessee Tech; 1973: LA, rnd 2; B2/23/1950 Union, SC **1973**†LARm 14 **1974**†LARm 14 **1975**†LARm 14 **1976**†LARm 14 (11, LLB) **1977**†LARm 14 (14, MLB/llb) **1978**†LARm☆16 (16, LLB) **1979**†LARm★16 (16, LLB) **1980**†LARm 15 (15, LLB) **1981** LARm 16 (16, LLB) **1982** LARm 7 (7, MLB) **1983**†LARm 7 (3) **1984**†Was 4 (0) **1984** LARm 5 (0) **NFL** 156 (98) [12 yrs]

YOUNGELMAN, SID Sidney, DT-DE, 6´3˝/257 lbs; Alabama; 1954: SF, rnd 7; B12/1/1931 Newark, NJ, D12/21/1991 Lake Hiawatha, NY **1955** SF 10 **1956** Phi 12 **1958** Phi 5 **1959** Cle 12 (RDT) **1960** NYT-A☆14 **1961** NYT-A☆14 (RDE) **1962** Buf-A 14 (LDT) **1963**†Buf-A 14 (LDE/rde)

YEAR	TEAM	G(GS, POS)	RUSH	YD	AVG(LG)	TD	REC	YD	AVG(LG)	TD	PASS	COMP	PCT	YD	AVG(LG)	TD	INT	SK	YD	QBR	KPR	OTD	PTS	TAY
1957	Phi	12(RDT)	0	3	(3)	0	—	—	—	—	—	—	—	—	—	—	—	—	—	—	—	—	0	3
NFL	9	107	0	3	(3)	0	—	—	—	—	—	—	—	—	—	—	—	—	—	—	—	—	0	3

YOUNGER, TANK Paul Lawrence, FB-LB-HB, 6´3˝/225 lbs; Grambling State; B6/25/1928 Grambling, LA, D9/15/2001 Inglewood, CA

YEAR	TEAM	G(GS, POS)	RUSH	YD	AVG(LG)	TD	REC	YD	AVG(LG)	TD	PASS	COMP	PCT	YD	AVG(LG)	TD	INT	SK	YD	QBR	KPR	OTD	PTS	TAY
1949	†LARm	12(8, RH)	52	191	3.7(16)	0	7	119	17.0(33)	0	—	—	—	—	—	—	—	—	—	—	—	—	0	251
1950	†LARm	12	8	28	3.5(6)	2	—	—	—	—	—	—	—	—	—	—	—	—	—	—	—	—	12	48
1951	†LARm★	12(LLB/fb)	36	223	6.2(24)	1	5	72	14.4(52)	0	—	—	—	—	—	—	—	—	—	—	i	—	6	264
1952	†LARm★	12(LLB/fb)	63	331	5.3(38)	1	12	73	6.1(12)	0	—	—	—	—	—	—	—	—	—	—	i	—	6	368
1953	LARm✧	12(fb)	84	350	4.2(39)	8	20	259	12.9(48)	1	—	—	—	—	—	—	—	—	—	—	k	—	54	574
1954	LARm☆	8(fb)	91	610	6.7(75)	8	8	76	9.5(21)	0	—	—	—	—	—	—	—	—	—	—	—	—	48	728
1955	LARm✧	8(FB)	138	644	4.7(54)	5	6	51	8.5(13)	0	—	—	—	—	—	—	—	—	—	—	—	—	30	720
1956	LARm	12(FB)	114	518	4.5(33)	3	18	268	14.9(54)	0	—	—	—	—	—	—	—	—	—	—	—	—	18	682
1957	LARm	12(fb)	96	401	4.2(29)	3	8	61	7.6(16)	0	1	0	0.0	0	0.0	0	1	—	—	—	—	—	18	422
1958	Pit	12(FB)	88	344	3.9(36)	3	16	188	11.8(51)	0	—	—	—	—	—	—	—	—	—	—	—	—	18	468
NFL	10	112(8)	770	3640	4.7(75)	34	100	1167	11.7(54)	1	1	0	0.0	0	0.0	0	1	—	—	—	ki	—	210	4523

YOUNGFLEISH, FRANK Frank Whiting, C-G, 5´9˝/190 lbs; Villanova; B5/7/1896 Pottsville, PA, D7/1958 Pottsville, PA **1926** Pot 9 (4) **1927** Pot 6 (5, C) **NFL** 15 (9) [2 yrs]

YOUNGSTROM, SWEDE Adolph Frederick, G-T-E-C, 6´1˝/187 lbs; Dartmouth; B5/24/1897 Waltham, MA, D8/5/1968 Boston, MA **[C]** **1920** Buf 11 (6, RG) **1921** Buf 12 (12, RG), 6 **1921** Can 1 (1) **1922** Buf 10 (10, RG) **1923** Buf☆12 (12, RG) **1924** Buf☆11 (11, RG) **1925** Buf 9 (9, RG) **1925** Cle☆1 (1) **1926** Fra 16 (7, lt), 12 **1927** Fra 13 (4) **NFL** 96 (73), 18 [8 yrs]

YOUNT, MIKE Myron Edwin, T, 6´1˝/205 lbs; Franklin (IN); B4/18/1894 Pleasant Township, IN, D1/25/1964 Indianapolis, IN **1921** Mun 2 (2, LT)

YOUSO, FRANK Frank Mitchell, T-DT, 6´4˝/257 lbs; Minnesota; 1958: NYG, rnd 2; B7/5/1936 International Falls, MN **1958**†NYG 12 (RT) **1959**†NYG 12 (RT) **1960** NYG 12 (RT) **1961** Min 14 (13, RT) **1962** Min 13 (13, RT) **1963** Oak-A 4 **1965** Oak-A 11 (rt)

YEAR	TEAM	G(GS, POS)	RUSH	YD	AVG(LG)	TD	REC	YD	AVG(LG)	TD	PASS	COMP	PCT	YD	AVG(LG)	TD	INT	SK	YD	QBR	KPR	OTD	PTS	TAY
1964	Oak-A	14(rt)	0	4	(4)	0	—	—	—	—	—	—	—	—	—	—	—	—	—	—	—	—	0	4
NFL	8	92(26)	0	4	(4)	0	—	—	—	—	—	—	—	—	—	—	—	—	—	—	k	—	0	-4

YEAR	TEAM	G (GS, POS)	RUSH	YD	AVG(LG)	TD	REC	YD	AVG(LG)	TD	PASS	COMP	PCT	YD	AVG(LG)	TD	INT	SK	YD	QBR	KPR	OTD	PTS	TAY

YOVANOVITS, DAVE   David, G, 6'3"/294 lbs; Temple; 2003: NYJ, rnd 7; B3/6/1981 Stanhope, NJ   **2004** NYJ 4 (0)   **2005** Cle 2 (1)   **NFL** 6 (1) [2 yrs]

YOVICSIN, JOHN   John Michael, DE, 6'3"/195 lbs; Gettysburg; B10/17/1918 Steelton, PA, D9/13/1989 Hyannis, MA   **1944** Phi 1 (0)

YOWARSKY, WALT   Walter Robert, DE-C-T, 6'2"/234 lbs; Kentucky; 1951: Was, rnd 3; B5/10/1928 Cleveland, OH   **1951** Was 11 (LDE)   **1954** Was 11 (LDE)   **1955** Det 2
1955 NYG 10 (LDE)   **1956**†NYG 11   **1957** NYG 11   **1958** SF 8 (C)   **NFL** 64 [6 yrs]

YURCHEY, JOHN   John Henry, HB-DB, 5'11"/188 lbs; Duquesne; B11/12/1917 Bridgeville, PA, D6/1/1944 Bridgeville, PA   **1940** Pit 1 (0)

ZABEL, STEVE   Steven Gregory, LB-TE, 6'4"/235 lbs; Oklahoma; 1970: Phi, rnd 1; B3/20/1948 Minneapolis, MN [K]   **1972** Phi 7 (6, mlb)   **1973** Phi 11 (LLB)   **1974** Phi 14 (LLB)
1975 NE 13 (9, ROLB)   **1976**†NE 14 (14, LOLB)   **1977** NE 11 (10, LOLB)   **1978**†NE 11 (11, LOLB)   **1979** Bal 15

1970	Phi	14(6, te)	—	—	—	—	8	119	14.9(29)	1	—	—	—	—	—	—	—	—	—	—	—	—	6	65
1971	Phi	14(LLB)	1	-5	-5.0(-5)	0	2	4	2.0(3)	2	—	—	—	—	—	—	—	—	—	—	ki	—	12	-9
NFL		10	124(56)	1	-5	-5.0(-5)	0	10	123	12.3(25)	3	—	—	—	—	—	—	—	—	Kki	—	19	56

ZACHARY, KEN   Kenneth R., RB, 6'0"/222 lbs; Oklahoma State; B11/19/1963 Sapulpa, OK

| **1987** | SD | 3(0) | 1 | 3 | 3.0(3) | 0 | — | — | — | — | — | — | — | — | — | — | — | — | — | — | k | — | 0 | -10 |

ZACKERY, TONY   Anthony Eugene, DB, 6'2"/195 lbs; Washington; 1989: NE, rnd 8; B11/20/1966 Seattle, WA   **1989** Atl 1 (0)   **1990** NE 2 (0)   **1991** NE 16 (0)   **NFL** 19 (0) [3 yrs]

ZADWORNEY, FRANK   Frank Stanley, HB-DB, 6'0"/202 lbs; Ohio State; 1940: Bkn, rnd 8; B11/2/1916, D3/24/1979 Westerville, OH

| **1940** | Bkn | 3(0) | 2 | 5 | 2.5 | 0 | — | — | — | — | — | — | — | — | — | — | — | — | — | — | — | — | 0 | 5 |

ZAESKE, PAUL   Paul Alan, WR, 6'2"/200 lbs; North Park; B12/4/1945 Sioux City, IA   **1969**†Hou-A 6   **1970** Hou 5   **NFL** 11 [2 yrs]

ZAGERS, BERT   Albert Aldon, DB-HB, 5'10"/185 lbs; Michigan State; 1955: Det, rnd 7; B1/30/1933 Fremont, MI, D9/2/1992 Traverse City, MI

1955	Was	11(RH)	89	395	4.4(41)	2	14	306	21.9(57)	0	—	—	—	—	—	—	—	—	—	—	kp	1	18	783
1957	Was	11(DB)	—	—	—	—	—	—	—	—	—	—	—	—	—	—	—	—	—	—	kpi	2	12	309
1958	Was	10(DB)	27	82	3.0(16)	1	3	50	16.7(19)	0	—	—	—	—	—	—	—	—	—	—	pi	—	6	172
NFL		3	32	116	477	4.1(41)	2	3	17	356	20.9(57)	0	—	—	—	—	—	—	—	kpi	3	36	1264

ZAHURSKY, STEVE   Steve, G-T, 6'6"/305 lbs; Kent State; B9/2/1976 Euclid, OH   **1999** Cle 9 (7, rg)   **2000** Cle 16 (16, RT/lg)   **2001** Jax 1 (0)   **NFL** 26 (23) [3 yrs]

ZALEJSKI, ERNIE   Ernest Raymond, DB-HB, 6'0"/185 lbs; Notre Dame; 1950: ChiB, rnd 5; B11/23/1925 South Bend, IN

| **1950** | Bal | 11 | 7 | -2 | -0.3(6) | 1 | 1 | 1 | 1.0(1) | 0 | — | — | — | — | — | — | — | — | — | — | kpi | 1 | 12 | 88 |

ZAMBERLIN, JOHN   John, LB, 6'2"/230 lbs; Pacific Lutheran; 1979: NE, rnd 5; B2/13/1956 Tacoma, WA   **1979** NE 16 (1)   **1980** NE 16 (13, RILB)   **1981** NE 16 (1)   **1982**†NE 8 (0)
1983 KC 14 (3)   **1984** KC 8 (7, LILB)   **NFL** 78 (25) [6 yrs]

ZANDER, CARL   Carl August, LB, 6'2"/235 lbs; Tennessee; 1985: Cin, rnd 2; B4/12/1963 Mendham, NJ   **1985** Cin 16 (7, lilb)   **1986** Cin 16 (16, LILB)   **1987** Cin 12 (12, LILB)
1988†Cin 16 (16, LILB)   **1989** Cin 16 (16, LILB)   **1990**†Cin 16 (13, LILB)   **1991** Cin 14 (14, RILB)   **NFL** 106 (94) [7 yrs]

ZANDERS, EMANUEL   Emanuel, G, 6'1"/251 lbs; Jackson State; B7/31/1951 Demopolis, AL   **1974** NO 10 (RG)   **1975** NO 14 (14, RG)   **1976** NO 14 (13, RG)   **1977** NO 14 (14, RG)
1978 NO 3 (3)   **1979** NO 16 (16, LG)   **1980** NO 16 (16, LG)

| **1981** | ChiB | 12(12, RG) | — | — | — | — | 1 | 7 | 7.0(7) | 0 | — | — | — | — | — | — | — | — | — | — | — | — | 0 | 4 |
| **NFL** | | 8 | 99(88) | — | — | — | — | 1 | 7 | 7.0(7) | 0 | — | — | — | — | — | — | — | — | — | — | — | 0 | 4 |

ZANDOFSKY, MIKE   Michael Leslie, G, 6'2"/300 lbs; Washington; 1989: Phx, rnd 3; B11/30/1965 Corvallis, OR   **1989** Phx 15 (6, lg)   **1990** SD 13 (0)   **1991** SD 10 (5, lg)
1992†SD 15 (0)   **1993** SD 16 (16, LG)   **1994** Atl 16 (16, RG)   **1995** Atl 12 (12, RG)   **1996** Atl 14 (14, RG)   **1997** Phi 5 (2)   **NFL** 116 (71) [9 yrs]

ZANINELLI, SILVIO   Silvio David, B, 5'10"/207 lbs; Duquesne; B12/9/1913 Reading, PA, D1/29/1979 Weirton, WV

1934	Pit	11(11, BB)	24	60	2.5	0	2	14	7.0	0	1	0	0.0	0	—	0	0	0	—	—	—	—	0	67
1935	Pit	11(6, FB)	22	15	0.7	0	1	7	7.0(7)	0	8	1	12.5	4	0.5(4)	0	2	—	—	—	—	—	0	-60
1936	Pit	12(3)	31	61	2.0	1	2	12	6.0	0	6	1	16.7	2	0.3(2)	0	1	—	—	—	—	—	6	38
1937	Pit	10(5, BB)	4	14	3.5	0	2	12	6.0	0	—	—	—	—	—	—	—	—	—	—	—	—	0	20
NFL		4	44(25)	81	150	1.9	1	7	45	6.4(7)	0	15	2	13.3	6	0.4(4)	0	3	—	—	—	—	6	66

ZAPALAC, WILLIE   William Frank, LB-DE, 6'4"/225 lbs; Texas; 1971: NYJ, rnd 4; B9/1/1948 Bellville, TX   **1971** NYJ 14   **1972** NYJ 6   **1973** NYJ 13   **NFL** 33 [3 yrs]

ZAPUSTAS, JOE   Joseph John, E, 6'0"/198 lbs; Fordham; B5/25/1907 South Boston, MA, D1/14/2001 Randolph, MA

| **1933** | NYG | 2(0) | — | — | — | — | 1 | 26 | 26.0(26) | 0 | — | — | — | — | — | — | — | — | — | — | — | — | 0 | 13 |

ZARNAS, GUST   Gustave Constantine, G, 5'10"/220 lbs; Ohio State; 1938: ChiB, rnd 5; B12/16/1913 Ikaris, Greece   **1938** ChiB 10 (1)   **1939** Bkn 4 (2)   **1939**†GB◇5 (2)
1940 GB 9 (2)   **NFL** 28 (7) [3 yrs]

ZARUBA, CARROLL   Carroll Robert, DB, 5'9"/210 lbs; Nebraska; 1960: DalT, rnd 1; B12/30/1933 Fullerton, NE, D5/10/2001 Sterling, CO   **1960** DalT-A 7

ZASTUDIL, DAVE   David Michael, P, 6'3"/210 lbs; Ohio University; 2002: Bal, rnd 4; B10/26/1978 Bay Village, OH [P]   **2003**†Bal 16 (0)   **2004** Bal 13 (0)

2002	Bal	16(0)	1	-12	-12.0(-12)	0	—	—	—	—	1	0	0.0	0	0.0(0)	0	0	—	—	P	—	0	-12
2005	Bal	16(0)	1	0	0.0(0)	0	—	—	—	—	1	0	0.0	0	0.0(0)	0	0	—	—	P	—	0	0
NFL		4	61(0)	2	-12	-6.0	0	—	—	—	—	1	0	0.0	0	0.0(0)	0	0	—	—	P	—	0	-12

ZATECHKA, ROB   Robert Brett, G, 6'4"/313 lbs; Nebraska; 1995: NYG, rnd 4; B12/1/1971 Lansing, MI   **1995** NYG 16 (3)   **1996** NYG 15 (6, lg)   **1997**†NYG 16 (0)   **NFL** 47 (9) [3 yrs]

ZATKOFF, ROGER   Roger, LB-DE, 6'2"/216 lbs; Michigan; 1953: GB, rnd 5; B3/25/1931 Hamtramck, MI   **1953** GB 12   **1954** GB★12 (RLB)   **1955** GB★12 (RLB)   **1956** GB★12
1957†Det 12 (RLB)   **1958** Det 12   **NFL** 72 [6 yrs]

ZAUNBRECHER, GODFREY   Godfrey William, C, 6'2"/240 lbs; LSU; 1970: Min, rnd 11; B12/17/1946 Crowley, LA   **1971**†Min 4   **1972** Min 7   **1973** Min 5   **NFL** 16 [3 yrs]

ZAWADZKAS, JERRY   Gerald A., TE, 6'4"/220 lbs; Columbia; 1967: Det, rnd 16; B1/3/1946 Torrington, CT   **1967** Det 2

ZAWATSON, DAVE   David Francis, G-T, 6'5"/275 lbs; California; 1989: Chi, rnd 2; B4/13/1966 Cleveland, OH   **1989** ChiB 4 (0)   **1990** NYJ 16 (0)   **1991** Mia 2 (0)   **NFL** 22 (0) [3 yrs]

ZECHER, RICH   Richard Frederick, DT-T, 6'2"/255 lbs; Utah State; 1965: Oak, rnd 9; B10/14/1943 Alameda, CA   **1965** Oak-A 14   **1966** Mia-A 14 (9, RDT)   **1967** Mia-A 7
1967 Buf-A 5   **NFL** 40 (9) [3 yrs]

ZEHRER, HENRY   Henry Christian, FB-WB, /175 lbs; none; B12/20/1905 New Britain, CT, D3/16/1955 Putnam, CT   **1926** Har 7 (1)

ZEIER, ERIC   Eric Royce, QB, 6'1"/205 lbs; Georgia; 1995: Cle, rnd 3; B9/6/1972 Pensacola, FL

1995	Cle	7(4, qb)	15	80	5.3(17)	0	—	—	—	—	161	82	50.9	864	5.4(59)	4	9	15	91	51.9	—	—	2	172
1996	Bal	1(0)	2	8	4.0(5)	0	—	—	—	—	21	10	47.6	97	4.6(15)	1	1	4	26	—	—	—	0	22
1997	Bal	5(3)	10	17	1.7(12)	0	—	—	—	—	116	67	57.8	958	8.3(92)	7	1	17	98	101.1	—	—	0	491
1998	Bal	10(4, qb)	11	17	1.5(7)	0	—	—	—	—	181	107	59.1	1312	7.2(73)	4	3	18	138	82.0	—	—	0	573
1999	TB	2(1)	3	7	2.3(8)	0	—	—	—	—	55	32	58.2	270	4.9(38)	0	1	5	36	—	—	—	0	102
2000	TB	3(0)	2	-2	-1.0(-1)	0	—	—	—	—	3	3	100.0	19	6.3(14)	0	0	—	—	—	—	—	0	8
NFL		6	28(12)	43	127	3.0(17)	0	—	—	—	—	537	301	56.1	3520	6.6(92)	16	15	59	389	74.4	—	—	2	1367

ZEIGLER, DUSTY   Curtis Dustin, C-G, 6'5"/298 lbs; Notre Dame; 1996: Buf, rnd 6; B9/27/1973 Savannah, GA   **1996** Buf 2 (0)   **1997** Buf 13 (13, C)   **1998**†Buf 16 (16, C)
1999†Buf 15 (15, RG)   **2000** NYG 16 (16, C)   **2001** NYG 16 (16, C)   **2002** NYG 2 (2)   **NFL** 80 (78) [7 yrs]

ZELE, MIKE   Michael Robert, NT-DT, 6'3"/239 lbs; Kent State; 1979: Atl, rnd 5; B7/3/1956 Cleveland, OH   **1979** Atl 13   **1980**†Atl 11 (4)   **1981** Atl 14 (0)   **1982**†Atl 9 (0)
1983 Atl 5 (4)   **NFL** 52 (8) [5 yrs]

ZELENCIK, CONNIE   Conrad James, C, 6'4"/245 lbs; Purdue; 1977: Chi, rnd 11; B4/3/1955 Calumet City, IL   **1977** Buf 14

ZELENCIK, FRANK   Frank, T, 6'1"/220 lbs; Oglethorpe; B11/11/1913 East Chicago, IN, D3/8/2003 Crown Point, IN   **1939** ChiC 9 (0)

ZELENKA, JOE   Joseph John, TE, 6'3"/261 lbs; Wake Forest; B3/9/1976 Cleveland, OH   **1999** SF 13 (0)   **2000** Was 16 (0)   **2001** Jax 16 (0)   **2002** Jax 16 (0)   **2003** Jax 16 (0)
2004 Jax 16 (0)   **2005**†Jax 16 (0)   **NFL** 109 (0) [7 yrs]

ZELLARS, RAY   Raymond Mark, RB, 5'11"/233 lbs; Notre Dame; 1995: NO, rnd 2; B3/25/1973 Pittsburgh, PA

1995	NO	12(0)	50	162	3.2(11)	2	7	33	4.7(9)	0	—	—	—	—	—	—	—	—	—	—	—	—	12	199
1996	NO	9(6, fb)	120	475	4.0(63)	4	9	45	5.0(12)	0	—	—	—	—	—	—	—	—	—	—	—	—	24	538
1997	NO	16(16, FB)	156	552	3.5(23)	4	31	263	8.5(38)	0	—	—	—	—	—	—	—	—	—	—	—	—	24	724
1998	NO	11(7, fb)	56	162	2.9(15)	1	10	50	5.0(14)	0	—	—	—	—	—	—	—	—	—	—	—	—	6	197
NFL		4	48(29)	382	1351	3.5(63)	11	57	391	6.9(38)	0	—	—	—	—	—	—	—	—	—	—	—	66	1657

YEAR	TEAM	G (GS, POS)	RUSH	YD	AVG (LG)	TD	REC	YD	AVG (LG)	TD	PASS	COMP	PCT	YD	AVG (LG)	TD	INT	SK	YD	QBR	KPR	OTD	PTS	TAY

ZELLER, JERRY Gerald T., WB-BB, 5´11˝/170 lbs; Purdue; Illinois; B6/3/1898, OH, D11/1968 Columbus, OH **1921** Evv 4 (2), 6

ZELLER, JOE Joseph Thomas, G-E, 6´1˝/203 lbs; Indiana; B5/2/1908 East Chicago, IN, D9/23/1983 Chicago, IL **1932** GB☆14 (8, RG) **1934** ChiB 11 (1) **1935** ChiB 12 (2)
1936 ChiB 11 (3) **1937**†ChiB 11 (2) **1938** ChiB 11 (0)

| 1933 | ChiB | 11(2) | — | — | — | — | 2 | 44 | 22.0 | 1 | — | — | — | — | — | — | — | — | — | — | — | — | 6 | 27 |
| NFL | 7 | 81(18) | — | — | — | — | 2 | 44 | 22.0 | 1 | — | — | — | — | — | — | — | — | — | — | — | 1 | 12 | 37 |

ZELLNER, PEPPI Hunndens Guiseppi, DE, 6´5˝/262 lbs; Fort Valley State (GA); 1999: Dal, rnd 4; B3/14/1975 Forsyth, GA **1999**†Dal 13 (0) **2000** Dal 12 (0) **2001** Dal 16 (15, RDE)
2002 Dal 16 (2) **2003** Was 16 (0) **2004** Arz 16 (14, LDE) **NFL** 89 (31) [6 yrs]

ZEMAN, BOB Edward Robert, DB, 6´1˝/200 lbs; Wisconsin; 1960: LAC, rnd 1/1959: Cle, rnd 10; B2/22/1937 Geneva, IL **1960**†LAC-A 12 (LS) **1961**†SD-A 14 (LS)
1962 Den-A★14 (LS) **1963** Den-A 14 (LS) **1965**†SD-A 14 **1966** SD-A 14 **NFL** 82 [6 yrs]

ZEMAN, ED Edward Robert, DB, 6´1˝/195 lbs; Fort Lewis; B9/25/1963 Denver, CO **1987** LARm 3 (0)

ZENDEJAS, JOAQUIN Joaquin, K, 5´11˝/176 lbs; La Verne; B1/14/1960 Curimeo, Mexico **[K]** **1983** NE 2 (0)

ZENDEJAS, LUIS Luis Fernando, K, 5´9˝/175 lbs; Arizona State; B10/22/1961 Mexico City, Mexico **[K]** **1987** Dal 2 (0) **1988** Dal 2 (0) **1988**†Phi 12 (0) **1989** Phi 8 (0)
1989 Dal 7 (0) **NFL** 31 (0) [3 yrs]

ZENDEJAS, MAX Maximiano Javier, K, 5´11˝/184 lbs; Arizona; 1986: Dal, rnd 4; B9/2/1963 Curimeo, Mexico **[K]** **1986** Was 9 (0) **1987** GB 10 (0) **1988** GB 8 (0) **NFL** 27 (0) [3 yrs]

ZENDEJAS, TONY Anthony Guerrero, K, 5´8˝/165 lbs; Nevada-Reno; 1984: Was, rnd S1; B5/15/1960 Curimeo, Mexico **[K]** **1986** Hou 15 (0) **1987**†Hou 13 (0) **1988**†Hou 16 (0)
1990 Hou 7 (0) **1991** LARm 16 (0) **1992** LARm 16 (0) **1993** LARm 16 (0) **1994** LARm 16 (0) **1995** Atl 1 (0) **1995** SF 3 (0)

1985	Hou	14(0)	—	—	—	—	—	—	—	—	1	1	100.0	7	-7.0(-7)	0	0	—	—	K	—	—	92	-4
1989	†Hou☆	16(0)	—	—	—	—	—	—	—	—	1	0	0.0	—	—	0	1	—	—	K	—	—	115	-40
NFL	11	149(0)	—	—	—	—	—	—	—	—	2	1	50.0	7	-3.5	0	1	—	—	KP	—	—	874	-44

ZENO, COLEMAN Joseph Coleman, WR, 6´4˝/210 lbs; Grambling State; 1971: NYG, rnd 17; B11/18/1946 New Orleans, LA

| 1971 | NYG | 2 | — | 2 | 10 | 5.0(7) | 0 | 5 | 97 | 19.4(53) | 0 | — | — | — | — | — | — | — | — | — | — | — | 0 | 59 |

ZENO, JOE Joseph H., G-T, 5´10˝/234 lbs; Holy Cross; 1942: Was, rnd 5; B6/14/1919 Brooklyn, NY, D1/8/1992 Sacramento, CA **1942** Was◇9 (0) **1943**†Was 10 (3)
1944 Was 10 (10, LT) **1946** Bos 11 (8, LG) **1947** Bos 2 (0) **NFL** 42 (21) [5 yrs]

ZENO, LANCE Lance Michael, C, 6´4˝/279 lbs; UCLA; B4/15/1967 Los Angeles, CA **1992** Cle 3 (0) **1993** Cle 2 (0) **1993**†GB 5 (0) **NFL** 10 (0) [2 yrs]

ZENTIC, MIKE Michael Lee, C, 6´3˝/255 lbs; Northwest Missouri State; Oklahoma State; B11/22/1963 **1987** Dal 3 (3)

ZERBE, HAROLD Harold, E, /165 lbs; none; B1901, deceased **1926** Can 1 (0)

ZEREOUE, AMOS Amos, RB, 5´8˝/212 lbs; West Virginia; 1999: Pit, rnd 3; B10/8/1976 Ivory Coast

1999	Pit	8(0)	18	48	2.7(8)	0	2	17	8.5(14)	0	—	—	—	—	—	—	—	—	—	—	k	—	0	121
2000	Pit	12(0)	6	14	2.3(11)	0	—	—	—	—	—	—	—	—	—	—	—	—	—	—	—	—	0	14
2001	†Pit	14(0)	85	441	5.2(32)	1	13	154	11.8(62)	1	—	—	—	—	—	—	—	—	—	—	—	—	12	533
2002	†Pit	16(5, rb)	193	762	3.9(42)	4	42	341	8.1(54)	0	—	—	—	—	—	—	—	—	—	—	—	—	24	973
2003	Pit	16(6, rb)	132	433	3.3(22)	2	40	310	7.8(29)	0	—	—	—	—	—	—	—	—	—	—	—	—	12	608
2004	Oak	15(6, rb)	112	425	3.8(55)	3	39	284	7.3(13)	0	—	—	—	—	—	—	—	—	—	—	—	—	18	597
2005	NE	3(0)	7	14	2.0(12)	0	1	5	5.0(5)	0	—	—	—	—	—	—	—	—	—	—	—	—	0	17
NFL	7	84(17)	553	2137	3.9(55)	10	137	1111	8.1(62)	1	—	—	—	—	—	—	—	—	—	—	k	—	66	2862

ZGONINA, JEFF Jeffrey Marc, DT, 6´2˝/285 lbs; Purdue; 1993: Pit, rnd 7; B5/24/1970 Chicago, IL **1993** Pit 5 (0) **1994**†Pit 16 (0) **1995** Car 2 (0) **1996** Atl 8 (0)
1997 SL 15 (0) **1998** Ind 2 (0) **1999**†SL 16 (0) **2000**†SL 16 (10, RDT) **2001** SL 13 (13, RDT) **2002** SL 16 (16, RDT) **2003** Mia 16 (3) **2004** Mia 16 (14, RDT) **2005** Mia 16 (3)
NFL 157 (59) [13 yrs]

ZIEGLER, FRANK Frank Richard, HB-DB, 5´11˝/175 lbs; Georgia Tech; 1949: Phi, rnd 3/1948: LAD-A, rnd 20; B10/1/1923 College Park, GA

1949	†Phi	10(4)	84	283	3.4(41)	1	3	33	11.0(24)	0	—	—	—	—	—	—	—	—	—	—	kpi	—	6	337
1950	Phi	12(RH)	172	733	4.3(52)	1	13	216	16.6(48)	2	—	—	—	—	—	—	—	—	—	—	kp	—	18	920
1951	Phi	12(RH)	113	418	3.7(34)	2	8	59	7.4(19)	0	—	—	—	—	—	—	—	—	—	—	—	—	12	468
1952	Phi	11(RH)	67	172	2.6(12)	2	8	120	15.0(37)	2	—	—	—	—	—	—	—	—	—	—	k	—	24	284
1953	Phi	12(RH)	83	320	3.9(52)	5	15	211	14.1(43)	0	1	0	0.0	0	0.0	0	0	—	—	—	—	30	476
NFL	5	57(4)	519	1926	3.7(52)	11	47	639	13.6(48)	4	1	0	0.0	0	0.0	0	0	—	—	kpi	—	90	2484

ZIEGLER, PAUL Paul K., B, 5´10˝/185 lbs; none; B9/1898 Kenton, OH, deceased **1922** Col 6 (2)

ZIEMAN, CHRIS Christopher Robert, T, 6´7˝/315 lbs; Michigan; B9/20/1976 Aurora, IL **2000** NYG 8 (0)

ZIFF, DAVE David, E, 6´0˝/195 lbs; Syracuse; Carson-Newman; B1/18/1902, MA, D10/17/1977 New York, NY **1925** Roc 4 (3, LE) **1926** Bkn 7 (7, RE) **NFL** 11 (10) [2 yrs]

ZILLY, JACK John Jynus, DE-E, 6´2˝/212 lbs; Notre Dame; 1945: Cle, rnd 4/1947: SF-A, rnd 6; B11/11/1921 Waterbury, CT **1950**†LARm 12 (RDE) **1951** LARm 4
1952 Phi 12 (LDE)

1947	LARm	12(7, LE)	—	—	—	—	7	75	10.7(19)	0	—	—	—	—	—	—	—	—	—	—	k	—	0	33
1948	LARm	12(6, RE)	—	—	—	—	13	169	13.0(30)	4	—	—	—	—	—	—	—	—	—	—	—	—	24	105
1949	†LARm	12(2)	—	—	—	—	3	35	11.7(14)	0	—	—	—	—	—	—	—	—	—	—	k	—	0	3
NFL	6	64(15)	—	—	—	—	23	279	12.1(30)	4	—	—	—	—	—	—	—	—	—	—	k	—	24	140

ZIMMERLINK, GENO Eugene Franklin, TE, 6´3˝/222 lbs; Virginia; B3/26/1963 Milltown, NJ **1987** Atl 3 (1)

ZIMMERMAN, CORL Corl James, G-T, 6´0˝/185 lbs; Mount Union; B2/22/1899 Akron, OH, D6/30/1959 Akron, OH **1927** Day 5 (3) **1928** Day 4 (2) **1929** Day 4 (2)
NFL 13 (7) [3 yrs]

ZIMMERMAN, DON Donald, WR, 6´3˝/195 lbs; Arkansas-Pine Bluff; Louisiana-Monroe; 1972: Phi, rnd 12; B11/22/1949 Monroe, LA

1973	Phi	14(11, WR)	—	—	—	—	22	220	10.0(30)	3	—	—	—	—	—	—	—	—	—	—	—	—	18	125
1974	Phi	14(14, WR)	—	—	—	—	30	368	12.3(64)	2	—	—	—	—	—	—	—	—	—	—	k	—	12	179
1975	Phi	10(2)	—	—	—	—	—	—	—	—	—	—	—	—	—	—	—	—	—	—	—	—	—	—
1976	Phi	1	—	—	—	—	—	—	—	—	—	—	—	—	—	—	—	—	—	—	—	—	—	—
1976	GB	2	1	3	3.0(3)	0	1	13	13.0(13)	0	—	—	—	—	—	—	—	—	—	—	—	—	0	10
NFL	4	41(27)	1	3	3.0(3)	0	53	601	11.3(64)	5	—	—	—	—	—	—	—	—	—	—	k	—	30	314

ZIMMERMAN, GARY Gary Wayne, T, 6´6˝/294 lbs; Oregon; 1984: NYG, rnd S1; B12/13/1961 Fullerton, CA **1986** Min☆16 (16, LT) **1987**†Min★12 (12, LT) **1988**†Min★16 (16, LT)
1989†Min★16 (16, LT) **1990** Min 16 (16, LT) **1991** Min 16 (16, LT) **1992**†Min★16 (16, LT) **1993** Den☆16 (16, LT) **1994** Den★16 (16, LT) **1995** Den★16 (16, LT)
1996†Den★14 (14, LT) **1997**†Den 16 (16, LT) **NFL** 184 (184) [12 yrs]

ZIMMERMAN, GIFF Gifford Guy, WB-TB, 5´10˝/180 lbs; Syracuse; B8/25/1900 Akron, OH, D11/27/1968 Akron, OH **1924** Akr 2 (1) **1925** Can 6 (3), 12 **NFL** 8 (4) [2 yrs]

ZIMMERMAN, JEFF Jeffrey Alan, G, 6´3˝/320 lbs; Florida; 1987: Dal, rnd 3; B1/10/1963 Enid, OK **1987** Dal 11 (1) **1988** Dal 1 (0) **1989** Dal 16 (1) **1990** Dal 6 (0)
NFL 34 (2) [4 yrs]

ZIMMERMAN, ROY Henry Leroy, QB-WB-K, 6´2˝/201 lbs; San Jose State; 1940: Was, rnd 7; B2/20/1918 Tonganoxie, KS, D8/22/1997 Madera, CA **[KP]**

1940	†Was	6(0)	31	127	4.1	0	—	—	—	—	12	4	33.3	53	4.4(19)	0	3	—	—	KP	—	0	34
1941	Was	9(5, wb)	20	54	2.7(12)	0	5	36	7.2(11)	0	1	0	0.0	0	0.0	0	2	—	—	P	—	0	72
1942	Was◇	7(1)	12	56	4.7(16)	0	—	—	—	—	10	2	20.0	13	1.3(9)	0	2	—	—	KPk	—	4	-8
1943	P-P☆	10(9, QB)	33	-41	-1.2(12)	1	—	—	—	—	124	43	34.7	846	6.8(60)	9	17	—	—	44.0 KPki	—	35	-239
1944	Phi☆	10(10, QB)	26	-84	-3.2(5)	0	—	—	—	—	105	39	37.1	785	7.5(75)	8	10	—	—	50.0 KPi	1	62	-16
1945	Phi	10(8, QB)	29	-11	-0.4(9)	1	—	—	—	—	127	67	52.8	991	7.8(74)	9	8	—	—	75.9 KPi	—	47	277
1946	Phi	11(7, QB)	23	43	1.9(12)	1	—	—	—	—	79	41	51.9	639	7.6(59)	4	8	—	—	KPi	—	14	95
1947	Det	12(7, QB)	13	28	2.2(10)	1	—	—	—	—	138	57	41.3	867	6.3(53)	7	9	—	—	52.4 KP	—	51	147
1948	Bos	9(2, QB)	13	72	5.5(18)	2	—	—	—	—	107	46	43.0	649	6.1(69)	7	13	—	—	45.4 KP	—	16	-89
NFL	9	84(49)	200	244	1.2(18)	6	5	36	7.2(11)	0	703	299	42.5	4801	6.8(75)	44	70	—	—	47.3 KPkpi	1	229	273

ZIMNY, BOB Robert John, T, 6´1˝/233 lbs; Indiana; 1944: Bkn, rnd 28; B12/11/1921 Chicago, IL **1945** ChiC★10 (3) **1946** ChiC 11 (6, RT) **1947** ChiC 7 (0)
1948†ChiC 12 (10, RT) **1949** ChiC 12 (4) **NFL** 52 (23) [5 yrs]

ZIRINSKY, WALT   Walter John, aka Walt Zwiezynski, HB, 5'11"/187 lbs; Lafayette; 1942: Cle, rnd 12; B8/1/1920 Northampton, PA, D11/30/2001 Catasauqua, PA

YEAR	TEAM	G(GS, POS)	RUSH	YD	AVG(LG)	TD	REC	YD	AVG(LG)	TD	PASS	COMP	PCT	YD	AVG(LG)	TD	INT	SK	YD	QBR	KPR	OTD	PTS	TAY
1945	Cle	5(0)	3	3	1.0(2)	0	—	—	—	—	—	—	—	—	—	—	—	—	—	—	—	—	0	3

ZIZAK, VINCE   Vincent Augustine, G-T, 5'8"/208 lbs; Villanova; B8/8/1908 Camden, NJ, D8/1973 Upper Darby, PA   **1934** ChiB 2 (0)   **1934** Phi 6 (1)   **1935** Phi 4 (1)   **1936** Phi 10 (3)   **1937** Phi 2 (1)   **NFL** 24 (6) [4 yrs]

ZOFKO, MICKEY   Michael Joseph, RB, 6'3"/195 lbs; Auburn; 1971: Det, rnd 9; B6/8/1949 Melbourne, FL [K]

YEAR	TEAM	G(GS, POS)	RUSH	YD	AVG(LG)	TD	REC	YD	AVG(LG)	TD	PASS	COMP	PCT	YD	AVG(LG)	TD	INT	SK	YD	QBR	KPR	OTD	PTS	TAY
1971	Det	11																						
1972	Det	14	-7	28	4.0(9)	0	2	14	7.0(17)	0	—	—	—	—	—	—	—	—	—	—	Kk	—	1	261
1973	Det	8	11	33	3.0(8)	0	2	16	8.0(9)	0	1	1	100.0	35	35.0(35)	0	0	—	—	—	k	—	0	51
1974	Det	4	3	6	2.0(3)	0	3	15	5.0(8)	0	—	—	—	—	—	—	—	—	—	—	k	—	0	3
1974	NYG	7																			k	—	0	-1
NFL	4	44	21	67	3.2(9)	0	7	45	6.4(17)	0	1	1	100.0	35	35.0(35)	0	0	—	—	—	Kk	—	1	313

ZOGG, JON   Jon Frederick, G, 6'4"/290 lbs; Boise State; **1987** LARd 1 (0)

ZOIA, CLYDE   Clyde John, G, 5'7"/175 lbs; Notre Dame; B5/1896, MN, deceased   **1920** ChiC 8 (3, LG)   **1921** ChiC 8 (6, LG)   **1922** ChiC 7 (7, LG)   **1923** ChiC☆11 (9, LG)   **NFL** 34 (25) [4 yrs]

ZOLAK, SCOTT   Scott David, QB, 6'5"/230 lbs; Maryland; 1991: NE, rnd 4; B12/13/1967 Pittsburgh, PA

YEAR	TEAM	G(GS, POS)	RUSH	YD	AVG(LG)	TD	REC	YD	AVG(LG)	TD	PASS	COMP	PCT	YD	AVG(LG)	TD	INT	SK	YD	QBR	KPR	OTD	PTS	TAY
1992	NE	6(4)	18	71	3.9(19)	0	—	—	—	—	100	52	52.0	561	5.6(65)	2	4	17	137	—	—		0	202
1993	NE	3(0)	1	0	0.0	0	—	—	—	—	2	0	0.0	0	0.0	0	0	0	0	—	—		0	0
1994	†NE	16(0)	1	-1	-1.0(-1)	0	—	—	—	—	8	5	62.5	28	3.5(13)	0	0	—	—	—	—		0	13
1995	NE	16(1)	4	19	4.8(12)	0	—	—	—	—	49	28	57.1	282	5.8(72)	1	0	4	28	—	—		0	165
1996	†NE	3(0)	4	-3	-0.8(0)	0	—	—	—	—	1	1	100.0	5	5.0(5)	0	0	—	—	—	—		0	-1
1997	NE	4(0)	3	-3	-1.0(-1)	0	—	—	—	—	9	6	66.7	67	7.4(20)	2	0	—	—	—	—		0	41
1998	†NE	6(2)	5	0	0.0(4)	0	—	—	—	—	75	32	42.7	371	4.9(61)	3	3	4	49	—	—		0	81
1999	Mia	1(0)	2	-2	-1.0(-1)	0	—	—	—	—	4	0	0.0	0	0.0	0	0	0	0	—	—		0	-2
NFL	8	55(7)	38	81	2.1(19)	0	—	—	—	—	248	124	50.0	1314	5.3(72)	8	7	25	214	—	—		0	498

ZOLL, CARL   Carl Francis, G, 5'9"/215 lbs; none; B1/28/1899 Howard, WI, D10/19/1973 Green Bay, WI   **1922** GB 1 (0)

ZOLL, DICK   Richard Archibald, G-T, 5'11"/218 lbs; Indiana; B12/10/1913 Green Bay, WI, D9/6/1985 Green Bay, WI [K]   **1937** Cle 11 (6, RG)   **1938** Cle 11 (6, LT)   **1939** GB 1 (0)   **NFL** 23 (12) [3 yrs]

ZOLL, MARTY   Martin A., G, 5'8"/185 lbs; none; B11/12/1900 Howard, WI, D10/14/1968 Green Bay, WI   **1921** GB 1 (0)

ZOMALT, ERIC   Eric Lee, DB, 5'11"/201 lbs; California; 1994: Phi, rnd 3; B8/9/1972 Los Angeles, CA   **1994** Phi 12 (0)   **1995**†Phi 15 (1)   **1996** Phi 3 (2)   **1996** NYJ 10 (1)   **NFL** 40 (4) [3 yrs]

ZOMBEK, JOE   Joseph A., DE-E, 6'1"/195 lbs; Pittsburgh; 1954: Pit, rnd 9; B12/24/1932, D1/13/1996 McDonald, PA   **1954** Pit 8 (rde)   **1955** Pit 1   **NFL** 9 [2 yrs]

ZONTINI, LOU   Louis Rogers, B, 5'9"/189 lbs; Notre Dame; B8/30/1917 Whitesville, WV, D8/6/1986 Cleveland, OH [K]

YEAR	TEAM	G(GS, POS)	RUSH	YD	AVG(LG)	TD	REC	YD	AVG(LG)	TD	PASS	COMP	PCT	YD	AVG(LG)	TD	INT	SK	YD	QBR	KPR	OTD	PTS	TAY
1940	ChiC	8(0)	1	1	1.0(1)	0	—	—	—	—	—	—	—	—	—	—	—	—	—	—	KPi	—	16	16
1941	ChiC	8(1)	1	-9	-9.0(-9)	0	1	22	22.0(22)	0	—	—	—	—	—	—	—	—	—	—	KP	—	5	2
1944	Cle	10(0)	33	105	3.2(16)	3	3	88	29.3(53)	1	2	2	100.0	18	9.0(18)	0	0	—	—	—	Kkpi	—	47	245
NFL	3	26(1)	35	97	2.8(16)	3	4	110	27.5(53)	1	2	2	100.0	18	9.0(18)	0	0	—	—	—	KPkpi	—	68	263
1946	Buf-A	14(5, fb)	13	36	2.8	0	—	—	—	—	—	—	—	—	—	—	—	—	—	—	—	—	42	37

ZOOK, JOHN   John Eldon, DE, 6'4"/243 lbs; Kansas; 1969: LA, rnd 4; B9/24/1947 Garden City, KS   **1969** Atl 14 (RDE)   **1970** Atl 14 (RDE)   **1971** Atl 14 (RDE)   **1972** Atl☆14 (RDE)   **1973** Atl☆14 (RDE)   **1974** Atl 14 (RDE)   **1975** Atl 14 (RDE)   **1976** SL 13 (12, LDE)   **1977** SL 12 (9, LDE)   **1978** SL 16 (RDE)   **1979** SL 5   **NFL** 144 (21) [11 yrs]

ZOPPETTI, FRANK   Frank, TB, 5'11"/185 lbs; Duquesne; B4/15/1916, D6/1985 Burgettstown, PA

YEAR	TEAM	G(GS, POS)	RUSH	YD	AVG(LG)	TD	REC	YD	AVG(LG)	TD	PASS	COMP	PCT	YD	AVG(LG)	TD	INT	SK	YD	QBR	KPR	OTD	PTS	TAY
1941	Pit	4(0)									0	0	0.0	0							—	—	0	0

ZORDICH, MIKE   Michael Edward, DB, 6'1"/207 lbs; Penn State; 1986: SD, rnd 9; B10/12/1963 Youngstown, OH [I]   **1987** NYJ 10 (0)   **1988** NYJ 16 (0)   **1989** Phx 16 (7, fs)   **1990** Phx 16 (1)   **1991** Phx 16 (16, FS)   **1992** Phx 16 (16, FS)   **1993** Phx 16 (9, FS)   **1994** Phi 16 (16, SS)   **1995**†Phi 15 (15, SS)   **1996**†Phi 16 (16, SS)   **1997** Phi 16 (16, SS)   **1998** Phi 16 (16, SS)   **NFL** 185 (128) [12 yrs]

ZORICH, CHRIS   Christopher Robert, DT, 6'1"/278 lbs; Notre Dame; 1991: Chi, rnd 2; B3/13/1969 Chicago, IL   **1991**†ChiB 12 (0)   **1992** ChiB 16 (2)   **1993** ChiB 16 (16, RDT)   **1994**†ChiB 16 (16, RDT)   **1995** ChiB 16 (15, RDT)   **1997** ChiB 3 (0)   **1997** Was 5 (0)   **NFL** 84 (49) [6 yrs]

ZORICH, GEORGE   George, G-LB, 6'2"/213 lbs; Northwestern; B11/24/1915 Wakefield, MA, D10/14/1962 Rensselaer, IN   **1944** ChiB☆10 (10, RG)   **1945** ChiB 8 (6, RG)   **NFL** 18 (16) [2 yrs]
1946 Mia-A 6 (0)   **1947** Bal-A 11 (1)   **AAFC** 17 (1) [2 yrs]

ZORN, JIM   James Arthur, QB, 6'2"/200 lbs; Cal Poly-Pomona; B5/10/1953 Whittier, CA

YEAR	TEAM	G(GS, POS)	RUSH	YD	AVG(LG)	TD	REC	YD	AVG(LG)	TD	PASS	COMP	PCT	YD	AVG(LG)	TD	INT	SK	YD	QBR	KPR	OTD	PTS	TAY
1976	Sea	14(14, QB)	52	246	4.7(19)	4	—	—	—	—	439	208	47.4	2571	5.9(80)	12	27	25	196	49.5	—	—	24	552
1977	Sea	10(10, QB)	25	141	5.6(15)	1	—	—	—	—	251	104	41.4	1687	6.7(82)	16	19	11	43	54.3	—	—	6	315
1978	Sea☆	16(16, QB)	59	290	4.9(23)	6	—	—	—	—	443	248	56.0	3283	7.4(64)	15	20	44	284	72.1	—	—	36	1267
1979	Sea	16(16, QB)	46	279	6.1(41)	2	—	—	—	—	505	285	56.4	3661	7.2(65)	20	18	23	201	77.7	—	—	12	1510
1980	Sea	16(16, QB)	44	214	4.9(25)	1	—	—	—	—	488	276	56.6	3346	6.9(77)	17	20	44	341	72.3	—	—	6	1182
1981	Sea	13(13, QB)	30	140	4.7(20)	1	—	—	—	—	397	236	59.4	2788	7.0(80)	13	9	24	201	82.4	—	—	6	1249
1982	Sea	9(7, QB)	15	113	7.5(35)	1	1	27	27.0(27)	0	245	126	51.4	1540	6.3(50)	7	11	20	152	61.9	—	—	6	502
1983	†Sea	16(8, qb)	30	71	2.4(18)	1	—	—	—	—	205	103	50.2	1166	5.7(43)	7	7	9	64	64.8	—	—	6	419
1984	†Sea	16(0)	7	-3	-0.4(7)	0	—	—	—	—	17	7	41.2	74	4.7(21)	0	2	1	8	—	—	—	0	-43
1985	GB	13(5, qb)	10	9	0.9(8)	0	—	—	—	—	123	56	45.5	794	6.5(56)	4	6	11	89	57.4	—	—	0	186
1987	TB	1(1)	4	4	1.0(5)	0	—	—	—	—	36	20	55.6	199	5.5(26)	0	2	1	24	—	—	—	0	24
NFL	11	140(106)	322	1504	4.7(41)	17	1	27	27.0(27)	0	3149	1669	53.0	21115	6.7(82)	111	141	213	1585	67.3	—	—	102	7160

ZUCCO, VIC   Victor A., DB, 6'0"/187 lbs; Wayne State (MI); Michigan State; 1957: ChiB, rnd 5; B9/4/1935 Renton, PA   **1957** ChiB 12 (DB)   **1958** ChiB 12 (DB)   **1959** ChiB 2   **1960** ChiB 12   **NFL** 38 [4 yrs]

ZUIDMULDER, DAVE   David C., TB, 5'10"/175 lbs; St. Ambrose; Georgetown (DC); B2/4/1906 New Franken, WI, D6/8/1978 Green Bay, WI   **1929** GB 1 (0)   **1930** GB 4 (1)   **1931** GB 2 (0)   **NFL** 7 (1) [3 yrs]

ZUKAUSKAS, PAUL   Paul Malcolm, G-T, 6'5"/320 lbs; Boston College; 2001: Cle, rnd 7; B7/12/1979 Weymouth, MA   **2001** Cle 1 (0)   **2002**†Cle 16 (3)   **2003** Cle 12 (10, RG)   **2004** Cle 14 (5, lg)   **NFL** 43 (18) [4 yrs]

ZUNKER, CHARLIE   Charles A., T, 6'4"/227 lbs; Southwest Texas State; B8/24/1908 Hanley, TX, D6/11/1963 San Antonio, TX   **1934** Cin 3 (0)

ZUPEK, ALBERT   Albert Ernest, BB, 6'1"/205 lbs; Lawrence; B1/12/1922 Racine, WI, D6/16/1980 Burlington, IA   **1946** GB 3 (0)

ZUVER, MERLE   Merle Dale, G-C, 6'1"/198 lbs; Nebraska; B1/25/1905 Adams, NE, D3/25/1969 Phoenix, AZ   **1930** GB 10 (5, rg)

ZUZZIO, TONY   Anthony Joseph, G, 5'11"/210 lbs; Muhlenberg; B8/5/1916 Irvington, NJ, D4/7/2002 Lawrence, KS   **1942** Det 2 (0)

ZYNTELL, JIM   Ignatius James, G, 6'1"/200 lbs; Holy Cross; B4/27/1910 Boston, MA, D11/13/1992 Brighton, MA   **1933** NYG 2 (0)   **1933** Phi 8 (7, RG)   **1934** Phi 8 (5, RG)   **1935** Phi 7 (4)   **NFL** 25 (16) [3 yrs]

THE KICKING REGISTER

Kicker is the most taken granted and maligned position in football. In a game where men weighing 350 pounds apiece slug it out at the line for close to three hours on Sunday, there has long been resentment on many levels that a game should be decided by a man who might weigh half that of the right tackle. This outcast lines up seven yards away from bodies slamming into other at the snap of the ball, takes a couple of steps, and kicks the ball through the uprights with the least bit of contact on him by the opposition heavily penalized. Of course, he may miss. And then those same massive bodies eager to pat him on the head for winning the game will turn away from him and then grunt in reply when an old college buddy on the opposition says on the way off the field, "Too bad you guys worked your tails off only to have it blown by the @#$%^&* kicker!"

The specialization of the kicking game in the NFL has gotten to the point where the kicker is purposely ostracized from the team. He has a less strenuous routine than the others, practicing by himself mostly. He does spend a lot of time with the punter, who on most teams has inherited the old backup quarterback's job as the holder, the middle part of the precision three-man ritual that decides the valuable three-pointer. Recognition is hard to come by. While the top 20 scorers of all-time spent most of their careers as kickers, only one pure kicker is in the Pro Football Hall of Fame: Jan Stenerud. Other kickers enshrined in Canton are recognized for the positions they played at an All-Pro level: Lou Groza (tackle) and George Blanda (quarterback). The Hall of Fame begrudgingly admits Groza and Blanda were "also placekickers." No such admission is made for several other Hall of Famers who served as kickers during their career, including running back Paul Hornung, who scored 388 of his 760 career points as a kicker, and legends Don Hutson and Bob Waterfield, who scored 199 and 495 points, respectively, as kickers. Ken Strong, a Hall of Fame halfback, came out retirement during World War II to serve as kicker only for the New York Giants. While he helped the club during a severe manpower shortage, he didn't help the cause of the kicker by playing without shoulder pads and wearing his wristwatch on the field.

But no one hurt the kicker's cause as much as one of the more reliable kickers of the 1960s and 1970s, Garo Yepremian. The 5-foot, 8-inch left-footed kicker from the island of Cyprus did not go to college but debuted with the Lions in 1966, scoring 50 points in nine games. When he did not keep up that pace the next year, he was out of the league until 1970, when Don Shula signed him to kick for the Miami Dolphins. It was there that Yepremian sent back the notion of the kicker as an athlete to a level it has yet to recover from. With the Dolphins trying to put style points on an undefeated season, Yepremian's fourth-quarter kick was blocked by the Redskins. The ball bounced back to Yepremian, who tried to throw it. Showing the form of a person wholly unfamiliar with the science of throwing any type of ball, it slipped out of his hand and he then batted it in the air. Redskin Mike Bass, seemingly putting in half the effort of Yepremian, glided by him, plucked the ball out of the air, and ran 49 yards for a touchdown. It briefly put Miami's unblemished record in jeopardy and spoiled what would have been the only shutout in Super Bowl history. Miami's defense stopped Washington cold once more and everyone could laugh at the kicker's expense after the game.

Yepremian was part of the new breed of soccer-style kickers that had started in 1964 with Hungarian-born, Cornell-educated Pete Gogolak of the Buffalo Bills in the American Football League. His "European-style" kicking was more reliable than the straight-ahead method that had been used since the drop-kick had fallen out of style before the NFL had even begun in 1920. Using the side of the foot as opposed to making contact with the toes, Gogolak was so successful that he was coveted by two leagues. His signing with the Giants in 1966 briefly threatened to overturn the imminent merger negotiations between the AFL and NFL. Giants owner Wellington Mara's luring of Gogolak—AFL commissioner Al Davis called it more than that—started a brief final skirmish between the leagues before they settled the merger. When the news of Gogolak's defection was announced at a meeting of NFL owners, Los Angeles Rams owner Carroll Rosenbloom was reported to have yelled, "If you'd wanted a kicker, why didn't you just ask me? I'd have given you one." Kickers, it seems, grew on trees. Maybe it was the California climate. That's where Tom Dempsey grew up. Dempsey is the best-known player with a physical disability in NFL history. Born with half a right foot and missing a right hand, Dempsey kicked the longest field goal in history for the New Orleans Saints to beat the Detroit Lions on the last play of the game on November 8, 1970. Kicking below sea level at outdoor Tulane Stadium, Dempsey's 63-yard kick has been equaled in the NFL only by Jason Elam, kicking a mile above sea level for Denver in 1998.

There has been one NFL Most Valuable Player Award given to a "pure kicker"—and a straight-ahead one at that—in Mark Moseley in 1982. Gary Anderson and Mike Vanderjagt each went entire regular seasons with missing, and Neil Rackers of the Arizona Cardinals set a record with 40 field goals in 2005. Yet the lasting glory usually goes to someone at another position, such as New England quarterback Tom Brady, who received two Super Bowl MVPs for setting up both of Adam Vinatieri's last-second, championship-winning kicks. Kickers still often earn more praise from announcers and fans alike for a tackle on the kickoff than for kicking the ball through the uprights minutes earlier, but they'll take the praise in whatever form it comes. It's a job that's a lot tougher than it looks—and one that get more tenuous with every miss.

KEY TO THE KICKING REGISTER

This section is simply about kickers. Every man to have ever kicked a recorded field goal is included here. The register covers the basics of kicking with field goals and extra points, plus the category TD for touchdowns. While that category seems like sheer flattery for the modern specialized kicker, in bygone eras many players simply went from the end zone back to the 10-yard line to line up for the extra point.

XPM	Extra Points Made
XPA	Extra Points Attempted
FGM	Field Goals Made
FGA	Field Goals Attempted
Points	Total Points Scored

YEAR	TEAM	TD	XPM	XPA	FGM	FGA	PTS
Abbott, Faye							
1925	Day	0	0	—	1	—	3
1928	Day	0	0	—	1	—	3
NFL	2	2	0	—	2	—	18
Abbott, Vince							
1987	SD	0	22	23	13	22	61
1988	SD	0	15	15	8	12	39
NFL	2	0	37	38	21	34	100
Abramson, George							
1925	GB	0	2	—	2	—	8
Absher, Dick							
1967	Was	0	4	4	0	1	4
Adams, Chet							
1946	Cle-A	2	5	5	0	0	17
1947	Cle-A	0	1	2	1	1	4
1949	Buf-A	0	32	32	4	11	44
1939	Cle	0	5	5	0	0	5
1940	Cle	0	7	9	1	5	10
1941	Cle	0	13	14	1	2	16
1942	Cle	0	14	15	3	6	23
1943	GB	0	0	0	1	6	3
1950	NYY	0	45	48	2	9	51
AAFC	3	2	38	39	5	12	65
NFL	6	0	84	91	8	28	108
Adkins, Bob							
1940	GB	2	1	2	0	1	13
1941	GB	0	3	3	0	0	3
NFL	2	2	4	5	0	1	16
Agajanian, Ben							
1947	LAD-A	0	39	40	**15**	**24**	84
1948	LAD-A	0	31	32	5	15	46
1945	Pit	0	1	2	4	4	13
1949	NYG	0	35	36	8	13	59
1953	LARm	0	36	37	10	24	66
1954	NYG	0	35	35	13	**25**	74
1955	NYG	0	32	33	10	15	62
1956	NYG	0	23	23	5	13	38
1957	NYG	0	32	32	10	18	62
1960	LAC-A	0	46	47	13	24	85
1961	DalT-A	0	7	7	3	9	16
1961	GB	0	8	8	1	2	11
1962	Oak-A	0	10	11	5	14	25
1964	SD-A	0	8	8	2	4	14
AAFC	2	0	70	72	20	39	130
NFL	11	0	273	279	84	165	525
Aguiar, Louie							
1991	NYJ	0	0	0	1	2	3
Aguirre, Joe							
1941	Was	2	8	9	2	5	26
1943	Was	7	6	9	0	2	48
1944	Was	4	15	18	4	8	51
1945	Was	0	23	24	**7**	**13**	44
1946	LAD-A	2	31	32	4	11	55
1948	LAD-A	9	2	3	0	0	56
AAFC	2	11	33	35	4	11	111
NFL	4	18	52	60	13	28	199
Akers, David							
1998	Was	0	2	2	0	2	2
1999	Phi	0	2	2	3	6	11
2000	Phi	0	34	36	29	33	121
2001	Phi	0	37	38	26	31	115
2002	Phi	0	43	43	30	34	133
2003	Phi	0	42	42	24	29	114
2004	Phi	0	41	42	**27**	**32**	**122**
2005	Phi	0	23	23	16	22	71
NFL	8	0	224	228	155	189	689
Albert, Frankie							
1947	SF-A	5	0	2	0	0	30
1948	SF-A	8	1	2	0	0	49
1949	SF-A	3	0	1	0	0	18
AAFC	3	16	1	5	0	0	97
Aldrich, Ki							
1941	Was	0	4	5	1	3	7
Alford, Bruce							
1967	Was	0	3	4	0	2	3
1968	Buf-A	0	15	15	14	24	57
1969	Buf-A	0	23	24	17	26	74
NFL	3	0	41	43	31	52	134
Alford, Gene							
1934	SL	0	3	—	1	—	6
Allegre, Raul							
1983	Bal	0	22	24	**30**	**35**	112
1984	Ind	0	14	14	11	18	47
1985	Ind	0	36	39	16	26	84
1986	NYG	0	33	33	24	32	105
1987	NYG	0	25	26	17	27	76
1988	NYG	0	14	14	10	11	44
1989	NYG	0	23	24	20	26	83

YEAR	TEAM	TD	XPM	XPA	FGM	FGA	PTS
1990	NYG	0	9	9	4	5	21
1991	NYG	0	5	5	2	2	11
1991	NYJ	0	2	2	3	4	11
NFL	9	0	183	190	137	186	594
Alvarez, Wilson							
1981	Sea	0	14	15	3	7	23
Andersen, Morten							
1982	NO	0	6	6	2	5	12
1983	NO	0	37	38	18	24	91
1984	NO	0	34	34	20	27	94
1985	NO	0	27	29	**31**	35	120
1986	NO	0	30	30	26	30	108
1987	NO	0	37	37	**28**	**36**	121
1988	NO	0	32	33	26	36	110
1989	NO	0	44	45	20	29	104
1990	NO	0	29	29	21	27	92
1991	NO	0	38	38	25	32	113
1992	NO	0	33	34	29	34	**120**
1993	NO	0	33	33	28	35	117
1994	NO	0	32	32	28	**39**	116
1995	Atl	0	29	30	**31**	37	122
1996	Atl	0	31	31	22	29	97
1997	Atl	0	35	35	23	27	104
1998	Atl	0	51	52	23	28	120
1999	Atl	0	34	34	15	21	79
2000	Atl	0	23	23	25	31	98
2001	NYG	0	29	30	23	28	98
2002	KC	0	**51**	**51**	22	26	117
2003	KC	0	**58**	**59**	16	20	106
2004	Min	0	45	45	18	22	99
NFL	23	0	798	808	520	658	2358
Anderson, Gary							
1982	Pit	0	22	22	10	12	52
1983	Pit	0	38	39	27	31	**119**
1984	Pit	0	45	45	**24**	32	**117**
1985	Pit	0	40	40	**33**	**42**	**139**
1986	Pit	0	32	32	21	32	95
1987	Pit	0	21	21	22	27	87
1988	Pit	0	34	35	28	36	118
1989	Pit	0	28	28	21	30	91
1990	Pit	0	32	32	20	25	92
1991	Pit	0	31	31	23	33	100
1992	Pit	0	29	31	28	36	113
1993	Pit	0	32	32	28	30	116
1994	Pit	0	32	32	24	29	104
1995	Phi	0	32	33	22	30	98
1996	Phi	0	40	40	25	29	115
1997	SF	0	38	38	29	36	125
1998	Min	0	**59**	**59**	**35**	**35**	**164**
1999	Min	0	46	46	19	30	103
2000	Min	0	**45**	**45**	22	23	111
2001	Min	0	29	30	15	18	74
2002	Min	0	36	37	18	23	90
2003	Ten	0	42	42	27	31	123
2004	Ten	0	37	37	17	22	88
NFL	23	0	820	827	538	672	2434
Anderson, John							
1979	GB	0	1	2	1	1	4
Andrews, Roy							
1924	KC	0	1	—	1	—	4
1925	KC	0	1	—	1	—	4
1926	KC	0	1	—	0	—	1
NFL	3	0	3	—	2	—	9
Annan, Dunc							
1922	Tol	5	1	—	0	—	31
Arians, Jake							
2001	Buf	0	16	17	12	21	52
Ariri, Obed							
1984	TB	0	38	40	19	26	95
1987	Was	0	6	6	3	5	15
NFL	2	0	44	46	22	31	110
Armstrong, Graham							
1947	Buf-A	0	8	10	0	1	8
1948	Buf-A	0	15	17	0	1	15
AAFC	2	0	23	27	0	2	23
Armstrong, John							
1924	RI	1	1	—	0	—	7
1925	RI	5	1	—	0	—	31
NFL	2	8	2	—	0	—	50
Arnold, Jay							
1938	Phi	4	3	3	0	1	27
Artoe, Lee							
1940	ChiB	0	1	2	1	1	4
1941	ChiB	0	3	4	1	7	6
1942	ChiB	0	20	22	0	1	20
1945	ChiB	0	0	0	0	1	0
1946	LAD-A	0	1	2	0	0	1
AAFC	1	0	1	2	0	0	1
NFL	4	0	24	28	2	10	30

YEAR	TEAM	TD	XPM	XPA	FGM	FGA	PTS
Ashmore, Roger							
1926	Mil	0	2	—	0	—	2
Atkins, Billy							
1960	Buf-A	0	27	33	6	13	45
1961	Buf-A	1	29	31	2	6	41
NFL	2	1	56	64	8	19	86
Atkinson, Jess							
1985	NYG	1	14	15	10	15	50
1985	SL	0	3	3	0	3	3
1986	Was	0	3	3	0	0	3
1987	Was	0	1	1	1	1	4
NFL	3	1	21	22	11	19	60
Aveni, John							
1959	ChiB	0	28	32	10	19	58
1960	ChiB	0	23	25	7	16	44
1961	Was	1	21	23	5	28	42
NFL	3	1	72	80	22	63	144
Bagdon, Ed							
1952	Was	0	4	6	1	3	7
Bahr, Chris							
1976	Cin	0	39	42	14	27	81
1977	Cin	0	25	26	19	27	82
1978	Cin	0	26	29	16	**30**	74
1979	Cin	0	40	42	13	23	79
1980	Oak	0	41	44	19	**37**	98
1981	Oak	0	27	33	14	24	69
1982	LARd	0	**32**	33	10	16	62
1983	LARd	0	**51**	**53**	21	27	114
1984	LARd	0	40	42	20	27	100
1985	LARd	0	40	42	20	32	100
1986	LARd	0	36	36	21	28	99
1987	LARd	0	27	28	19	29	84
1988	LARd	0	37	39	18	29	91
1989	SD	0	29	30	17	25	80
NFL	14	0	490	519	241	381	1213
Bahr, Matt							
1979	Pit	0	**50**	**52**	18	30	104
1980	Pit	0	39	42	19	28	96
1981	SF	0	12	12	2	6	18
1981	Cle	0	22	22	13	20	61
1982	Cle	0	17	17	7	15	38
1983	Cle	0	38	40	21	24	101
1984	Cle	0	25	25	**24**	32	97
1985	Cle	0	35	35	14	18	77
1986	Cle	0	30	30	20	26	90
1987	Cle	0	9	10	4	5	21
1988	Cle	0	32	33	24	29	104
1989	Cle	0	40	40	16	24	88
1990	NYG	0	29	30	17	23	80
1991	NYG	0	24	25	22	29	90
1992	NYG	0	29	29	16	21	77
1993	Phi	0	18	19	8	13	42
1993	NE	0	10	10	5	5	25
1994	NE	0	36	36	27	34	117
1995	NE	0	27	27	23	33	96
NFL	17	0	522	534	300	415	1422
Baker, Conway							
1937	ChiC	0	6	—	0	—	6
1938	ChiC	0	0	0	0	1	0
1943	ChiC	1	5	6	1	2	14
1944	C-P	0	11	15	0	0	11
1945	ChiC	0	0	1	0	1	0
NFL	5	1	22	22	1	4	31
Baker, Ralph							
1971	NYJ	0	1	1	0	0	1
Baker, Sam							
1956	Was	0	16	19	**17**	25	67
1957	Was	1	29	30	14	23	**77**
1958	Was	0	25	25	13	26	64
1959	Was	0	21	22	10	22	51
1960	Cle	0	**44**	**46**	12	20	80
1962	Dal	0	**50**	**51**	14	27	92
1963	Dal	0	38	38	9	20	65
1964	Phi	0	36	37	16	26	84
1965	Phi	0	38	40	9	23	65
1966	Phi	0	38	39	18	25	92
1967	Phi	0	45	45	12	19	81
1968	Phi	0	17	21	19	30	74
1969	Phi	0	31	31	16	30	79
NFL	13	2	428	444	179	316	977
Bakken, Jim							
1962	SL	0	0	0	0	1	0
1963	SL	0	44	44	11	21	77
1964	SL	0	40	40	**25**	**38**	115
1965	SL	0	33	33	21	31	96
1966	SL	0	27	28	23	40	96
1967	SL	0	36	36	**27**	39	**117**
1968	SL	0	40	40	15	24	85
1969	SL	0	38	40	12	24	74
1970	SL	0	37	38	20	32	97

YEAR	TEAM	TD	XPM	XPA	FGM	FGA	PTS
1971	SL	0	24	24	21	32	87
1972	SL	0	19	21	14	22	61
1973	SL	0	31	31	23	32	100
1974	SL	0	30	36	13	22	69
1975	SL	0	40	41	19	24	97
1976	SL	0	33	35	20	27	93
1977	SL	0	35	36	7	16	56
1978	SL	0	27	30	11	22	60
NFL	17	0	534	553	282	447	1380

BALASZ, FRANK

1941	GB	0	1	1	0	0	1

BALATTI, ED

1946	SF-A	1	2	2	0	0	8
1947	SF-A	2	1	1	0	0	13
AAFC	2	3	3	3	0	0	21

BALDWIN, AL

1948	Buf-A	8	0	1	0	0	48

BARKMAN, RALPH

1929	Ora	0	1	—	0	—	1

BARNES, LARRY

1960	Oak-A	0	37	39	6	25	55

BARNUM, LEN

1939	NYG	2	3	3	3	7	24
1940	NYG	0	6	7	1	4	9
1941	Phi	0	2	2	2	6	8
1942	Phi	0	7	8	3	7	16
NFL	4	3	18	20	9	24	63

BASCA, NICK

1941	Phi	1	9	9	1	2	18

BATEMAN, MARV

1973	Dal	0	1	1	0	0	1

BATTLES, CLIFF

1933	Bos	4	0	—	1	—	27
1934	Bos	7	1	—	0	—	43
NFL	2	31	1	—	1	—	190

BAUGH, SAMMY

1945	Was	0	1	1	0	0	1

BAUMANN, CHARLIE

1991	Mia	0	6	6	2	2	12
1991	NE	0	9	10	7	10	30
1992	NE	0	22	24	11	17	55
NFL	2	0	37	40	20	29	97

BEALS, ALYN

1946	SF-A	10	1	1	0	0	61
1949	SF-A	12	1	1	0	0	73
AAFC	2	22	2	2	0	0	134

BECK, BRADEN

1971	Hou	0	1	2	1	2	4

BECKLEY, ART

1926	Day	0	0	—	1	—	3

BEECHER, WILLIE

1987	Mia	0	12	12	3	4	21

BEHMAN, BULL

1925	Fra	2	12	—	5	—	39

BELL, BILL

1971	Atl	0	29	33	13	21	68
1972	Atl	0	31	31	16	30	79
1973	NE	0	4	5	1	4	7
NFL	3	0	64	69	30	55	154

BENIRSCHKE, ROLF

1977	SD	0	21	24	17	23	72
1978	SD	0	37	43	18	22	91
1979	SD	0	12	13	4	4	24
1980	SD	0	46	48	24	36	118
1981	SD	0	55	61	19	26	112
1982	SD	0	32	34	16	22	80
1983	SD	0	43	45	15	24	88
1984	SD	0	41	41	17	26	92
1985	SD	0	2	2	0	0	2
1986	SD	0	39	41	16	25	87
NFL	10	0	328	352	146	208	766

BENTLEY, SCOTT

1997	Den	0	4	4	2	3	10
2000	Was	0	0	0	1	1	3
NFL	2	0	4	4	3	4	13

BENYOLA, GEORGE

1987	NYG	0	3	3	3	5	12

BERRY, CHARLIE

1925	Pot	6	29	—	3	—	74

BERRY, HOWARD

1921	Roc	2	2	—	2	—	20

BERTELLI, ANGELO

1947	ChiR-A	0	0	0	0	1	0

BIASUCCI, DEAN

1984	Ind	0	13	14	3	5	22
1986	Ind	0	26	27	13	25	65
1987	Ind	0	24	24	24	27	96
1988	Ind	0	39	40	25	32	114
1989	Ind	0	31	32	21	27	94
1990	Ind	0	32	33	17	24	83
1991	Ind	0	14	14	15	26	59
1992	Ind	0	24	24	16	29	72
1993	Ind	0	15	16	26	31	93
1994	Ind	0	37	37	16	24	85
1995	SL	0	13	14	9	12	40
NFL	11	0	268	275	185	262	823

BIELSKI, DICK

1955	Phi	1	23	24	9	23	56
1956	Phi	1	0	0	0	1	6
1957	Phi	2	0	0	0	2	12
1959	Phi	1	0	0	0	5	6
1961	Dal	3	10	10	6	9	46
1962	Bal	2	25	28	11	25	70
NFL	6	12	58	62	26	65	208

BIRDWELL, DAN

1962	Oak-A	0	0	0	0	1	0

BIRNEY, TOM

1979	GB	0	7	10	7	9	28
1980	GB	0	14	18	6	12	32
NFL	2	0	21	28	13	21	60

BIRONAS, ROB

2005	Ten	0	30	32	23	29	99

BITTERLICH, DON

1976	Sea	0	7	7	1	4	10

BLACKLOCK, HUGH

1921	ChiS	0	2	—	0	—	2

BLAILOCK, RUSS

1925	Akr	0	2	—	1	—	5

BLAIR, GEORGE

1961	SD-A	0	42	47	13	27	81
1962	SD-A	0	31	35	17	20	82
1963	SD-A	0	44	48	17	28	95
1964	SD-A	0	5	6	3	5	14
NFL	4	0	122	136	50	80	272

BLANCHARD, CARY

1992	NYJ	0	17	17	16	22	65
1993	NYJ	0	31	31	17	26	82
1995	Ind	0	25	25	19	24	82
1996	Ind	0	27	27	36	40	135
1997	Ind	0	21	21	32	41	117
1998	Was	0	30	31	11	17	63
1999	NYG	0	19	19	18	21	73
2000	Arz	0	18	19	16	23	66
NFL	8	0	188	190	165	214	683

BLANDA, GEORGE

1949	ChiB	1	0	0	7	15	27
1950	ChiB	0	0	0	6	15	18
1951	ChiB	0	26	26	6	17	44
1952	ChiB	1	30	30	6	25	54
1953	ChiB	0	27	27	7	20	48
1954	ChiB	0	23	23	8	16	47
1955	ChiB	2	37	37	11	16	82
1956	ChiB	0	45	47	12	28	81
1957	ChiB	1	23	23	14	26	71
1958	ChiB	0	36	37	11	23	69
1960	Hou-A	4	46	47	15	33	115
1961	Hou-A	0	64	65	16	26	112
1962	Hou-A	0	48	49	11	26	81
1963	Hou-A	0	39	39	9	22	66
1964	Hou-A	0	37	38	13	29	76
1965	Hou-A	0	28	28	11	21	61
1966	Hou-A	0	39	40	16	30	87
1967	Oak-A	0	56	57	20	30	116
1968	Oak-A	0	54	54	21	34	117
1969	Oak-A	0	45	45	20	37	105
1970	Oak	0	36	36	16	29	84
1971	Oak	0	41	42	15	22	86
1972	Oak	0	44	44	17	26	95
1973	Oak	0	31	31	23	33	100
1974	Oak	0	44	46	11	17	77
1975	Oak	0	44	48	13	21	83
NFL	26	9	943	959	335	637	2002

BLANTON, SCOTT

1996	Was	0	40	40	26	32	118
1997	Was	0	34	34	16	24	82
1998	Was	0	4	4	2	4	10
NFL	3	0	78	78	44	60	210

BLISS, HARRY

1921	Col	0	1	—	0	—	1

BLOOD, JOHNNY

1928	Pot	3	1	—	0	—	19
1933	GB	3	1	—	0	—	19
1936	GB	3	1	—	0	—	19
1938	Pit	0	0	1	0	0	0
NFL	4	49	3	1	0	—	297

BLOODGOOD, AL

1925	KC	0	1	—	2	—	7
1926	KC	3	5	—	8	—	47
1927	Cle	6	6	—	1	—	45
NFL	3	10	12	—	11	—	105

BOGUE, GEORGE

1930	ChiC	0	1	—	0	—	1

BOJOVIC, NOVO

1985	SL	0	11	12	3	7	20

BOLKOVAC, NICK

1953	Pit	0	27	28	4	12	45
1954	Pit	0	3	3	3	4	12
NFL	2	0	30	31	7	16	57

BONDURANT, BOURBON

1921	Evv	0	6	—	0	—	6

BONIOL, CHRIS

1994	Dal	0	48	48	22	29	114
1995	Dal	0	46	48	27	28	127
1996	Dal	0	24	25	32	36	120
1997	Phi	0	33	33	22	31	99
1998	Phi	0	15	17	14	21	57
1999	ChiB	0	17	18	11	18	50
NFL	6	0	183	189	128	163	567

BOSTICK, LEW

1939	Cle	0	2	2	0	0	2

BOWSER, ARDA

1922	Can	2	2	—	0	—	14

BOYD, DANNY

2002	Jax	0	7	7	5	5	22

BOYNTON, BENNY

1921	Roc	2	8	—	1	—	23
1921	Was	1	3	—	0	—	9
1924	Buf	6	11	—	4	—	59
NFL	2	9	22	—	5	—	91

BRADY, KERRY

1987	Dal	0	1	1	0	0	1

BRAGG, MIKE

1974	Was	0	7	8	1	1	10

BREECH, JIM

1979	Oak	0	41	45	18	27	95
1980	Cin	0	11	12	4	7	23
1981	Cin	0	49	51	22	32	115
1982	Cin	0	25	26	14	18	67
1983	Cin	0	39	41	16	23	87
1984	Cin	0	37	37	22	31	103
1985	Cin	0	48	50	24	33	120
1986	Cin	0	50	51	17	32	101
1987	Cin	0	25	27	24	30	97
1988	Cin	0	56	59	11	16	89
1989	Cin	0	37	38	12	14	73
1990	Cin	0	41	44	17	21	92
1991	Cin	0	27	27	23	29	96
1992	Cin	0	31	31	19	27	88
NFL	14	0	517	539	243	340	1246

BRENNAN, MATT

1925	NYG	0	0	—	1	—	3
1926	Bkn	1	2	—	1	—	11
NFL	2	1	2	—	2	—	14

BRIEN, DOUG

1994	SF	0	60	62	15	20	105
1995	SF	0	19	19	7	12	40
1995	NO	0	16	16	12	17	52
1996	NO	0	18	18	21	25	81
1997	NO	0	22	22	23	27	91
1998	NO	0	31	31	20	22	91
1999	NO	0	20	21	24	29	92
2000	NO	0	37	37	23	29	106
2001	TB	0	2	2	5	6	17
2002	Min	0	5	7	5	6	20
2003	NYJ	0	24	24	27	32	105
2004	NYJ	0	33	34	24	29	105
2005	ChiB	0	7	7	1	4	10
NFL	12	0	294	300	207	258	915

BRITTON, EARL

1927	Day	0	0	—	1	—	3

BROCK, LOU

1942	GB	3	2	2	0		20

BROCKHAUS, JEFF

1987	SF	0	11	13	3	6	20

YEAR	TEAM	TD	XPM	XPA	FGM	FGA	PTS
Brooker, Tommy							
1962	DalT-A	3	33	33	12	22	87
1963	KC-A	0	20	20	6	14	38
1964	KC-A	0	**46**	**46**	8	17	70
1965	KC-A	0	37	37	13	30	76
1966	KC-A	0	13	13	2	2	19
NFL	5	3	149	149	41	85	290
Brovelli, Angelo							
1933	Pit	2	1	—	0	—	13
Brown, Ed							
1961	ChiB	0	1	1	1	2	4
Brown, Hardy							
1948	Bkn-A	2	25	29	0	1	37
1950	Bal	0	0	1	0	0	0
AAFC	1	2	25	29	0	1	37
NFL	1	1	0	1	0	0	6
Brown, Josh							
2003	Sea	0	48	48	22	30	114
2004	Sea	0	40	40	23	25	109
2005	Sea	0	**56**	**57**	18	25	110
NFL	3	0	144	145	63	80	333
Brown, Kris							
1999	Pit	0	30	31	25	29	105
2000	Pit	0	32	33	25	30	107
2001	Pit	0	34	37	30	**44**	124
2002	Hou	0	20	20	17	24	71
2003	Hou	0	27	27	18	22	81
2004	Hou	0	34	34	17	24	85
2005	Hou	0	24	24	26	34	102
NFL	7	0	201	206	158	207	675
Browner, Ross							
1983	Cin	0	1	1	0	0	1
Bruce, Gail							
1951	SF	0	1	1	0	0	1
Bruder, Doc							
1925	Fra	0	2	—	0	—	2
1926	Fra	3	1	—	0	—	19
NFL	2	4	3	—	0	—	27
Bruder, Hank							
1934	GB	3	4	—	0	—	22
Brumbaugh, Carl							
1930	ChiB	1	1	—	0	—	7
1934	ChiB	2	2	—	0	—	14
NFL	2	6	3	—	0	—	39
Bryan, Rick							
1985	Atl	0	1	1	0	0	1
Bryant, Matt							
2002	NYG	0	30	32	26	32	108
2003	NYG	0	17	17	11	14	50
2004	Ind	0	5	5	0	1	5
2004	Mia	0	7	7	3	3	16
2005	TB	0	31	31	21	25	94
NFL	4	0	90	92	61	75	273
Buck, Cub							
1922	GB	0	3	—	1	—	6
1923	GB	0	5	—	6	—	23
1924	GB	0	8	—	3	—	17
1925	GB	0	8	—	0	—	8
NFL	4	0	24	—	10	—	54
Buckler, Bill							
1926	ChiB	0	1	—	0	—	1
1932	ChiB	0	1	—	0	—	1
NFL	2	0	2	—	0	—	2
Budd, Johnny							
1926	Fra	0	12	—	6	—	30
1928	Pot	0	3	—	0	—	3
NFL	2	0	15	—	6	—	33
Buksar, George							
1952	Was	0	15	18	3	7	24
Bulger, Chet							
1943	ChiC	0	1	1	0	0	1
Burke, Mike							
1974	LARm	0	1	3	0	0	1
Burnett, Dale							
1930	NYG	6	4	—	0	—	40
Burnette, Tom							
1938	Pit	0	0	0	0	1	0
Burrow, Curtis							
1988	GB	0	2	4	0	1	2
Burrus, Harry							
1948	ChiR-A	0	2	3	0	0	2

YEAR	TEAM	TD	XPM	XPA	FGM	FGA	PTS
Burt, Russ							
1924	Buf	1	1	—	0	—	7
Busich, Sam							
1936	Bos	1	1	—	1	—	10
1943	Det	0	1	1	0	0	1
NFL	2	1	2	1	1	—	11
Butkus, Dick							
1971	ChiB	0	1	1	0	0	1
1972	ChiB	0	1	1	0	0	1
NFL	2	1	2	2	0	0	10
Butler, Kevin							
1985	ChiB	0	51	51	**31**	**37**	**144**
1986	ChiB	0	36	37	**28**	**41**	**120**
1987	ChiB	0	28	30	19	28	85
1988	ChiB	0	37	38	15	19	82
1989	ChiB	0	43	45	15	19	88
1990	ChiB	0	36	37	26	37	114
1991	ChiB	0	32	34	19	29	89
1992	ChiB	0	34	34	19	26	91
1993	ChiB	0	21	22	27	36	102
1994	ChiB	0	24	24	21	29	87
1995	ChiB	0	45	45	23	31	114
1996	Arz	0	17	19	14	17	59
1997	Arz	0	9	10	8	12	33
NFL	13	0	413	426	265	361	1208
Butler, Skip							
1971	NO	0	5	6	1	5	8
1972	Hou	0	15	16	12	19	51
1973	Hou	0	21	21	15	24	66
1974	Hou	0	29	29	9	19	56
1975	Hou	0	31	34	18	30	85
1976	Hou	0	24	24	16	27	72
1977	Hou	0	2	3	0	3	2
NFL	7	0	127	133	71	127	340
Caldwell, Bruce							
1928	NYG	1	0	—	1	—	9
Caldwell, Knute							
1925	Akr	0	5	—	0	—	5
Callihan, Bill							
1945	Det	1	25	27	0	0	31
Camarillo, Rich							
1992	Phx	0	0	1	0	0	0
Canale, Justin							
1967	Bos-A	0	1	1	0	0	1
Cannamela, Pat							
1952	DalT	0	8	10	0	1	8
Capece, Bill							
1981	TB	0	30	32	15	24	75
1982	TB	0	14	14	18	**23**	68
1983	TB	0	23	26	10	23	53
NFL	3	0	67	72	43	70	196
Cappelletti, Gino							
1960	Bos-A	0	30	32	8	21	60
1961	Bos-A	8	48	50	**17**	**32**	**147**
1962	Bos-A	5	38	40	20	37	128
1963	Bos-A	2	35	36	**22**	**38**	**113**
1964	Bos-A	7	36	36	**25**	**39**	**155**
1965	Bos-A	9	27	27	17	27	**132**
1966	Bos-A	6	35	36	16	32	**119**
1967	Bos-A	3	29	30	16	31	95
1968	Bos-A	2	26	26	15	27	83
1969	Bos-A	0	26	27	14	34	68
1970	Bos	0	12	13	6	15	30
NFL	11	42	342	353	176	333	1130
Carey, Bob							
1952	LARm	2	0	0	0	1	12
1954	LARm	0	2	2	1	1	5
NFL	2	3	2	2	1	2	23
Carman, Ed							
1925	Ham	0	1	—	0	—	1
Carnelly, Ray							
1939	Bkn	0	0	0	0	1	0
Carney, John							
1988	TB	0	6	6	2	5	12
1990	SD	0	27	28	19	21	84
1991	SD	0	31	31	19	29	88
1992	SD	0	35	35	26	32	113
1993	SD	0	31	33	31	40	124
1994	SD	0	33	33	**34**	**38**	**135**
1995	SD	0	32	33	21	26	95
1996	SD	0	31	31	29	36	118
1997	SD	0	5	5	7	7	26
1998	SD	0	19	19	26	30	97
1999	SD	0	22	23	31	36	115
2000	SD	0	27	27	18	25	81
2001	NO	0	32	32	27	31	113

YEAR	TEAM	TD	XPM	XPA	FGM	FGA	PTS
2002	NO	0	37	37	31	35	130
2003	NO	0	36	37	22	30	102
2004	NO	0	38	38	22	27	104
2005	NO	0	22	22	25	32	97
NFL	17	0	464	470	390	480	1634
Carroll, Bird							
1922	Can	1	1	—	0	—	7
1923	Can	2	1	—	0	—	13
NFL	2	4	2	—	0	—	26
Carter, Joe							
1933	Phi	2	1	—	0	—	13
Carter, Virgil							
1971	Cin	0	1	1	0	0	1
Case, Ernie							
1947	Bal-A	0	1	1	1	1	4
Cavosie, John							
1933	Por	1	1	—	1	—	10
Chandler, Bob							
1973	Buf	3	1	1	0	0	19
Chandler, Don							
1956	NYG	0	3	3	0	0	3
1959	NYG	0	2	2	0	1	2
1962	NYG	0	47	48	19	28	104
1963	NYG	0	**52**	**56**	18	29	**106**
1964	NYG	0	27	29	9	20	54
1965	GB	0	37	38	17	26	88
1966	GB	0	41	43	12	28	77
1967	GB	0	39	39	19	29	96
NFL	8	0	248	258	94	161	530
Chandler, Jeff							
2002	SF	0	14	14	8	12	38
2003	SF	0	7	8	6	7	25
2004	Car	0	8	8	0	2	8
2004	Was	0	6	6	5	6	21
NFL	3	0	35	36	19	27	92
Christensen, Frank							
1935	Det	1	2	—	0	—	8
Christie, Steve							
1990	TB	0	27	27	23	27	96
1991	TB	0	22	22	15	20	67
1992	Buf	0	**43**	**44**	24	30	115
1993	Buf	0	36	37	23	32	105
1994	Buf	0	**38**	**38**	24	28	110
1995	Buf	0	33	35	31	40	126
1996	Buf	0	33	33	24	29	105
1997	Buf	0	21	21	24	30	93
1998	Buf	0	41	41	33	**41**	**140**
1999	Buf	0	33	33	25	34	108
2000	Buf	0	31	31	26	35	109
2001	SD	0	6	6	9	11	33
2002	SD	0	35	36	18	26	89
2003	SD	0	36	36	15	20	81
2004	NYG	0	33	33	22	28	99
NFL	15	0	468	473	336	431	1476
Christopherson, Jim							
1962	Min	0	28	28	11	20	61
Clark, Algy							
1933	Cin	0	3	—	4	—	15
1934	Cin	0	0	—	1	—	3
NFL	2	3	3	—	5	—	36
Clark, Beryl							
1940	ChiC	0	3	3	0	0	3
Clark, Dutch							
1931	Por	9	6	—	0	—	60
1932	Por	6	**10**	—	**3**	—	**55**
1934	Det	8	13	—	4	—	73
1935	Det	6	**16**	—	1	—	**55**
1936	Det	7	**19**	—	4	—	**73**
1937	Det	6	6	—	1	—	45
1938	Det	0	2	2	2	2	8
NFL	7	42	72	2	15	2	369
Clark, Mike							
1963	Phi	0	29	32	7	15	50
1964	Pit	0	28	31	13	25	67
1965	Pit	0	19	24	11	19	52
1966	Pit	0	34	34	21	32	97
1967	Pit	0	35	35	12	22	71
1968	Dal	0	**54**	**54**	17	29	105
1969	Dal	0	43	44	20	36	103
1970	Dal	0	35	35	18	27	89
1971	Dal	0	**47**	**47**	13	25	86
1973	Dal	0	1	2	1	2	4
NFL	10	0	325	338	133	232	724
Clarke, Harry							
1941	ChiB	0	1	1	0	0	1

YEAR	TEAM	TD	XPM	XPA	FGM	FGA	PTS
CLAY, BOYD							
1940	Cle	0	0	0	0	1	0
1941	Cle	0	1	1	1	2	4
1942	Cle	0	4	4	0	0	4
NFL	3	0	5	5	1	3	8
CLAY, RANDY							
1950	NYG	2	0	1	1	1	15
1953	NYG	1	20	22	2	7	32
NFL	2	3	20	23	3	8	47
CLEMENS, CAL							
1936	GB	0	1	—	0	—	1
CLENDENEN, MIKE							
1987	Den	0	7	7	3	4	16
COCKROFT, DON							
1968	Cle	0	46	48	18	24	100
1969	Cle	0	45	45	12	23	81
1970	Cle	0	34	35	12	22	70
1971	Cle	0	34	34	15	28	79
1972	Cle	0	28	29	22	27	94
1973	Cle	0	24	24	22	31	90
1974	Cle	0	29	30	14	16	71
1975	Cle	0	21	24	17	23	72
1976	Cle	0	27	30	15	28	72
1977	Cle	0	30	31	17	23	81
1978	Cle	0	37	40	19	28	94
1979	Cle	0	38	43	17	29	89
1980	Cle	0	39	44	16	26	87
NFL	13	0	432	457	216	328	1080
CODY, ED							
1948	GB	0	11	13	0	0	11
COFER, MIKE							
1987	NO	0	5	7	1	1	8
1988	SF	0	40	41	27	38	121
1989	SF	0	49	51	29	36	136
1990	SF	0	39	39	24	36	111
1991	SF	0	49	50	14	28	91
1992	SF	0	53	54	18	27	107
1993	SF	0	59	61	16	26	107
1995	Ind	0	9	9	4	9	21
NFL	8	0	303	312	133	201	702
COLE, JOHN							
1940	Phi	0	3	5	1	1	6
COLELLA, TOM							
1944	Cle	3	0	0	1	1	21
CONDIT, MERL							
1941	Bkn	4	11	12	2	11	41
1942	Bkn	3	10	10	3	6	37
1943	Bkn	2	0	0	0	3	12
1945	Was	3	1	1	0	0	19
1946	Pit	1	4	4	0	2	10
NFL	5	14	26	27	5	22	125
CONE, FRED							
1951	GB	1	29	35	5	7	50
1952	GB	3	32	34	1	1	53
1953	GB	6	23	25	5	16	74
1954	GB	0	27	29	9	16	54
1955	GB	0	30	30	16	24	78
1956	GB	4	33	36	5	8	72
1957	GB	2	26	26	12	17	74
1960	Dal	0	21	23	6	13	39
NFL	8	16	221	238	59	102	494
CONERLY, CHARLIE							
1952	NYG	0	2	2	0	0	2
1954	NYG	1	1	1	0	0	7
1955	NYG	0	1	1	0	0	1
NFL	3	10	4	4	0	0	64
CONNOR, DUTCH							
1925	Pro	0	2	—	0	—	2
CONOVER, LARRY							
1923	Can	0	1	—	0	—	1
CONRAD, BOBBY JOE							
1958	ChiC	0	33	35	6	17	51
1959	ChiC	6	30	31	6	9	84
1960	SL	0	28	29	2	5	34
1961	SL	3	4	4	0	1	22
1962	SL	4	0	0	0	1	24
NFL	5	42	95	99	14	33	389
CONWAY, BRETT							
1999	Was	0	49	50	22	32	115
2000	Was	0	3	3	3	3	12
2000	Oak	0	3	3	1	1	6
2000	NYJ	0	2	2	2	2	8
2001	Was	0	22	22	26	33	100
2002	Was	0	4	4	1	1	7
2003	NYG	0	6	6	9	12	33
2003	Cle	0	3	3	5	7	18
NFL	5	0	92	93	69	91	299

YEAR	TEAM	TD	XPM	XPA	FGM	FGA	PTS
CONWAY, DAVE							
1971	GB	0	5	5	0	1	5
CONZELMAN, JIMMY							
1921	RI	2	0	—	1	—	15
1922	RI	7	0	—	2	—	48
1923	Mil	4	2	—	0	—	26
1926	Det	2	1	—	0	—	13
1928	Pro	2	1	—	0	—	13
NFL	5	26	4	—	3	—	169
COOK, DAVE							
1934	ChiC	0	1	—	0	—	4
COOPER, JOE							
1984	Hou	0	13	13	11	13	46
1986	NYG	0	4	4	2	4	10
NFL	2	0	17	17	13	17	56
COOPER, THURLOW							
1961	NYT-A	4	0	0	0	1	24
COPLEY, CHARLIE							
1921	Akr	0	10	—	0	—	10
1922	Mil	0	1	—	0	—	1
NFL	2	0	11	—	0	—	11
CORBETT, GEORGE							
1932	ChiB	1	0	—	0	—	7
1935	ChiB	0	0	—	1	—	3
NFL	2	3	1	—	1	—	22
CORGAN, CHUCK							
1924	KC	4	2	—	0	—	26
CORRAL, FRANK							
1978	LARm	0	31	33	29	43	118
1979	LARm	0	36	39	13	25	75
1980	LARm	0	51	52	16	30	99
1981	LARm	0	36	36	17	26	87
NFL	4	0	154	160	75	124	379
CORTEZ, JOSE							
2001	SF	0	47	47	18	25	101
2002	SF	0	25	25	18	24	79
2002	Was	0	9	9	5	8	24
2005	Dal	0	13	14	12	16	49
2005	Phi	0	3	3	0	0	3
2005	SF	0	2	2	0	1	2
NFL	5	0	99	100	53	74	258
COTHREN, PAIGE							
1957	LARm	0	38	38	11	19	71
1958	LARm	0	42	42	14	25	84
1959	Phi	0	1	1	8	18	25
NFL	3	0	81	81	33	62	180
COX, FRED							
1963	Min	0	39	39	12	24	75
1964	Min	0	40	42	21	33	103
1965	Min	0	44	44	23	35	113
1966	Min	0	34	34	18	33	88
1967	Min	0	26	26	17	33	77
1968	Min	0	31	32	19	29	88
1969	Min	0	43	43	26	37	121
1970	Min	0	35	35	30	46	125
1971	Min	0	25	25	22	32	91
1972	Min	0	34	34	21	33	97
1973	Min	0	33	33	21	35	96
1974	Min	0	32	39	12	20	68
1975	Min	0	46	48	13	17	85
1976	Min	0	32	36	19	31	89
1977	Min	0	25	29	8	17	49
NFL	15	0	519	539	282	455	1365
COX, STEVE							
1981	Cle	0	0	0	0	1	0
1982	Cle	0	0	0	0	1	0
1983	Cle	0	0	0	1	1	3
1984	Cle	0	0	0	1	3	3
1985	Was	0	0	0	0	1	0
1986	Was	0	0	0	3	6	9
1987	Was	0	3	3	1	2	6
NFL	7	0	3	3	6	15	21
CRAMER, CARL							
1921	Akr	5	1	—	0	—	31
1924	Akr	1	0	—	1	—	9
NFL	2	12	1	—	1	—	76
CRAWFORD, JIM							
1960	Bos-A	2	0	0	0	1	14
CRAYNE, DICK							
1936	Bkn	1	1	—	0	—	7
1937	Bkn	0	0	—	1	—	1
NFL	2	1	1	—	1	—	10
CRISWELL, RAY							
1988	TB	0	1	1	0	0	1
CRITTENDON, JACK							
1954	ChiC	0	0	0	0	1	0

YEAR	TEAM	TD	XPM	XPA	FGM	FGA	PTS
CROMWELL, NOLAN							
1980	LARm	1	1	1	0	0	7
CUDZIK, WALT							
1960	Bos-A	0	0	0	0	1	0
CUFF, WARD							
1937	NYG	4	0	—	2	—	30
1938	NYG	2	18	20	5	9	45
1939	NYG	2	6	6	7	16	39
1940	NYG	2	9	9	5	8	36
1941	NYG	2	19	20	5	13	46
1942	NYG	2	18	18	3	11	39
1943	NYG	3	26	27	3	9	53
1944	NYG	2	2	2	1	4	17
1946	ChiC	2	28	30	5	12	55
1947	GB	0	30	30	7	16	51
NFL	10	21	156	162	43	98	411
CUNDIFF, BILLY							
2002	Dal	0	25	25	12	19	61
2003	Dal	0	30	31	23	29	99
2004	Dal	0	31	31	20	26	91
2005	Dal	0	14	14	5	8	29
NFL	4	0	100	101	60	82	280
CUNNINGHAM, RICHIE							
1997	Dal	0	24	24	34	37	126
1998	Dal	0	40	40	29	35	127
1999	Dal	0	31	31	12	22	67
1999	Car	0	13	14	3	3	22
2000	Car	0	9	9	5	7	24
2002	Jax	0	2	2	1	1	5
NFL	5	0	119	120	84	105	371
CURRAN, PAT							
1975	SD	0	1	1	0	0	1
CURTIN, DON							
1926	Mil	0	1	—	2	—	7
DADDIO, BILL							
1941	ChiC	0	8	9	4	8	20
1942	ChiC	1	8	8	5	10	29
1946	Buf-A	0	3	3	0	0	3
AAFC	1	0	3	3	0	0	3
NFL	2	1	16	17	9	18	49
DALUISO, BRAD							
1991	Atl	0	2	2	2	3	8
1992	Den	0	0	0	0	1	0
1993	NYG	0	0	0	1	3	3
1994	NYG	0	5	5	11	11	38
1995	NYG	0	28	28	20	28	88
1996	NYG	0	22	22	24	27	94
1997	NYG	0	27	29	22	32	93
1998	NYG	0	32	32	21	27	95
1999	NYG	0	9	9	7	9	30
2000	NYG	0	34	34	17	23	85
2001	Oak	0	1	2	3	4	10
NFL	11	0	160	163	128	168	544
DANELO, JOE							
1975	GB	0	20	23	11	16	53
1976	NYG	0	20	21	8	21	44
1977	NYG	0	19	20	14	23	61
1978	NYG	0	27	29	21	29	90
1979	NYG	0	28	29	9	20	55
1980	NYG	0	27	28	16	24	75
1981	NYG	0	31	31	24	38	103
1982	NYG	0	18	18	12	21	54
1983	Buf	0	33	35	10	20	63
1984	Buf	0	17	17	8	16	41
NFL	10	0	240	251	133	228	639
DANMEIER, RICK							
1978	Min	0	36	37	12	19	72
1979	Min	0	28	31	13	22	67
1980	Min	0	33	38	16	26	81
1981	Min	0	34	37	21	25	97
1982	Min	0	23	23	8	14	47
NFL	5	0	154	166	70	106	364
DAVIDSON, COTTON							
1960	DalT-A	1	7	7	1	1	16
1961	DalT-A	1	20	20	0	2	26
1962	Oak-A	3	4	5	1	2	25
NFL	3	11	31	32	2	5	103
DAVIS, BOB							
1938	Cle	0	0	1	0	0	0
DAVIS, CORBY							
1938	Cle	3	1	1	0	0	19
1939	Cle	1	4	4	1	2	13
NFL	2	4	5	5	1	2	32
DAVIS, GREG							
1987	Atl	0	6	6	3	4	15
1988	Atl	0	25	27	19	30	82
1989	NE	0	13	16	16	23	61
1989	Atl	0	12	12	7	11	33

YEAR	TEAM	TD	XPM	XPA	FGM	FGA	PTS
1990	Atl	0	40	40	22	33	106
1991	Phx	0	19	19	21	30	82
1992	Phx	0	28	28	13	26	67
1993	Phx	0	37	37	21	28	100
1994	Arz	0	17	17	20	26	77
1995	Arz	0	19	19	30	39	109
1996	Arz	0	12	12	9	14	39
1997	Min	0	10	10	7	10	31
1997	SD	0	21	22	19	24	78
1998	Oak	0	31	31	17	27	82
NFL	12	0	290	296	224	325	962

DAVIS, JOE

YEAR	TEAM	TD	XPM	XPA	FGM	FGA	PTS
1946	Bkn-A	1	1	1	0	0	7

DAVIS, RED

1933	Phi	1	3	—	0	—	9

DAVIS, TOMMY

1959	SF	0	31	31	12	26	67
1960	SF	0	21	21	19	32	78
1961	SF	0	44	44	12	22	80
1962	SF	0	36	36	10	23	66
1963	SF	0	24	24	10	31	54
1964	SF	0	30	30	8	25	54
1965	SF	0	52	53	17	27	103
1966	SF	0	38	39	16	31	86
1967	SF	0	33	33	14	33	75
1968	SF	0	26	26	9	16	53
1969	SF	0	13	13	3	10	22
NFL	11	0	348	350	130	276	738

DAWSON, DALE

1987	Min	0	4	4	1	5	7
1988	Phi	0	3	3	0	1	3
1988	GB	0	1	2	3	5	10
NFL	2	0	8	9	4	11	20

DAWSON, LEN

1957	Pit	0	0	2	0	1	0

DAWSON, PHIL

1999	Cle	1	23	24	8	12	53
2000	Cle	0	17	17	14	17	59
2001	Cle	0	29	30	22	25	95
2002	Cle	0	34	35	22	28	100
2003	Cle	0	20	21	18	21	74
2004	Cle	0	28	28	24	29	100
2005	Cle	0	19	21	27	29	100
NFL	7	1	170	176	135	161	581

DEGREE, CY

1921	Det	0	0	—	1	—	3

DEL GRECO, AL

1984	GB	0	34	34	9	12	61
1985	GB	0	38	40	19	26	95
1986	GB	0	29	29	17	27	80
1987	GB	0	11	11	5	10	26
1987	SL	0	8	9	4	5	20
1988	Phx	0	42	44	12	21	78
1989	Phx	0	28	29	18	26	82
1990	Phx	0	31	31	17	27	82
1991	Hou	0	16	16	10	13	46
1992	Hou	0	41	41	21	27	104
1993	Hou	0	39	40	29	34	126
1994	Hou	0	18	18	16	20	66
1995	Hou	0	33	33	27	31	114
1996	Hou	0	35	35	32	38	131
1997	Ten	0	32	32	27	35	113
1998	Ten	0	28	28	36	39	136
1999	Ten	0	43	43	21	25	106
2000	Ten	0	37	38	27	33	118
NFL	17	0	543	551	347	449	1584

DELAUER, BOB

1946	LARm	0	0	0	0	2	0

DELINE, STEVE

1988	SD	0	12	12	6	8	30
1989	Phi	0	3	3	3	7	12
NFL	2	0	15	15	9	15	42

DEMPSEY, TOM

1969	NO	0	33	35	22	41	99
1970	NO	0	16	17	18	34	70
1971	Phi	0	13	14	12	17	49
1972	Phi	0	11	12	20	35	71
1973	Phi	0	34	34	24	40	106
1974	Phi	0	26	30	10	16	56
1975	LARm	0	31	36	21	26	94
1976	LARm	0	36	44	17	26	87
1977	Hou	0	8	11	4	6	20
1978	Buf	0	36	38	10	13	66
1979	Buf	0	8	11	1	4	11
NFL	11	0	252	282	159	258	729

DEPOYSTER, JERRY

1968	Det	0	18	20	3	15	27

DERBY, DEAN

YEAR	TEAM	TD	XPM	XPA	FGM	FGA	PTS
1957	Pit	1	3	3	2	4	15

DESANTIS, DAN

1941	Phi	0	1	1	0	0	1

DESHANE, CHUCK

1945	Det	2	0	0	0	2	12
1946	Det	0	10	10	0	1	10
NFL	2	2	10	10	0	3	22

DETERS, HAROLD

1967	Dal	0	9	10	1	4	12

DEWITZ, RUFE

1924	KC	0	1	—	1	—	4

DICKEY, LYNN

1973	Hou	0	1	1	0	0	1

DIETTRICH, JOHN

1987	Hou	0	5	5	6	6	23

DILWEG, LAVVIE

1931	GB	4	1	—	0	—	25
1932	GB	0	1	—	0	—	1
NFL	2	14	2	—	0	—	86

DONNELLY, RICK

1986	Atl	0	1	1	0	0	1

DORSEY, DEAN

1988	Phi	0	9	9	4	7	21
1988	GB	0	3	4	1	3	6

DOUGLASS, BOBBY

1971	Chi	3	1	1	0	0	19

DRAKE, JOHNNY

1940	Cle	9	2	5	0	1	56

DREWS, TED

1928	ChiB	0	1	—	0	—	1

DRISCOLL, PADDY

1921	ChiC	3	4	—	1	—	25
1922	ChiC	2	4	—	8	—	40
1923	ChiC	7	6	—	10	—	78
1924	ChiC	1	7	—	7	—	34
1925	ChiC	4	10	—	11	—	67
1926	ChiB	6	14	—	12	—	86
1927	ChiB	5	7	—	2	—	43
1928	ChiB	2	8	—	0	—	20
1929	ChiB	1	3	—	0	—	9
NFL	9	31	63	—	51	—	402

DUDLEY, BILL

1945	Pit	3	2	3	0	0	20
1946	Pit	5	12	14	2	7	48
1949	Det	6	30	32	5	14	81
1950	Was	3	31	31	5	10	64
1951	Was	3	21	22	10	13	69
1953	Was	0	25	25	11	22	58
NFL	6	44	121	127	33	66	484

DUFFY, PAT

1929	Day	0	1	—	0	—	1

DUNCAN, RICK

1967	Den-A	0	3	3	2	5	9

DUNCAN, TIM

2003	Arz	0	5	6	6	10	23

DUNN, RED

1924	Mil	2	14	—	7	—	47
1925	ChiC	3	10	—	0	—	28
1926	ChiC	0	3	—	4	—	15
1927	GB	1	7	—	0	—	13
1928	GB	0	1	—	0	—	1
1929	GB	0	11	—	2	—	17
1930	GB	0	14	—	0	—	14
1931	GB	0	15	—	0	—	15
NFL	8	6	75	—	13	—	150

DURKEE, CHARLIE

1967	NO	0	27	27	14	32	69
1968	NO	0	27	27	19	37	84
1971	NO	0	24	25	16	23	72
1972	NO	0	9	9	3	9	18
NFL	4	0	87	88	52	101	243

EAKIN, KAY

1941	NYG	1	0	0	0	1	6

ECKHARDT, OX

1935	NYG	2	1	—	0	—	13

EDINGER, PAUL

2000	ChiB	0	21	21	21	27	84
2001	ChiB	0	34	34	26	31	112
2002	ChiB	0	29	29	22	28	95
2003	ChiB	0	27	27	26	36	105
2004	ChiB	0	22	22	15	24	67

YEAR	TEAM	TD	XPM	XPA	FGM	FGA	PTS
2005	Min	0	31	31	25	34	106
NFL	6	0	164	164	135	180	569

EDWARDS, TURK

1939	Was	0	0	1	0	0	0

EISCHEID, MIKE

1966	Oak-A	0	37	37	11	26	70

ELAM, JASON

1993	Den	0	41	42	26	35	119
1994	Den	0	29	29	30	37	119
1995	Den	0	39	39	31	38	132
1996	Den	0	46	46	21	28	109
1997	Den	0	46	46	26	36	124
1998	Den	0	58	58	23	27	127
1999	Den	0	29	29	29	36	116
2000	Den	0	49	49	18	24	103
2001	Den	0	31	31	31	36	124
2002	Den	0	42	43	26	36	120
2003	Den	0	39	39	27	31	120
2004	Den	0	42	42	29	34	129
2005	Den	0	43	44	24	32	115
NFL	13	0	534	537	341	430	1557

ELIASON, DON

1946	Bos	0	0	1	0	0	0

ELKINS, CHIEF

1928	Fra	2	1	—	0	—	13
1929	ChiC	0	0	—	1	—	3
NFL	2	2	1	—	1	—	16

ELLING, AARON

2003	Min	0	48	48	18	25	102
2004	Ten	0	2	2	1	2	5
2005	Bal	0	0	0	0	1	0
NFL	3	0	50	50	19	28	107

ELLIOTT, AL

1924	Rac	1	0	—	1	—	9

ELLIOTT, DOC

1924	Cle	6	1	—	0	—	40
1925	Cle	2	6	—	3	—	27
NFL	2	17	7	—	4	—	121

ELLIOTT, LIN

1992	Dal	0	47	48	24	35	119
1993	Dal	0	2	3	2	4	8
1994	KC	0	30	30	25	30	105
1995	KC	0	34	37	24	30	106
NFL	4	0	113	118	75	99	338

ENGEBRETSEN, TINY

1932	ChiB	0	10	—	1	—	13
1933	Pit	0	1	—	0	—	1
1935	GB	0	1	—	0	—	1
1936	GB	0	2	—	5	—	17
1937	GB	0	5	—	1	—	8
1938	GB	0	9	9	2	4	15
1939	GB	0	18	19	4	8	30
1940	GB	0	8	8	1	5	11
1941	GB	0	0	0	1	3	3
NFL	9	0	54	36	15	20	99

EPSTEIN, HAYDEN

2002	Jax	0	13	13	5	9	28

ERDLITZ, DICK

1942	Phi	1	8	8	0	0	14
1946	Mia-A	1	22	22	2	7	34
AAFC	1	1	22	22	2	7	34
NFL	1	1	8	8	0	0	14

ERICKSON, HAL

1929	Min	0	1	—	1	—	4

ERNST, JACK

1925	Pot	3	1	—	0	—	19
1929	Bos	0	1	—	0	—	1
NFL	2	7	2	—	0	—	44

ERXLEBEN, RUSSELL

1979	NO	0	4	4	2	2	10
1980	NO	0	2	2	2	5	8
1982	NO	0	1	1	0	1	1
NFL	3	0	7	7	4	8	19

ETHRIDGE, JOE

1949	GB	0	1	1	1	2	4

ETTER, BOB

1968	Atl	0	17	19	11	21	50
1969	Atl	0	33	33	15	30	78
NFL	2	0	50	52	26	51	128

FAMIGLIETTI, GARY

1939	ChiB	0	1	—	0	—	1
1942	ChiB	8	0	—	0	—	48
1946	Bos	4	0	—	0	—	24
NFL	3	25	0	—	0	—	151

YEAR	TEAM	TD	XPM	XPA	FGM	FGA	PTS
FARKAS, ANDY							
1938	Was	6	1	1	0	0	37
1939	Was	11	2	3	0	1	68
1942	Was	6	3	3	0	0	39
NFL	3	37	6	7	0	1	228
FAUST, GEORGE							
1939	ChiC	0	1	1	0	1	1
FEAGLES, JEFF							
2003	NYG	0	0	0	0	1	0
FEAMSTER, TOM							
1956	Bal	0	24	26	0	3	24
FEARS, TOM							
1951	LARm	3	6	7	0	0	24
1953	LARm	4	5	6	1	1	32
1954	LARm	3	1	1	0	0	19
1955	LARm	2	0	0	0	3	12
NFL	4	39	12	14	1	4	249
FEATHERS, BEATTIE							
1934	ChiB	9	1	—	0	—	55
FEELY, JAY							
2001	Atl	0	28	28	29	37	115
2002	Atl	0	42	43	32	40	138
2003	Atl	0	32	33	19	27	89
2004	Atl	0	40	40	18	23	94
2005	NYG	0	43	43	35	42	148
NFL	5	0	185	187	133	169	584
FEENEY, AL							
1921	Can	0	6	—	0	—	6
FELLER, HAPPY							
1971	Phi	0	10	10	6	20	28
1972	NO	0	10	11	6	11	28
1973	NO	0	7	7	4	12	19
NFL	3	0	27	28	16	43	75
FELTON, RALPH							
1954	Was	0	16	17	1	2	19
FENNER, HAROLD							
1922	Day	0	0	—	1	—	3
FINN, JACK							
1924	Fra	2	2	—	2	—	20
FITZGIBBON, PAUL							
1931	GB	1	1	—	0	—	7
FLAHERTY, RAY							
1929	NYG	8	1	—	0	—	49
FLEMING, GEORGE							
1961	Oak-A	1	24	25	11	26	63
FLOWERS, KEITH							
1952	DalT	0	3	5	0	0	3
FLUTIE, DOUG							
2005	NE	0	1	1	0	0	1
FOLZ, ART							
1923	ChiC	1	1	—	0	—	7
FORD, COLE							
1995	Oak	0	17	18	8	9	41
1996	Oak	0	36	36	24	31	108
1997	Oak	0	33	35	13	22	72
NFL	3	0	86	89	45	62	221
FOSTER, WALLY							
1925	Buf	0	1	—	0	—	1
FRAHM, DICK							
1932	SI	0	2	—	0	—	2
1935	Bos	0	1	—	0	—	1
NFL	2	0	3	—	0	—	3
FRANCE, TODD							
2005	Phi	0	5	5	6	7	23
2005	TB	0	1	1	1	2	4
FRANCIS, SAM							
1937	ChiB	1	1	—	0	—	7
1938	ChiB	3	0	2	0	0	18
1940	Bkn	1	0	0	0	1	6
NFL	3	6	1	2	0	1	37
FRANCO, BRIAN							
1987	Cle	0	2	2	3	4	11
FRANKLIN, TONY							
1979	Phi	0	36	39	23	31	105
1980	Phi	0	48	48	16	31	96
1981	Phi	0	41	43	20	31	101
1982	Phi	0	23	25	6	9	41
1983	Phi	0	24	27	15	26	69
1984	NE	0	42	42	22	28	108
1985	NE	0	40	41	24	30	112
1986	NE	0	44	45	32	41	140
1987	NE	0	37	38	15	26	82
1988	Mia	0	6	7	4	11	18
NFL	10	0	341	355	177	264	872
FRASER, JIM							
1962	Den-A	0	2	2	0	0	2
FRIEDMAN, BENNY							
1927	Cle	2	11	—	0	—	23
1928	Det	6	19	—	0	—	55
1929	NYG	2	20	—	0	—	32
1930	NYG	6	10	—	1	—	49
1932	Bkn	0	5	—	1	—	8
1933	Bkn	0	6	—	0	—	6
NFL	6	18	71	—	2	—	185
FRITSCH, TED							
1942	GB	0	1	1	4	5	13
1943	GB	4	0	0	0	2	24
1945	GB	8	0	0	3	8	57
1946	GB	10	13	15	9	17	100
1947	GB	6	2	2	6	13	56
1948	GB	1	5	6	6	16	29
1949	GB	1	11	13	5	20	32
1950	GB	0	30	33	3	17	39
NFL	8	35	62	70	36	98	380
FRITSCH, TONI							
1971	Dal	0	2	2	5	8	17
1972	Dal	0	36	36	21	36	99
1973	Dal	0	43	43	18	28	97
1975	Dal	0	38	40	22	35	104
1976	SD	0	11	14	6	12	29
1977	Hou	0	19	20	12	16	55
1978	Hou	0	31	32	14	18	73
1979	Hou	0	41	43	21	25	104
1980	Hou	0	26	27	19	24	83
1981	Hou	0	32	34	15	22	77
1982	NO	0	8	9	4	7	20
NFL	11	0	287	300	157	231	758
FRY, WES							
1927	NYY	4	1	—	0	—	25
FULLER, MIKE							
1976	SD	0	1	1	0	0	1
GAFFNEY, JEFF							
1987	SD	0	4	5	3	6	13
GAIN, BOB							
1952	Cle	0	3	3	0	0	3
GALBREATH, TONY							
1978	NO	7	0	1	0	0	42
1979	NO	10	1	2	2	3	67
NFL	2	43	1	3	2	3	265
GALLERY, JIM							
1987	SL	0	30	31	9	19	57
1989	Cin	0	13	13	2	6	19
NFL	2	0	43	44	11	25	76
GANTT, GREG							
1974	NYJ	0	1	2	0	0	1
GARCIA, EDDIE							
1984	GB	0	14	15	3	9	23
GARCIA, TEDDY							
1988	NE	0	11	16	6	13	29
1989	Min	0	8	8	1	5	11
1990	Hou	0	26	28	14	20	68
NFL	3	0	45	52	21	38	108
GARVEY, FRANNY							
1926	Pro	0	1	—	0	—	1
GAVRIC, MOMCILO							
1969	SF	0	22	24	3	11	31
GEHRKE, FRED							
1947	LARm	1	4	4	1	1	13
1948	LARm	3	1	1	0	0	19
1949	LARm	5	2	3	0	1	32
NFL	3	24	7	8	1	2	154
GELATKA, CHUCK							
1938	NYG	2	0	1	0	0	12
GEORGE, BILL							
1953	ChiB	0	0	0	0	1	0
1954	ChiB	0	13	14	4	6	25
1958	ChiB	0	1	1	0	0	1
1961	ChiB	0	0	0	0	0	0
NFL	4	0	14	15	4	8	26
GEORGE, MATT							
1998	Pit	0	2	2	0	1	2
GERELA, ROY							
1969	Hou-A	0	29	29	19	40	86
1970	Hou	0	23	23	18	32	77
1971	Pit	0	27	27	17	27	78
1972	Pit	0	35	36	28	41	119
1973	Pit	0	36	37	29	43	123
1974	Pit	0	33	35	20	29	93
1975	Pit	0	44	46	17	21	95
1976	Pit	0	40	43	14	26	82
1977	Pit	0	34	37	9	14	61
1978	Pit	0	44	45	12	26	80
1979	SD	0	6	7	1	7	9
NFL	11	0	351	365	184	306	903
GERI, JOE							
1949	Pit	5	12	13	1	1	45
1950	Pit	3	22	22	8	14	64
1951	Pit	4	22	23	7	14	67
1952	ChiC	0	22	24	2	18	28
NFL	4	12	78	82	18	47	204
GIFFORD, FRANK							
1953	NYG	7	2	2	1	5	47
1956	NYG	9	8	9	1	2	65
NFL	2	78	10	11	2	7	484
GILBERT, WALLY							
1924	Dul	1	3	—	3	—	18
GILCHRIST, COOKIE							
1962	Buf-A	15	14	17	8	20	128
GILDEA, JOHNNY							
1938	NYG	0	0	0	0	2	0
GILLO, HANK							
1922	Rac	5	4	—	6	—	52
1923	Rac	2	8	—	8	—	44
1924	Rac	3	6	—	8	—	48
NFL	3	10	18	—	22	—	144
GIRARD, JUG							
1957	Pit	4	2	3	1	3	29
GLAMP, JOE							
1947	Pit	0	30	31	6	14	48
1948	Pit	3	26	27	4	10	56
1949	Pit	0	18	18	1	6	21
NFL	3	3	74	76	11	30	125
GLASGOW, BILL							
1930	Por	4	4	—	0	—	28
GLICK, GARY							
1956	Pit	0	16	17	4	7	28
1957	Pit	0	10	12	5	18	25
NFL	2	2	26	29	9	25	65
GODDARD, ED							
1937	Cle	1	1	—	0	—	7
1938	Cle	1	1	1	0	0	7
NFL	2	3	2	1	0	0	20
GOEBEL, PAUL							
1923	Col	1	2	—	0	—	8
GOGOLAK, CHARLIE							
1966	Was	0	39	41	22	34	105
1967	Was	0	3	3	1	4	6
1968	Was	0	30	31	9	19	57
1970	Bos	0	5	5	2	7	11
1971	NE	0	28	28	12	21	64
1972	NE	0	9	9	6	8	27
NFL	6	0	114	117	52	93	270
GOGOLAK, PETE							
1964	Buf-A	0	45	46	19	29	102
1965	Buf-A	0	31	31	28	46	115
1966	NYG	0	29	31	16	28	77
1967	NYG	0	28	29	6	10	46
1968	NYG	0	36	36	14	24	78
1969	NYG	0	33	33	11	21	66
1970	NYG	0	32	32	25	41	107
1971	NYG	0	30	30	6	17	48
1972	NYG	0	34	38	21	31	97
1973	NYG	0	25	25	17	28	76
1974	NYG	0	21	23	10	19	51
NFL	11	0	344	354	173	294	863
GOLEMBESKI, ARCHIE							
1926	Pro	1	1	—	0	—	7
GOSSETT, BRUCE							
1964	LARm	0	31	33	18	24	85
1965	LARm	0	30	32	15	26	75
1966	LARm	0	29	29	28	49	113
1967	LARm	0	48	48	20	43	108
1968	LARm	0	37	37	17	31	88
1969	LARm	0	36	36	22	34	102
1970	SF	0	39	41	21	31	102
1971	SF	0	32	32	23	36	101
1972	SF	0	41	42	18	29	95
1973	SF	0	26	26	26	33	104
1974	SF	0	25	27	11	24	58
NFL	11	0	374	383	219	360	1031
GOULD, ROBBIE							
2005	ChiB	0	19	20	21	27	82

YEAR	TEAM	TD	XPM	XPA	FGM	FGA	PTS
GOWIN, TOBY							
1997	Dal	0	0	0	0	1	0
GOWINS, BRIAN							
1999	ChiB	0	3	3	4	6	15
GRAHAM, SHAYNE							
2001	Buf	0	7	7	6	8	25
2002	Car	0	21	21	13	18	60
2003	Cin	0	40	40	22	25	106
2004	Cin	0	41	41	27	31	122
2005	Cin	0	47	47	28	32	**131**
NFL	5	0	156	156	96	114	444
GRAMATICA, BILL							
2001	Arz	0	25	25	16	20	73
2002	Arz	0	29	29	15	21	74
2003	Arz	0	6	6	3	4	15
2004	Mia	0	0	1	3	3	9
NFL	4	0	60	61	37	48	171
GRAMATICA, MARTIN							
1999	TB	0	25	25	**27**	**32**	106
2000	TB	0	42	42	28	34	126
2001	TB	0	28	28	23	29	97
2002	TB	0	32	32	**32**	39	128
2003	TB	0	33	34	16	26	81
2004	TB	0	21	22	11	19	54
NFL	6	0	181	183	137	179	592
GRANGE, GARDIE							
1930	ChiB	0	1	—	0	—	1
1931	ChiB	1	1	—	0	—	7
NFL	2	3	2	—	0	—	20
GRANGE, RED							
1929	ChiB	2	1	—	0	—	13
1930	ChiB	8	1	—	0	—	49
NFL	2	32	2	—	0	—	194
GRANT, DUCKY							
1928	ChiC	0	1	—	0	—	1
GRAVES, RAY							
1942	Phi	0	1	1	0	0	1
GREEN, ALLEN							
1961	Dal	0	19	19	5	15	34
GREEN, BOBBY JOE							
1961	Pit	0	0	0	0	1	0
GREEN, DAVE							
1975	Cin	0	40	45	10	21	70
1976	TB	0	11	14	8	14	35
1977	TB	0	5	6	4	7	17
1978	TB	0	0	0	1	1	3
NFL	4	0	56	65	23	43	125
GRIGG, TEX							
1925	Roc	0	2	—	0	—	2
GRIGG, CHUBBY							
1950	Cle	0	9	9	1	2	12
1952	DalT	0	9	12	0	3	9
NFL	2	0	18	21	1	5	21
GRIMES, GEORGE							
1948	Det	1	0	1	0	0	6
GROSSMAN, JACK							
1935	Bkn	2	1	—	0	—	13
GROSSMAN, REX							
1948	Bal-A	0	43	43	**10**	18	73
1949	Bal-A	0	19	19	6	11	37
1950	Bal	0	16	19	0	3	16
AAFC	2	0	62	62	16	29	110
NFL	1	0	16	19	0	3	16
GROVE, ROGER							
1931	GB	0	2	—	0	—	2
1932	GB	3	5	—	0	—	23
1933	GB	0	8	—	0	—	8
1934	GB	4	1	—	0	—	25
NFL	4	7	16	—	0	—	58
GROZA, LOU							
1946	Cle-A	0	**45**	**47**	13	**29**	84
1947	Cle-A	0	39	42	7	19	60
1948	Cle-A	0	51	52	8	**19**	75
1949	Cle-A	0	34	35	2	9	40
1950	Cle	1	29	29	**13**	**19**	74
1951	Cle	0	**43**	43	10	**23**	73
1952	Cle	0	32	32	**19**	33	89
1953	Cle	0	39	40	**23**	**26**	108
1954	Cle	0	37	38	**16**	24	85
1955	Cle	0	**44**	**45**	11	22	77
1956	Cle	0	18	18	11	20	51
1957	Cle	0	32	32	**15**	22	**77**
1958	Cle	0	36	38	8	19	60
1959	Cle	0	33	37	5	16	48
1961	Cle	0	37	38	16	23	85
1962	Cle	0	33	35	14	31	75
1963	Cle	0	40	43	15	23	85
1964	Cle	0	49	49	22	33	115
1965	Cle	0	45	45	16	25	93
1966	Cle	0	51	52	9	23	78
1967	Cle	0	43	43	11	23	76
AAFC	4	0	169	176	30	76	259
NFL	17	1	641	657	234	405	1349
GRUBE, FRANK							
1928	NYY	0	1	—	0	—	1
GUDAUSKAS, PETE							
1940	Cle	0	1	2	0	0	1
1944	ChiB	0	**36**	**37**	0	0	36
1945	ChiB	0	27	27	1	2	30
NFL	3	0	64	66	1	2	67
GUESMAN, DICK							
1961	NYT-A	0	24	26	5	15	39
1962	NYT-A	0	2	2	0	1	2
1963	NYJ-A	0	30	30	9	24	57
1964	Den-A	0	13	15	6	22	31
NFL	4	0	69	73	20	62	129
GUTHRIE, GRANT							
1970	Buf	0	24	25	10	19	54
1971	Buf	0	8	9	3	10	17
NFL	2	0	32	34	13	29	71
GUY, RAY							
1976	Oak	0	0	1	0	0	0
GUYON, JOE							
1921	Cle	3	10	—	0	—	28
1922	Oor	5	3	—	0	—	33
NFL	2	10	13	—	0	—	73
HAGERTY, JACK							
1932	NYG	0	2	—	0	—	2
HAGLER, SCOTT							
1987	Sea	0	4	4	2	2	10
HAJI-SHEIKH, ALI							
1983	NYG	0	22	23	**35**	42	127
1984	NYG	0	32	35	17	33	83
1985	NYG	0	5	5	2	5	11
1986	Atl	0	7	8	9	12	34
1987	Was	0	29	32	13	19	68
NFL	5	0	95	103	76	111	323
HALAS, GEORGE							
1922	ChiB	2	2	—	0	—	14
HALICKI, ED							
1929	Fra	6	6	—	1	—	45
1930	Fra	4	5	—	0	—	29
NFL	2	10	11	—	1	—	74
HALL, JEFF							
2000	SL	0	9	9	4	5	21
HALL, JOHN							
1997	NYJ	0	36	36	28	**41**	120
1998	NYJ	0	45	46	25	35	120
1999	NYJ	0	27	29	27	33	108
2000	NYJ	0	30	30	21	32	93
2001	NYJ	0	32	32	24	31	104
2002	NYJ	0	35	37	24	31	107
2003	Was	0	26	27	25	33	101
2004	Was	0	13	13	8	11	37
2005	Was	0	27	27	12	14	63
NFL	9	0	271	277	194	261	853
HAMER, TEX							
1925	Fra	7	3	—	0	—	45
1926	Fra	2	3	—	0	—	15
NFL	2	21	6	—	0	—	132
HAMILTON, REMY							
2005	Det	0	0	1	0	0	0
HAMRICK, JAMES							
1987	KC	0	4	4	2	2	10
HANNEMAN, CHUCK							
1939	Det	2	5	5	4	5	29
1940	Det	0	10	10	2	4	16
1941	Det	1	4	4	1	4	13
NFL	3	5	19	19	7	13	70
HANNY, DUKE							
1929	Pro	0	1	—	0	—	1
HANSON, JASON							
1992	Det	0	30	30	21	26	93
1993	Det	0	28	28	**34**	**43**	**130**
1994	Det	0	39	40	18	27	93
1995	Det	0	**48**	**48**	28	34	132
1996	Det	0	36	36	12	17	72
1997	Det	0	39	40	26	29	117
1998	Det	0	27	29	29	33	114
1999	Det	0	28	29	26	**32**	106
2000	Det	0	29	29	24	30	101
2001	Det	0	23	23	21	30	86
2002	Det	0	31	31	23	28	100
2003	Det	0	26	27	22	23	92
2004	Det	0	28	28	24	28	100
2005	Det	0	27	27	19	24	84
NFL	14	0	439	445	327	404	1420
HANSON, SWEDE							
1934	Phi	8	2	—	0	—	50
HARDER, PAT							
1946	ChiC	5	5	5	0	0	35
1947	ChiC	7	39	40	7	10	**102**
1948	ChiC	6	**53**	**53**	7	**17**	110
1949	ChiC	8	**45**	**47**	3	**5**	**102**
1950	ChiC	1	22	24	4	9	40
1951	Det	8	0	0	3	5	57
1952	Det	3	34	35	11	23	85
NFL	7	38	198	204	35	69	531
HARDY, DAVID							
1987	LARd	0	7	7	0	1	7
HARDY, JIM							
1952	Det	0	1	1	0	0	1
HARPER, DARRELL							
1960	Buf-A	0	1	2	2	3	7
HARRIS, WENDELL							
1962	Bal	0	6	9	1	3	9
1967	NYG	0	2	2	0	1	2
NFL	2	1	8	11	1	4	17
HATHAWAY, RUSS							
1921	Day	0	12	—	4	—	24
1922	Day	0	9	—	2	—	15
1923	Day	0	1	—	3	—	10
1924	Day	0	3	—	1	—	6
1926	Pot	0	3	—	0	—	3
NFL	5	0	28	—	10	—	58
HECKER, NORB							
1951	LARm	1	0	0	0	1	6
1955	Was	1	2	2	0	1	8
NFL	2	3	2	2	0	2	20
HEINEMAN, KEN							
1940	Cle	0	1	1	0	0	1
HELD, PAUL							
1954	Pit	0	14	16	3	5	23
HELMS, JACK							
1946	Det	0	4	6	3	4	13
HENDERSON, HERB							
1921	Evv	4	5	—	0	—	29
HENDRIAN, DUTCH							
1923	Akr	0	1	—	0	—	1
1924	GB	3	0	—	1	—	21
1925	NYG	2	1	—	3	—	22
NFL	3	6	2	—	4	—	50
HENRY, PETE							
1922	Can	0	4	—	2	—	10
1923	Can	1	25	—	9	—	58
1925	Can	0	5	—	1	—	8
1926	Can	0	3	—	0	—	3
1927	Pot	0	1	—	2	—	7
1928	Pot	0	2	—	0	—	2
NFL	6	1	40	—	14	—	88
HENTRICH, CRAIG							
1995	GB	0	5	5	3	5	14
1998	Ten	0	0	0	0	1	0
2000	Ten	0	0	0	0	1	0
2003	Ten	0	1	1	4	5	13
2004	Ten	0	0	0	1	3	3
NFL	5	0	6	6	8	15	30
HEPPNER, KRIS							
2000	Sea	0	8	8	6	9	26
2000	Was	0	9	9	4	6	21
HERBER, ARNIE							
1933	GB	0	1	—	0	—	1
1935	GB	0	1	—	0	—	1
1938	GB	2	0	—	0	1	12
NFL	3	7	2	—	0	1	44
HERGERT, JOE							
1960	Buf-A	1	0	—	2	4	12
1961	Buf-A	0	0	0	6	14	18
NFL	2	1	0	0	8	18	30
HERRERA, EFREN							
1974	Dal	0	**33**	33	8	13	57
1976	Dal	0	34	34	18	23	88
1977	Dal	0	**39**	**41**	18	29	93
1978	Sea	0	40	44	13	21	79
1979	Sea	0	43	46	19	23	100

YEAR	TEAM	TD	XPM	XPA	FGM	FGA	PTS
1980	Sea	0	33	33	20	31	93
1981	Sea	0	23	25	12	17	59
1982	Buf	0	11	12	8	14	35
NFL	8	0	256	268	116	171	604
HICKMAN, HERMAN							
1933	Bkn	0	2	—	2	—	8
HIGGINS, BOB							
1921	Can	2	2	—	0	—	14
HILBERT, JON							
2001	Dal	0	12	12	11	16	45
2002	Car	0	3	3	0	2	3
NFL	2	0	15	15	11	18	48
HILL, CHARLEY							
1925	KC	4	1	—	0	—	25
HILL, IRV							
1932	ChiC	3	4	—	0	—	22
HILL, JACK							
1961	Den-A	0	16	16	5	15	31
HILLEBRAND, JERRY							
1965	NYG	1	0	0	0	1	6
HINKLE, CLARKE							
1932	GB	3	1	—	0	—	19
1933	GB	4	0	—	2	—	30
1934	GB	2	6	—	3	—	27
1935	GB	2	0	—	2	—	18
1936	GB	5	1	—	0	—	31
1937	GB	7	9	—	2	—	57
1938	GB	7	7	7	3	9	58
1939	GB	5	2	3	1	10	35
1940	GB	3	3	3	9	14	48
1941	GB	6	2	2	6	14	56
NFL	10	44	31	15	28	47	379
HIRSCH, ELROY							
1946	ChiR-A	6	0	1	0	0	36
1950	LARm	7	5	5	0	0	47
1951	LARm	17	0	1	0	0	102
1953	LARm	4	4	5	0	0	28
AAFC	1	6	0	1	0	0	36
NFL	3	60	9	11	0	0	369
HOGAN, PAUL							
1924	Akr	0	2	—	1	—	5
1926	NYG	0	3	—	0	—	3
1926	Fra	0	2	—	0	—	2
NFL	2	1	7	—	1	—	16
HOKUF, STEVE							
1934	Bos	0	1	—	1	—	4
HOLLIDAY, RON							
1973	SD	0	1	1	0	0	1
HOLLIS, MIKE							
1995	Jax	0	27	28	20	27	87
1996	Jax	0	27	27	30	36	117
1997	Jax	0	41	41	31	36	134
1998	Jax	0	45	45	21	26	108
1999	Jax	0	37	37	31	38	130
2000	Jax	0	33	33	24	26	105
2001	Jax	0	29	31	18	28	83
2002	Buf	0	40	40	25	33	115
NFL	8	0	279	282	200	250	879
HOLMER, WALT							
1929	ChiB	0	0	—	1	—	3
1932	ChiC	1	2	—	0	—	8
NFL	2	5	2	—	1	—	35
HOLMES, JARET							
1999	ChiB	0	0	0	2	2	6
2000	NYG	0	3	3	2	2	9
2001	Jax	0	1	1	0	0	1
NFL	3	0	4	4	4	4	16
HORNUNG, PAUL							
1957	GB	3	0	0	0	4	18
1958	GB	2	22	23	11	21	67
1959	GB	7	31	32	7	17	94
1960	GB	15	41	41	15	28	176
1961	GB	10	41	41	15	22	146
1962	GB	7	14	14	6	10	74
1964	GB	5	41	43	12	38	107
NFL	7	62	190	194	66	140	760
HORWEEN, ARNIE							
1922	ChiC	4	0	—	1	—	27
1923	ChiC	0	3	—	2	—	9
NFL	2	4	3	—	3	—	36
HORWEEN, RALPH							
1921	ChiC	0	0	—	1	—	3
1922	ChiC	0	2	—	3	—	11
NFL	2	2	2	—	4	—	26
HOUSTON, JIM							
1966	Cle	1	1	1	0	0	7
HOWFIELD, BOBBY							
1968	Den-A	0	30	30	9	18	57
1969	Den-A	0	36	37	13	29	75
1970	Den	0	27	28	18	32	81
1971	NYJ	0	25	26	8	19	49
1972	NYJ	0	40	41	27	37	121
1973	NYJ	0	27	27	17	24	78
1974	NYJ	0	8	12	6	7	26
NFL	7	0	193	201	98	166	487
HOWFIELD, IAN							
1991	Hou	0	25	29	13	16	64
HUERTA, CARLOS							
1996	ChiB	0	3	3	4	7	15
1996	SL	0	2	2	0	0	2
HUGHES, DENNY							
1925	Pot	0	2	—	0	—	2
HUGHES, HONOLULU							
1932	Bos	0	5	—	0	—	5
HUGHITT, TOMMY							
1921	Buf	3	2	—	0	—	20
1923	Buf	1	0	—	1	—	9
NFL	2	6	2	—	1	—	41
HUMPHREYS, BOB							
1967	Den-A	0	18	19	7	15	39
1968	Den-A	0	1	1	1	5	4
NFL	2	0	19	20	8	20	43
HUNT, GEORGE							
1973	Bal	0	22	24	16	28	70
1975	NYG	0	24	29	6	11	42
NFL	2	0	46	53	22	39	112
HUSTED, MICHAEL							
1993	TB	0	27	27	16	22	75
1994	TB	0	20	20	23	35	89
1995	TB	0	25	25	19	26	82
1996	TB	0	18	19	25	32	93
1997	TB	0	32	35	13	17	71
1998	TB	0	29	30	21	28	92
1999	Oak	0	30	30	20	31	90
2000	Was	0	8	9	4	8	20
2002	KC	0	3	3	1	1	6
NFL	9	0	192	198	142	200	618
HUTSON, DON							
1935	GB	7	1	—	0	—	43
1938	GB	9	3	3	0	0	57
1939	GB	6	2	2	0	0	38
1940	GB	7	15	16	0	0	57
1941	GB	12	20	24	1	1	95
1942	GB	17	33	34	1	1	138
1943	GB	12	36	36	3	5	117
1944	GB	9	31	33	0	3	85
1945	GB	10	31	35	2	4	97
NFL	9	105	172	183	7	17	823
IGWEBUIKE, DONALD							
1985	TB	0	30	32	22	32	96
1986	TB	0	26	27	17	24	77
1987	TB	0	24	26	14	18	66
1988	TB	0	21	21	19	25	78
1989	TB	0	33	35	22	28	99
1990	Min	0	19	19	14	16	61
NFL	6	0	153	160	108	143	477
IRGENS, BILL							
1922	Min	0	1	—	0	—	1
IRWIN, DON							
1938	Was	1	0	1	0	0	6
ISBELL, CECIL							
1939	GB	2	3	3	0	0	15
IVY, POP							
1942	ChiC	0	2	2	0	0	2
1947	ChiC	0	0	0	0	1	0
NFL	2	3	2	2	0	1	20
JACKE, CHRIS							
1989	GB	0	42	42	22	28	108
1990	GB	0	28	29	23	30	97
1991	GB	0	31	31	18	24	85
1992	GB	0	30	30	22	29	96
1993	GB	0	35	35	31	37	128
1994	GB	0	41	43	19	26	98
1995	GB	0	43	43	17	23	94
1996	GB	0	51	53	21	27	114
1997	Was	0	5	5	0	0	5
1998	Arz	0	6	6	10	14	36
1999	Arz	0	26	26	19	27	83
NFL	11	0	338	343	202	265	944
JACOBS, DAVE							
1979	NYJ	0	10	11	5	9	25
1981	Cle	0	9	10	4	12	21
1987	Phi	0	2	4	3	5	11
NFL	3	0	21	25	12	26	57
JAEGER, JEFF							
1987	Cle	0	33	33	14	22	75
1989	LARd	0	34	34	23	34	103
1990	LARd	0	40	42	15	20	85
1991	LARd	0	29	30	29	34	116
1992	LARd	0	28	28	15	26	73
1993	LARd	0	27	29	35	44	132
1994	LARd	0	31	31	22	28	97
1995	Oak	0	22	22	13	18	61
1996	ChiB	0	23	23	19	23	80
1997	ChiB	0	20	20	21	26	83
1998	ChiB	0	27	28	21	26	90
1999	ChiB	0	7	7	2	2	13
NFL	12	0	321	327	229	309	1008
JAKOWENKO, GEORGE							
1976	Buf	0	21	24	12	17	57
JANIKOWSKI, SEBASTIAN							
2000	Oak	0	46	46	22	32	112
2001	Oak	0	42	42	23	28	111
2002	Oak	0	50	50	26	33	128
2003	Oak	0	28	29	22	25	94
2004	Oak	0	31	32	25	28	106
2005	Oak	0	30	30	20	30	90
NFL	6	0	227	229	138	176	641
JANKOWSKI, ED							
1937	GB	4	1	—	0	—	25
1938	GB	2	2	3	0	0	14
1941	GB	0	1	2	1	1	4
NFL	3	10	4	5	1	1	67
JANOWICZ, VIC							
1954	Was	0	9	9	4	8	21
1955	Was	7	28	31	6	20	88
NFL	2	7	37	40	10	28	109
JENCKS, BOB							
1963	ChiB	0	35	37	1	10	38
1964	ChiB	0	29	32	3	7	38
1965	Was	0	29	33	10	22	59
NFL	3	0	93	102	14	39	135
JENKINS, J.R.							
2002	Bal	0	0	0	0	1	0
JENKINS, JACK							
1943	Was	0	1	1	0	0	1
JENNINGS, LOU							
1929	Pro	0	4	—	0	—	4
JOHANSSON, OVE							
1977	Phi	0	1	3	1	4	4
JOHNSON, FARNHAM							
1948	ChiR-A	0	2	2	0	0	2
JOHNSON, HARVEY							
1946	NYY-A	0	36	36	6	8	54
1947	NYY-A	0	49	51	7	8	70
1948	NYY-A	0	37	37	2	7	43
1949	NYY-A	0	25	25	7	15	46
1951	NYY	0	31	31	6	14	49
AAFC	4	0	147	149	22	38	213
NFL	1	0	31	31	6	14	49
JOHNSON, JERRY							
1922	RI	1	6	—	0	—	15
JOHNSON, LEE							
1988	Cin	0	0	0	1	2	3
1989	Cin	0	0	1	0	0	0
1990	Cin	0	0	0	1	0	0
1991	Cin	0	0	0	0	3	3
1992	Cin	0	0	0	0	1	0
NFL	5	0	0	1	2	7	6
JOHNSON, NORM							
1982	Sea	0	13	14	10	14	43
1983	Sea	0	49	50	18	25	103
1984	Sea	0	50	51	20	24	110
1985	Sea	0	40	41	14	25	82
1986	Sea	0	42	42	22	35	108
1987	Sea	0	40	40	15	20	85
1988	Sea	0	39	39	22	28	105
1989	Sea	0	27	27	15	25	72
1990	Sea	0	33	34	23	32	102
1991	Atl	0	38	39	19	23	95
1992	Atl	0	39	39	18	22	93
1993	Atl	0	34	34	26	27	112
1994	Atl	0	32	32	21	25	95
1995	Pit	0	39	39	34	41	141
1996	Pit	0	37	37	23	30	106
1997	Pit	0	40	40	22	25	106

YEAR	TEAM	TD	XPM	XPA	FGM	FGA	PTS
1998	Pit	0	21	21	26	31	99
1999	Phi	0	25	25	18	25	79
NFL	18	0	638	644	366	477	1736

JOHNSOS, LUKE

YEAR	TEAM	TD	XPM	XPA	FGM	FGA	PTS
1930	ChiB	4	4	—	0	—	28
1931	ChiB	1	4	—	1	—	13
1932	ChiB	4	2	—	0	—	26
1933	ChiB	3	1	—	0	—	19
NFL	4	22	11	—	1	—	146

JOHNSTON, JIMMY

1939	Was	1	1	1	0	0	7

JOHNSTON, PRES

1946	Mia-A	0	1	1	0	0	1

JONES, BEN

1924	Cle	4	1	—	0	—	25

JONES, DEACON

1974	Was	0	1	1	0	0	1

JONES, THURMAN

1942	Bkn	0	1	1	0	0	1

JORDAN, STEVE

1987	Ind	0	7	7	3	5	16

JORGENSEN, BUD

1935	Phi	0	1	—	1	—	4

JURICH, TOM

1978	NO	0	2	2	0	3	2

JUZWIK, STEVE

1942	Was	2	3	3	0	0	15
1947	Buf-A	1	28	32	2	3	40
1948	ChiR-A	0	5	5	0	0	5
AAFC	2	1	33	37	2	3	45
NFL	1	9	3	3	0	0	57

KAEDING, NATE

2004	SD	0	54	55	20	25	114
2005	SD	0	49	49	21	24	112
NFL	2	0	103	104	41	49	226

KAKASIC, GEORGE

1936	Pit	1	1	—	2	—	13
1937	Pit	0	3	—	0	—	3
NFL	2	1	4	—	2	—	16

KAPLAN, AVE

1923	Min	1	3	—	3	—	18

KARAMATIC, GEORGE

1938	Was	1	2	3	1	2	11

KARCIS, BULL

1936	Pit	2	1	—	0	—	13

KARLIS, RICH

1982	Den	0	15	16	11	13	48
1983	Den	0	33	34	21	25	96
1984	Den	0	38	41	21	28	101
1985	Den	0	41	44	23	38	110
1986	Den	0	44	45	20	28	104
1987	Den	0	37	37	18	25	91
1988	Den	0	36	37	23	36	105
1989	Min	0	27	28	31	39	120
1990	Det	0	12	12	4	7	24
NFL	9	0	283	294	172	239	799

KASAY, JOHN

1991	Sea	0	27	28	25	31	102
1992	Sea	0	14	14	14	22	56
1993	Sea	0	29	29	23	28	98
1994	Sea	0	25	26	20	24	85
1995	Car	0	27	28	26	33	105
1996	Car	0	34	35	37	45	145
1997	Car	0	25	25	22	26	91
1998	Car	0	35	37	19	26	92
1999	Car	0	33	33	22	25	99
2001	Car	0	22	23	23	28	91
2002	Car	0	5	5	2	5	11
2003	Car	0	29	30	32	38	125
2004	Car	0	27	28	19	22	84
2005	Car	0	43	44	26	34	121
NFL	14	0	375	385	310	387	1305

KASKY, ED

1942	Phi	0	0	0	0	1	0

KAURIC, JERRY

1990	Cle	0	24	27	14	20	66

KAVANAUGH, KEN

1941	ChiB	6	1	1	0	0	37

KEANE, TOM

1955	ChiC	0	0	0	0	1	0

KECK, STAN

1923	Cle	0	1	—	2	—	7

KEEFER, JACK

1926	Pro	2	3	—	0	—	15

KEKERIS, JIM

1947	Phi	0	2	3	0	1	2

KELLEY, CHRIS

1987	Cle	0	1	1	0	0	1

KELLOGG, CLARENCE

1936	ChiC	0	6	—	1	—	9

KELLY, SHIPWRECK

1933	Bkn	7	1	—	0	—	43

KELSCH, MOSE

1933	Pit	0	2	—	3	—	11
1934	Pit	0	2	—	1	—	5
NFL	2	0	4	—	4	—	16

KEMPF, FLORIAN

1982	Hou	0	16	18	4	6	28
1983	Hou	0	33	34	17	21	84
1984	Hou	0	14	14	4	6	26
1987	NO	0	1	1	4	5	13
NFL	4	0	64	67	29	38	151

KENDRICK, JIM

1925	Ham	0	1	—	1	—	4
1925	Buf	1	2	—	2	—	14
1926	Buf	2	4	—	0	—	16
NFL	2	3	7	—	3	—	34

KENNEALLY, GEORGE

1929	Bos	0	1	—	0	—	1

KERCHEVAL, RALPH

1934	Bkn	3	7	—	4	—	37
1935	Bkn	2	8	—	5	—	35
1936	Bkn	3	4	—	5	—	37
1937	Bkn	1	1	—	2	—	13
1938	Bkn	1	7	9	5	13	28
1939	Bkn	0	3	3	6	13	21
1940	Bkn	0	3	3	4	11	15
NFL	7	10	33	15	31	37	186

KERKORIAN, GARY

1952	Pit	0	35	41	4	9	47
1954	Bal	1	11	12	5	10	32
1955	Bal	1	0	0	1	2	9
1956	Bal	0	1	2	0	0	1
NFL	4	2	47	55	10	21	89

KEYES, JIMMY

1968	Mia-A	0	30	30	7	16	51

KHAYAT, BOB

1960	Was	0	19	19	15	23	64
1962	Was	0	38	38	11	25	71
1963	Was	0	33	35	12	26	69
NFL	3	0	90	92	38	74	204

KIMRIN, OLA

2004	Was	0	6	6	6	10	24

KINARD, BRUISER

1939	Bkn	0	7	7	0	0	7
1941	Bkn	1	3	5	0	0	9
1943	Bkn	1	8	9	1	1	17
1944	Bkn	0	9	9	0	0	9
NFL	4	2	27	30	1	1	42

KINCAID, JIM

1954	Was	0	1	1	0	0	1

KING, DICK

1923	SL	0	2	—	0	—	2

KING, RIP

1921	Akr	2	3	—	0	—	15
1922	Akr	3	3	—	0	—	21
1923	ChiC	1	1	—	0	—	7
NFL	3	6	7	—	0	—	43

KIRKMAN, RED

1933	Phi	1	2	—	0	—	8
1934	Phi	1	5	—	0	—	11
1935	Phi	0	1	—	0	—	1
NFL	3	2	8	—	0	—	20

KIROUAC, LOU

1966	Atl	0	19	24	9	18	46

KISH, BEN

1944	Phi	1	1	—	0	—	7

KISSELL, ED

1952	Pit	0	0	0	0	2	0
1954	Pit	0	8	9	2	4	14
NFL		0	8	9	2	6	14

KISSELL, VITO

1950	Bal	0	11	11	0	1	11

KITZMILLER, DUTCH

1931	NYG	4	3	—	0	—	27

KNIGHT, CURT

1969	Was	0	35	36	16	27	83
1970	Was	0	33	34	20	27	93
1971	Was	0	27	27	**29**	**49**	**114**
1972	Was	0	40	41	14	30	82
1973	Was	0	37	37	22	42	103
NFL	5	0	172	175	101	175	475

KNORR, MICAH

2003	Den	0	2	2	1	1	5

KOEHLER, BOB

1921	ChiC	1	2	—	0	—	8

KOENEN, MICHAEL

2005	Atl	0	0	0	1	2	3

KOKEN, MIKE

1933	ChiC	0	1	—	0	—	1

KONZ, KEN

1954	Cle	2	3	3	0	0	15

KOPCHA, JOE

1935	ChiB	0	1	—	0	—	3

KOSTOS, TONY

1928	Fra	0	2	—	0	—	2
1930	Fra	1	1	—	0	—	7
NFL	2	2	3	—	0	—	15

KRAMER, JERRY

1962	GB	0	38	39	9	11	65
1963	GB	0	43	46	16	34	91
1968	GB	0	9	10	4	9	21
NFL	3	0	90	95	29	54	177

KRAUSE, MAX

1933	NYG	1	1	—	0	—	7

KREIDER, STEVE

1982	Cin	1	1	1	0	0	7
1985	Cin	1	1	1	0	0	7
NFL	2	9	2	2	0	0	56

KREINHEDER, WALT

1922	Akr	0	1	—	1	—	4

KREMSER, KARL

1969	Mia-A	0	26	27	13	22	65
1970	Mia	0	2	2	0	1	2
NFL	2	0	28	29	13	23	67

KRONER, GARY

1965	Den-A	0	32	32	13	29	71
1966	Den-A	0	20	20	14	25	62
1967	Den-A	0	5	6	2	2	11
NFL	3	0	57	58	29	56	144

KUEHL, WADDY

1922	Buf	3	1	—	0	—	19

KUHARICH, JOE

1940	ChiC	0	0	0	0	1	0
1945	ChiC	0	12	13	0	3	12
NFL	2	0	12	13	0	4	12

KULBITSKI, VIC

1947	Buf-A	5	1	1	0	0	31
1948	Buf-A	1	8	10	0	0	14
AAFC	2	6	9	11	0	0	45

LACH, STEVE

1942	ChiC	4	1	1	0	0	25

LAHAR, HAL

1941	ChiB	0	1	3	1	1	4

LAIRD, JIM

1925	Pro	3	2	—	3	—	29

LAMB, RODDY

1925	RI	4	3	—	0	—	27
1926	ChiC	1	1	—	0	—	7
NFL	2	6	4	—	0	—	40

LAMBEAU, CURLY

1921	GB	2	7	—	3	—	28
1922	GB	4	3	—	1	—	30
1924	GB	1	1	—	1	—	10
1925	GB	0	5	—	1	—	8
1926	GB	0	4	—	0	—	4
NFL	5	12	20	—	6	—	110

LANGHOFF, IRV

1922	Rac	1	2	—	0	—	8

LANSFORD, MIKE

1982	LARm	0	23	24	9	15	50
1983	LARm	0	9	9	6	9	27
1984	LARm	0	37	38	25	33	112
1985	LARm	0	38	39	22	29	104
1986	LARm	0	34	35	17	24	85

YEAR	TEAM	TD	XPM	XPA	FGM	FGA	PTS
1987	LARm	0	36	38	17	21	87
1988	LARm	0	45	48	24	32	117
1989	LARm	0	51	51	23	30	120
1990	LARm	0	42	43	15	24	87
NFL	9	0	315	325	158	217	789

LAPRESTA, BENNY

YEAR	TEAM	TD	XPM	XPA	FGM	FGA	PTS
1933	Bos	0	1	—	0	—	1

LARABA, BOB

| 1961 | SD-A | 3 | 1 | 2 | 0 | 0 | 19 |

LARGENT, STEVE

1985	Sea	6	1	1	0	0	37
1989	Sea	3	1	1	0	0	19
NFL	2	101	2	2	0	0	608

LASCARI, JOHN

| 1942 | NYG | 1 | 0 | 0 | 0 | 1 | 6 |

LASHAR, TIM

| 1987 | ChiB | 0 | 10 | 10 | 3 | 4 | 19 |

LAUER, DUTCH

| 1922 | RI | 5 | 1 | — | 0 | — | 31 |

LAUX, TED

| 1943 | P-P | 0 | 2 | 2 | 0 | 0 | 2 |

LAWLER, AL

| 1948 | ChiB | 0 | 3 | 3 | 1 | 1 | 6 |

LAYDEN, PETE

| 1950 | NYY | 0 | 3 | 3 | 0 | 0 | 3 |

LAYNE, BOBBY

1948	ChiB	1	0	0	0	1	6
1950	Det	4	1	2	0	0	25
1952	Det	1	2	2	0	0	8
1956	Det	5	33	33	12	15	99
1957	Det	3	25	25	6	11	43
1958	Det	0	1	3	0	0	1
1959	Pit	2	32	32	11	17	77
1960	Pit	2	21	22	5	6	48
1961	Pit	0	5	5	0	0	5
NFL	9	25	120	124	34	50	372

LEAHY, PAT

1974	NYJ	0	18	19	6	11	36
1975	NYJ	0	27	30	13	21	66
1976	NYJ	0	16	20	11	16	49
1977	NYJ	0	18	21	15	25	63
1978	NYJ	0	41	42	22	30	107
1979	NYJ	0	12	15	8	13	36
1980	NYJ	0	36	36	14	22	78
1981	NYJ	0	38	39	25	36	113
1982	NYJ	0	26	31	11	17	59
1983	NYJ	0	36	37	16	24	84
1984	NYJ	0	38	39	17	24	89
1985	NYJ	0	43	45	26	34	121
1986	NYJ	0	44	44	16	19	92
1987	NYJ	0	31	31	18	22	85
1988	NYJ	0	43	43	23	28	112
1989	NYJ	0	29	30	14	21	71
1990	NYJ	0	32	32	23	26	101
1991	NYJ	0	30	30	26	37	108
NFL	18	0	558	584	304	426	1470

LEAVITT, ALLAN

| 1977 | TB | 0 | 5 | 5 | 5 | 10 | 20 |

LEBARON, EDDIE

| 1952 | Was | 2 | 6 | 7 | 0 | 0 | 18 |

LECHLER, SHANE

| 2000 | Oak | 0 | 7 | 7 | 0 | 1 | 7 |

LECLERC, ROGER

1961	ChiB	0	40	41	10	24	70
1962	ChiB	0	36	40	13	27	75
1963	ChiB	0	0	0	13	23	39
1964	ChiB	0	0	0	10	16	30
1965	ChiB	0	52	52	11	26	85
1966	ChiB	0	24	25	18	30	78
1967	Den-A	0	2	2	1	6	5
NFL	7	0	154	160	76	152	382

LEE, BIFF

1933	Cin	0	0	—	1	—	3
1934	Cin	0	1	—	0	—	1
NFL	2	0	1	—	1	—	4

LEE, JOHN

| 1986 | SL | 0 | 14 | 17 | 8 | 13 | 38 |

LEWELLEN, VERNE

| 1925 | GB | 4 | 1 | — | 0 | — | 25 |

LEWIS, ART

| 1921 | Cin | 0 | 1 | — | 0 | — | 1 |

LEWIS, TINY

| 1930 | Por | 2 | 10 | — | 0 | — | 22 |

LEYPOLDT, JOHN

YEAR	TEAM	TD	XPM	XPA	FGM	FGA	PTS
1971	Buf	0	12	12	9	15	39
1972	Buf	0	29	30	16	24	77
1973	Buf	0	27	27	21	30	90
1974	Buf	0	25	29	19	33	82
1975	Buf	0	51	57	9	16	78
1976	Buf	0	3	3	0	3	3
1976	Sea	0	19	22	8	12	43
1977	Sea	0	33	37	9	18	60
1978	NO	0	4	5	2	3	10
NFL	8	0	203	222	93	154	482

LILLARD, JOE

1932	ChiC	0	2	—	0	—	2
1933	ChiC	2	1	—	2	—	19
NFL	2	2	3	—	2	—	21

LINCOLN, KEITH

| 1964 | SD-A | 6 | 16 | 17 | 5 | 12 | 67 |

LINDELL, RIAN

2000	Sea	0	25	25	15	17	70
2001	Sea	0	33	33	20	32	93
2002	Sea	0	38	38	23	29	107
2003	Buf	0	24	24	17	24	75
2004	Buf	0	45	45	24	28	117
2005	Buf	0	26	26	29	35	113
NFL	6	0	191	191	128	165	575

LINDSEY, STEVE

| 2000 | Jax | 0 | 5 | 5 | 5 | 7 | 20 |

LINHART, TONI

1972	NO	0	5	5	2	5	11
1974	Bal	0	22	22	12	20	58
1975	Bal	0	51	52	10	18	81
1976	Bal	0	49	50	20	27	109
1977	Bal	0	32	35	17	26	83
1978	Bal	0	27	31	8	17	51
1979	Bal	0	3	4	3	8	12
1979	NYJ	0	11	14	3	6	20
NFL	7	0	200	213	75	127	425

LIO, AUGIE

1941	Det	1	12	13	0	5	18
1942	Det	0	5	5	0	4	5
1943	Det	0	21	23	2	11	27
1944	Bos	0	10	11	2	8	16
1945	Bos	0	15	16	4	5	27
1946	Phi	1	27	27	6	11	51
1947	Bal-A	0	19	20	3	8	28
AAFC	1	0	19	20	3	8	28
NFL	6	2	90	95	14	44	144

LITTLE, STEVE

1979	SL	0	24	32	10	19	54
1980	SL	0	17	19	3	8	26
NFL	2	0	41	51	13	27	80

LITTLE TWIG, JOE

| 1923 | Oor | 0 | 1 | — | 0 | — | 1 |

LIVINGSTON, DALE

1968	Cin-A	0	20	20	13	26	59
1970	GB	0	19	21	15	28	64
NFL	2	0	39	41	28	54	123

LLOYD, DAVE

| 1965 | Phi | 0 | 7 | 7 | 1 | 2 | 10 |

LOHMILLER, CHIP

1988	Was	0	40	41	19	26	97
1989	Was	0	41	41	29	40	128
1990	Was	0	41	41	30	40	131
1991	Was	0	56	56	31	43	149
1992	Was	0	30	30	30	40	120
1993	Was	0	24	26	16	28	72
1994	Was	0	30	32	20	28	90
1995	NO	0	11	13	8	14	35
1996	SL	0	28	29	21	25	91
NFL	9	0	301	309	204	284	913

LONG, CARSON

| 1977 | Buf | 0 | 13 | 14 | 7 | 11 | 34 |

LONGWELL, RYAN

1997	GB	0	48	48	24	30	120
1998	GB	0	41	43	29	33	128
1999	GB	0	38	38	25	30	113
2000	GB	0	32	32	33	38	131
2001	GB	0	44	45	20	31	104
2002	GB	0	44	44	28	34	128
2003	GB	0	51	51	23	26	120
2004	GB	0	48	48	24	28	120
2005	GB	0	30	31	20	27	90
NFL	9	0	376	380	226	277	1054

LOVE, JOHN

| 1967 | Was | 3 | 10 | 11 | 2 | 7 | 34 |

LOWERY, NICK

YEAR	TEAM	TD	XPM	XPA	FGM	FGA	PTS
1978	NE	0	7	7	0	1	7
1980	KC	0	37	37	20	26	97
1981	KC	0	37	38	26	36	115
1982	KC	0	17	17	19	24	74
1983	KC	0	44	45	24	30	116
1984	KC	0	35	35	23	33	104
1985	KC	0	35	35	24	27	107
1986	KC	0	43	43	19	26	100
1987	KC	0	26	26	19	23	83
1988	KC	0	23	23	27	32	104
1989	KC	0	34	35	24	33	106
1990	KC	0	37	38	34	37	139
1991	KC	0	35	35	25	30	110
1992	KC	0	39	39	22	24	105
1993	KC	0	37	37	23	29	106
1994	NYJ	0	26	27	20	23	86
1995	NYJ	0	24	24	17	21	75
1996	NYJ	0	26	27	17	24	77
NFL	18	0	562	568	383	479	1711

LOWTHER, JACKIE

| 1945 | Pit | 0 | 0 | 1 | 0 | 0 | 0 |

LUCKHURST, MICK

1981	Atl	0	51	51	21	33	114
1982	Atl	0	21	22	10	14	51
1983	Atl	0	43	45	17	22	94
1984	Atl	0	31	31	20	27	91
1985	Atl	0	29	29	24	31	101
1986	Atl	0	21	21	14	24	63
1987	Atl	0	17	17	9	13	44
NFL	7	0	213	216	115	164	558

LUCKMAN, SID

| 1947 | ChiB | 1 | 1 | 1 | 0 | 0 | 7 |

LUJACK, JOHNNY

1948	ChiB	1	44	46	2	3	50
1949	ChiB	2	42	44	1	1	57
1950	ChiB	11	34	35	3	5	109
1951	ChiB	7	10	11	0	0	52
NFL	4	21	130	136	4	9	268

LUSTEG, BOOTH

1966	Buf-A	0	41	42	19	38	98
1967	Mia-A	0	18	18	7	12	39
1968	Pit	0	26	29	8	20	50
1969	GB	0	12	12	1	5	15
NFL	4	0	97	101	35	75	202

LYMAN, LINK

| 1924 | Cle | 4 | 1 | — | 0 | — | 25 |

MAHONEY, IKE

1925	ChiC	1	1	—	0	—	7
1926	ChiC	2	1	—	0	—	13
NFL	2	3	2	—	0	—	20

MALONE, CHARLEY

| 1939 | Was | 3 | 0 | 1 | 0 | 0 | 18 |

MALONEY, NED

| 1948 | SF-A | 1 | 1 | 1 | 0 | 0 | 7 |

MALONEY, RED

| 1925 | Pro | 1 | 4 | — | 0 | — | 19 |

MANCA, MASSIMO

| 1987 | Cin | 0 | 3 | 3 | 1 | 2 | 6 |

MANDERS, JACK

1933	ChiB	0	13	—	6	—	31
1934	ChiB	3	28	—	10	—	76
1935	ChiB	0	16	—	1	—	19
1936	ChiB	4	17	—	7	—	62
1937	ChiB	5	15	—	8	—	69
1938	ChiB	3	10	12	3	9	37
1939	ChiB	4	17	20	3	7	50
1940	ChiB	0	17	18	2	3	23
NFL	8	19	133	50	40	19	367

MANDERS, PUG

| 1944 | Bkn | 5 | 0 | 0 | 0 | 1 | 30 |

MANIACI, JOE

1937	Bkn	2	5	—	2	—	23
1938	ChiB	3	11	11	1	3	32
1939	ChiB	5	4	8	1	2	37
1940	ChiB	3	1	2	0	0	19
1941	ChiB	3	8	8	1	1	29
NFL	5	16	29	29	5	6	140

MANN, DAVE

| 1955 | ChiC | 5 | 0 | 2 | 1 | 1 | 33 |

MANN, ERROL

1968	GB	0	4	4	0	3	4
1969	Det	0	26	26	25	37	101
1970	Det	0	41	41	20	29	101
1971	Det	0	37	37	22	37	103
1972	Det	0	38	39	20	29	98

YEAR	TEAM	TD	XPM	XPA	FGM	FGA	PTS
1973	Det	0	14	14	13	19	53
1974	Det	0	23	26	23	32	92
1975	Det	0	25	29	14	21	67
1976	Det	0	9	10	4	10	21
1976	Oak	0	26	27	4	11	38
1977	Oak	0	**39**	**42**	**20**	**28**	**99**
1978	Oak	0	33	38	12	20	69
NFL	11	0	315	333	177	276	846
Manton, Tilly							
1936	NYG	1	15	—	0	—	21
1937	NYG	0	12	—	5	—	27
1938	NYG	0	0	1	0	0	0
1938	Was	0	2	2	1	4	5
1943	Bkn	0	0	0	0	1	0
NFL	4	1	29	3	6	5	53
Marcol, Chester							
1972	GB	0	29	29	**33**	**48**	**128**
1973	GB	0	19	20	21	35	82
1974	GB	0	19	19	**25**	**39**	**94**
1975	GB	0	0	0	1	1	3
1976	GB	0	24	27	10	19	54
1977	GB	0	11	14	13	21	50
1978	GB	0	30	30	11	19	63
1979	GB	0	16	18	4	10	28
1980	GB	1	7	7	2	3	19
1980	Hou	0	1	3	1	1	4
NFL	9	1	156	167	121	196	525
Mare, Olindo							
1997	Mia	0	33	33	28	36	117
1998	Mia	0	33	34	22	27	99
1999	Mia	0	27	27	**39**	**46**	144
2000	Mia	0	33	34	28	31	117
2001	Mia	0	39	40	19	21	96
2002	Mia	0	42	43	24	31	114
2003	Mia	0	33	34	22	29	99
2004	Mia	0	18	18	12	16	54
2005	Mia	0	33	33	25	30	108
NFL	9	0	291	296	219	267	948
Marefos, Andy							
1941	NYG	2	6	6	4	5	30
1942	NYG	1	0	0	0	2	6
1946	LAD-A	4	2	2	0	0	26
AAFC	1	4	2	2	0	0	26
NFL	2	3	6	6	4	7	36
Marek, Jodie							
1943	Bkn	0	0	0	0	1	0
Marler, Seth							
2003	Jax	0	30	30	20	33	90
Maronic, Steve							
1940	Det	0	0	0	0	1	0
Martin, Jim							
1953	Det	0	4	4	2	4	10
1954	Det	0	0	0	1	6	3
1955	Det	0	0	0	0	1	0
1956	Det	0	3	3	4	10	15
1957	Det	0	5	5	7	14	26
1958	Det	0	28	28	7	19	49
1959	Det	0	0	1	7	17	21
1960	Det	0	26	28	13	24	65
1961	Det	0	25	26	15	30	70
1963	Bal	0	32	35	**24**	39	104
1964	Was	0	35	39	12	28	71
NFL	11	0	158	169	92	192	434
Martinovich, Phil							
1939	Det	0	0	0	3	6	9
1940	ChiB	0	0	0	2	2	6
1946	Bkn-A	0	21	22	5	10	36
1947	Bkn-A	0	22	25	3	20	31
AAFC	2	0	43	47	8	30	67
NFL	2	0	0	0	5	8	15
Mason, Sam							
1925	Mil	0	1	—	0	—	1
Masterson, Bernie							
1934	ChiB	1	1	—	0	—	7
1940	ChiB	1	1	1	0	0	7
NFL	2	8	2	1	0	—	50
Masterson, Bob							
1938	Was	1	5	6	1	1	14
1939	Was	1	6	8	1	6	15
1940	Was	4	15	16	1	2	42
1941	Was	1	8	8	3	6	23
1942	Was	2	17	19	1	5	32
1943	Was	3	20	21	1	5	41
1944	Bkn	1	0	0	0	5	6
1945	Bos	0	0	0	0	1	0
1946	NYY-A	0	0	0	0	1	0
AAFC	1	0	0	0	0	1	0
NFL	8	13	71	78	8	31	173

YEAR	TEAM	TD	XPM	XPA	FGM	FGA	PTS
Mathews, Ray							
1952	Pit	7	1	1	0	0	43
Mathys, Charlie							
1921	Ham	0	0	—	1	—	3
1922	GB	2	0	—	1	—	15
NFL	2	5	0	—	2	—	36
Mattos, Harry							
1937	Cle	1	2	—	0	—	8
Maul, Tuffy							
1926	LA	2	3	—	2	—	21
May, Bill							
1937	ChiC	0	4	—	2	—	10
1938	ChiC	0	0	2	0	1	0
NFL	2	0	4	2	2	1	10
Maznicki, Frank							
1942	ChiB	2	21	22	4	5	45
1946	ChiB	0	25	26	4	9	37
1947	Bos	2	19	21	2	2	37
NFL	3	4	65	69	10	16	119
Mazzetti, Tim							
1978	Atl	0	18	18	13	16	57
1979	Atl	0	31	37	13	25	70
1980	Atl	0	46	49	19	27	103
NFL	3	0	95	104	45	68	230
McAdams, Dean							
1941	Bkn	0	3	3	2	3	9
1942	Bkn	0	2	2	0	0	2
NFL	2	0	5	5	2	3	11
McAfee, Wes							
1941	Phi	1	2	2	0	0	8
McBride, Jack							
1925	NYG	2	7	—	2	—	25
1926	NYG	5	15	—	1	—	48
1927	NYG	6	15	—	2	—	57
1928	NYG	1	2	—	0	—	8
1929	Pro	0	6	—	0	—	6
1930	Bkn	8	8	—	0	—	56
1931	Bkn	3	1	—	0	—	19
1933	NYG	0	7	—	0	—	7
1934	NYG	0	1	—	0	—	1
NFL	9	26	62	—	5	—	233
McCarthy, Jim							
1946	Bkn-A	3	5	7	0	1	23
1948	ChiR-A	0	21	21	2	3	27
1949	ChiH-A	0	21	23	6	13	39
AAFC	3	3	47	51	8	17	89
McCarthy, Vince							
1924	RI	1	1	—	0	—	7
McClard, Bill							
1972	SD	0	2	2	3	6	11
1973	NO	0	9	9	13	24	48
1974	NO	0	19	20	9	16	46
1975	NO	0	1	1	1	5	4
NFL	4	0	31	32	26	51	109
McCormick, Felix							
1929	Ora	0	0	—	1	—	3
McCullough, Hugh							
1940	ChiC	3	1	3	0	1	19
McDonald, Les							
1938	ChiB	1	1	1	0	0	7
McFadden, Paul							
1984	Phi	0	26	27	**30**	**37**	116
1985	Phi	0	29	29	25	30	104
1986	Phi	0	26	27	20	31	86
1987	Phi	0	36	36	16	26	84
1988	NYG	0	25	27	14	19	67
1989	Atl	0	18	18	15	20	63
NFL	6	0	160	164	120	163	520
McFadin, Bud							
1955	LARm	0	0	0	1	5	3
1956	LARm	1	0	0	1	4	9
NFL	2	3	0	0	2	9	24
McHan, Lamar							
1955	ChiC	2	0	2	0	0	12
McKay, Roy							
1946	GB	1	2	2	0	0	8
1947	GB	0	1	1	0	0	1
NFL	2	3	3	3	0	0	21
McLaughlin, Steve							
1995	SL	0	17	17	8	16	41
McLean, Ray							
1940	ChiB	4	1	1	0	0	25
1943	ChiB	3	0	1	0	0	18

YEAR	TEAM	TD	XPM	XPA	FGM	FGA	PTS
1947	ChiB	1	**44**	**52**	0	1	50
NFL	3	30	45	54	0	1	225
McLemore, Emmett							
1923	Oor	1	2	—	0	—	8
McNamara, Tom							
1923	Tol	0	0	—	1	—	3
McPhail, Buck							
1953	Bal	0	21	23	2	5	27
McPhail, Hal							
1934	Bos	3	4	—	0	—	22
Meeker, Butch							
1930	Pro	2	1	—	1	—	16
1931	Pro	0	1	—	0	—	1
NFL	2	2	2	—	1	—	17
Mellus, John							
1946	SF-A	0	1	2	0	1	1
Mercein, Chuck							
1965	NYG	2	0	0	0	2	12
1967	NYG	0	2	3	0	1	2
1968	GB	1	7	7	2	5	19
NFL	3	5	9	10	2	8	45
Mercer, Ken							
1927	Fra	3	6	—	5	—	39
1928	Fra	6	2	—	0	—	38
1929	Fra	1	6	—	2	—	18
NFL	3	10	14	—	7	—	95
Mercer, Mike							
1961	Min	0	36	37	9	21	63
1962	Min	0	3	3	0	5	3
1963	Oak-A	0	**47**	47	8	19	71
1964	Oak-A	0	34	34	15	24	79
1965	Oak-A	0	35	35	9	15	62
1966	Oak-A	0	2	3	**1**	4	5
1966	KC-A	0	33	35	**20**	26	93
1967	Buf-A	0	25	25	16	27	73
1968	Buf-A	0	4	4	0	4	4
1968	GB	0	12	14	7	12	33
1969	GB	0	23	23	5	17	38
1970	SD	0	34	35	12	19	70
NFL	10	0	288	295	102	193	594
Michaels, Al							
1923	Akr	0	0	—	1	—	3
Michaels, Lou							
1959	LARm	0	12	14	8	17	36
1960	LARm	0	1	1	2	3	7
1961	Pit	0	27	29	15	26	72
1962	Pit	0	32	33	**26**	**42**	110
1963	Pit	0	32	35	21	**41**	95
1964	Bal	0	**53**	**54**	17	35	104
1965	Bal	0	48	48	17	28	101
1966	Bal	0	35	36	21	39	98
1967	Bal	0	46	**48**	20	37	106
1968	Bal	0	48	50	18	28	102
1969	Bal	0	33	34	14	31	75
1971	GB	0	19	20	8	14	43
NFL	12	1	386	402	187	341	955
Michaels, Walt							
1951	GB	0	0	0	0	1	0
Michalik, Art							
1955	Pit	0	9	15	1	12	12
1956	Pit	0	0	0	0	1	0
NFL	2	0	9	15	1	13	12
Michel, Mike							
1977	Mia	0	0	1	0	0	0
1978	Phi	0	9	12	0	0	9
NFL	2	0	9	13	0	0	9
Mike-Mayer, Nick							
1973	Atl	0	34	34	26	38	112
1974	Atl	0	12	12	9	16	39
1975	Atl	0	30	33	4	10	42
1976	Atl	0	20	20	10	21	50
1977	Atl	0	7	7	7	19	28
1977	Phi	0	7	7	3	3	16
1978	Phi	0	21	22	8	17	45
1979	Buf	0	17	18	20	29	77
1980	Buf	0	37	39	13	23	76
1981	Buf	0	37	37	14	24	79
1982	Buf	0	4	5	1	4	7
NFL	10	0	226	234	115	204	571
Mike-Mayer, Steve							
1975	SF	0	27	31	14	28	69
1976	SF	0	26	30	16	28	74
1977	Det	0	19	21	8	19	43
1978	NO	0	18	18	6	13	36
1979	Bal	0	28	29	11	20	61
1980	Bal	0	43	46	12	23	79
NFL	6	0	161	175	67	131	362

YEAR	TEAM	TD	XPM	XPA	FGM	FGA	PTS
MILLER, CHRIS							
1989	Atl	0	0	0	1	1	3
MILLER, DAN							
1982	NE	0	4	5	2	3	10
1982	Bal	0	5	5	4	8	17
MILLS, JOE							
1922	Akr	1	1	—	0	—	7
MILSTEAD, CHARLIE							
1961	Hou-A	0	1	1	0	0	1
MINER, TOM							
1958	Pit	0	31	31	**14**	**28**	73
MINGO, GENE							
1960	Den-A	6	33	36	**18**	28	**123**
1961	Den-A	2	11	11	3	10	32
1962	Den-A	4	32	34	**27**	**39**	**137**
1963	Den-A	0	35	35	16	29	83
1964	Den-A	0	9	10	8	12	33
1965	Oak-A	0	0	0	8	19	24
1966	Mia-A	0	23	23	10	22	53
1967	Mia-A	0	9	9	1	6	12
1967	Was	0	20	22	4	10	32
1969	Pit	0	26	26	12	26	62
1970	Pit	0	17	17	5	18	32
NFL	10	13	215	223	112	219	629
MISHEL, DAVE							
1931	Cle	0	1	—	0	—	1
MOAN, KELLY							
1939	Cle	0	1	1	0	0	1
MOHR, CHRIS							
1989	TB	0	1	1	0	0	1
MOLENDA, BO							
1927	NYY	1	1	—	0	—	7
1928	NYY	0	3	—	0	—	3
1929	GB	3	3	—	0	—	21
1930	GB	3	4	—	0	—	22
1931	GB	3	3	—	0	—	21
1932	NYG	0	3	—	0	—	3
1934	NYG	0	2	—	0	—	2
1935	NYG	1	5	—	0	—	11
NFL	8	14	24	—	0	—	108
MOLESWORTH, KEITH							
1937	ChiB	0	1	—	0	—	1
MONAHAN, REGIS							
1937	Det	0	5	—	5	—	20
1938	Det	0	2	4	4	5	14
1939	ChiC	0	1	1	1	1	4
NFL	3	1	8	5	10	6	44
MONNETT, BOB							
1933	GB	4	10	—	0	—	34
1934	GB	2	5	—	4	—	29
1935	GB	1	2	—	1	—	11
1936	GB	0	3	—	0	—	3
1938	GB	0	7	8	0	0	7
NFL	5	8	27	8	5	—	90
MOONEY, JIM							
1930	Nwk	0	2	—	0	—	2
1931	Bkn	0	1	—	0	—	1
NFL	2	0	3	—	0	—	5
MORAN, HAP							
1926	Fra	5	3	—	0	—	33
1927	Fra	1	6	—	3	—	21
1930	NYG	4	3	—	0	—	27
1931	NYG	4	8	—	1	—	35
1932	NYG	1	2	—	0	—	8
NFL	5	22	22	—	4	—	166
MOREAU, DOUG							
1968	Mia-A	3	6	6	1	3	27
MORRIS, JACK							
1959	LARm	0	15	15	3	8	24
MORRISSEY, FRANK							
1922	Buf	0	8	—	2	—	14
1923	Buf	0	7	—	8	—	31
1924	Buf	0	0	—	2	—	6
NFL	3	0	15	—	12	—	51
MORROW, JIM							
1921	Can	1	1	—	0	—	7
MOSCRIP, MONK							
1938	Det	1	6	6	0	1	12
1939	Det	1	9	12	0	1	15
NFL	2	2	15	18	0	2	27
MOSELEY, MARK							
1970	Phi	0	25	28	14	25	67
1971	Hou	0	25	27	16	26	73
1972	Hou	0	2	2	1	2	5

YEAR	TEAM	TD	XPM	XPA	FGM	FGA	PTS
1974	Was	0	27	29	18	30	81
1975	Was	0	37	39	16	25	85
1976	Was	0	31	32	**22**	**34**	**97**
1977	Was	0	19	19	**21**	**37**	82
1978	Was	0	30	31	19	30	87
1979	Was	0	39	39	**25**	**33**	**114**
1980	Was	0	27	30	18	33	81
1981	Was	0	38	42	19	30	95
1982	Was	0	16	19	**20**	21	76
1983	Was	0	**62**	**63**	33	**47**	**161**
1984	Was	0	48	51	24	31	120
1985	Was	0	31	33	22	34	97
1986	Was	0	12	14	6	12	30
1986	Cle	0	13	14	6	7	31
NFL	16	0	482	512	300	457	1382
MOYNIHAN, DICK							
1927	Fra	0	0	—	1	—	3
MUHA, JOE							
1947	Phi	2	0	0	1	5	15
1948	Phi	1	0	0	0	5	6
1949	Phi	1	5	5	0	1	11
1950	Phi	1	0	0	0	5	6
NFL	4	5	5	5	1	16	38
MUHLMANN, HORST							
1969	Cin-A	0	32	33	16	24	80
1970	Cin	0	33	33	25	37	108
1971	Cin	0	31	31	20	36	91
1972	Cin	0	30	31	27	40	111
1973	Cin	0	31	32	21	31	94
1974	Cin	0	32	35	11	18	65
1975	Phi	0	21	24	20	29	81
1976	Phi	0	18	19	11	16	51
1977	Phi	0	17	19	3	8	26
NFL	9	0	245	257	154	239	707
MUNN, LYLE							
1929	NYG	0	1	—	0	—	1
MUNNS, GEORGE							
1921	Cin	0	1	—	0	—	1
MURDOCK, LES							
1967	NYG	0	13	15	4	9	25
MURRAY, EDDIE							
1980	Det	0	35	36	**27**	**42**	116
1981	Det	0	46	46	25	35	**121**
1982	Det	0	16	16	11	12	49
1983	Det	0	38	38	25	32	113
1984	Det	0	31	31	20	27	91
1985	Det	0	31	33	26	31	109
1986	Det	0	31	32	18	25	85
1987	Det	0	21	21	20	32	81
1988	Det	0	22	23	20	21	82
1989	Det	0	36	36	20	21	96
1990	Det	0	34	34	13	19	73
1991	Det	0	40	40	19	28	97
1992	KC	0	0	0	1	1	3
1992	TB	0	13	13	4	8	25
1993	Dal	0	38	38	28	33	122
1994	Phi	0	33	33	21	25	96
1995	Was	0	33	33	27	36	114
1997	Min	0	23	24	12	17	59
1999	Dal	0	10	10	7	9	31
2000	Was	0	7	8	8	12	31
NFL	19	0	538	545	352	466	1594
MURRAY, FRAN							
1939	Phi	2	8	12	2	4	26
1940	Phi	0	6	8	0	1	6
NFL	2	2	14	20	2	5	32
MURRAY, JAB							
1922	Rac	0	1	—	0	—	1
MUSICK, JIM							
1933	Bos	5	12	—	1	—	45
1935	Bos	2	2	—	0	—	14
NFL	2	8	14	—	1	—	65
MUTRYN, CHET							
1947	Buf-A	12	1	2	0	0	73
MYERS, TRUCK							
1922	Tol	0	1	—	—	—	1
MYHRA, STEVE							
1957	Bal	0	14	16	4	6	26
1958	Bal	0	**48**	**51**	4	10	60
1959	Bal	0	**50**	51	6	17	68
1960	Bal	0	35	37	9	19	62
1961	Bal	0	33	34	**21**	**39**	96
NFL	5	0	180	189	44	91	312
NAGURSKI, BRONKO							
1933	ChiB	1	1	—	0	—	7
1934	ChiB	7	2	—	0	—	44
1936	ChiB	3	1	—	0	—	19
NFL	3	25	4	—	0	—	154

YEAR	TEAM	TD	XPM	XPA	FGM	FGA	PTS
NAIOTI, JOHN							
1945	Pit	0	4	4	0	0	4
NEDNEY, JOE							
1996	Mia	0	35	36	18	29	89
1997	Arz	0	19	19	11	17	52
1998	Arz	0	30	30	13	19	69
1999	Oak	0	13	13	5	7	28
2000	Den	0	4	4	8	10	28
2000	Car	0	20	20	26	28	98
2001	Ten	0	34	35	20	28	94
2002	Ten	0	36	36	25	31	111
2003	Ten	0	0	1	1	1	3
2005	SF	0	19	19	26	28	97
NFL	9	0	210	213	153	198	669
NELSON, CHUCK							
1983	LARm	0	33	37	5	11	48
1984	Buf	0	14	14	3	5	23
1986	Min	0	**44**	**47**	22	28	110
1987	Min	0	36	37	13	24	75
1988	Min	0	**48**	**49**	20	25	108
NFL	5	0	175	184	63	93	364
NELSON, ROBERT							
1946	LAD-A	0	3	5	2	6	9
1949	LAD-A	0	34	35	3	6	43
1945	Det	0	0	0	1	4	3
AAFC	2	0	37	40	5	12	52
NFL	1	2	0	0	1	4	15
NEMETH, STEVE							
1946	ChiR-A	0	32	33	9	12	59
1947	Bal-A	0	1	1	0	1	1
AAFC	2	0	33	34	9	13	60
NESSER, FRANK							
1921	Col	1	1	—	0	—	7
NEUHEISEL, RICK							
1987	SD	0	1	1	1	0	7
NEVERS, ERNIE							
1926	Dul	8	11	—	4	—	71
1927	Dul	4	7	—	0	—	31
1929	ChiC	12	10	—	1	—	85
1930	ChiC	6	9	—	1	—	48
1931	ChiR-A	8	15	—	1	—	66
NFL	5	38	52	—	7	—	301
NEWMAN, HARRY							
1933	NYG	4	6	—	1	—	33
1934	NYG	4	4	—	3	—	37
1935	NYG	0	3	—	2	—	9
NFL	3	8	13	—	6	—	79
NEWMAN, OBIE							
1925	Akr	1	1	—	0	—	7
NEWMEYER, DON							
1926	LA	0	2	—	0	—	2
NICCOLAI, ARMAND							
1934	Pit	0	1	—	3	—	10
1935	Pit	0	10	—	**6**	—	28
1936	Pit	0	7	—	**7**	—	28
1937	Pit	0	5	—	4	—	17
1938	Pit	0	10	10	1	5	13
1939	Pit	0	15	15	3	8	24
1940	Pit	0	6	6	**14**	—	48
1941	Pit	0	8	9	2	4	14
1942	Pit	0	9	9	2	**14**	15
NFL	9	0	71	49	34	45	173
NIELSEN, HANS							
1981	ChiB	0	8	8	0	2	8
NITTMO, BJORN							
1989	NYG	0	12	13	9	12	39
NIX, JACK							
1950	SF	0	1	1	0	0	1
NORWOOD, SCOTT							
1985	Buf	0	23	23	13	17	62
1986	Buf	0	32	34	17	27	83
1987	Buf	0	31	31	10	15	61
1988	Buf	0	33	33	**32**	**37**	**129**
1989	Buf	0	**46**	**47**	23	30	115
1990	Buf	0	**50**	**52**	20	29	110
1991	Buf	0	**56**	**58**	18	29	110
NFL	7	0	271	278	133	184	670
NOVAK, EDDIE							
1924	Min	0	1	—	0	—	1
NOVAK, NICK							
2005	Was	0	15	15	5	7	30
2005	Arz	0	0	0	3	3	9
NOWASKEY, BOB							
1941	ChiB	2	1	2	0	0	13

YEAR	TEAM	TD	XPM	XPA	FGM	FGA	PTS
NUGENT, MIKE							
2005	NYJ	0	24	24	22	28	90
NYDALL, MALLY							
1929	Min	2	2	—	0	—	14
1930	Min	0	1	—	0	—	1
NFL	2	4	3	—	0	—	27
O'BOYLE, HARRY							
1928	GB	1	8	—	3	—	23
1932	GB	0	7	—	0	—	7
NFL	2	1	15	—	3	—	30
O'BRIEN, JIM							
1970	Bal	0	**36**	**38**	19	34	93
1971	Bal	0	35	36	20	29	95
1972	Bal	2	24	24	13	31	75
1973	Det	0	14	14	8	14	38
NFL	4	2	109	112	60	108	301
ODEN, CURLY							
1928	Pro	4	3	—	0	—	27
1930	Pro	0	1	—	0	—	1
NFL	2	17	4	—	0	—	106
O'DONAHUE, PAT							
1952	SF	1	1	1	0	0	7
O'DONOGHUE, NEIL							
1977	Buf	0	4	5	2	6	10
1978	TB	0	25	29	13	23	64
1979	TB	0	30	35	11	19	63
1980	SL	0	18	18	11	15	51
1981	SL	0	36	37	19	32	93
1982	SL	0	15	16	8	13	39
1983	SL	0	45	47	15	28	90
1984	SL	0	48	51	23	35	117
1985	SL	0	19	19	10	18	49
NFL	9	0	240	257	112	189	576
OGLESBY, CEDRIC							
2001	Arz	0	7	7	5	6	22
OLANDER, CLIFF							
1979	SD	0	1	1	0	1	1
OLIPHANT, ELMER							
1921	Buf	1	26	—	5	—	47
O'NEILL, PAT							
1994	NE	0	0	0	0	1	0
OWENS, BRIG							
1967	Was	1	2	3	0	2	8
PARDONNER, PAUL							
1934	ChiC	0	0	—	1	—	3
1935	ChiC	0	1	—	1	—	4
NFL	2	0	1	—	2	—	7
PARKER, ACE							
1937	Bkn	2	1	—	0	—	13
1938	Bkn	4	5	7	0	0	29
1939	Bkn	5	0	1	1	5	33
1940	Bkn	5	**19**	**22**	0	0	49
NFL	4	20	25	30	1	5	148
PARKER, BUDDY							
1937	ChiC	1	1	—	0	—	7
1940	ChiC	1	3	3	0	1	9
1941	ChiC	0	0	1	0	0	0
NFL	3	4	4	4	0	1	28
PARKS, MICKEY							
1939	Was	0	0	1	0	0	0
PARRIS, GARY							
1979	SL	0	1	1	0	0	1
PARTEE, DENNIS							
1968	SD-A	0	40	43	22	32	106
1969	SD-A	0	33	33	15	28	78
1971	SD	0	36	37	17	29	87
1972	SD	0	26	28	15	25	71
1973	SD	0	6	6	1	2	9
1974	SD	0	26	28	1	5	29
NFL	6	0	167	175	71	121	380
PASCHKA, GORDON							
1943	P-P	0	2	2	0	0	2
PASQUA, JOE							
1942	Cle	0	1	1	0	0	1
1943	Was	0	1	1	0	0	1
NFL	2	0	2	2	0	0	2
PASTORINI, DAN							
1977	Hou	2	0	1	0	0	12
PATERA, DENNIS							
1968	SF	0	10	13	2	8	16

YEAR	TEAM	TD	XPM	XPA	FGM	FGA	PTS
PATRICK, FRANK							
1938	ChiC	1	8	8	1	4	17
1939	ChiC	1	1	1	0	0	7
NFL	2	2	9	9	1	4	24
PATTERSON, BILLY							
1939	ChiB	0	1	1	0	0	1
PATTON, CLIFF							
1947	Phi	0	36	40	3	14	45
1948	Phi	0	50	50	**8**	12	74
1949	Phi	0	42	43	**9**	18	69
1950	Phi	0	32	33	8	17	56
1951	ChiC	0	19	19	5	8	34
NFL	5	0	179	185	33	69	278
PAVELEC, TED							
1942	Det	0	0	0	1	2	3
PEACE, LARRY							
1941	Bkn	0	1	1	0	0	1
PEDERSEN, WIN							
1941	NYG	0	0	0	1	1	3
PEEBLES, JIM							
1946	Was	1	0	0	0	2	6
1947	Was	0	0	0	0	1	0
1948	Was	0	1	2	0	0	1
NFL	3	1	1	2	0	3	7
PELFREY, DOUG							
1993	Cin	0	13	16	24	31	85
1994	Cin	0	24	25	28	33	108
1995	Cin	0	34	34	29	36	121
1996	Cin	0	41	41	23	28	110
1997	Cin	0	41	43	12	16	77
1998	Cin	0	21	21	19	27	78
1999	Cin	0	27	27	18	27	81
NFL	7	0	201	207	153	198	660
PENNINGTON, TOM							
1962	DalT-A	0	13	15	2	5	19
PERCIVAL, MAC							
1967	ChiB	0	26	29	13	26	65
1968	ChiB	0	25	25	**25**	36	100
1969	ChiB	0	26	26	8	21	50
1970	ChiB	0	28	28	20	34	88
1971	ChiB	0	18	18	15	33	63
1972	ChiB	0	26	26	12	24	62
1973	ChiB	0	10	10	6	8	28
1974	Dal	0	4	5	2	8	10
NFL	8	0	163	167	101	190	466
PERINI, PETE							
1954	ChiB	0	1	1	0	0	1
PERRIN, JACK							
1926	Har	0	3	—	1	—	6
PERRY, GERRY							
1958	Det	0	1	1	4	4	13
1959	Det	0	18	18	3	6	27
1960	SL	0	5	5	13	20	44
1961	SL	0	30	33	7	16	51
1962	SL	0	38	39	5	12	53
NFL	5	0	92	96	32	58	188
PERRY, JOE							
1953	SF	**13**	0	0	0	3	78
1954	SF	8	6	7	1	3	57
NFL	2	84	6	7	1	6	513
PETERS, FROSTY							
1930	Pro	2	7	—	2	—	25
1931	Bkn	2	2	—	0	—	2
NFL	2	2	9	—	2	—	27
PETERSON, NELS							
1938	Cle	2	2	2	2	2	20
PETERSON, TODD							
1994	Arz	0	4	4	2	4	10
1995	Sea	0	**40**	**40**	23	28	109
1996	Sea	0	27	27	28	34	111
1997	Sea	0	37	37	22	28	103
1998	Sea	0	41	41	19	24	98
1999	Sea	0	32	32	34	40	134
2000	KC	0	25	25	15	20	70
2001	KC	0	27	28	27	35	108
2002	Pit	0	25	26	12	21	61
2003	SF	0	22	23	12	15	58
2004	SF	0	23	23	18	22	77
2005	Atl	0	35	35	23	25	104
NFL	12	0	338	341	235	296	1043
PHARMER, ART							
1930	Min	1	2	—	0	—	8
1930	Fra	0	4	—	0	—	4
PLANSKY, TONY							
1929	NYG	0	2	—	2	—	62

YEAR	TEAM	TD	XPM	XPA	FGM	FGA	PTS
PLASMAN, DICK							
1937	ChiB	1	2	—	0	—	8
1939	ChiB	3	3	3	0	1	21
1940	ChiB	2	3	3	0	0	15
1941	ChiB	0	6	9	0	0	6
NFL	4	7	14	15	0	1	56
PLUM, MILT							
1958	Cle	4	2	2	0	0	26
1962	Det	1	0	0	5	12	21
1963	Det	0	13	13	1	4	16
1966	Det	0	1	1	0	0	1
NFL	4	13	16	16	6	16	112
POCHMAN, OWEN							
2001	NYG	0	0	0	0	2	0
2003	SF	0	9	10	8	15	33
NFL	2	0	9	10	8	17	33
POILLON, DICK							
1942	Was	0	2	2	1	2	5
1946	Was	1	21	21	6	16	45
1947	Was	6	37	41	4	6	85
1948	Was	3	33	38	5	7	66
1949	Was	0	34	37	4	7	46
NFL	5	10	127	139	20	38	247
POLLARD, AL							
1953	Phi	0	1	1	0	2	1
POLLARD, FRITZ							
1922	Mil	3	2	—	0	—	20
1923	Ham	0	1	—	0	—	1
NFL	2	12	3	—	0	—	75
POOLE, RAY							
1950	NYG	0	30	34	5	11	45
1951	NYG	0	30	31	12	16	66
1952	NYG	0	26	27	10	17	56
NFL	3	9	86	92	27	44	223
POSEY, DAVID							
1978	NE	0	29	31	11	22	62
PREGULMAN, MERV							
1948	Det	0	26	27	2	6	32
PRESNELL, GLENN							
1931	Por	4	8	—	1	—	35
1932	Por	2	1	—	0	—	13
1933	Por	6	**13**	—	5	—	**64**
1934	Det	7	9	—	4	—	63
1935	Det	2	4	—	4	—	28
1936	Det	1	6	—	1	—	15
NFL	6	22	41	—	15	—	218
PRICE, COTTON							
1940	Det	2	4	4	0	0	16
PRINDLE, MIKE							
1987	Det	0	6	6	6	7	24
PRITCHARD, BILL							
1927	Pro	1	3	—	0	—	9
1928	NYY	1	1	—	0	—	7
NFL	2	2	4	—	0	—	16
PUGH, MARION							
1941	NYG	0	0	1	0	0	0
PURDY, PID							
1926	GB	0	14	—	2	—	20
1927	GB	1	1	—	1	—	10
NFL	2	1	15	—	3	—	30
PUREIFORY, DAVE							
1975	GB	0	2	4	0	0	4
RACKERS, NEIL							
2000	Cin	0	21	21	12	21	57
2001	Cin	0	23	24	17	28	74
2002	Cin	0	30	32	15	18	75
2003	Arz	0	8	8	9	12	35
2004	Arz	0	28	28	22	29	94
2005	Arz	0	20	20	**40**	**42**	140
NFL	6	0	130	133	115	150	475
RADZIEVITCH, VIC							
1926	Har	0	2	—	1	—	5
RAGUSA, PAT							
1987	NYJ	0	7	7	2	4	13
RANSPOT, KEITH							
1944	Bos	3	0	0	0	1	18
RATTERMAN, GEORGE							
1947	Buf-A	1	0	1	0	0	6
RAY, DAVID							
1970	LARm	0	34	34	29	45	121
1971	LARm	0	37	37	18	29	91
1972	LARm	0	31	31	24	41	103
1973	LARm	0	40	42	**30**	**47**	130

YEAR	TEAM	TD	XPM	XPA	FGM	FGA	PTS
1974	LARm	0	25	31	9	16	52
NFL	5	0	167	175	110	178	497
Rayner, Dave							
2005	Ind	0	0	0	0	1	0
Rechichar, Bert							
1953	Bal	3	0	0	5	13	33
1954	Bal	0	1	1	6	13	19
1955	Bal	0	25	26	10	**24**	55
1956	Bal	0	8	10	3	13	17
1957	Bal	0	22	25	3	13	31
1958	Bal	1	0	0	1	4	9
1959	Bal	0	0	0	0	1	0
1960	Pit	0	6	6	3	7	15
NFL	8	4	62	68	31	88	179
Reed, Jeff							
2002	Pit	0	10	11	17	19	61
2003	Pit	0	31	32	23	32	100
2004	Pit	0	40	40	28	33	124
2005	Pit	0	45	45	24	29	117
NFL	4	0	126	128	92	113	402
Reese, Hank							
1935	Phi	0	4	—	1	—	7
1936	Phi	0	3	—	2	—	9
1937	Phi	0	3	—	0	—	3
1938	Phi	0	10	13	1	6	13
1939	Phi	0	1	1	2	4	7
NFL	5	0	21	14	6	10	39
Reeves, Dan							
1971	Dal	0	1	1	0	0	1
Reichardt, Bill							
1952	GB	1	5	5	5	20	26
Reichel, Lou							
1926	Col	0	2	—	0	—	2
Reissig, Bill							
1938	Bkn	0	0	0	2	2	6
1939	Bkn	0	0	1	1	1	3
NFL	2	0	0	1	3	3	9
Rentner, Pug							
1935	Bos	2	1	—	0	—	13
Reveiz, Fuad							
1985	Mia	0	50	52	22	27	116
1986	Mia	0	**52**	**55**	14	22	94
1987	Mia	0	28	30	9	11	55
1988	Mia	0	31	32	8	12	55
1990	SD	0	7	8	2	7	13
1990	Min	0	19	19	11	12	52
1991	Min	0	34	35	17	24	85
1992	Min	0	45	45	19	25	102
1993	Min	0	27	28	26	35	105
1994	Min	0	30	30	**34**	**39**	**132**
1995	Min	0	44	44	26	36	122
NFL	10	0	367	378	188	250	931
Ricardo, Benny							
1976	Buf	0	2	2	1	4	5
1976	Det	0	19	21	10	14	49
1978	Det	0	32	33	20	28	92
1979	Det	0	25	26	10	18	55
1980	NO	0	31	34	10	17	61
1981	NO	0	24	24	13	25	63
1983	Min	0	33	34	25	33	108
1984	SD	0	5	6	3	3	14
NFL	7	0	171	180	92	142	447
Richards, Kink							
1933	NYG	**7**	1	—	0	—	43
1934	NYG	2	1	—	0	—	13
1935	NYG	4	1	—	1	—	28
1938	NYG	0	2	2	0	0	2
NFL	4	19	5	2	1	—	122
Richey, Wade							
1998	SF	0	49	51	18	27	103
1999	SF	0	30	31	21	23	93
2000	SF	0	43	**45**	15	22	88
2001	SD	0	26	26	21	32	89
2003	Bal	0	0	0	1	2	3
NFL	5	0	148	153	76	106	376
Richter, Les							
1954	LARm	0	38	38	8	15	62
1955	LARm	0	30	31	13	**24**	69
1956	LARm	0	36	38	8	15	60
1959	LARm	0	0	0	0	1	0
1960	LARm	0	2	2	0	0	2
NFL	5	0	106	109	29	55	193
Riffle, Dick							
1942	Pit	4	1	1	0	0	25
Risley, Elliott							
1921	Ham	0	2	—	0	—	2

YEAR	TEAM	TD	XPM	XPA	FGM	FGA	PTS
Robb, Harry							
1926	Can	2	1	—	0	—	13
Roberts, Wooky							
1924	Cle	4	1	—	0	—	25
Robinson, Ed							
1923	Ham	1	1	—	0	—	7
1925	Ham	1	1	—	0	—	7
NFL	2	2	2	—	0	—	14
Robinson, Rex							
1982	NE	0	5	5	1	2	8
Robnett, Marshall							
1944	C-P	0	1	1	0	2	1
Roby, Doug							
1923	Cle	1	1	—	0	—	7
Roder, Mirro							
1973	ChiB	0	11	12	8	16	35
1974	ChiB	0	17	17	9	13	44
1976	TB	0	0	0	0	3	0
NFL	3	0	28	29	17	32	79
Roepke, Johnny							
1928	Fra	1	1	—	1	—	10
Rogalla, John							
1945	Phi	0	1	1	0	0	1
Rohleder, George							
1925	Col	0	1	—	3	—	10
1926	Akr	0	2	—	1	—	5
NFL	2	0	3	—	4	—	15
Rohrig, Herm							
1941	GB	0	1	1	1	1	4
Rokisky, John							
1946	Cle-A	0	1	1	0	0	1
1947	ChiR-A	0	33	35	4	8	45
AAFC	2	0	34	36	4	8	46
Romney, Milt							
1926	ChiB	4	1	—	0	—	25
1928	ChiB	2	1	—	0	—	13
NFL	2	9	2	—	0	—	56
Ronzani, Gene							
1935	ChiB	2	3	—	0	—	15
Rose, Gene							
1930	ChiC	4	1	—	0	—	25
Rouen, Tom							
1998	Den	0	0	1	0	0	0
Roveto, John							
1981	ChiB	0	19	20	10	18	49
1982	ChiB	0	10	10	4	13	22
NFL	2	0	29	30	14	31	71
Ruh, Emmett							
1921	Col	1	1	—	2	—	13
Russell, Andy							
1966	Pit	1	1	1	0	0	7
Russell, Bo							
1939	Was	1	15	16	1	6	24
1940	Was	0	11	12	1	1	14
NFL	2	1	26	28	2	7	38
Ruzek, Roger							
1987	Dal	0	26	26	22	25	92
1988	Dal	0	27	27	12	22	63
1989	Dal	0	14	15	5	11	29
1989	Phi	0	14	14	8	11	38
1990	Phi	0	**45**	**48**	21	29	108
1991	Phi	0	27	29	28	33	111
1992	Phi	0	40	44	16	25	88
1993	Phi	0	13	16	8	10	37
NFL	7	0	206	219	120	166	566
Ryan, Dave							
1945	Det	2	0	0	1	3	15
Ryan, Pat							
1983	NYJ	0	1	1	0	0	1
1984	NYJ	0	1	1	0	0	1
NFL	2	1	2	2	0	0	8
Rykovich, Julie							
1948	ChiR-A	1	0	0	0	1	6
1952	Was	2	1	1	0	0	13
AAFC	1	1	0	0	0	1	6
NFL	1	31	1	1	0	0	187
Saban, Lou							
1947	Cle-A	0	10	11	0	0	10
1949	Cle-A	1	11	11	0	2	17
AAFC	2	1	21	22	0	2	27

YEAR	TEAM	TD	XPM	XPA	FGM	FGA	PTS
Sanders, Jack							
1941	Pit	0	5	5	0	0	5
1942	Pit	0	7	8	0	0	7
NFL	2	0	12	13	0	0	12
Sanford, Sandy							
1940	Was	0	3	5	0	2	3
Sarausky, Tony							
1935	NYG	1	1	—	0	—	7
1936	NYG	1	1	—	1	—	10
NFL	2	2	2	—	1	—	17
Sauerbrun, Todd							
2004	Car	0	4	4	1	1	7
Scharer, Eddie							
1928	Det	0	1	—	0	—	1
Schell, Herb							
1924	Col	1	0	—	1	—	9
Schlopy, Todd							
1987	Buf	0	1	2	2	5	7
Schreiber, Larry							
1971	SF	1	1	1	0	0	7
Schubert, Eric							
1985	NYG	0	26	27	10	13	56
1986	SL	0	9	9	3	11	18
1987	NE	0	1	1	1	2	4
NFL	3	0	36	37	14	26	78
Schwammel, Ade							
1934	GB	0	0	—	1	—	3
1935	GB	0	3	—	4	—	15
1936	GB	0	5	—	1	—	8
NFL	3	0	8	—	6	—	26
Scobee, Josh							
2004	Jax	0	21	21	24	31	93
2005	Jax	0	38	39	23	30	107
NFL	2	0	59	60	47	61	200
Scollard, Nick							
1946	Bos	2	21	24	0	1	33
1947	Bos	0	2	2	1	4	5
1948	Bos	0	8	8	2	3	14
1949	NYB	2	18	21	3	10	39
NFL	4	4	49	55	6	18	91
Scott, Ralph							
1923	ChiB	0	1	—	0	—	1
Sechrist, Walt							
1924	Akr	0	1	—	0	—	1
1926	Ham	0	0	—	1	—	3
NFL	2	0	1	—	1	—	4
Seder, Tim							
2000	Dal	1	27	27	25	33	108
2001	Dal	1	12	12	11	17	51
2002	Jax	0	11	11	8	12	35
NFL	3	2	50	50	44	62	194
Senn, Bill							
1926	ChiB	7	3	—	0	—	45
1928	ChiB	6	1	—	0	—	37
1931	ChiB	1	1	—	0	—	7
1934	SL	0	0	—	1	—	3
NFL	4	25	5	—	1	—	158
Septien, Rafael							
1977	LARm	0	32	35	18	30	86
1978	Dal	0	**46**	**47**	16	26	94
1979	Dal	0	**40**	**44**	19	29	97
1980	Dal	0	**59**	**60**	11	17	92
1981	Dal	0	40	40	**27**	35	**121**
1982	Dal	0	**28**	**28**	10	14	58
1983	Dal	0	57	59	22	27	123
1984	Dal	0	33	34	23	29	102
1985	Dal	0	42	43	19	28	99
1986	Dal	0	43	43	15	21	88
NFL	10	0	420	433	180	256	960
Shaw, Ed							
1922	Can	4	8	—	2	—	38
Shaw, George							
1958	Bal	1	0	1	0	0	6
Sheard, Shag							
1924	Roc	0	1	—	0	—	1
Sheeks, Paul							
1921	Akr	1	1	—	2	—	13
1922	Akr	0	8	—	3	—	17
NFL	2	1	9	—	5	—	30
Shelley, Deck							
1931	Pro	0	4	—	0	—	4

YEAR	TEAM	TD	XPM	XPA	FGM	FGA	PTS
SHEPHERD, BILL							
1935	Bos	1	1	—	0	—	7
1936	Det	2	1	—	0	—	13
1937	Det	3	7	—	2	—	31
1938	Det	3	2	2	1	2	23
NFL	4	15	11	2	3	2	110
SHERMAN, ROD							
1968	Cin-A	1	4	4	0	1	10
SHLAPAK, BORIS							
1972	Bal	0	4	4	0	8	4
SHOCKLEY, BILL							
1960	NYT-A	2	**47**	**50**	9	21	86
1961	NYT-A	0	13	13	3	7	22
1961	Buf-A	0	0	0	1	2	3
1962	NYT-A	0	29	30	13	26	68
1968	Pit	0	2	3	0	1	2
NFL	4	2	91	96	26	57	181
SIEB, WALLY							
1922	Rac	2	1	—	0	—	13
SIES, HERB							
1923	RI	0	8	—	3	—	17
1924	Day	0	0	—	1	—	3
NFL	2	0	8	—	4	—	20
SIMINGTON, MILT							
1942	Pit	0	2	3	1	1	5
SIMONEAU, MARK							
2005	Phi	0	1	2	0	0	1
SIMONS, JOHN							
1924	Min	0	1	—	0	—	1
SIMPSON, JACKIE							
1962	Oak-A	0	6	7	3	10	15
SINKWICH, FRANKIE							
1943	Det	2	0	0	0	1	12
1944	Det	6	24	30	2	8	66
NFL	2	8	24	30	2	9	78
SIPE, BRIAN							
1976	Cle	0	1	1	0	0	1
SISSON, SCOTT							
1993	NE	0	15	15	14	26	57
1996	Min	0	30	30	22	29	96
NFL	2	0	45	45	36	55	153
SMITH, BILL							
1934	ChiC	3	4	—	1	—	25
1935	ChiC	2	5	—	**6**	—	35
1936	ChiC	1	2	—	1	—	11
1937	ChiC	1	3	—	0	—	9
1938	ChiC	1	4	5	2	2	16
1939	ChiC	4	6	8	2	8	36
NFL	6	12	24	13	12	10	132
SMITH, ED							
1936	Bos	0	0	—	1	—	3
SMITH, ERNIE							
1935	GB	0	11	—	1	—	14
1936	GB	0	17	—	4	—	29
1937	GB	0	11	—	1	—	14
1939	GB	0	3	4	0	0	3
NFL	4	0	42	4	6	—	60
SMITH, FLETCHER							
1966	KC-A	0	2	4	0	0	2
SMITH, GEORGE							
1942	Was	0	0	0	0	1	0
SMITH, JOHN							
1974	NE	0	42	43	16	22	90
1975	NE	0	33	33	9	17	60
1976	NE	0	42	46	15	25	87
1977	NE	0	33	33	15	21	78
1978	NE	0	6	7	1	1	9
1979	NE	0	46	49	**23**	**33**	115
1980	NE	0	**51**	**51**	**26**	34	**129**
1981	NE	0	37	39	15	24	82
1982	NE	0	6	7	5	8	21
1983	NE	0	12	15	3	6	21
NFL	10	0	308	323	128	191	692
SMITH, OLIN							
1924	Cle	1	2	—	0	—	8
SMITH, RED							
1928	NYY	3	2	—	0	—	20
1930	Nwk	0	1	—	0	—	1
1931	NYG	0	2	—	0	—	2
NFL	3	3	5	—	0	—	23
SMITH, RILEY							
1936	Bos	2	14	—	4	—	38
1937	Was	3	**22**	—	5	—	55

YEAR	TEAM	TD	XPM	XPA	FGM	FGA	PTS
1938	Was	1	3	6	2	5	15
NFL	3	6	39	6	11	5	108
SMUKLER, DAVE							
1936	Phi	0	2	—	1	—	5
1937	Phi	1	8	—	1	—	17
1938	Phi	2	6	0	0	0	18
NFL	3	3	16	—	2	—	40
SNYDER, BOB							
1937	Cle	1	7	—	1	—	16
1938	Cle	0	7	10	1	2	10
1939	ChiB	0	1	2	1	1	4
1940	ChiB	0	4	5	1	4	7
1941	ChiB	0	20	24	2	2	26
1943	ChiB	0	39	42	2	7	45
NFL	6	1	78	83	8	16	108
SOAR, HANK							
1937	NYG	2	2	—	1	—	17
1938	NYG	2	1	1	0	0	13
1939	NYG	3	2	2	0	1	20
1940	NYG	2	0	0	0	1	12
1941	NYG	0	3	3	0	0	3
1942	NYG	1	2	3	0	2	8
NFL	6	10	10	9	1	4	73
SOLTAU, GORDIE							
1950	SF	1	26	28	4	8	44
1951	SF	7	30	32	6	18	90
1952	SF	7	34	36	6	12	**94**
1953	SF	6	**48**	**49**	10	15	**114**
1954	SF	2	31	33	11	18	76
1955	SF	1	27	30	3	12	42
1956	SF	1	26	28	13	20	71
1957	SF	0	33	33	9	15	60
1958	SF	0	29	34	8	21	53
NFL	9	25	284	303	70	139	644
SOMERS, GEORGE							
1940	Phi	0	1	2	2	9	7
1941	Pit	0	0	0	0	2	0
1942	Pit	0	1	1	0	1	1
NFL	3	0	2	2	2	12	8
SOMMERS, JACK							
1947	Was	0	0	0	0	1	0
SONNENBERG, GUS							
1925	Det	0	12	—	5	—	27
1926	Det	0	7	—	9	—	34
1927	Pro	0	7	—	3	—	16
1928	Pro	0	7	—	1	—	10
NFL	4	1	33	—	18	—	93
SORENSON, GLEN							
1943	GB	0	0	0	0	2	0
1944	GB	0	1	1	0	1	1
1945	GB	0	0	0	0	1	0
NFL	3	0	1	1	0	4	1
SPADACCINI, VIC							
1939	Cle	1	12	16	0	0	18
1940	Cle	3	5	7	0	0	23
NFL	2	4	17	23	0	0	41
SPEEDIE, MAC							
1946	Cle-A	7	1	1	0	—	43
SPIKES, JACK							
1960	DalT-A	5	35	37	13	31	104
1961	DalT-A	5	10	14	4	13	54
1962	DalT-A	1	1	1	0	0	7
1963	KC-A	3	23	24	2	13	47
1965	Hou-A	3	6	6	1	2	27
NFL	5	21	75	82	20	59	263
STAUROVSKY, JASON							
1987	SL	0	6	6	1	3	9
1988	NE	0	14	15	7	11	35
1989	NE	0	14	14	14	17	56
1990	NE	0	19	19	16	22	67
1991	NE	0	10	11	13	19	49
1992	NYJ	0	6	6	3	8	15
NFL	6	0	69	71	54	80	231
STEELE, CLIFF							
1922	Roc	0	1	—	0	—	1
STEELE, ERNIE							
1942	Phi	2	1	1	0	0	13
STEFIK, BOB							
1948	Buf-A	0	0	1	0	0	0
STEIN, BOB							
1971	KC	0	0	0	0	1	0
STEIN, RUSS							
1922	Tol	0	2	—	1	—	5
1924	Fra	0	12	—	1	—	15
NFL	2	0	14	—	2	—	20

YEAR	TEAM	TD	XPM	XPA	FGM	FGA	PTS
STEINFORT, FRED							
1976	Oak	0	16	19	4	8	28
1977	Atl	0	13	13	6	11	31
1978	Atl	0	8	9	3	10	17
1980	Den	0	32	33	**26**	34	110
1981	Den	0	36	37	17	30	87
1983	Buf	0	1	1	1	6	4
1983	NE	0	16	17	6	15	34
NFL	6	0	122	129	63	114	311
STENERUD, JAN							
1967	KC-A	0	45	45	**21**	**36**	108
1968	KC-A	0	39	40	30	40	129
1969	KC-A	0	38	38	27	35	119
1970	KC	0	26	26	**30**	**42**	116
1971	KC	0	32	32	26	**44**	110
1972	KC	0	32	32	21	36	95
1973	KC	0	21	23	24	38	93
1974	KC	0	24	26	17	24	75
1975	KC	0	30	31	**22**	**32**	96
1976	KC	0	27	33	**21**	**38**	90
1977	KC	0	27	28	8	18	51
1978	KC	0	25	26	20	**30**	85
1979	KC	0	28	29	12	23	64
1980	GB	0	3	3	3	5	12
1981	GB	0	35	36	22	24	101
1982	GB	0	25	27	13	18	64
1983	GB	0	52	52	21	26	115
1984	Min	0	30	31	20	23	90
1985	Min	0	41	43	15	26	86
NFL	19	0	580	601	373	558	1699
STERNAMAN, DUTCH							
1921	ChiS	2	9	—	5	—	36
1922	ChiB	3	5	—	6	—	41
1923	ChiB	5	6	—	5	—	51
1924	ChiB	3	2	—	1	—	23
1926	ChiB	1	2	—	1	—	11
NFL	5	15	24	—	18	—	168
STERNAMAN, JOEY							
1922	ChiB	5	2	—	0	—	32
1923	Dul	0	2	—	5	—	17
1923	ChiB	2	2	—	1	—	17
1924	ChiB	6	12	—	9	—	75
1925	ChiB	6	17	—	3	—	62
1927	ChiB	2	4	—	0	—	16
1928	ChiB	4	6	—	0	—	30
1929	ChiB	0	8	—	0	—	8
1930	ChiB	1	5	—	0	—	11
NFL	8	26	58	—	18	—	268
STEUBER, BOB							
1948	Buf-A	3	20	23	1	2	41
STOKES, DIXIE							
1943	ChiC	0	5	6	1	3	8
STOVER, MATT							
1991	Cle	0	33	34	16	22	81
1992	Cle	0	29	30	21	29	92
1993	Cle	0	36	36	16	22	84
1994	Cle	0	32	32	26	28	110
1995	Cle	0	26	26	29	33	113
1996	Bal	0	34	35	19	25	91
1997	Bal	0	32	32	26	34	110
1998	Bal	0	24	24	21	28	87
1999	Bal	0	32	32	28	33	116
2000	Bal	0	30	30	**35**	**39**	**135**
2001	Bal	0	25	25	30	35	115
2002	Bal	0	33	33	21	25	96
2003	Bal	0	35	35	33	**38**	134
2004	Bal	0	30	30	29	32	117
2005	Bal	0	23	23	**30**	34	113
NFL	15	0	454	457	380	457	1594
STOYANOVICH, PETE							
1989	Mia	0	38	39	19	26	95
1990	Mia	0	37	37	21	25	100
1991	Mia	0	28	29	**31**	**37**	121
1992	Mia	0	34	36	**30**	**37**	**124**
1993	Mia	0	37	37	24	32	109
1994	Mia	0	35	35	24	31	107
1995	Mia	0	37	37	27	34	118
1996	KC	0	34	34	17	24	85
1997	KC	0	35	36	26	27	113
1998	KC	0	34	34	27	32	115
1999	KC	0	**45**	**45**	21	28	108
2000	KC	0	15	15	2	4	21
2000	SL	0	11	11	3	5	20
NFL	12	0	420	425	272	342	1236
STRAMIELLO, MIKE							
1930	Bkn	1	6	—	0	—	12
STRONG, KEN							
1929	SI	5	9	—	0	—	39
1930	SI	7	8	—	1	—	53
1931	SI	7	5	—	2	—	53

THE KICKING REGISTER

YEAR	TEAM	TD	XPM	XPA	FGM	FGA	PTS
1932	SI	2	3	—	0	—	15
1933	NYG	6	13	—	5	—	64
1934	NYG	6	8	—	4	—	56
1935	NYG	1	11	—	4	—	29
1939	NYG	0	7	7	4	8	19
1944	NYG	0	23	24	6	12	41
1945	NYG	0	23	23	6	13	41
1946	NYG	0	32	32	4	9	44
1947	NYG	0	24	25	2	5	30
NFL	12	34	166	111	38	47	484

STURTRIDGE, DICK

YEAR	TEAM	TD	XPM	XPA	FGM	FGA	PTS
1928	ChiB	3	1	—	0	—	19

STYDAHAR, JOE

1936	ChiB	0	3	—	0	—	3
1939	ChiB	0	4	6	0	0	4
1941	ChiB	0	4	4	0	0	4
1942	ChiB	0	5	8	0	0	5
1946	ChiB	0	12	13	0	2	12
NFL	5	0	28	31	0	2	28

STYNCHULA, ANDY

1964	NYG	0	1	1	0	0	1
1965	NYG	0	12	13	3	7	21
NFL	2	0	13	14	3	7	22

SUISHAM, SHAUN

2005	Dal	0	8	8	3	4	17

SUMMERALL, PAT

1953	ChiC	0	23	23	9	24	50
1954	ChiC	0	21	23	8	18	45
1955	ChiC	1	23	25	8	19	53
1956	ChiC	0	30	30	10	22	60
1957	ChiC	0	24	26	6	17	42
1958	NYG	0	28	30	12	23	64
1959	NYG	0	30	30	20	29	90
1960	NYG	0	32	32	13	26	71
1961	NYG	0	46	46	14	34	88
NFL	9	1	257	265	100	212	563

SUNTER, IAN

1980	Cin	0	15	15	11	20	48

SUTHERIN, DON

1959	Pit	0	0	0	0	1	0

SWANSON, EVAR

1926	ChiC	0	1	—	0	—	1
1927	ChiC	0	2	—	1	—	5
NFL	2	3	3	—	1	—	24

SWEET, FRED

1925	Pro	0	1	—	2	—	7

SZAKASH, PAUL

1939	Det	0	0	1	0	0	0

SZARO, RICH

1975	NO	0	17	17	10	16	47
1976	NO	0	25	29	18	23	79
1977	NO	0	29	31	5	12	44
1978	NO	0	9	9	4	6	21
1979	NYJ	0	2	2	0	2	2
NFL	5	0	82	88	37	59	193

TACKWELL, COOKIE

1930	Fra	1	1	—	0	—	7
1931	Fra	0	1	—	0	—	1
1931	ChiB	0	2	—	0	—	2
1932	ChiB	0	3	—	0	—	3
NFL	3	1	7	—	0	—	13

TANNER, JOHN

1923	Cle	1	2	—	0	—	8

TASSOS, DAMON

1946	Det	0	3	3	0	1	3

TAYLOR, JAY

2004	TB	0	11	11	4	5	23

TEBELL, GUS

1923	Col	3	7	—	4	—	37
1924	Col	0	3	—	1	—	6
NFL	2	3	10	—	5	—	43

TEVIS, LEE

1948	Bkn-A	0	4	4	2	7	10

THOMAS, BOB

1975	ChiB	0	18	22	13	23	57
1976	ChiB	0	27	30	12	25	63
1977	ChiB	0	27	30	14	27	69
1978	ChiB	0	26	28	17	22	77
1979	ChiB	0	34	37	16	27	82
1980	ChiB	0	35	37	13	18	74
1981	ChiB	0	2	3	2	3	8
1982	Det	0	3	3	5	5	18
1982	ChiB	0	6	6	5	7	21
1983	ChiB	0	35	38	14	25	77
1984	ChiB	0	35	37	22	28	101
1985	SD	0	51	55	18	28	105

YEAR	TEAM	TD	XPM	XPA	FGM	FGA	PTS
1986	NYG	0	4	4	0	1	4
NFL	12	0	303	330	151	239	756

THOMAS, REX

1926	Bkn	4	1	—	0	—	25
1930	Bkn	5	1	—	0	—	31
NFL	2	15	2	—	0	—	92

THOMASON, STUMPY

1936	Phi	1	1	—	0	—	7

THOMPSON, TED

1980	Hou	0	4	4	0	0	4

THORPE, JIM

1921	Cle	1	2	—	1	—	11
1923	Oor	0	0	—	1	—	3
1924	RI	0	1	—	2	—	7
NFL	3	6	3	—	4	—	51

TIFFIN, VAN

1987	TB	0	7	7	5	6	22
1987	Mia	0	4	4	0	1	4

TIMBERLAKE, BOB

1965	NYG	0	21	22	1	15	24

TOBIN, LEO

1921	Akr	0	1	—	0	—	1

TODD, DICK

1939	Was	6	2	3	0	0	38
1942	Was	4	2	3	0	0	26
NFL	2	34	4	6	0	0	208

TOIBIN, BRENDAN

1987	Was	0	4	4	0	2	4

TOMAINI, JOHNNY

1929	Ora	0	1	—	0	—	1

TOMASIC, ANDY

1942	Pit	1	0	1	0	0	6

TONNEMAKER, CLAYTON

1950	GB	0	1	1	0	0	1

TRACY, TOM

1960	Pit	9	0	0	3	6	63
1961	Pit	3	2	2	0	1	20
1963	Pit	0	2	2	0	0	2
NFL	3	31	4	4	3	7	199

TRAVENIO, HERB

1964	SD-A	0	10	12	2	5	16
1965	SD-A	0	40	40	18	30	94
NFL	2	0	50	52	20	35	110

TRAYNHAM, WADE

1966	Atl	0	2	2	0	1	2
1967	Atl	0	22	22	7	18	43
NFL	2	0	24	24	7	19	45

TREADWELL, DAVID

1989	Den	0	39	40	27	33	120
1990	Den	0	34	36	25	34	109
1991	Den	0	31	32	27	36	112
1992	Den	0	28	28	20	24	88
1993	NYG	0	28	29	25	31	103
1994	NYG	0	22	23	11	17	55
NFL	6	0	182	188	135	175	587

TROUT, DAVID

1981	Pit	0	38	46	12	17	74
1987	Pit	0	10	10	0	2	10
NFL	2	0	48	56	12	19	84

TRYON, EDDIE

1927	NYY	6	8	—	0	—	44

TUCKEY, DICK

1938	Was	0	0	1	0	0	0
1938	Cle	0	2	2	0	0	2

TURNBOW, GUY

1933	Phi	0	0	—	0	—	3

TURNER, JIM

1964	NYJ-A	0	33	33	13	27	72
1965	NYJ-A	0	31	31	20	34	91
1966	NYJ-A	0	34	35	18	35	88
1967	NYJ-A	0	36	39	17	32	87
1968	NYJ-A	0	43	43	34	46	145
1969	NYJ-A	0	33	33	32	47	129
1970	NYJ	0	28	28	19	35	85
1971	Den	0	18	18	25	38	93
1972	Den	0	37	37	20	29	97
1973	Den	0	40	40	22	33	106
1974	Den	0	35	38	11	21	68
1975	Den	0	23	26	21	28	86
1976	Den	0	36	39	15	21	81
1977	Den	1	31	34	13	19	76
1978	Den	0	31	35	11	22	64
1979	Den	0	32	34	13	21	71
NFL	16	1	521	543	304	488	1439

TUTHILL, JAMES

YEAR	TEAM	TD	XPM	XPA	FGM	FGA	PTS
2002	Was	0	20	21	10	16	50

TYNES, LAWRENCE

2004	KC	0	58	60	17	23	109
2005	KC	0	44	45	27	33	125
NFL	2	0	102	105	44	56	234

URAM, ANDY

1940	GB	3	1	1	0	0	19
1942	GB	5	1	1	0	0	31
NFL	2	16	2	2	0	0	98

URSELLA, RUBE

1921	Min	0	4	—	1	—	7
1924	RI	1	4	—	1	—	13
1925	RI	0	2	—	3	—	11
NFL	3	1	10	—	5	—	31

VACANTI, SAM

1949	Bal-A	0	3	3	0	2	3

VAN BUREN, STEVE

1945	Phi	18	2	2	0	0	110

VAN DYKE, JIMMY

1922	Lou	1	1	—	0	—	7

VAN RAAPHORST, DICK

1964	Dal	0	28	29	14	29	70
1966	SD-A	0	39	40	16	31	87
1967	SD-A	0	45	45	15	30	90
NFL	3	0	112	114	45	90	247

VANDERJAGT, MIKE

1998	Ind	0	23	23	27	31	104
1999	Ind	0	43	43	34	38	145
2000	Ind	0	46	46	25	27	121
2001	Ind	0	41	42	28	34	125
2002	Ind	0	34	34	23	31	103
2003	Ind	0	46	46	37	37	157
2004	Ind	0	59	60	20	25	119
2005	Ind	0	52	52	23	25	121
NFL	8	0	344	346	217	248	995

VENTURELLI, FRED

1948	ChiB	0	4	4	1	2	7

VETRANO, JOE

1946	SF-A	1	31	38	4	7	49
1947	SF-A	0	38	43	4	12	50
1948	SF-A	1	62	66	5	8	83
1949	SF-A	0	56	56	3	7	65
AAFC	4	2	187	203	16	34	247

VILLANUEVA, DANNY

1960	LARm	0	28	28	12	19	64
1961	LARm	0	32	32	13	27	71
1962	LARm	0	26	27	10	20	56
1963	LARm	0	25	26	9	17	52
1965	Dal	0	37	38	16	27	85
1966	Dal	0	56	56	17	31	107
1967	Dal	0	32	34	8	19	56
NFL	7	0	236	241	85	160	491

VINATIERI, ADAM

1996	NE	0	39	42	27	35	120
1997	NE	0	40	40	25	29	115
1998	NE	0	32	32	31	39	127
1999	NE	0	29	30	26	33	107
2000	NE	0	25	25	27	33	106
2001	NE	0	41	42	24	30	113
2002	NE	0	36	36	27	30	117
2003	NE	0	37	38	25	34	112
2004	NE	0	48	48	31	33	141
2005	NE	0	40	41	20	25	100
NFL	10	0	367	374	263	321	1158

VINYARD, KEN

1970	Atl	0	23	26	9	25	50

VITIELLO, SANDRO

1980	Cin	0	1	1	0	2	1

VON SCHAMANN, UWE

1979	Mia	0	36	40	21	29	99
1980	Mia	0	32	32	14	23	74
1981	Mia	0	37	38	24	31	109
1982	Mia	0	21	22	15	20	66
1983	Mia	0	45	48	18	27	99
1984	Mia	0	66	70	9	19	93
NFL	6	0	237	250	101	149	540

VOSS, TILLIE

1921	Det	1	2	—	0	—	8
1922	RI	2	6	—	0	—	18
1923	Tol	1	1	—	0	—	7
NFL	3	10	9	—	0	—	69

WALKER, DOAK

1950	Det	11	38	41	8	18	128
1951	Det	6	43	44	6	12	97
1952	Det	0	5	5	3	5	14

YEAR	TEAM	TD	XPM	XPA	FGM	FGA	PTS
1953	Det	5	27	29	12	19	93
1954	Det	5	**43**	**43**	11	17	106
1955	Det	7	27	29	9	16	**96**
NFL	6	34	183	191	49	87	534
Walker, Mike							
1972	NE	0	15	15	2	8	21
Walker, Wayne							
1968	Hou-A	0	26	26	8	16	50
Walker, Wayne							
1959	Det	0	5	6	0	0	5
1961	Det	0	6	6	0	3	6
1962	Det	0	37	37	9	22	64
1963	Det	0	29	29	9	22	56
1964	Det	0	32	34	14	25	74
1965	Det	0	33	33	8	22	57
1966	Det	0	11	11	2	8	17
1967	Det	0	11	11	5	15	26
1968	Det	0	6	6	6	14	24
1971	Det	0	2	2	0	0	2
NFL	10	2	172	175	53	131	345
Wallace, Dutch							
1924	Akr	0	2	—	0	—	2
Walquist, Laurie							
1930	ChiB	1	1	—	0	—	7
Walston, Bobby							
1951	Phi	8	28	31	6	11	94
1952	Phi	3	31	31	11	20	82
1953	Phi	5	45	48	4	13	87
1954	Phi	11	36	39	4	10	**114**
1955	Phi	3	6	7	2	3	30
1956	Phi	3	17	18	6	13	53
1957	Phi	1	20	21	9	12	53
1958	Phi	3	31	31	6	14	67
1959	Phi	3	33	34	0	1	51
1960	Phi	4	39	40	14	20	105
1961	Phi	2	43	**46**	14	25	97
1962	Phi	0	36	38	4	15	48
NFL	12	46	365	384	80	157	881
Warnke, David							
1983	TB	0	1	2	0	1	1
Waterfield, Bob							
1945	Cle	5	**31**	34	1	3	64
1946	LARm	1	**37**	**37**	6	9	61
1947	LARm	1	27	30	**7**	**16**	54
1948	LARm	0	38	44	6	11	56
1949	LARm	1	43	45	**9**	16	76
1950	LARm	1	**54**	**58**	7	14	81
1951	LARm	3	41	43	**13**	**23**	98
1952	LARm	1	**44**	**45**	11	18	83
NFL	8	13	315	336	60	110	573
Watkins, Foster							
1940	Phi	0	2	2	0	0	2
Watson, Allan							
1970	Pit	0	7	8	5	10	22
Watson, Rat							
1922	Tol	1	0	—	1	—	9
1923	Tol	0	1	—	0	—	1
NFL	2	1	1	—	1	—	10
Watson, Sid							
1956	Pit	4	10	12	1	1	37
Weaver, Red							
1923	Col	0	2	—	0	—	2
Webster, Tim							
1971	GB	0	8	8	6	11	26
Weed, Tad							
1955	Pit	0	12	12	3	6	21
Wehrli, Roger							
1975	SL	0	1	1	0	0	1
Weimer, Chuck							
1929	Buf	1	3	—	3	—	18
1930	Bkn	2	1	—	0	—	13
NFL	2	3	4	—	3	—	31
Weiner, Reds							
1934	Phi	0	3	—	1	—	6
Weinstock, Izzy							
1937	Pit	0	4	—	0	—	4
Weir, Ed							
1926	Fra	0	2	—	1	—	5
1927	Fra	0	1	—	0	—	1
1928	Fra	1	1	—	0	—	7
NFL	3	1	4	—	1	—	13
Weisgerber, Dick							
1942	GB	0	2	2	0	0	2

YEAR	TEAM	TD	XPM	XPA	FGM	FGA	PTS
Weldon, Larry							
1944	Was	0	4	4	0	0	4
1945	Was	0	1	1	0	0	1
NFL	2	0	5	5	0	0	5
Welker, Wes							
2004	Mia	1	1	1	1	1	10
Weller, Bub							
1927	ChiC	1	2	—	0	—	8
Welsh, Jim							
1924	Fra	0	17	—	7	—	38
1926	Pot	0	15	—	5	—	30
NFL	2	0	32	—	12	—	68
Wenig, Obe							
1921	RI	3	8	—	0	—	26
Wentworth, Cy							
1926	Pro	0	3	—	1	—	6
1929	Bos	3	6	—	0	—	24
NFL	2	6	9	—	1	—	48
Wentz, Barney							
1925	Pot	5	1	—	0	—	31
1927	Pot	2	2	—	1	—	17
NFL	2	17	3	—	1	—	108
Wersching, Ray							
1973	SD	0	13	15	11	25	46
1974	SD	0	0	0	5	11	15
1975	SD	0	20	21	12	24	56
1976	SD	0	14	16	4	8	26
1977	SF	0	23	23	10	17	53
1978	SF	0	24	25	15	23	69
1979	SF	0	32	35	20	24	92
1980	SF	0	33	39	15	19	78
1981	SF	0	30	30	17	23	81
1982	SF	0	23	25	12	17	59
1983	SF	0	51	51	25	30	126
1984	SF	0	**56**	**56**	25	35	**131**
1985	SF	0	**52**	**53**	13	21	91
1986	SF	0	41	42	25	35	116
1987	SF	0	**44**	**46**	13	17	83
NFL	15	0	456	477	222	329	1122
West, Belf							
1921	Can	0	4	—	1	—	7
West, Walter							
1944	Cle	1	6	8	0	0	12
Westfall, Ed							
1933	Pit	2	1	—	1	—	16
White, Jeff							
1973	NE	0	21	25	14	25	63
White, Phil							
1925	KC	2	1	—	1	—	16
1927	NYG	3	1	—	0	—	19
NFL	2	8	2	—	1	—	53
White, Whizzer							
1940	Det	5	2	4	0	1	32
White, Wilford							
1951	ChiB	2	1	1	1	2	16
1952	ChiB	0	1	1	2	3	7
NFL	2	2	2	2	3	5	23
Wiberg, Ossie							
1927	Cle	4	1	—	0	—	25
1928	Det	2	1	—	0	—	13
1930	NYG	4	6	—	0	—	30
1932	Bkn	0	1	—	0	—	1
NFL	4	10	9	—	0	—	69
Wilkes, Reggie							
1981	Phi	0	1	1	0	0	1
Wilkin, Willie							
1939	Was	0	0	1	0	0	0
Wilkins, Jeff							
1995	SF	0	27	29	12	13	63
1996	SF	0	40	40	30	34	130
1997	SL	0	32	32	25	**37**	107
1998	SL	0	25	26	20	26	85
1999	SL	0	**64**	**64**	20	28	**124**
2000	SL	0	38	38	17	17	89
2001	SL	0	**58**	**58**	23	29	127
2002	SL	0	37	37	19	25	94
2003	SL	0	46	46	**39**	**42**	**163**
2004	SL	0	32	32	19	24	89
2005	SL	0	36	36	27	31	117
NFL	11	0	435	438	251	306	1188
Williams, Frank							
1948	NYG	0	4	5	0	1	4

YEAR	TEAM	TD	XPM	XPA	FGM	FGA	PTS
Willis, Ken							
1990	Dal	0	26	26	18	25	80
1991	Dal	0	37	37	27	39	118
1992	TB	0	20	20	8	14	44
1992	NYG	0	7	7	2	2	13
NFL	3	0	90	90	55	80	255
Wilson, Jerrel							
1978	NE	0	0	1	0	0	0
Wilson, Mule							
1928	NYG	1	1	—	0	—	7
Wilson, Stu							
1932	SI	1	3	—	1	—	12
Wingo, Rich							
1981	GB	0	1	1	0	0	1
Winkelman, Ben							
1923	Mil	3	8	—	6	—	44
1924	Mil	2	0	—	1	—	15
NFL	2	5	8	—	7	—	59
Winters, Sonny							
1924	Col	1	5	—	1	—	14
Wittenborn, John							
1960	SF	0	0	0	0	3	0
1962	Phi	0	0	0	2	4	6
1967	Hou-A	0	30	30	14	28	72
1968	Hou-A	0	11	11	4	13	23
NFL	4	0	41	41	20	48	101
Wittum, Tom							
1977	SF	0	2	4	1	2	5
Wolfe, Red							
1938	NYG	0	0	1	0	0	0
Wood, Gary							
1965	NYG	0	1	1	0	0	1
Wood, Mike							
1979	SL	0	6	7	2	7	12
1979	SD	0	28	31	11	14	61
1981	Bal	0	29	33	10	18	59
1982	Bal	0	6	6	6	10	24
NFL	3	0	69	77	29	49	156
Wood, Willie							
1964	GB	1	1	1	0	1	7
Woodin, Whitey							
1926	GB	0	1	—	0	—	1
1931	GB	1	3	—	0	—	9
NFL	2	1	4	—	0	—	10
Woodruff, Lee							
1931	Pro	4	1	—	0	—	25
Workman, Hoge							
1924	Cle	0	16	—	3	—	25
1931	Cle	0	2	—	0	—	2
NFL	2	0	18	—	3	—	27
Wright, Ted							
1934	Bos	1	2	—	0	—	8
Wycoff, Doug							
1927	NYG	3	1	—	0	—	19
Yablonski, Vinnie							
1948	ChiC	0	0	0	1	4	3
1949	ChiC	0	1	1	5	6	16
1950	ChiC	1	7	7	2	3	19
1951	ChiC	0	8	8	2	5	14
NFL	4	1	16	16	10	18	52
Yarno, George							
1983	TB	0	1	1	0	0	1
Yepremian, Garo							
1966	Det	0	11	11	13	22	50
1967	Det	0	22	23	2	6	28
1970	Mia	0	31	31	22	29	97
1971	Mia	0	33	33	**28**	40	**117**
1972	Mia	0	43	**45**	24	37	115
1973	Mia	0	38	38	25	37	113
1974	Mia	0	43	43	8	15	67
1975	Mia	0	40	46	13	16	79
1976	Mia	0	29	31	16	23	77
1977	Mia	0	37	40	10	22	67
1978	Mia	0	41	**45**	19	23	98
1979	NO	0	39	40	12	16	75
1980	TB	0	31	32	16	23	79
1981	TB	0	6	6	2	4	12
NFL	14	0	444	464	210	313	1074
Yoho, Mack							
1960	Buf-A	1	0	0	2	5	12
1961	Buf-A	0	0	0	0	4	0
1962	Buf-A	0	20	22	1	3	23
1963	Buf-A	0	32	35	10	24	62
NFL	4	1	52	57	13	36	97

YEAR	TEAM	TD	XPM	XPA	FGM	FGA	PTS
YOUNCE, LEN							
1943	NYG	1	0	0	0	1	6
1947	NYG	0	1	1	1	1	4
1948	NYG	0	36	37	1	7	39
NFL	3	1	37	38	2	9	49
ZABEL, STEVE							
1976	NE	0	1	1	0	0	1
ZENDEJAS, JOAQUIN							
1983	NE	0	3	4	0	1	3
ZENDEJAS, LUIS							
1987	Dal	0	10	10	3	4	19
1988	Dal	0	5	5	1	3	8
1988	Phi	0	30	31	19	24	87
1989	Phi	0	23	23	9	15	50
1989	Dal	0	10	10	5	9	25
NFL	3	0	78	79	37	55	189
ZENDEJAS, MAX							
1986	Was	0	23	28	9	14	50
1987	GB	0	13	15	16	19	61

YEAR	TEAM	TD	XPM	XPA	FGM	FGA	PTS
1988	GB	0	17	19	9	16	44
NFL	3	0	53	62	34	49	155
ZENDEJAS, TONY							
1985	Hou	0	29	31	21	27	92
1986	Hou	0	28	29	22	27	94
1987	Hou	0	32	33	20	26	92
1988	Hou	0	48	50	22	34	114
1989	Hou	0	40	40	25	**37**	115
1990	Hou	0	20	21	7	12	41
1991	LARm	0	25	26	17	17	76
1992	LARm	0	38	38	15	20	83
1993	LARm	0	23	25	16	23	71
1994	LARm	0	28	28	18	23	82
1995	Atl	0	0	0	2	3	6
1995	SF	0	5	6	1	3	8
NFL	11	0	316	327	186	252	874
ZIMMERMAN, ROY							
1940	Was	0	0	1	0	0	0
1942	Was	0	1	1	1	1	4
1943	P-P	1	26	28	1	6	35
1944	Phi	3	32	34	4	8	62

YEAR	TEAM	TD	XPM	XPA	FGM	FGA	PTS
1945	Phi	1	29	33	4	8	47
1946	Phi	1	2	2	2	4	14
1947	Det	1	30	31	5	11	51
1948	Bos	0	13	15	1	4	16
NFL	8	7	133	145	18	42	229
ZOFKO, MICKEY							
1972	Det	0	1	1	0	0	1
ZOLL, DICK							
1938	Cle	0	1	1	0	0	1
ZONTINI, LOU							
1940	ChiC	0	10	10	2	5	16
1941	ChiC	0	5	7	0	4	5
1944	Cle	4	14	16	3	6	47
1946	Buf-A	0	30	31	4	8	42
AAFC	1	0	30	31	4	8	42
NFL	3	4	29	33	5	15	68

THE DEFENSE AND SPECIALIST REGISTER

The National Football League has many and varied statistics, but in the end it comes down to three things: running the ball, throwing the ball, and catching the ball. Someone is always trying to move the ball on offense, but what about the players on the other side of the line? What about special teams? It may even seem, at first glance, that this book too has forgotten about everybody except the quarterback, but the registers that follow highlight the people who make the QB's life challenging: the ones who chase and run down the quarterback, pick off his passes, punt the ball and return it when he can't get the first down, and bring the kickoff up the field after a successful touchdown drive.

You may have looked through the Player Register and noticed your favorite players were missing all but the most basic information. Herb Adderley, Night Train Lane, Reggie White, and Howie Long are limited to a couple of lines for their Hall of Fame careers. While players like Rick Upchurch and Dante Hall, with the ability to turn a game around immediately by taking an opponent's kickoff or punt and taking it deep into enemy territory, only have statistics from their limited roles as part-time wide receivers. And what about the great punters? Ray Guy, Horace Gillom, Reggie Roby, and look at what's missing from Sammy Baugh's line? Worry no more, you've come to the right place.

The Defense and Specialist Register is four registers for the price of one. In order to keep the player register from becoming a hodgepodge of different designs as the alphabetical register placed punter next to wide receiver next to defensive tackle next to cornerback, the editors of *The 2006 ESPN Pro Football Encyclopedia* decided it was better to set up separate registers. There is also a kicker register celebrating the point-scoring skills of the men who put the foot in football. This section features the exploits of the game's leading interceptors, punters, punt and kick returners, and sack artists. Listing everyone who performed these feats, however, would have stretched an already massive book hundreds of pages higher and maybe a pound heavier, so the editors made the tough call to list the best at their position who met a set of minimums.

Which players are in here? Finding out if a player appears in one of these registers is indicated in the Player Register with a code in brackets at the end of the player's bio line: P for punting (250 punts minimum), R for returns (75 or more for either kick returns or punt returns), I for interceptions (20 or more), and S for sacks (50 or more, only since 1982). Leaders for various years are bold faced.

RETURNS

Punt and kickoff return data started in 1941. However, George McAfee, the current fourth-ranked player in average, started in 1940.

His punt returns for that year are unknown. Fair catches of punts were first tabulated in 1963 in the NFL and 1967 in the AFL.

INTERCEPTIONS

Paul Krause is the leader with 81 career interceptions, edging out Emlen Tunnell. Night Train Lane, who is third on the all-time list has the NFL record with 14 as a rookie in 1952.

SACKS

The NFL has kept this data for individuals starting only in 1982. Researchers John Turney and Nick Webster calculated unofficial data from play-by-play accounts and have come up with a list that includes some of the game's great pass rushers who you will not find in this section. The numbers in italics have been adjusted for the longer 16-game schedule.

> Deacon Jones   173.5 (*198*)
> Jack Youngblood   151.5 (*167*)
> Alan Page   148.5 (*163*)
> Lawrence Taylor   142 (including 9.5 in 1981)
> Rickey Jackson   136 (including 8 in 1981)
> Carl Eller   133.5 (*153*)
> Coy Bacon   130 (*145*)
> Al Baker   128.5 (*140*)

There may be others with similar sack totals, not to mention, punts, returns, and even interceptions that have not yet been discovered by researchers. These registers are exclusive and reserved for the best at what they do.

PUNTS

Besides the traditional punting categories of punts, yards, average punt, longest punt, and blocks, additional statistics were compiled starting in 1976. This included the number of touchbacks (**TB**) and return yards (**RTYDS**), allowing a net punting total (**NET**) and net punting average (**AVG**) to be calculated. (Note that the second AVG category in the Punting Register refers to net yards.) In addition, the number of times the receiving team started inside their own 20-yard line was tallied. Punting for individuals was first tabulated in 1939. Sammy Baugh, currently ranked second, started his Hall of Fame career in 1937. His punting for 1937–38 is unknown.

YEAR	TEAM	KR	YDS	AVG (LG)	TD	PR	FC	YDS	AVG (LG)	TD
ADDERLEY, HERB
1961	GB	18	478	26.6(61)	0	0	—	—	—	—
1962	GB	15	418	27.9(**103**)	1	0	—	—	—	—
1963	GB	20	597	29.9(98)	1	0	—	—	—	—
1964	GB	19	508	26.7(43)	0	0	—	—	—	—
1965	GB	10	221	22.1(33)	0	1	0	0	0.0(0)	0
1966	GB	14	320	22.9(65)	0	0	—	—	—	—
1967	GB	10	207	20.7(37)	0	0	—	—	—	—
1968	GB	14	331	23.6(50)	0	0	—	—	—	—
NFL	8	120	3080	25.7(103)	2	1	0	0	0.0(0)	0
ADKINS, MARGENE
1970	Dal	7	149	21.3(27)	0	4	2	44	11.0(24)	0
1971	Dal	0	—	—	—	4	0	5	1.3(10)	0
1972	NO	43	**1020**	23.7(61)	0	7	2	0	0.0(4)	0
1973	NYJ	31	615	19.8(38)	0	0	—	—	—	—
NFL	4	81	1784	22.0(61)	0	15	4	49	3.3(24)	0
ALEXANDER, KERMIT
1963	SF	24	638	26.6(48)	0	0	—	—	—	—
1964	SF	20	483	24.1(44)	0	21	5	189	9.0(70)	0
1965	SF	32	**741**	23.2(46)	0	35	7	262	7.5(40)	0
1966	SF	37	984	26.6(56)	0	30	3	198	6.6(44)	1
1967	SF	1	18	18.0(18)	0	6	1	64	10.7(31)	0
1968	SF	20	360	18.0(35)	0	24	13	87	3.6(26)	0
1969	SF	3	47	15.7(24)	0	4	3	-18	-4.5(0)	0
1970	LARm	7	126	18.0(30)	0	7	1	38	5.4(49)	0
1971	LARm	0	—	—	—	1	3	5	5.0(5)	0
1973	Phi	9	189	21.0(25)	0	5	5	10	2.0(5)	0
NFL	10	153	3586	23.4(56)	0	133	41	835	6.3(70)	2
ALLEN, DAVID
2003	Jax	41	831	20.3(61)	0	27	15	324	12.0(52)	0
2004	Jax	11	210	19.1(25)	0	15	2	144	9.6(32)	0
2005	SL	23	472	20.5(32)	0	7	6	38	5.4(12)	0
NFL	3	75	1513	20.2(61)	0	49	23	506	10.3(52)	0
ANDERSON, GARY
1985	SD	13	302	23.2(**98**)	1	0	—	—	—	—
1986	SD	24	482	20.1(35)	0	25	10	227	9.1(30)	0
1987	SD	22	433	19.7(31)	0	0	—	—	—	—
1990	TB	6	123	20.5(37)	0	0	—	—	—	—
1991	TB	34	643	18.9(39)	0	0	—	—	—	—
1992	TB	29	564	19.4(39)	0	6	1	45	7.5(13)	0
1993	TB	12	181	15.1(24)	0	17	1	113	6.6(15)	0
1993	Det	3	51	17.0(24)	0	0	—	—	—	—
NFL	7	143	2779	19.4(98)	1	48	12	385	8.0(30)	0
ANDERSON, LARRY
1978	Pit	37	930	25.1(95)	1	0	—	—	—	—
1979	Pit	34	732	21.5(44)	0	0	—	—	—	—
1980	Pit	14	379	27.1(63)	0	0	—	—	—	—
1981	Pit	37	825	22.3(35)	0	20	8	208	10.4(33)	0
1982	Bal	27	517	19.1(33)	0	8	3	54	6.8(28)	0
1983	Bal	18	309	17.2(26)	0	20	4	138	6.9(20)	0
1984	Ind	22	525	23.9(69)	0	27	7	182	6.7(19)	0
NFL	7	189	4217	22.3(95)	1	75	22	582	7.8(33)	0
ANTHONY, REIDEL
1997	TB	25	592	23.7(51)	0	0	—	—	—	—
1998	TB	46	1118	24.3(60)	0	0	—	—	—	—
1999	TB	21	434	20.7(39)	0	0	—	—	—	—
2000	TB	3	88	29.3(45)	0	0	—	—	—	—
2001	TB	0	—	—	—	3	1	12	4.0(7)	0
NFL	5	95	2232	23.5(60)	0	3	1	12	4.0(7)	0
ARENAS, JOE
1951	SF	21	542	25.8(49)	0	21	—	272	13.0(51)	0
1952	SF	11	291	26.5(47)	0	7	—	40	5.7(13)	0
1953	SF	16	551	**34.4**(82)	0	8	—	93	11.6(50)	0
1954	SF	16	362	22.6(41)	0	23	—	117	5.1(23)	0
1955	SF	24	594	24.8(42)	0	21	—	55	2.6(7)	0
1956	SF	27	801	29.7(96)	1	19	—	117	6.2(67)	1
1957	SF	24	657	27.4(64)	0	25	—	80	3.2(26)	0
NFL	7	139	3798	27.3(96)	1	124	0	774	6.2(67)	1
ARNETT, JON
1957	LARm	18	504	**28.0**(98)	1	14	—	85	6.1(22)	0
1958	LARm	16	331	20.7(32)	0	18	—	**223**	**12.4**(58)	0
1959	LARm	14	320	22.9(42)	0	17	—	184	10.8(71)	0
1960	LARm	17	416	24.5(43)	0	10	—	60	6.0(29)	0
1961	LARm	25	653	26.1(**105**)	1	10	—	75	7.5(17)	0
1962	LARm	2	87	43.5(50)	0	5	—	49	9.8(21)	0
1963	LARm	12	279	23.3(34)	0	1	1	7	7.0(7)	0
1964	ChiB	15	331	22.1(44)	0	19	2	188	9.9(44)	0
1965	ChiB	5	150	30.0(77)	0	11	4	52	4.7(22)	0
1966	ChiB	2	39	19.5(25)	0	15	10	58	3.9(20)	0
NFL	10	126	3110	24.7(105)	2	120	17	981	8.2(71)	1
ATHAS, PETE
1971	NYG	0	—	—	—	3	1	21	7.0(10)	0
1972	NYG	0	—	—	—	8	6	95	11.9(48)	0
1973	NYG	0	—	—	—	20	14	153	7.7(28)	0
1974	NYG	0	—	—	—	20	1	180	9.0(22)	0
1975	Cle	6	95	15.8(23)	0	5	2	36	7.2(16)	0
1975	Min	0	—	—	—	1	1	1	1.0(1)	0
1976	NO	2	68	34.0(39)	0	35	10	332	9.5(67)	0
NFL	6	8	163	20.4(39)	0	92	35	818	8.9(67)	0

YEAR	TEAM	KR	YDS	AVG (LG)	TD	PR	FC	YDS	AVG (LG)	TD
ATKINS, PERVIS
1961	LARm	4	77	19.3(20)	0	0	—	—	—	—
1962	LARm	28	676	24.1(41)	0	11	—	94	8.5(45)	0
1963	LARm	19	429	22.6(35)	0	12	3	36	3.0(9)	0
1964	Was	14	319	22.8(33)	0	13	10	138	10.6(68)	0
1965	Was	1	15	15.0(15)	0	3	0	11	3.7(9)	0
1966	Oak-A	29	608	21.0(35)	0	1	—	13	13.0(13)	0
NFL	6	95	2124	22.4(41)	0	40	13	292	7.3(68)	0
ATKINSON, GEORGE
1968	Oak-A	32	802	**25.1**(60)	0	**36**	7	**490**	13.6(86)	**2**
1969	Oak-A	16	382	23.9(39)	0	25	8	153	6.1(30)	0
1970	Oak	23	574	25.0(62)	0	4	0	12	3.0(10)	0
1971	Oak	0	—	—	—	20	0	159	7.9(34)	0
1972	Oak	3	75	25.0(34)	0	10	1	33	3.3(8)	0
1973	Oak	0	—	—	—	41	6	336	8.2(63)	1
1974	Oak	0	—	—	—	4	1	31	7.8(13)	0
1975	Oak	2	60	30.0(45)	0	8	1	33	4.1(12)	0
NFL	8	76	1893	24.9(62)	0	148	24	1247	8.4(86)	3
AZUMAH, JERRY
2001	ChiB	4	65	16.3(23)	0	0	0	16	—	—
2003	ChiB	41	1191	29.0(89)	2	0	—	—	—	—
2004	ChiB	42	924	22.0(73)	0	0	—	—	—	—
2005	ChiB	32	705	22.0(40)	0	0	—	—	—	—
NFL	4	119	2885	24.2(89)	2	0	0	16	—	—
BAILEY, AARON
1995	Ind	21	495	23.6(95)	1	0	—	—	—	—
1996	Ind	43	1041	24.2(95)	1	0	—	—	—	—
1997	Ind	55	1206	21.9(61)	0	1	0	19	19.0(19)	0
1998	Ind	34	759	22.3(44)	0	19	4	176	9.3(33)	0
NFL	4	153	3501	22.9(95)	2	20	4	195	9.8(33)	0
BAILEY, JOHNNY
1990	ChiB	23	363	15.8(30)	0	36	13	399	**11.1**(95)	1
1991	ChiB	16	311	19.4(31)	0	36	11	281	7.8(37)	0
1992	Phx	28	690	24.6(63)	0	20	8	263	**13.1**(65)	0
1993	Phx	31	699	22.5(48)	0	35	5	282	8.1(58)	1
1994	LARm	12	260	21.7(32)	0	19	4	153	8.1(24)	0
1995	SL	5	97	19.4(31)	0	2	0	42	21.0(22)	0
NFL	6	115	2420	21.0(63)	0	148	41	1420	9.6(95)	2
BAIRD, BILL
1963	NYJ-A	0	—	—	—	4	—	143	35.8(**93**)	1
1964	NYJ-A	11	240	21.8(33)	0	18	—	170	9.4(27)	0
1965	NYJ-A	2	50	25.0(26)	0	14	—	88	6.3(23)	0
1966	NYJ-A	0	—	—	—	5	—	35	7.0(18)	0
1967	NYJ-A	0	—	—	—	25	3	219	8.8(33)	0
1968	NYJ-A	0	—	—	—	18	6	111	6.2(20)	0
1969	NYJ-A	0	—	—	—	4	2	21	5.3(7)	0
NFL	7	13	290	22.3(33)	0	88	11	787	8.9(93)	1
BALDWIN, RANDY
1991	Min	1	14	14.0(14)	0	0	—	—	—	—
1992	Cle	30	675	22.5(47)	0	0	—	—	—	—
1993	Cle	24	444	18.5(31)	0	0	—	—	—	—
1994	Cle	28	753	**26.9**(85)	1	0	—	—	—	—
1995	Car	14	316	22.6(36)	0	0	—	—	—	—
1996	Bal	20	405	20.3(34)	0	0	—	—	—	—
NFL	6	117	2607	22.3(85)	1	0	—	—	—	—
BALL, ERIC
1989	Cin	1	19	19.0(19)	0	0	—	—	—	—
1990	Cin	16	366	22.9(38)	0	0	—	—	—	—
1991	Cin	13	262	20.2(24)	0	0	—	—	—	—
1992	Cin	20	411	20.5(48)	0	0	—	—	—	—
1993	Cin	23	501	21.8(45)	0	0	—	—	—	—
1994	Cin	42	915	21.8(43)	0	0	—	—	—	—
NFL	6	115	2474	21.5(48)	0	0	—	—	—	—
BARBER, TIKI
1998	NYG	14	250	17.9(32)	0	0	—	—	—	—
1999	NYG	12	266	22.2(41)	0	**44**	13	**506**	11.5(**85**)	1
2000	NYG	1	28	28.0(28)	0	**39**	20	332	8.5(31)	0
2001	NYG	0	—	—	—	38	12	338	8.9(23)	0
2002	NYG	0	—	—	—	1	1	5	5.0(5)	0
NFL	5	27	544	20.1(41)	0	122	46	1181	9.7(85)	1
BARLOW, REGGIE
1997	Jax	10	267	26.7(92)	1	36	16	412	11.4(52)	0
1998	Jax	30	747	24.9(91)	0	43	14	**555**	12.9(85)	1
1999	Jax	19	396	20.8(56)	0	38	17	414	10.9(74)	1
2000	Jax	11	224	20.4(27)	0	29	14	200	6.9(21)	0
2003	TB	10	221	22.1(32)	0	12	6	58	4.8(17)	0
NFL	5	80	1855	23.2(92)	1	158	67	1639	10.4(85)	2
BARNES, LEW
1986	ChiB	3	94	31.3(85)	1	**57**	9	482	8.5(35)	0
1988	Atl	6	142	23.7(36)	0	34	8	307	9.0(68)	0
1989	KC	0	—	—	—	2	0	41	20.5(21)	0
NFL	3	9	236	26.2(85)	1	93	17	830	8.9(68)	0
BARNEY, LEM
1967	Det	5	87	17.4(25)	0	4	8	14	3.5(6)	0
1968	Det	25	670	26.8(98)	1	13	14	79	6.1(18)	0
1969	Det	7	154	22.0(32)	0	9	5	191	21.2(74)	1
1970	Det	2	96	48.0(74)	0	25	3	259	10.4(65)	1
1971	Det	9	222	24.7(48)	0	14	2	122	8.7(38)	0
1972	Det	1	17	17.0(17)	0	15	8	108	7.2(26)	0

YEAR	TEAM	KR	YDS	AVG (LG)	TD	PR	FC	YDS	AVG (LG)	TD
1973	Det	1	28	28.0 (28)	0	27	7	231	8.6 (42)	0
1974	Det	0	—	—	—	5	1	37	7.4 (11)	0
1975	Det	0	—	—	—	8	3	80	10.0 (30)	0
1976	Det	0	—	—	—	23	**22**	191	8.3 (30)	0
1977	Det	0	—	—	—	0	2	—	—	—
NFL	11	50	1274	25.5 (98)	1	143	75	1312	9.2 (74)	2
Baschnagel, Brian										
1976	ChiB	29	**754**	26.0 (48)	0	2	1	2	1.0 (3)	0
1977	ChiB	23	557	24.2 (84)	**1**	3	2	54	18.0 (42)	0
1978	ChiB	20	455	22.8 (6)	0	1	1	2	2.0 (2)	0
1979	ChiB	12	260	21.7 (32)	0	0	3	—	—	—
1981	ChiB	2	34	17.0 (23)	0	0	3	—	—	—
1983	ChiB	3	42	14.0 (19)	0	0	—	—	—	—
NFL	6	89	2102	23.6 (84)	1	6	10	58	9.7 (42)	0
Bates, Michael										
1993	Sea	30	603	20.1 (46)	0	0	—	—	—	—
1994	Sea	26	508	19.5 (38)	0	0	—	—	—	—
1995	Cle	9	176	19.6 (38)	0	0	—	—	—	—
1996	Car	33	998	**30.2 (93)**	1	0	—	—	—	—
1997	Car	47	1281	**27.3 (56)**	0	1	0	8	8.0 (8)	0
1998	Car	59	1480	25.1 (99)	1	0	—	—	—	—
1999	Car	52	1287	24.8 (100)	**2**	0	—	—	—	—
2000	Car	42	941	22.4 (92)	1	7	3	31	4.4 (12)	0
2001	Was	49	1150	23.5 (41)	0	2	2	5	2.5 (5)	0
2003	NYJ	22	596	27.1 (48)	0	0	—	—	—	—
2003	Dal	4	90	22.5 (30)	0	0	—	—	—	—
NFL	10	373	9110	24.4 (100)	5	10	5	44	4.4 (12)	0
Beebe, Don										
1989	Buf	16	353	22.1 (85)	0	0	—	—	—	—
1990	Buf	6	119	19.8 (27)	0	0	—	—	—	—
1991	Buf	7	121	17.3 (24)	0	0	—	—	—	—
1993	Buf	10	160	16.0 (22)	0	0	—	—	—	—
1994	Buf	12	230	19.2 (35)	0	0	—	—	—	—
1995	Car	9	215	23.9 (38)	0	0	—	—	—	—
1996	GB	15	403	26.9 (90)	1	0	—	—	—	—
1997	GB	6	134	22.3 (39)	0	0	—	—	—	—
NFL	8	81	1735	21.4 (90)	1	0	—	—	—	—
Bell, Ken										
1986	Den	23	531	23.1 (42)	0	0	—	—	—	—
1987	Den	15	323	21.5 (42)	0	0	—	—	—	—
1988	Den	36	762	21.2 (38)	0	1	0	4	4.0 (4)	0
1989	Den	30	602	20.1 (33)	0	21	3	143	6.8 (24)	0
NFL	4	104	2218	21.3 (42)	0	22	3	147	6.7 (24)	0
Bell, Theo										
1976	Pit	0	—	—	—	39	2	390	10.0 (35)	0
1978	Pit	0	—	—	—	21	2	152	7.2 (18)	0
1979	Pit	0	—	—	—	45	7	378	8.4 (27)	0
1980	Pit	3	50	16.7 (21)	0	34	6	339	10.0 (27)	0
1981	TB	0	—	—	—	27	0	132	4.9 (13)	0
1982	TB	0	—	—	—	9	1	62	6.9 (14)	0
1983	TB	0	—	—	—	10	2	48	4.8 (11)	0
1984	TB	0	—	—	—	4	1	10	2.5 (8)	0
NFL	8	3	50	16.7 (21)	0	189	21	1511	8.0 (35)	0
Bennett, Brandon										
1998	Cin	3	61	20.3 (21)	0	0	—	—	—	—
2001	Cin	4	60	15.0 (19)	0	0	—	—	—	—
2002	Cin	49	1231	25.1 (94)	1	0	—	—	—	—
2003	Cin	53	1146	21.6 (46)	0	0	—	—	—	—
2004	Car	8	177	22.1 (43)	0	0	—	—	—	—
NFL	5	117	2675	22.9 (94)	1	0	—	—	—	—
Bentley, Albert										
1985	Ind	27	674	25.0 (48)	0	0	—	—	—	—
1986	Ind	32	687	21.5 (37)	0	0	—	—	—	—
1987	Ind	22	500	22.7 (45)	0	0	—	—	—	—
1988	Ind	39	775	19.9 (40)	0	0	—	—	—	—
1989	Ind	17	328	19.3 (29)	0	0	—	—	—	—
1990	Ind	11	211	19.2 (36)	0	0	—	—	—	—
1992	Pit	1	17	17.0 (17)	0	0	—	—	—	—
NFL	7	149	3192	21.4 (48)	0	0	—	—	—	—
Betts, Ladell										
2002	Was	28	690	24.6 (60)	0	0	—	—	—	—
2003	Was	3	59	19.7 (26)	0	0	—	—	—	—
2004	Was	23	528	23.0 (70)	0	0	—	—	—	—
2005	Was	24	621	25.9 (94)	**1**	0	—	—	—	—
NFL	4	78	1898	24.3 (94)	1	0	—	—	—	—
Bieniemy, Eric										
1992	SD	15	257	17.1 (30)	0	30	3	229	7.6 (21)	0
1993	SD	7	110	15.7 (18)	0	0	—	—	—	—
1995	Cin	8	168	21.0 (34)	0	7	1	47	6.7 (10)	0
1997	Cin	34	789	23.2 (**102**)	**1**	0	—	—	—	—
1998	Cin	5	87	17.4 (22)	0	0	—	—	—	—
1999	Phi	10	210	21.0 (30)	0	0	—	—	—	—
NFL	6	79	1621	20.5 (102)	1	37	4	276	7.5 (21)	0
Bird, Rodger										
1966	Oak-A	19	390	20.5 (32)	0	**37**	—	**323**	8.7 (42)	0
1967	Oak-A	6	143	23.8 (27)	0	**46**	**16**	**612**	13.3 (**78**)	0
1968	Oak-A	0	—	—	—	11	4	128	11.6 (50)	0
NFL	3	25	533	21.3 (32)	0	94	20	1063	11.3 (78)	0

YEAR	TEAM	KR	YDS	AVG (LG)	TD	PR	FC	YDS	AVG (LG)	TD
Bivins, Charlie										
1960	ChiB	15	362	24.1 (45)	0	0	—	—	—	—
1961	ChiB	25	668	26.7 (78)	0	0	—	—	—	—
1962	ChiB	12	243	20.3 (37)	0	0	—	—	—	—
1963	ChiB	2	40	20.0 (22)	0	0	—	—	—	—
1964	ChiB	8	218	27.3 (41)	0	0	—	—	—	—
1967	Buf-A	16	380	23.8 (55)	0	0	—	—	—	—
NFL	6	78	1911	24.5 (78)	0	0	—	—	—	—
Blackwell, Will										
1997	Pit	32	791	24.7 (97)	**1**	23	6	149	6.5 (15)	0
1998	Pit	20	382	19.1 (43)	0	4	4	22	5.5 (13)	0
1999	Pit	14	282	20.1 (37)	0	1	1	39	39.0 (39)	0
2000	Pit	10	281	28.1 (**98**)	**1**	0	—	—	—	—
2001	Pit	2	36	18.0 (20)	0	0	—	—	—	—
NFL	5	78	1772	22.7 (98)	2	28	11	210	7.5 (39)	0
Bradley, Bill										
1969	Phi	21	467	22.2 (42)	0	28	5	181	6.5 (37)	0
1971	Phi	0	—	—	—	18	12	118	6.6 (33)	0
1972	Phi	2	22	11.0 (20)	0	22	7	155	7.0 (60)	0
1973	Phi	0	—	—	—	8	12	106	13.3 (43)	0
1974	Phi	0	—	—	—	22	5	248	11.3 (22)	0
1975	Phi	0	—	—	—	4	3	4	1.0 (6)	0
1976	Phi	0	—	—	—	9	5	64	7.1 (23)	0
1977	SL	4	75	18.8 (28)	0	11	0	77	7.0 (14)	0
NFL	8	27	564	20.9 (42)	0	122	49	953	7.8 (60)	0
Bright, Leon										
1981	NYG	25	481	19.2 (41)	0	52	0	410	7.9 (55)	0
1982	NYG	4	72	18.0 (20)	0	**37**	0	**325**	8.8 (33)	0
1983	NYG	21	475	22.6 (36)	0	17	0	117	6.9 (20)	0
1984	TB	16	303	18.9 (33)	0	23	1	173	7.5 (21)	0
1985	TB	11	213	19.4 (47)	0	12	2	124	10.3 (29)	0
NFL	5	77	1544	20.1 (47)	0	141	3	1149	8.1 (55)	0
Brooks, James										
1981	SD	**40**	**949**	23.7 (47)	0	22	6	290	**13.2 (42)**	0
1982	SD	**33**	**749**	22.7 (47)	0	12	4	138	11.5 (29)	0
1983	SD	32	607	19.0 (34)	0	18	4	137	7.6 (30)	0
1984	Cin	7	144	20.6 (37)	0	0	—	—	—	—
1985	Cin	3	38	12.7 (15)	0	0	—	—	—	—
1987	Cin	2	42	21.0 (23)	0	0	—	—	—	—
1988	Cin	1	-6	-6.0 (6)	0	0	—	—	—	—
1991	Cin	11	190	17.3 (35)	0	0	—	—	—	—
1992	TB	3	49	16.3 (24)	0	0	—	—	—	—
NFL	9	132	2762	20.9 (47)	0	52	14	565	10.9 (42)	0
Broussard, Steve										
1990	Atl	3	45	15.0 (23)	0	0	—	—	—	—
1994	Cin	7	115	16.4 (24)	0	0	—	—	—	—
1995	Sea	43	1064	24.7 (70)	0	0	—	—	—	—
1996	Sea	43	979	22.8 (86)	0	0	—	—	—	—
1997	Sea	50	1076	21.5 (43)	0	0	—	—	—	—
1998	Sea	29	781	26.9 (90)	**1**	0	—	—	—	—
NFL	6	175	4060	23.2 (90)	1	0	—	—	—	—
Brown, Eddie										
1974	Cle	6	138	23.0 (36)	0	2	1	0	0.0 (0)	0
1975	Cle	6	126	21.0 (27)	0	2	0	16	8.0 (9)	0
1975	Was	0	—	—	—	6	4	52	8.7 (14)	0
1976	Was	**30**	738	24.6 (67)	0	48	8	**646**	**13.5 (71)**	**1**
1977	Was	34	852	25.1 (46)	0	**57**	8	452	7.9 (43)	0
1978	LARm	0	—	—	—	1	0	13	13.0 (13)	0
1979	LARm	5	103	20.6 (28)	0	56	**19**	332	5.9 (30)	0
NFL	6	81	1957	24.2 (67)	0	172	40	1511	8.8 (71)	1
Brown, Ron										
1985	LARm	28	918	**32.8 (98)**	**3**	0	—	—	—	—
1986	LARm	36	794	22.1 (55)	0	0	—	—	—	—
1987	LARm	27	581	21.5 (95)	**1**	0	—	—	—	—
1988	LARm	19	401	21.1 (**73**)	0	0	—	—	—	—
1989	LARm	**47**	968	20.6 (74)	0	0	—	—	—	—
1990	LARd	30	575	19.2 (34)	0	0	—	—	—	—
1991	LARm	12	256	21.3 (39)	0	0	—	—	—	—
NFL	7	199	4493	22.6 (98)	4	0	—	—	—	—
Brown, Tim										
1988	LARd	**41**	**1098**	**26.8 (97)**	**1**	**49**	10	**444**	9.1 (36)	0
1989	LARd	3	63	21.0 (25)	0	4	0	43	10.8 (29)	0
1990	LARd	0	—	—	—	34	8	295	8.7 (39)	0
1991	LARd	1	29	29.0 (29)	0	29	10	**330**	11.4 (75)	**1**
1992	LARd	2	14	7.0 (14)	0	37	19	383	10.4 (40)	0
1993	LARd	0	—	—	—	40	20	**465**	11.6 (74)	1
1994	LARd	0	—	—	—	40	14	**487**	12.2 (48)	0
1995	Oak	0	—	—	—	36	9	364	10.1 (38)	0
1996	Oak	1	24	24.0 (24)	0	32	21	272	8.5 (36)	0
1997	Oak	1	7	7.0 (7)	0	0	—	—	—	—
1998	Oak	0	—	—	—	3	1	23	7.7 (8)	0
2001	Oak	0	—	—	—	6	21	111	18.5 (**88**)	1
2002	Oak	0	—	—	—	10	**17**	55	5.5 (11)	0
2004	TB	0	—	—	—	6	12	48	8.0 (14)	0
NFL	14	49	1235	25.2 (97)	1	326	162	3320	10.2 (88)	3
Brown, Timmy										
1960	Phi	11	295	26.8 (79)	0	10	—	47	4.7 (12)	0
1961	Phi	**29**	**811**	28.0 (**105**)	**1**	8	—	125	15.6 (66)	1
1962	Phi	30	831	27.7 (99)	**1**	6	—	81	13.5 (38)	0
1963	Phi	**33**	**945**	28.6 (100)	1	16	6	152	9.5 (22)	0

YEAR	TEAM	KR	YDS	AVG(LG)	TD	PR	FC	YDS	AVG(LG)	TD
1964	Phi	30	692	23.1(51)	0	10	6	96	9.6(53)	0
1965	Phi	3	46	15.3(22)	0	4	6	13	3.3(7)	0
1966	Phi	20	562	28.1(93)	2	1	0	0	0.0(0)	0
1967	Phi	13	301	23.2(41)	0	0	—	—	—	—
1968	Bal	15	298	19.9(29)	0	16	8	125	7.8(25)	0
NFL	9	184	4781	26.0(105)	5	71	26	639	9.0(66)	1
BROWN, TROY										
1993	NE	15	243	16.2(29)	0	25	9	224	9.0(19)	0
1994	NE	1	14	14.0(14)	0	24	10	202	8.4(38)	0
1995	NE	31	672	21.7(38)	0	—	—	—	—	—
1996	NE	29	634	21.9(51)	0	0	—	—	—	—
1998	NE	0	—	—	—	17	8	225	**13.2(39)**	0
1999	NE	8	271	33.9(54)	0	38	13	405	10.7(52)	0
2000	NE	2	15	7.5(9)	0	39	**19**	504	12.9(66)	1
2001	NE	1	13	13.0(13)	0	29	15	413	**14.2(85)**	2
2002	NE	0	—	—	—	24	10	175	7.3(27)	0
2003	NE	0	—	—	—	29	13	293	10.1(23)	0
2004	NE	0	—	—	—	12	3	83	6.9(23)	0
2005	NE	0	—	—	—	7	5	30	4.3(7)	0
NFL	12	87	1862	21.4(54)	0	244	105	2554	10.5(85)	3
BRUNSON, LARRY										
1974	KC	12	280	23.3(57)	0	19	2	111	5.8(29)	0
1975	KC	1	8	8.0(8)	0	1	0	4	4.0(4)	0
1976	KC	0	—	—	—	31	0	387	12.5(48)	0
1977	KC	11	216	19.6(32)	0	20	0	108	5.4(19)	0
1978	Oak	6	154	25.7(47)	0	0	—	—	—	—
1979	Oak	17	441	**25.9(89)**	0	2	0	8	4.0(7)	0
1980	Den	40	923	23.1(53)	0	2	0	12	6.0(12)	0
NFL	7	87	2022	23.2(89)	0	75	2	630	8.4(48)	0
BUCHANON, PHILLIP										
2002	Oak	0	—	—	—	15	8	178	11.9(83)	1
2003	Oak	2	25	12.5(17)	0	36	14	491	13.6(80)	2
2004	Oak	0	—	—	—	21	7	121	5.8(18)	0
2005	Hou	0	—	—	—	12	6	101	8.4(37)	0
NFL	4	2	25	12.5(17)	0	84	35	891	10.6(83)	3
BUCKLEY, TERRELL										
1992	GB	0	—	—	—	21	5	211	10.0(58)	1
1993	GB	0	—	—	—	11	5	76	6.9(39)	0
1995	Mia	1	16	16.0(16)	0	0	—	—	—	—
1996	Mia	1	48	48.0(48)	0	3	1	24	8.0(13)	0
1997	Mia	0	—	—	—	4	0	58	14.5(26)	0
1998	Mia	0	—	—	—	29	3	354	12.2(35)	0
1999	Mia	0	—	—	—	8	5	13	1.6(8)	0
2000	Den	0	—	—	—	2	1	10	5.0(11)	0
2003	Mia	0	—	—	—	1	0	2	2.0(2)	0
NFL	9	2	64	32.0(48)	0	79	20	748	9.5(58)	1
BURRIS, JEFF										
1994	Buf	0	—	—	—	32	6	332	10.4(57)	0
1995	Buf	0	—	—	—	20	1	229	11.4(40)	0
1996	Buf	0	—	—	—	27	7	286	10.6(45)	0
1997	Buf	1	10	10.0(10)	0	21	8	198	9.4(32)	0
2002	Cin	0	—	—	—	0	1	—	—	—
2003	Cin	0	—	—	—	5	0	58	11.6(34)	0
NFL	6	1	10	10.0(10)	0	105	23	1103	10.5(57)	0
BUTLER, BILL										
1959	GB	21	472	22.5(34)	0	18	—	163	9.1(61)	1
1960	Dal	20	399	20.0(60)	0	13	—	131	10.1(46)	0
1961	Pit	6	117	19.5(25)	0	2	—	11	5.5(9)	0
1962	Min	26	588	22.6(45)	0	12	—	169	14.1(46)	0
1963	Min	**33**	713	21.6(35)	0	21	8	220	10.5(60)	1
1964	Min	26	597	23.0(34)	0	22	3	156	7.1(32)	0
NFL	6	132	2886	21.9(60)	0	88	11	850	9.7(61)	2
BUTLER, CANNONBALL										
1965	Pit	25	509	20.4(36)	0	0	—	—	—	—
1966	Pit	17	454	26.7(93)	1	0	—	—	—	—
1967	Pit	10	223	22.3(32)	0	0	—	—	—	—
1968	Atl	37	799	21.6(42)	0	0	—	—	—	—
1969	Atl	13	405	31.2(61)	0	0	—	—	—	—
1970	Atl	14	284	20.3(29)	0	0	—	—	—	—
1971	Atl	13	372	28.6(82)	0	0	—	—	—	—
1972	SL	4	85	21.3(27)	0	0	—	—	—	—
NFL	8	133	3131	23.5(93)	1	0	—	—	—	—
BYNUM, KENNY										
1997	SD	38	814	21.4(57)	0	0	—	—	—	—
1998	SD	19	345	18.2(30)	0	0	—	—	—	—
1999	SD	37	781	21.1(37)	0	0	—	—	—	—
2000	SD	13	242	18.6(39)	0	0	—	—	—	—
NFL	4	107	2182	20.4(57)	0	0	—	—	—	—
BYRD, BUTCH										
1964	Buf-A	0	—	—	—	2	—	4	2.0(4)	0
1965	Buf-A	0	—	—	—	22	—	220	10.0(30)	0
1966	Buf-A	0	—	—	—	23	—	186	8.1(72)	1
1967	Buf-A	0	—	—	—	30	5	142	4.7(19)	0
1968	Buf-A	0	—	—	—	2	1	11	5.5(11)	0
1969	Buf-A	0	—	—	—	7	2	37	5.3(32)	0
NFL	6	0	—	—	—	86	8	600	7.0(72)	1
CANADEO, TONY										
1941	GB	4	110	27.5(55)	0	4	—	26	6.5(10)	0
1942	GB	6	137	22.8(35)	0	7	—	76	10.9(26)	0
1943	GB	10	242	24.2(43)	0	8	—	93	11.6(22)	0
1944	GB	1	12	12.0(12)	0	1	—	4	4.0(4)	0
1946	GB	6	163	27.2(38)	0	6	—	76	12.7(22)	0
1947	GB	15	312	20.8(35)	0	10	—	111	11.1(24)	0
1948	GB	9	166	18.4(28)	0	4	—	55	13.8(20)	0
1949	GB	2	20	10.0(12)	0	0	—	—	—	—
1950	GB	16	411	25.7(48)	0	5	—	68	13.6(21)	0
1951	GB	4	101	25.3(48)	0	0	—	—	—	—
1952	GB	2	62	31.0(40)	0	1	—	4	4.0(4)	0
NFL	11	75	1736	23.1(55)	0	46	0	513	11.2(26)	0
CARMICHAEL, AL										
1953	GB	26	641	24.7(43)	0	20	—	199	9.9(52)	0
1954	GB	20	531	26.5(49)	0	9	—	43	4.8(14)	0
1955	GB	14	418	**29.9(100)**	1	10	—	89	8.9(40)	0
1956	GB	**33**	**927**	28.1(**106**)	1	21	—	165	7.9(22)	0
1957	GB	**31**	**690**	22.3(33)	0	25	—	190	7.6(48)	0
1958	GB	29	700	24.1(60)	0	15	—	67	4.5(51)	0
1960	Den-A	22	581	26.4(58)	0	**15**	—	101	6.7(0)	0
1961	Den-A	16	310	19.4(31)	0	7	—	58	8.3(29)	0
NFL	8	191	4798	25.1(106)	2	122	0	912	7.5(52)	0
CARTER, DALE										
1992	KC	11	190	17.3(39)	0	38	6	398	10.5(86)	**2**
1993	KC	0	—	—	—	27	4	247	9.1(30)	0
1994	KC	0	—	—	—	16	4	124	7.8(42)	0
1996	KC	0	—	—	—	2	0	18	9.0(15)	0
NFL	4	11	190	17.3(39)	0	83	14	787	9.5(86)	2
CARTER, DEXTER										
1990	SF	41	783	19.1(35)	0	0	—	—	—	—
1991	SF	**37**	**839**	22.7(98)	**1**	0	—	—	—	—
1992	SF	2	55	27.5(32)	0	0	—	—	—	—
1993	SF	25	494	19.8(60)	0	34	20	411	12.1(72)	1
1994	SF	48	1105	23.0(96)	1	38	12	321	8.4(26)	0
1995	NYJ	33	705	21.4(57)	0	21	8	145	6.9(**20**)	**0**
1995	SF	23	522	22.7(46)	0	9	7	164	18.2(**78**)	1
1996	SF	41	909	22.2(71)	0	36	17	317	8.8(52)	0
NFL	7	250	5412	21.6(98)	2	138	64	1358	9.8(78)	2
CASANOVA, TOMMY										
1972	Cin	1	34	34.0(34)	0	30	**19**	289	9.6(**66**)	**1**
1973	Cin	0	—	—	—	15	6	119	7.9(27)	0
1974	Cin	1	48	48.0(48)	0	24	2	265	11.0(74)	0
1975	Cin	0	—	—	—	11	2	60	5.5(12)	0
1976	Cin	0	—	—	—	10	2	45	4.5(15)	0
1977	Cin	0	—	—	—	1	1	6	6.0(6)	0
NFL	6	2	82	41.0(48)	0	91	32	784	8.6(74)	1
CASSADY, HOWARD										
1956	Det	16	382	23.9(42)	0	13	—	83	6.4(34)	0
1957	Det	10	232	23.2(37)	0	0	—	—	—	—
1958	Det	6	126	21.0(39)	0	3	—	4	1.3(4)	0
1959	Det	8	163	20.4(34)	0	1	—	14	14.0(14)	0
1960	Det	4	82	20.5(28)	0	1	—	25	25.0(25)	0
1961	Det	9	127	14.1(23)	0	16	—	159	9.9(21)	0
1962	Cle	10	233	23.3(34)	0	7	—	47	6.7(13)	0
1962	Phi	14	249	17.8(34)	0	1	—	2	2.0(2)	0
1963	Det	0	—	—	—	1	0	7	7.0(7)	0
NFL	8	77	1594	20.7(42)	0	43	0	341	7.9(34)	0
CHANDNOIS, LYNN										
1950	Pit	12	351	29.3(60)	0	3	—	33	11.0(15)	0
1951	Pit	12	390	**32.5(55)**	0	12	—	55	4.6(20)	0
1952	Pit	17	599	**35.2(93)**	**2**	17	—	111	6.5(19)	0
1953	Pit	21	610	29.0(93)	1	26	—	101	3.9(15)	0
1954	Pit	13	256	19.7(34)	0	8	—	12	1.5(6)	0
1955	Pit	9	223	24.8(46)	0	0	—	—	—	—
1956	Pit	8	291	36.4(91)	0	0	—	—	—	—
NFL	7	92	2720	29.6(93)	3	66	0	312	4.7(20)	0
CHATMAN, ANTONIO										
2003	GB	36	804	22.3(46)	0	33	18	277	8.4(33)	0
2004	GB	25	565	22.6(59)	0	32	**27**	245	7.7(28)	0
2005	GB	5	91	18.2(29)	0	45	18	381	8.5(**85**)	1
NFL	3	66	1460	22.1(59)	0	110	63	903	8.2(85)	1
CHILDS, CLARENCE										
1964	NYG	34	987	**29.0(100)**	1	6	3	40	6.7(27)	0
1965	NYG	29	718	24.8(51)	0	0	—	—	—	—
1966	NYG	34	855	25.1(90)	1	0	1	—	—	—
1967	NYG	29	603	20.8(48)	0	0	—	—	—	—
1968	ChiB	8	291	36.4(88)	0	0	—	—	—	—
NFL	5	134	3454	25.8(100)	2	6	4	40	6.7(27)	0
CHRISTIANSEN, JACK										
1951	Det	11	270	24.5(45)	0	18	—	343	19.1(**89**)	4
1952	Det	16	409	25.6(46)	0	15	—	322	**21.5(79)**	2
1953	Det	10	183	18.3(34)	0	8	—	22	2.8(10)	0
1954	Det	5	102	20.4(27)	0	23	—	225	9.8(61)	1
1955	Det	7	169	24.1(35)	0	12	—	87	7.3(42)	0
1956	Det	6	116	19.3(22)	0	6	—	73	12.2(66)	1
1957	Det	4	80	20.0(22)	0	3	—	12	4.0(8)	0
NFL	7	59	1329	22.5(46)	0	85	0	1084	12.8(89)	8
CHRISTY, DICK										
1958	Pit	16	384	24.0(41)	0	17	—	153	9.0(43)	0
1960	Bos-A	24	617	25.7(46)	0	8	—	73	9.1(29)	0
1961	NYT-A	15	360	24.0(60)	0	18	—	**383**	21.3(70)	2
1962	NYT-A	**38**	**824**	21.7(43)	0	15	—	**250**	16.7(73)	2

YEAR	TEAM	KR	YDS	AVG(LG)	TD	PR	FC	YDS	AVG(LG)	TD
1963	NYJ-A	24	585	24.4(71)	0	9	—	46	5.1(13)	0
NFL	5	117	2770	23.7(71)	0	67	0	905	13.5(73)	4
CLACK, DARRYL										
1986	Dal	19	421	22.2(51)	0	0	—	—	—	—
1987	Dal	29	635	21.9(48)	0	0	—	—	—	—
1988	Dal	32	690	21.6(40)	0	0	—	—	—	—
1989	Dal	3	56	18.7(24)	0	0	—	—	—	—
NFL	4	83	1802	21.7(51)	0	0	—	—	—	—
COLE, CHRIS										
2000	Den	11	264	24.0(37)	0	0	—	—	—	—
2001	Den	48	1127	23.5(52)	0	0	—	—	—	—
2003	Den	30	714	23.8(34)	0	0	—	—	—	—
NFL	3	89	2105	23.7(52)	0	0	—	—	—	—
COLEMAN, ANDRE										
1994	SD	**49**	**1293**	26.4(90)	**2**	0	—	—	—	—
1995	SD	**62**	**1411**	22.8(92)	**2**	28	14	326	11.6(88)	**1**
1996	SD	**55**	1210	22.0(57)	0	0	—	—	—	—
1997	Sea	3	65	21.7(29)	0	0	—	—	—	—
1997	Pit	24	487	20.3(24)	0	5	2	5	1.0(5)	0
1998	Pit	0	—	—	—	10	3	53	5.3(12)	0
NFL	5	193	4466	23.1(92)	4	43	19	384	8.9(88)	1
COLZIE, NEAL										
1975	Oak	0	—	—	—	**48**	3	**655**	13.6(64)	0
1976	Oak	6	115	19.2(26)	0	41	3	448	10.9(32)	0
1977	Oak	0	—	—	—	32	6	334	10.4(23)	0
1978	Oak	1	15	15.0(15)	0	**47**	12	310	6.6(24)	0
1981	TB	0	—	—	—	2	0	12	6.0(12)	0
NFL	5	7	130	18.6(26)	0	170	24	1759	10.3(64)	0
COOPER, EVAN										
1984	Phi	17	299	17.6(48)	0	40	**19**	250	6.3(16)	0
1985	Phi	3	32	10.7(13)	0	43	10	364	8.5(56)	0
1986	Phi	2	42	21.0(24)	0	16	7	139	8.7(58)	0
1987	Phi	5	86	17.2(24)	0	0	—	—	—	—
1988	Atl	16	331	20.7(28)	0	2	1	10	5.0(10)	0
NFL	5	43	790	18.4(48)	0	101	37	763	7.6(58)	0
DAVIS, ANDRE'										
2002	Cle	50	1068	21.4(95)	1	7	4	33	4.7(15)	0
2003	Cle	38	803	21.1(69)	0	1	1	7	7.0(7)	0
2005	NE	3	108	36.0(65)	0	0	—	—	—	—
NFL	3	91	1979	21.7(95)	1	8	5	40	5.0(15)	0
DAVIS, CLARENCE										
1971	Oak	27	734	27.2(44)	0	0	—	—	—	—
1972	Oak	18	464	25.8(49)	0	0	2	—	—	—
1973	Oak	19	504	26.5(76)	0	0	—	—	—	—
1974	Oak	3	107	35.7(49)	0	0	—	—	—	—
1975	Oak	9	268	29.8(64)	0	0	—	—	—	—
1977	Oak	3	63	21.0(26)	0	0	—	—	—	—
NFL	6	79	2140	27.1(76)	0	0	2	—	—	—
DAVIS, GARY										
1976	Mia	26	617	23.7(47)	0	0	—	—	—	—
1977	Mia	14	414	29.6(73)	0	1	3	11	11.0(11)	0
1978	Mia	13	251	19.3(27)	0	2	1	36	18.0(25)	0
1979	Mia	2	27	13.5(16)	0	0	—	—	—	—
1980	TB	44	951	21.6(54)	0	0	—	—	—	—
1981	TB	5	81	16.2(21)	0	0	—	—	—	—
NFL	6	104	2341	22.5(73)	0	3	4	47	15.7(25)	0
DIXON, JAMES										
1989	Dal	**47**	**1181**	25.1(97)	**1**	0	—	—	—	—
1990	Dal	36	736	20.4(47)	0	0	—	—	—	—
1991	Dal	18	398	22.1(39)	0	0	—	—	—	—
NFL	3	101	2315	22.9(97)	1	0	—	—	—	—
DIXON, ZACHARY										
1979	Den	3	53	17.7(24)	0	0	—	—	—	—
1980	Phi	2	30	15.0(15)	0	0	—	—	—	—
1981	Bal	36	737	20.5(46)	0	0	—	—	—	—
1982	Bal	11	197	17.9(27)	0	0	—	—	—	—
1983	Bal	**2**	**23**	11.5(14)	**0**	0	—	—	—	—
1983	Sea	**49**	**1148**	23.4(94)	**1**	0	—	—	—	—
1984	Sea	25	446	17.8(36)	0	1	0	5	5.0(5)	0
NFL	6	128	2634	20.6(94)	1	1	0	5	5.0(5)	0
DODD, AL										
1967	ChiB	3	34	11.3(24)	0	3	4	8	2.7(6)	0
1969	NO	8	171	21.4(28)	0	15	9	106	7.1(21)	0
1970	NO	15	319	21.3(32)	0	14	3	129	9.2(41)	0
1971	NO	12	252	21.0(28)	0	13	4	88	6.8(14)	0
1973	Atl	0	—	—	—	8	1	69	8.6(28)	0
1974	Atl	0	—	—	—	27	0	344	12.7(57)	0
NFL	6	38	776	20.4(32)	0	80	21	744	9.3(57)	0
DREWREY, WILLIE										
1985	Hou	26	642	24.7(50)	0	24	10	215	9.0(23)	0
1986	Hou	25	500	20.0(32)	0	34	13	262	7.7(25)	0
1987	Hou	8	136	17.0(27)	0	3	1	11	3.7(5)	0
1988	Hou	1	10	10.0(10)	0	2	2	8	4.0(8)	0
1989	TB	1	26	26.0(26)	0	20	2	220	11.0(55)	0
1990	TB	14	244	17.4(29)	0	23	**15**	184	8.0(16)	0
1991	TB	12	246	20.5(43)	0	38	15	360	9.5(33)	0
1992	TB	0	—	—	—	7	6	62	8.9(17)	0
1993	Hou	15	293	19.5(34)	0	41	19	275	6.7(18)	0
NFL	9	102	2097	20.6(50)	0	192	83	1597	8.3(55)	0

YEAR	TEAM	KR	YDS	AVG(LG)	TD	PR	FC	YDS	AVG(LG)	TD
DRUMMOND, EDDIE										
2002	Det	40	1039	26.0(91)	0	18	8	138	7.7(73)	1
2003	Det	21	469	22.3(38)	0	12	4	151	12.6(57)	1
2004	Det	41	1092	26.6(**99**)	**2**	24	8	316	**13.2**(**83**)	**2**
2005	Det	49	1077	22.0(48)	0	26	11	157	6.0(38)	0
NFL	4	151	3677	24.4(99)	2	80	31	762	9.5(83)	4
DUDLEY, BILL										
1942	Pit	11	298	**27.1**(**84**)	**1**	20	—	**271**	13.6(47)	0
1945	Pit	3	65	21.7(35)	0	5	—	20	4.0(6)	0
1946	Pit	14	280	20.0(34)	0	**27**	—	**385**	**14.3**(**52**)	0
1947	Det	15	359	23.9(78)	0	11	—	182	16.5(84)	**1**
1948	Det	10	204	20.4(47)	0	8	—	67	8.4(18)	0
1949	Det	13	246	18.9(31)	0	11	—	199	18.1(67)	1
1950	Was	1	43	43.0(43)	0	12	—	185	15.4(**96**)	1
1951	Was	11	248	22.5(37)	0	22	—	172	7.8(27)	0
1953	Was	0	—	—	—	8	—	34	4.3(16)	0
NFL	9	78	1743	22.3(84)	1	124	0	1515	12.2(96)	3
DUNCAN, SPEEDY										
1964	SD-A	9	318	35.3(91)	0	4	—	19	4.8(9)	0
1965	SD-A	26	612	23.5(46)	0	30	—	**464**	**15.5**(**66**)	**2**
1966	SD-A	25	642	25.7(50)	0	18	—	238	**13.2**(**81**)	**1**
1967	SD-A	9	231	25.7(60)	0	36	6	434	12.1(50)	0
1968	SD-A	25	586	23.4(53)	0	18	5	206	11.4(**95**)	1
1969	SD-A	21	587	28.0(52)	0	27	7	280	10.4(38)	0
1970	SD	19	410	21.6(41)	0	5	4	10	2.0(8)	0
1971	Was	27	724	26.8(48)	0	22	9	233	**10.6**(**33**)	0
1972	Was	15	364	24.3(41)	0	11	6	70	6.4(18)	0
1973	Was	4	65	16.3(38)	0	28	11	228	8.1(18)	0
1974	Was	0	—	—	—	3	0	19	6.3(11)	0
NFL	11	180	4539	25.2(91)	0	202	48	2201	10.9(95)	4
DUNN, DAVID										
1995	Cin	50	1092	21.8(45)	0	0	—	—	—	—
1996	Cin	35	782	22.3(90)	**1**	7	1	54	7.7(20)	0
1997	Cin	19	487	25.6(85)	0	0	—	—	—	—
1998	Pit	21	525	25.0(44)	0	0	—	—	—	—
1999	Cle	9	180	20.0(27)	0	4	1	25	6.3(13)	0
2000	Oak	44	1073	24.4(88)	**1**	8	3	99	12.4(25)	0
2001	Oak	20	458	22.9(40)	0	19	11	169	8.9(23)	0
NFL	7	198	4597	23.2(90)	2	38	16	347	9.1(25)	0
DWIGHT, TIM										
1998	Atl	36	973	27.0(93)	1	31	13	263	8.5(23)	0
1999	Atl	44	944	21.5(40)	0	20	12	220	11.0(70)	**1**
2000	Atl	32	680	21.3(48)	0	33	17	309	9.4(70)	1
2001	SD	0	—	—	—	24	12	271	11.3(84)	1
2002	SD	8	166	20.8(26)	0	19	11	231	12.2(37)	0
2003	SD	22	488	22.2(32)	0	2	2	0	0.0(2)	0
2004	SD	50	1222	24.4(87)	1	1	5	6	6.0(6)	0
2005	NE	10	250	25.0(38)	0	32	13	273	8.5(29)	0
NFL	8	202	4723	23.4(93)	2	162	85	1573	9.7(84)	3
EDMONDS, BOBBY JOE										
1986	Sea	34	764	22.5(46)	0	34	14	419	**12.3**(**75**)	**1**
1987	Sea	27	564	20.9(43)	0	20	4	251	12.6(40)	0
1988	Sea	40	900	22.5(65)	0	35	8	340	9.7(41)	0
1989	LARd	14	271	19.4(43)	0	16	4	168	10.5(20)	0
1995	TB	58	1147	19.8(44)	0	29	10	293	10.1(45)	0
NFL	5	173	3646	21.1(65)	0	134	40	1471	11.0(75)	1
EDWARDS, GLEN										
1971	Pit	9	198	22.0(28)	0	1	0	0	0.0(0)	0
1972	Pit	1	18	18.0(18)	0	22	**19**	202	9.2(54)	0
1973	Pit	1	10	10.0(10)	0	34	5	336	9.9(44)	0
1974	Pit	2	31	15.5(19)	0	16	0	128	8.0(19)	0
1975	Pit	0	—	—	—	25	3	267	10.7(25)	0
1976	Pit	0	—	—	—	1	0	8	8.0(8)	0
1980	SD	0	—	—	—	4	1	17	4.3(8)	0
1981	SD	0	—	—	—	1	0	1	1.0(1)	0
NFL	8	13	257	19.8(28)	0	104	28	959	9.2(54)	0
ELDER, DONNIE										
1985	NYJ	3	42	14.0(25)	0	0	—	—	—	—
1986	Pit	21	425	20.2(36)	0	0	—	—	—	—
1986	Det	1	10	10.0(10)	0	0	—	—	—	—
1988	TB	34	772	**22.7**(**51**)	0	1	0	0	0.0(0)	0
1989	TB	40	685	17.1(30)	0	0	—	—	—	—
1990	SD	24	571	23.8(90)	0	0	—	—	—	—
1991	SD	27	535	19.8(42)	0	0	—	—	—	—
NFL	6	150	3040	20.3(90)	0	1	0	0	0.0(0)	0
ELLARD, HENRY										
1983	LARm	15	314	20.9(44)	0	16	4	217	**13.6**(**72**)	**1**
1984	LARm	2	24	12.0(12)	0	30	3	403	**13.4**(**83**)	**2**
1985	LARm	0	—	—	—	37	9	**501**	**13.5**(**80**)	**1**
1986	LARm	1	18	18.0(18)	0	14	10	127	9.1(20)	0
1987	LARm	1	8	8.0(8)	0	15	6	107	7.1(29)	0
1988	LARm	0	—	—	—	17	3	119	7.0(34)	0
1989	LARm	0	—	—	—	2	0	20	10.0(10)	0
1990	LARm	0	—	—	—	2	0	15	7.5(8)	0
1993	LARm	0	—	—	—	2	8	18	9.0(13)	0
NFL	9	19	364	19.2(44)	0	135	43	1527	11.3(83)	4
ENGRAM, BOBBY										
1996	ChiB	25	580	23.2(45)	0	31	19	282	9.1(34)	0
1997	ChiB	2	27	13.5(20)	0	1	0	4	4.0(4)	0
2001	Sea	1	6	6.0(6)	0	6	3	96	16.0(28)	0

YEAR	TEAM	KR	YDS	AVG(LG)	TD	PR	FC	YDS	AVG(LG)	TD
2002	Sea	0	—	—	—	21	**23**	224	10.7(61)	1
2003	Sea	1	18	18.0(18)	0	31	**22**	320	10.3(83)	1
2004	Sea	0	—	—	—	10	19	118	11.8(48)	0
2005	Sea	0	—	—	—	1	1	9	9.0(9)	0
NFL	7	29	631	21.8(45)	0	101	87	1053	10.4(83)	2
Epps, Phil										
1982	GB	0	—	—	—	20	5	150	7.5(35)	0
1983	GB	0	—	—	—	36	13	324	9.0(**90**)	**1**
1984	GB	12	232	19.3(47)	0	29	10	199	6.9(39)	0
1985	GB	12	279	23.3(48)	0	15	3	146	9.7(46)	0
1986	GB	1	21	21.0(21)	0	0	—	—	—	—
1989	NYJ	9	154	17.1(43)	0	0	—	—	—	—
NFL	6	34	686	20.2(48)	0	100	31	819	8.2(90)	1
Fair, Terry										
1998	Det	51	1428	**28.0(105)**	**2**	30	15	189	6.3(23)	0
1999	Det	34	752	22.1(91)	0	11	4	97	8.8(36)	0
2000	Det	6	149	24.8(31)	0	2	0	15	7.5(11)	0
2001	Det	10	187	18.7(32)	0	4	2	37	9.3(21)	0
2005	SL	10	182	18.2(35)	0	3	6	7	2.3(8)	0
NFL	5	111	2698	24.3(105)	2	50	27	345	6.9(36)	0
Faulk, Kevin										
1999	NE	39	943	24.2(95)	0	10	4	90	9.0(20)	0
2000	NE	38	816	21.5(40)	0	6	3	58	9.7(35)	0
2001	NE	33	662	20.1(42)	0	4	0	27	6.8(10)	0
2002	NE	26	725	**27.9(87)**	**2**	8	4	65	8.1(16)	0
2003	NE	10	207	20.7(30)	0	5	6	66	13.2(19)	0
2004	NE	4	73	18.3(24)	0	20	11	133	6.7(16)	0
2005	NE	4	81	20.3(26)	0	0	—	—	—	—
NFL	7	154	3507	22.8(95)	2	53	28	439	8.3(35)	0
Fisher, Jeff										
1981	ChiB	7	102	14.6(23)	0	43	**20**	509	11.8(88)	1
1982	ChiB	7	102	14.6(20)	0	7	6	53	7.6(17)	0
1983	ChiB	0	—	—	—	13	3	71	5.5(11)	0
1984	ChiB	0	—	—	—	**57**	11	492	8.6(28)	0
NFL	4	14	204	14.6(23)	0	120	40	1125	9.4(88)	1
Francis, Wallace										
1973	Buf	23	687	**29.9(101)**	**2**	0	—	—	—	—
1974	Buf	37	947	25.6(74)	0	0	—	—	—	—
1975	Atl	14	265	18.9(32)	0	0	—	—	—	—
1976	Atl	9	156	17.3(30)	0	0	—	—	—	—
1977	Atl	1	22	22.0(22)	0	0	—	—	—	—
NFL	5	84	2077	24.7(101)	2	0	—	—	—	—
Freeman, Phil										
1985	TB	48	1085	22.6(58)	0	0	—	—	—	—
1986	TB	31	582	18.8(33)	0	0	—	—	—	—
NFL	2	79	1667	21.1(58)	0	0	—	—	—	—
Fryar, Irving										
1984	NE	5	95	19.0(22)	0	36	10	347	9.6(55)	0
1985	NE	3	39	13.0(24)	0	37	**15**	520	**14.1(85)**	**2**
1986	NE	10	192	19.2(33)	0	35	10	366	10.5(59)	**1**
1987	NE	6	119	19.8(31)	0	18	**12**	174	9.7(36)	0
1988	NE	1	3	3.0(3)	0	38	8	398	10.5(30)	0
1989	NE	1	47	47.0(47)	0	12	1	107	8.9(20)	0
1990	NE	0	—	—	—	28	10	133	4.8(17)	0
1991	NE	0	—	—	—	2	4	10	5.0(10)	0
1992	NE	0	—	—	—	0	1	—	—	—
1993	Mia	1	10	10.0(10)	0	0	—	—	—	—
NFL	10	27	505	18.7(47)	0	206	71	2055	10.0(85)	3
Fuller, Mike										
1975	SD	31	725	23.4(34)	0	36	0	410	11.4(52)	1
1976	SD	20	420	21.0(47)	0	33	0	436	13.2(43)	0
1977	SD	0	—	—	—	28	2	360	12.9(88)	1
1978	SD	5	109	21.8(32)	0	39	10	436	11.2(34)	0
1979	SD	6	115	19.2(41)	0	46	7	448	9.7(27)	0
1980	SD	15	289	19.3(30)	0	30	12	298	9.9(31)	0
1981	Cin	1	34	34.0(34)	0	23	**13**	177	7.7(34)	0
1982	Cin	1	9	9.0(9)	0	17	8	95	5.6(13)	0
NFL	8	79	1701	21.5(47)	0	252	52	2660	10.6(88)	2
Futrell, Bobby										
1986	TB	5	115	23.0(30)	0	14	5	67	4.8(12)	0
1987	TB	31	609	19.6(40)	0	24	6	213	8.9(22)	0
1988	TB	2	38	19.0(20)	0	27	10	283	10.5(40)	0
1989	TB	4	58	14.5(22)	0	12	2	76	6.3(15)	0
NFL	4	42	820	19.5(40)	0	77	23	639	8.3(40)	0
Gabriel, Doug										
2003	Oak	29	646	22.3(85)	1	0	—	—	—	—
2004	Oak	53	1140	21.5(64)	0	2	2	7	3.5(7)	0
2005	Oak	4	64	16.0(21)	0	0	—	—	—	—
NFL	3	86	1850	21.5(85)	1	2	2	7	3.5(7)	0
Galloway, Joey										
1995	Sea	2	30	15.0(18)	0	36	12	360	10.0(**89**)	**1**
1996	Sea	0	—	—	—	15	5	158	10.5(**88**)	**1**
1998	Sea	0	—	—	—	25	5	251	10.0(74)	**2**
1999	Sea	0	—	—	—	3	1	54	18.0(21)	0
2000	Dal	0	—	—	—	1	0	2	2.0(2)	0
2001	Dal	0	—	—	—	1	0	6	6.0(6)	0
2002	Dal	0	—	—	—	15	8	181	12.1(71)	0
2003	Dal	2	38	19.0(22)	0	20	8	178	8.9(36)	0
2004	TB	0	—	—	—	20	8	142	7.1(59)	1
NFL	9	4	68	17.0(22)	0	136	47	1332	9.8(89)	5

YEAR	TEAM	KR	YDS	AVG(LG)	TD	PR	FC	YDS	AVG(LG)	TD
Garrett, Carl										
1969	Bos-A	28	792	28.3(63)	0	12	0	159	13.3(45)	0
1970	Bos	24	511	21.3(30)	0	17	0	168	9.9(62)	0
1971	NE	24	538	22.4(37)	0	8	2	124	15.5(50)	0
1972	NE	16	410	25.6(49)	0	6	0	36	6.0(27)	0
1973	ChiB	16	486	**30.4(67)**	0	0	—	—	—	—
1975	NYJ	7	159	22.7(33)	0	0	—	—	—	—
1976	Oak	18	388	21.6(36)	0	0	—	—	—	—
1977	Oak	21	420	20.0(31)	0	0	—	—	—	—
NFL	8	154	3704	24.1(67)	0	43	2	487	11.3(62)	0
Garron, Larry										
1960	Bos-A	1	21	21.0(21)	0	0	—	—	—	—
1961	Bos-A	16	438	27.4(89)	**1**	0	—	—	—	—
1962	Bos-A	24	686	28.6(95)	**1**	0	—	—	—	—
1963	Bos-A	28	693	24.8(58)	0	1	—	23	23.0(23)	0
1964	Bos-A	10	198	19.8(31)	0	0	—	—	—	—
1965	Bos-A	5	141	28.2(36)	0	0	—	—	—	—
1966	Bos-A	2	49	24.5(29)	0	0	—	—	—	—
1967	Bos-A	3	73	24.3(26)	0	0	—	—	—	—
NFL	8	89	2299	25.8(95)	2	1	0	23	23.0(23)	0
Gentry, Dennis										
1982	ChiB	9	161	17.9(23)	0	17	5	89	5.2(16)	0
1983	ChiB	7	130	18.6(28)	0	0	—	—	—	—
1984	ChiB	11	209	19.0(33)	0	0	—	—	—	—
1985	ChiB	18	466	25.9(94)	1	0	0	47	—	—
1986	ChiB	20	576	**28.8(91)**	**1**	0	—	—	—	—
1987	ChiB	25	621	24.8(88)	**1**	0	—	—	—	—
1988	ChiB	27	578	21.4(51)	0	0	—	—	—	—
1989	ChiB	28	667	23.8(63)	0	0	—	—	—	—
1990	ChiB	18	388	21.6(59)	0	0	—	—	—	—
1991	ChiB	13	227	17.5(27)	0	0	—	—	—	—
1992	ChiB	16	330	20.6(66)	0	0	—	—	—	—
NFL	11	192	4353	22.7(94)	3	17	5	136	8.0(47)	0
Gibson, Claude										
1961	SD-A	3	17	5.7(9)	0	14	—	209	14.9(39)	0
1962	SD-A	2	55	27.5(39)	0	10	—	89	8.9(27)	0
1963	Oak-A	2	10	5.0(5)	0	**26**	—	**307**	**11.8(85)**	**2**
1964	Oak-A	0	—	—	—	29	—	**419**	**14.4(58)**	0
1965	Oak-A	9	186	20.7(38)	0	**31**	—	357	11.5(58)	1
NFL	5	16	268	16.8(39)	0	110	0	1381	12.6(85)	3
Glasgow, Nesby										
1979	Bal	50	1126	22.5(58)	0	44	11	352	8.0(75)	1
1980	Bal	33	743	22.5(44)	0	23	**15**	187	8.1(20)	0
1981	Bal	1	35	35.0(35)	0	0	—	—	—	—
1982	Bal	0	—	—	—	4	5	24	6.0(8)	0
1983	Bal	0	—	—	—	1	1	9	9.0(9)	0
1984	Ind	0	—	—	—	7	2	79	11.3(35)	0
1988	Sea	0	—	—	—	1	0	0	0.0(0)	0
1990	Sea	1	2	2.0(2)	0	0	—	—	—	—
NFL	8	85	1906	22.4(58)	0	80	34	651	8.1(75)	1
Glenn, Aaron										
1994	NYJ	27	582	21.6(45)	0	0	—	—	—	—
1995	NYJ	1	12	12.0(12)	0	0	—	—	—	—
1996	NYJ	1	6	6.0(6)	0	0	—	—	—	—
1997	NYJ	28	741	**26.5(96)**	**1**	0	—	—	—	—
1998	NYJ	24	585	24.4(62)	0	0	—	—	—	—
1999	NYJ	27	601	22.3(46)	0	0	—	—	—	—
2000	NYJ	3	51	17.0(22)	0	0	—	—	—	—
2001	NYJ	0	—	—	—	2	1	6	3.0(4)	0
2002	Hou	0	—	—	—	0	0	47	—	—
2004	Hou	0	—	—	—	4	0	22	5.5(18)	0
2005	Dal	1	20	20.0(20)	0	0	—	—	—	—
NFL	11	112	2598	23.2(96)	1	6	1	75	12.5(47)	0
Gordon, Darrien										
1993	SD	0	—	—	—	31	15	395	12.7(54)	0
1994	SD	0	—	—	—	36	19	475	**13.2(90)**	**2**
1996	SD	0	—	—	—	36	13	537	**14.9(81)**	**1**
1997	Den	0	—	—	—	40	**22**	543	13.6(**94**)	**3**
1998	Den	0	—	—	—	34	6	379	11.1(44)	0
1999	Oak	0	—	—	—	42	14	397	9.5(78)	0
2000	Oak	1	17	17.0(17)	0	29	10	258	8.9(36)	0
2001	Atl	0	—	—	—	31	6	437	**14.1(74)**	0
2002	GB	4	53	13.3(19)	0	35	9	180	5.1(27)	0
NFL	9	5	70	14.0(19)	0	314	114	3601	11.5(94)	6
Gordon, Dick										
1965	ChiB	14	242	17.3(41)	0	1	0	-3	-3.0(3)	0
1966	ChiB	19	521	27.4(**94**)	0	4	2	-5	-1.3(0)	0
1967	ChiB	16	397	24.8(32)	0	12	12	82	6.8(43)	0
1968	ChiB	3	97	32.3(37)	0	1	0	5	5.0(5)	0
1969	ChiB	6	105	17.5(27)	0	1	0	11	11.0(11)	0
1972	LARm	4	141	35.3(53)	0	4	0	20	5.0(12)	0
1973	LARm	3	68	22.7(25)	0	0	—	—	—	—
1974	SD	14	354	25.3(39)	0	8	3	39	4.9(12)	0
NFL	8	79	1925	24.4(94)	0	31	17	149	4.8(43)	0
Gray, Johnnie										
1975	GB	0	—	—	—	1	0	27	27.0(27)	0
1976	GB	1	23	23.0(23)	0	37	7	307	8.3(27)	0
1977	GB	0	—	—	—	10	3	68	6.8(24)	0
1978	GB	0	—	—	—	11	6	95	8.6(22)	0
1979	GB	0	—	—	—	13	8	61	4.7(18)	0
1980	GB	5	63	12.6(18)	0	4	2	41	10.3(16)	0

YEAR	TEAM	KR	YDS	AVG (LG)	TD	PR	FC	YDS	AVG (LG)	TD
1981	GB	2	24	12.0(19)	0	1	1	0	0.0(0)	0
1982	GB	2	29	14.5(25)	0	6	1	48	8.0(15)	0
1983	GB	11	178	16.2(26)	0	2	0	9	4.5(5)	0
NFL	9	21	317	15.1(26)	0	85	28	656	7.7(27)	0
GRAY, MEL										
1986	NO	31	866	27.9(**101**)	**1**	0	—	—	—	—
1987	NO	30	636	21.2(43)	0	24	5	352	**14.7**(**80**)	0
1988	NO	32	670	20.9(39)	0	25	8	305	12.2(66)	1
1989	Det	24	640	**26.7**(**57**)	0	11	2	76	6.9(15)	0
1990	Det	41	939	22.9(65)	0	34	7	361	10.6(39)	0
1991	Det	36	**929**	**25.8**(**71**)	0	25	14	385	**15.4**(**78**)	1
1992	Det	**42**	1006	24.0(89)	1	18	9	175	9.7(58)	1
1993	Det	28	688	24.6(95)	**1**	23	14	197	8.6(35)	0
1994	Det	45	1276	**28.4**(**102**)	**3**	21	12	233	11.1(24)	0
1995	Hou	53	1183	22.3(54)	0	30	**20**	303	10.1(20)	0
1996	Hou	50	**1224**	24.5(88)	0	22	15	205	9.3(40)	0
1997	Ten	8	185	23.1(33)	0	17	10	144	8.5(30)	0
1997	Phi	1	8	8.0(8)	0	2	5	17	8.5(11)	0
NFL	12	421	10250	24.3(102)	6	252	121	2753	10.9(80)	3
GRAYSON, DAVE										
1961	DalT-A	16	453	**28.3**(**73**)	0	0	—	—	—	—
1962	DalT-A	18	535	29.7(59)	0	1	—	0	0.0(0)	0
1963	KC-A	20	564	28.2(**99**)	**1**	1	—	2	2.0(2)	0
1964	KC-A	30	679	22.6(80)	0	0	—	—	—	—
1965	Oak-A	1	34	34.0(34)	0	0	—	—	—	—
1966	Oak-A	6	128	21.3(29)	0	0	—	—	—	—
1967	Oak-A	19	405	21.3(29)	0	3	2	11	3.7(5)	0
1969	Oak-A	0	—	—	—	4	0	28	7.0(12)	0
NFL	8	110	2798	25.4(99)	1	9	2	41	4.6(12)	0
GREEN, ROY										
1979	SL	41	1005	24.5(**106**)	**1**	8	3	42	5.3(14)	0
1980	SL	32	745	23.3(37)	0	16	6	168	10.5(57)	1
1981	SL	8	135	16.9(28)	0	0	—	—	—	—
1982	SL	0	—	—	—	3	0	20	6.7(11)	0
1983	SL	1	14	14.0(14)	0	0	—	—	—	—
1984	SL	1	18	18.0(18)	0	0	1	—	—	—
1990	Phx	1	15	15.0(15)	0	0	—	—	—	—
1991	Phi	5	70	14.0(21)	0	0	—	—	—	—
NFL	8	89	2002	22.5(106)	1	27	10	230	8.5(57)	1
GRIMES, BILLY										
1949	LAD-A	16	411	25.7(0)	0	5	—	67	13.4(0)	0
1950	GB	26	600	23.1(36)	0	29	—	**555**	19.1(85)	**2**
1951	GB	23	582	25.3(47)	0	16	—	100	6.3(26)	0
1952	GB	18	422	23.4(34)	0	18	—	179	9.9(72)	0
AAFC	1	16	411	25.7(0)	0	5	0	67	13.4(0)	0
NFL	3	67	1604	23.9(47)	0	63	0	834	13.2(85)	2
GROTH, JEFF										
1979	Hou	1	21	21.0(21)	0	0	—	—	—	—
1980	Hou	12	216	18.0(27)	0	1	0	0	0.0(0)	0
1981	NO	3	50	16.7(21)	0	37	6	436	11.8(36)	0
1982	NO	0	—	—	—	21	**13**	144	6.9(18)	0
1983	NO	0	—	—	—	39	**15**	275	7.1(30)	0
1984	NO	0	—	—	—	6	12	32	5.3(9)	0
1985	NO	0	—	—	—	1	0	0	0.0(0)	0
NFL	7	16	287	17.9(27)	0	105	46	887	8.4(36)	0
GULIFORD, ERIC										
1993	Min	5	101	20.2(29)	0	29	15	212	7.3(50)	0
1994	Min	0	—	—	—	5	6	14	2.8(12)	0
1995	Car	0	—	—	—	43	**22**	**475**	11.0(62)	**1**
1997	NO	43	1128	26.2(**102**)	1	47	**26**	498	10.6(32)	0
1998	NO	18	431	23.9(34)	0	10	7	101	10.1(40)	0
NFL	5	66	1660	25.2(102)	1	134	76	1300	9.7(62)	1
HAKIM, AZ-ZAHIR										
1999	SL	2	35	17.5(20)	0	**44**	22	461	10.5(84)	**1**
2000	SL	1	2	2.0(2)	0	32	17	**489**	**15.3**(**86**)	1
2001	SL	0	—	—	—	36	12	330	9.2(32)	0
2002	Det	0	—	—	—	10	4	148	14.8(72)	1
2003	Det	0	—	—	—	9	0	85	9.4(20)	0
2005	NO	9	171	19.0(29)	0	34	4	260	7.6(42)	0
NFL	6	12	208	17.3(29)	0	165	59	1773	10.7(86)	3
HALL, ALVIN										
1981	Det	25	525	21.0(36)	0	0	—	—	—	—
1982	Det	16	426	**26.6**(**96**)	**1**	0	—	—	—	—
1983	Det	23	492	21.4(32)	0	8	4	109	13.6(66)	0
1984	Det	19	385	20.3(46)	0	7	1	30	4.3(11)	0
1985	Det	39	886	22.7(54)	0	0	—	—	—	—
1987	Det	6	105	17.5(25)	0	0	—	—	—	—
NFL	6	128	2819	22.0(96)	1	15	5	139	9.3(66)	0
HALL, DANTE										
2000	KC	17	358	21.1(36)	0	6	5	37	6.2(22)	0
2001	KC	43	969	22.5(71)	0	32	6	235	7.3(26)	0
2002	KC	57	1354	23.8(88)	1	29	11	390	13.4(90)	**2**
2003	KC	57	**1478**	25.9(**100**)	**2**	29	14	472	**16.3**(**93**)	**2**
2004	KC	**68**	**1718**	25.3(97)	2	23	**17**	232	10.1(46)	0
2005	KC	65	1560	24.0(96)	1	42	6	276	6.6(52)	0
NFL	6	307	7437	24.2(100)	6	161	59	1642	10.2(93)	4
HALL, DINO										
1979	Cle	50	1014	20.3(33)	0	29	5	295	10.2(47)	0
1980	Cle	32	691	21.6(40)	0	6	3	41	6.8(14)	0
1981	Cle	36	813	22.6(48)	0	33	6	248	7.5(40)	0

YEAR	TEAM	KR	YDS	AVG (LG)	TD	PR	FC	YDS	AVG (LG)	TD
1982	Cle	22	430	19.5(32)	0	4	0	33	8.3(10)	0
1983	Cle	11	237	21.5(28)	0	39	12	284	7.3(19)	0
NFL	5	151	3185	21.1(48)	0	111	26	901	8.1(47)	0
HAMPTON, DAVE										
1969	GB	22	582	26.5(87)	**1**	0	—	—	—	—
1970	GB	6	188	31.3(**101**)	1	0	—	—	—	—
1971	GB	**46**	**1314**	28.6(90)	1	0	—	—	—	—
1972	Atl	25	535	21.4(52)	0	0	—	—	—	—
1973	Atl	11	258	23.5(42)	0	0	—	—	—	—
1976	Phi	3	46	15.3(23)	0	0	—	—	—	—
NFL	6	113	2923	25.9(101)	3	0	—	—	—	—
HAMPTON, LORENZO										
1985	Mia	45	1020	22.7(46)	0	0	—	—	—	—
1986	Mia	9	182	20.2(25)	0	0	—	—	—	—
1987	Mia	16	304	19.0(32)	0	0	—	—	—	—
1988	Mia	9	216	24.0(37)	0	0	—	—	—	—
1989	Mia	17	303	17.8(34)	0	0	—	—	—	—
NFL	5	96	2025	21.1(46)	0	0	—	—	—	—
HARMON, RONNIE										
1986	Buf	18	321	17.8(32)	0	0	—	—	—	—
1987	Buf	1	30	30.0(30)	0	0	—	—	—	—
1988	Buf	11	249	22.6(37)	0	0	—	—	—	—
1989	Buf	18	409	22.7(49)	0	0	—	—	—	—
1991	SD	2	25	12.5(14)	0	0	—	—	—	—
1992	SD	7	96	13.7(30)	0	0	—	—	—	—
1993	SD	1	18	18.0(18)	0	0	—	—	—	—
1994	SD	9	157	17.4(25)	0	0	—	—	—	—
1995	SD	4	25	6.3(9)	0	0	—	—	—	—
1996	Hou	4	69	17.3(20)	0	0	—	—	—	—
1997	Ten	1	16	16.0(16)	0	0	—	—	—	—
NFL	11	76	1415	18.6(49)	0	0	—	—	—	—
HARPER, BRUCE										
1977	NYJ	**42**	**1035**	24.6(60)	0	34	5	425	12.5(49)	0
1978	NYJ	**55**	**1280**	23.3(40)	0	30	4	378	12.6(**82**)	**1**
1979	NYJ	**55**	**1158**	21.1(52)	0	33	9	290	8.8(51)	0
1980	NYJ	**49**	**1070**	21.8(35)	0	28	7	242	8.6(24)	0
1981	NYJ	23	480	20.9(42)	0	35	9	265	7.6(46)	0
1982	NYJ	18	368	20.4(37)	0	23	5	184	8.0(24)	0
1983	NYJ	1	16	16.0(16)	0	0	—	—	—	—
NFL	7	243	5407	22.3(60)	0	183	39	1784	9.7(82)	1
HARRELL, WILLARD										
1975	GB	3	78	26.0(39)	0	21	5	136	6.5(25)	0
1976	GB	0	—	—	—	3	1	-7	-2.3(1)	0
1977	GB	3	48	16.0(24)	0	28	10	253	9.0(75)	**1**
1978	SL	19	389	20.5(32)	0	21	6	196	9.3(70)	**1**
1979	SL	22	497	22.6(53)	0	32	12	205	6.4(68)	0
1980	SL	19	348	18.3(33)	0	11	4	31	2.8(15)	0
1981	SL	7	118	16.9(29)	0	1	1	8	8.0(8)	0
1982	SL	8	150	18.8(31)	0	1	1	1	1.0(1)	0
1983	SL	3	62	20.7(26)	0	5	1	31	6.2(11)	0
1984	SL	13	231	17.8(28)	0	0	—	—	—	—
NFL	10	97	1921	19.8(53)	0	123	41	854	6.9(75)	2
HARRIS, ARLEN										
2003	SL	51	1175	23.0(42)	0	7	0	36	5.1(13)	0
2004	SL	47	951	20.2(29)	0	0	—	—	—	—
2005	SL	1	21	21.0(21)	0	0	—	—	—	—
NFL	3	99	2147	21.7(42)	0	7	0	36	5.1(13)	0
HARRIS, COREY										
1992	Hou	10	206	20.6(42)	0	6	0	17	2.8(13)	0
1992	GB	23	485	21.1(50)	0	0	—	—	—	—
1993	GB	16	482	**30.1**(**65**)	0	0	—	—	—	—
1994	GB	29	618	21.3(59)	0	0	—	—	—	—
1995	Sea	19	397	20.9(35)	0	0	—	—	—	—
1996	Sea	7	166	23.7(41)	0	0	—	—	—	—
1997	Mia	11	224	20.4(34)	0	0	—	—	—	—
1998	Bal	35	965	**27.6**(**95**)	**1**	0	—	—	—	—
1999	Bal	38	843	22.2(66)	0	0	—	—	—	—
2000	Bal	39	907	23.3(41)	0	0	—	—	—	—
2001	Bal	11	235	21.4(34)	0	0	—	—	—	—
NFL	10	238	5528	23.2(95)	1	6	0	17	2.8(13)	0
HARRIS, RICKIE										
1965	Was	5	96	19.2(36)	0	31	5	377	12.2(57)	1
1966	Was	20	405	20.3(53)	0	18	8	108	6.0(52)	**1**
1967	Was	25	580	23.2(47)	0	23	12	208	9.0(51)	0
1968	Was	23	579	25.2(49)	0	19	2	144	7.6(20)	0
1969	Was	19	458	24.1(54)	0	14	2	158	11.3(**86**)	**1**
1970	Was	10	208	20.8(31)	0	14	3	10	0.7(8)	0
1971	NE	0	—	—	—	5	1	19	3.8(9)	0
1972	NE	0	—	—	—	4	3	5	1.3(5)	0
NFL	8	102	2326	22.8(54)	0	128	36	1029	8.0(86)	3
HARRIS, ROD										
1989	NO	19	378	19.9(39)	0	27	7	196	7.3(20)	0
1990	Dal	1	0	0.0(0)	0	12	6	63	5.3(12)	0
1990	Phi	1	44	44.0(44)	0	16	2	151	9.4(30)	0
1991	Phi	28	473	16.9(33)	0	**53**	9	416	7.8(40)	0
NFL	3	49	895	18.3(44)	0	108	24	826	7.6(40)	0
HASTINGS, ANDRE										
1993	Pit	12	177	14.8(22)	0	0	—	—	—	—
1994	Pit	0	—	—	—	2	0	15	7.5(12)	0
1995	Pit	0	—	—	—	48	8	474	9.9(72)	**1**

YEAR	TEAM	KR	YDS	AVG(LG)	TD	PR	FC	YDS	AVG(LG)	TD
1996	Pit	1	42	42.0(42)	0	37	12	242	6.5(33)	0
1997	NO	0	—	—	—	1	0	-2	-2.0(2)	0
1998	NO	1	16	16.0(16)	0	22	17	307	14.0(76)	0
2000	TB	0	—	—	—	5	1	50	10.0(16)	0
NFL	7	14	235	16.8(42)	0	115	38	1086	9.4(76)	1
Hayes, Bob										
1965	Dal	17	450	26.5(66)	0	12	2	153	12.8(47)	0
1966	Dal	0	—	—	—	17	4	106	6.2(18)	0
1967	Dal	1	17	17.0(17)	0	24	6	**276**	11.5(69)	**1**
1968	Dal	1	20	20.0(20)	0	15	10	312	**20.8(90)**	**2**
1969	Dal	3	80	26.7(46)	0	18	5	179	9.9(50)	0
1970	Dal	0	—	—	—	15	7	116	7.7(34)	0
1971	Dal	1	14	14.0(14)	0	1	0	5	5.0(5)	0
1974	Dal	0	—	—	—	2	0	11	5.5(6)	0
NFL	8	23	581	25.3(66)	0	104	34	1158	11.1(90)	3
Haymond, Alvin										
1964	Bal	1	0	0.0(0)	0	1	1	6	6.0(6)	0
1965	Bal	20	614	30.7(53)	0	**41**	9	**403**	9.8(55)	0
1966	Bal	10	223	22.3(29)	0	**40**	8	**347**	8.7(64)	0
1967	Bal	13	326	25.1(48)	0	26	4	155	6.0(32)	0
1968	Phi	28	677	24.2(98)	1	15	6	201	13.4(54)	1
1969	LARm	16	375	23.4(36)	0	33	8	**435**	**13.2(52)**	0
1970	LARm	**35**	**1022**	29.2(98)	1	**53**	15	376	7.1(30)	0
1971	LARm	9	207	23.0(34)	0	24	11	123	5.1(28)	0
1972	Was	10	291	29.1(41)	0	6	1	1	0.2(6)	0
1973	Hou	28	703	25.1(47)	0	14	6	101	7.2(44)	0
NFL	10	170	4438	26.1(98)	2	253	69	2148	8.5(64)	1
Haynes, Abner										
1960	DalT-A	19	434	22.8(82)	0	14	—	**215**	**15.4(46)**	0
1961	DalT-A	8	270	33.8(88)	**1**	19	—	196	10.3(44)	0
1962	DalT-A	1	27	27.0(27)	0	15	—	119	7.9(30)	0
1963	KC-A	12	317	26.4(45)	0	6	—	57	9.5(20)	0
1964	KC-A	12	278	23.2(45)	0	1	—	11	11.0(11)	0
1965	Den-A	**34**	**901**	**26.5(60)**	0	14	—	121	8.6(57)	1
1966	Den-A	9	229	25.4(43)	0	10	—	119	11.9(42)	0
1967	Mia-A	22	444	20.2(51)	0	6	2	37	6.2(20)	0
1967	NYJ-A	4	125	31.3(42)	0	0	—	—	—	—
NFL	8	121	3025	25.0(88)	1	85	2	875	10.3(57)	1
Haynes, Mike										
1976	NE	0	—	—	—	**45**	0	**608**	13.5(89)	2
1977	NE	0	—	—	—	24	2	200	8.3(46)	0
1978	NE	0	—	—	—	14	2	183	13.1(35)	0
1979	NE	0	—	—	—	5	1	16	3.2(5)	0
1980	NE	0	—	—	—	17	2	140	8.2(35)	0
1981	NE	0	—	—	—	6	1	12	2.0(6)	0
1985	LARd	0	—	—	—	1	0	9	9.0(9)	0
NFL	7	0	—	—	—	112	8	1168	10.4(89)	2
Hebron, Vaughn										
1993	Phi	3	35	11.7(18)	0	0	—	—	—	—
1994	Phi	21	443	21.1(33)	0	0	—	—	—	—
1996	Den	45	1099	24.4(59)	0	0	—	—	—	—
1997	Den	43	1009	23.5(46)	0	0	—	—	—	—
1998	Den	46	**1216**	26.4(95)	**1**	0	—	—	—	—
NFL	5	158	3802	24.1(95)	1	0	—	—	—	—
Henry, Wally										
1977	Phi	0	—	—	—	2	0	25	12.5(22)	0
1978	Phi	3	54	18.0(24)	0	11	1	165	15.0(57)	**1**
1979	Phi	28	668	23.9(53)	0	35	7	320	9.1(34)	0
1980	Phi	7	154	22.0(39)	0	26	1	222	8.5(30)	0
1981	Phi	25	533	21.3(43)	0	**54**	8	396	7.3(52)	0
1982	Phi	**24**	541	22.5(44)	0	20	2	103	5.2(11)	0
NFL	6	87	1950	22.4(53)	0	148	19	1231	8.3(57)	1
Herron, Mack										
1973	NE	**41**	**1092**	26.6(92)	1	27	8	282	10.4(54)	0
1974	NE	28	629	22.5(62)	0	35	4	517	14.8(66)	0
1975	NE	2	75	37.5(40)	0	12	2	89	7.4(24)	0
1975	Atl	11	189	17.2(30)	0	10	1	94	9.4(24)	0
NFL	3	82	1985	24.2(92)	1	84	15	982	11.7(66)	0
Hicks, Cliff										
1987	LARm	4	119	29.8(53)	0	13	1	110	8.5(26)	0
1988	LARm	0	—	—	—	25	0	144	5.8(13)	0
1989	LARm	0	—	—	—	4	3	39	9.8(15)	0
1991	Buf	0	—	—	—	12	7	203	16.9(59)	0
1992	Buf	1	5	5.0(5)	0	29	6	289	10.0(42)	0
1993	NYJ	0	—	—	—	17	4	157	9.2(20)	0
1994	NYJ	2	30	15.0(16)	0	38	5	342	9.0(26)	0
NFL	7	7	154	22.0(53)	0	138	26	1284	9.3(59)	0
Hill, Drew										
1979	LARm	40	803	20.1(39)	0	1	0	0	0.0(0)	0
1980	LARm	43	880	20.5(98)	**1**	0	—	—	—	—
1981	LARm	**60**	1170	19.5(50)	0	2	0	22	11.0(12)	0
1982	LARm	2	42	21.0(24)	0	0	—	—	—	—
1984	LARm	26	543	20.9(40)	0	0	—	—	—	—
1985	Hou	1	22	22.0(22)	0	0	—	—	—	—
NFL	6	172	3460	20.1(98)	1	3	0	22	7.3(12)	0
Hill, Ike										
1970	Buf	9	165	18.3(31)	0	19	2	102	5.4(54)	0
1971	Buf	12	280	23.3(36)	0	14	2	133	9.5(68)	**1**
1973	ChiB	27	637	23.6(95)	**1**	36	6	204	5.7(**72**)	**1**

YEAR	TEAM	KR	YDS	AVG(LG)	TD	PR	FC	YDS	AVG(LG)	TD
1974	ChiB	0	—	—	—	33	2	183	5.5(15)	0
NFL	4	48	1082	22.5(95)	1	102	12	622	6.1(72)	2
Holland, Jamie										
1987	SD	19	410	21.6(46)	0	0	—	—	—	—
1988	SD	31	810	26.1(94)	**1**	0	—	—	—	—
1989	SD	29	510	17.6(34)	0	0	—	—	—	—
1990	LARd	32	655	20.5(87)	0	0	—	—	—	—
1991	LARd	22	421	19.1(27)	0	0	—	—	—	—
NFL	5	133	2806	21.1(94)	1	0	—	—	—	—
Horne, Tony										
1998	SL	56	1306	23.3(102)	1	1	0	0	0.0(0)	0
1999	SL	30	892	**29.7(101)**	**2**	5	0	22	4.4(9)	0
2000	SL	57	1379	24.2(**103**)	1	1	0	16	16.0(16)	0
NFL	3	143	3577	25.0(103)	4	7	0	38	5.4(16)	0
Howard, Desmond										
1992	Was	22	462	21.0(42)	0	6	3	84	14.0(55)	1
1993	Was	21	405	19.3(33)	0	4	0	25	6.3(13)	0
1995	Jax	10	178	17.8(24)	0	24	8	246	10.3(40)	0
1996	GB	22	460	20.9(40)	0	**58**	16	**875**	15.1(**92**)	**3**
1997	Oak	**61**	**1318**	21.6(45)	0	27	20	210	7.8(32)	0
1998	Oak	**49**	1040	21.2(42)	0	**45**	13	541	12.0(75)	**2**
1999	GB	19	364	19.2(31)	0	12	7	93	7.8(20)	**0**
1999	Det	15	298	19.9(35)	0	6	3	115	19.2(68)	**1**
2000	Det	57	1401	24.6(70)	0	31	24	457	14.7(**95**)	1
2001	Det	57	1446	25.4(91)	0	22	19	201	9.1(34)	0
2002	Det	26	587	22.6(70)	0	9	5	48	5.3(14)	0
NFL	10	359	7959	22.2(91)	0	244	118	2895	11.9(95)	8
Hughes, Tyrone										
1993	NO	30	753	25.1(**99**)	**1**	**37**	**21**	**503**	**13.6(83)**	**2**
1994	NO	**63**	**1556**	24.7(98)	2	21	8	143	6.8(35)	0
1995	NO	**66**	**1617**	24.5(83)	0	28	**22**	262	9.4(74)	0
1996	NO	**70**	**1791**	25.6(58)	0	30	**20**	152	5.1(16)	0
1997	ChiB	43	1008	23.4(58)	0	36	7	258	7.2(19)	0
1998	Dal	11	274	24.9(36)	0	10	3	93	9.3(35)	0
NFL	6	283	6999	24.7(99)	3	162	81	1411	8.7(83)	2
Humphery, Bobby										
1984	NYJ	22	675	**30.7(97)**	**1**	0	—	—	—	—
1985	NYJ	17	363	21.4(56)	0	1	0	0	0.0(0)	0
1986	NYJ	28	655	23.4(96)	**1**	0	—	—	—	—
1987	NYJ	18	357	19.8(47)	0	0	—	—	—	—
1988	NYJ	21	510	24.3(48)	0	0	—	—	—	—
1989	NYJ	24	414	17.3(52)	0	0	—	—	—	—
NFL	6	130	2974	22.9(97)	2	1	0	0	0.0(0)	0
Hunter, Al										
1977	Sea	36	820	22.8(41)	0	0	—	—	—	—
1978	Sea	16	385	24.1(38)	0	0	—	—	—	—
1979	Sea	15	299	19.9(30)	0	0	—	—	—	—
1980	Sea	11	213	19.4(40)	0	0	—	—	—	—
NFL	4	78	1717	22.0(41)	0	0	—	—	—	—
Hunter, Herman										
1985	Phi	48	1047	21.8(51)	0	1	0	6	6.0(6)	0
1986	Det	**49**	**1007**	20.6(54)	0	0	—	—	—	—
1987	Hou	4	79	19.8(28)	0	0	—	—	—	—
NFL	3	101	2133	21.1(54)	0	1	0	6	6.0(6)	0
Irvin, LeRoy										
1980	LARm	1	5	5.0(5)	0	42	7	296	7.0(26)	0
1981	LARm	0	—	—	—	46	6	**615**	**13.4(84)**	**3**
1982	LARm	0	—	—	—	22	1	242	11.0(63)	**1**
1983	LARm	1	22	22.0(22)	0	25	3	212	8.5(20)	0
1984	LARm	2	33	16.5(22)	0	9	0	83	9.2(22)	0
1987	LARm	0	—	—	—	1	0	0	0.0(0)	0
1988	LARm	0	—	—	—	1	1	2	2.0(2)	0
1989	LARm	0	—	—	—	1	2	7	7.0(7)	0
NFL	8	4	60	15.0(22)	0	147	20	1457	9.9(84)	4
Ismail, Qadry										
1993	Min	**42**	902	21.5(47)	0	0	—	—	—	—
1994	Min	35	807	23.1(61)	0	0	—	—	—	—
1995	Min	42	1037	24.7(71)	0	0	—	—	—	—
1996	Min	28	527	18.8(32)	0	0	—	—	—	—
1997	Mia	8	166	20.8(27)	0	0	—	—	—	—
1998	NO	28	590	21.1(39)	0	0	—	—	—	—
1999	Bal	4	55	13.8(19)	0	0	—	—	—	—
2000	Bal	2	51	25.5(38)	0	0	—	—	—	—
NFL	8	189	4135	21.9(71)	0	0	—	—	—	—
Ismail, Rocket										
1993	LARd	25	605	**24.2(66)**	0	0	—	—	—	—
1994	LARd	43	923	21.5(51)	0	0	—	—	—	—
1995	Oak	36	706	19.6(43)	0	0	—	—	—	—
1996	Car	5	100	20.0(30)	0	0	—	—	—	—
2001	Dal	0	—	—	—	1	3	20	20.0(20)	0
NFL	5	109	2334	21.4(66)	0	1	3	20	20.0(20)	0
Jackson, Bernard										
1972	Cin	21	509	24.2(62)	0	0	—	—	—	—
1973	Cin	21	520	24.8(41)	0	0	—	—	—	—
1974	Cin	29	682	23.5(45)	0	0	—	—	—	—
1975	Cin	25	587	23.5(39)	0	0	—	—	—	—
1978	Den	9	209	23.2(40)	0	0	—	—	—	—
1979	Den	4	53	13.3(21)	0	0	—	—	—	—
1980	SD	9	149	16.6(32)	0	0	—	—	—	—
NFL	7	118	2709	23.0(62)	0	0	—	—	—	—

YEAR	TEAM	KR	YDS	AVG(LG)	TD	PR	FC	YDS	AVG(LG)	TD
JACQUET, NATE										
1997	Ind	8	156	19.5(27)	0	13	0	96	7.4(17)	0
1998	Mia	4	103	25.8(37)	0	0	—	—	—	—
1999	Mia	1	26	26.0(26)	0	28	0	351	12.5(45)	0
2000	SD	0	—	—	—	30	8	211	7.0(35)	0
2001	Min	46	1012	22.0(53)	0	29	6	219	7.6(23)	0
NFL	5	59	1297	22.0(53)	0	100	14	877	8.8(45)	0
JAMES, DICK										
1956	Was	9	181	20.1(27)	0	6	—	84	14.0(24)	0
1957	Was	12	259	21.6(38)	0	11	—	83	7.5(27)	0
1958	Was	9	212	23.6(39)	0	6	—	37	6.2(21)	0
1959	Was	23	503	21.9(38)	0	21	—	95	4.5(26)	0
1960	Was	19	458	24.1(48)	0	7	—	46	6.6(20)	0
1961	Was	21	617	29.4(48)	0	12	—	90	7.5(18)	0
1962	Was	32	889	27.8(72)	0	19	—	145	7.6(33)	0
1963	Was	30	830	27.7(48)	0	16	6	214	**13.4(39)**	0
1964	NYG	23	515	22.4(30)	0	21	10	153	7.3(31)	0
1965	Min	11	212	19.3(28)	0	1	3	5	5.0(5)	0
NFL	10	189	4676	24.7(72)	0	120	19	952	7.9(39)	0
JAMES, LIONEL										
1984	SD	**43**	**959**	22.3(55)	0	30	9	208	6.9(58)	1
1985	SD	36	779	21.6(46)	0	25	8	213	8.5(24)	0
1986	SD	18	315	17.5(31)	0	9	6	94	10.4(21)	0
1987	SD	2	41	20.5(21)	0	32	7	**400**	12.5(81)	1
1988	SD	0	—	—	—	28	**11**	278	9.9(24)	0
NFL	5	99	2094	21.2(55)	0	124	41	1193	9.6(81)	2
JANCIK, BOBBY										
1962	Hou-A	24	726	**30.3(61)**	0	14	—	116	8.3(21)	0
1963	Hou-A	**45**	**1317**	29.3(53)	0	13	—	145	11.2(56)	0
1964	Hou-A	21	488	23.2(42)	0	12	—	220	18.3(82)	1
1965	Hou-A	18	430	23.9(42)	0	12	—	85	7.1(25)	0
1966	Hou-A	**34**	**875**	25.7(53)	0	10	—	62	6.2(28)	0
1967	Hou-A	16	349	21.8(49)	0	6	2	19	3.2(19)	0
NFL	6	158	4185	26.5(61)	0	67	2	647	9.7(82)	1
JENKINS, KEN										
1983	Det	22	459	20.9(30)	0	23	1	230	10.0(43)	0
1984	Det	18	396	22.0(32)	0	1	0	1	1.0(1)	0
1985	Was	41	1018	24.8(95)	0	26	9	272	10.5(28)	0
1986	Was	27	554	20.5(37)	0	28	11	270	9.6(39)	0
NFL	4	108	2427	22.5(95)	0	78	21	773	9.9(43)	0
JENKINS, MARTAY										
2000	Arz	82	**2186**	26.7(98)	1	1	0	1	1.0(1)	0
2001	Arz	49	1120	22.9(70)	0	0	—	—	—	—
2002	Arz	20	559	**28.0(95)**	1	0	—	—	—	—
NFL	3	151	3865	25.6(98)	2	1	0	1	1.0(1)	0
JENKINS, RONNEY										
2000	SD	**67**	1531	22.9(93)	1	0	—	—	—	—
2001	SD	**58**	**1541**	26.6(93)	2	0	—	—	—	—
2002	SD	40	925	23.1(56)	0	0	—	—	—	—
2003	Oak	25	553	22.1(33)	0	0	—	—	—	—
NFL	4	190	4550	23.9(93)	3	0	—	—	—	—
JENNINGS, STANFORD										
1984	Cin	22	452	20.5(46)	0	0	—	—	—	—
1985	Cin	13	218	16.8(26)	0	0	—	—	—	—
1986	Cin	12	257	21.4(41)	0	0	—	—	—	—
1987	Cin	2	32	16.0(18)	0	0	—	—	—	—
1988	Cin	32	684	21.4(**98**)	1	0	—	—	—	—
1989	Cin	26	525	20.2(33)	0	0	—	—	—	—
1990	Cin	29	584	20.1(33)	0	0	—	—	—	—
1991	NO	12	213	17.8(24)	0	0	—	—	—	—
NFL	8	148	2965	20.0(98)	1	0	—	—	—	—
JOHNSON, BETHEL										
2003	NE	30	847	28.2(92)	1	1	0	2	2.0(2)	0
2004	NE	41	1016	24.8(93)	1	4	1	8	2.0(6)	0
2005	NE	31	694	22.4(54)	0	1	0	11	11.0(11)	0
NFL	3	102	2557	25.1(93)	2	6	1	21	3.5(11)	0
JOHNSON, BILLY										
1974	Hou	29	785	27.1(67)	0	30	3	409	13.6(49)	0
1975	Hou	33	798	24.2(81)	1	40	1	612	**15.3(83)**	3
1976	Hou	26	579	22.3(53)	0	38	**9**	403	10.6(46)	0
1977	Hou	25	630	25.2(76)	1	35	**8**	539	**15.4(87)**	2
1978	Hou	4	73	18.3(22)	0	8	0	60	7.5(20)	0
1979	Hou	4	37	9.3(12)	0	4	0	17	4.3(16)	0
1982	Atl	0	—	—	—	24	4	273	**11.4(71)**	0
1983	Atl	0	—	—	—	46	4	**489**	10.6(71)	1
1984	Atl	2	39	19.5(21)	0	15	1	152	10.1(37)	0
1985	Atl	0	—	—	—	10	0	82	8.2(18)	0
1986	Atl	0	—	—	—	8	8	87	10.9(30)	0
1987	Atl	0	—	—	—	21	6	168	8.0(45)	0
1988	Was	0	—	—	—	3	1	26	8.7(15)	0
NFL	13	123	2941	23.9(81)	2	282	45	3317	11.8(87)	6
JOHNSON, BUTCH										
1976	Dal	28	693	24.8(74)	0	45	11	489	10.9(55)	0
1977	Dal	22	536	24.4(64)	0	50	**15**	423	8.5(38)	0
1978	Dal	29	603	20.8(56)	0	51	12	401	7.9(23)	0
NFL	3	79	1832	23.2(74)	0	146	38	1313	9.0(55)	0
JOHNSON, KENNY										
1980	Atl	0	—	—	—	23	5	281	**12.2(56)**	0
1981	Atl	0	—	—	—	4	6	6	1.5(4)	0

YEAR	TEAM	KR	YDS	AVG(LG)	TD	PR	FC	YDS	AVG(LG)	TD
1983	Atl	11	224	20.4(28)	0	0	—	—	—	—
1984	Atl	19	359	18.9(27)	0	10	1	79	7.9(14)	0
1985	Atl	1	20	20.0(20)	0	0	—	—	—	—
1987	Hou	2	24	12.0(18)	0	24	5	196	8.2(26)	0
1988	Hou	6	157	26.2(56)	0	30	6	170	5.7(16)	0
1989	Hou	21	372	17.7(39)	0	19	**21**	122	6.4(19)	0
NFL	8	60	1156	19.3(56)	0	110	38	854	7.8(56)	0
JOHNSON, LEON										
1997	NYJ	12	319	26.6(101)	1	51	6	**619**	12.1(66)	1
1998	NYJ	16	366	22.9(37)	0	29	12	203	7.0(23)	0
1999	NYJ	2	31	15.5(17)	0	1	1	6	6.0(6)	0
2000	NYJ	6	117	19.5(27)	0	10	0	62	6.2(16)	0
2001	ChiB	14	286	20.4(33)	0	28	10	255	9.1(35)	0
2002	ChiB	21	418	19.9(36)	0	28	10	288	10.3(30)	0
2003	SD	50	1151	23.0(60)	0	24	5	184	7.7(21)	0
NFL	7	121	2688	22.2(101)	1	171	44	1617	9.5(66)	1
JOHNSON, VANCE										
1985	Den	30	740	24.7(39)	0	30	6	260	8.7(38)	0
1986	Den	2	21	10.5(21)	0	3	0	36	12.0(19)	0
1987	Den	7	140	20.0(34)	0	1	0	9	9.0(9)	0
1988	Den	0	—	—	—	0	1	—	—	—
1989	Den	0	—	—	—	12	6	118	9.8(34)	0
1990	Den	6	126	21.0(39)	0	11	11	92	8.4(29)	0
1991	Den	0	—	—	—	24	14	174	7.3(20)	0
NFL	7	45	1027	22.8(39)	0	81	38	689	8.5(38)	0
JONES, CLINT										
1967	Min	25	597	23.9(96)	1	0	—	—	—	—
1968	Min	4	60	15.0(22)	0	0	—	—	—	—
1969	Min	17	444	26.1(71)	0	0	—	—	—	—
1970	Min	19	452	23.8(41)	0	0	—	—	—	—
1971	Min	12	329	27.4(47)	0	0	—	—	—	—
1972	Min	12	327	27.3(49)	0	0	—	—	—	—
1973	SD	10	217	21.7(40)	0	0	—	—	—	—
NFL	7	99	2426	24.5(96)	1	0	—	—	—	—
JONES, JAMES										
1980	Dal	32	720	22.5(41)	0	54	4	**548**	10.1(52)	0
1981	Dal	27	517	19.1(33)	0	33	2	188	5.7(17)	0
1982	Dal	2	46	23.0(27)	0	0	—	—	—	—
1985	Dal	9	161	17.9(26)	0	0	—	—	—	—
NFL	4	70	1444	20.6(41)	0	87	6	736	8.5(52)	0
JONES, MARK										
2004	NYG	2	37	18.5(20)	0	34	11	227	6.7(29)	0
2005	TB	5	95	19.0(24)	0	**51**	18	**492**	9.6(31)	0
NFL	2	7	132	18.9(24)	0	85	29	719	8.5(31)	0
KASPER, KEVIN										
2001	Den	14	372	26.6(37)	0	0	—	—	—	—
2002	Den	15	393	26.2(56)	0	0	—	—	—	—
2002	Sea	8	185	23.1(34)	0	0	—	—	—	—
2002	Arz	32	722	22.6(40)	0	0	—	—	—	—
2003	Arz	5	136	27.2(37)	0	0	—	—	—	—
2004	NE	3	61	20.3(21)	0	0	—	—	—	—
NFL	4	77	1869	24.3(56)	0	0	—	—	—	—
KAUFMAN, NAPOLEON										
1995	Oak	22	572	26.0(84)	1	0	—	—	—	—
1996	Oak	25	548	21.9(39)	0	0	—	—	—	—
1999	Oak	42	831	19.8(48)	0	0	—	—	—	—
2000	Oak	9	198	22.0(31)	0	0	—	—	—	—
NFL	4	98	2149	21.9(84)	1	0	—	—	—	—
KELLY, LEROY										
1964	Cle	24	582	24.3(45)	0	9	7	171	19.0(68)	1
1965	Cle	24	621	25.9(51)	0	17	6	265	**15.6(67)**	2
1966	Cle	19	403	21.2(49)	0	13	6	104	8.0(52)	0
1967	Cle	5	131	26.2(32)	0	9	4	59	6.6(32)	0
1968	Cle	1	10	10.0(10)	0	1	0	9	9.0(9)	0
1969	Cle	2	26	13.0(14)	0	7	0	28	4.0(13)	0
1970	Cle	0	—	—	—	2	0	15	7.5(12)	0
1971	Cle	1	11	11.0(11)	0	30	4	292	**9.7(74)**	0
1972	Cle	0	—	—	—	5	3	40	8.0(14)	0
1973	Cle	0	—	—	—	1	0	7	7.0(7)	0
NFL	10	76	1784	23.5(51)	0	94	30	990	10.5(74)	3
KENNISON, EDDIE										
1996	SL	23	454	19.7(44)	0	29	16	423	14.6(78)	2
1997	SL	1	14	14.0(14)	0	34	20	247	7.3(43)	0
1998	SL	0	—	—	—	40	**25**	415	10.4(71)	1
1999	NO	0	—	—	—	35	**23**	258	7.4(18)	0
2003	KC	0	—	—	—	3	0	70	23.3(46)	0
2004	KC	1	36	36.0(36)	0	0	—	—	—	—
2005	KC	0	—	—	—	1	1	17	17.0(17)	0
NFL	7	25	504	20.2(44)	0	142	85	1430	10.1(78)	3
KINCHEN, TODD										
1992	LARm	4	63	15.8(19)	0	4	1	103	25.8(61)	**2**
1993	LARm	6	96	16.0(22)	0	7	4	32	4.6(8)	0
1994	LARm	21	510	24.3(46)	0	16	5	158	9.9(40)	0
1995	SL	35	743	21.2(50)	0	**53**	7	416	7.8(27)	0
1996	Den	0	—	—	—	26	4	300	11.5(40)	0
1997	Atl	1	18	18.0(18)	0	**52**	13	446	8.6(38)	0
1998	Atl	0	—	—	—	6	5	38	6.3(9)	0
NFL	7	67	1430	21.3(50)	0	164	39	1493	9.1(61)	2

YEAR	TEAM	KR	YDS	AVG (LG)	TD	PR	FC	YDS	AVG (LG)	TD
Kirby, Terry										
1993	Mia	4	85	21.3(26)	0	0	—	—	—	—
1996	SF	1	22	22.0(22)	0	1	4	3	3.0(3)	0
1997	SF	3	124	41.3(101)	1	0	—	—	—	—
1998	SF	17	340	20.0(33)	0	0	—	—	—	—
1999	Cle	11	230	20.9(28)	0	0	—	—	—	—
2001	Oak	46	1066	23.2(90)	1	0	—	—	—	—
2002	Oak	19	425	22.4(96)	1	0	0	79	—	—
NFL	7	101	2292	22.7(101)	3	1	4	82	82.0(79)	1
Laird, Bruce										
1972	Bal	29	**843**	**29.1**(**73**)	0	**34**	11	**303**	8.9(42)	0
1973	Bal	24	547	22.8(51)	0	15	6	72	4.8(13)	0
1974	Bal	19	499	26.3(55)	0	11	0	30	2.7(10)	0
1975	Bal	31	799	25.8(65)	0	0	—	—	—	—
1976	Bal	7	143	20.4(25)	0	0	—	—	—	—
1977	Bal	24	541	22.5(35)	0	0	—	—	—	—
1979	Bal	3	34	11.3(16)	0	0	—	—	—	—
1983	SD	15	342	22.8(41)	0	1	0	0	0.0(0)	0
NFL	8	152	3748	24.7(73)	0	61	17	405	6.6(42)	0
Lary, Yale										
1952	Det	12	303	25.3(41)	0	16	—	182	11.4(58)	1
1953	Det	6	116	19.3(33)	0	13	—	115	8.8(74)	**1**
1956	Det	4	76	19.0(29)	0	22	—	70	3.2(38)	0
1957	Det	0	—	—	—	25	—	139	5.6(36)	0
1958	Det	0	—	—	—	27	—	196	7.3(**71**)	**1**
1959	Det	0	—	—	—	21	—	43	2.0(12)	0
1960	Det	0	—	—	—	1	—	5	5.0(5)	0
1961	Det	0	—	—	—	1	—	8	8.0(8)	0
NFL	8	22	495	22.5(41)	0	126	0	758	6.0(74)	3
Lavette, Robert										
1985	Dal	34	682	20.1(34)	0	0	—	—	—	—
1986	Dal	36	699	19.4(37)	0	18	3	92	5.1(28)	0
1987	Dal	4	72	18.0(22)	0	0	1	—	—	—
1987	Phi	2	37	18.5(19)	0	0	—	—	—	—
NFL	3	76	1490	19.6(37)	0	18	4	92	5.1(28)	0
Lawrence, Rolland										
1973	Atl	3	71	23.7(28)	0	0	1	—	—	—
1975	Atl	4	80	20.0(24)	0	0	—	—	—	—
1976	Atl	21	521	24.8(36)	0	**54**	5	372	6.9(24)	0
1977	Atl	1	13	13.0(13)	0	51	10	352	6.9(37)	0
1978	Atl	0	—	—	—	1	1	17	17.0(17)	0
1980	Atl	0	—	—	—	3	0	-7	-2.3(6)	0
NFL	6	29	685	23.6(36)	0	109	17	734	6.7(37)	0
Leonard, Tony										
1976	SF	26	553	21.3(39)	0	35	5	293	8.4(60)	**1**
1977	SF	1	68	68.0(68)	0	22	2	154	7.0(19)	0
1978	SF	0	—	—	—	8	5	26	3.3(14)	0
1978	Det	0	—	—	—	10	0	114	11.4(24)	0
1979	Det	3	70	23.3(28)	0	1	0	7	7.0(7)	0
NFL	4	30	691	23.0(68)	0	76	12	594	7.8(60)	1
LeVias, Jerry										
1969	Hou-A	38	940	24.7(87)	0	**35**	11	**292**	8.3(46)	0
1970	Hou	26	598	23.0(37)	0	25	8	213	8.5(33)	0
1971	SD	24	559	23.3(71)	0	22	8	145	6.6(19)	0
1972	SD	0	—	—	—	1	0	-4	-4.0(4)	0
1974	SD	6	116	19.3(27)	0	5	0	41	8.2(22)	0
NFL	5	94	2213	23.5(87)	0	88	27	687	7.8(46)	0
Levy, Chuck										
1994	Arz	26	513	19.7(31)	0	0	—	—	—	—
1997	SF	36	793	22.0(59)	0	6	2	109	18.2(73)	**1**
1998	SF	22	383	17.4(30)	0	0	—	—	—	—
NFL	3	84	1689	20.1(59)	0	6	2	109	18.2(73)	1
Lewis, Cliff										
1946	Cle-A	3	70	23.3(0)	0	8	—	133	16.6(0)	0
1947	Cle-A	4	71	17.8(0)	0	7	—	84	12.0(0)	0
1948	Cle-A	7	147	21.0(0)	0	**26**	—	258	9.9(0)	0
1949	Cle-A	0	—	—	—	20	—	174	8.7(0)	0
1950	Cle	0	—	—	—	2	—	13	6.5(8)	0
1951	Cle	0	—	—	—	14	—	48	3.4(11)	0
AAFC	4	14	288	20.6(0)	0	61	0	649	10.6(0)	0
NFL	2	0	—	—	—	16	0	61	3.8(11)	0
Lewis, Jermaine										
1996	Bal	41	883	21.5(44)	0	36	13	339	9.4(46)	0
1997	Bal	41	905	22.1(51)	0	28	13	437	**15.6**(**89**)	2
1998	Bal	6	145	24.2(37)	0	32	10	405	12.7(**87**)	**2**
1999	Bal	8	158	19.8(25)	0	**57**	18	452	7.9(33)	0
2000	Bal	1	23	23.0(23)	0	36	9	578	16.1(**89**)	**2**
2001	Bal	42	1039	24.7(76)	0	**42**	9	**519**	12.4(62)	0
2002	Hou	46	961	20.9(45)	0	36	**17**	280	7.8(48)	0
2003	Jax	6	111	18.5(26)	0	5	0	45	9.0(14)	0
2004	Jax	21	386	18.4(26)	0	23	7	227	9.9(50)	0
NFL	9	212	4611	21.8(76)	0	295	96	3282	11.1(89)	6
Lewis, Leo										
1983	Min	1	25	25.0(25)	0	3	3	52	17.3(34)	0
1984	Min	1	31	31.0(31)	0	4	1	31	7.8(13)	0
1986	Min	0	—	—	—	7	4	53	7.6(13)	0
1987	Min	0	—	—	—	22	7	275	12.5(78)	1
1988	Min	1	12	12.0(12)	0	**58**	19	550	9.5(64)	0
1989	Min	2	30	15.0(15)	0	44	**27**	446	10.1(65)	0
1990	Cle	0	—	—	—	8	**7**	56	7.0(18)	0

YEAR	TEAM	KR	YDS	AVG (LG)	TD	PR	FC	YDS	AVG (LG)	TD
1990	Min	3	39	13.0(15)	0	25	**15**	180	7.2(30)	0
1991	Min	0	—	—	—	30	15	225	7.5(44)	0
NFL	8	8	137	17.1(31)	0	201	98	1868	9.3(78)	1
Lewis, Michael										
2001	NO	32	762	23.8(68)	0	14	0	81	5.8(32)	0
2002	NO	**70**	**1807**	25.8(97)	**2**	44	6	**625**	14.2(83)	1
2003	NO	45	1068	23.7(53)	0	30	10	275	9.2(27)	0
2004	NO	51	1215	23.8(96)	1	34	11	382	11.2(53)	0
2005	NO	8	137	17.1(20)	0	4	0	8	2.0(5)	0
NFL	5	206	4989	24.2(97)	3	126	27	1371	10.9(83)	1
Lewis, Nate										
1990	SD	17	383	22.5(39)	0	13	8	117	9.0(63)	**1**
1991	SD	23	578	**25.1**(**95**)	**1**	5	5	59	11.8(26)	0
1992	SD	19	402	21.2(62)	0	13	5	127	9.8(25)	0
1993	SD	33	684	20.7(60)	0	3	2	17	5.7(7)	0
1994	ChiB	35	874	25.0(55)	0	1	3	7	7.0(7)	0
1995	ChiB	42	904	21.5(52)	0	0	—	—	—	—
NFL	6	169	3825	22.6(95)	1	35	23	327	9.3(63)	1
Lewis, Woodley										
1950	LARm	2	47	23.5(27)	0	1	—	0	0.0(0)	0
1951	LARm	4	67	16.8(24)	0	1	—	12	12.0(12)	0
1952	LARm	16	345	21.6(47)	0	19	—	351	18.5(82)	**2**
1953	LARm	**32**	**830**	25.9(69)	0	35	—	**267**	7.6(**78**)	**1**
1954	LARm	**34**	**836**	24.6(88)	1	22	—	82	3.7(16)	0
1955	LARm	20	450	22.5(32)	0	29	—	105	3.6(22)	0
1956	ChiC	1	22	22.0(22)	0	5	—	22	4.4(7)	0
1957	ChiC	26	682	26.2(52)	0	24	—	175	7.3(31)	0
1958	ChiC	2	46	23.0(25)	0	2	—	12	6.0(9)	0
NFL	9	137	3325	24.3(88)	1	138	0	1026	7.4(82)	3
Lipps, Louis										
1984	Pit	0	—	—	—	**53**	2	**656**	12.4(**76**)	**1**
1985	Pit	13	237	18.2(26)	0	36	2	437	12.1(71)	**2**
1986	Pit	0	—	—	—	3	1	16	5.3(10)	0
1987	Pit	0	—	—	—	7	1	46	6.6(12)	0
1988	Pit	0	—	—	—	4	2	30	7.5(11)	0
1989	Pit	0	—	—	—	4	0	27	6.8(9)	0
1990	Pit	1	9	9.0(9)	0	0	—	—	—	—
1992	NO	0	—	—	—	5	1	22	4.4(16)	0
NFL	8	14	246	17.6(26)	0	112	9	1234	11.0(76)	3
Little, Floyd										
1967	Den-A	35	942	26.9(60)	0	16	6	270	**16.9**(**72**)	**1**
1968	Den-A	26	649	25.0(89)	0	24	5	261	10.9(67)	1
1969	Den-A	3	81	27.0(30)	0	6	3	70	11.7(52)	0
1970	Den	6	126	21.0(28)	0	22	3	187	8.5(24)	0
1971	Den	7	199	28.4(48)	0	0	—	—	—	—
1972	Den	3	48	16.0(22)	0	8	2	64	8.0(29)	0
1973	Den	0	—	—	—	1	0	7	7.0(7)	0
1974	Den	8	171	21.4(31)	0	4	1	34	8.5(17)	0
1975	Den	16	307	19.2(32)	0	0	—	—	—	—
NFL	9	104	2523	24.3(89)	0	81	20	893	11.0(72)	2
Livers, Virgil										
1975	ChiB	26	529	20.3(40)	0	42	0	**456**	10.9(39)	0
1976	ChiB	1	14	14.0(14)	0	28	0	205	7.3(51)	0
1977	ChiB	0	—	—	—	6	1	46	7.7(21)	0
1978	ChiB	0	—	—	—	10	0	31	3.1(13)	0
NFL	4	27	543	20.1(40)	0	86	1	738	8.6(51)	0
Logan, Marc										
1987	Cin	3	31	10.3(16)	0	0	—	—	—	—
1988	Cin	4	80	20.0(24)	0	0	—	—	—	—
1989	Mia	24	613	25.5(**97**)	**1**	0	—	—	—	—
1990	Mia	20	367	18.4(35)	0	0	—	—	—	—
1991	Mia	12	191	15.9(31)	0	0	—	—	—	—
1992	SF	22	478	21.7(82)	0	0	—	—	—	—
1997	Was	4	70	17.5(24)	0	0	—	—	—	—
NFL	7	89	1830	20.6(97)	1	0	—	—	—	—
Lyles, Lenny										
1958	Bal	11	398	36.2(**103**)	**2**	0	—	—	—	—
1959	SF	**25**	**565**	22.6(46)	0	0	—	—	—	—
1960	SF	17	526	**30.9**(**97**)	**1**	0	—	—	—	—
1961	Bal	28	672	24.0(64)	0	0	—	—	—	—
NFL	4	81	2161	26.7(103)	3	0	—	—	—	—
Mack, Tremain										
1998	Cin	45	1165	25.9(**97**)	**1**	0	—	—	—	—
1999	Cin	51	1382	**27.1**(**99**)	**1**	0	—	—	—	—
2000	Cin	50	1036	20.7(50)	0	0	—	—	—	—
NFL	3	146	3583	24.5(99)	2	0	—	—	—	—
Mandley, Pete										
1984	Det	22	390	17.7(32)	0	2	2	0	0.0(0)	0
1985	Det	6	152	25.3(35)	0	38	5	403	10.6(63)	**1**
1986	Det	2	37	18.5(37)	0	43	9	420	9.8(81)	1
1987	Det	0	—	—	—	23	6	250	10.9(54)	0
1988	Det	0	—	—	—	37	7	287	7.8(25)	0
1989	KC	1	0	0.0(0)	0	19	2	151	7.9(19)	0
1990	KC	4	51	12.8(23)	0	0	—	—	—	—
NFL	7	35	630	18.0(37)	0	162	31	1511	9.3(81)	2
Marion, Brock										
1994	Dal	2	39	19.5(21)	0	0	—	—	—	—
1995	Dal	1	16	16.0(16)	0	0	—	—	—	—
1996	Dal	3	68	22.7(37)	0	0	—	—	—	—
1997	Dal	10	311	31.1(49)	0	0	—	—	—	—

YEAR	TEAM	KR	YDS	AVG(LG)	TD	PR	FC	YDS	AVG(LG)	TD
1998	Mia	6	109	18.2(28)	0	0	—	—	—	—
1999	Mia	**62**	**1524**	24.6(93)	0	0	—	—	—	—
2000	Mia	22	513	23.3(47)	0	0	—	—	—	—
2001	Mia	17	371	21.8(55)	0	0	—	—	—	—
NFL	8	123	2951	24.0(93)	0	0	—	—	—	—
MARSHALL, LARRY										
1972	KC	23	651	28.3(48)	0	18	5	103	5.7(29)	0
1973	KC	14	391	27.9(38)	0	29	1	180	6.2(31)	0
1974	Min	4	56	14.0(24)	0	5	2	46	9.2(19)	0
1974	Phi	16	412	25.8(44)	0	8	0	72	9.0(21)	0
1975	Phi	22	557	25.3(33)	0	23	2	235	10.2(39)	0
1976	Phi	**30**	651	21.7(41)	0	27	9	290	10.7(29)	0
1977	Phi	20	455	22.8(44)	0	46	5	**489**	**10.6(48)**	0
1978	KC	7	173	24.7(40)	0	6	0	51	8.5(20)	0
1978	LARm	2	50	25.0(38)	0	0	—	—	—	—
NFL	7	138	3396	24.6(48)	0	162	24	1466	9.0(48)	0
MARTIN, KELVIN										
1987	Dal	12	237	19.8(38)	0	22	2	216	9.8(38)	0
1988	Dal	12	210	17.5(31)	0	44	15	360	8.2(21)	0
1989	Dal	0	—	—	—	4	5	32	8.0(12)	0
1990	Dal	0	—	—	—	5	3	46	9.2(17)	0
1991	Dal	3	47	15.7(25)	0	21	8	244	11.6(**85**)	1
1992	Dal	24	503	21.0(59)	0	**42**	**18**	**532**	12.7(79)	**2**
1993	Sea	3	38	12.7(15)	0	32	15	270	8.4(33)	0
1994	Sea	2	30	15.0(16)	0	33	**20**	280	8.5(23)	0
1995	Phi	20	388	19.4(38)	0	17	10	214	12.6(38)	0
1996	Dal	0	—	—	—	41	10	373	9.1(22)	0
NFL	10	76	1453	19.1(59)	0	261	106	2567	9.8(85)	3
MARTIN, MIKE										
1983	Cin	1	19	19.0(19)	0	23	3	227	9.9(19)	0
1984	Cin	19	386	20.3(44)	0	24	5	376	**15.7(55)**	0
1985	Cin	**48**	**1104**	23.0(45)	0	32	8	268	8.4(26)	0
1986	Cin	4	83	20.8(21)	0	13	6	96	7.4(14)	0
1987	Cin	3	51	17.0(20)	0	28	5	277	9.9(21)	0
1988	Cin	0	—	—	—	5	5	30	6.0(10)	0
1989	Cin	0	—	—	—	15	4	107	7.1(17)	0
NFL	7	75	1643	21.9(45)	0	140	36	1381	9.9(55)	0
MARTIN, ROBBIE										
1981	Det	25	509	20.4(34)	0	52	8	450	8.7(45)	1
1982	Det	16	268	16.8(27)	0	26	5	275	10.6(58)	0
1983	Det	8	140	17.5(51)	0	15	3	183	12.2(81)	**1**
1984	Det	10	144	14.4(23)	0	25	8	210	8.4(23)	0
1985	Ind	32	638	19.9(36)	0	40	7	443	11.1(70)	1
1986	Ind	21	385	18.3(27)	0	17	5	109	6.4(25)	0
NFL	6	112	2084	18.6(51)	0	175	36	1670	9.5(81)	3
MARTIN, SAMMY										
1988	NE	31	735	23.7(95)	**1**	0	—	—	—	—
1989	NE	24	584	24.3(38)	0	19	2	164	8.6(28)	0
1990	NE	25	515	20.6(38)	0	1	0	1	1.0(1)	0
1991	NE	8	178	22.3(26)	0	0	—	—	—	—
1991	Ind	12	305	25.4(38)	0	0	—	—	—	—
NFL	4	100	2317	23.2(95)	1	20	2	165	8.3(28)	0
MASON, DERRICK										
1997	Ten	26	551	21.2(54)	0	13	3	95	7.3(29)	0
1998	Ten	8	154	19.3(26)	0	31	11	228	7.4(25)	0
1999	Ten	41	805	19.6(41)	0	26	15	225	8.7(65)	1
2000	Ten	42	1132	**27.0(66)**	0	**51**	17	**662**	13.0(69)	1
2001	Ten	34	748	22.0(**101**)	1	20	19	128	6.4(20)	0
2002	Ten	0	—	—	—	9	12	60	6.7(21)	0
2003	Ten	5	106	21.2(34)	0	8	5	99	12.4(21)	0
2004	Ten	0	—	—	—	24	12	93	3.9(13)	0
NFL	8	156	3496	22.4(101)	1	182	94	1590	8.7(69)	2
MATHIS, TERANCE										
1990	NYJ	43	787	18.3(35)	0	11	7	165	15.0(**98**)	**1**
1991	NYJ	29	599	20.7(50)	0	23	10	157	6.8(25)	0
1992	NYJ	28	492	17.6(32)	0	2	0	24	12.0(12)	0
1993	NYJ	7	102	14.6(28)	0	14	8	99	7.1(16)	0
1996	Atl	0	—	—	—	3	1	19	6.3(10)	0
1998	Atl	0	—	—	—	1	0	0	0.0(0)	0
NFL	6	107	1980	18.5(50)	0	54	26	464	8.6(98)	1
MATSON, OLLIE										
1952	ChiC	20	624	31.2(**100**)	**2**	9	—	86	9.6(23)	0
1954	ChiC	17	449	26.4(91)	1	11	—	100	9.1(59)	**1**
1955	ChiC	15	368	24.5(37)	0	13	—	**245**	**18.8(78)**	**2**
1956	ChiC	13	362	27.8(105)	**1**	5	—	39	7.8(16)	0
1957	ChiC	7	154	22.0(32)	0	10	—	54	5.4(28)	0
1958	ChiC	14	497	**35.5(101)**	**2**	0	—	—	—	—
1959	LARm	16	367	22.9(48)	0	14	—	61	4.4(20)	0
1960	LARm	9	216	24.0(42)	0	1	—	0	0.0(0)	0
1963	Det	3	61	20.3(30)	0	0	—	—	—	—
1964	Phi	3	104	34.7(43)	0	2	0	10	5.0(9)	0
1966	Phi	26	544	20.9(31)	0	0	—	—	—	—
NFL	11	143	3746	26.2(105)	6	65	0	595	9.2(78)	3
MATTHEWS, IRA										
1979	Oak	35	873	24.9(**104**)	**1**	32	7	165	5.2(20)	0
1980	Oak	29	585	20.2(45)	0	**48**	7	421	8.8(34)	0
1981	Oak	7	144	20.6(39)	0	15	2	92	6.1(26)	0
NFL	3	71	1602	22.6(104)	1	95	16	678	7.1(34)	0

YEAR	TEAM	KR	YDS	AVG(LG)	TD	PR	FC	YDS	AVG(LG)	TD
MAUTI, RICH										
1977	NO	27	609	22.6(38)	0	37	10	281	7.6(33)	0
1978	NO	17	388	22.8(39)	0	0	3	—	—	—
1979	NO	36	801	22.3(39)	0	27	13	218	8.1(33)	0
1980	NO	31	798	**25.7(52)**	0	11	5	111	10.1(18)	0
1982	NO	5	93	18.6(22)	0	0	—	—	—	—
1983	NO	8	147	18.4(35)	0	0	—	—	—	—
1984	Was	1	16	16.0(16)	0	1	1	2	2.0(2)	0
NFL	7	125	2852	22.8(52)	0	76	32	612	8.1(33)	0
McAFEE, FRED										
1991	NO	1	14	14.0(14)	0	0	—	—	—	—
1992	NO	19	393	20.7(38)	0	0	—	—	—	—
1993	NO	28	580	20.7(55)	0	0	—	—	—	—
1994	Arz	7	113	16.1(29)	0	0	—	—	—	—
1995	Pit	5	56	11.2(25)	0	0	—	—	—	—
1998	Pit	1	10	10.0(25)	0	0	—	—	—	—
2000	NO	10	251	25.1(52)	0	0	—	—	—	—
2001	NO	6	144	24.0(34)	0	0	—	—	—	—
2002	NO	2	69	34.5(51)	0	0	—	—	—	—
2003	NO	9	140	15.6(23)	0	0	—	—	—	—
2004	NO	8	137	17.1(26)	0	0	—	—	—	—
2005	NO	22	485	22.0(34)	0	0	—	—	—	—
NFL	12	118	2392	20.3(55)	0	0	—	—	—	—
McAFEE, GEORGE										
1940	ChiB	—	—	—	—	—	—	—	—	—
1941	ChiB	7	223	31.9(97)	**1**	5	—	158	31.6(74)	**1**
1945	ChiB	5	98	19.6(25)	0	1	—	8	8.0(8)	0
1946	ChiB	3	96	32.0(46)	0	1	—	24	24.0(24)	0
1947	ChiB	1	23	23.0(23)	0	18	—	261	14.5(35)	0
1948	ChiB	1	25	25.0(25)	0	**30**	—	**417**	13.9(60)	1
1949	ChiB	0	—	—	—	24	—	279	11.6(33)	0
1950	ChiB	1	23	23.0(23)	0	**33**	—	284	8.6(25)	0
NFL	8	18	488	27.1(97)	2	112	0	1431	12.8(74)	2
McCONKEY, PHIL										
1984	NYG	28	541	19.3(33)	0	46	15	306	6.7(31)	0
1985	NYG	12	234	19.5(43)	0	**53**	**18**	442	8.3(37)	0
1986	NYG	24	471	19.6(27)	0	32	12	253	7.9(22)	0
1987	NYG	1	8	8.0(8)	0	42	**14**	394	9.4(37)	0
1988	NYG	2	30	15.0(17)	0	40	**25**	313	7.8(35)	0
1989	Phx	2	40	20.0(21)	0	1	0	13	13.0(13)	0
1989	SD	0	—	—	—	14	15	111	7.9(29)	0
NFL	6	69	1324	19.2(43)	0	228	99	1832	8.0(37)	0
McDUFFIE, O.J.										
1993	Mia	32	755	23.6(48)	0	28	**22**	317	11.3(72)	**2**
1994	Mia	36	767	21.3(46)	0	32	15	228	7.1(26)	0
1995	Mia	23	564	24.5(47)	0	24	12	163	6.8(24)	0
1996	Mia	0	—	—	—	22	**24**	212	9.6(19)	0
1997	Mia	0	—	—	—	2	1	4	2.0(3)	0
1998	Mia	0	—	—	—	12	8	141	11.8(39)	0
1999	Mia	1	17	17.0(17)	0	7	8	62	8.9(21)	0
2000	Mia	0	—	—	—	0	1	—	—	—
NFL	8	92	2103	22.9(48)	0	127	91	1127	8.9(72)	2
McELHENNY, HUGH										
1952	SF	18	396	22.0(40)	0	20	—	284	14.2(**94**)	1
1953	SF	15	368	24.5(55)	0	15	—	104	6.9(25)	0
1954	SF	8	210	26.3(51)	0	8	—	78	9.8(32)	0
1955	SF	9	189	21.0(31)	0	7	—	10	1.4(10)	0
1956	SF	13	300	23.1(36)	0	15	—	38	2.5(12)	0
1957	SF	0	—	—	—	10	—	41	4.1(13)	0
1958	SF	2	31	15.5(18)	0	24	—	93	3.9(49)	0
1961	Min	2	59	29.5(35)	0	8	—	155	19.4(81)	1
1962	Min	7	160	22.9(40)	0	5	—	43	8.6(14)	0
1963	NYG	6	136	22.7(51)	0	13	3	74	5.7(13)	0
1964	Det	3	72	24.0(27)	0	1	0	0	0.0(0)	0
NFL	11	83	1921	23.1(55)	0	126	3	920	7.3(94)	2
McGEE, TERRENCE										
2003	Buf	8	160	20.0(26)	0	0	—	—	—	—
2004	Buf	52	1370	**26.3(104)**	**3**	0	—	—	—	—
2005	Buf	46	1391	**30.2(99)**	1	0	—	—	—	—
NFL	3	106	2921	27.6(104)	4	0	—	—	—	—
McGILL, RALPH										
1972	SF	10	192	19.2(30)	0	22	0	219	10.0(33)	0
1973	SF	17	374	22.0(43)	0	22	1	186	8.5(54)	0
1974	SF	0	—	—	—	20	3	166	8.3(47)	0
1975	SF	0	—	—	—	31	0	290	9.4(34)	0
1976	SF	0	—	—	—	10	1	103	10.3(50)	**1**
1978	NO	0	—	—	—	1	0	5	5.0(5)	0
NFL	6	27	566	21.0(43)	0	106	5	969	9.1(54)	1
McKINNON, DENNIS										
1983	ChiB	2	42	21.0(25)	0	34	3	316	9.3(59)	**1**
1984	ChiB	0	—	—	—	5	0	62	12.4(18)	0
1985	ChiB	1	16	16.0(16)	0	4	0	44	11.0(17)	0
1987	ChiB	0	—	—	—	40	4	405	10.1(**94**)	**2**
1988	ChiB	0	—	—	—	34	8	277	8.1(23)	0
1989	ChiB	0	—	—	—	10	3	67	6.7(17)	0
1990	Dal	0	—	—	—	2	1	20	10.0(20)	0
NFL	7	3	58	19.3(25)	0	129	19	1191	9.2(94)	3
McLEMORE, DANA										
1982	SF	16	353	22.1(45)	0	7	0	156	22.3(**93**)	**1**
1983	SF	30	576	19.2(39)	0	31	6	331	10.7(56)	**1**

YEAR	TEAM	KR	YDS	AVG(LG)	TD	PR	FC	YDS	AVG(LG)	TD
1984	SF	3	80	26.7(50)	0	45	11	**521**	11.6(79)	1
1985	SF	4	76	19.0(26)	0	38	14	258	6.8(22)	0
1986	NO	2	39	19.5(22)	0	10	3	67	6.7(23)	0
1987	SF	1	23	23.0(23)	0	21	7	265	12.6(83)	1
NFL	6	56	1147	20.5(50)	0	152	41	1598	10.5(93)	4
McNeil, Gerald										
1986	Cle	**47**	997	21.2(**100**)	**1**	40	10	348	8.7(**84**)	**1**
1987	Cle	11	205	18.6(33)	0	**34**	9	386	11.4(40)	0
1988	Cle	2	38	19.0(22)	0	38	6	315	8.3(32)	0
1989	Cle	4	61	15.3(21)	0	**49**	15	**496**	10.1(49)	0
1990	Hou	27	551	20.4(64)	0	30	**20**	172	5.7(26)	0
NFL	5	91	1852	20.4(100)	1	191	60	1717	9.0(84)	1
McQuarters, R.W.										
1998	SF	17	339	19.9(45)	0	**47**	10	406	8.6(72)	1
1999	SF	26	568	21.8(37)	0	18	3	90	5.0(32)	0
2001	ChiB	0	—	—	—	12	1	96	8.0(16)	0
2003	ChiB	0	—	—	—	37	12	452	12.2(60)	1
2004	ChiB	2	46	23.0(37)	0	**44**	13	435	9.9(75)	1
2005	Det	16	381	23.8(73)	0	10	2	117	11.7(49)	0
NFL	6	61	1334	21.9(73)	0	168	41	1596	9.5(75)	3
Meggett, Dave										
1989	NYG	27	577	21.4(43)	0	**46**	14	**582**	12.7(**76**)	**1**
1990	NYG	21	492	23.4(58)	0	**43**	12	**467**	10.9(68)	**1**
1991	NYG	25	514	20.6(42)	0	28	9	287	10.3(70)	1
1992	NYG	20	455	22.8(92)	1	27	11	240	8.9(39)	0
1993	NYG	24	403	16.8(35)	0	32	20	331	10.3(75)	1
1994	NYG	29	548	18.9(30)	0	26	14	323	12.4(68)	**2**
1995	NE	38	964	25.4(62)	0	45	17	383	8.5(23)	0
1996	NE	34	781	23.0(54)	0	**52**	9	**588**	11.3(60)	**1**
1997	NE	33	816	24.7(61)	0	45	8	467	10.4(47)	0
1998	NYJ	1	16	16.0(16)	0	5	0	40	8.0(18)	0
NFL	10	252	5566	22.1(92)	1	349	114	3708	10.6(76)	7
Metcalf, Eric										
1989	Cle	31	718	23.2(49)	0	0	—	—	—	—
1990	Cle	**52**	**1052**	20.2(**101**)	**2**	0	—	—	—	—
1991	Cle	23	351	15.3(24)	0	12	1	100	8.3(30)	0
1992	Cle	9	157	17.4(30)	0	**44**	10	**429**	9.8(75)	1
1993	Cle	15	318	21.2(47)	0	36	11	464	**12.9**(**91**)	**2**
1994	Cle	9	210	23.3(32)	0	35	6	348	9.9(**92**)	**2**
1995	Atl	12	278	23.2(47)	0	39	14	383	9.8(66)	**1**
1996	Atl	49	1034	21.1(55)	0	27	9	296	11.0(39)	0
1997	SD	16	355	22.2(63)	0	45	8	489	10.9(85)	**3**
1998	Arz	57	1218	21.4(59)	0	43	7	295	6.9(24)	0
1999	Car	4	56	14.0(31)	0	34	18	238	7.0(30)	0
2001	Was	1	25	25.0(25)	0	33	5	412	12.5(**89**)	**1**
2002	GB	2	41	20.5(21)	0	3	0	-1	-0.3(0)	0
NFL	13	280	5813	20.8(101)	2	351	89	3453	9.8(92)	10
Metcalf, Terry										
1973	SL	4	124	31.0(48)	0	0	—	—	—	—
1974	SL	20	623	**31.1**(**94**)	**1**	26	3	340	13.1(43)	0
1975	SL	35	960	27.4(93)	**1**	23	3	285	**12.4**(**69**)	**1**
1976	SL	16	325	20.3(33)	0	17	1	188	11.1(39)	0
1977	SL	32	772	24.1(51)	0	14	0	108	7.7(23)	0
1981	Was	14	283	20.2(36)	0	4	0	15	3.8(13)	0
NFL	6	121	3087	25.5(94)	2	84	7	936	11.1(69)	1
Milburn, Glyn										
1993	Den	12	188	15.7(26)	0	40	11	425	10.6(54)	0
1994	Den	37	793	21.4(40)	0	41	4	379	9.2(44)	0
1995	Den	47	1269	27.0(86)	0	31	17	354	11.4(44)	0
1996	Det	64	1627	25.4(65)	0	34	19	284	8.4(33)	0
1997	Det	55	1315	23.9(69)	0	47	**26**	433	9.2(40)	0
1998	ChiB	**62**	**1550**	25.0(94)	**2**	25	15	291	11.6(93)	1
1999	ChiB	**61**	**1426**	23.4(93)	0	30	19	346	11.5(54)	0
2000	ChiB	63	1468	23.3(38)	0	35	26	300	8.6(25)	0
2001	ChiB	6	152	25.3(37)	0	4	3	33	8.3(20)	0
2001	SD	0	—	—	—	17	4	139	8.2(19)	0
NFL	9	407	9788	24.0(94)	2	304	144	2984	9.8(93)	1
Mills, Ernie										
1991	Pit	11	284	25.8(54)	0	1	0	0	0.0(0)	**1**
1992	Pit	1	11	11.0(11)	0	0	—	—	—	—
1994	Pit	2	6	3.0(6)	0	0	—	—	—	—
1995	Pit	54	1306	24.2(57)	0	0	—	—	—	—
1996	Pit	8	146	18.3(27)	0	0	—	—	—	—
1997	Car	4	65	16.3(33)	0	0	—	—	—	—
NFL	6	80	1818	22.7(57)	0	1	0	0	0.0(0)	1
Minor, Travis										
2002	Mia	46	1071	23.3(66)	0	0	—	—	—	—
2003	Mia	34	727	21.4(49)	0	0	—	—	—	—
2005	Mia	2	22	11.0(19)	0	0	—	—	—	—
NFL	3	82	1820	22.2(66)	0	0	—	—	—	—
Mitchell, Bobby										
1958	Cle	18	454	25.2(98)	1	14	—	165	11.8(68)	**1**
1959	Cle	11	236	21.5(31)	0	17	—	177	10.4(78)	1
1960	Cle	17	432	25.4(90)	**1**	9	—	101	11.2(34)	0
1961	Cle	16	428	26.8(91)	**1**	14	—	164	11.7(64)	1
1962	Was	12	398	33.2(92)	**1**	3	—	7	2.3(4)	0
1963	Was	9	343	38.1(92)	1	6	1	49	8.2(28)	0
1964	Was	3	58	19.3(28)	0	0	—	—	—	—
1965	Was	5	106	21.2(35)	0	1	1	15	15.0(15)	0
1966	Was	0	—	—	—	4	0	21	5.3(13)	0

YEAR	TEAM	KR	YDS	AVG(LG)	TD	PR	FC	YDS	AVG(LG)	TD
1968	Was	11	235	21.4(43)	0	1	1	0	0.0(0)	0
NFL	10	102	2690	26.4(98)	5	69	3	699	10.1(78)	3
Mitchell, Brian										
1990	Was	18	365	20.3(37)	0	12	4	107	8.9(26)	0
1991	Was	29	583	20.1(35)	0	45	**21**	**600**	13.3(69)	**2**
1992	Was	23	492	21.4(47)	0	29	9	271	9.3(84)	1
1993	Was	33	678	20.5(68)	0	29	7	193	6.7(48)	0
1994	Was	58	1478	25.5(86)	0	32	**24**	**452**	**14.1**(**78**)	**2**
1995	Was	55	1408	**25.6**(**59**)	0	25	15	315	12.6(59)	**1**
1996	Was	56	1258	22.5(50)	0	23	16	258	11.2(71)	0
1997	Was	47	1094	23.3(97)	1	38	23	442	11.6(63)	**1**
1998	Was	59	1337	22.7(101)	1	44	18	**506**	11.5(47)	0
1999	Was	43	893	20.8(45)	0	40	14	332	8.3(33)	0
2000	Phi	47	1124	23.9(89)	1	32	**33**	335	10.5(72)	1
2001	Phi	41	1025	25.0(94)	1	39	**22**	**467**	12.0(54)	0
2002	Phi	43	1162	27.0(57)	0	46	11	567	12.3(76)	1
2003	NYG	55	1117	20.3(29)	0	29	14	154	5.3(15)	0
NFL	14	607	14014	23.1(101)	4	463	231	4999	10.8(84)	9
Mitchell, Stump										
1981	SL	55	**1292**	23.5(67)	0	42	0	445	10.6(50)	1
1982	SL	16	364	22.8(33)	0	27	0	165	6.1(15)	0
1983	SL	36	778	21.6(**66**)	0	38	1	337	8.9(34)	0
1984	SL	35	804	23.0(56)	0	38	3	333	8.8(39)	0
1985	SL	19	345	18.2(35)	0	11	2	97	8.8(21)	0
1986	SL	6	203	33.8(53)	0	0	—	—	—	—
1988	Phx	10	221	22.1(41)	0	0	—	—	—	—
NFL	7	177	4007	22.6(67)	0	156	6	1377	8.8(50)	1
Monroe, Carl										
1983	SF	8	152	19.0(32)	0	0	—	—	—	—
1984	SF	27	561	20.8(44)	0	0	—	—	—	—
1985	SF	28	717	25.6(95)	1	0	—	—	—	—
1986	SF	8	139	17.4(25)	0	0	—	—	—	—
1987	SF	5	91	18.2(24)	0	0	—	—	—	—
NFL	5	76	1660	21.8(95)	1	0	—	—	—	—
Montgomery, Cleo										
1980	Cin	44	843	19.2(40)	0	31	7	223	7.2(42)	0
1981	Cle	14	334	23.9(38)	0	17	0	121	7.1(17)	0
1981	Oak	3	48	16.0(20)	0	0	—	—	—	—
1982	LARd	17	312	18.4(39)	0	0	—	—	—	—
1983	LARd	21	464	22.1(48)	0	0	—	—	—	—
1984	LARd	26	555	21.3(42)	0	14	1	194	13.9(69)	**1**
1985	LARd	7	150	21.4(30)	0	8	2	84	10.5(32)	0
NFL	6	132	2706	20.5(48)	0	70	10	622	8.9(69)	1
Moody, Keith										
1976	Buf	26	605	23.3(41)	0	16	8	166	10.4(67)	1
1977	Buf	30	636	21.2(45)	0	15	6	196	13.1(**91**)	1
1978	Buf	18	371	20.6(35)	0	19	5	240	12.6(**82**)	**1**
1979	Buf	27	556	20.6(35)	0	38	10	318	8.4(32)	0
1980	Oak	8	150	18.8(39)	0	0	—	—	—	—
NFL	5	109	2318	21.3(45)	0	88	29	920	10.5(91)	3
Moore, Manfred										
1974	SF	18	398	22.1(51)	0	5	0	149	29.8(88)	**1**
1975	SF	26	650	25.0(52)	0	16	0	160	10.0(17)	0
1976	TB	7	134	19.1(0)	0	14	0	106	7.6(21)	0
1976	Oak	1	28	28.0(28)	0	6	0	78	13.0(23)	0
1977	Min	24	524	21.8(48)	0	47	2	277	5.9(28)	0
NFL	4	76	1734	22.8(52)	0	88	2	770	8.8(88)	1
Morgan, Stanley										
1977	NE	0	—	—	—	16	2	220	13.8(53)	0
1978	NE	1	17	17.0(17)	0	32	5	335	10.5(48)	0
1979	NE	1	12	12.0(12)	0	29	**21**	289	10.0(80)	1
1981	NE	0	—	—	—	15	4	116	7.7(26)	0
NFL	4	2	29	14.5(17)	0	92	32	960	10.4(80)	1
Morris, Johnny										
1958	ChiB	16	399	24.9(45)	0	14	—	96	6.9(33)	0
1959	ChiB	17	438	25.8(58)	0	14	—	171	**12.2**(**78**)	1
1960	ChiB	19	384	20.2(32)	0	13	—	75	5.8(24)	0
1961	ChiB	2	46	23.0(25)	0	23	—	155	6.7(16)	0
1962	ChiB	0	—	—	—	20	—	208	10.4(33)	0
1963	ChiB	0	—	—	—	16	5	164	10.3(42)	0
1967	ChiB	0	—	—	—	4	4	24	6.0(15)	0
NFL	7	54	1267	23.5(58)	0	104	9	893	8.6(78)	1
Morris, Maurice										
2002	Sea	34	821	24.1(97)	1	0	—	—	—	—
2003	Sea	47	1007	21.4(56)	0	0	—	—	—	—
2004	Sea	47	994	21.1(34)	0	15	4	75	5.0(22)	0
2005	Sea	1	21	21.0(21)	0	0	—	—	—	—
NFL	4	129	2843	22.0(97)	1	15	4	75	5.0(22)	0
Morris, Mercury										
1969	Mia-A	**43**	**1136**	26.4(**105**)	**1**	25	3	172	6.9(38)	0
1970	Mia	28	812	29.0(96)	**1**	2	0	-1	-0.5(0)	0
1971	Mia	15	423	**28.2**(**94**)	**1**	0	—	—	—	—
1972	Mia	14	334	23.9(33)	0	0	—	—	—	—
1973	Mia	11	242	22.0(29)	0	0	—	—	—	—
NFL	5	111	2947	26.5(105)	3	27	3	171	6.3(38)	0
Morris, Randall										
1984	Sea	8	153	19.1(34)	0	0	—	—	—	—
1985	Sea	31	636	20.5(58)	0	0	—	—	—	—
1986	Sea	23	465	20.2(38)	0	0	—	—	—	—
1987	Sea	9	149	16.6(20)	0	0	—	—	—	—

YEAR	TEAM	KR	YDS	AVG(LG)	TD	PR	FC	YDS	AVG(LG)	TD
1988	Sea	11	218	19.8(30)	0	0	—	—	—	—
1988	Det	2	41	20.5(25)	0	0	—	—	—	—
NFL	5	84	1662	19.8(58)	0	0	—	—	—	—
MORTON, CHAD										
2000	NO	44	1029	23.4(68)	0	30	14	278	9.3(51)	0
2001	NYJ	12	247	20.6(33)	0	13	7	113	8.7(33)	0
2002	NYJ	58	**1509**	26.0(98)	**2**	4	4	51	12.8(21)	0
2003	Was	44	1029	23.4(94)	1	19	16	188	9.9(28)	0
2004	Was	16	358	22.4(49)	0	13	12	80	6.2(14)	0
2005	NYG	24	559	23.3(41)	0	47	16	453	9.6(58)	**1**
NFL	6	198	4731	23.9(98)	3	126	69	1163	9.2(58)	1
MORTON, MICHAEL										
1982	TB	21	361	17.2(26)	0	0	—	—	—	—
1983	TB	30	689	23.0(50)	0	0	—	—	—	—
1984	TB	38	835	22.0(43)	0	0	—	—	—	—
1985	Was	6	131	21.8(27)	0	0	—	—	—	—
NFL	4	95	2016	21.2(50)	0	0	—	—	—	—
MOSES, J.J.										
2002	GB	4	69	17.3(27)	0	5	0	12	2.4(8)	0
2003	Hou	**58**	1355	23.4(70)	0	36	7	244	6.8(40)	0
2004	Hou	59	1303	22.1(49)	0	36	13	309	8.6(27)	0
2005	Arz	7	177	25.3(35)	0	7	0	40	5.7(23)	0
NFL	4	128	2904	22.7(70)	0	84	20	605	7.2(40)	0
MOSS, SANTANA										
2001	NYJ	0	—	—	—	6	0	82	13.7(23)	0
2002	NYJ	0	—	—	—	25	8	**413**	**16.5(63)**	**2**
2003	NYJ	0	—	—	—	30	18	332	11.1(47)	0
2004	NYJ	0	—	—	—	27	7	225	8.3(46)	0
2005	Was	0	—	—	—	7	1	40	5.7(14)	0
NFL	5	0	—	—	—	95	34	1092	11.5(63)	2
MOULDS, ERIC										
1996	Buf	52	1205	23.2(**97**)	**1**	0	—	—	—	—
1997	Buf	43	921	21.4(53)	0	2	0	20	10.0(10)	0
2004	Buf	1	2	2.0(2)	0	0	—	—	—	—
NFL	3	96	2128	22.2(97)	1	2	0	20	10.0(10)	0
NELMS, MIKE										
1980	Was	38	810	21.3(51)	0	48	5	487	10.1(64)	0
1981	Was	37	1099	**29.7(84)**	0	45	1	492	10.9(75)	2
1982	Was	23	**557**	24.2(58)	0	32	0	252	7.9(28)	0
1983	Was	35	802	22.9(41)	0	38	0	289	7.6(35)	0
1984	Was	**42**	860	20.5(36)	0	49	1	428	8.7(46)	0
NFL	5	175	4128	23.6(84)	0	212	7	1948	9.2(75)	2
NELSON, AL										
1965	Phi	26	683	26.3(70)	0	0	—	—	—	—
1966	Phi	2	34	17.0(18)	0	1	0	3	3.0(3)	0
1968	Phi	11	308	28.0(69)	0	0	—	—	—	—
1969	Phi	3	63	21.0(27)	0	0	—	—	—	—
1970	Phi	10	187	18.7(27)	0	0	—	—	—	—
1971	Phi	13	358	27.5(51)	0	0	—	—	—	—
1972	Phi	25	728	29.1(78)	0	0	—	—	—	—
1973	Phi	11	264	24.0(53)	0	0	—	—	—	—
NFL	8	101	2625	26.0(78)	0	1	0	3	3.0(3)	0
NELSON, DARRIN										
1982	Min	6	132	22.0(33)	0	0	—	—	—	—
1983	Min	18	445	**24.7(50)**	0	0	—	—	—	—
1984	Min	39	**891**	22.8(47)	0	23	9	180	7.8(21)	0
1985	Min	3	51	17.0(26)	0	16	3	133	8.3(21)	0
1986	Min	3	105	35.0(40)	0	0	—	—	—	—
1987	Min	7	164	23.4(42)	0	0	—	—	—	—
1988	Min	9	210	23.3(30)	0	0	—	—	—	—
1989	Min	14	317	22.6(32)	0	0	—	—	—	—
1990	SD	4	36	9.0(26)	0	3	0	44	14.7(33)	0
1991	Min	31	682	22.0(50)	0	0	—	—	—	—
1992	Min	29	626	21.6(53)	0	0	—	—	—	—
NFL	11	163	3659	22.4(53)	0	42	12	357	8.5(33)	0
NORTHCUTT, DENNIS										
2000	Cle	0	—	—	—	27	12	289	10.7(30)	0
2001	Cle	1	26	26.0(26)	0	15	9	86	5.7(32)	0
2002	Cle	0	—	—	—	25	10	367	14.7(87)	**2**
2003	Cle	0	—	—	—	36	10	295	8.2(38)	0
2004	Cle	0	—	—	—	36	12	432	12.0(44)	0
2005	Cle	0	—	—	—	35	13	368	10.5(62)	1
NFL	6	1	26	26.0(26)	0	174	66	1837	10.6(87)	3
ODOM, STEVE										
1974	GB	31	713	23.0(52)	0	15	2	191	12.7(95)	**1**
1975	GB	42	1034	24.6(93)	**1**	1	0	0	0.0(0)	0
1976	GB	29	610	21.0(88)	0	0	—	—	—	—
1977	GB	23	468	20.3(37)	0	0	—	—	—	—
1978	GB	25	677	**27.1(95)**	**1**	33	7	298	9.0(48)	0
1979	GB	29	622	21.4(31)	0	15	5	80	5.3(19)	0
1979	NYG	15	327	21.8(75)	0	9	3	26	2.9(10)	0
NFL	6	194	4451	22.9(95)	2	73	17	595	8.2(95)	1
OLIVER, WINSLOW										
1996	Car	7	160	22.9(33)	0	52	17	598	11.5(84)	1
1997	Car	0	—	—	—	14	5	111	7.9(26)	0
1998	Car	2	43	21.5(25)	0	44	11	464	10.5(35)	0
1999	Atl	24	441	18.4(28)	0	12	5	152	12.7(58)	**1**
2000	Atl	2	15	7.5(11)	0	4	3	39	9.8(40)	0
NFL	5	35	659	18.8(33)	0	126	41	1364	10.8(84)	2

YEAR	TEAM	KR	YDS	AVG(LG)	TD	PR	FC	YDS	AVG(LG)	TD
O'NEAL, DELTHA										
2000	Den	46	1102	24.0(87)	**1**	34	11	354	10.4(64)	0
2001	Den	0	—	—	—	31	9	405	13.1(86)	1
2002	Den	1	15	15.0(15)	0	30	7	251	8.4(53)	0
2003	Den	8	128	16.0(24)	0	33	10	315	9.5(57)	1
2004	Cin	1	15	15.0(15)	0	7	6	33	4.7(17)	0
2005	Cin	1	14	14.0(14)	0	0	—	—	—	—
NFL	6	57	1274	22.4(87)	1	135	43	1358	10.1(86)	2
OWENS, ARTIE										
1976	SD	25	551	22.0(40)	0	0	—	—	—	—
1977	SD	8	132	16.5(19)	0	0	—	—	—	—
1978	SD	20	524	26.2(77)	0	1	0	20	20.0(20)	0
1979	SD	35	791	22.6(40)	0	0	—	—	—	—
1980	Buf	8	157	19.6(29)	0	0	—	—	—	—
NFL	5	96	2155	22.4(77)	0	1	0	20	20.0(20)	0
OWENS, JAMES										
1979	SF	41	1002	24.4(85)	**1**	0	—	—	—	—
1980	SF	31	726	23.4(**101**)	**1**	0	—	—	—	—
1981	TB	24	473	19.7(34)	0	0	—	—	—	—
1982	TB	3	52	17.3(27)	0	0	—	—	—	—
1983	TB	20	380	19.0(31)	0	0	—	—	—	—
1984	TB	8	168	21.0(36)	0	0	—	—	—	—
NFL	6	127	2801	22.1(101)	2	0	—	—	—	—
PALMER, DAVID										
1994	Min	0	—	—	—	30	9	193	6.4(20)	0
1995	Min	17	354	20.8(42)	0	26	13	342	**13.2(74)**	**1**
1996	Min	13	292	22.5(60)	0	22	**20**	216	9.8(69)	1
1997	Min	32	711	22.2(62)	0	34	19	444	**13.1(57)**	0
1998	Min	50	1176	23.5(88)	1	28	18	289	10.3(53)	0
1999	Min	27	621	23.0(51)	0	12	5	93	7.8(18)	0
2000	Min	6	120	20.0(24)	0	10	12	33	3.3(16)	0
NFL	7	145	3274	22.6(88)	1	162	96	1610	9.9(74)	2
PARRISH, LEMAR										
1970	Cin	16	482	30.1(95)	**1**	23	15	194	8.4(79)	**1**
1971	Cin	13	296	22.8(30)	0	12	9	93	7.8(47)	0
1972	Cin	15	348	23.2(45)	0	15	2	141	9.4(51)	**1**
1973	Cin	7	143	20.4(29)	0	25	1	200	8.0(47)	0
1974	Cin	2	36	18.0(21)	0	18	1	338	**18.8(90)**	**2**
1975	Cin	4	114	28.5(64)	0	13	1	83	6.4(34)	0
1976	Cin	3	62	20.7(28)	0	20	2	122	6.1(32)	0
1977	Cin	1	23	23.0(23)	0	4	0	30	7.5(11)	0
1978	Was	0	—	—	—	1	0	4	4.0(4)	0
NFL	9	61	1504	24.7(95)	1	131	31	1205	9.2(90)	4
PATTEN, DAVID										
1997	NYG	8	123	15.4(26)	0	0	—	—	—	—
1998	NYG	43	928	21.6(90)	1	0	—	—	—	—
1999	NYG	33	673	20.4(45)	0	0	—	—	—	—
2000	Cle	22	469	21.3(62)	0	0	—	—	—	—
2001	NE	2	44	22.0(24)	0	0	—	—	—	—
2004	NE	1	16	16.0(16)	0	0	—	—	—	—
NFL	6	109	2253	20.7(90)	1	0	—	—	—	—
PAUL, DON										
1950	ChiC	**28**	693	24.8(46)	0	18	—	194	10.8(82)	1
1951	ChiC	15	424	28.3(57)	0	19	—	143	7.5(23)	0
1952	ChiC	3	54	18.0(26)	0	10	—	97	9.7(22)	0
1953	ChiC	4	106	26.5(35)	0	18	—	85	4.7(22)	0
1954	Cle	1	31	31.0(31)	0	1	—	57	57.0(57)	0
1955	Cle	5	109	21.8(26)	0	19	—	148	7.8(60)	1
1956	Cle	0	—	—	—	17	—	103	6.1(17)	0
1957	Cle	0	—	—	—	9	—	75	8.3(32)	0
1958	Cle	1	0	0.0(0)	0	2	—	0	0.0(0)	0
NFL	9	57	1417	24.9(57)	0	113	0	902	8.0(82)	2
PAYTON, EDDIE										
1977	Cle	4	91	22.8(34)	**0**	3	0	17	5.7(**16**)	**0**
1977	Det	18	457	25.4(98)	**1**	27	0	273	10.1(**87**)	**1**
1978	KC	30	775	25.8(66)	0	32	2	364	11.4(39)	0
1980	Min	**53**	**1184**	22.3(59)	0	34	9	251	7.4(19)	0
1981	Min	39	898	23.0(**99**)	**1**	38	8	303	8.0(18)	0
1982	Min	12	271	22.6(32)	0	22	5	179	8.1(35)	0
NFL	5	156	3676	23.6(99)	2	156	24	1387	8.9(87)	1
PEARSON, PRESTON										
1968	Bal	15	527	**35.1(102)**	**2**	0	—	—	—	—
1969	Bal	**31**	706	22.8(51)	0	6	0	37	6.2(11)	0
1970	Pit	4	114	28.5(35)	0	0	—	—	—	—
1971	Pit	7	205	29.3(77)	0	0	—	—	—	—
1972	Pit	13	292	22.5(42)	0	1	0	3	3.0(3)	0
1973	Pit	16	308	19.3(28)	0	0	—	—	—	—
1974	Pit	12	258	21.5(29)	0	0	—	—	—	—
1975	Dal	16	391	24.4(42)	0	0	—	—	—	—
NFL	8	114	2801	24.6(102)	2	7	0	40	5.7(11)	0
PEGRAM, ERRIC										
1991	Atl	16	260	16.3(30)	0	0	—	—	—	—
1992	Atl	9	161	17.9(42)	0	0	—	—	—	—
1993	Atl	4	63	15.8(28)	0	0	—	—	—	—
1994	Atl	9	145	16.1(35)	0	0	—	—	—	—
1995	Pit	4	85	21.3(28)	0	0	—	—	—	—
1996	Pit	17	419	24.6(91)	**1**	0	—	—	—	—
1997	NYG	22	382	17.4(50)	0	0	—	—	—	—
NFL	7	81	1515	18.7(91)	1	0	—	—	—	—

YEAR	TEAM	KR	YDS	AVG(LG)	TD	PR	FC	YDS	AVG(LG)	TD
PICCONE, LOU										
1974	NYJ	**39**	**961**	24.6(46)	0	9	0	75	8.3(13)	0
1975	NYJ	26	637	24.5(53)	0	18	7	74	4.1(9)	0
1976	NYJ	31	699	22.5(58)	0	21	0	173	8.2(60)	1
1977	Buf	4	89	22.3(26)	0	0	1	—	—	—
1978	Buf	3	51	17.0(26)	0	14	4	88	6.3(13)	0
1979	Buf	3	41	13.7(17)	0	0	1	—	—	—
1980	Buf	0	—	—	—	2	3	15	7.5(8)	0
1981	Buf	2	31	15.5(16)	0	9	2	57	6.3(13)	0
1982	Buf	3	50	16.7(23)	0	0	—	—	—	—
NFL	9	111	2559	23.1(58)	0	73	18	482	6.6(60)	1
PINKETT, ALLEN										
1986	Hou	26	519	20.0(48)	0	1	2	-1	—	—
1987	Hou	17	322	18.9(30)	0	0	—	—	—	—
1988	Hou	7	137	19.6(29)	0	0	—	—	—	—
1990	Hou	4	91	22.8(28)	0	0	—	—	—	—
1991	Hou	26	508	19.5(41)	0	0	—	—	—	—
NFL	5	80	1577	19.7(48)	0	1	2	-1	—	—
PITTS, ELIJAH										
1961	GB	1	14	14.0(14)	0	0	—	—	—	—
1962	GB	0	—	—	—	7	—	17	2.4(7)	0
1963	GB	0	—	—	—	7	7	60	8.6(20)	0
1964	GB	0	—	—	—	15	7	191	12.7(65)	1
1965	GB	20	396	19.8(29)	0	8	6	27	3.4(12)	0
1966	GB	1	0	0.0(0)	0	7	4	9	1.3(6)	0
1967	GB	0	—	—	—	9	3	16	1.8(10)	0
1968	GB	2	40	20.0(27)	0	1	1	1	1.0(1)	0
1969	GB	1	22	22.0(22)	0	16	8	60	3.8(10)	0
1970	NO	1	22	22.0(22)	0	0	—	—	—	—
1971	GB	2	41	20.5(22)	0	5	2	13	2.6(5)	0
NFL	11	28	535	19.1(29)	0	75	41	394	5.3(65)	1
PODOLAK, ED										
1969	KC-A	7	165	23.6(28)	0	0	6	—	—	—
1970	KC	17	348	20.5(38)	0	23	**21**	311	**13.5(60)**	0
1971	KC	3	65	21.7(25)	0	14	9	84	6.0(23)	0
1972	KC	7	119	17.0(23)	0	8	10	11	1.4(12)	0
1973	KC	0	—	—	—	11	11	90	8.2(48)	0
1974	KC	0	—	—	—	15	2	134	8.9(54)	0
1975	KC	0	—	—	—	13	5	96	7.4(23)	0
1977	KC	0	—	—	—	2	1	13	6.5(7)	0
NFL	8	34	697	20.5(38)	0	86	65	739	8.6(60)	0
POTEAT, HANK										
2000	Pit	24	465	19.4(31)	0	36	7	467	13.0(54)	1
2001	Pit	16	250	15.6(30)	0	36	14	292	8.1(39)	0
2002	Pit	5	103	20.6(25)	0	4	2	29	7.3(11)	0
NFL	3	45	818	18.2(31)	0	76	23	788	10.4(54)	1
PRESTON, ROELL										
1995	Atl	30	627	20.9(44)	0	0	—	—	—	—
1996	Atl	32	681	21.3(50)	0	0	—	—	—	—
1997	GB	7	211	30.1(43)	0	1	0	0	0.0(0)	0
1998	GB	57	1497	26.3(101)	2	44	17	398	9.0(71)	1
1999	Ten	5	119	23.8(29)	0	8	2	59	7.4(12)	0
1999	Mia	0	—	—	—	1	1	6	6.0(6)	0
1999	SF	16	292	18.3(58)	0	3	8	6	2.0(6)	0
NFL	5	147	3427	23.3(101)	2	57	27	469	8.2(71)	0
PRITCHARD, BOSH										
1942	Cle	1	24	24.0(24)	**0**	0	—	—	—	—
1942	Phi	3	134	44.7(97)	1	11	—	107	9.7(19)	0
1946	Phi	8	164	20.5(42)	0	12	—	166	13.8(42)	0
1947	Phi	8	148	18.5(27)	0	24	—	271	11.3(30)	0
1948	Phi	9	249	27.7(50)	0	24	—	282	11.8(55)	1
1949	Phi	5	99	19.8(36)	0	13	—	99	7.6(23)	0
1951	Phi	5	81	16.2(20)	0	7	—	50	7.1(21)	0
1951	NYG	2	39	19.5(21)	0	4	—	97	24.3(81)	1
NFL	6	41	938	22.9(97)	1	95	0	1072	11.3(81)	2
PRUITT, GREG										
1973	Cle	16	453	28.3(54)	0	16	3	180	11.3(46)	0
1974	Cle	22	606	**27.5(88)**	1	27	0	349	12.9(72)	0
1975	Cle	14	302	21.6(40)	0	13	1	130	10.0(30)	0
1976	Cle	1	27	27.0(27)	0	0	—	—	—	—
1978	Cle	1	31	31.0(31)	0	0	—	—	—	—
1979	Cle	1	22	22.0(22)	0	0	—	—	—	—
1981	Cle	3	82	27.3(30)	0	0	—	—	—	—
1982	LARd	14	371	26.5(55)	0	**27**	7	209	7.7(25)	0
1983	LARd	31	604	19.5(42)	0	**58**	**18**	**666**	11.5(97)	1
1984	LARd	3	16	5.3(13)	0	**53**	**16**	473	8.9(38)	0
NFL	10	106	2514	23.7(88)	1	194	45	2007	10.3(97)	1
QUERY, JEFF										
1989	GB	6	125	20.8(28)	0	30	7	247	8.2(15)	0
1990	GB	0	—	—	—	32	7	308	9.6(25)	0
1991	GB	0	—	—	—	14	3	157	11.2(28)	0
1992	Cin	1	13	13.0(13)	0	0	—	—	—	—
1995	Cin	0	—	—	—	0	1	—	—	—
NFL	5	7	138	19.7(28)	0	76	18	712	9.4(28)	0
RANDLE EL, ANTWAAN										
2002	Pit	32	733	22.9(99)	1	**37**	11	257	6.9(29)	0
2003	Pit	24	466	19.4(34)	0	**45**	12	**542**	12.0(84)	2
2004	Pit	21	527	25.1(41)	0	42	13	347	8.3(60)	0
2005	Pit	1	16	16.0(16)	0	44	12	**448**	10.2(**81**)	2
NFL	4	78	1742	22.3(99)	1	168	48	1594	9.5(84)	4
RECHICHAR, BERT										
1952	Cle	4	70	17.5(19)	0	14	—	58	4.1(16)	0
1953	Bal	1	28	28.0(28)	0	1	—	0	0.0(0)	0
1954	Bal	3	26	8.7(12)	0	6	—	22	3.7(9)	0
1955	Bal	9	235	26.1(59)	0	**30**	—	121	4.0(24)	0
1956	Bal	0	—	—	—	5	—	10	2.0(7)	0
1957	Bal	1	0	0.0(0)	0	22	—	71	3.2(22)	0
1958	Bal	3	50	16.7(22)	0	7	—	29	4.1(11)	0
1959	Bal	2	39	19.5(27)	0	0	—	—	—	—
NFL	8	23	448	19.5(59)	0	85	0	311	3.7(24)	0
REECE, DANNY										
1976	TB	1	30	30.0(30)	0	20	0	143	7.2(30)	0
1977	TB	3	72	24.0(34)	0	31	2	274	8.8(36)	0
1978	TB	11	240	21.8(32)	0	44	3	393	8.9(50)	0
1979	TB	1	13	13.0(13)	0	**70**	1	**431**	6.2(17)	0
1980	TB	7	128	18.3(23)	0	**57**	1	313	5.5(19)	0
NFL	5	23	483	21.0(34)	0	222	7	1554	7.0(50)	0
RENFRO, MEL										
1964	Dal	**40**	**1017**	25.4(65)	0	**32**	9	**418**	13.1(69)	1
1965	Dal	21	630	30.0(100)	1	24	4	145	6.0(35)	0
1966	Dal	19	487	25.6(87)	1	21	6	123	5.9(38)	0
1967	Dal	5	112	22.4(30)	0	3	4	-1	-0.3(7)	0
1968	Dal	0	—	—	—	0	2	—	—	—
1969	Dal	0	—	—	—	15	7	80	5.3(34)	0
1970	Dal	0	—	—	—	13	6	77	5.9(29)	0
1971	Dal	0	—	—	—	0	1	—	—	—
1974	Dal	0	—	—	—	1	1	0	0.0(0)	0
NFL	9	85	2246	26.4(100)	2	109	40	842	7.7(69)	1
REYNOLDS, BILLY										
1953	Cle	4	74	18.5(21)	0	18	—	111	6.2(28)	0
1954	Cle	14	413	**29.5(51)**	0	25	—	138	5.5(39)	0
1957	Cle	7	152	21.7(29)	0	24	—	114	4.8(23)	0
1958	Pit	15	346	23.1(38)	0	25	—	143	5.7(22)	0
1960	Oak-A	0	—	—	—	7	—	24	3.4(0)	0
NFL	5	40	985	24.6(51)	0	99	0	530	5.4(39)	0
RHODES, DOMINIC										
2001	Ind	14	356	25.4(88)	1	0	—	—	—	—
2003	Ind	16	411	25.7(49)	0	0	—	—	—	—
2004	Ind	48	1188	24.8(88)	1	0	—	—	—	—
2005	Ind	41	855	20.9(39)	0	0	—	—	—	—
NFL	4	119	2810	23.6(88)	2	0	—	—	—	—
ROACHES, CARL										
1980	Hou	37	746	20.2(46)	0	47	6	384	8.2(68)	0
1981	Hou	28	769	**27.5(96)**	1	39	4	296	7.6(40)	0
1982	Hou	21	441	21.0(45)	0	19	4	104	5.5(25)	0
1983	Hou	34	641	18.9(**97**)	1	20	9	159	7.9(23)	0
1984	Hou	30	679	22.6(49)	0	26	8	152	5.8(18)	0
1985	NO	4	76	19.0(23)	0	4	2	21	5.3(10)	0
NFL	6	154	3352	21.8(97)	2	155	33	1116	7.2(68)	0
ROBERSON, BO										
1961	SD-A	13	207	15.9(32)	0	0	—	—	—	—
1962	Oak-A	27	748	27.7(87)	1	0	—	—	—	—
1963	Oak-A	38	809	21.3(58)	0	2	—	34	17.0(22)	0
1964	Oak-A	36	975	**27.1(59)**	0	1	—	20	20.0(20)	0
1965	Oak-A	12	259	21.6(29)	0	0	—	—	—	—
1965	Buf-A	4	59	14.8(22)	0	0	—	—	—	—
NFL	5	130	3057	23.5(87)	1	3	0	54	18.0(22)	0
ROBERTS, WALTER										
1964	Cle	24	661	27.5(60)	0	10	6	132	13.2(40)	0
1965	Cle	18	493	27.4(88)	0	18	13	162	9.0(51)	0
1966	Cle	20	454	22.7(57)	0	11	13	42	3.8(30)	0
1967	NO	28	737	26.3(91)	1	11	12	50	4.5(11)	0
1969	Was	17	383	22.5(42)	0	12	9	32	2.7(25)	0
1970	Was	0	—	—	—	10	6	28	2.8(9)	0
NFL	6	107	2728	25.5(91)	1	72	59	446	6.2(51)	0
ROBINSON, PATRICK										
1993	Cin	30	567	18.9(42)	0	**43**	6	305	7.1(36)	0
1994	Arz	12	231	19.3(33)	0	**41**	12	285	7.0(23)	0
NFL	2	42	798	19.0(42)	0	84	18	590	7.0(36)	0
RODGERS, DEL										
1982	GB	20	436	21.8(76)	0	0	—	—	—	—
1984	GB	39	843	21.6(**97**)	1	0	—	—	—	—
1987	SF	17	358	21.1(50)	0	0	—	—	—	—
1988	SF	6	98	16.3(24)	0	0	—	—	—	—
NFL	4	82	1735	21.2(97)	1	0	—	—	—	—
ROGERS, CHARLIE										
1999	Sea	18	465	25.8(49)	0	22	18	318	**14.5(94)**	1
2000	Sea	66	**1629**	24.7(61)	1	26	12	363	14.0(43)	0
2001	Sea	50	1120	22.4(64)	0	25	10	244	9.8(34)	0
2002	Buf	**64**	1280	20.0(90)	1	26	11	137	5.3(16)	0
2003	Mia	19	383	20.2(33)	0	21	13	186	8.9(48)	0
NFL	5	217	4877	22.5(90)	2	120	64	1248	10.4(94)	1
ROGERS, JIMMY										
1980	NO	41	930	22.7(88)	0	0	—	—	—	—
1981	NO	28	621	22.2(44)	0	0	—	—	—	—
1982	NO	1	24	24.0(24)	0	0	—	—	—	—
1983	NO	7	103	14.7(25)	0	0	—	—	—	—
NFL	4	77	1678	21.8(88)	0	0	—	—	—	—

YEAR	TEAM	KR	YDS	AVG(LG)	TD	PR	FC	YDS	AVG(LG)	TD
ROSSUM, ALLEN										
1998	Phi	44	1080	24.5(54)	0	22	7	187	8.5(25)	0
1999	Phi	54	1347	24.9(86)	1	28	17	250	8.9(39)	0
2000	GB	50	1288	25.8(92)	1	29	24	248	8.6(43)	0
2001	GB	23	431	18.7(27)	0	11	8	109	9.9(55)	1
2002	Atl	53	1164	22.0(91)	0	24	10	288	12.0(36)	0
2003	Atl	62	1291	20.8(52)	0	39	11	545	14.0(72)	1
2004	Atl	58	1250	21.6(49)	1	37	14	457	12.4(75)	1
2005	Atl	31	702	22.6(47)	0	17	12	145	8.5(29)	0
NFL 8		375	8553	22.8(92)	3	207	103	2229	10.8(75)	3
SAENZ, EDDIE										
1946	Was	11	264	24.0(55)	0	0	—	—	—	0
1947	Was	29	797	27.5(94)	2	24	—	308	12.8(30)	0
1948	Was	8	173	21.6(27)	0	2	—	26	13.0(16)	0
1949	Was	24	465	19.4(34)	0	17	—	178	10.5(32)	0
1950	Was	12	347	28.9(71)	0	14	—	125	8.9(24)	0
1951	Was	9	145	16.1(24)	0	2	—	6	3.0(6)	0
NFL 6		93	2191	23.6(94)	2	59	0	643	10.9(32)	0
SAMS, B.J.										
2004	Bal	59	1251	21.2(64)	0	55	12	575	10.5(78)	2
2005	Bal	44	998	22.7(87)	0	33	10	401	12.2(51)	0
NFL 2		103	2249	21.8(87)	0	88	22	976	11.1(78)	2
SANDERS, DEION										
1989	Atl	35	725	20.7(72)	0	28	7	307	11.0(68)	1
1990	Atl	39	851	21.8(50)	0	29	13	250	8.6(79)	1
1991	Atl	26	576	22.2(100)	1	21	9	170	8.1(23)	0
1992	Atl	40	1067	26.7(99)	2	13	9	41	3.2(14)	0
1993	Atl	7	169	24.1(31)	0	2	1	21	10.5(16)	0
1995	Dal	1	15	15.0(15)	0	1	1	54	54.0(43)	0
1996	Dal	0	—	—	—	1	1	4	4.0(4)	0
1997	Dal	1	18	18.0(18)	0	33	12	407	12.3(83)	1
1998	Dal	1	16	16.0(16)	0	24	8	375	15.6(69)	2
1999	Dal	4	87	21.8(31)	0	30	1	344	11.5(76)	1
2000	Was	1	-1	—	—	25	6	185	7.4(57)	0
2004	Bal	0	—	—	—	5	0	41	8.2(23)	0
2005	Bal	0	—	—	—	0	1	—	—	0
NFL 13		155	3523	22.7(100)	3	212	69	2199	10.4(83)	6
SANDERS, THOMAS										
1985	ChiB	1	10	10.0(10)	0	0	—	—	—	—
1986	ChiB	22	399	18.1(44)	0	0	—	—	—	—
1987	ChiB	20	349	17.5(42)	0	0	—	—	—	—
1988	ChiB	13	248	19.1(38)	0	0	—	—	—	—
1989	ChiB	23	491	21.3(96)	1	0	—	—	—	—
1990	Phi	15	299	19.9(37)	0	0	—	—	—	—
1991	Phi	10	160	16.0(31)	0	0	—	—	—	—
NFL 7		104	1956	18.8(96)	1	0	—	—	—	—
SAYERS, GALE										
1965	ChiB	21	660	31.4(96)	1	16	9	238	14.9(85)	1
1966	ChiB	23	718	31.2(93)	2	6	11	44	7.3(27)	0
1967	ChiB	16	603	37.7(103)	3	3	8	80	26.7(58)	1
1968	ChiB	17	461	27.1(48)	0	2	3	29	14.5(18)	0
1969	ChiB	14	339	24.2(52)	0	0	1	—	—	0
NFL 5		91	2781	30.6(103)	6	27	32	391	14.5(85)	2
SCHUBERT, STEVE										
1974	NE	5	112	22.4(32)	0	3	2	15	5.0(11)	0
1975	ChiB	9	146	16.2(25)	0	6	1	33	5.5(16)	0
1976	ChiB	1	3	3.0(3)	0	11	5	60	5.5(14)	0
1977	ChiB	0	—	—	—	31	9	291	9.4(70)	1
1978	ChiB	4	80	20.0(27)	0	27	21	229	8.5(73)	1
1979	ChiB	2	45	22.5(27)	0	25	10	238	9.5(77)	1
NFL 6		21	386	18.4(32)	0	103	48	866	8.4(77)	3
SCHWEDES, SCOTT										
1987	Mia	9	177	19.7(34)	0	24	6	203	8.5(31)	0
1988	Mia	3	49	16.3(25)	0	24	7	230	9.6(36)	0
1989	Mia	3	24	8.0(13)	0	18	3	210	11.7(70)	1
1990	Mia	2	52	26.0(30)	0	9	2	89	9.9(23)	0
1990	SD	0	—	—	—	5	1	33	6.6(12)	0
NFL 4		17	302	17.8(34)	0	80	19	765	9.6(70)	1
SCIARRA, JOHN										
1978	Phi	0	—	—	—	37	9	251	6.8(23)	0
1979	Phi	0	—	—	—	16	0	182	11.4(38)	0
1980	Phi	0	—	—	—	36	1	330	9.2(32)	0
1981	Phi	0	—	—	—	4	0	26	6.5(10)	0
1982	Phi	0	—	—	—	2	0	5	2.5(5)	0
1983	Phi	0	—	—	—	22	3	115	5.2(14)	0
NFL 6		0	—	—	—	117	13	909	7.8(38)	0
SCOBEY, JOSH										
2003	Arz	73	1684	23.1(100)	1	0	—	—	—	—
2004	Arz	32	723	22.6(71)	0	0	—	—	—	—
2005	Sea	59	1326	22.5(53)	0	0	—	—	—	—
NFL 3		164	3733	22.8(100)	1	0	—	—	—	—
SCOTT, JAKE										
1970	Mia	4	117	29.3(42)	0	27	15	290	10.7(77)	1
1971	Mia	0	—	—	—	33	18	318	9.6(31)	0
1972	Mia	0	—	—	—	13	2	100	7.7(15)	0
1973	Mia	2	20	10.0(20)	0	22	16	266	12.1(33)	0
1974	Mia	0	—	—	—	31	3	346	11.2(30)	0
1975	Mia	0	—	—	—	1	0	10	10.0(10)	0
1976	Was	0	—	—	—	3	0	27	9.0(11)	0
NFL 7		6	137	22.8(42)	0	130	55	1357	10.4(77)	1

YEAR	TEAM	KR	YDS	AVG(LG)	TD	PR	FC	YDS	AVG(LG)	TD
SENO, FRANK										
1943	Was	3	61	20.3(25)	0	2	—	27	13.5(20)	0
1944	Was	8	193	24.1(37)	0	10	—	129	12.9(60)	0
1945	ChiC	19	408	21.5(31)	0	10	—	103	10.3(25)	0
1946	ChiC	13	408	31.4(105)	1	17	—	176	10.4(21)	0
1947	Bos	27	636	23.6(79)	0	12	—	213	17.8(86)	1
1948	Bos	8	171	21.4(52)	0	13	—	99	7.6(30)	0
1949	Was	2	39	19.5(23)	0	0	—	—	—	—
NFL 7		80	1916	24.0(105)	1	64	0	747	11.7(86)	1
SHEPARD, DERRICK										
1987	Was	1	20	20.0(20)	0	6	0	146	24.3(73)	0
1988	Was	16	329	20.6(44)	0	12	2	104	8.7(23)	0
1989	NO	8	135	16.9(24)	0	7	1	91	13.0(56)	1
1989	Dal	19	394	20.7(32)	0	24	1	160	6.7(17)	0
1990	Dal	4	75	18.8(22)	0	20	1	121	6.1(13)	0
1991	Dal	3	54	18.0(21)	0	6	3	57	9.5(14)	0
NFL 5		51	1007	19.7(44)	0	75	8	679	9.1(73)	1
SHY, DON										
1967	Pit	21	473	22.5(45)	0	1	1	-5	-5.0(5)	0
1968	Pit	28	682	24.4(90)	0	0	—	—	—	—
1969	NO	16	447	27.9(57)	0	0	—	—	—	—
1973	SL	16	445	27.8(97)	1	0	—	—	—	—
NFL 4		81	2047	25.3(97)	1	1	1	-5	-5.0(0)	0
SIKAHEMA, VAI										
1986	SL	37	847	22.9(44)	0	43	16	522	12.1(71)	2
1987	SL	34	761	22.4(50)	0	44	7	550	12.5(76)	1
1988	Phx	23	475	20.7(39)	0	33	8	341	10.3(28)	0
1989	Phx	43	874	20.3(52)	0	37	13	433	11.7(53)	0
1990	Phx	27	544	20.1(32)	0	36	6	306	8.5(20)	0
1991	GB	15	325	21.7(35)	0	26	4	239	9.2(62)	0
1992	Phi	26	528	20.3(41)	0	40	10	503	12.6(87)	1
1993	Phi	30	579	19.3(35)	0	33	20	275	8.3(25)	0
NFL 8		235	4933	21.0(52)	0	292	84	3169	10.9(87)	4
SKANSI, PAUL										
1983	Pit	0	—	—	—	43	9	363	8.4(57)	0
1984	Sea	0	—	—	—	16	2	145	9.1(16)	0
1985	Sea	19	358	18.8(35)	0	31	7	312	10.1(32)	0
1986	Sea	1	21	21.0(21)	0	5	0	38	7.6(14)	0
1991	Sea	0	—	—	—	1	0	5	5.0(5)	0
NFL 5		20	379	19.0(35)	0	96	18	863	9.0(57)	0
SMART, ROD										
2003	Car	41	947	23.1(100)	1	0	—	—	—	—
2004	Car	8	169	21.1(33)	0	0	—	—	—	—
2005	Car	29	615	21.2(60)	0	0	—	—	—	—
NFL 3		78	1731	22.2(100)	1	0	—	—	—	—
SMITH, J.T.										
1978	Was	1	18	18.0(18)	0	4	1	33	8.3(12)	0
1979	KC	0	—	—	—	58	10	612	10.6(88)	2
1980	KC	0	—	—	—	40	8	581	14.5(75)	2
1981	KC	0	—	—	—	50	7	528	10.6(62)	0
1982	KC	0	—	—	—	3	1	26	8.7(16)	0
1983	KC	1	5	5.0(5)	0	26	5	210	8.1(19)	0
1984	KC	19	391	20.6(39)	0	39	14	332	8.5(27)	0
1985	SL	4	59	14.8(33)	0	26	10	283	10.9(31)	0
1986	SL	0	—	—	—	1	0	6	6.0(6)	0
1988	Phx	0	—	—	—	17	2	119	7.0(15)	0
1990	Phx	0	—	—	—	3	0	34	11.3(16)	0
NFL 11		25	473	18.9(39)	0	267	58	2764	10.4(88)	4
SMITH, JEFF										
1985	KC	33	654	19.8(39)	0	0	—	—	—	—
1986	KC	29	557	19.2(29)	0	29	11	245	8.4(48)	0
1987	TB	5	84	16.8(21)	0	0	—	—	—	—
1988	TB	10	180	18.0(26)	0	8	3	45	5.6(20)	0
NFL 4		77	1475	19.2(39)	0	37	14	290	7.8(48)	0
SMITH, JIM										
1977	Pit	16	381	23.8(37)	0	36	0	294	8.2(30)	0
1978	Pit	1	16	16.0(16)	0	9	0	65	7.2(13)	0
1979	Pit	0	—	—	—	16	1	146	9.1(38)	0
1980	Pit	0	—	—	—	7	0	28	4.0(11)	0
1981	Pit	0	—	—	—	30	1	204	6.8(28)	0
NFL 5		17	397	23.4(37)	0	98	2	737	7.5(38)	0
SMITH, NOLAND										
1967	KC-A	41	1148	28.0(106)	1	26	9	212	8.2(59)	0
1968	KC-A	23	549	23.9(37)	0	18	10	270	15.0(80)	1
1969	KC-A	4	125	31.3(37)	0	9	2	107	11.9(64)	0
1969	SF	14	315	22.5(60)	0	10	4	46	4.6(18)	0
NFL 3		82	2137	26.1(106)	1	63	25	635	10.1(80)	1
SMITH, REGGIE										
1980	Atl	25	512	20.5(35)	0	27	4	262	9.7(25)	0
1981	Atl	47	1143	24.3(52)	0	12	3	99	8.3(53)	0
1987	NYJ	4	60	15.0(20)	0	2	0	9	4.5(7)	0
NFL 3		76	1715	22.6(52)	0	41	7	370	9.0(53)	0
SMITH, RON										
1965	ChiB	1	17	17.0(17)	0	1	0	2	2.0(2)	0
1966	Atl	43	1013	23.6(80)	0	11	1	80	7.3(23)	0
1967	Atl	39	976	25.0(99)	1	20	2	92	4.6(26)	0
1968	LARm	26	718	27.6(94)	1	27	6	171	6.3(24)	0
1969	LARm	27	585	21.7(37)	0	23	6	122	5.3(21)	0
1970	ChiB	28	651	23.3(46)	0	33	1	126	3.8(15)	0

YEAR	TEAM	KR	YDS	AVG (LG)	TD	PR	FC	YDS	AVG (LG)	TD
1971	ChiB	26	671	25.8(41)	0	26	4	194	7.5(43)	0
1972	ChiB	30	924	**30.8(94)**	**1**	**26**	3	163	6.3(29)	0
1973	SD	36	947	26.3(70)	0	27	5	352	**13.0(84)**	**2**
1974	Oak	19	420	22.1(41)	0	41	2	486	11.9(55)	0
NFL	10	275	6922	25.2(99)	3	235	30	1788	7.6(84)	2
SMITH, STEVE										
2001	Car	56	1431	**25.6(99)**	**2**	34	10	364	10.7(70)	**1**
2002	Car	26	571	22.0(51)	0	**55**	13	470	8.5(87)	**2**
2003	Car	11	309	28.1(42)	0	**44**	14	439	10.0(53)	1
2004	Car	0	—	—	—	0	1	—	—	—
2005	Car	3	61	20.3(33)	0	27	6	286	10.6(44)	0
NFL	5	96	2372	24.7(99)	2	160	44	1559	9.7(87)	4
SMITH, VITAMIN										
1949	LARm	13	235	18.1(31)	0	**27**	—	**427**	15.8(**85**)	1
1950	LARm	22	**742**	**33.7(97)**	**3**	22	—	218	9.9(30)	0
1951	LARm	15	274	18.3(36)	0	12	—	139	11.6(37)	0
1952	LARm	5	158	31.6(55)	0	2	—	0	0.0(0)	0
1953	LARm	2	44	22.0(26)	0	12	—	30	2.5(21)	0
NFL	5	57	1453	25.5(97)	3	75	0	814	10.9(85)	1
SOLOMON, FREDDIE										
1975	Mia	17	348	20.5(31)	0	26	4	320	12.3(60)	1
1976	Mia	1	12	12.0(12)	0	13	0	205	15.8(79)	1
1977	Mia	10	273	27.3(90)	1	32	1	285	8.9(39)	0
1978	SF	0	—	—	—	9	5	35	3.9(11)	0
1979	SF	0	—	—	—	23	2	142	6.2(14)	0
1980	SF	4	61	15.3(32)	0	27	2	298	11.0(57)	**2**
1981	SF	0	—	—	—	29	6	173	6.0(19)	0
1982	SF	0	—	—	—	13	1	122	9.4(27)	0
1983	SF	0	—	—	—	5	3	34	6.8(11)	0
NFL	9	32	694	21.7(90)	1	177	24	1614	9.1(79)	4
SPIKES, IRVING										
1994	Mia	19	434	22.8(34)	0	0	—	—	—	—
1995	Mia	18	378	21.0(55)	0	0	—	—	—	—
1996	Mia	28	681	24.3(59)	0	0	—	—	—	—
1997	Mia	24	565	23.5(48)	0	0	—	—	—	—
NFL	4	89	2058	23.1(59)	0	0	—	—	—	—
STAGGERS, JON										
1970	Pit	14	333	23.8(46)	0	13	12	70	5.4(15)	0
1971	Pit	10	261	26.1(47)	0	31	14	262	8.5(67)	**1**
1972	GB	11	260	23.6(39)	0	9	**20**	148	16.4(**85**)	**1**
1973	GB	0	—	—	—	19	12	90	4.7(26)	0
1974	GB	0	—	—	—	22	6	222	10.1(68)	**1**
NFL	5	35	854	24.4(47)	0	94	64	792	8.4(85)	3
STAMPS, SYLVESTER										
1984	Atl	19	452	**23.8(50)**	0	0	—	—	—	—
1985	Atl	4	89	22.3(32)	0	0	—	—	—	—
1986	Atl	24	514	21.4(35)	0	1	0	8	8.0(8)	0
1987	Atl	24	660	**27.5(97)**	**1**	0	—	—	—	—
1988	Atl	12	219	18.3(27)	0	0	—	—	—	—
1989	TB	9	145	16.1(36)	0	0	—	—	—	—
NFL	6	92	2079	22.6(97)	1	1	0	8	8.0(8)	0
STANLEY, WALTER										
1985	GB	9	212	23.6(36)	0	14	3	179	12.8(27)	0
1986	GB	28	559	20.0(55)	0	33	7	316	9.6(**83**)	1
1987	GB	3	47	15.7(29)	0	28	4	173	6.2(48)	0
1988	GB	2	39	19.5(22)	0	12	3	52	4.3(15)	0
1989	Det	9	95	10.6(19)	0	36	5	496	**13.8(74)**	0
1990	Was	9	177	19.7(37)	0	24	8	176	7.3(30)	0
1992	NE	29	529	18.2(40)	0	28	17	227	8.1(50)	0
NFL	7	89	1658	18.6(55)	0	175	47	1619	9.3(83)	1
STARRING, STEPHEN										
1984	NE	0	—	—	—	10	1	73	7.3(16)	0
1985	NE	**48**	1012	21.1(53)	0	2	0	0	0.0(0)	0
1986	NE	36	802	22.3(52)	0	6	0	18	3.0(12)	0
1987	NE	23	445	19.3(43)	0	1	1	17	17.0(17)	0
1988	Det	8	130	16.3(22)	0	0	—	—	—	—
NFL	5	115	2389	20.8(53)	0	19	2	108	5.7(17)	0
STECKER, AARON										
2000	TB	29	663	22.9(48)	0	0	—	—	—	—
2001	TB	9	259	28.8(86)	0	0	—	—	—	—
2002	TB	37	934	25.2(67)	0	0	—	—	—	—
2003	TB	25	520	20.8(44)	0	0	—	—	—	—
2004	NO	18	469	26.1(98)	1	0	—	—	—	—
2005	NO	31	672	21.7(46)	0	0	—	—	—	—
NFL	6	149	3517	23.6(98)	1	0	—	—	—	—
STEVENS, HOWARD										
1973	NO	26	590	22.7(48)	0	17	15	171	10.1(37)	0
1974	NO	33	749	22.7(41)	0	**37**	**7**	**376**	10.2(40)	0
1975	Bal	3	71	23.7(31)	0	36	8	396	11.0(53)	0
1976	Bal	30	710	23.7(83)	0	39	**9**	315	8.1(44)	0
1977	Bal	11	216	19.6(37)	0	34	6	301	8.9(24)	0
NFL	5	103	2336	22.7(83)	0	163	45	1559	9.6(53)	0
STONE, DWIGHT										
1987	Pit	28	568	20.3(34)	0	0	—	—	—	—
1988	Pit	29	610	21.0(92)	**1**	0	—	—	—	—
1989	Pit	7	173	24.7(73)	0	0	—	—	—	—
1990	Pit	5	91	18.2(24)	0	0	—	—	—	—
1991	Pit	6	75	12.5(25)	0	0	—	—	—	—
1992	Pit	12	219	18.3(28)	0	0	—	—	—	—
1993	Pit	11	168	15.3(30)	0	0	—	—	—	—

YEAR	TEAM	KR	YDS	AVG (LG)	TD	PR	FC	YDS	AVG (LG)	TD
1994	Pit	11	182	16.5(31)	0	0	—	—	—	—
1995	Car	12	269	22.4(40)	0	0	—	—	—	—
1997	Car	3	76	25.3(37)	0	0	—	—	—	—
1998	Car	9	252	28.0(45)	0	0	—	—	—	—
1999	NYJ	28	689	24.6(50)	0	0	—	—	—	—
2000	NYJ	25	555	22.2(43)	0	0	—	—	—	—
NFL	13	186	3927	21.1(92)	1	0	—	—	—	—
STUDSTILL, PAT										
1961	Det	16	448	28.0(100)	**1**	8	—	75	9.4(26)	0
1962	Det	20	511	25.5(59)	0	**29**	—	**457**	**15.8(44)**	0
1964	Det	29	708	24.4(53)	0	17	4	137	8.1(36)	0
1965	Det	10	257	25.7(42)	0	5	6	47	9.4(17)	0
NFL	4	75	1924	25.7(100)	1	59	10	716	12.1(44)	0
SUTTON, MICKEY										
1986	LARm	5	91	18.2(0)	0	28	5	234	8.4(32)	0
1987	LARm	2	37	18.5(19)	0	0	2	—	—	—
1988	LARm	2	41	20.5(25)	0	3	6	52	17.3(46)	0
1989	GB	0	—	—	—	5	1	42	8.4(17)	0
1989	Buf	0	—	—	—	26	9	231	8.9(26)	0
1990	LARm	0	—	—	—	14	3	136	9.7(22)	0
NFL	5	9	169	18.8(25)	0	76	26	695	9.1(46)	0
SWINTON, REGGIE										
2001	Dal	56	1327	23.7(77)	0	31	8	414	13.4(65)	**1**
2002	Dal	28	697	24.9(**100**)	1	19	9	141	7.4(26)	0
2003	Dal	3	65	21.7(25)	0	1	3	0	0.0(**0**)	0
2003	Det	40	964	24.1(96)	1	23	9	318	13.8(**89**)	1
2004	Det	18	410	22.8(43)	0	16	9	104	6.5(18)	0
2005	Arz	**63**	**1456**	23.1(90)	0	42	14	334	8.0(32)	0
NFL	5	208	4919	23.6(100)	2	132	52	1311	9.9(89)	2
TALIAFERRO, GEORGE										
1949	LAD-A	13	313	24.1(0)	0	2	—	53	26.5(52)	**1**
1950	NYY	25	473	18.9(34)	0	9	—	129	14.3(27)	0
1951	NYY	**27**	**622**	23.0(47)	0	9	—	68	7.6(23)	0
1952	DalT	6	146	24.3(35)	0	1	—	4	4.0(4)	0
1953	Bal	16	331	20.7(39)	0	10	—	31	3.1(7)	0
1954	Bal	7	134	19.1(24)	0	5	—	34	6.8(18)	0
1955	Phi	1	16	16.0(16)	0	0	—	—	—	—
AAFC	1	13	313	24.1(0)	0	2	0	53	26.5(52)	1
NFL	6	82	1722	21.0(47)	0	34	0	266	7.8(0)	0
TASEFF, CARL										
1951	Cle	3	56	18.7(20)	0	1	—	6	6.0(6)	0
1953	Bal	4	87	21.8(35)	0	1	—	71	71.0(71)	**1**
1954	Bal	7	167	23.9(35)	0	8	—	52	6.5(13)	0
1955	Bal	7	162	23.1(38)	0	14	—	46	3.3(20)	0
1956	Bal	9	206	22.9(34)	0	**27**	—	**233**	8.6(90)	**1**
1957	Bal	0	—	—	—	7	—	60	8.6(40)	0
1958	Bal	1	50	50.0(50)	0	**29**	—	196	6.8(33)	0
1959	Bal	0	—	—	—	15	—	104	6.9(25)	0
1960	Bal	14	291	20.8(30)	0	6	—	25	4.2(7)	0
1961	Bal	0	—	—	—	5	—	39	7.8(23)	0
1962	Buf-A	0	—	—	—	4	—	18	4.5(7)	0
NFL	11	45	1019	22.6(50)	0	117	0	850	7.3(90)	2
TAYLOR, BRUCE										
1970	SF	12	190	15.8(25)	0	43	10	**516**	**12.0(76)**	0
1971	SF	0	—	—	—	**34**	10	**235**	6.9(38)	0
1972	SF	0	—	—	—	21	8	145	6.9(41)	0
1973	SF	0	—	—	—	15	6	207	**13.8(61)**	0
1974	SF	0	—	—	—	10	2	38	3.8(21)	0
1975	SF	0	—	—	—	16	1	166	10.4(66)	0
1976	SF	0	—	—	—	3	1	16	5.3(11)	0
NFL	7	12	190	15.8(25)	0	142	38	1323	9.3(76)	0
TAYLOR, JOHN										
1987	SF	0	—	—	—	1	0	9	9.0(9)	0
1988	SF	12	225	18.8(29)	0	44	7	**556**	**12.6(95)**	**2**
1989	SF	2	51	25.5(27)	0	36	20	417	11.6(37)	0
1990	SF	0	—	—	—	26	5	212	8.2(30)	0
1991	SF	0	—	—	—	31	14	267	8.6(24)	0
1995	SF	0	—	—	—	11	9	56	5.1(11)	0
NFL	6	14	276	19.7(29)	0	149	55	1517	10.2(95)	2
THOMPSON, BILL										
1969	Den-A	18	513	**28.5(63)**	0	25	4	288	**11.5(40)**	0
1970	Den	9	188	20.9(29)	0	23	1	233	10.1(45)	0
1971	Den	5	105	21.0(30)	0	29	4	274	9.4(28)	0
1972	Den	0	—	—	—	4	1	82	20.5(59)	0
1973	Den	1	25	25.0(25)	0	30	6	**366**	12.2(53)	0
1974	Den	13	325	25.0(37)	0	26	1	350	13.5(60)	0
1975	Den	0	—	—	—	13	1	158	12.2(24)	0
1976	Den	0	—	—	—	6	0	60	10.0(20)	0
1978	Den	0	—	—	—	1	0	3	3.0(3)	0
NFL	9	46	1156	25.1(63)	0	157	18	1814	11.6(60)	0
THRASH, JAMES										
1998	Was	6	129	21.5(39)	0	0	—	—	—	—
1999	Was	14	355	25.4(95)	1	0	—	—	—	—
2000	Was	45	1000	22.2(49)	0	10	6	106	10.6(25)	0
2001	Phi	5	101	20.2(34)	0	0	—	—	—	—
2003	Phi	34	815	24.0(54)	0	1	1	2	2.0(2)	0
2004	Was	9	186	20.7(36)	0	19	8	162	8.5(43)	0
2005	Was	7	170	24.3(31)	0	10	15	77	7.7(18)	0
NFL	7	120	2756	23.0(95)	1	40	30	347	8.7(43)	0

YEAR	TEAM	KR	YDS	AVG(LG)	TD	PR	FC	YDS	AVG(LG)	TD
TOOMER, AMANI										
1996	NYG	11	191	17.4(25)	0	18	10	298	**16.6(87)**	2
1997	NYG	0	—	—	—	47	19	455	9.7(53)	1
1998	NYG	4	66	16.5(31)	0	35	22	252	7.2(39)	0
1999	NYG	0	—	—	—	1	0	14	14.0(14)	0
2001	NYG	0	—	—	—	8	1	41	5.1(15)	0
NFL	5	15	257	17.1(31)	0	109	52	1060	9.7(87)	3
TOWNSELL, JO-JO										
1985	NYJ	2	42	21.0(23)	0	6	1	65	10.8(2)	0
1986	NYJ	13	322	24.8(93)	1	4	1	52	13.0(28)	0
1987	NYJ	11	272	24.7(60)	0	32	11	381	11.9**(91)**	1
1988	NYJ	31	601	19.4(40)	0	35	9	409	**11.7(59)**	1
1989	NYJ	34	653	19.2(69)	0	33	12	299	9.1(30)	0
1990	NYJ	7	158	22.6(38)	0	17	4	154	9.1(20)	0
NFL	6	98	2048	20.9(93)	1	127	38	1360	10.7(91)	2
TUNNELL, EMLEN										
1948	NYG	1	21	21.0(21)	0	12	—	115	9.6(25)	0
1949	NYG	2	26	13.0(23)	0	26	—	315	12.1(67)	1
1950	NYG	0	—	—	—	31	—	305	9.8(43)	0
1951	NYG	6	227	37.8**(100)**	1	34	—	**489**	14.4(81)	3
1952	NYG	15	364	24.3(39)	0	30	—	**411**	13.7(60)	0
1953	NYG	17	479	28.2(86)	0	**38**	—	223	5.9(37)	0
1954	NYG	5	98	19.6(25)	0	21	—	70	3.3(12)	0
1955	NYG	0	—	—	—	25	—	98	3.9(66)	1
1956	NYG	0	—	—	—	22	—	120	5.5(14)	0
1957	NYG	0	—	—	—	12	—	60	5.0(23)	0
1958	NYG	0	—	—	—	6	—	0	0.0(0)	0
1959	GB	0	—	—	—	1	—	3	3.0(3)	0
NFL	12	46	1215	26.4(100)	1	258	0	2209	8.6(81)	5
TURNER, BAKE										
1962	Bal	20	504	25.2(37)	0	10	—	95	9.5(43)	0
1963	NYJ-A	14	299	21.4(49)	0	0	—	—	—	—
1965	NYJ-A	18	402	22.3(32)	0	1	—	1	1.0(1)	0
1966	NYJ-A	2	50	25.0(26)	0	10	—	60	6.0(16)	0
1967	NYJ-A	4	40	10.0(21)	0	0	—	—	—	—
1968	NYJ-A	14	319	22.8(36)	0	0	—	—	—	—
1969	NYJ-A	3	74	24.7(28)	0	0	—	—	—	—
NFL	7	75	1688	22.5(49)	0	21	0	156	7.4(43)	0
TURNER, CECIL										
1968	ChiB	20	363	18.1(33)	0	9	**17**	19	2.1(12)	0
1969	ChiB	10	326	32.6(74)	0	8	2	32	4.0(12)	0
1970	ChiB	23	752	**32.7(96)**	4	1	0	0	0.0(0)	0
1971	ChiB	31	639	20.6(40)	0	9	5	63	7.0(21)	0
1972	ChiB	16	409	25.6(57)	0	0	—	—	—	—
1973	ChiB	8	127	15.9(28)	0	0	—	—	—	—
NFL	6	108	2616	24.2(96)	4	27	24	114	4.2(21)	0
TURNER, VERNON										
1991	LARm	24	457	19.0(36)	0	23	4	201	8.7(29)	0
1992	LARm	29	569	19.6(35)	0	28	6	207	7.4(23)	0
1993	Det	15	330	22.0(46)	0	17	4	152	8.9(53)	0
1993	TB	6	61	10.2(19)	0	0	—	—	—	—
1994	TB	43	886	20.6(77)	0	21	4	218	10.4(80)	1
1995	Det	17	323	19.0(43)	0	6	1	39	6.5(16)	0
NFL	5	134	2626	19.6(77)	0	95	19	817	8.6(80)	1
UPCHURCH, RICK										
1975	Den	40	1084	27.1(58)	0	27	4	312	11.6(51)	0
1976	Den	22	514	23.4(64)	0	39	3	536	**13.7(92)**	4
1977	Den	20	456	22.8(52)	0	**51**	6	**653**	12.8(87)	1
1978	Den	8	222	27.8(41)	0	36	2	**493**	13.7(75)	1
1979	Den	5	79	15.8(26)	0	30	4	304	10.1(44)	0
1980	Den	0	—	—	—	37	6	353	9.5(34)	0
1981	Den	0	—	—	—	9	1	63	7.0(15)	0
1982	Den	0	—	—	—	15	3	**242**	16.1(78)	2
1983	Den	0	—	—	—	4	1	52	13.0(17)	0
NFL	9	95	2355	24.8(64)	0	248	30	3008	12.1(92)	8
VAN BUREN, STEVE										
1944	Phi	8	266	33.3**(97)**	1	15	—	230	15.3(55)	1
1945	Phi	13	373	**28.7(98)**	1	14	—	154	11.0(24)	0
1946	Phi	11	319	29.0(63)	0	5	—	89	17.8(50)	1
1947	Phi	13	382	**29.4(95)**	1	0	—	—	—	—
1948	Phi	14	292	20.9(34)	0	0	—	—	—	—
1949	Phi	12	288	24.0(35)	0	0	—	—	—	—
1950	Phi	5	110	22.0(26)	0	0	—	—	—	—
NFL	7	76	2030	26.7(98)	3	34	0	473	13.9(55)	2
VANOVER, TAMARICK										
1995	KC	43	1095	25.5**(99)**	2	51	4	**540**	10.6(86)	1
1996	KC	33	854	25.9**(97)**	1	17	12	116	6.8(24)	0
1997	KC	51	1308	25.6(94)	1	35	14	383	10.9(82)	0
1998	KC	41	956	23.3(62)	0	27	11	264	9.8(37)	0
1999	KC	44	886	20.1(29)	0	51	18	**627**	12.3(84)	2
2002	SD	14	323	23.1(39)	0	16	4	86	5.4(16)	0
NFL	6	226	5422	24.0(99)	4	197	63	2016	10.2(86)	4
VAUGHN, DARRICK										
2000	Atl	39	1082	**27.7(100)**	3	0	—	—	—	—
2001	Atl	**61**	**1491**	24.4(96)	1	0	—	—	—	—
2003	Hou	3	47	15.7(22)	0	0	—	—	—	—
NFL	3	103	2620	25.4(100)	4	0	—	—	—	—
VAUGHN, JON										
1991	NE	34	717	21.1**(99)**	1	0	—	—	—	—
1992	NE	20	564	**28.2(100)**	1	0	—	—	—	—
1993	Sea	16	280	17.5(31)	0	0	—	—	—	—
1994	Sea	18	443	24.6(93)	1	0	—	—	—	—
1994	KC	15	386	25.7(91)	1	0	—	—	—	—
NFL	4	103	2390	23.2(100)	4	0	—	—	—	—
VERDIN, CLARENCE										
1986	Was	12	240	20.0(29)	0	0	—	—	—	—
1987	Was	12	244	20.3(38)	0	0	—	—	—	—
1988	Ind	7	145	20.7(32)	0	22	7	239	10.9**(73)**	**1**
1989	Ind	19	371	19.5(29)	0	23	5	296	**12.9(49)**	**1**
1990	Ind	18	350	19.4(44)	0	31	3	396	**12.8(36)**	0
1991	Ind	36	689	19.1(88)	1	25	10	165	6.6(22)	0
1992	Ind	**39**	**815**	20.9(42)	0	24	12	268	11.2(84)	**2**
1993	Ind	**50**	**1050**	21.0(38)	0	30	17	173	5.8(24)	0
1994	Atl	44	1026	23.3(69)	0	23	13	113	4.9(29)	0
NFL	9	237	4930	20.8(88)	1	178	67	1650	9.3(84)	4
VIGORITO, TOMMY										
1981	Mia	4	84	21.0(25)	0	36	12	379	10.5**(87)**	**1**
1982	Mia	0	—	—	—	20	5	192	9.6(59)	1
1983	Mia	0	—	—	—	0	—	62	62.0(62)	0
1985	Mia	0	—	—	—	22	5	197	9.0(21)	0
NFL	4	4	84	21.0(25)	0	79	22	830	10.5(87)	2
VOLK, RICK										
1967	Bal	0	—	—	—	11	4	88	8.0(24)	0
1968	Bal	0	—	—	—	25	7	198	7.9(24)	0
1969	Bal	0	—	—	—	10	6	58	5.8(14)	0
1970	Bal	0	—	—	—	3	4	15	5.0(6)	0
1971	Bal	0	—	—	—	22	**20**	118	5.4(18)	0
1972	Bal	0	—	—	—	5	7	25	5.0(8)	0
1973	Bal	2	16	8.0(16)	0	7	7	45	6.4(13)	0
1974	Bal	0	—	—	—	1	0	1	1.0(1)	0
NFL	8	2	16	8.0(16)	0	84	55	548	6.5(24)	0
WALKER, FULTON										
1981	Mia	38	932	24.5(90)	1	5	1	50	10.0(17)	—
1982	Mia	20	433	21.6(32)	0	0	—	—	—	—
1983	Mia	36	962	**26.7(78)**	0	8	0	86	10.8(23)	0
1984	Mia	29	617	21.3(41)	0	21	14	169	8.0(33)	0
1985	LARd	21	467	22.2(57)	0	**62**	6	**692**	11.2(32)	0
1986	LARd	23	368	16.0(27)	0	**49**	**15**	440	9.0(70)	**1**
NFL	6	167	3779	22.6(90)	1	145	36	1437	9.9(70)	1
WALKER, HERSCHEL										
1989	Min	13	374	28.8(93)	1	0	—	—	—	—
1990	Min	**44**	**966**	22.0(64)	0	0	—	—	—	—
1991	Min	5	83	16.6(21)	0	0	—	—	—	—
1992	Phi	3	69	23.0(34)	0	0	—	—	—	—
1993	Phi	11	184	16.7(30)	0	0	—	—	—	—
1994	Phi	21	581	27.7(94)	1	0	—	—	—	—
1995	NYG	41	881	21.5(67)	0	0	—	—	—	—
1996	Dal	27	779	28.9(89)	0	0	—	—	—	—
1997	Dal	50	1167	23.3(49)	0	0	—	—	—	—
NFL	9	215	5084	23.6(94)	2	0	—	—	—	—
WALLACE, JACKIE										
1974	Min	2	31	15.5(16)	0	25	4	191	7.6(20)	0
1975	Bal	1	0	0.0(0)	0	6	0	43	7.2(14)	0
1976	Bal	3	61	20.3(23)	0	0	3	—	—	—
1978	LARm	0	—	—	—	**52**	6	**618**	**11.9(58)**	0
NFL	4	6	92	15.3(23)	0	83	12	852	10.3(58)	0
WALTERS, TROY										
2000	Min	30	692	23.1(38)	0	15	16	217	14.5(63)	0
2001	Min	18	425	23.6(50)	0	11	3	69	6.3(16)	0
2002	Ind	53	1150	21.7(44)	0	35	15	270	7.7(34)	0
2003	Ind	6	126	21.0(34)	0	11	7	105	9.5(26)	0
2004	Ind	1	16	16.0(16)	0	7	6	40	5.7(14)	0
2005	Ind	1	13	13.0(13)	0	21	**25**	172	8.2(29)	0
NFL	6	109	2422	22.2(50)	0	100	72	873	8.7(63)	0
WARD, DEDRIC										
1997	NYJ	2	10	5.0(11)	0	8	2	55	6.9(12)	0
1998	NYJ	3	60	20.0(23)	0	8	3	72	9.0(20)	0
1999	NYJ	0	—	—	—	38	12	288	7.6(23)	0
2000	NYJ	0	—	—	—	27	**19**	214	7.9(19)	0
2001	Mia	0	—	—	—	9	2	88	9.8(18)	0
2002	Mia	0	—	—	—	16	11	169	10.6(34)	0
2003	Bal	1	20	20.0(20)	0	3	0	26	8.7(16)	0
2003	NE	0	—	—	—	0	2	—	—	—
2004	Dal	0	—	—	—	14	6	114	8.1(13)	0
NFL	8	6	90	15.0(23)	0	123	57	1026	8.3(34)	0
WARNER, CHARLEY										
1963	KC-A	9	215	23.9(33)	0	4	—	25	6.3(13)	0
1964	KC-A	7	180	25.7(44)	0	9	—	110	12.2(22)	0
1964	Buf-A	5	121	24.2(44)	0	3	—	55	18.3(40)	0
1965	Buf-A	32	825	25.8**(102)**	2	1	—	16	16.0(16)	0
1966	Buf-A	33	846	25.6(95)	1	0	—	—	—	—
NFL	4	86	2187	25.4(102)	3	17	0	206	12.1(40)	0
WARREN, CHRIS										
1990	Sea	23	478	20.8(71)	0	28	16	269	9.6(39)	0
1991	Sea	35	792	22.6(55)	0	**32**	14	298	9.3(59)	1
1992	Sea	28	524	18.7(34)	0	34	**25**	252	7.4(16)	0
1998	Dal	5	90	18.0(23)	0	2	1	11	5.5(6)	0
NFL	4	91	1884	20.7(71)	0	96	61	830	8.6(59)	1
WASHINGTON, VIC										
1971	SF	33	858	26.0(74)	0	0	—	—	—	—
1972	SF	27	771	28.6**(98)**	1	0	—	—	—	—
1973	SF	24	549	22.9(38)	0	0	—	—	—	—
1974	Hou	7	177	25.3(40)	0	0	—	—	—	—
1975	Buf	35	923	26.4(59)	0	0	—	—	—	—

YEAR	TEAM	KR	YDS	AVG(LG)	TD	PR	FC	YDS	AVG(LG)	TD
1976	Buf	3	63	21.0(27)	0	0	—	—	—	—
NFL	6	129	3341	25.9(98)	1	0	—	—	—	—
Watkins, Tom										
1961	Cle	9	226	25.1(47)	0	0	—	—	—	—
1962	Det	17	452	26.6(40)	0	8	—	42	5.3(20)	0
1963	Det	21	447	21.3(33)	0	**32**	12	**399**	12.5(**90**)	**1**
1964	Det	16	368	23.0(57)	0	16	6	238	**14.9**(**68**)	**2**
1965	Det	17	584	**34.4**(**94**)	0	23	11	234	10.2(41)	0
1967	Det	20	411	20.5(44)	0	15	3	57	3.8(18)	0
1968	Pit	1	22	22.0(22)	0	2	0	0	0.0(0)	0
NFL	7	101	2510	24.9(94)	0	96	32	970	10.1(90)	3
Watson, Chris										
1999	Den	48	1138	23.7(71)	0	44	8	334	7.6(81)	1
2000	Buf	44	894	20.3(37)	0	33	18	163	4.9(20)	0
2001	Buf	5	96	19.2(30)	0	0	—	—	—	—
NFL	3	97	2128	21.9(71)	0	77	26	497	6.5(81)	1
Welker, Wes										
2004	SD	4	102	25.5(33)	0	0	—	—	—	—
2004	Mia	57	1313	23.0(95)	1	43	12	464	10.8(71)	0
2005	Mia	61	1379	22.6(46)	0	43	23	390	9.1(47)	0
NFL	2	122	2794	22.9(95)	1	86	35	854	9.9(71)	0
West, Charlie										
1968	Min	22	576	26.2(82)	0	20	8	201	10.1(**98**)	1
1969	Min	9	240	26.7(78)	0	**39**	**19**	245	6.3(55)	0
1970	Min	11	319	29.0(66)	0	29	9	169	5.8(53)	0
1971	Min	24	556	23.2(36)	0	18	11	94	5.2(16)	0
1972	Min	9	196	21.8(31)	0	16	6	111	6.9(23)	0
1973	Min	3	104	34.7(42)	0	1	0	0	0.0(0)	0
1974	Det	4	71	17.8(25)	0	6	0	32	5.3(9)	0
1975	Det	2	41	20.5(25)	0	22	8	219	10.0(43)	0
1976	Det	0	—	—	—	3	2	9	3.0(4)	0
1978	Den	1	24	24.0(24)	0	3	2	20	6.7(12)	0
1979	Den	0	—	—	—	1	0	-1	—	—
NFL	11	85	2127	25.0(82)	0	158	65	1099	7.0(98)	1
Whittington, Arthur										
1978	Oak	23	473	20.6(34)	0	0	—	—	—	—
1979	Oak	5	46	9.2(19)	0	0	—	—	—	—
1980	Oak	21	392	18.7(90)	**1**	0	—	—	—	—
1981	Oak	25	563	22.5(47)	0	2	1	4	2.0(4)	0
1982	Buf	2	39	19.5(21)	0	0	—	—	—	—
NFL	5	76	1513	19.9(90)	1	2	1	4	2.0(4)	0
Wilkins, Terrence										
1999	Ind	51	1134	22.2(97)	**1**	41	17	388	9.5(39)	1
2000	Ind	15	279	18.6(30)	0	29	13	240	8.3(36)	0
2001	Ind	44	1007	22.9(50)	0	21	4	219	10.4(78)	1
2002	SL	47	1074	22.9(42)	0	25	13	242	9.7(55)	0
2003	Ind	14	325	23.2(42)	0	7	0	25	3.6(16)	0
NFL	5	171	3819	22.3(97)	1	123	47	1114	9.1(78)	2
Willhite, Gerald										
1982	Den	17	337	19.8(26)	0	6	4	63	10.5(23)	0
1984	Den	4	109	27.3(40)	0	20	9	200	10.0(35)	0
1985	Den	2	40	20.0(20)	0	16	5	169	10.6(18)	0
1986	Den	3	35	11.7(23)	0	42	8	**468**	11.1(70)	**1**
1987	Den	0	—	—	—	4	1	22	5.5(9)	0
1988	Den	0	—	—	—	13	2	90	6.9(12)	0
NFL	6	26	521	20.0(40)	0	101	29	1012	10.0(70)	1
Williams, Bobby										
1966	SL	7	132	18.9(34)	0	0	—	—	—	—
1967	SL	24	583	24.3(38)	0	0	—	—	—	—
1969	Det	17	563	**33.1**(**96**)	**1**	0	—	—	—	—
1970	Det	25	544	21.8(85)	1	0	—	—	—	—
1971	Det	4	112	28.0(40)	0	0	—	—	—	—
NFL	5	77	1934	25.1(96)	2	0	—	—	—	—
Williams, Dave										
1977	SF	4	122	30.5(80)	**1**	1	0	60	60.0(60)	0
1978	SF	34	745	21.9(89)	**1**	0	—	—	—	—
1980	ChiB	27	666	24.7(95)	**1**	0	—	—	—	—
1981	ChiB	23	486	21.1(42)	0	0	—	—	—	—
NFL	4	88	2019	22.9(95)	3	1	0	60	60.0(60)	0
Williams, Jimmy										
2002	SF	35	765	21.9(50)	0	20	8	336	**16.8**(**89**)	1
2003	SF	11	207	18.8(41)	0	35	10	240	6.9(20)	0
2004	SF	3	58	19.3(23)	0	0	—	—	—	—
2005	Sea	0	—	—	—	24	**22**	139	5.8(24)	0
NFL	4	49	1030	21.0(50)	0	79	40	715	9.1(89)	1
Williams, Karl										
1996	TB	14	383	27.4(63)	0	13	2	274	21.1(88)	1
1997	TB	15	277	18.5(28)	0	46	12	**597**	13.0(63)	**1**
1998	TB	0	—	—	—	10	6	83	8.3(18)	0
1999	TB	1	15	15.0(15)	0	20	12	153	7.7(30)	0
2000	TB	19	453	23.8(41)	0	31	18	286	9.2(73)	1
2001	TB	2	35	17.5(22)	0	35	13	366	10.5(84)	**1**
2002	TB	3	49	16.3(23)	0	43	20	410	9.5(56)	1
2003	TB	1	15	15.0(15)	0	15	10	110	7.3(19)	0
2004	Arz	1	18	18.0(18)	0	42	12	286	6.8(38)	0
NFL	9	56	1245	22.2(63)	0	255	105	2565	10.1(88)	5
Williams, Kevin										
1993	Dal	31	689	22.2(49)	0	36	14	381	10.6(64)	**2**
1994	Dal	43	1148	26.7(87)	1	39	13	349	8.9(83)	1
1995	Dal	49	1108	22.6(43)	0	18	15	166	9.2(30)	0
1996	Dal	21	471	22.4(39)	0	2	0	17	8.5(9)	0

YEAR	TEAM	KR	YDS	AVG(LG)	TD	PR	FC	YDS	AVG(LG)	TD
1997	Arz	**59**	**1458**	24.7(63)	0	40	15	462	11.6(50)	0
1998	Buf	47	1059	22.5(46)	0	37	11	369	10.0(73)	0
1999	Buf	42	840	20.0(62)	0	33	17	331	10.0(27)	0
2000	SF	30	536	17.9(33)	0	26	13	220	8.5(25)	0
NFL	8	322	7309	22.7(87)	1	231	98	2295	9.9(83)	3
Williams, Travis										
1967	GB	18	739	**41.1**(**104**)	**4**	0	—	—	—	—
1968	GB	28	599	21.4(60)	0	0	—	—	—	—
1969	GB	21	517	24.6(96)	**1**	8	3	189	23.6(83)	**1**
1970	GB	10	203	20.3(28)	0	4	2	20	5.0(11)	0
1971	LARm	25	743	**29.7**(**105**)	1	1	0	4	4.0(4)	0
NFL	5	102	2801	27.5(105)	6	13	5	213	16.4(83)	1
Wilson, Charles										
1990	GB	35	798	22.8(36)	0	0	—	—	—	—
1991	GB	23	522	22.7(82)	**1**	0	—	—	—	—
1992	TB	1	23	23.0(23)	0	0	—	—	—	—
1993	TB	23	454	19.7(42)	0	0	—	—	—	—
1994	TB	10	251	25.1(41)	0	0	—	—	—	—
NFL	5	92	2048	22.3(82)	1	0	—	—	—	—
Witherspoon, Derrick										
1995	Phi	18	459	25.5(86)	**1**	0	—	—	—	—
1996	Phi	53	1271	24.0(**97**)	**2**	0	—	—	—	—
1997	Phi	9	171	19.0(28)	0	0	—	—	—	—
NFL	3	80	1901	23.8(97)	3	0	—	—	—	—
Wood, Willie										
1960	GB	0	—	—	—	16	—	106	6.6(33)	0
1961	GB	0	—	—	—	14	—	225	**16.1**(**72**)	**2**
1962	GB	0	—	—	—	23	—	273	11.9(65)	0
1963	GB	1	20	20.0(20)	0	19	9	169	8.9(41)	0
1964	GB	0	—	—	—	19	11	252	13.3(64)	0
1965	GB	0	—	—	—	13	10	38	2.9(14)	0
1966	GB	1	0	0.0(0)	0	22	9	82	3.7(13)	0
1967	GB	1	0	0.0(0)	0	12	6	3	0.3(3)	0
1968	GB	0	—	—	—	26	11	126	4.8(16)	0
1969	GB	0	—	—	—	8	6	38	4.8(13)	0
1970	GB	0	—	—	—	11	**18**	58	5.3(12)	0
1971	GB	0	—	—	—	4	2	21	5.3(9)	0
NFL	12	3	20	6.7(20)	0	187	102	1391	7.4(72)	2
Woodson, Abe										
1958	SF	11	239	21.7(34)	0	7	—	53	7.6(38)	0
1959	SF	13	382	**29.4**(**105**)	**1**	15	—	143	9.5(65)	0
1960	SF	17	498	29.3(64)	0	13	—	**174**	13.4(**48**)	0
1961	SF	27	782	29.0(98)	**1**	16	—	172	10.8(80)	1
1962	SF	**37**	**1157**	**31.3**(**79**)	0	19	—	179	9.4(**85**)	**1**
1963	SF	29	935	**32.2**(**103**)	**3**	13	7	95	7.3(51)	0
1964	SF	32	880	27.5(70)	0	22	8	133	6.0(26)	0
1965	SL	27	665	24.6(65)	0	18	**18**	7	0.4(13)	0
NFL	8	193	5538	28.7(105)	5	123	33	956	7.8(85)	2
Woodson, Rod										
1987	Pit	13	290	22.3(36)	0	16	1	135	8.4(20)	0
1988	Pit	37	850	23.0(92)	**1**	33	6	281	8.5(28)	0
1989	Pit	**36**	**982**	**27.3**(**84**)	**1**	29	2	207	7.1(20)	0
1990	Pit	35	764	21.8(49)	0	**38**	8	**398**	10.5(52)	**1**
1991	Pit	**44**	**880**	20.0(47)	0	28	12	320	**11.4**(**40**)	0
1992	Pit	25	469	18.8(32)	0	32	13	364	11.4(80)	1
1993	Pit	15	294	19.6(44)	0	42	10	338	8.0(39)	0
1994	Pit	15	365	24.3(54)	0	39	9	319	8.2(42)	0
1997	SF	0	—	—	—	1	0	0	0.0(0)	0
1999	Bal	0	—	—	—	2	2	0	0.0(7)	0
NFL	10	220	4894	22.2(92)	2	260	63	2362	9.1(80)	2
Wright, Alexander										
1990	Dal	12	276	23.0(90)	**1**	0	—	—	—	—
1991	Dal	21	514	24.5(**102**)	**1**	0	1	—	—	—
1992	Dal	8	117	14.6(21)	0	0	—	—	—	—
1992	LARd	18	325	18.1(33)	0	0	—	—	—	—
1993	LARd	10	167	16.7(28)	0	0	—	—	—	—
1994	LARd	10	282	28.2(55)	0	0	—	—	—	—
NFL	5	79	1681	21.3(102)	2	0	1	—	—	—
Wright, Keith										
1978	Cle	30	789	**26.3**(**86**)	0	37	**16**	288	7.8(42)	0
1979	Cle	15	402	26.8(45)	0	12	6	50	4.2(13)	0
1980	Cle	25	576	23.0(50)	0	29	4	129	4.4(15)	0
NFL	3	70	1767	25.2(86)	0	78	26	467	6.0(42)	0
Young, Buddy										
1947	NYY-A	12	332	27.7(95)	**1**	8	—	127	15.9(0)	**1**
1948	NYY-A	12	303	25.3(0)	0	2	—	11	5.5(0)	0
1949	NYY-A	11	316	28.7(**91**)	**1**	9	—	171	19.0(0)	0
1950	NYY	20	536	26.8(50)	0	9	—	54	6.0(12)	0
1951	NYY	14	427	30.5(90)	**1**	12	—	231	**19.3**(**79**)	1
1952	DalT	**23**	**643**	28.0(63)	0	6	—	35	5.8(18)	0
1953	Bal	11	378	34.4(**104**)	**1**	6	—	9	1.5(9)	0
1954	Bal	13	308	23.7(30)	0	14	—	60	4.3(16)	0
1955	Bal	9	222	24.7(43)	0	1	—	0	0.0(0)	0
AAFC	3	35	951	27.2(186)	2	19	0	309	16.3(0)	1
NFL	6	90	2514	27.9(82)	2	48	0	389	8.1(79)	1
Young, Glen										
1983	Phi	26	547	21.0(52)	0	14	3	93	6.6(23)	0
1984	Cle	5	134	26.8(36)	0	0	—	—	—	—
1985	Cle	35	898	25.7(63)	0	0	—	—	—	—
1987	Cle	18	412	22.9(44)	0	0	—	—	—	—
1988	Cle	29	635	21.9(34)	0	0	—	—	—	—
NFL	5	113	2626	23.2(63)	0	14	3	93	6.6(23)	0

Abraham, Donnie

YEAR	TEAM	INT	YDS	AVG(LG)	TD
1996	TB	5	27	5.4(21)	0
1997	TB	5	16	3.2(16)	0
1998	TB	1	3	3.0(3)	0
1999	TB	**7**	115	16.4(55)	**2**
2000	TB	7	82	11.7(23)	0
2001	TB	6	98	16.3(46)	0
2002	NYJ	4	49	12.3(23)	0
2003	NYJ	1	12	12.0(12)	0
2004	NYJ	2	66	33.0(66)	1
NFL	9	38	468	12.3(66)	3

Adderley, Herb

YEAR	TEAM	INT	YDS	AVG(LG)	TD
1961	GB	1	9	9.0(9)	0
1962	GB	7	132	18.9(50)	1
1963	GB	5	86	17.2(39)	0
1964	GB	4	56	14.0(35)	0
1965	GB	6	**175**	29.2(44)	**3**
1966	GB	4	125	31.3(68)	1
1967	GB	4	16	4.0(12)	1
1968	GB	3	27	9.0(17)	0
1969	GB	5	**169**	33.8(80)	1
1970	Dal	3	69	23.0(30)	0
1971	Dal	6	182	30.3(46)	0
NFL	12	48	1046	21.8(80)	7

Alban, Dick

YEAR	TEAM	INT	YDS	AVG(LG)	TD
1952	Was	1	27	27.0(27)	0
1953	Was	4	13	3.3(11)	0
1954	Was	9	81	9.0(27)	0
1955	Was	2	48	24.0(25)	0
1956	Pit	2	21	10.5(21)	0
1957	Pit	1	35	35.0(35)	0
1958	Pit	5	25	5.0(16)	0
1959	Pit	6	119	19.8(46)	0
NFL	8	30	369	12.3(46)	0

Alexander, Brent

YEAR	TEAM	INT	YDS	AVG(LG)	TD
1995	Arz	2	14	7.0(14)	0
1996	Arz	2	3	1.5(3)	0
1999	Car	2	18	9.0(18)	0
2000	Pit	3	31	10.3(15)	0
2001	Pit	4	39	9.8(22)	0
2002	Pit	4	37	9.3(25)	0
2003	Pit	4	63	15.8(34)	0
2004	NYG	3	3	1.0(2)	0
2005	NYG	4	45	11.3(24)	0
NFL	10	28	253	9.0(34)	0

Alexander, Kermit

YEAR	TEAM	INT	YDS	AVG(LG)	TD
1963	SF	5	72	14.4(38)	0
1964	SF	5	65	13.0(24)	0
1965	SF	3	23	7.7(15)	0
1966	SF	4	73	18.3(55)	0
1967	SF	5	72	14.4(48)	0
1968	SF	9	155	17.2(66)	1
1969	SF	5	39	7.8(22)	0
1970	LARm	4	47	11.8(25)	1
1971	LARm	3	122	**40.7(82)**	1
NFL	10	43	668	15.5(82)	3

Alexander, Willie

YEAR	TEAM	INT	YDS	AVG(LG)	TD
1971	Hou	4	74	18.5(36)	0
1972	Hou	1	16	16.0(16)	0
1973	Hou	3	3	1.0(3)	0
1974	Hou	2	56	28.0(29)	0
1975	Hou	3	41	13.7(32)	0
1977	Hou	3	111	37.0(95)	1
1978	Hou	5	51	10.2(29)	0
1979	Hou	2	27	13.5(19)	0
NFL	8	23	379	16.5(95)	1

Allen, Chuck

YEAR	TEAM	INT	YDS	AVG(LG)	TD
1961	SD-A	5	111	22.2(59)	1
1962	SD-A	1	7	7.0(7)	0
1963	SD-A	5	37	7.4(26)	0
1964	SD-A	4	75	18.8(33)	0
1965	SD-A	1	0	0.0(0)	0
1966	SD-A	1	8	8.0(8)	0
1967	SD-A	2	2	1.0(2)	0
1968	SD-A	1	4	4.0(4)	0
1970	Pit	4	48	12.0(30)	0
1971	Pit	3	45	15.0(29)	0
1972	Phi	1	15	15.0(15)	0
NFL	12	28	352	12.6(59)	1

Allen, Eric

YEAR	TEAM	INT	YDS	AVG(LG)	TD
1988	Phi	5	76	15.2(21)	0
1989	Phi	**8**	38	4.8(18)	0
1990	Phi	3	37	12.3(35)	1
1991	Phi	5	20	4.0(8)	0
1992	Phi	4	49	12.3(36)	0
1993	Phi	6	**201**	33.5(**94**)	**4**
1994	Phi	3	61	20.3(33)	0
1995	NO	2	28	14.0(28)	0
1996	NO	1	33	33.0(33)	0
1997	NO	2	27	13.5(27)	0
1998	Oak	5	59	11.8(22)	0
1999	Oak	3	33	11.0(31)	0
2000	Oak	6	145	24.2(50)	**3**
2001	Oak	1	19	19.0(19)	0
NFL	14	54	826	15.3(94)	8

Allen, Jimmy

YEAR	TEAM	INT	YDS	AVG(LG)	TD
1975	Pit	2	0	0.0(0)	0
1977	Pit	5	76	15.2(48)	0
1978	Det	5	70	14.0(27)	0
1979	Det	4	0	0.0(0)	0
1980	Det	6	38	6.3(23)	0
1981	Det	9	123	13.7(34)	0
NFL	7	31	307	9.9(48)	0

Ambrose, Ashley

YEAR	TEAM	INT	YDS	AVG(LG)	TD
1994	Ind	2	50	25.0(42)	0
1995	Ind	3	12	4.0(7)	0
1996	Cin	8	63	7.9(69)	1
1997	Cin	3	56	18.7(29)	0
1998	Cin	2	0	0.0(0)	0
1999	NO	6	27	4.5(16)	0
2000	Atl	4	**139**	34.8(42)	1
2001	Atl	5	43	8.6(27)	0
2002	Atl	3	25	8.3(24)	0
2003	NO	3	78	26.0(73)	1
2004	NO	3	19	6.3(19)	0
NFL	12	42	512	12.2(73)	3

Anderson, Dick

YEAR	TEAM	INT	YDS	AVG(LG)	TD
1968	Mia-A	8	**230**	28.8(96)	1
1969	Mia-A	3	106	**35.3(40)**	0
1970	Mia	8	**191**	**23.9(86)**	0
1971	Mia	2	33	16.5(33)	0
1972	Mia	3	34	11.3(22)	0
1973	Mia	**8**	163	20.4(38)	**2**
1974	Mia	1	3	3.0(3)	0
1976	Mia	1	32	32.0(32)	0
NFL	9	34	792	23.3(96)	3

Anderson, John

YEAR	TEAM	INT	YDS	AVG(LG)	TD
1978	GB	5	27	5.4(12)	0
1981	GB	3	12	4.0(8)	0
1982	GB	3	22	7.3(9)	0
1983	GB	5	54	10.8(27)	1
1984	GB	3	24	8.0(22)	0
1985	GB	2	2	1.0(2)	0
1986	GB	1	3	3.0(3)	0
1987	GB	2	22	11.0(13)	0
1989	GB	1	1	1.0(1)	0
NFL	12	25	167	6.7(27)	1

Atkins, Billy

YEAR	TEAM	INT	YDS	AVG(LG)	TD
1958	SF	1	6	6.0(6)	0
1960	Buf-A	5	23	4.6(0)	0
1961	Buf-A	**10**	158	15.8(29)	0
1962	NYT-A	4	30	7.5(17)	0
NFL	4	20	217	10.9(29)	0

Atkins, Gene

YEAR	TEAM	INT	YDS	AVG(LG)	TD
1987	NO	3	12	4.0(8)	0
1988	NO	4	42	10.5(40)	0
1989	NO	1	-2	-2.0(-2)	0
1990	NO	2	15	7.5(15)	0
1991	NO	5	**198**	**39.6(79)**	0
1992	NO	3	0	0.0(0)	0
1993	NO	3	59	19.7(37)	0
1994	Mia	3	24	8.0(18)	0
1995	Mia	1	0	0.0(0)	0
NFL	9	25	348	13.9(79)	0

Atkinson, Al

YEAR	TEAM	INT	YDS	AVG(LG)	TD
1965	NYJ-A	1	2	2.0(2)	0
1966	NYJ-A	4	48	12.0(26)	0
1967	NYJ-A	5	59	11.8(36)	0
1968	NYJ-A	2	24	12.0(22)	0
1969	NYJ-A	2	4	2.0(4)	0
1970	NYJ	3	50	16.7(32)	0
1971	NYJ	2	19	9.5(17)	0
1972	NYJ	1	7	7.0(7)	0
1973	NYJ	1	11	11.0(11)	0
NFL	10	21	224	10.7(36)	0

Atkinson, George

YEAR	TEAM	INT	YDS	AVG(LG)	TD
1968	Oak-A	4	66	16.5(33)	1
1969	Oak-A	2	38	19.0(22)	1
1970	Oak	3	35	11.7(22)	0
1971	Oak	4	70	17.5(41)	0
1972	Oak	4	37	9.3(23)	0
1973	Oak	3	48	16.0(36)	0
1974	Oak	4	39	9.8(26)	0
1975	Oak	4	77	19.3(26)	0
1977	Oak	2	38	19.0(24)	0
NFL	9	30	448	14.9(41)	2

Atwater, Steve

YEAR	TEAM	INT	YDS	AVG(LG)	TD
1989	Den	3	34	11.3(30)	0
1990	Den	2	32	16.0(27)	0
1991	Den	5	104	20.8(49)	0
1992	Den	2	22	11.0(22)	0
1993	Den	2	81	40.5(68)	0
1994	Den	1	24	24.0(24)	0
1995	Den	3	54	18.0(25)	0
1996	Den	3	11	3.7(11)	0
1997	Den	2	42	21.0(22)	1
1998	Den	1	4	4.0(4)	0
NFL	10	24	408	17.0(68)	1

Bailey, Champ

YEAR	TEAM	INT	YDS	AVG(LG)	TD
1999	Was	5	55	11.0(59)	1
2000	Was	5	48	9.6(48)	0
2001	Was	3	17	5.7(12)	0
2002	Was	3	2	0.7(2)	0
2003	Was	2	2	1.0(2)	0
2004	Den	3	0	0.0(0)	0
2005	Den	8	139	17.4(65)	**2**
NFL	7	29	263	9.1(65)	3

Baird, Bill

YEAR	TEAM	INT	YDS	AVG(LG)	TD
1963	NYJ-A	6	31	5.2(26)	0
1964	NYJ-A	8	130	16.3(54)	1
1965	NYJ-A	3	9	3.0(9)	0
1966	NYJ-A	5	76	15.2(39)	1
1967	NYJ-A	3	27	9.0(17)	0
1968	NYJ-A	4	74	18.5(36)	0
1969	NYJ-A	5	10	2.0(7)	0
NFL	7	34	357	10.5(54)	2

Baker, Dave

YEAR	TEAM	INT	YDS	AVG(LG)	TD
1959	SF	5	75	15.0(29)	0
1960	SF	**10**	96	9.6(28)	0
1961	SF	6	123	20.5(40)	0
NFL	3	21	294	14.0(40)	0

Banfield, Tony

YEAR	TEAM	INT	YDS	AVG(LG)	TD
1960	Hou-A	3	22	7.3(22)	0
1961	Hou-A	8	136	17.0(58)	0
1962	Hou-A	6	17	2.8(11)	0
1963	Hou-A	7	21	3.0(14)	0
1965	Hou-A	3	28	9.3(28)	0
NFL	5	27	224	8.3(58)	0

Barbaro, Gary

YEAR	TEAM	INT	YDS	AVG(LG)	TD
1976	KC	3	27	9.0(16)	0
1977	KC	8	**165**	20.6(**102**)	1
1978	KC	3	92	30.7(35)	0
1979	KC	7	142	20.3(70)	1
1980	KC	10	163	16.3(39)	0
1981	KC	5	134	26.8(34)	0
1982	KC	3	48	16.0(43)	1
NFL	7	39	771	19.8(102)	3

Barber, Ronde

YEAR	TEAM	INT	YDS	AVG(LG)	TD
1998	TB	2	67	33.5(56)	0
1999	TB	2	60	30.0(43)	0
2000	TB	2	46	23.0(37)	1
2001	TB	**10**	86	8.6(36)	1
2002	TB	2	9	4.5(9)	0
2003	TB	2	53	26.5(29)	1
2004	TB	3	23	7.7(23)	0
2005	TB	5	105	21.0(42)	0
NFL	8	28	449	16.0(56)	3

Barnes, Erich

YEAR	TEAM	INT	YDS	AVG(LG)	TD
1958	ChiB	4	90	22.5(30)	1
1959	ChiB	5	67	13.4(29)	0
1961	NYG	7	**195**	27.9(**102**)	**2**
1962	NYG	6	61	10.2(22)	0
1963	NYG	3	0	0.0(0)	0
1964	NYG	2	26	13.0(26)	1
1965	Cle	1	35	35.0(35)	0
1966	Cle	4	128	32.0(54)	0
1967	Cle	4	47	11.8(40)	0
1968	Cle	3	64	21.3(40)	1
1969	Cle	1	55	55.0(55)	1
1970	Cle	5	85	17.0(38)	1
NFL	12	45	853	19.0(102)	7

Barney, Lem

YEAR	TEAM	INT	YDS	AVG(LG)	TD
1967	Det	**10**	**232**	23.2(71)	**3**
1968	Det	7	82	11.7(62)	0
1969	Det	8	126	15.8(32)	0
1970	Det	7	**168**	24.0(49)	**2**
1971	Det	3	78	26.0(28)	1
1972	Det	3	88	**29.3(64)**	0
1973	Det	4	130	32.5(38)	0
1974	Det	4	61	15.3(39)	0
1975	Det	5	23	4.6(13)	0
1976	Det	2	62	31.0(26)	1
1977	Det	3	27	9.0(22)	0
NFL	11	56	1077	19.2(71)	7

Bass, Mike

YEAR	TEAM	INT	YDS	AVG(LG)	TD
1969	Was	3	31	10.3(31)	0
1970	Was	4	37	9.3(22)	0
1971	Was	8	78	9.8(38)	1
1972	Was	3	53	17.7(29)	0
1973	Was	5	161	32.2(68)	1
1974	Was	3	33	11.0(28)	1
1975	Was	4	85	21.3(30)	0
NFL	7	30	478	15.9(68)	3

Baugh, Sammy

YEAR	TEAM	INT	YDS	AVG(LG)	TD
1940	Was	3	84	**28.0(44)**	0
1941	Was	4	83	20.8(35)	0
1942	Was	5	77	15.4(29)	0
1943	Was	**11**	112	10.2(23)	0
1944	Was	4	21	5.3(18)	0
1945	Was	4	114	28.5(**74**)	0
NFL	16	31	491	15.8(74)	0

Beasley, Aaron

YEAR	TEAM	INT	YDS	AVG(LG)	TD
1996	Jax	1	0	0.0(0)	0
1997	Jax	1	5	5.0(5)	0
1998	Jax	3	35	11.7(34)	0
1999	Jax	6	**200**	**33.3(93)**	**2**
2000	Jax	1	39	39.0(39)	0
2001	Jax	3	0	0.0(0)	0
2002	NYJ	2	29	14.5(24)	0
2003	NYJ	3	64	21.3(39)	0
2004	Atl	4	115	28.8(85)	0
NFL	9	24	487	20.3(93)	2

Beauchamp, Joe

YEAR	TEAM	INT	YDS	AVG(LG)	TD
1966	SD-A	2	24	12.0(21)	0
1967	SD-A	3	44	14.7(28)	0
1968	SD-A	5	114	22.8(35)	**2**
1970	SD	1	25	25.0(25)	0
1971	SD	4	95	23.8(52)	0
1972	SD	6	96	16.0(47)	1
1974	SD	1	35	35.0(35)	0
1975	SD	1	0	0.0(0)	0
NFL	9	23	433	18.8(52)	3

Bednarik, Chuck

YEAR	TEAM	INT	YDS	AVG(LG)	TD
1950	Phi	1	9	9.0(9)	0
1952	Phi	2	14	7.0(12)	0
1953	Phi	6	116	19.3(41)	1
1954	Phi	1	9	9.0(9)	0
1955	Phi	1	36	36.0(36)	0
1956	Phi	2	0	0.0(0)	0
1957	Phi	3	51	17.0(37)	0
1960	Phi	2	0	0.0(0)	0
1961	Phi	2	33	16.5(33)	0
NFL	13	20	268	13.4(41)	1

Bell, Bobby

YEAR	TEAM	INT	YDS	AVG(LG)	TD
1963	KC-A	1	20	20.0(20)	0
1964	KC-A	1	4	4.0(4)	0
1965	KC-A	4	73	18.3(38)	1
1966	KC-A	2	14	7.0(13)	0
1967	KC-A	4	82	20.5(32)	1
1968	KC-A	5	95	19.0(50)	1
1970	KC	3	57	19.0(45)	1
1971	KC	1	26	26.0(26)	1
1972	KC	3	56	18.7(61)	1
1973	KC	1	24	24.0(24)	0
1974	KC	1	28	28.0(28)	1
NFL	12	26	479	18.4(61)	6

Bellamy, Jay

YEAR	TEAM	INT	YDS	AVG(LG)	TD
1996	Sea	3	18	6.0(16)	0
1997	Sea	1	13	13.0(13)	0
1998	Sea	3	40	13.3(24)	0
1999	Sea	4	4	1.0(7)	0
2000	Sea	4	132	33.0(84)	1
2001	NO	3	21	7.0(21)	0
2002	NO	3	39	13.0(16)	0
2003	NO	3	19	6.3(10)	0
NFL	9	24	286	11.9(84)	1

Bergey, Bill

YEAR	TEAM	INT	YDS	AVG(LG)	TD
1969	Cin-A	2	62	31.0(58)	0
1970	Cin	3	35	11.7(26)	0
1971	Cin	1	16	16.0(16)	0
1973	Cin	3	50	16.7(22)	0
1974	Phi	5	57	11.4(27)	0
1975	Phi	3	48	16.0(20)	0
1976	Phi	2	48	24.0(37)	0
1977	Phi	2	4	2.0(4)	0
1978	Phi	4	70	17.5(50)	0
1979	Phi	1	0	0.0(0)	0
1980	Phi	1	7	7.0(7)	0
NFL	12	27	397	14.7(58)	0

Berry, Rex

YEAR	TEAM	INT	YDS	AVG(LG)	TD
1951	SF	4	77	19.3(38)	0
1952	SF	2	27	13.5(23)	0
1953	SF	7	142	20.3(29)	1
1954	SF	3	69	23.0(34)	1
1955	SF	3	69	23.0(44)	1
1956	SF	3	20	6.7(20)	0
NFL	6	22	404	18.4(44)	3

Bingham, Gregg

YEAR	TEAM	INT	YDS	AVG(LG)	TD
1973	Hou	2	22	11.0(18)	0
1974	Hou	4	36	9.0(18)	0
1975	Hou	4	57	14.3(26)	0
1976	Hou	2	18	9.0(15)	0
1977	Hou	2	36	18.0(30)	0
1979	Hou	3	78	26.0(54)	0

YEAR	TEAM	INT	YDS	AVG(LG)	TD
1981	Hou	2	20	10.0(17)	0
1982	Hou	1	8	8.0(8)	0
1983	Hou	1	4	4.0(4)	0
NFL	12	21	279	13.3(54)	0

Bishop, Don

YEAR	TEAM	INT	YDS	AVG(LG)	TD
1960	Dal	3	13	4.3(13)	0
1961	Dal	8	172	21.5(57)	0
1962	Dal	6	134	22.3(44)	0
1963	Dal	5	45	9.0(31)	0
NFL	8	22	364	16.5(57)	0

Blackwood, Glenn

YEAR	TEAM	INT	YDS	AVG(LG)	TD
1980	Mia	3	0	0.0(0)	0
1981	Mia	4	124	31.0(39)	0
1982	Mia	2	42	21.0(35)	1
1983	Mia	3	0	0.0(0)	0
1984	Mia	6	169	28.2(50)	0
1985	Mia	6	36	6.0(17)	0
1986	Mia	2	10	5.0(7)	0
1987	Mia	3	17	5.7(17)	0
NFL	8	29	398	13.7(50)	1

Blackwood, Lyle

YEAR	TEAM	INT	YDS	AVG(LG)	TD
1975	Cin	2	44	22.0(40)	0
1977	Bal	**10**	163	16.3(37)	0
1978	Bal	4	146	36.5(79)	**2**
1979	Bal	4	63	15.8(27)	0
1980	Bal	1	0	0.0(0)	0
1981	Mia	3	12	4.0(11)	0
1982	Mia	2	41	20.5(21)	0
1983	Mia	4	77	19.3(45)	0
1984	Mia	3	29	9.7(15)	0
1985	Mia	1	0	0.0(0)	0
1986	Mia	1	14	14.0(14)	0
NFL	14	35	589	16.8(79)	2

Blount, Mel

YEAR	TEAM	INT	YDS	AVG(LG)	TD
1970	Pit	1	4	4.0(4)	0
1971	Pit	2	16	8.0(16)	0
1972	Pit	3	75	25.0(34)	0
1973	Pit	4	82	20.5(24)	0
1974	Pit	2	74	37.0(52)	1
1975	Pit	**11**	121	11.0(47)	0
1976	Pit	6	75	12.5(28)	0
1977	Pit	6	65	10.8(37)	0
1978	Pit	4	55	13.8(35)	0
1979	Pit	3	1	0.3(1)	0
1980	Pit	4	28	7.0(17)	0
1981	Pit	6	106	17.7(50)	1
1982	Pit	1	2	2.0(2)	0
1983	Pit	4	32	8.0(21)	0
NFL	14	57	736	12.9(52)	2

Bly, Dre'

YEAR	TEAM	INT	YDS	AVG(LG)	TD
1999	SL	3	53	17.7(53)	1
2000	SL	3	44	14.7(22)	0
2001	SL	6	150	25.0(93)	**2**
2002	SL	2	0	0.0(0)	0
2003	Det	6	89	14.8(48)	1
2004	Det	4	107	26.8(55)	1
2005	Det	6	54	9.0(28)	0
NFL	7	30	497	16.6(93)	5

Bolton, Ron

YEAR	TEAM	INT	YDS	AVG(LG)	TD
1973	NE	6	65	10.8(56)	0
1974	NE	7	18	2.6(10)	0
1975	NE	5	33	6.6(15)	0
1976	Cle	3	76	25.3(39)	1
1977	Cle	3	50	16.7(43)	0
1979	Cle	3	20	6.7(13)	0
1980	Cle	6	62	10.3(29)	0
1981	Cle	1	3	3.0(3)	0
1982	Cle	1	0	0.0(0)	0
NFL	10	35	327	9.3(56)	1

Boyd, Bobby

YEAR	TEAM	INT	YDS	AVG(LG)	TD
1960	Bal	7	132	18.9(74)	0
1961	Bal	2	0	0.0(0)	0
1962	Bal	7	163	23.3(38)	0
1963	Bal	3	17	5.7(9)	0
1964	Bal	9	**185**	20.6(47)	0
1965	Bal	**9**	78	8.7(24)	1
1966	Bal	6	114	19.0(37)	1
1967	Bal	6	145	24.2(41)	1
1968	Bal	8	160	20.0(49)	1
NFL	9	57	994	17.4(74)	4

Bradley, Bill

YEAR	TEAM	INT	YDS	AVG(LG)	TD
1969	Phi	1	56	56.0(56)	1
1971	Phi	**11**	**248**	22.5(51)	0
1972	Phi	**9**	73	8.1(21)	0
1973	Phi	4	21	5.3(18)	0
1974	Phi	2	19	9.5(10)	0
1975	Phi	5	56	11.2(20)	0
1976	Phi	2	63	31.5(52)	0
NFL	9	34	536	15.8(56)	1

Braxton, Tyrone

YEAR	TEAM	INT	YDS	AVG(LG)	TD
1988	Den	2	6	3.0(6)	0
1989	Den	6	103	17.2(34)	1
1990	Den	1	10	10.0(10)	0
1991	Den	4	55	13.8(52)	1
1992	Den	2	54	27.0(40)	0
1993	Den	3	37	12.3(25)	0
1994	Mia	2	3	1.5(3)	0
1995	Den	2	36	18.0(36)	0
1996	Den	**9**	128	14.2(69)	1
1997	Den	4	113	28.3(43)	1
1998	Den	1	72	72.0(72)	0
NFL	12	36	617	17.1(72)	4

Breeden, Louis

YEAR	TEAM	INT	YDS	AVG(LG)	TD
1978	Cin	3	25	8.3(18)	0
1980	Cin	7	91	13.0(29)	0
1981	Cin	4	145	36.3(**102**)	1
1982	Cin	2	9	4.5(9)	0
1983	Cin	2	47	23.5(39)	0
1984	Cin	4	96	24.0(70)	0
1985	Cin	2	24	12.0(30)	0
1986	Cin	7	72	10.3(36)	1
1987	Cin	2	49	24.5(44)	0
NFL	9	33	558	16.9(102)	2

Brock, Charley

YEAR	TEAM	INT	YDS	AVG(LG)	TD
1939	GB	0	0	0.0(0)	**1**
1940	GB	3	7	2.3(6)	0
1942	GB	6	25	4.2(16)	0
1943	GB	4	61	15.3(41)	0
1944	GB	1	1	1.0(1)	0
1945	GB	4	**122**	**30.5(38)**	**2**
1947	GB	2	14	7.0(7)	0
NFL	8	20	230	11.5(41)	3

Brooks, Derrick

YEAR	TEAM	INT	YDS	AVG(LG)	TD
1996	TB	1	6	6.0(6)	0
1997	TB	2	13	6.5(13)	0
1998	TB	1	25	25.0(25)	0
1999	TB	4	61	15.3(38)	0
2000	TB	1	34	34.0(34)	1
2001	TB	3	65	21.7(53)	0
2002	TB	5	218	**43.6(97)**	**3**
2003	TB	2	56	28.0(44)	1
2004	TB	1	3	3.0(3)	0
2005	TB	1	0	0.0(0)	0
NFL	11	21	481	22.9(97)	5

Brookshier, Tom

YEAR	TEAM	INT	YDS	AVG(LG)	TD
1953	Phi	8	41	5.1(22)	0
1956	Phi	1	31	31.0(31)	0
1957	Phi	4	74	18.5(40)	0
1958	Phi	1	0	0.0(0)	0
1959	Phi	3	13	4.3(8)	0
1960	Phi	1	14	14.0(14)	0
1961	Phi	2	20	10.0(20)	0
NFL	7	20	193	9.6(40)	0

Brown, Cedric

YEAR	TEAM	INT	YDS	AVG(LG)	TD
1977	TB	2	66	33.0(27)	0
1978	TB	6	110	18.3(29)	0
1979	TB	3	79	26.3(72)	0
1980	TB	1	0	0.0(0)	0
1981	TB	9	215	23.9(81)	2
1982	TB	3	31	10.3(24)	0
1983	TB	4	78	19.5(36)	0
1984	TB	1	14	14.0(14)	0
NFL	8	29	593	20.4(81)	2

Brown, Dave

YEAR	TEAM	INT	YDS	AVG(LG)	TD
1976	Sea	4	70	17.5(33)	0
1977	Sea	4	68	17.0(29)	1
1978	Sea	3	44	14.7(44)	0
1979	Sea	5	46	9.2(23)	0
1980	Sea	6	32	5.3(24)	0
1981	Sea	2	2	1.0(2)	0
1982	Sea	1	3	3.0(3)	0
1983	Sea	6	83	13.8(37)	0
1984	Sea	8	179	22.4(90)	**2**
1985	Sea	6	58	9.7(28)	1
1986	Sea	5	58	11.6(24)	1
1987	GB	3	16	5.3(11)	0
1988	GB	3	27	9.0(15)	0
1989	GB	6	12	2.0(12)	0
NFL	15	62	698	11.3(90)	5

Brown, Ray

YEAR	TEAM	INT	YDS	AVG(LG)	TD
1971	Atl	3	32	10.7(23)	0
1972	Atl	2	46	23.0(46)	0
1973	Atl	6	99	16.5(24)	0
1974	Atl	**8**	164	20.5(**59**)	1
1975	Atl	4	119	29.8(41)	1
1976	Atl	3	58	19.3(21)	0
1977	Atl	5	56	11.2(24)	0
1978	NO	4	50	12.5(19)	0
1979	NO	1	2	2.0(2)	0
1980	NO	2	31	15.5(29)	0
NFL	10	38	657	17.3(59)	2

Brown, Willie

YEAR	TEAM	INT	YDS	AVG(LG)	TD
1963	Den-A	1	0	0.0(0)	0
1964	Den-A	9	140	15.6(45)	0
1965	Den-A	2	18	9.0(18)	0
1966	Den-A	3	37	12.3(31)	0
1967	Oak-A	7	33	4.7(25)	1
1968	Oak-A	2	27	13.5(27)	1
1969	Oak-A	5	111	22.2(30)	0
1970	Oak	3	0	0.0(0)	0
1971	Oak	2	2	1.0(2)	0
1972	Oak	4	26	6.5(13)	0
1973	Oak	3	-1	-0.3(-1)	0
1974	Oak	1	31	31.0(31)	0
1975	Oak	4	-1	-0.3(0)	0
1976	Oak	3	25	8.3(22)	0
1977	Oak	4	24	6.0(18)	0
1978	Oak	1	0	0.0(0)	0
NFL	16	54	472	8.7(45)	2

Browner, Joey

YEAR	TEAM	INT	YDS	AVG(LG)	TD
1983	Min	2	0	0.0(0)	0
1984	Min	1	20	20.0(20)	0
1985	Min	2	17	8.5(15)	1
1986	Min	4	62	15.5(39)	1
1987	Min	6	67	11.2(23)	0
1988	Min	5	29	5.8(18)	0
1989	Min	5	70	14.0(34)	0
1990	Min	7	103	14.7(31)	1
1991	Min	5	97	19.4(45)	0
NFL	9	37	465	12.6(45)	3

Bryant, Bobby

YEAR	TEAM	INT	YDS	AVG(LG)	TD
1968	Min	2	60	30.0(51)	1
1969	Min	8	97	12.1(56)	0
1970	Min	3	40	13.3(39)	1
1971	Min	3	51	17.0(19)	0
1972	Min	4	82	20.5(34)	0
1973	Min	**7**	105	15.0(46)	1
1975	Min	6	111	18.5(41)	0
1976	Min	2	30	15.0(25)	0
1977	Min	4	44	11.0(41)	0
1978	Min	7	69	9.9(23)	0
1979	Min	2	50	25.0(29)	0
1980	Min	3	10	3.3(7)	0
NFL	12	51	749	14.7(56)	3

Buchanan, Ray

YEAR	TEAM	INT	YDS	AVG(LG)	TD
1993	Ind	4	45	11.3(28)	0
1994	Ind	8	221	27.6(90)	**3**
1995	Ind	2	60	30.0(60)	0
1996	Ind	2	32	16.0(32)	0
1997	Atl	5	49	9.8(31)	0
1998	Atl	7	102	14.6(34)	0
1999	Atl	4	81	20.3(52)	1
2000	Atl	6	114	19.0(60)	0
2001	Atl	5	85	17.0(33)	0
2002	Atl	2	9	4.5(9)	0
2003	Atl	1	2	2.0(2)	0
2004	Oak	1	27	27.0(27)	0
NFL	12	47	827	17.6(90)	4

Buchanon, Willie

YEAR	TEAM	INT	YDS	AVG(LG)	TD
1972	GB	4	62	15.5(26)	0
1974	GB	4	10	2.5(8)	0
1976	GB	2	28	14.0(22)	0
1977	GB	2	41	20.5(29)	1
1978	GB	**9**	93	10.3(77)	1
1980	SD	2	13	6.5(7)	0
1981	SD	5	31	6.2(18)	0
NFL	10	28	278	9.9(77)	2

Buckley, Terrell

YEAR	TEAM	INT	YDS	AVG(LG)	TD
1992	GB	3	33	11.0(33)	1
1993	GB	2	31	15.5(31)	0
1994	GB	5	38	7.6(26)	0
1995	Mia	1	0	0.0(0)	0
1996	Mia	6	**164**	27.3(91)	1
1997	Mia	4	26	6.5(12)	0
1998	Mia	8	157	19.6(61)	1
1999	Mia	3	3	1.0(18)	0
2000	Den	6	110	18.3(33)	1
2001	NE	3	76	25.3(52)	1
2002	NE	4	50	12.5(39)	0
2003	Mia	2	75	37.5(74)	1
2004	NYJ	3	30	10.0(18)	0
NFL	13	50	793	15.9(91)	6

Buffone, Doug

YEAR	TEAM	INT	YDS	AVG(LG)	TD
1967	ChiB	3	39	13.0(22)	0
1968	ChiB	1	21	21.0(21)	0
1969	ChiB	2	12	6.0(12)	0
1970	ChiB	4	33	8.3(16)	0
1971	ChiB	2	27	13.5(18)	0
1972	ChiB	1	0	0.0(0)	0
1973	ChiB	3	22	7.3(22)	0
1974	ChiB	1	0	0.0(0)	0
1975	ChiB	1	12	12.0(12)	0
1977	ChiB	1	12	12.0(12)	0
1978	ChiB	3	22	7.3(16)	0
1979	ChiB	2	11	5.5(11)	0
NFL	13	24	211	8.8(22)	0

Buoniconti, Nick

YEAR	TEAM	INT	YDS	AVG(LG)	TD
1962	Bos-A	2	3	1.5(3)	0
1963	Bos-A	3	42	14.0(26)	0
1964	Bos-A	5	75	15.0(26)	0
1965	Bos-A	3	31	10.3(26)	0
1966	Bos-A	4	43	10.8(41)	0
1967	Bos-A	4	7	1.8(7)	0
1968	Bos-A	3	22	7.3(14)	0
1969	Mia-A	3	27	9.0(24)	0
1971	Mia	1	16	16.0(16)	0
1972	Mia	2	17	8.5(10)	0
1974	Mia	2	29	14.5(16)	0
NFL	12	32	312	9.8(41)	0

Burroughs, Don

YEAR	TEAM	INT	YDS	AVG(LG)	TD
1955	LARm	9	103	11.4(34)	0
1956	LARm	2	9	4.5(9)	0
1957	LARm	3	29	9.7(24)	0
1958	LARm	7	72	10.3(46)	0
1960	Phi	9	124	13.8(46)	0
1961	Phi	7	90	12.9(42)	0
1962	Phi	7	96	13.7(28)	0
1963	Phi	4	36	9.0(21)	0
1964	Phi	2	5	2.5(3)	0
NFL	10	50	564	11.3(46)	0

Burruss, Lloyd

YEAR	TEAM	INT	YDS	AVG(LG)	TD
1981	KC	4	75	18.8(46)	1
1982	KC	1	25	25.0(25)	0
1983	KC	4	46	11.5(27)	0
1984	KC	2	16	8.0(16)	0
1985	KC	1	0	0.0(0)	0
1986	KC	5	**193**	**38.6(72)**	**3**
1988	KC	2	57	28.5(32)	0
1989	KC	1	0	0.0(0)	0
1990	KC	1	14	14.0(14)	0
1991	KC	1	83	83.0(**83**)	0
NFL	10	22	509	23.1(83)	4

Butkus, Dick

YEAR	TEAM	INT	YDS	AVG(LG)	TD
1965	ChiB	5	84	16.8(38)	0
1966	ChiB	1	3	3.0(3)	0
1967	ChiB	1	24	24.0(24)	0
1968	ChiB	3	14	4.7(14)	0
1969	ChiB	2	13	6.5(11)	0
1970	ChiB	3	0	0.0(0)	0
1971	ChiB	4	9	2.3(9)	0
1972	ChiB	2	19	9.5(14)	0
1973	ChiB	1	0	0.0(0)	0
NFL	9	22	166	7.5(38)	0

Butler, Bobby

YEAR	TEAM	INT	YDS	AVG(LG)	TD
1981	Atl	5	86	17.2(41)	0
1982	Atl	2	0	0.0(0)	0
1983	Atl	4	12	3.0(12)	0
1984	Atl	2	25	12.5(25)	0
1985	Atl	5	-4	-0.8(0)	0
1986	Atl	1	33	33.0(33)	1
1987	Atl	4	48	12.0(31)	0
1988	Atl	1	22	22.0(22)	0
1990	Atl	3	0	0.0(0)	0
NFL	11	27	222	8.2(41)	1

Butler, Jack

YEAR	TEAM	INT	YDS	AVG(LG)	TD
1951	Pit	5	142	**28.4(52)**	1
1952	Pit	7	168	24.0(41)	0
1953	Pit	9	147	16.3(28)	1
1954	Pit	4	75	18.8(41)	**2**
1956	Pit	6	113	18.8(34)	0
1957	Pit	**10**	85	8.5(20)	0
1958	Pit	9	81	9.0(19)	0
1959	Pit	2	16	8.0(16)	0
NFL	9	52	827	15.9(52)	4

Butler, LeRoy

YEAR	TEAM	INT	YDS	AVG(LG)	TD
1990	GB	3	42	14.0(28)	0
1991	GB	3	6	2.0(6)	0
1992	GB	1	0	0.0(0)	0
1993	GB	6	131	21.8(39)	0
1994	GB	3	68	22.7(51)	0
1995	GB	5	105	21.0(76)	0
1996	GB	5	149	29.8(90)	1
1997	GB	5	4	0.8(2)	0
1998	GB	3	3	1.0(3)	0
1999	GB	2	0	0.0(0)	0
2000	GB	2	25	12.5(22)	0
NFL	12	38	533	14.0(90)	1

Byrd, Butch

YEAR	TEAM	INT	YDS	AVG(LG)	TD
1964	Buf-A	7	178	25.4(75)	1
1965	Buf-A	5	119	23.8(62)	0
1966	Buf-A	6	110	18.3(60)	1
1967	Buf-A	5	25	5.0(12)	0
1968	Buf-A	6	76	12.7(53)	1
1969	Buf-A	7	95	13.6(32)	1

YEAR	TEAM	INT	YDS	AVG(LG)	TD
1970	Buf	4	63	15.8(33)	1
NFL	7	40	666	16.6(75)	5

Byrd, Gill

YEAR	TEAM	INT	YDS	AVG(LG)	TD
1983	SD	1	0	0.0(0)	0
1984	SD	4	157	**39.3**(**99**)	**2**
1985	SD	1	25	25.0(25)	0
1986	SD	5	45	9.0(18)	0
1988	SD	7	82	11.7(42)	0
1989	SD	7	38	5.4(22)	0
1990	SD	7	63	9.0(24)	0
1991	SD	6	48	8.0(22)	0
1992	SD	4	88	22.0(44)	0
NFL	10	42	546	13.0(99)	2

Caroline, J.C.

YEAR	TEAM	INT	YDS	AVG(LG)	TD
1956	ChiB	6	182	30.3(59)	**2**
1957	ChiB	2	22	11.0(20)	0
1959	ChiB	5	14	2.8(8)	0
1960	ChiB	3	31	10.3(31)	0
1961	ChiB	3	48	16.0(28)	0
1962	ChiB	2	21	10.5(21)	0
1963	ChiB	1	3	3.0(3)	0
1964	ChiB	2	84	42.0(79)	0
NFL	9	24	405	16.9(79)	2

Carrier, Mark

YEAR	TEAM	INT	YDS	AVG(LG)	TD
1990	ChiB	**10**	39	3.9(14)	0
1991	ChiB	2	54	27.0(39)	0
1993	ChiB	4	94	23.5(34)	1
1994	ChiB	2	10	5.0(7)	0
1996	ChiB	2	0	0.0(0)	0
1997	Det	5	94	18.8(66)	0
1998	Det	3	33	11.0(33)	0
1999	Det	3	16	5.3(16)	0
2000	Was	1	30	30.0(30)	0
NFL	11	32	370	11.6(66)	1

Carrington, Darren

YEAR	TEAM	INT	YDS	AVG(LG)	TD
1989	Den	1	2	2.0(2)	0
1991	SD	3	30	10.0(19)	0
1992	SD	6	152	25.3(69)	1
1993	SD	7	104	14.9(28)	0
1994	SD	3	51	17.0(32)	0
1995	Jax	1	17	17.0(17)	0
1996	Oak	1	21	21.0(21)	0
NFL	8	22	377	17.1(69)	1

Carter, Dale

YEAR	TEAM	INT	YDS	AVG(LG)	TD
1992	KC	7	65	9.3(36)	1
1993	KC	1	0	0.0(0)	0
1994	KC	2	24	12.0(24)	0
1995	KC	4	45	11.3(29)	0
1996	KC	3	17	5.7(17)	0
1997	KC	2	9	4.5(9)	0
1998	KC	2	23	11.5(23)	0
1999	Den	2	48	24.0(34)	0
2002	NO	1	25	25.0(25)	0
NFL	10	24	256	10.7(36)	1

Carter, Tom

YEAR	TEAM	INT	YDS	AVG(LG)	TD
1993	Was	6	54	9.0(29)	0
1994	Was	3	58	19.3(40)	0
1995	Was	4	116	29.0(51)	1
1996	Was	5	24	4.8(24)	0
1997	ChiB	3	12	4.0(12)	0
1998	ChiB	2	20	10.0(19)	0
1999	ChiB	1	36	36.0(36)	0
1999	Cin	1	0	0.0(0)	0
2000	Cin	2	40	20.0(30)	0
NFL	8	27	360	13.3(51)	1

Case, Scott

YEAR	TEAM	INT	YDS	AVG(LG)	TD
1985	Atl	4	78	19.5(47)	0
1986	Atl	4	41	10.3(41)	0
1987	Atl	1	12	12.0(12)	0
1988	Atl	**10**	47	4.7(12)	0
1989	Atl	2	13	6.5(13)	0
1990	Atl	3	38	12.7(36)	1
1991	Atl	2	23	11.5(17)	0
1992	Atl	2	0	0.0(0)	0
1993	Atl	0	3	0.0(3)	0
1994	Atl	2	12	6.0(12)	0
NFL	11	30	267	8.9(47)	1

Cason, Jim

YEAR	TEAM	INT	YDS	AVG(LG)	TD
1948	SF-A	5	46	9.2(0)	0
1949	SF-A	**9**	**152**	16.9(0)	0
1950	SF	1	22	22.0(22)	0
1951	SF	8	147	18.4(65)	1
1952	SF	2	4	2.0(4)	0
1955	LARm	5	41	8.2(25)	1
1956	LARm	4	63	15.8(29)	0
AAFC	2	14	198	14.1(0)	0
NFL	6	20	277	13.9(65)	2

Cherry, Deron

YEAR	TEAM	INT	YDS	AVG(LG)	TD
1981	KC	1	4	4.0(4)	0
1983	KC	7	100	14.3(41)	0
1984	KC	7	140	20.0(67)	0
1985	KC	7	87	12.4(47)	1
1986	KC	**9**	150	16.7(49)	0
1987	KC	3	58	19.3(30)	0
1988	KC	7	51	7.3(24)	0
1989	KC	2	27	13.5(27)	0
1990	KC	3	40	13.3(21)	0
1991	KC	4	31	7.8(16)	0
NFL	11	50	688	13.8(67)	1

Christiansen, Jack

YEAR	TEAM	INT	YDS	AVG(LG)	TD
1951	Det	2	53	26.5(53)	0
1952	Det	2	47	23.5(32)	0
1953	Det	**12**	**238**	19.8(**92**)	1
1954	Det	8	84	10.5(30)	1
1955	Det	3	49	16.3(29)	0
1956	Det	8	109	13.6(33)	0
1957	Det	**10**	137	13.7(52)	1
1958	Det	1	0	0.0(0)	0
NFL	8	46	717	15.6(92)	3

Clark, Mario

YEAR	TEAM	INT	YDS	AVG(LG)	TD
1976	Buf	2	21	10.5(21)	0
1977	Buf	7	151	21.6(43)	0
1978	Buf	5	29	5.8(29)	0
1979	Buf	5	95	19.0(36)	0
1980	Buf	1	0	0.0(0)	0
1981	Buf	5	142	28.4(53)	0
1984	SF	1	0	0.0(0)	0
NFL	8	26	438	16.8(53)	0

Clay, Willie

YEAR	TEAM	INT	YDS	AVG(LG)	TD
1994	Det	3	54	18.0(28)	1
1995	Det	8	**173**	21.6(39)	0
1996	NE	4	50	12.5(35)	0
1997	NE	6	109	18.2(53)	1
1998	NE	3	19	6.3(19)	0
1999	NO	3	32	10.7(24)	0
NFL	7	27	437	16.2(53)	2

Clayborn, Raymond

YEAR	TEAM	INT	YDS	AVG(LG)	TD
1978	NE	4	72	18.0(44)	0
1979	NE	5	56	11.2(27)	0
1980	NE	5	87	17.4(29)	0
1981	NE	2	39	19.5(39)	0
1982	NE	1	26	26.0(26)	0
1984	NE	3	102	34.0(85)	0
1985	NE	6	80	13.3(38)	1
1986	NE	3	4	1.3(4)	0
1987	NE	2	24	12.0(24)	0
1988	NE	4	65	16.3(31)	0
1989	NE	1	0	0.0(0)	0
NFL	12	36	555	15.4(85)	1

Clements, Nate

YEAR	TEAM	INT	YDS	AVG(LG)	TD
2001	Buf	3	48	16.0(48)	1
2002	Buf	6	82	13.7(42)	1
2003	Buf	3	54	18.0(54)	1
2004	Buf	6	77	12.8(35)	1
2005	Buf	2	0	0.0(0)	0
NFL	5	20	261	13.1(54)	4

Colella, Tom

YEAR	TEAM	INT	YDS	AVG(LG)	TD
1942	Det	1	10	10.0(10)	0
1944	Cle	4	53	13.3(19)	0
1946	Cle-A	**10**	110	11.0(0)	0
1947	Cle-A	**6**	130	21.7(0)	1
1948	Cle-A	2	34	17.0(0)	0
1949	Buf-A	3	49	16.3(0)	0
AAFC	4	21	323	15.4(0)	1
NFL	4	5	63	12.6(19)	0

Coleman, Marcus

YEAR	TEAM	INT	YDS	AVG(LG)	TD
1996	NYJ	1	23	23.0(23)	0
1997	NYJ	1	24	24.0(24)	0
1999	NYJ	6	165	27.5(**98**)	1
2000	NYJ	4	6	1.5(7)	0
2001	NYJ	2	41	20.5(36)	0
2002	Hou	1	0	0.0(0)	0
2003	Hou	**7**	95	13.6(41)	0
2004	Hou	2	116	58.0(102)	1
2005	Hou	1	6	6.0(6)	0
NFL	9	25	476	19.0(102)	2

Collins, Mark

YEAR	TEAM	INT	YDS	AVG(LG)	TD
1986	NYG	1	0	0.0(0)	0
1987	NYG	2	28	14.0(28)	0
1988	NYG	1	13	13.0(13)	0
1989	NYG	2	12	6.0(12)	0
1990	NYG	2	0	0.0(0)	0
1991	NYG	4	77	19.3(41)	0
1992	NYG	1	0	0.0(0)	0
1993	NYG	4	77	19.3(50)	1
1994	KC	2	83	41.5(78)	1
1995	KC	1	8	8.0(8)	0
1996	KC	6	45	7.5(23)	0
1998	Sea	1	0	0.0(0)	0
NFL	12	27	343	12.7(78)	2

Colzie, Neal

YEAR	TEAM	INT	YDS	AVG(LG)	TD
1975	Oak	4	38	9.5(38)	0
1977	Oak	3	13	4.3(13)	0
1978	Oak	3	62	20.7(28)	0
1979	Mia	5	86	17.2(56)	0
1980	TB	1	39	39.0(39)	0
1981	TB	6	110	18.3(82)	1
1982	TB	3	64	21.3(51)	0
NFL	9	25	412	16.5(82)	1

Comp, Irv

YEAR	TEAM	INT	YDS	AVG(LG)	TD
1943	GB	10	149	14.9(35)	**1**
1944	GB	6	54	9.0(43)	0
1945	GB	2	67	33.5(54)	1
1946	GB	2	38	19.0(21)	0
1947	GB	6	65	10.8(30)	0
1948	GB	5	86	17.2(28)	0
1949	GB	3	24	8.0(14)	0
NFL	7	34	483	14.2(54)	2

Cook, Toi

YEAR	TEAM	INT	YDS	AVG(LG)	TD
1988	NO	1	0	0.0(0)	0
1989	NO	3	81	**27.0**(**63**)	1
1990	NO	2	55	27.5(50)	0
1991	NO	3	54	18.0(22)	0
1992	NO	6	90	15.0(48)	1
1993	NO	1	0	0.0(0)	0
1994	SF	1	18	18.0(18)	0
1996	Car	3	28	9.3(22)	0
NFL	10	20	326	16.3(63)	2

Costello, Vince

YEAR	TEAM	INT	YDS	AVG(LG)	TD
1957	Cle	2	19	9.5(12)	0
1959	Cle	0	14	0.0(14)	0
1962	Cle	3	40	13.3(22)	0
1963	Cle	7	118	16.9(31)	0
1964	Cle	2	21	10.5(20)	0
1965	Cle	3	33	11.0(23)	0
1966	Cle	1	0	0.0(0)	0
1967	NYG	4	54	13.5(26)	0
NFL	11	22	299	13.6(31)	0

Craft, Russ

YEAR	TEAM	INT	YDS	AVG(LG)	TD
1946	Phi	3	105	**35.0**(**49**)	0
1947	Phi	1	0	0.0(0)	0
1949	Phi	1	17	17.0(17)	0
1950	Phi	7	70	10.0(29)	0
1951	Phi	2	61	30.5(26)	0
1952	Phi	1	32	32.0(32)	1
1953	Phi	4	46	11.5(27)	0
1954	Pit	3	120	**40.0**(**81**)	1
NFL	9	22	451	20.5(81)	2

Crist, Chuck

YEAR	TEAM	INT	YDS	AVG(LG)	TD
1972	NYG	1	14	14.0(14)	0
1973	NYG	2	6	3.0(6)	0
1974	NYG	3	20	6.7(20)	0
1975	NO	3	69	23.0(42)	0
1976	NO	1	20	20.0(20)	0
1977	NO	4	6	1.5(6)	0
1978	SF	6	159	26.5(32)	0
NFL	7	20	294	14.7(42)	0

Crockett, Ray

YEAR	TEAM	INT	YDS	AVG(LG)	TD
1989	Det	1	5	5.0(5)	0
1990	Det	3	17	5.7(9)	0
1991	Det	**6**	141	23.5(96)	1
1992	Det	4	50	12.5(35)	0
1993	Det	2	31	15.5(31)	0
1994	Den	2	6	3.0(6)	0
1996	Den	2	34	17.0(34)	0
1997	Den	4	18	4.5(10)	0
1998	Den	3	105	35.0(80)	1
1999	Den	2	14	7.0(10)	0
2000	Den	4	31	7.8(26)	1
2001	KC	1	8	8.0(8)	0
2002	KC	2	0	0.0(0)	0
NFL	14	36	460	12.8(96)	3

Cromwell, Nolan

YEAR	TEAM	INT	YDS	AVG(LG)	TD
1978	LARm	1	31	31.0(31)	0
1979	LARm	5	109	21.8(34)	0
1980	LARm	**8**	**140**	17.5(34)	1
1981	LARm	5	94	18.8(94)	0
1982	LARm	3	33	11.0(21)	0
1983	LARm	3	76	25.3(43)	1
1984	LARm	3	54	18.0(33)	1
1985	LARm	2	5	2.5(5)	0
1986	LARm	5	101	20.2(80)	1
1987	LARm	2	28	14.0(28)	0
NFL	11	37	671	18.1(94)	4

Cross, Irv

YEAR	TEAM	INT	YDS	AVG(LG)	TD
1961	Phi	2	36	18.0(36)	0
1962	Phi	5	46	9.2(22)	0
1963	Phi	2	6	3.0(3)	0
1964	Phi	3	109	**36.3**(**94**)	1
1965	Phi	3	1	0.3(1)	0
1966	LARm	1	60	60.0(60)	1
1967	LARm	2	0	0.0(0)	0
1968	LARm	3	0	0.0(0)	0
1969	Phi	1	0	0.0(0)	0
NFL	9	22	258	11.7(94)	2

Crow, Lindon

YEAR	TEAM	INT	YDS	AVG(LG)	TD
1955	ChiC	3	11	3.7(11)	0
1956	ChiC	**11**	170	15.5(42)	0
1957	ChiC	1	0	0.0(0)	0
1958	NYG	3	40	13.3(34)	0
1959	NYG	5	54	10.8(30)	**1**
1960	NYG	3	3	1.0(3)	0
1961	LARm	6	117	19.5(31)	0
1962	LARm	5	100	20.0(65)	**1**
1964	LARm	1	23	23.0(23)	0
NFL	10	38	518	13.6(65)	2

Curtis, Mike

YEAR	TEAM	INT	YDS	AVG(LG)	TD
1967	Bal	1	6	6.0(6)	0
1968	Bal	2	38	19.0(38)	1
1970	Bal	5	50	10.0(18)	0
1971	Bal	3	44	14.7(31)	0
1972	Bal	4	74	18.5(33)	1
1973	Bal	2	9	4.5(7)	0
1974	Bal	3	24	8.0(11)	0
1975	Bal	1	3	3.0(3)	0
1976	Sea	2	40	20.0(26)	0
1977	Was	1	1	1.0(1)	0
1978	Was	1	0	0.0(0)	0
NFL	13	25	289	11.6(38)	2

Daniel, Eugene

YEAR	TEAM	INT	YDS	AVG(LG)	TD
1984	Ind	6	25	4.2(18)	0
1985	Ind	**8**	53	6.6(29)	0
1986	Ind	3	11	3.7(5)	0
1987	Ind	2	34	17.0(34)	0
1988	Ind	2	44	22.0(41)	1
1989	Ind	1	34	34.0(34)	0
1991	Ind	3	22	7.3(12)	0
1992	Ind	1	0	0.0(0)	0
1993	Ind	1	17	17.0(17)	0
1994	Ind	2	6	3.0(6)	0
1995	Ind	3	142	**47.3**(**97**)	1
1996	Ind	3	35	11.7(35)	1
1997	Bal	3	60	20.0(43)	0
NFL	14	38	483	12.7(97)	3

Darden, Thom

YEAR	TEAM	INT	YDS	AVG(LG)	TD
1972	Cle	3	64	21.3(20)	0
1973	Cle	1	36	36.0(36)	0
1974	Cle	8	105	13.1(31)	0
1976	Cle	7	73	10.4(21)	0
1977	Cle	6	107	17.8(49)	**1**
1978	Cle	**10**	**200**	20.0(46)	0
1979	Cle	5	125	25.0(39)	1
1980	Cle	2	42	21.0(23)	0
1981	Cle	3	68	22.7(45)	0
NFL	9	45	820	18.2(49)	2

David, Jim

YEAR	TEAM	INT	YDS	AVG(LG)	TD
1952	Det	7	48	6.9(15)	0
1953	Det	4	50	12.5(21)	0
1954	Det	7	74	10.6(25)	0
1955	Det	3	44	14.7(28)	0
1956	Det	7	4	0.6(3)	0
1957	Det	3	20	6.7(17)	0
1958	Det	3	12	4.0(7)	0
1959	Det	2	7	3.5(7)	0
NFL	8	36	259	7.2(28)	0

Davis, Eric

YEAR	TEAM	INT	YDS	AVG(LG)	TD
1990	SF	1	13	13.0(13)	0
1992	SF	3	52	17.3(37)	0
1993	SF	4	45	11.3(41)	1
1994	SF	1	8	8.0(8)	0
1995	SF	3	84	28.0(86)	1
1996	Car	5	57	11.4(36)	0
1997	Car	5	25	5.0(17)	0
1998	Car	5	81	16.2(56)	2
1999	Car	5	49	9.8(16)	0
2000	Car	5	14	2.8(8)	0
2002	Det	1	14	14.0(14)	0
NFL	12	38	442	11.6(86)	4

Davis, Jerry

YEAR	TEAM	INT	YDS	AVG(LG)	TD
1948	ChiC	4	47	11.8(18)	0
1949	ChiC	6	63	10.5(27)	0
1950	ChiC	9	40	4.4(15)	0
1951	ChiC	2	36	18.0(36)	0
1952	DalT	3	118	**39.3**(**66**)	1
NFL	5	24	304	12.7(66)	1

Davis, Milt

YEAR	TEAM	INT	YDS	AVG(LG)	TD
1957	Bal	**10**	**219**	21.9(75)	**2**
1958	Bal	4	40	10.0(28)	0
1959	Bal	**7**	119	17.0(57)	**1**
1960	Bal	6	32	5.3(19)	0
NFL	4	27	410	15.2(75)	3

DAWKINS, BRIAN

YEAR	TEAM	INT	YDS	AVG (LG)	TD
1996	Phi	3	41	13.7 (30)	0
1997	Phi	3	76	25.3 (64)	1
1998	Phi	2	39	19.5 (30)	0
1999	Phi	4	127	31.8 (67)	1
2000	Phi	4	62	15.5 (32)	0
2001	Phi	2	15	7.5 (15)	0
2002	Phi	2	27	13.5 (27)	0
2003	Phi	1	0	0.0 (0)	0
2004	Phi	4	40	10.0 (32)	0
2005	Phi	3	24	8.0 (24)	0
NFL	10	28	451	16.1 (67)	2

DEAN, VERNON

YEAR	TEAM	INT	YDS	AVG (LG)	TD
1982	Was	3	62	20.7 (26)	0
1983	Was	5	54	10.8 (26)	0
1984	Was	7	114	16.3 (36)	**2**
1985	Was	5	8	1.6 (8)	0
1986	Was	1	5	5.0 (5)	0
1988	Sea	1	31	31.0 (31)	0
NFL	7	22	274	12.5 (36)	2

DERBY, DEAN

YEAR	TEAM	INT	YDS	AVG (LG)	TD
1958	Pit	4	0	0.0 (0)	0
1959	Pit	**7**	127	18.1 (24)	0
1960	Pit	3	40	13.3 (25)	0
1961	Min	3	73	24.3 (30)	0
1962	Min	4	0	0.0 (0)	0
NFL	6	21	240	11.4 (30)	0

DILLON, BOBBY

YEAR	TEAM	INT	YDS	AVG (LG)	TD
1952	GB	4	35	8.8 (17)	0
1953	GB	9	112	12.4 (49)	1
1954	GB	7	111	15.9 (59)	1
1955	GB	9	153	17.0 (61)	0
1956	GB	7	**244**	**34.9 (45)**	1
1957	GB	9	180	20.0 (55)	1
1958	GB	6	134	22.3 (46)	1
1959	GB	1	7	7.0 (7)	0
NFL	8	52	976	18.8 (61)	5

DIMRY, CHARLES

YEAR	TEAM	INT	YDS	AVG (LG)	TD
1989	Atl	2	72	36.0 (40)	0
1990	Atl	3	16	5.3 (13)	0
1991	Den	3	35	11.7 (26)	1
1992	Den	1	2	2.0 (2)	0
1993	Den	1	0	0.0 (0)	0
1994	TB	1	0	0.0 (0)	0
1995	TB	1	0	0.0 (0)	0
1996	TB	2	1	0.5 (1)	0
1997	Phi	2	25	12.5 (25)	0
1998	SD	3	38	12.7 (30)	0
1999	SD	2	1	0.5 (1)	0
NFL	11	21	190	9.0 (40)	1

DISHMAN, CRIS

YEAR	TEAM	INT	YDS	AVG (LG)	TD
1989	Hou	4	31	7.8 (31)	0
1990	Hou	4	50	12.5 (42)	0
1991	Hou	6	61	10.2 (43)	0
1992	Hou	3	34	11.3 (17)	0
1993	Hou	6	74	12.3 (30)	0
1994	Hou	4	74	18.5 (38)	1
1995	Hou	3	17	5.7 (17)	0
1996	Hou	1	7	7.0 (7)	0
1997	Was	4	47	11.8 (29)	1
1998	Was	2	60	30.0 (49)	0
1999	KC	5	95	19.0 (47)	1
2000	Min	1	0	0.0 (0)	0
NFL	13	43	550	12.8 (49)	3

DIXON, HANFORD

YEAR	TEAM	INT	YDS	AVG (LG)	TD
1982	Cle	4	22	5.5 (22)	0
1983	Cle	3	41	13.7 (35)	0
1984	Cle	5	31	6.2 (18)	0
1985	Cle	3	65	21.7 (37)	0
1986	Cle	5	35	7.0 (19)	0
1987	Cle	3	5	1.7 (6)	0
1988	Cle	2	24	12.0 (24)	0
1989	Cle	1	2	2.0 (2)	0
NFL	8	26	225	8.7 (37)	0

DOLL, DON

YEAR	TEAM	INT	YDS	AVG (LG)	TD
1949	Det	11	**301**	**27.4 (95)**	1
1950	Det	12	163	13.6 (38)	1
1951	Det	1	0	0.0 (0)	0
1952	Det	2	0	0.0 (0)	0
1953	Was	10	102	10.2 (28)	0
1954	LARm	5	51	10.2 (26)	0
NFL	6	41	617	15.0 (95)	2

DOWNS, MICHAEL

YEAR	TEAM	INT	YDS	AVG (LG)	TD
1981	Dal	7	81	11.6 (25)	0
1982	Dal	1	22	22.0 (22)	0
1983	Dal	4	80	20.0 (28)	0
1984	Dal	7	126	18.0 (27)	1
1985	Dal	3	11	3.7 (11)	0
1986	Dal	6	54	9.0 (31)	0
1987	Dal	4	56	14.0 (27)	0
1988	Dal	2	3	1.5 (3)	0
1989	Phx	1	37	37.0 (37)	0
NFL	9	35	470	13.4 (37)	1

DUDLEY, BILL

YEAR	TEAM	INT	YDS	AVG (LG)	TD
1942	Pit	3	60	20.0 (25)	0
1945	Pit	2	47	23.5 (26)	0
1946	Pit	**10**	**242**	24.2 (80)	**1**
1947	Det	5	104	20.8 (41)	1
1948	Det	1	3	3.0 (3)	0
1950	Was	2	3	1.5 (3)	0
NFL	9	23	459	20.0 (80)	2

DUERSON, DAVE

YEAR	TEAM	INT	YDS	AVG (LG)	TD
1984	ChiB	1	9	9.0 (9)	0
1985	ChiB	5	53	10.6 (20)	0
1986	ChiB	6	139	23.2 (38)	0
1987	ChiB	3	0	0.0 (0)	0
1988	ChiB	2	18	9.0 (18)	0
1989	ChiB	1	2	2.0 (2)	0
1990	NYG	1	0	0.0 (0)	0
1991	Phx	1	5	5.0 (5)	0
NFL	9	20	226	11.3 (38)	0

DUNCAN, SPEEDY

YEAR	TEAM	INT	YDS	AVG (LG)	TD
1964	SD-A	1	3	3.0 (3)	0
1965	SD-A	4	30	7.5 (26)	0
1966	SD-A	7	67	9.6 (31)	0
1967	SD-A	2	100	50.0 (**100**)	1
1968	SD-A	1	4	4.0 (4)	0
1969	SD-A	6	118	19.7 (72)	1
1971	Was	1	46	46.0 (46)	1
1972	Was	1	8	8.0 (8)	0
1973	Was	1	6	6.0 (6)	0
NFL	11	24	382	15.9 (100)	3

EASLEY, KENNY

YEAR	TEAM	INT	YDS	AVG (LG)	TD
1981	Sea	3	155	**51.7 (82)**	1
1982	Sea	4	48	12.0 (44)	0
1983	Sea	7	106	15.1 (48)	0
1984	Sea	**10**	126	12.6 (58)	**2**
1985	Sea	2	22	11.0 (16)	0
1986	Sea	2	34	17.0 (24)	0
1987	Sea	4	47	11.8 (22)	0
NFL	7	32	538	16.8 (82)	3

EDGERSON, BOOKER

YEAR	TEAM	INT	YDS	AVG (LG)	TD
1962	Buf-A	6	111	18.5 (40)	0
1963	Buf-A	1	0	0.0 (0)	0
1964	Buf-A	4	130	32.5 (91)	0
1965	Buf-A	5	55	11.0 (19)	0
1967	Buf-A	2	25	12.5 (25)	0
1968	Buf-A	4	100	25.0 (45)	**2**
1969	Buf-A	1	0	0.0 (0)	0
NFL	8	23	421	18.3 (91)	2

EDWARDS, DONNIE

YEAR	TEAM	INT	YDS	AVG (LG)	TD
1996	KC	1	22	22.0 (22)	0
1997	KC	2	15	7.5 (12)	0
1999	KC	5	50	10.0 (28)	1
2000	KC	2	45	22.5 (42)	1
2002	SD	5	95	19.0 (46)	1
2003	SD	2	27	13.5 (15)	0
2004	SD	5	49	9.8 (30)	1
2005	SD	2	15	7.5 (14)	0
NFL	10	24	318	13.3 (46)	4

EDWARDS, GLEN

YEAR	TEAM	INT	YDS	AVG (LG)	TD
1971	Pit	1	20	20.0 (20)	0
1972	Pit	1	14	14.0 (14)	0
1973	Pit	6	**186**	31.0 (86)	1
1974	Pit	5	153	**30.6 (59)**	1
1975	Pit	3	68	22.7 (47)	0
1976	Pit	6	95	15.8 (55)	0
1977	Pit	3	116	38.7 (51)	0
1978	SD	3	43	14.3 (24)	0
1979	SD	4	99	24.8 (53)	0
1980	SD	5	122	24.4 (68)	1
1981	SD	2	45	22.5 (39)	0
NFL	11	39	961	24.6 (86)	3

EDWARDS, HERMAN

YEAR	TEAM	INT	YDS	AVG (LG)	TD
1977	Phi	6	9	1.5 (6)	0
1978	Phi	7	59	8.4 (25)	0
1979	Phi	3	6	2.0 (6)	0
1980	Phi	3	12	4.0 (9)	0
1981	Phi	3	1	0.3 (1)	0
1982	Phi	5	3	0.6 (3)	0
1983	Phi	1	0	0.0 (0)	0
1984	Phi	2	0	0.0 (0)	0
1985	Phi	3	8	2.7 (3)	1
NFL	9	33	98	3.0 (25)	1

ELLIS, ALLAN

YEAR	TEAM	INT	YDS	AVG (LG)	TD
1973	ChiB	1	12	12.0 (12)	0
1974	ChiB	3	32	10.7 (19)	0
1975	ChiB	2	4	2.0 (4)	0
1976	ChiB	6	47	7.8 (22)	1
1977	ChiB	6	23	3.8 (11)	0
1979	ChiB	3	67	22.3 (24)	0
1980	ChiB	1	0	0.0 (0)	0
NFL	7	22	185	8.4 (24)	1

ELLIS, KEN

YEAR	TEAM	INT	YDS	AVG (LG)	TD
1970	GB	3	69	23.0 (60)	0
1971	GB	6	10	1.7 (5)	0
1972	GB	4	106	26.5 (40)	1
1973	GB	3	53	17.7 (47)	1
1974	GB	3	56	18.7 (38)	1
1975	GB	1	0	0.0 (0)	0
1976	Mia	2	40	20.0 (40)	0
NFL	9	22	334	15.2 (60)	3

ELLSWORTH, PERCY

YEAR	TEAM	INT	YDS	AVG (LG)	TD
1996	NYG	3	62	20.7 (33)	0
1997	NYG	4	40	10.0 (25)	0
1998	NYG	5	92	18.4 (43)	2
1999	NYG	6	80	13.3 (26)	0
2000	Cle	1	33	33.0 (33)	1
2001	Cle	1	19	19.0 (19)	0
NFL	6	20	326	16.3 (43)	3

ELMENDORF, DAVE

YEAR	TEAM	INT	YDS	AVG (LG)	TD
1971	LARm	2	32	16.0 (32)	0
1972	LARm	3	29	9.7 (15)	0
1973	LARm	1	16	16.0 (16)	0
1974	LARm	7	186	26.6 (57)	**2**
1975	LARm	4	48	12.0 (26)	0
1976	LARm	2	0	0.0 (0)	0
1977	LARm	2	51	25.5 (27)	0
1978	LARm	3	20	6.7 (12)	0
1979	LARm	3	39	13.0 (32)	0
NFL	9	27	421	15.6 (57)	2

EVANS, DOUG

YEAR	TEAM	INT	YDS	AVG (LG)	TD
1993	GB	1	0	0.0 (0)	0
1994	GB	1	0	0.0 (0)	0
1995	GB	2	24	12.0 (24)	0
1996	GB	5	102	20.4 (63)	1
1997	GB	3	33	11.0 (27)	0
1998	Car	2	18	9.0 (18)	0
1999	Car	2	1	0.5 (1)	0
2000	Car	2	17	8.5 (17)	0
2001	Car	8	126	15.8 (49)	1
2002	Sea	1	0	0.0 (0)	0
2003	Det	1	2	2.0 (2)	0
NFL	11	28	323	11.5 (63)	2

EVERETT, THOMAS

YEAR	TEAM	INT	YDS	AVG (LG)	TD
1987	Pit	3	22	7.3 (21)	0
1988	Pit	3	31	10.3 (29)	0
1989	Pit	3	68	22.7 (32)	0
1990	Pit	3	2	0.7 (2)	0
1991	Pit	4	53	13.3 (27)	0
1992	Dal	2	28	14.0 (17)	0
1993	Dal	2	25	12.5 (17)	0
1994	TB	1	26	26.0 (26)	0
NFL	9	21	255	12.1 (32)	0

FARR, MILLER

YEAR	TEAM	INT	YDS	AVG (LG)	TD
1965	Den-A	2	22	11.0 (17)	0
1966	SD-A	3	68	22.7 (35)	0
1967	Hou-A	**10**	**264**	26.4 (67)	**3**
1968	Hou-A	3	104	34.7 (52)	**2**
1969	Hou-A	6	48	8.0 (35)	0
1970	SL	5	38	7.6 (19)	1
1971	SL	2	13	6.5 (13)	0
1972	SL	3	21	7.0 (21)	0
1973	Det	1	0	0.0 (0)	0
NFL	9	35	578	16.5 (67)	6

FENCIK, GARY

YEAR	TEAM	INT	YDS	AVG (LG)	TD
1977	ChiB	4	33	8.3 (23)	0
1978	ChiB	4	77	19.3 (59)	0
1979	ChiB	6	31	5.2 (17)	0
1980	ChiB	1	8	8.0 (8)	0
1981	ChiB	6	121	20.2 (69)	1
1982	ChiB	2	2	1.0 (2)	0
1983	ChiB	2	34	17.0 (20)	0
1984	ChiB	5	102	20.4 (61)	0
1985	ChiB	5	43	8.6 (22)	0
1986	ChiB	3	37	12.3 (24)	0
NFL	11	38	488	12.8 (69)	1

FICHTNER, ROSS

YEAR	TEAM	INT	YDS	AVG (LG)	TD
1962	Cle	7	76	10.9 (31)	0
1963	Cle	2	75	37.5 (39)	1
1964	Cle	2	67	33.5 (64)	0
1965	Cle	4	98	24.5 (48)	1
1966	Cle	8	152	19.0 (58)	1
1967	Cle	4	113	28.3 (88)	0
NFL	8	27	581	21.5 (88)	3

FISCHER, PAT

YEAR	TEAM	INT	YDS	AVG (LG)	TD
1962	SL	3	41	13.7 (25)	0
1963	SL	8	169	21.1 (53)	0
1964	SL	10	164	16.4 (39)	**2**
1965	SL	3	30	10.0 (16)	0
1966	SL	1	40	40.0 (40)	0
1967	SL	4	85	21.3 (69)	1
1968	Was	2	14	7.0 (13)	0
1969	Was	2	28	14.0 (27)	0
1970	Was	2	13	6.5 (10)	0
1971	Was	3	103	34.3 (53)	1
1972	Was	4	61	15.3 (35)	0
1973	Was	3	99	33.0 (67)	0
1974	Was	3	52	17.3 (30)	0
1975	Was	3	4	1.3 (4)	0
1976	Was	5	38	7.6 (32)	0
NFL	16	56	941	16.8 (69)	4

FOLEY, STEVE

YEAR	TEAM	INT	YDS	AVG (LG)	TD
1976	Den	4	95	23.8 (34)	0
1977	Den	3	22	7.3 (22)	0
1978	Den	6	84	14.0 (30)	0
1979	Den	6	14	2.3 (7)	0
1980	Den	4	115	28.8 (36)	0
1981	Den	5	81	16.2 (24)	0
1983	Den	5	28	5.6 (16)	0
1984	Den	6	97	16.2 (40)	1
1985	Den	3	47	15.7 (29)	0
1986	Den	2	39	19.5 (24)	0
NFL	10	44	622	14.1 (40)	1

FOLEY, TIM

YEAR	TEAM	INT	YDS	AVG (LG)	TD
1971	Mia	4	14	3.5 (18)	0
1972	Mia	3	25	8.3 (15)	0
1973	Mia	2	22	11.0 (15)	0
1974	Mia	2	-2	-1.0 (0)	0
1977	Mia	3	17	5.7 (17)	0
1978	Mia	6	12	2.0 (8)	0
1979	Mia	2	8	4.0 (8)	0
NFL	10	22	96	4.4 (18)	0

FORESTER, BILL

YEAR	TEAM	INT	YDS	AVG (LG)	TD
1953	GB	1	0	0.0 (0)	0
1954	GB	1	21	21.0 (21)	0
1955	GB	4	32	8.0 (17)	0
1956	GB	4	35	8.8 (13)	0
1957	GB	4	79	19.8 (37)	0
1959	GB	2	48	24.0 (34)	0
1960	GB	2	18	9.0 (15)	0
1961	GB	2	33	16.5 (33)	0
1963	GB	1	13	13.0 (13)	0
NFL	11	21	279	13.3 (37)	0

FORTE, BOB

YEAR	TEAM	INT	YDS	AVG (LG)	TD
1946	GB	2	23	11.5 (16)	0
1947	GB	9	140	15.6 (68)	1
1948	GB	5	56	11.2 (40)	0
1949	GB	2	17	8.5 (17)	0
1950	GB	1	5	5.0 (5)	0
1952	GB	4	50	12.5 (25)	0
NFL	7	23	291	12.7 (68)	1

FOX, TIM

YEAR	TEAM	INT	YDS	AVG (LG)	TD
1976	NE	3	67	22.3 (29)	0
1977	NE	3	39	13.0 (27)	0
1978	NE	2	10	5.0 (10)	0
1979	NE	2	38	19.0 (25)	0
1980	NE	4	41	10.3 (23)	0
1981	NE	3	20	6.7 (20)	0
1982	SD	4	103	25.8 (35)	0
1983	SD	2	14	7.0 (14)	0
1984	SD	1	36	36.0 (36)	0
1985	LARm	2	8	4.0 (8)	0
NFL	10	26	376	14.5 (36)	0

FRAZIER, LESLIE

YEAR	TEAM	INT	YDS	AVG (LG)	TD
1982	ChiB	2	0	0.0 (0)	0
1983	ChiB	7	135	19.3 (58)	1
1984	ChiB	5	89	17.8 (33)	0
1985	ChiB	6	119	19.8 (33)	1
NFL	5	20	343	17.1 (58)	2

FREEMAN, STEVE

YEAR	TEAM	INT	YDS	AVG (LG)	TD
1975	Buf	2	44	22.0 (30)	1
1977	Buf	1	4	4.0 (4)	0
1979	Buf	3	62	20.7 (50)	1
1980	Buf	7	107	15.3 (47)	1
1982	Buf	3	27	9.0 (14)	0
1983	Buf	3	40	13.3 (29)	0
1984	Buf	3	45	15.0 (45)	0
1986	Buf	1	0	0.0 (0)	0
NFL	10	23	329	14.3 (50)	3

FULCHER, DAVID

YEAR	TEAM	INT	YDS	AVG (LG)	TD
1986	Cin	4	20	5.0 (15)	0
1987	Cin	3	30	10.0 (28)	0
1988	Cin	5	38	7.6 (16)	1
1989	Cin	8	87	10.9 (22)	0
1990	Cin	4	20	5.0 (18)	0
1991	Cin	4	51	12.8 (27)	1
1992	Cin	3	0	0.0 (0)	0
NFL	7	31	246	7.9 (28)	2

GAECHTER, MIKE

YEAR	TEAM	INT	YDS	AVG (LG)	TD
1962	Dal	5	136	27.2 (100)	**1**
1963	Dal	3	140	**46.7 (86)**	0
1965	Dal	2	21	10.5 (19)	0

YEAR	TEAM	INT	YDS	AVG (LG)	TD
1966	Dal	3	28	9.3(23)	0
1967	Dal	2	0	0.0(0)	0
1968	Dal	3	23	7.7(17)	0
1969	Dal	3	72	24.0(37)	0
NFL	8	21	420	20.0(100)	1

Gibson, Claude

YEAR	TEAM	INT	YDS	AVG (LG)	TD
1961	SD-A	5	43	8.6(23)	0
1962	SD-A	8	85	10.6(37)	**1**
1963	Oak-A	3	18	6.0(18)	0
1964	Oak-A	2	74	37.0(39)	0
1965	Oak-A	4	53	13.3(22)	0
NFL	5	22	273	12.4(39)	1

Glenn, Aaron

YEAR	TEAM	INT	YDS	AVG (LG)	TD
1995	NYJ	1	17	17.0(17)	0
1996	NYJ	4	113	28.3(**100**)	**2**
1997	NYJ	1	5	5.0(5)	0
1998	NYJ	6	23	3.8(26)	0
1999	NYJ	3	20	6.7(12)	0
2000	NYJ	4	34	8.5(34)	0
2001	NYJ	5	82	16.4(60)	1
2002	Hou	5	181	36.2(70)	**2**
2003	Hou	1	0	0.0(0)	0
2004	Hou	5	40	8.0(23)	0
2005	Dal	4	10	2.5(10)	0
NFL	12	39	525	13.5(100)	5

Glenn, Vencie

YEAR	TEAM	INT	YDS	AVG (LG)	TD
1986	SD	2	31	15.5(31)	0
1987	SD	4	**166**	**41.5(103)**	1
1988	SD	1	0	0.0(0)	0
1989	SD	4	52	13.0(31)	0
1990	SD	1	0	0.0(0)	0
1991	NO	4	35	8.8(18)	0
1992	Min	5	65	13.0(39)	0
1993	Min	5	49	9.8(23)	0
1994	Min	4	55	13.8(32)	0
1995	NYG	5	91	18.2(75)	1
NFL	10	35	544	15.5(103)	2

Glick, Fred

YEAR	TEAM	INT	YDS	AVG (LG)	TD
1961	Hou-A	4	28	7.0(11)	0
1962	Hou-A	3	53	17.7(31)	0
1963	Hou-A	**12**	180	15.0(45)	1
1964	Hou-A	5	54	10.8(27)	0
1965	Hou-A	2	18	9.0(18)	0
1966	Hou-A	4	57	14.3(41)	0
NFL	6	30	390	13.0(45)	1

Gonsoulin, Goose

YEAR	TEAM	INT	YDS	AVG (LG)	TD
1960	Den-A	**11**	98	8.9(0)	0
1961	Den-A	6	76	12.7(38)	0
1962	Den-A	7	88	12.6(64)	**1**
1963	Den-A	6	64	10.7(42)	1
1964	Den-A	7	125	17.9(36)	0
1965	Den-A	6	91	15.2(32)	0
1967	SF	3	9	3.0(5)	0
NFL	7	46	551	12.0(64)	2

Gradishar, Randy

YEAR	TEAM	INT	YDS	AVG (LG)	TD
1975	Den	3	77	25.7(44)	1
1976	Den	3	44	14.7(31)	1
1977	Den	3	56	18.7(28)	0
1978	Den	4	19	4.8(8)	0
1980	Den	2	96	48.0(**93**)	1
1981	Den	4	38	9.5(16)	0
1983	Den	1	5	5.0(5)	0
NFL	9	20	335	16.8(93)	3

Graham, Kenny

YEAR	TEAM	INT	YDS	AVG (LG)	TD
1964	SD-A	4	24	6.0(9)	0
1965	SD-A	5	108	21.6(51)	1
1966	SD-A	5	70	14.0(32)	1
1967	SD-A	2	76	38.0(68)	1
1968	SD-A	5	87	17.4(42)	0
1969	SD-A	4	112	28.0(65)	**2**
1970	Cin	3	31	10.3(31)	0
NFL	7	28	508	18.1(68)	5

Grantham, Larry

YEAR	TEAM	INT	YDS	AVG (LG)	TD
1960	NYT-A	5	13	2.6(7)	0
1961	NYT-A	1	30	30.0(30)	0
1962	NYT-A	2	2	1.0(2)	0
1963	NYJ-A	3	89	29.7(41)	0
1964	NYJ-A	2	32	16.0(32)	0
1965	NYJ-A	1	0	0.0(0)	0
1966	NYJ-A	1	14	14.0(14)	0
1967	NYJ-A	5	77	15.4(36)	0
1970	NYJ	3	51	17.0(41)	1
1971	NYJ	1	0	0.0(0)	0
NFL	12	24	308	12.8(41)	1

Gray, Jerry

YEAR	TEAM	INT	YDS	AVG (LG)	TD
1986	LARm	8	101	12.6(28)	0
1987	LARm	2	35	17.5(35)	0
1988	LARm	3	83	27.7(47)	1
1989	LARm	6	48	8.0(27)	1
1991	LARm	3	83	27.7(59)	1

YEAR	TEAM	INT	YDS	AVG (LG)	TD
1992	Hou	6	24	4.0(22)	0
NFL	8	28	374	13.4(59)	3

Gray, Johnnie

YEAR	TEAM	INT	YDS	AVG (LG)	TD
1975	GB	1	7	7.0(7)	0
1976	GB	4	101	25.3(67)	1
1977	GB	1	12	12.0(12)	0
1978	GB	3	66	22.0(66)	0
1979	GB	5	66	13.2(35)	0
1980	GB	5	54	10.8(21)	0
1982	GB	1	21	21.0(21)	0
1983	GB	2	5	2.5(5)	0
NFL	9	22	332	15.1(67)	1

Grayson, Dave

YEAR	TEAM	INT	YDS	AVG (LG)	TD
1961	DalT-A	3	99	33.0(**99**)	1
1962	DalT-A	4	6	1.5(6)	0
1963	KC-A	5	17	3.4(11)	0
1964	KC-A	7	**187**	26.7(56)	0
1965	Oak-A	3	145	**48.3(79)**	**2**
1966	Oak-A	3	64	21.3(24)	0
1967	Oak-A	4	63	15.8(23)	0
1968	Oak-A	**10**	195	19.5(54)	1
1969	Oak-A	8	132	16.5(**76**)	1
1970	Oak	1	25	25.0(25)	0
NFL	10	48	933	19.4(99)	5

Green, Cornell

YEAR	TEAM	INT	YDS	AVG (LG)	TD
1963	Dal	7	211	30.1(55)	0
1965	Dal	3	49	16.3(43)	0
1966	Dal	4	88	22.0(41)	1
1967	Dal	7	52	7.4(28)	0
1968	Dal	4	74	18.5(55)	1
1969	Dal	2	0	0.0(0)	0
1970	Dal	1	59	59.0(59)	0
1971	Dal	2	16	8.0(12)	0
1972	Dal	2	1	0.5(1)	0
1974	Dal	2	2	1.0(2)	0
NFL	11	34	552	16.2(59)	2

Green, Darrell

YEAR	TEAM	INT	YDS	AVG (LG)	TD
1983	Was	2	7	3.5(7)	0
1984	Was	5	91	18.2(50)	1
1985	Was	2	0	0.0(0)	0
1986	Was	5	9	1.8(7)	0
1987	Was	3	65	21.7(56)	0
1988	Was	1	12	12.0(12)	0
1989	Was	2	0	0.0(0)	0
1990	Was	4	20	5.0(18)	1
1991	Was	5	47	9.4(24)	0
1992	Was	1	15	15.0(15)	0
1993	Was	4	10	2.5(6)	0
1994	Was	3	32	10.7(27)	1
1995	Was	3	42	14.0(22)	1
1996	Was	3	84	28.0(68)	1
1997	Was	1	83	83.0(83)	1
1998	Was	3	36	12.0(36)	0
1999	Was	3	33	11.0(25)	0
2000	Was	3	35	11.7(33)	0
2001	Was	1	0	0.0(0)	0
NFL	20	54	621	11.5(83)	6

Green, Gary

YEAR	TEAM	INT	YDS	AVG (LG)	TD
1977	KC	3	19	6.3(19)	0
1978	KC	1	0	0.0(0)	0
1979	KC	5	148	29.6(57)	0
1980	KC	2	25	12.5(25)	0
1981	KC	5	37	7.4(16)	0
1982	KC	2	42	21.0(42)	**1**
1983	KC	6	59	9.8(25)	0
1984	LARm	3	88	29.3(60)	0
1985	LARm	6	84	14.0(41)	1
NFL	9	33	502	15.2(60)	2

Green, Victor

YEAR	TEAM	INT	YDS	AVG (LG)	TD
1995	NYJ	1	2	2.0(2)	0
1996	NYJ	2	27	13.5(18)	0
1997	NYJ	3	89	29.7(39)	0
1998	NYJ	4	99	24.8(87)	0
1999	NYJ	5	92	18.4(32)	0
2000	NYJ	6	144	24.0(43)	1
2001	NYJ	3	76	25.3(63)	1
2002	NE	1	90	90.0(90)	1
2003	NO	0	24	0.0(24)	0
NFL	10	25	643	25.7(90)	3

Greene, Tony

YEAR	TEAM	INT	YDS	AVG (LG)	TD
1972	Buf	3	45	15.0(39)	1
1973	Buf	1	0	0.0(0)	0
1974	Buf	9	157	17.4(38)	0
1975	Buf	6	81	13.5(37)	0
1976	Buf	5	135	27.0(**101**)	1
1977	Buf	9	144	16.0(47)	0
1978	Buf	3	56	18.7(29)	0
1979	Buf	1	10	10.0(10)	0
NFL	9	37	628	17.0(101)	2

Gremminger, Hank

YEAR	TEAM	INT	YDS	AVG (LG)	TD
1956	GB	2	36	18.0(21)	0
1957	GB	5	93	18.6(45)	0
1958	GB	3	15	5.0(14)	0
1959	GB	1	45	45.0(45)	0
1960	GB	3	52	17.3(21)	0
1961	GB	5	54	10.8(41)	0
1962	GB	5	88	17.6(35)	0
1963	GB	3	25	8.3(16)	0
1964	GB	1	13	13.0(13)	0
1966	LARm	1	0	0.0(0)	0
NFL	10	29	421	14.5(45)	0

Griffin, Don

YEAR	TEAM	INT	YDS	AVG (LG)	TD
1986	SF	3	0	0.0(0)	0
1987	SF	5	1	0.2(1)	0
1989	SF	2	6	3.0(3)	0
1990	SF	3	32	10.7(23)	0
1991	SF	1	0	0.0(0)	0
1992	SF	5	4	0.8(2)	0
1993	SF	3	6	2.0(3)	0
1994	Cle	2	2	1.0(2)	0
1995	Cle	1	0	0.0(0)	0
NFL	11	25	51	2.0(23)	0

Griffith, Robert

YEAR	TEAM	INT	YDS	AVG (LG)	TD
1996	Min	4	67	16.8(41)	0
1997	Min	2	26	13.0(21)	0
1998	Min	5	25	5.0(17)	0
1999	Min	3	0	0.0(0)	0
2000	Min	1	25	25.0(25)	0
2001	Min	2	25	12.5(14)	0
2002	Cle	3	0	0.0(0)	0
2003	Cle	2	3	1.5(3)	0
2004	Cle	1	18	18.0(18)	0
2005	Arz	1	11	11.0(11)	0
NFL	11	24	200	8.3(41)	0

Hall, Ron

YEAR	TEAM	INT	YDS	AVG (LG)	TD
1959	Pit	1	0	0.0(0)	0
1961	Bos-A	2	12	6.0(12)	0
1962	Bos-A	3	94	31.3(47)	**1**
1963	Bos-A	3	24	8.0(14)	0
1964	Bos-A	11	148	13.5(50)	0
1965	Bos-A	3	35	11.7(29)	0
1966	Bos-A	6	159	26.5(**87**)	0
1967	Bos-A	1	4	4.0(4)	0
NFL	8	30	476	15.9(87)	1

Ham, Jack

YEAR	TEAM	INT	YDS	AVG (LG)	TD
1971	Pit	2	4	2.0(4)	0
1972	Pit	7	83	11.9(32)	1
1973	Pit	2	30	15.0(27)	0
1974	Pit	5	13	2.6(10)	0
1975	Pit	1	2	2.0(2)	0
1976	Pit	2	13	6.5(13)	0
1977	Pit	4	17	4.3(9)	0
1978	Pit	3	7	2.3(7)	0
1979	Pit	2	8	4.0(8)	0
1980	Pit	2	16	8.0(15)	0
1981	Pit	1	23	23.0(23)	0
1982	Pit	1	2	2.0(2)	0
NFL	12	32	218	6.8(32)	1

Hamilton, Harry

YEAR	TEAM	INT	YDS	AVG (LG)	TD
1985	NYJ	2	14	7.0(14)	0
1986	NYJ	1	29	29.0(29)	0
1987	NYJ	3	25	8.3(25)	0
1988	TB	6	**123**	20.5(58)	0
1989	TB	6	70	11.7(30)	0
1990	TB	5	39	7.8(27)	0
NFL	7	23	300	13.0(58)	0

Hanks, Merton

YEAR	TEAM	INT	YDS	AVG (LG)	TD
1992	SF	2	5	2.5(4)	0
1993	SF	3	104	34.7(67)	1
1994	SF	7	93	13.3(38)	0
1995	SF	5	31	6.2(23)	0
1996	SF	4	7	1.8(8)	0
1997	SF	6	103	17.2(55)	1
1998	SF	4	37	9.3(37)	0
1999	Sea	2	30	15.0(23)	1
NFL	9	33	410	12.4(67)	3

Harden, Mike

YEAR	TEAM	INT	YDS	AVG (LG)	TD
1981	Den	2	34	17.0(38)	0
1982	Den	2	3	1.5(3)	0
1983	Den	4	**127**	31.8(48)	0
1984	Den	6	79	13.2(45)	1
1985	Den	5	100	20.0(42)	**1**
1986	Den	6	179	29.8(52)	2
1987	Den	4	85	21.3(32)	0
1988	Den	4	36	9.0(34)	0
1989	LARd	2	1	0.5(1)	0
1990	LARd	3	19	6.3(15)	0
NFL	11	38	663	17.4(52)	4

Harper, Dwayne

YEAR	TEAM	INT	YDS	AVG (LG)	TD
1989	Sea	2	15	7.5(15)	0
1990	Sea	3	69	23.0(47)	0
1991	Sea	4	84	21.0(43)	0
1992	Sea	3	74	24.7(41)	0
1993	Sea	1	0	0.0(0)	0
1994	SD	3	28	9.3(15)	0
1995	SD	4	12	3.0(15)	0
1996	SD	1	0	0.0(0)	0
1997	SD	2	43	21.5(43)	0
1998	SD	1	12	12.0(12)	0
NFL	11	24	337	14.0(47)	0

Harris, Cliff

YEAR	TEAM	INT	YDS	AVG (LG)	TD
1970	Dal	2	66	33.0(60)	0
1971	Dal	2	0	0.0(0)	0
1972	Dal	3	40	13.3(23)	0
1973	Dal	2	9	4.5(5)	0
1974	Dal	3	8	2.7(8)	0
1975	Dal	3	58	19.3(27)	**1**
1976	Dal	3	32	10.7(29)	0
1977	Dal	5	7	1.4(7)	0
1978	Dal	4	26	6.5(23)	0
1979	Dal	2	35	17.5(20)	0
NFL	10	29	281	9.7(60)	1

Harris, Dick

YEAR	TEAM	INT	YDS	AVG (LG)	TD
1960	LAC-A	5	56	11.2(42)	1
1961	SD-A	7	140	20.0(56)	**3**
1962	SD-A	5	52	10.4(36)	0
1963	SD-A	8	83	10.4(22)	1
1964	SD-A	3	82	27.3(44)	0
1965	SD-A	1	0	0.0(0)	0
NFL	6	29	413	14.2(56)	5

Harris, Eric

YEAR	TEAM	INT	YDS	AVG (LG)	TD
1980	KC	7	54	7.7(41)	0
1981	KC	7	109	15.6(43)	0
1982	KC	3	66	22.0(56)	**1**
1983	LARm	4	100	25.0(45)	0
NFL	5	21	329	15.7(56)	1

Harris, John

YEAR	TEAM	INT	YDS	AVG (LG)	TD
1978	Sea	4	65	16.3(28)	0
1979	Sea	2	30	15.0(25)	0
1980	Sea	6	28	4.7(15)	0
1981	Sea	**10**	155	15.5(42)	**2**
1982	Sea	4	33	8.3(18)	0
1983	Sea	2	15	7.5(10)	0
1984	Sea	6	79	13.2(29)	0
1985	Sea	7	20	2.9(17)	0
1986	Min	3	69	23.0(28)	0
1987	Min	3	20	6.7(14)	0
1988	Min	3	46	15.3(27)	0
NFL	11	50	560	11.2(42)	2

Harris, Walt

YEAR	TEAM	INT	YDS	AVG (LG)	TD
1996	ChiB	2	0	0.0(0)	0
1997	ChiB	5	30	6.0(12)	0
1998	ChiB	4	41	10.3(26)	1
1999	ChiB	1	-1	-1.0(-1)	0
2000	ChiB	2	35	17.5(35)	1
2001	ChiB	1	45	45.0(39)	1
2002	Ind	2	0	0.0(0)	0
2004	Was	2	31	15.5(31)	0
2005	Was	1	0	0.0(0)	0
NFL	10	20	181	9.1(39)	3

Harrison, Rodney

YEAR	TEAM	INT	YDS	AVG (LG)	TD
1995	SD	5	22	4.4(17)	0
1996	SD	5	56	11.2(29)	0
1997	SD	2	75	37.5(75)	1
1998	SD	3	42	14.0(21)	0
1999	SD	1	0	0.0(0)	0
2000	SD	6	97	16.2(63)	1
2001	SD	2	51	25.5(22)	0
2002	SD	2	2	1.0(2)	0
2003	NE	3	0	0.0(2)	0
2004	NE	2	12	6.0(12)	0
NFL	11	31	357	11.5(75)	2

Hartley, Howard

YEAR	TEAM	INT	YDS	AVG (LG)	TD
1948	Was	3	76	25.3(53)	0
1949	Pit	6	63	10.5(41)	0
1950	Pit	5	84	16.8(38)	0
1951	Pit	10	69	6.9(23)	0
1952	Pit	4	51	12.8(24)	0
NFL	5	28	343	12.3(53)	0

Hasty, James

YEAR	TEAM	INT	YDS	AVG (LG)	TD
1988	NYJ	5	20	4.0(16)	0
1989	NYJ	5	62	12.4(34)	1
1990	NYJ	2	0	0.0(0)	0
1991	NYJ	3	39	13.0(39)	0
1992	NYJ	2	18	9.0(18)	0
1993	NYJ	2	22	11.0(22)	0
1994	NYJ	5	90	18.0(40)	0
1995	KC	3	89	29.7(64)	1
1997	KC	3	22	7.3(19)	0

YEAR	TEAM	INT	YDS	AVG (LG)	TD
1998	KC	4	42	10.5(21)	0
1999	KC	**7**	98	14.0(56)	**2**
2000	KC	4	53	13.3(38)	0
NFL	13	45	555	12.3(64)	4
Hayes, Lester					
1977	Oak	1	27	27.0(27)	0
1978	Oak	4	86	21.5(52)	0
1979	Oak	7	100	14.3(52)	**2**
1980	Oak	**13**	**273**	21.0(62)	1
1981	Oak	3	0	0.0(0)	0
1982	LARd	2	0	0.0(0)	0
1983	LARd	2	49	24.5(28)	0
1984	LARd	1	3	3.0(3)	0
1985	LARd	4	27	6.8(27)	**1**
1986	LARd	2	7	3.5(7)	0
NFL	10	39	572	14.7(62)	4
Haynes, Mike					
1976	NE	8	90	11.3(28)	0
1977	NE	5	54	10.8(22)	0
1978	NE	6	123	20.5(50)	1
1979	NE	3	66	22.0(33)	0
1980	NE	1	31	31.0(31)	0
1981	NE	1	3	3.0(3)	0
1982	NE	4	26	6.5(26)	0
1983	LARd	1	0	0.0(0)	0
1984	LARd	6	**220**	36.7(97)	1
1985	LARd	4	8	2.0(8)	0
1986	LARd	2	28	14.0(22)	0
1987	LARd	2	9	4.5(7)	0
1988	LARd	3	30	10.0(30)	0
NFL	13	46	688	15.0(97)	2
Hecker, Norb					
1951	LARm	3	74	24.7(36)	0
1952	LARm	1	50	50.0(50)	0
1953	LARm	7	91	13.0(24)	0
1955	Was	6	52	8.7(26)	0
1956	Was	8	26	3.3(14)	0
1957	Was	3	39	13.0(22)	0
NFL	6	28	332	11.9(50)	0
Hendricks, Ted					
1970	Bal	1	31	31.0(31)	0
1971	Bal	5	70	14.0(40)	0
1972	Bal	2	13	6.5(13)	0
1973	Bal	3	33	11.0(24)	0
1974	GB	5	74	14.8(44)	0
1975	Oak	2	40	20.0(33)	0
1976	Oak	1	9	9.0(9)	0
1978	Oak	3	29	9.7(16)	0
1979	Oak	1	23	23.0(23)	1
1980	Oak	3	10	3.3(5)	0
NFL	14	26	332	12.8(44)	1
Henry, Anthony					
2001	Cle	**10**	177	17.7(97)	1
2002	Cle	2	4	2.0(4)	0
2003	Cle	1	19	19.0(19)	0
2004	Cle	4	83	20.8(51)	0
2005	Dal	3	102	34.0(58)	1
NFL	5	20	385	19.3(97)	2
Hicks, Dwight					
1979	SF	5	57	11.4(29)	0
1980	SF	4	73	18.3(44)	0
1981	SF	9	**239**	26.6(72)	1
1982	SF	3	5	1.7(3)	0
1983	SF	2	102	51.0(62)	**2**
1984	SF	3	42	14.0(29)	0
1985	SF	4	68	17.0(25)	0
1986	Ind	2	16	8.0(16)	0
NFL	8	32	602	18.8(72)	3
Hicks, W.K.					
1964	Hou-A	5	89	17.8(62)	0
1965	Hou-A	**9**	**156**	17.3(31)	0
1966	Hou-A	3	12	4.0(12)	0
1967	Hou-A	3	122	**40.7(62)**	0
1968	Hou-A	3	42	14.0(28)	0
1969	Hou-A	4	36	9.0(20)	0
1970	NYJ	8	99	12.4(35)	0
1971	NYJ	4	46	11.5(26)	0
1972	NYJ	1	43	43.0(43)	0
NFL	9	40	645	16.1(62)	0
Hill, Jimmy					
1956	ChiC	5	21	4.2(12)	0
1957	ChiC	3	53	17.7(31)	0
1959	ChiC	2	4	2.0(4)	0
1961	SL	4	92	23.0(35)	1
1962	SL	2	15	7.5(15)	0
1963	SL	3	126	42.0(58)	1
1965	Det	1	9	9.0(9)	0
NFL	8	20	320	16.0(58)	2
Hoage, Terry					
1985	NO	4	79	19.8(52)	1
1986	Phi	1	18	18.0(18)	0

YEAR	TEAM	INT	YDS	AVG (LG)	TD
1987	Phi	2	3	1.5(3)	0
1988	Phi	8	116	14.5(38)	0
1990	Phi	1	0	0.0(0)	0
1994	Arz	3	64	21.3(41)	0
1995	Arz	2	0	0.0(0)	0
NFL	9	21	280	13.3(52)	1
Holmes, Jerry					
1981	NYJ	1	0	0.0(0)	0
1982	NYJ	3	2	0.7(2)	0
1983	NYJ	3	107	**35.7(43)**	1
1986	NYJ	6	29	4.8(28)	0
1987	NYJ	1	20	20.0(20)	0
1988	Det	1	32	32.0(32)	0
1989	Det	6	77	12.8(36)	1
1990	GB	3	39	13.0(24)	0
1991	GB	1	0	0.0(0)	0
NFL	9	25	306	12.2(43)	2
Holt, Issiac					
1985	Min	1	0	0.0(0)	0
1986	Min	8	54	6.8(27)	0
1987	Min	2	7	3.5(7)	0
1988	Min	2	15	7.5(15)	0
1989	Min	1	90	90.0(**90**)	1
1990	Dal	3	72	24.0(64)	1
1991	Dal	4	2	0.5(2)	0
1992	Dal	2	11	5.5(8)	0
NFL	8	23	251	10.9(90)	2
Hopkins, Wes					
1984	Phi	5	107	21.4(33)	0
1985	Phi	6	36	6.0(24)	1
1988	Phi	5	21	4.2(11)	0
1990	Phi	5	45	9.0(21)	0
1991	Phi	5	26	5.2(14)	0
1992	Phi	3	6	2.0(4)	0
1993	Phi	1	0	0.0(0)	0
NFL	10	30	241	8.0(33)	1
Houston, Ken					
1967	Hou-A	4	151	37.8(78)	2
1968	Hou-A	5	160	32.0(66)	**2**
1969	Hou-A	4	87	21.8(51)	1
1970	Hou	3	32	10.7(9)	0
1971	Hou	**9**	**220**	24.4(48)	**4**
1973	Was	6	32	5.3(32)	0
1974	Was	2	40	20.0(37)	0
1975	Was	4	33	8.3(19)	0
1976	Was	4	25	6.3(12)	0
1977	Was	5	69	13.8(31)	0
1978	Was	2	29	14.5(29)	0
1979	Was	1	20	20.0(20)	0
NFL	13	49	898	18.3(78)	9
Howard, Bob					
1968	SD-A	1	0	0.0(0)	0
1969	SD-A	6	50	8.3(19)	0
1970	SD	2	19	9.5(19)	0
1971	SD	4	47	11.8(29)	0
1973	SD	5	25	5.0(25)	0
1974	SD	3	52	17.3(23)	0
1975	NE	3	52	17.3(44)	1
1976	NE	3	28	9.3(15)	0
1977	NE	4	10	2.5(6)	0
1978	Phi	3	15	5.0(15)	0
1979	Phi	3	34	11.3(34)	0
NFL	11	37	332	9.0(44)	1
Howell, Mike					
1966	Cle	8	62	7.8(29)	0
1967	Cle	3	20	6.7(20)	0
1968	Cle	6	55	9.2(24)	0
1969	Cle	6	21	3.5(11)	0
1970	Cle	1	0	0.0(0)	0
1971	Cle	2	93	46.5(68)	0
1972	Cle	1	1	1.0(1)	0
NFL	8	27	252	9.3(68)	0
Howley, Chuck					
1958	ChiB	1	4	4.0(4)	0
1961	Dal	1	5	5.0(5)	0
1962	Dal	2	33	16.5(21)	0
1963	Dal	2	3	1.5(3)	0
1964	Dal	2	27	13.5(21)	0
1967	Dal	1	28	28.0(28)	1
1968	Dal	6	115	19.2(58)	1
1969	Dal	2	37	18.5(28)	0
1970	Dal	2	18	9.0(17)	0
1971	Dal	5	122	24.4(53)	0
1972	Dal	1	7	7.0(7)	0
NFL	14	25	399	16.0(58)	2
Huff, Sam					
1956	NYG	3	49	16.3(27)	0
1957	NYG	1	6	6.0(6)	0
1958	NYG	2	23	11.5(15)	0
1959	NYG	1	21	21.0(21)	0
1960	NYG	3	45	15.0(17)	0

YEAR	TEAM	INT	YDS	AVG (LG)	TD
1961	NYG	3	13	4.3(13)	0
1962	NYG	1	4	4.0(4)	0
1963	NYG	4	47	11.8(36)	1
1964	Was	4	34	8.5(14)	0
1965	Was	2	49	24.5(39)	0
1966	Was	1	17	17.0(17)	0
1967	Was	2	8	4.0(5)	0
1969	Was	3	65	21.7(32)	1
NFL	13	30	381	12.7(39)	2
Hunt, Bobby					
1962	DalT-A	8	101	12.6(17)	0
1963	KC-A	6	228	38.0(66)	0
1964	KC-A	7	133	19.0(59)	**1**
1965	KC-A	1	28	28.0(28)	0
1966	KC-A	**10**	113	11.3(33)	0
1967	KC-A	5	71	14.2(39)	0
1968	Cin-A	1	15	15.0(15)	0
1969	Cin-A	4	66	16.5(27)	0
NFL	8	42	755	18.0(66)	1
Hunter, James					
1976	Det	7	120	17.1(39)	1
1977	Det	6	104	17.3(26)	0
1978	Det	2	-4	-2.0(0)	0
1979	Det	3	6	2.0(6)	0
1980	Det	6	20	3.3(13)	0
1981	Det	1	-3	-3.0(-3)	0
1982	Det	2	36	18.0(36)	0
NFL	7	27	279	10.3(39)	1
Hurst, Maurice					
1989	NE	5	31	6.2(16)	1
1990	NE	4	61	15.3(36)	0
1991	NE	3	21	7.0(21)	0
1992	NE	3	29	9.7(27)	0
1993	NE	4	53	13.3(24)	0
1994	NE	7	68	9.7(24)	0
1995	NE	1	0	0.0(0)	0
NFL	7	27	263	9.7(36)	1
Hutson, Don					
1940	GB	**6**	24	4.0(0)	0
1941	GB	1	32	32.0(32)	0
1942	GB	7	71	10.1(27)	0
1943	GB	8	**197**	**24.6(84)**	**1**
1944	GB	4	50	12.5(43)	0
1945	GB	4	15	3.8(15)	0
NFL	11	30	389	13.0(84)	1
Irvin, LeRoy					
1980	LARm	2	80	40.0(80)	0
1981	LARm	3	18	6.0(18)	0
1983	LARm	4	42	10.5(22)	0
1984	LARm	5	**166**	**33.2(81)**	**2**
1985	LARm	6	83	13.8(34)	1
1986	LARm	6	**150**	25.0(50)	1
1987	LARm	2	47	23.5(47)	**1**
1988	LARm	3	25	8.3(22)	0
1989	LARm	3	43	14.3(18)	0
1990	Det	1	22	22.0(22)	0
NFL	11	35	676	19.3(81)	5
Jackson, Bobby					
1978	NYJ	5	26	5.2(13)	0
1979	NYJ	4	63	15.8(58)	1
1980	NYJ	1	7	7.0(7)	0
1982	NYJ	**5**	84	16.8(77)	**1**
1983	NYJ	2	8	4.0(8)	0
1985	NYJ	4	8	2.0(8)	0
NFL	6	21	196	9.3(77)	2
Jackson, Greg					
1990	NYG	5	8	1.6(5)	0
1991	NYG	1	3	3.0(3)	0
1992	NYG	4	71	17.8(36)	0
1993	NYG	4	32	8.0(29)	0
1994	Phi	6	86	14.3(55)	1
1995	Phi	1	18	18.0(18)	0
1996	NO	3	24	8.0(10)	0
1997	SD	2	37	18.5(36)	1
1998	SD	6	50	8.3(25)	0
NFL	11	32	329	10.3(55)	2
Jackson, Monte					
1975	LARm	2	13	6.5(10)	0
1976	LARm	**10**	173	17.3(46)	**3**
1977	LARm	5	73	14.6(33)	0
1978	Oak	2	25	12.5(25)	0
1979	Oak	2	5	2.5(5)	0
1980	Oak	1	0	0.0(0)	0
1982	LARd	1	0	0.0(0)	0
NFL	8	23	289	12.6(46)	3
Jackson, Terry					
1978	NYG	7	115	16.4(51)	1
1979	NYG	3	10	3.3(10)	0
1980	NYG	1	5	5.0(5)	0
1981	NYG	3	57	19.0(32)	1
1982	NYG	4	75	18.8(37)	0

YEAR	TEAM	INT	YDS	AVG (LG)	TD
1983	NYG	6	20	3.3(17)	0
1984	Sea	4	78	19.5(62)	1
NFL	8	28	360	12.9(62)	3
Jackson, Tom					
1974	Den	1	39	39.0(39)	0
1975	Den	2	0	0.0(0)	0
1976	Den	7	136	19.4(46)	1
1977	Den	4	95	23.8(73)	**1**
1978	Den	3	28	9.3(28)	1
1979	Den	1	34	34.0(34)	0
1982	Den	1	8	8.0(8)	0
1983	Den	1	0	0.0(0)	0
NFL	11	20	340	17.0(73)	3
James, Roland					
1980	NE	4	32	8.0(19)	0
1981	NE	2	29	14.5(21)	0
1982	NE	3	12	4.0(12)	0
1983	NE	5	99	19.8(46)	0
1984	NE	2	14	7.0(14)	0
1985	NE	4	51	12.8(39)	0
1986	NE	2	39	19.5(21)	0
1987	NE	1	27	27.0(27)	0
1988	NE	4	30	7.5(22)	0
1989	NE	2	50	25.0(28)	0
NFL	10	29	383	13.2(46)	0
James, Tommy					
1948	Cle-A	4	37	9.3(0)	0
1949	Cle-A	4	64	16.0(0)	**1**
1950	Cle	9	69	7.7(34)	0
1951	Cle	2	1	0.5(1)	0
1952	Cle	4	40	10.0(18)	0
1953	Cle	5	21	4.2(11)	0
1954	Cle	4	57	14.3(36)	0
1955	Cle	2	20	10.0(16)	0
AAFC	2	8	101	12.6(0)	1
NFL	7	26	208	8.0(36)	0
James, Tory					
1996	Den	2	15	7.5(15)	0
1999	Den	5	59	11.8(45)	0
2000	Oak	2	25	12.5(25)	0
2001	Oak	5	72	14.4(33)	0
2002	Oak	4	35	8.8(27)	0
2003	Cin	4	56	14.0(31)	0
2004	Cin	8	66	8.3(23)	0
2005	Cin	5	5	1.0(5)	0
NFL	9	35	333	9.5(45)	0
Janik, Tom					
1963	Den-A	2	32	16.0(31)	0
1964	Den-A	1	22	22.0(22)	**1**
1966	Buf-A	8	136	17.0(37)	**2**
1967	Buf-A	**10**	222	22.2(46)	2
1968	Buf-A	3	137	**45.7(100)**	1
1969	Bos-A	1	8	8.0(8)	0
NFL	8	25	557	22.3(100)	6
Jauron, Dick					
1973	Det	4	**208**	**52.0(95)**	1
1974	Det	1	26	26.0(26)	0
1975	Det	4	39	9.8(38)	0
1976	Det	2	0	0.0(0)	0
1977	Det	3	55	18.3(28)	0
1978	Cin	4	52	13.0(24)	1
1979	Cin	6	41	6.8(12)	0
1980	Cin	1	11	11.0(11)	0
NFL	8	25	432	17.3(95)	2
Jeter, Bob					
1965	GB	1	21	21.0(21)	0
1966	GB	5	142	28.4(75)	**2**
1967	GB	8	78	9.8(25)	0
1968	GB	3	35	11.7(29)	0
1969	GB	3	30	10.0(30)	0
1970	GB	3	27	9.0(18)	0
1971	ChiB	1	0	0.0(0)	0
1972	ChiB	2	0	0.0(0)	0
NFL	10	26	333	12.8(75)	2
Johnson, Curtis					
1970	Mia	3	29	9.7(21)	0
1971	Mia	2	34	17.0(34)	0
1972	Mia	3	20	6.7(13)	0
1973	Mia	2	19	9.5(17)	0
1975	Mia	4	41	10.3(17)	0
1976	Mia	1	14	14.0(14)	0
1977	Mia	4	35	8.8(19)	0
1978	Mia	3	-2	-0.7(0)	0
NFL	9	22	190	8.6(34)	0
Johnson, Jimmy					
1961	SF	5	116	23.2(63)	0
1963	SF	2	36	18.0(36)	0
1964	SF	3	65	21.7(43)	0
1965	SF	6	47	7.8(26)	0
1966	SF	4	57	14.3(35)	1
1967	SF	2	68	34.0(38)	0

YEAR	TEAM	INT	YDS	AVG(LG)	TD
1968	SF	1	25	25.0(25)	0
1969	SF	5	18	3.6(18)	0
1970	SF	2	36	18.0(36)	1
1971	SF	3	16	5.3(10)	0
1972	SF	4	18	4.5(15)	0
1973	SF	4	46	11.5(30)	0
1974	SF	3	50	16.7(37)	0
1975	SF	2	0	0.0(0)	0
1976	SF	1	17	17.0(17)	0
NFL	16	47	615	13.1(63)	2

Johnson, Johnnie

YEAR	TEAM	INT	YDS	AVG(LG)	TD
1980	LARm	3	102	34.0(**99**)	**1**
1982	LARm	1	7	7.0(7)	0
1983	LARm	4	115	**28.8**(**60**)	**2**
1984	LARm	2	21	10.5(21)	0
1985	LARm	5	96	19.2(46)	1
1986	LARm	1	13	13.0(13)	0
1987	LARm	1	0	0.0(0)	0
1988	LARm	4	18	4.5(11)	0
1989	Sea	1	18	18.0(18)	0
NFL	10	22	390	17.7(99)	4

Johnson, Levi

YEAR	TEAM	INT	YDS	AVG(LG)	TD
1973	Det	5	82	16.4(38)	0
1974	Det	5	139	27.8(55)	**2**
1975	Det	3	71	23.7(45)	0
1976	Det	6	**206**	34.3(76)	1
1977	Det	2	51	25.5(32)	0
NFL	5	21	549	26.1(76)	3

Jordan, Lee Roy

YEAR	TEAM	INT	YDS	AVG(LG)	TD
1963	Dal	3	41	13.7(23)	0
1964	Dal	1	3	3.0(3)	0
1966	Dal	1	49	49.0(49)	1
1967	Dal	3	85	28.3(40)	1
1968	Dal	3	17	5.7(7)	0
1969	Dal	2	38	19.0(38)	0
1970	Dal	1	6	6.0(6)	0
1971	Dal	2	34	17.0(23)	0
1972	Dal	2	18	9.0(12)	0
1973	Dal	6	78	13.0(31)	1
1974	Dal	2	23	11.5(13)	0
1975	Dal	6	80	13.3(38)	0
NFL	13	32	472	14.8(49)	3

Joyner, Seth

YEAR	TEAM	INT	YDS	AVG(LG)	TD
1986	Phi	1	4	4.0(4)	0
1987	Phi	2	42	21.0(29)	0
1988	Phi	4	96	24.0(30)	0
1989	Phi	1	0	0.0(0)	0
1990	Phi	1	9	9.0(9)	0
1991	Phi	3	41	13.7(41)	0
1992	Phi	4	88	22.0(43)	2
1993	Phi	1	6	6.0(6)	0
1994	Arz	3	2	0.7(2)	0
1995	Arz	3	9	3.0(11)	0
1996	Arz	1	10	10.0(10)	0
NFL	12	24	307	12.8(43)	2

Judson, William

YEAR	TEAM	INT	YDS	AVG(LG)	TD
1983	Mia	6	60	10.0(29)	0
1984	Mia	4	121	30.3(60)	1
1985	Mia	4	88	22.0(61)	**1**
1986	Mia	2	0	0.0(0)	0
1987	Mia	2	11	5.5(10)	0
1988	Mia	4	57	14.3(52)	0
1989	Mia	2	31	15.5(28)	0
NFL	7	24	368	15.3(61)	2

Keane, Tom

YEAR	TEAM	INT	YDS	AVG(LG)	TD
1950	LARm	6	50	8.3(25)	1
1951	LARm	2	2	1.0(2)	0
1952	DalT	10	93	9.3(39)	0
1953	Bal	11	118	10.7(35)	0
1954	Bal	5	22	4.4(9)	0
1955	ChiC	6	64	10.7(32)	0
NFL	8	40	349	8.7(39)	1

Kearney, Jim

YEAR	TEAM	INT	YDS	AVG(LG)	TD
1968	KC-A	3	23	7.7(23)	0
1969	KC-A	5	143	28.6(60)	1
1970	KC	4	28	7.0(15)	0
1971	KC	3	46	15.3(29)	0
1972	KC	5	**192**	**38.4**(**65**)	**4**
1973	KC	3	30	10.0(24)	0
NFL	8	23	462	20.1(65)	5

Kelly, Brian

YEAR	TEAM	INT	YDS	AVG(LG)	TD
1998	TB	1	4	4.0(4)	0
1999	TB	1	26	26.0(26)	0
2000	TB	1	9	9.0(9)	1
2002	TB	**8**	68	8.5(31)	0
2003	TB	1	0	0.0(0)	0
2004	TB	4	101	25.3(75)	0
2005	TB	4	19	4.8(14)	0
NFL	8	20	227	11.4(75)	1

Kelso, Mark

YEAR	TEAM	INT	YDS	AVG(LG)	TD
1987	Buf	**6**	25	4.2(12)	0
1988	Buf	7	**180**	25.7(78)	1
1989	Buf	6	101	16.8(43)	0
1990	Buf	2	0	0.0(0)	0
1991	Buf	2	0	0.0(0)	0
1992	Buf	7	21	3.0(13)	0
NFL	7	30	327	10.9(78)	1

Kinard, Terry

YEAR	TEAM	INT	YDS	AVG(LG)	TD
1983	NYG	3	49	16.3(25)	0
1984	NYG	2	29	14.5(29)	0
1985	NYG	5	100	20.0(31)	0
1986	NYG	4	52	13.0(25)	0
1987	NYG	5	**163**	32.6(70)	**1**
1988	NYG	3	46	15.3(39)	0
1989	NYG	5	135	**27.0**(**58**)	1
1990	Hou	4	75	18.8(47)	0
NFL	8	31	649	20.9(70)	2

Kindt, Don

YEAR	TEAM	INT	YDS	AVG(LG)	TD
1947	ChiB	3	19	6.3(10)	0
1948	ChiB	1	21	21.0(21)	0
1949	ChiB	2	3	1.5(3)	0
1951	ChiB	4	56	14.0(39)	0
1952	ChiB	3	49	16.3(26)	0
1953	ChiB	6	172	28.7(67)	**1**
1954	ChiB	2	28	14.0(25)	0
NFL	9	21	348	16.6(67)	1

Knight, Sammy

YEAR	TEAM	INT	YDS	AVG(LG)	TD
1997	NO	5	75	15.0(39)	0
1998	NO	6	171	28.5(**91**)	2
1999	NO	1	0	0.0(0)	0
2000	NO	5	68	13.6(37)	**2**
2001	NO	6	114	19.0(40)	0
2002	NO	5	36	7.2(17)	0
2003	Mia	3	98	32.7(70)	0
2004	Mia	4	32	8.0(32)	0
2005	KC	2	12	6.0(12)	0
NFL	9	37	606	16.4(91)	4

Konz, Ken

YEAR	TEAM	INT	YDS	AVG(LG)	TD
1953	Cle	5	15	3.0(9)	0
1954	Cle	7	133	19.0(54)	**2**
1955	Cle	5	32	6.4(15)	1
1956	Cle	4	34	8.5(28)	0
1957	Cle	4	20	5.0(16)	0
1958	Cle	4	123	30.8(46)	1
1959	Cle	1	35	35.0(21)	0
NFL	7	30	392	13.1(54)	4

Krause, Paul

YEAR	TEAM	INT	YDS	AVG(LG)	TD
1964	Was	**12**	140	11.7(35)	1
1965	Was	6	118	19.7(43)	0
1966	Was	2	0	0.0(0)	0
1967	Was	8	75	9.4(32)	0
1968	Min	7	82	11.7(29)	0
1969	Min	5	82	16.4(77)	1
1970	Min	6	90	15.0(40)	0
1971	Min	6	112	18.7(31)	0
1972	Min	6	109	18.2(35)	1
1973	Min	4	28	7.0(24)	0
1974	Min	2	53	26.5(45)	0
1975	Min	**10**	**201**	20.1(81)	0
1976	Min	2	21	10.5(19)	0
1977	Min	2	25	12.5(25)	0
1979	Min	3	49	16.3(18)	0
NFL	15	81	1185	14.6(81)	3

Lahr, Warren

YEAR	TEAM	INT	YDS	AVG(LG)	TD
1949	Cle-A	4	32	8.0(0)	0
1950	Cle	8	99	12.4(30)	**2**
1951	Cle	5	95	19.0(29)	**2**
1952	Cle	5	51	10.2(14)	0
1953	Cle	5	119	23.8(42)	0
1954	Cle	5	44	8.8(27)	1
1955	Cle	5	52	10.4(24)	0
1956	Cle	3	33	11.0(18)	0
1957	Cle	2	12	6.0(10)	0
1958	Cle	1	25	25.0(25)	0
1959	Cle	1	0	0.0(0)	0
AAFC	1	4	32	8.0(0)	0
NFL	10	40	530	13.3(42)	5

Lambert, Jack

YEAR	TEAM	INT	YDS	AVG(LG)	TD
1974	Pit	2	19	9.5(13)	0
1975	Pit	2	35	17.5(24)	0
1976	Pit	2	32	16.0(22)	0
1977	Pit	1	5	5.0(5)	0
1978	Pit	4	41	10.3(24)	0
1979	Pit	6	29	4.8(23)	0
1980	Pit	2	1	0.5(1)	0
1981	Pit	6	76	12.7(31)	0
1982	Pit	1	6	6.0(6)	0
1983	Pit	2	-1	-0.5(0)	0
NFL	10	28	243	8.7(31)	0

Landry, Tom

YEAR	TEAM	INT	YDS	AVG(LG)	TD
1949	NYY-A	1	44	44.0(44)	0
1950	NYG	2	0	0.0(0)	0
1951	NYG	8	121	15.1(55)	**2**
1952	NYG	8	99	12.4(30)	1
1953	NYG	3	55	18.3(30)	0
1954	NYG	8	71	8.9(27)	0
1955	NYG	2	14	7.0(10)	0
AAFC	1	1	44	44.0(44)	0
NFL	6	31	360	11.6(11)	3

Lane, Night Train

YEAR	TEAM	INT	YDS	AVG(LG)	TD
1952	LARm	**14**	**298**	21.3(80)	**2**
1953	LARm	3	9	3.0(8)	0
1954	ChiC	**10**	**181**	18.1(64)	0
1955	ChiC	6	69	11.5(26)	0
1956	ChiC	7	206	29.4(66)	1
1957	ChiC	2	47	23.5(33)	0
1958	ChiC	2	0	0.0(0)	0
1959	ChiC	3	125	**41.7**(**69**)	**1**
1960	Det	5	102	20.4(80)	1
1961	Det	6	73	12.2(32)	0
1962	Det	4	16	4.0(13)	0
1963	Det	5	70	14.0(33)	0
1964	Det	1	11	11.0(11)	0
NFL	14	68	1207	17.8(80)	5

Lanier, Willie

YEAR	TEAM	INT	YDS	AVG(LG)	TD
1968	KC-A	4	120	30.0(75)	1
1969	KC-A	4	70	17.5(44)	0
1970	KC	2	2	1.0(2)	0
1971	KC	2	38	19.0(21)	0
1972	KC	2	2	1.0(2)	0
1973	KC	3	47	15.7(29)	1
1974	KC	2	28	14.0(14)	0
1975	KC	5	105	21.0(61)	0
1976	KC	3	28	9.3(14)	0
NFL	11	27	440	16.3(75)	2

Lary, Yale

YEAR	TEAM	INT	YDS	AVG(LG)	TD
1952	Det	4	61	15.3(53)	0
1953	Det	5	98	19.6(32)	0
1956	Det	8	182	22.8(73)	1
1957	Det	2	64	32.0(63)	0
1958	Det	3	70	23.3(31)	0
1959	Det	3	0	0.0(0)	0
1960	Det	3	44	14.7(22)	0
1961	Det	6	95	15.8(42)	0
1962	Det	8	51	6.4(32)	0
1963	Det	2	21	10.5(21)	1
1964	Det	6	101	16.8(30)	0
NFL	11	50	787	15.7(73)	2

Lassiter, Kwamie

YEAR	TEAM	INT	YDS	AVG(LG)	TD
1996	Arz	1	20	20.0(20)	0
1997	Arz	1	10	10.0(10)	0
1998	Arz	**8**	80	10.0(29)	0
1999	Arz	2	110	55.0(78)	1
2000	Arz	1	11	11.0(11)	0
2001	Arz	9	80	8.9(25)	0
2002	Arz	2	7	3.5(7)	0
2003	SD	1	38	38.0(38)	1
NFL	9	25	356	14.2(78)	2

Lavender, Joe

YEAR	TEAM	INT	YDS	AVG(LG)	TD
1974	Phi	1	37	37.0(37)	1
1975	Phi	3	59	19.7(36)	**1**
1976	Was	8	77	9.6(28)	0
1977	Was	4	36	9.0(31)	0
1978	Was	1	0	0.0(0)	0
1979	Was	6	77	12.8(27)	0
1980	Was	6	96	16.0(51)	**1**
1981	Was	4	52	13.0(30)	0
NFL	9	33	434	13.2(51)	3

Law, Ty

YEAR	TEAM	INT	YDS	AVG(LG)	TD
1995	NE	3	47	15.7(38)	0
1996	NE	3	45	15.0(38)	1
1997	NE	3	70	23.3(40)	0
1998	NE	**9**	133	14.8(59)	1
1999	NE	2	20	10.0(27)	1
2000	NE	2	32	16.0(32)	0
2001	NE	3	91	30.3(46)	**2**
2002	NE	4	33	8.3(29)	0
2003	NE	6	112	18.7(65)	1
2004	NE	1	0	0.0(0)	0
2005	NYJ	**10**	**195**	19.5(74)	1
NFL	11	46	778	16.9(74)	7

Lawrence, Rolland

YEAR	TEAM	INT	YDS	AVG(LG)	TD
1973	Atl	1	81	81.0(81)	0
1974	Atl	1	0	0.0(0)	0
1975	Atl	9	163	18.1(87)	**1**
1976	Atl	6	43	7.2(22)	0
1977	Atl	**7**	138	19.7(36)	0
1978	Atl	6	76	12.7(44)	0
1979	Atl	6	120	20.0(38)	0
1980	Atl	3	37	12.3(37)	0
NFL	8	39	658	16.9(87)	1

LeBeau, Dick

YEAR	TEAM	INT	YDS	AVG(LG)	TD
1960	Det	4	58	14.5(43)	0
1961	Det	3	45	15.0(33)	0
1962	Det	4	67	16.8(31)	**1**
1963	Det	5	158	31.6(70)	1
1964	Det	5	45	9.0(18)	0
1965	Det	7	84	12.0(30)	1
1966	Det	4	66	16.5(37)	0
1967	Det	4	29	7.3(27)	0
1968	Det	5	23	4.6(16)	0
1969	Det	6	15	2.5(8)	0
1970	Det	**9**	96	10.7(43)	0
1971	Det	6	76	12.7(40)	0
NFL	14	62	762	12.3(70)	3

Lee, Carl

YEAR	TEAM	INT	YDS	AVG(LG)	TD
1983	Min	1	31	31.0(31)	0
1984	Min	1	0	0.0(0)	0
1985	Min	3	68	22.7(35)	0
1986	Min	3	10	3.3(10)	0
1987	Min	3	53	17.7(36)	0
1988	Min	8	118	14.8(58)	**2**
1989	Min	2	0	0.0(0)	0
1990	Min	2	29	14.5(25)	0
1991	Min	1	0	0.0(0)	0
1992	Min	2	20	10.0(20)	0
1993	Min	3	20	6.7(19)	0
1994	NO	2	3	1.5(3)	0
NFL	12	31	352	11.4(58)	2

Lee, Mark

YEAR	TEAM	INT	YDS	AVG(LG)	TD
1981	GB	6	50	8.3(25)	0
1982	GB	1	40	40.0(40)	0
1983	GB	4	23	5.8(15)	0
1984	GB	3	33	11.0(14)	0
1985	GB	1	23	23.0(23)	0
1986	GB	9	33	3.7(11)	0
1987	GB	1	0	0.0(0)	0
1988	GB	3	37	12.3(27)	0
1989	GB	2	10	5.0(10)	0
1990	GB	1	0	0.0(0)	0
1991	SF	1	5	5.0(5)	0
NFL	12	32	254	7.9(40)	0

Lewis, Albert

YEAR	TEAM	INT	YDS	AVG(LG)	TD
1983	KC	4	42	10.5(34)	0
1984	KC	4	57	14.3(31)	0
1985	KC	**8**	59	7.4(16)	0
1986	KC	4	18	4.5(13)	0
1987	KC	1	0	0.0(0)	0
1988	KC	1	19	19.0(19)	0
1989	KC	4	37	9.3(22)	0
1990	KC	2	15	7.5(15)	0
1991	KC	3	21	7.0(21)	0
1992	KC	1	0	0.0(0)	0
1993	KC	6	61	10.2(24)	0
1996	Oak	2	0	0.0(0)	0
1998	Oak	2	74	37.0(74)	1
NFL	16	42	403	9.6(74)	1

Lewis, Cliff

YEAR	TEAM	INT	YDS	AVG(LG)	TD
1946	Cle-A	5	41	8.2(0)	0
1947	Cle-A	4	19	4.8(0)	0
1948	Cle-A	9	103	11.4(0)	0
1949	Cle-A	6	53	8.8(0)	0
1950	Cle	1	4	4.0(4)	0
1951	Cle	5	46	9.2(20)	0
AAFC	4	24	216	9.0(0)	0
NFL	2	6	50	8.3(20)	0

Lewis, Darryll

YEAR	TEAM	INT	YDS	AVG(LG)	TD
1991	Hou	1	33	33.0(33)	1
1993	Hou	1	47	47.0(47)	1
1994	Hou	5	57	11.4(20)	0
1995	Hou	6	**145**	24.2(98)	1
1996	Hou	5	103	20.6(53)	1
1997	Ten	5	115	23.0(47)	1
1998	Ten	4	40	10.0(33)	0
1999	SD	4	9	2.3(5)	0
2000	SD	1	6	6.0(3)	0
NFL	10	32	555	17.3(98)	5

Lewis, Ray

YEAR	TEAM	INT	YDS	AVG(LG)	TD
1996	Bal	1	0	0.0(0)	0
1997	Bal	1	18	18.0(18)	0
1998	Bal	2	25	12.5(26)	0
1999	Bal	3	97	32.3(60)	0
2000	Bal	2	1	0.5(1)	0
2001	Bal	3	115	38.3(64)	0
2002	Bal	2	4	2.0(4)	0
2003	Bal	6	99	16.5(37)	1
2005	Bal	1	0	0.0(0)	0
NFL	10	21	359	17.1(64)	1

Lewis, Woodley

YEAR	TEAM	INT	YDS	AVG(LG)	TD
1950	LARm	12	**275**	22.9(36)	0
1951	LARm	3	34	11.3(20)	0
1952	LARm	1	20	20.0(20)	0
1953	LARm	7	87	12.4(45)	**1**

YEAR	TEAM	INT	YDS	AVG(LG)	TD
1956	ChiC	1	0	0.0(0)	0
1957	ChiC	2	34	17.0(30)	0
NFL	11	26	450	17.3(45)	1

Lippett, Ronnie

YEAR	TEAM	INT	YDS	AVG(LG)	TD
1984	NE	3	23	7.7(13)	0
1985	NE	3	93	31.0(58)	0
1986	NE	8	76	9.5(43)	0
1987	NE	3	103	34.3(45)	**2**
1988	NE	1	4	4.0(4)	0
1990	NE	4	94	23.5(**73**)	0
1991	NE	2	27	13.5(27)	0
NFL	8	24	420	17.5(73)	2

Livingston, Howie

YEAR	TEAM	INT	YDS	AVG(LG)	TD
1944	NYG	**9**	**172**	19.1(40)	1
1945	NYG	3	65	21.7(38)	0
1946	NYG	4	69	17.3(33)	0
1947	NYG	4	69	17.3(40)	0
1949	Was	4	53	13.3(21)	0
1950	Was	1	27	27.0(27)	0
1950	SF	4	99	24.8(35)	1
NFL	6	29	554	19.1(40)	2

Lockhart, Spider

YEAR	TEAM	INT	YDS	AVG(LG)	TD
1965	NYG	4	117	29.3(39)	0
1966	NYG	6	20	3.3(14)	0
1967	NYG	5	38	7.6(28)	0
1968	NYG	8	130	16.3(72)	**2**
1969	NYG	2	0	0.0(0)	0
1970	NYG	4	51	12.8(25)	0
1971	NYG	3	60	20.0(31)	0
1972	NYG	4	56	14.0(29)	1
1973	NYG	2	3	1.5(2)	0
1974	NYG	2	0	0.0(0)	0
1975	NYG	1	0	0.0(0)	0
NFL	11	41	475	11.6(72)	3

Logan, Jerry

YEAR	TEAM	INT	YDS	AVG(LG)	TD
1963	Bal	1	15	15.0(15)	0
1964	Bal	6	91	15.2(30)	1
1965	Bal	2	74	37.0(38)	2
1966	Bal	3	13	4.3(13)	0
1967	Bal	4	22	5.5(11)	0
1968	Bal	3	9	3.0(9)	0
1969	Bal	1	6	6.0(6)	0
1970	Bal	6	92	15.3(33)	**2**
1971	Bal	4	28	7.0(23)	0
1972	Bal	4	47	11.8(20)	0
NFL	10	34	397	11.7(38)	5

Logan, Randy

YEAR	TEAM	INT	YDS	AVG(LG)	TD
1973	Phi	5	38	7.6(30)	0
1974	Phi	2	2	1.0(2)	0
1975	Phi	1	4	4.0(4)	0
1976	Phi	1	38	38.0(38)	0
1977	Phi	5	124	24.8(45)	0
1978	Phi	2	15	7.5(9)	0
1979	Phi	3	57	19.0(35)	0
1980	Phi	1	16	16.0(16)	0
1981	Phi	2	-1	-0.5(0)	0
1983	Phi	1	0	0.0(0)	0
NFL	10	23	293	12.7(45)	0

Lott, Ronnie

YEAR	TEAM	INT	YDS	AVG(LG)	TD
1981	SF	7	117	16.7(41)	**3**
1982	SF	2	95	47.5(83)	**1**
1983	SF	4	22	5.5(22)	0
1984	SF	4	26	6.5(15)	0
1985	SF	6	68	11.3(25)	0
1986	SF	**10**	134	13.4(57)	1
1987	SF	5	62	12.4(34)	0
1988	SF	5	59	11.8(44)	0
1989	SF	5	34	6.8(28)	0
1990	SF	3	26	8.7(15)	0
1991	LARd	**8**	52	6.5(27)	0
1992	LARd	1	0	0.0(0)	0
1993	NYJ	3	35	11.7(29)	0
NFL	14	63	730	11.6(83)	5

Lowe, Gary

YEAR	TEAM	INT	YDS	AVG(LG)	TD
1956	Was	1	30	30.0(30)	0
1957	Det	1	3	3.0(3)	0
1958	Det	2	25	12.5(25)	0
1959	Det	5	**130**	26.0(42)	0
1960	Det	2	49	24.5(26)	0
1961	Det	5	16	3.2(11)	0
1962	Det	2	20	10.0(20)	0
1963	Det	2	14	7.0(14)	0
NFL	9	20	287	14.4(42)	0

Lowe, Woodrow

YEAR	TEAM	INT	YDS	AVG(LG)	TD
1976	SD	1	8	8.0(8)	0
1977	SD	1	28	28.0(28)	0
1978	SD	1	16	16.0(16)	0
1979	SD	5	150	30.0(77)	**2**
1980	SD	3	72	24.0(28)	1
1981	SD	3	0	0.0(0)	0
1982	SD	1	2	2.0(2)	0
1984	SD	3	61	20.3(32)	1
1985	SD	3	6	2.0(4)	0
NFL	11	21	343	16.3(77)	4

Lucci, Mike

YEAR	TEAM	INT	YDS	AVG(LG)	TD
1966	Det	5	118	23.6(63)	1
1967	Det	2	47	23.5(31)	1
1968	Det	1	1	1.0(1)	0
1970	Det	2	18	9.0(12)	0
1971	Det	5	74	14.8(27)	**2**
1972	Det	2	0	0.0(0)	0
1973	Det	4	50	12.5(21)	0
NFL	10	21	308	14.7(63)	4

Lyght, Todd

YEAR	TEAM	INT	YDS	AVG(LG)	TD
1991	LARm	1	0	0.0(0)	0
1992	LARm	3	80	26.7(39)	0
1993	LARm	2	0	0.0(0)	0
1994	LARm	1	14	14.0(14)	0
1995	SL	4	34	8.5(29)	1
1996	SL	5	43	8.6(25)	1
1997	SL	4	25	6.3(13)	0
1998	SL	3	30	10.0(17)	0
1999	SL	6	112	18.7(57)	1
2000	SL	2	21	10.5(21)	0
2001	Det	4	72	18.0(59)	1
2002	Det	2	31	15.5(31)	0
NFL	12	37	462	12.5(59)	4

Lyle, Keith

YEAR	TEAM	INT	YDS	AVG(LG)	TD
1994	LARm	2	1	0.5(1)	0
1995	SL	3	42	14.0(31)	0
1996	SL	**9**	**152**	16.9(68)	0
1997	SL	8	102	12.8(39)	0
1998	SL	3	20	6.7(20)	0
1999	SL	2	10	5.0(10)	0
2000	SL	1	9	9.0(9)	0
2001	Was	1	0	0.0(0)	0
2002	SD	2	26	13.0(26)	0
NFL	9	31	362	11.7(68)	0

Lynch, Dick

YEAR	TEAM	INT	YDS	AVG(LG)	TD
1958	Was	2	24	12.0(13)	0
1959	NYG	1	0	0.0(0)	0
1960	NYG	3	61	20.3(32)	1
1961	NYG	**9**	60	6.7(36)	0
1962	NYG	5	90	18.0(27)	0
1963	NYG	**9**	**251**	27.9(82)	**3**
1964	NYG	4	68	17.0(37)	0
1965	NYG	4	38	9.5(23)	0
NFL	8	37	592	16.0(82)	4

Lynch, John

YEAR	TEAM	INT	YDS	AVG(LG)	TD
1995	TB	3	3	1.0(3)	0
1996	TB	3	26	8.7(25)	0
1997	TB	2	28	14.0(28)	0
1998	TB	2	29	14.5(17)	0
1999	TB	2	32	16.0(28)	0
2000	TB	3	43	14.3(36)	0
2001	TB	3	21	7.0(15)	0
2002	TB	3	0	0.0(0)	0
2003	TB	2	18	9.0(18)	0
2004	Den	1	2	2.0(2)	0
2005	Den	2	2	1.0(1)	0
NFL	11	26	204	7.8(36)	0

Mack, Cedric

YEAR	TEAM	INT	YDS	AVG(LG)	TD
1983	SL	3	25	8.3(13)	0
1985	SL	2	10	5.0(10)	0
1986	SL	4	42	10.5(24)	0
1987	SL	2	0	0.0(0)	0
1988	Phx	3	33	11.0(12)	0
1989	Phx	4	15	3.8(9)	0
1990	Phx	2	53	26.5(39)	0
NFL	8	20	178	8.9(39)	0

Madison, Sam

YEAR	TEAM	INT	YDS	AVG(LG)	TD
1997	Mia	1	21	21.0(21)	0
1998	Mia	8	114	14.3(35)	0
1999	Mia	**7**	164	23.4(42)	1
2000	Mia	5	80	16.0(34)	0
2001	Mia	2	0	0.0(0)	0
2002	Mia	3	15	5.0(15)	0
2003	Mia	3	82	27.3(36)	1
2005	Mia	2	11	5.5(11)	0
NFL	9	31	487	15.7(42)	2

Maher, Bruce

YEAR	TEAM	INT	YDS	AVG(LG)	TD
1960	Det	1	19	19.0(19)	0
1961	Det	1	8	8.0(8)	0
1963	Det	1	0	0.0(0)	0
1964	Det	2	28	14.0(28)	0
1965	Det	4	76	19.0(35)	0
1966	Det	5	90	18.0(56)	0
1967	Det	2	14	7.0(14)	0
1968	NYG	1	89	89.0(89)	0
1969	NYG	5	112	22.4(48)	0
NFL	10	22	436	19.8(89)	0

Marion, Brock

YEAR	TEAM	INT	YDS	AVG(LG)	TD
1993	Dal	1	2	2.0(2)	0
1994	Dal	1	11	11.0(11)	0
1995	Dal	6	40	6.7(32)	1
1999	Mia	2	30	15.0(28)	0
2000	Mia	5	72	14.4(24)	0
2001	Mia	5	**227**	**45.4**(**100**)	**2**
2002	Mia	5	99	19.8(62)	0
2003	Mia	3	3	1.0(3)	0
2004	Det	3	43	14.3(24)	0
NFL	12	31	527	17.0(100)	3

Marion, Fred

YEAR	TEAM	INT	YDS	AVG(LG)	TD
1983	NE	2	4	2.0(4)	0
1984	NE	2	39	19.5(26)	0
1985	NE	7	**189**	27.0(**83**)	0
1986	NE	2	56	28.0(37)	1
1987	NE	4	53	13.3(25)	0
1988	NE	4	47	11.8(22)	0
1989	NE	2	19	9.5(18)	0
1990	NE	4	17	4.3(16)	0
1991	NE	2	33	16.5(33)	0
NFL	10	29	457	15.8(83)	1

Marshall, Wilber

YEAR	TEAM	INT	YDS	AVG(LG)	TD
1985	ChiB	4	23	5.8(14)	0
1986	ChiB	5	68	13.6(58)	1
1988	Was	3	61	20.3(43)	0
1989	Was	1	18	18.0(18)	0
1990	Was	1	6	6.0(6)	0
1991	Was	5	75	15.0(54)	**1**
1992	Was	2	20	10.0(20)	1
1994	Arz	0	13	0.0(13)	0
1995	NYJ	2	20	10.0(20)	0
NFL	11	23	304	13.2(58)	3

Martha, Paul

YEAR	TEAM	INT	YDS	AVG(LG)	TD
1966	Pit	3	44	14.7(35)	0
1967	Pit	4	41	10.3(23)	0
1968	Pit	3	43	14.3(23)	0
1969	Pit	5	37	7.4(15)	0
1970	Den	6	99	16.5(50)	0
NFL	7	21	264	12.6(50)	0

Matsos, Archie

YEAR	TEAM	INT	YDS	AVG(LG)	TD
1960	Buf-A	8	142	17.8(33)	1
1961	Buf-A	2	12	6.0(12)	0
1963	Oak-A	4	39	9.8(19)	0
1964	Oak-A	2	50	25.0(27)	0
1965	Oak-A	3	52	17.3(47)	0
1966	Den-A	2	10	5.0(5)	0
1966	SD-A	1	6	6.0(6)	0
NFL	6	22	311	14.1(47)	1

Maxie, Brett

YEAR	TEAM	INT	YDS	AVG(LG)	TD
1986	NO	2	15	7.5(15)	0
1987	NO	3	17	5.7(10)	0
1989	NO	3	41	13.7(26)	**1**
1990	NO	2	88	44.0(50)	1
1991	NO	3	33	11.0(31)	**1**
1992	NO	2	12	6.0(8)	0
1995	Car	6	59	9.8(49)	0
1996	Car	1	35	35.0(35)	0
1997	SF	1	0	0.0(0)	0
NFL	10	23	300	13.0(50)	3

Mayhew, Martin

YEAR	TEAM	INT	YDS	AVG(LG)	TD
1990	Was	7	20	2.9(15)	0
1991	Was	3	31	10.3(31)	**1**
1992	Was	3	58	19.3(33)	0
1994	TB	2	4	2.0(4)	0
1995	TB	5	81	16.2(40)	0
1996	TB	1	5	5.0(5)	0
NFL	7	21	199	9.5(40)	1

McAfee, George

YEAR	TEAM	INT	YDS	AVG(LG)	TD
1940	ChiB	4	50	12.5(0)	0
1941	ChiB	6	78	13.0(43)	**1**
1945	ChiB	1	13	13.0(7)	0
1946	ChiB	3	18	6.0(18)	0
1947	ChiB	1	49	49.0(49)	0
1948	ChiB	2	35	17.5(25)	0
1949	ChiB	6	76	12.7(54)	1
1950	ChiB	2	31	15.5(19)	0
NFL	8	25	350	14.0(54)	2

McCleon, Dexter

YEAR	TEAM	INT	YDS	AVG(LG)	TD
1997	SL	1	0	0.0(0)	0
1998	SL	2	29	14.5(15)	0
1999	SL	4	17	4.3(14)	0
2000	SL	8	28	3.5(23)	0
2001	SL	4	66	16.5(43)	0
2002	SL	1	0	0.0(0)	0
2003	KC	6	-3	-0.5(0)	0
2004	KC	2	23	11.5(23)	0
2005	KC	2	0	0.0(0)	0
NFL	9	30	160	5.3(43)	0

McDaniel, Terry

YEAR	TEAM	INT	YDS	AVG(LG)	TD
1989	LARd	3	21	7.0(20)	0
1990	LARd	3	20	6.7(15)	0
1992	LARd	4	180	**45.0**(**67**)	0
1993	LARd	5	87	17.4(36)	**1**
1994	LARd	7	103	14.7(35)	2
1995	Oak	6	46	7.7(42)	**1**
1996	Oak	5	150	30.0(56)	1
1997	Oak	1	17	17.0(17)	0
1998	Sea	1	43	43.0(43)	1
NFL	10	35	667	19.1(67)	6

McDonald, Tim

YEAR	TEAM	INT	YDS	AVG(LG)	TD
1988	Phx	2	11	5.5(11)	0
1989	Phx	7	**170**	24.3(53)	**1**
1990	Phx	4	63	15.8(38)	0
1991	Phx	5	36	7.2(13)	0
1992	Phx	2	35	17.5(20)	0
1993	SF	3	23	7.7(21)	0
1994	SF	2	79	39.5(73)	1
1995	SF	4	135	33.8(52)	**2**
1996	SF	2	14	7.0(14)	0
1997	SF	3	34	11.3(17)	0
1998	SF	4	22	5.5(18)	0
1999	SF	2	18	9.0(18)	0
NFL	12	40	640	16.0(73)	4

McElroy, Vann

YEAR	TEAM	INT	YDS	AVG(LG)	TD
1982	LARd	1	0	0.0(0)	0
1983	LARd	**8**	68	8.5(28)	0
1984	LARd	4	42	10.5(31)	0
1985	LARd	2	23	11.5(23)	0
1986	LARd	7	105	15.0(28)	0
1987	LARd	4	41	10.3(35)	1
1988	LARd	3	17	5.7(13)	0
1989	LARd	2	0	0.0(0)	0
NFL	9	31	296	9.5(35)	1

McKenzie, Mike

YEAR	TEAM	INT	YDS	AVG(LG)	TD
1999	GB	6	4	0.7(4)	0
2000	GB	1	26	26.0(26)	0
2001	GB	2	38	19.0(38)	1
2002	GB	2	0	0.0(0)	0
2003	GB	4	98	24.5(**90**)	1
2004	NO	5	19	3.8(14)	0
2005	NO	1	11	11.0(11)	0
NFL	7	21	196	9.3(90)	2

McKyer, Tim

YEAR	TEAM	INT	YDS	AVG(LG)	TD
1986	SF	6	33	5.5(21)	1
1987	SF	2	0	0.0(0)	0
1988	SF	7	11	1.6(7)	0
1989	SF	1	18	18.0(18)	0
1990	Mia	4	40	10.0(21)	0
1991	Atl	**6**	24	4.0(24)	0
1992	Atl	1	0	0.0(0)	0
1993	Det	2	10	5.0(10)	0
1995	Car	3	99	33.0(**96**)	1
1997	Den	1	0	0.0(0)	0
NFL	11	33	235	7.1(96)	2

McMillan, Erik

YEAR	TEAM	INT	YDS	AVG(LG)	TD
1988	NYJ	**8**	168	21.0(55)	**2**
1989	NYJ	6	180	30.0(**92**)	1
1990	NYJ	5	92	18.4(25)	0
1991	NYJ	3	**168**	**56.0**(**83**)	**2**
NFL	5	22	608	27.6(92)	5

McMillian, Mark

YEAR	TEAM	INT	YDS	AVG(LG)	TD
1992	Phi	1	0	0.0(0)	0
1993	Phi	2	25	12.5(17)	0
1994	Phi	2	2	1.0(5)	0
1995	Phi	3	27	9.0(19)	0
1996	NO	2	4	2.0(4)	0
1997	KC	**8**	**274**	**34.3**(**87**)	**3**
1998	KC	3	48	16.0(21)	0
1999	SF	1	0	0.0(0)	0
1999	Was	1	24	24.0(24)	0
NFL	8	23	404	17.6(87)	3

McNeil, Ryan

YEAR	TEAM	INT	YDS	AVG(LG)	TD
1993	Det	2	19	9.5(16)	0
1994	Det	1	14	14.0(14)	0
1995	Det	2	26	13.0(21)	0
1996	Det	5	14	2.8(15)	0
1997	SL	**9**	127	14.1(75)	1
1998	SL	1	37	37.0(37)	1
2000	Dal	2	4	2.0(4)	0
2001	SD	8	55	6.9(33)	0
2002	SD	1	16	16.0(16)	0
NFL	10	31	312	10.1(75)	2

McNorton, Bruce

YEAR	TEAM	INT	YDS	AVG(LG)	TD
1983	Det	7	30	4.3(15)	0
1984	Det	2	0	0.0(0)	0
1985	Det	2	14	7.0(10)	0
1986	Det	4	10	2.5(10)	0
1987	Det	3	20	6.7(20)	0
1988	Det	1	4	4.0(4)	0

YEAR	TEAM	INT	YDS	AVG(LG)	TD
1990	Det	1	33	33.0(33)	0
NFL	8	20	111	5.6(33)	0
McRae, Bennie					
1962	ChiB	1	47	47.0(47)	0
1963	ChiB	6	90	15.0(44)	1
1964	ChiB	2	44	22.0(26)	0
1965	ChiB	4	116	29.0(89)	1
1966	ChiB	3	53	17.7(53)	0
1967	ChiB	5	94	18.8(34)	2
1968	ChiB	4	41	10.3(22)	0
1969	ChiB	1	0	0.0(0)	0
1970	ChiB	1	0	0.0(0)	0
NFL	9	27	485	18.0(89)	4
Meador, Eddie					
1959	LARm	3	3	1.0(3)	0
1960	LARm	4	46	11.5(26)	1
1961	LARm	1	34	34.0(34)	0
1962	LARm	1	0	0.0(0)	0
1963	LARm	6	38	6.3(20)	0
1964	LARm	3	50	16.7(30)	0
1965	LARm	2	57	28.5(29)	0
1966	LARm	5	60	12.0(31)	0
1967	LARm	8	103	12.9(30)	2
1968	LARm	6	37	6.2(20)	0
1969	LARm	5	97	19.4(38)	**2**
1970	LARm	2	22	11.0(12)	0
NFL	12	46	547	11.9(38)	5
Milloy, Lawyer					
1996	NE	2	14	7.0(14)	0
1997	NE	3	15	5.0(15)	0
1998	NE	6	54	9.0(30)	1
1999	NE	4	17	4.3(17)	0
2000	NE	2	2	1.0(2)	0
2001	NE	2	21	10.5(21)	0
2004	Buf	2	20	10.0(11)	0
2005	Buf	1	0	0.0(0)	0
NFL	9	22	143	6.5(30)	1
Mincy, Charles					
1992	KC	4	128	32.0(39)	**2**
1993	KC	5	44	8.8(20)	0
1994	KC	3	49	16.3(31)	0
1995	Min	3	37	12.3(20)	0
1996	TB	1	26	26.0(26)	0
1997	TB	1	14	14.0(14)	0
1998	TB	4	58	14.5(22)	1
1999	Oak	2	23	11.5(21)	0
NFL	8	23	379	16.5(39)	3
Minnifield, Frank					
1984	Cle	1	26	26.0(26)	0
1985	Cle	1	3	3.0(3)	0
1986	Cle	3	20	6.7(20)	0
1987	Cle	4	24	6.0(27)	0
1988	Cle	4	16	4.0(13)	0
1989	Cle	3	29	9.7(25)	0
1990	Cle	2	0	0.0(0)	0
1992	Cle	2	6	3.0(5)	0
NFL	9	20	124	6.2(27)	0
Moegle, Dicky					
1955	SF	6	50	8.3(37)	0
1956	SF	6	75	12.5(31)	1
1957	SF	8	107	13.4(40)	0
1960	Pit	6	49	8.2(31)	0
1961	Dal	2	31	15.5(25)	0
NFL	6	28	312	11.1(40)	1
Moore, Zeke					
1969	Hou-A	4	71	17.8(51)	1
1970	Hou	6	85	14.2(32)	0
1971	Hou	3	29	9.7(26)	0
1974	Hou	2	38	19.0(22)	1
1975	Hou	5	**137**	27.4(**74**)	0
1976	Hou	1	28	28.0(28)	0
1977	Hou	3	56	18.7(34)	0
NFL	11	24	444	18.5(74)	2
Morrow, Tommy					
1962	Oak-A	10	141	14.1(36)	0
1963	Oak-A	9	104	11.6(35)	0
1964	Oak-A	4	101	25.3(77)	0
NFL	3	23	346	15.0(77)	0
Mumphord, Lloyd					
1969	Mia-A	5	102	20.4(51)	0
1970	Mia	5	35	7.0(32)	1
1972	Mia	4	50	12.5(28)	1
1975	Bal	4	58	14.5(28)	0
1976	Bal	1	22	22.0(22)	0
1978	Bal	2	20	10.0(19)	0
NFL	7	21	287	13.7(51)	2
Murphy, Mark					
1981	GB	3	57	19.0(50)	0
1984	GB	1	4	4.0(4)	0
1985	GB	2	50	25.0(50)	**1**

YEAR	TEAM	INT	YDS	AVG(LG)	TD
1988	GB	5	19	3.8(9)	0
1989	GB	3	31	10.3(20)	0
1990	GB	3	6	2.0(4)	0
1991	GB	3	27	9.0(16)	0
NFL	9	20	194	9.7(50)	1
Murphy, Mark					
1979	Was	3	29	9.7(16)	0
1980	Was	6	58	9.7(28)	0
1981	Was	7	68	9.7(29)	0
1982	Was	2	0	0.0(0)	0
1983	Was	**9**	127	14.1(48)	0
NFL	7	27	282	10.4(48)	0
Myers, Tom					
1972	NO	3	0	0.0(0)	0
1973	NO	3	33	11.0(20)	0
1974	NO	3	43	14.3(21)	0
1975	NO	5	83	16.6(29)	0
1976	NO	1	0	0.0(0)	0
1977	NO	1	2	2.0(2)	0
1978	NO	6	**167**	27.8(**97**)	1
1979	NO	7	**127**	18.1(52)	1
1980	NO	5	96	19.2(48)	0
1981	NO	2	70	35.0(54)	0
NFL	10	36	621	17.3(97)	2
Nelson, Andy					
1957	Bal	5	29	5.8(13)	0
1958	Bal	8	**199**	24.9(69)	1
1959	Bal	6	33	5.5(33)	**1**
1960	Bal	6	47	7.8(22)	0
1962	Bal	4	20	5.0(10)	0
1963	Bal	3	37	12.3(26)	1
1964	NYG	1	13	13.0(13)	0
NFL	8	33	378	11.5(69)	3
Nettles, Jim					
1965	Phi	3	84	28.0(56)	1
1966	Phi	3	57	19.0(34)	1
1967	Phi	4	52	13.0(34)	0
1969	LARm	2	37	18.5(25)	0
1970	LARm	3	54	18.0(32)	0
1971	LARm	5	97	19.4(44)	1
1972	LARm	6	**168**	28.0(43)	0
NFL	7	26	549	21.1(56)	3
Newman, Anthony					
1988	LARm	2	27	13.5(27)	0
1990	LARm	2	0	0.0(0)	0
1991	LARm	1	58	58.0(58)	0
1992	LARm	4	33	8.3(17)	0
1994	LARm	2	46	23.0(24)	1
1996	NO	3	40	13.3(21)	0
1997	NO	3	19	6.3(17)	0
1998	Oak	2	17	8.5(11)	0
1999	Oak	2	16	8.0(16)	0
NFL	10	21	256	12.2(58)	1
Nitschke, Ray					
1958	GB	1	2	2.0(2)	0
1960	GB	3	90	30.0(43)	1
1961	GB	2	41	20.5(14)	0
1962	GB	4	56	14.0(28)	0
1963	GB	2	8	4.0(8)	0
1964	GB	2	36	18.0(29)	0
1965	GB	1	21	21.0(21)	0
1966	GB	2	44	22.0(23)	0
1967	GB	3	35	11.7(20)	1
1968	GB	2	20	10.0(11)	0
1969	GB	2	32	16.0(20)	0
1971	GB	1	0	0.0(0)	0
NFL	15	25	385	15.4(43)	2
Nolan, Dick					
1954	NYG	6	48	8.0(17)	0
1955	NYG	1	20	20.0(20)	0
1956	NYG	2	17	8.5(17)	0
1957	NYG	1	12	12.0(12)	0
1958	ChiC	5	30	6.0(18)	0
1959	NYG	5	57	11.4(34)	0
1960	NYG	3	32	10.7(20)	0
NFL	8	23	216	9.4(34)	0
Norton, Jerry					
1954	Phi	5	110	22.0(69)	1
1955	Phi	1	0	0.0(0)	0
1956	Phi	2	34	17.0(23)	0
1957	Phi	4	155	**38.8**(**99**)	1
1958	Phi	1	0	0.0(0)	0
1959	ChiC	3	35	11.7(30)	0
1960	SL	**10**	96	9.6(26)	0
1961	SL	7	136	19.4(47)	**2**
1962	Dal	2	21	10.5(21)	0
NFL	11	35	587	16.8(99)	4
Norton, Jim					
1960	Hou-A	1	0	0.0(0)	0
1961	Hou-A	9	150	16.7(36)	0
1962	Hou-A	8	75	9.4(36)	0

YEAR	TEAM	INT	YDS	AVG(LG)	TD
1963	Hou-A	6	86	14.3(37)	0
1964	Hou-A	2	31	15.5(31)	0
1965	Hou-A	7	52	7.4(18)	0
1966	Hou-A	4	125	31.3(56)	0
1967	Hou-A	6	73	12.2(26)	1
1968	Hou-A	2	0	0.0(0)	0
NFL	9	45	592	13.2(56)	1
Odomes, Nate					
1988	Buf	1	0	0.0(0)	0
1989	Buf	5	20	4.0(13)	0
1990	Buf	1	0	0.0(0)	0
1991	Buf	5	120	24.0(48)	1
1992	Buf	5	19	3.8(10)	0
1993	Buf	**9**	65	7.2(25)	0
NFL	7	26	224	8.6(48)	1
Oliver, Louis					
1989	Mia	4	32	8.0(23)	0
1990	Mia	5	87	17.4(35)	0
1991	Mia	5	80	16.0(37)	0
1992	Mia	5	200	40.0(**103**)	1
1993	Mia	2	60	30.0(56)	**1**
1994	Cin	3	36	12.0(19)	0
1996	Mia	3	110	**36.7**(**60**)	0
NFL	7	27	605	22.4(103)	2
O'Neal, Deltha					
2001	Den	9	115	12.8(42)	0
2002	Den	5	70	14.0(28)	**2**
2003	Den	1	6	6.0(6)	0
2004	Cin	4	60	15.0(31)	1
2005	Cin	**10**	103	10.3(37)	0
NFL	6	29	354	12.2(42)	3
Owens, Brig					
1966	Was	7	165	23.6(60)	1
1967	Was	1	68	68.0(68)	1
1968	Was	8	109	13.6(38)	0
1969	Was	3	24	8.0(15)	0
1970	Was	4	86	21.5(32)	0
1971	Was	2	27	13.5(19)	0
1972	Was	1	0	0.0(0)	0
1973	Was	5	123	24.6(27)	1
1974	Was	4	59	14.8(24)	0
1975	Was	1	25	25.0(25)	0
NFL	11	36	686	19.1(68)	3
Owens, Burgess					
1973	NYJ	1	27	27.0(27)	0
1974	NYJ	3	68	22.7(39)	1
1975	NYJ	3	3	1.0(3)	0
1977	NYJ	3	18	6.0(12)	0
1978	NYJ	5	156	31.2(49)	1
1979	NYJ	6	41	6.8(15)	0
1980	Oak	3	59	19.7(58)	1
1981	Oak	2	30	15.0(30)	1
1982	LARd	4	56	14.0(35)	0
NFL	10	30	458	15.3(58)	4
Pardee, Jack					
1960	LARm	1	10	10.0(10)	0
1961	LARm	1	2	2.0(2)	0
1963	LARm	2	5	2.5(5)	0
1964	LARm	1	32	32.0(32)	0
1966	LARm	2	0	0.0(0)	0
1967	LARm	6	95	15.8(40)	2
1968	LARm	2	75	37.5(46)	**2**
1969	LARm	1	19	19.0(19)	0
1970	LARm	1	9	9.0(9)	0
1971	Was	5	58	11.6(20)	1
NFL	15	22	305	13.9(46)	5
Parrish, Bernie					
1959	Cle	5	83	16.6(37)	**1**
1960	Cle	6	**238**	**39.7**(**92**)	1
1961	Cle	7	40	5.7(16)	0
1962	Cle	2	37	18.5(37)	0
1964	Cle	4	98	24.5(54)	1
1965	Cle	4	45	11.3(35)	0
1966	Cle	1	16	16.0(16)	0
1966	Hou-A	2	0	0.0(0)	0
NFL	8	31	557	18.0(92)	3
Parrish, Lemar					
1970	Cin	5	28	5.6(19)	0
1971	Cin	7	105	15.0(65)	1
1972	Cin	5	90	18.0(33)	2
1973	Cin	2	10	5.0(10)	0
1975	Cin	1	26	26.0(26)	0
1976	Cin	2	0	0.0(0)	0
1977	Cin	3	95	31.7(47)	**1**
1978	Was	4	21	5.3(23)	0
1979	Was	**9**	65	7.2(23)	0
1980	Was	7	13	1.9(9)	0
1981	Was	1	1	1.0(1)	0
1982	Buf	1	8	8.0(8)	0
NFL	13	47	462	9.8(65)	4

YEAR	TEAM	INT	YDS	AVG(LG)	TD
Parrish, Tony					
1998	ChiB	1	8	8.0(8)	0
1999	ChiB	1	41	41.0(41)	0
2000	ChiB	3	81	27.0(38)	1
2001	ChiB	3	36	12.0(26)	0
2002	SF	7	204	29.1(60)	0
2003	SF	**9**	202	22.4(49)	0
2004	SF	4	64	16.0(26)	0
2005	SF	2	34	17.0(34)	1
NFL	8	30	670	22.3(60)	2
Patton, Jimmy					
1955	NYG	1	0	0.0(0)	0
1956	NYG	1	2	2.0(2)	0
1957	NYG	3	50	16.7(50)	1
1958	NYG	**11**	183	16.6(42)	0
1959	NYG	5	13	2.6(12)	0
1960	NYG	6	100	16.7(34)	0
1961	NYG	8	163	20.4(51)	1
1962	NYG	7	125	17.9(45)	0
1963	NYG	6	46	7.7(20)	0
1964	NYG	2	0	0.0(0)	0
1965	NYG	1	27	27.0(27)	0
1966	NYG	1	3	3.0(3)	0
NFL	12	52	712	13.7(51)	2
Paul, Don					
1950	ChiC	4	90	22.5(41)	0
1951	ChiC	3	52	17.3(36)	0
1953	ChiC	5	62	12.4(38)	0
1954	Cle	3	42	14.0(23)	0
1955	Cle	4	49	12.3(19)	0
1956	Cle	7	190	27.1(42)	1
1957	Cle	4	28	7.0(12)	0
1958	Cle	4	80	20.0(36)	0
NFL	9	34	593	17.4(42)	1
Paulson, Dainard					
1961	NYT-A	1	0	0.0(0)	0
1962	NYT-A	3	0	0.0(0)	0
1963	NYJ-A	6	114	19.0(47)	0
1964	NYJ-A	**12**	157	13.1(42)	**1**
1965	NYJ-A	7	72	10.3(22)	0
NFL	5	29	343	11.8(47)	1
Pellington, Bill					
1953	Bal	2	22	11.0(22)	0
1955	Bal	2	17	8.5(12)	0
1956	Bal	1	4	4.0(4)	0
1958	Bal	4	44	11.0(21)	0
1959	Bal	4	99	24.8(30)	**1**
1960	Bal	1	4	4.0(4)	0
1961	Bal	3	9	3.0(4)	0
1962	Bal	2	29	14.5(21)	0
1964	Bal	2	20	10.0(13)	0
NFL	11	21	248	11.8(30)	1
Perry, Darren					
1992	Pit	6	69	11.5(34)	0
1993	Pit	4	61	15.3(30)	0
1994	Pit	7	112	16.0(42)	0
1995	Pit	4	71	17.8(26)	0
1996	Pit	5	115	23.0(28)	1
1997	Pit	4	77	19.3(42)	0
1998	Pit	2	69	34.5(40)	0
2000	NO	3	3	1.0(3)	0
NFL	8	35	577	16.5(42)	1
Perry, Rod					
1976	LARm	8	79	9.9(43)	0
1977	LARm	1	0	0.0(0)	0
1978	LARm	8	117	14.6(44)	**3**
1980	LARm	5	115	23.0(83)	**1**
1981	LARm	3	18	6.0(10)	0
1982	LARm	3	57	19.0(33)	0
1983	Cle	1	21	21.0(21)	0
1984	Cle	1	17	17.0(17)	0
NFL	8	30	424	14.1(83)	4
Petitbon, Richie					
1959	ChiB	3	52	17.3(33)	**1**
1960	ChiB	2	0	0.0(0)	0
1961	ChiB	5	71	14.2(43)	0
1962	ChiB	6	**212**	**35.3**(**101**)	**1**
1963	ChiB	8	161	20.1(66)	1
1965	ChiB	2	22	11.0(18)	0
1966	ChiB	4	34	8.5(20)	0
1967	ChiB	5	73	14.6(35)	0
1968	ChiB	2	18	9.0(18)	0
1969	LARm	5	46	9.2(25)	0
1970	LARm	1	10	10.0(10)	0
1971	Was	5	102	20.4(42)	0
NFL	14	48	801	16.7(101)	3
Powers, Warren					
1964	Oak-A	5	65	13.0(33)	0
1965	Oak-A	5	56	11.2(21)	0
1966	Oak-A	5	88	17.6(35)	0
1967	Oak-A	6	154	25.7(70)	2

YEAR	TEAM	INT	YDS	AVG(LG)	TD
1968	Oak-A	1	3	3.0(3)	0
NFL	5	22	366	16.6(70)	2
Pridemore, Tom					
1978	Atl	1	0	0.0(0)	0
1979	Atl	2	20	10.0(20)	0
1980	Atl	2	2	1.0(2)	0
1981	Atl	7	221	31.6(**101**)	1
1982	Atl	1	28	28.0(28)	0
1983	Atl	4	56	14.0(25)	0
1984	Atl	2	0	0.0(0)	0
1985	Atl	2	45	22.5(36)	0
NFL	8	21	372	17.7(101)	1
Prior, Mike					
1987	Ind	**6**	57	9.5(38)	0
1988	Ind	3	46	15.3(23)	0
1989	Ind	6	88	14.7(58)	1
1990	Ind	3	66	22.0(36)	0
1991	Ind	3	50	16.7(37)	0
1992	Ind	6	44	7.3(19)	0
1993	GB	1	1	1.0(1)	0
1995	GB	1	9	9.0(9)	0
1996	GB	1	7	7.0(7)	0
1997	GB	4	72	18.0(49)	0
1998	GB	1	0	0.0(0)	0
NFL	13	35	440	12.6(58)	1
Ramsey, Nate					
1963	Phi	1	0	0.0(0)	0
1964	Phi	5	31	6.2(17)	0
1965	Phi	6	74	12.3(24)	0
1966	Phi	1	0	0.0(0)	0
1968	Phi	2	0	0.0(0)	0
1969	Phi	2	26	13.0(26)	1
1970	Phi	1	0	0.0(0)	0
1972	Phi	3	14	4.7(10)	0
NFL	10	21	145	6.9(26)	1
Ramsey, Ray					
1947	ChiR-A	5	66	13.2(0)	0
1948	Bkn-A	7	124	17.7(0)	0
1949	ChiH-A	2	79	39.5(0)	0
1950	ChiC	1	0	0.0(0)	0
1951	ChiC	5	90	18.0(39)	0
1952	ChiC	5	67	13.4(23)	0
1953	ChiC	10	237	23.7(46)	**1**
AAFC	3	14	269	19.2(0)	0
NFL	4	21	394	18.8(46)	1
Ray, Darrol					
1980	NYJ	6	132	22.0(71)	1
1981	NYJ	7	**227**	32.4(64)	**2**
1982	NYJ	3	91	**30.3**(**44**)	0
1983	NYJ	3	77	25.7(42)	0
1984	NYJ	2	54	27.0(28)	0
NFL	5	21	581	27.7(71)	3
Reagan, Frank					
1941	NYG	1	28	28.0(28)	0
1947	NYG	**10**	**203**	20.3(71)	0
1948	NYG	9	145	16.1(45)	0
1949	Phi	7	146	20.9(52)	0
1950	Phi	4	132	**33.0**(**47**)	1
1951	Phi	4	60	15.0(44)	0
NFL	7	35	714	20.4(71)	1
Reaves, Ken					
1966	Atl	1	16	16.0(16)	0
1967	Atl	7	153	21.9(42)	0
1968	Atl	1	90	90.0(90)	1
1969	Atl	3	14	4.7(14)	0
1970	Atl	6	44	7.3(28)	0
1971	Atl	6	43	7.2(31)	0
1972	Atl	3	59	19.7(28)	0
1973	Atl	2	20	10.0(11)	0
1974	SL	1	54	54.0(54)	0
1975	SL	3	7	2.3(9)	0
1976	SL	2	41	20.5(25)	0
1977	SL	2	17	8.5(10)	0
NFL	12	37	558	15.1(90)	1
Rechichar, Bert					
1952	Cle	6	79	13.2(25)	0
1953	Bal	7	64	9.1(36)	**1**
1954	Bal	2	27	13.5(21)	0
1955	Bal	6	109	18.2(40)	0
1956	Bal	4	63	15.8(42)	0
1957	Bal	5	33	6.6(31)	0
1960	Pit	1	10	10.0(10)	0
NFL	9	31	385	12.4(42)	1
Reed, Ed					
2002	Bal	5	167	33.4(59)	0
2003	Bal	**7**	132	18.9(54)	1
2004	Bal	**9**	**358**	39.8(**106**)	1
2005	Bal	1	23	23.0(23)	0
NFL	4	22	680	30.9(106)	2

YEAR	TEAM	INT	YDS	AVG(LG)	TD
Reinfeldt, Mike					
1976	Hou	1	19	19.0(19)	0
1977	Hou	5	78	15.6(30)	0
1978	Hou	1	0	0.0(0)	0
1979	Hou	**12**	**205**	17.1(39)	0
1980	Hou	4	36	9.0(23)	0
1981	Hou	2	18	9.0(16)	0
1983	Hou	1	19	19.0(19)	0
NFL	8	26	375	14.4(39)	0
Renfro, Mel					
1964	Dal	7	110	15.7(39)	1
1965	Dal	2	92	46.0(90)	1
1966	Dal	2	57	28.5(33)	0
1967	Dal	7	38	5.4(30)	0
1968	Dal	3	5	1.7(5)	0
1969	Dal	**10**	118	11.8(41)	0
1970	Dal	4	3	0.8(3)	0
1971	Dal	4	11	2.8(7)	0
1972	Dal	1	0	0.0(0)	0
1973	Dal	2	65	32.5(35)	1
1974	Dal	1	6	6.0(6)	0
1975	Dal	4	70	17.5(22)	0
1976	Dal	3	23	7.7(23)	0
1977	Dal	2	28	14.0(25)	0
NFL	14	52	626	12.0(90)	3
Reynolds, Ricky					
1988	TB	4	7	1.8(7)	0
1989	TB	5	87	17.4(68)	**1**
1990	TB	3	70	23.3(46)	0
1991	TB	2	7	3.5(7)	0
1992	TB	2	0	0.0(0)	0
1993	TB	1	3	3.0(3)	0
1994	NE	1	11	11.0(11)	1
1995	NE	3	6	2.0(4)	0
1996	NE	2	7	3.5(7)	0
NFL	9	23	198	8.6(68)	2
Rich, Herb					
1950	Bal	3	45	15.0(45)	1
1951	LARm	3	11	3.7(6)	0
1952	LARm	8	201	25.1(**97**)	1
1953	LARm	3	95	31.7(53)	**1**
1954	NYG	5	56	11.2(19)	0
1955	NYG	6	61	10.2(53)	0
1956	NYG	1	0	0.0(0)	0
NFL	7	29	469	16.2(97)	3
Richard, Stanley					
1991	SD	2	5	2.5(3)	0
1992	SD	3	26	8.7(20)	0
1993	SD	1	-2	-2.0(-2)	0
1994	SD	4	**224**	**56.0**(**99**)	2
1995	Was	3	24	8.0(24)	0
1996	Was	3	47	15.7(42)	0
1997	Was	4	28	7.0(23)	0
1998	Was	1	0	0.0(0)	0
NFL	8	21	352	16.8(99)	2
Richardson, Mike					
1983	ChiB	5	9	1.8(6)	0
1984	ChiB	2	7	3.5(7)	0
1985	ChiB	4	**174**	43.5(**90**)	**1**
1986	ChiB	7	69	9.9(32)	0
1988	ChiB	2	15	7.5(15)	0
NFL	5	20	274	13.7(90)	1
Riley, Ken					
1969	Cin-A	4	66	16.5(66)	0
1970	Cin	4	17	4.3(14)	0
1971	Cin	5	22	4.4(21)	0
1972	Cin	3	0	0.0(0)	0
1973	Cin	2	2	1.0(5)	0
1974	Cin	5	33	6.6(19)	0
1975	Cin	6	76	12.7(30)	1
1976	Cin	**9**	141	15.7(53)	1
1977	Cin	2	14	7.0(14)	0
1978	Cin	3	33	11.0(17)	0
1979	Cin	1	0	0.0(0)	0
1980	Cin	3	9	3.0(9)	0
1981	Cin	5	6	1.2(6)	0
1982	Cin	**5**	88	17.6(56)	**1**
1983	Cin	**8**	89	11.1(42)	**2**
NFL	15	65	596	9.2(66)	5
Riley, Lee					
1955	Det	2	38	19.0(23)	0
1956	Phi	3	57	19.0(31)	0
1958	Phi	1	8	8.0(8)	0
1959	Phi	1	0	0.0(0)	0
1960	NYG	1	2	2.0(2)	0
1961	NYT-A	4	59	14.8(41)	0
1962	NYT-A	**11**	122	11.1(30)	0
NFL	7	23	286	12.4(41)	0
Robertson, Isiah					
1971	LARm	4	32	8.0(20)	0
1973	LARm	3	57	19.0(49)	1

YEAR	TEAM	INT	YDS	AVG(LG)	TD
1974	LARm	2	11	5.5(6)	0
1975	LARm	4	118	29.5(76)	**1**
1976	LARm	4	28	7.0(14)	0
1977	LARm	1	20	20.0(20)	0
1979	Buf	2	29	14.5(23)	1
1980	Buf	2	39	19.5(39)	0
1981	Buf	2	15	7.5(15)	0
1982	Buf	1	0	0.0(0)	0
NFL	12	25	349	14.0(76)	3
Robertson, Marcus					
1992	Hou	1	27	27.0(27)	0
1993	Hou	7	137	19.6(69)	0
1994	Hou	3	90	30.0(41)	0
1996	Hou	4	44	11.0(27)	0
1997	Ten	5	127	25.4(48)	0
1998	Ten	1	0	0.0(0)	0
1999	Ten	1	3	3.0(3)	0
2001	Sea	2	30	15.0(25)	0
NFL	11	24	458	19.1(69)	0
Robinson, Dave					
1965	GB	3	141	**47.0**(**87**)	0
1966	GB	5	60	12.0(23)	0
1967	GB	4	16	4.0(12)	0
1968	GB	2	18	9.0(18)	0
1970	GB	2	33	16.5(20)	0
1971	GB	3	44	14.7(23)	0
1972	GB	2	10	5.0(7)	0
1973	Was	4	98	24.5(39)	1
1974	Was	2	29	14.5(29)	0
NFL	10	27	449	16.6(87)	1
Robinson, Eugene					
1985	Sea	2	47	23.5(47)	0
1986	Sea	3	39	13.0(25)	0
1987	Sea	3	75	25.0(44)	0
1988	Sea	1	0	0.0(0)	0
1989	Sea	5	24	4.8(20)	0
1990	Sea	3	89	29.7(39)	0
1991	Sea	5	56	11.2(27)	0
1992	Sea	7	126	18.0(49)	0
1993	Sea	**9**	80	8.9(28)	0
1994	Sea	3	18	6.0(18)	0
1995	Sea	1	32	32.0(21)	0
1996	GB	6	107	17.8(39)	0
1997	GB	1	26	26.0(26)	0
1998	Atl	4	36	9.0(25)	1
1999	Atl	3	7	2.3(7)	0
2000	Car	1	0	0.0(0)	0
NFL	16	57	762	13.4(49)	1
Robinson, Johnny					
1962	DalT-A	4	25	6.3(20)	0
1963	KC-A	3	41	13.7(19)	0
1964	KC-A	2	17	8.5(17)	0
1965	KC-A	5	99	19.8(50)	0
1966	KC-A	**10**	136	13.6(29)	1
1967	KC-A	5	17	3.4(10)	0
1968	KC-A	6	40	6.7(16)	0
1969	KC-A	8	**158**	19.8(33)	0
1970	KC	**10**	155	15.5(57)	0
1971	KC	4	53	13.3(29)	0
NFL	12	57	741	13.0(57)	1
Rolle, Samari					
1999	Ten	4	65	16.3(30)	0
2000	Ten	**7**	140	20.0(81)	1
2001	Ten	3	3	1.0(3)	0
2002	Ten	2	0	0.0(0)	0
2003	Ten	6	141	23.5(52)	0
2004	Ten	1	0	0.0(0)	0
2005	Bal	1	11	11.0(11)	0
NFL	8	24	360	15.0(81)	1
Romes, Charles					
1978	Buf	2	95	47.5(**85**)	1
1979	Buf	1	0	0.0(0)	0
1980	Buf	2	41	20.5(30)	0
1981	Buf	4	113	28.3(35)	0
1982	Buf	1	8	8.0(8)	0
1983	Buf	2	27	13.5(27)	0
1984	Buf	5	130	26.0(55)	0
1985	Buf	7	56	8.0(21)	0
1986	Buf	4	23	5.8(23)	0
NFL	10	28	493	17.6(85)	1
Ross, Kevin					
1984	KC	6	124	20.7(71)	1
1985	KC	3	47	15.7(27)	0
1986	KC	4	66	16.5(35)	0
1987	KC	3	40	13.3(40)	0
1988	KC	1	0	0.0(0)	0
1989	KC	4	29	7.3(23)	0
1990	KC	5	97	19.4(40)	0
1991	KC	1	0	0.0(0)	0
1992	KC	1	99	99.0(99)	1
1993	KC	2	49	24.5(48)	0
1994	Atl	3	26	8.7(16)	0

YEAR	TEAM	INT	YDS	AVG(LG)	TD
1995	Atl	3	70	23.3(33)	0
1996	SD	2	7	3.5(7)	0
NFL	13	38	654	17.2(99)	2
Rowser, John					
1970	Pit	3	27	9.0(12)	0
1971	Pit	4	94	23.5(**70**)	1
1972	Pit	4	30	7.5(23)	0
1973	Pit	6	131	21.8(71)	1
1974	Den	4	56	14.0(33)	0
1975	Den	1	2	2.0(2)	0
1976	Den	4	104	26.0(41)	**2**
NFL	8	26	444	17.1(71)	4
Saimes, George					
1963	Buf-A	4	29	7.3(16)	0
1964	Buf-A	6	56	9.3(32)	0
1965	Buf-A	4	24	6.0(20)	0
1966	Buf-A	1	32	32.0(32)	0
1967	Buf-A	2	14	7.0(14)	0
1968	Buf-A	2	36	18.0(19)	0
1969	Buf-A	3	47	15.7(28)	0
NFL	8	22	238	10.8(32)	0
Sample, Johnny					
1959	Bal	1	10	10.0(10)	0
1960	Bal	4	27	6.8(18)	0
1961	Pit	8	141	17.6(42)	1
1962	Pit	0	21	0.0(21)	0
1963	Was	1	0	0.0(0)	0
1964	Was	4	31	7.8(16)	1
1965	Was	6	57	9.5(28)	0
1966	NYJ-A	6	32	5.3(21)	0
1967	NYJ-A	4	53	13.3(41)	1
1968	NYJ-A	7	88	12.6(39)	1
NFL	11	41	460	11.2(42)	4
Sanders, Deion					
1989	Atl	5	52	10.4(22)	0
1990	Atl	3	153	**51.0**(**82**)	2
1991	Atl	**6**	119	19.8(55)	**1**
1992	Atl	3	105	**35.0**(**55**)	0
1993	Atl	**7**	91	13.0(41)	0
1994	SF	6	**303**	**50.5**(**93**)	**3**
1995	Dal	2	34	17.0(34)	0
1996	Dal	2	3	1.5(2)	0
1997	Dal	2	81	40.5(50)	1
1998	Dal	5	153	30.6(71)	1
1999	Dal	3	2	0.7(2)	0
2000	Was	4	91	22.8(32)	0
2004	Bal	3	87	29.0(48)	1
2005	Bal	2	57	28.5(33)	0
NFL	14	53	1331	25.1(93)	9
Sandifer, Dan					
1948	Was	**13**	**258**	19.8(54)	**2**
1949	Was	5	82	16.4(59)	0
1950	Det	2	27	13.5(27)	0
1951	Phi	1	28	28.0(28)	0
1952	GB	2	25	12.5(17)	0
NFL	6	23	420	18.3(59)	2
Scarpati, Joe					
1964	Phi	3	41	13.7(24)	1
1965	Phi	3	4	1.3(3)	0
1966	Phi	8	**182**	22.8(32)	0
1967	Phi	4	99	24.8(67)	1
1968	Phi	2	22	11.0(17)	0
1969	Phi	4	54	13.5(34)	1
1970	NO	1	4	4.0(4)	0
NFL	7	25	406	16.2(67)	3
Schmidt, Joe					
1953	Det	2	51	25.5(30)	0
1954	Det	2	13	6.5(13)	0
1956	Det	1	7	7.0(7)	0
1957	Det	1	8	8.0(8)	0
1958	Det	6	69	11.5(25)	0
1959	Det	1	17	17.0(17)	0
1960	Det	2	46	23.0(29)	1
1961	Det	4	38	9.5(26)	1
1962	Det	1	3	3.0(3)	0
1965	Det	4	42	10.5(14)	0
NFL	13	24	294	12.3(30)	2
Schmidt, Terry					
1974	NO	4	27	6.8(24)	1
1975	NO	1	37	37.0(37)	0
1978	ChiB	2	23	11.5(23)	0
1979	ChiB	6	44	7.3(20)	1
1980	ChiB	1	0	0.0(0)	0
1981	ChiB	2	4	2.0(4)	0
1982	ChiB	4	39	9.8(29)	0
1983	ChiB	5	31	6.2(32)	1
1984	ChiB	1	0	0.0(0)	0
NFL	9	26	205	7.9(37)	3
Schnellbacher, Otto					
1948	NYY-A	**11**	**239**	21.7(0)	**1**
1949	NYY-A	4	26	6.5(0)	0

YEAR	TEAM	INT	YDS	AVG(LG)	TD
1950	NYG	8	99	12.4(37)	0
1951	NYG	**11**	**194**	17.6(46)	**2**
AAFC	2	15	265	17.7(0)	1
NFL	2	19	293	15.4(46)	2

Schulz, Kurt

YEAR	TEAM	INT	YDS	AVG(LG)	TD
1995	Buf	6	48	8.0(32)	**1**
1996	Buf	4	24	6.0(19)	0
1997	Buf	2	23	11.5(21)	0
1998	Buf	6	48	8.0(24)	0
1999	Buf	3	26	8.7(26)	0
2000	Det	7	53	7.6(19)	0
2001	Det	2	22	11.0(19)	0
NFL	8	30	244	8.1(32)	1

Scott, Clarence

YEAR	TEAM	INT	YDS	AVG(LG)	TD
1971	Cle	4	47	11.8(21)	0
1973	Cle	5	71	14.2(45)	1
1974	Cle	4	42	10.5(25)	0
1975	Cle	2	4	2.0(4)	0
1976	Cle	4	11	2.8(5)	0
1977	Cle	3	72	24.0(49)	**1**
1978	Cle	3	15	5.0(7)	0
1979	Cle	3	56	18.7(29)	0
1980	Cle	2	14	7.0(9)	0
1981	Cle	4	46	11.5(26)	0
1982	Cle	3	29	9.7(24)	0
1983	Cle	2	0	0.0(0)	0
NFL	13	39	407	10.4(49)	2

Scott, Jake

YEAR	TEAM	INT	YDS	AVG(LG)	TD
1970	Mia	5	112	22.4(47)	0
1971	Mia	7	34	4.9(21)	0
1972	Mia	5	73	14.6(31)	0
1973	Mia	4	71	17.8(29)	0
1974	Mia	8	75	9.4(30)	0
1975	Mia	6	60	10.0(38)	0
1976	Was	4	12	3.0(6)	0
1977	Was	3	42	14.0(25)	0
1978	Was	7	72	10.3(39)	0
NFL	9	49	551	11.2(47)	0

Sensibaugh, Mike

YEAR	TEAM	INT	YDS	AVG(LG)	TD
1972	KC	**8**	65	8.1(35)	0
1973	KC	3	58	19.3(27)	0
1974	KC	4	85	21.3(33)	0
1975	KC	5	123	24.6(38)	0
1976	SL	4	60	15.0(35)	1
1977	SL	3	110	36.7(**79**)	**1**
NFL	8	27	501	18.6(79)	2

Sharockman, Ed

YEAR	TEAM	INT	YDS	AVG(LG)	TD
1962	Min	6	92	15.3(32)	0
1963	Min	5	93	18.6(47)	1
1964	Min	1	22	22.0(22)	0
1965	Min	6	118	19.7(40)	1
1966	Min	1	38	38.0(38)	0
1967	Min	3	94	31.3(37)	0
1968	Min	4	70	17.5(22)	0
1969	Min	1	36	36.0(36)	0
1970	Min	7	132	18.9(43)	1
1971	Min	6	109	18.2(33)	0
NFL	10	40	804	20.1(47)	3

Sharper, Darren

YEAR	TEAM	INT	YDS	AVG(LG)	TD
1997	GB	2	70	35.0(50)	**2**
1999	GB	3	12	4.0(9)	0
2000	GB	**9**	109	12.1(47)	0
2001	GB	6	78	13.0(23)	0
2002	GB	7	**233**	33.3(89)	1
2003	GB	5	78	15.6(50)	0
2004	GB	4	97	24.3(43)	**2**
2005	Min	**9**	**276**	30.7(92)	**2**
NFL	8	45	953	21.2(92)	7

Shell, Donnie

YEAR	TEAM	INT	YDS	AVG(LG)	TD
1974	Pit	1	0	0.0(0)	0
1975	Pit	1	29	29.0(29)	0
1976	Pit	1	4	4.0(4)	0
1977	Pit	3	14	4.7(8)	0
1978	Pit	3	21	7.0(20)	0
1979	Pit	5	10	2.0(8)	0
1980	Pit	7	135	19.3(67)	0
1981	Pit	5	52	10.4(25)	0
1982	Pit	**5**	27	5.4(18)	0
1983	Pit	5	18	3.6(18)	0
1984	Pit	7	61	8.7(52)	1
1985	Pit	4	40	10.0(26)	0
1986	Pit	3	29	9.7(17)	0
1987	Pit	1	50	50.0(50)	1
NFL	14	51	490	9.6(67)	2

Sherman, Will

YEAR	TEAM	INT	YDS	AVG(LG)	TD
1952	DalT	1	23	23.0(23)	0
1954	LARm	6	70	11.7(28)	0
1955	LARm	**11**	101	9.2(36)	0
1956	LARm	4	122	30.5(**95**)	1
1957	LARm	1	51	51.0(51)	0
1958	LARm	5	171	**34.2**(**70**)	**2**

YEAR	TEAM	INT	YDS	AVG(LG)	TD
1960	LARm	1	0	0.0(0)	0
NFL	8	29	538	18.6(95)	3

Shinnick, Don

YEAR	TEAM	INT	YDS	AVG(LG)	TD
1957	Bal	2	31	15.5(22)	0
1958	Bal	3	23	7.7(16)	0
1959	Bal	**7**	70	10.0(23)	0
1960	Bal	5	40	8.0(11)	0
1961	Bal	2	15	7.5(15)	0
1962	Bal	5	16	3.2(7)	0
1963	Bal	2	20	10.0(18)	0
1964	Bal	3	10	3.3(9)	0
1965	Bal	1	4	4.0(4)	0
1966	Bal	3	4	1.3(4)	0
1967	Bal	3	20	6.7(17)	0
1968	Bal	1	2	2.0(2)	0
NFL	12	37	255	6.9(23)	0

Shofner, Jim

YEAR	TEAM	INT	YDS	AVG(LG)	TD
1958	Cle	1	0	0.0(0)	0
1959	Cle	2	50	25.0(30)	0
1960	Cle	8	75	9.4(23)	0
1961	Cle	5	8	1.6(5)	0
1962	Cle	4	86	21.5(35)	0
NFL	6	20	219	10.9(35)	0

Shula, Don

YEAR	TEAM	INT	YDS	AVG(LG)	TD
1951	Cle	4	23	5.8(16)	0
1953	Bal	3	46	15.3(35)	0
1954	Bal	5	84	16.8(25)	0
1955	Bal	5	64	12.8(31)	0
1956	Bal	1	2	2.0(2)	0
1957	Was	3	48	16.0(30)	0
NFL	6	21	267	12.7(35)	0

Simpson, Bill

YEAR	TEAM	INT	YDS	AVG(LG)	TD
1974	LARm	1	0	0.0(0)	0
1975	LARm	6	90	15.0(29)	0
1976	LARm	4	62	15.5(30)	0
1977	LARm	6	**157**	26.2(42)	0
1978	LARm	5	82	16.4(28)	0
1980	Buf	4	36	9.0(14)	0
1981	Buf	4	42	10.5(42)	0
1982	Buf	4	45	11.3(24)	0
NFL	8	34	514	15.1(42)	0

Small, Gerald

YEAR	TEAM	INT	YDS	AVG(LG)	TD
1978	Mia	4	157	**39.3**(**46**)	1
1979	Mia	5	74	14.8(40)	0
1980	Mia	7	46	6.6(22)	0
1982	Mia	2	41	20.5(21)	0
1983	Mia	5	60	12.0(28)	0
1984	Atl	1	2	2.0(2)	0
NFL	7	24	380	15.8(46)	1

Smith, Bob

YEAR	TEAM	INT	YDS	AVG(LG)	TD
1948	Buf-A	1	18	18.0(18)	0
1948	Bkn-A	3	11	3.7(0)	0
1949	Det	9	218	24.2(**102**)	1
1950	Det	5	128	25.6(41)	1
1951	Det	3	70	23.3(42)	0
1952	Det	9	184	20.4(90)	1
1953	Det	3	119	**39.7**(**73**)	0
AAFC	2	4	29	7.3(18)	0
NFL	4	29	719	24.8(84)	3

Smith, Dennis

YEAR	TEAM	INT	YDS	AVG(LG)	TD
1981	Den	1	65	65.0(65)	0
1982	Den	1	29	29.0(29)	0
1983	Den	4	39	9.8(23)	0
1984	Den	3	13	4.3(10)	0
1985	Den	3	46	15.3(39)	0
1986	Den	1	0	0.0(0)	0
1987	Den	2	21	10.5(15)	0
1989	Den	2	78	39.0(50)	0
1990	Den	1	13	13.0(13)	0
1991	Den	5	60	12.0(39)	0
1992	Den	4	10	2.5(8)	0
1993	Den	3	57	19.0(36)	0
NFL	14	30	431	14.4(65)	0

Smith, Otis

YEAR	TEAM	INT	YDS	AVG(LG)	TD
1991	Phi	2	74	37.0(74)	**1**
1992	Phi	1	0	0.0(0)	0
1993	Phi	1	0	0.0(0)	0
1995	NYJ	6	101	16.8(49)	**1**
1996	NE	2	20	10.0(11)	0
1997	NYJ	6	158	26.3(51)	**3**
1998	NYJ	2	34	17.0(32)	0
2000	NE	1	56	56.0(56)	0
2001	NE	5	181	36.2(78)	**2**
2002	NE	2	21	10.5(22)	0
2003	Det	1	0	0.0(0)	0
NFL	12	29	645	22.2(78)	7

Sparks, Phillippi

YEAR	TEAM	INT	YDS	AVG(LG)	TD
1992	NYG	1	0	0.0(0)	0
1994	NYG	3	4	1.3(4)	0
1995	NYG	5	11	2.2(6)	0
1996	NYG	3	23	7.7(19)	0

YEAR	TEAM	INT	YDS	AVG(LG)	TD
1997	NYG	5	72	14.4(68)	0
1998	NYG	4	25	6.3(12)	0
1999	NYG	1	28	28.0(28)	0
2000	Dal	5	59	11.8(43)	0
NFL	8	27	222	8.2(68)	0

Spencer, Jimmy

YEAR	TEAM	INT	YDS	AVG(LG)	TD
1994	NO	5	24	4.8(11)	0
1995	NO	4	11	2.8(9)	0
1996	Cin	5	48	9.6(34)	0
1997	Cin	1	-2	-2.0(-2)	0
1998	SD	1	0	0.0(0)	0
1999	SD	4	1	0.3(1)	0
2000	Den	3	102	34.0(79)	2
2001	Den	3	25	8.3(18)	0
NFL	10	26	209	8.0(79)	2

Springs, Shawn

YEAR	TEAM	INT	YDS	AVG(LG)	TD
1997	Sea	1	0	0.0(0)	0
1998	Sea	7	142	20.3(56)	**2**
1999	Sea	5	77	15.4(42)	0
2000	Sea	2	8	4.0(8)	0
2001	Sea	1	0	0.0(0)	0
2002	Sea	3	0	0.0(0)	0
2003	Sea	1	8	8.0(8)	0
2004	Was	5	117	23.4(38)	0
2005	Was	1	2	2.0(2)	0
NFL	9	26	354	13.6(56)	2

Stacy, Billy

YEAR	TEAM	INT	YDS	AVG(LG)	TD
1959	ChiC	5	114	22.8(36)	0
1960	SL	4	42	10.5(25)	0
1961	SL	4	95	23.8(39)	**2**
1962	SL	6	72	12.0(53)	0
1963	SL	1	0	0.0(0)	0
NFL	5	20	323	16.1(53)	2

Starks, Duane

YEAR	TEAM	INT	YDS	AVG(LG)	TD
1998	Bal	5	3	0.6(2)	0
1999	Bal	5	59	11.8(43)	1
2000	Bal	6	125	20.8(64)	0
2001	Bal	4	9	2.3(9)	0
2002	Arz	2	3	1.5(3)	0
2004	Arz	3	46	15.3(41)	1
NFL	6	25	245	9.8(64)	2

Steele, Ernie

YEAR	TEAM	INT	YDS	AVG(LG)	TD
1942	Phi	2	49	24.5(29)	0
1944	Phi	6	113	18.8(62)	0
1945	Phi	1	15	15.0(15)	0
1946	Phi	3	69	23.0(30)	0
1947	Phi	6	103	17.2(43)	0
1948	Phi	6	55	9.2(33)	0
NFL	7	24	404	16.8(62)	0

Stone, Ken

YEAR	TEAM	INT	YDS	AVG(LG)	TD
1973	Buf	0	31	0.0(31)	0
1974	Was	5	95	19.0(31)	0
1976	TB	2	47	23.5(26)	0
1978	SL	**9**	139	15.4(33)	0
1979	SL	6	70	11.7(30)	0
1980	SL	5	63	12.6(20)	0
NFL	7	27	445	16.5(33)	0

Stratton, Mike

YEAR	TEAM	INT	YDS	AVG(LG)	TD
1962	Buf-A	6	99	16.5(18)	0
1963	Buf-A	3	31	10.3(26)	1
1964	Buf-A	1	0	0.0(0)	0
1965	Buf-A	2	19	9.5(19)	0
1966	Buf-A	3	37	12.3(23)	0
1967	Buf-A	1	3	3.0(3)	0
1968	Buf-A	1	15	15.0(15)	0
1972	Buf	1	0	0.0(0)	0
1973	SD	3	46	15.3(23)	0
NFL	10	21	250	11.9(26)	1

Stukes, Charlie

YEAR	TEAM	INT	YDS	AVG(LG)	TD
1967	Bal	2	13	6.5(13)	0
1968	Bal	1	60	60.0(60)	1
1969	Bal	1	6	6.0(6)	0
1970	Bal	3	52	17.3(47)	0
1971	Bal	8	95	11.9(40)	0
1972	Bal	5	23	4.6(11)	0
1973	LARm	5	104	20.8(42)	0
1974	LARm	7	90	12.9(41)	0
NFL	8	32	443	13.8(60)	1

Sumner, Charlie

YEAR	TEAM	INT	YDS	AVG(LG)	TD
1955	ChiB	7	162	23.1(63)	0
1958	ChiB	6	67	11.2(17)	0
1959	ChiB	3	22	7.3(15)	0
1961	Min	2	6	3.0(6)	0
1962	Min	3	46	15.3(32)	0
NFL	5	21	303	14.4(63)	0

Surtain, Patrick

YEAR	TEAM	INT	YDS	AVG(LG)	TD
1998	Mia	2	1	0.5(1)	0
1999	Mia	2	28	14.0(28)	0
2000	Mia	5	55	11.0(43)	0
2001	Mia	3	74	24.7(41)	1

YEAR	TEAM	INT	YDS	AVG(LG)	TD
2002	Mia	6	79	13.2(40)	1
2003	Mia	**7**	59	8.4(32)	0
2004	Mia	4	2	0.5(2)	0
2005	KC	4	57	14.3(53)	0
NFL	8	33	355	10.8(53)	2

Taseff, Carl

YEAR	TEAM	INT	YDS	AVG(LG)	TD
1953	Bal	3	36	12.0(29)	0
1954	Bal	2	15	7.5(15)	0
1955	Bal	1	0	0.0(0)	0
1956	Bal	2	13	6.5(8)	0
1957	Bal	1	7	7.0(7)	0
1958	Bal	7	52	7.4(17)	0
1959	Bal	2	60	30.0(33)	0
1961	Bal	1	15	15.0(15)	0
1962	Buf-A	2	21	10.5(17)	0
NFL	11	21	219	10.4(33)	0

Tatum, Jack

YEAR	TEAM	INT	YDS	AVG(LG)	TD
1971	Oak	4	136	**34.0**(**66**)	0
1972	Oak	4	91	22.8(56)	0
1973	Oak	1	26	26.0(26)	0
1974	Oak	4	84	21.0(40)	0
1975	Oak	4	67	16.8(28)	0
1976	Oak	2	0	0.0(0)	0
1977	Oak	6	146	24.3(41)	0
1978	Oak	3	60	20.0(27)	0
1979	Oak	2	26	13.0(13)	0
1980	Hou	7	100	14.3(35)	0
NFL	10	37	736	19.9(66)	0

Taylor, Rosey

YEAR	TEAM	INT	YDS	AVG(LG)	TD
1962	ChiB	2	64	32.0(43)	**1**
1963	ChiB	**9**	172	19.1(46)	1
1964	ChiB	2	45	22.5(26)	0
1965	ChiB	1	3	3.0(3)	0
1966	ChiB	1	15	15.0(15)	0
1967	ChiB	5	19	3.8(10)	0
1968	ChiB	3	96	32.0(**96**)	1
1969	SF	2	15	7.5(15)	0
1970	SF	3	27	9.0(19)	0
1971	SF	3	13	4.3(13)	0
1972	Was	1	17	17.0(17)	0
NFL	12	32	486	15.2(96)	3

Taylor, Terry

YEAR	TEAM	INT	YDS	AVG(LG)	TD
1984	Sea	3	63	21.0(37)	0
1985	Sea	4	75	18.8(75)	**1**
1986	Sea	2	0	0.0(0)	0
1987	Sea	1	11	11.0(11)	0
1988	Sea	5	53	10.6(27)	1
1989	Det	1	0	0.0(0)	0
1991	Det	4	26	6.5(23)	0
1992	Cle	1	0	0.0(0)	0
1994	Sea	1	0	0.0(0)	0
1995	Atl	3	31	10.3(31)	0
NFL	10	25	259	10.4(75)	2

Thomas, Clendon

YEAR	TEAM	INT	YDS	AVG(LG)	TD
1960	LARm	1	0	0.0(0)	0
1961	LARm	3	11	3.7(7)	0
1962	Pit	7	48	6.9(15)	0
1963	Pit	8	122	15.3(32)	0
1964	Pit	1	0	0.0(0)	0
1966	Pit	2	24	12.0(24)	0
1967	Pit	2	39	19.5(33)	0
1968	Pit	3	0	0.0(0)	0
NFL	11	27	244	9.0(33)	0

Thomas, Emmitt

YEAR	TEAM	INT	YDS	AVG(LG)	TD
1967	KC-A	4	60	15.0(57)	1
1968	KC-A	4	25	6.3(14)	0
1969	KC-A	**9**	146	16.2(45)	1
1970	KC	5	87	17.4(39)	0
1971	KC	8	145	18.1(36)	1
1972	KC	2	46	23.0(26)	0
1973	KC	3	65	21.7(33)	0
1974	KC	**12**	**214**	17.8(**73**)	**2**
1975	KC	6	119	19.8(36)	0
1976	KC	2	30	15.0(29)	0
1977	KC	1	0	0.0(0)	0
1978	KC	2	0	0.0(0)	0
NFL	13	58	937	16.2(73)	5

Thomas, J.T.

YEAR	TEAM	INT	YDS	AVG(LG)	TD
1973	Pit	1	10	10.0(10)	0
1974	Pit	5	22	4.4(14)	0
1975	Pit	3	44	14.7(33)	0
1976	Pit	2	43	21.5(38)	0
1977	Pit	2	10	5.0(12)	0
1980	Pit	2	0	0.0(0)	0
1981	Pit	4	18	4.5(16)	0
1982	Den	1	0	0.0(0)	0
NFL	8	20	147	7.3(38)	0

Thomas, Orlando

YEAR	TEAM	INT	YDS	AVG(LG)	TD
1995	Min	**9**	108	12.0(45)	1
1996	Min	5	57	11.4(34)	0
1997	Min	2	1	0.5(1)	0

YEAR	TEAM	INT	YDS	AVG(LG)	TD
1998	Min	2	27	13.5(27)	0
1999	Min	2	32	16.0(27)	1
2000	Min	1	0	0.0(0)	0
2001	Min	1	0	0.0(0)	0
NFL	7	22	225	10.2(45)	2

Thomas, Pat

YEAR	TEAM	INT	YDS	AVG(LG)	TD
1977	LARm	5	97	19.4(30)	0
1978	LARm	8	96	12.0(33)	1
1979	LARm	3	5	1.7(5)	0
1980	LARm	3	14	4.7(14)	0
1981	LARm	4	80	20.0(64)	0
1982	LARm	3	0	0.0(0)	0
NFL	7	26	292	11.2(64)	1

Thomas, William

YEAR	TEAM	INT	YDS	AVG(LG)	TD
1992	Phi	2	4	2.0(4)	0
1993	Phi	2	39	19.5(21)	0
1994	Phi	1	7	7.0(7)	0
1995	Phi	7	104	14.9(37)	1
1996	Phi	3	47	15.7(37)	0
1997	Phi	2	11	5.5(11)	0
1998	Phi	1	21	21.0(21)	0
2000	Oak	6	68	11.3(46)	1
2001	Oak	3	46	15.3(33)	0
NFL	11	27	347	12.9(46)	2

Thompson, Bill

YEAR	TEAM	INT	YDS	AVG(LG)	TD
1969	Den-A	3	92	30.7(57)	1
1970	Den	2	65	32.5(33)	0
1971	Den	5	83	16.6(42)	0
1972	Den	1	4	4.0(4)	0
1973	Den	3	96	**32.0(59)**	1
1974	Den	5	105	21.0(38)	1
1975	Den	2	97	48.5(49)	0
1977	Den	5	122	24.4(38)	0
1978	Den	4	0	0.0(0)	0
1979	Den	4	57	14.3(28)	0
1980	Den	2	49	24.5(36)	0
1981	Den	4	14	3.5(14)	0
NFL	13	40	784	19.6(59)	3

Thompson, Norm

YEAR	TEAM	INT	YDS	AVG(LG)	TD
1971	SL	4	45	11.3(25)	0
1972	SL	1	5	5.0(5)	0
1974	SL	6	**190**	**31.7(56)**	1
1975	SL	7	141	20.1(61)	**1**
1976	SL	4	83	20.8(38)	0
1977	Bal	3	39	13.0(20)	0
1978	Bal	6	52	8.7(31)	0
1979	Bal	2	38	19.0(26)	0
NFL	9	33	593	18.0(61)	2

Thurman, Dennis

YEAR	TEAM	INT	YDS	AVG(LG)	TD
1978	Dal	2	35	17.5(23)	0
1979	Dal	1	0	0.0(0)	0
1980	Dal	5	114	22.8(78)	**1**
1981	Dal	9	187	20.8(96)	0
1982	Dal	3	75	**25.0(60)**	**1**
1983	Dal	6	49	8.2(34)	0
1984	Dal	5	81	16.2(43)	1
1985	Dal	5	21	4.2(21)	**1**
NFL	9	36	562	15.6(96)	4

Tunnell, Emlen

YEAR	TEAM	INT	YDS	AVG(LG)	TD
1948	NYG	7	116	16.6(43)	1
1949	NYG	10	251	25.1(55)	**2**
1950	NYG	7	167	23.9(35)	0
1951	NYG	9	74	8.2(30)	0
1952	NYG	7	149	21.3(40)	0
1953	NYG	6	117	19.5(44)	0
1954	NYG	8	108	13.5(43)	0
1955	NYG	7	76	10.9(26)	0
1956	NYG	6	87	14.5(23)	0
1957	NYG	6	87	14.5(52)	1
1958	NYG	1	8	8.0(8)	0
1959	GB	2	20	10.0(18)	0
1960	GB	3	22	7.3(22)	0
NFL	13	79	1282	16.2(55)	4

Turner, Eric

YEAR	TEAM	INT	YDS	AVG(LG)	TD
1991	Cle	2	42	21.0(42)	1
1992	Cle	1	6	6.0(6)	0
1993	Cle	5	25	5.0(19)	0
1994	Cle	**9**	199	22.1(93)	1
1996	Bal	5	1	0.2(1)	0
1997	Oak	2	45	22.5(29)	0
1998	Oak	3	108	**36.0(94)**	1
1999	Oak	3	43	14.3(24)	0
NFL	8	30	469	15.6(94)	3

Turner, John

YEAR	TEAM	INT	YDS	AVG(LG)	TD
1978	Min	1	15	15.0(15)	0
1979	Min	2	48	24.0(36)	0
1980	Min	6	22	3.7(13)	0
1982	Min	2	43	21.5(33)	**1**
1983	Min	6	37	6.2(14)	0
1984	SD	2	43	21.5(43)	0
1985	Min	5	62	12.4(25)	0
NFL	7	24	270	11.3(43)	1

Van Pelt, Brad

YEAR	TEAM	INT	YDS	AVG(LG)	TD
1974	NYG	2	22	11.0(13)	0
1975	NYG	3	8	2.7(5)	0
1976	NYG	2	13	6.5(7)	0
1977	NYG	2	9	4.5(9)	0
1978	NYG	3	32	10.7(20)	0
1980	NYG	3	3	1.0(3)	0
1981	NYG	1	10	10.0(10)	0
1983	NYG	2	7	3.5(6)	0
1984	LARd	1	9	9.0(9)	0
1985	LARd	1	22	22.0(22)	0
NFL	13	20	135	6.8(22)	0

Vincent, Troy

YEAR	TEAM	INT	YDS	AVG(LG)	TD
1992	Mia	2	47	23.5(32)	0
1993	Mia	2	29	14.5(23)	0
1994	Mia	5	113	22.6(58)	1
1995	Mia	5	95	19.0(69)	**1**
1996	Phi	3	144	**48.0(90)**	1
1997	Phi	3	14	4.7(14)	0
1998	Phi	2	29	14.5(29)	0
1999	Phi	**7**	91	13.0(35)	0
2000	Phi	5	34	6.8(17)	0
2001	Phi	3	0	0.0(0)	0
2002	Phi	2	1	0.5(1)	0
2003	Phi	3	28	9.3(28)	0
2004	Buf	1	8	8.0(8)	0
2005	Buf	4	78	19.5(42)	0
NFL	14	47	711	15.1(90)	3

Volk, Rick

YEAR	TEAM	INT	YDS	AVG(LG)	TD
1967	Bal	6	145	24.2(**94**)	1
1968	Bal	6	154	25.7(90)	0
1969	Bal	4	36	9.0(23)	0
1970	Bal	4	61	15.3(31)	0
1971	Bal	4	36	9.0(21)	0
1972	Bal	4	86	21.5(23)	0
1973	Bal	1	0	0.0(0)	0
1974	Bal	2	0	0.0(0)	0
1976	NYG	2	14	7.0(11)	0
1977	Mia	1	0	0.0(0)	0
1978	Mia	4	42	10.5(24)	0
NFL	11	38	574	15.1(94)	1

Wagner, Lowell

YEAR	TEAM	INT	YDS	AVG(LG)	TD
1948	NYY-A	1	31	31.0(31)	0
1949	SF-A	6	121	20.2(**66**)	**1**
1950	SF	4	12	3.0(8)	0
1951	SF	9	115	12.8(40)	0
1952	SF	6	69	11.5(30)	0
1953	SF	6	135	22.5(32)	0
AAFC	4	7	152	21.7(97)	1
NFL	4	25	331	13.2(-31)	0

Wagner, Mike

YEAR	TEAM	INT	YDS	AVG(LG)	TD
1971	Pit	2	53	26.5(27)	0
1972	Pit	6	77	12.8(35)	0
1973	Pit	**8**	134	16.8(38)	0
1974	Pit	2	13	6.5(9)	0
1975	Pit	4	122	30.5(65)	0
1976	Pit	2	0	0.0(0)	0
1978	Pit	2	34	17.0(20)	0
1979	Pit	4	31	7.8(19)	0
1980	Pit	6	27	4.5(17)	0
NFL	9	36	491	13.6(65)	0

Walls, Everson

YEAR	TEAM	INT	YDS	AVG(LG)	TD
1981	Dal	**11**	133	12.1(33)	0
1982	Dal	**7**	61	8.7(37)	0
1983	Dal	4	70	17.5(37)	0
1984	Dal	3	12	4.0(12)	0
1985	Dal	**9**	31	3.4(19)	0
1986	Dal	3	46	15.3(24)	0
1987	Dal	5	38	7.6(30)	0
1988	Dal	2	0	0.0(0)	0
1990	NYG	6	80	13.3(40)	1
1991	NYG	4	7	1.8(5)	0
1992	NYG	1	0	0.0(0)	0
1992	Cle	2	26	13.0(24)	0
NFL	12	57	504	8.8(40)	1

Warfield, Eric

YEAR	TEAM	INT	YDS	AVG(LG)	TD
1999	KC	3	0	0.0(0)	0
2001	KC	4	61	15.3(51)	1
2002	KC	4	30	7.5(19)	0
2003	KC	4	39	9.8(20)	0
2004	KC	4	49	12.3(43)	1
2005	KC	1	57	57.0(57)	1
NFL	6	20	236	11.8(57)	3

Warren, Jimmy

YEAR	TEAM	INT	YDS	AVG(LG)	TD
1964	SD-A	2	28	14.0(28)	0
1965	SD-A	5	43	8.6(26)	0
1966	Mia-A	5	**198**	**39.6(70)**	1
1967	Mia-A	4	22	5.5(17)	0
1968	Mia-A	2	27	13.5(18)	0
1970	Oak	2	26	13.0(26)	0
1971	Oak	2	114	57.0(59)	2
1973	Oak	1	0	0.0(0)	0
1974	Oak	2	58	29.0(34)	0
NFL	11	25	516	20.6(70)	3

Washington, Brian

YEAR	TEAM	INT	YDS	AVG(LG)	TD
1988	Cle	3	104	**34.7(75)**	1
1990	NYJ	3	22	7.3(13)	0
1991	NYJ	1	0	0.0(0)	0
1992	NYJ	6	59	9.8(23)	1
1993	NYJ	6	128	21.3(62)	**1**
1994	NYJ	2	-3	-1.5(0)	0
1995	KC	3	100	33.3(74)	**1**
1996	KC	3	39	13.0(34)	0
NFL	8	27	449	16.6(75)	4

Washington, Dewayne

YEAR	TEAM	INT	YDS	AVG(LG)	TD
1994	Min	3	135	45.0(81)	2
1995	Min	1	25	25.0(25)	0
1996	Min	2	27	13.5(27)	1
1997	Min	4	71	17.8(27)	0
1998	Pit	5	**178**	35.6(78)	**2**
1999	Pit	4	1	0.3(1)	0
2000	Pit	5	59	11.8(31)	0
2001	Pit	1	15	15.0(15)	0
2002	Pit	3	51	17.0(28)	0
2003	Pit	1	7	7.0(7)	0
2004	Jax	2	0	0.0(0)	0
NFL	12	31	569	18.4(81)	5

Washington, Lionel

YEAR	TEAM	INT	YDS	AVG(LG)	TD
1983	SL	8	92	11.5(26)	0
1984	SL	5	42	8.4(18)	0
1985	SL	1	48	48.0(48)	**1**
1986	SL	2	19	9.5(19)	0
1988	LARd	1	0	0.0(0)	0
1989	LARd	3	46	15.3(32)	1
1990	LARd	1	2	2.0(2)	0
1991	LARd	5	22	4.4(16)	0
1992	LARd	2	21	10.5(18)	0
1993	LARd	2	0	0.0(0)	0
1994	LARd	3	65	21.7(31)	1
1996	Den	2	17	8.5(23)	0
1997	Oak	2	44	22.0(44)	1
NFL	14	37	418	11.3(48)	4

Washington, Mike

YEAR	TEAM	INT	YDS	AVG(LG)	TD
1977	TB	5	71	14.2(45)	**1**
1978	TB	5	43	8.6(24)	0
1979	TB	3	64	21.3(49)	1
1980	TB	4	30	7.5(16)	0
1981	TB	6	156	26.0(34)	1
1982	TB	3	13	4.3(13)	0
1983	TB	2	41	20.5(25)	0
NFL	7	28	418	14.9(49)	3

Waterfield, Bob

YEAR	TEAM	INT	YDS	AVG(LG)	TD
1945	Cle	6	92	15.3(29)	0
1946	LARm	5	72	14.4(28)	0
1947	LARm	5	56	11.2(35)	0
1948	LARm	4	8	2.0(5)	0
NFL	8	20	228	11.4(35)	0

Waters, Charlie

YEAR	TEAM	INT	YDS	AVG(LG)	TD
1970	Dal	5	45	9.0(20)	0
1971	Dal	2	37	18.5(30)	0
1972	Dal	6	132	22.0(56)	1
1973	Dal	5	112	22.4(44)	0
1974	Dal	2	26	13.0(24)	0
1975	Dal	3	55	18.3(35)	**1**
1976	Dal	3	6	2.0(5)	0
1977	Dal	3	11	3.7(6)	0
1978	Dal	4	61	15.3(22)	0
1980	Dal	5	78	15.6(29)	0
1981	Dal	3	21	7.0(21)	0
NFL	11	41	584	14.2(56)	2

Watkins, Bobby

YEAR	TEAM	INT	YDS	AVG(LG)	TD
1982	Det	5	22	4.4(20)	0
1983	Det	4	48	12.0(31)	0
1984	Det	6	0	0.0(0)	0
1985	Det	5	15	3.0(8)	0
NFL	4	20	85	4.3(31)	0

Waymer, Dave

YEAR	TEAM	INT	YDS	AVG(LG)	TD
1981	NO	4	54	13.5(31)	0
1984	NO	4	9	2.3(9)	0
1985	NO	6	49	8.2(28)	0
1986	NO	9	48	5.3(17)	0
1987	NO	5	78	15.6(35)	0
1988	NO	3	91	30.3(44)	0
1989	NO	6	66	11.0(42)	0
1990	SF	7	64	9.1(24)	0
1991	SF	4	77	19.3(42)	0
NFL	12	48	536	11.2(44)	0

Webb, Don

YEAR	TEAM	INT	YDS	AVG(LG)	TD
1961	Bos-A	5	153	30.6(59)	2
1964	Bos-A	6	43	7.2(25)	0
1965	Bos-A	2	45	22.5(45)	0
1966	Bos-A	1	0	0.0(0)	0
1967	Bos-A	4	91	22.8(41)	0
1969	Bos-A	2	32	16.0(32)	0
1970	Bos	1	2	2.0(2)	0
NFL	9	21	366	17.4(59)	2

Wehrli, Roger

YEAR	TEAM	INT	YDS	AVG(LG)	TD
1969	SL	3	44	14.7(44)	0
1970	SL	6	50	8.3(41)	0
1971	SL	2	11	5.5(6)	0
1973	SL	1	0	0.0(0)	0
1974	SL	2	54	27.0(53)	1
1975	SL	6	31	5.2(31)	0
1976	SL	4	31	7.8(26)	0
1977	SL	5	44	8.8(41)	0
1978	SL	4	3	0.8(3)	0
1979	SL	2	8	4.0(9)	1
1980	SL	1	25	25.0(25)	0
1981	SL	4	8	2.0(6)	0
NFL	14	40	309	7.7(53)	2

Wesley, Greg

YEAR	TEAM	INT	YDS	AVG(LG)	TD
2000	KC	2	28	14.0(28)	0
2001	KC	2	44	22.0(30)	0
2002	KC	6	170	28.3(50)	0
2003	KC	6	63	10.5(27)	0
2004	KC	4	92	23.0(65)	0
2005	KC	6	106	17.7(51)	0
NFL	6	26	503	19.3(65)	0

West, Willie

YEAR	TEAM	INT	YDS	AVG(LG)	TD
1961	SL	1	14	14.0(14)	0
1962	Buf-A	3	24	8.0(24)	0
1963	Buf-A	5	57	11.4(23)	0
1964	Den-A	1	0	0.0(0)	0
1964	NYJ-A	1	0	0.0(0)	0
1965	NYJ-A	6	57	9.5(28)	0
1966	Mia-A	8	62	7.8(31)	0
1967	Mia-A	1	16	16.0(16)	0
1968	Mia-A	4	102	25.5(32)	0
NFL	9	30	332	11.1(32)	0

Westmoreland, Dick

YEAR	TEAM	INT	YDS	AVG(LG)	TD
1964	SD-A	6	51	8.5(38)	0
1965	SD-A	1	28	28.0(28)	0
1966	Mia-A	4	104	26.0(42)	1
1967	Mia-A	**10**	127	12.7(29)	1
1968	Mia-A	1	0	0.0(0)	0
NFL	6	22	310	14.1(42)	2

White, Stan

YEAR	TEAM	INT	YDS	AVG(LG)	TD
1973	Bal	4	40	10.0(19)	1
1974	Bal	1	40	40.0(40)	0
1975	Bal	8	135	16.9(32)	1
1976	Bal	3	26	8.7(22)	0
1977	Bal	7	84	12.0(19)	0
1978	Bal	1	12	12.0(12)	0
1979	Bal	1	11	11.0(11)	0
1980	Det	2	22	11.0(15)	0
1981	Det	4	37	9.3(16)	0
1982	Det	3	21	7.0(18)	0
NFL	10	34	428	12.6(40)	2

White, William

YEAR	TEAM	INT	YDS	AVG(LG)	TD
1989	Det	1	0	0.0(0)	0
1990	Det	5	120	24.0(48)	1
1991	Det	2	35	17.5(28)	0
1992	Det	4	54	13.5(28)	0
1993	Det	1	5	5.0(5)	0
1994	KC	2	0	0.0(0)	0
1995	KC	2	48	24.0(30)	0
1997	Atl	1	11	11.0(11)	0
1998	Atl	2	36	18.0(36)	0
NFL	10	20	309	15.4(48)	1

Whitsell, Dave

YEAR	TEAM	INT	YDS	AVG(LG)	TD
1958	Det	1	29	29.0(29)	0
1961	ChiB	6	123	20.5(52)	0
1962	ChiB	5	45	9.0(26)	0
1963	ChiB	6	61	10.2(39)	1
1964	ChiB	2	57	28.5(41)	0
1965	ChiB	4	67	16.8(32)	1
1966	ChiB	3	44	14.7(21)	0
1967	NO	**10**	178	17.8(41)	2
1968	NO	6	44	7.3(32)	0
1969	NO	3	14	4.7(11)	0
NFL	10	46	662	14.4(52)	4

Whittenton, Jesse

YEAR	TEAM	INT	YDS	AVG(LG)	TD
1956	LARm	3	83	27.7(32)	1
1957	LARm	1	31	31.0(31)	0
1958	GB	1	0	0.0(0)	0
1960	GB	6	101	16.8(52)	0
1961	GB	5	98	19.6(41)	1
1962	GB	3	40	13.3(36)	0
1963	GB	4	90	22.5(33)	0
1964	GB	1	0	0.0(0)	0
NFL	9	24	443	18.5(52)	2

WILBURN, BARRY

YEAR	TEAM	INT	YDS	AVG (LG)	TD
1985	Was	1	10	10.0(10)	0
1986	Was	2	14	7.0(14)	0
1987	Was	9	135	15.0(100)	1
1988	Was	4	24	6.0(14)	0
1989	Was	3	13	4.3(13)	0
1995	Phi	1	0	0.0(0)	0
NFL	7	20	196	9.8(100)	1

WILLIAMS, AENEAS

YEAR	TEAM	INT	YDS	AVG (LG)	TD
1991	Phx	6	60	10.0(32)	0
1992	Phx	3	25	8.3(23)	0
1993	Phx	2	87	43.5(46)	1
1994	Arz	9	89	9.9(43)	0
1995	Arz	6	86	14.3(48)	2
1996	Arz	6	89	14.8(65)	1
1997	Arz	6	95	15.8(42)	2
1998	Arz	1	15	15.0(15)	0
1999	Arz	2	5	2.5(8)	0
2000	Arz	5	102	20.4(48)	0
2001	SL	4	69	17.3(42)	2
2002	SL	1	3	3.0(3)	0
2003	SL	4	82	20.5(46)	1
NFL	13	55	807	14.7(65)	9

WILLIAMS, CLANCY

YEAR	TEAM	INT	YDS	AVG (LG)	TD
1966	LARm	8	97	12.1(32)	1
1967	LARm	4	75	18.8(29)	0
1968	LARm	7	51	7.3(36)	0
1969	LARm	4	97	24.3(40)	0
1970	LARm	5	108	21.6(65)	1
NFL	6	28	428	15.3(65)	2

WILLIAMS, DARRYL

YEAR	TEAM	INT	YDS	AVG (LG)	TD
1992	Cin	4	65	16.3(30)	0
1993	Cin	2	126	63.0(97)	1
1994	Cin	2	45	22.5(33)	0
1995	Cin	1	1	1.0(1)	0
1996	Sea	5	148	29.6(79)	1
1997	Sea	8	172	21.5(44)	1
1998	Sea	3	41	13.7(28)	0
1999	Sea	4	41	10.3(21)	0
2000	Cin	1	36	36.0(36)	1
2001	Cin	1	16	16.0(16)	0
NFL	10	31	691	22.3(97)	4

WILLIAMS, MIKE

YEAR	TEAM	INT	YDS	AVG (LG)	TD
1975	SD	4	67	16.8(40)	0
1976	SD	4	76	19.0(35)	0
1977	SD	3	36	12.0(36)	0
1978	SD	3	23	7.7(23)	0
1979	SD	4	55	13.8(50)	0
1980	SD	1	0	0.0(0)	0
1981	SD	3	0	0.0(0)	0
1982	SD	2	12	6.0(6)	0
NFL	8	24	269	11.2(50)	0

WILLIAMS, WILLIE

YEAR	TEAM	INT	YDS	AVG (LG)	TD
1965	NYG	1	0	0.0(0)	0
1967	NYG	1	44	44.0(44)	0
1968	NYG	10	103	10.3(24)	0
1969	NYG	4	19	4.8(19)	0
1970	NYG	6	114	19.0(52)	0
1971	NYG	5	58	11.6(24)	0
1972	NYG	4	42	10.5(18)	0
1973	NYG	4	82	20.5(35)	0
NFL	9	35	462	13.2(52)	0

WILLIAMS, WILLIE

YEAR	TEAM	INT	YDS	AVG (LG)	TD
1995	Pit	7	122	17.4(63)	1
1996	Pit	1	1	1.0(1)	0
1997	Sea	1	0	0.0(0)	0
1998	Sea	2	36	18.0(28)	1
1999	Sea	5	43	8.6(40)	1
2000	Sea	4	74	18.5(69)	1
2001	Sea	4	24	6.0(24)	0
2002	Sea	1	2	2.0(2)	0
2004	Pit	1	0	0.0(0)	0
NFL	11	26	302	11.6(69)	4

WILLIAMSON, FRED

YEAR	TEAM	INT	YDS	AVG (LG)	TD
1961	Oak-A	5	58	11.6(26)	0
1962	Oak-A	8	151	18.9(91)	1
1963	Oak-A	6	44	7.3(17)	0
1964	Oak-A	6	40	6.7(28)	0
1965	KC-A	6	89	14.8(51)	0
1966	KC-A	4	20	5.0(19)	0
1967	KC-A	1	77	77.0(77)	1
NFL	8	36	479	13.3(91)	2

WILSON, LARRY

YEAR	TEAM	INT	YDS	AVG (LG)	TD
1960	SL	2	4	2.0(4)	0
1961	SL	3	36	12.0(25)	0
1962	SL	2	59	29.5(57)	1
1963	SL	4	67	16.8(36)	0
1964	SL	3	44	14.7(42)	1
1965	SL	6	153	25.5(96)	1
1966	SL	10	180	18.0(91)	2
1967	SL	4	75	18.8(44)	0
1968	SL	4	14	3.5(8)	0
1969	SL	2	15	7.5(15)	0
1970	SL	5	72	14.4(22)	0
1971	SL	4	46	11.5(23)	0
1972	SL	3	35	11.7(24)	0
NFL	13	52	800	15.4(96)	5

WILSON, NEMIAH

YEAR	TEAM	INT	YDS	AVG (LG)	TD
1965	Den-A	3	118	39.3(65)	1
1966	Den-A	2	2	2.0(2)	0
1967	Den-A	4	153	38.3(70)	2
1969	Oak-A	2	25	12.5(22)	0
1970	Oak	2	7	3.5(7)	0
1971	Oak	5	70	14.0(22)	0
1972	Oak	4	48	12.0(32)	0
1973	Oak	3	28	9.3(20)	0
1974	Oak	3	35	11.7(34)	0
NFL	10	27	486	18.0(70)	3

WILSON, STEVE

YEAR	TEAM	INT	YDS	AVG (LG)	TD
1980	Dal	4	82	20.5(35)	0
1981	Dal	2	0	0.0(0)	0
1982	Den	2	22	11.0(16)	0
1983	Den	5	91	18.2(36)	0
1984	Den	4	59	14.8(22)	0
1985	Den	3	8	2.7(8)	0
1986	Den	1	-5	-5.0(-5)	0
1988	Den	1	7	7.0(7)	0
NFL	10	22	264	12.0(36)	0

WOOD, DUANE

YEAR	TEAM	INT	YDS	AVG (LG)	TD
1960	DalT-A	4	85	21.3(64)	1
1961	DalT-A	4	31	7.8(31)	0
1962	DalT-A	4	81	20.3(33)	0
1963	KC-A	3	23	7.7(23)	0
1964	KC-A	5	27	5.4(12)	0
NFL	5	20	247	12.4(64)	1

WOOD, WILLIE

YEAR	TEAM	INT	YDS	AVG (LG)	TD
1961	GB	5	52	10.4(21)	0
1962	GB	9	132	14.7(37)	0
1963	GB	5	67	13.4(22)	0
1964	GB	3	73	24.3(42)	1
1965	GB	6	65	10.8(28)	0
1966	GB	3	38	12.7(20)	1
1967	GB	4	60	15.0(25)	0
1968	GB	2	54	27.0(35)	0
1969	GB	3	40	13.3(21)	0
1970	GB	7	110	15.7(24)	0
1971	GB	1	8	8.0(8)	0
NFL	12	48	699	14.6(42)	2

WOODRUFF, DWAYNE

YEAR	TEAM	INT	YDS	AVG (LG)	TD
1979	Pit	1	31	31.0(31)	0
1980	Pit	1	0	0.0(0)	0
1981	Pit	1	17	17.0(17)	0
1982	Pit	5	53	10.6(30)	0
1983	Pit	3	85	28.3(47)	0
1984	Pit	5	56	11.2(42)	1
1985	Pit	5	80	16.0(33)	0
1987	Pit	5	91	18.2(33)	1
1988	Pit	4	109	27.3(78)	1
1989	Pit	4	57	14.3(35)	0
1990	Pit	3	110	36.7(59)	0
NFL	11	37	689	18.6(78)	3

WOODSON, DARREN

YEAR	TEAM	INT	YDS	AVG (LG)	TD
1994	Dal	5	140	28.0(94)	1
1995	Dal	2	46	23.0(37)	1
1996	Dal	5	43	8.6(21)	0
1997	Dal	1	14	14.0(14)	0
1998	Dal	1	1	1.0(1)	0
1999	Dal	2	5	2.5(5)	0
2000	Dal	2	12	6.0(12)	0
2001	Dal	3	11	3.7(6)	0
2002	Dal	1	1	1.0(1)	0
2003	Dal	1	-2	-2.0(-2)	0
NFL	12	23	271	11.8(94)	2

WOODSON, ROD

YEAR	TEAM	INT	YDS	AVG (LG)	TD
1987	Pit	1	45	45.0(45)	1
1988	Pit	4	98	24.5(29)	0
1989	Pit	3	39	13.0(39)	0
1990	Pit	5	67	13.4(34)	0
1991	Pit	3	72	24.0(41)	0
1992	Pit	4	90	22.5(57)	0
1993	Pit	8	138	17.3(63)	1
1994	Pit	4	109	27.3(37)	2
1996	Pit	6	121	20.2(43)	1
1997	SF	3	81	27.0(41)	0
1998	Bal	6	108	18.0(60)	2
1999	Bal	7	195	27.9(66)	2
2000	Bal	4	20	5.0(18)	0
2001	Bal	3	57	19.0(47)	1
2002	Oak	8	225	28.1(98)	2
2003	Oak	2	18	9.0(13)	0
NFL	16	71	1483	20.9(98)	12

WOOLFORD, DONNELL

YEAR	TEAM	INT	YDS	AVG (LG)	TD
1989	ChiB	3	0	0.0(0)	0
1990	ChiB	3	18	6.0(9)	0
1991	ChiB	2	21	10.5(16)	0
1992	ChiB	7	67	9.6(32)	0
1993	ChiB	2	18	9.0(18)	0
1994	ChiB	5	30	6.0(25)	0
1995	ChiB	4	21	5.3(16)	0
1996	ChiB	6	37	6.2(28)	1
1997	Pit	4	91	22.8(34)	0
NFL	9	36	303	8.4(34)	1

WRIGHT, FELIX

YEAR	TEAM	INT	YDS	AVG (LG)	TD
1985	Cle	2	11	5.5(10)	0
1986	Cle	3	33	11.0(33)	0
1987	Cle	4	152	38.0(68)	1
1988	Cle	5	126	25.2(53)	0
1989	Cle	9	91	10.1(27)	1
1990	Cle	3	56	18.7(36)	0
1991	Min	2	3	1.5(3)	0
1992	Min	1	20	20.0(20)	0
NFL	8	29	492	17.0(68)	2

WRIGHT, LOUIS

YEAR	TEAM	INT	YDS	AVG (LG)	TD
1975	Den	2	9	4.5(9)	0
1976	Den	0	32	0.0(32)	0
1977	Den	3	128	42.7(59)	1
1978	Den	2	2	1.0(2)	0
1979	Den	2	20	10.0(15)	0
1982	Den	2	18	9.0(18)	0
1983	Den	6	50	8.3(34)	0
1984	Den	1	1	1.0(1)	0
1985	Den	5	44	8.8(24)	0
1986	Den	3	56	18.7(56)	0
NFL	11	26	360	13.8(59)	1

WRIGHT, NATE

YEAR	TEAM	INT	YDS	AVG (LG)	TD
1969	SL	2	41	20.5(21)	0
1970	SL	1	0	0.0(0)	0
1972	Min	1	10	10.0(10)	0
1973	Min	3	6	2.0(6)	0
1974	Min	6	91	15.2(44)	0
1976	Min	7	47	6.7(21)	0
1977	Min	3	0	0.0(0)	0
1978	Min	5	58	11.6(30)	0
1979	Min	4	44	11.0(32)	0
1980	Min	2	16	8.0(10)	0
NFL	10	34	313	9.2(44)	0

YOUNG, ROYNELL

YEAR	TEAM	INT	YDS	AVG (LG)	TD
1980	Phi	4	27	6.8(26)	0
1981	Phi	4	35	8.8(33)	0
1982	Phi	4	0	0.0(0)	0
1983	Phi	1	0	0.0(0)	0
1985	Phi	1	0	0.0(0)	0
1986	Phi	6	9	1.5(9)	0
1987	Phi	1	30	30.0(30)	0
1988	Phi	2	5	2.5(5)	0
NFL	8	23	106	4.6(33)	0

ZORDICH, MIKE

YEAR	TEAM	INT	YDS	AVG (LG)	TD
1988	NYJ	1	35	35.0(35)	1
1989	Phx	1	16	16.0(16)	1
1990	Phx	1	25	25.0(25)	0
1991	Phx	1	27	27.0(27)	0
1992	Phx	3	37	12.3(23)	0
1993	Phx	1	0	0.0(0)	0
1994	Phi	4	39	9.8(18)	1
1995	Phi	1	10	10.0(10)	0
1996	Phi	4	54	13.5(28)	0
1997	Phi	1	21	21.0(21)	0
1998	Phi	2	18	9.0(14)	0
NFL	12	20	282	14.1(35)	3

Abraham, John

YEAR	TEAM	SACKS
2000	NYJ	4.5
2001	NYJ	13
2002	NYJ	10
2003	NYJ	6
2004	NYJ	9.5
2005	NYJ	10.5
NFL	6	53.5

Armstrong, Trace

YEAR	TEAM	SACKS
1989	ChiB	5
1990	ChiB	10
1991	ChiB	1.5
1992	ChiB	6.5
1993	ChiB	11.5
1994	ChiB	7.5
1995	Mia	4.5
1996	Mia	12
1997	Mia	5.5
1998	Mia	10.5
1999	Mia	7.5
2000	Mia	**16.5**
2001	Oak	.5
2002	Oak	4
2003	Oak	3
NFL	15	106

Baker, Al

YEAR	TEAM	SACKS
1982	Det	8.5
1983	SL	13
1984	SL	10
1985	SL	4
1986	SL	10.5
1987	Cle	3.5
1988	Min	5.5
1989	Cle	7.5
1990	Cle	3
NFL	13	65.5

Bennett, Cornelius

YEAR	TEAM	SACKS
1987	Buf	8.5
1988	Buf	9.5
1989	Buf	5.5
1990	Buf	4
1991	Buf	9
1992	Buf	4
1993	Buf	5
1994	Buf	5
1995	Buf	2
1996	Atl	3
1997	Atl	7
1998	Atl	1
1999	Ind	5
2000	Ind	3
NFL	14	71.5

Bennett, Tony

YEAR	TEAM	SACKS
1990	GB	3
1991	GB	13
1992	GB	13.5
1993	GB	6.5
1994	Ind	9
1995	Ind	10.5
1996	Ind	6
1997	Ind	3
NFL	8	64.5

Bickett, Duane

YEAR	TEAM	SACKS
1985	Ind	6
1986	Ind	5
1987	Ind	8
1988	Ind	3.5
1989	Ind	8
1990	Ind	4.5
1991	Ind	5
1992	Ind	6.5
1993	Ind	3.5
1995	Sea	1
1996	Car	2
NFL	11	53

Boulware, Peter

YEAR	TEAM	SACKS
1997	Bal	11.5
1998	Bal	8.5
1999	Bal	10
2000	Bal	7
2001	Bal	**15**
2002	Bal	7
2003	Bal	8.5
2005	Bal	2.5
NFL	8	70

Brackens, Tony

YEAR	TEAM	SACKS
1996	Jax	7
1997	Jax	7
1998	Jax	3.5
1999	Jax	12
2000	Jax	7.5
2001	Jax	11
2002	Jax	1
2003	Jax	6
NFL	8	55

Bratzke, Chad

YEAR	TEAM	SACKS
1996	NYG	5
1997	NYG	3.5
1998	NYG	11
1999	Ind	12
2000	Ind	7.5
2001	Ind	8.5
2002	Ind	6
2003	Ind	3
NFL	8	56.5

Brown, Chad

YEAR	TEAM	SACKS
1993	Pit	3
1994	Pit	8.5
1995	Pit	5.5
1996	Pit	13
1997	Sea	6.5
1998	Sea	7.5
1999	Sea	5.5
2000	Sea	6
2001	Sea	8.5
2002	Sea	6
2003	Sea	7
2004	Sea	1
NFL	12	78

Brown, Greg

YEAR	TEAM	SACKS
1982	Phi	4
1983	Phi	8.5
1984	Phi	16
1985	Phi	13
1986	Phi	9
1987	Atl	2
NFL	7	52.5

Bryant, Jeff

YEAR	TEAM	SACKS
1982	Sea	3
1983	Sea	8
1984	Sea	14.5
1985	Sea	8.5
1986	Sea	4
1987	Sea	4
1988	Sea	3.5
1989	Sea	3.5
1990	Sea	5.5
1991	Sea	3
1992	Sea	4.5
1993	Sea	1
NFL	12	63

Burnett, Rob

YEAR	TEAM	SACKS
1990	Cle	2
1991	Cle	3
1992	Cle	9
1993	Cle	9
1994	Cle	10
1995	Cle	7.5
1996	Bal	3
1997	Bal	4
1998	Bal	2.5
1999	Bal	6.5
2000	Bal	10.5
2002	Mia	4
2003	Mia	2
NFL	14	73

Carter, Kevin

YEAR	TEAM	SACKS
1995	SL	6
1996	SL	9.5
1997	SL	7.5
1998	SL	12
1999	SL	**17**
2000	SL	10.5
2001	Ten	2
2002	Ten	10
2003	Ten	5.5
2004	Ten	6
2005	Mia	6
NFL	11	92

Childress, Ray

YEAR	TEAM	SACKS
1985	Hou	3.5
1986	Hou	5
1987	Hou	6
1988	Hou	8.5
1989	Hou	8.5
1990	Hou	8
1991	Hou	7
1992	Hou	13
1993	Hou	9
1994	Hou	6
1995	Hou	1
1996	Dal	1
NFL	12	76.5

Cofer, Mike

YEAR	TEAM	SACKS
1983	Det	4.5
1984	Det	7
1985	Det	1
1986	Det	7.5
1987	Det	8.5
1988	Det	12
1989	Det	9
1990	Det	10
1991	Det	1
1992	Det	2
NFL	10	62.5

Coleman, Marco

YEAR	TEAM	SACKS
1992	Mia	6
1993	Mia	5.5
1994	Mia	6
1995	Mia	6.5
1996	SD	4
1997	SD	2
1998	SD	3.5
1999	Was	6.5
2000	Was	12
2001	Was	4.5
2002	Jax	5
2003	Phi	.5
2004	Den	2.5
2005	Den	1
NFL	14	65.5

Coleman, Roderick

YEAR	TEAM	SACKS
2000	Oak	6
2001	Oak	6
2002	Oak	11
2003	Oak	5.5
2004	Atl	11.5
2005	Atl	10.5
NFL	6	50.5

Cox, Bryan

YEAR	TEAM	SACKS
1991	Mia	2
1992	Mia	14
1993	Mia	5
1994	Mia	3
1995	Mia	7.5
1996	ChiB	3
1997	ChiB	5
1998	NYJ	6
2000	NYJ	6
NFL	12	51.5

Cross, Jeff

YEAR	TEAM	SACKS
1989	Mia	10
1990	Mia	11.5
1991	Mia	7
1992	Mia	5
1993	Mia	10.5
1994	Mia	9.5
1995	Mia	6
NFL	7	59.5

Daniels, Phillip

YEAR	TEAM	SACKS
1996	Sea	2
1997	Sea	4
1998	Sea	6.5
1999	Sea	9
2000	ChiB	6
2001	ChiB	9
2002	ChiB	5.5
2003	ChiB	2.5
2004	Was	1
2005	Was	8
NFL	10	53.5

Dent, Richard

YEAR	TEAM	SACKS
1983	ChiB	3
1984	ChiB	**17.5**
1985	ChiB	**17**
1986	ChiB	11.5
1987	ChiB	12.5
1988	ChiB	10.5
1989	ChiB	9
1990	ChiB	12
1991	ChiB	10.5
1992	ChiB	8.5
1993	ChiB	12.5
1994	SF	2
1996	Ind	6.5
1997	Phi	4.5
NFL	14	137.5

Doleman, Chris

YEAR	TEAM	SACKS
1985	Min	.5
1986	Min	3
1987	Min	11
1988	Min	8
1989	Min	**21**
1990	Min	11
1991	Min	7
1992	Min	14.5
1993	Min	12.5
1994	Atl	7
1995	Atl	9
1996	SF	11
1997	SF	12
1998	SF	15
1999	Min	8
NFL	15	150.5

Douglas, Hugh

YEAR	TEAM	SACKS
1995	NYJ	10
1996	NYJ	8
1997	NYJ	4
1998	Phi	12.5
1999	Phi	2
2000	Phi	15
2001	Phi	9.5
2002	Phi	12.5
2003	Jax	3.5
2004	Phi	3
NFL	10	80

Ellis, Greg

YEAR	TEAM	SACKS
1998	Dal	3
1999	Dal	7.5
2000	Dal	3
2001	Dal	6
2002	Dal	7.5
2003	Dal	8
2004	Dal	9
2005	Dal	8
NFL	8	52

Fletcher, Simon

YEAR	TEAM	SACKS
1985	Den	1
1986	Den	5.5
1987	Den	4
1988	Den	9
1989	Den	12
1990	Den	11
1991	Den	13.5
1992	Den	16
1993	Den	13.5
1994	Den	7
1995	Den	5
NFL	11	97.5

Freeney, Dwight

YEAR	TEAM	SACKS
2002	Ind	13
2003	Ind	11
2004	Ind	**16**
2005	Ind	11
NFL	4	51

Fuller, William

YEAR	TEAM	SACKS
1986	Hou	1
1987	Hou	2
1988	Hou	8.5
1989	Hou	6.5
1990	Hou	8
1991	Hou	**15**
1992	Hou	8
1993	Hou	10
1994	Phi	9.5
1995	Phi	**13**
1996	Phi	13
1997	SD	3
1998	SD	3
NFL	13	100.5

Gastineau, Mark

YEAR	TEAM	SACKS
1982	NYJ	6
1983	NYJ	**19**
1984	NYJ	**22**
1985	NYJ	13.5
1986	NYJ	2
1987	NYJ	4.5
1988	NYJ	7
NFL	8	74

Gbaja-Biamila, Kabeer

YEAR	TEAM	SACKS
2000	GB	1.5
2001	GB	13.5
2002	GB	12
2003	GB	10
2004	GB	13.5
2005	GB	8
NFL	6	58.5

Geathers, Jumpy

YEAR	TEAM	SACKS
1984	NO	6
1985	NO	6.5
1986	NO	9
1988	NO	3.5
1989	NO	1
1990	Was	3
1991	Was	4.5
1992	Was	5
1993	Atl	3.5
1994	Atl	8
1995	Atl	7
1996	Den	5
NFL	12	62

Gildon, Jason

YEAR	TEAM	SACKS
1994	Pit	2
1995	Pit	3
1996	Pit	7
1997	Pit	5
1998	Pit	11
1999	Pit	8.5
2000	Pit	13.5
2001	Pit	12
2002	Pit	9
2003	Pit	6
2004	Jax	3
NFL	11	80

Glover, La'Roi

YEAR	TEAM	SACKS
1997	NO	6.5
1998	NO	10
1999	NO	8.5
2000	NO	**17**
2001	NO	8
2002	Dal	6.5
2003	Dal	5
2004	Dal	7
2005	Dal	3
NFL	9	71.5

Green, Jacob

YEAR	TEAM	SACKS
1982	Sea	3
1983	Sea	16
1984	Sea	13
1985	Sea	13.5
1986	Sea	12
1987	Sea	9.5
1988	Sea	9
1989	Sea	3
1990	Sea	12.5
1991	Sea	6
NFL	11	97.5

Greene, Kevin

YEAR	TEAM	SACKS
1986	LARm	7
1987	LARm	6.5
1988	LARm	16.5
1989	LARm	16.5
1990	LARm	13
1991	LARm	3
1992	LARm	10
1993	Pit	12.5
1994	Pit	**14**
1995	Pit	9
1996	Car	**14.5**
1997	SF	10.5
1998	Car	15
1999	Car	12
NFL	14	160

Greer, Curtis

YEAR	TEAM	SACKS
1982	SL	7.5
1983	SL	16
1984	SL	14
1985	SL	7
1987	SL	6
NFL	6	50.5

Haley, Charles

YEAR	TEAM	SACKS
1986	SF	12
1987	SF	6.5
1988	SF	11.5
1989	SF	10.5
1990	SF	**16**
1991	SF	7
1992	Dal	6
1993	Dal	4
1994	Dal	12.5
1995	Dal	10.5
1996	Dal	1
1999	SF	3
NFL	12	100.5

Hamilton, Keith

YEAR	TEAM	SACKS
1992	NYG	3.5
1993	NYG	11.5
1994	NYG	6.5
1995	NYG	2
1996	NYG	3
1997	NYG	8
1998	NYG	7
1999	NYG	4
2000	NYG	10
2001	NYG	6
2003	NYG	1.5
NFL	11	63

Hampton, Dan

YEAR	TEAM	SACKS
1982	ChiB	9
1983	ChiB	5
1984	ChiB	11.5
1985	ChiB	6.5
1986	ChiB	10
1987	ChiB	3.5
1988	ChiB	9.5
1989	ChiB	2
NFL	9	57

Hansen, Phil

YEAR	TEAM	SACKS
1991	Buf	2
1992	Buf	8
1993	Buf	3.5
1994	Buf	5.5
1995	Buf	10
1996	Buf	8
1997	Buf	6
1998	Buf	7.5
1999	Buf	6
2000	Buf	2
2001	Buf	3
NFL	11	61.5

Harris, Tim

YEAR	TEAM	SACKS
1986	GB	8
1987	GB	7
1988	GB	13.5
1989	GB	19.5
1990	GB	7
1991	SF	3
1992	SF	17
1994	SF	2
1995	SF	4
NFL	9	81

Harvey, Ken

YEAR	TEAM	SACKS
1988	Phx	6
1989	Phx	7
1990	Phx	10
1991	Phx	9
1992	Phx	6
1993	Phx	9.5
1994	Was	**13.5**
1995	Was	7.5
1996	Was	9
1997	Was	9.5
1998	Was	2
NFL	11	89

Jackson, Rickey

YEAR	TEAM	SACKS
1982	NO	4.5
1983	NO	12
1984	NO	12
1985	NO	11
1986	NO	9
1987	NO	9.5
1988	NO	7
1989	NO	7.5
1990	NO	6
1991	NO	11.5
1992	NO	13.5
1993	NO	11.5
1994	SF	3.5
1995	SF	9.5
NFL	15	128

Jeffcoat, Jim

YEAR	TEAM	SACKS
1983	Dal	2
1984	Dal	11.5
1985	Dal	12
1986	Dal	14
1987	Dal	5
1988	Dal	6.5
1989	Dal	11.5
1990	Dal	3.5
1991	Dal	4
1992	Dal	10.5
1993	Dal	6
1994	Dal	8
1995	Buf	2.5
1996	Buf	5
1997	Buf	.5
NFL	15	102.5

Jeter, Gary

YEAR	TEAM	SACKS
1983	LARm	6.5
1984	LARm	1
1985	LARm	11
1986	LARm	8
1987	LARm	7
1988	LARm	11.5
1989	NE	7
NFL	10	52

Johnson, Ellis

YEAR	TEAM	SACKS
1995	Ind	4.5
1997	Ind	4.5

YEAR	TEAM	SACKS
1998	Ind	8
1999	Ind	7.5
2000	Ind	5
2001	Ind	3.5
2002	Atl	7
2003	Atl	8
2004	Den	3
NFL	9	51

Johnson, Ezra

YEAR	TEAM	SACKS
1982	GB	5.5
1983	GB	14.5
1984	GB	7
1985	GB	9.5
1986	GB	3
1987	GB	2
1988	Ind	3
1989	Ind	8.5
1990	Hou	2.5
NFL	11	55.5

Johnson, Joe

YEAR	TEAM	SACKS
1994	NO	1
1995	NO	5.5
1996	NO	7.5
1997	NO	8.5
1998	NO	7
2000	NO	12
2001	NO	9
2002	GB	2
NFL	8	52.5

Johnstone, Lance

YEAR	TEAM	SACKS
1996	Oak	1
1997	Oak	3.5
1998	Oak	11
1999	Oak	10
2000	Oak	3.5
2001	Min	5.5
2002	Min	7
2003	Min	10
2004	Min	11
2005	Min	7.5
NFL	10	70

Jones, Rulon

YEAR	TEAM	SACKS
1982	Den	2
1983	Den	4
1984	Den	11
1985	Den	10
1986	Den	13.5
1987	Den	7
1988	Den	5
NFL	9	52.5

Jones, Sean

YEAR	TEAM	SACKS
1984	LARd	1
1985	LARd	8.5
1986	LARd	**15.5**
1987	LARd	6
1988	Hou	7.5
1989	Hou	6
1990	Hou	12.5
1991	Hou	10
1992	Hou	8.5
1993	Hou	13
1994	GB	10.5
1995	GB	9
1996	GB	5
NFL	13	113

Jones, Too Tall

YEAR	TEAM	SACKS
1982	Dal	6
1983	Dal	7
1984	Dal	8
1985	Dal	13
1986	Dal	5.5
1987	Dal	10
1988	Dal	7
1989	Dal	1
NFL	12	57.5

Joyner, Seth

YEAR	TEAM	SACKS
1986	Phi	2
1987	Phi	4
1988	Phi	3.5
1989	Phi	5
1990	Phi	7.5
1991	Phi	6.5
1992	Phi	6.5
1993	Phi	2
1994	Arz	6
1995	Arz	1
1996	Arz	5
1997	GB	3
NFL	12	52

Kearse, Jevon

YEAR	TEAM	SACKS
1999	Ten	**14.5**
2000	Ten	11.5
2001	Ten	10
2002	Ten	2
2003	Ten	9.5
2004	Phi	7.5
2005	Phi	7.5
NFL	7	62.5

Kennedy, Cortez

YEAR	TEAM	SACKS
1990	Sea	1
1991	Sea	6.5
1992	Sea	14
1993	Sea	6.5
1994	Sea	4
1995	Sea	6.5
1996	Sea	8
1997	Sea	2
1998	Sea	2
1999	Sea	6.5
2000	Sea	1
NFL	11	58

Kerney, Patrick

YEAR	TEAM	SACKS
1999	Atl	2.5
2000	Atl	2.5
2001	Atl	12
2002	Atl	10.5
2003	Atl	6.5
2004	Atl	13
2005	Atl	6.5
NFL	7	53.5

Lewis, Mo

YEAR	TEAM	SACKS
1991	NYJ	1
1992	NYJ	2
1993	NYJ	4
1994	NYJ	6
1995	NYJ	5
1996	NYJ	.5
1997	NYJ	8
1998	NYJ	7
1999	NYJ	5.5
2000	NYJ	10
2001	NYJ	3
2002	NYJ	.5
NFL	12	52.5

Little, Leonard

YEAR	TEAM	SACKS
1998	SL	.5
2000	SL	5
2001	SL	14.5
2002	SL	12
2003	SL	12.5
2004	SL	7
2005	SL	9.5
NFL	7	61

Lloyd, Greg

YEAR	TEAM	SACKS
1988	Pit	.5
1989	Pit	7
1990	Pit	4.5
1991	Pit	8
1992	Pit	6.5
1993	Pit	6
1994	Pit	10
1995	Pit	6.5
1996	Pit	1
1997	Pit	3.5
1998	Car	1
NFL	11	54.5

Long, Howie

YEAR	TEAM	SACKS
1982	LARd	5.5
1983	LARd	13
1984	LARd	12
1985	LARd	10
1986	LARd	7.5
1987	LARd	4
1988	LARd	3
1989	LARd	5
1990	LARd	6
1991	LARd	3
1992	LARd	9
1993	LARd	6
NFL	12	84

Manley, Dexter

YEAR	TEAM	SACKS
1982	Was	6.5
1983	Was	11
1984	Was	13.5
1985	Was	15
1986	Was	18.5
1987	Was	8.5
1988	Was	9
1989	Was	9
1991	TB	6.5
NFL	9	97.5

Mann, Charles

YEAR	TEAM	SACKS
1983	Was	3
1984	Was	7
1985	Was	14.5
1986	Was	10
1987	Was	9.5
1988	Was	5.5
1989	Was	10
1990	Was	5.5
1991	Was	11.5
1992	Was	4.5
1993	Was	1
1994	SF	1
NFL	12	83

Marshall, Leonard

YEAR	TEAM	SACKS
1983	NYG	.5
1984	NYG	6.5
1985	NYG	15.5
1986	NYG	12
1987	NYG	8
1988	NYG	8
1989	NYG	9.5
1990	NYG	4.5
1991	NYG	11
1992	NYG	4
1993	NYJ	2
1994	Was	2
NFL	12	83.5

Martin, Doug

YEAR	TEAM	SACKS
1982	Min	**11.5**
1983	Min	13
1984	Min	1
1985	Min	4
1986	Min	9
1987	Min	9
1988	Min	3
NFL	8	50.5

Martin, Wayne

YEAR	TEAM	SACKS
1989	NO	2.5
1990	NO	4
1991	NO	3.5
1992	NO	15.5
1993	NO	5
1994	NO	10
1995	NO	**13**
1996	NO	11
1997	NO	10.5
1998	NO	3
1999	NO	4.5
NFL	11	82.5

Matthews, Clay

YEAR	TEAM	SACKS
1983	Cle	6
1984	Cle	12
1985	Cle	6
1986	Cle	1
1987	Cle	2.5
1988	Cle	6
1989	Cle	4
1990	Cle	3.5
1991	Cle	6.5
1992	Cle	9
1993	Cle	5.5
1994	Atl	1
1996	Atl	6.5
NFL	18	69.5

McCrary, Michael

YEAR	TEAM	SACKS
1993	Sea	4
1994	Sea	1.5
1995	Sea	1
1996	Sea	**13.5**
1997	Bal	9
1998	Bal	14.5
1999	Bal	11.5
2000	Bal	6.5
2001	Bal	7.5
2002	Bal	2
NFL	10	71

McGinest, Willie

YEAR	TEAM	SACKS
1994	NE	4.5
1995	NE	11
1996	NE	9.5
1997	NE	2
1998	NE	3.5
1999	NE	9
2000	NE	6
2001	NE	6
2002	NE	5.5
2003	NE	5.5
2004	NE	9.5
2005	NE	6
NFL	12	78

McGlockton, Chester

YEAR	TEAM	SACKS
1992	LARd	3
1993	LARd	7
1994	LARd	9.5
1995	Oak	7.5
1996	Oak	8
1997	Oak	4.5
1998	KC	1
1999	KC	1.5
2000	KC	4.5
2001	Den	1
2002	Den	2.5
2003	NYJ	1
NFL	12	51

McMichael, Steve

YEAR	TEAM	SACKS
1982	ChiB	2.5
1983	ChiB	8.5
1984	ChiB	10
1985	ChiB	8
1986	ChiB	8
1987	ChiB	7
1988	ChiB	11.5
1989	ChiB	7.5
1990	ChiB	4
1991	ChiB	9
1992	ChiB	10.5
1993	ChiB	6
1994	GB	2.5
NFL	14	95

Mecklenburg, Karl

YEAR	TEAM	SACKS
1983	Den	2
1984	Den	7
1985	Den	13
1986	Den	9.5
1987	Den	7
1988	Den	1
1989	Den	7.5
1990	Den	5
1991	Den	9
1992	Den	7.5
1993	Den	9
1994	Den	1.5
NFL	12	79

Millard, Keith

YEAR	TEAM	SACKS
1985	Min	11
1986	Min	10.5
1987	Min	3.5
1988	Min	8
1989	Min	18
1990	Min	2
1992	Sea	1
1993	Phi	4
NFL	8	58

Nunn, Freddie Joe

YEAR	TEAM	SACKS
1985	SL	3
1986	SL	7
1987	SL	11
1988	Phx	14
1989	Phx	5
1990	Phx	9
1991	Phx	7
1992	Phx	4
1993	Phx	6.5
1994	Ind	1
NFL	10	67.5

O'Neal, Leslie

YEAR	TEAM	SACKS
1986	SD	12.5
1988	SD	4
1989	SD	12.5
1990	SD	13.5
1991	SD	9
1992	SD	**17**
1993	SD	12
1994	SD	12.5
1995	SD	12.5
1996	SL	7
1997	SL	10
1998	KC	4.5
1999	KC	5.5
NFL	13	132.5

Paup, Bryce

YEAR	TEAM	SACKS
1991	GB	7.5
1992	GB	6.5
1993	GB	11
1994	GB	7.5
1995	Buf	**17.5**
1996	Buf	6
1997	Buf	9.5
1998	Jax	6.5
1999	Jax	1
2000	Min	2
NFL	10	75

Perry, Michael Dean

YEAR	TEAM	SACKS
1988	Cle	6
1989	Cle	7
1990	Cle	11.5
1991	Cle	8.5
1992	Cle	8.5
1993	Cle	6
1994	Cle	4
1995	Den	6
1996	Den	3.5
NFL	9	61

Pickel, Bill

YEAR	TEAM	SACKS
1983	LARd	6
1984	LARd	12.5
1985	LARd	12.5
1986	LARd	11.5
1987	LARd	1
1988	LARd	5
1989	LARd	3
1990	LARd	1.5
1991	NYJ	2
1992	NYJ	1
NFL	11	56

Pleasant, Anthony

YEAR	TEAM	SACKS
1990	Cle	3.5
1991	Cle	2.5
1992	Cle	4
1993	Cle	11
1994	Cle	4.5
1995	Cle	8
1996	Bal	4
1997	Atl	.5
1998	NYJ	6
1999	NYJ	2
2000	SF	2
2001	NE	6
2002	NE	3
2003	NE	1
NFL	14	58

Porcher, Robert

YEAR	TEAM	SACKS
1992	Det	1
1993	Det	8.5
1994	Det	3
1995	Det	5
1996	Det	10
1997	Det	12.5
1998	Det	11.5
1999	Det	15
2000	Det	8
2001	Det	11
2002	Det	5.5
2003	Det	4.5
NFL	12	95.5

Porter, Joey

YEAR	TEAM	SACKS
1999	Pit	2
2000	Pit	10.5
2001	Pit	9
2002	Pit	9
2003	Pit	5
2004	Pit	7
2005	Pit	10.5
NFL	7	53

Pryce, Trevor

YEAR	TEAM	SACKS
1997	Den	2
1998	Den	8.5
1999	Den	13
2000	Den	12
2001	Den	7
2002	Den	9
2003	Den	8.5
2005	Den	4
NFL	8	64

Randle, John

YEAR	TEAM	SACKS
1990	Min	1
1991	Min	9.5
1992	Min	11.5
1993	Min	12.5
1994	Min	**13.5**
1995	Min	10.5
1996	Min	11.5
1997	Min	**15.5**
1998	Min	10.5
1999	Min	10
2000	Min	8
2001	Sea	11
2002	Sea	7
2003	Sea	5.5
NFL	14	137.5

Rice, Simeon

YEAR	TEAM	SACKS
1996	Arz	12.5
1997	Arz	5
1998	Arz	10
1999	Arz	16.5
2000	Arz	7.5
2001	TB	11
2002	TB	**15.5**
2003	TB	15
2004	TB	12
2005	TB	14
NFL	10	119

Sapp, Warren

YEAR	TEAM	SACKS
1995	TB	3
1996	TB	9
1997	TB	10.5
1998	TB	7
1999	TB	12.5
2000	TB	16.5
2001	TB	6
2002	TB	7.5
2003	TB	5
2004	Oak	2.5
2005	Oak	5
NFL	11	84.5

Scroggins, Tracy

YEAR	TEAM	SACKS
1992	Det	7.5
1993	Det	8
1994	Det	2.5
1995	Det	9.5
1996	Det	2
1997	Det	7.5
1998	Det	6.5
1999	Det	8.5
2000	Det	6.5
2001	Det	2
NFL	10	60.5

Seau, Junior

YEAR	TEAM	SACKS
1990	SD	1
1991	SD	7
1992	SD	4.5
1994	SD	5.5
1995	SD	2
1996	SD	7
1997	SD	7
1998	SD	3.5
1999	SD	3.5
2000	SD	3.5
2001	SD	1
2002	SD	1.5
2003	Mia	3
2004	Mia	1
2005	Mia	1
NFL	16	52

Simmons, Clyde

YEAR	TEAM	SACKS
1986	Phi	2
1987	Phi	6
1988	Phi	8
1989	Phi	15.5
1990	Phi	7.5
1991	Phi	13
1992	Phi	**19**
1993	Phi	5
1994	Arz	6
1995	Arz	11
1996	Jax	7.5
1997	Jax	8.5
1998	Cin	5
1999	ChiB	7
2000	ChiB	.5
NFL	15	121.5

Sinclair, Michael

YEAR	TEAM	SACKS
1992	Sea	1
1993	Sea	8
1994	Sea	4.5
1995	Sea	5.5
1996	Sea	13
1997	Sea	12
1998	Sea	**16.5**
1999	Sea	6
2000	Sea	3.5
2001	Sea	3.5
NFL	10	73.5

Slade, Chris

YEAR	TEAM	SACKS
1993	NE	9
1994	NE	9.5
1995	NE	4
1996	NE	7
1997	NE	9
1998	NE	4
1999	NE	4.5
2000	NE	4
2001	Car	2.5
NFL	9	53.5

SMITH, ANTHONY

YEAR	TEAM	SACKS
1991	LARd	10.5
1992	LARd	13
1993	LARd	12.5
1994	LARd	6
1995	Oak	7
1996	Oak	2
1997	Oak	6.5
NFL	7	57.5

SMITH, BRUCE

YEAR	TEAM	SACKS
1985	Buf	6.5
1986	Buf	15
1987	Buf	12
1988	Buf	11
1989	Buf	13
1990	Buf	19
1991	Buf	1.5
1992	Buf	14
1993	Buf	14
1994	Buf	10
1995	Buf	10.5
1996	Buf	**13.5**
1997	Buf	**14**
1998	Buf	10
1999	Buf	7
2000	Was	10
2001	Was	5
2002	Was	9
2003	Was	5
NFL	19	200

SMITH, CHUCK

YEAR	TEAM	SACKS
1992	Atl	2
1993	Atl	3.5
1994	Atl	11
1995	Atl	5.5
1996	Atl	6
1997	Atl	12
1998	Atl	8.5
1999	Atl	10
NFL	8	58.5

SMITH, NEIL

YEAR	TEAM	SACKS
1988	KC	2.5
1989	KC	6.5
1990	KC	9.5
1991	KC	8
1992	KC	14.5
1993	KC	**15**
1994	KC	11.5
1995	KC	12
1996	KC	6
1997	Den	8.5
1998	Den	4
1999	Den	6.5
NFL	12	104.5

STRAHAN, MICHAEL

YEAR	TEAM	SACKS
1993	NYG	1
1994	NYG	4.5
1995	NYG	7.5
1996	NYG	5
1997	NYG	14
1998	NYG	15
1999	NYG	5.5
2000	NYG	9.5
2001	NYG	**22.5**
2002	NYG	11
2003	NYG	**18.5**
2004	NYG	4
2005	NYG	11.5
NFL	13	129.5

STUBBLEFIELD, DANA

YEAR	TEAM	SACKS
1993	SF	10.5
1994	SF	8.5
1995	SF	4.5
1996	SF	1
1997	SF	15
1998	Was	1.5
1999	Was	3
2000	Was	2.5
2001	SF	4
2002	SF	3
NFL	11	53.5

STUBBS, DANNY

YEAR	TEAM	SACKS
1988	SF	6
1989	SF	4.5
1990	Dal	7.5
1991	Dal	1
1991	Cin	3
1992	Cin	9
1993	Cin	5
1995	Phi	5.5
1996	Mia	9
1997	Mia	1
NFL	9	51.5

SWILLING, PAT

YEAR	TEAM	SACKS
1986	NO	4
1987	NO	10.5
1988	NO	7
1989	NO	16.5
1990	NO	11
1991	NO	**17**
1992	NO	10.5
1993	Det	6.5
1994	Det	3.5
1995	Oak	13
1996	Oak	6
1998	Oak	2
NFL	12	107.5

TAYLOR, JASON

YEAR	TEAM	SACKS
1997	Mia	5
1998	Mia	9
1999	Mia	2.5
2000	Mia	14.5
2001	Mia	8.5
2002	Mia	**18.5**
2003	Mia	13
2004	Mia	9.5
2005	Mia	12
NFL	9	92.5

TAYLOR, LAWRENCE

YEAR	TEAM	SACKS
1982	NYG	7.5
1983	NYG	9
1984	NYG	11.5
1985	NYG	13
1986	NYG	**20.5**
1987	NYG	12
1988	NYG	15.5
1989	NYG	15
1990	NYG	10.5
1991	NYG	7
1992	NYG	5
1993	NYG	6
NFL	13	132.5

THOMAS, DERRICK

YEAR	TEAM	SACKS
1989	KC	10
1990	KC	**20**
1991	KC	13.5
1992	KC	14.5
1993	KC	8
1994	KC	11
1995	KC	8
1996	KC	13
1997	KC	9.5
1998	KC	12
1999	KC	7
NFL	11	126.5

THOMAS, HENRY

YEAR	TEAM	SACKS
1987	Min	2.5
1988	Min	6
1989	Min	9
1990	Min	8.5
1991	Min	8
1992	Min	6
1993	Min	9
1994	Min	7
1995	Det	10.5
1996	Det	6
1997	NE	7
1998	NE	6.5
1999	NE	3
2000	NE	4.5
NFL	14	93.5

TIPPETT, ANDRE

YEAR	TEAM	SACKS
1983	NE	8.5
1984	NE	18.5
1985	NE	**16.5**
1986	NE	9.5
1987	NE	**12.5**
1988	NE	7
1990	NE	3.5
1991	NE	8.5
1992	NE	7
1993	NE	8.5
NFL	11	100

TOLBERT, TONY

YEAR	TEAM	SACKS
1989	Dal	2
1990	Dal	6
1991	Dal	7
1992	Dal	8.5
1993	Dal	7.5
1994	Dal	5.5
1995	Dal	5.5
1996	Dal	12
1997	Dal	5
NFL	9	59

TOWNSEND, GREG

YEAR	TEAM	SACKS
1983	LARd	10.5
1984	LARd	7
1985	LARd	10
1986	LARd	11.5
1987	LARd	8.5
1988	LARd	**11.5**
1989	LARd	10.5
1990	LARd	12.5
1991	LARd	13
1992	LARd	5
1993	LARd	7.5
1994	Phi	2
NFL	12	109.5

WARREN, FRANK

YEAR	TEAM	SACKS
1982	NO	1
1983	NO	2
1984	NO	4
1985	NO	5.5
1986	NO	7.5
1987	NO	6
1988	NO	1
1989	NO	9.5
1991	NO	7
1992	NO	4
1993	NO	1
1994	NO	4
NFL	13	52.5

WHITE, RANDY

YEAR	TEAM	SACKS
1982	Dal	2.5
1983	Dal	12.5
1984	Dal	12.5
1985	Dal	10.5
1986	Dal	6.5
1987	Dal	6
1988	Dal	1.5
NFL	12	52

WHITE, REGGIE

YEAR	TEAM	SACKS
1985	Phi	13
1986	Phi	18
1987	Phi	**21**
1988	Phi	**18**
1989	Phi	11
1990	Phi	14
1991	Phi	15
1992	Phi	14
1993	GB	**13**
1994	GB	8
1995	GB	12
1996	GB	8.5
1997	GB	11
1998	GB	**16**
2000	Car	5.5
NFL	15	198

WILKINSON, DAN

YEAR	TEAM	SACKS
1994	Cin	5.5
1995	Cin	8
1996	Cin	6.5
1997	Cin	5
1998	Was	7.5
1999	Was	8
2000	Was	3.5
2001	Was	4
2003	Det	2
2004	Det	1.5
2005	Det	3
NFL	11	54.5

WILLIAMS, ALFRED

YEAR	TEAM	SACKS
1991	Cin	3
1992	Cin	10
1993	Cin	4
1994	Cin	9.5
1995	SF	4.5
1996	Den	13
1997	Den	8.5
1998	Den	3
1999	Den	4
NFL	9	59.5

WILLIAMS, LEE

YEAR	TEAM	SACKS
1984	SD	1
1985	SD	9
1986	SD	15
1987	SD	8
1988	SD	11
1989	SD	**14**
1990	SD	7.5
1991	Hou	3
1992	Hou	11
1993	Hou	3
NFL	10	82.5

WILLIS, KEITH

YEAR	TEAM	SACKS
1982	Pit	1
1983	Pit	14
1984	Pit	5
1985	Pit	5.5
1986	Pit	12
1987	Pit	3
1989	Pit	6.5
1990	Pit	5
1991	Pit	7
NFL	9	59

YOUNG, BRYANT

YEAR	TEAM	SACKS
1994	SF	6
1995	SF	6
1996	SF	11.5
1997	SF	4
1998	SF	9.5
1999	SF	11
2000	SF	9.5
2001	SF	3.5
2002	SF	2
2003	SF	3.5
2004	SF	3
2005	SF	8
NFL	12	77.5

Aguiar, Louie

YEAR	TEAM	PNT	YDS	AVG(LG)	BLK	TB	RTYDS	NET	AVG	IN20
1991	NYJ	64	2521	39.4(61)	0	7	164	2217	34.6	14
1992	NYJ	73	2993	41.0(65)	0	3	189	2744	37.6	21
1993	NYJ	73	2806	38.4(71)	0	7	156	2510	34.4	21
1994	KC	85	3582	42.1(61)	0	7	**506**	2936	**34.5**	15
1995	KC	91	3990	43.8(65)	0	**12**	433	**3317**	36.5	**29**
1996	KC	88	3667	41.7(68)	0	10	492	2975	33.8	25
1997	KC	82	3465	42.3(65)	0	4	255	3130	38.2	**28**
1998	KC	75	3226	43.0(59)	1	5	513	2613	34.4	20
1999	GB	75	2954	39.4(64)	0	4	330	2544	33.9	20
2000	ChiB	52	2017	38.8(56)	0	4	121	1816	34.9	8
NFL	10	758	31221	41.2(71)	1	63	3159	26802	35.4	201

Albert, Frankie

YEAR	TEAM	PNT	YDS	AVG(LG)	BLK	TB	RTYDS	NET	AVG	IN20
1946	SF-A	54	2214	41.0	0	—	—	—	—	—
1947	SF-A	40	1759	44.0	1	—	—	—	—	—
1948	SF-A	35	1568	44.8	0	—	—	—	—	—
1949	SF-A	31	1495	**48.2**	0	—	—	—	—	—
1950	SF	37	1424	38.5(64)	1	—	—	—	—	—
1951	SF	34	1507	44.3(66)	0	—	—	—	—	—
1952	SF	68	2899	42.6(70)	0	—	—	—	—	—
AAFC	4	160	7036	44.0	1	—	—	—	—	—
NFL	3	139	5830	41.9(70)	1	—	—	—	—	—

Anderson, Donny

YEAR	TEAM	PNT	YDS	AVG(LG)	BLK	TB	RTYDS	NET	AVG	IN20
1966	GB	2	89	44.5(49)	0	—	—	—	—	—
1967	GB	65	2378	36.6(63)	1	—	—	—	—	—
1968	GB	59	2359	40.0(65)	0	—	—	—	—	—
1969	GB	58	2329	40.2(58)	0	—	—	—	—	—
1970	GB	81	3302	40.8(62)	0	—	—	—	—	—
1971	GB	50	2022	40.4(58)	0	—	—	—	—	—
1972	SL	72	2847	39.5(61)	0	—	—	—	—	—
NFL	7	387	15326	39.6(65)	1	—	—	—	—	—

Araguz, Leo

YEAR	TEAM	PNT	YDS	AVG(LG)	BLK	TB	RTYDS	NET	AVG	IN20
1996	Oak	13	534	41.1(52)	0	2	45	449	34.5	4
1997	Oak	93	**4189**	45.0(63)	0	6	431	**3638**	**39.1**	**28**
1998	Oak	98	**4256**	43.4(64)	0	10	**787**	3269	**33.4**	29
1999	Oak	76	3045	40.1(56)	1	4	479	2486	32.3	25
2001	Det	17	713	41.9(55)	0	4	55	578	34.0	6
2003	Min	7	271	38.7(44)	0	0	77	194	27.7	1
2005	Sea	18	723	40.2(53)	0	1	78	625	34.7	4
NFL	7	322	13731	42.6(64)	1	27	1952	11239	34.9	97

Arnold, Jim

YEAR	TEAM	PNT	YDS	AVG(LG)	BLK	TB	RTYDS	NET	AVG	IN20
1983	KC	93	3710	39.9(64)	0	6	559	3031	**32.6**	21
1984	KC	98	**4397**	**44.9(63)**	0	**13**	461	**3676**	**37.5**	22
1985	KC	93	3827	41.2(62)	**2**	11	530	3077	**32.4**	15
1986	Det	36	1533	42.6(60)	1	4	267	1186	**32.1**	7
1987	Det	46	2007	43.6(60)	0	4	104	1823	39.6	17
1988	Det	97	**4110**	**42.4(69)**	0	7	**483**	3487	35.9	22
1989	Det	82	**3538**	43.1(64)	1	9	373	**2985**	36.0	14
1990	Det	63	2560	40.6(59)	0	5	233	2227	35.3	10
1991	Det	75	3092	41.2(63)	0	5	340	2652	35.4	27
1992	Det	65	2846	43.8(71)	1	10	356	2290	34.7	12
1993	Det	72	3207	**44.5(68)**	0	9	377	2650	36.8	15
1994	Mia	46	1810	39.3(53)	0	4	189	1541	33.5	14
NFL	12	866	36637	42.3(71)	5	87	4272	30625	35.4	196

Baker, Jason

YEAR	TEAM	PNT	YDS	AVG(LG)	BLK	TB	RTYDS	NET	AVG	IN20
2001	SF	69	2813	40.8(64)	0	4	290	2443	35.4	21
2002	Phi	13	445	34.2(44)	0	1	37	388	29.8	2
2002	SF	42	1688	40.2(51)	0	3	282	1346	32.0	12
2003	KC	80	3156	39.5(68)	1	7	327	2689	33.2	21
2004	Den	15	591	39.4(48)	0	1	55	516	34.4	7
2004	KC	9	340	37.8(52)	0	0	98	242	26.9	3
2005	Car	72	3118	43.3(59)	0	4	235	2803	38.9	23
NFL	5	300	12151	40.5(68)	1	20	1324	10427	34.8	89

Baker, Sam

YEAR	TEAM	PNT	YDS	AVG(LG)	BLK	TB	RTYDS	NET	AVG	IN20
1953	Was	17	614	36.1(51)	0	—	—	—	—	—
1956	Was	59	2510	42.5(56)	0	—	—	—	—	—
1957	Was	50	2139	42.8(63)	0	—	—	—	—	—
1958	Was	48	2181	**45.4(64)**	0	—	—	—	—	—
1959	Was	49	2229	45.5(66)	0	—	—	—	—	—
1960	Cle	55	2309	42.0(64)	0	—	—	—	—	—
1961	Cle	53	2296	43.3(62)	0	—	—	—	—	—
1962	Dal	57	2589	45.4(72)	0	—	—	—	—	—
1963	Dal	71	3138	44.2(64)	0	—	—	—	—	—
1964	Phi	49	2073	42.3(61)	**1**	—	—	—	—	—
1965	Phi	37	1551	41.9(60)	0	—	—	—	—	—
1966	Phi	42	1726	41.1(63)	0	—	—	—	—	—
1967	Phi	61	2335	38.3(53)	1	—	—	—	—	—
1968	Phi	55	2248	40.9(57)	0	—	—	—	—	—
NFL	14	703	29938	42.6(72)	2	—	—	—	—	—

Barker, Bryan

YEAR	TEAM	PNT	YDS	AVG(LG)	BLK	TB	RTYDS	NET	AVG	IN20
1990	KC	64	2479	38.7(56)	0	1	324	2135	33.4	16
1991	KC	57	2303	40.4(57)	0	6	190	1993	35.0	11
1992	KC	75	3245	43.3(65)	1	**13**	300	2685	35.3	16
1993	KC	76	3240	42.6(59)	1	8	352	2728	35.4	19
1994	Phi	66	2696	40.8(67)	0	7	158	2398	36.3	20
1995	Jax	82	3591	43.8(63)	0	5	323	3168	38.6	19
1996	Jax	69	3016	43.7(62)	0	8	400	2456	35.6	16
1997	Jax	66	2964	44.9(64)	0	8	241	2563	38.8	27
1998	Jax	85	3824	45.0(65)	0	11	332	3272	38.5	28
1999	Jax	78	3260	41.8(**83**)	0	6	259	2881	36.9	32
2000	Jax	76	3194	42.0(65)	0	5	478	2616	34.4	29
2001	Was	90	3747	41.6(59)	0	9	434	3133	34.8	27
2002	Was	48	1924	40.1(63)	0	5	386	1438	**30.0**	13
2003	Was	84	3377	40.2(**69**)	0	5	393	2884	34.3	24
2004	GB	66	2644	40.1(64)	0	7	301	2203	33.4	16
2005	SL	50	2137	42.7(63)	0	4	275	1782	35.6	13
NFL	16	1132	47641	42.1(83)	2	108	5146	40335	35.6	326

Barnhardt, Tommy

YEAR	TEAM	PNT	YDS	AVG(LG)	BLK	TB	RTYDS	NET	AVG	IN20
1987	NO	11	483	43.9(52)	0	1	64	399	36.3	4
1987	ChiB	6	236	39.3(50)	0	0	36	200	33.3	2
1988	Was	15	628	41.9(55)	0	2	74	514	34.3	1
1989	NO	55	2179	39.6(56)	0	4	174	1925	35.0	17
1990	NO	70	2990	42.7(65)	1	6	302	2568	36.2	20
1991	NO	86	**3743**	43.5(61)	1	10	470	**3073**	35.3	20
1992	NO	67	2947	44.0(62)	0	10	218	2529	37.7	19
1993	NO	77	3356	43.6(58)	0	6	348	2888	37.5	26
1994	NO	67	2920	43.6(57)	0	9	495	2245	33.5	14
1995	Car	95	**3906**	41.1(54)	0	11	342	**3344**	**35.2**	27
1996	TB	70	3015	43.1(62)	1	4	248	2687	37.8	24
1997	TB	29	1304	45.0(61)	0	3	110	1134	39.1	12
1998	TB	81	3340	41.2(55)	0	9	302	2858	35.3	19
1999	NO	82	3262	39.8(52)	0	5	283	2879	35.1	14
2000	Was	79	3160	40.0(53)	0	5	342	2718	34.4	23
NFL	14	890	37469	42.1(65)	3	85	3808	31961	35.9	242

Bateman, Marv

YEAR	TEAM	PNT	YDS	AVG(LG)	BLK	TB	RTYDS	NET	AVG	IN20
1972	Dal	51	1949	38.2(61)	0	—	—	—	—	—
1973	Dal	55	2290	41.6(62)	2	—	—	—	—	—
1974	Dal	33	1218	**36.9(55)**	0	—	—	—	—	—
1974	Buf	34	1494	**43.9(66)**	0	—	—	—	—	—
1975	Buf	61	2536	41.6(**74**)	2	—	—	—	—	—
1976	Buf	86	**3678**	**42.8(78)**	1	14	**878**	2520	**29.0**	16
1977	Buf	81	3229	39.9(**75**)	2	10	604	2425	29.2	14
NFL	6	401	16394	40.9(78)	7	24	1482	4945	29.6	30

Baugh, Sammy

YEAR	TEAM	PNT	YDS	AVG(LG)	BLK	TB	RTYDS	NET	AVG	IN20
1939	Was	26	998	38.4(69)	1	—	—	—	—	—
1940	Was	35	1799	**51.4(85)**	**1**	—	—	—	—	—
1941	Was	30	1462	**48.7(75)**	0	—	—	—	—	—
1942	Was	37	1785	**48.2(74)**	0	—	—	—	—	—
1943	Was	50	**2295**	**45.9(81)**	**3**	—	—	—	—	—
1944	Was	44	1787	40.6(**76**)	**1**	—	—	—	—	—
1945	Was	33	1429	**43.3(57)**	0	—	—	—	—	—
1946	Was	33	1488	45.1(60)	0	—	—	—	—	—
1947	Was	35	1528	**43.7(67)**	2	—	—	—	—	—
1949	Was	1	53	53.0(53)	0	—	—	—	—	—
1950	Was	9	352	39.1(58)	1	—	—	—	—	—
1951	Was	4	221	55.3(53)	0	—	—	—	—	—
1952	Was	1	48	48.0(48)	0	—	—	—	—	—
NFL	13	338	15245	45.1(85)	9	—	—	—	—	—

Bennett, Darren

YEAR	TEAM	PNT	YDS	AVG(LG)	BLK	TB	RTYDS	NET	AVG	IN20
1995	SD	72	3221	44.7(66)	0	8	429	2632	36.6	28
1996	SD	87	3967	45.6(66)	0	6	612	3235	37.2	23
1997	SD	89	3972	44.6(66)	1	8	416	3396	37.7	26
1998	SD	95	4174	43.9(65)	0	8	515	3499	36.8	27
1999	SD	89	3910	43.9(60)	0	6	343	3447	38.7	32
2000	SD	92	4248	**46.2(66)**	0	10	722	3326	36.2	23
2001	SD	78	3308	42.4(62)	0	4	346	2882	36.9	25
2002	SD	87	3540	40.7(63)	**2**	6	369	3051	34.3	31
2003	SD	82	3436	41.9(56)	0	3	409	2967	36.2	28
2004	Min	57	2240	39.3(61)	0	3	169	2011	35.3	18
2005	Min	8	300	37.5(53)	0	0	25	275	34.4	1
NFL	11	836	36316	43.4(66)	3	62	4355	30721	36.7	262

Berger, Mitch

YEAR	TEAM	PNT	YDS	AVG(LG)	BLK	TB	RTYDS	NET	AVG	IN20
1994	Phi	25	951	38.0(57)	0	2	128	783	31.3	8
1996	Min	88	3616	41.1(63)	**2**	6	**577**	2919	32.4	26
1997	Min	73	3133	42.9(65)	0	5	545	2488	34.1	22
1998	Min	55	2458	44.7(67)	0	5	325	2033	37.0	17
1999	Min	61	2769	**45.4(75)**	0	9	246	2343	38.4	18
2000	Min	62	2773	**44.7(60)**	0	11	310	2243	36.2	16
2001	Min	47	2046	43.5(67)	0	10	302	1544	**32.9**	10
2002	SL	72	3020	41.9(64)	0	10	463	2357	32.7	26
2003	NO	71	3144	44.3(59)	1	5	294	2750	38.2	28
2004	NO	85	3704	43.6(63)	0	4	310	3314	39.0	28
2005	NO	71	3066	43.2(**69**)	0	3	260	2746	38.7	28
NFL	11	710	30680	43.2(75)	3	70	3760	25520	35.9	227

Beverly, David

YEAR	TEAM	PNT	YDS	AVG(LG)	BLK	TB	RTYDS	NET	AVG	IN20
1974	Hou	79	3100	39.2(**69**)	0	—	—	—	—	—
1975	Hou	12	459	38.3(45)	0	—	—	—	—	—
1975	GB	66	2482	37.6(55)	0	—	—	—	—	—
1976	GB	83	3074	37.0(60)	1	5	268	2706	32.2	14
1977	GB	85	3391	39.9(59)	1	9	311	2900	33.7	16
1978	GB	106	3759	35.5(57)	0	9	286	3293	31.1	20
1979	GB	69	2785	40.4(65)	0	4	305	2400	34.8	11
1980	GB	86	3294	38.3(55)	0	6	342	2832	32.9	18
NFL	7	586	22344	38.1(69)	2	33	1512	14131	32.9	79

Bidwell, Josh

YEAR	TEAM	PNT	YDS	AVG(LG)	BLK	TB	RTYDS	NET	AVG	IN20
2000	GB	78	3003	38.5(53)	0	5	205	2698	34.6	22
2001	GB	82	3485	42.5(68)	0	10	288	2997	36.5	21
2002	GB	79	3296	41.7(57)	0	6	357	2819	35.7	26
2003	GB	69	2875	41.7(60)	0	7	316	2419	35.1	16
2004	TB	82	3472	42.3(60)	1	7	279	3053	36.8	23
2005	TB	90	4101	**45.6(61)**	0	**13**	466	3375	37.5	24
NFL	6	480	20232	42.2(68)	1	48	1911	17361	36.2	132

YEAR	TEAM	PNT	YDS	AVG (LG)	BLK	TB	RTYDS	NET	AVG	IN20
Birdsong, Carl										
1981	SL	69	2883	41.8(**75**)	0	8	276	2447	35.5	18
1982	SL	54	2365	**43.8(65)**	0	**6**	288	1957	36.2	8
1983	SL	85	3529	41.5(59)	0	7	307	3082	36.3	14
1984	SL	67	2594	38.7(59)	1	8	239	2195	32.3	19
1985	SL	85	3545	41.7(67)	**2**	8	456	2929	33.7	20
NFL	5	360	14916	41.4(75)	3	37	1566	12610	35.0	79
Black, Mike										
1983	Det	71	2911	41.0(60)	1	9	302	2429	33.7	17
1984	Det	76	3164	41.6(63)	0	8	516	2488	32.7	13
1985	Det	73	3054	41.8(60)	0	5	420	2534	34.7	17
1986	Det	46	1819	39.5(47)	1	5	250	1469	31.3	11
1987	Det	6	233	38.8(47)	0	0	12	221	36.8	1
NFL	5	272	11181	41.1(63)	2	27	1500	9141	33.6	59
Blanchard, Tom										
1971	NYG	66	2681	40.6(57)	0	—	—	—	—	—
1972	NYG	47	2006	42.7(58)	1	—	—	—	—	—
1973	NYG	56	2347	41.9(62)	1	—	—	—	—	—
1974	NO	88	3704	**42.1(71)**	0	—	—	—	—	—
1975	NO	92	**3776**	41.0(61)	**3**	—	—	—	—	—
1976	NO	101	3974	39.3(63)	0	5	**742**	3132	**31.0**	14
1977	NO	82	3474	**42.4(66)**	2	11	604	2650	**31.5**	11
1978	NO	84	3532	42.0(61)	**2**	10	539	2793	32.5	14
1979	TB	93	3679	39.6(58)	**2**	**25**	270	2909	30.6	14
1980	TB	88	3722	42.3(62)	**1**	12	529	2953	33.2	18
1981	TB	22	899	40.9(58)	0	2	259	600	27.3	4
NFL	11	819	33794	41.3(71)	12	65	2943	15037	32.0	75
Bracken, Don										
1985	GB	26	1052	40.5(54)	0	2	146	866	33.3	1
1986	GB	55	2203	40.1(63)	2	5	235	1868	32.8	6
1987	GB	72	2947	40.9(65)	1	5	354	2493	34.2	13
1988	GB	85	3287	38.7(62)	1	12	314	2733	31.8	20
1989	GB	66	2682	40.6(63)	0	**11**	416	2046	31.0	17
1990	GB	64	2431	38.0(59)	1	2	266	2125	32.7	17
1992	LARm	76	3122	41.1(59)	0	4	**522**	2520	33.2	20
1993	LARm	17	651	38.3(51)	0	0	86	565	33.2	3
NFL	8	461	18375	39.9(65)	5	41	2339	15216	33.0	97
Bragg, Mike										
1968	Was	76	3288	43.3(64)	**2**	—	—	—	—	—
1969	Was	70	2957	42.2(63)	**2**	—	—	—	—	—
1970	Was	61	2493	40.9(66)	1	—	—	—	—	—
1971	Was	58	2348	40.5(59)	1	—	—	—	—	—
1972	Was	59	2273	38.5(62)	0	—	—	—	—	—
1973	Was	64	2581	40.3(61)	0	—	—	—	—	—
1974	Was	74	2823	38.1(57)	1	—	—	—	—	—
1975	Was	72	2924	40.6(63)	0	—	—	—	—	—
1976	Was	90	3503	38.9(56)	0	11	323	2960	32.9	15
1977	Was	91	3502	38.5(56)	0	4	228	3194	35.1	**29**
1978	Was	103	4056	39.4(56)	1	10	328	3528	33.9	23
1979	Was	78	2998	38.4(**74**)	0	10	135	2663	34.1	12
1980	Bal	82	3203	39.1(59)	**2**	6	357	2726	32.5	22
NFL	13	978	38949	39.8(74)	10	41	1371	15071	33.9	101
Brown, Ed										
1954	ChiB	18	684	38.0(60)	0	—	—	—	—	—
1955	ChiB	44	1766	40.1(59)	1	—	—	—	—	—
1956	ChiB	42	1644	39.1(53)	**1**	—	—	—	—	—
1957	ChiB	34	1365	40.1(62)	1	—	—	—	—	—
1958	ChiB	27	1140	42.2(57)	0	—	—	—	—	—
1959	ChiB	64	2634	41.2(66)	0	—	—	—	—	—
1960	ChiB	56	2231	39.8(65)	**2**	—	—	—	—	—
1961	ChiB	58	2448	42.2(69)	0	—	—	—	—	—
1962	Pit	60	2400	40.0(78)	0	—	—	—	—	—
1963	Pit	57	2256	39.6(57)	0	—	—	—	—	—
1964	Pit	31	1346	43.4(54)	0	—	—	—	—	—
1965	Bal	2	80	40.0(40)	0	—	—	—	—	—
NFL	12	493	19994	40.6(78)	5	—	—	—	—	—
Buford, Maury										
1982	SD	21	868	41.3(71)	**2**	3	86	722	31.4	5
1983	SD	63	2763	43.9(60)	0	8	299	2304	36.6	13
1984	SD	66	2773	42.0(60)	0	3	399	2314	35.1	11
1985	ChiB	68	2870	42.2(69)	1	**14**	203	2387	34.6	18
1986	ChiB	69	2850	41.3(59)	1	8	110	2580	36.9	20
1988	NYG	73	3012	41.3(66)	2	10	296	2516	33.5	13
1989	ChiB	72	2844	39.5(60)	0	9	262	2402	33.4	21
1990	ChiB	76	3073	40.4(59)	**2**	7	322	2611	33.5	22
1991	ChiB	69	2814	40.8(64)	1	8	205	2449	35.0	13
NFL	9	577	23867	41.4(71)	9	70	2182	20285	35.2	136
Burk, Adrian										
1950	Bal	81	**3243**	40.0(68)	1	—	—	—	—	—
1951	Phi	67	2646	39.5(60)	0	—	—	—	—	—
1952	Phi	83	3335	40.2(68)	**2**	—	—	—	—	—
1953	Phi	41	1765	43.0(66)	0	—	—	—	—	—
1954	Phi	73	2918	40.0(58)	0	—	—	—	—	—
1955	Phi	61	2615	42.9(**75**)	0	—	—	—	—	—
1956	Phi	68	**2843**	41.8(62)	**1**	—	—	—	—	—
NFL	7	474	19365	40.9(75)	4	—	—	—	—	—
Camarillo, Rich										
1981	NE	47	1959	41.7(**75**)	0	9	209	1570	33.4	12
1982	NE	49	**2140**	43.7(**76**)	0	5	191	**1849**	**37.7**	10
1983	NE	81	3615	44.6(**70**)	0	**11**	392	3003	37.1	25
1984	NE	48	2020	42.1(61)	0	7	214	1666	34.7	12
1985	NE	92	**3953**	43.0(**75**)	0	13	**598**	3095	33.6	16
1986	NE	89	3746	42.1(64)	**3**	7	565	3041	33.1	16
1987	NE	62	2489	40.1(73)	1	8	333	1996	31.7	14
1988	LARm	40	1579	39.5(57)	0	2	145	1394	34.9	11
1989	Phx	76	3298	**43.4(58)**	0	6	330	2848	37.5	21
1990	Phx	67	2865	42.8(63)	0	5	258	2507	37.4	16
1991	Phx	76	3445	45.3(60)	1	7	313	2992	38.9	19
1992	Phx	54	2317	42.9(73)	0	2	141	2136	39.6	23
1993	Phx	73	3189	43.7(61)	0	8	267	2762	37.8	23
1994	Hou	96	**4115**	42.9(58)	0	9	438	**3497**	36.4	**35**
1995	Hou	77	3165	41.1(60)	**1**	8	288	2717	34.8	26
NFL	15	1027	43895	42.7(76)	6	107	4682	37073	36.1	279
Carrell, Duane										
1974	Dal	40	1591	39.8(59)	0	—	—	—	—	—
1975	LARm	73	2874	39.4(57)	0	—	—	—	—	—
1976	NYJ	81	3218	39.7(72)	0	6	458	2640	32.6	13
1977	SL	49	1757	35.9(56)	0	4	123	1554	31.7	11
1977	NYJ	14	557	39.8(56)	0	1	147	390	27.9	2
NFL	4	257	9997	38.9(72)	0	11	728	4584	31.8	26
Cater, Greg										
1980	Buf	73	2828	38.7(61)	1	**16**	204	2304	31.1	12
1981	Buf	80	3175	39.7(71)	0	12	220	2715	33.9	16
1982	Buf	35	1328	37.9(61)	0	1	30	1278	36.5	13
1983	Buf	89	3533	39.7(60)	0	7	403	2990	33.6	24
1986	SL	61	2271	37.2(52)	1	4	130	2061	33.2	16
1987	SL	39	1470	37.7(68)	1	2	204	1226	30.7	10
NFL	6	377	14605	38.7(71)	3	42	1191	12574	33.4	91
Chandler, Don										
1956	NYG	59	2473	41.9(63)	0	—	—	—	—	—
1957	NYG	60	2673	**44.6(61)**	0	—	—	—	—	—
1958	NYG	65	**2859**	44.0(**67**)	0	—	—	—	—	—
1959	NYG	55	2565	46.6(62)	0	—	—	—	—	—
1960	NYG	31	1256	40.5(58)	0	—	—	—	—	—
1961	NYG	68	2984	43.9(66)	**2**	—	—	—	—	—
1962	NYG	55	2233	40.6(65)	**2**	—	—	—	—	—
1963	NYG	59	2648	44.9(64)	0	—	—	—	—	—
1964	NYG	73	3328	45.6(74)	0	—	—	—	—	—
1965	GB	74	3176	42.9(**90**)	0	—	—	—	—	—
1966	GB	60	2452	40.9(58)	0	—	—	—	—	—
1967	GB	1	31	31.0(31)	0	—	—	—	—	—
NFL	12	660	28678	43.5(90)	4	—	—	—	—	—
Cockroft, Don										
1968	Cle	61	2297	37.7(59)	0	—	—	—	—	—
1969	Cle	57	2138	37.5(55)	1	—	—	—	—	—
1970	Cle	71	3023	42.6(71)	**1**	—	—	—	—	—
1971	Cle	62	2508	40.5(59)	**2**	—	—	—	—	—
1972	Cle	81	**3498**	43.2(65)	0	—	—	—	—	—
1973	Cle	82	3321	40.5(71)	1	—	—	—	—	—
1974	Cle	90	**3643**	40.5(64)	0	—	—	—	—	—
1975	Cle	82	3317	40.5(67)	1	—	—	—	—	—
1976	Cle	64	2487	38.9(51)	**3**	4	503	1904	28.4	9
1977	Cle	1	30	30.0(30)	0	1	0	10	10.0	0
NFL	10	651	26262	40.3(71)	9	5	503	1914	29.4	9
Coleman, Greg										
1977	Cle	61	2389	39.2(58)	0	2	558	1791	**29.4**	**23**
1978	Min	51	1991	39.0(61)	1	4	321	1590	30.6	12
1979	Min	90	3551	39.5(70)	1	9	354	3017	33.2	23
1980	Min	81	3139	38.8(65)	0	8	259	2720	33.6	20
1981	Min	88	3646	41.4(73)	0	11	399	3027	34.4	17
1982	Min	58	2384	41.1(67)	0	**6**	176	**2088**	**36.0**	7
1983	Min	91	3780	41.5(65)	0	8	297	**3323**	36.5	28
1984	Min	82	3473	42.4(62)	0	2	435	2998	36.6	16
1985	Min	67	2867	42.8(62)	0	4	328	2459	36.7	12
1986	Min	67	2774	41.4(69)	0	4	353	2341	34.9	15
1987	Min	45	1786	39.7(54)	1	3	323	1403	30.5	5
1988	Was	39	1505	38.6(53)	0	3	305	1140	**29.2**	8
NFL	12	820	33285	40.6(73)	3	64	4108	27897	34.0	186
Collins, Gary										
1962	Cle	45	1926	42.8(64)	0	—	—	—	—	—
1963	Cle	54	2160	40.0(**73**)	0	—	—	—	—	—
1964	Cle	48	2016	42.0(58)	0	—	—	—	—	—
1965	Cle	65	3035	**46.7(71)**	0	—	—	—	—	—
1966	Cle	57	2223	39.0(60)	0	—	—	—	—	—
1967	Cle	57	2078	36.5(52)	**2**	—	—	—	—	—
1968	Cle	2	52	26.0(28)	0	—	—	—	—	—
1969	Cle	3	112	37.3(59)	0	—	—	—	—	—
1971	Cle	5	162	32.4(42)	0	—	—	—	—	—
NFL	9	336	13764	41.0(73)	2	—	—	—	—	—
Colquitt, Craig										
1978	Pit	66	2642	40.0(58)	0	4	239	2323	35.2	14
1979	Pit	68	2733	40.2(61)	0	8	276	2297	33.8	19
1980	Pit	61	2483	40.7(54)	0	5	217	2166	35.5	13
1981	Pit	84	3641	43.3(74)	0	**16**	358	2963	35.3	5
1983	Pit	80	3352	41.9(58)	0	7	418	2794	34.9	20
1984	Pit	70	2883	41.2(62)	0	5	351	2432	34.7	21
1987	Ind	2	61	30.5(33)	1	0	7	54	18.0	0
NFL	7	431	17795	41.3(74)	1	45	1866	15029	34.9	92
Connell, Mike										
1978	SF	96	3583	37.3(59)	1	8	356	3067	31.6	15
1980	Was	85	3331	39.2(57)	0	7	351	2840	33.4	11

YEAR	TEAM	PNT	YDS	AVG (LG)	BLK	TB	RTYDS	NET	AVG	IN20
1981	Was	73	2923	40.0(57)	0	5	388	2435	33.4	13
NFL	3	254	9837	38.7(59)	1	20	1095	8342	32.8	39
COX, STEVE										
1981	Cle	68	2884	42.4(66)	**2**	12	253	2391	34.2	11
1982	Cle	48	1877	39.1(52)	1	6	216	1541	31.4	11
1984	Cle	74	3213	43.4(69)	**2**	8	489	2564	33.7	16
1985	Was	52	2175	41.8(57)	0	13	228	1687	32.4	14
1986	Was	75	3271	43.6(58)	0	**16**	220	2731	36.4	21
1987	Was	63	2571	40.8(**77**)	1	7	193	2238	35.0	14
1988	Was	6	221	36.8(55)	1	1	44	157	22.4	0
NFL	7	386	16212	42.0(77)	7	63	1643	13309	34.5	87
DAVIDSON, COTTON										
1954	Bal	72	2680	37.2(55)	**1**	—	—	—	—	—
1957	Bal	47	1664	35.4(56)	0	—	—	—	—	—
1960	DalT-A	58	2287	39.4(66)	0	—	—	—	—	—
1961	DalT-A	62	2479	40.0(62)	1	—	—	—	—	—
1962	Oak-A	38	1452	38.2(64)	**1**	—	—	—	—	—
1962	DalT-A	3	117	39.0(47)	**0**	—	—	—	—	—
NFL	5	280	10679	38.1(66)	3	—	—	—	—	—
DAVIS, TOMMY										
1959	SF	59	2694	45.7(**71**)	0	—	—	—	—	—
1960	SF	62	2737	44.1(**74**)	0	—	—	—	—	—
1961	SF	50	2269	45.4(67)	0	—	—	—	—	—
1962	SF	48	2188	**45.6(82)**	0	—	—	—	—	—
1963	SF	73	3311	45.4(64)	**2**	—	—	—	—	—
1964	SF	79	3599	45.6(68)	0	—	—	—	—	—
1965	SF	54	2471	45.8(65)	0	—	—	—	—	—
1966	SF	63	2609	41.4(60)	0	—	—	—	—	—
1969	SF	23	955	41.5(55)	0	—	—	—	—	—
NFL	9	511	22833	44.7(82)	2	—	—	—	—	—
DILTS, BUCKY										
1977	Den	90	**3525**	39.2(63)	0	5	397	**3028**	**33.6**	19
1978	Den	96	3494	36.4(73)	0	6	226	3148	**32.8**	23
1979	Bal	99	3657	36.9(53)	2	5	296	3261	**32.3**	21
NFL	3	285	10676	37.5(73)	2	16	919	9437	33.1	63
DONNELLY, RICK										
1985	Atl	59	2574	**43.6(68)**	0	5	260	2214	37.5	18
1986	Atl	78	3421	43.9(**71**)	1	9	477	2764	35.0	19
1987	Atl	61	2686	**44.0(62)**	**2**	**8**	501	2025	32.1	9
1988	Atl	98	3920	40.0(61)	0	6	297	**3503**	**35.7**	27
1990	Sea	67	2722	40.6(54)	0	**8**	254	2308	34.4	18
1991	Sea	13	505	38.8(57)	0	1	46	439	33.8	1
NFL	6	376	15828	42.1(71)	3	37	1835	13253	35.2	92
EISCHEID, MIKE										
1966	Oak-A	65	2703	41.6(56)	1	—	—	—	—	—
1967	Oak-A	76	3364	44.3(62)	**1**	—	—	—	—	—
1968	Oak-A	64	2788	43.6(72)	0	—	—	—	—	—
1969	Oak-A	69	2944	42.7(58)	0	—	—	—	—	—
1970	Oak	79	3121	39.5(57)	**1**	—	—	—	—	—
1971	Oak	11	461	41.9(57)	0	—	—	—	—	—
1972	Min	62	2651	42.8(61)	1	—	—	—	—	—
1973	Min	66	2628	39.8(57)	0	—	—	—	—	—
1974	Min	73	2636	36.1(50)	1	—	—	—	—	—
NFL	9	565	23296	41.2(72)	5	—	—	—	—	—
ERXLEBEN, RUSSELL										
1979	NO	4	148	37.0(40)	0	0	22	126	31.5	1
1980	NO	89	3499	39.3(57)	0	3	490	2949	33.1	23
1981	NO	66	2672	40.5(60)	0	6	282	2270	34.4	11
1982	NO	46	1976	43.0(60)	0	**6**	239	1617	35.2	6
1983	NO	74	3034	41.0(60)	0	9	571	2283	**30.9**	10
1987	Det	1	52	52.0(52)	0	0	0	52	52.0	0
NFL	6	280	11381	40.6(60)	0	24	1604	9297	33.2	51
FAGAN, JULIAN										
1970	NO	77	3269	**42.5(64)**	**2**	—	—	—	—	—
1971	NO	77	3188	41.4(**64**)	0	—	—	—	—	—
1972	NO	71	**2899**	40.8(**71**)	1	—	—	—	—	—
1973	NYJ	74	2744	37.1(58)	2	—	—	—	—	—
NFL	4	299	12100	40.5(71)	5	—	—	—	—	—
FEAGLES, JEFF										
1988	NE	91	3482	38.3(**74**)	0	8	217	3105	**34.1**	24
1989	NE	63	2392	38.0(64)	1	2	346	2006	31.3	13
1990	Phi	72	3026	42.0(60)	**2**	3	338	2628	35.5	20
1991	Phi	87	3640	41.8(**77**)	1	**11**	431	2989	**34.0**	**29**
1992	Phi	82	**3459**	42.2(68)	0	7	295	**3024**	**36.9**	**26**
1993	Phi	83	3323	40.0(60)	0	4	311	2932	35.3	31
1994	Arz	98	**3997**	40.8(54)	0	10	270	**3527**	**36.0**	**33**
1995	Arz	72	3150	43.8(60)	0	8	242	2748	38.2	20
1996	Arz	76	3328	43.8(68)	1	6	403	2805	36.4	23
1997	Arz	91	4028	44.3(62)	1	10	441	3387	36.8	24
1998	Sea	81	3568	44.0(59)	0	12	369	2959	36.5	27
1999	Sea	84	3425	40.8(59)	0	5	370	2955	35.2	34
2000	Sea	74	2960	40.0(57)	**1**	2	151	2769	36.9	24
2001	Sea	85	3730	43.9(68)	1	7	462	3128	36.4	26
2002	Sea	61	2542	41.7(58)	0	4	202	2260	37.0	22
2003	NYG	90	3641	40.5(59)	1	6	432	3089	33.9	**31**
2004	NYG	74	3069	41.5(55)	**2**	4	356	2633	34.6	23
2005	NYG	73	3070	42.1(56)	0	3	309	2701	37.0	26
NFL	18	1437	59830	41.6(77)	11	112	5945	51645	35.9	456

YEAR	TEAM	PNT	YDS	AVG (LG)	BLK	TB	RTYDS	NET	AVG	IN20
FRASER, JIM										
1962	Den-A	55	2400	**43.6(75)**	**1**	—	—	—	—	—
1963	Den-A	81	**3596**	**44.4(66)**	**3**	—	—	—	—	—
1964	Den-A	73	3225	**44.2(67)**	1	—	—	—	—	—
1965	KC-A	3	81	27.0(37)	0	—	—	—	—	—
1966	Bos-A	55	2044	37.2(68)	**2**	—	—	—	—	—
1968	NO	11	391	35.5(56)	0	—	—	—	—	—
NFL	6	278	11737	42.2(75)	7	—	—	—	—	—
FULHAGE, SCOTT										
1987	Cin	52	2168	41.7(58)	0	5	216	1852	35.6	10
1988	Cin	44	1672	38.0(53)	2	5	220	1352	29.4	13
1989	Atl	84	3472	41.3(65)	1	9	460	2832	**33.3**	**24**
1990	Atl	70	2913	41.6(59)	0	4	314	2519	36.0	15
1991	Atl	81	3470	42.8(60)	0	6	387	2963	36.6	21
1992	Atl	68	2818	41.4(56)	1	3	482	2276	33.0	11
NFL	6	399	16513	41.4(65)	4	32	2079	13794	34.6	94
GARCIA, FRANK										
1981	Sea	2	74	37.0(41)	0	0	0	74	37.0	0
1983	TB	95	**4008**	**42.2(64)**	1	**12**	**603**	3165	**33.0**	16
1984	TB	68	2849	41.9(60)	0	9	310	2359	34.7	12
1985	TB	77	3233	42.0(61)	**2**	6	**519**	2594	**32.8**	12
1986	TB	77	3089	40.1(60)	0	8	410	2519	32.7	19
1987	TB	62	2409	38.9(58)	0	5	553	1756	28.3	12
NFL	6	381	15662	41.1(64)	3	40	2395	12467	32.7	71
GARDOCKI, CHRIS										
1992	ChiB	79	3393	42.9(61)	0	9	351	2862	36.2	19
1993	ChiB	80	3080	38.5(58)	0	2	115	2925	36.6	28
1994	ChiB	76	2871	37.8(57)	0	9	225	2466	32.4	23
1995	Ind	63	2681	42.6(69)	0	7	436	2105	33.4	16
1996	Ind	68	3105	45.7(61)	0	2	413	2652	39.0	23
1997	Ind	67	3034	45.3(72)	0	6	**491**	2423	**36.2**	18
1998	Ind	79	3583	45.4(62)	0	10	451	2932	37.1	23
1999	Cle	106	**4645**	43.8(61)	0	11	**762**	3663	**34.6**	20
2000	Cle	108	**4919**	45.5(67)	0	5	**793**	**4026**	**37.3**	25
2001	Cle	99	**4249**	42.9(69)	0	9	**647**	**3422**	**34.6**	25
2002	Cle	81	3388	41.8(59)	0	6	408	2860	35.3	27
2003	Cle	72	3019	41.9(60)	0	10	316	2503	34.8	18
2004	Pit	67	2879	43.0(61)	0	6	252	2507	37.4	24
2005	Pit	67	2803	41.8(65)	0	7	336	2327	34.7	22
NFL	14	1112	47649	42.8(72)	0	99	5996	39673	35.7	311
GILLOM, HORACE										
1947	Cle-A	47	2096	44.6	0	—	—	—	—	—
1948	Cle-A	6	227	37.8	0	—	—	—	—	—
1949	Cle-A	54	2011	37.2	1	—	—	—	—	—
1950	Cle	66	2849	43.2(75)	1	—	—	—	—	—
1951	Cle	73	**3321**	**45.5(66)**	0	—	—	—	—	—
1952	Cle	61	2787	**45.7(73)**	1	—	—	—	—	—
1953	Cle	63	2760	43.8(67)	0	—	—	—	—	—
1954	Cle	52	2230	42.9(**80**)	0	—	—	—	—	—
1955	Cle	58	2389	41.2(56)	**3**	—	—	—	—	—
1956	Cle	12	536	44.7(53)	0	—	—	—	—	—
AAFC	3	107	4334	40.5	1	—	—	—	—	—
NFL	7	385	16872	43.8(80)	5	—	—	—	—	—
GIRARD, JUG										
1948	GB	8	320	40.0(49)	0	—	—	—	—	—
1949	GB	69	2694	39.0(72)	**3**	—	—	—	—	—
1950	GB	71	2715	38.2(63)	**2**	—	—	—	—	—
1951	GB	52	2101	40.4(66)	0	—	—	—	—	—
1954	Det	63	2585	41.0(65)	0	—	—	—	—	—
1955	Det	56	2310	41.3(65)	0	—	—	—	—	—
1956	Det	10	448	44.8(54)	0	—	—	—	—	—
1957	Pit	68	2754	40.5(56)	0	—	—	—	—	—
NFL	8	397	15927	40.1(72)	5	—	—	—	—	—
GOODBURN, KELLY										
1987	KC	59	2412	40.9(55)	0	5	**403**	1909	**32.4**	13
1988	KC	76	3059	40.3(59)	0	8	473	2426	31.9	10
1989	KC	67	2688	40.1(54)	0	5	325	2263	33.8	25
1990	KC	17	653	38.4(58)	0	2	87	526	30.9	6
1990	Was	11	377	34.3(48)	0	1	23	334	30.4	6
1991	Was	52	2070	39.8(61)	**3**	3	190	1820	33.1	16
1992	Was	64	2555	39.9(66)	1	5	332	2123	32.7	17
1993	Was	5	197	39.4(49)	0	0	0	197	39.4	3
NFL	7	351	14011	39.9(66)	4	29	1833	11598	33.0	96
GOSSETT, JEFF										
1981	KC	29	1141	39.3(55)	0	3	128	953	32.9	4
1982	KC	33	1366	41.4(56)	0	5	**247**	1019	**30.9**	6
1983	Cle	70	2854	40.8(60)	0	8	309	2385	34.1	17
1985	Cle	81	3261	40.3(64)	0	8	304	2797	34.5	18
1986	Cle	83	3423	41.2(61)	0	10	268	2955	35.6	21
1987	Hou	25	1008	40.3(53)	1	2	186	782	30.1	0
1987	Cle	19	769	40.5(55)	0	4	48	641	33.7	4
1988	LARd	91	**3804**	41.8(58)	0	8	397	**3247**	**35.7**	**27**
1989	LARd	67	2711	40.5(60)	0	7	301	2270	33.9	12
1990	LARd	60	2315	38.6(57)	2	4	153	2082	33.6	19
1991	LARd	67	2961	44.2(61)	0	2	341	2580	38.5	**26**
1992	LARd	77	3255	42.3(56)	0	3	385	2810	36.5	17
1993	LARd	71	2971	41.8(61)	0	9	301	2490	35.1	19
1994	LARd	77	3377	**43.9(65)**	0	**15**	366	2711	35.2	19
1995	Oak	75	3089	41.2(60)	**1**	8	294	2635	34.7	22
1996	Oak	57	2264	39.7(64)	0	5	192	1972	34.6	19
NFL	15	982	40569	41.3(65)	4	101	4220	34329	35.0	250

YEAR	TEAM	PNT	YDS	AVG(LG)	BLK	TB	RTYDS	NET	AVG	IN20
GOWIN, TOBY										
1997	Dal	86	3592	41.8(72)	0	9	365	3047	35.4	26
1998	Dal	77	3342	43.4(65)	**1**	**14**	210	2852	36.6	31
1999	Dal	81	3500	43.2(64)	0	10	459	2841	**35.1**	24
2000	NO	74	3043	41.1(58)	0	8	494	2389	**32.3**	22
2001	NO	76	3180	41.8(62)	0	7	316	2724	35.8	24
2002	NO	61	2553	41.9(59)	0	6	180	2253	36.9	15
2003	Dal	94	**3665**	39.0(59)	0	8	227	**3278**	**34.9**	25
2004	NYJ	80	3057	38.2(58)	0	8	221	2676	33.5	22
NFL	8	629	25932	41.2(72)	1	70	2472	22060	35.1	189
GREEN, BOBBY JOE										
1960	Pit	64	**2829**	44.2(**74**)	1	—	—	—	—	—
1961	Pit	73	3431	47.0(71)	0	—	—	—	—	—
1962	ChiB	69	3018	43.7(72)	0	—	—	—	—	—
1963	ChiB	64	2974	46.5(66)	0	—	—	—	—	—
1964	ChiB	71	3161	44.5(62)	0	—	—	—	—	—
1965	ChiB	58	2479	42.7(66)	0	—	—	—	—	—
1966	ChiB	80	**3358**	42.0(69)	0	—	—	—	—	—
1967	ChiB	79	3392	42.9(68)	0	—	—	—	—	—
1968	ChiB	27	1142	42.3(58)	1	—	—	—	—	—
1969	ChiB	76	2964	39.0(59)	1	—	—	—	—	—
1970	ChiB	83	**3395**	40.9(56)	0	—	—	—	—	—
1971	ChiB	77	3095	40.2(60)	0	—	—	—	—	—
1972	ChiB	67	2758	41.2(58)	0	—	—	—	—	—
1973	ChiB	82	3321	40.5(62)	0	—	—	—	—	—
NFL	14	970	41317	42.6(74)	3	—	—	—	—	—
GREEN, DAVE										
1973	Hou	22	868	39.5(61)	0	—	—	—	—	—
1974	Cin	66	2701	40.9(53)	0	—	—	—	—	—
1975	Cin	68	2655	39.0(57)	1	—	—	—	—	—
1976	TB	92	3619	39.3(56)	0	3	754	**2805**	**30.5**	12
1977	TB	98	3948	40.3(**70**)	1	6	469	3359	33.9	16
1978	TB	100	4092	40.9(61)	**2**	**14**	447	3365	33.0	20
NFL	6	446	17883	40.1(70)	4	23	1670	9529	32.9	48
GUY, RAY										
1973	Oak	69	3127	45.3(72)	0	—	—	—	—	—
1974	Oak	74	3124	42.2(66)	0	—	—	—	—	—
1975	Oak	68	2979	**43.8**(**64**)	0	—	—	—	—	—
1976	Oak	67	2785	41.6(66)	0	**15**	264	2221	33.1	13
1977	Oak	59	2552	**43.3**(**74**)	0	**14**	217	2055	34.8	11
1978	Oak	81	3462	42.7(69)	**2**	**14**	309	2873	34.6	23
1979	Oak	69	2939	42.6(71)	1	8	416	2363	33.8	16
1980	Oak	71	3099	43.6(**77**)	0	14	268	2551	35.9	18
1981	Oak	96	**4195**	43.7(69)	0	15	**514**	**3381**	**35.2**	23
1982	LARd	47	1839	39.1(57)	0	3	71	1708	36.3	12
1983	LARd	78	3336	42.8(67)	0	10	334	2802	35.9	17
1984	LARd	91	3809	41.9(63)	0	12	345	3224	35.4	**25**
1985	LARd	89	3627	40.8(68)	0	12	159	3228	36.3	32
1986	LARd	90	3620	40.2(64)	0	**11**	357	3043	33.8	20
NFL	14	1049	44493	42.4(77)	3	128	3254	29449	35.1	210
HANSEN, BRIAN										
1984	NO	69	3020	**43.8**(**66**)	1	7	**550**	2330	**33.3**	9
1985	NO	89	3763	42.3(58)	0	6	397	3246	36.5	14
1986	NO	81	3456	42.7(66)	1	11	234	3002	36.6	17
1987	NO	52	2104	40.5(60)	0	6	135	1849	35.6	19
1988	NO	72	2913	40.5(64)	1	8	248	2505	34.3	19
1990	NE	90	**3752**	41.7(69)	2	**8**	**503**	**3089**	**33.6**	18
1991	Cle	80	3397	42.5(65)	0	6	388	**2889**	36.1	20
1992	Cle	74	3083	41.7(**73**)	1	7	234	2709	36.1	28
1993	Cle	82	3632	44.3(72)	2	10	438	2994	35.6	15
1994	NYJ	84	3534	42.1(64)	0	12	260	3034	36.1	25
1995	NYJ	99	**4090**	41.3(67)	**1**	10	**703**	3187	**31.9**	23
1996	NYJ	74	3293	44.5(69)	0	8	429	2704	36.5	13
1997	NYJ	71	3068	43.2(58)	1	5	429	2539	35.3	20
1998	NYJ	31	1233	39.8(62)	0	2	178	1015	32.7	6
1999	Was	9	362	40.2(49)	0	1	120	222	24.7	1
NFL	15	1057	44700	42.3(73)	10	107	5246	37314	35.3	247
HANSON, CHRIS										
1999	GB	4	157	39.3(44)	0	0	3	154	38.5	0
2001	Jax	82	3577	43.6(59)	0	**12**	295	3042	37.1	24
2002	Jax	81	3583	**44.2**(**64**)	0	10	339	3044	37.6	27
2003	Jax	23	1001	43.5(58)	1	1	235	746	31.1	4
2004	Jax	84	3592	42.8(69)	0	9	**429**	2983	35.5	28
2005	Jax	82	3517	42.9(74)	**1**	11	236	3061	36.9	**33**
NFL	6	356	15427	43.3(74)	2	43	1537	13030	36.6	116
HARRIS, NICK										
2001	Cin	84	3372	40.1(57)	1	6	374	2878	33.9	21
2002	Cin	65	2608	40.1(57)	1	4	454	2074	**31.4**	11
2003	Cin	28	1084	38.7(53)	0	3	183	841	30.0	5
2003	Det	63	2531	40.2(51)	1	5	315	2116	33.1	11
2004	Det	92	3765	40.9(60)	1	7	441	3184	34.2	32
2005	Det	84	3656	43.5(60)	0	2	**520**	3096	36.9	**34**
NFL	5	416	17016	40.9(60)	4	27	2287	14189	34.1	114
HATCHER, DALE										
1985	LARm	87	3761	43.2(67)	1	6	297	**3344**	38.0	**32**
1986	LARm	97	3740	38.6(57)	1	5	416	3224	32.9	26
1987	LARm	76	**3140**	41.3(62)	1	4	317	**2743**	35.6	19
1988	LARm	36	1424	39.6(54)	0	1	202	1202	33.4	13
1989	LARm	73	2834	38.8(54)	1	7	315	2379	32.1	15
1991	LARm	63	2403	38.1(52)	0	5	231	2072	32.9	16
1993	Mia	58	2304	39.7(56)	0	4	359	1865	32.2	13
NFL	7	490	19606	40.0(67)	4	32	2137	16829	34.3	134

YEAR	TEAM	PNT	YDS	AVG(LG)	BLK	TB	RTYDS	NET	AVG	IN20
HAYES, JEFF										
1982	Was	51	1937	38.0(58)	**1**	5	106	1731	33.3	10
1983	Was	72	2796	38.8(56)	0	2	407	2349	32.6	**29**
1984	Was	72	2834	39.4(59)	1	5	187	2547	34.9	11
1985	Was	16	665	41.6(55)	0	2	47	578	36.1	4
1986	Cin	56	1965	35.1(52)	2	3	182	1723	29.7	11
1987	Mia	7	274	39.1(51)	1	0	33	241	30.1	1
NFL	6	274	10471	38.2(59)	5	17	962	9169	33.5	66
HENTRICH, CRAIG										
1994	GB	81	3351	41.4(70)	0	10	272	2879	35.5	24
1995	GB	65	2740	42.2(61)	**2**	7	279	2321	34.6	26
1996	GB	68	2886	42.4(65)	0	9	237	2469	36.3	28
1997	GB	75	3378	45.0(65)	0	**21**	255	2703	36.0	26
1998	Ten	69	3258	**47.2**(**71**)	0	11	332	2706	39.2	18
1999	Ten	90	3824	42.5(78)	0	3	335	3429	38.1	35
2000	Ten	76	3101	40.8(67)	0	9	160	2761	36.3	33
2001	Ten	85	3567	42.0(70)	0	8	264	3143	37.0	28
2002	Ten	65	2725	41.9(56)	1	5	390	2235	33.9	28
2003	Ten	71	3117	43.9(58)	0	8	276	2681	37.8	26
2004	Ten	73	3117	42.7(64)	0	8	184	2773	38.0	20
2005	Ten	78	3371	43.2(59)	0	**14**	144	2947	37.8	21
NFL	12	896	38435	42.9(78)	3	113	3128	33047	36.9	313
HILL, KING										
1959	ChiC	3	118	39.3(47)	0	—	—	—	—	—
1960	SL	5	198	39.6(50)	0	—	—	—	—	—
1961	Phi	55	2403	43.7(64)	0	—	—	—	—	—
1962	Phi	64	2747	42.9(80)	0	—	—	—	—	—
1963	Phi	69	2972	43.1(62)	0	—	—	—	—	—
1964	Phi	24	968	40.3(56)	0	—	—	—	—	—
1965	Phi	19	813	42.8(55)	0	—	—	—	—	—
1966	Phi	23	862	37.5(51)	0	—	—	—	—	—
1968	Min	33	1354	41.0(53)	0	—	—	—	—	—
1969	SL	73	2746	37.6(57)	1	—	—	—	—	—
NFL	10	368	15181	41.3(80)	1	—	—	—	—	—
HORAN, MIKE										
1984	Phi	92	**3880**	42.2(69)	0	6	486	**3274**	**35.6**	21
1985	Phi	91	**3777**	41.5(**75**)	0	10	462	3115	**34.2**	20
1986	Den	21	864	41.1(50)	0	2	99	725	34.5	8
1987	Den	44	1807	41.1(61)	**2**	5	186	1521	33.1	11
1988	Den	65	2861	44.0(70)	0	2	364	2457	37.8	19
1989	Den	77	3111	40.4(63)	0	5	370	2641	34.3	24
1990	Den	58	2575	44.4(67)	1	6	159	2296	38.9	14
1991	Den	72	3012	41.8(71)	1	**8**	170	2682	36.7	24
1992	Den	37	1681	45.4(62)	1	1	132	1529	40.2	7
1993	NYG	44	1882	42.8(60)	0	1	107	1755	39.9	13
1994	NYG	85	3521	41.4(63)	**2**	7	307	3074	35.3	25
1995	NYG	72	3063	42.5(60)	0	8	297	2606	36.2	15
1996	NYG	102	**4289**	42.0(63)	0	10	432	**3657**	**35.9**	**32**
1997	SL	53	2272	42.9(60)	0	4	266	1926	36.3	10
1998	ChiB	64	2643	41.3(57)	0	4	299	2264	35.4	12
1999	SL	26	1048	40.3(57)	0	4	51	917	35.3	7
NFL	16	1003	42286	42.2(75)	7	83	4187	36439	36.3	262
HUTTON, TOM										
1995	Phi	85	3682	43.3(63)	1	**13**	**527**	2895	33.7	20
1996	Phi	73	3107	42.6(60)	1	9	330	2597	35.1	17
1997	Phi	87	3660	42.1(61)	1	5	515	3045	34.6	19
1998	Phi	104	4339	41.7(61)	0	10	511	3628	**34.9**	21
1999	Mia	73	2978	40.8(63)	0	3	358	2560	35.1	22
NFL	5	422	17766	42.1(63)	3	40	2241	14725	34.9	99
JACKSON, RUSTY										
1976	LARm	77	3006	39.0(61)	2	6	281	2605	33.0	16
1978	Buf	87	3373	38.8(70)	**2**	9	442	2751	30.9	19
1979	Buf	96	3671	38.2(60)	0	11	555	2896	30.2	14
NFL	3	260	10050	38.7(70)	4	26	1278	8252	31.7	49
JAMES, JOHN										
1972	Atl	61	2609	42.8(59)	0	—	—	—	—	—
1973	Atl	63	2682	42.6(**72**)	0	—	—	—	—	—
1974	Atl	96	**3891**	40.5(65)	1	—	—	—	—	—
1975	Atl	89	3696	41.5(**75**)	1	—	—	—	—	—
1976	Atl	101	**4253**	**42.1**(**67**)	0	12	360	**3653**	**36.2**	**28**
1977	Atl	105	**4349**	41.4(61)	0	**13**	519	**3570**	**34.0**	19
1978	Atl	109	**4227**	38.8(57)	1	9	305	**3742**	**34.0**	24
1979	Atl	83	3296	39.7(62)	1	4	259	2957	35.2	12
1980	Atl	79	3087	39.1(59)	0	7	240	2707	34.3	**25**
1981	Atl	87	3543	40.7(62)	1	5	577	2866	32.6	13
1982	Hou	31	1260	40.6(56)	0	2	158	1062	34.3	4
1982	Det	12	481	40.1(50)	0	2	37	404	33.7	3
1983	Hou	79	3136	39.7(53)	1	8	354	2622	32.8	12
1984	Hou	88	3482	39.6(55)	0	5	**618**	2764	**31.4**	20
NFL	13	1083	43992	40.6(75)	6	67	3427	26347	34.0	160
JANIK, TOM										
1964	Den-A	10	374	37.4(49)	0	—	—	—	—	—
1969	Bos-A	70	2903	41.5(56)	0	—	—	—	—	—
1970	Bos	86	3364	39.1(57)	**1**	—	—	—	—	—
1971	NE	87	3249	37.3(58)	0	—	—	—	—	—
NFL	4	253	9890	39.1(58)	1	—	—	—	—	—
JENNINGS, DAVE										
1974	NYG	68	2709	39.8(64)	**2**	—	—	—	—	—
1975	NYG	76	3107	40.9(64)	0	—	—	—	—	—
1976	NYG	74	3054	41.3(61)	**3**	10	500	2354	30.6	11
1977	NYG	100	3993	39.9(58)	0	4	**680**	3233	32.3	19

YEAR	TEAM	PNT	YDS	AVG(LG)	BLK	TB	RTYDS	NET	AVG	IN20
1978	NYG	95	3995	42.1(68)	0	11	**624**	3151	33.2	19
1979	NYG	104	**4445**	**42.7**(**72**)	0	9	**447**	**3818**	**36.7**	19
1980	NYG	94	**4211**	**44.8**(**63**)	0	13	506	**3445**	36.6	16
1981	NYG	97	4198	43.3(62)	0	12	561	3397	35.0	19
1982	NYG	49	2096	42.8(73)	0	3	207	1829	37.3	**16**
1983	NYG	84	3386	40.3(66)	1	5	283	3003	35.3	**29**
1984	NYG	90	3598	40.0(54)	**4**	10	479	2919	31.1	22
1985	NYJ	74	2978	40.2(66)	0	8	319	2499	33.8	23
1986	NYJ	85	3353	39.4(55)	0	6	165	3068	36.1	**27**
1987	NYJ	64	2444	38.2(58)	0	6	100	2224	34.8	12
NFL	14	1154	47567	41.2(73)	10	97	4871	34940	34.6	232
Jett, John										
1993	Dal	56	2342	41.8(59)	0	3	169	2113	37.7	22
1994	Dal	70	2935	41.9(58)	0	4	378	2477	35.4	26
1995	Dal	53	2166	40.9(58)	0	6	216	1830	34.5	17
1996	Dal	74	3150	42.6(60)	0	9	249	2721	36.8	22
1997	Det	84	3576	42.6(60)	**2**	4	434	3062	35.6	24
1998	Det	66	2892	43.8(60)	0	6	398	2374	36.0	17
1999	Det	86	3637	42.3(62)	0	**12**	402	2995	34.8	27
2000	Det	93	**4044**	43.5(59)	**2**	**12**	**498**	**3306**	**34.8**	**33**
2001	Det	58	2512	43.3(62)	0	6	332	2060	35.5	16
2002	Det	91	3838	42.2(57)	0	7	239	3459	38.0	29
2003	Det	25	995	39.8(58)	0	3	45	890	35.6	8
NFL	11	756	32087	42.4(62)	4	72	3360	27287	36.1	241
Johnson, Curley										
1960	DalT-A	3	110	36.7(58)	0	—	—	—	—	—
1961	NYT-A	66	2821	42.7(70)	0	—	—	—	—	—
1962	NYT-A	50	1998	40.0(63)	0	—	—	—	—	—
1963	NYJ-A	72	3034	42.1(64)	1	—	—	—	—	—
1964	NYJ-A	79	3261	41.3(61)	**2**	—	—	—	—	—
1965	NYJ-A	72	3260	45.3(73)	0	—	—	—	—	—
1966	NYJ-A	62	2633	42.5(63)	0	—	—	—	—	—
1967	NYJ-A	65	2734	42.1(60)	0	—	—	—	—	—
1968	NYJ-A	68	2977	43.8(65)	1	—	—	—	—	—
1969	NYG	22	823	37.4(66)	**2**	—	—	—	—	—
NFL	10	559	23651	42.3(73)	6	—	—	—	—	—
Johnson, Lee										
1985	Hou	83	3464	41.7(65)	0	8	345	2959	35.7	22
1986	Hou	88	3623	41.2(66)	0	9	303	3140	35.7	26
1987	Hou	41	1652	40.3(59)	0	3	243	1349	32.9	5
1987	Cle	9	317	35.2(66)	0	1	6	291	32.3	3
1988	Cle	17	643	37.8(61)	0	1	103	520	30.6	6
1988	Cin	14	594	42.4(52)	0	1	60	514	36.7	4
1989	Cin	61	2446	40.1(62)	**2**	**11**	323	1903	30.2	14
1990	Cin	64	2705	42.3(**70**)	0	**8**	352	2193	34.3	12
1991	Cin	64	2795	43.7(62)	0	6	456	2219	**34.7**	15
1992	Cin	76	3196	42.1(64)	0	9	284	2732	35.9	15
1993	Cin	90	3954	43.9(60)	0	12	416	3298	**36.6**	24
1994	Cin	79	3461	43.8(64)	**1**	9	459	2822	35.3	19
1995	Cin	68	2861	42.1(61)	0	4	154	2627	38.6	26
1996	Cin	80	3630	45.4(67)	**1**	**17**	502	2788	34.4	16
1997	Cin	81	3471	42.9(66)	0	8	407	2904	35.9	27
1998	Cin	69	3083	44.7(69)	1	8	428	2495	35.6	14
1999	NE	90	3735	41.5(58)	0	14	345	3110	34.6	23
2000	NE	89	3798	42.7(62)	**1**	5	384	3314	36.8	31
2001	NE	24	1045	43.5(76)	0	3	65	920	38.3	3
2001	Min	25	983	39.3(59)	0	3	64	859	34.4	9
2002	Phi	14	523	37.4(53)	0	2	95	388	27.7	4
NFL	18	1226	51979	42.4(76)	6	142	5794	43345	35.4	318
Jones, Spike										
1970	Hou	84	3559	42.4(**73**)	**1**	—	—	—	—	—
1971	Buf	72	2966	41.2(62)	1	—	—	—	—	—
1972	Buf	80	3104	38.8(67)	1	—	—	—	—	—
1973	Buf	66	2660	40.3(62)	0	—	—	—	—	—
1974	Buf	35	1305	37.3(56)	0	—	—	—	—	—
1975	Phi	68	2742	40.3(64)	0	—	—	—	—	—
1976	Phi	94	3445	36.6(57)	**3**	7	405	2900	29.9	23
1977	Phi	93	3463	37.2(68)	2	5	244	3119	32.8	22
NFL	8	592	23244	39.3(73)	8	12	649	6019	32.2	45
Kidd, John										
1984	Buf	88	3696	42.0(63)	**2**	8	597	2939	32.7	16
1985	Buf	92	3818	41.5(67)	0	4	438	**3300**	35.9	**33**
1986	Buf	75	3031	40.4(57)	0	9	260	2591	34.5	14
1987	Buf	64	2495	39.0(67)	0	7	148	2207	34.5	**20**
1988	Buf	62	2451	39.5(60)	0	2	222	2189	35.3	13
1989	Buf	65	2564	39.4(60)	**2**	9	227	2157	32.2	15
1990	SD	61	2442	40.0(59)	1	2	131	2271	36.6	14
1991	SD	76	3064	40.3(60)	1	6	267	2677	34.8	22
1992	SD	68	2899	42.6(65)	0	9	244	2475	36.4	22
1993	SD	57	2431	42.6(67)	0	7	243	2048	35.9	16
1994	SD	7	246	35.1(53)	0	1	0	226	32.3	1
1994	Mia	14	602	43.0(58)	0	3	135	407	29.1	2
1995	Mia	57	2433	42.7(56)	0	5	265	2068	36.3	15
1996	Mia	78	3611	**46.3**(**63**)	0	11	368	3023	38.8	26
1997	Mia	52	2247	43.2(58)	0	4	243	1924	37.0	13
1998	NYJ	28	1166	41.6(57)	0	2	93	1033	36.9	8
1998	Det	13	520	40.0(54)	0	0	66	454	34.9	1
NFL	15	957	39716	41.5(67)	6	89	3947	33989	35.5	251
Knorr, Micah										
2000	Dal	58	2485	42.8(60)	0	8	248	2077	35.8	12
2001	Dal	78	3135	40.2(57)	**3**	6	493	2522	31.1	25
2002	Dal	47	1928	41.0(56)	0	4	199	1649	35.1	11

YEAR	TEAM	PNT	YDS	AVG(LG)	BLK	TB	RTYDS	NET	AVG	IN20
2002	Den	24	906	37.8(59)	0	2	47	819	34.1	8
2003	Den	68	2937	43.2(62)	**2**	6	560	2257	**32.2**	14
2004	Den	54	2243	41.5(66)	**1**	6	240	1883	34.2	12
NFL	5	329	13634	41.4(66)	6	32	1787	11207	34.1	82
Landeta, Sean										
1985	NYG	81	3472	42.9(68)	0	**14**	247	2945	36.4	20
1986	NYG	79	3539	**44.8**(**61**)	0	11	386	2933	37.1	24
1987	NYG	65	2773	42.7(64)	1	6	**606**	2047	**31.0**	13
1988	NYG	6	222	37.0(53)	0	0	7	215	35.8	1
1989	NYG	70	3019	**43.1**(71)	0	7	236	2643	37.8	19
1990	NYG	75	3306	**44.1**(**67**)	0	**11**	291	2795	37.3	**24**
1991	NYG	64	2768	43.3(61)	0	8	350	2258	35.3	16
1992	NYG	53	2317	43.7(71)	**2**	9	406	1731	**31.5**	13
1993	LARm	42	1825	43.5(66)	**0**	7	304	1381	**32.9**	7
1993	NYG	33	1390	42.1(57)	**1**	3	140	1190	**35.0**	11
1994	LARm	78	3494	**44.8**(**62**)	0	9	**637**	2677	**34.3**	23
1995	SL	83	3679	**44.3**(**63**)	0	12	393	3046	36.7	23
1996	SL	78	3491	44.8(70)	0	9	495	2816	36.1	23
1997	TB	54	2274	42.1(**74**)	1	6	278	1876	34.1	15
1998	GB	65	2788	42.9(**72**)	0	7	237	2411	37.1	30
1999	Phi	107	**4524**	42.3(60)	1	**12**	**490**	**3794**	**35.1**	21
2000	Phi	86	3635	42.3(60)	0	8	375	3100	36.0	23
2001	Phi	97	4221	43.5(64)	0	10	488	3533	**36.4**	26
2002	Phi	52	2229	42.9(63)	0	7	288	1801	34.6	19
2003	SL	59	2525	42.8(57)	0	5	484	1941	**32.9**	14
2004	SL	40	1733	43.3(63)	0	3	372	1301	**32.5**	9
2005	Phi	34	1484	43.6(56)	0	2	146	1298	38.2	7
NFL	21	1401	60708	43.3(74)	6	166	7656	49732	35.5	381
Landry, Tom										
1949	NYY-A	51	**2249**	44.1	**2**	—	—	—	—	—
1950	NYG	58	2136	36.8(61)	1	—	—	—	—	—
1951	NYG	15	638	42.5(59)	0	—	—	—	—	—
1952	NYG	82	**3363**	41.0(61)	1	—	—	—	—	—
1953	NYG	44	1772	40.3(60)	0	—	—	—	—	—
1954	NYG	64	2720	42.5(61)	0	—	—	—	—	—
1955	NYG	75	**3022**	40.3(69)	1	—	—	—	—	—
AAFC	1	51	2249	44.1	2	—	—	—	—	—
NFL	6	338	13651	40.4(69)	3	—	—	—	—	—
Lary, Yale										
1952	Det	5	181	36.2(43)	0	—	—	—	—	—
1953	Det	28	1112	39.7(61)	0	—	—	—	—	—
1956	Det	42	1698	40.4(41)	0	—	—	—	—	—
1957	Det	54	2156	39.9(66)	0	—	—	—	—	—
1958	Det	59	2524	42.8(62)	**1**	—	—	—	—	—
1959	Det	45	2121	**47.1**(**67**)	0	—	—	—	—	—
1960	Det	64	2802	43.8(63)	**2**	—	—	—	—	—
1961	Det	52	2519	**48.4**(**71**)	0	—	—	—	—	—
1962	Det	52	2354	45.3(68)	1	—	—	—	—	—
1963	Det	35	1713	**48.9**(**73**)	0	—	—	—	—	—
1964	Det	67	3099	46.3(73)	0	—	—	—	—	—
NFL	11	503	22279	44.3(73)	4	—	—	—	—	—
Lechler, Shane										
2000	Oak	65	2984	45.9(69)	**1**	10	279	2505	38.0	24
2001	Oak	73	3375	**46.2**(**65**)	1	**12**	502	2633	35.6	23
2002	Oak	53	2251	42.5(70)	0	**12**	276	1735	32.7	18
2003	Oak	96	**4503**	**46.9**(**73**)	0	**13**	**669**	**3574**	37.2	27
2004	Oak	73	3409	**46.7**(**67**)	0	**14**	413	2716	37.2	22
2005	Oak	82	3744	45.7(64)	0	9	460	3104	37.9	26
NFL	6	442	20266	45.9(73)	2	70	2599	16267	36.8	140
Lee, David										
1966	Bal	49	2233	**45.6**(**64**)	0	—	—	—	—	—
1967	Bal	49	2075	42.3(68)	0	—	—	—	—	—
1968	Bal	49	1935	39.5(59)	1	—	—	—	—	—
1969	Bal	57	2580	**45.3**(**66**)	0	—	—	—	—	—
1970	Bal	63	2819	44.7(62)	**1**	—	—	—	—	—
1971	Bal	62	2542	41.0(**76**)	0	—	—	—	—	—
1972	Bal	57	2400	42.1(60)	1	—	—	—	—	—
1973	Bal	62	2402	38.7(60)	2	—	—	—	—	—
1974	Bal	71	2634	37.1(58)	1	—	—	—	—	—
1975	Bal	86	**3402**	39.6(62)	1	—	—	—	—	—
1976	Bal	59	2342	39.7(56)	0	3	231	2051	34.8	21
1977	Bal	82	3142	38.3(59)	2	9	481	2481	29.5	19
1978	Bal	92	3513	38.2(67)	**2**	9	460	2873	30.6	17
NFL	13	838	34019	40.6(76)	11	21	1172	7405	31.8	57
Lewis, Dave										
1970	Cin	79	3651	**46.2**(**63**)	0	—	—	—	—	—
1971	Cin	72	3229	**44.8**(**56**)	0	—	—	—	—	—
1972	Cin	66	2777	42.1(60)	0	—	—	—	—	—
1973	Cin	68	2790	41.0(60)	0	—	—	—	—	—
NFL	4	285	12447	43.7(63)	0					
Lothridge, Billy										
1964	Dal	62	2501	40.3(**75**)	**1**	—	—	—	—	—
1965	LARm	42	1619	38.5(55)	**1**	—	—	—	—	—
1966	Atl	73	2968	40.7(60)	0	—	—	—	—	—
1967	Atl	87	**3801**	43.7(62)	0	—	—	—	—	—
1968	Atl	75	**3324**	**44.3**(**70**)	0	—	—	—	—	—
1969	Atl	69	2846	41.2(57)	0	—	—	—	—	—
1970	Atl	76	2944	38.7(59)	0	—	—	—	—	—
1971	Atl	44	1639	37.3(58)	1	—	—	—	—	—
1972	Mia	4	150	37.5(42)	0	—	—	—	—	—
NFL	9	532	21792	41.0(75)	3	—	—	—	—	—

YEAR	TEAM	PNT	YDS	AVG(LG)	BLK	TB	RTYDS	NET	AVG	IN20
Maguire, Paul										
1960	LAC-A	43	1743	**40.5(61)**	0	—	—	—	—	—
1961	SD-A	63	2615	41.5(**82**)	1	—	—	—	—	—
1962	SD-A	79	**3289**	41.6(66)	0	—	—	—	—	—
1963	SD-A	58	2241	38.6(60)	0	—	—	—	—	—
1964	Buf-A	65	2777	42.7(64)	0	—	—	—	—	—
1965	Buf-A	80	3437	43.0(68)	0	—	—	—	—	—
1966	Buf-A	69	2841	41.2(61)	0	—	—	—	—	—
1967	Buf-A	77	3320	43.1(64)	0	—	—	—	—	—
1968	Buf-A	100	**4175**	41.8(61)	1	—	—	—	—	—
1969	Buf-A	78	**3471**	44.5(78)	1	—	—	—	—	—
1970	Buf	83	3228	38.9(58)	**1**	—	—	—	—	—
NFL	11	795	33137	41.7(82)	4	—	—	—	—	—
Maynard, Brad										
1997	NYG	111	**4531**	40.8(57)	1	14	378	**3873**	**34.6**	**33**
1998	NYG	101	**4566**	45.2(63)	0	8	587	**3819**	37.8	**33**
1999	NYG	89	3651	41.0(63)	0	6	405	3126	35.1	**31**
2000	NYG	79	3210	40.6(64)	1	8	353	2697	33.7	26
2001	ChiB	87	3709	42.6(60)	0	8	327	3222	37.0	**36**
2002	ChiB	87	3679	42.3(**75**)	0	2	386	3253	37.4	26
2003	ChiB	79	3258	41.2(53)	2	9	277	2801	34.6	23
2004	ChiB	108	**4638**	42.9(58)	0	5	363	**4175**	**38.7**	**34**
2005	ChiB	96	3937	41.0(63)	**1**	11	292	3425	35.3	24
NFL	9	837	35179	42.0(75)	5	71	3368	30391	36.3	266
McGee, Max										
1954	GB	72	**2999**	41.7(63)	0	—	—	—	—	—
1958	GB	62	2625	42.3(61)	0	—	—	—	—	—
1959	GB	64	**2716**	42.4(61)	**1**	—	—	—	—	—
1960	GB	31	1291	41.6(58)	1	—	—	—	—	—
1961	GB	13	520	40.0(51)	0	—	—	—	—	—
1962	GB	14	496	35.4(56)	0	—	—	—	—	—
NFL	6	256	10647	41.6(63)	2	—	—	—	—	—
McInally, Pat										
1976	Cin	76	2999	39.5(61)	0	6	323	2556	33.6	12
1977	Cin	67	2802	41.8(67)	1	3	267	2475	36.4	16
1978	Cin	91	**3919**	**43.1(65)**	0	10	558	**3161**	34.7	**25**
1979	Cin	89	3678	41.3(61)	2	**12**	325	3113	34.2	19
1980	Cin	83	**3390**	40.8(61)	**2**	12	**476**	2674	31.5	21
1981	Cin	72	3272	**45.4(62)**	1	11	416	2636	**36.1**	17
1982	Cin	31	1201	38.7(53)	0	4	68	1053	34.0	7
1983	Cin	67	2804	41.9(60)	**2**	9	310	2314	33.5	13
1984	Cin	67	2832	42.3(61)	0	8	310	2362	35.3	19
1985	Cin	57	2410	42.3(64)	1	7	535	1735	**29.9**	8
NFL	10	700	29307	41.9(67)	9	82	3588	24079	34.4	157
McNeill, Tom										
1967	NO	74	3174	42.9(66)	0	—	—	—	—	—
1968	NO	49	2009	41.0(58)	1	—	—	—	—	—
1969	NO	7	312	44.6(**81**)	0	—	—	—	—	—
1970	Min	61	2309	37.9(64)	0	—	—	—	—	—
1971	Phi	73	3063	**42.0(64)**	1	—	—	—	—	—
1972	Phi	7	290	41.4(51)	0	—	—	—	—	—
1973	Phi	46	1881	40.9(66)	0	—	—	—	—	—
NFL	7	317	13038	41.1(81)	2	—	—	—	—	—
Mercer, Mike										
1961	Min	63	2458	39.0(59)	**2**	—	—	—	—	—
1962	Min	19	827	43.5(77)	0	—	—	—	—	—
1963	Oak-A	75	3007	40.1(53)	1	—	—	—	—	—
1964	Oak-A	59	2446	41.5(67)	1	—	—	—	—	—
1965	Oak-A	75	3079	41.1(70)	0	—	—	—	—	—
1966	Oak-A	9	373	41.4(59)	0	—	—	—	—	—
1970	SD	8	283	35.4(42)	0	—	—	—	—	—
NFL	7	308	12473	40.5(77)	4	—	—	—	—	—
Miller, Josh										
1996	Pit	55	2256	41.0(61)	0	8	248	1848	33.6	18
1997	Pit	64	2729	42.6(72)	0	11	271	2238	35.0	17
1998	Pit	81	3530	43.6(73)	0	12	310	2980	36.8	**34**
1999	Pit	84	3795	45.2(75)	0	10	392	3203	38.1	27
2000	Pit	90	3944	43.8(67)	**1**	8	371	3413	37.5	34
2001	Pit	59	2505	42.5(64)	1	5	310	2095	34.9	23
2002	Pit	55	2267	41.2(62)	1	5	346	1821	32.5	14
2003	Pit	84	3521	41.9(72)	1	8	299	3062	36.0	27
2004	NE	56	2350	42.0(69)	0	5	365	1885	33.7	19
2005	NE	76	3431	45.1(59)	**1**	4	405	2946	38.3	22
NFL	10	704	30328	43.1(75)	5	76	3317	25491	36.2	235
Mohr, Chris										
1989	TB	84	3311	39.4(58)	**2**	3	**492**	2759	**32.1**	10
1991	Buf	54	2085	38.6(58)	0	4	53	1952	36.1	12
1992	Buf	60	2531	42.2(61)	0	7	185	2206	36.8	12
1993	Buf	74	2991	40.4(58)	0	4	247	2664	36.0	19
1994	Buf	67	2799	41.8(**71**)	0	3	324	2415	36.0	13
1995	Buf	86	3473	40.4(60)	0	7	224	3109	36.2	23
1996	Buf	101	**4194**	41.5(**80**)	0	13	246	**3688**	**36.5**	**27**
1997	Buf	90	3764	41.8(59)	1	6	366	3278	36.0	24
1998	Buf	69	2882	41.8(57)	0	11	374	2288	33.2	18
1999	Buf	73	2840	38.9(60)	0	7	226	2474	33.9	20
2000	Buf	95	3661	38.5(57)	**1**	5	544	3017	31.4	19
2001	Atl	69	2680	38.8(55)	0	3	130	2490	36.1	25
2002	Atl	67	2804	41.9(59)	0	5	109	2595	38.7	21
2003	Atl	87	3473	39.9(54)	0	2	301	3132	36.0	19
2004	Atl	76	3082	40.6(56)	0	7	134	2808	36.9	19
NFL	15	1152	46570	40.4(80)	4	87	3955	40875	35.5	281

YEAR	TEAM	PNT	YDS	AVG(LG)	BLK	TB	RTYDS	NET	AVG	IN20
Mojsiejenko, Ralf										
1985	SD	68	2881	42.4(67)	0	9	274	2427	35.7	15
1986	SD	72	3026	42.0(62)	2	**11**	368	2438	32.9	15
1987	SD	67	**2875**	**42.9(57)**	0	12	392	**2243**	**33.5**	15
1988	SD	85	3745	44.1(62)	1	**11**	**558**	2967	**34.5**	22
1989	Was	62	2663	43.0(74)	1	9	383	2100	33.3	21
1990	Was	43	1687	39.2(53)	1	0	182	1505	34.2	17
1991	SF	16	656	41.0(55)	0	4	101	475	29.7	0
NFL	7	413	17533	42.5(74)	5	56	2258	14155	34.3	105
Montgomery, Greg										
1988	Hou	65	2523	38.8(61)	0	5	206	2217	34.1	12
1989	Hou	56	2422	**43.3(63)**	**2**	7	191	2091	36.1	15
1990	Hou	34	1530	**45.0(60)**	0	5	186	1244	36.6	7
1991	Hou	48	2105	43.9(60)	**2**	4	183	1842	36.8	13
1992	Hou	53	2487	**46.9(66)**	**2**	9	255	2052	37.3	14
1993	Hou	54	2462	**45.6(77)**	0	5	249	2113	39.1	13
1994	Det	63	2782	44.2(64)	1	8	431	2191	34.2	19
1996	Bal	68	2980	43.8(67)	**1**	5	273	2607	37.8	23
1997	Bal	83	3540	42.7(60)	0	2	460	3040	36.6	24
NFL	9	524	22831	43.6(77)	8	50	2434	19397	37.0	140
Moorman, Brian										
2001	Buf	80	3262	40.8(66)	0	7	418	2704	33.8	16
2002	Buf	66	2844	43.1(**84**)	1	7	294	2410	36.0	18
2003	Buf	85	3788	44.6(71)	0	3	577	3151	37.1	20
2004	Buf	77	3325	43.2(**80**)	0	9	315	2830	36.8	17
2005	Buf	71	3242	**45.7(68)**	0	9	285	2777	39.1	22
NFL	5	379	16461	43.4(84)	1	35	1889	13872	36.6	93
Morrison, Fred										
1950	ChiB	57	2470	**43.3(65)**	0	—	—	—	—	—
1951	ChiB	57	2227	39.1(67)	**1**	—	—	—	—	—
1952	ChiB	64	2707	42.3(65)	1	—	—	—	—	—
1953	ChiB	65	2766	42.6(65)	**2**	—	—	—	—	—
1956	Cle	38	1561	41.1(70)	0	—	—	—	—	—
NFL	5	281	11731	41.7(70)	4	—	—	—	—	—
Newsome, Harry										
1985	Pit	78	3088	39.6(59)	1	7	380	2568	32.5	17
1986	Pit	86	3447	40.1(64)	**3**	**11**	364	2863	32.2	18
1987	Pit	64	2678	41.8(57)	1	**13**	373	2045	31.5	8
1988	Pit	65	2950	**45.4(62)**	**6**	10	418	2332	32.8	9
1989	Pit	82	3368	41.1(57)	1	9	361	2827	34.1	15
1990	Min	78	3299	42.3(61)	1	8	**513**	2626	**33.2**	19
1991	Min	68	3095	**45.5(65)**	0	10	426	2469	36.3	17
1992	Min	72	3243	**45.0(84)**	1	**15**	339	2604	35.7	19
1993	Min	90	**3862**	42.9(64)	0	6	**560**	3182	35.4	25
NFL	9	683	29030	42.5(84)	14	89	3734	23516	34.4	147
Norton, Jerry										
1957	Phi	68	**2798**	41.1(63)	1	—	—	—	—	—
1959	ChiC	59	2650	44.9(60)	0	—	—	—	—	—
1960	SL	39	1777	**45.6(62)**	0	—	—	—	—	—
1961	SL	85	**3802**	44.7(**78**)	1	—	—	—	—	—
1963	GB	51	2279	44.7(61)	0	—	—	—	—	—
1964	GB	56	2365	42.2(61)	0	—	—	—	—	—
NFL	6	358	15671	43.8(78)	2	—	—	—	—	—
Norton, Jim										
1961	Hou-A	48	1952	40.7(63)	0	—	—	—	—	—
1962	Hou-A	56	2298	41.0(55)	**1**	—	—	—	—	—
1963	Hou-A	65	2792	43.0(68)	0	—	—	—	—	—
1964	Hou-A	55	2267	41.2(**79**)	**2**	—	—	—	—	—
1965	Hou-A	85	**3711**	43.7(65)	1	—	—	—	—	—
1966	Hou-A	69	2908	42.1(65)	0	—	—	—	—	—
1967	Hou-A	71	3025	42.6(58)	**1**	—	—	—	—	—
1968	Hou-A	73	3008	41.2(64)	**2**	—	—	—	—	—
NFL	8	522	21961	42.1(79)	7	—	—	—	—	—
O'Neal, Steve										
1969	NYJ-A	54	2393	44.3(**98**)	0	—	—	—	—	—
1970	NYJ	73	2925	40.1(64)	**1**	—	—	—	—	—
1971	NYJ	78	3026	38.8(58)	0	—	—	—	—	—
1972	NYJ	51	2006	39.3(57)	1	—	—	—	—	—
1973	NO	81	3375	41.7(71)	0	—	—	—	—	—
NFL	5	337	13725	40.7(98)	2	—	—	—	—	—
Parsley, Cliff										
1977	Hou	77	3030	39.4(55)	2	9	340	2510	31.8	12
1978	Hou	91	3539	38.9(59)	1	6	517	2902	31.5	20
1979	Hou	93	3777	40.6(59)	0	5	**726**	2951	**31.7**	14
1980	Hou	67	2727	40.7(57)	0	8	394	2173	32.4	19
1981	Hou	79	3137	39.7(62)	0	3	360	2717	34.4	17
1982	Hou	24	926	38.6(51)	0	2	136	750	31.3	3
NFL	6	431	17136	39.8(62)	3	33	2473	14003	32.5	85
Parsons, Bob										
1973	ChiB	4	106	26.5(33)	0	—	—	—	—	—
1974	ChiB	90	3408	37.9(59)	1	—	—	—	—	—
1975	ChiB	93	3625	39.0(60)	0	—	—	—	—	—
1976	ChiB	99	3726	37.6(62)	1	8	346	3220	32.2	20
1977	ChiB	80	3232	40.4(58)	2	7	216	2876	35.1	17
1978	ChiB	96	3549	37.0(54)	0	8	295	3094	32.2	18
1979	ChiB	92	3486	37.9(54)	1	6	404	2962	31.8	**26**
1980	ChiB	79	3207	40.6(61)	0	10	415	2592	32.8	16
1981	ChiB	114	**4531**	39.7(55)	0	7	594	**3797**	**33.3**	**31**
1982	ChiB	58	**2394**	41.3(**81**)	0	3	314	2020	**34.8**	10

YEAR	TEAM	PNT	YDS	AVG (LG)	BLK	TB	RTYDS	NET	AVG	IN20
1983	ChiB	79	2916	36.9(54)	0	5	261	2555	32.3	21
NFL	11	884	34180	38.7(81)	5	54	2845	23116	33.2	159
Partee, Dennis										
1968	SD-A	56	2281	40.7(60)	0	—	—	—	—	—
1969	SD-A	71	3169	**44.6**(**62**)	0	—	—	—	—	—
1970	SD	65	2852	43.9(62)	**1**	—	—	—	—	—
1971	SD	55	2392	43.5(73)	0	—	—	—	—	—
1972	SD	45	1813	40.3(65)	0	—	—	—	—	—
1973	SD	72	2958	41.1(62)	**3**	—	—	—	—	—
1974	SD	76	3042	40.0(65)	0	—	—	—	—	—
1975	SD	79	2910	36.8(56)	1	—	—	—	—	—
NFL	8	519	21417	41.3(73)	5	—	—	—	—	—
Pastorini, Dan										
1971	Hou	75	3044	40.6(62)	0	—	—	—	—	—
1972	Hou	82	3381	41.2(63)	1	—	—	—	—	—
1973	Hou	27	1087	40.3(59)	0	—	—	—	—	—
1975	Hou	62	2447	39.5(68)	0	—	—	—	—	—
1976	Hou	70	2571	36.7(74)	0	4	511	1980	28.3	12
NFL	5	316	12530	39.7(74)	1	4	511	1980	28.3	12
Player, Scott										
1998	Arz	81	3378	41.7(67)	**1**	6	313	2945	35.9	12
1999	Arz	94	3948	42.0(60)	0	8	340	3448	36.7	18
2000	Arz	65	2871	44.2(55)	0	5	347	2424	37.3	17
2001	Arz	67	2779	41.5(58)	0	7	377	2262	33.8	17
2002	Arz	88	3864	43.9(58)	**1**	10	547	3117	35.0	8
2003	Arz	82	3511	42.8(64)	1	9	472	2859	34.4	19
2004	Arz	98	4230	43.2(57)	1	7	487	3603	36.4	32
2005	Arz	73	3206	43.9(60)	**1**	7	328	2738	37.0	18
NFL	8	648	27787	42.9(67)	5	59	3211	23396	36.1	141
Prestridge, Luke										
1979	Den	89	3555	39.9(63)	0	7	480	2935	33.0	17
1980	Den	70	3075	**43.9**(**57**)	0	6	443	2512	35.9	10
1981	Den	86	3478	40.4(67)	0	5	388	2990	34.8	20
1982	Den	45	2026	**45.0**(**65**)	0	5	227	1699	37.8	**14**
1983	Den	87	3620	41.6(60)	0	7	524	2956	34.0	19
1984	NE	44	1884	42.8(**89**)	0	5	228	1556	35.4	8
NFL	6	421	17638	41.9(89)	0	35	2290	14648	34.8	88
Prokop, Joe										
1985	GB	56	2210	39.5(66)	0	6	265	1825	32.6	9
1987	SD	17	654	38.5(50)	0	1	37	597	35.1	1
1988	NYJ	85	3310	38.9(64)	0	10	201	2909	34.2	26
1989	NYJ	87	3426	39.4(**76**)	0	4	257	3089	35.5	29
1990	NYJ	59	2363	40.1(58)	0	3	257	2046	34.7	18
1991	SF	40	1541	38.5(58)	0	1	138	1383	34.6	8
1992	NYG	8	293	36.6(43)	0	0	59	234	29.3	0
1992	Mia	24	891	37.1(56)	0	0	199	692	28.8	2
NFL	7	376	14688	39.1(76)	0	25	1413	12775	34.0	93
Ramsey, Chuck										
1977	NYJ	62	2298	37.1(61)	0	8	301	1837	29.6	8
1978	NYJ	74	2964	40.1(**79**)	0	7	**609**	2215	**29.9**	9
1979	NYJ	73	2979	40.8(64)	0	10	260	2519	34.5	22
1980	NYJ	73	3096	42.4(59)	1	10	369	2527	34.1	15
1981	NYJ	81	3290	40.6(65)	0	13	149	2881	35.6	**27**
1982	NYJ	35	1348	38.5(54)	1	2	153	1155	32.1	8
1983	NYJ	81	3218	39.7(56)	1	5	367	2751	33.5	17
1984	NYJ	74	2935	39.7(64)	1	8	242	2533	33.8	19
NFL	8	553	22128	40.0(79)	4	63	2450	18418	33.3	125
Richardson, Kyle										
1997	Mia	11	480	43.6(54)	**0**	2	76	364	33.1	0
1997	Sea	8	324	40.5(52)	**2**	1	66	238	23.8	2
1998	Bal	90	3948	43.9(67)	**2**	7	284	**3524**	38.3	25
1999	Bal	103	4355	42.3(63)	1	10	468	**3687**	35.5	**39**
2000	Bal	86	3457	40.2(55)	0	8	382	2915	33.9	**35**
2001	Bal	85	3309	38.9(65)	**2**	10	183	2926	33.6	**29**
2002	Min	62	2474	39.9(59)	**1**	6	131	2223	35.3	21
2003	Cin	49	1961	40.0(58)	0	5	220	1641	33.5	9
2005	Cle	78	3181	40.8(61)	0	9	347	2654	34.0	22
NFL	8	572	23489	41.1(67)	8	58	2157	20172	35.3	182
Richter, Pat										
1963	Was	53	2210	41.7(61)	0	—	—	—	—	—
1964	Was	91	**3749**	41.2(63)	0	—	—	—	—	—
1965	Was	54	2364	43.8(72)	0	—	—	—	—	—
1966	Was	68	2884	42.4(60)	0	—	—	—	—	—
1967	Was	72	2976	41.3(58)	0	—	—	—	—	—
NFL	5	338	14183	42.0(72)	0	—	—	—	—	—
Roberts, George										
1978	Mia	81	3263	40.3(59)	0	9	303	2780	34.3	22
1979	Mia	69	2772	40.2(68)	1	11	131	2421	34.6	13
1980	Mia	77	3279	42.6(71)	**2**	8	339	2780	35.2	18
1981	SD	62	2540	41.0(61)	1	7	168	2232	35.4	16
1982	Atl	17	690	40.6(54)	0	3	118	512	30.1	3
NFL	5	306	12544	41.0(71)	4	38	1059	10725	35.0	72
Roby, Reggie										
1983	Mia	74	3189	43.1(64)	1	**11**	229	2740	36.5	**26**
1984	Mia	51	2281	44.7(69)	0	10	138	1943	38.1	15
1985	Mia	59	2576	43.7(63)	0	8	371	2045	34.7	19
1986	Mia	56	2476	44.2(**73**)	0	9	200	2096	37.4	13
1987	Mia	32	1371	42.8(**77**)	0	3	87	1224	38.3	8
1988	Mia	64	2754	43.0(64)	0	9	318	2256	35.3	18
1989	Mia	58	2458	42.4(58)	1	6	256	2082	35.3	18
1990	Mia	72	3022	42.0(62)	0	3	397	2565	35.6	20
1991	Mia	54	2466	**45.7**(**64**)	1	7	324	2002	36.4	17
1992	Mia	35	1443	41.2(60)	0	3	183	1200	**34.3**	11
1993	Was	78	3447	44.2(60)	0	**10**	343	2904	37.2	25
1994	Was	82	3639	44.4(65)	0	**12**	441	2958	36.1	21
1995	TB	77	3296	42.8(61)	1	7	335	2821	36.2	23
1996	Hou	67	2973	44.4(68)	**1**	7	251	2582	38.0	25
1997	Ten	73	3049	41.8(59)	0	1	430	2599	35.6	25
1998	SF	60	2511	41.9(66)	0	6	332	2059	34.3	14
NFL	16	992	42951	43.3(77)	5	112	4635	36076	36.4	298
Rouen, Tom										
1993	Den	67	3017	45.0(62)	1	8	337	2520	37.1	17
1994	Den	76	3258	42.9(59)	0	8	275	2823	37.1	23
1995	Den	52	2192	42.2(61)	**1**	3	137	1995	37.6	22
1996	Den	65	2714	41.8(57)	0	5	261	2353	36.2	16
1997	Den	60	2598	43.3(57)	0	4	235	2283	38.1	22
1998	Den	66	3097	46.9(**76**)	1	10	381	2516	37.6	14
1999	Den	84	3908	**46.5**(**65**)	0	**16**	600	2988	35.6	19
2000	Den	61	2455	40.2(62)	**1**	9	270	2005	32.3	18
2001	Den	81	3668	45.3(64)	1	8	517	2991	36.5	25
2002	Den	29	1239	42.7(63)	**2**	4	176	983	31.7	6
2002	NYG	8	333	41.6(55)	**0**	2	29	264	33.0	1
2002	Pit	7	316	45.1(55)	**0**	1	25	271	38.7	1
2003	Sea	67	2762	41.2(61)	2	3	140	2562	37.1	29
2004	Sea	26	1093	42.0(60)	0	1	91	982	37.8	10
2005	Sea	61	2539	41.6(62)	0	7	265	2134	35.0	20
NFL	13	810	35189	43.4(76)	9	89	3739	29670	36.6	243
Royals, Mark										
1987	SL	6	222	37.0(46)	0	0	119	103	17.2	2
1987	Phi	5	209	41.8(48)	0	1	36	153	30.6	1
1990	TB	72	2902	40.3(62)	0	5	352	2450	34.0	8
1991	TB	84	3389	40.3(56)	0	6	**559**	2710	**32.3**	22
1992	Pit	73	3119	42.7(58)	1	9	308	2631	35.6	22
1993	Pit	89	3781	42.5(61)	0	3	**678**	3043	**34.2**	**28**
1994	Pit	97	3849	39.7(64)	0	6	263	3466	**35.7**	**35**
1995	Det	57	2393	42.0(60)	**2**	6	442	1831	**31.0**	15
1996	Det	69	3020	43.8(60)	1	8	519	2341	**33.4**	11
1997	NO	88	4038	**45.9**(**66**)	0	13	706	3072	34.9	21
1998	NO	88	4017	**45.6**(**64**)	0	10	649	3168	**36.0**	26
1999	TB	90	3882	43.1(66)	0	8	360	3362	37.4	23
2000	TB	85	3551	41.8(63)	0	8	408	2983	35.1	17
2001	TB	83	3382	40.7(61)	0	8	380	2842	34.2	26
2002	Mia	69	2772	40.2(56)	0	6	273	2379	34.5	15
2003	Jax	45	1852	41.2(51)	0	5	185	1567	34.8	9
2003	Mia	16	643	40.2(50)	0	1	42	581	36.3	5
NFL	15	1116	47021	42.1(66)	4	103	6279	38682	34.7	286
Runager, Max										
1979	Phi	74	2927	39.6(57)	1	6	200	2607	34.8	13
1980	Phi	75	2947	39.3(58)	**1**	8	224	2563	33.7	16
1981	Phi	63	2567	40.7(64)	0	6	246	2201	34.9	18
1982	Phi	44	1784	40.5(53)	0	1	316	1448	32.9	8
1983	Phi	59	2459	41.7(55)	0	5	339	2020	34.2	12
1984	SF	56	2341	41.8(59)	1	**12**	176	1925	33.8	18
1985	SF	86	3422	39.8(57)	1	9	294	2948	33.9	30
1986	SF	83	3450	41.6(62)	2	8	373	2917	34.3	23
1987	SF	55	2157	39.2(56)	1	7	167	1850	33.0	13
1988	SF	1	24	24.0(24)	0	0	0	24	24.0	0
1988	Cle	48	1935	40.3(52)	2	2	201	1694	33.9	13
1989	Phi	17	568	33.4(52)	0	1	30	518	30.5	5
NFL	11	661	26581	40.2(64)	9	65	2566	22715	34.4	169
Sauerbrun, Todd										
1995	ChiB	55	2080	37.8(61)	0	6	248	1712	31.1	16
1996	ChiB	78	3491	44.8(**72**)	0	**12**	527	2724	34.9	15
1997	ChiB	95	4059	42.7(67)	0	11	**727**	3112	32.8	26
1998	ChiB	15	741	49.4(71)	0	3	50	631	42.1	6
1999	ChiB	85	3478	40.9(65)	0	10	266	3012	35.4	20
2000	KC	82	3656	44.6(68)	0	8	559	2937	35.8	28
2001	Car	93	**4419**	**47.5**(**73**)	1	**17**	425	**3654**	38.9	35
2002	Car	104	**4735**	**45.5**(**67**)	**1**	**12**	**554**	**3941**	**37.5**	**31**
2003	Car	77	3433	**44.6**(**64**)	**3**	9	402	2851	35.6	22
2004	Car	76	3351	44.1(65)	1	**8**	303	2888	37.5	25
2005	Den	72	3157	43.8(66)	**1**	6	266	2771	38.0	24
NFL	11	832	36600	44.0(73)	7	102	4327	30233	36.3	248
Saxon, Mike										
1985	Dal	81	3396	41.9(57)	1	10	286	2910	35.5	20
1986	Dal	86	3498	40.7(58)	1	10	301	2997	34.4	**28**
1987	Dal	68	2685	39.5(63)	0	5	260	2325	34.2	**20**
1988	Dal	80	3271	40.9(55)	0	**15**	239	2732	34.2	24
1989	Dal	79	3233	40.9(56)	**2**	6	334	2779	34.3	19
1990	Dal	79	**3413**	43.2(62)	0	8	438	**2815**	**35.6**	20
1991	Dal	57	2426	42.6(64)	0	5	231	2095	36.8	16
1992	Dal	61	2620	43.0(58)	0	9	397	2043	33.5	19
1993	NE	73	3096	42.4(59)	**3**	7	313	2643	34.8	25
1994	Min	77	3301	42.9(67)	0	5	410	2791	36.2	28
1995	Min	72	2948	40.9(60)	0	6	446	2382	33.1	21
NFL	11	813	33887	41.7(67)	7	86	3655	28512	35.1	240
Scarpitto, Bob										
1965	Den-A	67	2833	42.3(**74**)	0	—	—	—	—	—
1966	Den-A	77	**3480**	**45.2**(**70**)	1	—	—	—	—	—
1967	Den-A	105	**4713**	**44.9**(**73**)	**1**	—	—	—	—	—
1968	Bos-A	34	1382	40.6(**87**)	**2**	—	—	—	—	—
NFL	4	283	12408	43.8(87)	4	—	—	—	—	—

YEAR	TEAM	PNT	YDS	AVG (LG)	BLK	TB	RTYDS	NET	AVG	IN20
SCRIBNER, BUCKY										
1983	GB	69	2869	41.6 (**70**)	1	7	384	2345	33.5	11
1984	GB	85	3596	42.3 (61)	0	**12**	368	2988	35.2	18
1987	Min	20	827	41.4 (54)	0	1	79	728	36.4	4
1988	Min	84	3387	40.3 (55)	2	9	405	2802	32.6	23
1989	Min	72	2864	39.8 (55)	0	8	300	2404	33.4	16
NFL	5	330	13543	41.0 (70)	3	37	1536	11267	34.1	72
SEIPLE, LARRY										
1967	Mia-A	70	2909	41.6 (70)	**1**	—	—	—	—	—
1968	Mia-A	75	3044	40.6 (60)	0	—	—	—	—	—
1969	Mia-A	80	3263	40.8 (66)	**2**	—	—	—	—	—
1970	Mia	58	2392	41.2 (67)	0	—	—	—	—	—
1971	Mia	52	2087	40.1 (73)	1	—	—	—	—	—
1972	Mia	36	1437	39.9 (54)	0	—	—	—	—	—
1973	Mia	48	2031	42.3 (57)	0	—	—	—	—	—
1974	Mia	65	2511	38.6 (60)	0	—	—	—	—	—
1975	Mia	65	2506	38.6 (61)	0	—	—	—	—	—
1976	Mia	62	2366	38.2 (56)	0	5	272	1994	32.2	14
1977	Mia	22	801	36.4 (54)	1	1	65	716	31.1	5
NFL	11	633	25347	40.0 (73)	5	6	337	2710	32.3	19
SKLADANY, TOM										
1978	Det	86	3654	**42.5 (63)**	1	7	467	3047	35.0	19
1979	Det	10	406	40.6 (52)	0	0	5	401	40.1	2
1980	Det	72	3036	42.2 (**67**)	**1**	8	300	2576	35.3	16
1981	Det	64	2784	**43.5 (74)**	0	5	299	2385	37.3	21
1982	Det	36	1483	41.2 (59)	0	3	200	1223	34.0	6
1983	Phi	27	1062	39.3 (51)	0	2	172	850	31.5	5
NFL	6	295	12425	42.1 (74)	2	25	1443	10482	35.5	69
SMITH, HUNTER										
1999	Ind	58	2467	42.5 (61)	**2**	8	469	1838	**30.6**	16
2000	Ind	65	2906	44.7 (65)	0	9	357	2369	36.4	20
2001	Ind	68	3023	44.5 (65)	0	**12**	486	2297	**33.8**	12
2002	Ind	66	2672	40.5 (69)	1	9	156	2336	34.9	26
2003	Ind	62	2617	42.2 (55)	1	3	319	2238	35.5	20
2004	Ind	54	2443	45.2 (62)	0	3	395	1988	**36.8**	21
2005	Ind	52	2301	44.3 (58)	0	5	272	1929	37.1	23
NFL	7	425	18429	43.4 (69)	4	49	2454	14995	35.3	138
STANLEY, CHAD										
1999	SF	69	2737	39.7 (70)	**2**	9	374	2183	30.7	20
2000	SF	69	2727	39.5 (56)	1	7	332	2255	32.2	15
2001	Arz	19	751	39.5 (54)	0	1	82	649	34.2	4
2002	Hou	114	**4720**	41.4 (62)	**2**	6	328	**4272**	**36.8**	**36**
2003	Hou	97	4028	41.5 (58)	0	3	407	3561	**36.7**	**36**
2004	Hou	73	3009	41.2 (57)	0	7	265	2604	35.7	19
2005	Hou	77	2990	38.8 (61)	0	1	219	2751	35.7	29
NFL	7	518	20962	40.5 (70)	5	34	2007	18275	35.3	159
STARK, ROHN										
1982	Bal	46	2044	44.4 (60)	0	**12**	226	1578	34.3	8
1983	Bal	91	**4124**	**45.3 (68)**	0	9	**642**	**3302**	**36.3**	20
1984	Ind	98	4383	44.7 (72)	0	7	600	3643	**37.2**	21
1985	Ind	78	3584	**45.9 (68)**	**2**	**14**	572	2732	34.2	12
1986	Ind	76	3432	**45.2 (63)**	0	5	502	2830	**37.2**	22
1987	Ind	61	2440	40.0 (63)	**2**	7	353	1947	30.9	12
1988	Ind	64	2784	43.5 (65)	0	8	418	2206	34.5	15
1989	Ind	79	3392	42.9 (64)	1	10	**558**	2634	**32.9**	14
1990	Ind	71	3084	43.4 (61)	1	3	334	2690	37.4	**24**
1991	Ind	82	**3492**	42.6 (65)	0	6	**516**	2856	**34.8**	14
1992	Ind	83	3716	44.8 (64)	0	7	313	3263	39.3	22
1993	Ind	83	3595	43.3 (65)	0	**13**	352	2983	35.9	18
1994	Ind	73	3092	42.4 (60)	**1**	10	366	2526	34.1	22
1995	Pit	59	2368	40.1 (64)	0	11	186	1962	33.3	20
1996	Car	77	3128	40.6 (60)	0	9	173	2775	36.0	21
1997	Sea	20	813	40.7 (52)	0	2	236	537	26.9	7
NFL	16	1141	49471	43.4 (72)	7	133	6347	40464	35.5	272
STRYZINSKI, DAN										
1990	Pit	65	2454	37.8 (51)	1	5	105	2249	34.1	18
1991	Pit	74	2996	40.5 (63)	1	3	210	2726	36.3	10
1992	TB	74	3015	40.7 (57)	0	11	117	2678	36.2	15
1993	TB	93	3772	40.6 (57)	**1**	3	394	**3318**	**35.3**	24
1994	TB	72	2800	38.9 (53)	0	6	94	2586	35.9	20
1995	Atl	67	2759	41.2 (64)	0	5	236	2423	36.2	21
1996	Atl	75	3152	42.0 (58)	0	4	413	2659	35.5	22
1997	Atl	89	3498	39.3 (57)	0	9	55	3263	36.7	20
1998	Atl	74	2963	40.0 (55)	0	7	112	2711	36.6	25
1999	Atl	80	3163	39.5 (55)	0	4	119	2964	37.1	27
2000	Atl	84	3447	41.0 (60)	1	5	126	3221	37.9	27
2001	KC	73	2976	40.8 (76)	0	5	277	2599	35.6	27
2002	KC	64	2422	37.8 (56)	1	6	274	2028	31.2	15
2003	NYJ	71	2655	37.4 (55)	1	4	322	2253	31.3	22
NFL	14	1055	42072	39.9 (76)	6	77	2854	37678	35.7	293
STUDSTILL, PAT										
1961	Det	1	32	32.0 (32)	0	—	—	—	—	—
1965	Det	78	3335	42.8 (69)	0	—	—	—	—	—
1966	Det	72	2956	41.1 (66)	0	—	—	—	—	—
1967	Det	36	1602	**44.5 (78)**	0	—	—	—	—	—
1968	LARm	81	3207	39.6 (58)	0	—	—	—	—	—
1969	LARm	80	**3259**	40.7 (60)	0	—	—	—	—	—
1970	LARm	67	2618	39.1 (53)	0	—	—	—	—	—
1971	LARm	70	2896	41.4 (60)	0	—	—	—	—	—
1972	NE	75	2859	38.1 (57)	1	—	—	—	—	—
NFL	9	560	22764	40.7 (78)	1	—	—	—	—	—

YEAR	TEAM	PNT	YDS	AVG (LG)	BLK	TB	RTYDS	NET	AVG	IN20
SWIDER, LARRY										
1979	Det	88	3523	40.0 (72)	0	7	435	2948	**33.5**	13
1980	SL	99	4111	41.5 (66)	**1**	**15**	**645**	3166	**31.7**	12
1981	TB	58	2476	42.7 (62)	**2**	4	409	1987	33.1	13
1982	TB	39	1620	41.5 (59)	**1**	**6**	192	1308	32.7	6
NFL	4	284	11730	41.3 (72)	4	32	1681	9409	33.1	44
TELTSCHIK, JOHN										
1986	Phi	108	**4493**	41.6 (62)	1	10	**631**	**3662**	**33.6**	20
1987	Phi	82	3131	38.2 (60)	1	4	399	2652	**32.0**	13
1988	Phi	98	3958	40.4 (**70**)	**3**	8	375	3423	**33.9**	**28**
1989	Phi	57	2246	39.4 (58)	0	3	175	2011	35.3	12
NFL	4	345	13828	40.1 (70)	5	25	1580	11748	34.1	73
TUPA, TOM										
1989	Phx	6	280	46.7 (51)	0	0	41	239	39.8	2
1994	Cle	80	3211	40.1 (65)	0	8	220	2831	35.4	27
1995	Cle	65	2831	43.6 (64)	0	9	296	2355	36.2	18
1996	NE	63	2739	43.5 (62)	0	7	334	2265	36.0	14
1997	NE	78	3569	**45.8 (73)**	1	**14**	437	2852	36.1	24
1998	NE	74	3294	44.5 (64)	0	9	493	2621	35.4	13
1999	NYJ	81	3659	45.2 (69)	0	7	427	3092	38.2	25
2000	NYJ	83	3714	44.7 (**70**)	0	**15**	660	2754	**33.2**	18
2001	NYJ	67	2575	38.4 (59)	0	5	333	2142	32.0	21
2002	TB	90	3856	42.8 (71)	0	**12**	433	3183	35.4	30
2003	TB	83	3590	43.3 (60)	0	6	**489**	2981	35.9	26
2004	Was	103	4544	**44.1 (61)**	1	**8**	**727**	3657	35.2	30
NFL	12	873	37862	43.4 (73)	2	100	4890	30972	35.5	248
TURK, MATT										
1995	Was	74	3140	42.4 (60)	0	9	173	2787	37.7	**29**
1996	Was	75	3386	**45.1 (63)**	0	11	224	2942	39.2	24
1997	Was	84	3788	45.1 (62)	1	11	237	3331	39.2	32
1998	Was	93	4103	44.1 (69)	**1**	9	260	3663	39.0	**33**
1999	Was	62	2564	41.4 (57)	0	10	159	2205	35.6	16
2000	Mia	92	3870	42.1 (**70**)	0	14	258	3332	36.2	25
2001	Mia	81	3321	41.0 (**77**)	0	7	136	3045	37.6	28
2002	NYJ	63	2584	41.0 (65)	0	9	203	2201	34.9	13
2003	Mia	68	2631	38.7 (57)	0	7	143	2348	34.5	23
2004	Mia	98	**4088**	41.7 (67)	0	10	241	**3647**	**37.2**	**29**
NFL	10	790	33475	42.4 (77)	2	97	2034	29501	37.3	252
TUTEN, RICK										
1989	Phi	7	256	36.6 (45)	0	1	1	235	33.6	1
1990	Buf	53	2107	39.8 (55)	0	4	214	1813	34.2	12
1991	Sea	49	2106	43.0 (60)	0	3	239	1807	36.9	8
1992	Sea	108	**4760**	44.1 (65)	0	8	416	**4184**	**38.7**	**29**
1993	Sea	90	**4007**	44.5 (64)	1	7	475	**3392**	**37.3**	21
1994	Sea	91	3905	42.9 (64)	0	7	426	3339	36.7	33
1995	Sea	83	3735	**45.0 (73)**	0	8	549	3026	36.5	21
1996	Sea	85	3746	44.1 (66)	**1**	7	**640**	2966	**34.5**	20
1997	Sea	48	2007	41.8 (65)	0	5	161	1746	36.4	15
1998	SL	95	4202	44.2 (64)	0	10	**652**	3350	35.3	16
1999	SL	32	1359	42.5 (70)	0	7	101	1118	34.9	9
NFL	11	741	32190	43.4 (73)	2	67	3874	26976	36.4	185
VAN BROCKLIN, NORM										
1949	LARm	2	91	45.5 (46)	0	—	—	—	—	—
1950	LARm	11	466	42.4 (51)	0	—	—	—	—	—
1951	LARm	48	1992	41.5 (62)	**1**	—	—	—	—	—
1952	LARm	29	1250	43.1 (66)	0	—	—	—	—	—
1953	LARm	60	2529	42.2 (57)	0	—	—	—	—	—
1954	LARm	44	1874	42.6 (61)	0	—	—	—	—	—
1955	LARm	60	2676	**44.6 (61)**	0	—	—	—	—	—
1956	LARm	48	2070	**43.1 (72)**	0	—	—	—	—	—
1957	LARm	54	2392	44.3 (71)	0	—	—	—	—	—
1958	Phi	54	2225	41.2 (58)	**1**	—	—	—	—	—
1959	Phi	53	2263	42.7 (59)	**1**	—	—	—	—	—
1960	Phi	60	2585	43.1 (70)	0	—	—	—	—	—
NFL	12	523	22413	42.9 (72)	3	—	—	—	—	—
VAN HEUSEN, BILLY										
1968	Den-A	88	3853	43.8 (68)	0	—	—	—	—	—
1969	Den-A	25	1021	40.8 (61)	0	—	—	—	—	—
1970	Den	87	**3732**	42.9 (64)	0	—	—	—	—	—
1971	Den	76	3176	41.8 (62)	1	—	—	—	—	—
1972	Den	60	2408	40.1 (60)	1	—	—	—	—	—
1973	Den	69	3114	45.1 (**78**)	0	—	—	—	—	—
1974	Den	75	3024	40.3 (61)	1	—	—	—	—	—
1975	Den	63	2515	39.9 (64)	0	—	—	—	—	—
1976	Den	31	1093	35.3 (52)	1	2	146	907	28.3	4
NFL	9	574	23936	41.7 (78)	4	2	146	907	29.3	4
VILLANUEVA, DANNY										
1961	LARm	46	1845	40.1 (53)	0	—	—	—	—	—
1962	LARm	87	**3960**	45.5 (65)	1	—	—	—	—	—
1963	LARm	81	**3678**	45.4 (68)	0	—	—	—	—	—
1964	LARm	82	3616	44.1 (58)	0	—	—	—	—	—
1965	Dal	60	2505	41.8 (58)	0	—	—	—	—	—
1966	Dal	65	2551	39.2 (58)	**1**	—	—	—	—	—
1967	Dal	67	2707	40.4 (57)	0	—	—	—	—	—
NFL	7	488	20862	42.8 (68)	2	—	—	—	—	—
WAGNER, BRYAN										
1987	ChiB	36	1461	40.6 (71)	1	4	195	1186	32.1	9
1988	ChiB	79	3282	41.5 (**70**)	0	10	447	2635	33.4	18
1989	Cle	97	**3817**	39.4 (60)	0	6	418	**3279**	**33.8**	**32**
1990	Cle	74	2879	38.9 (65)	**4**	2	425	2414	**30.9**	13
1991	NE	14	548	39.1 (54)	0	0	140	408	29.1	0

YEAR	TEAM	PNT	YDS	AVG(LG)	BLK	TB	RTYDS	NET	AVG	IN20
1992	GB	30	1222	40.7(52)	0	5	73	1049	35.0	10
1993	GB	74	3174	42.9(60)	0	7	350	2684	36.3	19
1994	SD	65	2705	41.6(59)	0	3	348	2297	35.3	20
1995	NE	37	1557	42.1(57)	0	4	168	1309	35.4	13
NFL	9	506	20645	40.8(71)	5	41	2564	17261	34.1	134
WALDEN, BOBBY										
1964	Min	72	3341	46.4(73)	0	—	—	—	—	—
1965	Min	51	2146	42.1(61)	0					
1966	Min	60	2463	41.1(70)	0					
1967	Min	75	3117	41.6(76)	0					
1968	Pit	68	2745	40.4(57)	0					
1969	Pit	77	3254	42.3(61)	0					
1970	Pit	75	3393	45.2(66)	0					
1971	Pit	79	3455	43.7(57)	0					
1972	Pit	65	2846	43.8(72)	2					
1973	Pit	62	2548	41.1(57)	1					
1974	Pit	78	3040	39.0(65)	0					
1975	Pit	69	2717	39.4(67)	1					
1976	Pit	76	2982	39.2(58)	0	13	206	2516	33.1	22
1977	Pit	67	2482	37.0(65)	1	5	380	2002	29.4	13
NFL	14	974	40529	41.6(76)	5	18	586	4518	31.6	35
WALTER, KEN										
1997	Car	85	3604	42.4(62)	0	4	428	3096	36.4	29
1998	Car	77	3131	40.7(59)	0	5	94	2937	38.1	20
1999	Car	65	2562	39.4(56)	0	1	158	2384	36.7	18
2000	Car	64	2459	38.4(66)	2	2	187	2232	33.8	19
2001	NE	49	1964	40.1(58)	0	2	59	1865	38.1	24
2002	NE	70	2723	38.9(55)	1	9	181	2362	33.3	19
2003	NE	76	2865	37.7(52)	1	3	220	2585	33.6	25
2004	Sea	24	920	38.3(50)	1	1	74	826	33.0	4
NFL	8	510	20228	39.7(66)	5	27	1401	18287	35.9	158
WATERFIELD, BOB										
1945	Cle	39	1585	40.6(68)	1					
1946	LARm	39	1743	44.7(65)	0					
1947	LARm	59	2500	42.4(86)	1					
1948	LARm	43	1833	42.6(88)	0					
1949	LARm	49	2177	44.4(61)	1					
1950	LARm	52	2087	40.1(61)	2					
1951	LARm	4	166	41.5(52)	0					
1952	LARm	30	1276	42.5(59)	0					
NFL	8	315	13367	42.4(88)	5					
WEAVER, HERMAN										
1970	Det	62	2483	40.0(65)	1					
1971	Det	42	1752	41.7(63)	2					
1972	Det	43	1734	40.3(55)	1					
1973	Det	54	2333	43.2(66)	1					
1974	Det	72	2772	38.5(61)	2					
1975	Det	80	3361	42.0(61)	1					
1976	Det	83	3280	39.5(69)	1	6	278	2882	34.3	15
1977	Sea	58	2293	39.5(59)	1	4	336	1877	31.8	10
1978	Sea	66	2440	37.0(59)	0	6	371	1949	29.5	13
1979	Sea	66	2651	40.2(60)	3	3	289	2302	33.4	11
1980	Sea	67	2798	41.8(69)	2	7	476	2182	31.6	14
NFL	11	693	27897	40.3(69)	14	26	1750	11192	32.9	63
WEST, JEFF										
1975	SL	64	2412	37.7(58)	1					
1976	SD	38	1548	40.7(57)	0	5	223	1225	32.2	9
1977	SD	72	2707	37.6(59)	1	3	378	2269	31.1	10
1978	SD	73	2720	37.3(59)	2	8	356	2204	29.4	22
1979	SD	75	2736	36.5(62)	0	9	204	2352	31.4	23
1981	Sea	66	2578	39.1(56)	0	2	153	2385	36.1	16
1982	Sea	48	1835	38.2(52)	0	3	69	1706	35.5	8
1983	Sea	79	3118	39.5(56)	0	10	185	2733	34.6	25
1984	Sea	95	3567	37.5(60)	0	10	205	3162	33.3	24
1985	Sea	11	420	38.2(52)	0	3	49	311	28.3	0
NFL	10	621	23641	38.1(62)	4	53	1822	18347	32.9	137
WHITE, DANNY										
1976	Dal	70	2690	38.4(54)	2	12	252	2198	30.5	13
1977	Dal	80	3171	39.6(57)	1	10	280	2691	33.2	25
1978	Dal	76	3076	40.5(56)	1	11	311	2545	33.1	16
1979	Dal	76	3168	41.7(73)	0	9	252	2736	36.0	21
1980	Dal	71	2903	40.9(58)	0	11	215	2468	34.8	17
1981	Dal	79	3222	40.8(60)	0	7	231	2851	36.1	19

YEAR	TEAM	PNT	YDS	AVG(LG)	BLK	TB	RTYDS	NET	AVG	IN20
1982	Dal	37	1542	41.7(56)	0	2	118	1384	37.4	6
1983	Dal	38	1543	40.6(50)	1	3	233	1250	32.1	6
1984	Dal	82	3151	38.4(54)	0	8	156	2835	34.6	21
1985	Dal	1	43	43.0(43)	0	1	0	23	23.0	0
NFL	10	610	24509	40.2(73)	5	74	2048	20981	34.4	144
WIDBY, RON										
1968	Dal	59	2415	40.9(84)	0					
1969	Dal	63	2729	43.3(62)	0					
1970	Dal	69	2847	41.3(59)	1					
1971	Dal	56	2329	41.6(59)	1					
1972	GB	65	2714	41.8(64)	2					
1973	GB	56	2414	43.1(60)	0					
NFL	6	368	15448	42.0(84)	4					
WILMSMEYER, KLAUS										
1992	SF	49	1918	39.1(58)	0	2	177	1701	34.7	19
1993	SF	42	1718	40.9(61)	0	5	171	1447	34.5	11
1994	SF	54	2235	41.4(60)	0	3	242	1933	35.8	18
1995	NO	73	2965	40.6(53)	1	5	233	2632	35.6	21
1996	NO	87	3551	40.8(63)	0	9	546	2825	32.5	16
1998	Mia	93	3949	42.5(57)	1	13	339	3350	35.6	23
NFL	6	398	16336	41.0(63)	2	37	1708	13888	34.9	108
WILSON, JERREL										
1963	KC-A	61	2628	43.1(72)	1					
1964	KC-A	78	3326	42.6(70)	0					
1965	KC-A	69	3132	45.4(64)	1					
1966	KC-A	62	2715	43.8(69)	1					
1967	KC-A	41	1739	42.4(59)	1					
1968	KC-A	63	2841	45.1(70)	0					
1969	KC-A	68	3022	44.4(62)	0					
1970	KC	76	3415	44.9(68)	0					
1971	KC	64	2864	44.8(68)	1					
1972	KC	66	2960	44.8(69)	1					
1973	KC	80	3642	45.5(68)	1					
1974	KC	83	3462	41.7(64)	2					
1975	KC	54	2233	41.4(64)	1					
1976	KC	65	2729	42.0(62)	1	8	365	2204	33.4	14
1977	KC	88	3510	39.9(59)	1	5	703	2707	30.4	11
1978	NE	54	1921	35.6(57)	0	4	251	1590	29.4	14
NFL	16	1072	46139	43.0(72)	12	17	1319	6501	31.4	39
WITTUM, TOM										
1973	SF	79	3455	43.7(62)	0					
1974	SF	68	2800	41.2(67)	1					
1975	SF	67	2804	41.9(64)	3					
1976	SF	89	3634	40.8(68)	2	10	351	3083	33.9	15
1977	SF	77	2801	36.4(54)	3	4	444	2277	28.5	10
NFL	5	380	15494	40.8(68)	9	14	795	5360	32.3	25
YEWCIC, TOM										
1961	Bos-A	62	2406	38.8(64)	2					
1962	Bos-A	69	2654	38.5(56)	1					
1963	Bos-A	74	2880	38.9(65)	1					
1964	Bos-A	73	2787	38.2(63)	1					
1965	Bos-A	76	3094	40.7(70)	2					
1966	Bos-A	21	732	34.9(49)	1					
NFL	6	375	14553	38.8(70)	8					
ZASTUDIL, DAVE										
2002	Bal	81	3368	41.6(61)	2	5	471	2797	33.7	31
2003	Bal	89	3649	41.0(67)	0	8	354	3135	35.2	21
2004	Bal	73	2948	40.4(61)	0	12	181	2527	34.6	26
2005	Bal	84	3653	43.5(60)	1	7	481	3032	35.7	11
NFL	4	327	13618	41.6(67)	3	32	1487	11491	35.1	89
ZIMMERMAN, ROY										
1940	Was	7	256	36.6(47)	0					
1941	Was	14	594	42.4(65)	1					
1942	Was	4	202	50.5(52)	0					
1943	P-P	44	1521	34.6(53)	2					
1944	Phi	39	1531	39.3(61)	0					
1945	Phi	47	1778	37.8(64)	1					
1946	Phi	23	890	38.7(52)	0					
1947	Det	49	2078	42.4(62)	1					
1948	Bos	51	2215	43.4(67)	0					
NFL	9	278	11065	39.8(67)	5					

THE STARTERS

Anyone who makes it inside a National Football League stadium early enough on Sunday will see the starters for that day's game introduced. The crowd cheers long and loud for the home team—unless fans have taken to wearing paper bags on the heads from embarrassment, then watch out—and the starters rush out on the field to be congratulated by their teammates. With an announcer booming out the names, 70,000 fans screaming, dozens of reporters watching from the press box, and a team of statisticians standing by, figuring out who the starters are isn't much of a problem. This hasn't always been the case.

Historically, pro football has done a pretty poor job of keeping track of who's a regular and who isn't. Game starters have been kept and published in the league record books only since the mid 1980s, and in the team media guides from 1980 forward. This data is nearly complete since then. Before that, it gets a little murkier.

Data for the 1970s is from the team media guides and involves mostly players whose careers bridged the 1980s and have their totals traced back to their rookie years. Then there is the occasional mention of starter information in the player biographies of that period. Data for the 1950s and 1960s is virtually nonexistent and not even researchable. The official score sheets and team statistics packages for the NFL in those years did list the starting lineup, but that would usually just be the offensive players. The American Football League in the 1960s usually just recorded who played, not those who started.

Defensive players were usually listed along with the offensive positions, but there would be no way to tell a defensive starter from an offensive sub. In the 1950s and 1960s a few players still lined up on both offense and defense, making things yet more difficult to figure out. The main sources of starters from that era were the press guide biographies and newspaper box scores, which became less frequent in the 1960s and, as mentioned, showed only the offensive starters. The media guides in the early 1950s had very little information on how much a player actually played, and if a player retired, was released, or sent to another team, there would be no report of any of it.

As a result of some of the questionable record keeping practices of years gone by, many of the entries in the starters list are educated guesses. In addition, some players who did not start very many games ended up playing quite a bit, sometimes seeing more time than the starters. These can be determined for the players with stats, but not for players whose position have no statistics.

Tod Maher researched games started from newspaper lineups for the 1920–49 period, when there were only 11 starters per game. (A rule prohibited wholesale substitution, which was exempted for part of World War II because of the manpower shortage.) Again, in some cases, a player who did not start could wind up playing most of the game. This was especially true of quarterbacks like Sammy Baugh and Sid Luckman. For the first 30 years of the NFL, the player with the most activity as reflected by the stats are listed as starters.

The 1950 season was the beginning of modern football, with a rule change that allowed unlimited substitution. For the first time it was possible for teams to have offensive and defensive specialists. Before then, there would be a first and second team, each playing both offense and defense. This rule was tried on an experimental basis in 1949, but this book uses 1950, when the rule was officially adopted, as the starting point. Before then, the first team would play about 10 minutes both ways, and would then be replaced. The rules would not allow the first team back in until the end of the quarter. Hardly anyone played both ways for any length of time after that.

George Connor played quite a bit on both offense and defense for the Chicago Bears in the early 1950s. The legendary Chuck Bednarik of the Philadelphia Eagles played both ways in 1960, but he played only 400 of the 720 minutes, 350 on offense and 50 on defense, which amount to almost all the offensive plays and maybe 20 percent of the defensive ones. Even busier was Deion Sanders for the Dallas Cowboys in 1996. He played most of the defense and about 50 percent of the offense for Dallas. Sanders would be even busier in 1997; he played mostly defense that year, but he also played 135 baseball games for the Cincinnati Reds.

The positions in 1950 were pretty much the same as today, except some positions had different names. By then every team but one had adopted the T formation, which had been used by the Bears from their

beginning as the Decatur Staleys in 1920. The Eagles were the next to convert in 1940 and the last holdout was the Pittsburgh Steelers, who finally switched to the T in 1952. The receivers were still called ends, left and right, and the left end did not split out much. By the 1960s most teams had a split end and a tight end. The right halfback of the 1950s became the flanker back of the 1960s, although a few teams (notably the Rams) used flankers in the 1950s. By the 1970s, they were both called wide receivers. The left halfback became the running back. From the 1970s through the mid 1990s, the fullback was usually called a second running back, but in these tables, a fullback is identified. In some cases, though, there really was no difference.

Most teams played a 5–2 or 5–3 defense in the early 1950s, with a middle guard instead of a middle linebacker. In some cases, both positions were filled, with a three-man backfield. In the 1950s the defensive backs were usually called just backs, not categorized any more specifically. In the 1960s the defensive halfbacks were often called cornerbacks and the safeties were designated left and right. By the 1970s the left safety was the strong safety and the right safety became the weak safety, quickly changed to free safety. Strong meant lining up opposite the tight end, who usually set up on the right side of the offensive line. Some teams used strong and weak linebackers, instead of left and right, and the strong linebacker would follow the tight end on the occasions he was on the left side. Every team had converted to a 4–3 defensive front by the mid 1950s. In the 1970s a new defense—namely the 3–4 began to emerge. There were three lineman—two ends and a nose tackle—and four linebackers: left outside, left inside, right inside, and right outside. About 10 percent of the teams in the 1970s played this defense, up to 75 percent in the 1980s, and down to 30 percent in the 1990s and only 15 percent today.

KEY TO THE STARTERS

For the 1920–49 data, many of the positions are different than those listed for later years. As mentioned before, they are only listed as offensive players because the rules required teams to play both ways for almost this entire period. The coach leads off the column, followed by the position abbreviations.

LE Left End
LT Left Tackle
LG Left Guard
C Center
RG Right Guard
RT Right Tackle
RE Right End
TB/QB Tailback/Quarterback (if the team used the T formation, an asterisk after the player's name indicates he was a quarterback)
WB/HB/LH Wingback/Halfback/Left Halfback
BB/RH Blocking Back/Right Halfback
FB Fullback (for the Single Wing and its variants)

For lineups since 1950, teams sometimes used an alternate formation. On offense, the most common involved an extra tight end or wide receiver in place of the fullback. A plus after the player name indicates an extra wide receiver in the tight end or fullback column, while an asterisk indicates an extra tight end in the wide receiver or fullback column. The offensive abbreviations that are not the same as pre-1950 include:

WR/FL Wide Receiver/Flanker
TE Tight End/Right End
RB Running Back

The team's defensive starters continue across the next page for 1950 forward. These columns and abbreviations are:

LDE Left Defensive End
LDT/NT Left Defensive Tackle/Nose Tackle
RDT/RDE Right Defensive Tackle/Right Defensive End
RDE/LOLB Right Defensive End/Left Outside Linebacker
LLB/LILB Left Linebacker/Left Inside Linebacker

MLB/RILB   Middle Linebacker/Right Inside Linebacker
RLB/ROLB   Right Linebacker/Right Outside Linebacker
LCB   Left Cornerback
RCB   Right Cornerback
SS/LS   Strong Safety/Left Safety
FS/RS   Free Safety/Right Safety

On the right side of the page are two headings, depending on whether the team used a 4–3 (four lineman, three linebackers) or 3–4 alignment (three linemen, four linebackers). An asterisk after the player in the RDT/RE indicates a 3–4 alignment where the marked player was the RE and the linebackers were LOLB, LILB, RILB, and ROLB. A plus sign after the middle-linebacker player indicates his position was middle guard in a 5–2 defense. A plus sign after name in the fourth defensive back column indicates a middle guard in the 5–3 defense, which had only 3 defensive backs. A few teams used 5 defensive backs and no middle linebacker, with the nickel back in the MLB column with an asterisk. If there was more than one head coach for a team in a season, the one with the most games is shown.

The team's finish is shown to the right of their defensive starters. The FINISH column shows the following:

- First character: order of finish;
- Second character: league (1950–69) or conference code (1970–present);
- Third character: NFL conference code (1950–69) or AFL division code (1960–69), or division code (1970–present).

Intermediate games are **p** for playoff round (1949 AAFC, 1969 AFL, and 1982 NFL), **w** for wild card (since 1970), **d** division round, **c** conference championship, **l** league championship, **s** super bowl. The letter **e** is used for the divisional champ who played in the wild card round (since 1990). If the game was won, then another letter appears for the next round.

For 1920–49, the finish is shown in the team header line. Before 1933 there were no divisions, so there is a slash between the finish and the number of wins. From 1933-49, the letter after the order of finish indicates the division.

YEAR	COACH	LE	LT	LG	C	RG	RT	RE	TB/QB	WB/HB/LH	BB/RH	FB
AKRON (Pros 1920-25, Indians 1926) 1920 1/8-0-3, 1921 3/8-3-1, 1922 10/3-5-2, 1923 16/1-6, 1924 13/2-6, 1925 5/4-2-2, 1926 16/1-4-3												
1920	E.Tobin	B.Nash	P.Johnson	T.Tomlin	R.Bailey	A.Cobb	C.Copley	S.Bierce	F.Pollard	F.McCormick	H.Harris	R.King
1921	F.Pollard	J.Flower	P.Johnson	E.Tobin	R.Bailey	A.Nesser	C.Copley	S.Bierce	F.Pollard	C.Cramer	P.Sheeks	R.King
1922	U.Brewer	R.Daum	A.Jolley	W.LeJeune	J.Flower	A.Nesser	B.Spiers	B.Corcoran	J.Mills	C.Cramer	P.Sheeks	R.King
1923	D.Hendrian	R.Daum	L.Scott	W.LeJeune	J.Mills	D.Wallace	J.Flower	A.Nesser	W.Brenkert	C.Cramer	D.Hendrian	A.Michaels
1924	W.Brenkert	R.Daum	J.Flower	A.Nesser	J.Barrett	H.Newman	H.Sprinkle	J.Mills	A.Michaels	P.Hogan	W.Brenkert	C.Cramer
1925	S.Bierce	F.Bissell	K.Caldwell	A.Nesser	J.Barrett	G.Berry	D.Stahlman	O.Newman	F.Pollard	D.Annan	J.Robertson	G.Falcon
1926	F.Nied	R.Daum	K.Caldwell	R.Seidelson	G.Berry	N.McCombs	A.Casey	F.Bissell	O.Newman	H.Griggs	F.Pollard	C.Cramer
BALTIMORE COLTS (AAFC) 1947 4e/2-11-1, 1948 1e/7-7 d, 1949 7/1-11												
1947	C.Isbell	H.Bechtol	J.Mellus	B.French	M.Phillips	A.Lio	G.Perpich	E.Madar	B.Schwenk*	Hillenbrand	J.Vardian	B.Mertes
1948	C.Isbell	L.Davis	E.Blandin	D.Barwegan	B.Corley	D.Garrett	L.Artoe	J.North	Y.Tittle*	Hillenbrand	B.Pfohl	B.Mertes
1949	W.Driskill	L.Davis	E.Blandin	D.Barwegan	F.Prewitt	D.Garrett	J.Spruill	J.North	Y.Tittle*	J.Leicht	B.Pfohl	L.Gambino
BOSTON BULLDOGS 1929 4/4-4												
1929	C.Isbell	G.Kenneally	J.Carpe	F.Racis	A.Pierotti	E.McCrillis	J.Kozlowsky	R.Maloney	H.Stockton	A.Miller	J.Ernst	T.Latone
BOSTON YANKS (New York Bulldogs 1949) 1944 4e/2-8, 1945 3e/3-6-1, 1946 5e/2-8-1, 1947 3e/4-7-1, 1948 5e/3-9, 1949 5e/1-10-1												
1944	C.Isbell	K.Ranspot	E.Franco	A.Lio	J.Magee	B.Walker	E.McGee	J.Crowley	B.Davis*	T.Williams	J.Martin	G.Cafego
1945	H.Kopf	K.Ranspot	G.Sergienko	A.Lio	G.Smith	T.Leon	G.Doherty	D.Currivan	G.Cafego*	J.Grigas	B.Davis	P.Manders
1946	H.Kopf	S.Goldman	T.Dean	J.Zeno	Domnanovich	R.Canale	R.Calcagni	H.Crisler	P.Governali*	B.Dimancheff	M.Micka	J.Grigas
1947	C.Smith	S.Goldman	T.Dean	B.Kennedy	Domnanovich	Badaczewski	C.Vogelaar	N.Scollard	B.Dancewicz*	J.Golding	F.Seno	R.Romboli
1948	C.Smith	J.Tyree	M.Jarmoluk	Barzilauskas	Domnanovich	S.Batinski	C.Vogelaar	R.Heywood	R.Zimmerman*	B.Paschal	J.Golding	M.Micka
1949	C.Isbell	B.Chipley	J.Nolan	Barzilauskas	Domnanovich	J.Weaver	C.Vogelaar	N.Scollard	B.Layne*	P.Shoults	J.Golding	J.Osmanski
BROOKLYN (ns 1926, Dodgers 1930-43, Tigers 1944) 1926 14/3-8, 1930 4/7-4-1, 1931 9/2-12, 1932 6/3-9, 1933 2e/5-4-1, 1934 3e/4-7, 1935 2e/5-6-1, 1936 4e/3-8-1, 1937 4e/3-7-1, 1938 3e/4-4-3, 1939 3e/4-6-1, 1940 2e/8-3, 1941 2e/7-4, 1942 4e/3-8, 1943 4e/2-8, 1944 5e/0-10												
1926	C.Isbell	P.Jappe	J.Yeager	B.Morris	D.McGrath	C.Weber	H.Blacklock	D.Ziff	H.Bagby	R.Thomas	M.Brennan	G.Snell
1930	C.Isbell	M.Stramiello	S.Worden	H.Garvey	S.Hagberg	B.Gillson	H.Haines	B.Mahan	C.Weimer	S.Thomason	W.Kelly	J.McBride
1931	J.Depler	M.Stramiello	Lubratovich	D.Myers	A.Bultman	B.Gillson	J.Mooney	J.Nemecek	S.Thomason	B.Senn	F.Abruzzino	J.McBride
1932	B.Friedman	P.Riblett	Lubratovich	B.Jones	S.Mielziner	J.Bowdoin	Greenshields	E.Rowan	B.Friedman	O.Sansen	B.Karcis	J.Grossman
1933	C.McEwan	P.Riblett	Lubratovich	S.Worden	D.Morrison	H.Hickman	H.Ely	T.Nash	B.Friedman	S.Kelly	B.Karcis	D.Richards
1934	C.McEwan	P.Riblett	Lubratovich	S.Worden	D.Morrison	H.Hickman	H.Ely	W.Becker	C.Cagle	R.Kercheval	B.Karcis	O.Sansen
1935	P.Schissler	P.Riblett	C.Heldt	G.Bergerson	C.Oehler	B.Kirkland	B.Lee	R.Fuqua	R.Franklin	R.Kercheval	F.Lumpkin	B.Karcis
1936	P.Schissler	R.Badgro	C.Heldt	B.Kirkland	H.Krause	J.Rukas	B.Lee	R.Fuqua	B.Wilson	R.Kercheval	F.Lumpkin	D.Crayne
1937	P.Clark	J.Austin	J.Whatley	R.Leisk	W.Jorgensen	D.Nelson	J.Golemgeske	J.Barrett	A.Parker	R.Kercheval	T.Kaska	J.Maniaci
1938	P.Clark	P.Schwartz	B.Kinard	J.Golemgeske	L.Mark	O.Emerson	L.Disend	J.Druze	A.Parker	R.Kercheval	T.Kaska	S.Farrell
1939	P.Clark	P.Schwartz	L.Disend	B.Haak	L.Mark	C.Kaplanoff	B.Kinard	W.Young	A.Parker	R.Kercheval	W.Butcher	P.Manders
1940	J.Sutherland	P.Schwartz	B.Kinard	S.Petro	B.Svendsen	J.Sivell	W.Merrill	W.Young	A.Parker	B.McFadden	R.Shetley	P.Manders
1941	J.Sutherland	P.Schwartz	B.Kinard	W.Alfson	B.Svendsen	J.Sivell	W.Merrill	E.Rucinski	A.Parker	M.Condit	R.Shetley	P.Manders
1942	M.Getto	P.Schwartz	B.Kinard	G.Kinard	B.Robertson	J.Sivell	W.Merrill	E.Rucinski	D.McAdams	M.Condit	W.Butcher	P.Manders
1943	P.Cawthon	R.Wehba	B.Kinard	J.Fawcett	B.Svendsen	L.Jones	G.Sergienko	A.Kowalski	K.Heineman	M.Condit	J.Setcavage	P.Manders
1944	P.Cawthon	B.Masterson	B.Kinard	F.Rhea	G.Smith	T.Leon	G.Doherty	J.Carter	J.Butler	R.Hare	B.Brown	P.Manders
BROOKLYN DODGERS (AAFC) (merged with New York Yankees 1949) 1946 2e/3-10-1, 1947 3e/3-10-1, 1948 4e/2-12												
1946	C.Isbell	J.McCarthy	M.Ruby	G.Bernhardt	T.Warrington	H.Buffington	Mieszkowski	J.Davis	G.Dobbs	M.Colmer	W.McDonald	D.Principe
1947	C.Battles	J.McCarthy	M.Ruby	T.Warrington	E.Gustafson	H.Buffington	G.Williams	S.Judd	Hoernschemeyer	M.Gafford	W.McDonald	M.Colmer
1948	C.Voyles	H.Foldberg	J.Clowes	T.Warrington	E.Gustafson	J.Wozniak	R.Sazio	D.Edwards	B.Chappuis	M.Gafford	W.McDonald	M.Colmer
BUFFALO (All-Americans 1920-23, Bisons 1924-25, 1927, 1929, Rangers 1926) 1920 3/9-1-1, 1921 1/9-1-2, 1922 9/5-4-1, 1923 8/5-4-3, 1924 9/6-5, 1925 15/1-6-2, 1926 9/4-4-2, 1927 12/0-5, 1929 10/1-7-1												
1920	C.Isbell	M.Shelton	B.Spagna	B.Brace	L.Wray	S.Youngstrom	L.Little	H.Miller	O.Anderson	B.Weldon	T.Hughitt	P.Smith
1921	T.Hughitt	L.Urban	B.Nash	B.Brace	L.Wray	S.Youngstrom	L.Little	H.Miller	O.Anderson	E.Oliphant	T.Hughitt	P.Smith
1922	T.Hughitt	G.Goetz	C.Thomas	B.Brace	C.Guy	S.Youngstrom	F.Morrissey	L.Urban	O.Anderson	W.Kuehl	T.Hughitt	J.Laird
1923	T.Hughitt	G.Carberry	B.Nash	F.Morrissey	F.Culver	S.Youngstrom	M.Gulian	L.Urban	T.Holleran	M.Trainor	T.Hughitt	B.Roderick
1924	T.Hughitt	L.Watters	L.Feist	H.Collins	F.Culver	S.Youngstrom	I.Huffman	A.Guarnieri	E.Kaw	T.Hughitt	B.Boynton	P.Calac
1925	W.Koppisch	J.Noble	N.Harvey	C.Gay	M.Reed	S.Youngstrom	C.Van Dyne	L.Feist	W.Koppisch	J.Kendrick	W.Foster	F.Christman
1926	J.Kendrick	N.Allison	L.Caywood	J.Willson	G.Kirk	B.Irvin	F.Wilcox	R.Guffey	E.Slough	M.Wilson	J.Kendrick	B.Hobson
1927	D.Batterson	J.Underwood	N.Harvey	P.Minick	J.McArthur	F.McConnell	B.Irvin	L.Otte	B.Roderick	H.Carr	B.Hobson	K.Hauser
1929	C.Isbell	T.Voss	A.Jolley	N.McCombs	A.Dorfman	E.Comstock	W.Brewster	H.Bizer	C.Weimer	S.Hagberg	C.Ryan	B.Mahan
BUFFALO (AAFC) (Bisons 1946, Bills 1947-49) 1946 2e/3-10-1, 1947 2e/8-4-2, 1948 1e/7-7 dl, 1949 4/5-5-2 p												
1946	R.Dawson	R.Ebli	C.Stanley	J.Perko	F.Prewitt	R.Pirro	G.Doherty	H.Nelson	A.Dekdebrun*	C.Mutryn	S.Juzwik	V.Kulbitski
1947	R.Dawson	P.Gibson	G.Armstrong	H.Lahar	F.Prewitt	R.Pirro	G.Doherty	A.Coppage	G.Ratterman*	C.Mutryn	J.Rykovich	V.Kulbitski
1948	R.Dawson	A.Baldwin	G.Armstrong	H.Lahar	A.Statuto	R.Pirro	J.Kerns	P.Gibson	G.Ratterman*	C.Mutryn	B.Steuber	L.Tomasetti
1949	R.Dawson	A.Baldwin	J.Carpenter	A.Gibron	A.Statuto	R.Pirro	J.Kerns	J.Lukens	G.Ratterman*	C.Mutryn	R.Bumgardner	O.Cline
CANTON (Bulldogs 1920-23, 1925-26) 1920 8/7-4-2, 1921 4/5-2-3, 1922 1/10-0-2, 1923 1/11-0-1, 1925 11/4-4, 1926 20/1-9-3												
1920	R.Dawson	B.Higgins	C.Buck	C.Edwards	A.Feeney	J.Kellison	P.Henry	B.Lowe	Jim Thorpe	J.Guyon	T.Grigg	P.Calac
1921	C.Edwards	R.Steele	B.West	D.Speck	A.Feeney	D.Osborn	P.Henry	B.Higgins	T.Grigg	F.Slackford	H.Kempton	G.Falcon
1922	G.Chamberlin	G.Chamberlin	L.Lyman	T.Taylor	W.Murrah	D.Osborn	P.Henry	B.Carroll	H.Robb	N.Sacksteder	W.Roberts	D.Elliott
1923	G.Chamberlin	G.Chamberlin	L.Lyman	R.Comstock	L.Conover	D.Osborn	P.Henry	B.Carroll	L.Smyth	T.Grigg	H.Robb	D.Elliott
1925	R.Dawson	F.Culver	L.Lyman	W.Flattery	W.McRoberts	R.Comstock	P.Henry	B.Carroll	B.Jones	R.Redinger	H.Robb	P.Calac
1926	P.Henry	C.Marker	D.Nelson	J.Nichols	R.Kyle	W.Flattery	P.Henry	R.Stein	B.Roderick	D.Vick	H.Robb	P.Calac
CHICAGO BEARS (Decatur Staleys 1920, Chicago Staleys 1921) 1920 2/10-1-2, 1921 1/9-1-1, 1922 2/9-3, 1923 2/9-2-1, 1924 2/6-1-4, 1925 7/9-5-3, 1926 2/12-1-3, 1927 3/9-3-2, 1928 5/7-5-1, 1929 9/4-9-2, 1930 3/9-4-1, 1931 3/8-5, 1932 1/7-1-6, 1933 1w/10-2-1 l*, 1934 1w/13-0 l, 1935 3w/6-4-2, 1936 2w/9-3, 1937 1w/9-1-1 l, 1938 3w/6-5, 1939 2w/8-3, 1940 1w/8-3 l*, 1941 1w/10-1 dl*, 1942 1w/11-0 l, 1943 1w/8-1-1 l*, 1944 2w/6-3-1, 1945 4w/3-7, 1946 1w/8-2-1 l*, 1947 2w/8-4, 1948 2w/10-2, 1949 2w/9-3												
1920	R.Dawson	G.Chamberlin	B.Ingwersen	R.Petty	G.Trafton	J.Jones	H.Blacklock	G.Halas	P.Pearce*	D.Sternaman	J.Lanum	B.Koehler
1921	R.Dawson	G.Chamberlin	R.Scott	T.Taylor	G.Trafton	R.Smith	H.Blacklock	G.Halas	P.Pearce*	D.Sternaman	P.Stinchcomb	K.Huffine
1922	R.Dawson	H.Garvey	R.Scott	H.Anderson	O.Larson	R.Smith	H.Blacklock	G.Halas	J.Sternaman*	D.Sternaman	P.Stinchcomb	G.Bolan
1923	G.Halas	D.Hanny	E.Healey	H.Anderson	G.Trafton	H.Garvey	R.Scott	G.Halas	J.Bryan*	D.Sternaman	J.Lanum	O.Knop
1924	G.Halas	D.Hanny	E.Healey	H.Anderson	G.Trafton	J.McMillen	H.Blacklock	G.Halas	J.Sternaman*	D.Sternaman	L.Walquist	O.Knop
1925	G.Halas	D.Hanny	E.Healey	Fleckenstein	G.Trafton	J.McMillen	D.Murry	G.Halas	J.Sternaman*	D.Sternaman	L.Walquist	O.Knop
1926	G.Halas	D.Hanny	E.Healey	B.Buckler	G.Trafton	J.McMillen	D.Murry	G.Halas	M.Romney*	P.Driscoll	L.Walquist	O.Knop
1927	G.Halas	T.Voss	E.Healey	B.Buckler	G.Trafton	J.McMillen	L.Lyman	D.Hanny	D.Sternaman*	P.Driscoll	L.Walquist	O.Knop
1928	G.Halas	T.Voss	L.Lyman	B.Buckler	G.Trafton	J.McMillen	D.Murry	T.Drews	J.Sternaman*	P.Driscoll	L.Walquist	B.White
1929	G.Halas	C.Cunningham	P.Nelson	Z.Carlson	G.Trafton	J.Polisky	D.Murry	L.Johnsos	J.Sternaman*	G.Grange	L.Walquist	W.Holmer
1930	R.Jones	L.Johnsos	L.Lyman	Z.Carlson	B.Pearson	B.Frump	L.Steinbach	G.Grange	C.Brumbaugh*	R.Grange	J.Lintzenich	B.Nagurski
1931	R.Jones	L.Johnsos	L.Lyman	Z.Carlson	B.Pearson	B.Buckler	L.Burdick	H.Drury	C.Brumbaugh*	G.Grange	J.Lintzenich	B.Nagurski
1932	R.Jones	L.Johnsos	Engebretsen	Z.Carlson	O.Miller	J.Kopcha	L.Burdick	B.Hewitt	K.Molesworth*	R.Grange	D.Nesbitt	B.Nagurski
1933	G.Halas	B.Hewitt	L.Lyman	Z.Carlson	O.Miller	J.Kopcha	G.Musso	B.Karr	C.Brumbaugh*	K.Molesworth	J.Sisk	B.Nagurski
1934	G.Halas	B.Hewitt	L.Lyman	Z.Carlson	E.Kawal	J.Kopcha	G.Musso	B.Karr	C.Brumbaugh*	B.Feathers	G.Ronzani	B.Nagurski
1935	G.Halas	B.Hewitt	A.Buss	R.Richards	E.Kawal	J.Kopcha	G.Musso	B.Karr	B.Masterson*	B.Feathers	G.Ronzani	J.Manders
1936	G.Halas	B.Hewitt	J.Stydahar	E.Michaels	E.Kawal	D.Fortmann	G.Musso	B.Karr	B.Masterson*	B.Feathers	R.Nolting	B.Nagurski
1937	G.Halas	E.Manske	J.Stydahar	D.Fortmann	F.Bausch	G.Musso	R.Thompson	B.Karr	B.Masterson*	B.Feathers	J.Manders	B.Nagurski
1938	G.Halas	D.Plasman	J.Stydahar	D.Fortmann	F.Bausch	G.Musso	R.Thompson	L.McDonald	B.Masterson*	R.Nolting	J.Manders	B.Johnson
1939	G.Halas	L.McDonald	J.Stydahar	D.Fortmann	F.Bausch	G.Musso	R.Thompson	G.Wilson	B.Masterson*	S.Luckman	R.Nolting	J.Maniaci
1940	G.Halas	D.Plasman	J.Stydahar	D.Fortmann	B.Turner	G.Musso	L.Artoe	G.Wilson	S.Luckman*	R.Nolting	G.McAfee	B.Osmanski
1941	G.Halas	D.Plasman	E.Kolman	D.Fortmann	B.Turner	R.Bray	L.Artoe	J.Siegal	S.Luckman*	R.Nolting	H.Gallarneau	B.Osmanski
1942	H.Anderson	B.Nowaskey	E.Kolman	D.Fortmann	B.Turner	R.Bray	L.Artoe	G.Wilson	S.Luckman*	H.Clarke	H.Gallarneau	Famiglietti
1943	H.Anderson	J.Benton	Steinkemper	D.Fortmann	B.Turner	G.Musso	A.Hoptowit	G.Wilson	S.Luckman*	H.Clarke	D.Magnani	Famiglietti
1944	H.Anderson	C.Berry	A.Babartsky	P.Gudauskas	B.Turner	G.Zorich	A.Hoptowit	G.Wilson	S.Luckman*	B.Margarita	A.Grygo	J.Fordham

YEAR COACH	LE	LT	LG	C	RG	RT	RE	TB/QB	WB/HB/LH	BB/RH	FB
1945 H.Anderson	R.Smeja	A.Babartsky	P.Gudauskas	J.Schiechl	G.Zorich	L.Artoe	G.Wilson	S.Luckman*	B.Margarita	H.Gallarneau	J.Fordham
1946 G.Halas	K.Kavanaugh	F.Davis	C.Drulis	B.Turner	P.Preston	M.Jarmoluk	E.Sprinkle	S.Luckman*	D.Magnani	H.Gallarneau	J.Osmanski
1947 G.Halas	K.Kavanaugh	F.Davis	C.Drulis	B.Turner	R.Bray	W.Stickel	E.Sprinkle	S.Luckman*	D.Kindt	F.Minini	E.Allen
1948 G.Halas	K.Kavanaugh	F.Davis	C.Drulis	B.Turner	R.Bray	W.Stickel	E.Cifers	S.Luckman*	G.Gulyanics	G.McAfee	D.Kindt
1949 G.Halas	K.Kavanaugh	G.Connor	C.Drulis	B.Turner	R.Bray	W.Stickel	J.Keane	J.Lujack*	G.Gulyanics	G.McAfee	D.Kindt

CHICAGO CARDINALS (merged with Pittsburgh 1944) 1920 4/6-2-2, 1921 9/3-3-2, 1922 3/8-3, 1923 6/8-4, 1924 8/5-4-1, 1925 1/11-2-1, 1926 10/5-6-1, 1927 9/3-7-1, 1928 9/1-5, 1929 5/6-6-1, 1930 7/5-6-2, 1931 4/5-4, 1932 7/2-6-2, 1933 5w/1-9-1, 1934 4w/5-6, 1935 3w/6-4-2, 1936 4w/3-8-1, 1937 4w/5-5-1, 1938 5w/2-9, 1939 5w/1-10, 1940 5w/2-7-2, 1941 4w/3-7-1, 1942 4w/3-8, 1943 4w/0-10, 1944 5w/0-10, 1945 5w/1-9, 1946 3w/6-5, 1947 1w/9-3 l*, 1948 1w/11-1 l, 1949 3w/6-5-1

YEAR COACH	LE	LT	LG	C	RG	RT	RE	TB/QB	WB/HB/LH	BB/RH	FB
1920 R.Dawson	P.LaRosa	F.Gillies	C.Zoia	C.Knight	L.Chappell	W.Brennan	P.Florence	P.Driscoll*	B.Halstrom	H.Curran	N.McInerney
1921 P.Driscoll	L.Sachs	F.Gillies	C.Zoia	F.Rydzewski	G.Buckeye	N.McInerney	R.O'Connor	P.Driscoll*	B.Halstrom	P.Steger	B.Koehler
1922 P.Driscoll	D.Egan	S.Rundquist	C.Zoia	N.McInerney	G.Buckeye	F.Gillies	E.Anderson	A.Horween*	P.Driscoll	J.Mohardt	B.Koehler
1923 A.Horween	R.Kiley	S.Montgomery	C.Zoia	N.McInerney	W.Brennan	J.Leonard	E.Anderson	A.Horween*	P.Driscoll	R.King	J.Crangle
1924 A.Horween	P.McNulty	W.Brennan	G.Hartong	N.McInerney	G.Buckeye	F.Gillies	E.Anderson	A.Horween*	P.Driscoll	J.Hurlburt	B.Koehler
1925 N.Barry	W.Smith	E.Evans	J.Lunz	R.Claypool	W.Brennan	F.Gillies	E.Anderson	P.Driscoll	H.Erickson	R.Dunn	B.Koehler
1926 N.Barry	H.Blumer	B.Weller	J.Lunz	R.Claypool	W.Brennan	W.Ellis	N.McInerney	H.Erickson	R.Lamb	R.Dunn	B.Koehler
1927 G.Chamberlin	E.Swanson	B.Weller	T.Waldron	Springsteen	W.Brennan	D.Slater	J.Vesser	R.Lamb	M.MacDonnell	B.Jones	T.Bucklin
1928 F.Gillies	H.Blumer	C.Widerquist	C.Strack	R.Claypool	J.Davidson	D.Slater	C.Neacy	H.Erickson	M.MacDonnell	D.Grant	B.Jones
1929 D.Scanlon	P.Dowling	J.Tinsley	W.Kiesling	L.Larson	H.Blumer	D.Slater	C.Kassel	D.Hill	M.MacDonnell	G.Rose	E.Nevers
1930 E.Nevers	G.Kenneally	J.Tinsley	W.Kiesling	M.Erickson	H.Blumer	D.Slater	C.Kassel	B.Belden	G.Rose	B.Baker	E.Nevers
1931 E.Nevers	M.Creighton	J.Williams	W.Kiesling	F.McNally	C.Diehl	D.Slater	C.Kassel	W.Holmer	B.Glassgow	I.Hill	E.Nevers
1932 J.Chevigny	M.Creighton	J.Williams	W.Kiesling	T.Moynihan	A.Graham	L.Gordon	C.Kassel	J.Lillard	A.Martin	B.Simas	T.Holm
1933 P.Schissler	M.Creighton	J.Williams	G.Bergerson	F.McNally	P.Handler	L.Gordon	C.Kassel	J.Lillard	H.Moe	L.Malloy	C.Hinchman
1934 P.Schissler	M.Creighton	H.Field	B.Volok	B.Hughes	P.Handler	L.Gordon	H.Duggins	H.Griffith	D.Cook	F.Greene	M.Mikulak
1935 M.Creighton	B.Smith	T.Blazine	B.Cuppoletti	B.Hughes	P.Handler	T.Isaacson	B.Wilson	D.Russell	A.Nichelini	P.Sarboe	M.Mikulak
1936 M.Creighton	M.Creighton	C.Baker	B.Cuppoletti	B.Hughes	H.Tipton	H.Field	B.Wilson	G.Grosvenor	A.Nichelini	M.Mikulak	M.Dowell
1937 M.Creighton	G.Tinsley	T.Blazine	B.Cuppoletti	H.Harmon	R.Carter	J.Robinson	V.Deskin	G.Grosvenor	D.Russell	H.Tipton	H.Pangle
1938 M.Creighton	G.Tinsley	T.Blazine	B.Cuppoletti	P.Dougherty	R.Carter	A.Babartsky	B.Smith	D.Sloan	J.Lawrence	F.Patrick	B.Parker
1939 E.Nevers	J.Mason	T.Blazine	A.Sabados	K.Aldrich	R.Carter	A.Babartsky	B.Smith	F.Patrick	M.Popovich	E.Fisher	M.Goldberg
1940 J.Conzelman	J.Shirk	E.Beinor	A.Sabados	K.Aldrich	J.Kuharich	T.Blazine	A.Coppage	H.McCullough	J.Hall	B.Johnson	M.Goldberg
1941 J.Conzelman	B.Dewell	B.Davis	T.White	R.Apolskis	J.Kuharich	A.Babartsky	P.Ivy	R.Mallouf	J.Hall	B.Parker	M.Goldberg
1942 J.Conzelman	B.Daddio	G.Duggan	C.Baker	R.Apolskis	G.Wilson	C.Bulger	P.Ivy	B.Schwenk	S.Lach	B.Parker	M.Goldberg
1943 P.Handler	E.Rucinski	G.Duggan	C.Baker	V.Stewart	G.Wilson	C.Bulger	D.Currivan	W.Rankin*	J.Martin	B.Parker	J.Grigas
1944 R.Dawson	T.Bova	G.Duggan	C.Baker	M.Robnett	J.Perko	C.Bulger	W.Kichefski	W.Rankin*	G.Magulick	B.Thurbon	J.Grigas
1945 R.Dawson	B.Dewell	R.Foster	C.Baker	C.Speegle	J.Kuharich	C.Bulger	E.Rucinski	P.Christman*	L.Cantor	F.Seno	A.Drulis
1946 J.Conzelman	B.Dewell	R.Foster	L.Arms	V.Banonis	B.Ramsey	B.Zimny	M.Kutner	P.Christman*	M.Goldberg	F.Seno	P.Harder
1947 J.Conzelman	B.Dewell	C.Bulger	L.Arms	V.Banonis	B.Ramsey	S.Mauldin	M.Kutner	P.Christman*	C.Trippi	M.Goldberg	P.Harder
1948 J.Conzelman	B.Dewell	C.Bulger	P.Andros	V.Banonis	B.Ramsey	B.Zimny	M.Kutner	R.Mallouf*	C.Trippi	E.Angsman	P.Harder
1949 B.Parker	B.Dewell	B.Fischer	G.Petrovich	B.Blackburn	B.Ramsey	P.Andros	M.Kutner	P.Christman*	C.Trippi	E.Angsman	P.Harder

CHICAGO (AAFC) (Rockets 1946-48, Hornets 1949) 1946 4w/5-6-3, 1947 4w/1-13, 1948 4w/1-13, 1949 5/4-8

YEAR COACH	LE	LT	LG	C	RG	RT	RE	TB/QB	WB/HB/LH	BB/RH	FB
1946 R.Dawson	R.Heywood	W.Wilkin	E.Vogds	H.Coleman	T.Sumpter	C.Huneke	P.Lahey	Hoernschemeyer	E.Hirsch	Hillenbrand	E.Lewis
1947 J.Crowley	M.Morris	J.Kuzman	J.Pearcy	F.Negus	A.Agase	H.McCollum	J.Mulready	S.Vacanti*	F.Evans	R.Ramsey	B.Daley
1948 E.McKeever	J.McCarthy	J.Brutz	J.Pearcy	F.Negus	G.Bernhardt	F.Johnson	F.King	J.Freitas*	Livingstone	E.Prokop	D.Proctor
1949 R.Dawson	H.Foldberg	H.Paine	H.St. John	J.Rapacz	M.Wendell	Z.Czarobski	D.Edwards	Hoernschemeyer	R.Ramsey	B.Sweiger	E.Lewis

CHICAGO TIGERS 1920 11/2-5-1

YEAR COACH	LE	LT	LG	C	RG	RT	RE	TB/QB	WB/HB/LH	BB/RH	FB
1920 R.Dawson	J.Barrett	N.Mathews	E.Keefe	Des Jardien	G.Buckeye	S.Bennett	O.Knop	D.Annan	G.Malone	M.Ghee	G.Falcon

CINCINNATI (Celts 1921, Reds 1933-34) 1921 13/1-3, 1933 4w/3-6-1, 1934 5w/0-8

YEAR COACH	LE	LT	LG	C	RG	RT	RE	TB/QB	WB/HB/LH	BB/RH	FB
1921 R.Dawson	E.Hauser	A.Lewis	D.Dastillung	M.Doherty	C.Lynch	W.Schupp	P.Volz	G.Munns*	F.Beekley	K.Crawford	S.Knab
1933 R.Dawson	J.Mooney	G.Munday	B.Lee	J.Rogers	L.Caywood	L.Burdick	C.Tackwell	L.Pope	L.Mulleneaux	A.Clark	R.Corzine
1934 A.Clark	J.Mooney	G.Munday	L.Caywood	J.Rogers	B.Lee	E.Elser	C.Tackwell	T.Bushby	L.Pope	A.Clark	R.Corzine

CLEVELAND BROWNS (AAFC) 1946 1w/12-2 l*, 1947 1w/12-1-1 l*, 1948 1w/14-0 l*, 1949 1/9-1-2 pl*

YEAR COACH	LE	LT	LG	C	RG	RT	RE	TB/QB	WB/HB/LH	BB/RH	FB
1946 P.Brown	M.Speedie	J.Daniell	E.Ulinski	M.Scarry	B.Willis	L.Rymkus	D.Lavelli	O.Graham*	E.Jones	D.Greenwood	M.Motley
1947 P.Brown	M.Speedie	E.Blandin	W.Humble	M.Scarry	B.Willis	L.Rymkus	D.Lavelli	O.Graham*	T.Colella	D.Greenwood	M.Motley
1948 P.Brown	M.Speedie	L.Groza	E.Ulinski	F.Gatski	B.Gaudio	L.Rymkus	D.Lavelli	O.Graham*	E.Jones	B.Cowan	M.Motley
1949 P.Brown	M.Speedie	L.Groza	E.Ulinski	F.Gatski	L.Houston	L.Rymkus	D.Lavelli	O.Graham*	B.Boedeker	D.Jones	M.Motley

CLEVELAND (Tigers 1920, Indians 1921, 1923, 1931, Bulldogs 1924-1925, 1927) 1920 10/2-4-2, 1921 11/3-5, 1923 5/3-1-3, 1924 1/7-1-1, 1925 12/5-8-1, 1927 4/8-4-1, 1931 8/2-8

YEAR COACH	LE	LT	LG	C	RG	RT	RE	TB/QB	WB/HB/LH	BB/RH	FB
1920 P.Brown	B.Baston	T.Thornhill	T.Gormley	A.Pierotti	D.Haggerty	R.Pearlman	H.Baujan	G.Brickley	S.Cofall	J.Bryant	C.Cramer
1921 Jim Thorpe	B.Corcoran	D.O'Connor	R.Pearlman	R.Waldsmith	J.Murphy	B.Lowe	T.Whelan	B.Haas	J.Guyon	M.Ghee	P.Calac
1923 P.Brown	J.Work	R.Rosatti	E.Johns	C.Guy	R.Vince	I.Huffman	S.Bierce	D.Roby	J.Tanner	P.Bahan	J.Kyle
1924 G.Chamberlin	G.Chamberlin	L.Lyman	R.Comstock	D.Osborn	J.Jones	O.Smith	J.Work	H.Workman	D.Noble	W.Roberts	B.Jones
1925 C.Edwards	I.Williams	R.Meredith	A.Nesser	L.Conover	D.Wallace	H.Sprinkle	J.Work	A.Michaels	D.Noble	D.Wolf	D.Elliott
1927 P.Brown	C.Cunningham	T.Cobb	M.Rehnquist	C.Smith	D.Howard	B.Owen	C.Bacchus	B.Friedman	R.Thomas	T.Feather	J.Simmons
1931 P.Brown	J.Hurley	B.Lyon	B.Lee	Critchfield	M.Hutson	E.Jessen	C.Braidwood	H.Workman	R.Novotny	A.Clark	O.Vokaty

COLUMBUS (Panhandles 1920-22, Tigers 1923-26) 1920 13/2-6-2, 1921 17/1-8, 1922 18/0-8, 1923 8/5-4-1, 1924 10/4-4, 1925 20/0-9, 1926 19/1-6

YEAR COACH	LE	LT	LG	C	RG	RT	RE	TB/QB	WB/HB/LH	BB/RH	FB
1920 P.Brown	H.Ruh	O.Kuehner	F.Lone Star	W.Waite	O.Wolford	J.Mulbarger	J.Flower	L.Snoots	J.Schneider	H.Gaulke	Frank Nesser
1921 T.Nesser	M.Glassman	Fred Nesser	B.Houck	T.Nesser	O.Wolford	J.Mulbarger	H.Ruh	C.Nesser	E.Ruh	H.Bliss	Frank Nesser
1922 H.Dell	H.Ruh	J.Mulbarger	M.Stevenson	O.Wolford	Frank Nesser	B.Karch	M.Glassman	L.Snoots	E.Ruh	H.Gaulke	E.Krieger
1923 P.Stinchcomb	G.Tebell	G.Sonnenberg	J.Sack	R.Weaver	A.Nemecek	J.Mulbarger	P.Goebel	W.Isabel	B.Rapp	S.Winters	L.Snoots
1924 R.Weaver	H.Ruh	W.Ellis	E.Duvall	A.Nemecek	J.Mulbarger	B.Petcoff	P.Goebel	H.Stock	B.Rapp	S.Winters	B.Tynes
1925 R.Weaver	H.Ruh	W.Ellis	E.Duvall	A.Nemecek	J.Mulbarger	B.Petcoff	P.Goebel	B.Tynes	P.Lynch	B.Rapp	Frank Nesser
1926 J.Heldt	H.Pearce	B.Berrehsem	J.Heldt	L.Reichel	J.Mulbarger	B.Petcoff	F.Gorrill	P.Barnum	B.Rapp	T.Murphy	J.Bertoglio

DAYTON TRIANGLES 1920 6/5-2-2, 1921 8/4-4-1, 1922 7/4-3-1, 1923 16/1-6-1, 1924 13/2-6, 1925 19/0-7-1, 1926 16/1-4-1, 1927 10/1-6-1, 1928 10/0-7, 1929 12/0-6

YEAR COACH	LE	LT	LG	C	RG	RT	RE	TB/QB	WB/HB/LH	BB/RH	FB
1920 P.Brown	D.Thiele	H.Cutler	L.Dellinger	H.Kinderdine	C.Winston	E.Sauer	D.Reese	F.Bacon	N.Sacksteder	A.Mahrt	L.Partlow
1921 N.Talbot	D.Thiele	R.Hathaway	A.Sampson	H.Kinderdine	H.Sies	E.Sauer	D.Reese	F.Bacon	G.Redman	A.Mahrt	L.Partlow
1922 C.Storck	D.Thiele	R.Hathaway	B.Berns	H.Kinderdine	H.Sies	E.Sauer	D.Reese	L.Partlow	F.Bacon	A.Mahrt	K.Huffine
1923 C.Storck	D.Thiele	R.Hathaway	B.Berns	H.Kinderdine	J.Beasley	E.Sauer	D.Reese	L.Partlow	F.Bacon	F.Abbott	K.Huffine
1924 C.Storck	H.Fenner	R.Hathaway	E.Bonowitz	H.Kinderdine	S.Muirhead	E.Sauer	F.Bacon	A.Mahrt	L.Partlow	F.Abbott	K.Huffine
1925 C.Storck	H.Fenner	C.Drayer	E.Bonowitz	H.Kinderdine	A.Graham	E.Sauer	G.Mayl	A.Mahrt	F.Bacon	F.Abbott	K.Huffine
1926 C.Storck	H.Fenner	E.Calhoun	A.Graham	H.Kinderdine	P.Reiter	E.Sauer	G.Mayl	A.Beckley	D.Dobeleit	A.Mahrt	F.Abbott
1927 L.Mahrt	H.Fenner	B.Belanich	A.Graham	H.Kinderdine	E.DeWeese	J.Becker	R.Joseph	F.Abbott	F.Sillin	J.Tays	E.Britton
1928 F.Abbott	C.Mankat	B.Belanich	A.Graham	H.Kinderdine	J.Spencer	J.Becker	M.Hummon	W.Charles	C.Cook	A.Matsu	E.Britton
1929 F.Abbott	R.Carlson	B.Belanich	A.Graham	H.Kinderdine	J.Spencer	D.Faust	H.Fenner	J.Brewer	F.Sillin	S.Buchanan	E.Wynne

DETROIT (Heralds 1920, Tigers 1921, Panthers 1925-26, Wolverines 1928) 1920 9/2-3-3, 1921 16/1-5-1, 1925 3/8-2-2, 1926 12/4-6-2, 1928 3/7-2-1

YEAR COACH	LE	LT	LG	C	RG	RT	RE	TB/QB	WB/HB/LH	BB/RH	FB
1920 P.Brown	J.Fitzgerald	H.Lowery	C.Applegran	G.Runkel	C.Guy	S.Horning	R.Whipple	J.Kelly	B.Hanley	P.Wilson	P.Dunne
1921 B.Marshall	W.Clago	C.DeGree	C.Carman	C.Guy	M.Gardner	S.Horning	T.Voss	N.Sacksteder	W.Kuehl	B.Stobbs	N.DaPrato
1925 P.Brown	V.Hultman	G.Sonnenberg	T.McNamara	E.Vick	R.Smith	T.Hogan	T.Voss	J.Conzelman	A.Hadden	D.Vick	D.Marion
1926 J.Conzelman	D.Lauer	G.Sonnenberg	Fleischmann	J.Barrett	T.McNamara	T.Edwards	E.Lynch	B.Gregory	A.Hadden	E.Scharer	D.Marion
1928 P.Brown	L.Munn	T.Cobb	L.Caywood	J.Wostoupal	D.Howard	B.Owen	C.Bacchus	B.Friedman	L.Sedbrook	O.Wiberg	T.Feather

DETROIT LIONS (Portsmouth Spartans 1930-33) 1930 7/5-6-3, 1931 2/11-3, 1932 3/6-2-4, 1933 2w/6-5, 1934 2w/10-3, 1935 1w/7-3-2 l*, 1936 3w/8-4, 1937 2w/7-4, 1938 2w/7-4, 1939 3w/6-5, 1940 3w/5-5-1, 1941 3w/4-6-1, 1942 5w/0-11, 1943 3w/3-6-1, 1944 2w/6-3-1, 1945 2w/7-3, 1946 5w/1-10, 1947 5w/3-9, 1948 5w/2-10, 1949 4w/4-8

YEAR COACH	LE	LT	LG	C	RG	RT	RE	TB/QB	WB/HB/LH	BB/RH	FB
1930 H.Griffen	L.Jennings	V.Schleusner	E.Meyer	R.Brown	F.Roberts	D.Harris	Fleckenstein	C.Bennett	B.Glassgow	C.Kahl	F.Lumpkin
1931 P.Clark	B.McKalip	J.Douds	M.Bodenger	C.Randolph	O.Emerson	G.Christensen	H.Ebding	G.Presnell	G.Alford	F.Lumpkin	E.Schwartz
1932 P.Clark	B.McKalip	B.Armstrong	M.Bodenger	R.Davis	O.Emerson	G.Christensen	H.Ebding	D.Clark	G.Alford	F.Lumpkin	J.Cavosie
1933 P.Clark	J.Cavosie	B.Mitchell	M.Bodenger	C.Randolph	O.Emerson	G.Christensen	H.Ebding	G.Presnell	E.Caddel	F.Lumpkin	A.Gutowsky
1934 H.Griffen	B.McKalip	J.Johnson	M.Bodenger	C.Randolph	O.Emerson	G.Christensen	H.Ebding	D.Clark	E.Caddel	F.Lumpkin	F.Christensen
1935 P.Clark	E.Klewicki	J.Johnson	S.Knox	C.Randolph	O.Emerson	G.Christensen	J.Schneller	D.Clark	E.Caddel	F.Christensen	A.Gutowsky

YEAR	COACH	LE	LT	LG	C	RG	RT	RE	TB/QB	WB/HB/LH	BB/RH	FB
1936	P.Clark	E.Klewicki	J.Johnson	S.Knox	D.Ritchhart	J.Kopcha	G.Christensen	J.Schneller	D.Clark	E.Caddel	F.Christensen	A.Gutowsky
1937	D.Clark	E.Klewicki	J.Johnson	O.Emerson	D.Stokes	S.Wagner	B.Reynolds	B.Morse	D.Clark	E.Caddel	V.Huffman	A.Gutowsky
1938	D.Clark	E.Klewicki	J.Johnson	S.Wagner	D.Stokes	B.Feldhaus	B.Reynolds	M.Moscrip	V.Huffman	L.Cardwell	F.Vanzo	A.Gutowsky
1939	G.Henderson	M.Moscrip	J.Johnson	S.Wiethe	Wojciechowicz	B.Feldhaus	R.George	C.Hanneman	D.Sloan	L.Cardwell	F.Vanzo	B.Shepherd
1940	P.Clark	S.Rouse	J.Johnson	S.Wiethe	T.Calvelli	B.Feldhaus	H.Smith	C.Hanneman	W.White	L.Cardwell	F.Vanzo	H.Weiss
1941	B.Edwards	B.Fisk	J.Tripson	A.Lio	Wojciechowicz	S.Wiethe	T.Furst	P.Szakash	W.White	D.Booth	B.Callihan	H.Hopp
1942	B.Karcis	B.Fisk	A.Schibanoff	T.Pavelec	J.Schiechl	A.Lio	E.Uremovich	Wojciechowicz	H.Hopp	N.Mathews	B.Callihan	M.Sanzotta
1943	G.Dorais	B.Fisk	A.Lio	J.Matheson	Wojciechowicz	A.Rubino	A.Kaporch	B.Hightower	F.Sinkwich	N.Mathews	M.Evans	H.Hopp
1944	G.Dorais	D.Diehl	S.Batinski	J.Greene	Wojciechowicz	A.Kaporch	L.Lindon	J.Matheson	F.Sinkwich	A.Van Tone	B.Callihan	B.Westfall
1945	G.Dorais	J.Greene	B.Callihan	S.Batinski	R.Nelson	B.Radovich	E.Uremovich	J.Matheson	C.Fenenbock	A.Farkas	B.Trebotich	B.Westfall
1946	G.Dorais	T.Cremer	R.Thomas	S.Batinski	F.Szymanski	D.Tassos	E.Uremovich	J.Matheson	D.Ryan	E.Madarik	C.DeShane	C.Wilson
1947	G.Dorais	J.Greene	R.Thomas	S.Batinski	M.Pregulman	C.DeShane	M.Olenski	T.Cremer	R.Zimmerman*	B.Dudley	E.Madarik	C.Wilson
1948	B.McMillin	K.Mote	R.Thomas	H.Brown	M.Pregulman	B.Ward	J.Dugger	C.Souders	F.Enke*	B.Dudley	J.Margucci	C.Wilson
1949	B.McMillin	B.Mann	G.Hekkers	M.DeMarco	J.Simmons	B.Ward	H.Brown	J.Greene	F.Enke*	B.Dudley	W.Triplett	C.Wilson

DULUTH (Kelleys 1923-25, Eskimos 1926-27) 1923 7/4-3, 1924 4/5-1, 1925 16/0-3, 1926 8/6-5-3, 1927 11/1-8

YEAR	COACH	LE	LT	LG	C	RG	RT	RE	TB/QB	WB/HB/LH	BB/RH	FB
1923	H.Griffen	D.O'Donnell	A.Johnson	B.Stein	J.Madigan	D.Williams	H.Kieley	J.Rooney	B.Rooney	R.Method	J.Sternaman	K.Harris
1924	D.Scanlon	J.Underwood	B.Stein	A.Johnson	L.Strand	D.Williams	H.Kieley	J.Rooney	W.Gilbert	R.Method	C.Rooney	B.Rooney
1925	D.Scanlon	B.Marshall	A.Johnson	D.Williams	B.Stein	F.Denfeld	O.Carlson	J.Underwood	D.Kelley	M.MacDonnell	C.Rooney	B.Rooney
1926	D.Scanlon	J.Underwood	A.Johnson	O.Carlson	B.Stein	D.Williams	W.Kiesling	J.Rooney	J.Blood	R.Method	C.Rooney	E.Nevers
1927	E.Nevers	J.Rooney	R.Ashmore	W.Kiesling	B.Rooney	R.Suess	J.McCarthy	F.Cronin	J.Blood	R.Method	C.Rooney	E.Nevers

EVANSVILLE CRIMSON GIANTS 1921 6/3-2, 1922 15/0-3

YEAR	COACH	LE	LT	LG	C	RG	RT	RE	TB/QB	WB/HB/LH	BB/RH	FB
1921	H.Griffen	E.Goldsmith	B.Bondurant	A.Fishman	J.Windbiel	B.Garnjost	A.Spiegel	C.O'Neil	T.Williams	H.Henderson	M.Lindsey	F.Fausch
1922	F.Fausch	J.Reno	B.Bondurant	T.Ladson	D.Spain	J.Sanders	F.Fausch	P.Wathen	S.Sullivan	S.Rork	V.Endress	P.Lauer

FRANKFORD YELLOW JACKETS 1924 3/11-2-1, 1925 6/13-7, 1926 1/14-1-2, 1927 7/6-9-3, 1928 2/11-3-2, 1929 3/9-4-5, 1930 9/4-13-1, 1931 10/1-6-1

YEAR	COACH	LE	LT	LG	C	RG	RT	RE	TB/QB	WB/HB/LH	BB/RH	FB
1924	P.Berryman	W.Thomas	R.Stein	B.Spagna	H.Stein	B.Behman	M.Gulian	M.O'Connell	J.Storer	C.Way	L.Haws	T.Hamer
1925	G.Chamberlin	G.Chamberlin	B.Behman	B.Hoffman	Springsteen	B.Spagna	A.Harms	R.Crowther	G.Sullivan	T.Hamer	T.Homan	H.Stockton
1926	G.Chamberlin	Springsteen	D.Potts	B.Hoffman	M.Reed	R.Comstock	J.Budd	R.Crowther	H.Moran	T.Hamer	B.Jones	H.Stockton
1927	R.Daugherty	F.McGrath	E.Weir	R.Comstock	M.Reed	Connaughton	B.Behman	J.Weir	K.Mercer	C.Rogers	P.Fitzgibbon	N.Wilcox
1928	E.Weir	T.Kostos	B.Behman	H.Hanson	R.Mahoney	R.Comstock	B.Weller	C.Kassel	C.Rogers	A.Oehlrich	K.Mercer	W.Diehl
1929	B.Behman	M.Kostos	B.Behman	H.Hanson	R.Mahoney	R.Comstock	H.Malcolm	G.Barna	E.Halicki	A.Oehlrich	T.Homan	W.Diehl
1930	B.Behman	T.Kostos	R.Richards	H.Hanson	C.Havens	P.Jones	G.Watkins	C.Tackwell	E.Halicki	R.Goodbread	C.Crabtree	H.Joesting
1931	B.Behman	L.Wilson	F.Racis	H.Seborg	N.Barragar	P.Jones	B.Behman	T.Leary	M.Kaer	J.Pederson	J.Brumbaugh	H.Joesting

GREEN BAY PACKERS 1921 6/3-2-1, 1922 7/4-3-3, 1923 3/7-2-1, 1924 6/7-4, 1925 9/8-5, 1926 5/7-3-3, 1927 2/7-2-1, 1928 4/6-4-3, 1929 1/12-0-1, 1930 1/10-3-1, 1931 1/12-2, 1932 2/10-3-1, 1933 3w/5-7-1, 1934 3w/7-6, 1935 2w/8-4, 1936 1w/10-1-1 l*, 1937 2w/7-4, 1938 1w/8-3 l, 1939 1w/9-2 l*, 1940 2w/6-4-1, 1941 1w/10-1 d, 1942 2w/8-2-1, 1943 2w/7-2-1, 1944 1w/8-2 l*, 1945 3w/6-4, 1946 3w/6-5, 1947 3w/6-5-1, 1948 4w/3-9, 1949 5w/2-10

YEAR	COACH	LE	LT	LG	C	RG	RT	RE	TB/QB	WB/HB/LH	BB/RH	FB
1921	P.Berryman	B.DuMoe	F.Coughlin	J.Carey	J.Murray	M.Wilson	C.Buck	D.Hayes	C.Lambeau	G.Malone	N.Barry	A.Schmaehl
1922	C.Lambeau	D.Hayes	C.Buck	W.Woodin	W.Niemann	M.Gardner	J.Earp	T.Howard	C.Lambeau	E.Usher	C.Mathys	S.Mills
1923	C.Lambeau	C.Wheeler	C.Buck	W.Woodin	W.Niemann	M.Gardner	J.Earp	D.Lyle	C.Lambeau	M.Basing	C.Mathys	B.Gavin
1924	C.Lambeau	D.O'Donnell	C.Buck	W.Woodin	J.Earp	M.Gardner	R.Rosatti	T.Voss	C.Lambeau	M.Basing	C.Mathys	D.Hendrian
1925	C.Lambeau	D.O'Donnell	C.Buck	W.Woodin	O.Larson	M.Gardner	J.Earp	G.Vergara	C.Lambeau	V.Lewellen	C.Mathys	M.Basing
1926	C.Lambeau	D.O'Donnell	T.Cahoon	W.Woodin	J.Earp	M.Gardner	R.Rosatti	D.Flaherty	C.Lambeau	V.Lewellen	P.Purdy	C.Lidberg
1927	C.Lambeau	L.Dilweg	T.Cahoon	F.Mayer	J.Earp	B.Jones	R.Rosatti	D.O'Donnell	E.Kotal	V.Lewellen	R.Dunn	R.Enright
1928	C.Lambeau	L.Dilweg	C.Perry	J.Bowdoin	J.Earp	B.Jones	R.Ashmore	D.O'Donnell	V.Lewellen	E.Kotal	R.Dunn	H.O'Boyle
1929	C.Lambeau	L.Dilweg	B.Kern	M.Michalske	B.Darling	J.Bowdoin	C.Hubbard	D.O'Donnell	E.Kotal	J.Blood	R.Dunn	B.Molenda
1930	C.Lambeau	L.Dilweg	C.Hubbard	M.Michalske	B.Darling	J.Bowdoin	R.Sleight	D.O'Donnell	V.Lewellen	W.Engelmann	R.Dunn	B.Molenda
1931	C.Lambeau	L.Dilweg	D.Stahlman	M.Michalske	W.Don Carlos	J.Bowdoin	R.Sleight	T.Nash	J.Blood	H.Bruder	P.Fitzgibbon	H.McCrary
1932	C.Lambeau	A.Rose	C.Hubbard	M.Michalske	N.Barragar	J.Zeller	D.Stahlman	M.Gantenbein	V.Lewellen	H.Bruder	H.O'Boyle	C.Hinkle
1933	C.Lambeau	A.Rose	C.Hubbard	M.Michalske	A.Bultman	R.Comstock	J.Kurth	M.Gantenbein	B.Monnett	A.Herber	R.Grove	C.Hinkle
1934	C.Lambeau	M.Gantenbein	L.Evans	M.Michalske	N.Barragar	B.Jones	A.Schwammel	A.Norgard	A.Herber	J.Laws	H.Bruder	C.Hinkle
1935	C.Lambeau	D.Hutson	E.Smith	M.Michalske	N.Barragar	L.Evans	A.Schwammel	M.Gantenbein	A.Herber	J.Blood	B.Goldenberg	C.Hinkle
1936	C.Lambeau	D.Hutson	E.Smith	Engebretsen	G.Svendsen	L.Evans	A.Schwammel	M.Gantenbein	A.Herber	B.Monnett	H.Bruder	C.Hinkle
1937	C.Lambeau	D.Hutson	E.Smith	R.Letlow	G.Svendsen	L.Evans	L.Gordon	M.Gantenbein	B.Monnett	J.Laws	H.Bruder	C.Hinkle
1938	C.Lambeau	D.Hutson	C.Seibold	R.Letlow	O.Miller	B.Goldenberg	B.Lee	M.Gantenbein	B.Monnett	J.Laws	H.Schneidman	C.Hinkle
1939	C.Lambeau	D.Hutson	B.Ray	R.Letlow	B.Svendsen	B.Goldenberg	B.Lee	C.Mulleneaux	A.Herber	A.Uram	L.Craig	E.Jankowski
1940	C.Lambeau	D.Hutson	B.Ray	R.Letlow	C.Brock	B.Goldenberg	B.Lee	R.Riddick	C.Isbell	L.Brock	L.Craig	C.Hinkle
1941	C.Lambeau	H.Jacunski	B.Ray	L.McLaughlin	G.Svendsen	P.Tinsley	C.Schultz	R.Riddick	C.Isbell	C.Brock	L.Buhler	C.Hinkle
1942	C.Lambeau	J.Mason	B.Ray	B.Kuusisto	B.Ingalls	B.Goldenberg	P.Berezney	J.Carter	C.Isbell	J.Laws	L.Craig	T.Fritsch
1943	C.Lambeau	D.Hutson	B.Ray	B.Kuusisto	C.Brock	B.Goldenberg	P.Berezney	H.Jacunski	T.Canadeo	L.Brock	L.Craig	T.Fritsch
1944	C.Lambeau	D.Hutson	T.Croft	G.Sorenson	C.Brock	P.Tinsley	P.Berezney	H.Jacunski	I.Comp	L.Brock	L.Craig	T.Fritsch
1945	C.Lambeau	C.Goodnight	B.Ray	C.Tollefson	C.Brock	P.Tinsley	P.Lipscomb	J.Mason	I.Comp	J.Laws	L.Craig	T.Fritsch
1946	C.Lambeau	C.Goodnight	B.Ray	D.Wildung	C.Brock	M.Pregulman	P.Lipscomb	N.Luhn	T.Canadeo	H.Rohrig	L.Craig	T.Fritsch
1947	C.Lambeau	C.Goodnight	B.Ray	D.Wildung	C.Brock	D.Tassos	P.Lipscomb	N.Luhn	J.Jacobs*	T.Canadeo	B.Forte	T.Fritsch
1948	C.Lambeau	L.Craig	D.Wildung	E.Vogds	J.Rhodemyre	D.Tassos	P.Lipscomb	N.Luhn	J.Jacobs*	T.Canadeo	B.Forte	T.Fritsch
1949	C.Lambeau	L.Craig	D.Wildung	E.Vogds	J.Rhodemyre	D.Tassos	P.Lipscomb	N.Luhn	J.Girard*	T.Canadeo	B.Forte	T.Fritsch

HAMMOND PROS 1920 11/2-5, 1921 13/1-3-1, 1922 17/0-5-1, 1923 15/1-5-1, 1924 11/2-2-1, 1925 14/1-4, 1926 21/0-4

YEAR	COACH	LE	LT	LG	C	RG	RT	RE	TB/QB	WB/HB/LH	BB/RH	FB
1920	P.Berryman	C.Johnson	F.Seliger	R.Oltz	F.Moran	E.Davis	M.Bashaw	D.Kohl	.Ward	R.Specht	K.Meyers	H.Gillo
1921	M.Hicks	I.Williams	E.Risley	G.Hartong	J.Depler	R.Oltz	D.Tallant	C.Hanke	W.Hess	B.Derr	C.Mathys	D.King
1922	W.Hess	I.Williams	D.Tallant	P.Leatherman	F.Rydzewski	F.Tierney	G.Berry	E.Carman	L.Cearing	B.Giaver	W.Hess	J.Shelburne
1923	W.Hess	I.Williams	D.Tallant	G.Berry	R.Oltz	W.Smith	L.Usher	C.Hanke	W.Hess	L.Cearing	F.Pollard	O.Knop
1924	W.Hess	I.Williams	R.Neal	G.Berry	F.Rydzewski	B.Fortune	R.Oltz	S.Seyfrit	D.Annan	S.Butler	W.Hess	G.Falcon
1925	D.Young	I.Williams	R.Neal	G.Dahlgren	R.Oltz	B.Fortune	D.Tallant	L.Sachs	D.Annan	E.Robinson	W.Hess	B.Giaver
1926	D.Young	I.Williams	G.Dahlgren	R.Neal	F.Rydzewski	W.Sechrist	L.Usher	R.Hahn	D.Annan	H.Curzon	D.Hudson	B.Gavin

HARTFORD BLUES 1926 13/3-7

YEAR	COACH	LE	LT	LG	C	RG	RT	RE	TB/QB	WB/HB/LH	BB/RH	FB
1926	P.Berryman	D.Webber	M.Werwaiss	F.Flynn	R.O'Neil	E.Keenan	R.Nichols	G.O'Connell	J.Manning	J.Foley	C.Corgan	L.Smyth

KANSAS CITY (Blues 1924, Cowboys 1925-26) 1924 15/2-7, 1925 13/2-5-1, 1926 4/8-3

YEAR	COACH	LE	LT	LG	C	RG	RT	RE	TB/QB	WB/HB/LH	BB/RH	FB
1924	P.Berryman	D.Webber	R.Andrews	J.Berquist	C.Peterson	S.Owen	H.Bassett	J.Milton	C.Hill	R.DeWitz	C.Corgan	D.Strauss
1925	R.Andrews	D.Webber	S.Owen	M.Rehnquist	J.Mintun	D.Howard	A.Thompson	L.Munn	C.Hill	O.Bristow	A.Bloodgood	P.White
1926	R.Andrews	P.Randels	T.Cobb	J.Berquist	C.Smith	M.Rehnquist	B.Owen	L.Munn	O.Bristow	R.DeWitz	A.Bloodgood	G.Spear

KENOSHA MAROONS 1924 16/0-4-1

YEAR	COACH	LE	LT	LG	C	RG	RT	RE	TB/QB	WB/HB/LH	BB/RH	FB
1924	P.Berryman	W.Cassidy	B.Hurst	G.Dahlgren	M.Conrad	D.Stahlman	L.Usher	F.Heinisch	W.Wolter	D.Vick	J.Simpson	G.Seasholtz

LOS ANGELES BUCCANEERS 1926 7/6-3-1

YEAR	COACH	LE	LT	LG	C	RG	RT	RE	TB/QB	WB/HB/LH	BB/RH	FB
1926	P.Berryman	D.Hufford	J.Thurman	D.Thompson	J.McArthur	J.Nolan	D.Newmeyer	B.Muller	T.Imlay	E.White	B.Finch	T.Maul

LOS ANGELES DONS (AAFC) 1946 3w/7-5-2, 1947 3w/7-7, 1948 3w/7-7, 1949 5/4-8

YEAR	COACH	LE	LT	LG	C	RG	RT	RE	TB/QB	WB/HB/LH	BB/RH	FB
1946	D.DeGroot	J.Aguirre	B.Reinhard	A.Lolotai	R.Nelson	B.Radovich	L.Artoe	D.Gentry	C.O'Rourke*	B.Seymour	B.Nygren	J.Kimbrough
1947	D.DeGroot	J.Aguirre	E.Audet	L.Levy	R.Nelson	R.Frankowski	L.Artoe	D.Gentry	C.O'Rourke*	C.Fenenbock	B.Kelly	B.Reinhard
1948	J.Phelan	B.Baldwin	B.Reinhard	L.Levy	R.Nelson	K.Ramsey	E.Audet	L.Ford	G.Dobbs	H.Wedemeyer	W.Heap	J.Kimbrough
1949	J.Phelan	B.Baldwin	B.Reinhard	A.Lolotai	R.Nelson	K.Ramsey	B.Tinsley	L.Ford	G.Dobbs	H.Wedemeyer	G.Murphy	H.Rodgers

LOS ANGELES RAMS (Cleveland Rams 1937-42, 1944-45) 1937 5w/1-10, 1938 4w/4-7, 1939 4w/5-5-1, 1940 4w/4-6-1, 1941 5w/2-9, 1942 3w/5-6, 1944 4w/4-6, 1945 1w/9-1 l*, 1946 2w/6-4-1, 1947 4w/6-6, 1948 3w/6-5-1, 1949 1w/8-2-2 l

YEAR	COACH	LE	LT	LG	C	RG	RT	RE	TB/QB	WB/HB/LH	BB/RH	FB
1937	D.DeGroot	P.Bucklew	P.Miller	F.Burmeister	C.Cherundolo	D.Zoll	T.Livingston	S.Busich	B.Snyder	J.Alfonse	S.Pincura	J.Drake
1938	A.Lewis	J.Benton	D.Zoll	P.Ragazzo	C.Cherundolo	T.Hupke	T.Livingston	R.Hamilton	B.Snyder	J.Alfonse	C.Brazell	J.Drake
1939	D.Clark	J.Benton	C.Adams	T.Livingston	B.Conkright	B.McGarry	E.Dunstan	J.Wilson	P.Hall	G.Smith	V.Spadaccini	J.Drake
1940	D.Clark	J.Benton	C.Adams	B.McGarry	J.Haman	T.Livingston	E.Dunstan	P.McDonough	P.Hall	O.Cordill	G.Smith	J.Drake
1941	D.Clark	M.Patt	C.Adams	B.McGarry	B.Conkright	R.Matheson	E.Dunstan	P.McDonough	P.Hall	D.Magnani	C.Davis	J.Drake

YEAR COACH	LE	LT	LG	C	RG	RT	RE	TB/QB	WB/HB/LH	BB/RH	FB
1942 D.Clark	J.Benton	C.Adams	R.Matheson	B.Conkright	R.Stuart	J.Pasqua	J.Gibson	P.Hall	D.Magnani	D.Elston	G.Smith
1944 D.DeGroot	F.Konetsky	C.Pudloski	R.Matheson	M.Scarry	T.Corbo	J.Fawcett	S.Pritko	T.Colella	M.Kabealo	J.Karrs	H.Jones
1945 A.Walsh	J.Benton	E.Schultz	R.Matheson	M.Scarry	M.Lazetich	G.Bouley	S.Pritko	B.Waterfield*	F.Gehrke	J.Gillette	D.Greenwood
1946 D.DeGroot	B.Shaw	E.Schultz	R.Eason	B.deLauer	R.Matheson	G.Bouley	R.Hamilton	B.Waterfield*	F.Gehrke	J.Banta	P.West
1947 B.Snyder	J.Zilly	D.Huffman	R.Matheson	F.Naumetz	R.Eason	G.Bouley	R.Hamilton	B.Waterfield*	F.Gehrke	J.Banta	P.West
1948 Shaughnessy	F.Hubbell	D.Huffman	H.Dean	F.Naumetz	M.Lazetich	G.Bouley	J.Zilly	B.Waterfield*	F.Gehrke	J.Banta	D.Hoerner
1949 Shaughnessy	T.Fears	D.Huffman	H.Dean	J.Martin	R.Yagiello	E.Champagne	B.Shaw	B.Waterfield*	F.Gehrke	T.Younger	D.Hoerner
LOUISVILLE (Brecks 1921-23, Colonels 1926) 1921 19/0-2, 1922 13/1-3, 1923 19/0-3, 1926 21/0-4											
1921 D.DeGroot	H.Gruber	T.Ferguson	G.Wiggs	A.Higgins	B.Howser	H.Card	B.Netherton	C.Boldt	R.Chenoweth	J.Engelhard	K.Hower
1922 H.Wiggs	H.Gruber	H.Card	Brunklacher	A.Higgins	B.Otto	D.Gibson	E.Gregg	B.Padan	J.Van Dyke	C.Boldt	H.Wiggs
1923 J.Kendrick	J.Kendrick	D.Gibson	Brunklacher	B.Otto	C.Olmstead	A.Espie	J.Quast	J.Rowan	G.Wanless	E.Reiser	H.Wiggs
1926 D.DeGroot	L.Sachs	V.Green	B.McCaw	E.Berwick	D.Bernoske	G.Leaf	R.Bush	P.Stinchcomb	E.Robinson	C.Palmer	G.Golsen
MIAMI SEAHAWKS (AAFC) 1946 4e/3-11											
1946 D.DeGroot	H.Ulrich	M.Olenski	B.Jungmichel	K.Whitlow	C.Taylor	G.Ellenson	L.Blount	M.Pugh*	M.Gafford	D.Erdlitz	D.Reece
MILWAUKEE BADGERS 1922 12/2-4-3, 1923 3/7-2-3, 1924 12/5-8, 1925 17/0-6, 1926 15/2-7											
1922 D.DeGroot	B.Garrett	A.Webb	T.Tomlin	A.Pierotti	J.Dufft	J.Alexander	P.Robeson	F.Pollard	D.King	M.Purdy	D.Doane
1923 J.Conzelman	L.Sachs	R.Blailock	R.Smith	O.Larson	J.Underwood	A.Wenke	D.Reichle	B.Winkelman	H.Erickson	J.Conzelman	D.Doane
1924 H.Erickson	C.Neacy	C.Widerquist	W.LeJeune	O.Larson	L.McGinnis	B.Weller	E.Swanson	J.Conzelman	B.Winkelman	R.Dunn	D.Doane
1925 J.Bryan	C.Neacy	R.Brumm	P.Nadolney	B.Traynor	F.Tierney	P.Dunnigan	F.Roeseler	J.Bryan	J.Blood	S.Barr	S.Mason
1926 J.Bryan	L.Dilweg	O.Lane	S.Kuick	J.Burks	P.Dunnigan	R.Ashmore	C.Neacy	J.Bryan	J.Heimsch	S.Hallquist	H.Slater
MINNEAPOLIS (Marines 1921-24, Red Jackets 1929-30) 1921 13/1-3, 1922 13/1-3, 1923 13/2-5-2, 1924 17/0-6, 1929 11/1-9, 1930 10/1-7-1											
1921 D.DeGroot	Christianson	M.Palmer	D.Gaustad	H.Gunderson	R.Tersch	H.Erickson	S.Redeen	B.Dvorak	P.Regnier	R.Ursella	E.Sampson
1922 R.Tollefson	Christianson	R.Tersch	G.Kramer	J.Madigan	D.Gaustad	H.Erickson	R.Kraft	M.Norton	A.Cleve	B.Irgens	E.Sampson
1923 H.Mehre	L.Mohs	R.Tersch	F.Tierney	H.Mehre	B.Fosdick	A.Baril	P.Flinn	A.Cleve	L.Pahl	A.Kaplan	E.Sampson
1924 J.Brandy	L.Mohs	P.Dunnigan	G.Kramer	J.Madigan	F.Tierney	L.Scott	Christianson	M.Norton	A.Cleve	B.Houle	J.Simons
1929 D.DeGroot	K.Haycraft	C.Widerquist	F.Loven	L.Young	J.Chrape	C.Franta	B.Lundell	H.Erickson	H.Willegale	M.Nydall	H.Joesting
1930 G.Gibson	K.Haycraft	J.Ward	Steponovich	N.Barragar	G.Gibson	C.Franta	L.Wilson	A.Pharmer	M.Nydall	J.Pederson	H.Joesting
MUNCIE FLYERS 1920 14/0-1, 1921 19/0-2											
1920 D.DeGroot	J.Reno	B.Berns	E.Hole	O.Floyd	R.Hathaway	D.Davis	C.Helvie	M.Hole	A.Erehart	C.Checkaye	K.Huffine
1921 C.Checkaye	M.McIndoe	M.Yount	E.Hole	O.Floyd	K.Fulton	W.Smith	C.Helvie	C.Baldwin	G.Redman	C.Checkaye	M.Hole
NEW YORK BRICKLEY GIANTS 1921 19/0-2											
1921 D.DeGroot	P.Meyers	E.O'Hearn	H.Dadmun	A.Pierotti	D.Haggerty	T.Gormley	J.DuSossoit	G.Brickley	D.Maginnes	M.Devlin	D.Doane
NEW YORK GIANTS 1925 4/8-4, 1926 6/8-4-1, 1927 1/11-1-1, 1928 6/4-7-2, 1929 2/13-1-1, 1930 2/13-4, 1931 5/7-6-1, 1932 5/4-6-2, 1933 1e/11-3 l, 1934 1e/8-5 l*, 1935 1e/9-3 l, 1936 3e/5-6-1, 1937 2e/6-3-2, 1938 1e/8-2-1 l*, 1939 1e/9-1-1 l, 1940 3e/6-4-1, 1941 1e/8-3 l, 1942 3e/5-5-1, 1943 1e/6-3-1 d, 1944 1e/8-1-1 l, 1945 3e/3-6-1, 1946 1e/7-3-1 l, 1947 5e/2-8-2, 1948 3e/4-8, 1949 3e/6-6											
1925 D.DeGroot	P.Jappe	C.Milstead	A.Carney	D.Alexander	J.Williams	B.Parnell	L.Bomar	H.Haines	H.Benkert	D.Hendrian	J.McBride
1926 D.Alexander	T.Voss	S.Owen	D.Alexander	M.Murtagh	J.Williams	J.Alexander	L.Bomar	H.Haines	J.Hagerty	T.Grigg	J.McBride
1927 E.Potteiger	C.Corgan	S.Owen	H.Garvey	M.Murtagh	A.Nesser	C.Milstead	C.Hubbard	H.Haines	M.Wilson	D.Wycoff	J.McBride
1928 E.Potteiger	N.Allison	S.Owen	P.Jappe	M.Murtagh	H.Garvey	R.Rosatti	C.Hubbard	B.Caldwell	M.Wilson	J.Hagerty	J.McBride
1929 R.Andrews	R.Flaherty	S.Owen	D.McMullen	J.Wostoupal	L.Caywood	B.Owen	L.Munn	B.Friedman	L.Sedbrook	T.Feather	T.Plansky
1930 R.Andrews	R.Badgro	S.Owen	L.Caywood	J.Wostoupal	R.Comstock	B.Owen	G.Campbell	B.Friedman	L.Sedbrook	T.Feather	O.Wiberg
1931 S.Owen	R.Badgro	L.Grant	B.Gibson	M.Hein	L.Caywood	B.Owen	R.Flaherty	B.Friedman	H.Moran	D.Wycoff	C.Cagle
1932 S.Owen	R.Badgro	L.Grant	B.Gibson	M.Hein	P.Jones	B.Owen	R.Flaherty	J.McBride	D.Burnett	B.Molenda	C.Cagle
1933 S.Owen	R.Badgro	L.Grant	B.Gibson	M.Hein	P.Jones	B.Owen	R.Flaherty	H.Newman	D.Burnett	B.Molenda	K.Strong
1934 S.Owen	R.Badgro	L.Grant	P.Jones	M.Hein	B.Gibson	B.Owen	R.Flaherty	H.Newman	D.Burnett	B.Molenda	K.Strong
1935 S.Owen	W.Singer	B.Morgan	P.Jones	M.Hein	B.Bellinger	L.Grant	T.Goodwin	E.Danowski	D.Burnett	R.Corzine	K.Strong
1936 S.Owen	W.Singer	B.Morgan	J.Dell Isola	M.Hein	P.Jones	A.Lewis	T.Goodwin	E.Danowski	D.Burnett	T.Manton	T.Leemans
1937 S.Owen	J.Poole	J.Dennerlein	J.Dell Isola	M.Hein	O.Tuttle	L.Grant	J.Howell	E.Danowski	W.Cuff	R.Corzine	T.Leemans
1938 S.Owen	J.Poole	E.Widseth	K.Lunday	M.Hein	O.Tuttle	O.Parry	J.Howell	E.Danowski	W.Cuff	L.Shaffer	T.Leemans
1939 S.Owen	J.Poole	F.Cope	J.Dell Isola	M.Hein	O.Tuttle	J.Mellus	W.Walls	E.Danowski	W.Cuff	N.Falaschi	T.Leemans
1940 S.Owen	J.Poole	F.Cope	O.Tuttle	M.Hein	J.Dell Isola	J.Mellus	J.Howell	E.Miller	W.Cuff	N.Falaschi	T.Leemans
1941 S.Owen	J.Poole	J.Mellus	M.Edwards	M.Hein	D.Oldershaw	W.Pedersen	J.Howell	T.Leemans	W.Cuff	N.Falaschi	L.Eshmont
1942 S.Owen	N.Adams	F.Cope	M.Edwards	M.Hein	H.Buffington	A.Blozis	W.Walls	T.Leemans	W.Cuff	L.Shaffer	M.Hapes
1943 S.Owen	N.Adams	F.Cope	L.Younce	M.Hein	C.Avedisian	A.Blozis	W.Walls	T.Leemans	W.Cuff	L.Shaffer	B.Paschal
1944 S.Owen	N.Adams	F.Cope	L.Younce	M.Hein	J.Sivell	V.Carroll	F.Liebel	A.Herber	W.Cuff	L.Calligaro	B.Paschal
1945 S.Owen	S.Fox	F.Cope	L.Visnic	M.Hein	J.Sivell	P.Ragazzo	J.Weiss	A.Herber	W.Cuff	J.Sulaitis	S.Filipowicz
1946 S.Owen	J.Poole	T.Coulter	B.Dobelstein	C.Gladchuk	L.Younce	J.White	J.Howell	F.Filchock	H.Livingston	S.Filipowicz	B.Paschal
1947 S.Owen	T.Coulter	B.Schuler	B.Dobelstein	C.Gladchuk	L.Younce	J.White	R.Poole	P.Governali	H.Livingston	J.Sulaitis	K.Strong
1948 S.Owen	P.Walker	J.White	B.Dobelstein	J.Cannady	L.Younce	B.Schuler	R.Poole	C.Conerly*	J.Scott	S.Minisi	G.Roberts
1949 S.Owen	B.Swiacki	J.White	C.Butkus	T.Coulter	E.Royston	A.DeRogatis	R.Poole	C.Conerly*	G.Roberts	J.Scott	B.Greenhalgh
NEW YORK YANKEES 1927 6/7-8-1, 1928 7/4-8-1											
1927 R.Scott	R.Flaherty	N.Harvey	M.Michalske	R.Stephens	B.Oliver	D.Hall	R.Maloney	E.Tryon	B.Baker	W.Kelly	B.Molenda
1928 D.Rauch	F.Grube	E.Gallagher	M.Michalske	J.McArthur	M.Hogue	H.Levy	R.Flaherty	W.Kelly	R.Smith	G.Welch	B.Pritchard
NEW YORK YANKEES (AAFC) (merged with Brooklyn Dodgers 1949) 1946 1e/10-3-1 l, 1947 1e/11-2-1 l, 1948 3e/6-8, 1949 3/8-4 p											
1946 R.Scott	B.Masterson	B.Kinard	R.Piskor	T.Robertson	C.Riffle	H.Johnson	B.Alford	S.Sanders	L.Wagner	L.Cheatham	E.Prokop
1947 R.Flaherty	J.Russell	D.Palmer	R.Bentz	L.Sossamon	D.Barwegan	H.Johnson	B.Alford	S.Sanders	B.Sweiger	L.Cheatham	B.Young
1948 R.Strader	J.Russell	Weinmeister	D.Crawford	L.Sossamon	J.Signaigo	N.Greene	B.Alford	S.Sanders	B.Sweiger	L.Cheatham	B.Young
1949 R.Strader	J.Russell	M.Ruby	J.Wozniak	B.Ecklund	J.Signaigo	Weinmeister	B.Alford	D.Panciera*	B.Young	S.Howard	B.Kennedy
NEWARK TORNADOES 1930 11/1-10-1											
1930 R.Scott	P.Longua	B.Feaster	B.Ellor	T.Mitchell	A.Salata	J.Mooney	J.Tomaini	F.Kirkleski	N.Borelli	B.Finn	F.Briante
OORANG INDIANS 1922 11/3-6, 1923 18/1-10											
1922 R.Scott	S.Saunooke	St. Germaine	B.Hill	B.Winneshick	E.Busch	N.Lassa	P.Calac	J.Guyon	R.Attache	L.Boutwell	Eagle Feather
1923 Jim Thorpe	Little Twig	T.Buffalo	S.Powell	N.Lassa	Jack Thorpe	B.Newashe	P.Calac	Jim Thorpe	C.Lingrel	E.McLemore	Eagle Feather
ORANGE TORNADOES 1929 6/3-4-4											
1929 R.Scott	P.Scott	B.Feaster	E.Cuneo	T.Mitchell	A.Salata	B.Beattie	P.Longua	F.Kirkleski	H.Benkert	G.Pease	C.Waite
PHILADELPHIA EAGLES (merged with Pittsburgh 1943) 1933 4e/3-5-1, 1934 3e/4-7, 1935 5e/2-9, 1936 5e/1-11, 1937 5e/2-8-1, 1938 4e/5-6, 1939 4e/1-9-1, 1940 5e/1-10, 1941 4e/2-8-1, 1942 5e/2-9, 1943 3e/5-4-1, 1944 2e/7-1-2, 1945 2e/7-3, 1946 2e/6-5, 1947 1e/8-4 dl, 1948 1e/9-2-1 l*, 1949 1e/11-1 l*											
1933 R.Scott	G.Kenneally	P.Cuba	J.Kresky	J.Lipski	J.Zyntell	G.Turnbow	J.Carter	R.Davis	J.Roberts	R.Kirkman	S.Hanson
1934 L.Wray	G.Kenneally	P.Cuba	D.Willson	J.Lipski	J.Zyntell	J.MacMurdo	J.Carter	E.Matesic	S.Ellstrom	R.Kirkman	S.Hanson
1935 L.Wray	E.Manske	P.Cuba	J.Kresky	H.Reese	D.Willson	B.Brian	J.Carter	E.Matesic	S.Hanson	S.Thomason	J.Leonard
1936 B.Bell	E.Manske	A.Buss	J.Russell	H.Reese	F.McPherson	J.MacMurdo	J.Carter	S.Hanson	S.Thomason	J.Leonard	D.Smukler
1937 B.Bell	B.Hewitt	A.Buss	M.Stockton	H.Reese	B.Hughes	F.Ferko	J.Carter	E.Mortell	J.Arnold	G.Frey	D.Smukler
1938 B.Bell	B.Hewitt	D.Ellis	M.Stockton	M.Harper	G.Rado	C.Woltman	J.Carter	E.Mortell	J.Arnold	W.Dow	D.Smukler
1939 B.Bell	R.Ramsey	D.Ellis	T.Schmitt	M.Harper	B.Cuppoletti	C.Woltman	J.Carter	D.O'Brien*	J.Arnold	F.Murray	C.Newton
1940 B.Bell	R.Ramsey	R.Thompson	D.Bassi	M.Harper	B.Hughes	G.Somers	D.Looney	D.O'Brien*	J.Bukant	F.Murray	D.Riffle
1941 G.Neale	B.Krieger	J.Eibner	E.Conti	L.Graham	B.Suffridge	P.Ragazzo	D.Humbert	L.Barnum*	J.Banta	M.Landsberg	J.Castiglia
1942 G.Neale	L.Cabrelli	V.Sears	W.Gerber	R.Graves	E.Conti	J.Eibner	F.Meyer	T.Thompson*	B.Davis	L.Barnum	L.Tomasetti
1943 R.Scott	T.Bova	V.Sears	E.Schultz	R.Graves	E.Michaels	T.Doyle	L.Cabrelli	R.Zimmerman*	J.Butler	J.Hinkle	B.Kish
1944 R.Scott	J.Ferrante	B.Friedman	E.Conti	B.Manzini	B.Banducci	A.Wistert	L.Cabrelli	R.Zimmerman*	S.Van Buren	J.Hinkle	B.Kish
1945 G.Neale	J.Ferrante	V.Sears	E.Michaels	V.Lindskog	B.Banducci	A.Wistert	L.Cabrelli	R.Zimmerman*	S.Van Buren	M.Bleeker	B.Kish
1946 G.Neale	J.Ferrante	V.Sears	E.Michaels	V.Lindskog	D.Maronic	A.Wistert	L.Cabrelli	R.Zimmerman*	S.Van Buren	B.Pritchard	J.Muha
1947 G.Neale	J.Ferrante	V.Sears	C.Patton	Wojciechowicz	B.Kilroy	A.Wistert	P.Pihos	T.Thompson*	S.Van Buren	B.Pritchard	J.Muha

YEAR COACH	LE	LT	LG	C	RG	RT	RE	TB/QB	WB/HB/LH	BB/RH	FB
1948 G.Neale	J.Green	J.MacDowell	J.Magee	V.Lindskog	B.Kilroy	A.Wistert	P.Pihos	T.Thompson*	S.Van Buren	B.Pritchard	J.Muha
1949 G.Neale	J.Ferrante	V.Sears	C.Patton	C.Bednarik	B.Kilroy	A.Wistert	P.Pihos	T.Thompson*	S.Van Buren	B.Pritchard	J.Muha

PITTSBURGH (Pirates 1933-39, Steelers 1940-49, merged with Philadelphia 1943, merged with Chicago Cardinals 1944) 1933 5e/3-6-2, 1934 5e/2-10, 1935 3e/4-8, 1936 2e/6-6, 1937 3e/4-7, 1938 5e/2-9, 1939 4e/1-9-1, 1940 4e/2-7-2, 1941 5e/1-9-1, 1942 2e/7-4, 1943 3e/5-4-1, 1944 5w/0-10, 1945 5e/2-8, 1946 3e/5-5-1, 1947 1e/8-4 d, 1948 3e/4-8, 1949 2e/6-5-1

1933 R.Scott	P.Moss	D.Rhodes	Critchfield	C.Oehler	C.Janecek	C.Artman	R.Tesser	A.Brovelli	J.Clark	G.Shaffer	T.Holm
1934 L.DiMeolo	B.Smith	J.Quatse	J.Douds	C.Oehler	D.Ribble	A.Niccolai	J.Skladany	W.Heller	A.Rado	S.Zaninelli	A.Brovelli
1935 J.Bach	V.Vidoni	S.Sandberg	G.Rado	B.Ciccone	B.Hoel	A.Niccolai	B.Sortet	J.Gildea	A.Strutt	J.Turley	S.Zaninelli
1936 J.Bach	E.Skoronski	S.Sandberg	L.Mayhew	L.Mulleneaux	G.Kakasic	A.Niccolai	V.Sites	E.Matesic	W.Heller	J.Gildea	B.Karcis
1937 J.Blood	J.Brett	S.Sandberg	G.Kakasic	M.Basrak	J.Perko	A.Niccolai	B.Sortet	J.Gildea	B.Davidson	S.Zaninelli	S.Smith
1938 J.Blood	E.Manske	J.Cardwell	B.Gentry	M.Basrak	J.Perko	A.Niccolai	J.Tatum	W.White	T.Thompson	J.Blood	S.Smith
1939 W.Kiesling	G.Platukis	D.Campbell	B.Gentry	J.Maras	G.Kakasic	A.Niccolai	B.Sortet	H.McCullough	L.Tomasetti	R.Bond	Littlefield
1940 W.Kiesling	G.Platukis	D.Campbell	J.Sanders	T.Grabinski	J.Perko	A.Niccolai	B.Sortet	B.Patterson	L.Tomasetti	H.Bruder	G.Kiick
1941 A.Donelli	G.Platukis	J.Coomer	E.Schultz	C.Cherundolo	D.Bassi	J.Woudenberg	J.Wendlick	B.Brumbaugh	A.Jones	J.Patrick	D.Riffle
1942 W.Kiesling	T.Bova	E.Schultz	J.Sanders	C.Cherundolo	M.Simington	J.Woudenberg	W.Kichefski	B.Dudley	C.Sandig	V.Martin	D.Riffle
1943 R.Scott	T.Bova	V.Sears	E.Schultz	R.Graves	E.Michaels	T.Doyle	L.Cabrelli	R.Zimmerman*	J.Butler	J.Hinkle	B.Kish
1944 R.Scott	T.Bova	G.Duggan	C.Baker	M.Robnett	J.Perko	C.Bulger	W.Kichefski	W.Rankin*	G.Magulick	B.Thurbon	J.Grigas
1945 R.Scott	D.Dolly	G.Stough	E.Merkovsky	C.Cherundolo	J.Perko	T.Doyle	J.Pierre	B.Dudley	T.Bova	L.Pense	J.Lucente
1946 J.Sutherland	V.Jansante	J.Wiley	R.Fife	C.Cherundolo	R.Bucek	A.McCaffray	B.Davis	B.Dudley	M.Condit	C.Seabright	T.Compagno
1947 J.Sutherland	V.Jansante	J.Wiley	R.Moore	C.Cherundolo	N.Skorich	F.Wydo	B.Davis	J.Clement	J.Glamp	C.Seabright	S.Lach
1948 J.Michelosen	C.Mehelich	Mastrangelo	R.Moore	C.Cherundolo	B.Cregar	F.Wydo	E.Nickel	R.Evans	B.Cifers	C.Seabright	J.Shipkey
1949 J.Michelosen	V.Jansante	J.Wiley	R.Moore	B.Walsh	S.Suhey	F.Wydo	E.Nickel	J.Geri	J.Nuzum	C.Seabright	G.Papach

POTTSVILLE MAROONS 1925 2/10-2, 1926 3/10-2-2, 1927 8/5-8, 1928 8/2-8

1925 R.Scott	C.Berry	R.Hathaway	F.Racis	H.Stein	D.Osborn	R.Stein	F.Bucher	H.Flanagan	T.Latone	J.Ernst	B.Wentz
1926 D.Rauch	C.Berry	F.Racis	J.Welsh	H.Stein	D.Osborn	R.Hathaway	F.Bucher	J.Brown	H.Flanagan	J.Ernst	B.Wentz
1927 D.Rauch	G.Kenneally	W.Erickson	F.Racis	Youngfleish	J.Budd	P.Henry	V.Mullen	F.Kirkleski	T.Latone	J.Ernst	B.Wentz
1928 P.Henry	G.Kenneally	J.Budd	F.Racis	H.Stein	W.Kiesling	J.Carpe	J.Rooney	J.Blood	W.Norman	J.Ernst	T.Latone

PROVIDENCE STEAM ROLLER 1925 10/6-5-1, 1926 11/5-7-1, 1927 5/8-5-1, 1928 1/8-1-2, 1929 8/4-6-2, 1930 5/6-4-1, 1931 6/4-4-3

1925 R.Scott	F.Garvey	J.Kozlowsky	N.Share	D.Eckstein	A.Golembeski	M.Gulian	R.Maloney	C.Wentworth	A.McIntosh	C.Oden	J.Laird
1926 J.Laird	F.Garvey	J.Kozlowsky	J.Donahue	D.Eckstein	L.Young	M.Gulian	A.Golembeski	C.Wentworth	J.Spellman	C.Oden	J.Laird
1927 J.Conzelman	E.Lynch	G.Sonnenberg	Fleischmann	A.Pierotti	J.Laird	O.Smith	J.Spellman	A.Wilson	A.Hadden	C.Oden	B.Pritchard
1928 J.Conzelman	D.Hanny	G.Sonnenberg	M.Rehnquist	C.Smith	Fleischmann	P.Jackson	J.Spellman	W.Wilson	B.Cronin	C.Oden	A.Hadden
1929 J.Conzelman	A.Hadden	D.Hanny	H.Garvey	M.Rehnquist	Fleischmann	W.McGuirk	J.Spellman	A.Wilson	P.Williams	G.Welch	J.McBride
1930 J.Conzelman	A.Rose	J.Douds	M.Rehnquist	R.Smith	A.Graham	W.McGuirk	J.Spellman	F.Peters	P.Williams	C.Oden	T.Latone
1931 E.Robinson	A.Rose	T.Irvin	A.Graham	R.Smith	A.Sofish	J.Schein	J.Spellman	D.Shelley	O.Pape	H.Titmas	L.Woodruff

RACINE (Legion 1922-24, Tornadoes 1926) 1922 6/6-4-1, 1923 10/4-4-2, 1924 7/4-3-3, 1926 16/1-4

1922 R.Scott	N.Hayes	A.Braman	E.Gorman	J.Mintun	J.Murray	C.Miller	F.Roeseler	A.Elliott	I.Langhoff	C.Dressen	H.Gillo
1923 B.Ruetz	P.Meyers	A.Braman	E.Gorman	J.Mintun	G.Hartong	L.Smith	D.Halladay	A.Elliott	M.Romney	S.Barr	H.Gillo
1924 B.Ruetz	R.Brumm	D.Murry	A.Bentzin	J.Mintun	R.King	L.Smith	D.Halladay	A.Elliott	B.Giaver	M.Romney	H.Gillo
1926 R.Scott	J.Oldham	R.Hardy	Bieberstein	R.Brumm	G.Bernard	F.Hobscheid	B.Mathews	G.Kernwein	W.McIlwain	G.Sterr	C.Reichow

ROCHESTER JEFFERSONS 1920 7/6-3-2, 1921 10/2-3, 1922 16/0-4-1, 1923 20/0-4, 1924 18/0-7, 1925 17/0-6-1

1920 R.Scott	D.Lowery	B.Carroll	H.Smith	J.Bachmaier	A.Webb	L.Usher	H.Clark	R.Quigley	B.Argus	M.Purdy	J.Laird
1921 J.Forsyth	D.Lowery	J.Barron	H.Smith	D.Alexander	F.Morrissey	C.Thomas	R.Witter	H.Berry	B.Argus	J.Noonan	J.Laird
1922 D.Alexander	S.Roy	F.Matteo	J.Dooley	D.Alexander	T.Thompson	H.Smith	E.Anderson	D.King	B.Argus	L.Weltman	C.Wynne
1923 L.Lyons	S.Roy	J.Leonard	D.Lowery	J.Woods	J.Welsh	F.Matteo	H.Clark	G.Wallace	B.Argus	S.Sheard	M.Gavagan
1924 J.Murphy	S.Roy	F.Matteo	R.Martineau	H.Smith	D.Lowery	J.Dooley	H.Clark	J.Noonan	L.Peyton	S.Sheard	B.Argus
1925 T.Grigg	D.Ziff	J.Dooley	D.Lowery	H.Smith	R.Martineau	F.Matteo	E.Lynch	L.Smyth	S.Sheard	T.Grigg	B.Argus

ROCK ISLAND INDEPENDENDTS 1920 4/6-2-2, 1921 5/4-2-1, 1922 5/4-2-1, 1923 12/2-3-3, 1924 5/5-2-2, 1925 8/5-3-3

1920 R.Scott	O.Smith	E.Shaw	P.Wyland	F.Fitzgerald	D.Lyle	W.Buland	B.Marshall	F.Chicken	E.Novak	R.Ursella	A.Wyman
1921 J.Conzelman	O.Smith	E.Healey	E.Keefe	J.Earp	D.Lyle	W.Buland	O.Wenig	L.Bridgford	E.Novak	J.Conzelman	V.Vanderloo
1922 J.Conzelman	T.Voss	E.Healey	D.Lyle	L.Kolls	J.Jones	D.Slater	W.Clago	J.Johnson	D.Lauer	J.Conzelman	B.Gavin
1923 H.Sies	M.Kadesky	F.Cotton	G.Thompson	L.Kolls	H.Sies	D.Slater	M.Wilson	B.Giaver	W.Kuehl	J.Armstrong	B.Phelan
1924 J.Armstrong	F.Thomsen	N.Scott	G.Thompson	L.Kolls	J.Kraker	D.Slater	M.Wilson	Jim Thorpe	R.Ursella	J.Armstrong	B.Gavin
1925 R.Ursella	Little Twig	C.Widerquist	G.Thompson	L.Kolls	L.Burton	D.Slater	J.Rooney	R.Lamb	R.Ursella	J.Armstrong	E.Novak

SAN FRANCISCO 49ERS (AAFC) 1946 2w/9-5, 1947 2w/8-4-2, 1948 2w/12-2, 1949 2/9-3 pl

1946 R.Scott	B.Fisk	J.Mellus	D.Bassi	D.Elston	B.Banducci	J.Woudenberg	B.Titchenal	F.Albert*	L.Eshmont	Strzykalski	N.Standlee
1947 B.Shaw	N.Susoeff	B.Bryant	G.Gregory	J.Schiechl	B.Banducci	J.Woudenberg	A.Beals	F.Albert*	L.Eshmont	Strzykalski	N.Standlee
1948 B.Shaw	N.Susoeff	B.Bryant	D.Clark	J.Williams	V.Grgich	J.Woudenberg	A.Beals	F.Albert*	L.Eshmont	Strzykalski	N.Standlee
1949 B.Shaw	H.Shoener	B.Mike	D.Clark	B.Johnson	V.Grgich	J.Woudenberg	A.Beals	F.Albert*	L.Eshmont	V.Lillywhite	N.Standlee

STATEN ISLAND STAPLETONS 1929 6/3-4-3, 1930 6/5-5-2, 1931 7/4-6-1, 1932 8/2-7-3

1929 R.Scott	S.Stein	C.Williams	D.Skudin	B.Dunn	W.Godwin	B.Miller	T.Leary	I.Williams	K.Strong	D.Wycoff	F.Briante
1930 D.Wycoff	S.Stein	C.Williams	O.Satenstein	J.Fitzgerald	J.Bunyan	B.Miller	B.Lundell	B.Follet	K.Strong	R.Buckley	S.Snyder
1931 M.Brill	B.Barrabee	A.Kanya	H.Garvey	H.Rapp	O.Satenstein	B.Miller	C.Marshall	K.Strong	T.Feather	I.Yablock	D.Parkinson
1932 H.Hanson	L.Maynard	A.Kanya	J.Bunyan	M.Intrieri	R.Grant	L.Raskowski	S.Wilson	B.Campiglio	D.Frahm	D.Wycoff	K.Strong

ST. LOUIS (All-Stars 1923, Gunners 1934) 1923 14/1-4-2, 1934 6w/1-2

1923 R.Scott	O.Kraehe	B.Weller	W.Murrah	W.Kreinheder	R.Andrews	B.Travis	W.Meese	O.Siegfried	P.Casey	E.Simpson	D.King
1934 R.Scott	P.Moss	S.Sandberg	B.Montgomery	L.Mulleneaux	L.McGirl	B.Lyon	M.Gladden	M.Rapp	G.Alford	B.Workman	S.Johnston

TOLEDO MAROONS 1922 4/5-2-2, 1923 11/3-3-2

1922 R.Scott	T.Myers	R.Stein	C.Edwards	M.Conrad	H.Stein	S.Horning	D.Peabody	B.Phelan	D.Annan	R.Watson	G.Falcon
1923 G.Falcon	M.White	T.Voss	J.Jones	M.Conrad	T.McNamara	S.Horning	S.Seyfrit	C.Hill	D.Lauer	F.Fitzgerald	D.Strauss

TONAWANDA KARDEX 1921 18/0-1

1921 R.Scott	A.Goerke	G.Kuhrt	R.Kraft	R.Werder	B.MacDonald	C.Tallman	W.Sanborn	T.Rose	B.Meisner	F.Primeau	T.McLaughlin

WASHINGTON REDSKINS (Boston Braves 1932, Boston Redskins 1933-36) 1932 4/4-4-2, 1933 3e/5-5-2, 1934 2e/6-6, 1935 4e/2-8-1, 1936 1e/7-5 l, 1937 1e/8-3 l*, 1938 2e/6-3-2, 1939 2e/8-2-1, 1940 1e/9-2 l, 1941 3e/6-5, 1942 1e/10-1 l*, 1943 1e/6-3-1 dl, 1944 3e/6-3-1, 1945 1e/8-2 l, 1946 3e/5-5-1, 1947 4e/4-8, 1948 2e/7-5, 1949 4e/4-7-1

1932 R.Scott	G.Kenneally	J.MacMurdo	J.Kresky	M.Erickson	G.Hurley	D.Waters	P.Collins	C.Battles	E.Pinckert	H.Hughes	J.Musick
1933 L.Dietz	I.Frankian	T.Edwards	G.Hurley	O.Crow	J.MacMurdo	J.Riley	P.Collins	C.Battles	E.Pinckert	M.Apsit	J.Musick
1934 L.Dietz	C.Malone	T.Edwards	F.Walton	F.Bausch	L.Olsson	B.Boswell	P.Collins	C.Battles	E.Pinckert	S.Hokuf	H.McPhail
1935 E.Casey	C.Malone	T.Edwards	R.Concannon	F.Bausch	L.Olsson	G.O'Brien	P.Collins	C.Battles	E.Pinckert	B.Shepherd	J.Musick
1936 R.Flaherty	W.Millner	T.Edwards	L.Olsson	F.Bausch	J.Karcher	J.Barber	C.Malone	E.Britt	E.Pinckert	E.Smith	C.Battles
1937 R.Scott	W.Millner	T.Edwards	L.Olsson	E.Kawal	J.Karcher	J.Barber	C.Malone	S.Baugh	E.Pinckert	B.Smith	D.Irwin
1938 R.Flaherty	W.Millner	T.Edwards	L.Olsson	V.Carroll	J.Karcher	J.Barber	C.Malone	S.Baugh	E.Pinckert	R.Smith	A.Farkas
1939 R.Flaherty	W.Millner	T.Edwards	C.Stralka	M.Parks	J.Karcher	J.Barber	C.Malone	F.Filchock	J.Johnston	E.Pinckert	A.Farkas
1940 R.Flaherty	W.Millner	W.Wilkin	D.Farman	B.Titchenal	S.Slivinski	J.Barber	C.Malone	S.Baugh	E.Justice	M.Krause	J.Johnston
1941 R.Flaherty	B.Masterson	W.Wilkin	C.Stralka	G.Smith	C.Shugart	J.Barber	E.Cifers	S.Baugh	W.Moore	C.Hare	D.Todd
1942 R.Flaherty	B.Masterson	W.Wilkin	D.Farman	K.Aldrich	S.Slivinski	B.Young	E.Cifers	S.Baugh	E.Justice	C.Hare	A.Farkas
1943 D.Bergman	B.Masterson	L.Rymkus	D.Farman	G.Smith	S.Slivinski	J.Pasqua	J.Aguirre	S.Baugh	W.Moore	R.Hare	A.Farkas
1944 D.DeGroot	J.Aguirre	J.Zeno	A.Fiorentino	V.Foltz	E.Merkle	J.North	A.Piasecky	F.Filchock*	A.Farkas	W.Moore	B.Seymour
1945 D.DeGroot	J.Aguirre	J.Adams	A.Lolotai	K.Aldrich	Z.Hanna	J.Ungerer	D.Turley	S.Baugh*	S.Bagarus	deCorrevont	F.Akins
1946 T.Edwards	J.Peebles	Koniszewski	B.Ward	K.Aldrich	J.Steber	P.Stenn	E.Cifers	S.Baugh*	D.Todd	S.Bagarus	J.Jenkins
1947 T.Edwards	P.McKee	E.Williamson	J.Steber	K.Aldrich	F.Boensch	J.Peebles	Tereshinski	D.Poillon*	E.Saenz	T.Farmer	J.Jenkins
1948 T.Edwards	P.McKee	J.Sanchez	J.Steber	A.DeMao	F.Boensch	J.Adams	Tereshinski	S.Baugh*	T.Farmer	D.Sandifer	E.Quirk
1949 J.Whelchel	H.Crisler	L.Szafaryn	H.Siegert	A.DeMao	Badaczewski	J.Adams	H.Shoener	S.Baugh*	R.Goode	H.Livingston	D.Poillon

WASHINGTON SENATORS 1921 12/1-2

1921 R.Scott	G.Patterson	M.Smeach	C.McDonald	B.Crouch	T.Gormley	D.Ahern	D.McCarthy	B.Boynton	G.Beyers	B.Walson	J.Sullivan

YEAR	COACH	WR/LE	LT	LG	C	RG	RT	TE/RE	WR/FL	QB	RB/LH	FB
ARIZONA CARDINALS (Chicago 1950-59, St. Louis 1960-87, Phoenix 1988-1993)												
1950	C.Lambeau	F.Polsfoot	B.Fischer	G.Petrovich	B.Blackburn	B.Ramsey	J.Jennings	B.Shaw	E.Angsman	J.Hardy	C.Trippi	P.Harder
1951	C.Lambeau	F.Polsfoot	B.Fischer	E.Bagdon	J.Simmons	K.Ramsey	J.Jennings	D.Stonesifer	E.Angsman	C.Trippi	B.Cross	Pasquariello
1952	J.Kuharich	C.Anderson	M.Mergen	M.Sikora	J.Simmons	B.Fischer	J.Jennings	D.Stonesifer	E.Sitko	C.Trippi	B.Cross	O.Matson
1953	J.Stydahar	G.Nagler	T.Higgins	D.Suminski	J.Simmons	J.Watford	J.Jennings	D.Stonesifer	B.Cross	J.Root	C.Trippi	J.Olszewski
1954	J.Stydahar	D.Stonesifer	L.Teeuws	J.Hatley	J.Simmons	B.Lange	J.Jennings	J.Ladd	J.Olszewski	L.McHan	O.Matson	E.King
1955	R.Richards	D.Stonesifer	L.Teeuws	H.Thompson	J.Simmons	B.Lange	J.Jennings	G.Nagler	D.Mann	L.McHan	O.Matson	J.Olszewski
1956	R.Richards	D.Stonesifer	T.Dahms	D.Hogland	J.Simmons	J.Dittrich	J.Jennings	G.Nagler	D.Mann	L.McHan	O.Matson	J.Olszewski
1957	R.Richards	W.Lewis	D.Lunceford	D.Hogland	E.Putman	B.Konovsky	J.Jennings	G.Nagler	J.Childress	L.McHan	O.Matson	J.Olszewski
1958	P.Ivy	W.Lewis	B.Cross	D.Meinert	D.Gillis	B.Konovsky	J.McCusker	G.Nagler	J.Childress	L.McHan	O.Matson	M.Hammack
1959	P.Ivy	W.Lewis	D.Memmelaar	D.Meinert	D.Gillis	K.Gray	K.Panfil	J.Tracey	B.Conrad	K.Hill	J.Crow	M.Hammack
1960	P.Ivy	S.Randle	E.Cook	M.McGee	D.Gillis	K.Gray	K.Panfil	H.McInnis	J.Childress	J.Roach	J.Crow	M.Hammack
1961	P.Ivy	S.Randle	E.Cook	M.McGee	D.Gillis	K.Gray	E.McMillan	T.Anderson	B.Conrad	S.Etcheverry	P.Gautt	F.Mestnik
1962	W.Lemm	S.Randle	E.Cook	M.McGee	B.DeMarco	K.Gray	E.McMillan	T.Anderson	B.Conrad	C.Johnson	J.Crow	M.Hammack
1963	W.Lemm	S.Randle	I.Goode	E.Cook	B.DeMarco	K.Gray	E.McMillan	J.Smith	B.Conrad	C.Johnson	B.Triplett	J.Childress
1964	W.Lemm	S.Randle	B.Reynolds	I.Goode	B.DeMarco	K.Gray	E.McMillan	T.Anderson	B.Conrad	C.Johnson	J.Childress	J.Crow
1965	W.Lemm	S.Randle	B.Reynolds	I.Goode	B.DeMarco	K.Gray	E.McMillan	J.Smith	B.Conrad	C.Johnson	B.Triplett	W.Crenshaw
1966	C.Winner	S.Randle	B.Reynolds	I.Goode	B.DeMarco	K.Gray	E.McMillan	J.Smith	B.Conrad	C.Johnson	J.Roland	W.Crenshaw
1967	C.Winner	B.Gambrell	B.Reynolds	I.Goode	B.DeMarco	K.Gray	E.McMillan	J.Smith	B.Conrad	J.Hart	P.Gautt	J.Roland
1968	C.Winner	D.Williams	B.Reynolds	I.Goode	B.DeMarco	K.Gray	E.McMillan	J.Smith	B.Conrad	J.Hart	J.Roland	W.Crenshaw
1969	C.Winner	D.Williams	B.Reynolds	I.Goode	B.DeMarco	K.Gray	E.McMillan	J.Smith	J.Gilliam	C.Johnson	J.Roland	C.Edwards
1970	C.Winner	D.Williams	B.Reynolds	I.Goode	W.Mulligan	C.Williams	E.McMillan	J.Smith	J.Gilliam	J.Hart	M.Lane	C.Edwards
1971	B.Hollway	D.Williams	B.Reynolds	I.Goode	T.Banks	C.Williams	E.McMillan	J.Smith	J.Gilliam	J.Hart	J.Roland	M.Lane
1972	B.Hollway	A.Rashad	D.Dierdorf	C.Dobler	T.Banks	B.Young	W.Mulligan	J.Smith	W.Gillette	G.Cuozzo	D.Anderson	L.Burns
1973	D.Coryell	A.Rashad	D.Dierdorf	T.Banks	W.Mulligan	C.Dobler	E.McMillan	J.Smith	M.Gray	J.Hart	D.Anderson	J.Otis
1974	D.Coryell	E.Thomas	E.McMillan	B.Young	T.Brahaney	C.Dobler	D.Dierdorf	J.Smith	M.Gray	J.Hart	T.Metcalf	J.Otis
1975	D.Coryell	E.Thomas	R.Finnie	B.Young	T.Banks	C.Dobler	D.Dierdorf	J.Smith	M.Gray	J.Hart	T.Metcalf	J.Otis
1976	D.Coryell	M.Gray	R.Finnie	B.Young	T.Banks	C.Dobler	D.Dierdorf	J.Cain	I.Harris	J.Hart	T.Metcalf	J.Otis
1977	D.Coryell	I.Harris	R.Finnie	B.Young	T.Banks	C.Dobler	D.Dierdorf	J.Cain	M.Gray	J.Hart	T.Metcalf	W.Morris
1978	Wilkinson	P.Tilley	K.Wortman	B.Young	T.Banks	T.Stieve	D.Dierdorf	A.Chandler	M.Gray	J.Hart	W.Morris	J.Otis
1979	Wilkinson	P.Tilley	K.Wortman	B.Young	T.Banks	T.Stieve	J.Bostic	G.Parris	M.Gray	J.Hart	O.Anderson	W.Morris
1980	J.Hanifan	P.Tilley	G.Collins	B.Cotton	T.Brahaney	J.Bostic	D.Dierdorf	D.Marsh	M.Gray	J.Hart	O.Anderson	W.Morris
1981	J.Hanifan	P.Tilley	G.Collins	T.Stieve	T.Brahaney	J.Bostic	D.Dierdorf	G.LaFleur	M.Gray	J.Hart	O.Anderson	W.Morris
1982	J.Hanifan	P.Tilley	L.Sharpe	T.Stieve	D.Dierdorf	J.Bostic	T.Robbins	D.Marsh	R.Green	N.Lomax	O.Anderson	W.Morris
1983	J.Hanifan	P.Tilley	L.Sharpe	T.Stieve	R.Clark	J.Bostic	T.Robbins	D.Marsh	R.Green	N.Lomax	O.Anderson	W.Morris
1984	J.Hanifan	P.Tilley	L.Sharpe	T.Stieve	R.Clark	J.Bostic	T.Robbins	D.Marsh	R.Green	N.Lomax	O.Anderson	E.Ferrell
1985	J.Hanifan	P.Tilley	L.Sharpe	D.Dawson	R.Clark	J.Bostic	T.Robbins	D.Marsh	R.Green	N.Lomax	O.Anderson	E.Ferrell
1986	Stallings	J.Smith	L.Sharpe	D.Kennard	R.Clark	J.Bostic	La.Smith	D.Marsh	R.Green	N.Lomax	S.Mitchell	E.Ferrell
1987	Stallings	J.Smith	L.Sharpe	T.Peat	D.Kennard	La.Smith	T.Robbins	R.Awalt	R.Green	N.Lomax	S.Mitchell	E.Ferrell
1988	Stallings	J.Smith	L.Sharpe	T.Peat	D.Kennard	L.Smith	T.Robbins	R.Awalt	R.Green	N.Lomax	S.Mitchell	E.Ferrell
1989	Stallings	E.Jones	L.Sharpe	J.Wolf	D.Kennard	L.Smith	T.Robbins	R.Awalt	R.Green	G.Hogeboom	T.Jordan	E.Ferrell
1990	J.Bugel	E.Jones	L.Sharpe	D.Kennard	B.Lewis	L.Smith	T.Robbins	W.Reeves	R.Green	T.Rosenbach	J.Johnson	T.Jorden*
1991	J.Bugel	E.Jones	L.Sharpe	V.Smith	B.Lewis	L.Smith	T.Robbins	W.Reeves	R.Proehl	T.Tupa	J.Johnson	T.Jorden*
1992	J.Bugel	R.Hill	L.Sharpe	M.May	B.Lewis	L.Smith	D.Villa	W.Reeves	R.Proehl	C.Chandler	J.Johnson	B.Rolle*
1993	J.Bugel	G.Clark	L.Sharpe	M.May	E.Cunningham	L.Smith	R.Cunningham	W.Reeves	R.Proehl	S.Beuerlein	R.Moore	L.Centers
1994	B.Ryan	R.Hill	L.Sharpe	E.Dye	E.Cunningham	B.Coleman	R.Cunningham	D.Ware	R.Proehl	J.Schroeder	R.Moore	C.Fann*
1995	B.Ryan	R.Moore	E.Dye	D.Love	E.Cunningham	A.Redmon	L.Tharpe	W.Gaines	F.Sanders	D.Krieg	G.Hearst	L.Centers
1996	V.Tobin	R.Moore	L.Brown	D.Love	M.Devlin	A.Redmon	J.Wolf	P.Carter	F.Sanders	B.Esiason	L.Johnson	L.Centers
1997	V.Tobin	R.Moore	L.Brown	R.Selby	M.Devlin	A.Redmon	J.Dexter	P.Carter	F.Sanders	J.Plummer	L.McElroy	L.Centers
1998	V.Tobin	R.Moore	L.Brown	C.Dishman	A.Graham	L.Holmes	J.Dexter	J.McWilliams	F.Sanders	J.Plummer	A.Murrell	L.Centers
1999	V.Tobin	R.Moore	M.Joyce	C.Dishman	A.Graham	L.Holmes	A.Clement	T.Hardy	F.Sanders	J.Plummer	A.Murrell	J.Makovicka
2000	D.McGinnis	D.Boston	L.Shelton	M.Joyce	C.Dishman	L.Holmes	A.Clement	T.Hardy	F.Sanders	J.Plummer	M.Pittman	J.Makovicka
2001	D.McGinnis	D.Boston	L.Shelton	P.Kendall	Gruttadauria	L.Davis	A.Clement	S.Bush	F.Sanders	J.Plummer	M.Pittman	J.Makovicka
2002	D.McGinnis	J.McAddley	L.Shelton	P.Kendall	J.Starkey	C.Dishman	L.Davis	F.Jones	F.Sanders	J.Plummer	T.Jones	S.Bush*
2003	D.McGinnis	B.Gilmore	L.Shelton	C.Spikes	P.Kendall	L.Davis	A.Clement	F.Jones	A.Boldin	J.Blake	M.Shipp	J.Hodgins
2004	D.Green	B.Johnson	L.Davis	R.Wells	Stepanovich	C.Spikes	L.Shelton	F.Jones	L.Fitzgerald	J.McCown	E.Smith	A.Boldin+
2005	D.Green	A.Boldin	L.Davis	R.Wells	N.Leckey	E.Brown	O.Ross	A.Bergen	L.Fitzgerald	K.Warner	M.Shipp	E.Edwards*
ATLANTA FALCONS												
1966	N.Hecker	V.Burke	D.Talbert	E.Cook	Marchlewski	D.Grimm	E.Linden	B.Martin	A.Hawkins	R.Johnson	J.Coffey	Wheelwright
1967	N.Hecker	J.Simmons	D.Talbert	L.Kirouac	Marchlewski	J.Simon	E.Linden	R.Ogden	T.McDonald	R.Johnson	J.Coffey	T.Moore
1968	Van Brocklin	J.Simmons	D.Talbert	J.Simon	P.Sobocinski	D.Grimm	E.Linden	R.Ogden	P.Flatley	B.Berry	P.Dunn	C.Butler
1969	Van Brocklin	G.Cogdill	B.Sandeman	D.Enderle	B.Bosley	M.Snider	G.Kunz	J.Mitchell	P.Flatley	B.Berry	H.Wages	C.Butler
1970	Van Brocklin	T.Snyder	M.Snider	A.Maurer	J.Van Note	D.Enderle	G.Kunz	J.Mitchell	P.Flatley	B.Berry	H.Wages	C.Butler
1971	Van Brocklin	K.Burrow	B.Sandeman	A.Maurer	J.Van Note	M.Snider	G.Kunz	J.Mitchell	W.Chesson	B.Berry	A.Malone	C.Butler
1972	Van Brocklin	K.Burrow	B.Sandeman	A.Maurer	J.Van Note	D.Havig	G.Kunz	J.Mitchell	W.Chesson	B.Berry	A.Malone	D.Hampton
1973	Van Brocklin	A.Dodd	B.Sandeman	A.Maurer	J.Van Note	D.Havig	G.Kunz	J.Mitchell	T.Geredine	B.Lee	A.Malone	D.Hampton
1974	Van Brocklin	K.Burrow	L.Gotshalk	J.Miller	J.Van Note	D.Havig	G.Kunz	J.Mitchell	A.Dodd	B.Lee	A.Malone	D.Hampton
1975	M.Campbell	K.Burrow	B.Adams	L.Jackson	J.Van Note	D.Havig	L.Gotshalk	J.Mitchell	A.Jenkins	S.Bartkowski	H.Stanback	D.Hampton
1976	P.Peppler	J.Gilliam	B.Adams	L.Jackson	J.Van Note	G.Kindle	L.Gotshalk	J.Mitchell	A.Jenkins	S.Hunter	S.Collins	M.Esposito
1977	L.Bennett	W.Francis	B.Adams	D.Scott	J.Van Note	R.Thielemann	W.Bryant	J.Mitchell	A.Jenkins	S.Bartkowski	H.Stanback	W.Thompson
1978	L.Bennett	W.Francis	M.Kenn	D.Scott	J.Van Note	R.Thielemann	W.Bryant	J.Mitchell	B.Ryckman	S.Bartkowski	H.Stanback	B.Bean
1979	L.Bennett	W.Francis	M.Kenn	D.Scott	J.Van Note	R.Thielemann	W.Bryant	J.Mitchell	A.Jenkins	S.Bartkowski	B.Bean	W.Andrews
1980	L.Bennett	W.Francis	M.Kenn	D.Scott	J.Van Note	R.Thielemann	W.Bryant	J.Miller	A.Jenkins	S.Bartkowski	L.Cain	W.Andrews
1981	L.Bennett	W.Francis	M.Kenn	D.Scott	J.Van Note	R.Thielemann	W.Bryant	J.Miller	A.Jenkins	S.Bartkowski	L.Cain	W.Andrews
1982	L.Bennett	A.Jackson	M.Kenn	P.Howell	J.Van Note	R.Thielemann	W.Bryant	J.Miller	A.Jenkins	S.Bartkowski	L.Cain	W.Andrews
1983	D.Henning	S.Bailey	M.Kenn	R.Thielemann	J.Van Note	J.Scully	W.Bryant	A.Cox	A.Jenkins	S.Bartkowski	W.Andrews	B.Robinson*
1984	D.Henning	S.Bailey	M.Kenn	R.Thielemann	J.Van Note	J.Scully	B.Miller	A.Cox	A.Jackson	S.Bartkowski	G.Riggs	C.Benson*
1985	D.Henning	S.Bailey	M.Kenn	J.Kiewel	J.Van Note	B.Fralic	B.Miller	A.Cox	C.Brown	D.Archer	G.Riggs	C.Benson*
1986	D.Henning	C.Brown	M.Kenn	J.Scully	W.Radloff	B.Fralic	B.Miller	A.Cox	F.Dixon	D.Archer	G.Riggs	K.Whisenhunt*
1987	M.Campbell	S.Bailey	M.Kenn	J.Scully	W.Radloff	B.Fralic	L.Mitchell	A.Cox	F.Dixon	S.Campbell	G.Riggs	K.Whisenhunt*
1988	M.Campbell	S.Bailey	M.Kenn	J.Scully	W.Radloff	B.Fralic	H.Hoover	K.Whisenhunt	F.Dixon	C.Miller	G.Riggs	J.Settle
1989	M.Campbell	S.Collins	M.Kenn	S.Clayton	J.Dukes	B.Fralic	H.Hoover	R.Heller	M.Haynes	C.Miller	K.Jones	J.Settle
1990	Glanville	A.Rison	M.Kenn	H.Hoover	J.Dukes	B.Fralic	C.Hinton	G.Wilkins	M.Haynes	C.Miller	S.Broussard	K.Jones
1991	Glanville	A.Rison	M.Kenn	H.Hoover	J.Dukes	B.Fralic	C.Hinton	G.Thomas+	M.Haynes	C.Miller	E.Pegram	M.Pritchard+
1992	Glanville	A.Rison	M.Kenn	H.Hoover	J.Dukes	B.Fralic	C.Hinton	D.Hill+	M.Haynes	C.Miller	K.Jones	M.Pritchard+
1993	Glanville	A.Rison	M.Kenn	L.Kennedy	J.Dukes	C.Hinton	B.Whitfield	M.Lyons	M.Haynes	B.Hebert	E.Pegram	M.Pritchard+
1994	J.Jones	A.Rison	M.Kenn	D.Richards	R.Fortin	M.Zandofsky	B.Whitfield	T.Mathis+	R.Sanders	J.George	C.Heyward	B.Emanuel+
1995	J.Jones	J.Birden	B.Whitfield	R.Tobeck	R.Fortin	M.Zandofsky	D.Richards	T.Mathis+	E.Metcalf	J.George	C.Heyward	B.Emanuel+
1996	J.Jones	J.Birden	B.Whitfield	R.Tobeck	R.Fortin	M.Zandofsky	A.Davis	T.Mathis+	E.Metcalf	B.Hebert	J.Anderson	B.Emanuel+
1997	D.Reeves	T.Mathis	B.Whitfield	R.Tobeck	C.Collins	G.Williams	M.Willig	O.Santiago	B.Emanuel	C.Chandler	J.Anderson	B.Christian
1998	D.Reeves	T.Martin	B.Whitfield	C.Collins	R.Tobeck	G.Williams	E.Salaam	O.Santiago	T.Mathis	C.Chandler	J.Anderson	B.Christian
1999	D.Reeves	T.Mathis	B.Whitfield	B.Hallen	R.Tobeck	C.Collins	E.Salaam	O.Santiago	T.Dwight	C.Chandler	K.Oxendine	B.Christian
2000	D.Reeves	S.Jefferson	B.Whitfield	C.Collins	T.McClure	T.Claridge	E.Salaam	R.Kelly	T.Mathis	C.Chandler	J.Anderson	B.Christian
2001	D.Reeves	T.Martin	B.Whitfield	B.Hallen	T.McClure	T.Claridge	E.Salaam	R.Kelly	T.Mathis	C.Chandler	M.Smith	A.Crumpler*
2002	D.Reeves	B.Finneran	B.Whitfield	T.Claridge	T.McClure	K.Forney	T.Weiner	R.Kelly	A.Crumpler*	M.Vick	W.Dunn	B.Christian

YEAR	LDE	LDT/NT	RDT/RDE	RDE/LOLB	LLB/LILB	MLB/RILB	RLB/ROLB	LCB	RCB	SS/LS	FS/RS	FINISH	
1950	B.Dove	L.McDermott	J.Goldsberry	T.Wham	G.Cowhig	E.Bagdon+	B.Svoboda	D.Paul	M.Kutner	R.Ramsey	J.Davis	5na	5-7
1951	T.Bienemann	L.Ferry	D.Joyce	J.Hennessy	C.Patton	J.Groom+	L.Sanford	D.Paul	S.Whitman	R.Ramsey	J.Davis	6na	3-9
1952	B.Dove	V.Peters	D.Joyce	T.Bienemann	G.Polofsky	J.Groom+	L.Sanford	D.Paul	S.Whitman	R.Ramsey	R.Barni	5na	4-8
1953	P.Summerall	V.Peters	D.Joyce	T.Bienemann	N.Chickillo	J.Groom+	L.Sanford	D.Paul	J.Psaltis	R.Ramsey	T.Curcillo	6ne	1-10-1
1954	L.Sugar	C.Ulrich	J.Groom	T.Bienemann	F.Wallner	L.Sanford	G.Polofsky	C.Trippi	A.Brosky	N.Lane	B.Bredde	6ne	2-10
1955	L.Sugar	C.Ulrich	J.Groom	T.Bienemann	F.Wallner	T.Pasquesi+	L.Sanford	J.Psaltis	L.Crow	N.Lane	T.Keane	4ne	4-7-1
1956	L.Sugar	T.Pasquesi	L.Teeuws	P.Summerall	Brettschneider	S.West+	L.Sanford	W.Lewis	L.Crow	N.Lane	J.Hill	2ne	7-5
1957	L.Sugar	C.Ulrich	L.Teeuws	P.Summerall	Brettschneider	J.Tubbs	L.Sanford	F.Bernardi	L.Crow	N.Lane	J.Hill	6ne	3-9
1958	L.Sugar	C.Ulrich	E.Culpepper	L.Owens	Brettschneider	J.Patera	C.Weber	B.Conrad	D.Nolan	N.Lane	B.Gordon	5ne	2-9-1
1959	L.Sugar	E.Culpepper	F.Fuller	L.Owens	Brettschneider	T.Bates	B.Koman	B.Stacy	J.Norton	N.Lane	J.Hill	6ne	2-10
1960	L.Sugar	D.Owens	F.Fuller	L.Owens	J.Tracey	D.Meinert	B.Koman	J.Driskill	J.Hill	J.Norton	L.Wilson	4ne	6-5-1
1961	J.Robb	D.Owens	F.Fuller	E.Henke	T.Bates	D.Meinert	B.Koman	B.Stacy	J.Hill	J.Norton	L.Wilson	4ne	7-7
1962	J.Robb	D.Owens	F.Fuller	L.Owens	M.Rushing	G.Boyette	B.Koman	B.Stacy	J.Hill	N.Beal	L.Wilson	6ne	4-9-1
1963	J.Robb	D.Owens	L.Owens	D.Brumm	L.Stallings	D.Meinert	B.Koman	P.Fischer	J.Hill	J.Stovall	L.Wilson	3ne	9-5
1964	J.Robb	S.Silas	L.Owens	D.Brumm	L.Stallings	D.Meinert	B.Koman	P.Fischer	J.Burson	J.Stovall	L.Wilson	2ne	9-3-2
1965	J.Robb	S.Silas	L.Owens	D.Brumm	L.Stallings	D.Meinert	B.Koman	P.Fischer	J.Burson	J.Stovall	L.Wilson	5ne	5-9
1966	J.Robb	S.Silas	C.Walker	D.Brumm	L.Stallings	D.Meinert	B.Koman	J.Burson	A.Woodson	J.Stovall	L.Wilson	4ne	8-5-1
1967	J.Robb	S.Silas	C.Walker	D.Brumm	L.Stallings	D.Meinert	B.Koman	P.Fischer	J.Burson	J.Stovall	L.Wilson	3ncy	6-7-1
1968	D.Brumm	F.Heron	B.Rowe	C.Walker	L.Stallings	J.Rivers	D.Meggyesy	B.Atkins	L.Sanders	M.Barnes	L.Wilson	2ncy	9-4-1
1969	R.Krueger	F.Heron	B.Rowe	C.Walker	L.Stallings	J.Rivers	R.Rosema	R.Wehrli	N.Wright	J.Stovall	L.Wilson	3ncy	4-9-1
1970	R.Krueger	F.Heron	B.Rowe	C.Walker	L.Stallings	J.Rivers	D.Parish	M.Farr	R.Wehrli	J.Stovall	L.Wilson	3ne	8-5-1
1971	R.Yankowski	R.Krueger	B.Rowe	J.Schmiesing	L.Stallings	J.Rivers	M.McGill	M.Farr	R.Wehrli	J.Stovall	L.Wilson	4ne	4-9-1
1972	D.Brumm	J.Richardson	B.Rowe	R.Yankowski	L.Stallings	M.Arneson	T.Miller	N.Thompson	M.Farr	R.Wehrli	L.Wilson	4ne	4-9-1
1973	D.Butz	J.Richardson	B.Rowe	R.Yankowski	L.Stallings	M.Arneson	P.Barnes	D.Crump	R.Wehrli	J.Tolbert	C.Duren	4ne	4-9-1
1974	C.Rudolph	L.Brooks	B.Rowe	R.Yankowski	L.Stallings	M.Arneson	P.Barnes	N.Thompson	R.Wehrli	J.Tolbert	C.Duren	1ne	10-4 #d
1975	B.Bell	C.Davis	B.Rowe	R.Yankowski	L.Stallings	M.Arneson	P.Barnes	N.Thompson	R.Wehrli	K.Reaves	C.Duren	1ne	11-3 d
1976	J.Zook	C.Davis	M.Dawson	B.Bell	L.Stallings	T.Kearney	M.Arneson	N.Thompson	R.Wehrli	K.Reaves	M.Sensibaugh	3ne	10-4 #
1977	J.Zook	C.Davis	M.Dawson	R.Yankowski	E.Williams	T.Kearney	M.Arneson	L.Nelson	R.Wehrli	K.Reaves	M.Sensibaugh	3ne	7-7
1978	B.Pollard	M.Dawson	J.Zook*	S.Neils	T.Kearney	K.Allerman	M.Arneson	C.Allen	R.Wehrli	K.Greene	K.Stone	4ne	6-10
1979	B.Pollard	C.Davis	M.Dawson*	E.Williams	S.Neils	K.Allerman	M.Arneson	C.Allen	R.Wehrli	K.Greene	K.Stone	5ne	5-11
1980	B.Pollard	R.Brown	R.Yankowski*	S.Neils	E.Williams	T.Kearney	M.Arneson	C.Allen	R.Wehrli	L.Nelson	K.Stone	4ne	5-11
1981	B.Pollard	M.Dawson	R.Brown	C.Greer	E.Williams	D.Ahrens	E.Junior	J.Griffin	R.Wehrli	L.Nelson	K.Greene	5ne	7-9
1982	E.Grooms	M.Dawson	R.Brown	C.Greer	E.Junior	D.Ahrens	C.Baker	J.Griffin	C.Allen	L.Nelson	B.Perrin	4n	5-4 p
1983	A.Baker	E.Grooms	D.Galloway	C.Greer	B.Harris	E.Junior	C.Baker	L.Washington	W.Smith	L.Nelson	B.Perrin	3ne	8-7-1
1984	A.Baker	D.Galloway	M.Duda	C.Greer	T.Howard	K.Allerman	E.Junior	L.Washington	W.Smith	L.Smith	B.Perrin	3ne	9-7 #
1985	A.Baker	D.Galloway	M.Duda	C.Greer	N.Noga	E.Junior	F.Nunn	C.Mack	W.Smith	L.Smith	L.Young	5ne	5-11
1986	B.Clasby	D.Galloway	A.Baker*	F.Nunn	E.Junior	N.Noga	C.Baker	L.Washington	C.Mack	Le.Smith	L.Young	5ne	4-11-1
1987	F.Nunn	B.Clasby	S.Alvord	C.Greer	A.Bell	N.Noga	E.Junior	C.Carter	C.Mack	Le.Smith	L.Young	2ne	7-8
1988	R.Saddler	B.Clasby	S.Alvord	F.Nunn	A.Bell	N.Noga	E.Junior	C.Carter	C.Mack	T.McDonald	L.Young	3ne	7-9
1989	F.Nunn	R.Saddler	J.Wahler	D.Galloway	A.Bell	E.Hill	K.Harvey	C.Mack	C.Carter	T.McDonald	L.Young	4ne	5-11
1990	F.Nunn	J.Wahler	R.Saddler*	A.Bell	G.Jax	E.Hill	K.Harvey	J.Taylor	C.Mack	T.McDonald	L.Young	5ne	5-11
1991	J.Faulkner	J.Wahler	C.Patterson*	F.Nunn	G.Jax	E.Hill	K.Harvey	L.Lynch	A.Williams	T.McDonald	M.Zordich	5ne	4-12
1992	E.Swann	M.Bankston	M.Jones*	F.Nunn	T.Stowe	E.Hill	K.Harvey	R.Massey	A.Williams	T.McDonald	M.Zordich	5ne	4-12
1993	M.Bankston	E.Swann	K.Rucker	R.Davis	E.Hill	L.Lynch*	T.Stowe	A.Williams	R.Massey	J.Booty	M.Zordich	4ne	7-9
1994	M.Bankston	E.Swann	B.Wilson	C.Simmons	S.Joyner	E.Hill	W.Marshall	A.Williams	J.Williams	L.Lynch	T.Hoage	3ne	8-8
1995	M.Bankston	E.Swann	B.Wilson	C.Simmons	S.Joyner	E.Hill	J.Miller	A.Williams	L.Brown	L.Lynch	B.Alexander	5ne	4-12
1996	M.Bankston	E.Swann	B.Wilson	S.Rice	S.Joyner	E.Hill	J.Miller	A.Williams	R.Bradford	M.Darby	B.Alexander	4ne	7-9
1997	M.Bankston	E.Swann	B.Wilson	S.Rice	J.Miller	E.Hill	R.McKinnon	A.Williams	T.Knight	M.Darby	B.Alexander	5ne	4-12
1998	A.Wadsworth	R.Swinger	M.Smith	S.Rice	J.Miller	R.McKinnon	T.McCombs	A.Williams	J.Brown	T.Bennett	P.Tillman	2ne	9-7 wd
1999	A.Wadsworth	R.Swinger	J.Drake	S.Rice	Fredrickson	R.McKinnon	Z.Walz	A.Williams	T.Knight	T.Bennett	K.Lassiter	4ne	6-10
2000	B.Ottis	R.Davis	M.Tosi	S.Rice	R.Thompson	R.McKinnon	Fredrickson	A.Williams	T.Knight	P.Tillman	K.Lassiter	5ne	3-13
2001	F.Wakefield	R.Davis	B.Tanner	T.Burke	R.Thompson	R.McKinnon	Fredrickson	D.Barrett	C.Chavous	P.Tillman	K.Lassiter	3ne	7-9
2002	F.Wakefield	R.Davis	B.Tanner	Vanden Bosch	R.Thompson	R.McKinnon	Fredrickson	D.Starks	D.Barrett	A.Wilson	K.Lassiter	4nw	5-11
2003	D.Johnson	R.Davis	M.Bell	C.Pace	R.Thompson	R.McKinnon	L.Fisher	R.Hill	D.Barrett	A.Wilson	D.Jackson	4nw	4-12
2004	P.Zellner	R.Davis	D.Dockett	B.Berry	K.Dansby	R.McKinnon	J.Darling	R.Hill	D.Macklin	A.Wilson	I.Ohalete	3nw	6-10
2005	C.Okeafor	R.Kolodziej	D.Dockett	B.Berry	K.Dansby	J.Darling	O.Huff	R.Tate	D.Macklin	A.Wilson	R.Griffith	3nw	5-11

YEAR	LDE	LDT/NT	RDT/RDE	RDE/LOLB	LLB/LILB	MLB/RILB	RLB/ROLB	LCB	RCB	SS/LS	FS/RS	FINISH	
1966	B.Richards	K.Rubke	C.Sieminski	S.Williams	M.Rushing	T.Nobis	B.Jobko	R.Smith	L.Calland	J.Richardson	B.Riggle	7ne	3-11
1967	J.Norton	K.Rubke	J.Szczecko	S.Williams	M.Rushing	T.Nobis	R.Heck	K.Reaves	L.Calland	F.Hudlow	N.Rassas	4ncl	1-12-1
1968	C.Humphrey	J.Shay	C.Dabney	R.Cash	G.Allen	T.Nobis	R.Heck	K.Reaves	J.Burson	N.Rassas	B.Lothridge	4ncl	2-12
1969	C.Humphrey	J.Shay	D.Cahill	J.Zook	G.Allen	D.Hansen	G.Brezina	K.Reaves	R.Redmond	Weatherford	J.Mallory	3ncl	6-8
1970	C.Humphrey	G.Lens	G.Condren	J.Zook	G.Allen	T.Nobis	D.Hansen	K.Reaves	R.Redmond	J.Mallory	T.McCauley	3nw	4-8-2
1971	C.Humphrey	J.Small	G.Condren	J.Zook	R.Acks	D.Hansen	G.Brezina	K.Reaves	T.Hayes	J.Mallory	R.Brown	3nw	7-6-1
1972	C.Humphrey	C.Walker	M.Lewis	J.Zook	D.Hansen	T.Nobis	G.Brezina	K.Reaves	T.Hayes	R.Brown	C.Ellis	2nw	7-7
1973	C.Humphrey	C.Walker	M.Lewis	J.Zook	D.Hansen	T.Nobis	G.Brezina	K.Reaves	T.Hayes	R.Brown	C.Ellis	2nw	9-5
1974	C.Humphrey	M.Tilleman	M.Lewis	J.Zook	D.Hansen	T.Nobis	G.Brezina	R.Lawrence	T.Hayes	R.Brown	C.Ellis	4nw	3-11
1975	J.Merrow	M.Tilleman	M.Lewis	J.Zook	D.Hansen	T.Nobis	G.Brezina	R.Lawrence	T.Hayes	R.Easterling	R.Brown	3nw	4-10
1976	C.Humphrey	M.Tilleman	M.Lewis	J.Merrow	F.Kuykendall	T.Nobis	G.Brezina	R.Lawrence	F.Reed	R.Brown	R.Easterling	3nw	4-10
1977	C.Humphrey	J.Bailey	M.Lewis	J.Merrow	R.Pennywell	R.Ortega	G.Brezina	R.Lawrence	R.Byas	R.Brown	R.Easterling	2nw	7-7
1978	J.Yeates	J.Bailey	M.Lewis	J.Merrow	F.Kuykendall	R.Pennywell	G.Brezina	R.Lawrence	R.Byas	F.Reed	T.Pridemore	2nw	9-7 wd
1979	J.Yeates	W.Faumuina	E.Fields	D.Smith	F.Kuykendall	R.Pennywell	G.Brezina	R.Lawrence	R.Byas	F.Reed	R.Easterling	3nw	6-10
1980	J.Yeates	D.Smith	J.Merrow*	A.Richardson	F.Kuykendall	B.Curry	J.Williams	R.Lawrence	K.Johnson	B.Glazebrook	T.Pridemore	1nw	12-4 d
1981	J.Yeates	D.Smith	J.Merrow*	A.Richardson	F.Kuykendall	B.Curry	J.Williams	B.Butler	K.Johnson	B.Glazebrook	T.Pridemore	2nw	7-9
1982	J.Yeates	D.Smith	J.Merrow*	A.Richardson	F.Kuykendall	B.Curry	J.Williams	B.Butler	K.Johnson	B.Glazebrook	T.Pridemore	4n	5-4 p
1983	J.Yeates	A.Provence	D.Smith	J.Merrow	J.Rade	F.Kuykendall	B.Curry	B.Butler	K.Johnson	T.Pridemore	J.Britt	4nw	7-9
1984	M.Pitts	G.Burley	R.Bryan	D.Smith	D.Frye	B.Curry	A.Richardson	B.Butler	J.Britt	K.Johnson	T.Pridemore	4nw	4-12
1985	R.Bryan	M.Pitts	D.Benish	M.Gann	J.Rade	B.Curry	A.Richardson	B.Butler	W.Cason	S.Case	T.Greene	4nw	4-12
1986	M.Gann	T.Casillas	R.Bryan*	R.Wilkes	B.Curry	J.Rade	J.Williams	B.Butler	S.Case	R.Moore	B.Clark	3nw	7-8-1
1987	M.Gann	T.Casillas	R.Bryan*	T.Green	B.Curry	J.Rade	J.Williams	B.Butler	S.Case	R.Moore	T.Gordon	4nw	3-12
1988	M.Gann	T.Casillas	R.Bryan*	A.Bruce	J.Rade	J.Tuggle	J.Williams	B.Butler	S.Case	R.Moore	B.Clark	4nw	5-11
1989	M.Gann	T.Casillas	B.Thomas*	A.Bruce	J.Rade	J.Tuggle	T.Green	B.Butler	D.Sanders	E.Cooper	T.Gordon	4nw	3-13
1990	M.Gann	T.Epps	T.Green*	R.Lyles	J.Tuggle	J.Rade	D.Conner	C.Dimry	D.Sanders	B.Jordan	S.Case	3nw	5-11
1991	R.Bryan	M.Gardner	T.Green*	R.Lyles	J.Rade	J.Tuggle	D.Conner	T.McKyer	D.Sanders	B.Jordan	S.Case	2nw	10-6 #wd
1992	M.Gann	M.Gardner	T.Green*	K.Tippins	J.Solomon	J.Tuggle	D.Conner	T.McKyer	D.Sanders	J.Donaldson	S.Case	3nw	6-10
1993	M.Gann	P.Holt	M.Gardner	L.Archambeau	J.Solomon	J.Tuggle	D.Conner	D.Walker	D.Sanders	R.Harper	S.Case	3nw	6-10
1994	C.Smith	P.Holt	M.Gardner	L.Archambeau	C.Matthews	J.Tuggle	R.George	V.Clark	D.Johnson	K.Ross	R.Harper	2nw	7-9
1995	C.Smith	P.Holt	M.Gardner	C.Doleman	C.Matthews	J.Tuggle	D.Talley	D.Walker	D.Johnson	K.Ross	R.Harper	2nw	9-7 #w
1996	L.Archambeau	T.Hall	M.Gardner	C.Smith	C.Bennett	J.Tuggle	R.George	L.McGill	D.Walker	D.Bush	P.Bates	4nw	3-13
1997	L.Archambeau	T.Hall	D.Owens	C.Smith	C.Bennett	J.Tuggle	H.Crockett	R.Buchanan	R.Bradford	W.White	D.Bush	2nw	7-9
1998	L.Archambeau	T.Hall	S.Dronett	C.Smith	C.Bennett	J.Tuggle	H.Crockett	R.Buchanan	R.Bradford	W.White	E.Robinson	1nw	14-2 dcs
1999	L.Archambeau	T.Hall	S.Dronett	C.Smith	H.Crockett	J.Tuggle	K.Brooking	R.Buchanan	R.Bradford	M.Carter	E.Robinson	3nw	5-11
2000	P.Kerney	T.Hall	E.Jasper	B.Smith	C.Draft	J.Tuggle	H.Crockett	R.Buchanan	A.Ambrose	M.Carter	R.Bradford	5nw	4-12
2001	P.Kerney	T.Hall	S.Dronett	B.Smith	C.Draft	K.Brooking	H.Crockett	R.Buchanan	A.Ambrose	G.McBurrows	R.Bradford	3nw	7-9
2002	P.Kerney	E.Jasper	B.Smith*	S.Rogers	K.Brooking	J.Holecek	M.Stewart	R.Buchanan	A.Ambrose	G.McBurrows	K.Carpenter	2ns	9-6-1 wd

YEAR	COACH	WR/LE	LT	LG	C	RG	RT	TE/RE	WR/FL	QB	RB/LH	FB
2003	D.Reeves	P.Price	B.Whitfield	R.Garza	T.McClure	K.Forney	T.Weiner	A.Crumpler	B.Finneran	D.Johnson	T.Duckett	J.Griffith
2004	J.Mora	D.White	K.Shaffer	R.Garza	T.McClure	K.Forney	T.Weiner	A.Crumpler	P.Price	M.Vick	W.Dunn	J.Griffith
2005	J.Mora	R.White	K.Shaffer	M.Lehr	T.McClure	K.Forney	T.Weiner	A.Crumpler	M.Jenkins	M.Vick	W.Dunn	J.Griffith

Baltimore Colts

YEAR	COACH	WR/LE	LT	LG	C	RG	RT	TE/RE	WR/FL	QB	RB/LH	FB
1950	C.Crowe	P.Salata	E.Blandin	B.Murray	J.Williams	K.Cooper	B.French	H.Crisler	R.Collins	Y.Tittle	C.Mutryn	J.Spavital

Baltimore Ravens

YEAR	COACH	WR/LE	LT	LG	C	RG	RT	TE/RE	WR/FL	QB	RB/LH	FB
1996	Marchibroda	M.Jackson	T.Jones	J.Ogden	W.Williams	J.Blackshear	O.Brown	B.Kinchen	D.Alexander	V.Testaverde	E.Byner	F.Turner+
1997	Marchibroda	M.Jackson	J.Ogden	B.Cavil	W.Williams	J.Blackshear	O.Brown	E.Green	D.Alexander	V.Testaverde	B.Morris	J.Lewis+
1998	Marchibroda	M.Jackson	J.Ogden	W.Williams	J.Mitchell	J.Blackshear	O.Brown	E.Green	J.Lewis	J.Harbaugh	P.Holmes	R.Potts
1999	B.Billick	Q.Ismail	J.Ogden	E.Mulitalo	J.Mitchell	J.Blackshear	E.Lindsay	A.Pierce	J.Armour	T.Banks	E.Rhett	C.Evans
2000	B.Billick	Q.Ismail	J.Ogden	E.Mulitalo	J.Mitchell	M.Flynn	H.Swayne	S.Sharpe	P.Johnson	T.Dilfer	J.Lewis	T.Taylor+
2001	B.Billick	Q.Ismail	J.Ogden	E.Mulitalo	M.Flynn	B.Anderson	K.Vickers	S.Sharpe	T.Taylor	E.Grbac	T.Allen	T.Heap*
2002	B.Billick	T.Taylor	J.Ogden	E.Mulitalo	M.Flynn	B.Anderson	E.Brooks	T.Heap	T.Jones*	J.Blake	J.Lewis	A.Ricard
2003	B.Billick	T.Taylor	J.Ogden	E.Mulitalo	M.Flynn	B.Anderson	O.Brown	T.Heap	T.Jones*	K.Boller	J.Lewis	A.Ricard
2004	B.Billick	T.Taylor	J.Ogden	E.Mulitalo	C.Rabach	B.Anderson	O.Brown	T.Jones	R.Hymes	K.Boller	J.Lewis	A.Ricard
2005	B.Billick	M.Clayton	J.Ogden	E.Mulitalo	M.Flynn	K.Vincent	O.Brown	T.Heap	D.Mason	K.Boller	J.Lewis	O.Mughelli

Buffalo Bills

YEAR	COACH	WR/LE	LT	LG	C	RG	RT	TE/RE	WR/FL	QB	RB/LH	FB
1960	B.Ramsey	Chamberlain	H.Olson	P.Blazer	D.McGrew	C.Muelhaupt	D.Chelf	T.Rychlec	E.Dubenion	J.Green	W.Fowler	W.Carlton
1961	B.Ramsey	G.Bass	K.Rice	B.Shaw	A.Bemiller	C.Muelhaupt	H.Olson	T.Rychlec	E.Dubenion	M.Reynolds	W.Carlton	A.Baker
1962	L.Saban	G.Bass	S.Barber	B.Shaw	A.Bemiller	T.Day	H.Olson	E.Warlick	E.Dubenion	W.Rabb	M.Crockett	C.Gilchrist
1963	L.Saban	B.Miller	S.Barber	B.Shaw	A.Bemiller	T.Day	K.Rice	E.Warlick	E.Dubenion	J.Kemp	R.Kochman	C.Gilchrist
1964	L.Saban	G.Bass	S.Barber	B.Shaw	W.Cudzik	A.Bemiller	D.Hudson	E.Warlick	E.Dubenion	J.Kemp	B.Smith	C.Gilchrist
1965	L.Saban	E.Rutkowski	S.Barber	B.Shaw	D.Behrman	A.Bemiller	D.Hudson	P.Costa	B.Roberson	J.Kemp	W.Carlton	B.Joe
1966	J.Collier	B.Crockett	S.Barber	B.Shaw	A.Bemiller	J.O'Donnell	D.Hudson	P.Costa	E.Dubenion	J.Kemp	B.Burnett	W.Carlton
1967	J.Collier	B.Masters	S.Barber	B.Shaw	A.Bemiller	J.O'Donnell	D.Hudson	P.Costa	E.Dubenion	J.Kemp	K.Lincoln	W.Carlton
1968	H.Johnson	H.Moses	S.Barber	B.Shaw	A.Bemiller	B.Kalsu	D.Cunningham	P.Costa	R.Trapp	D.Darragh	M.Anderson	B.Gregory
1969	J.Rauch	H.Moses	M.Richey	A.Loukas	A.Bemiller	J.O'Donnell	P.Costa	B.Masters	M.Briscoe	J.Kemp	O.Simpson	W.Patrick
1970	J.Rauch	H.Moses	H.Kindig	R.Cheek	Marchlewski	J.O'Donnell	P.Costa	A.Denney	M.Briscoe	D.Shaw	O.Simpson	W.Patrick
1971	H.Johnson	H.Moses	W.Young	J.Reilly	B.Jarvis	J.O'Donnell	D.Green	J.White	M.Briscoe	D.Shaw	O.Simpson	W.Patrick
1972	L.Saban	B.Chandler	D.Foley	R.McKenzie	R.Prudhomme	B.Penchion	D.Green	J.White	J.Hill	D.Shaw	O.Simpson	J.Braxton
1973	L.Saban	B.Chandler	D.Foley	R.McKenzie	B.Jarvis	DeLamielleure	D.Green	P.Seymour	J.Hill	J.Ferguson	O.Simpson	L.Watkins
1974	L.Saban	A.Rashad	D.Foley	R.McKenzie	M.Montler	DeLamielleure	D.Green	P.Seymour	J.Hill	J.Ferguson	O.Simpson	J.Braxton
1975	L.Saban	B.Chandler	D.Foley	R.McKenzie	M.Montler	DeLamielleure	D.Green	P.Seymour	J.Hill	J.Ferguson	O.Simpson	J.Braxton
1976	J.Ringo	J.Holland	D.Foley	R.McKenzie	M.Montler	DeLamielleure	D.Green	P.Seymour	B.Chandler	G.Marangi	O.Simpson	J.Kinney
1977	J.Ringo	B.Chandler	D.Foley	R.McKenzie	W.Parker	DeLamielleure	J.Devlin	P.Seymour	L.Piccone	J.Ferguson	O.Simpson	J.Braxton
1978	C.Knox	B.Chandler	K.Jones	R.McKenzie	W.Parker	DeLamielleure	J.Devlin	R.Gant	F.Lewis	J.Ferguson	T.Miller	C.Brown
1979	C.Knox	J.Butler	K.Jones	R.McKenzie	W.Parker	DeLamielleure	J.Devlin	R.Gant	F.Lewis	J.Ferguson	T.Miller	C.Brown
1980	C.Knox	J.Butler	K.Jones	R.McKenzie	W.Grant	C.Dobler	J.Devlin	R.Gant	F.Lewis	J.Ferguson	J.Cribbs	C.Brown
1981	C.Knox	J.Butler	K.Jones	J.Borchardt	W.Grant	C.Dobler	J.Devlin	M.Brammer	F.Lewis	J.Ferguson	J.Cribbs	C.Brown
1982	C.Knox	J.Butler	K.Jones	R.McKenzie	W.Grant	J.Borchardt	J.Devlin	M.Brammer	F.Lewis	J.Ferguson	J.Cribbs	R.Leaks
1983	Stephenson	J.Butler	K.Jones	J.Ritcher	W.Grant	J.Borchardt	J.Cross	M.Brammer	F.Lewis	J.Ferguson	J.Cribbs	B.Moore
1984	Stephenson	P.Dennard	K.Jones	J.Ritcher	W.Grant	J.Borchardt	J.Devlin	T.Hunter	B.Franklin	J.Ferguson	G.Bell	B.Moore
1985	H.Bullough	J.Butler	K.Jones	J.Ritcher	W.Grant	T.Vogler	J.Devlin	E.Ramson	A.Reed	V.Ferragamo	J.Cribbs	G.Bell
1986	H.Bullough	C.Burkett	K.Jones	J.Ritcher	K.Hull	W.Wolford	J.Devlin	P.Metzelaars	A.Reed	J.Kelly	R.Riddick	R.Moore
1987	M.Levy	C.Burkett	W.Wolford	J.Ritcher	K.Hull	T.Vogler	J.Devlin	P.Metzelaars	A.Reed	J.Kelly	R.Harmon	C.Byrum
1988	M.Levy	T.Johnson	W.Wolford	J.Ritcher	K.Hull	T.Vogler	J.Devlin	P.Metzelaars	A.Reed	J.Kelly	T.Thomas	J.Mueller
1989	M.Levy	K.McKeller	W.Wolford	J.Ritcher	K.Hull	J.Devlin	H.Ballard	P.Metzelaars	A.Reed	J.Kelly	T.Thomas	L.Kinnebrew
1990	M.Levy	J.Lofton	W.Wolford	J.Ritcher	K.Hull	J.Davis	H.Ballard	K.McKeller	A.Reed	J.Kelly	T.Thomas	J.Mueller
1991	M.Levy	J.Lofton	W.Wolford	J.Ritcher	K.Hull	J.Davis	H.Ballard	K.McKeller	A.Reed	J.Kelly	T.Thomas	D.Beebe+
1992	M.Levy	J.Lofton	W.Wolford	J.Ritcher	K.Hull	G.Parker	H.Ballard	K.McKeller	A.Reed	J.Kelly	T.Thomas	D.Beebe+
1993	M.Levy	D.Beebe	J.Fina	J.Ritcher	K.Hull	J.Davis	H.Ballard	P.Metzelaars	A.Reed	J.Kelly	T.Thomas	B.Brooks+
1994	M.Levy	D.Beebe	J.Fina	C.Lacina	K.Hull	J.Davis	G.Parker	P.Metzelaars	A.Reed	J.Kelly	T.Thomas	B.Brooks+
1995	M.Levy	R.Copeland	J.Fina	R.Brown	K.Hull	J.Ostroski	G.Parker	L.Johnson	B.Brooks	J.Kelly	T.Thomas	J.Armour+
1996	M.Levy	Q.Early	J.Fina	R.Brown	K.Hull	J.Ostroski	G.Parker	L.Johnson	A.Reed	J.Kelly	T.Thomas	T.Cline*
1997	M.Levy	Q.Early	J.Fina	R.Brown	D.Zeigler	C.Lacina	J.Ostroski	L.Johnson	A.Reed	T.Collins	T.Thomas	E.Moulds+
1998	W.Phillips	E.Moulds	J.Fina	R.Brown	D.Zeigler	J.Panos	J.Ostroski	L.Johnson	A.Reed	D.Flutie	A.Smith	S.Gash
1999	W.Phillips	E.Moulds	J.Fina	R.Brown	J.Ostroski	D.Zeigler	R.Hicks	J.Riemersma	A.Reed	D.Flutie	J.Linton	S.Gash
2000	W.Phillips	E.Moulds	J.Fina	R.Brown	J.Ostroski	J.Nails	M.Spriggs	J.Riemersma	P.Price	R.Johnson	S.Morris	S.Jackson*
2001	G.Williams	E.Moulds	J.Fina	R.Brown	B.Conaty	C.Hulsey	J.Jennings	J.Riemersma	P.Price	R.Johnson	T.Henry	L.Centers
2002	G.Williams	E.Moulds	J.Jennings	R.Brown	T.Teague	M.Sullivan	M.Williams	J.Riemersma	P.Price	D.Bledsoe	T.Henry	L.Centers
2003	G.Williams	E.Moulds	J.Jennings	R.Brown	T.Teague	M.Pucillo	M.Williams	M.Campbell	J.Reed	D.Bledsoe	T.Henry	S.Gash
2004	M.Mularkey	E.Moulds	J.Jennings	R.Tucker	T.Teague	C.Villarrial	M.Williams	M.Campbell	L.Evans	D.Bledsoe	W.McGahee	D.Shelton
2005	M.Mularkey	E.Moulds	M.Gandy	B.Anderson	T.Teague	C.Villarrial	J.Peters	M.Campbell	L.Evans	K.Holcomb	W.McGahee	D.Shelton

Carolina Panthers

YEAR	COACH	WR/LE	LT	LG	C	RG	RT	TE/RE	WR/FL	QB	RB/LH	FB
1995	D.Capers	M.Carrier	Brockermeyer	F.Garcia	C.Whitley	M.Elliott	M.Dennis	P.Metzelaars	E.Guliford	K.Collins	D.Moore	B.Christian
1996	D.Capers	W.Green	Brockermeyer	M.Elliott	C.Whitley	G.Skrepenak	Davidds-Garrido	W.Walls	M.Carrier	K.Collins	A.Johnson	H.Griffith
1997	D.Capers	M.Carrier	Brockermeyer	M.Campbell	F.Garcia	G.Skrepenak	Davidds-Garrido	W.Walls	R.Carruth	K.Collins	F.Lane	S.Greene
1998	D.Capers	M.Muhammad	Brockermeyer	F.Garcia	Stoltenberg	C.Lacina	Davidds-Garrido	W.Walls	R.Ismail	S.Beuerlein	F.Lane	W.Floyd
1999	G.Seifert	M.Muhammad	C.Jones	M.Campbell	F.Garcia	A.Redmon	C.Terry	W.Walls	P.Jeffers	S.Beuerlein	Biakabutuka	W.Floyd
2000	G.Seifert	D.Hayes	C.Jones	M.Campbell	F.Garcia	J.Nesbit	C.Terry	W.Walls	M.Muhammad	S.Beuerlein	Biakabutuka	W.Floyd
2001	G.Seifert	M.Muhammad	T.Steussie	J.Nesbit	J.Mitchell	K.Donnalley	C.Terry	W.Walls	D.Hayes	C.Weinke	R.Huntley	K.Mangum*
2002	J.Fox	M.Muhammad	T.Steussie	J.Nesbit	J.Mitchell	K.Donnalley	C.Terry	W.Walls	S.Smith	R.Peete	L.Smith	B.Hoover
2003	J.Fox	M.Muhammad	T.Steussie	J.James	J.Mitchell	K.Donnalley	J.Gross	K.Mangum	S.Smith	J.Delhomme	S.Davis	J.Wiggins*
2004	J.Fox	M.Muhammad	J.Gross	T.Wharton	J.Mitchell	T.Reyes	M.Willig	K.Mangum	K.Colbert	J.Delhomme	N.Goings	B.Hoover
2005	J.Fox	S.Smith	T.Wharton	M.Wahle	J.Mitchell	T.Reyes	J.Gross	K.Mangum	K.Colbert	J.Delhomme	D.Foster	B.Hoover

Chicago Bears

YEAR	COACH	WR/LE	LT	LG	C	RG	RT	TE/RE	WR/FL	QB	RB/LH	FB
1950	G.Halas	K.Kavanaugh	G.Connor	D.Barwegan	B.Turner	R.Bray	P.Stenn	J.Keane	J.Rykovich	J.Lujack	G.Gulyanics	F.Morrison
1951	G.Halas	J.Hoffman	G.Connor	D.Barwegan	B.Turner	W.Serini	P.Stenn	J.Keane	J.Rykovich	J.Lujack	G.Gulyanics	J.Dottley
1952	G.Halas	B.McColl	G.Connor	D.Barwegan	W.Hansen	B.George	B.Turner	G.Schroeder	B.Stone	G.Blanda	C.Hunsinger	F.Morrison
1953	G.Halas	J.Dooley	G.Connor	Badaczewski	W.Hansen	B.George	K.Gilbert	B.McColl	J.Hoffman	G.Blanda	B.Stone	F.Morrison
1954	G.Halas	H.Hill	B.Wightkin	F.Williams	L.Strickland	K.Gilbert	S.Jones	B.McColl	J.Dooley	G.Blanda	B.Stone	C.Jagade
1955	G.Halas	H.Hill	B.Wightkin	H.Clark	L.Strickland	S.Jones	K.Gilbert	B.McColl	B.Watkins	E.Brown	John Hoffman	R.Casares
1956	P.Driscoll	H.Hill	B.Wightkin	H.Clark	L.Strickland	S.Jones	K.Gilbert	B.McColl	John Hoffman	E.Brown	B.Watkins	R.Casares
1957	P.Driscoll	H.Hill	B.Wightkin	H.Clark	L.Strickland	S.Jones	K.Gilbert	J.Dooley	B.McColl	E.Brown	W.Galimore	R.Casares
1958	G.Halas	H.Hill	H.Lee	A.Gibron	L.Strickland	S.Jones	B.Kilcullen	B.McColl	J.Morris	E.Brown	W.Galimore	R.Casares
1959	G.Halas	H.Hill	H.Lee	A.Gibron	J.Mellekas	S.Jones	D.Klein	B.McColl	J.Dooley	E.Brown	J.Morris	R.Casares
1960	G.Halas	A.Coia	H.Lee	S.Jones	J.Mellekas	T.Karras	S.Fanning	J.Dooley	J.Morris	E.Brown	W.Galimore	R.Casares
1961	G.Halas	B.Farrington	H.Lee	S.Jones	M.Pyle	R.Davis	A.Anderson	M.Ditka	J.Morris	B.Wade	W.Galimore	R.Casares
1962	G.Halas	B.Farrington	H.Lee	S.Jones	M.Pyle	R.Davis	A.Anderson	M.Ditka	J.Morris	B.Wade	R.Bull	J.Marconi
1963	G.Halas	B.Farrington	H.Lee	T.Karras	M.Pyle	R.Davis	B.Wetoska	M.Ditka	J.Morris	B.Wade	W.Galimore	J.Marconi
1964	G.Halas	R.Kreitling	H.Lee	M.Rabold	M.Pyle	J.Cadile	B.Wetoska	M.Ditka	J.Morris	B.Wade	J.Arnett	R.Bull
1965	G.Halas	J.Jones	H.Lee	M.Rabold	M.Pyle	J.Cadile	B.Wetoska	M.Ditka	J.Morris	R.Bukich	G.Sayers	R.Bull
1966	G.Halas	J.Jones	H.Lee	M.Rabold	M.Pyle	J.Cadile	B.Wetoska	M.Ditka	D.Gordon	R.Bukich	G.Sayers	R.Bull

YEAR	LDE	LDT/NT	RDT/RDE	RDE/LOLB	LLB/LILB	MLB/RILB	RLB/ROLB	LCB	RCB	SS/LS	FS/RS	FINISH	
2003	P.Kerney	E.Jasper	B.Smith*	K.Newman	K.Brooking	C.Draft	M.Stewart	J.Bolden	T.McBride	B.Scott	C.Hall	4ns	5-11
2004	P.Kerney	R.Coleman	E.Jasper	B.Smith	K.Brooking	C.Draft	M.Stewart	D.Hall	K.Mathis	B.Scott	C.Hall	1ns	11-5 dc
2005	P.Kerney	R.Coleman	C.Lavalais	J.Babineaux	M.Boley	K.Brooking	D.Williams	D.Hall	J.Webster	K.Carpenter	B.Scott	3ns	8-8
1950	B.Nowaskey	D.Colo	A.Donovan	B.Jensen	G.Buksar	S.Averno+	V.Kissell	Livingstone	C.Maggioli	H.Rich	B.Stone	7nn	1-11
1996	M.Frederick	J.Jones	A.Pleasant*	M.Croel	R.Lewis	M.Caldwell	K.Goganious	A.Langham	D.Brady	S.Moore	E.Turner	5ac	4-12
1997	R.Burnett	J.Jones	T.Siragusa	M.McCrary	P.Boulware	R.Lewis	J.Sharper	A.Langham	D.Jenkins	S.Moore	R.Jones	5ac	6-9-1
1998	R.Burnett	J.Jones	T.Siragusa	M.McCrary	P.Boulware	R.Lewis	J.Sharper	R.Woodson	D.Starks	S.Moore	K.Herring	4ac	6-10
1999	R.Burnett	L.Webster	T.Siragusa	M.McCrary	P.Boulware	R.Lewis	J.Sharper	C.McAlister	D.Jenkins	K.Herring	R.Woodson	3ac	8-8
2000	R.Burnett	S.Adams	T.Siragusa	M.McCrary	P.Boulware	R.Lewis	J.Sharper	D.Starks	C.McAlister	K.Herring	R.Woodson	2ac	12-4 wdcs*
2001	R.Burnett	S.Adams	T.Siragusa	M.McCrary	P.Boulware	R.Lewis	J.Sharper	D.Starks	C.McAlister	C.Harris	R.Woodson	2ac	10-6 wd
2002	A.Weaver	K.Gregg	A.Thomas*	C.Brown	E.Hartwell	B.Harris	P.Boulware	C.McAlister	G.Baxter	E.Reed	W.Demps	3an	7-9
2003	A.Weaver	K.Gregg	M.Douglas*	A.Thomas	E.Hartwell	R.Lewis	P.Boulware	C.McAlister	C.Fuller	E.Reed	G.Baxter	1an	10-6 e
2004	A.Weaver	K.Gregg	M.Douglas*	T.Suggs	E.Hartwell	R.Lewis	A.Thomas	C.McAlister	G.Baxter	E.Reed	W.Demps	2an	9-7
2005	J.Johnson	M.Kemoeatu	K.Gregg	T.Suggs	A.Thomas	T.Polley	B.Scott	C.McAlister	S.Rolle	E.Reed	W.Demps	3an	6-10
1960	M.Yoho	C.McMurtry	J.Sorey	L.Torczon	J.Laraway	A.Matsos	J.Schaffer	B.Atkins	B.Kinard	J.Wagstaff	R.McCabe	3ae	5-8-1
1961	M.Yoho	C.McMurtry	J.Sorey	L.Torczon	R.Felton	A.Matsos	S.Barber	R.McCabe	V.Valdez	J.Wagstaff	B.Atkins	4ae	6-8
1962	L.Moore	S.Youngelman	T.Sestak	M.Yoho	M.Matuszak	A.Matsos	M.Stratton	W.West	B.Edgerson	C.Taseff	C.Charon	3ae	7-6-1
1963	S.Youngelman	J.Dunaway	T.Sestak	M.Yoho	J.Tracey	H.Jacobs	M.Stratton	W.West	B.Edgerson	R.Abruzzese	G.Saimes	1ae	7-6-1 d
1964	R.McDole	J.Dunaway	T.Sestak	T.Day	J.Tracey	H.Jacobs	M.Stratton	B.Edgerson	B.Byrd	E.Sykes	G.Saimes	1ae	12-2 l*
1965	R.McDole	J.Dunaway	T.Sestak	T.Day	J.Tracey	H.Jacobs	M.Stratton	B.Edgerson	B.Byrd	H.Clarke	G.Saimes	1ae	10-3-1 l*
1966	R.McDole	J.Dunaway	T.Sestak	T.Day	J.Tracey	H.Jacobs	M.Stratton	T.Janik	B.Byrd	H.Clarke	G.Saimes	1ae	9-4-1 l
1967	R.McDole	J.Dunaway	T.Sestak	R.Prudhomme	J.Tracey	H.Jacobs	M.Stratton	B.Edgerson	B.Byrd	T.Janik	G.Saimes	3ae	4-10
1968	R.McDole	J.Dunaway	T.Sestak	T.Day	P.Guidry	H.Jacobs	M.Stratton	B.Edgerson	B.Byrd	T.Janik	G.Saimes	5ae	1-12-1
1969	R.McDole	J.Dunaway	B.Tatarek	M.McBath	P.Guidry	H.Jacobs	M.Stratton	B.Edgerson	B.Byrd	J.Pitts	G.Saimes	3ae	4-10
1970	R.McDole	J.Dunaway	W.Harvey	A.Cowlings	P.Guidry	E.Chandler	M.Stratton	R.James	B.Byrd	J.Pitts	P.Richardson	4ae	3-10-1
1971	A.Cowlings	J.Dunaway	B.Tatarek	C.Snowden	P.Guidry	E.Chandler	M.Stratton	R.James	A.Wyatt	J.Pitts	J.Allen	5ae	1-13
1972	W.Patulski	D.Croft	J.Patton	A.Cowlings	P.Guidry	K.Lee	M.Stratton	R.James	T.Greene	M.Tyler	J.Pitts	4ae	4-9-1
1973	W.Patulski	M.Kadish	J.Patton	E.Edwards	J.Skorupan	J.Cheyunski	R.Lewis	R.James	D.Harrison	E.Kellermann	T.Greene	2ae	9-5
1974	W.Patulski	M.Kadish	E.Edwards*	B.Cornell	D.Allen	J.Cheyunski	D.Washington	R.James	D.Harrison	N.Craig	T.Greene	2ae	9-5 w
1975	W.Patulski	M.Kadish	E.Edwards*	J.Skorupan	D.Allen	M.Krakau	B.Cornell	T.Greene	D.Harrison	E.Jones	S.Freeman	3ae	8-6
1976	K.Jones	M.Kadish	M.Smith	S.White	J.Skorupan	M.Krakau	D.Jilek	M.Clark	D.Harrison	D.Jones	T.Greene	5ae	2-12
1977	B.Williams	M.Kadish	B.Dunstan	S.White	S.Nelson	M.Krakau	D.Jilek	M.Clark	D.Harrison	D.Jones	T.Greene	4ae	3-11
1978	B.Williams	D.Hardison	P.Dokes	S.White	S.Nelson	R.McClanahan	L.Sanford	M.Clark	C.Romes	D.Jones	T.Greene	4ae	5-11
1979	B.Williams	M.Kadish	S.White*	I.Robertson	J.Haslett	S.Nelson	L.Sanford	M.Clark	C.Romes	S.Freeman	T.Greene	4ae	7-9
1980	B.Williams	F.Smerlas	S.White*	L.Sanford	J.Haslett	S.Nelson	I.Robertson	M.Clark	C.Romes	S.Freeman	B.Simpson	1ae	11-5 d
1981	B.Williams	F.Smerlas	S.White*	L.Sanford	J.Haslett	S.Nelson	I.Robertson	M.Clark	C.Romes	S.Freeman	B.Simpson	3ae	10-6 #wd
1982	B.Williams	F.Smerlas	S.White*	E.Parker	E.Marve	J.Haslett	I.Robertson	M.Clark	C.Romes	S.Freeman	B.Simpson	9a	4-5 #
1983	B.Williams	F.Smerlas	S.White*	L.Sanford	C.Keating	E.Marve	E.Parker	M.Clark	C.Romes	M.Kennedy	S.Freeman	2ae	8-8
1984	B.Williams	F.Smerlas	K.Johnson*	D.Talley	J.Haslett	E.Marve	L.Sanford	B.Carpenter	C.Romes	S.Freeman	D.Wilson	5ae	2-14
1985	B.Williams	F.Smerlas	B.Smith*	G.Frazier	E.Marve	J.Haslett	L.Sanford	D.Burroughs	C.Romes	S.Freeman	M.Bayless	5ae	2-14
1986	S.McNanie	F.Smerlas	B.Smith*	D.Talley	E.Marve	G.Cumby	L.Sanford	R.Bellinger	C.Romes	M.Bayless	S.Freeman	4ae	4-12
1987	S.McNanie	F.Smerlas	B.Smith*	C.Bennett	S.Conlan	S.Radecic	D.Talley	D.Burroughs	N.Odomes	D.Drane	M.Kelso	4ae	7-8
1988	A.Still	F.Smerlas	B.Smith*	C.Bennett	S.Conlan	R.Bentley	D.Talley	D.Burroughs	N.Odomes	L.Smith	M.Kelso	1ae	12-4 dc
1989	A.Still	F.Smerlas	B.Smith*	C.Bennett	S.Radecic	R.Bentley	D.Talley	K.Jackson	N.Odomes	L.Smith	M.Kelso	1ae	9-7 d
1990	L.Seals	J.Wright	B.Smith*	C.Bennett	S.Conlan	R.Bentley	D.Talley	K.Jackson	N.Odomes	L.Smith	J.Hagy	1ae	13-3 dcs
1991	L.Seals	J.Wright	P.Hansen*	C.Bennett	S.Conlan	C.Bailey	D.Talley	K.Jackson	N.Odomes	L.Smith	M.Kelso	1ae	13-3 dcs
1992	P.Hansen	J.Wright	B.Smith*	C.Bennett	S.Conlan	C.Bailey	D.Talley	K.Jackson	N.Odomes	H.Jones	M.Kelso	2ae	11-5 #wdcs
1993	P.Hansen	J.Wright	B.Smith*	C.Bennett	M.Patton	M.Maddox	D.Talley	J.Williams	N.Odomes	H.Jones	M.Kelso	1ae	12-4 dcs
1994	P.Hansen	J.Wright	B.Smith*	C.Bennett	M.Patton	M.Maddox	D.Talley	M.Washington	T.Smith	H.Jones	M.Darby	4ae	7-9
1995	P.Hansen	T.Washington	B.Smith*	B.Paup	M.Perry	C.Bennett	S.Rogers	J.Burris	T.Smith	H.Jones	K.Schulz	1ae	10-6 ed
1996	P.Hansen	T.Washington	B.Smith*	B.Paup	C.Spielman	M.Maddox	S.Rogers	J.Burris	T.Smith	M.Stevens	K.Schulz	2ae	10-6 w
1997	P.Hansen	T.Washington	B.Smith*	B.Paup	C.Spielman	D.Covington	S.Rogers	J.Burris	T.Smith	H.Jones	K.Schulz	4ae	6-10
1998	P.Hansen	T.Washington	B.Smith*	S.Rogers	J.Holecek	S.Cowart	G.Northern	K.Irvin	T.Smith	H.Jones	K.Schulz	2ae	10-6 w
1999	P.Hansen	T.Washington	B.Smith*	S.Rogers	J.Holecek	S.Cowart	G.Northern	K.Irvin	T.Smith	H.Jones	K.Schulz	2ae	11-5 w
2000	P.Hansen	T.Washington	M.Wiley*	K.Newman	J.Holecek	S.Cowart	S.Rogers	A.Winfield	K.Irvin	H.Jones	K.Carpenter	4ae	8-8
2001	P.Hansen	S.Price	P.Williams	A.Schobel	K.Newman	B.Spoon	J.Foreman	A.Winfield	N.Clements	R.Hill	K.Carpenter	5ae	3-13
2002	C.Ahanotu	R.Edwards	P.Williams	A.Schobel	K.Newman	L.Fletcher	E.Robinson	A.Winfield	N.Clements	C.Wire	P.Prioleau	4ae	8-8
2003	R.Denney	S.Adams	P.Williams	A.Schobel	J.Posey	L.Fletcher	T.Spikes	A.Winfield	N.Clements	L.Milloy	I.Reese	3ae	6-10
2004	C.Kelsay	S.Adams	P.Williams	A.Schobel	J.Posey	L.Fletcher	T.Spikes	T.McGee	N.Clements	L.Milloy	I.Reese	3ae	9-7
2005	C.Kelsay	S.Adams	T.Anderson	A.Schobel	J.Posey	L.Fletcher	A.Crowell	T.McGee	N.Clements	L.Milloy	T.Vincent	3ae	5-11
1995	M.Fox	G.Kragen	G.Williams*	L.Lathon	S.Mills	C.Bailey	D.Conner	T.Poole	T.McKyer	B.Maxie	P.Terrell	3nw	7-9
1996	M.Fox	G.Kragen	G.Williams*	K.Greene	S.Mills	C.Bailey	L.Lathon	E.Davis	T.Poole	B.Maxie	P.Terrell	1nw	12-4 #dc
1997	L.Miller	G.Kragen	R.Seals*	M.Barrow	S.Mills	A.Royal	L.Lathon	E.Davis	T.Poole	C.Cota	M.Minter	2nw	7-9
1998	J.Peter	T.Morabito	S.Gilbert*	K.Greene	J.Brady	M.Barrow	G.Lloyd	E.Davis	D.Evans	D.Richardson	B.Alexander	4nw	4-12
1999	J.Peter	T.Morabito	S.Gilbert	C.Wiley	K.Greene	D.Wells	M.Barrow	E.Davis	D.Evans	B.Alexander	M.Minter	2nw	8-8 #
2000	R.White	T.Morabito	S.Gilbert	J.Williams	D.Wells	L.Towns	L.Woodall	E.Davis	D.Evans	M.Minter	E.Robinson	3nw	7-9
2001	J.Williams	B.Buckner	K.Jenkins	M.Rucker	D.Morgan	L.Towns	D.Hambrick	R.Anderson	D.Evans	M.Minter	D.Grant	5nw	1-15
2002	J.Peppers	B.Buckner	K.Jenkins	M.Rucker	M.Fields	D.Morgan	H.Navies	T.Cousin	R.Howard	M.Minter	D.Grant	4ns	7-9
2003	J.Peppers	B.Buckner	K.Jenkins	M.Rucker	G.Favors	D.Morgan	Witherspoon	T.Cousin	R.Howard	M.Minter	D.Grant	1ns	11-5 edcs
2004	J.Peppers	B.Buckner	K.Moorehead	M.Rucker	M.Fields	D.Morgan	Witherspoon	R.Manning	C.Gamble	M.Minter	C.Branch	3ns	7-9
2005	J.Peppers	B.Buckner	J.Carstens	M.Rucker	B.Short	D.Morgan	Witherspoon	K.Lucas	C.Gamble	M.McCree	M.Minter	1ns	11-5 #edc
1950	B.Wightkin	F.Davis	A.Bauman	E.Sprinkle	S.Clarkson	W.Serini+	F.Negus	R.O'Quinn	D.Kindt	H.Davis	G.McAfee	1nn	9-3 c
1951	B.Wightkin	F.Davis	L.Cowan	E.Sprinkle	G.Connor	R.Bray+	S.Clarkson	D.Kindt	G.Schroeder	J.Lujack	B.Stone	4nn	7-5
1952	B.Wightkin	F.Williams	B.Bishop	E.Sprinkle	F.Dempsey	H.Clark+	G.Connor	D.Kindt	A.Campana	J.Lesane	J.Dooley	5nn	5-7
1953	B.Wightkin	F.Williams	B.Bishop	E.Sprinkle	J.Helwig	F.Dempsey+	B.Weatherly	D.Kindt	B.Anderson	S.Whitman	L.Lowe	4nw	3-8-1
1954	L.Brink	J.Kreamcheck	B.Bishop	E.Sprinkle	B.Weatherly	B.George+	G.Connor	D.Kindt	J.Helwig	S.Whitman	M.Moore	2nw	8-4
1955	Jack Hoffman	F.Williams	B.Bishop	D.Atkins	W.Hansen	B.George	J.Fortunato	K.Gorgal	D.Kindt	R.Smith	C.Sumner	2nw	8-4
1956	Jack Hoffman	F.Williams	B.Bishop	E.Meadows	W.Hansen	B.George	J.Fortunato	J.Caroline	M.Moore	R.Smith	S.Wallace	1nw	9-2-1 l
1957	J.Hoffman	F.Williams	B.Bishop	D.Atkins	W.Hansen	B.George	J.Fortunato	J.Caroline	M.Moore	V.Zucco	S.Wallace	5nw	5-7
1958	J.Hoffman	F.Williams	B.Bishop	D.Atkins	C.Howley	B.George	J.Fortunato	V.Zucco	E.Barnes	J.Johnson	C.Sumner	2nw	8-4
1959	E.Leggett	F.Williams	B.Bishop	D.Atkins	L.Morris	B.George	J.Fortunato	J.Caroline	E.Barnes	R.Petitbon	C.Sumner	2nw	8-4
1960	M.Youmans	E.Leggett	F.Williams	D.Atkins	J.Fortunato	B.George	L.Morris	J.Caroline	E.Barnes	R.Petitbon	C.Sumner	5nw	5-6-1
1961	M.Youmans	B.Kilcullen	F.Williams	D.Atkins	J.Fortunato	B.George	L.Morris	J.Caroline	D.Whitsell	R.Petitbon	R.Taylor	3nw	8-6
1962	O'Bradovich	B.Kilcullen	E.Leggett	D.Atkins	J.Fortunato	B.George	L.Morris	J.Caroline	D.Whitsell	R.Petitbon	R.Taylor	3nw	9-5
1963	B.Kilcullen	S.Jones	E.Leggett	D.Atkins	J.Fortunato	B.George	L.Morris	B.McRae	D.Whitsell	R.Petitbon	R.Taylor	1nw	11-1-2 l*
1964	D.Evey	S.Jones	B.Kilcullen	D.Atkins	J.Fortunato	B.George	L.Morris	B.McRae	D.Whitsell	R.Petitbon	R.Taylor	6nw	5-9
1965	D.Evey	J.Johnson	E.Leggett	D.Atkins	J.Fortunato	D.Butkus	L.Morris	B.McRae	D.Whitsell	R.Petitbon	R.Taylor	3nw	9-5
1966	O'Bradovich	J.Johnson	D.Evey	D.Atkins	J.Fortunato	D.Butkus	J.Purnell	B.McRae	D.Whitsell	R.Petitbon	R.Taylor	5nw	5-7-2

YEAR	COACH	WR/LE	LT	LG	C	RG	RT	TE/RE	WR/FL	QB	RB/LH	FB
1967	G.Halas	D.Gordon	R.Jackson	G.Seals	M.Pyle	J.Cadile	B.Wetoska	A.Denney	J.Morris	J.Concannon	G.Sayers	B.Piccolo
1968	J.Dooley	D.Gordon	R.Jackson	G.Seals	M.Pyle	J.Cadile	B.Wetoska	A.Denney	C.Turner	J.Concannon	G.Sayers	R.Bull
1969	J.Dooley	B.Wallace	R.Jackson	G.Seals	M.Pyle	J.Cadile	R.Mayes	A.Denney	D.Gordon	B.Douglass	G.Sayers	R.Bull
1970	J.Dooley	D.Gordon	R.Jackson	G.Holloway	B.Hyland	J.Cadile	W.Mass	R.Coady	G.Farmer	J.Concannon	R.Montgomery	R.Bull
1971	J.Dooley	D.Gordon	R.Jackson	G.Holloway	R.Coady	J.Cadile	S.Wright	B.Wallace	G.Farmer	B.Douglass	D.Shy	J.Grabowski
1972	A.Gibron	J.Seymour	R.Jackson	G.Holloway	R.Coady	B.Newton	B.Asher	E.Thomas	G.Farmer	B.Douglass	C.Pinder	J.Harrison
1973	A.Gibron	E.Thomas	R.Jackson	G.Holloway	R.Coady	B.Newton	B.Asher	C.Cotton	G.Farmer	B.Douglass	C.Garrett	J.Harrison
1974	A.Gibron	C.Wade	L.Antoine	E.Janet	R.Coady	B.Newton	B.Asher	F.Pagac	B.Rather	G.Huff	K.Grandberry	P.Williams
1975	J.Pardee	B.Grim	L.Antoine	N.Jackson	D.Peiffer	M.Nordquist	J.Sevy	B.Parsons	B.Rather	G.Huff	W.Payton	R.Harper
1976	J.Pardee	B.Baschnagel	L.Antoine	N.Jackson	D.Neal	R.Sorey	J.Sevy	G.Latta	J.Scott	B.Avellini	W.Payton	R.Harper
1977	J.Pardee	B.Rather	T.Albrecht	N.Jackson	D.Peiffer	R.Sorey	D.Lick	G.Latta	J.Scott	B.Avellini	W.Payton	R.Harper
1978	Armstrong	J.Scott	T.Albrecht	N.Jackson	D.Neal	R.Sorey	D.Lick	G.Latta	G.Richards	B.Avellini	W.Payton	R.Harper
1979	Armstrong	J.Scott	T.Albrecht	N.Jackson	D.Neal	R.Sorey	D.Lick	M.Cobb	B.Baschnagel	M.Phipps	W.Payton	D.Williams
1980	Armstrong	J.Scott	T.Albrecht	N.Jackson	D.Neal	R.Sorey	D.Lick	R.Earl	B.Baschnagel	V.Evans	W.Payton	R.Harper
1981	Armstrong	R.Watts	T.Albrecht	N.Jackson	D.Neal	E.Zanders	K.Van Horne	R.Earl	B.Baschnagel	V.Evans	W.Payton	M.Suhey
1982	M.Ditka	K.Margerum	P.McKinnely	N.Jackson	D.Neal	J.Williams	K.Van Horne	E.Moorehead	B.Baschnagel	J.McMahon	W.Payton	M.Suhey
1983	M.Ditka	W.Gault	J.Covert	N.Jackson	D.Neal	K.Becker	K.Van Horne	E.Moorehead	K.Margerum	J.McMahon	W.Payton	M.Suhey
1984	M.Ditka	W.Gault	J.Covert	M.Bortz	J.Hilgenberg	K.Becker	K.Van Horne	E.Moorehead	D.McKinnon	J.McMahon	W.Payton	M.Suhey
1985	M.Ditka	W.Gault	J.Covert	M.Bortz	J.Hilgenberg	T.Thayer	K.Van Horne	E.Moorehead	D.McKinnon	J.McMahon	W.Payton	M.Suhey
1986	M.Ditka	W.Gault	J.Covert	M.Bortz	J.Hilgenberg	T.Thayer	K.Van Horne	E.Moorehead	K.Ortego	M.Tomczak	W.Payton	M.Suhey
1987	M.Ditka	W.Gault	J.Covert	M.Bortz	J.Hilgenberg	T.Thayer	K.Van Horne	E.Moorehead	R.Morris	J.McMahon	W.Payton	N.Anderson
1988	M.Ditka	D.Gentry	Wojciechowski	M.Bortz	J.Hilgenberg	T.Thayer	K.Van Horne	J.Thornton	D.McKinnon	J.McMahon	N.Anderson	M.Suhey
1989	M.Ditka	R.Morris	J.Covert	M.Bortz	J.Hilgenberg	T.Thayer	K.Van Horne	J.Thornton	D.McKinnon	M.Tomczak	N.Anderson	B.Muster
1990	M.Ditka	W.Davis	J.Covert	M.Bortz	J.Hilgenberg	T.Thayer	K.Van Horne	J.Thornton	R.Morris	J.Harbaugh	N.Anderson	B.Muster
1991	M.Ditka	W.Davis	Wojciechowski	M.Bortz	J.Hilgenberg	T.Thayer	K.Van Horne	J.Thornton	T.Waddle	J.Harbaugh	N.Anderson	B.Muster
1992	M.Ditka	W.Davis	T.Auzenne	M.Bortz	J.Fontenot	T.Thayer	K.Van Horne	K.Jennings	T.Waddle	J.Harbaugh	N.Anderson	B.Muster
1993	Wannstedt	T.Waddle	T.Auzenne	M.Bortz	J.Fontenot	Wojciechowski	Leeuwenburg	K.Jennings	C.Conway	J.Harbaugh	N.Anderson	C.Heyward
1994	Wannstedt	J.Graham	A.Heck	M.Bortz	J.Fontenot	Leeuwenburg	J.Williams	M.Cook	C.Conway	S.Walsh	L.Tillman	R.Harris
1995	Wannstedt	J.Graham	A.Heck	T.Perry	J.Fontenot	Leeuwenburg	J.Williams	K.Jennings	C.Conway	E.Kramer	R.Salaam	T.Carter
1996	Wannstedt	C.Conway	A.Heck	T.Perry	J.Fontenot	T.Burger	J.Williams	K.Jennings	M.Timpson	D.Krieg	R.Harris	T.Carter
1997	Wannstedt	B.Engram	A.Heck	T.Perry	C.Villarrial	T.Burger	J.Williams	K.Jennings	R.Proehl	E.Kramer	R.Harris	Tony Carter
1998	Wannstedt	B.Engram	A.Heck	T.Perry	C.Wiegmann	C.Villarrial	J.Williams	A.Mayes	C.Conway	E.Kramer	E.Bennett	T.Hallock
1999	D.Jauron	B.Engram	Brockermeyer	T.Perry	O.Kreutz	C.Villarrial	J.Williams	A.Mayes	M.Robinson	S.Matthews	C.Enis	C.Conway+
2000	D.Jauron	E.Kennison	Brockermeyer	T.Perry	C.Wiegmann	C.Villarrial	J.Williams	K.Sinceno	M.Robinson	C.McNown	J.Allen	C.Enis
2001	D.Jauron	D.White	Brockermeyer	R.Tucker	O.Kreutz	C.Villarrial	J.Williams	F.Baxter	M.Booker	J.Miller	A.Thomas	D.Shelton
2002	D.Jauron	D.White	M.Gandy	K.Dogins	O.Kreutz	C.Villarrial	J.Williams	J.Davis	M.Booker	J.Miller	A.Thomas	D.Shelton
2003	D.Jauron	D.White	M.Gandy	S.Edwards	O.Kreutz	C.Villarrial	A.Gibson	D.Clark	M.Booker	K.Stewart	A.Thomas	S.Pritchett
2004	L.Smith	D.Terrell	Q.Mitchell	R.Brown	O.Kreutz	S.Edwards	J.Tait	D.Clark	B.Wade	C.Hutchinson	T.Jones	D.Lyman*
2005	L.Smith	M.Muhammad	J.Tait	R.Brown	O.Kreutz	T.Metcalf	F.Miller	D.Clark	J.Gage	K.Orton	T.Jones	B.Johnson

Cincinnati Bengals

YEAR	COACH	WR/LE	LT	LG	C	RG	RT	TE/RE	WR/FL	QB	RB/LH	FB
1968	P.Brown	W.McVea	E.Wright	D.Middendorf	B.Johnson	P.Matson	H.Fest	B.Trumpy	R.Sherman	J.Stofa	P.Robinson	T.Smiley
1969	P.Brown	E.Crabtree	E.Wright	E.Park	B.Johnson	P.Matson	H.Fest	B.Trumpy	S.Thomas	G.Cook	P.Robinson	J.Phillips
1970	P.Brown	E.Crabtree	E.Wright	R.Mayes	B.Johnson	P.Matson	M.Wilson	B.Trumpy	S.Thomas	V.Carter	P.Robinson	J.Phillips
1971	P.Brown	E.Crabtree	E.Wright	H.Fest	B.Johnson	P.Matson	V.Holland	B.Trumpy	S.Thomas	V.Carter	J.Phillips	F.Willis
1972	P.Brown	S.Thomas	S.Walters	H.Fest	B.Johnson	P.Matson	V.Holland	B.Trumpy	C.Myers	K.Anderson	E.Johnson	D.Dressler
1973	P.Brown	T.George	R.Mayes	H.Fest	B.Johnson	P.Matson	V.Holland	B.Trumpy	I.Curtis	K.Anderson	E.Johnson	B.Clark
1974	P.Brown	I.Curtis	R.Mayes	H.Fest	B.Johnson	J.Shinners	S.Walters	B.Trumpy	C.Joiner	K.Anderson	C.Davis	B.Clark
1975	P.Brown	I.Curtis	R.Mayes	H.Fest	B.Johnson	D.Lapham	V.Holland	B.Trumpy	C.Joiner	K.Anderson	S.Fritts	B.Clark
1976	B.Johnson	B.Brooks	R.Mayes	J.Shinners	B.Johnson	D.Lapham	V.Holland	B.Trumpy	I.Curtis	K.Anderson	A.Griffin	B.Clark
1977	B.Johnson	I.Curtis	R.Mayes	G.Bujnoch	B.Johnson	D.Lapham	V.Holland	B.Trumpy	B.Brooks	K.Anderson	A.Griffin	P.Johnson
1978	H.Rice	I.Curtis	M.Wilson	G.Bujnoch	B.Bush	D.Lapham	V.Holland	D.Bass	B.Brooks	K.Anderson	A.Griffin	P.Johnson
1979	H.Rice	D.Bass	M.Wilson	G.Bujnoch	B.Bush	D.Lapham	V.Holland	D.Ross	I.Curtis	K.Anderson	A.Griffin	P.Johnson
1980	F.Gregg	D.Bass	A.Munoz	G.Bujnoch	B.Bush	M.Montoya	M.Wilson	D.Ross	I.Curtis	K.Anderson	C.Alexander	P.Johnson
1981	F.Gregg	Collinsworth	A.Munoz	D.Lapham	B.Bush	M.Montoya	M.Wilson	D.Ross	I.Curtis	K.Anderson	C.Alexander	P.Johnson
1982	F.Gregg	Collinsworth	A.Munoz	D.Lapham	B.Bush	M.Montoya	M.Wilson	D.Ross	I.Curtis	K.Anderson	C.Alexander	P.Johnson
1983	F.Gregg	Collinsworth	A.Munoz	D.Lapham	D.Rimington	M.Montoya	M.Wilson	D.Ross	I.Curtis	K.Anderson	C.Alexander	P.Johnson
1984	S.Wyche	Collinsworth	A.Munoz	B.Blados	D.Rimington	M.Montoya	M.Wilson	M.Harris	I.Curtis	K.Anderson	J.Brooks	C.Alexander
1985	S.Wyche	Collinsworth	A.Munoz	B.Blados	D.Rimington	M.Montoya	M.Wilson	R.Holman	E.Brown	B.Esiason	J.Brooks	L.Kinnebrew
1986	S.Wyche	Collinsworth	A.Munoz	B.Kozerski	D.Rimington	M.Montoya	B.Blados	R.Holman	E.Brown	B.Esiason	J.Brooks	L.Kinnebrew
1987	S.Wyche	Collinsworth	A.Munoz	B.Reimers	D.Rimington	M.Montoya	J.Walter	R.Holman	E.Brown	B.Esiason	J.Brooks	L.Kinnebrew
1988	S.Wyche	T.McGee	A.Munoz	B.Reimers	B.Kozerski	M.Montoya	J.Walter	R.Holman	E.Brown	B.Esiason	J.Brooks	I.Woods
1989	S.Wyche	T.McGee	A.Munoz	B.Reimers	B.Kozerski	M.Montoya	B.Blados	R.Holman	E.Brown	B.Esiason	J.Brooks	E.Ball
1990	S.Wyche	T.McGee	A.Munoz	B.Reimers	B.Kozerski	K.Moyer	J.Walter	R.Holman	E.Brown	B.Esiason	J.Brooks	H.Green
1991	S.Wyche	T.McGee	A.Munoz	B.Reimers	B.Kozerski	K.Moyer	J.Walter	R.Holman	E.Brown	B.Esiason	J.Brooks	H.Green
1992	D.Shula	T.McGee	K.Sargent	B.Kozerski	M.Arthur	J.Melander	J.Walter	R.Holman	C.Pickens	B.Esiason	H.Green	E.Ball
1993	D.Shula	J.Query	T.Scott	K.Moyer	B.Kozerski	T.Rayam	J.Walter	T.McGee	C.Pickens	D.Klingler	H.Green	D.Fenner
1994	D.Shula	C.Pickens	K.Sargent	D.Cadigan	D.Brilz	K.Moyer	B.Kozerski	T.McGee	D.Scott	J.Blake	H.Green	D.Fenner
1995	D.Shula	C.Pickens	K.Sargent	S.Brumfield	D.Brilz	T.Kalis	J.Walter	T.McGee	D.Scott	J.Blake	H.Green	J.Cothran
1996	B.Coslet	C.Pickens	W.Anderson	R.Braham	D.Brilz	K.Blackman	J.Walter	T.McGee	D.Scott	J.Blake	G.Hearst	J.Cothran
1997	B.Coslet	C.Pickens	K.Sargent	R.Braham	D.Brilz	K.Blackman	W.Anderson	T.McGee	D.Scott	J.Blake	C.Dillon	B.Milne
1998	B.Coslet	C.Pickens	K.Sargent	R.Braham	D.Brilz	K.Blackman	W.Anderson	T.McGee	D.Scott	N.O'Donnell	C.Dillon	B.Milne
1999	B.Coslet	C.Pickens	R.Jones	M.O'Dwyer	R.Braham	Leeuwenburg	W.Anderson	T.McGee	D.Scott	J.Blake	C.Dillon	C.Groce
2000	D.LeBeau	C.Yeast	R.Jones	M.O'Dwyer	R.Braham	M.Goff	W.Anderson	T.McGee	P.Warrick	A.Smith	C.Dillon	M.Battaglia*
2001	D.LeBeau	D.Scott	R.Webb	M.O'Dwyer	R.Braham	M.Goff	W.Anderson	T.McGee	P.Warrick	J.Kitna	C.Dillon	L.Neal
2002	D.LeBeau	C.Johnson	L.Jones	M.O'Dwyer	R.Braham	M.Goff	W.Anderson	M.Schobel	P.Warrick	J.Kitna	C.Dillon	L.Neal
2003	M.Lewis	P.Warrick	L.Jones	E.Steinbach	R.Braham	M.Goff	W.Anderson	R.Kelly	C.Johnson	J.Kitna	R.Johnson	J.Johnson
2004	M.Lewis	C.Johnson	L.Jones	E.Steinbach	R.Braham	B.Williams	W.Anderson	R.Kelly	Houshmandzadeh	C.Palmer	R.Johnson	T.Stewart*
2005	M.Lewis	C.Johnson	L.Jones	E.Steinbach	R.Braham	B.Williams	W.Anderson	R.Kelly	Houshmandzadeh	C.Palmer	R.Johnson	J.Johnson

Cleveland Browns

YEAR	COACH	WR/LE	LT	LG	C	RG	RT	TE/RE	WR/FL	QB	RB/LH	FB
1950	P.Brown	M.Speedie	L.Groza	A.Gibron	F.Gatski	L.Houston	L.Rymkus	D.Lavelli	D.Jones	O.Graham	R.Bumgardner	M.Motley
1951	P.Brown	M.Speedie	L.Groza	A.Gibron	F.Gatski	B.Gaudio	L.Rymkus	D.Lavelli	D.Jones	O.Graham	K.Carpenter	M.Motley
1952	P.Brown	M.Speedie	L.Groza	A.Gibron	F.Gatski	L.Houston	J.Sandusky	P.Brewster	D.Jones	O.Graham	K.Carpenter	M.Motley
1953	P.Brown	P.Brewster	L.Groza	A.Gibron	F.Gatski	C.Noll	J.Sandusky	D.Lavelli	D.Jones	O.Graham	K.Carpenter	C.Jagade
1954	P.Brown	P.Brewster	L.Groza	A.Gibron	F.Gatski	H.Bradley	J.Sandusky	D.Lavelli	B.Reynolds	O.Graham	R.Renfro	M.Bassett
1955	P.Brown	P.Brewster	L.Groza	A.Gibron	F.Gatski	H.Bradley	M.McCormack	D.Lavelli	R.Renfro	O.Graham	F.Morrison	Modzelewski
1956	P.Brown	P.Brewster	L.Groza	A.Gibron	F.Gatski	H.Forester	M.McCormack	D.Lavelli	R.Renfro	T.O'Connell	P.Carpenter	Modzelewski
1957	P.Brown	P.Brewster	L.Groza	J.Smith	A.Hunter	F.Robinson	M.McCormack	P.Carpenter	R.Renfro	T.O'Connell	C.Hanulak	J.Brown
1958	P.Brown	P.Brewster	L.Groza	J.Smith	A.Hunter	C.Noll	M.McCormack	P.Carpenter	R.Renfro	M.Plum	B.Mitchell	J.Brown
1959	P.Brown	P.Carpenter	L.Groza	J.Smith	A.Hunter	G.Hickerson	M.McCormack	B.Howton	R.Renfro	M.Plum	B.Mitchell	J.Brown
1960	P.Brown	R.Kreitling	D.Schafrath	J.Smith	J.Morrow	G.Hickerson	M.McCormack	G.Nagler	R.Renfro	M.Plum	B.Mitchell	J.Brown
1961	P.Brown	R.Kreitling	D.Schafrath	J.Smith	J.Morrow	J.Wooten	M.McCormack	G.Nagler	R.Renfro	M.Plum	B.Mitchell	J.Brown
1962	P.Brown	R.Kreitling	D.Schafrath	J.Smith	J.Morrow	J.Wooten	M.McCormack	J.Brewer	R.Renfro	F.Ryan	T.Wilson	J.Brown
1963	B.Collier	R.Kreitling	D.Schafrath	J.Wooten	J.Morrow	G.Hickerson	Jo.Brown	J.Brewer	G.Collins	F.Ryan	E.Green	Ji.Brown
1964	B.Collier	P.Warfield	D.Schafrath	J.Wooten	J.Morrow	G.Hickerson	M.Clark	J.Brewer	G.Collins	F.Ryan	E.Green	J.Brown
1965	B.Collier	W.Roberts	D.Schafrath	J.Wooten	J.Morrow	G.Hickerson	M.Clark	J.Brewer	G.Collins	F.Ryan	E.Green	J.Brown

YEAR	LDE	LDT/NT	RDT/RDE	RDE/LOLB	LLB/LILB	MLB/RILB	RLB/ROLB	LCB	RCB	SS/LS	FS/RS	FINISH	
1967	O'Bradovich	F.Cornish	D.Evey	M.Amsler	D.Buffone	D.Butkus	J.Purnell	B.McRae	C.Gentry	R.Petitbon	R.Taylor	2nco	7-6-1
1968	O'Bradovich	J.Johnson	D.Evey	L.Phillips	D.Buffone	D.Butkus	J.Purnell	B.McRae	J.Taylor	R.Petitbon	R.Taylor	2nco	7-7
1969	D.Evey	F.Cornish	W.Holman	O'Bradovich	D.Buffone	D.Butkus	Kuechenberg	B.McRae	J.Taylor	G.Youngblood	D.Daniels	4nco	1-13
1970	W.Holman	G.Seals	B.Staley	O'Bradovich	D.Buffone	D.Butkus	L.Caffey	B.McRae	J.Taylor	P.Clark	D.Daniels	3nc	6-8
1971	W.Holman	G.Seals	B.Staley	O'Bradovich	D.Buffone	D.Butkus	R.Brupbacher	C.Ford	J.Taylor	R.Smith	J.Moore	3nc	6-8
1972	T.McGee	J.Osborne	B.Line	S.DeLong	D.Buffone	D.Butkus	R.Brupbacher	C.Ford	J.Taylor	R.Smith	J.Moore	4nc	4-9-1
1973	T.McGee	J.Osborne	W.Chambers	M.Tom	D.Buffone	D.Butkus	B.Pifferini	C.Ford	J.Taylor	C.Clemons	G.Lyle	4nc	3-11
1974	D.Gallagher	J.Osborne	W.Chambers	G.Hrivnak	D.Buffone	D.Rives	J.Gunn	A.Ellis	J.Taylor	C.Clemons	G.Lyle	4nc	4-10
1975	Hartenstine	R.Stillwell	W.Chambers	R.Harris	D.Buffone	L.Ely	W.Bryant	A.Ellis	V.Livers	D.Plank	C.Clemons	3nc	4-10
1976	Hartenstine	J.Osborne	W.Chambers	R.Stillwell	R.Brupbacher	D.Rives	W.Bryant	A.Ellis	V.Livers	D.Plank	C.Clemons	2nc	7-7
1977	Hartenstine	J.Osborne	R.Rydalch	B.Newsome	D.Buffone	T.Hicks	W.Bryant	A.Ellis	V.Livers	G.Fencik	D.Plank	2nc	9-5 #
1978	T.Hart	J.Osborne	A.Page	Hartenstine	D.Buffone	T.Hicks	G.Campbell	T.Schmidt	V.Livers	G.Fencik	D.Plank	3nc	7-9
1979	D.Hampton	J.Osborne	A.Page	Hartenstine	Muckensturm	T.Hicks	G.Campbell	T.Schmidt	V.Livers	G.Fencik	D.Plank	2nc	10-6 #w
1980	D.Hampton	J.Osborne	A.Page	Hartenstine	Muckensturm	T.Hicks	G.Campbell	T.Schmidt	A.Ellis	G.Fencik	D.Plank	3nc	7-9
1981	D.Hampton	J.Osborne	A.Page	A.Harris	O.Wilson	M.Singletary	G.Campbell	T.Schmidt	R.Henderson	G.Fencik	D.Plank	5nc	6-10
1982	Hartenstine	J.Osborne	D.Hampton	A.Harris	O.Wilson	M.Singletary	G.Campbell	T.Schmidt	L.Frazier	G.Fencik	Walterscheid	11n	3-6
1983	Hartenstine	J.Osborne	S.McMichael	D.Hampton	O.Wilson	M.Singletary	A.Harris	M.Richardson	L.Frazier	T.Bell	G.Fencik	2nc	8-8
1984	Hartenstine	S.McMichael	D.Hampton	R.Dent	O.Wilson	M.Singletary	A.Harris	M.Richardson	L.Frazier	T.Bell	G.Fencik	1nc	10-6 dc
1985	D.Hampton	S.McMichael	W.Perry	R.Dent	O.Wilson	M.Singletary	W.Marshall	M.Richardson	L.Frazier	D.Duerson	G.Fencik	1nc	15-1 dcs*
1986	D.Hampton	S.McMichael	W.Perry	R.Dent	O.Wilson	M.Singletary	W.Marshall	M.Richardson	V.Jackson	D.Duerson	G.Fencik	1nc	14-2 d
1987	D.Hampton	S.McMichael	W.Perry	R.Dent	O.Wilson	M.Singletary	W.Marshall	M.Richardson	V.Jackson	T.Bell	D.Duerson	1nc	11-4 d
1988	A.Harris	S.McMichael	D.Hampton	R.Dent	R.Rivera	M.Singletary	J.Morrissey	M.Richardson	V.Jackson	D.Duerson	M.Douglass	1nc	12-4 dc
1989	T.Armstrong	S.McMichael	W.Perry	R.Dent	R.Rivera	M.Singletary	J.Roper	D.Woolford	V.Jackson	D.Duerson	S.Gayle	4nc	6-10
1990	T.Armstrong	W.Perry	D.Hampton	R.Dent	J.Morrissey	M.Singletary	R.Rivera	D.Woolford	L.Stinson	S.Gayle	M.Carrier	1nc	11-5 ed
1991	T.Armstrong	S.McMichael	W.Perry	R.Dent	J.Morrissey	M.Singletary	J.Roper	D.Woolford	L.Stinson	S.Gayle	M.Carrier	2nc	11-5 w
1992	T.Armstrong	S.McMichael	W.Perry	R.Dent	J.Morrissey	M.Singletary	J.Roper	D.Woolford	L.Stinson	S.Gayle	M.Carrier	3nc	5-11
1993	T.Armstrong	S.McMichael	C.Zorich	R.Dent	J.Cain	D.Jones	V.Smith	D.Woolford	A.Blaylock	S.Gayle	M.Carrier	4nc	7-9
1994	T.Armstrong	A.Fontenot	C.Zorich	A.Spellman	J.Cain	D.Jones	V.Smith	D.Woolford	J.Lincoln	S.Gayle	M.Carrier	4nc	9-7 #wd
1995	A.Spellman	J.Flanigan	C.Zorich	J.Thierry	V.Smith	J.Cain	R.Cox	D.Woolford	J.Lincoln	M.Carter	M.Carrier	3nc	9-7 #
1996	A.Fontenot	J.Flanigan	C.Simpson	A.Spellman	J.Cain	B.Cox	V.Smith	D.Woolford	W.Harris	M.Carter	M.Carrier	3nc	7-9
1997	J.Thierry	J.Flanigan	C.Simpson	C.Reeves	R.Cox	B.Cox	B.Minter	Tom Carter	W.Harris	M.Carter	J.Mangum	5nc	4-12
1998	J.Thierry	J.Flanigan	M.Wells	S.Lee	R.McDonald	B.Minter	S.Harris	T.Cousin	W.Harris	M.Carter	T.Parrish	5nc	4-12
1999	B.Robinson	J.Flanigan	M.Wells	V.Tuinei	R.McDonald	S.Harris	B.Minter	W.Harris	T.Cousin	T.Parrish	C.Hudson	5nc	6-10
2000	B.Robinson	J.Flanigan	M.Wells	P.Daniels	S.Harris	B.Urlacher	W.Holdman	W.Harris	T.Smith	T.Parrish	M.Brown	5nc	5-11
2001	B.Robinson	T.Washington	K.Traylor	P.Daniels	R.Colvin	B.Urlacher	W.Holdman	W.Harris	R.McQuarters	T.Parrish	M.Brown	1nc	13-3 d
2002	P.Daniels	B.Robinson	K.Traylor	A.Brown	R.Colvin	B.Urlacher	B.Howard	R.McQuarters	J.Azumah	M.Green	M.Brown	3nn	4-12
2003	P.Daniels	K.Traylor	B.Robinson	A.Brown	L.Briggs	B.Urlacher	W.Holdman	C.Tillman	J.Azumah	B.Gray	M.Brown	3nn	7-9
2004	A.Ogunleye	T.Harris	I.Scott	A.Brown	Hillenmeyer	B.Urlacher	L.Briggs	R.McQuarters	J.Azumah	M.Green	T.Johnson	4nn	5-11
2005	A.Ogunleye	I.Scott	T.Harris	A.Brown	Hillenmeyer	B.Urlacher	L.Briggs	C.Tillman	N.Vasher	M.Brown	C.Harris	1nn	11-5 d

YEAR	LDE	LDT/NT	RDT/RDE	RDE/LOLB	LLB/LILB	MLB/RILB	RLB/ROLB	LCB	RCB	SS/LS	FS/RS	FINISH	
1968	J.Griffin	A.Rice	B.Staley	H.Gunner	A.Beauchamp	S.Headrick	F.Buncom	F.Smith	C.King	J.Phillips	B.Hunt	5aw	3-11
1969	R.Berry	A.Rice	B.Staley	S.Chomyszak	A.Beauchamp	B.Bergey	B.Peterson	F.Smith	K.Riley	A.Coleman	B.Hunt	5aw	4-9-1
1970	R.Berry	M.Reid	S.Chomyszak	R.Carpenter	A.Beauchamp	B.Bergey	K.Avery	L.Parrish	K.Riley	F.Smith	K.Dyer	1ac	8-6 d
1971	R.Berry	M.Reid	S.Chomyszak	R.Carpenter	A.Beauchamp	B.Bergey	K.Avery	L.Parrish	K.Riley	F.Smith	S.Durko	4ac	4-10
1972	R.Berry	M.Reid	S.Chomyszak	S.White	A.Beauchamp	B.Bergey	K.Avery	L.Parrish	K.Riley	N.Craig	T.Casanova	3ac	8-6
1973	R.Berry	M.Reid	R.Carpenter	S.White	A.Beauchamp	B.Bergey	R.Pritchard	L.Parrish	K.Riley	N.Craig	T.Casanova	1ac	10-4 #d
1974	K.Johnson	M.Reid	R.Carpenter	S.White	A.Beauchamp	D.Adams	R.Pritchard	L.Parrish	K.Riley	B.Jackson	T.Casanova	2ac	7-7
1975	K.Johnson	R.Brown	R.Carpenter	S.White	A.Beauchamp	J.LeClair	R.Pritchard	L.Parrish	K.Riley	T.Casanova	B.Jackson	2ac	11-3 w
1976	G.Burley	R.Brown	R.Carpenter	C.Bacon	B.Harris	J.LeClair	R.Williams	L.Parrish	K.Riley	T.Casanova	M.Cobb	2ac	10-4 #
1977	G.Burley	E.Edwards	W.Whitley	C.Bacon	B.Harris	J.LeClair	R.Williams	L.Parrish	K.Riley	T.Casanova	M.Cobb	2ac	8-6
1978	G.Burley	W.Whitley	E.Edwards	R.Browner	G.Cameron	J.LeClair	R.Williams	L.Breeden	K.Riley	M.Cobb	S.Perry	4ac	4-12
1979	G.Burley	E.Edwards	W.Whitley	R.Browner	B.Harris	J.LeClair	R.Williams	L.Breeden	K.Riley	M.Cobb	D.Jauron	4ac	4-12
1980	E.Edwards	W.Whitley	R.Browner*	T.Dinkel	J.LeClair	G.Cameron	R.Williams	R.Griffin	K.Riley	G.Bright	D.Jauron	4ac	6-10
1981	E.Edwards	W.Whitley	R.Browner*	B.Harris	J.LeClair	G.Cameron	R.Williams	L.Breeden	K.Riley	B.Kemp	B.Hicks	1ac	12-4 dcs
1982	E.Edwards	W.Whitley	R.Browner*	B.Harris	J.LeClair	G.Cameron	R.Williams	L.Breeden	K.Riley	B.Kemp	B.Hicks	2a	7-2 p
1983	E.Edwards	J.Boyarsky	R.Browner*	T.Dinkel	J.LeClair	G.Cameron	R.Williams	L.Breeden	K.Riley	B.Kemp	R.Jackson	3ac	7-9
1984	E.Edwards	T.Krumrie	R.Browner*	J.Schuh	R.Simpkins	G.Cameron	R.Williams	L.Breeden	R.Horton	B.Kemp	R.Jackson	2ac	8-8
1985	E.Edwards	T.Krumrie	R.Browner*	J.Schuh	R.Simpkins	G.Cameron	R.Williams	L.Breeden	R.Horton	B.Kemp	J.Griffin	2ac	7-9
1986	E.Edwards	T.Krumrie	R.Browner*	E.King	C.Zander	L.Barker	R.Williams	L.Breeden	L.Billups	D.Fulcher	B.Kemp	2ac	10-6 #
1987	E.Edwards	T.Krumrie	J.Skow*	E.King	C.Zander	J.Kelly	R.Williams	R.Horton	L.Billups	D.Fulcher	R.Jackson	4ac	4-11
1988	S.McClendon	T.Krumrie	J.Skow*	L.White	C.Zander	J.Kelly	R.Williams	L.Billups	E.Thomas	D.Fulcher	S.Wilcots	1ac	12-4 dcs
1989	J.Skow	T.Krumrie	J.Buck*	L.White	C.Zander	J.Kelly	R.Williams	L.Billups	E.Thomas	D.Fulcher	R.Dixon	4ac	8-8
1990	S.McClendon	T.Krumrie	D.Grant*	L.White	C.Zander	K.Walker	J.Francis	L.Billups	C.Carter	D.Fulcher	S.Wilcots	1ac	9-7 #ed
1991	A.Mitz	T.Krumrie	D.Grant*	J.Francis	L.Barker	C.Zander	A.Williams	W.Haddix	E.Thomas	D.Fulcher	R.Dixon	4ac	3-13
1992	L.Rogers	T.Krumrie	A.Mitz*	J.Francis	R.McDonald	G.Reasons	D.Stubbs	R.Jones	E.Thomas	D.Fulcher	D.Williams	4ac	5-11
1993	J.Copeland	T.Krumrie	G.Hinkle*	J.Francis	E.Shaw	R.McDonald	A.Williams	M.Brim	R.Jones	L.Gunn	D.Williams	4ac	3-13
1994	J.Copeland	K.Rucker	D.Wilkinson	A.Williams	J.Francis	S.Tovar	R.McDonald	M.Brim	R.Jones	L.Oliver	D.Williams	3ac	3-13
1995	J.Copeland	D.Wilkinson	K.Rucker	A.Smith	J.Francis	S.Tovar	R.McDonald	Roger Jones	Rod Jones	B.Walker	D.Williams	2ac	7-9
1996	J.Copeland	D.Wilkinson	T.Johnson	A.Smith	J.Francis	S.Tovar	R.McDonald	A.Ambrose	J.Spencer	B.Walker	B.Orlando	3ac	8-8
1997	J.Copeland	von Oelhoffen	D.Wilkinson*	J.Francis	T.Tumulty	R.McDonald	G.Dixon	A.Ambrose	J.Spencer	S.Shade	G.Myers	4ac	7-9
1998	M.Bankston	von Oelhoffen	C.Simmons*	J.Francis	B.Simmons	T.Spikes	R.Wilson	A.Ambrose	A.Hawkins	S.Shade	G.Myers	5ac	3-13
1999	J.Copeland	O.Gibson	M.Bankston*	S.Foley	B.Simmons	T.Spikes	A.Ross	R.Heath	A.Hawkins	M.Bell	C.Hall	5ac	4-12
2000	V.Booker	O.Gibson	J.Copeland	M.Bankston	S.Foley	A.Spearman	T.Spikes	T.Carter	R.Heath	C.Carter	D.Williams	5ac	4-12
2001	V.Booker	O.Gibson	T.Williams	J.Smith	S.Foley	B.Simmons	T.Spikes	M.Roman	A.Hawkins	J.Armour	C.Hall	5ac	6-10
2002	Whittington	O.Gibson	T.Williams	J.Smith	C.Curtis	B.Simmons	T.Spikes	J.Burris	A.Hawkins	J.Armour	C.Hall	4an	2-14
2003	D.Clemons	J.Thornton	T.Williams	J.Smith	A.Ross	K.Hardy	B.Simmons	A.Hawkins	T.James	R.Beckett	M.Roman	2an	8-8
2004	D.Clemons	J.Thornton	L.Moore	J.Smith	K.Hardy	L.Johnson	B.Simmons	D.O'Neal	T.James	K.Herring	M.Williams	3an	8-8
2005	J.Smith	B.Robinson	J.Thornton	R.Geathers	L.Johnson	O.Thurman	B.Simmons	D.O'Neal	T.James	I.Ohalete	K.Kaesviharn	1an	11-5 #e

YEAR	LDE	LDT/NT	RDT/RDE	RDE/LOLB	LLB/LILB	MLB/RILB	RLB/ROLB	LCB	RCB	SS/LS	FS/RS	FINISH	
1950	G.Young	C.Grigg	J.Kissell	L.Ford	T.Adamle	A.Agase	H.Herring	W.Lahr	T.James	C.Lewis	B.Willis+	1na	10-2 cl*
1951	G.Young	C.Grigg	J.Kissell	L.Ford	T.Adamle	A.Agase	H.Herring	W.Lahr	T.James	C.Lewis	B.Willis+	1na	11-1 l
1952	G.Young	B.Gain	D.Palmer	L.Ford	W.Michaels	T.Thompson	H.Herring	W.Lahr	T.James	B.Rechichar	B.Willis+	1na	8-4 l
1953	G.Young	D.Colo	D.Palmer	L.Ford	W.Michaels	B.Willis+	T.Thompson	W.Lahr	T.James	K.Gorgal	K.Konz	1ne	11-1 l
1954	C.Massey	J.Kissell	D.Colo	L.Ford	T.Catlin	M.McCormack+	W.Michaels	W.Lahr	D.Paul	K.Gorgal	T.James	1ne	9-3 l*
1955	C.Massey	J.Kissell	D.Colo	L.Ford	C.Noll	B.Gain+	W.Michaels	W.Lahr	D.Paul	K.Konz	J.Petitbon	1ne	9-2-1 l*
1956	C.Massey	J.Kissell	B.Gain	L.Ford	C.Noll	W.Michaels	G.Fiss	W.Lahr	D.Paul	K.Konz	J.Petitbon	4ne	5-7
1957	B.Quinlan	B.Gain	D.Colo	L.Ford	G.Fiss	V.Costello	W.Michaels	W.Lahr	D.Paul	K.Konz	J.Wren	1ne	9-2-1 l
1958	P.Wiggin	B.Gain	D.Colo	B.Quinlan	G.Fiss	V.Costello	W.Michaels	W.Lahr	D.Paul	K.Konz	J.Wren	1ne	9-3 c
1959	B.Gain	W.McClung	S.Youngelman	P.Wiggin	G.Fiss	V.Costello	W.Michaels	B.Parrish	J.Shofner	W.Lahr	J.Wren	2ne	7-5
1960	P.Wiggin	B.Gain	F.Peters	J.Marshall	G.Fiss	V.Costello	W.Michaels	B.Parrish	J.Shofner	D.Fleming	R.Mostardo	2ne	8-3-1
1961	J.Houston	B.Gain	F.Peters	P.Wiggin	V.Costello	D.Lloyd	W.Michaels	B.Parrish	J.Shofner	D.Fleming	B.Franklin	3ne	8-5-1
1962	P.Wiggin	B.Gain	F.Peters	B.Glass	G.Fiss	V.Costello	M.Lucci	B.Parrish	J.Shofner	R.Fichtner	B.Franklin	3ne	7-6-1
1963	P.Wiggin	B.Gain	F.Parker	B.Glass	J.Houston	V.Costello	G.Fiss	B.Parrish	J.Shofner	L.Benz	R.Fichtner	2ne	10-4
1964	P.Wiggin	Modzelewski	J.Kanicki	B.Glass	J.Houston	V.Costello	G.Fiss	B.Parrish	W.Beach	L.Benz	B.Franklin	1ne	10-3-1 l*
1965	P.Wiggin	Modzelewski	J.Kanicki	B.Glass	J.Houston	V.Costello	S.Williams	B.Parrish	W.Beach	R.Fichtner	L.Benz	1ne	11-3 l

YEAR	COACH	WR/LE	LT	LG	C	RG	RT	TE/RE	WR/FL	QB	RB/LH	FB
1966	B.Collier	P.Warfield	D.Schafrath	J.Wooten	J.Morrow	G.Hickerson	M.Clark	M.Morin	G.Collins	F.Ryan	L.Kelly	E.Green
1967	B.Collier	P.Warfield	D.Schafrath	J.Wooten	F.Hoaglin	G.Hickerson	M.Clark	R.Smith	G.Collins	F.Ryan	L.Kelly	E.Green
1968	B.Collier	P.Warfield	D.Schafrath	J.Demarie	F.Hoaglin	G.Hickerson	M.Clark	M.Morin	E.Barney	B.Nelsen	L.Kelly	E.Green
1969	B.Collier	P.Warfield	D.Schafrath	J.Demarie	F.Hoaglin	G.Hickerson	M.Clark	M.Morin	G.Collins	B.Nelsen	R.Johnson	L.Kelly
1970	B.Collier	F.Hooker	D.Schafrath	J.Demarie	F.Hoaglin	G.Hickerson	J.Taffoni	M.Morin	G.Collins	B.Nelsen	L.Kelly	B.Scott
1971	N.Skorich	F.Hooker	D.Schafrath	J.Demarie	F.Hoaglin	G.Hickerson	B.McKay	M.Morin	G.Collins	B.Nelsen	L.Kelly	B.Scott
1972	N.Skorich	F.Hooker	D.Dieken	G.Hickerson	B.DeMarco	J.Demarie	B.McKay	M.Morin	F.Pitts	M.Phipps	L.Kelly	B.Scott
1973	N.Skorich	F.Hooker	D.Dieken	G.Hickerson	B.DeMarco	J.Demarie	B.McKay	M.Morin	F.Pitts	M.Phipps	L.Kelly	K.Brown
1974	N.Skorich	F.Hooker	D.Dieken	P.Adams	B.DeMarco	J.Demarie	G.Sullivan	M.Morin	S.Holden	M.Phipps	G.Pruitt	H.McKinnis
1975	F.Gregg	R.Rucker	D.Dieken	C.Hutchison	T.DeLeone	B.McKay	G.Sullivan	O.Roan	S.Holden	M.Phipps	G.Pruitt	H.McKinnis
1976	F.Gregg	P.Warfield	D.Dieken	P.Adams	T.DeLeone	R.Jackson	B.Darrow	O.Roan	R.Rucker	B.Sipe	G.Pruitt	C.Miller
1977	F.Gregg	D.Logan	D.Dieken	H.Sheppard	T.DeLeone	R.Jackson	B.Darrow	O.Roan	R.Rucker	B.Sipe	G.Pruitt	C.Miller
1978	Rutigliano	D.Logan	D.Dieken	H.Sheppard	T.DeLeone	R.Jackson	B.Darrow	O.Newsome	R.Rucker	B.Sipe	G.Pruitt	M.Pruitt
1979	Rutigliano	D.Logan	D.Dieken	C.Risien	T.DeLeone	R.Jackson	H.Sheppard	O.Newsome	R.Rucker	B.Sipe	C.Hill	M.Pruitt
1980	Rutigliano	D.Logan	D.Dieken	H.Sheppard	T.DeLeone	DeLamielleure	C.Risien	O.Newsome	R.Rucker	B.Sipe	G.Pruitt	M.Pruitt
1981	Rutigliano	D.Logan	D.Dieken	R.E.Jackson	T.DeLeone	DeLamielleure	C.Risien	O.Newsome	R.Rucker	B.Sipe	C.White	M.Pruitt
1982	Rutigliano	D.Logan	D.Dieken	R.Jackson	T.DeLeone	DeLamielleure	C.Risien	O.Newsome	R.Feacher	B.Sipe	C.White	M.Pruitt
1983	Rutigliano	B.Jones	D.Dieken	R.Jackson	M.Baab	DeLamielleure	C.Risien	O.Newsome	D.Logan	B.Sipe	M.Pruitt	H.Holt*
1984	Schottenheimer	D.Harris	D.Dieken	R.Jackson	M.Baab	DeLamielleure	B.Contz	O.Newsome	H.Holt*	P.McDonald	B.Green	R.Bolden*
1985	Schottenheimer	C.Weathers	P.Farren	G.Lilja	M.Baab	D.Fike	C.Risien	O.Newsome	B.Brennan	B.Kosar	E.Byner	K.Mack
1986	Schottenheimer	W.Slaughter	P.Farren	L.Williams	M.Baab	D.Fike	C.Risien	O.Newsome	R.Langhorne	B.Kosar	C.Dickey	K.Mack
1987	Schottenheimer	R.Langhorne	P.Farren	L.Williams	M.Baab	D.Fike	C.Risien	O.Newsome	W.Slaughter	B.Kosar	E.Byner	K.Mack
1988	Schottenheimer	W.Slaughter	P.Farren	L.Williams	G.Rakoczy	D.Fike	C.Risien	O.Newsome	R.Langhorne	B.Kosar	E.Byner	K.Mack
1989	B.Carson	W.Slaughter	P.Farren	T.Banker	G.Rakoczy	D.Fike	C.Risien	O.Newsome	R.Langhorne	B.Kosar	E.Metcalf	T.Manoa
1990	B.Carson	W.Slaughter	P.Farren	R.Tamm	M.Baab	G.Rakoczy	T.Jones	O.Newsome	R.Langhorne	B.Kosar	E.Metcalf	K.Mack
1991	Belichick	W.Slaughter	T.Jones	J.Rienstra	M.Baab	E.King	D.Fike	S.Galbraith	R.Langhorne	B.Kosar	L.Hoard	K.Mack
1992	Belichick	M.Jackson	T.Jones	B.Dahl	J.Hilgenberg	E.King	D.Fike	M.Bavaro	L.Tillman	M.Tomczak	L.Hoard	T.Vardell
1993	Belichick	M.Jackson	T.Jones	H.Hoover	S.Everitt	B.Dahl	G.Williams	B.Kinchen	M.Carrier	V.Testaverde	E.Metcalf	T.Vardell
1994	Belichick	M.Jackson	T.Jones	D.Dawson	S.Everitt	B.Dahl	G.Williams	B.Kinchen	D.Alexander	V.Testaverde	E.Metcalf	L.Hoard
1995	Belichick	M.Jackson	T.Jones	W.Williams	S.Everitt	B.Dahl	O.Brown	B.Kinchen	A.Rison	V.Testaverde	L.Hoard	F.Hartley*
1999	C.Palmer	K.Johnson	L.Brown	J.Pyne	D.Wohlabaugh	S.Rehberg	O.Brown	I.Smith	D.Chiaverini	T.Couch	T.Kirby	M.Edwards
2000	C.Palmer	K.Johnson	R.Oben	J.Bundren	D.Wohlabaugh	E.Lindsay	S.Zahursky	M.Campbell	D.Patten	D.Pederson	T.Prentice	M.Edwards
2001	B.Davis	K.Johnson	R.Oben	R.Verba	D.Wohlabaugh	J.McKinney	R.Chanoine	O.Santiago	Q.Morgan	T.Couch	J.Jackson	M.Sellers*
2002	B.Davis	K.Johnson	R.Verba	B.Stokes	D.Wohlabaugh	S.O'Hara	R.Tucker	M.Campbell	Q.Morgan	T.Couch	W.Green	S.Heiden*
2003	B.Davis	Andre' Davis	B.Stokes	S.O'Hara	M.Fowler	P.Zukauskas	R.Tucker	S.Heiden	Q.Morgan	K.Holcomb	W.Green	D.Sanders*
2004	B.Davis	D.Northcutt	R.Verba	E.DeMar	J.Faine	K.Garmon	J.Gonzalez	S.Heiden	A.Bryant	J.Garcia	W.Green	T.Smith
2005	R.Crennel	D.Northcutt	L.Shelton	J.Andruzzi	J.Faine	C.Coleman	R.Tucker	S.Heiden	A.Bryant	T.Dilfer	R.Droughns	T.Smith

DALLAS COWBOYS

YEAR	COACH	WR/LE	LT	LG	C	RG	RT	TE/RE	WR/FL	QB	RB/LH	FB
1960	T.Landry	F.Dugan	B.Fry	D.Putnam	J.Houser	B.Guy	P.Dickson	J.Doran	B.Howton	E.LeBaron	D.McIlhenny	W.Kowalczyk
1961	T.Landry	B.Howton	B.Fry	A.Cvercko	M.Connelly	M.Falls	C.Granger	D.Bielski	F.Clarke	E.LeBaron	D.Perkins	A.Marsh
1962	T.Landry	B.Howton	B.Fry	A.Cvercko	M.Connelly	D.Memmelaar	M.Clark	L.Folkins	F.Clarke	E.LeBaron	D.Perkins	A.Marsh
1963	T.Landry	B.Howton	B.Fry	J.Smith	M.Connelly	D.Memmelaar	E.Nutting	L.Folkins	F.Clarke	D.Meredith	A.Marsh	D.Perkins
1964	T.Landry	T.McDonald	T.Liscio	J.Kupp	M.Connelly	J.Isbell	R.Schoenke	P.Norman	F.Clarke	D.Meredith	J.Stiger	D.Perkins
1965	T.Landry	B.Hayes	J.Boeke	J.Kupp	D.Manders	L.Donohue	R.Neely	F.Clarke	B.Dial	D.Meredith	P.Dunn	D.Perkins
1966	T.Landry	B.Hayes	J.Boeke	T.Liscio	D.Manders	L.Donohue	R.Neely	P.Norman	P.Gent	D.Meredith	D.Reeves	D.Perkins
1967	T.Landry	B.Hayes	T.Liscio	J.Niland	M.Connelly	L.Donohue	R.Neely	P.Norman	L.Rentzel	D.Meredith	D.Reeves	D.Perkins
1968	T.Landry	B.Hayes	T.Liscio	J.Niland	M.Walker	J.Wilbur	R.Neely	P.Norman	L.Rentzel	D.Meredith	C.Baynham	D.Perkins
1969	T.Landry	B.Hayes	T.Liscio	J.Niland	M.Walker	J.Wilbur	R.Neely	P.Norman	L.Rentzel	C.Morton	C.Hill	W.Garrison
1970	T.Landry	B.Hayes	T.Liscio	J.Niland	D.Manders	B.Nye	R.Wright	P.Norman	L.Rentzel	C.Morton	C.Hill	W.Garrison
1971	T.Landry	B.Hayes	R.Neely	J.Niland	D.Manders	B.Nye	R.Wright	B.Truax	L.Alworth	R.Staubach	D.Thomas	W.Garrison
1972	T.Landry	R.Sellers	R.Neely	J.Niland	D.Manders	B.Nye	R.Wright	M.Ditka	L.Alworth	C.Morton	C.Hill	W.Garrison
1973	T.Landry	B.Hayes	R.Neely	J.Niland	J.Fitzgerald	B.Nye	R.Wright	B.DuPree	O.Stowe	R.Staubach	C.Hill	W.Garrison
1974	T.Landry	G.Richards	R.Neely	J.Niland	J.Fitzgerald	B.Nye	R.Wright	B.DuPree	D.Pearson	R.Staubach	C.Hill	W.Garrison
1975	T.Landry	G.Richards	R.Neely	B.Lawless	J.Fitzgerald	B.Nye	R.Wright	J.Fugett	D.Pearson	R.Staubach	P.Pearson	R.Newhouse
1976	T.Landry	G.Richards	R.Neely	H.Scott	J.Fitzgerald	B.Nye	R.Wright	B.DuPree	D.Pearson	R.Staubach	D.Dennison	S.Laidlaw
1977	T.Landry	G.Richards	R.Neely	H.Scott	J.Fitzgerald	T.Rafferty	P.Donovan	B.DuPree	D.Pearson	R.Staubach	T.Dorsett	R.Newhouse
1978	T.Landry	T.Hill	P.Donovan	H.Scott	J.Fitzgerald	T.Rafferty	R.Wright	B.DuPree	D.Pearson	R.Staubach	T.Dorsett	R.Newhouse
1979	T.Landry	T.Hill	P.Donovan	H.Scott	J.Fitzgerald	T.Rafferty	J.Cooper	B.DuPree	D.Pearson	R.Staubach	T.Dorsett	R.Newhouse
1980	T.Landry	T.Hill	P.Donovan	H.Scott	J.Fitzgerald	T.Rafferty	J.Cooper	B.DuPree	D.Pearson	D.White	T.Dorsett	R.Newhouse
1981	T.Landry	T.Hill	P.Donovan	H.Scott	T.Rafferty	K.Petersen	J.Cooper	B.DuPree	D.Pearson	D.White	T.Dorsett	R.Springs
1982	T.Landry	T.Hill	P.Donovan	H.Richards	T.Rafferty	K.Petersen	J.Cooper	D.Cosbie	D.Pearson	D.White	T.Dorsett	R.Springs
1983	T.Landry	T.Hill	P.Donovan	H.Scott	T.Rafferty	K.Petersen	J.Cooper	D.Cosbie	D.Pearson	D.White	T.Dorsett	R.Springs
1984	T.Landry	T.Hill	P.Pozderac	G.Titensor	T.Rafferty	K.Petersen	J.Cooper	D.Cosbie	M.Renfro	G.Hogeboom	T.Dorsett	R.Springs
1985	T.Landry	T.Hill	P.Pozderac	G.Titensor	T.Rafferty	K.Petersen	J.Cooper	D.Cosbie	M.Renfro	D.White	T.Dorsett	T.Newsome
1986	T.Landry	T.Hill	M.Tuinei	G.Titensor	T.Rafferty	C.Ker	P.Pozderac	D.Cosbie	M.Renfro	S.Pelluer	T.Dorsett	T.Newsome
1987	T.Landry	K.Edwards	M.Tuinei	N.Newton	T.Rafferty	C.Ker	K.Gogan	D.Cosbie	M.Renfro	D.White	H.Walker	T.Newsome
1988	T.Landry	R.Alexander	D.Widell	N.Newton	T.Rafferty	C.Ker	K.Gogan	T.Chandler	M.Irvin	S.Pelluer	H.Walker	T.Newsome
1989	J.Johnson	K.Martin	M.Tuinei	N.Newton	T.Rafferty	C.Ker	K.Gogan	S.Folsom	D.Shepard	T.Aikman	P.Palmer	D.Johnston
1990	J.Johnson	M.Irvin	M.Tuinei	C.Ker	M.Stepnoski	J.Gesek	N.Newton	J.Novacek	K.Martin	T.Aikman	E.Smith	T.Agee
1991	J.Johnson	A.Roberts	M.Tuinei	K.Gogan	M.Stepnoski	J.Gesek	N.Newton	J.Novacek	M.Irvin	T.Aikman	E.Smith	D.Johnston
1992	J.Johnson	A.Harper	M.Tuinei	N.Newton	M.Stepnoski	J.Gesek	E.Williams	J.Novacek	M.Irvin	T.Aikman	E.Smith	D.Johnston
1993	J.Johnson	A.Harper	M.Tuinei	N.Newton	M.Stepnoski	K.Gogan	E.Williams	J.Novacek	M.Irvin	T.Aikman	E.Smith	D.Johnston
1994	B.Switzer	A.Harper	M.Tuinei	N.Newton	M.Stepnoski	D.Kennard	L.Allen	J.Novacek	M.Irvin	T.Aikman	E.Smith	D.Johnston
1995	B.Switzer	K.Williams	M.Tuinei	N.Newton	R.Donaldson	L.Allen	E.Williams	J.Novacek	M.Irvin	T.Aikman	E.Smith	D.Johnston
1996	B.Switzer	K.Williams	M.Tuinei	N.Newton	R.Donaldson	L.Allen	E.Williams	E.Bjornson	M.Irvin	T.Aikman	E.Smith	D.Johnston
1997	B.Switzer	A.Miller	G.Hegamin	N.Newton	C.Shiver	L.Allen	E.Williams	E.Bjornson	M.Irvin	T.Aikman	E.Smith	D.Johnston
1998	C.Gailey	B.Davis	L.Allen	N.Newton	C.Shiver	F.Adams	E.Williams	D.LaFleur	M.Irvin	T.Aikman	E.Smith	D.Johnston
1999	C.Gailey	R.Ismail	F.Adams	L.Allen	M.Stepnoski	E.McIver	E.Williams	D.LaFleur	E.Mills	T.Aikman	E.Smith	R.Thomas
2000	D.Campo	R.Ismail	F.Adams	L.Allen	M.Stepnoski	S.Page	E.Williams	D.LaFleur	J.McKnight	T.Aikman	E.Smith	R.Thomas
2001	D.Campo	R.Ismail	F.Adams	L.Allen	M.Stepnoski	K.Garmon	S.Page	J.Harris	J.Galloway	Q.Carter	E.Smith	T.Hambrick
2002	D.Campo	A.Bryant	F.Adams	R.Tucker	T.Walter	A.Gurode	S.Page	T.McGee	J.Galloway	C.Hutchinson	E.Smith	R.Thomas
2003	B.Parcells	J.Galloway	F.Adams	L.Allen	M.Lehr	A.Gurode	K.Vollers	D.Campbell	T.Glenn	Q.Carter	T.Hambrick	R.Anderson
2004	B.Parcells	K.Johnson	F.Adams	L.Allen	A.Johnson	A.Gurode	T.Tucker	J.Witten	Q.Morgan	V.Testaverde	J.Jones	D.Barnes
2005	B.Parcells	K.Johnson	T.Tucker	L.Allen	A.Johnson	M.Rivera	R.Petitti	J.Witten	T.Glenn	D.Bledsoe	J.Jones	D.Campbell*

DENVER BRONCOS

YEAR	COACH	WR/LE	LT	LG	C	RG	RT	TE/RE	WR/FL	QB	RB/LH	FB
1960	F.Filchock	L.Taylor	G.Holz	K.Adamson	M.Nichols	W.Smith	E.Danenhauer	B.Jessup	B.McNamara	F.Tripucka	H.Bell	D.Rolle
1961	F.Filchock	L.Taylor	J.Mattox	K.Adamson	M.Nichols	C.Larpenter	E.Danenhauer	G.Prebola	A.Frazier	F.Tripucka	D.Stone	F.Bukaty
1962	J.Faulkner	L.Taylor	J.Sturm	J.Denvir	J.Barton	B.McCullough	E.Danenhauer	G.Prebola	B.Scarpitto	F.Tripucka	D.Stone	B.Dickinson
1963	J.Faulkner	L.Taylor	H.Olson	B.McCullough	J.Sturm	E.Barnes	E.Danenhauer	G.Prebola	B.Scarpitto	M.Slaughter	D.Stone	B.Joe
1964	M.Speedie	L.Taylor	H.Olson	J.Perkins	J.Sturm	B.McCullough	E.Danenhauer	H.Dixon	B.Scarpitto	J.Lee	C.Mitchell	B.Joe
1965	M.Speedie	L.Taylor	Breitenstein	J.Sturm	R.Kubala	B.McCullough	E.Danenhauer	H.Dixon	B.Scarpitto	M.Slaughter	W.Hayes	C.Gilchrist
1966	R.Malavasi	L.Taylor	Breitenstein	J.Sturm	L.Kaminski	J.Gonzaga	L.Bernet	A.Denson	B.Scarpitto	J.McCormick	A.Haynes	W.Hayes
1967	L.Saban	E.Crabtree	S.Brunelli	G.Goeddeke	L.Kaminski	P.Matson	T.Cichowski	T.Beer	A.Denson	S.Tensi	F.Little	B.Hickey
1968	L.Saban	A.Denson	S.Brunelli	G.Goeddeke	L.Kaminski	B.Young	M.Current	T.Beer	E.Crabtree	M.Briscoe	F.Little	G.Ford
1969	L.Saban	A.Denson	S.Brunelli	G.Goeddeke	L.Kaminski	B.Young	M.Current	T.Beer	M.Haffner	S.Tensi	F.Little	T.Smiley

YEAR	LDE	LDT/NT	RDT/RDE	RDE/LOLB	LLB/LILB	MLB/RILB	RLB/ROLB	LCB	RCB	SS/LS	FS/RS	FINISH	
1966	P.Wiggin	W.Johnson	J.Kanicki	B.Glass	J.Houston	V.Costello	J.Brewer	E.Barnes	M.Howell	R.Fichtner	E.Kellermann	2ne	9-5
1967	P.Wiggin	W.Johnson	J.Kanicki	B.Glass	J.Houston	D.Lindsey	J.Brewer	E.Barnes	M.Howell	E.Kellermann	R.Fichtner	1ncy	9-5 c
1968	R.Snidow	W.Johnson	J.Kanicki	B.Glass	J.Houston	B.Matheson	D.Lindsey	E.Barnes	B.Davis	E.Kellermann	M.Howell	1ncy	10-4 cl
1969	R.Snidow	W.Johnson	M.Upshaw	J.Gregory	J.Houston	D.Lindsey	J.Garlington	E.Barnes	W.Sumner	E.Kellermann	M.Howell	1ncy	10-3-1 cl
1970	R.Snidow	W.Johnson	J.Sherk	J.Gregory	J.Houston	D.Lindsey	B.Andrews	E.Barnes	W.Sumner	E.Kellermann	M.Howell	2ac	7-7
1971	J.Jones	W.Johnson	J.Sherk	J.Gregory	J.Houston	D.Lindsey	B.Andrews	C.Scott	B.Davis	W.Sumner	M.Howell	1ac	9-5 d
1972	R.Jackson	W.Johnson	J.Sherk	B.Briggs	C.Hall	D.Lindsey	B.Andrews	C.Scott	B.Davis	T.Darden	W.Sumner	2ac	10-4 w
1973	J.Jones	W.Johnson	J.Sherk	N.Roman	C.Hall	B.Babich	J.Garlington	C.Scott	B.Davis	W.Sumner	T.Darden	3ac	7-5-2
1974	N.Roman	W.Johnson	J.Sherk	M.Seifert	C.Hall	B.Babich	J.Garlington	C.Scott	V.Green	W.Sumner	T.Darden	4ac	4-10
1975	R.East	W.Johnson	J.Sherk	M.Mitchell	C.Hall	D.Ambrose	B.Babich	C.Scott	T.Peters	V.Green	N.Craig	4ac	3-11
1976	J.Jones	W.Johnson	J.Sherk	M.Mitchell	C.Hall	B.Babich	G.Irons	C.Scott	R.Bolton	N.Craig	T.Darden	3ac	9-5
1977	J.Jones	E.Edwards	M.Sims	M.St. Clair	C.Hall	D.Ambrose	G.Irons	C.Scott	O.Davis	T.Peters	T.Darden	4ac	6-8
1978	M.St. Clair	E.Edwards	J.Sherk	M.Mitchell	C.Hall	D.Ambrose	G.Irons	C.Scott	O.Davis	T.Peters	T.Darden	3ac	8-8
1979	L.Alzado	M.Sims	J.Sherk	J.Gregory	C.Hall	D.Ambrose	C.Matthews	R.Bolton	O.Davis	C.Scott	T.Darden	3ac	9-7
1980	M.Harris	H.Bradley	L.Alzado*	C.Hall	R.Jackson	D.Ambrose	C.Matthews	R.Bolton	C.Burrell	C.Scott	T.Darden	1ac	11-5 #d
1981	M.Harris	H.Bradley	L.Alzado*	D.Goode	R.J.Jackson	D.Ambrose	C.Matthews	R.Bolton	H.Dixon	C.Scott	T.Darden	4ac	5-11
1982	M.Harris	H.Bradley	M.Robinson*	C.Banks	T.Cousineau	D.Ambrose	C.Weathers	L.Johnson	H.Dixon	C.Burrell	C.Scott	8a	4-5 #p
1983	R.Camp	B.Golic	K.Baldwin*	C.Banks	S.Nicolas	T.Cousineau	C.Matthews	L.Braziel	H.Dixon	C.Burrell	M.Whitwell	2ac	9-7 #
1984	R.Camp	B.Golic	K.Baldwin*	C.Banks	E.Johnson	T.Cousineau	C.Matthews	F.Minnifield	H.Dixon	A.Gross	D.Rogers	3ac	5-11
1985	R.Camp	B.Golic	C.Hairston*	C.Banks	E.Johnson	T.Cousineau	C.Matthews	F.Minnifield	H.Dixon	A.Gross	D.Rogers	1ac	8-8 d
1986	R.Camp	B.Golic	C.Hairston*	C.Banks	E.Johnson	A.Griggs	C.Matthews	F.Minnifield	H.Dixon	R.Ellis	C.Rockins	1ac	12-4 dc
1987	S.Clancy	B.Golic	C.Hairston*	L.Sanford	E.Johnson	M.Johnson	C.Matthews	F.Minnifield	H.Dixon	R.Ellis	F.Wright	1ac	10-5 dc
1988	S.Clancy	B.Golic	C.Hairston*	D.Grayson	M.Johnson	E.Johnson	C.Matthews	F.Minnifield	H.Dixon	B.Washington	F.Wright	2ac	10-6 w
1989	A.Baker	C.Hairston	M.Perry	R.Banks	C.Matthews	M.Johnson	D.Grayson	F.Minnifield	H.Dixon	F.Wright	T.Gash	1ac	9-6-1 dc
1990	A.Baker	C.Pike	M.Perry	R.Banks	C.Matthews	M.Johnson	D.Grayson	F.Minnifield	R.Clayborn	F.Wright	T.Gash	4ac	3-13
1991	R.Burnett	J.Jones	M.Perry	A.Pleasant	V.Waiters	R.Brown	C.Matthews	F.Minnifield	R.Hilliard	H.Barnett	V.Newsome	3ac	6-10
1992	R.Burnett	J.Jones	M.Perry	A.Pleasant	D.Brandon	M.Johnson	C.Matthews	F.Minnifield	T.Taylor	E.Turner	V.Newsome	3ac	7-9
1993	R.Burnett	J.Jones	M.Perry	A.Pleasant	P.Johnson	M.Johnson	C.Matthews	T.Taylor	N.Mustafaa	S.Moore	E.Turner	3ac	7-9
1994	R.Burnett	B.Johnson	M.Perry	A.Pleasant	C.Banks	P.Johnson	F.Stams	A.Langham	D.Griffin	S.Moore	E.Turner	2ac	11-5 wd
1995	R.Burnett	T.Goad	D.Footman	A.Pleasant	C.Banks	P.Johnson	G.Dixon	A.Langham	D.Griffin	S.Moore	E.Turner	4ac	5-11
1999	J.Thierry	D.Holland	J.Jurkovic	D.Alexander	R.Abdullah	W.Rainer	J.Miller	R.McNeil	D.McCutcheon	M.Pope	C.Fuller	6ac	2-14
2000	C.Brown	O.Roye	S.Colinet	K.McKenzie	J.Miller	W.Rainer	M.Moore	C.Fuller	D.McCutcheon	M.Smith	P.Ellsworth	6ac	3-13
2001	T.Rogers	G.Warren	M.Smith	K.McKenzie	J.Miller	W.Rainer	D.Rudd	C.Fuller	D.McCutcheon	E.Little	P.Ellsworth	3ac	7-9
2002	K.Lang	G.Warren	O.Roye	C.Brown	D.Hambrick	E.Holmes	D.Rudd	C.Fuller	D.McCutcheon	R.Griffith	D.Bush	2an	9-7 #w
2003	C.Brown	G.Warren	O.Roye	K.Lang	K.Bentley	Andra Davis	B.Taylor	A.Henry	D.McCutcheon	R.Griffith	E.Little	4an	5-11
2004	E.Ekuban	G.Warren	O.Roye	K.Lang	C.Thompson	A.Davis	W.Holdman	A.Henry	D.McCutcheon	R.Griffith	E.Little	4an	4-12
2005	O.Roye	J.Fisk	A.McKinley*	M.Stewart	A.Davis	B.Taylor	C.Thompson	D.McCutcheon	L.Bodden	C.Crocker	B.Russell	3an	6-10

1960	N.Borden	D.Healy	E.Husmann	J.Gonzaga	W.Hansen	J.Tubbs	G.Cronin	Franckhauser	D.Bishop	B.Bercich	B.Butler	7nw	0-11-1
1961	B.Lilly	D.Healy	B.Herchman	N.Borden	C.Howley	J.Tubbs	G.Babb	W.Livingston	D.Bishop	B.Bercich	D.Moegle	6ne	4-9-1
1962	B.Lilly	G.Reese	J.Meyers	G.Andrie	M.Dowdle	J.Tubbs	C.Howley	M.Gaechter	D.Bishop	J.Norton	D.Nolan	5ne	5-8-1
1963	B.Lilly	G.Reese	J.Meyers	G.Andrie	C.Howley	J.Tubbs	L.Jordan	C.Green	D.Bishop	M.Gaechter	W.Livingston	5ne	4-10
1964	G.Andrie	J.Colvin	B.Lilly	L.Stephens	C.Howley	J.Tubbs	L.Jordan	C.Green	D.Bishop	J.Ridlon	M.Renfro	5ne	5-8-1
1965	M.Youmans	J.Colvin	B.Lilly	G.Andrie	C.Howley	J.Tubbs	D.Edwards	C.Green	W.Livingston	O.Logan	M.Renfro	2ne	7-7
1966	W.Townes	J.Colvin	B.Lilly	G.Andrie	C.Howley	L.Jordan	D.Edwards	C.Green	W.Livingston	M.Gaechter	M.Renfro	1ne	10-3-1 l
1967	W.Townes	J.Pugh	B.Lilly	G.Andrie	C.Howley	L.Jordan	D.Edwards	C.Green	M.Johnson	M.Gaechter	M.Renfro	1nca	9-5 cl
1968	L.Cole	J.Pugh	B.Lilly	G.Andrie	C.Howley	L.Jordan	D.Edwards	C.Green	M.Johnson	M.Gaechter	M.Renfro	1nca	12-2 c
1969	L.Cole	J.Pugh	B.Lilly	G.Andrie	D.Edwards	L.Jordan	C.Howley	C.Green	P.Clark	M.Gaechter	M.Renfro	1nca	11-2-1 c
1970	L.Cole	J.Pugh	B.Lilly	G.Andrie	D.Edwards	L.Jordan	C.Howley	H.Adderley	M.Renfro	C.Green	C.Waters	1ne	10-4 dcs
1971	L.Cole	J.Pugh	B.Lilly	G.Andrie	D.Edwards	L.Jordan	C.Howley	H.Adderley	M.Renfro	C.Green	C.Harris	1ne	11-3 dcs*
1972	L.Cole	J.Pugh	B.Lilly	P.Toomay	D.Edwards	L.Jordan	C.Howley	H.Adderley	M.Renfro	C.Green	C.Harris	2ne	10-4 wc
1973	L.Cole	J.Pugh	B.Lilly	P.Toomay	D.Edwards	L.Jordan	D.Lewis	C.Waters	M.Renfro	C.Green	C.Harris	1ne	10-4 #dc
1974	L.Cole	J.Pugh	B.Lilly	P.Toomay	D.Edwards	L.Jordan	D.Lewis	C.Waters	M.Renfro	C.Green	C.Harris	3ne	8-6
1975	T.Jones	J.Pugh	L.Cole	H.Martin	D.Edwards	L.Jordan	D.Lewis	M.Washington	M.Renfro	C.Waters	C.Harris	2ne	10-4 wcs
1976	T.Jones	J.Pugh	L.Cole	H.Martin	B.Breunig	L.Jordan	D.Lewis	B.Barnes	M.Renfro	C.Waters	C.Harris	1ne	11-3 d
1977	T.Jones	J.Pugh	R.White	H.Martin	T.Henderson	B.Breunig	D.Lewis	B.Barnes	A.Kyle	C.Waters	C.Harris	1ne	12-2 dcs*
1978	T.Jones	J.Pugh	R.White	H.Martin	T.Henderson	B.Breunig	D.Lewis	B.Barnes	A.Kyle	C.Waters	C.Harris	1ne	12-4 dcs
1979	L.Cole	D.Stalls	R.White	H.Martin	T.Henderson	B.Breunig	D.Lewis	B.Barnes	A.Kyle	R.Hughes	C.Harris	1ne	11-5 #d
1980	T.Jones	L.Cole	R.White	H.Martin	M.Hegman	B.Breunig	D.Lewis	S.Wilson	A.Mitchell	C.Waters	D.Thurman	2ne	12-4 #wdc
1981	T.Jones	J.Dutton	R.White	H.Martin	M.Hegman	B.Breunig	D.Lewis	E.Walls	D.Thurman	C.Waters	M.Downs	1ne	12-4 dc
1982	T.Jones	J.Dutton	R.White	H.Martin	M.Hegman	B.Breunig	G.Brown	E.Walls	D.Thurman	B.Barnes	M.Downs	2n	6-3 pc
1983	T.Jones	J.Dutton	R.White	H.Martin	M.Hegman	B.Breunig	A.Dickerson	E.Walls	D.Thurman	D.Clinkscale	M.Downs	2ne	12-4 w
1984	T.Jones	J.Dutton	R.White	J.Jeffcoat	M.Hegman	B.Breunig	A.Dickerson	E.Walls	R.Fellows	D.Clinkscale	M.Downs	4ne	9-7 #
1985	T.Jones	J.Dutton	R.White	J.Jeffcoat	M.Hegman	E.Lockhart	J.Rohrer	E.Walls	R.Fellows	D.Clinkscale	M.Downs	1ne	10-6 #d
1986	T.Jones	J.Dutton	R.White	J.Jeffcoat	M.Hegman	E.Lockhart	J.Rohrer	E.Walls	R.Fellows	B.Bates	M.Downs	3ne	7-9
1987	T.Jones	K.Brooks	R.White	J.Jeffcoat	M.Hegman	E.Lockhart	J.Rohrer	E.Walls	R.Francis	B.Bates	M.Downs	2ne	7-8
1988	T.Jones	K.Brooks	D.Noonan	J.Jeffcoat	R.Burton	E.Lockhart	G.Cobb	E.Walls	R.Williams	B.Bates	M.Downs	5ne	3-13
1989	T.Jones	D.Hamel	W.Broughton	J.Jeffcoat	J.Del Rio	E.Lockhart	K.Norton	E.Walls	R.Williams	V.Albritton	R.Horton	5ne	1-15
1990	D.Stubbs	D.Hamel	D.Noonan	J.Jeffcoat	J.Del Rio	E.Lockhart	K.Norton	I.Holt	M.Hendrix	J.Washington	R.Horton	4ne	7-9
1991	T.Tolbert	T.Casillas	R.Maryland	J.Jeffcoat	K.Norton	J.Del Rio	V.Smith	I.Holt	L.Brown	J.Washington	R.Horton	2ne	11-5 wd
1992	T.Tolbert	T.Casillas	R.Maryland	C.Haley	V.Smith	R.Jones	K.Norton	I.Holt	L.Brown	T.Everett	J.Washington	1ne	13-3 dcs*
1993	T.Tolbert	T.Casillas	R.Maryland	C.Haley	D.Edwards	K.Norton	D.Smith	K.Smith	L.Brown	D.Woodson	T.Everett	1ne	12-4 dcs*
1994	T.Tolbert	R.Maryland	L.Lett	C.Haley	D.Edwards	R.Jones	D.Smith	K.Smith	L.Brown	D.Woodson	J.Washington	1ne	12-4 dc
1995	T.Tolbert	R.Maryland	L.Lett	C.Haley	D.Edwards	R.Jones	G.Myles	D.Sanders	L.Brown	D.Woodson	B.Marion	1ne	12-4 dcs*
1996	T.Tolbert	C.Hennings	L.Lett	S.Carver	B.Thomas	F.Strickland	D.Smith	K.Smith	D.Sanders	D.Woodson	B.Marion	1ne	10-6 #ed
1997	T.Tolbert	T.Casillas	C.Hennings	S.Carver	R.Godfrey	F.Strickland	D.Coakley	K.Smith	D.Sanders	D.Woodson	B.Marion	4ne	6-10
1998	K.Pittman	L.Lett	C.Hennings	G.Ellis	R.Godfrey	F.Strickland	D.Coakley	K.Smith	D.Sanders	D.Woodson	O.Stoutmire	1ne	10-6 e
1999	K.Pittman	A.Spellman	C.Hennings	G.Ellis	D.Hambrick	R.Godfrey	D.Coakley	K.Smith	D.Sanders	D.Woodson	G.Teague	2ne	8-8 w
2000	G.Ellis	B.Noble	L.Lett	A.Spellman	D.Hambrick	B.Wortham	D.Coakley	P.Sparks	R.McNeil	D.Woodson	G.Teague	4ne	5-11
2001	G.Ellis	B.Noble	M.Myers	P.Zellner	M.Steele	D.Nguyen	D.Coakley	D.Hawthorne	M.Edwards	D.Woodson	G.Teague	5ne	5-11
2002	G.Ellis	B.Noble	L.Glover	E.Ekuban	K.Hardy	D.Nguyen	D.Coakley	D.Ross	M.Edwards	D.Woodson	R.Williams	4ne	5-11
2003	G.Ellis	W.Blade	L.Glover	E.Ekuban	A.Singleton	D.Nguyen	D.Coakley	T.Newman	M.Edwards	D.Woodson	R.Williams	2ne	10-6 w
2004	G.Ellis	L.Carson	L.Glover	M.Wiley	A.Singleton	D.Nguyen	D.Coakley	T.Newman	L.Frazier	L.Scott	R.Williams	2ne	6-10
2005	M.Spears	L.Glover	G.Ellis*	S.Fujita	B.James	S.Shanle	D.Ware	T.Newman	A.Henry	R.Williams	K.Davis	3ne	9-7

1960	J.Young	B.McFadin	J.Hatley	C.Gavin	P.Mangum	H.Brown	A.Day	F.Bernardi	J.Pyeatt	A.Romine	G.Gonsoulin	4aw	4-9-1
1961	J.Cash	B.McFadin	G.Holz	C.Gavin	B.Hudson	W.McDaniel	J.Stalcup	B.McNamara	J.McMillin	P.Nugent	G.Gonsoulin	3aw	3-11
1962	C.Gavin	B.McFadin	G.Holz	J.Cash	J.Fraser	W.McDaniel	B.Roehnelt	J.McGeever	J.McMillin	B.Zeman	G.Gonsoulin	2aw	7-7
1963	R.Jacobs	B.McFadin	G.Holz	C.Gavin	J.Nocera	W.McDaniel	J.Fraser	J.McGeever	C.Mitchell	B.Zeman	G.Gonsoulin	4aw	2-11-1
1964	R.Jacobs	D.Guesman	C.Janerette	E.Cooke	J.Hopkins	M.Matuszak	J.Fraser	W.Brown	W.West	J.McGeever	G.Gonsoulin	4aw	2-11-1
1965	E.Cooke	R.Jacobs	C.Janerette	M.Leetzow	T.Erlandson	J.Hopkins	J.Bramlett	W.Brown	J.McGeever	M.Farr	G.Gonsoulin	4aw	4-10
1966	M.Leetzow	R.Jacobs	L.Cox	B.Young	G.Jeter	J.Hopkins	J.Bramlett	W.Brown	N.Wilson	L.Wright	G.Gonsoulin	4aw	4-10
1967	R.Mirich	J.Inman	D.Costa	R.Jackson	C.Cunningham	J.Huard	C.Myrtle	G.Sellers	N.Wilson	T.Cassese	J.Lentz	4aw	3-11
1968	P.Duranko	J.Inman	D.Costa	R.Jackson	C.Cunningham	J.Huard	F.Forsberg	C.Greer	D.Garrett	P.Jaquess	J.Lentz	4aw	5-9
1969	R.Jackson	J.Inman	D.Costa	P.Duranko	C.Cunningham	J.Huard	C.Myrtle	G.Cavness	B.Thompson	C.Greer	G.Burrell	4aw	5-8-1

YEAR	COACH	WR/LE	LT	LG	C	RG	RT	TE/RE	WR/FL	QB	RB/LH	FB
1970	L.Saban	A.Denson	S.Brunelli	G.Goeddeke	L.Kaminski	B.Young	M.Current	J.Whalen	M.Haffner	P.Liske	F.Little	W.Crenshaw
1971	L.Saban	J.Simmons	R.Shoals	L.Jackson	G.Goeddeke	M.Schnitker	M.Current	B.Masters	J.Gehrke	D.Horn	F.Little	B.Anderson
1972	J.Ralston	R.Sherman	M.Montgomery	L.Jackson	L.Kaminski	T.Lyons	M.Current	B.Masters	J.Simmons	C.Johnson	F.Little	B.Anderson
1973	J.Ralston	H.Moses	M.Montgomery	L.Jackson	B.Maples	T.Lyons	M.Current	R.Odoms	J.Simmons	C.Johnson	F.Little	J.Dawkins
1974	J.Ralston	B.Van Heusen	C.Minor	L.Jackson	B.Maples	T.Lyons	M.Current	R.Odoms	H.Moses	C.Johnson	F.Little	O.Armstrong
1975	J.Ralston	B.Van Heusen	C.Minor	T.Lyons	B.Maples	P.Howard	M.Current	R.Odoms	H.Moses	S.Ramsey	F.Little	J.Keyworth
1976	J.Ralston	H.Moses	B.Bain	T.Glassic	B.Maples	T.Lyons	C.Minor	R.Odoms	R.Upchurch	S.Ramsey	O.Armstrong	J.Keyworth
1977	R.Miller	J.Dolbin	A.Maurer	T.Glassic	M.Montler	P.Howard	C.Minor	R.Odoms	H.Moses	C.Morton	O.Armstrong	J.Keyworth
1978	R.Miller	J.Dolbin	C.Minor	T.Glassic	B.Bryan	P.Howard	T.Neville	R.Odoms	H.Moses	C.Morton	O.Armstrong	J.Keyworth
1979	R.Miller	R.Upchurch	C.Minor	T.Glassic	B.Bryan	P.Howard	D.Studdard	R.Odoms	H.Moses	C.Morton	R.Lytle	J.Keyworth
1980	R.Miller	R.Upchurch	C.Minor	T.Glassic	B.Bryan	P.Howard	D.Studdard	R.Odoms	H.Moses	C.Morton	D.Preston	J.Jensen
1981	D.Reeves	R.Upchurch	C.Minor	T.Glassic	B.Bryan	P.Howard	D.Studdard	R.Odoms	S.Watson	C.Morton	D.Preston	R.Parros
1982	D.Reeves	R.Upchurch	C.Minor	T.Glassic	B.Bryan	D.Studdard	K.Lanier	R.Odoms	S.Watson	S.DeBerg	D.Preston	R.Parros
1983	D.Reeves	R.Upchurch	D.Studdard	K.Bishop	B.Bryan	P.Howard	K.Lanier	R.Egloff	S.Watson	J.Elway	S.Winder	N.Poole
1984	D.Reeves	B.Johnson	D.Studdard	K.Bishop	B.Bryan	P.Howard	K.Lanier	C.Kay	S.Watson	J.Elway	S.Winder	J.Wright*
1985	D.Reeves	B.Johnson	D.Studdard	K.Bishop	B.Bryan	P.Howard	K.Lanier	C.Kay	S.Watson	J.Elway	S.Winder	J.Wright*
1986	D.Reeves	V.Johnson	D.Studdard	K.Bishop	B.Bryan	P.Howard	K.Lanier	C.Kay	S.Watson	J.Elway	S.Winder	G.Willhite
1987	D.Reeves	V.Johnson	D.Studdard	K.Bishop	M.Freeman	S.Humphries	K.Lanier	C.Kay	M.Jackson	J.Elway	S.Winder	G.Lang
1988	D.Reeves	V.Johnson	J.Juriga	K.Bishop	B.Bryan	K.Kartz	K.Lanier	C.Kay	R.Nattiel	J.Elway	T.Dorsett	S.Winder
1989	D.Reeves	V.Johnson	G.Perry	D.Widell	K.Kartz	J.Juriga	K.Lanier	C.Kay	M.Jackson	J.Elway	B.Humphrey	J.Alexander
1990	D.Reeves	V.Johnson	G.Perry	D.Widell	K.Kartz	J.Juriga	K.Lanier	C.Kay	M.Jackson	J.Elway	B.Humphrey	O.Mobley*
1991	D.Reeves	M.Young	J.Davidson	D.Widell	K.Kartz	C.Ker	K.Lanier	C.Kay	M.Jackson	J.Elway	G.Green	S.Sharpe*
1992	D.Reeves	V.Johnson	R.Freeman	J.Davidson	K.Kartz	D.Widell	K.Lanier	C.Kay	M.Jackson	J.Elway	G.Green	S.Sharpe*
1993	W.Phillips	A.Marshall	G.Zimmerman	D.Widell	K.Kartz	B.Habib	R.Freeman	S.Sharpe	D.Russell	J.Elway	R.Bernstine	R.Johnson*
1994	W.Phillips	A.Miller	G.Zimmerman	J.Melander	D.Widell	B.Habib	K.Scrafford	S.Sharpe	D.Russell	J.Elway	L.Russell	J.Evans*
1995	M.Shanahan	A.Miller	G.Zimmerman	M.Schlereth	T.Nalen	B.Habib	B.Thompson	S.Sharpe	M.Pritchard	J.Elway	T.Davis	A.Craver
1996	M.Shanahan	A.Miller	G.Zimmerman	M.Schlereth	T.Nalen	B.Habib	B.Thompson	S.Sharpe	E.McCaffrey	J.Elway	T.Davis	A.Craver
1997	M.Shanahan	R.Smith	G.Zimmerman	M.Schlereth	T.Nalen	B.Habib	T.Jones	S.Sharpe	E.McCaffrey	J.Elway	T.Davis	H.Griffith
1998	M.Shanahan	R.Smith	T.Jones	M.Schlereth	T.Nalen	D.Neil	H.Swayne	S.Sharpe	E.McCaffrey	J.Elway	T.Davis	H.Griffith
1999	M.Shanahan	R.Smith	T.Jones	M.Schlereth	T.Nalen	D.Neil	M.Lepsis	D.Carswell	E.McCaffrey	B.Griese	O.Gary	H.Griffith
2000	M.Shanahan	R.Smith	T.Jones	M.Schlereth	T.Nalen	D.Neil	M.Lepsis	D.Carswell	E.McCaffrey	B.Griese	M.Anderson	H.Griffith
2001	M.Shanahan	R.Smith	T.Teague	L.Friedman	T.Nalen	D.Neil	M.Lepsis	D.Carswell	E.Kennison	B.Griese	T.Davis	P.Hape
2002	M.Shanahan	R.Smith	E.Salaam	S.Herndon	B.Hamilton	D.Neil	M.Lepsis	S.Sharpe	E.McCaffrey	B.Griese	C.Portis	M.Anderson
2003	M.Shanahan	R.Smith	E.Salaam	B.Hamilton	T.Nalen	D.Neil	M.Lepsis	S.Sharpe	A.Lelie	J.Plummer	C.Portis	D.Carswell*
2004	M.Shanahan	R.Smith	M.Lepsis	B.Hamilton	T.Nalen	D.Neil	G.Foster	D.Carswell	A.Lelie	J.Plummer	R.Droughns	J.Putzier*
2005	M.Shanahan	R.Smith	M.Lepsis	B.Hamilton	T.Nalen	C.Carlisle	G.Foster	S.Alexander	A.Lelie	J.Plummer	M.Anderson	K.Johnson

Detroit Lions

YEAR	COACH	WR/LE	LT	LG	C	RG	RT	TE/RE	WR/FL	QB	RB/LH	FB
1950	B.McMillin	C.Box	F.Jaszewski	L.Creekmur	J.Simmons	J.Soboleski	G.Cifelli	L.Hart	Hoernschemeyer	B.Layne	D.Walker	O.Cline
1951	B.Parker	D.Dibble	F.Jaszewski	L.Creekmur	L.Torgeson	D.Rogas	G.Cifelli	L.Hart	Hoernschemeyer	B.Layne	D.Walker	P.Harder
1952	B.Parker	C.Box	L.Creekmur	J.Martin	V.Banonis	D.Stanfel	G.Cifelli	L.Hart	Hoernschemeyer	B.Layne	J.Girard	P.Harder
1953	B.Parker	C.Box	L.Creekmur	H.Sewell	V.Banonis	D.Stanfel	O.Spencer	L.Hart	Hoernschemeyer	B.Layne	D.Walker	O.Cline
1954	B.Parker	D.Dibble	L.Creekmur	H.Sewell	A.Miketa	J.Martin	C.Ane	L.Hart	Hoernschemeyer	B.Layne	L.Carpenter	B.Bowman
1955	B.Parker	J.Doran	C.Ane	H.Sewell	A.Miketa	D.Stanfel	J.Salsbury	J.Girard	D.Middleton	B.Layne	L.Carpenter	L.Hart
1956	B.Parker	D.Dibble	L.Creekmur	H.Sewell	C.Ane	J.Salsbury	O.Spencer	D.Middleton	G.Gedman	B.Layne	H.Cassady	L.Hart
1957	G.Wilson	S.Junker	L.Creekmur	H.Sewell	F.Gatski	S.Campbell	C.Ane	J.Doran	H.Cassady	B.Layne	G.Gedman	J.Johnson
1958	G.Wilson	J.Doran	L.Creekmur	H.Sewell	B.Glass	S.Campbell	C.Ane	D.Middleton	H.Cassady	T.Rote	G.Gedman	J.Johnson
1959	G.Wilson	J.Gibbons	L.Creekmur	H.Sewell	C.Ane	J.Gordy	O.Spencer	D.Middleton	H.Cassady	T.Rote	K.Webb	Pietrosante
1960	G.Wilson	G.Cogdill	O.Spencer	H.Sewell	B.Scholtz	J.Gordy	W.McClung	J.Gibbons	H.Cassady	J.Ninowski	D.Lewis	Pietrosante
1961	G.Wilson	G.Cogdill	J.Gonzaga	H.Sewell	B.Scholtz	J.Gordy	D.LaRose	J.Gibbons	T.Barr	J.Ninowski	D.Lewis	Pietrosante
1962	G.Wilson	G.Cogdill	J.Gonzaga	H.Sewell	B.Whitlow	J.Gordy	D.LaRose	J.Gibbons	P.Studstill	M.Plum	D.Lewis	Pietrosante
1963	G.Wilson	G.Cogdill	D.Sanders	J.Gonzaga	B.Whitlow	J.Gordy	L.Reeberg	J.Gibbons	T.Barr	E.Morrall	T.Watkins	D.Lewis
1964	G.Wilson	G.Cogdill	D.Sanders	J.Gonzaga	B.Whitlow	J.Gordy	J.Smith	J.Gibbons	T.Barr	M.Plum	T.Watkins	Pietrosante
1965	H.Gilmer	G.Cogdill	D.Sanders	T.Karras	E.Flanagan	J.Gordy	R.Shoals	J.Gibbons	T.Barr	M.Plum	J.Looney	Pietrosante
1966	H.Gilmer	G.Cogdill	D.Sanders	Kowalkowski	E.Flanagan	J.Gordy	J.Smith	R.Kramer	P.Studstill	K.Sweetan	A.Marsh	T.Nowatzke
1967	J.Schmidt	B.Malinchak	B.Cottrell	C.Walton	E.Flanagan	J.Gordy	C.Bradshaw	R.Kramer	P.Studstill	K.Sweetan	A.Marsh	M.Farr
1968	J.Schmidt	E.McCullouch	R.Shoals	C.Walton	E.Flanagan	F.Gallagher	C.Bradshaw	C.Sanders	B.Gambrell	B.Munson	M.Farr	B.Triplett
1969	J.Schmidt	E.McCullouch	R.Shoals	C.Walton	E.Flanagan	F.Gallagher	R.Freitas	C.Sanders	L.Walton	B.Munson	N.Eddy	B.Triplett
1970	J.Schmidt	E.McCullouch	R.Shoals	C.Walton	E.Flanagan	F.Gallagher	R.Freitas	C.Sanders	L.Walton	B.Munson	A.Taylor	M.Farr
1971	J.Schmidt	E.McCullouch	J.Yarbrough	C.Walton	E.Flanagan	Kowalkowski	R.Freitas	C.Sanders	L.Walton	G.Landry	A.Taylor	S.Owens
1972	J.Schmidt	R.Jessie	J.Yarbrough	C.Walton	E.Flanagan	Kowalkowski	R.Freitas	C.Sanders	L.Walton	G.Landry	A.Taylor	S.Owens
1973	McCafferty	R.Jessie	J.Yarbrough	G.Dennis	E.Flanagan	Kowalkowski	R.Freitas	C.Sanders	L.Walton	G.Landry	A.Taylor	S.Owens
1974	R.Forzano	R.Jessie	J.Yarbrough	C.Walton	E.Flanagan	Kowalkowski	R.Freitas	C.Sanders	L.Walton	B.Munson	A.Taylor	S.Owens
1975	R.Forzano	R.Jarvis	J.Yarbrough	L.Boden	J.Morris	Kowalkowski	R.Freitas	C.Sanders	M.Briscoe	J.Reed	A.Taylor	D.Bussey
1976	T.Hudspeth	R.Jarvis	C.Hertwig	L.Boden	J.Morris	Kowalkowski	R.Freitas	C.Sanders	L.Walton	G.Landry	D.Bussey	H.King
1977	T.Hudspeth	J.Hill	J.Yarbrough	R.Bolinger	J.Morris	L.Boden	C.Hertwig	D.Hill	R.Jarvis	G.Landry	R.Kane	H.King
1978	M.Clark	L.Blue	Baldischwiler	H.Elias	L.Tearry	L.Boden	B.Oates	D.Hill	F.Scott	G.Danielson	D.Bussey	H.King
1979	M.Clark	F.Scott	Baldischwiler	H.Elias	L.Tearry	R.Bolinger	K.Dorney	D.Hill	G.Washington	J.Komlo	D.Bussey	B.Robinson
1980	M.Clark	F.Scott	Baldischwiler	H.Elias	A.Fowler	R.Bolinger	K.Dorney	D.Hill	L.Thompson	G.Danielson	B.Sims	D.Bussey
1981	M.Clark	F.Scott	Baldischwiler	H.Elias	A.Fowler	R.Bolinger	K.Dorney	D.Hill	L.Thompson	E.Hipple	B.Sims	D.Bussey
1982	M.Clark	F.Scott	Baldischwiler	H.Elias	A.Fowler	R.Bolinger	K.Dorney	D.Hill	L.Thompson	G.Danielson	B.Sims	D.Bussey
1983	M.Clark	M.Nichols	C.Dieterich	H.Elias	S.Mott	D.Greco	K.Dorney	U.Norris	L.Thompson	E.Hipple	B.Sims	J.Jones
1984	M.Clark	M.Nichols	D.Laster	C.Dieterich	A.Fowler	D.Greco	K.Dorney	R.Rubick	L.Thompson	G.Danielson	B.Sims	J.Jones
1985	D.Rogers	M.Nichols	L.Brown	C.Dieterich	S.Mott	D.Jones	K.Dorney	D.Lewis	L.Thompson	E.Hipple	W.Montgomery	J.Jones
1986	D.Rogers	J.Chadwick	L.Brown	H.Salem	S.Mott	K.Dorney	R.Strenger	J.Giles	C.Bland	E.Hipple	G.James	J.Jones
1987	D.Rogers	P.Mandley	L.Brown	S.Barrows	S.Mott	K.Glover	H.Salem	R.Rubick	J.Chadwick	C.Long	G.James	J.Jones
1988	D.Rogers	P.Mandley	L.Brown	K.Glover	S.Mott	J.Milinchik	H.Salem	P.Carter	J.Chadwick	R.Hilger	G.James	J.Jones
1989	W.Fontes	R.Johnson	L.Brown	E.Andolsek	K.Glover	K.Dallafior	H.Salem	J.Phillips+	W.Stanley	R.Peete	B.Sanders	R.Clark+
1990	W.Fontes	R.Johnson	L.Brown	E.Andolsek	K.Glover	K.Dallafior	H.Salem	J.Campbell+	T.Greer	R.Peete	B.Sanders	R.Clark+
1991	W.Fontes	B.Perriman	L.Brown	E.Andolsek	K.Glover	M.Utley	E.Sanders	M.Farr+	R.Clark	R.Peete	B.Sanders	W.Green+
1992	W.Fontes	B.Perriman	L.Brown	S.Bouwens	K.Glover	K.Dallafior	S.Conover	M.Farr+	H.Moore	R.Peete	B.Sanders	W.Green+
1993	W.Fontes	B.Perriman	L.Brown	D.Richards	K.Glover	B.Fralic	D.Lutz	R.Holman	H.Moore	R.Peete	B.Sanders	W.Green+
1994	W.Fontes	B.Perriman	L.Brown	S.Bouwens	K.Glover	D.Widell	D.Lutz	R.Hall	H.Moore	S.Mitchell	B.Sanders	T.Hallock*
1995	W.Fontes	B.Perriman	L.Brown	D.Widell	K.Glover	D.Lutz	Z.Moss	D.Sloan	H.Moore	S.Mitchell	B.Sanders	J.Morton+
1996	W.Fontes	B.Perriman	R.Roberts	M.Compton	K.Glover	J.Hartings	Z.Moss	P.Metzelaars	H.Moore	S.Mitchell	B.Sanders	J.Morton+
1997	B.Ross	J.Morton	R.Roberts	M.Compton	K.Glover	J.Hartings	L.Tharpe	D.Sloan	H.Moore	S.Mitchell	B.Sanders	T.Vardell
1998	B.Ross	J.Morton	R.Roberts	M.Compton	J.Pyne	J.Hartings	L.Tharpe	W.Rasby	H.Moore	C.Batch	B.Sanders	T.Vardell
1999	B.Ross	J.Morton	R.Roberts	T.Semple	M.Compton	J.Hartings	B.Brooks	D.Sloan	G.Crowell	C.Batch	G.Hill	Schlesinger
2000	B.Ross	J.Morton	R.Roberts	T.Semple	M.Compton	J.Hartings	A.Gibson	D.Sloan	H.Moore	C.Batch	J.Stewart	Schlesinger
2001	Mornhinweg	J.Morton	J.Backus	T.Semple	E.Beverly	B.Stai	M.Joyce	D.Sloan	L.Foster	C.Batch	J.Stewart	Schlesinger
2002	Mornhinweg	B.Schroeder	J.Backus	T.Semple	D.Raiola	R.Brown	S.McDougle	M.Ricks	A.Hakim	J.Harrington	J.Stewart	Schlesinger
2003	S.Mariucci	B.Schroeder	J.Backus	E.Beverly	D.Raiola	R.Brown	S.McDougle	Fitzsimmons	A.Hakim	J.Harrington	S.Bryson	Schlesinger
2004	S.Mariucci	R.Williams	J.Backus	D.Loverne	D.Raiola	D.Woody	S.McDougle	S.Alexander	T.Streets	J.Harrington	K.Jones	Schlesinger
2005	S.Mariucci	R.Williams	J.Backus	K.Kosier	D.Raiola	D.Woody	K.Butler	M.Pollard	S.Vines	J.Harrington	K.Jones	Schlesinger

YEAR	LDE	LDT/NT	RDT/RDE	RDE/LOLB	LLB/LILB	MLB/RILB	RLB/ROLB	LCB	RCB	SS/LS	FS/RS	FINISH	
1970	R.Jackson	P.Smith	D.Costa	P.Duranko	C.Cunningham	F.Forsberg	D.Washington	C.Gordon	B.Thompson	C.Greer	P.Martha	4aw	5-8-1
1971	R.Jackson	D.Costa	P.Smith	L.Alzado	D.Washington	F.Forsberg	C.Myrtle	L.Mitchell	B.Thompson	C.Greer	G.Saimes	4aw	4-9-1
1972	L.Voss	P.Duranko	P.Smith	L.Alzado	F.Forsberg	T.Graham	C.Myrtle	L.Mitchell	R.Montgomery	C.Greer	S.Preece	3aw	5-9
1973	P.Duranko	P.Smith	B.Chavous	L.Alzado	B.Laskey	T.Graham	R.May	L.Mitchell	C.Jones	B.Thompson	C.Greer	2aw	7-5-2
1974	B.Chavous	J.Grant	P.Duranko	L.Alzado	B.Laskey	R.May	T.Jackson	J.Rowser	C.Jones	B.Thompson	C.Greer	2aw	7-6-1
1975	B.Chavous	J.Grant	P.Smith	L.Alzado	T.Jackson	R.Gradishar	R.May	L.Wright	C.Jones	B.Thompson	J.Rowser	2aw	6-8
1976	B.Chavous	R.Carter	P.Smith*	B.Swenson	J.Rizzo	R.Gradishar	T.Jackson	L.Wright	C.Jones	B.Thompson	J.Rowser	2aw	9-5
1977	B.Chavous	R.Carter	L.Alzado*	B.Swenson	J.Rizzo	R.Gradishar	T.Jackson	L.Wright	S.Foley	B.Thompson	B.Jackson	1aw	12-2 dcs
1978	B.Chavous	R.Carter	L.Alzado*	B.Swenson	J.Rizzo	R.Gradishar	T.Jackson	L.Wright	S.Foley	B.Thompson	B.Jackson	1aw	10-6 d
1979	B.Chavous	R.Carter	B.Manor*	B.Swenson	J.Rizzo	R.Gradishar	T.Jackson	L.Wright	S.Foley	B.Thompson	B.Jackson	2aw	10-6 w
1980	B.Chavous	R.Carter	B.Manor*	R.Nairne	L.Evans	R.Gradishar	T.Jackson	L.Wright	A.Kyle	B.Thompson	S.Foley	3aw	8-8
1981	B.Chavous	R.Carter	R.Jones*	B.Swenson	L.Evans	R.Gradishar	T.Jackson	L.Wright	A.Kyle	B.Thompson	S.Foley	2aw	10-6 #
1982	B.Chavous	R.Carter	R.Jones*	J.Ryan	L.Evans	R.Gradishar	T.Jackson	L.Wright	A.Kyle	D.Smith	M.Harden	12a	2-7
1983	B.Chavous	R.Carter	R.Jones*	J.Ryan	R.Gradishar	S.Busick	T.Jackson	L.Wright	M.Harden	D.Smith	S.Foley	3aw	9-7 #w
1984	B.Chavous	R.Carter	R.Jones*	J.Ryan	R.Dennison	S.Busick	T.Jackson	L.Wright	M.Harden	D.Smith	S.Foley	1aw	13-3 d
1985	B.Chavous	R.Carter	R.Jones*	J.Ryan	Mecklenburg	S.Busick	K.Woodard	L.Wright	M.Harden	D.Smith	S.Foley	2aw	11-5 #
1986	A.Townsend	G.Kragen	R.Jones*	J.Ryan	Mecklenburg	R.Hunley	T.Jackson	L.Wright	M.Harden	D.Smith	S.Foley	1aw	11-5 dcs
1987	A.Townsend	G.Kragen	R.Jones*	S.Fletcher	Mecklenburg	R.Hunley	J.Ryan	M.Haynes	M.Harden	D.Smith	T.Lilly	1aw	10-4-1 dcs
1988	W.Bowyer	G.Kragen	A.Townsend*	S.Fletcher	Mecklenburg	R.Dennison	J.Ryan	M.Haynes	J.Castille	D.Smith	M.Harden	2aw	8-8
1989	A.Carreker	G.Kragen	A.Townsend*	S.Fletcher	Mecklenburg	R.Dennison	M.Brooks	T.Braxton	W.Henderson	D.Smith	S.Atwater	1aw	11-5 dcs
1990	W.Powers	G.Kragen	R.Holmes*	S.Fletcher	Mecklenburg	M.Munford	M.Brooks	R.Robbins	W.Henderson	D.Smith	S.Atwater	5aw	5-11
1991	W.Powers	G.Kragen	R.Holmes*	S.Fletcher	Mecklenburg	M.Croel	M.Brooks	T.Braxton	W.Henderson	D.Smith	S.Atwater	1aw	12-4 dc
1992	B.Sochia	G.Kragen	K.Walker*	M.Croel	Mecklenburg	M.Brooks	S.Fletcher	T.Braxton	W.Henderson	D.Smith	S.Atwater	3aw	8-8
1993	D.Williams	G.Kragen	S.Dronett*	M.Croel	Mecklenburg	D.Wyman	S.Fletcher	T.Braxton	C.Dimry	D.Smith	S.Atwater	3aw	9-7 #w
1994	S.Dronett	T.Washington	H.Hasselbach	S.Fletcher	M.Croel	Mecklenburg	E.Alexander	B.Smith	R.Crockett	S.Atwater	D.Smith	4aw	7-9
1995	H.Hasselbach	J.Jones	M.Perry	S.Fletcher	E.Alexander	D.Wyman	A.Aldridge	R.Crockett	L.Washington	T.Braxton	S.Atwater	3aw	8-8
1996	D.Williams	M.Lodish	M.Perry	A.Williams	B.Romanowski	A.Aldridge	J.Mobley	R.Crockett	L.Washington	T.Braxton	S.Atwater	1aw	13-3 d
1997	N.Smith	K.Traylor	M.Perry	A.Williams	B.Romanowski	A.Aldridge	J.Mobley	R.Crockett	D.Gordon	T.Braxton	S.Atwater	2aw	12-4 wdcs*
1998	N.Smith	K.Traylor	T.Pryce	M.Tanuvasa	B.Romanowski	G.Cadrez	J.Mobley	R.Crockett	D.Gordon	E.Brown	S.Atwater	1aw	14-2 dcs*
1999	N.Smith	K.Traylor	T.Pryce	M.Tanuvasa	B.Romanowski	A.Wilson	G.Cadrez	R.Crockett	D.Carter	T.Braxton	E.Brown	5aw	6-10
2000	M.Tanuvasa	K.Traylor	T.Pryce	K.Pittman	B.Romanowski	A.Wilson	J.Mobley	R.Crockett	T.Buckley	B.Jenkins	E.Brown	2aw	11-5 w
2001	K.Washington	C.McGlockton	T.Pryce	K.Pittman	B.Romanowski	A.Wilson	J.Mobley	D.O'Neal	D.Walker	K.Kennedy	E.Brown	3aw	8-8
2002	T.Pryce	L.Dalton	C.McGlockton	K.Pittman	J.Mobley	A.Wilson	I.Gold	D.O'Neal	D.Walker	K.Kennedy	I.Reese	2aw	9-7 #
2003	T.Pryce	M.Fatafehi	D.Holland	B.Berry	J.Sykes	A.Wilson	D.Spragan	L.Walls	K.Herndon	K.Kennedy	N.Ferguson	2aw	10-6 #w
2004	M.Coleman	M.Fatafehi	M.Pope	R.Hayward	D.Spragan	A.Wilson	D.Williams	C.Bailey	K.Herndon	K.Kennedy	J.Lynch	2aw	10-6 w
2005	C.Brown	M.Myers	G.Warren	T.Pryce	D.J.Williams	A.Wilson	I.Gold	C.Bailey	D.Williams	N.Ferguson	J.Lynch	1aw	13-3 dc

1950	B.Hafen	T.McGraw	J.Prchlik	J.Cain	J.Lininger	L.Bingaman+	B.Schroll	B.Smith	C.Self	G.Krall	D.Doll	4nn	6-6
1951	J.Doran	T.McGraw	J.Prchlik	L.Hart	D.Flanagan	L.Bingaman+	L.Torgeson	C.Self	B.Smith	Christiansen	D.Doll	2nn	7-4-1
1952	J.Doran	T.McGraw	J.Prchlik	B.Earon	D.Flanagan	L.Bingaman+	L.Torgeson	J.David	B.Smith	Christiansen	Y.Lary	1nn	9-3 cl*
1953	J.Cain	T.McGraw	J.Prchlik	B.Earon	J.Schmidt	L.Bingaman+	L.Torgeson	J.David	B.Smith	Christiansen	Y.Lary	1nw	10-2 l*
1954	J.Doran	B.Miller	G.Mains	J.Cain	J.Schmidt	L.Bingaman+	L.Torgeson	J.David	C.Karilivacz	Christiansen	B.Stits	1nw	9-2-1 l
1955	G.Mains	B.Miller	D.McCord	J.Cain	J.Schmidt	L.Creekmur+	S.Gandee	J.David	C.Karilivacz	Christiansen	B.Stits	6nw	3-9
1956	D.McCord	R.Krouse	B.Miller	G.Mains	S.Gandee	J.Schmidt	B.Long	J.David	C.Karilivacz	Christiansen	Y.Lary	2nw	9-3
1957	D.McCord	B.Miller	G.Mains	G.Cronin	B.Long	J.Schmidt	R.Zatkoff	J.David	T.Barr	Christiansen	Y.Lary	1nw	8-4 cl*
1958	D.McCord	A.Karras	G.Mains	G.Cronin	B.Long	J.Schmidt	W.Walker	J.David	T.Barr	G.Lowe	Y.Lary	5nw	4-7-1
1959	D.McCord	A.Karras	G.Mains	B.Glass	B.Long	J.Schmidt	W.Walker	J.David	T.Barr	G.Lowe	Y.Lary	5nw	3-8-1
1960	D.McCord	A.Karras	R.Brown	B.Glass	Brettschneider	J.Schmidt	W.Walker	N.Lane	D.LeBeau	G.Lowe	Y.Lary	2nw	7-5
1961	D.McCord	A.Karras	R.Brown	B.Glass	Brettschneider	J.Schmidt	W.Walker	N.Lane	B.Maher	G.Lowe	Y.Lary	2nw	8-5-1
1962	D.McCord	A.Karras	R.Brown	S.Williams	Brettschneider	J.Schmidt	W.Walker	N.Lane	D.LeBeau	G.Lowe	Y.Lary	2nw	11-3
1963	D.McCord	F.Peters	R.Brown	S.Williams	M.Messner	D.Gaubatz	W.Walker	N.Lane	D.LeBeau	B.Maher	Y.Lary	4nw	5-8-1
1964	D.McCord	A.Karras	R.Brown	S.Williams	E.Clark	D.Gaubatz	W.Walker	D.LeBeau	B.Thompson	B.Maher	Y.Lary	4nw	7-5-2
1965	D.McCord	A.Karras	R.Brown	S.Williams	E.Clark	J.Schmidt	W.Walker	D.LeBeau	B.Thompson	B.Maher	W.Rasmussen	6nw	6-7-1
1966	D.McCord	A.Karras	R.Brown	L.Hand	M.Lucci	E.Clark	W.Hilgenberg	D.LeBeau	B.Smith	B.Maher	B.Thompson	6nw	4-9-1
1967	D.McCord	A.Karras	J.Rush	L.Hand	E.Clark	M.Lucci	W.Walker	L.Barney	D.LeBeau	B.Maher	T.Vaughn	3nco	5-7-2
1968	J.Baker	A.Karras	J.Rush	J.Robb	P.Naumoff	M.Lucci	W.Walker	L.Barney	D.LeBeau	M.Weger	T.Vaughn	4nco	4-8-2
1969	J.Robb	A.Karras	J.Rush	L.Hand	P.Naumoff	M.Lucci	W.Walker	L.Barney	D.LeBeau	M.Weger	T.Vaughn	2nco	9-4-1
1970	J.Mitchell	A.Karras	J.Rush	L.Hand	P.Naumoff	M.Lucci	W.Walker	L.Barney	D.LeBeau	M.Weger	W.Rasmussen	2nc	10-4 w
1971	J.Mitchell	D.Evey	J.Rush	L.Hand	P.Naumoff	M.Lucci	W.Walker	L.Barney	D.LeBeau	M.Weger	T.Vaughn	2nc	7-6-1
1972	J.Mitchell	L.Woods	B.Bell	L.Hand	P.Naumoff	M.Lucci	W.Walker	L.Barney	R.Redmond	M.Weger	D.LeBeau	2nc	8-5-1
1973	K.Sanders	H.Orvis	B.Bell	L.Hand	P.Naumoff	M.Lucci	C.Weaver	L.Barney	L.Johnson	M.Weger	D.Jauron	2nc	6-7-1
1974	K.Sanders	H.Orvis	J.Mitchell	L.Hand	P.Naumoff	J.Laslavic	C.Weaver	L.Barney	L.Johnson	C.West	D.Jauron	2nc	7-7
1975	K.Sanders	H.Orvis	L.Hand	B.Howard	P.Naumoff	J.Laslavic	C.Weaver	L.Barney	L.Johnson	C.West	D.Jauron	2nc	7-7
1976	K.Sanders	J.Mitchell	L.Hand	B.Howard	P.Naumoff	J.Laslavic	C.Weaver	L.Barney	L.Johnson	C.West	J.Hunter	3nc	6-8
1977	K.Sanders	H.Orvis	D.English	J.Mitchell	P.Naumoff	E.O'Neil	C.Weaver	J.Hunter	L.Barney	C.West	D.Jauron	3nc	6-8
1978	D.Pureifory	J.Woodcock	D.English	A.Baker	P.Naumoff	E.O'Neil	C.Weaver	W.Williams	L.Bradley	M.Burns	J.Allen	3nc	7-9
1979	D.Pureifory	D.Gallagher	D.English	A.Baker	E.O'Neil	C.Weaver	J.Harrell	W.Williams	L.Bradley	J.Allen	J.Hunter	5nc	2-14
1980	D.Pureifory	W.Gay	J.Mendenhall	A.Baker	C.Weaver	K.Fantetti	S.White	W.Smith	J.Hunter	J.Allen	R.Oldham	2nc	9-7 #
1981	D.Pureifory	W.Gay	D.English	A.Baker	G.Cobb	K.Fantetti	S.White	W.Smith	J.Hunter	R.Oldham	J.Allen	2nc	8-8
1982	D.Pureifory	W.Gay	D.English	A.Baker	G.Cobb	K.Fantetti	S.White	W.Smith	J.Hunter	R.Oldham	A.Hall	8n	4-5 #p
1983	C.Green	M.Dawson	D.English	W.Gay	G.Cobb	K.Fantetti	J.Williams	B.Watkins	A.Latimer	A.Hall	W.Graham	1nc	9-7 d
1984	M.Cofer	C.Green	D.English	W.Gay	G.Cobb	K.Fantetti	J.Williams	B.Watkins	B.McNorton	A.Hall	W.Graham	4nc	4-11-1
1985	E.Williams	D.English	W.Gay*	J.Williams	A.Curley	K.Allerman	A.King	B.Watkins	B.McNorton	D.Johnson	W.Graham	3nc	7-9
1986	K.Ferguson	E.Williams	W.Gay*	J.Williams	J.Harrell	V.Maxwell	M.Cofer	D.Galloway	B.McNorton	D.Johnson	D.Mitchell	3nc	5-11
1987	E.Williams	J.Ball	K.Ferguson*	J.Williams	S.Robinson	D.Gibson	M.Cofer	D.Galloway	B.McNorton	J.Griffin	R.Cherry	4nc	4-11
1988	E.Williams	J.Ball	K.Ferguson*	G.Jamison	C.Spielman	D.Gibson	M.Cofer	J.Holmes	B.McNorton	B.Blades	D.Mitchell	4nc	4-12
1989	E.Williams	J.Ball	K.Brooks*	J.Williams	C.Spielman	V.Jones	M.Cofer	T.Taylor	J.Holmes	B.Blades	W.White	3nc	7-9
1990	D.Owens	J.Ball	K.Ferguson*	J.Williams	C.Spielman	D.Gibson	M.Cofer	B.McNorton	L.Irvin	W.White	B.Blades	2nc	6-10
1991	M.Spindler	J.Ball	D.Owens*	G.Jamison	C.Spielman	D.Gibson	T.Hayworth	R.Crockett	M.Jenkins	W.White	B.Blades	1nc	12-4 dc
1992	M.Spindler	J.Ball	K.Pritchett*	G.Jamison	C.Spielman	D.Gibson	M.Cofer	R.Crockett	M.Jenkins	W.White	B.Blades	3nc	5-11
1993	M.Spindler	L.Pete	D.Owens*	G.Jamison	C.Spielman	D.Gibson	P.Swilling	R.Crockett	K.Scott	W.White	H.Colon	1nc	10-6 e
1994	R.Porcher	M.Spindler	K.Pritchett*	B.Thomas	C.Spielman	M.Johnson	T.Scroggins	R.McNeil	R.Massey	W.Clay	B.Blades	3nc	9-7 #w
1995	L.Elliss	H.Thomas	R.Porcher	T.Scroggins	T.Hayworth	C.Spielman	M.Johnson	R.McNeil	C.Raymond	W.Clay	B.Blades	2nc	10-6 w
1996	R.Porcher	H.Thomas	L.Elliss	K.Waldroup	A.London	P.Johnson	R.Brown	R.McNeil	C.Raymond	B.Blades	V.Malone	5nc	5-11
1997	R.Porcher	M.Wells	L.Elliss	K.Waldroup	G.Jamison	S.Boyd	R.Brown	B.Westbrook	C.Raymond	R.Rice	M.Carrier	3nc	9-7 w
1998	R.Porcher	D.Owens	L.Elliss	K.Waldroup	Fredrickson	S.Boyd	A.Aldridge	B.Westbrook	T.Fair	R.Rice	M.Carrier	4nc	5-11
1999	R.Porcher	J.Jones	L.Elliss	T.Scroggins	A.Aldridge	S.Boyd	C.Claiborne	R.Bailey	T.Fair	R.Rice	M.Carrier	3nc	8-8 #w
2000	R.Porcher	J.Jones	L.Elliss	T.Scroggins	A.Aldridge	S.Boyd	C.Claiborne	B.Westbrook	T.Fair	R.Rice	K.Schulz	3nc	9-7
2001	R.Porcher	S.Rogers	L.Elliss	T.Scroggins	A.Aldridge	C.Claiborne	B.Green	T.Lyght	T.Fair	L.Campbell	K.Schulz	5nc	2-14
2002	R.Porcher	S.Rogers	L.Elliss	J.Hall	B.Green	C.Claiborne	D.Curry	T.Lyght	C.Cash	C.Harris	B.Walker	4nn	3-13
2003	R.Porcher	D.Wilkinson	S.Rogers	J.Hall	B.Green	E.Holmes	B.Bailey	O.Smith	D.Bly	C.Harris	B.Walker	4nn	5-11
2004	C.Redding	D.Wilkinson	S.Rogers	J.Hall	J.Davis	T.Lehman	E.Holmes	F.Bryant	D.Bly	B.Walker	B.Marion	3nn	6-10
2005	C.Redding	S.Rogers	D.Wilkinson	J.Hall	B.Bailey	E.Holmes	J.Davis	A.Goodman	D.Bly	K.Kennedy	T.Holt	3nn	5-11

838 THE OFFENSIVE STARTERS: 1950–PRESENT

GREEN BAY PACKERS

YEAR	COACH	WR/LE	LT	LG	C	RG	RT	TE/RE	WR/FL	QB	RB/LH	FB
1950	G.Ronzani	A.Baldwin	D.Wildung	B.Burris	C.Tonnemaker	R.DiPierro	J.Spencer	T.Cook	B.Grimes	T.Rote	B.Reid	T.Canadeo
1951	G.Ronzani	B.Mann	W.Manley	B.Burris	J.Rhodemyre	H.Nichols	J.Spencer	R.Pelfrey	B.Grimes	T.Rote	T.Canadeo	F.Cone
1952	G.Ronzani	B.Mann	D.Afflis	S.Ruzich	J.Rhodemyre	D.Stephenson	S.Dowden	B.Howton	B.Reid	B.Parilli	T.Canadeo	F.Cone
1953	G.Ronzani	B.Mann	D.Afflis	S.Ruzich	D.Stephenson	B.Brown	G.Cifelli	B.Howton	A.Carmichael	B.Parilli	B.Reid	F.Cone
1954	Blackbourn	M.McGee	L.Szafaryn	A.Barry	J.Ringo	B.Brown	A.Hunter	B.Howton	A.Carmichael	T.Rote	B.Reid	H.Ferguson
1955	Blackbourn	G.Knafelc	L.Szafaryn	J.Skibinski	J.Ringo	B.Brown	T.Dahms	B.Howton	J.Johnson	T.Rote	B.Reid	H.Ferguson
1956	Blackbourn	G.Knafelc	B.Skoronski	J.Skibinski	J.Ringo	B.Brown	J.Sandusky	B.Howton	A.Carmichael	T.Rote	J.Johnson	H.Ferguson
1957	Blackbourn	R.Kramer	N.Masters	A.Barry	J.Ringo	J.Salsbury	O.Spencer	B.Howton	H.Ferguson	B.Starr	D.McIlhenny	P.Hornung
1958	R.McLean	M.McGee	N.Masters	J.Salsbury	J.Ringo	J.Kramer	O.Spencer	B.Howton	D.McIlhenny	B.Starr	P.Hornung	J.Taylor
1959	V.Lombardi	M.McGee	B.Skoronski	F.Thurston	J.Ringo	J.Kramer	F.Gregg	G.Knafelc	B.Dowler	L.McHan	P.Hornung	J.Taylor
1960	V.Lombardi	M.McGee	B.Skoronski	F.Thurston	J.Ringo	J.Kramer	F.Gregg	G.Knafelc	B.Dowler	B.Starr	P.Hornung	J.Taylor
1961	V.Lombardi	M.McGee	B.Skoronski	F.Thurston	J.Ringo	J.Kramer	F.Gregg	R.Kramer	B.Dowler	B.Starr	P.Hornung	J.Taylor
1962	V.Lombardi	M.McGee	B.Skoronski	F.Thurston	J.Ringo	J.Kramer	F.Gregg	R.Kramer	B.Dowler	B.Starr	P.Hornung	J.Taylor
1963	V.Lombardi	M.McGee	B.Skoronski	F.Thurston	J.Ringo	J.Kramer	F.Gregg	R.Kramer	B.Dowler	B.Starr	T.Moore	J.Taylor
1964	V.Lombardi	M.McGee	N.Masters	F.Thurston	B.Skoronski	D.Grimm	F.Gregg	R.Kramer	B.Dowler	B.Starr	P.Hornung	J.Taylor
1965	V.Lombardi	B.Dowler	B.Skoronski	F.Gregg	K.Bowman	J.Kramer	S.Wright	M.Fleming	C.Dale	B.Starr	P.Hornung	J.Taylor
1966	V.Lombardi	M.Fleming	B.Skoronski	F.Thurston	B.Curry	J.Kramer	F.Gregg	C.Dale	B.Dowler	B.Starr	P.Hornung	J.Taylor
1967	V.Lombardi	B.Dowler	B.Skoronski	G.Gillingham	K.Bowman	J.Kramer	F.Gregg	M.Fleming	C.Dale	B.Starr	E.Pitts	J.Grabowski
1968	P.Bengston	B.Dowler	B.Skoronski	G.Gillingham	K.Bowman	J.Kramer	F.Gregg	M.Fleming	C.Dale	B.Starr	D.Anderson	J.Grabowski
1969	P.Bengston	B.Dowler	F.Peay	B.Lueck	K.Bowman	G.Gillingham	F.Gregg	M.Fleming	C.Dale	B.Starr	T.Williams	J.Grabowski
1970	P.Bengston	C.Dale	F.Peay	B.Lueck	K.Bowman	G.Gillingham	D.Himes	J.Hilton	J.Clancy	B.Starr	D.Anderson	J.Grabowski
1971	D.Devine	C.Dale	F.Peay	B.Lueck	K.Bowman	G.Gillingham	D.Himes	R.McGeorge	J.Spilis	S.Hunter	D.Anderson	Brockington
1972	D.Devine	L.Glass	B.Hayhoe	B.Lueck	K.Bowman	M.Snider	D.Himes	L.Garrett	C.Dale	S.Hunter	M.Lane	Brockington
1973	D.Devine	J.Staggers	M.Snider	B.Lueck	K.Bowman	G.Gillingham	D.Himes	R.McGeorge	B.Smith	S.Hunter	M.Lane	Brockington
1974	D.Devine	J.Staggers	H.Schuh	B.Lueck	L.McCarren	G.Gillingham	D.Himes	R.McGeorge	B.Smith	J.Tagge	M.Lane	Brockington
1975	B.Starr	S.Odom	E.McMillan	B.Van Dyke	L.McCarren	K.Wortman	D.Himes	R.McGeorge	B.Smith	J.Hadl	W.Harrell	Brockington
1976	B.Starr	S.Odom	M.Koncar	B.Van Dyke	L.McCarren	G.Gillingham	D.Himes	R.McGeorge	K.Payne	L.Dickey	W.Harrell	Brockington
1977	B.Starr	S.Odom	M.Koncar	S.Knutson	L.McCarren	M.Jackson	D.Himes	R.McGeorge	O.Smith	L.Dickey	E.Torkelson	B.Smith
1978	B.Starr	J.Lofton	T.Stokes	D.Gofourth	L.McCarren	M.Jackson	G.Koch	R.McGeorge	A.Thompson	D.Whitehurst	T.Middleton	B.Smith
1979	B.Starr	J.Lofton	M.Koncar	D.Gofourth	L.McCarren	L.Harris	G.Koch	P.Coffman	A.Thompson	D.Whitehurst	T.Middleton	E.Torkelson
1980	B.Starr	J.Lofton	T.Stokes	D.Gofourth	L.McCarren	L.Harris	G.Koch	P.Coffman	A.Thompson	L.Dickey	E.Ivery	G.Ellis
1981	B.Starr	J.Lofton	M.Koncar	D.Gofourth	L.McCarren	L.Harris	G.Koch	P.Coffman	J.Jefferson	L.Dickey	H.Huckleby	G.Ellis
1982	B.Starr	J.Lofton	K.Swanke	D.Gofourth	L.McCarren	L.Harris	G.Koch	P.Coffman	J.Jefferson	L.Dickey	E.Ivery	G.Ellis
1983	B.Starr	J.Lofton	K.Swanke	D.Drechsler	L.McCarren	S.Kitson	G.Koch	P.Coffman	J.Jefferson	L.Dickey	E.Ivery	G.Ellis
1984	F.Gregg	J.Lofton	K.Swanke	T.Huffman	L.McCarren	R.Hallstrom	G.Koch	P.Coffman	J.Jefferson	L.Dickey	G.Ellis	J.Clark
1985	F.Gregg	J.Lofton	K.Swanke	R.Moran	M.Cannon	R.Hallstrom	G.Koch	P.Coffman	P.Epps	L.Dickey	E.Ivery	J.Clark
1986	F.Gregg	J.Lofton	K.Ruettgers	T.Neville	K.Swanke	R.Hallstrom	A.Veingard	D.Ross	P.Epps	R.Wright	K.Davis	P.Carruth
1987	F.Gregg	P.Epps	K.Ruettgers	R.Moran	M.Cannon	R.Hallstrom	K.Uecker	E.West	W.Stanley	R.Wright	K.Davis	J.Clark
1988	L.Infante	S.Sharpe	K.Ruettgers	R.Moran	M.Cannon	R.Hallstrom	K.Uecker	E.West	W.Stanley	D.Majkowski	K.Woodside	B.Fullwood
1989	L.Infante	P.Kemp	K.Ruettgers	R.Moran	B.Bush	R.Hallstrom	A.Veingard	E.West	S.Sharpe	D.Majkowski	K.Woodside	B.Fullwood
1990	L.Infante	P.Kemp	K.Ruettgers	B.Ard	J.Campen	K.Uecker	T.Mandarich	E.West	S.Sharpe	D.Majkowski	K.Woodside	M.Haddix
1991	L.Infante	P.Kemp	L.Cheek	R.Moran	J.Campen	R.Hallstrom	T.Mandarich	E.West	S.Sharpe	D.Majkowski	K.Woodside	D.Thompson
1992	M.Holmgren	S.Beach	K.Ruettgers	F.Winters	J.Campen	R.Hallstrom	T.Robbins	J.Harris	S.Sharpe	B.Favre	V.Workman	H.Sydney
1993	M.Holmgren	M.Clayton	K.Ruettgers	D.Widell	F.Winters	H.Galbreath	T.Robbins	J.Harris	S.Sharpe	B.Favre	D.Thompson	E.Bennett
1994	M.Holmgren	R.Brooks	K.Ruettgers	G.McIntyre	F.Winters	H.Galbreath	J.Sims	E.West	S.Sharpe	B.Favre	R.Cobb	E.Bennett
1995	M.Holmgren	M.Ingram	K.Ruettgers	A.Taylor	F.Winters	H.Galbreath	E.Dotson	M.Chmura	R.Brooks	B.Favre	D.Levens	E.Bennett
1996	M.Holmgren	A.Freeman	J.Michels	A.Taylor	F.Winters	A.Timmerman	E.Dotson	M.Chmura	R.Brooks	B.Favre	E.Bennett	W.Henderson
1997	M.Holmgren	A.Freeman	R.Verba	A.Taylor	F.Winters	A.Timmerman	E.Dotson	M.Chmura	R.Brooks	B.Favre	D.Levens	W.Henderson
1998	M.Holmgren	A.Freeman	R.Verba	M.Rivera	F.Winters	A.Timmerman	E.Dotson	M.Chmura	R.Brooks	B.Favre	T.Jervey	W.Henderson
1999	R.Rhodes	B.Schroeder	R.Verba	M.Wahle	F.Winters	M.Rivera	E.Dotson	T.Davis	A.Freeman	B.Favre	D.Levens	W.Henderson
2000	M.Sherman	B.Schroeder	C.Clifton	R.Verba	F.Winters	M.Rivera	M.Tauscher	B.Franks	A.Freeman	B.Favre	A.Green	T.Davis*
2001	M.Sherman	B.Schroeder	C.Clifton	M.Wahle	M.Flanagan	M.Rivera	M.Tauscher	B.Franks	A.Freeman	B.Favre	A.Green	W.Henderson
2002	M.Sherman	D.Driver	M.Flanagan	M.Wahle	F.Winters	M.Rivera	E.Dotson	B.Franks	T.Glenn	B.Favre	A.Green	W.Henderson
2003	M.Sherman	R.Ferguson	C.Clifton	M.Wahle	M.Flanagan	M.Rivera	M.Tauscher	B.Franks	D.Driver	B.Favre	A.Green	W.Henderson
2004	M.Sherman	D.Driver	C.Clifton	M.Wahle	G.Ruegamer	M.Rivera	M.Tauscher	B.Franks	J.Walker	B.Favre	A.Green	W.Henderson
2005	M.Sherman	R.Ferguson	C.Clifton	S.Wells	M.Flanagan	W.Whitticker	M.Tauscher	D.Martin	D.Driver	B.Favre	S.Gado	W.Henderson

HOUSTON TEXANS

YEAR	COACH	WR/LE	LT	LG	C	RG	RT	TE/RE	WR/FL	QB	RB/LH	FB
2002	D.Capers	J.Gaffney	C.Pitts	D.Graham	S.McKinney	F.Weary	R.Young	J.Holloway	C.Bradford	D.Carr	J.Wells	J.Baxter
2003	D.Capers	A.Johnson	C.Pitts	T.Washington	S.McKinney	Z.Wiegert	G.Randall	J.Holloway	J.Gaffney	D.Carr	D.Davis	M.Norris
2004	D.Capers	A.Johnson	S.Wand	C.Pitts	S.McKinney	Z.Wiegert	T.Wade	M.Bruener	C.Bradford	D.Carr	D.Davis	J.Gaffney+
2005	D.Capers	A.Johnson	C.Pitts	M.Brown	S.McKinney	Z.Wiegert	T.Wade	M.Bruener	J.Gaffney	D.Carr	D.Davis	M.Norris

INDIANAPOLIS COLTS (Baltimore 1953-69)

YEAR	COACH	WR/LE	LT	LG	C	RG	RT	TE/RE	WR/FL	QB	RB/LH	FB
1953	Molesworth	M.Embree	E.Blandin	D.Barwegan	B.Ecklund	B.Lange	J.Little	D.Edwards	B.Young	F.Enke	G.Taliaferro	J.Huzvar
1954	W.Ewbank	L.Colteryahn	K.Jackson	A.Spinney	B.Nutter	A.Sandusky	J.Little	D.Edwards	B.Young	G.Kerkorian	R.Womble	Z.Toth
1955	W.Ewbank	L.Colteryahn	G.Radosevich	A.Spinney	D.Szymanski	A.Sandusky	G.Preas	Mutscheller	B.Young	G.Shaw	L.Dupre	A.Ameche
1956	W.Ewbank	R.Berry	K.Jackson	A.Spinney	B.Nutter	A.Sandusky	G.Preas	Mutscheller	L.Moore	J.Unitas	L.Dupre	A.Ameche
1957	W.Ewbank	R.Berry	J.Parker	A.Spinney	B.Nutter	A.Sandusky	G.Preas	Mutscheller	L.Moore	J.Unitas	L.Dupre	A.Ameche
1958	W.Ewbank	R.Berry	J.Parker	A.Spinney	B.Nutter	A.Sandusky	G.Preas	Mutscheller	L.Moore	J.Unitas	L.Dupre	A.Ameche
1959	W.Ewbank	R.Berry	J.Parker	A.Spinney	B.Nutter	A.Sandusky	G.Preas	Mutscheller	L.Moore	J.Unitas	M.Sommer	A.Ameche
1960	W.Ewbank	R.Berry	J.Parker	A.Spinney	B.Nutter	A.Sandusky	G.Preas	Mutscheller	L.Moore	J.Unitas	A.Hawkins	A.Ameche
1961	W.Ewbank	R.Berry	J.Parker	P.Pyle	D.Szymanski	A.Sandusky	G.Preas	Mutscheller	L.Moore	J.Unitas	A.Hawkins	J.Perry
1962	W.Ewbank	R.Berry	T.Gilburg	J.Parker	D.Szymanski	A.Sandusky	G.Preas	D.Mackey	J.Orr	J.Unitas	L.Moore	J.Perry
1963	D.Shula	R.Berry	B.Vogel	J.Parker	D.Szymanski	A.Sandusky	G.Preas	J.Mackey	J.Orr	J.Unitas	T.Matte	J.Lockett
1964	D.Shula	R.Berry	B.Vogel	J.Parker	D.Szymanski	A.Sandusky	G.Preas	J.Mackey	J.Orr	J.Unitas	L.Moore	J.Hill
1965	D.Shula	R.Berry	B.Vogel	J.Parker	D.Szymanski	A.Sandusky	G.Preas	J.Mackey	J.Orr	J.Unitas	L.Moore	J.Hill
1966	D.Shula	R.Berry	B.Vogel	D.Sullivan	D.Szymanski	A.Sandusky	J.Parker	J.Mackey	J.Orr	J.Unitas	L.Moore	T.Lorick
1967	D.Shula	R.Berry	B.Vogel	G.Ressler	D.Szymanski	D.Sullivan	S.Ball	J.Mackey	W.Richardson	J.Unitas	T.Matte	T.Lorick
1968	D.Shula	J.Orr	B.Vogel	G.Ressler	B.Curry	D.Sullivan	S.Ball	J.Mackey	W.Richardson	E.Morrall	T.Matte	J.Hill
1969	D.Shula	J.Orr	B.Vogel	G.Ressler	B.Curry	D.Sullivan	S.Ball	J.Mackey	W.Richardson	J.Unitas	T.Matte	J.Hill
1984	F.Kush	T.Porter	S.Wright	B.Utt	R.Donaldson	R.Solt	J.Mills	D.Young	R.Butler	M.Pagel	C.Dickey	R.McMillan
1985	R.Dowhower	W.Capers	C.Hinton	B.Utt	R.Donaldson	R.Solt	Baldischwiler	P.Beach	R.Butler	M.Pagel	G.Wonsley	R.McMillan
1986	R.Dowhower	B.Brooks	C.Hinton	B.Utt	R.Donaldson	R.Solt	K.Call	P.Beach	M.Bouza	J.Trudeau	M.Boyer	R.McMillan
1987	R.Meyer	B.Brooks	C.Hinton	B.Utt	R.Donaldson	R.Solt	K.Call	P.Beach	M.Bouza	J.Trudeau	E.Dickerson	M.Boyer*
1988	R.Meyer	B.Brooks	C.Hinton	R.Dixon	R.Donaldson	B.Utt	J.Patten	P.Beach	C.Verdin	C.Chandler	E.Dickerson	M.Boyer*
1989	R.Meyer	B.Brooks	C.Hinton	R.Dixon	R.Donaldson	B.Utt	K.Call	P.Beach	A.Rison	J.Trudeau	E.Dickerson	A.Bentley
1990	R.Meyer	B.Brooks	Z.Moss	R.Dixon	R.Donaldson	P.Tomberlin	B.Baldinger	P.Beach	J.Hester	J.George	E.Dickerson	A.Bentley
1991	R.Venturi	B.Brooks	Z.Moss	R.Dixon	B.Baldinger	W.Schultz	K.Call	P.Beach	J.Hester	J.George	E.Dickerson	K.Clark*
1992	Marchibroda	R.Langhorne	Z.Moss	R.Dixon	R.Donaldson	R.Solt	K.Call	K.Cash	J.Hester	J.George	A.Johnson	B.Brooks+
1993	Marchibroda	R.Langhorne	W.Wolford	R.Dixon	K.Lowdermilk	W.Schultz	Z.Moss	K.Cash	J.Hester	J.George	R.Potts	A.Johnson
1994	Marchibroda	S.Dawkins	W.Wolford	R.Dixon	K.Lowdermilk	J.Staysniak	Z.Moss	K.Cash	F.Turner	J.Harbaugh	M.Faulk	R.Potts
1995	Marchibroda	S.Dawkins	W.Wolford	R.Dixon	K.Lowdermilk	J.Staysniak	J.Mathews	K.Dilger	F.Turner	J.Harbaugh	M.Faulk	R.Potts
1996	L.Infante	S.Dawkins	K.Vickers	D.Widell	K.Lowdermilk	E.Mahlum	J.Mathews	K.Dilger	M.Harrison	J.Harbaugh	M.Faulk	C.Groce
1997	L.Infante	S.Dawkins	A.Meadows	D.Widell	Leeuwenburg	T.Glenn	T.Mandarich	K.Dilger	M.Harrison	J.Harbaugh	M.Faulk	Z.Crockett

YEAR	LDE	LDT/NT	RDT/RDE	RDE/LOLB	LLB/LILB	MLB/RILB	RLB/ROLB	LCB	RCB	SS/LS	FS/RS	FINISH	
1950	D.Orlich	D.Stansauk	C.McGeary	S.Pritko	C.Schuette	E.Neal+	B.Summerhays	W.Dreyer	B.Forte	R.Steiner	A.Baldwin	5nn	3-9
1951	D.Orlich	D.Wildung	H.Ruetz	A.Wimberly	B.Schroll	D.Afflis+	B.Summerhays	J.Girard	A.Loomis	R.Steiner	H.Davis	5nn	3-9
1952	Martinkovic	D.Hanner	B.Dees	C.Elliott	D.Teteak	W.Serini+	B.Forte	A.Loomis	B.Dillon	C.Self	D.Sandifer	4nn	6-6
1953	Martinkovic	D.Wildung	D.Hanner	C.Elliott	C.Tonnemaker	B.Forester+	B.Forte	A.Loomis	B.Dillon	V.Walker	B.Aldridge	6nw	2-9-1
1954	Martinkovic	J.Helluin	D.Hanner	C.Elliott	C.Tonnemaker	B.Forester+	R.Zatkoff	C.Self	B.Dillon	V.Walker	J.Psaltis	5nw	4-8
1955	Martinkovic	J.Helluin	D.Hanner	N.Borden	T.Bettis	B.Forester+	R.Zatkoff	D.Nix	B.Dillon	V.Walker	B.Bookout	3nw	6-6
1956	Martinkovic	J.Helluin	D.Hanner	N.Borden	T.Bettis	B.Forester+	D.Teteak	H.Gremminger	B.Dillon	V.Walker	B.Bookout	5nw	4-8
1957	C.Massey	J.Helluin	D.Hanner	N.Borden	T.Bettis	S.Palumbo	B.Forester	H.Gremminger	B.Dillon	J.Symank	J.Petitbon	6nw	3-9
1958	N.Borden	D.Hanner	J.Kimmel	J.Temp	T.Bettis	R.Nitschke	B.Forester	H.Gremminger	B.Dillon	J.Whittenton	B.Kinard	6nw	1-10-1
1959	J.Temp	D.Hanner	H.Jordan	B.Quinlan	D.Currie	R.Nitschke	B.Forester	H.Gremminger	J.Whittenton	E.Tunnell	B.Freeman	3nw	7-5
1960	W.Davis	D.Hanner	H.Jordan	B.Quinlan	D.Currie	R.Nitschke	B.Forester	J.Symank	J.Whittenton	E.Tunnell	H.Gremminger	1nw	8-4 l
1961	W.Davis	D.Hanner	H.Jordan	B.Quinlan	D.Currie	R.Nitschke	B.Forester	H.Adderley	J.Whittenton	H.Gremminger	W.Wood	1nw	11-3 l*
1962	W.Davis	D.Hanner	H.Jordan	B.Quinlan	D.Currie	R.Nitschke	B.Forester	H.Adderley	J.Whittenton	H.Gremminger	W.Wood	1nw	13-1 l*
1963	W.Davis	R.Kostelnik	H.Jordan	L.Aldridge	D.Currie	R.Nitschke	B.Forester	H.Adderley	J.Whittenton	H.Gremminger	W.Wood	2nw	11-2-1
1964	W.Davis	R.Kostelnik	H.Jordan	L.Aldridge	D.Robinson	R.Nitschke	L.Caffey	H.Adderley	D.Hart	T.Brown	W.Wood	2nw	8-5-1
1965	W.Davis	R.Kostelnik	H.Jordan	L.Aldridge	D.Robinson	R.Nitschke	L.Caffey	H.Adderley	B.Jeter	W.Wood	T.Brown	1nw	10-3-1 cl*
1966	W.Davis	R.Kostelnik	H.Jordan	L.Aldridge	D.Robinson	R.Nitschke	L.Caffey	H.Adderley	B.Jeter	W.Wood	T.Brown	1nw	12-2 ls*
1967	W.Davis	R.Kostelnik	H.Jordan	L.Aldridge	D.Robinson	R.Nitschke	L.Caffey	H.Adderley	B.Jeter	T.Brown	W.Wood	1nco	9-4-1 cls*
1968	W.Davis	R.Kostelnik	H.Jordan	L.Aldridge	D.Robinson	R.Nitschke	L.Caffey	H.Adderley	B.Jeter	T.Brown	W.Wood	3nco	6-7-1
1969	W.Davis	R.Moore	H.Jordan	L.Aldridge	D.Robinson	R.Nitschke	L.Caffey	H.Adderley	B.Jeter	D.Hart	W.Wood	3nco	8-6
1970	S.Williams	R.Brown	M.McCoy	L.Aldridge	J.Carter	R.Nitschke	F.Carr	K.Ellis	B.Jeter	D.Hart	W.Wood	3nc	6-8
1971	S.Williams	M.McCoy	R.Brown	L.Aldridge	D.Robinson	J.Carter	F.Carr	K.Ellis	A.Matthews	D.Hart	W.Wood	4nc	4-8-2
1972	S.Williams	M.McCoy	R.Brown	A.Roche	D.Robinson	J.Carter	F.Carr	W.Buchanon	K.Ellis	A.Matthews	J.Hill	1nc	10-4 d
1973	S.Williams	M.McCoy	R.Brown	A.Roche	T.MacLeod	J.Carter	F.Carr	P.Smith	K.Ellis	A.Matthews	J.Hill	3nc	5-7-2
1974	S.Williams	M.McCoy	S.Okoniewski	A.Roche	T.Hendricks	J.Carter	F.Carr	W.Buchanon	K.Ellis	A.Matthews	J.Hill	3nc	6-8
1975	S.Williams	M.McCoy	D.Pureifory	A.Roche	T.Toner	J.Carter	F.Carr	P.Smith	K.Ellis	A.Matthews	J.Gray	3nc	4-10
1976	S.Williams	M.McCoy	D.Pureifory	A.Roche	G.Weaver	D.Hansen	F.Carr	W.Buchanon	P.Smith	S.Luke	J.Gray	4nc	5-9
1977	M.Butler	D.Roller	D.Pureifory	B.Barber	T.Toner	J.Carter	F.Carr	W.Buchanon	M.McCoy	S.Luke	J.Gray	4nc	4-10
1978	M.Butler	D.Roller	Barzilauskas	E.Johnson	G.Weaver	M.Hunt	J.Anderson	W.Buchanon	M.McCoy	S.Luke	J.Gray	2nc	8-7-1 #
1979	M.Butler	E.Edwards	C.Johnson	E.Johnson	G.Weaver	R.Wingo	M.Douglass	E.Hood	M.McCoy	S.Luke	J.Gray	4nc	5-11
1980	M.Butler	C.Johnson	E.Johnson*	J.Anderson	E.O'Neil	K.Allerman	M.Douglass	E.Hood	M.McCoy	S.Luke	J.Gray	4nc	5-10-1
1981	M.Butler	T.Jones	C.Merrill*	J.Anderson	R.Wingo	G.Cumby	M.Douglass	M.Lee	M.McCoy	J.Gray	M.Harvey	2nc	8-8
1982	M.Butler	T.Jones	E.Johnson*	J.Anderson	R.Wingo	G.Cumby	M.Douglass	M.Lee	M.McCoy	J.Gray	M.Harvey	3n	5-3-1 pd
1983	B.Braggs	C.Johnson	E.Johnson*	J.Anderson	R.Wingo	G.Cumby	M.Douglass	M.Lee	M.McCoy	J.Gray	M.Murphy	2nc	8-8
1984	A.Carreker	T.Jones	D.Humphrey*	J.Anderson	R.Scott	G.Cumby	M.Douglass	M.Lee	T.Lewis	M.Murphy	T.Flynn	2nc	8-8
1985	A.Carreker	C.Martin	E.Johnson*	J.Anderson	R.Scott	B.Noble	M.Douglass	M.Lee	T.Lewis	M.Murphy	T.Flynn	2nc	8-8
1986	A.Carreker	C.Martin	R.Brown*	T.Harris	R.Scott	J.Dorsey	B.Noble	M.Lee	M.Cade	T.Greene	K.Stills	4nc	4-12
1987	A.Carreker	J.Boyarsky	R.Brown*	J.Anderson	B.Noble	J.Holland	T.Harris	M.Lee	D.Brown	M.Murphy	K.Stills	3nc	5-9-1
1988	A.Carreker	B.Winter	R.Brown*	J.Anderson	B.Noble	J.Holland	T.Harris	M.Lee	D.Brown	M.Murphy	K.Stills	4nc	4-12
1989	B.Winter	B.Nelson	R.Brown*	J.Anderson	B.Noble	J.Holland	T.Harris	M.Lee	D.Brown	M.Murphy	K.Stills	2nc	10-6 #
1990	M.Brock	B.Nelson	R.Brown*	S.Stephen	B.Noble	J.Holland	T.Harris	M.Lee	J.Holmes	M.Murphy	C.Cecil	2nc	6-10
1991	M.Brock	E.Tuaolo	R.Brown*	S.Stephen	B.Noble	J.Holland	T.Bennett	J.Holmes	L.Butler	M.Murphy	C.Cecil	2nc	4-12
1992	M.Brock	J.Jurkovic	R.Brown*	G.Koonce	B.Noble	J.Holland	T.Bennett	T.Buckley	V.Clark	L.Butler	C.Cecil	2nc	9-7 #
1993	R.White	J.Jurkovic	M.Brock*	W.Simmons	G.Koonce	J.Holland	B.Paup	T.Buckley	R.Mitchell	L.Butler	G.Teague	2nc	9-7 wd
1994	R.White	J.Jurkovic	S.McMichael	S.Jones	B.Paup	F.Strickland	G.Koonce	T.Buckley	D.Evans	L.Butler	G.Teague	2nc	9-7 #wd
1995	R.White	J.Jurkovic	G.Wilkins	S.Jones	W.Simmons	F.Strickland	G.Koonce	C.Newsome	D.Evans	L.Butler	G.Teague	1nc	11-5 #edc
1996	R.White	G.Brown	S.Dotson	S.Jones	W.Simmons	G.Koonce	B.Williams	C.Newsome	D.Evans	L.Butler	E.Robinson	1nc	13-3 dcs*
1997	R.White	G.Brown	S.Dotson	G.Wilkins	S.Joyner	B.Harris	B.Williams	T.Williams	D.Evans	L.Butler	E.Robinson	1nc	13-3 dcs
1998	R.White	G.Brown	S.Dotson	V.Holliday	G.Koonce	B.Harris	B.Williams	C.Newsome	T.Williams	L.Butler	D.Sharper	2nc	11-5 w
1999	V.Booker	G.Brown	S.Dotson	V.Holliday	G.Koonce	B.Harris	J.Waddy	M.McKenzie	T.Williams	L.Butler	D.Sharper	4nc	8-8 #
2000	C.Hunt	R.Maryland	S.Dotson	J.Thierry	N.Diggs	B.Harris	N.Wayne	M.McKenzie	T.Williams	L.Butler	D.Sharper	3nc	9-7
2001	V.Holliday	G.Brown	S.Dotson	J.Thierry	N.Diggs	B.Harris	N.Wayne	M.McKenzie	T.Williams	L.Butler	D.Sharper	2nc	12-4 wd
2002	V.Holliday	G.Brown	C.Hunt	Gbaja-Biamila	N.Diggs	H.Nickerson	N.Wayne	M.McKenzie	T.Williams	M.Anderson	D.Sharper	1nn	12-4 e
2003	A.Kampman	G.Brown	C.Hunt	Gbaja-Biamila	H.Navies	N.Barnett	N.Diggs	M.McKenzie	A.Harris	A.Edwards	D.Sharper	1nn	10-6 ed
2004	A.Kampman	G.Jackson	C.Hunt	Gbaja-Biamila	H.Navies	N.Barnett	N.Diggs	A.Carroll	A.Harris	M.Roman	D.Sharper	1nn	10-6 e
2005	A.Kampman	G.Jackson	C.Jenkins	Gbaja-Biamila	P.Lenon	N.Barnett	R.Thomas	A.Carroll	A.Harris	M.Roman	N.Collins	4nn	4-12

2002	G.Walker	S.Payne	J.DeLoach*	K.Wong	J.Foreman	J.Sharper	J.Posey	A.Glenn	M.Coleman	E.Brown	M.Stevens	4as	4-12
2003	C.Sears	S.Martin	J.DeLoach*	K.Wong	J.Foreman	J.Sharper	C.Clemons	A.Glenn	M.Coleman	E.Brown	M.McCree	3as	5-11
2004	G.Walker	S.Payne	R.Smith*	J.Babin	J.Foreman	J.Sharper	K.Wong	A.Glenn	D.Robinson	G.Earl	M.Coleman	3as	7-9
2005	G.Walker	S.Payne	R.Smith*	S.Orr	D.Polk	M.Greenwood	A.Peek	D.Faggins	D.Robinson	C.Brown	M.Coleman	4as	2-14

1953	B.Poole	A.Donovan	T.Finnin	G.Marchetti	B.Pellington	S.Averno	A.Agase	B.Rechichar	D.Shula	C.Taseff	T.Keane	5nw	3-9
1954	G.Marchetti	A.Donovan	T.Finnin	D.Joyce	B.Pellington	J.Campanella	D.Eggers	C.Taseff	D.Shula	T.Keane	B.Rechichar	6nw	3-9
1955	G.Marchetti	A.Donovan	T.Finnin	D.Joyce	B.Pellington	J.Campanella	D.Eggers	B.Rechichar	D.Shula	C.Taseff	J.Thomas	4nw	5-6-1
1956	G.Marchetti	A.Donovan	T.Finnin	D.Joyce	B.Pellington	J.Campanella	D.Eggers	B.Rechichar	D.Shula	C.Taseff	J.Thomas	4nw	5-7
1957	G.Marchetti	A.Donovan	G.Lipscomb	D.Joyce	D.Shinnick	J.Patera	D.Eggers	A.DeCarlo	M.Davis	A.Nelson	B.Rechichar	3nw	7-5
1958	G.Marchetti	A.Donovan	G.Lipscomb	D.Joyce	L.Sanford	B.Pellington	D.Shinnick	C.Taseff	M.Davis	A.Nelson	R.Brown	1nw	9-3 l*
1959	G.Marchetti	A.Donovan	G.Lipscomb	D.Joyce	B.Pellington	D.Szymanski	D.Shinnick	C.Taseff	M.Davis	A.Nelson	R.Brown	1nw	9-3 l*
1960	G.Marchetti	A.Donovan	G.Lipscomb	O.Braase	B.Pellington	D.Szymanski	D.Shinnick	B.Boyd	M.Davis	A.Nelson	J.Sample	4nw	6-6
1961	G.Marchetti	A.Donovan	B.Smith	O.Braase	J.Burkett	B.Pellington	D.Shinnick	B.Boyd	G.Glick	A.Nelson	B.Harrison	3nw	8-6
1962	G.Marchetti	J.Colvin	B.Smith	O.Braase	B.Pellington	J.Burkett	D.Shinnick	B.Boyd	W.Harris	A.Nelson	J.Welch	4nw	7-7
1963	G.Marchetti	J.Colvin	F.Miller	O.Braase	J.Burkett	B.Pellington	D.Shinnick	B.Boyd	L.Lyles	A.Nelson	J.Welch	3nw	8-6
1964	G.Marchetti	F.Miller	B.Smith	O.Braase	Stonebreaker	B.Pellington	D.Shinnick	B.Boyd	L.Lyles	J.Logan	J.Welch	1nw	12-2 l
1965	L.Michaels	F.Miller	B.Smith	O.Braase	Stonebreaker	D.Gaubatz	D.Shinnick	B.Boyd	L.Lyles	J.Logan	W.Harris	1nw	10-3-1 c
1966	L.Michaels	B.Smith	F.Miller	O.Braase	M.Curtis	D.Gaubatz	D.Shinnick	B.Boyd	L.Lyles	J.Logan	A.Haymond	2nw	9-5
1967	R.Hilton	F.Miller	B.Smith	O.Braase	R.Porter	D.Gaubatz	D.Shinnick	B.Boyd	L.Lyles	J.Logan	R.Volk	1ncl	11-1-2 d
1968	Bubba Smith	B.R.Smith	F.Miller	O.Braase	M.Curtis	D.Gaubatz	D.Shinnick	B.Boyd	L.Lyles	J.Logan	R.Volk	1ncl	13-1 cls
1969	Bubba Smith	B.R.Smith	F.Miller	R.Hilton	B.Grant	M.Curtis	T.Hendricks	C.Stukes	T.Maxwell	J.Logan	R.Volk	2ncl	8-5-1
1984	D.Thompson	L.Wisniewski	B.Winter*	J.Cooks	C.Odom	B.Krauss	V.Maxwell	P.Davis	E.Daniel	M.Kafentzis	N.Glasgow	4ae	4-12
1985	D.Thompson	B.White	C.Scott*	J.Cooks	C.Odom	B.Krauss	D.Bickett	P.Davis	E.Daniel	N.Glasgow	A.Young	4ae	5-11
1986	D.Thompson	W.Broughton	J.Hand*	J.Cooks	C.Odom	D.Ahrens	D.Bickett	L.Coleman	E.Daniel	N.Glasgow	D.Hicks	5ae	3-13
1987	D.Thompson	J.Sally	J.Hand*	J.Cooks	C.Odom	B.Krauss	D.Bickett	W.Tullis	E.Daniel	N.Glasgow	F.Robinson	1ae	9-6 d
1988	D.Thompson	J.Klecko	J.Hand*	O.Alston	F.Young	B.Krauss	D.Bickett	W.Tullis	E.Daniel	F.Robinson	M.Prior	2ae	9-7
1989	D.Thompson	H.Armstrong	J.Hand*	C.Banks	J.Herrod	F.Young	D.Bickett	C.Goode	E.Daniel	M.Ball	M.Prior	2ae	8-8
1990	D.Thompson	H.Armstrong	J.Hand*	C.Banks	J.Herrod	F.Young	D.Bickett	C.Goode	E.Daniel	K.Taylor	M.Prior	3ae	7-9
1991	D.Thompson	T.Davis	J.Hand*	C.Banks	S.Radecic	J.Herrod	D.Bickett	C.Goode	E.Daniel	M.Ball	K.Taylor	5ae	1-15
1992	S.Emtman	T.Siragusa	J.Hand*	C.Banks	S.Radecic	J.Herrod	D.Bickett	C.Goode	E.Daniel	J.Baylor	M.Prior	3ae	9-7
1993	S.McClendon	S.Clancy	T.Siragusa	J.Hand	D.Bickett	Q.Coryatt	J.Herrod	C.Goode	E.Daniel	J.Baylor	J.Belser	5ae	4-12
1994	Whittington	T.McCoy	T.Siragusa	T.Bennett	S.Grant	J.Herrod	Q.Coryatt	D.Watts	E.Daniel	J.Belser	R.Buchanan	3ae	8-8
1995	Whittington	T.McCoy	T.Siragusa	T.Bennett	S.Grant	J.Herrod	Q.Coryatt	R.Buchanan	E.Daniel	D.Tate	J.Belser	2ae	9-7 wdc
1996	Whittington	T.McCoy	T.Siragusa	T.Bennett	S.Grant	J.Herrod	S.Morrison	R.Buchanan	E.Daniel	D.Tate	J.Belser	3ae	9-7 #w
1997	A.Fontenot	T.McCoy	E.Johnson	D.Footman	E.Alexander	S.Grant	Q.Coryatt	C.Gray	D.Watts	R.Blackmon	J.Belser	5ae	3-13

YEAR	COACH	WR/LE	LT	LG	C	RG	RT	TE/RE	WR/FL	QB	RB/LH	FB
1998	J.Mora	J.Pathon	T.Glenn	S.McKinney	Leeuwenburg	T.Mandarich	A.Meadows	K.Dilger	M.Harrison	P.Manning	M.Faulk	M.Pollard*
1999	J.Mora	T.Wilkins	T.Glenn	S.McKinney	L.Moore	W.Jackson	A.Meadows	K.Dilger	M.Harrison	P.Manning	E.James	M.Pollard*
2000	J.Mora	J.Pathon	T.Glenn	S.McKinney	J.Saturday	L.Moore	A.Meadows	K.Dilger	M.Harrison	P.Manning	E.James	M.Pollard*
2001	J.Mora	R.Wayne	T.Glenn	S.McKinney	J.Saturday	L.Moore	A.Meadows	K.Dilger	M.Harrison	P.Manning	D.Rhodes	M.Pollard*
2002	T.Dungy	Q.Ismail	T.Glenn	R.DeMulling	J.Saturday	R.Diem	A.Meadows	M.Pollard	M.Harrison	P.Manning	E.James	R.Wayne+
2003	T.Dungy	R.Wayne	T.Glenn	R.DeMulling	J.Saturday	S.Sciullo	R.Diem	M.Pollard	M.Harrison	P.Manning	E.James	D.Clark*
2004	T.Dungy	R.Wayne	T.Glenn	R.DeMulling	J.Saturday	J.Scott	R.Diem	M.Pollard	M.Harrison	P.Manning	E.James	D.Clark*
2005	T.Dungy	R.Wayne	T.Glenn	R.Lilja	J.Saturday	J.Scott	R.Diem	D.Clark	M.Harrison	P.Manning	E.James	B.Fletcher*

JACKSONVILLE JAGUARS

YEAR	COACH	WR/LE	LT	LG	C	RG	RT	TE/RE	WR/FL	QB	RB/LH	FB
1995	T.Coughlin	E.Givins	T.Boselli	S.Bouwens	D.Widell	T.Myslinski	B.DeMarco	R.Griffith	W.Jackson	M.Brunell	J.Stewart	L.Maston
1996	T.Coughlin	J.Smith	T.Boselli	B.Coleman	D.Widell	B.DeMarco	L.Searcy	D.Brown	K.McCardell	M.Brunell	J.Stewart	L.Maston
1997	T.Coughlin	J.Smith	T.Boselli	B.Coleman	D.Widell	R.Tylski	L.Searcy	P.Mitchell	K.McCardell	M.Brunell	N.Means	T.Hallock
1998	T.Coughlin	J.Smith	T.Boselli	B.Coleman	Q.Neujahr	B.DeMarco	L.Searcy	P.Mitchell	K.McCardell	M.Brunell	F.Taylor	D.Shelton
1999	T.Coughlin	J.Smith	T.Boselli	B.Coleman	J.Wade	Z.Wiegert	L.Searcy	K.Brady	K.McCardell	M.Brunell	J.Stewart	D.Shelton
2000	T.Coughlin	Jimmy Smith	T.Boselli	B.Meester	Jeff Smith	B.Stai	Z.Wiegert	K.Brady	K.McCardell	M.Brunell	F.Taylor	D.Shelton
2001	T.Coughlin	Jimmy Smith	T.Fordham	B.Meester	Jeff Smith	Z.Wiegert	M.Williams	K.Brady	K.McCardell	M.Brunell	S.Mack	P.Washington
2002	T.Coughlin	J.Smith	M.Pearson	B.Meester	J.Wade	C.Naeole	T.Fordham	K.Brady	B.Shaw	M.Brunell	F.Taylor	P.Mitchell*
2003	J.Del Rio	J.Smith	M.Pearson	V.Manuwai	B.Meester	C.Naeole	M.Williams	K.Brady	T.Edwards	B.Leftwich	F.Taylor	M.Edwards
2004	J.Del Rio	J.Smith	E.Salaam	V.Manuwai	B.Meester	C.Naeole	M.Williams	K.Brady	R.Williams	B.Leftwich	F.Taylor	M.Edwards
2005	J.Del Rio	J.Smith	K.Barnes	V.Manuwai	B.Meester	C.Naeole	M.Williams	K.Brady	E.Wilford	B.Leftwich	F.Taylor	G.Jones

KANSAS CITY CHIEFS (Dallas Texans 1960-62)

YEAR	COACH	WR/LE	LT	LG	C	RG	RT	TE/RE	WR/FL	QB	RB/LH	FB
1960	H.Stram	C.Burford	C.Diamond	S.Fournet	J.Barton	B.Krisher	J.Cornelison	B.Bryant	J.Robinson	C.Davidson	A.Haynes	J.Spikes
1961	H.Stram	C.Burford	C.Diamond	S.Fournet	J.Gilliam	B.Krisher	J.Cornelison	M.Boydston	J.Robinson	C.Davidson	A.Haynes	F.Jackson
1962	H.Stram	C.Burford	J.Tyrer	M.Terrell	J.Gilliam	A.Reynolds	C.Diamond	F.Arbanas	F.Jackson	L.Dawson	A.Haynes	C.McClinton
1963	H.Stram	C.Burford	J.Tyrer	M.Terrell	J.Gilliam	A.Reynolds	D.Hill	F.Arbanas	F.Jackson	L.Dawson	A.Haynes	C.McClinton
1964	H.Stram	C.Burford	J.Tyrer	E.Budde	J.Gilliam	A.Reynolds	D.Hill	F.Arbanas	F.Jackson	L.Dawson	A.Haynes	M.Hill
1965	H.Stram	C.Burford	J.Tyrer	E.Budde	J.Gilliam	C.Merz	D.Hill	F.Arbanas	F.Jackson	L.Dawson	M.Hill	C.McClinton
1966	H.Stram	C.Burford	J.Tyrer	E.Budde	W.Frazier	C.Merz	D.Hill	F.Arbanas	O.Taylor	L.Dawson	M.Garrett	C.McClinton
1967	H.Stram	C.Burford	J.Tyrer	E.Budde	J.Gilliam	C.Merz	D.Hill	F.Arbanas	O.Taylor	L.Dawson	M.Garrett	C.McClinton
1968	H.Stram	F.Pitts	J.Tyrer	E.Budde	E.Holub	M.Moorman	D.Hill	F.Arbanas	O.Taylor	L.Dawson	M.Garrett	R.Holmes
1969	H.Stram	F.Pitts	J.Tyrer	E.Budde	E.Holub	M.Moorman	D.Hill	F.Arbanas	O.Taylor	L.Dawson	M.Garrett	R.Holmes
1970	H.Stram	F.Pitts	J.Tyrer	E.Budde	J.Rudnay	M.Moorman	D.Hill	F.Arbanas	O.Taylor	L.Dawson	E.Podolak	W.Hayes
1971	H.Stram	E.Wright	J.Tyrer	E.Budde	J.Rudnay	M.Moorman	D.Hill	M.Stroud	O.Taylor	L.Dawson	E.Podolak	W.Hayes
1972	H.Stram	D.Homan	J.Tyrer	E.Budde	J.Rudnay	M.Moorman	D.Hill	M.Stroud	O.Taylor	L.Dawson	E.Podolak	W.Hayes
1973	H.Stram	E.Wright	J.Tyrer	E.Budde	J.Rudnay	M.Moorman	F.Peay	M.Stroud	O.Taylor	M.Livingston	E.Podolak	W.Hayes
1974	H.Stram	E.Wright	C.Getty	E.Budde	J.Rudnay	G.Daney	J.Nicholson	M.Stroud	O.Taylor	L.Dawson	E.Podolak	W.Green
1975	P.Wiggin	B.Pearson	C.Getty	R.Rasley	J.Rudnay	T.Condon	J.Nicholson	B.Masters	L.Brunson	M.Livingston	E.Podolak	W.Green
1976	P.Wiggin	H.Marshall	M.Herkenhoff	C.Getty	J.Rudnay	T.Condon	J.Nicholson	B.Masters	L.Brunson	M.Livingston	W.Green	M.Lane
1977	P.Wiggin	H.Marshall	M.Herkenhoff	B.Simmons	J.Rudnay	T.Condon	J.Nicholson	W.White	L.Brunson	M.Livingston	T.Reed	Brockington
1978	M.Levy	H.Marshall	M.Herkenhoff	B.Simmons	J.Rudnay	T.Condon	C.Getty	W.White	T.McKnight	M.Livingston	T.Reed	A.Morgado
1979	M.Levy	H.Marshall	C.Getty	B.Simmons	J.Rudnay	T.Condon	J.Nicholson	T.Samuels	J.Smith	S.Fuller	T.Reed	T.McKnight
1980	M.Levy	H.Marshall	M.Herkenhoff	B.Simmons	J.Rudnay	T.Condon	J.Rourke	M.Williams	J.Smith	S.Fuller	T.Reed	T.McKnight
1981	M.Levy	H.Marshall	M.Herkenhoff	B.Budde	J.Rudnay	T.Condon	C.Getty	A.Dixon	J.Smith	B.Kenney	J.Delaney	J.Hadnot
1982	M.Levy	H.Marshall	M.Herkenhoff	B.Budde	J.Rudnay	T.Condon	C.Getty	W.Scott	C.Carson	B.Kenney	J.Delaney	B.Jackson
1983	J.Mackovic	C.Carson	M.Herkenhoff	B.Budde	B.Rush	T.Condon	D.Lutz	W.Scott	H.Marshall	B.Kenney	B.Jackson	T.Brown
1984	J.Mackovic	C.Carson	M.Herkenhoff	B.Budde	B.Rush	T.Condon	D.Lutz	W.Scott	H.Marshall	B.Kenney	H.Heard	T.Brown
1985	J.Mackovic	C.Carson	M.Herkenhoff	B.Budde	B.Rush	B.Olderman	D.Lutz	W.Arnold	H.Marshall	B.Kenney	H.Heard	M.Pruitt
1986	J.Mackovic	C.Carson	I.Eatman	B.Budde	R.Donnalley	M.Adickes	D.Lutz	W.Arnold	S.Paige	B.Kenney	H.Heard	M.Pruitt
1987	F.Gansz	C.Carson	J.Alt	R.Baldinger	T.Baugh	M.Adickes	I.Eatman	J.Hayes	S.Paige	B.Kenney	H.Heard	C.Okoye
1988	F.Gansz	C.Carson	J.Alt	R.Baldinger	T.Baugh	M.Adickes	I.Eatman	J.Hayes	S.Paige	S.DeBerg	P.Palmer	C.Okoye
1989	Schottenheimer	P.Mandley	J.Alt	M.Adickes	M.Webster	D.Lutz	I.Eatman	J.Hayes	S.Paige	S.DeBerg	H.Heard	C.Okoye
1990	Schottenheimer	R.Thomas	J.Alt	D.Szott	T.Grunhard	D.Lutz	R.Baldinger	A.Roberts	S.Paige	S.DeBerg	B.Word	C.Okoye
1991	Schottenheimer	R.Thomas	J.Alt	D.Szott	T.Grunhard	D.Lutz	R.Baldinger	J.Hayes	T.Barnett	S.DeBerg	B.Word	C.Okoye
1992	Schottenheimer	J.Birden	J.Alt	D.Szott	T.Grunhard	D.Lutz	R.Baldinger	J.Hayes	W.Davis	D.Krieg	B.Word	C.Okoye
1993	Schottenheimer	J.Birden	J.Alt	D.Szott	T.Grunhard	W.Shields	R.Siglar	J.Hayes	W.Davis	J.Montana	M.Allen	K.Anders
1994	Schottenheimer	J.Birden	J.Alt	D.Szott	T.Grunhard	W.Shields	D.Graham	D.Walker	W.Davis	J.Montana	M.Allen	K.Anders
1995	Schottenheimer	L.Dawson	J.Alt	D.Szott	T.Grunhard	W.Shields	R.Siglar	K.Cash	W.Davis	S.Bono	M.Allen	K.Anders
1996	Schottenheimer	C.Penn	J.Alt	D.Szott	T.Grunhard	W.Shields	R.Siglar	D.Walker	S.LaChapelle	S.Bono	M.Allen	K.Anders
1997	Schottenheimer	A.Rison	J.Criswell	D.Szott	T.Grunhard	W.Shields	G.Parker	T.Popson	L.Dawson	E.Grbac	G.Hill	K.Anders
1998	Schottenheimer	A.Rison	J.Criswell	G.Parker	T.Grunhard	W.Shields	V.Riley	T.Gonzalez	D.Alexander	R.Gannon	D.Bennett	K.Anders
1999	Cunningham	A.Rison	G.Parker	D.Szott	T.Grunhard	W.Shields	V.Riley	T.Gonzalez	D.Alexander	E.Grbac	B.Morris	T.Richardson
2000	Cunningham	S.Morris	J.Tait	J.Blackshear	T.Grunhard	W.Shields	V.Riley	T.Gonzalez	D.Alexander	E.Grbac	K.Anders	T.Richardson
2001	D.Vermeil	S.Minnis	J.Tait	B.Waters	C.Wiegmann	W.Shields	M.Spears	T.Gonzalez	D.Alexander	T.Green	P.Holmes	T.Richardson
2002	D.Vermeil	E.Kennison	W.Roaf	B.Waters	C.Wiegmann	W.Shields	J.Tait	T.Gonzalez	J.Morton	T.Green	P.Holmes	T.Richardson
2003	D.Vermeil	J.Morton	W.Roaf	B.Waters	C.Wiegmann	W.Shields	J.Tait	T.Gonzalez	E.Kennison	T.Green	P.Holmes	T.Richardson
2004	D.Vermeil	J.Morton	W.Roaf	B.Waters	C.Wiegmann	W.Shields	J.Welbourn	T.Gonzalez	E.Kennison	T.Green	P.Holmes	T.Richardson
2005	D.Vermeil	S.Parker	W.Roaf	B.Waters	C.Wiegmann	W.Shields	J.Welbourn	T.Gonzalez	E.Kennison	T.Green	L.Johnson	T.Richardson

MIAMI DOLPHINS

YEAR	COACH	WR/LE	LT	LG	C	RG	RT	TE/RE	WR/FL	QB	RB/LH	FB
1966	G.Wilson	F.Jackson	M.Williams	E.Park	T.Goode	B.Neighbors	N.Evans	D.Kocourek	B.Roberson	D.Wood	J.Auer	B.Joe
1967	G.Wilson	J.Clancy	M.Williams	F.Woodson	T.Goode	B.Neighbors	N.Evans	D.Moreau	F.Jackson	B.Griese	J.Harper	S.Price
1968	G.Wilson	K.Noonan	D.Crusan	C.Fowler	T.Goode	B.Neighbors	N.Evans	D.Moreau	H.Twilley	B.Griese	J.Kiick	L.Csonka
1969	G.Wilson	J.Clancy	D.Crusan	M.Williams	T.Goode	L.Little	N.Evans	L.Seiple	K.Noonan	B.Griese	J.Kiick	L.Csonka
1970	D.Shula	P.Warfield	D.Crusan	M.Williams	B.DeMarco	L.Little	N.Evans	M.Fleming	H.Twilley	B.Griese	J.Kiick	L.Csonka
1971	D.Shula	P.Warfield	D.Crusan	Kuechenberg	B.DeMarco	L.Little	N.Evans	M.Fleming	H.Twilley	B.Griese	J.Kiick	L.Csonka
1972	D.Shula	P.Warfield	D.Crusan	Kuechenberg	J.Langer	L.Little	N.Evans	M.Fleming	H.Twilley	E.Morrall	M.Morris	L.Csonka
1973	D.Shula	P.Warfield	W.Moore	Kuechenberg	J.Langer	L.Little	N.Evans	M.Fleming	M.Briscoe	B.Griese	M.Morris	L.Csonka
1974	D.Shula	P.Warfield	T.Funchess	Kuechenberg	J.Langer	L.Little	N.Evans	J.Mandich	N.Moore	B.Griese	J.Kiick	L.Csonka
1975	D.Shula	H.Twilley	W.Moore	Kuechenberg	J.Langer	L.Little	N.Evans	A.Tillman	N.Moore	B.Griese	M.Morris	D.Nottingham
1976	D.Shula	N.Moore	W.Moore	Kuechenberg	J.Langer	L.Little	D.Carlton	A.Tillman	F.Solomon	B.Griese	B.Malone	D.Nottingham
1977	D.Shula	N.Moore	W.Moore	Kuechenberg	J.Langer	L.Little	M.Current	A.Tillman	F.Solomon	B.Griese	B.Malone	N.Bulaich
1978	D.Shula	D.Harris	W.Moore	Kuechenberg	J.Langer	L.Little	M.Current	A.Tillman	N.Moore	B.Griese	D.Williams	L.Harris
1979	D.Shula	D.Harris	Kuechenberg	E.Newman	J.Langer	L.Little	M.Current	B.Hardy	N.Moore	B.Griese	D.Williams	L.Csonka
1980	D.Shula	N.Moore	J.Giesler	Kuechenberg	M.Dennard	E.Newman	E.Laakso	R.Lee	B.Hardy	D.Woodley	D.Williams	S.Howell
1981	D.Shula	D.Harris	J.Giesler	Kuechenberg	M.Dennard	E.Newman	E.Laakso	R.Lee	N.Moore	D.Woodley	T.Nathan	A.Franklin
1982	D.Shula	J.Cefalo	J.Giesler	Kuechenberg	D.Stephenson	E.Newman	E.Laakso	B.Hardy	D.Harris	D.Woodley	T.Nathan	A.Franklin
1983	D.Shula	M.Duper	J.Giesler	Kuechenberg	D.Stephenson	E.Newman	E.Laakso	D.Johnson	N.Moore	D.Marino	T.Nathan	A.Franklin
1984	D.Shula	M.Duper	J.Giesler	R.Foster	D.Stephenson	E.Newman	C.Green	D.Johnson	M.Clayton	D.Marino	T.Nathan	W.Bennett
1985	D.Shula	M.Duper	J.Giesler	R.Foster	D.Stephenson	R.Lee	C.Green	B.Hardy	M.Clayton	D.Marino	T.Nathan	W.Bennett
1986	D.Shula	M.Duper	J.Giesler	R.Foster	D.Stephenson	R.Lee	G.Koch	B.Hardy	M.Clayton	D.Marino	L.Hampton	W.Bennett
1987	D.Shula	M.Duper	J.Giesler	R.Foster	D.Stephenson	T.Toth	R.Lee	B.Hardy	M.Clayton	D.Marino	L.Hampton	W.Bennett
1988	D.Shula	M.Duper	J.Giesler	R.Foster	J.Dellenbach	H.Galbreath	R.Lee	F.Edmunds	M.Clayton	D.Marino	L.Hampton	W.Bennett
1989	D.Shula	M.Duper	J.Dellenbach	R.Foster	J.Uhlenhake	H.Galbreath	R.Lee	F.Edmunds	M.Clayton	D.Marino	S.Smith	T.Brown
1990	D.Shula	M.Duper	R.Webb	K.Sims	J.Uhlenhake	H.Galbreath	M.Dennis	F.Edmunds	M.Clayton	D.Marino	S.Smith	T.Paige
1991	D.Shula	M.Duper	R.Webb	K.Sims	J.Uhlenhake	H.Galbreath	M.Dennis	G.Baty	M.Clayton	D.Marino	M.Higgs	T.Paige

YEAR	LDE	LDT/NT	RDT/RDE	RDE/LOLB	LLB/LILB	MLB/RILB	RLB/ROLB	LCB	RCB	SS/LS	FS/RS	FINISH	
1998	Whittington	T.McCoy	E.Johnson	B.Berry	S.Morrison	M.Barber	E.Alexander	J.Burris	T.Poole	R.Blackmon	J.Belser	5ae	3-13
1999	S.King	Whittington	E.Johnson	C.Bratzke	C.Bennett	M.Barber	M.Peterson	J.Burris	T.Poole	C.Cota	J.Belser	1ae	13-3 d
2000	B.Holsey	Whittington	E.Johnson	C.Bratzke	C.Bennett	D.Hollier	M.Peterson	J.Burris	T.Poole	C.Cota	J.Belser	2ae	10-6 w
2001	B.Scioli	J.Williams	E.Johnson	C.Bratzke	M.Washington	R.Morris	M.Peterson	J.Burris	D.Macklin	C.Cota	I.Bashir	4ae	6-10
2002	C.Bratzke	B.Scioli	L.Tripplett	D.Freeney	M.Peterson	R.Morris	M.Washington	W.Harris	D.Macklin	D.Gibson	I.Bashir	2as	10-6 w
2003	R.Brock	L.Tripplett	M.Reagor	D.Freeney	M.Washington	R.Morris	D.Thornton	W.Harris	N.Harper	M.Doss	I.Bashir	1as	12-4 #edc
2004	R.Brock	M.Reagor	J.Williams	D.Freeney	D.Thornton	R.Morris	C.June	N.Harper	J.David	M.Doss	I.Bashir	1as	12-4 ed
2005	R.Brock	C.Simon	M.Reagor	D.Freeney	D.Thornton	G.Brackett	C.June	N.Harper	J.David	M.Doss	B.Sanders	1as	14-2 d
1995	J.Smeenge	K.Pritchett	D.Davey	J.Lageman	K.Goganious	B.Schwartz	M.Williams	V.Clark	M.Washington	H.Colon	M.Dumas	5ac	4-12
1996	J.Smeenge	D.Davey	J.Jurkovic	C.Simmons	E.Robinson	T.McManus	K.Hardy	A.Beasley	M.Washington	D.Hall	C.Hudson	2ac	9-7 #wdc
1997	J.Lageman	R.Wynn	D.Davey	C.Simmons	K.Hardy	B.Schwartz	E.Robinson	D.Thomas	D.Figures	T.Davis	C.Hudson	2ac	11-5 #w
1998	J.Smeenge	K.Pritchett	J.Jurkovic	R.Wynn	B.Paup	B.Schwartz	K.Hardy	A.Beasley	D.Thomas	D.Darius	C.Hudson	1ac	11-5 ed
1999	R.Wynn	G.Walker	S.Payne	T.Brackens	B.Paup	L.Marts	K.Hardy	F.Bryant	A.Beasley	D.Darius	C.Lake	1ac	14-2 dcs
2000	R.Wynn	G.Walker	S.Payne	T.Brackens	K.Hardy	T.Slaughter	B.Boyer	F.Bryant	A.Beasley	D.Darius	M.Logan	4ac	7-9
2001	R.Wynn	G.Walker	S.Payne	T.Brackens	K.Hardy	H.Nickerson	T.Slaughter	F.Bryant	A.Beasley	D.Darius	M.McCree	5ac	6-10
2002	M.Coleman	M.Stroud	J.Henderson	R.Meier	D.Clark	W.Rainer	T.Slaughter	F.Bryant	J.Craft	D.Darius	M.McCree	3as	6-10
2003	T.Brackens	M.Stroud	J.Henderson	H.Douglas	A.Ayodele	M.Peterson	D.Clark	F.Bryant	R.Mathis	D.Darius	D.Cooper	3as	5-11
2004	R.Meier	M.Stroud	J.Henderson	G.Favors	D.Smith	M.Peterson	A.Ayodele	R.Mathis	D.Washington	D.Darius	D.Grant	2as	9-7
2005	R.Hayward	M.Stroud	J.Henderson	P.Spicer	A.Ayodele	M.Peterson	D.Smith	R.Mathis	K.Wright	D.Cooper	D.Grant	2as	12-4 w
1960	P.Miller	W.Napier	R.Collins	M.Branch	W.Corey	S.Headrick	S.Stover	D.Wood	D.Webster	D.Flynn	J.Harris	2aw	8-6
1961	P.Miller	P.Rochester	R.Collins	M.Branch	E.Holub	S.Headrick	S.Stover	D.Wood	D.Grayson	D.Nix	D.Webster	2aw	6-8
1962	C.Merz	P.Rochester	J.Mays	M.Branch	E.Holub	S.Headrick	W.Corey	D.Wood	D.Grayson	B.Hunt	J.Robinson	1aw	11-3 l*
1963	B.Bell	B.Buchanan	J.Mays	M.Branch	E.Holub	S.Headrick	W.Corey	D.Wood	D.Grayson	B.Hunt	J.Robinson	3aw	5-7-2
1964	B.Bell	J.Mays	B.Buchanan	M.Branch	E.Holub	S.Headrick	W.Corey	D.Wood	D.Grayson	B.Hunt	J.Robinson	2aw	7-7
1965	J.Mays	E.Lothamer	B.Buchanan	M.Branch	B.Bell	S.Headrick	E.Holub	F.Williamson	W.Mitchell	B.Hunt	J.Robinson	3aw	7-5-2
1966	J.Mays	A.Rice	B.Buchanan	C.Hurston	B.Bell	S.Headrick	E.Holub	F.Williamson	W.Mitchell	B.Hunt	J.Robinson	1aw	11-2-1 ls
1967	J.Mays	E.Lothamer	B.Buchanan	C.Hurston	B.Bell	S.Headrick	W.Lanier	F.Williamson	W.Mitchell	B.Hunt	J.Robinson	2aw	9-5
1968	J.Mays	E.Lothamer	B.Buchanan	A.Brown	B.Bell	W.Lanier	J.Lynch	E.Thomas	W.Mitchell	J.Kearney	J.Robinson	1aw	12-2 d
1969	J.Mays	C.Culp	B.Buchanan	A.Brown	B.Bell	W.Lanier	J.Lynch	J.Marsalis	E.Thomas	J.Kearney	J.Robinson	2aw	11-3 pls*
1970	J.Mays	C.Culp	B.Buchanan	A.Brown	B.Bell	W.Lanier	J.Lynch	J.Marsalis	E.Thomas	J.Kearney	J.Robinson	2aw	7-5-2
1971	M.Upshaw	C.Culp	B.Buchanan	A.Brown	B.Bell	W.Lanier	J.Lynch	J.Marsalis	E.Thomas	J.Kearney	J.Robinson	1aw	10-3-1 d
1972	M.Upshaw	C.Culp	B.Buchanan	W.Young	B.Bell	W.Lanier	J.Lynch	J.Marsalis	E.Thomas	J.Kearney	M.Sensibaugh	2aw	8-6
1973	M.Upshaw	C.Culp	B.Buchanan	W.Young	B.Bell	W.Lanier	J.Lynch	N.Allen	E.Thomas	J.Kearney	M.Sensibaugh	2aw	7-5-2
1974	M.Upshaw	T.Keating	B.Buchanan	W.Young	B.Bell	W.Lanier	J.Lynch	N.Allen	E.Thomas	J.Kearney	M.Sensibaugh	3aw	5-9
1975	J.Matuszak	J.Lohmeyer	B.Buchanan	W.Young	B.Peterson	W.Lanier	J.Lynch	K.Reardon	E.Thomas	J.Kearney	M.Sensibaugh	3aw	5-9
1976	W.Paul	J.Lohmeyer	B.Maddox	W.Young	B.Andrews	W.Lanier	J.Lynch	K.Reardon	E.Thomas	T.Gray	G.Barbaro	4aw	5-9
1977	W.Paul	W.Lee	K.Simons	W.Young	B.Andrews	W.Lanier	J.Lynch	G.Green	E.Thomas	T.Gray	G.Barbaro	5aw	2-12
1978	A.Still	D.Parrish	S.Hicks*	W.Paul	D.Rozumek	G.Spani	T.Howard	G.Green	E.Thomas	T.Gray	G.Barbaro	5aw	4-12
1979	A.Still	D.Parrish	S.Hicks*	W.Paul	Manumaleuga	G.Spani	T.Howard	G.Green	T.Collier	J.Reese	G.Barbaro	5aw	7-9
1980	A.Still	D.Parrish	D.Lindstrom*	T.Howard	Manumaleuga	G.Spani	W.Paul	G.Green	E.Harris	Christopher	G.Barbaro	3aw	8-8
1981	A.Still	D.Parrish	M.Bell*	W.Paul	J.Blanton	G.Spani	C.Jackson	G.Green	E.Harris	L.Burruss	G.Barbaro	3aw	9-7
1982	A.Still	K.Kremer	M.Bell*	T.Howard	J.Blanton	G.Spani	C.Jackson	G.Green	E.Harris	L.Burruss	G.Barbaro	11a	3-6
1983	A.Still	D.Mangiero	M.Bell*	T.Howard	J.Blanton	G.Spani	C.Jackson	G.Green	L.Smith	L.Burruss	D.Cherry	4aw	6-10
1984	A.Still	B.Maas	M.Bell*	K.McAlister	J.Zamberlin	G.Spani	C.Daniels	A.Lewis	K.Ross	L.Burruss	D.Cherry	4aw	8-8
1985	A.Still	B.Maas	M.Bell*	C.Daniels	S.Radecic	G.Spani	K.Jolly	A.Lewis	K.Ross	L.Burruss	D.Cherry	5aw	6-10
1986	A.Still	B.Maas	P.Koch*	L.Cooper	D.Hackett	S.Radecic	T.Cofield	A.Lewis	K.Ross	L.Burruss	D.Cherry	2aw	10-6 #w
1987	A.Still	B.Maas	M.Bell*	L.Cooper	A.Pearson	D.Hackett	J.Del Rio	A.Lewis	K.Ross	L.Burruss	D.Cherry	5aw	4-11
1988	L.Griffin	B.Maas	M.Bell*	J.Del Rio	A.Pearson	D.Hackett	T.Cofield	A.Lewis	K.Ross	L.Burruss	D.Cherry	5aw	4-11-1
1989	N.Smith	B.Maas	L.Griffin*	C.Martin	W.Ashley	D.Hackett	D.Thomas	A.Lewis	K.Ross	K.Porter	D.Cherry	2aw	8-7-1
1990	N.Smith	D.Saleaumua	B.Maas*	C.Martin	P.Snow	D.Hackett	D.Thomas	A.Lewis	K.Ross	K.Porter	J.Donaldson	2aw	11-5 w
1991	N.Smith	D.Saleaumua	B.Maas*	C.Martin	T.Simien	D.Hackett	D.Thomas	J.Pearson	K.Ross	K.Porter	D.Cherry	2aw	10-6 wd
1992	N.Smith	J.Phillips	D.Saleaumua	L.Griffin	C.Martin	T.Simien	D.Thomas	K.Ross	D.Carter	M.Bayless	C.Mincy	2aw	10-6 w
1993	N.Smith	J.Phillips	D.Saleaumua*	T.Rogers	T.Simien	L.Marts	D.Thomas	A.Lewis	D.Carter	M.Bayless	K.Ross	1aw	11-5 edc
1994	N.Smith	J.Phillips	D.Saleaumua	D.Mickell	G.Jamison	T.Simien	D.Thomas	M.Collins	D.Carter	D.Whitmore	W.White	2aw	9-7 #w
1995	V.Booker	J.Phillips	D.Saleaumua	N.Smith	G.Jamison	T.Simien	D.Thomas	D.Carter	J.Hasty	B.Washington	M.Collins	1aw	13-3 d
1996	N.Smith	J.Phillips	D.Saleaumua	V.Booker	D.Thomas	T.Simien	A.Davis	D.Carter	J.Hasty	B.Washington	M.Collins	2aw	9-7 #
1997	V.Booker	J.Phillips	J.Browning*	D.Thomas	T.Wooden	D.Edwards	A.Davis	D.Carter	J.Hasty	R.Tongue	J.Woods	1aw	13-3 d
1998	L.O'Neal	T.Barndt	C.McGlockton*	D.Thomas	W.Simmons	D.Edwards	A.Davis	M.McMillian	J.Hasty	R.Tongue	J.Woods	4aw	7-9
1999	E.Hicks	C.McGlockton	T.Barndt	L.O'Neal	D.Thomas	M.Patton	D.Edwards	C.Dishman	J.Hasty	R.Tongue	J.Woods	2aw	9-7 #
2000	E.Hicks	C.McGlockton	J.Browning	D.Clemons	L.Bush	M.Patton	D.Edwards	P.Dennis	J.Hasty	G.Wesley	J.Woods	3aw	7-9
2001	E.Hicks	E.Downing	D.Ransom	D.Clemons	L.Bush	M.Patton	D.Edwards	R.Crockett	E.Warfield	G.Wesley	J.Woods	4aw	6-10
2002	E.Hicks	J.Browning	D.Ransom	D.Clemons	S.Fujita	M.Patton	M.Maslowski	E.Warfield	W.Bartee	G.Wesley	S.Harts	3aw	8-8
2003	E.Hicks	J.Browning	R.Sims	V.Holliday	S.Fujita	M.Maslowski	S.Barber	E.Warfield	D.McCleon	G.Wesley	J.Woods	1aw	13-3 d
2004	E.Hicks	R.Sims	L.Dalton	J.Allen	S.Fujita	K.Mitchell	S.Barber	E.Warfield	W.Bartee	G.Wesley	J.Woods	3aw	7-9
2005	E.Hicks	J.Browning	L.Dalton	J.Allen	D.Johnson	K.Mitchell	K.Bell	P.Surtain	E.Warfield	S.Knight	G.Wesley	2aw	10-6
1966	E.Cooke	T.Nomina	R.Zecher	L.Torczon	T.Erlandson	F.Emanuel	W.McDaniel	J.Warren	Westmoreland	P.Jaquess	W.West	4ae	3-11
1967	E.Cooke	R.Jacobs	J.Richardson	M.Branch	T.Erlandson	F.Emanuel	J.Bramlett	J.Warren	Westmoreland	W.West	B.Neff	3ae	4-10
1968	J.Riley	T.Nomina	R.Jacobs	M.Fernandez	R.Edmunds	F.Emanuel	J.Bramlett	J.Warren	Westmoreland	B.Petrella	D.Anderson	3ae	5-8-1
1969	J.Riley	M.Fernandez	J.Richardson	B.Stanfill	R.Edmunds	N.Buoniconti	E.Weisacosky	J.Warren	L.Mumphord	T.Beier	D.Anderson	5ae	3-10-1
1970	J.Riley	M.Fernandez	J.Richardson	B.Stanfill	D.Swift	N.Buoniconti	M.Kolen	C.Johnson	L.Mumphord	D.Anderson	J.Scott	2ae	10-4 w
1971	J.Riley	M.Fernandez	B.Heinz	B.Stanfill	D.Swift	N.Buoniconti	M.Kolen	T.Foley	C.Johnson	D.Anderson	J.Scott	1ae	10-3-1 dcs
1972	V.Den Herder	M.Fernandez	B.Heinz	B.Stanfill	D.Swift	N.Buoniconti	M.Kolen	T.Foley	C.Johnson	J.Scott	D.Anderson	1ae	14-0 dcs*
1973	V.Den Herder	M.Fernandez	B.Heinz	B.Stanfill	D.Swift	N.Buoniconti	M.Kolen	T.Foley	C.Johnson	J.Scott	D.Anderson	1ae	12-2 dcs*
1974	V.Den Herder	M.Fernandez	B.Heinz	B.Stanfill	B.Matheson	N.Buoniconti	M.Kolen	T.Foley	C.Johnson	D.Anderson	J.Scott	1ae	11-3 d
1975	V.Den Herder	R.Crowder	D.Reese	B.Stanfill	D.Swift	M.Kolen	B.Matheson	T.Foley	C.Johnson	C.Babb	J.Scott	2ae	10-4 #
1976	V.Den Herder	R.Crowder	D.Reese	J.Andrews	L.Gordon	S.Towle	B.Matheson	J.White	C.Johnson	C.Babb	B.Hill	3ae	6-8
1977	V.Den Herder	B.Baumhower	A.Duhe*	K.Bokamper	S.Towle	B.Matheson	L.Gordon	N.Thomas	C.Johnson	T.Foley	V.Roberson	2ae	10-4 #
1978	V.Den Herder	B.Baumhower	A.Duhe*	K.Bokamper	S.Towle	R.Chambers	L.Gordon	N.Thomas	C.Johnson	T.Foley	R.Volk	2ae	11-5 #w
1979	V.Den Herder	B.Baumhower	D.Betters*	K.Bokamper	S.Towle	R.Chambers	L.Gordon	N.Thomas	G.Small	T.Foley	N.Colzie	1ae	10-6 d
1980	V.Den Herder	B.Baumhower	D.Betters*	K.Bokamper	R.Chambers	A.Duhe	L.Gordon	D.McNeal	G.Small	G.Blackwood	D.Bessillieu	3ae	8-8
1981	D.Betters	B.Baumhower	V.Den Herder*	B.Brudzinski	A.Duhe	E.Rhone	L.Gordon	D.McNeal	G.Small	G.Blackwood	L.Blackwood	1ae	11-4-1 d
1982	D.Betters	B.Baumhower	K.Bokamper*	B.Brudzinski	A.Duhe	E.Rhone	L.Gordon	D.McNeal	G.Small	G.Blackwood	L.Blackwood	2a	7-2 pdcs
1983	D.Betters	B.Baumhower	K.Bokamper*	B.Brudzinski	A.Duhe	E.Rhone	C.Bowser	W.Judson	G.Small	G.Blackwood	L.Blackwood	1ae	12-4 d
1984	D.Betters	B.Baumhower	K.Bokamper*	B.Brudzinski	A.Duhe	M.Brown	C.Bowser	D.McNeal	W.Judson	G.Blackwood	L.Blackwood	1ae	14-2 dcs
1985	D.Betters	M.Charles	K.Bokamper*	B.Brudzinski	J.Shipp	M.Brown	H.Green	P.Lankford	W.Judson	G.Blackwood	B.Brown	1ae	12-4 dc
1986	T.Turner	B.Baumhower	G.Little*	B.Brudzinski	J.Shipp	J.Offerdahl	M.Brown	W.Judson	P.Lankford	G.Blackwood	B.Brown	3ae	8-8
1987	T.Turner	B.Sochia	J.Bosa*	B.Brudzinski	J.Shipp	J.Offerdahl	M.Brown	P.Lankford	W.Judson	G.Blackwood	B.Brown	2ae	8-7
1988	T.Turner	B.Sochia	J.Cline*	R.Graf	M.Brown	J.Offerdahl	H.Green	P.Lankford	W.Judson	L.Hobley	J.Williams	5ae	6-10
1989	T.Turner	B.Sochia	J.Cross*	E.Junior	J.Offerdahl	B.Krauss	H.Green	P.Lankford	W.Judson	J.Williams	L.Oliver	2ae	8-8
1990	T.Turner	S.Lee	J.Cross*	D.Griggs	J.Offerdahl	C.Odom	H.Green	T.McKyer	J.Brown	J.Williams	L.Oliver	2ae	12-4 wd
1991	T.Turner	A.Oglesby	J.Cross*	D.Griggs	C.Odom	Reichenbach	B.Cox	V.Jackson	J.Brown	J.Williams	L.Oliver	3ae	8-8 #

YEAR	COACH	WR/LE	LT	LG	C	RG	RT	TE/RE	WR/FL	QB	RB/LH	FB
1992	D.Shula	M.Duper	R.Webb	K.Sims	J.Uhlenhake	H.Galbreath	J.Dellenbach	K.Jackson	M.Clayton	D.Marino	M.Higgs	T.Paige
1993	D.Shula	I.Fryar	R.Webb	K.Sims	J.Dellenbach	B.Weidner	R.Heller	K.Jackson	M.Ingram	S.Mitchell	M.Higgs	K.Byars
1994	D.Shula	I.Fryar	R.Webb	K.Sims	J.Dellenbach	B.Weidner	R.Heller	K.Jackson	M.Ingram	D.Marino	B.Parmalee	K.Byars
1995	D.Shula	I.Fryar	R.Webb	K.Sims	T.Ruddy	C.Gray	B.Milner	E.Green	O.McDuffie	D.Marino	B.Parmalee	K.Byars
1996	J.Johnson	F.Barnett	R.Webb	K.Sims	T.Ruddy	C.Gray	J.Brown	T.Drayton	O.McDuffie	D.Marino	Abdul-Jabbar	S.Pritchett
1997	J.Johnson	L.Thomas	R.Webb	J.Buckey	T.Ruddy	E.McIver	J.Brown	T.Drayton	O.McDuffie	D.Marino	Abdul-Jabbar	S.Pritchett
1998	J.Johnson	O.Gadsden	R.Webb	M.Dixon	T.Ruddy	K.Donnalley	J.Brown	T.Drayton	O.McDuffie	D.Marino	Abdul-Jabbar	S.Pritchett
1999	J.Johnson	T.Martin	R.Webb	M.Dixon	T.Ruddy	K.Donnalley	J.Brown	T.Drayton	O.McDuffie	D.Marino	C.Collins	R.Konrad
2000	Wannstedt	L.Shepherd	R.Webb	M.Dixon	T.Ruddy	K.Donnalley	T.Wade	H.Goodwin	O.Gadsden	J.Fiedler	L.Smith	R.Konrad
2001	Wannstedt	O.Gadsden	S.Folau	M.Dixon	T.Ruddy	T.Perry	T.Wade	H.Goodwin	J.McKnight	J.Fiedler	L.Smith	R.Konrad
2002	Wannstedt	J.McKnight	M.Dixon	J.Nails	T.Ruddy	T.Perry	T.Wade	R.McMichael	C.Chambers	J.Fiedler	R.Williams	R.Konrad
2003	Wannstedt	D.Thompson	W.Smith	J.Nails	T.Ruddy	T.Perry	T.Wade	R.McMichael	C.Chambers	J.Fiedler	R.Williams	R.Konrad
2004	Wannstedt	M.Booker	D.McIntosh	J.James	S.McKinney	T.Whitley	J.St. Clair	R.McMichael	C.Chambers	A.Feeley	S.Morris	D.Lee*
2005	N.Saban	M.Booker	D.McIntosh	J.James	S.McKinney	R.Hadnot	V.Carey	R.McMichael	C.Chambers	G.Frerotte	R.Brown	L.Diamond*
MINNESOTA VIKINGS												
1961	Van Brocklin	D.Middleton	G.Alderman	J.Huth	B.Lapham	M.Rabold	F.Youso	G.Smith	J.Reichow	F.Tarkenton	H.McElhenny	M.Triplett
1962	Van Brocklin	C.Ferguson	G.Alderman	J.Huth	M.Tingelhoff	M.Rabold	F.Youso	Stonebreaker	J.Reichow	F.Tarkenton	T.Mason	D.Mayberry
1963	Van Brocklin	P.Flatley	G.Alderman	J.Huth	M.Tingelhoff	L.Bowie	E.Linden	R.Poage	J.Reichow	F.Tarkenton	T.Mason	B.Brown
1964	Van Brocklin	P.Flatley	G.Alderman	P.Pyle	M.Tingelhoff	L.Bowie	E.Linden	H.Bedsole	J.Reichow	F.Tarkenton	T.Mason	B.Brown
1965	Van Brocklin	P.Flatley	G.Alderman	M.Sunde	M.Tingelhoff	L.Bowie	E.Linden	G.Smith	R.Phillips	F.Tarkenton	T.Mason	B.Brown
1966	Van Brocklin	P.Flatley	G.Alderman	M.Sunde	M.Tingelhoff	J.Vellone	D.Davis	P.Carpenter	R.Phillips	F.Tarkenton	T.Mason	B.Brown
1967	B.Grant	P.Flatley	G.Alderman	M.Sunde	M.Tingelhoff	L.Bowie	D.Davis	M.McKeever	R.Phillips	J.Kapp	D.Osborn	B.Brown
1968	B.Grant	G.Washington	G.Alderman	J.Vellone	M.Tingelhoff	L.Bowie	D.Davis	B.Martin	T.Hall	J.Kapp	C.Jones	B.Brown
1969	B.Grant	G.Washington	G.Alderman	J.Vellone	M.Tingelhoff	M.Sunde	D.Davis	J.Beasley	J.Henderson	J.Kapp	D.Osborn	B.Brown
1970	B.Grant	G.Washington	G.Alderman	J.Vellone	M.Tingelhoff	M.Sunde	R.Yary	J.Beasley	B.Grim	G.Cuozzo	D.Osborn	B.Brown
1971	B.Grant	G.Washington	G.Alderman	E.White	M.Tingelhoff	M.Sunde	R.Yary	S.Voigt	B.Grim	G.Cuozzo	C.Jones	D.Osborn
1972	B.Grant	G.Washington	G.Alderman	E.White	M.Tingelhoff	M.Sunde	R.Yary	J.Beasley	J.Gilliam	F.Tarkenton	O.Reed	E.Marinaro
1973	B.Grant	C.Dale	G.Alderman	E.White	M.Tingelhoff	M.Sunde	R.Yary	S.Voigt	J.Gilliam	F.Tarkenton	O.Reed	C.Foreman
1974	B.Grant	J.Lash	C.Goodrum	E.White	M.Tingelhoff	A.Maurer	R.Yary	S.Voigt	J.Gilliam	F.Tarkenton	D.Osborn	C.Foreman
1975	B.Grant	J.Lash	C.Goodrum	A.Maurer	M.Tingelhoff	E.White	R.Yary	S.Voigt	J.Gilliam	F.Tarkenton	C.Foreman	E.Marinaro
1976	B.Grant	A.Rashad	S.Riley	C.Goodrum	M.Tingelhoff	E.White	R.Yary	S.Voigt	S.White	F.Tarkenton	C.Foreman	B.McClanahan
1977	B.Grant	A.Rashad	S.Riley	C.Goodrum	M.Tingelhoff	E.White	R.Yary	S.Voigt	S.White	F.Tarkenton	C.Foreman	B.McClanahan
1978	B.Grant	A.Rashad	F.Myers	C.Goodrum	M.Tingelhoff	W.Hamilton	R.Yary	B.Tucker	S.White	F.Tarkenton	R.Young	C.Foreman
1979	B.Grant	A.Rashad	S.Riley	C.Goodrum	D.Swilley	W.Hamilton	R.Yary	B.Tucker	S.White	T.Kramer	R.Young	T.Brown
1980	B.Grant	A.Rashad	S.Riley	J.Hough	D.Swilley	W.Hamilton	R.Yary	B.Tucker	S.White	T.Kramer	R.Young	T.Brown
1981	B.Grant	A.Rashad	S.Riley	J.Hough	D.Swilley	W.Hamilton	R.Yary	J.Senser	S.White	T.Kramer	R.Young	T.Brown
1982	B.Grant	A.Rashad	S.Riley	J.Hough	D.Swilley	W.Hamilton	T.Irwin	J.Senser	S.White	T.Kramer	D.Nelson	T.Brown
1983	B.Grant	T.LeCount	S.Riley	J.Hough	D.Swilley	W.Hamilton	T.Irwin	B.Bruer	S.White	S.Dils	D.Nelson	T.Brown
1984	L.Steckel	S.White	S.Riley	C.Rouse	R.Sams	T.Tausch	T.Irwin	S.Jordan	M.Jones	T.Kramer	T.Brown	A.Anderson
1985	B.Grant	L.Lewis	C.Rouse	B.Boyd	D.Swilley	T.Tausch	T.Irwin	S.Jordan	A.Carter	T.Kramer	D.Nelson	T.Brown
1986	J.Burns	A.Carter	G.Zimmerman	J.Hough	D.Swilley	T.Tausch	T.Irwin	S.Jordan	L.Lewis	T.Kramer	D.Nelson	A.Anderson
1987	J.Burns	A.Carter	G.Zimmerman	D.Huffman	K.Lowdermilk	G.Koch	T.Irwin	S.Jordan	L.Lewis	W.Wilson	D.Nelson	A.Anderson
1988	J.Burns	A.Carter	G.Zimmerman	R.McDaniel	K.Lowdermilk	T.Tausch	T.Irwin	S.Jordan	H.Jones	W.Wilson	D.Nelson	A.Anderson
1989	J.Burns	A.Carter	G.Zimmerman	R.McDaniel	K.Lowdermilk	T.Kalis	T.Irwin	S.Jordan	H.Jones	W.Wilson	H.Walker	A.Anderson
1990	J.Burns	A.Carter	G.Zimmerman	R.McDaniel	K.Lowdermilk	T.Kalis	T.Irwin	S.Jordan	H.Jones	R.Gannon	H.Walker	A.Anderson
1991	J.Burns	A.Carter	G.Zimmerman	R.McDaniel	K.Lowdermilk	T.Kalis	T.Irwin	S.Jordan	C.Carter	R.Gannon	H.Walker	T.Allen
1992	D.Green	A.Carter	G.Zimmerman	R.McDaniel	K.Lowdermilk	B.Habib	T.Irwin	S.Jordan	C.Carter	R.Gannon	T.Allen	M.Tice*
1993	D.Green	A.Carter	E.Lindsay	R.McDaniel	A.Schreiber	S.Adams	T.Irwin	S.Jordan	C.Carter	J.McMahon	B.Word	M.Tice*
1994	D.Green	J.Reed	T.Steussie	R.McDaniel	J.Christy	B.Dafney	C.Hinton	A.Jordan	C.Carter	W.Moon	T.Allen	A.Cooper*
1995	D.Green	J.Reed	T.Steussie	R.McDaniel	J.Christy	J.Gerak	K.Stringer	A.Cooper	C.Carter	W.Moon	R.Smith	C.Evans
1996	D.Green	J.Reed	T.Steussie	R.McDaniel	J.Christy	J.Gerak	K.Stringer	A.Jordan	C.Carter	W.Moon	R.Smith	G.DeLong*
1997	D.Green	J.Reed	T.Steussie	R.McDaniel	J.Christy	D.Dixon	K.Stringer	A.Glover	C.Carter	B.Johnson	R.Smith	C.Evans
1998	D.Green	J.Reed	T.Steussie	R.McDaniel	J.Christy	D.Dixon	K.Stringer	A.Glover	C.Carter	R.Cunningham	R.Smith	R.Moss+
1999	D.Green	R.Moss	T.Steussie	R.McDaniel	J.Christy	D.Dixon	K.Stringer	A.Glover	C.Carter	J.George	R.Smith	J.Reed+
2000	D.Green	R.Moss	T.Steussie	C.Lacina	M.Birk	D.Dixon	K.Stringer	J.Davis	C.Carter	D.Culpepper	R.Smith	Kleinsasser
2001	D.Green	R.Moss	B.Badger	C.Lacina	M.Birk	D.Dixon	C.Liwienski	Chamberlain	C.Carter	D.Culpepper	M.Bennett	Kleinsasser
2002	M.Tice	R.Moss	B.McKinnie	C.Lacina	M.Birk	D.Dixon	C.Liwienski	Chamberlain	D.Bates	D.Culpepper	M.Bennett	Kleinsasser*
2003	M.Tice	R.Moss	B.McKinnie	C.Liwienski	M.Birk	D.Dixon	M.Rosenthal	Kleinsasser	N.Burleson	D.Culpepper	M.Williams	K.Campbell+
2004	M.Tice	R.Moss	B.McKinnie	C.Liwienski	M.Birk	D.Dixon	N.Dorsey	J.Wiggins	N.Burleson	D.Culpepper	M.Bennett	S.Berton*
2005	M.Tice	T.Taylor	B.McKinnie	C.Liwienski	M.Fowler	A.Goldberg	M.Rosenthal	Kleinsasser	N.Burleson	B.Johnson	M.Moore	J.Wiggins*
NEW ENGLAND PATRIOTS (Boston 1960-70)												
1960	L.Saban	O.Lofton	G.McGee	C.Leo	W.Cudzik	J.Davis	J.DeLucca	T.Stephens	J.Colclough	B.Songin	D.Christy	A.Miller
1961	M.Holovak	Cappelletti	C.Long	T.Sardisco	W.Cudzik	C.Leo	J.DeLucca	T.Stephens	J.Colclough	B.Parilli	R.Burton	B.Lott
1962	M.Holovak	Cappelletti	C.Long	T.Sardisco	W.Cudzik	B.Neighbors	M.Graham	T.Romeo	J.Colclough	B.Parilli	R.Burton	L.Garron
1963	M.Holovak	Cappelletti	D.Oakes	C.Long	W.Cudzik	B.Neighbors	M.Graham	T.Romeo	J.Colclough	B.Parilli	J.Crawford	L.Garron
1964	M.Holovak	A.Graham	D.Oakes	C.Long	J.Morris	B.Neighbors	B.Schmidt	T.Romeo	Cappelletti	B.Parilli	R.Burton	L.Garron
1965	M.Holovak	J.Colclough	D.Oakes	C.Long	J.Morris	B.Neighbors	T.Neville	J.Whalen	Cappelletti	B.Parilli	L.Garron	J.Nance
1966	M.Holovak	A.Graham	D.Oakes	C.Long	J.Morris	L.St. Jean	T.Neville	J.Whalen	Cappelletti	B.Parilli	L.Garron	J.Nance
1967	M.Holovak	A.Graham	D.Oakes	C.Long	J.Morris	L.St. Jean	T.Neville	J.Whalen	Cappelletti	B.Parilli	L.Garron	J.Nance
1968	M.Holovak	A.Graham	T.Funchess	J.Canale	J.Morris	L.St. Jean	T.Neville	J.Whalen	A.Marsh	M.Taliaferro	R.Gamble	J.Nance
1969	C.Rush	C.Frazier	T.Funchess	M.Montler	J.Morris	L.St. Jean	T.Neville	J.Whalen	R.Sellers	M.Taliaferro	C.Garrett	J.Nance
1970	C.Rush	B.Turner	T.Funchess	M.Montler	J.Morris	L.St. Jean	T.Neville	B.Brown	R.Sellers	J.Kapp	C.Garrett	J.Nance
1971	J.Mazur	R.Vataha	M.Montler	H.Hagen	J.Morris	L.St. Jean	T.Neville	T.Beer	R.Sellers	J.Plunkett	C.Garrett	J.Nance
1972	J.Mazur	R.Vataha	B.Reynolds	M.Montler	J.Morris	L.St. Jean	T.Neville	B.Windsor	R.Rucker	J.Plunkett	C.Garrett	J.Ashton
1973	Fairbanks	D.Stingley	S.Adams	J.Hannah	B.Lenkaitis	L.St. Jean	T.Neville	B.Windsor	R.Rucker	J.Plunkett	J.Ashton	S.Cunningham
1974	Fairbanks	R.Rucker	L.Gray	J.Hannah	B.Lenkaitis	S.Adams	T.Neville	B.Windsor	R.Vataha	J.Plunkett	M.Herron	S.Cunningham
1975	Fairbanks	R.Vataha	L.Gray	J.Hannah	B.Lenkaitis	S.Adams	S.Jordan	R.Francis	D.Stingley	S.Grogan	A.Johnson	S.Cunningham
1976	Fairbanks	R.Vataha	L.Gray	J.Hannah	B.Lenkaitis	S.Adams	B.McKay	R.Francis	D.Stingley	S.Grogan	A.Johnson	S.Cunningham
1977	Fairbanks	S.Morgan	L.Gray	J.Hannah	B.Lenkaitis	S.Adams	T.Neville	R.Francis	D.Stingley	S.Grogan	D.Calhoun	S.Cunningham
1978	Fairbanks	S.Morgan	L.Gray	J.Hannah	B.Lenkaitis	S.Adams	S.Jordan	R.Francis	H.Jackson	S.Grogan	A.Johnson	S.Cunningham
1979	R.Erhardt	S.Morgan	D.Wheeler	J.Hannah	B.Lenkaitis	S.Adams	S.Jordan	R.Francis	H.Jackson	S.Grogan	H.Ivory	S.Cunningham
1980	R.Erhardt	S.Morgan	D.Wheeler	J.Hannah	B.Lenkaitis	S.Adams	S.Jordan	R.Francis	H.Jackson	S.Grogan	V.Ferguson	D.Calhoun
1981	R.Erhardt	S.Morgan	D.Wheeler	J.Hannah	P.Brock	B.Cryder	S.Jordan	D.Hasselbeck	H.Jackson	M.Cavanaugh	T.Collins	S.Cunningham
1982	R.Meyer	S.Morgan	B.Holloway	J.Hannah	P.Brock	R.Wooten	S.Jordan	D.Hasselbeck	M.Bradshaw	S.Grogan	T.Collins	M.van Eeghen
1983	R.Meyer	S.Morgan	B.Holloway	J.Hannah	P.Brock	R.Wooten	B.Cryder	L.Dawson	C.Jones	S.Grogan	T.Collins	M.van Eeghen
1984	R.Meyer	S.Morgan	B.Holloway	J.Hannah	P.Brock	R.Wooten	D.Haley	L.Dawson	S.Starring	T.Eason	C.James	D.Ramsey*
1985	R.Berry	S.Morgan	B.Holloway	J.Hannah	P.Brock	R.Wooten	S.Moore	L.Dawson	I.Fryar	T.Eason	T.Collins	C.James
1986	R.Berry	S.Morgan	B.Holloway	P.Fairchild	P.Brock	R.Wooten	S.Moore	G.Hawthorne	I.Fryar	T.Eason	T.Collins	C.James
1987	R.Berry	S.Morgan	D.Villa	S.Farrell	G.Morriss	R.Wooten	B.Armstrong	L.Dawson	I.Fryar	S.Grogan	T.Collins	M.Tatupu
1988	R.Berry	S.Morgan	D.Villa	S.Farrell	M.Baab	R.Wooten	B.Armstrong	R.Francis	I.Fryar	D.Flutie	J.Stephens	B.Perryman
1989	R.Berry	S.Morgan	D.Villa	S.Farrell	M.Baab	P.Fairchild	B.Armstrong	L.Dawson	C.Jones	S.Grogan	J.Stephens	B.Perryman
1990	R.Rust	I.Fryar	B.Armstrong	C.Gambol	D.Douglas	D.Johnson	D.Villa	M.Cook	H.Dykes	M.Wilson	J.Stephens	B.Perryman
1991	MacPherson	I.Fryar	B.Armstrong	E.Crawford	G.Chilton	D.Villa	P.Harlow	M.Cook	G.McMurtry	H.Millen	L.Russell	I.Hunter
1992	MacPherson	I.Fryar	B.Armstrong	R.Redding	G.Chilton	E.Chung	P.Harlow	M.Cook	G.McMurtry	H.Millen	L.Russell	J.Stephens
1993	B.Parcells	V.Brisby	B.Armstrong	E.Chung	M.Arthur	R.Baldinger	P.Harlow	M.Cook	B.Coates*	D.Bledsoe	L.Russell	K.Turner

YEAR	LDE	LDT/NT	RDT/RDE	RDE/LOLB	LLB/LILB	MLB/RILB	RLB/ROLB	LCB	RCB	SS/LS	FS/RS	FINISH	
1992	D.Griggs	C.Klingbeil	J.Cross*	M.Coleman	J.Grimsley	J.Offerdahl	B.Cox	T.Vincent	J.Brown	J.Williams	L.Oliver	1ae	11-5 #dc
1993	J.Cross	L.Webster	C.Klingbeil	M.Coleman	J.Grimsley	J.Offerdahl	B.Cox	T.Vincent	J.Brown	J.Williams	L.Oliver	2ae	9-7 #
1994	J.Cross	T.Bowens	C.Klingbeil	M.Coleman	C.Singleton	B.Cox	D.Hollier	T.Vincent	J.Brown	M.Stewart	G.Atkins	1ae	10-6 #ed
1995	J.Cross	T.Bowens	C.Klingbeil	M.Coleman	C.Singleton	B.Cox	D.Hollier	T.Vincent	J.Brown	M.Stewart	G.Atkins	2ae	9-7 w
1996	T.Armstrong	D.Gardener	T.Bowens	D.Stubbs	D.Hollier	Z.Thomas	C.Singleton	T.Buckley	C.Jackson	L.Oliver	S.Wooden	4ae	8-8
1997	T.Armstrong	T.Bowens	D.Gardener	J.Taylor	A.Harris	Z.Thomas	D.Rodgers	T.Buckley	C.Jackson	S.Wooden	C.Harris	2ae	9-7 #w
1998	K.Mixon	T.Bowens	D.Gardener	J.Taylor	D.Rodgers	Z.Thomas	R.Jones	T.Buckley	S.Madison	C.Jackson	B.Marion	2ae	10-6 wd
1999	R.Owens	T.Bowens	D.Gardener	J.Taylor	D.Rodgers	Z.Thomas	R.Jones	T.Buckley	S.Madison	C.Jackson	B.Marion	3ae	9-7 wd
2000	K.Mixon	T.Bowens	D.Gardener	J.Taylor	D.Rodgers	Z.Thomas	R.Jones	P.Surtain	S.Madison	B.Walker	B.Marion	1ae	11-5 ed
2001	K.Mixon	T.Bowens	D.Gardener	J.Taylor	D.Rodgers	Z.Thomas	M.Greenwood	P.Surtain	S.Madison	B.Walker	B.Marion	2ae	11-5 #w
2002	A.Ogunleye	T.Bowens	L.Chester	J.Taylor	D.Rodgers	Z.Thomas	M.Greenwood	P.Surtain	S.Madison	A.Freeman	B.Marion	2ae	9-7 #
2003	A.Ogunleye	T.Bowens	L.Chester	J.Taylor	J.Seau	Z.Thomas	M.Greenwood	P.Surtain	S.Madison	S.Knight	B.Marion	2ae	10-6 #
2004	D.Bowens	B.Robinson	J.Zgonina	J.Taylor	J.Seau	Z.Thomas	M.Greenwood	P.Surtain	S.Madison	S.Knight	A.Freeman	4ae	4-12
2005	K.Carter	K.Traylor	V.Holliday	J.Taylor	D.Spragan	Z.Thomas	C.Crowder	T.Daniels	S.Madison	T.Tillman	L.Schulters	2ae	9-7
1961	J.Marshall	J.Prestel	E.Culpepper	D.Joyce	C.Osborne	R.Hawkins	K.Rubke	J.Morris	D.Pesonen	R.Mostardo	C.Sumner	7nw	3-11
1962	J.Leo	J.Prestel	P.Dickson	J.Marshall	C.Livingston	R.Hawkins	C.Osborne	D.Derby	E.Sharockman	C.Lamson	B.Butler	6nw	2-11-1
1963	D.Hultz	J.Prestel	P.Dickson	J.Marshall	R.Winston	R.Hawkins	Stonebreaker	L.Calland	E.Sharockman	K.Kassulke	C.Lamson	4nw	5-8-1
1964	C.Eller	J.Prestel	P.Dickson	J.Marshall	R.Winston	R.Hawkins	B.Jobko	G.Rose	E.Sharockman	K.Kassulke	L.Vargo	2nw	8-5-1
1965	C.Eller	G.Larsen	P.Dickson	J.Marshall	R.Winston	R.Hawkins	B.Jobko	G.Rose	E.Sharockman	K.Kassulke	L.Vargo	5nw	7-7
1966	C.Eller	G.Larsen	P.Dickson	J.Marshall	R.Winston	L.Warwick	J.Kirby	E.Mackbee	E.Sharockman	K.Kassulke	D.Hackbart	6nw	4-9-1
1967	C.Eller	A.Page	P.Dickson	J.Marshall	R.Winston	L.Warwick	J.Kirby	E.Mackbee	E.Sharockman	K.Kassulke	D.Hackbart	4nco	3-8-3
1968	C.Eller	G.Larsen	A.Page	J.Marshall	R.Winston	L.Warwick	J.Kirby	E.Mackbee	E.Sharockman	K.Kassulke	P.Krause	1nco	8-6 c
1969	C.Eller	G.Larsen	A.Page	J.Marshall	R.Winston	L.Warwick	W.Hilgenberg	E.Mackbee	B.Bryant	K.Kassulke	P.Krause	1nco	12-2 cls
1970	C.Eller	G.Larsen	A.Page	J.Marshall	R.Winston	L.Warwick	W.Hilgenberg	B.Bryant	E.Sharockman	K.Kassulke	P.Krause	1nc	12-2 d
1971	C.Eller	G.Larsen	A.Page	J.Marshall	R.Winston	C.Gersbach	W.Hilgenberg	C.West	E.Sharockman	K.Kassulke	P.Krause	1nc	11-3 d
1972	C.Eller	G.Larsen	A.Page	J.Marshall	R.Winston	J.Siemon	W.Hilgenberg	C.West	B.Bryant	K.Kassulke	P.Krause	3nc	7-7
1973	C.Eller	G.Larsen	A.Page	J.Marshall	R.Winston	J.Siemon	W.Hilgenberg	N.Wright	B.Bryant	J.Wright	P.Krause	1nc	12-2 dcs
1974	C.Eller	D.Sutherland	A.Page	J.Marshall	R.Winston	J.Siemon	W.Hilgenberg	N.Wright	J.Wallace	J.Wright	P.Krause	1nc	10-4 dcs
1975	C.Eller	D.Sutherland	A.Page	J.Marshall	R.Winston	J.Siemon	W.Hilgenberg	N.Wright	B.Bryant	T.Brown	P.Krause	1nc	12-2 d
1976	C.Eller	D.Sutherland	A.Page	J.Marshall	M.Blair	J.Siemon	W.Hilgenberg	N.Wright	N.Allen	J.Wright	P.Krause	1nc	11-2-1 dcs
1977	C.Eller	D.Sutherland	A.Page	J.Marshall	M.Blair	J.Siemon	F.McNeill	N.Wright	B.Bryant	J.Wright	P.Krause	1nc	9-5 #dc
1978	M.Mullaney	D.Sutherland	J.White	J.Marshall	M.Blair	J.Siemon	F.McNeill	N.Wright	B.Bryant	P.Wise	T.Hannon	1nc	8-7-1 #d
1979	M.Mullaney	D.Sutherland	J.White	J.Marshall	M.Blair	J.Siemon	F.McNeill	J.Turner	B.Bryant	T.Hannon	P.Krause	3nc	7-9
1980	M.Mullaney	D.Sutherland	J.White	R.Holloway	M.Blair	S.Studwell	F.McNeill	J.Turner	B.Bryant	T.Hannon	K.Knoff	1nc	9-7 #d
1981	M.Mullaney	J.White	D.Martin*	M.Blair	J.Siemon	S.Studwell	F.McNeill	J.Turner	W.Teal	T.Hannon	K.Knoff	4nc	7-9
1982	D.Martin	C.Johnson	M.Mullaney*	M.Blair	D.Johnson	S.Studwell	F.McNeill	J.Swain	W.Teal	T.Hannon	J.Turner	4n	5-4 pd
1983	D.Martin	C.Johnson	N.Elshire*	M.Blair	S.Studwell	D.Johnson	F.McNeill	J.Swain	W.Teal	T.Hannon	J.Turner	2nc	8-8
1984	N.Elshire	C.Johnson	M.Mullaney*	M.Blair	S.Studwell	D.Johnson	F.McNeill	J.Swain	R.Bess	T.Hannon	C.Lee	5nc	3-13
1985	D.Martin	T.Newton	M.Mullaney*	C.Doleman	S.Studwell	D.Fowlkes	C.Martin	W.Teal	R.Bess	J.Browner	K.Nord	3nc	7-9
1986	D.Martin	T.Newton	K.Millard	M.Mullaney	C.Martin	S.Studwell	D.Howard	I.Holt	C.Lee	J.Browner	J.Harris	2nc	9-7
1987	D.Martin	H.Thomas	K.Millard	C.Doleman	J.Solomon	S.Studwell	D.Howard	W.Henderson	C.Lee	J.Browner	J.Harris	2nc	8-7 wdc
1988	D.Martin	H.Thomas	K.Millard	C.Doleman	J.Solomon	S.Studwell	D.Howard	I.Holt	C.Lee	J.Browner	J.Harris	2nc	11-5 wd
1989	A.Noga	H.Thomas	K.Millard	C.Doleman	R.Berry	S.Studwell	Merriweather	N.Mustafaa	C.Lee	J.Browner	T.Curtis	1nc	10-6 #d
1990	A.Noga	H.Thomas	K.Clarke	C.Doleman	M.Dusbabek	S.Studwell	Merriweather	C.Lee	N.Mustafaa	J.Browner	D.Fullington	2nc	6-10
1991	A.Noga	K.Clarke	H.Thomas	C.Doleman	J.Williams	R.Berry	Merriweather	C.Lee	N.Mustafaa	J.Browner	F.Wright	3nc	8-8
1992	A.Noga	H.Thomas	J.Randle	C.Doleman	C.Jenkins	J.Del Rio	Merriweather	C.Lee	A.McMillian	T.Scott	F.Wright	1nc	11-5 e
1993	R.Barker	H.Thomas	J.Randle	C.Doleman	C.Jenkins	J.Del Rio	F.Strickland	C.Lee	A.McMillian	T.Scott	V.Glenn	2nc	9-7 w
1994	R.Barker	H.Thomas	J.Randle	J.Harris	C.Jenkins	J.Del Rio	E.McDaniel	A.Parker	D.Washington	T.Scott	V.Glenn	1nc	10-6 e
1995	R.Barker	E.Tuaolo	J.Randle	D.Alexander	B.Thomas	J.Del Rio	E.McDaniel	C.Fuller	D.Washington	H.Barnett	O.Thomas	4nc	8-8
1996	F.Smith	E.Tuaolo	J.Randle	D.Alexander	D.Talley	J.Brady	D.Edwards	C.Fuller	D.Washington	R.Griffith	O.Thomas	2nc	9-7 #w
1997	F.Smith	J.Fisk	J.Randle	D.Alexander	E.McDaniel	J.Brady	D.Edwards	C.Fuller	D.Washington	R.Griffith	O.Thomas	3nc	9-7 wd
1998	D.Alexander	J.Ball	T.Williams	J.Randle	D.Edwards	E.McDaniel	D.Rudd	C.Fuller	J.Hitchcock	R.Griffith	O.Thomas	1nc	15-1 d
1999	J.Randle	J.Ball	T.Williams	C.Doleman	K.Wong	E.McDaniel	D.Rudd	K.Wright	J.Hitchcock	R.Griffith	O.Thomas	2nc	10-6 wd
2000	J.Randle	C.Hovan	T.Williams	T.Sawyer	D.Rudd	K.Wong	E.McDaniel	C.Dishman	R.Tate	R.Griffith	O.Thomas	1nc	11-5 dc
2001	S.Colinet	F.Robbins	C.Hovan	T.Sawyer	L.Hall	K.Wong	E.McDaniel	D.Carter	E.Kelly	R.Griffith	O.Thomas	4nc	5-11
2002	K.Mixon	F.Robbins	C.Hovan	L.Johnstone	N.Rogers	G.Biekert	H.Crockett	B.Williams	E.Kelly	C.Chavous	R.Bradford	2nn	6-10
2003	K.Williams	F.Robbins	C.Hovan	K.Mixon	H.Crockett	G.Biekert	C.Claiborne	B.Williams	K.Irvin	C.Chavous	B.Russell	2nn	9-7
2004	K.Mixon	C.Hovan	K.Williams	K.Udeze	K.Newman	E.Henderson	C.Claiborne	A.Winfield	B.Williams	C.Chavous	B.Russell	2nn	8-8 #wd
2005	D.Scott	P.Williams	K.Williams	E.James	K.Newman	S.Cowart	E.Henderson	A.Winfield	B.Williams	C.Chavous	D.Sharper	2nn	9-7
1960	B.Dee	H.Jagielski	H.Smith	T.Sardisco	T.Addison	B.Brown	J.Rudolph	C.Washington	Cappelletti	F.Bruney	R.O'Hanley	4ae	5-9
1961	B.Dee	D.Klein	J.Hunt	L.Eisenhauer	T.Addison	H.Jacobs	R.Loudd	D.Webb	C.Shonta	R.Hall	F.Bruney	2ae	9-4-1
1962	B.Dee	J.Richardson	H.Antwine	L.Eisenhauer	T.Addison	N.Buoniconti	J.Rudolph	C.Shonta	D.Felt	R.O'Hanley	R.Hall	2ae	9-4-1
1963	B.Dee	J.Richardson	H.Antwine	L.Eisenhauer	T.Addison	N.Buoniconti	J.Rudolph	B.Suci	D.Felt	R.O'Hanley	R.Hall	1ae	7-6-1 dl
1964	B.Dee	J.Hunt	H.Antwine	L.Eisenhauer	T.Addison	N.Buoniconti	J.Rudolph	D.Webb	D.Felt	R.O'Hanley	R.Hall	2ae	10-3-1
1965	B.Dee	J.Hunt	H.Antwine	L.Eisenhauer	T.Addison	N.Buoniconti	J.Rudolph	C.Shonta	T.Hennessey	R.O'Hanley	R.Hall	3ae	4-8-2
1966	B.Dee	J.Hunt	H.Antwine	L.Eisenhauer	T.Addison	N.Buoniconti	L.Farmer	D.Webb	T.Hennessey	C.Shonta	R.Hall	2ae	8-4-2
1967	B.Dee	J.Hunt	H.Antwine	L.Eisenhauer	E.Philpott	N.Buoniconti	D.Satcher	L.Mitchell	J.Charles	D.Webb	C.Shonta	5ae	3-10-1
1968	D.Byrd	J.Hunt	H.Antwine	L.Eisenhauer	E.Philpott	N.Buoniconti	D.Satcher	L.Mitchell	D.Johnson	J.Charles	D.Webb	4ae	4-10
1969	K.Henke	J.Hunt	H.Antwine	L.Eisenhauer	E.Philpott	J.Cheyunski	J.Bramlett	L.Carwell	D.Johnson	J.Charles	D.Webb	3ae	4-10
1970	M.Witt	J.Hunt	R.Berger	H.Antwine	E.Philpott	J.Cheyunski	J.Bramlett	L.Carwell	D.Johnson	C.Scott	D.Webb	5ae	2-12
1971	I.Lassiter	D.Rowe	J.Adams	D.Wirgowski	E.Weisacosky	J.Cheyunski	S.Kiner	L.Carwell	J.Outlaw	R.Harris	D.Webb	3ae	6-8
1972	J.Adams	D.Rowe	R.Cash	D.Wirgowski	E.Weisacosky	J.Cheyunski	R.Acks	L.Carwell	J.Outlaw	H.Jackson	R.Harris	5ae	3-11
1973	R.Hamilton	D.Rowe	J.Adams	R.Cash	S.Kiner	E.Chandler	R.Acks	G.Hoey	R.Bolton	S.Durko	R.Anderson	3ae	5-9
1974	M.Lunsford	R.Hamilton	J.Adams*	G.Webster	S.Nelson	S.Hunt	S.King	J.Sanders	R.Bolton	J.Mildren	P.McCray	3ae	7-7
1975	T.McGee	R.Hamilton	J.Adams*	G.Webster	S.Nelson	S.Hunt	S.Zabel	B.Howard	R.Bolton	P.McCray	J.Sanders	4ae	3-11
1976	T.McGee	R.Hamilton	J.Adams*	S.Zabel	S.Nelson	S.Hunt	S.King	B.Howard	M.Haynes	P.McCray	T.Fox	2ae	11-3 #w
1977	M.Lunsford	R.Hamilton	J.Adams*	S.Zabel	S.Nelson	S.Hunt	P.Barnes	B.Howard	M.Haynes	P.McCray	T.Fox	3ae	9-5
1978	M.Lunsford	R.Hamilton	R.Bishop*	S.Zabel	S.Nelson	S.Hunt	R.Shoate	R.Clayborn	M.Haynes	D.Beaudoin	T.Fox	1ae	11-5 #d
1979	M.Lunsford	R.Hamilton	R.Bishop*	M.Hawkins	S.Nelson	S.Hunt	R.Shoate	R.Clayborn	M.Haynes	D.Beaudoin	T.Fox	2ae	9-7
1980	M.Lunsford	R.Hamilton	J.Adams*	M.Hawkins	S.Nelson	J.Zamberlin	R.Shoate	R.Clayborn	M.Haynes	R.James	T.Fox	2ae	10-6
1981	T.McGee	R.Bishop	J.Adams*	M.Hawkins	S.Nelson	B.Matthews	R.Shoate	R.Clayborn	M.Haynes	R.Sanford	T.Fox	4ae	2-14
1982	K.Sims	L.Williams	J.Adams*	L.McGrew	S.Nelson	C.Weishuhn	D.Blackmon	M.Haynes	R.Clayborn	R.James	R.Sanford	7a	5-4 p
1983	T.Williams	D.Owens	J.Adams*	A.Tippett	J.Rembert	C.Weishuhn	D.Blackmon	R.Lippett	R.Clayborn	R.James	R.Sanford	2ae	8-8
1984	K.Sims	D.Owens	T.Williams*	A.Tippett	S.Nelson	L.McGrew	D.Blackmon	E.Gibson	R.Clayborn	R.James	F.Marion	2ae	9-7
1985	K.Sims	D.Owens	J.Adams*	A.Tippett	S.Nelson	L.McGrew	D.Blackmon	R.Lippett	R.Clayborn	R.James	F.Marion	3ae	11-5 #wdcs
1986	B.Williams	T.Williams	G.Veris*	A.Tippett	S.Nelson	L.McGrew	D.Blackmon	R.Lippett	R.Clayborn	R.James	F.Marion	1ae	11-5 d
1987	K.Sims	T.Williams	G.Veris*	A.Tippett	S.Nelson	L.McGrew	E.Williams	R.Lippett	R.Clayborn	J.Bowman	F.Marion	2ae	8-7
1988	B.Williams	T.Goad	G.Veris*	A.Tippett	E.Reynolds	J.Rembert	L.McGrew	R.Lippett	R.Clayborn	R.James	F.Marion	2ae	9-7
1989	K.Sims	T.Goad	B.Williams*	J.Rembert	E.Reynolds	V.Brown	L.McGrew	M.Hurst	R.Clayborn	R.James	F.Marion	4ae	5-11
1990	B.Williams	T.Goad	R.Agnew*	V.Brown	R.Harvey	E.Reynolds	A.Tippett	R.Lippett	M.Hurst	R.McSwain	F.Marion	5ae	1-15
1991	R.Agnew	T.Goad	B.Williams*	A.Tippett	E.Lockhart	V.Brown	C.Singleton	R.Lippett	M.Hurst	H.Colon	F.Marion	4ae	6-10
1992	R.Agnew	T.Goad	B.Williams*	A.Tippett	V.Brown	J.Rembert	D.Howard	D.Pool	M.Hurst	T.Gordon	R.Robbins	5ae	2-14
1993	M.Pitts	T.Goad	J.Washington*	A.Tippett	V.Brown	T.Collins	D.Sabb	R.Smith	M.Hurst	C.Brown	H.Barnett	4ae	5-11

YEAR	COACH	WR/LE	LT	LG	C	RG	RT	TE/RE	WR/FL	QB	RB/LH	FB
1994	B.Parcells	V.Brisby	B.Armstrong	B.Kratch	M.Arthur	T.Rucci	P.Harlow	B.Coates	M.Timpson	D.Bledsoe	M.Butts	K.Turner
1995	B.Parcells	V.Brisby	B.Armstrong	W.Roberts	D.Wohlabaugh	B.Kratch	M.Lane	B.Coates	W.Moore	D.Bledsoe	C.Martin	S.Gash
1996	B.Parcells	S.Jefferson	B.Armstrong	W.Roberts	D.Wohlabaugh	T.Rucci	M.Lane	B.Coates	T.Glenn	D.Bledsoe	C.Martin	S.Gash
1997	P.Carroll	S.Jefferson	B.Armstrong	M.Lane	D.Wohlabaugh	T.Rucci	Z.Moss	B.Coates	T.Glenn	D.Bledsoe	C.Martin	K.Byars
1998	P.Carroll	S.Jefferson	B.Armstrong	M.Lane	D.Wohlabaugh	T.Rucci	Z.Moss	B.Coates	T.Glenn	D.Bledsoe	R.Edwards	T.Carter
1999	P.Carroll	S.Jefferson	B.Armstrong	H.Irwin	D.Woody	T.Rucci	Z.Moss	B.Coates	T.Glenn	D.Bledsoe	T.Allen	T.Carter
2000	Belichick	T.Brown	B.Armstrong	J.Andruzzi	D.Woody	S.Isaia	G.Williams	R.Rutledge	T.Glenn	D.Bledsoe	K.Faulk	T.Carter
2001	Belichick	T.Brown	M.Light	M.Compton	D.Woody	J.Andruzzi	G.Randall	R.Rutledge	D.Patten	T.Brady	A.Smith	M.Edwards
2002	Belichick	T.Brown	M.Light	M.Compton	D.Woody	J.Andruzzi	K.Jones	C.Fauria	D.Patten	T.Brady	A.Smith	M.Edwards
2003	Belichick	T.Brown	M.Light	D.Woody	D.Koppen	J.Andruzzi	T.Ashworth	C.Fauria	D.Branch	T.Brady	K.Faulk	D.Graham*
2004	Belichick	D.Branch	M.Light	J.Andruzzi	D.Koppen	S.Neal	B.Gorin	D.Graham	D.Givens	T.Brady	C.Dillon	D.Patten+
2005	Belichick	D.Branch	N.Kaczur	L.Mankins	D.Koppen	S.Neal	T.Ashworth	B.Watson	D.Givens	T.Brady	C.Dillon	C.Fauria*

New Orleans Saints

YEAR	COACH	WR/LE	LT	LG	C	RG	RT	TE/RE	WR/FL	QB	RB/LH	FB
1967	T.Fears	D.Abramowicz	R.Rissmiller	R.Schmidt	Wendryhoski	D.Williams	J.Jones	K.Kramer	R.Poage	G.Cuozzo	Wheelwright	J.Taylor
1968	T.Fears	D.Parks	J.Sturm	J.Kupp	Wendryhoski	D.Williams	J.Jones	M.Stickles	D.Abramowicz	B.Kilmer	D.McCall	T.Lorick
1969	T.Fears	A.Dodd	D.Talbert	J.Kupp	J.Sturm	D.Williams	E.Linden	D.Parks	D.Abramowicz	B.Kilmer	A.Livingston	T.Baker
1970	J.Roberts	A.Dodd	D.Talbert	J.Kupp	J.Sturm	D.Williams	E.Linden	D.Parks	D.Abramowicz	B.Kilmer	T.Barrington	J.Otis
1971	J.Roberts	A.Dodd	D.Morrison	J.Kupp	J.Didion	D.Williams	G.Hines	D.Parks	D.Abramowicz	A.Manning	B.Gresham	J.Strong
1972	J.Roberts	B.Newland	D.Morrison	C.Johnson	J.Didion	R.Smith	G.Hines	D.Parks	D.Abramowicz	A.Manning	B.Gresham	B.Butler
1973	J.North	B.Newland	C.Johnson	J.Kupp	J.Didion	D.Williams	D.Morrison	J.Beasley	J.Dunbar	A.Manning	J.Phillips	J.Profit
1974	J.North	J.Parker	D.Thompson	J.Kupp	J.Didion	E.Zanders	D.Morrison	P.Seal	B.Newland	A.Manning	A.Maxson	J.Phillips
1975	E.Hefferle	J.Parker	D.Thompson	J.Kupp	J.Hill	E.Zanders	D.Morrison	P.Seal	L.Burton	A.Manning	M.Strachan	A.Maxson
1976	H.Stram	D.Herrmann	T.Wickert	K.Schumacher	J.Hill	E.Zanders	D.Morrison	H.Childs	L.Burton	B.Scott	T.Galbreath	C.Muncie
1977	H.Stram	D.Herrmann	M.Montgomery	T.Stieve	J.Hill	E.Zanders	D.Morrison	H.Childs	J.Gilliam	A.Manning	C.Muncie	T.Galbreath
1978	D.Nolan	T.Owens	J.Taylor	F.Sturt	J.Hill	D.Lafary	R.Woods	H.Childs	I.Harris	A.Manning	C.Muncie	T.Galbreath
1979	D.Nolan	W.Chandler	J.Taylor	E.Zanders	J.Hill	C.Dobler	R.Woods	H.Childs	I.Harris	A.Manning	C.Muncie	T.Galbreath
1980	D.Nolan	W.Chandler	J.Taylor	E.Zanders	J.Hill	F.Sturt	S.Brock	B.Williams	I.Harris	A.Manning	J.Rogers	W.Wilson
1981	B.Phillips	G.Merkens	J.Taylor	F.Sturt	J.Hill	S.Adams	S.Brock	L.Hardy	J.Groth	A.Manning	G.Rogers	J.Holmes
1982	B.Phillips	L.Scott	D.Lafary	B.Edelman	J.Hill	L.Oubre	S.Brock	H.Brenner	J.Groth	K.Stabler	G.Rogers	W.Wilson
1983	B.Phillips	E.Goodlow	D.Lafary	B.Edelman	J.Hill	L.Oubre	S.Brock	H.Brenner	J.Groth	K.Stabler	G.Rogers	H.Gajan
1984	B.Phillips	J.Groth	K.Clark	B.Edelman	J.Hill	S.Korte	S.Brock	H.Brenner	T.Young	R.Todd	G.Rogers	H.Gajan
1985	B.Phillips	E.Goodlow	D.Lafary	B.Edelman	S.Korte	R.Williams	S.Brock	H.Brenner	E.Martin	D.Wilson	E.Campbell	W.Wilson
1986	J.Mora	M.Jones	B.Contz	B.Edelman	S.Korte	C.Commiskey	S.Brock	H.Brenner	E.Martin	D.Wilson	R.Mayes	J.Tice*
1987	J.Mora	E.Martin	J.Dombrowski	B.Edelman	J.Hilgenberg	S.Trapilo	S.Brock	H.Brenner	M.Jones	B.Hebert	R.Mayes	J.Tice*
1988	J.Mora	E.Martin	J.Dombrowski	B.Edelman	S.Korte	J.Hilgenberg	S.Brock	H.Brenner	L.Hill	B.Hebert	D.Hilliard	J.Tice*
1989	J.Mora	E.Martin	J.Dombrowski	B.Edelman	J.Hilgenberg	S.Trapilo	S.Brock	H.Brenner	L.Hill	B.Hebert	D.Hilliard	B.Jordan
1990	J.Mora	E.Martin	K.Haverdink	J.Dombrowski	J.Hilgenberg	S.Trapilo	S.Brock	H.Brenner	B.Perriman	S.Walsh	R.Mayes	C.Heyward
1991	J.Mora	E.Martin	R.Cooper	J.Dombrowski	J.Hilgenberg	C.Port	S.Brock	H.Brenner	Q.Early	B.Hebert	G.Fenerty	J.Tice*
1992	J.Mora	E.Martin	R.Cooper	J.Dombrowski	J.Hilgenberg	D.Kennard	S.Brock	H.Brenner	Q.Early	B.Hebert	V.Dunbar	C.Heyward
1993	J.Mora	E.Martin	R.Cooper	C.Port	J.Hilgenberg	D.Kennard	W.Roaf	H.Brenner	Q.Early	W.Wilson	D.Brown	B.Muster
1994	J.Mora	Q.Early	W.Roaf	J.Dombrowski	J.Uhlenhake	C.Port	R.Cooper	I.Smith	M.Haynes	J.Everett	D.Brown	W.Walls*
1995	J.Mora	Q.Early	W.Roaf	J.Dombrowski	J.Uhlenhake	A.McCollum	R.Cooper	I.Smith	M.Haynes	J.Everett	M.Bates	W.Walls*
1996	R.Venturi	M.Haynes	W.Roaf	J.Dombrowski	A.McCollum	E.King	C.Jones	I.Smith	T.Small	J.Everett	M.Bates	L.Neal
1997	M.Ditka	R.Hill	W.Roaf	A.McCollum	J.Fontenot	M.Verstegen	C.Jones	I.Smith	A.Hastings	H.Shuler	M.Bates	R.Zellars
1998	M.Ditka	A.Hastings	W.Roaf	K.Turley	T.Ackerman	C.Naeole	C.Jones	C.Cleeland	S.Dawkins	K.Collins	L.Smith	A.Craver
1999	M.Ditka	K.Poole	W.Roaf	T.Ackerman	J.Fontenot	C.Naeole	K.Turley	C.Cleeland	E.Kennison	B.Tolliver	R.Williams	A.Craver
2000	J.Haslett	W.Jackson	W.Roaf	W.Williams	J.Fontenot	C.Naeole	K.Turley	A.Glover	J.Horn	J.Blake	R.Williams	T.Smith
2001	J.Haslett	W.Jackson	D.Terrell	W.Williams	J.Fontenot	C.Naeole	K.Turley	C.Cleeland	J.Horn	A.Brooks	R.Williams	T.Smith
2002	J.Haslett	J.Horn	K.Turley	K.Jacox	J.Fontenot	L.Bentley	S.Folau	D.Sloan	J.Pathon	A.Brooks	D.McAllister	T.Smith
2003	J.Haslett	J.Horn	W.Gandy	K.Jacox	J.Fontenot	L.Bentley	V.Riley	E.Conwell	J.Pathon	A.Brooks	D.McAllister	T.Smith
2004	J.Haslett	J.Horn	W.Gandy	K.Jacox	L.Bentley	M.Holland	V.Riley	E.Conwell	D.Stallworth	A.Brooks	D.McAllister	M.Karney
2005	J.Haslett	D.Stallworth	W.Gandy	K.Jacox	L.Bentley	M.Holland	J.Brown	E.Conwell	J.Horn	A.Brooks	A.Smith	M.Karney

New York Giants

YEAR	COACH	WR/LE	LT	LG	C	RG	RT	TE/RE	WR/FL	QB	RB/LH	FB
1950	S.Owen	B.Swiacki	J.White	J.Sulaitis	J.Rapacz	B.Austin	J.Sanchez	B.McChesney	R.Clay	C.Conerly	G.Roberts	E.Price
1951	S.Owen	B.McChesney	T.Coulter	J.Sulaitis	J.Rapacz	B.Murray	H.Hannah	B.Stribling	J.Scott	C.Conerly	F.Griffith	E.Price
1952	S.Owen	B.McChesney	T.Coulter	R.Beck	J.Rapacz	G.Kennard	D.Yelvington	B.Stribling	J.Scott	C.Conerly	K.Rote	E.Price
1953	S.Owen	C.Anderson	R.Brown	G.Kennard	J.Rapacz	B.Austin	D.Yelvington	B.Stribling	K.Rote	C.Conerly	S.Grandelius	E.Price
1954	J.Howell	B.Schnelker	R.Brown	B.Austin	R.Wietecha	G.Kennard	D.Yelvington	K.MacAfee	K.Rote	C.Conerly	F.Gifford	E.Price
1955	J.Howell	K.Rote	R.Brown	B.Austin	R.Wietecha	J.Stroud	D.Yelvington	B.Schnelker	A.Webster	C.Conerly	F.Gifford	B.Epps
1956	J.Howell	K.Rote	R.Brown	B.Austin	R.Wietecha	J.Stroud	D.Yelvington	K.MacAfee	A.Webster	C.Conerly	F.Gifford	M.Triplett
1957	J.Howell	K.Rote	R.Brown	D.Yelvington	R.Wietecha	J.Stroud	J.Spinks	B.Schnelker	A.Webster	C.Conerly	F.Gifford	M.Triplett
1958	J.Howell	K.Rote	R.Brown	A.Barry	R.Wietecha	J.Stroud	F.Youso	B.Schnelker	A.Webster	C.Conerly	F.Gifford	M.Triplett
1959	J.Howell	K.Rote	R.Brown	D.Dess	R.Wietecha	J.Stroud	F.Youso	B.Schnelker	A.Webster	C.Conerly	F.Gifford	M.Triplett
1960	J.Howell	K.Rote	R.Brown	D.Dess	R.Wietecha	J.Stroud	F.Youso	B.Schnelker	J.Morrison	C.Conerly	F.Gifford	M.Triplett
1961	A.Sherman	D.Shofner	R.Brown	D.Dess	R.Wietecha	J.Stroud	G.Larson	J.Walton	J.Morrison	Y.Tittle	K.Rote	A.Webster
1962	A.Sherman	D.Shofner	R.Brown	D.Dess	R.Wietecha	G.Larson	J.Stroud	J.Walton	F.Gifford	Y.Tittle	P.King	A.Webster
1963	A.Sherman	D.Shofner	R.Brown	D.Dess	G.Larson	B.Bolin	J.Stroud	J.Walton	F.Gifford	Y.Tittle	P.King	A.Webster
1964	A.Sherman	D.Shofner	R.Brown	D.Dess	G.Larson	B.Bolin	R.Anderson	A.Thomas	F.Gifford	Y.Tittle	D.James	Wheelwright
1965	A.Sherman	D.Shofner	R.Brown	P.Case	B.Scholtz	B.Bolin	F.Lasky	A.Thomas	J.Morrison	E.Morrall	S.Thurlow	Frederickson
1966	A.Sherman	H.Jones	W.Young	P.Case	G.Larson	B.Bolin	F.Peay	A.Thomas	E.Koy	E.Morrall	J.Morrison	C.Mercein
1967	A.Sherman	H.Jones	W.Young	P.Case	G.Larson	D.Dess	C.Harper	A.Thomas	D.Shofner	F.Tarkenton	E.Koy	Frederickson
1968	A.Sherman	H.Jones	W.Young	P.Case	G.Larson	D.Dess	S.Wright	A.Thomas	J.Morrison	F.Tarkenton	E.Koy	B.Duhon
1969	A.Webster	H.Jones	W.Young	P.Case	G.Larson	D.Van Horn	R.Buzin	F.White	D.Herrmann	F.Tarkenton	E.Koy	J.Morrison
1970	A.Webster	C.McNeil	W.Young	C.Harper	G.Larson	D.Van Horn	R.Buzin	B.Tucker	D.Herrmann	F.Tarkenton	R.Johnson	Frederickson
1971	A.Webster	D.Herrmann	W.Young	B.Hyland	G.Larson	D.Van Horn	C.Harper	B.Tucker	R.Houston	F.Tarkenton	B.Duhon	Frederickson
1972	A.Webster	D.Herrmann	W.Young	D.Enderle	G.Larson	D.Van Horn	J.Taffoni	B.Tucker	R.Houston	N.Snead	R.Johnson	C.Evans
1973	A.Webster	D.Herrmann	W.Young	D.Enderle	G.Larson	D.Van Horn	J.Taffoni	B.Tucker	B.Grim	N.Snead	R.Johnson	J.Roland
1974	Arnsbarger	W.Gillette	W.Young	T.Mullen	B.Hyland	J.Hicks	D.Van Horn	B.Tucker	B.Grim	C.Morton	D.Kotar	J.Dawkins
1975	Arnsbarger	R.Rhodes	W.Young	T.Mullen	B.Hyland	J.Hicks	D.Van Horn	B.Tucker	W.Gillette	C.Morton	R.Johnson	J.Dawkins
1976	J.McVay	J.Robinson	T.Mullen	A.Simpson	K.Chandler	J.Hicks	D.Van Horn	B.Tucker	R.Rhodes	C.Morton	D.Kotar	L.Csonka
1977	J.McVay	J.Robinson	G.Gravelle	D.Van Horn	K.Chandler	J.Hicks	Mikolajczyk	G.Shirk	E.Moorehead	J.Pisarcik	D.Kotar	L.Csonka
1978	J.McVay	J.Perkins	G.Gravelle	D.Van Horn	J.Clack	J.Turner	Mikolajczyk	A.Dixon	J.Robinson	J.Pisarcik	D.Kotar	L.Csonka
1979	R.Perkins	J.Robinson	B.Benson	D.Van Horn	J.Clack	J.Turner	T.Neville	G.Shirk	E.Gray	P.Simms	D.Kotar	B.Taylor
1980	R.Perkins	D.Pittman	B.Benson	R.Simmons	J.Clack	J.Turner	G.King	G.Shirk	E.Gray	P.Simms	B.Taylor	B.Matthews
1981	R.Perkins	M.Friede	B.Benson	R.Simmons	E.Hughes	J.Turner	G.King	G.Shirk	J.Perkins	P.Simms	L.Perry	R.Carpenter
1982	R.Perkins	E.Gray	B.Benson	B.Ard	R.Umphrey	J.Turner	G.King	T.Mullady	J.Perkins	S.Brunner	B.Woolfolk	R.Carpenter
1983	B.Parcells	E.Gray	B.Benson	B.Ard	R.Umphrey	J.Turner	G.King	Z.Mowatt	J.Mistler	S.Brunner	B.Woolfolk	R.Carpenter
1984	B.Parcells	E.Gray	W.Roberts	B.Ard	K.Belcher	B.Benson	K.Nelson	Z.Mowatt	B.Johnson	P.Simms	J.Morris	R.Carpenter
1985	B.Parcells	B.Johnson	B.Benson	B.Ard	B.Oates	C.Godfrey	K.Nelson	M.Bavaro	L.Manuel	P.Simms	J.Morris	R.Carpenter
1986	B.Parcells	B.Johnson	B.Benson	B.Ard	B.Oates	C.Godfrey	K.Nelson	M.Bavaro	S.Robinson	P.Simms	J.Morris	M.Carthon
1987	B.Parcells	L.Manuel	B.Benson	B.Ard	B.Oates	D.Johnson	W.Roberts	M.Bavaro	S.Baker	P.Simms	J.Morris	G.Adams
1988	B.Parcells	L.Manuel	W.Roberts	B.Ard	B.Oates	E.Moore	D.Riesenberg	M.Bavaro	S.Baker	P.Simms	J.Morris	M.Carthon
1989	B.Parcells	O.Turner	J.Elliott	W.Roberts	B.Oates	E.Moore	D.Riesenberg	Z.Mowatt	L.Manuel	P.Simms	O.Anderson	M.Carthon
1990	B.Parcells	M.Ingram	E.Moore	W.Roberts	B.Oates	B.Kratch	D.Riesenberg	M.Bavaro	S.Baker	P.Simms	O.Anderson	M.Carthon
1991	R.Handley	M.Ingram	J.Elliott	W.Roberts	B.Oates	E.Moore	D.Riesenberg	H.Cross	S.Baker	J.Hostetler	R.Hampton	M.Carthon

YEAR	LDE	LDT/NT	RDT/RDE	RDE/LOLB	LLB/LILB	MLB/RILB	RLB/ROLB	LCB	RCB	SS/LS	FS/RS	FINISH
1994	M.Pitts	T.Goad	M.Jones*	D.Sabb	V.Brown	T.Collins	C.Slade	R.Reynolds	M.Hurst	H.Barnett	M.Guyton	2ae 10-6 #w
1995	T.Roberts	R.White	T.Barnett*	W.McGinest	V.Brown	T.Johnson	C.Slade	R.Reynolds	M.Hurst	T.Ray	M.Guyton	4ae 6-10
1996	M.Jones	M.Wheeler	Sagapolutele	W.McGinest	T.Collins	T.Johnson	D.Sabb	T.Law	R.Reynolds	L.Milloy	W.Clay	1ae 11-5 dcs
1997	C.Sullivan	M.Wheeler	H.Thomas	W.McGinest	C.Slade	T.Johnson	T.Collins	T.Law	J.Hitchcock	L.Milloy	W.Clay	1ae 10-6 ed
1998	F.Collons	C.Eaton	H.Thomas	W.McGinest	C.Slade	T.Johnson	T.Collins	T.Law	C.Canty	L.Milloy	W.Clay	4ae 9-7 w
1999	B.Mitchell	C.Eaton	H.Thomas	W.McGinest	C.Slade	Katzenmoyer	T.Bruschi	T.Law	S.Israel	L.Milloy	C.Carter	4ae 8-8
2000	B.Mitchell	C.Eaton	B.Hamilton*	W.McGinest	C.Slade	T.Johnson	T.Bruschi	T.Law	O.Smith	L.Milloy	T.Jones	5ae 5-11
2001	B.Hamilton	B.Mitchell	A.Pleasant	R.Seymour	M.Vrabel	T.Bruschi	R.Phifer	T.Law	O.Smith	L.Milloy	T.Jones	1ae 11-5 #dcs*
2002	W.McGinest	B.Hamilton	A.Pleasant	R.Seymour	M.Vrabel	T.Johnson	R.Phifer	T.Law	O.Smith	L.Milloy	T.Jones	3ae 9-7 #
2003	B.Hamilton	T.Washington	R.Seymour	W.McGinest	R.Phifer	T.Bruschi	M.Vrabel	T.Law	T.Poole	R.Harrison	E.Wilson	1ae 14-2 dcs*
2004	T.Warren	K.Traylor	R.Seymour*	W.McGinest	T.Johnson	T.Bruschi	M.Vrabel	T.Law	R.Gay	R.Harrison	E.Wilson	1ae 14-2 dcs*
2005	T.Warren	V.Wilfork	R.Seymour*	W.McGinest	T.Bruschi	M.Vrabel	R.Colvin	A.Samuel	E.Hobbs	A.Hawkins	E.Wilson	1ae 10-6 ed

1967	D.Atkins	M.Tilleman	D.Rowe	B.Schweda	Stonebreaker	Whittingham	J.Burkett	D.Whitsell	J.Douglas	J.Heidel	O.Logan	4nca 3-11
1968	D.Atkins	M.Tilleman	D.Rowe	B.Schweda	T.Davis	Whittingham	J.Brewer	G.Howard	J.Douglas	B.Burris	D.Whitsell	3ncy 4-9-1
1969	D.Atkins	M.Tilleman	D.Rowe	D.Long	M.Morgan	D.Absher	J.Brewer	G.Howard	E.Nevett	B.Thompson	D.Whitsell	3nca 5-9
1970	R.Neal	M.Tilleman	D.Rowe	D.Long	M.Morgan	D.Absher	J.Burkett	D.Wyatt	D.Howell	H.Hollas	J.Scarpati	4nw 2-11-1
1971	R.Neal	B.Pollard	D.Long	J.Owens	T.Roussel	J.Flanigan	W.Colman	D.Martin	D.Howell	H.Hollas	D.Wyatt	4nw 4-8-2
1972	R.Neal	B.Pollard	D.Long	J.Owens	T.Roussel	J.Federspiel	W.Colman	E.Jackson	D.Howell	H.Hollas	D.Wyatt	4nw 2-11-1
1973	B.Newsome	B.Pollard	E.Price	J.Owens	W.Hall	J.Federspiel	W.Colman	E.Jackson	B.Lee	J.Fuller	T.Myers	3nw 5-9
1974	B.Newsome	E.Price	D.Moore	B.Pollard	J.Merlo	J.Federspiel	W.Colman	E.Jackson	T.Schmidt	J.Fuller	T.Myers	3nw 5-9
1975	A.Dorris	B.Pollard	D.Moore	Baumgartner	D.Coleman	J.Federspiel	R.Middleton	E.Jackson	T.Schmidt	T.Myers	J.Fuller	4nw 2-12
1976	B.Pollard	E.Price	D.Moore	Baumgartner	J.Merlo	J.Federspiel	G.Westbrooks	E.Jackson	M.Spencer	C.Crist	T.Myers	3nw 4-10
1977	E.Grooms	E.Price	D.Moore	B.Pollard	J.Merlo	J.Federspiel	P.Hughes	E.Jackson	C.Chapman	C.Crist	T.Myers	4nw 3-11
1978	E.Grooms	E.Price	D.Moore	J.Campbell	J.Merlo	J.Federspiel	P.Hughes	C.Chapman	M.Spencer	R.Brown	T.Myers	3nw 7-9
1979	E.Grooms	B.Bennett	D.Moore	D.Reese	K.Bordelon	J.Federspiel	P.Hughes	C.Chapman	E.Felton	R.Brown	T.Myers	2nw 8-8
1980	E.Grooms	M.Fultz	D.Moore	T.Hart	K.Bordelon	J.Federspiel	R.Mathis	C.Chapman	D.Waymer	R.Brown	T.Myers	4nw 1-15
1981	D.Moore	J.Boyarsky	E.Grooms*	R.Jackson	G.Redd	J.Kovach	R.Nairne	D.Waymer	J.Poe	R.Gary	T.Myers	4nw 4-12
1982	B.Clark	D.Moore	J.Wilks*	R.Jackson	J.Kovach	D.Winston	R.Nairne	D.Waymer	J.Poe	R.Gary	F.Wattelet	9n 4-5 #
1983	B.Clark	D.Moore	J.Wilks*	R.Jackson	J.Kovach	D.Winston	W.Paul	D.Waymer	J.Poe	R.Gary	F.Wattelet	3nw 8-8
1984	B.Clark	D.Moore	J.Wilks*	R.Jackson	D.Winston	J.Kovach	W.Paul	D.Waymer	J.Poe	R.Gary	F.Wattelet	3nw 7-9
1985	B.Clark	T.Elliott	J.Wilks*	R.Jackson	G.Redd	J.Del Rio	W.Paul	D.Waymer	J.Poe	T.Hoage	F.Wattelet	3nw 5-11
1986	B.Clark	T.Elliott	J.Wilks*	R.Jackson	S.Mills	A.Toles	J.Haynes	D.Waymer	J.Poe	A.Gibson	F.Wattelet	4nw 7-9
1987	B.Clark	T.Elliott	J.Wilks*	R.Jackson	S.Mills	V.Johnson	P.Swilling	D.Waymer	V.Jakes	A.Gibson	B.Maxie	2nw 12-3 w
1988	F.Warren	T.Elliott	J.Wilks*	R.Jackson	S.Mills	V.Johnson	P.Swilling	D.Waymer	V.Jakes	A.Gibson	B.Maxie	3nw 10-6 #
1989	F.Warren	J.Wilks	J.Geathers*	R.Jackson	S.Mills	V.Johnson	P.Swilling	R.Massey	T.Cook	G.Atkins	D.Waymer	3nw 9-7
1990	W.Martin	R.Goff	J.Wilks*	R.Jackson	S.Mills	V.Johnson	P.Swilling	R.Massey	T.Cook	B.Maxie	G.Atkins	2nw 8-8 w
1991	W.Martin	J.Wilks	F.Warren*	R.Jackson	S.Mills	V.Johnson	P.Swilling	V.Buck	T.Cook	B.Maxie	G.Atkins	1nw 11-5 e
1992	W.Martin	J.Wilks	F.Warren*	R.Jackson	S.Mills	V.Johnson	P.Swilling	T.Cook	R.Jones	B.Maxie	G.Atkins	2nw 12-4 w
1993	W.Martin	L.Miller	R.Goff*	R.Jackson	J.Williams	V.Johnson	R.Turnbull	V.Buck	T.Cook	K.Taylor	G.Atkins	2nw 8-8
1994	W.Martin	F.Warren	J.Johnson*	D.Conner	S.Mills	W.Tubbs	R.Turnbull	J.Spencer	C.Lee	S.Lumpkin	V.Buck	2nw 7-9
1995	J.Johnson	W.Broughton	W.Martin	R.Turnbull	R.Porter	B.Jones	R.Harvey	J.Spencer	E.Allen	S.Lumpkin	V.Buck	3nw 7-9
1996	D.Mickell	W.Martin	A.Robbins	J.Johnson	R.Porter	W.Tubbs	M.Fields	M.McMillian	E.Allen	A.Newman	G.Jackson	4nw 3-13
1997	D.Mickell	W.Martin	Sagapolutele	J.Johnson	R.Harvey	W.Tubbs	M.Fields	A.Molden	E.Allen	A.Newman	S.Knight	4nw 6-10
1998	J.Tomich	W.Martin	L.Glover	J.Johnson	Kei.Mitchell	Kev.Mitchell	M.Fields	A.Molden	T.Drakeford	C.Cota	S.Knight	3nw 6-10
1999	J.Tomich	W.Martin	L.Glover	B.Smith	K.Mitchell	C.Bordano	M.Fields	A.Ambrose	F.Weary	S.Knight	W.Clay	5nw 3-13
2000	D.Howard	N.Hand	L.Glover	J.Johnson	K.Mitchell	D.Smith	M.Fields	K.Mathis	F.Weary	S.Knight	D.Perry	1nw 10-6 #ed
2001	D.Howard	N.Hand	L.Glover	J.Johnson	K.Mitchell	C.Clemons	D.Smith	K.Mathis	F.Thomas	S.Knight	J.Bellamy	3nw 7-9
2002	W.Whitehead	G.Jackson	N.Hand	D.Howard	D.Smith	C.Clemons	S.Hodge	K.Irvin	F.Thomas	J.Bellamy	S.Knight	3ns 9-7
2003	C.Grant	J.Sullivan	K.Smith	W.Whitehead	S.Hodge	D.Smith	D.Rodgers	A.Ambrose	F.Thomas	J.Bellamy	T.Jones	2ns 8-8
2004	C.Grant	H.Green	B.Young	D.Howard	J.Allen	C.Watson	D.Rodgers	M.McKenzie	F.Brown	J.Bellamy	T.Jones	2ns 8-8 #
2005	D.Howard	B.Young	W.Whitehead	C.Grant	S.Hodge	R.McKinnon	C.Bockwoldt	M.McKenzie	F.Thomas	D.Smith	J.Bullocks	4ns 3-13

1950	J.Duncan	Weinmeister	A.DeRogatis	R.Poole	D.Woodard	J.Baker+	J.Cannady	Schnellbacher	H.Rowe	E.Tunnell	T.Landry	1na 10-2 c
1951	J.Duncan	Weinmeister	A.DeRogatis	R.Poole	D.Woodard	J.Baker+	J.Cannady	Schnellbacher	J.Amberg	E.Tunnell	T.Landry	2na 9-2-1
1952	J.Duncan	Weinmeister	R.Krouse	R.Poole	J.Sulaitis	J.Baker+	J.Cannady	J.Amberg	D.Menasco	E.Tunnell	T.Landry	2na 7-5
1953	J.Duncan	Weinmeister	R.Krouse	J.Sulaitis	B.Peviani	J.Cannady	D.Woodard	B.Long	R.Clay	E.Tunnell	T.Landry	5ne 3-9
1954	B.Poole	R.Krouse	R.Collins	C.Livingston	B.Svoboda	P.Knight	J.Cannady	H.Rich	D.Nolan	E.Tunnell	T.Landry	3ne 7-5
1955	W.Yowarsky	R.Krouse	R.Boggan	R.Grier	B.Svoboda	P.Knight	H.Svare	H.Rich	D.Nolan	E.Tunnell	T.Landry	3ne 6-5-1
1956	J.Katcavage	Modzelewski	R.Grier	A.Robustelli	B.Svoboda	S.Huff	H.Svare	E.Hughes	D.Nolan	E.Tunnell	J.Patton	1ne 8-3-1 l*
1957	Martinkovic	Modzelewski	J.Katcavage	A.Robustelli	B.Svoboda	S.Huff	H.Svare	E.Hughes	D.Nolan	E.Tunnell	J.Patton	2ne 7-5
1958	J.Katcavage	Modzelewski	R.Grier	A.Robustelli	B.Svoboda	S.Huff	H.Svare	E.Hughes	C.Karilivacz	E.Tunnell	J.Patton	1ne 9-3 cl
1959	J.Katcavage	Modzelewski	R.Grier	A.Robustelli	C.Livingston	S.Huff	H.Svare	L.Crow	D.Lynch	D.Nolan	J.Patton	1ne 10-2 l
1960	J.Katcavage	Modzelewski	R.Grier	A.Robustelli	C.Livingston	S.Huff	H.Svare	L.Crow	D.Lynch	D.Nolan	J.Patton	3ne 6-4-2
1961	J.Katcavage	Modzelewski	R.Grier	A.Robustelli	C.Livingston	S.Huff	T.Scott	E.Barnes	D.Lynch	D.Nolan	J.Patton	1ne 10-3-1 l
1962	J.Katcavage	Modzelewski	R.Grier	A.Robustelli	B.Winter	S.Huff	T.Scott	E.Barnes	D.Lynch	A.Webb	J.Patton	1ne 12-2 l
1963	J.Katcavage	Modzelewski	J.LoVetere	A.Robustelli	B.Winter	S.Huff	T.Scott	E.Barnes	D.Lynch	A.Webb	J.Patton	1ne 11-3 l
1964	J.Katcavage	A.Stynchula	J.LoVetere	A.Robustelli	B.Winter	L.Slaby	T.Scott	E.Barnes	D.Lynch	J.Patton	D.Pesonen	7ne 2-10-2
1965	J.Katcavage	R.LaLonde	M.Bundra	A.Stynchula	J.Carroll	J.Hillebrand	O.Underwood	S.Lockhart	D.Lynch	H.Carr	J.Patton	2ne 7-7
1966	J.Katcavage	J.Prestel	D.Davis	R.Davis	J.Hillebrand	M.Ciccolella	L.Vargo	S.Lockhart	C.Childs	W.Harris	H.Carr	8ne 1-12-1
1967	J.Katcavage	J.Moran	B.Lurtsema	G.Condren	B.Swain	V.Costello	K.Avery	S.Eaton	H.Carr	W.Harris	S.Lockhart	2ncy 7-7
1968	J.Katcavage	R.Anderson	B.Lurtsema	B.Anderson	T.Crutcher	H.Davis	K.Avery	S.Eaton	W.Williams	B.Maher	S.Lockhart	2nca 7-7
1969	B.Anderson	J.Szczecko	B.Lurtsema	F.Dryer	H.Davis	R.Heck	T.Crutcher	S.Eaton	W.Williams	B.Maher	S.Lockhart	2ncy 6-8
1970	B.Lurtsema	J.Shay	J.Kanicki	F.Dryer	R.Heck	J.Files	M.Hazeltine	S.Eaton	W.Williams	T.Longo	S.Lockhart	2ne 9-5
1971	H.Reed	J.Kanicki	R.Lakes	F.Dryer	R.Heck	J.Files	J.Douglas	O.Brown	W.Williams	S.Eaton	S.Lockhart	5ne 4-10
1972	H.Reed	L.Jacobson	J.Mendenhall	J.Gregory	J.Files	R.Hornsby	P.Hughes	P.Athas	W.Williams	R.Flowers	S.Lockhart	3ne 8-6
1973	C.Campbell	D.Goich	J.Mendenhall	J.Gregory	J.Douglas	J.Files	P.Hughes	P.Athas	W.Williams	R.Flowers	S.Lockhart	5ne 2-11-1
1974	R.Hilton	G.Pettigrew	J.Mendenhall	J.Gregory	B.Van Pelt	B.Kelley	P.Hughes	P.Athas	E.Small	C.Crist	S.Lockhart	5ne 2-12
1975	D.Gallagher	R.Dvorak	J.Mendenhall	J.Gregory	P.Hughes	B.Kelley	B.Van Pelt	B.Brooks	J.Stienke	C.Powers	S.Lockhart	4ne 5-9
1976	G.Martin	D.Gallagher	J.Mendenhall	J.Gregory	B.Van Pelt	H.Carson	B.Kelley	B.Bryant	J.Stienke	C.Powers	R.Volk	5ne 3-11
1977	G.Martin	J.Mendenhall	T.Archer	J.Gregory	B.Van Pelt	H.Carson	B.Kelley	B.Bryant	R.Rhodes	C.Powers	J.Stienke	4ne 5-9
1978	G.Martin	J.Mendenhall	T.Archer	J.Gregory	B.Van Pelt	H.Carson	B.Kelley	T.Jackson	R.Rhodes	B.Reece	E.Jones	4ne 6-10
1979	G.Martin	J.Mendenhall	G.Jeter*	B.Van Pelt	D.Lloyd	H.Carson	B.Kelley	T.Jackson	R.Rhodes	B.Reece	R.Oldham	4ne 6-10
1980	G.Martin	C.McGriff	G.Jeter*	B.Van Pelt	F.Marion	H.Carson	J.Skorupan	M.Haynes	M.Dennis	B.Reece	G.Woolford	5ne 4-12
1981	C.McGriff	B.Neill	G.Jeter*	B.Van Pelt	B.Kelley	H.Carson	L.Taylor	M.Haynes	T.Jackson	B.Currier	B.Reece	3ne 9-7 wd
1982	C.McGriff	B.Neill	P.Tabor*	B.Van Pelt	B.Kelley	H.Carson	L.Taylor	M.Haynes	T.Jackson	B.Currier	B.Reece	10n 4-5 #
1983	C.McGriff	J.Sally	D.Hardison*	B.Van Pelt	B.Kelley	H.Carson	L.Taylor	M.Haynes	T.Jackson	B.Currier	T.Kinard	5ne 3-12-1
1984	C.McGriff	J.Burt	L.Marshall*	B.Hunt	G.Reasons	H.Carson	L.Taylor	M.Haynes	P.Williams	B.Currier	T.Kinard	2ne 9-7 #wd
1985	C.McGriff	J.Burt	L.Marshall*	B.Hunt	G.Reasons	H.Carson	L.Taylor	E.Patterson	P.Williams	K.Hill	T.Kinard	2ne 10-6 #wd
1986	G.Martin	J.Burt	L.Marshall*	C.Banks	G.Reasons	H.Carson	L.Taylor	M.Collins	P.Williams	K.Hill	T.Kinard	1ne 14-2 dcs*
1987	G.Martin	J.Burt	L.Marshall*	C.Banks	P.Johnson	H.Carson	L.Taylor	M.Collins	P.Williams	K.Hill	T.Kinard	5ne 6-9
1988	E.Dorsey	J.Burt	L.Marshall*	C.Banks	P.Johnson	H.Carson	L.Taylor	M.Collins	P.Williams	K.Hill	T.Kinard	2ne 10-6 #
1989	J.Washington	E.Howard	L.Marshall*	C.Banks	G.Reasons	J.Cooks	L.Taylor	M.Collins	P.Williams	M.Guyton	T.Kinard	1ne 12-4 d
1990	E.Dorsey	E.Howard	J.Washington*	C.Banks	S.DeOssie	P.Johnson	L.Taylor	M.Collins	E.Walls	G.Jackson	M.Guyton	1ne 13-3 dcs*
1991	E.Dorsey	J.Washington	L.Marshall*	C.Banks	G.Reasons	P.Johnson	L.Taylor	M.Collins	E.Walls	G.Jackson	M.Guyton	4ne 8-8

846 THE OFFENSIVE STARTERS: 1950–PRESENT

YEAR	COACH	WR/LE	LT	LG	C	RG	RT	TE/RE	WR/FL	QB	RB/LH	FB
1992	R.Handley	M.Ingram	J.Elliott	W.Roberts	B.Oates	E.Moore	D.Riesenberg	H.Cross	S.Baker	J.Hostetler	R.Hampton	J.Bunch
1993	D.Reeves	M.Jackson	J.Elliott	W.Roberts	B.Oates	B.Kratch	D.Riesenberg	H.Cross	C.Calloway	P.Simms	R.Hampton	J.Bunch
1994	D.Reeves	M.Sherrard	J.Elliott	W.Roberts	B.Williams	L.Smith	D.Riesenberg	H.Cross	C.Calloway	D.Brown	R.Hampton	A.Pierce*
1995	D.Reeves	M.Sherrard	J.Elliott	G.Bishop	B.Williams	L.Smith	D.Riesenberg	H.Cross	C.Calloway	D.Brown	R.Hampton	A.Pierce*
1996	D.Reeves	C.Calloway	G.Bishop	L.Smith	B.Williams	R.Stone	S.Gragg	H.Cross	T.Lewis	D.Brown	R.Hampton	C.Way
1997	J.Fassel	C.Calloway	R.Oben	G.Bishop	L.Scott	R.Stone	S.Gragg	H.Cross	K.Alexander	D.Kanell	T.Wheatley	C.Way
1998	J.Fassel	C.Calloway	R.Oben	G.Bishop	L.Scott	R.Stone	S.Gragg	H.Cross	I.Hilliard	D.Kanell	G.Brown	C.Way
1999	J.Fassel	A.Toomer	R.Oben	L.Petitgout	B.Williams	R.Stone	S.Gragg	H.Cross	I.Hilliard	K.Graham	J.Montgomery	C.Way
2000	J.Fassel	A.Toomer	L.Brown	G.Parker	D.Zeigler	R.Stone	L.Petitgout	H.Cross	I.Hilliard	K.Collins	T.Barber	G.Comella
2001	J.Fassel	A.Toomer	L.Brown	G.Parker	D.Zeigler	R.Stone	L.Petitgout	D.Campbell	I.Hilliard	K.Collins	T.Barber	G.Comella
2002	J.Fassel	A.Toomer	L.Petitgout	R.Seubert	C.Bober	J.Whittle	M.Rosenthal	D.Campbell	I.Hilliard	K.Collins	T.Barber	J.Shockey*
2003	J.Fassel	A.Toomer	L.Petitgout	W.Lucier	C.Bober	D.Diehl	I.Allen	J.Shockey	I.Hilliard	K.Collins	T.Barber	J.Finn
2004	T.Coughlin	A.Toomer	L.Petitgout	J.Whittle	S.O'Hara	C.Snee	D.Diehl	J.Shockey	I.Hilliard	K.Warner	T.Barber	J.Finn
2005	T.Coughlin	P.Burress	L.Petitgout	D.Diehl	S.O'Hara	C.Snee	K.McKenzie	J.Shockey	A.Toomer	E.Manning	T.Barber	J.Finn

New York Jets (New York Titans 1960-62)

YEAR	COACH	WR/LE	LT	LG	C	RG	RT	TE/RE	WR/FL	QB	RB/LH	FB
1960	S.Baugh	A.Powell	J.Klotz	B.Mischak	M.Hudock	J.McMullan	G.Cockrell	T.Cooper	D.Maynard	A.Dorow	D.Bohling	B.Mathis
1961	S.Baugh	A.Powell	J.Klotz	B.Mischak	M.Hudock	J.McMullan	G.Cockrell	T.Cooper	D.Maynard	A.Dorow	D.Christy	B.Mathis
1962	B.Turner	A.Powell	A.Kroll	B.Mischak	M.Hudock	S.Fournet	G.Cockrell	T.Cooper	D.Maynard	J.Green	D.Christy	B.Mathis
1963	W.Ewbank	B.Turner	W.Hill	D.Ficca	M.Hudock	S.Fournet	S.Plunkett	G.Heeter	D.Maynard	D.Wood	D.Christy	M.Smolinski
1964	W.Ewbank	B.Turner	W.Hill	D.Ficca	M.Hudock	S.DeLuca	S.Plunkett	G.Heeter	D.Maynard	D.Wood	B.Mathis	M.Snell
1965	W.Ewbank	G.Sauer	W.Hill	S.DeLuca	M.Hudock	D.Herman	S.Plunkett	D.Mackey	D.Maynard	J.Namath	B.Mathis	M.Snell
1966	W.Ewbank	G.Sauer	W.Hill	S.DeLuca	J.Schmitt	D.Herman	S.Plunkett	P.Lammons	D.Maynard	J.Namath	E.Boozer	M.Snell
1967	W.Ewbank	G.Sauer	W.Hill	R.Rasmussen	J.Schmitt	D.Herman	S.Plunkett	P.Lammons	D.Maynard	J.Namath	E.Boozer	M.Snell
1968	W.Ewbank	G.Sauer	W.Hill	B.Talamini	J.Schmitt	D.Herman	S.Walton	P.Lammons	D.Maynard	J.Namath	E.Boozer	M.Snell
1969	W.Ewbank	G.Sauer	W.Hill	R.Rasmussen	J.Schmitt	D.Herman	R.Finnie	P.Lammons	D.Maynard	J.Namath	E.Boozer	M.Snell
1970	W.Ewbank	G.Sauer	W.Hill	R.Rasmussen	J.Schmitt	D.Herman	D.Foley	P.Lammons	D.Maynard	A.Woodall	G.Nock	E.Boozer
1971	W.Ewbank	R.Caster	B.Svihus	R.Rasmussen	J.Schmitt	D.Herman	W.Hill	P.Lammons	D.Maynard	B.Davis	E.Boozer	J.Riggins
1972	W.Ewbank	E.Bell	B.Svihus	R.Rasmussen	J.Schmitt	D.Herman	W.Hill	R.Caster	D.Maynard	J.Namath	E.Boozer	J.Riggins
1973	W.Ewbank	J.Barkum	R.Woods	R.Rasmussen	J.Schmitt	D.Herman	W.Hill	R.Caster	E.Bell	A.Woodall	E.Boozer	J.Riggins
1974	C.Winner	J.Barkum	R.Woods	R.Rasmussen	W.Mulligan	G.Puetz	W.Hill	R.Caster	D.Knight	J.Namath	E.Boozer	J.Riggins
1975	C.Winner	J.Barkum	R.Woods	R.Rasmussen	W.Mulligan	G.Puetz	W.Hill	R.Caster	E.Bell	J.Namath	C.Garrett	J.Riggins
1976	L.Holtz	L.Piccone	R.Woods	R.Rasmussen	J.Fields	D.Austin	G.Puetz	R.Caster	D.Knight	J.Namath	S.Davis	C.Gaines
1977	W.Michaels	W.Walker	G.Puetz	R.Rasmussen	J.Fields	D.Alexander	M.Powell	J.Barkum	R.Caster	R.Todd	S.Dierking	C.Gaines
1978	W.Michaels	W.Walker	C.Ward	R.Rasmussen	J.Fields	D.Alexander	M.Powell	J.Barkum	D.Gaffney	M.Robinson	S.Dierking	K.Long
1979	W.Michaels	W.Walker	C.Ward	R.Rasmussen	J.Fields	D.Alexander	M.Powell	J.Barkum	D.Gaffney	R.Todd	S.Dierking	C.Gaines
1980	W.Michaels	W.Walker	C.Ward	R.Rasmussen	J.Fields	D.Alexander	M.Powell	J.Barkum	L.Jones	R.Todd	S.Dierking	M.Shuler*
1981	W.Michaels	W.Walker	C.Ward	R.Rasmussen	J.Fields	D.Alexander	M.Powell	J.Barkum	D.Gaffney	R.Todd	F.McNeil	Augustyniak
1982	W.Michaels	W.Walker	C.Ward	S.Waldemore	J.Fields	D.Alexander	M.Powell	J.Barkum	L.Jones	R.Todd	F.McNeil	Augustyniak
1983	J.Walton	W.Walker	C.Ward	J.Pellegrini	J.Fields	D.Alexander	M.Powell	J.Barkum	D.Gaffney	R.Todd	F.McNeil	Crutchfield
1984	J.Walton	W.Walker	R.McElroy	S.Waldemore	J.Fields	D.Alexander	M.Powell	M.Shuler	L.Jones	P.Ryan	F.McNeil	M.Barber
1985	J.Walton	A.Toon	R.McElroy	J.Sweeney	J.Fields	D.Alexander	M.Powell	M.Shuler	W.Walker	K.O'Brien	F.McNeil	T.Paige
1986	J.Walton	A.Toon	J.Sweeney	T.Banker	J.Fields	D.Alexander	R.McElroy	M.Shuler	W.Walker	K.O'Brien	F.McNeil	T.Paige
1987	J.Walton	A.Toon	J.Sweeney	T.Banker	G.Bingham	J.Fields	D.Alexander	M.Shuler	R.Klever*	K.O'Brien	F.McNeil	R.Vick
1988	J.Walton	A.Toon	J.Criswell	M.Haight	J.Sweeney	D.Alexander	R.McElroy	M.Shuler	W.Walker	K.O'Brien	F.McNeil	R.Vick
1989	J.Walton	A.Toon	J.Criswell	M.Haight	J.Sweeney	D.Alexander	R.McElroy	M.Shuler	J.Townsell	K.O'Brien	J.Hector	R.Vick
1990	B.Coslet	R.Moore	J.Criswell	M.Haight	J.Sweeney	D.Cadigan	B.Miller	M.Boyer	A.Toon	K.O'Brien	B.Thomas	B.Baxter
1991	B.Coslet	R.Moore	J.Criswell	D.Cadigan	J.Sweeney	D.White	I.Eatman	M.Boyer	A.Toon	K.O'Brien	B.Thomas	B.Baxter
1992	B.Coslet	R.Moore	J.Criswell	D.Cadigan	J.Sweeney	D.White	I.Eatman	M.Boyer	A.Toon	B.Nagle	B.Thomas	B.Baxter
1993	B.Coslet	C.Burkett	J.Criswell	D.Cadigan	J.Sweeney	D.White	S.Malamala	J.Mitchell	R.Moore	B.Esiason	J.Johnson	B.Baxter
1994	P.Carroll	A.Monk	J.Criswell	R.Duffy	J.Sweeney	D.White	S.Malamala	J.Mitchell	R.Moore	B.Esiason	J.Johnson	B.Baxter
1995	R.Kotite	W.Chrebet	M.Willig	R.Duffy	C.Dixon	C.Haselrig	J.Brown	K.Brady	C.Wilson	B.Esiason	A.Murrell	B.Baxter
1996	R.Kotite	W.Chrebet	J.Elliott	H.Galbreath	R.Duffy	M.O'Dwyer	D.Williams	K.Brady	K.Johnson	F.Reich	A.Murrell	R.Anderson
1997	B.Parcells	J.Graham	J.Elliott	L.Palelei	R.Duffy	M.O'Dwyer	D.Williams	K.Brady	K.Johnson	N.O'Donnell	A.Murrell	L.Neal
1998	B.Parcells	W.Chrebet	J.Elliott	T.Burger	K.Mawae	M.O'Dwyer	J.Fabini	K.Brady	K.Johnson	V.Testaverde	C.Martin	K.Byars
1999	B.Parcells	W.Chrebet	J.Elliott	K.Jenkins	K.Mawae	R.Thomas	J.Fabini	F.Baxter	K.Johnson	R.Lucas	C.Martin	R.Anderson
2000	A.Groh	W.Chrebet	J.Fabini	K.Jenkins	K.Mawae	R.Thomas	R.Young	A.Becht	D.Ward	V.Testaverde	C.Martin	R.Anderson
2001	H.Edwards	W.Chrebet	J.Fabini	K.Jenkins	K.Mawae	R.Thomas	R.Young	A.Becht	L.Coles	V.Testaverde	C.Martin	R.Anderson
2002	H.Edwards	W.Chrebet	J.Fabini	J.Machado	K.Mawae	R.Thomas	K.McKenzie	A.Becht	L.Coles	C.Pennington	C.Martin	R.Anderson
2003	H.Edwards	C.Conway	J.Fabini	D.Szott	K.Mawae	B.Smith	K.McKenzie	A.Becht	S.Moss	C.Pennington	C.Martin	J.Sowell
2004	H.Edwards	J.McCareins	J.Fabini	P.Kendall	K.Mawae	B.Moore	K.McKenzie	A.Becht	S.Moss	C.Pennington	C.Martin	J.Sowell
2005	H.Edwards	L.Coles	A.Jones	J.Goodwin	P.Kendall	B.Moore	J.Fabini	C.Baker	J.McCareins	B.Bollinger	C.Martin	J.Sowell

New York Yanks (Dallas Texans 1952)

YEAR	COACH	WR/LE	LT	LG	C	RG	RT	TE/RE	WR/FL	QB	RB/LH	FB
1950	R.Strader	A.Weiner	M.Ruby	J.Signaigo	B.Ecklund	J.Wozniak	N.Johnson	D.Edwards	B.Young	G.Ratterman	G.Taliaferro	Z.Toth
1951	R.Strader	D.Garza	P.Mitchell	J.Clowes	B.Ecklund	J.Wozniak	M.McCormack	D.Edwards	S.Howard	B.Celeri	B.Young	Z.Toth
1952	J.Phelan	D.Wilkins	J.Lansford	W.Humble	B.Ecklund	J.Wozniak	K.Jackson	R.Pelfrey	B.Young	F.Tripucka	G.Taliaferro	Z.Toth

Oakland Raiders (Los Angeles 1982-94)

YEAR	COACH	WR/LE	LT	LG	C	RG	RT	TE/RE	WR/FL	QB	RB/LH	FB
1960	E.Erdelatz	C.Hardy	R.Sabal	D.Manoukian	J.Otto	W.Hawkins	P.Oglesby	G.Prebola	A.Goldstein	T.Flores	T.Teresa	B.Lott
1961	M.Feldman	C.Hardy	R.Sabal	W.Smith	J.Otto	W.Hawkins	J.Stone	D.Asad	B.Coolbaugh	T.Flores	W.Crow	A.Miller
1962	Conkright	D.Dorsey	C.Brown	S.Campbell	J.Otto	W.Hawkins	J.Stone	M.Boydston	D.Craig	C.Davidson	C.Daniels	A.Miller
1963	A.Davis	A.Powell	P.Jacobs	W.Hawkins	J.Otto	S.Bishop	D.Klein	K.Herock	B.Roberson	T.Flores	C.Daniels	A.Miller
1964	A.Davis	A.Powell	K.Rice	B.Mischak	J.Otto	W.Hawkins	D.Klein	K.Herock	B.Roberson	T.Flores	C.Daniels	B.Cannon
1965	A.Davis	A.Powell	B.Svihus	K.Rice	J.Otto	W.Hawkins	H.Schuh	B.Cannon	Biletnikoff	T.Flores	C.Daniels	A.Miller
1966	J.Rauch	A.Powell	B.Svihus	W.Hawkins	J.Otto	J.Harvey	H.Schuh	B.Cannon	Biletnikoff	T.Flores	C.Daniels	R.Hagberg
1967	J.Rauch	B.Miller	B.Svihus	G.Upshaw	J.Otto	W.Hawkins	H.Schuh	B.Cannon	R.Sherman	D.Lamonica	C.Daniels	H.Dixon
1968	J.Rauch	W.Wells	B.Svihus	G.Upshaw	J.Otto	J.Harvey	H.Schuh	B.Cannon	Biletnikoff	D.Lamonica	P.Banaszak	H.Dixon
1969	J.Madden	W.Wells	B.Svihus	G.Upshaw	J.Otto	J.Harvey	H.Schuh	B.Cannon	Biletnikoff	D.Lamonica	C.Smith	H.Dixon
1970	J.Madden	W.Wells	A.Shell	G.Upshaw	J.Otto	J.Harvey	H.Schuh	R.Chester	Biletnikoff	D.Lamonica	C.Smith	H.Dixon
1971	J.Madden	R.Sherman	A.Shell	G.Upshaw	J.Otto	G.Buehler	B.Brown	R.Chester	Biletnikoff	D.Lamonica	P.Banaszak	M.Hubbard
1972	J.Madden	M.Siani	A.Shell	G.Upshaw	J.Otto	G.Buehler	B.Brown	R.Chester	Biletnikoff	D.Lamonica	C.Smith	M.Hubbard
1973	J.Madden	M.Siani	A.Shell	G.Upshaw	J.Otto	G.Buehler	B.Brown	B.Moore	Biletnikoff	K.Stabler	C.Smith	M.Hubbard
1974	J.Madden	C.Branch	A.Shell	G.Upshaw	J.Otto	G.Buehler	J.Vella	B.Moore	Biletnikoff	K.Stabler	C.Davis	M.Hubbard
1975	J.Madden	C.Branch	A.Shell	G.Upshaw	D.Dalby	G.Buehler	J.Vella	B.Moore	Biletnikoff	K.Stabler	C.Davis	M.van Eeghen
1976	J.Madden	C.Branch	A.Shell	G.Upshaw	D.Dalby	G.Buehler	J.Vella	D.Casper	Biletnikoff	K.Stabler	C.Davis	M.van Eeghen
1977	J.Madden	C.Branch	A.Shell	G.Upshaw	D.Dalby	G.Buehler	H.Lawrence	D.Casper	Biletnikoff	K.Stabler	C.Davis	M.van Eeghen
1978	J.Madden	C.Branch	A.Shell	G.Upshaw	D.Dalby	M.Marvin	H.Lawrence	D.Casper	M.Bradshaw	K.Stabler	Whittington	M.van Eeghen
1979	T.Flores	C.Branch	A.Shell	G.Upshaw	D.Dalby	S.Sylvester	H.Lawrence	R.Chester	D.Casper*	K.Stabler	Whittington	M.van Eeghen
1980	T.Flores	C.Branch	A.Shell	G.Upshaw	D.Dalby	M.Marvin	H.Lawrence	R.Chester	B.Chandler	J.Plunkett	K.King	M.van Eeghen
1981	T.Flores	C.Branch	A.Shell	C.Marsh	S.Sylvester	M.Marvin	H.Lawrence	D.Ramsey	M.Bradshaw	M.Wilson	K.King	D.Jensen
1982	T.Flores	C.Branch	B.Davis	C.Marsh	D.Dalby	M.Marvin	H.Lawrence	Christensen	M.Barnwell	J.Plunkett	M.Allen	K.King
1983	T.Flores	C.Branch	B.Davis	C.Hannah	D.Dalby	M.Marvin	H.Lawrence	Christensen	M.Barnwell	J.Plunkett	M.Allen	K.King
1984	T.Flores	C.Branch	B.Davis	C.Hannah	D.Dalby	D.Mosebar	H.Lawrence	Christensen	M.Barnwell	M.Wilson	M.Allen	K.King
1985	T.Flores	J.Hester	B.Davis	C.Hannah	D.Mosebar	M.Marvin	H.Lawrence	Christensen	D.Williams	M.Wilson	M.Allen	F.Hawkins
1986	T.Flores	R.Barksdale	B.Davis	C.Hannah	D.Mosebar	M.Marvin	H.Lawrence	Christensen	D.Williams	J.Plunkett	M.Allen	F.Hawkins
1987	T.Flores	J.Lofton	B.Holloway	B.Lewis	D.Mosebar	D.Miraldi	J.Clay	Christensen	M.Fernandez	M.Wilson	M.Allen	B.Jackson

YEAR	LDE	LDT/NT	RDT/RDE	RDE/LOLB	LLB/LILB	MLB/RILB	RLB/ROLB	LCB	RCB	SS/LS	FS/RS	FINISH
1992	E.Dorsey	E.Howard	L.Marshall*	C.Banks	P.Johnson	S.DeOssie	L.Taylor	M.Collins	P.Williams	L.McGriggs	G.Jackson	4ne 6-10
1993	K.Hamilton	S.Dillard	M.Fox*	C.Miller	C.Bailey	M.Brooks	L.Taylor	M.Collins	C.Raymond	M.Guyton	G.Jackson	2ne 11-5 wd
1994	K.Hamilton	M.Fox	E.Howard	M.Strahan	M.Brooks	C.Bailey	C.Miller	P.Sparks	T.Randolph	J.Williams	J.Campbell	2ne 9-7 #
1995	M.Strahan	K.Hamilton	R.Agnew	R.Harris	M.Croel	M.Brooks	C.Miller	P.Sparks	T.Randolph	J.Campbell	V.Glenn	4ne 5-11
1996	M.Strahan	R.Harris	K.Hamilton	C.Bratzke	J.Armstead	C.Widmer	C.Miller	P.Sparks	J.Sehorn	J.Campbell	T.Wooten	5ne 6-10
1997	M.Strahan	R.Harris	K.Hamilton	C.Bratzke	J.Armstead	C.Widmer	C.Miller	P.Sparks	J.Sehorn	S.Garnes	T.Wooten	1ne 10-5-1 e
1998	M.Strahan	R.Harris	K.Hamilton	C.Bratzke	J.Armstead	C.Widmer	M.Buckley	P.Sparks	C.Hamilton	S.Garnes	T.Wooten	3ne 8-8
1999	M.Strahan	C.Peter	K.Hamilton	C.Jones	R.Phillips	C.Widmer	J.Armstead	P.Sparks	J.Sehorn	S.Garnes	P.Ellsworth	3ne 7-9
2000	M.Strahan	C.Peter	K.Hamilton	C.Jones	R.Phillips	M.Barrow	J.Armstead	D.Thomas	J.Sehorn	S.Garnes	S.Williams	1ne 12-4 dcs
2001	M.Strahan	C.Griffin	K.Hamilton	K.Holmes	B.Short	M.Barrow	J.Armstead	W.Allen	J.Sehorn	S.Garnes	S.Williams	3ne 7-9
2002	M.Strahan	C.Griffin	L.LeGree	K.Holmes	B.Short	M.Barrow	D.Jones	W.Allen	W.Peterson	S.Williams	O.Stoutmire	2ne 10-6 w
2003	M.Strahan	C.Griffin	K.Hamilton	K.Holmes	B.Short	M.Barrow	D.Jones	W.Allen	F.Walker	S.Williams	O.Stoutmire	4ne 4-12
2004	M.Strahan	N.Hand	F.Robbins	K.Washington	C.Emmons	K.Lewis	B.Green	W.Allen	W.Peterson	G.Wilson	B.Alexander	2ne 6-10
2005	M.Strahan	K.Clancy	W.Joseph	O.Umenyiora	R.Torbor	A.Pierce	N.Greisen	W.Allen	C.DeLoatch	G.Wilson	B.Alexander	1ne 11-5 e

1960	B.Reifsnyder	T.Saidock	D.Guesman	N.Mumley	L.Grantham	R.Ellis	E.Bell	R.Donnahoo	D.Felt	F.Julian	C.Tharp	2ae 7-7
1961	N.Mumley	T.Saidock	D.Guesman	S.Youngelman	E.Cooke	H.Bobo	L.Grantham	J.Bookman	D.Paulson	D.Felt	L.Riley	3ae 7-7
1962	B.Watters	G.Strugar	D.Guesman	L.Torczon	E.Cooke	H.Bobo	L.Grantham	D.Paulson	P.Hynes	B.Atkins	L.Riley	4ae 5-9
1963	B.Watters	C.Janerette	D.Guesman	L.Torczon	J.Price	D.Yohn	L.Grantham	T.Stricker	C.Washington	D.Paulson	B.Baird	4ae 5-8-1
1964	B.Wilder	P.Rochester	G.Holz	L.Torczon	R.Baker	W.McDaniel	L.Grantham	M.Johnston	C.Washington	D.Paulson	B.Baird	3ae 5-8-1
1965	G.Philbin	P.Rochester	J.Harris	V.Biggs	R.Baker	W.McDaniel	L.Grantham	B.Baird	C.Washington	D.Paulson	R.Abruzzese	2ae 5-8-1
1966	G.Philbin	P.Rochester	J.Harris	V.Biggs	P.Crane	A.Atkinson	L.Grantham	J.Sample	B.Baird	R.Abruzzese	J.Hudson	3ae 6-6-2
1967	G.Philbin	P.Rochester	J.Harris	V.Biggs	R.Baker	A.Atkinson	L.Grantham	J.Sample	R.Beverly	J.Hudson	B.Baird	2ae 8-5-1
1968	G.Philbin	P.Rochester	J.Elliott	V.Biggs	R.Baker	A.Atkinson	L.Grantham	J.Sample	R.Beverly	J.Hudson	B.Baird	1ae 11-3 ls*
1969	G.Philbin	S.Thompson	J.Elliott	V.Biggs	R.Baker	A.Atkinson	L.Grantham	J.Dockery	C.Gordon	J.Richards	B.Baird	1ae 10-4 p
1970	G.Philbin	M.Lomas	J.Elliott	V.Biggs	R.Baker	A.Atkinson	L.Grantham	S.Tannen	E.Thomas	G.Hollomon	W.Hicks	3ae 4-10
1971	G.Philbin	J.Little	C.Hinton	M.Lomas	R.Baker	A.Atkinson	L.Grantham	J.Dockery	E.Thomas	P.Wise	W.Hicks	3ae 6-8
1972	G.Philbin	J.Little	J.Elliott	M.Lomas	R.Baker	A.Atkinson	L.Grantham	S.Tannen	E.Thomas	G.Hollomon	Farasopoulos	2ae 7-7
1973	E.Galigher	J.Little	J.Elliott	M.Lomas	R.Baker	J.Ebersole	B.Ferguson	D.Howell	E.Thomas	B.Owens	Farasopoulos	4ae 4-10
1974	E.Galigher	Barzilauskas	J.Schmiesing	M.Lomas	R.Baker	J.Rivers	J.Ebersole	R.Sowells	R.Word	B.Owens	S.Tannen	3ae 7-7
1975	B.Newsome	Barzilauskas	E.Galigher	R.Neal	G.Turk	J.Ebersole	R.Lewis	R.Sowells	R.Word	B.Owens	E.Taylor	4ae 3-11
1976	L.Pillers	Barzilauskas	E.Galigher	R.Neal	G.Buttle	J.Ebersole	B.Martin	S.Suggs	E.Taylor	P.Wise	B.Owens	4ae 3-11
1977	L.Pillers	Barzilauskas	A.Salaam	R.Neal	G.Buttle	J.Ebersole	L.Keller	B.Hardee	E.Taylor	S.Suggs	B.Owens	4ae 3-11
1978	L.Pillers	A.Salaam	J.Klecko*	L.Keller	J.Hennessy	M.Hennigan	B.Martin	B.Jackson	E.Taylor	S.Suggs	B.Owens	3ae 8-8
1979	L.Pillers	A.Salaam	J.Klecko	M.Lyons	G.Buttle	S.Blinka	M.McKibben	B.Jackson	J.Lynn	S.Suggs	B.Owens	3ae 8-8
1980	M.Gastineau	A.Salaam	M.Lyons	J.Klecko	G.Buttle	S.Blinka	R.Crosby	B.Jackson	D.Dykes	K.Schroy	D.Ray	5ae 4-12
1981	M.Gastineau	A.Salaam	M.Lyons	J.Klecko	G.Buttle	S.Blinka	L.Mehl	B.Jackson	J.Holmes	K.Schroy	D.Ray	2ae 10-5-1 w
1982	M.Gastineau	A.Salaam	M.Lyons	K.Neil	G.Buttle	S.Blinka	L.Mehl	B.Jackson	J.Holmes	K.Schroy	D.Ray	4a 6-3 pdc
1983	M.Gastineau	J.Klecko	M.Lyons	K.Neil	G.Buttle	B.Crable	L.Mehl	B.Jackson	J.Holmes	K.Schroy	D.Ray	4ae 7-9
1984	M.Gastineau	B.Bennett	M.Lyons	R.Faurot	G.Buttle	K.Clifton	L.Mehl	D.Mullen	J.Lynn	K.Springs	D.Ray	3ae 7-9
1985	M.Gastineau	J.Klecko	B.Bennett*	C.Jackson	K.Clifton	L.Mehl	R.Guilbeau	B.Jackson	R.Carter	K.Springs	H.Hamilton	2ae 11-5 #w
1986	M.Lyons	J.Klecko	B.Bennett*	C.Jackson	K.Clifton	L.Mehl	B.Crable	J.Holmes	R.Carter	L.Lyles	H.Hamilton	2ae 10-6 #wd
1987	M.Lyons	J.Klecko	B.Bennett*	A.Gordon	T.Benson	K.Clifton	B.Crable	J.Holmes	C.Howard	R.Miano	H.Hamilton	5ae 6-9
1988	M.Gastineau	S.Mersereau	M.Lyons*	A.Gordon	T.Benson	K.Clifton	K.McArthur	B.Humphery	J.Hasty	R.Miano	E.McMillan	4ae 8-7-1
1989	P.Frase	S.Mersereau	M.Lyons*	A.Gordon	T.Benson	K.Clifton	J.Lageman	B.Humphery	J.Hasty	Radachowsky	E.McMillan	5ae 4-12
1990	R.Stallworth	S.Mersereau	D.Byrd	J.Lageman	J.Mott	K.Clifton	J.Kelly	T.Stargell	J.Hasty	B.Washington	E.McMillan	4ae 6-10
1991	M.Washington	S.Mersereau	D.Byrd	J.Lageman	M.Lewis	K.Clifton	J.Kelly	M.Brim	J.Hasty	B.Washington	L.Young	2ae 8-8 #w
1992	M.Gunn	S.Mersereau	P.Frase	M.Washington	B.Houston	K.Clifton	M.Lewis	M.Brim	J.Hasty	B.Washington	L.Young	4ae 4-12
1993	M.Washington	S.Mersereau	L.Marshall	J.Lageman	B.Houston	K.Clifton	M.Lewis	E.Thomas	J.Hasty	B.Washington	R.Lott	3ae 8-8
1994	M.Washington	D.Evans	T.Casillas	J.Lageman	B.Houston	M.Jones	M.Lewis	A.Glenn	J.Hasty	B.Washington	R.Lott	5ae 6-10
1995	E.Howard	T.Casillas	M.Brock	M.Washington	B.Houston	M.Jones	M.Lewis	A.Glenn	O.Smith	V.Green	T.Scott	5ae 3-13
1996	B.Hamilton	M.Washington	M.Brock	H.Douglas	B.Houston	M.Jones	M.Lewis	A.Glenn	R.Mickens	V.Green	G.Jones	5ae 1-15
1997	R.Lyle	E.Logan	H.Douglas*	M.Lewis	D.Gordon	M.Jones	J.Farrior	A.Glenn	O.Smith	V.Green	J.Henderson	3ae 9-7 #
1998	R.Lyle	J.Ferguson	E.Logan	A.Pleasant	M.Lewis	P.Johnson	B.Cox	A.Glenn	O.Smith	V.Green	J.Henderson	1ae 12-4 dc
1999	R.Lyle	J.Ferguson	A.Pleasant*	M.Lewis	B.Cox	M.Jones	R.Phifer	A.Glenn	M.Coleman	V.Green	S.Atwater	4ae 8-8
2000	R.Lyle	J.Ferguson	S.Burton*	M.Lewis	B.Cox	M.Jones	R.Phifer	A.Glenn	M.Coleman	V.Green	C.Hayes	3ae 9-7
2001	S.Ellis	S.Burton	S.Martin	J.Abraham	M.Lewis	M.Jones	J.Farrior	A.Glenn	M.Coleman	V.Green	D.Robinson	3ae 10-6 w
2002	S.Ellis	J.Ferguson	J.Evans	J.Abraham	M.Lewis	M.Jones	S.Cowart	D.Abraham	A.Beasley	S.Garnes	D.Robinson	1ae 9-7 #ed
2003	S.Ellis	D.Robertson	J.Ferguson	B.Thomas	M.Lewis	M.Jones	S.Cowart	R.Mickens	A.Beasley	S.Garnes	T.Carter	3ae 6-10
2004	S.Ellis	D.Robertson	J.Ferguson	J.Abraham	V.Hobson	J.Vilma	E.Barton	D.Abraham	D.Barrett	R.Tongue	E.Coleman	2ae 10-6 wd
2005	S.Ellis	J.Reed	D.Robertson	J.Abraham	V.Hobson	J.Vilma	M.Brown	T.Law	D.Barrett	E.Coleman	K.Rhodes	4ae 4-12

1950	J.Russell	C.Vogelaar	P.Mitchell	B.Poole	L.Kusserow	Domnanovich	E.Sharkey	P.Layden	D.Iverson	S.Sanders	J.Golding	3nn 7-5
1951	A.Tait	A.Donovan	D.Colo	B.Poole	S.Averno	H.Johnson	J.Champion	B.Griffin	B.Aldridge	P.Crowe	J.Golding	6nn 1-9-2
1952	G.Marchetti	A.Donovan	J.Campanella	B.Poole	P.Cannamela	S.Averno+	J.Reid	J.Petitbon	J.Davis	T.Keane	S.Williams	6nn 1-11

1960	C.Cavalli	G.Fields	D.Deskins	C.Powell	B.Dougherty	T.Louderback	R.Morris	E.Macon	J.Cannavino	A.Bravo	W.Crow	3aw 6-8
1961	G.Finneran	B.Voight	H.Smith	C.Powell	B.Dougherty	T.Louderback	R.Morris	F.Williamson	B.Garner	J.Cannavino	A.Bravo	4aw 2-12
1962	J.Jelacic	O.Trask	C.McMurtry	D.Allen	B.Dougherty	J.Simpson	C.Rieves	F.Williamson	B.Garner	V.Valdez	T.Morrow	4aw 1-13
1963	D.Allen	C.McMurtry	D.Costa	J.Jelacic	J.Simpson	A.Matsos	C.Osborne	F.Williamson	C.Gibson	J.Krakoski	T.Morrow	2aw 10-4
1964	D.Allen	R.Mirich	D.Costa	D.Birdwell	B.Budness	A.Matsos	C.Osborne	F.Williamson	H.Williams	J.Krakoski	T.Morrow	3aw 5-7-2
1965	I.Lassiter	R.Mirich	D.Costa	B.Davidson	J.Williamson	A.Matsos	G.Otto	K.McCloughan	D.Grayson	J.Krakoski	H.Williams	2aw 8-5-1
1966	I.Lassiter	D.Birdwell	T.Keating	B.Davidson	J.Williamson	B.Budness	G.Otto	K.McCloughan	D.Grayson	W.Powers	H.Williams	2aw 8-5-1
1967	I.Lassiter	D.Birdwell	T.Keating	B.Davidson	B.Laskey	D.Conners	G.Otto	K.McCloughan	W.Brown	H.Williams	R.Bird	1aw 13-1 ls
1968	I.Lassiter	D.Birdwell	C.Oats	B.Davidson	C.Oliver	D.Conners	G.Otto	K.McCloughan	W.Brown	R.Bird	D.Grayson	1aw 12-2 dl
1969	I.Lassiter	C.Oats	T.Keating	B.Davidson	B.Laskey	D.Conners	G.Otto	N.Wilson	W.Brown	G.Atkinson	D.Grayson	1aw 12-1-1 pl
1970	T.Cline	C.Oats	T.Keating	B.Davidson	B.Laskey	D.Conners	G.Otto	K.McCloughan	N.Wilson	G.Atkinson	D.Grayson	1aw 8-4-2 dc
1971	H.Jones	A.Thoms	C.Oats	B.Davidson	P.Villapiano	D.Conners	G.Otto	N.Wilson	W.Brown	G.Atkinson	J.Tatum	2aw 8-4-2
1972	T.Cline	O.Sistrunk	A.Thoms	H.Jones	P.Villapiano	D.Conners	G.Irons	N.Wilson	W.Brown	G.Atkinson	J.Tatum	1aw 10-3-1 d
1973	B.Smith	O.Sistrunk	A.Thoms	T.Cline	P.Villapiano	D.Conners	G.Irons	N.Wilson	W.Brown	G.Atkinson	J.Tatum	1aw 9-4-1 dc
1974	B.Smith	O.Sistrunk	A.Thoms	H.Jones	P.Villapiano	D.Conners	G.Irons	S.Thomas	W.Brown	G.Atkinson	J.Tatum	1aw 12-2 dc
1975	T.Cline	O.Sistrunk	A.Thoms	H.Jones	P.Villapiano	M.Johnson	G.Irons	S.Thomas	W.Brown	G.Atkinson	J.Tatum	1aw 11-3 dc
1976	J.Matuszak	D.Rowe	O.Sistrunk*	P.Villapiano	W.Hall	M.Johnson	T.Hendricks	S.Thomas	W.Brown	G.Atkinson	J.Tatum	1aw 13-1 dcs*
1977	J.Matuszak	D.Rowe	O.Sistrunk*	F.Rice	M.Johnson	W.Hall	T.Hendricks	S.Thomas	W.Brown	G.Atkinson	J.Tatum	2aw 11-3 wc
1978	J.Matuszak	O.Sistrunk	D.Browning*	T.Hendricks	M.Johnson	W.Hall	P.Villapiano	L.Hayes	M.Jackson	C.Phillips	J.Tatum	2aw 9-7
1979	P.Toomay	D.Pear	D.Browning*	T.Hendricks	M.Johnson	P.Villapiano	R.Martin	L.Hayes	H.Williams	M.Davis	J.Tatum	3aw 9-7
1980	J.Matuszak	R.Kinlaw	D.Browning*	T.Hendricks	M.Millen	R.McClanahan	R.Martin	L.Hayes	M.Jackson	M.Davis	B.Owens	2aw 11-5 #wdcs*
1981	J.Matuszak	J.Robinson	D.Browning*	T.Hendricks	M.Millen	R.McClanahan	R.Martin	L.Hayes	M.Jackson	O.McKinney	B.Owens	4aw 7-9
1982	H.Long	R.Kinlaw	L.Alzado*	T.Hendricks	M.Millen	B.Nelson	R.Martin	L.Hayes	T.Watts	M.Davis	B.Owens	1a 8-1 pd
1983	H.Long	R.Kinlaw	L.Alzado*	T.Hendricks	M.Millen	B.Nelson	R.Martin	L.Hayes	T.Watts	M.Davis	V.McElroy	1aw 12-4 dcs*
1984	H.Long	R.Kinlaw	L.Alzado*	B.Van Pelt	M.Millen	B.Nelson	R.Martin	L.Hayes	M.Haynes	M.Davis	V.McElroy	3aw 11-5 w
1985	H.Long	B.Pickel	L.Alzado*	B.Van Pelt	M.Millen	R.McKenzie	R.Martin	L.Hayes	M.Haynes	M.Davis	V.McElroy	1aw 12-4 d
1986	H.Long	B.Pickel	S.Jones*	J.Robinson	M.Millen	R.McKenzie	R.Martin	L.Hayes	M.Haynes	S.Toran	V.McElroy	4aw 8-8
1987	H.Long	B.Pickel	S.Jones*	L.King	M.Millen	J.Robinson	R.Martin	L.Washington	M.Haynes	S.Toran	V.McElroy	4aw 5-10

848 THE OFFENSIVE STARTERS: 1950–PRESENT

YEAR COACH	WR/LE	LT	LG	C	RG	RT	TE/RE	WR/FL	QB	RB/LH	FB
1988 M.Shanahan	T.Brown	D.Mosebar	C.Hannah	B.Lewis	B.Wilkerson	R.Graves	A.Parker	J.Lofton	J.Schroeder	M.Allen	B.Jackson
1989 A.Shell	W.Gault	R.Graves	J.Gesek	D.Mosebar	S.Wisniewski	B.Wilkerson	M.Dyal	M.Fernandez	J.Schroeder	B.Jackson	S.Smith
1990 A.Shell	W.Gault	R.Graves	S.Wisniewski	D.Mosebar	M.Montoya	S.Wright	E.Horton	M.Fernandez	J.Schroeder	M.Allen	S.Smith
1991 A.Shell	W.Gault	B.Wilkerson	S.Wisniewski	D.Mosebar	M.Montoya	S.Wright	E.Horton	M.Fernandez	J.Schroeder	R.Craig	S.Smith
1992 A.Shell	W.Gault	B.Wilkerson	S.Wisniewski	D.Mosebar	M.Montoya	R.McElroy	E.Horton	T.Brown	J.Schroeder	E.Dickerson	S.Smith
1993 A.Shell	A.Wright	G.Perry	S.Wisniewski	D.Mosebar	M.Montoya	B.Wilkerson	E.Horton	T.Brown	J.Hostetler	G.Robinson	S.Smith
1994 A.Shell	A.Wright	G.Perry	S.Wisniewski	D.Mosebar	K.Gogan	G.Skrepenak	A.Glover	T.Brown	J.Hostetler	H.Williams	T.Rathman
1995 M.White	R.Ismail	R.Jenkins	S.Wisniewski	D.Turk	K.Gogan	G.Skrepenak	K.Cash	T.Brown	J.Hostetler	H.Williams	D.Fenner
1996 M.White	J.Jett	P.Harlow	S.Wisniewski	B.Robbins	K.Gogan	L.Kennedy	R.Dudley	T.Brown	J.Hostetler	N.Kaufman	D.Fenner
1997 J.Bugel	J.Jett	P.Harlow	S.Wisniewski	B.Robbins	L.Holmes	L.Kennedy	R.Dudley	T.Brown	J.George	N.Kaufman	D.Fenner
1998 J.Gruden	J.Jett	M.Collins	S.Wisniewski	B.Robbins	D.Graham	L.Kennedy	R.Dudley	T.Brown	J.George	N.Kaufman	J.Ritchie
1999 J.Gruden	T.Brown	M.Collins	S.Wisniewski	B.Robbins	G.DiNapoli	L.Kennedy	R.Dudley	J.Jett	R.Gannon	T.Wheatley	J.Ritchie
2000 J.Gruden	T.Brown	M.Stinchcomb	S.Wisniewski	B.Robbins	M.Collins	L.Kennedy	R.Dudley	J.Jett	R.Gannon	T.Wheatley	J.Ritchie
2001 J.Gruden	T.Brown	B.Sims	S.Wisniewski	A.Treu	F.Middleton	L.Kennedy	R.Williams	J.Rice	R.Gannon	C.Garner	J.Ritchie
2002 B.Callahan	T.Brown	B.Sims	M.Collins	B.Robbins	F.Middleton	L.Kennedy	R.Williams	J.Rice	R.Gannon	C.Garner	J.Porter+
2003 B.Callahan	T.Brown	B.Sims	F.Middleton	B.Robbins	M.Collins	L.Kennedy	D.Jolley	J.Rice	R.Mirer	C.Garner	Z.Crockett
2004 N.Turner	D.Gabriel	B.Sims	B.Badger	A.Treu	J.Grove	R.Gallery	D.Jolley	J.Porter	K.Collins	T.Wheatley	Z.Crockett
2005 N.Turner	R.Moss	B.Sims	B.Badger	A.Treu	R.Stone	R.Gallery	C.Anderson	J.Porter	K.Collins	L.Jordan	Z.Crockett

Philadelphia Eagles

YEAR COACH	WR/LE	LT	LG	C	RG	RT	TE/RE	WR/FL	QB	RB/LH	FB
1950 G.Neale	J.Ferrante	V.Sears	D.Maronic	V.Lindskog	B.Kilroy	A.Wistert	P.Pihos	F.Ziegler	T.Thompson	S.Van Buren	J.Myers
1951 W.Millner	B.Walston	V.Sears	A.Wistert	V.Lindskog	J.Magee	B.Kilroy	P.Pihos	F.Ziegler	A.Burk	S.Van Buren	J.Parmer
1952 J.Trimble	B.Walston	F.Wydo	M.Nipp	K.Farragut	J.Magee	L.Snyder	B.Grant	F.Ziegler	B.Thomason	R.Goldston	J.Huzvar
1953 J.Trimble	B.Walston	F.Wydo	M.Nipp	K.Farragut	J.Magee	L.Snyder	P.Pihos	F.Ziegler	B.Thomason	J.Williams	J.Parmer
1954 J.Trimble	B.Walston	F.Wydo	K.Huxhold	C.Bednarik	J.Magee	L.Snyder	P.Pihos	J.Williams	A.Burk	T.Ledbetter	J.Parmer
1955 J.Trimble	B.Stribling	F.Wydo	B.Lansford	B.Kelley	K.Huxhold	L.Snyder	P.Pihos	B.Walston	A.Burk	Giancanelli	R.Goode
1956 H.Devore	B.Walston	B.Lansford	K.Huxhold	B.Kelley	B.Pellegrini	F.Wydo	J.Bredice	Giancanelli	B.Thomason	K.Keller	D.Schaefer
1957 H.Devore	B.Walston	B.Lansford	A.Gibron	J.Simerson	K.Huxhold	B.Gaona	B.Stribling	P.Retzlaff	B.Thomason	B.Barnes	C.Peaks
1958 B.Shaw	B.Walston	P.Jacobs	H.Bradley	C.Bednarik	K.Huxhold	L.Snyder	D.Bielski	P.Retzlaff	Van Brocklin	B.Barnes	C.Peaks
1959 B.Shaw	B.Walston	J.DeLucca	J.Huth	C.Bednarik	M.Campbell	J.Smith	P.Retzlaff	T.McDonald	Van Brocklin	B.Barnes	C.Peaks
1960 B.Shaw	P.Retzlaff	J.McCusker	J.Wittenborn	C.Bednarik	S.Campbell	J.Smith	B.Walston	T.McDonald	Van Brocklin	B.Barnes	T.Dean
1961 N.Skorich	P.Retzlaff	J.McCusker	J.Wittenborn	C.Bednarik	S.Campbell	J.Smith	B.Walston	T.McDonald	S.Jurgensen	B.Barnes	C.Peaks
1962 N.Skorich	P.Retzlaff	J.McCusker	J.Wittenborn	J.Schrader	R.Hord	J.Smith	D.Lucas	T.McDonald	S.Jurgensen	T.Brown	C.Peaks
1963 N.Skorich	R.Goodwin	D.Graham	E.Blaine	J.Schrader	P.Case	J.Smith	P.Retzlaff	T.McDonald	S.Jurgensen	T.Brown	T.Dean
1964 J.Kuharich	R.Poage	D.Graham	E.Blaine	J.Ringo	L.Hoyem	B.Brown	P.Retzlaff	R.Goodwin	N.Snead	T.Brown	E.Gros
1965 J.Kuharich	R.Poage	L.Howell	E.Blaine	J.Ringo	J.Skaggs	B.Brown	P.Retzlaff	R.Goodwin	N.Snead	T.Brown	E.Gros
1966 J.Kuharich	F.Hill	L.Howell	E.Blaine	J.Ringo	J.Skaggs	B.Brown	P.Retzlaff	R.Goodwin	N.Snead	T.Brown	E.Gros
1967 J.Kuharich	B.Hawkins	L.Howell	D.Hart	J.Ringo	J.Skaggs	B.Brown	M.Ditka	G.Ballman	N.Snead	I.Lang	T.Woodeshick
1968 J.Kuharich	G.Ballman	L.Howell	D.Hart	G.Ceppetelli	M.Nordquist	B.Brown	F.Hill	B.Hawkins	N.Snead	I.Lang	T.Woodeshick
1969 J.Williams	B.Hawkins	L.Howell	D.Hart	M.Evans	J.Skaggs	J.Carollo	G.Ballman	H.Jackson	N.Snead	L.Keyes	T.Woodeshick
1970 J.Williams	B.Hawkins	W.Key	D.Hart	M.Evans	J.Skaggs	J.Carollo	G.Ballman	H.Jackson	N.Snead	C.Pinder	L.Bouggess
1971 E.Khayat	H.Jackson	W.Key	H.Allison	M.Evans	M.Nordquist	S.Smith	G.Ballman	B.Hawkins	P.Liske	R.Bull	L.Bouggess
1972 E.Khayat	H.Jackson	W.Key	T.Luken	M.Evans	M.Nordquist	S.Smith	K.Kramer	B.Hawkins	P.Liske	P.James	L.Watkins
1973 McCormack	D.Zimmerman	S.Smith	W.Key	G.Morriss	M.Nordquist	J.Sisemore	C.Young	H.Carmichael	R.Gabriel	T.Sullivan	N.Bulaich
1974 McCormack	H.Carmichael	S.Smith	W.Key	G.Morriss	M.Nordquist	J.Sisemore	C.Young	D.Zimmerman	R.Gabriel	T.Sullivan	N.Bulaich
1975 McCormack	H.Carmichael	S.Walters	J.Niland	G.Morriss	B.Lueck	J.Sisemore	C.Young	C.Smith	R.Gabriel	T.Sullivan	A.Malone
1976 D.Vermeil	H.Carmichael	S.Walters	W.Key	G.Morriss	J.Sisemore	E.George	C.Young	C.Smith	M.Boryla	T.Sullivan	M.Hogan
1977 D.Vermeil	H.Carmichael	S.Walters	W.Key	G.Morriss	J.Sisemore	E.George	K.Krepfle	C.Smith	R.Jaworski	T.Sullivan	M.Hogan
1978 D.Vermeil	H.Carmichael	S.Walters	W.Key	G.Morriss	W.Peoples	J.Sisemore	K.Krepfle	K.Payne	R.Jaworski	W.Montgomery	M.Hogan
1979 D.Vermeil	H.Carmichael	S.Walters	W.Key	G.Morriss	W.Peoples	J.Sisemore	K.Krepfle	C.Smith	R.Jaworski	W.Montgomery	L.Harris
1980 D.Vermeil	H.Carmichael	S.Walters	P.Perot	G.Morriss	W.Peoples	J.Sisemore	K.Krepfle	C.Smith	R.Jaworski	W.Montgomery	L.Harris
1981 D.Vermeil	H.Carmichael	S.Walters	S.Kenney	G.Morriss	R.Baker	J.Sisemore	K.Krepfle	C.Smith	R.Jaworski	W.Montgomery	H.Oliver
1982 D.Vermeil	H.Carmichael	S.Walters	S.Kenney	G.Morriss	R.Baker	J.Sisemore	J.Spagnola	R.Smith	R.Jaworski	W.Montgomery	P.Harrington
1983 M.Campbell	H.Carmichael	S.Walters	S.Kenney	G.Morriss	R.Baker	J.Sisemore	V.Kab	M.Quick	R.Jaworski	M.Williams	H.Oliver
1984 M.Campbell	K.Jackson	D.Miraldi	S.Kenney	M.Dennard	R.Baker	L.Mitchell	J.Spagnola	M.Quick	R.Jaworski	W.Montgomery	H.Oliver
1985 M.Campbell	K.Jackson	K.Reeves	S.Kenney	M.Dennard	R.Baker	L.Mitchell	J.Spagnola	M.Quick	R.Jaworski	E.Jackson	M.Haddix
1986 B.Ryan	M.Quick	T.Jelesky	K.Reeves	M.Darwin	R.Baker	L.Mitchell	J.Spagnola	K.Jackson	R.Jaworski	K.Byars	M.Haddix
1987 B.Ryan	M.Quick	M.Darwin	A.Schreiber	G.Feehery	R.Baker	J.Conwell	J.Spagnola	K.Jackson	R.Cunningham	K.Byars	A.Toney
1988 B.Ryan	M.Quick	M.Darwin	D.Alexander	D.Rimington	R.Singletary	R.Heller	K.Jackson	C.Carter	R.Cunningham	K.Byars	A.Toney
1989 B.Ryan	R.Johnson	M.Darwin	M.Schad	D.Alexander	R.Solt	R.Heller	K.Jackson	C.Carter	R.Cunningham	K.Byars	A.Toney
1990 B.Ryan	F.Barnett	R.Heller	M.Schad	D.Alexander	R.Solt	R.Singletary	K.Jackson	C.Williams	R.Cunningham	K.Byars	A.Toney
1991 R.Kotite	F.Barnett	R.Heller	D.McKnight	D.Alexander	R.Solt	A.Davis	K.Jackson	C.Williams	J.McMahon	H.Sherman	K.Byars
1992 R.Kotite	F.Barnett	R.Heller	M.Schad	D.Alexander	E.Floyd	A.Davis	K.Byars	C.Williams	R.Cunningham	H.Walker	H.Sherman
1993 R.Kotite	V.Bailey	B.Thompson	M.Schad	D.Alexander	R.Hallstrom	A.Davis	M.Bavaro	C.Williams	B.Brister	H.Walker	H.Sherman
1994 R.Kotite	F.Barnett	B.Williams	A.Davis	D.Alexander	L.Holmes	B.Thompson	M.Bavaro	C.Williams	R.Cunningham	H.Walker	M.Johnson*
1995 R.Rhodes	F.Barnett	B.Brooks	G.McIntyre	R.McKenzie	J.Panos	A.Davis	E.West	C.Williams	R.Peete	R.Watters	F.McCrary
1996 R.Rhodes	I.Fryar	B.Brooks	J.Panos	R.McKenzie	L.Holmes	R.Cooper	J.Dunn	C.Jones	T.Detmer	R.Watters	K.Turner
1997 R.Rhodes	I.Fryar	J.Mayberry	J.Panos	S.Everitt	I.Beckles	B.Brooks	J.Johnson	M.Timpson	T.Detmer	R.Watters	K.Turner
1998 R.Rhodes	I.Fryar	T.Thomas	J.Mayberry	S.Everitt	I.Beckles	R.Cooper	J.Dunn	J.Graham	B.Hoying	D.Staley	K.Turner
1999 A.Reid	T.Small	T.Thomas	D.Brzezinski	S.Everitt	J.Dellenbach	L.Palelei	J.Weaver	C.Johnson	D.Pederson	D.Staley	K.Turner
2000 A.Reid	T.Small	T.Thomas	J.Welbourn	B.Miller	J.Mayberry	J.Runyan	C.Lewis	C.Johnson	D.McNabb	D.Autry	C.Martin
2001 A.Reid	T.Pinkston	T.Thomas	J.Welbourn	H.Fraley	J.Mayberry	J.Runyan	C.Lewis	J.Thrash	D.McNabb	D.Staley	C.Martin
2002 A.Reid	T.Pinkston	T.Thomas	J.Welbourn	H.Fraley	J.Mayberry	J.Runyan	C.Lewis	J.Thrash	D.McNabb	D.Staley	C.Martin
2003 A.Reid	T.Pinkston	T.Thomas	J.Welbourn	H.Fraley	B.Williams	J.Runyan	C.Lewis	J.Thrash	D.McNabb	B.Westbrook	J.Ritchie
2004 A.Reid	T.Pinkston	T.Thomas	A.Hicks	H.Fraley	J.Mayberry	J.Runyan	C.Lewis	T.Owens	D.McNabb	B.Westbrook	F.Mitchell+
2005 A.Reid	G.Lewis	T.Thomas	A.Hicks	H.Fraley	S.Andrews	J.Runyan	L.Smith	R.Brown	D.McNabb	B.Westbrook	J.Parry

Pittsburgh Steelers

YEAR COACH	WR/LE	LT	LG	C	RG	RT	TE/RE	WR/FL	QB	RB/LH	FB
1950 Michelosen	V.Jansante	L.Allen	D.Tomlinson	B.Walsh	G.Hughes	F.Wydo	E.Nickel	L.Chandnois*	J.Geri*	C.Seabright*	F.Rogel
1951 Michelosen	H.Minarik	L.Allen	D.Tomlinson	B.Walsh	G.Hughes	F.Wydo	E.Nickel	L.Chandnois*	C.Ortmann*	T.Smith*	F.Rogel
1952 J.Bach	D.Hensley	D.Fugler	J.Schweder	B.Walsh	P.Ladygo	G.Hughes	E.Nickel	L.Chandnois	J.Finks	R.Mathews	F.Rogel
1953 J.Bach	E.Barker	B.Gaona	J.Schweder	B.Walsh	M.McFadden	G.Hughes	E.Nickel	L.Chandnois	J.Finks	R.Mathews	F.Rogel
1954 W.Kiesling	G.Sulima	B.Gaona	J.Schweder	B.Walsh	P.Ladygo	G.Hughes	E.Nickel	J.Lattner	J.Finks	R.Mathews	F.Rogel
1955 W.Kiesling	E.Bernet	B.Gaona	J.Schweder	L.Tepe	E.Stautner	Varrichione	E.Nickel	L.Chandnois	J.Finks	R.Mathews	F.Rogel
1956 W.Kiesling	L.Perry	B.Gaona	B.O'Neil	J.Taylor	M.McFadden	Varrichione	R.Mathews	E.Nickel	Marchibroda	S.Watson	F.Rogel
1957 B.Parker	J.Girard	W.McClung	M.Sandusky	E.Beatty	J.Nisby	Varrichione	J.McClairen	R.Mathews	E.Morrall	B.Wells	F.Rogel
1958 B.Parker	J.Orr	T.Karras	M.Sandusky	E.Beatty	J.Nisby	Varrichione	J.McClairen	R.Mathews	B.Layne	T.Tracy	T.Younger
1959 B.Parker	P.Brewster	T.Karras	M.Sandusky	E.Beatty	J.Nisby	Varrichione	J.Orr	T.Barnett	B.Layne	T.Tracy	L.Krutko
1960 B.Parker	B.Dial	D.James	M.Sandusky	E.Beatty	J.Nisby	Varrichione	P.Carpenter	J.Orr	B.Layne	T.Tracy	J.Johnson
1961 B.Parker	B.Dial	C.Bradshaw	M.Sandusky	B.Nutter	J.Nisby	D.James	P.Carpenter	D.Hoak	B.Layne	T.Tracy	J.Johnson
1962 B.Parker	B.Dial	C.Bradshaw	M.Sandusky	B.Nutter	R.Lemek	D.James	P.Carpenter	D.Hoak	B.Layne	J.Womack	J.Johnson
1963 B.Parker	B.Dial	C.Bradshaw	M.Sandusky	B.Nutter	R.Lemek	D.James	R.Mack	G.Ballman	E.Brown	D.Hoak	J.Johnson
1964 B.Parker	C.Thomas	C.Bradshaw	R.Stehouwer	B.Nutter	R.Lemek	D.James	J.Powers	G.Ballman	E.Brown	D.Hoak	J.Johnson
1965 M.Nixon	C.Thomas	C.Bradshaw	M.Sandusky	A.Hunter	M.Magac	D.James	J.Hilton	G.Ballman	B.Nelsen	D.Hoak	M.Lind
1966 B.Austin	R.Jefferson	C.Bradshaw	L.Gagner	R.Mansfield	M.Magac	D.James	J.Hilton	G.Ballman	R.Smith	D.Hoak	W.Asbury
1967 B.Austin	D.Compton	M.Haggerty	L.Gagner	R.Mansfield	B.Van Dyke	J.Brown	J.Hilton	J.Wilburn	K.Nix	D.Shy	W.Asbury
1968 B.Austin	R.Jefferson	F.O'Brien	L.Gagner	R.Mansfield	B.Van Dyke	J.Brown	J.Hilton	J.Wilburn	D.Shiner	D.Hoak	E.Gros

YEAR	LDE	LDT/NT	RDT/RDE	RDE/LOLB	LLB/LILB	MLB/RILB	RLB/ROLB	LCB	RCB	SS/LS	FS/RS	FINISH	
1988	G.Townsend	B.Pickel	M.Wise*	L.King	M.Millen	J.Robinson	R.Martin	R.Fellows	M.Haynes	R.Carter	V.McElroy	3aw	7-9
1989	H.Long	B.Golic	S.Davis*	L.King	T.Benson	J.Robinson	G.Townsend	T.McDaniel	L.Washington	M.Harden	E.Anderson	3aw	8-8
1990	H.Long	B.Golic	S.Davis	G.Townsend	J.Robinson	R.Ellison	T.Benson	T.McDaniel	L.Washington	M.Harden	E.Anderson	1aw	12-4 dc
1991	H.Long	B.Golic	S.Davis	G.Townsend	W.Moss	R.Ellison	T.Benson	T.McDaniel	L.Washington	R.Lott	E.Anderson	3aw	9-7 w
1992	H.Long	W.Broughton	N.Harrison	G.Townsend	A.Wallace	R.Ellison	W.Moss	T.McDaniel	L.Washington	R.Lott	E.Anderson	4aw	7-9
1993	H.Long	C.McGlockton	N.Harrison	G.Townsend	A.Wallace	J.Kelly	W.Moss	T.McDaniel	L.Washington	D.Hoskins	E.Anderson	2aw	10-6 wd
1994	N.Harrison	J.Ball	C.McGlockton	A.Smith	Fredrickson	G.Biekert	W.Moss	T.McDaniel	A.Lewis	D.Hoskins	E.Anderson	3aw	9-7 #
1995	A.Smith	J.Ball	C.McGlockton	P.Swilling	Fredrickson	G.Biekert	M.Jones	T.McDaniel	A.Lewis	D.Hoskins	E.Anderson	3aw	8-8
1996	L.Johnstone	R.Maryland	C.McGlockton	P.Swilling	Fredrickson	G.Biekert	M.Jones	T.McDaniel	A.Lewis	L.Lynch	D.Carrington	4aw	7-9
1997	D.Russell	R.Maryland	C.McGlockton	A.Smith	Fredrickson	G.Biekert	M.Morton	T.McDaniel	A.Lewis	J.Trapp	E.Turner	4aw	4-12
1998	J.Harris	D.Russell	R.Maryland	L.Johnstone	T.Wooden	G.Biekert	R.Harvey	C.Woodson	E.Allen	A.Newman	A.Lewis	2aw	8-8
1999	J.Harris	R.Maryland	D.Russell	L.Johnstone	K.Williams	G.Biekert	R.Harvey	C.Woodson	E.Allen	A.Newman	E.Turner	3aw	8-8
2000	T.Bryant	G.Jackson	D.Russell	L.Johnstone	W.Thomas	G.Biekert	E.Alexander	C.Woodson	E.Allen	M.Pope	A.Dorsett	1aw	12-4 dc
2001	R.Upshaw	D.Russell	G.Jackson	T.Bryant	W.Thomas	G.Biekert	E.Alexander	C.Woodson	E.Allen	M.Pope	A.Dorsett	1aw	10-6 ed
2002	D.Grant	S.Adams	J.Parrella	T.Bryant	B.Romanowski	N.Harris	E.Barton	C.Woodson	T.James	D.Gibson	R.Woodson	1aw	11-5 dcs
2003	T.Armstrong	C.Cooper	R.Coleman	T.Brayton	T.Smith	N.Harris	E.Barton	C.Woodson	P.Buchanon	D.Gibson	R.Woodson	3aw	4-12
2004	T.Brayton	T.Washington	W.Sapp	B.Hamilton	D.Grant	D.Clark	N.Harris	P.Buchanon	C.Woodson	M.Anderson	R.Buchanan	4aw	5-11
2005	B.Hamilton	T.Washington	W.Sapp	D.Burgess	K.Morrison	R.Hill*	D.Clark	N.Asomugha	F.Washington	J.Cooper	S.Schweigert	4aw	4-12

1950	J.Green	W.Stickel	M.Jarmoluk	N.Willey	J.Muha	M.Gianelli+	C.Bednarik	P.McHugh	J.Sutton	R.Craft	F.Reagan	3na	6-6
1951	P.Pihos	W.Stickel	M.Jarmoluk	N.Willey	K.Farragut	M.Gianelli+	C.Bednarik	P.McHugh	J.Sutton	R.Craft	F.Reagan	5na	4-8
1952	J.Zilly	V.Sears	M.Jarmoluk	N.Willey	W.Robinson	B.Kilroy+	C.Bednarik	N.Ferris	B.Bawel	R.Craft	J.Sutton	2na	7-5
1953	T.Scott	V.Sears	M.Jarmoluk	N.Willey	W.Robinson	B.Kilroy+	C.Bednarik	E.Van Buren	T.Brookshier	R.Craft	B.Hudson	2ne	7-4-1
1954	T.Scott	J.Richardson	M.Jarmoluk	N.Willey	W.Robinson	B.Kilroy+	C.Bednarik	H.Dowda	R.Barni	J.Norton	B.Hudson	2ne	7-4-1
1955	T.Scott	J.Richardson	M.Jarmoluk	N.Willey	W.Robinson	J.Ricca+	C.Bednarik	H.Dowda	B.Bawel	E.Bell	B.Hudson	4ne	4-7-1
1956	T.Scott	J.Richardson	J.Weatherall	N.Willey	W.Robinson	M.Campbell+	C.Bednarik	R.Ryan	T.Brookshier	E.Bell	L.Riley	6ne	3-8-1
1957	T.Scott	J.Weatherall	S.Youngelman	N.Willey	C.Bednarik	B.Hudson	B.Koman	J.Norton	T.Brookshier	E.Bell	J.Harris	5ne	4-8
1958	E.Meadows	J.Richardson	D.Owens	M.Campbell	B.Koman	B.Pellegrini	T.Louderback	J.Norton	T.Brookshier	E.Bell	L.Riley	5ne	2-9-1
1959	J.Robb	J.Richardson	D.Owens	E.Khayat	B.Pellegrini	C.Weber	T.Catlin	J.Carr	T.Brookshier	A.Powell	L.Riley	2ne	7-5
1960	J.Robb	J.Richardson	E.Khayat	M.Campbell	B.Pellegrini	C.Weber	M.Baughan	J.Carr	T.Brookshier	D.Burroughs	B.Freeman	1ne	10-2 I*
1961	L.Sugar	J.Richardson	E.Khayat	M.Campbell	J.Nocera	C.Weber	M.Baughan	J.Carr	T.Brookshier	D.Burroughs	B.Freeman	2ne	10-4
1962	J.Baker	R.Gunnels	J.Lewis	B.Richards	B.Harrison	C.Bednarik	M.Baughan	B.Scotti	I.Cross	J.Carr	D.Burroughs	7ne	3-10-1
1963	G.Tarasovic	R.Gunnels	J.Mellekas	B.Richards	L.Caffey	D.Lloyd	M.Baughan	B.Scotti	I.Cross	J.Carr	D.Burroughs	7ne	2-10-2
1964	G.Tarasovic	F.Peters	J.Meyers	B.Richards	M.Morgan	D.Lloyd	M.Baughan	N.Ramsey	I.Cross	J.Scarpati	D.Burroughs	3ne	6-8
1965	D.Hultz	F.Peters	J.Meyers	B.Richards	M.Morgan	D.Lloyd	M.Baughan	A.Nelson	I.Cross	N.Ramsey	J.Scarpati	5ne	5-9
1966	D.Hultz	F.Peters	J.Meyers	G.Pettigrew	M.Morgan	D.Lloyd	H.Wells	A.Nelson	J.Nettles	N.Ramsey	J.Scarpati	2ne	9-5
1967	D.Hultz	F.Peters	J.Meyers	G.Pettigrew	M.Morgan	D.Lloyd	H.Wells	A.Martin	J.Nettles	N.Ramsey	J.Scarpati	2nca	6-7-1
1968	T.Rossovich	R.Beisler	G.Pettigrew	M.Tom	R.Medved	D.Lloyd	H.Wells	A.Nelson	A.Haymond	N.Ramsey	J.Scarpati	4nca	2-12
1969	T.Rossovich	F.Peters	E.Calloway	M.Tom	T.Guillory	D.Lloyd	R.Porter	A.Nelson	I.Cross	N.Ramsey	J.Scarpati	4nca	4-9-1
1970	E.Calloway	D.Hultz	G.Pettigrew	M.Tom	A.Young	T.Rossovich	R.Porter	R.Jones	A.Nelson	N.Ramsey	S.Preece	5ne	3-10-1
1971	R.Harris	D.Hultz	E.Calloway	M.Tom	S.Zabel	T.Rossovich	R.Porter	A.Nelson	N.Ramsey	L.Keyes	B.Bradley	3ne	6-7-1
1972	R.Harris	D.Hultz	H.Antwine	M.Tom	R.Porter	C.Allen	B.Creech	A.Nelson	N.Ramsey	L.Keyes	B.Bradley	5ne	2-11-1
1973	D.Wirgowski	G.Pettigrew	R.Harris	W.Wynn	S.Zabel	M.McKeever	J.Sodaski	J.Outlaw	J.Lavender	R.Logan	B.Bradley	3ne	5-8-1
1974	W.Wynn	B.Dunstan	J.Patton	J.Jones	S.Zabel	B.Bergey	J.Bunting	J.Outlaw	J.Lavender	R.Logan	B.Bradley	4ne	7-7
1975	W.Wynn	R.Glover	B.Dunstan	B.Gay	F.LeMaster	B.Bergey	J.Bunting	J.Outlaw	J.Lavender	R.Logan	B.Bradley	5ne	4-10
1976	B.Gay	M.Sistrunk	C.Hairston	W.Wynn	F.LeMaster	B.Bergey	J.Bunting	J.Outlaw	A.Clark	R.Logan	B.Bradley	4ne	4-10
1977	M.Sistrunk	C.Johnson	C.Hairston*	J.Bunting	B.Bergey	F.LeMaster	D.Mahalic	J.Outlaw	H.Edwards	R.Logan	J.Sanders	4ne	5-9
1978	M.Sistrunk	C.Johnson	C.Hairston*	R.Wilkes	B.Bergey	F.LeMaster	D.Mahalic	J.Outlaw	H.Edwards	R.Logan	J.Sanders	2ne	9-7 w
1979	C.Humphrey	C.Johnson	C.Hairston*	J.Bunting	T.Tautolo	F.LeMaster	R.Wilkes	B.Howard	H.Edwards	R.Logan	B.Wilson	2ne	11-5 #wd
1980	D.Harrison	C.Johnson	C.Hairston*	J.Bunting	B.Bergey	F.LeMaster	J.Robinson	R.Young	H.Edwards	R.Logan	B.Wilson	1ne	12-4 #dcs
1981	D.Harrison	C.Johnson	C.Hairston*	J.Bunting	A.Chesley	F.LeMaster	J.Robinson	R.Young	H.Edwards	R.Logan	B.Wilson	2ne	10-6 w
1982	D.Harrison	K.Clarke	C.Hairston*	J.Bunting	J.Robinson	F.LeMaster	R.Wilkes	R.Young	H.Edwards	R.Logan	B.Wilson	11n	3-6
1983	D.Harrison	K.Clarke	C.Hairston*	R.Wilkes	J.Robinson	A.Griggs	J.Williams	R.Young	H.Edwards	R.Logan	W.Hopkins	4ne	5-11
1984	D.Harrison	K.Clarke	G.Brown*	R.Wilkes	J.Robinson	A.Griggs	J.Williams	E.Foules	H.Edwards	R.Ellis	W.Hopkins	5ne	6-9-1
1985	R.White	K.Clarke	G.Brown*	R.Wilkes	Reichenbach	A.Griggs	G.Cobb	R.Young	H.Edwards	R.Ellis	W.Hopkins	4ne	7-9
1986	B.Darby	K.Clarke	R.White	G.Brown	G.Cobb	Reichenbach	A.Johnson	R.Young	E.Cooper	A.Waters	T.Hoage	4ne	5-10-1
1987	R.White	K.Clarke	J.Brown	C.Simmons	S.Joyner	Reichenbach	G.Cobb	R.Young	E.Foules	A.Waters	T.Hoage	2ne	7-8
1988	R.White	M.Pitts	J.Brown	C.Simmons	S.Joyner	Reichenbach	T.Bell	R.Young	E.Allen	A.Waters	W.Hopkins	1ne	10-6 #d
1989	R.White	M.Pitts	J.Brown	C.Simmons	S.Joyner	B.Evans	A.Harris	I.Jenkins	E.Allen	A.Waters	W.Hopkins	2ne	11-5 w
1990	R.White	M.Golic	J.Brown	C.Simmons	S.Joyner	B.Evans	J.Small	B.Smith	E.Allen	A.Waters	W.Hopkins	2ne	10-6 w
1991	R.White	M.Pitts	J.Brown	C.Simmons	S.Joyner	B.Evans	J.Small	B.Smith	E.Allen	A.Waters	W.Hopkins	3ne	10-6 #
1992	R.White	A.Harmon	M.Golic	C.Simmons	S.Joyner	B.Evans	W.Thomas	J.Booty	E.Allen	R.Miano	W.Hopkins	2ne	11-5 wd
1993	M.Flores	A.Harmon	W.Perry	C.Simmons	S.Joyner	B.Evans	W.Thomas	M.McMillian	E.Allen	A.Waters	R.Miano	3ne	8-8
1994	W.Fuller	A.Harmon	W.Perry	G.Townsend	B.Romanowski	B.Evans	W.Thomas	M.McMillian	E.Allen	M.Zordich	G.Jackson	4ne	7-9
1995	W.Fuller	A.Harmon	R.Dixon	M.Mamula	B.Romanowski	K.Gouveia	W.Thomas	M.McMillian	B.Taylor	M.Zordich	G.Jackson	2ne	10-6 wd
1996	W.Fuller	K.Johnson	R.Hall	M.Mamula	R.Farmer	J.Willis	W.Thomas	T.Vincent	B.Taylor	M.Zordich	B.Dawkins	2ne	10-6 #w
1997	G.Jefferson	H.Thomas	R.Hall	M.Mamula	D.Smith	J.Willis	W.Thomas	T.Vincent	C.Dimry	M.Zordich	B.Dawkins	3ne	6-9-1
1998	G.Jefferson	H.Thomas	B.Johnson	H.Douglas	J.Darling	J.Willis	W.Thomas	T.Vincent	B.Taylor	M.Zordich	B.Dawkins	5ne	3-13
1999	G.Jefferson	H.Thomas	S.Martin	M.Mamula	J.Darling	J.Trotter	W.Thomas	T.Vincent	B.Taylor	T.Hauck	B.Dawkins	5ne	5-11
2000	B.Whiting	C.Simon	H.Thomas	H.Douglas	B.Gardner	J.Trotter	C.Emmons	T.Vincent	B.Taylor	D.Moore	B.Dawkins	2ne	11-5 wd
2001	B.Whiting	C.Simon	H.Thomas	H.Douglas	M.Caldwell	J.Trotter	C.Emmons	T.Vincent	B.Taylor	D.Moore	B.Dawkins	1ne	11-5 edc
2002	B.Whiting	C.Simon	D.Walker	H.Douglas	S.Barber	L.Kirkland	C.Emmons	T.Vincent	B.Taylor	B.Bishop	B.Dawkins	1ne	12-4 dc
2003	B.Whiting	C.Simon	D.Walker	N.Kalu	N.Wayne	M.Simoneau	C.Emmons	T.Vincent	L.Sheppard	M.Lewis	C.Hart	1ne	12-4 dc
2004	J.Kearse	C.Simon	D.Walker	D.Burgess	M.Simoneau	J.Trotter	D.Jones	L.Sheppard	S.Brown	M.Lewis	B.Dawkins	1ne	13-3 dcs
2005	J.Kearse	H.Thomas	D.Walker	N.Kalu	D.Jones	J.Trotter	K.Adams	L.Sheppard	S.Brown	M.Lewis	B.Dawkins	4ne	6-10

1950	C.Mehelich	E.Stautner	C.Samuelson	B.McPeak	F.Sinkovitz	G.Nicksich+	D.Hogan	B.Gage	H.Hartley	J.Finks	S.McWilliams	3na	6-6
1951	G.Hays	P.Lea	E.Stautner	B.McPeak	F.Sinkovitz	J.Schweder+	D.Hogan	H.Hartley	J.Finks	J.Butler	J.Shipkey	4na	4-7-1
1952	G.Tarasovic	L.Ferry	E.Stautner	B.McPeak	D.Hogan	J.Shipkey	F.Sinkovitz	H.Hartley	J.Butler	C.Hipps	D.Dodrill+	4na	5-7
1953	G.Tarasovic	L.Ferry	E.Stautner	B.McPeak	D.Flanagan	M.Matuszak	D.Hogan	J.Brandt	J.Butler	A.DeCarlo	D.Dodrill+	4ne	6-6
1954	D.Brundage	L.Ferry	E.Stautner	B.McPeak	L.Tepe	D.Dodrill+	S.Sheriff	R.Craft	D.McConnell	J.Butler	P.Cameron	4ne	5-7
1955	E.Meadows	Modzelewski	W.McClung	B.McPeak	D.Flanagan	D.Dodrill+	J.Reger	D.Doyle	J.Butler	J.Hill	R.McCabe	6ne	4-8
1956	J.O'Malley	W.McClung	E.Stautner	B.McPeak	M.Matuszak	D.Dodrill+	J.Reger	G.Glick	J.Butler	D.Alban	A.Davis	4ne	5-7
1957	B.O'Neil	J.Krupa	E.Stautner	B.McPeak	G.Tarasovic	D.Dodrill	J.Reger	F.Bruney	J.Butler	G.Glick	D.Alban	3ne	6-6
1958	B.Smith	J.Lewis	J.Krupa	E.Stautner	B.Dougherty	D.Dodrill	J.Reger	D.Derby	J.Butler	G.Glick	D.Alban	3ne	7-4-1
1959	G.Tarasovic	J.Krupa	R.Fisher	E.Stautner	D.Lasse	D.Dodrill	J.Reger	D.Derby	J.Butler	B.Luna	D.Alban	4ne	6-5-1
1960	G.Tarasovic	E.Stautner	J.Krupa	B.Smith	R.Hayes	D.Campbell	J.Reger	J.Scudero	J.Wren	D.Derby	D.Moegle	5ne	5-6-1
1961	L.Michaels	G.Lipscomb	J.Krupa	E.Stautner	G.Tarasovic	M.Pottios	J.Reger	J.Sample	B.Keys	B.Butler	W.Daniel	5ne	6-8
1962	L.Michaels	G.Lipscomb	J.Krupa	E.Stautner	G.Tarasovic	B.Schmitz	J.Reger	D.Haley	B.Keys	C.Thomas	W.Daniel	2ne	9-5
1963	L.Michaels	F.Atkinson	J.Krupa	J.Baker	B.Schmitz	M.Pottios	A.Russell	D.Haley	B.Keys	C.Thomas	G.Glass	4ne	7-4-3
1964	B.McGee	R.Mansfield	C.Hinton	J.Baker	M.Messner	M.Pottios	B.Harrison	D.Haley	B.Keys	J.Bradshaw	W.Daniel	6ne	5-9
1965	B.McGee	R.Mansfield	C.Hinton	J.Baker	J.Campbell	M.Pottios	G.Breen	M.Woodson	B.Keys	J.Bradshaw	W.Daniel	7ne	2-12
1966	B.McGee	K.Kortas	C.Hinton	L.Voss	J.Campbell	B.Saul	A.Russell	M.Woodson	B.Keys	C.Thomas	P.Martha	6ne	5-8-1
1967	B.McGee	K.Kortas	C.Hinton	L.Voss	J.Campbell	B.Saul	A.Russell	M.Woodson	B.Hohn	C.Thomas	P.Martha	4ncy	4-9-1
1968	L.Voss	K.Kortas	C.Hinton	B.McGee	J.Hillebrand	R.May	A.Russell	M.Woodson	B.Wade	C.Thomas	P.Martha	4ncy	2-11-1

YEAR	COACH	WR/LE	LT	LG	C	RG	RT	TE/RE	WR/FL	QB	RB/LH	FB
1969	C.Noll	R.Jefferson	M.Taylor	L.Gagner	R.Mansfield	B.Van Dyke	J.Brown	J.Hilton	J.Wilburn	D.Shiner	D.Hoak	E.Gros
1970	C.Noll	D.Smith	M.Haggerty	S.Davis	R.Mansfield	B.Van Dyke	J.Brown	D.Hughes	R.Shanklin	T.Bradshaw	P.Pearson	J.Fuqua
1971	C.Noll	D.Smith	J.Kolb	S.Davis	R.Mansfield	B.Van Dyke	J.Brown	B.Adams	R.Shanklin	T.Bradshaw	P.Pearson	J.Fuqua
1972	C.Noll	F.Lewis	J.Kolb	S.Davis	R.Mansfield	B.Van Dyke	G.Mullins	J.McMakin	R.Shanklin	T.Bradshaw	F.Harris	J.Fuqua
1973	C.Noll	F.Lewis	J.Kolb	S.Davis	R.Mansfield	B.Van Dyke	G.Hines	J.McMakin	R.Shanklin	T.Bradshaw	F.Harris	P.Pearson
1974	C.Noll	F.Lewis	J.Kolb	S.Davis	R.Mansfield	G.Mullins	G.Gravelle	L.Brown	R.Shanklin	T.Bradshaw	R.Bleier	F.Harris
1975	C.Noll	F.Lewis	J.Kolb	J.Clack	R.Mansfield	G.Mullins	G.Gravelle	L.Brown	L.Swann	T.Bradshaw	R.Bleier	F.Harris
1976	C.Noll	F.Lewis	J.Kolb	S.Davis	M.Webster	J.Clack	G.Mullins	L.Brown	L.Swann	T.Bradshaw	R.Bleier	F.Harris
1977	C.Noll	J.Stallworth	J.Kolb	S.Davis	M.Webster	J.Clack	L.Brown	B.Cunningham	L.Swann	T.Bradshaw	R.Bleier	F.Harris
1978	C.Noll	J.Stallworth	J.Kolb	S.Davis	M.Webster	G.Mullins	R.Pinney	R.Grossman	L.Swann	T.Bradshaw	R.Bleier	F.Harris
1979	C.Noll	J.Stallworth	J.Kolb	S.Davis	M.Webster	S.Courson	L.Brown	B.Cunningham	L.Swann	T.Bradshaw	S.Thornton	F.Harris
1980	C.Noll	J.Smith	T.Petersen	R.Pinney	M.Webster	T.McGriff	L.Brown	R.Grossman	L.Swann	T.Bradshaw	R.Bleier	F.Harris
1981	C.Noll	J.Stallworth	R.Pinney	C.Wolfley	M.Webster	S.Courson	L.Brown	B.Cunningham	L.Swann	T.Bradshaw	F.Pollard	F.Harris
1982	C.Noll	J.Stallworth	R.Pinney	C.Wolfley	M.Webster	S.Courson	L.Brown	B.Cunningham	L.Swann	T.Bradshaw	F.Pollard	F.Harris
1983	C.Noll	J.Stallworth	T.Petersen	C.Wolfley	M.Webster	S.Courson	T.Ilkin	B.Cunningham	C.Sweeney	C.Stoudt	Abercrombie	F.Harris
1984	C.Noll	J.Stallworth	T.Ilkin	C.Wolfley	M.Webster	B.Wingle	L.Brown	D.Nelson	L.Lipps	M.Malone	R.Erenberg	F.Pollard
1985	C.Noll	J.Stallworth	R.Pinney	C.Wolfley	M.Webster	T.Long	T.Ilkin	B.Cunningham	L.Lipps	M.Malone	Abercrombie	F.Pollard
1986	C.Noll	J.Stallworth	R.Pinney	C.Wolfley	M.Webster	T.Long	T.Ilkin	P.Gothard	L.Lipps	M.Malone	Abercrombie	E.Jackson
1987	C.Noll	J.Stallworth	R.Pinney	C.Wolfley	M.Webster	T.Long	T.Ilkin	D.Lee	C.Sweeney	M.Malone	Abercrombie	E.Jackson
1988	C.Noll	W.Thompson	C.Wolfley	Blankenship	M.Webster	T.Long	T.Ilkin	P.Gothard	L.Lipps	B.Brister	W.Williams	M.Hoge
1989	C.Noll	D.Hill	J.Jackson	J.Rienstra	D.Dawson	T.Long	T.Ilkin	M.Mularkey	L.Lipps	B.Brister	T.Worley	M.Hoge
1990	C.Noll	L.Lipps	J.Jackson	Blankenship	D.Dawson	T.Long	T.Ilkin	M.Mularkey	D.Hill	B.Brister	T.Worley	M.Hoge
1991	C.Noll	L.Lipps	J.Jackson	T.Ricketts	D.Dawson	C.Haselrig	T.Ilkin	E.Green	D.Stone	N.O'Donnell	B.Foster	M.Hoge
1992	B.Cowher	J.Graham	J.Jackson	D.Love	D.Dawson	C.Haselrig	T.Ilkin	A.Cooper	D.Stone	N.O'Donnell	B.Foster	M.Hoge
1993	B.Cowher	J.Graham	J.Jackson	D.Love	D.Dawson	J.Strzelczyk	L.Searcy	E.Green	D.Stone	N.O'Donnell	B.Foster	M.Hoge
1994	B.Cowher	A.Hastings	J.Jackson	D.Love	D.Dawson	T.Kalis	L.Searcy	E.Green	C.Johnson	N.O'Donnell	B.Foster	J.Williams
1995	B.Cowher	Y.Thigpen	J.Jackson	T.Newberry	D.Dawson	J.Strzelczyk	L.Searcy	M.Bruener	C.Johnson	N.O'Donnell	E.Pegram	J.Williams
1996	B.Cowher	C.Johnson	J.Jackson	W.Wolford	D.Dawson	B.Stai	J.Strzelczyk	M.Bruener	A.Hastings	M.Tomczak	J.Bettis	T.Lester
1997	B.Cowher	Y.Thigpen	J.Jackson	W.Wolford	D.Dawson	B.Stai	J.Strzelczyk	M.Bruener	C.Johnson	K.Stewart	J.Bettis	T.Lester
1998	B.Cowher	C.Hawkins	W.Wolford	A.Faneca	D.Dawson	B.Stai	J.Stephens	M.Bruener	C.Johnson	K.Stewart	J.Bettis	J.Witman
1999	B.Cowher	C.Hawkins	W.Gandy	A.Faneca	R.Duffy	B.Stai	A.Brown	M.Bruener	H.Ward	K.Stewart	J.Bettis	J.Witman
2000	B.Cowher	P.Burress	W.Gandy	A.Faneca	D.Dawson	R.Tylski	M.Smith	M.Bruener	H.Ward	K.Stewart	J.Bettis	D.Kreider
2001	B.Cowher	P.Burress	W.Gandy	A.Faneca	J.Hartings	R.Tylski	M.Smith	M.Bruener	H.Ward	K.Stewart	J.Bettis	J.Witman
2002	B.Cowher	P.Burress	W.Gandy	A.Faneca	J.Hartings	K.Simmons	M.Smith	M.Bruener	H.Ward	T.Maddox	J.Bettis	D.Kreider
2003	B.Cowher	P.Burress	A.Faneca	K.Vincent	J.Hartings	K.Simmons	O.Ross	J.Tuman	H.Ward	T.Maddox	J.Bettis	D.Kreider
2004	B.Cowher	P.Burress	M.Smith	A.Faneca	J.Hartings	K.Vincent	O.Ross	J.Tuman	H.Ward	Roethlisberger	J.Bettis	D.Kreider
2005	B.Cowher	A.Randle El	M.Smith	A.Faneca	J.Hartings	K.Simmons	M.Starks	H.Miller	H.Ward	Roethlisberger	W.Parker	D.Kreider
SAINT LOUIS RAMS (Los Angeles 1950-81)												
1950	J.Stydahar	T.Fears	D.Huffman	J.Finlay	F.Naumetz	H.Thompson	B.Reinhard	E.Hirsch	V.Smith	Van Brocklin	G.Davis	D.Hoerner
1951	J.Stydahar	T.Fears	D.Simensen	D.Daugherty	L.McLaughlin	B.Lange	T.Dahms	E.Hirsch	V.Smith	Van Brocklin	G.Davis	D.Towler
1952	H.Pool	E.Hirsch	D.Simensen	D.Daugherty	L.McLaughlin	H.Thompson	T.Dahms	T.Fears	V.Smith	Van Brocklin	S.Quinlan	D.Towler
1953	H.Pool	E.Hirsch	B.Fry	D.Putnam	L.McLaughlin	H.Thompson	T.Dahms	B.Boyd	T.Fears	Van Brocklin	S.Quinlan	D.Towler
1954	H.Pool	E.Hirsch	B.Cross	D.Putnam	L.McLaughlin	H.Thompson	C.Toogood	B.Boyd	T.Fears	Van Brocklin	S.Quinlan	D.Towler
1955	S.Gillman	T.Fears	B.Cross	D.Putnam	L.McLaughlin	J.Hock	C.Toogood	E.Hirsch	B.Boyd	Van Brocklin	R.Waller	T.Younger
1956	S.Gillman	E.Hirsch	B.Fry	D.Putnam	D.Daugherty	J.Hock	G.Holtzman	L.Clarke	B.Boyd	B.Wade	R.Waller	T.Younger
1957	S.Gillman	E.Hirsch	B.Fry	D.Putnam	B.Griffin	J.Hock	K.Panfil	L.Clarke	B.Boyd	Van Brocklin	T.Wilson	J.Marconi
1958	S.Gillman	L.Lundy	B.Fry	D.Putnam	J.Morrow	B.Lansford	K.Panfil	R.Phillips	D.Shofner	B.Wade	J.Arnett	J.Marconi
1959	S.Gillman	D.Shofner	B.Fry	D.Putnam	J.Morrow	J.Houser	C.Bradshaw	S.Williams	R.Phillips	B.Wade	J.Arnett	O.Matson
1960	Waterfield	R.Phillips	J.Boeke	B.Lansford	A.Hunter	R.Hord	C.Bradshaw	C.Dale	O.Matson	B.Wade	J.Arnett	J.Marconi
1961	Waterfield	R.Phillips	J.Boeke	C.Cowan	A.Hunter	R.Hord	Varrichione	C.Dale	O.Matson	Z.Bratkowski	J.Arnett	D.Bass
1962	Waterfield	R.Phillips	J.Carollo	C.Cowan	L.Hayes	D.Putnam	Varrichione	C.Dale	P.Atkins	Z.Bratkowski	J.Arnett	D.Bass
1963	H.Svare	R.Phillips	J.Carollo	C.Cowan	A.Hunter	D.Chuy	Varrichione	J.Adams	C.Dale	R.Gabriel	D.Bass	B.Wilson
1964	H.Svare	R.Phillips	J.Carollo	C.Cowan	A.Hunter	D.Chuy	Varrichione	M.McKeever	B.Pope	B.Munson	B.Wilson	L.Josephson
1965	H.Svare	J.Snow	J.Carollo	D.Chuy	K.Iman	J.Scibelli	C.Cowan	M.McKeever	T.McDonald	R.Gabriel	L.Josephson	D.Bass
1966	G.Allen	J.Snow	J.Carollo	T.Mack	K.Iman	J.Scibelli	C.Cowan	B.Truax	T.McDonald	R.Gabriel	T.Moore	D.Bass
1967	G.Allen	J.Snow	J.Carollo	T.Mack	K.Iman	J.Scibelli	C.Cowan	B.Truax	B.Casey	R.Gabriel	L.Josephson	D.Bass
1968	G.Allen	J.Snow	J.Carollo	T.Mack	K.Iman	J.Scibelli	C.Cowan	B.Truax	B.Casey	R.Gabriel	W.Ellison	D.Bass
1969	G.Allen	J.Snow	C.Cowan	T.Mack	K.Iman	J.Scibelli	B.Brown	B.Truax	W.Tucker	R.Gabriel	L.Smith	L.Josephson
1970	G.Allen	J.Snow	C.Cowan	T.Mack	K.Iman	J.Scibelli	B.Brown	B.Truax	W.Tucker	R.Gabriel	L.Smith	L.Josephson
1971	T.Protho	J.Snow	C.Cowan	T.Mack	K.Iman	J.Scibelli	H.Schuh	B.Klein	L.Rentzel	R.Gabriel	W.Ellison	L.Josephson
1972	T.Protho	J.Snow	C.Cowan	T.Mack	K.Iman	J.Scibelli	H.Schuh	B.Klein	L.Rentzel	R.Gabriel	J.Bertelsen	W.Ellison
1973	C.Knox	H.Jackson	C.Cowan	T.Mack	K.Iman	J.Scibelli	J.Williams	B.Klein	J.Snow	J.Hadl	L.McCutcheon	J.Bertelsen
1974	C.Knox	H.Jackson	C.Cowan	T.Mack	K.Iman	J.Scibelli	J.Williams	B.Klein	J.Snow	J.Harris	L.McCutcheon	J.Bertelsen
1975	C.Knox	H.Jackson	C.Cowan	T.Mack	R.Saul	J.Scibelli	J.Williams	B.Klein	R.Jessie	J.Harris	L.McCutcheon	C.Bryant
1976	C.Knox	H.Jackson	D.France	T.Mack	R.Saul	D.Harrah	J.Williams	B.Klein	R.Jessie	J.Harris	L.McCutcheon	Cappelletti
1977	C.Knox	H.Jackson	D.France	T.Mack	R.Saul	D.Harrah	J.Williams	T.Nelson	B.Waddy	P.Haden	L.McCutcheon	Cappelletti
1978	R.Malavasi	R.Jessie	D.France	T.Mack	R.Saul	D.Harrah	J.Williams	T.Nelson	W.Miller	P.Haden	C.Bryant	Cappelletti
1979	R.Malavasi	P.Dennard	D.France	K.Hill	R.Saul	D.Harrah	J.Slater	T.Nelson	B.Waddy	P.Haden	W.Tyler	C.Bryant
1980	R.Malavasi	P.Dennard	D.France	K.Hill	R.Saul	D.Smith	J.Slater	V.Hicks	B.Waddy	V.Ferragamo	E.Peacock	C.Bryant
1981	R.Malavasi	P.Dennard	I.Pankey	K.Hill	R.Saul	D.Harrah	D.Smith	W.Arnold	B.Waddy	P.Haden	W.Tyler	C.Bryant
1982	R.Malavasi	P.Dennard	I.Pankey	K.Hill	D.Smith	D.Harrah	J.Slater	M.Barber	W.Miller	V.Ferragamo	W.Tyler	M.Guman
1983	J.Robinson	P.Dennard	B.Bain	K.Hill	D.Smith	D.Harrah	J.Slater	M.Barber	G.Farmer	V.Ferragamo	E.Dickerson	M.Guman
1984	J.Robinson	H.Ellard	B.Bain	K.Hill	D.Smith	D.Harrah	I.Pankey	Da.Hill	Dr.Hill	J.Kemp	E.Dickerson	M.Guman
1985	J.Robinson	H.Ellard	I.Pankey	K.Hill	D.Smith	D.Harrah	J.Slater	D.Hill	R.Brown	D.Brock	E.Dickerson	T.Hunter*
1986	J.Robinson	H.Ellard	I.Pankey	T.Newberry	D.Smith	D.Harrah	J.Slater	D.Hill	R.Brown	S.Bartkowski	E.Dickerson	B.Redden
1987	J.Robinson	H.Ellard	I.Pankey	T.Newberry	D.Smith	D.Harrah	J.Slater	D.Hill	R.Brown	J.Everett	C.White	M.Guman
1988	J.Robinson	H.Ellard	I.Pankey	T.Newberry	D.Smith	D.Love	J.Slater	D.Johnson	A.Cox	J.Everett	G.Bell	B.McGee
1989	J.Robinson	H.Ellard	I.Pankey	T.Newberry	D.Smith	T.Slaton	J.Slater	D.Johnson	F.Anderson	J.Everett	G.Bell	B.McGee
1990	J.Robinson	H.Ellard	I.Pankey	T.Newberry	D.Smith	D.Love	J.Slater	P.Holohan	F.Anderson	J.Everett	C.Gary	B.McGee
1991	J.Robinson	H.Ellard	G.Perry	B.Brostek	T.Newberry	D.Love	J.Slater	D.Johnson	F.Anderson	J.Everett	R.Delpino	J.Price*
1992	C.Knox	F.Anderson	G.Perry	T.Newberry	B.Brostek	J.Milinchik	J.Slater	P.Carter	H.Ellard	J.Everett	C.Gary	D.Lang
1993	C.Knox	F.Anderson	I.Eatman	T.Newberry	B.Brostek	L.Goeas	J.Slater	P.Carter	H.Ellard	J.Everett	J.Bettis	T.Lester
1994	C.Knox	F.Anderson	C.Jones	T.Newberry	B.Brostek	L.Goeas	W.Gandy	T.Drayton	J.Hester	C.Miller	J.Bettis	H.Griffith
1995	R.Brooks	J.Hester	W.Gandy	L.Goeas	B.Brostek	D.White	D.Ashmore	T.Drayton	I.Bruce	C.Miller	J.Bettis	M.Cook*
1996	R.Brooks	E.Kennison	W.Gandy	L.Goeas	B.Brostek	D.White	Z.Wiegert	E.Conwell	I.Bruce	T.Banks	L.Phillips	D.Harris
1997	D.Vermeil	E.Kennison	O.Pace	J.Gerak	Gruttadauria	Z.Wiegert	W.Gandy	E.Conwell	I.Bruce	T.Banks	L.Phillips	C.Heyward
1998	D.Vermeil	E.Kennison	O.Pace	F.Miller	J.Flannery	Z.Wiegert	W.Gandy	R.Williams	R.Proehl	T.Banks	R.Holcombe	D.Harris
1999	D.Vermeil	T.Holt	O.Pace	T.Nutten	Gruttadauria	A.Timmerman	F.Miller	R.Williams	I.Bruce	K.Warner	M.Faulk	J.Robinson*
2000	M.Martz	T.Holt	O.Pace	T.Nutten	A.McCollum	A.Timmerman	R.Tucker	R.Williams	I.Bruce	K.Warner	M.Faulk	R.Holcombe
2001	M.Martz	T.Holt	O.Pace	T.Nutten	A.McCollum	A.Timmerman	R.Tucker	E.Conwell	I.Bruce	K.Warner	M.Faulk	J.Hodgins
2002	M.Martz	T.Holt	O.Pace	T.Nutten	A.McCollum	A.Timmerman	J.St. Clair	E.Conwell	I.Bruce	M.Bulger	M.Faulk	Manumaleuna*
2003	M.Martz	T.Holt	O.Pace	A.McCollum	D.Wohlabaugh	A.Timmerman	K.Turley	Manumaleuna	I.Bruce	M.Bulger	M.Faulk	C.Cleeland*
2004	M.Martz	T.Holt	O.Pace	T.Nutten	A.McCollum	A.Timmerman	G.Williams	Manumaleuna	I.Bruce	M.Bulger	M.Faulk	C.Cleeland*
2005	J.Vitt	T.Holt	O.Pace	C.Terrell	A.McCollum	A.Timmerman	A.Barron	Manumaleuna	I.Bruce	M.Bulger	S.Jackson	K.Curtis+

YEAR	LDE	LDT/NT	RDT/RDE	RDE/LOLB	LLB/LILB	MLB/RILB	RLB/ROLB	LCB	RCB	SS/LS	FS/RS	FINISH	
1969	L.Voss	J.Greene	C.Hinton	B.McGee	J.Hillebrand	R.May	A.Russell	B.Hohn	J.Shorter	C.Beatty	P.Martha	4ncy	1-13
1970	L.Voss	J.Greene	C.Hinton	B.McGee	J.Hillebrand	C.Allen	A.Russell	M.Blount	L.Calland	C.Beatty	O.Austin	3ac	5-9
1971	L.Greenwood	J.Greene	L.Voss	D.White	J.Ham	C.Allen	A.Russell	J.Rowser	M.Blount	M.Wagner	G.Edwards	2ac	6-8
1972	L.Greenwood	J.Greene	B.McGee	D.White	J.Ham	H.Davis	A.Russell	J.Rowser	M.Blount	M.Wagner	R.Anderson	1ac	11-3 dc
1973	L.Greenwood	J.Greene	E.Holmes	D.White	J.Ham	H.Davis	A.Russell	J.Rowser	M.Blount	M.Wagner	G.Edwards	2ac	10-4 #w
1974	L.Greenwood	J.Greene	E.Holmes	D.White	J.Ham	J.Lambert	A.Russell	J.Thomas	M.Blount	M.Wagner	G.Edwards	1ac	10-3-1 dcs*
1975	L.Greenwood	J.Greene	E.Holmes	D.White	J.Ham	J.Lambert	A.Russell	J.Thomas	M.Blount	M.Wagner	G.Edwards	1ac	12-2 dcs*
1976	L.Greenwood	J.Greene	E.Holmes	D.White	J.Ham	J.Lambert	A.Russell	J.Thomas	M.Blount	M.Wagner	G.Edwards	1ac	10-4 #dc
1977	L.Greenwood	J.Greene	S.Furness	D.White	J.Ham	J.Lambert	L.Toews	J.Thomas	M.Blount	D.Shell	G.Edwards	1ac	9-5 d
1978	L.Greenwood	J.Greene	J.Banaszak	D.White	J.Ham	J.Lambert	L.Toews	R.Johnson	M.Blount	D.Shell	M.Wagner	1ac	14-2 dcs*
1979	L.Greenwood	J.Greene	G.Dunn	J.Banaszak	J.Ham	J.Lambert	D.Winston	R.Johnson	M.Blount	D.Shell	J.Thomas	1ac	12-4 dcs*
1980	L.Greenwood	J.Greene	S.Furness	J.Banaszak	J.Ham	J.Lambert	R.Cole	R.Johnson	M.Blount	D.Shell	M.Wagner	3ac	9-7
1981	J.Goodman	T.Beasley	G.Dunn	J.Banaszak	J.Ham	J.Lambert	R.Cole	D.Woodruff	M.Blount	D.Shell	J.Thomas	2ac	8-8
1982	J.Goodman	G.Dunn	T.Beasley*	J.Ham	L.Toews	J.Lambert	R.Cole	D.Woodruff	M.Blount	D.Shell	R.Johnson	4a	6-3 p
1983	J.Goodman	G.Dunn	T.Beasley*	Merriweather	L.Toews	J.Lambert	R.Cole	D.Woodruff	M.Blount	D.Shell	R.Woods	1ac	10-6 d
1984	J.Goodman	G.Dunn	K.Gary*	Merriweather	D.Little	R.Cole	B.Hinkle	D.Woodruff	S.Washington	D.Shell	E.Williams	1ac	9-7 dc
1985	K.Willis	G.Dunn	K.Gary*	Merriweather	D.Little	R.Cole	B.Hinkle	D.Woodruff	H.Clayton	D.Shell	E.Williams	2ac	7-9
1986	K.Willis	G.Dunn	E.Nelson*	Merriweather	D.Little	R.Cole	B.Hinkle	J.Swain	H.Clayton	D.Shell	E.Williams	3ac	6-10
1987	K.Willis	G.Dunn	E.Nelson*	Merriweather	D.Little	R.Cole	B.Hinkle	D.Woodruff	D.Hall	D.Shell	T.Everett	3ac	8-7
1988	T.Johnson	G.Williams	K.Gary*	B.Hinkle	D.Little	H.Nickerson	A.Jones	D.Woodruff	R.Woodson	C.Gowdy	T.Everett	4ac	5-11
1989	K.Willis	G.Williams	T.Johnson*	B.Hinkle	D.Little	H.Nickerson	G.Lloyd	D.Woodruff	R.Woodson	C.Lake	T.Everett	2ac	9-7 wd
1990	K.Willis	G.Williams	D.Evans*	B.Hinkle	H.Nickerson	D.Little	G.Lloyd	D.Johnson	R.Woodson	C.Lake	T.Everett	3ac	9-7 #
1991	A.Jones	G.Williams	D.Evans*	B.Hinkle	H.Nickerson	D.Little	G.Lloyd	D.Johnson	R.Woodson	C.Lake	T.Everett	2ac	7-9
1992	K.Davidson	G.Williams	D.Evans*	J.Williams	H.Nickerson	D.Little	G.Lloyd	R.Woodson	D.Johnson	C.Lake	D.Perry	1ac	11-5 d
1993	K.Davidson	J.Steed	D.Evans*	K.Greene	L.Kirkland	C.Brown	G.Lloyd	R.Woodson	D.Johnson	C.Lake	D.Perry	2ac	9-7 #w
1994	G.Williams	J.Steed	R.Seals*	K.Greene	L.Kirkland	C.Brown	G.Lloyd	R.Woodson	D.Figures	C.Lake	D.Perry	1ac	12-4 dc
1995	B.Buckner	J.Steed	R.Seals*	K.Greene	L.Kirkland	C.Brown	G.Lloyd	W.Williams	C.Lake	M.Bell	D.Perry	1ac	11-5 dcs
1996	B.Buckner	J.Steed	K.Henry*	J.Gildon	L.Kirkland	J.Olsavsky	C.Brown	R.Woodson	W.Williams	C.Lake	D.Perry	1ac	10-6 ed
1997	N.Harrison	J.Steed	K.Henry*	J.Gildon	L.Kirkland	E.Holmes	G.Lloyd	D.Woolford	C.Lake	M.Bell	D.Perry	1ac	11-5 #dc
1998	O.Roye	J.Steed	K.Henry*	J.Gildon	L.Kirkland	E.Holmes	C.Emmons	C.Lake	D.Washington	L.Flowers	D.Perry	3ac	7-9
1999	O.Roye	J.Steed	K.Henry*	J.Gildon	L.Kirkland	E.Holmes	C.Emmons	C.Scott	D.Washington	L.Flowers	T.Davis	4ac	6-10
2000	A.Smith	von Oelhoffen	K.Henry*	J.Gildon	L.Kirkland	E.Holmes	J.Porter	C.Scott	D.Washington	L.Flowers	B.Alexander	3ac	9-7
2001	A.Smith	C.Hampton	von Oelhoffen*	J.Gildon	E.Holmes	K.Bell	J.Porter	C.Scott	D.Washington	L.Flowers	B.Alexander	1ac	13-3 dc
2002	A.Smith	C.Hampton	von Oelhoffen*	J.Gildon	K.Bell	J.Farrior	J.Porter	C.Scott	D.Washington	L.Flowers	B.Alexander	1an	10-5-1 ed
2003	A.Smith	C.Hampton	von Oelhoffen*	J.Gildon	J.Farrior	K.Bell	J.Porter	C.Scott	D.Washington	M.Logan	B.Alexander	3an	6-10
2004	A.Smith	C.Hoke	von Oelhoffen*	C.Haggans	J.Farrior	L.Foote	J.Porter	W.Williams	D.Townsend	T.Polamalu	C.Hope	1an	15-1 dc
2005	A.Smith	C.Hampton	von Oelhoffen*	C.Haggans	J.Farrior	L.Foote	J.Porter	I.Taylor	D.Townsend	T.Polamalu	C.Hope	2an	11-5 #wdcs*

1950	L.Brink	E.Champagne	G.Bouley	J.Zilly	V.Vasicek	D.Paul	M.Lazetich	J.Williams	W.Lewis	T.Keane	S.West+	1nn	9-3 cl
1951	L.Brink	J.Winkler	C.Toogood	A.Robustelli	T.Younger	S.West+	D.Paul	N.Hecker	W.Lewis	J.Williams	H.Rich	1nn	8-4 l*
1952	L.Brink	C.Toogood	J.Winkler	A.Robustelli	T.Younger	S.West+	D.Paul	W.Lewis	N.Lane	J.Williams	H.Rich	1nn	9-3 c
1953	L.Brink	C.Toogood	L.Teeuws	A.Robustelli	B.McFadin	S.West+	D.Paul	N.Hecker	N.Lane	W.Lewis	H.Rich	3nw	8-3-1
1954	D.Wardlow	A.Hauser	G.Lipscomb	A.Robustelli	B.Griffin	B.McFadin+	D.Paul	H.Haynes	J.Dwyer	D.Doll	W.Sherman	4nw	6-5-1
1955	P.Miller	B.McFadin	A.Hauser	A.Robustelli	L.Richter	D.Paul+	B.Griffin	J.Cason	E.Hughes	D.Burroughs	W.Sherman	1nw	8-3-1 l
1956	P.Miller	B.McFadin	A.Hauser	D.Wardlow	H.Pitts	L.Richter+	L.Morris	J.Cason	J.Whittenton	D.Burroughs	W.Sherman	5nw	4-8
1957	P.Miller	A.Hauser	F.Fuller	B.Smith	B.Dougherty	L.Richter+	D.Daugherty	J.Whittenton	D.Shofner	D.Burroughs	W.Sherman	4nw	6-6
1958	G.Holtzman	G.Strugar	F.Fuller	L.Michaels	J.Pardee	L.Richter	D.Daugherty	J.Harris	J.Morris	D.Burroughs	W.Sherman	2nw	8-4
1959	L.Lundy	G.Strugar	J.LoVetere	L.Michaels	J.Pardee	L.Richter	B.Jobko	E.Meador	Franckhauser	D.Burroughs	J.Morris	6nw	2-10
1960	G.Brito	G.Strugar	J.LoVetere	L.Lundy	J.Pardee	L.Richter	B.Jobko	E.Meador	C.Britt	W.Sherman	C.Thomas	6nw	4-7-1
1961	D.Jones	U.Henry	J.LoVetere	L.Lundy	J.Pardee	L.Richter	B.Jobko	E.Meador	A.Hall	L.Crow	C.Thomas	6nw	4-10
1962	D.Jones	M.Olsen	J.LoVetere	L.Lundy	M.McKeever	M.Henry	J.Pardee	E.Meador	C.Shannon	L.Crow	C.Britt	7nw	1-12-1
1963	D.Jones	M.Olsen	R.Grier	L.Lundy	M.McKeever	M.Henry	J.Pardee	E.Meador	B.Smith	L.Crow	C.Shannon	6nw	5-9
1964	D.Jones	M.Olsen	R.Grier	L.Lundy	J.Pardee	M.Henry	C.Livingston	J.Richardson	A.Martin	B.Smith	E.Meador	5nw	5-7-2
1965	D.Jones	M.Olsen	R.Grier	L.Lundy	T.Guillory	D.Woodlief	D.Currie	C.Williams	D.McIlhany	C.Lamson	E.Meador	7nw	4-10
1966	D.Jones	M.Olsen	R.Grier	L.Lundy	J.Pardee	B.George	M.Baughan	C.Williams	I.Cross	C.Lamson	E.Meador	3nw	8-6
1967	D.Jones	M.Olsen	R.Brown	L.Lundy	J.Pardee	M.Pottios	M.Baughan	C.Williams	I.Cross	C.Lamson	E.Meador	1ncl	11-1-2 dc
1968	D.Jones	M.Olsen	R.Brown	G.Schumacher	J.Pardee	M.Pottios	M.Baughan	C.Williams	I.Cross	R.Smith	E.Meador	2ncl	10-3-1
1969	D.Jones	M.Olsen	C.Bacon	D.Talbert	J.Pardee	D.Woodlief	M.Baughan	C.Williams	R.Smith	R.Petitbon	E.Meador	1ncl	11-3 c
1970	D.Jones	M.Olsen	D.Talbert	C.Bacon	J.Pardee	M.Pottios	M.Baughan	C.Williams	K.Alexander	R.Petitbon	E.Meador	2nw	9-4-1
1971	D.Jones	M.Olsen	P.Olsen	C.Bacon	J.Purnell	M.McKeever	I.Robertson	J.Nettles	G.Howard	K.Alexander	D.Elmendorf	2nw	8-5-1
1972	Ja.Youngblood	M.Olsen	L.Brooks	C.Bacon	J.Purnell	M.McKeever	I.Robertson	A.Clark	G.Howard	D.Elmendorf	J.Nettles	3nw	6-7-1
1973	Ja.Youngblood	L.Brooks	M.Olsen	F.Dryer	K.Geddes	J.Reynolds	I.Robertson	E.McMillan	C.Stukes	D.Elmendorf	S.Preece	1nw	12-2 d
1974	Ja.Youngblood	L.Brooks	M.Olsen	F.Dryer	K.Geddes	J.Reynolds	I.Robertson	E.McMillan	C.Stukes	D.Elmendorf	S.Preece	1nw	10-4 dc
1975	Ja.Youngblood	L.Brooks	M.Olsen	F.Dryer	K.Geddes	J.Reynolds	I.Robertson	E.McMillan	M.Jackson	D.Elmendorf	B.Simpson	1nw	12-2 dc
1976	Ja.Youngblood	L.Brooks	M.Olsen	F.Dryer	Ji.Youngblood	J.Reynolds	I.Robertson	R.Perry	M.Jackson	D.Elmendorf	B.Simpson	1nw	10-3-1 dc
1977	Ja.Youngblood	L.Brooks	C.Jones	F.Dryer	B.Brudzinski	Ji.Youngblood	I.Robertson	P.Thomas	M.Jackson	D.Elmendorf	B.Simpson	1nw	10-4 d
1978	Ja.Youngblood	L.Brooks	C.Jones	F.Dryer	Ji.Youngblood	J.Reynolds	B.Brudzinski	P.Thomas	R.Perry	D.Elmendorf	B.Simpson	1nw	12-4 dc
1979	Ja.Youngblood	L.Brooks	M.Fanning	F.Dryer	Ji.Youngblood	J.Reynolds	B.Brudzinski	D.O'Steen	R.Perry	D.Elmendorf	N.Cromwell	1nw	9-7 dcs
1980	Ja.Youngblood	L.Brooks	C.Jones	F.Dryer	Ji.Youngblood	J.Reynolds	B.Brudzinski	P.Thomas	R.Perry	J.Johnson	N.Cromwell	2nw	11-5 w
1981	Ja.Youngblood	M.Fanning	L.Brooks	C.Jones	Ji.Youngblood	C.Ekern	G.Andrews	P.Thomas	R.Perry	J.Johnson	N.Cromwell	3nw	6-10
1982	Ja.Youngblood	M.Fanning	C.Jones	R.Doss	C.Ekern	Ji.Youngblood	G.Andrews	P.Thomas	R.Perry	J.Johnson	N.Cromwell	14n	2-7
1983	Ja.Youngblood	G.Meisner	R.Doss*	M.Owens	C.Ekern	J.Collins	G.Andrews	E.Harris	L.Irvin	N.Cromwell	J.Johnson	2nw	9-7 wd
1984	Ja.Youngblood	G.Meisner	R.Doss*	M.Owens	C.Ekern	J.Collins	G.Andrews	G.Green	L.Irvin	N.Cromwell	J.Johnson	2nw	10-6 w
1985	D.Reed	C.DeJurnett	R.Doss*	M.Owens	C.Ekern	J.Collins	M.Wilcher	G.Green	L.Irvin	N.Cromwell	J.Johnson	1nw	11-5 dc
1986	D.Reed	S.Miller	R.Doss*	M.Owens	C.Ekern	M.Jerue	M.Wilcher	J.Gray	L.Irvin	N.Cromwell	V.Newsome	2nw	10-6 w
1987	D.Reed	G.Meisner	R.Doss*	M.Owens	C.Ekern	J.Collins	M.Wilcher	J.Gray	L.Irvin	V.Newsome	N.Cromwell	3nw	6-9
1988	D.Reed	A.Wright	S.Miller*	K.Greene	C.Ekern	M.Jerue	M.Wilcher	J.Gray	L.Irvin	M.Stewart	J.Johnson	2nw	10-6 #w
1989	D.Reed	A.Wright	S.Miller*	K.Greene	M.Owens	F.Strickland	M.Wilcher	J.Gray	L.Irvin	M.Stewart	V.Newsome	2nw	11-5 wdc
1990	D.Reed	A.Wright	M.Piel*	K.Greene	L.Kelm	F.Stams	M.Wilcher	J.Gray	B.Humphery	V.Newsome	M.Stewart	3nw	5-11
1991	K.Wilson	A.Wright	R.Young	K.Greene	B.Faryniarz	L.Kelm	F.Strickland	J.Gray	D.Henley	M.Stewart	P.Terrell	4nw	3-13
1992	G.Robinson	M.Boutte	S.Gilbert	B.Hawkins	K.Greene	L.Kelm	R.Phifer	T.Lyght	D.Henley	A.Newman	P.Terrell	3nw	6-10
1993	T.Woods	M.Boutte	S.Gilbert	F.Stokes	H.Rolling	S.Conlan	R.Phifer	T.Lyght	S.Israel	M.Stewart	A.Newman	4nw	5-11
1994	R.Young	J.Jones	S.Gilbert	F.Stokes	J.Kelly	S.Conlan	R.Phifer	D.Henley	T.Lyght	M.Pope	A.Newman	4nw	4-12
1995	K.Carter	J.Jones	D.Farr	S.Gilbert	C.Jenkins	S.Conlan	R.Phifer	T.Lyght	A.Parker	T.Wright	K.Lyle	3nw	7-9
1996	K.Carter	J.Jones	D.Farr	L.O'Neal	C.Jenkins	R.Jones	R.Phifer	T.Lyght	A.Parker	T.Wright	K.Lyle	3nw	6-10
1997	K.Carter	B.Johnson	D.Farr	L.O'Neal	M.Jones	R.Jones	R.Phifer	T.Lyght	R.McNeil	T.Wright	K.Lyle	5nw	5-11
1998	K.Carter	R.Agnew	D.Farr	M.D.Jones	M.A.Jones	E.Hill	R.Phifer	T.Lyght	R.McNeil	B.Jenkins	K.Lyle	4nw	4-12
1999	K.Carter	R.Agnew	D.Farr	G.Wistrom	M.Jones	L.Fletcher	T.Collins	T.Lyght	D.McCleon	B.Jenkins	K.Lyle	1nw	13-3 dcs*
2000	K.Carter	R.Agnew	J.Zgonina	G.Wistrom	M.Jones	L.Fletcher	T.Collins	T.Lyght	D.McCleon	D.Bush	K.Lyle	2nw	10-6 #w
2001	C.Ahanotu	B.Young	J.Zgonina	G.Wistrom	T.Polley	L.Fletcher	M.Fields	A.Williams	D.McCleon	A.Archuleta	K.Herring	1nw	14-2 dcs
2002	L.Little	R.Pickett	J.Zgonina	G.Wistrom	R.Thomas	J.Duncan	T.Polley	T.Fisher	D.Bly	A.Archuleta	K.Herring	2nw	7-9
2003	L.Little	R.Pickett	B.Young	G.Wistrom	P.Tinoisamoa	R.Thomas	T.Polley	J.Butler	T.Fisher	A.Archuleta	A.Williams	1nw	12-4 d
2004	L.Little	R.Pickett	D.Lewis	B.Fisher	T.Polley	R.Thomas	P.Tinoisamoa	J.Butler	T.Fisher	A.Archuleta	A.Williams	2nw	8-8 #wd
2005	L.Little	R.Pickett	J.Kennedy	A.Hargrove	P.Tinoisamoa	C.Claiborne	D.Coakley	D.Groce	T.Fisher	A.Archuleta	M.Furrey	2nw	6-10

San Diego Chargers (Los Angeles 1960)

YEAR	COACH	WR/LE	LT	LG	C	RG	RT	TE/RE	WR/FL	QB	RB/LH	FB
1960	S.Gillman	R.Anderson	E.Wright	O.Ferrante	D.Rogers	F.Cole	R.Mix	H.Clark	D.Kocourek	J.Kemp	P.Lowe	H.Ferguson
1961	S.Gillman	D.Norton	E.Wright	O.Ferrante	D.Rogers	S.DeLuca	R.Mix	H.Clark	D.Kocourek	J.Kemp	P.Lowe	C.Flowers
1962	S.Gillman	D.Norton	E.Wright	D.Rogers	W.Frazier	R.Mix	S.Plunkett	D.Kocourek	J.Robinson	J.Hadl	K.Lincoln	B.Jackson
1963	S.Gillman	D.Norton	E.Wright	S.Gruneisen	D.Rogers	P.Shea	R.Mix	D.Kocourek	L.Alworth	T.Rote	P.Lowe	K.Lincoln
1964	S.Gillman	D.Norton	E.Wright	P.Shea	D.Rogers	W.Sweeney	R.Mix	D.Kocourek	L.Alworth	J.Hadl	P.Lowe	K.Lincoln
1965	S.Gillman	D.Norton	E.Wright	E.Park	S.Gruneisen	W.Sweeney	R.Mix	D.Kocourek	L.Alworth	J.Hadl	P.Lowe	G.Foster
1966	S.Gillman	G.Garrison	E.Wright	E.Mitchell	S.Gruneisen	W.Sweeney	R.Mix	J.MacKinnon	L.Alworth	J.Hadl	P.Lowe	G.Foster
1967	S.Gillman	G.Garrison	E.Wright	G.Kirner	S.Gruneisen	W.Sweeney	R.Mix	W.Frazier	L.Alworth	J.Hadl	D.Post	B.Hubbert
1968	S.Gillman	G.Garrison	T.Owens	G.Kirner	S.Gruneisen	W.Sweeney	R.Mix	J.MacKinnon	L.Alworth	J.Hadl	D.Post	G.Foster
1969	S.Gillman	G.Garrison	T.Owens	B.Lenkaitis	S.Gruneisen	W.Sweeney	G.Ferguson	W.Frazier	L.Alworth	J.Hadl	D.Post	B.Hubbert
1970	C.Waller	G.Garrison	T.Owens	B.Lenkaitis	S.Gruneisen	W.Sweeney	R.Washington	W.Frazier	L.Alworth	J.Hadl	D.Post	J.Queen
1971	S.Gillman	B.Parks	T.Owens	D.Wilkerson	C.Mauck	W.Sweeney	R.Washington	P.Norman	G.Garrison	J.Hadl	M.Garrett	J.Queen
1972	H.Svare	C.Dicus	T.Owens	D.Wilkerson	C.Mauck	W.Sweeney	R.Washington	P.Norman	G.Garrison	J.Hadl	M.Garrett	C.Edwards
1973	H.Svare	R.Holliday	T.Owens	D.Wilkerson	C.Mauck	W.Sweeney	R.Washington	P.Norman	J.LeVias	D.Fouts	M.Garrett	C.Edwards
1974	T.Protho	H.Davis	T.Owens	D.Wilkerson	C.Mauck	I.Gordon	R.Washington	W.Stewart	G.Garrison	D.Fouts	D.Woods	B.Matthews
1975	T.Protho	D.McDonald	T.Owens	D.Wilkerson	E.Flanagan	I.Gordon	R.Washington	P.Curran	G.Garrison	D.Fouts	R.Young	B.Matthews
1976	T.Protho	D.McDonald	B.Shields	D.Wilkerson	E.Flanagan	D.Macek	R.Washington	P.Curran	C.Joiner	D.Fouts	D.Woods	R.Young
1977	T.Protho	J.Rodgers	B.Shields	D.Wilkerson	R.Perretta	D.Macek	R.Washington	B.Klein	C.Joiner	J.Harris	D.Woods	R.Young
1978	D.Coryell	J.Jefferson	B.Shields	D.Wilkerson	D.Macek	E.White	R.Washington	B.Klein	C.Joiner	D.Fouts	L.Mitchell	D.Woods
1979	D.Coryell	J.Jefferson	B.Shields	D.Wilkerson	B.Rush	E.White	R.Washington	B.Klein	C.Joiner	D.Fouts	M.Thomas	C.Williams
1980	D.Coryell	C.Joiner	B.Shields	D.Wilkerson	D.Macek	E.White	D.Audick	K.Winslow	J.Jefferson	D.Fouts	C.Williams	Cappelletti
1981	D.Coryell	C.Joiner	B.Shields	D.Wilkerson	D.Macek	E.White	R.Washington	K.Winslow	W.Chandler	D.Fouts	C.Muncie	E.Sievers*
1982	D.Coryell	C.Joiner	B.Shields	D.Wilkerson	D.Macek	E.White	R.Washington	K.Winslow	W.Chandler	D.Fouts	C.Muncie	Cappelletti
1983	D.Coryell	C.Joiner	B.Shields	D.Wilkerson	D.Macek	E.White	A.Gissinger	K.Winslow	W.Chandler	D.Fouts	C.Muncie	E.Sievers*
1984	D.Coryell	C.Joiner	S.Claphan	D.Wilkerson	D.Macek	D.McKnight	E.White	K.Winslow	W.Chandler	D.Fouts	E.Jackson	E.Sievers*
1985	D.Coryell	C.Joiner	J.Lachey	E.White	D.Macek	D.McKnight	S.Claphan	E.Sievers	W.Chandler	D.Fouts	L.James	T.Spencer
1986	A.Saunders	C.Joiner	J.Lachey	S.Claphan	D.Macek	D.McKnight	G.Kowalski	K.Winslow	W.Chandler	D.Fouts	G.Anderson	T.Spencer
1987	A.Saunders	L.James	J.Lachey	FitzPatrick	D.Macek	D.McKnight	G.Kowalski	K.Winslow	W.Chandler	D.Fouts	G.Anderson	T.Spencer
1988	A.Saunders	A.Miller	K.Dallafior	B.Thompson	D.Rosado	D.McKnight	D.Richards	A.Cox	Q.Early	M.Malone	G.Anderson	R.Bernstine*
1989	D.Henning	A.Miller	J.Patten	B.Thompson	C.Hall	D.Richards	B.Miller	A.Cox	J.Holland	J.McMahon	T.Spencer	J.Caravello*
1990	D.Henning	A.Miller	L.Goeas	C.Hall	F.Cornish	D.Richards	B.Thompson	D.Walker	A.Cox*	B.Tolliver	M.Butts	J.Caravello*
1991	D.Henning	A.Miller	H.Swayne	E.Moten	C.Hall	D.Richards	B.Thompson	D.Walker	N.Lewis	J.Friesz	R.Bernstine	A.Cox*
1992	B.Ross	A.Miller	H.Swayne	E.Moten	C.Hall	D.Richards	B.Thompson	D.Young	N.Lewis	S.Humphries	M.Butts	D.Walker*
1993	B.Ross	A.Miller	H.Swayne	M.Zandofsky	C.Hall	J.Milinchik	S.Brock	D.Young	N.Lewis	S.Humphries	M.Butts	D.Walker*
1994	B.Ross	S.Jefferson	H.Swayne	J.Cocozzo	C.Hall	J.Milinchik	S.Brock	D.Young	M.Seay	S.Humphries	N.Means	A.Pupunu*
1995	B.Ross	S.Jefferson	H.Swayne	E.Moten	C.Hall	I.Davis	S.Brock	D.Young	T.Martin	S.Humphries	N.Means	A.Pupunu*
1996	B.Ross	A.Coleman	V.Parker	E.Moten	G.Engel	J.Cocozzo	T.Berti	D.May	T.Martin	S.Humphries	L.Russell	S.Mitchell*
1997	K.Gilbride	T.Martin	V.Parker	J.Cocozzo	R.McKenzie	I.Davis	T.Berti	F.Hartley	C.Jones	S.Humphries	G.Brown	F.Jones*
1998	J.Jones	B.Still	J.Jackson	A.Taylor	R.Fortin	R.McKenzie	V.Parker	F.Jones	C.Jones	C.Whelihan	N.Means	W.Davis*
1999	M.Riley	J.Graham	J.Jackson	A.Taylor	R.Fortin	D.Graham	V.Parker	F.Jones	M.Ricks	J.Harbaugh	N.Means	F.McCrary
2000	M.Riley	J.Graham	B.Coleman	R.Roundtree	R.Fortin	K.Gogan	V.Parker	F.Jones	C.Conway	R.Leaf	J.Fazande	F.McCrary
2001	M.Riley	J.Graham	D.McIntosh	R.Roundtree	K.Jacox	D.Graham	V.Parker	S.Heiden	C.Conway	D.Flutie	L.Tomlinson	F.McCrary
2002	Schottenheimer	C.Conway	D.McIntosh	B.Hallen	J.Ball	T.Fonoti	V.Parker	S.Alexander	T.Dwight	D.Brees	L.Tomlinson	F.McCrary
2003	Schottenheimer	D.Boston	D.McIntosh	K.Garmon	J.Ball	P.Bogle	C.Van Buren	A.Gates	J.Peelle*	D.Brees	L.Tomlinson	L.Neal
2004	Schottenheimer	E.Parker	R.Oben	T.Fonoti	N.Hardwick	M.Goff	S.Olivea	A.Gates	K.Osgood	D.Brees	L.Tomlinson	L.Neal
2005	Schottenheimer	E.Parker	L.Jordan	K.Dielman	N.Hardwick	M.Goff	S.Olivea	A.Gates	K.McCardell	D.Brees	L.Tomlinson	L.Neal

San Francisco 49ers

YEAR	COACH	WR/LE	LT	LG	C	RG	RT	TE/RE	WR/FL	QB	RB/LH	FB
1950	B.Shaw	A.Loyd	D.Campora	H.Hobbs	B.Johnson	B.Banducci	C.Matthews	A.Beals	Strzykalski	F.Albert	J.Cason	J.Perry
1951	B.Shaw	G.Soltau	R.Collins	N.Feher	B.Johnson	B.Banducci	L.Nomellini	B.Wilson	Strzykalski	F.Albert	V.Lillywhite	J.Perry
1952	B.Shaw	G.Soltau	B.Toneff	J.Smith	B.Johnson	B.Banducci	L.Nomellini	B.Wilson	H.McElhenny	Y.Tittle	J.Arenas	J.Perry
1953	B.Shaw	G.Soltau	D.Hogland	J.Smith	B.Johnson	B.Banducci	B.St. Clair	B.Wilson	H.McElhenny	Y.Tittle	J.Arenas	J.Perry
1954	B.Shaw	G.Soltau	D.Hogland	N.Feher	B.Johnson	B.Banducci	B.St. Clair	B.Wilson	H.McElhenny	Y.Tittle	J.Johnson	J.Perry
1955	R.Strader	G.Soltau	L.Nomellini	D.Hogland	B.Johnson	L.Palatella	B.St. Clair	B.Wilson	H.McElhenny	Y.Tittle	J.Arenas	J.Perry
1956	F.Albert	G.Soltau	B.Cross	B.Toneff	B.Johnson	E.Henke	B.St. Clair	B.Wilson	J.Arenas	Y.Tittle	H.McElhenny	J.Perry
1957	F.Albert	C.Conner	J.Gonzaga	L.Palatella	F.Morze	T.Connolly	B.Cross	B.Wilson	R.Owens	Y.Tittle	H.McElhenny	G.Babb
1958	F.Albert	C.Conner	J.Gonzaga	B.Bosley	W.Yowarsky	T.Connolly	B.St. Clair	B.Wilson	R.Owens	Y.Tittle	H.McElhenny	J.Perry
1959	R.Hickey	C.Conner	J.Thomas	B.Bosley	F.Morze	T.Connolly	B.St. Clair	B.Wilson	H.McElhenny	Y.Tittle	J.Smith	J.Perry
1960	R.Hickey	C.Conner	J.Thomas	B.Bosley	F.Morze	M.Magac	B.St. Clair	M.Stickles	R.Owens	J.Brodie	H.McElhenny	J.Smith
1961	R.Hickey	A.Thomas	J.Thomas	B.Bosley	F.Morze	T.Connolly	B.St. Clair	M.Stickles	R.Owens	J.Brodie	J.Smith	C.Roberts
1962	R.Hickey	C.Conner	R.Lakes	M.Magac	B.Bosley	T.Connolly	B.St. Clair	M.Stickles	B.Casey	J.Brodie	B.Kilmer	J.Smith
1963	Christiansen	C.Conner	L.Rohde	J.Thomas	B.Bosley	L.Donohue	B.St. Clair	M.Stickles	B.Casey	L.McHan	D.Lisbon	J.Smith
1964	Christiansen	D.Parks	L.Rohde	J.Thomas	B.Bosley	L.Donohue	W.Rock	M.Stickles	B.Casey	J.Brodie	D.Lisbon	M.Lind
1965	Christiansen	D.Parks	L.Rohde	J.Thomas	B.Bosley	H.Mudd	W.Rock	M.Stickles	B.Casey	J.Brodie	J.Crow	K.Willard
1966	Christiansen	D.Parks	L.Rohde	J.Thomas	B.Bosley	H.Mudd	W.Rock	M.Stickles	B.Casey	J.Brodie	J.Crow	K.Willard
1967	Christiansen	D.Parks	L.Rohde	E.Collett	B.Bosley	H.Mudd	W.Rock	M.Stickles	D.Witcher	J.Brodie	J.Crow	K.Willard
1968	D.Nolan	D.Witcher	L.Rohde	E.Collett	B.Bosley	H.Mudd	C.Banaszek	J.Crow	C.McNeil	J.Brodie	G.Lewis	K.Willard
1969	D.Nolan	G.Washington	L.Rohde	E.Collett	F.Blue	W.Peoples	C.Banaszek	B.Windsor	D.Witcher	S.Spurrier	D.Cunningham	K.Willard
1970	D.Nolan	D.Witcher	L.Rohde	R.Beisler	F.Blue	W.Peoples	C.Banaszek	B.Windsor	G.Washington	J.Brodie	D.Cunningham	K.Willard
1971	D.Nolan	D.Witcher	L.Rohde	R.Beisler	F.Blue	W.Peoples	C.Banaszek	T.Kwalick	G.Washington	J.Brodie	V.Washington	K.Willard
1972	D.Nolan	G.Washington	L.Rohde	R.Beisler	F.Blue	W.Peoples	C.Banaszek	T.Kwalick	P.Riley	S.Spurrier	V.Washington	K.Willard
1973	D.Nolan	D.Abramowicz	L.Rohde	J.Watson	F.Blue	W.Peoples	C.Banaszek	T.Kwalick	G.Washington	J.Brodie	V.Washington	K.Willard
1974	D.Nolan	G.Washington	L.Rohde	J.Watson	F.Blue	W.Peoples	C.Banaszek	T.Mitchell	D.Abramowicz	T.Owen	W.Jackson	L.Schreiber
1975	D.Nolan	G.Washington	J.Watson	B.Penchion	B.Reid	W.Peoples	C.Banaszek	T.Mitchell	T.Beasley	S.Spurrier	D.Williams	L.Schreiber
1976	M.Clark	G.Washington	J.Barrett	S.Lawson	R.Cross	A.Maurer	C.Banaszek	T.Mitchell	J.Lash	J.Plunkett	D.Williams	W.Jackson
1977	K.Meyer	G.Washington	J.Barrett	S.Lawson	R.Cross	W.Peoples	K.Fahnhorst	T.Mitchell	K.Harrison	J.Plunkett	D.Williams	W.Jackson
1978	P.McCulley	K.Harrison	J.Ayers	E.Hughes	R.Cross	W.Downing	K.Fahnhorst	K.MacAfee	F.Solomon	S.DeBerg	O.Simpson	G.Boykin
1979	B.Walsh	F.Solomon	R.Singleton	J.Ayers	F.Quillan	R.Cross	K.Fahnhorst	K.MacAfee	M.Shumann	S.DeBerg	O.Simpson	W.Jackson
1980	B.Walsh	D.Clark	R.Singleton	J.Ayers	F.Quillan	R.Cross	K.Fahnhorst	C.Young	F.Solomon	S.DeBerg	P.Hofer	E.Cooper
1981	B.Walsh	D.Clark	D.Audick	J.Ayers	F.Quillan	R.Cross	K.Fahnhorst	C.Young	F.Solomon	J.Montana	R.Patton	E.Cooper
1982	B.Walsh	D.Clark	L.Mason	J.Ayers	F.Quillan	R.Cross	K.Fahnhorst	C.Young	F.Solomon	J.Montana	J.Moore	E.Cooper
1983	B.Walsh	D.Clark	B.Paris	J.Ayers	F.Quillan	R.Cross	K.Fahnhorst	R.Francis	F.Solomon	J.Montana	W.Tyler	R.Craig
1984	B.Walsh	D.Clark	B.Paris	J.Ayers	F.Quillan	R.Cross	K.Fahnhorst	E.Cooper	F.Solomon	J.Montana	W.Tyler	R.Craig
1985	B.Walsh	D.Clark	B.Paris	J.Ayers	F.Quillan	R.Cross	K.Fahnhorst	R.Francis	F.Solomon	J.Montana	W.Tyler	R.Craig
1986	B.Walsh	D.Clark	B.Paris	J.Ayers	F.Quillan	R.Cross	K.Fahnhorst	R.Francis	J.Rice	J.Montana	J.Cribbs	R.Craig
1987	B.Walsh	M.Wilson	B.Paris	J.Sapolu	R.Cross	B.Collie	H.Barton	R.Francis	J.Rice	J.Montana	R.Craig	T.Rathman
1988	B.Walsh	M.Wilson	S.Wallace	J.Sapolu	R.Cross	G.McIntyre	H.Barton	R.Heller	J.Rice	J.Montana	R.Craig	T.Rathman
1989	G.Seifert	J.Taylor	B.Paris	G.McIntyre	J.Sapolu	B.Collie	H.Barton	B.Jones	J.Rice	J.Montana	R.Craig	T.Rathman
1990	G.Seifert	J.Taylor	B.Paris	G.McIntyre	J.Sapolu	H.Barton	S.Wallace	B.Jones	J.Rice	J.Montana	R.Craig	T.Rathman
1991	G.Seifert	J.Taylor	S.Wallace	G.McIntyre	J.Sapolu	R.Foster	H.Barton	B.Jones	J.Rice	S.Young	D.Carter	T.Rathman
1992	G.Seifert	J.Taylor	S.Wallace	G.McIntyre	J.Sapolu	R.Foster	H.Barton	B.Jones	J.Rice	S.Young	R.Watters	T.Rathman
1993	G.Seifert	J.Taylor	S.Wallace	G.McIntyre	J.Sapolu	R.Tamm	H.Barton	B.Jones	J.Rice	S.Young	R.Watters	M.Logan
1994	G.Seifert	J.Taylor	S.Wallace	J.Sapolu	B.Oates	D.Deese	H.Barton	B.Jones	J.Rice	S.Young	R.Watters	W.Floyd
1995	G.Seifert	J.Taylor	S.Wallace	J.Sapolu	B.Oates	R.Milstead	H.Barton	B.Jones	J.Rice	S.Young	D.Loville	W.Floyd
1996	G.Seifert	T.Owens	S.Wallace	R.Brown	J.Sapolu	C.Dalman	H.Barton	B.Jones	J.Rice	S.Young	T.Kirby	W.Floyd

YEAR	LDE	LDT/NT	RDT/RDE	RDE/LOLB	LLB/LILB	MLB/RILB	RLB/ROLB	LCB	RCB	SS/LS	FS/RS	FINISH	
1960	M.Schleicher	V.Peters	D.Chorovich	R.Nery	R.Loudd	E.Karas	P.Maguire	D.Nix	D.Harris	B.Zeman	C.McNeil	1aw	10-4 l
1961	E.Faison	B.Hudson	E.Ladd	R.Nery	E.Karas	C.Allen	P.Maguire	C.Gibson	D.Harris	B.Zeman	C.McNeil	1aw	12-2 l
1962	E.Faison	B.Hudson	E.Ladd	R.Nery	E.Karas	C.Allen	P.Maguire	C.Gibson	D.Harris	B.Whitehead	B.Bethune	3aw	4-10
1963	E.Faison	H.Schmidt	G.Gross	B.Petrich	E.Karas	C.Allen	P.Maguire	B.Whitehead	D.Harris	G.Blair	G.Glick	1aw	11-3 l*
1964	E.Faison	E.Ladd	G.Gross	B.Petrich	R.Carpenter	F.Buncom	C.Allen	Westmoreland	J.Warren	K.Graham	B.Whitehead	1aw	8-5-1 l
1965	E.Faison	G.Gross	E.Ladd	B.Petrich	H.Travenio	C.Allen	F.Buncom	J.Warren	S.Duncan	K.Graham	B.Whitehead	1aw	9-2-3 l
1966	H.Kindig	G.Gross	S.DeLong	B.Petrich	D.Degen	R.Redman	F.Buncom	M.Farr	S.Duncan	K.Graham	B.Whitehead	3aw	7-6-1
1967	H.Kindig	H.Ridge	S.Appleton	Billingsley	J.Staggs	R.Redman	F.Buncom	J.Beauchamp	S.Duncan	K.Graham	B.Whitehead	3aw	8-5-1
1968	H.Ridge	R.Washington	S.Appleton	S.DeLong	J.Staggs	C.Allen	T.Erlandson	B.Howard	S.Duncan	K.Graham	J.Beauchamp	3aw	9-5
1969	B.Briggs	R.Washington	Billingsley	S.DeLong	J.Staggs	R.Redman	P.Barnes	B.Howard	S.Duncan	K.Graham	J.Hill	3aw	8-6
1970	J.Owens	B.Briggs	Billingsley	S.DeLong	J.Staggs	B.Babich	P.Barnes	B.Howard	J.Beauchamp	J.Hill	J.Tolbert	3aw	5-6-3
1971	T.Williams	R.East	K.Hardy	S.DeLong	R.Redman	B.Babich	P.Barnes	B.Howard	J.Beauchamp	B.Salter	C.Fletcher	3aw	6-8
1972	D.Jones	R.East	D.Costa	L.Aldridge	B.Babich	T.Rossovich	R.Redman	J.Beauchamp	L.Dunlap	B.Salter	C.Detwiler	4aw	4-9-1
1973	D.Jones	R.East	D.Costa	C.Bacon	M.Stratton	C.Gersbach	R.Redman	B.Howard	L.Dunlap	R.Smith	J.Beauchamp	4aw	2-11-1
1974	P.Lazetich	D.Rowe	R.Brown	C.Bacon	D.Goode	C.Anthony	F.Rice	B.Howard	S.Williams	C.Fletcher	J.Beauchamp	3aw	5-9
1975	F.Dean	L.Kelcher	G.Johnson	C.Bacon	D.Goode	T.Graham	F.Rice	J.Beauchamp	M.Williams	S.Williams	C.Fletcher	4aw	2-12
1976	L.Jones	L.Kelcher	G.Johnson	F.Dean	D.Goode	T.Graham	W.Lowe	D.Colbert	M.Williams	M.Fuller	C.Fletcher	3aw	6-8
1977	L.Jones	L.Kelcher	G.Johnson	F.Dean	D.Goode	T.Graham	W.Lowe	H.Stringert	M.Williams	M.Fuller	C.Duren	3aw	7-7
1978	L.Jones	L.Kelcher	G.Johnson	F.Dean	D.Goode	B.Horn	W.Lowe	H.Stringert	M.Williams	M.Fuller	P.Shaw	2aw	9-7
1979	L.Jones	W.Young	G.Johnson	F.Dean	R.Preston	B.Horn	W.Lowe	W.Buchanon	M.Williams	M.Fuller	G.Edwards	1aw	12-4 d
1980	L.Jones	L.Kelcher	G.Johnson	F.Dean	R.Preston	B.Horn	W.Lowe	W.Buchanon	M.Williams	P.Shaw	G.Edwards	1aw	11-5 #dc
1981	L.Jones	L.Kelcher	G.Johnson	J.Woodcock	L.King	B.Horn	W.Lowe	W.Buchanon	M.Williams	P.Shaw	G.Edwards	1aw	10-6 #dc
1982	L.Jones	L.Kelcher	G.Johnson	K.Ferguson	L.King	C.Thrift	W.Lowe	J.Allen	M.Williams	B.Laird	T.Fox	4a	6-3 pd
1983	K.Ferguson	R.Ackerman	G.Johnson*	L.King	M.Green	B.Smith	W.Lowe	G.Byrd	D.Walters	A.Young	K.Greene	4aw	6-10
1984	C.Ehin	B.Elko	K.Ferguson*	L.King	M.Green	B.Smith	W.Lowe	G.Byrd	D.Walters	K.Greene	T.Fox	5aw	7-9
1985	L.Williams	C.Ehin	E.Wilson*	L.King	M.Green	B.Smith	W.Lowe	J.Hendy	D.Walters	G.Byrd	J.Dale	3aw	8-8
1986	L.Williams	C.Ehin	L.O'Neal*	B.Smith	G.Plummer	T.Benson	W.Lowe	K.Taylor	D.Brown	J.Dale	G.Byrd	5aw	4-12
1987	L.Williams	M.Charles	J.Phillips*	B.Smith	G.Plummer	T.Benson	C.Banks	E.Patterson	G.Byrd	M.Bayless	V.Glenn	3aw	8-7
1988	L.Williams	M.Charles	J.Phillips*	K.Browner	C.Faucette	G.Plummer	T.Keys	S.Seale	G.Byrd	M.Bayless	V.Glenn	4aw	6-10
1989	L.Williams	J.Phillips	B.Grossman*	B.Smith	G.Plummer	C.Figaro	L.O'Neal	G.Byrd	S.Seale	M.Bayless	V.Glenn	5aw	6-10
1990	L.Williams	L.Miller	B.Grossman*	B.Smith	G.Plummer	J.Seau	L.O'Neal	G.Byrd	S.Seale	M.Bayless	V.Glenn	4aw	6-10
1991	G.Hinkle	J.Phillips	B.Grossman*	H.Rolling	G.Plummer	J.Seau	L.O'Neal	G.Byrd	S.Seale	M.Bayless	S.Richard	5aw	4-12
1992	B.Grossman	B.Winter	G.Thornton	L.O'Neal	H.Rolling	G.Plummer	J.Seau	G.Byrd	A.Blaylock	F.Fields	S.Richard	1aw	11-5 ed
1993	B.Grossman	S.Lee	B.Winter	L.O'Neal	Hendrickson	G.Plummer	J.Seau	D.Frank	S.Vanhorse	D.Carrington	S.Richard	4aw	8-8
1994	C.Mims	S.Lee	R.Davis	L.O'Neal	D.Griggs	D.Gibson	J.Seau	D.Gordon	D.Harper	D.Carrington	S.Richard	1aw	11-5 dcs
1995	C.Mims	S.Lee	R.Davis	L.O'Neal	L.Bush	D.Gibson	J.Seau	D.Harper	T.Shaw	S.Gayle	B.Orlando	2aw	9-7 w
1996	C.Mims	J.Parrella	R.Davis	M.Coleman	L.Bush	K.Gouveia	J.Seau	D.Harper	T.Shaw	R.Harrison	K.Ross	3aw	8-8
1997	W.Fuller	J.Parrella	S.Lee	M.Coleman	P.Sapp	L.Bush	J.Seau	D.Harper	T.Shaw	R.Harrison	M.Dumas	4aw	4-12
1998	W.Fuller	N.Hand	J.Parrella	M.Coleman	L.Bush	K.Gouveia	J.Seau	C.Dimry	T.Shaw	R.Harrison	G.Jackson	5aw	5-11
1999	A.Fontenot	N.Hand	J.Parrella	R.Johnson	L.Bush	E.Hill	J.Seau	D.Lewis	T.Shaw	G.Jackson	M.Dumas	3aw	8-8
2000	A.Fontenot	J.Williams	J.Parrella	D.Mickell	G.Dixon	O.Ruff	J.Seau	F.Brown	D.Jenkins	R.Harrison	M.Dumas	5aw	1-15
2001	M.Wiley	L.Carson	J.Parrella	R.Johnson	G.Dixon	O.Ruff	J.Seau	T.Cody	R.McNeil	R.Harrison	R.Beckett	5aw	5-11
2002	M.Wiley	J.Williams	J.Fisk	R.Johnson	B.Leber	D.Edwards	J.Seau	A.Molden	R.McNeil	R.Harrison	R.Beckett	3aw	8-8
2003	M.Wiley	J.Williams	J.Fisk	A.Dingle	B.Leber	Z.Moreno	D.Edwards	Q.Jammer	S.Davis	K.Lassiter	J.Wilson	3aw	4-12
2004	J.Cesaire	J.Williams	I.Olshansky*	B.Leber	D.Edwards	R.Godfrey	S.Foley	S.Davis	Q.Jammer	T.Kiel	J.Wilson	1aw	12-4 e
2005	L.Castillo	J.Williams	I.Olshansky*	S.Merriman	D.Edwards	R.Godfrey	S.Foley	Q.Jammer	D.Florence	T.Kiel	B.Jue	3aw	9-7

1950	H.Shoener	L.Nomellini	R.Collins	G.Bruce	V.Lillywhite	P.Wissman	N.Standlee	S.Cathcart	L.Wagner	J.Powers	V.Grgich+	5nn	3-9
1951	E.Henke	L.Nomellini	A.Carapella	G.Bruce	N.Standlee	H.Brown	P.Wissman	J.Powers	L.Wagner	J.Cason	V.Grgich+	2nn	7-4-1
1952	E.Henke	L.Nomellini	A.Carapella	P.O'Donahue	J.Powers	H.Brown	D.Burke	R.Berry	L.Wagner	J.Cason	B.Momsen+	3nn	7-5
1953	C.Matthews	L.Nomellini	A.Carapella	C.Powell	J.Morton	H.Brown	J.Manley	R.Berry	L.Wagner	F.Bruney	A.Michalik+	2nw	9-3
1954	C.Matthews	L.Nomellini	M.Campbell	J.Brumfield	H.Brown	A.Carapella+	B.Toneff	R.Berry	J.Arenas	J.Williams	J.Cason	3nw	7-4-1
1955	C.Matthews	B.Toneff	M.Campbell	C.Powell	M.Hazeltine	A.Carapella+	H.Brown	G.Maderos	B.Luna	R.Berry	D.Moegle	5nw	4-8
1956	B.Bosley	L.Nomellini	B.Herchman	C.Powell	S.Sheriff	E.Beatty	M.Hazeltine	G.Maderos	P.Carr	R.Berry	D.Moegle	3nw	5-6-1
1957	E.Henke	L.Nomellini	B.Herchman	B.Toneff	M.Hazeltine	M.Matuszak	C.Powell	J.Smith	B.Stits	B.Holladay	D.Moegle	1nw	8-4 c
1958	E.Henke	L.Nomellini	B.Herchman	B.Toneff	M.Matuszak	K.Rubke	M.Hazeltine	J.Mertens	B.Stits	J.Ridlon	B.Atkins	4nw	6-6
1959	E.Henke	L.Nomellini	M.Clark	C.Krueger	K.Rubke	J.Tubbs	M.Hazeltine	J.Mertens	A.Woodson	D.Baker	E.Dove	3nw	7-5
1960	D.Colchico	L.Nomellini	M.Clark	C.Krueger	G.Kelley	B.Harrison	M.Hazeltine	J.Mertens	A.Woodson	D.Baker	E.Dove	2nw	7-5
1961	D.Colchico	L.Nomellini	M.Clark	C.Krueger	G.Kelley	B.Harrison	M.Hazeltine	J.Mertens	A.Woodson	D.Baker	E.Dove	5nw	7-6-1
1962	D.Colchico	L.Nomellini	C.Krueger	C.Miller	E.Pine	J.Thomas	M.Hazeltine	J.Mertens	A.Woodson	E.Kimbrough	E.Dove	5nw	6-8
1963	D.Colchico	C.Krueger	R.Lakes	C.Miller	E.Pine	M.Dowdle	M.Hazeltine	K.Alexander	A.Woodson	E.Kimbrough	J.Johnson	7nw	2-12
1964	D.Colchico	C.Krueger	R.Lakes	C.Miller	D.Wilcox	M.Dowdle	M.Hazeltine	J.Johnson	A.Woodson	E.Kimbrough	K.Alexander	7nw	4-10
1965	K.Rubke	C.Krueger	R.Lakes	C.Miller	D.Wilcox	M.Dowdle	M.Hazeltine	J.Johnson	J.Mertens	E.Kimbrough	K.Alexander	4nw	7-6-1
1966	J.Norton	C.Krueger	R.Lakes	C.Miller	D.Wilcox	E.Beard	M.Hazeltine	J.Johnson	K.Alexander	E.Kimbrough	G.Donnelly	4nw	6-6-2
1967	S.Hindman	C.Krueger	R.Lakes	C.Miller	D.Wilcox	E.Beard	M.Hazeltine	J.Johnson	K.Alexander	A.Randolph	G.Gonsoulin	3ncl	7-7
1968	S.Hindman	C.Krueger	R.Lakes	C.Miller	D.Wilcox	E.Beard	M.Hazeltine	J.Johnson	K.Alexander	A.Randolph	J.Fuller	3ncl	7-6-1
1969	S.Hindman	C.Krueger	R.Lakes	B.Belk	D.Wilcox	F.Nunley	Vanderbundt	J.Johnson	K.Alexander	A.Randolph	M.Phillips	4ncl	4-8-2
1970	T.Hart	C.Krueger	R.Lakes	B.Belk	D.Wilcox	F.Nunley	Vanderbundt	J.Johnson	B.Taylor	M.Phillips	R.Taylor	1nw	10-3-1 dc
1971	T.Hart	C.Krueger	E.Edwards	C.Hardman	D.Wilcox	F.Nunley	Vanderbundt	J.Johnson	B.Taylor	M.Phillips	R.Taylor	1nw	9-5 dc
1972	T.Hart	C.Krueger	E.Edwards	C.Hardman	D.Wilcox	F.Nunley	Vanderbundt	J.Johnson	B.Taylor	M.Phillips	M.Simpson	1nw	8-5-1 d
1973	T.Hart	C.Krueger	B.Hoskins	C.Hardman	D.Wilcox	J.Sniadecki	W.Harper	J.Johnson	B.Taylor	M.Phillips	M.Simpson	3nw	5-9
1974	T.Hart	B.Belk	B.Hoskins	C.Hardman	D.Wilcox	F.Nunley	W.Harper	J.Johnson	B.Taylor	M.Phillips	W.Hall	2nw	6-8
1975	T.Hart	B.Sandifer	B.Hoskins	C.Hardman	Vanderbundt	F.Nunley	D.Washington	J.Johnson	B.Taylor	M.Phillips	R.McGill	2nw	5-9
1976	T.Hart	J.Webb	C.Elam	C.Hardman	Vanderbundt	F.Nunley	D.Washington	J.Johnson	B.Taylor	M.Phillips	R.McGill	2nw	8-6
1977	T.Hart	J.Webb	C.Elam	C.Hardman	Vanderbundt	B.Elia	D.Washington	T.Leonard	B.Taylor	M.Phillips	R.McGill	3nw	5-9
1978	A.Reese	J.Webb	E.Galigher	C.Hardman	J.Harris	D.Bunz	E.Bradley	T.Leonard	E.Lewis	C.Crist	V.Roberson	4nw	2-14
1979	A.Reese	T.Vincent	J.Webb	C.Hardman	S.Hilton	D.Bunz	W.Harper	C.Cornelius	G.Williams	T.Gray	T.Dungy	4nw	2-14
1980	J.Webb	A.Reese	T.Vincent	L.Pillers	W.Harper	D.Bunz	B.Leopold	R.Rhodes	C.Johnson	R.Churchman	D.Hicks	3nw	6-10
1981	J.Stuckey	A.Reese	D.Board*	W.Harper	D.Bunz	J.Reynolds	K.Turner	R.Lott	E.Wright	C.Williamson	D.Hicks	1nw	13-3 dcs*
1982	J.Stuckey	J.Harty	L.Pillers*	W.Harper	J.Reynolds	B.Horn	K.Turner	R.Lott	E.Wright	C.Williamson	D.Hicks	11n	3-6
1983	L.Pillers	P.Kugler	D.Board*	W.Harper	R.Ellison	J.Reynolds	K.Turner	R.Lott	E.Wright	C.Williamson	D.Hicks	1nw	10-6 dc
1984	J.Stuckey	M.Tuiasosopo	D.Board*	D.Bunz	R.Ellison	J.Reynolds	K.Turner	R.Lott	E.Wright	C.Williamson	D.Hicks	1nw	15-1 dcs*
1985	J.Stover	M.Carter	D.Board*	T.Shell	R.Ellison	M.Walter	K.Turner	R.Lott	E.Wright	C.Williamson	D.Hicks	2nw	10-6 #w
1986	J.Stover	M.Carter	D.Board*	M.McColl	R.Ellison	J.Fahnhorst	K.Turner	T.McKyer	D.Griffin	C.Williamson	R.Lott	1nw	10-5-1 d
1987	P.Kugler	M.Carter	D.Board*	M.McColl	J.Fahnhorst	M.Walter	K.Turner	T.McKyer	D.Griffin	J.Fuller	R.Lott	1nw	13-2 d
1988	L.Roberts	M.Carter	K.Fagan*	C.Haley	R.Ellison	M.Walter	K.Turner	T.McKyer	E.Wright	J.Fuller	R.Lott	1nw	10-6 #dcs*
1989	P.Holt	M.Carter	K.Fagan*	C.Haley	M.Millen	M.Walter	K.Turner	D.Pollard	D.Griffin	C.Brooks	R.Lott	1nw	14-2 dcs*
1990	P.Holt	M.Carter	K.Fagan*	C.Haley	M.Millen	K.DeLong	B.Romanowski	D.Pollard	D.Griffin	C.Brooks	R.Lott	1nw	14-2 dc
1991	P.Holt	M.Carter	L.Roberts*	C.Haley	K.DeLong	M.Walter	B.Romanowski	M.Hanks	D.Griffin	D.Waymer	T.Bowles	3nw	10-6 #
1992	P.Holt	M.Carter	K.Fagan*	T.Harris	K.DeLong	M.Walter	B.Romanowski	E.Davis	D.Griffin	D.Whitmore	D.Hall	1nw	14-2 dc
1993	D.Brown	Stubblefield	T.Washington	K.Fagan	J.Johnson	M.Walter	B.Romanowski	E.Davis	D.Griffin	T.McDonald	M.Hanks	1nw	10-6 dc
1994	D.Brown	B.Young	Stubblefield	R.Jackson	L.Woodall	G.Plummer	K.Norton	E.Davis	D.Sanders	T.McDonald	M.Hanks	1nw	13-3 dcs*
1995	D.Brown	B.Young	Stubblefield	R.Jackson	L.Woodall	K.Norton	G.Plummer	E.Davis	M.Pope	T.McDonald	M.Hanks	1nw	11-5 #d
1996	R.Barker	B.Young	Stubblefield	C.Doleman	L.Woodall	K.Norton	G.Plummer	T.Drakeford	M.Pope	T.McDonald	M.Hanks	2nw	12-4 #wd

854 THE OFFENSIVE STARTERS: 1950–PRESENT

YEAR	COACH	WR/LE	LT	LG	C	RG	RT	TE/RE	WR/FL	QB	RB/LH	FB
1997	S.Mariucci	J.Stokes	D.Deese	R.Brown	C.Dalman	K.Gogan	K.Scrafford	B.Jones	T.Owens	S.Young	G.Hearst	W.Floyd
1998	S.Mariucci	J.Stokes	D.Deese	R.Brown	C.Dalman	K.Gogan	K.Scrafford	G.Clark	J.Rice	S.Young	G.Hearst	M.Edwards
1999	S.Mariucci	T.Owens	D.Fiore	R.Brown	C.Dalman	J.Newberry	D.Deese	G.Clark	J.Rice	J.Garcia	C.Garner	F.Beasley
2000	S.Mariucci	T.Owens	D.Deese	R.Brown	J.Newberry	D.Fiore	S.Gragg	G.Clark	J.Rice	J.Garcia	C.Garner	F.Beasley
2001	S.Mariucci	T.Owens	D.Deese	R.Brown	J.Newberry	D.Fiore	S.Gragg	E.Johnson	J.Stokes	J.Garcia	G.Hearst	F.Beasley
2002	S.Mariucci	T.Owens	D.Deese	E.Heitmann	J.Newberry	R.Stone	S.Gragg	E.Johnson	T.Streets	J.Garcia	G.Hearst	F.Beasley
2003	D.Erickson	T.Owens	D.Deese	K.Kosier	J.Newberry	R.Stone	S.Gragg	J.Weaver	T.Streets	J.Garcia	G.Hearst	F.Beasley
2004	D.Erickson	C.Wilson	K.Kosier	E.Heitmann	B.Gutierrez	J.Smiley	S.Gragg	E.Johnson	B.Lloyd	T.Rattay	K.Barlow	F.Beasley
2005	M.Nolan	J.Morton	A.Snyder	J.Smiley	J.Newberry	E.Heitmann	K.Harris	B.Bajema	B.Lloyd	A.Smith	K.Barlow	F.Beasley

SEATTLE SEAHAWKS

YEAR	COACH	WR/LE	LT	LG	C	RG	RT	TE/RE	WR/FL	QB	RB/LH	FB
1976	J.Patera	S.McCullum	N.Bebout	B.Penchion	F.Hoaglin	J.Demarie	N.Evans	R.Howard	S.Largent	J.Zorn	S.Smith	D.Testerman
1977	J.Patera	D.Fergerson	N.Bebout	G.Jolley	A.Kuehn	R.Coder	N.Evans	R.Howard	S.Largent	J.Zorn	S.Smith	D.Testerman
1978	J.Patera	S.McCullum	N.Bebout	T.Lynch	J.Yarno	B.Newton	S.August	R.Howard	S.Largent	J.Zorn	S.Smith	D.Sims
1979	J.Patera	S.McCullum	N.Bebout	T.Lynch	J.Yarno	B.Newton	S.August	B.Peets	S.Largent	J.Zorn	S.Smith	D.Doornink
1980	J.Patera	S.McCullum	L.Bullard	T.Lynch	J.Yarno	B.Newton	S.August	J.Sawyer	S.Largent	J.Zorn	D.Doornink	J.Jodat
1981	J.Patera	S.McCullum	R.Essink	E.Bailey	J.Yarno	B.Newton	S.August	J.Sawyer	S.Largent	J.Zorn	S.Smith	D.Doornink
1982	McCormack	P.Johns	R.Essink	E.Bailey	J.Yarno	R.Pratt	S.August	M.Tice	S.Largent	J.Zorn	S.Smith	D.Doornink
1983	C.Knox	P.Johns	R.Essink	R.McKenzie	B.Bush	R.Pratt	S.August	C.Young	S.Largent	D.Krieg	C.Warner	P.Metzelaars*
1984	C.Knox	D.Turner	R.Essink	R.McKenzie	B.Bush	R.Pratt	B.Cryder	C.Young	S.Largent	D.Krieg	E.Lane	M.Tice*
1985	C.Knox	D.Turner	R.Essink	E.Bailey	B.Bush	R.Pratt	B.Cryder	C.Young	S.Largent	D.Krieg	C.Warner	D.Hughes
1986	C.Knox	D.Turner	R.Mattes	E.Bailey	B.Bush	B.Millard	M.Wilson	M.Tice	S.Largent	D.Krieg	C.Warner	J.Williams
1987	C.Knox	D.Turner	R.Mattes	E.Bailey	B.Bush	B.Millard	M.Wilson	M.Tice	S.Largent	D.Krieg	C.Warner	J.Williams
1988	C.Knox	B.Blades	R.Mattes	E.Bailey	B.Bush	B.Millard	M.Wilson	M.Tice	S.Largent	D.Krieg	C.Warner	J.Williams
1989	C.Knox	B.Blades	A.Heck	E.Bailey	G.Feasel	B.Millard	M.Wilson	R.Tyler	S.Largent	D.Krieg	C.Warner	J.Williams
1990	C.Knox	T.Kane	A.Heck	E.Bailey	G.Feasel	B.Millard	R.Lee	T.McNeal	B.Blades	D.Krieg	D.Fenner	J.Williams
1991	C.Knox	T.Kane	A.Heck	W.Wheat	G.Feasel	B.Millard	B.Hitchcock	M.Tice	B.Blades	D.Krieg	D.Fenner	J.Williams
1992	T.Flores	T.Kane	R.Roberts	A.Heck	J.Tofflemire	D.Brilz	B.Hitchcock	R.Heller	L.Clark	S.Gelbaugh	C.Warren	J.Williams
1993	T.Flores	K.Martin	R.Roberts	D.Brilz	R.Donaldson	B.Hitchcock	A.Heck	F.Edmunds	B.Blades	R.Mirer	C.Warren	J.Williams
1994	T.Flores	K.Martin	R.Roberts	J.Blackshear	R.Donaldson	K.Mawae	H.Ballard	P.Green	B.Blades	R.Mirer	C.Warren	T.Johnson
1995	D.Erickson	J.Galloway	J.Atkins	M.Joyce	J.Sweeney	K.Mawae	H.Ballard	C.Fauria	B.Blades	R.Mirer	C.Warren	S.Smith
1996	D.Erickson	J.Galloway	J.Atkins	P.Kendall	K.Mawae	D.Graham	H.Ballard	C.Fauria	B.Blades	R.Mirer	C.Warren	M.Strong
1997	D.Erickson	J.Galloway	W.Jones	P.Kendall	K.Mawae	D.Graham	H.Ballard	C.Crumpler	M.Pritchard	W.Moon	C.Warren	M.Strong
1998	D.Erickson	J.Galloway	W.Jones	P.Kendall	K.Glover	B.Habib	H.Ballard	C.Fauria	M.Pritchard	W.Moon	R.Watters	B.Blades+
1999	M.Holmgren	S.Dawkins	W.Jones	P.Kendall	C.Gray	B.Habib	G.Williams	C.Fauria	D.Mayes	J.Kitna	R.Watters	R.Brown
2000	M.Holmgren	S.Dawkins	W.Jones	P.Kendall	C.Gray	F.Wedderburn	C.McIntosh	C.Fauria	D.Jackson	J.Kitna	R.Watters	M.Strong
2001	M.Holmgren	K.Robinson	W.Jones	S.Hutchinson	R.Tobeck	C.Gray	T.Weiner	C.Fauria	D.Jackson	M.Hasselbeck	S.Alexander	M.Strong
2002	M.Holmgren	K.Robinson	W.Jones	C.Gray	R.Tobeck	F.Wedderburn	F.Womack	I.Mili	D.Jackson	M.Hasselbeck	S.Alexander	M.Strong
2003	M.Holmgren	K.Robinson	W.Jones	S.Hutchinson	R.Tobeck	C.Gray	C.Terry	I.Mili	D.Jackson	M.Hasselbeck	S.Alexander	M.Strong
2004	M.Holmgren	J.Rice	W.Jones	S.Hutchinson	R.Tobeck	C.Gray	C.Terry	B.Engram+	D.Jackson	M.Hasselbeck	S.Alexander	M.Strong
2005	M.Holmgren	B.Engram	W.Jones	S.Hutchinson	R.Tobeck	C.Gray	S.Locklear	J.Stevens	J.Jurevicius	M.Hasselbeck	S.Alexander	M.Strong

TAMPA BAY BUCCANEERS

YEAR	COACH	WR/LE	LT	LG	C	RG	RT	TE/RE	WR/FL	QB	RB/LH	FB
1976	J.McKay	J.McKay	S.Young	H.Fest	D.Ryczek	T.Alward	M.Current	B.Moore	M.Owens	S.Spurrier	L.Carter	E.Williams
1977	J.McKay	J.McKay	D.Reavis	J.Winans	D.Ryczek	D.Medlin	D.Carlton	D.Nafziger	M.Owens	G.Huff	R.Bell	J.DuBose
1978	J.McKay	J.McKay	D.Reavis	G.Horton	S.Wilson	G.Puetz	D.Carlton	J.Giles	M.Owens	D.Williams	R.Bell	J.Davis
1979	J.McKay	I.Hagins	D.Reavis	G.Horton	S.Wilson	G.Roberts	C.Hannah	J.Giles	M.Owens	D.Williams	J.Eckwood	R.Bell
1980	J.McKay	G.Jones	D.Reavis	G.Yarno	S.Wilson	R.Snell	C.Hannah	J.Giles	I.Hagins	D.Williams	J.Eckwood	R.Bell
1981	J.McKay	T.Bell	G.Sanders	R.Snell	S.Wilson	G.Roberts	C.Hannah	J.Giles	K.House	D.Williams	J.Eckwood	J.Wilder
1982	J.McKay	G.Jones	D.Reavis	R.Snell	S.Wilson	G.Roberts	S.Farrell	J.Giles	K.House	D.Williams	J.Owens	J.Wilder
1983	J.McKay	G.Carter	D.Reavis	R.Grimes	S.Wilson	S.Farrell	K.Thomas	J.Giles	K.House	J.Thompson	M.Carver	J.Wilder
1984	J.McKay	K.House	G.Sanders	S.Courson	S.Wilson	S.Farrell	R.Heller	J.Giles	G.Carter	S.DeBerg	J.Wilder	J.Bell*
1985	L.Bennett	K.House	G.Yarno	S.Courson	R.Grimes	S.Farrell	R.Heller	J.Giles	G.Carter	S.DeBerg	J.Wilder	J.Bell*
1986	L.Bennett	K.House	R.Taylor	G.Yarno	R.Grimes	S.Farrell	R.Heller	C.Magee	G.Carter	S.Young	J.Wilder	R.Springs
1987	R.Perkins	M.Carrier	R.Taylor	G.Yarno	R.Grimes	R.Mallory	R.Heller	C.Magee	G.Carter	S.DeBerg	J.Smith	J.Wilder
1988	R.Perkins	M.Carrier	P.Gruber	R.Mallory	R.Grimes	D.Turk	R.Taylor	R.Hall	B.Hill	V.Testaverde	L.Tate	W.Howard
1989	R.Perkins	M.Carrier	P.Gruber	T.McHale	R.Grimes	J.Bruhin	R.Taylor	R.Hall	B.Hill	V.Testaverde	L.Tate	W.Howard
1990	R.Perkins	M.Carrier	P.Gruber	T.McHale	R.Grimes	I.Beckles	R.Taylor	R.Hall	B.Hill	V.Testaverde	G.Anderson	R.Cobb
1991	Williamson	M.Carrier	P.Gruber	T.McHale	T.Mayberry	I.Beckles	R.Taylor	R.Hall	L.Dawsey	V.Testaverde	R.Cobb	R.Wilson
1992	S.Wyche	M.Carrier	P.Gruber	B.Reimers	T.Mayberry	I.Beckles	C.McRae	R.Hall	L.Dawsey	V.Testaverde	R.Cobb	A.McDowell
1993	S.Wyche	C.Hawkins	P.Gruber	B.Reimers	T.Mayberry	I.Beckles	S.Dill	R.Hall	H.Copeland	C.Erickson	R.Cobb	V.Workman
1994	S.Wyche	C.Hawkins	P.Gruber	C.McRae	T.Mayberry	I.Beckles	S.Dill	J.Harris	C.Wilson	C.Erickson	E.Rhett	A.McDowell
1995	S.Wyche	A.Harper	P.Gruber	J.Pyne	T.Mayberry	I.Beckles	S.Dill	J.Harris	L.Dawsey	T.Dilfer	E.Rhett	D.Moore*
1996	T.Dungy	R.Thomas	P.Gruber	J.Pyne	T.Mayberry	I.Beckles	D.Riesenberg	J.Harris	C.Hawkins	T.Dilfer	E.Rhett	M.Alstott
1997	T.Dungy	R.Anthony	P.Gruber	J.Pyne	T.Mayberry	J.Diaz	J.Odom	J.Harris	H.Copeland	T.Dilfer	W.Dunn	M.Alstott
1998	T.Dungy	R.Anthony	P.Gruber	J.Diaz	T.Mayberry	F.Middleton	J.Odom	D.Moore	B.Emanuel	T.Dilfer	W.Dunn	M.Alstott
1999	T.Dungy	J.Green	P.Gruber	J.Diaz	T.Mayberry	F.Middleton	J.Wunsch	D.Moore	B.Emanuel	T.Dilfer	W.Dunn	M.Alstott
2000	T.Dungy	J.Green	P.Pierson	R.McDaniel	J.Christy	F.Middleton	J.Wunsch	D.Moore	K.Johnson	S.King	W.Dunn	M.Alstott
2001	T.Dungy	J.Green	K.Walker	R.McDaniel	J.Christy	C.Coleman	J.Wunsch	D.Moore	K.Johnson	B.Johnson	W.Dunn	M.Alstott
2002	J.Gruden	K.Johnson	R.Oben	K.Jenkins	J.Christy	C.Coleman	K.Walker	K.Dilger	K.McCardell	B.Johnson	M.Pittman	M.Alstott
2003	J.Gruden	K.Johnson	R.Oben	K.Jenkins	J.Wade	C.Coleman	K.Walker	K.Dilger	K.McCardell	B.Johnson	M.Pittman	J.Cook
2004	J.Gruden	J.Galloway	D.Deese	M.Stinchcomb	J.Wade	C.Coleman	K.Walker	K.Dilger	M.Clayton	B.Griese	M.Pittman	M.Alstott
2005	J.Gruden	J.Galloway	A.Davis	D.Buenning	J.Wade	S.Mahan	K.Walker	A.Becht	M.Clayton	C.Simms	C.Williams	A.Smith*

TENNESSEE TITANS (Houston Oilers 1960-96, Tennessee Oilers 1997-98)

YEAR	COACH	WR/LE	LT	LG	C	RG	RT	TE/RE	WR/FL	QB	RB/LH	FB
1960	L.Rymkus	B.Groman	A.Jamison	B.Talamini	G.Belotti	H.Wharton	R.Michael	J.Carson	C.Hennigan	G.Blanda	B.Cannon	D.Smith
1961	W.Lemm	B.Groman	A.Jamison	B.Talamini	B.Schmidt	H.Wharton	R.Michael	J.White	C.Hennigan	G.Blanda	B.Cannon	C.Tolar
1962	P.Ivy	W.Dewveall	A.Jamison	B.Talamini	B.Schmidt	H.Wharton	R.Michael	B.McLeod	C.Hennigan	G.Blanda	B.Cannon	C.Tolar
1963	P.Ivy	W.Dewveall	W.Suggs	B.Talamini	B.Schmidt	H.Wharton	R.Michael	B.McLeod	C.Hennigan	G.Blanda	B.Tobin	C.Tolar
1964	S.Baugh	C.Frazier	W.Suggs	B.Talamini	T.Goode	J.Wittenborn	S.Bishop	W.Dewveall	C.Hennigan	G.Blanda	S.Blanks	C.Tolar
1965	H.Taylor	C.Frazier	W.Suggs	B.Talamini	J.Frongillo	S.Bishop	N.Evans	W.Frazier	C.Hennigan	G.Blanda	O.Burrell	C.Tolar
1966	W.Lemm	C.Frazier	W.Suggs	B.Talamini	B.Maples	S.Bishop	G.Hines	B.McLeod	C.Hennigan	G.Blanda	O.Burrell	C.Tolar
1967	W.Lemm	C.Frazier	W.Suggs	B.Talamini	B.Maples	S.Bishop	G.Hines	A.Reed	O.Burrell	P.Beathard	W.Campbell	H.Granger
1968	W.Lemm	J.Beirne	W.Suggs	T.Regner	B.Maples	S.Bishop	G.Hines	A.Reed	M.Haik	P.Beathard	S.Blanks	H.Granger
1969	W.Lemm	J.Beirne	W.Suggs	T.Regner	B.Maples	S.Bishop	G.Hines	A.Reed	M.Haik	P.Beathard	R.Hopkins	H.Granger
1970	W.Lemm	C.Joiner	W.Suggs	K.Gray	B.Maples	E.Drungo	G.Hines	A.Reed	J.LeVias	C.Johnson	M.Richardson	J.Dawkins
1971	E.Hughes	J.Beirne	G.Ferguson	B.Young	W.Suggs	E.Drungo	S.Walton	A.Reed	C.Joiner	D.Pastorini	W.Campbell	R.Holmes
1972	B.Peterson	C.Joiner	T.Funchess	T.Regner	C.Hunt	R.Saul	L.Carr	A.Reed	K.Burrough	D.Pastorini	P.Robinson	F.Willis
1973	S.Gillman	K.Burrough	T.Funchess	S.Freelon	S.Gruneisen	A.Jenkins	E.Drungo	M.Alston	B.Parks	D.Pastorini	B.Gresham	F.Willis
1974	S.Gillman	K.Burrough	G.Sampson	H.Jones	S.Smith	B.Goodman	E.Drungo	M.Alston	B.Parks	D.Pastorini	V.Washington	W.Rodgers
1975	B.Phillips	K.Burrough	G.Sampson	R.Saul	C.Mauck	E.Fisher	E.Drungo	M.Alston	B.Johnson	D.Pastorini	R.Coleman	D.Hardeman
1976	B.Phillips	K.Burrough	G.Sampson	C.Hayman	C.Mauck	E.Fisher	E.Drungo	M.Alston	B.Johnson	D.Pastorini	R.Coleman	F.Willis
1977	B.Phillips	K.Burrough	G.Sampson	G.Reihner	C.Mauck	E.Drungo	K.Hunt	M.Barber	E.Foster	D.Pastorini	R.Coleman	R.Carpenter
1978	B.Phillips	K.Burrough	G.Sampson	G.Reihner	C.Mauck	E.Fisher	C.Hayman	M.Barber	M.Renfro	D.Pastorini	E.Campbell	T.Wilson
1979	B.Phillips	K.Burrough	L.Gray	C.Hayman	C.Mauck	E.Fisher	M.Towns	M.Barber	R.Caster	D.Pastorini	E.Campbell	T.Wilson
1980	B.Phillips	B.Johnson	L.Gray	B.Young	C.Mauck	E.Fisher	M.Towns	M.Barber	M.Renfro	K.Stabler	E.Campbell	T.Wilson
1981	E.Biles	K.Burrough	L.Gray	Schuhmacher	D.Carter	E.Fisher	M.Towns	D.Casper	M.Renfro	K.Stabler	E.Campbell	T.Wilson

YEAR	LDE	LDT/NT	RDT/RDE	RDE/LOLB	LLB/LILB	MLB/RILB	RLB/ROLB	LCB	RCB	SS/LS	FS/RS	FINISH
1997	R.Barker	B.Young	Stubblefield	C.Doleman	L.Woodall	G.Plummer	K.Norton	R.Woodson	D.Walker	T.McDonald	M.Hanks	1nw 13-3 dc
1998	R.Barker	B.Young	J.Bryant	C.Doleman	L.Woodall	W.Tubbs	K.Norton	D.Walker	R.McQuarters	T.McDonald	M.Hanks	2nw 12-4 wdc
1999	J.Posey	B.Young	J.Bryant	G.Wilkins	L.Woodall	W.Tubbs	K.Norton	D.Walker	R.McDonald	T.McDonald	L.Schulters	4nw 4-12
2000	A.Pleasant	B.Young	B.Buckner	Engelberger	J.Posey	K.Norton	W.Tubbs	A.Plummer	J.Webster	L.Schulters	Z.Bronson	4nw 6-10
2001	A.Carter	B.Young	Stubblefield	Engelberger	J.Peterson	D.Smith	J.Ulbrich	A.Plummer	J.Webster	L.Schulters	Z.Bronson	2nw 12-4 w
2002	A.Carter	B.Young	Stubblefield	C.Okeafor	J.Peterson	D.Smith	J.Ulbrich	A.Plummer	J.Webster	T.Parrish	R.Heard	1nw 10-6 ed
2003	Engelberger	B.Young	T.Kirschke	A.Carter	J.Peterson	D.Smith	J.Ulbrich	A.Plummer	M.Rumph	T.Parrish	Z.Bronson	3nw 7-9
2004	Engelberger	A.Adams	B.Young	A.Carter	J.Ulbrich	D.Smith	J.Winborn	A.Plummer	S.Spencer	T.Parrish	R.Heard	4nw 2-14
2005	B.Young	A.Adams	M.Douglas*	J.Peterson	B.Moore	D.Smith	A.Carter	B.Thornton	S.Spencer	T.Parrish	M.Adams	4nw 4-12
1976	D.Tipton	S.Niehaus	R.Harris	B.Lurtsema	K.Geddes	E.Bradley	M.Curtis	E.McMillan	R.Woolsey	A.Matthews	D.Brown	5nw 2-12
1977	R.Harris	R.East	B.Lurtsema	A.Roche	S.Green	T.Beeson	K.Geddes	E.McMillan	D.Brown	A.Beamon	S.Preece	4aw 5-9
1978	E.Price	D.Boyd	B.Sandifer	B.Gregory	S.Green	T.Beeson	K.Butler	C.Webster	D.Brown	A.Beamon	J.Harris	2aw 9-7
1979	C.Eller	R.Hardy	M.Tuiasosopo	B.Gregory	S.Green	T.Beeson	K.Butler	C.Webster	D.Brown	K.Simpson	A.Beamon	3aw 9-7
1980	J.Green	R.Hardy	M.Tuiasosopo	B.Gregory	M.Jackson	T.Beeson	K.Butler	K.Justin	D.Brown	K.Simpson	J.Harris	5aw 4-12
1981	J.Green	R.Hardy	M.White	M.Tuiasosopo	M.Jackson	J.Norman	K.Butler	K.Simpson	D.Brown	K.Easley	J.Harris	5aw 6-10
1982	J.Green	R.Hardy	M.Tuiasosopo	J.Bryant	B.Scholtz	M.Jackson	K.Butler	K.Simpson	D.Brown	K.Easley	J.Harris	10a 4-5 #
1983	J.Green	J.Nash	J.Bryant*	B.Scholtz	S.Robinson	K.Butler	M.Jackson	K.Justin	D.Brown	K.Easley	J.Harris	2aw 9-7 #wdc
1984	J.Green	J.Nash	J.Bryant*	B.Scholtz	S.Robinson	K.Butler	G.Gaines	K.Simpson	D.Brown	K.Easley	J.Harris	2aw 12-4 wd
1985	J.Green	J.Nash	J.Bryant*	B.Scholtz	F.Young	K.Butler	M.Jackson	T.Taylor	D.Brown	K.Easley	J.Harris	3aw 8-8
1986	J.Green	J.Nash	J.Bryant*	B.Scholtz	F.Young	K.Butler	G.Gaines	T.Taylor	D.Brown	K.Easley	E.Robinson	3aw 10-6 #
1987	J.Green	J.Nash	J.Bryant*	B.Scholtz	F.Young	B.Bosworth	G.Gaines	T.Taylor	P.Hunter	K.Easley	E.Robinson	2aw 9-6 w
1988	J.Green	J.Nash	J.Bryant*	B.Scholtz	B.Bosworth	D.Wyman	T.Woods	T.Taylor	M.Jenkins	P.Moyer	E.Robinson	1aw 9-7 d
1989	J.Green	J.Nash	J.Bryant*	T.Woods	D.Comeaux	D.Wyman	M.Johnson	D.Harper	P.Hunter	N.Glasgow	E.Robinson	4aw 7-9
1990	J.Green	J.Nash	J.Bryant	T.Woods	T.Wooden	D.Comeaux	R.Porter	D.Harper	P.Hunter	N.Glasgow	E.Robinson	3aw 9-7 #
1991	J.Green	J.Bryant	C.Kennedy	T.Woods	T.Wooden	D.Comeaux	R.Porter	D.Harper	P.Hunter	R.Blackmon	E.Robinson	4aw 7-9
1992	J.Bryant	J.Nash	C.Kennedy	T.Woods	T.Wooden	D.Wyman	R.Porter	D.Harper	P.Hunter	R.Blackmon	E.Robinson	5aw 2-14
1993	J.Bryant	J.Nash	C.Kennedy	N.Tuatagaloa	T.Wooden	R.Stephens	K.Murphy	D.Harper	P.Hunter	R.Blackmon	E.Robinson	5aw 6-10
1994	A.Edwards	J.Nash	C.Kennedy	B.Williams	T.Wooden	R.Stephens	R.Porter	C.Gray	O.Watters	R.Blackmon	E.Robinson	5aw 6-10
1995	M.Sinclair	J.Nash	C.Kennedy	B.Williams	T.Wooden	D.Wells	W.Moss	C.Gray	C.Harris	R.Blackmon	E.Robinson	3aw 8-8
1996	M.Sinclair	S.Adams	C.Kennedy	M.McCrary	T.Wooden	D.Wells	W.Moss	C.Gray	C.Harris	R.Blackmon	D.Williams	4aw 7-9
1997	M.Sinclair	S.Adams	D.Saleaumua	P.Daniels	W.Moss	D.Wells	C.Brown	S.Springs	W.Williams	B.Blades	D.Williams	3aw 8-8
1998	M.Sinclair	S.Adams	C.Kennedy	P.Daniels	D.Smith	D.Wells	C.Brown	S.Springs	W.Williams	J.Bellamy	D.Williams	2aw 8-8
1999	M.Sinclair	S.Adams	C.Kennedy	P.Daniels	D.Smith	A.Simmons	C.Brown	S.Springs	W.Williams	D.Williams	J.Bellamy	1aw 9-7 #e
2000	M.Sinclair	R.Parker	C.Kennedy	L.King	A.Simmons	G.Koonce	C.Brown	S.Springs	W.Williams	K.Joseph	J.Bellamy	4aw 6-10
2001	M.Sinclair	C.Eaton	J.Randle	L.King	A.Simmons	L.Kirkland	C.Brown	K.Lucas	W.Williams	R.Tongue	M.Robertson	2aw 9-7
2002	L.King	C.Eaton	J.Randle	A.Cochran	M.Bell	I.Kacyvenski	C.Brown	S.Springs	K.Lucas	R.Tongue	M.Robertson	2nw 7-9
2003	A.Cochran	C.Woodard	J.Randle	C.Okeafor	A.Simmons	R.Godfrey	C.Brown	S.Springs	M.Trufant	R.Tongue	K.Hamlin	2nw 10-6 w
2004	C.Okeafor	C.Woodard	R.Moore	G.Wistrom	I.Kacyvenski	O.Huff	C.Brown	M.Trufant	K.Lucas	T.Bierria	K.Hamlin	1nw 9-7 e
2005	B.Fisher	C.Darby	M.Tubbs	G.Wistrom	J.Sharper	L.Tatupu	D.Lewis	K.Herndon	M.Trufant	M.Boulware	M.Manuel	1nw 13-3 dcs
1976	C.Rudolph	D.Pear	L.Selmon	P.Toomay	J.Gunn	S.Reese	R.Wood	C.Jordan	D.Reece	M.Cotney	K.Stone	5aw 0-14
1977	C.Rudolph	D.Pear	L.Selmon*	D.Lewis	D.Selmon	R.Wood	C.Johnson	J.White	M.Washington	M.Cotney	C.Brown	5nc 2-12
1978	C.Hannah	D.Pear	L.Selmon*	D.Lewis	D.Selmon	R.Wood	C.Johnson	J.White	M.Washington	M.Cotney	C.Brown	5nc 5-11
1979	W.Chambers	R.Crowder	L.Selmon*	D.Lewis	D.Selmon	R.Wood	C.Johnson	J.White	M.Washington	M.Cotney	C.Brown	1nc 10-6 #dc
1980	B.Kollar	D.Logan	L.Selmon*	D.Lewis	D.Selmon	R.Wood	C.Johnson	C.Jordan	M.Washington	M.Cotney	C.Brown	4nc 5-10-1
1981	B.Kollar	D.Logan	L.Selmon*	A.Hawkins	C.Johnson	R.Wood	H.Green	N.Thomas	M.Washington	N.Colzie	C.Brown	1nc 9-7 d
1982	D.Stalls	D.Logan	L.Selmon*	A.Hawkins	C.Johnson	S.Brantley	H.Green	N.Thomas	M.Washington	N.Colzie	C.Brown	4n 5-4 p
1983	J.Cannon	D.Logan	L.Selmon*	E.Judie	J.Davis	S.Brantley	H.Green	J.Holt	M.Washington	M.Cotney	B.Reece	5nc 2-14
1984	J.Cannon	D.Logan	L.Selmon*	K.Browner	J.Davis	S.Brantley	H.Green	J.Castille	J.Holt	M.Cotney	B.Reece	3nc 6-10
1985	J.Cannon	D.Logan	R.Holmes*	E.Randle	J.Davis	S.Brantley	C.Washington	J.Castille	J.Holt	D.Greenwood	I.Sully	5nc 2-14
1986	B.Nelson	D.Logan	R.Holmes*	K.Browner	J.Davis	S.Brantley	C.Washington	V.McKeever	R.Jones	C.Swoope	C.Curry	5nc 2-14
1987	J.Cannon	M.Stensrud	R.Holmes*	J.Walker	J.Davis	E.Randle	C.Washington	R.Reynolds	R.Jones	B.Kemp	R.Isom	4nc 4-11
1988	R.Davis	C.Jarvis	R.Holmes*	K.Murphy	E.Marve	S.Coleman	W.Moss	R.Reynolds	B.Futrell	M.Robinson	H.Hamilton	3nc 5-11
1989	R.Davis	C.Jarvis	R.Goff*	K.Murphy	E.Marve	E.Randle	W.Moss	R.Reynolds	R.Jones	M.Robinson	H.Hamilton	5nc 5-11
1990	R.Davis	C.Jarvis	J.Skow*	B.Thomas	E.Marve	W.Moss	K.Murphy	R.Reynolds	W.Haddix	M.Robinson	H.Hamilton	2nc 6-10
1991	R.Seals	T.Newton	R.Davis	K.McCants	K.Murphy	J.Solomon	B.Thomas	R.Reynolds	C.Carter	T.Covington	M.Carter	5nc 3-13
1992	R.Seals	M.Wheeler	S.Dotson	K.McCants	J.Williams	D.Brownlow	B.Thomas	R.Reynolds	M.Mack	M.Carter	D.Fullington	3nc 5-11
1993	R.Seals	M.Wheeler	S.Dotson	E.Curry	J.Williams	H.Nickerson	B.Bussey	M.Mayhew	R.Reynolds	M.Carter	J.King	5nc 5-11
1994	C.Ahanotu	B.Culpepper	S.Dotson	E.Curry	L.Marts	H.Nickerson	B.Bussey	M.Mayhew	C.Dimry	M.Carter	T.Everett	5nc 6-10
1995	C.Ahanotu	M.Wheeler	W.Sapp	E.Curry	L.Marts	H.Nickerson	D.Brooks	M.Mayhew	C.Dimry	J.Lynch	T.Everett	5nc 7-9
1996	C.Ahanotu	B.Culpepper	W.Sapp	R.Upshaw	L.Marts	H.Nickerson	D.Brooks	M.Mayhew	D.Abraham	J.Lynch	M.Johnson	4nc 6-10
1997	C.Ahanotu	B.Culpepper	W.Sapp	R.Upshaw	R.Porter	H.Nickerson	D.Brooks	D.Abraham	A.Parker	J.Lynch	C.Mincy	2nc 10-6 wd
1998	T.Jackson	B.Culpepper	W.Sapp	R.Upshaw	J.Gooch	H.Nickerson	D.Brooks	D.Abraham	R.Barber	J.Lynch	C.Mincy	3nc 8-8
1999	C.Ahanotu	B.Culpepper	W.Sapp	S.White	S.Quarles	H.Nickerson	D.Brooks	D.Abraham	R.Barber	J.Lynch	D.Robinson	1nc 11-5 dc
2000	C.Ahanotu	A.McFarland	W.Sapp	M.Jones	S.Quarles	J.Duncan	D.Brooks	D.Abraham	R.Barber	J.Lynch	D.Robinson	2nc 10-6 w
2001	M.Jones	A.McFarland	W.Sapp	S.Rice	S.Quarles	J.Duncan	D.Brooks	B.Kelly	R.Barber	J.Lynch	D.Jackson	3nc 9-7 w
2002	G.Spires	A.McFarland	W.Sapp	S.Rice	A.Singleton	S.Quarles	D.Brooks	B.Kelly	R.Barber	J.Lynch	D.Jackson	1ns 12-4 dcs*
2003	G.Spires	A.McFarland	W.Sapp	S.Rice	R.Nece	S.Quarles	D.Brooks	R.Barber	D.Smith	J.Lynch	J.Phillips	3ns 7-9
2004	G.Spires	C.Darby	A.McFarland	S.Rice	I.Gold	S.Quarles	D.Brooks	B.Kelly	R.Barber	D.Smith	J.Phillips	4ns 5-11
2005	G.Spires	C.Hovan	A.McFarland	S.Rice	R.Nece	S.Quarles	D.Brooks	B.Kelly	R.Barber	J.Phillips	D.Jackson	2ns 11-5 #w
1960	D.Allen	O.Trask	J.Helluin	D.Floyd	D.Cline	D.Morris	M.Dukes	J.Norton	M.Johnston	B.Gordon	J.Spence	1ae 10-4 l*
1961	D.Allen	O.Trask	E.Husmann	D.Floyd	D.Cline	D.Morris	M.Dukes	T.Banfield	M.Johnston	J.Norton	F.Glick	1ae 10-3-1 l*
1962	G.Cutsinger	E.Culpepper	E.Husmann	D.Floyd	D.Cline	G.Babb	M.Dukes	T.Banfield	M.Johnston	J.Norton	F.Glick	1ae 11-3 l
1963	G.Cutsinger	D.Meredith	E.Husmann	D.Floyd	D.Cline	G.Babb	M.Dukes	T.Banfield	B.Jancik	J.Norton	F.Glick	3ae 6-8
1964	S.Appleton	B.McFadin	E.Husmann	D.Floyd	D.Brabham	D.Cline	J.Baker	P.Jaquess	B.Jancik	W.Hicks	F.Glick	4ae 4-10
1965	G.Cutsinger	B.McFadin	E.Husmann	D.Floyd	J.Baker	D.Cline	D.Brabham	T.Banfield	W.Hicks	J.Norton	F.Glick	4ae 4-10
1966	G.Cutsinger	P.Holmes	E.Ladd	D.Floyd	J.Baker	D.Cline	J.Meyer	T.Viltz	W.Hicks	F.Glick	J.Norton	4ae 3-11
1967	P.Holmes	W.Parker	G.Rice	D.Floyd	G.Webster	G.Boyette	O.Underwood	M.Farr	W.Hicks	K.Houston	J.Norton	1ae 9-4-1 l
1968	P.Holmes	W.Parker	G.Rice	E.Bethea	G.Webster	G.Boyette	O.Underwood	M.Farr	L.Carwell	K.Houston	W.Hicks	2ae 7-7
1969	P.Holmes	C.Stith	T.Domres	E.Bethea	G.Webster	G.Boyette	O.Underwood	M.Farr	Z.Moore	K.Houston	W.Hicks	2ae 6-6-2 p
1970	P.Holmes	W.Parker	T.Domres	E.Bethea	O.Underwood	G.Boyette	R.Pritchard	L.Mitchell	Z.Moore	K.Houston	J.Peacock	4ac 3-10-1
1971	P.Holmes	M.Tilleman	Billingsley	E.Bethea	G.Webster	G.Boyette	R.Pritchard	Z.Moore	W.Alexander	K.Houston	J.Charles	3ac 4-9-1
1972	P.Holmes	M.Tilleman	L.Brooks	E.Bethea	F.Rice	R.Pritchard	P.Croyle	W.Alexander	B.Johnson	K.Houston	J.Charles	4ac 1-13
1973	T.Smith	A.Cowlings	J.Matuszak	E.Bethea	F.Rice	G.Bingham	G.Roberts	Z.Moore	W.Alexander	J.Severson	B.Atkins	4ac 1-13
1974	T.Smith	C.Culp	E.Bethea*	A.Cowlings	G.Bingham	S.Kiner	T.Washington	W.Alexander	Z.Moore	A.Johnson	B.Atkins	2ac 7-7
1975	T.Smith	C.Culp	E.Bethea*	T.Washington	S.Kiner	G.Bingham	R.Brazile	W.Alexander	Z.Moore	W.Germany	B.Atkins	3ac 10-4
1976	T.Smith	C.Culp	E.Bethea*	T.Washington	S.Kiner	G.Bingham	R.Brazile	W.Alexander	Z.Moore	M.Reinfeldt	Whittington	4ac 5-9
1977	J.Young	C.Culp	E.Bethea*	T.Washington	S.Kiner	G.Bingham	R.Brazile	W.Alexander	Z.Moore	B.Currier	M.Reinfeldt	2ac 8-6
1978	J.Young	C.Culp	E.Bethea*	T.Washington	S.Kiner	G.Bingham	R.Brazile	W.Alexander	G.Stemrick	B.Currier	M.Reinfeldt	2ac 10-6 wdc
1979	A.Dorris	C.Culp	E.Bethea*	T.Washington	G.Bingham	A.Stringer	R.Brazile	J.Wilson	G.Stemrick	V.Perry	M.Reinfeldt	2ac 11-5 wdc
1980	A.Dorris	K.Kennard	E.Bethea*	T.Washington	A.Stringer	G.Bingham	R.Brazile	J.Wilson	G.Stemrick	V.Perry	M.Reinfeldt	2ac 11-5 #w
1981	A.Dorris	K.Kennard	E.Bethea*	T.Washington	G.Bingham	D.Hunt	R.Brazile	J.Wilson	G.Stemrick	V.Perry	M.Reinfeldt	3ac 7-9

YEAR	COACH	WR/LE	LT	LG	C	RG	RT	TE/RE	WR/FL	QB	RB/LH	FB
1982	E.Biles	H.Bailey	Schuhmacher	R.Williams	D.Carter	E.Fisher	M.Towns	D.Casper	M.Holston	A.Manning	E.Campbell	S.Edwards
1983	C.Studley	M.Renfro	D.France	M.Munchak	D.Carter	B.Matthews	H.Salem	C.Dressel	T.Smith	G.Nielsen	E.Campbell	L.Moriarty
1984	H.Campbell	T.Smith	H.Salem	M.Munchak	B.Matthews	Schuhmacher	Steinkuhler	J.Williams	H.Walls	W.Moon	L.Moriarty	C.Dressel*
1985	H.Campbell	T.Smith	H.Salem	M.Munchak	J.Romano	Schuhmacher	B.Matthews	J.Williams	D.Hill	W.Moon	B.Woolfolk	L.Moriarty
1986	Glanville	D.Hill	B.Matthews	M.Munchak	J.Pennison	K.Hill	Steinkuhler	J.Williams	E.Givins	W.Moon	M.Rozier	B.Woolfolk
1987	Glanville	D.Hill	B.Davis	M.Munchak	J.Pennison	B.Matthews	Steinkuhler	J.Williams	E.Givins	W.Moon	M.Rozier	R.Wallace
1988	Glanville	D.Hill	B.Davis	M.Munchak	J.Pennison	B.Matthews	Steinkuhler	J.Williams	E.Givins	W.Moon	M.Rozier	A.Highsmith
1989	Glanville	D.Hill	B.Davis	M.Munchak	J.Pennison	B.Matthews	Steinkuhler	B.Mrosko	E.Givins	W.Moon	M.Rozier	A.Highsmith
1990	J.Pardee	D.Hill	D.Maggs	M.Munchak	J.Pennison	B.Matthews	D.Williams	E.Givins	C.Duncan	W.Moon	L.White	H.Jeffires+
1991	J.Pardee	D.Hill	D.Maggs	M.Munchak	B.Matthews	D.Dawson	D.Williams	E.Givins	C.Duncan	W.Moon	A.Pinkett	H.Jeffires+
1992	J.Pardee	W.Slaughter	D.Maggs	M.Munchak	B.Matthews	D.Dawson	D.Williams	E.Givins	C.Duncan	W.Moon	L.White	H.Jeffires+
1993	J.Pardee	W.Slaughter	B.Hopkins	M.Munchak	B.Matthews	D.Dawson	D.Williams	E.Givins	C.Duncan	W.Moon	G.Brown	H.Jeffires+
1994	J.Pardee	W.Slaughter	B.Hopkins	J.Flannery	B.Matthews	K.Donnalley	D.Williams	P.Carter	E.Givins	B.Tolliver	L.White	H.Jeffires+
1995	J.Fisher	H.Jeffires	B.Hopkins	B.Matthews	M.Stepnoski	K.Donnalley	D.Williams	F.Wycheck	C.Sanders	C.Chandler	R.Thomas	R.Lewis*
1996	J.Fisher	C.Sanders	B.Hopkins	B.Matthews	M.Stepnoski	K.Donnalley	I.Eatman	R.Lewis	W.Davis	C.Chandler	E.George	F.Wycheck*
1997	J.Fisher	C.Sanders	B.Hopkins	B.Matthews	M.Stepnoski	K.Donnalley	J.Runyan	F.Wycheck	W.Davis	S.McNair	E.George	M.Roan*
1998	J.Fisher	W.Davis	B.Hopkins	B.Matthews	M.Stepnoski	J.Layman	J.Runyan	J.Harris	Y.Thigpen	S.McNair	E.George	F.Wycheck*
1999	J.Fisher	K.Dyson	B.Hopkins	B.Matthews	K.Long	B.Olson	J.Runyan	F.Wycheck	Y.Thigpen	S.McNair	E.George	L.Neal
2000	J.Fisher	D.Mason	B.Hopkins	B.Matthews	K.Long	B.Olson	F.Miller	F.Wycheck	C.Sanders	S.McNair	E.George	E.Kinney*
2001	J.Fisher	D.Mason	B.Hopkins	Z.Piller	B.Matthews	B.Olson	F.Miller	F.Wycheck	K.Dyson	S.McNair	E.George	E.Kinney*
2002	J.Fisher	D.Mason	B.Hopkins	Z.Piller	G.DiNapoli	B.Olson	F.Miller	F.Wycheck	K.Dyson	S.McNair	E.George	E.Kinney*
2003	J.Fisher	D.Mason	B.Hopkins	Z.Piller	J.Hartwig	B.Olson	F.Miller	E.Kinney	D.Bennett	S.McNair	E.George	J.McCareins+
2004	J.Fisher	D.Mason	B.Hopkins	J.Bell	J.Hartwig	B.Olson	F.Miller	E.Kinney	D.Bennett	S.McNair	C.Brown	R.Holcombe
2005	J.Fisher	B.Jones	B.Hopkins	Z.Piller	J.Hartwig	B.Olson	M.Roos	E.Kinney	D.Bennett	S.McNair	C.Brown	B.Troupe*

WASHINGTON REDSKINS

YEAR	COACH	WR/LE	LT	LG	C	RG	RT	TE/RE	WR/FL	QB	RB/LH	FB
1950	H.Ball	H.Taylor	L.Niemi	J.Steber	A.DeMao	H.Siegert	B.Hendren	Tereshinski	B.Dudley	S.Baugh	C.Justice	R.Goode
1951	D.Todd	H.Taylor	L.Niemi	H.Siegert	A.DeMao	C.Witucki	P.Lipscomb	G.Brito	L.Heath	S.Baugh	B.Dudley	R.Goode
1952	C.Lambeau	H.Taylor	L.Niemi	G.Pepper	A.DeMao	B.Brown	J.Moss	G.Brito	J.Rykovich	E.LeBaron	H.Gilmer	L.Heath
1953	C.Lambeau	H.Taylor	D.Boll	K.Ramsey	H.Ulinski	C.Witucki	J.Clark	P.Dekker	J.Rykovich	E.LeBaron	C.Justice	P.Barry
1954	J.Kuharich	E.Barker	D.Boll	M.Berschet	H.Ulinski	C.Witucki	K.Barfield	H.Taylor	B.Wells	A.Dorow	C.Justice	R.Goode
1955	J.Kuharich	J.Carson	D.Boll	W.Houston	H.Ulinski	R.Stephens	F.Miller	R.Thomas	B.Zagers	E.LeBaron	V.Janowicz	D.Atkeson
1956	J.Kuharich	J.Carson	D.Boll	R.Stephens	J.Allen	D.Stanfel	J.Miller	S.Meilinger	D.James	A.Dorow	T.Runnels	L.Elter
1957	J.Kuharich	J.Carson	D.Boll	R.Stephens	J.Schrader	D.Stanfel	R.Lemek	S.Meilinger	J.Podoley	E.LeBaron	E.Sutton	D.Bosseler
1958	J.Kuharich	B.Anderson	D.Boll	R.Stephens	J.Schrader	D.Stanfel	R.Lemek	J.Walton	J.Podoley	E.LeBaron	E.Sutton	J.Olszewski
1959	M.Nixon	B.Anderson	D.Lawrence	D.Boll	J.Schrader	R.Stephens	R.Lemek	J.Walton	D.James	E.LeBaron	J.Olszewski	D.Bosseler
1960	M.Nixon	B.Anderson	F.O'Brien	R.Stephens	J.Schrader	V.Promuto	R.Lemek	J.Walton	D.James	R.Guglielmi	J.Olszewski	D.Bosseler
1961	B.McPeak	B.Anderson	R.Mattson	R.Lemek	J.Schrader	V.Promuto	F.O'Brien	F.Dugan	D.James	N.Snead	S.Horner	D.Bosseler
1962	B.McPeak	B.Anderson	R.Mattson	J.Nisby	F.Hageman	V.Promuto	F.O'Brien	F.Dugan	B.Mitchell	N.Snead	B.Barnes	D.Bosseler
1963	B.McPeak	P.Richter	R.Mattson	J.Nisby	F.Hageman	V.Promuto	F.O'Brien	F.Dugan	B.Mitchell	N.Snead	D.James	D.Bosseler
1964	B.McPeak	A.Coia	R.Mattson	J.Nisby	L.Hauss	V.Promuto	F.O'Brien	P.Carpenter	B.Mitchell	S.Jurgensen	C.Taylor	J.Lockett
1965	B.McPeak	P.Richter	J.Snowden	D.Croftcheck	L.Hauss	V.Promuto	F.O'Brien	P.Carpenter	B.Lewis	S.Jurgensen	C.Taylor	D.Lewis
1966	O.Graham	C.Taylor	M.Johnson	R.Schoenke	L.Hauss	V.Promuto	J.Snowden	J.Smith	B.Mitchell	S.Jurgensen	A.Whitfield	S.Thurlow
1967	O.Graham	C.Taylor	M.Johnson	R.Schoenke	L.Hauss	V.Promuto	J.Snowden	J.Smith	B.Mitchell	S.Jurgensen	A.Whitfield	G.Allen
1968	O.Graham	C.Taylor	W.Rock	R.Schoenke	L.Hauss	J.Wooten	J.Snowden	P.Richter	J.Smith	S.Jurgensen	G.Allen	S.Thurlow
1969	V.Lombardi	C.Taylor	J.Snowden	R.Schoenke	L.Hauss	V.Promuto	W.Rock	J.Smith	B.Long	S.Jurgensen	L.Brown	C.Harraway
1970	B.Austin	C.Taylor	J.Snowden	R.Schoenke	L.Hauss	P.Laaveg	W.Rock	J.Smith	W.Roberts	S.Jurgensen	L.Brown	C.Harraway
1971	G.Allen	C.Taylor	J.Snowden	R.Schoenke	L.Hauss	J.Wilbur	W.Rock	J.Smith	B.Dowler	B.Kilmer	L.Brown	C.Harraway
1972	G.Allen	C.Taylor	T.Hermeling	P.Laaveg	L.Hauss	J.Wilbur	W.Rock	J.Smith	R.Jefferson	B.Kilmer	L.Brown	C.Harraway
1973	G.Allen	C.Taylor	T.Hermeling	P.Laaveg	L.Hauss	J.Wilbur	G.Starke	J.Smith	R.Jefferson	B.Kilmer	L.Brown	C.Harraway
1974	G.Allen	C.Taylor	R.Schoenke	P.Laaveg	L.Hauss	W.Sweeney	G.Starke	J.Smith	R.Jefferson	B.Kilmer	L.Brown	M.Denson
1975	G.Allen	C.Taylor	T.Hermeling	R.Schoenke	L.Hauss	W.Sweeney	G.Starke	J.Smith	F.Grant	B.Kilmer	M.Thomas	M.Denson
1976	G.Allen	F.Grant	T.Stokes	R.Saul	L.Hauss	T.Hermeling	G.Starke	J.Fugett	R.Jefferson	B.Kilmer	M.Thomas	J.Riggins
1977	G.Allen	C.Taylor	T.Stokes	R.Saul	L.Hauss	T.Hermeling	G.Starke	J.Fugett	F.Grant	B.Kilmer	M.Thomas	C.Harmon
1978	J.Pardee	J.McDaniel	T.Hermeling	R.Saul	B.Kuziel	D.Nugent	G.Starke	J.Fugett	D.Buggs	J.Theismann	M.Thomas	J.Riggins
1979	J.Pardee	D.Buggs	T.Hermeling	R.Saul	B.Kuziel	J.Williams	G.Starke	D.Warren	R.Thompson	J.Theismann	B.Malone	J.Riggins
1980	J.Pardee	R.Thompson	T.Hermeling	R.Saul	B.Kuziel	J.Williams	G.Starke	D.Warren	A.Monk	J.Theismann	W.Jackson	C.Harmon
1981	J.Gibbs	V.Seay	J.Jacoby	R.Grimm	J.Bostic	M.Jones	G.Starke	D.Warren	A.Monk	J.Theismann	J.Washington	R.Walker*
1982	J.Gibbs	C.Brown	J.Jacoby	R.Grimm	J.Bostic	M.May	G.Starke	D.Warren	A.Monk	J.Theismann	J.Riggins	R.Walker*
1983	J.Gibbs	C.Brown	J.Jacoby	R.Grimm	J.Bostic	M.May	G.Starke	R.Walker	A.Monk	J.Theismann	J.Riggins	D.Warren*
1984	J.Gibbs	C.Muhammad	J.Jacoby	R.Grimm	J.Bostic	K.Huff	M.May	D.Warren	A.Monk	J.Theismann	J.Riggins	R.Walker*
1985	J.Gibbs	G.Clark	J.Jacoby	R.Grimm	R.Donnalley	K.Huff	M.May	D.Warren	A.Monk	J.Theismann	J.Riggins	C.Didier*
1986	J.Gibbs	A.Monk	J.Jacoby	R.Grimm	J.Bostic	R.Thielemann	M.May	D.Warren	G.Clark	J.Schroeder	G.Rogers	C.Didier*
1987	J.Gibbs	A.Monk	J.Jacoby	R.McKenzie	R.Grimm	R.Thielemann	M.May	D.Warren	G.Clark	J.Schroeder	G.Rogers	C.Didier*
1988	J.Gibbs	A.Monk	J.Jacoby	R.McKenzie	J.Bostic	M.May	J.Lachey	D.Warren	G.Clark	D.Williams	C.McEwen	T.Smith
1989	J.Gibbs	A.Monk	J.Lachey	R.Grimm	J.Bostic	M.May	J.Lachey	D.Warren	G.Clark	M.Rypien	E.Byner	R.Sanders+
1990	J.Gibbs	A.Monk	J.Lachey	R.Grimm	J.Bostic	R.McKenzie	E.Simmons	D.Warren	G.Clark	M.Rypien	E.Byner	R.Sanders+
1991	J.Gibbs	G.Clark	J.Lachey	R.McKenzie	J.Bostic	M.Schlereth	J.Jacoby	R.Middleton	A.Monk	M.Rypien	E.Byner	D.Warren*
1992	J.Gibbs	G.Clark	J.Jacoby	J.Jacoby	R.McKenzie	M.Schlereth	E.Simmons	R.Middleton	A.Monk	M.Rypien	E.Byner	D.Warren*
1993	R.Petitbon	T.McGee	M.Elewonibi	R.Brown	J.Bostic	R.McKenzie	E.Simmons	R.Middleton	R.Sanders	M.Rypien	R.Brooks	F.Wycheck*
1994	N.Turner	D.Howard	J.Lachey	R.Brown	J.Gesek	R.McKenzie	E.Simmons	E.Horton	H.Ellard	H.Shuler	R.Ervins	C.Smith
1995	N.Turner	M.Westbrook	J.Patton	R.Brown	J.Gesek	T.Johnson	E.Simmons	S.Galbraith	H.Ellard	G.Frerotte	T.Allen	M.Logan
1996	N.Turner	M.Westbrook	J.Patton	T.Johnson	J.Uhlenhake	B.Dahl	E.Simmons	J.Asher	H.Ellard	G.Frerotte	T.Allen	M.Logan
1997	N.Turner	M.Westbrook	S.Pourdanesh	J.Patton	J.Uhlenhake	T.Johnson	E.Simmons	J.Asher	H.Ellard	G.Frerotte	T.Allen	L.Bowie
1998	N.Turner	M.Westbrook	B.Badger	J.Patton	C.Raymer	R.Milstead	S.Pourdanesh	J.Asher	L.Shepherd	T.Green	T.Allen	S.Davis
1999	N.Turner	M.Westbrook	A.Heck	K.Sims	C.Raymer	T.Johnson	J.Jansen	S.Alexander	A.Connell	B.Johnson	S.Davis	L.Centers
2000	N.Turner	J.Thrash	C.Samuels	K.Sims	M.Fischer	Leeuwenburg	J.Jansen	S.Alexander	A.Connell	B.Johnson	S.Davis	M.Sellers*
2001	Schottenheimer	R.Gardner	C.Samuels	D.Szott	C.Raymer	B.Coleman	J.Jansen	W.Rasby	M.Westbrook	T.Banks	S.Davis	D.Bennett
2002	S.Spurrier	R.Gardner	C.Samuels	D.Loverne	L.Moore	W.Brown	J.Jansen	W.Rasby	D.Thompson	S.Matthews	S.Davis	B.Johnson
2003	S.Spurrier	L.Coles	C.Samuels	D.Dockery	L.Moore	R.Thomas	J.Jansen	Z.Flemister	R.Gardner	P.Ramsey	T.Canidate	B.Johnson
2004	J.Gibbs	R.Gardner	C.Samuels	D.Dockery	C.Raymer	R.Thomas	R.Brown	R.Royal	L.Coles	M.Brunell	C.Portis	C.Cooley*
2005	J.Gibbs	D.Patten	C.Samuels	D.Dockery	C.Rabach	R.Thomas	J.Jansen	R.Royal	S.Moss	M.Brunell	C.Portis	C.Cooley*

YEAR	LDE	LDT/NT	RDT/RDE	RDE/LOLB	LLB/LILB	MLB/RILB	RLB/ROLB	LCB	RCB	SS/LS	FS/RS	FINISH	
1982	K.Kennard	M.Stensrud	J.Baker*	A.Riley	G.Bingham	D.Hunt	R.Brazile	J.Wilson	G.Stemrick	V.Perry	M.Reinfeldt	13a	1-8
1983	B.Hamm	B.Sochia	J.Baker*	A.Riley	G.Bingham	R.Abraham	R.Brazile	S.Brown	W.Tullis	K.Bostic	C.Hartwig	4ac	2-14
1984	B.Hamm	M.Stensrud	J.Baker*	A.Riley	G.Bingham	R.Abraham	R.Brazile	S.Brown	W.Tullis	K.Bostic	C.Hartwig	4ac	3-13
1985	R.Childress	M.Stensrud	J.Baker*	R.Lyles	A.Riley	R.Abraham	F.Bush	S.Brown	P.Allen	K.Bostic	B.Eason	4ac	5-11
1986	R.Childress	M.Golic	R.Byrd*	R.Lyles	J.Grimsley	R.Abraham	J.Meads	S.Brown	P.Allen	K.Bostic	B.Eason	4ac	5-11
1987	R.Childress	D.Smith	R.Byrd*	R.Lyles	J.Grimsley	A.Smith	J.Meads	S.Brown	P.Allen	K.Bostic	J.Donaldson	2ac	9-6 wd
1988	R.Childress	D.Smith	W.Fuller*	R.Lyles	J.Grimsley	A.Smith	J.Meads	S.Brown	P.Allen	K.Bostic	J.Donaldson	2ac	10-6 wd
1989	R.Childress	D.Smith	R.Byrd*	R.Lyles	J.Grimsley	A.Smith	J.Meads	S.Brown	P.Allen	B.McDowell	J.Donaldson	2ac	9-7 w
1990	W.Fuller	R.Childress	D.Smith	S.Jones	J.Grimsley	A.Smith	J.Meads	C.Dishman	R.Johnson	B.McDowell	T.Kinard	2ac	9-7 #w
1991	W.Fuller	R.Childress	D.Smith	S.Jones	L.Lathon	A.Smith	J.Meads	C.Dishman	R.Johnson	B.McDowell	B.Orlando	1ac	11-5 ed
1992	W.Fuller	R.Childress	J.Alm	S.Jones	L.Lathon	A.Smith	E.Robinson	C.Dishman	J.Gray	B.McDowell	M.Robertson	2ac	10-6 w
1993	W.Fuller	R.Childress	G.Montgomery	S.Jones	E.Robinson	A.Smith	W.Marshall	C.Dishman	S.Jackson	B.McDowell	M.Robertson	1ac	12-4 d
1994	K.Davidson	R.Childress	G.Montgomery	L.Lathon	E.Robinson	A.Smith	M.Barrow	C.Dishman	D.Lewis	B.Bishop	M.Robertson	4ac	2-14
1995	K.Davidson	G.Walker	G.Montgomery	H.Ford	E.Robinson	M.Barrow	J.Bowden	C.Dishman	D.Lewis	B.Bishop	C.Cecil	2ac	7-9
1996	A.Cook	G.Walker	H.Ford	R.Young	J.Bowden	B.Wortham	M.Barrow	C.Dishman	D.Lewis	B.Bishop	M.Robertson	3ac	8-8
1997	A.Cook	G.Walker	H.Ford	J.Roberson	J.Bowden	B.Wortham	L.Marts	D.Walker	D.Lewis	B.Bishop	M.Robertson	3ac	8-8
1998	P.Lyons	G.Walker	J.Evans	K.Holmes	E.Robinson	J.Bowden	L.Marts	D.Walker	D.Lewis	B.Bishop	M.Robertson	2ac	8-8
1999	J.Kearse	J.Evans	J.Fisk	H.Ford	E.Robinson	B.Wortham	J.Bowden	D.Walker	S.Rolle	B.Bishop	M.Robertson	2ac	13-3 wdc
2000	J.Kearse	J.Thornton	J.Fisk	K.Holmes	G.Favors	R.Godfrey	E.Robinson	D.Walker	S.Rolle	B.Bishop	M.Robertson	1ac	13-3 d
2001	K.Carter	J.Evans	J.Fisk	J.Kearse	G.Favors	R.Godfrey	E.Robinson	A.Dyson	S.Rolle	A.Morris	P.Phenix	3ac	7-9
2002	K.Carter	J.Thornton	H.Ford	C.Hall	P.Sirmon	D.Mitchell*	K.Bulluck	A.Dyson	S.Rolle	T.Williams	L.Schulters	1as	11-5 dc
2003	K.Carter	R.Smith	Haynesworth	J.Kearse	P.Sirmon	R.Calmus	K.Bulluck	A.Dyson	S.Rolle	T.Williams	L.Schulters	2as	12-4 #w
2004	A.Odom	K.Carter	Haynesworth	C.Hall	R.Boiman	B.Kassell	K.Bulluck	A.Dyson	S.Rolle	T.Williams	L.Thompson	4as	5-11
2005	Vanden Bosch	R.Starks	Haynesworth	A.Odom	P.Sirmon	B.Kassell	K.Bulluck	R.Hill	P.Jones	T.Williams	L.Thompson	3as	4-12
1950	E.Berrang	L.Karras	P.Lipscomb	D.Brown	Drazenovich	E.Quirk+	H.Brown	H.Dowda	J.Bartos	H.Haynes	E.Saenz	6na	3-9
1951	W.Yowarsky	L.Karras	B.Hendren	Tereshinski	Drazenovich	J.Ricca+	G.Buksar	H.Dowda	N.Ferris	E.Salem	J.Dwyer	3na	5-7
1952	B.Cox	E.Ecker	P.Lipscomb	Tereshinski	Drazenovich	J.Ricca+	G.Buksar	H.Dowda	J.Williams	D.Alban	A.Davis	5na	4-8
1953	G.Brito	Modzelewski	P.Lipscomb	Tereshinski	Drazenovich	J.Ricca+	J.Cloud	H.Dowda	J.Williams	D.Doll	D.Alban	3ne	6-5-1
1954	W.Yowarsky	V.Peters	B.Morgan	C.Ostrowski	Drazenovich	J.Ricca+	N.Adduci	J.Scudero	R.Felton	G.Rosso	D.Alban	5ne	3-9
1955	G.Brito	V.Peters	J.Kimmel	C.Ostrowski	L.Torgeson	Drazenovich	R.Felton	J.Scudero	R.Barni	D.Alban	N.Hecker	2ne	8-4
1956	G.Brito	V.Peters	J.Kimmel	C.Ostrowski	L.Torgeson	Drazenovich	B.Fulcher	J.Scudero	R.Barni	A.DeCarlo	N.Hecker	3ne	6-6
1957	G.Brito	V.Peters	D.Owens	C.Ostrowski	L.Torgeson	Drazenovich	R.Felton	B.Zagers	D.James	D.Shula	N.Hecker	4ne	5-6-1
1958	G.Brito	J.Weatherall	W.Renfro	C.Ostrowski	R.Felton	Drazenovich	J.Allen	B.Zagers	L.Walters	D.Nix	D.James	4ne	4-7-1
1959	J.Paluck	B.Toneff	D.Churchwell	A.Gob	R.Felton	Drazenovich	T.Braatz	D.Nix	B.Scotti	G.Glick	D.Haley	5ne	3-9
1960	J.Paluck	B.Toneff	D.Lawrence	A.Stynchula	D.Lasse	R.Felton	B.Roehnelt	B.Scotti	P.Heenan	G.Glick	B.Brewer	6ne	1-9-2
1961	J.Paluck	B.Toneff	J.Rutgens	A.Stynchula	R.Wilkins	F.Hageman	R.Breedlove	J.Krakoski	J.Steffen	J.Kerr	D.Hackbart	7ne	1-12-1
1962	E.Khayat	B.Toneff	J.Rutgens	A.Stynchula	G.Kelley	B.Pellegrini	R.Breedlove	C.Crabb	J.Steffen	J.Kerr	D.Hackbart	4ne	5-7-2
1963	J.Paluck	B.Toneff	J.Rutgens	A.Stynchula	B.Pellegrini	C.Kammerer	R.Breedlove	J.Steffen	L.Sanders	C.Crabb	D.Hackbart	6ne	3-11
1964	J.Paluck	B.Toneff	J.Rutgens	R.Snidow	J.Reger	S.Huff	R.Breedlove	J.Sample	L.Sanders	J.Steffen	P.Krause	3ne	6-8
1965	R.Snidow	F.Williams	J.Rutgens	C.Kammerer	J.Reger	S.Huff	B.Pellegrini	J.Sample	L.Sanders	J.Steffen	P.Krause	4ne	6-8
1966	R.Snidow	W.Barnes	S.Jones	C.Kammerer	J.Reger	S.Huff	C.Hanburger	R.Harris	J.Shorter	B.Owens	P.Krause	5ne	7-7
1967	R.Snidow	W.Barnes	J.Rutgens	C.Kammerer	J.Carroll	S.Huff	C.Hanburger	R.Harris	J.Shorter	B.Owens	P.Krause	3nca	5-6-3
1968	S.Musgrove	D.Crane	J.Rutgens	C.Kammerer	T.Roussel	E.Breding	C.Hanburger	P.Fischer	R.Harris	B.Owens	A.Martin	3nca	5-9
1969	L.Carroll	D.Crane	J.Rutgens	C.Kammerer	T.Roussel	S.Huff	C.Hanburger	P.Fischer	M.Bass	B.Owens	R.Harris	2nca	7-5-2
1970	J.Hoffman	F.Peters	B.Brundige	B.Anderson	H.McLinton	M.McKeever	C.Hanburger	P.Fischer	M.Bass	B.Owens	R.Harris	4ne	6-8
1971	R.McDole	M.Sistrunk	D.Talbert	V.Biggs	J.Pardee	M.Pottios	C.Hanburger	P.Fischer	M.Bass	R.Petitbon	B.Owens	2ne	9-4-1 w
1972	R.McDole	B.Brundige	D.Talbert	V.Biggs	J.Pardee	H.McLinton	C.Hanburger	P.Fischer	M.Bass	B.Owens	R.Taylor	1ne	11-3 dcs
1973	R.McDole	B.Brundige	D.Talbert	V.Biggs	D.Robinson	H.McLinton	C.Hanburger	P.Fischer	M.Bass	K.Houston	B.Owens	2ne	10-4 #w
1974	R.McDole	B.Brundige	D.Talbert	V.Biggs	D.Robinson	H.McLinton	C.Hanburger	P.Fischer	M.Bass	K.Houston	B.Owens	2ne	10-4 #w
1975	R.McDole	B.Brundige	D.Talbert	D.Johnson	B.Dusek	H.McLinton	C.Hanburger	P.Fischer	M.Bass	K.Houston	B.Salter	3ne	8-6
1976	R.McDole	D.Butz	D.Talbert	D.Johnson	B.Dusek	H.McLinton	C.Hanburger	P.Fischer	J.Lavender	K.Houston	J.Scott	2ne	10-4 #w
1977	R.McDole	D.Butz	D.Talbert	D.Johnson	B.Dusek	H.McLinton	M.Curtis	G.Williams	J.Lavender	K.Houston	J.Scott	2ne	9-5 #
1978	R.McDole	D.Butz	D.Talbert	C.Bacon	B.Dusek	H.McLinton	C.Hanburger	L.Parrish	J.Lavender	K.Houston	J.Scott	3ne	8-8
1979	K.Lorch	D.Butz	D.Talbert	C.Bacon	B.Dusek	N.Olkewicz	P.Wysocki	L.Parrish	J.Lavender	K.Houston	M.Murphy	3ne	10-6 #
1980	K.Lorch	D.Butz	P.Brooks	C.Bacon	B.Dusek	N.Olkewicz	M.Coleman	L.Parrish	J.Lavender	T.Peters	M.Murphy	3ne	6-10
1981	K.Lorch	D.Butz	P.Brooks	D.Manley	B.Dusek	N.Olkewicz	M.Coleman	L.Parrish	J.Lavender	T.Peters	M.Murphy	4ne	8-8
1982	M.Mendenhall	D.Butz	P.Brooks	D.Manley	M.Kaufman	N.Olkewicz	R.Milot	J.White	V.Dean	T.Peters	M.Murphy	1n	8-1 pdcs*
1983	Liebenstein	D.Butz	D.Grant	D.Manley	M.Kaufman	N.Olkewicz	R.Milot	D.Green	V.Dean	C.Jordan	M.Murphy	1ne	14-2 dcs
1984	C.Mann	D.Butz	D.Grant	D.Manley	M.Kaufman	N.Olkewicz	R.Milot	D.Green	V.Dean	K.Coffey	C.Jordan	1ne	11-5 d
1985	C.Mann	D.Butz	D.Grant	D.Manley	M.Kaufman	N.Olkewicz	R.Milot	D.Green	V.Dean	T.Peters	C.Jordan	3ne	10-6 #
1986	C.Mann	D.Butz	D.Grant	D.Manley	C.Daniels	N.Olkewicz	R.Milot	D.Green	V.Dean	K.Coffey	C.Jordan	2ne	12-4 wdc
1987	C.Mann	D.Butz	D.Grant	D.Manley	M.Kaufman	N.Olkewicz	M.Coleman	D.Green	B.Wilburn	A.Walton	T.Bowles	1ne	11-4 dcs*
1988	C.Mann	D.Butz	D.Grant	D.Manley	M.Coleman	N.Olkewicz	W.Marshall	B.Wilburn	D.Green	A.Walton	T.Bowles	3ne	7-9
1989	C.Mann	T.Rocker	D.Grant	D.Manley	R.Caldwell	N.Olkewicz	W.Marshall	B.Davis	A.Johnson	A.Walton	T.Bowles	3ne	10-6
1990	C.Mann	E.Williams	D.Grant	M.Koch	A.Collins	G.Manusky	W.Marshall	M.Mayhew	D.Green	A.Walton	T.Bowles	2ne	10-6 wd
1991	C.Mann	E.Williams	T.Johnson	F.Stokes	W.Marshall	M.Millen	A.Collins	M.Mayhew	D.Green	D.Copeland	B.Edwards	1ne	14-2 dcs*
1992	C.Mann	E.Williams	T.Johnson	F.Stokes	W.Marshall	K.Gouveia	A.Collins	M.Mayhew	A.Johnson	D.Copeland	B.Edwards	3ne	9-7 #wd
1993	C.Mann	B.Wilson	T.Johnson	S.Palmer	C.Banks	K.Gouveia	A.Collins	T.Carter	D.Green	D.Copeland	B.Edwards	5ne	4-12
1994	T.Woods	B.Wilson	T.Johnson	S.Palmer	K.Harvey	T.Stowe	A.Collins	T.Carter	D.Green	M.Bayless	D.Morrison	5ne	3-13
1995	T.Woods	M.Boutte	W.Gaines	S.Palmer	K.Harvey	R.Stephens	M.Patton	T.Carter	D.Green	J.Washington	S.Richard	3ne	6-10
1996	T.Woods	M.Boutte	S.Gilbert	R.Owens	K.Harvey	R.Stephens	M.Patton	T.Carter	D.Green	D.Morrison	S.Richard	3ne	9-7 #
1997	K.Lang	C.Mims	M.Boutte	R.Owens	K.Harvey	M.Patton	D.Smith	C.Dishman	D.Green	J.Campbell	S.Richard	2ne	8-7-1
1998	K.Lang	D.Wilkinson	D.Brown	K.Kinney	K.Harvey	M.Patton	D.Smith	C.Dishman	D.Green	L.Evans	S.Richard	4ne	6-10
1999	K.Lang	D.Wilkinson	Stubblefield	M.Coleman	G.Jones	D.Smith	S.Barber	C.Bailey	D.Green	S.Shade	L.Evans	1ne	10-6 ed
2000	M.Coleman	D.Wilkinson	Stubblefield	B.Smith	S.Barber	D.Smith	L.Arrington	C.Bailey	D.Sanders	S.Shade	M.Carrier	3ne	8-8
2001	M.Coleman	D.Wilkinson	K.Lang	B.Smith	L.Arrington	K.Mitchell	R.Jones	C.Bailey	F.Smoot	S.Shade	D.Terrell	2ne	8-8
2002	R.Wynn	D.Wilkinson	D.Gardener	B.Smith	L.Arrington	J.Trotter	J.Armstead	C.Bailey	F.Smoot	I.Ohalete	D.Terrell	3ne	7-9
2003	B.Smith	B.Holsey	L.Dalton	R.Wynn	L.Arrington	J.Trotter	J.Armstead	C.Bailey	F.Smoot	I.Ohalete	M.Bowen	3ne	5-11
2004	R.Wynn	J.Salave'a	C.Griffin	D.Evans	M.Washington	A.Pierce	L.Marshall	S.Springs	F.Smoot	R.Clark	S.Taylor	2ne	6-10
2005	R.Wynn	C.Griffin	J.Salave'a	P.Daniels	M.Washington	L.Marshall	L.Arrington	W.Harris	S.Springs	R.Clark	S.Taylor	2ne	10-6 wd

Head coach in the National Football League is probably the most scrutinized management position in sports. Even with assistant coaches handling different aspects of the game, the head coach's head is never far from the chopping block. Although head coaches get perks like their own paid radio programs and endorsements, it is their name that goes next to the won–loss record. The head coach has to meet with the press daily and football's six-day wait between games gives everyone who watched the game—and even those who didn't—the opportunity to go over costly plays again and again. A coach can't gloat too much over his last win or agonize too much on each loss because there is always a game to prepare for, like 16 final exams each fall; if the team is lucky and good, there's harder work ahead with the playoffs and the ultimate test of a coach's ability to keep his team focused: the Super Bowl. Even the relatively sane assignment of coaching the Pro Bowl comes with the stigma that the coach is there because he lost the championship game.

Unlike baseball, where there is a game the next day to wipe away even the hardest loss and a pitcher to share the win or defeat, the head coach of a football team has the pressure of living up to or living down the last game for almost a week. The pressure of a losing season multiplies as the season progresses, but barely missing the playoffs can be the most agonizing scenario of all. And when the day comes that he is not wanted as head coach any more, he has to tell his friends and colleagues, the assistant coaches he's spent countless hours with breaking down film and discussing players and game plans, that they're fired, too. Or he may have to pat his assistant on the back who's been asked to take his place as head coach; the veteran head coach knows all too well what the new guy is in for. There are 21 men in the Hall of Fame as head coaches and many of them were fired at least once.

In the early days of the league, the head coach was usually a player. Fritz Pollard, credited with being the first African American coach in the NFL—and the last until Art Shell was hired by the Raiders in 1989—took over the league's first defending champion, the Akron Pros, in 1921. George Halas, Curly Lambeau, Guy Chamberlin, Jimmy Conzelman and Steve Owen, among others, served as both player and coach for their clubs, usually calling the signals from the field as opposed to the sidelines. As these men became older and their playing skills diminished, it made sense for them to shift to the sidelines, as college coaches did, not to mention many NFL coaches as well.

For many years head coaches were in charge of most of the team's operations, as well as those of a scout. The playing of NFL games on Sundays allowed for some scouting of college games on Saturdays, but the only thing harder than traveling to a campus the day before a game was trying to convince a college player that he could make a good living in the early pro game. Halas and Lambeau were especially convincing, and they relied on their contacts and former players to tell them when they saw someone they might not know about or confirm reports on players they knew of already. Halas also refined the practice that allowed coaches to think big picture: assistant coaches. Trusted assistants could handle the more mundane—though no less important—aspects of the game while also providing a sounding board for different ideas and new schemes. Paul Brown came a generation after the NFL's first groundbreakers but his coaching innovations are still felt today. He started two franchises—the Cleveland Browns and Cincinnati Bengals—from scratch, melded them into cohesive units, and made them win.

The traditional image of the coach is that of a crusty older man perpetually wearing a hat with a whistle around his neck, but the stress of the job is shared by both young and old. With his 2006 coaching debut, Chuck Mangini—one of 10 head coaches in new locations since the end of 2005—becomes the 15th youngest coach in NFL history since 1940, joining Jon Gruden, Bill Cowher, John Madden, Al Davis, Norm Van Brocklin, and two Shulas, Don and David, plus a handful of others who signed their first NFL head coaching contracts at age 34 or younger. Harland Svare was the youngest since the player–coach days when he took over the Los Angeles Rams at age 31 in 1960. On the other end, Halas and Marv Levy both coached until they were 72. Bill Parcells and Joe Gibbs continue coaching legacies after several years away from the game. It seems the coach can leave the game, but the game never leaves the coach.

KEY TO THE HEAD COACHES REGISTER

Many other great coaches not mentioned here are legends in the game, including Hall of Famers Greasy Neale, Ray Flaherty, Weeb Ewbank, Vince Lombardi, Sid Gillman, Hank Stram, Bud Grant, George Allen, Tom Landry, Chuck Noll, and Bill Walsh. All men elected to the Hall of Fame as head coaches are designated with **HOF**. Every head coach's birth date is also included, and biographical data is listed if it is not already under an entry in the Player Register. Also included are wins, losses, and ties in the regular season. **WP** and **LP** refer to a head coach's record in playoff games. The record as well as years coached is totaled at the bottom of each entry. As for how the team finished, the team's place in the standings is listed in the far right column. The symbols and letters next to the NFL, AAFC, AFL, NFC, and AFC stand for the following:

   *   After the name means biographical data is in player register.
   †   After the team means the coach was a co-coach.
   ◆   Before the place of finish means the coach started in midseason.
   ◇   Before the place of finish means the coach ended in midseason.
   #   Indicates if the team was involved in a tiebreaker, and each letter indicates a playoff game corresponding with the letters below.
   ‡   Shows the final playoff game was won (league championship for 1933–1965, Super Bowl for 1966–present).
   P   Intermediate games or playoff round used by the AAFC (1949), AFL (1969), and NFL (1982).
   W   Wild card (1970–present),
   D   Division round
   C   Conference championship
   L   League championship
   S   Super Bowl
   E   Used for the divisional champ who played in the wild-card round (1990–present). If the team won the game, that is indicated by the presence of another of these letters for the next round.

YEAR TEAM	W-L-T	WP-LP	FINISH PLAYOFFS
Abbott, Faye* B8/16/1895			
1928 Day	0-7-0	—	10 NFL
1929 Day	0-6-0	—	12 NFL
NFL 2	0-13-0	—	—
Albert, Frankie* B1/27/1920			
1956 SF	5-6-1	—	3 NFL-W
1957 SF	8-4-0	0-1	1 NFL-W C
1958 SF	6-6-0	—	4 NFL-W
NFL 3	19-16-1	0-1	—
Alexander, Doc* B4/1/1898			
1922 Roc	0-4-1	—	15 NFL
1926 NYG	8-4-1	—	6 NFL
NFL 2	8-8-2	—	—
Allen, George George Herbert; Marquette, Alma, Michigan; B4/29/1922 Grosse Point Woods, MI, D12/31/1990 Rancho Palos Verdes, CA; HOF 2002			
1966 LARm	8-6-0	—	3 NFL-W
1967 LARm	11-1-2	0-1	1 NFL-Cnl DC
1968 LARm	10-3-1	—	2 NFL-Cnl
1969 LARm	11-3-0	0-1	1 NFL-Cnl C
1970 LARm	9-4-1	—	2 NFC-W
1971 Was	9-4-1	0-1	2 NFC-E W
1972 Was	11-3-0	2-1	1 NFC-E DCS
1973 Was	10-4-0	0-1	2 NFC-E #W
1974 Was	10-4-0	0-1	2 NFC-E #W
1975 Was	8-6-0	—	3 NFC-E
1976 Was	10-4-0	0-1	2 NFC-E #W
1977 Was	9-5-0	—	2 NFC-E #
NFL 12	116-47-5	2-7	—
Anderson, Hunk* B9/22/1898			
1942 ChiB†	6-0-0	0-1	◆1 NFL-W L
1943 ChiB†	8-1-1	1-0	1 NFL-W L‡
1944 ChiB†	6-3-1	—	2 NFL-W
1945 ChiB†	3-7-0	—	4 NFL-W
NFL 4	23-11-2	1-1	—
Andrews, Roy* B1898			
1924 KC	2-7-0	—	15 NFL
1925 KC	2-5-1	—	13 NFL
1926 KC	8-3-0	—	4 NFL
1927 Cle	8-4-1	—	4 NFL
1928 Det	7-2-1	—	3 NFL
1929 NYG	13-1-1	—	2 NFL
1930 NYG	11-4-0	—	◇2 NFL
1931 ChiC	0-2-0	—	◆4 NFL
NFL 8	51-28-4	—	—
Armstrong, John* B1894			
1924 RI	5-2-2	—	5 NFL
Armstrong, Neill* B3/9/1926			
1978 ChiB	7-9-0	—	3 NFC-C
1979 ChiB	10-6-0	0-1	2 NFC-C #W
1980 ChiB	7-9-0	—	3 NFC-C
1981 ChiB	6-10-0	—	5 NFC-C
NFL 4	30-34-0	0-1	—
Arnsbarger, Bill William Stephen; Miami (OH); B12/16/1926 Paris, KY			
1974 NYG	2-12-0	—	5 NFC-E
1975 NYG	5-9-0	—	4 NFC-E
1976 NYG	0-7-0	—	◇5 NFC-E
NFL 3	7-28-0	—	—
Austin, Bill* B10/18/1928			
1966 Pit	5-8-1	—	6 NFL-E
1967 Pit	4-9-1	—	4 NFL-Cny
1968 Pit	2-11-1	—	4 NFL-Cny
1970 Was	6-8-0	—	4 NFC-E
NFL 4	17-36-3	—	—
Bach, Joe Joseph Anthony; Notre Dame; B1/17/1901 Tower, MN, D10/24/1966 Pittsburgh, PA			
1935 Pit	4-8-0	—	3 NFL-E
1936 Pit	6-6-0	—	2 NFL-E
1952 Pit	5-7-0	—	4 NFL-A
1953 Pit	6-6-0	—	4 NFL-E
NFL 4	21-27-0	—	—
Ball, Herman R. Herman; Davis & Elkins; B4/9/1910 Kingsville, WV, D1/12/1998 Paoli, PA			
1949 Was	1-4-0	—	◆4 NFL-E
1950 Was	3-9-0	—	6 NFL-A
1951 Was	0-3-0	—	◇3 NFL-A
NFL 3	4-16-0	—	—
Barr, Shorty* B11/30/1897			
1926 Rac	1-2-0	—	◇16 NFL
Barry, Norm* B12/25/1897			
1925 ChiC	11-2-1	—	1 NFL
1926 ChiC	5-6-1	—	10 NFL
NFL 2	16-8-2	—	—
Bates, Jim James Ira; Tennessee; B5/31/1946 Pontiac, MI			
2004 Mia	3-4-0	—	◆4 AFC-E

YEAR TEAM	W-L-T	WP-LP	FINISH PLAYOFFS
Batterson, Dim George Walder; none; B10/3/1881, NY, D12/3/1935 Buffalo, NY			
1927 Buf	0-5-0	—	12 NFL
Battles, Cliff* B5/1/1910			
1946 Bkn-A†	1-6-0	—	◆2 AAFC-E
1947 Bkn-A	3-10-1	—	3 AAFC-E
NFL 2	4-16-1	—	—
Baugh, Sammy* B3/17/1914			
1960 NYT-A	7-7-0	—	2 AFL-E
1961 NYT-A	7-7-0	—	3 AFL-E
1964 Hou-A	4-10-0	—	4 AFL-E
NFL 3	18-24-0	—	—
Behman, Bull* B1/15/1900			
1929 Fra	10-4-5	—	3 NFL
1930 Fra	2-10-1	—	◇9 NFL
1931 Fra	1-6-1	—	10 NFL
NFL 3	13-20-7	—	—
Belichick, Bill William Stephen; Wesleyan; B4/16/1952 Nashville, TN			
1991 Cle	6-10-0	—	3 AFC-C
1992 Cle	7-9-0	—	3 AFC-C
1993 Cle	7-9-0	—	3 AFC-C
1994 Cle	11-5-0	1-1	2 AFC-C WD
1995 Cle	5-11-0	—	4 AFC-C
2000 NE	5-11-0	—	5 AFC-E
2001 NE	11-5-0	3-0	1 AFC-E #DCS‡
2002 NE	9-7-0	—	3 AFC-E #
2003 NE	14-2-0	3-0	1 AFC-E DCS‡
2004 NE	14-2-0	3-0	1 AFC-E DCS‡
2005 NE	10-6-0	1-1	1 AFC-E ED
NFL 11	99-77-0	11-2	—
Bell, Bert DeBenneville; Pennsylvania; B2/25/1895 Philadelphia, PA, D10/11/1959 Philadelphia, PA; HOF 1963			
1936 Phi	1-11-0	—	5 NFL-E
1937 Phi	2-8-1	—	5 NFL-E
1938 Phi	5-6-0	—	4 NFL-E
1939 Phi	1-9-1	—	4 NFL-E
1940 Phi	1-10-0	—	5 NFL-E
1941 Pit	0-2-0	—	◇5 NFL-E
NFL 6	10-46-2	—	—
Bengston, Phil John Phillip; Minnesota; B7/17/1913 Rousseau, MN, D12/18/1994 San Diego, CA			
1968 GB	6-7-1	—	3 NFL-Coa
1969 GB	8-6-0	—	3 NFL-Coa
1970 GB	6-8-0	—	3 NFC-C
1972 NE	1-4-0	—	◆5 AFC-E
NFL 4	21-25-1	—	—
Bennett, Leeman Leeman; Kentucky; B6/20/1938 Paducah, KY			
1977 Atl	7-7-0	—	2 NFC-W
1978 Atl	9-7-0	1-1	2 NFC-W WD
1979 Atl	6-10-0	—	3 NFC-W
1980 Atl	12-4-0	0-1	1 NFC-W D
1981 Atl	7-9-0	—	2 NFC-W
1982 Atl	5-4-0	0-1	4 NFC P
1985 TB	2-14-0	—	5 NFC-C
1986 TB	2-14-0	—	5 NFC-C
NFL 8	50-69-0	1-3	—
Bergman, Dutch Arthur J.; Notre Dame; B2/23/1895 Peru, IN, D8/18/1972 Washington, DC			
1943 Was	6-3-1	1-1	1 NFL-E DL
Berry, Raymond* B2/27/1933			
1984 NE	4-4-0	—	◆2 AFC-E
1985 NE	11-5-0	3-1	3 AFC-E #WDCS
1986 NE	11-5-0	0-1	1 AFC-E D
1987 NE	8-7-0	—	2 AFC-E
1988 NE	9-7-0	—	2 AFC-E
1989 NE	5-11-0	—	4 AFC-E
NFL 6	48-39-0	3-2	—
Berryman, Punk Robert Norman; Penn State; B12/13/1893, D5/20/1988 Philadelphia, PA			
1924 Fra	11-2-1	—	3 NFL
1926 Bkn	3-8-0	—	14 NFL
NFL 2	14-10-1	—	—
Bettis, Tom* B3/17/1933			
1977 KC	1-6-0	—	◆5 AFC-W
Bezdek, Hugo Hugo Francis; Chicago; B3/1/1883 Prague, Austria-Hungary, D9/19/1952 Atlantic City, NJ			
1937 Cle	1-10-0	—	5 NFL-W
1938 Cle	0-3-0	—	◇4 NFL-W
NFL 2	1-13-0	—	—
Bierce, Scotty* B9/3/1896			
1925 Akr	4-2-2	—	5 NFL
Biles, Ed Edward G.; Miami (OH); B10/18/1931 Cincinnati, OH			
1981 Hou	7-9-0	—	3 AFC-C
1982 Hou	1-8-0	—	13 AFC

YEAR TEAM	W-L-T	WP-LP	FINISH PLAYOFFS
1983 Hou	0-6-0	—	◇4 AFC-C
NFL 3	8-23-0	—	—
Billick, Brian Brian Harold; Air Force, Brigham Young; B2/28/1954 Fairborn, OH			
1999 Bal	8-8-0	—	3 AFC-C
2000 Bal	12-4-0	4-0	2 AFC-C WDCS‡
2001 Bal	10-6-0	1-1	2 AFC-C WD
2002 Bal	7-9-0	—	3 AFC-N
2003 Bal	10-6-0	0-1	1 AFC-N E
2004 Bal	9-7-0	—	2 AFC-N
2005 Bal	6-10-0	—	3 AFC-N
NFL 7	62-50-0	5-2	—
Blackbourn, Lisle Lisle William; Lawrence; B6/3/1899 Beetown, WI, D6/14/1963 Lancaster, WI			
1954 GB	4-8-0	—	5 NFL-W
1955 GB	6-6-0	—	3 NFL-W
1956 GB	4-8-0	—	5 NFL-W
1957 GB	3-9-0	—	6 NFL-W
NFL 4	17-31-0	—	—
Blood, Johnny* B11/27/1903			
1937 Pit	4-7-0	—	3 NFL-E
1938 Pit	2-9-0	—	5 NFL-E
1939 Pit	0-3-0	—	◇4 NFL-E
NFL 3	6-19-0	—	—
Boland, Pat Patrick Henry; Minnesota; B10/12/1906 Duluth, MN, D7/2/1971 Duluth, MN			
1946 ChiR-A	2-3-1	—	◆4 AAFC-W
Brandy, Joe Joseph H.; Notre Dame; B11/6/1897 Ogdensburg, NY, DJul 1971 Ogdensburg, NY			
1924 Min	0-6-0	—	17 NFL
Brenkert, Wayne* B3/5/1898			
1923 Akr	1-1-0	—	◆16 NFL
1924 Akr	2-6-0	—	13 NFL
NFL 2	3-7-0	—	—
Brewer, Untz* B11/21/1894			
1922 Akr	3-5-2	—	10 NFL
Brickley, Charlie Charles Edward; Harvard; B11/24/1891 Boston, MA, D12/28/1949 New York, NY			
1921 NYG	0-2-0	—	19 NFL
Bridges, Frank Frank D.; Baylor; B7/4/1890 Savannah, GA, D6/10/1970 San Antonio, TX			
1944 Bkn†	0-5-0	—	◆5 NFL-E
Brill, Marty Martin; Notre Dame; B3/13/1906 Philadelphia, PA, D4/30/1973 Whittier, CA			
1931 SI	3-3-1	—	◆7 NFL
Brooks, Rich Richard Llewellyn; Oregon State; B8/10/1941 Forest, CA			
1995 SL	7-9-0	—	3 NFC-W
1996 SL	6-10-0	—	3 NFC-W
NFL 2	13-19-0	—	—
Brown, Paul Paul Eugene; Miami (OH), Ohio State; B9/7/1908 Norwalk, OH, D8/5/1991 Cincinnati, OH; HOF 1967			
1946 Cle-A	12-2-0	1-0	1 AAFC-W L‡
1947 Cle-A	12-1-1	1-0	1 AAFC-W L‡
1948 Cle-A	14-0-0	1-0	1 AAFC-W L‡
1949 Cle-A	9-1-2	2-0	1 AAFC PL‡
AAFC 4	47-4-3	5-0	—
1950 Cle	10-2-0	2-0	1 NFL-A CL‡
1951 Cle	11-1-0	0-1	1 NFL-A L
1952 Cle	8-4-0	0-1	1 NFL-A L
1953 Cle	11-1-0	0-1	1 NFL-E L
1954 Cle	9-3-0	1-0	1 NFL-E L‡
1955 Cle	9-2-1	1-0	1 NFL-E L‡
1956 Cle	5-7-0	—	4 NFL-E
1957 Cle	9-2-1	0-1	1 NFL-E L
1958 Cle	9-3-0	0-1	1 NFL-E C
1959 Cle	7-5-0	—	2 NFL-E
1960 Cle	8-3-1	—	2 NFL-E
1961 Cle	8-5-1	—	3 NFL-E
1962 Cle	7-6-1	—	3 NFL-E
1968 Cin-A	3-11-0	—	5 AFL-W
1969 Cin-A	4-9-1	—	5 AFL-W
1970 Cin	8-6-0	0-1	1 AFL-C D
1971 Cin	4-10-0	—	4 AFC-C
1972 Cin	8-6-0	—	3 AFC-C
1973 Cin	10-4-0	0-1	1 AFC-C #D
1974 Cin	7-7-0	—	2 AFC-C
1975 Cin	11-3-0	0-1	2 AFC-C W
NFL 26	166-100-6	4-8	—
Bruney, Fred* B12/30/1931			
1985 Phi	1-0-0	—	◆4 NFC-E
Bryan, Johnny* B2/28/1897			
1925 Mil	0-6-0	—	17 NFL
1926 Mil	2-7-0	—	15 NFL
NFL 2	2-13-0	—	—

YEAR TEAM	W-L-T	WP-LP	FINISH PLAYOFFS
BUGEL, JOE Joseph John; Western Kentucky; B3/10/1940 Pittsburgh, PA			
1990 Phx	5-11-0	—	5 NFC-E
1991 Phx	4-12-0	—	5 NFC-E
1992 Phx	4-12-0	—	5 NFC-E
1993 Phx	7-9-0	—	4 NFC-E
1997 Oak	4-12-0	—	4 AFC-W
NFL 5	24-56-0	—	
BULLOUGH, HANK* B1/24/1934			
1978 NE†	0-1-0	—	◆1 AFC-E #D
1985 Buf	2-10-0	—	◆5 AFC-E
1986 Buf	2-7-0	—	◇4 AFC-E
NFL 3	4-18-0	—	
BURNS, JERRY Jerome Monahan; Michigan; B1/24/1927 Detroit, MI			
1986 Min	9-7-0	—	2 NFC-C
1987 Min	8-7-0	2-1	2 NFC-C WDC
1988 Min	11-5-0	1-1	2 NFC-C WD
1989 Min	10-6-0	0-1	1 NFC-C #D
1990 Min	6-10-0	—	2 NFC-C
1991 Min	8-8-0	—	3 NFC-C
NFL 6	52-43-0	3-3	
CALLAHAN, BILL Bill; Illinois Benedictine; B7/31/1956 Chicago, IL			
2002 Oak	11-5-0	2-1	1 AFC-W DCS
2003 Oak	4-12-0	—	3 AFC-W
NFL 2	15-17-0	2-1	
CAMPBELL, HUGH Hugh Thomas; Washington State; B5/21/1941 San Jose, CA			
1984 Hou	3-13-0	—	4 AFC-C
1985 Hou	5-9-0	—	◇4 AFC-C
NFL 2	8-22-0	—	
CAMPBELL, MARION* B5/25/1929			
1974 Atl	1-5-0	—	◆4 NFC-W
1975 Atl	4-10-0	—	3 NFC-W
1976 Atl	1-4-0	—	◇3 NFC-W
1983 Phi	5-11-0	—	4 NFC-E
1984 Phi	6-9-1	—	5 NFC-E
1985 Phi	6-9-0	—	◇4 NFC-E
1987 Atl	3-12-0	—	4 NFC-W
1988 Atl	5-11-0	—	4 NFC-W
1989 Atl	3-9-0	—	◇4 NFC-W
NFL 9	34-80-1	—	
CAMPO, DAVE David Cross; Central Connecticut State; B7/18/1947 New London, CT			
2000 Dal	5-11-0	—	4 NFC-E
2001 Dal	5-11-0	—	4 NFC-E
2002 Dal	5-11-0	—	4 NFC-E
NFL 3	15-33-0	—	
CAPERS, DOM Dominic; Mount Union; B8/7/1950 Cambridge, OH			
1995 Car	7-9-0	—	3 NFC-W
1996 Car	12-4-0	1-1	1 NFC-W #DC
1997 Car	7-9-0	—	2 NFC-W
1998 Car	4-12-0	—	4 NFC-W
2002 Hou	4-12-0	—	4 AFC-S
2003 Hou	5-11-0	—	3 AFC-S
2004 Hou	7-9-0	—	3 AFC-S
2005 Hou	2-14-0	—	4 AFC-S
NFL 8	48-80-0	1-1	
CARROLL, PETE Peter Clay; Pacific; B9/15/1951 San Francisco, CA			
1994 NYJ	6-10-0	—	5 AFC-E
1997 NE	10-6-0	1-1	1 AFC-E ED
1998 NE	9-7-0	0-1	4 AFC-E W
1999 NE	8-8-0	—	4 AFC-E
NFL 4	33-31-0	1-2	
CARSON, BUD Leon H.; North Carolina; B4/28/1931 Brackenridge, PA, D12/7/2005 Sarasota, FL			
1989 Cle	9-6-1	1-1	1 AFC-C DC
1990 Cle	2-7-0	—	◇4 AFC-C
NFL 2	11-13-1	1-1	
CASEY, EDDIE* B5/16/1894			
1935 Bos	2-8-1	—	4 NFL-E
CAWTHON, PETE Peter Willis; Southwestern (TX); B3/24/1898 Houston, TX, D12/31/1962 Houston, TX			
1943 Bkn	2-8-0	—	4 NFL-E
1944 Bkn	0-5-0	—	◇5 NFL-E
NFL 2	2-13-0	—	
CHAMBERLIN, GUY* B1/16/1894			
1922 Can	10-0-2	—	1 NFL
1923 Can	11-0-1	—	1 NFL
1924 Cle	7-1-1	—	1 NFL
1925 Fra	13-7-0	—	6 NFL
1926 Fra	14-1-2	—	1 NFL
1927 ChiC	3-7-1	—	9 NFL
NFL 6	58-16-7	—	

YEAR TEAM	W-L-T	WP-LP	FINISH PLAYOFFS
CHECKAYE, COONIE* B1/6/1893			
1921 Mun	0-2-0	—	19 NFL
CHEVIGNY, JACK John Edward; Notre Dame; B8/14/1906 Hammond, IN, D2/19/1945			
1932 ChiC	2-6-2	—	7 NFL
CHRISTIANSEN, JACK* B12/20/1928			
1963 SF	2-9-0	—	◆7 NFL-W
1964 SF	4-10-0	—	7 NFL-W
1965 SF	7-6-1	—	4 NFL-W
1966 SF	6-6-2	—	4 NFL-W
1967 SF	7-7-0	—	3 NFL-Cnl
NFL 5	26-38-3	—	
CLARK, ALGY* B1904			
1934 Cin	0-8-0	—	5 NFL-W
CLARK, DUTCH* B10/11/1906			
1937 Det	7-4-0	—	2 NFL-W
1938 Det	7-4-0	—	2 NFL-W
1939 Cle	5-5-1	—	4 NFL-W
1940 Cle	4-6-1	—	4 NFL-W
1941 Cle	2-9-0	—	5 NFL-W
1942 Cle	5-6-0	—	3 NFL-W
NFL 6	30-34-2	—	
CLARK, MONTE* B1/24/1937			
1976 SF	8-6-0	—	2 NFC-W
1978 Det	7-9-0	—	3 NFC-C
1979 Det	2-14-0	—	5 NFC-C
1980 Det	9-7-0	—	2 NFC-C #
1981 Det	8-8-0	—	2 NFC-C
1982 Det	4-5-0	0-1	8 NFC #P
1983 Det	9-7-0	0-1	1 NFC-C D
1984 Det	4-11-1	—	4 NFC-C
NFL 8	51-67-1	0-2	
CLARK, POTSY George M.; William & Vashti; B3/20/1894 Carthage, IL, D11/8/1972 La Jolla, CA			
1931 Por	11-3-0	—	2 NFL
1932 Por	6-2-4	—	3 NFL
1933 Por	6-5-0	—	2 NFL-W
1934 Det	10-3-0	—	2 NFL-W
1935 Det	7-3-2	1-0	1 NFL-W L‡
1936 Det	8-4-0	—	3 NFL-W
1937 Bkn	3-7-1	—	4 NFL-E
1938 Bkn	4-4-3	—	3 NFL-E
1939 Bkn	4-6-1	—	3 NFL-E
1940 Det	5-5-1	—	3 NFL-W
NFL 10	64-42-12	1-0	
COFALL, STAN* B5/5/1894			
1920 Cle	0-2-1	—	◇6 NFL
COLLIER, BLANTON Blanton Long; Georgetown (KY); B7/2/1906 Millersburg, KY, D3/22/1983 Houston, TX			
1963 Cle	10-4-0	—	2 NFL-E
1964 Cle	10-3-1	1-0	1 NFL-E L‡
1965 Cle	11-3-0	0-1	1 NFL-E L
1966 Cle	9-5-0	—	2 NFL-E
1967 Cle	9-5-0	0-1	1 NFL-Cny C
1968 Cle	10-4-0	1-1	1 NFL-Cny CL
1969 Cle	10-3-1	1-1	1 NFL-Cny CL
1970 Cle	7-7-0	—	2 AFL-C
NFL 8	76-34-2	3-4	
COLLIER, JOE Joel D.; Northwestern; B6/7/1932 Rock Island, IL			
1966 Buf-A	9-4-1	0-1	1 AFL-E L
1967 Buf-A	4-10-0	—	3 AFL-E
1968 Buf-A	0-2-0	—	◇5 AFL-E
NFL 3	13-16-1	0-1	
CONKRIGHT, BILL* B4/17/1914			
1962 Oak-A	1-8-0	—	◆4 AFL-W
CONZELMAN, JIMMY* B3/6/1898			
1921 RI	1-4-0	—	◆5 NFL
1922 RI	4-2-1	—	5 NFL
1922 Mil	0-3-0	—	◆12 NFL
1923 Mil	7-2-3	—	3 NFL
1925 Det	8-2-2	—	3 NFL
1926 Det	4-6-2	—	12 NFL
1927 Pro	8-5-1	—	5 NFL
1928 Pro	8-1-2	—	1 NFL
1929 Pro	4-6-2	—	8 NFL
1930 Pro	6-4-1	—	5 NFL
1940 ChiC	2-7-2	—	5 NFL-W
1941 ChiC	3-7-1	—	4 NFL-W
1942 ChiC	3-8-0	—	4 NFL-W
1946 ChiC	6-5-0	—	3 NFL-W
1947 ChiC	9-3-0	1-0	1 NFL-W L‡
1948 ChiC	11-1-0	0-1	1 NFL-W L
NFL 15	87-63-17	1-1	
CORNSWEET, AL* B7/16/1906			
1931 Cle†	2-8-0	—	8 NFL

YEAR TEAM	W-L-T	WP-LP	FINISH PLAYOFFS
CORYELL, DON Donald David; Washington; B10/17/1924 Seattle, WA			
1973 SL	4-9-1	—	4 NFC-E
1974 SL	10-4-0	0-1	1 NFC-E #D
1975 SL	11-3-0	0-1	1 NFC-E D
1976 SL	10-4-0	—	3 NFC-E #
1977 SL	7-7-0	—	3 NFC-E
1978 SD	8-4-0	—	◆2 AFC-W
1979 SD	12-4-0	0-1	1 AFC-W D
1980 SD	11-5-0	1-1	1 AFC-W #DC
1981 SD	10-6-0	1-1	1 AFC-W #DC
1982 SD	6-3-0	1-1	4 AFC PD
1983 SD	6-10-0	—	4 AFC-W
1984 SD	7-9-0	—	5 AFC-W
1985 SD	8-8-0	—	3 AFC-W
1986 SD	1-7-0	—	◇5 AFC-W
NFL 14	111-83-1	3-6	
COSLET, BRUCE* B8/5/1946			
1990 NYJ	6-10-0	—	4 AFC-E
1991 NYJ	8-8-0	0-1	2 AFC-E #W
1992 NYJ	4-12-0	—	4 AFC-E
1993 NYJ	8-8-0	—	3 AFC-E
1996 Cin	7-2-0	—	◆3 AFC-C
1997 Cin	7-9-0	—	4 AFC-C
1998 Cin	3-13-0	—	5 AFC-C
1999 Cin	4-12-0	—	5 AFC-C
2000 Cin	0-3-0	—	◇5 AFC-C
NFL 9	47-77-0	0-1	
COUGHLIN, FRANK* B2/28/1896			
1921 RI	0-1-1	—	◇5 NFL
COUGHLIN, TOM Thomas Richard; Syracuse; B8/31/1946 Waterloo, NY			
1995 Jax	4-12-0	—	5 AFC-C
1996 Jax	9-7-0	2-1	2 AFC-C #WDC
1997 Jax	11-5-0	0-1	2 AFC-C #W
1998 Jax	11-5-0	1-1	1 AFC-C ED
1999 Jax	14-2-0	1-1	1 AFC-C DCS
2000 Jax	7-9-0	—	4 AFC-C
2001 Jax	6-10-0	—	5 AFC-C
2002 Jax	6-10-0	—	3 AFC-S
2004 NYG	6-10-0	—	2 NFC-E
2005 NYG	11-5-0	0-1	1 NFC-E E
NFL 10	85-75-0	4-5	
COWHER, BILL* B5/8/1957			
1992 Pit	11-5-0	0-1	1 AFC-C D
1993 Pit	9-7-0	0-1	2 AFC-C #W
1994 Pit	12-4-0	1-1	1 AFC-C DC
1995 Pit	11-5-0	2-1	1 AFC-C DCS
1996 Pit	10-6-0	1-1	1 AFC-C ED
1997 Pit	11-5-0	1-1	1 AFC-C #DC
1998 Pit	7-9-0	—	3 AFC-C
1999 Pit	6-10-0	—	4 AFC-C
2000 Pit	9-7-0	—	3 AFC-C
2001 Pit	13-3-0	1-1	1 AFC-C DC
2002 Pit	10-5-1	1-1	1 AFC-N ED
2003 Pit	6-10-0	—	3 AFC-N
2004 Pit	15-1-0	1-1	1 AFC-N DC
2005 Pit	11-5-0	4-0	2 AFC-N #WDCS
NFL 14	141-82-1	12-9	
CREIGHTON, MILAN* B1/21/1908			
1935 ChiC	6-4-2	—	3 NFL-W
1936 ChiC	3-8-1	—	4 NFL-W
1937 ChiC	5-5-1	—	4 NFL-W
1938 ChiC	2-9-0	—	5 NFL-W
NFL 4	16-26-4	—	
CRENNEL, ROMEO Romeo; Western Kentucky; B6/18/1947 Lynchbug, VA			
2005 Cle	6-10-0	—	3 AFC-N
CROWE, CLEM Clem Frederick; Notre Dame; B10/18/1903 Lafayette, IN, D4/13/1983 Rochester, NY			
1949 Buf-A	4-1-1	0-1	◆4 AAFC P
1950 Bal	1-11-0	—	7 NFL-N
CROWLEY, JIM* B9/10/1902			
1947 ChiR-A	0-10-0	—	◇4 AAFC-W
CUNNINGHAM, GUNTHER Gunther; Oregon; B6/19/1946 Munich, Germany			
1999 KC	9-7-0	—	2 AFC-W #
2000 KC	7-9-0	—	3 AFC-W
NFL 2	16-16-0	—	
DAUGHERTY, RUSS* B1/31/1902			
1927 Fra†	4-4-2	—	◆7 NFL
DAVIS, AL Allen R.; Wittenberg, Syracuse; B7/4/1929 Brockton, MA; HOF 1992			
1963 Oak-A	10-4-0	—	2 AFL-W
1964 Oak-A	5-7-2	—	3 AFL-W
1965 Oak-A	8-5-1	—	2 AFL-W
NFL 3	23-16-3	—	

YEAR TEAM	W-L-T	WP-LP	FINISH PLAYOFFS
DAVIS, BUTCH Paul Hilton; Arkansas; B11/17/1951 Tahlequah, OK			
2001 Cle	7-9-0	—	3 AFC-C
2002 Cle	9-7-0	0-1	2 AFC-N #W
2003 Cle	5-11-0	—	4 AFC-N
2004 Cle	3-7-0	—	◇4 AFC-N
NFL 4	24-34-0	0-1	—
DAWSON, RED Lowell Potter; Tulane; B12/20/1906 Minneapolis, MN, D6/10/1983 Ocala, FL			
1946 Buf-A	3-10-1	—	2 AAFC-E
1947 Buf-A	8-4-2	—	2 AAFC-E
1948 Buf-A	7-7-0	1-1	1 AAFC-E DL
1949 Buf-A	1-4-1	—	◇4 AAFC P
AAFC 4	19-25-4	1-1	
DEGROOT, DUDLEY Dudley S.; Stanford; B11/20/1899 Chicago, IL, D5/5/1970 El Cajon, CA			
1944 Was	6-3-1	—	3 NFL-E
1945 Was	8-2-0	0-1	1 NFL-E L
NFL 2	14-5-1	0-1	—
1946 LAD-A	7-5-2	—	3 AAFC-W
1947 LAD-A	5-6-0	—	◇3 AAFC-W
AAFC 5	12-11-2	—	
DELL, HERB Herbert Edward; Oberlin; B1/28/1889 Columbus, OH, DJan 1964 Pinellas County, FL			
1922 Col	0-8-0	—	18 NFL
DEL RIO, JACK* B4/4/1963			
2003 Jax	5-11-0	—	3 AFC-S
2004 Jax	9-7-0	—	2 AFC-S
2005 Jax	12-4-0	0-1	2 AFC-S W
NFL 3	26-22-0	0-1	—
DEPLER, JACK* B1/6/1899			
1929 Ora	3-5-4	—	6 NFL
1930 Bkn	7-4-1	—	4 NFL
1931 Bkn	2-12-0	—	9 NFL
NFL 3	12-21-5	—	
DEVINE, DAN Daniel John; Minnesota-Duluth; B12/23/1924 Augusta, WI, D5/9/2002 Tempe, AZ			
1971 GB	4-8-2	—	4 NFC-C
1972 GB	10-4-0	0-1	1 NFC-C D
1973 GB	5-7-2	—	3 NFC-C
1974 GB	6-8-0	—	3 NFC-C
NFL 4	25-27-4	0-1	—
DEVORE, HUGH Hugh John; Notre Dame; B11/25/1910 Newark, NJ, D12/8/1992 Edmond, OK			
1953 GB†	0-2-0	—	◆6 NFL-W
1956 Phi	3-8-1	—	6 NFL-E
1957 Phi	4-8-0	—	5 NFL-E
NFL 3	7-18-1	—	
DIETZ, LONE STAR William; Macalester, Carlisle Indian; B8/17/1884 Pine Ridge, SD, D7/20/1964 Reading, PA			
1933 Bos	5-5-2	—	3 NFL-E
1934 Bos	6-6-0	—	2 NFL-E
NFL 2	11-11-2	—	
DIMEOLO, LUBY Albert; Pittsburgh; B10/27/1903 Youngstown, OH, DJun 1966			
1934 Pit	2-10-0	—	5 NFL-E
DITKA, MIKE* B10/18/1939			
1982 ChiB	3-6-0	—	11 NFC
1983 ChiB	8-8-0	—	2 NFC-C
1984 ChiB	10-6-0	1-1	1 NFC-C DC
1985 ChiB	15-1-0	3-0	1 NFC-C DCS‡
1986 ChiB	14-2-0	0-1	1 NFC-C D
1987 ChiB	11-4-0	0-1	1 NFC-C D
1988 ChiB	12-4-0	1-1	1 NFC-C DC
1989 ChiB	6-10-0	—	4 NFC-C
1990 ChiB	11-5-0	1-1	1 NFC-C ED
1991 ChiB	11-5-0	0-1	2 NFC-C W
1992 ChiB	5-11-0	—	3 NFC-C
1997 NO	6-10-0	—	4 NFC-W
1998 NO	6-10-0	—	3 NFC-W
1999 NO	3-13-0	—	5 NFC-W
NFL 14	121-95-0	6-6	
DOHERTY, MEL Melvin; Marietta; deceased Cincinnati, OH			
1921 Cin	1-3-0	—	13 NFL
DONELLI, ALDO Aldo T.; Duquesne; B7/22/1907 Morgan, PA, D8/9/1994 Fort Lauderdale, FL			
1941 Pit	0-5-0	—	◆◇5 NFL-E
1944 Cle	4-6-0	—	4 NFL-W
NFL 2	4-11-0	—	
DOOLEY, JIM* B2/8/1930			
1968 ChiB	7-7-0	—	2 NFL-Coa
1969 ChiB	1-13-0	—	4 NFL-Coa
1970 ChiB	6-8-0	—	3 NFC-C
1971 ChiB	6-8-0	—	3 NFC-C
NFL 4	20-36-0	—	

YEAR TEAM	W-L-T	WP-LP	FINISH PLAYOFFS
DORAIS, GUS Charles Emile; Notre Dame; B7/2/1891 Chippewa Falls, WI, D1/3/1954 Birmingham, AL			
1943 Det	3-6-1	—	3 NFL-W
1944 Det	6-3-1	—	2 NFL-W
1945 Det	7-3-0	—	2 NFL-W
1946 Det	1-10-0	—	5 NFL-W
1947 Det	3-9-0	—	5 NFL-W
NFL 5	20-31-2	—	
DOUDS, JAP* B4/21/1905			
1933 Pit	3-6-2	—	5 NFL-E
DOVE, BOB* B2/21/1921			
1946 ChiR-A†	2-2-1	—	◆◇4 AAFC-W
DOWHOWER, ROD Rodney Douglas; San Diego State; B4/15/1943 Ord, NE			
1985 Ind	5-11-0	—	4 AFC-E
1986 Ind	0-13-0	—	◇5 AFC-E
NFL 2	5-24-0	—	
DRISCOLL, PADDY* B1/11/1895			
1920 ChiC	6-2-2	—	4 NFL
1921 ChiC	3-3-2	—	9 NFL
1922 ChiC	8-3-0	—	3 NFL
1956 ChiB	9-2-1	0-1	1 NFL-W L
1957 ChiB	5-7-0	—	5 NFL-W
NFL 5	31-17-5	0-1	—
DRISKILL, WALT Walter Scott; Colorado; B9/20/1913, D7/25/1998 Delray Beach, CA			
1949 Bal-A	1-7-0	—	◆7 AAFC
DRULIS, CHUCK* B3/8/1918			
1961 SL†	2-0-0	—	◆4 NFL-E
DUNGY, TONY B10/6/1955			
1996 TB	6-10-0	—	4 NFC-C
1997 TB	10-6-0	1-1	2 NFC-C WD
1998 TB	8-8-0	—	3 NFC-C
1999 TB	11-5-0	1-1	1 NFC-C DC
2000 TB	10-6-0	0-1	2 NFC-C W
2001 TB	9-7-0	0-1	3 NFC-C W
2002 Ind	10-6-0	0-1	2 AFC-S W
2003 Ind	12-4-0	2-1	1 AFC-S #EDC
2004 Ind	12-4-0	1-1	1 AFC-S ED
2005 Ind	14-2-0	0-1	1 AFC-S D
NFL 10	102-58-0	5-8	—
EDWARDS, BILL William Miller; Ohio State, Wittenberg; B6/21/1905 Massillon, OH, D6/12/1987 Springfield, OH			
1941 Det	4-6-1	—	3 NFL-W
1942 Det	0-3-0	—	◇5 NFL-W
NFL 2	4-9-1	—	
EDWARDS, CAP* BMay 1888			
1921 Can	5-2-3	—	4 NFL
1923 Cle	3-1-3	—	5 NFL
1925 Cle	5-8-1	—	12 NFL
NFL 3	13-11-7	—	
EDWARDS, HERMAN* B4/27/1954			
2001 NYJ	10-6-0	0-1	3 AFC-E W
2002 NYJ	9-7-0	1-1	1 AFC-E #ED
2003 NYJ	6-10-0	—	3 AFC-E
2004 NYJ	10-6-0	1-1	2 AFC-E WD
2005 NYJ	4-12-0	—	4 AFC-E
NFL 5	39-41-0	2-3	—
EDWARDS, TURK* B9/28/1907			
1946 Was	5-5-1	—	3 NFL-E
1947 Was	4-8-0	—	4 NFL-E
1948 Was	7-5-0	—	2 NFL-E
NFL 3	16-18-1	—	
ERDELATZ, EDDIE Edward J.; St. Mary's (CA); B4/21/1913 San Francisco, CA, D11/11/1966 Burlingame, CA			
1960 Oak-A	6-8-0	—	3 AFL-W
1961 Oak-A	0-2-0	—	◇4 AFL-W
NFL 2	6-10-0	—	
ERHARDT, RON Ronald Peter; Jamestown (ND); B2/27/1932 Mandan, ND			
1978 NE†	0-1-0	—	◆1 AFC-E #D
1979 NE	9-7-0	—	2 AFC-E
1980 NE	10-6-0	—	2 AFC-E
1981 NE	2-14-0	—	4 AFC-E
NFL 4	21-28-0	—	
ERICKSON, DENNIS Dennis; Montana State; B3/24/1947 Everett, WA			
1995 Sea	8-8-0	—	3 AFC-W
1996 Sea	7-9-0	—	4 AFC-W
1997 Sea	8-8-0	—	3 AFC-W
1998 Sea	8-8-0	—	2 AFC-W
2003 SF	7-9-0	—	3 NFC-W
2004 SF	2-14-0	—	4 NFC-W
NFL 6	40-56-0	—	
ERICKSON, HAL* B3/10/1899			
1924 Mil	5-8-0	—	12 NFL

YEAR TEAM	W-L-T	WP-LP	FINISH PLAYOFFS
EWART, CHARLEY Charles Diven; Yale; B10/16/1915 Lynn, MA, D4/30/1990 Elk Grove, IL			
1949 NYB	1-10-1	—	5 NFL-E
EWBANK, WEEB Wilbur Charles; Miami (OH); B5/6/1907 Richmond, IN, D11/17/1998 Oxford, OH; HOF 1978			
1954 Bal	3-9-0	—	6 NFL-W
1955 Bal	5-6-1	—	4 NFL-W
1956 Bal	5-7-0	—	4 NFL-W
1957 Bal	7-5-0	—	3 NFL-W
1958 Bal	9-3-0	1-0	1 NFL-W L‡
1959 Bal	9-3-0	1-0	1 NFL-W L‡
1960 Bal	6-6-0	—	4 NFL-W
1961 Bal	8-6-0	—	3 NFL-W
1962 Bal	7-7-0	—	4 NFL-W
1963 NYJ-A	5-8-1	—	4 AFL-E
1964 NYJ-A	5-8-1	—	3 AFL-E
1965 NYJ-A	5-8-1	—	2 AFL-E
1966 NYJ-A	6-6-2	—	3 AFL-E
1967 NYJ-A	8-5-1	—	2 AFL-E
1968 NYJ-A	11-3-0	2-0	1 AFL-E LS‡
1969 NYJ-A	10-4-0	0-1	1 AFL-E P
1970 NYJ	4-10-0	—	3 AFL-E
1971 NYJ	6-8-0	—	3 AFC-E
1972 NYJ	7-7-0	—	2 AFC-E
1973 NYJ	4-10-0	—	4 AFC-E
NFL 20	130-129-7	4-1	—
FAIRBANKS, CHUCK Charles Leo; Michigan State; B6/10/1933 Detroit, MI			
1973 NE	5-9-0	—	3 AFC-E
1974 NE	7-7-0	—	3 AFC-E
1975 NE	3-11-0	—	4 AFC-E
1976 NE	11-3-0	0-1	2 AFC-E #W
1977 NE	9-5-0	—	3 AFC-E
1978 NE	11-4-0	0-1	◇1 AFC-E #D
NFL 6	46-39-0	0-2	—
FALCON, GUIL* B12/15/1892			
1920 ChiT	2-5-1	—	5 NFL
1922 Tol	5-2-2	—	4 NFL
1923 Tol	3-3-2	—	11 NFL
NFL 3	10-10-5	—	
FASSEL, JIM James Edward; USC, Long Beach State; B8/31/1949 Anaheim, CA			
1997 NYG	10-5-1	0-1	1 NFC-E E
1998 NYG	8-8-0	—	3 NFC-E
1999 NYG	7-9-0	—	3 NFC-E
2000 NYG	12-4-0	2-1	1 NFC-E DCS
2001 NYG	7-9-0	—	3 NFC-E
2002 NYG	10-6-0	0-1	2 NFC-E W
2003 NYG	4-12-0	—	4 NFC-E
NFL 7	58-53-1	2-3	—
FAULKNER, JACK Jack T.; Miami (OH); B4/4/1926 Youngstown, OH			
1962 Den-A	7-7-0	—	2 AFL-W
1963 Den-A	2-11-1	—	4 AFL-W
1964 Den-A	0-4-0	—	◇4 AFL-W
NFL 3	9-22-1	—	
FAUSCH, FRANK* B6/13/1895			
1921 Evv	3-2-0	—	6 NFL
1922 Evv	0-3-0	—	17 NFL
NFL 2	3-5-0	—	
FEARS, TOM* B12/3/1923			
1967 NO	3-11-0	—	4 NFL-Cap
1968 NO	4-9-1	—	3 NFL-Cny
1969 NO	5-9-0	—	3 NFL-Cap
1970 NO	1-5-1	—	◇4 NFC-W
NFL 4	13-34-2	—	
FELDMAN, MARTY Martin; Oregon, Stanford; B9/12/1922 Los Angeles, CA			
1961 Oak-A	2-10-0	—	◆4 AFL-W
1962 Oak-A	0-5-0	—	◇4 AFL-W
NFL 2	2-15-0	—	
FILCHOCK, FRANK* B10/18/1916			
1960 Den-A	4-9-1	—	4 AFL-W
1961 Den-A	3-11-0	—	3 AFL-W
NFL 2	7-20-1	—	
FISH, JACK John; none; B,			
1930 Nwk	1-4-1	—	◇11 NFL
FISHER, JEFF* B2/25/1958			
1994 Hou	1-5-0	—	◆4 AFC-C
1995 Hou	7-9-0	—	2 AFC-C
1996 Hou	8-8-0	—	3 AFC-C
1997 Ten	8-8-0	—	3 AFC-C
1998 Ten	8-8-0	—	2 AFC-C
1999 Ten	13-3-0	3-1	2 AFC-C WDC
2000 Ten	13-3-0	0-1	1 AFC-C D
2001 Ten	7-9-0	—	3 AFC-C
2002 Ten	11-5-0	1-1	1 AFC-S DC
2003 Ten	12-4-0	1-1	2 AFC-S #W
2004 Ten	5-11-0	—	4 AFC-S

YEAR TEAM	W-L-T	WP-LP	FINISH PLAYOFFS
2005 Ten	4-12-0	—	3 AFC-S
NFL 12	97-85-0	5-4	—

Flaherty, Ray* B9/1/1903

YEAR TEAM	W-L-T	WP-LP	FINISH PLAYOFFS
1936 Bos	7-5-0	0-1	1 NFL-E L
1937 Was	8-3-0	1-0	1 NFL-E L‡
1938 Was	6-3-2	—	2 NFL-E
1939 Was	8-2-1	—	2 NFL-E
1940 Was	9-2-0	0-1	1 NFL-E L
1941 Was	6-5-0	—	3 NFL-E
1942 Was	10-1-0	1-0	1 NFL-E L‡
NFL 7	54-21-3	2-2	—
1946 NYY-A	10-3-1	0-1	1 AAFC-E L
1947 NYY-A	11-2-1	0-1	1 AAFC-E L
1948 NYY-A	1-3-0	—	✧3 AAFC-E
1949 ChiH-A	4-8-0	—	5 AAFC
AAFC 12	26-16-2	0-2	—

Flores, Tom* B3/21/1937

YEAR TEAM	W-L-T	WP-LP	FINISH PLAYOFFS
1979 Oak	9-7-0	—	3 AFC-W
1980 Oak	11-5-0	4-0	2 AFC-W #WDCS
1981 Oak	7-9-0	—	4 AFC-W
1982 LARd	8-1-0	1-1	1 AFC PD
1983 LARd	12-4-0	3-0	1 AFC-W DCS‡
1984 LARd	11-5-0	0-1	3 AFC-W W
1985 LARd	12-4-0	0-1	1 AFC-W D
1986 LARd	8-8-0	—	4 AFC-W
1987 LARd	5-10-0	—	4 AFC-W
1992 Sea	2-14-0	—	5 AFC-W
1993 Sea	6-10-0	—	5 AFC-W
1994 Sea	6-10-0	—	5 AFC-W
NFL 12	97-87-0	8-3	—

Folwell, Bob Robert Cook; Pennsylvania; B2/17/1885 Mullica Hill, NJ, D1/8/1928 Philadelphia, PA

YEAR TEAM	W-L-T	WP-LP	FINISH PLAYOFFS
1925 NYG	8-4-0	—	4 NFL

Fontes, Wayne* B2/2/1940

YEAR TEAM	W-L-T	WP-LP	FINISH PLAYOFFS
1988 Det	2-3-0	—	◆4 NFC-C
1989 Det	7-9-0	—	3 NFC-C
1990 Det	6-10-0	—	2 NFC-C
1991 Det	12-4-0	1-1	1 NFC-C DC
1992 Det	5-11-0	—	3 NFC-C
1993 Det	10-6-0	0-1	1 NFC-C E
1994 Det	9-7-0	0-1	3 NFC-C #W
1995 Det	10-6-0	0-1	2 NFC-C W
1996 Det	5-11-0	—	5 NFC-C
NFL 9	66-67-0	1-4	—

Forsyth, Jack Walter Scott; Rochester; B5/4/1892 Rochester, NY, D12/19/1966 Rochester, NY

YEAR TEAM	W-L-T	WP-LP	FINISH PLAYOFFS
1920 Roc	6-3-2	—	13 NFL
1921 Roc	2-3-0	—	10 NFL
NFL 2	8-6-2	—	—

Forzano, Rick Richard Edward; Kent State; B11/20/1928 Akron, OH

YEAR TEAM	W-L-T	WP-LP	FINISH PLAYOFFS
1974 Det	7-7-0	—	2 NFC-C
1975 Det	7-7-0	—	2 NFC-C
1976 Det	1-3-0	—	✧3 NFC-C
NFL 3	15-17-0	—	—

Fox, John John; San Diego State; B2/8/1955 Virginia Beach, VA

YEAR TEAM	W-L-T	WP-LP	FINISH PLAYOFFS
2002 Car	7-9-0	—	4 NFC-S
2003 Car	11-5-0	3-1	1 NFC-S EDCS
2004 Car	7-9-0	—	3 NFC-S
2005 Car	11-5-0	2-1	1 NFC-S #EDC
NFL 4	36-28-0	5-2	—

Friedman, Benny* B3/18/1905

YEAR TEAM	W-L-T	WP-LP	FINISH PLAYOFFS
1930 NYG	2-0-0	—	◆2 NFL
1932 Bkn	3-9-0	—	6 NFL
NFL 2	5-9-0	—	—

Gailey, Chan Thomas Chandler; Florida; B1/5/1952 Gainesville, GA

YEAR TEAM	W-L-T	WP-LP	FINISH PLAYOFFS
1998 Dal	10-6-0	0-1	1 NFC-E E
1999 Dal	8-8-0	0-1	2 NFC-E W
NFL 2	18-14-0	0-2	—

Gansz, Frank Francis von Renssalaer; Navy; B11/22/1938 Altoona, PA

YEAR TEAM	W-L-T	WP-LP	FINISH PLAYOFFS
1987 KC	4-11-0	—	5 AFC-W
1988 KC	4-11-1	—	5 AFC-W
NFL 2	8-22-1	—	—

Garrett, Budge* B4/17/1893

YEAR TEAM	W-L-T	WP-LP	FINISH PLAYOFFS
1922 Mil	2-1-3	—	✧12 NFL

Getto, Mike Michael J.; Pittsburgh; B9/18/1905 Irwin, PA, D8/27/1960 Lawrence, KS

YEAR TEAM	W-L-T	WP-LP	FINISH PLAYOFFS
1942 Bkn	3-8-0	—	4 NFL-E

Gibbs, Joe Joe Jackson; San Diego State; B11/25/1940 Mocksville, NC; HOF 1996

YEAR TEAM	W-L-T	WP-LP	FINISH PLAYOFFS
1981 Was	8-8-0	—	4 NFC-E
1982 Was	8-1-0	4-0	1 NFC PDCS‡
1983 Was	14-2-0	2-1	1 NFC-E DCS
1984 Was	11-5-0	0-1	1 NFC-E D
1985 Was	10-6-0	—	3 NFC-E #
1986 Was	12-4-0	2-1	2 NFC-E WDC
1987 Was	11-4-0	3-0	1 NFC-E DCS‡
1988 Was	7-9-0	—	3 NFC-E
1989 Was	10-6-0	—	3 NFC-E
1990 Was	10-6-0	1-1	2 NFC-E WD
1991 Was	14-2-0	3-0	1 NFC-E DCS‡
1992 Was	9-7-0	1-1	3 NFC-E #WD
2004 Was	6-10-0	-	2 NFC-E
2005 Was	10-6-0	1-1	2 NFC-E WD
NFL 14	140-76-0	17-6	—

Gibron, Abe* B9/22/1925

YEAR TEAM	W-L-T	WP-LP	FINISH PLAYOFFS
1972 ChiB	4-9-1	—	4 NFC-C
1973 ChiB	3-11-0	—	4 NFC-C
1974 ChiB	4-10-0	—	4 NFC-C
NFL 3	11-30-1	—	—

Gibson, George* B10/2/1905

YEAR TEAM	W-L-T	WP-LP	FINISH PLAYOFFS
1930 Min	1-7-1	—	10 NFL
1930 Fra	2-3-0	—	◆9 NFL
NFL 1	3-10-1	—	—

Gilbride, Kevin Kevin; Southern Connecticut State; B8/27/1951 New Haven, CT

YEAR TEAM	W-L-T	WP-LP	FINISH PLAYOFFS
1997 SD	4-12-0	—	4 AFC-W
1998 SD	2-4-0	—	✧5 AFC-W
NFL 2	6-16-0	—	—

Gillies, Fred* B12/9/1895

YEAR TEAM	W-L-T	WP-LP	FINISH PLAYOFFS
1928 ChiC	1-5-0	—	9 NFL

Gillman, Sid Sidney; Ohio State; B10/26/1911 Minneapolis, MN, D1/3/2003 Carlsbad, CA; HOF 1983

YEAR TEAM	W-L-T	WP-LP	FINISH PLAYOFFS
1955 LARm	8-3-1	0-1	1 NFL-W L
1956 LARm	4-8-0	—	5 NFL-W
1957 LARm	6-6-0	—	4 NFL-W
1958 LARm	8-4-0	—	2 NFL-W
1959 LARm	2-10-0	—	6 NFL-W
1960 LAC-A	10-4-0	0-1	1 AFL-W L
1961 SD-A	12-2-0	0-1	1 AFL-W L
1962 SD-A	4-10-0	—	3 AFL-W
1963 SD-A	11-3-0	1-0	1 AFL-W L‡
1964 SD-A	8-5-1	0-1	1 AFL-W L
1965 SD-A	9-2-3	0-1	1 AFL-W L
1966 SD-A	7-6-1	—	3 AFL-W
1967 SD-A	8-5-1	—	3 AFL-W
1968 SD-A	9-5-0	—	3 AFL-W
1969 SD-A	4-5-0	—	✧3 AFL-W
1971 SD	4-6-0	—	✧3 AFC-W
1973 Hou	1-8-0	—	◆4 AFC-C
1974 Hou	7-7-0	—	2 AFC-C
NFL 18	122-99-7	1-5	—

Gillo, Hank* B10/5/1894

YEAR TEAM	W-L-T	WP-LP	FINISH PLAYOFFS
1920 Ham	2-5-0	—	11 NFL

Gilmer, Harry* B4/14/1926

YEAR TEAM	W-L-T	WP-LP	FINISH PLAYOFFS
1965 Det	6-7-1	—	6 NFL-W
1966 Det	4-9-1	—	6 NFL-W
NFL 2	10-16-2	—	—

Glanville, Jerry Jerry Michael; Montana State, Northern Michigan; B10/14/1941 Detroit, MI

YEAR TEAM	W-L-T	WP-LP	FINISH PLAYOFFS
1985 Hou	0-2-0	—	◆4 AFC-C
1986 Hou	5-11-0	—	4 AFC-C
1987 Hou	9-6-0	1-1	2 AFC-C WD
1988 Hou	10-6-0	1-1	2 AFC-C WD
1989 Hou	9-7-0	0-1	2 AFC-C W
1990 Atl	5-11-0	—	3 NFC-W
1991 Atl	10-6-0	1-1	2 NFC-W #WD
1992 Atl	6-10-0	—	3 NFC-W
1993 Atl	6-10-0	—	3 NFC-W
NFL 9	60-69-0	3-4	—

Golembeski, Archie* B5/25/1900

YEAR TEAM	W-L-T	WP-LP	FINISH PLAYOFFS
1925 Pro	6-5-1	—	10 NFL

Graham, Otto* B12/6/1921

YEAR TEAM	W-L-T	WP-LP	FINISH PLAYOFFS
1966 Was	7-7-0	—	5 NFL-E
1967 Was	5-6-3	—	3 NFL-Cap
1968 Was	5-9-0	—	3 NFL-Cap
NFL 3	17-22-3	—	—

Grant, Bud* B5/20/1927

YEAR TEAM	W-L-T	WP-LP	FINISH PLAYOFFS
1967 Min	3-8-3	—	4 NFL-Coa
1968 Min	8-6-0	0-1	1 NFL-Coa C
1969 Min	12-2-0	2-1	1 NFL-Coa CLS
1970 Min	12-2-0	0-1	1 NFC-C D
1971 Min	11-3-0	0-1	1 NFC-C D
1972 Min	7-7-0	—	3 NFC-C
1973 Min	12-2-0	2-1	1 NFC-C DCS
1974 Min	10-4-0	2-1	1 NFC-C DCS
1975 Min	12-2-0	0-1	1 NFC-C D
1976 Min	11-2-1	2-1	1 NFC-C DCS
1977 Min	9-5-0	1-1	1 NFC-C #DC
1978 Min	8-7-1	0-1	1 NFC-C #D
1979 Min	7-9-0	—	3 NFC-C
1980 Min	9-7-0	0-1	1 NFC-C #D
1981 Min	7-9-0	—	4 NFC-C
1982 Min	5-4-0	1-1	4 NFC PD
1983 Min	8-8-0	—	2 NFC-C
1985 Min	7-9-0	—	3 NFC-C
NFL 18	158-96-5	10-12	—

Green, Dennis Dennis; Iowa; B2/17/1949 Harrisburg, PA

YEAR TEAM	W-L-T	WP-LP	FINISH PLAYOFFS
1992 Min	11-5-0	0-1	1 NFC-C E
1993 Min	9-7-0	0-1	2 NFC-C W
1994 Min	10-6-0	0-1	1 NFC-C E
1995 Min	8-8-0	—	4 NFC-C
1996 Min	9-7-0	0-1	2 NFC-C #W
1997 Min	9-7-0	1-1	3 NFC-C WD
1998 Min	15-1-0	1-1	1 NFC-C D
1999 Min	10-6-0	1-1	2 NFC-C WD
2000 Min	11-5-0	1-1	1 NFC-C DC
2001 Min	5-10-0	—	✧4 NFC-C
2004 Arz	6-10-0	—	3 NFC-W
2005 Arz	5-11-0	—	3 NFC-W
NFL 12	108-83-0	4-8	—

Gregg, Forrest* B10/18/1933

YEAR TEAM	W-L-T	WP-LP	FINISH PLAYOFFS
1975 Cle	3-11-0	—	4 AFC-C
1976 Cle	9-5-0	—	3 AFC-C
1977 Cle	6-7-0	—	✧4 AFC-C
1980 Cin	6-10-0	—	4 AFC-C
1981 Cin	12-4-0	2-1	1 AFC-C DCS
1982 Cin	7-2-0	0-1	2 AFC P
1983 Cin	7-9-0	—	3 AFC-C
1984 GB	8-8-0	—	2 NFC-C
1985 GB	8-8-0	—	2 NFC-C
1986 GB	4-12-0	—	4 NFC-C
1987 GB	5-9-1	—	3 NFC-C
NFL 11	75-85-1	2-2	—

Griffen, Hal* B3/1/1902

YEAR TEAM	W-L-T	WP-LP	FINISH PLAYOFFS
1930 Por	5-6-3	—	7 NFL

Grigg, Tex* B2/15/1891

YEAR TEAM	W-L-T	WP-LP	FINISH PLAYOFFS
1925 Roc	0-6-1	—	17 NFL

Groh, Al Albert; Virginia; B7/13/1944 New York, NY

YEAR TEAM	W-L-T	WP-LP	FINISH PLAYOFFS
2000 NYJ	9-7-0	—	3 AFC-E

Gruden, Jon Jon; Dayton, Tennessee; B8/17/1963 Sandusky, OH

YEAR TEAM	W-L-T	WP-LP	FINISH PLAYOFFS
1998 Oak	8-8-0	—	2 AFC-W
1999 Oak	8-8-0	—	3 AFC-W
2000 Oak	12-4-0	1-1	1 AFC-W DC
2001 Oak	10-6-0	1-1	1 AFC-W ED
2002 TB	12-4-0	3-0	1 NFC-S DCS‡
2003 TB	7-9-0	—	3 NFC-S
2004 TB	5-11-0	—	4 NFC-S
2005 TB	11-5-0	0-1	2 NFC-S #W
NFL 8	73-55-0	5-3	—

Haines, Hinkey* B12/23/1898

YEAR TEAM	W-L-T	WP-LP	FINISH PLAYOFFS
1931 SI	1-3-0	—	✧7 NFL

Halas, George* B2/2/1895

YEAR TEAM	W-L-T	WP-LP	FINISH PLAYOFFS
1920 Dec	10-1-2	—	9 NFL
1921 ChiS	9-1-1	—	1 NFL
1922 ChiB	9-3-0	—	2 NFL
1923 ChiB	9-2-1	—	2 NFL
1924 ChiB	6-1-4	—	2 NFL
1925 ChiB	9-5-3	—	7 NFL
1926 ChiB	12-1-3	—	2 NFL
1927 ChiB	9-3-2	—	3 NFL
1928 ChiB	7-5-1	—	5 NFL
1929 ChiB	4-9-2	—	9 NFL
1933 ChiB	10-2-1	1-0	1 NFL-W L‡
1934 ChiB	13-0-0	0-1	1 NFL-W L
1935 ChiB	6-4-2	—	3 NFL-W
1936 ChiB	9-3-0	—	2 NFL-W
1937 ChiB	9-1-1	0-1	1 NFL-W L
1938 ChiB	6-5-0	—	3 NFL-W
1939 ChiB	8-3-0	—	2 NFL-W
1940 ChiB	8-3-0	1-0	1 NFL-W L‡
1941 ChiB	10-1-0	2-0	1 NFL-W DL‡
1942 ChiB	5-0-0	—	✧1 NFL-W L
1946 ChiB	8-2-1	1-0	1 NFL-W L‡
1947 ChiB	8-4-0	—	2 NFL-W
1948 ChiB	10-2-0	—	2 NFL-W
1949 ChiB	9-3-0	—	2 NFL-W
1950 ChiB	9-3-0	0-1	1 NFL-N C
1951 ChiB	7-5-0	—	4 NFL-N
1952 ChiB	5-7-0	—	5 NFL-N
1953 ChiB	3-8-1	—	4 NFL-W
1954 ChiB	8-4-0	—	2 NFL-W
1955 ChiB	8-4-0	—	2 NFL-W
1958 ChiB	8-4-0	—	2 NFL-W
1959 ChiB	8-4-0	—	2 NFL-W
1960 ChiB	5-6-1	—	5 NFL-W
1961 ChiB	8-6-0	—	3 NFL-W
1962 ChiB	9-5-0	—	3 NFL-W
1963 ChiB	11-1-2	1-0	1 NFL-W L‡
1964 ChiB	5-9-0	—	6 NFL-W
1965 ChiB	9-5-0	—	3 NFL-W
1966 ChiB	5-7-2	—	5 NFL-W
1967 ChiB	7-6-1	—	2 NFL-Coa
NFL 40	318-148-31	6-3	—

YEAR TEAM	W-L-T	WP-LP	FINISH PLAYOFFS
HANDLER, PHIL* B7/21/1908			
1943 ChiC	0-10-0	—	4 NFL-W
1944 C-P†	0-10-0	—	5 NFL-W
1945 ChiC	1-9-0	—	5 NFL-W
1949 ChiC†	2-4-0	—	◇3 NFL-W
1951 ChiC†	1-1-0	—	◆6 NFL-A
NFL 5	4-34-0		
HANDLEY, RAY Robert Ray; Stanford; B10/8/1944 Artesia, NM			
1991 NYG	8-8-0	—	4 NFC-E
1992 NYG	6-10-0	—	4 NFC-E
NFL 2	14-18-0		
HANIFAN, JIM James Martin Michael; California; B9/21/1933 Compton, CA			
1980 SL	5-11-0	—	4 NFC-E
1981 SL	7-9-0	—	5 NFC-E
1982 SL	5-4-0	0-1	4 NFC P
1983 SL	8-7-1	—	3 NFC-E
1984 SL	9-7-0	—	3 NFC-E #
1985 SL	5-11-0	—	5 NFC-E
1989 Atl	0-4-0	—	◆4 NFC-W
NFL 7	39-53-1	0-1	
HANLEY, BO* B12/14/1887			
1924 Ken†	0-4-1	—	16 NFL
HANLEY, DICK* B11/19/1894			
1946 ChiR-A	1-1-1	—	◇4 AAFC-W
HANSON, HAL* B11/18/1895			
1932 SI	2-7-3	—	8 NFL
HASLETT, JIM B12/9/1955			
2000 NO	10-6-0	1-1	1 NFC-W #ED
2001 NO	7-9-0	—	3 NFC-W
2002 NO	9-7-0	—	3 NFC-S
2003 NO	8-8-0	—	2 NFC-S
2004 NO	8-8-0	—	2 NFC-S #
2005 NO	3-13-0	—	4 NFC-S
NFL 6	45-51-0	1-1	
HECKER, NORB* B5/26/1927			
1966 Atl	3-11-0	—	7 NFL-E
1967 Atl	1-12-1	—	4 NFL-Cnl
1968 Atl	0-3-0	—	◇4 NFL-Cnl
NFL 3	4-26-1		
HEGARTY, JACK John Edward; Holy Cross, Georgetown; B6/9/1888 Newburyport, MA, deceased			
1921 Was	1-2-0	—	12 NFL
HEIN, MEL* B8/22/1909			
1947 LAD-A†	2-1-0	—	◆3 AAFC-W
HEFFERLE, ERNIE Ernest Edward; Duquesne; B1/12/1915 Herminie, PA			
1975 NO	1-7-0	—	◆4 NFC-W
HELDT, JACK* B12/2/1899			
1926 Col	1-6-0	—	19 NFL
HENDERSON, GUS Elmer Clinton; Oberlin; B3/10/1889 Oberlin, OH, D12/16/1965 Desert Hot Springs, GA			
1939 Det	6-5-0	—	3 NFL-W
HENDRIAN, DUTCH* B1/19/1896			
1923 Akr	0-5-0	—	◇16 NFL
HENNING, DAN* B6/21/1942			
1983 Atl	7-9-0	—	4 NFC-W
1984 Atl	4-12-0	—	4 NFC-W
1985 Atl	4-12-0	—	4 NFC-W
1986 Atl	7-8-1	—	3 NFC-W
1989 SD	6-10-0	—	5 AFC-W
1990 SD	6-10-0	—	4 AFC-W
1991 SD	4-12-0	—	5 AFC-W
NFL 7	38-73-1		
HENRY, PETE* B10/31/1897			
1926 Can†	1-9-3	—	20 NFL
1928 Pot	2-8-0	—	8 NFL
NFL 2	3-17-3		
HESS, WALLY* B10/28/1894			
1922 Ham	0-5-1	—	16 NFL
1923 Ham	1-5-1	—	15 NFL
1924 Ham	2-2-1	—	11 NFL
NFL 3	3-12-3		
HICKEY, RED* B2/14/1917			
1959 SF	7-5-0	—	3 NFL-W
1960 SF	7-5-0	—	2 NFL-W
1961 SF	7-6-1	—	5 NFL-W
1962 SF	6-8-0	—	5 NFL-W
1963 SF	0-3-0	—	◇7 NFL-W
NFL 5	27-27-1		
HICKS, MAX* B7/1/1894			
1921 Ham	1-3-1	—	13 NFL
HIGGINS, AUSTIN* B11/29/1897			
1921 Lou	0-2-0	—	19 NFL

YEAR TEAM	W-L-T	WP-LP	FINISH PLAYOFFS
HOLLWAY, BOB Robert; Michigan; B1/29/1926 Ann Arbor, MI			
1971 SL	4-9-1	—	4 NFC-E
1972 SL	4-9-1	—	4 NFC-E
NFL 2	8-18-2		
HOLMGREN, MIKE Michael George; USC; B6/15/1948 San Francisco, CA			
1992 GB	9-7-0	—	2 NFC-C #
1993 GB	9-7-0	1-1	2 NFC-C WD
1994 GB	9-7-0	1-1	2 NFC-C #WD
1995 GB	11-5-0	2-1	1 NFC-C #EDC
1996 GB	13-3-0	3-0	1 NFC-C DCS‡
1997 GB	13-3-0	2-1	1 NFC-C DCS
1998 GB	11-5-0	0-1	2 NFC-C W
1999 Sea	9-7-0	0-1	1 AFC-W #E
2000 Sea	6-10-0	—	4 AFC-W
2001 Sea	9-7-0	—	2 AFC-W
2002 Sea	7-9-0	—	2 NFC-W
2003 Sea	10-6-0	0-1	2 NFC-W W
2004 Sea	9-7-0	0-1	1 NFC-W E
2005 Sea	13-3-0	2-1	1 NFC-W DCS
NFL 14	138-86-0	11-9	—
HOLOVAK, MIKE* B9/19/1919			
1961 Bos-A	7-1-1	—	◆2 AFL-E
1962 Bos-A	9-4-1	—	2 AFL-E
1963 Bos-A	7-6-1	1-1	1 AFL-E DL
1964 Bos-A	10-3-1	—	2 AFL-E
1965 Bos-A	4-8-2	—	3 AFL-E
1966 Bos-A	8-4-2	—	2 AFL-E
1967 Bos-A	3-10-1	—	5 AFL-E
1968 Bos-A	4-10-0	—	4 AFL-E
1976 NYJ	0-1-0	—	◆4 AFC-E
NFL 9	52-47-9	1-1	
HOLTZ, LOU Louis Leo; Kent State; B1/16/1937 Follansbee, WV			
1976 NYJ	3-10-0	—	◇4 AFC-E
HORWEEN, ARNIE* B7/7/1898			
1923 ChiC	8-4-0	—	6 NFL
1924 ChiC	5-4-1	—	8 NFL
NFL 2	13-8-1		—
HOWELL, JIM LEE* B3/9/1915			
1954 NYG	7-5-0	—	3 NFL-E
1955 NYG	6-5-1	—	3 NFL-E
1956 NYG	8-3-1	1-0	1 NFL-E L‡
1957 NYG	7-5-0	—	2 NFL-E
1958 NYG	9-3-0	1-1	1 NFL-E CL
1959 NYG	10-2-0	0-1	1 NFL-E L
1960 NYG	6-4-2	—	3 NFL-E
NFL 7	53-27-4	2-2	
HUDSPETH, TOMMY Tommy Joe; Tulsa; B9/14/1931 Cherryvale, KS			
1976 Det	5-5-0	—	◆3 NFC-C
1977 Det	6-8-0	—	3 NFC-C
NFL 2	11-13-0		—
HUFFINE, KEN* B12/22/1897			
1920 Mun	0-1-0	—	12 NFL
HUGHES, ED* B10/23/1927			
1971 Hou	4-9-1	—	3 AFC-C
HUGHITT, TOMMY* B12/27/1892			
1920 Buf	9-1-1	—	2 NFL
1921 Buf	9-1-2	—	1 NFL
1922 Buf	5-4-1	—	9 NFL
1923 Buf	5-4-3	—	8 NFL
1924 Buf	6-5-0	—	9 NFL
NFL 5	34-15-7		
HUNTER, HAL Harold; Pittsburgh; B6/3/1934 Canonsburg, PA			
1984 Ind	0-1-0	—	◆4 AFC-E
IMLAY, TUT* B3/20/1902			
1926 LA†	6-3-1	—	7 NFL
INFANTE, LINDY Gelindo; Florida; B3/27/1940 Miami, FL			
1988 GB	4-12-0	—	4 NFC-C
1989 GB	10-6-0	—	2 NFC-C #
1990 GB	6-10-0	—	2 NFC-C
1991 GB	4-12-0	—	4 NFC-C
1996 Ind	9-7-0	0-1	3 AFC-E #W
1997 Ind	3-13-0	—	5 AFC-E
NFL 6	36-60-0	0-1	—
ISBELL, CECIL* B7/11/1915			
1947 Bal-A	2-11-1	—	4 AAFC-E
1948 Bal-A	7-7-0	0-1	1 AAFC-E D
1949 Bal-A	0-4-0	—	◇7 AAFC
AAFC 3	9-22-1	0-1	—
1951 ChiC†	1-1-0	—	◆6 NFL-A
IVY, POP* B1/25/1916			
1958 ChiC	2-9-1	—	5 NFL-E
1959 ChiC	2-10-0	—	6 NFL-E

YEAR TEAM	W-L-T	WP-LP	FINISH PLAYOFFS
1960 SL	6-5-1	—	4 NFL-E
1961 SL	5-7-0	—	◇4 NFL-E
1962 Hou-A	11-3-0	0-1	1 AFL-E L
1963 Hou-A	6-8-0	—	3 AFL-E
NFL 6	32-42-2	0-1	
JAURON, DICK* B10/7/1950			
1999 ChiB	6-10-0	—	5 NFC-C
2000 ChiB	5-11-0	—	5 NFC-C
2001 ChiB	13-3-0	0-1	1 NFC-C D
2002 ChiB	4-12-0	—	3 NFC-N
2003 ChiB	7-9-0	—	3 NFC-N
2005 Det	1-4-0	—	◆3 NFC-N
NFL 6	36-49-0	0-1	
JOESTING, HERB* B4/17/1905			
1929 Min	1-9-0	—	11 NFL
JOHNSON, BILL* B7/14/1926			
1976 Cin	10-4-0	—	2 AFC-C #
1977 Cin	8-6-0	—	2 AFC-C
1978 Cin	0-5-0	—	◇4 AFC-C
NFL 3	18-15-0		
JOHNSON, HARVEY* B6/22/1919			
1968 Buf-A	1-10-1	—	◆5 AFL-E
1971 Buf	1-13-0	—	5 AFC-E
NFL 2	2-23-1		
JOHNSON, JIMMY James William; Arkansas; B7/16/1943 Port Arthur, TX; HOF 1994			
1989 Dal	1-15-0	—	5 NFC-E
1990 Dal	7-9-0	—	4 NFC-E WD
1991 Dal	11-5-0	1-1	2 NFC-E WD
1992 Dal	13-3-0	3-0	1 NFC-E DCS‡
1993 Dal	12-4-0	3-0	1 NFC-E DCS‡
1996 Mia	8-8-0	—	4 AFC-E
1997 Mia	9-7-0	0-1	2 AFC-E #W
1998 Mia	10-6-0	1-1	2 AFC-E WD
1999 Mia	9-7-0	1-1	3 AFC-E WD
NFL 9	80-64-0	9-4	—
JOHNSOS, LUKE* B12/6/1905			
1942 ChiB†	6-0-0	0-1	◆1 NFL-W L
1943 ChiB†	8-1-1	1-0	1 NFL-W L‡
1944 ChiB†	6-3-1	—	2 NFL-W
1945 ChiB†	3-7-0	—	4 NFL-W
NFL 4	23-11-2	1-1	—
JOLLEY, AL* B9/29/1899			
1929 Buf	1-7-1	—	10 NFL
1933 Cin	0-3-0	—	◇4 NFL-W
NFL 2	1-10-1		—
JONES, JUNE* B2/19/1953			
1994 Atl	7-9-0	—	2 NFC-W
1995 Atl	9-7-0	0-1	2 NFC-W #W
1996 Atl	3-13-0	—	4 NFC-W
1998 SD	3-7-0	—	◆5 AFC-W
NFL 4	22-36-0	0-1	
JONES, RALPH Ralph Robert; Wabash; B1880, D7/25/1951 Boulder, CO			
1930 ChiB	9-4-1	—	3 NFL
1931 ChiB	8-5-0	—	3 NFL
1932 ChiB	7-1-6	—	1 NFL
NFL 3	24-10-7		
KARCIS, BULL* B12/3/1908			
1942 Det	0-8-0	—	◆5 NFL-W
KENDRICK, JIM* B8/22/1893			
1923 Lou	0-3-0	—	19 NFL
1926 Buf	4-4-2	—	9 NFL
NFL 2	4-7-2		—
KEOGH, JACK John Joseph; Pennsylvania; B6/17/1886 South Hadley Falls, PA, D2/13/1955 Holyoke, MA			
1926 Har	3-7-0	—	13 NFL
KHAYAT, ED* B9/14/1935			
1971 Phi	6-4-1	—	◆3 NFC-E
1972 Phi	2-11-1	—	5 NFC-E
NFL 2	8-15-2		—
KIESLING, WALT* B3/27/1903			
1939 Pit	1-6-1	—	◆4 NFL-E
1940 Pit	2-7-2	—	4 NFL-E
1941 Pit	1-2-1	—	◆5 NFL-E
1942 Pit	7-4-0	—	2 NFL-E
1943 P-P†	5-4-1	—	3 NFL-E
1944 C-P†	0-10-0	—	5 NFL-W
1954 Pit	5-7-0	—	4 NFL-E
1955 Pit	4-8-0	—	6 NFL-E
1956 Pit	5-7-0	—	4 NFL-E
NFL 9	30-55-5		
KNOX, CHUCK Charles Robert; Juniata; B4/27/1932 Sewickley, PA			
1973 LARm	12-2-0	0-1	1 NFC-W D
1974 LARm	10-4-0	1-1	1 NFC-W DC
1975 LARm	12-2-0	1-1	1 NFC-W DC

YEAR TEAM	W-L-T	WP-LP	FINISH PLAYOFFS
1976 LARm	10-3-1	1-1	1 NFC-W DC
1977 LARm	10-4-0	0-1	1 NFC-W D
1978 Buf	5-11-0	—	4 AFC-E
1979 Buf	7-9-0	—	4 AFC-E
1980 Buf	11-5-0	0-1	1 AFC-E D
1981 Buf	10-6-0	1-1	3 AFC-E #WD
1982 Buf	4-5-0	—	9 AFC #
1983 Sea	9-7-0	2-1	2 AFC-W #WDC
1984 Sea	12-4-0	1-1	2 AFC-W WD
1985 Sea	8-8-0	—	3 AFC-W
1986 Sea	10-6-0	—	3 AFC-W #
1987 Sea	9-6-0	0-1	2 AFC-W W
1988 Sea	9-7-0	0-1	1 AFC-W D
1989 Sea	7-9-0	—	4 AFC-W
1990 Sea	9-7-0	—	3 AFC-W #
1991 Sea	7-9-0	—	4 AFC-W
1992 LARm	6-10-0	—	3 NFC-W
1993 LARm	5-11-0	—	4 NFC-W
1994 LARm	4-12-0	—	4 NFC-W
NFL 22	186-147-1	7-11	—

KOPF, HERB Herbert M.; Washington & Jefferson; B2/3/1895 Winsted, CT, DJan 1967 Caldwell, NJ

YEAR TEAM	W-L-T	WP-LP	FINISH PLAYOFFS
1944 Bos	2-8-0	—	4 NFL-E
1945 Bos	3-6-1	—	3 NFL-E
1946 Bos	2-8-1	—	5 NFL-E
NFL 3	7-22-2	—	—

KOPPISCH, WALT* B6/6/1901

YEAR TEAM	W-L-T	WP-LP	FINISH PLAYOFFS
1925 Buf	1-6-2	—	15 NFL

KOTITE, RICH* B10/13/1942

YEAR TEAM	W-L-T	WP-LP	FINISH PLAYOFFS
1991 Phi	10-6-0	—	3 NFC-E #
1992 Phi	11-5-0	1-1	2 NFC-E WD
1993 Phi	8-8-0	—	3 NFC-E
1994 Phi	7-9-0	—	4 NFC-E
1995 NYJ	3-13-0	—	5 AFC-E
1996 NYJ	1-15-0	—	5 AFC-E
NFL 6	40-56-0	1-1	—

KRAEHE, OLLIE* B8/22/1898

YEAR TEAM	W-L-T	WP-LP	FINISH PLAYOFFS
1923 SL	1-4-2	—	14 NFL

KUBALE, ED Edwin A.; Centre; B11/22/1899 South Bend, IN, D2/4/1971 Danville, KY

YEAR TEAM	W-L-T	WP-LP	FINISH PLAYOFFS
1944 Bkn†	0-5-0	—	◆5 NFL-E

KUHARICH, JOE* B4/14/1917

YEAR TEAM	W-L-T	WP-LP	FINISH PLAYOFFS
1952 ChiC	4-8-0	—	5 NFL-A
1954 Was	3-9-0	—	5 NFL-E
1955 Was	8-4-0	—	2 NFL-E
1956 Was	6-6-0	—	3 NFL-E
1957 Was	5-6-1	—	4 NFL-E
1958 Was	4-7-1	—	4 NFL-E
1964 Phi	6-8-0	—	3 NFL-E
1965 Phi	5-9-0	—	5 NFL-E
1966 Phi	9-5-0	—	2 NFL-E
1967 Phi	6-7-1	—	2 NFL-Cap
1968 Phi	2-12-0	—	4 NFL-Cap
NFL 11	58-81-3	—	—

KUHLMANN, HANK Henry Norman; Missouri; B10/6/1937 St. Louis, MO

YEAR TEAM	W-L-T	WP-LP	FINISH PLAYOFFS
1989 Phx	0-5-0	—	◆4 NFC-E

KUSH, FRANK Frank Joseph; Michigan State; B1/20/1929 Windber, PA

YEAR TEAM	W-L-T	WP-LP	FINISH PLAYOFFS
1982 Bal	0-8-1	—	14 AFC
1983 Bal	7-9-0	—	4 AFC-E
1984 Ind	4-11-0	—	✧4 AFC-E
NFL 3	11-28-1	—	—

LAIRD, JIM* B9/10/1897

YEAR TEAM	W-L-T	WP-LP	FINISH PLAYOFFS
1926 Pro	5-7-1	—	11 NFL

LAMBEAU, CURLY* B4/9/1898

YEAR TEAM	W-L-T	WP-LP	FINISH PLAYOFFS
1921 GB	3-2-1	—	6 NFL
1922 GB	4-3-3	—	7 NFL
1923 GB	7-2-1	—	3 NFL
1924 GB	7-4-0	—	6 NFL
1925 GB	8-5-0	—	9 NFL
1926 GB	7-3-3	—	5 NFL
1927 GB	7-2-1	—	2 NFL
1928 GB	6-4-3	—	4 NFL
1929 GB	12-0-1	—	1 NFL
1930 GB	10-3-1	—	1 NFL
1931 GB	12-2-0	—	1 NFL
1932 GB	10-3-1	—	2 NFL
1933 GB	5-7-1	—	3 NFL-W
1934 GB	7-6-0	—	3 NFL-W
1935 GB	8-4-0	—	2 NFL-W
1936 GB	10-1-1	1-0	1 NFL-W L‡
1937 GB	7-4-0	—	2 NFL-W
1938 GB	8-3-0	0-1	1 NFL-W L
1939 GB	9-2-0	1-0	1 NFL-W L‡
1940 GB	6-4-1	—	2 NFL-W
1941 GB	10-1-0	0-1	1 NFL-W D
1942 GB	8-2-1	—	2 NFL-W
1943 GB	7-2-1	—	2 NFL-W
1944 GB	8-2-0	1-0	1 NFL-W L‡
1945 GB	6-4-0	—	3 NFL-W
1946 GB	6-5-0	—	3 NFL-W
1947 GB	6-5-1	—	3 NFL-W
1948 GB	3-9-0	—	4 NFL-W
1949 GB	2-10-0	—	5 NFL-W
1950 ChiC	5-7-0	—	5 NFL-A
1951 ChiC	2-8-0	—	✧6 NFL-A
1952 Was	4-8-0	—	5 NFL-A
1953 Was	6-5-1	—	3 NFL-E
NFL 33	226-132-22	3-2	—

LANDRY, TOM* B9/11/1924

YEAR TEAM	W-L-T	WP-LP	FINISH PLAYOFFS
1960 Dal	0-11-1	—	7 NFL-W
1961 Dal	4-9-1	—	6 NFL-E
1962 Dal	5-8-1	—	5 NFL-E
1963 Dal	4-10-0	—	5 NFL-E
1964 Dal	5-8-1	—	5 NFL-E
1965 Dal	7-7-0	—	2 NFL-E
1966 Dal	10-3-1	0-1	1 NFL-E L
1967 Dal	9-5-0	1-1	1 NFL-Cap CL
1968 Dal	12-2-0	0-1	1 NFL-Cap C
1969 Dal	11-2-1	0-1	1 NFL-Cap C
1970 Dal	10-4-0	2-1	1 NFC-E DCS
1971 Dal	11-3-0	3-0	1 NFC-E DCS‡
1972 Dal	10-4-0	1-1	2 NFC-E WC
1973 Dal	10-4-0	1-1	1 NFC-E #DC
1974 Dal	8-6-0	—	3 NFC-E
1975 Dal	10-4-0	2-1	2 NFC-E WCS
1976 Dal	11-3-0	0-1	1 NFC-E D
1977 Dal	12-2-0	3-0	1 NFC-E DCS‡
1978 Dal	12-4-0	2-1	1 NFC-E DCS
1979 Dal	11-5-0	0-1	1 NFC-E #D
1980 Dal	12-4-0	2-1	2 NFC-E #WDC
1981 Dal	12-4-0	1-1	1 NFC-E DC
1982 Dal	6-3-0	2-1	2 NFC PC
1983 Dal	12-4-0	0-1	2 NFC-E W
1984 Dal	9-7-0	—	4 NFC-E #
1985 Dal	10-6-0	0-1	1 NFC-E #D
1986 Dal	7-9-0	—	3 NFC-E
1987 Dal	7-8-0	—	2 NFC-E
1988 Dal	3-13-0	—	5 NFC-E
NFL 29	250-162-6	20-16	—

LEBEAU, DICK* B9/9/1937

YEAR TEAM	W-L-T	WP-LP	FINISH PLAYOFFS
2000 Cin	4-9-0	—	◆5 AFC-C
2001 Cin	6-10-0	—	5 AFC-C
2002 Cin	2-14-0	—	4 AFC-N

LEMM, WALLY Walter Horner; Carroll (WI); B10/23/1919 Chicago, IL, D10/2/1988 Waukesha, WI

YEAR TEAM	W-L-T	WP-LP	FINISH PLAYOFFS
1961 Hou-A	9-0-0	1-0	◆1 AFL-E L‡
1962 SL	4-9-1	—	6 NFL-E
1963 SL	9-5-0	—	3 NFL-E
1964 SL	9-3-2	—	2 NFL-E
1965 SL	5-9-0	—	5 NFL-E
1966 Hou-A	3-11-0	—	4 AFL-E
1967 Hou-A	9-4-1	0-1	1 AFL-E L
1968 Hou-A	7-7-0	—	2 AFL-E
1969 Hou-A	6-6-2	0-1	2 AFL-E P
1970 Hou	3-10-1	—	4 AFL-C
NFL 10	64-64-7	1-2	—

LEONARD, JIM* B2/14/1910

YEAR TEAM	W-L-T	WP-LP	FINISH PLAYOFFS
1945 Pit	2-8-0	—	5 NFL-E

LEVY, MARV Marvin Daniel; Coe College (IA), Harbard; B8/3/1925 Chicago, IL; HOF 2001

YEAR TEAM	W-L-T	WP-LP	FINISH PLAYOFFS
1978 KC	4-12-0	—	5 AFC-W
1979 KC	7-9-0	—	5 AFC-W
1980 KC	8-8-0	—	3 AFC-W
1981 KC	9-7-0	—	3 AFC-W
1982 KC	3-6-0	—	11 AFC
1986 Buf	2-5-0	—	◆4 AFC-E
1987 Buf	7-8-0	—	4 AFC-E
1988 Buf	12-4-0	1-1	1 AFC-E DC
1989 Buf	9-7-0	0-1	1 AFC-E D
1990 Buf	13-3-0	2-1	1 AFC-E DCS
1991 Buf	13-3-0	2-1	1 AFC-E DCS
1992 Buf	11-5-0	3-1	2 AFC-E #WDCS
1993 Buf	12-4-0	2-1	1 AFC-E DCS
1994 Buf	7-9-0	—	4 AFC-E
1995 Buf	10-6-0	1-1	1 AFC-E ED
1996 Buf	10-6-0	0-1	2 AFC-E W
1997 Buf	6-10-0	—	4 AFC-E
NFL 17	143-112-0	11-8	—

LEWIS, ART* B2/18/1911

YEAR TEAM	W-L-T	WP-LP	FINISH PLAYOFFS
1938 Cle	4-4-0	—	◆4 NFL-W

LEWIS, MARVIN Marvin; Idaho State; B9/23/1958 McDonald, PA

YEAR TEAM	W-L-T	WP-LP	FINISH PLAYOFFS
2003 Cin	8-8-0	—	2 AFC-N
2004 Cin	8-8-0	—	3 AFC-N
2005 Cin	11-5-0	0-1	1 AFC-N #E
NFL 3	27-21-0	0-1	—

LOMBARDI, VINCE Vincent Thomas; Fordham; B6/11/1913 Brooklyn, NY, D9/3/1970 Washington, DC; HOF 1971

YEAR TEAM	W-L-T	WP-LP	FINISH PLAYOFFS
1959 GB	7-5-0	—	3 NFL-W
1960 GB	8-4-0	0-1	1 NFL-W L
1961 GB	11-3-0	1-0	1 NFL-W L‡
1962 GB	13-1-0	1-0	1 NFL-W L‡
1963 GB	11-2-1	—	2 NFL-W
1964 GB	8-5-1	—	2 NFL-W
1965 GB	10-3-1	2-0	1 NFL-W CL‡
1966 GB	12-2-0	2-0	1 NFL-W LS‡
1967 GB	9-4-1	3-0	1 NFL-Coa CLS‡
1969 Was	7-5-2	—	2 NFL-Cap
NFL 10	96-34-6	9-1	—

LYONS, LEO Leo V.; none; B3/11/1892 Fairport, NY, D5/18/1976 Rochester, NY

YEAR TEAM	W-L-T	WP-LP	FINISH PLAYOFFS
1923 Roc	0-4-0	—	20 NFL
1924 Roc	0-3-0	—	◆18 NFL
NFL 2	0-7-0	—	—

MACKOVIC, JOHN John; Wake Forest; B10/1/1943 Barberton, OH

YEAR TEAM	W-L-T	WP-LP	FINISH PLAYOFFS
1983 KC	6-10-0	—	4 AFC-W
1984 KC	8-8-0	—	4 AFC-W
1985 KC	6-10-0	—	5 AFC-W
1986 KC	10-6-0	0-1	2 AFC-W #W
NFL 4	30-34-0	0-1	—

MACPHERSON, DICK Richard F.; Maine Maritime, Springfield; B11/4/1930 Old Town, ME

YEAR TEAM	W-L-T	WP-LP	FINISH PLAYOFFS
1991 NE	6-10-0	—	4 AFC-E
1992 NE	2-14-0	—	5 AFC-E
NFL 2	8-24-0	—	—

MADDEN, JOHN John Earl; Cal Poly-San Luis Obispo; B4/10/1936 Daly City, CA; HOF 2006

YEAR TEAM	W-L-T	WP-LP	FINISH PLAYOFFS
1969 Oak-A	12-1-1	1-1	1 AFL-W PL
1970 Oak	8-4-2	1-1	1 AFL-W DC
1971 Oak	8-4-2	—	2 AFC-W
1972 Oak	10-3-1	0-1	1 AFC-W D
1973 Oak	9-4-1	1-1	1 AFC-W DC
1974 Oak	12-2-0	1-1	1 AFC-W DC
1975 Oak	11-3-0	1-1	1 AFC-W DC
1976 Oak	13-1-0	3-0	1 AFC-W DCS‡
1977 Oak	11-3-0	1-1	2 AFC-W WC
1978 Oak	9-7-0	—	2 AFC-W
NFL 10	103-32-7	9-7	—

MAHRT, LOU* B7/30/1904

YEAR TEAM	W-L-T	WP-LP	FINISH PLAYOFFS
1927 Day	1-6-1	—	10 NFL

MALAVASI, RAY Raymondo Giuseppi Giovanni Baptiste; Army, Mississippi State; B11/8/1930 Passaic, NJ, D12/15/1987 Santa Ana, CA

YEAR TEAM	W-L-T	WP-LP	FINISH PLAYOFFS
1966 Den-A	4-8-0	—	◆4 AFL-W
1978 LARm	12-4-0	1-1	1 NFC-W DC
1979 LARm	9-7-0	2-1	1 NFC-W DCS
1980 LARm	11-5-0	0-1	2 NFC-W W
1981 LARm	6-10-0	—	3 NFC-W
1982 LARm	2-7-0	—	14 NFC
NFL 6	44-41-0	3-3	—

MARCHIBRODA, TED* B3/15/1931

YEAR TEAM	W-L-T	WP-LP	FINISH PLAYOFFS
1975 Bal	10-4-0	0-1	1 AFC-E #D
1976 Bal	11-3-0	0-1	1 AFC-E #D
1977 Bal	10-4-0	0-1	1 AFC-E #D
1978 Bal	5-11-0	—	4 AFC-E
1979 Bal	5-11-0	—	5 AFC-E
1992 Ind	9-7-0	—	3 AFC-E
1993 Ind	4-12-0	—	5 AFC-E
1994 Ind	8-8-0	—	3 AFC-E
1995 Ind	9-7-0	2-1	2 AFC-E WDC
1996 Bal	4-12-0	—	5 AFC-C
1997 Bal	6-9-1	—	5 AFC-C
1998 Bal	6-10-0	—	4 AFC-C
NFL 12	87-98-1	2-4	—

MARIUCCI, STEVE Steven; Northern Michigan; B11/4/1955 Iron Mountain, MI

YEAR TEAM	W-L-T	WP-LP	FINISH PLAYOFFS
1997 SF	13-3-0	1-1	1 NFC-W DC
1998 SF	12-4-0	1-1	2 NFC-W WDC
1999 SF	4-12-0	—	4 NFC-W
2000 SF	6-10-0	—	4 NFC-W
2001 SF	12-4-0	0-1	2 NFC-W W
2002 SF	10-6-0	1-1	1 NFC-W ED
2003 Det	5-11-0	—	4 NFC-N
2004 Det	6-10-0	—	3 NFC-N
2005 Det	4-7-0	—	✧3 NFC-N
NFL 9	72-67-0	3-4	—

MARSHALL, BILLY William H.; Detroit Mercy;

YEAR TEAM	W-L-T	WP-LP	FINISH PLAYOFFS
1920 Det	2-3-3	—	10 NFL
1921 Det	1-5-1	—	16 NFL
NFL 2	3-8-4	—	—

MARTZ, MIKE Mike; California-Santa Barbara, Fresno State; B5/13/1951 Sioux Falls, SD

YEAR TEAM	W-L-T	WP-LP	FINISH PLAYOFFS
2000 SL	10-6-0	0-1	2 NFC-W #W
2001 SL	14-2-0	2-1	1 NFC-W DCS

YEAR TEAM	W-L-T	WP-LP	FINISH PLAYOFFS
2002 SL	7-9-0	—	2 NFC-W
2003 SL	12-4-0	0-1	1 NFC-W D
2004 SL	8-8-0	1-1	2 NFC-W #WD
2005 SL	2-2-0	—	✧2 NFC-W
NFL 6	53-31-0	3-4	

MATHEWS, NED* B8/11/1918

| **1946** ChiR-A† | 2-2-1 | — | ◆✧4 AAFC-W |

MAZUR, JOHN John Edward; Notre Dame; B6/17/1930 Plymouth, PA

1970 Bos	1-6-0	—	◆5 AFL-E
1971 NE	6-8-0	—	3 AFC-E
1972 NE	2-7-0	—	✧5 AFC-E
NFL 3	9-21-0	—	

McCAFFERTY, DON* B3/12/1921

1970 Bal	11-2-1	3-0	1 AFL-E DCS‡
1971 Bal	10-4-0	1-1	2 AFC-E WC
1972 Bal	1-4-0	—	✧3 AFC-E
1973 Det	6-7-1	—	2 NFC-C
NFL 4	28-17-2	4-1	

McCORMACK, MIKE* B6/21/1930

1973 Phi	5-8-1	—	3 NFC-E
1974 Phi	7-7-0	—	4 NFC-E
1975 Phi	4-10-0	—	5 NFC-E
1980 Bal	7-9-0	—	4 AFC-E
1981 Bal	2-14-0	—	4 AFC-E
1982 Sea	4-3-0	—	◆10 AFC #
NFL 6	29-51-1	—	

McCULLEY, PETE Peter; Louisiana Tech; B11/29/1931 Franklin, MS, D11/25/1992 Pensacola Beach, FL

| **1978** SF | 1-8-0 | — | ✧4 NFC-W |

McEWAN, CAP John James; Minnesota, Army; B2/18/1893 Alexandria, MN, D8/9/1970 New York, NY

1933 Bkn	5-4-1	—	2 NFL-E
1934 Bkn	4-7-0	—	3 NFL-E
NFL 2	9-11-1	—	

McGALL, ALFRED Alfred

| **1930** Nwk | 0-3-0 | — | ◆✧11 NFL |

McGINNIS, DAVE David; TCU; B8/7/1951 Independence, KS

2000 Arz	1-8-0	—	◆5 NFC-E
2001 Arz	7-9-0	—	3 NFC-E
2002 Arz	5-11-0	—	4 NFC-W
2003 Arz	4-12-0	—	4 NFC-W
NFL 4	17-40-0	—	

McILWAIN, WALLY* B1/20/1903

| **1926** Rac | 0-2-0 | — | ◆16 NFL |

McKAY, JOHN John Harvey; Purdue, Oregon; B7/5/1923 Everettsville, WV, D6/10/2001 Tampa, FL

1976 TB	0-14-0	—	5 AFC-W
1977 TB	2-12-0	—	5 NFC-C
1978 TB	5-11-0	—	5 NFC-C
1979 TB	10-6-0	1-1	1 NFC-C #DC
1980 TB	5-10-1	—	4 NFC-C
1981 TB	9-7-0	0-1	1 NFC-C D
1982 TB	5-4-0	0-1	4 NFC P
1983 TB	2-14-0	—	5 NFC-C
1984 TB	6-10-0	—	3 NFC-C
NFL 9	44-88-1	1-3	

McKEEVER, ED Edward Clark Timothy; Notre Dame, Texas Tech; B8/25/1910 San Antonio, TX, D9/12/1974 Baton Rouge, LA

| **1948** ChiR-A | 1-13-0 | — | 4 AAFC-W |

McLEAN, RAY* B12/6/1915

1953 GB†	0-2-0	—	◆6 NFL-W
1958 GB	1-10-1	—	6 NFL-W
NFL 2	1-12-1	—	

McMILLIN, BO* B1/12/1895

1948 Det	2-10-0	—	5 NFL-W
1949 Det	4-8-0	—	4 NFL-W
1950 Det	6-6-0	—	4 NFL-N
1951 Phi	2-0-0	—	✧5 NFL-A
NFL 4	14-24-0	—	

McPEAK, BILL* B7/24/1926

1961 Was	1-12-1	—	7 NFL-E
1962 Was	5-7-2	—	4 NFL-E
1963 Was	3-11-0	—	6 NFL-E
1964 Was	6-8-0	—	3 NFL-E
1965 Was	6-8-0	—	4 NFL-E
NFL 5	21-46-3	—	

McVAY, JOHN John E.; Miami (OH); B1/5/1931 Bellaire, OH

1976 NYG	3-4-0	—	✧5 NFC-E
1977 NYG	5-9-0	—	4 NFC-E
1978 NYG	6-10-0	—	4 NFC-E
NFL 3	14-23-0	—	

MEAGHER, JACK* B10/1/1896

| **1946** Mia-A | 1-5-0 | — | ✧4 AAFC-E |

YEAR TEAM	W-L-T	WP-LP	FINISH PLAYOFFS
MEHRE, HARRY* B9/18/1901			
1923 Min	2-5-2	—	13 NFL

MEYER, KEN Ken; Denison; B7/14/1926 Erie, PA

| **1977** SF | 5-9-0 | — | 3 NFC-W |

MEYER, RON Ronald Shaw; Purdue; B2/17/1941 Westerville, OH

1982 NE	5-4-0	0-1	7 AFC P
1983 NE	8-8-0	—	2 AFC-E
1984 NE	5-3-0	—	✧2 AFC-E
1986 Ind	3-0-0	—	◆5 AFC-E
1987 Ind	9-6-0	0-1	1 AFC-E D
1988 Ind	9-7-0	—	2 AFC-E
1989 Ind	8-8-0	—	2 AFC-E
1990 Ind	7-9-0	—	3 AFC-E
1991 Ind	0-5-0	—	✧5 AFC-E
NFL 9	54-50-0	0-2	

MICHAELS, WALT* B10/16/1929

1977 NYJ	3-11-0	—	4 AFC-E
1978 NYJ	8-8-0	—	3 AFC-E
1979 NYJ	8-8-0	—	3 AFC-E
1980 NYJ	4-12-0	—	5 AFC-E
1981 NYJ	10-5-1	0-1	2 AFC-E W
1982 NYJ	6-3-0	2-1	4 AFC PDC
NFL 6	39-47-1	2-2	

MICHELOSEN, JOHN John Pollock; Pittsburgh; B2/13/1916 Ambridge, PA, D10/17/1982 San Diego, CA

1948 Pit	4-8-0	—	3 NFL-E
1949 Pit	6-5-1	—	2 NFL-E
1950 Pit	6-6-0	—	3 NFL-A
1951 Pit	4-7-1	—	4 NFL-A
NFL 4	20-26-2	—	

MILLER, RED Robert N.; Western Illinois; B10/31/1927 Macomb, IL

1977 Den	12-2-0	2-1	1 AFC-W DCS
1978 Den	10-6-0	0-1	1 AFC-W D
1979 Den	10-6-0	0-1	2 AFC-W W
1980 Den	8-8-0	—	3 AFC-W
NFL 4	40-22-0	2-3	

MILLNER, WAYNE* B1/31/1913

| **1951** Phi | 2-8-0 | — | ◆5 NFL-A |

MODZELEWSKI, DICK* B2/16/1931

| **1977** Cle | 0-1-0 | — | ◆4 AFC-C |

MOELLER, GARY Gary O.; Ohio State; B1/26/1941 Lima, OH

| **2000** Det | 4-3-0 | — | ◆3 NFC-C |

MOLESWORTH, KEITH* B10/20/1905

| **1953** Bal | 3-9-0 | — | 5 NFL-W |

MORA, JIM James Ernest; Occidental, USC; B5/24/1935 Glendale, CA

1986 NO	7-9-0	—	4 NFC-W
1987 NO	12-3-0	0-1	2 NFC-W W
1988 NO	10-6-0	—	3 NFC-W #
1989 NO	9-7-0	—	3 NFC-W
1990 NO	8-8-0	0-1	2 NFC-W W
1991 NO	11-5-0	0-1	1 NFC-W E
1992 NO	12-4-0	0-1	2 NFC-W
1993 NO	8-8-0	—	2 NFC-W
1994 NO	7-9-0	—	2 NFC-W
1995 NO	7-9-0	—	3 NFC-W
1996 NO	2-6-0	—	✧4 NFC-W
1998 Ind	3-13-0	—	5 AFC-E
1999 Ind	13-3-0	0-1	1 AFC-E D
2000 Ind	10-6-0	0-1	2 AFC-E W
2001 Ind	6-10-0	—	4 AFC-E
NFL 15	125-106-0	0-6	

MORA, JIM JR. James Ernest; Washington; B11/19/1961 Los Angeles, CA

2004 Atl	11-5-0	1-1	1 NFC-S DC
2005 Atl	8-8-0	—	3 NFC-S
NFL 2	19-13-0	1-1	

MORAN, CHARLEY Charles Barthell; Bethel (KY); B2/22/1878 Nashville, TN, D6/14/1949 Horse Cave, KY

| **1927** Fra | 2-5-1 | — | ✧7 NFL |

MORNHINWEG, MARTY Marty; Montana; B3/29/1962 Edmond, OK

2001 Det	2-14-0	—	5 NFC-C
2002 Det	3-13-0	—	4 NFC-N
NFL 2	5-27-0	—	

MULARKEY, MIKE Michael Rene; Florida; B11/19/1961 Fort Lauderdale, FL

2004 Buf	9-7-0	—	3 AFC-E
2005 Buf	5-11-0	—	3 AFC-E
NFL 2	14-18-0	—	

MULLER, BRICK* B6/12/1901

| **1926** LA† | 6-3-1 | — | 7 NFL |

YEAR TEAM	W-L-T	WP-LP	FINISH PLAYOFFS
MURPHY, JOHNNY Johnny			
1924 Roc	0-4-0	—	✧18 NFL

NEALE, GREASY Alfred Earle; West Virginia Wesleyan; B11/5/1891 Parkersburg, WV, D11/2/1973 Lake Worth, FL; HOF 1969

1941 Phi	2-8-1	—	4 NFL-E
1942 Phi	2-9-0	—	5 NFL-E
1943 P-P†	5-4-1	—	3 NFL-E
1944 Phi	7-1-2	—	2 NFL-E
1945 Phi	7-3-0	—	2 NFL-E
1946 Phi	6-5-0	—	2 NFL-E
1947 Phi	8-4-0	1-1	1 NFL-E DL
1948 Phi	9-2-1	1-0	1 NFL-E L‡
1949 Phi	11-1-0	1-0	1 NFL-E L‡
1950 Phi	6-6-0	—	3 NFL-A
NFL 10	63-43-5	3-1	

NESSER, AL* B6/6/1893

| **1926** Akr | 0-1-1 | — | ✧16 NFL |

NESSER, TED* B4/5/1883

1920 Col	2-6-2	—	7 NFL
1921 Col	1-8-0	—	17 NFL
NFL 2	3-14-2	—	

NEVERS, ERNIE* B6/11/1903

1927 Dul	1-8-0	—	11 NFL
1930 ChiC	5-6-2	—	7 NFL
1931 ChiC	5-2-0	—	✧4 NFL
1939 ChiC	1-10-0	—	5 NFL-W
NFL 4	12-26-2	—	

NIED, FRANK Francis Theodore; none; B8/14/1894 Akron, OH, D5/13/1969 Fort Lauderdale, FL

| **1926** Akr | 1-3-2 | — | ◆16 NFL |

NIXON, MIKE* B11/21/1911

1959 Was	3-9-0	—	5 NFL-E
1960 Was	1-9-2	—	6 NFL-E
1965 Pit	2-12-0	—	7 NFL-E
NFL 3	6-30-2	—	

NOLAN, DICK* B3/26/1932

1968 SF	7-6-1	—	3 NFL-Cnl
1969 SF	4-8-2	—	4 NFL-Cnl
1970 SF	10-3-1	1-1	1 NFC-W DC
1971 SF	9-5-0	1-1	1 NFC-W DC
1972 SF	8-5-1	0-1	1 NFC-W D
1973 SF	5-9-0	—	3 NFC-W
1974 SF	6-8-0	—	2 NFC-W
1975 SF	5-9-0	—	2 NFC-W
1978 NO	7-9-0	—	3 NFC-W
1979 NO	8-8-0	—	2 NFC-W
1980 NO	0-12-0	—	✧4 NFC-W
NFL 11	69-82-5	2-3	

NOLAN, MIKE Michael; Oregon; B3/7/1959 Baltimore, MD

| **2005** SF | 4-12-0 | — | 4 NFC-W |

NOLL, CHUCK* B1/5/1932

1969 Pit	1-13-0	—	4 NFL-Cny
1970 Pit	5-9-0	—	3 AFL-C
1971 Pit	6-8-0	—	2 AFC-C
1972 Pit	11-3-0	1-1	1 AFC-C DC
1973 Pit	10-4-0	0-1	2 AFC-C #W
1974 Pit	10-3-1	3-0	1 AFC-C DCS‡
1975 Pit	12-2-0	3-0	1 AFC-C DCS‡
1976 Pit	10-4-0	1-1	1 AFC-C #DC
1977 Pit	9-5-0	0-1	1 AFC-C D
1978 Pit	14-2-0	3-0	1 AFC-C DCS‡
1979 Pit	12-4-0	3-0	1 AFC-C DCS‡
1980 Pit	9-7-0	—	3 AFC-C
1981 Pit	8-8-0	—	2 AFC-C
1982 Pit	6-3-0	0-1	4 AFC P
1983 Pit	10-6-0	0-1	1 AFC-C D
1984 Pit	9-7-0	1-1	1 AFC-C DC
1985 Pit	7-9-0	—	2 AFC-C
1986 Pit	6-10-0	—	3 AFC-C
1987 Pit	8-7-0	—	3 AFC-C
1988 Pit	5-11-0	—	4 AFC-C
1989 Pit	9-7-0	1-1	2 AFC-C WD
1990 Pit	9-7-0	—	3 AFC-C #
1991 Pit	7-9-0	—	2 AFC-C
NFL 23	193-148-1	16-8	

NORTH, JOHN* B6/17/1921

1973 NO	5-9-0	—	3 NFC-W
1974 NO	5-9-0	—	3 NFC-W
1975 NO	1-5-0	—	✧4 NFC-W
NFL 3	11-23-0	—	

O'CONNOR, FRED Fred; East Stroudsburg State; B9/1/1939 Brooklyn, NY

| **1978** SF | 1-6-0 | — | ◆4 NFC-W |

OWEN, STEVE* B4/21/1898

1931 NYG	7-6-1	—	5 NFL
1932 NYG	4-6-2	—	5 NFL
1933 NYG	11-3-0	0-1	1 NFL-E L
1934 NYG	8-5-0	1-0	1 NFL-E L‡

YEAR TEAM	W-L-T	WP-LP	FINISH PLAYOFFS
1935 NYG	9-3-0	0-1	1 NFL-E L
1936 NYG	5-6-1	—	3 NFL-E
1937 NYG	6-3-2	—	2 NFL-E
1938 NYG	8-2-1	1-0	1 NFL-E L‡
1939 NYG	9-1-1	—	1 NFL-E L
1940 NYG	6-4-1	—	3 NFL-E
1941 NYG	8-3-0	0-1	1 NFL-E L
1942 NYG	5-5-1	—	3 NFL-E
1943 NYG	6-3-1	0-1	1 NFL-E D
1944 NYG	8-1-1	0-1	1 NFL-E L
1945 NYG	3-6-1	—	3 NFL-E
1946 NYG	7-3-1	0-1	1 NFL-E L
1947 NYG	2-8-2	—	5 NFL-E
1948 NYG	4-8-0	—	3 NFL-E
1949 NYG	6-6-0	—	3 NFL-E
1950 NYG	10-2-0	0-1	1 NFL-A C
1951 NYG	9-2-1	—	2 NFL-A
1952 NYG	7-5-0	—	2 NFL-A
1953 NYG	3-9-0	—	5 NFL-E
NFL 23	151-100-17	2-8	—

PALM, MIKE* B11/26/1899

YEAR TEAM	W-L-T	WP-LP	FINISH PLAYOFFS
1933 Cin	3-3-1	—	◆4 NFL-W

PALMER, CHRIS Christopher J.; Southern Connecticut State; B9/23/1949 Brewster, NY

YEAR TEAM	W-L-T	WP-LP	FINISH PLAYOFFS
1999 Cle	2-14-0	—	6 AFC-C
2000 Cle	3-13-0	—	6 AFC-C
NFL 2	5-27-0	—	

PARCELLS, BILL Duane Charles; Colgate, Wichita State; B8/22/1941 Englewood, NJ

YEAR TEAM	W-L-T	WP-LP	FINISH PLAYOFFS
1983 NYG	3-12-1	—	5 NFC-E
1984 NYG	9-7-0	1-1	2 NFC-E #WD
1985 NYG	10-6-0	1-1	2 NFC-E #WD
1986 NYG	14-2-0	3-0	1 NFC-E DCS‡
1987 NYG	6-9-0	—	5 NFC-E
1988 NYG	10-6-0	—	2 NFC-E #
1989 NYG	12-4-0	0-1	1 NFC-E D
1990 NYG	13-3-0	3-0	1 NFC-E DCS‡
1993 NE	5-11-0	—	4 AFC-E
1994 NE	10-6-0	0-1	2 AFC-E #W
1995 NE	6-10-0	—	4 AFC-E
1996 NE	11-5-0	2-1	1 AFC-E DCS
1997 NYJ	9-7-0	—	3 AFC-E #
1998 NYJ	12-4-0	1-1	1 AFC-E DC
1999 NYJ	8-8-0	—	4 AFC-E
2003 Dal	10-6-0	0-1	2 NFC-E W
2004 Dal	6-10-0	—	2 NFC-E
2005 Dal	9-7-0	—	3 NFC-E
NFL 18	163-123-1	11-7	—

PARDEE, JACK* B4/19/1936

YEAR TEAM	W-L-T	WP-LP	FINISH PLAYOFFS
1975 ChiB	4-10-0	—	3 NFC-C
1976 ChiB	7-7-0	—	2 NFC-C
1977 ChiB	9-5-0	0-1	2 NFC-C #
1978 Was	8-8-0	—	3 NFC-E
1979 Was	10-6-0	—	3 NFC-E #
1980 Was	6-10-0	—	3 NFC-E
1990 Hou	9-7-0	0-1	2 AFC-C #W
1991 Hou	11-5-0	1-1	1 AFC-C ED
1992 Hou	10-6-0	0-1	2 AFC-C W
1993 Hou	12-4-0	0-1	1 AFC-C D
1994 Hou	1-9-0	—	◇4 AFC-C
NFL 11	87-77-0	1-5	—

PARKER, BUDDY* B12/16/1913

YEAR TEAM	W-L-T	WP-LP	FINISH PLAYOFFS
1949 ChiC†	2-4-0	—	◆◇3 NFL-W
1949 ChiC	4-1-1	—	3 NFL-W
1951 Det	7-4-1	—	2 NFL-N
1952 Det	9-3-0	2-0	1 NFL-N CL‡
1953 Det	10-2-0	1-0	1 NFL-W L‡
1954 Det	9-2-1	0-1	1 NFL-W L
1955 Det	3-9-0	—	6 NFL-W
1956 Det	9-3-0	—	2 NFL-W
1957 Pit	6-6-0	—	3 NFL-E
1958 Pit	7-4-1	—	3 NFL-E
1959 Pit	6-5-1	—	4 NFL-E
1960 Pit	5-6-1	—	5 NFL-E
1961 Pit	6-8-0	—	5 NFL-E
1962 Pit	9-5-0	—	2 NFL-E
1963 Pit	7-4-3	—	4 NFL-E
1964 Pit	5-9-0	—	6 NFL-E
NFL 15	104-75-9	3-1	—

PATERA, JACK* B8/1/1933

YEAR TEAM	W-L-T	WP-LP	FINISH PLAYOFFS
1976 Sea	2-12-0	—	5 NFC-W
1977 Sea	5-9-0	—	4 AFC-W
1978 Sea	9-7-0	—	2 AFC-W
1979 Sea	9-7-0	—	3 AFC-W
1980 Sea	4-12-0	—	5 AFC-W
1981 Sea	6-10-0	—	5 AFC-W
1982 Sea	0-2-0	—	◇10 AFC #
NFL 7	35-59-0	—	—

PEPPLER, PAT Albert; Michigan State; B4/16/1922 Baltimore, MD

YEAR TEAM	W-L-T	WP-LP	FINISH PLAYOFFS
1976 Atl	3-6-0	—	◆3 NFC-W

PERKINS, RAY* B12/6/1941

YEAR TEAM	W-L-T	WP-LP	FINISH PLAYOFFS
1979 NYG	6-10-0	—	4 NFC-E
1980 NYG	4-12-0	—	5 NFC-E
1981 NYG	9-7-0	1-1	3 NFC-E WD
1982 NYG	4-5-0	—	10 NFC #
1987 TB	4-11-0	—	4 NFC-C
1988 TB	5-11-0	—	3 NFC-C
1989 TB	5-11-0	—	5 NFC-C
1990 TB	5-8-0	—	◇2 NFC-C
NFL 8	42-75-0	1-1	—

PETERSON, BILL William E.; Ohio Northern; B5/14/1923 Toronto, OH, D8/5/1993 Tallahassee, FL

YEAR TEAM	W-L-T	WP-LP	FINISH PLAYOFFS
1972 Hou	1-13-0	—	4 AFC-C
1973 Hou	0-5-0	—	◇4 AFC-C
NFL 2	1-18-0		

PETITBON, RICHIE* B4/18/1938

YEAR TEAM	W-L-T	WP-LP	FINISH PLAYOFFS
1993 Was	4-12-0	—	5 NFC-E

PHELAN, JIMMY James Michael; Notre Dame; B12/5/1893 Portland, OR, D11/14/1974 Honolulu, HI

YEAR TEAM	W-L-T	WP-LP	FINISH PLAYOFFS
1948 LAD-A	7-7-0	—	3 AAFC-W
1949 LAD-A	4-8-0	—	5 AAFC
AAFC 2	11-15-0	—	—
1952 DalT	1-11-0	—	6 NFL-N

PHILLIPS, BUM Oail Andrews; Stephen F. Austin; B9/29/1923 Orange, TX

YEAR TEAM	W-L-T	WP-LP	FINISH PLAYOFFS
1975 Hou	10-4-0	—	3 AFC-C
1976 Hou	5-9-0	—	4 AFC-C
1977 Hou	8-6-0	—	2 AFC-C
1978 Hou	10-6-0	2-1	2 AFC-C WDC
1979 Hou	11-5-0	2-1	2 AFC-C WDC
1980 Hou	11-5-0	0-1	2 AFC-C #W
1981 NO	4-12-0	—	4 NFC-W
1982 NO	4-5-0	—	9 NFC #
1983 NO	8-8-0	—	3 NFC-W
1984 NO	7-9-0	—	3 NFC-W
1985 NO	4-8-0	—	◇3 NFC-W
NFL 11	82-77-0	4-3	—

PHILLIPS, WADE Harold Wade; Houston; B6/21/1947 Orange, TX

YEAR TEAM	W-L-T	WP-LP	FINISH PLAYOFFS
1985 NO	1-3-0	—	◆3 NFC-W
1993 Den	9-7-0	0-1	3 AFC-W #W
1994 Den	7-9-0	—	4 AFC-W
1998 Buf	10-6-0	0-1	2 AFC-E W
1999 Buf	11-5-0	0-1	2 AFC-E W
2000 Buf	8-8-0	—	4 AFC-E
NFL 6	46-38-0	0-3	—

PIEROTTI, AL* B10/24/1895

YEAR TEAM	W-L-T	WP-LP	FINISH PLAYOFFS
1920 Cle	2-2-1	—	◆6 NFL

POLLARD, FRITZ* B1/27/1894

YEAR TEAM	W-L-T	WP-LP	FINISH PLAYOFFS
1921 Akr†	8-3-1	—	3 NFL
1925 Ham	0-1-0	—	◇14 NFL
NFL 2	8-4-1	—	—

POOL, HAMPTON* B3/11/1915

YEAR TEAM	W-L-T	WP-LP	FINISH PLAYOFFS
1946 Mia-A	2-6-0	—	◆4 AAFC-E
1947 ChiR-A	1-3-0	—	◆4 AAFC-W
AAFC 2	3-9-0	—	—
1952 LARm	9-2-0	0-1	◆1 NFL-N C
1953 LARm	8-3-1	—	3 NFL-W
1954 LARm	6-5-1	—	4 NFL-W
NFL 6	23-10-2	0-1	—

POTTEIGER, EARL* B1/11/1891

YEAR TEAM	W-L-T	WP-LP	FINISH PLAYOFFS
1924 Kent†	0-4-1	—	16 NFL
1927 NYG	11-1-1	—	1 NFL
1928 NYG	4-7-2	—	6 NFL
NFL 3	15-12-4	—	—

PROCHASKA, RAY* B8/9/1919

YEAR TEAM	W-L-T	WP-LP	FINISH PLAYOFFS
1961 SL†	2-0-0	—	◆4 NFL-E

PROTHO, TOMMY James Thompson; Duke; B7/20/1920 Memphis, TN, D5/14/1995 Memphis, TN

YEAR TEAM	W-L-T	WP-LP	FINISH PLAYOFFS
1971 LARm	8-5-1	—	2 NFC-W
1972 LARm	6-7-1	—	3 NFC-W
1974 SD	5-9-0	—	3 AFC-W
1975 SD	2-12-0	—	4 AFC-W
1976 SD	6-8-0	—	3 AFC-W
1977 SD	7-7-0	—	3 AFC-W
1978 SD	1-3-0	—	◇2 AFC-W
NFL 7	35-51-2	—	—

RALSTON, JOHN John R.; California; B4/26/1927 Oakland, CA

YEAR TEAM	W-L-T	WP-LP	FINISH PLAYOFFS
1972 Den	5-9-0	—	3 AFC-W
1973 Den	7-5-2	—	2 AFC-W
1974 Den	7-6-1	—	2 AFC-W
1975 Den	6-8-0	—	2 AFC-W
1976 Den	9-5-0	—	2 AFC-W
NFL 5	34-33-3	—	—

RAMSEY, BUSTER* B3/16/1920

YEAR TEAM	W-L-T	WP-LP	FINISH PLAYOFFS
1960 Buf-A	5-8-1	—	3 AFL-E
1961 Buf-A	6-8-0	—	4 AFL-E
NFL 2	11-16-1	—	

RAUCH, DICK* B7/15/1893

YEAR TEAM	W-L-T	WP-LP	FINISH PLAYOFFS
1925 Pot	10-2-0	—	2 NFL
1926 Pot	10-2-2	—	3 NFL
1927 Pot	5-8-0	—	8 NFL
1928 NYY	4-8-1	—	7 NFL
1929 Bos	4-4-0	—	4 NFL
NFL 5	33-24-3	—	—

RAUCH, JOHN* B8/20/1927

YEAR TEAM	W-L-T	WP-LP	FINISH PLAYOFFS
1966 Oak-A	8-5-1	—	2 AFL-W
1967 Oak-A	13-1-0	1-1	1 AFL-W LS
1968 Oak-A	12-2-0	1-1	1 AFL-W DL
1969 Buf-A	4-10-0	—	3 AFL-E
1970 Buf	3-10-1	—	4 AFL-E
NFL 5	40-28-2	2-2	—

REEVES, DAN* B1/19/1944

YEAR TEAM	W-L-T	WP-LP	FINISH PLAYOFFS
1981 Den	10-6-0	—	2 AFC-W #
1982 Den	2-7-0	—	12 AFC
1983 Den	9-7-0	0-1	3 AFC-W #W
1984 Den	13-3-0	0-1	1 AFC-W D
1985 Den	11-5-0	—	2 AFC-W #
1986 Den	11-5-0	2-1	1 AFC-W DCS
1987 Den	10-4-1	2-1	1 AFC-W DCS
1988 Den	8-8-0	—	2 AFC-W
1989 Den	11-5-0	2-1	1 AFC-W DCS
1990 Den	5-11-0	—	5 AFC-W
1991 Den	12-4-0	1-1	1 AFC-W DC
1992 Den	8-8-0	—	3 AFC-W
1993 NYG	11-5-0	1-1	2 NFC-E WD
1994 NYG	9-7-0	—	2 NFC-E #
1995 NYG	5-11-0	—	4 NFC-E
1996 NYG	6-10-0	—	5 NFC-E
1997 Atl	7-9-0	—	2 NFC-W
1998 Atl	14-2-0	2-1	1 NFC-W DCS
1999 Atl	5-11-0	—	3 NFC-W
2000 Atl	4-12-0	—	5 NFC-W
2001 Atl	7-9-0	—	3 NFC-W
2002 Atl	9-6-1	1-1	2 NFC-S WD
2003 Atl	5-11-0	—	4 NFC-S
NFL 23	192-166-2	11-9	—

REID, ANDY Andrew Walter; Brigham Young; B3/19/1958 Los Angeles, CA

YEAR TEAM	W-L-T	WP-LP	FINISH PLAYOFFS
1999 Phi	5-11-0	—	5 NFC-E
2000 Phi	11-5-0	1-1	2 NFC-E WD
2001 Phi	11-5-0	2-1	1 NFC-E EDC
2002 Phi	12-4-0	1-1	1 NFC-E DC
2003 Phi	12-4-0	1-1	1 NFC-E DC
2004 Phi	13-3-0	2-1	1 NFC-E DCS
2005 Phi	6-10-0	—	4 NFC-E
NFL 7	70-42-0	7-5	—

RHODES, RAY* B10/20/1950

YEAR TEAM	W-L-T	WP-LP	FINISH PLAYOFFS
1995 Phi	10-6-0	1-1	2 NFC-E WD
1996 Phi	10-6-0	0-1	2 NFC-E #W
1997 Phi	6-9-1	—	3 NFC-E
1998 Phi	3-13-0	—	5 NFC-E
1999 GB	8-8-0	—	4 NFC-C #
NFL 5	37-42-1	1-2	—

RICE, HOMER Homer C.; Centre; B2/20/1927 Bellevue, KY

YEAR TEAM	W-L-T	WP-LP	FINISH PLAYOFFS
1978 Cin	4-7-0	—	◆4 AFC-C
1979 Cin	4-12-0	—	4 AFC-C
NFL 2	8-19-0	—	—

RICHARDS, RAY* B7/16/1906

YEAR TEAM	W-L-T	WP-LP	FINISH PLAYOFFS
1955 ChiC	4-7-1	—	4 NFL-E
1956 ChiC	7-5-0	—	2 NFL-E
1957 ChiC	3-9-0	—	6 NFL-E
NFL 3	14-21-1	—	—

RILEY, MIKE Michael Joseph; Alabama, Whitworth College; B7/6/1953 Wallace, ID

YEAR TEAM	W-L-T	WP-LP	FINISH PLAYOFFS
1999 SD	8-8-0	—	3 AFC-W
2000 SD	1-15-0	—	5 AFC-W
2001 SD	5-11-0	—	5 AFC-W
NFL 3	14-34-0	—	—

RINGO, JIM* B11/21/1931

YEAR TEAM	W-L-T	WP-LP	FINISH PLAYOFFS
1976 Buf	0-9-0	—	◆5 AFC-E
1977 Buf	3-11-0	—	4 AFC-E
NFL 2	3-20-0	—	

ROBB, HARRY* B5/11/1897

YEAR TEAM	W-L-T	WP-LP	FINISH PLAYOFFS
1925 Can	4-4-0	—	11 NFL
1926 Can†	1-9-0	—	20 NFL
NFL 2	5-13-0	—	

ROBERTS, J.D. John David; Oklahoma; B10/24/1932 Oklahoma City, OK

YEAR TEAM	W-L-T	WP-LP	FINISH PLAYOFFS
1970 NO	1-6-0	—	◆4 NFC-W
1971 NO	4-8-2	—	4 NFC-W
1972 NO	2-11-1	—	4 NFC-W
NFL 3	7-25-3	—	

YEAR TEAM	W-L-T	WP-LP	FINISH PLAYOFFS
ROBINSON, ED Edward North; Brown; B10/15/1873 Lynn, MA, D3/10/1995 Boston, MA			
1931 Pro	4-4-3	—	6 NFL
ROBINSON, JOHN John Alexander; Oregon; B7/25/1935 Chicago, IL			
1983 LARm	9-7-0	1-1	2 NFC-W WD
1984 LARm	10-6-0	0-1	2 NFC-W W
1985 LARm	11-5-0	1-1	1 NFC-W DC
1986 LARm	10-6-0	0-1	2 NFC-W W
1987 LARm	6-9-0	—	3 NFC-W
1988 LARm	10-6-0	0-1	2 NFC-W #W
1989 LARm	11-5-0	2-1	2 NFC-W WDC
1990 LARm	5-11-0	—	3 NFC-W
1991 LARm	3-13-0	—	4 NFC-W
NFL 9	75-68-0	4-6	—
ROBISKIE, TERRY* B11/12/1954			
2000 Was	1-2-0	—	◆3 NFC-E
2004 Cle	1-5-0	—	◆4 AFC-N
NFL 2	2-7-0	—	
ROGERS, CHARLEY* B1903			
1927 Fra†	4-4-2	—	◆7 NFL
ROGERS, DARRYL Darryl Dale; Fresno State; B5/28/1935 Los Angeles, CA			
1985 Det	7-9-0	—	3 NFC-C
1986 Det	5-11-0	—	3 NFC-C
1987 Det	4-11-0	—	4 NFC-C
1988 Det	2-9-0	—	◇4 NFC-C
NFL 4	18-40-0	—	
RONZANI, GENE* B3/28/1909			
1950 GB	3-9-0	—	5 NFL-N
1951 GB	3-9-0	—	5 NFL-N
1952 GB	6-6-0	—	4 NFL-N
1953 GB	2-7-1	—	◇6 NFL-W
NFL 4	14-31-1	—	
ROSE, TAM* B6/20/1889			
1921 Ton	0-1-0	—	18 NFL
ROSS, BOBBY Robert Joseph; VMI; B12/23/1935 Richmond, VA			
1992 SD	11-5-0	1-1	1 AFC-W ED
1993 SD	8-8-0	—	4 AFC-W
1994 SD	11-5-0	2-1	1 AFC-W DCS
1995 SD	9-7-0	0-1	2 AFC-W W
1996 SD	8-8-0	—	3 AFC-W
1997 Det	9-7-0	0-1	3 NFC-C W
1998 Det	5-11-0	—	4 NFC-C
1999 Det	8-8-0	0-1	3 NFC-C #W
2000 Det	5-4-0	—	◇3 NFC-C
NFL 9	74-63-0	3-5	—
RUETZ, BABE George Gerhard; B9/23/1893 Racine, WI, D5/24/1997 Racine, WI			
1922 Rac	6-4-1	—	6 NFL
1923 Rac	4-4-2	—	10 NFL
1924 Rac	4-3-3	—	7 NFL
NFL 3	14-11-6	—	
RUSH, CLIVE* B2/14/1931			
1969 Bos-A	4-10-0	—	3 AFL-E
1970 Bos	1-6-0	—	◇5 AFL-E
NFL 2	5-16-0	—	
RUST, ROD Rodney A.; Iowa State; B8/2/1928 Webster City, IA			
1990 NE	1-15-0	—	5 AFC-E
RUTIGLIANO, SAM San; Tennessee, Tulsa; B7/1/1932 Brooklyn, NY			
1978 Cle	8-8-0	—	3 AFC-C
1979 Cle	9-7-0	—	3 AFC-C
1980 Cle	11-5-0	0-1	1 AFC-C #D
1981 Cle	5-11-0	—	4 AFC-C
1982 Cle	4-5-0	0-1	8 AFC #P
1983 Cle	9-7-0	—	2 AFC-C #
1984 Cle	1-7-0	—	◇3 AFC-C
NFL 7	47-50-0	0-2	—
RYAN, BUDDY James David; Oklahoma State; B2/16/1934 Frederick, OK			
1986 Phi	5-10-1	—	4 NFC-E
1987 Phi	7-8-0	—	2 NFC-E
1988 Phi	10-6-0	0-1	1 NFC-E #D
1989 Phi	11-5-0	0-1	2 NFC-E W
1990 Phi	10-6-0	0-1	2 NFC-E W
1994 Arz	8-8-0	—	3 NFC-E
1995 Arz	4-12-0	—	5 NFC-E
NFL 7	55-55-1	0-3	—
RYMKUS, LOU* B11/6/1919			
1960 Hou-A	10-4-0	1-0	1 AFL-E L‡
1961 Hou-A	1-3-1	—	◇1 AFL-E L‡
NFL 2	11-7-1	1-0	—
SABAN, LOU* B10/13/1921			
1960 Bos-A	5-9-0	—	4 AFL-E
1961 Bos-A	2-3-0	—	◇2 AFL-E

YEAR TEAM	W-L-T	WP-LP	FINISH PLAYOFFS
1962 Buf-A	7-6-1	—	3 AFL-E
1963 Buf-A	7-6-1	0-1	1 AFL-E D
1964 Buf-A	12-2-0	1-0	1 AFL-E L‡
1965 Buf-A	10-3-1	1-0	1 AFL-E L‡
1967 Den-A	3-11-0	—	4 AFL-W
1968 Den-A	5-9-0	—	4 AFL-W
1969 Den-A	5-8-1	—	4 AFL-W
1970 Den	5-8-1	—	4 AFC-W
1971 Den	2-6-1	—	◇4 AFC-W
1972 Buf	4-9-1	—	4 AFC-E
1973 Buf	9-5-0	—	2 AFC-E
1974 Buf	9-5-0	0-1	2 AFC-E W
1975 Buf	8-6-0	—	3 AFC-E
1976 Buf	2-3-0	—	◇5 AFC-E
NFL 16	95-99-7	2-2	—
SABAN, NICK Nick Lou; Kent State; B10/31/1951 Fairmont, WV			
2005 Mia	9-7-0	—	2 AFC-E
SACHS, LENNY Leonard David; Loyola (IL), DePaul; B8/7/1897 Chicago, IL, D10/27/1942 Chicago, IL			
1926 Lou	0-4-0	—	21 NFL
SALATA, ANDY* B9/30/1905			
1930 Nwk	0-3-0	—	◆11 NFL
SANDUSKY, JOHN* B12/28/1925			
1972 Bal	4-5-0	—	◆3 AFC-E
SAUNDERS, AL Alan Keith; San Jose State; B2/1/1947 London, England			
1986 SD	3-5-0	—	◆5 AFC-W
1987 SD	8-7-0	—	3 AFC-W
1988 SD	6-10-0	—	4 AFC-W
NFL 3	17-22-0	—	
SCANLON, DEWEY* B8/16/1899			
1924 Dul	5-1-0	—	4 NFL
1925 Dul	0-3-0	—	16 NFL
1926 Dul	6-5-3	—	8 NFL
1929 ChiC	6-6-1	—	5 NFL
NFL 4	17-15-4	—	
SCHISSLER, PAUL Paul John; Doane, Hastings, St. Viator; B11/11/1893 Hastings, NE, D4/17/1968 Hastings, NE			
1933 ChiC	1-9-1	—	5 NFL-W
1934 ChiC	5-6-0	—	4 NFL-W
1935 Bkn	5-6-1	—	2 NFL-E
1936 Bkn	3-8-1	—	4 NFL-E
NFL 4	14-29-3	—	
SCHMIDT, JOE* B1/19/1932			
1967 Det	5-7-2	—	3 NFL-Coa
1968 Det	4-8-2	—	4 NFL-Coa
1969 Det	9-4-1	—	2 NFL-Coa
1970 Det	10-4-0	0-1	2 NFC-C W
1971 Det	7-6-1	—	2 NFC-C
1972 Det	8-5-1	—	2 NFC-C
NFL 6	43-34-7	0-1	—
SCHNELLENBERGER, HOWARD Howard Leslie; Kentucky; B3/16/1934 Louisville, KY			
1973 Bal	4-10-0	—	4 AFC-E
1974 Bal	0-3-0	—	◇5 AFC-E
NFL 2	4-13-0	—	
SCHOTTENHEIMER, MARTY* B9/23/1943			
1984 Cle	4-4-0	—	◆3 AFC-C
1985 Cle	8-8-0	0-1	1 AFC-C D
1986 Cle	12-4-0	1-1	1 AFC-C DC
1987 Cle	10-5-0	1-1	1 AFC-C DC
1988 Cle	10-6-0	0-1	2 AFC-C W
1989 KC	8-7-1	—	2 AFC-W
1990 KC	11-5-0	1-1	2 AFC-W W
1991 KC	10-6-0	1-1	2 AFC-W WD
1992 KC	10-6-0	2-1	2 AFC-W W
1993 KC	11-5-0	0-1	1 AFC-W EDC
1994 KC	9-7-0	0-1	2 AFC-W #W
1995 KC	13-3-0	0-1	1 AFC-W D
1996 KC	9-7-0	—	2 AFC-W #
1997 KC	13-3-0	0-1	1 AFC-W D
1998 KC	7-9-0	—	4 AFC-W
2001 Was	8-8-0	—	2 NFC-E
2002 SD	8-8-0	—	3 AFC-W
2003 SD	4-12-0	—	3 AFC-W
2004 SD	12-4-0	0-1	1 AFC-W E
2005 SD	9-7-0	—	3 AFC-W
NFL 20	186-124-1	5-12	—
SCOTT, RALPH* B9/26/1894			
1927 NYY	7-8-1	—	6 NFL
SCOTT, TOM Tom			
1946 Bkn-A†	1-6-0	—	◆2 AAFC-E
SEIFERT, GEORGE George Gerald; Utah; B1/22/1940 San Francisco, CA			
1989 SF	14-2-0	3-0	1 NFC-W DCS‡
1990 SF	14-2-0	1-1	1 NFC-W DC
1991 SF	10-6-0	—	3 NFC-W #

YEAR TEAM	W-L-T	WP-LP	FINISH PLAYOFFS
1992 SF	14-2-0	1-1	1 NFC-W DC
1993 SF	10-6-0	1-1	1 NFC-W DC
1994 SF	13-3-0	3-0	1 NFC-W DCS‡
1995 SF	11-5-0	0-1	1 NFC-W #D
1996 SF	12-4-0	1-1	2 NFC-W #WD
1999 Car	8-8-0	—	2 NFC-W #
2000 Car	7-9-0	—	3 NFC-W
2001 Car	1-15-0	—	5 NFC-W
NFL 11	114-62-0	10-5	—
SHANAHAN, MIKE Michael Edward; Eastern Illinois; B8/24/1952 Oak Park, IL			
1988 LARd	7-9-0	—	3 AFC-W
1989 LARd	1-3-0	—	◇3 AFC-W
1995 Den	8-8-0	—	4 AFC-W
1996 Den	13-3-0	0-1	1 AFC-W D
1997 Den	12-4-0	4-0	2 AFC-W WDCS‡
1998 Den	14-2-0	3-0	1 AFC-W DCS‡
1999 Den	6-10-0	—	5 AFC-W
2000 Den	11-5-0	0-1	2 AFC-W W
2001 Den	8-8-0	—	3 AFC-W
2002 Den	9-7-0	—	2 AFC-W #
2003 Den	10-6-0	0-1	2 AFC-W #W
2004 Den	10-6-0	0-1	2 AFC-W W
2005 Den	13-3-0	1-1	1 AFC-W DC
NFL 13	122-74-0	8-5	—
SHAUGHNESSY, CLARK Clark David; Minnesota; B3/6/1892 St. Cloud, MN, D3/15/1970 Santa Monica, CA			
1948 LARm	6-5-1	—	3 NFL-W
1949 LARm	8-2-2	0-1	1 NFL-W L
NFL 2	14-7-3	0-1	—
SHAW, BUCK Lawrence Timothy; Notre Dame; B3/28/1899 Mitchellville, IA, D3/19/1977 Menlo Park, CA			
1946 SF-A	9-5-0	—	2 AAFC-W
1947 SF-A	8-4-2	—	2 AAFC-W
1948 SF-A	12-2-0	—	2 AAFC-W
1949 SF-A	9-3-0	1-1	2 AAFC PL
AAFC 4	38-14-2	1-1	
1950 SF	3-9-0	—	5 NFL-N
1951 SF	7-4-1	—	2 NFL-N
1952 SF	7-5-0	—	3 NFL-N
1953 SF	9-3-0	—	2 NFL-W
1954 SF	7-4-1	—	3 NFL-W
1958 Phi	2-9-1	—	5 NFL-E
1959 Phi	7-5-0	—	2 NFL-E
1960 Phi	10-2-0	1-0	1 NFL-E L‡
NFL 13	52-41-3	1-0	—
SHELL, ART* B11/26/1946			
1989 LARd	7-5-0	—	◆3 AFC-W
1990 LARd	12-4-0	1-1	1 AFC-W DC
1991 LARd	9-7-0	0-1	3 AFC-W W
1992 LARd	7-9-0	—	4 AFC-W
1993 LARd	10-6-0	1-1	2 AFC-W WD
1994 LARd	9-7-0	—	3 AFC-W #
NFL 6	54-38-0	2-3	—
SHERMAN, ALLIE* B2/10/1923			
1961 NYG	10-3-1	0-1	1 NFL-E L
1962 NYG	12-2-0	0-1	1 NFL-E L
1963 NYG	11-3-0	0-1	1 NFL-E L
1964 NYG	2-10-2	—	7 NFL-E
1965 NYG	7-7-0	—	2 NFL-E
1966 NYG	1-12-1	—	8 NFL-E
1967 NYG	7-7-0	—	2 NFL-Cny
1968 NYG	7-7-0	—	2 NFL-Cap
NFL 8	57-51-4	0-3	—
SHERMAN, MIKE Michael Francis; Central Connecticut State; B12/19/1954 Norwood, MA			
2000 GB	9-7-0	—	3 NFC-C
2001 GB	12-4-0	1-1	2 NFC-C WD
2002 GB	12-4-0	0-1	1 NFC-N E
2003 GB	10-6-0	1-1	1 NFC-N ED
2004 GB	10-6-0	0-1	1 NFC-N E
2005 GB	4-12-0	—	4 NFC-N
NFL 6	57-39-0	2-4	—
SHIPKEY, TED Theodore Edwin; Stanford; B9/23/1904 Great Falls, MT, D7/18/1978 Palcentia, CA			
1947 LAD-A†	2-1-0	—	◆3 AAFC-W
SHIPP, KEN Kenneth; Middle Tennessee State; B2/3/1929 Old Hickory, TN			
1975 NYJ	1-4-0	—	◆4 AFC-E
SHOFNER, JIM* B12/18/1935			
1990 Cle	1-6-0	—	◆4 AFC-C
SHULA, DAVID* B5/28/1959			
1992 Cin	5-11-0	—	4 AFC-C
1993 Cin	3-13-0	—	4 AFC-C
1994 Cin	3-13-0	—	3 AFC-C
1995 Cin	7-9-0	—	2 AFC-C
1996 Cin	1-6-0	—	◇3 AFC-C
NFL 5	19-52-0	—	

THE HEAD COACHES

SHULA, DON* B1/4/1930

YEAR TEAM	W-L-T	WP-LP	FINISH PLAYOFFS
1963 Bal	8-6-0	—	3 NFL-W
1964 Bal	12-2-0	0-1	1 NFL-W L
1965 Bal	10-3-1	0-1	1 NFL-W C
1966 Bal	9-5-0	—	2 NFL-W
1967 Bal	11-1-2	—	1 NFL-Cnl D
1968 Bal	13-1-0	2-1	1 NFL-Cnl CLS
1969 Bal	8-5-1	—	2 NFL-Cnl
1970 Mia	10-4-0	0-1	2 AFL-E W
1971 Mia	10-3-1	2-1	1 AFC-E DCS
1972 Mia	14-0-0	3-0	1 AFC-E DCS‡
1973 Mia	12-2-0	3-0	1 AFC-E DCS‡
1974 Mia	11-3-0	0-1	1 AFC-E D
1975 Mia	10-4-0	—	2 AFC-E #
1976 Mia	6-8-0	—	3 AFC-E
1977 Mia	10-4-0	—	2 AFC-E #
1978 Mia	11-5-0	0-1	2 AFC-E #W
1979 Mia	10-6-0	0-1	1 AFC-E D
1980 Mia	8-8-0	—	3 AFC-E
1981 Mia	11-4-1	0-1	1 AFC-E D
1982 Mia	7-2-0	3-1	2 AFC PDCS
1983 Mia	12-4-0	0-1	1 AFC-E D
1984 Mia	14-2-0	2-1	1 AFC-E DCS
1985 Mia	12-4-0	1-1	1 AFC-E DC
1986 Mia	8-8-0	—	3 AFC-E
1987 Mia	8-7-0	—	2 AFC-E
1988 Mia	6-10-0	—	5 AFC-E
1989 Mia	8-8-0	—	2 AFC-E
1990 Mia	12-4-0	1-1	2 AFC-E WD
1991 Mia	8-8-0	—	3 AFC-E #
1992 Mia	11-5-0	1-1	1 AFC-E #DC
1993 Mia	9-7-0	—	2 AFC-E #
1994 Mia	10-6-0	1-1	1 AFC-E #ED
1995 Mia	9-7-0	0-1	2 AFC-E W
NFL 33	328-156-6	19-17	—

SIES, HERB* B1/2/1893

YEAR TEAM	W-L-T	WP-LP	FINISH PLAYOFFS
1923 RI	2-3-3	—	12 NFL

SKORICH, NICK* B6/26/1921

1961 Phi	10-4-0	—	2 NFL-E
1962 Phi	3-10-1	—	7 NFL-E
1963 Phi	2-10-2	—	7 NFL-E
1971 Cle	9-5-0	0-1	1 AFC-C D
1972 Cle	10-4-0	0-1	2 AFC-C W
1973 Cle	7-5-2	—	3 AFC-C
1974 Cle	4-10-0	—	4 AFC-C
NFL 7	45-48-5	0-2	—

SMITH, JERRY* B9/9/1930

1971 Den	2-3-0	—	◆4 AFC-W

SMITH, LOVIE Lovie; Tulsa; B5/8/1958 Gladewater, TX

2004 ChiB	5-11-0	—	4 NFC-N
2005 ChiB	11-5-0	0-1	1 NFC-N D
NFL 2	16-16-0	0-1	—

SMITH, CLIPPER Maurice Francis; Notre Dame; B10/15/1898 Manteno, IL, D3/18/1984 Laguna Beach, CA

1947 Bos	4-7-1	—	3 NFL-E
1948 Bos	3-9-0	—	5 NFL-E
NFL 2	7-16-1	—	—

SNYDER, BOB* B2/6/1913

1947 LARm	6-6-0	—	4 NFL-W

SPEEDIE, MAC* B1/12/1920

1964 Den-A	2-7-1	—	◆4 AFL-W
1965 Den-A	4-10-0	—	4 AFL-W
1966 Den-A	0-2-0	—	◇4 AFL-W
NFL 3	6-19-1	—	—

SPURRIER, STEVE* B4/20/1945

2002 Was	7-9-0	—	3 NFC-E
2003 Was	5-11-0	—	3 NFC-E
NFL 2	12-20-0	—	—

STALLINGS, GENE Eugene Clifton; Texas A&M; B3/2/1935 Paris, TX

1986 SL	4-11-1	—	5 NFC-E
1987 SL	7-8-0	—	2 NFC-E
1988 Phx	7-9-0	—	3 NFC-E
1989 Phx	5-6-0	—	◇4 NFC-E
NFL 4	23-34-1	—	—

STANFEL, DICK* B7/20/1927

1980 NO	1-3-0	—	◆4 NFC-W

STARR, BART* B1/9/1934

1975 GB	4-10-0	—	3 NFC-C
1976 GB	5-9-0	—	4 NFC-C
1977 GB	4-10-0	—	4 NFC-C
1978 GB	8-7-1	—	2 NFC-C #
1979 GB	5-11-0	—	4 NFC-C
1980 GB	5-10-1	—	4 NFC-C
1981 GB	8-8-0	—	2 NFC-C
1982 GB	5-3-1	1-1	3 NFC PD
1983 GB	8-8-0	—	2 NFC-C
NFL 9	52-76-3	1-1	—

STECKEL, LES Leslie Todd; Kansas; B7/1/1946 Whitehall, PA

YEAR TEAM	W-L-T	WP-LP	FINISH PLAYOFFS
1984 Min	3-13-0	—	5 NFC-C

STEPHENSON, KAY* B12/17/1944

1983 Buf	8-8-0	—	2 AFC-E
1984 Buf	2-14-0	—	5 AFC-E
1985 Buf	0-4-0	—	◇5 AFC-E
NFL 3	10-26-0	—	—

STERNAMAN, JOEY* B2/1/1900

1923 Dul	4-3-0	—	7 NFL

STEVENS, MAL Marvin Allen; Washburn, Yale; B4/14/1900 Stockton, KS, D12/6/1979 New York, NY

1946 Bkn-A	2-4-1	—	◇2 AAFC-E

STINCHCOMB, PETE* B6/24/1895

1923 Col	3-4-0	—	◆8 NFL

STORCK, CARL Carl H.; none; B11/14/1892 Dayton, OH, D3/13/1950 Dayton, OH

1922 Day	4-3-1	—	7 NFL
1923 Day	1-6-1	—	16 NFL
1924 Day	2-6-0	—	13 NFL
1925 Day	0-7-1	—	19 NFL
1926 Day	1-4-1	—	16 NFL
NFL 5	8-26-4	—	—

STRADER, RED Norman Parker; St. Mary's (CA); B12/21/1904 Newton, NJ, D5/26/1956 Berkeley, CA

1948 NYY-A	5-5-0	—	◆3 AAFC-E
1949 NYY-A	8-4-0	0-1	3 AAFC P
AAFC 2	13-9-0	0-1	—
1950 NYY	7-5-0	—	3 NFL-N
1951 NYY	1-9-2	—	6 NFL-N
1955 SF	4-8-0	—	5 NFL-W
NFL 6	12-22-2	—	—

STRAM, HANK Henry Louis; Purdue; B1/3/1924 Chicago, IL, D7/4/2005 Covington, LA; HOF 2003

1960 DalT-A	8-6-0	—	2 AFL-W
1961 DalT-A	6-8-0	—	2 AFL-W
1962 DalT-A	11-3-0	1-0	1 AFL-W L‡
1963 KC-A	5-7-2	—	3 AFL-W
1964 KC-A	7-7-0	—	2 AFL-W
1965 KC-A	7-5-2	—	3 AFL-W
1966 KC-A	11-2-1	1-1	1 AFL-W LS
1967 KC-A	9-5-0	—	2 AFL-W
1968 KC-A	12-2-0	0-1	1 AFL-W D
1969 KC-A	11-3-0	3-0	2 AFL-W PLS‡
1970 KC	7-5-2	—	2 AFL-W
1971 KC	10-3-1	0-1	1 AFC-W D
1972 KC	8-6-0	—	2 AFC-W
1973 KC	7-5-2	—	2 AFC-W
1974 KC	5-9-0	—	3 AFC-W
1976 NO	4-10-0	—	3 NFC-W
1977 NO	3-11-0	—	4 NFC-W
NFL 17	131-97-10	5-3	—

STUDLEY, CHUCK Charles B.; Illinois; B1/17/1929 Maywood, IL

1983 Hou	2-8-0	—	◆4 AFC-C

STYDAHAR, JOE* B3/16/1912

1950 LARm	9-3-0	1-0	1 NFL-N CL
1951 LARm	8-4-0	1-0	1 NFL-N L‡
1952 LARm	0-1-0	—	◇1 NFL-N C
1953 ChiC	1-10-1	—	6 NFL-E
1954 ChiC	2-10-0	—	6 NFL-E
NFL 5	20-28-1	2-1	—

SUTHERLAND, JOCK John Bain; Pittsburgh; B3/21/1889 Coupar-Angus, Scotland, D4/11/1948 Pittsburgh, PA

1940 Bkn	8-3-0	—	2 NFL-E
1941 Bkn	7-4-0	—	2 NFL-E
1946 Pit	5-5-1	—	3 NFL-E
1947 Pit	8-4-0	0-1	1 NFL-E D
NFL 4	28-16-1	0-1	—

SVARE, HARLAND* B11/15/1930

1962 LARm	0-5-1	—	◆7 NFL-W
1963 LARm	5-9-0	—	6 NFL-W
1964 LARm	5-7-2	—	5 NFL-W
1965 LARm	4-10-0	—	7 NFL-W
1971 SD	2-2-0	—	◆3 AFC-W
1972 SD	4-9-1	—	4 AFC-W
1973 SD	1-6-1	—	◇4 AFC-W
NFL 7	21-48-5	—	—

SWITZER, BARRY Barry; Arkansas; B10/5/1937 Crossett, AR

1994 Dal	12-4-0	1-1	1 NFC-E DC
1995 Dal	12-4-0	3-0	1 NFC-E DCS‡
1996 Dal	10-6-0	1-1	1 NFC-E #ED
1997 Dal	6-10-0	—	4 NFC-E
NFL 4	40-24-0	5-2	—

TALBOT, NELSON Nelson Strobridge; Yale; B6/10/1892 Dayton, OH, D7/6/1952 Dayton, OH

YEAR TEAM	W-L-T	WP-LP	FINISH PLAYOFFS
1920 Day	5-2-2	—	8 NFL
1921 Day	4-4-1	—	8 NFL
NFL 2	9-6-3	—	—

TAYLOR, HUGH* B7/6/1923

1965 Hou-A	4-10-0	—	4 AFL-E

TEBELL, GUS* B9/6/1897

1923 Col	2-0-1	—	◆8 NFL

THOMAS, JOE Joseph; Ohio Northern; B3/18/1921 Warren, OH

1974 Bal	2-9-0	—	◆5 AFC-E

THORPE, JIM* B5/28/1888

1920 Can	7-4-2	—	3 NFL
1921 Cle	3-5-0	—	11 NFL
1922 Oor	3-6-0	—	11 NFL
1923 Oor	1-10-0	—	18 NFL
NFL 4	14-25-2	—	—

TICE, MIKE* B2/2/1959

2001 Min	0-1-0	—	◆4 NFC-C
2002 Min	6-10-0	—	2 NFC-N
2003 Min	9-7-0	—	2 NFC-N
2004 Min	8-8-0	1-1	2 NFC-N #WD
2005 Min	9-7-0	—	2 NFC-N
NFL 5	32-33-0	1-1	—

TOBIN, ELGIE* BMay 1885

1920 Akr	8-0-3	—	1 NFL
1921 Akr†	8-3-1	—	3 NFL
NFL 2	16-3-4	—	—

TOBIN, VINCE Vincent Michael; Missouri; B9/29/1943 Burlington Junction, MO

1996 Arz	7-9-0	—	4 NFC-E
1997 Arz	4-12-0	—	5 NFC-E
1998 Arz	9-7-0	1-1	2 NFC-E WD
1999 Arz	6-10-0	—	4 NFC-E
2000 Arz	2-5-0	—	◇5 NFC-E
NFL 5	28-43-0	1-1	—

TODD, DICK* B10/2/1914

1951 Was	5-4-0	—	◆3 NFL-A

TOLLEFSON, RUSSELL Russell I.; Minnesota; B9/27/1891 Minneapolis, MN, D5/13/1962 Glendale, CA

1922 Min	1-3-0	—	13 NFL

TRIMBLE, JIM James William; Indiana; B5/29/1918 McKeesport, PA

1952 Phi	7-5-0	—	2 NFL-A
1953 Phi	7-4-1	—	2 NFL-E
1954 Phi	7-4-1	—	2 NFL-E
1955 Phi	4-7-1	—	4 NFL-E
NFL 4	25-20-3	—	—

TURNER, BULLDOG* B3/10/1919

1962 NYT-A	5-9-0	—	4 AFL-E

TURNER, NORV Norval Eugene; Oregon; B5/17/1952 Camp LeJeune, NC

1994 Was	3-13-0	—	5 NFC-E
1995 Was	6-10-0	—	3 NFC-E
1996 Was	9-7-0	—	3 NFC-E #
1997 Was	8-7-1	—	2 NFC-E
1998 Was	6-10-0	—	4 NFC-E
1999 Was	10-6-0	1-1	1 NFC-E ED
2000 Was	7-6-0	—	◇3 NFC-E
2004 Oak	5-11-0	—	4 AFC-W
2005 Oak	4-12-0	—	4 AFC-W
NFL 9	58-82-1	1-1	—

URSELLA, RUBE* B1/11/1890

1920 RI	6-2-1	—	14 NFL
1921 Min	1-3-0	—	13 NFL
1925 RI	5-3-3	—	8 NFL
NFL 3	12-8-4	—	—

VAN BROCKLIN, NORM* B3/15/1926

1961 Min	3-11-0	—	7 NFL-W
1962 Min	2-11-1	—	6 NFL-W
1963 Min	5-8-1	—	4 NFL-W
1964 Min	8-5-1	—	2 NFL-W
1965 Min	7-7-0	—	5 NFL-W
1966 Min	4-9-1	—	6 NFL-W
1968 Atl	2-9-0	—	◆4 NFL-Cnl
1969 Atl	6-8-0	—	3 NFL-Cnl
1970 Atl	4-8-2	—	3 NFC-W
1971 Atl	7-6-1	—	3 NFC-W
1972 Atl	7-7-0	—	2 NFC-W
1973 Atl	9-5-0	—	2 NFC-W
1974 Atl	2-6-0	—	◇4 NFC-W
NFL 13	66-100-7	—	—

VENTURI, RICK Rick J.; Northwestern; B2/23/1946 Taylorville, IL

YEAR TEAM	W-L-T	WP-LP	FINISH PLAYOFFS
1991 Ind	1-10-0	—	♦5 AFC-E
1996 NO	1-7-0	—	♦4 NFC-W
NFL 2	2-17-0	—	

VERMEIL, DICK Richard Albert; San Jose State; B10/30/1936 Calistoga, CA

YEAR TEAM	W-L-T	WP-LP	FINISH PLAYOFFS
1976 Phi	4-10-0	—	4 NFC-E
1977 Phi	5-9-0	—	4 NFC-E
1978 Phi	9-7-0	0-1	2 NFC-E W
1979 Phi	11-5-0	1-1	2 NFC-E #WD
1980 Phi	12-4-0	2-1	1 NFC-E #DCS
1981 Phi	10-6-0	0-1	2 NFC-E W
1982 Phi	3-6-0	—	11 NFC
1997 SL	5-11-0	—	5 NFC-W
1998 SL	4-12-0	—	4 NFC-W
1999 SL	13-3-0	3-0	1 NFC-W DCS‡
2001 KC	6-10-0	—	4 AFC-W
2002 KC	8-8-0	—	3 AFC-W
2003 KC	13-3-0	0-1	1 AFC-W D
2004 KC	7-9-0	—	3 AFC-W
2005 KC	10-6-0	—	2 AFC-W
NFL 15	120-109-0	6-5	

VITT, JOE Joe; Towson State; B8/23/1954 Syracuse, NY

YEAR TEAM	W-L-T	WP-LP	FINISH PLAYOFFS
2005 SL	4-8-0	—	♦2 NFC-W

VOYLES, CARL Carl Marvin; Oklahoma State; B8/11/1902 McLoud, OK, D1/11/1982 Fort Myers, FL

YEAR TEAM	W-L-T	WP-LP	FINISH PLAYOFFS
1948 Bkn-A	2-12-0	—	4 AAFC-E

WALLER, CHARLIE Charles Fletcher; Georgia, Oglethorpe; B12/26/1921 Griffin, GA

YEAR TEAM	W-L-T	WP-LP	FINISH PLAYOFFS
1969 SD-A	4-1-0	—	♦3 AFL-W
1970 SD	5-6-3	—	3 AFL-W
NFL 2	9-7-3	—	

WALLER, RON* B2/14/1933

YEAR TEAM	W-L-T	WP-LP	FINISH PLAYOFFS
1973 SD	1-5-0	—	♦4 AFC-W

WALSH, ADAM Adam James; Notre Dame; B12/4/1901 Churchville, IA, D1/13/1985 Los Angeles, CA

YEAR TEAM	W-L-T	WP-LP	FINISH PLAYOFFS
1945 Cle	9-1-0	1-0	1 NFL-W L‡
1946 LARm	6-4-1	—	2 NFL-W
NFL 2	15-5-1	1-0	

WALSH, BILL William Ernest; San Jose State; B11/30/1931 Los Angeles, CA; HOF 1993

YEAR TEAM	W-L-T	WP-LP	FINISH PLAYOFFS
1979 SF	2-14-0	—	4 NFC-W
1980 SF	6-10-0	—	3 NFC-W
1981 SF	13-3-0	3-0	1 NFC-W DCS‡
1982 SF	3-6-0	—	11 NFC
1983 SF	10-6-0	1-1	1 NFC-W DC
1984 SF	15-1-0	3-0	1 NFC-W DCS‡
1985 SF	10-6-0	0-1	2 NFC-W #W
1986 SF	10-5-1	0-1	1 NFC-W D
1987 SF	13-2-0	0-1	1 NFC-W D
1988 SF	10-6-0	3-0	1 NFC-W #DCS‡
NFL 10	92-59-1	10-4	

WALSH, CHILE Charles Francis; Notre Dame; B2/4/1903 Des Moines, IA, D9/4/1971 Los Angeles, CA

YEAR TEAM	W-L-T	WP-LP	FINISH PLAYOFFS
1934 SL	1-2-0	—	6 NFL-W

WALTON, JOE* B12/15/1935

YEAR TEAM	W-L-T	WP-LP	FINISH PLAYOFFS
1983 NYJ	7-9-0	—	4 AFC-E
1984 NYJ	7-9-0	—	3 AFC-E
1985 NYJ	11-5-0	0-1	2 AFC-E #W
1986 NYJ	10-6-0	1-1	2 AFC-E #WD
1987 NYJ	6-9-0	—	5 AFC-E
1988 NYJ	8-7-1	—	4 AFC-E
1989 NYJ	4-12-0	—	5 AFC-E
NFL 7	53-57-1	1-2	

WANNSTEDT, DAVE David Raymond; Pittsburgh; B5/21/1952 Pittsburgh, PA

YEAR TEAM	W-L-T	WP-LP	FINISH PLAYOFFS
1993 ChiB	7-9-0	—	4 NFC-C
1994 ChiB	9-7-0	1-1	4 NFC-C #WD
1995 ChiB	9-7-0	—	3 NFC-C #
1996 ChiB	7-9-0	—	3 NFC-C
1997 ChiB	4-12-0	—	5 NFC-C
1998 ChiB	4-12-0	—	5 NFC-C
2000 Mia	11-5-0	1-1	1 AFC-E ED
2001 Mia	11-5-0	0-1	2 AFC-E #W
2002 Mia	9-7-0	—	2 AFC-E #
2003 Mia	10-6-0	—	2 AFC-E #
2004 Mia	1-8-0	—	♦4 AFC-E
NFL 11	82-87-0	2-3	

WATERFIELD, BOB* B7/26/1920

YEAR TEAM	W-L-T	WP-LP	FINISH PLAYOFFS
1960 LARm	4-7-1	—	6 NFL-W
1961 LARm	4-10-0	—	6 NFL-W
1962 LARm	1-7-0	—	♦7 NFL-W
NFL 3	9-24-1	—	

WEAVER, RED* B7/19/1897

YEAR TEAM	W-L-T	WP-LP	FINISH PLAYOFFS
1924 Col	4-4-0	—	10 NFL
1925 Col	0-9-0	—	20 NFL
NFL 2	4-13-0	—	

WEBSTER, ALEX* B4/19/1931

YEAR TEAM	W-L-T	WP-LP	FINISH PLAYOFFS
1969 NYG	6-8-0	—	2 NFL-Cny
1970 NYG	9-5-0	—	2 NFC-E
1971 NYG	4-10-0	—	5 NFC-E
1972 NYG	8-6-0	—	3 NFC-E
1973 NYG	2-11-1	—	5 NFC-E
NFL 5	29-40-1	—	

WEIR, ED* B3/14/1903

YEAR TEAM	W-L-T	WP-LP	FINISH PLAYOFFS
1927 Fra†	4-4-2	—	♦7 NFL
1928 Fra	11-3-2	—	2 NFL
NFL 2	15-7-4	—	

WHELCHEL, JOHN John Esten; Navy; B4/1/1898 Hogansville, GA, D11/5/1973 Portsmouth, VA

YEAR TEAM	W-L-T	WP-LP	FINISH PLAYOFFS
1949 Was	3-3-1	—	♦4 NFL-E

WHITE, MIKE Michael Kavanaugh; California; B1/4/1936 Berkeley, CA

YEAR TEAM	W-L-T	WP-LP	FINISH PLAYOFFS
1995 Oak	8-8-0	—	3 AFC-W
1996 Oak	7-9-0	—	4 AFC-W
NFL 2	15-17-0	—	

WIGGIN, PAUL* B11/18/1934

YEAR TEAM	W-L-T	WP-LP	FINISH PLAYOFFS
1975 KC	5-9-0	—	3 AFC-W
1976 KC	5-9-0	—	4 AFC-W
1977 KC	1-6-0	—	♦5 AFC-W
NFL 3	11-24-0	—	

WIGGS, HUBERT* B9/29/1893

YEAR TEAM	W-L-T	WP-LP	FINISH PLAYOFFS
1922 Lou	1-2-0	—	13 NFL

WILKIN, WILLIE* B4/21/1916

YEAR TEAM	W-L-T	WP-LP	FINISH PLAYOFFS
1946 ChiR-A†	2-2-1	—	♦♦4 AAFC-W

WILKINSON, BUD Charles Burnham; Minnesota; B4/23/1916 Minneapolis, MN, D2/9/1994 St. Louis, MO

YEAR TEAM	W-L-T	WP-LP	FINISH PLAYOFFS
1978 SL	6-10-0	—	4 NFC-E
1979 SL	3-10-0	—	♦5 NFC-E
NFL 2	9-20-0	—	

WILLIAMS, GREGG Gregg; Truman State, Central Missouri State; B7/15/1958 Excelsior Springs, MO

YEAR TEAM	W-L-T	WP-LP	FINISH PLAYOFFS
2001 Buf	3-13-0	—	5 AFC-E
2002 Buf	8-8-0	—	4 AFC-E
2003 Buf	6-10-0	—	3 AFC-E
NFL 3	17-31-0	—	

WILLIAMS, JERRY* B11/1/1923

YEAR TEAM	W-L-T	WP-LP	FINISH PLAYOFFS
1969 Phi	4-9-1	—	4 NFL-Cap
1970 Phi	3-10-1	—	5 NFC-E
1971 Phi	0-3-0	—	♦3 NFC-E
NFL 3	7-22-2	—	

WILLIAMSON, RICHARD Richard Alan; Alabama; B4/13/1941 Fort Deposit, AL

YEAR TEAM	W-L-T	WP-LP	FINISH PLAYOFFS
1990 TB	1-2-0	—	♦2 NFC-C
1991 TB	3-13-0	—	5 NFC-C
NFL 2	4-15-0	—	

WILLSEY, RAY Raymond; California; B9/30/1928 Regina, Canada

YEAR TEAM	W-L-T	WP-LP	FINISH PLAYOFFS
1961 SL†	2-0-0	—	♦4 NFL-E

WILSON, GEORGE* B2/3/1914

YEAR TEAM	W-L-T	WP-LP	FINISH PLAYOFFS
1957 Det	8-4-0	2-0	1 NFL-W CL‡
1958 Det	4-7-1	—	5 NFL-W
1959 Det	3-8-1	—	5 NFL-W
1960 Det	7-5-0	—	2 NFL-W
1961 Det	8-5-1	—	2 NFL-W
1962 Det	11-3-0	—	2 NFL-W
1963 Det	5-8-1	—	4 NFL-W
1964 Det	7-5-2	—	4 NFL-W
1966 Mia-A	3-11-0	—	4 AFL-E
1967 Mia-A	4-10-0	—	3 AFL-E
1968 Mia-A	5-8-1	—	3 AFL-E
1969 Mia-A	3-10-1	—	5 AFL-E
NFL 12	68-84-8	2-0	—

WILSON, LARRY* B3/24/1938

YEAR TEAM	W-L-T	WP-LP	FINISH PLAYOFFS
1979 SL	2-1-0	—	♦5 NFC-E

WINNER, CHARLEY Charles Height; Southeast Missouri State, Washington-St. Louis; B7/1/1924 Somerville, NJ

YEAR TEAM	W-L-T	WP-LP	FINISH PLAYOFFS
1966 SL	8-5-1	—	4 NFL-E
1967 SL	6-7-1	—	3 NFL-Cny
1968 SL	9-4-1	—	2 NFL-Cny
1969 SL	4-9-1	—	3 NFL-Cny
1970 SL	8-5-1	—	3 NFC-E
1974 NYJ	7-7-0	—	3 AFC-E
1975 NYJ	2-7-0	—	♦4 AFC-E
NFL 7	44-44-5	—	

WORKMAN, HOGE* B9/25/1899

YEAR TEAM	W-L-T	WP-LP	FINISH PLAYOFFS
1931 Cle†	2-8-0	—	8 NFL

WRAY, LUD* B2/7/1894

YEAR TEAM	W-L-T	WP-LP	FINISH PLAYOFFS
1932 Bos	4-4-2	—	4 NFL
1933 Phi	3-5-1	—	4 NFL-E
1934 Phi	4-7-0	—	3 NFL-E
1935 Phi	2-9-0	—	5 NFL-E
NFL 4	13-25-3	—	

WYCHE, SAM* B1/5/1945

YEAR TEAM	W-L-T	WP-LP	FINISH PLAYOFFS
1984 Cin	8-8-0	—	2 AFC-C
1985 Cin	7-9-0	—	2 AFC-C
1986 Cin	10-6-0	—	2 AFC-C #
1987 Cin	4-11-0	—	4 AFC-C
1988 Cin	12-4-0	2-1	1 AFC-C DCS
1989 Cin	8-8-0	—	4 AFC-C
1990 Cin	9-7-0	1-1	1 AFC-C #ED
1991 Cin	3-13-0	—	4 AFC-C
1992 TB	5-11-0	—	3 NFC-C
1993 TB	5-11-0	—	5 NFC-C
1994 TB	6-10-0	—	5 NFC-C
1995 TB	7-9-0	—	5 NFC-C
NFL 12	84-107-0	3-2	—

WYCOFF, DOUG* B9/16/1903

YEAR TEAM	W-L-T	WP-LP	FINISH PLAYOFFS
1929 SI	3-4-3	—	6 NFL
1930 SI	5-5-2	—	6 NFL
NFL 2	8-9-5	—	

YOUNG, DOC Alva Andrew; Indiana University Medical College; B12/18/1891 Hamilton County, IN, D7/2/1971 Chicago, IL

YEAR TEAM	W-L-T	WP-LP	FINISH PLAYOFFS
1925 Ham	1-3-0	—	♦14 NFL
1926 Ham	0-4-0	—	21 NFL
NFL 2	1-7-0	—	

YOUNGSTROM, SWEDE* B5/24/1897

YEAR TEAM	W-L-T	WP-LP	FINISH PLAYOFFS
1927 Fra†	4-4-2	—	♦7 NFL

THE GAMES

One of the widest appeals of the National Football League is that every game means so much. Because of the intense physical nature of the game and the need for preparation and recuperation, only 16 games are played per season. There are no throwaway games. In a league where only the best teams have a playoff spot clinched before the last week of the season, there aren't any games that can be taken lightly. And in a league that has long embraced the concept of parity, one team can defeat any other on "any given Sunday."

The schedule itself has undergone many transformations over the years. It took until 1936 for every team to play the same number of games—12—and the season was immediately reduced to 11 the next year. It dropped to 10 games in 1943 until the end of World War II. The number increased to 11 in 1946 and went back to 12 the next year with the rival All-America Football Conference playing a 14-game schedule. The NFL stayed at 12, even as it absorbed three AAFC teams in 1950, and didn't change until 1961, when the league followed its new rival, the American Football League, in playing 14 games per season. With the 1970 merger came games between the two conferences and the adoption of sudden death (limited to one extra quarter) in the regular season. The first regular-season overtime game seemed somewhat pointless as the Chiefs and Broncos still ended in a tie on September 22, 1974, but they were 15 minutes late for supper. The season was extended to 16 games in 1978, and in 1990 a bye week was added for every team. Strikes truncated the 1982 and 1987 schedule.

The calendar changed like the fall colors. A season that began in October in the early years of the league eventually moved to the second weekend of September, which generally meant the season ended before the weather turned poor in the East or Midwest, where all the teams were located until after World War II. Even with the inclusion of an NFL Championship Game starting in 1933, the season generally ended before Christmas (not counting the Pro Bowl). The AFL first extended the pro football season into the next calendar year, playing its first championship on New Year's Day, 1961. The NFL followed suit in 1965. With the expansion of the schedule and the playoffs, the NFL has gone later and later into January of the next year, and finally breaking into February in 2001 with Super Bowl XXXVI.

The generally small number of games through history—13,609 games and 423 playoff games (counting all games with independents in 1920 and AAFC games, but not the Playoff Bowl)—makes keeping track of every game possible to include in this book. Games are predominantly played one day per week, although a game has been played every Monday night since 1970 and NFL games have been played sporadically on every other day of the week over the years. Still, it takes about 10 years for the NFL to play as many games as in one major league baseball season.

The 2006 ESPN Football Encyclopedia goes beyond just giving the scores. Through exhaustive efforts we have been able to find quarter by quarter scoring, as well as offensive statistics for each team starting in 1940, and players who achieved 300 yards passing, or have surpassed 100 yards rushing or receiving dating from 1932, although early data is incomplete for defunct teams.

Note that this section only tracks the regular season. Playoff and Super Bowl games are in separate sections.

KEY TO GAME SCORES

The visiting team is listed first and the home team second. The team in bold for each game is the winner. Following the score by quarter is a second line with the same teams listed that includes the information that follows.

D   First Downs
R/   Rushing Attempts and Yards
P   Passing Attempts, Completions, and Interceptions

Underneath the team statistical information for each game is a list of the standout performers. For many games there are no players listed because no runner, receiver, or returner exceeded 100 yards and no quarterbacks totaled 300 yards passing or more. Players are listed by team with a designation showing which category they reached a superlative in for that day.

R   Rushing
P   Passing
C   Receiving

To show all this in a working model, take the 2005 game between the New York Giants and Philadelphia Eagles on Sunday, December 11. It was played in Philadelphia and won in overtime on a field goal by the Giants, with the extra period displayed in the box score. New York had 28 first downs on the day, ran 40 times for 138 yards, and passed 44 times, completed 28, and threw 3 interceptions, totaling 299 yards through the air (including yardage lost on sacks). For the Giants, Tiki Barber had 124 yards rushing, Jeremy Shockey had 107 receiving yards, and Eli Manning passed for 321 yards. On the Eagles' side of the ball, rookie Ryan Moats had 114 yards rushing. All this is represented below.

NYG	7	10	3	3	3	**26**
Phi	7	10	0	6	0	23

NYG   D28 R40/138   P(44-28-3) 299
Phi   D17 R25/175   P(32-14-0) 162
NYG-Barber 124R, Shockey 107C,
Manning 312P; Phi-Moats 114R

APFA PLAYS ALL COMERS

The American Professional Football Association, forerunner of the NFL, wasn't picky about who was on the schedule. Besides the teams in the league, 35 other opponents played against the APFA clubs, including the St. Paul Ideals, who played the first game in the history of the new league on Sunday, September 26, 1920. The Ideals were drubbed by the Rock Island Independents, 48–0, and the league was on. A list of all the non-league clubs that faced the APFA follows, along with the abbreviations used for those clubs in this section. These games are counted in the 1920 APFA standings, located in the Historical Record portion of the book. (Abbreviations for the APFA as well as NFL teams can be found on the inside back cover.)

ABu   All Buffalo
ATn   All Tonawanda
Cha   Champaign Legion
ChB   Chicago Boosters
ChS   Chicago Stayms
ClP   Cleveland Panthers
Cin   Cincinnati Celts
CWP   Columbus Wagner Pirates
DtM   Detroit Maroons
Ely   Elyria Athletics
FtP   Fort Porter (NY)
FtW   Fort Wayne Friars
Gar   Gary Elks
Kew   Kewanee (IL) Walworths
Lan   Lansing Oldsmobile
Log   Logan Square
McK   McKeesport Olympics
Min   Minneapolis Marines
Mol   Moline Universal Tractors
PtQ   Pitcairn (PA) Quakers
Pul   Pullman Thorns
Rck   Rockford (IL) A.C.
Ric   Richmond Athletics
RoS   Rochester Scalpers
StP   St. Paul Ideals
Syr   Syracuse Stars
Tho   Thorn Tornadoes (of Chicago)
Tol   Toledo Maroons
UAA   Union A.A. (of Philadelphia)
Uti   Utica K. of C.
WBu   West Buffalo
WGC   Washington Glee Club (of New Haven)
Whe   Wheeling Stogies
WJC   Washington & Jefferson Collegians
Zan   Zanesville Mark Grays

1920 APFA

SUNDAY, SEPTEMBER 26

StP	0	0	0	0	0
RI	14	14	14	6	**48**

SUNDAY, OCTOBER 3

Col	0	0	0	0	0
Day	0	0	7	7	**14**
Mun	0	0	0	0	0
RI	21	10	7	7	**45**
PtQ	0	0	0	0	0
Can	34	0	0	14	**48**
Mol	0	0	0	0	0
Dec	7	7	0	6	**20**
Whe	0	0	0	0	0
Akr	8	21	7	7	**43**
WBu	0	0	6	0	6
Buf	6	13	6	7	**32**
ABu	0	0	0	0	0
Roc	0	3	7	0	**10**

SUNDAY, OCTOBER 10

Ham	0	0	0	0	0
RI	0	13	0	13	**26**
ChiC	0	0	0	0	0
ChiT	0	0	0	0	0
Cle	0	0	0	0	0
Day	0	0	0	0	0
Col	0	0	0	0	0
Akr	7	14	14	2	**37**
Tol	0	0	0	0	0
Can	7	14	14	7	**42**
ABu	0	0	0	0	0
Buf	7	20	7	17	**51**
Kew	0	0	7	0	7
Dec	13	12	0	0	**25**
ClP	0	0	7	7	14
Det	6	13	14	7	**40**
FtP	0	0	0	0	0
Roc	26	13	21	6	**66**

SUNDAY, OCTOBER 17

Dec	0	7	0	0	**7**
RI	0	0	0	0	0
Cle	0	0	0	0	0
Can	7	0	0	0	**7**
Det	0	0	0	0	0
ChiT	6	0	6	0	**12**
Ham	0	0	0	0	0
Day	7	20	3	14	**44**
Cin	0	0	0	0	0
Akr	7	0	0	6	**13**
McK	0	0	7	0	7
Buf	7	7	0	14	**28**
Mol	?	?	?	?	3
ChiC	?	?	?	?	**33**
Col	0	0	0	0	0
FtW	7	0	7	0	**14**
Uti	0	0	0	0	0
Roc	0	0	0	0	0

SUNDAY, OCTOBER 24

Can	7	7	3	3	20
Day	0	14	6	0	20
Cle	0	0	0	0	0
Akr	7	0	0	0	**7**
ChiC	0	0	0	0	0
RI	0	7	0	0	**7**
Dec	0	7	3	0	**10**
ChiT	0	0	0	0	0
Col	0	0	0	0	0
Det	0	6	0	0	**6**
Tol	0	0	0	0	0
Buf	14	10	7	7	**38**
Syr	7	0	0	0	7
Roc	0	14	7	0	**21**

SUNDAY, OCTOBER 31

Col	0	0	0	0	0
Cle	0	7	0	0	**7**
Akr	3	7	0	0	**10**
Can	0	0	0	0	0
ChiT	0	7	0	0	7
RI	6	0	7	7	**20**
Roc	0	3	0	3	6
Buf	10	7	0	0	**17**
Det	0	0	0	0	0
ChiC	0	0	21	0	**21**
Cin	0	7	0	0	7
Day	7	9	7	0	**23**
Dec	13	3	13	0	**29**
Rck	0	0	0	0	0
Ham	?	?	?	?	**14**
Log	?	?	?	?	9

SUNDAY, NOVEMBER 7

ChiC	0	6	0	0	**6**
ChiT	3	0	0	0	3
Can	0	14	2	2	**18**
Cle	0	0	0	0	0
Dec	0	0	0	0	0
RI	0	0	0	0	0
ATn	0	0	0	0	0
Buf	7	21	7	0	**35**
Col	10	0	0	0	**10**
Zan	0	0	0	0	0
Uti	0	0	0	7	7
Roc	6	7	0	14	**27**
Ham	?	?	?	?	**14**
Pul	?	?	?	?	13

THURSDAY, NOVEMBER 11

RI	0	0	0	7	7
Tho	0	0	0	7	7
Dec	6	7	7	0	**20**
Cha	0	0	0	0	0

SUNDAY, NOVEMBER 14

Akr	0	7	0	0	7
Cle	0	0	7	0	7
Day	7	0	0	14	**21**
RI	0	0	0	0	0
Dec	0	0	3	0	**3**
Min	0	0	0	0	0
ChiT	0	0	0	0	0
Can	0	14	7	0	**21**
Col	7	0	0	0	7
Buf	6	23	7	7	**43**
Cin	0	0	0	0	0
ChiC	6	14	0	0	**20**
Det	0	0	0	0	0
FtW	0	0	0	0	0
Ham	6	0	0	0	6
Gar	0	0	0	7	**7**
ATn	0	0	6	0	**6**
Roc	0	0	0	0	0

SUNDAY, NOVEMBER 21

Can	0	0	0	3	**3**
Buf	0	0	0	0	0
Day	0	0	0	0	0
Akr	0	0	0	13	**13**
Ham	0	0	7	0	7
Dec	7	14	0	7	**28**
Lan	0	0	0	0	0
ChiC	0	7	7	0	**14**
Tol	0	0	0	0	0
Cle	7	0	0	7	**14**
RoS	0	0	0	0	0
Roc	2	0	0	14	**16**
Col	0	0	0	0	0
Zan	0	0	0	0	0

THURSDAY, NOVEMBER 25

Can	0	0	0	0	0
Akr	7	0	0	0	**7**
Dec	0	0	3	3	**6**
ChiT	0	0	0	0	0
Det	0	0	0	0	0
Day	14	14	0	0	**28**
Ham	0	0	0	0	0
ChB	?	?	?	?	**27**
ATn	0	7	0	7	**14**
Roc	3	0	0	0	3
Col	0	0	0	0	0
Ely	0	0	0	0	0

SUNDAY, NOVEMBER 28

Dec	6	0	0	0	6
ChiC	0	0	7	0	**7**
Akr	0	0	7	7	**14**
Day	0	0	0	0	0
Cle	0	0	0	0	0
Buf	0	7	0	0	**7**
Lan	0	0	0	0	0
Det	0	0	0	0	0
Tho	0	0	0	0	0
ChiT	?	?	?	?	**27**
Roc	0	7	0	0	**7**
RoS	0	0	0	6	6
WJC	0	0	7	0	7
RI	14	20	7	7	**48**

SATURDAY, DECEMBER 4

Can	0	0	3	0	3
Buf	0	0	7	0	**7**

SUNDAY, DECEMBER 5

Akr	0	0	0	0	0
Buf	0	0	0	0	0
Dec	0	7	0	3	**10**
ChiC	0	0	0	0	0
Can	0	0	0	0	0
WGC	0	0	0	0	0
Roc	0	0	0	0	0
RoS	0	0	0	0	0
DtM	0	0	0	7	7
Det	0	0	7	0	7
CWP	0	0	0	0	0
Col	3	0	14	7	**24**

SATURDAY, DECEMBER 11

Can	0	7	0	0	7
UAA	0	7	6	0	**13**

SUNDAY, DECEMBER 12

Akr	0	0	0	0	0
Dec	0	0	0	0	0

SATURDAY, DECEMBER 18

Can	13	0	13	13	**39**
Ric	0	0	0	0	0

SUNDAY, DECEMBER 19

ChiC	?	?	?	?	14
ChS	?	?	?	?	14

1921 APFA

SUNDAY, SEPTEMBER 25

Col	0	0	0	0	0
Akr	0	7	7	0	**14**

SUNDAY, OCTOBER 2

Ham	0	0	0	0	0
Buf	0	3	7	7	**17**
Cin	0	0	0	0	0
Akr	7	7	21	6	**41**
Min	0	0	0	0	0
ChiC	?	?	?	?	**20**
Col	0	0	13	0	13
Day	14	7	0	21	**42**
Det	0	0	0	0	0
RI	0	0	0	0	0
Lou	0	0	0	0	0
Evv	?	?	?	0	**21**

SUNDAY, OCTOBER 9

Akr	17	0	0	6	**23**
ChiC	0	0	0	0	0
Col	0	0	0	0	0
Buf	17	14	7	0	**38**
Ham	0	7	0	0	7
Can	0	0	7	0	7
Day	0	0	0	7	7
Det	0	3	7	0	**10**
Mun	0	0	0	0	0
Evv	0	7	0	7	**14**

MONDAY, OCTOBER 10

RI	0	3	0	7	10
ChiS	0	0	7	7	**14**

SUNDAY, OCTOBER 16

RI	0	14	0	0	**14**
ChiC	7	0	0	0	7
Can	0	0	7	7	14
Day	14	0	0	0	14
Akr	7	0	6	7	**20**
Det	0	0	0	0	0
Roc	3	0	7	3	13
ChiS	0	3	6	7	**16**
Col	0	2	0	7	9
Cle	14	21	0	0	**35**
NYG	0	0	0	0	0
Buf	17	21	7	10	**55**
Ham	0	3	0	0	**3**
Evv	0	0	0	0	0
Cin	0	7	0	7	**14**
Mun	0	0	0	0	0

SUNDAY, OCTOBER 23

Akr	3	0	0	0	**3**
Can	0	0	0	0	0
Col	0	6	0	0	6
ChiC	0	0	7	10	**17**
Roc	0	0	0	0	0
Buf	7	7	14	0	**28**
Cin	0	0	0	0	0
Cle	0	7	14	7	**28**
Min	6	0	0	0	6
GB	0	0	0	7	**7**
RI	7	7	0	0	**14**
Det	0	0	0	0	0
Day	0	0	0	0	0
ChiS	0	0	0	7	**7**

SUNDAY, OCTOBER 30

Roc	0	0	0	0	0
Akr	0	6	0	13	**19**
Det	0	0	0	0	0
Buf	14	7	0	0	**21**
Cle	0	2	0	0	2
Day	0	0	3	0	**3**
RI	7	0	0	6	**13**
GB	3	0	0	0	3
Col	0	0	0	0	0
Min	7	7	7	7	**28**

SUNDAY, NOVEMBER 6

Cle	6	0	0	0	6
Buf	7	0	3	0	**10**
Ham	0	0	0	0	0
ChiC	7	0	0	0	**7**
Akr	0	14	7	0	**21**
Col	0	0	0	0	0
Det	0	7	0	2	9
ChiS	6	0	7	7	**20**
Evv	0	0	0	6	6
GB	7	15	14	7	**43**
Day	0	0	0	0	0
Can	0	7	7	0	**14**
Min	3	0	0	0	3
RI	0	0	7	7	**14**
Ton	0	0	0	0	0
Roc	7	14	0	24	**45**

SUNDAY, NOVEMBER 13

Akr	0	0	0	0	0
Buf	0	0	0	0	0
RI	0	0	0	0	0
ChiS	0	3	0	0	**3**
Det	0	0	0	0	0
Day	6	0	0	21	**27**
Ham	0	0	7	0	7
GB	14	0	0	0	**14**
Can	0	0	7	0	**7**
Cle	0	0	0	0	0

SUNDAY, NOVEMBER 20

GB	0	0	3	0	3
ChiC	0	0	0	3	3
Akr	0	0	0	0	0
Day	0	0	3	0	**3**
Col	6	0	0	7	13
Roc	0	7	0	20	**27**
Cle	0	0	7	0	7
ChiS	6	13	3	0	**22**
Can	0	0	0	7	7
Buf	7	0	0	0	7

THURSDAY, NOVEMBER 24

Can	0	7	0	7	**14**
Akr	0	0	0	0	0
Buf	0	0	7	0	**7**
ChiS	6	0	0	0	6

SUNDAY, NOVEMBER 27

Can	3	6	0	6	**15**
Wss	0	0	0	0	0
Day	0	0	0	0	0
Buf	7	0	0	0	**7**
GB	0	0	0	0	0
ChiS	0	14	0	6	**20**
Cin	0	0	0	0	0
Evv	?	?	?	?	**48**

SATURDAY, DECEMBER 3

Akr	0	0	0	0	0
Buf	7	7	0	0	**14**
Cle	7	3	0	7	**17**
NYG	0	0	0	0	0

SUNDAY, DECEMBER 4

Akr	0	0	0	7	**7**
ChiC	0	0	0	0	0
Buf	0	0	7	0	7
ChiS	7	0	3	0	**10**
Col	0	0	0	6	**6**
Lou	0	0	0	0	0

SUNDAY, DECEMBER 11

Can	0	0	0	0	0
ChiS	0	0	3	7	**10**
Cle	0	0	0	0	0
Wss	0	0	0	7	**7**

SUNDAY, DECEMBER 18

ChiC	0	0	0	0	0
ChiS	0	0	0	0	0
Can	14	0	0	14	**28**
Wss	0	7	7	0	14

1922 NFL

SUNDAY, OCTOBER 1

Col	0	0	0	0	0
Akr	7	7	9	13	**36**
Ham	0	0	0	0	0
Buf	0	7	0	0	**7**
Lou	0	0	0	0	0
Can	6	13	6	13	**38**
Mil	0	0	0	0	0
ChiC	3	0	0	0	**3**
Oor	0	0	0	0	0
Day	9	7	7	13	**36**
ChiB	3	0	0	3	**6**
Rac	0	0	0	0	0
GB	0	7	0	7	14
RI	6	10	0	3	**19**
Evv	0	0	0	0	0
Tol	0	0	3	12	**15**

SUNDAY, OCTOBER 8

Can	0	0	0	0	0
Day	0	0	0	0	0
Rac	0	10	0	0	**10**
GB	6	0	0	0	6
Col	0	0	6	0	6
Oor	0	7	0	13	**20**
ChiB	0	7	0	3	**10**
RI	0	0	6	0	6

Mil	6	6	0	0	12
Tol	0	6	0	6	12

THURSDAY, OCTOBER 12

Roc	0	0	13	0	13
Akr	0	6	0	7	13

SUNDAY, OCTOBER 15

Ham	0	0	0	0	0
Tol	7	7	0	0	**14**
Evv	0	0	0	0	0
RI	6	27	7	20	**60**
Rac	0	0	0	0	0
Mil	7	6	0	7	**20**
Min	0	0	0	0	0
Day	7	3	0	7	**17**
Roc	0	0	0	0	0
ChiB	0	0	0	7	**7**
Col	0	0	0	0	0
Buf	0	6	7	6	**19**
Oor	0	0	0	0	0
Can	0	0	14	0	**14**
GB	0	3	0	0	3
ChiC	3	0	7	6	**16**

SUNDAY, OCTOBER 22

Buf	0	0	0	0	0
ChiB	7	0	0	0	**7**
Can	0	9	6	7	**22**
Akr	0	0	0	0	0
Tol	0	0	7	0	**7**
Rac	0	0	0	0	0
Roc	0	0	0	0	0
RI	0	6	7	13	**26**
Ham	0	0	0	0	0
Day	3	0	14	3	**20**
GB	0	0	0	0	0
Mil	0	0	0	0	0
Min	0	0	0	0	0
ChiC	0	3	0	0	**3**

SUNDAY, OCTOBER 29

Buf	0	0	7	0	**7**
Day	0	0	0	0	0
Can	7	0	0	0	**7**
ChiB	0	0	0	6	6
Col	0	0	0	6	6
ChiC	3	21	6	7	**37**
RI	0	0	0	0	0
GB	0	0	0	0	0
Ham	0	0	0	0	0
Mil	0	0	0	0	0
Roc	0	0	0	0	0
Rac	0	0	6	3	**9**
Oor	0	0	0	0	0
Akr	20	7	14	21	**62**
Lou	0	0	0	0	0
Tol	13	7	6	13	**39**

SUNDAY, NOVEMBER 5

Tol	0	0	0	0	0
Can	0	0	0	0	0
Day	0	0	0	0	0
ChiB	3	0	0	6	**9**
Buf	0	7	0	0	7
ChiC	6	0	3	0	**9**
Oor	0	6	0	0	6
Min	0	0	7	6	**13**
Lou	0	0	0	0	0
Rac	13	18	?	?	**57**
Col	0	0	0	0	0
GB	0	0	3	0	**3**
Ham	0	0	0	0	0
Akr	0	3	7	12	**22**

SATURDAY, NOVEMBER 11

Col	0	0	0	0	0
Rac	13	0	7	14	**34**

SUNDAY, NOVEMBER 12

Day	0	0	0	0	0
RI	7	10	7	19	**43**
Buf	0	0	0	0	0
Can	0	3	0	0	**3**
Min	0	6	0	0	6
GB	0	0	0	14	**14**
Akr	0	0	0	0	0
ChiC	0	7	0	0	**7**
Oor	0	0	0	6	6
ChiB	13	7	13	0	**33**
Evv	?	?	?	?	6
Lou	?	?	?	?	**13**

SUNDAY, NOVEMBER 19

Can	0	0	0	7	**7**
ChiC	0	0	0	0	0
GB	0	0	0	3	3
Rac	0	0	0	3	3
RI	0	0	0	0	0
ChiB	0	0	0	3	**3**
Akr	0	3	0	0	3
Buf	0	0	3	0	3
Oor	0	0	0	0	0
Mil	6	0	7	0	**13**

SUNDAY, NOVEMBER 26

ChiC	3	0	0	0	3
Can	0	0	0	20	**20**
Akr	0	0	3	7	10
ChiB	13	0	0	7	**20**
Col	0	6	0	0	6
Tol	0	7	0	0	**7**
Ham	0	0	0	0	0
Rac	6	0	0	0	**6**
Mil	0	0	0	0	0
GB	0	7	0	6	**13**
Oor	0	6	0	13	**19**
Buf	7	0	0	0	7

THURSDAY, NOVEMBER 30

Buf	?	?	?	?	**21**
Roc	0	0	0	0	0
ChiB	0	0	0	0	0
ChiC	0	3	0	3	**6**
Mil	0	0	0	0	0
Rac	0	3	0	0	**3**
Oor	6	0	12	0	**18**
Col	0	0	0	6	6
Akr	0	0	0	0	0
Can	7	7	0	0	**14**

SUNDAY, DECEMBER 3

Mil	0	0	6	0	6
Can	13	20	0	7	**40**
Tol	0	0	0	0	0
ChiB	7	9	6	0	**22**
GB	0	7	0	7	**14**
Rac	0	0	0	0	0
Day	0	0	0	7	**7**
ChiC	0	3	0	0	3
Akr	0	0	0	0	0
Buf	6	3	7	0	**16**

SUNDAY, DECEMBER 10

Can	3	7	0	9	**19**
Tol	0	0	0	0	0
ChiB	0	0	0	0	0
ChiC	3	3	3	0	**9**

1923 NFL

SUNDAY, SEPTEMBER 30

Ham	0	0	0	0	0
Can	0	3	7	7	**17**
ChiB	0	0	0	0	0
RI	0	3	0	0	**3**
Min	0	0	0	0	0
GB	0	0	6	6	**12**
Oor	0	0	2	0	2
Mil	0	0	13	0	**13**
Buf	0	0	0	0	0
ChiC	0	0	0	3	**3**
Akr	0	0	0	7	7
Dul	0	7	3	0	**10**
Col	6	0	0	0	6
Day	0	0	0	7	**7**
Tol	0	0	0	7	7
Rac	0	0	0	7	7

SUNDAY, OCTOBER 7

Lou	0	0	0	0	0
Can	13	10	7	7	**37**
ChiB	0	3	0	0	**3**
Rac	0	0	0	0	0
SL	0	0	0	0	0
GB	0	0	0	0	0
Col	0	0	0	0	0
Mil	0	0	0	0	0
Cle	0	0	0	0	0
RI	0	0	0	0	0
Roc	0	0	0	0	0
ChiC	?	?	?	?	**60**
Dul	0	0	7	3	**10**
Min	0	0	0	0	0
Akr	0	0	0	0	0
Buf	0	9	0	0	**9**
Oor	0	0	0	0	0
Tol	0	0	0	7	**7**
Day	0	0	0	0	0
Ham	?	?	?	?	**7**

SUNDAY, OCTOBER 14

Day	0	0	0	0	0
Can	3	10	3	14	**30**
ChiB	0	3	0	0	**3**
GB	0	0	0	0	0
Rac	0	0	0	7	7
Mil	7	0	0	0	7
Akr	0	0	0	0	0
ChiC	0	?	?	?	**19**
Buf	0	0	0	3	**3**
Col	0	0	0	0	0
Roc	0	0	0	0	0
RI	14	14	0	28	**56**
Oor	0	0	0	0	0
Min	0	10	7	6	**23**
Ham	0	0	0	0	0
SL	0	0	0	0	0

SUNDAY, OCTOBER 21

Can	0	0	0	6	**6**
ChiB	0	0	0	0	0
Mil	0	0	0	0	0
GB	3	0	7	2	**12**
SL	0	0	0	0	0
Cle	0	0	6	0	**6**
Min	0	0	0	0	0
ChiC	0	0	3	6	**9**
Ham	0	0	0	0	0
Dul	3	0	0	0	**3**
Lou	0	0	0	0	0
Col	13	14	0	7	**34**
Oor	0	0	0	0	0
Buf	13	10	7	27	**57**
Akr	0	7	0	0	7
Rac	?	?	?	?	**9**
Day	?	?	?	?	3
Tol	0	0	0	6	**6**

SUNDAY, OCTOBER 28

Akr	0	3	0	0	3
Can	0	0	0	7	**7**
Buf	0	3	0	0	3
ChiB	0	9	0	9	**18**
Rac	0	10	7	7	**24**
GB	0	0	3	0	3
SL	0	0	0	0	0
Mil	0	0	6	0	**6**
Oor	0	0	0	0	0
Cle	0	7	7	13	**27**
Day	3	0	0	0	3
ChiC	0	3	3	7	**13**
Min	0	0	0	0	0
Dul	0	9	0	0	**9**
Col	3	0	0	0	**3**
Tol	0	0	0	0	0

SUNDAY, NOVEMBER 4

Can	0	0	0	7	**7**
ChiC	3	0	0	0	3
Oor	0	0	0	0	0
ChiB	13	13	0	0	**26**
GB	0	0	3	0	**3**
SL	0	0	0	0	0
Mil	0	0	7	7	**14**
RI	3	0	0	0	3
Buf	0	0	0	0	0
Cle	0	0	0	0	0
Rac	3	3	0	0	6
Min	0	6	0	7	**13**

SUNDAY, NOVEMBER 11

Can	0	0	0	3	3
Buf	3	0	0	0	3
Akr	0	0	6	0	6
ChiB	7	7	0	6	**20**
GB	6	0	3	7	**16**
Rac	0	0	0	0	0
Dul	0	3	0	0	3
Mil	0	0	3	3	**6**
Day	0	0	0	0	0
Cle	0	0	0	0	0
Ham	0	0	0	0	0
ChiC	6	0	0	0	**6**
Tol	0	0	0	0	0
Col	0	9	0	7	**16**
RI	0	0	6	0	6
Min	0	6	0	0	6
Oor	0	0	7	0	7
SL	7	7	0	0	**14**

SUNDAY, NOVEMBER 18

Oor	0	0	0	0	0
Can	7	6	21	7	**41**
RI	0	0	3	0	3
ChiB	0	0	0	7	**7**
GB	3	0	7	0	**10**
Mil	0	7	0	0	7
Col	0	0	0	3	3
Cle	0	0	6	3	**9**
Dul	0	0	0	0	0
ChiC	3	0	0	7	**10**
Day	0	0	0	0	0
Buf	3	0	0	0	**3**

SATURDAY, NOVEMBER 24

Tol	6	0	6	0	**12**
Roc	0	6	0	0	6
Mil	7	7	3	0	**17**
SL	0	0	0	0	0

SUNDAY, NOVEMBER 25

Can	6	14	13	13	**46**
Cle	3	0	7	0	10
Ham	0	0	0	7	7
ChiB	0	7	0	7	**14**
Dul	0	0	0	0	0
GB	0	10	0	0	**10**
Rac	0	0	3	7	**10**
ChiC	0	2	0	2	4
Oor	3	0	0	0	3
Col	13	14	0	0	**27**
Tol	0	0	0	3	3
Buf	0	0	3	0	3
Min	6	0	0	0	6
RI	0	0	0	6	6

THURSDAY, NOVEMBER 29

Tol	0	0	0	0	0
Can	14	0	7	7	**28**
ChiC	0	0	0	0	0
ChiB	3	0	0	0	**3**
Ham	0	0	0	0	0
GB	6	0	7	6	**19**
Mil	7	3	0	6	**16**
Rac	0	0	0	0	0
Buf	0	0	0	0	0
Akr	0	0	2	0	**2**

SATURDAY, DECEMBER 1

Buf	?	?	?	?	**13**
Roc	0	0	0	0	0

SUNDAY, DECEMBER 2

Buf	0	0	0	0	0
Can	0	14	0	0	**14**
Mil	0	0	0	0	0
ChiB	0	0	0	0	0
Oor	6	0	0	13	19
ChiC	7	12	3	0	**22**
Day	3	0	0	0	3
Col	0	10	6	14	**30**
Min	0	0	0	0	0
Rac	0	3	20	0	**23**

SUNDAY, DECEMBER 9

Can	0	3	7	0	**10**
Col	0	0	0	0	0
RI	0	7	0	0	7
ChiB	7	9	7	6	**29**
Mil	0	7	7	0	**14**
ChiC	3	0	0	9	12
Oor	?	?	?	?	**19**
Lou	0	0	0	0	0

1924 NFL

SATURDAY, SEPTEMBER 27

Roc	0	0	0	0	0
Fra	0	7	0	14	**21**

SUNDAY, SEPTEMBER 28

ChiB	0	0	0	0	0
RI	0	0	0	0	0
GB	0	0	3	0	3
Dul	0	0	0	6	**6**
Ham	0	0	0	0	0
Rac	7	0	0	3	**10**
Mil	0	0	7	0	7
ChiC	0	3	7	7	**17**

SATURDAY, OCTOBER 4

Ken	0	0	0	6	6
Fra	0	14	3	14	**31**

SUNDAY, OCTOBER 5

Akr	0	0	3	0	**3**
Roc	0	0	0	0	0
ChiB	7	0	0	7	14
Cle	3	0	13	0	**16**
Col	0	0	0	0	0
Buf	0	0	3	10	**13**
Dul	0	3	0	0	**3**
Min	0	0	0	0	0
Fra	0	0	7	0	7
Day	0	7	3	9	**19**
GB	0	0	0	0	0
ChiC	3	0	0	0	**3**
KC	0	0	0	0	0
Mil	0	0	3	0	**3**
Rac	0	0	0	0	0
RI	0	0	0	9	**9**

SATURDAY, OCTOBER 11

Cle	0	0	0	3	3
Fra	0	0	3	0	3

SUNDAY, OCTOBER 12

Akr	7	7	0	0	14
Cle	9	13	0	7	**29**
Col	2	6	7	0	**15**
Roc	0	0	0	7	7
Day	0	0	0	7	**7**
Buf	0	0	0	0	0
KC	0	0	0	0	0
GB	7	0	9	0	**16**
Ken	0	0	0	0	0
Mil	0	14	7	0	**21**
Min	0	0	0	0	0
ChiC	7	0	0	6	**13**
Rac	3	0	7	0	10
ChiB	0	0	10	0	10

Ham	0	0	0	0	0
RI	6	7	0	13	**26**

SATURDAY, OCTOBER 18

Col	7	0	0	0	7
Fra	6	7	0	10	**23**

SUNDAY, OCTOBER 19

ChiC	0	0	0	0	0
ChiB	3	0	0	3	**6**
Mil	0	0	0	0	0
GB	0	0	0	17	**17**
Ham	0	0	0	6	6
Ken	0	0	6	0	6
KC	0	0	0	3	3
Rac	7	3	0	3	**13**
Roc	0	0	0	0	0
Buf	0	13	6	7	**26**
Day	0	0	0	0	0
RI	6	0	7	7	**20**

SUNDAY, OCTOBER 26

Akr	0	7	0	6	13
Buf	10	0	7	0	**17**
Col	3	0	7	7	**17**
Day	6	0	0	0	6
Fra	3	0	0	0	3
ChiB	0	10	9	14	**33**
Min	0	0	0	0	0
GB	0	13	0	6	**19**
Rac	0	10	0	0	**10**
Mil	0	0	0	0	0
Ham	6	0	0	0	**6**
ChiC	0	3	0	0	3
RI	0	7	0	0	7
KC	3	0	0	20	**23**
Ken	0	0	0	0	0
Dul	9	3	6	14	**32**
Roc	0	0	0	0	0
Cle	6	27	7	19	**59**

SATURDAY, NOVEMBER 1

Akr	0	0	0	0	0
Fra	0	20	0	3	**23**

SUNDAY, NOVEMBER 2

Akr	0	0	0	0	0
Col	6	10	7	7	**30**
Day	0	0	0	0	0
Cle	14	0	7	14	**35**
Dul	0	0	6	0	**6**
Min	0	0	0	0	0
Fra	0	7	7	10	**24**
Buf	0	0	0	0	0
Rac	3	0	0	0	3
GB	0	0	0	6	**6**
Ham	6	0	0	0	**6**
KC	0	0	0	0	0
Mil	7	3	7	0	**17**
ChiC	0	6	2	0	8
RI	0	3	0	0	3
ChiB	0	0	0	3	3

SATURDAY, NOVEMBER 8

KC	0	0	0	7	7
Fra	12	14	10	6	**42**

SUNDAY, NOVEMBER 9

Cle	13	7	0	0	**20**
Akr	0	0	7	0	7
Col	6	0	0	0	6
ChiB	6	3	0	3	**12**
Day	0	0	0	0	0
ChiC	6	10	7	0	**23**
Dul	0	0	0	0	0
GB	7	6	0	0	**13**
Min	0	7	0	0	7
Mil	7	10	3	8	**28**
Ken	0	0	0	0	0
Buf	7	13	0	7	**27**
RI	0	0	6	0	**6**
Rac	3	0	0	0	3

TUESDAY, NOVEMBER 11

Mil	0	3	0	0	3
KC	7	0	0	0	**7**

SATURDAY, NOVEMBER 15

Min	0	0	0	7	7
Fra	13	20	6	0	**39**

SUNDAY, NOVEMBER 16

Akr	0	0	0	0	0
ChiC	7	3	0	3	**13**
Day	6	0	0	0	6
Buf	7	0	7	0	**14**
Fra	3	3	6	0	**12**
Cle	0	0	0	7	7
GB	3	0	7	7	**17**
Mil	0	3	0	7	10
Rac	3	0	0	0	3
ChiB	0	3	0	0	3
Roc	0	0	0	0	0
Col	6	3	0	7	**16**
KC	0	0	0	0	0
RI	3	0	7	7	**17**

SATURDAY, NOVEMBER 22

Buf	9	0	7	0	**16**
Roc	0	0	0	0	0
Mil	0	6	0	0	6
Fra	7	0	7	7	**21**

SUNDAY, NOVEMBER 23

GB	0	0	0	0	0
ChiB	0	0	3	0	**3**
Col	0	0	0	0	0
Cle	0	7	0	0	**7**
Dul	0	9	0	0	**9**
RI	0	0	0	0	0
Rac	0	0	7	3	10
ChiC	7	3	0	0	10
Mil	0	6	10	7	**23**
Buf	0	0	0	0	0

THURSDAY, NOVEMBER 27

Buf	0	0	0	0	0
Akr	0	3	6	13	**22**
ChiB	7	14	0	0	**21**
ChiC	0	0	0	0	0
Day	0	0	0	7	7
Fra	13	6	13	0	**32**
Mil	7	3	0	0	10
Cle	7	14	7	25	**53**
GB	3	0	7	7	**17**
KC	0	0	0	6	6

SATURDAY, NOVEMBER 29

Buf	0	0	7	0	7
Fra	21	10	0	14	**45**

SUNDAY, NOVEMBER 30

GB	0	0	0	0	0
Rac	0	7	0	0	**7**
Mil	0	7	0	7	14
ChiB	0	14	3	14	**31**

1925 NFL

SUNDAY, SEPTEMBER 20

ChiB	0	0	0	0	0
RI	0	0	0	0	0
Ham	0	0	0	0	0
GB	0	7	0	7	**14**

SATURDAY, SEPTEMBER 26

Buf	7	0	0	0	7
Fra	0	13	7	7	**27**

SUNDAY, SEPTEMBER 27

Buf	0	0	0	0	0
Pot	7	7	7	7	**28**
ChiB	0	0	10	0	10
GB	0	7	0	7	**14**
Col	0	0	0	0	0
Det	0	0	0	7	**7**

Ham	3	7	0	0	**10**
ChiC	3	3	0	0	6
Cle	0	0	0	0	0
Akr	7	0	0	0	**7**
KC	3	0	0	0	**3**
Dul	0	0	0	0	0
Roc	0	0	0	7	7
Can	0	14	0	0	**14**
Day	0	0	0	0	0
RI	0	0	0	0	0

SATURDAY, OCTOBER 3

Pro	0	0	0	0	0
Fra	7	0	0	0	**7**

SUNDAY, OCTOBER 4

ChiB	0	0	0	0	0
Det	0	0	0	0	0
Col	0	0	0	0	0
Cle	0	0	3	0	**3**
Day	0	0	0	0	0
Can	0	0	7	7	**14**
GB	0	0	0	0	0
RI	0	0	0	3	**3**
KC	0	0	7	0	7
Akr	7	7	0	0	**14**
Mil	0	0	0	0	0
ChiC	0	14	7	13	**34**
Pro	0	0	6	0	**6**
Pot	0	0	0	0	0
Roc	0	0	0	0	0
Buf	0	0	0	0	0

SATURDAY, OCTOBER 10

Can	0	0	0	7	7
Fra	0	6	0	6	**12**

SUNDAY, OCTOBER 11

Col	3	0	6	0	9
ChiC	3	10	3	3	**19**
Can	0	0	0	0	0
Pot	0	7	14	7	**28**
Fra	0	0	0	0	0
Det	0	3	0	0	**3**
KC	6	0	0	7	13
Cle	0	7	3	6	**16**
Ham	0	7	0	0	7
ChiB	7	14	0	7	**28**
NYG	0	0	0	0	0
Pro	0	14	0	0	**14**
Mil	0	0	0	0	0
GB	3	14	7	7	**31**
RI	0	12	0	0	**12**
Dul	0	0	0	0	0
Akr	0	0	0	0	0
Buf	0	0	0	0	0

SATURDAY, OCTOBER 17

NYG	0	3	0	0	3
Fra	2	0	3	0	**5**

SUNDAY, OCTOBER 18

Akr	0	0	14	6	**20**
Can	0	3	0	0	3
KC	0	7	0	0	7
ChiC	0	13	7	0	**20**
Cle	0	0	0	0	0
ChiB	7	0	0	0	**7**
Col	0	0	0	6	6
Buf	10	0	0	7	**17**
Day	0	0	0	0	0
Det	0	3	0	3	**6**
Fra	7	7	0	0	**14**
NYG	0	0	0	0	0
Pot	0	14	0	20	**34**
Pro	0	0	0	0	0
RI	0	0	0	0	0
GB	0	0	7	13	**20**

SATURDAY, OCTOBER 24

Day	0	0	0	0	0
Fra	0	0	0	3	**3**

SUNDAY, OCTOBER 25

Akr	0	0	0	0	0
Det	0	0	0	0	0
ChiB	0	0	0	0	0
ChiC	0	6	0	3	**9**
Roc	0	0	0	13	13
GB	0	0	7	26	**33**
KC	0	0	0	3	3
RI	0	0	0	3	3

SATURDAY, OCTOBER 31

Col	0	0	0	0	0
Fra	13	0	0	6	**19**

SUNDAY, NOVEMBER 1

Cle	0	0	0	0	0
NYG	6	7	0	6	**19**
Col	0	0	0	0	0
Pot	7	7	6	0	**20**
Day	3	0	0	0	3
Akr	0	0	7	10	**17**
Dul	0	6	0	0	6
ChiC	0	0	0	10	**10**
Fra	0	12	0	0	**12**
Buf	3	0	0	0	3
GB	0	6	0	0	**6**
Mil	0	0	0	0	0
Ham	0	0	0	6	6
Det	7	7	6	6	**26**
Roc	0	0	0	0	0
Pro	0	8	6	3	**17**
RI	0	0	0	0	0
ChiB	3	0	3	0	**6**

TUESDAY, NOVEMBER 3

Buf	0	0	0	0	0
NYG	0	7	0	0	**7**

SATURDAY, NOVEMBER 7

Akr	0	0	0	7	7
Fra	10	7	0	0	**17**

SUNDAY, NOVEMBER 8

Akr	0	0	0	0	0
Pot	7	7	0	7	**21**
Buf	0	0	0	0	0
Pro	0	0	0	10	**10**
Cle	0	0	0	0	0
Can	6	0	0	0	**6**
Col	0	0	0	0	0
NYG	7	0	0	12	**19**
Mil	0	0	0	0	0
Det	7	7	7	0	**21**
Fra	0	0	0	0	0
ChiB	13	0	6	0	**19**
GB	0	0	0	6	6
ChiC	0	0	0	9	**9**

WEDNESDAY, NOVEMBER 11

Cle	0	7	6	0	13
Det	13	6	3	0	**22**
Roc	0	0	0	0	0
NYG	10	3	0	0	**13**

SATURDAY, NOVEMBER 14

Pot	0	0	0	0	0
Fra	0	3	10	7	**20**

SUNDAY, NOVEMBER 15

Buf	6	0	0	0	6
ChiC	9	7	0	7	**23**
Day	0	0	0	0	0
GB	0	0	0	7	**7**
Det	0	0	0	0	0
ChiB	0	0	7	7	**14**
KC	0	12	0	0	12
RI	3	0	7	25	**35**
Pro	0	3	0	9	12
NYG	7	0	6	0	**13**
Roc	0	6	0	0	6
Pot	0	7	7	0	**14**

SATURDAY, NOVEMBER 21

Cle	0	7	0	7	**14**
Fra	0	0	0	0	0

SUNDAY, NOVEMBER 22

Day	0	0	0	0	0
ChiC	14	0	0	0	**14**
Col	0	0	0	0	0
Can	6	0	0	0	**6**
Cle	0	0	0	6	6
Pot	7	0	7	10	**24**
Fra	0	0	0	7	7
Pro	7	3	10	0	**20**
GB	0	0	0	0	0
ChiB	0	7	0	14	**21**
KC	0	3	0	0	3
NYG	6	0	3	0	**9**
Roc	0	0	0	0	0
Det	7	0	0	13	**20**
Mil	0	7	0	0	7
RI	6	6	7	21	**40**

THURSDAY, NOVEMBER 26

ChiC	0	0	0	0	0
ChiB	0	0	0	0	0
KC	7	3	0	7	**17**
Cle	0	0	0	0	0
RI	0	0	0	6	**6**
Det	0	3	0	0	3
GB	0	0	0	0	0
Pot	10	14	0	7	**31**

SATURDAY, NOVEMBER 28

GB	0	7	0	0	7
Fra	7	0	0	6	**13**

SUNDAY, NOVEMBER 29

Cle	0	0	7	0	7
Pro	0	0	0	7	7
Day	0	0	0	0	0
NYG	7	10	6	0	**23**
Fra	0	0	0	0	0
Pot	9	7	12	21	**49**
Col	0	7	0	6	13
ChiB	0	14	0	0	**14**
RI	0	0	0	0	0
ChiC	7	0	0	0	**7**

SATURDAY, DECEMBER 5

ChiB	0	7	0	7	**14**
Fra	0	0	7	0	7

SUNDAY, DECEMBER 6

Can	0	0	0	0	0
Cle	0	0	6	0	**6**
GB	0	0	6	7	**13**
Pro	7	0	0	3	10
Pot	0	14	0	7	**21**
ChiC	0	7	0	0	7
ChiB	12	0	0	7	**19**
NYG	0	7	0	0	7

WEDNESDAY, DECEMBER 9

ChiB	0	0	0	6	6
Pro	2	7	0	0	**9**

THURSDAY, DECEMBER 10

Mil	0	0	0	0	0
ChiC	?	?	?	?	**59**

SATURDAY, DECEMBER 12

Cle	0	3	0	0	**3**
Fra	0	0	0	0	0
ChiB	0	0	0	0	0
Det	7	0	14	0	**21**
Ham	0	0	0	0	0
ChiC	0	7	0	6	**13**

SUNDAY, DECEMBER 13

Fra	0	7	7	0	**14**
Pro	0	0	3	3	6
NYG	3	0	0	6	**9**
ChiB	0	0	0	0	0

THE GAMES

SUNDAY, DECEMBER 20
Fra 6 0 0 7 13
Cle 0 0 0 7 7

1926 NFL

SUNDAY, SEPTEMBER 19
Col 0 0 0 0 0
ChiC 7 0 0 7 14

Det 0 0 0 0 0
GB 0 7 7 7 21

ChiB 3 7 0 0 10
Mil 0 0 0 7 7

KC 0 0 0 0 0
Dul 0 7 0 0 7

SATURDAY, SEPTEMBER 25
Akr 0 6 0 0 6
Fra 0 6 0 0 6

SUNDAY, SEPTEMBER 26
NYG 0 7 14 0 21
Har 0 0 0 0 0

Bkn 0 0 0 0 0
Pro 0 6 0 7 13

Akr 0 0 0 0 0
Buf 0 7 0 0 7

Col 7 7 0 0 14
Can 0 0 0 2 2

LA 0 0 0 0 0
ChiC 9 0 6 0 15

Ham 3 0 0 0 3
Rac 6 0 0 0 6

ChiB 0 0 0 6 6
GB 0 0 6 0 6

Det 0 0 0 0 0
Mil 0 6 0 0 6

SATURDAY, OCTOBER 2
Har 0 0 0 0 0
Fra 6 7 0 0 13

SUNDAY, OCTOBER 3
Fra 0 10 0 0 10
Har 0 0 0 0 0

Day 0 3 0 0 3
Buf 0 0 0 0 0

Col 0 0 0 0 0
Pot 0 0 0 3 3

NYG 0 7 0 0 7
Pro 0 0 6 0 6

Ham 0 0 0 0 0
Akr 0 10 7 0 17

Lou 0 0 0 0 0
Can 0 0 6 7 13

ChiB 7 0 0 3 10
Det 0 0 0 7 7

Rac 0 0 0 0 0
ChiC 7 6 0 7 20

LA 0 6 0 0 6
Mil 0 0 0 0 0

Dul 0 0 0 0 0
GB 0 0 0 0 0

SATURDAY, OCTOBER 9
Buf 0 0 0 0 0
Fra 3 7 6 14 30

SUNDAY, OCTOBER 10
KC 0 0 0 0 0
Det 0 7 0 3 10

Har 0 0 0 0 0
Bkn 0 0 0 6 6

Day 0 0 0 6 6
Pot 0 10 7 7 24

NYG 0 0 0 0 0
ChiB 0 0 7 0 7

Can 0 0 0 0 0
Akr 0 0 0 0 0

Col 0 0 0 0 0
Pro 0 7 12 0 19

Mil 0 7 0 6 13
Rac 2 0 0 0 2

ChiC 0 7 3 3 13
GB 7 0 0 0 7

Dul 0 6 13 7 26
Ham 0 0 0 0 0

SATURDAY, OCTOBER 16
KC 0 9 0 0 9
Col 0 0 0 0 0

Pot 0 7 0 14 21
Bkn 0 0 0 0 0

NYG 0 0 0 0 0
Fra 0 6 0 0 6

SUNDAY, OCTOBER 17
Lou 0 0 0 0 0
Det 10 9 7 21 47

Buf 0 7 0 0 7
Day 6 0 0 0 6

Fra 0 6 0 0 6
NYG 0 0 0 0 0

Bkn 0 0 0 0 0
Pot 0 7 7 0 14

LA 0 6 7 3 16
Can 0 7 6 0 13

ChiB 3 13 0 0 16
ChiC 0 0 0 0 0

Dul 0 14 7 0 21
Rac 0 0 0 0 0

Mil 0 0 0 0 0
GB 0 0 0 7 7

SATURDAY, OCTOBER 23
Col 6 0 6 0 12
Bkn 0 14 0 6 20

Can 0 0 0 0 0
Fra 0 0 7 10 17

SUNDAY, OCTOBER 24
Bkn 0 0 6 0 6
Har 0 7 0 9 16

LA 0 0 0 0 0
Buf 0 0 0 0 0

KC 0 0 0 0 0
NYG 0 0 7 6 13

Pot 0 0 0 0 0
Pro 0 7 0 7 14

Akr 0 0 0 0 0
Det 9 6 0 10 25

Dul 0 0 0 6 6
ChiB 0 3 21 0 24

ChiC 3 0 0 0 3
Mil 0 0 0 2 2

Rac 0 0 0 0 0
GB 14 7 0 14 35

SATURDAY, OCTOBER 30
Pro 0 0 7 0 7
Fra 0 0 0 6 6

SUNDAY, OCTOBER 31
GB 3 0 0 0 3
ChiC 0 0 0 0 0

Buf 0 0 0 0 0
Pot 7 0 7 0 14

Fra 0 6 0 0 6
Pro 3 0 0 0 3

Dul 0 0 0 7 7
Mil 0 0 0 7 7

Akr 0 0 0 0 0
ChiB 3 7 7 0 17

Can 0 0 0 0 0
Det 0 3 0 3 6

KC 7 0 0 0 7
Har 0 2 0 0 2

TUESDAY, NOVEMBER 2
Can 0 0 0 7 7
NYG 0 0 7 0 7

SATURDAY, NOVEMBER 6
ChiC 0 7 0 0 7
Fra 0 0 14 19 33

SUNDAY, NOVEMBER 7
KC 3 0 0 7 10
Bkn 0 6 0 3 9

ChiC 0 0 0 0 0
NYG 6 0 7 7 20

Akr 0 0 0 0 0
Pot 14 6 7 7 34

Dul 0 0 0 0 0
Det 0 0 0 0 0

LA 7 0 0 0 7
Pro 0 0 6 0 6

GB 0 0 7 14 21
Mil 0 0 0 0 0

Lou 0 0 0 0 0
ChiB 7 13 7 7 34

Col 0 0 0 0 0
Buf 7 7 6 6 26

Can 0 0 0 7 7
Har 0 6 3 7 16

THURSDAY, NOVEMBER 11
Dul 7 0 0 6 13
NYG 7 0 7 0 14

LA 0 0 0 0 0
Pot 3 0 7 0 10

ChiC 0 0 0 0 0
ChiB 0 10 0 0 10

Can 0 2 0 0 2
Pro 7 7 7 0 21

SATURDAY, NOVEMBER 13
Dul 0 0 0 0 0
Fra 7 0 3 0 10

SUNDAY, NOVEMBER 14
Day 0 0 0 0 0
Det 0 0 0 0 0

LA 0 6 0 0 6
NYG 0 0 0 0 0

Mil 7 0 0 0 7
ChiB 0 0 10 0 10

Can 0 0 0 0 0
Bkn 0 13 6 0 19

Dul 0 0 0 0 0
Pot 0 0 7 6 13

Lou 0 0 0 0 0
GB 0 0 7 7 14

Buf 7 6 0 0 13
Har 0 0 0 7 7

KC 7 6 6 3 22
Pro 0 0 0 0 0

SATURDAY, NOVEMBER 20
Day 0 0 0 0 0
Fra 7 14 0 14 35

SUNDAY, NOVEMBER 21
Dul 10 0 0 0 10
Can 0 2 0 0 2

KC 0 0 2 0 2
Buf 0 0 0 0 0

LA 0 7 13 0 20
Bkn 0 0 0 0 0

Pro 0 0 0 0 0
NYG 7 0 0 14 21

Ham 0 0 0 0 0
Pot 0 7 0 0 7

Day 0 0 0 0 0
Har 0 7 2 7 16

GB 6 7 0 0 13
ChiB 6 3 3 7 19

THURSDAY, NOVEMBER 25
NYG 0 3 14 0 17
Bkn 0 0 0 0 0

LA 0 2 0 7 9
Det 0 0 6 0 6

ChiC 0 0 0 0 0
ChiB 0 0 0 0 0

GB 0 7 0 7 14
Fra 13 0 0 7 20

Pro 0 0 0 0 0
Pot 0 0 3 5 8

Akr 0 0 0 0 0
Can 0 0 0 0 0

SATURDAY, NOVEMBER 27
Det 0 3 3 0 6
Fra 0 0 0 7 7

Dul 3 0 6 7 16
Har 0 0 0 0 0

SUNDAY, NOVEMBER 28
GB 7 0 0 0 7
Det 0 0 0 0 0

Bkn 0 0 0 0 0
NYG 7 7 6 7 27

KC 7 0 0 0 7
ChiC 0 0 0 2 2

Buf 0 0 0 0 0
Pot 0 0 0 0 0

Dul 0 0 0 0 0
Pro 0 0 0 0 0

Can 0 0 0 0 0
ChiB 7 7 7 14 35

SATURDAY, DECEMBER 4
ChiB 0 0 0 6 6
Fra 0 0 0 7 7

SUNDAY, DECEMBER 5
LA 3 0 0 0 3
KC 0 0 7 0 7

SATURDAY, DECEMBER 11
Pro 0 0 0 0 0
Fra 7 3 7 7 24

SUNDAY, DECEMBER 12
Dul 0 0 7 0 7
KC 3 3 3 3 12

Pot 0 0 0 7 7
ChiB 0 3 6 0 9

SATURDAY, DECEMBER 18
Pot 0 0 0 0 0
Fra 0 0 0 0 0

SUNDAY, DECEMBER 19
GB 0 0 3 0 3
ChiB 0 0 3 0 3

1927 NFL

SUNDAY, SEPTEMBER 18
Day 0 0 0 0 0
GB 0 0 7 7 14

SATURDAY, SEPTEMBER 24
Day 0 6 0 0 6
Fra 3 0 0 0 3

SUNDAY, SEPTEMBER 25
ChiB 0 0 0 9 9
ChiC 0 0 0 0 0

Buf 0 0 0 0 0
Pot 12 10 0 0 22

NYG 0 8 0 0 8
Pro 0 0 0 0 0

Cle 0 0 0 7 7
GB 0 0 12 0 12

SUNDAY, OCTOBER 2
NYY 0 0 6 0 6
Day 0 3 0 0 3

Buf 0 0 0 0 0
Pro 0 5 0 0 5

Pot 7 0 0 0 7
ChiC 0 6 7 6 19

ChiB 0 7 0 0 7
GB 0 0 6 0 6

NYG 0 0 0 0 0
Cle 0 0 0 0 0

SATURDAY, OCTOBER 8
Day 0 0 0 0 0
Fra 0 0 0 0 0

SUNDAY, OCTOBER 9
Day 0 0 0 0 0
ChiC 0 0 0 7 7

NYG 0 3 9 7 19
Pot 0 0 0 0 0

Dul 0 0 0 0 0
GB 0 7 0 13 20

NYY 0 13 0 0 13
Cle 0 0 7 0 7

WEDNESDAY, OCTOBER 12
NYY 7 0 6 6 19
Buf 0 2 0 6 8

SATURDAY, OCTOBER 15
Buf 0 0 0 0 0
Fra 10 24 0 20 54

SUNDAY, OCTOBER 16
Fra 13 0 0 10 23
Buf 0 0 0 0 0

Cle 0 0 6 0 6
NYG 0 0 0 0 0

Pot 0 0 0 6 6
Pro 0 3 0 0 3

ChiC 0 0 0 0 0
GB 0 6 0 7 13

NYY 0 0 0 0 0
ChiB 0 12 0 0 12

SATURDAY, OCTOBER 22
NYG 0 0 6 7 13
Fra 0 0 0 0 0

SUNDAY, OCTOBER 23
Fra 0 0 0 0 0
NYG 0 20 0 7 27

Day 0 0 0 0 0
Pro 0 0 7 0 7

NYY 0 0 0 0 0
GB 0 13 0 0 13

Cle 6 0 0 6 12
ChiB 2 6 6 0 14

Dul 7 20 0 0 27
Pot 0 0 0 0 0

SATURDAY, OCTOBER 29
Pro 0 14 6 0 20
Fra 7 0 0 0 7

SUNDAY, OCTOBER 30
Day 0 0 6 0 6
ChiB 0 0 0 14 14

Fra 0 0 0 0 0
Pro 0 7 7 0 14

NYY 0 7 0 0 7
ChiC 0 6 0 0 6

Dul 7 0 0 13 20
Cle 13 6 2 0 21

Pot 0 0 0 0 0
NYG 8 0 0 8 16

SATURDAY, NOVEMBER 5
Pot 0 0 0 0 0
Fra 0 3 7 0 10

SUNDAY, NOVEMBER 6
GB 0 0 0 6 6
ChiC 0 6 0 0 6

Fra 0 0 0 0 0
Pot 0 3 6 0 9

Pro 0 0 0 0 0
ChiB 0 0 0 0 0

NYY 0 0 0 0 0
Cle 0 8 0 7 15

Dul 0 0 0 0 0
NYG 7 7 0 7 21

TUESDAY, NOVEMBER 8
ChiB 0 6 0 0 **6**
NYY 6 7 0 13 **26**
Pro 0 0 0 0 **0**
NYG 7 6 6 6 **25**

FRIDAY, NOVEMBER 11
NYY 6 6 7 0 **19**
Pot 3 7 2 0 **12**

SATURDAY, NOVEMBER 12
Cle 0 0 0 0 **0**
Fra 0 15 0 7 **22**

SUNDAY, NOVEMBER 13
Pot 6 0 0 6 **12**
ChiB 2 8 20 0 **30**
Day 0 0 0 0 **0**
GB 0 6 0 0 **6**
Fra 0 0 0 0 **0**
Cle 2 7 14 14 **37**
ChiC 0 0 0 6 **6**
NYY 7 7 0 6 **20**
Dul 7 0 0 0 **7**
Pro 7 0 0 6 **13**

SATURDAY, NOVEMBER 19
ChiC 0 6 2 0 **8**
Fra 3 2 0 7 **12**

SUNDAY, NOVEMBER 20
ChiC 0 0 7 0 **7**
NYG 21 0 0 7 **28**
GB 0 0 6 0 **6**
ChiB 0 7 0 7 **14**
Dul 0 0 0 0 **0**
Pot 0 6 0 0 **6**
Cle 0 0 10 12 **22**
Pro 0 0 0 0 **0**

THURSDAY, NOVEMBER 24
ChiC 3 0 0 0 **3**
ChiB 0 0 0 0 **0**
Pro 0 0 0 0 **0**
Pot 0 6 0 0 **6**
GB 0 7 3 7 **17**
Fra 6 3 0 0 **9**
Cle 7 7 2 14 **30**
NYY 13 0 0 6 **19**

SATURDAY, NOVEMBER 26
Dul 0 0 0 0 **0**
Fra 0 6 0 0 **6**

SUNDAY, NOVEMBER 27
ChiB 0 0 0 7 **7**
NYG 0 0 13 0 **13**
NYY 0 0 7 7 **14**
Pro 0 0 7 7 **14**
Cle 6 6 20 0 **32**
ChiC 0 7 0 0 **7**

SATURDAY, DECEMBER 3
ChiB 0 0 0 0 **0**
Fra 0 0 0 0 **0**
Pro 0 9 0 0 **9**
NYY 0 0 0 0 **0**
Dul 0 0 0 0 **0**
Cle 7 7 6 0 **20**

SUNDAY, DECEMBER 4
Pot 0 0 0 0 **0**
Pro 0 0 13 7 **20**
Fra 0 0 0 0 **0**
ChiB 3 0 0 6 **9**
NYY 0 0 0 0 **0**
NYG 7 0 7 0 **14**

SATURDAY, DECEMBER 10
NYY 0 0 6 0 **6**
Fra 0 6 0 0 **6**

SUNDAY, DECEMBER 11
Dul 0 0 7 7 **14**
ChiB 7 0 0 20 **27**

NYG 0 0 7 6 **13**
NYY 0 0 0 0 **0**

1928 NFL

SUNDAY, SEPTEMBER 23
Fra 12 7 0 0 **19**
GB 3 6 0 0 **9**
ChiB 9 0 0 6 **15**
ChiC 0 0 0 0 **0**

SUNDAY, SEPTEMBER 29
Day 0 0 0 0 **0**
Fra 0 0 0 6 **6**

SUNDAY, SEPTEMBER 30
ChiB 6 6 0 0 **12**
GB 0 0 6 6 **12**
NYG 6 6 0 0 **12**
Pot 0 0 6 0 **6**
NYY 7 0 0 0 **7**
Pro 7 13 0 0 **20**

SUNDAY, OCTOBER 7
NYY 0 0 0 7 **7**
Pot 0 2 7 0 **9**
NYG 0 0 6 0 **6**
GB 0 0 0 0 **0**
Day 0 0 0 0 **0**
ChiC 0 0 7 0 **7**
Fra 0 0 0 10 **10**
Pro 0 6 0 0 **6**

SATURDAY, OCTOBER 13
NYY 0 7 6 0 **13**
Fra 0 0 0 0 **0**

SUNDAY, OCTOBER 14
ChiC 0 0 0 0 **0**
GB 0 13 0 7 **20**
Day 0 0 0 0 **0**
Pro 7 7 7 7 **28**
Det 14 7 0 14 **35**
NYY 0 12 0 0 **12**
NYG 0 0 0 0 **0**
ChiB 6 0 7 0 **13**

SATURDAY, OCTOBER 20
Day 3 0 0 6 **9**
Fra 0 0 7 6 **13**

SUNDAY, OCTOBER 21
Pro 0 0 0 12 **12**
NYY 0 0 6 0 **6**
GB 3 7 0 6 **16**
ChiB 0 0 6 6
NYG 0 0 0 0 **0**
Det 14 0 0 14 **28**

SUNDAY, OCTOBER 28
Day 0 0 0 0 **0**
GB 3 7 0 7 **17**
Pot 0 0 0 6 **6**
Pro 6 7 0 0 **13**
Det 0 0 0 6 **6**
ChiB 0 0 0 0 **0**
NYG 7 0 3 0 **10**
NYY 0 0 0 7 **7**

SATURDAY, NOVEMBER 3
Det 0 0 7 0 **7**
Fra 13 6 0 6 **25**

SUNDAY, NOVEMBER 4
Det 0 0 0 0 **0**
Pro 0 0 7 0 **7**
GB 6 13 0 7 **26**
Pot 0 0 7 7 **14**
NYY 0 0 0 0 **0**
ChiB 7 7 6 7 **27**
Fra 0 0 0 0 **0**
NYG 0 0 0 0 **0**

TUESDAY, NOVEMBER 6
Pot 0 0 0 7 **7**
NYG 0 6 7 0 **13**

SATURDAY, NOVEMBER 10
Pot 0 0 0 0 **0**
Fra 6 6 7 0 **19**

SUNDAY, NOVEMBER 11
Day 0 0 0 0 **0**
ChiB 7 13 7 0 **27**
Fra 0 18 0 6 **24**
Pot 0 0 0 0 **0**
NYY 0 0 0 0 **0**
GB 0 0 0 0 **0**
Det 7 0 0 12 **19**
NYG 6 7 6 0 **19**

SATURDAY, NOVEMBER 17
Pro 0 0 0 6 **6**
Fra 0 0 6 0 **6**

SUNDAY, NOVEMBER 18
Fra 0 0 0 0 **0**
Pro 6 0 0 0 **6**
Pot 0 6 0 6 **6**
ChiB 0 7 6 0 **13**
NYY 0 0 0 0 **0**
Det 7 0 6 0 **13**
GB 0 7 0 0 **7**
NYG 0 0 0 0 **0**

SATURDAY, NOVEMBER 24
ChiC 0 0 0 0 **0**
Fra 0 6 13 0 **19**

SUNDAY, NOVEMBER 25
ChiC 0 0 0 0 **0**
NYY 7 0 0 12 **19**
GB 0 0 0 0 **0**
Pot 6 7 6 7 **26**
ChiB 0 7 0 0 **7**
Det 0 0 7 7 **14**
NYG 0 0 0 0 **0**
Pro 0 9 0 7 **16**

THURSDAY, NOVEMBER 29
Pro 0 7 0 0 **7**
Pot 0 0 0 0 **0**
Day 0 0 0 0 **0**
Det 7 7 6 13 **33**
GB 0 0 0 0 **0**
Fra 2 0 0 0 **2**
ChiC 0 0 0 0 **0**
ChiB 0 28 0 6 **34**

SUNDAY, DECEMBER 2
Fra 6 0 0 0 **6**
ChiB 0 21 7 0 **28**
NYY 0 6 0 13 **19**
NYG 0 0 0 13 **13**
GB 0 0 7 0 **7**
Pro 0 0 7 0 **7**

SATURDAY, DECEMBER 8
NYY 0 0 0 0 **0**
Fra 0 7 0 0 **7**

SUNDAY, DECEMBER 9
GB 0 0 0 6 **6**
ChiC 0 0 0 0 **0**
Det 6 7 7 14 **34**
NYY 6 0 0 0 **6**

SATURDAY, DECEMBER 15
ChiB 0 0 0 0 **0**
Fra 0 0 6 13 **19**

SUNDAY, DECEMBER 16
NYG 0 0 6 0 **6**
NYY 0 0 0 7 **7**

1929 NFL

SUNDAY, SEPTEMBER 22
Day 0 0 0 0 **0**
GB 0 0 9 0 **9**
ChiB 0 0 12 7 **19**
Min 6 0 0 0 **6**

SATURDAY, SEPTEMBER 28
Day 0 0 7 0 **7**
Fra 7 7 0 0 **14**

SUNDAY, SEPTEMBER 29
ChiB 0 0 0 0 **0**
GB 0 14 9 0 **23**
NYY 0 0 0 0 **0**
Ora 0 0 0 0 **0**
Day 0 0 0 0 **0**
Pro 13 21 0 7 **41**
ChiC 3 0 6 0 **9**
Buf 0 0 3 0 **3**

SATURDAY, OCTOBER 5
Buf 0 0 0 0 **0**
Fra 0 0 0 19 **19**

SUNDAY, OCTOBER 6
ChiB 7 0 0 0 **7**
Min 0 0 6 0 **6**
Fra 6 7 0 0 **13**
Buf 0 0 0 0 **0**
Bos 0 0 0 0 **0**
Ora 0 0 7 0 **7**
NYG 0 0 0 7 **7**
Pro 0 0 0 0 **0**
Day 0 0 0 0 **0**
Sta 0 6 0 6 **12**
ChiC 2 0 0 0 **2**
GB 0 0 3 6 **9**

SUNDAY, OCTOBER 13
Fra 0 2 0 0 **2**
GB 7 0 0 0 **7**
ChiB 2 7 7 0 **16**
Buf 0 0 0 0 **0**
ChiC 0 0 7 0 **7**
Min 0 0 7 7 **14**
Ora 0 0 0 0 **0**
Pro 0 7 0 0 **7**
Sta 2 7 0 0 **9**
NYG 0 6 6 7 **19**
Day 0 0 0 0 **0**
Bos 0 14 7 20 **41**

SATURDAY, OCTOBER 19
Ora 0 0 6 0 **6**
Fra 0 6 0 0 **6**

SUNDAY, OCTOBER 20
Fra 0 0 0 0 **0**
NYG 0 19 7 6 **32**
Min 0 0 0 0 **0**
GB 0 12 6 6 **24**
Buf 0 0 7 0 **7**
Pro 0 7 0 0 **7**
Ora 0 6 7 6 **19**
Bos 6 7 0 0 **13**
ChiC 0 0 0 0 **0**
ChiB 0 0 0 0 **0**

SATURDAY, OCTOBER 26
Sta 0 6 0 0 **6**
Fra 6 0 0 0 **6**

SUNDAY, OCTOBER 27
Fra 0 3 0 0 **3**
Sta 0 0 0 0 **0**
Min 0 0 0 0 **0**
ChiB 13 0 7 7 **27**
Buf 0 6 0 0 **6**
Bos 0 14 0 0 **14**
Pro 0 0 0 0 **0**
NYG 7 0 6 6 **19**

GB 0 7 0 0 **7**
ChiC 0 0 0 6 **6**

TUESDAY, OCTOBER 29
Ora 0 0 0 0 **0**
Bos 0 0 0 6 **6**

SATURDAY, NOVEMBER 2
ChiC 0 0 0 0 **0**
Fra 6 0 2 0 **8**

SUNDAY, NOVEMBER 3
GB 6 0 0 10 **16**
Min 0 0 6 0 **6**
Ora 0 0 0 0 **0**
Sta 0 0 0 0 **0**
NYG 6 0 20 0 **26**
ChiC 7 0 0 7 **14**

TUESDAY, NOVEMBER 5
NYY 14 25 0 6 **45**
Buf 0 6 0 0 **6**
Pro 7 0 0 0 **7**
Sta 0 7 0 0 **7**

WEDNESDAY, NOVEMBER 6
ChiC 0 10 0 6 **16**
Pro 0 0 0 0 **0**

SATURDAY, NOVEMBER 9
Pro 0 0 0 0 **0**
Fra 0 7 0 0 **7**

SUNDAY, NOVEMBER 10
Fra 0 0 0 7 **7**
Pro 6 0 0 0 **6**
Ora 0 0 0 0 **0**
NYG 13 3 6 0 **22**
Bos 0 6 0 0 **6**
Sta 7 0 7 0 **14**
GB 0 0 14 0 **14**
ChiB 0 0 0 0 **0**
Min 0 0 0 0 **0**
ChiC 0 2 0 6 **8**

SATURDAY, NOVEMBER 16
ChiB 7 0 0 7 **14**
Fra 13 0 0 7 **20**

SUNDAY, NOVEMBER 17
Fra 0 0 0 0 **0**
Ora 0 0 0 0 **0**
Buf 0 0 7 0 **7**
Bos 0 12 0 0 **12**
ChiB 0 0 0 0 **0**
NYG 0 7 20 7 **34**
Min 7 3 0 6 **16**
Pro 7 0 6 0 **19**
GB 6 0 0 6 **12**
ChiC 0 0 0 0 **0**

SATURDAY, NOVEMBER 23
Min 0 0 0 0 **0**
Fra 0 10 14 0 **24**

SUNDAY, NOVEMBER 24
GB 7 0 13 0 **20**
NYG 0 0 6 0 **6**
Bos 0 0 0 6 **6**
Pro 7 7 0 6 **20**
Buf 0 7 0 12 **19**
ChiB 0 7 0 0 **7**
Day 0 0 0 0 **0**
ChiC 6 6 7 0 **19**
Min 0 0 0 0 **0**
Sta 21 6 0 7 **34**

THURSDAY, NOVEMBER 28
NYG 14 0 0 7 **21**
Sta 0 0 7 0 **7**
GB 0 0 0 0 **0**
Fra 0 0 0 0 **0**
ChiC 13 7 7 13 **40**
ChiB 0 0 6 0 **6**

880 THE GAMES

SUNDAY, DECEMBER 1

Fra	0	0	0	0	0
ChiB	0	0	0	0	0
GB	6	0	6	13	**25**
Pro	0	0	0	0	0
Sta	0	0	0	0	0
Ora	0	0	3	0	**3**
ChiC	0	9	6	6	21
NYG	7	7	0	10	**24**

SATURDAY, DECEMBER 7

NYG	6	0	0	6	**12**
Fra	0	0	0	0	0

SUNDAY, DECEMBER 8

Fra	0	0	0	0	0
NYG	6	19	0	6	**31**
GB	6	0	19	0	**25**
ChiB	0	0	0	0	0
ChiC	0	20	0	6	**26**
Ora	0	0	0	0	0

SATURDAY, DECEMBER 14

Ora	0	0	0	0	0
Fra	3	7	0	0	**10**

SUNDAY, DECEMBER 15

NYG	7	0	0	7	**14**
ChiB	6	0	3	0	9

1930 NFL

SUNDAY, SEPTEMBER 14

Nwk	0	0	0	6	6
Por	0	0	7	6	**13**

WEDNESDAY, SEPTEMBER 17

NYG	7	6	13	6	**32**
Nwk	0	0	0	0	0

SUNDAY, SEPTEMBER 21

Bkn	0	0	0	0	0
ChiB	0	0	0	0	0
ChiC	0	0	0	0	0
GB	0	7	7	0	**14**
Nwk	0	0	0	6	6
Sta	6	6	0	0	**12**

WEDNESDAY, SEPTEMBER 23

Fra	6	0	7	0	**13**
Nwk	0	0	0	6	6

THURSDAY, SEPTEMBER 24

Bkn	0	0	0	0	0
Por	6	0	0	6	**12**

SATURDAY, SEPTEMBER 27

Sta	0	3	0	0	3
Fra	0	0	7	0	**7**

SUNDAY, SEPTEMBER 28

ChiB	0	0	0	0	0
GB	0	7	0	0	**7**
NYG	7	7	7	6	**27**
Pro	0	0	0	7	7
ChiC	0	0	0	7	7
Min	0	0	7	0	7
Fra	0	0	0	0	0
Sta	7	7	0	7	**21**

WEDNESDAY, OCTOBER 1

Sta	0	0	7	0	7
Nwk	0	7	0	0	7
Fra	0	0	0	0	0
Pro	0	14	0	0	**14**

SATURDAY, OCTOBER 4

Nwk	12	7	0	0	**19**
Fra	0	0	0	0	0

SUNDAY, OCTOBER 5

ChiC	0	0	0	0	0
Por	0	0	0	0	0
ChiB	7	0	13	0	**20**
Min	0	0	0	0	0
NYG	0	7	0	0	7
GB	0	7	0	7	**14**
Nwk	0	0	0	0	0
Pro	0	7	0	7	**14**
Bkn	0	13	0	7	**20**
Sta	0	0	0	0	0

WEDNESDAY, OCTOBER 8

Fra	7	0	0	0	7
Por	0	13	14	12	**39**
ChiC	0	13	0	0	**13**
Nwk	0	0	0	0	0

SUNDAY, OCTOBER 12

Por	0	0	0	0	0
Min	0	6	7	0	**13**
Nwk	0	0	0	0	0
Bkn	6	19	7	0	**32**
NYG	0	12	0	0	**12**
ChiB	0	0	0	0	0
ChiC	0	0	0	7	7
Pro	0	3	6	0	**9**
Fra	0	0	6	6	12
GB	20	0	0	7	**27**

THURSDAY, OCTOBER 16

ChiC	0	6	0	6	12
NYG	0	13	0	12	**25**

SATURDAY, OCTOBER 18

Bkn	0	7	7	0	**14**
Fra	0	0	0	7	7

SUNDAY, OCTOBER 19

Bkn	0	14	0	0	**14**
Nwk	0	0	0	0	0
Fra	0	0	0	0	0
NYG	0	26	13	14	**53**
GB	7	0	0	6	**13**
Min	0	0	0	0	0
Sta	0	0	0	6	6
Pro	7	0	0	0	**7**
ChiB	12	0	7	13	**32**
ChiC	0	0	6	0	6

WEDNESDAY, OCTOBER 22

ChiB	0	0	6	0	6
Por	0	7	0	0	**7**

SATURDAY, OCTOBER 25

ChiC	6	7	0	21	**34**
Fra	0	7	0	0	7

SUNDAY, OCTOBER 26

Por	7	6	0	0	13
ChiC	0	13	0	10	**23**
Pro	0	0	0	0	0
NYG	0	6	7	12	**25**
Sta	0	0	6	0	**6**
Nwk	0	0	0	0	0
Fra	0	7	0	0	7
ChiB	7	0	6	0	**13**
Min	0	0	0	0	0
GB	6	6	7	0	**19**

THURSDAY, OCTOBER 30

Nwk	0	7	0	0	7
NYG	14	6	0	14	**34**

SUNDAY, NOVEMBER 2

Por	0	0	6	7	13
GB	7	13	13	14	**47**
Fra	0	0	0	0	0
ChiC	0	0	6	0	**6**
Sta	0	0	7	0	7
NYG	6	0	0	3	**9**
Bkn	0	0	0	0	0
Pro	0	0	3	0	**3**
Min	0	0	7	0	7
ChiB	0	13	7	0	**20**

SUNDAY, NOVEMBER 5

NYG	0	13	0	6	**19**
Por	0	0	0	6	6

SATURDAY, NOVEMBER 8

Pro	0	0	0	7	7
Fra	0	13	7	0	**20**

SUNDAY, NOVEMBER 9

Por	0	0	7	6	13
Sta	0	6	7	0	13
NYG	0	0	0	13	**13**
ChiC	0	7	0	0	7
Fra	0	7	0	0	7
Pro	7	0	0	0	7
Min	0	0	0	0	0
Bkn	13	7	14	0	**34**
GB	0	6	0	7	**13**
ChiB	0	0	6	6	12

SATURDAY, NOVEMBER 15

Por	6	0	0	0	6
Fra	7	0	0	0	**7**

SUNDAY, NOVEMBER 16

GB	0	0	6	0	6
ChiC	0	6	0	7	**13**
ChiB	0	0	0	12	**12**
NYG	0	0	0	0	0

SATURDAY, NOVEMBER 22

ChiB	7	6	0	0	**13**
Fra	0	0	6	0	6

SUNDAY, NOVEMBER 23

GB	0	0	6	0	6
NYG	0	7	6	0	**13**
Min	0	0	0	0	0
Pro	3	0	0	7	**10**
Sta	0	0	0	6	**6**
Bkn	0	0	0	0	0

THURSDAY, NOVEMBER 27

NYG	0	6	0	0	6
Sta	0	0	7	0	**7**
Pro	0	6	0	6	12
Bkn	6	7	13	7	**33**
GB	6	6	0	13	**25**
Fra	0	0	7	0	7
ChiC	0	0	0	0	0
ChiB	0	6	0	0	**6**

SUNDAY, NOVEMBER 30

Por	0	6	0	0	6
ChiB	7	7	0	0	**14**
Bkn	0	0	0	7	**7**
NYG	0	6	0	0	6
GB	6	12	13	6	**37**
Sta	0	7	0	0	7

SATURDAY, DECEMBER 6

NYG	0	0	7	7	**14**
Fra	6	0	0	0	6

SUNDAY, DECEMBER 7

Min	0	0	0	0	0
Por	14	14	7	7	**42**
GB	0	0	0	0	0
ChiB	0	7	0	14	**21**
NYG	0	7	0	6	**13**
Bkn	0	0	0	0	0

SUNDAY, DECEMBER 14

GB	6	0	0	0	6
Por	0	6	0	0	6

1931 NFL

SUNDAY, SEPTEMBER 13

Bkn	0	0	0	0	0
Por	0	14	0	0	**14**
Cle	0	0	0	0	0
GB	7	6	6	7	**26**

FRIDAY, SEPTEMBER 18

Cle	0	0	0	0	0
ChiB	7	7	0	7	**21**

SUNDAY, SEPTEMBER 20

Bkn	0	0	0	6	6
GB	0	12	14	6	**32**

WEDNESDAY, SEPTEMBER 23

ChiC	0	3	0	0	3
Por	0	0	13	0	**13**

SATURDAY, SEPTEMBER 26

Bkn	0	0	0	0	0
Cle	0	0	6	0	**6**

SUNDAY, SEPTEMBER 27

ChiB	0	0	0	0	0
GB	0	7	0	0	**7**
NYG	0	14	0	0	**14**
Pro	0	6	0	0	6

WEDNESDAY, SEPTEMBER 30

NYG	0	0	6	0	6
Por	0	0	0	14	**14**

FRIDAY, OCTOBER 2

Bkn	0	7	6	7	**20**
Fra	0	0	0	0	0

SUNDAY, OCTOBER 4

Fra	0	0	0	0	0
Pro	0	0	0	0	0
NYG	7	0	0	0	7
GB	14	6	0	7	**27**
Bkn	0	0	0	7	7
Sta	0	0	3	6	**9**

WEDNESDAY, OCTOBER 7

Cle	0	0	0	0	0
Por	0	6	0	0	**6**

SATURDAY, OCTOBER 10

Pro	0	0	0	6	**6**
Fra	0	0	0	0	0

SUNDAY, OCTOBER 11

Sta	0	0	0	6	6
Bkn	6	12	0	0	**18**
ChiC	0	7	0	0	7
GB	0	0	13	13	**26**
NYG	0	0	0	0	0
ChiB	0	0	6	0	**6**

THURSDAY, OCTOBER 15

Fra	0	0	0	0	0
Por	0	0	6	13	**19**

SUNDAY, OCTOBER 18

Fra	0	0	0	0	0
GB	2	6	7	0	**15**
Cle	7	0	0	6	**13**
Pro	0	0	0	6	6
ChiC	7	0	0	6	13
ChiB	0	0	14	12	**26**
Sta	0	0	0	0	0
NYG	0	0	0	7	**7**
Por	0	19	0	0	**19**
Bkn	0	0	0	0	0

SUNDAY, OCTOBER 25

Por	0	7	0	13	**20**
Sta	7	0	0	0	7
Pro	0	7	13	0	20
GB	21	7	0	20	**48**
Bkn	0	0	0	0	0
NYG	13	0	7	7	**27**
Fra	0	6	7	0	**13**
ChiB	0	6	0	6	12

SATURDAY, OCTOBER 31

Por	0	0	7	7	**14**
Fra	0	0	0	0	0

SUNDAY, NOVEMBER 1

Por	0	0	0	0	0
NYG	0	14	0	0	**14**
ChiC	0	7	7	0	**14**
Bkn	0	7	0	0	7
Pro	0	0	0	7	7
Sta	7	0	0	0	7
GB	0	6	0	0	**6**
ChiB	0	0	2	0	2

WEDNESDAY, NOVEMBER 4

Bkn	0	0	0	0	0
Sta	6	0	7	0	**13**

SUNDAY, NOVEMBER 8

Fra	0	0	0	0	0
NYG	7	6	0	0	**13**
Bkn	0	0	0	0	0
Pro	0	7	0	0	**7**
Sta	0	0	0	0	0
GB	7	6	7	6	**26**
ChiC	0	14	0	0	**14**
Cle	0	0	6	0	6
Por	0	0	0	6	6
ChiB	0	0	3	6	**9**

WEDNESDAY, NOVEMBER 11

Sta	0	0	6	6	12
Por	2	0	12	0	**14**

SUNDAY, NOVEMBER 15

ChiB	0	0	6	6	**12**
NYG	0	6	0	0	6
Cle	6	0	0	0	6
Por	7	7	0	0	**14**
Sta	0	0	0	0	0
Pro	0	0	0	6	**6**
GB	0	6	0	7	13
ChiC	7	0	7	7	**21**

SATURDAY, NOVEMBER 21

Cle	7	0	0	0	7
Pro	0	6	0	7	**13**

SUNDAY, NOVEMBER 22

Por	7	0	6	6	19
ChiC	0	13	0	7	**20**
Cle	0	7	0	0	7
Sta	6	0	0	10	**16**
ChiB	7	0	6	13	**26**
Bkn	0	0	0	0	0
GB	7	0	0	7	**14**
NYG	0	10	0	0	10

THURSDAY, NOVEMBER 26

GB	13	19	0	6	**38**
Pro	0	7	0	0	7
NYG	0	6	0	0	6
Sta	7	0	0	2	**9**
ChiC	0	0	7	0	7
ChiB	0	12	6	0	**18**

SATURDAY, NOVEMBER 28

Cle	0	0	0	0	0
ChiC	0	14	0	7	**21**

SUNDAY, NOVEMBER 29

ChiB	0	0	0	0	0
Por	0	3	0	0	**3**
Pro	0	0	0	0	0
NYG	0	0	0	0	0
GB	7	0	0	0	**7**
Bkn	0	0	0	0	0

SUNDAY, DECEMBER 6

GB	0	6	0	0	6
ChiB	7	0	0	0	**7**
NYG	7	6	0	6	**19**
Bkn	0	0	6	0	6

SUNDAY, DECEMBER 13

NYG	0	7	12	6	**25**
ChiB	0	0	0	6	6

1932 NFL

SUNDAY, SEPTEMBER 18

ChiC	0	0	0	7	7
GB	2	0	13	0	**15**

SUNDAY, SEPTEMBER 25

NYG	0	0	0	0	0
Por	0	7	0	0	7
ChiB	0	0	0	0	0
GB	0	0	0	0	0
Bkn	0	0	0	7	7
Sta	0	0	0	0	0

SUNDAY, OCTOBER 2

ChiC	0	0	7	0	7
Por	0	7	0	0	7
NYG	0	0	0	0	0
GB	7	0	0	6	13
ChiB	0	0	0	0	0
Sta	0	0	0	0	0
Bkn	7	0	7	0	14
Bos	0	0	0	0	0

SUNDAY, OCTOBER 9

Por	0	0	10	0	10
GB	7	0	0	8	15
ChiB	0	0	0	0	0
ChiC	0	0	0	0	0
NYG	0	6	0	0	6
Bos	0	7	0	7	14
Sta	0	7	0	0	7
Bkn	6	0	0	0	6

SUNDAY, OCTOBER 16

Por	0	0	0	7	7
Sta	0	7	0	0	7
GB	0	2	0	0	2
ChiB	0	0	0	0	0
ChiC	9	0	0	0	9
Bos	0	0	0	0	0
Bkn	0	0	0	12	12
NYG	14	0	0	6	20

THURSDAY, OCTOBER 20

Por	0	7	0	6	13
Sta	0	6	0	0	6

SUNDAY, OCTOBER 23

Sta	0	0	0	7	7
ChiB	7	6	7	7	27
Bkn	0	0	0	0	0
GB	6	0	0	7	13
Bos	0	0	0	0	0
NYG	0	0	0	0	0

SUNDAY, OCTOBER 30

Por	6	0	0	0	6
NYG	0	0	0	0	0
ChiB	7	0	0	0	7
Bos	7	0	0	0	7

Bos-Battles 144R

Sta	0	0	0	0	0
GB	6	0	14	6	26
Bkn	0	0	7	0	7
ChiC	0	0	7	20	27

SUNDAY, NOVEMBER 6

Por	0	7	0	10	17
Bkn	7	0	0	0	7
ChiB	7	14	0	7	28
NYG	6	0	0	2	8
GB	7	6	0	6	19
ChiC	0	7	2	0	9
Sta	0	0	0	6	6
Bos	6	7	0	6	19

Bos-Pape 122R

SUNDAY, NOVEMBER 13

Por	0	13	0	0	13
ChiB	7	0	0	6	13
GB	7	14	0	0	21
Bos	0	0	0	0	0
Sta	0	7	0	0	7
NYG	0	14	7	6	27
ChiC	0	0	0	0	0
Bkn	3	0	0	0	3

SUNDAY, NOVEMBER 20

Bos	0	0	0	0	0
Por	0	7	3	0	10
Bkn	0	0	0	0	0
ChiB	0	7	6	7	20
GB	0	0	0	0	0
NYG	0	6	0	0	6
ChiC	0	0	7	0	7
Sta	14	0	0	7	21

THURSDAY, NOVEMBER 24

ChiC	0	0	0	0	0
ChiB	6	14	14	0	34
GB	0	7	0	0	7
Bkn	0	0	0	0	0
NYG	7	6	0	0	13
Sta	7	0	6	0	13

SUNDAY, NOVEMBER 27

ChiB	0	7	0	0	7
Por	0	0	0	7	7
GB	0	0	7	14	21
Sta	0	3	0	0	3
Bos	0	0	2	6	8
ChiC	6	0	0	0	6
NYG	0	0	0	13	13
Bkn	0	7	0	0	7

SUNDAY, DECEMBER 4

GB	0	0	0	0	0
Por	7	6	0	6	19
NYG	0	0	0	0	0
ChiB	6	0	0	0	6
Bos	7	0	0	0	7
Bkn	0	0	0	0	0

SUNDAY, DECEMBER 11

GB	0	0	0	0	0
ChiB	0	0	0	9	9

SUNDAY, DECEMBER 18

Por	0	0	0	0	0
ChiB	0	0	0	9	9

1933 NFL

SUNDAY, SEPTEMBER 17

Bos	0	0	0	7	7
GB	0	0	7	0	7
Cin	0	0	0	0	0
Por	0	14	0	7	21

WEDNESDAY, SEPTEMBER 20

NYG	0	7	0	16	23
Pit	0	0	2	0	2

SUNDAY, SEPTEMBER 24

ChiB	0	0	0	14	14
GB	0	0	7	0	7
NYG	0	0	0	7	7
Por	0	7	10	0	17

WEDNESDAY, SEPTEMBER 27

ChiC	6	7	0	0	13
Pit	0	7	0	7	14

SUNDAY, OCTOBER 1

NYG	3	7	0	0	10
GB	0	0	0	7	7
Bos	0	0	0	0	0
ChiB	0	0	0	7	7
ChiC	0	6	0	0	6
Por	0	7	0	0	7

ChiC-Battles 115R

WEDNESDAY, OCTOBER 4

Bos	7	0	7	7	21
Pit	0	0	0	6	6

SUNDAY, OCTOBER 8

Por	0	0	0	0	0
GB	7	0	3	7	17
ChiB	0	7	3	0	10
Bkn	0	0	0	0	0
NYG	7	0	6	7	20
Bos	0	14	7	0	21

NYG-Newman 108R;
Bos-Battles 215R

ChiC	0	3	0	0	3
Cin	0	0	0	0	0

WEDNESDAY, OCTOBER 11

Cin	3	0	0	0	3
Pit	7	0	0	10	17

SUNDAY, OCTOBER 15

Pit	0	0	0	0	0
GB	7	20	13	7	47
ChiC	0	9	0	0	9
ChiB	0	0	7	5	12
Por	7	0	6	0	13
Bos	0	0	0	0	0
Phi	0	0	0	0	0
NYG	21	7	7	21	56
Cin	0	0	0	0	0
Bkn	7	7	13	0	27

WEDNESDAY, OCTOBER 18

Por	0	9	6	10	25
Phi	0	0	0	0	0

SUNDAY, OCTOBER 22

GB	0	7	0	0	7
ChiB	0	0	0	10	10
ChiC	0	0	0	0	0
Bos	0	0	10	0	10
Bkn	0	0	0	7	7
NYG	7	7	7	0	21

NYG-Richards 107R

Pit	0	0	0	0	0
Cin	0	0	0	0	0

SUNDAY, OCTOBER 29

Phi	0	7	2	0	9
GB	14	0	0	21	35
Pit	0	9	7	0	16
Bos	7	0	7	0	14

Bos-Musick 132R

NYG	7	0	0	3	10
ChiB	0	7	0	7	14
ChiC	0	0	0	0	0
Bkn	0	7	0	0	7

SUNDAY, NOVEMBER 5

GB	0	0	7	7	14
ChiC	0	0	6	0	6
ChiB	0	0	0	0	0
Bos	7	0	0	3	10
Phi	0	0	0	6	6
Cin	0	0	0	0	0
Por	3	7	0	0	10
NYG	0	0	0	13	13
Pit	0	0	0	3	3
Bkn	3	0	0	0	3

SUNDAY, NOVEMBER 12

GB	0	0	0	0	0
Por	0	0	7	0	7
ChiB	0	3	0	0	3
Phi	0	0	0	3	3
Bos	0	0	0	0	0
NYG	0	7	0	0	7
Bkn	6	7	13	6	32
Pit	0	0	0	0	0
Cin	7	5	0	0	12
ChiC	0	0	0	9	9

ChiC-Musick 132R

SUNDAY, NOVEMBER 19

GB	0	0	7	0	7
Bos	0	6	7	7	20
ChiB	0	0	0	0	0
NYG	0	3	0	0	3
Pit	0	0	0	6	6
Phi	6	0	13	6	25
Bkn	0	3	0	0	3
ChiC	0	0	0	0	0
Por	0	0	0	7	7
Cin	0	10	0	0	10

SUNDAY, NOVEMBER 26

GB	0	0	0	6	6
NYG	7	0	10	0	17
Por	0	7	0	7	14
ChiB	10	0	0	7	17

ChiB-Nagurski 124R

Bos	0	0	0	0	0
Bkn	7	0	0	7	14
Cin	3	0	0	0	3
Phi	0	7	6	7	20

THURSDAY, NOVEMBER 30

ChiB	6	9	0	7	22
ChiC	0	0	0	6	6
NYG	0	0	3	7	10
Bkn	0	0	0	0	0

NYG-Hinkle 116R

SUNDAY, DECEMBER 3

GB	0	3	0	7	10
Phi	0	0	0	0	0
ChiB	7	0	3	7	17
Por	7	0	0	0	7
Bos	0	0	0	0	0
ChiC	0	0	0	0	0
Pit	0	3	0	0	3
NYG	0	0	7	20	27
Bkn	0	0	0	0	0
Cin	0	0	3	7	10

SUNDAY, DECEMBER 10

GB	0	0	0	6	6
ChiB	0	7	0	0	7
NYG	0	7	6	7	20
Phi	0	0	7	7	14

1934 NFL

SUNDAY, SEPTEMBER 9

Cin	0	0	0	0	0
Pit	0	7	0	6	13

Cin-Hanson 116R

SUNDAY, SEPTEMBER 16

Phi	0	0	6	0	6
GB	3	13	3	0	19
Bos	0	0	7	0	7
Pit	0	0	0	0	0

SUNDAY, SEPTEMBER 23

ChiC	6	0	3	0	9
Cin	0	0	0	0	0
NYG	0	0	0	0	0
Det	0	3	0	6	9
ChiB	3	0	7	14	24
GB	0	3	7	0	10

WEDNESDAY, SEPTEMBER 26

Phi	0	7	7	3	17
Pit	0	0	0	0	0

SUNDAY, SEPTEMBER 30

NYG	0	0	0	6	6
GB	0	3	10	7	20
Bos	0	0	6	0	6
Bkn	0	3	0	7	10
ChiC	0	0	0	0	0
Det	6	0	0	0	6
ChiB	0	7	0	14	21
Cin	0	3	0	0	3

ChiB-Feathers 140R

WEDNESDAY, OCTOBER 3

NYG	7	0	7	0	14
Pit	6	6	0	0	12

SUNDAY, OCTOBER 7

NYG	10	0	0	6	16
Bos	0	0	13	0	13
Pit	3	0	0	6	9
Phi	0	0	0	7	7
ChiC	7	0	9	0	16
Cin	0	0	0	0	0
Det	0	3	0	0	3
GB	0	0	0	0	0
ChiB	7	0	7	7	21
Bkn	7	0	0	0	7

ChiB-Feathers 132R
ChiB-Feathers 101R

WEDNESDAY, OCTOBER 10

ChiB	7	7	0	14	28
Pit	0	0	0	0	0

SUNDAY, OCTOBER 14

Bkn	0	0	0	0	0
NYG	7	0	7	0	14
Det	0	7	0	3	10
Phi	0	0	0	0	0
Cin	0	0	0	0	0
GB	7	7	6	21	41
ChiB	0	13	0	7	20
ChiC	0	0	0	0	0
Pit	0	0	0	0	0
Bos	13	6	20	0	39

WEDNESDAY, OCTOBER 17

Bos	0	0	0	0	0
Det	0	3	14	7	24

Det-Battles 122R

SUNDAY, OCTOBER 21

Phi	0	0	0	0	0
Bos	0	0	6	0	6
Pit	0	0	0	7	7
NYG	3	0	7	7	17
ChiC	0	0	0	0	0
GB	7	0	0	8	15
Cin	0	7	0	0	7
ChiB	21	13	7	0	41

ChiB-Feathers 114R

MONDAY, OCTOBER 22

Bkn	0	0	0	0	0
Det	0	0	21	7	28

SUNDAY, OCTOBER 28

Phi	0	0	0	0	0
NYG	0	7	0	10	17
ChiC	0	0	0	0	0
Bos	0	9	0	0	9
Det	3	10	19	6	38
Cin	0	0	0	0	0

Det-Clark 194R

Pit	3	0	0	0	3
Bkn	7	0	0	14	21
GB	0	7	0	7	14
ChiB	7	3	7	10	27

ChiB-Feathers 155R

SUNDAY, NOVEMBER 4

NYG	0	0	0	7	7
ChiB	14	0	7	6	27
GB	0	3	7	0	10
Bos	0	0	0	0	0
Pit	7	0	0	0	7
Det	7	13	13	7	40

Det-Hanson 190R

TUESDAY, NOVEMBER 6

Cin	0	0	0	0	0
Phi	26	6	12	20	64
ChiC	7	0	7	7	21
Bkn	0	0	0	0	0

Bkn-Newman 114R

SUNDAY, NOVEMBER 11

GB	3	0	0	0	3
NYG	3	0	14	0	17
Pit	0	0	0	0	0
SL	0	6	0	0	6
ChiB	7	7	0	7	21
Bos	0	0	0	0	0

Bkn 3 7 0 0 **10**
Phi 0 0 7 0 7
Phi-Hanson 118R

Det 7 3 7 0 **17**
ChiC 0 0 0 13 13

SUNDAY, NOVEMBER 18

ChiC 0 0 6 3 **9**
GB 0 0 0 0 0

Bos 7 0 0 7 **14**
Phi 0 7 0 0 7

ChiB 0 0 0 10 **10**
NYG 0 7 2 0 9

Bkn 0 0 10 0 **10**
Pit 0 0 0 0 0

SL 0 0 7 0 7
Det 14 13 6 7 **40**
Det-Danowski 105R

SUNDAY, NOVEMBER 25

Bos 0 0 0 0 0
NYG 0 3 0 0 **3**

Phi 0 7 6 0 **13**
Bkn 0 0 0 0 0

ChiC 0 0 0 6 6
ChiB 10 0 0 7 **17**

GB 0 0 0 3 **3**
Det 0 0 0 0 0

THURSDAY, NOVEMBER 29

NYG 13 14 0 0 **27**
Bkn 0 0 0 0 0

ChiB 0 7 6 6 **19**
Det 7 9 0 0 16

GB 0 0 0 0 0
ChiC 0 0 0 6 **6**

SUNDAY, DECEMBER 2

Bkn 0 3 0 0 3
Bos 7 0 0 6 **13**

NYG 0 0 0 0 0
Phi 0 6 0 0 **6**

Det 0 0 0 7 7
ChiB 7 3 0 0 **10**

GB 7 7 0 7 **21**
SL 0 0 7 7 14

1935 NFL

FRIDAY, SEPTEMBER 13

Pit 14 0 0 3 **17**
Phi 7 0 0 0 7

SUNDAY, SEPTEMBER 15

ChiC 7 0 0 0 **7**
GB 0 6 0 0 6

FRIDAY, SEPTEMBER 20

Phi 0 0 0 0 0
Det 0 14 0 21 **35**

SUNDAY, SEPTEMBER 22

ChiB 0 0 0 0 0
GB 7 0 0 0 **7**

NYG 7 21 0 14 **42**
Pit 0 0 0 7 7

SUNDAY, SEPTEMBER 29

Bkn 0 3 0 0 3
Bos 0 0 0 7 **7**

ChiC 0 3 0 7 10
Det 0 0 7 3 10

NYG 0 7 0 0 7
GB 0 0 6 10 **16**

ChiB 0 23 0 0 **23**
Pit 0 0 7 0 7
ChiB-Hutson 109C

SUNDAY, OCTOBER 6

NYG 6 14 0 0 **20**
Bos 0 6 6 0 12

Det 3 0 0 7 10
Bkn 3 3 6 0 **12**

Pit 0 0 0 0 0
GB 0 20 0 7 **27**
GB-Hutson 109C

WEDNESDAY, OCTOBER 9

Phi 10 0 0 7 **17**
Pit 0 0 0 6 6

SUNDAY, OCTOBER 13

Det 3 0 7 7 **17**
Bos 0 0 0 7 7

GB 0 0 0 0 0
ChiC 0 3 0 0 **3**

Bkn 0 0 0 7 7
NYG 7 0 0 3 **10**

ChiB 0 27 6 6 **39**
Phi 0 0 0 0 0

SUNDAY, OCTOBER 20

Bkn 0 0 14 0 14
ChiB 14 7 3 0 **24**

Det 3 0 0 6 9
GB 0 0 10 3 **13**

Bos 0 0 6 0 6
NYG 17 0 0 0 **17**

ChiC 0 7 0 6 13
Pit 7 3 0 7 **17**

SUNDAY, OCTOBER 27

Phi 0 0 6 0 6
Bkn 3 0 7 7 **17**

GB 0 3 0 14 **17**
ChiB 0 0 7 7 14
GB-Hutson 103C

ChiC 0 0 7 7 14
NYG 6 0 7 0 13

Bos 0 0 0 0 0
Pit 0 3 3 0 **6**

WEDNESDAY, OCTOBER 30

Bos 0 0 0 0 0
Det 7 0 0 7 **14**
Det-Shepherd 129R

SUNDAY, NOVEMBER 3

Phi 0, 7 0 0 7
Bos 6 0 0 0 **6**

Det 7 0 0 0 **7**
ChiC 0 6 0 0 6

ChiB 0 0 7 13 **20**
NYG 3 0 0 0 3

Bkn 7 6 0 0 **13**
Pit 0 0 7 0 7

TUESDAY, NOVEMBER 5

Bkn 0 0 3 0 **3**
Phi 0 0 0 0 0

SUNDAY, NOVEMBER 10

ChiB 7 20 0 3 **30**
Bos 7 0 0 7 14

Pit 6 0 3 7 **16**
Bkn 7 0 0 0 7

Phi 0 0 3 0 **3**
ChiC 0 0 0 12 12

Det 0 7 0 0 7
GB 3 7 7 14 **31**
GB-Blood 100C

SUNDAY, NOVEMBER 17

NYG 0 0 3 0 **3**
ChiC 0 0 0 0 0

GB 3 0 7 0 10
Det 0 6 0 14 **20**

ChiC 3 6 3 0 12
Bkn 0 7 0 7 **14**

SUNDAY, NOVEMBER 24

ChiC 3 0 0 3 **6**
Bos 0 0 0 0 0

Det 7 6 7 0 20
ChiB 0 13 7 0 20

Phi 0 0 0 0 0
NYG 0 0 7 3 **10**

GB 6 14 0 14 **34**
Pit 0 7 7 0 14
GB-Monnett 107R

THURSDAY, NOVEMBER 28

NYG 0 7 7 7 **21**
Bkn 0 0 0 0 0

GB 7 0 0 0 **7**
ChiC 3 6 0 0 9
GB-Monnett 107R

ChiB 0 2 0 0 2
Det 7 0 7 0 **14**

SUNDAY, DECEMBER 1

Pit 0 3 0 0 3
Bos 0 0 0 13 **13**

ChiC 0 0 0 7 7
ChiB 0 7 0 0 7
ChiC-Russell 100R

Bkn 0 0 14 0 14
Det 0 3 9 16 **28**

NYG 0 14 0 7 **21**
Phi 7 7 0 0 14

SUNDAY, DECEMBER 8

Bos 0 0 0 0 0
Bkn 0 0 0 0 0

Pit 0 0 0 0 0
NYG 3 7 0 3 **13**

GB 0 3 7 3 **13**
Phi 0 6 0 0 6

ChiB 6 0 0 7 **13**
ChiC 0 0 0 0 0

1936 NFL

SUNDAY, SEPTEMBER 13

ChiC 0 0 7 0 7
GB 0 0 7 3 **10**

Bos 0 0 0 0 0
Pit 0 7 0 3 **10**

NYG 0 0 0 7 7
Phi 7 0 0 3 **10**
Phi-Hanson 107R

SUNDAY, SEPTEMBER 20

ChiB 3 7 6 14 **30**
GB 0 3 0 0 3

Bos 3 7 7 9 **26**
Phi 3 0 0 0 3
Bos-Battles 125R

WEDNESDAY, SEPTEMBER 23

Pit 7 3 0 0 **10**
Bkn 0 0 0 6 6

SUNDAY, SEPTEMBER 27

Bos 7 0 7 0 **14**
Bkn 3 0 0 0 3

NYG 0 0 7 0 7
Pit 0 7 0 3 **10**
NYG-Leemans 102R

ChiB 7 0 10 0 **17**
Phi 0 0 0 0 0

MONDAY, SEPTEMBER 28

ChiC 0 0 0 0 0
Det 7 20 12 0 **39**

SUNDAY, OCTOBER 4

ChiC 0 0 0 0 0
GB 0 14 3 7 **24**

Phi 0 0 0 0 0
Bkn 0 9 9 0 **18**

ChiB 7 7 13 0 **27**
Pit 0 0 0 9 9

NYG 0 7 0 0 **7**
Bos 0 0 0 0 0

SUNDAY, OCTOBER 11

Bos 0 0 2 0 2
GB 10 7 7 7 **31**

ChiC 0 0 0 0 0
ChiB 0 7 0 0 **7**

Bkn 0 0 10 0 10
NYG 7 3 0 0 10

Det 0 14 0 9 **23**
Phi 0 0 0 0 0

WEDNESDAY, OCTOBER 14

Det 0 7 0 7 **14**
Bkn 0 7 0 0 7

Phi 0 0 0 0 0
Pit 7 0 10 0 **17**

SUNDAY, OCTOBER 18

Det 0 0 9 9 18
GB 3 7 0 10 **20**

Pit 0 7 0 0 7
ChiB 6 6 0 14 **26**

ChiC 6 0 0 0 6
NYG 0 0 7 7 **14**
NYG-Leemans 117R

SUNDAY, OCTOBER 25

Pit 3 0 0 7 10
GB 7 21 14 0 **42**

Det 0 10 0 0 10
ChiB 3 9 0 0 **12**

Phi 7 10 0 0 17
NYG 0 7 0 14 **21**
NYG-Leemans 117R

ChiC 0 0 0 0 0
Bkn 3 6 0 0 **9**
ChiC-Hinkle 109R

SUNDAY, NOVEMBER 1

GB 0 14 0 7 **21**
ChiB 10 0 0 0 10

Det 0 0 0 7 7
NYG 7 0 7 0 **14**
Det-Gutowsky 137R

Bkn 0 0 0 7 7
Pit 3 0 7 0 **10**

ChiC 3 0 7 0 10
Bos 7 6 0 0 **13**

THURSDAY, NOVEMBER 5

Pit 0 0 0 6 **6**
Phi 0 0 0 0 0

SUNDAY, NOVEMBER 8

Pit 3 0 0 3 6
ChiC 6 0 7 0 **13**

ChiB 13 6 6 0 **25**
NYG 0 7 0 0 7

GB 0 0 0 7 **7**
Bos 3 0 0 0 3
Bos-Caddel 153R

SUNDAY, NOVEMBER 15

NYG 0 0 0 0 0
Det 7 10 14 7 **38**

Pit 0 6 0 0 6
ChiC 7 7 0 0 **14**

GB 3 14 21 0 **38**
Bkn 0 0 7 0 7

ChiB 7 3 7 9 **26**
Bos 0 0 0 0 0

SUNDAY, NOVEMBER 22

Det 0 0 0 14 **14**
ChiC 0 7 0 0 7

GB 3 0 14 9 **26**
NYG 0 0 7 7 14

Bkn 0 0 0 6 6
Bos 3 0 14 13 **30**

ChiB 0 21 0 7 **28**
Phi 0 0 0 0 0
Phi-Caddel 136R, Clark 118R

THURSDAY, NOVEMBER 26

ChiC 0 0 0 7 7
Det 6 0 0 7 **13**

NYG 0 14 0 0 **14**
Bkn 0 0 0 0 0

SUNDAY, NOVEMBER 29

GB 14 6 3 3 **26**
Det 7 7 3 0 17

ChiB 7 0 0 0 7
ChiC 0 0 0 14 **14**
ChiC-Grosvenor 126R

Pit 0 0 0 0 0
Bos 7 10 0 13 **30**

Bkn 0 6 7 0 **13**
Phi 0 0 0 7 7
Bkn-Wilson 162R
Phi-Gutowsky 100R

SUNDAY, DECEMBER 6

Bkn 0 0 0 6 6
Det 7 7 0 0 **14**

GB 0 0 0 0 0
ChiC 0 0 0 0 0
ChiC-Grosvenor 100R

Bos 0 7 7 0 **14**
NYG 0 0 0 0 0

1937 NFL

SUNDAY, SEPTEMBER 5

Phi 0 7 0 7 14
Pit 7 0 7 13 **27**

FRIDAY, SEPTEMBER 10

Bkn 0 6 0 7 **13**
Phi 0 7 0 0 7

Det 7 14 7 0 **28**
Cle 0 0 0 0 0

SUNDAY, SEPTEMBER 12

ChiC 7 0 7 0 **14**
GB 0 7 0 0 7

THURSDAY, SEPTEMBER 16

NYG 0 0 3 0 3
Was 3 0 0 10 **13**

SUNDAY, SEPTEMBER 19

ChiB 0 0 14 0 **14**
GB 0 0 2 0 2

ChiC 0 0 0 7 7
Det 0 13 0 3 **16**

Pit 0 7 7 7 **21**
Bkn 0 0 0 0 0

TUESDAY, SEPTEMBER 21

Cle 0 7 0 14 **21**
Phi 0 3 0 0 3
Cle-Tinsley 167C; Phi-Millner 117C

FRIDAY, SEPTEMBER 24

ChiC 14 0 0 7 **21**
Was 7 0 7 0 14

SUNDAY, SEPTEMBER 26

NYG 0 7 0 3 **10**
Pit 0 0 7 0 7

Cle 7 0 0 0 7
Bkn 6 0 0 3 **9**

ChiC 6 0 0 0 **6**
Phi 0 0 0 6 6
ChiC-Soar 118R

SUNDAY, OCTOBER 3

NYG 3 7 0 6 **16**
Phi 7 0 0 0 7

Det 0 6 0 0 6
GB 6 0 6 14 **26**

Bkn 0 0 0 7 7
Was 0 6 3 2 **11**

ChiC 0 6 0 0 **6**
Cle 0 0 0 0 0

MONDAY, OCTOBER 4

ChiB 0 0 7 0 **7**
Pit 0 0 0 0 0
Pit-Battles 132R

SUNDAY, OCTOBER 10

Phi	7	0	0	7	**14**
Was	0	0	0	0	0
ChiC	0	7	0	6	13
GB	3	21	10	0	**34**

ChiC-Tinsley 148C

ChiB	0	10	3	7	**20**
Cle	0	0	0	2	2
Pit	0	3	0	0	3
Det	0	0	7	0	**7**

SUNDAY, OCTOBER 17

Phi	0	0	0	0	0
NYG	7	7	0	7	**21**
Pit	0	13	0	7	20
Was	7	0	13	14	**34**

Was-Battles 135R

ChiC	0	0	0	7	7
ChiB	6	0	10	0	**16**
GB	0	14	7	14	**35**
Cle	0	3	0	7	10
Bkn	0	0	0	0	0
Det	7	16	7	0	**30**

SUNDAY, OCTOBER 24

Bkn	0	0	0	0	0
NYG	7	7	7	0	**21**
Was	0	0	7	3	**10**
Phi	0	7	0	0	7

Was-Battles 103R

ChiC	0	0	7	6	**13**
Pit	0	0	0	7	7
Cle	0	7	0	0	7
GB	14	0	7	14	**35**
Det	0	13	0	7	20
ChiB	7	14	0	7	**28**

SUNDAY, OCTOBER 31

GB	0	0	7	7	**14**
Det	0	0	13	0	13
ChiB	0	3	0	0	3
NYG	3	0	0	0	3
Phi	7	0	0	0	7
Pit	6	3	7	0	**16**
Was	7	0	14	0	**21**
Bkn	0	0	0	0	0
Cle	0	0	0	7	7
ChiC	7	0	6	0	**13**

SUNDAY, NOVEMBER 7

Pit	0	0	0	0	0
NYG	0	7	3	7	**17**
GB	0	17	0	7	**24**
ChiB	0	0	14	0	14

GB-Hutson 140C

Phi	0	7	0	7	**14**
Bkn	0	3	7	0	10
Cle	0	7	0	0	7
Det	0	14	7	6	**27**

SUNDAY, NOVEMBER 14

Det	0	3	7	7	**17**
NYG	0	0	0	0	0
Bkn	0	0	7	0	7
ChiB	0	16	7	6	**29**
Was	6	0	0	7	13
Pit	7	2	3	9	**21**
Phi	0	0	0	7	7
GB	6	10	0	21	**37**

Phi-Carter 139C

SUNDAY, NOVEMBER 21

Bkn	0	0	13	10	**23**
Pit	0	0	0	0	0
GB	0	0	0	0	0
NYG	0	3	7	0	**10**
Det	7	3	6	0	**16**
ChiC	0	0	0	7	7
Was	6	0	10	0	**16**
Cle	0	7	0	0	7

THURSDAY, NOVEMBER 25

ChiB	6	0	0	7	**13**
Det	0	0	0	0	0
NYG	7	0	3	3	13
Bkn	7	3	0	3	13

SUNDAY, NOVEMBER 28

GB	6	0	0	0	6
Was	0	0	7	7	**14**
Cle	0	0	7	0	7
ChiB	6	6	3	0	**15**

Cle-McDonald 115C, Buivid 164P; ChiB-Tinsley 155C, Coffee 306P

SUNDAY, DECEMBER 5

ChiB	0	13	27	2	**42**
ChiC	14	0	0	14	28
Was	14	7	7	21	**49**
NYG	0	0	14	0	14

Was-Battles 165R

Was-Millner 181C, Baugh 358P

1938 NFL

FRIDAY, SEPTEMBER 9

Pit	0	0	0	7	7
Det	9	7	0	0	**16**

SUNDAY, SEPTEMBER 11

ChiC	7	6	0	0	13
ChiB	0	7	6	3	**16**
Cle	3	7	0	7	17
GB	3	17	0	6	**26**
Was	7	7	12	0	**26**
Phi	3	13	7	0	23

Was-Krause 132R; Phi-Carter 114C

NYG	6	14	0	7	**27**
Pit	7	7	0	0	14

FRIDAY, SEPTEMBER 16

Phi	7	13	7	0	**27**
Pit	0	0	0	7	7

SATURDAY, SEPTEMBER 17

ChiC	7	0	0	0	**7**
Cle	0	0	0	6	6

SUNDAY, SEPTEMBER 18

ChiB	0	0	0	2	**2**
GB	0	0	0	0	0
Bkn	10	0	0	6	16
Was	0	13	0	3	16

FRIDAY, SEPTEMBER 23

Pit	0	0	7	10	**17**
Bkn	3	0	0	0	3

SUNDAY, SEPTEMBER 25

NYG	0	7	3	0	10
Phi	0	7	0	7	**14**
Cle	0	0	0	13	13
Was	3	7	21	6	**37**
ChiC	0	0	7	0	7
GB	0	14	14	0	**28**

WEDNESDAY, SEPTEMBER 28

GB	0	14	7	3	**24**
ChiC	0	6	7	9	22

SUNDAY, OCTOBER 2

ChiB	7	14	7	0	**28**
Phi	0	0	0	6	6
Det	0	10	7	0	17
Cle	7	0	0	14	**21**
ChiC	0	0	0	0	0
Bkn	0	13	0	0	**13**

MONDAY, OCTOBER 3

Pit	0	7	0	6	**13**
NYG	7	0	3	0	10

SUNDAY, OCTOBER 9

NYG	3	0	0	7	**10**
Was	0	7	0	0	7
Det	3	0	7	7	**17**
GB	0	0	0	7	7
Bkn	0	10	0	7	**17**
Pit	0	7	0	0	7

Bkn-Parker 103R; Pit-White 116R

ChiB	0	0	7	0	7
Cle	7	0	7	0	**14**

SUNDAY, OCTOBER 16

ChiB	7	13	14	0	**34**
ChiC	7	0	14	7	28
Was	0	0	7	0	**7**
Det	5	0	0	0	5
Phi	0	0	7	0	7
NYG	0	14	3	0	**17**
Bkn	0	7	0	0	7
GB	14	7	14	0	**35**

SUNDAY, OCTOBER 23

ChiC	0	0	0	0	0
Det	0	3	7	0	**10**
Cle	6	3	7	7	**23**
ChiB	0	7	7	7	21

ChiB-Manske 117C

Phi	0	0	7	7	14
Was	7	0	7	6	**20**

Was-Farkas 126R

Pit	0	0	0	0	0
GB	7	0	6	7	**20**
Bkn	0	0	0	14	14
NYG	7	21	0	0	**28**

WEDNESDAY, OCTOBER 26

Phi	0	7	0	0	**7**
ChiC	0	0	0	0	0

Phi-Shepherd 152R

SUNDAY, OCTOBER 30

Det	0	6	0	7	**13**
ChiB	0	0	0	7	7
GB	7	14	7	0	**28**
Cle	0	0	7	0	7

GB-Hutson 148C

Was	3	0	0	3	6
Bkn	6	0	0	0	6

SUNDAY, NOVEMBER 6

GB	14	7	3	0	**24**
ChiB	10	7	0	0	17
Cle	0	0	0	0	0
Det	6	0	0	0	**6**
Bkn	0	10	0	0	**10**
Phi	0	0	7	0	7
ChiC	0	0	0	0	0
NYG	0	0	0	6	**6**
Was	0	0	0	7	**7**
Pit	0	0	0	0	0

SUNDAY, NOVEMBER 13

GB	0	14	7	7	**28**
Det	0	0	7	0	7
Was	0	0	0	7	7
ChiB	0	17	2	12	**31**
Phi	0	0	14	0	14
Bkn	7	13	0	12	**32**
Cle	0	0	0	0	0
NYG	7	14	7	0	**28**

NYG-White 133R

SUNDAY, NOVEMBER 20

Phi	7	0	0	7	**14**
Pit	0	0	7	0	7
GB	0	0	3	0	3
NYG	0	0	9	6	**15**

NYG-Leemans 159R

ChiB	7	10	0	7	**24**
Bkn	0	6	0	0	6
Det	7	0	0	0	**7**
ChiC	3	0	0	0	3

THURSDAY, NOVEMBER 24

ChiB	0	0	7	0	7
Det	0	7	0	7	**14**
NYG	0	0	0	7	7
Bkn	7	0	0	0	7

Bkn-Tinsley 167C

SUNDAY, NOVEMBER 27

Cle	3	7	0	7	17
ChiC	7	7	17	0	**31**
Pit	0	0	0	0	0
Was	3	0	0	12	**15**

SUNDAY, DECEMBER 4

Phi	14	0	7	0	**21**
Det	0	0	0	7	7
Cle	7	0	6	0	**13**
Pit	0	0	0	7	7
Was	0	0	0	0	0
NYG	14	0	10	12	**36**

1939 NFL

SUNDAY, SEPTEMBER 10

ChiC	0	0	0	13	13
Det	14	0	0	7	**21**

THURSDAY, SEPTEMBER 14

Pit	0	7	0	0	7
Bkn	3	7	0	2	**12**

FRIDAY, SEPTEMBER 15

Cle	7	0	7	7	21
ChiB	0	20	0	10	**30**

SUNDAY, SEPTEMBER 17

Was	0	0	0	7	**7**
Phi	0	0	0	0	0
ChiC	0	0	7	3	10
GB	0	14	0	0	**14**

WEDNESDAY, SEPTEMBER 20

Cle	6	0	0	6	12
Bkn	14	3	0	6	**23**

SUNDAY, SEPTEMBER 24

ChiC	7	0	0	3	**10**
Pit	0	0	0	0	0
ChiB	0	13	0	3	16
GB	0	0	21	0	**21**
Bkn	0	0	7	0	7
Det	0	0	6	21	**27**
NYG	0	6	0	7	**13**
Phi	3	0	0	0	3

SUNDAY, OCTOBER 1

Cle	0	7	7	13	**27**
GB	3	7	14	0	24
Bkn	0	0	0	0	0
Phi	0	0	0	0	0
Det	0	10	7	0	**17**
ChiC	3	0	0	0	3
NYG	0	0	0	0	0
Was	0	0	0	0	0

NYG-Maniaci 141R

MONDAY, OCTOBER 2

ChiB	0	13	13	6	**32**
Pit	0	0	0	0	0

SUNDAY, OCTOBER 8

ChiB	0	21	14	0	**35**
Cle	14	0	0	7	21
Bkn	0	6	7	0	13
Was	7	7	7	20	**41**
NYG	0	0	14	0	**14**
Pit	0	7	0	0	7
ChiC	0	0	0	20	20
GB	7	7	7	6	**27**

ChiC-Smith 128C; GB-Uram 108R, Hutson 126C

SUNDAY, OCTOBER 15

Phi	3	7	0	0	10
NYG	0	7	10	10	**27**
ChiC	0	7	0	0	7
ChiB	17	7	0	20	**44**

ChiB-Osmanski 119R

Pit	7	7	0	0	14
Was	13	6	19	6	**44**

Was-Farkas 112C

Cle	0	7	0	0	7
Det	2	6	0	7	**15**

SUNDAY, OCTOBER 22

Cle	7	7	0	10	**24**
ChiC	0	0	0	0	0
Det	7	0	0	0	7
GB	0	17	0	9	**26**

GB-Hutson 111C

Was	14	0	7	0	**21**
Pit	0	7	0	7	14
ChiB	0	0	0	13	13
NYG	3	7	0	6	**16**

ChiB-Maniaci 102R

Phi	0	7	0	7	14
Bkn	7	0	10	6	**23**

Bkn-Manders 139R, Schwartz 100C

SUNDAY, OCTOBER 29

Det	0	3	7	0	**10**
ChiB	0	0	0	0	0
Was	0	7	0	7	14
GB	7	10	0	7	**24**
NYG	0	7	0	0	**7**
Bkn	3	0	3	0	6
Pit	0	7	7	0	14
Cle	7	0	0	7	14

Cle-Hall 131R

SUNDAY, NOVEMBER 5

GB	13	7	0	7	27
ChiB	7	10	6	7	**30**
Phi	0	6	0	0	6
Was	7	0	0	0	**7**
NYG	0	0	14	0	14
Det	3	3	3	9	**18**
ChiC	0	0	0	0	0
Cle	14	0	0	0	**14**

Cle-Manders 106R

MONDAY, NOVEMBER 6

Pit	0	3	3	7	13
Bkn	0	7	7	3	**17**

SUNDAY, NOVEMBER 12

ChiC	0	7	0	0	7
NYG	10	7	0	0	**17**
GB	7	6	7	3	**23**
Phi	3	0	7	6	16

GB-Hutson 112C

ChiB	0	14	3	6	**23**
Det	0	7	0	6	13

ChiB-Osmanski 111R

Was	7	14	7	14	**42**
Bkn	0	0	0	0	0

Was-Farkas 124R

SUNDAY, NOVEMBER 19

Det	3	0	0	0	3
Cle	0	14	0	0	**14**
Phi	0	7	0	7	14
ChiB	6	14	7	0	**27**

Phi-Ramsey 131C; ChiB-Manske 110C

ChiC	0	0	7	0	7
Was	7	6	6	9	**28**

Was-Farkas 145C

GB	14	7	7	0	**28**
Bkn	0	0	0	0	0

GB-Hutson 149C

Pit	0	0	0	7	7
NYG	7	6	3	7	**23**

THURSDAY, NOVEMBER 23

Pit	0	0	0	14	14
Phi	0	7	3	7	**17**

Pit-Manders 101R

SUNDAY, NOVEMBER 26

Bkn	0	0	0	7	7
NYG	0	7	7	14	**28**

```
Det    0   7   0   0    7
Was    7   0  14  10   31

ChiB   0  13  21  14   48
ChiC   0   0   0   7    7

GB     0   0   0   7    7
Cle    0   0   6   0    6

Phi    0   0   6   6   12
Pit    3  14   7   0   24
```

SUNDAY, DECEMBER 3
```
Was    0   0   0   7    7
NYG    3   3   3   0    9

Phi    0   0   0  13   13
Cle    7   7   7  14   35

GB     0   3   2   7   12
Det    0   7   0   0    7
```

1940 NFL
SUNDAY, SEPTEMBER 8
```
ChiC   0   0   7   0    7
Pit    0   7   0   0    7
ChiC  D9 R?/64   P(21-9-1) 128
Pit   D3 R?/65   P(13-4-2)  64
```

SUNDAY, SEPTEMBER 15
```
Phi    0   6   0  14   20
GB    21   0   6   0   27
Phi  D11 R24/7   P(40-18-4) 225
GB   D9 R44/148  P(23-10-1) 118
Phi-Looney 115C

NYG    0   0   7   3   10
Pit   10   0   0   0   10
NYG  D9 R?/104   P(16-4-1) 111
Pit  D8 R?/137   P(15-3-2)  60

Det    0   0   0   0    0
ChiC   0   0   0   0    0
Det  D5 R?/-10   P(6-1-2)   26
ChiC D2 R?/14    P(2-0-1)    0

Bkn    0   0  10   7   17
Was    7  10   0   7   24
Bkn  D10 R?/120  P(25-12-2) 156
Was  D15 R?/195  P(20-14-0) 174
```

SUNDAY, SEPTEMBER 22
```
Phi    0   7   0   6   13
Cle   13   6   0   2   21
Phi  D11 R?/43   P(28-14-3) 196
Cle  D9 R?/122   P(19-9-1)  107
Phi-Looney 129C

ChiB   7   7  14  13   41
GB     3   0   7   0   10
ChiB D6 R?/97    P(14-6-2) 191
GB   D15 R?/149  P(30-12-7) 192
ChiB-Swisher 106C

Pit    0   0   3   7   10
Det    0   7   0   0    7
Pit  D11 R?/172  P(9-4-1)   37
Det  D13 R?/187  P(15-4-1)  44

NYG    0   0   7   0    7
Was    7   7   0   7   21
NYG  D15 R?/145  P(26-10-2) 140
Was  D8 R?/74    P(19-9-1)   99
```

WEDNESDAY, SEPTEMBER 25
```
ChiB   0   7   0   0    7
ChiC   7   7   0   7   21
ChiB D17 R?/135  P(24-6-2) 121
ChiC D12 R?/173  P(12-7-1)  83
```

SATURDAY, SEPTEMBER 28
```
NYG   10   3   7   0   20
Phi    7   0   7   0   14
NYG  D8 R?/153   P(4-3-0)  82
Phi  D15 R?/43   P(34-14-1) 170
```

SUNDAY, SEPTEMBER 29
```
Bkn    7   0   3   0   10
Pit    0   3   0   0    3
Bkn  D14 R?/259  P(13-2-1) 56
Pit  D7 R?/77    P(16-5-1) 111
Bkn-McFadden 104R

Cle    0   0   0   0    0
Det    0   0   6   0    6
Cle  D5 R?/40    P(16-8-2) 106
Det  D13 R?/172  P(18-7-4)  54
```

```
ChiC   0   6   0   0    6
GB    17   0  14   0   31
ChiC D14 R?/137  P(31-10-6) 87
GB   D13 R?/155  P(27-10-3) 177
```

FRIDAY, OCTOBER 4
```
Phi    3   0   7   7   17
Bkn    0  17   0  13   30
Phi  D9 R?/52    P(19-8-1) 100
Bkn  D14 R?/178  P(9-6-1)   71
```

SATURDAY, OCTOBER 5
```
ChiC   7   0   7   0   14
Det    0  20   7  16   43
ChiC D9 R?/120   P(17-3-7)  25
Det  D9 R?/194   P(11-5-2)  49
```

SUNDAY, OCTOBER 6
```
Was   14   7  13   6   40
Pit    3   0   7   0   10
Was  D14 R?/147  P(21-12-1) 186
Pit  D15 R?/95   P(29-8-4)   93

ChiB   0  14   7   0   21
Cle    0   0  14   0   14
ChiB D13 R?/187  P(13-4-2)  53
Cle  D10 R?/75   P(30-13-3) 158
```

SUNDAY, OCTOBER 13
```
Phi    0   0   0   7    7
NYG    0   0  10   7   17
Phi  D9 R?/15    P(21-9-0) 102
NYG  D15 R?/189  P(15-9-2)  87

Det    0   0   0   0    0
ChiB   7   0   0   0    7
Det  D13 R?/107  P(15-7-1)  66
ChiB D10 R?/195  P(7-3-2)   15

Pit    0   0   0   0    0
Bkn   14   0   0   7   21
Pit  D12 R?/137  P(24-9-3)  76
Bkn  D8 R?/119   P(16-6-1) 121

ChiC  14   7   0   0   21
Was   14   0   7   7   28
ChiC D5 R?/82    P(14-5-1) 127
Was  D20 R?/115  P(29-18-4) 325
Was-Todd 101C

Cle    0   0   7   14  14
GB     3  14   7   7   31
Cle  D16 R?/77   P(42-17-4) 265
GB   D18 R?/86   P(37-18-4) 327
GB-Mulleneaux 111C
```

SUNDAY, OCTOBER 20
```
Was    7  14   6   7   34
Phi    3  14   0   0   17
Was  D14 R?/97   P(27-20-1) 283
Phi  D10 R?/38   P(35-13-4) 238

Pit    0   0   0   0    0
NYG    7   3   0   2   12
Pit  D7 R?/40    P(25-7-4) 108
NYG  D14 R?/158  P(14-9-1) 142

Bkn    0   0   7   0    7
ChiB   0   0   7   9   16
Bkn  D9 R?/74    P(19-9-1) 187
ChiB D18 R?/300  P(19-7-2) 117

Det    0   7  16   0   23
GB     0   7   7   0   14
Det  D13 R?/109  P(20-8-4) 168
GB   D12 R?/80   P(32-15-7) 221
Det-Hanneman 101C

ChiC   0   0   7  14   14
Cle   13   0   0  13   26
ChiC D12 R?/196  P(23-7-3)  63
Cle  D7 R?/153   P(18-4-2) 177
```

SATURDAY, OCTOBER 26
```
Bkn    7   0   7   7   21
Phi    0   0   0   7    7
Bkn  D7 R?/199   P(12-5-0)  71
Phi  D13 R?/29   P(42-15-2) 228
Phi-McDonald 102C
```

SUNDAY, OCTOBER 27
```
Was    7   6   0   7   20
Det    0   7   0   7   14
Was  D8 R?/206   P(16-6-5)  65
Det  D18 R?/137  P(29-15-3) 193
```

```
ChiB   7  23   7   0   37
NYG    0   7  14   0   21
ChiB D12 R?/74   P(18-9-0) 171
NYG  D21 R?/74   P(38-19-5) 252
NYG-Cuff 104C

Pit    3   0   0   0    3
GB     7   3   0  14   24
Pit  D9 R?/61    P(18-3-5)  34
GB   D13 R?/176  P(20-7-1) 120

Cle    7   0   0   0    7
ChiC   7   0   7   3   17
Cle  D8 R?/93    P(20-6-3)  54
ChiC D14 R?/146  P(16-6-2)  77
```

SUNDAY, NOVEMBER 3
```
NYG    0   3   0   7   10
Bkn    0   0   0   7    7
NYG  D11 R?/137  P(10-5-1)  37
Bkn  D13 R?/73   P(26-14-1) 190

Det    0   0   0   0    0
Cle    0  14   0  10   24
Det  D12 R?/112  P(24-9-5) 149
Cle  D16 R?/177  P(13-10-1) 131

GB     0   7   0   0    7
ChiB   7   7   0   0   14
GB   D11 R?/52   P(31-13-3) 156
ChiB D13 R?/187  P(10-3-1)  59

Pit    3   0   7   0   10
Was    6   7   7  17   37
Pit  D10 R?/95   P(19-10-1) 194
Was  D11 R?/167  P(16-14-0) 204
Was-Johnston 106C
```

SUNDAY, NOVEMBER 10
```
ChiB   0   7   7   0   14
Det    3   0   7   7   17
ChiB D14 R?/132  P(9-7-1) 167
Det  D14 R?/98   P(25-12-0) 155

Phi    3   0   0   0    3
Pit    0   0   7   0    7
Phi  D8 R?/70    P(20-8-1)  59
Pit  D8 R?/145   P(5-1-1)   26

GB     7   7  14   0   28
ChiC   0   7   0   0    7
GB   D16 R?/274  P(19-6-0) 114
ChiC D12 R?/92   P(24-8-5)  97
GB-Isbell 118R

Cle    0   6   0   7   13
NYG    0   0   0   0    0
Cle  D4 R?/84    P(6-1-1)  36
NYG  D15 R?/202  P(26-8-2)  44
NYG-Leemans 101R

Was    0   0  14   0   14
Bkn    7   2   7   0   16
Was  D20 R?/19   P(47-25-2) 312
Bkn  D7 R?/73    P(14-6-0)  94
Was-Todd 126C
```

SUNDAY, NOVEMBER 17
```
GB     0   0   0   3    3
NYG    7   0   0   0    7
GB   D16 R?/132  P(27-10-2)  95
NYG  D5 R?/95    P(5-3-1)   25

Det    7   0  14   0   21
Phi    0   0   0   0    0
Det  D14 R?/266  P(18-8-0) 131
Phi  D9 R?/-23   P(38-13-2) 152

ChiB   3   0   0   0    3
Was    0   7   0   0    7
ChiB D16 R?/149  P(29-9-2) 148
Was  D11 R?/44   P(19-13-1) 125

Cle    0   7   0   7   14
Bkn    0   6  16   7   29
Cle  D15 R?/140  P(32-14-2) 145
Bkn  D9 R?/126   P(20-6-2) 114
```

SUNDAY, NOVEMBER 24
```
ChiC   3   0   0   0    3
Bkn    0   0  14   0   14
ChiC D15 R?/199  P(17-6-3)  88
Bkn  D9 R?/116   P(14-6-2) 106

Was    0   0   7   0    7
NYG   14   0   0   7   21
Was  D12 R?/116  P(21-8-5)  78
NYG  D6 R?/141   P(7-3-0)   80
```

```
GB    13  14   3  20   50
Det    0   0   0   7    7
GB   D11 R?/202  P(13-7-0) 112
Det  D11 R?/96   P(24-10-5) 157

Cle    7   0   6  12   25
ChiB  13   0  14  10   47
Cle  D11 R?/73   P(27-14-2) 209
ChiB D15 R?/134  P(21-10-1) 295
ChiB-Kavanaugh 100C
```

THURSDAY, NOVEMBER 28
```
Pit    0   0   0   0    0
Phi    0   0   0   7    7
Pit  D5 R?/65    P(10-4-3)  65
Phi  D8 R?/53    P(26-8-0)  67
```

SUNDAY, DECEMBER 1
```
Bkn    7   0   0   7   14
NYG    6   0   0   0    6
Bkn  D15 R?/210  P(22-8-3) 130
NYG  D8 R?/106   P(13-5-1)  57

ChiC   0   0   0   0    0
ChiB  17  14   0   0   31
ChiC D11 R?/101  P(25-14-2) 139
ChiB D8 R?/191   P(5-3-0)   63

Phi    0   0   0   6    6
Was    0   6   0   7   13
Phi  D19 R?/16   P(60-33-0) 316
Was  D12 R?/220  P(9-5-2)   36
Phi-Looney 180C, O'Brien 316P

GB     3   0   0  10   13
Cle    0   7   6   0   13
GB   D18 R?/208  P(27-11-2) 156
Cle  D10 R?/80   P(25-11-3) 148
```

1941 NFL
SUNDAY, SEPTEMBER 7
```
Pit    0  14   0   0   14
Cle   10   7   0   0   17
Pit  D8 R?/141   P(12-4-5)  58
Cle  D10 R?/69   P(26-10-2) 125
```

SATURDAY, SEPTEMBER 13
```
NYG    3  14   0   7   24
Phi    0   0   0   0    0
NYG  D8 R?/134   P(13-6-0)  94
Phi  D11 R?/26   P(35-14-5) 144
```

SUNDAY, SEPTEMBER 14
```
Det    0   0   0   0    0
GB     0   6   3  14   23
Det  D5 R?/77    P(24-4-4)  56
GB   D16 R?/156  P(25-12-0) 151
```

TUESDAY, SEPTEMBER 16
```
Cle    0  10   0   0   10
ChiC   0   0   6   0    6
Cle  D4 R?/80    P(13-5-2)  90
ChiC D11 R?/118  P(23-9-2) 114
```

SUNDAY, SEPTEMBER 21
```
Cle    0   0   0   7    7
GB     7   0   0  17   24
Cle  D6 R?/75    P(17-6-5)  85
GB   D15 R?/238  P(12-4-1)  46

Phi    0   3   7   0   10
Pit    0   0   0   7    7
Phi  D8 R?/127   P(13-4-2)  65
Pit  D7 R?/124   P(20-4-2)  45

Det    0   0   0   7    7
Bkn    0   0   7   7   14
Det  D10 R?/88   P(17-6-2)  54
Bkn  D15 R?/115  P(23-13-1) 197
```

SATURDAY, SEPTEMBER 27
```
Bkn   14   0   0  10   24
Phi    0   7   0   6   13
Bkn  D7 R?/125   P(12-4-1)  33
Phi  D17 R?/93   P(35-18-1) 248

Det    0   0   0   7    7
ChiC   0  14   0   0   14
Det  D5 R?/96    P(14-2-0)  66
ChiC D8 R?/100   P(15-8-0)  71
```

SUNDAY, SEPTEMBER 28
```
ChiB   6   9   7   3   25
GB     0  10   7   0   17
ChiB D11 R?/258  P(6-1-0)   44
GB   D15 R?/77   P(28-14-2) 217

NYG    7   0   7   3   17
Was    0   7   0   3   10
NYG  D10 R?/129  P(17-6-1) 114
Was  D5 R?/90    P(12-7-4)  64
```

SUNDAY, OCTOBER 5
```
NYG    3   0  14  20   37
Pit    3   0   7   0   10
NYG  D9 R?/76    P(10-6-1) 131
Pit  D7 R?/64    P(14-6-4) 113

ChiB   7  28   7   6   48
Cle    0   7   7   7   21
ChiB D11 R?/147  P(17-9-1) 242
Cle  D14 R?/80   P(31-14-3) 145

ChiC   6   0   0   0    6
GB     7   0   7   0   14
ChiC D7 R?/79    P(8-5-0) 195
GB   D9 R?/114   P(18-9-1)  71

Bkn    0   0   0   0    0
Was    0   0   3   0    3
Bkn  D13 R?/161  P(21-8-2)  80
Was  D9 R?/106   P(19-8-2)  93
```

SUNDAY, OCTOBER 12
```
Phi    0   0   0   0    0
NYG    7   3   0   6   16
Phi  D9 R?/45    P(18-10-2) 124
NYG  D9 R?/147   P(10-5-1)   54

Was    7   3  14   0   24
Pit    0   7   0  13   20
Was  D5 R?/73    P(13-5-1)  83
Pit  D9 R?/27    P(22-8-3) 163

ChiC   0   0   0   7    7
ChiB  20  13  14   6   53
ChiC D11 R?/103  P(27-10-2) 100
ChiB D17 R?/237  P(22-15-0) 376

Bkn    0   0   7   0    7
GB    13   3   7   7   30
Bkn  D11 R?/75   P(33-13-2) 181
GB   D14 R?/164  P(21-14-1) 126
GB-Hutson 126C

Cle    0   0   0   7    7
Det    7   0   3   7   17
Cle  D9 R?/74    P(17-6-1)  54
Det  D10 R?/132  P(12-6-1) 119
```

SUNDAY, OCTOBER 19
```
GB     7   0   7   3   17
Cle    7   0   0   7   14
GB   D16 R?/109  P(35-19-0) 285
Cle  D15 R?/102  P(33-20-2) 188

Pit    0   0   0   0    0
NYG    0   7   7  14   28
Pit  D5 R?/100   P(15-6-4) 114
NYG  D13 R?/150  P(14-3-1)  56

Det    0   0   0   0    0
ChiB   7  21  14   7   49
Det  D10 R?/84   P(15-2-4)  24
ChiB D17 R?/174  P(19-9-0) 209

ChiC   6   7   7   0   20
Bkn    0   0   6   0    6
ChiC D13 R?/159  P(14-9-0) 159
Bkn  D11 R?/113  P(19-5-3)  63

Was    0  14   0   7   21
Phi   14   0   3   0   17
Was  D18 R?/162  P(30-12-5) 154
Phi  D12 R?/52   P(19-11-2) 107
```

SUNDAY, OCTOBER 26
```
ChiC   0   0   7   7   14
Phi    0  14   7   0   21
ChiC D14 R?/80   P(36-18-4) 217
Phi  D9 R?/69    P(12-10-0)  99

NYG    0  10   3   0   13
Bkn    0   3   6   7   16
NYG  D10 R?/112  P(15-5-1)  56
Bkn  D12 R?/226  P(16-7-0)  97
NYG-Uram 103R
```

Pit   0   0   0   0   7
ChiB   7 14   7   6   34
Pit   D9 R?/117   P(19-3-3)   42
ChiB D17 R?/281 P(12-5-3) 129

GB   7 10   0   7   24
Det   0   0   0   7   7
GB   D18 R?/227 P(25-15-0) 211
Det D12 R?/77   P(20-7-2)   115
  GB-Uram 103R

Cle   0   6   0   7   13
Was   10   7   0   0   17
Cle D12 R?/44   P(33-14-2) 133
Was D9 R?/62   P(14-7-1)   79

SUNDAY, NOVEMBER 2

ChiC   0   7   3   0   10
NYG   7   0   0   0   7
ChiC D?R?/74   P(24-13-2) 200
NYG D8 R?/82   P(15-6-1)   65
  ChiC-Dewell 131C

GB   6   0 10   0   16
ChiB   0   0 14 14   28
GB   D16 R?/123 P(19-10-2) 153
ChiB D10 R?/65   P(32-9-0)   94

Pit   0   3   0   0   3
Was   7 10   0   6   23
Pit D4 R?/23   P(16-4-3)   24
Was D16 R?/208 P(22-14-7) 132

Det   7   0   0   7   14
Cle   0   0   0   0   0
Det D6 R?/96   P(16-4-0)   25
Cle D9 R?/50   P(24-11-4) 151

Phi   0   6   0   0   6
Bkn   5   3   0   7   15
Phi D11 R?/78   P(17-8-1)   90
Bkn D13 R?/152 P(15-10-1) 101

SUNDAY, NOVEMBER 9

Det   0   6   0   7   13
NYG   7   3   3   7   20
Det D6 R?/53   P(15-9-0)   65
NYG D9 R?/114   P(13-5-2)   128

Cle   0   7   6   0   13
ChiB   0 16   6   9   31
Cle D12 R?/137 P(26-9-3)   140
ChiB D24 R?/247 P(16-10-1) 201

Pit   0   0   0   7   7
Phi   7   0   0   0   7
Pit D5 R?/145   P(13-2-0)   10.
Phi D10 R?/173 P(18-7-1)   75

Was   0   7   0   0   7
Bkn   0   7   0   6   13
Was D8 R?/45   P(17-11-2) 150
Bkn D17 R?/170 P(18-10-2) 149

SUNDAY, NOVEMBER 16

Cle   7   7   0   0   14
NYG   14 21   7   7   49
Cle D14 R?/176 P(31-14-5) 141
NYG D13 R?/187 P(15-10-2) 198
  Cle-Hall 104R

ChiC   3   0   6   0   9
GB   7   3   0   7   17
ChiC D16 R?/100 P(28-13-4) 148
GB   D13 R?/145 P(22-9-2)   127

Bkn   7   0   0   0   7
Pit   0   7   0   7   14
Bkn D9 R?/103   P(25-13-3) 175
Pit D5 R?/205   P(0-0-0)   0

Phi   0   3   7   7   17
Det   0   7   0 14   21
Phi D14R?/65   P(28-10-3) 136
Det D11 R?/105 P(24-9-1)   246

Was   0   7   7   7   21
ChiB   7 21   0   7   35
Was D18 R?/71   P(34-19-2) 263
ChiB D9 R?/170   P(12-7-1)   136

SUNDAY, NOVEMBER 23

Was   0   0   0 13   13
NYG   0   0 10 10   20
Was D15 R?/57   P(34-17-2) 160
NYG D13 R?/116 P(18-9-0)   87

ChiC   0   0   7   0   7
Cle   0   0   0   0   0
ChiC D7 R?/48   P(28-8-1)   83
Cle D6 R?/103 P(29-10-5)   91

ChiB   7   7   7   3   24
Det   7   0   0   8   15
ChiB D25 R?/224 P(26-9-2) 166
Det   D3 R?/78   P(17-1-5)   15

GB   0 26   7 21   54
Pit   7   0   0   0   7
GB   D13 R?/155 P(19-11-0) 116
Pit D11 R?/210 P(10-3-4)   56

SUNDAY, NOVEMBER 30

Pit   0   7   0   0   7
Bkn   14   7   7   7   35
Pit D5 R?/87   P(17-2-6)   25
Bkn D8 R?/190 P(16-6-2)   123

GB   0   0 13   9   22
Was   10   7   0   0   17
GB   D14 R?/118 P(25-15-3) 270
Was D18 R?/142 P(28-19-2) 189
  GB-Hutson 135C

ChiB   0   0 21 28   49
Phi   7   7   0   0   14
ChiB D21 R?/274 P(29-13-1) 249
Phi D12 R?/116 P(27-13-4) 156

ChiC   3   0   0   0   3
Det   7   0 14   0   21
ChiC D13 R?/88 P(29-12-4) 147
Det D9 R?/93   P(17-7-1)   94

SUNDAY, DECEMBER 7

ChiB   0 14   7 13   34
ChiC   7 10   0   7   24
ChiB D16 R?/204 P(16-11-1) 158
ChiC D18 R?/103 P(22-10-1) 226

Bkn   0   7   7   7   21
NYG   0   0   0   7   7
Bkn D16 R?/262 P(4-1-1)   5
NYG D8 R?/73   P(16-7-3)   123

Phi   7   0   7   0   14
Was   0   7   0 13   20
Phi D15 R?/145 P(27-11-5) 145
Was D14 R?/72   P(35-17-5) 186

1942 NFL
SUNDAY, SEPTEMBER 13

Phi   7   7   3   7   24
Pit   7   0   0   7   14
Phi D14 R42/159 P(18-12-1) 169
Pit D15 R38/118 P(21-8-1)   75
  Pit-Dudley 107R

Cle   0   0   0   0   0
ChiC   7   0   0   0   7
Cle D11 R?/160 P(28-11-2) 161
ChiC D10 R?/150 P(16-7-1)   99

SUNDAY, SEPTEMBER 20

Det   0   0   0   0   0
ChiC   0   6   0   7   13
Det D9 R?/58   P(17-6-2)   59
ChiC D11 R?/99 P(23-9-0)   109

Phi   7   0   0   7   14
Cle   7 10   7   0   24
Phi D14 R45/145 P(19-8-2)   90
Cle D12 R33/96   P(15-9-1)   200

Pit   0   0 14   0   14
Was   0   7   7 14   28
Pit D13 R44/129 P(22-3-3)   34
Was D10 R27/93   P(26-13-1) 112

SUNDAY, SEPTEMBER 27

ChiB   7   6 14 17   44
GB   0 21   7   0   28
ChiB D14 R52/225 P(11-5-2)   85
GB   D16 R32/104 P(30-16-4) 233
  GB-Hutson 147C

Cle   7   0   7   0   14
Det   0   0   0   0   0
Cle D11 R?/116 P(20-7-2)   106
Det D9 R?/107   P(22-5-1)   57

NYG   0   7   0   7   14
Was   0   7   0   0   7
NYG D0 R26/1   P(1-1-0)   5
Was D15 R49/120 P(25-12-2) 113

Bkn   14   7 14   0   35
Phi   0   7   0   7   14
Bkn D14 R50/213 P(13-8-2) 100
Phi D9 R42/86   P(22-11-1) 206
  Bkn-Condit 105R

SUNDAY, OCTOBER 4

ChiB   7   0   7   7   21
Cle   0   0   0   7   7
ChiB D12 R35/118 P(19-10-3) 179
Cle D7 R23/20   P(22-8-3)   128
  ChiB-McLean 126C

GB   3   0   0 14   17
ChiC   7   6   0   0   13
GB   D9 R40/141 P(19-5-4)   88
ChiC D11 R21/105 P(24-10-3) 95

Bkn   14   0   7   7   28
Det   0   7   0   0   7
Bkn D4 R32/120 P(10-6-2)   80
Det D13 R33/121 P(26-9-3) 115

NYG   3   7   0   0   10
Pit   0   6   0   7   13
NYG D9 R30/123 P(10-4-1)   27
Pit D13 R50/168 P(11-4-1)   41

Was   7   0   0   7   14
Phi   3   7   0   0   10
Was D11 R35/64 P(23-11-2) 206
Phi D10 R36/83 P(17-6-1)   108

SUNDAY, OCTOBER 11

ChiC   7   7   0   0   14
ChiB   21 13   0   7   41
ChiC D8 R26/43   P(31-16-2) 156
ChiB D11 R29/80 P(20-9-3)   252

Det   7   0   0   7   14
GB   10 14   7   7   38
Det D13 R31/184 P(26-7-3)   70
GB   D17 R53/107 P(31-16-1) 305
  GB-Hutson 149C

Cle   0   0 14   0   14
Was   7   7 19   0   33
Cle D5 R22/-29 P(22-10-0) 132
Was D15 R52/187 P(17-10-2) 143

Phi   3   0   7   7   17
NYG   14   0 14   7   35
Phi D14 R35/69 P(25-9-3)   147
NYG. D6 R39/77   P(12-6-1)   99

Pit   0   7   0   0   7
Bkn   0   0   0   0   0
Pit D9 R51/167 P(7-0-2)   0
Bkn D7 R36/86   P(15-6-3)   43

SUNDAY, OCTOBER 18

NYG   7   0   0   0   7
ChiB   6   0   7 13   26
NYG D10 R32/78   P(16-8-1) 142
ChiB D18 R51/244 P(9-3-2)   91

ChiC   0   0   0   7   7
Det   0   0   0   0   0
ChiC D12 R42/123 P(26-7-1) 138
Det D9 R34/114   P(14-6-3)   65

Cle   0 21   0   7   28
GB   10   7 14 14   45
Cle D15 R20/134 P(28-16-2) 254
GB   D26 R45/209 P(39-27-0) 330
  GB-Hutson 209C

Was   0 14   0   7   21
Bkn   0 10   0   0   10
Was D13 R33/151 P(22-10-0) 128
Bkn D14 R35/154 P(27-11-2) 158
  Bkn-Condit 116R

Pit   0   0   7   7   14
Phi   0   0   0   7   7
Pit D9 R56/208 P(5-1-0)   13
Phi D11 R32/101 P(18-10-1) 106

SUNDAY, OCTOBER 25

Phi   0   7   0   7   14
ChiB   7 14 14 10   45
Phi D7 R34/15   P(24-7-2)   68
ChiB D16 R41/151 P(23-11-4) 227

ChiC   3   0   0   0   3
Cle   0   0   7   0   7
ChiC D13 R37/100 P(30-11-4) 114
Cle D9 R32/60   P(23-8-3)   93

GB   7   7   7   7   28
Det   0   0   0   7   7
GB   D9 R32/48   P(19-8-0)   118
Det D16 R39/151 P(22-8-3) 128

NYG   7   0   0   0   7
Bkn   0   7   3   7   17
NYG D10 R35/68 P(18-8-3)   88
Bkn D11 R48/123 P(7-3-0)   106

Was   0   7   0   7   14
Pit   0   0   0   0   0
Was D11 R29/67 P(18-10-1) 126
Pit D14 R37/113 P(24-11-0) 134

SUNDAY, NOVEMBER 1

Det   0   0   0   0   0
ChiB   0   6   7   3   16
Det D6 R29/82   P(17-5-2)   43
ChiB D16 R48/160 P(16-8-3) 161

ChiC 10   0   7   7   24
GB   7 14 13 21   55
ChiC D16 R40/104 P(25-11-4) 138
GB   D13 R33/116 P(27-13-1) 423
  GB-Hutson 207C, Uram 174C,
  Isbell 333P

Cle   0   7 10   0   17
Bkn   0   0   0   0   0
Cle D8 R30/45   P(17-11-1) 159
Bkn D14 R41/174 P(21-5-4)   94

Pit   0 10   0   7   17
NYG   3   0   0   7   10
Pit D12 R50/195 P(10-4-1)   40
NYG D10 R36/136 P(19-6-3)   80
  Pit-Dudley 135R

Phi   0   6 14   7   27
Was   7   0 20   3   30
Phi D13 R36/77 P(17-11-1) 198
Was D16 R39/262 P(27-12-2) 134
  Phi-Meyer 119C; Was-Farkas 166R

SUNDAY, NOVEMBER 8

ChiB   14   7   7   7   35
Bkn   0   0   0   0   0
ChiB D22 R51/260 P(24-12-1) 164
Bkn D9 R23/60   P(21-6-3)   60

ChiC   0   0   0   0   0
Was   14   7   7   0   28
ChiC D17 R43/159 P(37-11-4) 105
Was D10 R27/145 P(29-16-2) 181

GB   6 10   0 14   30
Cle   0   0   5   7   12
GB   D21 R45/140 P(37-20-2) 197
Cle D14 R25/138 P(31-11-7)   96

Pit   0 14 14   7   35
Det   7   0   0   0   7
Pit D15 R51/267 P(12-4-1)   48
Det D6 R23/112   P(17-4-3)   77
  Det-Hackney 108R

SUNDAY, NOVEMBER 15

GB   0   0   0   0   0
ChiB   7 14 10   7   38
GB   D14 R26/43   P(41-21-3) 165
ChiB D12 R43/181 P(18-7-3) 161
  GB-Hutson 117C

Det   7   0   0   0   7
Cle   7   0   6 14   27
Det D17 R44/232 P(22-9-3) 114
Cle D8 R31/125   P(19-11-2) 160

Was   0   0   0 14   14
NYG   0   0   0   7   7
Was D18 R35/118 P(26-19-1) 211
NYG D8 R34/52   P(16-4-1)   48

Phi   0   0   0   7   7
Bkn   0   0   0   7   7
Phi D15 R33/243 P(18-7-1)   77
Bkn D11 R41/219 P(16-4-4)   40
  Phi-Pritchard 104R

SUNDAY, NOVEMBER 22

ChiB   14 14   7   7   42
Det   0   0   0   0   0
ChiB D8 R32/92   P(21-13-4) 270
Det D10 R25/81   P(25-7-7)   63

ChiC   3   0   0   0   3
Pit   7   3   0   9   19
ChiC D12 R33/75   P(33-16-5) 183
Pit D8 R41/226   P(14-2-1)   40
  Pit-Riffle 104R

GB   0 14   0   7   21
Pit   7   7   7   0   21
GB   D23 R37/202 P(40-24-1) 221
NYG D14 R35/150 P(20-9-2) 151
  GB-Fritsch 111R, Hutson 134C

Bkn   3   0   0   0   3
Was   0   6   7 10   23
Bkn D10 R37/90 P(19-6-4)   32
Was D12 R37/149 P(22-10-2) 118

SUNDAY, NOVEMBER 29

Cle   0   0   0   0   0
ChiB   0 21 12 14   47
Cle D6 R25/10   P(24-7-4)   48
ChiB D14 R39/183 P(20-13-1) 323
  ChiB-Famiglietti 101R,
  McLean 109C, Pool 118C

ChiC   0   7   0   0   7
NYG   14   0   7   0   21
ChiC D17 R27/80   P(42-23-3) 222
NYG D13 R40/183 P(10-5-1)   79

GB   7   0   0   0   7
Phi   0   0   0   0   0
GB   D11 R42/110 P(12-3-0)   67
Phi D7 R35/91   P(10-3-3)   39

Was   0   0   8   7   15
Det   3   0   0   0   3
Was D18 R50/165 P(22-14-2) 128
Det D7 R17/19   P(14-7-3)   94

Bkn   0   0   0   0   0
Pit   0   7   0   6   13
Bkn D7 R41/100 P(2-0-0)   0
Pit D5 R37/174 P(8-1-0)   7

SUNDAY, DECEMBER 6

ChiB   7   0 14   0   21
ChiC   0   0   0   7   7
ChiB D12 R49/187 P(13-3-3)   61
ChiC D5 R19/-17 P(29-10-2)   73

Pit   0   0   7 14   21
GB   7   3   0 14   24
Pit D7 R35/86   P(27-13-1) 254
GB   D17 R37/154 P(35-19-2) 260

Bkn   0   0   0   0   0
NYG   0   0   0 10   10
Bkn D8 R47/126 P(8-1-0)   1
NYG D15 R44/136 P(15-10+0) 113

1943 NFL
SUNDAY, SEPTEMBER 19

ChiC   3   7   0   7   17
Det   7 14 14   0   35
ChiC D9 R24/0   P(36-16-4) 157
Det D14 R34/168 P(24-9-4) 120

SUNDAY, SEPTEMBER 26

Bkn   0   0   0   0   0
Det   7 13   0   7   27
Bkn D8 R26/-2   P(24-11-3)   84
Det D12 R34/94 P(28-7-3)   132

ChiB   7   0   7   7   21
GB   0   7   7   7   21
ChiB D12 R40/146 P(18-9-1) 102
GB   D12 R40/224 P(17-4-3)   55

SATURDAY, OCTOBER 2

Bkn   0   0   0   0   0
P-P   10   7   0   0   17
Bkn D8 R23/-33 P(35-15-3) 126
P-P D10 R50/202 P(17-4-0)   98

SUNDAY, OCTOBER 3

GB   14   7   7   0   28
ChiC   0   0   0   0   0
GB   D13 R45/184 P(19-12-1) 155
ChiC D14 R30/102 P(22-12-6) 153

ChiB   7   0 13   7   27
Det   0 14   0   7   21
ChiB D13 R38/129 P(20-10-3) 267
Det D14 R34/105 P(24-7-2)   77
  ChiB-Geyer 113C

1944 NFL

SATURDAY, OCTOBER 9
NYG 14 0 0 0 14
P-P 0 7 0 21 28
NYG D6 R33/42 P(14-6-3) 50
P-P D14 R43/191 P(13-6-3) 112

SUNDAY, OCTOBER 10
ChiC 0 0 0 0 0
ChiB 0 0 13 7 20
ChiC D13 R38/117 P(20-8-6) 99
ChiB D12 R38/86 P(21-10-1) 211

Det 0 0 7 7 14
GB 14 7 7 7 35
Det D8 R25/71 P(24-8-5) 137
GB D22 R54/239 P(22-11-1) 206

Bkn 0 0 0 0 0
Was 14 0 6 7 27
Bkn D7 R33/48 P(25-11-1) 116
Was D16 R42/186 P(27-14-1) 245
Was-Moore 121C

SUNDAY, OCTOBER 17
NYG 13 0 0 7 20
Bkn 0 0 0 0 0
NYG D12 R48/215 P(6-2-0) 41
Bkn D6 R27/-24 P(17-6-2) 72
NYG-Paschal 101R

Det 0 0 7 0 7
ChiC 0 0 0 0 0
Det D9 R33/-53 P(22-11-0) 189
ChiC D10 R38/38 P(19-5-3) 46

Was 13 7 6 7 33
GB 0 0 0 7 7
Was D16 R48/153 P(30-16-3) 146
GB D7 R30/61 P(31-9-5) 115
Was-Baugh 146P

P-P 7 0 0 14 21
ChiB 7 28 7 6 48
P-P D12 R30/117 P(22-7-2) 181
ChiB D17 R46/210 P(24-13-2) 186

SUNDAY, OCTOBER 24
Bkn 0 0 7 14 21
ChiB 9 10 7 7 33
Bkn D6 R31/64 P(16-5-1) 116
ChiB D21 R48/203 P(27-17-0) 243

GB 3 7 7 10 27
Det 6 0 0 0 6
GB D18 R43/120 P(39-21-1) 326
Det D9 R16/44 P(29-12-9) 118

P-P 0 0 0 14 14
NYG 14 14 14 0 42
P-P D12 R38/64 P(32-13-1) 178
NYG D10 R30/72 P(17-10-0) 127

ChiC 0 0 0 7 7
Was 0 0 13 0 13
ChiC D12 R49/77 P(15-9-3) 92
Was D7 R21/101 P(14-7-1) 78

SUNDAY, OCTOBER 31
GB 7 14 0 14 35
NYG 7 0 7 7 21
GB D15 R39/158 P(22-15-1) 271
NYG D16 R40/114 P(36-17-0) 174
GB-Canadeo 122R, Hutson 103C, Jacunski 124C

Was 7 14 13 14 48
Bkn 10 0 0 0 10
Was D9 R23/86 P(29-16-3) 376
Bkn D8 R45/123 P(20-9-1) 111
Was-Aguirre 100C, Moore 213C, Baugh 376P

Det 0 0 14 0 14
ChiB 7 7 7 14 35
Det D12 R29/132 P(29-11-4) 125
ChiB D18 R41/240 P(20-9-1) 241

ChiC 0 13 0 0 13
P-P 21 0 0 13 34
ChiC D9 R28/31 P(21-8-3) 175
P-P D16 R54/167 P(10-4-1) 74

SUNDAY, NOVEMBER 7
GB 7 0 0 0 7
ChiB 0 7 7 7 21
GB D11 R34/122 P(23-6-1) 112
ChiB D14 R44/155 P(16-8-1) 186

NYG 0 0 0 0 0
Det 0 0 0 0 0
NYG D3 R40/81 P(4-1-0) 3
Det D6 R37/102 P(12-5-1) 28

ChiC 0 0 0 0 0
Bkn 0 0 0 7 7
ChiC D8 R30/82 P(24-7-3) 56
Bkn D12 R40/104 P(18-10-3) 96

Was 0 7 0 7 14
P-P 0 7 0 7 14
Was D11 R23/62 P(30-15-3) 147
P-P D10 R44/80 P(17-5-3) 89

SUNDAY, NOVEMBER 14
Det 0 0 13 7 20
Was 7 14 7 14 42
Det D10 R21/80 P(34-13-5) 170
Was D12 R29/106 P(30-18-2) 180
Was-Baugh 180P

P-P 7 0 0 0 7
Bkn 0 7 6 0 13
P-P D18 R48/197 P(20-6-2) 52
Bkn D5 R39/102 P(7-2-0) 74

ChiB 14 14 14 14 56
NYG 0 7 0 0 7
ChiB D23 R44/194 P(38-22-2) 488
NYG D7 R23/84 P(25-7-1) 73
ChiB-Luckman 433P

ChiC 0 0 0 7 14
GB 7 14 14 0 35
ChiC D13 R36/78 P(26-11-5) 131
GB D15 R33/31 P(26-16-2) 296
GB-Jacunski 120C

SUNDAY, NOVEMBER 21
ChiC 0 0 0 13 13
NYG 7 3 14 0 24
ChiC D9 R31/80 P(18-8-2) 88
NYG D14 R41/179 P(23-12-1) 147

GB 14 3 7 7 31
Bkn 0 0 0 7 7
GB D13 R41/128 P(31-11-2) 270
Bkn D10 R31/107 P(23-11-6) 97
GB-Hutson 237C

ChiB 0 0 0 7 7
Was 7 0 14 0 21
ChiB D12 R29/89 P(24-9-4) 145
Was D8 R45/213 P(9-5-0) 44

Det 0 13 7 14 34
P-P 7 7 7 14 35
Det D12 R33/74 P(22-10-4) 194
P-P D17 R48/262 P(13-7-1) 96
P-P-Hinkle 132R

SUNDAY, NOVEMBER 28
P-P 7 0 7 13 27
Was 0 0 7 7 14
P-P D19 R64/308 P(13-6-1) 82
Was D10 R20/58 P(28-14-2) 211
P-P-Hinkle 117R

Bkn 0 0 7 0 7
NYG 7 10 7 0 24
Bkn D10 R38/121 P(20-10-1) 77
NYG D9 R40/169 P(10-2-1) 39

ChiB 0 14 0 21 35
ChiC 7 3 14 0 24
ChiB D19 R56/199 P(21-10-2) 241
ChiC D5 R30/104 P(18-4-4) 98
ChiB-Luckman 241P

SUNDAY, DECEMBER 5
GB 14 3 7 14 38
P-P 14 0 0 14 28
GB D8 R38/175 P(23-9-2) 103
P-P D10 R40/142 P(18-7-6) 176
P-P-Bova 106C

Was 3 0 7 0 10
NYG 0 0 7 7 14
Was D14 R41/69 P(27-16-0) 154
NYG D14 R43/270 P(7-2-2) 7
NYG-Paschal 188R

SUNDAY, DECEMBER 12
NYG 0 14 10 7 31
Was 0 7 0 0 7
NYG D11 R48/194 P(7-4-1) 99
Was D9 R28/51 P(30-18-5) 256

SUNDAY, SEPTEMBER 17
Bkn 0 0 7 0 7
GB 7 0 0 7 14
Bkn D16 R44/138 P(27-10-3) 120
GB D15 R35/116 P(22-8-3) 102

SUNDAY, SEPTEMBER 24
Cle 3 13 0 14 30
C-P 0 7 14 7 28
Cle D6 R?/96 P(18-12-3) 136
C-P D11 R?/128 P(16-8-3) 182
Cle-Benton 111C

ChiB 0 7 7 14 28
GB 14 14 0 14 42
ChiB D15 R27/79 P(33-15-5) 194
GB D16 R42/214 P(18-7-2) 150

TUESDAY, SEPTEMBER 26
Phi 7 7 7 7 28
Bos 0 0 0 7 7
Phi D11 R?/205 P(8-2-0) 23
Bos D6 R?/8 P(14-8-3) 58

SUNDAY, OCTOBER 1
Det 6 0 0 0 6
GB 0 7 13 7 27
Det D10 R37/84 P(18-7-2) 77
GB D17 R40/185 P(30-15-2) 144

SUNDAY, OCTOBER 8
NYG 0 10 12 0 22
Bos 3 0 0 7 10
NYG D7 R?/148 P(7-1-3) 12
Bos D11 R?/119 P(11-7-2) 80
NYG-Hutson 207C

Bkn 0 0 0 7 14
Det 0 7 12 0 19
Bkn D13 R?/113 P(21-7-3) 148
Det D9 R?/160 P(17-7-3) 158
Det-Sinkwich 135R

C-P 0 0 0 7 7
GB 7 14 0 13 34
C-P D8 R27/61 P(27-8-4) 126
GB D15 R38/147 P(31-15-1) 241
GB-Hutson 207C

ChiB 0 0 0 0 7
Cle 0 10 6 3 19
ChiB D6 R?/77 P(21-7-2) 143
Cle D11 R?/157 P(17-6-3) 65

Was 6 6 12 7 31
Phi 7 14 3 7 31
Was D15 R?/103 P(33-25-0) 291
Phi D11 R?/159 P(11-8-1) 154
Was-Filchock 291P

SUNDAY, OCTOBER 15
Was 7 7 0 7 21
Bos 0 0 0 7 7
Was D14 R?/139 P(18-10-0) 145
Bos D9 R?/96 P(23-8-1) 109

NYG 0 0 0 7 14
Bkn 0 0 0 0 0
NYG D4 R?/73 P(14-6-1) 123
Bkn D8 R?/86 P(16-4-6) 89

C-P 0 0 0 0 0
ChiB 7 13 0 14 34
C-P D4 R?/89 P(18-3-3) 26
ChiB D13 R?/131 P(19-10-1) 154

Cle 0 6 7 7 20
Det 14 3 0 0 17
Cle D6 R?/71 P(19-7-0) 106
Det D8 R?/101 P(18-8-1) 136

SUNDAY, OCTOBER 22
Bos 0 0 0 0 0
Phi 10 14 7 7 38
Bos D7 R?/-10 P(20-8-3) 121
Phi D8 R?/156 P(13-6-0) 135

Bkn 0 0 7 0 14
Was 0 14 0 3 17
Bkn D12 R?/132 P(20-10-2) 142
Was D16 R?/87 P(41-22-1) 234

C-P 0 0 0 0 0
NYG 0 9 7 7 23
C-P D10 R?/112 P(28-7-6) 103
NYG D15 R?/224 P(20-7-2) 109

Det 0 0 7 14 21
ChiB 7 7 0 7 21
Det D15 R?/189 P(17-7-2) 129
ChiB D15 R?/205 P(14-10-1) 199

Cle 7 7 0 7 21
GB 7 14 7 2 30
Cle D14 R41/212 P(23-12-0) 125
GB D24 R45/294 P(22-10-3) 158
Cle-Colella 147R; GB-Canadeo 107R

SUNDAY, OCTOBER 29
Bos 0 7 7 3 17
Bkn 7 7 0 0 14
Bos D6 R?/22 P(16-4-1) 104
Bkn D9 R?/152 P(12-1-3) 12

C-P 0 0 7 13 20
Was 7 7 7 21 42
C-P D19 R?/187 P(30-13-6) 180
Was D8 R?/140 P(19-10-1) 211
C-P-Grigas 100R; Was-Aguirre 117C

Cle 0 7 14 0 21
ChiB 7 14 0 7 28
Cle D8 R?/29 P(18-6-0) 94
ChiB D16 R?/274 P(18-10-0) 114
ChiB-Grygo 144R

GB 7 0 7 0 14
Det 0 0 0 0 0
GB D11 R40/115 P(26-8-1) 112
Det D10 R37/103 P(19-8-3) 93

Phi 3 7 7 7 24
NYG 7 10 0 0 17
Phi D16 R?/145 P(14-7-1) 74
NYG D8 R?/157 P(14-6-4) 116
NYG-Paschal 139R

SUNDAY, NOVEMBER 5
Bos 0 0 0 0 0
NYG 10 0 14 7 31
Bos D13 R?/54 P(26-11-3) 119
NYG D13 R?/223 P(6-2-2) 32
NYG-Paschal 113R

Phi 14 7 0 0 21
Bkn 0 0 0 0 0
Phi D4 R?/203 P(9-2-0) 60
Bkn D6 R?/26 P(27-7-5) 106
Phi-Van Buren 129R

Det 21 0 6 0 27
C-P 0 0 0 6 6
Det D12 R?/83 P(22-11-4) 194
C-P D13 R?/172 P(30-12-6) 112
C-P-Grigas 117R

GB 7 0 7 7 21
ChiB 7 0 14 0 21
GB D8 R28/49 P(22-8-4) 97
ChiB D13 R46/138 P(23-11-2) 182

Cle 3 0 0 7 10
Was 0 14 0 0 14
Cle D21 R?/320 P(26-9-2) 87
Was D7 R?/62 P(22-10-1) 137

SUNDAY, NOVEMBER 12
Bos 0 0 7 0 7
ChiB 0 7 7 7 21
Bos D11 R?/86 P(20-8-2) 94
ChiB D17 R?/129 P(25-16-2) 258
ChiB-McLean 146C

Was 0 0 0 10 10
Bkn 0 0 0 0 0
Was D11 R?/20 P(22-12-1) 155
Bkn D16 R?/104 P(29-12-2) 174

C-P 0 0 0 0 0
Det 7 7 0 7 21
C-P D17 R?/161 P(30-13-4) 177
Det D8 R?/78 P(13-4-1) 41
C-P-Grigas 123R

GB 7 14 7 14 42
Cle 0 0 0 0 0
GB D10 R46/177 P(17-6-3) 133
Cle D10 R31/98 P(31-11-7) 133
GB-Hutson 107C

NYG 7 0 0 14 21
Phi 7 7 0 7 21
NYG D6 R?/109 P(24-9-3) 148
Phi D11 R?/172 P(19-6-3) 102

SUNDAY, NOVEMBER 19
Bkn 0 0 6 0 6
Bos 6 0 0 7 13
Bkn D13 R?/154 P(18-8-2) 72
Bos D6 R?/134 P(10-6-0) 87
Bos-Davis 131R

ChiB 0 14 0 7 21
Det 7 14 20 0 41
ChiB D19 R?/147 P(23-14-2) 167
Det D10 R?/154 P(20-7-3) 170
Det-Sinkwich 170P

Cle 6 6 7 14 33
C-P 0 0 6 0 6
Cle D9 R?/135 P(12-6-1) 196
C-P D12 R?/90 P(31-10-5) 120

GB 0 0 0 0 0
NYG 0 7 3 14 24
GB D18 R45/131 P(34-14-5) 152
NYG D9 R40/221 P(6-1-1) 36
NYG-Cuff 103R

Phi 7 13 3 14 37
Was 7 0 0 0 7
Phi D10 R?/192 P(10-6-1) 114
Was D10 R?/21 P(38-24-3) 266

SUNDAY, NOVEMBER 26
Bos 0 0 7 0 7
Was 7 0 0 7 14
Bos D7 R?/31 P(24-12-4) 97
Was D15 R?/145 P(17-11-1) 124

Bkn 0 0 0 0 0
NYG 7 0 0 0 7
Bkn D8 R?/65 P(24-11-0) 124
NYG D11 R?/102 P(19-9-1) 161

GB 7 7 7 14 35
C-P 7 6 0 7 20
GB D11 R37/87 P(29-14-1) 190
C-P D5 R32/19 P(17-6-3) 138

ChiB 14 0 14 0 28
Phi 0 0 0 7 7
ChiB D9 R?/91 P(20-5-2) 85
Phi D13 R?/2 P(26-9-5) 94

Det 0 6 6 14 26
Cle 7 0 7 0 14
Det D8 R?/61 P(27-12-7) 176
Cle D10 R?/73 P(22-7-4) 93
Det-Diehl 114C

SUNDAY, DECEMBER 3
Bos 0 0 7 0 7
Det 10 14 14 0 38
Bos D8 R35/-12 P(30-12-3) 163
Det D17 R29/106 P(36-19-4) 308

Bkn 0 0 0 0 0
Phi 7 6 14 7 34
Bkn D6 R29/13 P(22-6-3) 16
Phi D11 R59/253 P(11-2-1) 47

ChiB 7 7 7 28 49
C-P 0 7 0 0 7
ChiB D12 R43/308 P(20-8-1) 104
C-P D10 R29/-2 P(30-6-1) 96
ChiB-Margarita 129R

Was 0 10 3 3 16
NYG 10 0 0 6 16
Was D20 R?/55 P(37-26-2) 273
NYG D13 R?/160 P(9-3-1) 42
NYG-Cuff 100R

SUNDAY, DECEMBER 10
Cle 0 6 0 7 13
Phi 7 13 0 6 26
Cle D7 R28/37 P(22-7-6) 179
Phi D13 R49/177 P(15-7-1) 140

NYG 14 0 7 10 31
Was 0 0 0 0 0
NYG D6 R?/113 P(6-3-0) 77
Was D17 R?/123 P(49-20-6) 178

1945 NFL

SUNDAY, SEPTEMBER 23
```
Det     0   7   3   0   10
ChiC    0   0   0   0    0
Det  D11 R?/83   P(20-6-3)  109
ChiC D2  R?/26   P(20-3-3)   57
```

TUESDAY, SEPTEMBER 25
```
Pit     0   0   0   7    7
Bos     7   7   7   7   28
Pit  D12 R?/22   P(25-9-6)  113
Bos  D10 R?/214  P(14-7-1)  117
```

SUNDAY, SEPTEMBER 30
```
ChiB    0   0   7  14   21
GB     10   0   7  14   31
ChiB D26 R46/182 P(33-18-1) 227
GB   D14 R41/198 P(16-5-0)   94

ChiC    0   0   0   0    0
Cle     0   7  14   0   21
ChiC D6  R?/25   P(21-6-3)   70
Cle  D14 R?/254  P(18-5-4)  119
```

SUNDAY, OCTOBER 7
```
Det     0   7   7   7   21
GB      0  41   9   7   57
Det  D15 R42/141 P(34-13-5) 244
GB   D7  R27/51  P(17-8-1)  242
Det-Greene 123C; GB-Hutson 144C,
  McKay 151P

ChiB    0   0   0   0    0
Cle    14   3   0   0   17
ChiB D16 R?/95   P(30-14-2) 227
Cle  D14 R?/236  P(14-3-2)   53

ChiC    0   0   0   6    6
Phi     7   7   0   7   21
ChiC D14 R?/43   P(36-10-0) 170
Phi  D9  R?/164  P(7-3-0)    76

Was     0   6   7   7   20
Bos     0  14   7   7   28
Was  D16 R?/163  P(32-12-2) 164
Bos  D15 R?/174  P(10-6-1)  150

NYG     6  28   0   0   34
Pit     0   6   0   0    6
NYG  D14 R?/91   P(20-12-0) 246
Pit  D12 R?/106  P(11-4-2)   28
```

SUNDAY, OCTOBER 14
```
ChiC    0   7   7   2   16
ChiB    7   0   0   0    7
ChiC D17 R?/241  P(11-3-1)   86
ChiB D8  R?/17   P(26-13-1) 196

Cle     6   0   0  21   27
GB      0   7   0   7   14
Cle  D12 R45/154 P(16-8-3)  135
GB   D16 R39/81  P(30-10-3) 151
GB-Hutson 110C

Phi     7   3   7   7   24
Det     7   7   7   7   28
Phi  D8  R?/136  P(21-8-4)  100
Det  D9  R?/53   P(25-7-3)  125

NYG     0   7   3   3   13
Bos     7   3   0   3   13
NYG  D7  R?/60   P(14-5-3)  118
Bos  D15 R?/146  P(13-10-1)  92
NYG-Hutson 110C

Was     0   7   0   7   14
Pit     0   0   0   0    0
Was  D22 R?/149  P(26-20-1) 227
Pit  D6  R?/86   P(11-4-0)   33
```

SUNDAY, OCTOBER 21
```
Cle     6  14   7  14   41
ChiB    0   7  14   0   21
Cle  D19 R?/137  P(23-16-1) 270
ChiB D22 R?/239  P(19-8-2)  104
Cle-Benton 151C

Bos     7   7   0   0   14
GB      7  14  17   0   38
Bos  D12 R31/67  P(24-11-0) 183
GB   D16 R46/277 P(21-7-3)  179
GB-Hutson 169C

ChiC    0   0   0   0    0
Det     7  13   0   6   26
ChiC D8  R?/31   P(37-7-3)   82
Det  D9  R?/75   P(27-12-1) 251
```

```
Pit     7  14   0   0   21
NYG     0   0   7   0    7
Pit  D10 R?/96   P(11-6-0)  128
NYG  D11 R?/94   P(27-12-2) 128

Phi     0   7   0   7   14
Was     3   7   7   7   24
Phi  D15 R?/149  P(16-8-3)   50
Was  D19 R?/252  P(13-10-0) 161
Was-Akins 168R
```

SUNDAY, OCTOBER 28
```
ChiC    0   7   0   7   14
GB      7  20   0   6   33
ChiC D15 R32/151 P(31-17-1) 223
GB   D14 R40/136 P(13-10-1) 233
GB-Hutson 141C

ChiB    7   0   3   0   10
Det     0   7   7   2   16
ChiB D16 R?/131  P(21-10-1)  84
Det  D4  R?/15   P(16-9-2)  133

Was     0  10   7   7   24
NYG     0   7   0   7   14
Was  D18 R?/182  P(25-19-0) 231
NYG  D11 R?/30   P(27-13-2) 207
Was-Bagarus 162C

Cle     0   7   0   7   14
Phi     0   7   7  14   28
Cle  D10 R?/72   P(25-10-1) 171
Phi  D6  R?/41   P(16-7-0)  144

Bos     3   0   0   7   10
Pit     0   3   0   3    6
Bos  D3  R?/14   P(7-3-1)    59
Pit  D11 R?/60   P(27-14-4) 133
```

SUNDAY, NOVEMBER 4
```
GB     14  10   0   0   24
ChiB    0  21   7   0   28
GB   D9  R28/29  P(22-8-2)  151
ChiB D19 R52/271 P(15-8-2)  125
ChiB-Margarita 116R

Cle     7   0   7   7   21
NYG    10   7   0   0   17
Cle  D17 R?/225  P(20-11-1) 174
NYG  D9  R?/194  P(12-4-2)   57
Cle-Benton 111C;
NYG-Paschal 143R

Det     0   0   3   7   10
Bos     0   3   0   6    9
Det  D5  R?/76   P(15-2-3)   23
Bos  D6  R?/66   P(17-6-4)   77

Phi     6   7  13  19   45
Pit     3   0   0   0    3
Phi  D12 R?/200  P(21-12-0) 225
Pit  D5  R?/33   P(15-7-3)  108

ChiC    0   7   7   7   21
Was    14   7   0   3   24
ChiC D14 R?/168  P(20-12-1) 156
Was  D15 R?/135  P(31-19-0) 249
```

SUNDAY, NOVEMBER 11
```
Det     7   0  14  14   35
ChiB    0  14  14   0   28
Det  D12 R?/140  P(21-9-5)  186
ChiB D15 R?/54   P(30-15-0) 279
Det-Greene 120C;
ChiB-Luckman 279P

GB      7   0   0   0    7
Cle    20   0   0   0   20
GB   D12 R37/108 P(38-12-7) 177
Cle  D6  R36/265 P(11-4-3)  102
Cle-Gehrke 132R

NYG     3   0   0  14   17
Phi     7  17   0  14   38
NYG  D7  R?/22   P(17-8-1)  131
Phi  D15 R?/261  P(17-9-2)  176
Phi-Van Buren 129R, Ferrante 135C

ChiC    0   0   7   0    7
Pit     0   3   0  20   23
ChiC D5  R?/57   P(17-6-3)   26
Pit  D4  R?/171  P(8-0-1)     0

Bos     0   0   0   7    7
Was     3   3  14  14   34
Bos  D5  R?/30   P(17-6-5)   55
Was  D11 R?/192  P(21-13-1) 150
```

SUNDAY, NOVEMBER 18
```
Cle    14   7   7   7   35
ChiC    0  14   0   7   21
Cle  D10 R?/96   P(20-12-0) 242
ChiC D19 R?/51   P(45-19-2) 294
Cle-Benton 128C;
ChiC-Rucinski 100C

Det     7   0   0   7   14
NYG     7  14   0  14   35
Det  D8  R?/60   P(28-9-5)  161
NYG  D15 R?/120  P(20-11-1) 235
NYG-Liebel 150C

Pit     6   0   0   0    6
Phi     7   6  10   7   30
Pit  D13 R?/142  P(16-7-2)   52
Phi  D15 R?/171  P(17-9-1)  106
Phi-Van Buren 107R

GB      7  14   0   7   28
Bos     0   0   0   0    0
GB   D11 R42/177 P(19-7-2)  109
Bos  D5  R40/12  P(14-4-2)   36

ChiB    7  14   0   0   21
Was     7   7   0  14   28
ChiB D18 R?/109  P(37-19-0) 233
Was  D11 R?/210  P(21-13-1) 129
ChiB-Kavanaugh 138C;
Was-Bagarus 103C
```

THURSDAY, NOVEMBER 22
```
Cle     7  14   7   0   28
Det     7   0  14   0   21
Cle  D15 R?/115  P(21-12-3) 329
Det  D13 R?/158  P(19-6-5)  101
Cle-Benton 303C, Waterfield 329P
```

SUNDAY, NOVEMBER 25
```
Pit     7   0   0   0    7
ChiB   14   7   0   7   28
Pit  D9  R?/122  P(21-3-2)    9
ChiB D14 R?/282  P(24-14-2) 243
ChiB-McAfee 105R, Margarita 104C

GB      0   7  16   0   23
NYG     7   0   0   0    7
GB   D12 R39/111 P(15-4-1)   79
NYG  D12 R34/51  P(25-14-4) 180

Was     0   0   0   0    0
Phi     0   7   0   9   16
Was  D11 R?/23   P(23-16-4) 101
Phi  D14 R?/111  P(28-13-1) 157
```

SUNDAY, DECEMBER 2
```
ChiB    7  14   7   0   28
ChiC    7   0   0  13   20
ChiB D12 R?/123  P(13-9-1)  134
ChiC D16 R?/122  P(29-16-0) 171

Bos     0   0   0   7    7
Cle     7   6   7   0   20
Bos  D11 R?/36   P(25-9-2)  146
Cle  D15 R?/265  P(28-18-3) 228
Cle-Benton 119C

GB      0   3   0   0    3
Det     0   0  14   0   14
GB   D15 R38/157 P(28-9-4)   80
Det  D16 R30/55  P(27-15-1) 249

Phi     7   7   7   0   21
NYG     0   0  21   7   28
Phi  D18 R?/159  P(24-15-1) 148
NYG  D8  R?/71   P(19-10-0) 187
Phi-Van Buren 100R;
NYG-Liebel 134C, Herber 187P

Pit     0   0   0   0    0
Was     7   7   0  10   24
Pit  D10 R?/110  P(22-8-1)   46
Was  D10 R?/109  P(13-9-2)  211
```

SUNDAY, DECEMBER 9
```
Bos     0   0   0   7    7
Phi     0   7   7  21   35
Bos  D8  R?/98   P(16-4-4)   33
Phi  D18 R?/227  P(25-13-2) 139
Phi-Van Buren 100R

NYG     0   0   0   0    0
Was     3   0   7   7   17
NYG  D4  R?/27   P(20-5-1)   35
Was  D19 R?/296  P(20-11-0) 150
Was-Akins 150R
```

1946 AAFC

FRIDAY, SEPTEMBER 6
```
Mia     0   0   0   0    0
Cle    10  17   0  17   44
Mia  D5  R?/-1   P(18-5-2)   28
Cle  D13 R?/178  P(22-8-1)  167
```

SUNDAY, SEPTEMBER 8
```
Bkn     0   7   7  13   27
Buf     0   0   0  14   14
Bkn  D9  R?/160  P(12-5-1)  137
Buf  D12 R?/118  P(19-10-0) 186

NYY     0   7   7   7   21
SF      7   0   0   0    7
NYY  D13 R?/132  P(17-8-0)   62
SF   D6  R?/86   P(14-7-2)   94
```

FRIDAY, SEPTEMBER 13
```
Cle     7   0  13   0   20
ChiR    0   0   6   0    6
Cle  D8  R?/225  P(13-6-0)   31
ChiR D8  R?/147  P(22-7-4)   81

Bkn     0   7   0   7   14
LAD     7   7   0   6   20
Bkn  D15 R?/183  P(24-9-1)   92
LAD  D14 R?/196  P(18-9-1)  132
```

SATURDAY, SEPTEMBER 14
```
Buf     7   3   0   0   10
NYY     7   0   0  14   21
Buf  D5  R?/64   P(12-2-1)   38
NYY  D14 R?/228  P(10-4-1)   58
```

SUNDAY, SEPTEMBER 15
```
Mia     7   0   0   7   14
SF      7   7   7   0   21
Mia  D6  R?/12   P(20-10-1) 159
SF   D15 R?/169  P(18-13-2) 135
```

FRIDAY, SEPTEMBER 20
```
NYY     0  10   0   7   17
ChiR    3   0   7   7   17
NYY  D10 R?/105  P(21-11-3) 133
ChiR D9  R?/57   P(26-11-1) 170

Mia     0  14   0   0   14
LAD     3   7  13   7   30
Mia  D7  R?/-17  P(36-12-5) 250
LAD  D9  R?/108  P(24-11-3) 128
```

SUNDAY, SEPTEMBER 22
```
Cle    21   0   0   7   28
Buf     0   0   0   0    0
Cle  D9  R?/139  P(21-8-1)  190
Buf  D14 R?/115  P(24-8-3)   49

Bkn     7   0   0   6   13
SF      7  12  13   0   32
Bkn  D14 R?/33   P(44-25-0) 231
SF   D10 R?/141  P(17-10-1) 211
```

WEDNESDAY, SEPTEMBER 25
```
Buf     7   7  14   7   35
ChiR    7   7   7  17   38
Buf  D9  R?/235  P(14-6-2)  161
ChiR D13 R?/142  P(29-17-0) 260
```

SUNDAY, SEPTEMBER 29
```
LAD     0   0  14   7   21
Buf     7   0   0  14   21
LAD  D14 R?/94   P(23-11-3) 146
Buf  D6  R?/139  P(8-3-0)    29

SF      0   0   7   0    7
ChiR    0   3  14   7   24
SF   D12 R?/93   P(25-13-3) 170
ChiR D12 R?/170  P(20-10-1)  86

NYY     7   0   0   0    7
Cle    14   0   0  10   24
NYY  D7  R?/36   P(22-8-4)  113
Cle  D11 R?/151  P(15-10-1) 144
```

FRIDAY, OCTOBER 4
```
NYY     0   7   0  14   21
Buf     0   0  13   0   13
NYY  D7  R?/118  P(13-7-1)   75
Buf  D11 R?/131  P(19-8-1)   92
```

SATURDAY, OCTOBER 5
```
LAD     0   0   7  14   21
ChiR    6   3   0   0    9
LAD  D16 R?/120  P(28-17-3) 186
ChiR D7  R?/44   P(17-8-2)  109
```

SUNDAY, OCTOBER 6
```
Bkn     0   0   7   0    7
Cle    12   7   0   7   26
Bkn  D12 R?/37   P(30-16-4) 140
Cle  D11 R?/152  P(10-8-0)  107
```

TUESDAY, OCTOBER 8
```
SF      7   7   7  13   34
Mia     0   0   0   7    7
SF   D11 R?/204  P(16-7-0)   80
Mia  D8  R?/41   P(20-11-1) 110
```

FRIDAY, OCTOBER 11
```
ChiR    0   7   7   7   21
Bkn    16   0   2   3   21
ChiR D22 R?/172  P(26-14-1) 328
Bkn  D5  R?/71   P(9-4-2)    86

Mia    14   0   0   3   17
Buf     7   0   7   0   14
Mia  D11 R?/100  P(28-12-3) 205
Buf  D7  R?/160  P(20-9-3)   63
```

SATURDAY, OCTOBER 12
```
Cle     0   0   7   0    7
NYY     0   0   0   0    0
Cle  D5  R?/24   P(11-5-0)   43
NYY  D10 R?/190  P(13-5-1)   47

SF     10   0   7   6   23
LAD     0   7   7   0   14
SF   D10 R?/94   P(21-10-2) 135
LAD  D8  R?/0    P(34-15-2) 178
```

FRIDAY, OCTOBER 18
```
Mia     0   0   0   7    7
ChiR    0   7  14   7   28
Mia  D4  R?/-28  P(23-9-2)   83
ChiR D10 R?/210  P(16-9-2)  102
```

SATURDAY, OCTOBER 19
```
Bkn     0   0  10   0   10
NYY     7   0   0  14   21
Bkn  D8  R?/15   P(18-11-1) 150
NYY  D17 R?/149  P(24-15-0) 179

SF      0  14   0   0   14
Buf     3   7   0   7   17
SF   D15 R?/193  P(22-10-2)  88
Buf  D6  R?/57   P(19-7-0)  173
```

SUNDAY, OCTOBER 20
```
LAD     7   0   0   7   14
Cle     0   7   3  21   31
LAD  D21 R?/274  P(20-10-1) 121
Cle  D10 R?/224  P(10-4-1)  129
LAD-Benton 144C
```

FRIDAY, OCTOBER 25
```
Mia     0   0   0   7    7
Bkn    10   7   7   6   30
Mia  D10 R?/54   P(27-13-3) 188
Bkn  D8  R?/46   P(19-13-1) 272
```

SUNDAY, OCTOBER 27
```
ChiR    0   3   7   7   17
Buf     0  28  14   7   49
ChiR D12 R?/49   P(35-13-3) 132
Buf  D14 R?/217  P(9-4-1)    50

SF      3  17   7   7   34
Cle     0   6   0  14   20
SF   D16 R?/177  P(21-14-1) 180
Cle  D15 R?/54   P(19-14-1) 284

NYY    10   7   7   7   31
LAD    14   0   3   0   17
NYY  D9  R?/132  P(24-9-2)  152
LAD  D11 R?/101  P(26-12-4) 198
```

SATURDAY, NOVEMBER 2
```
Bkn    14   0   7   0   21
ChiR    0  14   0   0   14
Bkn  D6  R?/156  P(17-6-2)   84
ChiR D8  R?/107  P(14-3-3)   45
```

```
Buf    0   7   0   7  14
SF     0   0   7  20  27
Buf  D7 R?/71   P(18-5-2)  56
SF   D13 R?/209 P(18-8-3) 149
```

SUNDAY, NOVEMBER 3
```
Cle    3  13   0   0  16
LAD    7   0   0  10  17
Cle  D13 R?/43  P(19-12-0) 241
LAD  D12 R?/220 P(15-8-1)   71
LAD-Benton 109C

Mia    7   0   0  14  21
NYY   17   0   0   7  24
Mia  D10 R?/132 P(13-5-0)   82
NYY  D15 R?/210 P(26-11-1) 165
```

SUNDAY, NOVEMBER 10
```
Buf   10   0   7   0  17
Bkn    0   7   0   7  14
Buf  D12 R?/316 P(12-5-0)   28
Bkn  D11 R?/27  P(26-13-1) 280

Cle    7   7   0   0  14
SF     0   0   0   7   7
Cle  D9 R?/97   P(15-6-1) 174
SF   D14 R?/143 P(15-6-2)  69

LAD    0  12   0   0  12
NYY    0   7  10   0  17
LAD  D10 R?/61  P(24-12-2) 149
NYY  D7 R?/43   P(13-5-1)   87
LAD-Benton 113C
```

MONDAY, NOVEMBER 11
```
ChiR   7   0   3  10  20
Mia    0   0   0   7   7
ChiR D8 R?/185  P(7-5-1)   47
Mia  D8 R?/33   P(19-8-2) 134
```

SUNDAY, NOVEMBER 17
```
LAD    7   7   0   5  19
Bkn    0  14   0   0  14
LAD  D13 R?/199 P(15-9-2)   98
Bkn  D16 R?/29  P(35-21-0) 263

ChiR   7   7   0   0  14
Cle    7  10  14  20  51
ChiR D9 R?/41   P(24-11-5) 115
Cle  D8 R?/209  P(20-8-0)  151

SF     0   9   0   0   9
NYY    0   3   0   7  10
SF   D9 R?/119  P(14-7-2)   55
NYY  D13 R?/75  P(25-16-0) 178
```

MONDAY, NOVEMBER 18
```
Buf    0   7   0   7  14
Mia    0   7  14   0  21
Buf  D9 R?/249  P(12-5-3) 104
Mia  D12 R?/152 P(16-9-2) 138
```

SUNDAY, NOVEMBER 24
```
SF    14   9   0   7  30
Bkn    0  14   0   0  14
SF   D20 R?/265 P(13-6-0)   82
Bkn  D8 R?/65   P(28-13-2) 118

Buf   10   0   0   7  17
Cle    7   7  14  14  42
Buf  D19 R?/133 P(26-11-2) 123
Cle  D10 R?/292 P(18-10-0) 163

ChiR   7   3  14  14  38
NYY    7  14   7   0  28
ChiR D9 R?/87   P(15-8-0)  177
NYY  D14 R?/160 P(28-15-4) 154
```

MONDAY, NOVEMBER 25
```
LAD   14   0   7  13  34
Mia   14   7   0   0  21
LAD  D14 R?/168 P(18-12-1) 155
Mia  D4 R?/59   P(14-7-0)   74
```

THURSDAY, NOVEMBER 28
```
NYY    7   0   0  14  21
Bkn    0   0   0   7   7
NYY  D11 R?/171 P(18-5-0)  48
Bkn  D5 R?/4    P(19-7-0)  82
```

SATURDAY, NOVEMBER 30
```
ChiR   0   0   0   0   0
SF     0  14   0   0  14
ChiR D9 R?/42   P(30-15-4) 123
SF   D7 R?/108  P(13-3-3)   46
```

SUNDAY, DECEMBER 1
```
Buf    0   7   7   0  14
LAD   14  14  14  20  62
Buf  D12 R?/68  P(25-14-2) 200
LAD  D20 R?/288 P(19-17-1) 337
LAD-Benton 202C, Waterfield 312P
```

TUESDAY, DECEMBER 3
```
Cle    7  10   7  10  34
Mia    0   0   0   0   0
Cle  D11 R?/159 P(15-6-1)  74
Mia  D5 R?/8    P(23-7-8)  38
```

SUNDAY, DECEMBER 8
```
Cle   14  14  17  21  66
Bkn    0   7   0   7  14
Cle  D13 R?/93  P(28-18-1) 358
Bkn  D8 R?/86   P(25-9-4)  153

LAD    7   0   0   0   7
SF    21   0   7  20  48
LAD  D14 R?/33  P(34-20-2) 180
SF   D14 R?/236 P(15-10-2) 152
```

MONDAY, DECEMBER 9
```
NYY    3  14   7   7  31
Mia    0   0   0   0   0
NYY  D11 R?/107 P(16-10-1) 187
Mia  D11 R?/22  P(24-13-2)  92
```

FRIDAY, DECEMBER 13
```
Bkn    7   7   3   3  20
Mia   10   7   0  14  31
Bkn  D10 R?/143 P(20-9-1) 187
Mia  D15 R?/354 P(14-5-4)  98
```

SUNDAY, DECEMBER 15
```
ChiR   0   7   7   3  17
LAD    7   3   0   7  17
ChiR D13 R?/94  P(22-10-1) 132
LAD  D8 R?/87   P(19-7-3)  110
```

1946 NFL
FRIDAY, SEPTEMBER 20
```
ChiC   0   0   7   0   7
Pit    7   7   0   0  14
ChiC D11 R?/107 P(14-6-1) 79
Pit  D8 R?/112  P(4-2-0)  25
```

SUNDAY, SEPTEMBER 29
```
ChiB   3  14   7   6  30
GB     0   0   0   0   0
ChiB D22 R51/301 P(17-5-1) 131
GB   D6 R36/99   P(10-2-2)  15

Phi    6   0  10   9  25
LARm   7   7   0   0  14
Phi  D16 R44/141 P(21-11-0) 175
LARm D15 R31/116 P(32-10-3) 117

Pit    0   0   0  14  14
Was    7   7   0   0  14
Pit  D14 R?/109 P(18-8-1)  122
Was  D18 R?/159 P(20-12-1) 165
```

MONDAY, SEPTEMBER 30
```
Det    0   0   7   7  14
ChiC   7  21   3   3  34
Det  D12 R?/-17 P(27-11-6) 173
ChiC D19 R?/227 P(9-5-0)   116
```

TUESDAY, OCTOBER 1
```
NYG    7   3   0   7  17
Bos    0   0   0   0   0
NYG  D17 R44/184 P(17-9-1) 87
Bos  D8 R33/112  P(18-3-1) 27
```

SUNDAY, OCTOBER 6
```
LARm   7   0   7   7  21
GB     0  10   0   7  17
LARm D22 R35/157 P(18-11-3) 105
GB   D15 R54/179 P(20-7-1)  226

ChiB   0   7   7  20  34
ChiC   0   7   3   7  17
ChiB D22 R45/179 P(24-13-1) 179
ChiC D12 R27/133 P(20-10-1) 218

Det    0   0   0   9  16
Was    0   7  10   0  17
Det  D8 R?/24   P(30-14-5) 135
Was  D15 R?/187 P(16-7-2)  142
```

```
Bos   12   0   6   7  25
Phi   14  14   7  14  49
Bos  D17 R26/59  P(24-13-3) 282
Phi  D21 R37/197 P(18-14-1) 208

NYG    0  17   0   0  17
Pit    0   0   0   0   0
NYG  D10 R32/208 P(8-3-1)  41
Pit  D17 R37/151 P(20-9-3) 218
NYG-Filchock 108R
```

SUNDAY, OCTOBER 13
```
LARm   7   7  14   0  28
ChiB  14   7   0   7  28
LARm D18 R39/241 P(25-10-2) 155
ChiB D17 R30/64  P(26-11-2) 248
LARm-Harmon 114R; ChiB-McLean 141C

ChiC   7  20   0   9  36
Det    0   0   0   7  14
ChiC D23 R37/131 P(35-20-2) 263
Det  D8 R15/-24  P(28-12-3) 182
ChiC-Dewell 132C, Christman 263P

NYG    0   0   7   7  14
Was    7   0   7  10  24
NYG  D13 R29/66  P(26-12-5) 145
Was  D15 R39/180 P(17-11-2) 187

GB     0   7   5   7  19
Phi    7   0   0   0   7
GB   D10 R35/35  P(22-8-1)  99
Phi  D15 R32/50  P(29-17-3) 204

Bos    0   0   0   7   7
Pit    0  16   0   0  16
Bos  D16 R35/130 P(24-5-1) 93
Pit  D15 R47/217 P(14-3-1) 100
Pit-Dudley 112R
```

SUNDAY, OCTOBER 20
```
Phi    0   7   0   7  14
ChiB   7   0  14   0  21
Phi  D11 R27/45  P(22-10-4) 154
ChiB D17 R50/152 P(17-7-1)  145

Pit    0   7   0   0   7
GB     0   3   0  14  17
Pit  D11 R34/154 P(11-3-1) 59
GB   D24 R63/288 P(15-6-2) 94
Pit-Dudley 133R

Det    0   0  14   0  14
LARm   7  14   7   7  35
Det  D10 R24/16  P(18-6-2)  95
LARm D20 R40/122 P(30-16-3) 312
LARm-Benton 144C

ChiC   7  10   0   7  24
NYG    7   0   7  14  28
ChiC D16 R36/133 P(23-8-2)  170
NYG  D17 R29/34  P(27-18-3) 294
ChiC-Kutner 118C

Was    0   7   0   7  14
Bos    6   0   0   0   6
Was  D16 R51/137 P(23-10-1) 119
Bos  D7 R31/51   P(11-5-3)   82
```

SUNDAY, OCTOBER 27
```
Det    0   7   0   0   7
GB     0   3   7   0  10
Det  D11 R34/74  P(23-11-3) 84
GB   D13 R52/111 P(19-5-1)  47

LARm   0  10   0   0  10
ChiC  14   6   7   7  34
LARm D19 R38/163 P(44-14-4) 173
ChiC D21 R30/121 P(34-17-1) 238
ChiC-Dewell 119C

Phi    0   0  14  14  28
Was   10  14   0   0  24
Phi  D18 R31/34  P(27-19-3) 228
Was  D11 R42/66  P(11-8-2)   61

ChiB   0   0   0   0   0
NYG    0   7   7   0  14
ChiB D15 R37/115 P(40-23-5) 227
NYG  D9 R31/63   P(12-5-2)   87

Pit    6   0  14  13  33
Bos    0   7   0   0   7
Pit  D13 R35/160 P(14-4-1) 121
Bos  D14 R35/126 P(20-8-2)  64
```

SUNDAY, NOVEMBER 3
```
GB     0   0   0   7   7
ChiB   0   0  10   0  10
GB   D9 R36/78   P(21-4-0) 47
ChiB D14 R47/123 P(9-4-1)  36

LARm   0  17   0  17  41
Det    6   0   0  14  20
LARm D19 R31/107 P(29-15-0) 224
Det  D16 R26/61  P(32-12-4) 232
LARm-Benton 109C

NYG    0   0   7   7  14
Phi    7  10   7   0  24
NYG  D18 R36/103 P(32-14-4) 148
Phi  D11 R36/135 P(12-5-0)   62

Was    0   0   0   0   7
Pit    7   0   0   0   7
Was  D14 R44/138 P(22-9-3) 139
Pit  D5 R40/100  P(4-1-0)    8

ChiC   7   7   7   7  28
Bos    0   0   0   7   7
ChiC D20 R38/157 P(29-15-1) 236
Bos  D18 R40/167 P(25-8-3)  109
ChiC-Dewell 109C
```

SUNDAY, NOVEMBER 10
```
GB     3  14   0   2  19
ChiC   0   0   0   7   7
GB   D19 R62/220 P(10-3-1) 50
ChiC D10 R15/12  P(32-12-5) 225
ChiC-Kutner 127C

Pit    0   0   0   7   7
Det    0  10   0   7  17
Pit  D12 R29/28  P(31-16-0) 174
Det  D7 R39/111  P(13-6-0)  182

ChiB  14   6   7   0  27
LARm   7   0   7   7  21
ChiB D19 R55/147 P(22-12-3) 243
LARm D20 R33/134 P(30-16-4) 180
ChiB-Kavanaugh 146C; LARm-Benton 113C

Bos    0   7   0   7  14
Was    0   3   7   7  17
Bos  D15 R41/101 P(24-12-0) 114
Was  D16 R44/241 P(15-3-1)   77
Was-Todd 117R

Phi   10   0   0   7  17
NYG    7  17   7  14  45
Phi  D14 R34/75  P(29-13-1) 198
NYG  D19 R59/251 P(12-5-3)   90
NYG-Franck 107R
```

SUNDAY, NOVEMBER 17
```
Was    7   3   7   3  20
ChiB   0  17   0   7  24
Was  D10 R26/36  P(27-15-3) 201
ChiB D15 R36/77  P(23-9-1)  189

GB     0   0   3   6   9
Det    0   0   0   0   0
GB   D20 R61/224 P(18-8-1) 95
Det  D6 R24/32   P(17-6-1) 49

ChiC   0  14   0   0  14
LARm   3   0   7   7  17
ChiC D12 R32/103 P(29-9-4)  165
LARm D16 R39/142 P(33-14-0) 162

Bos    7   7   0  14  28
NYG    7  14   7   0  28
Bos  D13 R35/68  P(21-11-0) 129
NYG  D17 R40/96  P(16-11-2) 197

Phi    0   0   7   0   7
Pit    0   0   0  10  10
Phi  D9 R40/161  P(13-3-2) 29
Pit  D6 R39/69   P(15-5-2) 53
```

SUNDAY, NOVEMBER 24
```
Det    6   0   0   0   6
ChiB  14   0  21   7  42
Det  D11 R15/27  P(33-11-4) 178
ChiB D24 R62/261 P(14-6-0)  101

ChiC   0   3   0  21  24
GB     3   0   3   0   6
ChiC D16 R30/243 P(21-6-1) 106
GB   D11 R54/131 P(10-2-4)  24

Pit    0   0   0   0   0
NYG    0   7   0   0   7
Pit  D10 R37/86  P(14-5-1) 53
NYG  D10 R45/115 P(10-5-1) 39
```

```
Was    7   7   0  13  27
Phi    3   0   0   7  10
Was  D18 R45/177 P(17-11-0) 168
Phi  D15 R41/110 P(27-10-4) 161
Phi-Van Buren 130R

LARm   0   0   7   7  21
Bos    7  14   6  13  40
LARm D20 R41/217 P(37-15-3) 165
Bos  D15 R34/180 P(22-11-0) 224
```

THURSDAY, NOVEMBER 28
```
Bos    7   7   6  14  34
Det    7   0   3   0  10
Bos  D31 R?/142  P(28-15-2) 282
Det  D15 R32/142 P(28-11-3) 124
```

SUNDAY, DECEMBER 1
```
ChiC   0  21   7   7  35
ChiB   0   7   7  14  28
ChiC D15 R40/162 P(20-7-2)  135
ChiB D26 R45/142 P(41-20-1) 232
ChiC-Harder 112R

GB     0   7   6   7  20
Was    0   0   0   7   7
GB   D19 R64/301 P(12-2-1) 16
Was  D11 R25/83  P(20-9-4) 114

LARm  14   0  10   7  31
NYG    7   0   7   7  21
LARm D25 R37/141 P(31-22-1) 312
NYG  D15 R30/214 P(20-9-2)  180
LARm-Benton 202C, Waterfield 312P; NYG-Reagan 133R

Pit    0   0   7   0   7
Phi    7   3   0   0  10
Pit  D9 R31/121  P(16-2-3) 37
Phi  D14 R58/211 P(3-2-0)  14
```

SUNDAY, DECEMBER 8
```
ChiB  17  14  14   0  45
Det    3   7   7   7  24
ChiB D20 R38/158 P(20-10-2) 219
Det  D16 R24/26  P(37-18-3) 240

GB     7   3   0   7  17
LARm   7   7   7  17  38
GB   D14 R43/99  P(21-7-4)  128
LARm D20 R40/143 P(17-10-1) 175

Was    0   7   0   0   7
NYG    3  14  14   0  31
Was  D17 R33/93  P(33-17-3) 240
NYG  D18 R39/130 P(14-9-1)  142

Phi    0  24  16   0  40
Bos    7   0   0   7  14
Phi  D12 R43/104 P(16-11-2) 208
Bos  D6 R24/-26  P(22-12-4) 160
```

1947 AAFC
FRIDAY, AUGUST 29
```
LAD    7   7   3   7  24
ChiR   7   7   7   0  21
LAD  D13 R?/139 P(17-11-1) 140
ChiR D12 R?/129 P(27-13-1) 175
```

SUNDAY, AUGUST 31
```
Bkn    7   0   0   0   7
SF     7   6   3   7  23
Bkn  D7 R?/74   P(25-9-1)  91
SF   D12 R?/131 P(33-10-2) 144

NYY    7   7   7   3  24
Buf    7   7   7   7  28
NYY  D7 R?/170  P(20-14-1) 229
Buf  D11 R?/137 P(13-9-0)  121
```

FRIDAY, SEPTEMBER 5
```
Buf    0   0  14   0  14
Cle   13  14   0   3  30
Buf  D17 R?/308 P(16-3-4)  24
Cle  D11 R?/193 P(29-12-1) 139

ChiR   6   0  13   7  26
NYY   14  13   7  14  48
ChiR D8 R?/119  P(22-9-0)  102
NYY  D11 R?/235 P(20-10-2) 146
```

SUNDAY, SEPTEMBER 7
```
Bkn    7   0   0   0   7
Bal    6   0   7   3  16
Bkn  D8 R?/99   P(11-3-0)  19
Bal  D9 R?/59   P(19-11-2) 111
```

```
LAD     0   0   7   7   14
SF      7   7   0   3   17
LAD  D10 R?/71    P(12-7-2)  123
SF   D18 R?/262   P(16-8-1)  154
```

FRIDAY, SEPTEMBER 12
```
Cle    20   0  21  14   55
Bkn     0   7   0   0    7
Cle  D13 R?/223   P(18-12-0) 194
Bkn  D11 R?/138   P(15-5-4)   39

NYY    13   3   7   7   30
LAD    14   0   0   0   14
NYY  D8 R?/99     P(17-10-0) 195
LAD  D5 R?/24     P(18-9-1)  128
```

SUNDAY, SEPTEMBER 14
```
Bal     0   7   0   0    7
SF      7   0   7   0   14
Bal  D8 R?/-35    P(20-11-2) 144
SF   D18 R?/259   P(17-7-0)   84

ChiR    0   0   6  14   20
Buf     0   7  14   7   28
ChiR D16 R?/155   P(25-13-2) 175
Buf  D11 R?/163   P(13-6-0)  102
```

FRIDAY, SEPTEMBER 19
```
Bkn     0   7  14   0   21
LAD     3  21   7  17   48
Bkn  D9 R?/32     P(40-21-3) 117
LAD  D8 R?/142    P(20-9-2)  215

Buf    10   7   7   7   31
ChiR    0  14   0   0   14
Buf  D15 R?/144   P(33-19-1) 304
ChiR D9 R?/83     P(16-10-0) 162
```

SUNDAY, SEPTEMBER 21
```
Bal     0   0   0   0    0
Cle    21   7   0   0   28
Bal  D14 R?/138   P(30-10-3) 159
Cle  D11 R?/173   P(13-8-0)  122

NYY     0  14   7   0   21
SF      3   0   7   6   16
NYY  D10 R?/72    P(12-7-1)   94
SF   D17 R?/153   P(25-13-3) 184
```

FRIDAY, SEPTEMBER 26
```
Cle    10  17   0  14   41
ChiR    0   0  14   7   21
Cle  D14 R?/232   P(17-7-2)  163
ChiR D9 R?/127    P(20-11-5) 195
```

SUNDAY, SEPTEMBER 28
```
SF      0   7  14  20   41
Buf     7  10   7   0   24
SF   D22 R?/277   P(26-10-1) 131
Buf  D8 R?/145    P(18-9-0)  134

NYY    14   7   0   0   21
Bal     0   7   0   0    7
NYY  D10 R?/111   P(16-9-2)  120
Bal  D14 R?/75    P(35-20-2) 189
```

FRIDAY, OCTOBER 3
```
Bkn     0   7   7  21   35
ChiR    7  10   0  14   31
Bkn  D16 R?/256   P(15-5-0)   63
ChiR D17 R?/202   P(19-9-0)  212
```

SUNDAY, OCTOBER 5
```
Buf    20   0   7   0   27
LAD     7   0  14   4   25
Buf  D10 R?/87    P(15-9-1)  185
LAD  D16 R?/129   P(20-13-2) 227

NYY     3   0  14   0   17
Cle     0  17   6   3   26
NYY  D11 R?/111   P(20-11-3) 111
Cle  D14 R?/212   P(22-11-1) 161

SF      7   7   0  14   28
Bal     7   7  14   0   28
SF   D15 R?/165   P(16-12-2) 217
Bal  D17 R?/159   P(30-18-3) 241
```

SUNDAY, OCTOBER 12
```
Bal     3  12   0   0   15
Buf     0   7   7   6   20
Bal  D13 R?/69    P(24-15-0) 197
Buf  D14 R?/239   P(9-6-0)    96
```

```
Bkn     0   7   0   0    7
NYY    14   0  14   3   31
Bkn  D4 R?/23     P(18-7-1)   63
NYY  D11 R?/239   P(13-6-1)  100

ChiR    0   7   0  21   28
SF     21   7  14   0   42
ChiR D7 R?/36     P(29-15-2) 273
SF   D16 R?/241   P(24-11-4) 116

LAD     0   7   3   3   13
Cle    10   0   0   0   10
LAD  D10 R?/105   P(22-6-0)   56
Cle  D22 R?/162   P(29-19-1) 233
```

FRIDAY, OCTOBER 17
```
Buf     7   7   0   0   14
Bkn     7   0   0   7   14
Buf  D13 R?/202   P(13-7-0)   81
Bkn  D12 R?/274   P(7-1-2)    12
```

SUNDAY, OCTOBER 19
```
ChiR    0   7   0  21   28
Cle     3   7  14   7   31
ChiR D17 R?/105   P(32-17-2) 260
Cle  D16 R?/159   P(18-11-0) 297

LAD     0  14   7  17   38
Bal    10   0   0   0   10
LAD  D10 R?/128   P(16-8-2)  117
Bal  D7 R?/48     P(26-10-4) 136
```

FRIDAY, OCTOBER 24
```
NYY     7   0  21   0   28
ChiR    0   0   0   7    7
NYY  D16 R?/395   P(14-5-2)   62
ChiR D4 R?/-20    P(21-9-1)  152
```

SUNDAY, OCTOBER 26
```
Bkn     7   0   0   0    7
Buf     0  14  21   0   35
Bkn  D6 R?/112    P(10-2-0)   28
Buf  D22 R?/255   P(27-12-0) 171

Cle     7   7   0   0   14
SF      0   0   0   7    7
Cle  D22 R?/137   P(25-19-0) 278
SF   D15 R?/166   P(15-7-1)   85
```

FRIDAY, OCTOBER 31
```
ChiR    0   3   0   0    3
Bkn     0   0   7   0    7
ChiR D11 R?/160   P(19-6-2)   47
Bkn  D9 R?/112    P(15-7-0)   88
```

SUNDAY, NOVEMBER 2
```
Bal     0   7   7   7   21
NYY    14   0   7  14   35
Bal  D9 R?/14     P(28-15-0) 236
NYY  D11 R?/286   P(14-6-2)   62

Cle     7   7   7   7   28
Buf     0   0   0   7    7
Cle  D13 R?/136   P(16-13-2) 256
Buf  D13 R?/85    P(29-13-0) 167

SF      7   7   6   6   26
LAD     0  10   0   6   16
SF   D21 R?/205   P(24-14-2) 202
LAD  D10 R?/76    P(22-11-2) 120
LAD-Washington 145R
```

FRIDAY, NOVEMBER 7
```
Bal     7   0   0  14   21
ChiR    0  24   0   3   27
Bal  D17 R?/74    P(40-22-2) 274
ChiR D7 R?/148    P(8-2-1)    53
```

SUNDAY, NOVEMBER 9
```
Bkn     6   0   0   6   12
Cle     7   6   0   0   13
Bkn  D10 R?/251   P(12-3-0)   22
Cle  D13 R?/166   P(14-4-2)   95

LAD     0   0   0   0    0
Buf     6   0  13   6   25
LAD  D8 R?/138    P(19-5-0)   42
Buf  D6 R?/80     P(9-4-0)    10
```

```
SF      3  13   0   0   16
NYY     0   7  10   7   24
SF   D7 R?/61     P(25-11-1)  78
NYY  D18 R?/231   P(20-13-0) 180
```

SUNDAY, NOVEMBER 16
```
Bal     0   7   0   7   14
Bkn     0   7   7   7   21
Bal  D10 R?/75    P(26-13-0) 255
Bkn  D11 R?/228   P(11-5-0)   52

LAD     0  10   3   0   13
NYY     2   7   0   7   16
LAD  D6 R?/81     P(15-3-1)   22
NYY  D16 R?/218   P(20-6-2)  160

SF      0   7   0   7   14
Cle     9   7  14   7   37
SF   D17 R?/170   P(22-12-2) 159
Cle  D18 R?/156   P(25-16-0) 284
```

FRIDAY, NOVEMBER 21
```
SF     14  20   7   0   41
ChiR    0   7   2   7   16
SF   D16 R?/219   P(19-10-0) 213
ChiR D15 R?/117   P(35-14-3) 170
```

SUNDAY, NOVEMBER 23
```
Buf     7   6  13   7   33
Bal     0   7   0   7   14
Buf  D16 R?/232   P(18-6-3)   93
Bal  D11 R?/97    P(21-10-3) 143

Cle     0   7  14   7   28
NYY    14  14   0   0   28
Cle  D19 R?/99    P(28-15-3) 325
NYY  D19 R?/269   P(9-5-1)    62

LAD     3   0   3  10   16
Bkn     0   9   3   0   12
LAD  D13 R?/149   P(23-12-3) 209
Bkn  D9 R?/81     P(22-12-1) 201
```

THURSDAY, NOVEMBER 27
```
Cle     7   7   6   7   27
LAD    10   0   0   7   17
Cle  D9 R?/126    P(23-13-2) 204
LAD  D19 R?/204   P(37-19-2) 258

SF      7  14   0   0   21
Bkn     0   0   0   7    7
SF   D12 R?/295   P(17-8-1)  120
Bkn  D14 R?/98    P(17-9-3)  129
```

SUNDAY, NOVEMBER 30
```
Buf     0   6   0   7   13
NYY    14   0  14   7   35
Buf  D10 R?/87    P(21-9-4)  115
NYY  D17 R?/254   P(8-4-1)   106

ChiR    0   0   7   0    7
Bal     7   0   0   7   14
ChiR D13 R?/76    P(39-19-2) 239
Bal  D17 R?/209   P(14-8-2)  109

Buf     0   7   0  14   21
SF      0   7   0  14   21
Buf  D14 R?/121   P(30-17-4) 176
SF   D11 R?/131   P(24-11-1)  98
```

SUNDAY, DECEMBER 7
```
ChiR    0   0   7   0    7
LAD     7   7  20   0   34
ChiR D8 R?/76     P(27-9-3)  137
LAD  D13 R?/183   P(29-8-4)  131

Cle    14   7  14   7   42
Bal     0   0   0   0    0
Cle  D21 R?/334   P(22-13-0) 225
Bal  D10 R?/85    P(24-7-2)  101

NYY     7  10   0   3   20
Bkn     3   7   0   0   10
NYY  D12 R?/183   P(13-5-0)  175
Bkn  D11 R?/156   P(12-3-0)   30
```

1947 NFL
SUNDAY, SEPTEMBER 21
```
Det     0   7   0   3   10
Pit     0   7   0  10   17
Det  D14 R31/113  P(22-10-2) 165
Pit  D14 R?/89    P(26-12-4) 194
```

SUNDAY, SEPTEMBER 28
```
Was     0  14  14  14   42
Phi    10  14  14   7   45
Was  D19 R21/14   P(36-22-2) 373
Phi  D26 R?/199   P(17-12-0) 202
Was-Taylor 212C, Baugh 364P

ChiB    6   7   0   7   20
GB      3  14   2  10   29
ChiB D21 R37/164  P(25-13-5) 150
GB   D17 R40/236  P(12-5-1)  101

Det     0  14   0   7   21
ChiC    7  14  14  10   45
Det  D20 R28/148  P(30-18-2) 167
ChiC D26 R33/134  P(31-21-0) 430
ChiC-Kutner 160C, Christman 320P
```

MONDAY, SEPTEMBER 29
```
NYG     7   0   0   7    7
Bos     0   0   0   7    7
NYG  D11 R37/116  P(16-6-3)  122
Bos  D10 R?/62    P(24-13-2) 150

LARm    6  14   7  21   48
Pit     7   0   0   0    7
LARm D20 R38/197  P(27-14-0) 258
Pit  D10 R30/75   P(25-8-2)   74
```

SUNDAY, OCTOBER 5
```
NYG     0   0   0   0    0
Phi     7   7   6   3   23
NYG  D4 R17/39    P(19-5-1)   62
Phi  D21 R?/261   P(19-6-2)   70
Phi-Van Buren 105R

Pit     3   7  14   2   26
Was     0   7  13   7   27
Pit  D16 R?/206   P(20-10-1) 167
Was  D15 R26/109  P(28-13-2) 275

Det    14   0   0   7   21
Bos     0   0   0   7    7
Det  D11 R23/99   P(21-9-3)  161
Bos  D13 R?/119   P(21-11-4) 161

ChiB    7   0   0   0    7
ChiC    0   7  14  10   31
ChiB D11 R23/98   P(29-11-4) 131
ChiC D19 R41/146  P(26-13-3) 157

LARm    0   0   0  14   14
GB      0   0  14   3   17
LARm D14 R35/130  P(17-6-0)  105
GB   D17 R52/244  P(12-4-1)   36
```

SUNDAY, OCTOBER 12
```
NYG     7   0   0  13   20
Was     7   7   7   7   28
NYG  D9 R24/64    P(24-9-1)  159
Was  D19 R47/142  P(19-13-1) 214

Pit     7   7   7   9   30
Bos     0   0   0  14   14
Pit  D19 R50/276  P(14-9-1)  127
Bos  D8 R24/26    P(15-5-1)   86

Phi     0   0   0   7    7
ChiB    0  21  12   7   40
Phi  D15 R18/58   P(34-18-4) 215
ChiB D21 R39/142  P(35-17-0) 364
ChiB-Kavanaugh 144C, Luckman 314P

ChiC    0   7   0   7   14
GB      0   3   7   0   10
ChiC D21 R47/217  P(26-8-3)  125
GB   D12 R41/151  P(20-5-1)  110

LARm   13   0   7   7   27
Det     0   0   7   7   14
LARm D19 R47/296  P(16-8-3)  110
Det  D17 R22/98   P(36-18-3) 285
```

SUNDAY, OCTOBER 19
```
Bos     7   7   0   0   14
NYG     0   0   0   0    0
Bos  D8 R35/89    P(14-5-1)  103
NYG  D15 R34/138  P(27-13-4) 120

Phi    10  14   0   0   24
Pit     0   7   7  21   35
Phi  D16 R32/175  P(20-7-2)  168
Pit  D25 R52/229  P(14-6-1)  177
Phi-Van Buren 133R
```

```
Was     0   7   3   0   10
GB     10   0   0   7   17
Was  D18 R24/96   P(39-19-2) 234
GB   D20 R41/170  P(24-13-1) 182
GB-Luhn 140C

Det     7   3   0  14   24
ChiB    7  20   0   6   33
Det  D21 R29/109  P(38-19-3) 262
ChiB D21 R28/106  P(31-19-2) 354
ChiB-Keane 122C, Luckman 342P

ChiC    0   0   0   7    7
LARm    0  14  13   0   27
ChiC D15 R32/80   P(31-14-1) 134
LARm D22 R47/260  P(24-11-0) 106
```

SUNDAY, OCTOBER 26
```
Pit     7  17   7   7   38
NYG     0   7   0   0    7
Pit  D14 R42/158  P(13-5-1)  155
NYG  D14 R32/120  P(25-6-3)  130

ChiB   14   0  21  21   56
Was     0   7   6   7   20
ChiB D26 R29/166  P(38-25-3) 320
Was  D23 R20/52   P(46-26-1) 411
ChiB-Keane 102C;
Was-Duckworth 102C, Saenz 143C

Bos     0   0   0   0    0
ChiC    7   6   7   7   27
Bos  D8 R23/91    P(20-6-2)  123
ChiC D26 R42/174  P(33-21-3) 253
ChiC-Dewell 116C

LARm    0   0   0   7    7
Phi     0   0   7   7   14
LARm D20 R31/138  P(35-18-3) 145
Phi  D14 R41/50   P(12-6-1)   98

Det     0   3   7   7   17
GB      7   7  13   7   34
Det  D17 R38/142  P(14-7-2)   88
GB   D23 R50/366  P(17-7-1)  119
GB-Cody 111R
```

SUNDAY, NOVEMBER 2
```
NYG     0   0   0   7    7
Det     0  14   7  14   35
NYG  D17 R31/120  P(47-19-3) 283
Det  D15 R24/66   P(24-15-4) 278

Pit     3   6   7   2   18
GB     10   0   7   0   17
Pit  D14 R41/133  P(19-9-0)  128
GB   D12 R36/125  P(14-7-1)  165

Phi    14   3  14   7   38
Was     7   0   7   0   14
Phi  D14 R43/204  P(12-8-0)   97
Was  D19 R29/120  P(40-17-2) 211
Phi-Van Buren 138R

ChiB    7   7   0  14   28
Bos     0  14   7   3   24
ChiB D22 R33/110  P(46-23-3) 271
Bos  D14 R33/127  P(20-8-3)  156
ChiB-Kavanaugh 129C, Luckman 278P

LARm    7   3   0   0   10
ChiC    0   0   7  10   17
LARm D15 R39/222  P(21-6-3)  109
ChiC D22 R48/155  P(26-13-2) 238
LARm-Washington 145R;
ChiC-Kutner 108C
```

SUNDAY, NOVEMBER 9
```
Phi     6   7  14  14   41
NYG     3   7   0  14   24
Phi  D16 R44/216  P(15-10-1) 164
NYG  D15 R23/65   P(35-16-2) 341
NYG-Governali 341P

Was     0   7   0   7   14
Pit     7   7   7   0   21
Was  D16 R40/133  P(19-10-0) 183
Pit  D15 R49/171  P(12-4-2)   89

Bos     0   6   7  14   27
LARm    6   0  10   0   16
Bos  D10 R36/123  P(13-6-1)  165
LARm D24 R57/249  P(27-12-4) 118
Bos-Currivan 100C
```

```
GB     0   10   0   7   17
ChiB   0   14   6   0   20
GB   D14 R43/124  P(23-12-0) 175
ChiB D14 R43/148  P(20-11-4) 172
  ChiB-Kavanaugh 103C

ChiC  10    0   0   7   17
Det    0    7   0   0    7
ChiC D11 R47/172  P(17-4-2)   74
Det  D11 R24/106  P(31-13-4)  92

SUNDAY, NOVEMBER 16
NYG    0    0   7   0    7
Pit    3    0   0  21   24
NYG  D6  R38/47   P(10-3-3)   35
Pit  D13 R41/145  P(17-6-1)   94

Was    0    7   0  14   21
Det   14   10   7   7   38
Was  D22 R29/110  P(39-24-1) 256
Det  D18 R38/138  P(24-15-2) 317
  Det-LeForce 317P

Bos    0    0   0   0    0
Phi   13    7   6   6   32
Bos  D6  R21/21   P(27-10-2) 138
Phi  D16 R46/178  P(22-9-1)  102

ChiB   7    7   6  21   41
LARm   7    0   7   7   21
ChiB D27 R44/195  P(28-14-2) 193
LARm D18 R29/82   P(40-16-5) 214

GB     3   10   0   7   20
ChiC   7    0  14   0   21
GB   D15 R38/77   P(24-12-1) 172
ChiC D16 R32/112  P(26-9-3)  157
  ChiC-Kutner 100C

SUNDAY, NOVEMBER 23
GB     7    3   7   7   24
NYG   14    3   7   0   24
GB   D16 R42/148  P(25-9-5)  193
NYG  D15 R38/97   P(17-10-1) 124

Pit    0    7   0   0    7
ChiB   7   14   7  21   49
Pit  D17 R46/224  P(20-6-3)   92
ChiB D26 R41/280  P(27-11-1) 242

ChiC   0    7   7   7   21
Was    7   10   7  14   45
ChiC D21 R24/62   P(44-21-5) 291
Was  D26 R33/133  P(33-25-2) 355
  ChiC-Kutner 133C;
  Was-McKee 103C, Baugh 355P

Phi    0    7   0   7   14
Bos    7    7   7   0   21
Phi  D14 R39/164  P(14-6-4)   79
Bos  D15 R41/134  P(16-8-2)  140

Det    3    7   0   7   17
LARm   7   14   0   7   28
Det  D18 R36/95   P(36-16-2) 197
LARm D9  R34/97   P(16-6-2)   89

THURSDAY, NOVEMBER 27
ChiB   7    7  20   0   34
Det    0    0   0  14   14
ChiB D23 R44/184  P(27-14-3) 253
Det  D13 R17/35   P(36-15-2) 237
  Det-Greene 110C

SUNDAY, NOVEMBER 30
ChiC   3    7  14   7   31
NYG    7    7  14   7   35
ChiC D26 R36/216  P(37-15-2) 280
NYG  D18 R42/249  P(17-8-1)  180

Pit    0    0   0   0    0
Phi    7    0   0  14   21
Pit  D6  R31/75   P(16-5-2)   45
Phi  D15 R42/219  P(12-5-0)   32

Was    0    3  14   7   24
Bos    3   10   7   7   27
Was  D20 R35/118  P(29-20-0) 278
Bos  D10 R31/80   P(20-9-3)  242
  Was-Nussbaumer 113C;
  Bos-Currivan 181C

GB     2    0  14  14   30
LARm   7    0   0   3   10
GB   D21 R43/159  P(21-11-1) 167
LARm D12 R33/104  P(19-6-4)   90
  GB-Goodnight 107C
```

```
SUNDAY, DECEMBER 7
Was    3    0   0   7   10
NYG   14    0   7  14   35
Was  D17 R31/85   P(47-17-4) 203
NYG  D14 R27/81   P(24-13-0) 267
  Was-Saenz 118C;
  NYG-Governali 255P

Bos    0    7   0   0    7
Pit   10    0   0   7   17
Bos  D8  R23/78   P(25-7-3)  108
Pit  D13 R48/167  P(13-5-1)   68

ChiC   3    0  14  28   45
Phi    7    0   0  14   21
ChiC D21 R44/185  P(22-11-0) 194
Phi  D19 R21/69   P(27-17-3) 314

LARm   0   10   0   7   17
ChiB  14    0   0   0   14
LARm D18 R34/148  P(29-13-1) 182
ChiB D27 R46/211  P(34-20-4) 296
  ChiB-McAfee 157C

GB     7    7  14   7   35
Det    0    0  14   0   14
GB   D22 R53/182  P(22-11-0) 107
Det  D14 R23/85   P(36-12-5) 197
  Det-Heywood 128C

SUNDAY, DECEMBER 14
NYG    3    7   0   0   10
LARm  10   14   3   7   34
NYG  D11 R23/59   P(32-15-4) 176
LARm D15 R35/248  P(22-7-3)  134

Bos    6    0   0   7   13
Was    6   14   6  14   40
Bos  D7  R19/23   P(23-7-3)   89
Was  D28 R49/231  P(41-25-1) 343
  Was-Castiglia 136R, Baugh 343P

GB     0    7   7   0   14
Phi    7    7  14   0   28
GB   D17 R31/167  P(39-16-6) 220
Phi  D17 R42/178  P(19-12-1) 220
  GB-Luhn 135C; Phi-Pihos 108C

ChiC  14   13   0   3   30
ChiB   7    0   0  14   21
ChiC D17 R42/82   P(21-10-1) 247
ChiB D24 R41/155  P(38-16-4) 347
  ChiB-Keane 161C
```

1948 AAFC

```
FRIDAY, AUGUST 27
LAD    0    7   0   0    7
ChiR   0    0   0   0    0
LAD  D6  R?/77    P(7-3-1)    20
ChiR D14 R?/165   P(26-8-3)   77

NYY    0    0  21   0   21
Bkn    0    3   0   0    3
NYY  D15 R?/250   P(22-11-1)  83
Bkn  D11 R?/136   P(29-10-2)  97

SUNDAY, AUGUST 29
Buf    0    7   0   0    7
SF     7   21   0   7   35
Buf  D18 R?/271   P(36-17-2) 196
SF   D12 R?/225   P(20-13-1) 186

FRIDAY, SEPTEMBER 3
LAD    0    0   0  14   14
Cle    3    7   9   0   19
LAD  D15 R?/69    P(28-16-2) 145
Cle  D14 R?/141   P(17-9-2)  122

SUNDAY, SEPTEMBER 5
NYY    0    7  14   7   28
Bal   14    7  14  10   45
NYY  D14 R?/93    P(28-14-1) 149
Bal  D13 R?/142   P(21-11-2) 346

Bkn    0    7   6   7   20
SF     6   16   7   7   36
Bkn  D10 R?/160   P(14-6-2)   82
SF   D21 R?/216   P(30-19-0) 269

MONDAY, SEPTEMBER 6
ChiR   0    0   0   7    7
Buf   14   14  14   0   42
ChiR D17 R?/32    P(49-21-4) 258
Buf  D20 R?/199   P(16-10-2) 185
```

```
FRIDAY, SEPTEMBER 10
Bal    0    0   7   7   14
ChiR   7    7   0   7   21
Bal  D12 R?/142   P(25-9-0)  110
ChiR D17 R?/310   P(16-7-1)   87

Bkn    0    0   0   7    7
LAD    7    3   0   7   17
Bkn  D15 R?/161   P(23-12-4) 160
LAD  D8  R?/172   P(14-11-1) 103

SUNDAY, SEPTEMBER 12
Cle   14    7   7  14   42
Buf    0   13   0   0   13
Cle  D20 R?/268   P(26-14-0) 236
Buf  D13 R?/216   P(12-3-0)   20

NYY    0    0   0   0    0
SF    13   14   7   7   41
NYY  D13 R?/88    P(21-9-3)  111
SF   D7  R?/128   P(14-9-2)  139

THURSDAY, SEPTEMBER 16
Bal    0    7   7  13   27
NYY    7    0   0   7   14
Bal  D19 R?/161   P(19-10-0) 241
NYY  D19 R?/99    P(22-11-3) 197

FRIDAY, SEPTEMBER 17
Cle    7    7  14   0   28
ChiR   0    7   0   0    7
Cle  D16 R?/142   P(20-12-1) 157
ChiR D12 R?/125   P(25-7-3)  117

SUNDAY, SEPTEMBER 19
LAD    0    7   0  14   21
SF     7   13   2  14   36
LAD  D7  R?/89    P(20-6-0)   95
SF   D18 R?/295   P(22-15-0) 213

SUNDAY, SEPTEMBER 26
Bkn    0    7   0  13   20
Bal   14    7  14   0   35
Bkn  D15 R?/134   P(31-14-3) 177
Bal  D14 R?/232   P(14-6-3)   99

ChiR   7    3   0   0   10
Cle    0    0  14   7   21
ChiR D9  R?/45    P(19-9-2)  159
Cle  D14 R?/126   P(23-11-1) 216

SF     7   10  14   7   38
Buf    7   14   0   7   28
SF   D18 R?/268   P(25-14-0) 268
Buf  D14 R?/105   P(35-23-2) 299

WEDNESDAY, SEPTEMBER 29
NYY    0    0   3  10   10
LAD    0    0   0  20   20
NYY  D6  R?/104   P(19-4-0)   75
LAD  D17 R?/156   P(36-15-3) 262

FRIDAY, OCTOBER 1
SF     7   14  10   0   31
ChiR   0    7   0   0    7
SF   D19 R?/230   P(31-14-2) 170
ChiR D11 R?/112   P(20-9-3)  128

SUNDAY, OCTOBER 3
Bkn    0    7   7   7   21
Buf    3   14   7   7   31
Bkn  D7  R?/9     P(29-15-2) 144
Buf  D17 R?/222   P(23-13-3) 176

TUESDAY, OCTOBER 5
Cle    7    0   7   0   14
Bal    0    0   3   0    3
Cle  D13 R?/228   P(17-7-0)  146
Bal  D8  R?/87    P(17-10-1) 103

FRIDAY, OCTOBER 8
ChiR   7    0  14   7   28
LAD    7   14   7  21   49
ChiR D13 R?/95    P(25-13-3) 271
LAD  D17 R?/131   P(33-19-1) 356

SUNDAY, OCTOBER 10
Bkn    0   10   7   0   17
Cle   10    0   7  13   30
Bkn  D15 R?/94    P(29-11-2) 165
Cle  D23 R?/262   P(31-14-1) 170
```

```
NYY    0    0   7   7   14
Buf    7    6   0   0   13
NYY  D13 R?/99    P(18-9-1)  207
Buf  D12 R?/131   P(20-7-2)  186

SF     7   21  14  14   56
Bal    7    0   0   7   14
SF   D19 R?/330   P(20-16-0) 163
Bal  D16 R?/187   P(21-9-3)  120

FRIDAY, OCTOBER 15
Bal    0    7   7  15   29
LAD    7    7   0   0   14
Bal  D19 R?/169   P(26-14-2) 269
LAD  D9  R?/69    P(28-10-2) 166

ChiR   0    0   7   0    7
Bkn    7    0   7   7   21
ChiR D9  R?/80    P(17-6-2)   82
Bkn  D20 R?/316   P(26-12-3) 110

SUNDAY, OCTOBER 17
Buf    7    0   0   7   14
Cle   17    0   7   7   31
Buf  D14 R?/82    P(35-19-2) 260
Cle  D21 R?/209   P(28-12-0) 219

SF     0   14   0   7   21
NYY    0    0   7   0    7
SF   D15 R?/229   P(13-6-1)   79
NYY  D15 R?/160   P(18-8-3)   89

SUNDAY, OCTOBER 24
Bal    0   10   0   0   10
SF     0    0   7  14   21
Bal  D14 R?/42    P(33-21-0) 266
SF   D20 R?/390   P(21-8-2)  104

Bkn    0   14   7  14   35
ChiR   0    0   7   0    7
Bkn  D14 R?/154   P(25-10-3) 177
ChiR D13 R?/152   P(27-11-4) 142

Buf    0   14   7  14   35
LAD    7    7   0   0   14
Buf  D16 R?/173   P(28-17-3) 310
LAD  D17 R?/167   P(41-21-0) 219
  LAD-Keane 137C

NYY    0    0   0   7    7
Cle    7   14   7   7   35
NYY  D10 R?/107   P(29-13-2) 128
Cle  D18 R?/149   P(33-22-3) 337

SUNDAY, OCTOBER 31
Bal    0    7   3   0   10
Buf    7    7   7  14   35
Bal  D16 R?/111   P(31-18-0) 269
Buf  D20 R?/218   P(21-13-1) 295

LAD    0    3   7   7   17
Bkn    0    0   0   0    0
LAD  D16 R?/161   P(23-11-2) 101
Bkn  D10 R?/80    P(27-9-2)  113
  LAD-Hickey 120C, Hardy 406P

ChiR   0    0   0   7    7
NYY    0   21   7  14   42
ChiR D8  R?/104   P(13-4-2)  102
NYY  D15 R?/244   P(22-12-1) 240

SUNDAY, NOVEMBER 7
Bal    0    0   0   7    7
Cle    7    7   7   7   28
Bal  D15 R?/89    P(34-16-0) 183
Cle  D23 R?/190   P(27-15-2) 224

Buf   13    0   6   7   26
Bkn    0    0  14   0   14
Buf  D16 R?/419   P(13-3-1)   20
Bkn  D14 R?/54    P(53-26-1) 211

ChiR   0    0  21   0   21
SF    10   20   7   7   44
ChiR D17 R?/170   P(25-14-2) 168
SF   D19 R?/328   P(20-10-0) 138

LAD    0    0   0   6    6
NYY    7   14   3  14   38
LAD  D17 R?/88    P(41-17-3) 220
NYY  D15 R?/180   P(23-8-2)  173

SUNDAY, NOVEMBER 14
Bkn    0    0   0   0    0
NYY    7    7   0   7   21
Bkn  D15 R?/158   P(31-15-2) 136
NYY  D11 R?/186   P(15-8-2)   72
```

```
ChiR   3    7   0  14   24
Bal    0   10  14  14   38
ChiR D11 R?/46    P(31-13-2) 270
Bal  D21 R?/229   P(30-17-2) 223

LAD    0    6  14   7   27
Buf    0    6   7   0   13
LAD  D14 R?/133   P(29-16-0) 149
Buf  D15 R?/189   P(35-14-3) 208

SF     7    0   0   0    7
Cle    7    0   7   0   14
SF   D11 R?/145   P(15-6-3)   32
Cle  D20 R?/144   P(26-12-1) 147

SUNDAY, NOVEMBER 21
Cle   14   13   7   0   34
NYY    0   14   0   7   21
Cle  D10 R?/133   P(23-9-1)  211
NYY  D12 R?/138   P(31-12-3) 109

LAD    0   14   0   3   17
Bal    7    0   7   0   14
LAD  D9  R?/69    P(28-12-1) 119
Bal  D19 R?/191   P(29-18-0) 215
  LAD-Fears 123C

SF    14   14  21  14   63
Bkn    7    7   7  19   40
SF   D22 R?/328   P(23-15-1) 219
Bkn  D15 R?/158   P(25-12-4) 312

THURSDAY, NOVEMBER 25
Buf    6   13   7  13   39
ChiR  14    7   7   7   35
Buf  D14 R?/179   P(19-8-3)  181
ChiR D16 R?/190   P(25-13-3) 263

Cle    0   14  17   0   31
LAD    7    7   0   0   14
Cle  D18 R?/156   P(32-16-0) 239
LAD  D12 R?/111   P(22-11-1) 137

SUNDAY, NOVEMBER 28
Bal   14    3   7  14   38
Bkn   13    0   0   0   20
Bal  D21 R?/242   P(26-20-0) 249
Bkn  D18 R?/134   P(32-17-2) 244

Buf    7   14   0   0   35
NYY    0    7   0   7   14
Buf  D15 R?/190   P(25-11-2) 205
NYY  D9  R?/70    P(26-11-2) 141

Cle   10    0  21   0   31
SF     0   14   7   7   28
Cle  D12 R?/126   P(23-11-1) 234
SF   D11 R?/172   P(22-11-2) 117

SATURDAY, DECEMBER 4
NYY    7   14   7   0   28
ChiR   0    0   0   7    7
NYY  D11 R?/117   P(21-9-0)  190
ChiR D15 R?/99    P(24-12-4) 210

SUNDAY, DECEMBER 5
Buf    6    2   0   7   15
Bal    7    7   7  14   35
Buf  D19 R?/155   P(42-17-2) 140
Bal  D12 R?/140   P(14-8-0)  163

Cle    7   14  10   0   31
Bkn    0    0  14   7   21
Cle  D20 R?/246   P(18-10-3) 194
Bkn  D14 R?/27    P(36-18-1) 387

SF    21    0  10   7   38
LAD    0    7   7   7   21
SF   D17 R?/369   P(12-6-0)  121
LAD  D22 R?/46    P(56-27-7) 405
  LAD-Waterfield 142P
```

1948 NFL

```
FRIDAY, SEPTEMBER 17
GB    10    7   7   7   31
Bos    0    0   0   0    0
GB   D20 R46/257  P(26-11-1)  85
Bos  D9  R17/20   P(27-11-4) 101

WEDNESDAY, SEPTEMBER 22
Det    0    0   7   0    7
LARm  14    7   3  20   44
Det  D14 R34/108  P(29-12-4) 168
LARm D23 R42/216  P(25-10-2) 191
```

THURSDAY, SEPTEMBER 23
NYG 0 14 6 7 **27**
Bos 0 0 0 7 7
NYG D13 R33/88 P(21-11-0) 211
Bos D10 R27/91 P(29-12-5) 137

FRIDAY, SEPTEMBER 24
Phi 0 7 7 0 14
ChiC 7 7 0 7 **21**
Phi D15 R34/124 P(30-12-1) 207
ChiC D14 R41/189 P(23-6-1) 151

SUNDAY, SEPTEMBER 26
ChiB 14 17 7 7 **45**
GB 0 0 0 7 7
ChiB D21 R54/240 P(11-6-1) 57
GB D15 R35/108 P(25-10-4) 78

Pit 7 7 0 0 14
Was 7 0 0 10 **17**
Pit D23 R48/233 P(15-7-1) 111
Was D18 R35/142 P(24-13-0) 257
Pit-Clement 127R; Was-Crisler 130C

SUNDAY, OCTOBER 3
Bos 7 0 0 0 14
Pit 0 7 3 14 **24**
Bos D5 R32/106 P(10-3-2) 31
Pit D24 R60/291 P(13-3-1) 48

Det 7 0 0 14 21
GB 0 13 10 10 **33**
Det D14 R32/64 P(21-12-1) 148
GB D23 R47/268 P(19-11-1) 155
GB-Canadeo 118R

NYG 3 0 7 0 10
Was 0 14 7 20 **41**
NYG D4 R23/10 P(17-6-4) 92
Was D24 R52/159 P(27-18-3) 336

Phi 7 14 7 0 28
LARm 0 0 21 7 28
Phi D12 R36/138 P(21-13-1) 142
LARm D21 R32/108 P(50-21-1) 295

MONDAY, OCTOBER 4
ChiB 7 7 14 0 **28**
ChiC 0 10 7 0 17
ChiB D15 R40/206 P(14-6-1) 124
ChiC D15 R29/101 P(33-17-3) 199

SATURDAY, OCTOBER 9
Bos 10 7 0 0 **17**
Det 0 0 0 14 14
Bos D9 R33/144 P(15-4-1) 40
Det D27 R38/176 P(44-19-2) 284
Det-Greene 106C

SUNDAY, OCTOBER 10
ChiC 7 7 0 3 **17**
GB 0 0 7 0 7
ChiC D16 R56/320 P(14-6-3) 35
GB D12 R39/115 P(25-10-4) 122
ChiC-Angsman 146R

LARm 0 0 14 7 21
ChiB 0 21 14 7 **42**
LARm D19 R21/82 P(33-15-4) 218
ChiB D24 R44/170 P(28-20-1) 243

NYG 0 0 0 0 0
Phi 14 7 3 21 **45**
NYG D6 R24/61 P(20-8-2) 64
Phi D19 R47/198 P(25-13-1) 168

Was 0 0 0 7 7
Pit 0 7 0 3 **10**
Was D15 R38/122 P(24-13-3) 121
Pit D17 R42/97 P(24-8-2) 113

SUNDAY, OCTOBER 17
ChiC 14 28 7 14 **63**
NYG 7 7 7 14 35
ChiC D23 R34/299 P(20-15-0) 280
NYG D26 R37/145 P(31-18-1) 247
ChiC-Kutner 128C, Mallouf 252P;
NYG-Roberts 125R, Conerly 257P

Det 0 0 0 0 0
ChiB 7 7 0 14 **28**
Det D5 R30/33 P(23-7-3) 76
ChiB D21 R52/259 P(23-10-2) 138

LARm 0 0 0 0 0
GB 6 7 3 0 **16**
LARm D17 R34/84 P(38-20-7) 244
GB D16 R45/157 P(15-6-1) 132
GB-Canadeo 105R

Phi 14 10 14 7 **45**
Was 0 0 0 0 0
Phi D28 R56/218 P(19-13-0) 198
Was D11 R27/81 P(30-14-3) 132

Pit 0 0 0 7 7
Bos 6 0 0 7 **13**
Pit D11 R34/92 P(25-5-6) 113
Bos D9 R43/80 P(20-8-1) 162

SUNDAY, OCTOBER 24
Bos 6 0 0 21 27
ChiC 0 14 35 0 **49**
Bos D12 R24/76 P(24-10-4) 147
ChiC D20 R52/300 P(18-6-1) 142
Bos-Golding 101C; ChiC-Trippi 104R

ChiB 0 0 7 0 7
Phi 7 0 0 5 **12**
ChiB D14 R46/121 P(24-8-2) 102
Phi D15 R43/104 P(20-9-2) 71

LARm 0 0 13 21 **34**
Det 0 21 0 6 27
LARm D19 R30/121 P(40-24-1) 264
Det D16 R30/66 P(22-15-2) 224
LARm-Keane 137C

Pit 6 7 14 0 27
NYG 13 7 7 7 **34**
Pit D14 R36/83 P(30-12-4) 204
NYG D13 R35/144 P(15-6-1) 192

Was 6 7 0 10 **23**
GB 0 0 0 7 7
Was D23 R62/247 P(10-5-1) 60
GB D16 R37/174 P(23-7-2) 135
GB-Goodnight 117C

SUNDAY, OCTOBER 31
Bos 14 0 7 0 21
Was 14 14 10 21 **59**
Bos D22 R31/109 P(40-19-6) 224
Was D20 R30/124 P(34-22-1) 501
Was-Farmer 103C, Todd 158C,
Baugh 446P

ChiC 3 10 14 0 **27**
LARm 3 0 7 12 22
ChiC D27 R51/178 P(32-16-0) 299
LARm D19 R17/54 P(54-28-2) 406
ChiC-Dewell 144C;
LARm-Hickey 120C, Hardy 406P

GB 7 7 0 6 20
Det 0 7 10 7 **24**
GB D17 R37/159 P(14-6-0) 147
Det D17 R39/208 P(27-11-3) 175
Det-Margucci 100C

NYG 0 0 0 14 14
ChiB 7 7 14 7 **35**
NYG D14 R24/67 P(30-11-2) 137
ChiB D22 R48/292 P(23-10-3) 169

Phi 3 14 0 17 **34**
Pit 0 7 7 0 14
Phi D20 R40/157 P(26-18-1) 177
Pit D15 R32/110 P(30-11-3) 144
Phi-Van Buren 109R

SUNDAY, NOVEMBER 7
ChiB 7 0 0 14 **21**
LARm 0 0 6 0 6
ChiB D16 R45/204 P(16-7-0) 124
LARm D16 R35/117 P(32-12-1) 125

Det 6 7 0 7 20
ChiC 7 21 7 21 **56**
Det D15 R32/105 P(30-16-1) 252
ChiC D23 R35/233 P(29-16-1) 251
Det-Greene 122C; ChiC-Trippi 103R,
Kutner 143C

GB 0 0 0 7 7
Pit 7 17 7 7 **38**
GB D13 R32/98 P(24-10-2) 152
Pit D19 R49/221 P(14-7-2) 80

Phi 7 7 14 7 **35**
NYG 0 0 7 7 14
Phi D21 R43/269 P(19-9-4) 189
NYG D19 R28/115 P(40-18-1) 261
Phi-Van Buren 143R, Pihos 128C

Was 9 0 7 7 **23**
Bos 0 0 0 7 7
Was D22 R40/196 P(32-18-2) 190
Bos D9 R30/113 P(18-8-1) 129

SUNDAY, NOVEMBER 14
Bos 0 0 0 0 0
Phi 0 24 7 14 **45**
Bos D7 R29/101 P(21-9-2) 61
Phi D22 R43/220 P(29-14-0) 269
Phi-Van Buren 137R,
Thompson 197P

ChiC 14 7 0 3 **24**
Pit 7 0 0 0 7
ChiC D18 R42/184 P(27-14-1) 184
Pit D14 R37/141 P(22-11-3) 186
ChiC-Kutner 126C

Det 7 7 0 7 21
Was 3 0 16 27 **46**
Det D16 R35/122 P(26-10-4) 199
Was D29 R41/184 P(33-23-2) 266
Det-Mann 147C; Was-Crisler 119C,
Baugh 266P

GB 0 0 0 6 6
ChiB 0 0 7 0 **7**
GB D12 R34/111 P(27-14-2) 109
ChiB D10 R42/112 P(16-7-2) 87

LARm 7 14 10 21 **52**
NYG 7 9 21 0 37
LARm D25 R52/223 P(21-13-3) 167
NYG D14 R24/92 P(33-14-3) 141

SUNDAY, NOVEMBER 21
ChiB 10 7 21 13 **51**
Bos 7 3 0 7 17
ChiB D26 R54/281 P(40-19-1) 187
Bos D9 R34/153 P(17-5-2) 98

LARm 0 17 0 7 24
ChiC 7 10 3 7 **27**
LARm D14 R28/92 P(35-18-1) 323
ChiC D22 R47/170 P(25-13-0) 216
LARm-Fears 123C

NYG 0 21 14 14 **49**
GB 3 0 0 0 3
NYG D28 R36/109 P(36-24-1) 334
GB D11 R32/93 P(27-9-8) 139

Pit 7 0 0 7 14
Det 0 10 0 7 **17**
Pit D22 R48/202 P(21-9-3) 86
Det D11 R36/124 P(15-7-0) 68

Was 0 14 0 7 21
Phi 14 7 7 14 **42**
Was D10 R21/44 P(25-11-2) 210
Phi D28 R60/376 P(18-13-2) 199
Was-Crisler 109C;
Phi-Van Buren 171R

THURSDAY, NOVEMBER 25
ChiC 7 7 7 7 **28**
Det 7 0 0 7 14
ChiC D10 R32/104 P(25-10-0) 159
Det D19 R36/184 P(26-10-1) 186
Det-Wilson 125R

SUNDAY, NOVEMBER 28
Bos 14 0 0 0 14
NYG 0 21 7 0 **28**
Bos D11 R27/59 P(29-10-5) 98
NYG D21 R42/166 P(27-16-0) 237

GB 0 10 0 0 10
LARm 7 7 7 3 **24**
GB D8 R24/97 P(34-14-3) 100
LARm D23 R46/239 P(28-18-3) 206

Pit 0 0 0 0 0
Phi 7 10 0 0 **17**
Pit D12 R38/87 P(32-11-2) 113
Phi D15 R37/183 P(23-12-1) 167
Phi-Pihos 112C

Was 0 0 0 6 13
ChiB 20 21 0 7 **48**
Was D21 R30/89 P(46-19-4) 246
ChiB D24 R38/185 P(28-8-2) 132

SUNDAY, DECEMBER 5
ChiB 7 14 0 21 **42**
Det 0 0 7 7 14
ChiB D29 R48/230 P(34-22-1) 221
Det D13 R27/96 P(29-12-2) 170

GB 0 7 0 0 7
ChiC 7 7 7 21 **42**
GB D9 R38/122 P(15-1-1) 10
ChiC D25 R70/289 P(18-7-1) 99

LARm 7 20 14 0 **41**
Was 0 7 6 0 13
LARm D23 R49/199 P(21-13-0) 196
Was D19 R23/79 P(33-21-2) 188
LARm-Waterfield 142P

NYG 7 0 7 14 28
Pit 7 10 0 21 **38**
NYG D31 R23/100 P(53-36-1) 363
Pit D23 R48/266 P(19-11-0) 165
NYG-Conerly 363P; Pit-Papach 148R

Phi 7 0 0 7 14
Bos 10 21 0 6 **37**
Phi D18 R39/129 P(47-17-3) 196
Bos D9 R38/118 P(11-2-1) 80

SUNDAY, DECEMBER 12
ChiC 3 0 7 14 **24**
ChiB 7 7 0 7 21
ChiC D20 R42/193 P(21-8-1) 119
ChiB D20 R46/152 P(30-19-3) 310

Det 0 7 7 7 21
Phi 3 14 7 21 **45**
Det D20 R20/74 P(32-20-3) 338
Phi D28 R50/262 P(24-16-0) 258
Det-Greene 132C;
Phi-Ferrante 184C, Thompson 258P

Pit 0 0 7 7 14
LARm 0 14 7 10 **31**
Pit D16 R38/111 P(21-13-2) 166
LARm D20 R41/208 P(18-9-0) 113
Pit-Jansante 104C

Was 0 7 14 7 **28**
NYG 7 7 0 7 21
Was D24 R35/136 P(42-25-3) 354
NYG D23 R33/122 P(40-23-0) 225
Was-Taylor 194C, Baugh 354P

1949 AAFC

FRIDAY, AUGUST 26
Buf 7 0 0 7 14
ChiH 0 14 0 3 **17**
Buf D9 R?/127 P(18-8-2) 66
ChiH D7 R?/107 P(22-9-2) 198

SUNDAY, AUGUST 28
Bal 0 0 17 0 17
SF 10 7 0 14 **31**
Bal D8 R?/59 P(30-14-2) 142
SF D17 R?/227 P(33-14-1) 140

FRIDAY, SEPTEMBER 2
Bal 0 17 0 0 17
LAD 14 7 7 21 **49**
Bal D13 R?/109 P(29-13-3) 219
LAD D21 R?/304 P(21-12-0) 224

SUNDAY, SEPTEMBER 4
ChiH 0 0 0 0 0
SF 28 0 7 7 **42**
ChiH D17 R?/101 P(32-14-6) 173
SF D15 R?/348 P(18-10-1) 104

MONDAY, SEPTEMBER 5
Cle 7 0 0 21 28
Buf 0 0 21 0 28
Cle D17 R?/177 P(40-27-1) 330
Buf D13 R?/80 P(12-7-1) 95

FRIDAY, SEPTEMBER 9
ChiH 7 13 0 3 **23**
LAD 0 7 7 7 21
ChiH D11 R?/112 P(28-13-1) 155
LAD D15 R?/81 P(19-9-2) 229

SUNDAY, SEPTEMBER 11
Bal 0 0 0 0 0
Cle 7 7 0 7 **21**
Bal D11 R?/81 P(21-8-2) 75
Cle D17 R?/172 P(20-14-1) 234

NYY 0 0 10 7 **17**
Buf 0 0 0 0 14
NYY D15 R?/158 P(28-8-0) 181
Buf D11 R?/140 P(23-13-3) 173

FRIDAY, SEPTEMBER 16
Bal 0 7 0 0 7
ChiH 7 14 7 7 **35**
Bal D15 R?/127 P(25-15-2) 233
ChiH D13 R?/195 P(19-10-0) 237

SUNDAY, SEPTEMBER 18
NYY 3 0 0 0 3
Cle 7 0 0 7 **14**
NYY D15 R?/184 P(24-6-1) 127
Cle D5 R?/89 P(11-4-2) 36

LAD 7 0 0 7 14
SF 0 21 21 0 **42**
LAD D17 R?/92 P(44-16-5) 175
SF D9 R?/244 P(14-4-4) 164

THURSDAY, SEPTEMBER 22
LAD 7 0 0 0 7
NYY 0 0 0 10 **10**
LAD D5 R?/69 P(19-7-2) 38
NYY D7 R?/212 P(10-2-2) 30

SUNDAY, SEPTEMBER 25
Cle 0 0 7 21 28
Bal 0 13 0 7 20
Cle D13 R?/107 P(24-9-1) 104
Bal D14 R?/139 P(34-13-1) 181

SF 3 0 14 0 17
Buf 7 7 7 7 **28**
SF D9 R?/133 P(22-9-0) 97
Buf D20 R?/221 P(20-15-0) 224

FRIDAY, SEPTEMBER 30
SF 14 14 7 7 **42**
ChiH 10 7 0 7 24
SF D17 R?/347 P(19-8-1) 136
ChiH D10 R?/91 P(26-10-3) 274

SUNDAY, OCTOBER 2
Bal 0 14 7 14 **35**
Buf 7 0 7 14 28
Bal D11 R?/90 P(20-12-0) 276
Buf D23 R?/213 P(28-16-2) 165

LAD 0 0 0 7 7
Cle 0 14 14 14 **42**
LAD D12 R?/179 P(35-10-1) 126
Cle D22 R?/242 P(31-19-1) 308

FRIDAY, OCTOBER 7
NYY 10 7 14 7 **38**
ChiH 7 3 7 7 24
NYY D16 R?/243 P(13-10-0) 179
ChiH D8 R?/30 P(25-15-1) 178

SUNDAY, OCTOBER 9
Buf 7 14 7 0 28
LAD 0 21 14 7 **42**
Buf D16 R?/187 P(35-18-3) 319
LAD D19 R?/187 P(27-18-0) 283

Cle 7 14 0 7 28
SF 21 14 7 14 **56**
Cle D10 R?/86 P(26-13-3) 281
SF D17 R?/258 P(31-18-4) 249

FRIDAY, OCTOBER 14
Cle 14 20 14 13 **61**
LAD 7 0 0 7 14
Cle D15 R?/184 P(28-17-1) 423
LAD D13 R?/181 P(28-8-5) 81

SUNDAY, OCTOBER 16
NYY 0 10 7 7 **24**
Bal 7 7 7 0 21
NYY D14 R?/183 P(16-5-1) 65
Bal D17 R?/131 P(34-17-3) 344

Buf 7 0 0 0 7
SF 14 23 7 7 **51**
Buf D10 R?/11 P(36-21-0) 167
SF D16 R?/310 P(23-9-0) 140

SUNDAY, OCTOBER 23

ChiH 3 14 0 0 **17**
Bal 0 0 0 7 7
ChiH D12 R?/125 P(24-10-1) 174
Bal D14 R?/193 P(16-10-2) 142

SF 0 3 0 0 3
NYY 0 0 17 7 **24**
SF D8 R?/49 P(31-13-4) 137
NYY D7 R?/158 P(11-2-2) 15

LAD 0 0 7 7 14
Buf 14 3 0 0 **17**
LAD D7 R?/110 P(17-6-1) 78
Buf D23 R?/325 P(19-14-0) 138

FRIDAY, OCTOBER 28

LAD 7 7 0 10 **24**
ChiH 7 0 0 7 14
LAD D17 R?/149 P(25-13-1) 226
ChiH D11 R?/72 P(23-10-3) 138

SUNDAY, OCTOBER 30

Bal 0 0 14 0 14
NYY 7 14 0 0 **21**
Bal D12 R?/15 P(28-17-1) 216
NYY D12 R?/224 P(9-3-2) 64

SF 0 14 0 14 28
Cle 0 14 7 9 **30**
SF D19 R?/224 P(27-14-0) 253
Cle D17 R?/129 P(25-14-0) 271

SUNDAY, NOVEMBER 6

SF 0 7 7 14 **28**
Bal 3 0 7 0 10
SF D18 R?/295 P(20-9-2) 120
Bal D13 R?/118 P(27-13-3) 109

Buf 7 0 0 10 **17**
NYY 14 0 0 0 14
Buf D13 R?/117 P(26-15-0) 190
NYY D9 R?/226 P(14-6-1) 60

ChiH 0 0 0 2 2
Cle 7 7 7 14 **35**
ChiH D10 R?/46 P(29-12-4) 184
Cle D19 R?/246 P(22-14-1) 296

SUNDAY, NOVEMBER 13

ChiH 0 10 0 0 10
NYY 14 0 0 0 **14**
ChiH D7 R?/61 P(32-14-2) 157
NYY D8 R?/148 P(9-3-2) 13

Buf 0 7 0 0 7
Cle 7 0 0 0 7
Buf D14 R?/158 P(20-6-2) 82
Cle D15 R?/114 P(26-11-0) 176

SF 7 14 7 13 **41**
LAD 0 17 0 7 24
SF D12 R?/188 P(20-14-0) 220
LAD D13 R?/211 P(19-4-4) 74
LAD-Hoerner 100R

SUNDAY, NOVEMBER 20

LAD 14 7 0 0 **21**
Bal 7 3 0 0 10
LAD D7 R?/131 P(10-3-0) 57
Bal D19 R?/135 P(36-17-1) 193
LAD-Fears 110C

Cle 17 14 0 0 **31**
NYY 0 0 0 0 0
Cle D16 R?/79 P(34-19-1) 382
NYY D12 R?/140 P(26-10-5) 137

ChiH 0 0 0 0 0
Buf 0 7 0 3 **10**
ChiH D7 R?/55 P(17-5-2) 55
Buf D7 R?/153 P(4-1-1) 20

THURSDAY, NOVEMBER 24

Cle 14 0 0 0 **14**
ChiH 0 6 0 0 6
Cle D10 R?/147 P(9-6-0) 88
ChiH D9 R?/111 P(19-8-3) 87

NYY 0 0 0 17 **17**
LAD 7 0 0 9 16
NYY D13 R?/138 P(17-7-2) 107
LAD D10 R?/151 P(22-8-2) 95

SUNDAY, NOVEMBER 27

Buf 7 10 14 7 **38**
Bal 0 7 0 7 14
Buf D22 R?/227 P(31-22-2) 234
Bal D7 R?/46 P(26-12-2) 231

NYY 7 0 7 0 14
SF 7 0 21 7 **35**
NYY D7 R?/110 P(22-4-4) 54
SF D17 R?/165 P(30-17-3) 243

1949 NFL

THURSDAY, SEPTEMBER 22

Phi 7 0 0 0 **7**
NYB 0 0 0 0 0
Phi D8 R57/170 P(9-5-0) 66
NYB D1 R37/34 P(1-0-0) 0

FRIDAY, SEPTEMBER 23

Det 7 7 0 10 24
LARm 10 7 0 10 **27**
Det D18 R25/65 P(38-18-2) 233
LARm D20 R45/168 P(27-12-3) 163

SUNDAY, SEPTEMBER 25

ChiB 0 0 3 14 **17**
GB 0 0 0 0 0
ChiB D19 R51/206 P(23-13-1) 183
GB D7 R40/187 P(13-0-4) 0

NYG 0 0 0 7 7
Pit 0 21 0 7 **28**
NYG D13 R29/105 P(35-18-1) 154
Pit D18 R46/223 P(22-10-0) 149

MONDAY, SEPTEMBER 26

Was 0 7 0 0 7
ChiC 7 7 7 17 **38**
Was D20 R34/102 P(37-17-2) 217
ChiC D21 R45/265 P(20-12-2) 150
ChiC-Trippi 130R

FRIDAY, SEPTEMBER 30

NYG 10 0 14 14 **38**
NYB 0 14 0 0 14
NYG D21 R38/186 P(18-8-1) 67
NYB D21 R38/117 P(32-17-1) 160
NYG-Roberts 108R

SUNDAY, OCTOBER 2

ChiB 10 7 0 0 **17**
ChiC 0 0 7 0 7
ChiB D16 R38/111 P(31-15-2) 202
ChiC D11 R30/87 P(29-16-1) 122

LARm 10 7 14 17 **48**
GB 0 0 0 7 7
LARm D23 R38/247 P(27-11-0) 173
GB D16 R41/197 P(20-4-3) 80

MONDAY, OCTOBER 3

Phi 0 5 0 17 **22**
Det 7 7 0 0 14
Phi D25 R57/236 P(26-10-2) 91
Det D13 R28/102 P(22-7-2) 33
Phi-Van Buren 135R

Was 6 0 14 7 **27**
Pit 0 14 0 0 14
Was D17 R42/228 P(16-8-0) 182
Pit D19 R44/193 P(21-9-1) 110
Was-Taylor 111C

FRIDAY, OCTOBER 7

GB 0 9 3 7 **19**
NYB 0 0 0 0 0
GB D20 R41/231 P(30-9-1) 154
NYB D17 R34/72 P(25-12-1) 117
GB-Canadeo 100R

SATURDAY, OCTOBER 8

Det 0 0 0 7 7
Pit 0 7 7 0 **14**
Det D17 R23/52 P(35-21-2) 210
Pit D18 R55/206 P(9-3-3) 66

ChiC 3 0 0 0 3
Phi 7 7 7 7 **28**
ChiC D13 R31/156 P(26-7-3) 57
Phi D20 R56/269 P(11-7-2) 107

SUNDAY, OCTOBER 9

LARm 3 14 7 7 **31**
ChiB 7 9 0 0 16
LARm D18 R38/125 P(33-16-2) 211
ChiB D17 R33/76 P(33-12-7) 251

NYG 14 10 21 0 **45**
Was 14 7 0 14 35
NYG D17 R35/152 P(19-12-2) 217
Was D22 R31/117 P(38-17-5) 335
Was-Taylor 136C

SUNDAY, OCTOBER 16

ChiC 17 6 14 2 **39**
GB 3 7 0 7 17
ChiC D14 R49/213 P(16-5-3) 31
GB D17 R37/130 P(32-12-4) 179

LARm 0 7 7 7 **21**
Det 3 7 0 0 10
LARm D15 R35/86 P(31-14-3) 208
Det D17 R34/114 P(36-16-3) 180

NYB 0 7 7 0 14
Was 7 14 10 7 **38**
NYB D16 R33/257 P(29-14-0) 132
Was D16 R38/182 P(24-18-0) 287
Was-Crisler 118C, Baugh 254P

Phi 7 7 7 0 21
ChiB 7 14 7 10 **38**
Phi D14 R32/42 P(29-16-2) 213
ChiB D28 R45/200 P(26-16-1) 257
ChiB-Keane 127C

Pit 7 0 7 7 **21**
NYG 0 17 0 0 17
Pit D13 R48/131 P(15-5-1) 63
NYG D14 R45/145 P(25-10-2) 99

SUNDAY, OCTOBER 23

ChiB 0 0 14 14 28
NYG 7 7 14 7 **35**
ChiB D28 R27/77 P(59-34-2) 358
NYG D10 R41/94 P(15-8-0) 273
ChiB-Keane 193C, Lujack 319P;
NYG-Roberts 201C, Conerly 273P

Det 7 0 0 17 **24**
ChiC 7 0 0 0 7
Det D16 R35/126 P(35-14-2) 210
ChiC D10 R32/159 P(30-12-6) 117
ChiC-Angsman 116R

GB 0 0 7 0 7
LARm 14 0 14 7 **35**
GB D18 R55/183 P(24-8-2) 106
LARm D14 R44/171 P(13-6-3) 77
GB-Canadeo 122R

NYB 10 3 0 0 13
Pit 10 7 7 0 **24**
NYB D19 R28/71 P(41-19-3) 244
Pit D24 R53/356 P(15-5-1) 46
NYB-Chipley 116C;
Pit-Nuzum 117R, Papach 113R

Was 7 0 7 0 14
Phi 14 21 7 7 **49**
Was D15 R33/159 P(34-10-4) 135
Phi D28 R55/331 P(27-13-1) 188
Phi-Pritchard 128R

SUNDAY, OCTOBER 30

ChiB 3 7 0 14 24
LARm 3 14 3 7 **27**
ChiB D18 R43/167 P(25-9-5) 225
LARm D27 R40/82 P(42-24-3) 303
LARm-Fears 143C, Waterfield 303P

Det 7 0 0 7 14
GB 3 0 6 7 **16**
Det D23 R38/215 P(33-16-2) 197
GB D16 R47/251 P(15-5-2) 61
Det-Triplett 109R;
GB-Canadeo 117R

NYG 7 0 20 14 **41**
ChiC 14 14 3 7 38
NYG D18 R41/181 P(22-9-1) 139
ChiC D23 R52/308 P(14-7-1) 82
NYG-Roberts 108R;
ChiC-Trippi 125R

Phi 3 14 7 14 **38**
Pit 0 0 7 0 7
Phi D21 R51/237 P(17-8-1) 128
Pit D14 R31/81 P(30-11-3) 143
Phi-Van Buren 103R

Was 0 7 7 0 14
NYB 7 0 0 7 14
Was D20 R45/133 P(30-17-3) 285
NYB D13 R31/130 P(20-11-1) 157
Was-Crisler 144C, Taylor 109C

SUNDAY, NOVEMBER 6

ChiC 0 14 14 14 **42**
Det 0 6 7 6 19
ChiC D16 R39/155 P(22-8-3) 162
Det D20 R40/189 P(33-13-0) 172
Det-Mann 127C

GB 0 0 3 0 3
ChiB 3 7 0 14 **24**
GB D15 R51/188 P(18-5-1) 85
ChiB D17 R42/160 P(24-9-1) 177

LARm 7 0 0 7 14
Phi 3 14 14 7 **38**
LARm D13 R10/27 P(36-20-2) 197
Phi D25 R64/264 P(16-11-0) 175

NYB 0 7 14 10 **31**
NYG 14 10 0 0 24
NYB D21 R25/54 P(39-23-1) 333
NYG D18 R35/124 P(38-21-2) 201
NYB-Chipley 143C, Layne 333P;
NYG-Poole 104C

Pit 0 7 7 0 14
Was 0 7 0 20 **27**
Pit D20 R57/230 P(22-6-2) 89
Was D16 R27/175 P(27-12-3) 208
Was-Stout 107R

SUNDAY, NOVEMBER 13

ChiC 7 31 14 13 **65**
NYB 7 0 6 7 20
ChiC D32 R47/319 P(36-17-1) 253
NYB D20 R20/139 P(36-15-7) 254
ChiC-Harder 117R

Det 7 3 0 14 24
ChiB 7 7 6 7 **27**
Det D15 R24/64 P(34-16-3) 243
ChiB D24 R52/213 P(31-16-4) 216

LARm 0 0 0 7 7
Pit 0 7 0 0 7
LARm D23 R54/195 P(25-13-2) 167
Pit D7 R37/138 P(0-0-0) 0
LARm-Hoerner 100R

NYG 10 0 14 6 **30**
GB 0 3 0 7 10
NYG D19 R39/99 P(32-16-4) 352
GB D17 R35/137 P(35-12-3) 151
NYG-Roberts 212C, Conerly 357P

Phi 14 16 14 0 **44**
Was 7 0 7 7 21
Phi D26 R55/256 P(28-14-1) 294
Was D17 R25/95 P(30-15-5) 276
Phi-Scott 127C, Thompson 269P

SUNDAY, NOVEMBER 20

ChiB 7 17 7 0 **31**
Was 7 0 0 14 21
ChiB D20 R41/149 P(38-16-1) 315
Was D13 R38/99 P(29-12-1) 140
ChiB-Hoffman 100R,
Kavanaugh 115C

Det 7 10 14 14 **45**
NYG 0 7 14 0 21
Det D22 R43/141 P(39-20-5) 261
NYG D11 R30/45 P(25-16-3) 194
Det-Mann 124C

LARm 0 14 0 14 28
ChiC 7 7 14 0 28
LARm D22 R32/187 P(41-21-3) 278
ChiC D19 R45/169 P(29-13-2) 89
LARm-Fears 110C

NYB 0 0 0 0 0
Phi 7 14 21 0 **42**
NYB D7 R27/97 P(18-6-3) 38
Phi D22 R56/216 P(20-10-3) 140
Phi-Van Buren 174R

Pit 0 7 7 16 **30**
GB 0 0 0 7 7
Pit D19 R51/295 P(14-8-2) 154
GB D16 R51/188 P(18-6-2) 99
Pit-Nuzum 168R; GB-Canadeo 116R

THURSDAY, NOVEMBER 24

ChiB 7 7 7 7 **28**
Det 0 0 0 7 7
ChiB D18 R39/144 P(24-16-1) 202
Det D9 R29/40 P(25-10-4) 70

SUNDAY, NOVEMBER 27

GB 0 21 0 0 21
ChiC 27 7 0 7 **41**
GB D19 R35/155 P(36-12-3) 164
ChiC D17 R40/145 P(19-12-1) 199
GB-Canadeo 122R;
ChiC-Ravensberg 114C

NYB 0 7 6 7 20
LARm 14 0 14 14 **42**
NYB D19 R43/142 P(23-13-1) 221
LARm D23 R29/108 P(31-20-0) 354
NYB-Heywood 161C;
LARm-Fears 131C, Waterfield 267P

Pit 7 3 0 7 17
Phi 10 7 7 10 **34**
Pit D6 R22/62 P(19-6-0) 134
Phi D26 R61/296 P(30-16-1) 190
Phi-Van Buren 205R

Was 7 0 0 0 7
NYG 0 10 0 13 **23**
Was D19 R32/69 P(43-28-2) 207
NYG D15 R22/69 P(32-14-1) 184
NYG-Swiacki 116C

SUNDAY, DECEMBER 4

ChiC 3 0 7 21 **31**
LARm 10 7 7 3 27
ChiC D14 R30/106 P(35-10-1) 171
LARm D19 R45/157 P(28-15-4) 222

GB 0 0 0 0 0
Was 0 13 17 0 **30**
GB D10 R34/105 P(28-7-4) 122
Was D17 R40/162 P(30-13-0) 157

NYB 0 7 7 13 27
Det 7 14 0 7 **28**
NYB D20 R24/55 P(41-25-2) 223
Det D17 R43/181 P(32-9-1) 145
NYB-Heywood 151C

Phi 0 7 14 3 **24**
NYG 3 0 0 0 3
Phi D16 R49/171 P(17-9-0) 127
NYG D11 R21/43 P(38-14-3) 69

Pit 0 7 0 14 21
ChiB 7 10 6 7 **30**
Pit D14 R38/140 P(22-10-4) 207
ChiB D19 R39/154 P(30-13-2) 201
Pit-Nickel 192C

SUNDAY, DECEMBER 11

ChiC 7 0 7 7 21
ChiB 14 17 7 14 **52**
ChiC D17 R27/48 P(31-19-2) 280
ChiB D24 R33/128 P(41-24-3) 468
ChiC-Trippi 123C;
ChiB-Hoffman 174C,
Kavanaugh 137C, Lujack 468P

GB 0 7 0 0 7
Det 7 0 0 14 **21**
GB D11 R36/109 P(30-11-0) 80
Det D19 R35/92 P(36-17-2) 301
Det-Mann 182C

NYG 0 0 3 0 3
Phi 0 10 0 7 **17**
NYG D10 R43/161 P(23-9-3) 78
Phi D12 R39/119 P(21-11-1) 131

Pit 0 6 14 7 **27**
NYB 0 0 0 0 0
Pit D17 R53/154 P(20-8-1) 135
NYB D9 R13/16 P(38-17-3) 146

Was 7 0 7 13 27
LARm 20 14 6 13 **53**
Was D25 R22/58 P(56-30-4) 320
LARm D28 R35/179 P(32-20-2) 405
Was-Baugh 308P;
LARm-Fears 159C, Shaw 137C,
Van Brocklin 152P

1950 NFL

SATURDAY, SEPTEMBER 16

Cle 7 7 7 14 **35**
Phi 3 0 0 7 10
Cle D23 R24/141 P(38-21-2) 307
Phi D24 R44/148 P(32-11-3) 100
Cle-Speedie 109C, Graham 346P

SUNDAY, SEPTEMBER 17

ChiB 0 3 14 7 **24**
LARm 0 7 0 13 20
ChiB D19 R60/201 P(19-8-1) 137
LARm D15 R32/54 P(29-16-2) 255
ChiB-Gulyanics 121R

Det 9 13 16 7 **45**
GB 7 0 0 0 7
Det D14 R31/38 P(24-12-1) 266
GB D11 R32/78 P(25-7-7) 86

NYG 0 2 0 16 **18**
Pit 0 0 0 7 7
NYG D10 R51/167 P(13-3-1) 30
Pit D10 R32/34 P(18-9-3) 104

NYY 14 0 7 0 **21**
SF 0 10 0 7 17
NYY D17 R46/153 P(18-10-1) 59
SF D16 R42/193 P(17-7-1) 64
NYY-Toth 108R

Was 7 7 10 14 **38**
Bal 0 0 14 0 14
Was D16 R?/120 P(26-14-1) 288
Bal D23 R?/120 P(42-22-2) 267
Was-Taylor 150C

FRIDAY, SEPTEMBER 22

NYY 0 7 14 7 28
LARm 7 21 7 10 **45**
NYY D14 R27/227 P(28-12-2) 220
LARm D28 R40/201 P(40-21-1) 328
NYY-Toth 138R, Edwards 110C;
LARm-Davis 103C, Hoerner 105C

SUNDAY, SEPTEMBER 24

Cle 17 0 7 7 **31**
Bal 0 0 0 0 0
Cle D15 R?/295 P(24-12-4) 180
Bal D11 R?/63 P(28-13-4) 156
Cle-Carpenter 100R, Lavelli 115C

ChiB 3 9 17 3 **32**
SF 7 7 0 6 20
ChiB D20 R40/188 P(33-16-2) 172
SF D17 R44/195 P(23-11-2) 74

Phi 10 21 14 0 **45**
ChiC 0 0 7 0 7
Phi D26 R59/276 P(28-10-3) 163
ChiC D12 R20/110 P(42-12-8) 155

Pit 0 0 7 0 7
Det 0 0 0 10 **10**
Pit D8 R19/54 P(30-12-1) 122
Det D24 R53/265 P(27-11-3) 107
Det-Layne 118R

Was 7 0 7 7 21
GB 0 14 14 7 **35**
Was D19 R29/204 P(42-21-3) 296
GB D21 R46/175 P(28-6-0) 123
Was-Goode 102R, Livingston 141C

FRIDAY, SEPTEMBER 29

Det 7 0 0 14 21
NYY 7 14 9 14 **44**
Det D14 R20/88 P(34-12-3) 179
NYY D16 R32/95 P(29-15-2) 264
NYY-Ratterman 264P

SUNDAY, OCTOBER 1

ChiB 0 7 7 7 21
GB 3 7 21 0 **31**
ChiB D23 R39/162 P(38-18-4) 240
GB D8 R33/179 P(13-5-2) 44
ChiB-Keane 129C; GB-Coutre 101R

LARm 14 0 14 7 **35**
SF 0 0 0 0 0
LARm D21 R39/209 P(23-14-0) 132
SF D23 R32/130 P(51-24-1) 282
SF-Beals 106C

NYG 6 0 0 0 **6**
Cle 0 0 0 0 0
NYG D8 R?/136 P(13-4-0) 61
Cle D12 R?/123 P(31-12-4) 127

Pit 3 7 7 9 **26**
Was 7 0 0 0 7
Pit D15 R43/101 P(17-8-1) 137
Was D12 R29/132 P(26-9-1) 157
Was-Taylor 102C

MONDAY, OCTOBER 2

Bal 0 13 0 0 13
ChiC 7 0 20 28 **55**
Bal D11 R34/43 P(28-13-3) 307
ChiC D27 R51/272 P(30-13-2) 281
ChiC-Shaw 165C, Hardy 281P

SATURDAY, OCTOBER 7

LARm 0 0 13 7 20
Phi 14 14 14 14 **56**
LARm D23 R27/126 P(55-24-5) 329
Phi D20 R42/298 P(20-8-0) 175
LARm-Fears 123C;
Phi-Ziegler 106R, Ferrante 101C

Cle 7 14 2 7 **30**
Pit 3 0 7 7 17
Cle D15 R39/191 P(17-10-0) 75
Pit D19 R42/214 P(20-10-1) 131

SUNDAY, OCTOBER 8

ChiC 0 0 6 0 6
ChiB 0 14 6 7 **27**
ChiC D7 R22/66 P(18-6-1) 69
ChiB D23 R56/241 P(15-9-2) 93

NYY 3 14 20 7 **44**
GB 3 0 21 7 31
NYY D17 R38/190 P(24-10-2) 210
GB D23 R40/312 P(31-9-3) 101
GB-Grimes 167R

NYG 0 7 7 7 **21**
Was 7 7 0 3 17
NYG D15 R?/120 P(18-7-0) 168
Was D18 R?/155 P(15-7-1) 105

SF 0 0 7 0 7
Det 3 7 7 7 **24**
SF D14 R30/59 P(32-15-4) 141
Det D12 R32/92 P(33-15-0) 205

THURSDAY, OCTOBER 12

SF 10 0 7 7 24
NYY 0 15 0 14 **29**
SF D14 R26/109 P(34-22-2) 254
NYY D17 R28/109 P(35-18-3) 280
SF-Cason 124C

SUNDAY, OCTOBER 15

ChiC 10 7 7 0 24
Cle 7 3 7 17 **34**
ChiC D15 R27/137 P(28-8-2) 126
Cle D21 R31/43 P(36-22-3) 369
Cle-Lavelli 131C, Speedie 106C,
Graham 369P

GB 7 0 0 7 14
ChiB 0 7 14 7 **28**
GB D11 R40/171 P(23-8-1) 80
ChiB D13 R40/128 P(19-10-0) 87

LARm 6 0 14 10 **30**
Det 7 0 7 14 28
LARm D23 R33/68 P(46-24-3) 354
Det D12 R30/58 P(34-13-2) 204

Phi 7 0 7 10 **24**
Bal 7 7 0 0 14
Phi D28 R64/254 P(25-12-3) 206
Bal D6 R19/65 P(21-4-1) 160
Phi-Ledbetter 107R, Ferrante 103C;
Bal-Stone 156C

Pit 7 3 0 7 **17**
NYG 0 0 6 0 6
Pit D17 R49/150 P(19-10-2) 178
NYG D12 R37/97 P(19-9-2) 76

THURSDAY, OCTOBER 19

GB 0 10 7 0 17
NYY 14 7 7 7 **35**
GB D14 R32/147 P(39-16-3) 240
NYY D16 R35/106 P(23-12-2) 244
GB-Baldwin 106C

SUNDAY, OCTOBER 22

Bal 13 0 7 7 27
LARm 21 14 14 21 **70**
Bal D25 R41/143 P(39-16-4) 280
LARm D28 R36/188 P(25-17-3) 347

ChiC 10 28 0 0 **38**
Was 7 7 7 7 28
ChiC D18 R38/140 P(30-14-2) 289
Was D21 R27/125 P(33-17-3) 275

Cle 0 13 0 0 13
NYG 3 0 7 7 **17**
Cle D16 R32/83 P(18-10-3) 47
NYG D18 R56/211 P(12-2-1) 6
NYG-Scott 121C

Det 0 7 14 6 27
SF 14 7 7 0 **28**
Det D17 R30/138 P(36-14-3) 189
SF D18 R47/190 P(21-14-1) 105

Phi 0 0 7 10 **17**
Pit 0 0 10 0 10
Phi D17 R48/187 P(19-12-1) 175
Pit D13 R29/101 P(26-7-5) 205
Phi-Ferrante 118C

SUNDAY, OCTOBER 29

Bal 0 7 0 7 14
SF 0 0 7 10 **17**
Bal D14 R21/21 P(45-22-4) 271
SF D20 R56/269 P(16-7-3) 43
Bal-Crisler 117C; SF-Perry 142R

ChiB 13 0 14 0 27
NYY 7 14 0 17 **38**
ChiB D25 R30/108 P(46-22-6) 364
NYY D15 R40/191 P(19-10-1) 276
ChiB-Kavanaugh 177C, Lujack 331P

Det 3 7 7 7 24
LARm 7 17 41 0 **65**
Det D11 R31/65 P(29-13-3) 148
LARm D20 R32/67 P(28-20-0) 427
Det-Greene 124C;
LARm-Smith 109C,
Van Brocklin 293P

NYG 0 3 0 0 3
ChiC 0 0 14 3 **17**
NYG D10 R37/98 P(20-8-1) 73
ChiC D16 R47/194 P(23-14-1) 110

Pit 0 0 0 7 7
Cle 7 10 14 14 **45**
Pit D19 R40/129 P(36-13-6) 220
Cle D22 R44/338 P(10-6-0) 195
Cle-Motley 188R

Was 3 0 0 0 3
Phi 0 14 0 21 **35**
Was D13 R33/237 P(24-8-3) 54
Phi D18 R41/222 P(26-9-1) 186
Was-Dudley 101R

SUNDAY, NOVEMBER 5

ChiB 14 7 0 14 **35**
Det 0 7 0 14 21
ChiB D25 R60/324 P(13-8-1) 131
Det D24 R23/93 P(45-23-1) 374
Det-Hart 154C, Walker 116C,
Layne 374P

Cle 10 0 0 0 **10**
ChiC 0 0 0 7 7
Cle D16 R53/237 P(21-10-2) 114
ChiC D12 R24/73 P(25-13-4) 194
ChiC-Shaw 111C

GB 7 7 7 0 21
Bal 7 0 27 7 **41**
GB D13 R32/118 P(35-15-5) 171
Bal D19 R38/229 P(31-14-3) 277
Bal-Spavital 176R

Pit 3 3 3 0 **9**
Phi 3 3 0 0 6
Pit D13 R55/207 P(11-1-1) 10
Phi D19 R41/112 P(27-12-5) 146
Pit-Geri 113R

Was 0 7 14 0 21
NYG 7 0 7 10 **24**
Was D13 R42/130 P(17-9-0) 106
NYG D16 R38/126 P(25-13-0) 131

SUNDAY, NOVEMBER 12

Bal 0 0 7 0 7
Pit 10 7 0 0 **17**
Bal D20 R31/110 P(44-25-1) 206
Pit D15 R40/133 P(17-8-0) 96

ChiC 0 7 7 7 21
NYG 3 21 13 14 **51**
ChiC D18 R27/95 P(38-18-3) 231
NYG D22 R44/309 P(22-11-1) 243
NYG-Roberts 218R

LARm 3 21 14 7 **45**
GB 0 0 14 0 14
LARm D13 R30/87 P(39-15-3) 283
GB D17 R30/97 P(43-11-5) 200
LARm-Fears 128C

NYY 7 7 0 6 20
ChiB 7 0 7 14 **28**
NYY D18 R32/93 P(29-13-1) 225
ChiB D20 R54/236 P(19-10-2) 120
ChiB-Hunsinger 119R

Phi 3 7 13 10 **33**
Was 0 0 0 0 0
Phi D21 R53/267 P(24-11-3) 207
Was D6 R28/85 P(19-6-5) 42
Phi-Van Buren 108R

SF 7 7 0 0 14
Cle 7 7 3 17 **34**
SF D14 R37/123 P(22-11-3) 168
Cle D16 R46/155 P(20-7-0) 74
SF-Loyd 102C; Cle-Motley 114R

SUNDAY, NOVEMBER 19

ChiC 0 0 14 0 **14**
Phi 7 3 0 0 10
ChiC D16 R40/190 P(26-12-1) 133
Phi D16 R46/203 P(18-9-1) 89
Phi-Ziegler 113R

GB 0 14 0 7 21
Det 0 10 7 7 **24**
GB D16 R34/125 P(31-15-4) 184
Det D19 R30/135 P(36-15-4) 241

LARm 7 9 10 17 **43**
NYY 0 7 21 7 35
LARm D32 R38/266 P(49-28-2) 370
NYY D25 R28/185 P(39-19-6) 312
LARm-Hoerner 129R, Hirsch 157C;
NYY-Weiner 137C

NYG 0 7 21 27 **55**
Bal 6 14 0 0 20
NYG D25 R56/423 P(11-6-3) 55
Bal D12 R31/96 P(34-19-2) 209
NYG-Price 145R

SF 0 0 0 0 0
ChiB 0 7 0 10 **17**
SF D12 R29/129 P(27-13-2) 141
ChiB D19 R62/257 P(21-4-1) 105

Was 0 7 0 7 14
Cle 0 3 0 17 **20**
Was D18 R30/93 P(31-20-2) 171
Cle D19 R53/258 P(13-6-2) 65
Cle-Motley 178R

THURSDAY, NOVEMBER 23

Pit 7 7 7 7 **28**
ChiC 3 0 0 14 17
Pit D19 R58/220 P(8-5-0) 131
ChiC D16 R26/114 P(31-15-2) 169
Pit-Geri 101R

NYY 0 7 0 7 14
Det 14 7 14 14 **49**
NYY D18 R20/85 P(48-26-2) 356
Det D25 R40/377 P(25-13-2) 214
Det-Hoernschemeyer 198R,
Box 123C

SUNDAY, NOVEMBER 26

Bal 7 0 7 14 28
Was 0 17 7 14 **38**
Bal D16 R21/140 P(42-18-0) 222
Was D23 R37/249 P(36-22-2) 281

LARm 0 0 0 14 14
ChiB 7 3 7 7 **24**
LARm D20 R25/71 P(50-29-2) 263
ChiB D21 R53/188 P(18-10-1) 174
LARm-Hoerner 106C

Phi 3 0 0 0 3
NYG 0 0 0 7 **7**
Phi D17 R57/169 P(20-8-2) 89
NYG D6 R34/134 P(4-2-0) 30
NYG-Clay 101R

SF 7 0 14 0 21
GB 7 6 0 12 **25**
SF D17 R54/184 P(23-9-2) 97
GB D13 R35/134 P(23-11-2) 170

SUNDAY, DECEMBER 3

ChiB 0 7 3 0 10
ChiC 3 7 0 10 **20**
ChiB D14 R43/140 P(18-7-1) 112
ChiC D18 R36/120 P(33-19-0) 255

Det 0 14 17 14 **45**
Bal 0 7 7 7 21
Det D24 R37/193 P(35-19-6) 372
Bal D17 R23/87 P(41-22-3) 224
Det-Box 302C, Layne 341P

GB 0 0 0 7 7
LARm 0 16 21 14 **51**
GB D13 R29/139 P(38-17-3) 85
LARm D31 R23/199 P(47-32-2) 324
LARm-Fears 189C

NYY 0 7 0 7 14
NYG 14 10 14 13 **51**
NYY D12 R21/52 P(39-18-2) 169
NYG D24 R48/377 P(19-11-1) 222
NYG-Price 156R

Phi 0 0 0 0 0
Cle 7 3 3 0 **13**
Phi D10 R42/86 P(23-8-2) 81
Cle D1 R41/69 P(0-0-0) 0

Was 7 10 0 7 **24**
Pit 0 0 0 0 0
Was D12 R33/83 P(23-13-1) 167
Pit D12 R33/119 P(31-8-7) 124

SUNDAY, DECEMBER 10

Bal 0 14 0 0 14
NYY 14 7 14 16 **51**
Bal D14 R24/31 P(43-18-4) 250
NYY D25 R50/343 P(24-11-2) 187
Bal-Salata 155C

ChiC 7 0 0 0 7
Pit 0 14 7 7 **28**
ChiC D19 R28/93 P(44-21-5) 274
Pit D17 R37/197 P(22-9-2) 211
ChiC-Shaw 128C

Cle 0 14 14 17 **45**
Was 7 7 7 0 21
Cle D23 R29/156 P(32-23-1) 321
Was D16 R38/160 P(22-8-3) 118
Cle-Jones 161C, Graham 321P

Det 0 0 3 0 3
ChiB 3 0 3 0 **6**
Det D13 R32/84 P(45-16-1) 166
ChiB D14 R37/135 P(37-13-3) 145

GB 0 0 0 0 0
SF 10 14 0 6 **30**
GB D14 R15/31 P(38-20-2) 291
SF D19 R35/223 P(33-17-1) 197
SF-Perry 135R

NYG 9 0 0 0 **9**
Phi 0 7 0 0 7
NYG D9 R41/138 P(11-5-0) 66
Phi D15 R44/106 P(23-11-4) 156
NYG-Price 103R

1951 NFL

FRIDAY, SEPTEMBER 28

NYY 0 7 0 7 14
LARm 21 13 7 13 **54**
NYY D13 R34/103 P(35-10-0) 8
LARm D34 R29/181 P(42-27-3) 541
LARm-Fears 162C, Hirsch 173C,
Smith 103C, Van Brocklin 554P

SUNDAY, SEPTEMBER 30

ChiB 10 7 7 7 **31**
GB 0 6 7 7 20
ChiB D22 R50/177 P(21-13-1) 152
GB D17 R21/68 P(41-22-2) 214

Cle 7 0 3 0 10
SF 7 3 7 7 **24**
Cle D11 R19/55 P(30-18-2) 172
SF D18 R48/237 P(17-10-1) 107
Cle-Jones 143C; SF-Lillywhite 145R

Phi 0 10 7 0 **17**
ChiC 0 0 7 7 14
Phi D12 R?/112 P(16-5-3) 109
ChiC D12 R?/138 P(16-8-2) 109

Was 3 7 7 0 17
Det 7 7 7 14 **35**
Was D18 R?/187 P(19-7-0) 99
Det D30 R?/205 P(26-20-0) 310
Det-Swiacki 127C, Layne 310P

MONDAY, OCTOBER 1

NYG 3 7 3 0 13
Pit 3 7 3 0 13
NYG D11 R33/170 P(18-9-1) 133
Pit D12 R40/96 P(22-10-3) 155

SATURDAY, OCTOBER 6

SF 7 0 0 7 14
Phi 7 0 7 7 **21**
SF D14 R37/174 P(24-11-2) 89
Phi D13 R34/97 P(28-14-2) 228

SUNDAY, OCTOBER 7

ChiB 0 0 7 7 14
ChiC 0 14 14 0 **28**
ChiB D19 R?/59 P(45-21-5) 262
ChiC D15 R?/216 P(24-11-1) 144

Cle 7 0 21 10 **38**
LARm 10 0 7 6 23
Cle D26 R49/293 P(19-10-2) 157
LARm D18 R28/88 P(33-12-3) 224
Cle-Jones 110R, Motley 106R

NYG 14 7 7 7 **35**
Was 0 7 0 7 14
NYG D20 R?/123 P(27-13-4) 153
Was D18 R?/127 P(26-13-4) 148

Pit 0 23 10 0 33
GB 21 7 0 7 **35**
Pit D16 R46/151 P(20-8-1) 96
GB D17 R45/141 P(24-12-2) 252

MONDAY, OCTOBER 8

NYY 10 0 0 0 10
Det 10 7 0 20 **37**
NYY D18 R?/107 P(44-14-2) 151
Det D16 R?/159 P(26-9-0) 148

SUNDAY, OCTOBER 14

ChiC 0 17 0 0 17
NYG 7 7 0 14 **28**
ChiC D17 R?/96 P(41-19-2) 187
NYG D16 R?/179 P(22-8-5) 90
NYG-Price 107R

LARm 10 7 10 0 **27**
Det 0 14 0 7 21
LARm D20 R32/150 P(32-16-1) 272
Det D14 R39/127 P(20-6-4) 70
LARm-Hirsch 147C

NYY 0 0 0 21 21
ChiB 3 7 0 14 **24**
NYY D17 R?/191 P(26-10-1) 130
ChiB D21 R?/311 P(24-8-0) 141

Phi 0 7 3 14 24
GB 7 0 10 20 **37**
Phi D16 R38/66 P(32-14-3) 184
GB D20 R37/111 P(33-14-1) 197

SF 7 0 21 0 **28**
Pit 0 10 0 14 24
SF D18 R38/158 P(30-18-2) 216
Pit D20 R44/134 P(22-12-2) 192
SF-Soltau 120C

Was 0 0 0 0 0
Cle 7 7 17 14 **45**
Was D15 R42/105 P(22-12-3) 150
Cle D21 R39/192 P(19-11-0) 184

SUNDAY, OCTOBER 21

ChiC 0 0 3 0 3
Was 0 7 0 0 **7**
ChiC D22 R?/231 P(29-13-2) 134
Was D14 R?/232 P(7-3-1) 58
Was-Goode 104R

LARm 0 0 7 21 **28**
GB 0 0 0 0 0
LARm D21 R50/323 P(25-10-1) 173
GB D15 R20/77 P(50-22-1) 230
LARm-Towler 144R, Hirsch 111C

NYY 0 10 7 7 24
Det 3 7 14 0 24
NYY D19 R?/64 P(33-14-0) 178
Det D24 R?/81 P(45-21-2) 326
Det-Dibble 125C, Layne 306P

Phi 7 10 0 7 24
NYG 0 0 23 3 **26**
Phi D13 R?/49 P(28-14-3) 195
NYG D16 R?/157 P(20-11-3) 95
Phi-Walston 118C; NYG-Price 101R

Pit 0 0 0 0 0
Cle 0 10 7 0 **17**
Pit D12 R36/105 P(32-11-2) 96
Cle D17 R46/197 P(15-9-1) 46
Cle-Cole 126R

SF 0 0 0 7 7
ChiB 6 0 7 0 **13**
SF D18 R31/70 P(31-15-3) 174
ChiB D16 R48/247 P(21-8-2) 134
SF-Soltau 109C; ChiB-Dottley 112R

SUNDAY, OCTOBER 28

ChiB 0 14 7 7 **28**
Det 0 7 14 2 23
ChiB D17 R48/141 P(17-9-1) 243
Det D19 R27/119 P(31-15-3) 299
ChiB-Dottley 105R; Det-Doran 140C

GB 0 6 0 23 **29**
NYY 14 7 0 6 27
GB D18 R16/64 P(45-21-3) 276
NYY D17 R35/99 P(27-14-2) 319
GB-Girard 130C; NYY-Celeri 319P

LARm 3 7 7 0 17
SF 10 28 0 6 **44**
LARm D23 R34/131 P(46-20-6) 240
SF D19 R43/194 P(12-8-0) 127
LARm-Hirsch 163C; SF-Soltau 132C

NYG 7 6 0 0 13
Cle 14 0 0 0 **14**
NYG D13 R38/110 P(14-9-2) 86
Cle D15 R33/51 P(24-16-3) 184
Cle-Jones 116C

Pit 0 7 0 21 **28**
ChiC 0 0 14 0 14
Pit D11 R31/128 P(18-7-1) 159
ChiC D23 R45/165 P(40-22-6) 227

Was 0 14 3 10 **27**
Phi 3 7 7 6 23
Was D19 R57/211 P(17-8-0) 203
Phi D15 R37/123 P(21-6-3) 152
Was-Goode 123R

SUNDAY, NOVEMBER 4

ChiB 3 14 7 3 **27**
Was 0 0 0 0 0
ChiB D21 R53/303 P(15-5-0) 89
Was D10 R32/80 P(19-7-3) 95

Cle 14 10 7 3 **34**
ChiC 7 3 0 7 17
Cle D25 R44/238 P(21-15-0) 174
ChiC D25 R28/91 P(29-17-1) 227
Cle-Carpenter 118R;
ChiC-Polsfoot 129C

Det 0 3 7 14 **24**
GB 3 0 0 14 17
Det D16 R44/196 P(16-7-2) 151
GB D18 R27/42 P(44-28-0) 213

NYY 7 7 10 7 31
NYG 13 10 7 7 **37**
NYY D24 R24/71 P(48-20-2) 215
NYG D12 R33/54 P(24-14-3) 235
NYY-Edwards 105C

Phi 0 14 13 7 **34**
Pit 3 7 3 0 13
Phi D15 R40/119 P(16-8-2) 123
Pit D14 R37/119 P(27-6-1) 68

SF 0 7 6 3 16
LARm 10 3 0 10 **23**
SF D15 R49/234 P(16-5-2) 19
LARm D16 R43/155 P(25-12-2) 202
SF-Perry 115R; LARm-Hirsch 103C

SUNDAY, NOVEMBER 11

ChiC 7 0 0 14 21
LARm 0 7 28 10 **45**
ChiC D16 R39/128 P(24-9-3) 214
LARm D23 R38/237 P(25-13-1) 281
LARm-Towler 109R, Hirsch 195C

Det 7 17 7 10 **41**
ChiB 0 7 7 14 28
Det D24 R33/177 P(32-16-1) 259
ChiB D21 R33/94 P(32-19-3) 283
Det-Layne 259P

GB 0 0 0 7 7
Pit 14 7 0 7 **28**
GB D16 R22/59 P(29-18-4) 159
Pit D21 R51/176 P(21-11-3) 148

NYY 0 14 0 0 14
SF 7 0 3 9 **19**
NYY D12 R34/106 P(25-10-2) 139
SF D23 R48/245 P(28-19-2) 223

Phi 3 7 7 0 17
Cle 0 0 10 10 **20**
Phi D23 R52/234 P(26-8-2) 76
Cle D10 R22/18 P(30-14-1) 186

Was 0 7 0 7 14
NYG 14 0 7 7 **28**
Was D13 R34/56 P(35-14-6) 247
NYG D16 R47/199 P(15-9-2) 91

SUNDAY, NOVEMBER 18

ChiC 7 17 3 0 **27**
SF 7 0 7 7 21
ChiC D17 R45/248 P(16-8-1) 189
SF D26 R43/231 P(29-13-2) 148
SF-Soltau 110C

Cle 10 0 0 0 **10**
NYG 0 0 0 0 0
Cle D6 R29/56 P(18-8-3) 127
NYG D11 R40/98 P(23-13-1) 101

Det 0 7 14 7 **28**
Phi 3 7 0 0 10
Det D20 R38/242 P(28-11-3) 161
Phi D20 R44/102 P(29-13-3) 123
Det-Hoernschemeyer 118R

GB 0 13 0 0 13
ChiB 3 7 7 7 **24**
GB D18 R24/173 P(33-10-2) 67
ChiB D25 R56/256 P(22-10-1) 167
GB-Rote 150R; ChiB-Dottley 117R

NYY 0 21 0 0 21
LARm 20 14 0 14 **48**
NYY D24 R24/224 P(43-19-2) 255
LARm D24 R44/371 P(23-12-1) 203
NYY-Taliaferro 166R;
LARm-Towler 155R

Was 0 6 3 13 **22**
Pit 0 7 0 0 7
Was D19 R64/271 P(10-5-2) 50
Pit D5 R22/70 P(22-3-0) 45
Was-Goode 108R

THURSDAY, NOVEMBER 22

GB 14 7 7 7 35
Det 10 21 21 0 **52**
GB D20 R28/179 P(40-17-3) 279
Det D19 R25/172 P(40-21-1) 306
GB-Rote 131R, Pelfrey 103C;
Det-Layne 296P

SUNDAY, NOVEMBER 25

Pit 10 7 0 0 **17**
Phi 0 6 0 7 13
Pit D17 R38/156 P(29-13-3) 167
Phi D18 R46/164 P(28-11-4) 136

ChiB 0 0 7 14 21
Cle 0 14 14 14 **42**
ChiB D22 R30/74 P(41-15-2) 163
Cle D22 R34/273 P(19-12-1) 243
Cle-Jones 116R, Speedie 144C

LARm 7 0 0 14 21
Was 7 14 10 0 **31**
LARm D23 R28/61 P(43-22-2) 315
Was D26 R65/352 P(12-7-1) 117
LARm-Hirsch 104C;
Was-Goode 148R

NYG 0 10 0 0 **10**
ChiC 0 0 0 0 0
NYG D7 R46/107 P(10-4-1) 46
ChiC D13 R36/65 P(28-12-0) 87

SF 7 3 0 0 10
NYY 0 0 0 10 10
SF D22 R53/234 P(24-14-1) 103
NYY D14 R31/134 P(28-12-4) 149

SUNDAY, DECEMBER 2

ChiC 0 0 14 14 28
Cle 14 14 14 7 **49**
ChiC D22 R29/156 P(37-19-3) 192
Cle D20 R29/79 P(29-14-3) 191
Cle-Graham 217P

LARm 7 14 7 14 **42**
ChiB 17 0 0 0 17
LARm D25 R27/206 P(19-13-0) 290
ChiB D24 R56/266 P(26-10-0) 85
LARm-Hirsch 106C

NYY 0 7 3 21 **31**
GB 7 0 14 7 28
NYY D18 R22/83 P(43-20-3) 288
GB D23 R31/195 P(42-21-5) 242
NYY-Edwards 124C

Phi 14 7 7 7 **35**
Was 0 7 7 7 21
Phi D32 R64/307 P(13-9-0) 103
Was D17 R33/181 P(18-7-0) 94
Phi-Ziegler 136R; Was-Goode 100R

Pit 0 0 0 0 0
NYG 0 7 0 7 **14**
Pit D14 R32/79 P(39-14-3) 120
NYG D10 R49/137 P(12-4-2) 34

SF 6 0 7 7 **20**
Det 0 3 7 0 10
SF D20 R52/200 P(22-12-1) 158
Det D11 R23/78 P(36-12-2) 102
SF-Perry 126R

SUNDAY, DECEMBER 9

ChiB 3 21 14 7 **45**
NYY 0 7 7 7 21
ChiB D30 R60/336 P(23-13-1) 149
NYY D20 R25/112 P(31-16-1) 248

Cle 0 21 0 7 **28**
Pit 0 0 0 0 0
Cle D15 R39/160 P(18-12-0) 91
Pit D13 R27/91 P(32-16-2) 118

Det 0 10 7 7 **24**
LARm 3 6 7 6 22
Det D19 R39/163 P(16-7-2) 91
LARm D27 R47/156 P(33-17-0) 247

GB 3 10 6 0 19
SF 3 7 7 14 **31**
GB D16 R21/42 P(41-19-4) 145
SF D27 R53/302 P(19-14-2) 105
SF-Arenas 108R

NYG 0 10 7 6 **23**
Phi 0 7 0 0 7
NYG D9 R48/213 P(16-4-1) 52
Phi D14 R41/124 P(23-9-4) 83
NYG-Price 171R

Was 10 0 0 10 **20**
ChiC 7 7 0 3 17
Was D21 R54/231 P(15-8-1) 103
ChiC D19 R31/156 P(19-10-0) 178
Was-Goode 108R;
ChiC-Polsfoot 121C

SUNDAY, DECEMBER 16

ChiC 0 0 10 14 **24**
ChiB 0 7 7 0 14
ChiC D23 R38/273 P(31-13-3) 135
ChiB D18 R35/144 P(28-12-4) 254
ChiC-Trippi 145R;
ChiB-Schroeder 150C

Cle 7 3 7 7 **24**
Phi 0 0 2 7 9
Cle D15 R32/96 P(29-12-1) 147
Phi D9 R30/65 P(24-9-0) 8

Det 3 7 7 0 17
SF 0 14 0 7 **21**
Det D19 R41/122 P(35-13-4) 209
SF D17 R28/87 P(29-15-1) 178

GB 7 7 0 0 14
LARm 14 0 14 14 **42**
GB D20 R21/45 P(56-27-2) 358
LARm D18 R26/151 P(27-15-2) 245
GB-Mann 123C, Rote 335P;
LARm-Towler 102R, Hirsch 146C,
Waterfield 204P

NYG 3 14 7 3 **27**
NYY 3 7 0 7 17
NYG D10 R45/166 P(9-3-1) 71
NYY D15 R20/43 P(45-13-8) 331
NYG-Price 138R

Pit 0 0 0 20 **20**
Was 3 7 0 0 10
Pit D17 R21/123 P(46-19-5) 288
Was D9 R32/118 P(26-8-4) 97
Pit-Minarik 121C; Was-Goode 107R

1952 NFL

SUNDAY, SEPTEMBER 28

ChiB 3 0 7 14 **24**
GB 0 7 0 7 14
ChiB D19 R35/141 P(33-17-1) 237
GB D11 R31/110 P(17-7-1) 100

Det 0 3 0 0 3
SF 7 0 7 3 **17**
Det D13 R26/98 P(32-16-3) 149
SF D19 R42/160 P(27-16-1) 164

LARm 0 0 0 7 7
Cle 10 13 7 7 **37**
LARm D11 R22/100 P(27-6-3) 58
Cle D23 R46/291 P(16-10-1) 128
Cle-Carpenter 145R

NYG 7 3 7 7 **24**
DalT 6 0 0 0 6
NYG D17 R43/259 P(15-7-0) 78
DalT D16 R27/132 P(29-13-0) 74
NYG-Price 130R

Phi 14 3 7 7 **31**
Pit 0 12 0 13 25
Phi D18 R40/119 P(27-16-0) 275
Pit D20 R36/130 P(24-13-2) 190
Phi-Grant 135C

MONDAY, SEPTEMBER 29

Was 3 14 0 6 **23**
ChiC 0 0 7 0 7
Was D21 R59/196 P(17-11-1) 87
ChiC D7 R30/86 P(12-4-1) 18

FRIDAY, OCTOBER 3

Det 0 14 3 0 **17**
LARm 0 7 7 0 14
Det D22 R44/166 P(37-18-4) 195
LARm D12 R23/39 P(25-10-3) 157

SATURDAY, OCTOBER 4

Cle 7 0 14 0 **21**
Pit 6 7 7 0 20
Cle D19 R27/58 P(49-21-4) 401
Pit D15 R31/75 P(34-12-0) 183
Cle-Graham 401P

NYG 7 14 7 3 **31**
Phi 7 0 0 0 7
NYG D15 R39/208 P(26-10-1) 108
Phi D13 R31/129 P(28-12-3) 161
NYG-Price 119R

SUNDAY, OCTOBER 5

ChiB 0 10 0 0 10
ChiC 0 7 0 14 **21**
ChiB D17 R41/155 P(28-10-3) 142
ChiC D13 R40/165 P(19-7-1) 51
ChiB-Dottley 121R

SF 14 3 0 20 **37**
DalT 0 7 0 7 14
SF D18 R38/273 P(27-14-2) 227
DalT D10 R33/157 P(23-6-1) 26
SF-McElhenny 170R

Was 7 0 7 6 20
GB 7 14 7 7 **35**
Was D15 R36/153 P(20-9-1) 125
GB D16 R36/178 P(16-8-1) 242
GB-Howton 128C

SUNDAY, OCTOBER 12

ChiC 7 0 0 10 **17**
Was 0 0 6 0 6
ChiC D18 R45/211 P(22-12-2) 95
Was D13 R37/110 P(26-13-1) 77

DalT 0 7 0 13 20
ChiB 14 17 7 0 **38**
DalT D14 R38/138 P(20-8-2) 139
ChiB D23 R43/272 P(24-13-2) 123

LARm 0 6 0 24 **30**
GB 7 7 14 0 28
LARm D22 R29/158 P(27-15-2) 147
GB D20 R46/189 P(18-12-1) 219
GB-Rote 106R, Howton 156C

NYG 0 7 0 10 **17**
Cle 0 3 6 0 9
NYG D12 R48/201 P(9-4-2) 86
Cle D10 R23/21 P(35-14-1) 190
Cle-Speedie 161C

Pit 0 7 7 7 21
Phi 3 10 0 13 **26**
Pit D8 R27/38 P(25-9-3) 140
Phi D14 R38/113 P(34-11-1) 188
Phi-Grant 111C

SF 0 14 7 7 **28**
Det 0 0 0 0 0
SF D21 R52/179 P(24-16-0) 86
Det D4 R17/40 P(26-8-2) 25

SATURDAY, OCTOBER 18

GB 7 0 10 7 **24**
DalT 0 14 0 0 14
GB D19 R45/187 P(30-15-1) 131
DalT D12 R20/86 P(29-10-2) 146
DalT-Taliaferro 129C

SUNDAY, OCTOBER 19

ChiC 3 14 0 7 **24**
NYG 7 7 7 2 23
ChiC D17 R53/155 P(18-11-2) 161
NYG D10 R33/92 P(24-9-2) 146

Cle 14 7 21 7 **49**
Phi 0 0 0 7 7
Cle D28 R46/234 P(31-19-2) 273
Phi D11 R21/45 P(41-13-2) 117
Cle-Jones 121C, Graham 290P

LARm 6 7 3 0 16
Det 0 7 14 3 **24**
LARm D16 R31/91 P(29-17-4) 194
Det D14 R31/80 P(31-15-4) 193
LARm-Carey 132C

SF 14 7 10 9 **40**
ChiB 2 7 0 7 16
SF D26 R51/237 P(20-12-1) 183
ChiB D10 R27/99 P(25-7-2) 92
SF-McElhenny 103R, Soltau 107C;
ChiB-Schroeder 115C

Was 14 0 7 7 **28**
Pit 7 10 0 7 24
Was D14 R44/137 P(16-8-2) 133
Pit D19 R42/188 P(26-10-0) 123
Was-Taylor 111C

SUNDAY, OCTOBER 26

ChiB 0 7 0 0 7
LARm 3 0 0 28 **31**
ChiB D12 R37/1 P(25-12-2) 158
LARm D19 R43/201 P(25-15-2) 173
LARm-Towler 134R

DalT 0 7 0 14 21
SF 14 13 7 14 **48**
DalT D15 R31/112 P(28-10-2) 122
SF D15 R24/263 P(25-13-1) 71

Det 14 14 14 10 **52**
GB 7 3 7 0 17
Det D21 R39/162 P(22-12-1) 216
GB D21 R21/53 P(45-26-5) 352
GB-Howton 151C

Phi 0 14 0 0 **14**
NYG 3 0 7 0 10
Phi D15 R42/105 P(24-11-0) 120
NYG D12 R34/54 P(28-17-0) 55

Pit 0 20 7 7 **34**
ChiC 0 0 7 21 28
Pit D13 R36/114 P(26-15-1) 199
ChiC D19 R47/209 P(24-9-0) 208
ChiC-Matson 121C

Was 0 13 0 2 15
Cle 3 3 3 10 **19**
Was D23 R48/220 P(21-10-0) 106
Cle D16 R25/84 P(30-11-1) 152

SUNDAY, NOVEMBER 2

ChiB 0 10 0 10 **20**
SF 3 7 7 0 17
ChiB D13 R36/117 P(24-8-0) 89
SF D14 R33/170 P(28-16-1) 147

Cle 3 0 3 0 6
Det 0 10 0 7 **17**
Cle D15 R26/107 P(32-13-3) 107
Det D20 R38/142 P(34-15-3) 161
Det-Hart 109C

DalT 0 0 6 14 20
LARm 14 21 7 0 **42**
DalT D17 R39/146 P(26-8-2) 106
LARm D17 R31/173 P(28-14-4) 259
LARm-Towler 111R, Fears 112C

NYG 7 14 0 7 **28**
ChiC 6 0 0 0 6
NYG D9 R44/150 P(16-6-3) 108
ChiC D17 R34/164 P(36-13-6) 147
NYG-Price 116R

Phi 3 0 0 7 10
GB 6 0 0 6 **12**
Phi D9 R33/56 P(31-7-2) 18
GB D13 R45/137 P(34-10-2) 116

Pit 7 10 7 0 **24**
Was 7 0 0 16 23
Pit D12 R31/134 P(18-7-2) 41
Was D22 R38/159 P(24-15-2) 230
Was-Taylor 139C

SUNDAY, NOVEMBER 9

ChiC 6 7 0 0 13
Cle 7 7 14 0 **28**
ChiC D12 R37/180 P(20-5-1) 15
Cle D22 R38/184 P(28-19-1) 239
Cle-Speedie 157C

Det 3 7 7 14 **31**
Pit 0 0 6 0 6
Det D25 R59/321 P(17-4-0) 70
Pit D15 R19/-3 P(35-19-2) 195
Det-Hoernschemeyer 107R

GB 7 10 7 17 **41**
ChiB 7 0 7 14 28
GB D19 R46/218 P(25-15-1) 172
ChiB D12 R25/75 P(27-11-1) 89

LARm 3 7 3 14 **27**
DalT 0 6 0 0 6
LARm D10 R37/174 P(17-5-3) -5
DalT D13 R41/174 P(26-12-6) 33

SF 7 0 0 7 14
NYG 0 10 10 3 **23**
SF D16 R21/37 P(35-18-4) 303
NYG D17 R47/189 P(22-12-0) 158
SF-McElhenny 118C, Soltau 196C,
Tittle 341P; NYG-Price 106R

Was 0 7 6 7 20
Phi 14 14 7 3 **38**
Was D15 R36/120 P(23-12-2) 126
Phi D23 R46/213 P(27-12-0) 156

SUNDAY, NOVEMBER 16

ChiC 0 7 0 0 7
Phi 0 10 0 0 **10**
ChiC D20 R48/132 P(31-16-0) 94
Phi D8 R23/66 P(22-11-3) 117

DalT 0 0 13 0 13
Det 10 19 0 14 **43**
DalT D11 R29/68 P(32-13-4) 98
Det D15 R32/158 P(25-11-3) 214

GB 0 7 7 3 **17**
NYG 0 3 0 0 3
GB D9 R37/90 P(14-6-0) 31
NYG D13 R40/139 P(31-10-3) 47

LARm 10 7 16 7 **40**
ChiB 3 7 0 14 24
LARm D15 R34/165 P(27-15-1) 351
ChiB D22 R35/196 P(35-13-3) 113
LARm-Hirsch 191C,
Van Brocklin 308P

Pit 0 0 14 14 28
Cle 9 6 7 7 **29**
Pit D18 R16/50 P(48-21-2) 329
Cle D25 R43/201 P(41-21-2) 209
Pit-Mathews 126C, Nickel 120C,
Finks 296P; Cle-Lavelli 107C

SF 3 0 6 14 **23**
Was 7 7 3 0 17
SF D18 R34/145 P(28-13-2) 172
Was D17 R43/163 P(24-13-2) 127

SUNDAY, NOVEMBER 23

ChiC 0 7 0 7 14
Pit 10 0 0 7 **17**
ChiC D19 R47/184 P(21-9-0) 94
Pit D14 R38/104 P(23-12-3) 122

DalT 7 0 7 0 14
GB 7 14 14 7 **42**
DalT D13 R30/45 P(40-22-4) 108
GB D13 R20/73 P(29-10-5) 227

Det 3 13 0 7 23
ChiB 10 0 7 7 **24**
Det D17 R44/149 P(27-9-3) 110
ChiB D18 R37/179 P(33-11-0) 216
ChiB-Stone 148C

NYG 0 0 7 7 **14**
Was 3 0 7 0 10
NYG D15 R35/159 P(19-10-1) 132
Was D18 R31/108 P(30-14-4) 189

Phi 14 0 0 14 **28**
Cle 7 3 10 0 20
Phi D20 R57/176 P(23-9-3) 189
Cle D13 R18/82 P(36-14-2) 227
Phi-Walston 121C;
Cle-Speedie 156C

SF 0 0 0 9 9
LARm 0 7 7 21 **35**
SF D14 R33/111 P(34-12-2) 89
LARm D18 R38/134 P(38-18-2) 256
LARm-Carey 115C

THURSDAY, NOVEMBER 27

GB 3 14 7 0 24
Det 3 21 7 17 **48**
GB D17 R20/103 P(29-14-2) 196
Det D23 R41/132 P(34-19-3) 262
GB-Howton 123C; Det-Box 116C

ChiB 0 2 0 21 23
DalT 0 13 7 7 **27**
ChiB D15 R31/122 P(27-15-4) 195
DalT D22 R38/130 P(27-17-2) 204

SUNDAY, NOVEMBER 30

Cle 7 14 13 14 **48**
Was 14 3 0 7 24
Cle D22 R39/255 P(22-10-4) 193
Was D17 R31/75 P(33-15-2) 122
Cle-Jagade 147R, Lavelli 106C

LARm 7 3 17 7 **34**
SF 0 7 0 14 21
LARm D19 R45/251 P(25-15-2) 137
SF D14 R27/67 P(32-12-3) 141
LARm-Towler 132R

NYG 0 0 7 0 7
Pit 14 14 7 28 **63**
NYG D8 R20/15 P(39-11-7) 147
Pit D20 R35/123 P(31-15-3) 292
Pit-Hensley 154C, Finks 254P

Phi 0 3 12 7 22
ChiC 0 14 14 0 **28**
Phi D21 R28/111 P(45-19-2) 243
ChiC D11 R34/97 P(21-10-1) 81
Phi-Grant 186C

SUNDAY, DECEMBER 7

ChiB 7 7 0 7 21
Det 14 7 10 14 **45**
ChiB D18 R21/37 P(36-14-6) 171
Det D25 R32/116 P(42-25-1) 312
Det-Box 172C, Layne 296P

Cle 7 0 3 0 **10**
ChiC 0 0 0 0 0
Cle D13 R35/157 P(22-14-2) 175
ChiC D9 R29/52 P(31-14-4) 98

DalT 0 7 0 14 21
Phi 17 7 14 0 **38**
DalT D17 R23/77 P(37-17-3) 164
Phi D15 R38/164 P(28-17-2) 227
Phi-Grant 203C

GB 0 14 0 13 27
LARm 7 10 21 7 **45**
GB D23 R36/83 P(32-14-5) 264
LARm D19 R45/167 P(18-13-1) 207
GB-Howton 200C

Pit 7 3 14 0 **24**
SF 7 0 0 0 7
Pit D15 R47/142 P(27-11-0) 133
SF D14 R24/70 P(34-18-5) 232
SF-Boone 116C

Was 0 13 7 7 **27**
NYG 3 7 7 0 17
Was D16 R42/127 P(25-16-2) 238
NYG D9 R26/100 P(24-8-3) 102
Was-Taylor 196C, LeBaron 260P

SATURDAY, DECEMBER 13

DalT 0 0 0 6 6
Det 0 14 10 17 **41**
DalT D12 R32/132 P(35-13-2) 164
Det D20 R39/216 P(35-19-1) 301
Det-Box 202C

SUNDAY, DECEMBER 14

ChiC 0 0 0 7 7
ChiB 3 7 0 0 **10**
ChiC D14 R33/122 P(34-14-4) 149
ChiB D15 R43/149 P(30-10-3) 110
ChiC-Stonesifer 111C

Cle 7 6 7 14 34
NYG 7 6 21 3 **37**
Cle D22 R28/112 P(32-18-3) 272
NYG D18 R33/70 P(27-17-0) 225
Cle-Jagade 103C; NYG-Conerly 184P

GB 0 7 7 0 14
SF 7 7 7 3 **24**
GB D16 R22/64 P(48-24-1) 324
SF D24 R42/193 P(28-17-1) 160
GB-Howton 162C; SF-Perry 109R,
Boone 108C

Phi 7 7 0 7 21
Was 7 7 0 13 **27**
Phi D14 R37/73 P(31-16-1) 154
Was D15 R22/87 P(27-10-2) 180

Pit 0 0 7 7 14
LARm 0 14 7 7 **28**
Pit D18 R26/109 P(48-23-5) 244
LARm D27 R33/158 P(43-24-4) 358
Pit-Nickel 202C; LARm-Fears 122C,
Hirsch 108C

1953 NFL

SUNDAY, SEPTEMBER 27

ChiB 7 0 0 2 9
Bal 0 10 0 3 **13**
ChiB D20 R44/109 P(34-19-4) 225
Bal D9 R37/90 P(20-12-1) 74

Cle 7 10 10 0 **27**
GB 0 0 0 0 0
Cle D19 R32/96 P(26-20-1) 270
GB D12 R31/93 P(27-8-3) 55

NYG 0 0 0 7 7
LARm 0 7 7 7 **21**
NYG D13 R29/104 P(27-11-3) 88
LARm D16 R34/148 P(27-13-2) 186

Phi 7 0 7 7 21
SF 14 3 7 7 **31**
Phi D21 R36/139 P(31-18-1) 171
SF D20 R39/261 P(17-8-2) 122
SF-Perry 145R

Pit 7 7 0 7 21
Det 7 17 7 7 **38**
Pit D18 R25/96 P(41-20-1) 223
Det D20 R31/57 P(37-19-0) 375
Det-Layne 364P

Was 7 0 0 17 **24**
ChiC 7 3 3 0 13
Was D10 R35/135 P(16-5-2) 90
ChiC D17 R28/162 P(37-26-2) 172

FRIDAY, OCTOBER 2

Was 7 7 7 0 21
Phi 7 7 0 7 21
Was D13 R26/85 P(20-9-0) 143
Phi D23 R46/141 P(24-13-4) 174
Was-Taylor 113C

SATURDAY, OCTOBER 3

Det 7 3 17 0 **27**
Bal 7 10 0 0 17
Det D14 R38/197 P(17-6-5) 74
Bal D14 R25/83 P(32-14-2) 203

NYG 7 7 0 0 14
Pit 7 3 0 14 **24**
NYG D8 R27/49 P(30-15-2) 156
Pit D14 R45/106 P(33-13-0) 102

SUNDAY, OCTOBER 4

ChiB 3 7 0 7 **17**
GB 6 7 0 0 13
ChiB D16 R37/81 P(31-12-4) 139
GB D13 R26/82 P(27-11-2) 188
GB-Bailey 100C

Cle 14 6 0 7 **27**
ChiC 7 0 0 0 7
Cle D12 R31/71 P(22-15-0) 272
ChiC D17 R24/111 P(42-16-4) 128
Cle-Lavelli 137C, Graham 310P

LARm 10 10 7 3 30
SF 0 7 14 10 **31**
LARm D21 R34/115 P(34-20-1) 272
SF D21 R32/106 P(32-17-2) 190
LARm-Boyd 107C, Hirsch 107C

SATURDAY, OCTOBER 10

Phi 6 0 7 0 13
Cle 6 14 7 10 **37**
Phi D20 R31/187 P(37-15-3) 228
Cle D20 R21/125 P(31-21-0) 291
Phi-Walston 110C;
Cle-Brewster 122C, Graham 328P

SUNDAY, OCTOBER 11

Bal 0 3 6 7 **16**
ChiB 7 0 0 7 14
Bal D19 R34/111 P(33-14-1) 216
ChiB D15 R32/101 P(26-14-2) 134
Bal-Taliaferro 126C

ChiC 7 14 7 0 28
Pit 0 7 7 17 **31**
ChiC D16 R33/72 P(37-12-4) 161
Pit D24 R31/86 P(44-23-3) 268

LARm 7 14 10 7 **38**
GB 3 7 3 7 20
LARm D16 R28/92 P(31-17-0) 320
GB D18 R28/106 P(38-16-4) 172
LARm-Hirsch 168C; GB-Rush 101C

NYG 2 7 0 0 9
Was 10 0 3 0 **13**
NYG D11 R30/102 P(30-12-5) 37
Was D14 R46/215 P(14-4-2) 94

(continued)

SF   7   7   7   0   **21**
Det 10   7   7   0   **24**
SF   D11 R33/76 P(19-9-3) 59
Det D14 R36/117 P(19-10-3) 174

SATURDAY, OCTOBER 17
Pit   0   0   7   0   **7**
Phi 0   0   6 17   **23**
Pit   D12 R28/54 P(33-16-1) 114
Phi   D17 R35/67 P(38-20-1) 259

SUNDAY, OCTOBER 18
Bal   0   0   7   7   **14**
GB 0 13 14 10   **37**
Bal   D10 R18/65 P(30-10-5) 128
GB   D21 R56/303 P(19-7-2) 34

ChiC 0   0   0   7   **7**
NYG 14 0   7   0   **21**
ChiC D14 R20/-1 P(39-16-2) 156
NYG   D10 R41/64 P(17-10-3) 155
ChiC-Stonesifer 112C

Cle   3 10   0 17   **30**
Was   0   7   0   7   **14**
Cle   D24 R32/197 P(33-16-1) 206
Was   D12 R34/159 P(21-5-1) 87
Cle-Renfro 101R

LARm 7 10   7   7   **31**
Det   0   9 10   0   **19**
LARm D18 R38/183 P(27-12-1) 208
Det   D23 R31/163 P(33-16-2) 263
LARm-Hirsch 103C

SF   7   0 14 14   **35**
ChiB 21   0   0   7   **28**
SF   D20 R42/251 P(31-11-1) 128
ChiB D17 R34/74 P(37-13-1) 191
SF-Perry 113R

SATURDAY, OCTOBER 24
GB   0   0   7   7   **14**
Pit 7 10 14   0   **31**
GB   D11 R16/34 P(39-20-1) 91
Pit   D24 R55/282 P(20-9-1) 69
Pit-Rogel 168R

SUNDAY, OCTOBER 25
ChiB 7   3   0 14   **24**
LARm 3 21 0 14   **38**
ChiB D24 R18/80 P(47-23-4) 296
LARm D19 R39/213 P(26-15-0) 312
ChiB-Dooley 164C, Blanda 334P;
LARm-Towler 154C, Boyd 130C,
Van Brocklin 323P

Cle 0   7   0   0   **7**
NYG   0   0   0   0   **0**
Cle   D12 R48/169 P(5-2-1)   9
NYG   D8 R21/67   P(19-9-3) 66

Det 0   7   0   7   **14**
SF   7   3   0   0   **10**
Det   D13 R30/121 P(21-9-0) 118
SF   D25 R56/227 P(23-11-2) 124
SF-Perry 148R

Phi 7 21   7 21   **56**
ChiC 3   0   0 14   **17**
Phi   D32 R33/205 P(41-25-1) 337
ChiC D12 R20/59 P(37-12-1) 136
Phi-Pihos 156C

Was   7   3   0   7   **17**
Bal 3   7 10   7   **27**
Was   D17 R32/167 P(27-10-4) 129
Bal   D17 R42/214 P(25-9-1) 115

SATURDAY, OCTOBER 31
GB 7 14   7   7   **35**
Bal   7   7   3   7   **24**
GB   D25 R45/231 P(29-12-1) 173
Bal   D11 R33/171 P(15-5-1) 97
GB-Reid 120R

SUNDAY, NOVEMBER 1
ChiB 7   7   0   0   **14**
SF 14   7   0   3   **24**
ChiB D19 R5/29   P(50-30-2) 244
SF   D29 R41/217 P(44-25-2) 278
SF-Soltau 102C, Tittle 304P

Det 10   7   0   7   **24**
LARm 0   9 21   7   **37**
Det   D19 R37/139 P(31-12-4) 116
LARm D14 R33/222 P(22-12-3) 170
LARm-Quinlan 130R

NYG 17 0   0   6   **23**
ChiC 7   3   0 10   **20**
NYG   D9 R33/118 P(23-6-5) 110
ChiC D19 R26/62 P(47-23-4) 249
ChiC-Nagler 124C

Phi 14 7   0 14   **35**
Pit   0   7   0   0   **7**
Phi   D19 R34/166 P(36-22-1) 256
Pit   D15 R21/55 P(49-21-5) 207

Was   0   3   0   0   **3**
Cle 3   3   7 14   **27**
Was   D15 R27/93 P(35-14-4) 205
Cle   D17 R39/190 P(22-14-1) 189

SATURDAY, NOVEMBER 7
Bal   7   0   0   0   **7**
Det 0   7   3   7   **17**
Bal   D14 R37/179 P(15-4-5) 54
Det   D19 R39/180 P(25-11-0) 138
Bal-Huzvar 117R

SUNDAY, NOVEMBER 8
ChiC 7 10   0   0   **17**
Was 7   7   0 14   **28**
ChiC D11 R29/162 P(25-8-2) 79
Was   D18 R48/262 P(17-6-0) 105
Was-Justice 120R

GB   14   0   0   7   **21**
ChiB 7   7   7   0   **21**
GB   D15 R35/94 P(35-19-1) 237
ChiB D17 R30/54 P(45-19-1) 234
GB-Mann 101C

NYG   0   0   0   7   **7**
Phi 3 14   6   7   **30**
NYG   D10 R30/64 P(27-10-2) 28
Phi   D21 R23/54 P(48-24-1) 460
Phi-Pihos 145C, Walston 176C,
Thomason 437P

Pit   9   0   0   7   **16**
Cle 0 24   0 10   **34**
Pit   D22 R39/147 P(46-17-2) 209
Cle   D16 R33/204 P(18-12-2) 218
Pit-Mathews 113C

SF 0 17   7   7   **31**
LARm 3 10   7   7   **27**
SF   D17 R32/113 P(32-18-3) 301
LARm D18 R49/281 P(19-9-1) 52
SF-Tittle 301P; LARm-Quinlan 119R,
Younger 101R

SUNDAY, NOVEMBER 15
Bal   7   0   0   7   **14**
Phi 7 14   0 24   **45**
Bal   D15 R26/53 P(34-18-3) 169
Phi   D21 R28/166 P(41-20-6) 331
Phi-Johnson 100R, Pihos 118C,
Walston 110C, Thomason 329P

ChiB 7   6   7   7   **27**
Was   0 14 10   0   **24**
ChiB D25 R55/237 P(25-10-2) 117
Was   D14 R28/114 P(24-9-2) 177
Was-Taylor 100C

Det 7   0   0   7   **14**
GB   0   7   0   7   **14**
Det   D11 R36/132 P(25-8-4) 163
GB   D19 R29/133 P(46-18-4) 228
Det-Walker 105C

LARm 0 10   7   7   **24**
ChiC 10   0   7   7   **24**
LARm D17 R38/174 P(29-14-3) 117
ChiC D20 R32/200 P(23-14-1) 149

Pit 7   0   0   7   **14**
NYG   0   0   7   3   **10**
Pit   D8 R24/105 P(29-11-1) 142
NYG   D18 R42/107 P(40-19-1) 216

SF   0   7   0 14   **21**
Cle 3   3   3 14   **23**
SF   D18 R27/134 P(27-17-0) 202
Cle   D22 R43/177 P(27-17-0) 280
Cle-Lavelli 137C

SATURDAY, NOVEMBER 21
ChiC 0   0   0   0   **0**
Phi 14 10   7   7   **38**
ChiC D10 R24/58 P(31-8-4) 53
Phi   D27 R43/211 P(40-20-4) 280
Phi-Pihos 113C

SUNDAY, NOVEMBER 22
Cle 7 10   3   0   **20**
Pit   9   0   0   7   **16**
Cle   D13 R23/60 P(29-16-1) 175
Pit   D17 R45/216 P(24-9-2) 72

Det 3   7   7   3   **20**
ChiB 3   6   7   0   **16**
Det   D28 R47/177 P(44-21-0) 240
ChiB D27 R23/110 P(39-16-4) 225

LARm 0   0   7 14   **21**
Bal   7   0   6   0   **13**
LARm D14 R39/303 P(21-12-1) 192
Bal   D12 R42/245 P(21-6-2) 95
LARm-Towler 205R;
Bal-Taliaferro 136R

SF 13   7 10   7   **37**
GB   0   7   0   0   **7**
SF   D20 R44/290 P(18-8-0) 63
GB   D14 R38/184 P(20-8-4) 32
SF-Perry 153R

Was 0   0   7 17   **24**
NYG   0 14   0   7   **21**
Was   D17 R28/75 P(26-13-3) 178
NYG   D25 R50/160 P(26-17-2) 211

THURSDAY, NOVEMBER 26
GB   15   0   0   0   **15**
Det 7   0 14 13   **34**
GB   D13 R48/154 P(13-7-3) 73
Det   D17 R30/210 P(18-8-5) 141
Det-Box 110C

SUNDAY, NOVEMBER 29
ChiC 0   0 14   2   **16**
Cle 0 10   0 17   **27**
ChiC D18 R30/133 P(36-15-0) 241
Cle   D18 R30/115 P(28-19-0) 243
Cle-Renfro 105C

LARm 7   0   7   7   **21**
ChiB 7 14   0   3   **24**
LARm D19 R35/141 P(32-17-0) 215
ChiB D10 R33/126 P(27-12-0) 177
LARm-Fears 104C

Phi   7   7 14   0   **28**
NYG 7   7 13 10   **37**
Phi   D18 R31/174 P(40-17-5) 209
NYG   D20 R37/77 P(31-13-0) 230
Phi-Johnson 121R

SF 14 10 14   0   **38**
Bal   0   0   7 14   **21**
SF   D16 R32/188 P(14-10-1) 180
Bal   D18 R42/160 P(28-11-3) 74
SF-Soltau 123C

Was 0   0 10   7   **17**
Pit   2   0   7   0   **9**
Was   D17 R40/139 P(22-11-1) 77
Pit   D16 R24/43 P(46-24-3) 242

SATURDAY, DECEMBER 5
Bal   0   0   0   2   **2**
LARm 14 17 14   0   **45**
Bal   D6 R24/31   P(31-11-1) 39
LARm D19 R27/118 P(24-15-1) 216

SUNDAY, DECEMBER 6
ChiB 0   0   0   7   **7**
Det 3   0 10   0   **13**
ChiB D13 R25/54 P(42-16-5) 193
Det   D12 R41/172 P(18-7-2) 137

GB   0   7   0   7   **14**
SF 14 17 10   7   **48**
GB   D17 R35/94 P(35-16-5) 190
SF   D15 R32/115 P(21-11-1) 176

NYG   0   7   0   7   **14**
Cle 10 21 24   7   **62**
NYG   D16 R26/74 P(40-16-3) 209
Cle   D20 R29/106 P(32-20-0) 389
NYG-Long 118C; Cle-Brewster 182C

Phi   0   0   0   0   **0**
Was 14 10   7   7   **38**
Phi   D6 R31/66   P(27-7-4) 71
Was   D19 R41/159 P(34-12-4) 116

Pit 0   0   7 14   **21**
ChiC 7   0   3   7   **17**
Pit   D18 R46/147 P(21-11-2) 63
ChiC D14 R24/47 P(24-18-1) 165

SATURDAY, DECEMBER 12
GB   7   0   7   3   **17**
LARm 26 0   7   0   **33**
GB   D11 R37/157 P(24-5-4) 82
LARm D23 R32/158 P(32-17-5) 305
LARm-Hirsch 196C

SUNDAY, DECEMBER 13
Bal   0   7   0   7   **14**
SF 7 24   7   7   **45**
Bal   D12 R16/57 P(35-12-2) 79
SF   D31 R33/252 P(44-29-2) 345
SF-Perry 108R, Wilson 127C,
Tittle 371P

ChiC 3 14   7   0   **24**
ChiB 0 10   0   7   **17**
ChiC D16 R32/114 P(30-13-2) 174
ChiB D21 R31/74 P(43-22-1) 324
ChiC-Nagler 109C;
ChiB-Dooley 119C, Hensley 117C,
Blanda 306P

Cle 10   3   7   7   **27**
Phi 0 14 14 14   **42**
Cle   D20 R18/67 P(30-19-2) 272
Phi   D31 R39/146 P(35-23-0) 313
Cle-Brewster 103C;
Phi-Thomason 331P

Det 7   7   6   7   **27**
NYG   7   0   0   9   **16**
Det   D16 R31/147 P(28-17-2) 207
NYG   D18 R32/63 P(35-20-5) 205

Pit 0   0   0 14   **14**
Was   7   3   3   0   **13**
Pit   D18 R49/212 P(30-15-0) 139
Was   D15 R28/123 P(22-9-6) 107

1954 NFL
SUNDAY, SEPTEMBER 26
ChiB 10   7   6   0   **23**
Det 10 7 24   7   **48**
ChiB D19 R28/39 P(45-14-6) 348
Det   D19 R34/117 P(36-16-3) 257
ChiB-Hill 140C

Cle   0   0 10   0   **10**
Phi 0 14   7   7   **28**
Cle   D9 R19/47   P(23-9-1) 95
Phi   D24 R47/182 P(30-19-1) 215

LARm 13 14   7 14   **48**
Bal   0   0   0   0   **0**
LARm D26 R37/160 P(26-19-0) 403
Bal   D14 R17/19 P(31-16-4) 177
LARm-Boyd 121C, Quinlan 135C

NYG 10 14 10   7   **41**
ChiC 3   0   0   7   **10**
NYG   D20 R47/155 P(25-16-1) 226
ChiC D7 R27/105 P(25-11-1) 71

Pit 7   7   0   7   **21**
GB   7 10   3   0   **20**
Pit   D23 R35/128 P(40-27-1) 316
GB   D9 R29/161 P(18-5-2) 91
Pit-Finks 327P

Was   0   0   0   7   **7**
SF 13 14   0 14   **41**
Was   D13 R36/110 P(22-8-3) 74
SF   D24 R36/208 P(38-19-1) 206

SATURDAY, OCTOBER 2
NYG   7   0   0   7   **14**
Bal 0 20   0   0   **20**
NYG   D21 R38/152 P(33-14-2) 101
Bal   D14 R31/61 P(19-13-0) 269
Bal-Young 125C

Was   0   0   0   7   **7**
Pit 13 14   7   3   **37**
Was   D18 R31/121 P(29-16-3) 132
Pit   D26 R32/152 P(30-18-0) 277
Was-Taylor 111C; Pit-Mathews 117C

SUNDAY, OCTOBER 3
ChiB 0   0   0 10   **10**
GB   0   0   0   3   **3**
ChiB D14 R29/81 P(39-15-3) 142
GB   D15 R36/95 P(35-13-4) 179
GB-Howton 100C

Phi 7 14 14   0   **35**
ChiC 16   0   0   0   **16**
Phi   D19 R23/29 P(48-20-3) 422
ChiC D11 R28/38 P(34-11-5) 91
Phi-Walston 110C, Williams 166C

SF   7   3   7   7   **24**
LARm 3   7   7   7   **24**
SF   D22 R26/181 P(35-23-0) 268
LARm D16 R32/148 P(26-12-2) 222
SF-Wilson 158C; LARm-Boyd 157C

SATURDAY, OCTOBER 9
Pit   3   9   7   3   **22**
Phi 14 3   0   7   **24**
Pit   D18 R35/99 P(46-18-1) 132
Phi   D17 R34/110 P(28-13-5) 178

SUNDAY, OCTOBER 10
Bal   7   2   0   0   **9**
ChiB 14 0   7   7   **28**
Bal   D8 R32/54   P(26-13-2) 85
ChiB D14 R31/81 P(21-8-2) 161
ChiB-Hill 144C

ChiC 0   0   0   7   **7**
Cle 14 17   0   0   **31**
ChiC D20 R26/78 P(30-13-2) 183
Cle   D21 R30/98 P(27-19-1) 333

LARm 3   0   0   0   **3**
Det 7   0   7   7   **21**
LARm D20 R27/61 P(42-18-4) 297
Det   D21 R42/250 P(16-9-2) 124
LARm-Boyd 128C, Hirsch 105C;
Det-Carpenter 119R

NYG 17 14   3 17   **51**
Was   0 14   7   0   **21**
NYG   D28 R37/166 P(38-20-0) 278
Was   D13 R26/164 P(20-7-3) 73
NYG-Schnelker 136C, Conerly 237P

SF 10   0   0 13   **23**
GB   0   0   0 17   **17**
SF   D21 R56/271 P(18-11-1) 101
GB   D9 R14/52   P(32-13-2) 94
SF-Perry 100R

SATURDAY, OCTOBER 16
Bal   0   0   0   0   **0**
Det 0 14 14   7   **35**
Bal   D11 R43/155 P(13-5-2) 58
Det   D20 R28/37 P(35-22-1) 335

SUNDAY, OCTOBER 17
ChiC 0   3   0 14   **17**
NYG 14 0   7 10   **31**
ChiC D18 R46/181 P(27-8-2) 121
NYG   D13 R23/149 P(22-10-3) 171

Cle 14   6   0   7   **27**
Pit 7 27 14   7   **55**
Cle   D23 R27/167 P(29-22-6) 269
Pit   D22 R42/184 P(17-13-1) 257
Cle-Lavelli 134C; Pit-Mathews 152C,
Finks 239P

LARm 3   0   7   7   **17**
GB 0   7   7 21   **35**
LARm D15 R30/168 P(21-11-1) 277
GB   D28 R32/175 P(37-21-1) 273
LARm-Boyd 149C; GB-Howton 105C

Phi 7 14 14 14   **49**
Was   7   0 14   0   **21**
Phi   D30 R37/172 P(33-23-1) 260
Was   D9 R20/28   P(15-7-4) 87
Phi-Pihos 132C, Burk 232P

SF 7   7 17   0   **31**
ChiB 14   3   0   7   **24**
SF   D12 R38/294 P(24-9-0) 62
ChiB D19 R25/50 P(51-22-6) 387
SF-McElhenny 114R, Perry 119R;
ChiB-Dooley 133C, Hill 116C,
Blanda 359P

SATURDAY, OCTOBER 23

Phi 0 0 0 7 7
Pit 0 3 7 7 17
Phi D15 R30/121 P(34-18-2) 157
Pit D11 R29/64 P(22-12-2) 149
Phi-Pihos 111C

SUNDAY, OCTOBER 24

ChiB 7 14 3 14 38
LARm 7 14 14 7 42
ChiB D28 R24/105 P(46-28-2) 338
LARm D30 R43/314 P(26-17-1) 243
ChiB-McColl 110C, Blanda 338P;
LARm-Towler 123R, Younger 186R,
Boyd 131C

Cle 7 14 14 0 35
ChiC 3 0 0 0 3
Cle D23 R36/92 P(35-23-1) 235
ChiC D8 R25/60 P(21-6-2) 100

Det 0 10 7 14 31
SF 17 7 7 6 37
Det D27 R28/104 P(53-31-0) 339
SF D23 R34/270 P(25-12-0) 154
Det-Walker 129C;
SF-McElhenny 126R

GB 0 0 7 0 7
Bal 3 0 0 3 6
GB D14 R26/102 P(38-20-1) 192
Bal D14 R28/131 P(32-19-0) 90
GB-Howton 147C

Was 0 0 7 0 7
NYG 3 14 0 7 24
Was D17 R43/84 P(23-12-5) 144
NYG D20 R30/156 P(22-13-3) 203

SATURDAY, OCTOBER 30

GB 10 7 13 7 37
Phi 0 7 0 7 14
GB D12 R26/66 P(20-11-0) 89
Phi D15 R31/102 P(32-14-2) 101
GB-McGee 104C

SUNDAY, OCTOBER 31

Bal 0 7 7 7 21
Was 7 14 0 3 24
Bal D21 R21/83 P(38-22-2) 231
Was D20 R51/172 P(13-8-1) 129
Bal-Edwards 105C

ChiB 7 0 7 17 31
SF 7 14 0 6 27
ChiB D21 R31/127 P(35-21-1) 342
SF D21 R31/147 P(31-17-2) 241
ChiB-Hill 214C

Det 3 14 3 7 27
LARm 14 0 7 3 24
Det D19 R37/163 P(30-12-3) 188
LARm D25 R46/285 P(21-9-1) 170
LARm-Quinlan 115R, Younger 140R

NYG 0 7 0 7 14
Cle 7 7 3 7 24
NYG D10 R34/116 P(17-6-2) 135
Cle D20 R46/167 P(26-14-3) 146

Pit 7 0 0 7 14
ChiC 0 7 3 7 17
Pit D15 R21/45 P(36-22-3) 206
ChiC D18 R60/171 P(18-9-0) 140

SATURDAY, NOVEMBER 6

Det 7 3 10 7 27
Bal 3 0 0 0 3
Det D20 R31/120 P(37-20-1) 234
Bal D6 R21/39 P(27-8-2) 30

SUNDAY, NOVEMBER 7

ChiC 0 7 0 7 14
Phi 10 7 7 6 30
ChiC D18 R38/122 P(28-10-1) 52
Phi D22 R43/140 P(27-16-2) 221
Phi-Moselle 100C

GB 0 13 3 7 23
ChiB 7 7 0 14 28
GB D21 R27/153 P(42-17-0) 182
ChiB D21 R23/104 P(46-24-2) 278
ChiB-Hoffman 110C

LARm 7 14 14 7 42
SF 17 3 14 0 34
LARm D21 R35/178 P(18-16-1) 276
SF D23 R30/221 P(31-19-1) 193
LARm-Younger 104R, Hirsch 145C;
SF-Perry 124R, Soltau 105C

NYG 9 14 7 0 30
Pit 0 6 0 0 6
NYG D20 R42/245 P(21-13-2) 137
Pit D20 R27/82 P(39-19-5) 229

Was 0 3 0 0 3
Cle 13 14 21 14 62
Was D4 R25/33 P(20-5-3) 31
Cle D33 R47/226 P(28-18-1) 289
Cle-Brewster 114C

SATURDAY, NOVEMBER 13

Bal 10 3 0 0 13
GB 0 0 7 7 14
Bal D12 R30/240 P(24-10-3) 84
GB D22 R37/188 P(28-15-1) 154
Bal-Taseff 122R; GB-Ferguson 112R

SUNDAY, NOVEMBER 14

ChiC 10 0 0 7 17
LARm 14 7 0 7 28
ChiC D23 R37/191 P(40-22-3) 189
LARm D15 R33/189 P(20-6-1) 54

Cle 3 3 17 16 39
ChiB 0 3 0 7 10
Cle D21 R50/222 P(23-11-1) 94
ChiB D10 R22/37 P(32-11-3) 169
ChiB-Hill 117C

Phi 0 7 0 7 14
NYG 3 7 17 0 27
Phi D19 R28/22 P(44-19-4) 220
NYG D23 R34/149 P(42-16-1) 256

Pit 0 7 0 7 14
Was 0 3 7 7 17
Pit D15 R22/66 P(28-16-2) 180
Was D24 R54/258 P(18-9-1) 156

SF 0 0 0 7 7
Det 20 7 14 7 48
SF D16 R35/104 P(38-15-3) 245
Det D17 R33/172 P(21-11-0) 302
SF-Perry 110C; Det-Walker 119C

SATURDAY, NOVEMBER 20

SF 3 21 0 7 31
Pit 3 0 0 0 3
SF D25 R43/262 P(29-18-1) 210
Pit D13 R26/118 P(30-8-1) 84
SF-Johnson 124R, Perry 122R

SUNDAY, NOVEMBER 21

ChiB 7 0 14 7 28
Bal 0 6 7 0 13
ChiB D19 R45/160 P(23-13-1) 173
Bal D21 R32/181 P(28-13-4) 156

Det 0 14 7 0 21
GB 7 3 7 0 17
Det D23 R41/188 P(31-19-2) 230
GB D23 R21/74 P(42-20-3) 277
GB-Howton 101C

LARm 3 7 7 0 17
NYG 7 9 0 0 16
LARm D24 R46/210 P(33-16-1) 275
NYG D11 R24/66 P(27-14-0) 220
LARm-Boyd 103C, Fears 136C;
NYG-Schnelker 171C

Phi 0 0 0 0 0
Cle 3 0 3 0 6
Phi D10 R32/57 P(23-10-2) 53
Cle D14 R44/111 P(21-11-2) 185

Was 7 7 2 0 16
ChiC 7 10 14 7 38
Was D15 R31/186 P(23-13-3) 163
ChiC D19 R40/288 P(25-11-1) 136
Was-Wells 100R; ChiC-Matson 163R

THURSDAY, NOVEMBER 25

GB 7 7 10 0 24
Det 0 14 14 0 28
GB D16 R31/133 P(38-13-2) 217
Det D15 R25/85 P(34-20-2) 214

SUNDAY, NOVEMBER 28

ChiC 0 14 3 0 17
Pit 0 10 0 10 20
ChiC D13 R36/219 P(18-11-3) 218
Pit D22 R43/165 P(33-17-1) 174
ChiC-Matson 115R, Matson 161C;
Pit-Rogel 102R

Cle 10 3 3 0 16
NYG 0 0 7 0 7
Cle D19 R39/116 P(27-16-2) 210
NYG D8 R21/4 P(27-11-1) 64
Cle-Brewster 126C

LARm 7 6 0 0 13
ChiB 14 3 7 0 24
LARm D15 R40/136 P(26-14-2) 292
ChiB D16 R36/175 P(29-15-4) 236
LARm-Fears 134C,
Van Brocklin 308P; ChiB-Hill 109C

SF 7 0 0 6 13
Bal 0 7 3 7 17
SF D22 R43/205 P(24-12-1) 120
Bal D15 R34/161 P(14-9-1) 136

Was 10 7 7 9 33
Phi 6 7 21 7 41
Was D17 R29/136 P(32-12-2) 119
Phi D24 R39/133 P(36-20-2) 374
Phi-Williams 163C, Burk 345P

SATURDAY, DECEMBER 4

Bal 3 10 6 3 22
LARm 0 7 0 14 21
Bal D16 R42/55 P(34-18-1) 166
LARm D18 R27/155 P(26-10-7) 104
LARm-Quinlan 101R

SUNDAY, DECEMBER 5

ChiB 13 9 0 7 29
ChiC 0 0 0 7 7
ChiB D16 R23/63 P(37-19-3) 346
ChiC D18 R35/81 P(40-17-7) 175
ChiB-Dooley 144C, Hill 117C

Cle 7 10 10 7 34
Was 0 7 0 7 14
Cle D24 R39/160 P(28-18-2) 285
Was D13 R34/113 P(19-7-2) 143
Cle-Lavelli 126C

GB 0 0 0 0 0
SF 21 7 0 7 35
GB D19 R21/55 P(45-25-1) 216
SF D25 R39/237 P(21-15-0) 212
SF-Perry 137R

Phi 0 7 6 0 13
Det 0 3 7 3 13
Phi D12 R26/71 P(35-17-5) 242
Det D20 R32/159 P(33-17-5) 197

Pit 3 0 0 0 3
NYG 7 7 7 3 24
Pit D10 R25/83 P(38-12-6) 94
NYG D14 R30/80 P(31-21-3) 303
NYG-Rote 147C

SATURDAY, DECEMBER 11

Bal 7 0 0 0 7
SF 0 7 0 3 10
Bal D17 R33/96 P(27-17-1) 177
SF D18 R31/98 P(26-17-2) 194

SUNDAY, DECEMBER 12

ChiC 0 13 0 7 20
Was 13 17 7 0 37
ChiC D18 R20/78 P(43-19-3) 186
Was D25 R47/221 P(23-12-2) 243
ChiC-Stonesifer 144C;
Was-Taylor 106C

Det 0 3 0 21 24
ChiB 7 14 0 7 28
Det D20 R29/123 P(32-20-1) 222
ChiB D22 R36/180 P(25-18-2) 184

GB 7 13 0 7 27
LARm 14 7 7 7 35
GB D19 R21/74 P(37-22-2) 195
LARm D30 R36/136 P(36-23-2) 434
GB-McGee 105C; LARm-Boyd 106C,
Hirsch 119C

NYG 0 0 14 0 14
Phi 7 14 0 9 30
NYG D9 R20/44 P(29-9-4) 232
Phi D14 R31/57 P(31-17-1) 164
NYG-Rote 122C; Phi-Pihos 119C

Pit 0 0 7 0 7
Cle 7 21 0 14 42
Pit D10 R31/96 P(27-7-3) 75
Cle D25 R50/278 P(22-12-2) 186

SUNDAY, DECEMBER 19

Det 0 0 7 7 14
Cle 7 0 3 0 10
Det D15 R33/90 P(37-18-1) 183
Cle D6 R49/109 P(6-1-0) 4

1955 NFL

SATURDAY, SEPTEMBER 24

NYG 10 7 0 0 17
Phi 7 0 10 10 27
NYG D12 R33/135 P(24-9-1) 57
Phi D17 R36/150 P(28-14-1) 252

SUNDAY, SEPTEMBER 25

ChiB 0 7 3 7 17
Bal 10 10 3 0 23
ChiB D23 R33/122 P(43-21-2) 239
Bal D14 R45/226 P(12-7-0) 80
ChiB-Hill 107C; Bal-Ameche 194R

Det 0 7 3 7 17
GB 0 6 7 7 20
Det D16 R36/171 P(20-8-1) 140
GB D18 R35/172 P(27-15-1) 122

LARm 9 7 0 7 23
SF 0 0 7 7 14
LARm D19 R43/114 P(21-11-3) 95
SF D22 R38/168 P(28-11-5) 119

Was 6 7 7 7 27
Cle 0 3 14 0 17
Was D13 R27/95 P(16-8-1) 165
Cle D23 R46/221 P(28-15-2) 178
Cle-Morrison 117R

MONDAY, SEPTEMBER 26

ChiC 0 0 0 7 7
Pit 0 0 7 7 14
ChiC D8 R29/61 P(17-5-2) 25
Pit D23 R44/119 P(34-20-5) 236

SATURDAY, OCTOBER 1

Det 6 7 0 0 13
Bal 7 7 0 14 28
Det D18 R18/42 P(45-22-2) 279
Bal D19 R48/238 P(19-10-1) 106
Bal-Ameche 153R

Was 0 0 28 3 31
Phi 7 10 7 6 30
Was D16 R36/118 P(15-10-0) 136
Phi D27 R33/121 P(38-25-0) 344
Phi-Thomason 349P

SUNDAY, OCTOBER 2

ChiB 0 0 3 0 3
GB 0 7 0 7 14
ChiB D11 R37/132 P(19-6-4) 85
GB D19 R33/223 P(30-14-0) 163
GB-Ferguson 153R

Cle 7 17 7 7 38
SF 0 3 0 0 3
Cle D21 R60/210 P(12-8-0) 147
SF D8 R27/67 P(18-6-2) 72

NYG 3 14 0 0 17
ChiC 7 0 7 3 17
NYG D21 R42/245 P(34-13-4) 120
ChiC D9 R30/152 P(24-9-3) 201
NYG-Webster 139R

Pit 0 0 13 13 26
LARm 0 17 0 10 27
Pit D16 R41/155 P(22-12-2) 103
LARm D20 R36/156 P(30-18-1) 190
LARm-Boyd 114C

SATURDAY, OCTOBER 8

Bal 21 0 0 3 24
GB 3 7 3 7 20
Bal D8 R33/103 P(16-6-3) 152
GB D17 R40/136 P(39-19-0) 186

SUNDAY, OCTOBER 9

ChiC 7 3 7 7 24
Was 3 0 0 7 10
ChiC D16 R51/187 P(17-6-1) 45
Was D17 R29/113 P(40-13-3) 189

LARm 7 3 7 0 17
Det 0 3 0 7 10
LARm D18 R42/155 P(23-12-2) 129
Det D26 R29/90 P(47-27-4) 280

Phi 7 3 7 6 23
Pit 0 6 10 14 30
Phi D11 R29/65 P(23-13-2) 225
Pit D26 R47/162 P(34-14-1) 297
NYG-Rote 114C

Phi 7 0 0 7 17
Cle 0 14 0 7 21
Phi D14 R29/43 P(30-13-0) 136
Cle D21 R42/165 P(21-16-0) 207
Cle-Lavelli 108C

SF 6 7 7 0 20
ChiB 0 10 7 2 19
SF D16 R29/159 P(23-13-2) 131
ChiB D25 R49/239 P(32-15-1) 202
ChiB-Hoffman 135R

SATURDAY, OCTOBER 15

Phi 0 7 0 0 7
Pit 7 0 6 0 13
Phi D6 R31/8 P(25-11-3) 140
Pit D17 R57/201 P(24-11-2) 105

SUNDAY, OCTOBER 16

Bal 3 0 0 7 10
ChiB 3 14 14 7 38
Bal D18 R36/215 P(28-11-3) 57
ChiB D19 R46/254 P(18-5-2) 123

ChiC 0 0 0 0 0
NYG 3 0 7 0 10
ChiC D10 R39/112 P(21-9-1) 22
NYG D9 R42/167 P(7-4-0) 48

Cle 7 3 14 0 24
Was 7 0 0 7 14
Cle D14 R33/92 P(18-9-1) 118
Was D16 R34/131 P(25-7-2) 51
Cle-Brewster 109C

LARm 7 0 7 14 28
GB 10 7 7 6 30
LARm D16 R33/151 P(31-12-3) 109
GB D20 R36/112 P(40-19-5) 231
GB-Howton 158C

SF 0 6 0 21 27
Det 7 10 7 0 24
SF D15 R38/114 P(32-15-2) 316
Det D13 R44/153 P(23-8-3) 47
SF-Tittle 316P

SUNDAY, OCTOBER 23

ChiB 0 10 14 10 34
SF 10 7 0 6 23
ChiB D28 R56/252 P(25-17-2) 168
SF D15 R27/132 P(19-12-2) 200
SF-Wilson 192C

Det 0 3 7 3 13
LARm 7 3 0 14 24
Det D20 R28/130 P(35-21-2) 219
LARm D19 R27/152 P(28-19-2) 274
LARm-Waller 127R, Boyd 111C

GB 0 0 0 10 10
Cle 0 14 7 20 41
GB D9 R32/139 P(22-6-2) 22
Cle D21 R49/204 P(15-10-0) 250

Phi 0 7 7 10 24
ChiC 7 3 7 7 24
Phi D14 R40/190 P(30-12-3) 193
ChiC D18 R42/180 P(21-8-2) 242

Pit 6 7 6 0 19
NYG 7 7 3 0 17
Pit D22 R44/147 P(28-16-0) 212
NYG D16 R28/95 P(26-20-0) 189

Was 0 0 7 7 14
Bal 0 3 10 0 13
Was D16 R42/172 P(14-5-2) 105
Bal D12 R31/84 P(21-9-3) 84

SATURDAY, OCTOBER 29

GB 0 3 0 7 10
Bal 7 0 7 0 14
GB D17 R34/142 P(24-13-3) 163
Bal D17 R50/202 P(13-5-4) 55
Bal-Ameche 117R

SUNDAY, OCTOBER 30

ChiB 7 10 7 7 31
LARm 7 0 6 7 20
ChiB D21 R41/157 P(25-16-2) 248
LARm D22 R29/115 P(38-19-3) 231
ChiB-Hill 151C

Cle 7 14 5 0 26
ChiC 3 3 7 7 20
Cle D15 R47/196 P(12-4-0) 62
ChiC D16 R39/134 P(34-10-2) 148
Cle-Modzelewski 121R

Det 0 7 7 7 21
SF 14 17 0 7 38
Det D25 R31/115 P(46-22-2) 286
SF D26 R48/249 P(20-13-1) 189
Det-Middleton 144C; SF-Perry 149R

Pit 0 0 0 0 0
Phi 0 0 14 10 24
Pit D11 R30/57 P(29-13-3) 119
Phi D18 R44/159 P(25-11-0) 86

Was 0 0 7 0 7
NYG 7 0 21 7 35
Was D17 R36/189 P(43-17-4) 203
NYG D12 R27/130 P(21-8-2) 143

SATURDAY, NOVEMBER 5

Bal 0 7 7 0 14
Det 3 7 0 14 24
Bal D15 R29/64 P(22-12-1) 173
Det D22 R40/178 P(24-13-4) 187

Pit 3 10 0 0 13
ChiC 10 14 3 0 27
Pit D21 R31/145 P(49-23-3) 321
ChiC D12 R41/183 P(22-9-0) 78
Pit-Mathews 156C, Finks 337P; ChiC-Matson 130R

SUNDAY, NOVEMBER 6

GB 0 3 0 28 31
ChiB 14 14 10 14 52
GB D19 R25/151 P(31-12-0) 168
ChiB D25 R54/406 P(16-8-5) 98
GB-Ferguson 120R; ChiB-Casares 115R, Watkins 115R

NYG 0 14 0 0 14
Cle 3 0 7 14 24
NYG D17 R26/110 P(31-13-3) 222
Cle D17 R44/122 P(25-15-3) 195

Phi 0 7 0 14 21
Was 0 17 10 7 34
Phi D19 R17/35 P(51-25-0) 345
Was D14 R48/163 P(18-6-0) 125
Phi-Pihos 119C

SF 0 7 0 7 14
LARm 3 0 7 17 27
SF D15 R26/75 P(24-10-3) 148
LARm D23 R54/232 P(30-10-1) 130

SUNDAY, NOVEMBER 13

Bal 0 0 0 7 7
NYG 3 0 7 7 17
Bal D18 R33/133 P(28-16-0) 173
NYG D19 R38/196 P(23-9-0) 140

ChiC 0 0 0 14 14
GB 7 17 7 0 31
ChiC D10 R27/112 P(24-8-4) 221
GB D24 R48/203 P(29-10-2) 122

Cle 17 0 0 0 17
Phi 0 10 6 17 33
Cle D12 R35/141 P(20-8-3) 131
Phi D18 R34/148 P(28-12-2) 183
Phi-Stribling 123C

Det 0 14 10 7 31
Pit 0 0 7 21 28
Det D12 R39/65 P(23-13-0) 169
Pit D26 R32/84 P(47-28-3) 367
Det-Middleton 102C; Pit-Chandnois 108C

LARm 0 0 0 3 3
ChiB 10 14 0 0 24
LARm D18 R24/138 P(46-19-1) 146
ChiB D23 R44/233 P(22-12-0) 230
LARm-Fears 129C; ChiB-Hill 113C

SF 0 0 0 0 0
Was 0 0 7 0 7
SF D15 R30/76 P(30-14-3) 136
Was D15 R43/166 P(13-6-4) 59

SUNDAY, NOVEMBER 20

ChiB 7 3 14 0 24
Det 7 7 0 0 14
ChiB D21 R39/158 P(25-19-0) 264
Det D14 R19/61 P(32-20-2) 309
Det-Middleton 168C, Layne 319P

LARm 3 0 7 7 17
Bal 0 10 7 0 17
LARm D24 R44/197 P(24-12-0) 222
Bal D22 R39/130 P(23-14-2) 202
LARm-Younger 109R

Phi 0 0 0 7 7
NYG 7 3 21 0 31
Phi D14 R23/42 P(37-15-6) 101
NYG D15 R41/118 P(25-10-1) 160

Pit 7 7 0 0 14
Cle 7 14 13 7 41
Pit D16 R23/65 P(32-14-4) 173
Cle D18 R49/199 P(11-8-0) 68
Cle-Morrison 140R

SF 7 7 7 0 21
GB 0 13 0 14 27
SF D19 R37/186 P(28-15-1) 212
GB D26 R46/251 P(32-14-2) 187
SF-Hardy 122C

Was 14 0 0 17 31
ChiC 0 0 0 0 0
Was D18 R51/252 P(24-6-1) 77
ChiC D7 R27/72 P(26-9-3) 34

THURSDAY, NOVEMBER 24

GB 10 0 0 0 10
Det 0 10 0 14 24
GB D11 R32/108 P(24-10-2) 120
Det D19 R39/190 P(21-11-1) 92
Det-Carpenter 120R

SUNDAY, NOVEMBER 27

ChiB 0 7 0 7 14
ChiC 21 6 13 13 53
ChiB D12 R15/25 P(46-15-4) 186
ChiC D20 R53/301 P(21-12-2) 173
ChiC-Mann 108R

Cle 0 7 14 14 35
NYG 7 7 7 14 35
Cle D25 R38/106 P(31-17-1) 289
NYG D21 R28/147 P(34-18-1) 228
Cle-Brewster 107C, Renfro 130C, Graham 319P

LARm 14 0 0 9 23
Phi 0 7 0 14 21
LARm D14 R34/97 P(28-17-0) 233
Phi D19 R29/93 P(28-16-2) 237
Phi-Pihos 103C

SF 0 0 7 14 21
Bal 3 10 6 7 26
SF D14 R20/148 P(25-14-2) 148
Bal D22 R47/192 P(22-12-2) 200
SF-Wilson 143C

Was 7 7 9 0 23
Pit 0 7 0 7 14
Was D20 R62/332 P(9-1-0) -32
Pit D15 R28/65 P(34-18-2) 243
Was-Elter 136R; Pit-Watson 128C

SUNDAY, DECEMBER 4

Bal 0 0 0 14 14
LARm 7 3 3 7 20
Bal D21 R31/120 P(25-17-2) 148
LARm D26 R52/273 P(21-13-1) 145
LARm-Waller 138R, Younger 132R

ChiC 0 3 0 0 3
Phi 3 7 10 7 27
ChiC D9 R24/48 P(26-9-3) 1
Phi D27 R42/156 P(41-21-3) 268
Phi-Pihos 127C

Cle 10 10 10 0 30
Pit 0 0 10 0 10
Cle D19 R59/273 P(16-7-0) 70
Pit D8 R16/26 P(26-7-4) 97
Cle-Morrison 104R

Det 0 13 7 0 20
ChiB 0 7 7 7 21
Det D20 R44/207 P(35-15-0) 163
ChiB D12 R40/196 P(14-4-0) 7

GB 0 21 7 0 28
SF 7 0 0 0 7
GB D13 R31/85 P(18-9-0) 151
SF D20 R47/164 P(36-16-4) 117

NYG 7 10 3 7 27
Was 0 20 0 0 20
NYG D19 R41/134 P(25-14-1) 131
Was D15 R23/51 P(25-15-2) 183

SUNDAY, DECEMBER 11

Bal 3 0 7 14 24
SF 7 21 0 7 35
Bal D20 R34/126 P(37-15-1) 201
SF D19 R41/175 P(20-12-1) 150

ChiC 6 6 12 0 24
Cle 14 0 0 21 35
ChiC D15 R36/84 P(27-12-2) 155
Cle D18 R34/91 P(25-13-1) 235
Cle-Renfro 110C

GB 3 7 0 7 17
LARm 7 14 3 7 31
GB D20 R41/161 P(32-18-2) 144
LARm D14 R33/153 P(20-13-1) 157

NYG 7 14 3 0 24
Det 3 2 7 7 19
NYG D17 R39/151 P(19-6-0) 97
Det D19 R25/75 P(49-24-1) 239

Phi 3 0 0 0 3
ChiB 7 7 0 3 17
Phi D21 R34/172 P(39-23-4) 236
ChiB D15 R33/214 P(21-7-1) 78
Phi-Pihos 114C

Pit 0 14 3 0 17
Was 7 0 7 14 28
Pit D10 R27/58 P(31-13-1) 114
Was D16 R47/218 P(15-7-2) 87
Was-Monachino 104R

1956 NFL
SUNDAY, SEPTEMBER 30

Cle 7 0 0 0 7
ChiC 3 3 0 3 9
Cle D8 R27/108 P(13-7-2) 106
ChiC D20 R53/276 P(16-7-3) 68
ChiC-Matson 144R

NYG 17 7 7 7 38
SF 0 7 7 7 21
NYG D15 R36/167 P(19-8-0) 133
SF D27 R23/107 P(46-28-3) 301

Phi 7 0 0 0 7
LARm 7 3 7 10 27
Phi D12 R35/91 P(25-11-5) 97
LARm D18 R38/234 P(18-8-2) 60
Phi-Walston 115C; LARm-Waller 166R

Was 0 6 0 7 13
Pit 7 7 9 7 30
Was D10 R28/75 P(26-15-2) 117
Pit D17 R42/142 P(13-6-1) 83

ChiB 7 0 0 7 14
Bal 0 14 14 0 28
ChiB D19 R30/154 P(29-16-0) 137
Bal D21 R38/128 P(25-19-1) 231
ChiB-Hill 102C

Det 3 7 0 10 20
GB 0 3 6 7 16
Det D23 R51/175 P(24-15-2) 200
GB D10 R23/72 P(24-9-2) 88

SATURDAY, OCTOBER 6

Cle 0 7 0 7 14
Pit 0 10 0 0 10
Cle D17 R41/214 P(17-14-0) 122
Pit D14 R33/92 P(25-13-0) 153

Was 0 6 3 0 9
Phi 0 7 0 6 13
Was D13 R51/146 P(10-6-2) 48
Phi D13 R40/108 P(11-8-1) 99

Det 14 7 0 10 31
Bal 7 0 7 0 14
Det D25 R49/218 P(26-16-1) 247
Bal D10 R21/68 P(20-8-4) 138
Det-Dibble 106C

SUNDAY, OCTOBER 7

NYG 6 7 0 14 27
ChiC 0 14 14 7 35
NYG D17 R34/157 P(31-16-2) 176
ChiC D18 R57/223 P(8-5-1) 136

ChiB 10 10 7 10 37
GB 7 7 0 7 21
ChiB D25 R52/278 P(17-11-1) 184
GB D20 R23/127 P(34-14-0) 140
ChiB-Casares 139R

LARm 7 3 13 7 30
SF 3 9 7 14 33
LARm D21 R26/71 P(40-23-2) 361
SF D15 R48/208 P(15-7-0) 11
LARm-Boyd 119C, Hirsch 150C

SUNDAY, OCTOBER 14

ChiC 7 7 7 10 31
Was 0 0 3 0 3
ChiC D13 R36/225 P(9-4-1) 55
Was D15 R41/136 P(23-12-2) 100

NYG 0 7 7 7 21
Cle 0 7 0 2 9
NYG D24 R52/256 P(13-9-2) 74
Cle D14 R25/40 P(25-17-1) 94

Phi 7 21 0 7 35
Pit 0 0 7 14 21
Phi D12 R33/97 P(20-11-2) 168
Pit D17 R28/77 P(34-17-3) 247
Phi-Walston 108C

Bal 6 14 6 7 33
GB 7 17 14 0 38
Bal D17 R35/206 P(23-12-3) 124
GB D19 R42/184 P(22-11-0) 187

SF 0 0 0 7 7
ChiB 0 14 10 7 31
SF D13 R29/96 P(22-9-2) 172
ChiB D23 R56/308 P(15-8-1) 86
ChiB-Casares 112R

LARm 0 0 7 14 21
Det 10 7 0 7 24
LARm D14 R17/128 P(30-14-2) 253
Det D23 R47/175 P(27-14-2) 193
LARm-Hirsch 107C

SUNDAY, OCTOBER 21

ChiC 0 3 0 17 20
Phi 0 3 3 0 6
ChiC D14 R47/125 P(15-6-0) 119
Phi D20 R41/229 P(30-14-6) 120

Cle 3 6 0 0 9
Was 0 7 7 6 20
Cle D13 R31/111 P(20-10-2) 105
Was D18 R43/200 P(10-4-2) 35

Pit 3 0 0 7 10
NYG 0 17 14 7 38
Pit D10 R22/91 P(32-11-0) 91
NYG D25 R46/247 P(28-15-0) 213
NYG-Gifford 100C

Bal 0 0 6 21 27
ChiB 0 20 17 21 58
Bal D13 R27/130 P(24-13-1) 148
ChiB D26 R49/209 P(21-16-1) 268
Bal-Mutscheller 109C; ChiB-Casares 124R, Hill 198C

SF 7 3 7 0 17
Det 3 7 3 7 20
SF D15 R31/190 P(19-8-2) 67
Det D25 R46/244 P(28-15-1) 149
SF-McElhenny 119R; Det-McIlhenny 104R

LARm 7 3 7 0 17
GB 7 14 7 14 42
LARm D18 R23/153 P(30-14-4) 232
GB D27 R37/158 P(32-17-0) 334
LARm-Younger 106R; GB-Howton 257C

SUNDAY, OCTOBER 28

Was 0 3 14 0 17
ChiC 14 0 0 0 14
Was D17 R48/193 P(11-8-0) 141
ChiC D19 R44/138 P(18-11-1) 161

Pit 0 21 0 3 24
Cle 13 0 0 3 16
Pit D18 R33/139 P(20-12-3) 219
Cle D11 R39/176 P(16-7-3) 108
Pit-Perry 112C

Phi 3 0 0 0 3
NYG 0 13 0 7 20
Phi D7 R30/65 P(22-11-2) 67
NYG D12 R45/159 P(15-6-0) 85

GB 7 0 7 7 21
Bal 0 21 0 7 28
GB D14 R18/20 P(38-20-1) 253
Bal D16 R40/318 P(16-8-1) 100
Bal-Moore 185R

ChiB 14 10 7 7 38
SF 0 14 0 7 21
ChiB D27 R49/233 P(24-14-1) 207
SF D20 R28/211 P(23-13-1) 190
ChiB-Jeter 108C; SF-McElhenny 101R, Soltau 114C

Det 0 3 7 7 16
LARm 0 0 0 7 7
Det D16 R41/116 P(16-11-0) 177
LARm D18 R38/159 P(22-12-4) 225
LARm-Waller 105R

SUNDAY, NOVEMBER 4

Phi 3 0 0 14 17
ChiC 0 7 14 7 28
Phi D18 R38/126 P(23-11-2) 109
ChiC D17 R41/154 P(17-11-0) 108
ChiC-McHan 123P

Cle 7 0 7 10 24
GB 0 0 0 7 7
Cle D15 R54/222 P(4-2-1) 50
GB D13 R26/127 P(29-14-0) 145

NYG 7 3 7 0 17
Pit 0 0 7 7 14
NYG D18 R46/119 P(23-12-0) 110
Pit D18 R34/137 P(31-13-1) 118

ChiB 7 14 7 7 35
LARm 14 7 3 0 24
ChiB D16 R52/232 P(17-7-1) 138
LARm D17 R29/101 P(32-13-5) 163
ChiB-Casares 132R

Det 0 10 0 7 17
SF 0 10 3 0 13
Det D19 R47/194 P(18-7-2) 89
SF D15 R31/93 P(21-11-1) 153

SUNDAY, NOVEMBER 11

ChiC 0 3 0 7 10
NYG 2 7 7 7 23
ChiC D15 R37/127 P(26-12-0) 157
NYG D22 R47/187 P(22-13-1) 175
NYG-Gifford 116C

Bal 7 0 0 14 21
Cle 7 0 0 0 7
Bal D11 R43/305 P(14-5-0) 5
Cle D14 R36/135 P(24-11-1) 129
Bal-Ameche 108R, Moore 120R; Cle-Renfro 100C

Pit 7 0 0 0 7
Phi 7 0 7 0 14
Pit D14 R25/54 P(36-14-3) 95
Phi D13 R46/122 P(9-6-0) 130

Det 0 3 7 7 17
Was 3 10 0 5 18
Det D16 R22/52 P(40-15-4) 260
Was D15 R55/203 P(18-7-0) 83

```
GB    0  7  7  0  14
ChiB  7 21  7  3  38
GB   D12 R21/62  P(32-13-5) 249
ChiB D21 R47/195 P(20-13-2) 299
GB-Howton 151C;
ChiB-Hoffman 108R, Hill 121C

SF    3  3  0  0   6
LARm  3 10  7 10  30
SF   D14 R31/67  P(33-16-3) 197
LARm D17 R44/259 P(19-9-2) 139
```

SUNDAY, NOVEMBER 18

```
ChiC  0  0  0  7   7
Pit   7  0  7  0  14
ChiC D15 R42/151 P(22-7-3) 103
Pit  D15 R45/241 P(19-5-4) 39
Pit-Baldacci 110R, Rogel 112R

Cle   0  3  7  6  16
Phi   0  0  0  0   0
Cle  D17 R54/233 P(11-4-0) 41
Phi  D7 R29/68 P(12-4-2) 3
Cle-Carpenter 133R

NYG   0  0  7  0   7
Was   7 17  3  6  33
NYG  D15 R17/74 P(32-14-3) 175
Was  D23 R58/231 P(18-10-1) 160

Bal   0  3  0  0   3
Det   7  6 14  0  27
Bal  D15 R24/58 P(32-17-2) 298
Det  D26 R48/240 P(21-12-1) 153
Bal-Berry 155C, Unitas 314P

LARm  0  0 14  7  21
ChiB  3  7 14  6  30
LARm D20 R28/100 P(33-18-1) 226
ChiB D21 R45/166 P(24-15-2) 267
ChiB-Casares 104R, Hill 121C

SF    0  7  7  3  17
GB    6  3  0  7  16
SF   D24 R41/226 P(24-15-1) 149
GB   D16 R34/138 P(16-9-1) 181
SF-McElhenny 140R;
GB-Howton 121C
```

THURSDAY, NOVEMBER 22

```
GB    3  0  0 21  24
Det   7  0  6  7  20
GB   D21 R24/84 P(40-21-3) 289
Det  D17 R42/206 P(22-9-3) 146
GB-Ferguson 106C, Rote 301P;
Det-Gedman 103R
```

SUNDAY, NOVEMBER 25

```
Pit   7  0  0 20  27
ChiC  7 17  7  7  38
Pit  D25 R36/146 P(41-16-4) 206
ChiC D19 R48/242 P(17-11-1) 128
Pit-Mathews 119C;
ChiC-Matson 159R

Was   7  0  6  7  20
Cle   7  0  7  3  17
Was  D14 R36/97 P(20-10-1) 140
Cle  D13 R46/136 P(12-6-1) 48

ChiB  0  0  3 14  17
NYG   3  7  7  0  17
ChiB D11 R30/12 P(25-12-2) 232
NYG  D18 R53/176 P(24-7-2) 85
ChiB-Hill 195C

SF    7  0  0  3  10
Phi   0  3  7  0  10
SF   D19 R39/107 P(30-15-3) 178
Phi  D13 R39/120 P(23-10-3) 170
SF-Wilson 120C

LARm  7  0  7  7  21
Bal  14 28  0 14  56
LARm D23 R24/163 P(40-21-4) 260
Bal  D29 R39/258 P(26-20-1) 316
LARm-Boyd 117C;
Bal-Ameche 162R,
Mutscheller 112C
```

SUNDAY, DECEMBER 2

```
GB    0  3 14  7  24
ChiC  7  7  0  7  21
GB   D25 R40/194 P(28-13-3) 157
ChiC D14 R30/80 P(28-13-2) 129

Phi   7  0  7  0  14
Cle   7  7  0  3  17
Phi  D20 R33/148 P(28-13-3) 104
Cle  D19 R47/177 P(18-9-2) 115
Cle-Carpenter 116R

Was   7  0  0  7  14
NYG  14  0  7  7  28
Was  D13 R27/144 P(22-9-4) 75
NYG  D22 R43/193 P(26-15-2) 174
NYG-Gifford 108R

LARm  6  0  7  0  13
Pit   0 10  7 13  30
LARm D7 R27/100 P(16-10-1) 63
Pit  D16 R38/130 P(18-9-1) 134

SF    0  7  7  6  20
Bal   7  3  7  0  17
SF   D16 R35/120 P(18-14-0) 240
Bal  D22 R38/152 P(30-18-2) 150
SF-Wilson 148C

Det   0 10  0  0  10
ChiB  0 14  7 21  42
ChiB D15 R30/114 P(26-12-3) 70
Det  D25 R48/214 P(23-14-3) 254
Det-Middleton 146C
```

SATURDAY, DECEMBER 8

```
GB    7  7  0  6  20
SF   10  0  7 21  38
GB   D16 R21/74 P(30-15-1) 201
SF   D23 R48/246 P(25-14-1) 181
SF-McElhenny 132R, Conner 125C
```

SUNDAY, DECEMBER 9

```
ChiC  0  3  0  0   3
ChiB  0  3  7  0  10
ChiC D11 R33/91 P(30-11-1) 174
ChiB D16 R50/258 P(15-3-3) 44
ChiB-Casares 117R

Cle   7 10  7  0  24
NYG   0  7  0  0   7
Cle  D19 R49/193 P(11-7-1) 106
NYG  D13 R23/103 P(31-14-1) 126
Cle-Morrison 112R

Phi  10  0  7  0  17
Was   0  3  7  9  19
Phi  D12 R31/130 P(15-9-0) 109
Was  D21 R41/136 P(28-14-0) 196

Pit   0  7  0  0   7
Det  14 24  7  0  45
Pit  D9 R33/25 P(28-11-3) 104
Det  D15 R39/130 P(26-17-3) 166

Bal   0  7  0  0   7
LARm 14  0  0 17  31
Bal  D16 R32/162 P(29-14-1) 124
LARm D24 R41/196 P(22-10-1) 140
```

SATURDAY, DECEMBER 15

```
NYG   0 14  7  0  21
Phi   0  0  0  0   0
NYG  D22 R57/291 P(11-4-1) 41
Phi  D13 R23/73 P(31-14-1) 101
NYG-Webster 132R
```

SUNDAY, DECEMBER 16

```
ChiC  0 14  3  7  24
Cle   7  0  0  0   7
ChiC D16 R59/221 P(8-2-1) 31
Cle  D13 R31/100 P(31-11-4) 151

Pit   0  7  0 16  23
Was   0  0  0  0   0
Pit  D11 R44/76 P(21-9-1) 177
Was  D5 R33/70 P(14-3-3) 15

Bal   0 10  0  7  17
SF    7  0  3 20  30
Bal  D22 R45/232 P(21-12-1) 104
SF   D20 R35/165 P(21-12-2) 138

Det   0  7  7  7  21
ChiB  3 14  7 14  38
Det  D17 R27/47 P(30-15-1) 161
ChiB D24 R46/309 P(17-8-2) 137
ChiB-Casares 190R

GB    0  7  7  7  21
LARm 14 21 14  0  49
GB   D19 R28/181 P(28-15-2) 173
LARm D33 R49/314 P(27-18-0) 297
LARm-Wilson 223R, Boyd 146C
```

SUNDAY, DECEMBER 23

```
Was   3  7  7  0  17
Bal   0  6 13  0  19
Was  D12 R40/112 P(15-6-1) 108
Bal  D24 R50/185 P(23-13-1) 183
Bal-Mutscheller 128C
```

1957 NFL

SUNDAY, SEPTEMBER 29

```
ChiB  7  7  3  0  17
GB    0 14  0  7  21
ChiB D19 R35/141 P(28-14-5) 221
GB   D16 R39/97 P(22-12-2) 200
GB-Howton 165C

ChiC  7  7  3  3  20
SF    3  7  0  0  10
ChiC D22 R46/173 P(20-9-0) 173
SF   D16 R29/212 P(24-14-2) 112
SF-McElhenny 125R

Det   0  7  0  7  14
Bal   7 17 10  0  34
Det  D13 R24/23 P(27-15-4) 178
Bal  D18 R34/151 P(23-14-3) 241
Bal-Unitas 241P

NYG   0  0  0  0   0
Cle   0  3  0  3   6
NYG  D12 R39/155 P(16-3-2) 39
Cle  D10 R41/122 P(10-4-0) 40

Phi   0  0  7  0   7
LARm  0 14  0  3  17
Phi  D13 R40/125 P(14-8-2) 63
LARm D17 R42/188 P(20-8-1) 82
LARm-Wilson 135R

Was   0  0  7  0   7
Pit   0  7 14  7  28
Was  D13 R28/89 P(24-12-4) 153
Pit  D16 R33/73 P(32-15-0) 228
```

SATURDAY, OCTOBER 5

```
ChiB  7  3  0  0  10
Bal   7  0  7  7  21
ChiB D8 R24/29 P(23-8-2) 133
Bal  D22 R45/177 P(27-17-1) 162

Cle   0 10  3 10  23
Pit   0  6  6  0  12
Cle  D12 R36/106 P(19-11-0) 134
Pit  D14 R21/63 P(25-17-1) 173

NYG   7  7  7  3  24
Phi  10  0 10  0  20
NYG  D24 R50/183 P(22-13-1) 193
Phi  D6 R29/57 P(12-5-2) 16
```

SUNDAY, OCTOBER 6

```
Det  14  3  0  7  24
GB    0  0 14  0  14
Det  D19 R56/249 P(20-9-1) 78
GB   D11 R18/98 P(29-11-5) 107
Det-Johnson 109R

LARm  7  0  7  6  20
SF    0 16  0  7  23
LARm D19 R41/184 P(24-12-1) 217
SF   D16 R44/196 P(15-7-0) 122
LARm-Wilson 125R;
SF-McElhenny 109R

Was   6  7 14 10  37
ChiC  7  7  0  0  14
Was  D21 R53/247 P(13-8-0) 180
ChiC D9 R23/76 P(17-7-1) 147
Was-Carson 104C;
ChiC-Nagler 153C
```

SUNDAY, OCTOBER 13

```
Bal   7  0 17 21  45
GB    3  7  0  7  17
Bal  D22 R49/243 P(19-9-2) 145
GB   D12 R22/47 P(28-15-5) 145

ChiC  3  0  0 14  20
Pit  12  3  0  3  29
ChiC D15 R36/189 P(23-9-3) 126
Pit  D16 R40/152 P(17-6-2) 79

LARm  0  7  0  0   7
Det   0 10  0  0  10
LARm D14 R40/167 P(18-5-6) 74
Det  D12 R37/126 P(25-8-1) 82
```

```
NYG   7  7  7  3  24
Was   7  7  0  6  20
NYG  D17 R42/176 P(15-12-0) 179
Was  D17 R33/117 P(23-13-0) 229
NYG-Epps 115R, Schnelker 122C;
Was-Carson 100C, Podoley 104C

Phi   0  0  0  7   7
Cle  14  3  0  7  24
Phi  D10 R29/63 P(23-10-3) 44
Cle  D11 R41/165 P(11-5-1) 79
Cle-Brewster 105C

SF    0  0 14  7  21
ChiB  0  0  7 10  17
SF   D18 R32/105 P(27-17-0) 269
ChiB D14 R43/216 P(19-6-2) 77
SF-Conner 142C
```

SUNDAY, OCTOBER 20

```
Bal   7 14  6  0  27
Det   0  3  7 21  31
Bal  D15 R35/117 P(21-16-1) 205
Det  D20 R32/178 P(34-12-2) 191
Bal-Moore 100C, Mutscheller 107C,
Unitas 239P; Det-Cassady 113C

ChiC 21 10  6  7  44
Was   0  7  0  7  14
ChiC D20 R37/256 P(16-8-1) 182
Was  D20 R48/169 P(22-11-2) 168
ChiC-Matson 155R, Lewis 107C

Cle   0  0  0  7   7
Phi   3  7  0  7  17
Cle  D14 R31/103 P(25-13-4) 182
Phi  D13 R45/186 P(10-6-0) 84

LARm  3  0 10 13  26
ChiB  3 14  7 10  34
LARm D13 R30/79 P(18-12-1) 142
ChiB D22 R44/218 P(19-11-2) 223
LARm-Arnett 137C;
ChiB-Galimore 153R

Pit   0  0  0  0   0
NYG   7  7  7 14  35
Pit  D10 R26/54 P(28-14-3) 118
NYG  D17 R41/128 P(21-14-0) 212

SF    3  7  7  7  24
GB    0  7  0  7  14
SF   D15 R32/78 P(26-13-4) 150
GB   D15 R39/194 P(20-10-2) 61
```

SUNDAY, OCTOBER 27

```
ChiB 14  3  0  0  17
SF    0  7  7  7  21
ChiB D19 R38/103 P(31-15-5) 202
SF   D14 R30/94 P(21-13-1) 102
ChiB-Hill 102C

Cle   3  0  7  7  17
ChiC  3  0  0  0   3
Cle  D13 R50/162 P(12-5-1) 42
ChiC D7 R29/103 P(13-4-1) 54

Det   0  0 10  0  10
LARm 14  7  0 14  35
Det  D24 R23/88 P(44-23-3) 220
LARm D21 R53/224 P(16-12-1) 133

GB    0  0  0 24  24
Bal   3  7  7  7  24
GB   D14 R35/48 P(22-11-1) 229
Bal  D20 R33/152 P(31-16-2) 179

Phi   0  0  0  0   0
Pit   0  6  0  0   6
Phi  D5 R31/70 P(13-4-2) 0
Pit  D15 R37/107 P(28-14-1) 227

Was  14  7  3  7  31
NYG   7  7  0  0  14
Was  D15 R41/147 P(8-6-0) 107
NYG  D18 R29/158 P(30-19-3) 166
```

SUNDAY, NOVEMBER 3

```
ChiB  7  3  3  3  16
LARm 10  0  0  0  10
ChiB D17 R40/74 P(29-14-0) 227
LARm D17 R28/84 P(35-14-2) 70
ChiB-Hill 111C

Det   7  3  0 21  31
SF    0 14  7 14  35
Det  D22 R25/157 P(36-20-0) 259
SF   D26 R37/153 P(28-21-1) 226
Det-Doran 150C, Rote 212P
```

```
NYG   7 17  0  7  31
GB    7  0  7  7  21
NYG  D16 R36/123 P(22-9-1) 153
GB   D17 R41/225 P(32-11-2) 157
GB-Hornung 112R, Howton 111C

Phi  17  0  0 21  38
ChiC  0  7  7  7  21
Phi  D20 R39/165 P(21-12-2) 199
ChiC D19 R21/73 P(33-17-4) 281
ChiC-Nagler 152C

Pit   0  7  7  5  19
Bal   6  0  7  0  13
Pit  D12 R30/15 P(30-18-1) 256
Bal  D17 R38/168 P(15-6-4) 87
Pit-Mathews 165C

Was   7  3  0  7  17
Cle   7  0 14  0  21
Was  D13 R32/106 P(12-5-1) 58
Cle  D21 R58/231 P(12-8-1) 122
Cle-Brown 109R, Brewster 103C
```

SUNDAY, NOVEMBER 10

```
Bal   7  7  0  7  21
Was   0  7  7  3  17
Bal  D15 R27/71 P(30-17-0) 230
Was  D21 R47/179 P(21-10-1) 108
Bal-Berry 224C

ChiC  0  0  7  7  14
NYG   7  3  7 10  27
ChiC D17 R29/120 P(22-7-1) 61
NYG  D21 R43/170 P(22-11-0) 203
NYG-Gifford 126R

Det   0 21  3  3  27
Phi   3  6  0  7  16
Det  D18 R48/199 P(24-11-1) 177
Phi  D13 R28/157 P(25-9-3) 44

GB    7  0  0  7  14
ChiB  0  0  7  7  21
GB   D11 R37/137 P(22-12-0) 138
ChiB D18 R35/154 P(27-16-2) 198

Pit   0  0  0  0   0
Cle   3  7  7  7  24
Pit  D18 R30/90 P(37-17-2) 186
Cle  D11 R36/123 P(12-8-1) 168

SF    7 10  0  7  24
LARm 14 14  2  7  37
SF   D15 R37/128 P(27-15-0) 133
LARm D25 R47/193 P(24-14-0) 207
LARm-Boyd 117C
```

SUNDAY, NOVEMBER 17

```
Bal  13  0  0 16  29
ChiB  0 14  0  0  14
Bal  D12 R29/48 P(23-11-0) 180
ChiB D16 R37/139 P(30-11-5) 70

Cle   3  7  3 17  30
Was   6  3 14  7  30
Cle  D17 R32/82 P(24-16-1) 343
Was  D14 R42/153 P(10-7-0) 177
Cle-Brewster 124C, Carpenter 112C,
Renfro 113C, O'Connell 349P

LARm  0  3 14 14  31
GB   10 14  0  7  31
LARm D27 R43/271 P(32-14-3) 241
GB   D16 R33/120 P(22-13-0) 156
LARm-Arnett 149R, Hirsch 106C

Phi   0  0  0  0   0
NYG   0  6  0  7  13
Phi  D16 R49/213 P(13-5-1) 40
NYG  D13 R32/110 P(17-8-0) 79

SF    0  0  7  3  10
Det   0 21  3  7  31
SF   D16 R21/73 P(26-19-1) 150
Det  D28 R34/145 P(43-24-2) 370
SF-Wilson 105C; Det-Doran 137C
```

SUNDAY, NOVEMBER 24

```
ChiB  0 17  7  3  27
Det   0  0  7  0   7
ChiB D17 R54/200 P(14-7-1) 79
Det  D14 R26/106 P(35-12-2) 110
ChiB-Casares 116R

GB    0 21  0  6  27
Pit   0  3  0  7  10
GB   D15 R39/151 P(33-10-2) 102
Pit  D11 R23/59 P(37-14-4) 108
```

```
LARm    0  21   7   3  31
Cle     7  10  14  14  45
LARm D16 R35/174  P(20-7-3)  112
Cle  D21 R58/330  P(13-6-2)   48
Cle-Brown 237R

NYG    14  14   0   0  28
ChiC    0   7   0  14  21
NYG  D18 R50/202  P(17-7-0)  205
ChiC D14 R25/89   P(36-13-5) 266
ChiC-Matson 137C

SF      0  14   0   7  21
Bal     0  14   6   7  27
SF   D26 R26/129  P(32-24-2) 281
Bal  D23 R40/225  P(27-16-0) 230

Was     3   6   3   0  12
Phi     0   7   7   7  21
Was  D14 R35/107  P(24-12-2) 123
Phi  D12 R31/122  P(14-9-2)  186
```

THURSDAY, NOVEMBER 28
```
GB      3   3   0   0   6
Det     0   3  12   3  18
GB   D19 R23/58   P(38-21-1) 228
Det  D13 R38/215  P(15-7-2)  134
Det-Johnson 105R
```

SUNDAY, DECEMBER 1
```
ChiC    0   0   0   0   0
Cle     7  14   3   7  31
ChiC D10 R38/150  P(21-5-3)   16
Cle  D15 R39/167  P(17-6-1)  167
Cle-Renfro 109C

LARm    0   7   7   0  14
Bal    14   0   3  14  31
LARm D13 R29/125  P(25-10-2) 132
Bal  D23 R46/164  P(31-18-1) 261

Pit     3   0   3   0   6
Phi     0   7   0   0   7
Pit  D13 R37/171  P(17-10-0)  87
Phi  D10 R40/153  P(8-5-0)    67

SF      7  10   7   3  27
NYG     0  10   0   7  17
SF   D19 R41/193  P(16-11-3) 123
NYG  D21 R24/70   P(26-18-1) 195
NYG-Gifford 105C

Was    14   0   0   0  14
ChiB    0   3   0   0   3
Was  D15 R53/212  P(15-7-1)   80
ChiB D9  R30/135  P(20-6-2)   27
```

SATURDAY, DECEMBER 7
```
NYG     0   7   3   0  10
Pit     7   7   0   7  21
NYG  D16 R27/66   P(29-16-1) 194
Pit  D12 R42/142  P(10-4-0)   47
```

SUNDAY, DECEMBER 8
```
Bal     0   6   7   0  13
SF      7   3   0   7  17
Bal  D16 R30/82   P(37-23-2) 288
SF   D23 R25/111  P(37-22-2) 215
Bal-Moore 180C;
SF-McElhenny 165C

ChiB    7   7   0   0  14
ChiC    0   0   6   6  12
ChiB D15 R48/223  P(18-9-1)  151
ChiC D10 R31/70   P(26-11-1) 125

Cle     0   0   7   0   7
Det     3   0   7  10  20
Cle  D14 R34/69   P(24-15-1) 197
Det  D15 R27/151  P(23-7-0)   75

GB      0   3   0  14  17
LARm    7  14  14  14  42
GB   D18 R27/161  P(32-16-0) 146
LARm D27 R42/302  P(31-17-2) 297
LARm-Waller 105R,
Van Brocklin 253P

Phi     0   0   0   7   7
Was     7  14   7  14  42
Phi  D13 R26/107  P(29-11-5) 140
Was  D20 R42/203  P(16-9-1)  173
```

SATURDAY, DECEMBER 14
```
ChiC    0  10   7  14  31
Phi    14   0  10   0  27
ChiC D21 R35/105  P(20-13-1) 286
Phi  D18 R37/164  P(22-15-1) 272
ChiC-Lewis 162C
```

SUNDAY, DECEMBER 15
```
Bal     7   0   7   7  21
LARm   10   0   0  17  37
Bal  D19 R28/137  P(30-14-3) 199
LARm D26 R44/151  P(33-19-1) 294
Bal-Berry 146C;
LARm-Van Brocklin 328P

Cle     7  10   7  10  34
NYG    14   7   0   7  28
Cle  D21 R45/298  P(16-11-1) 190
NYG  D23 R28/108  P(32-17-3) 282
Cle-Carpenter 117R, Renfro 120C

Det     0   0  14   7  21
ChiB    3   7   0   3  13
Det  D23 R39/174  P(35-15-4) 155
ChiB D14 R29/54   P(28-13-1) 160

GB      0  20   0   0  20
SF     10   0  10   7  27
GB   D15 R27/105  P(25-15-3) 122
SF   D19 R40/172  P(26-15-2) 153
SF-Perry 130R

Pit     0   0   0   3   3
Was     0   3   0   7  10
Pit  D7  R26/80   P(23-7-0)   78
Was  D15 R45/144  P(13-9-1)   65
```

SUNDAY, DECEMBER 22
```
Pit    14   0   3  10  27
ChiC    0   0   2   0   2
Pit  D19 R45/168  P(28-13-0) 129
ChiC D10 R15/38   P(24-8-1)   58
```

1958 NFL
SUNDAY, SEPTEMBER 28
```
ChiB    7  14   7   6  34
GB     10   3   0   7  20
ChiB D16 R40/146  P(15-9-2)  154
GB   D12 R26/123  P(24-11-1)  94

Cle     0   7   7  16  30
LARm    3  14  10   0  27
Cle  D23 R38/257  P(25-13-2) 116
LARm D20 R31/202  P(22-17-0) 268
Cle-Brown 171R;
LARm-Wilson 108R, Shofner 149C

Det     0   9   6   0  15
Bal     7   7   0  14  28
Det  D12 R24/73   P(30-12-3) 109
Bal  D26 R36/166  P(43-23-1) 250
Bal-Berry 149C

NYG    14  13   7   3  37
ChiC    0   7   0   0   7
NYG  D17 R41/252  P(10-4-1)   43
ChiC D16 R34/123  P(35-19-2) 207

Pit     0   7  13   0  20
SF      7   0   6  10  23
Pit  D10 R23/117  P(24-9-3)  100
SF   D18 R30/88   P(33-20-3) 234
SF-Owens 103C

Was     0  10   0  14  24
Phi     7   0   0   0   7
Was  D25 R54/212  P(15-10-1) 134
Phi  D11 R27/60   P(25-12-0) 109
```

SATURDAY, OCTOBER 4
```
ChiB    3   7  21   7  38
Bal    27   7   7  10  51
ChiB D20 R31/140  P(35-16-5) 176
Bal  D18 R38/147  P(25-11-0) 178
Bal-Moore 118C, Unitas 198P

Was     0   0   3   7  10
ChiC    7  10   7  13  37
Was  D13 R28/133  P(24-9-0)  114
ChiC D26 R39/261  P(32-18-2) 270
Was-Carson 142C
```

SUNDAY, OCTOBER 5
```
Cle     7  17  14   7  45
Pit     0  10   0   2  12
Cle  D20 R36/192  P(21-16-2) 219
Pit  D12 R26/100  P(25-8-4)  169
Cle-Brown 129R, Carpenter 131C

Det     0   6   7   0  13
GB      3  10   0   0  13
Det  D13 R26/33   P(30-16-1) 245
GB   D15 R36/114  P(34-19-2) 173
Det-Doran 133C

LARm    3   7   9  14  33
SF      0   3   0   0   3
LARm D23 R37/227  P(29-16-2) 135
SF   D11 R22/85   P(25-15-4) 101
LARm-Arnett 129R

NYG     7  10   7   0  24
Phi    10   7   3   7  27
NYG  D21 R31/102  P(33-18-1) 212
Phi  D15 R32/70   P(34-16-3) 238
NYG-Gifford 113C
```

SUNDAY, OCTOBER 12
```
Bal     0   7   7  10  24
GB     14   3   0   0  17
Bal  D19 R27/152  P(36-17-1) 230
GB   D21 R26/61   P(47-26-4) 299
Bal-Moore 108C; GB-Starr 320P

ChiC    0   7   7  14  28
Cle    14   7   7   7  35
ChiC D18 R22/148  P(28-12-2) 241
Cle  D26 R54/332  P(15-7-1)  122
ChiC-Crow 152C; Cle-Brown 182R,
Mitchell 147R

LARm    0  21   0  21  42
Det     0  21   0   7  28
LARm D14 R24/205  P(23-10-1) 142
Det  D26 R50/230  P(28-12-3) 206
Det-Doran 102C

NYG    14   0   0   7  21
Was     0   0   0  14  14
NYG  D15 R45/195  P(19-7-2)  149
Was  D13 R32/69   P(26-14-2) 248

Phi     3   0   0   0   3
Pit    14   7   3   0  24
Phi  D16 R22/59   P(37-16-3) 148
Pit  D19 R50/214  P(21-10-1)  72

SF      6   0   0   0   6
ChiB    7   7   0  14  28
SF   D19 R15/101  P(33-19-3) 127
ChiB D21 R44/219  P(26-12-0) 115
```

SUNDAY, OCTOBER 19
```
Bal     6   7   7  20  40
Det     0   0   7   7  14
Bal  D25 R49/316  P(18-11-0) 219
Det  D14 R23/79   P(25-9-1)  141
Bal-Moore 136R

ChiC    0   6   0  17  23
NYG     0   0   6   0   6
ChiC D23 R49/176  P(24-14-1) 245
NYG  D13 R26/97   P(26-9-1) -118

GB      0   0   0  21  21
Was    10  10  14   3  37
GB   D16 R28/137  P(26-7-1)  288
Was  D23 R50/292  P(16-7-0)  154
GB-Ferguson 100R, Howton 130C;
Was-Olszewski 165R

LARm    7   0   3   0  10
ChiB   10   7   0  14  31
LARm D11 R23/73   P(31-13-4) 142
ChiB D15 R33/114  P(29-13-2) 192
LARm-Shofner 114C

Pit     7   0   0   3  10
Cle     7  14   0   6  27
Pit  D14 R32/87   P(28-15-1) 172
Cle  D19 R36/264  P(20-9-2)  145
Cle-Brown 153R, Mitchell 108R

SF     14   0   3  13  30
Phi    10   7   0   7  24
SF   D18 R37/111  P(24-13-1) 269
Phi  D25 R30/107  P(33-18-1) 202
```

SUNDAY, OCTOBER 26
```
ChiB    0  13   7   7  27
SF      7   0   0   7  14
ChiB D17 R33/112  P(24-13-1) 236
SF   D20 R28/68   P(36-25-2) 251
SF-Wilson 121C

Cle    10   7  14   7  38
ChiC    7  14   3   0  24
Cle  D14 R43/266  P(14-10-0) 110
ChiC D17 R37/136  P(22-10-1) 114
Cle-Brown 180R, Renfro 108C

Det     7  14   7  13  41
LARm    3   7  14   0  24
Det  D21 R34/152  P(26-13-2) 170
LARm D14 R18/48   P(36-16-7) 225

Phi     0  14   0  21  35
GB      3  14  21   0  38
Phi  D19 R21/118  P(39-22-2) 293
GB   D19 R37/127  P(25-14-0) 191
Phi-Retzlaff 121C; GB-McGee 100C,
Parilli 199P

Pit     0   3   0   3   6
NYG     7   3   0   7  17
Pit  D10 R25/45   P(33-14-1) 194
NYG  D12 R46/146  P(10-2-0)   29
Pit-Younger 109C

Was     0   7   0   3  10
Bal     7  14  14   0  35
Was  D11 R38/167  P(16-4-2)   16
Bal  D21 R41/186  P(20-12-1) 204
```

SUNDAY, NOVEMBER 2
```
ChiB    7   7   7  14  35
LARm   17  14  10   0  41
ChiB D26 R38/171  P(45-18-2) 167
LARm D14 R32/145  P(23-12-3) 172
ChiB-Casares 113R

Det     7   0  14   0  21
SF      0  17   0   7  24
Det  D12 R29/130  P(26-9-1)   41
SF   D15 R36/234  P(29-16-4) 177
SF-Perry 174R

GB      0   0   0   0   0
Bal     7  21  14  14  56
GB   D8  R24/95   P(26-5-5)   49
Bal  D30 R49/220  P(29-15-1) 170

NYG     0   7   7   7  21
Cle     3  14   0   0  17
NYG  D22 R45/161  P(23-12-3) 196
Cle  D11 R32/184  P(14-4-2)   17
NYG-Triplett 116R; Cle-Brown 113R

Phi     0   7   0  14  21
ChiC    0   7   7   7  21
Phi  D27 R35/118  P(48-25-3) 281
ChiC D13 R26/200  P(33-14-3) 184
ChiC-Lewis 150C

Was     3   3   0  10  16
Pit     0  14   0  10  24
Was  D15 R34/80   P(26-14-4) 216
Pit  D20 R36/146  P(26-13-0) 252
Was-Walton 106C; Pit-Orr 133C
```

SUNDAY, NOVEMBER 9
```
Bal     7   7   0   7  21
NYG     0   7  14   3  24
Bal  D19 R32/146  P(30-12-1) 238
NYG  D18 R39/167  P(20-13-1) 174
Bal-Moore 181C

ChiC    3   7  14   7  31
Was    14  24   0   7  45
ChiC D23 R30/91   P(21-14-2) 293
Was  D27 R42/242  P(23-15-0) 258
ChiC-Lewis 132C, McHan 276P;
Was-Olszewski 136C, Podoley 121C,
LeBaron 267P

Det     3  17   7   3  30
GB      0   3   0   7  10
Det  D18 R27/91   P(30-17-0) 246
GB   D13 R37/129  P(17-10-1) 118

GB      3   0   0   7  10
ChiB    0   7  14   3  24
GB   D9  R24/52   P(26-11-2)  93
ChiB D15 R43/273  P(18-8-2)   89
ChiB-Casares 113R
```

```
Pit     3  14  14   0  31
Phi     7   3   7   7  24
Pit  D15 R36/96   P(25-11-2) 290
Phi  D23 R34/125  P(35-19-0) 197
Pit-Mathews 115C, Tracy 116C,
Layne 225P

SF      0   7   7   7  21
LARm   21  14  14   7  56
SF   D20 R32/114  P(37-14-4) 168
LARm D27 R39/324  P(27-17-1) 253
LARm-Marconi 119R,
Shofner 136C, Wade 256P
```

SUNDAY, NOVEMBER 16
```
Bal     0  14   0   3  17
ChiB    0   0   0   0   0
Bal  D14 R42/159  P(23-10-1) 126
ChiB D8  R28/107  P(26-8-3)   54
Bal-Ameche 142R

ChiC    0  14   0   7  21
Phi     7  21  14   7  49
ChiC D19 R35/105  P(45-17-2) 216
Phi  D28 R30/102  P(35-23-2) 412
ChiC-Lewis 130C; Phi-Barnes 109C,
Van Brocklin 318P

Cle     7   3   0  10  20
Was     7   3   0   0  10
Cle  D20 R45/237  P(27-12-3) 186
Was  D11 R26/65   P(21-9-2)  150
Cle-Brown 152R, Carpenter 115C

LARm   10   0   3   7  20
GB      7   0   0   0   7
LARm D22 R35/132  P(42-19-2) 352
GB   D14 R22/81   P(36-18-4) 203
LARm-Phillips 208C, Wade 372P

NYG     0   0   3   7  10
Pit     0   7  14  10  31
NYG  D13 R32/88   P(26-11-0) 103
Pit  D17 R37/129  P(22-9-2)  168

SF      0   0   0   7   7
Det    14  14   0   7  35
SF   D22 R26/78   P(34-21-2) 217
Det  D23 R29/153  P(25-15-0) 293
```

SUNDAY, NOVEMBER 23
```
ChiB    3   3  14   0  20
Det     0   7   0   0   7
ChiB D15 R43/138  P(18-10-1) 169
Det  D13 R22/67   P(25-10-0) 104
ChiB-McColl 123C

LARm    0   0   7   0   7
Bal     7   6   0  21  34
LARm D19 R18/75   P(45-25-4) 344
Bal  D19 R40/151  P(20-14-0) 218
LARm-Lundy 103C, Shofner 110C,
Wade 356P; Bal-Moore 157C

Phi     0   7   0   7  14
Cle    14   7   0   7  28
Phi  D20 R35/115  P(30-18-0) 210
Cle  D15 R39/135  P(11-8-0)  143

Pit    10  10   0   7  27
ChiC   10   3   7   0  20
Pit  D18 R29/84   P(30-18-0) 374
ChiC D18 R32/73   P(39-20-2) 242
Pit-Orr 116C, Tracy 125C,
Layne 352P

SF      6   3   3  21  33
GB      9   0   3   0  12
SF   D26 R42/256  P(35-20-0) 283
GB   D11 R20/149  P(25-8-1)   58
SF-McElhenny 159R, Wilson 128C

Was     0   0   0   0   0
NYG     6  10   7   7  30
Was  D11 R30/125  P(32-11-2)  90
NYG  D19 R38/186  P(22-13-0) 173
```

THURSDAY, NOVEMBER 27
```
GB      7   0   7   0  14
Det     0  10   7   7  24
GB   D14 R25/104  P(30-15-1) 138
Det  D15 R34/94   P(22-7-1)  104
```

SUNDAY, NOVEMBER 30

ChiB 0 0 0 10 10
Pit 7 3 0 14 24
ChiB D19 R34/127 P(34-18-2) 143
Pit D12 R35/194 P(16-7-1) 202
Pit-Tracy 156R, Orr 163C

LARm 3 3 7 7 20
ChiC 0 7 7 0 14
LARm D18 R39/145 P(30-16-0) 161
ChiC D17 R13/60 P(51-28-1) 234

Phi 7 3 0 0 10
NYG 3 14 0 7 24
Phi D13 R28/83 P(29-17-3) 212
NYG D16 R37/151 P(23-9-1) 131

SF 7 20 0 0 27
Bal 7 0 7 21 35
SF D22 R30/155 P(29-15-5) 158
Bal D24 R39/219 P(33-17-1) 196
SF-Perry 113R; Bal-Moore 114R, Berry 114C

Was 7 0 7 0 14
Cle 7 0 0 14 21
Was D21 R40/150 P(18-13-1) 160
Cle D15 R29/130 P(19-10-0) 206
Cle-Renfro 100C

SATURDAY, DECEMBER 6

Bal 14 0 7 7 28
LARm 3 13 7 7 30
Bal D26 R39/156 P(41-23-3) 203
LARm D12 R19/44 P(26-11-2) 235
LARm-Shofner 175C

SUNDAY, DECEMBER 7

ChiC 0 0 0 14 14
ChiB 10 20 0 0 30
ChiC D12 R31/50 P(35-10-4) 84
ChiB D17 R41/151 P(30-11-4) 162
ChiB-Casares 102R

Cle 14 0 7 0 21
Phi 7 7 0 0 14
Cle D21 R49/250 P(11-5-1) 92
Phi D16 R26/129 P(28-16-2) 144
Cle-Brown 138R, Carpenter 100R

GB 0 7 7 7 21
SF 27 7 14 0 48
GB D21 R33/172 P(31-15-5) 163
SF D23 R30/210 P(30-21-1) 258
GB-Taylor 137R; SF-Smith 113R

NYG 5 7 0 7 19
Det 0 3 14 0 17
NYG D13 R48/116 P(17-6-2) 135
Det D13 R31/140 P(20-6-2) 14

Pit 0 0 7 7 14
Was 0 14 0 0 14
Pit D20 R24/98 P(34-18-3) 287
Was D19 R49/216 P(11-6-1) -28
Pit-Orr 123C, Layne 309P; Was-Bosseler 145R

SATURDAY, DECEMBER 13

ChiC 0 7 14 0 21
Pit 0 17 7 14 38
ChiC D17 R18/33 P(42-22-5) 244
Pit D35 R41/211 P(52-24-3) 472
ChiC-Childress 118C; Pit-Younger 106R, McClairen 139C, Orr 205C, Tracy 106C, Layne 409P

SUNDAY, DECEMBER 14

Bal 3 3 0 6 12
SF 0 7 7 7 21
Bal D13 R24/109 P(38-14-0) 180
SF D23 R31/128 P(38-24-0) 240

Cle 7 3 0 0 10
NYG 0 3 0 10 13
Cle D9 R37/150 P(12-6-0) 107
NYG D12 R22/64 P(37-15-0) 162
Cle-Brown 148R

Det 3 10 3 0 16
ChiB 0 7 0 14 21
Det D15 R35/118 P(32-15-0) 196
ChiB D13 R29/72 P(21-10-0) 154

GB 7 7 3 3 20
LARm 0 24 3 7 34
GB D17 R44/206 P(18-7-1) 73
LARm D15 R30/114 P(24-14-0) 243

Phi 0 0 0 0 0
Was 3 10 0 7 20
Phi D9 R14/7 P(29-12-2) 251
Was D24 R57/226 P(23-9-2) 184
Phi-McDonald 148C; Was-Anderson 105C

1959 NFL

SATURDAY, SEPTEMBER 26

NYG 3 14 0 6 23
LARm 0 7 14 0 21
NYG D17 R31/86 P(31-21-0) 321
LARm D20 R28/124 P(23-15-1) 234
NYG-Schnelker 171C, Conerly 321P; LARm-Shofner 130C

Cle 0 7 0 0 7
Pit 0 0 10 7 17
Cle D20 R32/139 P(23-13-1) 135
Pit D18 R32/121 P(21-13-2) 202

SUNDAY, SEPTEMBER 27

ChiB 0 3 0 3 6
GB 0 0 0 9 9
ChiB D10 R30/75 P(23-10-0) 89
GB D16 R48/177 P(14-4-1) 85

Det 3 0 6 0 9
Bal 0 0 14 7 21
Det D19 R29/155 P(29-12-5) 179
Bal D19 R37/117 P(31-13-0) 222

Phi 0 0 0 14 14
SF 7 7 7 3 24
Phi D15 R29/104 P(40-21-0) 174
SF D18 R41/170 P(18-10-1) 121

Was 0 0 14 7 21
ChiC 7 14 14 14 49
Was D23 R40/193 P(25-15-1) 226
ChiC D25 R26/250 P(28-17-1) 319
Was-Anderson 123C; ChiC-Conrad 140R, Lewis 115C

SATURDAY, OCTOBER 3

ChiB 9 14 3 0 26
Bal 0 0 0 21 21
ChiB D13 R35/110 P(25-12-1) 155
Bal D19 R26/74 P(38-17-3) 183
Bal-Berry 123C

SUNDAY, OCTOBER 4

Cle 7 14 7 6 34
ChiC 0 0 7 0 7
Cle D20 R45/160 P(14-11-0) 139
ChiC D21 R20/101 P(38-17-1) 172
Cle-Brown 147R; ChiC-Lewis 106C

Det 0 7 3 0 10
GB 14 0 0 14 28
Det D14 R26/82 P(34-18-3) 142
GB D10 R33/113 P(17-8-1) 150
GB-McGee 124C, McHan 146P

LARm 0 0 0 0 0
SF 10 14 0 10 34
LARm D12 R19/87 P(36-15-3) 90
SF D19 R47/235 P(15-8-1) 61
SF-Smith 103R

NYG 0 7 0 14 21
Phi 7 14 21 7 49
NYG D21 R27/110 P(33-19-2) 223
Phi D18 R36/76 P(25-15-0) 223
Phi-McDonald 133C

Was 3 6 14 0 23
Pit 0 0 10 7 17
Was D14 R31/84 P(23-12-1) 238
Pit D23 R26/113 P(43-22-2) 268
Was-Anderson 106C; Pit-Brewster 123C

SUNDAY, OCTOBER 11

Bal 7 7 7 10 31
Det 3 14 7 0 24
Bal D20 R39/164 P(26-13-2) 245
Det D16 R28/190 P(30-10-4) 102

ChiC 7 0 0 7 14
Was 7 0 7 9 23
ChiC D20 R26/104 P(32-20-0) 194
Was D17 R46/168 P(15-8-1) 112

LARm 7 7 7 7 28
ChiB 0 21 0 0 21
LARm D22 R54/245 P(17-12-0) 175
ChiB D16 R15/21 P(29-14-1) 285
LARm-Matson 199R; ChiB-Hill 147C, Brown 323P

NYG 0 7 0 3 10
Cle 0 0 0 6 6
NYG D14 R34/156 P(17-9-0) 94
Cle D23 R36/139 P(37-18-1) 204

Pit 7 3 7 7 24
Phi 7 7 7 7 28
Pit D15 R21/66 P(35-18-2) 203
Phi D18 R40/109 P(28-13-2) 172

SF 3 3 14 0 20
GB 7 7 0 7 21
SF D13 R31/122 P(23-8-0) 117
GB D25 R55/284 P(14-6-1) 87
GB-Hornung 138R

SUNDAY, OCTOBER 18

Bal 7 0 0 14 21
ChiB 0 0 7 0 7
Bal D18 R36/122 P(30-16-2) 208
ChiB D18 R22/103 P(34-19-5) 237

ChiC 0 0 7 0 7
Cle 14 0 3 0 17
ChiC D13 R30/98 P(20-7-2) 122
Cle D18 R44/169 P(22-12-0) 126
Cle-Brown 123R

LARm 11 3 7 24 45
GB 0 6 0 0 6
LARm D23 R43/258 P(21-16-0) 198
GB D16 R25/117 P(28-14-2) 145
LARm-Matson 121R

Phi 7 0 0 0 7
NYG 7 10 7 0 24
Phi D16 R29/68 P(27-16-2) 179
NYG D20 R34/163 P(20-13-1) 269
NYG-Gifford 117C

Pit 14 7 0 6 27
Was 6 0 0 0 6
Pit D13 R33/134 P(15-8-2) 53
Was D12 R40/195 P(16-3-2) -13
Was-Bosseler 136R

SF 7 13 7 7 34
Det 0 0 7 6 13
SF D20 R39/299 P(18-7-0) 108
Det D14 R28/117 P(26-12-1) 185
SF-Perry 145R, Smith 152R

SUNDAY, OCTOBER 25

ChiB 3 0 7 7 17
SF 0 7 3 10 20
ChiB D17 R25/90 P(32-15-3) 230
SF D18 R41/175 P(28-13-1) 157

Det 0 10 0 7 17
LARm 0 7 0 0 7
Det D18 R39/172 P(18-7-1) 87
LARm D23 R34/126 P(31-20-3) 219
LARm-Clarke 100C

GB 0 7 7 7 21
Bal 0 14 21 3 38
GB D16 R22/139 P(29-15-4) 205
Bal D25 R37/118 P(29-19-0) 191
GB-McGee 110C; Bal-Berry 117C

NYG 14 0 0 7 21
Pit 10 0 3 3 16
NYG D10 R39/80 P(19-9-2) 199
Pit D9 R31/33 P(27-10-4) 210
NYG-Gifford 135C; Pit-Dial 146C

Phi 0 0 21 7 28
ChiC 7 10 7 0 24
Phi D22 R38/168 P(28-16-1) 231
ChiC D14 R38/163 P(23-9-4) 150
Phi-Barnes 111R, McDonald 122C

Was 0 0 7 0 7
Cle 6 7 7 14 34
Was D14 R35/153 P(19-8-4) 91
Cle D20 R31/172 P(23-16-0) 240
Cle-Brown 122R, Mitchell 107C, Plum 253P

SUNDAY, NOVEMBER 1

ChiB 7 0 19 0 26
LARm 7 0 7 7 21
ChiB D20 R42/143 P(27-14-0) 196
LARm D17 R21/166 P(32-15-2) 237

Cle 3 14 14 7 38
Bal 3 7 7 14 31
Cle D22 R42/197 P(23-14-2) 200
Bal D28 R19/45 P(41-23-3) 381
Cle-Brown 178R; Bal-Berry 156C, Moore 115C, Unitas 397P

Det 7 0 0 0 7
SF 14 7 5 7 33
Det D11 R21/84 P(29-12-1) 99
SF D20 R38/196 P(25-12-4) 198
SF-Smith 115R

GB 0 3 0 0 3
NYG 7 3 10 0 20
GB D9 R26/69 P(26-7-1) 91
NYG D15 R40/80 P(31-15-1) 135

Pit 0 10 7 7 24
ChiC 14 21 0 10 45
Pit D20 R36/175 P(23-8-3) 154
ChiC D20 R46/266 P(11-3-2) 70

Was 0 9 0 14 23
Phi 10 20 0 0 30
Was D21 R44/254 P(22-9-2) 124
Phi D17 R31/212 P(19-13-1) 142
Was-Bosseler 168R; Phi-Barnes 163R

SUNDAY, NOVEMBER 8

Bal 3 0 7 14 24
Was 0 7 3 17 27
Bal D19 R25/96 P(36-16-2) 271
Was D16 R26/56 P(34-17-1) 222
Bal-Moore 109C, Mutscheller 103C

ChiC 0 3 0 0 3
NYG 3 0 3 3 9
ChiC D6 R28/114 P(21-8-3) 49
NYG D11 R40/130 P(20-11-2) 144

Det 7 0 0 3 10
Pit 0 0 3 7 10
Det D16 R40/183 P(20-8-3) 131
Pit D14 R25/66 P(27-12-3) 123

GB 0 10 0 7 17
ChiB 14 7 7 0 28
GB D16 R39/158 P(15-5-1) 72
ChiB D15 R42/172 P(17-10-1) 107

Phi 0 0 0 7 7
Cle 7 14 0 7 28
Phi D15 R23/67 P(41-23-2) 247
Cle D16 R36/183 P(20-12-0) 128
Cle-Brown 125R

SF 7 10 7 0 24
LARm 0 3 7 6 16
SF D16 R44/169 P(14-8-0) 131
LARm D28 R33/175 P(35-21-1) 261
SF-Wilson 100C; LARm-Matson 105R

SUNDAY, NOVEMBER 15

Bal 7 14 0 7 28
GB 3 0 14 7 24
Bal D23 R36/192 P(34-19-0) 317
GB D22 R30/218 P(40-14-3) 237
Bal-Unitas 324P; GB-Dowler 147C

ChiC 7 7 0 3 17
Phi 0 14 3 10 27
ChiC D11 R32/129 P(15-6-2) 52
Phi D18 R43/159 P(21-10-2) 218
Phi-Retzlaff 137C

Cle 14 0 10 7 31
Was 7 7 3 0 17
Cle D19 R32/276 P(25-17-0) 154
Was D15 R35/255 P(17-7-2) 98
Cle-Mitchell 232R; Was-Olszewski 190R

LARm 0 10 0 7 17
Det 7 6 7 3 23
LARm D14 R30/82 P(26-16-0) 220
Det D10 R39/135 P(14-6-0) 87
LARm-Shofner 169C

Pit 0 7 0 7 14
NYG 0 6 3 0 9
Pit D20 R41/155 P(31-13-3) 167
NYG D9 R30/78 P(24-7-1) 109

SF 0 3 0 0 3
ChiB 7 0 7 0 14
SF D16 R29/82 P(35-18-5) 181
ChiB D14 R37/215 P(19-10-1) 142

SUNDAY, NOVEMBER 22

ChiB 0 17 0 7 24
Det 0 0 0 14 14
ChiB D13 R34/116 P(18-6-1) 14
Det D18 R37/143 P(35-11-4) 196
ChiB-Casares 111R

LARm 3 7 0 10 20
Phi 0 13 7 3 23
LARm D14 R24/177 P(30-12-2) 93
Phi D21 R36/112 P(38-19-0) 278
LARm-Arnett 108R

NYG 0 13 7 10 30
ChiC 0 0 14 6 20
NYG D12 R30/118 P(23-12-1) 268
ChiC D9 R34/96 P(12-6-0) 0
NYG-Webster 120C

Pit 0 14 0 7 21
Cle 0 6 0 14 20
Pit D21 R47/182 P(21-13-0) 156
Cle D16 R22/126 P(29-17-0) 261
Cle-Brown 111R, Renfro 161C

SF 0 7 7 0 14
Bal 0 21 7 17 45
SF D3 R16/35 P(17-11-2) 98
Bal D29 R60/271 P(23-12-1) 168
Bal-Ameche 120R

Was 0 0 0 0 0
GB 0 14 7 0 21
Was D17 R43/200 P(24-7-2) 38
GB D22 R35/186 P(23-12-2) 150

THURSDAY, NOVEMBER 26

GB 17 7 0 0 24
Det 3 14 0 0 17
GB D12 R36/73 P(15-10-0) 169
Det D21 R40/190 P(29-13-2) 164
GB-Dowler 107C; Det-Pietrosante 134R, Gibbons 103C

SUNDAY, NOVEMBER 29

ChiB 7 10 7 7 31
ChiC 0 0 7 0 7
ChiB D15 R36/93 P(27-12-1) 180
ChiC D13 R37/171 P(25-8-2) 99
ChiB-Dewveall 105C

LARm 0 14 7 0 21
Bal 14 14 7 0 35
LARm D16 R23/92 P(26-16-2) 282
Bal D23 R42/188 P(24-14-1) 208
LARm-Shofner 113C, Wade 304P; Bal-Berry 168C

Phi 0 0 0 0 0
Pit 3 7 7 14 31
Phi D9 R19/29 P(32-15-4) 196
Pit D24 R46/228 P(28-12-1) 165
Pit-Tracy 122R, Layne 182P

SF 0 21 0 0 21
Cle 7 3 3 7 20
SF D9 R29/59 P(22-10-0) 141
Cle D21 R43/182 P(26-11-2) 99
Cle-Brown 114R

Was 0 0 7 7 14
NYG 14 24 0 7 45
Was D9 R21/102 P(19-8-3) 28
NYG D26 R58/351 P(18-9-1) 126
NYG-Gifford 159R

SATURDAY, DECEMBER 5

Bal 7 7 6 14 34
SF 0 7 0 7 14
Bal D25 R42/135 P(36-21-0) 260
SF D13 R23/115 P(27-14-6) 139
Bal-Moore 115C; SF-Smith 100R

SUNDAY, DECEMBER 6
ChiC 0 7 0 14 21
Det 10 14 7 14 **45**
ChiC D16 R23/71 P(26-14-0) 218
Det D24 R44/219 P(28-12-2) 158

Cle 0 0 0 7 7
NYG 7 17 24 0 **48**
Cle D9 R35/110 P(20-6-3) 26
NYG D21 R31/125 P(40-23-1) 401
NYG-Gifford 129C, Schnelker 102C

GB 14 14 0 10 **38**
LARm 7 0 13 0 20
GB D21 R31/143 P(22-13-1) 192
LARm D22 R33/99 P(42-21-3) 187

Phi 3 17 0 14 **34**
Was 0 0 7 7 14
Phi D26 R42/151 P(31-18-1) 275
Was D16 R27/129 P(34-12-3) 188
Phi-McDonald 153C;
Was-Anderson 108C

Pit 0 7 7 7 21
ChiB 6 14 7 0 **27**
Pit D18 R33/148 P(28-10-0) 166
ChiB D24 R39/161 P(31-18-2) 230
Pit-Tracy 109R, Dial 108C

SATURDAY, DECEMBER 12
Bal 7 10 7 21 **45**
LARm 10 6 10 0 26
Bal D19 R36/183 P(27-13-0) 99
LARm D21 R29/147 P(37-17-5) 286

SUNDAY, DECEMBER 13
ChiC 6 0 7 7 20
Pit 0 28 7 0 **35**
ChiC D11 R27/50 P(29-10-2) 114
Pit D12 R35/122 P(20-11-1) 185
Pit-Layne 201P

Cle 7 7 0 14 **28**
Phi 0 21 0 0 21
Cle D30 R59/296 P(14-12-0) 154
Phi D16 R25/60 P(22-15-1) 237
Cle-Brown 152R, Mitchell 127R

Det 0 0 14 0 14
ChiB 9 6 7 3 **25**
Det D17 R28/122 P(36-15-1) 134
ChiB D15 R35/139 P(28-16-0) 208

GB 0 14 16 6 **36**
SF 14 0 0 0 14
GB D27 R41/230 P(25-20-0) 249
SF D17 R29/182 P(22-13-2) 97
GB-Carpenter 113R; SF-Smith 106R

NYG 7 0 10 7 **24**
Was 7 3 0 0 10
NYG D22 R39/169 P(26-17-1) 238
Was D19 R34/175 P(36-15-1) 171
NYG-Rote 108C

1960 AFL
FRIDAY, SEPTEMBER 9
Den 0 7 6 0 **13**
Bos 3 0 7 0 10
Den D15 R44/149 P(15-10-1) 174
Bos D13 R25/79 P(27-13-2) 140
Den-Carmichael 130C

SATURDAY, SEPTEMBER 10
DalT 6 14 0 0 20
LAC 0 7 0 14 **21**
DalT D21 R31/84 P(41-22-1) 210
LAC D22 R26/59 P(42-25-0) 295
LAC-Anderson 103C

SUNDAY, SEPTEMBER 11
Hou 7 0 13 17 **37**
Oak 0 7 7 8 22
Hou D25 R37/164 P(37-19-1) 267
Oak D11 R27/50 P(36-15-0) 245
Hou-Smith 104R, Groman 115C,
Blanda 279P; Oak-Larscheid 105C,
Teresa 116C

Buf 3 0 0 0 3
NYT 0 17 3 7 **27**
Buf D9 R23/74 P(23-5-2) 39
NYT D20 R37/164 P(30-15-1) 176
NYT-Maynard 116C

FRIDAY, SEPTEMBER 16
DalT 10 7 3 14 **34**
Oak 0 10 0 6 16
DalT D19 R31/202 P(25-14-0) 186
Oak D22 R26/119 P(43-23-5) 187

SATURDAY, SEPTEMBER 17
Bos 7 0 0 21 **28**
NYT 3 14 7 0 24
Bos D19 R29/109 P(38-18-2) 191
NYT D17 R30/116 P(29-12-1) 181

SUNDAY, SEPTEMBER 18
LAC 7 7 0 14 28
Hou 14 7 10 7 **38**
LAC D22 R15/28 P(45-27-2) 329
Hou D22 R48/284 P(21-7-1) 93
LAC-Kemp 337P

Den 0 6 14 7 **27**
Buf 0 13 8 0 21
Den D17 R44/117 P(27-14-2) 147
Buf D14 R33/68 P(25-13-6) 211
Buf-Dubenion 112C

FRIDAY, SEPTEMBER 23
Buf 6 7 0 0 **13**
Bos 0 0 0 0 0
Buf D14 R36/112 P(17-6-1) 121
Bos D18 R28/173 P(33-12-4) 111

Den 0 10 7 7 24
NYT 7 0 14 7 **28**
Den D25 R46/209 P(31-14-1) 204
NYT D17 R33/184 P(22-9-2) 90
Den-Taylor 125C

SUNDAY, SEPTEMBER 25
Oak 7 0 0 7 **14**
Hou 10 0 3 0 13
Oak D20 R40/105 P(25-15-1) 164
Hou D20 R29/112 P(36-17-3) 222

LAC 0 0 0 0 0
DalT 0 7 0 10 **17**
LAC D16 R27/151 P(30-11-4) 60
DalT D20 R33/91 P(37-17-2) 167

SUNDAY, OCTOBER 2
LAC 0 7 7 10 **24**
Buf 0 3 7 0 10
LAC D12 R27/98 P(15-9-1) 61
Buf D18 R33/142 P(25-13-4) 96

NYT 14 13 7 3 **37**
DalT 7 7 7 14 35
NYT D27 R37/137 P(35-18-1) 267
DalT D24 R21/109 P(31-19-1) 333
NYT-Powell 134C, Dorow 281P;
DalT-Robinson 120C,
Davidson 333P

Oak 7 7 0 0 14
Den 3 21 7 0 **31**
Oak D21 R32/216 P(40-19-3) 172
Den D18 R30/165 P(29-14-2) 206
Den-Taylor 101C

SATURDAY, OCTOBER 8
Bos 18 7 10 0 **35**
LAC 0 0 0 0 0
Bos D17 R45/177 P(16-9-1) 176
LAC D14 R16/33 P(36-21-2) 167

SUNDAY, OCTOBER 9
NYT 0 14 0 7 21
Hou 6 7 7 7 **27**
NYT D25 R23/63 P(51-25-2) 304
Hou D21 R37/168 P(29-13-0) 376
NYT-Maynard 174C;
Hou-Groman 106C

Oak 0 0 20 0 **20**
DalT 0 7 0 12 19
Oak D15 R36/126 P(27-14-1) 160
DalT D19 R31/140 P(31-13-3) 152

SUNDAY, OCTOBER 16
Bos 6 0 8 0 14
Oak 7 14 0 6 **27**
Bos D18 R33/143 P(31-11-3) 136
Oak D17 R35/225 P(28-16-5) 174

DalT 0 10 0 0 10
Hou 14 3 3 0 **20**
DalT D21 R29/111 P(34-16-5) 192
Hou D17 R33/67 P(36-17-2) 233
Hou-Groman 140C

NYT 7 3 0 7 **17**
Buf 0 6 0 7 13
NYT D23 R40/157 P(36-16-3) 134
Buf D8 R21/123 P(24-10-2) 81

LAC 7 3 13 0 **23**
Den 6 3 0 10 19
LAC D16 R33/140 P(29-16-1) 178
Den D14 R22/104 P(33-16-2) 129

SUNDAY, OCTOBER 23
Bos 10 7 0 7 24
Den 0 0 14 17 **31**
Bos D16 R34/211 P(33-15-3) 223
Den D19 R35/65 P(38-20-2) 261

Hou 14 21 0 7 **42**
NYT 7 14 7 0 28
Hou D17 R29/77 P(34-18-2) 287
NYT D23 R26/124 P(44-24-4) 329
Hou-Groman 102C, Blanda 287P;
NYT-Maynard 156C

Oak 0 7 0 2 9
Buf 14 14 3 7 **38**
Oak D13 R22/85 P(40-16-3) 134
Buf D12 R26/91 P(34-15-3) 248
Buf-Carlton 110C, Green 243P

FRIDAY, OCTOBER 28
LAC 7 21 7 10 **45**
Bos 0 0 0 16 16
LAC D15 R32/219 P(27-14-2) 237
Bos D16 R20/46 P(35-17-2) 185
LAC-Lowe 137R, Anderson 124C

Oak 7 7 0 14 **28**
NYT 14 7 3 3 27
Oak D17 R37/175 P(27-13-1) 222
NYT D17 R27/127 P(34-15-3) 164
NYT-Powell 123C

SUNDAY, OCTOBER 30
Hou 7 7 10 0 24
Buf 9 10 6 0 **25**
Hou D13 R30/171 P(32-9-4) 156
Buf D17 R24/59 P(49-18-1) 293
Hou-Smith 107R; Buf-Carlton 177C,
Green 334P

DalT 7 7 3 0 **17**
Den 7 0 0 7 14
DalT D19 R45/131 P(23-12-2) 177
Den D13 R22/147 P(31-14-2) 155

FRIDAY, NOVEMBER 4
Oak 0 7 14 0 28
Bos 14 6 7 7 **34**
Oak D18 R37/188 P(27-14-2) 146
Bos D17 R24/100 P(37-16-0) 261
Bos-Christy 124C

LAC 0 7 7 7 **21**
NYT 0 0 0 7 7
LAC D16 R31/160 P(33-13-1) 177
NYT D12 R24/89 P(33-12-3) 127

SUNDAY, NOVEMBER 6
Hou 7 10 14 14 **45**
Den 3 12 10 0 25
Hou D24 R31/191 P(35-18-0) 276
Den D26 R25/121 P(54-31-2) 371
Hou-Cannon 105R, Groman 155C,
Blanda 276P; Den-Carmichael 117C,
Taylor 140C, Tripucka 375P

DalT 14 3 21 7 **45**
Buf 0 7 7 14 28
DalT D15 R42/169 P(24-10-0) 45
Buf D18 R21/52 P(42-17-4) 300
Buf-Dubenion 161C

FRIDAY, NOVEMBER 11
NYT 0 14 7 0 21
Bos 7 10 7 14 **38**
NYT D15 R31/110 P(28-16-1) 176
Bos D20 R21/142 P(35-20-0) 235
NYT-Maynard 100C;
Bos-Christy 105R

SUNDAY, NOVEMBER 13
Hou 0 14 0 7 **21**
LAC 0 0 12 7 19
Hou D24 R17/49 P(55-31-4) 337
LAC D26 R28/151 P(38-18-2) 261
Hou-Hennigan 110C, Blanda 366P;
LAC-Kocourek 105C

Buf 0 0 0 7 7
Oak 10 3 7 0 **20**
Buf D18 R22/90 P(44-22-1) 192
Oak D14 R28/181 P(24-15-0) 155
Buf-Rychlec 123C; Oak-Teresa 141R

Den 0 0 0 0 0
DalT 0 17 0 17 **34**
Den D13 R24/45 P(33-18-4) 114
DalT D20 R39/271 P(25-12-0) 185
DalT-Haynes 114R

FRIDAY, NOVEMBER 18
DalT 0 7 0 7 14
Bos 13 7 22 0 **42**
DalT D18 R20/48 P(43-20-1) 177
Bos D22 R27/120 P(39-27-0) 219

SUNDAY, NOVEMBER 20
Den 3 0 7 0 10
Hou 7 13 0 0 **20**
Den D20 R29/81 P(52-26-2) 248
Hou D9 R30/95 P(14-6-1) 265
Den-Taylor 138C; Hou-Groman 182C

Buf 6 13 0 13 **32**
LAC 0 3 0 0 3
Buf D14 R31/83 P(28-14-1) 165
LAC D11 R18/78 P(35-14-6) 107
LAC-Anderson 109C

THURSDAY, NOVEMBER 24
DalT 0 10 3 22 35
NYT 14 14 0 13 **41**
DalT D18 R27/210 P(37-14-1) 205
NYT D24 R34/106 P(33-21-1) 293
DalT-Haynes 157R;
NYT-Maynard 179C, Powell 110C,
Dorow 301P

FRIDAY, NOVEMBER 25
Hou 0 7 7 10 **24**
Bos 0 3 7 0 10
Hou D22 R36/95 P(39-22-0) 316
Bos D18 R14/8 P(35-11-3) 243
Hou-Groman 171C, Hennigan 113C,
Lee 331P; Bos-Johnson 123C

SUNDAY, NOVEMBER 27
Buf 10 7 21 0 38
Den 0 7 7 24 38
Buf D14 R48/220 P(24-10-0) 157
Den D18 R31/81 P(41-19-5) 303
Buf-Fowler 120R, Dubenion 134C;
Den-Taylor 199C, Tripucka 328P

Oak 7 0 7 14 28
LAC 14 17 7 14 **52**
Oak D22 R19/100 P(44-21-1) 180
LAC D31 R52/241 P(24-13-2) 298
LAC-Lowe 149R, Norton 119C,
Kemp 307P

SUNDAY, DECEMBER 4
Bos 7 7 0 0 14
Buf 7 7 10 14 **38**
Bos D13 R19/66 P(33-10-1) 101
Buf D18 R36/149 P(37-11-0) 122

Hou 0 0 0 0 0
DalT 14 0 10 0 **24**
Hou D14 R23/27 P(33-19-3) 120
DalT D19 R53/270 P(15-8-0) 74

LAC 0 14 0 27 **41**
Oak 0 14 3 0 17
LAC D16 R31/131 P(25-17-0) 268
Oak D21 R32/165 P(36-19-1) 227
LAC-Kocourek 123C, Norton 105C,
Phillips 114C; Oak-Hardy 123C

NYT 14 7 0 9 **30**
Den 0 7 13 7 27
NYT D20 R42/186 P(23-12-3) 187
Den D20 R18/40 P(47-27-4) 209
NYT-Powell 122C

SATURDAY, DECEMBER 10
Den 10 13 7 3 33
LAC 14 10 0 17 **41**
Den D20 R30/110 P(35-17-2) 281
LAC D22 R32/181 P(32-15-2) 166
Den-Taylor 171C; LAC-Lowe 106R

SUNDAY, DECEMBER 11
Bos 0 0 0 0 0
DalT 3 7 14 10 **34**
Bos D13 R20/51 P(39-18-4) 133
DalT D17 R29/99 P(32-14-3) 201

Buf 0 10 0 13 23
Hou 0 14 0 10 **31**
Buf D20 R38/159 P(35-11-3) 181
Hou D16 R40/112 P(22-8-3) 206
Hou-Groman 101C

NYT 7 7 10 7 **31**
Oak 0 14 7 7 28
NYT D28 R32/106 P(48-29-0) 365
Oak D14 R24/88 P(31-16-3) 187
NYT-Powell 162C, Dorow 375P

SATURDAY, DECEMBER 17
Den 3 7 0 0 10
Oak 3 14 0 31 **48**
Den D10 R8/33 P(42-19-4) 173
Oak D29 R49/233 P(35-19-2) 299

SUNDAY, DECEMBER 18
Bos 0 0 21 0 21
Hou 3 7 10 17 **37**
Bos D14 R26/54 P(44-18-0) 283
Hou D18 R32/121 P(33-14-4) 289
Bos-Songin 327P;
Hou-Groman 150C

Buf 0 0 0 7 7
DalT 0 3 7 14 **24**
Buf D17 R25/122 P(40-19-1) 150
DalT D22 R32/72 P(37-18-0) 334
DalT-Robinson 130C,
Davidson 334P

NYT 7 14 15 7 43
LAC 10 6 17 17 **50**
NYT D18 R29/148 P(28-12-3) 184
LAC D24 R29/230 P(30-16-4) 209
LAC-Ford 109R

1960 NFL
FRIDAY, SEPTEMBER 23
SL 0 10 19 14 **43**
LARm 7 0 7 7 21
SL D20 R33/149 P(31-14-3) 281
LARm D16 R20/50 P(39-20-3) 188
SL-Crow 125C, Randle 159C,
Roach 205P; LARm-Dale 106C

SATURDAY, SEPTEMBER 24
Pit 7 7 14 7 **35**
Dal 0 14 7 7 28
Pit D20 R34/122 P(28-17-1) 353
Dal D17 R24/72 P(28-15-3) 323
Pit-Carpenter 116C, Layne 288P;
Dal-Doran 154C, LeBaron 345P

SUNDAY, SEPTEMBER 25
ChiB 0 0 0 17 17
GB 0 7 7 14 **28**
ChiB D19 R35/155 P(27-13-3) 151
GB D15 R32/153 P(24-9-2) 77

Cle 14 10 7 10 **41**
Phi 3 7 0 14 24
Cle D21 R44/329 P(11-9-0) 67
Phi D24 R33/106 P(36-21-3) 300
Cle-Brown 153R, Mitchell 156R

NYG 0 7 7 7 **21**
SF 14 0 3 2 19
NYG D19 R39/138 P(18-10-0) 140
SF D20 R27/119 P(34-21-0) 216
SF-Stickles 123C

Was 0 0 0 0 0
Bal 0 7 10 3 **20**
Was D9 R16/35 P(26-10-2) 78
Bal D20 R36/125 P(35-17-1) 219

FRIDAY, SEPTEMBER 30
Phi 3 10 0 14 **27**
Dal 3 3 6 13 25
Phi D16 R35/162 P(24-11-4) 139
Dal D18 R33/154 P(29-10-5) 185

SUNDAY, OCTOBER 2
ChiB 0 0 0 7 7
Bal 14 14 7 7 **42**
ChiB D20 R35/160 P(29-12-7) 158
Bal D17 R22/85 P(27-14-0) 290
Bal-Berry 113C, Moore 140C, Unitas 307P

Det 3 6 0 0 9
GB 0 7 7 14 **28**
Det D14 R24/69 P(32-18-1) 203
GB D23 R52/255 P(17-7-2) 109
GB-Taylor 151R

LARm 0 3 0 6 9
SF 0 7 6 0 **13**
LARm D11 R34/102 P(18-12-1) 97
SF D19 R39/137 P(24-13-1) 147

NYG 0 14 7 14 **35**
SL 7 0 0 7 14
NYG D18 R36/137 P(33-19-1) 268
SL D11 R27/107 P(27-8-3) 115
NYG-Rote 135C, Shaw 240P

Pit 0 0 7 13 20
Cle 7 14 0 7 **28**
Pit D18 R33/110 P(23-16-1) 296
Cle D17 R40/132 P(14-10-0) 296
Pit-Carpenter 100C;
Cle-Kreitling 157C, Plum 308P

SUNDAY, OCTOBER 9
Bal 0 7 0 14 21
GB 0 7 7 21 **35**
Bal D27 R35/199 P(33-17-4) 210
GB D18 R36/159 P(15-6-0) 58

Dal 7 0 7 0 14
Was 3 10 3 10 **26**
Dal D22 R21/56 P(37-21-3) 275
Was D13 R38/149 P(16-10-1) 213
Dal-Doran 134C

LARm 0 6 14 7 27
ChiB 17 10 7 0 **34**
LARm D16 R21/83 P(24-11-1) 19
ChiB D21 R47/145 P(21-13-1) 312
ChiB-Dewveall 115C, Morris 124C, Brown 333P

NYG 0 12 0 7 **19**
Pit 7 0 7 3 17
NYG D18 R31/77 P(35-14-4) 246
Pit D16 R41/169 P(23-8-4) 143
NYG-Rote 116C

SL 7 7 3 10 27
Phi 7 14 0 10 **31**
SL D20 R41/219 P(27-10-4) 145
Phi D14 R26/94 P(23-17-1) 199
SL-Crow 134R; Phi-Retzlaff 132C

SF 0 0 0 14 **14**
Det 7 0 0 3 10
SF D17 R29/95 P(34-18-1) 188
Det D13 R34/97 P(22-13-1) 135
Det-Cogdill 115C

SUNDAY, OCTOBER 16
Cle 7 21 14 6 **48**
Dal 0 0 0 7 7
Cle D18 R34/200 P(21-14-0) 82
Dal D8 R25/88 P(27-9-4) 79

Det 0 3 7 0 10
Phi 7 14 0 7 **28**
Det D14 R25/154 P(37-14-4) 122
Phi D16 R40/139 P(23-10-2) 190

LARm 0 3 7 7 17
Bal 0 14 10 7 **31**
LARm D21 R40/159 P(26-13-3) 188
Bal D15 R27/156 P(24-12-2) 170
Bal-Moore 118R

SL 0 0 0 14 14
Pit 6 7 7 7 **27**
SL D20 R36/141 P(36-16-3) 154
Pit D12 R35/91 P(15-9-0) 146

SF 0 10 0 0 10
ChiB 7 13 7 0 **27**
SF D23 R47/229 P(31-16-0) 69
ChiB D6 R23/150 P(9-4-0) 81
SF-McElhenny 122R;
ChiB-Morris 114R

Dal 0 3 7 14 24
NYG 3 14 7 0 24
Was D24 R50/135 P(23-16-0) 94
NYG D21 R22/76 P(33-17-2) 210

SUNDAY, OCTOBER 23
Bal 3 14 0 0 17
Det 3 7 7 13 **30**
Bal D22 R27/85 P(40-20-2) 247
Det D11 R33/168 P(17-7-0) 132
Bal-Berry 186C

ChiB 0 3 7 14 24
LARm 7 3 7 7 24
ChiB D20 R31/85 P(44-21-2) 252
LARm D13 R28/136 P(24-12-1) 84

Dal 0 3 0 7 10
SL 9 0 3 12
Dal D9 R23/51 P(24-10-1) 124
SL D17 R45/226 P(22-4-1) 80
SL-Crow 143R

Phi 0 7 14 10 **31**
Cle 3 12 7 7 29
Phi D18 R24/136 P(26-17-1) 292
Cle D21 R36/202 P(26-12-1) 249
Phi-Peaks 102R; Cle-Brown 167R

Pit 3 7 10 7 27
Was 7 3 7 10 27
Pit D21 R26/119 P(28-14-0) 265
Was D18 R43/117 P(23-16-0) 250
Pit-Dial 187C

SF 0 0 7 7 14
GB 14 10 3 14 **41**
SF D14 R26/71 P(37-15-1) 92
GB D27 R44/249 P(26-12-0) 206
GB-McGee 110C

SUNDAY, OCTOBER 30
Bal 7 24 7 7 **45**
Dal 0 0 7 0 7
Bal D23 R45/217 P(25-12-0) 276
Dal D9 R21/83 P(24-8-4) 64
Bal-Berry 195C, Unitas 270P

ChiB 0 7 0 0 7
SF 6 14 0 5 **25**
ChiB D14 R25/172 P(28-10-1) 83
SF D18 R43/224 P(20-12-0) 96

Cle 0 14 17 0 **31**
Was 0 3 0 7 10
Cle D18 R24/135 P(20-15-0) 146
Was D18 R38/105 P(28-15-3) 154

Det 0 21 7 7 35
LARm 10 24 0 14 **48**
Det D25 R36/241 P(45-22-5) 242
LARm D19 R30/113 P(26-13-1) 169
Det-Lewis 128R;
LARm-Phillips 108C

GB 9 3 0 7 **19**
Pit 0 7 0 6 13
GB D20 R44/163 P(35-15-0) 180
Pit D16 R30/119 P(24-12-0) 189
GB-Taylor 105R

SL 3 7 10 0 **20**
NYG 0 7 0 6 13
SL D15 R50/185 P(10-4-1) 75
NYG D16 R28/109 P(31-12-5) 116

SUNDAY, NOVEMBER 6
Det 0 10 0 14 **24**
SF 0 0 0 0 0
Det D15 R25/134 P(30-14-0) 179
SF D14 R29/106 P(31-19-3) 126

GB 0 7 10 24
Bal 14 7 3 14 **38**
GB D26 R38/151 P(33-24-4) 275
Bal D19 R26/95 P(29-20-1) 309
Bal-Berry 137C, Moore 137C,
Unitas 324P

LARm 10 14 7 7 **38**
Dal 3 10 0 0 13
LARm D20 R35/281 P(32-14-1) 219
Dal D15 R28/164 P(28-9-3) 61
LARm-Marconi 115R, Phillips 151C

NYG 0 10 7 0 **17**
Cle 0 6 7 0 13
NYG D16 R46/209 P(18-6-0) 105
Cle D9 R24/6 P(25-13-0) 89
NYG-Triplett 137R

Pit 0 0 0 7 7
Phi 14 3 7 10 **34**
Pit D11 R27/104 P(26-9-3) 108
Phi D24 R39/167 P(35-21-0) 320
Phi-McDonald 141C

Was 0 0 7 0 7
SL 7 16 7 14 **44**
Was D9 R31/139 P(19-7-2) 39
SL D25 R40/261 P(24-17-0) 238

SUNDAY, NOVEMBER 13
Bal 10 7 0 7 **24**
ChiB 7 7 3 3 20
Bal D18 R29/76 P(33-16-2) 222
ChiB D17 R34/159 P(26-14-4) 133
Bal-Berry 104C

Dal 0 0 0 7 7
GB 7 20 7 7 **41**
Dal D14 R29/99 P(35-16-3) 161
GB D20 R37/165 P(27-13-2) 226
GB-Taylor 121R

LARm 3 0 0 7 10
Det 0 3 6 3 **12**
LARm D15 R25/62 P(33-18-1) 183
Det D19 R33/103 P(32-16-3) 129

Pit 0 14 10 0 24
NYG 7 7 3 10 **27**
Pit D16 R35/127 P(26-10-3) 203
NYG D20 R35/132 P(32-18-1) 233
Pit-Dial 121C

SL 0 7 10 10 27
Cle 0 7 14 7 **28**
SL D18 R33/170 P(21-13-2) 215
Cle D20 R40/234 P(15-11-0) 168
SL-Randle 104C; Cle-Brown 173R

Was 3 0 7 3 13
Phi 0 13 0 6 **19**
Was D16 R38/108 P(27-14-3) 129
Phi D12 R29/81 P(24-9-3) 166

SUNDAY, NOVEMBER 20
Cle 0 0 3 7 10
Pit 7 0 0 7 **14**
Cle D24 R28/121 P(37-23-0) 292
Pit D18 R37/149 P(24-10-2) 174
Cle-Nagler 177C, Plum 328P

Det 0 0 7 0 7
ChiB 0 7 0 14 **28**
Det D11 R32/133 P(26-10-2) 14
ChiB D12 R30/129 P(29-15-2) 204
Det-Pietrosante 106R;
ChiB-Dewveall 163C

LARm 7 13 10 3 **33**
GB 10 0 7 14 31
LARm D12 R27/73 P(29-15-1) 132
GB D20 R37/203 P(25-11-2) 181
GB-Moore 105R

Phi 0 0 7 10 **17**
NYG 7 3 0 0 10
Phi D14 R30/61 P(24-13-0) 203
NYG D17 R40/154 P(25-12-1) 204
Phi-Walston 119C

SL 3 7 10 6 **26**
Was 0 0 0 7 7
SL D28 R46/267 P(29-17-1) 248
Was D8 R21/37 P(33-15-5) 117
SL-Crow 157R, Randle 146C

SF 3 3 3 17 **26**
Dal 0 0 7 0 7
SF D17 R35/172 P(33-15-2) 141
Dal D13 R22/54 P(29-16-4) 228

THURSDAY, NOVEMBER 24
GB 0 0 10 0 10
Det 9 7 7 0 **23**
GB D12 R22/118 P(26-8-0) 63
Det D19 R37/109 P(34-19-1) 182

SUNDAY, NOVEMBER 27
Cle 0 17 0 0 17
SL 3 7 7 0 17
Cle D17 R37/186 P(19-13-0) 88
SL D21 R40/195 P(20-10-5) 127
Cle-Brown 132R

Dal 0 0 0 7 7
ChiB 7 7 0 3 **17**
Dal D12 R26/44 P(31-14-0) 174
ChiB D16 R38/221 P(24-11-2) 58

NYG 17 3 3 0 23
Phi 0 17 0 14 **31**
NYG D13 R35/144 P(21-11-4) 193
Phi D20 R29/64 P(23-13-3) 147
NYG-Rote 124C

SF 3 7 7 13 **30**
Bal 0 13 7 2 22
SF D18 R31/119 P(27-15-0) 237
Bal D19 R25/67 P(32-17-5) 361
SF-Owens 152C; Bal-Berry 181C,
Moore 139C, Unitas 356P

Was 0 0 7 0 7
Pit 6 7 3 6 **22**
Was D9 R26/66 P(24-12-3) 115
Pit D20 R45/208 P(26-10-2) 186
Pit-Johnson 109R

SUNDAY, DECEMBER 4
Dal 7 10 0 14 31
NYG 14 7 3 7 31
Dal D19 R30/70 P(35-17-2) 258
NYG D19 R31/114 P(27-13-1) 213

Det 3 0 0 17 **20**
Bal 2 6 0 7 15
Det D18 R32/133 P(28-13-2) 169
Bal D19 R23/54 P(40-22-3) 333
Bal-Berry 117C, Moore 139C,
Unitas 357P

GB 0 13 14 14 **41**
ChiB 0 6 0 7 13
GB D28 R43/225 P(23-17-0) 218
ChiB D15 R26/82 P(27-15-2) 239
GB-Taylor 140R, McGee 121C;
ChiB-Coia 104C

Phi 3 7 3 7 **20**
SL 0 0 6 0 6
Phi D10 R25/54 P(27-13-1) 214
SL D13 R44/165 P(16-5-2) 25
Phi-Retzlaff 123C

SF 0 10 10 3 **23**
LARm 0 0 0 7 7
SF D16 R43/186 P(16-11-0) 158
LARm D18 R29/134 P(28-14-4) 129
SF-Roberts 100R;
LARm-Phillips 114C

Was 10 3 0 3 16
Cle 7 17 0 3 **27**
Was D16 R38/121 P(26-17-1) 57
Cle D18 R20/139 P(28-10-1) 187
Cle-Brown 135R

SATURDAY, DECEMBER 10
GB 0 3 0 10 **13**
SF 0 0 0 0 0
GB D16 R48/251 P(17-6-1) 41
SF D6 R22/71 P(25-9-2) 0
GB-Taylor 161R

SUNDAY, DECEMBER 11
Bal 3 0 0 0 3
LARm 0 0 7 0 **10**
Bal D19 R35/91 P(38-17-1) 181
LARm D9 R21/113 P(23-12-2) 135

ChiB 0 0 0 0 0
Cle 7 21 0 14 **42**
ChiB D12 R26/103 P(32-11-7) 90
Cle D15 R39/131 P(12-7-0) 84
ChiB-Dooley 101C; Cle-Brown 100R

Dal 0 7 0 7 14
Det 0 16 0 7 **23**
Dal D24 R30/114 P(27-18-1) 172
Det D17 R40/213 P(14-12-0) 130
Det-Pietrosante 142R

NYG 0 0 7 10 **17**
Was 0 0 0 0 0
NYG D4 R31/-1 P(11-6-2) 52
Was D6 R36/109 P(7-0-2) -6

Phi 0 0 0 21 21
Pit 13 14 0 0 **27**
Phi D16 R19/34 P(40-16-2) 274
Pit D21 R46/275 P(20-14-3) 209
Phi-Brown 112C; Pit-Johnson 182R

SATURDAY, DECEMBER 17
GB 7 21 0 7 **35**
LARm 7 0 14 0 21
GB D16 R30/58 P(11-9-0) 241
LARm D24 R33/143 P(33-23-3) 279
GB-McGee 125C;
LARm-Thomas 137C

SUNDAY, DECEMBER 18
Bal 0 10 0 0 10
SF 7 13 7 7 **34**
Bal D9 R15/39 P(36-12-3) 138
SF D19 R42/152 P(24-10-2) 99

ChiB 0 0 0 0 0
Det 13 16 0 7 **36**
ChiB D11 R23/78 P(28-7-1) 65
Det D16 R41/160 P(16-8-2) 41
Det-Pietrosante 104R

Cle 7 14 0 27 **48**
NYG 14 13 7 0 34
Cle D21 R17/115 P(40-19-4) 296
NYG D21 R32/151 P(38-18-2) 274
Cle-Brown 110R, Mitchell 133C,
Plum 296P; NYG-Schnelker 180C

Phi 7 10 7 14 **38**
Was 7 7 7 7 28
Phi D14 R22/36 P(26-16-0) 372
Was D20 R40/192 P(22-15-1) 191
Phi-Brown 128C, McDonald 116C,
Retzlaff 110C

Pit 7 0 0 0 7
SL 0 7 17 14 **38**
Pit D9 R22/30 P(22-10-2) 150
SL D21 R49/271 P(22-8-0) 108
SL-Crow 203R, Randle 115C

1961 AFL
SATURDAY, SEPTEMBER 9
NYT 7 7 0 7 **21**
Bos 0 7 10 3 20
NYT D15 R27/93 P(26-15-1) 183
Bos D14 R32/131 P(26-11-1) 86

Oak 0 0 0 0 0
Hou 7 21 10 17 **55**
Oak D7 R25/65 P(22-7-3) 34
Hou D25 R55/203 P(27-13-1) 279
Hou-Tolar 101R, Hennigan 113C

SUNDAY, SEPTEMBER 10
SD 6 6 0 14 **26**
DalT 0 0 10 0 10
SD D17 R29/198 P(34-16-0) 167
DalT D16 R32/209 P(24-10-4) 83
SD-Lowe 100R; DalT-Spikes 109R

Den 7 8 0 7 **22**
Buf 8 0 0 2 10
Den D12 R33/100 P(21-13-1) 179
Buf D31 R31/166 P(27-11-2) 118
Den-Taylor 132C

SATURDAY, SEPTEMBER 16
Den 3 0 7 7 17
Bos 3 7 21 14 **45**
Den D10 R20/69 P(49-20-0) 201
Bos D19 R21/46 P(35-18-0) 346
Bos-Colclough 123C, Songin 250P

SUNDAY, SEPTEMBER 17
Oak 0 0 0 0 0
SD 14 16 0 14 **44**
Oak D13 R23/85 P(27-14-5) 21
SD D23 R36/203 P(29-17-0) 183

NYT 17 7 7 0 31
Buf 7 21 7 6 41
NYT D22 R28/66 P(44-24-3) 250
Buf D15 R38/168 P(19-8-2) 120
NYT-Maynard 107C, Powell 125C,
Dorow 281P

SATURDAY, SEPTEMBER 23
Bos 3 3 14 3 23
Buf 7 7 7 0 21
Bos D15 R22/166 P(37-13-1) 163
Buf D14 R26/63 P(32-14-1) 112

SUNDAY, SEPTEMBER 24
Hou 3 0 7 14 24
SD 3 28 3 0 34
Hou D19 R27/72 P(55-25-6) 300
SD D7 R33/50 P(22-7-0) 108
Hou-Hennigan 109C, White 112C

DalT 7 7 13 15 42
Oak 3 17 8 8 35
DalT D21 R33/189 P(26-12-1) 273
Oak D17 R29/92 P(30-17-0) 215
DalT-Burford 101C

Den 7 0 7 14 28
NYT 14 14 7 0 35
Den D18 R16/63 P(54-28-1) 223
NYT D13 R23/108 P(25-9-3) 95
Den-Taylor 126C

SATURDAY, SEPTEMBER 30
SD 13 0 6 0 19
Buf 0 11 0 0 11
SD D15 R31/162 P(26-14-1) 140
Buf D15 R28/102 P(28-15-1) 137
SD-Lowe 128R

SUNDAY, OCTOBER 1
Den 0 3 0 16 19
Oak 7 19 7 0 33
Den D14 R33/111 P(27-13-2) 164
Oak D14 R36/153 P(19-10-0) 103
Den-Taylor 118C; Oak-Crow 107R

Hou 7 0 0 14 21
DalT 6 14 0 6 26
Hou D15 R20/104 P(38-15-3) 249
DalT D27 R56/398 P(21-8-0) 130
Hou-Hennigan 101C;
DalT-Haynes 117R, Spikes 146R

Bos 9 0 14 7 30
NYT 0 20 3 14 37
Bos D11 R18/80 P(34-15-1) 159
NYT D26 R35/157 P(31-16-0) 196
NYT-Mathis 109R

SATURDAY, OCTOBER 7
SD 7 24 0 7 38
Bos 0 14 7 6 27
SD D19 R28/84 P(25-12-2) 315
Bos D17 R21/105 P(32-16-2) 148
SD-Kocourek 160C, Kemp 315P

SUNDAY, OCTOBER 8
DalT 9 7 3 0 19
Den 0 0 0 12 12
DalT D18 R50/191 P(17-5-1) 39
Den D19 R25/57 P(27-16-3) 214
DalT-Haynes 139R; Den-Taylor 120C

Buf 0 7 0 15 22
Hou 0 10 2 0 12
Buf D18 R38/206 P(26-10-2) 176
Hou D8 R21/48 P(27-10-2) 146
Buf-Crockett 102C;
Hou-Hennigan 109C

FRIDAY, OCTOBER 13
Hou 0 14 7 10 31
Bos 7 3 14 7 31
Hou D25 R27/92 P(41-27-2) 448
Bos D21 R31/129 P(24-14-2) 254
Hou-Groman 109C, Hennigan 272C,
Lee 457P; Bos-Cappelletti 131C

SUNDAY, OCTOBER 15
SD 7 10 0 8 25
NYT 0 7 3 0 10
SD D19 R36/123 P(38-15-1) 299
NYT D14 R20/62 P(43-18-4) 140
SD-Norton 111C, Kemp 302P

Oak 0 10 7 7 24
Den 7 7 0 13 27
Oak D14 R33/141 P(33-16-2) 247
Den D14 R23/82 P(34-18-3) 212
Den-Frazier 166C

DalT 3 0 0 21 24
Buf 3 7 7 10 27
DalT D11 R17/29 P(28-10-2) 164
Buf D15 R46/165 P(15-10-1) 197
Buf-Bass 159C

SUNDAY, OCTOBER 22
Buf 0 0 0 21 21
Bos 17 21 7 7 52
Buf D23 R22/51 P(40-20-2) 224
Bos D18 R33/235 P(22-13-2) 202
Buf-Richards 107C;
Bos-Garron 116R, Lott 108C

SD 20 14 7 0 41
Oak 0 3 0 10 10
SD D20 R44/218 P(33-10-1) 116
Oak D6 R20/2 P(25-10-4) 56
SD-Lowe 106R

NYT 0 10 0 0 10
Den 7 0 3 17 27
NYT D17 R28/78 P(46-19-3) 281
Den D20 R31/133 P(38-17-3) 205
NYT-Powell 160C; Den-Frazier 126C

DalT 7 0 0 0 7
Hou 0 21 3 14 38
DalT D13 R25/126 P(39-13-1) 170
Hou D23 R40/160 P(35-17-0) 315
Hou-Groman 123C, Hennigan 108C

SUNDAY, OCTOBER 29
Den 0 0 0 0 0
SD 3 14 10 10 37
Den D14 R23/76 P(45-21-4) 228
SD D13 R25/101 P(33-13-4) 211
SD-Norton 103C

NYT 7 0 0 7 14
Oak 0 3 3 0 6
NYT D16 R42/210 P(20-8-1) 77
Oak D9 R33/105 P(26-8-2) 32

Bos 0 7 0 11 18
DalT 0 3 7 7 17
Bos D17 R28/144 P(28-17-1) 168
DalT D16 R28/67 P(23-14-0) 169
Bos-Norton 103C

Hou 7 7 7 7 28
Buf 3 7 0 6 16
Hou D17 R34/46 P(32-18-4) 464
Buf D22 R21/99 P(51-19-4) 252
Hou-Groman 100C, Hennigan 232C,
Blanda 464P; Buf-Bass 123C

FRIDAY, NOVEMBER 3
DalT 7 7 7 0 21
Bos 14 0 14 0 28
DalT D17 R25/64 P(33-18-2) 300
Bos D19 R26/84 P(30-16-1) 145
DalT-Burford 137C, Davidson 313P

SUNDAY, NOVEMBER 5
NYT 7 6 0 0 13
SD 0 7 28 13 48
NYT D16 R38/90 P(30-12-5) 111
SD D17 R31/184 P(23-12-2) 169
SD-Lowe 110R

Oak 14 0 14 3 31
Buf 0 15 0 7 22
Oak D16 R30/125 P(28-15-0) 256
Buf D18 R28/124 P(29-12-2) 241
Buf-Dubenion 100C

Hou 3 24 14 14 55
Den 0 0 7 14 21
Hou D24 R34/234 P(37-19-1) 348
Den D19 R17/74 P(47-20-4) 130
Hou-Cannon 118R, Groman 134C

SATURDAY, NOVEMBER 11
Oak 0 6 0 6 12
NYT 0 13 7 3 23
Oak D19 R36/131 P(28-11-3) 179
NYT D19 R40/165 P(35-15-3) 188
NYT-Mathis 127R

SUNDAY, NOVEMBER 12
SD 0 0 12 7 19
Den 7 2 0 7 16
SD D13 R26/56 P(31-11-3) 153
Den D32 R32/86 P(49-23-5) 272
Den-Frazier 125C, Taylor 119C

Buf 3 7 0 20 30
DalT 3 14 0 3 20
Buf D15 R33/100 P(27-9-2) 69.
DalT D16 R24/85 P(34-18-4) 195

Bos 0 6 3 6 15
Hou 7 13 0 7 27
Bos D16 R15/44 P(44-21-2) 208
Hou D16 R36/169 P(31-14-2) 177
Hou-Groman 117C

FRIDAY, NOVEMBER 17
Oak 0 14 3 0 17
Bos 7 6 0 7 20
Oak D15 R18/39 P(32-17-1) 164
Bos D14 R32/94 P(22-11-2) 131

SUNDAY, NOVEMBER 19
DalT 0 0 7 7 14
SD 0 17 0 7 24
DalT D17 R28/108 P(36-16-3) 180
SD D13 R20/3 P(28-15-1) 335
SD-Kocourek 169C, Norton 120C,
Kemp 357P

Buf 0 10 0 13 23
Den 7 0 3 0 10
Buf D13 R36/80 P(31-15-0) 155
Den D11 R17/112 P(41-14-6) 161

NYT 0 0 7 6 13
Hou 21 14 7 7 49
NYT D25 R23/107 P(47-21-3) 240
Hou D24 R31/148 P(38-21-1) 407
NYT-Christy 103C;
Hou-Cannon 122C, Groman 152C,
Hennigan 123C, Blanda 418P

THURSDAY, NOVEMBER 23
Buf 7 0 0 7 14
NYT 7 7 7 7 28
Buf D22 R23/63 P(46-22-2) 214
NYT D12 R23/59 P(28-13-0) 157
NYT-Renn 117C

SUNDAY, NOVEMBER 26
Oak 0 3 0 8 11
DalT 14 7 22 0 43
Oak D14 R21/67 P(44-23-5) 187
DalT D20 R27/284 P(29-10-2) 211
DalT-Haynes 158R

Den 0 7 0 14 21
Hou 7 14 0 24 45
Den D11 R13/44 P(42-17-6) 115
Hou D21 R34/60 P(33-18-3) 251

SUNDAY, DECEMBER 3
SD 7 0 0 6 13
Hou 13 6 14 0 33
SD D14 R17/35 P(42-24-3) 77
Hou D22 R30/122 P(34-20-1) 351
Hou-Hennigan 214C, Blanda 351P

Buf 6 6 7 7 26
Oak 0 7 7 7 21
Buf D22 R30/120 P(34-16-1) 149
Oak D20 R22/97 P(37-20-1) 220
Buf-Bass 110C

Bos 14 0 0 14 28
Den 0 7 3 14 24
Bos D11 R28/71 P(31-11-2) 173
Den D19 R32/64 P(48-22-3) 217
Den-Stone 137C

DalT 0 0 7 0 7
NYT 0 14 7 3 28
DalT D16 R28/86 P(39-15-4) 271
NYT D16 R34/127 P(33-17-1) 266
DalT-Burford 105C, Haynes 127C;
NYT-Christy 145C

SATURDAY, DECEMBER 9
Bos 7 14 7 7 35
Oak 7 7 0 7 21
Bos D29 R43/207 P(32-19-2) 200
Oak D14 R10/27 P(34-19-1) 186

SUNDAY, DECEMBER 10
Buf 10 0 0 0 10
SD 0 14 14 0 28
Buf D18 R38/99 P(34-13-3) 180
SD D7 R19/47 P(25-11-2) 190
Buf-Baker 117R; SD-Kocourek 175C

Den 0 0 14 7 21
DalT 7 14 14 14 49
Den D19 R18/20 P(46-23-4) 199
DalT D23 R30/148 P(35-19-2) 265
DalT-Jackson 106R, Robinson 112C

Hou 10 10 7 21 48
NYT 7 7 0 7 21
Hou D26 R35/266 P(38-19-1) 307
NYT D17 R27/152 P(28-9-2) 152
Hou-Cannon 216R, Cannon 114C,
Groman 101C; NYT-Powell 122C

SUNDAY, DECEMBER 17
Bos 17 10 7 7 41
SD 0 0 0 0 0
Bos D18 R39/139 P(23-11-2) 156
SD D11 R16/2 P(34-13-5) 190
SD-Hayes 100C

Hou 0 26 14 7 47
Oak 0 9 7 0 16
Hou D25 R28/172 P(32-18-2) 350
Oak D19 R24/105 P(38-22-1) 151
Hou-Cannon 145R, Dewveall 108C,
Hennigan 123C, Blanda 350P

NYT 0 21 0 3 24
DalT 14 14 0 7 35
NYT D19 R41/204 P(24-8-3) 51
DalT D16 R36/199 P(15-9-1) 126
DalT-Haynes 107R

1961 NFL
SUNDAY, SEPTEMBER 17
ChiB 0 6 0 7 13
Min 3 7 14 13 37
ChiB D20 R35/134 P(17-8-4) 136
Min D17 R29/79 P(27-19-0) 257
Min-Reichow 103C, Tarkenton 250P

Cle 10 0 3 7 20
Phi 10 7 3 7 27
Cle D20 R30/103 P(30-18-1) 329
Phi D15 R33/147 P(17-11-1) 158
Cle-Renfro 104C, Plum 329P

Det 7 7 0 3 17
GB 7 3 0 3 13
Det D15 R38/128 P(23-11-1) 138
GB D17 R28/132 P(27-14-2) 162
GB-McGee 127C

LARm 10 14 0 0 24
Bal 7 10 7 3 27
LARm D21 R35/185 P(23-12-1) 123
Bal D19 R35/213 P(27-14-2) 113
LARm-Wilson 118R; Bal-Perry 106R

Pit 0 14 0 10 24
Dal 7 3 7 10 27
Pit D15 R34/105 P(26-16-3) 237
Dal D20 R29/96 P(39-19-2) 307
Pit-Dial 137C; Dal-Howton 138C

SL 0 7 0 14 21
NYG 0 3 0 7 10
SL D15 R38/163 P(24-11-0) 76
NYG D12 R28/83 P(32-12-2) 74

Was 3 0 0 0 3
SF 14 14 0 7 35
Was D9 R21/37 P(34-8-3) 98
SF D23 R26/112 P(31-22-3) 287
SF-Stickles 116C, Brodie 237P

SATURDAY, SEPTEMBER 23
ChiB 7 0 7 7 21
LARm 3 7 0 7 17
ChiB D15 R32/134 P(22-13-2) 194
LARm D13 R30/80 P(31-18-2) 219
ChiB-Ditka 130C;
LARm-Phillips 163C

SUNDAY, SEPTEMBER 24
Det 3 0 10 3 16
Bal 3 2 3 7 15
Det D15 R37/184 P(18-9-2) 90
Bal D7 R25/83 P(19-11-2) 103

Min 0 7 0 0 7
Dal 7 7 0 7 21
Min D16 R25/125 P(31-13-3) 126
Dal D22 R36/208 P(30-17-2) 229
Dal-Perkins 108R

NYG 0 7 10 0 17
Pit 7 0 7 0 14
NYG D18 R33/142 P(28-16-0) 136
Pit D19 R38/124 P(24-10-2) 128

SL 7 7 3 0 17
Cle 0 0 10 10 20
SL D18 R26/95 P(30-13-2) 90
Cle D14 R30/111 P(32-16-3) 134

SF 7 3 0 0 10
GB 7 13 3 7 30
SF D15 R30/137 P(25-10-3) 96
GB D19 R37/124 P(16-11-1) 151
SF-Smith 102R

Was 0 0 7 0 7
Phi 0 0 0 14 14
Was D15 R29/106 P(29-13-1) 219
Phi D11 R26/64 P(28-11-3) 196
Was-Dugan 168C

SUNDAY, OCTOBER 1
ChiB 0 0 0 0 0
GB 3 7 7 7 24
ChiB D16 R32/124 P(29-13-4) 131
GB D18 R33/198 P(23-13-2) 83
GB-Taylor 130R

Dal 0 0 0 7 7
Cle 3 8 7 7 25
Dal D9 R26/52 P(25-12-2) 100
Cle D18 R41/216 P(17-8-1) 100

Min 3 10 10 10 33
Bal 3 13 7 11 34
Min D21 R37/124 P(30-17-0) 137
Bal D16 R16/82 P(33-14-3) 284
Bal-Moore 143C

NYG 7 7 3 7 24
Was 21 0 0 0 21
NYG D30 R32/91 P(46-27-3) 325
Was D8 R23/42 P(24-12-1) 103
NYG-Rote 105C, Shofner 103C,
Tittle 315P

Pit 0 14 0 0 14
LARm 7 7 0 10 24
Pit D14 R36/94 P(26-12-5) 142
LARm D17 R25/42 P(28-17-1) 216

SL 0 14 0 16 30
Phi 14 6 7 0 27
SL D19 R35/223 P(16-13-1) 145
Phi D20 R26/80 P(36-24-2) 371
SL-Gautt 135R;
Phi-McDonald 187C, Walston 127C,
Jurgensen 399P

SF 14 7 21 7 49
Det 0 0 0 0 0
SF D23 R41/178 P(20-8-1) 139
Det D16 R25/55 P(43-18-4) 236
SF-Kilmer 103R

SUNDAY, OCTOBER 8
Bal 0 7 0 0 7
GB 7 10 14 14 45
Bal D18 R32/153 P(29-12-6) 136
GB D25 R30/211 P(29-13-1) 146
GB-Hornung 111R

```
ChiB   0   7   3  21  31
Det    0   0   7   0  17
ChiB  D15 R29/173  P(25-13-1)  281
Det   D13 R30/165  P(30-11-3)  174
ChiB-Ditka 120C, Farrington 105C,
Wade 330P; Det-Pietrosante 113R,
Barr 101C

Dal    0   7   7   7  28
Min    0   0   0   0   0
Dal   D18 R37/117  P(27-14-0)  180
Min   D14 R20/83   P(26-12-3)  100

LARm   0   0   0   0   0
SF    14   7   7   7  35
LARm  D11 R23/83   P(23-11-1)   83
SF    D29 R40/259  P(26-20-0)  262
SF-Kilmer 131R

NYG    7   0  17   0  24
SL     2   0   7   0   9
NYG   D15 R32/71   P(34-16-2)  153
SL    D5  R17/28   P(22-6-4)   132
SL-Stacy 161C

Pit    3   7   0   6  16
Phi    0   7   7   7  21
Pit   D19 R40/141  P(29-19-1)  140
Phi   D14 R29/124  P(22-11-3)  103

Was    0   7   0   0   7
Cle    3  14   0  14  31
Was   D16 R21/44   P(29-15-2)  201
Cle   D13 R27/91   P(27-17-0)  194
Was-Dugan 120C
```

SUNDAY, OCTOBER 15

```
Bal    0   7   0   3  10
ChiB   3   7   0  14  24
Bal   D20 R28/106  P(36-19-1)  256
ChiB  D14 R29/90   P(19-12-1)  194
Bal-Mutscheller 112C;
ChiB-Galimore 149C

GB    14   7   7  21  49
Cle    0   3   7   7  17
GB    D23 R35/216  P(17-15-0)  266
Cle   D33 R33/125  P(26-17-1)  165
GB-Taylor 158R, McGee 120C;
Cle-Renfro 100C

LARm   3   0   7   3  13
Det    0   7   7   0  14
LARm  D11 R24/80   P(27-12-3)  164
Det   D14 R39/152  P(24-10-4)  159
LARm-Phillips 107C

NYG    0  10  14   7  31
Dal    7   3   0   0  10
NYG   D21 R34/258  P(24-9-4)   117
Dal   D15 R30/192  P(28-14-4)  139
NYG-Gaiters 129R

Phi    7   6   7   0  20
SL     0   0   7   0   7
Phi   D14 R23/57   P(32-17-0)  212
SL    D14 R28/79   P(32-17-2)  121

SF     7   7  10  14  38
Min    7  10   7   0  24
SF    D31 R51/324  P(16-13-2)  231
Min   D12 R24/118  P(29-13-0)   84
SF-Kilmer 115R, Smith 100C,
Stickles 102C

Was    0   0   0   0   0
Pit   17   0   0   3  20
Was   D13 R22/65   P(43-12-6)  126
Pit   D12 R43/95   P(18-8-2)    90
```

SUNDAY, OCTOBER 22

```
Bal    0   7   0  10  17
Det    0   0  14   0  14
Bal   D18 R31/88   P(37-22-4)  225
Det   D11 R29/76   P(23-9-0)   132

Cle    3   7   3  17  30
Pit    0   0  14  14  28
Cle   D21 R47/229  P(20-12-2)  149
Pit   D17 R26/87   P(24-15-1)  222
Cle-Brown 114R, Mitchell 119R;
Pit-Dial 235C

GB    10   3   3  17  33
Min    0   7   0   0   7
GB    D22 R35/241  P(20-10-1)  226
Min   D18 R34/149  P(35-19-4)  179
GB-Moore 159R, Dowler 100C
```

```
LARm   0   0  14   0  14
NYG    3   7   0  14  24
LARm  D15 R39/218  P(25-10-3)  154
NYG   D21 R38/204  P(29-11-2)  171
LARm-Arnett 118R, Phillips 154C

Phi    9   7  20   7  43
Dal    0   0   7   0   7
Phi   D23 R39/289  P(19-12-0)  191
Dal   D26 R30/177  P(29-20-1)  169

SL     0   7   3  14  24
Was    0   0   7   0   7
SL    D14 R27/87   P(24-16-0)  155
Was   D11 R19/41   P(29-11-2)   48

SF     0   0   0   0   0
ChiB   0  10  14   7  31
SF    D6  R27/92   P(18-5-3)    40
ChiB  D17 R35/149  P(22-13-1)  156
ChiB-Ditka 107C, Wade 171P
```

SUNDAY, OCTOBER 29

```
ChiB   0   7   7   7  21
Bal    7   7   6   0  20
ChiB  D17 R33/142  P(28-11-2)  199
Bal   D19 R25/80   P(37-20-2)  292
Bal-Moore 155C, Unitas 302P

Cle   14   7   0   0  21
SL     0   0   7  14  14
Cle   D15 R51/224  P(9-5-0)    102
SL    D13 R24/77   P(24-10-1)  118
Cle-Brown 109R, Mitchell 104R

Dal    7   7   0   3  17
NYG    0  10   3   3  16
Dal   D17 R35/146  P(28-15-1)  187
NYG   D15 R32/112  P(23-10-3)  150

Det    7   0  14   7  28
LARm   7   0   0   0   7
Det   D23 R34/168  P(23-11-0)  241
LARm  D18 R28/109  P(25-14-1)  149
Det-Pietrosante 112R, Cogdill 103C;
LARm-Phillips 117C

Min    0   0   3   7  10
GB    14   7   0   7  28
Min   D13 R27/142  P(24-10-1)  121
GB    D24 R38/157  P(25-19-0)  310
GB-Dowler 121C, McGee 102C,
Starr 311P

Phi    7   7   3  10  27
Was    7  10   0   7  24
Phi   D19 R15/-12  P(41-27-2)  413
Was   D17 R28/77   P(31-21-1)  258
Phi-McDonald 141C, Retzlaff 125C,
Jurgensen 436P

SF     0   0   3   0   3
Pit   17   0   3   0  20
SF    D12 R25/52   P(30-12-1)  164
Pit   D8  R37/156  P(12-6-1)    48
SF-Owens 122C; Pit-Johnson 103R
```

SUNDAY, NOVEMBER 5

```
ChiB   7   7   0   7  21
Phi    3   7   6   0  16
ChiB  D9  R35/126  P(12-4-0)    89
Phi   D19 R34/105  P(33-18-3)  237
Phi-McDonald 109C

Det    0  17   0   3  20
SF     0   0   7  13  20
Det   D22 R28/137  P(36-19-3)  265
SF    D14 R27/113  P(26-16-2)  213
SF-Owens 131C

GB     7   7   0   7  21
Bal    7  14  14  10  45
GB    D10 R22/161  P(18-7-0)    64
Bal   D29 R42/189  P(36-22-2)  218
Bal-Perry 105R, Unitas 218P

Min    7   3   7   0  17
LARm  14   3   0  14  31
Min   D21 R39/253  P(22-12-2)  146
LARm  D23 R42/295  P(28-10-1)   97

Pit    0   0  10   7  17
Cle    7  14   0   7  28
Pit   D18 R42/160  P(18-12-2)  196
Cle   D14 R32/148  P(19-10-1)  104
Pit-Johnson 105R, Schnelker 160C;
Cle-Brown 110R
```

```
SL     7  14   0  10  31
Dal    0   3   7   7  17
SL    D13 R32/122  P(17-6-0)    71
Dal   D18 R33/136  P(33-14-5)  238

Was    0   0   0   0   0
NYG    9  16   7  21  53
Was   D7  R25/31   P(26-9-4)    51
NYG   D24 R33/147  P(37-17-4)  236
NYG-Shofner 122C
```

SUNDAY, NOVEMBER 12

```
Bal    0  14   3   3  20
Min    7   7   7   7  28
Bal   D21 R43/216  P(31-14-2)  138
Min   D19 R34/159  P(18-11-1)  116
Bal-Perry 100R

Cle    3   7   7   0  17
Was    0   0   6   0   6
Cle   D16 R29/179  P(16-13-0)  124
Was   D16 R25/96   P(29-17-1)  144
Cle-Brown 133R

Dal    0   7   0   0   7
Pit    3   7   0   7  17
Dal   D8  R20/63   P(33-13-2)  122
Pit   D22 R39/167  P(23-11-1)  204
Pit-Dial 148C

Det    3  14  14  14  45
SL     0  14   0   0  14
Det   D16 R33/201  P(31-13-1)  171
SL    D21 R24/35   P(33-16-3)  179
Det-Barr 113C

GB     0  21   3   7  31
ChiB   0   7   7  14  28
GB    D20 R38/162  P(23-11-1)  160
ChiB  D15 R21/73   P(30-17-1)  169
ChiB-Burford 107C, Ditka 190C

Phi    0   0  14   7  21
NYG   14  10  14   0  38
Phi   D23 R27/132  P(40-19-4)  240
NYG   D22 R37/164  P(24-18-0)  270
NYG-Webster 100R, Shofner 137C,
Tittle 307P

SF     0   0   7   0   7
LARm   0   0   3  14  17
SF    D10 R27/110  P(15-8-0)    57
LARm  D20 R44/184  P(25-13-0)  183
```

SUNDAY, NOVEMBER 19

```
ChiB   7   3   7  14  31
SF    17   3  21   0  41
ChiB  D21 R23/133  P(35-19-1)  295
SF    D15 R34/218  P(19-11-0)  318
ChiB-Morris 123C, Wade 323P;
SF-Roberts 107C, Owens 107C,
Thomas 131C, Brodie 322P

Det    0  14   9  14  37
Min   10   0   0   0  10
Det   D20 R39/172  P(23-15-1)  179
Min   D8  R21/69   P(24-13-2)   57

LARm   0   7   3   7  17
GB     0  14   7  14  35
LARm  D19 R33/111  P(29-19-0)  201
GB    D17 R31/76   P(15-10-1)  173
GB-Taylor 186R

Phi    3   7   0  14  24
Cle    0  14  10  21  45
Phi   D19 R19/97   P(32-18-1)  230
Cle   D30 R44/259  P(22-16-0)  246
Cle-Brown 237R

Pit    7   0   0  14  21
NYG    7   7  14  14  42
Pit   D20 R30/?    P(30-18-1)  187
NYG   D21 R33/121  P(33-20-1)  304
Pit-Dial 117C; NYG-Rote 129C,
Tittle 314P

SL     0   0   0   0   0
Bal    7   3   6   0  16
SL    D8  R20/80   P(22-8-1)    49
Bal   D24 R48/179  P(37-21-0)  227

Was    7  14   0   7  28
Dal    0  14   7   7  28
Was   D18 R25/82   P(23-16-1)  210
Dal   D27 R31/170  P(33-22-2)  271
Was-Anderson 168C,
Kocourek 169C, Norton 120C,
Kemp 357P
```

THURSDAY, NOVEMBER 23

```
GB     0   7   0  10  17
Det    3   3   3   0   9
GB    D13 R36/126  P(22-13-1)  151
Det   D18 R24/107  P(36-16-4)  172
```

SUNDAY, NOVEMBER 26

```
Bal   14   3   7   3  27
Was    0   0   6   0   6
Bal   D20 R35/207  P(33-18-3)  208
Was   D7  R19/34   P(32-9-3)    63
Bal-Moore 122R

Dal    3   0   3   7  13
Phi   14  14   0   7  35
Dal   D21 R30/118  P(44-22-2)  240
Phi   D20 R24/117  P(25-16-3)  337
Dal-Howton 102C;
Phi-McDonald 131C,
Jurgensen 351P

LARm   0   3  14   7  24
ChiB   7  14   0   7  28
LARm  D19 R18/70   P(36-17-3)  287
ChiB  D24 R42/172  P(19-15-1)  199
LARm-Matson 115C,
Bratkowski 322P

Min    0  14   7   7  28
SF    14  10   7   7  38
Min   D20 R28/121  P(24-16-1)  243
SF    D21 R35/196  P(24-14-0)  246
Min-Smith 123C; SF-Smith 168R,
Owens 138C

NYG    0  14   6  17  37
Cle    7   7   0   7  21
NYG   D24 R34/116  P(27-18-1)  253
Cle   D20 R23/66   P(35-19-2)  268
Cle-Renfro 166C

SL     0   0  14  13  27
Pit    0  13  14   3  30
SL    D12 R24/59   P(28-14-3)  165
Pit   D19 R49/160  P(26-10-5)  187
SL 1-Randle 113C
```

SUNDAY, DECEMBER 3

```
Cle   21   3   0  14  38
Dal    0  10   0   7  17
Cle   D23 R35/230  P(13-10-0)  143
Dal   D19 R32/174  P(37-11-3)  202
Cle-Mitchell 140R; Dal-Perkins 123R

Det    0   9   0   7  16
ChiB   3   3   6   3  15
Det   D17 R24/73   P(34-18-2)  172
ChiB  D12 R32/127  P(24-9-2)    66

LARm   0  14   0   7  21
Min    7  14  14   7  42
LARm  D13 R20/200  P(27-13-3)  148
Min   D27 R44/210  P(31-21-1)  231
LARm-Bass 113R; Min-Hayes 123R,
Reichow 112C, Tarkenton 252P

NYG    7  10   0   0  17
GB    13   0   0   7  20
NYG   D18 R20/69   P(28-14-0)  193
GB    D25 R42/270  P(24-10-2)  134
GB-Taylor 186R

Phi    7  14   7   7  35
Pit    7   3   7   7  24
Phi   D12 R22/92   P(31-14-0)  192
Pit   D20 R47/161  P(34-14-6)  200

SF     0   7   0  10  17
Bal    7   3   0  10  20
SF    D17 R32/148  P(28-13-2)  161
Bal   D18 R33/154  P(27-15-1)  192

Was    7  10   0   7  24
SL     7   0  10  21  38
Was   D13 R34/140  P(17-10-0)  222
SL    D21 R32/149  P(26-14-3)  301
SL-Conrad 128C
```

SATURDAY, DECEMBER 9

```
Bal   10   0   0   7  17
LARm   7   3  10  14  34
Bal   D24 R35/272  P(27-15-1)  142
LARm  D22 R35/182  P(24-14-0)  203
LARm-Dale 118C
```

SUNDAY, DECEMBER 10

```
Cle   14   0   0   0  14
ChiB   7   0   0  10  17
Cle   D15 R27/75   P(29-17-1)  245
ChiB  D19 R28/108  P(31-16-2)  216

Dal    6   0   0   7  13
SL     0  10  14   7  31
Dal   D8  R30/110  P(16-6-0)    16
SL    D14 R28/74   P(30-14-3)  260
SL-Randle 116C

GB     0   7   7   7  21
SF     0  14   2   6  22
GB    D20 R33/153  P(20-15-2)  177
SF    D17 R27/68   P(29-19-0)  328
GB-Taylor 122R; SF-Casey 118C,
Owens 127C, Brodie 328P

Min    0   0   7   0   7
Det    0   7   3   3  13
Min   D18 R33/116  P(34-15-3)  135
Det   D15 R36/120  P(28-10-1)  175

NYG    7   7   7   7  28
Phi    0  10   0  14  24
NYG   D17 R38/143  P(25-13-0)  228
Phi   D16 R23/124  P(31-16-2)  331
NYG-Walton 100C;
Phi-McDonald 237C,
Jurgensen 367P

Pit    7   3  14   6  30
Was    0   7   0   7  14
Pit   D20 R39/110  P(19-13-0)  214
Was   D21 R24/96   P(45-21-3)  247
Pit-Layne 226P
```

SATURDAY, DECEMBER 16

```
Bal    3  17   0   7  27
SF    10   0   7   7  24
Bal   D21 R28/97   P(34-19-0)  269
SF    D25 R26/93   P(39-16-2)  262
Bal-Orr 105C, Unitas 314P;
SF-Owens 100C, Stickles 143C
```

SUNDAY, DECEMBER 17

```
Cle    0   0   0   7   7
NYG    7   0   0   0   7
Cle   D7  R27/107  P(25-7-1)    71
NYG   D17 R40/136  P(28-14-1)  130
Cle-Brown 102R

Dal    0   3  14   7  24
Was    7   0  21   6  34
Dal   D11 R17/60   P(30-13-1)  261
Was   D22 R46/181  P(29-15-0)  185
Dal-Clarke 159C; Was-James 146R

GB     7   7   0  10  24
LARm   0   3   7   7  17
GB    D21 R36/123  P(27-16-2)  161
LARm  D14 R19/119  P(35-19-2)  110
LARm-Phillips 101C

Min   14  14   7   7  35
ChiB   7  14  24   7  52
Min   D12 R24/149  P(22-12-1)   57
ChiB  D25 R30/205  P(36-23-2)  347
Min-Triplett 121R, Tarkenton 161P;
ChiB-Ditka 102C, Wade 355P

Phi    3   7   7  10  27
Det    3   0   7  14  24
Phi   D27 R33/91   P(42-27-2)  394
Det   D18 R23/130  P(26-16-1)  266
Phi-Retzlaff 105C, Jurgensen 403P;
Det-Cogdill 171C

Pit    0   0   0   0   0
SL     7   0   6   7  20
Pit   D16 R41/83   P(25-12-2)  155
SL    D15 R31/134  P(23-10-0)  111
Pit-Mack 101C
```

1962 AFL

FRIDAY, SEPTEMBER 7

```
SD     0   7   7   7  21
Den   10  14   6   0  30
SD    D14 R24/96   P(28-9-1)   112
Den   D28 R29/121  P(50-29-3)  384
Den-Tripucka 376P
```

SATURDAY, SEPTEMBER 8
Bos 0 14 0 14 28
DalT 0 21 7 14 42
Bos D22 R23/113 P(31-16-1) 209
DalT D27 R42/265 P(23-16-0) 156
DalT-Haynes 122R

SUNDAY, SEPTEMBER 9
Hou 7 14 7 0 28
Buf 3 0 6 14 23
Hou D26 R41/204 P(31-16-6) 216
Buf D15 R26/134 P(26-10-3) 86
Hou-Tolar 109R, Hennigan 145C

NYT 0 14 14 0 28
Oak 0 3 7 7 17
NYT D13 R22/163 P(25-12-3) 261
Oak D20 R37/184 P(35-12-2) 129
NYT-Christy 106R, Powell 175C;
Oak-Daniels 101R

SATURDAY, SEPTEMBER 15
Den 3 0 7 13 23
Buf 6 14 0 0 20
Den D22 R10/27 P(56-29-3) 428
Buf D18 R36/211 P(34-16-2) 174
Den-Frazier 125C, Taylor 133C,
Tripucka 447P; Buf-Gilchrist 131R

SUNDAY, SEPTEMBER 16
Hou 7 14 0 0 21
Bos 7 17 0 10 34
Hou D18 R24/69 P(37-21-4) 392
Bos D17 R34/223 P(35-15-0) 207
Hou-Hennigan 202C, Blanda 386P;
Bos-Burton 118R

NYT 0 0 0 14 14
SD 7 14 10 9 40
NYT D20 R21/83 P(41-20-3) 165
SD D13 R33/110 P(20-6-2) 187

FRIDAY, SEPTEMBER 21
Den 0 3 0 13 16
Bos 3 14 10 14 41
Den D18 R14/41 P(56-27-2) 372
Bos D22 R25/170 P(23-12-3) 171
Den-Tarr 152C, Taylor 119C;
Bos-Romeo 121C

SATURDAY, SEPTEMBER 22
NYT 7 7 3 0 17
Buf 0 6 0 0 6
NYT D12 R24/84 P(27-17-1) 151
Buf D16 R27/172 P(35-14-4) 155

SUNDAY, SEPTEMBER 23
Hou 14 14 7 7 42
SD 7 3 0 7 17
Hou D27 R42/277 P(22-12-1) 155
SD D15 R17/45 P(38-17-2) 292
Hou-Tolar 142R; SD-Kocourek 140C

DalT 13 3 0 10 26
Oak 3 7 0 6 16
DalT D14 R28/82 P(23-15-0) 203
Oak D16 R15/55 P(42-20-4) 181

SUNDAY, SEPTEMBER 30
SD 7 21 14 0 42
Oak 7 7 3 16 33
SD D15 R31/205 P(21-10-3) 199
Oak D14 R25/141 P(31-14-2) 125
SD-Lincoln 166R

Den 3 10 0 19 32
NYT 7 3 0 0 10
Den D16 R25/60 P(32-23-3) 273
NYT D11 R16/78 P(44-21-3) 166

Buf 0 0 7 14 21
DalT 14 0 20 7 41
Buf D14 R26/77 P(39-14-3) 158
DalT D24 R44/320 P(19-12-1) 231
DalT-Haynes 164R

FRIDAY, OCTOBER 5
Oak 0 0 0 7 7
Den 0 14 7 23 44
Oak D14 R37/74 P(22-7-3) 123
Den D19 R30/190 P(26-10-4) 113

SATURDAY, OCTOBER 6
Bos 3 21 13 6 43
NYT 0 7 7 0 14
Bos D16 R32/117 P(27-16-0) 238
NYT D13 R16/48 P(46-24-2) 325
Bos-Colclough 142C;
NYT-Maynard 117C, Powell 162C

SUNDAY, OCTOBER 7
DalT 0 14 0 14 28
SD 9 14 0 9 32
DalT D10 R15/74 P(24-12-2) 139
SD D22 R40/138 P(31-15-0) 233

Buf 7 0 7 0 14
Hou 3 0 0 14 17
Buf D13 R33/77 P(31-12-3) 129
Hou D12 R22/71 P(37-13-5) 251

FRIDAY, OCTOBER 12
DalT 3 7 0 17 27
Bos 0 0 7 0 7
DalT D17 R31/112 P(31-17-2) 302
Bos D14 R23/63 P(32-17-2) 253
DalT-Burford 171C, Dawson 306P

SATURDAY, OCTOBER 13
SD 0 3 0 7 10
Buf 7 14 7 7 35
SD D12 R21/43 P(32-10-4) 72
Buf D17 R48/303 P(12-5-1) 136
Buf-Crow 115R, Gilchrist 124R

SUNDAY, OCTOBER 14
NYT 3 7 7 0 17
Hou 14 21 14 7 56
NYT D12 R19/47 P(34-15-3) 93
Hou D24 R40/185 P(28-16-1) 252
Hou-Smith 114R, Blanda 190P

Den 6 0 10 7 23
Oak 0 0 6 0 6
Den D15 R21/87 P(32-16-3) 242
Oak D15 R30/79 P(34-14-2) 150

FRIDAY, OCTOBER 19
SD 10 10 0 0 20
Bos 3 0 14 7 24
SD D11 R24/90 P(31-12-4) 170
Bos D20 R41/175 P(26-14-2) 137
SD-Norton 107C

SATURDAY, OCTOBER 20
Oak 0 0 6 0 6
Buf 0 7 0 7 14
Oak D13 R29/147 P(28-9-2) 143
Buf D12 R39/201 P(11-3-1) 51
Buf-Gilchrist 143R

SUNDAY, OCTOBER 21
Hou 0 3 7 0 10
Den 3 3 0 14 20
Hou D15 R21/67 P(46-24-0) 201
Den D21 R23/86 P(40-26-1) 301
Den-Tripucka 308P

NYT 0 10 7 0 17
DalT 7 3 7 3 20
NYT D13 R28/98 P(26-13-3) 178
DalT D22 R28/137 P(27-19-1) 205
NYT-Maynard 102C;
DalT-Haynes 121C

FRIDAY, OCTOBER 26
Oak 7 6 0 3 16
Bos 7 3 0 16 26
Oak D11 R23/94 P(27-11-1) 185
Bos D18 R37/253 P(23-16-0) 177
Bos-Garron 140R

SUNDAY, OCTOBER 28
DalT 14 7 7 3 31
Hou 0 0 7 0 7
DalT D18 R38/134 P(21-15-1) 179
Hou D17 R21/70 P(34-17-6) 205

SD 0 3 0 0 3
NYT 0 0 0 23 23
SD D10 R22/38 P(40-14-3) 145
NYT D13 R21/70 P(31-18-1) 275
NYT-Maynard 157C, Powell 105C,
Green 313P

Buf 7 6 10 22 45
Den 10 14 0 14 38
Buf D19 R40/199 P(16-9-0) 253
Den D21 R37/196 P(24-14-2) 167
Den-Tripucka 168P

SATURDAY, NOVEMBER 3
Bos 14 0 7 7 28
Buf 14 7 7 0 28
Bos D18 R20/88 P(33-20-1) 287
Buf D19 R45/194 P(17-4-1) 46
Bos-Cappelletti 103C;
Buf-Gilchrist 107R

SUNDAY, NOVEMBER 4
Oak 0 7 7 7 21
NYT 3 0 14 14 31
Oak D12 R21/33 P(34-12-2) 167
NYT D24 R43/163 P(35-17-4) 242
NYT-Powell 100C

Hou 0 7 7 0 14
DalT 0 0 0 6 6
Hou D19 R42/141 P(20-13-1) 194
DalT D18 R22/104 P(31-19-2) 159
Hou-Tolar 110R

Den 7 0 7 9 23
SD 0 17 3 0 20
Den D21 R30/51 P(35-18-2) 200
SD D16 R33/151 P(26-10-2) 162
SD-Robinson 125C

SUNDAY, NOVEMBER 11
DalT 21 7 10 14 52
NYT 14 6 8 3 31
DalT D23 R47/226 P(12-5-0) 111
NYT D16 R18/53 P(37-21-2) 189
DalT-Haynes 107R, McClinton 102R;
NYT-Powell 102C

Bos 3 17 3 10 33
Den 0 9 7 13 29
Bos D25 R39/171 P(23-15-0) 225
Den D23 R28/130 P(38-16-2) 213
Bos-MacKinnon 102R,
Colclough 123C, Kocourek 126C

Hou 7 0 7 14 28
Oak 7 6 7 0 20
Hou D20 R44/152 P(43-17-4) 203
Oak D8 R20/80 P(32-9-3) 193
Hou-Tolar 105R;
Oak-Roberson 107C

Buf 17 20 3 0 40
SD 0 0 6 14 20
Buf D20 R40/211 P(16-6-2) 124
SD D21 R34/164 P(28-15-3) 206
SD-MacKinnon 102R,
Kocourek 126C

SUNDAY, NOVEMBER 18
DalT 0 7 0 17 24
Den 0 0 0 3 3
DalT D17 R43/180 P(17-11-0) 267
Den D12 R19/98 P(29-13-0) 81
DalT-Arbanas 117C

Bos 7 3 7 0 17
Hou 7 7 0 7 21
Bos D15 R30/106 P(35-16-0) 238
Hou D19 R39/99 P(29-16-5) 228

Buf 0 3 7 0 10
Oak 3 3 0 0 6
Buf D17 R48/306 P(27-9-1) 99
Oak D6 R27/86 P(31-9-3) 28
Buf-Gilchrist 103R

THURSDAY, NOVEMBER 22
NYT 14 10 8 14 46
Den 0 13 14 18 45
NYT D25 R27/113 P(46-22-3) 208
Den D19 R22/115 P(41-21-3) 179
NYT-Maynard 105C, Green 292P

FRIDAY, NOVEMBER 23
Buf 7 0 3 0 10
Bos 0 14 0 7 21
Buf D11 R23/63 P(26-15-1) 192
Bos D15 R30/99 P(17-12-0) 220

SUNDAY, NOVEMBER 25
SD 14 7 3 3 27
Hou 0 12 7 14 33
SD D18 R36/153 P(39-15-3) 241
Hou D10 R25/47 P(31-12-5) 228
Hou-Dewveall 139C

Oak 0 7 0 0 7
DalT 14 7 0 14 35
Oak D18 R22/53 P(29-17-0) 165
DalT D19 R44/281 P(13-9-1) 119
DalT-Haynes 112R, McClinton 109R

FRIDAY, NOVEMBER 30
NYT 7 3 7 0 17
Bos 0 3 7 14 24
NYT D13 R25/64 P(39-16-0) 209
Bos D12 R36/170 P(20-6-1) 171
NYT-Maynard 113C;
Bos-Colclough 127C

SUNDAY, DECEMBER 2
DalT 0 0 7 7 14
Buf 6 7 3 7 23
DalT D16 R19/131 P(34-19-2) 162
Buf D24 R30/91 P(35-21-0) 230
Buf-Warlick 117C

Den 0 14 3 0 17
Hou 10 7 7 10 34
Den D16 R14/39 P(53-22-8) 206
Hou D19 R25/52 P(44-21-5) 280
Hou-Cannon 107C

Oak 0 0 7 14 21
SD 14 0 7 10 31
Oak D12 R21/76 P(34-14-2) 296
SD D23 R44/185 P(24-11-1) 150
Oak-Dorsey 155C;
SD-McDougall 108R

SATURDAY, DECEMBER 8
Buf 3 3 7 7 20
NYT 3 0 0 0 3
Buf D23 R40/241 P(26-12-4) 151
NYT D11 R15/27 P(43-20-3) 180
Buf-Gilchrist 143R

SUNDAY, DECEMBER 9
Oak 0 17 0 0 17
Hou 10 10 7 5 32
Oak D22 R28/219 P(40-16-2) 197
Hou D13 R29/90 P(33-11-2) 181
Oak-Daniels 187R;
Hou-McLeod 114C

Den 3 0 0 7 10
DalT 14 0 3 0 17
Den D19 R20/57 P(47-28-4) 245
DalT D14 R43/227 P(20-11-3) 118
Den-Taylor 110C;
DalT-McClinton 105R

Bos 7 10 0 3 20
SD 0 3 3 8 14
Bos D15 R44/140 P(22-7-1) 147
SD D10 R27/86 P(23-10-0) 101

SATURDAY, DECEMBER 15
Hou 14 10 14 6 44
NYT 7 3 0 0 10
Hou D27 R42/218 P(40-18-3) 243
NYT D9 R22/122 P(31-6-4) 40
Hou-Cannon 103R, Tolar 107C

SUNDAY, DECEMBER 16
SD 7 0 10 0 17
DalT 3 20 0 3 26
SD D17 R24/143 P(35-14-6) 184
DalT D19 R35/134 P(27-15-2) 104

Bos 0 0 0 0 0
Oak 3 7 7 3 20
Bos D11 R18/82 P(35-13-2) 86
Oak D10 R32/71 P(27-11-1) 217

1962 NFL

SUNDAY, SEPTEMBER 16
ChiB 10 7 7 6 30
SF 0 0 7 7 14
ChiB D12 R40/258 P(13-5-0) 13
SF D14 R23/121 P(24-12-2) 72
ChiB-Galimore 181R

LARm 0 7 13 7 27
Bal 7 9 0 14 30
LARm D15 R31/112 P(32-15-2) 112
Bal D15 R29/50 P(36-19-2) 209
LARm-Dale 139C; Bal-Unitas 245P

Min 0 0 0 7 7
GB 14 3 10 7 34
Min D14 R29/129 P(23-11-5) 48
GB D15 R37/185 P(16-8-0) 123

NYG 0 0 0 7 7
Cle 3 7 3 4 17
NYG D19 R27/87 P(31-17-3) 207
Cle D19 R40/216 P(19-8-1) 131
Cle-Brown 134R

Pit 0 7 0 0 7
Det 0 21 7 17 45
Pit D10 R26/44 P(22-9-1) 129
Det D26 R37/159 P(30-21-0) 236

SL 0 13 7 7 27
Phi 0 7 0 7 21
SL D23 R48/175 P(26-14-0) 179
Phi D13 R19/28 P(25-15-2) 257
SL-Randle 122C; Phi-Retzlaff 126C

Was 7 7 7 14 35
Dal 7 7 14 7 35
Was D17 R26/75 P(26-14-1) 211
Dal D22 R27/142 P(39-23-2) 341
Was-Mitchell 135C; Dal-Clarke 241C

SUNDAY, SEPTEMBER 23
Bal 7 7 3 17 34
Min 0 0 0 7 7
Bal D20 R46/153 P(26-16-2) 195
Min D13 R20/51 P(34-17-2) 122

ChiB 0 14 13 0 27
LARm 0 7 6 10 23
ChiB D18 R36/137 P(30-15-0) 227
LARm D18 R27/149 P(31-16-3) 249
LARm-Bass 107R, Dale 101C

NYG 10 7 3 9 29
Phi 7 6 0 0 13
NYG D13 R31/87 P(26-15-2) 268
Phi D23 R13/37 P(57-33-3) 381
NYG-Shofner 135C;
Phi-Brown 160C, Jurgensen 396P

Pit 0 21 0 9 30
Dal 7 0 7 14 28
Pit D22 R41/210 P(26-10-1) 144
Dal D19 R28/126 P(30-19-2) 225
Dal-Perkins 108R

SL 0 0 0 0 0
GB 3 7 7 0 17
SL D11 R18/16 P(33-17-2) 115
GB D20 R37/171 P(27-15-2) 163
GB-Taylor 122R

SF 7 3 14 0 24
Det 10 14 7 14 45
SF D16 R23/75 P(30-20-1) 267
Det D22 R32/174 P(22-16-0) 250
SF-Casey 126C; Det-Cogdill 147C,
Plum 272P

Was 7 0 3 7 17
Cle 3 10 0 3 16
Was D12 R24/95 P(18-8-3) 114
Cle D23 R34/131 P(34-19-1) 224

SUNDAY, SEPTEMBER 30
ChiB 0 0 0 0 0
GB 0 14 21 14 49
ChiB D7 R28/85 P(20-7-5) 91
GB D21 R42/244 P(13-10-1) 165
GB-Taylor 126R

Cle 7 0 0 0 7
Phi 7 7 7 14 35
Cle D16 R26/104 P(33-14-3) 126
Phi D23 R35/110 P(27-19-3) 288
Phi-McDonald 140C

Dal	7	3	7	10	**27**
LARm	0	3	0	14	17
Dal	D13	R36/177	P(21-10-0)	226	
LARm	D15	R16/40	P(40-19-1)	234	

Dal-Clarke 130C; LARm-Phillips 118C

Det	10	7	7	5	**29**
Bal	7	10	3	0	20
Det	D14	R33/156	P(31-16-4)	260	
Bal	D14	R25/84	P(33-16-3)	174	

Det-Barr 165C

Min	0	0	0	7	7
SF	7	7	7	0	**21**
Min	D15	R26/143	P(28-16-3)	116	
SF	D16	R39/204	P(19-5-2)	57	

NYG	3	14	7	7	**31**
Pit	14	3	3	7	27
NYG	D19	R27/95	P(29-17-1)	332	
Pit	D23	R44/175	P(24-12-3)	142	

NYG-Webster 101C, Tittle 332P; Pit-Johnson 113R

SL	0	0	7	7	14
Was	7	7	0	10	**24**
SL	D23	R24/66	P(32-20-4)	285	
Was	D14	R38/89	P(23-13-1)	205	

SL-Randle 122C; Was-Mitchell 147C

SATURDAY, OCTOBER 6

Phi	0	0	7	0	7
Pit	10	3	0	0	**13**
Phi	D11	R15/44	P(33-13-2)	153	
Pit	D18	R52/236	P(18-11-2)	132	

Pit-Johnson 128R

SUNDAY, OCTOBER 7

ChiB	0	0	10	3	**13**
Min	0	0	0	0	0
ChiB	D12	R27/114	P(29-13-0)	135	
Min	D16	R33/129	P(24-12-3)	130	

Dal	0	3	7	0	10
Cle	7	0	9	3	**19**
Dal	D12	R28/101	P(21-11-0)	138	
Cle	D12	R28/62	P(25-15-1)	169	

Det	0	7	0	0	7
GB	3	0	3	3	**9**
Det	D12	R27/107	P(26-11-1)	92	
GB	D20	R34/129	P(28-18-2)	190	

LARm	0	7	0	7	14
Was	10	10	0	0	**20**
LARm	D15	R20/98	P(21-14-1)	143	
Was	D19	R38/144	P(22-15-0)	205	

LARm-Phillips 103C

NYG	7	14	7	3	**31**
SL	7	7	0	0	14
NYG	D21	R31/101	P(34-20-1)	231	
SL	D15	R25/104	P(25-12-2)	120	

SL-Conrad 105C

SF	7	0	7	7	**21**
Bal	0	0	0	13	13
SF	D25	R45/224	P(19-15-0)	111	
Bal	D18	R29/123	P(21-11-1)	138	

SF-Smith 145R

SUNDAY, OCTOBER 14

Bal	13	10	0	13	**36**
Cle	0	0	7	7	14
Bal	D25	R35/171	P(34-19-1)	219	
Cle	D13	R18/20	P(32-16-2)	216	

GB	10	17	7	14	**48**
Min	0	7	0	14	21
GB	D29	R42/209	P(29-20-0)	297	
Min	D15	R19/46	P(29-18-3)	260	

GB-Taylor 164R, Dowler 124C, McGee 159C; Min-McElhenny 118C

LARm	0	3	0	7	10
Det	7	3	3	0	**13**
LARm	D8	R20/160	P(16-4-1)	26	
Det	D21	R44/200	P(27-17-1)	132	

LARm-Bass 140R

Phi	6	0	0	13	19
Dal	0	17	7	17	**41**
Phi	D21	R27/78	P(32-17-2)	250	
Dal	D13	R32/155	P(12-10-0)	199	

Phi-McDonald 131C; Dal-Clarke 118C

Pit	0	7	10	3	**20**
NYG	3	0	7	7	17
Pit	D16	R56/250	P(10-5-0)	72	
NYG	D18	R17/97	P(40-18-3)	194	

Pit-Johnson 123R

SF	10	14	3	7	**34**
ChiB	10	7	3	7	27
SF	D16	R42/194	P(16-6-1)	105	
ChiB	D17	R18/86	P(35-19-2)	381	

SF-Smith 115R; ChiB-Ditka 132C, Morris 122C, Wade 356P

Was	7	0	7	3	17
SL	0	3	0	14	17
Was	D15	R25/62	P(30-18-1)	259	
SL	D16	R23/58	P(33-19-2)	251	

Was-Mitchell 158C

SUNDAY, OCTOBER 21

Bal	6	0	9	0	15
ChiB	0	7	7	21	**35**
Bal	D19	R32/84	P(35-20-3)	331	
ChiB	D18	R29/102	P(26-13-2)	306	

Bal-Orr 155C; ChiB-Ditka 100C, Wade 318P

Cle	6	14	0	14	**34**
SL	0	0	7	0	7
Cle	D26	R31/136	P(31-20-0)	351	
SL	D16	R19/90	P(35-13-3)	101	

Cle-Renfro 152C, Ninowski 339P

Dal	14	7	7	14	**42**
Pit	7	3	3	14	27
Dal	D19	R38/107	P(26-13-3)	295	
Pit	D21	R34/123	P(30-15-2)	250	

Dal-Folkins 123C, LeBaron 158P; Pit-Dial 157C

Det	7	7	0	0	14
NYG	7	0	10	0	**17**
Det	D16	R35/91	P(23-13-2)	187	
NYG	D13	R35/67	P(21-11-1)	124	

Det-Cogdill 144C

Min	14	17	0	7	**38**
LARm	0	0	14	0	14
Min	D23	R44/214	P(24-14-0)	193	
LARm	D12	R18/41	P(30-12-3)	129	

SF	3	3	7	0	13
GB	0	10	14	7	**31**
SF	D14	R36/163	P(15-6-3)	19	
GB	D19	R34/251	P(12-10-0)	85	

SF-Smith 119R; GB-Taylor 160R

Was	0	17	3	7	**27**
Phi	0	7	7	7	21
Was	D15	R26/49	P(25-17-2)	276	
Phi	D24	R28/154	P(39-24-4)	308	

Was-Mitchell 147C; Phi-Cassady 133C

SUNDAY, OCTOBER 28

ChiB	0	0	0	3	3
Det	0	6	2	3	**11**
ChiB	D8	R25/60	P(21-10-1)	15	
Det	D13	R34/79	P(24-12-1)	109	

Cle	7	0	17	17	**41**
Pit	0	0	7	7	14
Cle	D21	R40/200	P(25-12-2)	154	
Pit	D17	R37/164	P(16-9-1)	41	

GB	0	10	0	7	**17**
Bal	0	3	3	0	6
GB	D14	R29/111	P(19-11-2)	141	
Bal	D18	R38/155	P(31-18-2)	154	

LARm	7	14	0	7	**28**
SF	0	7	0	7	14
LARm	D18	R43/159	P(18-11-0)	155	
SF	D20	R27/154	P(36-19-2)	157	

Phi	7	0	7	7	21
Min	0	21	3	7	**31**
Phi	D18	R26/90	P(27-15-2)	314	
Min	D17	R44/187	P(17-8-1)	172	

Phi-Brown 174C; Min-Mason 113C

SL	7	7	7	7	**28**
Dal	3	7	7	7	24
SL	D14	R26/110	P(20-10-1)	239	
Dal	D20	R39/201	P(30-16-2)	178	

SL-Randle 144C; Dal-Perkins 137R

Was	7	6	7	14	34
NYG	7	14	21	7	**49**
Was	D19	R19/59	P(40-17-3)	316	
NYG	D25	R28/97	P(39-27-0)	505	

Was-Mitchell 158C, Snead 346P; NYG-Gifford 127C, Shofner 269C, Tittle 505P

SUNDAY, NOVEMBER 4

Bal	5	0	7	10	**22**
SF	0	3	0	0	3
Bal	D15	R42/172	P(18-9-0)	139	
SF	D11	R31/81	P(19-10-2)	70	

Bal-Orr 110C

Dal	3	7	14	14	**38**
Was	3	0	0	7	10
Dal	D21	R36/224	P(23-13-1)	164	
Was	D17	R23/68	P(34-16-1)	225	

Dal-Marsh 109R

Det	0	0	7	5	**12**
LARm	0	0	3	0	3
Det	D15	R34/139	P(24-12-2)	150	
LARm	D9	R18/22	P(26-14-1)	102	

GB	7	3	7	21	**38**
ChiB	0	7	0	0	7
GB	D25	R44/215	P(27-14-0)	161	
ChiB	D16	R27/65	P(26-13-3)	147	

GB-Taylor 124R

Min	0	14	7	10	31
Pit	7	7	12	13	**39**
Min	D15	R17/79	P(21-13-1)	240	
Pit	D29	R48/212	P(28-16-1)	227	

Min-Ferguson 106C, Tarkenton 273P; Pit-Dial 103C

Phi	7	0	7	0	14
Cle	0	7	0	7	14
Phi	D15	R26/65	P(27-15-3)	124	
Cle	D16	R39/182	P(24-10-3)	119	

SL	0	14	0	14	28
NYG	7	3	0	21	**31**
SL	D29	R38/141	P(42-27-3)	353	
NYG	D15	R21/85	P(32-9-1)	181	

SL-Randle 256C, Johnson 365P

SUNDAY, NOVEMBER 11

Bal	7	0	7	0	**14**
LARm	0	2	0	0	2
Bal	D16	R38/96	P(27-16-2)	224	
LARm	D12	R29/95	P(28-13-1)	120	

Cle	0	0	9	0	9
Was	0	10	7	0	**17**
Cle	D12	R21/89	P(18-11-2)	102	
Was	D20	R38/142	P(23-14-2)	79	

Det	10	14	7	7	**38**
SF	7	10	0	7	24
Det	D21	R39/180	P(27-16-1)	257	
SF	D18	R19/62	P(33-20-2)	226	

SF-Johnson 181C

GB	7	28	14	0	**49**
Phi	0	0	0	0	0
GB	D37	R55/294	P(31-19-1)	334	
Phi	D3	R13/30	P(25-9-1)	24	

GB-Taylor 141R, Dowler 101C, McGee 174C

Min	7	10	10	3	30
ChiB	0	7	14	10	**31**
Min	D13	R33/143	P(24-6-2)	147	
ChiB	D22	R26/88	P(42-26-5)	259	

Min-Ferguson 130C

NYG	0	24	3	14	**41**
Dal	0	0	3	7	10
NYG	D22	R31/106	P(31-21-1)	340	
Dal	D16	R26/89	P(38-17-2)	173	

NYG-Shofner 158C, Tittle 315P

Pit	3	6	0	17	**26**
SL	7	3	7	0	17
Pit	D16	R47/194	P(14-8-0)	59	
SL	D17	R28/115	P(27-11-3)	220	

Pit-Johnson 138R; SL-Conrad 101C

SUNDAY, NOVEMBER 18

Bal	3	7	3	0	13
GB	10	0	0	7	**17**
Bal	D19	R44/189	P(28-17-1)	193	
GB	D8	R27/87	P(13-8-0)	29	

Bal-Orr 100C

ChiB	0	10	7	17	**34**
Dal	0	13	13	7	33
ChiB	D28	R22/67	P(47-28-2)	437	
Dal	D14	R23/157	P(28-11-0)	144	

ChiB-Ditka 133C, Morris 201C, Wade 466P

Det	0	3	14	0	**17**
Min	3	3	0	0	6
Det	D18	R34/135	P(35-19-2)	223	
Min	D13	R22/73	P(25-10-1)	107	

Phi	14	0	0	0	14
NYG	10	3	3	3	**19**
Phi	D8	R21/115	P(24-8-0)	84	
NYG	D16	R45/186	P(19-8-3)	82	

NYG-Webster 107R

SL	0	0	0	14	14
Cle	0	7	17	14	**38**
SL	D20	R35/210	P(32-15-2)	149	
Cle	D22	R38/136	P(21-13-0)	225	

SF	0	7	10	7	**24**
LARm	3	0	0	14	17
SF	D22	R47/207	P(21-17-1)	263	
LARm	D13	R19/60	P(24-11-2)	187	

SF-Kilmer 101R, Stickles 107C

Was	0	7	14	0	21
Pit	3	3	0	17	**23**
Was	D14	R32/97	P(31-11-2)	174	
Pit	D18	R30/96	P(35-17-4)	251	

THURSDAY, NOVEMBER 22

GB	0	0	0	14	14
Det	7	16	3	0	**26**
GB	D11	R27/73	P(19-11-2)	49	
Det	D14	R40/157	P(18-10-2)	147	

SUNDAY, NOVEMBER 25

ChiB	7	13	16	21	**57**
Bal	0	0	0	0	0
ChiB	D27	R33/98	P(40-26-0)	407	
Bal	D10	R15/61	P(26-11-1)	57	

ChiB-Coia 128C, Wade 328P

Dal	0	7	7	0	14
Phi	14	7	0	7	**28**
Dal	D19	R27/92	P(29-16-1)	208	
Phi	D22	R31/140	P(21-13-2)	313	

Phi-Brown 107R, McDonald 108C, Retzlaff 113C, Jurgensen 342P

LARm	3	7	0	14	24
Min	3	14	0	7	24
LARm	D22	R34/172	P(28-18-0)	278	
Min	D21	R36/160	P(24-14-4)	253	

LARm-Phillips 141C; Min-Mason 119C

NYG	7	21	7	7	**42**
Was	3	7	0	14	24
NYG	D22	R36/149	P(24-12-3)	256	
Was	D17	R22/39	P(44-21-2)	277	

NYG-Shofner 125C; Was-James 117C

Pit	0	0	7	7	14
Cle	0	14	0	21	**35**
Pit	D18	R38/144	P(23-13-1)	144	
Cle	D24	R30/155	P(33-21-0)	263	

Cle-Brown 110R

SF	7	10	0	7	**24**
SL	0	7	3	7	17
SF	D15	R42/118	P(18-9-0)	97	
SL	D18	R31/164	P(25-10-2)	150	

SUNDAY, DECEMBER 2

Bal	0	0	0	14	14
Det	7	0	0	14	**21**
Bal	D16	R19/43	P(33-19-2)	227	
Det	D22	R41/104	P(31-20-2)	229	

Det-Cogdill 137C

Cle	7	7	0	7	21
Dal	3	14	14	14	**45**
Cle	D18	R13/61	P(32-19-1)	234	
Dal	D28	R41/217	P(20-16-1)	181	

Cle-Kreitling 125C; Dal-Marsh 117R

LARm	3	0	0	7	10
GB	10	14	3	14	**41**
LARm	D14	R29/146	P(28-18-1)	91	
GB	D24	R34/146	P(24-16-1)	218	

NYG	10	7	6	3	**26**
ChiB	14	0	3	7	24
NYG	D22	R29/173	P(29-12-1)	170	
ChiB	D23	R22/106	P(39-21-4)	274	

ChiB-Morris 112C

Phi	0	14	14	9	**37**
Was	7	7	0	0	14
Phi	D21	R31/120	P(22-15-1)	252	
Was	D26	R22/75	P(39-22-2)	272	

Phi-Retzlaff 135C; Was-Mitchell 114C

SL	0	0	0	7	7
Pit	7	0	6	6	**19**
SL	D14	R18/58	P(38-18-2)	213	
Pit	D23	R40/238	P(27-12-1)	174	

SL-Conrad 106C; Pit-Dial 186C

SF	7	0	7	21	**35**
Min	3	7	2	0	12
SF	D15	R28/105	P(22-13-0)	255	
Min	D18	R35/116	P(25-15-0)	234	

SF-Casey 123C, Brodie 272P

SATURDAY, DECEMBER 8

Was	7	7	7	0	21
Bal	0	14	0	20	**34**
Was	D19	R21/72	P(33-18-3)	321	
Bal	D24	R32/95	P(36-25-1)	354	

Was-Jackson 122C, Mitchell 107C, Snead 350P; Bal-Berry 122C, Orr 133C, Unitas 367P

SUNDAY, DECEMBER 9

Cle	0	3	10	0	13
NYG	0	7	7	3	**17**
Cle	D16	R23/89	P(33-17-0)	147	
NYG	D19	R45/215	P(14-7-0)	99	

Dal	7	13	0	0	20
SL	0	14	17	21	**52**
Dal	D14	R24/86	P(31-13-2)	188	
SL	D22	R42/217	P(31-15-2)	310	

SL-Crow 118R, Conrad 128C, Randle 105C, Johnson 302P

GB	3	7	7	14	**31**
SF	7	14	0	0	21
GB	D20	R43/164	P(18-10-1)	130	
SF	D18	R20/36	P(31-20-2)	269	

SF-Casey 134C

LARm	7	0	0	7	14
ChiB	13	10	0	7	**30**
LARm	D14	R36/228	P(28-12-3)	105	
ChiB	D11	R25/87	P(28-16-3)	186	

LARm-Bass 169R; ChiB-Ditka 155C

Min	14	0	0	9	23
Det	10	14	13	0	**37**
Min	D15	R32/203	P(26-8-5)	168	
Det	D16	R34/145	P(27-12-4)	180	

Min-Mason 138R; Det-Cogdill 103C

Pit	0	17	0	9	**26**
Phi	7	0	10	0	17
Pit	D16	R38/130	P(29-15-4)	138	
Phi	D16	R19/65	P(35-17-3)	218	

Phi-Retzlaff 122C

SATURDAY, DECEMBER 15

Cle	6	7	0	0	**13**
SF	7	3	0	0	10
Cle	D14	R33/191	P(10-5-0)	73	
SF	D19	R38/129	P(20-13-1)	100	

Cle-Brown 135R

SUNDAY, DECEMBER 16

Dal	3	21	0	7	31
NYG	7	21	7	6	**41**
Dal	D16	R29/166	P(32-12-1)	212	
NYG	D23	R27/153	P(42-21-2)	318	

Dal-Clarke 114C, Howton 108C; NYG-Webster 155C, Tittle 341P

Det	0	0	0	0	0
ChiB	0	0	0	3	**3**
Det	D13	R25/96	P(34-16-2)	129	
ChiB	D9	R28/136	P(34-17-1)	182	

ChiB-Marconi 121R

GB	7	6	0	7	**20**
LARm	3	7	0	7	17
GB	D18	R33/181	P(35-17-1)	246	
LARm	D16	R36/207	P(22-12-0)	96	

GB-Taylor 156R; LARm-Arnett 103R

Min   7 3 0 7 17
Bal   7 0 7 28 **42**
Min D15 R36/191 P(24-8-1) 26
Bal D22 R24/125 P(39-21-4) 451
Min-Mason 143R; Bal-Berry 131C,
Unitas 385P

Phi   7 21 7 0 35
SL   14 17 7 7 **45**
Phi D17 R20/79 P(34-15-3) 419
SL   D30 R41/174 P(35-19-2) 415
Phi-Brown 199C,
McDonald 162C, Jurgensen 419P;
SL 1-Anderson 175C, Randle 134C,
Johnson 386P

Pit   7 7 6 7 **27**
Was   3 0 7 14 24
Pit D14 R41/117 P(17-8-2) 166
Was D17 R17/22 P(40-19-4) 289
Pit-Dial 101C; Was-James 140C

1963 AFL
SATURDAY, SEPTEMBER 7

KC   14 14 21 10 **59**
Den   0 7 0 0 7
KC   D20 R32/120 P(28-19-1) 358
Den D12 R20/86 P(35-15-5) 95
KC-Jackson 149C, Dawson 278P

Oak   0 0 10 14 **24**
Hou   6 0 0 7 13
Oak D16 R19/79 P(46-13-2) 249
Hou D16 R23/112 P(42-17-6) 206
Oak-Powell 181C;
Hou-Hennigan 101C

SUNDAY, SEPTEMBER 8

Buf   0 3 0 7 10
SD   0 7 7 0 **14**
Buf D19 R27/116 P(33-17-3) 190
SD   D17 R23/131 P(29-18-1) 239

NYJ   7 7 0 0 14
Bos   7 7 3 21 **38**
NYJ D15 R18/117 P(43-18-5) 155
Bos D24 R28/120 P(35-19-1) 268
NYJ-Smolinski 100R, Turner 103C

SATURDAY, SEPTEMBER 14

Bos   3 7 0 3 13
SD   0 14 0 3 **17**
Bos D19 R43/164 P(35-16-2) 139
SD   D11 R21/76 P(21-8-1) 164

Den   0 7 0 7 14
Hou   0 13 7 0 **20**
Den D13 R28/106 P(22-11-3) 76
Hou D17 R27/82 P(31-15-1) 208
Hou-Hennigan 133C

SUNDAY, SEPTEMBER 15

Buf   0 10 7 0 17
Oak   0 21 7 7 **35**
Buf D23 R29/97 P(48-26-2) 336
Oak D27 R23/120 P(35-17-2) 372
Buf-Dubenion 131C, Miller 108C;
Oak-Daniels 172C, Davidson 315P

SUNDAY, SEPTEMBER 22

Hou   7 0 10 0 17
NYJ   7 7 0 10 **24**
Hou D18 R29/85 P(38-25-2) 308
NYJ D17 R21/60 P(34-15-2) 191
Hou-Hennigan 186C, Blanda 308P

Bos   7 10 3 0 **20**
Oak   0 0 0 14 14
Bos D11 R42/160 P(13-7-2) 72
Oak D13 R10/24 P(31-12-2) 133
Oak-Powell 150C

KC   10 0 9 8 **27**
Buf   6 14 7 0 27
KC   D20 R22/49 P(38-25-3) 241
Buf D17 R32/114 P(26-15-1) 242
KC-Burford 106C;
Buf-Dubenion 100C

SATURDAY, SEPTEMBER 28

Oak   7 0 0 0 7
NYJ   7 0 3 0 **10**
Oak D14 R16/63 P(37-15-4) 164
NYJ D11 R25/65 P(28-12-5) 173

Hou   14 14 3 0 **31**
Buf   17 3 0 0 20
Hou D23 R29/116 P(26-18-1) 237
Buf D19 R38/188 P(27-11-2) 123
Hou-Hennigan 123C

SUNDAY, SEPTEMBER 29

KC   0 3 0 7 10
SD   7 14 0 3 **24**
KC   D12 R14/27 P(34-18-3) 137
SD   D17 R34/154 P(19-12-1) 140

Bos   3 0 7 0 10
Den   0 0 7 7 **14**
Bos D11 R22/133 P(20-8-3) 79
Den D20 R39/104 P(25-11-2) 154
Den-Taylor 169C

SATURDAY, OCTOBER 5

Oak   0 0 0 0 0
Buf   3 0 9 0 **12**
Oak D10 R7/24 P(37-12-2) 119
Buf D18 R38/135 P(33-15-1) 140
Buf-Miller 152C

Bos   0 10 0 14 24
NYJ   14 7 3 7 **31**
Bos D22 R31/105 P(39-18-5) 304
NYJ D16 R23/46 P(22-14-0) 172
Bos-Graham 156C, Yewcic 311P

SUNDAY, OCTOBER 6

Hou   0 0 0 7 7
KC   0 14 7 7 **28**
Hou D12 R15/46 P(39-20-4) 241
KC   D21 R43/125 P(23-14-0) 212
KC-Dawson 225P

SD   13 7 0 14 34
Den   3 14 9 24 **50**
SD   D15 R16/95 P(24-14-3) 317
Den D24 R40/205 P(37-18-1) 229
SD-Alworth 114C; Den-Stone 104R,
Taylor 142C

FRIDAY, OCTOBER 11

Oak   7 0 7 0 14
Bos   3 0 10 7 **20**
Oak D12 R20/59 P(32-15-3) 118
Bos D12 R36/93 P(21-5-3) 93

SUNDAY, OCTOBER 13

NYJ   7 3 10 0 20
SD   3 0 14 7 **24**
NYJ D16 R24/63 P(31-15-0) 203
SD   D22 R40/287 P(27-19-2) 223
SD-Lowe 161R

Hou   17 9 7 0 **33**
Den   3 7 7 7 24
Hou D24 R40/118 P(43-21-0) 274
Den D13 R23/96 P(32-15-5) 217
Den-Scarpitto 134C

Buf   7 14 7 7 **35**
KC   10 3 13 0 26
Buf D16 R29/97 P(24-12-2) 300
KC   D21 R28/123 P(46-23-1) 176
Buf-Kemp 300P; KC-Burford 100C

FRIDAY, OCTOBER 18

Den   7 7 7 0 21
Bos   10 13 3 14 **40**
Den D18 R18/95 P(39-19-1) 250
Bos D19 R27/53 P(31-21-1) 331
Bos-Colclough 110C, Parilli 358P

SUNDAY, OCTOBER 20

SD   0 3 14 21 **38**
KC   0 7 3 7 17
SD   D18 R25/147 P(26-17-0) 255
KC   D17 R33/78 P(29-18-2) 247
SD-Lincoln 127R, Alworth 232C;
KC-Haynes 149C

NYJ   7 6 0 13 26
Oak   21 14 7 7 **49**
NYJ D17 R17/91 P(44-16-2) 223
Oak D28 R34/223 P(23-13-1) 282
Oak-Daniels 200R

Buf   0 0 7 7 14
Hou   0 21 7 0 **28**
Buf D22 R28/140 P(43-18-4) 241
Hou D13 R25/82 P(32-12-1) 205
Hou-Frazier 106C

SATURDAY, OCTOBER 26

Den   7 7 14 7 **35**
NYJ   14 7 7 7 35
Den D16 R32/116 P(32-16-1) 201
NYJ D16 R25/69 P(36-14-1) 225
NYJ-Maynard 159C, Wood 231P

Bos   0 0 14 7 21
Buf   0 7 7 14 **28**
Bos D15 R21/104 P(31-12-2) 201
Buf D19 R27/83 P(36-18-1) 221
Buf-Ferguson 109C, Kemp 317P

SUNDAY, OCTOBER 27

Oak   7 7 7 13 **34**
SD   10 7 9 7 33
Oak D13 R36/179 P(21-8-3) 117
SD   D18 R31/234 P(21-9-5) 146
Oak-Daniels 125R;
SD-Lincoln 130R, MacKinnon 111C

KC   0 7 0 0 7
Hou   0 0 14 0 **14**
KC   D20 R35/223 P(36-16-4) 129
Hou D19 R26/92 P(31-20-1) 218

FRIDAY, NOVEMBER 1

Hou   0 3 0 0 3
Bos   14 14 7 10 **45**
Hou D13 R12/19 P(45-19-6) 187
Bos D15 R40/143 P(22-8-1) 168

SATURDAY, NOVEMBER 2

SD   7 17 14 15 **53**
NYJ   0 0 0 7 7
SD   D25 R31/157 P(31-22-0) 371
NYJ D15 R14/39 P(41-19-2) 196
SD-Alworth 180C, Rote 369P

SUNDAY, NOVEMBER 3

Buf   7 0 16 7 **30**
Den   0 14 0 14 28
Buf D20 R43/152 P(28-16-0) 307
Den D11 R18/59 P(27-11-1) 242
Buf-Gilchrist 125R, Dubenion 119C;
Den-Breaux 239P

KC   0 7 0 0 7
Oak   0 3 0 7 **10**
KC   D16 R26/143 P(27-16-0) 112
Oak D20 R25/89 P(40-18-1) 243
KC-McClinton 101R

FRIDAY, NOVEMBER 8

Oak   3 19 0 0 **22**
KC   0 0 7 0 7
Oak D16 R41/163 P(23-12-0) 123
KC   D9 R18/83 P(25-6-2) -22
Oak-Daniels 122R

SATURDAY, NOVEMBER 9

Den   0 3 0 14 17
Buf   0 6 14 7 **27**
Den D17 R18/77 P(42-21-1) 168
Buf D20 R31/94 P(36-16-1) 267
Buf-Rutkowski 100C

SUNDAY, NOVEMBER 10

SD   7 0 0 0 **7**
Bos   0 0 6 0 6
SD   D12 R21/32 P(32-18-1) 239
Bos D15 R28/103 P(30-14-2) 188
SD-Alworth 210C

NYJ   0 7 13 7 27
Hou   7 7 3 14 **31**
NYJ D21 R24/72 P(40-20-5) 282
Hou D23 R36/120 P(32-19-0) 189
NYJ-Turner 210C, Wood 312P

SUNDAY, NOVEMBER 17

NYJ   0 14 0 0 **14**
Den   3 3 3 0 9
NYJ D16 R30/109 P(34-16-0) 238
Den D14 R38/163 P(21-6-0) 52
Den-Joe 105R

SD   10 0 7 6 **23**
Buf   7 3 3 0 13
SD   D16 R27/199 P(22-10-2) 156
Buf D22 R23/119 P(37-23-3) 239
SD-Lincoln 101R;
Buf-Dubenion 112C

KC   7 3 7 7 **24**
Bos   0 15 2 7 24
KC   D20 R26/96 P(32-20-0) 234
Bos D25 R29/108 P(48-26-1) 366
Bos-Colclough 137C, Romeo 149C,
Parilli 354P

THURSDAY, NOVEMBER 28

Oak   2 0 14 10 **26**
Den   0 3 0 7 10
Oak D16 R33/172 P(26-10-0) 119
Den D9 R20/29 P(32-16-3) 136

SUNDAY, DECEMBER 1

Hou   0 0 0 0 0
SD   7 13 0 7 **27**
Hou D14 R21/102 P(32-13-3) 141
SD   D24 R37/212 P(31-14-4) 137
SD-Lincoln 102R

Buf   0 7 0 0 7
Bos   0 0 14 3 **17**
Buf D15 R23/73 P(46-19-2) 166
Bos D10 R25/64 P(37-13-0) 186

KC   0 0 0 0 0
NYJ   7 3 0 7 **17**
KC   D13 R29/119 P(35-13-2) 177
NYJ D10 R29/82 P(29-13-0) 97
KC-Jackson 110C

SUNDAY, DECEMBER 8

Den   3 11 0 7 21
KC   17 7 14 14 **52**
Den D27 R42/216 P(34-18-2) 197
KC   D23 R30/159 P(25-11-1) 212

SD   7 13 7 0 27
Oak   3 7 0 31 **41**
SD   D17 R18/45 P(31-14-1) 291
Oak D24 R37/154 P(41-18-0) 252
SD-Norton 119C; Oak-Powell 132C

Bos   10 21 10 5 **46**
Hou   7 7 7 7 28
Bos D22 R43/194 P(21-8-1) 131
Hou D22 R18/60 P(39-24-3) 214
Bos-Garron 107R;
Hou-Hennigan 122C

NYJ   0 0 7 7 14
Buf   10 14 7 14 **45**
NYJ D14 R15/38 P(37-15-2) 130
Buf D22 R44/285 P(16-10-0) 85
Buf-Gilchrist 243R

SATURDAY, DECEMBER 14

Buf   3 0 6 10 **19**
NYJ   7 3 0 0 10
Buf D20 R41/158 P(24-11-2) 150
NYJ D17 R20/49 P(33-11-2) 168
Buf-Gilchrist 114R

Bos   0 0 0 3 3
KC   0 7 14 14 **35**
Bos D7 R18/74 P(27-9-5) 31
KC   D22 R34/224 P(34-15-2) 174

SUNDAY, DECEMBER 15

Den   7 3 14 7 31
Oak   14 7 7 7 **35**
Den D20 R22/67 P(43-24-1) 316
Oak D14 R26/83 P(21-11-1) 250
Den-Prebola 106C, Taylor 116C;
Oak-Daniels 127C, Flores 272P

SD   0 17 3 0 **20**
Hou   0 7 0 7 14
SD   D14 R39/162 P(18-10-1) 85
Hou D13 R15/42 P(39-18-3) 247

SUNDAY, DECEMBER 22

NYJ   0 0 0 0 0
KC   21 0 14 13 **48**
NYJ D12 R21/78 P(28-11-3) 79
KC   D16 R30/128 P(27-17-1) 264
KC-Dawson 222P

Hou   14 21 14 0 49
Oak   7 28 7 10 **52**
Hou D27 R25/133 P(32-20-2) 335
Oak D21 R28/181 P(29-17-2) 359
Hou-Dewveall 137C, Blanda 342P;
Oak-Daniels 158R, Powell 247C,
Flores 407P

Den   0 10 0 10 20
SD   10 16 10 22 **58**
Den D16 R23/77 P(32-16-2) 154
SD   D23 R32/270 P(25-12-2) 181
SD-Lowe 183R

1963 NFL
SATURDAY, SEPTEMBER 14

Det   10 10 0 3 **23**
LARm   0 0 2 0 2
Det D13 R32/99 P(20-12-3) 111
LARm D9 R25/90 P(29-13-4) 138

SL   0 20 7 7 **34**
Dal   0 7 0 0 7
SL   D20 R45/206 P(23-11-1) 133
Dal D16 R26/111 P(31-14-1) 143

SUNDAY, SEPTEMBER 15

ChiB   3 0 7 0 **10**
GB   3 0 0 0 3
ChiB D15 R35/107 P(24-18-1) 124
GB   D9 R21/77 P(22-11-4) 73

Min   7 3 0 14 **24**
SF   10 7 3 0 20
Min D27 R43/156 P(29-20-1) 262
SF   D10 R21/126 P(23-11-1) 120

NYG   3 21 13 0 **37**
Bal   14 14 0 0 28
NYG D22 R37/119 P(25-16-1) 243
Bal D17 R24/91 P(33-19-2) 204
NYG-King 101C

Pit   0 6 0 15 **21**
Phi   7 0 7 7 21
Pit D21 R37/109 P(34-18-0) 206
Phi D14 R23/58 P(26-16-2) 295
Pit-Dial 116C; Phi-McDonald 179C,
Jurgensen 322P

Was   0 7 7 0 14
Cle   10 14 3 10 **37**
Was D14 R22/71 P(32-13-2) 201
Cle D23 R29/217 P(32-21-2) 326
Was-Mitchell 122C;
Cle-Brown 162R, Brown 100C,
Ryan 334P

SATURDAY, SEPTEMBER 21

Was   7 6 7 17 **37**
LARm   7 7 0 0 14
Was D21 R36/177 P(24-12-2) 227
LARm D16 R19/75 P(30-15-1) 173

SUNDAY, SEPTEMBER 22

Bal   3 0 7 10 **20**
SF   0 7 7 0 14
Bal D27 R40/132 P(45-23-0) 263
SF   D14 R19/56 P(20-12-1) 138

ChiB   7 7 0 14 **28**
Min   7 7 0 0 14
ChiB D24 R27/106 P(33-23-0) 253
Min D20 R34/152 P(27-16-3) 174
ChiB-Ditka 124C

Cle   14 10 3 14 **41**
Dal   7 10 7 0 24
Cle D19 R31/265 P(19-11-2) 188
Dal D19 R31/118 P(26-15-2) 189
Cle-Brown 232R

Det   0 0 3 7 10
GB   3 7 7 14 **31**
Det D7 R26/67 P(27-7-4) 80
GB   D15 R43/204 P(23-10-3) 112
GB-Moore 122R

NYG   0 0 0 0 0
Pit   0 10 0 21 **31**
NYG D7 R16/59 P(26-8-4) 116
Pit D18 R57/223 P(16-8-1) 63
Pit-Johnson 123R

```
SL    0   14   7   7   28
Phi   3   14   7   0   24
SL    D27 R46/196  P(31-19-2)  209
Phi   D12 R21/63   P(24-12-0)  156
SL-Childress 136R
```

SUNDAY, SEPTEMBER 29

```
Bal   0   7   10   3   20
GB    0   0   14   17   31
Bal   D16 R30/80   P(30-19-2)  253
GB    D21 R44/168  P(27-13-2)  187

ChiB  7   28   0   2   37
Det   0   0   14   7   21
ChiB  D22 R33/104  P(35-18-1)  203
Det   D10 R16/40   P(30-11-3)  238
Det-Cogdill 119C

Dal   0   7   10   0   17
Was   7   0   7   7   21
Dal   D22 R38/164  P(30-14-3)  185
Was   D19 R34/123  P(26-13-1)  150
Dal-Perkins 105R

LARm  3   0   0   3   6
Cle   0   7   6   7   20
LARm  D12 R31/85   P(24-14-2)  129
Cle   D16 R36/131  P(16-9-1)  152

NYG   0   14   16   7   37
Phi   0   0   7   7   14
NYG   D17 R27/176  P(25-15-0)  176
Phi   D18 R30/125  P(28-18-5)  191
NYG-Morrison 120R

SL    7   0   3   0   10
Pit   3   3   0   17   23
SL    D13 R27/137  P(28-15-3)  166
Pit   D14 R49/179  P(19-7-1)  38

SF    7   7   0   0   14
Min   0   28   7   10   45
SF    D14 R24/103  P(33-15-3)  134
Min   D22 R36/140  P(39-18-2)  256
Min-Poage 137C
```

SATURDAY, OCTOBER 5

```
Pit   3   17   3   0   23
Cle   7   7   14   7   35
Pit   D23 R35/97   P(36-19-1)  303
Cle   D19 R33/219  P(21-9-0)  138
Pit-Dial 144C, Mack 130C;
Cle-Brown 175R
```

SUNDAY, OCTOBER 6

```
Bal   0   0   3   0   3
ChiB  0   0   0   10   10
Bal   D11 R22/45   P(36-21-1)  165
ChiB  D15 R34/147  P(28-11-1)  134

Dal   0   7   0   14   21
Phi   0   14   10   0   24
Dal   D11 R26/74   P(19-9-0)  129
Phi   D20 R42/192  P(22-12-1)  193
Phi-Retzlaff 107C

LARm  0   0   3   0   3
GB    9   6   20   7   42
LARm  D13 R25/102  P(29-11-0)  61
GB    D20 R38/214  P(21-12-0)  204

NYG   14   3   0   7   24
Was   0   14   0   0   14
NYG   D26 R39/155  P(34-19-1)  302
Was   D16 R26/125  P(29-11-0)  126
NYG-Shofner 107C, Tittle 324P

SL    7   14   7   28   56
Min   0   7   0   7   14
SL    D26 R31/186  P(30-20-0)  334
Min   D17 R26/73   P(35-14-1)  145
SL-Randle 159C, Johnson 301P

SF    0   0   0   3   3
Det   14   0   5   7   26
SF    D7 R27/71    P(22-10-1)  -10
Det   D10 R27/112  P(25-6-1)  119
```

SUNDAY, OCTOBER 13

```
ChiB  7   21   3   21   52
LARm  0   7   0   7   14
ChiB  D22 R34/85   P(30-20-1)  201
LARm  D14 R23/66   P(30-19-6)  137
ChiB-Ditka 110C; LARm-Dale 111C
```

```
Cle   7   7   14   7   35
NYG   14   3   0   7   24
Cle   D21 R39/210  P(16-12-1)  130
NYG   D17 R23/72   P(31-17-0)  139
Cle-Brown 123R

Det   0   0   0   14   14
Dal   0   7   0   10   17
Det   D16 R29/105  P(38-14-3)  254
Dal   D10 R32/173  P(22-8-2)  63
Det-Cogdill 150C

GB    17   7   3   10   37
Min   7   0   7   14   28
GB    D21 R34/153  P(35-20-2)  282
Min   D14 R31/98   P(23-14-2)  240
GB-McGee 104C; Min-Poage 106C

Phi   0   16   14   7   37
Was   3   14   7   0   24
Phi   D21 R34/108  P(29-17-2)  303
Was   D13 R23/90   P(29-10-4)  207
Phi-McDonald 139C,
Jurgensen 315P; Was-Mitchell 112C

Pit   3   17   3   0   23
SL    3   0   7   14   24
Pit   D14 R36/106  P(23-8-1)  215
SL    D23 R34/117  P(42-21-1)  408
Pit-Mack 124C; SL-Smith 212C,
Johnson 428P

SF    3   0   0   0   3
Bal   7   0   10   3   20
SF    D5 R22/40    P(26-10-1)  80
Bal   D18 R36/158  P(28-12-0)  144
```

SUNDAY, OCTOBER 20

```
Bal   3   7   6   9   25
Det   7   14   0   0   21
Bal   D14 R33/143  P(25-10-1)  113
Det   D12 R27/91   P(19-8-1)  70

ChiB  0   7   0   7   14
SF    10   7   3   0   20
ChiB  D20 R17/71   P(40-26-3)  243
SF    D22 R49/192  P(20-10-1)  134
ChiB-Morris 107C

Dal   0   7   14   0   21
NYG   7   10   13   7   37
Dal   D19 R21/60   P(31-20-2)  257
NYG   D22 R25/87   P(33-19-1)  273
Dal-Clarke 168C; NYG-Walton 105C,
Tittle 279P

GB    10   10   3   7   30
SL    0   0   0   7   7
GB    D21 R56/225  P(18-7-2)  99
SL    D12 R12/40   P(40-16-4)  208
SL-Conrad 112C

Min   0   10   14   0   24
LARm  7   7   7   6   27
Min   D13 R25/107  P(24-14-2)  104
LARm  D18 R34/99   P(26-12-1)  180
LARm-Phillips 133C

Phi   0   7   0   7   14
Cle   6   14   0   17   37
Phi   D10 R18/81   P(21-9-3)  80
Cle   D29 R43/218  P(28-19-1)  282
Cle-Brown 144R, Ryan 203P

Was   3   14   7   3   27
Pit   7   10   7   14   38
Was   D23 R26/97   P(29-13-3)  300
Pit   D24 R43/130  P(19-13-0)  219
Was-Mitchell 173C, Snead 309P;
Pit-Dial 155C
```

SUNDAY, OCTOBER 27

```
Dal   7   7   7   0   21
Pit   0   6   7   14   27
Dal   D22 R36/126  P(30-18-2)  290
Pit   D19 R29/114  P(31-15-3)  370
Dal-Howton 103C; Pit-Dial 162C,
Mack 129C, Brown 377P

GB    0   17   3   14   34
Bal   3   0   7   10   20
GB    D18 R37/179  P(20-9-2)  133
Bal   D10 R25/86   P(24-11-2)  214
GB-Taylor 107R

Min   3   0   7   0   10
Det   7   7   7   7   28
Min   D10 R24/86   P(25-15-0)  80
Det   D21 R38/216  P(16-12-1)  203
Det-Watkins 102R, Barr 101C
```

```
NYG   17   6   10   0   33
Cle   0   0   0   6   6
NYG   D26 R44/182  P(33-22-1)  205
Cle   D6 R14/63    P(20-5-2)  79
NYG-Shofner 108C

Phi   0   7   0   0   7
ChiB  10   0   6   0   16
Phi   D11 R28/88   P(25-10-4)  123
ChiB  D17 R37/113  P(35-20-0)  241

SL    0   7   7   7   21
Was   0   0   0   0   0
SL    D21 R36/134  P(32-18-3)  270
Was   D16 R23/94   P(31-15-3)  89
SL-Randle 102C

SF    0   7   14   0   21
LARm  7   7   0   14   28
SF    D14 R33/69   P(17-11-0)  213
LARm  D24 R38/158  P(25-15-0)  232
```

SUNDAY, NOVEMBER 3

```
ChiB  7   0   7   3   17
Bal   0   0   7   0   7
ChiB  D18 R48/164  P(12-9-0)  112
Bal   D14 R22/102  P(19-11-1)  90

Cle   7   9   7   0   23
Phi   3   7   0   7   17
Cle   D15 R40/274  P(9-4-1)  52
Phi   D20 R33/152  P(30-14-2)  201
Cle-Brown 223R

Det   0   10   14   21   45
SF    7   0   0   0   7
Det   D27 R40/201  P(36-24-3)  308
SF    D9 R20/67    P(21-6-4)  66
Det-Watkins 107R, Barr 135C,
Morrall 330P

LARm  10   0   0   3   13
Min   7   0   14   0   21
LARm  D16 R21/77   P(36-16-1)  139
Min   D14 R27/128  P(19-13-0)  113

NYG   3   21   7   7   38
SL    0   7   7   7   21
NYG   D19 R36/116  P(32-18-1)  310
SL    D19 R28/129  P(32-16-4)  185
NYG-Tittle 295P; SL-Childress 118C

Pit   7   0   0   7   14
GB    3   6   14   10   33
Pit   D17 R32/123  P(28-12-2)  155
GB    D24 R52/248  P(17-7-1)  151
GB-Taylor 141R

Was   0   10   3   7   20
Dal   7   7   14   7   35
Was   D23 R32/150  P(38-16-4)  318
Dal   D17 R27/97   P(20-13-2)  124
Was-Mitchell 100C;
Dal-Meredith 153P
```

SUNDAY, NOVEMBER 10

```
Cle   0   7   0   0   7
Pit   0   2   0   7   9
Cle   D14 R30/134  P(26-11-0)  93
Pit   D23 R49/187  P(27-13-1)  195
Pit-Johnson 131R, Dial 114C

Dal   7   14   0   3   24
SF    7   3   14   7   31
Dal   D31 R21/113  P(48-30-1)  419
SF    D23 R39/155  P(25-15-1)  239
Dal-Clarke 190C, Folkins 112C,
Howton 107C, Meredith 460P;
SF-Lisbon 102C

Det   0   14   7   0   21
Bal   17   7   0   0   24
Det   D21 R25/73   P(34-22-0)  257
Bal   D24 R32/123  P(24-17-1)  351
Det-Barr 101C; Bal-Berry 148C,
Unitas 376P

LARm  0   0   0   0   0
ChiB  3   0   3   0   6
LARm  D10 R32/59   P(23-7-0)  29
ChiB  D18 R34/108  P(34-16-1)  168

Min   0   7   0   0   7
GB    0   7   7   14   28
Min   D13 R29/117  P(35-17-2)  175
GB    D18 R27/146  P(22-14-0)  228
GB-Dowler 134C
```

```
Phi   7   0   0   7   14
NYG   7   21   7   7   42
Phi   D6 R17/20    P(23-11-3)  81
NYG   D25 R35/117  P(31-21-1)  300
NYG-Shofner 119C

Was   0   6   0   14   20
SL    3   7   7   7   24
Was   D16 R23/44   P(27-15-1)  224
SL    D18 R34/103  P(29-17-0)  185
```

SUNDAY, NOVEMBER 17

```
Bal   16   0   0   21   37
Min   0   13   7   14   34
Bal   D18 R26/105  P(31-19-0)  303
Min   D16 R34/276  P(20-14-0)  150
Bal-Unitas 248P; Min-Mason 146R,
Flatley 156C

GB    0   0   0   7   7
ChiB  13   0   3   10   26
GB    D16 R20/71   P(30-11-5)  161
ChiB  D19 R57/248  P(14-6-0)  69

LARm  7   7   0   14   28
Det   0   0   7   7   21
LARm  D14 R27/74   P(31-17-1)  269
Det   D19 R25/87   P(41-21-4)  288
LARm-Dale 207C; Det-Barr 100C,
Cogdill 107C, Morrall 312P

Phi   6   0   7   7   20
Dal   7   10   7   3   27
Phi   D16 R19/76   P(37-19-1)  264
Dal   D25 R35/151  P(33-25-0)  297
Dal-Meredith 302P

Pit   3   7   10   14   34
Was   7   7   0   14   28
Pit   D22 R49/144  P(28-13-1)  246
Was   D22 R12/38   P(41-24-2)  404
Pit-Johnson 105R, Ballman 161C;
Was-Mitchell 218C, Snead 424P

SL    3   10   0   7   20
Cle   7   0   7   0   14
SL    D17 R23/70   P(34-25-2)  278
Cle   D19 R31/157  P(28-15-2)  145
Cle-Brown 154R

SF    0   7   0   7   14
NYG   10   10   21   7   48
SF    D10 R21/30   P(31-14-2)  194
NYG   D24 R40/207  P(32-16-1)  361
SF-Casey 127C; NYG-King 101C,
Shofner 159C, Tittle 284P
```

SUNDAY, NOVEMBER 24

```
Bal   3   10   3   0   16
LARm  7   7   3   0   17
Bal   D19 R24/112  P(35-20-1)  228
LARm  D16 R33/199  P(21-10-1)  91
LARm-Bass 120R

ChiB  7   7   0   3   17
Pit   0   7   3   7   17
ChiB  D19 R27/87   P(32-17-3)  241
Pit   D19 R45/166  P(25-10-1)  125
ChiB-Ditka 146C

Dal   3   7   0   7   17
Cle   10   3   0   14   27
Dal   D13 R24/125  P(35-13-4)  82
Cle   D14 R28/175  P(27-13-3)  162

Det   0   21   7   3   31
Min   10   7   10   7   34
Det   D19 R31/119  P(34-21-0)  242
Min   D17 R34/137  P(24-16-1)  214
Det-Barr 119C; Min-Flatley 174C

SL    3   0   14   7   24
NYG   0   10   0   7   17
SL    D13 R32/120  P(21-7-0)  57
NYG   D21 R31/128  P(39-23-2)  208
NYG-Shofner 106C

SF    0   3   0   7   10
GB    7   21   0   0   28
SF    D13 R35/155  P(23-9-0)  80
GB    D20 R35/246  P(21-15-0)  119
GB-Taylor 119R

Was   3   10   0   0   13
Phi   0   0   0   10   10
Was   D16 R24/85   P(23-16-2)  160
Phi   D13 R21/92   P(37-19-1)  203
```

THURSDAY, NOVEMBER 28

```
GB    0   6   0   7   13
Det   0   6   0   7   13
GB    D15 R21/31   P(35-18-0)  263
Det   D16 R27/88   P(37-19-0)  188
GB-Dowler 178C
```

SUNDAY, DECEMBER 1

```
Bal   3   13   3   17   36
Was   0   7   6   7   20
Bal   D24 R26/125  P(40-25-0)  343
Was   D18 R21/80   P(34-18-2)  305
Bal-Matte 116C, Orr 111C,
Unitas 355P; Was-Snead 332P

Cle   7   14   0   3   24
SL    0   3   7   0   10
Cle   D23 R44/240  P(18-10-1)  163
SL    D13 R28/179  P(26-9-0)  19
Cle-Brown 179R, Collins 100C;
SL-Triplett 102R

LARm  0   14   7   0   21
SF    0   7   3   7   17
LARm  D15 R40/106  P(24-10-1)  191
SF    D13 R26/68   P(35-13-3)  244
SF-Casey 127C

Min   3   14   0   0   17
ChiB  7   3   7   0   17
Min   D9 R38/116   P(13-6-1)  86
ChiB  D15 R33/67   P(32-16-0)  154

NYG   7   7   7   13   34
Dal   14   13   0   0   27
NYG   D15 R29/73   P(27-16-3)  191
Dal   D18 R40/226  P(16-6-2)  70

Phi   0   14   3   3   20
Pit   0   3   0   17   20
Phi   D8 R28/114   P(24-9-3)  107
Pit   D22 R34/159  P(31-13-4)  215
Pit-Ballman 128C
```

SATURDAY, DECEMBER 7

```
GB    7   3   14   7   31
LARm  0   14   0   0   14
GB    D19 R32/181  P(26-14-0)  197
LARm  D14 R28/94   P(25-10-3)  76
GB-Taylor 113R, McGee 105C
```

SUNDAY, DECEMBER 8

```
Cle   0   10   0   0   10
Det   7   7   17   7   38
Cle   D12 R23/160  P(32-11-3)  115
Det   D23 R44/176  P(25-13-1)  271
Det-Barr 118C

Min   0   0   3   0   3
Bal   3   21   10   7   41
Min   D14 R24/93   P(26-12-2)  110
Bal   D22 R27/121  P(26-20-0)  318
Bal-Berry 127C, Mackey 144C,
Unitas 344P

Phi   0   7   7   0   14
SL    0   17   14   7   38
Phi   D17 R35/160  P(27-13-2)  109
SL    D11 R19/60   P(31-14-0)  298
SL-Conrad 122C, Johnson 315P

Pit   0   17   0   7   24
Dal   9   0   10   0   19
Pit   D19 R45/211  P(18-8-1)  215
Dal   D15 R39/151  P(16-6-0)  112
Pit-Sapp 119R, Dial 103C

SF    0   7   0   7   14
ChiB  14   0   7   6   27
SF    D15 R34/141  P(29-9-4)  105
ChiB  D17 R40/171  P(25-7-1)  130

Was   0   7   0   7   14
NYG   3   20   14   7   44
Was   D15 R24/59   P(39-16-7)  240
NYG   D16 R35/143  P(27-12-4)  143
Was-Mitchell 197C
```

SATURDAY, DECEMBER 14

```
GB    7   7   0   7   21
SF    0   14   0   3   17
GB    D22 R35/105  P(28-18-0)  324
SF    D14 R36/181  P(24-11-0)  90
GB-Dowler 188C, Starr 306P;
SF-Smith 126R
```

SUNDAY, DECEMBER 15
```
Cle   10   10    0    7   27
Was    0    7    7    6   20
Cle   D22 R39/176 P(30-14-1) 192
Was   D12 R18/56  P(28-12-1) 183
Cle-Brown 125R
```
```
Dal    0   14   14    0   28
SL     0   14   10    0   24
Dal   D10 R24/106 P(18-9-0) 108
SL    D21 R28/162 P(39-20-1) 281
```
```
Det    0    7    0    7   14
ChiB   3    0   14    7   24
Det   D16 R28/127 P(24-12-2) 94
ChiB  D16 R31/101 P(30-14-2) 220
ChiB-Morris 171C
```
```
LARm   0    3    6    7   16
Bal   10    3    0    6   19
LARm  D18 R29/109 P(36-17-1) 232
Bal   D23 R29/219 P(37-21-1) 307
Bal-Matte 120R, Berry 130C, Unitas 323P
```
```
Min    0   13    7   14   34
Phi    6    0    7    0   13
Min   D17 R40/163 P(16-8-0) 64
Phi   D17 R27/109 P(27-14-2) 108
```
```
Pit    0    3   14    0   17
NYG    9    7   14    3   33
Pit   D17 R38/188 P(33-13-3) 212
NYG   D21 R36/143 P(26-17-1) 280
Pit-Johnson 104R, Ballman 104C;
NYG-Shofner 110R, Tittle 308P
```

1964 AFL
SATURDAY, SEPTEMBER 12
```
Den    3    0    0    3    6
NYJ    7    6    0   17   30
Den   D14 R22/97 P(33-18-4) 95
NYJ   D15 R35/103 P(19-9-0) 144
NYJ-Maynard 101C
```
```
Hou    0    7    7    7   21
SD     6   14    0    7   27
Hou   D28 R33/121 P(48-28-0) 240
SD    D22 R24/93 P(26-15-1) 235
Hou-Blanks 128C; SD-Alworth 119C
```
SUNDAY, SEPTEMBER 13
```
KC     0    3   14    0   17
Buf    3   14    0   17   34
KC    D11 R22/70 P(26-16-1) 234
Buf   D18 R36/123 P(34-15-3) 208
KC-Arbanas 113C
```
```
Bos    0    7    7    3   17
Oak    7    0    0    7   14
Bos   D11 R28/87 P(21-9-0) 151
Oak   D17 R24/49 P(32-16-0) 180
Oak-Powell 135C
```
SATURDAY, SEPTEMBER 19
```
Oak    7    7    0   14   28
Hou   14   14   14    0   42
Oak   D23 R20/93 P(45-17-5) 271
Hou   D21 R27/172 P(27-13-3) 206
Oak-Powell 115C; Hou-Blanks 127R, Hennigan 119C
```
SUNDAY, SEPTEMBER 20
```
Den    3    7    3    0   13
Buf    3   10    7   10   30
Den   D12 R27/69 P(37-14-2) 157
Buf   D24 R45/230 P(23-10-4) 177
```
```
Bos   10    3   10   10   33
SD     0    0   18    0   18
Bos   D18 R33/116 P(33-15-0) 97
SD    D13 R22/84 P(36-17-3) 194
```
SATURDAY, SEPTEMBER 26
```
SD     0    3    0    0    3
Buf    7    7    3   13   30
SD    D15 R31/128 P(33-13-2) 120
Buf   D14 R33/109 P(21-10-1) 163
SD-Norton 112C; Buf-Dubenion 123C
```

SUNDAY, SEPTEMBER 27
```
NYJ    3    7    0    0   10
Bos    0   13   10    3   26
NYJ   D13 R19/46 P(43-19-6) 169
Bos   D14 R34/58 P(34-13-2) 220
```
```
Hou   14   17    0    7   38
Den    0   10    0    7   17
Hou   D24 R27/124 P(40-23-0) 312
Den   D24 R30/113 P(38-21-3) 258
Hou-Hennigan 188C; Den-Taylor 149C
```
```
KC     0    7    0   14   21
Oak    0    0    9    0    9
KC    D15 R31/182 P(18-12-0) 153
Oak   D11 R23/96 P(33-16-2) 160
KC-Haynes 106R, Haynes 117C
```
SATURDAY, OCTOBER 3
```
SD     3    7    0    7   17
NYJ    0    3    7    7   17
SD    D17 R31/88 P(29-15-2) 205
NYJ   D14 R16/47 P(43-19-2) 273
NYJ-Maynard 113C, Wood 302P
```
```
Oak    3    0    7   10   20
Buf    0    7    9    7   23
Oak   D18 R23/90 P(32-17-3) 160
Buf   D22 R29/113 P(36-17-2) 299
```
SUNDAY, OCTOBER 4
```
Bos    9   10    6   14   39
Den    0    0    3    7   10
Bos   D17 R32/207 P(33-15-0) 152
Den   D12 R20/53 P(34-21-3) 79
Bos-Garrett 121R
```
```
Hou    0    0    0    7    7
KC     0   14    7    7   28
Hou   D12 R19/72 P(45-19-5) 182
KC    D12 R32/104 P(36-19-3) 309
KC-Arbanas 131C, Burford 143C, Dawson 320P
```
FRIDAY, OCTOBER 9
```
SD     0   10   13    3   26
Bos    3    0    7    7   17
SD    D21 R31/123 P(37-20-1) 252
Bos   D18 R27/105 P(35-17-4) 156
SD-Alworth 124C; Bos-Cappelletti 101C
```
SATURDAY, OCTOBER 10
```
Oak    0    0   13    0   13
NYJ   14    7   14    0   35
Oak   D22 R17/17 P(49-23-3) 389
NYJ   D16 R46/231 P(14-3-1) 82
Oak-Cannon 110C, Powell 141C; NYJ-Snell 168R
```
SUNDAY, OCTOBER 11
```
KC     0   13    0   14   27
Den    6    6   14    7   33
KC    D20 R27/102 P(27-15-3) 191
Den   D17 R39/117 P(23-13-1) 165
KC-Arbanas 103C, Burford 108C
```
```
Buf   14   17    7   10   48
Hou    3    7    0    7   17
Buf   D22 R37/160 P(29-16-3) 405
Hou   D8 R16/44 P(32-10-2) 93
Buf-Bass 147C, Dubenion 183C, Kemp 378P
```
FRIDAY, OCTOBER 16
```
Oak    3   21   10    9   43
Bos    0   14    7   22   43
Oak   D17 R25/110 P(34-16-1) 321
Bos   D28 R26/95 P(47-25-4) 400
Oak-Powell 121C, Roberson 115C, Davidson 337P; Bos-Parilli 422P
```
SATURDAY, OCTOBER 17
```
Hou    0    0   14    7   21
NYJ    7   17    0    0   24
Hou   D19 R19/100 P(41-20-1) 238
NYJ   D18 R48/218 P(17-10-1) 152
Hou-Hennigan 138C; NYJ-Snell 180R, Maynard 102C
```

SUNDAY, OCTOBER 18
```
Buf    7   14    7    7   35
KC     0    0   22    0   22
Buf   D20 R35/121 P(25-15-4) 274
KC    D15 R30/130 P(24-14-1) 168
Buf-Dubenion 122C
```
```
Den    0    0    7    7   14
SD     7   14   14    7   42
Den   D14 R27/107 P(32-16-2) 79
SD    D26 R39/272 P(32-19-1) 214
SD-Kocourek 113C
```
FRIDAY, OCTOBER 23
```
KC     0    0    0    7    7
Bos    7    0   10    7   24
KC    D7 R26/52 P(28-12-0) 118
Bos   D11 R35/106 P(18-13-1) 153
```
SATURDAY, OCTOBER 24
```
NYJ    7    7   10    0   24
Buf    0   10    7   17   34
NYJ   D15 R29/66 P(41-16-0) 179
Buf   D20 R37/180 P(27-12-2) 347
Buf-Dubenion 218C
```
SUNDAY, OCTOBER 25
```
SD     0   20    0    0   20
Hou    7   10    0    0   17
SD    D22 R26/102 P(33-20-2) 243
Hou   D22 R27/94 P(40-24-2) 304
Hou-Hennigan 145C, Blanda 312P
```
```
Den    0    0    7    7   14
Oak   17    7    7    9   40
Den   D12 R21/65 P(30-14-3) 157
Oak   D29 R37/199 P(39-25-1) 427
Oak-Daniels 167R, Cannon 103C, Powell 152C, Davidson 427P
```
SATURDAY, OCTOBER 31
```
Bos    0    0    7    7   14
NYJ    7   14    7    7   35
Bos   D13 R17/34 P(40-18-5) 284
NYJ   D22 R30/148 P(37-22-2) 316
Bos-Cappelletti 147C, Parilli 304P; NYJ-Maynard 109C, Turner 143C, Wood 325P
```
SUNDAY, NOVEMBER 1
```
Den    3    7    7   22   39
KC    14   14   14    7   49
Den   D14 R27/78 P(33-16-2) 269
KC    D24 R19/137 P(38-23-3) 383
Den-Denson 113C, Dixon 121C; KC-Haynes 106C, McClinton 103C, Dawson 435P
```
```
Oak    3    7    0    7   17
SD    14    3    0   14   31
Oak   D18 R20/61 P(45-19-6) 270
SD    D20 R24/99 P(40-18-3) 331
Oak-Davidson 317P; SD-Alworth 203C
```
```
Hou   10    0    0    0   10
Buf    0    7    0   17   24
Hou   D27 R21/35 P(68-37-3) 393
Buf   D18 R38/290 P(18-7-3) 107
Hou-Hennigan 160C, Blanda 393P; Buf-Gilchrist 139R
```
FRIDAY, NOVEMBER 6
```
Hou    7    0    7   10   24
Bos    7    6    3    9   25
Hou   D22 R23/84 P(45-21-1) 329
Bos   D21 R37/193 P(29-14-1) 247
Hou-Frazier 143C, Frazier 102C, Blanda 328P; Bos-Graham 167C
```
SUNDAY, NOVEMBER 8
```
Buf    0    7    3   10   20
NYJ    7    0    0    0    7
Buf   D13 R25/140 P(31-13-2) 254
NYJ   D15 R13/31 P(49-23-5) 338
Buf-Bass 231C; NYJ-Maynard 100C, Turner 165C, Wood 367P
```
```
Oak    0    7    0    0    7
KC    14   14    7    7   42
Oak   D12 R16/50 P(38-20-1) 119
KC    D20 R32/164 P(19-8-1) 186
KC-Dawson 222P
```

```
SD     7    3    7   14   31
Den    0    9   11    0   20
SD    D19 R31/70 P(36-14-2) 127
Den   D13 R33/121 P(23-12-3) 158
SD-Lincoln 100R
```
SUNDAY, NOVEMBER 15
```
Bos    0   14    7   15   36
Buf   10    3   15    0   28
Bos   D14 R21/44 P(35-18-1) 210
Buf   D20 R21/70 P(53-20-3) 316
Bos-Parilli 240P; Buf-Bass 141C, Rutkowski 127C
```
```
NYJ    7    0    0    9   16
Den    0    7    0    0    7
NYJ   D16 R21/111 P(38-11-6) 104
Den   D11 R43/171 P(21-7-2) 6
NYJ-Turner 109C; Den-Joe 108R
```
```
SD     0   28    0    0   28
KC     0    7    0    7   14
SD    D12 R36/95 P(19-11-0) 238
KC    D19 R25/72 P(34-17-2) 149
SD-Alworth 168C
```
```
Hou    0    3    0    7   10
Oak    0    0   10   10   20
Hou   D18 R23/100 P(46-21-1) 288
Oak   D13 R27/187 P(30-9-1) 94
Hou-Hennigan 104C; Oak-Daniels 104R
```
FRIDAY, NOVEMBER 20
```
Den    7    0    0    0    7
Bos    2    7    3    0   12
Den   D16 R24/70 P(35-16-3) 144
Bos   D15 R25/116 P(33-13-5) 180
```
SUNDAY, NOVEMBER 22
```
KC     7   14    7    0   28
Hou    3    7    3    6   19
KC    D20 R37/184 P(21-15-0) 188
Hou   D20 R19/45 P(46-23-3) 266
KC-Haynes 156R; Hou-Hennigan 111C
```
```
NYJ   10   10    0    6   26
Oak    7    7    7   14   35
NYJ   D21 R23/83 P(42-21-2) 229
Oak   D16 R29/77 P(35-20-3) 353
Oak-Davidson 358P
```
THURSDAY, NOVEMBER 26
```
Buf    0   14    0   13   27
SD    10    0    7    7   24
Buf   D18 R44/140 P(27-12-1) 133
SD    D11 R19/52 P(24-12-5) 282
SD-Alworth 185C
```
SUNDAY, NOVEMBER 29
```
KC     0    0   14    0   14
NYJ    3    3   14    7   27
KC    D18 R26/208 P(42-23-4) 211
NYJ   D11 R29/98 P(21-12-1) 119
KC-Haynes 120R, Jackson 175C
```
```
Bos    7   10   14    3   34
Hou    7    3    7    0   17
Bos   D15 R27/88 P(36-20-1) 333
Hou   D18 R18/44 P(48-27-4) 312
Bos-Graham 104C, Parilli 336P; Hou-Hennigan 181C
```
```
Oak    7    3    0   10   20
Den    7    3    7    3   20
Oak   D16 R28/160 P(27-14-3) 213
Den   D19 R34/141 P(30-15-1) 124
Oak-Powell 143C; Den-Taylor 112C
```
SUNDAY, DECEMBER 6
```
Bos   10    0    7   14   31
KC     3    7    7    7   24
Bos   D17 R25/83 P(41-20-1) 292
KC    D17 R29/115 P(42-22-1) 202
Bos-Parilli 300P; KC-Jackson 144C
```
```
NYJ    0    3    0    0    3
SD    10   14    7    7   38
NYJ   D9 R15/36 P(36-13-3) 77
SD    D23 R37/144 P(31-16-2) 322
SD-Alworth 101C
```

```
Buf    0    0    7    6   13
Oak    0    7    3    6   16
Buf   D12 R33/112 P(24-9-2) 133
Oak   D18 R15/79 P(43-20-1) 261
Oak-Powell 106C
```
SUNDAY, DECEMBER 13
```
KC    11   14    7   17   49
SD     0    0    6    0    6
KC    D22 R39/178 P(30-17-1) 213
SD    D13 R13/73 P(33-13-3) 110
KC-Jackson 142C, Dawson 220P
```
```
Buf    9   14    0    7   30
Den    0    3   13    3   19
Buf   D13 R38/157 P(21-6-1) 64
Den   D7 R20/47 P(31-12-0) 70
```
```
NYJ   10    0    0    7   17
Hou   10    9    7    7   33
NYJ   D13 R30/82 P(22-11-3) 178
Hou   D21 R37/236 P(31-15-1) 141
NYJ-Turner 120C; Hou-Blanks 179R
```
SUNDAY, DECEMBER 20
```
Buf    7   10    3    7   24
Bos    6    0    0    8   14
Buf   D17 R41/94 P(24-12-3) 286
Bos   D15 R11/33 P(40-19-2) 286
Buf-Bass 103C, Dubenion 127C; Bos-Colclough 134C
```
```
NYJ    0    0    7    0    7
KC     3    7    7    7   24
NYJ   D10 R29/157 P(29-12-1) 72
KC    D17 R36/130 P(27-15-1) 176
NYJ-Snell 103R
```
```
Den    0    0    7    8   15
Hou   17    7    7    3   34
Den   D26 R24/67 P(55-35-3) 260
Hou   D16 R17/80 P(35-18-3) 218
Den-Scarpitto 111C
```
```
SD     3    7   10    0   20
Oak    0   14    0    7   21
SD    D18 R20/109 P(36-21-3) 255
Oak   D22 R25/215 P(39-21-3) 206
Oak-Daniels 144R
```

1964 NFL
SATURDAY, SEPTEMBER 12
```
SL     3    7    3    3   16
Dal    6    0    0    0    6
SL    D14 R34/72 P(25-12-1) 199
Dal   D14 R22/124 P(31-16-2) 151
Dal-Clarke 145C
```
SUNDAY, SEPTEMBER 13
```
Bal    7    0   14    3   24
Min    7   10    7   10   34
Bal   D11 R18/60 P(26-11-0) 170
Min   D27 R49/153 P(33-13-2) 150
Min-Brown 103R, Mason 137R
```
```
ChiB   0    3    0    9   12
GB     7   10    3    3   23
ChiB  D10 R22/46 P(28-11-2) 83
GB    D18 R36/197 P(18-9-0) 97
```
```
Cle    0   13    7    7   27
Was    0   10    0    3   13
Cle   D17 R37/143 P(19-8-3) 112
Was   D13 R22/96 P(30-17-0) 211
Was-Mitchell 115C
```
```
Det    3   13    7    3   26
SF     7    0   10    0   17
Det   D17 R37/138 P(34-15-1) 234
SF    D13 R19/63 P(33-15-0) 156
Det-Barr 108C, Cogdill 116C; SF-Casey 119C
```
```
LARm   0   13   13    0   26
Pit    0    7    0    7   14
LARm  D9 R38/148 P(23-8-0) 27
Pit   D11 R29/119 P(32-9-5) 48
```
```
NYG    0    0    0    7    7
Phi    7    7   10   14   38
NYG   D14 R29/81 P(34-18-2) 123
Phi   D14 R30/94 P(22-12-0) 159
Phi-Retzlaff 139C
```

SATURDAY, SEPTEMBER 19
```
Det    3   7   0   7  17
LARm   0  14   3   0  17
Det   D11 R21/40   P(32-15-3) 147
LARm  D16 R33/118  P(34-18-2) 191
Det-Barr 109C
```

SUNDAY, SEPTEMBER 20
```
Bal    7  14   0   0  21
GB     7   6   7   0  20
Bal   D13 R37/116  P(12-7-0) 145
GB    D20 R32/174  P(22-17-3) 134

ChiB   0  14  13   7  34
Min    0  14   7   7  28
ChiB  D24 R27/88   P(33-24-1) 344
Min   D20 R23/108  P(34-22-1) 305
ChiB-Morris 135C, Wade 341P;
Min-Tarkenton 311P

NYG   14   0   7   3  24
Pit    0  13   7   7  27
NYG   D24 R38/147  P(34-14-2) 209
Pit   D14 R42/137  P(10-5-2) 77

SL    10   3  10  10  33
Cle    6  10   7  10  33
SL    D17 R27/114  P(27-14-1) 230
Cle   D18 R30/115  P(26-12-2) 166
SL 1-Randle 121C; e 6-Collins 105C

SF     7   7   7   7  28
Phi    0   3   7  14  24
SF    D21 R34/99   P(28-12-1) 253
Phi   D26 R29/94   P(46-21-2) 270
SF-Casey 169C; Phi-Retzlaff 121C

Was    3   6   0   9  18
Dal    0  14   3   7  24
Was   D12 R20/59   P(36-11-2) 148
Dal   D19 R35/180  P(23-11-3) 155
```

FRIDAY, SEPTEMBER 25
```
Was    3   7   0   0  10
NYG    0   0   3  10  13
Was   D13 R34/128  P(25-14-0) 143
NYG   D14 R37/93   P(29-12-2) 142
```

SUNDAY, SEPTEMBER 27
```
ChiB   0   0   0   0   0
Bal    7  17  14  14  52
ChiB  D14 R20/60   P(29-15-2) 181
Bal   D20 R41/213  P(15-13-1) 243
ChiB-Ditka 106C

Cle    0  14   7   7  28
Phi    7   6   0   7  20
Cle   D15 R34/169  P(26-11-1) 193
Phi   D20 R33/171  P(28-19-2) 166
Cle-Brown 104R

Dal    3   7   0   7  17
Pit    3   6  14   0  23
Dal   D19 R28/150  P(40-19-2) 170
Pit   D16 R34/131  P(22-10-0) 160
Dal-Clarke 110C; Pit-Ballman 135C

Min    0   7   0   6  13
LARm   6   7   6   3  22
Min   D15 R29/103  P(22-10-0) 111
LARm  D19 R41/223  P(18-9-1) 156

SL     0  13   7   3  23
SF     0   0   6   7  13
SL    D22 R37/83   P(32-21-1) 213
SF    D14 R22/93   P(31-15-1) 142
```

MONDAY, SEPTEMBER 28
```
GB     0  14   0   0  14
Det    0   3   0   7  10
GB    D20 R38/115  P(22-14-1) 174
Det   D16 R25/99   P(22-16-1) 97
```

SUNDAY, OCTOBER 4
```
ChiB   0   7  14   0  21
SF    10  14   0   7  31
ChiB  D16 R21/100  P(39-22-0) 153
SF    D22 R31/68   P(33-15-0) 252
ChiB-Morris 109C

Dal    0   6   0   0   6
Cle    7   6   7   7  27
Dal   D17 R33/132  P(26-13-0) 107
Cle   D18 R30/116  P(26-15-1) 251
Cle-Warfield 123C
```

```
LARm   7   6   0   7  20
Bal    7   0  21   7  35
LARm  D17 R27/52   P(32-18-1) 205
Bal   D18 R33/160  P(19-10-0) 229
LARm-McKeever 103C;
Bal-Orr 145C

Min    0  14   7   3  24
GB     0  13   7   3  23
Min   D21 R48/179  P(16-11-0) 153
GB    D17 R24/128  P(23-11-0) 197
GB-Dowler 128C

NYG    3   0   0   0   3
Det    7  19   0   0  26
NYG   D12 R26/95   P(28-11-3) 72
Det   D20 R34/169  P(35-16-0) 244
Det-Barr 118C

Pit    0   0   0   7   7
Phi    7   7   0   7  21
Pit   D18 R25/86   P(34-17-0) 207
Phi   D20 R42/272  P(17-9-0) 180
Phi-Brown 116R, Gros 129R,
Brown 110C

SL    14   0   0   2   7  23
Was    3   7   0   7  17
SL    D20 R41/174  P(25-15-3) 280
Was   D13 R14/96   P(27-13-2) 112
SL 1-Randle 139C
```

SATURDAY, OCTOBER 10
```
Pit   10   6   7   0  23
Cle    0   7   0   7  14
Pit   D28 R64/354  P(11-9-0) 123
Cle   D14 R12/96   P(29-13-0) 121
Pit-Johnson 200R
```

SUNDAY, OCTOBER 11
```
Det    7   7   3   7  24
Min    3   7   7   3  20
Det   D14 R32/139  P(21-10-2) 133
Min   D17 R36/100  P(22-13-3) 141

LARm   0   3   7   7  17
ChiB   7  17  14   0  38
LARm  D17 R13/24   P(48-18-5) 239
ChiB  D21 R29/93   P(47-23-0) 235
LARm-Phillips 110C, Pope 108C;
ChiB-Morris 147C, Wade 249P

NYG    0  13   0   0  13
Dal    3   3  10   0  13
NYG   D9  R29/95   P(18-6-2) 33
Dal   D27 R37/218  P(41-21-3) 245
Dal-Perkins 137R, Clarke 120C,
McDonald 108C

Phi    0   0  20   0  20
Was   14   7   0  14  35
Phi   D16 R26/126  P(35-12-1) 95
Was   D17 R33/73   P(33-22-2) 361
Phi-Brown 101R;
Was-Mitchell 183C, Jurgensen 385P

SF     0   7   0   0   7
GB     0   7   3  14  24
SF    D18 R29/92   P(31-16-0) 178
GB    D17 R39/198  P(22-13-0) 138
GB-Taylor 133R
```

MONDAY, OCTOBER 12
```
Bal   17  10  10  10  47
SL     0   7   6  14  27
Bal   D19 R39/266  P(26-10-0) 116
SL    D18 R30/154  P(29-15-1) 94
```

SUNDAY, OCTOBER 18
```
Cle    7   6   0   7  20
Dal    6  10   0   0  16
Cle   D12 R37/195  P(20-9-1) 69
Dal   D20 R30/96   P(43-19-2) 236
Cle-Brown 188R

Det    0  10   0   0  10
ChiB   0   0   0   0   0
Det   D9  R34/103  P(22-10-0) 104
ChiB  D16 R17/29   P(44-24-3) 178

GB     0  14   0   7  21
Bal    0   7   0   7  14
GB    D20 R33/147  P(33-18-0) 254
Bal   D16 R31/129  P(27-14-0) 129
GB-McGee 123C
```

```
Phi   13  10   0   0  23
NYG    7   3   0   7  17
Phi   D8  R37/149  P(14-5-0) 18
NYG   D18 R33/89   P(34-17-2) 105
Phi-Matson 100R

Pit    3   7   0   0  10
Min    6   7   7  10  30
Pit   D15 R37/110  P(21-8-1) 117
Min   D20 R40/219  P(13-7-0) 91
Min-Mason 114R

SF     7   0   0   7  14
LARm   7  21   0  14  42
SF    D19 R20/117  P(44-20-7) 321
LARm  D17 R36/126  P(22-8-1) 165
SF-Parks 112C; LARm-Pope 141C,
Gabriel 170P

Was    0   0   0  10  24
SL    10  14   0  14  38
Was   D9  R23/105  P(27-11-2) 159
SL    D26 R41/190  P(30-17-3) 176
```

SUNDAY, OCTOBER 25
```
Bal    7  14  13   0  34
Det    0   0   0   0   0
Bal   D17 R37/133  P(25-12-2) 182
Det   D14 R24/53   P(38-22-3) 194

ChiB   0   6   7   7  20
Was    0  13   0  14  27
ChiB  D22 R24/16   P(58-33-2) 305
Was   D10 R17/48   P(32-16-1) 166
ChiB-Ditka 168C, Wade 321P;
Was-Jurgensen 205P

Dal    7   7   0  17  31
SL     0   3   3   7  13
Dal   D18 R36/146  P(19-12-1) 130
SL    D17 R28/119  P(33-14-2) 145
Dal-Clarke 103C

LARm   0  14   7   6  27
GB     0   7   0  10  17
LARm  D12 R32/161  P(16-9-2) 120
GB    D14 R31/119  P(26-12-0) 60

Min    3   7   3  14  27
SF     7  10   0   5  22
Min   D15 R29/110  P(22-11-1) 105
SF    D18 R27/116  P(41-20-5) 276
SF-Parks 146C

NYG    6   0   7   7  20
Cle    7   3  18  14  42
NYG   D23 R38/166  P(36-24-3) 260
Cle   D15 R23/97   P(20-10-3) 128

Phi    7  10   3  14  34
Pit    7   7   0   0  14
Phi   D21 R41/154  P(22-13-1) 237
Pit   D11 R29/187  P(29-10-2) 118
Phi-Mack 104C; Pit-Peaks 101R
```

SUNDAY, NOVEMBER 1
```
Cle    0  10  10  10  30
Pit    0   0   0  17  17
Cle   D24 R43/250  P(28-15-0) 162
Pit   D16 R35/165  P(23-8-2) 86
Cle-Brown 149R; Pit-Johnson 100R

Dal    7  10   0   7  24
ChiB   0   0   7   3  10
Dal   D19 R35/129  P(19-10-0) 142
ChiB  D19 R35/95   P(33-15-3) 168

GB     7  21   0  14  42
Min    7   3   3   0  13
GB    D19 R39/186  P(18-12-0) 164
Min   D8  R28/72   P(20-12-0) 95
GB-Taylor 108R, Starr 186P

LARm   0   7   3   7  17
Det    3  13   7  14  37
LARm  D16 R24/82   P(31-17-1) 264
Det   D23 R33/93   P(24-16-0) 302
LARm-Dale 109C, McKeever 100C;
Det-Cogdill 165C, Plum 347P

SL    10   0   0   7  17
NYG    7  17   7   3  34
SL    D20 R25/132  P(29-15-3) 210
NYG   D23 R43/153  P(34-20-1) 281
SL 1-Conrad 124C, Smith 124C,
Johnson 306P; YG-Morrison 122C,
Tittle 285P
```

```
SF     0   0   0   7   7
Bal    9  14   0  14  37
SF    D14 R21/71   P(34-17-1) 150
Bal   D21 R37/151  P(31-16-1) 233

Was   14   0   7   0  21
Phi    0   0   3   7  10
Was   D11 R37/74   P(19-7-1) 135
Phi   D12 R23/94   P(36-17-3) 150
```

SUNDAY, NOVEMBER 8
```
Bal   10   6  10  14  40
ChiB   0   3   7  14  24
Bal   D22 R38/261  P(33-16-0) 218
ChiB  D17 R20/112  P(27-20-1) 265
Bal-Lorick 126R, Orr 123C;
ChiB-Morris 183C

Dal   14   0   0  17  31
NYG    0   7   7   7  21
Dal   D14 R34/81   P(26-13-2) 161
NYG   D20 R23/52   P(38-19-2) 249

Det    0   0   0   7   7
GB    14   6   7   3  30
Det   D14 R15/50   P(33-18-1) 164
GB    D13 R34/232  P(20-14-0) 175
GB-Taylor 145R

Phi    0   3   7   0  10
LARm   7  10   3   0  20
Phi   D15 R22/54   P(35-18-0) 223
LARm  D20 R44/261  P(13-6-1) 121
Phi-Retzlaff 105C;
LARm-Josephson 138R

Pit    3  10   3  14  30
SL     3  10   3  14  34
Pit   D21 R28/116  P(34-17-2) 239
SL    D24 R35/124  P(29-18-0) 227
Pit-Ballman 125C

SF     0   0   0   7   7
Min   14  10   0   0  24
SF    D11 R18/82   P(29-9-1) 155
Min   D24 R44/142  P(35-21-1) 254

Was    0   7  14   3  24
Cle    0  13  14   7  34
Was   D20 R24/101  P(37-21-1) 261
Cle   D13 R34/210  P(20-11-0) 175
Was-Mitchell 113C; Cle-Brown 121R
```

SUNDAY, NOVEMBER 15
```
ChiB   7  14  13   0  34
LARm   7   3   7   7  24
ChiB  D21 R38/127  P(38-23-0) 267
LARm  D13 R31/110  P(31-11-0) 283
ChiB-Morris 107C;
LARm-Pope 105C

Det   14   7   0   0  21
Cle    3  13   7  14  37
Det   D17 R28/106  P(29-16-2) 225
Cle   D25 R37/218  P(25-15-2) 152
Cle-Brown 147R

GB     7   7   0   0  14
SF     0  10  14   0  24
GB    D20 R30/125  P(33-18-1) 238
SF    D15 R42/139  P(17-10-0) 73
GB-McGee 139C

Min    3   7   0   3  13
Bal    0   0  10   7  17
Min   D22 R34/221  P(21-11-3) 85
Bal   D18 R31/107  P(31-15-0) 274
Min-Brown 106R; Bal-Moore 107C

NYG    7   0   0   3  10
SL     0   3   7   0  10
NYG   D12 R35/81   P(16-10-2) 131
SL    D12 R22/38   P(30-13-2) 105

Phi    7   3   0   7  17
Dal    0   0   7   7  14
Phi   D13 R32/152  P(26-11-0) 148
Dal   D14 R29/71   P(27-16-1) 152
Phi-Gros 118R

Was    7  13  10   0  30
Pit    0   0   0   0   0
Was   D13 R33/102  P(12-8-2) 184
Pit   D16 R25/111  P(35-13-4) 156
```

SUNDAY, NOVEMBER 22
```
Bal    7   0   7  10  24
LARm   0   0   0   7   7
Bal   D15 R34/144  P(19-7-0) 141
LARm  D14 R28/77   P(21-13-0) 54
Bal-Mackey 103C

Cle   14   0   0   7  21
GB     7   0  14   7  28
Cle   D20 R28/138  P(28-17-2) 164
GB    D18 R41/156  P(18-13-0) 129
Cle-Warfield 126C

Dal    6   0   0  10  16
Was    7   0  14   7  28
Dal   D11 R24/136  P(34-10-4) 60
Was   D16 R29/59   P(35-20-1) 307
Was-Coia 107C, Jurgensen 307P

Min    7   3  10   3  23
Det    0   6   7  10  23
Min   D15 R42/157  P(22-13-1) 73
Det   D13 R24/65   P(30-17-4) 224
Det-Barr 165C

Pit    3  14  20   7  44
NYG    0   3   0  14  17
Pit   D26 R48/238  P(17-11-0) 191
NYG   D22 R28/79   P(34-18-0) 226
Pit-Johnson 106R, Ballman 117C

SL     3  14   7  14  38
Phi    3   3   7   0  13
SL    D18 R33/235  P(29-14-0) 225
Phi   D18 R32/128  P(31-17-3) 215
SL-Thornton 128C, Conrad 110C;
Phi-Gros 103R

SF     7   7   0   7  21
ChiB  14   3   3   3  23
SF    D21 R31/116  P(27-19-0) 207
ChiB  D19 R28/119  P(33-22-0) 251
```

THURSDAY, NOVEMBER 26
```
ChiB   0  21   3   3  27
Det    3  14   7   0  24
ChiB  D26 R34/116  P(29-22-2) 197
Det   D26 R26/100  P(26-13-1) 120
ChiB-Morris 100C
```

SUNDAY, NOVEMBER 29
```
Bal    0   7   0   7  14
SF     3   0   0   0   3
Bal   D16 R30/59   P(27-14-2) 180
SF    D15 R30/139  P(35-14-5) 107

GB     7  10  14  14  45
Dal    0  14   0   7  21
GB    D17 R41/116  P(23-11-0) 130
Dal   D8  R28/78   P(20-7-3) 54

LARm   0   3  10   4  17
Min    7  10   7  10  34
LARm  D13 R25/151  P(27-11-2) 158
Min   D15 R31/72   P(32-15-0) 185

NYG    0  14   7   0  21
Was    7   3  13  13  36
NYG   D15 R24/83   P(26-12-3) 160
Was   D25 R32/148  P(44-24-0) 316
Was-Carpenter 117C,
Jurgensen 319P

Phi    3   0   7  14  24
Cle    7  14  10   7  38
Phi   D22 R25/129  P(34-20-3) 254
Cle   D16 R32/157  P(25-13-1) 145
Phi-Retzlaff 100C; Cle-Brown 133R

SL     7   0   0  14  21
Pit    3   7   0   0  10
SL    D14 R26/80   P(33-12-4) 199
Pit   D16 R42/131  P(23-10-3) 148
Pit-Thomas 113C
```

SATURDAY, DECEMBER 5
```
GB     0   7   7   3  17
ChiB   0   3   0   0   3
GB    D15 R39/170  P(13-9-0) 64
ChiB  D14 R27/118  P(32-17-3) 79
```

SUNDAY, DECEMBER 6
```
Cle    3   3   3  10  19
SL     0  21   7   0  28
Cle   D18 R22/106  P(33-15-2) 231
SL    D25 R45/150  P(22-15-1) 159
```

```
Dal     7  0  7  0  14
Phi     0  7  0 17  24
Dal  D13 R21/59  P(26-11-1)  73
Phi  D16 R32/165 P(20-10-1)  92

Det     7 10  7  7  31
Bal     0  7  7  0  14
Det  D21 R47/159 P(18-11-1) 143
Bal  D18 R24/90  P(28-15-2) 272
Bal-Orr 138C

LARm    7  0  0  0   7
SF      0 14  7  7  28
LARm D13 R14/15  P(36-19-2) 183
SF   D15 R31/47  P(35-20-1) 274
LARm-Dale 117C; SF-Stickles 147C

Min     3 17  0 10  30
NYG     7  7  7  0  21
Min  D17 R34/137 P(29-13-0) 193
NYG  D15 R32/114 P(33-14-0) 221
Min-Brown 102R;
NYG-Thomas 121C

Pit     7  0  0  7  14
Was     0  7  0  0   7
Pit  D13 R43/139 P(10-5-1)   41
Was  D12 R21/82  P(35-17-1) 102
```

SATURDAY, DECEMBER 12

```
Cle     3 21 21  7  52
NYG     0  7  0 13  20
Cle  D22 R36/153 P(19-16-0) 254
NYG  D19 R20/76  P(37-22-2) 263
Cle-Warfield 103C, Ryan 202P;
NYG-Morrison 147C
```

SUNDAY, DECEMBER 13

```
GB      0  7  3 14  24
LARm   14  7  0  3  24
GB   D22 R38/213 P(30-15-1) 151
LARm D12 R25/115 P(16-8-2)  113
GB-Taylor 165R

Min    14 17  7  3  41
ChiB    0  0  7  7  14
Min  D22 R52/250 P(15-7-1)  182
ChiB D9  R14/47  P(24-11-2) 135
Min-Brown 128C

Phi     7 20  0  7  34
SL      3 27  3  3  36
Phi  D22 R26/140 P(31-15-2) 271
SL   D28 R32/105 P(49-28-2) 360
Phi-Retzlaff 106C, Snead 301P;
SL-Smith 145C, Johnson 371P

Pit     0  0  7  7  14
Dal    10  0  0  7  17
Pit  D12 R35/78  P(22-9-2)  147
Dal  D17 R29/91  P(29-14-0) 177
Dal-Dial 100C

SF      0  0  7  0   7
Det     7 10  0  7  24
SF   D17 R28/90  P(43-23-0) 197
Det  D12 R32/100 P(22-11-2) 227
Det-Gibbons 161C

Was     7  3  7  0  17
Bal     3  7 14 21  45
Was  D9  R27/66  P(23-13-1) 116
Bal  D21 R26/118 P(26-16-1) 240
```

1965 AFL

SATURDAY, SEPTEMBER 11

```
Bos     0  7  0  0   7
Buf     0  7 10  7  24
Bos  D13 R24/104 P(35-10-5) 111
Buf  D17 R27/77  P(42-19-2) 271

Den    14  3  0 14  31
SD      3 24  0  7  34
Den  D21 R33/151 P(27-16-0) 179
SD   D19 R32/166 P(27-13-1) 293
Den-Scarpitto 108C; SD-Lowe 124R,
Alworth 211C
```

SUNDAY, SEPTEMBER 12

```
KC      7  0  3  0  10
Oak     0 10 10 17  37
KC   D11 R28/112 P(27-6-1)   42
Oak  D12 R33/116 P(26-13-0) 172
```

```
NYJ    14  0  7  0  21
Hou     7  7  0 13  27
NYJ  D12 R32/179 P(21-4-1)   49
Hou  D14 R46/172 P(24-11-3) 120
NYJ-Snell 102R
```

SATURDAY, SEPTEMBER 18

```
KC      0  7  0  7  14
NYJ     3  0  0  7  10
KC   D9  R29/143 P(20-10-0)  81
NYJ  D14 R25/98  P(35-15-0) 133
```

SUNDAY, SEPTEMBER 19

```
SD      7  3  0  7  17
Oak     0  6  0  6   6
SD   D18 R43/180 P(28-11-0) 136
Oak  D12 R19/36  P(30-10-3)  97
SD-Foster 104R

Buf     3 10  7 10  30
Den     0  0  7  8  15
Buf  D20 R28/88  P(52-21-2) 276
Den  D17 R24/69  P(42-22-5) 291
Buf-Dubenion 103C;
Den-Taylor 172C

Bos     0 10  0  0  10
Hou     7  7 10  7  31
Bos  D22 R29/57  P(50-20-5) 150
Hou  D17 R17/100 P(34-18-2) 320
Hou-Frazier 182C
```

FRIDAY, SEPTEMBER 24

```
Den     7  3 14  3  27
Bos     0  3  0  7  10
Den  D22 R49/220 P(25-11-2)  42
Bos  D9  R19/34  P(23-9-2)   91
Den-Gilchrist 142R
```

SUNDAY, SEPTEMBER 26

```
KC      0  0  7  3  10
SD      0  3  0  7  10
KC   D8  R25/122 P(29-14-3)  87
SD   D12 R27/92  P(32-13-3)  94

Hou     7  0  7  7  21
Oak     7  0  7  7  21
Hou  D14 R30/86  P(36-15-2) 183
Oak  D15 R28/146 P(29-14-1) 180
Oak-Daniels 115R

NYJ     0 10  0 11  21
Buf     7  6 10 10  33
NYJ  D18 R12/44  P(40-19-2) 263
Buf  D27 R36/104 P(42-25-0) 304
```

SUNDAY, OCTOBER 3

```
Hou     0  0  0 14  14
SD      0 10 14  7  31
Hou  D12 R16/47  P(35-13-1) 146
SD   D26 R44/271 P(26-14-0) 222
SD-Lowe 157R, Alworth 145C

NYJ     0  6  0 13  13
Den     0  6  3  7  16
NYJ  D12 R22/64  P(34-18-2) 140
Den  D21 R43/175 P(32-18-1) 170

Bos     3  0  7  7  17
KC      7 13  0  7  27
Bos  D16 R22/32  P(36-16-2) 174
KC   D19 R39/119 P(25-13-2) 144

Oak     0 10  2  0  12
Buf     3  7  0  7  17
Oak  D12 R24/93  P(26-7-1)   69
Buf  D14 R38/140 P(21-10-2) 123
```

FRIDAY, OCTOBER 8

```
Oak     7  3  7  7  24
Bos     0  3  0  0   3
Oak  D20 R33/149 P(35-21-0) 269
Bos  D15 R25/72  P(31-13-0) 138
Oak-Daniels 113R, Powell 206C
```

SUNDAY, OCTOBER 10

```
KC      7 10  7  7  31
Den     0  7 10  6  23
KC   D15 R32/82  P(22-13-0) 172
Den  D20 R47/192 P(31-12-1)  98
```

```
SD      0 14 17  3  34
Buf     3  0  0  0   3
SD   D18 R34/89  P(32-21-1) 369
Buf  D8  R15/57  P(37-15-4)  93
SD-Alworth 168C, Norton 107C,
Hadl 314P
```

SATURDAY, OCTOBER 16

```
Oak     0 14  7  3  24
NYJ     3  0  0  7  10
Oak  D18 R30/75  P(40-18-1) 191
NYJ  D14 R30/102 P(31-9-1)  191
NYJ-Maynard 149C
```

SUNDAY, OCTOBER 17

```
Hou     7  7  3  0  17
Den     0  7 14  7  28
Hou  D23 R21/87  P(56-19-5) 241
Den  D15 R38/110 P(26-10-2) 170
Hou-Hennigan 130C

Buf     0  3  0 20  23
KC      0  0  0  7   7
Buf  D7  R27/47  P(29-14-2)  80
KC   D12 R27/70  P(34-17-4) 161

SD      3 10  0  0  13
Bos     3  0  7  3  13
SD   D15 R42/116 P(22-10-1) 168
Bos  D7  R21/37  P(31-7-2)  141
SD-Alworth 109C
```

SATURDAY, OCTOBER 23

```
SD      0 10 14 10  34
NYJ     3  3  0  3   9
SD   D17 R30/152 P(30-18-1) 190
NYJ  D15 R21/79  P(39-19-0) 222
SD-Lowe 110R, Alworth 142C
```

SUNDAY, OCTOBER 24

```
Bos     0  0  7 14  21
Oak     3  3 10 14  30
Bos  D14 R23/73  P(39-18-2) 220
Oak  D21 R27/100 P(36-15-0) 220
Bos-Whalen 109C;
Oak-Biletnikoff 118C

KC     14  3  0 19  36
Hou     0  0 28 10  38
KC   D32 R41/302 P(42-17-4) 240
Hou  D21 R20/64  P(43-22-0) 302
KC-Hill 130R; Hou-Blanda 304P

Den     0  6  0  7  13
Buf     7 14 10  0  31
Den  D19 R29/95  P(40-20-1) 264
Buf  D21 R23/76  P(27-16-0) 262
Buf-Joe 156C
```

SUNDAY, OCTOBER 31

```
Bos     9  0  3 10  22
SD      0  0  0  6   6
Bos  D10 R29/133 P(21-7-2)  120
SD   D17 R25/80  P(40-19-4) 150
SD-Norton 106C

Oak     7  0  0  0   7
KC      0  7  0  7  14
Oak  D11 R18/39  P(29-15-0) 128
KC   D16 R38/171 P(17-9-0)   47

Hou     7  6  3  3  19
Buf    14  0  0  3  17
Hou  D16 R27/124 P(34-13-1) 148
Buf  D19 R37/121 P(27-12-4) 162

Den     3  0  0  7  10
NYJ     0 24  7 14  45
Den  D10 R25/57  P(34-13-5) 148
NYJ  D13 R34/123 P(18-9-2)   80
```

SUNDAY, NOVEMBER 7

```
SD      0 14  7 14  35
Den     0  7 14  0  21
SD   D21 R32/176 P(24-14-2) 264
Den  D22 R27/74  P(41-20-3) 202
SD-Lowe 112R; Den-Taylor 114C

NYJ     3  3  7  0  13
KC      0  0  0  0   0
NYJ  D15 R27/92  P(33-16-2) 183
KC   D18 R27/81  P(35-16-2) 233
```

```
Oak     3 17  7  6  33
Hou     0  7 14  0  21
Oak  D23 R16/21  P(61-27-3) 296
Oak-Todd 149R, Daniels 109C;
Hou-Blanda 308P
```

```
Buf     3 17  3  0  23
Bos     0  7  0  0   7
Buf  D9  R27/62  P(23-7-0)   99
Bos  D15 R29/28  P(39-18-2) 236
Bos-Colclough 114C
```

SUNDAY, NOVEMBER 14

```
Buf     0  7  0 10  17
Oak     0  7  0  7  14
Buf  D9  R31/94  P(33-11-2) 129
Oak  D9  R27/137 P(27-10-3) 158

SD      0  7  0  0   7
KC     10  7  0 14  31
SD   D14 R25/78  P(35-15-6) 252
KC   D14 R30/149 P(22-13-1) 129
SD-Alworth 181C

Den     0  7  7 17  31
Hou     7  7  0  7  21
Den  D12 R32/173 P(28-5-3)   20
Hou  D21 R27/100 P(49-19-6) 234
Den-Gilchrist 119R

NYJ    17  3  7  3  30
Bos     0 17  3  0  20
NYJ  D13 R36/98  P(25-10-0) 155
Bos  D18 R22/28  P(50-22-3) 259
NYJ-Maynard 122C
```

SUNDAY, NOVEMBER 21

```
Oak     0 14  0 14  28
Den     0  7  7  0  14
Oak  D16 R31/72  P(31-16-1) 179
Den  D22 R21/109 P(46-20-4) 272
Den-Taylor 141C

Hou     0  0 14 14  14
NYJ    10 10  0 21  41
Hou  D17 R17/62  P(46-18-4) 213
NYJ  D23 R38/284 P(32-18-2) 238
NYJ-Mathis 129R, Snell 132R,
Namath 221P

KC      0  7  0  3  10
Bos     3  0  7  0  10
KC   D16 R27/104 P(33-17-2) 222
Bos  D14 R30/115 P(23-13-1) 169
KC-Burford 120C
```

THURSDAY, NOVEMBER 25

```
Buf     7  0 10  3  20
SD      0  0 10 10  20
Buf  D13 R18/47  P(38-18-1) 194
SD   D23 R35/52  P(37-18-2) 309
SD-Alworth 127C, Hadl 315P
```

SUNDAY, NOVEMBER 28

```
Hou     0  0  7 14  21
KC     10 14  7 21  52
Hou  D13 R29/167 P(27-12-1) 122
KC   D23 R36/234 P(23-16-0) 277
Hou-Burrell 112R;
KC-McClinton 123R, Jackson 118C

Bos     3  0 17  7  27
NYJ     0 10  0 13  23
Bos  D16 R28/83  P(36-12-1) 168
NYJ  D18 R33/131 P(30-16-1) 251
NYJ-Maynard 121C, Turner 118C
```

SATURDAY, DECEMBER 4

```
NYJ     0  0  7  0   7
SD      0 17 14  7  38
NYJ  D12 R16/41  P(39-19-3) 156
SD   D23 R39/174 P(21-14-2) 229
SD-Alworth 147C
```

SUNDAY, DECEMBER 5

```
Den     3  7  0  3  13
Oak     0 14 10  0  24
Den  D17 R30/99  P(37-18-1) 342
Oak  D16 R30/138 P(27-9-1)  177
Den-Hayes 126C, Taylor 164C,
Lee 370P; Oak-Daniels 103R
```

```
Buf    13  0  3 13  29
Hou     7  3  0  8  18
Buf  D11 R33/202 P(24-5-2)   82
Hou  D15 R28/86  P(34-12-2) 214
Buf-Carlton 148R, Roberson 106C
```

SUNDAY, DECEMBER 12

```
NYJ     0  0 14  0  14
Oak     0 14  0 10  24
NYJ  D16 R18/81  P(38-20-4) 289
Oak  D16 R31/146 P(30-12-2) 219
NYJ-Maynard 112C, Turner 120C;
Oak-Daniels 110R, Powell 116C

Bos     7 14  7  0  28
Den     6  0  0 14  20
Bos  D17 R31/131 P(22-11-1) 189
Den  D21 R27/135 P(35-19-2) 213

SD      7  7  3 20  37
Hou     2 10  7  0  19
SD   D18 R42/225 P(25-11-1) 136
Hou  D13 R14/19  P(45-14-2) 202

KC      7  0  3 15  25
Buf    10 10 14  0  34
KC   D18 R17/63  P(37-23-1) 346
Buf  D16 R23/74  P(34-22-2) 249
KC-Dawson 355P;
Buf-Roberson 127C
```

SATURDAY, DECEMBER 18

```
Hou     0  0  8  6  14
Bos    10 16  3 13  42
Hou  D7  R16/40  P(26-11-3)  72
Bos  D22 R41/190 P(37-17-1) 341
Bos-Cappelletti 151C
```

SUNDAY, DECEMBER 19

```
Oak     7  7  0  0  14
SD      7 10  7 10  34
Oak  D20 R22/102 P(39-21-3) 198
SD   D18 R36/147 P(22-12-2) 291
SD-Alworth 160C

Den     7 14  7  7  35
KC     21  7 10  7  45
Den  D15 R28/170 P(38-18-0) 229
KC   D17 R22/0   P(29-15-0) 362
KC-McClinton 213C, Taylor 110C

Buf     6  0  0  6  12
NYJ     7  0  7  0  14
Buf  D11 R29/99  P(32-13-1) 137
NYJ  D14 R23/60  P(44-17-2) 239
NYJ-Maynard 180C
```

1965 NFL

SUNDAY, SEPTEMBER 19

```
ChiB    3  0  0 21  24
SF      0 24 21  7  52
ChiB D16 R26/77  P(39-18-0) 186
SF   D26 R35/197 P(28-16-0) 288
SF-Brodie 269P

Cle     3  7  7  0  17
Was     0  0  0  7   7
Cle  D18 R41/180 P(19-8-1)  133
Was  D14 R18/24  P(33-15-1) 208

GB      0  7 13 21  41
Pit     0  9  0  0   9
GB   D21 R35/134 P(23-17-0) 220
Pit  D15 R29/92  P(30-8-3)  101
GB-Dowler 104C

LARm    0  0  0  0   0
Det     3  0  0 17  20
LARm D9  R27/65  P(19-8-3)   54
Det  D14 R37/96  P(25-15-1) 228
Det-Barr 133C

Min    10  0  6  0  16
Bal     0 14  7 14  35
Min  D16 R28/103 P(27-11-2) 160
Bal  D20 R32/107 P(22-14-2) 203

NYG     0  0  2  0   2
Dal    10  7  7  7  31
NYG  D8  R22/99  P(29-8-2)   40
Dal  D19 R41/142 P(18-9-0)  128
```

SL 17 3 0 7 27
Phi 10 10 7 7 34
SL D19 R18/32 P(43-20-1) 325
Phi D23 R32/132 P(33-17-0) 226
SL 1-Smith 115C, Johnson 383P;
hi 1-Brown 129C

SATURDAY, SEPTEMBER 25
ChiB 0 14 14 0 28
LARm 0 6 3 21 30
ChiB D10 R19/51 P(25-15-1) 173
LARm D24 R28/123 P(45-27-0) 266
ChiB-Morris 116C;
LARm-McDonald 131C

SUNDAY, SEPTEMBER 26
Bal 3 7 0 7 17
GB 0 10 0 10 20
Bal D15 R29/112 P(32-14-2) 197
GB D11 R38/106 P(18-11-0) 78

Det 7 14 0 10 31
Min 7 3 12 7 29
Det D18 R29/76 P(29-14-1) 148
Min D15 R35/157 P(23-9-2) 129

NYG 0 7 6 3 16
Phi 7 0 7 0 14
NYG D14 R30/131 P(18-12-0) 149
Phi D18 R25/76 P(32-17-0) 220
Phi-Brown 106C

Pit 7 0 0 10 17
SF 7 6 7 7 27
Pit D16 R28/77 P(23-11-2) 173
SF D26 R44/191 P(20-16-0) 210

SL 7 28 14 0 49
Cle 3 7 3 0 13
SL D23 R44/169 P(24-13-2) 320
Cle D19 R21/122 P(32-13-6) 168
SL-Randle 198C, Johnson 310P;
Cle-Brown 110R, Collins 116C

Was 0 0 0 7 7
Dal 7 13 0 7 27
Was D13 R18/89 P(30-13-1) 185
Dal D16 R41/160 P(21-6-0) 137

SUNDAY, OCTOBER 3
ChiB 0 0 7 7 14
GB 14 6 3 0 23
ChiB D23 R40/192 P(29-17-1) 221
GB   D14 R27/78 P(20-11-0) 221
ChiB-Sayers 104C

Cle 0 7 7 21 35
Phi 0 10 0 7 17
Cle D22 R43/239 P(20-9-0) 75
Phi D21 R24/163 P(31-14-5) 182
Cle-Brown 133R

Min 7 21 7 3 38
LARm 0 14 7 14 35
Min D18 R34/151 P(25-17-1) 241
LARm D20 R23/121 P(28-18-1) 240

NYG 7 7 0 9 23
Pit 0 3 7 3 13
NYG D17 R32/112 P(18-11-0) 232
Pit D18 R33/73 P(28-17-2) 250

SF 0 7 7 10 24
Bal 10 14 0 3 27
SF D15 R18/39 P(37-19-3) 313
Bal D20 R40/110 P(30-18-1) 231
SF-Parks 231C

Was 0 0 0 10 10
Det 0 7 7 0 14
Was D11 R29/77 P(27-14-6) 119
Det D10 R35/105 P(23-7-4) 13
Was-Lowe 157R, Alworth 145C

MONDAY, OCTOBER 4
Dal 0 7 0 6 13
SL 14 0 3 3 20
Dal D9 R23/85 P(25-9-2) 96
SL D20 R47/197 P(26-14-2) 156

SATURDAY, OCTOBER 9
Pit 0 6 6 7 19
Cle 10 0 7 7 24
Pit D16 R36/175 P(20-9-0) 77
Cle D21 R45/232 P(23-12-0) 143
Pit-Hoak 107R; Cle-Brown 168R

SUNDAY, OCTOBER 10
Det 0 0 7 0 7
Bal 14 14 0 3 31
Det D14 R26/66 P(30-13-4) 89
Bal D17 R28/69 P(28-19-1) 294
Bal-Orr 167C, Unitas 319P

LARm 0 3 3 0 6
ChiB 0 10 7 14 31
LARm D17 R19/73 P(45-19-2) 211
ChiB D17 R35/89 P(23-17-0) 301

NYG 7 0 0 7 14
Min 7 10 21 2 40
NYG D13 R23/61 P(26-14-1) 184
Min D22 R37/173 P(24-14-0) 187
NYG-Thomas 117C

Phi 7 7 14 7 35
Dal 7 3 7 7 24
Phi D22 R36/142 P(26-16-0) 254
Dal D14 R26/64 P(25-15-2) 234
Dal-Hayes 177C

SL 7 3 13 14 37
Was 0 3 7 6 16
SL D24 R40/197 P(35-15-1) 206
Was D12 R21/65 P(33-14-1) 175
SL-Conrad 121C; Was-Mitchell 164C

SF 0 7 3 0 10
GB 7 6 7 7 27
SF D15 R27/103 P(38-21-1) 176
GB D20 R33/186 P(27-17-1) 153

SUNDAY, OCTOBER 17
Bal 10 14 14 0 38
Was 0 7 0 0 7
Bal D14 R32/69 P(21-13-1) 204
Was D14 R24/87 P(41-21-2) 181

ChiB 14 3 7 21 45
Min   0 13 10 14 37
ChiB D16 R30/182 P(20-10-1) 134
Min D26 R46/304 P(20-10-2) 109
Min-Brown 117R

Dal 0 0 0 17 17
Cle 10 7 6 0 23
Dal D15 R21/79 P(39-15-1) 185
Cle D16 R35/105 P(27-14-0) 230

GB   3 0 21 7 31
Det 14 0 7 0 21
GB D17 R28/83 P(23-15-1) 291
Det D18 R29/131 P(33-14-3) 165
GB-Dale 108C, Long 106C,
Starr 301P; Det-Barr 112C

Phi 7 7 13 7 27
NYG 7 21 7 0 35
Phi D21 R28/129 P(41-23-4) 311
NYG D14 R33/111 P(15-10-0) 287
Phi-Retzlaff 133C, Hill 321P;
NYG-Jones 102C, Thomas 145C,
Morrall 296P

SL 7 0 3 10 20
Pit 7 0 0 0 7
SL D12 R32/69 P(33-20-1) 275
Pit D9 R27/158 P(20-6-1) -16

SF   7 21 0 17 45
LARm 0 7 7 7 21
SF   D16 R30/106 P(31-21-2) 280
LARm D17 R24/92 P(36-18-1) 129

SUNDAY, OCTOBER 24
Cle 3 14 14 7 38
NYG 7 0 0 7 14
Cle D26 R43/243 P(24-15-0) 283
NYG D22 R27/120 P(28-13-1) 192
Cle-Brown 177R, Collins 121C

Dal 0 0 0 3 3
GB 0 3 10 0 13
Dal D13 R33/193 P(20-10-2) -1
GB D7 R29/73 P(19-4-0) -10
Dal-Perkins 133R

Det 3 0 7 0 10
ChiB 10 14 7 7 38
Det D14 R34/122 P(31-14-2) 138
ChiB D16 R28/142 P(16-12-0) 148

LARm 3 7 10 0 20
Bal 7 7 7 10 31
LARm D13 R27/64 P(25-13-1) 162
Bal D26 R30/133 P(28-19-0) 223
Bal-Orr 100C

Min 0 14 21 7 42
SF 14 21 3 3 41
Min D27 R35/154 P(35-21-0) 395
SF D21 R32/179 P(29-19-1) 259
Min-Flatley 202C, Tarkenton 407P;
SF-Parks 108C

Pit 6 7 7 0 20
Phi 7 0 0 7 14
Pit D8 R30/60 P(16-6-1) 72
Phi D20 R36/199 P(36-16-4) 189

Was 3 7 7 7 24
SL 0 10 0 10 20
Was D15 R32/74 P(15-12-0) 177
SL D22 R36/121 P(28-17-2) 188

SUNDAY, OCTOBER 31
Bal 3 14 10 7 34
SF 7 14 0 7 28
Bal D25 R33/108 P(34-23-0) 310
SF D26 R25/114 P(36-25-1) 329
Bal-Unitas 324P; SF-Crow 101C

Dal 6 0 7 0 13
Pit 0 19 0 3 22
Dal D14 R28/90 P(34-12-1) 165
Pit D15 R20/78 P(35-18-1) 245
Pit-Ballman 120C

Det 14 0 7 10 31
LARm 0 0 7 0 7
Det D16 R34/116 P(26-13-0) 227
LARm D18 R18/80 P(31-18-3) 223
Det-Barr 103C;
LARm-McKeever 111C

GB   7 3 0 0 10
ChiB 0 17 7 7 31
GB   D14 R35/121 P(26-13-3) 98
ChiB D20 R46/212 P(11-5-2) 53

Min 7 14 0 6 27
Cle 3 7 0 7 17
Min D25 R41/196 P(27-17-0) 212
Cle D11 R28/34 P(23-9-0) 133
Min-Brown 138R; Cle-Collins 116C

Phi 0 0 7 14 21
Was 7 3 0 13 23
Phi D13 R25/55 P(28-14-1) 213
Was D21 R29/66 P(36-23-1) 293

SL 3 7 0 0 10
NYG 0 0 7 7 14
SL D21 R39/209 P(37-17-2) 229
NYG D19 R30/137 P(25-10-1) 122
SL-Triplett 176R

SUNDAY, NOVEMBER 7
Bal 0 10 14 2 26
ChiB 0 0 7 14 21
Bal D18 R33/94 P(25-15-2) 308
ChiB D25 R27/74 P(45-24-2) 266

Det 0 7 0 5 12
GB 0 0 0 0 0
Det D12 R43/128 P(16-6-3) 52
GB D8 R24/70   P(14-9-1) -2

LARm 0 7 0 6 13
Min 0 10 7 7 24
LARm D26 R20/120 P(40-23-1) 200
Min D18 R34/172 P(21-12-1) 187
Min-Flatley 105C

Phi 14 3 10 7 34
Cle 0 14 7 17 38
Phi D24 R30/230 P(36-18-2) 352
Cle D21 R29/187 P(24-16-1) 182
Phi-Brown 186R, Retzlaff 151C,
Snead 362P; Cle-Brown 131R,
Collins 128C

Pit 3 0 0 14 17
SL 0 7 7 7 21
Pit D18 R33/138 P(26-15-1) 201
SL D16 R25/105 P(27-10-0) 171
SL-Gambrell 100C

SF 10 0 14 7 31
Dal 7 20 3 9 39
SF D26 R46/173 P(30-14-2) 238
Dal D9 R16/41   P(20-11-2) 201
SF-Parks 120C; Dal-Hayes 108C

Was 14 3 0 6 23
NYG 0 7 0 0 7
Was D11 R32/135 P(21-11-1) 148
NYG D17 R31/129 P(28-14-2) 95

SUNDAY, NOVEMBER 14
Bal 0 10 21 10 41
Min 0 7 7 7 21
Bal D20 R31/192 P(26-16-0) 201
Min D20 R32/164 P(21-12-0) 85
Bal-Cuozzo 208P

LARm 3 0 0 0 3
GB   3 0 0 3 6
LARm D9 R28/116 P(16-7-1) 26
GB   D10 R38/102 P(13-7-0) 75

NYG 7 7 0 7 21
Cle 14 3 7 10 34
NYG D21 R32/107 P(30-18-2) 240
Cle D22 R32/232 P(24-13-1) 227
NYG-Jones 118C; Cle-Brown 156R,
Green 160C

Pit 7 0 10 0 17
Dal 7 3 0 14 24
Pit D12 R27/50 P(29-11-5) 147
Dal D15 R29/123 P(32-14-2) 218
Pit-Jefferson 108C

SL   7 6 0 0 13
ChiB 10 0 7 17 34
SL   D15 R20/78 P(38-14-1) 217
ChiB D23 R44/189 P(26-15-0) 274
ChiB-Morris 123C

SF 10 10 0 7 27
Det 0 0 7 14 21
SF D18 R33/127 P(34-21-3) 197
Det D17 R24/89 P(33-14-1) 104

Was 0 0 7 0 7
Phi 7 0 7 7 21
Was D14 R18/82 P(29-16-1) 137
Phi D21 R27/128 P(28-21-1) 285
Phi-Retzlaff 204C, Snead 311P

SUNDAY, NOVEMBER 21
ChiB 0 10 7 0 17
Det 7 3 0 0 10
ChiB D14 R39/201 P(16-9-0) 29
Det D11 R28/66 P(23-12-1) 118

Cle 0 17 0 7 24
Dal 0 3 7 7 17
Cle D15 R30/135 P(18-9-0) 65
Dal D18 R29/124 P(29-17-3) 169

GB 7 3 0 28 38
Min 3 3 7 7 20
GB D16 R38/180 P(19-9-2) 159
Min D19 R42/183 P(24-13-2) 181
GB-Taylor 111R; Min-Flatley 133C

LARm 0 17 3 7 27
SF   0 10 3 17 30
LARm D20 R30/105 P(39-16-2) 249
SF   D19 R23/55 P(37-23-2) 214

NYG 0 7 7 14 28
SL 2 3 3 7 15
NYG D11 R32/87 P(20-9-1) 140
SL D20 R26/54 P(39-22-3) 282
SL-Smith 105C, Humphrey 320P

Phi 0 0 7 0 7
Bal 14 3 3 14 34
Phi D12 R24/76 P(26-13-2) 174
Bal D22 R34/126 P(29-17-2) 277
Bal-Moore 163C, Unitas 305P

Was 0 10 14 7 31
Pit 3 0 0 0 3
Was D12 R38/118 P(23-9-1) 81
Pit D7 R24/61   P(18-7-4) 54

THURSDAY, NOVEMBER 25
Bal 7 3 0 14 24
Det 7 14 3 0 24
Bal D22 R29/126 P(34-14-2) 154
Det D17 R36/187 P(23-9-1) 77
Bal-Mackey 102C; Det-Marsh 146R

SUNDAY, NOVEMBER 28
ChiB 7 0 14 14 35
NYG 0 0 7 7 14
ChiB D21 R37/170 P(25-15-1) 200
NYG D14 R21/54 P(31-15-2) 148
ChiB-Sayers 113R

Cle 0 7 14 21 42
Pit 0 0 7 14 21
Cle D20 R42/241 P(13-6-0) 119
Pit D13 R26/137 P(22-9-0) 221
Cle-Brown 146R; Pit-Ballman 118C

Dal 14 7 3 7 31
Was 0 7 7 20 34
Dal D17 R30/82 P(28-14-1) 202
Was D28 R22/51 P(43-26-2) 364
Was-Taylor 139C, Jurgensen 411P

GB   0 7 0 3 10
LARm 7 6 0 8 21
GB   D12 R16/22 P(35-19-1) 232
LARm D19 R38/102 P(29-15-1) 242
GB-Pitts 111C

Phi 7 14 0 7 28
SL 10 0 7 7 24
Phi D24 R34/229 P(31-15-1) 248
SL D17 R27/128 P(37-15-5) 169
Phi-Brown 180R, Retzlaff 148C

SF 14 21 10 0 45
Min 3 7 0 14 24
SF D20 R39/194 P(21-10-0) 209
Min D18 R24/92 P(42-16-1) 195
SF-Willard 113R, Brodie 209P

SUNDAY, DECEMBER 5
ChiB 7 3 3 0 13
Bal 0 0 0 0 0
ChiB D18 R45/202 P(24-16-1) 216
Bal D15 R20/59 P(39-15-2) 163
ChiB-Sayers 118R

Dal 7 7 7 0 21
Phi 7 6 6 0 19
Dal D18 R35/185 P(23-12-2) 156
Phi D22 R22/64 P(45-21-1) 370
Dal-Hayes 106C; Phi-Poage 142C,
Retzlaff 118C, Snead 320P

Det 0 14 0 0 14
SF 3 0 0 14 17
Det D16 R34/145 P(27-10-1) 155
SF D20 R32/148 P(35-18-1) 209
Det-Marsh 109R

LARm 7 10 3 7 27
SL   3 0 0 0 3
LARm D22 R38/177 P(31-17-0) 203
SL   D11 R21/62 P(26-13-1) 104

Min 7 9 3 0 19
GB 7 7 7 3 24
Min D21 R45/251 P(30-11-0) 85
GB D16 R28/113 P(22-9-3) 153
Min-Mason 101R

Pit 0 0 0 10 10
NYG 7 21 0 7 35
Pit D13 R22/85 P(27-11-2) 99
NYG D21 R37/243 P(24-11-0) 171

Was 6 10 0 0 16
Cle 0 7 3 14 24
Was D16 R23/63 P(35-18-2) 138
Cle D24 R38/200 P(22-9-3) 84
Cle-Brown 141R

SATURDAY, DECEMBER 11
SL 10 3 0 0 13
Dal 3 10 0 14 27
SL D17 R28/88 P(31-18-0) 251
Dal D18 R36/79 P(30-16-0) 324
SL 1-Conrad 126C; al-Hayes 103C,
Meredith 326P

SUNDAY, DECEMBER 12
Cle 0 7 0 0 7
LARm 7 14 7 14 42
Cle D6 R19/40   P(27-11-1) 79
LARm D23 R33/169 P(31-15-1) 300
LARm-McDonald 200C,
Gabriel 323P

GB 14 7 14 7 42
Bal 3 10 0 7 20
GB D18 R35/144 P(17-10-1) 222
Bal D21 R27/74 P(41-20-3) 190
GB-Hornung 115C; Bal-Berry 125C

Min 8 14 0 7 29
Det 0 7 0 0 7
Min D15 R38/75 P(24-13-0) 199
Det D8 R22/29 P(23-11-3) 106

```
NYG   7  13   0   7   27
Was  10   0   0   0   10
NYG  D21 R45/151  P(12-7-2) 217
Was  D18 R24/74   P(35-16-0) 220
  NYG-Jones 182C;
  Was-Mitchell 118C

Phi  27   7   6   7   47
Pit   0  13   0   0   13
Phi  D17 R34/191  P(21-7-2) 111
Pit  D17 R25/58   P(43-24-9) 266
  Pit-Ballman 163C

SF    0  13   0   7   20
ChiB 13  14  13  21   61
SF   D19 R20/58   P(44-23-2) 272
ChiB D21 R29/183  P(33-17-0) 401
  SF-Parks 129C; ChiB-Sayers 113R,
  Jones 113C, Bukich 347P
```

SATURDAY, DECEMBER 18
```
Bal  10   0   0  10   20
LARm  0   7   3   7   17
Bal  D10 R47/214  P(7-3-0) 50
LARm D14 R25/57   P(30-16-2) 210
  LARm-McDonald 110C
```

SUNDAY, DECEMBER 19
```
Cle   7  10   0  10   27
SL    0   7  10   7   24
Cle  D16 R30/141  P(33-16-3) 146
SL   D14 R28/110  P(34-13-4) 50

Dal  10   7   0  21   38
NYG   0   7   7   6   20
Dal  D16 R28/161  P(18-8-0) 173
NYG  D18 R28/109  P(38-19-2) 213

Det  14   7   7   7   35
Phi   0  14  14   0   28
Det  D19 R42/113  P(32-18-1) 214
Phi  D10 R21/40   P(20-11-3) 53

GB    0   7   7  10   24
SF    0   3   7  14   24
GB   D17 R28/76   P(30-15-1) 223
SF   D20 R24/99   P(34-26-3) 293
  GB-Dowler 117C; SF-Parks 149C

Min   0   0   3  21   24
ChiB  0   0   7  10   17
Min  D17 R34/103  P(29-13-1) 181
ChiB D17 R33/167  P(29-11-3) 164

Pit   0  14   0   0   14
Was  14  14   7   0   35
Pit  D14 R35/145  P(17-9-4) 86
Was  D11 R26/32   P(26-12-1) 145
```

1966 AFL

FRIDAY, SEPTEMBER 2
```
Oak   0  10   7   6   23
Mia   7   0   0   7   14
Oak  D16 R22/16   P(39-18-4) 241
Mia  D22 R23/94   P(32-11-5) 88
  Oak-Powell 104C
```

SATURDAY, SEPTEMBER 3
```
Den   7   0   0   0    7
Hou   7  10   7  21   45
Den  D0 R16/33    P(20-2-0) -7
Hou  D28 R47/213  P(31-17-0) 259
  Hou-Frazier 100C
```

SUNDAY, SEPTEMBER 4
```
Buf   0   0   0   7    7
SD    0   7   3  17   27
Buf  D15 R27/117  P(27-9-3) 150
SD   D15 R36/137  P(18-14-0) 153
```

FRIDAY, SEPTEMBER 9
```
NYJ   9   0  10   0   19
Mia   0   0   0  14   14
NYJ  D14 R35/96   P(36-12-2) 151
Mia  D9 R19/50    P(35-10-3) 61
```

SATURDAY, SEPTEMBER 10
```
Oak   0   0   0   0    0
Hou   0  14   3  14   31
Oak  D23 R17/73   P(48-23-4) 199
Hou  D20 R32/72   P(35-18-2) 197
```

```
Bos   0   0   0   0    0
SD    3  14   0   7   24
Bos  D15 R21/130  P(41-14-4) 122
SD   D12 R31/138  P(28-10-0) 141
```

SUNDAY, SEPTEMBER 11
```
KC   21   0  14   7   42
Buf   0  10   3   7   20
KC   D17 R37/165  P(17-11-0) 223
Buf  D15 R27/79   P(38-11-0) 116
  KC-Coan 101R
```

SUNDAY, SEPTEMBER 18
```
KC   10   0   7  15   32
Oak   7   3   0   0   10
KC   D11 R26/139  P(22-9-0) 85
Oak  D17 R29/96   P(50-23-2) 245
  Oak-Powell 133C

Mia   3   7   0  14   24
Buf  21  27   3   7   58
Mia  D17 R32/111  P(40-13-4) 202
Buf  D25 R34/179  P(33-17-2) 329
  Mia-Roberson 128C;
  Buf-Dubenion 101C

Hou   3   3   7   0   13
NYJ   7  14  17  14   52
Hou  D16 R28/71   P(41-19-4) 136
NYJ  D23 R24/126  P(39-18-0) 340
  NYJ-Maynard 156C, Namath 283P

Bos   3   6   0  15   24
Den   3   7   0   0   10
Bos  D16 R33/145  P(23-9-2) 116
Den  D12 R31/101  P(25-10-3) 72
  Bos-Nance 126R
```

SUNDAY, SEPTEMBER 25
```
KC   17   0   6  20   43
Bos   0  14   7   3   24
KC   D22 R26/76   P(41-23-2) 319
Bos  D17 R32/144  P(30-13-3) 164
  KC-Burford 155C, Dawson 291P

SD    3   9  10   7   29
Oak   3   0   7  10   20
SD   D12 R35/133  P(21-10-1) 143
Oak  D18 R25/109  P(31-11-4) 153

NYJ   0   0   6  10   16
Den   0   7   0   0    7
NYJ  D20 R38/153  P(35-16-2) 206
Den  D7 R21/77    P(26-8-1) 105
  NYJ-Maynard 101C

Hou   0   6   0  14   20
Buf   3  17   0   7   27
Hou  D15 R21/24   P(54-23-5) 276
Buf  D14 R33/136  P(26-11-2) 140
  Hou-Frazier 128C, Blanda 303P
```

SUNDAY, OCTOBER 2
```
Hou   0  17  14   7   38
Den   6  17  14   3   40
Hou  D20 R22/95   P(37-15-2) 289
Den  D17 R38/150  P(31-13-1) 212
  Hou-Frazier 154C, Blanda 300P;
  Den-Denson 158C

NYJ   0   7   0  17   24
Bos   7   3  14   0   24
NYJ  D20 R18/29   P(56-28-3) 338
Bos  D13 R33/86   P(29-14-1) 138
  NYJ-Sauer 106C, Namath 338P

Mia   3   7   0   0   10
SD    6  17   7  14   44
Mia  D16 R42/187  P(27-9-0) 89
SD   D14 R25/40   P(24-16-1) 321
  SD-Alworth 119C, Foster 134C,
  Tensi 223P

Buf   6   6   3  14   29
KC    0  14   0   0   14
Buf  D20 R33/147  P(36-19-1) 214
KC   D11 R20/51   P(34-12-2) 214
  KC-Taylor 125C
```

SATURDAY, OCTOBER 8
```
Bos  10   3   7   0   20
Buf   0   3   0   7   10
Bos  D12 R33/109  P(26-12-0) 177
Buf  D15 R24/52   P(38-18-0) 269
  Buf-Dubenion 104C
```

```
Den   0   3   0   7   10
KC   21   0   3  13   37
Den  D11 R21/79   P(35-12-2) 133
KC   D21 R31/234  P(26-14-0) 145
  KC-Taylor 103C

SD    3   6   0   7   16
NYJ   7   3   0   7   17
SD   D23 R26/95   P(51-24-1) 350
NYJ  D12 R30/119  P(22-11-3) 129
  SD-Alworth 149C, Hadl 331P
```

SUNDAY, OCTOBER 9
```
Mia   3   7   0   0   10
Oak   0  14   0   7   21
Mia  D12 R34/77   P(21-12-1) 115
Oak  D19 R26/106  P(24-14-1) 251
```

SUNDAY, OCTOBER 16
```
Den   7   0   0   0    7
Mia  10   0   7   7   24
Den  D11 R22/65   P(27-10-4) 53
Mia  D10 R34/71   P(18-9-1) 146

Oak   0  28   3   3   34
KC    3   3   0   7   13
Oak  D14 R31/83   P(25-14-1) 288
KC   D15 R23/76   P(21-12-3) 133
  Oak-Dixon 129C, Flores 301P

NYJ   0   0   0   0    0
Hou  10   7   0   7   24
NYJ  D11 R16/53   P(44-21-4) 163
Hou  D17 R43/141  P(24-13-1) 198

SD    7  10   0   0   17
Buf   0   3   7   7   17
SD   D12 R23/50   P(21-12-0) 169
Buf  D22 R42/213  P(26-11-2) 107
  SD-Lincoln 123C; Buf-Burnett 138R
```

SUNDAY, OCTOBER 23
```
Mia   7   7   3   3   20
Hou   0   3  10   0   13
Mia  D13 R48/201  P(13-9-0) 139
Hou  D13 R23/100  P(34-14-4) 201

Oak   0   7   0  17   24
NYJ   7   7   0   7   21
Oak  D17 R24/129  P(33-16-2) 205
NYJ  D27 R32/137  P(32-19-0) 260
  Oak-Daniels 104R, Powell 109C

KC   14   7  14  21   56
Den   0   3   7   0   10
KC   D26 R41/380  P(22-13-1) 234
Den  D12 R14/28   P(34-18-5) 183
  KC-Coan 111R

SD    7   3   7   0   17
Bos   0  14   7  14   35
SD   D16 R21/40   P(39-19-2) 289
Bos  D22 R46/172  P(24-13-2) 242
  SD-Alworth 177C; Bos-Nance 108R,
  Garron 106C
```

SUNDAY, OCTOBER 30
```
Buf   0  13  17   3   33
NYJ   0   0  20   3   23
Buf  D17 R31/134  P(40-16-3) 134
NYJ  D17 R9/5     P(53-24-5) 323
  NYJ-Sauer 114C, Namath 343P

Oak   0   0   7  14   21
Bos  14   3   7   0   24
Oak  D14 R19/43   P(34-12-2) 200
Bos  D16 R55/281  P(11-4-2) 58
  Oak-Daniels 112C; Bos-Nance 208R

Den   7  10   0   0   17
SD    7  14   0   3   24
Den  D15 R30/125  P(31-15-0) 155
SD   D21 R33/154  P(26-19-0) 180

Hou   0   3   0  14   17
KC    0  24  14  10   48
Hou  D22 R31/94   P(40-20-3) 174
KC   D15 R27/151  P(22-12-0) 290
  KC-Garrett 102R, Taylor 187C
```

SUNDAY, NOVEMBER 6
```
Hou  10   0   0  13   23
Oak   7  14  10   7   38
Hou  D8 R24/120   P(26-9-1) 126
Oak  D14 R36/141  P(26-10-2) 249
```

```
SD    7   0   7   0   14
KC    7  17   0   0   24
SD   D14 R20/84   P(31-17-2) 203
KC   D24 R44/159  P(24-12-2) 143
  SD-Alworth 101C

Den   0   3   7   7   17
Bos   0   3   0   0    3
Den  D16 R41/97   P(20-12-2) 143
Bos  D11 R25/43   P(26-14-0) 67

Buf   0  10  10   9   29
Mia   0   0   0   0    0
Buf  D18 R27/114  P(46-16-3) 271
Mia  D11 R21/48   P(39-15-3) 123
```

SUNDAY, NOVEMBER 13
```
Oak   7  21   7   6   41
SD   10   0   3   6   19
Oak  D20 R33/219  P(34-19-0) 258
SD   D16 R19/151  P(37-16-1) 167
  Oak-Daniels 104R; SD-Lowe 125R

Mia   0  10   0   6   16
KC   17  14   0   3   34
Mia  D11 R22/81   P(40-12-6) 79
KC   D17 R36/160  P(21-12-3) 236
  KC-Taylor 113C

Hou   7   7   0   7   21
Bos   7  13   7   0   27
Hou  D20 R30/72   P(46-23-0) 302
Bos  D20 R37/149  P(30-12-0) 242
  Hou-Frazier 158C, Trull 329P;
  Bos-Nance 104R, Cappelletti 118C

NYJ   0   0   0   3    3
Buf   0   0   0  14   14
NYJ  D15 R27/55   P(37-19-1) 274
Buf  D10 R32/92   P(23-10-0) 132
  NYJ-Sauer 134C
```

SUNDAY, NOVEMBER 20
```
Bos   0  17   7   3   27
KC   10   0  17   0   27
Bos  D19 R29/116  P(34-19-2) 245
KC   D21 R17/73   P(39-25-2) 286
  Bos-Nance 107R, Graham 134C;
  KC-Taylor 133C, Dawson 324P

Buf   0  14  14  14   42
Hou   3  10   0   7   20
Buf  D23 R38/156  P(38-18-0) 352
Hou  D11 R16/87   P(35-10-3) 228
  Hou-Frazier 119C

Oak   0  14   0   3   17
Den   0   3   0   0    3
Oak  D8 R31/66    P(19-6-0) 94
Den  D10 R22/71   P(36-10-3) 31
  Oak-Cannon 109C

Mia   6   0   7   0   13
NYJ   0  10  13   7   30
Mia  D12 R20/63   P(30-11-1) 141
NYJ  D18 R37/78   P(31-17-0) 236
  NYJ-Sauer 142C
```

THURSDAY, NOVEMBER 24
```
Buf   0  17   7   7   31
Oak   7   3   0   0   10
Buf  D25 R46/226  P(32-14-0) 239
Oak  D11 R18/58   P(30-17-2) 257
  Oak-Powell 116C
```

SUNDAY, NOVEMBER 27
```
KC    7   9  13   3   32
NYJ   7   3   0  14   24
KC   D27 R36/128  P(33-20-0) 311
NYJ  D15 R12/31   P(36-18-1) 252
  KC-Burford 109C, Taylor 136C;
  NYJ-Sauer 121C

SD    0   3   0  14   17
Den   3   0   3  14   20
SD   D16 R23/86   P(33-15-1) 200
Den  D16 R38/170  P(26-12-2) 173
  SD-Alworth 111C

Bos   0  10  10   0   20
Mia   0   0   7   7   14
Bos  D18 R27/159  P(32-14-2) 232
Mia  D19 R20/68   P(52-17-3) 105
  Bos-Nance 133R; Mia-Auer 104C
```

SATURDAY, DECEMBER 3
```
NYJ   3   7  10   8   28
Oak  14   0   0  14   28
NYJ  D16 R22/173  P(42-20-5) 316
Oak  D17 R27/154  P(31-15-1) 261
  NYJ-Mathis 128C, Namath 327P
```

SUNDAY, DECEMBER 4
```
Mia   0   7   0   0    7
Den   0  10   7   0   17
Mia  D19 R23/48   P(40-16-0) 207
Den  D17 R39/91   P(25-14-2) 262
  Mia-Roberson 161C;
  Den-Mitchell 126C

SD    7   7   0  14   28
Hou   0  10   9   3   22
SD   D15 R17/76   P(36-20-3) 302
Hou  D23 R45/243  P(28-16-1) 152
  SD-Alworth 147C, Hadl 341P;
  Hou-Granger 183R

Buf   3   0   0   0    3
Bos   7   0   7   0   14
Buf  D17 R26/40   P(40-19-2) 274
Bos  D12 R33/107  P(22-9-1) 119
  Bos-Nance 109R
```

SUNDAY, DECEMBER 11
```
NYJ   9   3   7   8   27
SD    0  14  14  14   42
NYJ  D20 R31/146  P(30-14-3) 189
SD   D25 R27/222  P(26-13-1) 203
  NYJ-Snell 102R, Lammons 123C;
  SD-Lowe 126R, Alworth 127C

Bos   3  21   7   7   38
Hou   7   0   0   7   14
Bos  D31 R46/240  P(27-18-0) 272
Hou  D13 R20/65   P(30-17-1) 170
  Bos-Nance 146R, Garron 113C

Den   0   3   0   7   10
Oak  14   7   0   7   28
Den  D11 R25/42   P(26-16-2) 160
Oak  D18 R25/134  P(30-19-1) 243
  Oak-Powell 109C

KC    3   3   0  13   19
Mia   0  11   0   7   18
KC   D17 R32/188  P(29-12-2) 128
Mia  D14 R27/163  P(29-13-3) 123
```

SATURDAY, DECEMBER 17
```
Bos   7   0   6  15   28
NYJ   7  10  14   7   38
Bos  D21 R21/82   P(38-21-2) 379
NYJ  D26 R45/241  P(21-14-0) 287
  Bos-Cappelletti 111C, Parilli 379P;
  NYJ-Boozer 117R, Snell 124R,
  Maynard 129C
```

SUNDAY, DECEMBER 18
```
KC   14   3   3   7   27
SD    3   7   7   0   17
KC   D22 R43/294  P(15-9-1) 93
SD   D19 R25/131  P(36-17-2) 195
  KC-Garrett 161R; SD-Alworth 156C

Hou   7  14   0   7   28
Mia   0   8   7  14   29
Hou  D20 R31/118  P(24-12-1) 189
Mia  D25 R29/148  P(38-22-2) 269
  Mia-Jackson 110C, Stofa 307P

Den   0   7   0  14   21
Buf  14  10   7   7   38
Den  D16 R18/44   P(40-14-3) 320
Buf  D19 R35/207  P(30-10-3) 129
  Den-Scarpitto 123C,
  McCormick 328P
```

1966 NFL

SATURDAY, SEPTEMBER 10
```
Bal   0   3   0   3    6
GB    0  14  10   0   24
Bal  D11 R32/112  P(21-14-3) .101
GB   D17 R35/155  P(19-14-1) 137
```

```
SUNDAY, SEPTEMBER 11
Min     0   7  10   3   20
SF      6  14   0   0   20
Min   D20 R40/226  P(28-10-1)  72
SF    D18 R30/104  P(39-22-1)  203
SF-Casey 107C

Phi     3   7   0   3   13
SL      0   3   3  10   16
Phi   D18 R31/133  P(25-9-0)  121
SL    D20 R30/120  P(26-19-1)  158

LARm    3  13   3   0   19
Atl     0   7   7   0   14
LARm  D23 R37/146  P(35-21-1)  275
Atl   D10 R19/121  P(25-9-2)  116
LARm-McDonald 114C

NYG     7  10   0  17   34
Pit     7   7  17   3   34
NYG   D8 R20/32  P(18-10-2)  247
Pit   D25 R38/138  P(28-17-0)  266
NYG-Jones 173C; Pit-Ballman 114C

Cle     7   0  10  21   38
Was    14   0   0   0   14
Cle   D18 R34/148  P(25-13-0)  159
Was   D17 R25/103  P(35-17-5)  212

ChiB    3   0   0   0   3
Det     0  14   0   0   14
ChiB  D17 R36/147  P(27-15-2)  109
Det   D14 R36/123  P(15-7-1)  85

FRIDAY, SEPTEMBER 16
ChiB   10   7   0   0   17
LARm    7   7   7  10   31
ChiB  D12 R30/121  P(35-11-1)  118
LARm  D17 R32/99  P(21-14-0)  195
LARm-Snow 105C

SUNDAY, SEPTEMBER 18
Atl     0   3   7   0   10
Phi     3   7   3  10   23
Atl   D16 R26/96  P(31-14-3)  202
Phi   D20 R43/205  P(20-11-1)  135
Atl-Hawkins 144C; Phi-Lang 114R

Bal     0  10  14  14   38
Min    13   3   0   7   23
Bal   D14 R27/109  P(22-14-2)  237
Min   D18 R39/180  P(28-16-1)  157
Bal-Mackey 143C, Unitas 241P

Det     0   0   0   3   3
Pit     3   0   7   7   17
Det   D9 R21/69  P(24-11-3)  89
Pit   D15 R33/113  P(23-13-1)  143

NYG     0   7   0   0   7
Dal     7  24  14   7   52
NYG   D18 R22/137  P(37-13-4)  120
Dal   D24 R34/144  P(33-16-1)  374
Dal-Hayes 195C, Reeves 120C,
Meredith 358P

Was     0   0   0   7   7
SL      0   3   3  17   23
Was   D14 R20/27  P(32-18-0)  190
SL    D21 R32/145  P(34-19-1)  237
Was-Mitchell 119C; SL-Smith 136C

GB      0   7   7   7   21
Cle     7   0   0   3   20
GB    D22 R38/118  P(30-20-0)  238
Cle   D16 R22/110  P(24-15-0)  156

SUNDAY, SEPTEMBER 25
LARm    0   6   7   0   13
GB      7  10   0   7   24
LARm  D12 R31/106  P(28-14-1)  67
GB    D14 R33/94  P(21-13-0)  233

Was     9   0  21   3   33
Pit     0  14  10   3   27
Was   D17 R30/92  P(33-20-2)  228
Pit   D15 R25/72  P(24-12-3)  206
Pit-Ballman 128C

Atl     0   7   3   0   10
Det     7  14   0   7   28
Atl   D13 R33/155  P(24-9-0)  104
Det   D18 R30/136  P(27-19-2)  208

SF      0   7   0   0   7
Bal     6  10   6  14   36
SF    D14 R22/95  P(32-18-1)  155
Bal   D23 R33/168  P(31-14-1)  211
Bal-Lorick 110R

SL      7   7  14   6   34
Cle    14   7   7   7   35
SL    D13 R28/107  P(20-11-2)  206
Cle   D25 R32/143  P(41-21-1)  230
Cle-Kelly 109R

Min     3   7   7   0   17
Dal     0   7   7  14   28
Min   D25 R34/142  P(42-19-1)  247
Dal   D18 R33/148  P(23-9-0)  166
Min-Brown 115R

NYG     0   3   7   7   17
Phi     7  14   0  14   35
NYG   D19 R28/150  P(36-20-1)  236
Phi   D17 R36/110  P(19-10-0)  161
Phi-Retzlaff 120C

FRIDAY, SEPTEMBER 30
SF      0   3   0   0   3
LARm   10  10  14   0   34
SF    D15 R19/53  P(41-16-4)  198
LARm  D20 R34/163  P(34-15-1)  193

SUNDAY, OCTOBER 2
ChiB    3   0   0  10   13
Min     0   0   7   3   10
ChiB  D11 R30/104  P(25-13-1)  179
Min   D16 R37/115  P(29-15-1)  169
Min-Flatley 118C

SL     14   3  10  14   41
Phi     0   0  14   0   14
SL    D8 R28/84  P(17-8-0)  63
Phi   D17 R19/62  P(45-16-5)  168

Dal     3  14  16  14   47
Atl     7   0   7   0   14
Dal   D22 R28/143  P(26-16-0)  220
Atl   D20 R30/106  P(27-16-2)  170
Dal-Clarke 125C

Pit     0  10   0   0   10
Was    10   0   7   7   24
Pit   D16 R25/69  P(42-16-3)  180
Was   D11 R32/84  P(22-14-0)  249
Was-Mitchell 150C

Det     0   7   0   7   14
GB     10   0   7   3   23
Det   D17 R37/174  P(24-15-2)  175
GB    D10 R29/66  P(19-11-0)  185

Cle     7   0   7  14   28
NYG     0   7   0   0   7
Cle   D23 R46/258  P(24-14-1)  160
NYG   D12 R18/50  P(29-13-4)  224
Cle-Kelly 138R

SATURDAY, OCTOBER 8
Pit     0   0  10   0   10
Cle    14   7   0  20   41
Pit   D12 R16/22  P(38-18-5)  182
Cle   D31 R43/241  P(28-19-0)  226
Cle-Green 103R, Kelly 113R

SUNDAY, OCTOBER 9
Phi     0   0   0   7   7
Dal    21   7  14  14   56
Phi   D11 R18/38  P(40-19-1)  179
Dal   D32 R32/212  P(38-25-0)  440
Dal-Hayes 107C, Meredith 394P

Bal     0   3   7   7   17
ChiB   10   0  10   7   27
Bal   D19 R23/108  P(38-18-2)  256
ChiB  D19 R52/219  P(15-8-1)  96
ChiB-Sayers 106R

LARm    7   0   7   0   14
Det     0   0   0   7   7
LARm  D21 R35/166  P(34-21-2)  203
Det   D14 R30/89  P(31-15-4)  194
LARm-Bass 137R;
Det-Studstill 142C

NYG    10   3   0   6   19
SL      0   0   7  17   24
NYG   D20 R37/126  P(35-19-2)  145
SL    D15 R26/91  P(18-9-2)  177

Atl     7  10   3   0   20
Was     7  13   6   7   33
Atl   D19 R27/122  P(27-14-2)  146
Was   D26 R36/146  P(26-17-0)  286
Was-Taylor 105C

GB      3   0  10   7   20
SF      0   7   7   7   21
GB    D17 R34/106  P(26-18-1)  262
SF    D17 R30/154  P(25-12-1)  94

SUNDAY, OCTOBER 16
GB      0   0  10   7   17
ChiB    0   0   0   0   0
GB    D12 R35/121  P(19-8-1)  59
ChiB  D6 R30/42  P(23-12-3)  52

Was     3   7   0   0   10
NYG     0   3   0  10   13
Was   D9 R25/81  P(23-9-2)  107
NYG   D17 R29/97  P(31-16-1)  228
NYG-Jones 146C

LARm    0   0   0   7   7
Min     0  21   7   7   35
LARm  D13 R23/84  P(33-16-3)  146
Min   D20 R37/65  P(32-22-1)  313
Min-Phillips 142C, Tarkenton 327P

Phi     0  14   0  17   31
Pit     7   7   0   0   14
Phi   D22 R49/188  P(24-12-2)  93
Pit   D14 R26/87  P(28-10-2)  91
Phi-Brown 100R

Dal     3   0   0   7   10
SL      0   7   0   3   10
Dal   D17 R33/135  P(34-15-3)  191
SL    D13 R27/45  P(30-15-0)  130

Det     0   0   7   7   14
Bal    17   7  14   7   45
Det   D17 R28/78  P(39-20-2)  215
Bal   D21 R33/137  P(32-22-0)  283
Det-Studstill 141C; Bal-Unitas 218P

SF      7  17  13   7   44
Atl     0   7   0   0   7
SF    D29 R37/176  P(36-21-1)  328
Atl   D14 R17/59  P(33-18-3)  156

SUNDAY, OCTOBER 23
Dal     7   0   0  14   21
Cle    10   3  17   0   30
Dal   D30 R31/156  P(45-26-4)  257
Cle   D17 R31/105  P(24-9-0)  159
Dal-Hayes 108C

LARm    0  10   0   0   10
ChiB    7  10   0   0   17
LARm  D14 R33/108  P(34-15-2)  95
ChiB  D15 R39/152  P(21-9-1)  135

Min     0   7   3   7   17
Bal     0  10   3   7   20
Min   D24 R38/136  P(36-23-0)  181
Bal   D20 R27/146  P(29-17-1)  201

Phi     0  24   0   7   31
NYG     7   0   0   0   7
Phi   D18 R46/202  P(14-9-1)  114
NYG   D13 R19/76  P(33-15-4)  152

Atl     0   0   0   3   3
GB      7  21   7  21   56
Atl   D15 R29/140  P(29-11-4)  76
GB    D19 R28/126  P(19-10-0)  231
Atl-Coffey 117R; GB-Dale 110C

SL      7   3   3   7   20
Was     3   6  14   3   26
SL    D17 R35/164  P(24-13-2)  87
Was   D15 R23/56  P(35-20-1)  235
SL-Roland 109R

Det     0   0   0  14   14
SF      3   7   3  14   27
Det   D17 R30/112  P(34-19-0)  202
SF    D23 R32/171  P(36-18-4)  188
Det-Studstill 128C

SUNDAY, OCTOBER 30
Pit     7   7   7   0   21
Dal     0  24  21   7   52
Pit   D6 R12/7  P(30-10-2)  112
Dal   D24 R43/192  P(33-14-3)  233
Dal-Meredith 226P

Cle    14   7   7  21   49
Atl     0  10   0   7   17
Cle   D22 R31/213  P(25-16-1)  295
Atl   D23 R36/204  P(25-14-1)  117
Cle-Ryan 223P

SF      0   0   3   0   3
Min     7   0   7  14   28
SF    D10 R22/49  P(26-13-2)  105
Min   D29 R51/246  P(36-21-1)  313

Was     3   7   3  14   27
Phi     0   3   7   3   13
Was   D17 R34/101  P(31-18-2)  159
Phi   D14 R24/105  P(37-17-1)  152

Bal    10   7   0   0   17
LARm    0   3   0   0   3
Bal   D13 R29/92  P(22-13-1)  230
LARm  D21 R31/115  P(39-23-3)  225
Bal-Mackey 132C

GB      0  17   7   7   31
Det     0   0   0   0   0
GB    D19 R43/174  P(15-13-0)  170
Det   D19 R22/84  P(45-21-3)  233
Det-Studstill 164C

MONDAY, OCTOBER 31
ChiB    0   7   3   7   17
SL     14   0   0  10   24
ChiB  D16 R32/109  P(29-13-3)  173
SL    D11 R41/119  P(16-4-1)  47

SUNDAY, NOVEMBER 6
SL      0   3  14   3   20
NYG     0   7   0  10   17
SL    D16 R47/148  P(28-8-2)  116
NYG   D11 R17/42  P(33-15-1)  168
SL-Smith 103C

Was     3   0   7   0   10
Bal     3  20   7   7   37
Was   D14 R17/76  P(32-21-2)  196
Bal   D28 R37/126  P(36-25-2)  394
Was-Taylor 111C; Bal-Berry 131C,
Orr 131C, Unitas 342P

Cle     0   6   0   0   6
Pit     0   3   3  10   16
Cle   D19 R29/131  P(37-19-5)  176
Pit   D12 R32/135  P(19-11-0)  132

Dal    10   7   3   3   23
Phi     7  17   0   0   24
Dal   D16 R37/112  P(30-12-0)  128
Phi   D5 R27/58  P(17-5-0)  22

Det     0   7   0   3   10
ChiB    0   7   3   0   10
Det   D17 R32/88  P(34-17-1)  167
ChiB  D15 R35/176  P(16-9-0)  106
Det-Studstill 125C;
ChiB-Sayers 124R

LARm    0   7   6   0   13
SF      0   7   7   7   21
LARm  D11 R16/26  P(26-11-1)  116
SF    D21 R33/81  P(31-21-2)  277
LARm-Bass 106R

Min     0  10   0  10   20
GB      7   0   0  10   17
Min   D20 R46/126  P(26-16-0)  164
GB    D18 R35/158  P(18-11-0)  134

SUNDAY, NOVEMBER 13
Bal     3   3  10   3   19
Atl     0   7   0   0   7
Bal   D13 R29/95  P(25-10-2)  105
Atl   D17 R40/89  P(28-14-5)  152
Bal-McKeever 115C

Det     0  12   6  14   32
Min    10   0  14   7   31
Det   D16 R22/50  P(42-24-2)  218
Min   D15 R37/149  P(24-11-5)  83
Det-Studstill 116C

Phi     0   0   0   7   7
Cle     0   7  13   7   27
Phi   D17 R26/115  P(31-18-2)  175
Cle   D17 R30/169  P(32-15-0)  176

SL      9   0   0   0   9
Pit     3  10   3  14   30
SL    D14 R29/98  P(35-13-0)  195
Pit   D6 R28/48  P(24-9-1)  102
SL-Smith 106C; Pit-Jefferson 105C

NYG     0   0   7   7   14
LARm   14  10  10  21   55
NYG   D25 R36/111  P(33-20-5)  278
LARm  D38 R43/223  P(40-28-1)  349
LARm-McKeever 115C

SF      7   3   7  13   30
ChiB   10  20   0   0   30
SF    D28 R31/112  P(54-28-1)  311
ChiB  D12 R26/100  P(22-8-1)  120
SF-Casey 225C, Brodie 327P

Dal     7   7   7  10   31
Was     6   0  17   7   30
Dal   D24 R34/132  P(30-21-1)  383
Was   D19 R16/23  P(46-26-0)  318
Dal-Hayes 246C, Meredith 406P;
Was-Taylor 199C, Jurgensen 347P

SUNDAY, NOVEMBER 20
Atl     7   6   7   7   27
NYG     0   3   7   6   16
Atl   D19 R38/122  P(26-15-1)  167
NYG   D21 R27/151  P(33-19-2)  152

Bal     0   0   0  14   14
Det     7   0  10   3   20
Bal   D16 R25/81  P(37-21-5)  208
Det   D16 R34/154  P(32-16-2)  127

Phi     0   7  14  14   35
SF      3  17  14   0   34
Phi   D15 R31/120  P(30-15-3)  169
SF    D24 R34/166  P(40-22-2)  238
SF-Willard 124R

ChiB    0   0   0   6   6
GB      0   7   0   6   13
ChiB  D9 R26/75  P(22-9-3)  85
GB    D15 R33/69  P(31-17-1)  227

Dal     0  10   7   3   20
Pit     0   7   0   0   7
Dal   D16 R32/124  P(29-11-1)  134
Pit   D16 R26/53  P(29-14-2)  110

Min     0   0   3   3   6
LARm    6   3   0  12   21
Min   D10 R37/143  P(20-7-1)  43
LARm  D15 R34/98  P(37-15-0)  130

Was     0   0   3   0   3
Cle     7   0   7   0   14
Was   D20 R35/168  P(38-27-2)  159
Cle   D10 R24/159  P(17-9-0)  112
Cle-Kelly 100R

THURSDAY, NOVEMBER 24
Cle     0  14   0   0   14
Dal     6   7   6   7   26
Cle   D18 R26/157  P(26-12-0)  164
Dal   D25 R42/173  P(24-16-0)  131
Cle-Kelly 115R; Dal-Perkins 111R

SF     10  10  14   7   41
Det     7   7   0   0   14
SF    D22 R40/214  P(28-15-3)  273
Det   D10 R18/47  P(31-14-1)  149
SF-Willard 114R, Parks 102C

SUNDAY, NOVEMBER 27
Atl     0   0   0   6   6
ChiB    7   3   3  10   23
Atl   D6 R22/66  P(19-7-0)  101
ChiB  D23 R47/299  P(23-16-2)  177
ChiB-Sayers 172R

GB      7  14   0   7   28
Min     3   0   6   7   16
GB    D20 R31/164  P(31-20-0)  140
Min   D18 R40/128  P(27-15-1)  194

LARm    3  10   3   7   23
Bal     0   0   0   7   7
LARm  D17 R42/162  P(23-13-1)  148
Bal   D7 R18/33  P(32-9-2)  107
LARm-Bass 126R, McDonald 106C

Pit     3   0   0   0   3
SL      0   3   0   3   6
Pit   D8 R20/32  P(25-10-2)  46
SL    D15 R47/199  P(17-4-0)  29

NYG     0  14  14  13   41
Was    13  21  14  24   72
NYG   D25 R36/111  P(33-20-5)  278
Was   D16 R24/209  P(18-10-1)  132
Was-Taylor 124C

SUNDAY, DECEMBER 4
Atl     0  20   0   0   20
Min     3   3   0  13   19
Atl   D10 R34/73  P(22-11-0)  114
Min   D16 R33/109  P(33-12-5)  161
```

```
ChiB  0   7   3   6   16
Bal   7   7   0   7   21
ChiB  D18 R27/51  P(39-23-2) 245
Bal   D16 R31/112 P(21-13-1) 148

SL    10  0   0   7   17
Dal   7   14  0   10  31
SL    D21 R29/94  P(43-21-2) 201
Dal   D11 R30/108 P(21-7-0) 82

NYG   14  17  6   3   40
Cle   7   7   14  21  49
NYG   D23 R50/212 P(20-10-0) 123
Cle   D21 R18/130 P(27-16-3) 317
Cle-Kelly 126R, Collins 120C,
Ryan 326P

Det   3   0   0   0   3
LARm  7   3   3   10  23
Det   D16 R26/93  P(46-23-3) 212
LARm  D14 R31/146 P(28-20-0) 147
LARm-Bass 107R

SF    0   0   0   7   7
GB    7   0   0   13  20
SF    D17 R32/140 P(33-14-2) 181
GB    D20 R36/107 P(24-13-0) 204
SF-Parks 138C; GB-Dale 142C

Pit   0   13  3   7   23
Phi   3   10  7   7   27
Pit   D15 R25/95  P(25-11-0) 155
Phi   D19 R44/180 P(25-13-0) 124
Phi-Concannon 129R
```

SATURDAY, DECEMBER 10
```
GB    7   0   0   7   14
Bal   0   10  0   0   10
GB    D14 R30/97  P(23-12-0) 145
Bal   D15 R43/153 P(25-11-4) 130
```

SUNDAY, DECEMBER 11
```
ChiB  7   0   0   7   14
SF    10  21  0   10  41
ChiB  D9 R17/65  P(29-10-3) 64
SF    D25 R35/149 P(39-22-1) 262
SF-Parks 103C

Cle   0   7   7   7   21
Phi   6   21  0   6   33
Cle   D21 R24/118 P(40-17-3) 231
Phi   D17 R44/203 P(23-7-4) 117

Min   7   14  7   0   28
Det   0   6   3   7   16
Min   D19 R37/111 P(20-12-2) 206
Det   D16 R28/132 P(32-18-2) 150

SL    0   3   0   7   10
Atl   7   6   0   3   16
SL    D16 R30/101 P(37-20-2) 195
Atl   D11 R30/87  P(32-8-1) 105

Was   0   10  7   17  34
Dal   7   10  14  0   31
Was   D13 R22/104 P(33-18-1) 295
Dal   D17 R36/241 P(23-11-0) 129
Was-Lowe 126R, Alworth 127C,
Taylor 145C, Jurgensen 308P;
Dal-Reeves 108R

Pit   5   14  21  7   47
NYG   0   14  7   7   28
Pit   D20 R33/95  P(35-18-1) 297
NYG   D15 R25/119 P(27-14-0) 191
Pit-Nelsen 322P; NYG-Jones 111C,
Kennedy 229P
```

SATURDAY, DECEMBER 17
```
Cle   0   10  14  14  38
SL    0   0   0   10  10
Cle   D20 R25/84  P(32-17-1) 344
SL    D12 R29/128 P(29-13-1) 99
Cle-Collins 126C, Warfield 161C,
Ryan 367P; SL-Gambrell 111C
```

SUNDAY, DECEMBER 18
```
Min   14  0   14  0   28
ChiB  14  17  3   7   41
Min   D29 R45/215 P(36-17-2) 245
ChiB  D14 R36/267 P(12-3-0) 113
Min-Osborn 118R;
ChiB-Sayers 197R
```

```
Bal   0   13  7   10  30
SF    0   7   0   7   14
Bal   D21 R31/84  P(30-20-1) 319
SF    D19 R25/126 P(40-19-1) 179
Bal-Orr 108C, Unitas 339P;
SF-Parks 117C

Phi   7   3   7   20  37
Was   7   7   7   7   28
Phi   D20 R40/140 P(28-18-2) 170
Was   D17 R17/107 P(39-20-2) 248
Phi-Woodeshick 105R;
Was-Smith 137C, Jurgensen 249P

Pit   6   23  21  7   57
Atl   0   7   14  12  33
Pit   D27 R36/126 P(31-19-0) 332
Atl   D18 R24/79  P(33-15-3) 291
Pit-Jefferson 142C, Nelsen 334P;
Atl-Hawkins 104C

Dal   7   0   0   10  17
NYG   0   0   0   7   7
Dal   D11 R26/102 P(24-15-1) 155
NYG   D19 R36/107 P(33-15-2) 155
NYG-Morrison 131C

GB    7   10  0   10  27
LARm  3   6   0   14  23
GB    D14 R35/118 P(23-13-1) 237
LARm  D19 R26/100 P(38-23-1) 251
GB-Dale 121C
```

1967 AFL

SUNDAY, SEPTEMBER 3
```
Bos   7   0   14  0   21
Den   7   3   6   10  26
Bos   D20 R21/90  P(30-16-6) 212
Den   D11 R40/92  P(19-8-0) 117
Den-Denson 131C
```

SATURDAY, SEPTEMBER 9
```
KC    0   17  8   0   25
Hou   0   14  0   6   20
KC    D20 R35/141 P(19-17-1) 171
Hou   D17 R33/178 P(25-16-2) 158
Hou-Granger 101R

Bos   7   7   0   0   14
SD    7   7   0   14  28
Bos   D17 R36/128 P(35-19-2) 194
SD    D14 R28/62  P(30-16-1) 268
Bos-Graham 116C; SD-Frazier 105C
```

SUNDAY, SEPTEMBER 10
```
NYJ   0   14  3   0   17
Buf   0   0   0   20  20
NYJ   D14 R36/152 P(23-11-0) 135
Buf   D15 R22/89  P(34-18-2) 159
NYJ-Maynard 106C

Den   0   0   0   0   0
Oak   7   13  14  17  51
Den   D3 R24/48  P(16-2-1) -53
Oak   D19 R43/208 P(21-11-1) 180
```

SUNDAY, SEPTEMBER 17
```
Den   0   0   14  7   21
Mia   7   7   7   14  35
Den   D13 R31/97  P(20-6-2) 29
Mia   D19 R33/202 P(21-14-2) 233
Mia-Haynes 151R, Auer 113C

Bos   7   0   0   0   7
Oak   7   14  14  0   35
Bos   D15 R18/65  P(38-20-3) 191
Oak   D13 R31/132 P(27-17-0) 235
Oak-Cannon 114C

Hou   0   10  0   10  20
Buf   3   0   0   0   3
Hou   D9 R37/113 P(18-8-2) 26
Buf   D9 R19/43  P(31-14-2) 150
```

SUNDAY, SEPTEMBER 24
```
NYJ   7   14  3   14  38
Den   10  14  0   0   24
NYJ   D27 R29/79  P(37-22-2) 399
Den   D15 R24/117 P(30-14-1) 242
NYJ-Lammons 141C,
Maynard 141C, Namath 399P;
Den-Denson 134C
```

```
Hou   0   3   0   0   3
SD    3   3   0   7   13
Hou   D13 R32/76  P(30-12-0) 90
SD    D17 R31/119 P(40-20-1) 206
SD-Alworth 121C

Bos   6   7   0   10  23
Buf   0   0   0   0   0
Bos   D13 R42/183 P(24-9-0) 82
Buf   D11 R21/42  P(33-13-5) 199
Bos-Nance 185R

KC    0   14  0   10  24
Mia   0   0   0   0   0
KC    D20 R43/252 P(16-7-0) 97
Mia   D8 R18/23  P(32-15-3) 101
KC-Garrett 131R
```

SUNDAY, OCTOBER 1
```
KC    0   7   0   14  21
Oak   0   10  3   10  23
KC    D12 R28/93  P(26-13-1) 150
Oak   D16 R29/100 P(38-23-1) 206

Den   3   3   0   0   6
Hou   3   0   7   0   10
Den   D15 R43/189 P(22-6-3) 49
Hou   D14 R32/166 P(19-8-1) 76
Hou-Granger 138R

SD    7   14  13  3   37
Buf   3   0   7   7   17
SD    D26 R43/202 P(32-18-0) 282
Buf   D12 R13/54  P(31-10-2) 193
SD-Post 121R, Frazier 106C

Mia   0   7   0   0   7
NYJ   0   16  13  0   29
Mia   D13 R23/114 P(29-12-3) 94
NYJ   D22 R22/57  P(43-25-1) 427
NYJ-Boozer 109C, Maynard 121C,
Sauer 120C, Namath 415P
```

SATURDAY, OCTOBER 7
```
Oak   0   0   7   7   14
NYJ   7   10  3   7   27
Oak   D10 R22/55  P(38-16-4) 155
NYJ   D15 R37/151 P(28-9-2) 146
```

SUNDAY, OCTOBER 8
```
Bos   7   14  10  0   31
SD    7   10  0   14  31
Bos   D21 R34/123 P(34-17-1) 264
SD    D17 R26/61  P(31-17-0) 224
Bos-Nance 127R

Buf   0   3   0   14  17
Den   0   2   7   7   16
Buf   D21 R24/87  P(39-15-3) 210
Den   D13 R39/83  P(19-11-0) 107

Mia   0   0   0   0   0
KC    10  17  7   7   41
Mia   D17 R19/93  P(44-20-5) 113
KC    D15 R29/115 P(23-13-0) 220
Mia-Clancy 102C; KC-Dawson 250P
```

SUNDAY, OCTOBER 15
```
Hou   0   7   21  0   28
NYJ   7   10  3   8   28
Hou   D8 R28/80  P(28-9-3) 51
NYJ   D25 R24/72  P(49-27-6) 295
NYJ-Maynard 157C

KC    7   7   3   14  31
SD    14  10  14  7   45
KC    D20 R27/121 P(37-24-3) 324
SD    D24 R36/145 P(42-25-4) 307
KC-Taylor 134C, Dawson 364P;
SD-Post 116R, Garrison 108C,
Hadl 307P

Mia   3   0   7   0   10
Bos   7   20  7   7   41
Mia   D11 R18/39  P(46-19-2) 184
Bos   D20 R29/178 P(21-16-3) 272
Bos-Nance 113R, Whalen 134C,
Parilli 281P

Oak   0   17  0   7   24
Buf   7   0   7   6   20
Oak   D13 R30/144 P(23-9-4) 79
Buf   D10 R16/38  P(33-13-2) 120
```

SUNDAY, OCTOBER 22
```
SD    7   7   14  10  38
Den   7   0   7   7   21
SD    D22 R34/155 P(36-15-2) 335
Den   D11 R23/49  P(36-15-0) 206
SD-Alworth 142C, Hadl 345P;
Den-Crabtree 123C

Oak   14  6   7   21  48
Bos   0   0   7   7   14
Oak   D23 R37/134 P(41-17-0) 261
Bos   D11 R21/43  P(37-10-0) 40
Oak-Biletnikoff 109C,
Lamonica 240P

NYJ   17  7   6   3   33
Mia   0   0   7   7   14
NYJ   D20 R32/133 P(21-15-0) 202
Mia   D17 R22/78  P(38-21-2) 168
NYJ-Sauer 139C

Hou   10  14  0   0   24
KC    0   3   0   16  19
Hou   D7 R23/84  P(14-3-0) 43
KC    D19 R40/157 P(31-17-3) 166
```

SUNDAY, OCTOBER 29
```
Buf   3   0   0   0   3
Hou   0   3   7   0   10
Buf   D14 R39/115 P(23-10-2) 100
Hou   D10 R31/120 P(14-6-3) 61

Den   0   0   0   0   0
KC    14  28  0   10  52
Den   D10 R21/53  P(34-14-3) 215
KC    D22 R40/176 P(27-14-1) 268
Den-Denson 107C; KC-Garrett 101R

Bos   10  10  3   0   23
NYJ   0   14  9   7   30
Bos   D11 R21/72  P(36-13-2) 98
NYJ   D20 R27/81  P(43-22-2) 328
NYJ-Maynard 132C, Namath 362P

SD    0   10  0   0   10
Oak   9   7   14  21  51
SD    D16 R22/54  P(45-19-4) 287
Oak   D18 R33/127 P(35-14-2) 310
SD-Alworth 213C, Hadl 318P;
Oak-Daniels 101C, Lamonica 316P
```

SUNDAY, NOVEMBER 5
```
Hou   0   0   0   7   7
Bos   3   3   5   7   18
Hou   D11 R19/72  P(28-12-1) 128
Bos   D19 R49/208 P(23-12-0) 137
Hou-Campbell 101R;
Bos-Nance 108R

Oak   3   15  3   0   21
Den   0   0   7   10  17
Oak   D15 R35/132 P(40-16-1) 195
Den   D7 R25/67  P(21-7-1) 52

Mia   0   0   6   0   6
Buf   14  7   7   7   35
Mia   D16 R20/47  P(37-16-1) 80
Buf   D18 R37/182 P(19-9-2) 128

NYJ   0   0   9   9   18
KC    10  3   22  7   42
NYJ   D22 R14/66  P(52-28-3) 274
KC    D24 R29/214 P(31-17-1) 178
NYJ-Mathis 135C; KC-Garrett 192R
```

SUNDAY, NOVEMBER 12
```
Buf   0   0   0   10  10
NYJ   10  0   3   7   20
Buf   D16 R32/121 P(30-10-2) 136
NYJ   D15 R24/67  P(35-23-2) 293
NYJ-Maynard 103C, Sauer 170C,
Namath 338P

Mia   0   0   0   0   0
SD    0   7   0   17  24
Mia   D13 R26/121 P(39-13-0) 122
SD    D17 R30/103 P(29-15-4) 229
SD-Alworth 125C

Hou   10  0   3   7   20
Den   0   0   0   18  18
Hou   D26 R43/253 P(39-14-1) 133
Den   D14 R24/78  P(39-14-0) 144
Hou-Granger 142R

KC    7   23  0   3   33
Bos   3   7   0   0   10
KC    D20 R35/111 P(26-19-1) 186
Bos   D12 R18/92  P(36-15-2) 226
```

SUNDAY, NOVEMBER 19
```
Den   7   14  0   0   21
Buf   0   7   13  0   20
Den   D13 R21/40  P(33-14-2) 154
Buf   D21 R32/138 P(37-19-1) 229
Den-Denson 102C; Buf-Costa 138C

Mia   3   7   0   7   17
Oak   0   7   17  7   31
Mia   D12 R23/81  P(29-17-2) 199
Oak   D22 R33/146 P(33-21-2) 250
Mia-Clancy 114C

SD    7   3   0   7   17
KC    6   3   7   0   16
SD    D20 R31/188 P(23-11-1) 139
KC    D16 R30/75  P(31-18-0) 222
SD-Post 108R

NYJ   3   13  7   6   29
Bos   0   3   0   21  24
NYJ   D16 R34/105 P(23-15-1) 285
Bos   D16 R29/96  P(28-12-2) 180
NYJ-Maynard 164C
```

THURSDAY, NOVEMBER 23
```
Oak   17  6   7   14  44
KC    10  0   7   10  27
Oak   D26 R32/156 P(41-23-2) 303
KC    D13 R18/56  P(40-15-4) 136
Oak-Biletnikoff 158C

Den   7   10  3   0   20
SD    0   7   3   14  24
Den   D21 R35/112 P(41-18-2) 246
SD    D14 R28/112 P(28-14-1) 204
Den-Crabtree 107C;
SD-Garrison 119C
```

SUNDAY, NOVEMBER 26
```
Bos   3   0   3   0   6
Hou   0   7   3   17  27
Bos   D14 R24/109 P(36-13-2) 123
Hou   D16 R34/178 P(23-9-2) 72
Bos-Nance 109R;
Hou-Granger 124R

Buf   0   14  0   0   14
Mia   7   3   0   7   17
Buf   D19 R30/106 P(31-17-4) 245
Mia   D18 R24/116 P(33-17-3) 202
```

SUNDAY, DECEMBER 3
```
Mia   0   0   7   7   14
Hou   7   3   0   7   17
Mia   D9 R16/34  P(30-15-0) 182
Hou   D26 R49/279 P(31-17-2) 175
Mia-Clancy 126C;
Hou-Campbell 141R, Granger 111R

Oak   17  14  7   3   41
SD    7   14  0   0   21
Oak   D21 R34/135 P(35-22-0) 325
SD    D19 R28/115 P(40-18-3) 303
Oak-Lamonica 349P; SD-Hadl 315P

Buf   7   6   0   0   13
KC    6   0   7   10  23
Buf   D8 R16/31  P(37-16-3) 211
KC    D18 R38/129 P(30-15-1) 128

Den   0   26  7   0   33
NYJ   0   0   10  14  24
Den   D9 R45/124 P(16-7-0) 18
NYJ   D23 R11/40  P(62-25-5) 305
NYJ-Lammons 106C
```

SATURDAY, DECEMBER 9
```
Buf   14  14  10  6   44
Bos   0   0   2   7   9
Buf   D17 R39/133 P(23-10-2) 119
Bos   D9 R20/53  P(29-7-6) 97
```

SUNDAY, DECEMBER 10
```
Oak   0   0   3   16  19
Hou   0   0   0   7   7
Oak   D23 R36/167 P(35-23-1) 254
Hou   D14 R30/118 P(27-10-2) 120

KC    0   0   14  7   21
NYJ   0   0   0   7   7
KC    D13 R31/124 P(22-13-2) 80
NYJ   D17 R28/83  P(25-14-2) 84
```

SD   3   7 14   0 24
Mia   0 13 14 14 **41**
SD   D15 R29/87 P(23-10-5) 182
Mia D24 R36/161 P(30-16-0) 164

SATURDAY, DECEMBER 16
SD   0   7   0 10 17
Hou   3   7   7   7 **24**
SD   D19 R24/98 P(41-23-0) 198
Hou D21 R42/158 P(24-14-1) 176
Hou-Granger 107R

SUNDAY, DECEMBER 17
NYJ   7   7   0 15 29
Oak   3   7 14 14 **38**
NYJ D23 R31/108 P(46-27-3) 356
Oak D17 R31/119 P(32-16-2) 336
NYJ-Maynard 159C, Sauer 146C,
Namath 370P; Oak-Biletnikoff 110C,
Lamonica 336P

Bos 14   3   9   6 32
Mia   7 28   3   3 **41**
Bos D27 R29/163 P(27-12-3) 307
Mia D19 R28/108 P(30-17-0) 251
Bos-Nance 164R, Colclough 112C,
Whalen 122C

KC   14 14   7   3 **38**
Den   0   7 10   7 24
KC   D19 R39/254 P(23-11-1) 146
Den D17 R25/116 P(28-14-3) 156
KC-Garrett 169R; Den-Crabtree 129C

SATURDAY, DECEMBER 23
Hou   7   7 17 10 **41**
Mia   0   3   0   7 10
Hou D15 R43/247 P(12-5-0) 72
Mia D16 R20/106 P(42-17-5) 243
Hou-Granger 160R

SUNDAY, DECEMBER 24
NYJ 14 14 14   0 **42**
SD   7 17   0   7 31
NYJ D23 R40/113 P(26-18-0) 316
SD   D19 R27/230 P(32-17-1) 246
NYJ-Maynard 141C, Sauer 118C,
Namath 343P; SD-Hubbert 189R,
Garrison 115C

Buf 10   0   3   8 21
Oak   7   7   7   7 **28**
Buf D12 R31/92 P(33-9-2) 118
Oak D14 R32/173 P(25-8-3) 99
Buf-Costa 163C

1967 NFL
SUNDAY, SEPTEMBER 17
Dal   7   7   7   0 **21**
Cle   0   0   7   7 14
Dal D19 R43/181 P(23-14-1) 189
Cle D12 R17/11 P(37-17-3) 210
Dal-Reeves 114R, Hayes 125C

Det 10   7   0   0 17
GB   0   7   0 10 17
Det D10 R39/192 P(17-7-0) 41
GB   D13 R20/43 P(23-14-4) 263
GB-Dale 109C, Starr 321P

Atl   0 10   0 14 31
Bal 10 21   0   7 **38**
Atl D13 R27/104 P(30-18-4) 199
Bal D20 R31/89 P(33-23-1) 419
Bal-Mackey 126C, Unitas 401P

Was 10   7   7   0 24
Phi 14   7   7   7 **35**
Was D21 R21/84 P(46-25-0) 304
Phi D18 R27/150 P(27-18-0) 276
Was-Taylor 144C, Jurgensen 324P;
Phi-Ballman 105C, Hawkins 100C,
Snead 301P

ChiB 13   0   0   0 13
Pit   10   7 17   7 **41**
ChiB D6 R18/16 P(16-8-2) 79
Pit   D23 R42/195 P(25-15-1) 198
Pit-Asbury 107R

NYG   0   0 14 16 **37**
SL   7   3   7   0 17
NYG D15 R35/104 P(20-7-0) 232
SL   D20 R37/205 P(30-10-4) 153
NYG-Jones 175C; SL-Roland 124R

LARm 3 10   7   7 **27**
NO   0   7   3   0 13
LARm D23 R34/170 P(37-17-0) 292
NO   D17 R22/125 P(40-19-2) 174
LARm-Casey 107C, Gabriel 302P

SF   7 17   3   0 **27**
Min   0   0   0 21 21
SF   D20 R42/240 P(26-11-1) 120
Min D19 R27/148 P(36-18-2) 187

FRIDAY, SEPTEMBER 22
Min   0   0   0   3   3
LARm 6 19   7   7 **39**
Min D13 R21/48 P(34-13-4) 176
LARm D16 R36/116 P(29-9-1) 121

SUNDAY, SEPTEMBER 24
SL   13   6   0   9 **28**
Pit   0   7   0   7 14
SL   D12 R37/146 P(26-8-1) 137
Pit D17 R28/94 P(30-11-3) 143

NYG 10   0   7   7 24
Dal   7 14   7 10 **38**
NYG D15 R12/76 P(35-18-3) 190
Dal D23 R42/178 P(29-16-0) 236
Dal-Hayes 118C, Meredith 243P

Cle   7   0   0   7 14
Det   3   7   7 14 **31**
Cle D15 R25/191 P(19-9-2) 78
Det D29 R51/238 P(27-16-0) 223
Cle-Kelly 141R; Det-Watkins 115R

ChiB 0   0   3   7 10
GB   0 10   0   3 **13**
ChiB D6 R30/140 P(12-5-1) 19
GB   D24 R51/233 P(20-11-5) 132
GB-Grabowski 111R

Bal   0 14 14 10 **38**
Phi   0   6   0   0   6
Bal D21 R28/72 P(35-22-0) 273
Phi D16 R17/58 P(38-22-4) 241
Bal-Richardson 184C

Atl   0   7   0   0   7
SF   14   7 10   7 **38**
Atl D10 R19/64 P(21-10-1) 33
SF   D25 R34/180 P(37-22-2) 337

Was   6 14   0 10 **30**
NO   3   7   0   0 10
Was D17 R31/158 P(20-13-1) 211
NO   D13 R22/81 P(38-19-0) 209

SUNDAY, OCTOBER 1
Cle   7 14   7 14 **42**
NO   0   0   0   7   7
Cle D23 R45/198 P(26-13-3) 223
NO   D17 R21/68 P(40-19-4) 198
Cle-Kelly 110R, Warfield 107C

ChiB 7   0 10   0 **17**
Min   0   0   0   7   7
ChiB D17 R49/194 P(11-7-0) 27
Min D12 R27/63 P(21-10-1) 137

Atl   0   0   0   0   0
GB   0   7   9   7 **23**
Atl D8 R19/39   P(23-12-2) 19
GB   D23 R38/177 P(34-17-2) 205
GB-Dowler 105C

Det 14   7   0   7 28
SL   0 17 14   7 **38**
Det D20 R26/116 P(26-17-1) 194
SL   D21 R35/90 P(27-19-1) 313
Det-Studstill 107C;
SL-Gambrell 117C, Hart 313P

SF   0   0   7   0   7
Bal 10 17   7   7 **41**
SF   D15 R21/69 P(32-16-2) 171
Bal D26 R34/142 P(40-24-0) 382
Bal-Perkins 110C, Unitas 353P

Pit   7   7   3   7 24
Phi   0   7 10 14 **34**
Pit D19 R30/153 P(27-13-3) 165
Phi D17 R29/48 P(25-17-0) 271
Phi-Hawkins 187C, Snead 258P

LARm 0   7 14 14 **35**
Dal   0   6   0   7 13
LARm D25 R37/221 P(27-14-1) 135
Dal D20 R24/51 P(41-21-3) 221
Dal-Rentzel 102C

NYG 10   3   7 14 34
Was   3 14   7 14 **38**
NYG D20 R26/226 P(30-19-0) 294
Was D23 R29/129 P(36-22-1) 276
NYG-Koy 160R, Jones 196C;
Was-Mitchell 110R, Taylor 106C

SATURDAY, OCTOBER 7
Pit   3   0   7   0 10
Cle   0   7 14   0 **21**
Pit D20 R25/70 P(35-23-3) 208
Cle D24 R38/178 P(25-11-3) 183
Pit-Compton 108C; Cle-Green 108R

SUNDAY, OCTOBER 8
GB   0   7   3 17 **27**
Det   3   7   0   7 59
GB   D16 R45/118 P(19-12-2) 131
Det D7 R18/63   P(25-10-3) 59

SL   13   7   3 21 **34**
Min   7 10   0   7 24
SL   D18 R34/165 P(27-14-2) 247
Min D16 R31/101 P(22-12-2) 236
SL-Roland 122R; Min-Brown 109C

Bal   0   3   7 14 **24**
ChiB 3   0   0   0   3
Bal D15 R18/70 P(37-19-3) 149
ChiB D15 R36/71 P(31-18-4) 201

SF   3 17   0   7 **27**
LARm 0   0 21   3 24
SF   D14 R30/66 P(35-18-3) 269
LARm D16 R32/125 P(22-13-3) 128

Dal   0   3   0 14 **17**
Was   0   7   0   7 14
Dal D18 R36/115 P(31-17-2) 205
Was D14 R19/16 P(33-20-1) 237
Dal-Rentzel 104C

NO   7   7   0   7 21
NYG   7   7   6   7 **27**
NO   D16 R17/72 P(28-14-1) 138
NYG D28 R45/187 P(28-14-3) 348
NYG-Thomas 123C, Tarkenton 348P

Phi 24   0   7   7 **38**
Atl   0   0   0   7   7
Phi D18 R36/201 P(21-10-0) 179
Atl D17 R21/85 P(41-21-4) 223
Phi-Woodeshick 129R

SUNDAY, OCTOBER 15
Det   0   0   0   3   3
ChiB 0   7   0   7 **14**
Det D9 R20/42   P(32-13-2) 126
ChiB D14 R55/237 P(4-3-1) 28
ChiB-Sayers 142R

Min   0   0   0 10 **10**
GB   0   7   0   0   7
Min D10 R45/158 P(11-2-2) 25
GB   D10 R26/42 P(25-15-3) 226

LARm 0   7   7   7 24
Bal   3   7   7   7 **24**
LARm D19 R31/128 P(31-19-1) 282
Bal D20 R24/98 P(34-21-1) 270
LARm-Snow 151C

NO   0   0   3   0 10
Dal   7   7   0   0 **14**
NO   D12 R19/42 P(40-20-1) 165
Dal D18 R35/125 P(30-11-2) 109

NYG   7   7   0 13 **27**
Pit   7 10   7   0 24
NYG D18 R32/76 P(30-19-1) 305
Pit D16 R28/62 P(27-13-1) 197
NYG-Morrison 125C

SL   0   6   3   3 16
Cle 10   7   0   3 **20**
SL   D18 R39/132 P(35-15-3) 217
Cle D8 R31/109 P(18-7-1) 114

SF   7 14   0   7 **28**
Phi   3   7 14   3 27
SF   D24 R43/170 P(28-17-0) 216
Phi D15 R12/43 P(30-15-0) 201
Phi-Hawkins 150C

Was   0   7   7   6 20
Atl   0   7   7   6 20
Was D23 R32/81 P(42-29-2) 334
Atl D15 R26/108 P(30-18-0) 215
Was-Mitchell 114C, Jurgensen 326P

SUNDAY, OCTOBER 22
ChiB 0   0   0   0   0
Cle   0   0   7 17 **24**
ChiB D9 R22/20   P(27-15-1) 116
Cle D23 R37/189 P(29-14-0) 158
Cle-Kelly 111R, Collins 106C

Dal   7   7   0 10 **24**
Pit   0   7   0 14 21
Dal D14 R26/88 P(25-17-1) 290
Pit D29 R29/81 P(46-28-1) 298
Dal-Hayes 170C; Pit-Wilburn 142C,
Nix 313P

Phi 14   0   0   0 14
SL   3 17 21   7 **48**
Phi D17 R22/71 P(32-16-2) 248
SL   D22 R35/149 P(32-16-0) 267
Phi-Hawkins 197C, Snead 321P;
SL-Conrad 115C, Smith 116C,
Hart 267P

GB   7   3 10 28 **48**
NYG   0 14   0   7 21
GB   D28 R45/249 P(21-9-0) 148
NYG D20 R30/143 P(28-14-3) 181
GB-Grabowski 123R

Was   7   7   7   7 28
LARm 0 14   7   7 28
Was D17 R17/49 P(41-18-0) 305
LARm D24 R33/189 P(37-21-1) 249
Was-Smith 102C, Taylor 148C,
Jurgensen 334P; LARm-Casey 127C

NO   0   6   0   7 13
SF   3   7   7 10 **27**
NO   D12 R21/72 P(29-14-2) 128
SF   D20 R32/136 P(40-20-0) 182

Bal   0   6   0 14 20
Min   0   3 10   7 20
Bal D22 R35/118 P(34-20-1) 225
Min D19 R33/115 P(25-15-0) 195

Atl   0   3   0   0   3
Det   7   3   0 14 **24**
Atl D12 R32/136 P(26-11-1) 87
Det D15 R35/140 P(22-11-1) 110

SUNDAY, OCTOBER 29
Bal   0   7   0 10 **17**
Was   3   7   0   3 13
Bal D21 R31/115 P(33-19-1) 236
Was D19 R27/96 P(35-25-1) 226

Cle 10   0   7 10 34
NYG   0 21 14   3 **38**
Cle D17 R25/110 P(29-15-1) 259
NYG D22 R34/137 P(30-18-1) 249
Cle-Warfield 126C;
NYG-Thomas 110C

Dal   0   7   7   0 21
Phi   7 14   0   0 **21**
Dal D13 R29/114 P(29-14-3) 192
Phi D23 R35/176 P(33-20-2) 165
Dal-Hayes 131C;
Phi-Woodeshick 101R

Det   7   7 10 21 **45**
SF   0   3   0   0   3
Det D24 R44/229 P(33-17-0) 162
SF   D10 R22/82 P(33-10-5) 91

LARm 7   7   0 14 **28**
ChiB 0   7   3   7 17
LARm D20 R45/165 P(19-8-1) 144
ChiB D11 R28/92 P(29-8-3) 88

Min   0 10   0   3 20
Atl   7   7   0   7 **21**
Min D22 R41/177 P(29-13-2) 137
Atl D12 R25/95 P(17-9-0) 91
Min-Osborn 103R

Pit   0   0   0 14 **14**
NO   3   7   0   0 10
Pit D19 R34/179 P(26-13-4) 88
NO   D19 R27/83 P(35-19-1) 225
Pit-Shy 108R; NO-Abramowicz 156C

MONDAY, OCTOBER 30
GB   7   7   3 14 **31**
SL   3 17   0   3 23
GB   D16 R24/129 P(26-11-2) 117
SL   D19 R37/116 P(29-16-2) 289
SL-Williams 147C, Hart 317P

SUNDAY, NOVEMBER 5
GB   0   3   0   7 10
Bal   0   0 13   0 **13**
GB   D15 R25/126 P(25-16-1) 139
Bal D17 R35/134 P(33-15-1) 103

Atl   0   0   7   0   7
Dal   7   9 14   7 **37**
Atl D13 R14/66 P(35-18-3) 157
Dal D21 R37/171 P(26-10-2) 153
Dal-Perkins 111R, Reeves 114C

LARm 0   7   7   3 **17**
SF   0   7   0   7 14
LARm D9 R33/105 P(14-8-0) 47
SF   D14 R27/99 P(34-17-2) 158

NYG 14   0   3   7 24
Min   7   7   0 13 **27**
NYG D17 R36/165 P(23-12-0) 238
Min D17 R38/189 P(20-11-2) 115
NYG-Jones 149C; Min-Osborn 115R

Cle 14   0   7   3 **34**
Pit   0   7   0   7 14
Cle D21 R40/181 P(26-14-0) 132
Pit D14 R28/72 P(30-14-2) 229

ChiB 14   6   0   7 **27**
Det   0   0   6   0 13
ChiB D9 R36/120 P(18-7-1) 60
Det D12 R27/91 P(34-6-1) 83

Phi   0 10   0 14 24
NO   7   7 10   7 **31**
Phi D20 R26/96 P(36-19-2) 263
NO   D13 R35/112 P(16-9-2) 137

SL   0 10   3 14 **27**
Was   0   0   7   7 21
SL   D22 R47/178 P(33-16-2) 236
Was D9 R21/102 P(18-6-1) 117
SL-Roland 130R, Smith 103C

SUNDAY, NOVEMBER 12
Bal 21 14   7   7 **49**
Atl   0   0   0   7   7
Bal D30 R41/169 P(32-22-1) 426
Atl D9 R29/115 P(16-6-2) 62
Bal-Perkins 134C, Unitas 370P

Cle   7   0   0   0   7
GB   35 10   3   7 **55**
Cle D11 R21/162 P(22-7-4) 66
GB   D28 R45/235 P(24-15-1) 221
GB-Wilson 100R, Anderson 103C

Dal   7   7 10   3 **27**
NO   7   0   3   0 10
Dal D18 R40/202 P(21-9-1) 178
NO   D14 R18/43 P(37-18-2) 168

Det   0   0 10   0 **10**
Min   0 10   0   0 10
Det D17 R43/277 P(19-10-1) 89
Min D7 R30/137 P(15-6-0) 40
Det-Farr 197R

Pit   0   7   0   7 14
SL   0   0   7   0 14
Pit D21 R35/82 P(32-17-1) 192
SL   D19 R28/113 P(29-15-3) 145

SF   7   7   7   7 28
Was   0   3 14 14 **31**
SF   D24 R34/124 P(38-20-1) 170
Was D30 R27/132 P(42-23-1) 288
Was-Mitchell 103C, Smith 101C

NYG   7   0   0   0   7
ChiB 0 20   7   7 **34**
NYG D14 R30/83 P(26-9-3) 78
ChiB D16 R34/147 P(24-13-0) 117

Phi   0   7   0   7 17
LARm 3 20   3   7 **33**
Phi D11 R16/42 P(35-19-3) 215
LARm D23 R42/161 P(37-15-2) 233

SUNDAY, NOVEMBER 19
Det   0   0   0   7   7
Bal   7 13   7 14 **41**
Det D16 R33/170 P(23-9-3) 91
Bal D29 R43/190 P(24-13-1) 161
Bal-Matte 110R

LARm 0   7   0 24 **31**
Atl   0   3   0   0   3
LARm D15 R29/121 P(28-17-2) 284
Atl D13 R33/98 P(28-12-4) 140

```
Min    7   3   0   0   10
Cle    0   0   7   7   14
Min  D12 R32/99  P(25-11-1) 105
Cle  D18 R41/210 P(21-11-0)  25
Cle-Kelly 123R

SF     0   0   0   0    0
GB     3   7   3   0   13
SF   D16 R26/140 P(49-20-2) 168
GB   D13 R36/168 P(26-13-1) 129

NO     0   0  14   7   21
Phi    3  28  10   7   48
NO   D15 R22/72  P(33-16-2) 237
Phi  D21 R26/90  P(34-21-2) 331
NO-Roberts 109C; Phi-Snead 309P

SL     3   0   0   0    3
ChiB   7  20   3   0   30
SL   D15 R20/76  P(42-14-7) 154
ChiB D13 R30/111 P(25-11-2) 320
ChiB-Gordon 179C,
Concannon 336P

Pit    6   7   0   7   20
NYG    0  14  14   0   28
Pit  D18 R21/71  P(42-16-1) 210
NYG  D18 R32/67  P(26-16-3) 171
Pit-Jefferson 129C

Was    0  14   6   7   27
Dal    0   6   0  14   20
Was  D16 R25/49  P(33-23-1) 265
Dal  D27 R28/104 P(45-26-4) 342
Was-Post 108R, Jurgensen 265P;
Dal-Hayes 135C, Rentzel 223C
```

THURSDAY, NOVEMBER 23

```
SL    14   0   7   0   21
Dal   14   9  14   9   46
SL   D15 R34/95  P(27-13-3) 222
Dal  D18 R36/136 P(24-13-1) 300
SL 1-Smith 116C; al 1-Hayes 110C,
Rentzel 145C

LARm   0  14   0  17   31
Det    7   0   0   0    7
LARm D15 R36/92  P(21-9-1)  171
Det  D10 R35/70  P(25-10-2)  38
```

SUNDAY, NOVEMBER 26

```
Atl    0  21   0   3   24
NO     3   7   7  10   27
Atl  D21 R37/183 P(20-9-0)   86
NO   D24 R31/141 P(36-18-0) 230

Bal    0   3  17   6   26
SF     3   3   0   3    9
Bal  D17 R36/169 P(28-16-1) 174
SF   D8  R21/81  P(25-11-3)  84

GB     7   7   3   0   17
ChiB   7   3   0   3   13
GB   D15 R29/71  P(17-11-0) 174
ChiB D14 R38/193 P(14-7-2)   56
GB-Dowler 105C; ChiB-Sayers 117R

Min    3  14   0  24   41
Pit    7   6   7   7   27
Min  D16 R29/110 P(32-14-3) 102
Pit  D7  R28/65  P(25-6-4)   52

Phi    0   7   0   0    7
NYG   17  17   3   7   44
Phi  D15 R13/38  P(38-17-3) 134
NYG  D26 R36/176 P(34-22-0) 268

Was    0  14   7  13   34
Cle   14  14   7   7   42
Was  D33 R29/108 P(50-32-1) 373
Cle  D19 R34/203 P(17-11-0) 221
Was-Mitchell 106C, Taylor 123C,
Whitfield 102C, Jurgensen 418P;
Cle-Kelly 163R
```

SUNDAY, DECEMBER 3

```
NO     3   3   7   7   20
SL     0   7  10  14   31
NO   D18 R26/92  P(43-17-1) 146
SL   D12 R31/185 P(19-8-3) 125
SL-Roland 106R

NYG    0   0   7   7   14
Cle   10   7   0   7   24
NYG  D26 R29/161 P(43-26-2) 182
Cle  D17 R30/183 P(14-6-0)  32
```

```
Phi    7   7  21   0   35
Was    0  14  14   7   35
Phi  D18 R28/89  P(34-21-3) 276
Was  D28 R22/94  P(50-30-2) 366
Phi-Hawkins 151C, Snead 288P;
Was-Smith 145C, Jurgensen 366P

GB     3  10  14   3   30
Min    3   7  10   7   27
GB   D15 R32/133 P(15-10-1) 143
Min  D15 R38/219 P(17-8-1)  57
GB-Dowler 100C; Min-Osborn 155R

Atl    3   0   0   0    3
LARm   3   7  10   0   20
Atl  D10 R25/79  P(18-7-1)  75
LARm D21 R39/140 P(30-18-1) 169

ChiB   7   7  14   0   28
SF     0   7   0   7   14
ChiB D15 R39/113 P(15-11-1) 107
SF   D9  R22/71  P(32-12-2) 155
ChiB-Gordon 105C

Dal    0  14   3   0   17
Bal    3   7   0  13   23
Dal  D13 R33/134 P(27-10-4)  89
Bal  D16 R25/50  P(39-22-3) 260
Bal-Hawkins 124C

Pit    7  14   0   3   24
Det    0   0   7   7   14
Pit  D19 R39/97  P(29-14-0) 233
Det  D18 R29/87  P(34-16-2) 167
Pit-Wilburn 135C
```

SATURDAY, DECEMBER 9

```
GB     7   3   7   7   24
LARm   0   7  10  10   27
GB   D12 R32/98  P(20-10-2) 120
LARm D20 R34/102 P(36-20-2) 222
```

SUNDAY, DECEMBER 10

```
Phi    0   3   0  14   17
Dal   10   7  14   7   38
Phi  D12 R17/23  P(34-15-3)  79
Dal  D22 R39/167 P(33-16-2) 158

Cle    0   7   6   7   20
SL     0   9   0   7   16
Cle  D8  R29/82  P(15-8-0)  49
SL   D16 R37/121 P(37-18-2) 174

Det    7  14   2   7   30
NYG    0   0   0   7    7
Det  D16 R36/98  P(17-13-1) 208
NYG  D15 R23/120 P(24-7-1)  29

Min    0   7   0   3   10
ChiB   3   0   7   0   10
Min  D11 R32/105 P(19-8-1) 107
ChiB D16 R36/190 P(25-10-0) 108
ChiB-Sayers 131R

NO     0   0  10   0   10
Bal    7  10   3  10   30
NO   D15 R25/73  P(35-18-3) 195
Bal  D17 R35/125 P(24-10-1) 127

SF    17   7   3   7   34
Atl    0   7  14   7   28
SF   D23 R42/174 P(34-20-1) 294
Atl  D14 R18/54  P(34-14-2) 243
SF-Witcher 186C, Mira 324P

Was    0   9   0   6   15
Pit    3   0   0   7   10
Was  D11 R27/91  P(32-9-3) 155
Pit  D20 R31/54  P(47-19-4) 226
Pit-Wilburn 133C
```

SATURDAY, DECEMBER 16

```
Dal    3   0   0  13   16
SF     7  14   3   0   24
Dal  D17 R29/134 P(33-16-2) 137
SF   D20 R38/132 P(26-14-2) 239
```

SUNDAY, DECEMBER 17

```
Min    0   0   3   0    3
Det    0  14   0   0   14
Min  D10 R30/142 P(30-9-3)  48
Det  D12 R37/94  P(17-5-2)  40

NO     0   7   9  14   30
Was    0   0   7   7   14
NO   D15 R28/116 P(28-17-2) 248
Was  D19 R18/58  P(49-26-2) 273
NO-Abramowicz 144C
```

```
Bal    7   0   0   3   10
LARm   3  14   3  14   34
Bal  D18 R27/104 P(31-19-2) 158
LARm D16 R29/71  P(22-18-0) 257

SL     0   0   0  14   14
NYG    7   7  16   7   37
SL   D19 R21/68  P(38-22-2) 262
NYG  D20 R36/143 P(29-16-2) 275
SL-Smith 152C; NYG-Jones 125C,
Tarkenton 275P

ChiB   7  10   3   3   23
Atl    7   0   0   7   14
ChiB D14 R38/178 P(17-8-0) 115
Atl  D13 R19/77  P(31-14-1)  80
ChiB-Sayers 120R

Pit    7  10   7   0   24
GB     0  10   0   7   17
Pit  D10 R33/122 P(21-12-1)  72
GB   D15 R26/93  P(36-18-3) 216

Cle    7   3   0  14   24
Phi    0   7   7  14   28
Cle  D22 R31/132 P(39-19-1) 192
Phi  D17 R24/125 P(28-14-0) 215
```

1968 AFL

FRIDAY, SEPTEMBER 6

```
Cin    7   3   3   0   13
SD    10   0  13   6   29
Cin  D13 R30/122 P(26-14-1) 104
SD   D27 R33/229 P(37-20-0) 325
SD-Post 140R, Garrison 101C,
Hadl 325P
```

SUNDAY, SEPTEMBER 8

```
Bos    0   3  10   3   16
Buf    7   0   0   0    7
Bos  D9  R43/150 P(13-5-1)  45
Buf  D11 R30/76  P(25-13-2) 115
```

MONDAY, SEPTEMBER 9

```
KC     3  14   3   6   26
Hou    7   0   0  14   21
KC   D17 R49/204 P(18-10-0)  61
Hou  D19 R16/55  P(48-23-3) 385
```

SATURDAY, SEPTEMBER 14

```
Hou    3  21   0   0   24
Mia    3   0   0   7   10
Hou  D18 R37/164 P(26-13-3) 232
Mia  D12 R32/130 P(28-13-3) 165
Mia-Noonan 104C
```

SUNDAY, SEPTEMBER 15

```
NYJ    7  10   0   3   20
KC     3   0  10   6   19
NYJ  D18 R30/101 P(29-17-1) 296
KC   D11 R28/118 P(20-12-0)  83
NYJ-Maynard 203C, Namath 302P

Oak   21  10   3  14   48
Buf    0   0   6   0    6
Oak  D20 R35/210 P(32-11-0) 201
Buf  D14 R38/210 P(26-5-0)  -19
Oak-Dixon 104R

Den    0   0   3  10   10
Cin    0   0  10  14   24
Den  D15 R25/78  P(33-14-1) 121
Cin  D11 R27/104 P(22-12-0) 185
Den-Denson 115C;
Cin-Trumpy 114C
```

SATURDAY, SEPTEMBER 21

```
Hou    0   7   7   0   14
SD     3   6   0  21   30
Hou  D19 R33/124 P(30-18-3) 161
SD   D20 R29/97  P(29-17-2) 234
SD-Alworth 183C

Oak   14  19   7   7   47
Mia    0  14   0   7   21
Oak  D25 R35/213 P(24-15-0) 329
Mia  D22 R19/37  P(48-26-5) 312
Oak-Wells 106C, Lamonica 344P
```

SUNDAY, SEPTEMBER 22

```
Den    2   0   0   0    2
KC     3   3   7  21   34
Den  D13 R27/51  P(30-17-3) 194
KC   D17 R27/145 P(23-17-0) 196
Den-Crabtree 113C

NYJ   14   6  17  10   47
Bos    3   7   7  14   31
NYJ  D14 R29/79  P(29-14-2) 189
Bos  D15 R28/55  P(37-20-4) 304
Bos-Marsh 140C

Buf    0   7   7   9   23
Cin   10   0  10  14   34
Buf  D17 R24/92  P(36-15-2) 123
Cin  D9  R29/149 P(18-8-1)  52
```

SATURDAY, SEPTEMBER 28

```
KC    24  14   3   7   48
Mia    3   0   0   0    3
KC   D17 R32/163 P(24-15-0) 268
Mia  D12 R20/96  P(36-11-5) 138
KC-Holmes 123R, Taylor 113C
```

SUNDAY, SEPTEMBER 29

```
Bos    7   3   7   3   20
Den    3   7   0   7   17
Bos  D14 R41/69  P(30-11-0) 143
Den  D15 R32/149 P(23-7-2)  85
Bos-Garrison 121C

Oak    0  10   7   7   24
Hou    7   2   0   6   15
Oak  D17 R44/253 P(22-7-1)  52
Hou  D18 R31/151 P(41-17-2) 173
Oak-Dixon 187R; Hou-Reed 122C

SD     0  17   0  14   31
Cin    3   0   7   0   10
SD   D18 R37/101 P(24-11-1) 201
Cin  D14 R25/66  P(29-17-2) 129
SD-Garrison 121C

NYJ    7  14   0  14   35
Buf   10  10   3  14   37
NYJ  D17 R22/170 P(43-19-5) 257
Buf  D19 R39/140 P(19-8-1)  57
NYJ-Snell 124R, Maynard 114C,
Sauer 113C, Namath 280P
```

SATURDAY, OCTOBER 5

```
SD     0   7   6   7   20
NYJ    3   6   7   7   23
SD   D15 R20/28  P(37-17-3) 319
NYJ  D19 R40/82  P(34-16-0) 220
SD-Alworth 137C, Garrison 163C,
Hadl 326P

KC     6   6   3   3   18
Buf    7   0   0   0    7
KC   D20 R49/212 P(18-9-2) 141
Buf  D11 R23/115 P(20-8-2) 136
Buf-Moses 108C
```

SUNDAY, OCTOBER 6

```
Cin    0   7   0   0    7
Den    0   0   3   7   10
Cin  D15 R37/111 P(38-15-0) 136
Den  D11 R23/99  P(34-14-0) 112

Mia    7   7  10   0   24
Hou    0   0   0   7    7
Mia  D18 R53/187 P(12-6-0)  70
Hou  D10 R24/86  P(23-7-4) 126
Mia-Kiick 104R

Bos    7   3   0   0   10
Oak    0   7  21  13   41
Bos  D13 R20/48  P(39-14-2)  98
Oak  D28 R36/197 P(41-19-1) 254
Oak-Biletnikoff 107C
```

SATURDAY, OCTOBER 12

```
Buf    3   3   0   8   14
Mia    0   7   0   7   14
Buf  D12 R28/144 P(27-14-2)  93
Mia  D14 R37/112 P(22-9-2)  59
```

SUNDAY, OCTOBER 13

```
SD    10   0   7   6   23
Oak    0  14   0   0   14
SD   D20 R49/170 P(34-15-1) 214
Oak  D11 R19/45  P(32-13-2) 215
SD-Foster 104R, Alworth 182C
```

```
Den    7   7   7   0   21
NYJ    7   3   0   3   13
Den  D12 R29/48  P(23-10-0) 174
NYJ  D18 R25/129 P(41-20-5) 331
Den-Crabtree 148C;
NYJ-Maynard 140C, Sauer 191C,
Namath 341P

Cin    0   0   3   0    3
KC     0   3   3   7   13
Cin  D7  R28/99  P(19-7-1)  17
KC   D15 R40/136 P(17-11-1) 129

Hou    0  10   3   3   16
Bos    0   0   0   0    0
Hou  D15 R50/161 P(25-10-1) 119
Bos  D12 R17/60  P(39-9-3)   54
```

SUNDAY, OCTOBER 20

```
Den    3   7   7   7   24
SD     3  28  10  14   55
Den  D26 R32/181 P(44-23-3) 295
SD   D20 R32/211 P(24-13-1) 370
Den-Jones 128C; SD-Post 121R,
Alworth 131C, MacKinnon 172C,
Hadl 321P

Buf    3   3   0   0    6
Bos    3   3  17   0   23
Buf  D9  R23/49  P(33-16-4) 154
Bos  D11 R46/203 P(12-4-1)  96

Oak    0   0   3   7   10
KC     7  10   7   0   24
Oak  D10 R19/53  P(27-12-1) 169
KC   D19 R60/294 P(3-2-0)   16
KC-Garrett 109R

Mia   10   0   0  14   24
Cin    0   2  14   6   22
Mia  D21 R38/139 P(29-16-0) 157
Cin  D14 R30/143 P(21-14-1) 184

NYJ    2   8   0  10   20
Hou    0   6   0   8   14
NYJ  D15 R37/94  P(27-12-0) 137
Hou  D16 R22/79  P(31-12-1)  62
```

SUNDAY, OCTOBER 27

```
SD     0  10   3   7   20
KC     7  10   0  10   27
SD   D22 R27/98  P(36-19-4) 297
KC   D15 R40/194 P(13-8-0) 180
SD-Alworth 169C

Bos    0   0   0  14   14
NYJ    7   3  10  28   48
Bos  D8  R17/44  P(28-13-5) 182
NYJ  D16 R48/174 P(20-11-2) 182
Bos-Whalen 113C

Mia    0   0   0  14   14
Den    0   0  14   7   21
Mia  D17 R24/124 P(26-16-2) 216
Den  D20 R43/196 P(22-8-3) 127
Den-Little 126R

Cin    0   7   3   0   10
Oak    7   7  14   3   31
Cin  D8  R28/169 P(19-11-1)  59
Oak  D26 R42/265 P(34-17-1) 174
Cin-Robinson 159R; Oak-Wells 118C

Hou   10   0  10  10   30
Buf    7   0   0   0    7
Hou  D13 R45/133 P(18-9-0) 199
Buf  D8  R23/50  P(32-9-3)  63
Hou-Reed 132C
```

SUNDAY, NOVEMBER 3

```
Mia    7   7   7   7   28
SD     7  10   7  10   34
Mia  D19 R24/114 P(27-20-1) 238
SD   D28 R40/239 P(30-18-2) 240
Mia-Twilley 124C; SD-Post 151R

Den   14   7   7   7   35
Bos    0   7   0   7   14
Den  D18 R47/238 P(19-12-2) 232
Bos  D15 R30/77  P(32-11-4)  98
Den-Little 147R

Buf    7   0   0  14   21
NYJ    3  13   3   6   25
Buf  D10 R24/62  P(29-12-3) 134
NYJ  D11 R36/110 P(28-10-1) 164
```

Hou	10	7	7	3	**27**
Cin	0	3	7	7	17
Hou	D21	R37/159	P(23-14-0)	202	
Cin	D21	R26/179	P(25-20-0)	195	

Cin-Robinson 156R

KC	7	0	7	7	21
Oak	7	24	7	0	**38**
KC	D14	R24/98	P(30-15-2)	229	
Oak	D25	R38/70	P(47-29-2)	469	

KC-Richardson 121C; Oak-Biletnikoff 144C, Wells 125C, Lamonica 352P

SUNDAY, NOVEMBER 10

Hou	7	0	0	0	7
NYJ	13	3	7	3	**26**
Hou	D9	R25/119	P(25-8-3)	47	
NYJ	D16	R40/135	P(20-7-0)	176	

NYJ-Sauer 128C

KC	3	3	0	10	**16**
Cin	0	3	6	0	9
KC	D16	R39/255	P(15-5-1)	49	
Cin	D15	R30/157	P(21-12-2)	126	

KC-Holmes 158R; Cin-Robinson 115R

Mia	0	0	7	14	**21**
Buf	0	17	0	0	17
Mia	D22	R36/149	P(28-13-1)	156	
Buf	D12	R26/133	P(25-12-2)	141	

Mia-Kiick 111R

Oak	12	14	7	10	**43**
Den	7	0	0	0	7
Oak	D22	R41/207	P(28-15-1)	280	
Den	D11	R24/90	P(36-11-3)	85	

Oak-Wells 127C, Blanda 295P

SD	7	10	10	0	**27**
Bos	3	0	0	14	17
SD	D11	R38/144	P(24-6-2)	175	
Bos	D11	R34/121	P(36-12-3)	107	

SUNDAY, NOVEMBER 17

SD	7	14	0	0	**21**
Buf	3	0	3	0	6
SD	D15	R28/76	P(23-11-3)	206	
Buf	D7	R24/90	P(38-16-1)	61	

SD-MacKinnon 103C

NYJ	6	6	7	13	32
Oak	7	7	8	21	**43**
NYJ	D18	R32/68	P(37-19-0)	345	
Oak	D21	R31/146	P(34-21-2)	291	

NYJ-Maynard 228C, Namath 381P; Oak-Biletnikoff 120C, Lamonica 311P

Den	0	3	7	7	17
Hou	7	10	7	14	**38**
Den	D11	R26/102	P(28-11-2)	126	
Hou	D22	R36/157	P(29-17-0)	220	

Cin	0	17	0	21	**38**
Mia	7	0	14	0	21
Cin	D17	R38/179	P(17-9-0)	243	
Mia	D16	R23/122	P(31-16-1)	204	

Cin-Robinson 134R

Bos	10	0	7	0	17
KC	14	10	0	7	**31**
Bos	D15	R29/78	P(48-21-2)	184	
KC	D12	R26/27	P(31-17-3)	312	

KC-Pitts 126C, Dawson 333P

SUNDAY, NOVEMBER 24

NYJ	10	17	3	7	**37**
SD	0	7	0	8	15
NYJ	D22	R40/142	P(32-18-1)	368	
SD	D12	R12/45	P(46-19-4)	190	

NYJ-Maynard 166C, Sauer 124C, Namath 337P; SD-Foster 100C

Buf	0	7	7	18	32
Den	0	21	7	6	**34**
Buf	D14	R26/88	P(38-17-2)	132	
Den	D15	R33/84	P(29-12-2)	302	

Den-Denson 107C, Little 165C, Briscoe 335P

Oak	7	7	6	14	**34**
Cin	0	0	0	0	0
Oak	D33	R46/208	P(34-26-0)	396	
Cin	D7	R25/116	P(14-7-1)	32	

Oak-Smith 118R, Biletnikoff 137C, Wells 133C, Lamonica 368P

Mia	0	13	7	14	**34**
Bos	10	0	0	0	10
Mia	D22	R28/128	P(39-21-0)	263	
Bos	D18	R23/112	P(30-15-2)	225	

THURSDAY, NOVEMBER 28

Buf	0	3	0	7	10
Oak	0	3	10	0	**13**
Buf	D17	R44/199	P(25-10-2)	144	
Oak	D11	R25/75	P(32-12-1)	111	

Hou	0	3	7	0	10
KC	0	7	7	10	**24**
Hou	D12	R31/93	P(31-13-2)	151	
KC	D15	R32/79	P(23-17-1)	242	

Hou-Beirne 103C; KC-Pitts 124C

SUNDAY, DECEMBER 1

Cin	0	0	7	7	14
Bos	2	24	0	7	**33**
Cin	D14	R30/106	P(37-18-1)	106	
Bos	D20	R37/129	P(25-12-1)	142	

Mia	0	10	0	7	17
NYJ	0	14	0	21	**35**
Mia	D21	R31/163	P(33-17-0)	178	
NYJ	D19	R28/113	P(32-18-0)	267	

NYJ-Maynard 160C

SD	21	10	0	16	**47**
Den	3	14	6	0	23
SD	D27	R35/161	P(38-22-1)	335	
Den	D15	R23/110	P(33-15-0)	177	

SD-Smith 106R, Alworth 171C, Hadl 325P

SATURDAY, DECEMBER 7

Buf	6	0	0	0	6
Hou	0	7	7	21	**35**
Buf	D7	R28/79	P(32-13-2)	10	
Hou	D23	R41/188	P(24-11-2)	215	

Hou-Haik 129C

SUNDAY, DECEMBER 8

Bos	0	7	0	0	7
Mia	7	21	0	10	**38**
Bos	D11	R30/161	P(16-6-2)	16	
Mia	D19	R28/162	P(30-17-0)	150	

Bos-Nance 111R

Cin	0	7	7	14	14
NYJ	14	3	3	7	**27**
Cin	D6	R38/107	P(7-3-0)	51	
NYJ	D19	R29/85	P(39-21-1)	286	

NYJ-Maynard 103C

Den	14	6	0	7	27
Oak	7	13	10	3	**33**
Den	D16	R19/63	P(41-15-4)	204	
Oak	D24	R33/159	P(42-22-4)	338	

Den-Denson 131C; Oak-Wells 163C, Lamonica 354P

KC	7	14	14	5	**40**
SD	3	0	0	0	3
KC	D20	R48/183	P(17-9-1)	188	
SD	D17	R19/75	P(37-15-7)	136	

SATURDAY, DECEMBER 14

KC	6	17	7	0	**30**
Den	0	7	0	0	7
KC	D15	R43/119	P(18-9-0)	183	
Den	D19	R28/125	P(32-10-2)	124	

KC-Taylor 119C; Den-Haffner 122C

SUNDAY, DECEMBER 15

Bos	0	7	10	0	17
Hou	7	14	7	17	**45**
Bos	D9	R26/55	P(24-7-3)	71	
Hou	D25	R34/135	P(40-19-1)	255	

Hou-Granger 104R

NYJ	10	7	7	7	**31**
Mia	0	7	0	0	7
NYJ	D19	R31/126	P(25-15-1)	221	
Mia	D12	R24/41	P(34-15-2)	96	

NYJ-Turner 157C

Oak	3	7	14	10	**34**
SD	3	10	6	8	27
Oak	D14	R27/67	P(39-18-2)	249	
SD	D18	R29/91	P(53-22-2)	365	

Oak-Wells 113C; SD-Garrison 128C, Hadl 359P

1968 NFL

SATURDAY, SEPTEMBER 14

Atl	0	0	7	0	7
Min	3	28	3	13	**47**
Atl	D14	R21/81	P(35-16-1)	153	
Min	D21	R41/186	P(23-19-0)	218	

Min-Jones 101R

SUNDAY, SEPTEMBER 15

Det	6	0	7	0	13
Dal	7	24	7	21	**59**
Det	D15	R21/68	P(31-15-4)	189	
Dal	D29	R38/161	P(36-25-0)	381	

Det-McCullouch 132C

Cle	0	10	0	14	**24**
NO	0	10	0	0	10
Cle	D16	R35/153	P(20-10-1)	185	
NO	D14	R28/85	P(31-15-3)	123	

Cle-Kelly 107R

NYG	7	21	0	6	**34**
Pit	13	7	0	0	20
NYG	D21	R46/165	P(22-12-0)	166	
Pit	D20	R25/130	P(32-15-3)	194	

NYG-Jones 101C; Pit-Jefferson 113C

SF	7	3	0	0	10
Bal	7	7	10	3	**27**
SF	D15	R21/83	P(42-23-3)	189	
Bal	D22	R36/161	P(31-16-1)	185	

Was	14	14	7	3	**38**
ChiB	7	14	0	7	28
Was	D18	R29/74	P(21-14-0)	263	
ChiB	D18	R32/165	P(30-17-2)	151	

Was-Allen 121C, Jurgensen 276P; ChiB-Sayers 105R

Phi	3	3	0	7	13
GB	7	14	6	3	**30**
Phi	D15	R19/91	P(35-16-1)	187	
GB	D18	R37/185	P(18-14-1)	193	

GB-Dowler 110C

MONDAY, SEPTEMBER 16

LARm	7	3	14	0	**24**
SL	0	3	3	7	13
LARm	D15	R34/154	P(22-9-0)	84	
SL	D18	R25/75	P(40-17-3)	169	

SUNDAY, SEPTEMBER 22

ChiB	0	0	0	0	0
Det	7	21	7	7	**42**
ChiB	D11	R21/61	P(36-11-8)	106	
Det	D22	R33/173	P(24-16-1)	295	

Bal	14	7	0	7	**28**
Atl	7	3	3	7	20
Bal	D22	R34/125	P(23-16-3)	263	
Atl	D12	R28/86	P(24-11-1)	164	

Bal-Casey 108C, Orr 160C, Gabriel 262P

SL	7	3	0	7	17
SF	7	7	7	14	**35**
SL	D13	R25/105	P(24-11-0)	123	
SF	D22	R45/132	P(29-17-2)	263	

Pit	3	7	0	0	10
LARm	7	24	7	7	**45**
Pit	D16	R24/56	P(36-16-2)	202	
LARm	D20	R28/87	P(32-21-0)	291	

LARm-Casey 108C, Gabriel 262P

NYG	7	10	10	7	**34**
Phi	12	0	7	6	25
NYG	D24	R46/201	P(20-14-1)	176	
Phi	D12	R25/201	P(14-4-2)	125	

Phi-Woodeshick 129R

Was	0	3	7	7	17
NO	14	6	7	10	**37**
Was	D12	R22/81	P(27-14-1)	147	
NO	D17	R32/183	P(25-15-1)	183	

NO-McCall 127R

Min	7	9	10	0	**26**
GB	0	0	6	7	13
Min	D20	R39/124	P(15-9-1)	118	
GB	D18	R27/105	P(22-14-2)	137	

Cle	0	7	0	0	7
Dal	0	14	7	7	**28**
Cle	D12	R26/87	P(19-12-0)	163	
Dal	D24	R44/203	P(17-10-0)	143	

SUNDAY, SEPTEMBER 29

Was	7	7	0	7	21
NYG	3	21	17	7	**48**
Was	D23	R23/99	P(42-27-3)	277	
NYG	D20	R36/151	P(20-11-1)	226	

NYG-Jones 179C

ChiB	14	6	0	7	**27**
Min	0	3	0	14	17
ChiB	D20	R43/278	P(20-14-0)	131	
Min	D17	R26/158	P(25-12-2)	121	

ChiB-Sayers 108R; Min-Brown 109R

Det	0	7	10	6	**23**
GB	10	0	0	7	17
Det	D20	R43/153	P(22-15-1)	190	
GB	D15	R26/105	P(20-9-3)	219	

GB-Dale 205C

Dal	7	7	14	17	**45**
Phi	3	10	0	0	13
Dal	D21	R31/137	P(25-16-1)	281	
Phi	D14	R21/40	P(31-16-5)	223	

Dal-Meredith 231P; Phi-Hawkins 103C

LARm	10	0	0	14	**24**
Cle	0	6	0	0	6
LARm	D22	R42/188	P(34-17-1)	176	
Cle	D6	R20/66	P(16-4-2)	63	

LARm-Bass 134R

Atl	0	10	3	0	13
SF	7	7	7	7	**28**
Atl	D14	R21/71	P(32-14-1)	156	
SF	D24	R46/189	P(20-17-1)	185	

SL	0	0	0	21	**21**
NO	3	7	7	3	20
SL	D14	R26/122	P(32-11-1)	97	
NO	D18	R34/96	P(27-19-1)	227	

Bal	3	21	3	14	**41**
Pit	0	0	0	7	7
Bal	D18	R33/123	P(24-14-1)	153	
Pit	D11	R20/49	P(36-15-3)	164	

SATURDAY, OCTOBER 5

Pit	3	7	7	7	24
Cle	7	10	7	7	**31**
Pit	D19	R27/116	P(27-13-1)	156	
Cle	D24	R38/184	P(25-16-1)	190	

Cle-Kelly 128R

SUNDAY, OCTOBER 6

ChiB	0	7	0	0	7
Bal	0	21	7	0	**28**
ChiB	D7	R25/145	P(18-7-1)	80	
Bal	D22	R36/154	P(28-15-2)	306	

ChiB-Sayers 105R; Bal-Mackey 104C, Orr 104C, Morrall 302P

Dal	10	0	3	14	**27**
SL	0	3	7	0	10
Dal	D22	R40/194	P(20-11-1)	103	
SL	D14	R25/78	P(33-17-2)	173	

GB	7	3	21	7	**38**
Atl	0	7	0	0	7
GB	D26	R37/158	P(36-24-0)	312	
Atl	D7	R26/78	P(19-5-4)	76	

GB-Anderson 101R

Phi	0	0	0	14	14
Was	0	10	7	0	**17**
Phi	D13	R27/83	P(26-13-4)	138	
Was	D17	R33/124	P(29-21-1)	196	

Phi-Hawkins 105C

SF	0	7	3	0	10
LARm	7	7	7	3	**24**
SF	D12	R22/62	P(23-13-1)	96	
LARm	D19	R39/121	P(24-12-1)	154	

SF-McNeil 113C

Det	3	0	0	7	10
Min	0	7	3	14	**24**
Det	D9	R21/79	P(18-13-0)	168	
Min	D18	R38/135	P(22-11-0)	130	

NO	7	7	7	0	21
NYG	7	17	7	7	**38**
NO	D23	R19/95	P(42-24-3)	219	
NYG	D19	R30/95	P(22-11-0)	166	

NO-Abramowicz 101C; NYG-Jones 116C

SUNDAY, OCTOBER 13

Min	0	0	17	0	17
NO	14	0	0	6	**20**
Min	D15	R39/139	P(28-9-2)	51	
NO	D10	R30/121	P(17-9-3)	86	

LARm	0	3	10	3	**16**
GB	0	7	0	7	14
LARm	D11	R38/93	P(20-7-0)	97	
GB	D15	R29/84	P(28-13-3)	113	

Det	7	7	7	7	**28**
ChiB	7	3	0	0	10
Det	D24	R51/244	P(23-13-0)	161	
ChiB	D12	R28/130	P(22-6-0)	111	

Det-Farr 138R

Bal	7	14	0	21	**42**
SF	0	7	0	7	14
Bal	D18	R24/96	P(25-14-1)	182	
SF	D28	R37/156	P(36-19-3)	236	

SF-Witcher 112C

NYG	7	7	0	7	21
Atl	7	7	3	7	**24**
NYG	D23	R33/179	P(24-16-1)	242	
Atl	D17	R37/136	P(15-10-0)	186	

NYG-Jones 108C

SL	3	17	7	0	**27**
Cle	0	7	7	7	21
SL	D20	R39/147	P(24-9-2)	135	
Cle	D15	R17/22	P(40-17-2)	311	

Cle-Morin 151C, Nelsen 324P

Phi	0	0	7	7	14
Dal	7	7	7	13	**34**
Phi	D11	R24/92	P(22-9-4)	72	
Dal	D27	R35/151	P(39-22-0)	263	

Dal-Rentzel 152C, Meredith 306P

Pit	0	10	0	3	13
Was	6	3	7	0	**16**
Pit	D17	R29/183	P(20-9-1)	104	
Was	D19	R39/116	P(29-15-1)	178	

Pit-Hoak 115R

SUNDAY, OCTOBER 20

Cle	7	7	7	9	**30**
Bal	0	7	6	7	20
Cle	D19	R43/179	P(23-15-0)	126	
Bal	D13	R24/81	P(29-11-4)	131	

Cle-Kelly 130R

Was	7	0	7	0	14
SL	3	21	7	10	**41**
Was	D21	R22/56	P(33-22-1)	257	
SL	D24	R39/173	P(22-14-0)	148	

Atl	7	7	0	0	14
LARm	0	17	0	10	**27**
Atl	D7	R22/32	P(16-7-2)	101	
LARm	D24	R35/173	P(38-23-2)	246	

LARm-Truax 111C

ChiB	7	6	3	13	**29**
Phi	3	10	3	0	16
ChiB	D16	R36/171	P(24-10-1)	94	
Phi	D12	R27/89	P(20-12-2)	101	

GB	0	0	7	7	14
Det	14	0	0	0	14
GB	D16	R32/134	P(17-10-0)	79	
Det	D18	R48/212	P(13-9-0)	70	

Det-Farr 145R

NO	3	7	3	3	**16**
Pit	0	6	6	0	12
NO	D16	R34/103	P(25-12-0)	170	
Pit	D16	R39/210	P(20-8-1)	91	

Pit-Hoak 166R

SF	3	13	7	3	**26**
NYG	0	3	0	7	10
SF	D22	R39/214	P(24-15-0)	179	
NYG	D19	R29/156	P(26-13-2)	116	

SF-Lewis 101R

Dal	3	3	7	7	**20**
Min	0	7	0	0	7
Dal	D9	R26/84	P(16-10-1)	93	
Min	D16	R39/130	P(26-16-2)	144	

SUNDAY, OCTOBER 27

NYG	0	3	3	7	**13**
Was	0	3	7	0	10
NYG	D22	R47/173	P(26-14-2)	124	
Was	D9	R18/69	P(25-7-1)	73	

```
NO    7   0   7   3   17
SL    3   0   7  21   31
NO   D16 R32/116  P(31-16-1)  185
SL   D18 R28/166  P(22-9-0)   226
SL-Smith 147C

Min   7   7   0  10   24
ChiB  7   6   7   6   26
Min  D17 R28/97   P(27-16-1)  177
ChiB D20 R33/240  P(29-12-1)  171
Min-Washington 133C;
ChiB-Sayers 143R

LARm  3   0   7   0   10
Bal  13   7   7   0   27
LARm D12 R22/70   P(29-16-2)  78
Bal  D17 R40/159  P(27-11-3)  205

SF    7   0   0   7   14
Det   0   0   0   7    7
SF   D16 R36/116  P(37-22-0)  216
Det  D10 R24/78   P(35-15-1)  141
SF-McNeil 143C

Atl   0   0   0   7    7
Cle   7  13   3   7   30
Atl  D17 R26/147  P(26-15-2)  137
Cle  D24 R33/196  P(27-18-0)  248
Cle-Kelly 112R, Kelly 174R

Phi   0   3   0   0    3
Pit   0   0   0   6    6
Phi  D15 R31/116  P(35-17-1)  171
Pit  D13 R35/123  P(28-9-1)   126
Phi-Hawkins 108C
```

MONDAY, OCTOBER 28
```
GB    0   7  14   7   28
Dal   7   3   0   7   17
GB   D20 R31/105  P(25-17-1)  217
Dal  D20 R34/159  P(33-13-3)  206
GB-Starr 260P
```

SUNDAY, NOVEMBER 3
```
Dal   0  10   0   7   17
NO    0   0   3   0    3
Dal  D22 R30/185  P(36-16-2)  220
NO   D13 R28/59   P(39-15-4)  184
Dal-Hayes 108C

Cle   3  13  10   7   33
SF    7   7   0   7   21
Cle  D22 R38/224  P(33-11-2)  138
SF   D21 R24/70   P(37-23-2)  241

SL    7   7  14  17   45
Phi   0  10   7   0   17
SL   D21 R45/186  P(14-8-0)   176
Phi  D17 R21/112  P(35-19-1)  230
SL-Williams 100C

Was   0   0   0  14   14
Min   3   7   0  17   27
Was  D9  R21/41   P(23-15-1)  92
Min  D15 R36/215  P(20-9-2)   102

Bal   3  13   0  10   26
NYG   0   0   0   0    0
Bal  D20 R41/144  P(26-16-1)  184
NYG  D12 R16/55   P(31-14-3)  160

ChiB  0   3   7   3   13
GB    0   0   7   3   10
ChiB D18 R47/291  P(14-5-2)   37
GB   D12 R26/107  P(18-10-0)  135
ChiB-Sayers 205R

Pit  14   7  13   7   41
Atl   0   7  14   0   21
Pit  D25 R34/114  P(32-22-0)  288
Atl  D16 R25/86   P(26-15-4)  257
Pit-Jefferson 199C

Det   7   0   0   0    7
LARm  3   0   0   7   10
Det  D15 R28/72   P(34-14-2)  144
LARm D9  R31/101  P(25-7-2)   185
LARm-Casey 131C
```

SUNDAY, NOVEMBER 10
```
LARm  0   7   3   7   17
Atl   0   0   3   7   10
LARm D18 R45/179  P(26-11-1)  71
Atl  D9  R25/92   P(21-11-1)  140

NYG   7   7   7   6   27
Dal   0   0   7   0    7
NYG  D13 R28/112  P(24-16-0)  181
Dal  D24 R32/99   P(35-20-3)  250
```

```
Pit  14   7   7   0   28
Bal   7   7   0   7   21
Pit  D17 R32/83   P(30-20-0)  280
SL   D17 R24/88   P(40-17-2)  337
Pit-Wilburn 117C; SL-Conrad 133C,
Smith 105C, Williams 114C,
Hart 353P

SF    0   6  13   0   19
ChiB  7  17   3   0   27
SF   D11 R16/56   P(26-9-4)   199
ChiB D26 R55/215  P(30-16-1)  234

Was   3   6   0   7   16
Phi   0   3   0   7   10
Was  D17 R41/175  P(21-8-1)   92
Phi  D13 R26/69   P(33-18-2)  207
Phi-Hill 114C

Bal   7   3  10   7   27
Det   0   0   0   7    7
Bal  D17 R30/116  P(19-10-1)  238
Det  D20 R23/83   P(37-26-0)  225
Bal-Orr 160C

NO    3   0   7   7   17
Cle   0  14  14   7   35
NO   D18 R30/161  P(43-15-3)  123
Cle  D17 R35/222  P(24-10-3)  245
Cle-Kelly 127R, Kelly 104C,
Warfield 107C, Nelsen 262P

GB    3   0   7   0   10
Min   7   7   0   0   14
GB   D21 R32/172  P(23-13-1)  91
Min  D15 R42/160  P(16-8-0)   66
```

SUNDAY, NOVEMBER 17
```
LARm  3   7   3  10   20
SF    7   6   0   7   20
LARm D22 R30/129  P(44-21-2)  270
SF   D18 R33/167  P(24-10-1)  171
LARm-Casey 109C; SF-Willard 128R

NO    0   7   0   0    7
GB   17   6   0   6   29
NO   D11 R27/74   P(26-8-2)   62
GB   D18 R35/132  P(22-13-0)  157
GB-Dale 161C

Cle  14  10   0  21   45
Pit   7   3   0  14   24
Cle  D18 R27/47   P(35-22-3)  352
Pit  D21 R25/165  P(36-17-6)  188
Cle-Morin 103C; Pit-Gros 109R

Dal   7   6  17  14   44
Was   0  10   7  14   31
Dal  D24 R38/220  P(32-20-1)  295
Was  D13 R22/82   P(29-14-0)  207
Dal-Perkins 103R, Hayes 105C;
Was-Taylor 114C

Min   3   0   7   3   13
Det   0   0   6   0    6
Min  D15 R47/139  P(10-6-3)   113
Det  D6  R22/93   P(20-6-1)   38

Phi   3   3   0   0    6
NYG   0   7   0   0    7
Phi  D9  R21/68   P(21-8-3)   39
NYG  D16 R40/138  P(23-12-2)  136

SL    0   0   0   0    0
Bal   3   6   7   7   27
SL   D16 R24/58   P(48-17-5)  144
Bal  D17 R32/170  P(27-15-2)  256
Bal-Mackey 105C, Richardson 126C

Atl   6  10   0   0   16
ChiB  3  10   0   0   13
Atl  D14 R35/157  P(13-8-0)   143
ChiB D16 R28/117  P(28-16-1)  185
```

SUNDAY, NOVEMBER 24
```
SF   14  21   3   7   45
Pit   0   0  14   0   14
SF   D18 R31/130  P(25-16-1)  269
Pit  D22 R24/71   P(45-26-5)  280
SF-Willard 110R, Crow 144C;
Pit-Jefferson 132C, Shiner 287P

Atl   3   0   6   3   12
SL    0   7  10   0   17
Atl  D10 R21/60   P(20-9-1)   102
SL   D17 R44/133  P(22-10-2)  127

Dal  14  10   0  10   34
ChiB  0   3   0   0    3
Dal  D26 R35/113  P(32-15-1)  230
ChiB D9  R27/67   P(28-17-1)  80
```

```
Min   0   3   3   3    9
Bal   7  14   0   0   21
Min  D15 R21/88   P(25-15-2)  141
Bal  D22 R42/170  P(24-17-2)  243
Bal-Richardson 150C

GB    7   7  10   3   27
Was   0   7   0   0    7
GB   D23 R47/158  P(24-18-2)  230
Was  D13 R19/33   P(29-18-0)  134

Phi   0   6   0   7   13
Cle  10  10  14  13   47
Phi  D21 R20/57   P(48-27-3)  285
Cle  D22 R37/201  P(27-14-0)  237
Cle-Kelly 108R, Morin 108C

NO    3   7   7   3   20
Det   7   3   7   3   20
NO   D17 R36/126  P(30-11-3)  136
Det  D15 R25/85   P(41-14-1)  189

NYG   0  14   0   7   21
LARm  0   0  14  10   24
NYG  D18 R35/146  P(28-14-2)  127
LARm D19 R36/168  P(20-9-2)   143
```

THURSDAY, NOVEMBER 28
```
Phi   3   3   3   3   12
Det   0   0   0   0    0
Phi  D12 R44/112  P(16-7-0)   49
Det  D8  R29/102  P(15-7-3)   66

Was   0   7   7   6   20
Dal   3  14   2  10   29
Was  D20 R22/28   P(34-18-3)  220
Dal  D17 R38/147  P(23-12-1)  138
Was-Smith 116C
```

SUNDAY, DECEMBER 1
```
Atl   0   0   0   0    0
Bal  14  14   6  10   44
Atl  D12 R27/56   P(31-15-4)  87
Bal  D23 R29/108  P(33-22-0)  278

LARm  7  10   0  14   31
Min   0   0   0   3    3
LARm D19 R52/201  P(16-10-2)  123
Min  D9  R23/80   P(18-7-1)   47

ChiB  3  13   0   7   23
NO    3   7   0   7   17
ChiB D15 R45/213  P(19-5-0)   46
NO   D17 R25/114  P(32-13-4)  178
ChiB-Piccolo 112R

GB    3   7  10   0   20
SF    0   7   0  20   27
GB   D17 R34/173  P(23-9-1)   44
SF   D17 R23/60   P(39-24-1)  292
SF-Brodie 301P

SL    3   0   0  17   20
Pit   7   3   0   0   10
SL   D18 R36/185  P(32-13-2)  137
Pit  D13 R27/77   P(33-11-0)  90

NYG   0   3   0   7   10
Cle   0  17  21   7   45
NYG  D12 R26/105  P(25-11-2)  77
Cle  D25 R35/172  P(29-14-1)  206
Cle-Warfield 137C
```

SATURDAY, DECEMBER 7
```
Bal   7   6   3   0   16
GB    3   0   0   0    3
Bal  D14 R38/138  P(20-10-0)  104
GB   D9  R29/66   P(24-13-1)  97
```

SUNDAY, DECEMBER 8
```
NO    7   7   3   0   17
Phi   0  13   0  14   29
NO   D21 R32/109  P(34-20-1)  202
Phi  D15 R25/151  P(18-10-1)  167
Phi-Woodeshick 122R

ChiB  3   7   0   7   17
LARm  0   7   2   7   16
ChiB D17 R47/150  P(19-12-1)  98
LARm D16 R32/103  P(26-8-1)   107

Cle   3   0   7  14   24
Was   7   7   0   7   21
Cle  D15 R36/149  P(22-12-1)  205
Was  D17 R27/114  P(40-21-3)  212
Cle-Morin 133C; Was-Smith 103C
```

```
Det   7   0   7  10   24
Atl   0   7   0   0    7
Det  D18 R32/130  P(28-21-0)  212
Atl  D14 R28/172  P(21-9-2)   58
Det-Gambrell 105C

Min   7  10   7   6   30
SF    3   3   0  14   20
Min  D15 R42/125  P(17-10-1)  122
SF   D15 R23/101  P(26-18-1)  179

Pit   0   7   0   0    7
Dal   7  14   0   7   28
Pit  D19 R33/193  P(41-17-0)  120
Dal  D11 R27/109  P(26-12-1)  232
Pit-Hoak 114R; Dal-Rentzel 100C

SL   14   7   0   7   28
NYG   7   7   0   0   21
SL   D19 R42/277  P(10-7-1)   74
NYG  D22 R39/157  P(29-16-1)  284
SL 1-Crenshaw 162R;
YG-Jones 142C, Morrison 109C,
Tarkenton 325P
```

SATURDAY, DECEMBER 14
```
Cle   3   3   7   3   16
SL    7   6   7   7   27
Cle  D13 R27/129  P(23-9-0)   189
SL   D16 R41/203  P(22-9-0)   121
Cle-Warfield 104C
```

SUNDAY, DECEMBER 15
```
GB    7  14   7   0   28
ChiB 10   0   0  17   27
GB   D12 R28/65   P(18-11-0)  251
ChiB D14 R33/134  P(26-10-2)  157
GB-Dowler 182C;
ChiB-Gordon 147C

Min   0   7   7  10   24
Phi   0   7   3   7   17
Min  D15 R39/145  P(10-7-0)   135
Phi  D18 R38/130  P(26-18-0)  156

Det   0   0   0   3    3
Was   0   0   0  14   14
Det  D21 R33/130  P(36-20-1)  238
Was  D13 R22/72   P(26-13-2)  136
Det-Sanders 133C

Pit   7   0   0   7   14
NO    7  14   0   3   24
Pit  D16 R25/151  P(35-13-3)  199
NO   D13 R22/85   P(37-18-0)  258
Pit-Jefferson 139C; NO-Parks 103C

SF    7   7   0   0   14
Atl   9   3   0   0   12
SF   D21 R47/248  P(29-13-3)  210
Atl  D11 R24/51   P(27-13-1)  99
SF-Willard 162R, Witcher 114C

Bal  14   0   0  14   28
LARm  7   7   0  10   24
Bal  D13 R24/64   P(25-13-1)  144
LARm D19 R39/165  P(28-18-1)  114
LARm-Ellison 111R, Snow 106C

Dal   0   7  14   7   28
NYG   3   0   7   0   10
Dal  D21 R32/129  P(29-15-3)  191
NYG  D15 R22/54   P(46-21-0)  265
Dal-Rentzel 130C;
NYG-Thomas 107C
```

1969 AFL
SUNDAY, SEPTEMBER 14
```
Bos   0   0   0   7    7
Den  14  14   7   0   35
Bos  D21 R23/89   P(38-19-4)  237
Den  D16 R33/135  P(15-10-0)  186
Den-Little 105R

NYJ   6  10   3  14   33
Buf   3   0   6  10   19
NYJ  D15 R41/178  P(19-7-3)   146
Buf  D13 R20/59   P(30-12-4)  122
NYJ-Snell 106R, Maynard 118C

Mia   0   0   7   0    7
Cin   7  14   6   0   27
Mia  D19 R23/79   P(39-19-2)  281
Cin  D11 R35/101  P(21-11-1)  126
Mia-Griese 327P; Cin-Crabtree 113C
```

```
Hou   0   3   7   7   17
Oak   7   0   7   7   21
Hou  D17 R31/102  P(38-14-2)  176
Oak  D17 R41/137  P(31-10-3)  148

KC    3  10   7   7   27
SD    0   0   6   0    6
KC   D14 R20/67   P(34-19-2)  206
SD   D16 R22/45   P(43-22-4)  250
KC-Taylor 111C
```

SATURDAY, SEPTEMBER 20
```
Mia   7  10   0   0   17
Oak   7  10   0   3   20
Mia  D17 R39/119  P(34-9-3)   186
Oak  D19 R27/115  P(42-23-3)  258
Oak-Biletnikoff 132C
```

SUNDAY, SEPTEMBER 21
```
Hou   0   7   3   7   17
Buf   3   0   0   0    3
Hou  D15 R36/123  P(20-10-0)  122
Buf  D10 R27/93   P(21-12-3)  40

SD    3  10   0   7   20
Cin   7  10  14   3   34
SD   D17 R25/180  P(33-13-1)  215
Cin  D19 R33/180  P(22-14-1)  292
SD-Post 147R, Garrison 109C;
Cin-Trumpy 118C, Cook 327P

NYJ  13   0   0   6   19
Den   0  14   0   7   21
NYJ  D22 R30/108  P(37-19-0)  262
Den  D18 R29/151  P(24-12-2)  141
Den-Little 104R

KC   14   7   0  10   31
Bos   0   0   0   0    0
KC   D25 R48/232  P(22-13-2)  163
Bos  D6  R15/43   P(23-12-0)  39
```

SUNDAY, SEPTEMBER 28
```
Den  14   0   7   7   28
Buf   7  17  21   0   41
Den  D20 R17/69   P(45-17-5)  233
Buf  D28 R35/159  P(42-21-0)  247
Den-Denson 138C;
Buf-Simpson 110R

NYJ   0  10   3  14   27
SD    7  17   3   7   34
NYJ  D24 R19/81   P(51-29-2)  333
SD   D22 R38/150  P(31-19-0)  268
NYJ-Sauer 118C, Namath 344P;
SD-Garrison 188C

Oak   7   3  21   7   38
Bos   0  10   0  13   23
Oak  D21 R46/210  P(23-13-1)  213
Bos  D10 R22/52   P(29-12-2)  118
Oak-Lamonica 226P

KC    6   0   7   6   19
Cin   7   3   0  14   24
KC   D17 R35/126  P(35-20-1)  139
Cin  D7  R23/92   P(23-14-3)  209
Cin-Trumpy 100C

Mia   0  10   0   0   10
Hou   0   6  10   6   22
Mia  D13 R22/62   P(30-14-1)  154
Hou  D17 R33/120  P(31-18-0)  178
```

SATURDAY, OCTOBER 4
```
Oak   3   0   7  10   20
Mia  10   0   7   0   17
Oak  D15 R22/74   P(43-19-1)  206
Mia  D17 R26/110  P(27-13-2)  104
Oak-Biletnikoff 119C
```

SUNDAY, OCTOBER 5
```
Cin   7   0   7   0   14
SD    7   0   7   7   21
Cin  D8  R27/151  P(18-7-0)   70
SD   D23 R37/199  P(28-17-1)  214
Cin-Phillips 103R; SD-Post 123R,
Alworth 125C

KC    3   6   3  14   26
Den   0   3   0  10   13
KC   D19 R35/168  P(27-14-0)  182
Den  D15 R21/80   P(30-15-1)  132

Buf   0   0   7   0    7
Hou   7   7   7   7   28
Buf  D12 R19/44   P(47-21-4)  237
Hou  D15 R38/113  P(28-10-3)  139
```

NYJ · 3 7 10 3 **23**
Bos 0 7 0 7 14
NYJ D10 R45/164 P(21-15-1) 145
Bos D11 R16/35 P(27-15-2) 168

SATURDAY, OCTOBER 11
SD 0 14 0 7 **21**
Mia 0 0 7 7 14
SD D15 R33/126 P(28-13-1) 155
Mia D22 R22/67 P(31-18-2) 138
SD-Garrison 103C

Bos 6 0 7 3 16
Buf 7 3 3 10 **23**
Bos D14 R24/100 P(31-13-1) 148
Buf D14 R34/204 P(26-13-2) 160
Buf-Patrick 131R

SUNDAY, OCTOBER 12
Hou 0 0 0 0 0
KC 14 10 0 0 **24**
Hou D7 R20/31 P(35-10-5) 70
KC D14 R43/163 P(17-9-1) 81

Oak 0 10 7 7 **24**
Den 0 7 0 7 14
Oak D20 R29/79 P(37-19-0) 244
Den D18 R27/121 P(34-12-2) 113

NYJ 0 14 7 0 **21**
Cin 0 0 7 0 7
NYJ D21 R45/222 P(26-14-1) 154
Cin D15 R18/89 P(31-14-2) 169
NYJ-Boozer 129R;
Cin-Crabtree 133C

SUNDAY, OCTOBER 19
SD 0 3 3 7 **13**
Bos 7 0 0 3 10
SD D24 R44/171 P(27-15-0) 163
Bos D11 R26/127 P(25-11-2) 90

Mia 0 0 3 7 10
KC 7 10 0 0 **17**
Mia D14 R23/83 P(45-21-3) 153
KC D17 R27/105 P(34-17-1) 298
KC-Taylor 131C, Livingston 308P

Den 13 17 0 0 **30**
Cin 0 6 14 3 23
Den D17 R46/272 P(16-7-1) 149
Cin D20 R23/97 P(29-17-1) 159
Den-Little 166R; Cin-Thomas 155C

Buf 0 0 14 7 21
Oak 14 14 8 14 **50**
Buf D19 R27/146 P(42-16-2) 246
Oak D20 R25/84 P(41-24-2) 320
Buf-Briscoe 119C; Oak-Wells 101C,
Lamonica 313P

MONDAY, OCTOBER 20
Hou 0 7 10 0 17
NYJ 3 14 3 6 **26**
Hou D20 R19/70 P(47-23-3) 307
NYJ D18 R41/141 P(24-12-3) 306
Hou-Reed 119C, Beathard 314P;
NYJ-Maynard 212C, Namath 306P

SUNDAY, OCTOBER 26
Cin 0 12 7 3 22
KC 14 7 14 7 **42**
Cin D7 R16/65 P(21-11-0) 131
KC D26 R50/313 P(26-15-2) 195
KC-McVea 141R, Garrett 101C

Den 7 7 7 0 21
Hou 14 0 0 10 **24**
Den D17 R22/96 P(33-14-0) 218
Hou D19 R43/219 P(28-14-2) 239
Den-Haffner 102C;
Hou-Hopkins 107R, LeVias 122C

Buf 3 0 3 0 6
Mia 0 14 3 7 **24**
Buf D13 R27/56 P(36-20-3) 220
Mia D17 R36/136 P(18-9-2) 217
Mia-Kiick 109C

Oak 7 7 7 3 **24**
SD 3 0 3 6 12
Oak D19 R41/171 P(26-19-3) 228
SD D20 R21/71 P(52-15-4) 182
Oak-Banaszak 123R

Bos 10 7 0 0 17
NYJ 7 3 3 10 **23**
NYJ D10 R20/82 P(24-12-1) 129
NYJ D21 R43/210 P(21-10-1) 108
NYJ-Snell 109R

SUNDAY, NOVEMBER 2
Hou 0 0 0 0 0
Bos 0 17 7 0 **24**
Hou D17 R22/83 P(42-26-2) 203
Bos D14 R32/153 P(23-12-0) 162
Bos-Sellers 124C

KC 0 3 3 23 **29**
Buf 7 0 0 0 7
KC D14 R31/147 P(22-9-1) 98
Buf D14 R30/105 P(25-10-4) 39

SD 0 0 0 0 0
Den 0 0 13 0 **13**
SD D10 R20/50 P(30-11-0) 20
Den D19 R33/114 P(32-15-2) 199

Oak 0 0 3 14 17
Cin 7 17 0 7 **31**
Oak D24 R23/119 P(44-21-5) 275
Cin D15 R37/134 P(19-11-1) 186
Oak-Wells 136C; Cin-Phillips 120R

Mia 7 14 3 7 31
NYJ 10 0 6 18 **34**
Mia D23 R34/203 P(30-20-1) 218
NYJ D15 R26/94 P(26-13-1) 221
Mia-Kiick 106R, Seiple 102C,
Griese 222P; NYJ-Maynard 121C

SUNDAY, NOVEMBER 9
Cin 7 7 7 10 31
Hou 0 14 7 10 31
Cin D12 R22/93 P(25-15-0) 298
Hou D26 R44/219 P(33-16-2) 237
Cin-Crabtree 117C, Trumpy 159C,
Cook 298P; Hou-Granger 104R,
Beirne 114C

SD 3 0 0 0 3
KC 0 10 10 7 **27**
SD D10 R16/70 P(31-10-5) 104
KC D17 R31/99 P(29-20-3) 209

Den 0 7 3 0 10
Oak 7 14 14 10 **41**
Den D21 R31/125 P(36-19-1) 177
Oak D20 R29/89 P(25-12-0) 270
Oak-Biletnikoff 110C

Mia 3 7 0 7 **17**
Buf 0 0 0 16 16
Mia D8 R34/145 P(10-7-0) 63
Bos D7 R37/183 P(9-2-1) 28
Mia-Csonka 121R; Bos-Nance 109R

Buf 0 3 3 0 6
NYJ 0 7 3 6 **16**
Buf D13 R24/106 P(24-14-1) 191
NYJ D16 R38/104 P(22-10-1) 169
Buf-Moses 147C

SUNDAY, NOVEMBER 16
Hou 0 3 0 17 20
Den 10 0 0 0 10
Hou D19 R24/90 P(51-24-2) 364
Den D8 R40/99 P(21-7-1) 113
Hou-LeVias 150C, Beathard 338P

SD 0 7 3 6 16
Oak 0 14 0 7 **21**
SD D17 R37/117 P(32-12-0) 107
Oak D13 R28/74 P(29-15-3) 235
SD-Post 113R; Oak-Wells 105C

Mia 3 0 0 0 3
Buf 7 7 7 7 **28**
Mia D16 R18/50 P(41-20-0) 198
Buf D18 R33/122 P(24-12-0) 187
Mia-Seiple 106C

Bos 19 3 0 3 **25**
Cin 0 7 0 7 14
Bos D13 R44/210 P(18-9-0) 88
Cin D14 R22/114 P(24-14-3) 191
Bos-Nance 125R

KC 10 10 7 7 **34**
NYJ 3 7 0 6 16
KC D23 R28/139 P(38-23-1) 285
NYJ D22 R17/77 P(41-25-3) 333
KC-McVea 102R;
NYJ-Maynard 137C, Namath 327P

SUNDAY, NOVEMBER 23
Cin 0 0 0 7 7
NYJ 6 13 14 7 **40**
Cin D9 R19/50 P(21-9-1) 108
NYJ D34 R34/115 P(29-18-1) 213
NYJ-Maynard 137C

Den 7 10 7 0 24
SD 14 3 21 7 **45**
Den D23 R11/34 P(36-26-3) 329
SD D27 R40/235 P(22-11-2) 227
Den-Denson 140C, Embree 122C,
Tensi 301P; SD-Post 128R

Hou 0 10 7 15 **32**
Mia 7 0 0 15 22
Hou D23 R39/187 P(35-14-2) 258
Mia D9 R20/119 P(27-8-5) 22
Hou-LeVias 101C

Buf 7 7 7 0 21
Bos 14 7 0 14 **35**
Buf D24 R36/177 P(32-18-4) 248
Bos D16 R30/139 P(19-12-1) 234
Buf-Moses 130C; Bos-Sellers 102C

Oak 3 14 3 7 **27**
KC 7 10 7 0 24
Oak D15 R31/120 P(24-9-0) 142
KC D26 R41/198 P(24-13-5) 238
KC-Taylor 103C

THURSDAY, NOVEMBER 27
Den 0 3 0 14 17
KC 3 14 0 14 **31**
Den D17 R22/85 P(33-12-2) 151
KC D17 R47/152 P(14-9-1) 133

SD 0 7 7 7 **21**
Hou 7 10 0 0 17
SD D20 R36/139 P(28-16-2) 186
Hou D18 R36/109 P(26-15-2) 103

SUNDAY, NOVEMBER 30
Bos 6 16 0 16 **38**
Mia 9 7 7 0 23
Bos D10 R35/81 P(17-8-0) 135
Mia D19 R41/144 P(27-12-3) 99

Cin 3 3 0 7 13
Buf 0 10 0 6 **16**
Cin D11 R37/227 P(7-2-0) 35
Buf D8 R32/100 P(26-10-1) 84
Cin-Robinson 117R

Oak 7 14 3 3 **27**
NYJ 7 7 0 0 14
Oak D18 R38/82 P(28-19-1) 322
NYJ D13 R19/99 P(32-11-1) 139
Oak-Wells 152C, Lamonica 333P

SATURDAY, DECEMBER 6
NYJ 14 7 6 7 **34**
Hou 0 10 0 16 26
NYJ D12 R44/132 P(18-7-0) 81
Hou D18 R16/60 P(44-23-6) 160
Hou-LeVias 110C

SUNDAY, DECEMBER 7
Cin 0 7 3 7 17
Oak 7 14 3 13 **37**
Cin D10 R32/102 P(17-5-1) 108
Oak D26 R44/309 P(26-13-2) 235
Cin-Abramowicz 105C;
Oak-Wells 102C

Den 0 7 10 7 24
Mia 7 7 3 10 **27**
Den D13 R21/68 P(31-13-2) 176
Mia D20 R39/146 P(27-14-1) 76

Buf 6 6 0 7 19
KC 7 6 3 6 **22**
Buf D17 R23/93 P(32-18-0) 144
KC D17 R38/146 P(23-13-0) 131

Bos 0 3 0 15 18
SD 7 7 14 0 **28**
Bos D16 R22/110 P(29-15-4) 183
SD D24 R41/190 P(27-15-1) 240
Bos-Sellers 102C; SD-Alworth 147C

SATURDAY, DECEMBER 13
KC 0 0 0 6 6
Oak 0 3 0 7 **10**
KC D12 R48/165 P(6-2-0) 29
Oak D14 R35/102 P(20-11-2) 175

SUNDAY, DECEMBER 14
Bos 13 3 7 0 23
Hou 0 7 7 13 **27**
Bos D7 R21/85 P(26-10-0) 171
Hou D25 R39/180 P(31-22-0) 269
Bos-Sellers 158C;
Hou-Granger 139R

Cin 3 6 7 0 16
Den 0 7 13 7 **27**
Cin D14 R19/28 P(30-19-1) 272
Den D21 R41/188 P(17-13-1) 207
Cin-Thomas 177C

Buf 0 0 0 6 6
SD 10 14 7 14 **45**
Buf D15 R17/58 P(35-18-2) 180
SD D30 R45/242 P(32-19-0) 295
SD-Post 106R, Alworth 122C

NYJ 14 10 3 0 **27**
Mia 0 3 0 6 9
NYJ D13 R27/57 P(27-13-2) 191
Mia D16 R24/50 P(38-17-4) 168
NYJ-Turner 105C

1969 NFL
SUNDAY, SEPTEMBER 21
LARm 3 7 10 7 **27**
Bal 0 10 7 3 20
LARm D15 R28/87 P(33-20-0) 252
Bal D19 R20/54 P(42-20-3) 283

Was 0 14 7 5 **26**
NO 7 3 7 3 20
Was D22 R25/74 P(23-10-0) 229
NO D20 R43/217 P(21-11-0) 111
NO-Livingston 142R

Min 3 14 3 3 23
NYG 0 7 7 14 **24**
Min D13 R33/97 P(28-13-1) 230
NYG D13 R28/115 P(34-19-0) 205
Min-Washington 152C;
NYG-Jones 100C

Cle 7 6 14 0 **27**
Phi 7 6 0 13 20
Cle D19 R37/173 P(28-13-2) 196
Phi D12 R24/88 P(31-12-2) 158
Cle-Johnson 118R

SL 0 0 0 0 0
Dal 7 0 7 10 **24**
SL D10 R21/58 P(35-17-2) 199
Dal D14 R37/152 P(16-8-0) 210
SL-Williams 104C; Dal-Rentzel 128C

ChiB 0 0 0 0 0
GB 7 0 0 10 **17**
ChiB D22 R24/90 P(26-13-2) 114
GB D18 R43/196 P(14-9-0) 90

SF 3 0 2 7 12
Atl 3 7 0 14 **24**
SF D19 R32/131 P(39-21-3) 200
Atl D13 R36/229 P(12-7-1) 79

Det 3 0 3 7 13
Pit 3 6 0 7 **16**
Det D14 R30/80 P(34-19-1) 156
Pit D12 R30/109 P(26-10-1) 128

SUNDAY, SEPTEMBER 28
Was 0 7 3 13 23
Cle 0 10 7 10 **27**
Was D15 R26/177 P(18-14-0) 98
Cle D22 R45/199 P(21-12-1) 140
Cle-Morrison 131R

Pit 13 0 7 0 20
Phi 0 17 14 10 **41**
Pit D19 R29/101 P(34-16-0) 254
Phi D19 R33/142 P(30-22-1) 318
Pit-Jefferson 123C;
Phi-Hawkins 145C, Snead 335P

NYG 0 0 0 0 0
Det 7 7 3 7 **24**
NYG D10 R31/86 P(25-8-0) 101
Det D18 R28/122 P(26-12-1) 119

Bal 0 7 0 7 14
Min 12 15 14 11 **52**
Bal D15 R16/56 P(42-20-3) 179
Min D34 R27/92 P(56-36-2) 530
Min-Washington 172C, Kapp 449P

Atl 0 0 0 7 7
LARm 7 10 0 0 **17**
Atl D13 R33/156 P(15-7-1) 22
LARm D16 R30/107 P(33-18-0) 162

ChiB 0 7 10 0 17
SL 13 0 0 7 **20**
ChiB D26 R33/129 P(42-27-1) 242
SL D11 R29/84 P(17-9-2) 86

SF 0 0 0 7 7
GB 0 0 7 7 **14**
SF D17 R31/112 P(33-15-1) 264
GB D17 R32/135 P(25-15-1) 134
SF-McNeil 109C

Dal 0 14 0 7 **21**
NO 7 10 0 0 17
Dal D17 R42/213 P(15-8-0) 81
NO D17 R18/41 P(39-23-3) 269
Dal-Hill 138R

SUNDAY, OCTOBER 5
Det 0 7 7 14 **28**
Cle 7 14 0 0 21
Det D17 R36/144 P(23-13-2) 157
Cle D14 R25/79 P(29-13-3) 185
Cle-Warfield 106C

Was 0 0 3 14 17
SF 7 3 7 0 17
Was D20 R21/54 P(40-27-2) 250
SF D19 R34/127 P(29-18-1) 144

SL 0 20 0 7 **27**
Pit 7 0 7 0 14
SL D17 R25/103 P(27-16-2) 241
Pit D20 R29/100 P(43-22-4) 245
SL-Gilliam 197C; Pit-Jefferson 115C

NO 7 10 0 0 17
LARm 12 10 14 0 **36**
NO D17 R27/53 P(42-14-3) 262
LARm D16 R29/122 P(33-14-0) 228
LARm-Snow 133C, Gabriel 228P

Dal 7 21 7 3 **38**
Phi 7 0 0 0 7
Dal D27 R40/182 P(27-20-1) 344
Phi D15 R14/54 P(40-18-2) 198
Dal-Rentzel 128C; Phi-Ballman 108C

Bal 7 7 0 7 **21**
Atl 7 7 0 0 14
Bal D17 R35/106 P(24-18-1) 154
Atl D19 R33/134 P(26-16-0) 168
Bal-Snow 133C, Gabriel 228P

GB 0 0 0 0 0
Min 6 7 3 3 **19**
GB D16 R24/108 P(31-18-1) 65
Min D12 R38/157 P(21-7-0) 73

MONDAY, OCTOBER 6
ChiB 0 14 7 3 24
NYG 14 0 7 7 **28**
ChiB D22 R40/179 P(35-20-1) 201
NYG D16 R24/88 P(25-14-0) 179
NYG-Tarkenton 227P

SUNDAY, OCTOBER 12
Pit 0 0 0 7 7
NYG 7 0 0 3 **10**
Pit D19 R34/147 P(24-14-2) 84
NYG D14 R27/76 P(29-16-0) 132

LARm 0 13 0 14 **27**
SF 0 7 7 7 21
LARm D19 R30/92 P(41-18-0) 177
SF D19 R25/76 P(51-20-3) 241

Dal 14 3 7 0 **24**
Atl 3 0 7 7 17
Dal D19 R42/165 P(21-15-0) 232
Atl D14 R27/88 P(27-11-1) 125

Cle 0 20 0 7 **27**
NO 0 10 7 0 17
Cle D18 R37/92 P(26-15-0) 214
NO D21 R31/161 P(19-13-1) 116

GB 14 0 7 7 **28**
Det 0 10 0 7 17
GB D23 R37/121 P(20-13-0) 187
Det D15 R26/145 P(24-11-3) 82
GB-Dale 167C

SL	3	0	7	7	17
Was	10	13	0	10	**33**
SL	D14	R27/99	P(30-13-5)	127	
Was	D23	R38/155	P(34-19-0)	222	

Was-Long 110C

Min	7	0	7	17	**31**
ChiB	0	0	0	0	0
Min	D19	R37/185	P(19-9-1)	71	
ChiB	D8	R22/54	P(27-14-3)	65	

Min-Osborn 106R

MONDAY, OCTOBER 13

Phi	3	7	7	3	20
Bal	0	10	7	7	**24**
Phi	D18	R21/59	P(43-21-1)	261	
Bal	D24	R39/113	P(35-19-2)	250	

Phi-Jackson 138C

SATURDAY, OCTOBER 18

Pit	0	10	0	21	31
Cle	7	7	7	21	**42**
Pit	D20	R27/137	P(33-16-4)	183	
Cle	D16	R34/144	P(28-12-4)	139	

Pit-Jefferson 110C; Cle-Collins 103C

SUNDAY, OCTOBER 19

Atl	14	0	0	7	**21**
SF	0	7	0	0	7
Atl	D17	R34/191	P(23-12-2)	93	
SF	D19	R28/90	P(42-26-3)	205	

NYG	0	7	7	0	14
Was	0	0	7	13	**20**
NYG	D20	R39/179	P(28-18-0)	139	
Was	D16	R31/172	P(21-11-1)	108	

Was-Brown 105R

Bal	13	3	7	7	**30**
NO	0	0	7	3	10
Bal	D25	R35/182	P(28-20-0)	309	
NO	D23	R18/78	P(42-24-2)	247	

Bal-Orr 113C, Unitas 319P; NO-Abramowicz 115C

GB	0	14	0	7	21
LARm	7	20	7	0	**34**
GB	D15	R19/38	P(23-13-0)	151	
LARm	D21	R37/137	P(28-17-0)	175	

GB-Dowler 100C

Phi	7	0	0	7	14
Dal	28	14	0	7	**49**
Phi	D8	R15/58	P(26-12-1)	122	
Dal	D24	R48/171	P(27-16-1)	276	

Phi-Jackson 107C; Dal-Morton 247P

ChiB	0	7	0	0	7
Det	0	7	3	3	**13**
ChiB	D12	R33/120	P(17-8-0)	33	
Det	D12	R37/155	P(21-9-1)	97	

Min	7	7	7	6	**27**
SL	3	7	0	0	10
Min	D19	R35/116	P(31-14-1)	216	
SL	D7	R26/79	P(28-12-1)	90	

SUNDAY, OCTOBER 26

SF	0	10	14	0	**24**
Bal	0	7	7	7	21
SF	D20	R33/143	P(30-18-0)	188	
Bal	D21	R24/108	P(38-19-3)	300	

Bal-Orr 146C, Unitas 300P

SL	7	0	7	7	21
Cle	7	0	7	7	21
SL	D19	R31/139	P(30-15-1)	306	
Cle	D19	R29/106	P(30-20-1)	230	

SL-Gilliam 192C, Johnson 306P

NO	3	0	0	7	10
Phi	0	6	7	0	**13**
NO	D13	R17/31	P(46-22-3)	236	
Phi	D20	R36/122	P(36-17-2)	244	

Phi-Jackson 105C

Was	0	0	14	0	**14**
Pit	7	0	0	0	7
Was	D14	R30/97	P(29-14-2)	117	
Pit	D17	R40/171	P(28-11-2)	130	

Atl	0	3	7	0	10
GB	7	7	0	14	**28**
Atl	D19	R35/164	P(19-9-1)	55	
GB	D26	R43/241	P(15-9-2)	96	

GB-Anderson 114R

Det	0	3	0	7	10
Min	3	21	0	0	**24**
Det	D13	R33/107	P(28-14-4)	60	
Min	D13	R28/52	P(19-11-1)	149	

LARm	0	6	3	0	**9**
ChiB	7	0	0	0	7
LARm	D14	R33/126	P(23-11-1)	110	
ChiB	D14	R28/154	P(22-8-1)	5	

ChiB-Sayers 109R

MONDAY, OCTOBER 27

NYG	3	0	0	0	3
Dal	0	3	3	19	**25**
NYG	D8	R15/40	P(32-13-1)	126	
Dal	D21	R44/217	P(27-12-2)	153	

SUNDAY, NOVEMBER 2

GB	0	14	10	14	**38**
Pit	10	7	7	10	34
GB	D14	R27/82	P(24-13-3)	236	
Pit	D19	R41/142	P(27-15-3)	204	

GB-Dale 134C; Pit-Jefferson 164C

Det	6	7	10	3	**26**
SF	0	7	0	7	14
Det	D12	R41/124	P(14-3-0)	1	
SF	D14	R18/86	P(32-20-4)	196	

Phi	3	10	3	7	**23**
NYG	3	3	7	7	20
Phi	D17	R37/131	P(28-13-4)	164	
NYG	D13	R24/104	P(26-14-1)	188	

NO	7	16	21	7	**51**
SL	7	7	7	21	42
NO	D26	R37/163	P(34-22-1)	345	
SL	D19	R21/104	P(37-20-2)	374	

NO-Baker 110R, Dodd 145C, Kilmer 345P; SL-Gilliam 106C, Williams 164C, Johnson 374P

LARm	7	10	7	14	**38**
Atl	0	3	3	0	6
LARm	D17	R24/134	P(30-20-0)	296	
Atl	D15	R35/107	P(29-13-3)	172	

Atl-Flatley 113C

Was	3	0	7	7	17
Bal	3	10	14	14	**41**
Was	D21	R25/45	P(38-28-3)	312	
Bal	D23	R36/187	P(21-11-1)	172	

Was-Jurgensen 339P; Bal-Matte 117R

ChiB	0	7	0	7	14
Min	7	10	7	7	**31**
ChiB	D14	R36/185	P(16-10-1)	26	
Min	D15	R27/192	P(21-9-2)	104	

ChiB-Sayers 116R

Dal	0	3	0	7	10
Cle	14	14	0	14	**42**
Dal	D20	R29/140	P(33-17-3)	183	
Cle	D20	R33/95	P(26-18-1)	230	

Cle-Morin 101C, Nelsen 255P

SUNDAY, NOVEMBER 9

GB	6	0	0	0	6
Bal	7	7	0	0	**14**
GB	D16	R29/93	P(28-13-2)	205	
Bal	D17	R36/120	P(25-15-3)	131	

Atl	0	7	7	7	21
Det	7	17	0	3	**27**
Atl	D15	R32/157	P(14-11-1)	122	
Det	D15	R41/171	P(14-9-1)	70	

NO	0	10	7	0	17
Dal	10	7	0	16	**33**
NO	D20	R32/141	P(30-16-2)	162	
Dal	D18	R29/187	P(23-13-2)	251	

Dal-Hill 109R, Rentzel 119C

SF	6	3	7	14	30
LARm	17	3	7	14	**41**
SF	D21	R21/61	P(42-25-2)	338	
LARm	D15	R23/96	P(23-13-0)	310	

SF-Brodie 356P; LARm-Tucker 118C, Gabriel 319P

Phi	7	0	7	14	28
Was	0	7	7	14	28
Phi	D25	R38/173	P(33-18-2)	199	
Was	D18	R20/117	P(32-22-0)	222	

Phi-Jackson 112C

Pit	0	0	0	7	7
ChiB	16	13	9	0	**38**
Pit	D10	R19/31	P(25-8-3)	55	
ChiB	D25	R54/272	P(17-9-1)	107	

ChiB-Sayers 112R

Cle	0	3	0	0	3
Min	10	17	7	17	**51**
Cle	D8	R10/42	P(27-12-4)	109	
Min	D31	R39/188	P(33-20-0)	266	

Min-Washington 119C

NYG	7	3	0	7	17
SL	14	7	7	14	**42**
NYG	D21	R19/103	P(47-23-1)	240	
SL	D23	R45/197	P(18-10-0)	206	

NYG-Thomas 127C; SL 1-Smith 101C

SUNDAY, NOVEMBER 16

SL	0	0	0	0	0
Det	0	3	7	10	**20**
SL	D16	R24/89	P(36-15-3)	150	
Det	D14	R25/65	P(22-15-0)	232	

Det-McCullouch 117C

ChiB	0	10	14	7	31
Atl	10	17	14	7	**48**
ChiB	D23	R37/223	P(28-12-0)	123	
Atl	D16	R30/162	P(14-10-1)	194	

Atl-Johnson 202P

Cle	7	3	0	14	**24**
Pit	3	0	0	0	3
Cle	D23	R34/127	P(32-18-2)	263	
Pit	D15	R27/171	P(22-11-1)	107	

Cle-Warfield 132C

Dal	17	10	7	7	**41**
Was	7	14	7	0	28
Dal	D23	R43/218	P(17-8-1)	147	
Was	D19	R20/57	P(35-24-4)	320	

Dal-Hill 150R; Was-Taylor 155C, Jurgensen 338P

NO	3	16	3	3	**25**
NYG	3	14	0	7	24
NO	D16	R34/151	P(19-10-0)	145	
NYG	D18	R26/108	P(29-18-1)	256	

LARm	0	0	20	3	**23**
Phi	3	7	0	7	17
LARm	D13	R34/103	P(30-15-0)	134	
Phi	D15	R33/153	P(26-11-2)	175	

Phi-Woodeshick 130R

Min	3	0	3	3	**9**
GB	0	7	0	0	7
Min	D18	R44/156	P(27-15-2)	114	
GB	D10	R26/87	P(21-12-2)	138	

Bal	0	0	10	7	17
SF	6	7	0	7	**20**
Bal	D14	R28/72	P(28-12-2)	187	
SF	D23	R33/132	P(37-29-1)	276	

SUNDAY, NOVEMBER 23

Bal	7	0	7	10	**24**
ChiB	0	7	7	7	21
Bal	D15	R31/107	P(27-16-2)	238	
ChiB	D14	R37/153	P(19-11-3)	99	

Det	3	13	0	0	**16**
GB	0	0	0	10	10
Det	D15	R39/188	P(24-12-1)	97	
GB	D17	R23/70	P(30-17-1)	210	

Atl	7	13	0	0	20
Was	7	10	7	3	**27**
Atl	D17	R32/133	P(24-10-0)	118	
Was	D24	R31/148	P(32-26-1)	263	

Was-Brown 102R, Harraway 110C, Long 108C, Jurgensen 300P

Dal	3	7	3	10	23
LARm	7	3	7	7	**24**
Dal	D20	R30/130	P(33-15-3)	222	
LARm	D16	R30/88	P(30-16-2)	202	

LARm-Tucker 101C

Pit	0	7	7	0	14
Min	7	10	14	21	**52**
Pit	D10	R25/48	P(25-12-4)	97	
Min	D25	R35/114	P(32-18-3)	215	

NYG	0	10	7	0	17
Cle	14	7	0	7	**28**
NYG	D20	R28/117	P(32-22-3)	259	
Cle	D14	R28/153	P(18-7-1)	115	

Cle-Kelly 124R

SF	7	14	7	10	38
NO	0	7	21	15	**43**
SF	D23	R36/161	P(25-16-1)	272	
NO	D26	R22/135	P(28-16-0)	267	

SF-Thomas 106C; NO-Abramowicz 113C

Phi	0	10	10	14	**34**
SL	6	0	7	17	30
Phi	D19	R29/76	P(33-18-1)	254	
SL	D23	R35/132	P(41-23-1)	282	

Phi-Jackson 127C

THURSDAY, NOVEMBER 27

Min	7	3	7	10	**27**
Det	0	0	0	0	0
Min	D9	R34/88	P(16-8-1)	85	
Det	D9	R23/74	P(32-17-2)	82	

SF	14	0	10	0	24
Dal	0	7	10	7	24
SF	D15	R22/92	P(33-18-0)	227	
Dal	D21	R34/137	P(37-16-3)	168	

SUNDAY, NOVEMBER 30

Cle	0	14	7	7	**28**
ChiB	7	14	0	3	24
Cle	D19	R31/68	P(30-16-0)	290	
ChiB	D23	R38/237	P(27-10-0)	97	

Cle-Collins 126C; ChiB-Sayers 126R

NYG	3	7	0	0	10
GB	7	6	7	0	**20**
NYG	D17	R36/143	P(31-13-0)	182	
GB	D16	R39/141	P(14-8-1)	133	

Phi	0	10	0	7	17
NO	10	10	3	3	**26**
Phi	D15	R14/90	P(36-14-4)	214	
NO	D23	R40/184	P(33-18-0)	201	

Phi-Ballman 119C

Atl	3	0	0	3	6
Bal	3	3	0	7	**13**
Atl	D14	R29/114	P(25-15-0)	169	
Bal	D20	R41/161	P(23-13-0)	151	

Atl-Flatley 101C

LARm	0	10	0	14	**24**
Was	3	3	0	7	13
LARm	D18	R32/166	P(29-16-0)	128	
Was	D20	R20/72	P(39-21-2)	154	

Pit	0	3	0	7	10
SL	6	6	7	28	**47**
Pit	D10	R22/77	P(28-8-3)	110	
SL	D25	R37/196	P(36-22-2)	205	

SL-Edwards 128R

SATURDAY, DECEMBER 6

ChiB	0	7	7	7	21
SF	7	21	7	7	**42**
ChiB	D24	R24/68	P(49-31-3)	300	
SF	D14	R29/186	P(24-11-0)	174	

ChiB-Gordon 108C, Wallace 100C, Carter 301P; SF-Thomas 118R

SUNDAY, DECEMBER 7

Was	7	6	14	7	**34**
Phi	7	9	3	10	29
Was	D20	R31/172	P(34-19-0)	159	
Phi	D19	R32/118	P(36-17-1)	265	

Was-Brown 138R; Phi-Woodeshick 102R, Hawkins 112C

GB	0	0	0	7	7
Cle	0	13	7	0	**20**
GB	D12	R29/99	P(23-10-1)	119	
Cle	D17	R38/210	P(24-10-0)	137	

Cle-Kelly 151R

Dal	3	7	0	0	**10**
Pit	0	0	0	7	7
Dal	D13	R35/93	P(25-11-2)	109	
Pit	D14	R29/77	P(31-12-0)	140	

NO	0	10	0	7	17
Atl	14	14	7	10	**45**
NO	D17	R24/83	P(39-23-2)	204	
Atl	D15	R29/163	P(21-11-0)	213	

NO-Abramowicz 105C; Atl-Wages 105C

Det	0	14	0	3	17
Bal	0	3	7	7	17
Det	D11	R27/84	P(31-13-0)	161	
Bal	D14	R26/69	P(30-11-1)	220	

Bal-Hinton 134C

SL	3	3	0	0	6
NYG	7	14	21	7	**49**
SL	D10	R17/45	P(31-12-2)	136	
NYG	D33	R39/190	P(40-25-0)	327	

NYG-Jones 110C, Tarkenton 252P

Min	7	10	0	3	**20**
LARm	0	3	3	7	13
Min	D15	R41/177	P(16-8-0)	69	
LARm	D15	R22/61	P(38-21-1)	186	

SATURDAY, DECEMBER 13

Bal	0	10	0	0	10
Dal	3	7	10	7	**27**
Bal	D8	R14/60	P(33-12-4)	164	
Dal	D18	R41/133	P(27-14-0)	275	

Dal-Hayes 181C

SUNDAY, DECEMBER 14

Cle	7	6	14	0	**27**
SL	7	0	0	14	21
Cle	D17	R34/104	P(31-16-1)	237	
SL	D16	R21/61	P(37-15-1)	158	

Cle-Warfield 119C

Atl	3	0	14	10	**27**
Phi	0	0	3	0	3
Atl	D17	R38/199	P(20-11-0)	173	
Phi	D13	R34/147	P(26-11-3)	87	

Atl-Flatley 120C

GB	0	0	21	0	**21**
ChiB	0	0	0	3	3
GB	D14	R29/173	P(17-9-2)	190	
ChiB	D11	R37/158	P(24-8-2)	38	

NO	0	0	7	7	14
Was	7	10	0	0	**17**
NO	D20	R32/174	P(25-13-2)	162	
Was	D15	R36/91	P(28-15-0)	157	

NYG	7	7	0	7	**21**
Pit	0	14	0	3	17
NYG	D18	R30/113	P(31-17-1)	184	
Pit	D14	R24/105	P(23-12-2)	206	

Pit-Jefferson 112C

LARm	0	0	0	0	0
Det	7	12	3	6	**28**
LARm	D4	R12/41	P(21-10-2)	55	
Det	D16	R47/149	P(17-8-1)	183	

SF	0	0	0	7	7
Min	0	3	0	7	**10**
SF	D15	R14/12	P(48-26-3)	279	
Min	D7	R38/111	P(10-4-1)	82	

SUNDAY, DECEMBER 21

SL	14	0	7	7	28
GB	7	24	7	7	**45**
SL	D14	R23/60	P(27-17-1)	179	
GB	D28	R32/108	P(34-23-1)	422	

B-Dale 195C, Dowler 102C, Horn 410P

Phi	6	7	0	0	13
SF	0	0	7	7	**14**
Phi	D16	R35/152	P(34-12-2)	123	
SF	D15	R35/127	P(31-15-4)	154	

Phi-Pinder 128R

Bal	3	3	7	0	**13**
LARm	0	7	0	0	7
Bal	D23	R36/95	P(33-19-2)	249	
LARm	D10	R18/53	P(24-13-1)	106	

Was	0	3	0	7	10
Dal	10	3	0	7	**20**
Was	D19	R23/101	P(41-25-1)	173	
Dal	D20	R38/138	P(27-16-0)	195	

Pit	14	0	7	3	24
NO	0	10	7	10	**27**
Pit	D11	R24/126	P(22-9-0)	141	
NO	D23	R24/93	P(36-20-1)	247	

NO-Abramowicz 129C

Min	3	0	0	0	3
Atl	0	7	3	0	**10**
Min	D9	R33/125	P(17-4-3)	42	
Atl	D5	R32/61	P(13-6-1)	50	

```
Det     7   6   0   7  20
ChiB    0   0   0   3   3
Det  D15 R41/147  P(19-10-1)  103
ChiB D9  R19/56   P(35-12-3)   40

Cle     7   0   7   0  14
NYG     0  13   0  14  27
Cle  D24 R32/196  P(28-17-1)  155
NYG  D14 R31/131  P(26-14-0)  257
NYG-Morrison 134C
```

1970 NFL

FRIDAY, SEPTEMBER 18
```
SL      3   0   3   7  13
LARm    3  14   7  10  34
SL   D15 R18/99   P(41-12-1)  228
LARm D17 R40/157  P(27-16-0)  185
SL-Gilliam 133C, Smith 102C
```

SATURDAY, SEPTEMBER 19
```
ChiB    7   3   7   7  24
NYG    10   3   0   3  16
ChiB D18 R37/98   P(30-16-1)  158
NYG  D16 R21/58   P(39-23-2)  253
```

SUNDAY, SEPTEMBER 20
```
Atl     0   0   0  14  14
NO      3   0   0   0   3
Atl  D14 R33/149  P(20-11-1)  116
NO   D9  R31/85   P(27-17-1)  150

Dal     0   7   7   3  17
Phi     7   0   0   0   7
Dal  D20 R40/198  P(17-11-1)   99
Phi  D13 R30/104  P(23-10-3)  121
Dal-Hill 117R, Rentzel 100C

KC      0   7   3   0  10
Min     0  17   0  10  27
KC   D8  R21/63   P(27-18-2)  155
Min  D17 R43/132  P(20-12-2)   88
KC-Taylor 100C

Den     0   5   7  13  25
Buf     7   3   0   0  10
Den  D11 R32/136  P(26-8-1)   146
Buf  D8  R30/93   P(23-10-1)   56

Mia     7   0   7   0  14
Bos     3  17   0   7  27
Mia  D15 R25/95   P(32-13-2)  119
Bos  D18 R36/184  P(23-12-1)  117

Oak     7   0  14   0  21
Cin    14   3  14   0  31
Oak  D13 R22/48   P(36-17-2)  243
Cin  D14 R40/247  P(18-8-0)   117
Oak-Biletnikoff 113C, Taylor 100C;
Cin-Phillips 130R

Det    10   3  10  17  40
GB      0   0   0   0   0
Det  D19 R46/266  P(22-12-0)  132
GB   D5  R20/50   P(26-12-1)   64

Bal     0   3   7   6  16
SD      0   0   7   7  14
Bal  D19 R28/101  P(32-16-1)  202
SD   D22 R32/83   P(37-17-0)  205
SD-Garrison 122C

Hou     7   7   2   3  19
Pit     0   0   0   7   7
Hou  D17 R41/172  P(25-11-0)  133
Pit  D11 R22/71   P(30-10-1)  143

Was     7   3   0   7  17
SF      7   9   7   3  26
Was  D13 R22/124  P(30-16-1)   85
SF   D21 R40/150  P(21-17-0)  174
```

MONDAY, SEPTEMBER 21
```
NYJ     0   7   7   7  21
Cle    14   0  10   7  31
NYJ  D31 R34/168  P(33-19-3)  286
Cle  D20 R30/76   P(27-12-0)  145
NYJ-Snell 108R, Sauer 172C
```

SUNDAY, SEPTEMBER 27
```
Cle     7  10   7   7  31
SF     14   7   0  13  34
Cle  D20 R31/122  P(28-15-2)  326
SF   D24 R38/158  P(31-20-0)  277
Cle-Hooker 157C, Nelsen 308P;
SF-Willard 105R
```

```
Atl     0   3   7  14  24
GB      7  13   0   7  27
Atl  D19 R28/112  P(44-28-3)  272
GB   D15 R33/86   P(21-10-2)  258
Atl-Berry 302P; GB-Dale 186C

NYG     3   7   0   0  10
Dal     0   0  14  14  28
NYG  D15 R25/99   P(36-14-2)  139
Dal  D24 R41/199  P(24-14-1)  161
Dal-Hayes 112C

LARm    3  13   0   3  19
Buf     0   0   0   0   0
LARm D21 R39/169  P(29-15-1)  195
Buf  D12 R19/52   P(31-17-3)  125
LARm-Snow 138C

Pit     0  10   3   0  13
Den     7   0   9   0  16
Pit  D14 R28/18   P(31-16-1)  227
Den  D12 R35/82   P(25-12-2)  144
Pit-Shanklin 123C

Phi     6   3   0   7  16
ChiB    7  10   0   3  20
Phi  D19 R34/91   P(33-24-0)  232
ChiB D12 R19/37   P(29-19-0)  144

Was     7   3   0   7  17
SL      0  13  14   0  27
Was  D20 R31/147  P(26-12-2)  107
SL   D22 R41/174  P(21-10-2)  123
Was-Brown 114R; SL-Lane 146R

Cin     0   0   0   3   3
Det     7  24   0   7  38
Cin  D6  R24/76   P(13-7-2)    64
Det  D21 R44/191  P(15-11-0)   94

NO      0   0   0   0   0
Min     7   6   3  10  26
NO   D8  R25/60   P(35-15-2)   71
Min  D12 R41/106  P(28-12-1)  185

Mia     3   3   7   7  20
Hou     0   0   7   0   7
Mia  D20 R44/157  P(17-10-1)  127
Hou  D19 R22/126  P(32-16-0)  181

NYJ     7  14   7   3  31
Bos     0   7  14   0  21
NYJ  D18 R45/187  P(20-9-0)    96
Bos  D12 R18/70   P(24-11-3)  139

Oak     3  17   0   7  27
SD      3   7   3  14  27
Oak  D23 R37/138  P(38-23-0)  267
SD   D17 R30/133  P(25-10-2)  211
Oak-Wells 127C
```

MONDAY, SEPTEMBER 28
```
KC     10  21   3  10  44
Bal     0   7   3  14  24
KC   D11 R36/153  P(12-9-1)   142
Bal  D26 R24/81   P(51-22-5)  228
KC-Dawson 152P; Bal-Hinton 190C
```

SATURDAY, OCTOBER 3
```
Pit     0   7   0   0   7
Cle     2   0  13   0  15
Pit  D17 R26/134  P(29-13-3)  129
Cle  D8  R34/69   P(21-4-2)   130
```

SUNDAY, OCTOBER 4
```
Dal     0   0   0   7   7
SL      3   3   7   7  20
Dal  D17 R33/141  P(22-9-2)   128
SL   D15 R32/145  P(22-12-2)  164

Min     0   0   0  10  10
GB      3   0   3   7  13
Min  D13 R21/57   P(38-19-2)  159
GB   D9  R39/141  P(15-8-1)    32

NYG     7   3   0   0  10
NO      0   7   0   7  14
NYG  D22 R36/151  P(33-19-3)  210
NO   D10 R26/91   P(16-9-2)    92

Bal     0   7   0   7  14
Bos     0   7   0   7  14
Bal  D14 R32/98   P(24-14-0)  138
Bos  D12 R17/60   P(38-17-0)  180
Bos-Sellers 108C
```

```
KC      0   3  10   0  13
Den    10   7   0   9  26
KC   D14 R23/88   P(26-10-3)   33
Den  D17 R36/140  P(25-15-0)  100

Hou     3   0   7  10  20
Cin     0   0   7   3  10
Hou  D14 R29/73   P(28-17-4)  166
Cin  D12 R27/71   P(32-14-2)  177

NYJ    17   7   7   0  31
Buf     7   6   7  14  34
NYJ  D11 R32/109  P(26-12-0)  228
Buf  D20 R36/149  P(21-12-2)  252
NYJ-Caster 138C; Buf-Briscoe 120C,
Moses 118C, Shaw 317P

SD      0   0   7   3  10
LARm   10  20   0   7  37
SD   D12 R19/54   P(25-15-4)   93
LARm D12 R34/155  P(19-11-0)  122

SF      0   7  10   3  20
Atl     0   7   0  14  21
SF   D18 R41/163  P(27-16-0)  163
Atl  D18 R30/152  P(32-17-0)  204
Atl-Butler 127R

Was     0  13   6  14  33
Phi     7   0   0  14  21
Was  D21 R39/177  P(28-14-0)  139
Phi  D15 R24/136  P(23-11-2)  101
Was-Brown 110R, Smith 104C
```

MONDAY, OCTOBER 5
```
ChiB    7   0   0   7  14
Det     0   0  21   7  28
ChiB D8  R21/38   P(18-10-2)  139
Det  D22 R41/140  P(19-13-0)  210
```

SATURDAY, OCTOBER 10
```
Mia     7   0   3  10  20
NYJ     3   0   0   3   6
Mia  D20 R38/117  P(24-14-1)  195
NYJ  D14 R12/39   P(40-17-3)  224
Mia-Warfield 122C
```

SUNDAY, OCTOBER 11
```
Atl     0   0   0   0   0
Dal     3   3   0   7  13
Atl  D9  R32/84   P(18-10-0)   44
Dal  D13 R54/218  P(11-4-2)    39
Dal-Hill 117R

SF      0  10   7   3  20
LARm    0   6   0   0   6
SF   D12 R37/50   P(20-13-0)  193
LARm D11 R23/104  P(35-14-2)  101
SF-Washington 145C

Bos     3   0   0   7  10
KC      0  10   0  13  23
Bos  D6  R21/76   P(23-5-6)    29
KC   D20 R49/272  P(17-8-2)    74

NO      0   7   3   7  17
SL      0   3   7  14  24
NO   D19 R27/130  P(38-13-2)  212
SL   D17 R30/196  P(31-18-2)  236
NO-Parks 114C; SL-Lane 132R,
Smith 149C

Bal     7  10   0   7  24
Hou     0   7   6   7  20
Bal  D18 R27/74   P(30-15-1)  227
Hou  D24 R33/94   P(34-20-0)  271

Det     0   3   0   7  10
Was     7  10   7   7  31
Det  D16 R28/99   P(25-14-0)  152
Was  D21 R36/127  P(20-14-1)  225
Was-Brown 101R, Taylor 124C

Cin    10   7   3   7  27
Cle     2  14   0  14  30
Cin  D15 R20/54   P(28-20-1)  182
Cle  D23 R41/130  P(29-17-1)  216

Den    10   7   6   0  23
Oak     7  14   0  14  35
Den  D13 R23/145  P(32-17-1)  140
Oak  D25 R31/174  P(37-20-1)  348
Den-Parks 114C; Oak-Wells 198C,
Lamonica 364P
```

```
Phi     0   9   7   7  23
NYG    17   3   7   3  30
Phi  D16 R27/94   P(38-14-3)  273
NYG  D17 R30/174  P(30-16-1)  156
Phi-Jackson 194C;
NYG-Johnson 142R

Buf     3   0   7   0  10
Pit     3   7   3  10  23
Buf  D16 R24/85   P(37-17-3)  200
Pit  D12 R40/171  P(22-7-0)    38
Buf-Moses 122C

Min     7  10   7   0  24
ChiB    0   0   0   0   0
Min  D17 R34/142  P(33-17-1)  200
ChiB D9  R18/62   P(35-19-3)   75
Min-Washington 122C
```

MONDAY, OCTOBER 12
```
GB      3   3  13   3  22
SD      0   6   0  14  20
GB   D19 R41/200  P(24-18-1)  141
SD   D14 R31/217  P(23-7-4)    40
GB-Williams 109R
```

SUNDAY, OCTOBER 18
```
Bal    17   3   6   3  29
NYJ     3   2  14   3  22
Bal  D14 R31/78   P(24-12-3)  176
NYJ  D22 R17/37   P(62-34-6)  361
NYJ-Bell 151C, Maynard 148C,
Namath 397P

SD      0   7  13   0  20
ChiB    0   0   0   7   7
SD   D20 R31/83   P(27-17-0)  274
ChiB D15 R29/100  P(34-17-1)  117
SD-Garrison 165C

KC      0  17   3   7  27
Cin     3   6   0  10  19
KC   D14 R31/116  P(22-9-0)   158
Cin  D15 R22/82   P(47-23-1)  174

NO      3   0  14   0  17
SF      3   0  10   7  20
NO   D14 R30/80   P(34-15-2)  203
SF   D14 R32/73   P(37-17-3)  264
SF-Washington 126C

LARm   14   0   0  17  31
GB      0   7   0  14  21
LARm D18 R32/142  P(25-11-0)  135
GB   D19 R29/137  P(29-16-2)  182

Mia    10   3   7  13  33
Buf     0   7   7   0  14
Mia  D20 R35/147  P(23-15-1)  154
Buf  D14 R22/53   P(32-24-2)  337
Buf-Briscoe 145C, Patrick 111C,
Shaw 348P

Pit     7   0   0   0   7
Hou     3   0   7  10  20
Pit  D11 R28/55   P(22-10-4)  186
Hou  D17 R36/135  P(36-20-3)  124

Det    14  24   3   0  41
Cle     7   7   0  10  24
Det  D13 R29/115  P(21-11-1)  200
Cle  D19 R33/147  P(29-12-5)  171
Det-Walton 158C; Cle-Kelly 106R

SL      0  28   0   7  35
Phi    10   0   3   7  20
SL   D17 R33/198  P(25-7-1)   101
Phi  D17 R28/146  P(40-18-1)  132
SL-Lane 125R

NYG     3   7   0   6  16
Bos     0   0   0   0   0
NYG  D13 R41/122  P(14-8-0)   102
Bos  D14 R27/93   P(22-10-1)   62
```

MONDAY, OCTOBER 19
```
Was     3  10   0   7  20
Oak    14   6  14   0  34
Was  D20 R22/77   P(32-24-0)  224
Oak  D25 R35/226  P(27-19-1)  232
Was-Taylor 102C; Oak-Dixon 164R,
Chester 110C
```

SUNDAY, OCTOBER 25
```
Det     0   3   3  10  16
ChiB    7   0   0   3  10
Det  D13 R43/108  P(23-11-0)   79
ChiB D10 R24/75   P(32-14-3)  235
ChiB-Farmer 147C

Phi     3   7   7   0  17
GB     10  14   3   3  30
Phi  D15 R37/148  P(27-13-3)  163
GB   D15 R32/127  P(20-9-0)   114

Cin     0   0   0   0   0
Was    10   0   7   3  20
Cin  D14 R25/120  P(28-11-1)  101
Was  D20 R39/212  P(24-13-0)  112
Was-Brown 110R

Dal     3  10  14   0  27
KC      7   3   0   6  16
Dal  D15 R39/195  P(15-7-0)   132
KC   D12 R18/53   P(38-17-2)  183
Dal-Thomas 134R, Hayes 100C

SL      3   7   7   0  17
NYG    14  14   7   0  35
SL   D19 R27/126  P(40-15-2)  203
NYG  D20 R32/103  P(19-16-0)  268
SL-Gilliam 119C; NYG-McNeil 110C,
Tucker 150C, Tarkenton 280P

Den     7   7   0   0  14
SF      3   3  10   3  19
Den  D15 R33/162  P(27-12-3)  121
SF   D16 R34/128  P(35-16-0)  234
Den-Little 140R

Buf     0   3   0   7  10
NYJ     0   0   6   0   6
Buf  D15 R25/89   P(24-10-2)  104
NYJ  D10 R35/86   P(16-7-1)    33
Buf-Briscoe 100C

Hou     0  17  14   0  31
SD      0  14   7  10  31
Hou  D25 R45/185  P(36-21-0)  263
SD   D16 R25/76   P(22-8-2)   157
Hou-Joiner 100C; SD-Alworth 124C

NO      0   7   0   7  14
Atl     3   6  10  13  32
NO   D12 R22/96   P(28-15-1)  176
Atl  D20 R41/127  P(22-16-1)  147

Cle     0  14   7   7  28
Mia     0   0   0   0   0
Cle  D21 R34/87   P(29-23-1)  232
Mia  D8  R25/119  P(20-7-3)    46

Bos     3   0   3   0   6
Bal     3  14   3   7  27
Bos  D12 R17/45   P(32-17-4)  125
Bal  D14 R27/101  P(25-14-0)  157
Bos-Sellers 101C

Pit     0   7   7   0  14
Oak     7  17   7   0  31
Pit  D14 R29/128  P(37-15-4)  138
Oak  D15 R38/162  P(17-10-1)  184
Oak-Dixon 106R, Chester 107C
```

MONDAY, OCTOBER 26
```
LARm    0   0   3   0   3
Min     7   3   0   3  13
LARm D5  R23/66   P(22-10-1)   34
Min  D12 R51/146  P(9-5-0)     26
```

SUNDAY, NOVEMBER 1
```
Mia     0   0   0   0   0
Bal     7   7  14   7  35
Mia  D20 R33/201  P(38-19-3)  182
Bal  D14 R24/82   P(21-13-1)  157

Hou     0   0   0   0   0
SL      3  17  10  14  44
Hou  D9  R23/79   P(30-13-2)   81
SL   D20 R39/180  P(27-16-0)  274
```

```
Was    3  10   0   6  19
Den    0   0   0   3   3
Was  D12 R31/97  P(17-9-0)  102
Den  D14 R32/140 P(34-14-3) 106

Phi    0   0  10   7  17
Dal    0  14   7   0  21
Phi  D20 R40/151 P(38-16-4) 245
Dal  D8  R25/46  P(20-10-0) 232
Phi-Hawkins 105C;
Dal-Rentzel 142C

NYG    0   3  16   3  22
NYJ    0   7   3   0  10
NYG  D15 R37/100 P(22-11-0) 140
NYJ  D16 R29/102 P(17-13-2) 135

Min   10  14   3   3  30
Det    7  10   0   0  17
Min  D17 R38/136 P(22-13-2) 251
Det  D13 R28/68  P(32-17-3) 186

Buf   10  21   0  14  45
Bos    0   0   0   3   3
Buf  D18 R34/215 P(17-11-0) 149
Bos  D19 R26/100 P(38-18-2) 151
Buf-Simpson 123R

LARm   7  13   3   7  30
NO    14   0   3   0  17
LARm D21 R32/148 P(36-23-2) 260
NO   D11 R18/67  P(30-14-1) 145
LARm-Truax 124C

GB     3   7   0   0  10
SF     0  10   6  10  26
GB   D15 R32/173 P(26-8-4)  135
SF   D10 R31/126 P(21-11-0) 132
GB-Anderson 105R

ChiB  10   3   7   3  23
Atl    0   7   0   7  14
ChiB D10 R29/89  P(20-6-1)  65
Atl  D17 R31/147 P(26-15-1) 131

SD     0  14   7   6  27
Cle    3   7   0   0  10
SD   D16 R31/131 P(21-13-0) 190
Cle  D19 R34/158 P(24-12-1) 151

Oak    0   7   7   3  17
KC     0   7   3   7  17
Oak  D22 R36/163 P(28-13-0) 115
KC   D16 R34/164 P(14-8-1)  157
KC-Podolak 108R, Taylor 129C
```

MONDAY, NOVEMBER 2

```
Cin    0   7   3   0  10
Pit    0   7   0  14  21
Cin  D18 R32/139 P(30-16-2) 143
Pit  D13 R32/86  P(24-12-0) 195
```

SUNDAY, NOVEMBER 8

```
SF     3   7  14  13  37
ChiB  13   0   3   0  16
SF   D19 R26/47  P(30-23-0) 340
ChiB D14 R30/91  P(25-13-2) 87
SF-Washington 119C, Brodie 317P

Hou    3   3   0   0   6
KC     7   7   0  10  24
Hou  D14 R21/74  P(43-21-3) 252
KC   D11 R37/133 P(14-5-0)  88
Hou-Hopkins 101C

NYJ    3   0   7   7  17
Pit    7   7   7   0  21
NYJ  D20 R29/104 P(44-15-2) 142
Pit  D14 R38/154 P(21-7-0)  123

Cin    3  20  13   7  43
Buf    7   7   0   0  14
Cin  D17 R41/156 P(24-12-0) 163
Buf  D17 R23/103 P(31-15-2) 274
Buf-Briscoe 109C

Min    3   7   3   6  19
Was    7   0   3   0  10
Min  D14 R36/110 P(21-5-0)  53
Was  D21 R33/155 P(25-18-0) 179

Den    0   7   7   7  21
SD     3  14   0   7  24
Den  D21 R39/190 P(22-14-1) 155
SD   D18 R30/91  P(21-14-0) 144

Mia    0   0   0  17  17
Phi    0  17   7   0  24
Mia  D14 R24/117 P(29-11-4) 128
Phi  D17 R40/113 P(29-15-1) 178
```


```
Atl    0   0  10   0  10
LARm   0   3   0   7  10
Atl  D7  R31/85  P(11-5-1)  109
LARm D20 R28/145 P(38-24-2) 219

Cle    0  10   7   3  20
Oak    3  10   0  10  23
Cle  D12 R33/130 P(28-9-3)  110
Oak  D21 R41/160 P(32-14-1) 134
Cle-Scott 101R

Bos    0   0   0   0   0
SL    14   7   3   7  31
Bos  D19 R21/36  P(47-20-3) 159
SL   D15 R32/151 P(22-10-1) 132

Det    0   7   7   3  17
NO     3   3   3  10  19
Det  D18 R35/135 P(25-13-3) 143
NO   D15 R33/131 P(28-16-0) 141

Dal   10   7   3   0  20
NYG    3   6   7   7  23
Dal  D9  R25/102 P(22-10-0) 161
NYG  D20 R41/202 P(26-15-0) 136
Dal-Hayes 129C;
NYG-Johnson 140R
```

MONDAY, NOVEMBER 9

```
Bal    0   7   6   0  13
GB     3   0   0   7  10
Bal  D14 R36/127 P(18-10-1) 163
GB   D16 R37/130 P(23-10-4) 88
```

SUNDAY, NOVEMBER 15

```
Atl    7   3   3   0  13
Phi    3   3   0   7  13
Atl  D15 R32/124 P(16-10-1) 112
Phi  D15 R26/78  P(28-17-0) 152

Buf    7   7   0   3  17
Bal    0   7   3   7  17
Buf  D16 R35/181 P(20-10-2) 90
Bal  D21 R30/136 P(29-15-1) 209

Det   10   0  10   0  20
Min    3   7   0  14  24
Det  D15 R34/126 P(17-10-2) 59
Min  D17 R28/85  P(30-13-1) 204

KC     3   7   7  14  31
Pit    0   0   7   7  14
KC   D21 R45/167 P(24-19-1) 257
Pit  D15 R21/103 P(31-11-5) 99

Cle    7   3   0   0  10
Cin    0   7   7   0  14
Cle  D15 R35/153 P(25-11-1) 143
Cin  D14 R33/210 P(17-10-0) 123
Cin-Carter 110R

SD     0   0   7   9  16
Bos    0   7   0   7  14
SD   D15 R28/29  P(36-16-0) 238
Bos  D15 R33/95  P(17-9-0)  84

ChiB   0   0  10   9  19
GB     3   0   7   3  20
ChiB D12 R28/110 P(26-9-0)  172
GB   D18 R33/123 P(35-23-1) 196
ChiB-Gordon 158C

SF     7   0   9  14  30
Hou    3   0   7   3  13
SF   D17 R35/171 P(26-15-1) 205
Hou  D16 R28/103 P(35-18-0) 165

NO    10   0   0   0  10
Mia    7   0   7   7  21
NO   D18 R36/128 P(23-13-2) 191
Mia  D20 R35/181 P(19-15-0) 225

Was    0  12  21   0  33
NYG    7   7   0  21  35
Was  D17 R28/167 P(27-14-1) 244
NYG  D29 R38/186 P(34-23-2) 299
Was-Taylor 100C;
NYG-Johnson 106R,
Frederickson 165C, Tarkenton 320P

Oak    7   3   7   7  24
Den    0   3   3  13  19
Oak  D16 R28/67  P(29-15-1) 258
Den  D20 R33/116 P(39-14-3) 196

NYJ    0  17   7   7  31
LARm   0   7   6   7  20
NYJ  D15 R44/153 P(17-10-0) 233
LARm D12 R20/51  P(48-16-3) 274
NYJ-Maynard 102C
```


MONDAY, NOVEMBER 16

```
SL     7  10   0  21  38
Dal    0   0   0   0   0
SL   D19 R39/242 P(30-14-1) 150
Dal  D14 R32/103 P(34-10-4) 140
```

SUNDAY, NOVEMBER 22

```
GB     0   3   0   0   3
Min    0   3   7   0  10
GB   D15 R37/124 P(28-14-1) 158
Min  D11 R38/98  P(16-8-0)  104

Bos    0   3   0   0   3
NYJ    3   0   7   7  17
Bos  D5  R17/23  P(22-5-0)  57
NYJ  D19 R44/152 P(22-13-2) 141

Den    0  14  10   7  31
NO     0   6   0   0   6
Den  D25 R37/150 P(33-18-1) 302
NO   D11 R19/49  P(34-20-2) 214

SF     0   0   0   7   7
Det    7   7   7   7  28
SF   D15 R22/56  P(25-18-3) 134
Det  D19 R35/187 P(17-11-0) 111
Det-Farr 117R

Bal    3   7   0   7  17
Mia    7  14   7   3  34
Bal  D19 R23/109 P(36-22-2) 187
Mia  D12 R39/115 P(16-10-0) 136

LARm   3   0  14   0  17
Atl    0   7   0   0   7
LARm D10 R42/123 P(16-8-1)  99
Atl  D14 R33/87  P(30-17-3) 185
Atl-Gipson 110C

SL     0   0   3   3   6
KC     3   3   0   0   6
SL   D17 R36/153 P(23-13-1) 119
KC   D11 R43/169 P(15-5-2)  43
C-Podolak 112R

Dal    3  21  14   7  45
Was    7   0  14   0  21
Dal  D22 R33/181 P(21-14-1) 189
Was  D20 R32/169 P(30-18-0) 135
Dal-Thomas 104R;
Was-Brown 119R

SD     7   0   7   3  17
Oak    0   7   7   6  20
SD   D20 R30/176 P(27-12-2) 155
Oak  D22 R38/183 P(23-14-0) 213
SD-Garrison 114C;
Oak-Biletnikoff 115C

Buf    6   0   0   7  13
ChiB   0  14   7  10  31
Buf  D14 R29/134 P(22-14-2) 119
ChiB D12 R33/91  P(20-8-1)  150
ChiB-Gordon 107C, Douglass 196P

Pit    0   0   7   0   7
Cin    6   7   7  14  34
Pit  D23 R26/138 P(43-16-4) 183
Cin  D17 R41/186 P(18-10-0) 146
Pit-Fuqua 119R; Cin-Robinson 119R

Hou    0   7   0   7  14
Cle    7   7  14   0  28
Hou  D23 R35/178 P(37-20-3) 148
Cle  D18 R37/126 P(20-10-0) 222
Hou-Dawkins 143R; Cle-Glass 102C
```

MONDAY, NOVEMBER 23

```
NYG    3  10   7   0  20
Phi    0   9   7   7  23
NYG  D17 R30/109 P(30-15-0) 178
Phi  D18 R39/117 P(17-12-0) 164
```

THURSDAY, NOVEMBER 26

```
Oak   14   0   0   0  14
Det    0  14   0  14  28
Oak  D18 R26/100 P(33-13-2) 148
Det  D25 R44/262 P(15-10-0) 137
Oak-Biletnikoff 109C; Det-Farr 104R

GB     3   0   0   0   3
Dal    3   0   3  10  16
GB   D9  R28/78  P(21-9-1)  51
Dal  D15 R39/151 P(20-12-0) 201
Dal-Hayes 105C
```


SUNDAY, NOVEMBER 29

```
Bos    0   7   7   0  14
Buf    0   7   0   7  14
Bos  D10 R33/58  P(18-8-3)  109
Buf  D12 R23/95  P(37-18-1) 230

Min    0   3   0   7  10
NYJ    7   3   3   7  20
Min  D11 R18/59  P(27-10-4) 108
NYJ  D15 R51/187 P(12-8-0)  74
NYJ-Nock 117R

NO     0   3   0   0   3
Cin   13   7   3   3  26
NO   D15 R25/70  P(37-20-2) 292
Cin  D17 R34/149 P(27-12-1) 148
NO-Abramowicz 165C

NYG    0  10  14   3  27
Was    3   0   7  14  24
NYG  D23 R33/150 P(36-24-1) 251
Was  D18 R27/167 P(29-18-2) 189
Was-Brown 139R, Roberts 109C

SD     0   0   7   7  14
KC     0   7   6  13  26
SD   D10 R17/35  P(33-18-2) 161
KC   D16 R35/138 P(24-17-1) 191

LARm   0   6  10  14  30
SF     3  10   0   0  13
LARm D14 R30/155 P(22-7-0)  65
SF   D16 R29/125 P(36-18-2) 160

Phi    0   7   7   0  14
SL     6   0  17   0  23
Phi  D19 R33/106 P(28-17-1) 170
SL   D17 R40/156 P(21-12-1) 181

Den    0   0   0  21  21
Hou   14  10   0   7  31
Den  D14 R20/83  P(32-10-3) 164
Hou  D17 R35/98  P(25-15-1) 234
Hou-LeVias 101C

ChiB  17   0   0   3  20
Bal    0  14   0   7  21
ChiB D14 R29/103 P(37-21-0) 132
Bal  D18 R25/50  P(40-23-5) 258

Cle    3   3   3   0   9
Pit    7   7   7   7  28
Cle  D16 R23/42  P(39-15-1) 129
Pit  D15 R38/168 P(17-10-0) 257
Pit-Fuqua 116C, Shanklin 121C
```

MONDAY, NOVEMBER 30

```
Mia    3  10   0   7  20
Atl    0   0   0   7   7
Mia  D16 R38/218 P(11-8-1)  86
Atl  D15 R33/111 P(24-18-1) 160
Mia-Csonka 108R
```

SATURDAY, DECEMBER 5

```
ChiB   0   6   0  13  13
Min    3   3   7   3  16
ChiB D9  R15/41  P(29-10-3) 88
Min  D16 R53/202 P(12-5-0)  79
Min-Osborn 139R
```

SUNDAY, DECEMBER 6

```
NO     3   3   3   7  16
LARm   7  14   3  10  34
NO   D15 R22/75  P(32-17-0) 180
LARm D25 R29/109 P(46-23-0) 336
LARm-Snow 103C

Den    0   0   0   0   0
KC    10   0   0   3  16
Den  D7  R20/76  P(21-9-5)  70
KC   D8  R32/204 P(19-7-0)  18
KC-Podolak 139R

Buf    0   6   0   0   6
NYG    0   3  14   3  20
Buf  D13 R24/73  P(31-15-1) 107
NYG  D15 R35/151 P(19-11-0) 119
NYG-Johnson 100R

Bos    0   7   6   7  20
Mia   17  10   7   3  37
Bos  D19 R23/67  P(35-22-0) 176
Mia  D18 R40/208 P(19-11-0) 93
Mia-Csonka 115R
```


```
SL     3   0   0   0   3
Det    0   9   0   7  16
SL   D6  R18/38  P(26-10-2) 108
Det  D18 R40/160 P(21-11-1) 119
SL-Gilliam 105C

GB     6   0   7   7  20
Pit    3   0   6   3  12
GB   D14 R33/82  P(32-14-2) 235
Pit  D13 R33/131 P(34-8-5)  143
Pit-Smith 111C

Was    0   0   0   0   0
Dal    0   7  14  13  34
Was  D9  R21/67  P(25-14-2) 99
Dal  D24 R48/276 P(24-11-0) 148
Dal-Thomas 123R

Oak    0   0   7   7  14
NYJ    0   3   7   3  13
Oak  D16 R24/71  P(44-15-2) 179
NYJ  D12 R44/158 P(22-9-1)  99
NYJ-Boozer 115R

Phi    0   3   7   0  10
Bal   13  10   3   3  29
Phi  D9  R27/97  P(29-14-3) 89
Bal  D13 R39/148 P(18-10-1) 101

Atl   13   0   7   0  20
SF     7   7  10  10  34
Atl  D13 R39/153 P(18-8-0)  52
SF   D20 R29/95  P(30-20-1) 259
SF-Washington 115C

Cin    0  10   0   7  17
SD     0   7   0   7  14
Cin  D11 R38/136 P(19-8-1)  0
SD   D21 R29/113 P(36-17-3) 167
```

MONDAY, DECEMBER 7

```
Cle    0   7   7   7  21
Hou    3   0   0   7  10
Cle  D20 R45/194 P(27-15-2) 150
Hou  D11 R23/110 P(28-11-1) 113
Cle-Kelly 108R
```

SATURDAY, DECEMBER 12

```
KC     3   0   3   0   6
Oak    0   6   7   7  20
KC   D7  R23/62  P(12-6-1)  59
Oak  D23 R47/204 P(19-9-1)  120

Dal    0   0   3   3   6
Cle    2   0   0   0   2
Dal  D12 R41/122 P(17-8-0)  52
Cle  D13 R19/63  P(39-23-3) 236
```

SUNDAY, DECEMBER 13

```
SF     7  10  14   7  38
NO    14   7   0   6  27
SF   D19 R34/113 P(22-15-0) 217
NO   D17 R34/105 P(22-15-1) 248
SF-Washington 131C;
NO-Abramowicz 140C

Phi    0   7   7   0  14
Was    0   7   7  10  24
Phi  D13 R30/51  P(28-16-0) 155
Was  D17 R40/194 P(15-10-0) 122
Was-Henderson 120C

NYG    7  14   3  10  34
SL     0   3   7   7  17
NYG  D22 R46/144 P(21-14-0) 217
SL   D13 R19/71  P(30-13-1) 273
SL-Lane 106C, Smith 115C

Pit    6  10   0   0  16
Atl    0   7  10   7  27
Pit  D14 R37/99  P(28-8-5)  94
Atl  D11 R41/147 P(16-7-2)  74

Cin    0   6  14  10  30
Hou    3   3   7   7  20
Cin  D17 R39/194 P(21-11-0) 144
Hou  D19 R21/43  P(54-27-2) 310
Hou-Joiner 143C, Rhome 315P

SD     7  10   0   0  17
Den    3   0   0  14  17
SD   D15 R37/86  P(25-11-0) 145
Den  D14 R28/112 P(28-11-2) 152

NYJ    3   7   0   0  10
Mia    0   6   0  10  16
NYJ  D14 R26/128 P(24-10-2) 86
Mia  D19 R40/144 P(18-10-2) 125
NYJ-Boozer 114R
```

Bal 10 0 7 3 **20**
Buf 7 7 0 0 14
Bal D15 R29/49 P(31-13-0) 226
Buf D18 R27/97 P(43-23-2) 236
Bal-Jefferson 125C;
Buf-Moses 100C

Min 14 7 14 0 **35**
Bos 0 7 0 7 14
Min D28 R38/112 P(32-22-0) 317
Bos D15 R24/66 P(29-15-3) 116
Min-Henderson 137C,
Washington 101C

GB 3 0 0 14 17
ChiB 14 7 7 7 **35**
GB D16 R35/98 P(24-11-1) 82
ChiB D20 R21/53 P(36-22-1) 339
GB-Dale 128C; ChiB-Farmer 142C,
Concannon 338P

MONDAY, DECEMBER 14
Det 7 7 7 7 **28**
LARm 0 3 3 17 23
Det D22 R35/179 P(23-16-1) 164
LARm D20 R15/47 P(42-27-1) 334
LARm-Snow 150C, Gabriel 334P

SATURDAY, DECEMBER 19
NYJ 7 7 3 3 20
Bal 0 14 7 14 **35**
NYJ D13 R31/43 P(31-17-0) 169
Bal D23 R36/102 P(37-20-1) 355
Bal-Morrall 348P

SUNDAY, DECEMBER 20
GB 0 0 0 0 0
Det 3 0 3 14 **20**
GB D9 R24/46 P(27-15-3) 78
Det D9 R32/91 P(19-7-1) 71

ChiB 0 7 3 14 **24**
NO 0 3 0 0 3
ChiB D19 R20/104 P(51-26-4) 272
NO D9 R23/48 P(31-14-4) 143
ChiB-Gordon 119C

Cle 0 10 17 0 **27**
Den 3 3 0 7 13
Cle D15 R33/82 P(25-12-2) 201
Den D16 R37/179 P(26-10-3) 101

SF 3 21 0 14 **38**
Oak 7 0 0 0 7
SF D16 R43/125 P(22-7-0) 171
Oak D17 R28/88 P(33-16-5) 270

Min 3 21 7 6 **37**
Atl 7 0 0 0 7
Min D21 R38/136 P(30-19-2) 262
Atl D12 R19/46 P(33-19-3) 85
Min-Henderson 129C

KC 0 10 3 0 13
SD 3 14 7 7 **31**
KC D14 R21/76 P(25-16-0) 161
SD D22 R35/143 P(29-17-0) 323
SD-Garrison 149C

Bos 0 0 0 7 7
Cin 14 24 7 0 **45**
Bos D8 R21/67 P(24-7-2) 82
Cin D23 R45/237 P(17-10-0) 187

Pit 7 7 3 3 20
Phi 6 14 0 10 **30**
Pit D10 R34/259 P(15-7-0) 82
Phi D23 R35/107 P(29-21-2) 276
Pit-Fuqua 218R

Hou 3 0 0 7 10
Dal 17 7 14 3 **41**
Hou D12 R27/86 P(27-8-4) 65
Dal D22 R41/208 P(22-15-1) 341
Dal-Thomas 115R, Hayes 187C,
Morton 349P

Buf 0 0 0 7 7
Mia 21 10 7 7 **45**
Buf D10 R16/46 P(33-17-3) 151
Mia D19 R44/159 P(17-8-0) 166

SL 7 3 3 14 27
Was 14 7 0 7 **28**
SL D14 R25/69 P(31-16-2) 181
Was D20 R43/141 P(14-9-1) 146
SL-Gilliam 125C

LARm 7 17 7 0 **31**
NYG 3 0 0 0 3
LARm D18 R43/192 P(21-13-0) 149
NYG D20 R20/50 P(44-21-1) 166
LARm-Josephson 106R

1971 NFL
SUNDAY, SEPTEMBER 19
KC 7 7 0 0 14
SD 0 0 7 14 **21**
KC D17 R34/116 P(23-12-2) 115
SD D21 R26/102 P(38-18-1) 254

LARm 0 3 14 3 20
NO 0 3 14 7 **24**
LARm D11 R26/118 P(30-11-0) 144
NO D21 R41/122 P(29-16-1) 154

Phi 0 7 0 7 14
Cin 0 10 17 10 **37**
Phi D17 R18/39 P(40-20-3) 276
Cin D23 R35/236 P(33-24-0) 296
Phi-Hawkins 118C, Liske 301P;
Cin-Johnson 113R, Thomas 122C

Pit 0 6 6 3 15
ChiB 0 3 0 14 **17**
Pit D15 R43/223 P(24-10-4) 129
ChiB D8 R21/45 P(29-16-1) 96
Pit-Fuqua 114R, Shanklin 113C

Mia 3 0 0 7 10
Den 3 0 7 0 10
Mia D15 R31/118 P(24-13-1) 121
Den D13 R32/104 P(21-12-1) 157
Mia-Warfield 146C

Hou 0 0 0 0 0
Cle 7 10 7 7 **31**
Hou D11 R15/35 P(39-17-5) 208
Cle D21 R34/108 P(39-19-1) 269

NYG 0 28 14 0 **42**
GB 7 7 10 16 40
NYG D12 R31/102 P(21-13-1) 221
GB D17 R30/124 P(26-15-1) 224
NYG-Houston 151C, Tarkenton 236P

Was 0 14 3 7 **24**
SL 0 10 0 7 17
Was D10 R38/148 P(17-6-0) 276
SL D13 R38/117 P(27-10-4) 138

SF 0 7 0 10 17
Atl 3 7 10 0 **20**
SF D22 R30/166 P(34-17-4) 206
Atl D16 R36/101 P(21-16-0) 165

Dal 7 21 7 14 **49**
Buf 14 10 6 7 37
Dal D19 R40/160 P(14-10-0) 211
Buf D18 R22/66 P(30-18-3) 335
Buf-Briscoe 113C, Shaw 353P

NYJ 0 0 0 0 0
Bal 10 9 0 3 **22**
NYJ D7 R18/43 P(24-12-0) 75
Bal D16 R43/253 P(17-7-0) 66
Bal-Bulaich 198R

Oak 0 6 0 0 6
NE 0 0 14 6 **20**
Oak D20 R36/205 P(31-11-1) 99
NE D12 R37/134 P(15-6-1) 127

MONDAY, SEPTEMBER 20
Min 0 3 7 6 **16**
Det 10 3 0 0 13
Min D14 R29/43 P(32-19-2) 232
Det D15 R38/160 P(26-8-0) 61
Min-Grim 126C

SUNDAY, SEPTEMBER 26
ChiB 0 0 3 17 **20**
Min 0 7 10 0 17
ChiB D19 R25/76 P(42-26-1) 239
Min D11 R28/84 P(26-11-1) 146
ChiB-Gordon 115C

Atl 0 13 0 7 20
LARm 10 0 7 3 20
Atl D20 R39/104 P(22-15-1) 287
LARm D20 R37/192 P(30-16-0) 125
Atl-Mitchell 143C, Berry 301P;
LARm-Ellison 138R

Cle 0 7 0 7 14
Bal 0 3 7 3 13
Cle D18 R40/118 P(27-13-2) 149
Bal D12 R31/137 P(19-3-5) 41

Was 14 3 3 10 **30**
NYG 3 0 0 0 3
Was D19 R30/126 P(32-23-0) 301
NYG D13 R25/68 P(30-14-2) 88
Was-Taylor 125C, Kilmer 309P

SF 3 7 14 14 **38**
NO 0 7 0 13 20
SF D17 R36/194 P(22-10-2) 125
NO D16 R28/90 P(30-14-1) 173
NO-Abramowicz 110C

KC 10 3 0 7 **20**
Hou 0 3 6 7 16
KC D19 R39/79 P(24-14-0) 207
Hou D15 R20/26 P(28-13-3) 172

Mia 3 9 7 10 **29**
Buf 7 0 7 0 14
Mia D20 R45/226 P(18-10-0) 150
Buf D14 R18/131 P(23-17-2) 136
Mia-Csonka 103R, Kiick 108R

Cin 3 0 0 7 10
Pit 7 7 7 0 **21**
Cin D15 R18/28 P(43-23-1) 225
Pit D15 R29/80 P(30-18-1) 208
Pit-Smith 162C

Det 3 14 3 14 **34**
NE 0 0 7 0 7
Det D19 R37/164 P(21-13-0) 204
NE D10 R29/145 P(17-6-2) 101

Oak 3 3 14 14 **34**
SD 0 0 0 0 0
Oak D20 R40/212 P(19-12-0) 163
SD D13 R22/73 P(29-14-5) 153

Den 0 3 0 7 13
GB 7 13 14 0 **34**
Den D19 R27/81 P(41-23-6) 246
GB D15 R40/214 P(19-5-3) 89

Dal 0 21 7 14 **42**
Phi 0 0 0 7 7
Dal D23 R43/150 P(29-19-3) 219
Phi D12 R19/32 P(36-14-7) 138

MONDAY, SEPTEMBER 27
NYJ 0 0 7 3 10
SL 7 10 0 0 **17**
NYJ D18 R31/118 P(28-16-0) 121
SL D15 R36/118 P(23-11-1) 222
SL-Gilliam 136C

SUNDAY, OCTOBER 3
SF 3 14 7 7 **31**
Phi 0 0 3 0 3
SF D21 R31/202 P(30-15-0) 308
Phi D17 R28/89 P(30-17-0) 172
SF-Washington 112C

ChiB 0 3 0 0 3
LARm 7 3 7 0 **17**
ChiB D10 R18/68 P(38-9-4) 45
LARm D21 R43/263 P(31-13-2) 159

NYG 14 7 0 0 **21**
SL 3 7 3 7 20
NYG D16 R32/81 P(32-20-2) 220
SL D14 R30/129 P(22-10-1) 176
SL-Gray 124C

SD 3 7 7 0 17
Pit 7 0 7 7 **21**
SD D28 R39/169 P(36-25-2) 258
Pit D16 R27/125 P(24-15-0) 157
SD-Parks 111C

Atl 7 17 7 7 38
Det 14 14 10 3 **41**
Atl D16 R21/47 P(23-13-3) 295
Det D23 R57/223 P(12-7-1) 95
Atl-Burrow 190C, Berry 309P

NYJ 0 0 0 14 **14**
Mia 10 0 0 0 10
NYJ D13 R42/134 P(21-9-1) 87
Mia D14 R32/163 P(23-9-1) 134
Mia-Warfield 104C

NO 0 0 6 7 13
Hou 3 0 0 10 13
NO D16 R36/184 P(20-8-2) 79
Hou D13 R26/107 P(25-9-3) 156

Buf 0 0 0 0 0
Min 0 12 0 7 **19**
Buf D7 R18/56 P(20-12-2) 8
Min D23 R52/193 P(21-12-2) 133

Cin 0 0 10 7 17
GB 3 7 0 10 **20**
Cin D10 R24/90 P(23-11-1) 88
GB D18 R50/256 P(12-4-2) 62
GB-Brockington 120R

Bal 14 3 0 6 **23**
NE 0 7 0 0 7
Bal D24 R36/136 P(24-19-2) 222
NE D9 R24/89 P(20-9-1) 62

Was 7 7 3 3 **20**
Dal 0 0 7 0 7
Was D14 R41/200 P(10-5-1) 85
Dal D20 R29/82 P(35-17-0) 185
Was-Harraway 111R, Parks 111C

KC 0 10 0 6 **16**
Den 0 0 0 3 3
KC D11 R33/93 P(21-9-1) 66
Den D9 R27/62 P(28-14-4) 160

MONDAY, OCTOBER 4
Oak 0 10 0 24 **34**
Cle 0 14 3 3 20
Oak D20 R27/168 P(21-11-1) 160
Cle D20 R43/156 P(25-15-2) 178
Oak-Hubbard 103R

SUNDAY, OCTOBER 10
Pit 0 7 3 7 17
Cle 10 10 0 7 **27**
Pit D11 R20/110 P(28-13-1) 112
Cle D20 R40/131 P(27-18-1) 219
Cle-Morin 126C

Bal 14 8 0 21 **43**
Buf 0 0 0 0 0
Bal D19 R43/214 P(26-13-2) 187
Buf D4 R11/4 P(21-10-4) 45
Bal-Mitchell 111C

NO 0 7 0 7 14
ChiB 7 28 0 0 **35**
NO D18 R20/75 P(33-16-2) 188
ChiB D26 R47/202 P(28-16-1) 225
ChiB-Gordon 139C

Hou 0 10 3 0 13
Was 6 10 0 6 **22**
Hou D13 R21/46 P(35-16-3) 146
Was D11 R40/115 P(21-10-0) 136

NYJ 0 0 0 0 0
NE 3 7 3 7 **20**
NYJ D11 R33/113 P(25-4-0) 8
NE D15 R36/207 P(22-10-0) 130
NE-Garrett 111R

SL 6 10 7 3 **26**
Atl 0 3 0 6 9
SL D16 R42/151 P(27-12-0) 112
Atl D15 R26/94 P(27-13-4) 119

SD 3 7 0 0 10
KC 0 10 7 14 **31**
SD D11 R21/54 P(23-12-2) 125
KC D21 R38/221 P(23-16-0) 167

LARm 0 3 7 10 **20**
SF 0 0 0 13 13
LARm D9 R34/219 P(12-2-1) -18
SF D14 R31/120 P(34-17-2) 152

GB 0 7 14 7 **28**
Det 0 7 0 7 14
GB D14 R24/126 P(19-11-2) 137
Det D26 R41/178 P(29-18-1) 287
Det-Walton 103C, Landry 302P

Mia 7 3 7 6 **23**
Cin 3 3 7 0 13
Mia D16 R34/131 P(23-12-1) 181
Cin D19 R33/214 P(19-11-0) 116

Oak 3 3 14 7 **27**
Den 0 0 7 0 7
Oak D20 R42/156 P(28-11-1) 113
Den D11 R29/99 P(24-11-2) 220

Min 3 10 0 0 **13**
Phi 0 0 0 0 0
Min D15 R43/135 P(24-11-0) 60
Phi D9 R25/50 P(32-14-2) 122

MONDAY, OCTOBER 11
NYG 3 3 0 7 13
Dal 3 10 7 0 **20**
NYG D18 R21/67 P(46-26-0) 265
Dal D21 R45/222 P(23-11-1) 179
NYG-Duhon 111C

SUNDAY, OCTOBER 17
ChiB 0 0 0 0 0
SF 3 3 0 7 **13**
ChiB D13 R18/62 P(41-15-4) 158
SF D20 R42/161 P(35-20-2) 193

SL 0 0 0 0 0
Was 10 0 3 7 **20**
SL D11 R14/25 P(30-15-4) 180
Was D21 R47/229 P(17-9-1) 120
Was-Brown 150R

Det 0 14 3 14 **31**
Hou 0 7 0 0 7
Det D20 R43/230 P(16-9-1) 155
Hou D13 R24/86 P(40-15-4) 209
Det-Taylor 122C

NE 0 3 0 0 3
Mia 21 10 7 3 **41**
NE D11 R18/35 P(35-14-2) 82
Mia D19 R34/215 P(22-11-0) 216
Mia-Griese 185P

Phi 7 3 0 0 10
Oak 0 0 13 21 **34**
Phi D11 R23/62 P(27-14-1) 164
Oak D20 R35/176 P(30-18-1) 236
Oak-Biletnikoff 148C

LARm 0 10 0 14 **24**
Atl 6 0 3 7 16
LARm D18 R36/124 P(24-14-0) 182
Atl D14 R33/114 P(19-10-4) 135

Bal 3 21 7 0 **31**
NYG 7 0 0 0 7
Bal D19 R37/241 P(22-10-0) 122
NYG D15 R23/87 P(33-18-3) 164
Bal-Bulaich 108R

Buf 0 7 10 0 17
NYJ 14 0 7 7 **28**
Buf D14 R23/83 P(33-11-2) 188
NYJ D20 R52/191 P(12-7-0) 140
Buf-Moses 151C; NYJ-Boozer 116R

SD 3 3 7 3 16
Den 7 13 0 0 **20**
SD D15 R16/76 P(44-18-1) 212
Den D17 R55/225 P(18-7-1) 71
SD-Garrison 105C;
Den-Anderson 106R

Min 7 0 7 10 **24**
GB 0 7 6 0 13
Min D17 R28/98 P(33-17-1) 172
GB D19 R37/121 P(25-12-3) 221
Min-Grim 101C; GB-Dale 151C

Cle 0 6 7 14 **27**
Cin 3 7 7 7 24
Cle D17 R26/64 P(35-18-2) 205
Cin D15 R40/232 P(22-10-1) 107

Dal 0 0 0 7 14
NO 0 0 7 0 **24**
Dal D20 R31/96 P(34-17-3) 204
NO D10 R31/108 P(15-6-1) 49

MONDAY, OCTOBER 18
Pit 9 0 0 7 16
KC 0 28 0 10 **38**
Pit D18 R26/71 P(39-20-2) 251
KC D15 R35/63 P(26-14-1) 285
KC-Taylor 190C

SATURDAY, OCTOBER 23
Buf 0 0 0 3 3
SD 7 3 3 7 **20**
Buf D11 R27/152 P(24-8-2) 37
SD D22 R42/198 P(29-15-1) 248
Buf-Simpson 106R;
SD-Garrison 106C

SUNDAY, OCTOBER 24
Cin 0 0 17 10 27
Oak 10 7 0 14 **31**
Cin D17 R35/111 P(23-15-1) 139
Oak D19 R37/202 P(18-10-2) 114

THE GAMES

```
Was    7  10   0   3   20
KC     3   3   7  14   27
Was  D16 R25/99   P(38-15-1) 205
KC   D20 R39/162  P(23-10-2) 163
Was-Taylor 125C; KC-Podolak 110R,
Taylor 105C

Den    7  17   3   0   27
Cle    0   0   0   0    0
Den  D18 R57/280  P(16-8-0)   85
Cle  D6  R15/24   P(27-7-3)   36
Den-Little 113R

Mia    0  10   7   0   30
NYJ    7   0   0   7   14
Mia  D19 R44/302  P(18-5-0)   59
NYJ  D16 R32/132  P(24-8-0)  101
Mia-Csonka 137R, Kiick 121R

GB     0   6   0   7   13
LARm   7   6   7  10   30
GB   D14 R27/93   P(26-11-3) 144
LARm D20 R40/164  P(23-12-1) 167

SF     0  10   3  13   26
SL     0   7   0   7   14
SF   D16 R37/140  P(32-16-0) 226
SL   D15 R24/108  P(26-11-1) 176
SL-Smith 103C

NO     0   3   3   0    6
Atl   14  14   0   0   28
NO   D15 R15/58   P(41-14-2) 144
Atl  D25 R53/284  P(16-9-1)   80
Atl-Butler 114R

ChiB   7  14   0   7   28
Det    6  14   3   0   23
ChiB D17 R34/173  P(21-15-0) 150
Det  D17 R28/116  P(26-11-2) 145

Hou    7   3   6   0   16
Pit    3   3   3  14   23
Hou  D19 R26/92   P(34-17-1) 180
Pit  D26 R37/165  P(33-21-4) 254
Pit-Fuqua 113R

NYG    0   7   0   0    7
Phi    7   6   0  10   23
NYG  D16 R29/165  P(26-11-1)  71
Phi  D15 R40/169  P(20-6-1)   43

NE     7   0   0  14   21
Dal   10  24   0  10   44
NE   D17 R24/76   P(29-16-1) 183
Dal  D20 R34/168  P(25-16-0) 238
NE-Vataha 107C
```

MONDAY, OCTOBER 25

```
Bal    0   0   0   3    3
Min    7   0   3   0   10
Bal  D16 R35/129  P(33-19-3) 147
Min  D9  R29/67   P(15-7-1)   86
```

SUNDAY, OCTOBER 31

```
NYJ    7   7   7   0   21
SD     0  21   7  21   49
NYJ  D19 R30/169  P(23-11-3)  94
SD   D16 R31/165  P(28-19-1) 358
SD-Garrison 162C, Hadl 358P

Min    7   0   3   7   17
NYG    3   7   0   0   10
Min  D13 R25/101  P(33-16-1) 161
NYG  D13 R37/125  P(30-20-0) 127

Dal    7   2   0  10   19
ChiB  10   3   3   7   23
Dal  D26 R34/139  P(47-27-4) 342
ChiB D7  R31/82   P(19-7-1)  112

SL    14   0   7   7   28
Buf    0   9   7   7   23
SL   D24 R41/142  P(27-15-0) 163
Buf  D19 R23/62   P(34-18-2) 247

Mia    7   7   3   3   20
LARm   0   0   0  14   14
Mia  D13 R29/127  P(19-13-0) 185
LARm D22 R30/114  P(35-23-0) 245
Mia-Warfield 108C;
LARm-Snow 107C

NO     0   0   0  14   14
Was    0  17   0   7   24
NO   D16 R31/106  P(27-12-1) 106
Was  D21 R37/173  P(22-13-2) 204
Was-Brown 113R
```

```
Den    0   7   6   3   16
Phi    3  14   0   0   17
Den  D19 R39/170  P(28-14-2) 102
Phi  D9  R26/46   P(17-7-1)   77
Den-Little 123R

NE     0   0   7   3   10
SF     0   0   6  14   27
NE   D11 R31/177  P(20-7-0)   69
SF   D13 R36/71   P(21-10-3) 176
SF-Washington 160C

Atl   14   7   7   3   31
Cle    0   0   7  14   14
Atl  D17 R54/175  P(10-7-0)  142
Cle  D10 R20/65   P(19-9-4)   88

KC     7   7   3   3   20
Oak    3   7  10   0   20
KC   D18 R37/161  P(13-7-1)   87
Oak  D19 R28/111  P(25-12-2) 141
Oak-Biletnikoff 128C

Pit    7   7   7   0   21
Bal    7  20   7   0   34
Pit  D14 R16/26   P(35-20-1) 155
Bal  D19 R32/71   P(34-18-1) 312
Bal-Perkins 124C, Richardson 100C

Cin    0   3   0   3    6
Hou    0   3   7   0   10
Cin  D9  R31/135  P(20-6-1)  -52
Hou  D9  R34/94   P(20-7-4)   83
```

MONDAY, NOVEMBER 1

```
Det    7   7   0   0   14
GB     7   0   0   0    7
Det  D18 R48/190  P(14-6-1)  101
GB   D13 R40/218  P(5-1-0)     0
GB-Brockington 111R
```

SUNDAY, NOVEMBER 7

```
Buf    0   0   0   0    0
Mia    7   7   7  13   34
Buf  D19 R29/206  P(30-18-2) 158
Mia  D23 R38/302  P(19-9-0)   89
Mia-Morris 116R

Phi    0   0   7   0    7
Was    0   0   0   7    7
Phi  D10 R31/77   P(22-10-1)  95
Was  D14 R31/61   P(24-12-4) 136

Atl    3   0   0   6    9
Cin    3   0   0   3    6
Atl  D15 R45/155  P(15-7-0)  112
Cin  D10 R30/94   P(24-10-2)  73

SD     0   3  14   0   17
NYG    7  14   0  14   35
SD   D18 R21/92   P(35-19-3) 227
NYG  D21 R37/157  P(20-16-0) 260

Dal    3   0   3  10   16
SL     0   0   0  13   13
Dal  D20 R38/173  P(31-20-0) 199
SL   D11 R16/36   P(23-12-0) 192
Dal-Thomas 101R

SF     3   3   0   7   13
Min    3   0   3   3    9
SF   D14 R36/119  P(30-13-2) 103
Min  D10 R26/91   P(25-6-1)   76

Oak    0   7   7   7   21
NO     0   0   7  14   21
Oak  D13 R34/134  P(12-6-1)  106
NO   D26 R48/212  P(29-14-1) 161

Cle    0   0   2   7    9
Pit   10   6   0  10   26
Cle  D11 R32/129  P(22-10-2)  81
Pit  D21 R48/230  P(21-7-1)  163
Cle-Kelly 102R; Pit-Fuqua 131R

Det    0   0  17   7   24
Den    0   3   3   7   13
Det  D19 R37/228  P(16-7-1)  190
Den  D20 R43/203  P(20-13-0) 157
Det-Owens 109R

KC     0   3   0   7   10
NYJ    7   3   0   3   13
KC   D10 R31/95   P(25-13-2)  95
NYJ  D11 R37/136  P(9-3-0)     9

Hou    0   6   7   7   20
NE     7   7   0  14   28
Hou  D16 R27/71   P(36-18-3) 260
NE   D21 R36/99   P(31-15-0) 154
```

```
GB     0  14   0   3   17
ChiB   0   0   0  14   14
GB   D13 R43/171  P(14-7-1)  133
ChiB D16 R22/75   P(18-19-3) 205
GB-Brockington 142R
```

MONDAY, NOVEMBER 8

```
LARm   3   7   0   7   17
Bal    0   7   0  17   24
LARm D12 R23/108  P(27-12-1) 154
Bal  D17 R36/155  P(30-10-2)  94
```

SUNDAY, NOVEMBER 14

```
NYG    7   0   7   7   21
Atl    3   7   0   7   17
NYG  D19 R39/172  P(26-14-1) 152
Atl  D13 R28/80   P(20-11-2) 139

Hou    0   0   0  21   21
Oak   21  17   3   0   41
Hou  D16 R28/59   P(32-11-4) 130
Oak  D12 R33/82   P(17-8-4)  163

Pit   14   0   7   0   21
Mia    3  14   0   7   24
Pit  D17 R24/69   P(37-25-3) 219
Mia  D11 R33/120  P(16-9-2)  189
Mia-Warfield 158C

Buf    7  13  10   3   33
NE     7  21   7   3   38
Buf  D15 R24/89   P(36-15-0) 128
NE   D9  R27/119  P(16-9-1)  180
NE-Plunkett 218P

Cle    0   3   0   7   10
KC     3  10   0   0   13
Cle  D15 R19/45   P(33-16-2) 247
KC   D23 R43/183  P(24-15-0) 201
Cle-Pitts 129C

Bal    0   0  14   0   14
NYJ    0   7   0   6   13
Bal  D15 R37/119  P(25-9-0)   70
NYJ  D9  R29/75   P(21-9-3)  113

LARm   0  14   0   7   21
Det    3   0   3   7   13
LARm D19 R30/141  P(22-17-1) 170
Det  D21 R38/177  P(25-15-0) 140
Det-Taylor 101R

Phi    0   0   0   7    7
Dal    3   7   7   3   20
Phi  D14 R18/44   P(39-23-2) 242
Dal  D21 R40/179  P(29-14-0) 129

Was    6   6   3   0   20
ChiB   0   3   3  10   16
Was  D15 R28/88   P(36-24-0) 195
ChiB D20 R34/205  P(33-15-0) 180

Cin    7   7   3   7   24
Den    0   0   3   7   10
Cin  D19 R42/213  P(23-15-0) 260
Den  D10 R29/122  P(18-7-1)   99
Cin-Coslet 102C; Den-Little 101R

NO     0   9  10   7   26
SF    10   0   3   7   20
NO   D17 R31/122  P(21-13-0) 216
SF   D23 R33/143  P(28-20-2) 190

GB     0   0   0   3    3
Min    0   0   0   3    3
GB   D15 R54/245  P(11-6-3)   56
Min  D5  R31/66   P(11-5-0)   21
GB-Brockington 149R
```

MONDAY, NOVEMBER 15

```
SL     7   3   0   7   17
SD     0   3   7  10   20
SL   D21 R31/132  P(35-17-3) 214
SD   D21 R32/140  P(30-21-1) 249
```

SUNDAY, NOVEMBER 21

```
SD    10  14   0   9   33
Oak    3  14  10   7   34
SD   D22 R31/96   P(36-20-1) 312
Oak  D21 R35/170  P(26-16-0) 190
SD-Hadl 321P

SF     3   3   0   0    7
LARm   0  14   3   0   17
SF   D21 R34/96   P(42-23-4) 286
LARm D8  R30/124  P(16-5-1)   49
```

```
Dal    7   0   3   3   13
Was    0   0   0   0    0
Dal  D16 R37/146  P(21-11-0) 133
Was  D15 R21/65   P(32-19-2) 167

Den    3   0   0   7   10
KC    14   7   7   0   28
Den  D15 R27/129  P(37-17-3) 190
KC   D16 R32/132  P(22-12-1) 255
Den-Simmons 153C

NYJ    0  17   0   3   20
Buf    7   0   0   0    7
NYJ  D10 R42/153  P(14-6-1)   78
Buf  D12 R23/78   P(33-13-5) 119

Min    3   3   7  10   23
NO     0   0   3   7   10
Min  D20 R42/172  P(25-14-1)  95
NO   D11 R26/91   P(32-15-2) 167

NYG    7   6   0   0   13
Pit    3   7   7   0   17
NYG  D22 R29/146  P(41-27-2) 273
Pit  D11 R24/115  P(20-12-0)  60
NYG-Tucker 108C, Tarkenton 302P

Phi    7  10   6  14   37
SL     0  17   3   0   20
Phi  D17 R36/133  P(26-15-0) 134
SL   D15 R21/85   P(36-19-4) 248
Phi-Jackson 117C; SL-Gilliam 166C

Hou    0   3   3   7   13
Cin   14   7   0   7   28
Hou  D13 R19/70   P(27-12-1) 171
Cin  D19 R44/120  P(16-13-0) 143

NE     0   0   7   0    7
Cle    0  10   7  10   27
NE   D19 R27/123  P(32-13-4) 169
Cle  D19 R43/175  P(26-12-0) 146
Cle-Kelly 113R

Det    7  14   7   0   28
ChiB   3   0   0   0    3
Det  D14 R35/186  P(15-9-0)   70
ChiB D8  R26/112  P(26-6-4)    6

Bal    7   0   7   0   14
Mia    0   0  14   3   17
Bal  D14 R29/100  P(26-15-3) 168
Mia  D16 R36/168  P(16-10-0)  81
```

MONDAY, NOVEMBER 22

```
GB     0  14   0   7   21
Atl    6   6   7   9   28
GB   D7  R20/103  P(8-3-1)    40
Atl  D27 R55/204  P(21-16-0) 182
```

THURSDAY, NOVEMBER 25

```
LARm  14   0   7   0   21
Dal    7   7   7   7   28
LARm D21 R33/86   P(36-20-1) 227
Dal  D15 R33/114  P(14-8-0)  166

KC     0   7   7   7   21
Det    0  17  12   3   32
KC   D19 R25/119  P(23-14-1) 139
Det  D22 R35/158  P(22-15-2) 223
```

SUNDAY, NOVEMBER 28

```
Atl    0   7   0   0    7
Min    0   7  10   7   24
Atl  D4  R22/68   P(23-11-3)  55
Min  D19 R47/257  P(23-10-2)  47
Min-Jones 155R

Den    0  10   0  12   22
Pit    0   0   0  10   10
Den  D14 R37/126  P(25-14-1) 150
Pit  D12 R33/158  P(29-9-1)   67

SL    17   0   0   7   24
NYG    0   0   0   7    7
SL   D21 R41/207  P(17-7-2)  137
NYG  D15 R24/74   P(34-18-4) 211
SL 1-Roland 116R

Was    0  13   0   7   20
Phi    0   6   0   7   13
Was  D10 R28/102  P(19-10-0) 155
Phi  D16 R27/100  P(28-13-2) 180
Phi-Hawkins 126C

NE     3   3   7   7   20
Buf    0  17   0  10   27
NE   D15 R36/189  P(22-10-3) 105
Buf  D16 R34/147  P(17-9-0)  117
NE-Garrett 127R
```

```
SF     0  10   7   7   24
NYJ    0   0   7  14   21
SF   D20 R45/263  P(13-5-0)   88
NYJ  D21 R30/118  P(30-12-2) 275
SF-Washington 125R, Willard 129R;
NYJ-Caster 126C

SD     0   0   0   0    0
Cin    7  14   7   3   31
SD   D8  R16/47   P(27-9-6)   83
Cin  D28 R44/173  P(36-26-1) 238

Cle    3  10  14  10   37
Hou    0  17   0   7   24
Cle  D19 R41/160  P(24-11-2) 151
Hou  D10 R20/46   P(28-14-3) 170
Cle-Kelly 107R

Bal    7  13  10   7   37
Oak    0   0   0  14   14
Bal  D19 R39/210  P(16-10-0)  96
Oak  D20 R25/65   P(41-22-6) 246

NO     3   3   6  17   29
GB     7   0   0   0    7
NO   D18 R50/163  P(25-11-0) 110
GB   D15 R27/95   P(25-11-2) 167
NO-Gresham 113R
```

MONDAY, NOVEMBER 29

```
ChiB   0   0   3   0    3
Mia   10  10   7   7   34
ChiB D9  R16/96   P(28-9-3)  101
Mia  D23 R42/208  P(22-16-1) 238
Mia-Csonka 104R
```

SATURDAY, DECEMBER 4

```
NYJ    0   3   7   0   10
Dal   28  10   7   7   52
NYJ  D12 R34/130  P(20-6-3)   19
Dal  D26 R37/218  P(21-14-0) 221
Dal-Thomas 112R
```

SUNDAY, DECEMBER 5

```
Phi    7   9   0   7   23
Det    0   0  10  10   20
Phi  D20 R38/145  P(23-15-0) 214
Det  D20 R30/125  P(27-15-1) 225

NO     7   0  14   7   28
LARm  21  14   0  10   45
NO   D20 R23/56   P(36-19-1) 207
LARm D22 R39/293  P(18-10-0) 128
LARm-Ellison 247R

GB     3   3  10   0   16
SL     0   9   0   7   16
GB   D19 R35/211  P(28-15-2) 146
SL   D12 R32/80   P(24-11-0) 225
SL-Gray 102C

Cin   10  10   0   7   27
Cle    7   7  10   7   31
Cin  D15 R34/232  P(23-13-1) 114
Cle  D22 R38/182  P(28-14-2) 224
Cin-Johnson 109R; Cle-Kelly 127R;
Pitts 103C

ChiB   0   0   3   0    3
Den    0   3   0   3    6
ChiB D9  R19/73   P(31-7-3)   -7
Den  D10 R42/159  P(16-8-2)   54
Den-Little 125R

NYG    0   0   0   7    7
Was   13   7   3   0   23
NYG  D15 R27/89   P(33-16-5) 165
Was  D9  R36/155  P(14-4-1)   35
Was-Brown 129R

Mia    7   3   3   0   13
NE    17   3  14   0   34
Mia  D12 R29/98   P(22-9-2)   99
NE   D14 R33/85   P(23-16-0) 223
NE-Vataha 129C

Buf    0   0   0   0    0
Bal    0  14  10   0   24
Buf  D8  R21/76   P(34-16-4) 106
Bal  D16 R43/180  P(21-11-1) 130

Pit    0   3   0   0    3
Hou   16   6   0   7   29
Pit  D10 R20/73   P(33-14-3)  59
Hou  D15 R41/147  P(23-13-0) 128

Min    7   7   0   0   14
SD     3   3   0  24   30
Min  D19 R34/142  P(28-12-4) 173
SD   D21 R32/149  P(29-20-1) 165
```

Oak 3 0 10 0 13
Atl 7 10 0 7 **24**
Oak D20 R42/208 P(31-12-2) 120
Atl D17 R38/113 P(18-12-1) 214
Oak-Hubbard 143R

MONDAY, DECEMBER 6

KC 0 16 7 3 **26**
SF 3 7 0 7 17
KC D20 R37/172 P(28-16-0) 255
SF D18 R24/112 P(32-20-1) 219

SATURDAY, DECEMBER 11

Mia 0 0 3 0 3
Bal 7 7 0 0 **14**
Mia D14 R23/96 P(30-17-2) 151
Bal D19 R37/104 P(19-16-0) 121

Det 3 0 7 0 10
Min 7 7 3 12 **29**
Det D17 R32/107 P(32-15-3) 129
Min D7 R32/113 P(15-4-2) 21

SUNDAY, DECEMBER 12

Cle 7 0 7 7 **21**
NO 0 10 0 7 17
Cle D20 R42/132 P(21-11-2) 152
NO D18 R33/159 P(23-7-0) 66

ChiB 7 0 3 0 10
GB 7 0 14 10 **31**
ChiB D13 R24/61 P(29-11-1) 186
GB D15 R43/115 P(14-7-1) 180

Dal 14 14 14 0 **42**
NYG 0 7 0 7 14
Dal D23 R33/197 P(22-12-2) 242
NYG D17 R20/64 P(43-25-2) 183
Dal-Hayes 154C

SL 0 0 7 0 7
Phi 13 0 3 3 **19**
SL D10 R25/112 P(25-8-4) 161
Phi D19 R49/177 P(23-15-0) 205
Phi-Jackson 109C

Atl 0 3 0 0 3
SF 7 14 0 3 **24**
Atl D8 R22/61 P(23-9-2) 69
SF D18 R46/171 P(18-9-1) 119

Pit 0 7 0 14 **21**
Cin 0 7 6 0 13
Pit D16 R36/126 P(27-10-1) 146
Cin D14 R25/126 P(30-18-2) 222

Oak 0 7 0 7 14
KC 7 6 0 3 **16**
Oak D18 R29/93 P(31-17-2) 114
KC D17 R31/110 P(31-18-2) 194
KC-Taylor 113C

Den 0 3 7 7 17
SD 7 7 14 17 **45**
Den D19 R29/167 P(25-10-3) 163
SD D24 R30/155 P(37-22-0) 343
SD-Hadl 332P

Hou 3 3 7 7 **20**
Buf 0 0 0 14 14
Hou D16 R28/92 P(33-17-0) 176
Buf D14 R24/85 P(31-20-2) 207

NE 0 3 0 3 6
NYJ 3 0 10 0 **13**
NE D16 R27/100 P(31-18-1) 150
NYJ D17 R44/166 P(12-7-2) 95

MONDAY, DECEMBER 13

Was 7 17 7 7 **38**
LARm 10 0 7 7 24
Was D15 R40/79 P(19-14-1) 240
LARm D17 R27/104 P(44-17-3) 214
Was-Jefferson 137C

SATURDAY, DECEMBER 18

SL 0 6 6 0 12
Dal 7 14 0 10 **31**
SL D14 R26/88 P(43-12-2) 127
Dal D18 R38/205 P(16-10-1) 118

SUNDAY, DECEMBER 19

Cle 3 7 3 7 **20**
Was 0 13 0 0 13
Cle D13 R28/69 P(23-15-2) 154
Was D22 R35/117 P(33-18-2) 229

SD 0 23 7 3 33
Hou 0 7 28 14 **49**
SD D20 R31/88 P(29-12-3) 147
Hou D22 R32/135 P(23-15-3) 220
Hou-Burrough 122C

Buf 3 6 0 0 9
KC 3 6 10 3 **22**
Buf D15 R23/102 P(35-17-2) 158
KC D14 R33/137 P(31-13-0) 118

Cin 7 0 7 7 21
NYJ 7 21 7 0 **35**
Cin D23 R27/138 P(30-19-0) 155
NYJ D18 R35/210 P(15-9-1) 164
NYJ-Maynard 114C

Den 3 0 0 10 13
Oak 7 7 0 7 **21**
Den D23 R39/155 P(41-17-1) 211
Oak D16 R30/148 P(18-8-3) 163

GB 3 0 3 0 6
Mia 3 3 14 7 **27**
GB D14 R30/137 P(22-13-0) 86
Mia D17 R36/155 P(21-13-0) 90

Phi 7 17 17 0 **41**
NYG 7 7 0 14 28
Phi D15 R29/85 P(27-17-0) 261
NYG D24 R20/64 P(47-30-2) 314
Phi-Jackson 145C;
NYG-Morrison 160C, Tucker 116C,
Johnson 372P

Det 3 10 14 0 27
SF 7 10 7 7 **31**
Det D18 R33/134 P(18-9-1) 176
SF D20 R37/171 P(20-14-1) 186

LARm 13 3 7 0 **23**
Pit 0 7 7 0 14
LARm D14 R32/89 P(22-13-0) 148
Pit D24 R33/187 P(34-20-4) 144

Min 10 7 7 3 **27**
ChiB 0 0 10 0 10
Min D16 R38/117 P(23-13-0) 232
ChiB D14 R30/104 P(40-15-2) 206
ChiB-Farmer 128C

Atl 7 3 0 14 **24**
NO 7 3 7 3 20
Atl D14 R22/57 P(27-18-0) 262
NO D20 R39/165 P(26-17-0) 135
Atl-Burrow 190C

NE 0 14 0 7 **21**
Bal 0 3 7 7 17
NE D11 R34/91 P(17-10-0) 152
Bal D17 R34/100 P(32-16-2) 146
NE-Vataha 100C

1972 NFL

SUNDAY, SEPTEMBER 17

GB 7 10 3 6 **26**
Cle 3 7 0 0 10
GB D15 R48/145 P(17-7-0) 145
Cle D13 R23/62 P(33-14-3) 126

NYJ 14 14 3 10 **41**
Buf 0 7 7 10 24
NYJ D19 R47/191 P(16-6-1) 102
Buf D16 R25/80 P(26-16-4) 207
NYJ-Riggins 125R

NYG 0 10 0 6 16
Det 0 13 7 10 **30**
NYG D14 R27/112 P(25-16-1) 133
Det D18 R37/192 P(17-9-0) 200
Det-Owens 113R, Hilton 120C

SL 0 3 7 0 **10**
Bal 0 0 3 0 3
SL D5 R28/46 P(15-10-0) 88
Bal D20 R27/117 P(36-22-2) 247

Phi 3 3 0 0 6
Dal 0 7 14 7 **28**
Phi D17 R30/70 P(36-20-3) 245
Dal D22 R39/154 P(29-13-2) 235
Phi-Jackson 161C

Oak 0 7 0 21 28
Pit 14 3 10 7 **34**
Oak D20 R30/97 P(33-17-3) 273
Pit D17 R41/141 P(17-7-3) 106
Oak-Siani 111C

Hou 0 10 0 7 17
Den 10 7 6 7 **30**
Hou D12 R19/54 P(33-14-1) 142
Den D18 R36/239 P(24-11-1) 239
Den-Little 101R, Sherman 110C

Mia 7 10 3 0 **20**
KC 0 0 3 7 10
Mia D19 R42/196 P(15-8-1) 100
KC D16 R27/134 P(33-22-2) 198
Mia-Csonka 118R

Cin 7 3 7 14 **31**
NE 0 7 0 0 7
Cin D21 R47/246 P(17-11-0) 111
NE D9 R21/54 P(17-9-2) 83

NO 0 7 0 7 14
LARm 13 21 0 0 **34**
NO D20 R18/69 P(46-21-1) 218
LARm D20 R36/254 P(22-11-1) 139
LARm-Thomas 144R

Atl 10 21 3 3 **37**
ChiB 7 0 7 7 21
Atl D16 R37/173 P(9-6-1) 146
ChiB D15 R43/214 P(12-4-1) 69
ChiB-Harrison 113R

SD 3 0 0 0 3
SF 7 17 7 3 **34**
SD D13 R31/87 P(30-13-4) 171
SF D18 R35/117 P(25-13-2) 178
SF-Washington 140C

MONDAY, SEPTEMBER 18

Was 7 3 0 14 **24**
Min 0 7 7 7 21
Was D11 R31/146 P(17-7-1) 57
Min D26 R43/182 P(31-18-0) 200
Was-Brown 105R

SUNDAY, SEPTEMBER 24

NYJ 6 21 3 14 **44**
Bal 7 13 0 14 34
NYJ D19 R25/83 P(28-15-1) 490
Bal D28 R27/80 P(45-26-0) 332
NYJ-Bell 197C, Caster 204C,
Namath 496P; Bal-Havrilak 115C,
Mitchell 114C, Unitas 376P

Dal 7 3 3 10 **23**
NYG 0 7 0 7 14
Dal D18 R36/139 P(28-15-0) 158
NYG D14 R26/84 P(28-19-1) 271
NYG-Houston 175C

SL 0 3 7 0 10
Was 7 10 7 0 **24**
SL D16 R25/79 P(28-16-2) 140
Was D19 R37/181 P(22-13-0) 91
Was-Brown 148R

Den 7 0 0 7 14
SD 13 21 0 3 **37**
Den D17 R20/95 P(37-20-6) 218
SD D18 R35/142 P(32-15-1) 175
SD-Garrett 104R

Min 3 14 17 0 **34**
Det 3 0 0 7 10
Min D13 R36/130 P(16-8-0) 156
Det D16 R25/89 P(40-17-4) 124
Min-Gilliam 109C

Hou 0 0 13 0 13
Mia 13 7 7 7 **34**
Hou D7 R21/63 P(21-9-1) 104
Mia D30 R53/274 P(17-12-1) 161

Cle 3 17 7 0 **27**
Phi 0 3 7 7 17
Cle D15 R36/155 P(20-9-1) 142
Phi D20 R24/66 P(39-22-2) 248
Phi-Jackson 131C

SF 3 7 3 7 20
Buf 0 6 7 14 **27**
SF D10 R20/33 P(30-11-3) 169
Buf D17 R43/177 P(21-8-1) 56
Buf-Simpson 138R

Pit 0 10 0 0 10
Cin 3 0 6 6 **15**
Pit D14 R24/74 P(34-18-0) 131
Cin D13 R39/121 P(27-13-1) 148

Atl 3 3 14 0 20
NE 0 7 0 14 **21**
Atl D20 R40/182 P(23-14-0) 217
NE D19 R26/103 P(29-12-0) 184

LARm 7 3 3 0 13
ChiB 0 0 3 10 13
LARm D8 R34/106 P(17-7-2) 65
ChiB D11 R33/144 P(15-3-2) 26

Oak 10 0 10 0 **20**
GB 7 7 0 0 14
Oak D21 R46/196 P(21-8-0) 117
GB D15 R36/143 P(13-5-0) 64
Oak-Hubbard 125R

MONDAY, SEPTEMBER 25

KC 0 10 0 10 **20**
NO 0 10 7 0 17
KC D20 R33/139 P(29-21-1) 185
NO D10 R24/59 P(24-10-0) 93

SUNDAY, OCTOBER 1

LARm 0 0 3 0 3
Atl 10 7 7 7 **31**
LARm D13 R24/112 P(32-10-6) 137
Atl D17 R51/297 P(9-2-1) 61
Atl-Hampton 161R, Malone 103R

Cin 0 3 0 3 6
Cle 10 0 3 14 **27**
Cin D19 R30/128 P(43-21-2) 203
Cle D14 R34/109 P(24-12-0) 180
Cle-Pitts 105C

Dal 3 3 7 0 13
GB 3 7 3 3 **16**
Dal D16 R32/138 P(29-16-3) 131
GB D11 R40/124 P(18-4-0) 44

KC 3 7 14 21 **45**
Den 7 3 7 7 24
KC D14 R32/130 P(23-11-1) 175
Den D21 R31/148 P(36-13-3) 184

SF 0 10 10 17 **37**
NO 0 0 2 0 2
SF D14 R36/126 P(28-20-1) 192
NO D8 R16/7 P(35-13-4) 77

Was 0 14 0 9 23
NE 0 7 10 7 **24**
Was D15 R28/136 P(30-14-1) 213
NE D23 R34/127 P(34-17-1) 253
Was-Brown 113R, Taylor 134C;
NE-Ashton 108R

Mia 0 0 6 10 **16**
Min 7 0 0 7 14
Mia D14 R26/120 P(34-17-2) 134
Min D12 R35/131 P(23-10-3) 109

Det 7 14 7 10 **38**
ChiB 0 10 0 14 24
Det D21 R43/197 P(12-8-0) 115
ChiB D21 R41/253 P(16-8-2) 74

Pit 3 12 0 10 **25**
SL 0 6 6 7 19
Pit D20 R32/153 P(40-25-1) 209
SL D15 R22/58 P(35-15-4) 190

Bal 10 7 0 0 **17**
Buf 0 0 0 0 0
Bal D17 R41/159 P(29-12-2) 180
Buf D11 R32/118 P(28-11-3) 111
Buf-Hill 115C

SD 0 7 0 10 17
Oak 14 0 0 3 17
SD D20 R50/196 P(13-9-1) 149
Oak D15 R25/90 P(26-14-1) 142
SD-Edwards 100C

NYJ 10 3 0 7 20
Hou 0 14 9 3 **26**
NYJ D19 R24/97 P(38-18-2) 301
Hou D19 R42/150 P(28-14-0) 262
NYJ-Barkum 102C, Namath 301P

MONDAY, OCTOBER 2

NYG 7 14 0 6 **27**
Phi 3 3 6 0 12
NYG D21 R46/157 P(19-12-2) 164
Phi D21 R29/182 P(26-14-2) 212
NYG-Johnson 124R;
Phi-Jackson 138C

SUNDAY, OCTOBER 8

SF 0 7 0 0 7
LARm 0 14 10 7 **31**
SF D13 R27/119 P(18-10-2) 131
LARm D22 R43/302 P(23-12-0) 211
LARm-Thomas 142R, Snow 130C

Den 7 3 0 0 10
Cin 0 7 7 7 **21**
Den D11 R31/130 P(19-6-0) 37
Cin D13 R30/90 P(20-12-0) 109

Phi 0 0 0 0 0
Was 0 0 14 0 **14**
Phi D12 R26/60 P(31-16-1) 176
Was D22 R33/147 P(24-14-3) 224

NE 7 0 0 7 14
Buf 3 28 7 0 **38**
NE D23 R34/110 P(39-17-3) 244
Buf D19 R45/145 P(13-9-0) 160
NE-Rucker 103C

Mia 0 14 3 10 **27**
NYJ 7 0 3 7 17
Mia D23 R38/174 P(27-15-0) 220
NYJ D16 R31/123 P(25-12-1) 147
Mia-Csonka 102R

ChiB 0 3 7 7 17
GB 7 10 0 3 **20**
ChiB D13 R45/139 P(15-7-0) 119
GB D17 R31/101 P(30-15-0) 240

Pit 6 7 0 0 13
Dal 3 7 7 0 **17**
Pit D14 R26/130 P(39-12-1) 142
Dal D21 R40/191 P(30-12-2) 176
Dal-Hill 108R

SL 3 3 6 7 **19**
Min 0 7 0 10 17
SL D12 R31/109 P(23-12-0) 153
Min D21 R45/179 P(23-15-1) 113

KC 7 14 7 3 **31**
Cle 0 7 0 0 7
KC D18 R48/221 P(18-8-1) 62
Cle D10 R23/97 P(28-12-4) 112

Det 3 10 7 6 **26**
Atl 3 0 7 13 23
Det D15 R37/180 P(17-5-3) 134
Atl D15 R38/199 P(17-10-1) 79
Det-Jessie 102C

SD 7 3 0 13 **23**
Bal 0 3 17 0 20
SD D24 R49/213 P(20-12-3) 137
Bal D19 R33/145 P(22-14-0) 120
SD-Garrett 132R

NO 0 7 0 14 21
NYG 17 14 14 0 **45**
NO D15 R12/58 P(31-18-4) 228
NYG D20 R43/208 P(19-13-1) 149
NO-Parks 120C

MONDAY, OCTOBER 9

Oak 3 7 3 21 **34**
Hou 0 0 0 0 0
Oak D19 R38/164 P(27-13-0) 138
Hou D7 R22/90 P(25-4-5) -1

SUNDAY, OCTOBER 15

LARm 3 14 10 7 **34**
Phi 0 3 0 0 3
LARm D18 R40/166 P(22-11-0) 147
Phi D14 R21/47 P(33-14-2) 90

Dal 0 7 7 7 **21**
Bal 0 0 0 0 0
Dal D21 R37/125 P(30-22-2) 265
Bal D14 R23/105 P(26-13-1) 70
Dal-Sellers 113C

NYG 0 13 0 10 **23**
SF 3 7 0 7 17
NYG D18 R41/140 P(16-11-0) 129
SF D18 R21/85 P(30-21-2) 257
SF-Kwalick 126C

Min 3 3 10 7 **23**
Den 0 7 0 13 20
Min D21 R31/128 P(30-19-0) 177
Den D15 R33/161 P(27-15-2) 175
Den-Little 100R

Atl 7 0 7 7 **21**
NO 14 0 0 0 14
Atl D17 R41/147 P(26-16-0) 175
NO D8 R30/101 P(18-6-0) 20

ChiB 7 0 3 7 **17**
Cle 0 0 0 0 0
ChiB D13 R48/256 P(9-2-1) 54
Cle D9 R23/37 P(29-13-0) 126
ChiB-Douglass 117R

NYJ 7 14 0 20 41
NE 0 6 7 0 13
NYJ D24 R54/333 P(9-5-1) 63
NE D18 R23/136 P(31-18-2) 175
NYJ-Boozer 150R, Riggins 168R

Cin 3 0 7 13 23
KC 0 3 10 3 16
Cin D11 R24/69 P(25-14-0) 182
KC D22 R31/123 P(40-22-2) 197
KC-Taylor 149C

Was 3 7 6 17 33
SL 0 0 3 0 3
Was D20 R43/160 P(20-15-1) 230
SL D10 R21/66 P(24-9-2) 85
Was-Brown 110R

Buf 3 10 0 3 16
Oak 0 0 7 21 28
Buf D16 R45/181 P(23-15-1) 114
Oak D22 R34/215 P(26-10-2) 181
Buf-Simpson 144R;
Oak-Hubbard 122R

Hou 7 0 0 0 7
Pit 0 10 7 7 24
Hou D7 R25/108 P(22-10-1) 0
Pit D18 R48/249 P(19-9-0) 46
Pit-Harris 115R

SD 3 0 0 7 10
Mia 3 14 7 0 24
SD D15 R36/133 P(22-12-2) 110
Mia D14 R39/153 P(13-9-0) 86

MONDAY, OCTOBER 16

GB 0 7 10 7 24
Det 7 10 3 3 23
GB D16 R35/125 P(18-11-1) 140
Det D18 R36/146 P(19-9-2) 83

SUNDAY, OCTOBER 22

Atl 0 7 3 0 10
GB 6 3 0 0 9
Atl D19 R45/107 P(25-14-0) 137
GB D10 R29/112 P(15-6-0) 103

Buf 0 13 0 10 23
Mia 7 0 10 7 24
Buf D11 R32/164 P(18-7-0) 24
Mia D20 R52/230 P(10-6-1) 80
Mia-Csonka 107R

NO 7 0 3 10 20
SF 7 10 0 3 20
NO D19 R34/94 P(27-17-1) 273
SF D14 R21/66 P(35-19-3) 274
NO-Parks 110C; SF-Kwalick 102C

Cin 0 0 10 2 12
LARm 7 3 2 3 15
Cin D20 R46/173 P(29-18-0) 110
LARm D9 R22/55 P(23-9-2) 94

Cle 0 13 3 7 23
Hou 7 0 7 3 17
Cle D13 R39/135 P(19-9-0) 119
Hou D17 R36/143 P(27-17-0) 221

Dal 10 3 7 0 20
Was 0 7 10 7 24
Dal D18 R26/116 P(27-14-2) 160
Was D17 R37/133 P(16-11-0) 172
Was-Brown 100C

SL 0 21 0 0 21
NYG 0 7 14 6 27
SL D13 R26/83 P(25-13-2) 108
NYG D16 R36/107 P(26-15-1) 209

SD 6 0 0 14 20
Det 6 7 14 7 34
SD D17 R21/82 P(27-12-2) 143
Det D24 R44/182 P(24-12-1) 142
SD-Garrison 119C; Det-Walton 101C

NE 0 0 3 0 3
Pit 10 7 13 3 33
NE D17 R24/127 P(32-16-3) 149
Pit D19 R40/243 P(14-9-0) 183
Pit-Fuqua 111R, Shanklin 111C

Den 7 17 0 6 30
Oak 0 3 10 10 23
Den D15 R24/13 P(29-21-0) 396
Oak D23 R27/127 P(40-22-0) 189
Den-Parks 110C, Simmons 118C,
Johnson 361P

Phi 14 7 0 0 21
KC 0 6 7 7 20
Phi D12 R45/153 P(12-8-2) 196
KC D17 R32/92 P(29-17-1) 152

Bal 3 7 3 7 20
NYJ 14 3 0 7 24
Bal D23 R46/179 P(34-19-0) 227
NYJ D10 R30/119 P(16-5-3) 228
Bal-McCauley 112R

MONDAY, OCTOBER 23

Min 7 0 3 0 10
ChiB 0 10 0 3 13
Min D12 R19/51 P(25-17-1) 231
ChiB D17 R53/195 P(6-4-1) 46
ChiB-Harrison 103R

SUNDAY, OCTOBER 29

Phi 0 3 0 0 3
NO 7 0 7 7 21
Phi D13 R32/152 P(21-8-2) 57
NO D23 R35/148 P(35-20-1) 284

Pit 0 17 7 14 38
Buf 0 0 7 14 21
Pit D18 R33/216 P(17-9-1) 93
Buf D24 R38/254 P(29-18-4) 164
Pit-Harris 138R; Buf-Simpson 189R

Hou 0 0 0 7 7
Cin 10 3 7 10 30
Hou D10 R15/98 P(17-7-1) 47
Cin D29 R46/244 P(31-23-1) 252
Cin-Dressler 110R, Johnson 103R

Cle 3 7 3 14 27
Den 10 0 7 3 20
Cle D26 R39/172 P(33-15-1) 171
Den D17 R22/146 P(24-14-1) 126

ChiB 0 17 0 10 27
SL 0 3 7 0 10
ChiB D15 R40/149 P(10-8-1) 180
SL D17 R32/150 P(36-15-3) 119
ChiB-Farmer 141C;
SL-Anderson 102R

SF 14 7 14 14 49
Atl 7 7 0 0 14
SF D19 R46/189 P(18-8-1) 159
Atl D13 R20/55 P(35-12-4) 97

KC 0 3 10 13 26
SD 0 7 0 7 14
KC D15 R34/134 P(27-14-2) 134
SD D16 R22/81 P(36-18-3) 199

LARm 0 3 7 7 17
Oak 28 7 0 10 45
LARm D16 R27/154 P(35-11-6) 163
Oak D23 R44/213 P(24-10-0) 149

Mia 7 9 7 0 23
Bal 0 0 0 0 0
Mia D24 R52/286 P(16-10-1) 89
Bal D12 R24/114 P(21-13-0) 78

Min 0 3 7 17 27
GB 10 0 3 0 13
Min D15 R37/152 P(22-13-0) 192
GB D12 R32/102 P(22-9-4) 130
Min-Gilliam 106C

Was 3 6 7 7 23
NYG 0 6 3 7 16
Was D16 R36/210 P(17-9-1) 127
NYG D19 R25/112 P(37-25-0) 248
Was-Brown 191R

NE 3 0 0 7 10
NYJ 3 14 10 7 34
NE D14 R17/66 P(36-11-3) 128
NYJ D21 R40/191 P(25-13-1) 201

MONDAY, OCTOBER 30

Det 0 14 3 7 24
Dal 14 7 0 7 28
Det D14 R28/59 P(21-12-0) 224
Dal D19 R43/159 P(19-11-1) 206

SUNDAY, NOVEMBER 5

SL 0 6 0 0 6
Phi 3 0 0 3 6
SL D14 R32/146 P(15-7-2) 82
Phi D17 R38/99 P(26-16-0) 200

Hou 0 0 0 0 0
Cle 3 0 3 14 20
Hou D11 R29/119 P(24-15-0) 93
Cle D15 R38/152 P(20-9-0) 146

Dal 10 14 7 3 34
SD 0 0 7 21 28
Dal D17 R33/100 P(23-16-1) 169
SD D17 R29/144 P(26-11-3) 202
SD-Hadl 211P

NO 0 0 3 3 6
Min 7 13 7 10 37
NO D16 R21/123 P(35-19-3) 147
Min D23 R32/148 P(31-22-1) 233
Min-Gilliam 111C

Mia 10 6 7 7 30
Buf 6 7 3 0 16
Mia D21 R45/254 P(14-5-1) 73
Buf D12 R25/73 P(23-12-2) 99
Mia-Morris 106R

ChiB 0 0 0 0 0
Det 7 7 0 0 14
ChiB D9 R29/122 P(12-4-0) 24
Det D21 R46/191 P(22-12-4) 135

Atl 0 7 0 0 7
LARm 7 3 7 3 20
Atl D19 R30/117 P(20-11-2) 120
LARm D17 R49/202 P(11-8-0) 93
Atl-Chesson 120C;
LARm-Ellison 114R

Oak 0 0 7 7 14
KC 0 17 3 7 27
Oak D20 R23/73 P(38-23-1) 220
KC D22 R50/190 P(18-10-0) 181
Oak-Biletnikoff 114C;
KC-Podolak 115R

Den 0 0 10 7 17
NYG 6 13 0 10 29
Den D17 R24/183 P(30-14-3) 147
NYG D23 R41/138 P(24-12-1) 178
Den-Little 124R

Cin 0 0 14 3 17
Pit 10 16 7 7 40
Cin D21 R33/145 P(28-17-1) 221
Pit D20 R30/230 P(24-11-0) 185
Pit-Harris 101R

SF 7 0 3 14 24
GB 7 7 10 10 34
SF D16 R19/21 P(37-19-1) 306
GB D13 R41/197 P(16-6-0) 141
SF-Washington 164C,
Spurrier 315P;
GB-Brockington 133R

Was 7 14 7 7 35
NYJ 7 3 0 7 17
Was D7 R28/89 P(16-7-1) 222
NYJ D19 R29/106 P(28-15-3) 116

MONDAY, NOVEMBER 6

Bal 7 3 14 0 24
NE 3 0 7 7 17
Bal D19 R41/178 P(19-10-0) 89
NE D21 R32/127 P(29-18-2) 154

SUNDAY, NOVEMBER 12

Buf 3 0 0 0 3
NYJ 7 17 7 10 41
Buf D11 R31/143 P(20-9-3) 67
NYJ D17 R41/148 P(16-9-1) 141

KC 0 7 0 0 7
Pit 0 0 3 13 16
KC D16 R29/75 P(36-17-1) 108
Pit D15 R40/238 P(20-8-3) 80
Pit-Harris 134R

Det 0 0 14 0 14
Min 3 0 7 6 16
Det D9 R24/102 P(18-11-0) 126
Min D17 R40/177 P(27-15-0) 121
Min-Reed 124R

NO 3 0 10 7 20
Atl 7 19 7 3 36
NO D19 R22/109 P(31-13-0) 155
Atl D21 R41/189 P(21-12-1) 163

Phi 6 9 0 3 18
Hou 0 3 7 7 17
Phi D12 R36/153 P(20-8-0) 84
Hou D18 R39/236 P(25-15-3) 112
Hou-Willis 119R

SL 0 10 7 7 24
Dal 10 13 7 3 33
SL D16 R18/54 P(38-15-2) 274
Dal D23 R48/230 P(28-16-1) 197
SL-Smith 110C; Dal-Sellers 111C

Bal 7 0 0 14 21
SF 7 7 3 7 24
Bal D18 R26/84 P(27-14-0) 213
SF D19 R48/205 P(14-10-1) 105
Bal-Havrilak 136C;
SF-Schreiber 104R

Oak 0 3 7 10 20
Cin 0 7 0 7 14
Oak D24 R48/293 P(24-13-1) 88
Cin D14 R26/89 P(29-12-1) 144
Oak-Smith 146R

GB 14 3 3 3 23
ChiB 7 0 3 7 17
GB D8 R34/123 P(10-4-2) 40
ChiB D19 R40/179 P(24-11-1) 117

NYG 0 7 3 3 13
Was 0 6 7 14 27
NYG D14 R29/118 P(26-14-2) 117
Was D21 R39/143 P(23-15-1) 237
Was-Brown 106R

Den 0 7 0 9 16
LARm 0 0 10 0 10
Den D13 R38/133 P(23-11-2) 112
LARm D9 R24/73 P(23-13-2) 110

NE 0 0 0 0 0
Mia 17 14 7 14 52
NE D11 R26/92 P(28-11-3) 77
Mia D21 R38/181 P(19-11-0) 301
Mia-Briscoe 128C

MONDAY, NOVEMBER 13

Cle 0 7 0 14 21
SD 0 3 7 7 17
Cle D18 R30/124 P(21-13-1) 175
SD D24 R44/191 P(21-12-1) 136

SUNDAY, NOVEMBER 19

Dal 2 10 7 9 28
Phi 7 0 0 0 7
Dal D20 R35/163 P(24-12-2) 158
Phi D12 R27/120 P(17-10-1) 6
Dal-Hill 100R

Bal 0 10 0 10 20
Cin 7 3 3 6 19
Bal D17 R33/143 P(20-12-0) 163
Cin D17 R33/81 P(28-16-0) 186

NYG 0 3 0 10 13
SL 0 7 0 0 7
NYG D16 R41/150 P(24-13-0) 97
SL D12 R37/186 P(8-5-1) 21
NYG-Johnson 134R;
SL-Anderson 121R

SD 7 17 3 0 27
KC 7 0 3 7 17
SD D17 R34/108 P(28-17-0) 186
KC D22 R22/99 P(41-25-4) 264

NYJ 7 10 7 0 24
Mia 7 7 7 7 28
NYJ D14 R32/108 P(23-14-2) 175
Mia D20 R45/214 P(17-8-1) 132
Mia-Morris 107R

NO 0 0 0 14 14
Det 7 7 3 10 27
NO D17 R22/77 P(30-20-2) 242
Det D21 R34/123 P(26-17-0) 207

GB 0 14 0 9 23
Hou 0 7 0 3 10
GB D14 R40/210 P(13-6-0) 100
Hou D16 R32/114 P(27-13-0) 126
GB-Lane 126R

SF 7 7 13 7 34
ChiB 0 0 14 7 21
SF D20 R38/110 P(27-17-0) 266
ChiB D15 R30/133 P(21-10-0) 223
SF-Washington 114C, Spurrier 275P

Min 3 7 14 21 45
LARm 7 13 7 14 41
Min D14 R22/56 P(28-14-0) 319
LARm D25 R39/191 P(33-25-1) 235
Min-Brown 116C,
Gilliam 105C, Tarkenton 319P;
LARm-Ellison 104R, Snow 112C

Pit 3 7 7 7 24
Cle 10 10 3 3 26
Pit D15 R29/211 P(21-10-1) 103
Cle D24 R38/217 P(25-14-2) 172
Pit-Harris 136R, Shanklin 108C;
Cle-Kelly 107R

Buf 0 17 0 10 27
NE 7 0 14 3 24
Buf D19 R35/179 P(26-12-0) 116
NE D15 R39/115 P(23-9-3) 183
Buf-Simpson 103R

Oak 7 13 3 14 37
Den 10 3 0 7 20
Oak D25 R47/197 P(24-13-0) 140
Den D13 R19/38 P(31-16-1) 170
Oak-Smith 101R

MONDAY, NOVEMBER 20

Atl 7 3 0 3 13
Was 0 7 14 3 24
Atl D14 R33/151 P(21-11-1) 105
Was D18 R42/159 P(19-10-1) 109

THURSDAY, NOVEMBER 23

SF 0 14 7 10 31
Dal 7 3 0 0 10
SF D17 R34/123 P(24-16-0) 157
Dal D19 R26/107 P(39-19-2) 201

NYJ 0 10 10 0 20
Det 3 17 0 17 37
NYJ D19 R36/229 P(23-9-1) 165
Det D19 R41/260 P(18-6-0) 125
NYJ-McClain 121R, Riggins 105R;
Det-Taylor 123R

SUNDAY, NOVEMBER 26

GB 3 3 0 10 16
Was 0 14 0 7 21
GB D12 R35/120 P(21-7-1) 67
Was D16 R35/132 P(21-14-0) 149

Min 3 0 0 7 10
Pit 7 0 3 13 23
Min D16 R38/95 P(44-24-1) 225
Pit D12 R34/206 P(19-7-1) 86
Pit-Harris 128R

Phi 3 7 0 0 10
NYG 14 24 10 14 62
Phi D8 R15/38 P(26-11-2) 184
NYG D28 R53/246 P(21-13-0) 257
Phi-Jackson 152C;
NYG-Johnson 123R, Tucker 100C

KC 0 3 0 0 3
Oak 10 13 0 3 26
KC D11 R25/98 P(23-10-3) 61
Oak D24 R53/255 P(21-14-1) 165

LARm 3 3 7 3 16
NO 0 7 9 3 19
LARm D17 R34/186 P(30-11-0) 123
NO D17 R29/102 P(30-15-0) 158

Buf 10 0 0 0 10
Cle 0 10 7 10 27
Buf D12 R44/147 P(12-5-1) 28
Cle D16 R36/132 P(22-11-2) 121

NE 0 0 0 0 0
Bal 0 17 14 0 31
NE D12 R32/131 P(26-11-3) 75
Bal D15 R38/164 P(27-11-2) 98

Den 10 3 0 7 20
Atl 0 16 7 0 23
Den D17 R36/102 P(25-14-0) 213
Atl D13 R29/80 P(16-13-0) 170

Cin 0 10 0 3 13
ChiB 0 0 3 0 3
Cin D13 R44/158 P(20-12-2) 113
ChiB D9 R24/110 P(25-8-2) 106

Hou 0 3 0 17 20
SD 10 10 7 7 34
Hou D18 R22/51 P(40-19-1) 162
SD D23 R42/230 P(26-13-0) 137
SD-Garrett 102R

MONDAY, NOVEMBER 27

SL 0 3 0 7 10
Mia 7 3 14 7 31
SL D12 R20/51 P(31-14-3) 173
Mia D24 R43/200 P(21-14-0) 226
Mia-Csonka 114R, Stowe 140C

SUNDAY, DECEMBER 3

Den 7 7 0 7 21
KC 0 10 14 0 **24**
Den D22 R32/137 P(36-19-2) 191
KC D12 R30/113 P(20-7-1) 76

NYG 0 3 0 7 10
Cin 3 3 7 0 **13**
NYG D16 R29/155 P(25-12-3) 112
Cin D15 R29/105 P(34-17-1) 212
NYG-Johnson 119R

Cle 0 0 0 0 0
Pit 3 7 7 13 **30**
Cle D11 R29/99 P(20-9-1) 27
Pit D19 R43/184 P(17-9-0) 153
Pit-Harris 102R, McMakin 113C

NO 3 7 0 7 17
NYJ 3 3 3 9 **18**
NO D22 R33/139 P(31-20-1) 194
NYJ D18 R20/64 P(40-21-2) 259

Buf 0 0 0 7 7
Bal 14 0 7 14 **35**
Buf D13 R29/100 P(24-14-3) 144
Bal D22 R44/189 P(26-14-0) 202

ChiB 0 3 0 7 10
Min 3 10 7 3 **23**
ChiB D5 R27/90 P(13-2-1) 1
Min D19 R35/80 P(39-21-1) 261
Min-Gilliam 111C

Det 0 0 0 7 7
GB 9 14 7 3 **33**
Det D6 R11/27 P(22-11-3) 162
GB D19 R55/233 P(15-8-0) 76

Mia 3 10 17 7 **37**
NE 0 7 0 14 21
Mia D29 R51/304 P(21-11-2) 197
NE D14 R15/110 P(29-15-2) 107
Mia-Morris 113R

Dal 3 7 7 10 **27**
SL 0 0 6 0 6
Dal D18 R48/209 P(23-11-2) 140
SL D10 R19/52 P(36-14-1) 89
Dal-Hill 120R

Hou 0 0 10 0 10
Atl 10 3 7 0 **20**
Hou D13 R30/88 P(30-14-5) 154
Atl D17 R42/161 P(24-13-1) 167
Hou-Burrough 106C

Was 3 7 3 10 **23**
Phi 7 0 0 0 7
Was D19 R50/170 P(15-12-0) 155
Phi D9 R20/66 P(21-7-0) 54

Oak 7 7 0 7 **21**
SD 0 10 6 3 19
Oak D17 R27/96 P(23-14-2) 202
SD D26 R53/233 P(26-15-2) 207
SD-Garrett 145R

MONDAY, DECEMBER 4

LARm 3 13 7 3 **26**
SF 6 3 7 0 16
LARm D15 R35/138 P(26-11-0) 175
SF D19 R20/58 P(46-27-3) 246

SATURDAY, DECEMBER 9

Cle 0 14 10 3 **27**
Cin 0 10 14 0 24
Cle D15 R29/109 P(26-11-2) 150
Cin D25 R38/194 P(26-13-2) 140
Cin-Myers 116C

Was 0 3 7 14 24
Dal 14 14 3 3 **34**
Was D19 R39/143 P(29-14-2) 169
Dal D14 R36/246 P(17-7-0) 61
Dal-Garrison 121R, Hill 111R

SUNDAY, DECEMBER 10

SD 0 3 3 7 13
Den 7 14 17 0 **38**
SD D20 R28/99 P(44-22-2) 236
Den D15 R32/172 P(12-6-2) 85
SD-Garrison 156C

Mia 10 7 0 6 **23**
NYG 6 7 0 0 13
Mia D16 R41/204 P(17-9-1) 163
NYG D21 R35/121 P(26-15-2) 222
Mia-Warfield 132C

ChiB 7 0 7 7 **21**
Phi 0 12 0 0 12
ChiB D13 R47/214 P(9-1-1) 36
Phi D18 R25/83 P(40-16-3) 147

GB 0 0 17 6 **23**
Min 0 7 0 0 7
GB D18 R45/214 P(14-7-1) 56
Min D9 R21/54 P(21-11-3) 90
GB-Brockington 114R

Atl 0 0 0 0 0
SF 3 3 0 14 **20**
Atl D14 R22/149 P(25-12-1) 116
SF D19 R47/210 P(18-9-0) 66

Det 0 7 7 7 21
Buf 0 7 7 7 21
Det D14 R31/116 P(25-8-0) 144
Buf D23 R43/187 P(32-18-0) 231
Buf-Simpson 116R, Hill 129C

LARm 0 0 14 0 14
SL 3 14 0 7 **24**
LARm D29 R40/151 P(39-24-1) 240
SL D11 R23/77 P(18-7-0) 192
LARm-Bertelsen 107C;
SL-Rashad 113C

NE 0 14 3 0 **17**
NO 3 0 7 0 10
NE D18 R36/109 P(24-16-1) 180
NO D20 R20/94 P(52-24-3) 243

Pit 3 0 6 0 **9**
Hou 0 3 0 0 3
Pit D12 R38/130 P(19-10-0) 63
Hou D11 R30/72 P(24-13-0) 87

Bal 0 10 0 0 10
KC 3 7 7 7 **24**
Bal D14 R29/106 P(24-11-2) 148
KC D21 R40/185 P(21-15-0) 137
KC-Hayes 104R

MONDAY, DECEMBER 11

NYJ 7 6 0 3 16
Oak 3 7 7 7 **24**
NYJ D20 R15/36 P(48-25-2) 365
Oak D19 R44/169 P(17-10-2) 197
NYJ-Maynard 131C, Namath 403P;
Oak-Hubbard 118R

SATURDAY, DECEMBER 16

Bal 0 0 0 0 0
Mia 3 7 3 3 **16**
Bal D13 R30/131 P(25-12-3) 126
Mia D16 R48/170 P(18-9-1) 114

Min 7 0 10 0 17
SF 0 6 0 14 **20**
Min D17 R38/177 P(25-11-2) 96
SF D18 R33/154 P(30-17-5) 229
SF-Washington 119C

SUNDAY, DECEMBER 17

NYG 6 14 0 3 **23**
Dal 0 3 0 0 3
NYG D25 R52/174 P(28-16-1) 175
Dal D10 R20/47 P(21-12-3) 85
NYG-Clements 105R

KC 0 3 7 7 **17**
Atl 0 7 0 7 14
KC D19 R43/182 P(26-18-1) 108
Atl D16 R31/85 P(25-11-2) 166

Cle 7 3 7 9 **26**
NYJ 7 0 3 0 10
Cle D16 R36/193 P(17-7-2) 149
NYJ D15 R37/182 P(12-5-1) 24
NYJ-Boozer 106R

NE 0 7 0 14 21
Den 3 21 7 14 **45**
NE D22 R27/125 P(35-18-0) 135
Den D26 R31/141 P(31-21-0) 341

Det 3 14 7 10 **34**
LARm 3 7 7 0 17
Det D24 R36/157 P(24-18-1) 213
LARm D20 R25/119 P(35-21-1) 214

Pit 7 7 3 7 **24**
SD 2 0 0 0 2
Pit D15 R39/115 P(24-12-1) 131
SD D12 R30/56 P(26-11-4) 116

ChiB 7 0 7 7 21
Oak 7 0 7 14 **28**
ChiB D15 R36/162 P(18-6-0) 33
Oak D25 R35/191 P(26-17-2) 168
ChiB-Douglass 127R

Buf 10 0 0 14 **24**
Was 0 7 10 0 17
Buf D17 R45/184 P(21-10-2) 80
Was D15 R35/133 P(15-4-3) 38
Buf-Simpson 101R

Cin 3 13 17 28 **61**
Hou 3 7 0 7 17
Cin D24 R26/153 P(27-20-0) 190
Hou D17 R35/132 P(32-17-5) 164

GB 7 10 7 6 **30**
NO 0 7 6 7 20
GB D15 R43/178 P(15-6-0) 66
NO D12 R21/50 P(24-14-1) 102

Phi 0 6 3 14 23
SL 14 0 7 3 **24**
Phi D18 R30/104 P(27-14-0) 171
SL D18 R27/72 P(31-19-1) 324
Phi-Carmichael 100C;
SL 1-Gillette 108C, Hart 334P

1973 NFL

SUNDAY, SEPTEMBER 16

Atl 0 24 21 17 **62**
NO 0 0 7 0 7
Atl D32 R52/218 P(22-17-0) 278
NO D11 R31/152 P(24-8-6) 35
Atl-Hampton 104R, Mitchell 111C

SL 21 3 0 10 **34**
Phi 3 3 10 7 23
SL D20 R32/197 P(29-17-1) 195
Phi D18 R27/109 P(37-22-1) 143
SL 2-Metcalf 133R

LARm 6 14 3 0 **23**
KC 0 0 0 13 13
LARm D22 R55/278 P(10-8-0) 80
KC D16 R21/40 P(27-20-1) 230
LARm-Bertelsen 143R,
McCutcheon 120R

Buf 7 3 7 14 **31**
NE 6 0 7 0 13
Buf D23 R51/360 P(12-9-1) 99
NE D17 R26/107 P(27-16-1) 190
Buf-Simpson 250R, Watkins 105R

Cin 0 3 7 0 10
Den 14 7 0 7 **28**
Cin D22 R24/133 P(39-19-1) 211
Den D23 R38/153 P(25-11-1) 190

SD 0 0 0 0 0
Was 21 0 7 10 **38**
SD D10 R36/128 P(20-7-4) 7
Was D13 R39/83 P(18-10-0) 128

SF 3 7 3 0 13
Mia 3 3 0 15 **21**
SF D16 R30/98 P(35-18-0) 154
Mia D15 R36/171 P(24-11-2) 108
Mia-Csonka 104R

Hou 0 0 14 0 14
NYG 6 21 0 7 **34**
Hou D6 R22/96 P(17-8-4) 59
NYG D29 R53/218 P(29-17-3) 154

Oak 0 13 3 0 16
Min 10 0 7 7 **24**
Oak D19 R39/200 P(30-13-2) 153
Min D16 R35/103 P(31-13-1) 170
Oak-Siani 111C

Bal 0 7 7 0 14
Cle 7 10 7 0 **24**
Bal D10 R36/125 P(22-6-1) 4
Cle D20 R42/147 P(26-12-0) 150

Det 0 0 10 0 10
Pit 0 3 7 14 **24**
Det D17 R28/108 P(27-11-3) 193
Pit D29 R60/241 P(23-15-1) 154
Det-Jessie 131C; Pit-Fuqua 100R

Dal 0 17 0 3 **20**
ChiB 3 0 7 7 17
Dal D17 R46/188 P(22-9-2) 84
ChiB D12 R44/172 P(13-6-1) 30
Dal-Hill 130R

MONDAY, SEPTEMBER 17

NYJ 0 0 0 7 7
GB 3 10 3 7 **23**
NYJ D16 R17/69 P(38-18-1) 200
GB D14 R48/155 P(14-6-0) 98

SUNDAY, SEPTEMBER 23

Mia 0 0 0 7 7
Oak 3 3 3 3 **12**
Mia D10 R24/105 P(25-12-0) 90
Oak D12 R46/187 P(10-7-1) 63

Atl 0 0 0 0 0
LARm 0 14 3 14 **31**
Atl D2 R22/66 P(9-2-1) 4
LARm D24 R55/209 P(15-12-0) 142

Hou 7 0 3 0 10
Cin 0 10 0 14 **24**
Hou D10 R29/157 P(23-11-2) 57
Cin D23 R40/218 P(26-15-0) 154
Cin-Johnson 131R

KC 0 10 0 0 **10**
NE 0 0 0 7 7
KC D16 R42/149 P(14-11-0) 156
NE D18 R25/40 P(29-16-1) 162
KC-Taylor 115C

Phi 6 0 10 7 23
NYG 7 3 0 13 23
Phi D16 R28/128 P(28-14-2) 216
NYG D24 R40/134 P(35-19-1) 272
Phi-Sullivan 100R, Carmichael 103C;
NYG-Johnson 112R, Tucker 136C

NYJ 3 0 10 21 **34**
Bal 3 7 0 0 10
NYJ D16 R36/108 P(25-20-1) 168
Bal D14 R23/89 P(35-17-8) 188
Bal-Doughty 105C

Det 0 3 0 10 13
GB 0 10 0 3 13
Det D12 R37/110 P(15-8-3) 82
GB D17 R40/176 P(20-9-0) 101
GB-Brockington 118R

Was 0 7 3 17 27
SL 7 0 10 17 **34**
Was D22 R26/69 P(40-26-0) 291
SL D20 R35/65 P(30-17-0) 278
Was-Taylor 132C; SL-Smith 129C

Min 0 13 0 9 **22**
ChiB 7 3 0 3 13
Min D13 R35/188 P(18-12-1) 121
ChiB D16 R43/200 P(19-10-0) 174
Min-Foreman 116R

SF 0 20 10 6 **36**
Den 10 3 7 14 34
SF D16 R39/135 P(35-14-1) 212
Den D22 R32/115 P(36-17-5) 240

Cle 3 0 0 3 6
Pit 10 6 10 7 **33**
Cle D16 R35/84 P(30-15-3) 124
Pit D14 R35/196 P(15-6-1) 173

Buf 0 7 0 0 7
SD 7 7 14 6 **34**
Buf D16 R36/148 P(32-12-4) 139
SD D17 R30/105 P(23-14-1) 249
Buf-Simpson 103R, Hill 118C

MONDAY, SEPTEMBER 24

NO 0 3 0 0 3
Dal 12 0 21 7 **40**
NO D17 R38/138 P(21-13-1) 98
Dal D24 R36/169 P(22-15-1) 186

SUNDAY, SEPTEMBER 30

NYG 0 10 0 0 10
Cle 0 0 6 6 **12**
NYG D8 R25/49 P(19-9-3) 74
Cle D15 R46/141 P(22-10-2) 98

Was 7 0 7 14 **28**
Phi 0 7 0 0 7
Was D15 R36/81 P(29-16-1) 195
Phi D14 R22/53 P(38-19-2) 206
Phi-Bulaich 109C

NE 0 3 13 7 23
Mia 0 20 3 21 **44**
NE D21 R39/143 P(30-16-1) 213
Mia D16 R38/301 P(12-8-0) 53
Mia-Morris 197R

Oak 0 3 0 0 3
KC 0 6 3 7 **16**
Oak D8 R25/77 P(18-8-3) 72
KC D13 R49/169 P(13-10-0) 64

NO 0 7 0 3 10
Bal 14 0 0 0 **14**
NO D12 R24/62 P(33-18-1) 250
Bal D19 R51/248 P(16-7-4) 91
Bal-McCauley 109R, Mitchell 133R

SL 0 0 3 7 10
Dal 14 10 7 14 **45**
SL D17 R20/44 P(38-23-2) 246
Dal D31 R42/250 P(25-20-0) 328

NYJ 0 0 0 7 7
Buf 3 0 0 6 **9**
NYJ D17 R26/102 P(31-12-0) 148
Buf D15 R44/208 P(17-7-1) 64
Buf-Simpson 123R

Cin 7 6 7 0 **20**
SD 3 0 0 10 13
Cin D19 R44/202 P(17-10-0) 215
SD D17 R32/114 P(31-15-2) 177
Cin-Johnson 121R, Johnson 116C;
SD-Garrison 117C

GB 0 3 0 0 3
Min 0 5 3 3 **11**
GB D10 R30/90 P(20-7-1) 70
Min D17 R43/206 P(16-12-1) 78

LARm 10 17 0 13 **40**
SF 7 3 3 7 20
LARm D24 R55/223 P(12-9-0) 128
SF D17 R18/99 P(30-15-3) 199

Pit 3 3 13 17 **36**
Hou 0 7 0 0 7
Pit D14 R39/125 P(19-9-2) 130
Hou D13 R28/63 P(33-19-3) 115

ChiB 6 10 14 3 **33**
Den 0 0 0 14 14
ChiB D19 R52/202 P(22-8-1) 123
Den D25 R22/71 P(40-24-2) 295
Den-Anderson 143C, Johnson 326P

MONDAY, OCTOBER 1

Atl 3 0 3 0 6
Det 7 14 3 7 **31**
Atl D15 R23/118 P(30-15-2) 70
Det D15 R47/258 P(12-6-0) 39

SUNDAY, OCTOBER 7

Cin 3 0 0 7 10
Cle 0 7 7 3 **17**
Cin D11 R24/96 P(23-11-1) 167
Cle D21 R52/216 P(18-9-0) 72

Bal 3 0 3 10 16
NE 3 7 7 7 **24**
Bal D11 R36/111 P(19-8-0) 81
NE D19 R43/146 P(13-6-0) 45

SF 0 10 3 0 **13**
Atl 0 6 0 3 9
SF D16 R37/151 P(24-13-0) 139
Atl D15 R26/133 P(38-17-1) 138

NYJ 0 0 0 3 3
Mia 14 10 7 0 **31**
NYJ D12 R39/156 P(20-6-4) 42
Mia D18 R32/151 P(21-12-1) 219

Den 0 7 0 7 14
KC 0 6 7 3 **16**
Den D10 R27/158 P(19-10-1) 112
KC D19 R41/179 P(29-18-0) 170

SD 0 0 0 21 21
Pit 17 21 0 0 **38**
SD D20 R36/167 P(35-13-4) 181
Pit D15 R38/154 P(23-9-2) 132

Min 14 6 0 3 **23**
Det 3 3 3 0 9
Min D17 R31/147 P(24-17-2) 179
Det D15 R30/154 P(31-18-3) 91
Min-Foreman 114R

LARm 7 14 10 0 **31**
Hou 6 3 3 14 26
LARm D21 R46/169 P(16-10-0) 179
Hou D16 R23/76 P(38-25-2) 204

Oak 0 3 7 7 **17**
SL 7 0 0 3 10
Oak D32 R43/247 P(31-19-1) 199
SL D17 R28/120 P(27-12-0) 88

```
GB    7   0   6   3   16
NYG   7   0   0   7   14
GB  D11 R37/125 P(11-7-2) 75
NYG D13 R25/57  P(28-21-2) 174

Phi   6  10   7   3   26
Buf  10  14   0   3   27
Phi D28 R44/275 P(29-16-0) 176
Buf D16 R36/229 P(9-6-0) 47
Phi-Bulaich 104R, Sullivan 155R;
Buf-Simpson 171R

ChiB  0   0   3  13   16
NO    7   0   7   7   21
ChiB D13 R30/74  P(30-13-1) 179
NO   D19 R41/163 P(18-10-0) 119
```

MONDAY, OCTOBER 8
```
Dal   0   7   0   0    7
Was   0   0   0  14   14
Dal D20 R39/182 P(32-13-1) 87
Was D13 R28/71  P(20-14-0) 103
Dal-Hill 103R
```

SUNDAY, OCTOBER 14
```
Den   7  17  14  10   48
Hou   0  10  10   0   20
Den D21 R43/233 P(20-9-0) 214
Hou D20 R29/117 P(27-21-1) 98
Den-Little 123R, Johnson 214P

Pit   0   0   0   7    7
Cin   6   3   7   3   19
Pit D6  R22/71  P(14-9-1) 67
Cin D19 R55/172 P(21-9-0) 78
Cin-Clark 112R

Det   0   3   7   3   13
NO    0   3   3  14   20
Det D19 R36/186 P(19-9-1) 173
NO  D21 R45/171 P(15-9-1) 163

Phi   0   7   3  17   27
SL    0   3  14   7   24
Phi D20 R27/102 P(45-29-0) 351
SL  D24 R22/65  P(38-26-1) 278
Phi-Carmichael 187R, Gabriel 379P;
SL-Rashad 104C

Dal   7   7   7  10   31
LARm 14  20   3   0   37
Dal  D17 R26/114 P(25-15-3) 150
LARm D16 R40/104 P(22-12-2) 279
LARm-Jackson 238C, Hadl 279P

NYJ   3   0   3   3    9
NE    0   7   0   0    7
NYJ D13 R58/232 P(7-1-0) 0
NE  D9  R26/114 P(18-8-2) 58
NYJ-Riggins 132R

Bal   3   3   0   7   13
Buf   0  10   7  14   31
Bal D13 R41/143 P(15-7-2) 60
Buf D18 R44/259 P(13-7-1) 52
Buf-Simpson 166R

Min   7   7   0   3   17
SF    3   3   7   0   13
Min D14 R30/96  P(22-10-1) 124
SF  D28 R28/110 P(48-31-2) 320
Min-Gilliam 107C;
SF-Washington 118C, Spurrier 320P

KC    7   0   0   3   10
GB    0  10   0   0   10
KC D9  R33/96  P(19-10-1) 53
GB D16 R41/169 P(23-12-2) 146
GB-Brockington 106R

ChiB  0   6   0   0    6
Atl   0  17  21   8   46
ChiB D13 R31/137 P(19-9-1) 21
Atl  D21 R39/175 P(20-17-0) 247

Oak   0   6   7  14   27
SD    3   0  14   0   17
Oak D20 R42/180 P(22-13-1) 187
SD  D18 R32/90  P(30-12-1) 179

Was   7   7   0   7   21
NYG   0   3   0   0    3
Was D12 R36/116 P(13-8-3) 32
NYG D12 R33/92  P(32-19-4) 138
```

MONDAY, OCTOBER 15
```
Mia   0   3   7   7   17
Cle   0   6   3   0    9
Mia D11 R40/212 P(11-3-2) 38
Cle D12 R38/154 P(16-8-1) 57
Mia-Csonka 114R
```

SUNDAY, OCTOBER 21
```
NYG   0   7   7  14   28
Dal   7  10   7  21   45
NYG D21 R31/116 P(34-18-1) 219
Dal D22 R40/234 P(11-8-1) 126
Dal-Hill 123R

SL    0   6   7   0   13
Was   7  14   0  10   31
SL  D12 R17/46  P(39-15-3) 202
Was D23 R47/142 P(33-20-3) 286
Was-Taylor 153C

KC    0   3   0   6    9
Cin   0   7   0   7   14
KC  D12 R26/104 P(21-15-2) 163
Cin D19 R39/196 P(22-12-2) 138
Cin-Clark 104R, Curtis 106C

NYJ   7   7   0   0   14
Pit   0   9   3  14   26
NYJ D9  R31/72  P(15-6-3) 46
Pit D19 R49/214 P(22-10-1) 146
Pit-Harris 102R

Bal   0  10   6  13   29
Det   0   6   7  14   27
Bal D19 R45/165 P(13-9-0) 172
Det D24 R35/170 P(29-20-0) 227
Bal-Doughty 109C

Buf   3   0   0   3    6
Mia   3  21   3   0   27
Buf D8  R32/75  P(18-6-1) 1
Mia D18 R40/183 P(21-10-2) 127

Atl   7  10  10  14   41
SD    0   0   0   0    0
Atl D25 R46/196 P(19-11-1) 142
SD  D11 R22/89  P(36-13-4) 88

NE    3   3   7   0   13
ChiB  0   7   3   0   10
NE   D14 R44/177 P(16-7-0) 54
ChiB D13 R38/193 P(13-6-2) 44

Hou   0   0  13   0   13
Cle  14  14   0  14   42
Hou D4  R18/23  P(22-8-1) 83
Cle D26 R52/264 P(21-12-1) 102

NO    0   0   0   0    0
SF    0  10  21   9   40
NO D2  R27/97  P(18-5-1) -15
SF D21 R43/203 P(31-17-2) 221
SF-Abramowicz 101C

GB    0   0   7   0    7
LARm  0  10   3  11   24
GB   D6  R25/35  P(12-5-1) 28
LARm D21 R50/244 P(19-10-0) 134

Phi   0   7   7   7   21
Min   7   7   7   7   28
Phi D19 R26/126 P(32-23-0) 189
Min D25 R44/217 P(21-16-0) 192
Min-Gilliam 116C
```

MONDAY, OCTOBER 22
```
Oak   0  13   7   3   23
Den   7   0  10   6   23
Oak D21 R32/147 P(25-17-0) 270
Den D13 R33/114 P(25-11-2) 102
Oak-Biletnikoff 116C, Siani 116C,
Stabler 313P
```

SUNDAY, OCTOBER 28
```
Was   0   0   0   3    3
NO   10   6   0   3   19
Was D15 R18/24  P(37-19-2) 155
NO  D19 R52/203 P(17-7-0) 39

Oak   3   0  14  17   34
Bal   0   0   7  14   21
Oak D28 R39/182 P(29-25-0) 260
Bal D22 R31/117 P(28-15-2) 209
Oak-Stabler 304P
```

```
Den  21   9   7   3   40
NYJ   7   0  21   0   28
Den D20 R50/197 P(22-14-1) 235
NYJ D17 R14/86  P(36-13-3) 229

Hou   0   7   0   7   14
ChiB  7  14   7   7   35
Hou  D19 R37/157 P(31-15-2) 54
ChiB D19 R35/115 P(26-13-0) 154

Atl   7   7   3   0   17
SF    0   0   0   3    3
Atl D19 R48/183 P(13-11-1) 194
SF  D13 R22/93  P(37-16-0) 85
Atl-Hampton 100R, Burrow 164C

Dal   0  13   9  10   32
Phi  10  17   0   3   30
Dal D27 R36/130 P(39-24-2) 232
Phi D19 R27/69  P(34-20-0) 203
Dal-Garrison 102R, Hill 100R

SD    0  10   3   3   16
Cle   0  10   0   0   10
SD  D16 R44/204 P(16-8-1) 135
Cle D13 R31/118 P(21-10-2) 66
SD-Garrett 130R

Cin   0   6   0   7   13
Pit   3   7   0  10   20
Cin D17 R32/101 P(38-20-3) 217
Pit D10 R35/86  P(14-7-2) 156
Pit-Shanklin 104C

Mia   7   6  10   7   30
NE    7   7   0   0   14
Mia D19 R45/238 P(18-7-0) 73
NE  D12 R29/94  P(23-13-0) 142
Mia-Morris 100R

NYG   3   7   0  17   27
SL    7   7   7  14   35
NYG D29 R31/95  P(44-28-1) 332
SL  D19 R32/160 P(31-13-0) 220
NYG-Grim 137C, Johnson 348P;
SL-Anderson 130R, Gray 125C,
Hart 235P

GB    0   0   0   0    0
Det  10   7   0  17   34
GB  D7  R25/60  P(19-6-1) 3
Det D23 R56/263 P(12-7-1) 66
Det-Taylor 160R

LARm  0   3   3   3    9
Min   3   7   0   0   10
LARm D11 R30/89  P(20-10-2) 68
Min  D19 R45/182 P(16-8-0) 71
```

MONDAY, OCTOBER 29
```
KC    0   7   0   7   14
Buf  14   0   9   0   23
KC  D8  R17/38  P(29-8-2) 67
Buf D21 R65/246 P(12-6-1) 63
Buf-Simpson 157R
```

SUNDAY, NOVEMBER 4
```
Cin   0   0  10   0   10
Dal  17   7  14   0   38
Cin D16 R30/125 P(22-14-3) 146
Dal D17 R36/119 P(21-14-0) 181

NE    7   3   7   6   23
Phi   0   0  21   3   24
NE  D20 R40/161 P(25-18-1) 129
Phi D19 R28/132 P(36-24-3) 234
Phi-Young 108C

Den   0   7   0  10   17
SL    0   7   3   7   17
Den D15 R30/104 P(23-15-1) 190
SL  D18 R27/93  P(31-18-2) 168
Den-Odoms 114C

Hou   7  14   0  10   31
Bal   3   0  14  10   27
Hou D20 R36/104 P(33-22-3) 340
Bal D16 R34/104 P(26-12-1) 155
Hou-Burrough 117C, Parks 127C,
Dickey 340P

Cle   0   0   0   3    3
Min   3   6   7  10   26
Cle D4  R16/70  P(23-12-2) 75
Min D23 R51/201 P(24-14-0) 152
```

```
KC    6   3   3   7   19
SD    0   0   0   0    0
KC D17 R43/188 P(20-10-0) 144
SD D11 R26/91  P(30-12-3) 99

ChiB  7   3  14   7   31
GB    7  10   0   0   17
ChiB D21 R52/230 P(15-10-0) 107
GB   D8  R32/110 P(16-3-1) -12
ChiB-Douglass 100R

LARm 10   0   0   3   13
Atl   3   6   0   6   15
LARm D14 R35/126 P(19-6-1) 100
Atl  D18 R32/93  P(31-19-1) 168

SF    0  20   0   0   20
Det  14  10   3   3   30
SF  D16 R23/70  P(47-23-6) 254
Det D18 R38/159 P(27-14-2) 232
SF-Kwalick 133C

Buf   0   0   0   0    0
NO    3  10   0   0   13
Buf D10 R31/124 P(19-9-0) 66
NO  D19 R34/115 P(33-16-0) 166

NYG   0   0   0   0    0
Oak  14  14   7   7   42
NYG D11 R24/57  P(36-11-4) 128
Oak D28 R37/211 P(26-18-2) 228

Mia   7   7  10   0   24
NYJ   0  14   0   0   14
Mia D21 R35/153 P(19-13-1) 193
NYJ D16 R33/113 P(30-19-1) 168
Mia-Csonka 107R
```

MONDAY, NOVEMBER 5
```
Was   3   3   3   7   16
Pit   7   0   7   7   21
Was D14 R33/117 P(22-9-2) 73
Pit D18 R49/153 P(19-8-4) 102
```

SUNDAY, NOVEMBER 11
```
SL    7   0   0  14   21
GB   10  12   0   3   25
SL D19 R19/71  P(30-19-0) 187
GB D21 R52/243 P(14-7-0) 62
GB-Brockington 137R

Bal   0   0   0   0    0
Mia  17  10  10   7   44
Bal D4  R28/112 P(22-7-2) 20
Mia D17 R41/315 P(20-9-2) 97
Mia-Morris 144R

Dal   6   7   3   7   23
NYG   0  10   0   0   10
Dal D14 R36/141 P(16-7-0) 54
NYG D18 R30/81  P(31-18-4) 186

NE    6   0   7   0   13
NYJ   7  13   3  10   33
NE  D10 R18/41  P(40-17-3) 108
NYJ D16 R51/267 P(15-6-1) 59

Pit   0   7   3   7   17
Oak   0   3   0   6    9
Pit D8  R35/112 P(19-6-1) 82
Oak D26 R39/172 P(38-17-4) 223
Oak-Biletnikoff 105C

Cin   6   7   0   3   16
Buf   3   3   7   0   13
Cin D18 R46/161 P(22-9-2) 120
Buf D10 R34/150 P(16-5-2) 30

Atl   7  10   3  24   44
Phi   7   6   7   7   27
Atl D22 R43/170 P(25-13-1) 122
Phi D20 R26/128 P(33-21-2) 205
Phi-Carmichael 105C

Cle  17   0   3   3   23
Hou   0   3   3   7   13
Cle D13 R37/180 P(17-8-1) 119
Hou D16 R27/106 P(38-20-1) 203

Det   7   0   0   0    7
Min   7   7  14   0   28
Det D17 R24/127 P(34-16-1) 119
Min D23 R48/248 P(16-11-1) 155
Min-Brown 101R, Gilliam 129C

SF    0   9   0   0    9
Was   7   3  13  10   33
SF  D22 R29/123 P(36-20-2) 199
Was D22 R28/86  P(40-23-0) 257
```

```
SD    3  13   0   3   19
Den  10   0   6  14   30
SD  D14 R30/120 P(22-12-1) 101
Den D21 R39/179 P(30-16-2) 234
Den-Little 109R

NO    0   0   0   7    7
LARm  0  16  13   0   29
NO   D9  R29/124 P(15-9-0) 96
LARm D25 R53/212 P(25-13-1) 212
LARm-McCutcheon 115R
```

MONDAY, NOVEMBER 12
```
ChiB  0   0   7   0    7
KC    3   9   0   7   19
ChiB D9  R23/80  P(21-9-1) 66
KC   D19 R48/197 P(22-11-2) 130
KC-Podolak 134R
```

SUNDAY, NOVEMBER 18
```
NYJ   0   7   7   0   14
Cin   0  17   0   3   20
NYJ D21 R30/93  P(44-26-2) 264
Cin D11 R33/132 P(19-10-0) 76
NYJ-Caster 131C

SL    3   7   0   3   13
NYG   0   7  14   3   24
SL  D14 R22/68  P(30-16-1) 214
NYG D21 R45/172 P(23-16-1) 186

SF    3   3   0   7   13
LARm  7   7  10   7   31
SF  D12 R21/66  P(31-12-2) 129
LARm D21 R48/185 P(24-13-0) 229
LARm-Jackson 117C

Hou   0   0   7   7   14
KC    7   7  10  14   38
Hou D13 R23/46  P(41-17-2) 216
KC  D18 R46/119 P(19-13-1) 147

Cle   0   7   0   0    7
Oak   0   0   0   7    7
Cle D14 R43/158 P(17-9-0) 68
Oak D13 R26/97  P(33-17-0) 75

GB   14   3   7   0   24
NE    0   7   7  19   33
GB D15 R30/75  P(23-17-1) 263
NE D23 R33/116 P(32-18-1) 340
NE-Rucker 108C, Plunkett 348P

Phi   3   7   0   0   10
Dal   0  14   7  10   31
Phi D12 R29/118 P(33-13-1) 133
Dal D16 R40/286 P(17-7-3) 107
Phi-Young 113C

Det   7  13  10   0   30
ChiB  7   0   0   0    7
Det  D10 R36/162 P(14-7-2) 66
ChiB D15 R36/139 P(31-14-5) 119
Det-Taylor 106R

Den   3   3   7  10   23
Pit   3   3   0   7   13
Den D20 R49/184 P(20-13-0) 73
Pit D12 R24/83  P(19-10-0) 217

Bal   0   0   0   0    0
Was   7   6   3   6   22
Bal D22 R35/120 P(30-14-2) 122
Was D14 R32/104 P(20-10-1) 140

Mia   7  10   0   0   17
Buf   0   0   0   0    0
Mia D17 R42/154 P(20-11-0) 123
Buf D15 R39/238 P(22-6-1) 71
Buf-Braxton 119R, Simpson 120R

NO    0   0   0   0    0
SD    0  10   0   7   17
NO D22 R34/142 P(37-21-1) 199
SD D14 R35/186 P(24-9-1) 102
NO-Beasley 127C
```

MONDAY, NOVEMBER 19
```
Min   0   7   0   7   14
Atl   0  17   3   0   20
Min D17 R32/82  P(30-17-1) 209
Atl D18 R42/176 P(23-11-1) 171
Atl-Hampton 108R
```

THURSDAY, NOVEMBER 22

Was 10 3 7 0 **20**
Det 0 0 0 0 **0**
Was D20 R45/202 P(22-12-0) 96
Det D11 R23/74 P(26-13-1) 134
Was-Harraway 107R

Mia 14 0 0 0 **14**
Dal 0 0 0 7 **7**
Mia D16 R41/157 P(10-6-0) 103
Dal D16 R34/131 P(24-15-1) 136

SUNDAY, NOVEMBER 25

Buf 3 7 0 14 **24**
Bal 7 0 0 10 **17**
Buf D16 R37/215 P(19-11-1) 169
Bal D15 R36/152 P(25-8-2) 69
Buf-Simpson 124R

SD 0 0 0 3 **3**
Oak 7 17 7 0 **31**
SD D13 R32/117 P(21-10-1) 118
Oak D22 R39/155 P(24-13-1) 165

NE 10 14 3 5 **32**
Hou 0 0 0 0 **0**
NE D22 R42/141 P(32-17-1) 176
Hou D11 R22/101 P(29-14-2) 83

SL 3 7 7 7 **24**
Cin 7 7 14 14 **42**
SL D24 R37/195 P(29-14-1) 160
Cin D25 R37/199 P(24-13-0) 167
SL-Anderson 105R

Pit 7 3 3 3 **16**
Cle 7 7 0 7 **21**
Pit D16 R44/170 P(30-13-1) 210
Cle D10 R34/104 P(17-5-3) 146

NYG 3 0 0 13 **16**
Phi 10 3 7 0 **20**
NYG D19 R25/113 P(26-18-0) 257
Phi D22 R49/253 P(15-10-0) 127
NYG-Johnson 101R;
Phi-Sullivan 156R

Atl 7 14 0 7 **28**
NYJ 7 6 7 0 **20**
Atl D15 R44/147 P(18-8-1) 141
NYJ D15 R29/117 P(32-15-3) 173

ChiB 3 0 3 7 **13**
Min 3 7 14 7 **31**
ChiB D16 R35/141 P(20-10-1) 57
Min D20 R39/203 P(18-13-0) 172
Min-Gilliam 139C

LARm 0 10 7 7 **24**
NO 0 10 3 0 **13**
LARm D31 R55/340 P(26-12-2) 110
NO D15 R29/150 P(26-12-0) 109
LARm-McCutcheon 152R

KC 3 0 3 7 **10**
Den 0 14 0 0 **14**
KC D17 R37/139 P(32-13-2) 103
Den D12 R29/82 P(21-10-1) 137
Den-Moses 108C

MONDAY, NOVEMBER 26

GB 0 3 0 3 **6**
SF 0 10 0 10 **20**
GB D16 R36/131 P(26-14-3) 124
SF D18 R39/174 P(21-9-0) 94

SUNDAY, DECEMBER 2

Cle 0 3 3 14 **20**
KC 7 0 3 10 **20**
Cle D14 R31/144 P(28-13-1) 121
KC D17 R52/208 P(22-11-0) 137
Cle-Pruitt 110R; KC-Ellison 108R

Phi 0 0 7 21 **28**
SF 7 21 3 7 **38**
Phi D22 R23/92 P(55-28-1) 317
SF D22 R38/178 P(24-15-1) 211
Phi-Young 112C, Gabriel 322P;
SF-Willard 117R

Dal 7 3 3 9 **22**
Den 0 0 3 7 **10**
Dal D14 R39/74 P(19-14-0) 189
Den D12 R24/82 P(30-13-1) 147

NYG 7 14 0 3 **24**
Was 3 10 0 14 **27**
NYG D13 R37/120 P(23-13-0) 146
Was D18 R31/99 P(30-18-1) 260

Buf 7 3 7 0 **17**
Atl 0 6 0 0 **6**
Buf D17 R54/239 P(12-7-1) 95
Atl D12 R32/125 P(22-9-0) 147
Buf-Simpson 137R

Min 0 0 0 0 **0**
Cin 0 10 10 7 **27**
Min D13 R26/81 P(29-16-1) 120
Cin D17 R39/227 P(17-12-0) 105

LARm 10 3 0 13 **26**
ChiB 0 0 0 0 **0**
LARm D24 R53/296 P(21-8-1) 90
ChiB D6 R24/53 P(19-9-0) 47
LARm-McCutcheon 152R

SD 0 14 0 0 **14**
NE 3 13 7 7 **30**
SD D11 R31/187 P(15-10-2) 44
NE D22 R40/184 P(27-13-2) 175

Bal 0 0 0 17 **17**
NYJ 3 14 0 3 **20**
Bal D19 R39/168 P(21-11-0) 151
NYJ D18 R36/134 P(21-15-1) 219
NYJ-Boozer 105R

Oak 0 0 3 14 **17**
Hou 0 3 0 3 **6**
Oak D19 R34/235 P(26-15-3) 140
Hou D15 R30/94 P(36-22-0) 191
Oak-Hubbard 121R

NO 0 3 7 0 **10**
GB 3 10 7 10 **30**
NO D16 R29/100 P(36-18-4) 156
GB D13 R42/154 P(13-9-0) 105

Det 3 10 0 7 **20**
SL 0 10 3 3 **16**
Det D17 R30/92 P(24-14-0) 211
SL D19 R34/169 P(25-12-1) 132

MONDAY, DECEMBER 3

Pit 0 3 7 16 **26**
Mia 20 10 0 0 **30**
Pit D19 R35/178 P(42-14-6) 90
Mia D8 R37/123 P(13-8-0) 66
Pit-Harris 105R

SATURDAY, DECEMBER 8

Min 14 14 3 0 **31**
GB 0 0 0 7 **7**
Min D10 R37/138 P(19-10-0) 83
GB D17 R36/152 P(32-14-4) 148
Min-Foreman 100R;
GB-Brockington 124R

KC 0 0 0 7 **7**
Oak 7 13 3 14 **37**
KC D8 R12/24 P(24-12-2) 82
Oak D24 R61/259 P(21-11-0) 94
Oak-Hubbard 115R

SUNDAY, DECEMBER 9

NE 3 3 7 0 **13**
Buf 7 10 17 3 **37**
NE D20 R30/98 P(41-17-2) 292
Buf D13 R40/293 P(7-2-0) 31
NE-Adams 100C;
Buf-Simpson 219R

Mia 0 0 0 3 **3**
Bal 3 7 6 0 **16**
Mia D11 R27/93 P(23-11-2) 135
Bal D15 R51/166 P(8-5-0) 35
Bal-Mitchell 104R

ChiB 0 7 0 0 **7**
Det 3 21 9 7 **40**
ChiB D9 R17/46 P(28-9-2) 33
Det D22 R38/124 P(35-17-0) 182

SF 3 0 7 0 **10**
NO 7 6 3 0 **16**
SF D18 R27/116 P(34-17-1) 152
NO D14 R45/120 P(24-13-1) 154

Cle 0 3 14 0 **17**
Cin 3 14 10 3 **34**
Cle D10 R23/78 P(27-13-2) 70
Cin D21 R46/173 P(19-11-0) 201
Cin-Curtis 117C

SL 0 10 9 13 **32**
Atl 10 0 0 0 **10**
SL D15 R60/243 P(10-2-1) 9
Atl D9 R22/89 P(31-8-2) 31
SL-Metcalf 100R

Hou 7 0 0 0 **7**
Pit 3 14 10 6 **33**
Hou D5 R23/58 P(17-6-4) 25
Pit D19 R49/188 P(26-13-4) 132

NYJ 14 3 3 3 **23**
Phi 0 7 17 0 **24**
NYJ D24 R42/276 P(29-11-2) 156
Phi D20 R35/155 P(25-14-0) 203
NYJ-Boozer 160R;
Phi-Carmichael 146C

Den 7 13 19 3 **42**
SD 7 7 0 14 **28**
Den D23 R44/192 P(29-18-0) 231
SD D14 R22/126 P(31-13-2) 215
SD-LeVias 149C

Was 0 0 0 7 **7**
Dal 0 3 14 10 **27**
Was D9 R22/59 P(24-11-0) 96
Dal D22 R47/193 P(25-16-2) 221
Was-LeVias 149C; Dal-Hill 110R

MONDAY, DECEMBER 10

NYG 3 0 3 0 **6**
LARm 0 14 16 10 **40**
NYG D8 R25/62 P(24-12-4) 141
LARm D24 R39/219 P(24-14-2) 146

SATURDAY, DECEMBER 15

Pit 7 7 13 10 **37**
SF 0 7 0 7 **14**
Pit D18 R41/172 P(24-11-0) 136
SF D16 R28/127 P(33-13-5) 112

Det 0 0 0 7 **7**
Mia 14 11 3 6 **34**
Det D17 R38/146 P(22-11-2) 98
Mia D18 R29/165 P(19-12-0) 157
Det-Owens 113R;
Mia-Warfield 103C, Griese 141P

SUNDAY, DECEMBER 16

Buf 7 14 7 6 **34**
NYJ 7 0 0 7 **14**
Buf D21 R62/304 P(5-3-0) 70
NYJ D12 R11/39 P(30-13-0) 184
Buf-Simpson 200R;
NYJ-Barkum 102C

NE 0 0 7 6 **13**
Bal 9 0 0 9 **18**
NE D10 R19/50 P(27-13-2) 147
Bal D19 R50/211 P(20-11-1) 118
Bal-Mitchell 142R

Cle 7 3 0 7 **17**
LARm 13 14 3 0 **30**
Cle D12 R26/110 P(25-16-2) 105
LARm D16 R45/231 P(18-7-0) 84

Dal 3 10 7 10 **30**
SL 3 0 0 0 **3**
Dal D24 R45/207 P(23-15-0) 252
SL D10 R31/135 P(20-6-2) 6
Dal-Newhouse 124R, Pearson 140C

Cin 3 10 14 0 **27**
Hou 0 10 0 14 **24**
Cin D14 R26/101 P(23-15-0) 281
Hou D25 R39/190 P(26-17-0) 191
Cin-Curtis 144C;
Hou-Robinson 100R

NO 0 0 10 0 **10**
Atl 7 7 0 0 **14**
NO D11 R39/105 P(21-6-2) 90
Atl D17 R47/148 P(19-10-0) 148

Min 7 10 14 0 **31**
NYG 0 0 0 7 **7**
Min D19 R42/183 P(14-10-0) 130
NYG D13 R32/112 P(28-11-2) 154

Phi 10 3 7 0 **20**
Was 0 24 7 7 **38**
Phi D18 R26/51 P(39-22-1) 295
Was D22 R38/186 P(24-13-1) 246
Phi-Carmichael 111C, Young 104C,
Gabriel 302P; Was-Brown 150R,
Brown 105C, Kilmer 251P

GB 7 7 0 7 **21**
ChiB 0 0 0 0 **0**
GB D16 R53/298 P(12-3-1) 72
ChiB D12 R36/125 P(27-10-1) 68
GB-Brockington 142R, Lane 101R

SD 3 0 3 0 **6**
KC 0 12 3 10 **33**
SD D12 R23/90 P(29-13-3) 113
KC D19 R44/143 P(22-11-0) 97

Den 0 3 7 7 **17**
Oak 7 7 3 14 **21**
Den D16 R27/90 P(38-15-3) 119
Oak D16 R45/161 P(20-12-0) 134

1974 NFL

SUNDAY, SEPTEMBER 15

Mia 0 10 7 7 **24**
NE 7 17 7 3 **34**
Mia D18 R29/89 P(30-19-1) 221
NE D22 R44/196 P(24-14-1) 177
Mia-Briscoe 113C, Warfield 104C

NYJ 6 10 0 0 **16**
KC 0 14 3 7 **24**
NYJ D17 R33/138 P(30-14-4) 210
KC D16 R44/180 P(21-9-2) 110
NYJ-Riggins 116R

Det 0 0 2 7 **9**
ChiB 0 14 3 0 **17**
Det D9 R26/89 P(28-13-2) 67
ChiB D13 R42/98 P(19-10-2) 175
ChiB-Wade 116C

Min 3 7 13 9 **32**
GB 0 10 0 7 **17**
Min D20 R46/165 P(23-14-1) 97
GB D12 R33/96 P(20-9-3) 95

Phi 3 0 0 0 **3**
SL 7 0 0 0 **7**
Phi D20 R28/113 P(39-23-1) 174
SL D18 R37/126 P(27-13-1) 192

Dal 7 10 0 7 **24**
Atl 0 0 0 0 **0**
Dal D21 R44/205 P(29-15-0) 206
Atl D7 R21/64 P(28-8-2) 44

SD 0 7 7 0 **14**
Hou 14 0 0 7 **21**
SD D23 R40/216 P(26-13-2) 195
Hou D19 R36/156 P(27-19-1) 193
SD-Edwards 100R;
Hou-Coleman 123R

LARm 0 10 7 0 **17**
Den 0 0 3 7 **10**
LARm D14 R44/145 P(20-10-1) 127
Den D11 R20/52 P(26-13-0) 104

Bal 0 0 0 0 **0**
Pit 3 7 13 7 **30**
Bal D11 R34/118 P(20-9-2) 48
Pit D18 R29/103 P(37-18-1) 289

Was 7 6 0 0 **13**
NYG 3 0 7 0 **10**
Was D13 R39/128 P(23-13-1) 109
NYG D12 R36/98 P(22-9-2) 60

SF 7 0 7 3 **17**
NO 0 10 3 0 **13**
SF D15 R36/158 P(15-7-3) 56
NO D22 R40/129 P(28-16-2) 149

Cle 0 0 0 0 **0**
Cin 0 7 16 10 **33**
Cle D15 R35/200 P(22-9-1) 3
Cin D18 R34/166 P(18-10-0) 176
Cin-Curtis 117C

MONDAY, SEPTEMBER 16

Oak 0 3 7 10 **20**
Buf 0 7 0 14 **21**
Oak D18 R35/152 P(22-9-1) 100
Buf D22 R45/200 P(20-10-0) 106

SUNDAY, SEPTEMBER 22

NO 0 0 0 0 **0**
LARm 7 10 0 7 **24**
NO D14 R30/109 P(29-12-2) 130
LARm D20 R39/157 P(23-10-1) 150
LARm-McCutcheon 102R

GB 3 10 7 0 **20**
Bal 3 3 0 7 **13**
GB D13 R43/84 P(16-10-1) 109
Bal D19 R29/133 P(36-15-4) 149

NE 7 7 7 7 **28**
NYG 7 7 0 6 **20**
NE D18 R35/173 P(17-11-0) 145
NYG D20 R32/54 P(35-28-1) 254

NYJ 6 14 0 3 **23**
ChiB 0 0 14 7 **21**
NYJ D22 R46/146 P(23-16-0) 235
ChiB D20 R22/67 P(38-18-0) 248

Min 0 7 0 0 **7**
Det 0 3 0 3 **6**
Min D14 R30/134 P(24-12-0) 119
Det D9 R34/123 P(18-12-0) 39

SF 13 0 0 3 **16**
Atl 7 0 0 3 **10**
SF D17 R48/200 P(22-7-1) 72
Atl D15 R36/127 P(23-10-3) 82

Cle 3 7 10 0 **20**
Hou D13 R23/35 P(27-9-3) 133
Cle D22 R43/216 P(29-15-0) 126

Pit 0 0 7 7 **35**
Den 21 0 7 7 **35**
Pit D33 R40/160 P(50-31-2) 324
Den D20 R37/156 P(27-12-2) 176
Pit-Gilliam 348P;
Den-Armstrong 131R

KC 0 0 7 0 **7**
Oak 7 13 0 7 **27**
KC D11 R34/124 P(26-10-5) 48
Oak D14 R36/119 P(26-12-2) 176

Mia 0 7 10 0 **24**
Buf 0 3 7 6 **16**
Mia D16 R39/176 P(13-10-2) 72
Buf D16 R30/107 P(22-17-0) 157

SL 7 7 3 0 **17**
Was 0 0 0 0 **0**
SL D12 R29/175 P(17-9-0) 49
Was D21 R39/132 P(33-19-1) 200

SD 7 6 0 7 **20**
Cin 0 7 10 0 **17**
SD D20 R42/130 P(24-13-0) 173
Cin D23 R32/210 P(28-17-1) 163
SD-Garrison 116C

MONDAY, SEPTEMBER 23

Dal 0 7 0 3 **10**
Phi 0 0 7 6 **13**
Dal D20 R41/168 P(33-19-2) 107
Phi D5 R29/98 P(14-6-1) 67
Dal-Pearson 161C

SUNDAY, SEPTEMBER 29

Cle 0 0 0 7 **7**
SL 0 7 22 0 **29**
Cle D11 R29/93 P(29-14-1) 155
SL D14 R42/171 P(11-4-0) 107

Bal 0 0 0 7 **7**
Phi 10 3 14 3 **30**
Bal D17 R21/46 P(48-29-2) 261
Phi D19 R36/137 P(28-17-0) 206

KC 0 0 3 14 **17**
Hou 0 0 0 0 **0**
KC D13 R23/20 P(26-20-0) 152
Hou D17 R27/55 P(33-19-2) 151

ChiB 0 0 0 7 **7**
Min 2 6 3 0 **11**
ChiB D18 R32/117 P(27-16-2) 162
Min D16 R35/138 P(25-16-2) 165
ChiB-Wade 112C

Oak 7 0 0 0 **7**
Pit 0 0 0 0 **0**
Oak D17 R47/177 P(12-5-0) 70
Pit D16 R27/117 P(33-9-3) 86

NYJ 0 6 6 0 **12**
Buf 7 3 0 6 **16**
NYJ D7 R33/106 P(18-2-3) 33
Buf D17 R61/223 P(2-0-0) 0
Buf-Simpson 117R

Atl 0 7 3 3 **13**
NO 0 7 0 7 **14**
Atl D12 R38/167 P(20-7-1) 63
NO D15 R47/172 P(14-6-1) 24

Cin 0 7 7 7 **21**
SF 0 3 0 0 **3**
Cin D19 R38/205 P(20-12-2) 168
SF D14 R34/171 P(22-11-2) 55

LARm 7 0 0 7 **14**
NE 0 7 6 7 **20**
LARm D20 R31/109 P(32-13-2) 196
NE D13 R35/98 P(25-14-1) 151
LARm-Jackson 102C

Mia 0 7 0 21 **28**
SD 0 7 14 0 **21**
Mia D25 R39/173 P(27-14-2) 218
SD D19 R36/203 P(22-14-0) 189
Mia-Csonka 106R, Mandich 101C;
SD-Woods 157R

Det 3 10 6 0 **19**
GB 0 8 10 3 **21**
Det D11 R26/71 P(31-17-0) 219
GB D19 R32/154 P(38-18-1) 200

NYG 0 14 0 0 **14**
Dal 0 0 0 6 **6**
NYG D16 R47/179 P(17-11-0) 128
Dal D18 R23/112 P(37-20-3) 221
Dal-Pearson 116C

MONDAY, SEPTEMBER 30
Den 0 0 0 3 **3**
Was 7 6 0 17 **30**
Den D10 R23/53 P(24-12-1) 106
Was D21 R42/100 P(26-20-0) 245

SUNDAY, OCTOBER 6
Was 0 3 0 14 **17**
Cin 7 7 7 7 **28**
Was D24 R34/110 P(41-24-0) 227
Cin D14 R30/99 P(18-12-0) 132

Den 3 0 7 7 **17**
KC 7 7 0 0 **14**
Den D13 R48/131 P(16-5-2) 90
KC D11 R38/89 P(19-10-1) 81

Atl 0 7 0 7 **14**
NYG 7 0 0 0 **7**
Atl D17 R38/157 P(17-10-3) 128
NYG D13 R29/172 P(26-12-2) 89
NYG-Kotar 119R

Bal 0 3 0 0 **3**
NE 7 14 14 7 **42**
Bal D15 R24/85 P(41-22-1) 180
NE D23 R38/186 P(23-12-2) 198

Buf 7 6 7 7 **27**
GB 0 0 0 7 **7**
Buf D22 R41/148 P(16-13-1) 157
GB D18 R25/100 P(31-17-2) 131

SL 0 7 24 3 **34**
SF 6 3 0 0 **9**
SL D21 R49/223 P(19-11-2) 184
SF D12 R28/186 P(20-7-2) 120
SL-Gray 124C

Min 3 10 7 3 **23**
Dal 0 0 14 0 **14**
Min D18 R35/111 P(27-17-0) 265
Dal D16 R32/144 P(20-9-4) 129
Min-Foreman 131C

Phi 6 7 0 0 **13**
SD 0 7 0 0 **7**
Phi D19 R34/143 P(33-18-1) 112
SD D19 R31/160 P(33-13-4) 126
SD-Woods 133R

Pit 0 3 3 7 **13**
Hou 0 7 0 0 **7**
Pit D18 R38/184 P(32-16-2) 202
Hou D10 R24/119 P(23-12-1) 121
Pit-Pearson 117R

NO 0 0 0 3 **10**
ChiB 7 10 0 7 **24**
NO D14 R28/70 P(26-15-0) 98
ChiB D18 R36/131 P(25-12-1) 117

Det 0 0 0 13 **13**
LARm 0 10 6 0 **16**
Det D17 R24/65 P(28-18-1) 226
LARm D26 R47/207 P(24-14-0) 127
Det-Jessie 149C;
LARm-McCutcheon 124R

Oak 7 16 14 3 **40**
Cle 17 0 0 7 **24**
Oak D14 R49/222 P(37-20-4) 223
Cle D14 R22/124 P(21-10-5) 120
Oak-Davis 116R

MONDAY, OCTOBER 7
NYJ 0 0 10 7 **17**
Mia 7 7 0 7 **21**
NYJ D14 R16/41 P(39-17-3) 280
Mia D23 R49/159 P(23-17-0) 167
NYJ-Caster 117C

SUNDAY, OCTOBER 13
NO 10 0 7 0 **17**
Den 7 19 7 0 **33**
NO D19 R29/137 P(36-17-3) 196
Den D24 R36/123 P(27-17-2) 274
Den-Moses 132C

ChiB 0 0 0 10 **10**
Atl 0 7 3 3 **13**
ChiB D13 R36/88 P(25-14-2) 124
Atl D15 R34/121 P(18-10-2) 93
ChiB-Rather 114C

NE 7 3 0 14 **24**
NYJ 0 0 0 0 **0**
NE D18 R46/206 P(21-11-1) 115
NYJ D11 R27/139 P(26-8-4) 34
NYJ-Riggins 100R

Oak 0 7 0 7 **14**
SD 0 0 0 0 **0**
Oak D21 R42/202 P(19-12-1) 162
SD D18 R35/184 P(24-11-1) 112
Oak-Branch 124C; SD-Woods 118R

Pit 7 17 10 0 **34**
KC 3 7 7 0 **24**
Pit D19 R41/119 P(36-14-1) 202
KC D19 R25/58 P(49-16-7) 199

Cin 13 7 7 7 **34**
Cle 0 3 7 7 **24**
Cin D26 R37/189 P(29-19-1) 263
Cle D19 R33/263 P(28-11-1) 87

Buf 0 17 0 10 **27**
Bal 0 7 0 14 **21**
Buf D15 R36/181 P(27-11-1) 125
Bal D11 R42/161 P(16-6-1) 1
Buf-Simpson 127R

Mia 0 7 3 7 **17**
Was 0 0 3 17 **20**
Mia D16 R39/107 P(24-11-2) 126
Was D18 R18/26 P(39-26-3) 299
Was-Jefferson 111C,
Jurgensen 303P

Hou 3 0 7 0 **10**
Min 16 14 7 14 **51**
Hou D11 R22/56 P(32-16-4) 129
Min D25 R35/145 P(37-27-0) 357
Min-Gilliam 102C

Dal 7 7 0 14 **28**
SL 0 21 7 3 **31**
Dal D24 R34/146 P(29-19-1) 224
SL D17 R34/138 P(21-9-0) 236
Dal-Pearson 118C; SL-Smith 110C

LARm 3 0 0 3 **6**
GB 0 7 3 7 **17**
LARm D16 R42/157 P(28-9-4) 94
GB D10 R44/143 P(9-2-1) -1
LARm-McCutcheon 109R

NYG 7 0 0 0 **7**
Phi 0 14 14 7 **35**
NYG D11 R29/120 P(23-8-3) 123
Phi D28 R46/186 P(38-22-2) 201

MONDAY, OCTOBER 14
SF 3 0 3 7 **13**
Det 0 7 0 10 **17**
SF D17 R31/139 P(40-17-3) 171
Det D13 R22/99 P(32-15-1) 130

SUNDAY, OCTOBER 20
SD 0 0 0 7 **7**
Den 7 10 7 3 **27**
SD D16 R24/84 P(29-14-3) 149
Den D20 R42/189 P(13-10-0) 165
Den-Little 127C

NE 7 7 7 7 **28**
Buf 20 0 7 3 **30**
NE D19 R28/189 P(21-1-1) 131
Buf D19 R52/180 P(12-8-0) 135
NE-Cunningham 125R;
Buf-Simpson 122R

Cin 0 14 0 13 **27**
Oak 3 3 14 10 **30**
Cin D17 R33/121 P(23-14-2) 166
Oak D28 R36/138 P(41-19-0) 221

Cle 0 13 0 3 **16**
Pit 7 7 3 3 **20**
Cle D16 R35/135 P(23-10-1) 127
Pit D15 R45/165 P(18-5-0) 66

Bal 7 14 0 14 **35**
NYJ 0 7 0 13 **20**
Bal D24 R58/266 P(17-11-0) 89
NYJ D11 R18/60 P(20-12-1) 128
Bal-Mitchell 156R

KC 0 3 0 0 **3**
Mia 0 2 0 7 **9**
KC D11 R37/136 P(11-5-1) 64
Mia D23 R40/189 P(25-11-3) 107

Det 0 6 7 7 **20**
Min 0 3 13 0 **16**
Det D23 R29/82 P(32-22-0) 276
Min D25 R31/161 P(30-18-1) 210
Det-Jessie 116C

SF 0 0 14 0 **14**
LARm 14 13 0 10 **37**
SF D12 R21/67 P(30-12-3) 112
LARm D19 R44/122 P(16-12-0) 276

NO 0 10 3 0 **13**
Atl 0 0 3 0 **3**
NO D15 R55/232 P(24-7-2) 89
Atl D10 R16/64 P(38-18-2) 110

NYG 0 3 0 0 **3**
Was 0 7 14 3 **24**
NYG D10 R28/57 P(29-15-5) 114
Was D18 R29/80 P(36-20-1) 166

SL 7 14 3 7 **31**
Hou 10 0 14 0 **27**
SL D23 R45/211 P(25-14-0) 134
Hou D21 R26/85 P(41-26-0) 348
Hou-Montgomery 179C,
Pastorini 354P

Phi 0 17 7 0 **24**
Dal 0 14 10 7 **31**
Phi D20 R17/50 P(36-21-1) 250
Dal D29 R49/246 P(27-18-0) 174
Dal-Hill 140R

MONDAY, OCTOBER 21
GB 0 0 6 3 **9**
ChiB 10 0 0 0 **10**
GB D16 R33/91 P(32-14-2) 140
ChiB D13 R41/159 P(16-7-2) 85
ChiB-Garrett 101R

SUNDAY, OCTOBER 27
Oak 7 7 14 7 **35**
SF 7 3 14 0 **24**
Oak D18 R42/164 P(11-6-0) 133
SF D20 R36/193 P(26-15-2) 179
Oak-Hubbard 117R

NE 3 7 0 7 **17**
Min 0 0 0 14 **14**
NE D18 R41/176 P(28-15-2) 218
Min D20 R30/114 P(39-19-3) 257
NE-Cunningham 129R;
Min-Gilliam 117C

Den 0 7 0 0 **7**
Cle 0 3 6 14 **23**
Den D18 R32/186 P(27-14-0) 172
Cle D14 R26/72 P(32-13-1) 187
Den-Armstrong 142R;
Cle-McKinnis 111C

ChiB 0 3 0 3 **6**
Buf 10 0 0 6 **16**
ChiB D17 R28/99 P(37-16-1) 159
Buf D16 R37/126 P(17-8-0) 100

Hou 3 3 14 14 **34**
Cin 0 7 0 14 **21**
Hou D12 R37/112 P(18-11-0) 142
Cin D26 R18/85 P(45-31-1) 330
Cin-Anderson 352P

Bal 0 0 7 0 **7**
Mia 0 3 7 7 **17**
Bal D10 R23/89 P(20-8-1) 69
Mia D24 R53/252 P(18-12-1) 119
Mia-Malone 104R,
Nottingham 102R

LARm 6 0 0 14 **20**
NYJ 0 7 6 0 **13**
LARm D17 R45/264 P(15-6-1) 41
NYJ D18 R26/136 P(32-19-2) 155
LARm-McCutcheon 139R

KC 0 7 7 10 **24**
SD 7 0 0 7 **14**
KC D20 R46/262 P(20-12-1) 149
SD D20 R33/193 P(27-14-2) 211
KC-Green 146R; SD-Woods 154R

Was 0 0 0 0 **0**
SL 9 7 7 0 **23**
Was D19 R30/116 P(29-20-1) 176
SL D15 R27/115 P(20-15-0) 190
SL-Thomas 106C

Dal 0 14 0 7 **21**
NYG 0 0 0 7 **7**
Dal D22 R49/184 P(20-11-2) 160
NYG D13 R23/62 P(26-13-3) 165

GB 0 7 3 7 **17**
Det 3 6 7 3 **19**
GB D22 R35/97 P(30-17-1) 216
Det D18 R25/115 P(33-18-0) 249
Det-Sanders 146C

Phi 0 7 3 0 **10**
NO 0 0 7 7 **14**
Phi D16 R25/105 P(33-22-1) 153
NO D20 R32/134 P(26-14-1) 164
NO-Seal 115C

MONDAY, OCTOBER 28
Atl 0 14 0 3 **17**
Pit 14 0 3 7 **24**
Atl D13 R33/108 P(20-8-2) 59
Pit D21 R52/235 P(21-9-2) 120
Pit-Harris 141R

SUNDAY, NOVEMBER 3
Hou 14 3 3 7 **27**
NYJ 13 6 0 3 **22**
Hou D20 R31/111 P(29-19-1) 214
NYJ D18 R23/77 P(31-19-2) 235
Hou-Burrough 145C

Oak 14 7 0 7 **28**
Den 0 7 10 0 **17**
Oak D16 R47/180 P(19-12-0) 207
Den D11 R32/113 P(24-13-1) 223
Oak-Hubbard 107R, Branch 108C,
Stabler 217P

Was 0 3 7 7 **17**
GB 3 3 0 0 **6**
Was D14 R36/100 P(24-14-2) 137
GB D15 R30/96 P(35-17-3) 158

Cin 0 17 0 7 **24**
Bal 0 0 7 7 **14**
Cin D17 R38/125 P(22-17-0) 279
Bal D24 R33/153 P(32-19-1) 157
Cin-Curtis 166C

SL 7 0 7 0 **14**
Dal 7 0 0 10 **17**
SL D19 R33/134 P(28-11-0) 82
Dal D22 R34/132 P(27-15-0) 146

NYG 7 13 3 10 **33**
KC 7 7 0 13 **27**
NYG D19 R41/94 P(33-17-0) 252
KC D29 R42/139 P(41-29-1) 264

Min 3 0 7 7 **17**
ChiB 0 0 0 0 **0**
Min D17 R53/190 P(20-10-1) 79
ChiB D10 R16/58 P(41-15-2) 100

Buf 6 13 7 3 **29**
NE 7 14 7 0 **28**
Buf D22 R27/103 P(25-16-2) 224
NE D20 R38/155 P(28-12-3) 200
Buf-Rashad 115C

Cle 14 0 14 0 **35**
SD 0 7 12 17 **36**
Cle D20 R40/108 P(23-16-1) 186
SD D16 R37/103 P(21-12-1) 321
SD-Davis 142C, Woods 119C,
Fouts 333P

NO 0 14 0 0 **14**
Det 10 6 0 3 **19**
NO D17 R27/94 P(37-22-3) 186
Det D10 R25/58 P(22-11-1) 137

Phi 0 0 0 0 **0**
Pit 7 10 10 0 **27**
Phi D10 R22/66 P(31-9-2) 77
Pit D20 R48/238 P(22-12-0) 137

Atl 0 7 0 0 **7**
Mia 0 14 21 7 **42**
Atl D13 R25/103 P(26-13-2) 93
Mia D22 R53/194 P(16-11-1) 161
Mia-Malone 108R

MONDAY, NOVEMBER 4
LARm 6 6 0 3 **15**
SF 0 3 3 7 **13**
LARm D18 R46/158 P(20-12-0) 145
SF D11 R22/65 P(29-15-1) 201

SUNDAY, NOVEMBER 10
SD 0 7 0 7 **14**
KC 0 0 0 7 **7**
SD D13 R47/143 P(21-7-2) 111
KC D17 R30/81 P(45-26-1) 347
KC-Brunson 193C, Dawson 381P

Den 7 7 3 0 **17**
Bal 0 3 3 0 **6**
Den D12 R30/133 P(16-9-0) 38
Bal D24 R39/147 P(43-19-4) 176
Den-Armstrong 110R

SF 0 0 7 7 **14**
Dal 10 0 3 7 **20**
SF D20 R29/64 P(35-21-0) 262
Dal D21 R46/221 P(14-9-0) 158
SF-Washington 121C; Dal-Hill 153R,
Pearson 100C

Det 0 3 7 3 **13**
Oak 14 7 14 0 **35**
Det D14 R21/63 P(35-19-2) 185
Oak D31 R41/284 P(27-20-0) 228
Oak-Hubbard 111R, Branch 102C

NYJ 7 3 3 7 **26**
NYG 3 10 7 0 **20**
NYJ D27 R45/189 P(31-20-0) 236
NYG D22 R33/124 P(32-21-0) 216
NYJ-Burns 101R

Pit 0 3 0 7 **10**
Cin 0 10 7 0 **17**
Pit D20 R39/161 P(35-13-1) 128
Cin D22 R35/136 P(22-20-0) 193

Mia 14 7 0 0 **21**
NO 0 0 0 0 **0**
Mia D16 R37/141 P(18-11-0) 81
NO D16 R30/157 P(32-17-1) 116

Cle 14 0 0 7 **21**
NE 0 14 0 0 **14**
Cle D10 R34/100 P(18-10-0) 83
NE D17 R45/164 P(21-9-4) 123

Was 7 0 10 10 **27**
Phi 7 7 6 0 **20**
Was D15 R23/46 P(42-21-1) 225
Phi D23 R31/84 P(48-24-2) 183
Was-Taylor 155C

ChiB 3 0 0 0 **3**
GB 0 10 0 10 **20**
ChiB D16 R23/86 P(34-18-1) 149
GB D9 R39/96 P(20-9-1) 119

Hou 14 0 7 0 **21**
Buf 0 6 3 0 **9**
Hou D10 R37/115 P(11-6-2) 59
Buf D16 R40/133 P(28-10-6) 91

Atl 0 0 0 0 **0**
LARm 7 0 7 7 **21**
Atl D11 R32/119 P(24-11-0) 45
LARm D19 R46/189 P(13-5-1) 123
LARm-McCutcheon 140R

MONDAY, NOVEMBER 11
Min 14 0 7 7 **28**
SL 7 10 7 0 **24**
Min D18 R38/178 P(29-14-1) 126
SL D23 R25/95 P(43-28-1) 341
SL-Hart 353P

SUNDAY, NOVEMBER 17

Buf 0 0 7 21 28
Mia 0 14 0 14 35
Buf D16 R31/132 P(23-13-1) 139
Mia D21 R39/160 P(18-11-0) 222
Mia-Warfield 139C

Dal 0 0 7 14 21
Was 7 21 0 0 28
Dal D18 R31/152 P(38-16-1) 144
Was D13 R37/100 P(19-11-0) 152

LARm 0 0 0 7 7
NO 3 10 7 0 20
LARm D18 R23/61 P(38-21-1) 200
NO D13 R36/146 P(23-11-1) 175

SF 0 20 7 7 34
ChiB 0 0 0 0 0
SF D22 R36/114 P(26-15-3) 299
ChiB D8 R27/99 P(28-14-2) 71
SF-Owen 316P

SD 0 3 0 7 10
Oak 7 0 7 3 17
SD D17 R37/164 P(21-9-0) 144
Oak D21 R42/132 P(32-16-1) 240
SD-Woods 117R; Oak-Branch 125C

NYG 3 3 7 6 19
Det 10 0 0 10 20
NYG D15 R35/159 P(25-12-0) 133
Det D21 R31/100 P(29-19-1) 194

Bal 0 10 0 7 17
Atl 0 7 0 0 7
Bal D18 R58/252 P(11-4-1) 74
Atl D15 R31/124 P(22-12-1) 112
Bal-Mitchell 151R

Pit 7 6 0 13 26
Cle 3 3 10 0 16
Pit D10 R41/233 P(19-3-3) 81
Cle D13 R31/80 P(35-15-3) 138
Pit-Harris 156R

GB 0 6 3 10 19
Min 0 0 0 7 7
GB D20 R52/202 P(19-10-0) 191
Min D14 R20/74 P(31-15-1) 210
GB-Brockington 137R;
Min-Lash 136C

SL 7 0 0 6 13
Phi 0 0 3 0 3
SL D16 R40/188 P(23-10-1) 100
Phi D13 R23/71 P(32-19-2) 134
Phi-Young 101C

Cin 3 0 0 0 3
Hou 7 0 7 6 20
Cin D16 R23/89 P(36-21-2) 149
Hou D14 R36/124 P(13-11-1) 90

NYJ 7 7 7 0 21
NE 0 3 10 3 16
NYJ D15 R34/123 P(20-8-2) 99
NE D18 R37/163 P(32-11-4) 120
NE-Cunningham 113R

MONDAY, NOVEMBER 18

KC 7 10 19 6 42
Den 7 14 0 13 34
KC D24 R37/194 P(30-19-1) 170
Den D34 R22/73 P(49-32-3) 459
KC-Green 114R; Den-Odoms 125C,
Johnson 445P

SUNDAY, NOVEMBER 24

SL 6 0 7 10 23
NYG 0 7 7 7 21
SL D20 R23/82 P(42-25-0) 259
NYG D20 R29/104 P(35-21-1) 257
SL-Gray 102C

Buf 0 12 0 3 15
Cle 0 3 0 7 10
Buf D10 R40/188 P(7-1-0) 9
Cle D19 R37/147 P(29-16-3) 130
Buf-Simpson 115R

Phi 0 0 7 0 7
Was 3 10 7 6 26
Phi D14 R24/79 P(29-18-2) 135
Was D19 R41/131 P(24-18-0) 172

Min 0 17 0 0 17
LARm 0 6 0 14 20
Min D18 R26/87 P(35-19-1) 214
LARm D25 R33/112 P(39-25-0) 268

KC 0 6 0 0 6
Cin 7 20 0 6 33
KC D9 R15/34 P(31-14-0) 140
Cin D28 R37/170 P(35-20-1) 268
Cin-Anderson 262P

Den 7 3 10 0 20
Oak 3 7 0 7 17
Den D22 R48/292 P(18-9-1) 118
Oak D20 R28/128 P(34-22-3) 220
Den-Armstrong 146R,
Keyworth 148R;
Oak-Biletnikoff 121C

Mia 0 0 7 7 14
NYJ 0 7 0 10 17
Mia D13 R27/116 P(20-9-1) 120
NYJ D17 R43/131 P(22-13-3) 139
NYJ-Caster 100C

Atl 0 0 0 0 0
SF 7 7 0 13 27
Atl D10 R15/75 P(34-15-3) 117
SF D18 R46/202 P(19-8-1) 89
SF-Schreiber 106R

ChiB 0 0 3 14 17
Det 10 10 7 7 34
ChiB D14 R28/101 P(31-14-1) 75
Det D18 R39/180 P(19-9-1) 127

SD 0 0 0 0 0
GB 3 10 14 7 34
SD D13 R31/109 P(28-9-2) 84
GB D15 R29/73 P(26-17-1) 224

NE 0 17 0 10 27
Bal 0 3 7 7 17
NE D19 R42/130 P(26-17-0) 172
Bal D15 R27/117 P(34-18-2) 205

Dal 7 0 3 0 10
Hou 0 0 0 0 0
Dal D15 R47/214 P(15-8-0) 38
Hou D6 R18/26 P(27-13-1) 55

MONDAY, NOVEMBER 25

Pit 7 7 14 0 28
NO 0 0 7 0 7
Pit D18 R43/272 P(19-8-2) 62
NO D15 R33/109 P(32-10-3) 69
Pit-Harris 114R

THURSDAY, NOVEMBER 28

Was 3 6 7 7 23
Dal 3 0 14 7 24
Was D11 R33/105 P(17-8-0) 102
Dal D23 R38/134 P(32-15-1) 239
Dal-Pearson 108C

Den 0 10 21 0 31
Det 3 14 3 7 27
Den D23 R44/240 P(22-11-2) 121
Det D16 R31/121 P(20-14-0) 131
Den-Armstrong 144R

SUNDAY, DECEMBER 1

NO 3 6 0 0 9
Min 6 6 3 14 29
NO D13 R33/145 P(21-10-0) 81
Min D19 R33/97 P(29-20-0) 308
Min-Gilliam 109C, Lash 112C,
Tarkenton 317P

GB 0 7 7 0 14
Phi 9 20 0 7 36
GB D17 R29/81 P(41-16-1) 221
Phi D15 R36/92 P(32-16-1) 122

SF 0 0 0 0 0
Cle 0 0 0 7 7
SF D14 R42/159 P(23-6-5) 33
Cle D11 R35/157 P(20-9-1) 26

SD 0 0 0 14 14
NYJ 10 14 3 0 27
SD D14 R30/153 P(24-11-2) 150
NYJ D21 R35/114 P(29-19-0) 261
SD-Woods 142R, Garrison 109C;
NYJ-Caster 137C

NYG 6 7 0 0 13
ChiB 13 0 0 3 16
NYG D14 R31/90 P(26-9-3) 79
ChiB D15 R53/160 P(13-5-0) 66

NE 6 7 6 7 26
Oak 7 13 7 14 41
NE D20 R29/105 P(34-17-3) 266
Oak D21 R41/129 P(21-16-2) 251
Oak-Branch 138C, Stabler 251P

KC 0 0 7 10 17
SL 6 0 0 7 13
KC D13 R39/156 P(22-13-1) 84
SL D15 R23/82 P(39-19-2) 170

Bal 0 0 0 0 0
Buf 0 6 0 0 6
Bal D10 R21/46 P(27-11-1) 98
Buf D9 R46/138 P(13-5-0) 46

LARm 6 7 17 0 30
Atl 0 7 0 0 7
LARm D14 R40/150 P(22-9-0) 159
Atl D11 R15/19 P(41-20-5) 218
Atl-Mitchell 109C

Hou 0 7 3 3 13
Pit 3 7 0 0 10
Hou D11 R43/97 P(19-10-0) 61
Pit D6 R20/75 P(25-6-3) 9

MONDAY, DECEMBER 2

Cin 0 3 0 0 3
Mia 7 3 7 7 24
Cin D8 R18/66 P(25-14-0) 96
Mia D19 R49/196 P(13-11-0) 114
Mia-Csonka 123R

SATURDAY, DECEMBER 7

Cle 0 10 7 0 17
Dal 14 6 21 0 41
Cle D19 R27/87 P(29-15-4) 170
Dal D25 R46/252 P(25-15-1) 217

Atl 0 7 0 3 10
Min 7 3 6 7 23
Atl D15 R28/116 P(25-11-2) 75
Min D18 R43/148 P(22-14-1) 104

SUNDAY, DECEMBER 8

Mia 7 7 3 0 17
Bal 0 3 3 10 16
Mia D18 R44/178 P(15-9-2) 84
Bal D13 R23/123 P(26-14-0) 145
Mia-Malone 104R

Phi 0 13 7 0 20
NYG 0 0 7 0 7
Phi D23 R32/74 P(34-23-0) 228
NYG D12 R12/35 P(33-18-2) 191
Phi-Young 103C; NYG-Gillette 100C

GB 3 0 3 0 6
SF 0 0 0 7 7
GB D14 R28/133 P(30-16-2) 95
SF D17 R31/103 P(31-16-1) 180

SL 0 0 0 0 0
NO 7 0 0 7 14
SL D12 R23/64 P(39-16-0) 150
NO D17 R48/228 P(17-7-0) 87
NO-Maxson 148R

Det 0 9 7 7 23
Cin 6 3 3 7 19
Det D17 R37/189 P(18-8-2) 70
Cin D15 R31/147 P(24-14-2) 105

ChiB 7 0 14 0 21
SD 0 7 7 14 28
ChiB D18 R34/144 P(26-14-2) 136
SD D16 R42/106 P(19-9-1) 149

Pit 0 12 7 2 21
NE 7 3 0 7 17
Pit D16 R46/184 P(18-10-1) 69
NE D12 R32/79 P(18-8-1) 105
Pit-Harris 136R

Hou 0 7 0 7 14
Den 7 10 6 14 37
Hou D16 R19/88 P(38-20-1) 180
Den D27 R45/243 P(21-15-1) 168
Den-Armstrong 183R

Buf 0 0 7 3 10
NYJ 0 0 6 14 20
Buf D12 R38/126 P(19-7-1) 94
NYJ D12 R33/95 P(19-8-0) 131

Oak 0 0 0 7 7
KC 3 3 0 0 6
Oak D13 R41/181 P(9-3-3) 12
KC D14 R32/164 P(23-12-2) 102
KC-Kinney 124R

MONDAY, DECEMBER 9

Was 0 20 3 0 23
LARm 10 0 7 0 17
Was D19 R29/87 P(30-19-1) 263
LARm D18 R32/117 P(27-12-2) 157

SATURDAY, DECEMBER 14

Dal 9 0 7 7 23
Oak 3 14 7 3 27
Dal D21 R28/144 P(39-17-0) 256
Oak D15 R34/126 P(25-14-1) 141

Min 0 14 7 14 35
KC 3 9 0 3 15
Min D22 R33/114 P(29-19-1) 244
KC D17 R27/83 P(31-16-2) 198
Min-McCullum 118C

Cin 0 0 3 0 3
Pit 7 10 7 3 27
Cin D11 R41/170 P(8-3-1) 23
Pit D21 R37/171 P(21-12-0) 183
Pit-Stallworth 105C

SUNDAY, DECEMBER 15

Cle 7 0 10 7 24
Hou 0 7 14 7 28
Cle D20 R34/142 P(29-16-2) 189
Hou D20 R42/182 P(25-12-2) 101
Cle-Pruitt 102R

NO 0 7 0 14 21
SF 7 7 0 21 35
NO D23 R35/121 P(44-21-2) 197
SF D18 R37/160 P(23-13-1) 178

Den 0 0 0 0 0
SD 7 7 0 3 17
Den D13 R27/173 P(19-12-2) 114
SD D21 R43/163 P(30-16-2) 190
Den-Armstrong 142R;
SD-Woods 105R

GB 0 0 3 0 3
Atl 7 3 0 0 10
GB D14 R30/125 P(38-15-2) 138
Atl D10 R38/129 P(20-7-3) 68

NYG 0 14 0 0 14
SL 0 0 20 6 26
NYG D18 R36/148 P(31-13-4) 132
SL D22 R36/152 P(37-17-1) 164

Det 0 3 7 7 17
Phi 14 0 7 7 28
Det D15 R27/78 P(32-21-0) 170
Phi D19 R32/87 P(34-20-1) 170

ChiB 0 0 0 0 0
Was 0 21 7 14 42
ChiB D10 R16/73 P(36-12-4) 53
Was D27 R40/182 P(30-21-0) 329
Was-Thomas 102R, Grant 119C

Buf 0 7 0 7 14
LARm 0 0 13 6 19
Buf D8 R21/109 P(20-9-3) 109
LARm D21 R54/177 P(21-11-0) 144

NE 21 3 0 3 27
Mia 0 17 7 10 34
NE D18 R30/114 P(41-15-0) 219
Mia D18 R33/61 P(23-15-3) 272
Mia-Baker 121C

NYJ 7 21 7 10 45
Bal 0 10 14 14 38
NYJ D24 R32/130 P(29-19-0) 260
Bal D33 R18/82 P(54-36-4) 373
NYJ-Riggins 107R, Knight 117C;
Bal-Chester 102C, Jones 385P

1975 NFL

SUNDAY, SEPTEMBER 21

NO 3 0 0 0 3
Was 10 10 0 21 41
NO D9 R21/71 P(35-18-2) 137
Was D19 R35/136 P(26-14-1) 179
Was-Kilmer 199P

KC 7 10 13 3 33
Den 0 17 7 13 37
KC D18 R40/146 P(27-13-0) 166
Den D15 R31/127 P(20-12-2) 298
Den-Upchurch 153C, Johnson 329P

SF 0 10 0 7 17
Min 3 10 0 14 27
SF D16 R28/100 P(27-14-0) 145
Min D17 R38/126 P(26-14-2) 153

Atl 7 6 7 0 20
SL 7 6 0 10 23
Atl D19 R51/236 P(16-8-1) 58
SL D18 R36/167 P(23-12-2) 150
Atl-Hampton 135R

Pit 10 10 3 14 37
SD 0 0 0 0 0
Pit D24 R45/205 P(29-22-0) 238
SD D9 R23/88 P(23-12-3) 58

Cle 0 3 14 0 17
Cin 14 3 7 0 24
Cle D17 R32/105 P(22-14-0) 125
Cin D24 R40/127 P(27-17-0) 252
Cin-Curtis 127C

NYG 0 13 0 10 23
Phi 0 7 0 7 14
NYG D15 R40/96 P(28-14-1) 240
Phi D24 R32/99 P(44-28-2) 264

Bal 0 21 7 7 35
ChiB 0 0 7 0 7
Bal D26 R49/168 P(24-15-0) 136
ChiB D6 R18/47 P(20-8-2) 74

Det 10 7 7 6 30
GB 0 3 7 6 16
Det D10 R40/117 P(12-8-0) 113
GB D15 R31/93 P(33-13-2) 124

NYJ 7 7 0 0 14
Buf 14 7 14 7 42
NYJ D17 R21/111 P(36-14-4) 150
Buf D26 R64/309 P(13-7-0) 52
NYJ-Caster 103C;
Buf-Simpson 173R

Hou 7 0 0 0 7
NE 0 0 0 0 0
Hou D7 R33/116 P(16-6-1) 53
NE D17 R52/179 P(24-12-1) 100

LARm 0 0 0 7 7
Dal 0 9 3 6 18
LARm D11 R33/128 P(17-4-3) 20
Dal D18 R49/197 P(24-10-0) 80

MONDAY, SEPTEMBER 22

Oak 7 10 7 7 31
Mia 0 7 0 14 21
Oak D17 R45/159 P(15-8-3) 102
Mia D21 R33/118 P(32-15-4) 164

SUNDAY, SEPTEMBER 28

Det 0 7 3 7 17
Atl 0 7 7 0 14
Det D20 R44/184 P(27-14-0) 173
Atl D13 R37/156 P(22-7-1) 94

Buf 0 10 13 7 30
Pit 0 0 7 14 21
Buf D21 R46/310 P(20-9-0) 124
Pit D19 R30/122 P(29-14-2) 231
Buf-Simpson 227R;
Pit-Stallworth 103C

Oak 0 10 14 7 31
Bal 10 3 7 0 20
Oak D18 R34/143 P(28-15-2) 143
Bal D20 R29/77 P(43-21-1) 252
Oak-Branch 132C;
Bal-Doughty 106C, Jones 307P

SD 7 3 0 7 17
Hou 3 13 7 10 33
SD D12 R25/60 P(26-13-1) 144
Hou D24 R56/251 P(25-13-1) 151
Hou-Coleman 112R,
Hardeman 107R

Cin 7 7 7 0 21
NO 0 0 0 0 0
Cin D17 R33/92 P(26-18-1) 202
NO D12 R24/67 P(32-13-2) 122

SL 0 3 14 14 31
Dal 0 7 21 3 37
SL D19 R32/118 P(32-15-2) 314
Dal D28 R44/160 P(34-23-1) 288
SL-Gray 114C, Hart 314P;
Dal-Dupree 100C, Staubach 307P

LARm	3	0	10	10	**23**
SF	0	14	0	0	14
LARm	D15	R33/115	P(26-15-1)	183	
SF	D14	R35/129	P(23-13-0)	107	

LARm-Jackson 109C

Min	7	14	7	14	**42**
Cle	0	3	0	7	10
Min	D26	R38/137	P(32-19-2)	215	
Cle	D14	R23/130	P(29-14-4)	120	

NYJ	14	3	6	7	**30**
KC	7	7	7	3	24
NYJ	D24	R47/291	P(15-8-2)	127	
KC	D25	R35/131	P(33-20-1)	208	

NYJ-Garrett 135R, Riggins 145R

Mia	0	0	9	13	**22**
NE	7	7	0	0	14
Mia	D17	R43/210	P(15-9-3)	47	
NE	D12	R33/78	P(19-9-3)	109	

Mia-Nottingham 120R

Phi	3	3	0	7	13
ChiB	0	9	0	6	**15**
Phi	D21	R29/128	P(41-24-2)	199	
ChiB	D14	R33/133	P(28-19-2)	161	

NYG	7	0	6	0	13
Was	0	28	0	21	**49**
NYG	D17	R33/96	P(25-16-0)	65	
Was	D25	R37/168	P(30-20-1)	249	

Was-Jefferson 106C

MONDAY, SEPTEMBER 29

GB	0	0	0	13	13
Den	0	6	7	10	**23**
GB	D22	R27/71	P(36-23-2)	242	
Den	D18	R38/162	P(23-14-1)	175	

GB-Payne 167C

SUNDAY, OCTOBER 5

NYG	0	0	7	7	14
SL	7	16	0	3	**26**
NYG	D19	R33/126	P(24-17-0)	138	
SL	D18	R46/254	P(20-8-1)	125	

SL-Metcalf 109R, Otis 101R

Bal	7	6	0	0	13
LARm	0	7	3	14	**24**
Bal	D13	R28/88	P(25-14-2)	151	
LARm	D21	R38/153	P(22-16-1)	271	

LARm-Jackson 108C

NO	0	0	7	0	7
Atl	7	7	0	0	**14**
NO	D14	R31/120	P(31-15-2)	125	
Atl	D13	R39/137	P(23-11-1)	94	

Atl-Hampton 101R

Den	0	7	7	0	14
Buf	10	14	14	0	**38**
Den	D13	R15/47	P(36-15-3)	258	
Buf	D29	R60/293	P(18-9-0)	143	

Buf-Braxton 102R, Simpson 138R

NE	0	0	0	7	7
NYJ	0	19	10	7	**36**
NE	D15	R24/72	P(32-13-3)	248	
NYJ	D24	R46/173	P(24-17-1)	207	

NYJ-Caster 110C, Namath 218P

Was	3	7	0	0	10
Phi	6	3	7	10	**26**
Was	D10	R18/66	P(34-17-3)	127	
Phi	D21	R53/213	P(20-11-1)	182	

ChiB	0	3	0	0	3
Min	14	7	0	7	**28**
ChiB	D10	R31/103	P(27-15-1)	89	
Min	D23	R38/140	P(31-19-1)	215	

Cin	0	7	0	14	**21**
Hou	0	10	7	2	19
Cin	D18	R37/86	P(28-19-1)	176	
Hou	D13	R34/83	P(23-11-2)	93	

SF	0	10	3	7	**20**
KC	0	3	0	0	3
SF	D15	R36/107	P(20-12-0)	108	
KC	D13	R30/89	P(27-17-1)	123	

Oak	0	3	0	3	**6**
SD	0	0	0	0	0
Oak	D17	R51/192	P(23-10-1)	72	
SD	D5	R29/115	P(13-3-2)	-22	

Mia	7	14	10	0	**31**
GB	0	0	0	7	7
Mia	D25	R58/281	P(13-7-0)	133	
GB	D10	R23/104	P(19-13-0)	101	

Mia-Morris 125R, Nottingham 102R

Pit	7	21	0	14	**42**
Cle	0	0	0	6	6
Pit	D23	R40/134	P(23-18-0)	367	
Cle	D19	R31/122	P(31-16-2)	99	

Pit-Stallworth 109C, Swann 126C

MONDAY, OCTOBER 6

Dal	3	6	6	21	**36**
Det	0	3	7	0	10
Dal	D14	R26/94	P(20-12-2)	250	
Det	D16	R40/183	P(23-9-0)	27	

Dal-Pearson 188C

SUNDAY, OCTOBER 12

GB	14	2	0	3	19
NO	0	7	7	6	**20**
GB	D8	R27/98	P(20-11-0)	63	
NO	D26	R45/223	P(39-17-0)	169	

NO-Strachan 105R

Atl	7	7	3	0	**17**
SF	0	0	3	0	3
Atl	D14	R38/140	P(22-10-0)	95	
SF	D19	R31/107	P(41-22-4)	231	

Dal	3	0	3	7	**13**
NYG	0	0	7	0	7
Dal	D14	R49/196	P(22-8-0)	66	
NYG	D10	R29/96	P(23-8-3)	77	

NYJ	7	0	7	7	21
Min	3	3	14	9	**29**
NYJ	D17	R32/115	P(21-12-2)	190	
Min	D25	R42/174	P(28-18-1)	233	

Min-Foreman 105C

Hou	3	17	13	7	**40**
Cle	3	7	0	0	10
Hou	D20	R46/250	P(21-12-0)	119	
Cle	D15	R27/102	P(30-17-4)	144	

Hou-Coleman 110R

NE	0	7	3	0	10
Cin	0	7	17	3	**27**
NE	D12	R31/208	P(20-6-1)	42	
Cin	D26	R43/174	P(33-17-0)	272	

NE-Herron 119R

Buf	10	14	7	7	**38**
Bal	14	7	7	3	31
Buf	D26	R43/178	P(26-14-1)	246	
Bal	D19	R36/196	P(23-11-1)	153	

Buf-Simpson 159R, Holland 121C;
Bal-Mitchell 107R

Den	3	6	0	0	9
Pit	7	10	0	3	**20**
Den	D17	R36/124	P(36-12-3)	153	
Pit	D14	R39/137	P(26-16-0)	190	

ChiB	0	0	0	7	7
Det	0	14	6	7	**27**
ChiB	D16	R23/45	P(37-21-3)	193	
Det	D21	R33/127	P(35-20-0)	193	

Oak	3	0	0	7	10
KC	21	7	0	14	**42**
Oak	D23	R27/91	P(42-20-3)	269	
KC	D25	R52/224	P(16-10-1)	146	

KC-Green 101R

Phi	6	3	0	7	16
Mia	0	10	7	7	**24**
Phi	D13	R24/100	P(26-18-1)	169	
Mia	D18	R45/207	P(21-15-0)	132	

LARm	0	3	7	0	**13**
SD	0	0	10	0	10
LARm	D24	R46/224	P(26-15-1)	199	
SD	D16	R35/128	P(26-17-0)	144	

LARm-McCutcheon 112R;
SD-Woods 105R

MONDAY, OCTOBER 13

SL	0	3	14	0	17
Was	3	7	7	10	**27**
SL	D13	R19/68	P(41-20-3)	220	
Was	D21	R39/158	P(30-16-0)	189	

Was-Thomas 100R

SUNDAY, OCTOBER 19

Phi	3	7	0	10	20
SL	7	7	10	7	**31**
Phi	D16	R29/102	P(40-16-1)	148	
SL	D22	R53/278	P(20-9-2)	125	

SL-Otis 116R

Mia	6	20	14	3	**43**
NYJ	0	0	0	0	0
Mia	D22	R51/261	P(18-13-2)	176	
NYJ	D12	R22/116	P(33-8-6)	60	

Mia-Morris 114R

KC	0	9	0	3	**12**
SD	3	0	7	0	10
KC	D15	R34/137	P(23-14-0)	219	
SD	D16	R39/155	P(21-10-1)	61	

KC-White 105C

GB	3	0	6	10	**19**
Dal	0	0	14	3	17
GB	D14	R32/142	P(28-15-2)	149	
Dal	D20	R38/206	P(31-16-1)	168	

Dal-Pearson 101R

Atl	0	0	0	7	7
LARm	10	6	6	0	**22**
Atl	D18	R16/63	P(36-15-3)	163	
LARm	D25	R53/218	P(25-14-1)	166	

Oak	0	7	0	3	10
Cin	0	7	7	0	**14**
Oak	D18	R48/188	P(24-8-4)	91	
Cin	D10	R33/109	P(19-4-4)	75	

Oak-White 105C

Det	3	0	0	16	19
Min	0	13	12	0	**25**
Det	D21	R27/104	P(37-22-1)	186	
Min	D20	R35/158	P(24-15-0)	121	

Det-Jarvis 100C; Min-Foreman 107R

Was	0	7	3	0	10
Hou	0	0	6	7	**13**
Was	D17	R30/58	P(29-12-2)	197	
Hou	D14	R41/121	P(17-10-1)	107	

Cle	3	6	3	3	15
Den	3	3	0	10	**16**
Cle	D17	R45/144	P(33-14-1)	127	
Den	D18	R26/108	P(35-20-1)	217	

Bal	7	0	3	0	10
NE	0	14	0	7	**21**
Bal	D10	R32/117	P(24-12-0)	13	
NE	D18	R51/241	P(14-6-1)	41	

NE-Johnson 124R

NO	0	7	0	14	21
SF	21	7	0	7	**35**
NO	D18	R29/127	P(33-19-2)	114	
SF	D15	R31/89	P(23-13-2)	178	

ChiB	0	3	0	0	3
Pit	0	10	10	14	**34**
ChiB	D16	R30/196	P(22-8-0)	46	
Pit	D25	R47/157	P(23-12-0)	146	

ChiB-Adamle 110R

MONDAY, OCTOBER 20

NYG	0	7	0	10	**17**
Buf	7	7	0	0	14
NYG	D16	R41/135	P(21-15-1)	214	
Buf	D18	R47/171	P(19-11-2)	138	

Buf-Simpson 126R

SATURDAY, OCTOBER 25

SL	10	0	3	7	**20**
NYG	0	0	0	13	13
SL	D14	R39/125	P(22-12-0)	189	
NYG	D22	R30/82	P(41-19-3)	199	

SL 1-Gray 187C; YG-Gillette 100C

SUNDAY, OCTOBER 26

SD	0	0	0	0	0
Oak	2	7	14	2	**25**
SD	D12	R32/140	P(28-8-1)	17	
Oak	D23	R50/177	P(24-14-1)	177	

SF	0	0	10	6	16
NE	3	14	0	7	**24**
SF	D14	R17/31	P(42-22-2)	212	
NE	D20	R42/155	P(27-16-0)	151	

NE-Johnson 103R

Mia	0	14	7	14	**35**
Buf	13	10	0	7	30
Mia	D25	R45/229	P(21-13-2)	148	
Buf	D21	R33/128	P(29-20-2)	217	

Mia-Morris 124R

Cin	0	14	0	7	**21**
Atl	7	0	0	7	14
Cin	D17	R32/130	P(26-18-0)	170	
Atl	D17	R40/176	P(25-10-5)	130	

Bal	14	10	7	14	**45**
NYJ	0	14	7	7	28
Bal	D24	R36/212	P(25-17-0)	188	
NYJ	D17	R28/82	P(28-19-1)	259	

Bal-Johnson 105C;
NYJ-Caster 115C, Namath 333P

Was	0	6	3	14	**23**
Cle	0	0	7	0	7
Was	D23	R43/190	P(33-15-0)	205	
Cle	D12	R27/100	P(20-11-0)	100	

Was-Thomas 124R

Dal	0	10	0	10	**20**
Phi	7	7	0	3	17
Dal	D21	R25/78	P(50-27-1)	300	
Phi	D13	R34/111	P(23-9-0)	156	

Dal-Staubach 314P

Pit	3	10	0	3	**16**
GB	0	6	7	0	13
Pit	D23	R59/248	P(23-12-0)	84	
GB	D11	R21/63	P(22-14-1)	98	

Pit-Bleier 163R

Det	6	0	0	2	8
Hou	3	7	14	0	**24**
Det	D22	R37/157	P(40-24-1)	179	
Hou	D14	R31/88	P(16-9-1)	212	

Hou-Burrough 111C

Den	0	0	0	13	13
KC	3	3	3	17	**26**
Den	D22	R38/151	P(32-17-3)	201	
KC	D17	R37/197	P(23-10-1)	106	

NO	0	0	7	7	14
LARm	10	14	0	14	**38**
NO	D17	R29/96	P(20-11-1)	77	
LARm	D27	R53/223	P(22-13-0)	118	

MONDAY, OCTOBER 27

Min	0	10	3	0	**13**
ChiB	7	0	2	0	9
Min	D18	R40/150	P(30-16-0)	181	
ChiB	D11	R31/137	P(22-10-2)	79	

Min-Foreman 102R

SATURDAY, NOVEMBER 1

SD	7	7	7	3	24
NYG	14	7	7	7	**35**
SD	D18	R31/182	P(25-13-1)	167	
NYG	D22	R37/165	P(26-18-1)	183	

SUNDAY, NOVEMBER 2

Pit	0	10	13	7	**30**
Cin	3	0	0	21	24
Pit	D20	R47/239	P(24-13-2)	130	
Cin	D17	R20/69	P(43-19-3)	298	

Pit-Harris 157R, Swann 116C;
Cin-Joiner 114C, Anderson 331P

Min	7	7	0	14	**28**
GB	7	3	7	0	17
Min	D23	R37/101	P(30-24-1)	266	
GB	D15	R30/132	P(21-14-3)	113	

Buf	7	0	10	7	**24**
NYJ	3	13	7	0	23
Buf	D22	R33/148	P(29-15-2)	287	
NYJ	D25	R41/199	P(31-16-1)	167	

NYJ-Riggins 108R

NE	3	7	7	0	17
SL	0	7	3	14	**24**
NE	D17	R32/122	P(34-14-2)	152	
SL	D18	R44/115	P(32-20-1)	158	

Hou	7	0	7	3	**17**
KC	3	10	0	0	13
Hou	D13	R40/144	P(19-11-1)	181	
KC	D22	R36/137	P(36-17-3)	208	

Hou-Burrough 177C

Cle	0	0	0	7	7
Bal	7	14	0	0	**21**
Cle	D17	R29/125	P(44-17-2)	153	
Bal	D15	R33/117	P(26-16-1)	111	

Dal	0	17	0	7	24
Was	3	7	7	7	**30**
Dal	D22	R43/172	P(30-18-1)	213	
Was	D29	R32/102	P(39-21-4)	301	

Dal-Pearson 114C; Was-Grant 105C,
Kilmer 301P

Mia	10	10	12	14	**46**
ChiB	0	6	7	0	13
Mia	D20	R41/123	P(23-15-0)	316	
ChiB	D16	R24/93	P(31-19-2)	190	

Mia-Moore 113C

Oak	7	0	14	21	**42**
Den	0	10	7	0	17
Oak	D21	R48/184	P(17-11-2)	144	
Den	D24	R35/150	P(35-13-3)	177	

Atl	0	0	0	7	7
NO	0	10	10	3	**23**
Atl	D19	R25/95	P(37-14-3)	210	
NO	D19	R50/175	P(19-8-3)	177	

Atl-Jenkins 102C;
NO-Strachan 109R, Burton 159C

Det	0	0	21	7	**28**
SF	3	7	7	0	17
Det	D17	R41/174	P(15-9-0)	112	
SF	D19	R32/128	P(32-14-2)	168	

MONDAY, NOVEMBER 3

LARm	7	14	14	7	**42**
Phi	0	3	0	0	3
LARm	D20	R47/208	P(20-10-0)	207	
Phi	D15	R25/97	P(38-16-4)	168	

LARm-McCutcheon 101R

SUNDAY, NOVEMBER 9

Atl	0	0	0	0	0
Min	7	17	7	7	**38**
Atl	D6	R15/43	P(26-5-5)	17	
Min	D23	R63/220	P(23-12-0)	59	

Min-Foreman 102R

Hou	0	7	3	7	17
Pit	10	7	0	7	**24**
Hou	D18	R29/92	P(35-16-2)	206	
Pit	D22	R40/183	P(28-17-1)	169	

Cle	0	0	3	7	10
Det	7	7	0	7	**21**
Cle	D13	R31/126	P(32-10-1)	74	
Det	D15	R41/128	P(19-11-1)	154	

GB	0	7	0	7	14
ChiB	10	7	10	0	**27**
GB	D13	R23/41	P(42-21-1)	268	
ChiB	D15	R47/148	P(16-10-1)	113	

Cin	7	0	10	0	**17**
Den	0	13	0	3	16
Cin	D20	R45/163	P(27-18-0)	181	
Den	D19	R26/92	P(40-21-0)	213	

NE	10	13	7	3	**33**
SD	3	3	10	3	19
NE	D24	R39/120	P(28-17-1)	224	
SD	D18	R23/79	P(42-25-2)	279	

SD-Garrison 108C, Fouts 329P

SF	0	0	14	10	**24**
LARm	14	0	0	9	23
SF	D19	R28/104	P(38-19-0)	290	
LARm	D25	R37/132	P(35-22-2)	211	

SF-Washington 144C

Was	7	0	0	14	**21**
NYG	0	10	3	0	13
Was	D20	R37/147	P(23-13-3)	230	
NYG	D15	R34/117	P(30-14-1)	156	

Was-Thomas 123R, Grant 109C

Bal	0	21	0	21	**42**
Buf	7	21	0	7	35
Bal	D25	R46/199	P(23-15-1)	299	
Buf	D20	R27/179	P(31-14-2)	239	

Bal-Mitchell 112R, Carr 136C,
Doughty 102C, Jones 306P;
Buf-Simpson 123R, Chandler 118C

NO	3	0	0	7	10
Oak	7	14	20	7	**48**
NO	D10	R30/95	P(16-6-3)	45	
Oak	D34	R53/260	P(27-20-1)	263	

NYJ	7	0	0	0	7
Mia	0	7	13	7	**27**
NYJ	D15	R35/147	P(28-11-2)	122	
Mia	D14	R35/128	P(15-9-0)	214	

Mia-Moore 102C

SL 7 0 7 10 **24**
Phi 10 10 3 0 23
SL D23 R34/153 P(30-19-1) 208
Phi D17 R34/87 P(30-22-1) 239
Phi-Smith 102C

MONDAY, NOVEMBER 10

KC 3 21 3 7 **34**
Dal 0 17 14 0 31
KC D21 R45/164 P(28-13-0) 132
Dal D26 R40/204 P(31-17-2) 232

SUNDAY, NOVEMBER 16

GB 0 0 3 7 10
Det 7 0 0 6 **13**
GB D20 R35/127 P(30-17-2) 150
Det D17 R48/166 P(21-8-2) 104

Cle 7 3 7 0 17
Oak 7 10 7 14 **38**
Cle D16 R30/135 P(30-14-3) 95
Oak D22 R46/217 P(25-16-1) 210
Cle-Pruitt 103R; Oak-Davis 120R,
Stabler 220P

Min 7 13 0 0 **20**
NO 0 0 7 0 7
Min D23 R40/160 P(39-25-2) 310
NO D6 R27/67 P(18-5-0) -7
Min-Foreman 117R, Gilliam 139C,
Tarkenton 310P

Was 0 7 7 3 17
SL 0 3 0 14 **20**
Was D16 R38/145 P(27-14-3) 252
SL D31 R47/230 P(37-19-2) 197
SL-Otis 109R, Gray 109C

KC 3 0 0 0 3
Pit 0 7 14 7 **28**
KC D12 R25/78 P(28-13-2) 123
Pit D23 R39/239 P(24-16-1) 181
Pit-Harris 119R

NYJ 3 3 7 6 19
Bal 14 17 7 14 **52**
NYJ D19 R26/82 P(41-15-3) 237
Bal D26 R42/225 P(22-16-1) 277

Den 7 10 0 10 **27**
SD 3 7 7 0 17
Den D22 R33/112 P(36-24-2) 225
SD D17 R29/105 P(25-14-1) 202

Mia 0 6 7 6 19
Hou 3 3 7 7 **20**
Mia D23 R38/114 P(29-21-2) 236
Hou D15 R31/169 P(22-11-0) 70

Dal 10 7 7 10 **34**
NE 0 10 7 14 31
Dal D16 R41/171 P(20-11-0) 165
NE D20 R29/99 P(30-12-2) 125

LARm 0 6 3 7 **16**
Atl 0 0 0 7 7
LARm D18 R38/96 P(37-19-2) 235
Atl D15 R28/99 P(28-13-1) 106
LARm-Jessie 151C

Phi 0 7 3 3 **13**
NYG 3 0 0 7 10
Phi D14 R38/184 P(25-12-0) 110
NYG D15 R38/129 P(23-9-1) 81

ChiB 0 3 0 0 3
SF 0 10 0 21 **31**
ChiB D11 R37/156 P(20-10-0) 44
SF D21 R42/233 P(22-11-2) 102
ChiB-Payton 105R;
SF-Williams 106R

MONDAY, NOVEMBER 17

Buf 3 7 7 7 24
Cin 6 14 3 10 **33**
Buf D20 R38/242 P(18-9-0) 93
Cin D34 R38/112 P(46-30-0) 441
Buf-Simpson 197R;
Cin-Curtis 139C, Myers 108C,
Anderson 447P

SUNDAY, NOVEMBER 23

SF 7 0 0 9 **16**
NO 0 0 3 6 9
SF D11 R31/90 P(22-13-0) 138
NO D18 R24/104 P(52-25-2) 176

NYG 0 0 14 0 14
GB 14 10 0 16 **40**
NYG D17 R34/119 P(37-16-1) 260
GB D26 R40/210 P(30-19-1) 298
GB-Payne 103C

Den 7 0 7 7 21
Atl 0 14 7 14 **35**
Den D17 R27/102 P(32-13-5) 131
Atl D20 R42/148 P(25-12-3) 129
Atl-Hampton 106R, Jenkins 106C

SD 0 7 0 6 13
Min 7 0 7 14 **28**
SD D13 R24/81 P(23-15-1) 147
Min D25 R43/162 P(32-24-2) 191
Min-Foreman 127R

NE 7 14 7 3 31
Buf 14 10 7 14 **45**
NE D28 R31/138 P(46-25-3) 360
Buf D23 R40/153 P(32-16-1) 263
NE-Cunningham 100R,
Francis 125C, Grogan 365P;
Buf-Hill 147C, Ferguson 276P

Bal 2 7 10 14 **33**
Mia 7 7 0 3 17
Bal D14 R43/180 P(14-6-0) 42
Mia D15 R38/128 P(21-8-3) 39
Bal-Mitchell 106R

ChiB 3 0 7 0 10
LARm 14 7 10 7 **38**
ChiB D12 R33/105 P(30-16-2) 111
LARm D17 R38/199 P(23-10-1) 141
LARm-McCutcheon 114R

Cin 13 7 3 0 23
Cle 9 3 3 20 **35**
Cin D17 R28/74 P(31-17-1) 328
Cle D24 R33/166 P(36-23-0) 273
Cin-Joiner 200C; Cle-Pruitt 121R,
Pruitt 106C

Phi 0 3 0 14 17
Dal 3 14 3 7 **27**
Phi D23 R29/111 P(42-21-2) 216
Dal D22 R48/205 P(15-11-2) 146
Dal-Pearson 109C

Oak 6 14 0 6 **26**
Was 0 9 7 7 23
Oak D26 R51/190 P(32-20-2) 216
Was D19 R26/122 P(40-19-2) 215
Oak-Biletnikoff 113C

SL 20 10 7 0 **37**
NYJ 3 3 0 0 6
SL D23 R43/209 P(17-14-0) 267
NYJ D22 R27/157 P(41-14-3) 166
SL 2-Gray 116C

Det 0 8 3 10 21
KC 14 0 7 3 **24**
Det D21 R49/228 P(26-10-1) 138
KC D20 R40/251 P(25-17-1) 169
KC-Green 135R, Lane 108R

MONDAY, NOVEMBER 24

Pit 2 13 3 14 **32**
Hou 0 3 0 6 9
Pit D22 R45/228 P(16-13-2) 139
Hou D13 R23/126 P(32-17-2) 131
Pit-Harris 149R

THURSDAY, NOVEMBER 27

LARm 7 0 6 7 **20**
Det 0 0 0 0 0
LARm D20 R40/177 P(24-11-0) 143
Det D12 R29/121 P(26-11-2) 93
LARm-Jackson 106C

Buf 6 7 6 13 **32**
SL 7 0 0 7 14
Buf D25 R59/264 P(22-11-2) 128
SL D16 R21/54 P(31-13-4) 156
Buf-Braxton 160R

SUNDAY, NOVEMBER 30

NYG 3 0 0 0 3
Dal 14 0 0 0 **14**
NYG D11 R28/74 P(24-8-3) 84
Dal D19 R44/181 P(23-13-2) 208

Pit 0 10 0 10 **20**
NYJ 0 0 0 7 7
Pit D21 R39/213 P(23-9-0) 113
NYJ D16 R41/141 P(21-8-4) 129

Hou 3 0 7 9 19
Cin 0 16 0 7 **23**
Hou D20 R39/206 P(34-10-1) 107
Cin D18 R35/135 P(23-13-0) 154

NO 3 7 6 0 **16**
Cle 0 0 7 0 7
NO D18 R51/177 P(10-6-0) 60
Cle D19 R29/99 P(29-17-1) 150

GB 7 21 0 0 **28**
ChiB 0 0 7 0 7
ChiB D11 R25/88 P(25-9-3) 44
GB D22 R52/193 P(21-12-2) 116
GB-Brockington 111R

KC 0 0 0 14 14
Bal 0 14 14 0 **28**
KC D18 R21/66 P(36-25-2) 263
Bal D19 R38/216 P(17-16-0) 207
KC-Dawson 307P; Bal-Mitchell 178R

SD 0 10 0 0 10
Den 7 0 3 3 **13**
SD D3 R17/59 P(24-8-1) 64
Den D24 R60/328 P(20-8-6) 8
Den-Keyworth 132R

SF 0 0 3 14 17
Phi 3 10 7 7 **27**
SF D23 R25/82 P(49-28-3) 323
Phi D18 R38/66 P(36-23-1) 211
SF-Washington 101C

Min 0 7 7 16 30
Was 7 14 3 7 **31**
Min D28 R33/143 P(38-27-0) 345
Was D21 R26/145 P(25-13-0) 228
Min-Tarkenton 357P

Atl 13 7 0 14 34
Oak 21 0 3 13 **37**
Atl D20 R43/150 P(26-12-1) 170
Oak D33 R62/286 P(33-18-2) 248
Atl-Jenkins 106C;
Oak-Banaszak 116R, Branch 155C,
Stabler 264P

MONDAY, DECEMBER 1

NE 0 0 0 7 7
Mia 7 3 7 3 **20**
NE D15 R21/72 P(32-15-0) 172
Mia D16 R48/199 P(20-15-0) 129

SUNDAY, DECEMBER 7

SD 7 0 7 14 **28**
KC 3 3 14 0 20
SD D21 R50/247 P(18-8-3) 165
KC D17 R30/63 P(30-17-0) 169
SD-Young 124R

GB 3 0 0 0 3
Min 14 10 0 0 **24**
GB D6 R20/51 P(30-11-3) 71
Min D19 R42/161 P(36-23-0) 226

Dal 3 0 7 17 27
SL 14 14 0 3 **31**
Dal D28 R25/118 P(41-25-3) 255
SL D22 R43/169 P(18-11-1) 199

NYJ 6 7 7 10 **30**
NE 0 7 14 7 28
NYJ D21 R53/205 P(18-14-0) 156
NE D21 R29/163 P(30-15-4) 261
NYJ-Riggins 152R;
NE-Calhoun 103R, Vataha 149C

Bal 14 7 0 0 **21**
NYG 0 0 0 0 0
Bal D15 R39/148 P(18-11-0) 75
NYG D22 R29/121 P(28-12-3) 133
Bal-Mitchell 119R

Buf 0 14 0 7 21
Mia 7 14 3 7 **31**
Buf D21 R29/130 P(41-20-2) 255
Mia D19 R44/197 P(15-12-0) 99
Buf-Simpson 117C

Cin 7 17 0 7 **31**
Phi 0 0 0 0 0
Cin D34 R48/258 P(37-21-2) 226
Phi D13 R24/118 P(41-13-4) 107

Hou 3 3 7 14 **27**
SF 0 0 3 10 13
Hou D25 R51/170 P(23-11-0) 109
SF D11 R25/5 P(32-18-1) 195

Det 7 0 7 7 21
ChiB 10 0 9 6 **25**
Det D19 R39/153 P(34-14-1) 192
ChiB D15 R42/140 P(19-11-2) 173
Det-Briscoe 119C; ChiB-Rather 123C

LARm 0 2 9 3 **14**
NO 0 0 0 7 7
LARm D14 R38/132 P(18-11-2) 100
NO D12 R30/76 P(23-14-2) 142

Cle 3 14 0 0 17
Pit 7 3 14 7 **31**
Cle D15 R32/122 P(37-14-3) 115
Pit D17 R39/160 P(25-11-0) 98
Pit-Harris 103R

Was 3 7 7 13 **30**
Atl 0 14 3 10 27
Was D22 R30/91 P(38-25-1) 314
Atl D16 R30/127 P(26-14-3) 261
Was-Grant 135C, Kilmer 320P

MONDAY, DECEMBER 8

Den 3 0 0 7 10
Oak 0 7 7 3 **17**
Den D18 R42/147 P(27-11-4) 107
Oak D16 R40/100 P(16-7-2) 78

SATURDAY, DECEMBER 13

Was 10 0 0 0 10
Dal 0 14 0 17 **31**
Was D12 R27/81 P(33-14-2) 114
Dal D19 R46/207 P(20-10-1) 136

Cin 0 7 0 7 14
Pit 14 7 7 7 **35**
Cin D16 R26/123 P(33-19-1) 194
Pit D21 R38/191 P(23-13-1) 128
Pit-Harris 118R

SUNDAY, DECEMBER 14

KC 0 0 0 14 14
Cle 7 3 16 14 **40**
KC D15 R29/47 P(31-13-1) 99
Cle D27 R44/278 P(21-15-0) 203
Cle-Pruitt 214R, Rucker 130C

Buf 6 7 14 7 **34**
NE 0 0 7 7 14
Buf D26 R53/349 P(19-11-1) 119
NE D16 R30/86 P(30-17-2) 185
Buf-Braxton 101R, Simpson 185R;
NE-Calhoun 100C

Mia 0 0 7 0 7
Bal 0 0 3 7 **10**
Mia D15 R43/192 P(19-8-1) 86
Bal D22 R46/146 P(39-23-0) 206

SL 10 7 17 0 **34**
ChiB 0 7 0 20 27
SL D19 R47/190 P(20-9-0) 172
ChiB D18 R25/67 P(36-20-1) 259
SL 1-Otis 147R

Phi 0 7 0 3 10
Den 3 7 6 9 **25**
Phi D17 R25/114 P(34-16-3) 170
Den D20 R49/197 P(28-11-1) 172

NO 0 7 0 7 14
NYG 0 7 14 7 **28**
NO D19 R43/176 P(34-14-2) 79
NYG D13 R31/124 P(19-11-0) 119

Min 0 3 0 10 13
Det 14 3 0 0 **17**
Min D16 R26/74 P(34-18-2) 127
Det D14 R43/204 P(17-9-2) 54

GB 2 3 0 0 5
LARm 0 9 3 10 **22**
GB D9 R24/53 P(29-13-2) 117
LARm D22 R43/195 P(26-15-2) 139

SF 0 9 0 0 9
Atl 0 10 14 7 **31**
SF D23 R28/212 P(49-21-2) 194
Atl D21 R35/100 P(39-21-0) 362
SF-Williams 104C; Atl-Jenkins 147C,
Bartkowski 305P

Hou 3 14 3 7 **27**
Oak 6 14 0 6 26
Hou D19 R28/86 P(41-17-3) 174
Oak D23 R44/140 P(25-15-3) 237
Hou-Burrough 112C

MONDAY, DECEMBER 15

NYJ 0 3 7 6 16
SD 7 7 0 10 **24**
NYJ D24 R41/139 P(34-16-3) 182
SD D23 R48/249 P(16-8-0) 109
SD-Young 111R

SATURDAY, DECEMBER 20

Min 14 7 14 0 **35**
Buf 0 7 6 0 13
Min D28 R41/168 P(43-27-1) 219
Buf D20 R26/120 P(37-16-4) 189

Pit 3 0 0 0 3
LARm 0 3 0 7 **10**
Pit D14 R34/177 P(21-5-3) 40
LARm D14 R48/171 P(13-6-1) 62
Pit-Harris 126R

Den 3 0 7 3 13
Mia 0 7 0 7 **14**
Den D21 R34/146 P(27-19-0) 206
Mia D16 R32/113 P(17-10-0) 90

SUNDAY, DECEMBER 21

KC 3 10 0 7 20
Oak 7 14 0 7 **28**
KC D23 R33/117 P(32-18-3) 229
Oak D24 R44/246 P(19-14-1) 141
KC-Pearson 103C

Cle 0 0 3 7 10
Hou 14 0 0 7 **21**
Cle D22 R27/96 P(43-24-2) 179
Hou D14 R44/166 P(23-11-2) 156
Hou-Burrough 129C

SD 0 10 7 0 17
Cin 27 14 0 6 **47**
SD D15 R29/113 P(27-11-0) 75
Cin D27 R41/167 P(34-25-1) 272

NE 7 7 0 7 21
Bal 7 3 14 10 **34**
NE D18 R28/112 P(35-16-5) 168
Bal D18 R39/128 P(31-18-1) 171
NE-Johnson 103C

Dal 0 14 10 7 **31**
NYJ 14 0 0 7 21
Dal D21 R53/243 P(15-6-1) 86
NYJ D13 R41/121 P(13-2-1) -1
Dal-Newhouse 108R

NYG 7 6 7 6 **26**
SF 0 10 6 7 23
NYG D23 R45/175 P(30-16-0) 153
SF D20 R33/181 P(30-14-1) 169

Atl 6 0 0 7 13
GB 3 9 10 0 **22**
Atl D14 R26/124 P(37-13-2) 178
GB D20 R46/169 P(33-16-1) 162

SL 7 7 7 3 **24**
Det 0 0 7 6 13
SL D20 R51/272 P(12-6-1) 73
Det D16 R21/101 P(30-14-1) 199
SL-Latin 112R

ChiB 7 14 7 14 **42**
NO 0 10 0 7 17
ChiB D19 R42/195 P(23-15-2) 263
NO D17 R29/68 P(30-10-3) 129
ChiB-Payton 134R

Phi 3 7 10 6 **26**
Was 3 0 0 0 3
Phi D12 R47/172 P(18-9-1) 101
Was D18 R26/143 P(41-16-7) 90

1976 NFL
SUNDAY, SEPTEMBER 12

Pit 0 7 7 14 28
Oak 0 7 0 24 **31**
Pit D24 R42/196 P(27-15-1) 242
Oak D28 R36/116 P(38-21-4) 324
Oak-Casper 124C, Stabler 342P

Det 0 0 0 0 0
ChiB 0 0 7 3 **10**
Det D15 R27/109 P(35-15-0) 134
ChiB D12 R43/114 P(17-8-0) 126

```
SL     3  10  10   7  30
Sea    3   0   7  14  24
SL    D25 R47/281  P(23-15-1) 175
Sea   D17 R22/73   P(37-17-2) 279
  SL-Metcalf 113R, Otis 140R;
  Sea-McCullum 112C

Min   13  17   7   3  40
NO     0   3   6   0   9
Min   D28 R47/173  P(36-22-0) 276
NO    D9  R16/50   P(26-10-0)  82
  Min-Foreman 106C

NYG    3   7   0   7  17
Was    0   3   9   7  19
NYG   D14 R40/96   P(26-13-4) 221
Was   D17 R31/89   P(36-17-1) 233
  NYG-Gillette 105C

Phi    0   0   0   7   7
Dal    6  14   7   0  27
Phi   D18 R30/136  P(32-14-2) 144
Dal   D24 R40/180  P(35-24-1) 265
  Dal-Laidlaw 104R

Den    0   0   7   0   7
Cin    0   0   3  14  17
Den   D12 R34/115  P(22-7-2)   46
Cin   D14 R33/118  P(25-17-1) 135

SF     0  13   6   7  26
GB     7   0   0   7  14
SF    D17 R45/210  P(12-8-1)  104
GB    D17 R36/125  P(36-14-0) 102
  SF-Williams 121R

SD     6   7  14   3  30
KC     6  10   0   0  16
SD    D27 R47/267  P(30-17-0) 217
KC    D19 R26/113  P(34-20-3) 217

Bal    3  14   3   7  27
NE     3   3   0   7  13
Bal   D20 R38/122  P(23-17-0) 150
NE    D17 R37/149  P(22-12-4) 168

LARm   0   6   7  17  30
Atl    0   0   7  14  21
LARm  D17 R51/232  P(16-8-1)  137
Atl   D12 R22/62   P(33-16-3) 148
  LARm-Cappelletti 102R,
  McCutcheon 115R

TB     0   0   0   0   0
Hou    0   7   3  10  20
TB    D8  R26/52   P(26-9-2)   58
Hou   D21 R42/190  P(29-19-1) 182
  Hou-Coleman 142R

NYJ   10   0   0   7  17
Cle    0  21  10   7  38
NYJ   D17 R28/111  P(36-19-2) 147
Cle   D21 R42/207  P(25-18-0) 183
  Cle-Pruitt 124R
```

MONDAY, SEPTEMBER 13

```
Mia    7  10  10   3  30
Buf    0  14   0   7  21
Mia   D25 R48/204  P(21-13-1) 197
Buf   D16 R30/108  P(30-13-0) 275
  Mia-Bulaich 107R;
  Buf-Holland 111C
```

SUNDAY, SEPTEMBER 19

```
ChiB   7  12   0   0  19
SF     3   2   0   7  12
ChiB  D15 R43/167  P(16-8-1)   92
SF    D16 R35/78   P(29-19-2) 112
  ChiB-Payton 148R

Mia    0   7   0   7  14
NE     0   3   7  10  30
Mia   D17 R22/108  P(32-17-3) 146
NE    D23 R51/278  P(27-16-0) 152
  NE-Cunningham 106R

GB     0   0   0   0   0
SL     6   6   3  14  29
GB    D7  R24/62   P(26-10-3)  69
SL    D22 R46/208  P(30-16-0) 212

Hou    0   3   0  10  13
Buf    0   3   0   0   3
Hou   D11 R39/208  P(24-9-1)   52
Buf   D13 R33/89   P(30-11-0)  79
```

```
Cin    7  13   7   0  27
Bal    0   7   7   7  28
Cin   D14 R25/126  P(29-15-2) 177
Bal   D21 R43/129  P(29-14-3) 270
  Bal-Mitchell 106R, Carr 198C,
  Jones 301P

LARm   0   0   0  10  10
Min    0   3   0   7  10
LARm  D25 R65/261  P(22-11-2) 133
Min   D20 R26/74   P(43-27-2) 289
  LARm-Cappelletti 128R,
  McCutcheon 110R; Min-White 139C

Atl    0   7   0   0  10
Det    0   0  24  24  24
Atl   D13 R42/177  P(16-5-3)   59
Det   D15 R41/198  P(20-8-0)   97

SD     3   3   0  17  23
SD    D16 R41/195  P(22-14-0) 131
TB    D5  R33/129  P(18-3-3)   -4

NYG    0   0   0   0   7
Phi    0   3   7  10  20
NYG   D11 R28/82   P(31-17-0) 132
Phi   D17 R50/211  P(14-10-1)  89

Dal    3  14   0   7  24
NO     0   0   0   6   6
Dal   D22 R41/198  P(22-15-0) 225
NO    D11 R20/69   P(29-16-1)  94
  Dal-Dupree 108C
```

MONDAY, SEPTEMBER 20

```
Oak    7  10   0   7  24
KC     0   0   7  14  21
Oak   D25 R47/211  P(29-23-1) 235
KC    D18 R25/115  P(21-12-0) 165
```

SUNDAY, SEPTEMBER 26

```
Atl    0   0   0  10  10
ChiB   0   0   0   0   0
Atl   D19 R43/137  P(32-14-0) 133
ChiB  D10 R32/116  P(22-10-3) 110

Cle    0   7   0   6  13
Den   17   0  20   7  44
Cle   D17 R33/83   P(37-20-2) 144
Den   D18 R32/55   P(21-11-2) 171

SL    10   0   7   7  24
SD     6  27   3   7  43
SL    D22 R28/124  P(33-20-1) 240
SD    D24 R45/206  P(18-15-0) 245
  D-Joiner 134C, Fouts 259P

Buf    0   7   0   7  14
TB     6   0   0   3   9
Buf   D14 R35/109  P(22-12-0) 186
TB    D15 R40/170  P(28-13-1) 168
  Buf-Chandler 110C

NYG   10   0   0   0  10
LARm   0   7   3  14  24
NYG   D20 R42/168  P(26-14-4) 119
LARm  D18 R44/189  P(23-14-1) 179
  NYG-Kotar 108R

Min    0   0   3   7  10
Det    0   0   3   6   9
Min   D10 R35/116  P(20-10-0)  52
Det   D14 R33/101  P(24-13-0) 150

SF    17  14   0   6  37
Sea    0   7   0   7  21
SF    D19 R32/142  P(29-16-1) 239
Sea   D29 R35/130  P(44-21-2) 291
  SF-McGee 104C; Sea-Largent 128C

NYJ    0   0   0   0   0
Mia    0   3  10   3  16
NYJ   D10 R20/65   P(26-16-1) 159
Mia   D23 R47/211  P(24-12-0) 123
```

```
NO     7   3   0  17  27
KC     7   7   3   0  17
NO    D19 R44/299  P(21-12-2) 126
KC    D18 R44/165  P(20-10-0) 105
  NO-Galbreath 146R, Muncie 126R

NE     6   3  14   7  30
Pit    7   6   7   7  27
NE    D18 R40/142  P(32-13-2) 257
Pit   D24 R37/169  P(39-20-0) 247
  NE-Francis 139C

Bal    7   3   7  10  27
Dal    7   0  10  13  30
Bal   D25 R39/184  P(31-13-0) 216
Dal   D21 R32/92   P(29-23-0) 365
  Bal-Mitchell 115R;
  Dal-Staubach 339P

Oak    0   7   0   7  14
Hou    6   0   0   0   6
Oak   D13 R36/106  P(22-13-1) 128
Hou   D17 R32/79   P(36-16-1) 189

GB     7   0   0   0   7
Cin    0  14   7   7  28
GB    D7  R25/71   P(23-5-3)  -35
Cin   D19 R48/222  P(24-11-0)  64
```

MONDAY, SEPTEMBER 27

```
Was    0  10   0   7  20
Phi    3   7   0   7  17
Was   D11 R37/140  P(33-11-3)  90
Phi   D19 R56/252  P(37-14-5) 166
  Phi-Hogan 100R
```

SUNDAY, OCTOBER 3

```
NYG    0   7   7   7  21
SL    10   7   3   7  27
NYG   D23 R33/137  P(28-18-1) 207
SL    D25 R45/187  P(22-16-0) 117
  NYG-Kotar 132C

NYJ    0   0   6   0   6
SF     0   0   3  14  17
NYJ   D19 R35/170  P(26-14-0)  91
SF    D16 R38/126  P(23-12-2) 121
  NYJ-Marinaro 111R

Dal    0  14   7   7  28
Sea    7   6   0   0  13
Dal   D25 R45/211  P(20-14-1) 200
Sea   D19 R24/103  P(41-19-1) 140
  Dal-Newhouse 120R

TB     0   3   0  14  17
Bal    0  24   9   9  42
TB    D6  R24/76   P(15-4-1)   33
Bal   D31 R50/238  P(33-19-0) 220

SD     0   0   0   0   0
Den    0  10   6  10  26
SD    D12 R27/88   P(27-14-2) 152
Den   D17 R44/141  P(17-10-1) 170
  SD-Joiner 105C

Was    0   0   0   7   7
ChiB  10  10   7   6  33
Was   D10 R24/71   P(21-10-3)  48
ChiB  D25 R57/260  P(20-10-0) 132
  ChiB-Payton 104R

Oak    0  10   0   7  17
NE     7  14  14  13  48
Oak   D25 R24/114  P(44-24-1) 207
NE    D27 R52/296  P(17-11-1) 172
  Oak-Casper 136C;
  NE-Cunningham 101R

Cin   21  10   0  14  45
Cle    7  10   7   0  24
Cin   D25 R36/133  P(27-19-2) 265
Cle   D26 R27/127  P(42-26-0) 290
  Cin-Anderson 265P;
  Cle-Rucker 141C

Phi    0   0   7   7  14
Atl    0  13   0   0  13
Phi   D14 R34/157  P(22-10-0)  53
Atl   D18 R30/126  P(32-18-2) 162

LARm   0   0  14  17  31
Mia    7   7   7   7  28
LARm  D23 R41/167  P(29-17-1) 426
Mia   D21 R42/219  P(11-6-2) 100
  LARm-Jessie 220C, Harris 436P;
  Mia-Malone 111R
```

```
Hou    7   3  21   0  31
NO     0   6   3  17  26
Hou   D14 R25/87   P(29-18-1) 168
NO    D22 R32/105  P(44-22-1) 270

Det    0  14   0   0  14
GB     0  10   0  14  24
Det   D20 R39/155  P(17-12-1)  61
GB    D15 R48/212  P(11-4-0)   35
  GB-Harrell 111R

KC     0  10   0   7  17
Buf   16   7   7  20  50
KC    D22 R33/161  P(33-18-3) 341
Buf   D25 R44/266  P(24-14-0) 180
  KC-Brunson 106C, Adams 319P;
  Buf-Kinney 114R, Simpson 130R
```

MONDAY, OCTOBER 4

```
Pit    6   0   0   0   6
Min    0   7   0  10  17
Pit   D12 R40/173  P(22-10-4)  52
Min   D11 R40/152  P(11-4-2)   26
  Min-Foreman 148R
```

SUNDAY, OCTOBER 10

```
NE     0   3   7   0  10
Det   13   7   0  10  30
NE    D10 R22/96   P(25-11-5) 103
Det   D20 R48/196  P(18-15-0) 133
  Det-King 100R

Atl    0   0   0   0   0
NO     6  14   0  10  30
Atl   D12 R29/100  P(31-11-2)  68
NO    D20 R39/144  P(31-19-1) 168

Pit    7   3   0   6  16
Cle    3   3   9   3  18
Pit   D13 R25/111  P(23-13-1)  85
Cle   D15 R48/147  P(25-10-0) 179

Buf    0   0   0   7  14
NYJ    7   7   0   3  17
Buf   D11 R33/125  P(24-11-1)  80
NYJ   D20 R51/207  P(22-7-1)   63
  NYJ-Marinaro 119R

Den    3   0   0   3   3
Hou    0   0   7   7  17
Den   D8  R26/87   P(23-6-1)   67
Hou   D18 R31/95   P(40-24-0) 217
  Hou-Burrough 107C

Mia    0   0   0   7  14
Bal    0  21   7   0  28
Mia   D14 R28/88   P(31-13-1) 180
Bal   D22 R49/169  P(31-14-0) 163
  Mia-Moore 124C; Bal-Chester 106C

ChiB   0   0  13   6  19
Min    7  10   0   3  20
ChiB  D19 R40/235  P(20-13-1)  94
Min   D16 R40/111  P(30-18-0) 176
  ChiB-Payton 141R;
  Min-Rashad 109C

Sea    0  13   0   0  13
GB     7   0   7  13  27
Sea   D17 R23/58   P(33-18-1) 169
GB    D24 R44/187  P(24-16-2) 193

KC     6  10   7  10  33
Was    0   7   0  20  30
KC    D20 R39/119  P(29-15-0) 324
Was   D26 R39/174  P(38-20-2) 264
  KC-Livingston 332P;
  Was-Grant 138C

TB     0   0   0   0   0
Cin   14   0   0   7  21
TB    D12 R33/114  P(23-12-2)  86
Cin   D17 R39/188  P(15-10-0)  89

Dal    7  10   0   7  24
NYG    0   0   7   7  14
Dal   D18 R42/163  P(15-13-0) 168
NYG   D18 R33/138  P(16-12-1) 153

Oak    7   0   0  13  27
SD     7   0   3   7  17
Oak   D22 R38/153  P(20-16-1) 323
SD    D22 R38/154  P(31-16-1) 229
  Oak-Branch 167C, Casper 104C,
  Stabler 339P; SD-Joiner 108C

Phi    7   0   0   7  14
SL     0  19   7   7  33
Phi   D14 R24/58   P(24-12-2) 117
SL    D29 R59/198  P(17-13-0) 186
  SL-Gray 103C
```

MONDAY, OCTOBER 11

```
SF     0   0  16   0  16
LARm   0   0   0   0   0
SF    D15 R37/108  P(21-11-2) 162
LARm  D13 R28/92   P(27-16-0) 104
```

SUNDAY, OCTOBER 17

```
Cin    3   0   3   0   6
Pit    0  13   0  10  23
Cin   D11 R24/75   P(31-13-2)  96
Pit   D16 R55/201  P(12-5-1)   52
  Pit-Harris 143R

Dal    0  10   0   7  17
SL     0   7   7   7  21
Dal   D23 R30/151  P(42-21-1) 229
SL    D26 R40/90   P(34-22-2) 346
  SL-Gray 152C, Hart 346P

ChiB   0   0   6   0  12
LARm  10   0   0  10  20
ChiB  D14 R41/173  P(31-14-3) 152
LARm  D17 R46/185  P(22-8-2)   94
  ChiB-Payton 145R

Det    0   0   0   7   7
Was    0   0  10  10  20
Det   D13 R34/103  P(28-11-2) 144
Was   D14 R40/109  P(20-9-1)   98

Cle   14   0   6   0  20
Atl    0  14   3   0  17
Cle   D23 R57/321  P(18-12-2) 111
Atl   D13 R26/89   P(28-15-1) 169
  Cle-Pruitt 191R

Bal    3  14   0  14  31
Buf    3  10   0   0  13
Bal   D24 R40/213  P(22-13-0) 202
Buf   D17 R32/145  P(28-13-0) 199

NO     0   0   0   3   3
SF     2  21   9   3  33
NO    D9  R25/95   P(19-7-1)   43
SF    D18 R45/133  P(17-11-0) 176

Hou    3   3   7  14  27
SD     0   7  10  13  30
Hou   D16 R23/51   P(39-25-1) 329
SD    D24 R41/223  P(24-19-0) 245
  Hou-Burrough 136C, Pastorini 329P;
  SD-Joiner 106C

KC     7   3   0   7  20
Mia    0   0   7  10  17
KC    D21 R39/186  P(33-20-1) 267
Mia   D27 R37/179  P(35-25-2) 262
  Mia-Moore 106C, Twilley 104C;
  Griese 306P

Sea    0  13   0   0  13
TB     3   0   7   0  10
Sea   D14 R29/90   P(29-12-1) 163
TB    D18 R33/145  P(31-19-0) 140

Phi    3   3   0   7  13
GB     7  14   0   7  28
Phi   D16 R33/96   P(32-19-0) 143
GB    D17 R40/130  P(20-12-1) 226

Oak    0   3  14   0  17
Den    0   0   0  10  10
Oak   D20 R43/131  P(20-16-1) 158
Den   D16 R27/88   P(29-15-0) 173

NYG    0   7   0   0   7
Min    0   3   7   7  24
NYG   D12 R28/87   P(24-15-2) 122
Min   D23 R40/109  P(30-21-1) 252
  Min-Foreman 118C
```

MONDAY, OCTOBER 18

```
NYJ    0   0   7   0   7
NE     7  13  21   0  41
NYJ   D20 R25/116  P(46-25-1) 193
NE    D29 R47/330  P(25-14-1) 145
  NE-Grogan 103R
```

SATURDAY, OCTOBER 23

```
Atl    0   0   0   0   0
SF     2   3   7   3  15
Atl   D7  R28/83   P(29-8-2)  -39
SF    D14 R47/169  P(20-11-1)  76
```

SUNDAY, OCTOBER 24

```
ChiB   0   7  14   0  21
Dal    3  14   7   7  31
ChiB  D8  R28/93   P(16-6-0)   17
Dal   D29 R55/241  P(31-19-2) 288
```

```
Det    13   7  14   7  41
Sea     0  14   0   0  14
Det  D22 R38/152 P(31-19-0) 217
Sea  D20 R30/97  P(38-18-6) 242

Cin    10  10   7   0  27
Hou     0   0   0   7   7
Cin  D18 R40/162 P(24-16-0) 166
Hou  D12 R9/28   P(42-23-3) 148

Mia     3  14   3   3  23
TB      7   6   7   0  20
Mia  D19 R42/200 P(15-8-1)  90
TB   D20 R30/143 P(28-19-1) 191
Mia-Malone 118R

GB      7   0   0   7  14
Oak     0  18   0   0  18
GB   D21 R30/108 P(34-22-2) 264
Oak  D15 R33/115 P(21-13-1) 161
GB-Payne 120C, Dickey 303P;
Oak-Branch 135C

SD      0  14   3   0  17
Cle    14   0   0   7  21
SD   D19 R27/78  P(36-24-1) 232
Cle  D22 R34/137 P(28-23-2) 237

Bal     7   6   0   7  20
NYJ     0   0   0   0   0
Bal  D18 R42/136 P(27-16-1) 281
NYJ  D15 R19/123 P(37-17-2) 154
Bal-Carr 210R; NYJ-Gaines 102R

LARm    0  10   0   6  16
NO      0   0   7   3  10
LARm D14 R42/122 P(15-5-2)  57
NO   D21 R31/114 P(40-24-0) 214

Pit     0  10   0  17  27
NYG     0   0   0   0   0
Pit  D18 R47/230 P(19-12-0) 101
NYG  D10 R29/88  P(26-11-1)  63
Pit-Harris 106R

Min     0   7  10  14  31
Phi     9   0   0   3  12
Min  D27 R43/242 P(33-23-1) 249
Phi  D17 R31/161 P(25-11-0) 121
Min-Foreman 200R

Den    14   7  14   0  35
KC      7  10   3   6  26
Den  D24 R38/192 P(25-16-2) 203
KC   D29 R42/169 P(39-25-1) 298
Den-Armstrong 101R

NE      0   6  13   7  26
Buf     0   3   6  13  22
NE   D18 R41/184 P(21-8-1)  93
Buf  D21 R42/209 P(29-11-1) 100
NE-Cunningham 118R;
Buf-Simpson 110R
```

MONDAY, OCTOBER 25

```
SL      0   7   0   3  10
Was     6   0   0  14  20
SL   D15 R32/100 P(31-17-2) 206
Was  D15 R39/117 P(18-9-1)   23
```

SUNDAY, OCTOBER 31

```
KC      3   3  14   8  28
TB      0  19   0   0  19
KC   D22 R43/136 P(30-17-2) 182
TB   D16 R21/14  P(36-20-0) 182

Den     6   0   0   0   6
Oak     3   3  13   0  19
Den  D16 R29/131 P(30-13-1) 134
Oak  D20 R45/160 P(27-16-2) 222
Oak-Branch 103C

Min     0   3   3   7  13
ChiB    7   0   7   0  14
Min  D23 R38/106 P(46-24-2) 248
ChiB D7  R33/135 P(13-4-0)   38

Phi     0  10   0   0  10
NYG     0   0   0   0   0
Phi  D14 R39/150 P(23-13-0)  95
NYG  D14 R30/114 P(28-17-0) 177
NYG-Robinson 102C

SF      0  13   0   7  20
SL      7   0   7   6  23
SF   D23 R54/265 P(17-8-1)  117
SL   D17 R34/148 P(31-16-1) 225
SF-Williams 194R; SL-Otis 109R,
Gray 115C
```


```
Dal     7   0  10   3  20
Was     0   0   0   7   7
Dal  D18 R49/135 P(25-13-0) 118
Was  D10 R23/88  P(24-12-2)  58

NO      0  14   0   6  20
Atl     0   0   7  16  23
NO   D18 R42/138 P(21-12-2) 115
Atl  D18 R38/105 P(21-14-1) 150

Sea     0   3   3   0   6
LARm   24   7   0  14  45
Sea  D9  R19/50  P(32-13-2) 144
LARm D25 R46/206 P(28-16-0) 223

GB      0   3   3   0   6
Det    10  14   0   3  27
GB   D11 R25/87  P(26-11-2)  76
Det  D21 R43/222 P(20-12-1) 187
Det-Jarvis 163C

SD      0   0   0   0   0
Pit     0   3   0  20  23
SD   D7  R26/44  P(28-10-1)  90
Pit  D20 R52/255 P(25-11-1) 106
Pit-Harrison 108R

NYJ     0  16   0   3  19
Buf     0   0  14   0  14
NYJ  D16 R33/155 P(20-6-2)   79
Buf  D17 R48/224 P(30-10-3)  87
NYJ-Gaines 119R;
Buf-Simpson 166R

Cle     3   3   0   0   6
Cin     7   7   0   7  21
Cle  D19 R31/182 P(27-12-1) 137
Cin  D24 R41/203 P(24-15-2) 182
Cle-Pruitt 124R; Cin-Clark 100R,
Curtis 116C

NE      0   3   0   0   3
Mia     0  10   0   0  10
NE   D11 R27/130 P(31-10-1)  96
Mia  D18 R37/157 P(22-12-0) 100
Mia-Malone 119R
```

MONDAY, NOVEMBER 1

```
Hou     0   0   0  14  14
Bal     7  14   3  14  38
Hou  D12 R14/83  P(31-11-1) 107
Bal  D25 R53/268 P(30-19-0) 190
Bal-Mitchell 136R
```

SUNDAY, NOVEMBER 7

```
SL      0   0  14   3  17
Phi     7   0   0   7  14
SL   D20 R47/185 P(25-14-0) 132
Phi  D14 R32/127 P(28-15-1) 143
SL-Otis 115R

Atl     0   3   3   7  13
Sea     3  14  16   0  30
Atl  D12 R33/148 P(32-10-4)  90
Sea  D19 R39/196 P(28-15-0) 153
Atl-Collins 100R; Sea-Smith 124R

Was     0  14   7   3  24
SF      0  14   0   7  21
Was  D23 R35/120 P(32-20-2) 283
SF   D19 R41/273 P(21-8-2)  112
Was-Grant 200C, Theismann 302P;
SF-Williams 180R

Det     3   6   7   7  23
Min     7   3   7  14  31
Det  D26 R39/208 P(27-19-0) 191
Min  D19 R34/83  P(25-17-1) 347
Det-Gaines 116R; Min-White 210C,
Tarkenton 347P

NYG     3   0   0   0   3
Dal     0   3   0   6   9
NYG  D18 R53/186 P(16-9-1)   83
Dal  D12 R30/96  P(25-13-1) 161

TB      0  10   3   0  13
Den    10   0  14  24  48
TB   D17 R33/112 P(37-16-2) 122
Den  D18 R40/193 P(21-10-2) 222
Den-Armstrong 116R

NO      0  13  14   0  27
GB      6  10   7   9  32
NO   D21 R33/136 P(35-15-2) 161
GB   D19 R47/175 P(25-10-1) 123

Cle     5   3   0  13  21
Hou     0   7   0   7  14
Cle  D13 R44/200 P(19-9-0)   62
Hou  D11 R31/125 P(21-13-1)  63
```


```
Buf     0   3   0   7  10
NE      3  10   7   0  20
Buf  D20 R42/149 P(34-15-4) 224
NE   D16 R39/172 P(18-8-2)  126
Buf-Chandler 104C;
NE-Cunningham 141R

Mia     7  10   3   7  27
NYJ     0   0   0   7   7
Mia  D18 R42/142 P(21-16-0) 181
NYJ  D16 R28/116 P(24-12-1) 154

Bal     7  14   7   9  37
SD      0   0  14   7  21
Bal  D26 R39/181 P(26-19-1) 300
SD   D23 R21/63  P(36-22-0) 230
Bal-Mitchell 125C

Pit     7   3  21  14  45
KC      0   0   0   0   0
Pit  D26 R54/330 P(17-8-1)  121
KC   D14 R22/34  P(35-15-4) 223
Pit-Bleier 102R, Harris 117R;
KC-White 105C

Oak     0  14   7   7  28
ChiB    7   0  20   0  27
Oak  D13 R27/118 P(17-11-0) 204
ChiB D20 R55/181 P(18-10-1) 184
Oak-Branch 163C, White 105C
```

MONDAY, NOVEMBER 8

```
LARm    3   3   0   6  12
Cin     0   0  20   0  20
LARm D21 R41/182 P(28-16-1) 160
Cin  D15 R31/167 P(26-11-1) 132
```

SUNDAY, NOVEMBER 14

```
Det     0   6   0  10  16
NO      0   3   7   7  17
Det  D26 R39/171 P(38-27-0) 284
NO   D6  R24/79  P(19-8-0)  104
Det-Jarvis 111C, Landry 310P

TB      0   0   0   0   0
NYJ     7   7   0   7  34
TB   D18 R28/106 P(40-18-2) 171
NYJ  D24 R47/211 P(22-10-0) 133
NYJ-Gaines 103R

Den     0   7   3   7  17
SD      0   0   0   0   0
Den  D13 R33/61  P(34-19-1) 194
SD   D8  R22/33  P(29-13-5)  95

SF      0   3   7   6  16
Atl     7   0   0  14  21
SF   D21 R32/159 P(31-14-2) 143
Atl  D15 R52/199 P(15-7-0)   90
Atl-Collins 107R

NE      7  14   0   0  21
Bal     0   7   0   7  14
NE   D19 R51/205 P(17-12-0) 121
Bal  D13 R29/107 P(25-10-2)  95
NE-Calhoun 141R

GB      0  10   3   0  13
ChiB   14   0   7   3  24
GB   D16 R33/82  P(28-15-1) 179
ChiB D16 R45/202 P(19-9-2)   47
ChiB-Payton 109R

Mia     0   7   0   7  14
Pit     0   7   0   7  14
Mia  D14 R32/116 P(21-9-0)  108
Pit  D19 R48/218 P(8-4-0)    96
Pit-Bleier 110R, Harris 110R

Was     3   3   3   0   9
NYG     3   3   3   3  12
Was  D20 R36/174 P(30-12-1) 141
NYG  D10 R49/144 P(14-3-2)  161
Was-Thomas 106R

KC      0   7   3   0  10
Oak     0   7   7   7  21
KC   D17 R34/115 P(29-16-0) 174
Oak  D20 R40/211 P(18-10-4) 128

Sea     7   0   7   7  21
Min     7   7   6   7  27
Sea  D15 R23/108 P(29-17-3) 278
Min  D29 R43/180 P(31-26-0) 244
Sea-Raible 112C;
Min-Foreman 100R

Phi     0   0   0   0   0
Cle     0  10   0  14  24
Phi  D12 R26/143 P(24-14-4)  21
Cle  D18 R37/131 P(25-17-0) 205
```


```
Hou     3  10   7   7  27
Cin     3  14  14   0  31
Hou  D20 R48/141 P(25-12-2) 111
Cin  D15 R28/85  P(30-14-0) 215
Cin-Curtis 116C

SL      3   3  14  10  30
LARm    7   7   7   7  28
SL   D23 R36/93  P(33-20-2) 324
LARm D15 R32/122 P(17-10-1) 161
SL-Harris 130C, Tilley 120C,
Hart 324P; LARm-Jackson 107C
```

MONDAY, NOVEMBER 15

```
Buf     0   7   0   3  10
Dal     0  14   0   3  17
Buf  D19 R42/147 P(28-10-1) 103
Dal  D14 R26/63  P(34-15-0) 165
Dal-Pearson 135C
```

SUNDAY, NOVEMBER 21

```
Min     3   7   0   7  17
GB      3   0   7   0  10
Min  D17 R30/100 P(43-23-0) 151
GB   D13 R38/146 P(27-12-4)  82

SD     14  13   7   0  34
Buf     3   7   3   0  13
SD   D20 R35/184 P(29-19-3) 198
Buf  D14 R38/148 P(30-8-3)   71
Buf-Simpson 118R

Was     3   3   7   3  16
SL      7   0   3   0  10
Was  D20 R56/247 P(20-9-1)  110
SL   D16 R31/82  P(31-9-1)  155
Was-Thomas 195R

Hou     3   0   7   6  16
Pit    10   5  10   7  32
Hou  D12 R33/101 P(23-9-2)  124
Pit  D17 R48/143 P(13-8-1)  105

Cin    14   0   7   6  27
KC      0   7   7  10  24
Cin  D21 R41/269 P(17-9-1)  104
KC   D19 R39/126 P(25-12-0) 125
Cin-Griffin 139R

Cle     0   7   7  10  24
TB      0   0   7   0   7
Cle  D21 R41/149 P(23-12-0) 133
TB   D18 R28/102 P(32-18-1) 125

NYG     0   6   0   7  13
Den     7   7   0   0  14
NYG  D13 R38/121 P(24-11-2) 122
Den  D15 R44/136 P(16-10-0) 103

NE     14   7   7  10  38
NYJ    10   7   0   7  24
NE   D15 R41/154 P(22-10-1)  83
NYJ  D20 R30/130 P(42-18-7) 184
NE-Calhoun 109R

LARm    0   6  17   0  23
SF      0   3   0   0   3
LARm D8  R47/124 P(8-3-0)    26
SF   D7  R29/70  P(28-9-4)   18

Dal     7   0   3   0  10
Atl     0   0   0  17  17
Dal  D15 R36/182 P(28-13-3) 125
Atl  D13 R43/141 P(20-8-1)   89

ChiB    7   0   0   3  10
Det     0  14   0   0  14
ChiB D7  R37/177 P(29-8-1)  110
Det  D23 R41/203 P(26-15-2) 146

NO      3  17  28   3  51
Sea     6   0   7  14  27
NO   D28 R24/105 P(24-14-2) 141
Sea  D28 R24/105 P(34-17-3) 164
Sea-Largent 101C

Oak    12   0   7   7  26
Phi     7   0   0   0   7
Oak  D23 R47/250 P(18-14-0) 133
Phi  D14 R33/97  P(25-12-1) 110
Oak-van Eeghen 133R
```

MONDAY, NOVEMBER 22

```
Bal     7   7   0   3  17
Mia     0  10   0   6  16
Bal  D20 R44/163 P(20-13-0) 177
Mia  D16 R26/87  P(28-17-2) 251
Mia-Harris 116C
```


THURSDAY, NOVEMBER 25

```
SL      0   7   0   7  14
Dal     7   7   0   5  19
SL   D24 R31/128 P(46-20-2) 249
Dal  D16 R41/169 P(22-11-2) 126
SL-Harris 113C

Buf     0   0   7   7  14
Det     0  10  10   7  27
Buf  D19 R41/307 P(21-4-1)   15
Det  D17 R41/193 P(20-8-1)  111
Buf-Simpson 273R;
Det-Bussey 137R
```

SUNDAY, NOVEMBER 28

```
Phi     0   0   0   0   0
Was     7   7  10   0  24
Phi  D13 R32/88  P(35-14-2) 106
Was  D8  R38/87  P(18-10-0) 119

Pit     0   0   7   0   7
Cin     3   0   0   0   3
Pit  D20 R49/204 P(15-10-1) 143
Cin  D9  R30/110 P(26-10-1) 115

TB      0   3   0   6   9
Oak     7  14  21   7  49
TB   D16 R29/111 P(30-13-2) 107
Oak  D28 R42/179 P(31-19-1) 307
Oak-Branch 110C

ChiB   10   0   3   3  16
GB      0   3   7   0  10
ChiB D16 R53/201 P(12-7-0)   72
GB   D15 R25/9   P(28-5-2)  177
ChiB-Payton 110R; GB-Smith 121C

Den     0   0   0   7   7
NE      7  24   0   7  38
Den  D12 R13/44  P(34-15-3) 145
NE   D25 R62/332 P(14-8-1)   82
NE-Calhoun 177R

KC     10   0   3  10  23
SD      7   6   0   7  20
KC   D20 R38/177 P(27-14-1) 191
SD   D24 R37/210 P(32-18-3) 190
KC-Podolak 127R

Sea     9   0   7   0  16
NYG     0  14   7   7  28
Sea  D15 R35/128 P(32-14-3) 116
NYG  D20 R45/164 P(21-15-2) 115

NYJ     9   0   0   7  16
Bal    14   3   3  13  33
NYJ  D14 R32/159 P(23-9-1)   96
Bal  D19 R41/198 P(35-23-0) 189

Atl     0   7   7   0  14
Hou     3   7  10   0  20
Atl  D15 R36/118 P(19-10-2) 155
Hou  D17 R40/159 P(26-18-1) 200
Atl-Jenkins 102C;
Hou-Johnson 104C

Mia     0   7   0   7  14
Cle     0   7   7   3  17
Mia  D23 R33/134 P(33-22-0) 190
Cle  D18 R30/133 P(23-15-3) 178

NO      0   0   0   0   0
LARm    6  20   0   7  33
NO   D18 R23/116 P(30-11-2) 146
LARm D25 R49/323 P(27-17-1) 150
NO-Muncie 119R;
LARm-McCutcheon 119R
```

MONDAY, NOVEMBER 29

```
Min     0  13   3   0  16
SF      7  10   0   3  20
Min  D16 R30/113 P(37-16-0) 169
SF   D17 R54/317 P(8-3-1)    14
Min-Rashad 103C;
SF-Jackson 156R, Williams 153R
```

SATURDAY, DECEMBER 4

```
Bal     7   3   0   7  17
SL     14   7   0   3  24
Bal  D12 R20/62  P(23-13-1) 217
SL   D20 R51/177 P(22-13-0) 198
SL 1-Otis 107R

Atl     0   0   0   0   0
LARm    9  15  14  21  59
Atl  D8  R21/59  P(22-11-2)  12
LARm D30 R41/210 P(31-18-1) 359
LARm-McCutcheon 121R,
Jessie 112C, Scales 102C
```

938 THE GAMES

SUNDAY, DECEMBER 5

```
GB     6   0   0   3    9
Min    0   3   3  14   20
GB  D8  R21/59  P(26-8-0)  85
Min D29 R48/218 P(32-23-1) 195

Det    0  10   0   0   10
NYG    0  17   7   0   24
Det D16 R24/111 P(31-15-2) 163
NYG D17 R43/196 P(24-12-2) 187

Hou    0   0   3   7   10
Cle    0   7   3   3   13
Hou D9  R23/58  P(29-17-3) 117
Cle D15 R44/176 P(22-9-2)   89

Was   17   7  10   3   37
NYJ    0   3   6   7   16
Was D29 R49/238 P(25-17-0) 188
NYJ D12 R32/232 P(15-5-2)   52
  Was-Riggins 104R;
  NYJ-Gaines 109R

Dal    9   3   7   7   26
Phi    0   7   0   0    7
Dal D22 R35/117 P(40-23-0) 248
Phi D13 R31/134 P(28-12-0)  42

ChiB   0   6  21   7   34
Sea    0   7   0   0    7
ChiB D23 R48/259 P(28-14-1) 250
Sea D16 R23/105 P(34-15-3) 181
  ChiB-Payton 183R, Scott 106C

KC     3  13   0   0   16
Den    7   7   0   3   17
KC  D13 R30/59  P(29-17-1) 129
Den D13 R37/82  P(28-12-2) 187

TB     0   0   0   0    0
Pit    7  21  14   0   42
TB  D8  R30/94  P(14-5-2)   11
Pit D26 R58/222 P(15-12-0) 163
  Pit-Bleier 118R

Buf   10   3   7   7   27
Mia    3  14  14  14   45
Buf D23 R42/269 P(29-13-2) 155
Mia D19 R29/218 P(22-11-1) 207
  Buf-Simpson 203R;
  Mia-Solomon 114C

NO     0   3   0   3    6
NE     0  13   0  14   27
NO  D14 R30/118 P(31-18-0) 118
NE  D21 R42/220 P(24-9-0)  108
  NE-Calhoun 113R

SF     0   0   0   7    7
SD     0   0   0   7   13
SF  D18 R45/185 P(22-11-1)  96
SD  D19 R39/170 P(21-12-0)  97
  SF-Williams 104R
```

MONDAY, DECEMBER 6

```
Cin    6   7   7   0   20
Oak   14   7   7   7   35
Cin D22 R25/107 P(37-16-3) 251
Oak D26 R54/228 P(23-16-1) 217
  Cin-McDaniel 201C;
  Oak-Branch 112C, Stabler 217P
```

SATURDAY, DECEMBER 11

```
Min    0  15  14   0   29
Mia    0   0   0   7    7
Min D26 R46/226 P(25-16-0) 181
Mia D13 R26/55  P(30-12-2) 133
  Min-White 120C

LARm   3   0  17   0   20
Det   10   7   0   0   17
LARm D14 R40/117 P(22-12-2) 132
Det D11 R29/91  P(21-12-3) 122

Pit    0   7   7   7   21
Hou    0   0   0   0    0
Pit D20 R53/258 P(19-8-1)   76
Hou D9  R24/93  P(29-13-1)  65
  Pit-Bleier 107R, Harris 104R
```

SUNDAY, DECEMBER 12

```
Was    0  10   3  14   27
Dal    0   7   7   0   14
Was D24 R47/184 P(30-14-2) 175
Dal D10 R36/149 P(22-5-2)   54
```

```
SL     0   7   3   7   17
NYG    7   0   0   7   14
SL  D23 R53/230 P(14-9-1)   70
NYG D16 R39/183 P(22-8-2)   67
  SL-Otis 119R; NYG-Kotar 103R

Sea    0   3   0   7   10
Phi    7   7  10   3   27
Sea D20 R21/71  P(49-24-1) 226
Phi D25 R54/270 P(20-12-0) 142
  Phi-Hogan 104R, Sullivan 121R

SF     0   7  10  10   27
NO     0   7   0   0    7
SF  D22 R42/212 P(28-14-1) 148
NO  D11 R20/54  P(33-18-0) 245

Buf    3   3   7   7   20
Bal    7  13  28  10   58
Buf D21 R46/271 P(24-11-1)  84
Bal D25 R38/133 P(23-15-2) 263

Cin    6  21  10   5   42
NYJ    0   3   0   0    3
Cin D14 R40/144 P(25-11-0) 200
NYJ D6  R32/64  P(28-7-6)    8

NE     0   7   7  17   31
TB     0  14   0   0   14
NE  D13 R39/260 P(14-4-1)   40
TB  D16 R45/135 P(18-12-1) 133
  NE-Johnson 127R

Cle    0   7   7   0   14
KC     0  15  17   7   39
Cle D16 R29/157 P(25-11-3) 114
KC  D26 R44/198 P(35-18-1) 188
  KC-Podolak 137R

SD     0   0   0   0    0
Oak    7  10   7   0   24
SD  D11 R27/125 P(25-10-2)  82
Oak D25 R45/193 P(27-16-0) 158

GB     0  10   0  14   24
Atl    0  10   0  10   20
GB  D24 R43/196 P(26-16-1) 154
Atl D16 R27/145 P(24-10-1) 108
  Atl-Jenkins 101C

Den    0   0   7  21   28
ChiB   7   0   0   7   14
Den D26 R59/356 P(25-8-5)   97
ChiB D5 R31/116 P(17-2-2)   56
  Den-Armstrong 116R, Weese 120R
```

1977 NFL

SUNDAY, SEPTEMBER 18

```
Dal    0   3   0   7   6   16
Min    7   0   0   3   0   10
Dal D16 R35/131 P(30-18-0) 166
Min D20 R43/156 P(32-13-3) 138

GB    14  10   0   0   24
NO     0   0  14   6   20
GB  D11 R34/81  P(20-11-1) 123
NO  D19 R32/153 P(30-18-1) 162

TB     0   0   3   0    3
Phi    0   7   6   0   13
TB  D8  R27/92  P(27-11-0)  26
Phi D15 R38/144 P(25-15-2) 137

SL     0   0   0   0    0
Den    0   0   7   0    7
SL  D12 R30/69  P(36-19-1) 204
Den D15 R40/136 P(20-12-1) 122

Det    7   3   3   7   20
ChiB   7  20   0   3   30
Det D20 R30/168 P(25-17-0) 195
ChiB D16 R48/260 P(9-4-0)   40
  ChiB-Payton 160R

Mia    0   3   0  10   13
Buf    0   0   0   0    0
Mia D10 R32/96  P(19-9-0)   52
Buf D16 R40/127 P(37-19-1) 197

SD     0   0   0   0    0
Oak   14   0   0  10   24
SD  D7  R20/59  P(22-11-1)  62
Oak D21 R59/178 P(20-13-1) 139

KC    14   0   0   3   17
NE     7   7   0   7   21
KC  D21 R37/180 P(26-13-0) 155
NE  D19 R46/241 P(16-10-2) 140
  NE-Cunningham 105R
```

```
Cle    3  10   0   0   13
Cin    0   0   3   0    3
Cle D16 R37/112 P(22-15-1) 173
Cin D16 R33/104 P(34-16-1) 141

Bal    7   7   5  10   29
Sea    0   3   0   7   10
Bal D23 R50/206 P(26-17-0) 220
Sea D16 R25/104 P(35-14-4) 151
  Bal-Mitchell 114R

Was    0   0   0  17   17
NYG    7   0   3  10   20
Was D19 R38/122 P(26-13-1) 139
NYG D13 R41/166 P(14-7-1)  113

NYJ    0   0   0   0    0
Hou    0   7   0  13   20
NYJ D11 R26/102 P(26-10-1)  77
Hou D19 R33/109 P(32-20-0) 130

LARm   6   0   0   0    6
Atl    0  10   7   0   17
LARm D9 R21/59  P(30-15-0) 108
Atl D14 R52/156 P(17-10-0) 108
```

MONDAY, SEPTEMBER 19

```
SF     0   0   0   0    0
Pit    0  10   3  14   27
SF  D8  R33/82  P(18-4-2)   19
Pit D19 R45/175 P(24-12-0) 133
  Pit-Harris 100R
```

SATURDAY, SEPTEMBER 24

```
Min    0   2   7   0    9
TB     0   3   0   0    3
Min D17 R32/104 P(38-25-2) 211
TB  D8  R34/104 P(17-5-3)   34
```

SUNDAY, SEPTEMBER 25

```
Mia    7   6   6   0   19
SF     3   6   0   6   15
Mia D22 R45/208 P(17-10-0) 153
SF  D13 R34/162 P(21-11-1) 118
  Mia-Moore 114C

Phi    0   0   0   0    0
LARm   7   7   3   3   20
Phi D6  R16/31  P(29-13-3)  81
LARm D21 R56/220 P(23-12-1) 136
  LARm-McCutcheon 106R

Atl    0   0   3   3    6
Was    0   3   7   0   10
Atl D16 R45/107 P(33-16-0) 234
Was D15 R30/105 P(29-13-2) 147
  Atl-Jenkins 152C

Sea    0   7  13   0   20
Cin   21   7   0  14   42
Sea D15 R31/110 P(30-19-0) 172
Cin D27 R40/199 P(30-18-1) 225
  Sea-Sims 105C; Cin-Curtis 100C

Bal    7   7   6   0   20
NYJ    0   3   0   9   12
Bal D15 R50/152 P(15-9-1)   60
NYJ D14 R34/80  P(22-13-2) 132

SD     7   9   0   7   23
KC     0   0   0   7    7
SD  D20 R48/214 P(25-11-3)  73
KC  D9  R27/75  P(23-8-3)   96

NO     0  14   0   5   19
Det    7   3  13   0   23
NO  D9  R17/39  P(22-10-1)  53
Det D26 R53/306 P(28-13-0) 123
  Det-Bussey 150R

Buf    0   6   0   0    6
Den    0   3  13   3   19
Buf D8  R24/66  P(28-13-3)  63
Den D17 R46/203 P(20-9-0)   93

Hou    0  10   0   6   16
GB     7   3   0   0   10
Hou D18 R34/90  P(30-18-0) 137
GB  D15 R32/95  P(26-16-3) 184

ChiB   3   0   3   7   13
SL     3  10   3   0   16
ChiB D18 R25/101 P(39-19-2) 184
SL  D17 R40/133 P(24-16-2) 215

Oak    0   9   0   7   16
Pit    0   0   0   7    7
Oak D13 R46/140 P(19-8-0)  107
Pit D31 R31/152 P(32-16-3) 217
```

```
NYG    0   7  14   0   21
Dal   14  17   3   7   41
NYG D14 R27/69  P(26-10-3)  92
Dal D25 R45/185 P(36-21-0) 259
```

MONDAY, SEPTEMBER 26

```
NE     0  17  10   0   27
Cle    7   0  10  13   30
NE  D21 R40/141 P(23-15-1) 122
Cle D25 R44/198 P(27-19-2) 195
  Cle-Pruitt 151R
```

SUNDAY, OCTOBER 2

```
NYG    0   0   0   3    3
Atl    0   7   3   7   17
NYG D10 R29/105 P(23-7-2)   72
Atl D18 R48/151 P(24-16-0) 144
  NYG-Robinson 118C

TB     0   0   0   0    0
Dal   17   3   3   0   23
TB  D10 R32/76  P(23-8-2)   87
Dal D23 R42/205 P(24-15-1) 210

NO     7  14   7  14   42
ChiB   7   3   0  14   24
NO  D18 R46/146 P(17-8-0)  168
ChiB D19 R31/197 P(38-18-2) 218
  ChiB-Payton 140R; Rather 113C

Cin    0   3   0   0    3
SD     7   7   7   3   24
Cin D15 R22/92  P(33-15-3) 127
SD  D25 R43/165 P(24-17-1) 220

SF     7   0   7   0   14
LARm   3  14   0  17   34
SF  D12 R25/48  P(25-15-2) 183
LARm D17 R49/150 P(14-7-0)  95

SL     0   0   0  14   14
Was    7   0   7  10   24
SL  D19 R32/106 P(31-17-2) 223
Was D16 R41/163 P(21-12-0) 198

Pit    7   7   7   7   28
Cle    7   7   0   0   14
Pit D21 R56/218 P(17-10-2) 143
Cle D16 R29/80  P(24-10-3)  85

Buf    0   0   7   0    7
Bal    0  10   7   0   17
Buf D18 R23/77  P(39-19-2) 225
Bal D22 R41/155 P(30-20-0) 154

GB     0   7   0   0    7
Min    7   6   0   6   19
GB  D8  R21/81  P(20-8-0)  127
Min D24 R49/194 P(27-19-0) 131

NE    14   3   7   7   31
NYJ   14   0   0  16   30
NE  D20 R38/125 P(34-16-3) 231
NYJ D10 R37/107 P(21-12-3) 144

Den    0  10   0  14   24
Sea    7   0   6   0   13
Den D19 R39/153 P(21-12-1) 177
Sea D19 R32/81  P(31-21-1) 191

Phi    0   7   6   0   13
Det    7   3   7   0   17
Phi D19 R35/137 P(26-13-1) 193
Det D18 R45/140 P(18-13-0)  95

Hou    0   7   0   0    7
Mia   21   0   0   6   27
Hou D13 R27/68  P(31-16-2) 137
Mia D29 R51/217 P(20-13-1) 180
```

MONDAY, OCTOBER 3

```
Oak    7   6  21   3   37
KC     0  21   0   7   28
Oak D29 R49/242 P(28-19-3) 297
KC  D14 R27/194 P(20-9-0)  128
  Oak-Davis 102R, van Eeghen 116R,
  Casper 101C; KC-Reed 119R
```

SUNDAY, OCTOBER 9

```
Atl    0   0   7   0    7
SF     0   0   0   0    0
Atl D11 R44/113 P(14-9-0)  130
SF  D12 R39/153 P(18-5-1)   35

Mia   14  14   0   0   28
Bal   14  14  14   3   45
Mia D16 R29/182 P(34-18-2) 213
Bal D19 R35/207 P(30-18-0) 190
  Mia-Malone 139R, Harris 127C;
  Bal-Mitchell 142R, Jones 205P
```

```
Phi    7  14   7   0   28
NYG    0   3   0   7   10
Phi D14 R43/179 P(17-8-1)  147
NYG D15 R32/94  P(38-12-4) 165
  Phi-Lusk 117R

Det    0   0   0   7    7
Min   14   0   0   0   14
Det D19 R27/59  P(47-26-1) 222
Min D13 R27/58  P(31-21-0) 256
  Min-White 104C

Cin    0   7   7   3   17
GB     0   7   0   0    7
Cin D21 R42/159 P(20-15-1) 174
GB  D15 R37/112 P(25-13-2) 115

Was   10   0   0   0   10
TB     0   0   0   0    0
Was D14 R47/121 P(22-11-1) 118
TB  D11 R26/97  P(28-10-3)  39

SD     7   0   0   7   14
NO     0   0   0   0    0
SD  D14 R31/132 P(21-11-0) 137
NO  D18 R36/157 P(26-16-1)  43

Dal    3  10   3  14   30
SL    10   7   7   0   24
Dal D22 R39/264 P(29-18-0) 124
SL  D15 R31/146 P(34-10-2) 174
  Dal-Dorsett 141R

NYJ    0   7  10   7   24
Buf    7   0   0  12   19
NYJ D17 R44/172 P(15-10-0) 194
Buf D21 R37/172 P(33-18-1) 199
  Buf-Simpson 122R

Sea    0   0   0   0    0
NE     7   7  17   0   31
Sea D6  R31/95  P(23-5-4)   50
NE  D19 R55/196 P(15-9-1)  137
  NE-Cunningham 101R

Oak    3   6  10   7   26
Cle    0   0   3   7   10
Oak D17 R48/171 P(20-9-2)   88
Cle D14 R26/113 P(27-12-2) 137
  Oak-van Eeghen 114R

KC     0   0   0   7    7
Den   10   6   7   0   23
KC  D14 R29/86  P(27-15-4)  80
Den D16 R39/124 P(30-18-0) 188

Pit    3   7   0   0   10
Hou    0  10  10   7   27
Pit D21 R45/178 P(33-12-6) 211
Hou D15 R29/98  P(24-13-2) 169
  Pit-Swann 102C
```

MONDAY, OCTOBER 10

```
LARm  13   3   0   7   23
ChiB   0   7   0  10   24
LARm D22 R40/177 P(46-19-4) 239
ChiB D14 R46/200 P(18-12-1) 231
  ChiB-Payton 126R, Scott 142C
```

SUNDAY, OCTOBER 16

```
GB     3   0   0   3    6
Det    0   3   0   7   10
GB  D11 R29/67  P(25-11-4)  82
Det D17 R38/133 P(26-18-0) 129

SL     0  14   0   7   21
Phi    3   0   0  14   17
SL  D16 R41/128 P(25-17-0) 209
Phi D14 R23/96  P(38-17-3) 258

Bal   14   0   3   0   17
KC     0   6   0   0    6
Bal D16 R45/161 P(20-11-0)  80
KC  D13 R31/102 P(23-11-2) 117

Cle   14   7   0   3   24
Hou   10  10   0   3   23
Cle D11 R31/109 P(20-9-1)   61
Hou D18 R37/109 P(29-14-2) 119

SF     0   0  14   0   14
NYG    0  17   0   3   20
SF  D16 R39/92  P(22-15-1) 183
NYG D9  R41/131 P(6-2-0)    23

ChiB   6   0  10   0   0   16
Min   10   3   0   3   6   22
ChiB D17 R44/170 P(22-14-0) 133
Min D24 R41/195 P(31-17-1) 201
  ChiB-Payton 122R;
  Min-Foreman 150R
```

```
Atl    0   0   0   0    0
Buf    0   3   0   0    3
Atl  D15 R39/114 P(30-9-2)   86
Buf  D15 R45/218 P(21-8-0)   96
Buf-Simpson 138R

Den    7  14   6   3   30
Oak    7   0   0   0    7
Den  D8  R37/102 P(17-8-0)   98
Oak  D21 R30/87  P(42-22-7) 239

Was    6   3   0   7   16
Dal    0  14   6  14   34
Was  D12 R32/115 P(25-7-1)    1
Dal  D23 R50/171 P(29-16-0) 264
Was-Woods 111C;
Dal-Pearson 157C

NE     7   0   7  10   24
SD     6   0   7   7   20
NE   D22 R51/256 P(22-12-1)  69
SD   D16 R19/53  P(26-18-1) 230
NE-Cunningham 141R;
SD-Woods 111C

NO     0   7   0   0    7
LARm   0   7   0   7   14
NO   D12 R23/77  P(34-15-0) 155
LARm D24 R61/243 P(16-9-1)  165
LARm-McCutcheon 126R

TB     6   7   3   7   23
Sea    7  10   0  13   30
TB   D22 R34/167 P(32-18-4) 217
Sea  D21 R35/134 P(30-20-2) 241
TB-Owens 166C; Sea-Myer 252P

NYJ    0   3   7   7   17
Mia    7  14   0   0   21
NYJ  D14 R25/123 P(26-16-0) 191
Mia  D23 R42/212 P(24-17-0) 128
Mia-Malone 105R
```

MONDAY, OCTOBER 17

```
Cin    0   7   0   7   14
Pit    0   7   0   7   ...
Cin  D20 R35/103 P(36-15-4) 208
Pit  D18 R50/166 P(9-6-0)    87
```

SUNDAY, OCTOBER 23

```
Sea    3   7   0   3   13
Mia    0  24   0   7   31
Sea  D14 R27/79  P(33-17-3) 143
Mia  D19 R39/136 P(18-11-1)  86

Hou    0   7   0   3   10
Pit    0   7   6  14   27
Hou  D10 R38/133 P(15-5-5)  -14
Pit  D14 R40/125 P(25-16-1) 234
Hou-Coleman 114R

KC     0   0   7  14   21
SD     3   7   3   3   16
KC   D19 R37/115 P(26-15-0) 170
SD   D19 R35/116 P(35-18-2) 226

Atl    0   6   3   7   16
ChiB   3   0   0   7   10
Atl  D11 R44/127 P(22-8-0)   90
ChiB D17 R33/118 P(28-11-3) 131

Bal    0   0   3   0    3
NE     7   0  10   0   17
Bal  D8  R23/75  P(18-6-0)   11
NE   D20 R52/169 P(16-11-0) 201
NE-Stingley 116C

Oak   14   0   0  14   28
NYJ   13  14   0   0   27
Oak  D29 R55/210 P(26-19-1) 213
NYJ  D17 R20/67  P(29-17-2) 375
Oak-van Eeghen 143R;
NYJ-Walker 178C, Todd 396P

NO     0  21   3   7   31
SL    14   7   7  21   49
NO   D23 R26/165 P(35-16-2) 275
SL   D31 R52/244 P(26-19-0) 243
NO-Muncie 102R

Dal    0   6   0  10   16
Phi    0   7   0   3   10
Dal  D17 R41/149 P(26-15-0) 139
Phi  D15 R32/114 P(23-10-2)  72

NYG    0   0   7  10   17
Was    3   3   0   0    6
NYG  D12 R43/104 P(20-11-0) 162
Was  D19 R27/71  P(39-20-1) 156
```


```
Cle    0  13   7   7   27
Buf    7   3   6   0   16
Cle  D26 R48/219 P(24-15-2) 127
Buf  D20 R25/162 P(29-11-2) 185
Cle-Miller 117R; Buf-Gant 111C

Det    0   7   0   0    7
SF     7  14   7   0   28
Det  D16 R27/69  P(37-12-2)  50
SF   D16 R46/193 P(14-8-0)  107
SF-Williams 106R,
Washington 112C

Den    7  10   0   7   24
Cin    7   3   0   3   13
Den  D16 R42/180 P(15-9-0)  155
Cin  D14 R31/177 P(28-15-1) 159
Cin-Johnson 108R

GB     0   6   7   0   13
TB     0   0   0   0    0
GB   D14 R41/125 P(15-11-1)  93
TB   D13 R26/75  P(35-15-2) 113
```

MONDAY, OCTOBER 24

```
Min    0   0   0   3    3
LARm   7  14   7   7   35
Min  D16 R29/98  P(31-13-2) 108
LARm D21 R50/283 P(21-12-0) 114
LARm-Tyler 102R
```

SUNDAY, OCTOBER 30

```
Pit    0   0   7  14   21
Bal    3  14   7   7   31
Pit  D18 R33/164 P(26-11-5) 219
Bal  D22 R48/160 P(20-10-0) 158

Phi    7   3   0   7   17
Was   14   6   3   0   23
Phi  D16 R29/131 P(27-9-3)  150
Was  D19 R34/118 P(34-16-1) 194
Phi-Carmichael 116C

Buf    3   0   7   7   17
Sea   14  28   7   7   56
Buf  D17 R28/115 P(37-17-3) 221
Sea  D30 R39/226 P(29-15-3) 333
Sea-Fergerson 113C, Largent 134C,
Zorn 296P

SD     0   0   7   7   14
Mia    6   0   0   7   13
SD   D14 R35/90  P(31-15-3) 122
Mia  D15 R37/178 P(16-9-3)   63

ChiB  13   3   0  10   26
GB     0   0   0   0    0
ChiB D21 R54/375 P(10-4-1)   44
GB   D17 R31/101 P(30-12-1)  96
ChiB-Payton 205R

KC     0   0   0   7    7
Cle   13  17   7   7   44
KC   D16 R26/137 P(32-14-3) 119
Cle  D34 R53/322 P(31-16-2) 204
Cle-Pruitt 153R

Oak    7  10   7   0   24
Den    0   0   0  14   14
Oak  D17 R57/200 P(14-7-0)   70
Den  D19 R23/98  P(32-19-1) 180
Oak-Davis 105R

Det    0   0   0   0    0
Dal    3  20   7   7   37
Det  D7  R18/74  P(30-10-2)  46
Dal  D20 R47/176 P(27-16-1) 168

Min    0   7   0   7   14
Atl    0   7   0   0    7
Min  D17 R41/145 P(26-16-3) 212
Atl  D10 R34/134 P(21-8-2)   78

LARm   7  13   0   6   26
NO     3  14   7   3   27
LARm D19 R34/134 P(26-17-0) 242
NO   D19 R50/253 P(19-9-0)   90
LARm-McCutcheon 107R,
Jackson 127C; NO-Galbreath 100R

TB     0   0   3   7   10
SF     7   7   6   0   20
TB   D18 R36/104 P(31-12-1) 146
SF   D20 R43/205 P(20-12-1) 101

Hou    0   7   0   0    7
Cin    0   7   3   3   13
Hou  D15 R38/107 P(26-14-1)  79
Cin  D15 R38/89  P(29-17-2) 173
```


```
NYJ    3   7   0   3   13
NE     3   7  14   0   24
NYJ  D15 R35/134 P(32-16-0) 158
NE   D20 R40/147 P(23-16-1) 228
NE-Stingley 121C
```

MONDAY, OCTOBER 31

```
NYG    0   0   0   0    0
SL     0  14   7   7   28
NYG  D18 R35/158 P(35-17-3) 143
SL   D18 R36/145 P(14-9-1)  113
```

SUNDAY, NOVEMBER 6

```
Cin    7   0   3   0   10
Cle    0   7   0   0    7
Cin  D15 R29/84  P(19-14-1) 153
Cle  D19 R31/131 P(28-20-2) 159

GB     0   0   3   7   10
KC    10   0   0  10   20
GB   D15 R27/84  P(28-15-0) 115
KC   D20 R44/177 P(21-11-0) 124

SD     0   0   0   0    0
Det    0   0   7  13   20
SD   D14 R25/111 P(27-15-0) 118
Det  D15 R49/197 P(7-5-0)    67
Det-Kane 105R

SF     0   0  10   0   10
Atl    0   0   0   3    3
SF   D8  R40/72  P(12-5-0)   25
Atl  D13 R34/126 P(26-12-2)  29

Dal    7   7   7   3   24
NYG    0   0   7   3   10
Dal  D13 R31/83  P(26-15-0) 171
NYG  D13 R36/119 P(17-6-1)    2

Sea    0   0   7   0    7
Oak    3  24  10   7   44
Sea  D13 R27/126 P(23-8-3)   51
Oak  D29 R53/248 P(26-16-0) 149
Oak-Davis 100R

ChiB   0   0   0   0    0
Hou    3  14  14  16   47
ChiB D10 R39/141 P(17-9-0)  -16
Hou  D19 R39/255 P(19-11-0) 234
Hou-Burrough 180C

SL     7  13   7   0   27
Min    0   0   7   0    7
SL   D23 R51/316 P(14-10-3) 143
Min  D20 R20/107 P(33-19-3) 130
SL-Morris 182R

Buf   14   3   0   7   24
NE     7   0   0   7   14
Buf  D21 R53/224 P(22-15-1) 175
NE   D14 R24/89  P(27-9-4)  113
Buf-Hooks 155R

TB     0   0   0   0    0
LARm   3  14   7   7   31
TB   D9  R9/109  P(21-8-2)   43
LARm D21 R52/177 P(23-12-0) 153

Pit    0   0   7   7   14
Den   14   7   0   0   21
Pit  D19 R35/119 P(27-13-0)  97
Den  D12 R38/99  P(14-6-0)   75

Mia    0   7   0   7   14
NYJ    3   0   0   7   10
Mia  D15 R31/109 P(15-12-0) 105
NYJ  D18 R31/130 P(35-20-0) 117

NO     0   0   0   7    7
Phi    0  14   0  14   28
NO   D9  R24/78  P(21-13-4)  88
Phi  D21 R48/145 P(22-13-1) 150
```

MONDAY, NOVEMBER 7

```
Was    0   3   0   0    3
Bal    3   0   0   7   10
Was  D13 R22/93  P(27-11-2) 113
Bal  D21 R51/190 P(27-13-2) 163
Bal-Mitchell 111R
```

SUNDAY, NOVEMBER 13

```
Sea    7   0   7   3   17
NYJ    0   0   0   0    0
Sea  D26 R44/232 P(37-16-0) 213
NYJ  D8  R27/99  P(18-6-3)   25
```


```
LARm   0  17   0   7   24
GB     0   0   6   0    6
LARm D23 R56/190 P(17-10-0) 146
GB   D17 R31/93  P(36-18-2) 246
GB-Odom 115C

Bal   10  14   7   0   31
Buf    7   3   0   3   13
Bal  D18 R48/145 P(23-12-2) 171
Buf  D12 R19/86  P(33-14-3) 120

Was    0   7  10   0   17
Phi    0   7   0   7   14
Was  D18 R33/140 P(27-15-2) 132
Phi  D15 R48/212 P(21-7-0)   72

NYG    7   3   0   0   10
TB     0   0   0   0    0
NYG  D13 R44/123 P(12-6-1)   74
TB   D19 R39/105 P(26-13-3) 182
TB-Owens 113C

Det    6   0   0   0    6
Atl    0   0   0  17   17
Det  D12 R42/112 P(14-5-2)   33
Atl  D13 R38/110 P(16-6-3)   61

Hou    3  13  13   0   29
Oak   10   7  14   3   34
Hou  D13 R29/156 P(27-11-4) 196
Oak  D24 R48/110 P(31-23-2) 255
Hou-Carpenter 120R;
Oak-Branch 115C

Den    3   0   7   7   17
SD     7   7   0   0   14
Den  D14 R32/102 P(32-12-1) 120
SD   D13 R42/128 P(33-14-1) 192

NE     0   0   0   5    5
Mia    0   7   0  10   17
NE   D17 R39/134 P(31-15-1) 140
Mia  D14 R29/71  P(20-11-0) 102

SF     0   0   7   3   10
NO     7   0   0   0    7
SF   D21 R52/243 P(21-7-2)   44
NO   D12 R50/161 P(7-3-0)    33
SF-Jackson 123R, Williams 110R

Cin    0  10   0   0   10
Min    7   7   7  21   42
Cin  D13 R20/61  P(32-12-1) 187
Min  D30 R49/207 P(24-21-0) 216
Cin-Brooks 198C;
Min-Foreman 133R

Cle    3   0   7  21   31
Pit    7  21   0   7   35
Cle  D23 R31/138 P(40-21-3) 283
Pit  D25 R46/171 P(23-15-0) 249
Cle-Pruitt 108R, Rucker 104R;
Pit-Stallworth 126C, Swann 129C

KC    14   3   3   7   27
ChiB   0   0   7  21   28
KC   D24 R45/174 P(27-16-2) 184
ChiB D24 R49/247 P(23-11-2) 184
KC-Podolak 102R;
ChiB-Payton 192R
```

MONDAY, NOVEMBER 14

```
SL     3   0   7  14   24
Dal    0  14   0   3   17
SL   D19 R43/158 P(24-10-1) 137
Dal  D16 R36/156 P(20-11-2)  80
```

SUNDAY, NOVEMBER 20

```
TB     0   7   0   0    7
Det    0   0   3  13   16
TB   D8  R33/76  P(21-7-3)   71
Det  D14 R40/147 P(25-10-3)  69

LARm   0  10   7   6   23
SF     0   7   0   3   10
LARm D10 R38/130 P(13-5-0)   86
SF   D19 R39/148 P(26-11-3) 121
LARm-McCutcheon 100R

Dal    6   7   0   0   13
Pit    0  14  14   0   28
Dal  D20 R27/136 P(36-18-2) 201
Pit  D17 R47/228 P(12-7-0)   92
Pit-Harris 179R

Hou    0   9   0  13   22
Sea    0   3   0   7   10
Hou  D25 R50/195 P(36-21-2) 237
Sea  D12 R29/102 P(24-5-2)   27
```


```
Phi    0   9   0   7   16
SL     0   0  14   7   21
Phi  D19 R35/142 P(30-16-1) 175
SL   D27 R35/142 P(27-13-1) 226
SL-Gray 142C

Min    0   0   0   7    7
ChiB   0  10   0   0   10
Min  D11 R27/86  P(25-12-3) 102
ChiB D18 R63/343 P(7-4-1)    23
ChiB-Payton 275R

Mia    7   0   7   3   17
Cin    3   7   6   7   23
Mia  D17 R35/192 P(29-10-3)  93
Cin  D19 R42/173 P(26-14-0)  96
Mia-Harris 108R

Atl    3  17   0   0   20
NO     0   7   7   7   21
Atl  D18 R46/210 P(16-6-2)   35
NO   D19 R40/212 P(26-13-3)  84
Atl-Thompson 123R

Cle    7   0   7   7   21
NYG    0   7   0   0    7
Cle  D14 R39/140 P(24-13-1) 129
NYG  D14 R30/116 P(26-12-3) 105

Oak    0   0   7   0    7
SD     0   6   3   3   12
Oak  D10 R30/112 P(16-5-1)   30
SD   D18 R58/263 P(13-5-2)   47

Den    0   7   0   7   14
KC     0   7   0   7   14
Den  D21 R53/249 P(18-8-2)  127
KC   D14 R32/140 P(33-20-1) 160
Den-Armstrong 120R

NYJ    3   0   3   6   12
Bal    6  13   7   7   33
NYJ  D13 R29/111 P(33-10-3) 185
Bal  D21 R58/140 P(38-23-2) 315
Bal-Chester 102C, Jones 322P

NE     3   0  14   3   20
Buf    0   0   7   0    7
NE   D19 R54/256 P(17-8-1)   73
Buf  D11 R26/126 P(22-10-1)  83
```

MONDAY, NOVEMBER 21

```
GB     0   3   3   3    9
Was    0   3   0   7   10
GB   D17 R35/89  P(24-12-3) 107
Was  D15 R38/159 P(21-10-1)  95
```

THURSDAY, NOVEMBER 24

```
Mia   14  14  20   7   55
SL     0   7   0   7   14
Mia  D34 R55/295 P(25-17-1) 208
SL   D13 R22/54  P(29-16-1) 156
Mia-Davis 104R, Griese 207P

ChiB   0   0  17  14   31
Det    0   7   0   7   14
ChiB D18 R37/172 P(21-14-2) 253
Det  D15 R31/68  P(39-20-1) 150
ChiB-Payton 137R, Payton 107C
```

SUNDAY, NOVEMBER 27

```
Min    0  13   0   0   13
GB     0   0   0   6    6
Min  D12 R55/158 P(8-5-0)    60
GB   D9  R32/108 P(23-6-2)   61
Min-Foreman 101R

LARm   6   3   0   0    9
Cle    0   0   0   0    0
LARm D24 R49/216 P(29-21-3) 147
Cle  D11 R22/90  P(27-13-3)  91
LARm-McCutcheon 104R

NYG    0   6   0   7   13
Cin   20   7   0   3   30
NYG  D15 R29/70  P(35-19-0) 170
Cin  D15 R43/176 P(11-5-0)  154

NO     3  14   0   0   17
SF     3   7   7   3   20
NO   D13 R40/164 P(8-4-1)    19
SF   D16 R46/282 P(8-5-0)    61
SF-Jackson 190R

Atl   10   0   7   0   17
TB     0   0   0   0    0
Atl  D18 R58/175 P(15-9-0)   47
TB   D8  R20/62  P(23-5-4)   16
```

THE GAMES

SD 10 3 3 14 **30**
Sea 0 14 7 7 **28**
SD D21 R27/111 P(26-19-1) 192
Sea D20 R29/109 P(26-16-2) 281
Sea-Largent 116C, Zorn 291P

KC 0 6 0 14 **20**
Hou 7 7 6 14 **34**
KC D18 R29/91 P(38-17-2) 246
Hou D21 R40/296 P(25-11-2) 74
Hou-Carpenter 149R, Coleman 101R

Phi 0 0 0 6 **6**
NE 7 7 0 0 **14**
Phi D17 R35/78 P(33-15-2) 139
NE D11 R37/109 P(20-10-1) 173

Bal 0 3 10 0 **13**
Den 0 14 0 13 **27**
Bal D23 R33/90 P(46-27-3) 240
Den D11 R33/174 P(14-8-1) 143
Bal-McCauley 112C

Dal 0 0 7 7 **14**
Was 0 7 0 0 **7**
Dal D19 R39/150 P(24-10-1) 132
Was D18 R32/133 P(35-17-1) 201

Pit 6 14 0 3 **23**
NYJ 6 7 0 7 **20**
Pit D15 R32/114 P(28-10-1) 124
NYJ D21 R46/209 P(25-9-5) 59
NYJ-Dierking 107R

MONDAY, NOVEMBER 28
Buf 3 7 3 0 **13**
Oak 13 7 14 0 **34**
Buf D18 R19/65 P(43-18-1) 239
Oak D26 R64/307 P(13-7-2) 166
Buf-Chandler 120C;
Oak-van Eeghen 143R

SUNDAY, DECEMBER 4
NYJ 7 3 0 6 **16**
NO 0 0 6 4 **10**
NYJ D16 R38/141 P(21-8-1) 141
NO D18 R35/188 P(24-13-0) 115
NYJ-Gaines 103R; NO-Muncie 107R

Was 0 7 0 3 **10**
Buf 0 0 0 0 **0**
Was D18 R46/128 P(28-12-1) 136
Buf D19 R32/146 P(42-17-2) 180

SF 0 10 14 3 **27**
Min 0 0 7 21 **28**
SF D19 R59/196 P(13-5-1) 47
Min D18 R25/52 P(32-20-2) 257
SF-Williams 107R;
Min-Rashad 121C

Sea 3 10 7 0 **20**
Pit 7 6 0 17 **30**
Sea D17 R33/166 P(30-10-1) 210
Pit D22 R49/236 P(21-13-1) 157
Pit-Harris 103R

Oak 0 7 0 7 **14**
LARm 0 3 10 7 **20**
Oak D27 R37/198 P(38-16-4) 153
LARm D19 R40/137 P(22-13-0) 165

Phi 0 7 7 0 **14**
Dal 7 7 3 7 **24**
Phi D14 R25/72 P(23-18-2) 171
Dal D19 R45/268 P(26-13-2) 164
Dal-Dorsett 206R

SL 0 7 0 0 **7**
NYG 7 7 0 13 **27**
SL D15 R20/91 P(27-16-2) 161
NYG D20 R60/236 P(10-3-0) 84

Cin 7 10 3 7 **27**
KC 10 0 7 0 **17**
Cin D24 R55/224 P(24-9-0) 102
KC D10 R22/72 P(26-12-2) 167

Det 0 0 0 9 **9**
GB 0 3 0 7 **10**
Det D13 R31/100 P(25-14-2) 95
GB D11 R52/164 P(9-4-2) 65

Den 0 14 3 7 **24**
Hou 0 7 0 7 **14**
Den D23 R45/169 P(26-15-1) 163
Hou D11 R30/112 P(26-10-0) 139

Cle 0 0 0 14 **14**
SD 14 13 3 7 **37**
Cle D17 R27/111 P(31-19-1) 208
SD D23 R37/167 P(23-16-0) 258
SD-Dorsey 108C

NE 3 3 3 7 **16**
Atl 0 0 7 3 **10**
NE D13 R41/97 P(26-12-3) 170
Atl D9 R28/67 P(18-7-4) 57

ChiB 0 0 0 10 **10**
TB 0 0 0 0 **0**
ChiB D17 R44/141 P(27-12-1) 133
TB D9 R42/114 P(15-4-2) 21
ChiB-Payton 101R

MONDAY, DECEMBER 5
Bal 6 0 0 0 **6**
Mia 3 7 0 7 **17**
Bal D17 R33/122 P(34-18-0) 189
Mia D17 R31/207 P(22-13-1) 145
Mia-Harris 140R

SATURDAY, DECEMBER 10
Was 10 3 3 10 **26**
SL 0 10 3 7 **20**
Was D16 R42/151 P(28-14-0) 115
SL D13 R37/176 P(26-7-3) 133
SL-Metcalf 119R

Pit 0 10 0 0 **10**
Cin 7 0 10 0 **17**
Pit D21 R32/123 P(39-20-1) 139
Cin D17 R30/111 P(34-16-1) 302
Cin-Brooks 166C, Anderson 303P

SUNDAY, DECEMBER 11
NYG 0 7 0 7 **14**
Phi 0 3 7 7 **17**
NYG D15 R48/153 P(16-10-2) 65
Phi D10 R34/121 P(10-4-0) -13

Min 0 7 0 6 **13**
Oak 21 0 0 14 **35**
Min D11 R20/67 P(34-16-3) 147
Oak D17 R57/182 P(15-10-0) 124
Oak-van Eeghen 112R

SD 3 3 3 0 **9**
Den 7 0 0 10 **17**
SD D17 R23/64 P(41-24-2) 160
Den D20 R32/156 P(27-15-3) 142

Hou 7 6 6 0 **19**
Cle 0 6 2 7 **15**
Hou D10 R36/111 P(12-7-1) 56
Cle D22 R41/178 P(35-19-4) 222
Cle-Rucker 101C

Buf 7 0 7 0 **14**
NYJ 0 3 0 7 **10**
Buf D26 R53/174 P(32-17-1) 216
NYJ D10 R22/57 P(27-10-3) 140
Buf-Chandler 108C

GB 0 10 0 0 **10**
ChiB 7 7 0 7 **21**
GB D16 R35/161 P(24-10-0) 115
ChiB D25 R49/234 P(20-12-2) 114
ChiB-Payton 163R

Mia 0 3 0 7 **10**
NE 14 0 0 0 **14**
Mia D18 R19/25 P(38-22-1) 223
NE D16 R51/177 P(10-6-0) 106

Det 0 3 0 10 **13**
Bal 0 0 3 7 **10**
Det D12 R27/83 P(33-17-1) 122
Bal D20 R35/148 P(38-21-2) 201

TB 3 10 7 13 **33**
NO 0 0 0 14 **14**
TB D14 R48/135 P(10-8-0) 103
NO D17 R28/96 P(33-17-6) 154

Sea 14 20 0 0 **34**
KC 21 0 3 7 **31**
Sea D21 R47/209 P(14-8-2) 133
KC D21 R39/145 P(26-15-3) 189

Atl 0 0 0 7 **7**
LARm 9 0 7 7 **23**
Atl D10 R23/64 P(28-15-1) 149
LARm D20 R46/265 P(25-15-1) 121
LARm-McCutcheon 152R

MONDAY, DECEMBER 12
Dal 0 21 7 14 **42**
SF 7 7 7 14 **35**
Dal D24 R45/183 P(19-14-0) 215
SF D19 R35/93 P(30-16-0) 269
SF-Washington 130C, Plunkett 263P

SATURDAY, DECEMBER 17
Buf 0 0 0 14 **14**
Mia 7 14 3 7 **31**
Buf D24 R26/103 P(40-25-3) 331
Mia D18 R42/238 P(14-10-1) 210
Buf-Ferguson 331P;
Mia-Davis 172R, Moore 144C

LARm 0 0 0 14 **14**
Was 3 14 0 0 **17**
LARm D20 R29/194 P(34-15-1) 99
Was D17 R40/133 P(21-12-2) 118

Min 7 10 13 0 **30**
Det 0 7 7 7 **21**
Min D18 R52/194 P(16-11-0) 199
Det D14 R21/50 P(30-11-2) 122
Min-Foreman 156R, Rashad 139C

SUNDAY, DECEMBER 18
NE 0 14 10 0 **24**
Bal 0 3 13 14 **30**
NE D17 R35/166 P(25-11-2) 104
Bal D24 R36/172 P(30-19-0) 311
Bal-Chester 122C, Doughty 110C,
Jones 340P

KC 0 7 13 0 **20**
Oak 3 3 12 3 **21**
KC D15 R31/155 P(26-14-4) 180
Oak D25 R48/242 P(16-10-1) 79

Cin 3 3 0 7 **13**
Hou 0 13 2 6 **21**
Cin D17 R28/109 P(29-11-0) 132
Hou D21 R49/150 P(21-10-0) 182
Hou-Johnson 138C

Den 0 0 3 3 **6**
Dal 7 0 7 0 **14**
Den D12 R24/98 P(27-12-1) 80
Dal D15 R42/112 P(20-15-1) 150

Cle 6 10 0 3 **19**
Sea 0 7 0 13 **20**
Cle D23 R51/259 P(17-7-4) 101
Sea D21 R32/191 P(24-10-2) 132
Cle-Pruitt 127R

NYJ 0 0 0 0 **0**
Phi 17 3 0 7 **27**
NYJ D11 R23/86 P(30-13-3) 64
Phi D16 R45/161 P(16-9-0) 124
Phi-Montgomery 103R

SL 0 7 0 0 **7**
TB 7 7 3 0 **17**
SL D17 R37/134 P(29-16-2) 162
TB D11 R39/108 P(12-7-1) 171
TB-Owens 138C

NO 0 7 0 7 **14**
Atl 0 14 14 7 **35**
NO D17 R37/135 P(19-11-2) 134
Atl D22 R49/236 P(17-9-0) 108
Atl-Stanback 129R

Pit 0 0 0 10 **10**
SD 6 3 0 0 **9**
Pit D13 R40/89 P(25-12-1) 192
SD D14 R30/68 P(22-12-3) 107

SF 7 0 7 0 **14**
GB 9 7 0 0 **16**
SF D20 R34/117 P(29-17-3) 195
GB D19 R32/103 P(22-17-0) 219

ChiB 3 0 0 6 3 **12**
NYG 0 6 0 0 0 **6**
ChiB D13 R37/112 P(26-17-1) 172
NYG D20 R53/253 P(33-12-2) 117
NYG-Csonka 100R

1978 NFL

SATURDAY, SEPTEMBER 2
NYG 7 3 6 3 **19**
TB 3 0 7 3 **13**
NYG D12 R35/76 P(25-12-1) 162
TB D16 R39/165 P(28-10-3) 86
NYG-Perkins 110C

SUNDAY, SEPTEMBER 3
SL 0 3 0 7 **10**
ChiB 3 0 0 14 **17**
SL D16 R28/99 P(33-17-2) 137
ChiB D19 R45/124 P(19-8-0) 49
ChiB-Payton 101R

SD 7 3 7 7 **24**
Sea 6 7 0 7 **20**
SD D16 R28/89 P(22-14-1) 186
Sea D22 R38/138 P(32-21-1) 308
Sea-Largent 127C, Zorn 329P

Pit 0 14 0 14 **28**
Buf 0 10 7 0 **17**
Pit D21 R43/142 P(19-14-1) 217
Buf D16 R29/100 P(26-13-1) 164

Min 7 10 0 7 **24**
NO 14 10 0 7 **31**
Min D24 R32/155 P(49-28-4) 269
NO D19 R34/138 P(22-15-0) 183
Min-Foreman 122R, Young 134C

Oak 0 0 3 3 **6**
Den 0 7 0 7 **14**
Oak D16 R37/117 P(29-12-2) 201
Den D13 R41/144 P(13-5-1) 8

Was 3 0 6 7 **16**
NE 0 7 0 7 **14**
Was D14 R37/149 P(24-10-1) 175
NE D21 R40/161 P(31-12-2) 165
NE-Jackson 124C

KC 7 10 7 0 **24**
Cin 0 9 0 14 **23**
KC D26 R69/267 P(20-14-0) 121
Cin D12 R17/77 P(24-10-2) 128
KC-Bailey 106R

GB 6 0 0 7 **13**
Det 0 0 0 7 **7**
GB D16 R55/181 P(9-3-0) 31
Det D11 R26/82 P(19-10-1) 40

Mia 0 6 7 7 **20**
NYJ 10 0 6 7 6 **33**
Mia D16 R25/154 P(29-15-2) 175
NYJ D23 R43/153 P(25-17-1) 227
Mia-Williams 119R;
NYJ-Walker 108C

LARm 3 3 0 10 **16**
Phi 0 0 14 0 **14**
LARm D15 R33/103 P(33-14-0) 117
Phi D10 R30/128 P(17-7-1) 80

SF 0 7 0 0 **7**
Cle 7 7 0 10 **24**
SF D18 R40/131 P(32-16-3) 164
Cle D18 R41/213 P(26-12-0) 180
Cle-Pruitt 106R, Rucker 113C

Hou 7 0 7 0 **14**
Atl 0 14 3 3 **20**
Hou D13 R21/156 P(36-19-2) 105
Atl D11 R35/100 P(23-10-0) 71
Hou-Campbell 137R

MONDAY, SEPTEMBER 4
Bal 0 0 0 0 **0**
Dal 0 21 14 3 **38**
Bal D9 R27/99 P(20-9-2) 82
Dal D25 R45/278 P(27-19-2) 305
Dal-Dorsett 147R, Dorsett 107C,
Staubach 280P

SUNDAY, SEPTEMBER 10
NYJ 0 7 7 7 **21**
Buf 0 7 6 7 **20**
NYJ D18 R39/117 P(26-14-2) 171
Buf D17 R25/101 P(32-20-1) 213
NYJ-Gaffney 108C; Buf-Gant 100C

Oak 0 0 7 14 **21**
SD 0 13 0 7 **20**
Oak D18 R18/84 P(35-15-3) 280
SD D24 R53/197 P(29-17-0) 175
Oak-Bradshaw 107C, Casper 100C,
Stabler 307P

SATURDAY, SEPTEMBER 9
Det 9 3 0 3 **15**
TB 7 0 0 0 **7**
Det D11 R46/149 P(14-9-0) 47
TB D10 R29/140 P(14-6-1) -31

SUNDAY, SEPTEMBER 10
Cin 7 3 0 0 **10**
Cle 0 0 3 3 **13**
Cin D14 R36/115 P(26-15-1) 162
Cle D20 R37/169 P(32-16-1) 186
Cle-Pruitt 120R

Atl 0 0 0 0 **0**
LARm 0 3 0 7 **10**
Atl D7 R28/70 P(15-5-1) 3
LARm D23 R46/142 P(36-19-2) 216

Phi 7 3 6 14 **30**
Was 7 14 7 7 **35**
Phi D18 R27/128 P(23-14-1) 139
Was D19 R35/117 P(24-14-1) 199

NO 3 0 7 7 **17**
GB 7 7 7 7 **28**
NO D25 R23/100 P(53-33-1) 295
GB D20 R37/220 P(15-10-0) 156
NO-Galbreath 122C, Manning 303P;
GB-Middleton 114R, Lofton 107C,
Whitehurst 161P

NE 3 13 0 0 **16**
SL 0 0 6 0 **6**
NE D21 R52/269 P(21-13-2) 172
SL D9 R20/57 P(28-12-1) 136
NE-Calhoun 143R

Dal 7 14 6 7 **34**
NYG 0 7 10 7 **24**
Dal D32 R49/189 P(28-18-1) 212
NYG D22 R24/100 P(37-15-3) 243
Dal-Dorsett 111R;
NYG-Robinson 100C

Sea 0 7 3 0 **10**
Pit 0 14 0 7 **21**
Sea D18 R28/93 P(22-11-1) 154
Pit D26 R40/151 P(33-17-0) 185

ChiB 3 3 3 7 **16**
SF 7 3 0 3 **13**
ChiB D11 R37/111 P(22-7-1) 101
SF D19 R41/195 P(32-12-3) 112
SF-Simpson 108R

Mia 14 0 14 14 **42**
Bal 0 0 0 0 **0**
Mia D20 R42/292 P(22-14-1) 148
Bal D18 R26/96 P(37-17-6) 151

Hou 3 0 3 14 **20**
KC 6 0 7 4 **17**
Hou D15 R41/179 P(13-7-0) 47
KC D19 R41/261 P(14-9-1) 34
Hou-Campbell 107R; KC-Reed 141R

MONDAY, SEPTEMBER 11
Den 0 0 0 9 0 **9**
Min 3 0 6 0 3 **12**
Den D18 R29/102 P(32-15-3) 129
Min D13 R36/101 P(34-15-3) 105

SUNDAY, SEPTEMBER 17
Dal 0 7 0 7 **14**
LARm 7 7 0 13 **27**
Dal D21 R29/96 P(46-22-4) 223
LARm D16 R36/98 P(25-14-2) 219
LARm-Jessie 144C

Phi 0 7 10 7 **24**
NO 0 7 0 3 **17**
Phi D22 R42/207 P(23-14-1) 166
NO D14 R21/88 P(32-17-3) 220
Phi-Montgomery 104R

Oak 0 14 0 14 **28**
GB 0 3 0 0 **3**
Oak D28 R58/348 P(16-6-4) 72
GB D13 R27/79 P(33-12-1) 117
Oak-van Eeghen 151R

ChiB 0 7 12 0 **19**
Det 0 0 0 7 **7**
ChiB D15 R45/185 P(12-9-1) 141
Det D15 R27/143 P(27-13-0) 94

TB 3 6 7 0 **16**
Min 7 0 0 0 **7**
TB D10 R40/92 P(19-5-0) 63
Min D15 R28/73 P(37-25-3) 146

Cle 0 17 0 7 **24**
Atl 3 7 0 6 **16**
Cle D17 R34/110 P(35-20-0) 198
Atl D17 R30/87 P(28-11-4) 147

```
SF    0   6   6   7   19
Hou   7   7   3   3   20
SF    D18 R26/61  P(32-20-1) 321
Hou   D23 R50/151 P(24-15-1) 179
SF-Solomon 110C, DeBerg 321P

Sea   0   14  3   7   24
NYJ   7   7   3   0   17
Sea   D28 R40/153 P(26-19-1) 181
NYJ   D17 R32/177 P(24-13-3) 201
Sea-Sims 121R

Buf   0   7   3   14  24
Mia   7   7   10  7   31
Buf   D17 R36/128 P(24-14-0) 221
Mia   D18 R46/285 P(14-7-0) 88
Buf-Lewis 153C; Mia-Williams 135R

Was   7   14  7   0   28
SL    3   0   0   7   10
Was   D16 R46/255 P(14-6-0) 47
SL    D19 R26/132 P(41-17-1) 196
Was-Riggins 108R; SL-Tilley 123C

Pit   14  7   7   0   28
Cin   0   3   0   0   3
Pit   D26 R49/212 P(20-14-1) 235
Cin   D9  R19/56  P(36-17-2) 123
Pit-Cunningham 107C

SD    0   14  0   0   14
Den   7   0   6   14  27
SD    D6  R27/101 P(33-19-2) 214
Den   D21 R34/137 P(31-18-0) 177

KC    0   7   0   3   10
NYG   14  6   3   3   26
KC    D19 R37/215 P(28-15-1) 150
NYG   D16 R39/172 P(25-15-0) 167
KC-Reed 114R
```

MONDAY, SEPTEMBER 18

```
Bal   0   7   0   27  34
NE    6   7   0   14  27
Bal   D15 R36/96  P(16-11-1) 265
NE    D23 R48/206 P(33-11-3) 223
Bal-Carr 187C; NE-Johnson 109R, Morgan 125C
```

SUNDAY, SEPTEMBER 24

```
NO    0   10  0   10  20
Cin   3   10  0   5   18
NO    D12 R29/74  P(25-14-1) 180
Cin   D14 R46/166 P(17-9-0) 117

Cle   0   6   3   0   9
Pit   3   0   6   6   15
Cle   D19 R32/97  P(32-14-2) 102
Pit   D18 R37/139 P(32-14-2) 200

LARm  7   3   0   0   10
Hou   3   0   3   0   6
LARm  D26 R50/175 P(26-17-0) 213
Hou   D10 R23/112 P(20-10-1) 120

Mia   3   0   0   0   3
Phi   0   7   0   10  17
Mia   D9  R23/82  P(17-6-3) 61
Phi   D20 R50/222 P(19-13-0) 115
Phi-Montgomery 111R

Atl   2   0   7   0   9
TB    7   0   0   7   14
Atl   D13 R40/148 P(24-12-3) 69
TB    D10 R34/94  P(24-7-0) 82
Atl-Stanback 112R

NYJ   3   0   0   0   3
Was   0   13  7   3   23
NYJ   D11 R25/102 P(23-10-2) 113
Was   D26 R45/256 P(30-21-0) 171
Was-Riggins 114R

Bal   0   14  3   0   17
Buf   14  10  0   0   24
Bal   D16 R35/182 P(27-10-3) 125
Buf   D12 R41/129 P(14-9-0) 118

GB    0   7   10  7   24
SD    0   7   0   3   10
GB    D9  R33/118 P(14-7-1) 9
SD    D20 R30/91  P(37-22-5) 154

NE    0   7   7   7   21
Oak   14  0   0   0   14
NE    D22 R41/207 P(25-14-3) 197
Oak   D14 R34/83  P(21-13-3) 153
NE-Francis 126C
```

```
SL    7   3   2   0   12
Dal   7   0   14  0   21
SL    D16 R36/115 P(30-15-0) 195
Dal   D21 R37/216 P(26-16-0) 173
SL-Gray 107C; Dal-Dorsett 154R

Den   7   3   7   0   6   23
KC    7   3   7   0   0   17
Den   D25 R58/228 P(21-12-1) 129
KC    D13 R41/155 P(10-7-1) 89

Det   3   3   10  0   16
Sea   0   7   0   21  28
Det   D15 R30/132 P(26-16-0) 129
Sea   D21 R36/87  P(17-12-1) 158
Det-Bussey 120R

SF    0   3   0   7   10
NYG   14  3   10  0   27
SF    D13 R29/104 P(33-11-4) 87
NYG   D22 R52/256 P(26-12-2) 126
```

MONDAY, SEPTEMBER 25

```
Min   14  0   7   3   24
ChiB  7   3   3   7   20
Min   D17 R39/153 P(20-14-1) 142
ChiB  D23 R36/90  P(37-22-2) 188
```

SUNDAY, OCTOBER 1

```
SL    0   10  0   0   10
Mia   10  0   7   7   24
SL    D19 R36/140 P(33-21-0) 211
Mia   D16 R34/123 P(21-12-1) 144

SD    0   13  7   3   23
NE    7   0   7   14  28
SD    D18 R38/160 P(20-14-1) 162
NE    D19 R32/101 P(29-17-1) 198
NE-Jackson 106C

Pit   7   7   14  0   28
NYJ   0   10  7   0   17
Pit   D20 R39/138 P(26-17-1) 189
NYJ   D18 R36/155 P(23-9-1) 142
Pit-Swann 100C

Cin   0   0   9   3   12
SF    7   14  0   7   28
Cin   D18 R32/103 P(35-17-5) 219
SF    D11 R42/113 P(17-8-2) 66

Sea   0   0   0   7   7
Den   0   0   14  14  28
Sea   D19 R25/92  P(39-25-3) 231
Den   D24 R41/204 P(23-16-3) 169

Oak   3   3   3   10  6   25
ChiB  0   9   0   10  0   19
Oak   D26 R39/156 P(43-25-0) 255
ChiB  D17 R37/156 P(18-12-2) 122
Oak-Lane 144R; ChiB-Payton 123R

Det   0   0   7   7   14
GB    7   14  7   7   35
Det   D14 R31/126 P(25-14-1) 101
GB    D16 R32/221 P(20-15-2) 261
GB-Middleton 148R, Thompson 111C

LARm  6   14  0   6   26
NO    0   7   6   7   20
LARm  D15 R33/124 P(21-10-1) 157
NO    D19 R31/143 P(28-17-1) 172

NYG   14  0   0   6   20
Atl   0   9   7   7   23
NYG   D8  R25/87  P(21-7-0) 59
Atl   D22 R51/152 P(26-14-0) 198
Atl-Francis 153C

KC    0   0   0   7   13
Buf   0   21  7   0   28
KC    D15 R38/238 P(21-9-0) 70
Buf   D17 R39/117 P(18-15-1) 175
KC-Lane 144R; Buf-Chandler 116C

Min   7   10  0   7   24
TB    0   7   0   0   7
Min   D19 R37/111 P(31-20-1) 208
TB    D18 R24/87  P(35-16-3) 283
TB-Owens 132C, Williams 311P

Hou   0   0   6   10  16
Cle   3   7   0   3   13
Hou   D20 R46/164 P(29-14-1) 215
Cle   D11 R23/78  P(32-12-3) 104
```

```
Phi   0   0   0   17  17
Bal   0   14  0   0   14
Phi   D21 R43/245 P(19-12-0) 117
Bal   D13 R32/89  P(24-13-1) 145
Phi-Montgomery 144R
```

MONDAY, OCTOBER 2

```
Dal   0   0   3   2   5
Was   3   3   0   3   9
Dal   D19 R33/109 P(30-13-1) 200
Was   D16 R36/127 P(22-11-1) 124
```

SUNDAY, OCTOBER 8

```
Den   0   0   0   0   0
SD    7   7   6   3   23
Den   D11 R16/76  P(30-8-3) 80
SD    D19 R45/128 P(34-22-1) 170

Atl   0   0   0   7   7
Pit   3   14  7   7   31
Atl   D20 R34/113 P(33-17-2) 144
Pit   D28 R44/181 P(18-13-0) 206
Pit-Harris 104R, Stallworth 114C

NYG   0   3   0   0   3
Dal   7   7   7   3   24
NYG   D10 R28/102 P(20-6-1) 40
Dal   D21 R34/157 P(33-17-1) 200
Dal-Hill 112C

Bal   7   14  3   6   30
SL    3   7   7   0   17
Bal   D14 R35/156 P(17-10-1) 66
SL    D21 R39/145 P(32-19-1) 198
SL-Gray 112C

ChiB  0   0   0   14  14
GB    0   3   14  7   24
ChiB  D21 R40/147 P(37-23-3) 210
GB    D8  R36/98  P(12-6-0) 68
ChiB-Scott 113C

Phi   0   7   0   7   14
NE    10  7   7   0   24
Phi   D17 R24/107 P(39-18-0) 186
NE    D22 R50/205 P(24-12-1) 189
NE-Morgan 104C

Buf   7   0   0   7   14
NYJ   14  21  10  0   45
Buf   D16 R35/137 P(28-12-2) 185
NYJ   D18 R45/231 P(10-4-0) 47

Hou   0   10  7   0   17
Oak   0   7   7   7   21
Hou   D20 R51/205 P(17-9-1) 168
Oak   D22 R33/123 P(23-14-3) 156
Hou-Campbell 104R

Was   0   7   0   14  21
Det   3   6   3   7   19
Was   D12 R25/76  P(27-12-2) 208
Det   D19 R46/231 P(30-15-1) 143

TB    0   10  0   20  30
KC    3   0   0   10  13
TB    D21 R39/121 P(23-14-0) 226
KC    D15 R40/120 P(28-15-2) 136

SF    0   3   7   0   10
LARm  7   10  7   3   27
SF    D13 R32/132 P(26-7-1) 83
LARm  D23 R41/227 P(29-14-2) 177

Min   0   14  14  0   28
Sea   13  6   0   10  29
Min   D28 R31/117 P(37-27-0) 274
Sea   D23 R32/184 P(28-17-2) 248

Cle   7   7   3   7   24
NO    0   9   0   7   16
Cle   D20 R44/179 P(17-11-1) 92
NO    D21 R22/67  P(39-24-1) 231
```

MONDAY, OCTOBER 9

```
Cin   0   0   0   0   0
Mia   7   14  0   0   21
Cin   D15 R24/94  P(35-19-2) 153
Mia   D18 R41/183 P(24-14-0) 152
Mia-Williams 107R
```

SUNDAY, OCTOBER 15

```
Pit   6   7   14  7   34
Cle   0   7   0   7   14
Pit   D20 R38/168 P(21-10-0) 153
Cle   D19 R38/132 P(35-19-2) 228
```

```
KC    0   0   0   6   6
Oak   7   7   14  0   28
KC    D14 R28/92  P(30-17-1) 163
Oak   D20 R39/136 P(22-16-0) 218

Buf   3   7   0   0   10
Hou   0   7   3   7   17
Buf   D15 R38/149 P(22-9-0) 80
Hou   D17 R39/178 P(22-12-0) 152
Hou-Campbell 105R

Sea   0   14  7   7   28
GB    28  3   14  0   45
Sea   D23 R39/194 P(31-17-2) 289
GB    D20 R36/190 P(19-12-1) 179
Sea-Sims 104R, Largent 127C; Zorn 308P; GB-Middleton 121R

TB    0   0   0   14  14
NYG   3   0   0   14  17
TB    D20 R43/163 P(27-7-2) 100
NYG   D16 R41/170 P(15-6-2) 48
TB-DuBose 109R

LARm  0   13  0   21  34
Min   3   7   0   7   17
LARm  D23 R43/180 P(27-13-2) 146
Min   D13 R24/42  P(34-17-1) 125

NYJ   10  10  0   13  33
Bal   0   0   3   7   10
NYJ   D17 R49/204 P(13-8-0) 199
Bal   D23 R29/149 P(41-23-3) 211
NYJ-Long 136R, Walker 154C; Bal-Doughty 101C

Mia   7   14  7   0   28
SD    0   7   14  0   21
Mia   D17 R35/139 P(21-13-0) 122
SD    D20 R34/117 P(30-22-2) 287
SD-Fouts 313P

NO    7   0   0   7   14
SF    0   0   0   7   7
NO    D12 R55/175 P(4-2-0) 31
SF    D12 R27/74  P(37-16-2) 101

Dal   0   7   14  0   21
SL    7   7   0   7   21
Dal   D24 R32/131 P(41-23-2) 287
SL    D17 R47/134 P(29-17-2) 236
Dal-Pearson 101C

Det   0   0   0   0   0
Atl   0   7   0   7   14
Det   D13 R26/22  P(29-14-2) 147
Atl   D15 R35/126 P(17-11-0) 122

NE    3   0   0   7   10
Cin   0   3   0   0   3
NE    D19 R35/136 P(27-13-2) 162
Cin   D17 R25/73  P(42-24-3) 206

Was   0   3   0   7   10
Phi   7   3   0   7   17
Was   D14 R33/135 P(21-8-2) 138
Phi   D17 R42/180 P(15-7-1) 82
Phi-Montgomery 125R
```

MONDAY, OCTOBER 16

```
ChiB  0   0   7   0   7
Den   3   0   0   13  16
ChiB  D15 R40/210 P(26-15-2) 137
Den   D18 R36/135 P(24-15-1) 173
ChiB-Payton 157R
```

SUNDAY, OCTOBER 22

```
Den   3   3   0   0   6
Bal   0   7   0   0   7
Den   D17 R38/151 P(33-20-0) 190
Bal   D11 R30/106 P(21-13-1) 131

Cin   0   0   0   0   0
Buf   0   3   0   2   5
Cin   D16 R33/141 P(27-13-3) 103
Buf   D12 R37/170 P(21-12-0) 56
Buf-Brown 100R

NO    0   3   0   7   10
LARm  3   0   0   0   3
NO    D12 R27/40  P(22-11-0) 78
LARm  D20 R40/158 P(30-15-3) 184

SL    0   0   3   0   3
NYJ   3   7   13  0   23
SL    D13 R32/160 P(27-10-2) 144
NYJ   D21 R49/170 P(22-11-0) 123
SL-Gray 105C
```

```
ChiB  0   10  6   3   19
TB    7   6   14  1   28
ChiB  D15 R29/120 P(29-15-3) 203
TB    D21 R48/146 P(20-11-1) 173
ChiB-Scott 105C

Atl   7   0   0   13  20
SF    7   7   0   6   20
Atl   D16 R34/114 P(20-15-0) 216
SF    D21 R44/208 P(22-8-0) 53
Atl-Jackson 113C

Was   0   6   0   0   6
NYG   10  0   0   7   17
Was   D15 R31/118 P(39-16-3) 165
NYG   D12 R45/179 P(10-3-0) 105

Oak   0   0   0   7   7
Sea   7   14  6   0   27
Oak   D18 R19/70  P(31-19-4) 177
Sea   D27 R44/204 P(27-14-1) 170

SD    0   0   7   7   14
Det   17  14  0   0   31
SD    D16 R20/89  P(30-13-4) 215
Det   D29 R39/273 P(32-22-1) 188
SD-Joiner 110C

Cle   3   0   0   0   3
KC    3   7   0   7   17
Cle   D11 R32/111 P(18-10-2) 51
KC    D17 R47/190 P(13-8-0) 48

Mia   7   7   3   7   24
NE    0   17  7   9   33
Mia   D20 R26/144 P(36-22-2) 189
NE    D24 R46/225 P(22-10-1) 168
Mia-Williams 116R; NE-Ivory 113R

GB    0   7   0   7   14
Min   0   14  0   7   21
GB    D14 R25/129 P(32-20-1) 118
Min   D22 R32/60  P(43-26-0) 234

Phi   0   0   7   0   7
Dal   0   14  0   0   14
Phi   D15 R31/117 P(27-14-0) 145
Dal   D15 R34/191 P(22-10-0) 87
Phi-Krepfle 100C
```

MONDAY, OCTOBER 23

```
Hou   0   10  7   7   24
Pit   0   10  0   7   17
Hou   D22 R43/169 P(19-13-0) 160
Pit   D21 R31/113 P(33-17-1) 215
Pit-Grossman 116C
```

THURSDAY, OCTOBER 26

```
Min   14  7   0   0   21
Dal   0   3   7   0   10
Min   D21 R38/144 P(32-18-0) 137
Dal   D13 R24/92  P(27-12-2) 147
Min-Foreman 101R
```

SUNDAY, OCTOBER 29

```
TB    0   0   0   7   7
GB    0   0   0   9   9
TB    D7  R34/72  P(17-5-1) 98
GB    D18 R45/91  P(33-16-1) 158

SL    0   13  0   3   16
Phi   0   10  0   0   10
SL    D15 R35/94  P(24-12-3) 260
Phi   D19 R28/132 P(40-21-3) 220
Phi-Carmichael 126C

NYJ   7   0   0   14  21
NE    21  20  7   7   55
NYJ   D20 R27/104 P(33-17-2) 172
NE    D26 R43/240 P(21-16-0) 289
NE-Jackson 118C, Grogan 281P

Bal   0   6   0   2   8
Mia   2   24  0   0   26
Bal   D13 R33/192 P(14-7-4) 39
Mia   D14 R39/120 P(23-15-2) 189
Bal-Washington 126R

Buf   6   7   0   7   20
Cle   7   13  14  7   41
Buf   D28 R25/82  P(38-17-2) 201
Cle   D28 R47/309 P(17-14-0) 223
Buf-Chandler 114C; Cle-Pruitt 173R

KC    7   0   7   0   14
Pit   7   13  7   0   27
KC    D20 R39/181 P(28-15-2) 141
Pit   D17 R40/135 P(15-8-2) 80
```

```
Hou   0  0  0 13  13
Cin   7  0 14  7  28
Hou D15 R27/137 P(27-13-0) 119
Cin D18 R48/189 P(16-11-0) 247
   Hou-Campbell 102R;
   Cin-Curtis 130C

SF    7  6  0  7  20
Was   0 14 14 10  38
SF  D24 R34/125 P(33-19-3) 201
Was D21 R44/119 P(23-12-0) 177

Det   7 14  0  0  21
ChiB  3  7  0  7  17
Det D23 R38/134 P(33-20-1) 181
ChiB D21 R34/167 P(27-15-1) 191
   ChiB-Payton 119C

SD    7  0  7 13  27
Oak   0 20  0  3  23
SD  D22 R42/161 P(28-11-1) 163
Oak D15 R37/147 P(17-11-1)  87

NYG   0 10  0  0  10
NO    0  7  7 14  28
NYG D17 R38/204 P(26-10-3) 129
NO  D22 R43/161 P(21-13-0) 139

Den   3  7  7  3  20
Sea   7  7  0  3  17
Den D25 R57/278 P(28-11-0) 145
Sea D19 R32/118 P(40-15-4) 140
```

MONDAY, OCTOBER 30
```
LARm  0  7  0  0   7
Atl   0  6  0  9  15
LARm D14 R33/94 P(27-15-3) 140
Atl  D9 R39/98 P(17-8-1)  87
```

SUNDAY, NOVEMBER 5
```
Det   0  7  0  0   7
Min   0  3  7  7  17
Det D11 R18/70 P(30-18-0) 105
Min D22 R48/124 P(29-18-4) 188

GB    3  0  0  0   3
Phi   0  7  3  0  10
GB  D15 R36/174 P(33-18-3) 211
Phi D10 R30/51 P(20-13-1)  97

NE    0  7  0  7  14
Buf   3  0  0  7  10
NE  D20 R47/279 P(17-5-1)  53
Buf D15 R34/140 P(23-14-1) 107
   NE-Ivory 128R

Cle   0  7  3  0  10
Hou   0  0  7  7  14
Cle D10 R22/28 P(29-15-1) 166
Hou D18 R41/156 P(25-17-2) 236
   Cle-Newsome 124C

SF    3  0  0  7  10
Atl   0  7  7  7  21
SF  D13 R39/118 P(21-6-1)  50
Atl D16 R34/62 P(29-16-1) 184

TB    0  6  3 14  23
LARm  3 14  3  6  26
TB  D18 R35/209 P(22-11-3) 132
LARm D15 R30/124 P(27-15-0) 220
   TB-Bell 104R; LARm-Miller 105C

NYG   0  0  3  7  10
SL    7 13  0  0  20
NYG D22 R38/142 P(32-12-3) 169
SL  D17 R37/139 P(23-12-0) 211
   SL-Tilley 101C

Cin   0  0 13  0  13
SD    3  3 13  3  22
Cin D12 R25/156 P(26-11-3)  92
SD  D20 R49/173 P(25-13-0) 149
   Cin-Turner 116R; SD-Mitchell 101R

NO    0  7  0  7  14
Pit   3  0 10  7  20
NO  D23 R32/81 P(32-22-1) 340
Pit D20 R34/145 P(23-16-1) 200
   NO-Manning 344P

Sea   7  7 14  3  31
ChiB  0  6 10 13  29
Sea D23 R38/224 P(24-13-0) 165
ChiB D26 R33/174 P(40-21-3) 227
   Sea-Smith 152R, Largent 126C;
   ChiB-Payton 109R

Dal   0  3  6  7  16
Mia  17  3  0  3  23
Dal D19 R26/89 P(30-19-2) 239
Mia D13 R28/54 P(18-12-0) 152
```

```
Oak   0  7  0 13  20
KC    0  0  3  7  10
Oak D20 R44/176 P(24-17-3) 153
KC  D12 R32/107 P(27-9-3)  95
   Oak-Whittington 134R, Casper 112C

NYJ   0 17  7  7  31
Den  14 14  0  0  28
NYJ D19 R43/202 P(27-12-2) 201
Den D15 R34/133 P(29-15-3) 173
   NYJ-Walker 133C
```

MONDAY, NOVEMBER 6
```
Was   3  7  7  0  17
Bal   0  7  7  7  21
Was D13 R36/139 P(23-8-2) 116
Bal D16 R45/145 P(19-10-1) 160
   Bal-Carr 124C
```

SUNDAY, NOVEMBER 12
```
Bal   7  3  0  7  17
Sea   0  0  0  7   7
Bal D14 R40/133 P(19-13-0) 115
Sea D18 R31/168 P(24-10-1)  95
   Sea-Sims 106R

NYG   0  3  3  7  0  13
Was   0  3  3  7  3  16
NYG D17 R44/153 P(20-12-2) 147
Was D23 R32/99 P(35-22-0) 219

NYJ   0  3  6  0   9
Phi   0  7  3  7  17
NYJ D15 R33/108 P(23-10-2) 140
Phi D19 R43/154 P(23-13-1) 129

Pit   0  0  7  0   7
LARm  3  0  7  0  10
Pit D12 R25/59 P(25-11-3) 115
LARm D14 R44/192 P(27-14-0) 121
   LARm-Cappelletti 106R

TB    0 13  0 10  23
Det   7 14  7  6  34
TB  D18 R26/113 P(23-13-0)  89
Det D20 R38/211 P(24-15-1) 193
   Det-King 104R, Hill 106C

Atl   0  3  3 14  20
NO    3 14  0  0  17
Atl D16 R22/74 P(33-16-1) 210
NO  D22 R49/166 P(31-17-0) 181
   NO-Chandler 117C

ChiB  0  7  0  7  14
Min   7 10  0  0  17
ChiB D15 R42/186 P(18-8-3)  47
Min D18 R33/90 P(37-24-1) 223
   ChiB-Payton 127R

Dal   7 14 14  7  42
GB    7  0  0  7  14
Dal D32 R58/313 P(34-21-0) 224
GB  D9 R17/66 P(26-7-2)  76
   Dal-Dorsett 149R, Newhouse 101R

Den   0  7  6  6  19
Cle   0  0  0  7   7
Den D17 R36/109 P(28-18-0) 214
Cle D14 R30/110 P(27-16-2) 145
   Den-Moses 115C

SL    3  6  7  0  16
SF    3  0  7  0  10
SL  D21 R41/114 P(38-17-2) 221
SF  D16 R37/118 P(27-10-2) 146

KC    0  6  7 10  23
SD    6  7  7  3  29
KC  D26 R53/205 P(28-19-0) 198
SD  D24 R50/197 P(20-13-0) 188
   KC-Morgado 115R;
   SD-Mitchell 144R, Jefferson 130C

Hou   0  0  7 19  26
NE    6 17  0  0  23
Hou D24 R46/128 P(28-15-1) 194
NE  D16 R35/144 P(18-9-2) 130

Mia   7 15  3  0  25
Buf   7 10  0  7  24
Mia D20 R42/193 P(21-13-0)  96
Buf D28 R28/170 P(27-15-0) 114
   Mia-Williams 144R;
   Buf-Brown 114R
```

MONDAY, NOVEMBER 13
```
Oak   6 14  7  7  34
Cin   0  0  7 14  21
Oak D11 R29/98 P(19-9-0) 103
Cin D27 R30/93 P(51-30-4) 355
   Cin-Curtis 101C, Anderson 388P
```

SUNDAY, NOVEMBER 19
```
NO    7  0  0  0   7
Dal   0 14  7  6  27
NO  D15 R17/62 P(39-24-3) 215
Dal D17 R42/198 P(15-9-0) 106
   Dal-Dorsett 152R

SL   14 10  3  0  27
Was   0 10  7  0  17
SL  D18 R47/166 P(29-13-2) 137
Was D14 R16/18 P(39-16-3) 193
   SL 1-Morris 123R;
   as-McDaniel 119C

NE    0 10  0  9  19
NYJ   7  0  3  7  17
NE  D18 R52/225 P(18-10-1)  99
NYJ D12 R24/69 P(23-14-3) 139

Sea   3  7  3  0  13
KC    0  3  0  7  10
Sea D13 R29/132 P(23-14-0) 125
KC  D20 R41/124 P(33-18-0) 231

Atl   0  7  0  7  14
ChiB  0  3 10  0  13
Atl D21 R42/149 P(32-16-1) 195
ChiB D13 R42/111 P(14-7-0)  72
   Atl-Ryckman 107C

Cle   0 17 14 14  45
Bal   7  3  7  7  24
Cle D20 R40/171 P(22-15-0) 309
Bal D22 R23/62 P(38-24-1) 267
   Cle-Hill 113C, Rucker 123C,
   Sipe 309P

Buf   0  0  3  7  10
TB    7  3  7 14  31
Buf D18 R26/79 P(38-18-4) 132
TB  D20 R46/205 P(14-7-1) 107

Det   0 14  3  0  17
Oak   6  7 14  2  29
Det D18 R29/120 P(31-18-2) 208
Oak D24 R46/161 P(22-13-0) 119

Phi   0  6  0 13  19
NYG  14  0  3  0  17
Phi D23 R45/150 P(31-15-3) 164
NYG D14 R31/100 P(23-13-1) 181
   Phi-Carmichael 105C

LARm  7  7  7 10  31
SF    0  7  7 14  28
LARm D21 R37/131 P(25-17-0) 255
SF  D16 R45/165 P(15-9-1)  83
   LARm-Jessie 116C; SF-Hofer 104R

Cin   3  3  0  0   6
Pit   0  7  0  0   7
Cin D15 R31/97 P(29-14-2) 149
Pit D14 R34/70 P(30-12-4)  84

SD    7  0  6  0  13
Min   7  0  0  0   7
SD  D19 R43/124 P(23-13-2) 163
Min D17 R21/63 P(42-27-2) 209

GB    3  0  0  0   3
Den   0  0 14  2  16
GB  D13 R31/84 P(17-9-1) 179
Den D19 R46/215 P(17-12-0) 144
   Den-Lytle 110R, Moses 101C
```

MONDAY, NOVEMBER 20
```
Mia   7  7  7  9  30
Hou   7  7  7 14  35
Mia D27 R32/127 P(33-23-1) 327
Hou D23 R42/265 P(15-10-1) 141
   Mia-Griese 349P;
   Hou-Campbell 199R
```

THURSDAY, NOVEMBER 23
```
Den   7  0  7  0  14
Det   7  0  3  7  17
Den D16 R31/128 P(22-11-0) 105
Det D15 R37/139 P(18-10-1) 105
```

```
Was   0  0  3  7  10
Dal  13  7 10  7  37
Was D11 R29/81 P(24-10-0) 120
Dal D26 R54/289 P(19-9-1) 218
   Dal-Laidlaw 122R, Pearson 116C
```

SUNDAY, NOVEMBER 26
```
NO    7  7  3  0  17
Atl   3  0 10  0  13
NO  D13 R33/130 P(24-13-1) 205
Atl D25 R35/130 P(44-23-3) 255
   NO-Childs 100C

NYG   7  3  7  0  17
Buf   7  0  7 27  41
NYG D15 R33/99 P(24-15-1) 222
Buf D27 R49/366 P(15-9-1)  99
   NYG-Middleton 110R;
   Buf-Hooks 115R, Miller 208R

SD    0  0  0  0   0
KC    0 17  3  3  23
SD  D11 R20/75 P(41-15-5) 164
KC  D19 R47/238 P(21-13-0) 115
   KC-McKnight 104R

Phi   0  7  0  7  14
SL    3  0  0  7  10
Phi D15 R37/95 P(25-13-0) 149
SL  D17 R25/102 P(37-20-2) 192

TB    0  3  0  0   3
ChiB  0  0  7  7  14
TB  D6 R22/99 P(13-5-0)  -7
ChiB D17 R60/251 P(7-4-1)  50
   ChiB-Harper 144R, Payton 105R

NYJ   0  3 14  7  24
Mia   0  6  0  7  13
NYJ D18 R35/85 P(26-17-1) 222
Mia D18 R27/106 P(34-20-3) 150
   NYJ-Walker 126C

Sea   7  0  0 10  17
Oak   0 10  0  6  16
Sea D20 R34/84 P(44-23-1) 263
Oak D20 R34/133 P(31-17-0) 198

Min   3  0  0  7  10
GB    0  7  3  0  10
Min D15 R42/111 P(37-20-4) 182
GB  D16 R54/154 P(23-11-0) 164
   GB-Middleton 110R

LARm  3  6  0 10  19
Cle  10  7  7  6  30
LARm D24 R31/148 P(45-22-4) 215
Cle D16 R32/130 P(24-15-1) 227

NE   14  7  7  7  35
Bal   7  0  0  0   7
NE  D15 R36/228 P(20-9-1) 232
Bal D18 R34/145 P(28-15-2) 155
   NE-Morgan 170C

Cin   7  0  0  3  10
Hou   0 14  3  0  17
Cin D19 R36/142 P(25-17-0)  95
Hou D17 R37/153 P(20-9-2) 147
   Hou-Campbell 122R
```

MONDAY, NOVEMBER 27
```
Pit   3 14  0  7  24
SF    0  0  7  0   7
Pit D22 R53/212 P(21-13-1) 168
SF  D12 R29/67 P(28-10-5)  74
   Pit-Swann 134C
```

SUNDAY, DECEMBER 3
```
GB   10  7  0  0  17
TB    0  7  0  0   7
GB  D11 R30/65 P(19-13-1) 108
TB  D20 R40/177 P(32-14-2) 144

Phi   7 20  0  0  27
Min  14  0  7  7  28
Phi D18 R35/163 P(29-13-1) 213
Min D23 R25/80 P(56-30-3) 289
   Phi-Montgomery 115R,
   Carmichael 115C;
   Min-Rashad 107C, Tarkenton 289P

LARm  3  7  0 10  20
NYG   0  7  3  7  17
LARm D13 R36/98 P(25-12-0)  94
NYG D18 R38/185 P(34-12-4) 148
```

```
Bal   3  7  6  0  16
NYJ   7  7  7  3  24
Bal D17 R34/169 P(27-14-1)  75
NYJ D19 R42/202 P(18-7-2) 175
   NYJ-Long 107R

Buf   0  7  0  0   7
KC    7  0  7  0  14
Buf D16 R34/136 P(25-14-3) 207
KC  D21 R47/241 P(21-12-1)  99
   Buf-Lewis 126C

Cle   0 10  7  7  24
Sea  14  9  7 17  47
Cle D24 R24/193 P(41-21-3) 259
Sea D28 R42/183 P(27-17-1) 255
   Cle-Pruitt 113R; Sea-Largent 108C

Det   0  7  0  7  14
SL    0  7  7  7  21
Det D16 R32/105 P(28-12-5) 119
SL  D18 R36/133 P(24-12-1) 151

SF    0  7  0  7  14
NO    3 14  0  7  24
SF  D14 R38/159 P(27-9-1) 128
NO  D24 R39/193 P(34-22-1) 190
   NO-Chandler 103C

Den   0  7  7  7  21
Oak   0  6  0  0   6
Den D16 R43/147 P(11-6-0)  45
Oak D16 R30/101 P(24-34-3) 178
   Den-Chandler 103C

Atl   0  7  0  0   7
Cin   3  7 14 13  37
Atl D10 R22/83 P(29-10-3)  91
Cin D20 R38/223 P(30-14-0) 137

NE    7  3  0  0  10
Dal   3  0  7  7  17
NE  D16 R36/213 P(29-13-2) 150
Dal D17 R35/99 P(27-15-0) 230

Pit   3  0  3  7  13
Hou   0  0  0  3   3
Pit D17 R48/177 P(24-11-1)  74
Hou D9 R26/81 P(27-10-3)  83
   Pit-Harris 102R

Mia   0  6 10  0  16
Was   0  0  0  0   0
Mia D19 R43/153 P(27-14-1) 142
Was D16 R27/123 P(28-12-4) 167
```

MONDAY, DECEMBER 4
```
ChiB  0  0  7  0   7
SD   17  6 10  7  40
ChiB D7 R27/80 P(17-5-2)  32
SD  D24 R43/150 P(30-19-3) 331
   SD-Jefferson 155C
```

SATURDAY, DECEMBER 9
```
Bal   0  7  6  0  13
Pit   7 14  7  7  35
Bal D12 R27/86 P(19-8-2)  43
Pit D20 R48/139 P(21-12-2) 234

Min   0  0  7  0   7
Det  14 14  3 14  45
Min D16 R18/22 P(36-20-2) 213
Det D22 R30/157 P(33-26-1) 350
   Det-Danielson 352P
```

SUNDAY, DECEMBER 10
```
KC    3  0  0  0   3
Den   7  0 10  7  24
KC  D13 R27/99 P(29-19-1) 100
Den D20 R35/190 P(23-20-1) 271
   Den-Odoms 165C

Oak   0  0  6  0   6
Mia   3  0  3 17  23
Oak D21 R30/85 P(38-24-5) 234
Mia D13 R29/97 P(26-14-2) 163

Buf   0 10  7  7  24
NE    7  0  7 12  26
Buf D16 R35/184 P(24-9-1) 123
NE  D24 R51/249 P(21-13-0) 154

GB    0  0  0  0   0
ChiB  0  7  7  0  14
GB  D11 R27/78 P(25-8-1)  83
ChiB D17 R47/174 P(19-9-1) 119
```

SL 0 0 0 0 0
NYG 10 0 0 7 **17**
SL D17 R33/143 P(38-15-1) 198
NYG D14 R51/231 P(14-8-1) 24
NYG-Kotar 118R

TB 0 3 0 0 3
SF 0 3 0 3 **6**
TB D13 R28/113 P(27-13-1) 83
SF D17 R32/90 P(32-21-4) 149

Dal 14 0 10 7 **31**
Phi 7 0 0 6 13
Dal D17 R41/146 P(20-13-0) 169
Phi D11 R28/139 P(26-9-2) 85

Was 0 10 0 7 17
Atl 7 3 7 3 **20**
Was D15 R34/146 P(34-13-0) 165
Atl D17 R34/113 P(37-16-0) 140

NYJ 0 10 0 24 0 34
Cle 7 10 10 7 3 **37**
NYJ D20 R21/103 P(44-22-4) 266
Cle D29 R46/236 P(32-20-1) 283
Cle-Pruitt 138R

Hou 7 3 0 7 **17**
NO 0 0 7 5 12
Hou D16 R43/125 P(18-12-0) 119
NO D18 R19/56 P(37-25-1) 241

Sea 7 3 0 0 10
SD 3 17 0 17 **37**
Sea D17 R28/136 P(33-14-2) 103
SD D20 R29/95 P(34-23-1) 286

MONDAY, DECEMBER 11

Cin 0 14 3 3 **20**
LARm 13 3 3 0 19
Cin D18 R38/161 P(27-13-2) 206
LARm D21 R32/136 P(37-16-2) 279

SATURDAY, DECEMBER 16

Pit 7 14 0 0 **21**
Den 0 0 7 10 17
Pit D14 R38/116 P(19-13-2) 144
Den D19 R26/74 P(26-15-1) 226
Den-Moses 116C

ChiB 7 0 7 0 **14**
Was 0 3 0 7 10
ChiB D10 R40/170 P(10-6-3) 44
Was D16 R31/124 P(31-21-2) 181

SUNDAY, DECEMBER 17

KC 3 7 7 2 19
Sea 7 13 0 3 **23**
KC D18 R36/253 P(19-5-3) 44
Sea D26 R45/204 P(30-19-1) 252
KC-Reed 121R; Sea-Hunter 133R

SD 0 21 10 14 **45**
Hou 0 17 0 7 24
SD D24 R39/149 P(41-21-2) 368
Hou D14 R27/117 P(33-16-2) 153
SD-Jefferson 149C, Fouts 369P

Dal 7 3 13 7 **30**
NYJ 0 0 0 7 7
Dal D23 R52/190 P(24-15-1) 156
NYJ D11 R19/68 P(28-8-3) 69
Dal-Dorsett 121R

Atl 7 7 7 0 21
SL 0 28 7 7 **42**
Atl D18 R18/41 P(42-21-3) 270
SL D24 R36/79 P(42-23-1) 348
Atl-Jackson 102C; SL-Stief 183C, Tilley 105C, Hart 333P

GB 0 0 7 7 14
LARm 7 0 14 10 **31**
GB D17 R29/75 P(27-13-3) 166
LARm D18 R44/178 P(26-9-1) 121
LARm-Bryant 121R

NO 3 0 7 7 **17**
TB 3 0 0 7 10
NO D24 R38/171 P(36-25-2) 250
TB D10 R22/102 P(23-7-0) 75

NYG 3 0 0 0 3
Phi 13 0 0 7 **20**
NYG D11 R18/48 P(30-18-3) 175
Phi D16 R52/238 P(13-4-1) 64
Phi-Hogan 100R, Montgomery 130R

Buf 0 7 7 7 **21**
Bal 0 7 0 7 14
Buf D16 R45/193 P(13-3-0) 53
Bal D18 R46/139 P(16-5-1) 33
Buf-Miller 123R

Cle 6 0 10 0 16
Cin 0 17 7 24 **48**
Cle D17 R37/222 P(23-6-2) 106
Cin D27 R48/245 P(24-16-1) 249
Cle-Pruitt 182R; Cin-Johnson 160R, Curtis 138C

SF 7 0 0 7 14
Det 3 17 7 6 **33**
SF D20 R49/231 P(21-8-3) 138
Det D17 R32/69 P(30-15-1) 152

Min 0 6 0 14 20
Oak 21 0 3 3 **27**
Min D21 R21/90 P(38-23-5) 299
Oak D16 R50/168 P(27-16-0) 143
Min-Rashad 115C, Tarkenton 316P

MONDAY, DECEMBER 18

NE 0 0 0 3 3
Mia 7 6 7 3 **23**
NE D16 R27/77 P(34-19-3) 219
Mia D12 R36/114 P(13-12-0) 171

1979 NFL

SATURDAY, SEPTEMBER 1

Det 0 7 0 9 16
TB 10 14 0 7 **31**
Det D16 R32/142 P(36-13-0) 89
TB D18 R48/229 P(20-5-0) 105
TB-Eckwood 121R

SUNDAY, SEPTEMBER 2

Dal 3 7 3 9 **22**
SL 0 7 7 7 21
Dal D24 R41/161 P(35-21-0) 294
SL D17 R32/237 P(29-12-2) 105
Dal-Newhouse 108R, Hill 113C; SL-Anderson 193R

Cle 7 3 9 3 3 **25**
NYJ 3 7 3 9 0 22
Cle D24 R38/131 P(36-21-3) 292
NYJ D24 R51/229 P(31-17-2) 161
Cle-Logan 115C, Sipe 302P

Atl 0 20 7 7 6 **40**
NO 7 21 3 3 0 34
Atl D35 R47/257 P(38-22-1) 295
NO D23 R32/188 P(31-15-2) 324
Atl-Andrews 167R, Jenkins 131C, Bartkowski 312P; NO-Muncie 161R, Chandler 205C

GB 0 0 3 0 3
ChiB 0 6 0 0 **6**
GB D9 R21/77 P(24-10-0) 72
ChiB D17 R51/183 P(25-15-1) 117
ChiB-Payton 125R

Bal 0 0 0 0 0
KC 0 7 0 7 **14**
Bal D15 R25/83 P(43-24-1) 225
KC D12 R36/166 P(18-9-0) 45
Bal-Washington 130C

Mia 0 0 3 6 **9**
Buf 0 7 0 0 7
Mia D20 R40/175 P(27-14-1) 118
Buf D5 R25/45 P(13-7-1) 76

Oak 0 10 14 0 **24**
LARm 7 10 0 0 17
Oak D16 R35/130 P(26-11-0) 110
LARm D21 R32/123 P(41-21-3) 217

Hou 6 0 7 16 **29**
Was 0 17 7 3 27
Hou D21 R45/199 P(30-12-3) 166
Was D14 R34/142 P(14-7-1) 104
Hou-Campbell 166R

SF 0 6 3 13 22
Min 0 0 14 14 **28**
SF D22 R27/98 P(42-29-2) 254
Min D22 R27/110 P(34-21-0) 287
SF-Solomon 107C; Min-Rashad 152C, Kramer 297P

Cin 0 0 0 0 0
Den 0 3 7 0 **10**
Cin D16 R30/95 P(27-17-0) 137
Den D22 R40/199 P(21-13-0) 200

SD 0 13 10 10 **33**
Sea 3 7 0 6 16
SD D22 R33/139 P(30-21-1) 217
Sea D19 R31/181 P(28-16-3) 153

NYG 3 0 7 7 17
Phi 0 23 0 0 **23**
NYG D18 R26/63 P(40-20-2) 222
Phi D16 R34/154 P(21-12-0) 161

MONDAY, SEPTEMBER 3

Pit 0 6 0 7 3 **16**
NE 7 6 0 0 0 13
Pit D20 R38/118 P(29-15-0) 191
NE D16 R37/162 P(33-11-2) 82

THURSDAY, SEPTEMBER 6

LARm 6 0 0 7 **13**
Den 0 2 7 0 9
LARm D15 R37/96 P(32-23-0) 181
Den D12 R25/73 P(29-13-1) 106

SUNDAY, SEPTEMBER 9

Cle 10 7 3 7 **27**
KC 0 0 7 17 24
Cle D23 R37/164 P(35-19-1) 238
KC D19 R32/101 P(35-16-1) 147

Sea 0 3 7 0 10
Mia 0 9 3 7 **19**
Sea D19 R28/119 P(46-21-3) 226
Mia D15 R30/117 P(27-15-0) 198
Mia-Harris 117C

Hou 0 0 0 7 7
Pit 7 3 14 14 **38**
Hou D12 R39/102 P(27-8-5) 22
Pit D17 R29/82 P(29-12-2) 174

Cin 0 10 7 7 24
Buf 0 10 21 20 **51**
Cin D16 R33/134 P(27-13-2) 201
Buf D23 R36/209 P(21-16-0) 246
Cin-Brooks 156C; Buf-Butler 116C

Dal 3 3 7 8 **21**
SF 3 7 0 3 13
Dal D19 R36/98 P(34-20-0) 249
SF D16 R24/63 P(33-19-1) 231

Was 0 17 7 3 **27**
Det 3 0 0 21 24
Was D23 R44/182 P(20-14-0) 139
Det D20 R39/217 P(22-11-3) 157

SL 0 14 13 0 **27**
NYG 14 0 0 0 14
SL D23 R53/189 P(24-12-2) 159
NYG D10 R18/40 P(36-14-2) 88
SL-Anderson 109R

Min 0 7 0 0 7
ChiB 0 10 9 7 **26**
Min D13 R29/88 P(19-10-1) 71
ChiB D15 R39/236 P(19-9-1) 93
ChiB-Payton 182R

TB 0 13 0 13 3 **29**
Bal 17 0 0 9 0 26
TB D17 R34/98 P(29-10-2) 196
Bal D18 R35/92 P(37-22-2) 114

NO 3 9 0 7 19
GB 0 0 21 7 **28**
NO D29 R36/185 P(45-28-2) 289
GB D21 R30/194 P(15-9-1) 115
NO-Childs 112C; GB-Atkins 110R

NYJ 3 0 0 0 3
NE 14 21 7 14 **56**
NYJ D12 R23/89 P(24-12-3) 45
NE D30 R45/232 P(25-18-1) 365
NE-Jackson 121C, Morgan 102C, Grogan 315P

Oak 0 3 7 0 10
SD 14 7 2 7 **30**
Oak D16 R26/97 P(41-20-2) 186
SD D20 R38/140 P(30-15-0) 209

MONDAY, SEPTEMBER 10

Atl 0 7 0 7 **14**
Phi 3 7 0 0 10
Atl D14 R33/145 P(16-10-1) 102
Phi D16 R28/57 P(37-16-2) 184
Atl-Andrews 121R; Phi-Carmichael 127C

SUNDAY, SEPTEMBER 16

Bal 10 0 0 0 10
Cle 0 3 7 3 **13**
Bal D13 R33/98 P(29-17-0) 185
Cle D16 R32/124 P(32-14-2) 197

KC 0 6 0 0 6
Hou 7 10 0 3 **20**
KC D16 R34/183 P(27-11-4) 97
Hou D16 R44/172 P(18-12-0) 173
Hou-Campbell 131R

TB 0 7 14 0 **21**
GB 3 0 0 7 10
TB D19 R45/235 P(25-12-1) 132
GB D18 R30/89 P(34-24-0) 185

Den 7 3 7 0 3 **20**
Atl 0 10 0 7 0 17
Den D18 R43/168 P(22-13-1) 201
Atl D19 R28/56 P(29-20-0) 326
Atl-Francis 138C, Jenkins 129C, Bartkowski 326P

Pit 7 0 0 17 **24**
SL 9 6 6 0 21
Pit D25 R42/164 P(35-17-2) 234
SL D12 R31/106 P(25-12-0) 106

Buf 6 6 7 0 19
SD 7 6 7 7 **27**
Buf D14 R26/60 P(29-16-0) 238
SD D18 R36/245 P(13-8-0) 94
Buf-Brown 157C; SD-Williams 157R

Mia 0 7 0 20 **27**
Min 3 6 3 0 12
Mia D22 R42/136 P(22-15-2) 183
Min D14 R28/137 P(25-14-3) 106

Oak 0 0 7 3 10
Sea 7 3 10 7 **27**
Oak D25 R25/102 P(39-25-2) 329
Sea D19 R37/103 P(23-14-0) 316
Oak-Branch 156C, Stabler 343P; Sea-Largent 139C

ChiB 7 0 6 7 20
Dal 7 3 7 7 **24**
ChiB D14 R36/200 P(16-5-1) 118
Dal D26 R46/214 P(31-18-0) 206
ChiB-Payton 134R; Dal-Dorsett 108R

SF 10 0 0 14 24
LARm 0 14 7 6 **27**
SF D17 R30/119 P(30-16-0) 120
LARm D25 R45/222 P(29-17-1) 165
LARm-Bryant 106R

Phi 3 10 3 10 **26**
NO 0 7 0 7 14
Phi D18 R43/199 P(23-12-0) 162
NO D12 R21/75 P(25-15-2) 160

Det 0 7 0 3 10
NYJ 0 14 3 14 **31**
Det D12 R23/53 P(30-19-1) 176
NYJ D22 R48/209 P(13-9-0) 178
NYJ-Walker 177C

NE 0 7 7 6 **20**
Cin 0 0 7 7 14
NE D18 R42/165 P(27-11-0) 167
Cin D17 R32/166 P(21-7-0) 32

MONDAY, SEPTEMBER 17

NYG 0 0 0 0 0
Was 3 14 7 3 **27**
NYG D13 R29/113 P(24-7-2) 93
Was D22 R43/141 P(29-18-2) 141

SUNDAY, SEPTEMBER 23

ChiB 0 6 3 7 16
Mia 3 0 14 14 **31**
ChiB D16 R28/85 P(25-16-2) 155
Mia D23 R39/193 P(17-12-0) 196
Mia-Moore 121C

Atl 0 3 13 7 23
Det 7 3 0 14 **24**
Atl D11 R28/144 P(25-12-1) 126
Det D22 R36/151 P(36-19-0) 249

GB 0 14 0 7 0 21
Min 7 0 7 7 6 **27**
GB D14 R37/141 P(15-10-0) 108
Min D24 R43/161 P(26-19-2) 215
Min-Rashad 136C

SD 0 14 0 7 21
NE 17 3 0 7 **27**
SD D15 R18/39 P(35-21-2) 193
NE D20 R43/151 P(23-13-2) 140

NYJ 3 21 0 7 31
Buf 6 13 21 6 **46**
NYJ D22 R42/265 P(21-11-3) 151
Buf D25 R38/149 P(30-19-0) 348
Buf-Butler 255C, Ferguson 367P

Oak 0 0 0 7 7
KC 14 0 7 14 **35**
Oak D10 R14/31 P(24-13-3) 90
KC D22 R55/222 P(17-9-2) 70

Hou 0 10 17 0 3 **30**
Cin 14 10 0 3 0 27
Hou D19 R44/177 P(33-15-2) 184
Cin D21 R47/165 P(21-11-1) 100
Hou-Campbell 158R

Was 14 0 0 3 **17**
SL 0 0 7 0 7
Was D11 R40/100 P(16-8-1) 91
SL D23 R33/95 P(43-24-1) 281
SL-Stief 125C, Tilley 114C, Hart 306P

Sea 10 10 14 0 34
Den 0 10 21 6 **37**
Sea D22 R36/153 P(34-17-3) 197
Den D23 R31/90 P(27-17-2) 254
Sea-Largent 110C; Den-Odoms 125C

LARm 6 0 0 0 6
TB 0 21 0 0 **21**
LARm D11 R27/110 P(35-17-1) 76
TB D15 R45/148 P(20-5-1) 101

Phi 7 7 3 0 **17**
NYG 3 3 0 7 13
Phi D19 R44/187 P(19-11-1) 139
NYG D14 R32/146 P(22-10-2) 83
Phi-Montgomery 126R

Bal 10 0 3 0 13
Pit 7 3 0 7 **17**
Bal D17 R36/97 P(34-17-2) 188
Pit D17 R26/157 P(30-19-3) 235
Pit-Thornton 129R

NO 0 13 14 3 **30**
SF 7 7 0 7 21
NO D28 R43/174 P(28-20-0) 338
SF D17 R20/78 P(33-18-3) 263
NO-Chandler 127C, Manning 355P; SF-Solomon 144C

MONDAY, SEPTEMBER 24

Dal 7 0 0 0 7
Cle 20 0 0 6 **26**
Dal D20 R30/123 P(39-21-2) 271
Cle D15 R33/82 P(28-15-1) 229
Dal-Pearson 109C, Staubach 303P

SUNDAY, SEPTEMBER 30

SL 0 0 0 0 0
LARm 7 7 0 7 **21**
SL D9 R25/82 P(33-14-3) 149
LARm D24 R46/186 P(29-16-0) 206

Cle 0 10 0 0 10
Hou 10 14 7 0 **31**
Cle D24 R24/108 P(43-20-3) 201
Hou D17 R42/194 P(13-8-0) 76

NYG 0 0 7 7 14
NO 0 10 7 7 **24**
NYG D13 R34/122 P(29-12-2) 163
NO D21 R35/167 P(34-17-2) 195

Was 3 10 3 0 **16**
Atl 7 0 0 0 7
Was D20 R48/131 P(26-19-1) 228
Atl D14 R22/70 P(26-6-3) 86
Was-Buggs 134C

Min 0 3 7 3 **13**
Det 0 0 3 7 10
Min D18 R40/137 P(23-13-2) 150
Det D11 R25/96 P(25-13-2) 97
Min-White 100C

Den 0 3 0 0 3
Oak 7 7 0 13 **27**
Den D21 R22/81 P(41-19-1) 210
Oak D16 R37/90 P(18-11-0) 187

SF 0 3 6 0 9
SD 0 17 0 14 **31**
SF D14 R26/120 P(23-13-2) 122
SD D22 R30/71 P(34-26-1) 246

Cin 3 3 7 0 13
Dal 7 14 10 7 **38**
Cin D20 R28/104 P(36-19-3) 181
Dal D24 R42/194 P(26-13-1) 176
Cin-Bass 108C; Dal-Dorsett 119R

KC 0 10 0 14 **24**
Sea 0 3 0 3 6
KC D11 R32/215 P(12-8-1) 15
Sea D18 R32/134 P(38-23-1) 178
KC-McKnight 147R

Buf 0 14 17 0 **31**
Bal 3 3 0 7 13
Buf D16 R30/66 P(23-14-1) 308
Bal D18 R36/84 P(38-22-1) 265
Buf-Lewis 120C, Ferguson 317P

TB 0 10 0 7 **17**
ChiB 0 3 3 7 13
TB D18 R45/214 P(31-14-2) 159
ChiB D11 R25/82 P(23-12-2) 152
TB-Eckwood 120R

Pit 0 0 7 7 14
Phi 0 7 10 0 **17**
Pit D19 R29/139 P(26-12-2) 169
Phi D18 R44/159 P(20-11-2) 148
Pit-Stallworth 102C

Mia 10 0 0 17 27
NYJ 7 13 6 7 **33**
Mia D21 R23/68 P(45-22-1) 286
NYJ D16 R47/168 P(10-6-1) 186
Mia-Moore 127C; NYJ-Gaffney 104C

MONDAY, OCTOBER 1
NE 7 7 0 0 14
GB 7 13 7 0 **27**
NE D26 R33/162 P(37-18-5) 239
GB D19 R35/118 P(29-17-2) 199

SUNDAY, OCTOBER 7
Dal 3 20 7 6 **36**
Min 7 3 10 0 20
Dal D25 R46/279 P(23-15-0) 167
Min D14 R22/61 P(34-18-0) 179
Dal-Dorsett 145R; Min-White 131C

LARm 0 28 0 7 **35**
NO 0 0 3 7 17
LARm D22 R46/141 P(25-12-2) 154
NO D13 R25/102 P(32-15-5) 132

ChiB 0 0 0 7 **7**
Buf 0 0 0 0 0
ChiB D15 R62/240 P(8-4-0) 18
Buf D7 R24/64 P(21-5-1) 42
ChiB-Payton 155R

SD 0 0 0 0 0
Den 0 0 7 0 **7**
SD D19 R26/69 P(45-27-3) 305
Den D11 R34/160 P(14-8-0) 33
SD-Joiner 115C, Fouts 305P

NYJ 0 3 3 2 8
Bal 10 0 0 0 **10**
NYJ D19 R43/184 P(29-12-3) 174
Bal D14 R22/44 P(36-23-1) 232

KC 0 10 0 0 **10**
Cin 0 7 0 0 7
KC D11 R36/99 P(12-7-0) 101
Cin D14 R41/155 P(23-12-0) 66

Was 0 0 10 0 10
Phi 7 7 14 0 **28**
Was D22 R38/161 P(32-19-1) 157
Phi D29 R39/209 P(12-8-0) 143
Was-Riggins 115R; Phi-Montgomery 127R

TB 0 7 0 7 14
NYG 0 14 0 3 **17**
TB D15 R27/91 P(38-14-3) 182
NYG D15 R54/202 P(12-6-0) 18
NYG-Taylor 148R

GB 0 7 0 0 7
Atl 10 5 3 7 **25**
GB D17 R24/117 P(30-13-2) 158
Atl D19 R41/152 P(29-14-0) 134

SL 0 7 3 14 **24**
Hou 0 14 0 3 17
SL D26 R43/194 P(39-24-3) 253
Hou D13 R15/57 P(29-15-2) 165
SL-Anderson 109R

Det 0 3 14 0 17
NE 0 14 0 10 **24**
Det D9 R27/55 P(24-8-2) 156
NE D22 R45/140 P(23-11-1) 111

Pit 21 9 7 14 **51**
Cle 0 14 7 14 35
Pit D21 R45/361 P(21-12-0) 161
Cle D24 R24/93 P(42-23-3) 365
Pit-Harris 153R; Cle-Sipe 351R

Sea 14 7 7 7 **35**
SF 7 3 0 14 24
Sea D21 R36/148 P(20-13-0) 162
SF D29 R34/172 P(40-31-1) 292
SF-DeBerg 306P

MONDAY, OCTOBER 8
Mia 0 0 3 0 3
Oak 0 0 13 0 **13**
Mia D18 R35/169 P(19-10-2) 57
Oak D13 R30/97 P(22-12-0) 112

SUNDAY, OCTOBER 14
SF 3 0 7 6 16
NYG 2 27 0 3 **32**
SF D21 R30/116 P(48-27-2) 237
NYG D21 R27/97 P(33-18-0) 280
SF-Hofer 104C; NYG-Gray 169C, Simms 300P

NO 0 0 21 21 **42**
TB 0 0 7 7 14
NO D22 R48/234 P(15-12-0) 163
TB D16 R25/161 P(40-16-3) 213
TB-Bell 101R

Det 0 9 7 0 16
GB 0 10 7 7 **24**
Det D13 R31/93 P(27-14-1) 154
GB D18 R42/189 P(17-9-1) 109
GB-Simpson 121R

Atl 0 0 12 7 19
Oak 10 9 10 21 **50**
Atl D27 R22/121 P(44-25-3) 313
Oak D25 R40/156 P(23-17-0) 191
Atl-Cain 110C

Pit 3 0 0 7 10
Cin 7 20 0 7 **34**
Pit D16 R18/64 P(40-21-2) 263
Cin D19 R45/170 P(20-9-2) 114
Pit-Stallworth 126C

NE 14 0 3 10 **27**
ChiB 0 0 0 7 7
NE D25 R47/142 P(35-21-2) 218
ChiB D5 R22/73 P(15-8-0) 96

Phi 7 7 10 0 **24**
SL 3 3 7 7 20
Phi D18 R39/139 P(23-14-2) 123
SL D18 R37/131 P(26-14-2) 191
Phi-Montgomery 117R

Hou 7 7 14 0 **28**
Bal 3 3 7 3 16
Hou D16 R49/220 P(16-6-2) 174
Bal D16 R31/107 P(27-13-3) 82
Hou-Campbell 149R

Was 0 3 3 7 **13**
Cle 0 6 3 0 9
Was D13 R32/89 P(24-14-1) 221
Cle D21 R35/167 P(25-13-1) 137

Buf 0 7 0 0 7
Mia 7 10 0 0 **17**
Buf D11 R22/70 P(21-11-1) 108
Mia D14 R46/178 P(12-7-1) 101

Sea 0 3 0 7 10
SD 7 0 7 6 **20**
Sea D19 R25/133 P(43-19-1) 147
SD D19 R29/96 P(35-28-0) 295
SD-Jefferson 137C, Fouts 318P

LARm 0 6 0 0 6
Dal 14 0 7 0 **30**
LARm D11 R15/59 P(30-10-2) 99
Dal D23 R50/201 P(22-15-0) 202
Dal-Dorsett 103R

Den 3 7 7 7 **24**
KC 0 0 10 0 10
Den D21 R39/137 P(30-17-1) 207
KC D16 R27/98 P(29-13-1) 68
Den-Moses 107C

MONDAY, OCTOBER 15
Min 0 0 0 7 7
NYJ 0 7 0 7 **14**
Min D20 R23/54 P(48-28-4) 256
NYJ D16 R41/183 P(13-9-0) 62

SUNDAY, OCTOBER 21
Det 0 0 7 0 7
NO 7 3 7 0 **17**
Det D13 R16/80 P(31-14-4) 117
NO D18 R44/159 P(22-17-3) 125

SD 7 7 17 9 **40**
LARm 7 0 0 9 16
SD D17 R35/65 P(32-17-2) 326
LARm D24 R27/104 P(42-21-4) 233
SD-Jefferson 112C, Joiner 168C, Fouts 326P

SL 6 7 0 0 13
Dal 3 14 2 3 **22**
SL D18 R33/137 P(38-16-0) 98
Dal D12 R32/155 P(25-11-2) 164
SL-Anderson 105R; Dal-Dorsett 111R

Hou 0 7 0 7 14
Sea 7 7 6 14 **34**
Hou D16 R21/83 P(38-20-1) 160
Sea D21 R35/151 P(26-18-1) 240
Sea-Largent 135C

NYG 0 0 14 7 21
KC 3 7 7 0 17
NYG D13 R28/100 P(26-12-1) 126
KC D28 R42/169 P(38-22-2) 294
NYG-Gray 107C; KC-Reed 106R, Reed 103C

Phi 0 0 0 7 7
Was 0 7 7 3 **17**
Phi D12 R16/61 P(27-12-2) 139
Was D20 R49/211 P(24-15-2) 116
Was-Riggins 120R

GB 0 0 3 0 3
TB 7 7 0 7 **21**
GB D16 R24/38 P(35-22-3) 261
TB D15 R48/228 P(10-6-0) 85
GB-Coffman 106C; TB-Bell 167R

Oak 0 10 3 6 19
NYJ 7 0 7 14 **28**
Oak D25 R27/113 P(47-29-5) 346
NYJ D16 R33/167 P(18-9-1) 161
Oak-van Eeghen 108C, Stabler 360P

Mia 10 3 0 0 13
NE 0 0 7 14 **28**
Mia D13 R29/135 P(27-12-3) 69
NE D17 R44/129 P(25-17-0) 170

Cin 7 0 13 7 28
Cle 7 0 7 14 **28**
Cin D20 R29/102 P(32-20-0) 293
Cle D22 R32/124 P(34-18-3) 191
Cin-Bass 100C, Curtis 108C, Anderson 318P; Cle-Pruitt 135R, Sipe 197P

Bal 0 0 7 7 **14**
Buf 0 0 7 6 13
Bal D12 R35/110 P(25-8-1) 151
Buf D20 R24/82 P(39-19-0) 242
Buf-Lewis 158C

ChiB 7 7 3 10 27
Min 3 7 7 13 **30**
ChiB D23 R49/204 P(30-16-3) 292
Min D15 R21/54 P(43-19-1) 213
ChiB-Payton 111R, Baschnagel 104C; Min-Kramer 218P

Atl 0 9 0 6 15
SF 7 0 7 6 **20**
SF D13 R26/95 P(28-14-1) 119
Atl D22 R38/160 P(38-25-1) 237

MONDAY, OCTOBER 22
Den 7 0 0 0 7
Pit 7 21 0 14 **42**
Den D16 R17/53 P(36-18-2) 276
Pit D27 R42/236 P(27-21-1) 294
Den-Moses 133C; Pit-Harris 121R

THURSDAY, OCTOBER 25
SD 6 0 16 0 22
Oak 14 10 7 14 **45**
SD D22 R22/82 P(42-23-3) 298
Oak D19 R39/137 P(17-13-0) 202
SD-Jefferson 109C, Joiner 107C, Fouts 303P

SUNDAY, OCTOBER 28
Dal 0 3 0 3 3
Pit 0 7 7 0 **14**
Dal D16 R23/79 P(42-18-1) 199
Pit D16 R35/173 P(25-11-0) 115
Pit-Harris 102R

Cle 10 0 7 21 **38**
SL 6 7 0 7 20
Cle D27 R42/226 P(28-20-0) 192
SL D16 R25/109 P(31-16-2) 173

NO 7 7 0 0 **14**
Was 3 7 0 0 10
NO D14 R38/102 P(16-11-0) 131
Was D15 R36/178 P(16-8-1) 47

Buf 0 0 6 14 **20**
Det 14 0 3 0 17
Buf D18 R20/105 P(35-17-2) 319
Det D20 R41/208 P(18-14-0) 169
Buf-Lewis 190C, Ferguson 339P; Det-Bussey 139R

NE 13 0 6 7 26
Bal 14 3 7 7 **31**
NE D19 R31/110 P(36-15-1) 298
Bal D23 R37/140 P(31-18-1) 256
NE-Morgan 151C, Grogan 317P

NYJ 7 3 0 14 0 24
Hou 0 17 0 3 **27**
NYJ D20 R38/132 P(34-13-2) 225
Hou D17 R33/112 P(36-18-1) 199
NYJ-Walker 111C

TB 3 0 3 6 **12**
Min 0 10 0 0 10
TB D20 R40/102 P(25-12-0) 258
Min D21 R33/111 P(36-22-1) 219
TB-Hagins 149C; Min-Rashad 117C

KC 0 0 0 0 0
Den 7 7 6 0 **20**
KC D12 R28/102 P(32-18-2) 108
Den D20 R29/112 P(36-22-1) 86
Den-Odoms 114C

Phi 3 0 3 7 13
Cin 17 7 10 3 **37**
Phi D17 R24/73 P(34-19-1) 187
Cin D17 R37/198 P(21-12-0) 92
Cin-Griffin 103R

ChiB 7 7 7 7 **28**
SF 3 14 3 7 27
ChiB D20 R37/207 P(19-10-1) 145
SF D28 R30/107 P(41-26-2) 348
ChiB-Payton 162R; SF-DeBerg 348P

NYG 3 7 3 7 **20**
LARm 0 0 7 7 14
NYG D10 R35/110 P(23-9-1) 124
LARm D20 R31/95 P(36-21-4) 271

GB 0 0 7 0 7
Mia 0 13 14 0 **27**
GB D9 R14/53 P(20-12-1) 143
Mia D28 R50/195 P(28-19-0) 280
GB-Coffman 116C; Mia-Harris 180C

MONDAY, OCTOBER 29
Sea 0 21 3 7 **31**
Atl 7 7 0 14 28
Sea D19 R46/205 P(26-14-0) 206
Atl D19 R26/153 P(26-16-2) 162
Sea-Doornink 122R, Largent 127C

SUNDAY, NOVEMBER 4
SD 10 0 3 7 **20**
KC 0 0 0 14 14
SD D23 R30/86 P(44-28-2) 229
KC D17 R26/119 P(26-15-2) 164

Min 0 0 0 0 0
SL 3 7 14 13 **37**
Min D23 R23/70 P(49-27-3) 263
SL D29 R45/325 P(24-14-2) 142
SL-Anderson 164R

NYJ 0 21 3 3 **27**
GB 6 9 7 0 22
NYJ D20 R52/246 P(16-8-1) 136
GB D22 R26/108 P(37-22-2) 287
NYJ-Gaines 125R; GB-Lofton 114C

Cle 7 3 0 14 **24**
Phi 6 7 6 0 19
Cle D23 R39/154 P(35-20-3) 187
Phi D21 R40/236 P(23-16-2) 199
Cle-Pruitt 104R, Rucker 106C; Phi-Montgomery 197R

Det 0 0 0 7 7
ChiB 7 7 14 7 **35**
Det D11 R25/82 P(27-11-4) 117
ChiB D21 R45/161 P(28-18-0) 147
ChiB-Payton 113R

TB 7 0 0 7 14
Atl 0 3 0 14 **17**
TB D26 R26/74 P(24-11-1) 194
Atl D18 R46/212 P(20-11-1) 54

Dal 3 3 10 0 **16**
NYG 0 7 0 7 14
Dal D19 R32/106 P(30-20-0) 238
NYG D12 R32/116 P(16-10-1) =133
Dal-Pearson 124C

LARm 14 7 3 0 **24**
Sea 0 0 0 0 0
LARm D20 R63/303 P(30-20-1) 172
Sea D1 R12/23 P(17-2-0) -30

NO 0 0 0 7 7
Den 3 0 0 7 **10**
NO D13 R30/102 P(26-13-1) 117
Den D19 R36/148 P(26-17-3) 201

NE 0 6 10 10 **26**
Buf 6 0 0 0 6
NE D20 R37/111 P(35-19-1) 327
Buf D15 R22/83 P(33-16-2) 181
NE-Morgan 158C, Grogan 350P

Cin 0 21 0 7 28
Bal 7 10 7 14 **38**
Cin D15 R25/67 P(28-17-2) 284
Bal D23 R37/140 P(31-18-0) 215
Cin-Curtis 144C, Ross 102C, Anderson 320P; Bal-Washington 106R

SF 0 10 0 0 10
Oak 9 7 7 0 **23**
SF D19 R25/156 P(43-21-2) 207
Oak D19 R43/134 P(24-16-1) 175
SF-Hofer 106R

Was 0 7 0 0 7
Pit 7 17 7 7 **38**
Was D19 R24/88 P(34-15-2) 149
Pit D26 R40/173 P(34-20-1) 372
Pit-Stallworth 126C, Swann 106C, Bradshaw 311P

MONDAY, NOVEMBER 5
Hou 0 3 6 0 **9**
Mia 3 0 0 3 6
Hou D10 R46/179 P(10-6-0) 11
Mia D13 R26/102 P(26-14-2) 138
Hou-Campbell 120R

SUNDAY, NOVEMBER 11
LARm 9 7 7 0 23
ChiB 0 7 7 13 **27**
LARm D16 R40/245 P(15-7-2) 76
ChiB D19 R35/82 P(33-16-0) 190
LARm-Tyler 129R; ChiB-Watts 147C

SL 7 0 0 21 28
Was 0 7 10 13 **30**
SL D23 R37/147 P(37-17-3) 184
Was D22 R47/154 P(28-16-0) 173
SL-Anderson 105R

```
Atl    0   0   3   0    3
NYG    0  10   7   7   24
Atl  D16 R30/120  P(32-13-2) 129
NYG  D15 R27/75   P(33-14-0) 144
Atl-Jenkins 105C

Sea    7   9   0  13   29
Cle    3   3  14   7   24
Sea  D24 R42/189  P(28-16-0) 238
Cle  D21 R31/215  P(29-13-2) 158
Cle-Pruitt 141R

Oak    7   7   0   3   17
Hou    7   7  14   3   31
Oak  D21 R27/81   P(35-21-2) 213
Hou  D16 R38/143  P(14-8-0)  205
Hou-Campbell 107R,
Burrough 109C

TB     0   3   3  10   16
Det    7   0   7   0   14
TB   D17 R34/104  P(34-17-1) 182
Det  D16 R27/38   P(32-19-1) 229
Det-Scott 148C

Bal    0   0   0   0    0
Mia    7   6   3   3   19
Bal  D11 R30/82   P(30-18-2) 149
Mia  D13 R32/124  P(25-12-2) 123
Bal-Washington 121C

Buf    0   7   0   7   14
NYJ    0   6   0   6   12
Buf  D15 R44/138  P(17-11-0) 132
NYJ  D16 R27/67   P(25-16-3) 170

Min    0   0   0   7    7
GB     7   6   0   6   19
Min  D23 R25/117  P(38-27-2) 230
GB   D19 R40/178  P(19-11-3) 115
GB-Middleton 135R

Pit   10  10   7   3   30
KC     0   0   3   0    3
Pit  D20 R44/127  P(29-17-2) 228
KC   D8  R26/65   P(20-9-1)   62

SF     3   3  10   7   20
NO    17   7   7   0   31
SF   D26 R29/195  P(39-22-1) 198
NO   D27 R37/215  P(22-15-0) 153
SF-Hofer 147R; NO-Muncie 117R

NE     3   0   3   0   10
Den   24  14   0   7   45
NE   D8  R23/58   P(30-11-1)  34
Den  D21 R44/107  P(19-13-0) 182

SD     0  13   3  10   26
Cin   14   0   0   0   14
SD   D19 R21/54   P(40-21-4) 270
Cin  D19 R46/194  P(22-9-0)   60
```

MONDAY, NOVEMBER 12

```
Phi    7  10   7   7   31
Dal    0   0  14   0   21
Phi  D17 R38/170  P(35-14-0) 158
Dal  D17 R27/123  P(35-19-1) 285
Phi-Montgomery 127R;
Dal-Hill 213C, Staubach 308P
```

SUNDAY, NOVEMBER 18

```
Pit    0   0   7   0    7
SD     7  14   7   7   35
Pit  D14 R29/66   P(38-20-5) 125
SD   D14 R30/98   P(25-11-2) 120
SD-Jefferson 106C

NYG    0   0   3   0    3
TB     0  14  10   7   31
NYG  D14 R23/95   P(33-17-2) 105
TB   D20 R39/187  P(24-12-0) 176
TB-Bell 152R

KC     3   7  14   0   24
Oak    0   7   7   7   21
KC   D20 R49/241  P(16-11-0) 122
Oak  D21 R17/68   P(44-27-2) 271
KC-Williams 109R

NO     7   7   3   7   24
Sea    7  17   0  14   38
NO   D24 R26/134  P(24-21-0) 286
Sea  D28 R33/130  P(34-25-0) 391
NO-Childs 121C; Sea-Largent 146C,
Zorn 384P

Det    0   0   7   0    7
Min    0   0  14   0   14
Det  D13 R19/65   P(32-14-2) 102
Min  D20 R49/174  P(30-14-0) 121
```

```
SL     0   6   7   0   13
Phi    3   3   3   7   16
SL   D12 R24/134  P(32-19-0) 172
Phi  D14 R40/157  P(27-11-0) 130
SL-Anderson 112R;
Phi-Montgomery 118R

GB     3   9   0   0   12
Buf    3   3   6   7   19
GB   D14 R28/95   P(26-13-3) 195
Buf  D20 R42/187  P(28-17-0) 213
GB-Lofton 112C; Buf-Lewis 116C

Dal    0   3   3  14   20
Was    7   7  10  10   34
Dal  D27 R28/85   P(28-9-0)  299
Was  D19 R33/104  P(24-15-0) 202
Dal-Pearson 134C; Was-Buggs 111C

Cin    0   7   7   7   21
Hou    7  28   0   7   42
Cin  D17 R31/200  P(30-14-5) 106
Hou  D26 R39/163  P(30-20-1) 322
Cin-Johnson 113R;
Hou-Campbell 112R,
Burrough 123C

NYJ    6   0   0   7   13
ChiB   7   7   6   3   23
NYJ  D20 R36/140  P(24-15-2) 180
ChiB D19 R44/146  P(18-12-0) 108

Den    3  14  21   0   38
SF     0  21   0   7   28
Den  D22 R28/144  P(35-19-1) 225
SF   D18 R34/74   P(41-23-0) 166

Bal    7   7   0   7   21
NE     6  27  10   7   50
Bal  D24 R24/89   P(37-26-0) 174
NE   D22 R42/248  P(20-14-0) 169
NE-Ivory 116R

Mia    0   3   7  14   24
Cle    7   0   7  16   30
Mia  D15 R30/121  P(31-16-3) 196
Cle  D25 R31/148  P(42-23-0) 345
Mia-Harris 119C; Cle-Rucker 177C,
Sipe 358P
```

MONDAY, NOVEMBER 19

```
Atl    0   0   7   7   14
LARm   7   7   6   0   20
Atl  D19 R36/201  P(25-11-2) 135
LARm D18 R41/179  P(22-9-1)  160
Atl-Bean 104R; LARm-Tyler 111R
```

THURSDAY, NOVEMBER 22

```
Hou    7  10   6   7   30
Dal   14   7   0   3   24
Hou  D17 R41/224  P(17-9-0)  154
Dal  D20 R30/92   P(30-21-2) 279
Hou-Campbell 195R;
Dal-Pearson 118C

ChiB   0   0   0   0    0
Det    3  10   0   7   20
ChiB D14 R23/78   P(39-19-2) 142
Det  D18 R34/106  P(30-16-3) 225
```

SUNDAY, NOVEMBER 25

```
Phi    7   0   7   7   21
GB     3   0   0   7   10
Phi  D16 R36/229  P(18-8-0)  118
GB   D25 R34/118  P(49-24-0) 213
Phi-Harris 137R

Min    0  14   9   0   23
TB     6   3   7   6   22
Min  D16 R29/110  P(26-15-0) 158
TB   D22 R42/183  P(38-19-0) 242
TB-Bell 101R

Cle   10  10   7   3   30
Pit    3  10   0  17   33
Cle  D22 R24/62   P(38-23-1) 283
Pit  D36 R45/255  P(44-30-1) 351
Cle-Logan 135C, Sipe 333P;
Pit-Harris 151R, Bradshaw 364P

KC     7   0   0   0    7
SD     0   0   7   0   28
KC   D9  R21/65   P(22-14-1) 125
SD   D30 R32/135  P(43-27-1) 325
SD-Joiner 123C, Fouts 350P
```

```
Mia    7   7   7   7   28
Bal    7   7   0  10   24
Mia  D16 R32/100  P(24-12-0) 165
Bal  D27 R31/119  P(43-25-2) 297
Mia-Harris 116C; Bal-Landry 304P

SL     0   7  14   7   28
Cin    7  21   3   3   34
SL   D26 R27/163  P(38-23-2) 317
Cin  D20 R41/189  P(24-15-0) 153
SL-Tilley 134C, Hart 329P;
Cin-Griffin 105R

NO     7  20   0  10   37
Atl    0   6   0   0    6
NO   D18 R36/139  P(33-16-0) 276
Atl  D13 R20/102  P(24-18-1) 135
NO-Chandler 103C, Childs 117C

Oak    0   7   0   7   14
Den    0   0   0  14   14
Oak  D15 R30/173  P(28-16-1) 203
Den  D22 R37/215  P(35-13-3) 167
Oak-Russell 100R; Den-Lytle 102R

LARm   3  10  13   0   26
SF     3   0   3   0   20
LARm D18 R41/124  P(24-12-2) 198
SF   D22 R36/136  P(34-21-2) 238

Buf    0   3   3   7   16
NE     0   0   0  13   10
Buf  D18 R33/80   P(33-17-2) 201
NE   D21 R49/173  P(25-9-4)  136

Was    0   3   3   0    6
NYG    7   0   0   7   14
Was  D27 R30/121  P(23-11-0) 104
NYG  D16 R50/193  P(14-7-1)   74
NYG-Taylor 126R
```

MONDAY, NOVEMBER 26

```
NYJ    0   0   7   0    7
Sea    3  13  14   0   30
NYJ  D21 R33/139  P(36-19-0) 226
Sea  D25 R31/86   P(40-27-0) 313
NYJ-Barkum 103C
```

THURSDAY, NOVEMBER 29

```
NE     0  17   0   7   24
Mia    3  10  16  10   39
NE   D21 R26/93   P(39-21-2) 327
Mia  D22 R41/170  P(22-11-2) 152
NE-Jackson 105C, Morgan 124C,
Grogan 350P
```

SUNDAY, DECEMBER 2

```
Atl    7   7   7   7   28
SD     7   3   7   9   26
Atl  D22 R32/153  P(30-17-1) 222
SD   D22 R26/86   P(37-28-1) 324
Atl-Andrews 131R;
SD-Jefferson 103C, Fouts 338P

ChiB   7   7   0   0   14
TB     0   0   0   0    0
ChiB D10 R48/147  P(15-6-0)   17
TB   D13 R33/107  P(31-11-5) 131

Hou    7   0   0   0    7
Cle    0   0   0   7   14
Hou  D13 R26/121  P(31-16-1) 128
Cle  D23 R40/198  P(26-13-1) 137
Hou-Campbell 108R;
Cle-Pruitt 111R

GB     0  21   0   0   21
Was    7   0   7  24   38
GB   D19 R31/96   P(33-13-2) 178
Was  D24 R40/195  P(34-21-1) 242
Was-Theismann 256P

Det    0   0   7   0    7
Phi    0  24  13   7   44
Det  D5  R18/53   P(28-11-1) 127
Phi  D29 R43/167  P(26-16-0) 217
Phi-Montgomery 108R

NYG    7   0   0   0    7
Dal   14   0   7   7   28
NYG  D14 R31/99   P(15-9-1)   98
Dal  D21 R44/166  P(19-11-0) 150
Dal-Dorsett 108R

SF     0   3   0   7   10
SL     0   0   7   6   13
SF   D16 R32/119  P(29-16-1) 171
SL   D16 R41/211  P(17-9-0)   75
SL-Anderson 129R
```

```
Cin    0  10   7   0   17
Pit   10  14  10   3   37
Cin  D21 R28/131  P(36-20-0) 209
Pit  D24 R32/154  P(29-17-1) 324
Cin-Curtis 119C; Pit-Swann 192C,
Bradshaw 339P

Min    7   7   0   7   21
LARm   7   7   7   6   27
Min  D26 R38/141  P(42-21-3) 268
LARm D14 R38/126  P(25-12-2) 174
Min-Rashad 102C

Bal    3   0  14   0   17
NYJ    3  17   7   3   30
Bal  D21 R24/103  P(49-29-0) 240
NYJ  D21 R45/178  P(26-12-1) 190

Den    3   0  13   3   19
Buf    0  10   0   6   16
Den  D11 R32/97   P(23-9-1)  129
Buf  D19 R35/100  P(46-27-1) 298
Buf-Ferguson 316P

Sea    0   0   7  14   21
KC    14  10   6   7   37
Sea  D21 R19/44   P(46-22-3) 231
KC   D20 R53/194  P(23-10-0) 137
Sea-Largent 120C
```

MONDAY, DECEMBER 3

```
Oak    7   7   7  21   42
NO     0  28   7   0   35
Oak  D31 R36/142  P(44-26-2) 264
NO   D33 R42/187  P(28-17-0) 141
Oak-Branch 126C, Stabler 295P;
NO-Muncie 128R, Galbreath 106C
```

SATURDAY, DECEMBER 8

```
Dal   10   0   7   7   24
Phi    3   0   7   7   17
Dal  D19 R41/185  P(21-11-0) 194
Phi  D18 R28/80   P(36-13-1) 204

Den    0  20   3   0   23
Sea    7   7   7   7   28
Den  D27 R38/141  P(41-22-2) 222
Sea  D21 R26/74   P(39-22-2) 308
Sea-McCullum 102C, Zorn 308P
```

SUNDAY, DECEMBER 9

```
Mia   14   0   7   7   28
Det    0   3   0   7   10
Mia  D22 R41/142  P(23-18-1) 179
Det  D10 R20/82   P(25-9-2)  100

NE     0  12   7   7   26
NYJ    7  10   7   3   27
NE   D19 R36/107  P(35-15-0) 213
NYJ  D20 R41/154  P(27-10-0) 127
NE-Morgan 129C

Cin   14   0   0   0   14
Was    7  14   0   7   28
Cin  D22 R29/113  P(36-20-0) 232
Was  D23 R32/125  P(34-23-2) 295

Cle    0   0   7   7   14
Oak    7   6   0   6   19
Cle  D22 R29/88   P(30-14-2) 105
Oak  D20 R37/130  P(34-23-1) 196
Cle-Pruitt 149R

TB     0   7   0   0    7
SF    10   3   0  10   23
TB   D13 R16/52   P(32-14-5) 211
SF   D21 R36/113  P(34-25-0) 214

LARm   0  28   3   3   34
Atl    0   6   0   7   13
LARm D15 R35/171  P(15-10-2) 177
Atl  D24 R32/108  P(41-24-2) 239
LARm-Tyler 138R; Atl-Francis 108C

ChiB   3   3   0   9   15
GB     0   0   7   7   14
ChiB D16 R38/161  P(25-10-1) 106
GB   D19 R23/55   P(37-20-2) 251
ChiB-Payton 115R; GB-Lofton 112C

SD    14  21   0   0   35
NO     0   0   0   0    0
SD   D31 R42/166  P(27-20-0) 234
NO   D12 R14/56   P(33-20-1) 175
SD-Jefferson 104C
```

```
Buf    0   0   0   3    3
Min    7   3   0   0   10
Buf  D18 R29/105  P(45-18-2) 186
Min  D12 R28/85   P(32-12-1) 104
Buf-Lewis 111C

NYG    0   0   6  14   20
SL     9   3   7  10   29
NYG  D15 R24/86   P(30-18-1) 171
SL   D26 R54/232  P(24-15-0) 174
SL-Anderson 140R

KC     7   0   0   3   10
Bal    7   0   0   0    7
KC   D16 R50/219  P(21-11-0)  83
Bal  D16 R29/75   P(36-16-2) 223
```

MONDAY, DECEMBER 10

```
Pit    0   0   3  14   17
Hou    0   0  10  10   20
Pit  D15 R22/120  P(29-14-2) 218
Hou  D20 R54/190  P(17-10-0) 160
Hou-Campbell 109R
```

SATURDAY, DECEMBER 15

```
NYJ    6  14   7   0   27
Mia    7   7   3   7   24
NYJ  D14 R34/96   P(22-12-3) 226
Mia  D22 R25/62   P(41-26-2) 322
Mia-Moore 102C, Strock 322P

GB     6   3   9   0   18
Det    7   0   0   6   13
GB   D20 R44/195  P(24-11-0)  92
Det  D18 R28/156  P(29-13-1)  72
```

SUNDAY, DECEMBER 16

```
Buf    0   0   0   0    0
Pit    7   7   7   7   28
Buf  D8  R24/78   P(31-11-2)  78
Pit  D24 R45/214  P(27-14-2) 201
Pit-Harris 100R

Phi    9   3   7   7   26
Hou    0  10   0  10   20
Phi  D20 R31/168  P(29-16-0) 198
Hou  D19 R40/235  P(27-12-3) 104
Hou-Campbell 134R

KC     0   0   0   0    0
TB     0   0   0   3    3
KC   D4  R22/58   P(13-7-1)   22
TB   D16 R62/224  P(13-5-2)   45
TB-Bell 137R

Was   10   7   0  17   34
Dal    0  14  14   7   35
Was  D21 R39/206  P(23-12-0) 167
Dal  D27 R30/114  P(42-24-1) 320
Was-Riggins 151R; Dal-Hill 113C,
Pearson 108C, Staubach 336P

SL     0   0   0   0    0
ChiB  14   7   7  14   42
SL   D11 R26/90   P(32-7-2)   23
ChiB D27 R45/201  P(35-19-2) 255
ChiB-Payton 157R, Watts 103C

NO     0  14   6   9   29
LARm   7   0   0   7   14
NO   D23 R54/276  P(15-10-3) 146
LARm D16 R38/176  P(26-14-2) 114
LARm-Tyler 141R

Min    6   7   3   7   23
NE     7   0  20   0   27
Min  D30 R29/154  P(61-35-1) 299
NE   D14 R24/69   P(27-13-1) 222
Min-Young 116C, Kramer 308P;
NE-Jackson 147C

Cle    6   0   0   6   12
Cin    0   6   7   3   16
Cle  D21 R26/116  P(42-20-1) 234
Cin  D15 R38/146  P(22-13-0)  50

Sea   10   7   9   3   29
Oak    7  10   0   7   24
Sea  D19 R31/94   P(35-23-1) 314
Oak  D29 R28/82   P(47-31-2) 336
Sea-McCullum 173C, Zorn 314P;
Oak-Branch 109C, Stabler 342P

Bal   10   7   7   7   31
NYG    0   7   0   0    7
Bal  D23 R50/211  P(24-17-1) 176
NYG  D10 R28/163  P(15-7-4)   32
```

SF 7 7 7 0 **21**
Atl 3 7 7 14 **31**
SF D28 R29/106 P(54-29-1) 343
Atl D20 R31/111 P(28-18-2) 152
SF-Hofer 130C, DeBerg 345P

MONDAY, DECEMBER 17
Den 7 0 0 0 7
SD 0 7 7 3 **17**
Den D20 R30/111 P(41-27-4) 224
SD D17 R33/97 P(29-17-3) 230

1980 NFL
SUNDAY, SEPTEMBER 7
ChiB 3 0 3 0 6
GB 0 6 0 0 6 **12**
ChiB D18 R43/101 P(30-17-3) 167
GB D12 R30/114 P(22-10-1) 100

NYG 7 7 17 10 **41**
SL 7 7 14 7 35
NYG D19 R40/104 P(31-16-1) 274
SL D20 R24/132 P(31-18-3) 287
NYG-Gray 174C, Simms 280P; SL-Hart 322P

TB 0 10 0 7 **17**
Cin 0 3 2 7 12
TB D13 R34/91 P(23-11-0) 155
Cin D9 R36/112 P(21-6-1) 16

Atl 6 0 7 10 23
Min 7 7 7 3 **24**
Atl D20 R32/158 P(28-14-1) 156
Min D28 R23/77 P(42-30-1) 371
Atl-Cain 123R; Min-Rashad 160C, Kramer 395P

Det 10 7 10 14 **41**
LARm 6 14 0 0 20
Det D27 R46/330 P(19-10-0) 164
LARm D24 R24/86 P(29-17-3) 169
Det-Bussey 111R, Sims 153R

SD 3 21 7 3 **34**
Sea 0 0 3 7 13
SD D22 R44/197 P(31-21-0) 224
Sea D13 R17/47 P(33-18-2) 202
SD-Cappelletti 112R, Jefferson 103C, Fouts 230P

Hou 0 0 17 0 17
Pit 17 0 0 14 **31**
Hou D16 R15/60 P(44-25-5) 232
Pit D20 R39/119 P(24-12-2) 237
Pit-Stallworth 125C

SF 0 14 6 6 **26**
NO 0 7 6 10 23
SF D21 R31/154 P(29-21-1) 196
NO D19 R22/90 P(41-25-0) 304
SF-Hofer 114C; NO-Hardy 103C, Manning 314P

Den 0 0 6 0 6
Phi 7 13 0 7 **27**
Den D14 R23/93 P(41-18-2) 140
Phi D21 R35/137 P(30-19-0) 284
Phi-Carmichael 135C

Oak 7 0 14 6 **27**
KC 7 0 0 7 14
Oak D18 R28/91 P(37-19-0) 285
KC D17 R32/113 P(28-16-3) 163
Oak-Pastorini 317P

Cle 0 3 0 14 17
NE 3 10 14 7 **34**
Cle D16 R17/48 P(35-22-0) 215
NE D27 R49/186 P(26-17-1) 266
NE-Morgan 102C

Bal 0 7 7 3 **17**
NYJ 0 0 14 0 14
Bal D23 R41/113 P(42-24-1) 239
NYJ D7 R15/39 P(26-11-4) 187

Mia 0 0 7 0 7
Buf 0 3 0 14 **17**
Mia D13 R22/90 P(26-15-4) 110
Buf D22 R43/144 P(33-21-5) 213

MONDAY, SEPTEMBER 8
Dal 7 3 0 7 **17**
Was 0 0 0 3 3
Dal D18 R44/177 P(18-10-2) 107
Was D14 R20/58 P(34-19-1) 181

THURSDAY, SEPTEMBER 11
LARm 0 3 3 3 9
TB 0 3 0 7 **10**
LARm D16 R33/169 P(29-17-4) 191
TB D12 R27/100 P(23-10-1) 83

SUNDAY, SEPTEMBER 14
NO 0 3 0 0 3
ChiB 10 3 2 7 **22**
NO D13 R22/91 P(31-17-2) 128
ChiB D15 R37/218 P(24-7-0) 115
ChiB-Payton 183R

Sea 3 10 0 4 **17**
KC 0 7 6 3 16
Sea D19 R37/122 P(27-17-1) 187
KC D17 R26/83 P(31-20-0) 155

Dal 0 10 3 7 20
Den 7 17 14 3 **41**
Dal D20 R29/110 P(34-20-1) 276
Den D19 R40/153 P(21-10-0) 190
Dal-Hill 117C

Det 3 13 6 7 **29**
GB 0 7 0 0 7
Det D19 R43/230 P(20-12-1) 229
GB D17 R23/59 P(36-18-2) 183
Det-Sims 134R

SL 0 0 14 7 21
SF 0 7 14 3 **24**
SL D21 R37/86 P(38-28-1) 256
SF D19 R25/132 P(42-25-3) 260
SF-Hofer 135C

Pit 3 10 0 7 **20**
Bal 0 7 10 0 17
Pit D22 R37/119 P(35-20-1) 273
Bal D25 R24/97 P(34-19-1) 250
Bal-Carr 108C

Cin 0 7 2 7 16
Mia 0 0 0 17 **17**
Cin D18 R40/169 P(32-17-1) 145
Mia D14 R30/118 P(25-13-1) 131

NYJ 3 0 0 7 10
Buf 0 10 10 0 **20**
NYJ D17 R26/137 P(34-19-1) 166
Buf D22 R36/155 P(29-18-0) 207

Oak 3 7 7 7 24
SD 3 7 0 14 6 **30**
Oak D25 R41/186 P(34-16-3) 249
SD D30 R32/76 P(44-29-5) 372
SD-Jefferson 110C, Winslow 132C, Fouts 387P

Phi 14 0 14 14 **42**
Min 0 7 0 0 7
Phi D28 R40/249 P(27-21-1) 280
Min D16 R14/32 P(44-20-1) 175
Phi-Montgomery 169R

Was 6 14 0 3 **23**
NYG 0 14 0 7 21
Was D18 R46/208 P(21-10-0) 118
NYG D15 R31/87 P(29-12-3) 163

Atl 14 14 3 6 **37**
NE 7 14 0 0 21
Atl D22 R41/167 P(30-19-0) 237
NE D21 R28/107 P(31-17-1) 153
Atl-Andrews 124R, Miller 117C

MONDAY, SEPTEMBER 15
Hou 0 3 7 6 **16**
Cle 0 7 0 0 7
Hou D23 R48/192 P(28-23-0) 177
Cle D13 R16/75 P(25-12-1) 106
Hou-Campbell 106R

SUNDAY, SEPTEMBER 21
Pit 0 14 7 7 28
Cin 10 3 0 17 **30**
Pit D18 R28/128 P(25-14-2) 265
Cin D17 R39/136 P(28-17-0) 173

SL 0 7 0 0 7
Det 0 10 0 10 **20**
SL D20 R18/82 P(36-22-1) 242
Det D19 R45/181 P(24-12-0) 139
SL-Tilley 128C

KC 0 6 7 0 13
Cle 0 7 13 0 **20**
KC D14 R34/94 P(26-15-0) 157
Cle D26 R33/103 P(36-23-1) 282
Cle-White 100C

TB 7 10 0 0 17
Dal 7 7 7 7 **28**
TB D22 R32/204 P(30-17-2) 238
Dal D26 R36/146 P(33-24-0) 244
TB-Giles 105C; Dal-Dorsett 100R

LARm 7 37 0 7 **51**
GB 0 0 0 7 7
GB D16 R28/60 P(31-15-5) 132
LARm D21 R41/161 P(23-16-0) 220

Buf 7 7 7 14 **35**
NO 0 19 0 7 26
Buf D26 R37/129 P(31-22-2) 281
NO D15 R17/38 P(35-24-0) 278
Buf-Butler 133C

Min 14 7 7 6 **34**
ChiB 0 0 0 14 14
Min D12 R38/161 P(17-8-1) 121
ChiB D16 R25/93 P(40-17-2) 173
Min-Brown 113R; ChiB-Watts 104C

SF 14 10 6 7 **37**
NYJ 0 3 3 21 27
SF D24 R31/144 P(29-21-0) 232
NYJ D30 R11/47 P(60-42-1) 413
NYJ-Gaines 160C, Todd 447P

Bal 0 9 0 7 16
Hou 7 7 0 7 **21**
Bal D14 R26/139 P(29-11-0) 101
Hou D27 R47/210 P(21-18-2) 182
Hou-Carpenter 114R

SD 3 24 3 0 **30**
Den 3 3 7 0 13
SD D16 R33/92 P(27-13-3) 211
Den D22 R27/153 P(43-25-6) 221
Den-Moses 103C

Was 0 7 7 7 21
Oak 7 7 7 3 **24**
Was D23 R27/84 P(36-19-1) 156
Oak D24 R46/227 P(33-17-3) 164
Oak-King 136R

Mia 3 0 0 17 **20**
Atl 0 7 3 7 17
Mia D19 R31/60 P(36-20-1) 186
Atl D18 R21/49 P(36-18-0) 310
Atl-Jenkins 136C, Bartkowski 332P

NE 3 7 7 10 **37**
Sea 3 14 0 14 31
NE D23 R49/203 P(24-15-1) 271
Sea D22 R27/134 P(37-20-1) 299
NE-Morgan 108C; Sea-Largent 127C, Zorn 312P

MONDAY, SEPTEMBER 22
NYG 3 0 0 0 3
Phi 7 14 7 7 **35**
NYG D19 R25/83 P(49-21-2) 169
Phi D23 R27/148 P(31-19-1) 234

SUNDAY, SEPTEMBER 28
NO 0 9 7 0 16
Mia 0 0 21 0 **21**
NO D17 R31/80 P(36-20-2) 183
Mia D22 R31/128 P(38-20-3) 296
Mia-Nathan 118C

LARm 14 7 0 7 **28**
NYG 0 0 0 7 7
LARm D22 R45/165 P(18-14-1) 203
NYG D13 R18/62 P(36-15-1) 160
LARm-Hill 109C

Oak 0 0 7 0 7
Buf 7 10 0 7 **24**
Oak D12 R17/70 P(20-10-2) 109
Buf D25 R49/165 P(22-17-1) 160

SD 3 14 3 0 **34**
KC 0 7 0 0 7
SD D18 R33/108 P(30-15-0) 188
KC D16 R31/92 P(34-18-1) 101

Cle 0 17 7 10 **34**
TB 6 7 0 14 27
Cle D22 R31/92 P(32-22-1) 308
TB D24 R25/80 P(56-30-2) 337
Cle-Sipe 318P; TB-Eckwood 101C, Jones 106C, Williams 343P

Phi 0 7 0 7 14
SL 7 3 7 7 **24**
Phi D19 R30/109 P(36-16-3) 210
SL D19 R41/195 P(21-11-0) 108
Phi-Carmichael 108C; SL-Anderson 151R

NYJ 0 14 0 7 21
Bal 7 14 7 7 **35**
NYJ D21 R29/116 P(36-16-2) 220
Bal D23 R48/172 P(25-18-2) 275

ChiB 3 0 0 0 3
Pit 7 17 7 7 **38**
ChiB D13 R26/99 P(27-12-4) 101
Pit D23 R38/163 P(27-17-1) 280
Pit-Smith 131C, Bradshaw 217P

Hou 0 0 6 7 13
Cin 7 3 0 0 **10**
Hou D20 R26/37 P(34-26-0) 222
Cin D14 R34/116 P(24-14-1) 134

Atl 3 0 3 14 **20**
SF 0 3 0 14 17
Atl D19 R38/159 P(17-11-0) 233
SF D15 R25/93 P(51-32-2) 318
SF-Solomon 132C, DeBerg 345P

Min 0 7 0 0 7
Det 7 0 3 17 **27**
Min D16 R16/59 P(34-21-5) 217
Det D23 R47/260 P(26-13-1) 150
Det-Sims 157R

Dal 7 7 7 7 **28**
GB 0 0 0 7 7
Dal D24 R43/194 P(20-16-0) 200
GB D17 R23/132 P(31-13-1) 132

Sea 0 7 0 7 **14**
Was 0 0 7 0 7
Sea D20 R47/235 P(19-7-2) 80
Was D15 R25/78 P(36-17-4) 205
Sea-Jodat 117R

MONDAY, SEPTEMBER 29
Den 7 0 7 0 14
NE 3 7 7 6 **23**
Den D8 R27/108 P(12-8-1) 62
NE D23 R47/157 P(24-17-1) 200

SUNDAY, OCTOBER 5
Det 3 3 0 22 28
Atl 17 17 2 7 **43**
Det D17 R27/72 P(36-23-1) 298
Atl D19 R36/191 P(22-11-2) 174
Det-Scott 107C, Thompson 129C, Danielson 348P; Atl-Cain 102R

SL 7 20 3 10 **40**
NO 0 0 0 7 7
SL D29 R62/330 P(18-13-0) 103
NO D3 R9/15 P(22-10-2) 65
SL-Anderson 126R, Morris 102R

Buf 3 9 0 14 **26**
SD 7 10 7 0 24
Buf D14 R38/119 P(28-14-0) 83
SD D19 R29/86 P(35-20-1) 214

Den 3 10 3 3 **19**
Cle 3 10 0 3 16
Den D17 R34/82 P(26-14-1) 157
Cle D18 R23/103 P(40-20-1) 255

KC 14 17 0 0 **31**
Oak 0 3 0 14 17
KC D10 R42/175 P(11-6-1) 45
Oak D23 R23/73 P(60-26-5) 259

Cin 6 0 0 3 9
GB 7 7 0 0 **14**
Cin D14 R24/92 P(30-15-2) 124
GB D21 R42/130 P(26-18-0) 183
GB-Lofton 114C

Was 7 0 0 7 14
Phi 7 14 3 0 **24**
Was D14 R32/97 P(33-19-1) 232
Phi D18 R37/139 P(20-11-1) 173

SF 0 14 6 6 26
LARm 17 17 7 7 **48**
SF R18/75 P(49-28-3) 344
LARm D24 R36/158 P(27-20-0) 304
LARm-Peacock 114R, Ferragamo 304P

NYG 0 0 0 3 3
Dal 3 14 0 7 **24**
NYG D14 R24/137 P(34-13-3) 155
Dal D20 R32/85 P(33-22-1) 250

NE 7 7 7 0 **21**
NYJ 6 0 0 5 11
NE D16 R33/80 P(24-15-1) 174
NYJ D20 R20/92 P(36-22-2) 211

Bal 10 0 7 13 **30**
Mia 3 14 0 0 17
Bal D25 R40/154 P(26-18-0) 282
Mia D20 R22/78 P(39-23-0) 278

Pit 6 10 7 0 **23**
Min 3 0 0 14 17
Pit D23 R40/180 P(28-16-1) 231
Min D20 R29/107 P(36-18-5) 211
Pit-Harris 102R, Swann 107C

Sea 3 20 3 0 **26**
Hou 0 0 0 7 7
Sea D14 R36/118 P(23-13-0) 185
Hou D16 R20/79 P(50-23-5) 163

MONDAY, OCTOBER 6
TB 0 0 0 0 0
ChiB 0 3 10 10 **23**
TB D13 R24/79 P(32-11-1) 68
ChiB D18 R45/173 P(21-10-0) 100
ChiB-Payton 133R

SUNDAY, OCTOBER 12
SD 7 3 7 7 24
Oak 7 10 7 14 **38**
SD D30 R28/90 P(39-23-2) 345
Oak D14 R37/217 P(16-12-0) 157
SD-Jefferson 114C, Joiner 135C, Fouts 388P; Oak-King 138R

NYJ 7 0 0 7 **14**
Atl 0 0 0 7 7
NYJ D19 R46/190 P(19-8-0) 89
Atl D18 R23/97 P(32-20-3) 143
NYJ-Long 100R

Phi 0 3 14 14 **31**
NYG 7 9 0 0 16
Phi D23 R39/124 P(28-18-0) 205
NYG D13 R32/82 P(33-14-2) 79

SF 0 7 0 7 14
Dal 14 24 14 7 **59**
SF D14 R13/78 P(35-12-5) 147
Dal D28 R59/234 P(23-16-0) 226
SF-Clark 148C; Dal-White 239P

Mia 0 0 0 0 0
NE 10 7 0 17 **34**
Mia D8 R20/61 P(35-14-4) 27
NE D21 R44/180 P(24-15-3) 180

Cle 7 6 7 7 **27**
Sea 0 3 0 0 3
Cle D24 R38/176 P(24-12-0) 211
Sea D20 R27/118 P(29-23-0) 205
Cle-Pruitt 116R

Bal 10 7 0 0 **17**
Buf 0 9 0 3 12
Bal D22 R42/149 P(21-10-1) 206
Buf D24 R39/162 P(36-17-1) 201

NO 3 0 7 3 13
Det 0 3 7 14 **24**
NO D21 R21/57 P(36-25-0) 276
Det D18 R34/226 P(19-13-0) 154
NO-Chandler 106C, Manning 314P

Cin 10 7 0 0 **17**
Pit 0 0 16 0 16
Cin D17 R32/120 P(36-18-1) 184
Pit D15 R28/123 P(35-14-1) 208

Hou 3 7 3 7 20
KC 0 0 14 7 **21**
Hou D21 R45/199 P(17-11-2) 131
KC D14 R29/149 P(18-11-1) 132
Hou-Campbell 178R

ChiB 0 0 7 0 7
Min 3 0 3 7 **13**
ChiB D12 R38/161 P(20-12-4) 73
Min D16 R34/92 P(33-15-1) 144
ChiB-Payton 102R

GB 7 7 0 0 0 14
TB 0 7 0 7 0 14
GB D32 R47/154 P(51-35-2) 415
TB D15 R35/180 P(25-6-0) 82
GB-Coffman 109C, Ivery 128C, Thompson 102C, Dickey 418P

LARm 0 14 0 7 **21**
SL 0 0 7 6 13
LARm D24 R55/244 P(23-12-0) 91
SL D18 R24/82 P(38-17-1) 152
LARm-Bryant 115R

MONDAY, OCTOBER 13

Was 3 0 7 7 17
Den 7 3 3 7 **20**
Was D15 R35/184 P(23-18-0) 130
Den D19 R37/165 P(19-11-1) 132
Was-Jackson 104R; Den-Armstrong 107R

SUNDAY, OCTOBER 19

Sea 3 0 7 17 **27**
NYJ 0 7 7 3 17
Sea D17 R24/85 P(27-17-0) 244
NYJ D19 R42/149 P(27-17-2) 189
Sea-McCullum 107C

NE 7 3 17 10 **37**
Bal 7 7 7 0 21
NE D21 R35/117 P(24-15-0) 264
Bal D21 R34/146 P(21-15-2) 160
NE-Jackson 127C

GB 0 0 14 7 21
Cle 0 10 3 13 **26**
GB D19 R37/90 P(22-17-3) 222
Cle D23 R26/87 P(39-24-0) 384
GB-Lofton 136C; Cle-Sipe 391P

Min 0 0 0 0 0
Cin 7 0 0 7 **14**
Min D10 R18/55 P(25-13-2) 113
Cin D25 R43/169 P(28-21-1) 263
Cin-Johnson 115R, Bass 110C

SL 0 0 0 0 0
Was 10 13 0 0 **23**
SL D17 R25/82 P(32-13-2) 147
Was D21 R41/137 P(32-22-1) 316
Was-Theismann 307P

Dal 7 3 0 0 10
Phi 0 10 0 7 **17**
Dal D19 R23/46 P(38-20-3) 203
Phi D15 R32/68 P(25-13-1) 180
Dal-Pearson 107C

NYG 0 0 7 0 7
SD 0 21 7 16 **44**
NYG D13 R25/82 P(31-15-2) 124
SD D31 R32/111 P(42-27-1) 456
SD-Jefferson 107C, Joiner 171C, Winslow 102C, Fouts 444P

LARm 0 14 10 7 **31**
SF 0 3 0 14 17
LARm D18 R38/138 P(27-18-1) 281
SF D22 R28/123 P(37-21-2) 230
LARm-Ferragamo 291P

Atl 7 6 21 7 **41**
NO 7 7 0 0 14
Atl D24 R41/162 P(28-16-0) 193
NO D17 R17/36 P(32-23-3) 302
Atl-Bartkowski 202P; NO-Chandler 140C, Manning 323P

TB 0 7 0 7 14
Hou 3 10 7 0 **20**
TB D12 R21/67 P(28-16-2) 126
Hou D23 R46/245 P(26-19-1) 222
Hou-Campbell 203R

KC 3 10 7 3 **23**
Den 7 7 3 0 17
KC D19 R44/178 P(20-14-0) 183
Den D17 R22/86 P(32-18-2) 182
KC-Marshall 103C

Det 0 0 0 7 7
ChiB 7 3 7 7 **24**
Det D13 R22/65 P(27-15-0) 176
ChiB D16 R50/170 P(8-5-1) 171
ChiB-Payton 101R, Scott 140C

Buf 0 0 7 7 14
Mia 7 7 3 0 **17**
Buf D18 R23/68 P(42-24-0) 221
Mia D15 R44/149 P(17-11-1) 83

MONDAY, OCTOBER 20

Oak 7 21 7 10 **45**
Pit 10 14 10 0 34
Oak D20 R39/143 P(21-13-0) 247
Pit D27 R26/117 P(38-24-2) 350
Oak-Branch 123C; Pit-Bell 114C, Smith 102C

SUNDAY, OCTOBER 26

Pit 10 3 13 0 26
Cle 0 7 7 13 **27**
Pit D21 R34/87 P(37-18-1) 306
Cle D26 R25/91 P(46-28-1) 348
Pit-Bell 125C, Stoudt 310P; Cle-Logan 131C, Sipe 349P

NE 3 0 10 0 13
Buf 0 14 0 17 **31**
NE D8 R17/39 P(29-13-4) 109
Buf D21 R50/181 P(28-12-2) 176
Buf-Cribbs 118R

SD 3 21 0 7 31
Dal 7 7 21 7 **42**
SD D21 R18/97 P(44-21-4) 352
Dal D29 R49/198 P(34-22-1) 227
SD-Jefferson 160C, Winslow 110C, Fouts 371P

Den 0 7 7 0 **14**
NYG 3 6 0 0 9
Den D21 R47/212 P(20-8-0) 64
NYG D15 R27/127 P(36-19-1) 188
Den-Armstrong 106R

Min 0 0 3 0 3
GB 0 0 3 13 **16**
Min D15 R29/85 P(38-19-1) 212
GB D18 R40/147 P(32-16-3) 183

TB 7 0 14 3 **24**
SF 7 6 7 3 23
TB D17 R44/174 P(18-10-1) 89
SF D15 R26/99 P(32-25-1) 206

SL 7 0 10 0 **17**
Bal 0 0 0 10 10
SL D13 R32/95 P(32-18-1) 171
Bal D21 R21/48 P(43-19-2) 177
SL-Gray 101C; Bal-Carr 120C

Sea 0 0 0 14 14
Oak 3 3 10 17 **33**
Sea D14 R18/25 P(33-17-2) 238
Oak D19 R40/138 P(25-16-0) 201
Sea-Largent 142C

NO 0 7 0 7 14
Was 3 6 10 3 **22**
NO D23 R34/220 P(24-12-3) 83
Was D20 R38/183 P(29-15-0) 185
NO-Rogers 114R

ChiB 0 0 14 0 14
Phi 7 0 7 3 **17**
ChiB D17 R35/132 P(18-10-2) 106
Phi D21 R36/138 P(26-15-0) 167

Det 0 3 7 7 17
KC 0 10 0 10 **20**
Det D18 R38/231 P(19-7-2) 91
KC D18 R39/119 P(18-12-0) 174
Det-Sims 155R

LARm 0 3 7 0 10
Atl 6 0 0 7 **13**
LARm D15 R28/118 P(36-18-2) 199
Atl D15 R29/121 P(22-12-2) 151
LARm-Hill 117C; Atl-Andrews 111R

Cin 3 0 0 0 3
Hou 0 3 10 10 **23**
Cin D13 R18/102 P(36-23-3) 157
Hou D17 R38/251 P(23-13-1) 122
Hou-Campbell 202R

MONDAY, OCTOBER 27

Mia 0 0 0 14 14
NYJ 0 14 0 3 **17**
Mia D20 R22/71 P(42-22-2) 208
NYJ D21 R43/159 P(20-11-3) 164

SUNDAY, NOVEMBER 2

Atl 0 10 10 10 **30**
Buf 7 7 0 0 14
Atl D19 R42/150 P(24-13-3) 161
Buf D20 R29/94 P(37-20-3) 270
Buf-Butler 122C

Hou 0 7 6 7 **20**
Den 6 3 0 7 16
Hou D23 R45/173 P(19-11-0) 157
Den D18 R29/96 P(22-17-0) 156
Hou-Campbell 157R

Dal 0 10 3 14 **27**
SL 7 3 7 7 24
Dal D16 R24/58 P(38-23-1) 252
SL D18 R36/143 P(24-12-2) 217
Dal-Pearson 103C; SL-Tilley 145C

Min 7 16 7 9 **39**
Was 0 7 7 0 14
Min D30 R44/201 P(29-18-0) 200
Was D20 R23/74 P(34-20-2) 174

NYG 0 0 6 7 13
TB 7 16 0 7 **30**
NYG D16 R25/73 P(34-22-2) 147
TB D23 R49/244 P(26-13-0) 135
TB-Bell 130R

Phi 0 7 10 10 **27**
Sea 6 0 7 7 20
Phi D22 R31/115 P(31-20-1) 248
Sea D20 R26/103 P(36-20-0) 220
Phi-Smith 109C; Sea-Largent 101C

Mia 0 3 7 0 10
Oak 6 10 0 0 **16**
Mia D10 R24/63 P(25-14-3) 103
Oak D20 R43/192 P(26-16-3) 137

NYJ 0 14 0 7 21
NE 17 14 3 0 **34**
NYJ D18 R30/113 P(35-19-3) 222
NE D16 R34/88 P(27-13-1) 185

NO 0 7 17 7 31
LARm 24 7 7 7 **45**
NO D21 R18/79 P(48-24-1) 243
LARm D22 R43/225 P(26-15-1) 261
LARm-Ferragamo 270P

GB 7 7 0 6 20
Pit 2 7 6 7 **22**
GB D18 R25/77 P(39-20-3) 266
Pit D18 R37/160 P(28-12-2) 121
GB-Ellis 106C

SD 10 7 14 0 **31**
Cin 0 7 0 7 14
SD D21 R31/126 P(41-22-0) 263
Cin D21 R24/113 P(39-24-3) 207
SD-Winslow 153C

Bal 7 7 14 3 **31**
KC 3 14 7 0 24
Bal D22 R41/192 P(29-17-2) 211
KC D17 R28/101 P(29-15-1) 150

SF 7 0 3 3 13
Det 7 3 0 7 **17**
SF D13 R22/63 P(42-21-1) 178
Det D21 R30/146 P(33-24-2) 265

MONDAY, NOVEMBER 3

ChiB 0 0 7 14 21
Cle 3 7 3 14 **27**
ChiB D20 R21/86 P(33-18-1) 189
Cle D31 R38/170 P(39-23-2) 262
Cle-Pruitt 129R

SUNDAY, NOVEMBER 9

Dal 7 14 14 0 35
NYG 7 21 0 10 **38**
Dal D21 R36/239 P(23-10-5) 155
NYG D26 R40/117 P(33-18-1) 345
Dal-Dorsett 183R; NYG-Friede 137C, Simms 351P

Atl 3 3 14 7 6 **33**
SL 17 7 3 0 0 27
Atl D34 R38/209 P(47-31-1) 354
SL D19 R16/86 P(43-25-5) 329
Atl-Andrews 115R, Bartkowski 378P; SL 1-Tilley 120C, Hart 344P

Den 0 7 6 7 **20**
SD 0 6 0 7 13
Den D11 R28/88 P(24-12-0) 131
SD D26 R29/135 P(45-29-1) 324
SD-Muncie 115R, Joiner 127C, Fouts 363P

Was 0 0 14 7 21
ChiB 21 14 0 0 **35**
Was D22 R30/127 P(34-24-2) 281
ChiB D17 R41/154 P(18-11-1) 210
Was-Monk 124C, Theismann 305P; ChiB-Payton 107R

Cin 3 7 0 7 17
Oak 0 14 7 7 **28**
Cin D20 R25/69 P(46-23-4) 195
Oak D19 R35/104 P(25-19-2) 244
Cin-Chandler 139C, Harris 119C, Manning 306P

Mia 7 14 7 7 **35**
LARm 0 7 0 7 14
Mia D27 R44/280 P(29-17-0) 161
LARm D20 R18/108 P(42-19-4) 176
Mia-Williams 151R

Det 0 0 0 0 0
Min 0 10 14 10 **34**
Det D12 R21/48 P(25-14-1) 130
Min D23 R35/100 P(40-27-0) 346
Min-Brown 140C

SF 13 0 0 3 16
GB 0 13 0 10 **23**
SF D17 R25/114 P(35-18-1) 262
GB D24 R40/180 P(33-24-1) 235
SF-Solomon 104C; GB-Lofton 146C

Phi 0 17 7 10 **34**
NO 7 7 7 0 21
Phi D26 R32/134 P(32-21-0) 320
NO D22 R19/84 P(48-28-2) 327
Phi-Smith 137C, Jaworski 323P; NO-Chandler 139C, Harris 119C, Manning 306P

Buf 10 7 7 7 **31**
NYJ 0 10 0 14 24
Buf D17 R38/147 P(28-16-0) 127
NYJ D18 R29/103 P(27-17-1) 164

Cle 14 7 0 7 **28**
Bal 0 6 7 14 27
Cle D25 R39/211 P(29-22-0) 192
Bal D26 R21/110 P(39-27-1) 246
Cle-Pruitt 103R

KC 3 0 7 21 **31**
Sea 0 17 6 7 30
KC D17 R30/81 P(26-19-2) 216
Sea D23 R36/130 P(38-19-5) 192

Pit 10 14 0 0 **24**
TB 7 7 7 0 21
Pit D14 R36/135 P(26-11-1) 94
TB D23 R29/75 P(45-21-1) 294
TB-Giles 128C, Williams 302P

MONDAY, NOVEMBER 10

NE 0 6 14 14 34
Hou 3 21 0 14 **38**
NE D27 R26/99 P(39-25-2) 374
Hou D20 R39/148 P(18-15-1) 242
NE-Grogan 374P; Hou-Campbell 130R, Barber 105C

SUNDAY, NOVEMBER 16

Phi 14 3 7 0 **24**
Was 0 0 0 0 0
Phi D18 R39/157 P(23-13-1) 139
Was D13 R21/81 P(37-17-3) 137

LARm 7 0 10 0 **17**
NE 7 0 0 7 14
LARm D13 R40/107 P(26-14-2) 150
NE D14 R29/103 P(24-11-2) 99

NYJ 7 10 0 7 24
Den 3 7 7 14 **31**
NYJ D14 R30/99 P(25-14-1) 201
Den D29 R27/115 P(39-27-2) 275
NYJ-Jones 103C; Den-Morton 306P

SL 14 7 0 0 21
Dal 7 10 7 7 **31**
SL D16 R28/141 P(30-12-1) 188
Dal D26 R40/184 P(37-20-1) 276
SL 1-Anderson 100R; al-Dorsett 122R, Hill 126C

SF 7 0 6 0 13
Mia 3 7 7 0 **17**
SF D20 R17/29 P(45-32-1) 260
Mia D23 R39/166 P(25-18-1) 212

Bal 7 3 0 0 **10**
Det 0 0 3 6 9
Bal D14 R36/137 P(17-9-3) 150
Det D26 R45/203 P(25-11-1) 108
Det-Sims 126R

Hou 0 7 3 0 **10**
ChiB 0 6 0 0 6
Hou D20 R41/237 P(24-13-1) 93
ChiB D14 R31/178 P(23-12-1) 148
Hou-Campbell 206R

NO 7 0 0 6 13
Atl 3 7 7 14 **31**
NO D17 R23/82 P(36-22-2) 235
Atl D22 R45/206 P(24-13-0) 164

TB 6 7 10 7 30
Min 14 10 7 7 **38**
TB D27 R23/87 P(56-30-2) 486
Min D26 R26/124 P(40-25-0) 326
TB-Jones 121C, Williams 486P; Min-White 120C, Kramer 324P

Cle 0 13 0 0 13
Pit 0 7 0 9 **16**
Cle D14 R24/95 P(34-15-1) 171
Pit D21 R27/79 P(35-19-4) 240
Pit-Swann 138C

KC 7 0 0 0 7
SD 0 6 7 7 **20**
KC D10 R22/75 P(22-15-0) 108
SD D30 R47/171 P(39-22-1) 212
SD-Thomas 109R

GB 0 7 7 7 21
NYG 7 7 6 7 **27**
GB D24 R27/121 P(36-20-2) 289
NYG D19 R35/112 P(33-17-0) 294
GB-Lofton 175C, Dickey 331P; NYG-Friede 108C, Gray 119C, Simms 322P

Buf 0 7 0 7 **14**
Cin 0 0 0 0 0
Buf D22 R43/137 P(24-15-2) 169
Cin D9 R22/89 P(28-15-1) 124

MONDAY, NOVEMBER 17

Oak 0 0 7 12 **19**
Sea 0 7 7 3 17
Oak D12 R29/117 P(22-9-1) 110
Sea D23 R40/158 P(35-19-2) 233

THURSDAY, NOVEMBER 20

SD 7 10 7 0 3 **27**
Mia 7 10 0 7 0 24
SD D22 R29/142 P(41-25-0) 221
Mia D21 R39/103 P(34-22-2) 222
Mia-Nathan 102C

SUNDAY, NOVEMBER 23

Pit 7 3 0 3 13
Buf 7 7 7 7 **28**
Pit D16 R21/84 P(35-20-0) 155
Buf D23 R40/178 P(28-16-1) 201
Buf-Cribbs 110R

Hou 0 0 0 28 0 28
NYJ 14 7 0 7 3 **31**
Hou D28 R26/123 P(51-33-4) 349
NYJ D17 R36/104 P(26-13-2) 223
Hou-Stabler 388P

GB 0 10 6 9 **25**
Min 0 6 7 0 13
GB D25 R40/246 P(21-13-0) 197
Min D17 R24/89 P(34-18-0) 187
GB-Ellis 101R, Ivery 145R

Was 0 3 0 7 10
Dal 7 0 0 7 **14**
Was D14 R46/184 P(18-9-1) 38
Dal D12 R35/115 P(16-7-4) 84
Was-Jackson 128R

ChiB 7 3 7 0 17
Atl 0 14 0 14 **28**
ChiB D18 R33/132 P(35-19-0) 151
Atl D18 R27/87 P(32-17-1) 239

KC 0 0 7 14 **21**
SL 10 0 3 0 13
KC D23 R44/129 P(32-18-2) 192
SL D16 R23/125 P(39-14-1) 194
KC-Marshall 117C; SL 1-Anderson 107R

Sea 0 10 0 10 20
Den 7 10 3 16 36
Sea D14 R25/69 P(26-16-3) 151
Den D17 R32/76 P(30-20-2) 200

NYG 0 0 0 0 0
SF 0 12 0 0 12
NYG D12 R20/80 P(28-15-1) 51
SF D16 R38/120 P(28-16-2) 206

Det 0 14 3 7 24
TB 3 7 0 0 10
Det D19 R40/129 P(29-22-0) 133
TB D15 R16/45 P(34-18-1) 155

Oak 0 0 0 7 7
Phi 0 3 7 0 10
Oak D12 R28/100 P(36-10-2) 175
Phi D13 R32/107 P(32-14-1) 164
Oak-Branch 125C

Cin 7 0 0 0 7
Cle 0 14 14 3 31
Cin D25 R31/150 P(40-25-2) 247
Cle D21 R16/31 P(36-27-1) 301
Cle-Sipe 310P

Bal 0 0 7 14 21
NE 7 3 10 27 47
Bal D18 R28/155 P(28-17-3) 172
NE D23 R48/245 P(21-10-1) 141
Bal-Dickey 102R; NE-Calhoun 106R, Ferguson 100R

MONDAY, NOVEMBER 24
LARm 0 14 3 10 27
NO 0 0 0 7 7
LARm D21 R45/215 P(26-15-0) 178
NO D9 R11/34 P(35-15-2) 62

THURSDAY, NOVEMBER 27
Sea 0 0 0 7 7
Dal 9 21 0 21 51
Sea D18 R26/148 P(34-13-3) 84
Dal D24 R45/200 P(19-12-2) 125
Dal-Dorsett 107R

ChiB 0 3 0 14 6 23
Det 3 7 7 0 0 17
ChiB D21 R29/178 P(24-11-0) 124
Det D19 R41/149 P(22-10-0) 164
ChiB-Payton 123R, Scott 106C

SUNDAY, NOVEMBER 30
Was 0 3 0 3 6
Atl 0 0 7 3 10
Was D11 R32/85 P(18-14-1) 108
Atl D18 R31/131 P(32-14-0) 210
Atl-Andrews 111R

SL 7 0 6 10 23
NYG 0 0 0 7 7
SL D19 R51/225 P(17-10-1) 136
NYG D13 R24/106 P(30-12-2) 83
SL-Anderson 168R

Cle 7 7 3 0 17
Hou 0 7 0 7 14
Cle D11 R31/121 P(21-13-1) 73
Hou D17 R31/114 P(26-17-2) 208
Hou-Campbell 109R, Casper 150C

Cin 7 0 0 13 20
KC 3 0 3 0 6
Cin D18 R37/205 P(23-13-2) 97
KC D17 R29/82 P(37-21-1) 173
Cin-Johnson 112R

Min 3 13 7 0 23
NO 0 0 13 7 20
Min D23 R40/153 P(29-13-2) 115
NO D18 R21/103 P(32-19-2) 236

Phi 0 0 7 14 21
SD 0 3 0 19 22
Phi D20 R27/92 P(36-23-0) 171
SD D17 R30/73 P(29-20-1) 330
SD-Jefferson 164C, Fouts 342P

Mia 0 3 0 7 10
Pit 0 13 3 7 23
Mia D14 R23/81 P(26-14-1) 143
Pit D20 R42/168 P(31-13-1) 267
Pit-Harris 116R, Bell 173C

TB 10 0 3 7 20
GB 0 3 0 14 17
TB D19 R41/138 P(32-16-0) 235
GB D18 R24/74 P(36-24-0) 183

NYJ 0 13 0 0 13
LARm 10 14 0 14 38
NYJ D13 R17/85 P(35-14-1) 139
LARm D26 R44/226 P(37-23-4) 284
LARm-Peacock 152R, Ferragamo 284P

Buf 7 7 3 7 24
Bal 0 14 7 7 28
Buf D24 R41/120 P(28-17-1) 164
Bal D14 R40/113 P(24-8-2) 88

NE 0 3 7 7 17
SF 0 14 7 0 21
NE D16 R31/81 P(32-16-6) 262
SF D15 R35/101 P(29-17-2) 128
NE-Morgan 142C

MONDAY, DECEMBER 1
Den 3 0 0 0 3
Oak 0 0 6 3 9
Den D12 R22/95 P(35-18-4) 119
Oak D15 R43/164 P(19-9-0) 51

THURSDAY, DECEMBER 4
Pit 0 0 0 0 0
Hou 0 0 3 3 6
Pit D18 R29/160 P(26-10-3) 118
Hou D13 R32/91 P(27-15-1) 177

SUNDAY, DECEMBER 7
SD 7 3 0 7 17
Was 14 6 6 14 40
SD D17 R23/105 P(27-14-5) 181
Was D23 R37/149 P(37-26-0) 241
Was-Harmon 118C

Det 0 13 10 0 23
SL 7 7 0 10 24
Det D16 R36/121 P(28-15-1) 183
SL D14 R42/126 P(22-12-1) 99

Atl 3 7 7 3 20
Phi 0 14 0 3 17
Atl D23 R30/182 P(33-13-2) 193
Phi D20 R27/86 P(36-17-2) 190
Atl-Andrews 101R

LARm 0 0 7 0 0 7
Buf 0 0 7 3 10
LARm D14 R42/181 P(23-8-1) 34
Buf D15 R43/150 P(25-10-0) 122

NYJ 0 0 7 7 14
Cle 0 3 7 7 17
NYJ D17 R19/93 P(28-19-2) 205
Cle D27 R27/79 P(41-30-1) 319
Cle-Rucker 108C, Sipe 340P

Bal 0 6 0 27 33
Cin 7 17 3 7 34
Bal D23 R21/94 P(40-21-1) 219
Cin D26 R42/148 P(38-21-1) 361
Bal-Carr 133C; Cin-Johnson 118R, Curtis 176C

Min 0 0 7 14 21
TB 3 7 0 0 10
Min D19 R24/118 P(31-22-0) 247
TB D19 R32/128 P(36-18-0) 220

NO 14 21 0 0 0 35
SF 0 7 14 14 3 38
NO D17 R36/143 P(39-24-1) 193
SF D24 R33/176 P(36-24-0) 254
NO-Childs 144C, Manning 377P; SF-Elliott 125R, Clark 155C

GB 0 7 0 0 7
ChiB 0 28 13 20 61
GB D19 R22/81 P(31-14-2) 185
ChiB D33 R48/267 P(24-20-0) 327
GB-Lofton 111C; ChiB-Payton 130R, Watts 126C, Evans 316P

Dal 7 9 3 0 19
Oak 7 3 3 0 13
Dal D17 R39/128 P(26-14-0) 132
Oak D16 R22/83 P(36-16-2) 165

Den 0 0 7 7 14
KC 0 28 0 3 31
Den D21 R26/132 P(35-20-1) 216
KC D22 R49/199 P(18-12-1) 132

NYG 3 10 0 14 27
Sea 0 7 7 7 21
NYG D14 R39/150 P(18-8-1) 161
Sea D22 R28/116 P(37-20-0) 221
NYG-Taylor 103R, Gray 114C; Sea-Largent 139C

MONDAY, DECEMBER 8
NE 0 6 0 7 13
Mia 0 0 6 7 3 16
NE D15 R33/120 P(17-13-0) 155
Mia D17 R29/118 P(25-15-0) 173

SATURDAY, DECEMBER 13
Sea 0 0 7 7 14
SD 0 21 0 0 21
Sea D16 R18/79 P(42-22-0) 152
SD D25 R27/90 P(42-28-2) 330
SD-Jefferson 113C, Fouts 339P

NYG 0 10 0 3 13
Was 0 0 7 9 16
NYG D18 R39/143 P(27-11-2) 110
Was D16 R29/113 P(32-16-1) 119

SUNDAY, DECEMBER 14
SF 0 3 0 7 10
Atl 7 0 14 14 35
SF D15 R21/106 P(42-25-2) 204
Atl D26 R43/171 P(34-24-1) 292
Atl-Andrews 105R, Francis 148C

NO 7 0 0 14 21
NYJ 0 7 0 7 14
NO D20 R24/121 P(30-20-0) 191
NYJ D20 R43/227 P(28-11-2) 64
NYJ-Newton 117R

Cin 7 7 0 3 17
ChiB 0 7 0 7 14
Cin D17 R35/154 P(25-13-0) 140
ChiB D17 R31/116 P(28-13-4) 100
Cin-Johnson 134R

KC 0 3 13 0 16
Pit 7 0 0 14 21
KC D16 R40/132 P(23-8-1) 66
Pit D16 R32/115 P(22-14-2) 170

SL 0 0 0 3 3
Phi 0 0 7 10 17
SL D8 R28/67 P(23-8-1) 59
Phi D18 R40/108 P(34-17-0) 236
Phi-Smith 134C

TB 0 7 0 7 14
Det 7 7 3 10 27
TB D11 R17/40 P(37-13-2) 173
Det D19 R27/76 P(44-29-0) 332
Det-Thompson 106C, Danielson 360P

Oak 7 10 0 7 24
Den 0 0 7 0 7
Oak D15 R36/97 P(21-13-1) 179
Den D26 R26/76 P(42-26-3) 431
Den-Moses 141C, Odoms 128C, Morton 338P

Buf 0 0 2 0 2
NE 7 7 7 3 24
Buf D8 R22/108 P(22-11-1) 53
NE D21 R47/195 P(19-12-2) 129

Cle 7 6 3 7 23
Min 0 0 9 19 28
Cle D21 R33/134 P(33-20-1) 232
Min D29 R16/75 P(49-38-0) 455
Min-Rashad 142C, Kramer 456P

Hou 6 3 0 13 22
GB 0 3 0 0 3
Hou D22 R41/257 P(22-15-1) 114
GB D16 R20/54 P(37-18-3) 283
Hou-Campbell 181R; GB-Dickey 309P

Mia 7 7 0 10 24
Bal 7 0 7 0 14
Mia D19 R42/175 P(29-9-1) 143
Bal D14 R29/136 P(35-16-2) 140

MONDAY, DECEMBER 15
Dal 0 0 0 14 14
LARm 7 21 10 0 38
Dal D13 R23/96 P(33-13-3) 175
LARm D21 R46/242 P(25-15-0) 275
Dal-Hill 121C; LARm-Thomas 147R, Waddy 124C

SATURDAY, DECEMBER 20
NYJ 7 7 7 3 24
Mia 10 0 0 7 17
NYJ D18 R34/120 P(19-12-3) 152
Mia D22 R30/135 P(41-20-2) 212

ChiB 0 7 7 0 14
TB 10 0 0 3 13
ChiB D21 R46/182 P(31-15-2) 140
TB D16 R28/107 P(29-16-2) 344
ChiB-Payton 130R; TB-House 138C, Williams 350P

SUNDAY, DECEMBER 21
Cle 0 10 14 3 27
Cin 3 7 14 0 24
Cle D18 R19/57 P(44-24-2) 256
Cin D20 R31/125 P(36-16-2) 248
Cle-Sipe 308P

Oak 10 10 7 6 33
NYG 0 10 0 7 17
Oak D17 R34/144 P(25-14-0) 167
NYG D22 R39/185 P(32-17-1) 106
Oak-van Eeghen 115R

Den 10 9 6 0 25
Sea 0 0 3 14 17
Den D15 R33/135 P(26-10-0) 101
Sea D27 R24/96 P(41-26-2) 203

Phi 0 0 10 17 27
Dal 7 14 7 7 35
Phi D21 R23/84 P(30-18-0) 323
Dal D24 R38/168 P(24-16-1) 172
Phi-Jaworski 331P; Dal-Hill 110C, White 202P

NE 3 14 7 14 38
NO 10 3 7 7 27
NE D27 R38/240 P(28-16-1) 233
NO D23 R23/89 P(41-26-0) 359
NE-Calhoun 113R; NO-Manning 301P

Buf 6 7 5 0 18
SF 6 0 7 0 13
Buf D16 R32/165 P(20-12-0) 102
SF D19 R29/146 P(36-25-0) 152
Buf-Cribbs 128R

KC 21 0 7 10 38
Bal 0 28 0 0 28
KC D23 R33/71 P(28-17-0) 301
Bal D22 R35/123 P(40-23-1) 212
KC-Marshall 176C, Smith 129C, Kenney 316P

Min 3 6 0 7 16
Hou 3 0 10 7 20
Min D24 R23/114 P(53-26-4) 248
Hou D33 R23/219 P(33-19-2) 116
Hou-Campbell 203R, Casper 120C

GB 0 0 0 3 3
Det 0 10 0 14 24
GB D11 R25/87 P(27-14-1) 103
Det D22 R30/132 P(27-18-2) 225

Atl 7 7 0 3 17
LARm 3 0 14 3 20
Atl D21 R42/165 P(26-13-1) 184
LARm D23 R37/256 P(34-20-0) 191
LARm-Thomas 144R

Was 0 21 3 7 31
SL 0 0 0 7 7
Was D20 R35/174 P(32-19-0) 217
SL D14 R32/186 P(26-6-3) -12
Was-Hammond 135R; SL-Anderson 122R

MONDAY, DECEMBER 22
Pit 0 3 7 7 17
SD 3 6 10 7 26
Pit D16 R18/49 P(32-16-0) 253
SD D27 R44/180 P(38-21-0) 308
Pit-Bell 127C; SD-Muncie 115R, Winslow 171C, Fouts 308P

1981 NFL

SATURDAY, SEPTEMBER 5
Min 0 0 6 7 13
TB 7 0 0 14 21
Min D27 R27/100 P(63-37-2) 343
TB D10 R28/111 P(22-8-0) 108
Min-Dils 361P

SUNDAY, SEPTEMBER 6
Hou 3 3 14 7 27
LARm 10 10 0 0 20
Hou D13 R37/140 P(20-13-0) 169
LARm D17 R32/137 P(28-16-4) 248
Hou-Campbell 122R

KC 10 3 10 14 37
Pit 6 13 7 7 33
KC D17 R40/139 P(26-14-1) 214
Pit D29 R34/89 P(36-21-2) 319
Pit-Stallworth 107C, Bradshaw 319P

Oak 7 0 0 0 7
Den 6 3 0 0 9
Oak D12 R24/81 P(24-14-2) 84
Den D21 R45/176 P(25-12-0) 182

Phi 0 10 7 7 24
NYG 3 0 7 0 7
Phi D21 R43/178 P(26-16-1) 147
NYG D14 R23/55 P(37-20-0) 175

Bal 10 3 3 13 29
NE 0 14 0 14 28
Bal D21 R43/249 P(20-12-0) 97
NE D22 R28/114 P(29-16-2) 274
Bal-McMillan 146R; NE-Hasselbeck 111C

SF 0 0 3 14 17
Det 0 10 0 14 24
SF D19 R33/121 P(28-18-1) 176
Det D21 R30/127 P(27-16-1) 168

Dal 0 14 6 6 26
Was 0 7 3 0 10
Dal D20 R44/206 P(24-12-0) 140
Was D20 R18/44 P(49-23-4) 280
Dal-Dorsett 132R; Was-Washington 124C

NO 0 0 0 0 0
Atl 7 7 7 6 27
NO D14 R20/76 P(41-23-1) 173
Atl D21 R38/164 P(26-16-2) 135
NO-Chandler 117C

NYJ 0 0 0 0 0
Buf 3 7 21 0 31
NYJ D8 R25/102 P(25-16-2) 129
Buf D25 R44/182 P(24-15-1) 236
Buf-Butler 123C

GB 3 7 0 6 16
ChiB 3 6 0 0 9
GB D20 R46/193 P(23-10-1) 153
ChiB D20 R30/145 P(35-17-0) 161

Sea 21 0 0 0 21
Cin 0 10 10 7 27
Sea D17 R23/60 P(41-21-1) 230
Cin D24 R45/210 P(33-14-2) 165
Sea-Largent 114C

Mia 0 13 7 0 20
SL 0 0 0 7 7
Mia D14 R33/151 P(24-14-1) 141
SL D14 R29/61 P(35-17-1) 142

MONDAY, SEPTEMBER 7
SD 10 10 14 10 44
Cle 0 7 7 0 14
SD D28 R41/205 P(25-19-0) 330
Cle D27 R14/53 P(57-31-2) 366
SD-Muncie 161R, Fouts 330P; Cle-Sipe 375P

THURSDAY, SEPTEMBER 10
Pit 3 7 0 0 10
Mia 0 13 14 3 30
Pit D15 R26/117 P(33-15-2) 183
Mia D25 R36/185 P(34-14-1) 161

SUNDAY, SEPTEMBER 13

```
SL      7   7   0   3   17
Dal    14  13   3   0   30
SL   D18 R27/142 P(41-14-2) 262
Dal  D24 R35/181 P(29-21-1) 210
Dal-Dorsett 129R

Cin     0  10   7  14   31
NYJ     0  17   3  10   30
Cin  D22 R29/77  P(34-22-1) 233
NYJ  D19 R30/164 P(29-18-0) 224
Cin-Curtis 108C

Buf     7  14   7   7   35
Bal     0   3   0   0    3
Buf  D26 R39/169 P(28-16-1) 261
Bal  D11 R26/73  P(28-12-2)  74
Buf-Ferguson 261P

ChiB    0  10   7   0   17
SF      7   7   7   7   28
ChiB D18 R36/123 P(33-19-1) 216
SF   D20 R32/125 P(32-20-0) 287
SF-Solomon 113C

Atl     0   0   0  31   31
GB      7   7   3   0   17
Atl  D19 R31/116 P(32-17-4) 219
GB   D22 R23/96  P(44-30-3) 300
GB-Lofton 179C, Dickey 342P

NE      3   0   0   0    3
Phi     0   3  10   0   13
NE   D14 R32/146 P(31-11-5) 137
Phi  D18 R40/220 P(25-11-0) 142
Phi-Montgomery 137R

Den     3   7   0   0   10
Sea     7   3   3   0   13
Den  D16 R24/110 P(25-14-1) 142
Sea  D18 R29/111 P(34-24-2) 156

Det     3   0  10  10   23
SD      0   7   7  14   28
Det  D26 R41/178 P(27-19-1) 207
SD   D17 R24/57  P(25-18-1) 310
SD-Joiner 166C, Fouts 316P

Hou     3   0   3   3    9
Cle     0   7   0   0    7
Hou  D8  R30/91  P(18-10-1) 118
Cle  D20 R24/99  P(53-25-1) 203

NYG     0   0   7  10   17
Was     0   0   7   0    7
NYG  D10 R35/71  P(27-8-1)   86
Was  D19 R22/65  P(48-27-1) 284
Was-Theismann 318P

LARm    0   3   7   7   17
NO      6  10   0   7   23
LARm D17 R24/88  P(34-20-2) 167
NO   D19 R50/226 P(18-4-3)   78
NO-Rogers 162R

TB      7   3   0   0   10
KC      7   3   3   6   19
TB   D17 R23/12  P(43-20-0) 286
KC   D13 R41/157 P(25-12-0)  99
```

MONDAY, SEPTEMBER 14

```
Oak     3  13   7  13   36
Min     0   7   3   0   10
Oak  D14 R33/149 P(25-12-1) 161
Min  D19 R19/42  P(50-23-1) 227
Min-White 140C
```

THURSDAY, SEPTEMBER 17

```
Phi     0  10   7   3   20
Buf     0  14   0   0   14
Phi  D24 R38/160 P(32-20-1) 236
Buf  D17 R31/90  P(30-14-2) 187
Phi-Montgomery 125R;
Buf-Lewis 108C
```

SUNDAY, SEPTEMBER 20

```
SF      0  10   0   7   17
Atl    17   7  10   0   34
SF   D23 R30/113 P(34-24-2) 273
Atl  D18 R34/163 P(23-14-0) 200

Mia     6   3   0   7   16
Hou     0   7   0   7   ...
Mia  D16 R33/124 P(32-18-1) 133
Hou  D9  R21/85  P(26-16-1) 117
```


```
Bal     0   0  10   0   10
Den     0  14  14   0   28
Bal  D10 R26/161 P(19-7-1)   48
Den  D27 R35/127 P(33-24-4) 315
Bal-Dickey 115R; Den-Watson 143C,
Morton 291P

SD     14  14   7   7   42
KC      7   7  14   3   31
SD   D23 R24/114 P(43-22-3) 284
KC   D29 R37/148 P(41-22-5) 278
KC-Smith 140C, Kenney 303P

Det     0  14   3   7   24
Min     7  10   6   3   26
Det  D19 R42/172 P(43-25-2) 232
Min  D18 R21/94  P(43-25-2) 312
Det-Sims 112R, Scott 113C;
Min-Brown 115C, Kramer 333P

NYJ     0   3   0   7   10
Pit     7  10  14   7   38
NYJ  D16 R21/84  P(33-14-2) 174
Pit  D33 R56/343 P(30-15-0) 223
Pit-Davis 100R, Stallworth 134C

Cle     3  10   0   7   20
Cin     0   0   3  14   17
Cle  D31 R45/185 P(35-24-0) 237
Cin  D15 R14/48  P(25-16-0) 233

Was    10   7   0  13   30
SL      9  17   0  14   40
Was  D24 R27/133 P(37-25-1) 388
SL   D18 R37/107 P(22-12-0) 208
Was-Jackson 104R, Monk 128C,
Thompson 106C, Theismann 388P;
SL-Green 115C

GB      0  10   6   7   23
LARm   14  14   7   7   35
GB   D19 R33/122 P(34-15-1)  78
LARm D19 R43/177 P(12-6-1)   26
LARm-Tyler 108R

NO      0   0   0   7    7
NYG     0  13   7   0   20
NO   D18 R28/109 P(39-16-2) 190
NYG  D26 R33/106 P(42-28-0) 315
NYG-Perkins 118C, Shirk 101C,
Simms 324P

TB      7   0   7   3   17
ChiB    0  14   7   7   28
TB   D22 R30/141 P(40-17-2) 309
ChiB D15 R38/121 P(24-13-1) 126
TB-Eckwood 114R, Giles 109C,
Williams 324P

Sea     0   3   7   0   10
Oak     7   6   0   7   20
Sea  D18 R16/82  P(43-24-1) 308
Oak  D26 R41/190 P(30-20-2) 242
Sea-McCullum 122C, Zorn 327P
```

MONDAY, SEPTEMBER 21

```
Dal     7  10   7  11   35
NE      7   7   7   0   21
Dal  D22 R46/237 P(34-24-0) 218
NE   D16 R22/108 P(27-14-4) 225
Dal-Dorsett 162R
```

SUNDAY, SEPTEMBER 27

```
NO      7   0   0   7   14
SF      0   7   7   7   21
NO   D18 R37/163 P(38-21-2) 250
SF   D15 R39/146 P(22-16-1) 168
NO-Rogers 115R

Min     0  20  10   0   30
GB     10   0   3   0   13
Min  D28 R32/157 P(34-19-0) 253
GB   D22 R19/71  P(40-22-0) 245
Min-Brown 109R;
GB-Jefferson 121C, Lofton 101C

SD      0   0  10  14   24
Den    21   7   7   7   42
SD   D23 R23/82  P(47-26-3) 267
Den  D20 R37/103 P(24-21-0) 350
SD-Winslow 106C;
Den-Watson 178C, Morton 308P

NYG     0   0   3   7   10
Dal     3   7   0   8   18
NYG  D16 R24/85  P(35-18-3) 258
Dal  D16 R41/124 P(27-14-0) 193
NYG-Perkins 129C
```


```
Oak     0   0   0   0    0
Det     0   3   0  13   16
Oak  D14 R32/86  P(21-11-1)  45
Det  D20 R35/181 P(27-12-2)  79
Det-Sims 133R

SL      0   3   7   0   10
TB      6   0   0  14   20
SL   D18 R38/176 P(19-12-1)  79
TB   D18 R34/167 P(30-17-0) 154

NE      0   7  14   0   21
Pit     7   7   7   6   27
NE   D24 R32/115 P(43-23-1) 323
Pit  D27 R45/251 P(30-15-0) 247
NE-Jackson 126C, Cavanaugh 325P

Atl     3   7   0   7   17
Cle     0  21   7   0   28
Atl  D14 R23/112 P(30-12-2) 150
Cle  D26 R44/178 P(34-21-2) 207
Atl-Jenkins 136C

Hou     0   0   3   0   17
NYJ     7  14   5   7   33
Hou  D16 R23/116 P(30-15-3) 105
NYJ  D25 R46/171 P(29-25-0) 307
NYJ-Walker 128C, Todd 312P

Mia     7   7   7  10   31
Bal     0   7  14   7   28
Mia  D22 R33/119 P(30-19-0) 309
Bal  D20 R32/166 P(27-20-1) 348
Mia-Woodley 309P; Bal-Butler 145C,
Jones 357P

Was     0   6   0   7   13
Phi     0   7   7  22   36
Was  D23 R33/109 P(34-22-1) 228
Phi  D15 R25/70  P(27-15-1) 151
Was-Metcalf 123C

KC      7  13   0   0   20
Sea     0   7   7   0   14
KC   D26 R42/154 P(25-16-0) 227
Sea  D23 R19/82  P(47-31-0) 277
Sea-Hughes 103C, Zorn 308P

Buf     0  14   0  10   24
Cin     0  10   0  14   3  27
Buf  D25 R30/102 P(46-25-0) 287
Cin  D30 R31/113 P(40-28-0) 316
Buf-Lewis 132C;
Cin-Collinsworth 111C,
Anderson 328P
```

MONDAY, SEPTEMBER 28

```
LARm    7   3   7   7   24
ChiB    0   0   0   7    7
LARm D20 R35/134 P(29-13-0) 195
ChiB D17 R30/88  P(34-16-1) 135
ChiB-Payton 111C
```

SUNDAY, OCTOBER 4

```
NYJ    14   0   0  14   0  28
Mia     7   7   7   7   0  28
NYJ  D32 R51/242 P(39-28-1) 304
Mia  D17 R29/98  P(34-21-0) 301
NYJ-Walker 112C, Todd 310P;
Mia-Moore 210C

KC      0   3   7   7   17
NE      7   7  10   9   33
KC   D22 R37/219 P(21-9-4)  108
NE   D25 R49/240 P(26-11-2) 211
KC-Delaney 101R; NE-Morgan 118C

Den     0   7  10   0   17
Oak     0   0   0   0    0
Den  D17 R45/162 P(17-10-0)  90
Oak  D12 R21/78  P(28-14-2)  90

Bal     0   3   0  14   17
Buf    14   0   3   6   23
Bal  D23 R31/133 P(36-22-1) 245
Buf  D22 R36/229 P(29-14-1) 137
Buf-Cribbs 159R

Pit     7   6   0   7   20
NO      0   3   0   3    6
Pit  D19 R33/137 P(29-19-0) 269
NO   D16 R35/78  P(24-15-4) 102
Pit-Stallworth 158C

Sea     0   7   0   3   10
SD      0  10   7   7   24
Sea  D15 R23/92  P(34-16-1) 200
SD   D25 R28/99  P(41-30-0) 272
Sea-Largent 118C; SD-Fouts 302P
```


```
Det    10   0   0   0   10
TB      0   3   0   0    3
Det  D18 R35/93  P(40-18-4) 239
TB   D14 R25/49  P(29-13-1) 162
TB-Williams 168P

SF     14  10   6   0   30
Was     0   3   0  14   17
SF   D16 R35/128 P(28-15-1) 168
Was  D19 R23/83  P(46-22-4) 221

Cle     3   0   7   6   16
LARm    7   7   0  13   27
Cle  D16 R26/78  P(28-14-1) 240
LARm D29 R46/213 P(31-21-0) 197

ChiB    0   7   7   7   21
Min    10   7   0   7   24
ChiB D24 R31/89  P(43-26-1) 307
Min  D22 R34/134 P(38-20-1) 211
ChiB-Margerum 140C, Evans 307P

Cin     3   0   7   0   10
Hou     0   7   7   3   17
Cin  D20 R23/75  P(52-30-1) 282
Hou  D11 R44/191 P(6-1-0)    -4
Hou-Campbell 182R

GB      3  10   7   7   27
NYG     0   0   7   7   14
GB   D27 R49/148 P(23-18-1) 215
NYG  D17 R16/41  P(32-20-2) 221

Dal     7   3   0   7   17
SL     10   0   7   3   20
Dal  D17 R33/140 P(28-15-1) 166
SL   D18 R29/115 P(29-16-1) 184
Dal-Johnson 101C
```

MONDAY, OCTOBER 5

```
Atl     0   0  10   3   13
Phi     6   7   0   3   16
Atl  D22 R29/112 P(46-23-2) 227
Phi  D14 R26/107 P(26-17-0) 161
```

SUNDAY, OCTOBER 11

```
Min     0  14  10   9   33
SD      7   7   0   7   21
Min  D29 R30/93  P(43-27-2) 433
SD   D29 R29/120 P(38-20-0) 305
Min-Brown 109C, LeCount 120C,
Senser 100C, Kramer 444P;
SD-Muncie 102R, Fouts 310P

SL      0   0   7   7   14
NYG     0  17  10   7   34
SL   D19 R26/101 P(29-19-1) 184
NYG  D27 R36/198 P(33-19-0) 179
NYG-Carpenter 103R

Dal     0   7   0   7   14
SF     21   3  14   7   45
Dal  D10 R21/83  P(29-12-2) 109
SF   D23 R46/150 P(33-20-0) 290
SF-Clark 135C

NE      0  14   7   3   24
NYJ     0   0  21   7   28
NE   D25 R27/86  P(52-27-4) 368
NYJ  D18 R24/141 P(29-16-1) 156
NE-Hasselbeck 139C, Grogan 330P

Was    10   7   0   7   24
ChiB    0   0   0   7    7
Was  D16 R47/227 P(25-12-1)  74
ChiB D13 R18/51  P(41-11-4) 153
Was-Riggins 126R

Det     0  14   0   7   21
Den    10   7   3   7   27
Det  D18 R49/262 P(16-7-1)   63
Den  D20 R37/135 P(12-6-2)  266
Det-Sims 185R; Den-Watson 182C

Phi    14  10   7   0   31
NO      7   0   0   7   14
Phi  D21 R36/169 P(28-15-2) 200
NO   D18 R31/190 P(24-10-1)  50
NO-Rogers 134R

LARm   13   7  10   7   37
Atl     0  21   7   7   35
LARm D14 R33/87  P(31-14-1) 165
Atl  D14 R33/152 P(38-17-2) 197
Atl-Andrews 119R

Sea    10   0   0   7   17
Hou     0   7  21   7   35
Sea  D19 R16/75  P(40-25-2) 214
Hou  D21 R48/216 P(19-12-0) 156
Hou-Campbell 186R
```


```
Cle     0   7   0   0    7
Pit     7   3   0   3   13
Cle  D26 R32/166 P(42-20-2) 279
Pit  D19 R28/166 P(33-19-1) 199
Cle-Newsome 120C

TB      0   7  14   0   21
GB      3   7   0   0   10
TB   D22 R45/172 P(23-15-1) 199
GB   D19 R22/95  P(33-19-4) 203

Cin     3  14   7  17   41
Bal     0   5   0  14   19
Cin  D24 R35/121 P(28-21-0) 257
Bal  D22 R26/56  P(33-25-2) 294
Cin-Ross 106C; Bal-Jones 310P

Oak     0   0   0   0    0
KC      3   7  10   7   27
Oak  D13 R22/79  P(40-14-3) 151
KC   D20 R48/176 P(23-15-0) 278
KC-Delaney 106R, Delaney 104C,
Marshall 110C
```

MONDAY, OCTOBER 12

```
Mia     0   7   7   7   21
Buf    10  21   0   0   31
Mia  D22 R18/99  P(44-26-4) 225
Buf  D20 R49/166 P(29-20-0) 338
Buf-Lewis 106C, Ferguson 338P
```

SUNDAY, OCTOBER 18

```
NO      7   7   3   0   17
Cle    10   0   3   7   20
NO   D14 R24/142 P(29-17-0) 192
Cle  D23 R32/94  P(42-25-0) 261
NO-Rogers 122R; Cle-Pruitt 113C

Buf     0   7   0   7   14
NYJ     6   0  21   6   33
Buf  D14 R16/46  P(36-15-2) 242
NYJ  D21 R43/200 P(27-17-0) 174
NYJ-Lewis 109C

SD      9  16   7  13   43
Bal     7   0   7   0   14
SD   D30 R37/172 P(43-26-0) 298
Bal  D18 R16/68  P(37-20-2) 196

SF      0   3   0  10   13
GB      0   3   0   0    3
SF   D21 R47/126 P(32-23-0) 211
GB   D19 R19/78  P(24-14-1) 163

Pit     0   0   0   7    7
Cin    10   3  14   7   34
Pit  D10 R19/65  P(27-14-0) 140
Cin  D25 R32/164 P(28-16-0) 330
Cin-Anderson 346P

Den     0   0   7   7   14
KC     14   0   0  14   28
Den  D20 R29/77  P(43-28-3) 319
KC   D13 R45/224 P(12-6-2)  100
Den-Upchurch 138C, Morton 342P;
KC-Delaney 149R

Was     0   0   7   3   10
Mia     0   3   7   3   13
Was  D20 R38/162 P(23-17-1) 139
Mia  D20 R31/149 P(28-15-0) 296

NYG     3  10  13   6   32
Sea     0   0   0   7    7
NYG  D20 R44/213 P(28-12-1)  88
Sea  D10 R14/29  P(34-20-2)  98
NYG-Carpenter 116R

LARm    0  10   7   0   17
Dal    12  14   0   3   29
LARm D22 R34/171 P(30-13-3) 203
Dal  D24 R42/221 P(33-15-2) 215
Dal-Dorsett 159R

TB      0   0   9   7   16
Oak    12   3   0   3   18
TB   D11 R16/29  P(30-16-0) 327
Oak  D24 R51/194 P(34-17-3) 176
TB-House 178C, Williams 335P

Hou     0   0   0  10   10
NE      7   0  17  14   38
Hou  D18 R33/120 P(35-18-4) 189
NE   D21 R41/244 P(21-12-1) 192

SL      7   7   0   6   20
Atl     0  20   7  14   41
SL   D22 R25/120 P(51-24-3) 263
Atl  D17 R29/114 P(32-18-0) 280
SL-Tilley 100C; Atl-Andrews 132C,
Jenkins 101C, Bartkowski 288P
```

Phi 6 3 0 14 23
Min 0 21 7 7 **35**
Phi D26 R26/105 P(44-29-2) 298
Min D20 R23/94 P(46-24-0) 240
Phi-Carmichael 109C, Montgomery 143C, Jaworski 330P; Min-Kramer 257P

MONDAY, OCTOBER 19

ChiB 7 7 0 3 17
Det 10 17 7 14 **48**
ChiB D24 R37/133 P(33-20-1) 316
Det D23 R32/159 P(25-14-0) 326
ChiB-Anderson 176C; Det-Kane 101R, Scott 110C, Thompson 118C, Hipple 336P

SUNDAY, OCTOBER 25

GB 7 3 10 7 27
Det 7 10 7 7 **31**
GB D23 R21/75 P(43-24-1) 307
Det D24 R38/171 P(36-20-1) 238

LARm 0 10 7 0 17
SF 14 3 3 0 **20**
LARm D25 R37/145 P(39-20-1) 256
SF D14 R28/60 P(32-18-0) 265
LARm-Dennard 119C, Haden 310P; SF-Clark 109C

NYG 0 7 10 7 3 **27**
Atl 7 7 3 7 0 24
NYG D12 R28/76 P(32-19-0) 213
Atl D23 R36/141 P(48-24-1) 289
NYG-Perkins 126C; Atl-Bartkowski 311P

TB 7 0 0 3 10
Phi 0 7 0 13 **20**
TB D24 R30/109 P(45-19-3) 238
Phi D17 R42/189 P(15-9-1) 109
Phi-Montgomery 119R

SD 0 3 0 14 0 17
ChiB 7 3 0 7 3 **20**
SD D15 R20/61 P(43-13-2) 295
ChiB D28 R61/195 P(39-17-0) 219
SD-Joiner 124C; ChiB-Payton 107R

Den 0 7 0 0 7
Buf 0 3 3 3 **9**
Den D10 R24/64 P(25-10-0) 97
Buf D17 R29/119 P(42-21-1) 204
Buf-Cribbs 123R

Sea 0 7 6 6 **19**
NYJ 0 0 3 0 3
Sea D26 R50/217 P(21-13-0) 163
NYJ D15 R25/118 P(29-14-2) 101
Sea-Brown 104R

Cin 0 0 0 7 7
NO 0 0 7 10 **17**
Cin D15 R19/34 P(41-19-1) 171
NO D18 R37/166 P(25-16-1) 170
NO-Rogers 113R

Min 0 3 7 7 17
SL 13 0 7 10 **30**
Min D22 R17/69 P(55-25-2) 318
SL D18 R40/138 P(26-13-2) 182
Min-Senser 100C, White 120C, Kramer 343P

Bal 0 7 14 7 28
Cle 7 21 7 7 **42**
Bal D18 R32/118 P(37-17-2) 239
Cle D30 R33/131 P(41-30-2) 431
Cle-Pruitt 104C, Sipe 444P

KC 0 0 7 21 **28**
Oak 7 10 0 0 17
KC D22 R34/119 P(35-17-3) 211
Oak D21 R37/117 P(47-19-4) 225

NE 6 9 0 7 22
Was 7 7 10 0 **24**
NE D23 R39/126 P(30-17-2) 283
Was D15 R32/85 P(23-14-0) 145
NE-Collins 103R, Hasselbeck 112C, Grogan 306P

Mia 0 6 7 14 27
Dal 7 7 0 14 **28**
Mia D25 R34/148 P(37-21-5) 381
Dal D23 R36/139 P(32-22-1) 327
Mia-Cefalo 164C, Harris 165C, Woodley 408P; Dal-Dorsett 122R, Hill 106C, White 354P

MONDAY, OCTOBER 26

Hou 0 3 0 10 13
Pit 10 3 0 13 **26**
Hou D13 R28/76 P(24-16-1) 231
Pit D22 R37/167 P(28-14-1) 196
Pit-Smith 100C

SUNDAY, NOVEMBER 1

Hou 7 0 0 14 21
Cin 0 24 3 7 **34**
Hou D21 R26/132 P(37-25-3) 301
Cin D25 R36/156 P(30-21-0) 266
Cin-Johnson 114R

SL 0 0 0 21 21
Was 14 7 7 14 **42**
SL D29 R22/130 P(47-27-4) 319
Was D25 R39/160 P(19-14-0) 201
SL-Anderson 122R, Hart 305P

NE 3 7 7 0 17
Oak 3 10 0 14 **27**
NE D15 R28/77 P(31-18-1) 205
Oak D24 R36/185 P(36-22-1) 275
NE-Hasselbeck 100C; Oak-King 102R

NYJ 0 13 3 10 **26**
NYG 0 0 7 0 7
NYJ D13 R35/114 P(30-13-0) 185
NYG D10 R15/55 P(36-22-1) 111
NYJ-Walker 142C

KC 7 0 7 6 20
SD 7 12 0 3 **22**
KC D26 R40/184 P(22-13-0) 155
SD D21 R25/82 P(39-24-1) 297
KC-Delaney 117R

Atl 10 14 10 7 **41**
NO 0 10 0 0 10
Atl D20 R39/144 P(22-15-1) 262
NO D14 R22/58 P(38-22-1) 204
Atl-Jenkins 179C

SF 0 10 0 7 **17**
Pit 0 0 14 0 14
SF D25 R39/130 P(38-23-2) 200
Pit D16 R28/144 P(23-12-3) 125
Pit-Harris 104R

Bal 0 10 0 0 10
Mia 7 7 10 3 **27**
Bal D19 R21/68 P(37-23-2) 240
Mia D19 R33/146 P(25-14-0) 164
Mia-Franklin 101R

Cle 0 3 3 7 13
Buf 6 7 2 7 **22**
Cle D14 R20/71 P(38-14-3) 140
Buf D21 R44/172 P(30-14-1) 297
Buf-Cribbs 163C

Sea 7 14 3 0 24
GB 7 14 7 6 **34**
Sea D15 R26/119 P(28-14-1) 102
GB D25 R43/182 P(31-19-2) 195
GB-Ellis 127R

ChiB 3 0 0 7 10
TB 0 10 7 3 **20**
ChiB D18 R30/92 P(36-21-2) 233
TB D15 R37/209 P(21-9-1) 183
TB-Eckwood 110R

Det 10 3 0 0 13
LARm 7 0 0 13 **20**
Det D13 R33/125 P(25-7-2) 168
LARm D17 R37/178 P(24-14-2) 143
LARm-Tyler 136R, Dennard 119C

Dal 0 3 0 14 **17**
Phi 0 7 7 0 14
Dal D19 R37/141 P(24-13-2) 176
Phi D17 R24/94 P(27-12-1) 197
Dal-Hill 121C; Phi-Carmichael 151C

MONDAY, NOVEMBER 2

Min 0 3 0 14 17
Den 0 3 3 13 **19**
Min D19 R22/102 P(36-22-1) 223
Den D17 R37/147 P(30-16-1) 182

SUNDAY, NOVEMBER 8

Phi 7 10 14 21 **52**
SL 7 3 0 0 10
Phi D30 R45/197 P(35-19-1) 255
SL D13 R19/81 P(29-14-2) 158
Phi-Montgomery 118R, Carmichael 103C, Jaworski 235P

Cle 0 7 7 6 0 20
Den 3 7 3 7 3 **23**
Cle D20 R22/82 P(42-20-2) 280
Den D22 R36/116 P(33-21-0) 246

Oak 0 3 10 3 16
Hou 3 7 0 7 **17**
Oak D16 R28/149 P(32-16-2) 167
Hou D17 R41/108 P(31-17-0) 190

ChiB 7 3 0 3 3 **16**
KC 3 3 0 7 0 13
ChiB D15 R61/201 P(30-7-0) 77
KC D18 R39/165 P(34-12-1) 84

Cin 10 21 0 9 **40**
SD 0 10 0 7 17
Cin D29 R40/124 P(33-21-1) 337
SD D25 R22/136 P(41-20-2) 311
Cin-Curtis 147C; SD-Chandler 194C, Scales 102C, Fouts 352P

Pit 7 14 0 0 21
Sea 3 7 0 14 **24**
Pit D17 R38/162 P(22-13-2) 205
Sea D19 R33/96 P(25-18-0) 260

Atl 0 0 7 7 14
SF 0 10 0 7 **17**
Atl D19 R26/76 P(42-20-3) 216
SF D17 R34/82 P(30-16-1) 205
Atl-Jenkins 134C; SF-Clark 128C

Det 7 14 0 10 31
Was 10 10 3 10 **33**
Det D24 R35/222 P(22-14-3) 277
Was D25 R41/193 P(32-19-2) 271
Det-Sims 159R, Scott 156C; Was-Washington 144R, Seay 145C

Mia 0 6 14 7 3 **30**
NE 7 10 0 10 0 27
Mia D24 R41/203 P(37-22-2) 216
NE D23 R32/141 P(40-23-4) 351
Mia-Harris 145C; NE-Morgan 182C, Grogan 355P

NYG 0 14 0 10 24
GB 20 3 0 3 **26**
NYG D17 R31/88 P(46-23-4) 233
GB D13 R30/82 P(31-14-2) 185

TB 0 0 3 7 10
Min 3 13 7 2 **25**
TB D10 R15/43 P(27-13-0) 150
Min D26 R46/205 P(41-24-2) 221
Min-Brown 129R, Senser 101C

NO 0 7 7 7 **21**
LARm 3 10 0 0 13
NO D26 R52/307 P(19-11-0) 155
LARm D16 R23/113 P(33-15-4) 191
NO-Rogers 161R

NYJ 10 14 7 10 **41**
Bal 7 7 0 0 14
NYJ D28 R37/122 P(31-21-0) 271
Bal D21 R24/114 P(33-24-1) 218

MONDAY, NOVEMBER 9

Buf 7 7 0 0 14
Dal 7 0 20 0 **27**
Buf D18 R17/55 P(43-20-4) 310
Dal D21 R47/196 P(17-9-1) 202
Buf-Butler 118C, Ferguson 301P; Dal-Dorsett 117R

SUNDAY, NOVEMBER 15

Pit 7 7 13 7 **34**
Atl 0 7 3 10 20
Pit D13 R32/72 P(23-14-1) 221
Atl D24 R22/61 P(50-33-2) 380
Pit-Stallworth 127C, Bradshaw 253P; Atl-Andrews 124C, Jackson 109C, Bartkowski 416P

Cle 2 3 0 10 **15**
SF 0 6 6 0 12
Cle D14 R26/106 P(33-16-1) 161
SF D21 R35/118 P(42-24-2) 187

NYJ 0 10 7 0 **17**
NE 0 3 3 0 6
NYJ D17 R53/166 P(17-7-1) 60
NE D15 R23/92 P(34-14-1) 105

Buf 0 0 0 0 0
SL 3 7 0 14 **24**
Buf D17 R19/85 P(37-21-4) 226
SL D22 R41/258 P(23-13-1) 80
SL-Anderson 177R

Bal 6 0 0 7 13
Phi 7 14 10 7 **38**
Bal D9 R18/36 P(26-12-1) 172
Phi D34 R49/235 P(31-21-1) 339
Phi-Montgomery 115R

Dal 7 10 0 7 24
Det 0 7 10 10 **27**
Dal D19 R27/98 P(30-20-2) 225
Det D23 R35/198 P(24-14-1) 231
Det-Sims 119R

ChiB 10 0 0 7 17
GB 7 14 0 0 **21**
ChiB D20 R39/165 P(29-13-3) 88
GB D18 R34/114 P(32-11-1) 133
ChiB-Payton 105R

Den 7 0 7 10 **24**
TB 0 0 7 0 7
Den D22 R41/153 P(29-20-1) 128
TB D10 R14/41 P(31-14-2) 168

NO 0 3 0 7 10
Min 0 10 10 0 **20**
NO D23 R39/116 P(39-19-2) 198
Min D17 R23/70 P(40-19-0) 287

LARm 0 3 0 7 10
Cin 10 0 0 14 **24**
LARm D21 R27/107 P(47-21-4) 189
Cin D17 R36/146 P(26-11-1) 87

Was 7 3 7 10 3 **30**
NYG 7 6 7 7 0 27
Was D29 R50/184 P(38-25-1) 234
NYG D17 R27/96 P(24-9-1) 152

Oak 7 14 3 9 **33**
Mia 0 3 7 7 17
Oak D19 R32/143 P(39-16-0) 161
Mia D22 R20/70 P(47-26-1) 236

Hou 0 3 0 7 10
KC 7 3 7 6 **23**
Hou D19 R28/146 P(37-18-3) 224
KC D19 R47/258 P(12-6-1) 25
KC-Delaney 193R

MONDAY, NOVEMBER 16

SD 7 10 0 6 23
Sea 0 24 14 6 **44**
SD D26 R30/195 P(43-24-1) 291
Sea D24 R37/156 P(22-11-0) 212
SD-Muncie 151R, Winslow 106C

SUNDAY, NOVEMBER 22

Mia 0 12 0 3 15
NYJ 3 3 0 10 **16**
Mia D13 R31/146 P(22-10-2) 41
NYJ D21 R29/120 P(38-21-0) 165

Den 0 7 0 14 21
Cin 14 14 0 10 **38**
Den D17 R19/68 P(34-21-2) 269
Cin D25 R33/184 P(38-25-0) 387
Den-Watson 102C, DeBerg 305P; Cin-Ross 123C, Anderson 396P

NYG 3 7 0 10 **20**
Phi 7 3 0 0 10
NYG D14 R29/120 P(27-10-2) 172
Phi D20 R35/139 P(45-20-1) 154
NYG-Carpenter 111R; Phi-Montgomery 102R

Det 3 6 7 7 **23**
ChiB 0 7 0 0 7
Det D20 R49/229 P(29-10-1) 127
ChiB D4 R17/44 P(30-7-3) -20
Det-Sims 117R

Pit 12 0 6 14 **32**
Cle 3 7 0 0 10
Pit D25 R43/139 P(32-17-2) 223
Cle D22 R28/146 P(39-18-6) 219

Was 0 7 3 0 10
Dal 7 3 7 7 **24**
Was D17 R25/125 P(34-14-1) 131
Dal D27 R47/258 P(27-13-0) 212
Was-Winslow 144C, Fouts 296P; Dal-Dorsett 115R, Pearson 111C

NE 7 0 3 7 17
Buf 3 10 0 7 **20**
NE D11 R39/116 P(13-7-0) 181
Buf D19 R43/185 P(34-15-1) 249
NE-Morgan 141C; Buf-Hooks 111C

NO 0 10 14 3 **27**
Hou 0 3 7 14 24
NO D20 R45/181 P(14-10-0) 140
Hou D16 R26/99 P(23-15-1) 161
NO-Rogers 142R

SF 3 7 17 6 **33**
LARm 0 17 7 7 31
SF D19 R28/71 P(30-19-1) 259
LARm D27 R47/203 P(32-18-1) 208
SF-Solomon 124C

SD 7 21 20 7 **55**
Oak 7 14 0 0 21
SD D32 R38/148 P(47-30-1) 317
Oak D18 R17/59 P(43-20-3) 283
SD-Winslow 144C, Fouts 296P; Oak-Ramsey 122C

Sea 3 3 7 0 13
KC 3 17 7 13 **40**
Sea D21 R23/83 P(30-19-1) 256
KC D29 R43/269 P(22-17-0) 181
KC-Hadnot 106R

GB 0 0 0 3 3
TB 3 24 0 10 **37**
GB D14 R20/70 P(38-21-4) 212
TB D23 R43/210 P(24-13-1) 138
GB-Lofton 102C; TB-Owens 112R

SL 14 7 7 7 **35**
Bal 10 0 7 7 24
SL D24 R48/241 P(21-12-0) 211
Bal D22 R28/155 P(45-23-2) 230
SL 1-Anderson 130R, Tilley 158C

MONDAY, NOVEMBER 23

Min 7 14 0 9 30
Atl 7 0 14 10 **31**
Min D25 R22/130 P(47-24-4) 330
Atl D19 R37/149 P(32-21-0) 193
Min-Brown 108R, Rashad 151C, Kramer 330P

THURSDAY, NOVEMBER 26

ChiB 0 3 0 6 9
Dal 3 0 0 7 **10**
ChiB D15 R50/229 P(19-6-1) 43
Dal D11 R31/95 P(23-9-1) 178
ChiB-Payton 179R; Dal-Hill 117C

SUNDAY, NOVEMBER 29

Oak 0 3 8 21 **32**
Sea 0 10 14 7 31
Oak D28 R36/181 P(33-20-1) 156
Sea D18 R32/69 P(36-19-0) 314

Atl 10 14 7 0 **31**
Hou 0 13 0 14 27
Atl D18 R33/111 P(25-18-1) 348
Hou D23 R20/83 P(48-25-3) 235
Atl-Andrews 101R, Jenkins 122C, Bartkowski 371P; Hou-Holston 101C

TB 0 10 7 14 **31**
NO 7 7 0 0 14
TB D22 R38/127 P(24-16-1) 218
NO D20 R27/137 P(31-19-2) 204
TB-House 107C; NO-Rogers 120R

Was 0 14 0 0 14
Buf 7 7 7 0 **21**
Was D19 R27/91 P(34-22-1) 202
Buf D18 R39/188 P(18-6-0) 41
Buf-Hooks 109R

Cin 14 14 0 13 **41**
Cle 0 7 0 14 21
Cin D24 R29/130 P(34-27-0) 226
Cle D23 R29/125 P(34-22-0) 224
Cin-Johnson 105R, Anderson 235P

Den 0 10 0 7 **17**
SD 14 13 7 0 **34**
Den D19 R17/67 P(46-26-3) 322
SD D20 R38/148 P(34-21-1) 260
SD-Chandler 111C

THURSDAY, NOVEMBER 26
KC 7 0 3 0 10
Det 7 10 3 7 **27**
KC D14 R28/116 P(25-14-2) 129
Det D21 R41/171 P(22-10-0) 114

SUNDAY, NOVEMBER 29
GB 0 14 14 7 **35**
Min 14 0 6 3 23
GB D24 R41/115 P(33-18-2) 294
Min D23 R11/28 P(55-38-5) 376
GB-Lofton 159C; Min-Kramer 384P

SL 3 3 7 14 **27**
NE 7 0 6 7 20
SL D25 R41/157 P(28-20-0) 255
NE D19 R27/127 P(25-17-2) 226

Bal 0 0 0 0 0
NYJ 7 6 9 3 **25**
Bal D11 R24/49 P(24-10-1) 103
NYJ D22 R41/161 P(29-16-0) 139

LARm 0 0 0 0 0
Pit 7 14 3 0 **24**
LARm D12 R21/71 P(37-15-4) 103
Pit D18 R44/211 P(19-10-0) 170
Pit-Harris 114R

NYG 0 3 0 7 10
SF 7 7 0 3 **17**
NYG D12 R22/80 P(34-13-3) 143
SF D19 R39/123 P(40-27-0) 214

MONDAY, NOVEMBER 30
Phi 7 0 3 0 10
Mia 0 3 0 10 **13**
Phi D11 R31/136 P(24-12-1) 80
Mia D14 R34/73 P(30-15-0) 132
Mia-Harris 114C

THURSDAY, DECEMBER 3
Cle 3 3 0 7 13
Hou 0 14 0 3 **17**
Cle D28 R43/190 P(31-21-2) 177
Hou D7 R20/34 P(20-12-1) 120
Cle-Pruitt 155R

SUNDAY, DECEMBER 6
Buf 7 7 14 0 **28**
SD 7 14 3 3 27
Buf D19 R34/84 P(29-13-0) 234
SD D28 R32/145 P(42-28-1) 337
Buf-Lewis 113C; SD-Muncie 119R,
Joiner 106C, Winslow 126C,
Fouts 343P

KC 0 6 7 0 13
Den 7 9 0 0 **16**
KC D18 R24/74 P(34-18-1) 233
Den D16 R29/77 P(24-16-0) 265
Den-Watson 103C

Dal 17 10 0 10 **37**
Bal 6 0 7 0 13
Dal D29 R66/354 P(19-8-1) 110
Bal D9 R20/156 P(24-7-2) 82
Dal-Dorsett 175R; Bal-Dickey 130R

NE 0 7 0 7 14
Mia 0 14 7 3 **24**
NE D17 R30/134 P(20-12-0) 122
Mia D19 R42/212 P(24-11-1) 128
Mia-Nathan 119R

SF 7 7 0 7 **21**
Cin 0 3 0 0 3
SF D24 R35/146 P(36-23-1) 179
Cin D24 R20/155 P(38-21-3) 190

Min 0 0 0 9 9
ChiB 0 3 0 7 **10**
Min D16 R19/38 P(36-21-2) 254
ChiB D13 R51/175 P(11-4-2) 69
Min-White 112C; ChiB-Payton 112R

LARm 7 0 0 0 7
NYG 0 0 7 3 **10**
LARm D16 R47/172 P(21-8-1) 68
NYG D10 R39/87 P(22-5-0) 60

NYJ 0 9 7 7 23
Sea 6 7 7 7 **27**
NYJ D23 R28/119 P(51-27-2) 276
Sea D18 R35/127 P(27-20-3) 256
Sea-Largent 169C

Det 3 7 7 0 17
GB 0 14 7 10 **31**
Det D20 R31/143 P(33-17-2) 217
GB D24 R34/68 P(31-20-0) 265
GB-Jefferson 113C

Atl 3 6 7 7 23
TB 7 7 3 7 **24**
Atl D23 R27/137 P(34-24-1) 236
TB D22 R28/93 P(29-19-0) 327
TB-House 126C, Williams 336P

Phi 0 13 0 0 13
Was 6 0 0 9 **15**
Phi D25 R37/161 P(35-16-3) 255
Was D11 R32/108 P(22-13-2) 68
Phi-Montgomery 116R

NO 3 0 0 0 3
SL 7 10 0 13 **30**
NO D11 R29/117 P(18-7-3) 59
SL D19 R41/155 P(19-13-1) 135

MONDAY, DECEMBER 7
Pit 7 7 6 7 27
Oak 7 0 7 16 **30**
Pit D24 R30/96 P(36-21-2) 235
Oak D22 R38/214 P(29-18-1) 257
Oak-King 102R

SATURDAY, DECEMBER 12
Min 0 7 0 0 7
Det 14 17 7 14 **45**
Min D16 R22/72 P(44-17-4) 144
Det D29 R35/205 P(29-18-1) 271
Det-Sims 110R

NYJ 0 14 0 0 **14**
Cle 0 3 7 3 13
NYJ D18 R34/164 P(28-15-2) 150
Cle D17 R24/74 P(35-20-0) 260

SUNDAY, DECEMBER 13
Hou 0 0 0 6 6
SF 0 0 21 7 **28**
Hou D11 R22/56 P(30-21-0) 130
SF D22 R29/148 P(35-25-0) 266

SD 7 7 0 10 **24**
TB 7 0 3 13 23
SD D27 R31/94 P(36-22-0) 351
TB D18 R19/114 P(36-22-2) 290
SD-Chandler 112C, Fouts 351P;
TB-Williams 321P

Sea 0 3 7 13 23
Den 7 3 6 7 **23**
Sea D18 R27/86 P(40-18-0) 199
Den D23 R41/237 P(30-15-2) 136

GB 14 7 7 7 **35**
NO 0 0 0 7 7
GB D17 R29/116 P(21-19-0) 202
NO D16 R34/87 P(21-14-4) 165
GB-Dickey 218P

ChiB 0 7 14 2 **23**
Oak 6 0 0 0 6
ChiB D19 R38/150 P(32-15-1) 228
Oak D15 R17/46 P(46-20-1) 217

Bal 7 0 7 0 14
Was 7 21 10 0 **38**
Bal D21 R33/120 P(25-14-2) 217
Was D27 R34/147 P(36-23-1) 339
Bal-Casper 114C; Was-Monk 148C,
Seay 104C, Theismann 339P

NYG 7 3 7 3 **20**
SL 3 0 0 7 7
NYG D16 R39/175 P(24-12-1) 77
SL D12 R24/92 P(32-16-2) 130
NYG-Carpenter 117R

Mia 7 3 0 7 **17**
KC 0 7 0 0 7
Mia D16 R40/93 P(28-14-3) 160
KC D16 R28/91 P(37-21-1) 185

Buf 14 3 2 0 **19**
NE 0 3 0 7 10
Buf D20 R47/192 P(18-10-0) 137
NE D16 R27/97 P(28-12-2) 107
Buf-Cribbs 153R

Phi 3 7 0 0 10
Dal 0 7 7 7 **21**
Phi D14 R23/90 P(32-11-4) 135
Dal D23 R43/148 P(30-17-0) 264
Dal-Dorsett 101R

Cin 0 10 7 0 **17**
Pit 0 3 0 10 13
Cin D19 R33/103 P(35-21-1) 215
Pit D14 R25/87 P(30-15-2) 120

MONDAY, DECEMBER 14
Atl 7 3 3 3 16
LARm 0 14 0 7 **21**
Atl D16 R30/122 P(36-14-2) 130
LARm D19 R45/162 P(22-11-2) 111
Atl-Andrews 115R

SATURDAY, DECEMBER 19
Buf 0 3 0 6 9
Mia 7 3 3 3 **16**
Buf D15 R23/111 P(30-14-2) 129
Mia D18 R47/157 P(22-11-0) 125

Dal 0 0 0 10 10
NYG 0 3 7 3 **13**
Dal D16 R34/90 P(33-17-1) 164
NYG D15 R40/139 P(27-13-1) 158

SUNDAY, DECEMBER 20
GB 0 3 0 0 3
NYJ 7 14 0 7 **28**
GB D8 R15/45 P(33-12-1) 39
NYJ D22 R49/153 P(33-15-1) 240

SF 7 7 0 7 **21**
NO 14 0 3 0 17
SF D19 R31/154 P(25-17-1) 195
NO D15 R36/133 P(23-14-1) 89
NO-Rogers 107R

Cin 10 17 0 3 **30**
Atl 0 21 0 7 28
Cin D23 R27/133 P(35-19-1) 300
Atl D26 R28/91 P(47-25-1) 237
Cin-Collinsworth 128C

SL 0 0 0 0 0
Phi 7 21 10 0 **38**
SL D11 R32/139 P(26-11-3) 72
Phi D25 R39/259 P(24-15-2) 185
SL-Anderson 102R;
Phi-Montgomery 108R

Cle 0 7 7 7 21
Sea 14 14 14 0 **42**
Cle D16 R37/110 P(22-14-1) 182
Sea D16 R37/110 P(22-14-1) 182
Cle-Logan 101C

KC 3 0 7 0 **10**
Min 3 0 0 0 3
KC D13 R37/140 P(16-12-1) 133
Min D16 R23/84 P(38-17-1) 161
KC-Jackson 102R

Den 3 0 14 7 24
ChiB 0 14 14 7 **35**
Den D19 R19/76 P(49-22-3) 222
ChiB D15 R41/170 P(20-10-2) 111
Den-Upchurch 102C

NE 0 7 0 7 14
Bal 10 7 6 0 **23**
NE D20 R23/77 P(38-20-3) 273
Bal D19 R41/128 P(28-17-1) 255

Pit 3 3 14 0 20
Hou 7 7 0 7 **21**
Pit D17 R36/126 P(30-13-1) 151
Hou D18 R19/41 P(37-24-2) 335
Hou-Casper 119C, Holston 128C,
Nielsen 377P

Was 6 10 14 0 **30**
LARm 0 7 0 0 7
Was D25 R44/241 P(25-15-1) 261
LARm D14 R28/78 P(27-10-2) 87

TB 3 7 0 10 **20**
Det 0 7 3 7 17
TB D11 R33/104 P(19-8-0) 172
Det D21 R35/159 P(28-18-2) 181

MONDAY, DECEMBER 21
Oak 0 3 7 0 10
SD 7 10 3 3 **23**
Oak D20 R28/107 P(38-14-1) 229
SD D21 R39/147 P(27-14-0) 214
Oak-Chandler 128C

1982 NFL
SUNDAY, SEPTEMBER 12
SD 3 3 10 7 **23**
Den 0 3 0 7 10
SD D23 R38/140 P(34-19-0) 253
Den D17 R25/101 P(36-23-2) 222
SD-Chandler 120C

Mia 14 10 21 0 **45**
NYJ 7 7 0 14 28
Mia D25 R55/210 P(23-15-1) 113
NYJ D20 R23/144 P(30-18-3) 197
Mia-Franklin 103C;
NYJ-McNeil 116R

LARd 3 10 0 10 **23**
SF 0 14 3 0 17
LARd D17 R43/161 P(20-10-2) 94
SF D18 R22/60 P(41-21-1) 192
LARd-Allen 116R; SF-Clark 106C

LARm 10 13 0 0 23
GB 0 0 14 21 **35**
LARm D12 R28/105 P(37-16-0) 166
GB D22 R35/149 P(27-17-3) 228
GB-Ivery 109R, Jefferson 116C

Cle 0 14 0 7 **21**
Sea 0 0 0 7 7
Cle D25 R47/200 P(23-11-0) 130
Sea D18 R15/40 P(39-22-1) 140
Cle-Pruitt 136R

KC 3 3 0 3 9
Buf 7 7 0 0 **14**
KC D17 R29/104 P(30-14-1) 125
Buf D17 R34/101 P(31-18-0) 158

Was 0 14 0 20 3 **37**
Phi 10 3 14 7 0 34
Was D26 R30/114 P(39-28-0) 373
Phi D25 R27/101 P(38-27-0) 325
Was-Monk 134C, Theismann 382P;
Phi-Jaworski 371P

TB 0 3 0 7 10
Min 0 7 7 3 **17**
TB D16 R22/65 P(38-21-3) 290
Min D22 R32/101 P(28-16-0) 115
TB-Giles 100C

Hou 0 0 0 6 6
Cin 7 3 14 3 **27**
Hou D9 R23/89 P(17-11-0) 82
Cin D26 R29/103 P(40-29-0) 316
Cin-Anderson 354P

ChiB 0 7 0 3 10
Det 0 7 3 7 **17**
ChiB D14 R26/50 P(26-12-0) 104
Det D14 R32/67 P(28-13-1) 145

NE 3 7 7 7 **24**
Bal 3 7 0 3 13
NE D15 R44/227 P(16-7-1) 103
Bal D22 R35/131 P(46-20-3) 221
NE-Collins 137R

Atl 0 7 0 9 **16**
NYG 0 7 0 7 14
Atl D17 R33/118 P(27-15-1) 154
NYG D17 R24/76 P(41-25-1) 302
NYG-Brunner 310P

SL 7 0 7 7 **21**
NO 0 0 0 7 7
SL D15 R37/96 P(18-10-0) 54
NO D16 R24/107 P(34-20-2) 183
NO-Scott 103C

MONDAY, SEPTEMBER 13
Pit 6 7 17 6 **36**
Dal 0 7 7 7 21
Pit D23 R35/147 P(28-17-0) 241
Dal D28 R22/95 P(38-26-2) 341
Pit-Harris 103R, Stallworth 137C;
Dal-Cosbie 102C, Hill 130C,
White 347P

THURSDAY, SEPTEMBER 16
Min 2 17 3 0 22
Buf 0 7 6 10 **23**
Min D22 R17/113 P(46-20-1) 258
Buf D26 R30/134 P(45-25-1) 317
Min-White 142C; Buf-Butler 111C,
Ferguson 330P

SUNDAY, SEPTEMBER 19
Was 9 9 0 3 **21**
TB 0 6 0 7 13
Was D18 R45/177 P(20-12-0) 71
TB D14 R28/101 P(27-14-0) 177
Was-Riggins 136R; TB-House 105C

Sea 0 7 0 14 21
Hou 0 6 0 17 **23**
Sea D17 R27/80 P(38-24-0) 223
Hou D18 R35/170 P(38-17-2) 112
Hou-Campbell 142R

Det 0 9 7 3 **19**
LARm 0 0 14 0 14
Det D19 R38/148 P(34-17-1) 207
LARm D21 R30/111 P(34-19-2) 264
Det-Sims 119R, Sims 103C;
LARm-Miller 131C

LARd 7 17 7 7 **38**
Atl 7 0 0 7 14
LARd D18 R31/100 P(30-16-0) 264
Atl D26 R21/63 P(56-34-3) 322
LARd-Branch 138C, Miller 131C;
Atl-Bartkowski 375P

Bal 0 17 0 3 20
Mia 14 0 10 0 **24**
Bal D14 R42/160 P(17-9-0) 96
Mia D21 R34/142 P(25-16-0) 161

NYJ 0 10 7 14 **31**
NE 0 0 0 0 0
NYJ D30 R52/254 P(27-17-0) 142
NE D5 R21/61 P(17-6-3) -4
NYJ-McNeil 106R

Phi 0 3 0 21 **24**
Cle 7 0 0 14 21
Phi D25 R25/93 P(41-25-1) 330
Cle D23 R30/139 P(41-20-2) 227
Phi-Carmichael 100C,
Jaworski 334P; Cle-Newsome 122C

Dal 0 7 7 10 **24**
SL 0 0 0 7 7
Dal D19 R30/133 P(32-20-2) 246
SL D19 R23/62 P(39-22-1) 249
Dal-Hill 101R; SL-Green 170C

NO 7 0 3 0 **10**
ChiB 0 0 0 0 0
NO D17 R53/182 P(17-11-1) 135
ChiB D13 R16/48 P(35-17-3) 135
NO-Wilson 138R

Cin 0 3 7 10 20
Pit 7 3 13 3 **26**
Cin D24 R25/69 P(38-27-3) 310
Pit D20 R17/26 P(42-29-0) 269
Cin-Collinsworth 144C,
Anderson 323P

SF 14 0 0 7 21
Den 7 7 0 10 **24**
SF D20 R31/88 P(37-26-2) 221
Den D17 R31/100 P(26-17-1) 183
SF-Clark 127C, Solomon 109C,
Montana 336P

SD 0 0 3 12 15
KC 7 9 3 0 **19**
SD D16 R15/78 P(38-22-1) 204
KC D20 R34/100 P(30-22-1) 182

MONDAY, SEPTEMBER 20
GB 0 7 7 13 **27**
NYG 9 3 7 0 19
GB D16 R41/198 P(20-13-0) 163
NYG D15 R25/76 P(33-15-2) 191
GB-Lofton 101C

SUNDAY, NOVEMBER 21
TB 3 3 3 0 9
Dal 0 7 7 0 **14**
TB D21 R34/135 P(42-23-0) 247
Dal D13 R26/78 P(16-11-1) 107

```
NE     0   0   0   7    7
Cle    0   0   0  10   10
NE  D13 R38/169  P(11-3-0)    96
Cle D19 R33/97   P(32-13-0)  128

Mia    0   6   0   3    9
Buf    0   7   0   0    7
Mia D13 R32/122  P(29-12-2)  127
Buf D18 R34/132  P(29-12-6)  126

Bal    0   0   0   0    0
NYJ   10  17   7   3   37
Bal D17 R25/88   P(34-17-2)  230
NYJ D29 R42/227  P(31-16-0)  249
NYJ-McNeil 123R

Pit    3   7   7   7   24
Hou    0   0   0  10   10
Pit D20 R31/163  P(40-16-2)  199
Hou D16 R23/93   P(44-18-3)  199

Min    7   0   0   0    7
GB     0  13  13   0   26
Min D12 R17/25   P(41-19-0)  159
GB  D21 R34/136  P(32-19-0)  223

Det   14   0   3   0   17
ChiB   3   7   7   3   20
Det D17 R27/95   P(32-15-2)   57
ChiB D21 R34/144 P(27-16-3)  221

Cin    3   8   0   7   18
Phi    0   0   0  14   14
Cin D18 R27/113  P(32-19-2)  197
Phi D19 R22/62   P(43-24-2)  213

KC     0   7   0  10   17
NO    10   0   7  10   27
KC  D14 R19/94   P(25-15-1)  192
NO  D21 R44/149  P(19-14-1)  144
KC-Smith 101C; NO-Rogers 123R

SF     3   7   7  14   31
SL     0   7   6   7   20
SF  D22 R26/77   P(39-26-1)  371
SL  D15 R27/108  P(34-17-0)  146
SF-Clark 103C, Montana 408P

Was    7  14   3   3   27
NYG    3   7   7   7   24
Was D19 R40/139  P(24-16-0)  173
NYG D20 R31/136  P(28-14-1)  151

LARm  14   0   3   0   17
Atl    3   7  14   4   34
LARm D14 R23/123 P(28-17-0)  151
Atl D24 R39/174  P(24-19-0)  213
Atl-Andrews 119R

Sea    0   0   7  10   17
Den    0   7   3   0   10
Sea D21 R30/84   P(41-22-1)  303
Den D10 R25/136  P(27-12-2)  114
Sea-Johns 103C, Zorn 318P
```

MONDAY, NOVEMBER 22
```
SD    10  14   0   0   24
LARd   0   7  14   7   28
SD  D26 R23/72   P(42-25-2)  339
LARd D23 R37/181 P(25-18-2)  145
SD-Chandler 118C, Winslow 105C,
Fouts 357P
```

THURSDAY, NOVEMBER 25
```
NYG    0   0   6   7   13
Det    3   3   0   0    6
NYG D10 R27/88   P(28-12-2)  118
Det D19 R38/171  P(32-15-3)  150
Det-Sims 114R

Cle    0   0  14  14   14
Dal    0  17  14   0   31
Cle D17 R20/82   P(38-20-4)  198
Dal D27 R52/299  P(24-13-2)  197
Dal-Dorsett 116R
```

SUNDAY, NOVEMBER 28
```
Hou    7   0   0  14   21
NE    14   6   0   9   29
Hou D18 R21/71   P(33-19-1)  169
NE  D17 R42/190  P(16-10-0)  188
Hou-Casper 100C; NE-Collins 161R,
Morgan 122C

ChiB   0   0   0   7    7
Min    0  14   7  14   35
ChiB D12 R25/94  P(35-15-3)  103
Min D20 R22/63   P(35-26-2)  151
Min-White 177C, Kramer 342P
```

```
Phi    0   0   9   0    9
Was    3   7   3   0   13
Phi D17 R23/101  P(42-18-4)  218
Was D15 R31/61   P(28-14-2)  234
Phi-Carmichael 109C;
Was-Brown 124C

NO     7   6  10   0   23
SF     0   6   0  14   20
NO  D17 R45/170  P(20-11-1)  154
SF  D21 R16/55   P(42-27-1)  321
SF-Montana 334P

SL     7   7   3   6   23
Atl    3   3   7   7   20
SL  D20 R45/203  P(15-10-0)   96
Atl D20 R31/131  P(25-15-1)  143
SL-Anderson 122R, Tyler 138R

LARd   0  10   7   0   17
Cin   14   7   7   3   31
LARd D21 R20/33  P(44-27-4)  302
Cin D21 R35/137  P(26-14-0)  210
LARd-Tyler 138R, Plunkett 318P;
Cin-Johnson 129R

Pit    0   0   0   0    0
Sea    3   6   7   0   16
Pit D12 R23/83   P(27-14-3)  135
Sea D21 R38/124  P(22-14-0)  166
Sea-Largent 109C

Bal    0   0   0   0    0
Buf    3  14   0   3   20
Bal D6 R20/36    P(17-3-0)    52
Buf D21 R56/245  P(17-7-0)    67

GB     6   7   0   0   13
NYJ    0   6   9   0   15
GB  D17 R24/52   P(30-19-0)  211
NYJ D20 R35/134  P(36-20-1)  221

Den    3   7   3   7   20
SD     0  17   3  10   30
Den D20 R26/119  P(28-19-2)  175
SD  D28 R37/106  P(40-27-1)  330
SD-Joiner 121C, Winslow 107C,
Fouts 337P

KC     7   0   0   7   14
LARm   0  14   6   0   20
KC  D18 R35/139  P(27-12-1)  139
LARm D19 R46/237 P(12-6-1)    44
LARm-Tyler 138R
```

MONDAY, NOVEMBER 29
```
Mia    0   3   0  14   17
TB     3   3  10   7   23
Mia D18 R22/103  P(47-24-5)  227
TB  D15 R38/154  P(19-7-0)    61
```

THURSDAY, DECEMBER 2
```
SF     3  17   0  10   30
LARm   0   0   7   7   24
SF  D21 R29/49   P(38-27-0)  326
LARm D18 R22/64  P(43-20-2)  277
SF-Moore 102C, Montana 305P
```

SUNDAY, DECEMBER 5
```
SD    14  13   0   3   30
Cle    3   0  10   0   13
SD  D24 R36/130  P(23-18-2)  252
Cle D24 R21/90   P(48-33-2)  308
Cle-Newsome 140C, Sipe 338P

KC     0   7   0   7   14
Pit   14  14   0   7   35
KC  D16 R20/59   P(31-18-1)  179
Pit D20 R35/101  P(25-18-2)  275
Pit-Stallworth 107C

Sea    0   7   0  16   23
LARd   7  21   0   0   28
Sea D19 R19/80   P(45-16-3)  251
LARd D15 R42/194 P(19-10-1)   41
LARd-Allen 156R

SL    10  13   0   0   23
Phi    7   0   6   7   20
SL  D25 R50/231  P(23-14-0)  129
Phi D14 R22/100  P(24-15-0)  145
SL-Mitchell 145R

Buf    0   0  14   7   21
GB     6   7   7  13   33
Buf D23 R34/142  P(36-18-2)  194
GB  D21 R35/106  P(23-14-1)  195
```

```
Atl    7   7  10  10   34
Den   14   3   3   7   27
Atl D19 R37/137  P(23-14-1)  205
Den D23 R27/101  P(44-24-2)  249
Atl-Andrews 106C;
Den-Watson 101C

Min    0   7   7   0   14
Mia    6   3   3  10   22
Min D13 R19/93   P(28-16-3)   89
Mia D17 R46/178  P(21-13-0)  123
Mia-Franklin 129R

NE     0   6   7   0   13
ChiB  14   9   0   3   26
NE  D15 R21/46   P(28-13-2)  203
ChiB D23 R45/166 P(21-15-1)  176
NE-Morgan 130C

Cin    0   6   7   7   20
Bal    7   3   0   7   17
Cin D24 R30/106  P(29-22-0)  184
Bal D19 R39/210  P(20-11-0)  123

TB     0   3  10   0   13
NO     7   0   3   0   10
TB  D14 R27/93   P(24-15-0)  178
NO  D25 R27/69   P(43-29-0)  311
NO-Stabler 333P

Hou    0   7   0   7   14
NYG    3   0   0  14   17
Hou D12 R25/77   P(22-17-0)  191
NYG D20 R29/112  P(30-18-0)  250
NYG-Woolfolk 102C

Dal    0   7  10   7   24
Was    0   0   0  10   10
Dal D22 R38/160  P(30-21-2)  202
Was D15 R17/66   P(30-20-3)  209
Was-Monk 100C
```

MONDAY, DECEMBER 6
```
NYJ    7  14   0   7   28
Det    3   0   7   3   13
NYJ D21 R35/87   P(32-23-1)  350
Det D15 R25/104  P(37-14-3)  170
NYJ-Walker 164C, Todd 384P
```

SATURDAY, DECEMBER 11
```
SD     7  17   7  10   41
SF     7  10   0  20   37
SD  D28 R20/94   P(48-33-0)  444
SF  D29 R22/99   P(47-32-2)  366
SD-Chandler 125C, Joiner 145C,
Winslow 101C, Fouts 444P;
SF-Clark 135C, Montana 356P

Phi    7   0   0   0    7
NYG    3  14   3   3   23
Phi D9 R14/41    P(30-17-2)  157
NYG D19 R40/103  P(26-17-0)  250
NYG-Eddings 148C
```

SUNDAY, DECEMBER 12
```
ChiB   7   0   0   7   14
Sea    3  14   0   3   20
ChiB D19 R29/97  P(30-20-1)  213
Sea D17 R29/126  P(32-22-0)  164
Sea-Largent 111C

NO     0   0   0   0    0
Atl    0  14  14   0   35
NO  D13 R20/70   P(33-12-3)   21
Atl D26 R45/189  P(32-21-1)  140

Pit    0   0   0   0    0
Buf    0  10   3   0   13
Pit D6 R22/96    P(23-4-3)    -2
Buf D20 R46/184  P(25-12-2)  155
Pit-Wilder 116C; Buf-Cribbs 143R

Mia    0   0   0   3    3
NE     0   0   0   3    3
Mia D16 R38/176  P(18-9-2)    59
NE  D13 R43/199  P(5-2-1)     13
Mia-Franklin 107R;
NE-van Eeghen 100R

Was    3   3   3   3   12
SL     0   0   0   7    7
Was D18 R35/122  P(26-17-0)  170
SL  D19 R25/131  P(26-15-0)  225
SL-Anderson 109R
```

```
LARd   0   7   0  14   21
KC     3   3   7   3   16
LARd D18 R24/59  P(33-18-1)  284
KC  D21 R31/79   P(36-19-0)  206
LARd-Branch 111C, Plunkett 303P;
KC-Dixon 102C

TB     0   3   7   7   17
NYJ   14   0   9   9   32
TB  D15 R22/47   P(38-18-2)  204
NYJ D22 R39/138  P(29-17-0)  169
TB-Wilder 116C

Det   17   6   7   0   30
GB     0   0   3   7   10
Det D21 R43/155  P(32-15-3)  141
GB  D17 R14/44   P(52-19-5)  156
Det-Sims 109R

Bal    0   7   3   0   10
Min    7   0   3   3   13
Bal D15 R32/82   P(32-14-2)  116
Min D16 R31/87   P(35-19-1)  258

Cle    0   3   0   0    ?
Cin    0  14   3   6   23
Cle D12 R19/64   P(31-18-3)  146
Cin D19 R35/97   P(28-18-1)  159

Den    0   0  14   3   27
LARm   7  14   0   3   24
Den D22 R34/127  P(31-23-1)  258
LARm D14 R26/92  P(33-17-1)  161
Den-Watson 183C, DeBerg 307P
```

MONDAY, DECEMBER 13
```
Dal    0  17  10  10   37
Hou    7   0   0   0    7
Dal D20 R33/121  P(33-24-0)  295
Hou D10 R17/39   P(33-12-0)  160
```

SATURDAY, DECEMBER 18
```
NYJ    6  10   0   3   19
Mia   10   7   0   3   20
NYJ D17 R30/108  P(32-18-2)  166
Mia D16 R27/120  P(33-19-2)  184

LARm  14   7   0  10   31
LARd   0   7   7  23   37
LARm D21 R28/69  P(35-20-2)  203
LARd D26 R36/134 P(34-22-4)  297
LARd-Branch 128C, Plunkett 321P
```

SUNDAY, DECEMBER 19
```
Atl    0  10   0   7   17
SF     0   7   0   0    7
Atl D23 R57/231  P(21-12-2)  160
SF  D11 R16/55   P(31-16-1)  164
Atl-Andrews 108R; SF-Clark 101C

NE     3   7   3   3   16
Sea    0   0   0   0    0
NE  D25 R60/249  P(20-14-0)  144
Sea D12 R14/53   P(35-15-4)  118
NE-Collins 103R

Pit    0   7   0   2    9
Cle    3   0   7   0   10
Pit D15 R25/98   P(39-12-4)  124
Cle D15 R27/38   P(40-19-1)  186

SL     0   7   0   3   10
ChiB   0   0   0   0    0
SL  D17 R33/147  P(26-9-1)    93
ChiB D14 R32/118 P(35-16-0)  155

Buf    6   3   7   7   23
TB     3   0   7   7   24
Buf D21 R32/166  P(25-17-3)  152
TB  D22 R35/138  P(36-20-3)  204

GB     0  10   3   7   20
Bal    3   3  14   0   20
GB  D24 R40/138  P(35-17-1)  224
Bal D19 R39/110  P(40-23-0)  185
GB-Jefferson 101C

Hou    0   0   7   7   14
Phi    7  14   7   7   35
Hou D14 R26/43   P(30-18-4)  175
Phi D17 R26/198  P(21-12-1)  164
Hou-Casper 102C;
Phi-Montgomery 147R

Min    7  17   0  10   34
Det    7   0   3  21   31
Min D17 R34/116  P(29-20-0)  216
Det D19 R18/42   P(39-20-2)  304
Det-Thompson 161C,
Danielson 347P
```

```
KC     3   7  10  17   37
Den    0  13   3   0   16
KC  D17 R33/98   P(26-12-1)  172
Den D17 R26/74   P(30-19-2)  146
KC-Carson 110C

NO     0   0   0   7    7
Dal    0  21   0   0   21
NO  D18 R46/238  P(22-6-3)    63
Dal D16 R33/121  P(22-14-2)  195
NO-Rogers 166R; Dal-Dorsett 105R

NYG    7   7   0   0   14
Was    3   6   6   0   15
NYG D10 R20/55   P(26-10-0)   84
Was D20 R41/134  P(38-25-4)  241
```

MONDAY, DECEMBER 20
```
Cin   10  14  10   0   34
SD     7  10  23  10   50
Cin D22 R11/44   P(56-40-1)  397
SD  D34 R35/175  P(41-26-2)  486
Cin-Collinsworth 156C,
Anderson 416P; SD-Brooks 105R,
Chandler 260C, Winslow 116C,
Fouts 435P
```

SUNDAY, DECEMBER 26
```
SF     3   0   6  17   26
KC     3   7   0   3   13
SF  D23 R33/133  P(35-20-2)  237
KC  D18 R33/124  P(31-15-1)  151
SF-Clark 104C

NYJ    7  14   7  14   42
Min    0   7   0   7   14
NYJ D15 R25/92   P(23-16-0)  232
Min D28 R35/155  P(58-33-3)  329
Min-Senser 115C, Kramer 328P

ChiB  17   3   7   7   34
LARm   6  10   3   7   26
ChiB D37 R37/158 P(28-18-0)  263
LARm D27 R23/77  P(46-30-2)  506
ChiB-Payton 104R, Payton 102C;
LARm-Dennard 122C, Farmer 183C,
Tyler 102C, Ferragamo 509P

Det    0   7   7   7   21
TB     0   6   7  10   23
Det D13 R30/113  P(16-7-2)    97
TB  D24 R41/120  P(34-21-1)  257

Phi    0   7   7  10   24
Dal    7  10   0   3   20
Phi D16 R30/83   P(23-14-2)  153
Dal D17 R34/109  P(31-17-2)  136

Den    0   0   0  10   10
LARd   3  24   0   0   27
Den D25 R22/61   P(56-26-5)  284
LARd D16 R30/61  P(34-16-1)  251
LARd-Dennard 122C, Farmer 183C,
Tyler 102C, Ferragamo 509P

NE     0   0   0   7   14
Pit   10  10   0   7   37
NE  D14 R15/48   P(40-18-1)  283
Pit D28 R52/212  P(27-17-0)  282
NE-Morgan 127C; Pit-Harris 101R

GB     7  14   7  10   38
Atl    0   7   0   0    7
GB  D22 R30/164  P(22-12-1)  247
Atl D19 R22/58   P(43-30-1)  277
GB-Lofton 146C

SL     7   7   3   7   24
NYG    0   0  14   0   21
NYG D22 R17/78   P(51-29-0)  316
SL  D47 R47/190  P(25-14-1)  186
NYG-Brunner 326P;
SL-Anderson 110R

Bal    0   3  10  13   26
SD     7  16  14   7   44
Bal D20 R25/70   P(44-29-1)  300
SD  D25 R30/169  P(34-20-2)  338
SD-Muncie 126R, Chandler 118C,
Winslow 120C, Fouts 298P

Was    7  10   0  10   27
NO     0   7   3   0   10
Was D16 R37/198  P(23-14-0)  250
NO  D14 R35/120  P(24-9-1)    77
Was-Brown 156C
```

Cle	0	10	0	10	20
Hou	7	0	7	0	14

Cle D21 R39/111 P(34-18-0) 229
Hou D21 R31/105 P(37-19-4) 264

Sea	0	14	0	10	24
Cin					

Sea D16 R24/79 P(35-19-2) 200
Cin D24 R35/133 P(29-22-2) 256

MONDAY, DECEMBER 27

Buf	10	0	0	0	10
Mia	0	7	13	7	27

Buf D17 R28/138 P(33-21-2) 163
Mia D17 R38/161 P(18-7-1) 81
Buf-Cribbs 108R

SUNDAY, JANUARY 2

Atl 0 3 3 0 6
NO 0 14 0 21 35
Atl D16 R25/80 P(24-16-1) 168
NO D32 R37/152 P(36-25-2) 310

SL 0 0 0 0 0
Was 7 7 7 7 28
SL D10 R20/41 P(34-18-3) 155
Was D18 R39/129 P(25-16-0) 124

Den 2 0 7 2 11
Sea 3 0 0 7 10
Den D19 R41/199 P(33-18-2) 188
Sea D18 R31/129 P(39-22-2) 234

NYJ 6 0 0 7 13
KC 7 20 0 10 37
NYJ D19 R23/133 P(39-20-2) 175
KC D22 R35/146 P(28-18-1) 209

ChiB 3 17 3 0 0 23
TB 0 6 7 10 3 26
ChiB D14 R32/113 P(30-12-0) 135
TB D22 R21/99 P(50-25-2) 325
ChiB-Payton 109R;
TB-Williams 367P

LARd 0 10 10 21 41
SD 3 0 17 14 34
LARd D21 R29/157 P(28-17-0) 197
SD D29 R33/157 P(38-18-2) 281
LARd-Allen 126R; SD-Muncie 129R,
Chandler 138C, Fouts 303P

Buf 0 13 3 3 19
NE 3 7 6 14 30
Buf D17 R25/129 P(28-17-1) 224
NE D29 R40/158 P(34-20-1) 260
Buf-Cribbs 104R, Lewis 113C;
NE-Morgan 141C

Cle 7 0 0 14 21
Pit 7 6 7 17 37
Cle D20 R20/52 P(47-22-4) 293
Pit D27 R49/261 P(24-14-2) 260
Cle-Feacher 109C, Newsome 123C,
McDonald 313P; Pit-Harris 120R,
Swann 114C

GB 7 7 10 0 24
Det 14 3 3 7 27
GB D17 R30/94 P(26-13-4) 182
Det D23 R32/127 P(35-20-1) 241
GB-Lofton 128C

NYG 3 10 10 3 26
Phi 7 7 0 10 24
NYG D20 R31/118 P(35-21-3) 186
Phi D15 R22/50 P(26-16-1) 151

Cin 14 7 7 7 35
Hou 3 10 0 14 27
Cin D29 R42/147 P(32-28-0) 310
Hou D20 R24/112 P(33-21-2) 222
Cin-Ross 101C, Anderson 323P

Mia 10 7 7 10 34
Bal 0 7 0 0 7
Mia D22 R41/132 P(24-14-0) 239
Bal D20 R36/157 P(33-16-2) 116

LARm 7 0 7 7 21
SF 7 13 0 0 20
LARm D17 R25/147 P(35-23-0) 227
SF D18 R24/124 P(38-20-1) 200

MONDAY, JANUARY 3

Dal 3 7 3 14 27
Min 0 10 7 14 31
Dal D18 R28/197 P(32-14-1) 167
Min D23 R38/159 P(34-18-2) 222
Dal-Dorsett 153R; Min-Brown 100R

1983 NFL
SATURDAY, SEPTEMBER 3

Phi 0 3 16 3 22
SF 0 10 0 7 17
Phi D20 R41/125 P(19-15-0) 156
SF D17 R28/126 P(30-15-1) 210

SUNDAY, SEPTEMBER 4

Atl 6 0 7 7 20
ChiB 0 10 0 7 17
Atl D18 R31/132 P(23-14-0) 185
ChiB D21 R36/150 P(30-21-1) 251
ChiB-Payton 103R

Bal 3 10 7 3 6 29
NE 0 13 3 7 23
Bal D21 R36/172 P(31-17-1) 283
NE D19 R35/222 P(26-13-1) 200
NE-Weathers 100R

Den 0 0 0 7 14
Pit 0 7 3 0 10
Den D14 R38/138 P(16-5-1) 1
Pit D21 R29/123 P(32-18-3) 191

Det 5 0 3 3 11
TB
Det D16 R31/77 P(34-22-1) 236
TB D16 R22/60 P(33-21-1) 171

GB 7 21 3 7 3 41
Hou 10 0 7 21 38
GB D22 R26/135 P(34-30-1) 344
Hou D28 R36/150 P(34-22-2) 348
GB-Lofton 154C, Dickey 333P;
Hou-Campbell 123R, Smith 197C,
Manning 348P

LARd 7 10 0 3 20
Cin 0 0 3 7 10
LARd D22 R40/124 P(30-14-1) 133
Cin D17 R16/58 P(35-26-1) 203

LARm 3 7 6 0 16
NYG 0 6 0 0 6
LARm D20 R42/116 P(28-17-2) 279
NYG D13 R26/122 P(35-16-3) 137
NYG-Carpenter 113R

Mia 0 6 3 3 12
Buf 0 0 0 0 0
Mia D13 R36/151 P(23-9-0) 26
Buf D14 R21/86 P(36-21-2) 172

Min 7 10 10 0 27
Cle 0 7 7 7 21
Min D24 R39/189 P(33-22-1) 198
Cle D17 R24/116 P(34-20-3) 186

NYJ 0 13 7 21 41
SD 7 0 9 13 29
NYJ D25 R51/251 P(29-17-1) 140
SD D23 R23/134 P(36-20-2) 354
NYJ-McNeil 120R;
SD-Duckworth 110C, Joiner 106C,
Fouts 354P

SL 7 3 0 7 17
NO 0 7 14 7 28
SL D20 R27/115 P(36-22-1) 225
NO D15 R40/272 P(12-7-1) 111
NO-Rogers 206R

Sea 3 0 3 7 13
KC 7 0 7 3 17
Sea D13 R20/110 P(43-19-2) 198
KC D18 R33/120 P(33-20-0) 245
KC-Carson 104C

MONDAY, SEPTEMBER 5

Dal 0 3 14 14 31
Was 10 13 0 7 30
Dal D16 R30/183 P(21-9-0) 173
Was D26 R36/148 P(38-28-1) 299
Dal-Dorsett 151R, Hill 133C;
Was-Garrett 101C, Theismann 325P

THURSDAY, SEPTEMBER 8

SF 13 28 0 7 48
Min 7 3 7 0 17
SF D21 R43/197 P(24-17-0) 216
Min D18 R11/45 P(48-28-5) 272
SF-Tyler 107R, Montana 230P;
Min-LeCount 107C

SUNDAY, SEPTEMBER 11

Buf 0 3 7 0 10
Cin 0 3 0 3 6
Buf D21 R31/110 P(34-22-0) 157
Cin D15 R25/80 P(25-16-0) 201

Cle 7 7 10 7 31
Det 7 7 3 9 26
Cle D21 R34/160 P(29-18-0) 222
Det D24 R25/106 P(42-25-3) 329
Cle-Pruitt 137R, Sipe 234P;
Det-Thompson 179C

Dal 0 17 7 10 34
SL 10 0 0 7 17
Dal D19 R30/115 P(27-19-0) 214
SL D16 R20/53 P(40-23-4) 260
SL 1-Tilley 105C

Den 0 3 0 14 17
Bal 3 0 0 7 10
Den D15 R30/104 P(32-18-1) 223
Bal D13 R36/150 P(27-11-3) 121
Den-Watson 161C

Hou 0 3 0 3 6
LARd 6 7 0 7 20
Hou D7 R27/153 P(19-6-2) 70
LARd D26 R36/186 P(28-19-2) 200

NE 3 0 0 21 24
Mia 7 10 10 7 34
NE D19 R27/127 P(20-14-1) 187
Mia D21 R45/201 P(20-11-0) 195
Mia-Harris 109C

NO 3 7 10 7 27
LARm 0 7 7 16 30
NO D20 R41/121 P(31-16-1) 220
LARm D21 R25/104 P(30-17-2) 255

NYG 3 7 3 3 16
Atl 0 3 7 3 13
NYG D19 R44/156 P(30-18-1) 187
Atl D14 R20/63 P(35-23-0) 235
NYG-Carpenter 111R

Pit 7 6 3 9 25
GB 7 7 0 7 21
Pit D27 R59/285 P(19-12-0) 186
GB D17 R19/87 P(21-15-0) 276
Pit-Harris 118R; GB-Lofton 169C

Sea 0 10 0 7 17
NYJ 3 0 7 7 17
Sea D19 R57/196 P(15-7-0) 76
NYJ D16 R29/174 P(28-12-3) 205
Sea-Warner 128R;
NYJ-McNeil 140R, Walker 116C

TB 0 3 7 0 10
ChiB 0 10 7 0 17
TB D17 R29/85 P(42-22-1) 262
ChiB D16 R35/241 P(24-16-2) 263
ChiB-Payton 115C

Was 7 0 3 13 23
Phi 0 3 7 3 13
Was D14 R32/150 P(26-15-0) 135
Phi D17 R21/35 P(37-24-2) 277
Was-Riggins 100R;
Phi-Carmichael 108C, Quick 106C,
Jaworski 326P

MONDAY, SEPTEMBER 12

SD 3 0 7 7 17
KC 0 7 0 7 14
SD D27 R51/192 P(25-17-1) 251
KC D13 R18/45 P(31-24-1) 222
SD-Muncie 110R

THURSDAY, SEPTEMBER 15

Cin 0 7 0 0 7
Cle 7 3 7 0 17
Cin D18 R21/102 P(40-26-2) 199
Cle D18 R28/84 P(32-22-2) 218

SUNDAY, SEPTEMBER 18

Atl 3 21 0 6 30
Det 0 7 7 0 14
Atl D26 R43/185 P(35-24-0) 350
Det D18 R11/45 P(44-21-1) 235
Atl-Andrews 150R, Jackson 123C,
Bartkowski 366P

Bal 6 3 7 7 23
Buf 7 7 14 0 28
Bal D17 R31/147 P(26-12-0) 225
Buf D27 R42/145 P(27-18-0) 177

ChiB 7 3 7 14 0 31
NO 7 3 14 7 3 34
ChiB D21 R34/189 P(33-20-3) 304
NO D21 R28/84 P(40-26-3) 248
ChiB-Payton 161R, Gault 103C;
NO-Brenner 105C

KC 3 9 0 0 12
Was 0 0 17 10 27
KC D17 R17/33 P(46-20-2) 297
Was D17 R38/180 P(28-12-2) 153
KC-Carson 109C, Kenney 330P

LARm 0 3 21 0 24
GB 10 7 0 10 27
LARm D15 R26/93 P(30-20-1) 245
GB D23 R28/110 P(36-22-3) 253

Min 7 6 0 3 16
TB 0 6 3 7 3 19
Min D18 R33/90 P(42-24-0) 264
TB D20 R42/114 P(30-17-2) 192

NYG 3 0 10 0 13
Dal 0 14 0 14 28
NYG D16 R33/131 P(27-13-3) 203
Dal D18 R28/89 P(32-24-2) 220
NYG-Gray 124C

NYJ 0 0 0 13 13
NE 13 3 7 0 23
NYJ D19 R27/89 P(33-17-0) 177
NE D22 R47/328 P(11-9-0) 70
NE-Collins 212R

Phi 7 0 0 6 13
Den 0 0 3 7 10
Phi D19 R43/133 P(28-18-0) 274
Den D16 R21/69 P(33-18-2) 176
Phi-Quick 152C

Pit 6 6 14 14 40
Hou 7 0 0 21 28
Pit D25 R49/275 P(27-16-1) 176
Hou D16 R18/57 P(35-16-4) 254
Pit-Harris 115R; Hou-Manning 300P

SD 7 3 0 21 31
Sea 14 3 10 7 34
SD D23 R22/99 P(41-21-3) 332
Sea D24 R56/206 P(24-15-1) 162
SD-Sievers 115C, Fouts 338P;
Sea-Warner 109R, Largent 116C

SF 7 14 7 14 42
SL 7 3 10 7 27
SF D24 R31/191 P(32-20-1) 336
SL D22 R32/213 P(35-21-2) 172
SF-Tyler 108R, Solomon 121C,
Montana 341P; SL-Mitchell 123R,
Green 133C

MONDAY, SEPTEMBER 19

Mia 0 0 0 14 14
LARd 7 6 7 7 27
Mia D19 R29/101 P(35-21-1) 207
LARd D21 R38/152 P(15-11-0) 119
LARd-Allen 105R

SUNDAY, SEPTEMBER 25

Atl 0 7 6 7 20
SF 7 7 7 3 24
Atl D19 R31/135 P(24-19-0) 184
SF D28 R31/157 P(32-27-2) 261
Atl-Andrews 126R;
SF-Solomon 103C

ChiB 3 3 13 0 19
Bal 0 13 0 6 3 22
ChiB D15 R22/103 P(36-16-2) 227
Bal D20 R50/216 P(30-19-2) 245
ChiB-Gault 130C

Cin 14 0 0 3 23...
Cin 14 0 0 3 23
TB 0 7 3 7 17
Cin D19 R30/121 P(30-15-1) 146
TB D22 R23/52 P(40-30-3) 291
TB-Wilder 126C, Thompson 316P

Cle 7 7 3 6 3 30
SD 3 7 14 0 0 24
Cle D29 R29/103 P(45-27-1) 307
SD D23 R26/70 P(38-24-0) 351
Cle-Logan 121C, Sipe 327P;
SD-Chandler 134C, Winslow 108C,
Fouts 351P

Det 0 7 10 0 17
Min 3 14 0 3 20
Det D24 R36/154 P(42-18-5) 217
Min D14 R26/40 P(31-18-1) 141
Det-Nichols 100C

Hou 3 3 7 0 13
Buf 7 6 3 14 30
Hou D23 R37/181 P(29-19-0) 201
Buf D21 R32/228 P(22-11-1) 105
Hou-Campbell 142R, Smith 147C;
Buf-Cribbs 166R

KC 3 3 0 0 6
Mia 0 7 7 0 14
KC D8 R25/63 P(22-10-4) 92
Mia D20 R47/179 P(18-11-2) 100

LARd 0 7 13 2 22
Den 0 0 0 7 7
LARd D11 R37/82 P(24-13-1) 132
Den D16 R30/130 P(33-14-2) 138
LARd-Dickerson 192R;
Den-Winder 119R

LARm 14 0 3 7 24
NYJ 7 7 7 7 28
LARm D19 R32/203 P(37-22-4) 222
NYJ D25 R27/81 P(50-37-2) 403
LARm-Dickerson 192R;
NYJ-Walker 135C, Todd 446P

NE 7 7 7 7 28
Pit 7 6 0 10 23
NE D12 R28/88 P(15-9-1) 208
Pit D30 R46/210 P(35-21-3) 238
NE-Starring 108C; Pit-Harris 106R

NO 0 10 3 7 20
Dal 7 6 0 8 21
NO D17 R38/115 P(34-18-1) 183
Dal D16 R26/173 P(31-15-4) 99
NO-Wilson 108R; Dal-Dorsett 124R

SL 0 7 0 7 14
Phi 3 0 8 0 11
SL D17 R43/195 P(19-12-0) 89
Phi D15 R22/78 P(28-17-1) 180
SL-Anderson 133R; Phi-Quick 133C

Was 7 13 0 7 27
Sea 3 7 0 7 17
Was D17 R39/131 P(16-9-0) 162
Sea D20 R27/74 P(40-20-1) 234
Sea-Largent 130C

MONDAY, SEPTEMBER 26

GB 3 0 0 0 3
NYG 0 10 17 0 27
GB D15 R21/53 P(31-18-1) 272
NYG D19 R45/208 P(19-8-0) 104
NYG-Carpenter 116R

SUNDAY, OCTOBER 2

Bal 7 7 10 10 34
Cin 10 14 7 0 31
Bal D30 R38/166 P(20-12-0) 98
Cin D21 R23/80 P(31-21-3) 313
Cin-Collinsworth 206C,
Anderson 330P

Dal 3 10 14 10 37
Min 7 17 0 0 24
Dal D28 R47/200 P(40-22-2) 200
Min D14 R16/44 P(39-17-3) 272
Dal-Dorsett 141R; Min-White 107C

Den 0 0 7 7 14
ChiB 14 10 0 7 31
Den D16 R15/46 P(40-21-2) 200
ChiB D22 R39/177 P(26-16-4) 246

Det 3 7 0 0 10
LARm 0 14 0 7 21
Det D17 R24/65 P(41-19-1) 200
LARm D23 R40/239 P(20-14-1) 116
LARm-Dickerson 199R

Hou 0 3 7 0 10
Pit 0 7 0 10 17
Hou D19 R39/123 P(28-13-3) 147
Pit D14 R38/137 P(12-5-0) 88

LARd 0 14 14 7 35
Was 7 10 3 17 37
LARd D19 R24/105 P(30-16-4) 326
Was D25 R32/98 P(40-23-0) 361
LARd-Dickerson 199R,
Muhammad 112C, Plunkett 372P;
Was-Brown 180C, Theismann 417P

Mia 0 0 0 7 **7**
NO 0 7 10 0 **17**
Mia D19 R22/66 P(34-16-2) 178
NO   D21 R45/199 P(18-12-0) 124
NO-Wilson 160R

Phi 14 7 0 7 **28**
Atl 0 7 10 24
Phi D16 R27/95 P(28-16-0) 220
Atl D21 R37/191 P(34-20-0) 174
Phi-Quick 122C; Atl-Andrews 150R;
Bailey 106C

SL   7 0 0 7 **14**
KC   14 0 3 21 **38**
SL   D10 R31/123 P(25-10-5) 71
KC   D17 R30/106 P(38-21-2) 183
SL-Anderson 106R

SD   13 14 7 7 **41**
NYG 0 17 7 10 34
SD   D28 R27/120 P(41-24-3) 302
NYG D23 R28/54 P(51-31-1) 387
NYG-Gray 159C, Brunner 395P

SF   7 10 3 13 **33**
NE   6 0 0 7 13
SF   D29 R42/174 P(38-25-0) 252
NE   D14 R18/75 P(29-16-1) 220

Sea 3 0 7 14 **24**
Cle 0 3 0 6 9
Sea D15 R35/137 P(17-11-1) 122
Cle D22 R28/125 P(40-25-3) 280
Cle-Pruitt 107R, Sipe 310P

TB   0 7 0 7 **14**
GB   14 35 0 6 **55**
TB   D18 R14/20 P(47-24-2) 273
GB   D23 R42/164 P(28-18-1) 355
GB-Lofton 112C

MONDAY, OCTOBER 3

NYJ 0 7 10 17 **34**
Buf 0 0 10 0 10
NYJ D24 R38/210 P(31-20-1) 206
Buf D16 R19/65 P(41-25-3) 151
NYJ-Harper 118R

SUNDAY, OCTOBER 9

Buf 7 7 7 14 3 **38**
Mia 0 7 14 14 0 35
Buf D28 R23/76 P(55-38-1) 407
Mia D31 R43/153 P(30-20-2) 335
Buf-Ferguson 419P;
Mia-Duper 202C, Marino 322P

Den 7 13 3 3 **26**
Hou 0 14 0 0 14
Den D22 R44/253 P(21-11-0) 148
Hou D19 R26/126 P(32-15-0) 167
Den-Winder 165R;
Hou-Campbell 101R

GB   0 0 7 7 **14**
Det 10 14 7 7 **38**
GB   D20 R16/87 P(38-21-2) 201
Det D26 R42/171 P(29-21-0) 255

KC   14 3 0 3 **20**
LARd 0 7 7 7 **21**
KC   D20 R21/55 P(45-25-0) 236
LARd D21 R35/114 P(30-17-2) 157
LARd-Dickerson 142R

LARm 0 0 10 0 **10**
SF   7 0 7 7 21
LARm D13 R28/189 P(26-13-1) 118
SF   D20 R25/78 P(42-28-0) 303
LARm-Dickerson 142R;
SF-Montana 316P

Min 7 3 10 3 **23**
ChiB 0 7 0 7 14
Min D15 R30/191 P(29-14-1) 177
ChiB D23 R37/239 P(32-15-2) 186
Min-Galbreath 104R;
ChiB-Payton 102R

NE   7 0 0 0 **7**
Bal 0 0 7 5 **12**
NE   D20 R33/161 P(34-19-2) 242
Bal D13 R39/176 P(17-7-1) 126
NE-Morgan 136C

NO   3 0 3 13 **19**
Atl 0 3 7 7 17
NO   D19 R33/163 P(29-15-1) 148
Atl D20 R28/89 P(37-20-1) 203
NO-Wilson 103R; Atl-Bailey 109C

NYJ 0 0 0 7 **7**
Cle 0 7 0 3 **10**
NYJ D19 R27/124 P(31-22-1) 188
Cle D18 R25/66 P(36-22-2) 267

Phi 0 7 7 3 **17**
NYG 3 3 0 7 13
Phi D20 R28/98 P(31-16-0) 206
NYG D20 R33/127 P(32-17-1) 251

Sea 7 14 0 0 **21**
SD   0 7 14 7 **28**
Sea D20 R31/110 P(41-25-1) 288
SD   D27 R23/94 P(38-29-2) 318
Sea-Young 140C; SD-Fouts 331P

TB   10 0 7 7 **24**
Dal 7 3 7 3 7 **27**
TB   D13 R23/87 P(30-19-1) 248
Dal D25 R37/104 P(44-29-3) 340
Dal-Springs 126C, White 377P

Was 7 17 14 0 **38**
SL   0 7 7 0 14
Was D22 R37/182 P(25-14-0) 138
SL   D18 R23/82 P(32-21-1) 228
Was-Riggins 115R

MONDAY, OCTOBER 10

Pit 7 3 0 14 **24**
Cin 0 0 14 0 14
Pit D9 R20/56 P(23-10-1) 112
Cin D22 R32/105 P(34-21-3) 176

SUNDAY, OCTOBER 16

Atl 7 7 7 0 **21**
LARm 0 7 7 13 **27**
Atl D15 R29/110 P(22-13-0) 158
LARm D29 R34/103 P(36-23-1) 218
Atl-Bailey 106C

Buf 7 17 3 3 **30**
Bal 7 0 0 0 7
Buf D23 R39/171 P(31-21-0) 230
Bal D13 R30/211 P(20-8-3) 73
Buf-Cribbs 105R

ChiB 0 10 0 7 **17**
Det 7 10 7 7 **31**
ChiB D25 R20/118 P(46-28-0) 309
Det D21 R34/171 P(28-11-0) 195
ChiB-Evans 336P

Cin 7 3 7 0 **17**
Den 7 0 7 10 **24**
Cin D22 R29/105 P(33-20-1) 252
Den D22 R28/110 P(37-25-1) 276
Cin-Collinsworth 149C;
Den-Watson 119C

Cle 0 0 7 10 **17**
Pit 20 14 0 10 **44**
Cle D27 R31/159 P(49-27-6) 290
Pit D19 R39/146 P(18-14-0) 186
Cle-Green 137R, Newsome 103C,
Sipe 310P

Hou 7 0 7 0 **14**
Min 7 3 10 14 **34**
Hou D17 R34/145 P(31-17-2) 163
Min D17 R28/120 P(34-20-0) 209
Hou-Campbell 130R

LARd 7 10 5 14 **36**
Sea 7 0 17 14 38
LARd D24 R30/183 P(34-23-3) 199
Sea D13 R44/151 P(16-4-0) 2
LARd-Christensen 152C

Mia 7 13 10 2 **32**
NYJ 7 0 0 7 14
Mia D12 R29/51 P(30-17-0) 215
NYJ D23 R25/121 P(48-24-6) 221

NYG 0 14 13 0 **27**
KC   0 10 14 14 **38**
NYG D16 R24/78 P(37-18-3) 246
KC   D25 R32/97 P(36-25-1) 335
NYG-Gray 111C; KC-Marshall 131C,
Kenney 342P

Phi 7 0 0 0 **7**
Dal 3 14 3 17 **37**
Phi D9 R12/44 P(25-8-2) 165
Dal D32 R49/212 P(40-26-1) 310

SL   3 10 14 7 **34**
TB   6 0 14 7 27
SL   D17 R37/136 P(22-17-1) 143
TB   D17 R21/74 P(30-20-2) 196

SD   7 14 0 0 **21**
NE   3 7 3 24 **37**
SD   D27 R29/86 P(37-25-1) 341
NE   D24 R37/169 P(33-17-0) 178
SD-Fouts 357P

SF   6 0 16 10 **32**
NO   0 10 0 3 13
SF   D15 R35/194 P(27-17-1) 134
NO   D20 R25/90 P(37-22-3) 198

MONDAY, OCTOBER 17

Was 10 10 13 14 **47**
GB   10 14 7 17 **48**
Was D33 R43/184 P(39-27-0) 368
GB   D20 R18/70 P(32-23-1) 403
Was-Monk 105C, Theismann 398P;
GB-Coffman 124C, Ellis 105C,
Dickey 387P

SUNDAY, OCTOBER 23

Atl 0 0 7 20 **27**
NYJ 0 7 14 0 21
Atl D19 R26/130 P(36-25-2) 277
NYJ D19 R30/183 P(37-20-1) 221
Atl-Bartkowski 313P

ChiB 7 0 0 0 **7**
Phi 0 0 3 3 6
ChiB D15 R49/186 P(18-9-0) 86
Phi D14 R25/109 P(30-11-0) 116

Cle 0 14 7 0 **21**
Cin 0 7 7 14 **28**
Cle D16 R20/74 P(36-20-2) 198
Cin D17 R42/134 P(20-16-0) 154

Det 0 3 7 7 **17**
Was 14 14 3 7 **38**
Det D12 R18/81 P(34-13-2) 95
Was D26 R46/209 P(23-15-0) 232
Was-Washington 147R

KC   0 10 0 3 **13**
Hou 7 0 3 0 10
KC   D19 R24/112 P(44-26-0) 241
Hou D19 R42/172 P(24-14-1) 108

LARd 10 21 3 6 **40**
Dal 3 17 0 14 38
LARd D31 R37/219 P(50-26-1) 300
Dal D17 R27/81 P(39-20-2) 238
LARd-Dickerson 144R,
Hawkins 118R, Barber 113C,
Ferragamo 327P, Wilson 318P

Mia 7 14 0 0 **21**
Bal 0 0 0 7 7
Mia D14 R43/115 P(18-11-0) 157
Bal D17 R27/138 P(31-15-2) 173

Min 7 3 7 3 **20**
GB   0 3 0 14 17
Min D24 R43/211 P(27-16-0) 199
GB   D27 R25/87 P(41-23-3) 327
Min-Brown 179R; GB-Dickey 383P

NE   0 0 7 24 **31**
Buf 0 0 0 0 0
NE   D21 R43/200 P(29-17-0) 244
Buf D14 R19/93 P(44-17-3) 199
NE-Collins 147R; Buf-Lewis 116C

NO   0 10 14 0 **24**
TB   14 7 0 0 21
NO   D19 R40/179 P(29-12-4) 60
TB   D12 R25/74 P(36-16-3) 61

Pit 7 17 0 3 **27**
Sea 0 0 7 14 21
Pit D26 R60/182 P(20-12-0) 158
Sea D14 R17/57 P(28-14-1) 197
Pit-Harris 132R; Sea-Johns 118C

SD   0 3 3 0 **6**
Den 0 0 0 14 **14**
SD   D17 R23/106 P(48-22-3) 193
Den D21 R39/128 P(26-14-1) 133

SF   0 14 3 28 **45**
LARm 0 21 7 7 35
SF   D22 R27/102 P(39-25-0) 358
LARm D28 R32/139 P(35-26-2) 302
SF-Montana 358P;
LARm-Dickerson 144R,
Barber 113C, Ferragamo 327P

MONDAY, OCTOBER 24

NYG 7 7 3 3 **20**
SL   3 7 7 3 **20**
NYG D18 R36/112 P(46-20-2) 162
SL   D23 R43/200 P(33-16-3) 184
SL-Mitchell 108R, Green 100C

SUNDAY, OCTOBER 30

Bal 3 13 3 3 **22**
Phi 7 7 7 0 21
Bal D17 R53/233 P(18-8-0) 73
Phi D16 R24/101 P(24-14-2) 183
Bal-McMillan 109R

Dal 7 10 7 14 **38**
NYG 7 7 6 0 20
Dal D27 R46/197 P(34-16-2) 288
NYG D17 R21/94 P(34-15-3) 296
Dal-Hill 106C, White 304P;
NYG-Woolfolk 135C, Rutledge 325P

Det 14 3 14 7 **38**
ChiB 3 0 14 17
Det D21 R37/192 P(19-12-0) 204
ChiB D25 R31/139 P(39-22-2) 243

GB   7 0 0 7 **14**
Cin 6 21 0 7 **34**
GB   D17 R19/73 P(32-17-2) 210
Cin D30 R49/223 P(29-20-0) 241
Cin-Johnson 112R

Hou 7 3 9 0 **19**
Cle 3 7 9 6 **25**
Hou D11 R35/120 P(27-11-1) 138
Cle D19 R36/188 P(41-19-2) 189
Cle-Green 107R

KC   0 17 3 7 **27**
Den 0 17 3 7 **27**
KC   D21 R17/35 P(52-27-2) 327
Den D23 R32/75 P(42-21-0) 329
KC-Kenney 365P;
Den-Upchurch 143C, Watson 121C,
DeBerg 350P

LARm 7 0 0 0 **7**
Mia 7 7 10 6 **30**
LARm D19 R21/105 P(38-23-3) 204
Mia D20 R32/173 P(39-25-1) 279
LARm-Dickerson 101R;
Mia-Duper 134C

Min 0 10 0 21 **31**
SL   14 6 14 7 **41**
Min D23 R19/59 P(38-27-3) 289
SL   D24 R40/182 P(29-20-0) 238
Min-Dils 314P; SL 1-Anderson 136R

NE   0 0 0 13 **13**
Atl 3 14 7 0 **24**
NE   D22 R25/169 P(36-22-1) 248
Atl D28 R42/195 P(33-22-0) 235
Atl-Andrews 125R

NO   0 7 0 14 **21**
Buf 7 13 7 0 **27**
NO   D20 R30/133 P(37-23-2) 256
Buf D22 R37/132 P(26-14-0) 169
NO-Rogers 114R;
Buf-Ferguson 173P

NYJ 0 17 0 10 **27**
SF   0 10 3 0 13
NYJ D21 R35/186 P(28-20-0) 170
SF   D17 R25/85 P(36-21-2) 227

Sea 0 17 7 10 **34**
LARd 0 7 7 7 21
Sea D20 R40/183 P(23-14-1) 169
LARd D22 R27/125 P(34-22-4) 255
Sea-Warner 101R;
LARd-Dickerson 101R, Allen 104C

TB   6 3 3 0 **12**
Pit 0 0 0 17 **17**
TB   D13 R45/131 P(29-14-0) 105
Pit D21 R29/129 P(39-20-3) 209
TB-Wilder 126R

MONDAY, OCTOBER 31

Was 7 3 7 10 **27**
SD   0 0 7 17 24
Was D24 R36/169 P(46-25-1) 313
SD   D21 R28/121 P(38-19-6) 307
Was-Brown 101C,
Monk 106C, Theismann 324P;
SD-Chandler 103C, Luther 314P

SUNDAY, NOVEMBER 6

Atl 0 10 0 0 **10**
NO   0 7 7 13 **27**
Atl D14 R29/93 P(28-17-1) 120
NO   D17 R43/238 P(14-9-1) 128
NO-Rogers 137R

Bal 3 0 7 7 **17**
NYJ 7 0 7 0 14
Bal D15 R41/132 P(17-9-0) 99
NYJ D18 R27/102 P(39-22-2) 196

Buf 0 0 0 7 **7**
NE   0 14 0 7 **21**
Buf D20 R17/77 P(48-20-4) 186
NE   D19 R41/199 P(28-15-2) 251
NE-Collins 100R

ChiB 0 0 7 7 **14**
LARm 0 14 0 7 **21**
ChiB D15 R26/114 P(30-20-1) 170
LARm D18 R42/161 P(23-12-0) 123
LARm-Dickerson 127R

Cin 24 10 14 7 **55**
Hou 0 0 14 0 14
Cin D22 R50/207 P(13-8-0) 117
Hou D20 R25/72 P(45-25-3) 230

Cle 7 0 14 0 **21**
GB   7 7 14 7 **35**
Cle D24 R25/119 P(50-27-2) 337
GB   D26 R40/154 P(33-20-3) 216
GB-Jefferson 102C, Dickey 228P

Den 0 3 6 10 **19**
Sea 6 0 14 7 **27**
Den D23 R29/135 P(36-18-2) 222
Sea D18 R37/183 P(23-14-1) 216
Den-Watson 110C;
Sea-Warner 134R

LARd 7 0 0 21 **28**
KC   0 6 7 7 20
LARd D22 R33/91 P(32-16-1) 232
KC   D20 R24/81 P(45-24-2) 276
LARd-Dickerson 127R;
KC-Carson 103C

Mia 7 7 3 3 **20**
SF   7 7 0 3 17
Mia D18 R36/133 P(29-15-0) 183
SF   D20 R34/184 P(26-16-0) 210

Dal 0 10 0 17 **27**
Phi 7 3 3 7 20
Dal D22 R32/114 P(24-21-1) 249
Phi D16 R30/130 P(35-13-1) 223
Phi-Quick 120C

SL   0 0 7 0 **7**
Was 7 10 21 7 **45**
SL   D15 R19/79 P(35-17-1) 188
Was D23 R45/209 P(25-14-1) 165

SD   0 3 0 0 **3**
Pit 17 3 3 3 **26**
SD   D11 R20/59 P(34-17-2) 159
Pit D19 R43/156 P(23-11-1) 132

TB   0 7 7 3 **17**
Min 7 2 0 3 12
TB   D11 R34/208 P(19-11-1) 67
Min D18 R26/68 P(42-22-0) 179
TB-Wilder 219R;
Min-Galbreath 110C

MONDAY, NOVEMBER 7

NYG 3 3 3 0 **9**
Det 7 5 0 3 **15**
NYG D21 R43/176 P(26-13-3) 108
Det D15 R33/134 P(24-15-2) 141

SUNDAY, NOVEMBER 13

Buf 0 0 14 10 **24**
NYJ 3 0 7 7 17
Buf D20 R20/69 P(44-25-1) 245
NYJ D18 R28/89 P(36-25-1) 236
NYJ-Harper 102C

Cin 3 3 3 6 **15**
KC   3 10 7 0 **20**
Cin D19 R26/107 P(32-19-2) 170
KC   D16 R24/58 P(34-23-0) 234
Cin-Collinsworth 118C

```
Dal    0   6   3  14  23
SD     7  10   7   0  24
Dal  D25 R28/98  P(47-31-0) 291
SD   D21 R20/23  P(43-26-1) 332
   Dal-White 300P; SD-Luther 340P

Den   10   0   0  10  20
LARd   0   6   7   9  22
Den  D14 R25/63  P(31-11-1) 169
LARd D23 R29/140 P(43-26-0) 200
   LARd-Christensen 114C

Det    0  10   7   0  17
Hou    3   7  14   3  27
Det  D24 R25/118 P(36-20-4) 207
Hou  D20 R33/121 P(26-18-1) 189
   Det-Sims 105R;
   Hou-Campbell 107R

GB    10   9   3   7  29
Min    0   0  14   7  21
GB   D20 R42/163 P(27-13-1) 180
Min  D23 R26/158 P(37-21-1) 261
   Min-Nelson 119R, Nelson 137C,
   Dils 303P

Mia    0   6   0   0   6
NE     7   7   3   0  17
Mia  D13 R25/81  P(37-14-1) 126
NE   D20 R44/224 P(26-12-0) 162

NO     0   0   0   0   0
SF     7  10   7   3  27
NO   D10 R20/74  P(29-16-2)  55
SF   D28 R34/124 P(44-26-2) 273

Phi    7   0   7   0  14
ChiB   0  14   0   3  17
Phi  D14 R32/120 P(21-12-1) 143
ChiB D19 R42/223 P(20-10-0) 112
   ChiB-Payton 131R

Pit    7  10   0   7  24
Bal    3   3   7   0  13
Pit  D24 R48/214 P(23-13-1) 152
Bal  D16 R28/135 P(31-15-2) 199
   Pit-House 110C, Sweeney 104C

Sea    7  14   0   7  28
SL     7  21   0   5  33
Sea  D15 R22/84  P(26-13-1) 165
SL   D22 R39/177 P(27-21-0) 231
   Sea-Largent 155C;
   SL-Anderson 130R, Green 130C,
   Lomax 253P

TB     0   0   0   0   0
Cle   10   0   3   7  20
TB   D11 R21/66  P(31-17-0) 166
Cle  D39 R30/101 P(26-14-0) 174
   TB-House 110C

Was   13   3  10   7  33
NYG    3   0   0  14  17
Was  D18 R43/140 P(28-18-0) 138
NYG  D16 R14/25  P(38-20-1) 281
   NYG-Gray 145C
```

MONDAY, NOVEMBER 14

```
LARm   7   7  13   9  36
Atl    3   0   0   7  13
LARm D23 R42/269 P(22-15-0) 173
Atl  D17 R29/93  P(30-14-1) 116
   LARm-Dickerson 146R,
   Redden 110R
```

SUNDAY, NOVEMBER 20

```
Bal    0   0   0   0   0
Mia    0  24   7   6  37
Bal  D9  R24/89  P(19-9-2)   70
Mia  D23 R43/169 P(21-14-0) 240
   Mia-Duper 121C

ChiB   0  14   6   7  27
TB     0   0   0   0   0
ChiB D22 R56/273 P(13-8-1)   73
TB   D8  R20/72  P(21-7-2)   60
   ChiB-Payton 106R, Suhey 112R

Cle    3  17   3   7  30
NE     0   0   0   0   0
Cle  D16 R38/176 P(20-9-1)   51
NE   D12 R23/114 P(31-13-5)  76
   Cle-Pruitt 136R

Det    3   0  10   7  23
GB     7  13   0   0  20
Det  D23 R54/254 P(36-14-3) 129
GB   D16 R23/95  P(35-16-2) 144
   Det-Sims 189R
```

```
Hou    3   0   0   7  10
Cin   17  21   0   0  38
Hou  D12 R17/41  P(30-15-3) 158
Cin  D22 R45/195 P(18-10-0) 166
   Cin-Johnson 137R

KC     0   0  14   7  21
Dal    0  10   7  14  41
KC   D29 R19/43  P(59-33-2) 391
Dal  D18 R33/192 P(31-18-1) 229
   KC-Carson 135C, Marshall 115C,
   Kenney 337P; Dal-Dorsett 108R

LARd   7   3   7  10  27
Buf    0   3   0  21  24
LARd D27 R45/169 P(32-24-0) 232
Buf  D15 R22/68  P(21-12-2) 116

Min    7   0  10   0  17
Pit    7   0   0   7  14
Min  D20 R42/150 P(27-16-2) 188
Pit  D14 R28/108 P(30-13-0) 128

NYG    3  10   3   7  23
Phi    0   0   0   0   0
NYG  D22 R60/215 P(25-13-0) 117
Phi  D4  R9/10   P(27-7-1)   69
   NYG-Woolfolk 159R

SD     0   7   0   7  14
SL     7  30   7   0  44
SD   D16 R19/34  P(50-24-3) 281
SL   D18 R40/173 P(20-12-1) 205
   SD-Winslow 117C, Luther 338P;
   SL-Anderson 113R

SF     7   7   3   7  24
Atl    0  14   0  14  28
SF   D22 R30/134 P(28-21-0) 174
Atl  D19 R25/98  P(39-28-0) 275
   Atl-Johnson 104C, Bartkowski 301P

Sea    0   7  10   7  24
Den   10  10   7  11  38
Sea  D29 R27/94  P(42-31-4) 380
Den  D17 R39/184 P(18-10-1) 145
   Sea-Johns 116C, Krieg 418P;
   Den-Watson 119C

Was   10  19  10   3  42
LARm   6   0   0  14  20
Was  D28 R47/191 P(30-18-0) 276
LARm D18 R24/83  P(32-12-4) 108
   Was-Brown 140C
```

MONDAY, NOVEMBER 21

```
NYJ    7   7   0  17  31
NO    14   0  14   0  28
NYJ  D18 R23/84  P(30-20-1) 205
NO   D20 R47/239 P(20-12-1) 162
   NYJ-Walker 110C; NO-Gajan 113R
```

THURSDAY, NOVEMBER 24

```
Pit    0   3   0   0   3
Det   17   7   7  14  45
Pit  D10 R24/134 P(33-11-5)  84
Det  D25 R47/199 P(21-12-0) 129
   Det-Sims 106R

SL     7   0   3   7  17
Dal    7  14   0  14  35
SL   D14 R22/89  P(30-18-0) 189
Dal  D17 R25/132 P(31-24-0) 230
   Dal-Dorsett 102R
```

SUNDAY, NOVEMBER 27

```
Bal    3  14   0   6  23
Cle   14  14  10   3  41
Bal  D23 R41/195 P(26-15-2) 146
Cle  D22 R26/110 P(33-20-0) 307
   Cle-Pruitt 110R, Newsome 108C,
   Sipe 313P

Buf    0   7   7   3  17
LARm   0  14  10  17  41
Buf  D22 R17/74  P(49-22-5) 271
LARm D24 R37/153 P(31-18-0) 202
   Buf-Franklin 106C;
   LARm-Dickerson 125R

Den    7   0   0   0   7
SD    14   7   0  10  31
Den  D15 R23/83  P(28-14-3) 112
SD   D31 R40/141 P(33-24-1) 287
   SD-Joiner 102C, Winslow 103C
```

```
GB    14  10   7  10   0  41
Atl    0  21   3  17   6  47
GB   D32 R29/134 P(37-25-3) 366
Atl  D25 R28/152 P(35-22-1) 293
   GB-Lofton 161C, Dickey 366P;
   Atl-Andrews 129R, Moroski 303P

Hou    0   3   7  14  24
TB     0  12   7  14  33
Hou  D21 R25/92  P(31-19-3) 165
TB   D19 R38/135 P(29-17-0) 210
   TB-Thompson 224P

KC     7  21   7  13   0  48
Sea    7   7  17  17   3  51
KC   D26 R26/127 P(38-21-0) 304
Sea  D33 R47/280 P(32-17-1) 251
   KC-Carson 149C, Kenney 311P;
   Sea-Warner 207R

Min    3   7   3   3  16
NO     7   3   0   7  17
Min  D17 R33/121 P(30-13-1) 124
NO   D18 R42/153 P(22-13-3) 171

NE     0   0   3   0   3
NYJ    3  13  10   0  26
NE   D12 R28/96  P(27-13-1) 112
NYJ  D21 R34/116 P(36-22-1) 305
   NYJ-Todd 305P

NYG    2   3   0   7  12
LARd   0  13   7   7  27
NYG  D20 R24/58  P(41-19-3) 283
LARd D22 R32/138 P(32-19-0) 243
   NYG-Gray 134C,
   Williams 119C, Brunner 346P;
   LARd-Dickerson 125R

Phi    0  21   3   0  24
Was    7  21   0   0  28
Phi  D18 R21/77  P(36-19-1) 311
Was  D21 R43/171 P(26-16-1) 248
   Phi-Hoover 128C, Quick 104C,
   Jaworski 333P; Was-Brown 147C

SF     3   0   0   0   3
ChiB   3   7   0   3  13
SF   D20 R25/72  P(43-26-2) 218
ChiB D16 R41/191 P(19-11-0) 133
```

MONDAY, NOVEMBER 28

```
Cin    0  14   0  14  28
Mia    7  10   7  14  38
Cin  D17 R21/48  P(36-23-2) 325
Mia  D21 R32/123 P(30-19-0) 236
   Cin-Collinsworth 127C, Curtis 114C,
   Anderson 342P
```

THURSDAY, DECEMBER 1

```
LARd   0  14  28   0  42
SD     7   3   0   0  10
LARd D19 R37/142 P(29-15-1) 181
SD   D21 R21/74  P(48-26-2) 248
   LARd-Christensen 140C
```

SUNDAY, DECEMBER 4

```
Atl    0   0   0  21  21
Was    7  13  14   3  37
Atl  D24 R21/129 P(37-24-4) 269
Was  D21 R38/155 P(28-17-0) 215
   Atl-Bailey 159C

Buf    0   7   0   7  14
KC     0   3   3   3   9
Buf  D16 R40/188 P(15-6-1)   76
KC   D23 R24/57  P(43-22-2) 284
   Buf-Cribbs 185R; KC-Kenney 306P

ChiB   7   7   0  14  28
GB    14   7   0  10  31
ChiB D16 R29/84  P(35-21-0) 274
GB   D20 R33/184 P(35-16-2) 328
   ChiB-Gault 129C; GB-Ellis 141R,
   Lofton 120C, Dickey 345P

Cin   14   3   3   3  23
Pit    0   3   0   7  10
Cin  D21 R55/195 P(19-13-0) 159
Pit  D9  R22/84  P(19-8-2)   70
   Cin-Johnson 126R

Cle    3   3   0   0   6
Den    0  21   3   3  27
Cle  D19 R16/65  P(48-22-3) 216
Den  D24 R41/127 P(24-16-1) 284
   Den-Sampson 101C
```

```
Dal    7   7   7  14  35
Sea    0   3   0   7  10
Dal  D25 R38/132 P(30-23-1) 286
Sea  D14 R17/28  P(30-16-2) 188
   Dal-Dorsett 117R

LARm   0   6   0   3   9
Phi    6   0   0   7  13
LARm D17 R34/112 P(33-17-0) 232
Phi  D21 R25/75  P(39-21-3) 211
   LARm-Dickerson 103R

Mia    0   7   3  14  24
Hou    7   7   3   0  17
Mia  D23 R32/148 P(26-17-1) 195
Hou  D17 R33/168 P(26-13-1) 160
   Hou-Campbell 138R

NO     0   0   0   0   0
NE     7   0   0   0   7
NO   D15 R39/159 P(27-15-0) 119
NE   D14 R44/191 P(10-3-0)   16
   NE-Tatupu 128R

NYJ    0  10   0   0  10
Bal    0   3   0   3   6
NYJ  D20 R35/151 P(28-15-3) 132
Bal  D19 R40/160 P(24-13-2) 164
   NYJ-McNeil 102R; Bal-Dickey 123R

SL     0   7   0   3  10
NYG    6   0   0   0   6
SL   D10 R36/80  P(25-11-1)  81
NYG  D9  R28/61  P(35-10-4)  81

TB     0   7   7   7  21
SF     0  14  14   7  35
TB   D19 R19/38  P(46-25-2) 321
SF   D29 R40/227 P(32-22-0) 233
   TB-House 156C, Thompson 337P;
   SF-Tyler 102R
```

MONDAY, DECEMBER 5

```
Min    0   0   0   2   2
Det    0   0   0  13  13
Min  D19 R31/94  P(33-20-1) 130
Det  D14 R34/167 P(17-9-0)  101
   Det-Sims 137R
```

SATURDAY, DECEMBER 10

```
Atl    0   3   7  14  24
Mia    0  14   3  14  31
Atl  D21 R32/186 P(27-16-0) 179
Mia  D22 R34/124 P(22-18-0) 229
   Atl-Andrews 161R

Pit    7  13   7   7  34
NYJ    0   0   0  14  14
Pit  D22 R48/242 P(23-13-1) 138
NYJ  D13 R18/36  P(38-17-3) 215
   Pit-Harris 103R; NYJ-Jones 146C
```

SUNDAY, DECEMBER 11

```
Bal    3  13   3   0  19
Den    0   0  21   0  21
Bal  D19 R48/187 P(27-13-1) 201
Den  D19 R12/45  P(45-23-0) 307
   Bal-Henry 169C; Den-Elway 345P

ChiB  10   6   0   3  19
Min    6   0   7   0  13
ChiB D16 R40/210 P(17-9-0)   93
Min  D18 R26/49  P(36-16-1) 206
   ChiB-Suhey 101R

Hou    3  10  14   7  34
Cle    0   0  14   0  14
Hou  D21 R41/152 P(25-14-0) 168
Cle  D23 R34/162 P(26-18-1) 223
   Cle-Pruitt 153R;
   Hou-Campbell 130R, Smith 150C

Det    0   6   3   0   9
Cin    7   7   0   3  17
Det  D16 R30/116 P(31-10-1) 105
Cin  D21 R47/203 P(26-10-2) 123
   Cin-Johnson 118R

KC     7   7  10  14  38
SD     3  10   7  21  41
KC   D25 R20/131 P(41-31-1) 406
SD   D30 R30/100 P(49-31-2) 376
   KC-Carson 165C, Kenney 411P;
   SD-Winslow 162C
```

```
NE     0   7   7   7  21
LARd   0   0   0   7   7
NE   D15 R39/130 P(21-12-1) 145
LARd D18 R32/106 P(37-22-1) 264
   LARm-Farmer 122C

NO     0   7   3  10  20
Phi    0   3   0  14  17
NO   D16 R37/100 P(24-16-0) 183
Phi  D21 R30/173 P(33-20-0) 159

SL     0  20   7   7  34
LARd  17   7   0   0  24
SL   D26 R33/149 P(24-17-0) 217
LARd D23 R26/115 P(31-19-3) 212
   SL-Anderson 119R;
   LARd-Farmer 122C

SF     3   3  14   3  23
Buf    0  10   0   0  10
SF   D19 R37/127 P(28-18-0) 183
Buf  D16 R24/120 P(35-23-3) 183
   Buf-Cribbs 100R

Sea    7  10   0   0  17
NYG    3   3   3   3  12
Sea  D12 R30/56  P(28-18-1) 127
NYG  D24 R23/98  P(52-29-2) 342
   NYG-Williams 103C, Rutledge 349P

Was   14   0   7  10  31
Dal    7   0   0   0   7
Was  D20 R42/166 P(17-11-1) 170
Dal  D13 R20/33  P(35-20-3) 172
   Was-Monk 119C, Winslow 162C
```

MONDAY, DECEMBER 12

```
GB     3   3   3   3  12
TB     0   3   0   6   9
GB   D21 R33/95  P(36-24-3) 268
TB   D12 R28/93  P(23-12-3) 146
```

FRIDAY, DECEMBER 16

```
NYJ    7   0   7   0  14
Mia    7   7   3  17  34
NYJ  D14 R20/71  P(37-20-2) 197
Mia  D25 R40/182 P(30-16-1) 144
```

SATURDAY, DECEMBER 17

```
Cin    0   7   7   0  14
Min    0   7  13   0  20
Cin  D24 R31/141 P(43-26-1) 238
Min  D16 R33/156 P(29-16-2) 102
   Cin-Kreider 109C

NYG    3   9   7   3  22
Was    0   7   7  17  31
NYG  D23 R24/79  P(47-24-1) 306
Was  D18 R32/142 P(28-16-4) 141
   NYG-Williams 124C, Rutledge 324P;
   Was-Riggins 122R
```

SUNDAY, DECEMBER 18

```
Buf    0   7   0   7  14
Atl    3  14   7   7  31
Buf  D14 R12/34  P(43-22-2) 243
Atl  D25 R41/243 P(32-20-0) 151
   Buf-Tuttle 103C; Atl-Andrews 158R

Den    0   0  14   3  17
KC    21   7  10  10  48
Den  D15 R25/94  P(37-15-4) 164
KC   D17 R33/91  P(34-17-0) 268

GB     7   0   7   7  21
ChiB   7   0   7   9  23
GB   D18 R25/116 P(30-10-4) 222
ChiB D23 R50/236 P(26-14-3) 133
   GB-Coffman 122C;
   ChiB-Payton 148R

Hou    3   0   0   7  10
Bal    3   7   3   7  20
Hou  D25 R34/125 P(40-23-3) 236
Bal  D14 R39/188 P(13-5-1)   27
   Bal-Dickey 110R

LARm   2   7   7  10  26
NO     7   0  10   7  24
LARm D11 R20/78  P(31-15-1) 160
NO   D18 R47/142 P(22-11-2) 111
   NO-Rogers 124R

NE     0   0   0   6   6
Sea    3   7   7   7  24
NE   D19 R26/112 P(36-16-2) 147
Sea  D21 R39/170 P(21-13-0) 198
   Sea-Warner 116R, Largent 133C
```

THE GAMES

```
Phi    0    0    0    7    7
SL     7    7   10    7   31
Phi   D13 R12/14  P(45-21-4) 224
SL    D24 R40/231 P(28-14-1) 147
Phi-Carmichael 102C;
SL-Anderson 156R

Pit    3    7    0    7   17
Cle    9   14    7    0   30
Pit   D22 R32/129 P(33-14-2) 156
Cle   D18 R32/114 P(22-14-0) 196
Cle-Sipe 199P

SD     7    0    7    0   14
LARd   7    6    3   14   30
SD    D18 R21/83  P(36-20-1) 229
LARd  D23 R36/155 P(30-21-1) 325
LARd-Christensen 136C,
Plunkett 332P

TB     7    6    0    7   20
Det    0   10    3   10   23
TB    D21 R24/44  P(42-28-1) 349
Det   D19 R32/131 P(28-18-0) 207
TB-House 136C, Thompson 373P
```

MONDAY, DECEMBER 19
```
Dal    3    7    0    7   17
SF    21    0    7   14   42
Dal   D24 R23/62  P(48-29-3) 303
SF    D13 R24/85  P(27-15-1) 209
SF-Montana 223P
```

1984 NFL
SUNDAY, SEPTEMBER 2
```
Atl    5   14    7   10   36
NO     7   14    0    7   28
Atl   D22 R46/249 P(21-14-2) 173
NO    D23 R31/120 P(32-16-3) 148
Atl-Riggs 202R; NO-Rogers 102R

TB     0    7    0    7   14
ChiB   3   10   14    7   34
TB    D11 R18/89  P(27-9-6) 165
ChiB  D20 R49/183 P(23-17-1) 144

Cin    0    3    7    7   17
Den    0   13    0    7   20
Cin   D29 R38/111 P(50-26-1) 322
Den   D19 R30/121 P(29-18-1) 202
Cin-Collinsworth 141C,
Anderson 323P

SL     7    0    6   10   23
GB     0   14   10    0   24
SL    D19 R29/157 P(35-25-1) 260
GB    D21 R32/102 P(22-16-1) 164
GB-Lofton 134C

KC     7   17   13    0   37
Pit    3   14    3    7   27
KC    D18 R31/94  P(37-19-0) 170
Pit   D20 R24/46  P(41-22-2) 419
Pit-Lipps 183C, Stallworth 167C

LARd   0    0   13   11   24
Hou    0    7    0    7   14
LARd  D20 R35/142 P(37-15-0) 174
Hou   D18 R36/120 P(29-12-0) 156

Mia    7    7   21    0   35
Was    0   10    0    7   17
Mia   D18 R30/86  P(28-21-0) 311
Was   D23 R29/156 P(36-21-2) 193
Mia-Duper 178C, Marino 311P

NE    14    7    0    0   21
Buf    0    3    7    7   17
NE    D16 R29/102 P(22-12-1) 213
Buf   D24 R29/94  P(40-27-0) 232
NE-Starring 105C

Phi    3    3   14    7   27
NYG    7   14    0    7   28
Phi   D17 R21/62  P(33-19-0) 252
NYG   D23 R41/109 P(30-23-0) 388
Phi-Quick 147C;
NYG-Johnson 137C, Williams 167C,
Simms 409P

NYJ    0    7    9    7   23
Ind    0    7    0    7   14
NYJ   D23 R43/155 P(29-14-2) 153
Ind   D19 R30/122 P(26-17-1) 172
NYJ-McNeil 112R
```

```
SD    14    7   21    0   42
Min    7    0    3    3   13
SD    D27 R36/130 P(35-27-0) 396
Min   D12 R26/115 P(30-11-3) 91
SD-Duckworth 115C

SF     7    7    3   13   30
Det    7    6    7    7   27
SF    D24 R32/124 P(25-16-0) 174
Det   D19 R28/132 P(24-17-0) 166
```

MONDAY, SEPTEMBER 3
```
Cle    0    0    0    0    0
Sea    7   13   13    0   33
Cle   D10 R18/52  P(28-9-2) 68
Sea   D20 R46/145 P(28-14-1) 162

Dal    0    7    3   10   20
LARm  13    0    0    0   13
Dal   D26 R34/115 P(47-33-1) 321
LARm  D11 R24/137 P(34-11-5) 67
Dal-Donley 137C, Hogeboom 343P;
LARm-Dickerson 138R
```

THURSDAY, SEPTEMBER 6
```
Pit    7    6    7    3   23
NYJ    0    0    0   10   17
Pit   D19 R40/121 P(25-14-1) 172
NYJ   D11 R19/73  P(27-11-3) 95
```

SUNDAY, SEPTEMBER 9
```
Den    0    0    0    0    0
ChiB  10   17    0    0   27
Den   D8  R22/53  P(27-9-2) 77
ChiB  D15 R50/302 P(17-10-1) 104
ChiB-Payton 179R

Det   10    7    0    3   27
Atl    0   10    7    7   24
Det   D28 R42/208 P(32-21-0) 241
Atl   D22 R25/91  P(28-24-0) 289
Det-Sims 140R; Atl-Johnson 116C

Ind    0   21    7    7   35
Hou    0    7    0    7   21
Ind   D25 R48/168 P(20-15-0) 215
Hou   D24 R20/72  P(43-23-0) 343
Hou-Smith 102C, Moon 365P

KC     7    7   10    3   27
Cin    0   14    3    7   24
KC    D17 R22/74  P(35-18-1) 249
Cin   D22 R32/123 P(37-24-0) 275
KC-Hancock 109C; Cin-Anderson 310P

GB     0    7    0    0    7
LARd   7    0    7   14   28
GB    D15 R25/104 P(38-17-2) 105
LARd  D18 R32/121 P(22-14-1) 112
LARd-Dickerson 102R

Cle    7    3    7    0   17
LARm   7    3    0   10   20
Cle   D16 R30/82  P(35-18-1) 251
LARm  D14 R33/136 P(20-12-2) 90
LARm-Dickerson 102R

NE     0    7    0    0    7
Mia    7    7   14    7   28
NE    D18 R28/127 P(42-20-4) 205
Mia   D17 R30/74  P(28-17-2) 269

TB     7    3    3    0   13
NO     0    7    0   10   17
TB    D20 R37/130 P(22-15-0) 134
NO    D17 R29/130 P(23-13-0) 203

Dal    0    0    7    0    7
NYG   14    7    0    7   28
Dal   D23 R24/138 P(43-21-1) 206
NYG   D15 R37/120 P(20-10-0) 164

Min    3    0    0   14   17
Phi    3    6    3    7   19
Min   D14 R27/118 P(21-12-1) 113
Phi   D11 R33/152 P(37-27-0) 224
Min-Anderson 105R

Buf    0    0    7    0    7
SL    17    7    7    6   37
Buf   D9  R8/54   P(32-13-3) 117
SL    D28 R46/221 P(33-21-0) 265

SD    10    0    0    7   17
Sea    3   14    0   14   31
SD    D21 R21/97  P(40-23-4) 318
Sea   D21 R43/173 P(38-18-1) 257
SD-Holohan 133C, Fouts 332P
```

MONDAY, SEPTEMBER 10
```
Was    0    3   14   14   31
SF    14   13    0   10   37
Was   D20 R21/62  P(43-24-0) 309
SF    D30 R40/167 P(40-24-0) 367
Was-Monk 200C, Theismann 331P;
SF-Clark 105C, Montana 381P
```

SUNDAY, SEPTEMBER 16
```
ChiB   3    3    0    3    9
GB     0    7    0    0    7
ChiB  D15 R47/180 P(24-15-1) 165
GB    D10 R19/32  P(23-11-1) 122
ChiB-Payton 110R

Phi    0   10    0    7   17
Dal    3   10   10    0   23
Phi   D20 R20/56  P(48-22-3) 243
Dal   D21 R34/95  P(41-23-0) 352
Dal-Donley 122C, Hogeboom 320P

Den    0   17    0    7   24
Cle    7    0    7    0   14
Den   D18 R27/133 P(35-15-1) 164
Cle   D21 R29/79  P(42-22-3) 231
Cle-Harris 104C

LARd   0    3    6   13   22
KC     3   10    0    7   20
LARd  D27 R33/77  P(48-28-4) 306
KC    D19 R22/92  P(37-17-2) 187
LARd-Barnwell 129C, Hill 152C,
Plunkett 313P

Atl    3    3    7    7   20
Min    0   14    3   10   27
Atl   D13 R25/111 P(24-14-1) 147
Min   D23 R37/180 P(32-16-0) 234
Atl-Bailey 102C

Sea    9   14    0    0   23
NE     0    7   14   17   38
Sea   D16 R28/37  P(35-17-2) 215
NE    D22 R45/189 P(26-12-1) 102
Sea-Johns 105C; NE-Collins 107R

Cin    9    0    7    7   23
NYJ    6    7   10   20   43
Cin   D20 R23/86  P(31-20-4) 339
NYJ   D25 R36/178 P(33-20-0) 219
Cin-Harris 148C, Anderson 316P;
NYJ-McNeil 150R

LARm   7    0    7    0   14
Pit    3   14    0    7   24
LARm  D15 R27/83  P(30-15-3) 215
Pit   D20 R35/119 P(30-20-0) 226
LARm-Hill 152C;
Pit-Stallworth 100C

SL     0   14    3   17   34
Ind    7   10    9    7   33
SL    D19 R26/132 P(39-16-3) 265
Ind   D22 R38/189 P(26-12-0) 210
SL-Anderson 119R, Green 183C;
Ind-Dickey 121R, Porter 120C

Hou    0    7    0    7   14
SD    14   14    0    3   31
Hou   D14 R12/27  P(35-15-0) 257
SD    D29 R39/147 P(40-27-1) 330
Hou-Smith 159C;
SD-Winslow 146C, Fouts 336P

NO     0    0    7    7   14
SF     7   10    0   13   30
NO    D20 R31/119 P(34-16-5) 149
SF    D19 R32/148 P(26-13-1) 159

Det    0    7    7    3   17
TB     0    7    7    7   21
Det   D13 R26/102 P(36-15-0) 168
TB    D23 R26/89  P(40-24-1) 236

NYG    0    7    0    7   14
Was    7    6    0   17   30
NYG   D20 R21/47  P(45-22-3) 302
Was   D20 R40/131 P(31-15-2) 129
NYG-Johnson 117C, Simms 347P
```

MONDAY, SEPTEMBER 17
```
Mia    7    7    7    0   21
Buf    0    3    7    7   17
Mia   D23 R34/72  P(35-26-1) 296
Buf   D16 R19/68  P(38-23-0) 228
```

SUNDAY, SEPTEMBER 23
```
Hou    0   10    0    0   10
Atl   21    0   14    7   42
Hou   D20 R34/90  P(28-17-1) 187
Atl   D18 R31/138 P(17-13-0) 193
Atl-Riggs 120R

Pit    0    7    3    0   10
Cle    0    0   10   10   20
Pit   D12 R28/71  P(25-9-1) 148
Cle   D17 R45/128 P(28-15-1) 285

GB     0    0    6    0    6
Dal    7    6    0    7   20
GB    D15 R28/127 P(35-11-4) 77
Dal   D19 R37/100 P(35-17-1) 200
Dal-Cosbie 103C

KC     0    0    0    0    0
Den    0   14    7    0   21
KC    D16 R16/50  P(48-23-2) 287
Den   D21 R36/210 P(29-17-2) 157
KC-Marshall 148C; Den-Winder 139R

LARm   0    7    7   10   24
Cin    0    0    7    7   14
LARm  D17 R38/136 P(23-13-0) 205
Cin   D19 R34/129 P(32-18-2) 166

Ind    0    7    0    0    7
Mia    7   16   14    7   44
Ind   D15 R30/152 P(24-11-3) 71
Mia   D24 R40/139 P(30-15-0) 260
Mia-Duper 173C

Min    7    9   10    3   29
Det    7    7    7    7   28
Min   D23 R42/205 P(26-15-0) 215
Det   D17 R21/114 P(31-25-0) 222
Min-Anderson 120R, Lewis 101C;
Det-Danielson 218P

SL     0    7    7   10   24
NO    10    3    7   14   34
SL    D22 R20/113 P(33-23-0) 224
NO    D25 R36/152 P(30-15-1) 298
NO-Brenner 131C

TB     0    0    7    7   14
NYG    0   10    0    7   17
TB    D22 R29/137 P(31-18-1) 189
NYG   D17 R33/129 P(34-17-0) 161
TB-Wilder 112R

NYJ    0   21    0    7   28
Buf   10    0    9    7   26
NYJ   D23 R33/143 P(26-17-1) 248
Buf   D24 R21/87  P(51-31-1) 304
NYJ-McNeil 112R, Walker 128C;
Buf-Ferguson 340P

SF     7    7    7    0   21
Phi    0    6    3    0    9
SF    D23 R37/177 P(34-17-0) 221
Phi   D15 R20/72  P(41-16-1) 169
SF-Tyler 113R

ChiB   0    7    0    0    7
Sea    7    3   21    7   38
ChiB  D20 R35/136 P(39-20-3) 165
Sea   D12 R35/93  P(16-6-0) 110
ChiB-Payton 116R

Was    7    3   13    3   26
NE     0    0    7    3   10
Was   D23 R54/235 P(19-11-0) 97
NE    D13 R11/17  P(31-21-0) 225
Was-Riggins 140R
```

MONDAY, SEPTEMBER 24
```
SD     7    3    3   17   30
LARd   6    7    7   13   33
SD    D23 R32/147 P(37-19-1) 196
LARd  D26 R27/49  P(33-24-1) 348
SD-Jackson 155R, Winslow 119C;
LARd-Christensen 120C,
Plunkett 363P
```

SUNDAY, SEPTEMBER 30
```
Dal   10    7    3    3   23
ChiB   7    7    0    0   14
Dal   D17 R25/59  P(29-18-0) 254
ChiB  D26 R47/283 P(23-11-1) 117
ChiB-Payton 155R
```

```
LARd   0    7    3    3   13
Den    0    6   10    0   16
LARd  D12 R19/70  P(32-15-2) 211
Den   D26 R49/231 P(26-14-1) 121
LARd-Dickerson 120R

Buf    0   10    7    0   17
Ind    7    3    7   14   31
Buf   D23 R40/175 P(35-15-3) 173
Ind   D21 R34/188 P(23-14-0) 142
Buf-Bell 144R; Ind-McMillan 114R

Cle    0    3    3    0    6
KC     0    3    0    7   10
Cle   D16 R26/78  P(38-17-4) 108
KC    D17 R31/95  P(33-15-2) 139

NYG    6    0    0    6   12
LARm   0   17   16    0   33
NYG   D19 R13/8   P(49-25-0) 244
LARm  D19 R41/204 P(17-8-0) 105
NYG-Gray 112C;
LARm-Dickerson 120R

Mia    6   20    0   10   36
SL     0   14    7    7   28
Mia   D26 R29/132 P(37-24-0) 420
SL    D24 R26/137 P(37-22-0) 308
Mia-Clayton 143C, Duper 164C,
Marino 429P; SL-Mitchell 109R,
Lomax 308P

NE     7    7   14    0   28
NYJ    7    7    0    7   21
NE    D26 R30/122 P(42-28-0) 354
NYJ   D19 R26/115 P(31-20-1) 258
NE-Eason 354P

NO    14    0    3   10   27
Hou    0    0    3    7   10
NO    D20 R46/197 P(22-14-1) 160
Hou   D8  R25/84  P(18-7-2) 49

Det    0    7   14    3   24
SD     7   10    3    7   27
Det   D21 R23/147 P(25-20-0) 236
SD    D30 R39/114 P(35-22-0) 261
Det-Sims 119R

Atl    3    0    0    2    5
SF     0   14    0    0   14
Atl   D22 R35/161 P(41-22-2) 257
SF    D17 R32/161 P(25-13-0) 149
Atl-Riggs 136R

Sea    7    3    0   10   20
Min    3    3    3    3   12
Sea   D19 R30/192 P(27-17-3) 217
Min   D20 R35/138 P(31-16-1) 196
Sea-Lane 113R, Largent 130C

GB     3    8    7    7   27
TB     7   10    3   10   30
GB    D18 R39/167 P(31-16-3) 216
TB    D25 R47/180 P(41-21-3) 226
TB-Wilder 172R

Phi    0    7    0    0    7
Was    0   10    7    3   20
Phi   D14 R19/76  P(35-18-1) 136
Was   D19 R45/232 P(20-9-1) 86
Was-Riggins 104R
```

MONDAY, OCTOBER 1
```
Cin    0   10    0    7   17
Pit    0   14   10   14   38
Cin   D15 R26/125 P(32-19-5) 155
Pit   D22 R36/151 P(30-19-3) 241
Pit-Stallworth 119C
```

SUNDAY, OCTOBER 7
```
Atl    0   10    7   13   30
LARm   0    7   14    7   28
Atl   D18 R37/147 P(19-14-0) 209
LARm  D17 R29/156 P(23-13-0) 167
Atl-Cain 145R, Bailey 158C;
LARm-Dickerson 107R

NO     0    7    0    0    7
ChiB   6    0    7    7   20
NO    D14 R31/176 P(26-7-0) 145
ChiB  D19 R49/246 P(14-10-0) 97
ChiB-Payton 154R

Hou    0    0    3    0    3
Cin    0    3    7    3   13
Hou   D13 R25/85  P(33-15-0) 150
Cin   D20 R38/169 P(24-13-2) 159
```

```
Den     14   7   0   7   28
Det      0   7   0   0    7
Den  D20 R32/108  P(22-16-1) 179
Det  D23 R23/92   P(50-23-7) 256
Den-Watson 111C

Sea      0   7   0   7   14
LARd     0  14   0  14   28
Sea  D17 R40/131  P(19-8-2)   61
LARd D13 R31/79   P(23-12-1) 296
LARd-Dickerson 107R, Allen 173C,
Wilson 309P

Mia      0  21   3   7   31
Pit      0   0   7   0    7
Mia  D20 R35/116  P(24-16-1) 226
Pit  D17 R26/79   P(44-19-2) 208
Mia-Clayton 110C

NE       3   0   7   7   17
Cle      0   9   7   0   16
NE   D14 R26/109  P(21-14-0) 145
Cle  D23 R24/44   P(37-23-1) 305
Cle-Harris 136C, McDonald 320P

NYJ      0  10   0   7   17
KC       6   3   0   7   16
NYJ  D21 R40/172  P(23-13-1) 158
KC   D20 R32/205  P(25-15-0) 125
NYJ-McNeil 107R

Phi      7  10   3   7   27
Buf      0   3   7   7   17
Phi  D23 R30/111  P(38-24-0) 228
Buf  D20 R28/128  P(38-14-1) 150

SL       7   7  17   0   31
Dal      7   6   0   7   20
SL   D23 R40/152  P(30-20-0) 325
Dal  D19 R20/121  P(36-18-2) 177
SL-Anderson 110R, Green 189C,
Lomax 354P

SD       7   7  10  10   34
GB       7   7   7   7   28
SD   D29 R38/107  P(50-31-0) 352
GB   D18 R12/47   P(40-25-2) 368
SD-Winslow 157C, Fouts 376P;
GB-Coffman 104C, Lofton 158C,
Dickey 384P

Min     14   7   0  10   31
TB       7  14   7   7   35
Min  D30 R32/169  P(49-28-2) 374
TB   D18 R31/102  P(29-16-0) 212
Min-Jones 110C, Kramer 386P;
TB-House 126C

Was      7  21   7   0   35
Ind      7   0   0   0    7
Was  D25 R49/178  P(22-18-1) 268
Ind  D12 R20/71   P(29-11-2) 115
Was-Monk 141C, Theismann 267P
```

MONDAY, OCTOBER 8
```
SF      21   7   3   0   31
NYG      3   0   0   7   10
SF   D18 R32/167  P(27-16-0) 217
NYG  D23 R23/113  P(44-25-2) 276
SF-Tyler 101R
```

SUNDAY, OCTOBER 14
```
TB       7   0   0   0    7
Det      0   7   0   6   13
TB   D19 R38/97   P(29-25-0) 259
Det  D16 R31/176  P(23-11-0) 137
Det-Sims 100R

SD       3   3   7   0   13
KC      10   0   7  14   31
SD   D17 R19/77   P(48-23-2) 243
KC   D24 R22/146  P(41-23-3) 360
KC-Carson 165C

Min     13   0   7   0   20
LARd     7   3   3  10   23
Min  D16 R31/104  P(19-11-0) 122
LARd D24 R32/142  P(37-21-1) 251
Min-Jones 132C;
LARd-Dickerson 175R

LARm     0  21   0   7   28
NO       3   0   0   7   10
LARm D17 R34/215  P(19-8-0)  138
NO   D23 R30/95   P(47-25-3) 204
LARm-Dickerson 175R
```

```
Hou      0   0   3   7   10
Mia      0   7   7  14   28
Hou  D16 R26/83   P(28-19-1) 156
Mia  D28 R34/208  P(32-25-0) 307
Mia-Carter 105R, Marino 321P

Cin      7   7   0   0   14
NE       3   0   7  10   20
Cin  D20 R43/155  P(26-13-0) 154
NE   D17 R37/175  P(22-11-1) 173
NE-Morgan 102C

NYG      6   0   0   3   19
Atl      0   0   7   0    7
NYG  D16 R39/90   P(25-16-0) 247
Atl  D16 R27/103  P(31-19-3) 179
NYG-Manuel 120C

NYJ      7  10   0   7   24
Cle      7   7   3   3   20
NYJ  D19 R33/192  P(25-11-2) 144
Cle  D26 R32/117  P(37-25-0) 267
Cle-Newsome 191C

Ind      0   0   0   7    7
Phi      7   6   0   3   16
Ind  D13 R33/127  P(22-11-1)  72
Phi  D19 R27/49   P(43-29-1) 252

Pit      7   3   0  10   20
SF       0   7   0  10   17
Pit  D23 R47/175  P(18-11-1) 149
SF   D22 R20/117  P(35-24-1) 241
Pit-Pollard 105R

ChiB     7   7   7   0   21
SL      10   7   7  14   38
ChiB D20 R37/178  P(26-13-1) 192
SL   D23 R28/124  P(24-14-1) 230
ChiB-Payton 100R; SL 1-Green 166C

Buf      0  14   7   7   28
Sea      7   0   7   7   21
Buf  D19 R35/142  P(32-14-2) 214
Sea  D15 R22/41   P(29-17-2) 197
Buf-Bell 113R; Sea-Largent 106C

Dal      7   0   0   7   14
Was      7  10  10   7   34
Dal  D21 R24/90   P(44-26-3) 269
Was  D19 R45/241  P(17-11-0) 182
Dal-Hill 134C; Was-Riggins 165R,
Muhammad 104C
```

MONDAY, OCTOBER 15
```
GB       0   0   7  14   14
Den     14   3   0   0   17
GB   D25 R26/74   P(39-27-1) 349
Den  D10 R31/92   P(20-11-1) 101
GB-Lofton 206C, Dickey 371P
```

SUNDAY, OCTOBER 21
```
ChiB    14   6   7  17   44
TB       0   0   0   6    6
ChiB D23 R39/169  P(19-13-0) 258
TB   D17 R15/45   P(39-24-1) 247
TB-Carter 109C

Cle      3   3   0   3    9
Cin      3   3   0   6   12
Cle  D24 R19/56   P(47-27-2) 268
Cin  D18 R33/120  P(34-18-1) 176
Cle-McDonald 300P

NO       0   0   0   0   27
Dal      3   3   0  21   3   30
NO   D17 R44/235  P(25-7-3)  107
Dal  D22 R29/98   P(43-26-2) 194

Den      3  20   7   7   37
Buf      0   0   0   7    7
Den  D24 R27/107  P(40-21-0) 232
Buf  D10 R19/71   P(32-17-4) 155

Det      0   0  10   6   16
Min      7   7   0   0   14
Det  D20 R43/175  P(28-19-1) 260
Min  D14 R22/33   P(35-22-1) 157
Det-Sims 103R, Nichols 117C

Pit      3  10   0   3   16
Ind      0   0   0  17   17
Pit  D18 R32/127  P(30-14-1) 278
Ind  D21 R32/127  P(31-18-1) 174
Pit-Stallworth 101C
```

```
LARd     7   7  20  10   44
SD       7  13   0  17   37
LARd D23 R34/170  P(37-24-1) 328
SD   D30 R23/85   P(45-24-3) 379
LARd-Allen 107R, Wilson 332P;
SD-Winslow 107C, Fouts 410P

Mia      3  13  14  14   44
NE       3   7  14   7   24
Mia  D33 R37/236  P(39-24-1) 316
NE   D18 R27/102  P(29-19-0) 306
Mia-Marino 316P; NE-Morgan 114C,
Eason 313P

KC       0   0   0   7    7
NYJ      7   7   7   7   28
KC   D16 R24/121  P(25-12-1)  84
NYJ  D23 R38/115  P(32-22-0) 258

NYG      0   7   0   3   10
Phi      7   3   0  14   24
NYG  D16 R30/59   P(33-16-1) 216
Phi  D17 R24/86   P(37-17-0) 239

Was      7   0  14   3   24
SL       9   7   3   7   26
Was  D21 R35/103  P(29-15-0) 193
SL   D22 R24/120  P(38-20-0) 336
SL-Green 163C, Lomax 361P

SF      10   7   3  14   34
Hou      0   7   7   7   21
SF   D25 R38/164  P(35-25-1) 353
Hou  D22 R18/82   P(33-25-2) 350
SF-Tyler 108R, Clark 127C,
Montana 353P; Hou-Smith 101C,
Moon 356P

Sea      7  13   7   3   30
GB      17   0   7   0   24
Sea  D22 R29/97   P(35-22-2) 281
GB   D22 R21/92   P(38-24-3) 312
Sea-Largent 129C, Krieg 310P;
GB-Lofton 162C, Dickey 364P
```

MONDAY, OCTOBER 22
```
LARm     0  21   0   3   24
Atl      0   3   0   7   10
LARm D16 R41/189  P(19-14-0) 113
Atl  D11 R25/86   P(31-20-0) 138
LARm-Dickerson 145R
```

SUNDAY, OCTOBER 28
```
Min      0   0   0   7    7
ChiB     6  10   0   0   16
Min  D16 R16/41   P(36-20-2) 126
ChiB D18 R40/129  P(27-16-0) 178

Cin      0  17   7   7   31
Hou      7   0   0   3   10
Cin  D26 R47/219  P(24-18-1) 154
Hou  D20 R22/98   P(28-17-3) 218

Ind      0   0   0   3    3
Dal      3   6   0  13   22
Ind  D9 R24/73    P(22-9-2)   82
Dal  D27 R39/135  P(32-21-0) 262
Dal-Dorsett 104R, Hill 125C

Den      0   6   0  13   3   22
LARd     9   3   0   0   7   19
Den  D24 R46/182  P(34-21-0) 178
LARd D20 R37/122  P(36-19-3) 234
Den-Winder 126R

Det      0   3   6   0    9
GB      14  14  10   3   41
Det  D20 R14/65   P(48-25-3) 243
GB   D30 R38/195  P(26-18-0) 244
GB-Ivery 116R, Dickey 248P

TB       0   7   6   7   20
KC       0   7   7  10   24
TB   D23 R29/106  P(54-29-3) 244
KC   D23 R23/53   P(29-... )  313
TB-House 100C; KC-Carson 131C,
Kenney 332P

Buf      0   0   0   7    7
Mia      7  17   0  14   38
Buf  D15 R16/103  P(40-27-1) 170
Mia  D28 R31/191  P(32-22-3) 302
Mia-Clayton 106C

NYJ     10  10   0   0   20
NE       0   7   0   7   14
NYJ  D19 R30/166  P(25-15-2) 132
NE   D23 R28/122  P(35-23-1) 244
NYJ-McNeil 110R
```

```
NO       0  10   0   6   16
Cle      0   7   0   0    7
NO   D18 R31/111  P(27-21-0) 262
Cle  D17 R31/83   P(23-16-0) 179
NO-Young 101C

Was      0   6   0   7   13
NYG     14   9   7   7   37
Was  D15 R23/79   P(46-23-1) 248
NYG  D25 R34/130  P(29-18-0) 294
Was-Monk 104C; NYG-Gray 128C,
Simms 339P

Atl      0   3   0   7   10
Pit      7  14   7   7   35
Atl  D15 R31/193  P(28-22-1) 193
Pit  D17 R34/173  P(22-11-2) 141
Pit-Pollard 111R

SL       0  17   7  10   34
Phi      7   3   0   4   14
SL   D23 R40/156  P(26-20-1) 271
Phi  D15 R13/47   P(42-23-3) 290
Phi-Quick 170C, Jaworski 340P

SF       3  16   7   7   33
LARm     0   0   0   0    0
SF   D23 R39/111  P(32-22-0) 361
LARm D12 R19/72   P(30-14-2) 134
SF-Montana 365P
```

MONDAY, OCTOBER 29
```
Sea      7  10   7   0   24
SD       7  13   0  17   37
Sea  D18 R33/81   P(29-23-1) 274
SD   D16 R23/48   P(40-24-3) 153
```

SUNDAY, NOVEMBER 4
```
LARd     0   3   3   0    6
ChiB     7   7   0   3   17
LARd D12 R23/75   P(28-13-3) 106
ChiB D13 R47/175  P(16-7-1)   84
LARd-Dickerson 208R;
ChiB-Payton 111R

Cle      3   3   0   7   13
Buf      0   7   0   3   10
Cle  D16 R43/211  P(18-7-1)   73
Buf  D13 R29/106  P(24-16-2)  77
Cle-Green 156R

NE       3   3   7   6   19
Den      0   6   6  14   26
NE   D25 R36/195  P(38-21-1) 289
Den  D18 R18/28   P(40-26-1) 291
NE-James 120R, Morgan 122C,
Eason 313P; Den-Johnson 156C,
Watson 134C, Elway 315P

GB       0  10  10   3   23
NO       7   3   0   3   13
GB   D20 R36/207  P(28-15-0) 166
NO   D23 R34/186  P(32-18-2) 141

LARm     3   0  10   3   16
SL       0   0   0  13   13
LARm D11 R28/201  P(14-5-0)   60
SL   D20 R22/69   P(52-34-2) 293
LARm-Dickerson 208R;
SL-Green 105C, Lomax 341P

Mia      0   7  17   7   31
NYJ      7   3   0   7   17
Mia  D24 R28/100  P(42-23-2) 407
NYJ  D14 R29/200  P(28-12-2)  86
Mia-Duper 155C, Moore 105C,
Marino 422P; NYJ-McNeil 132C

TB       7   7   0  10   24
Min      3   7   7  10   27
TB   D23 R32/153  P(36-17-1) 183
Min  D24 R34/144  P(36-24-2) 218
TB-Wilder 146R

NYG      6   0   7   6   19
Dal      0   7   0   0    7
NYG  D18 R37/121  P(37-16-1) 227
Dal  D13 R28/116  P(31-14-2) 140
NYG-Manuel 102C

Phi      3   3   7  10   23
Det      7  10   0   6   23
Phi  D18 R23/64   P(39-20-2) 230
Det  D25 R38/164  P(40-25-2) 258
Phi-Quick 110C; Det-Jenkins 128C
```

```
Hou      0   0   7   0    7
Pit      7  14  14   0   35
Hou  D17 R26/97   P(32-18-0) 176
Pit  D17 R46/191  P(15-9-2)  131
Pit-Stallworth 109C

SD       7  10   7  14   38
Ind      3   0   7   0   10
SD   D24 R33/119  P(38-27-2) 283
Ind  D13 R22/90   P(32-18-4) 205
SD-Joiner 119C

Cin      3  14   0   0   17
SF       0   7   3  13   23
Cin  D21 R25/116  P(34-21-2) 230
SF   D26 R31/91   P(42-27-4) 294
SF-Clark 124C, Montana 301P

KC       0   0   0   0    0
Sea      3  28   7   7   45
KC   D17 R23/78   P(51-23-6) 196
Sea  D17 R34/132  P(21-12-1) 129
```

MONDAY, NOVEMBER 5
```
Atl      0   7   0   7   14
Was      0  14   6   7   27
Atl  D16 R29/148  P(25-13-1) 124
Was  D24 R40/126  P(25-19-1) 129
Atl-Riggs 134R; Was-Riggins 100R
```

SUNDAY, NOVEMBER 11
```
Pit      0  13   0   7   20
Cin      3   0  12   7   22
Pit  D20 R38/160  P(31-16-3) 133
Cin  D15 R30/116  P(18-12-0) 166

Dal      7   0   7   0   14
SL       0   7  10   0   17
Dal  D16 R30/116  P(33-12-2) 134
SL   D25 R26/78   P(52-27-2) 357
SL-Lomax 388P

Den      3   3   0  10   16
SD       7   3   0   3   13
Den  D17 R28/62   P(35-19-0) 177
SD   D20 R25/112  P(38-22-0) 254

Min      0  10   7   0   17
GB       7  10  14  14   45
Min  D14 R28/110  P(37-19-1) 162
GB   D26 R36/211  P(41-23-1) 302
GB-Ellis 110R, Lofton 119C,
Dickey 303P

Hou      0   7   0  10   17
KC       3   3   7   3   16
Hou  D18 R38/157  P(26-19-0) 140
KC   D21 R23/131  P(41-20-0) 191
Hou-Moriarty 117R, Smith 107C

ChiB     7   6   0   0   13
LARm     0   6   6  17   29
ChiB D15 R25/94   P(27-21-0) 227
LARm D17 R35/195  P(15-7-0)  175
LARm-Dickerson 149R

Ind      3   3   0   3    9
NYJ      0   2   0   7    9
Ind  D11 R57/153  P(15-6-0)   50
NYJ  D7 R24/78    P(28-12-1)  65

Phi     14   0   3   6   23
Mia      0   7  10   7   24
Phi  D19 R35/177  P(25-14-2) 187
Mia  D21 R33/97   P(34-20-1) 234

Buf      7   0   3   0   10
NE       0  14  14  10   38
Buf  D12 R18/77   P(48-13-3) 112
NE   D21 R33/68   P(34-23-2) 210

NO      10   0   0   7   17
Atl      0   3   0   7   10
NO   D17 R31/87   P(31-15-1) 235
Atl  D20 R35/120  P(33-20-0) 160

SF       6   7  14  14   41
Cle      0   7   0   7   14
SF   D23 R39/213  P(30-24-1) 255
Cle  D10 R20/43   P(33-13-1) 208
SF-Solomon 105C

Det     14   0   0   0   14
Was      0   7   7  14   28
Det  D21 R22/169  P(42-18-3) 181
Was  D24 R41/122  P(36-17-0) 168
Was-Griffin 114R, Muhammad 105C
```

```
NYG   3  0  7  7  17
TB    0  3  7 10  20
NYG  D14 R20/65  P(33-21-1) 173
TB   D24 R41/116 P(28-16-2) 223
```

MONDAY, NOVEMBER 12
```
LARd  0  7  0  7  14
Sea   0  0 17  0  17
LARd D19 R36/141 P(34-16-3) 169
Sea  D11 R27/85  P(25-11-1) 122
```

SUNDAY, NOVEMBER 18
```
Dal   0  3  0  0   3
Buf   7  0  0  7  14
Dal  D19 R24/78  P(46-22-2) 219
Buf  D14 R33/203 P(30-13-2) 104
Buf-Bell 206R
```
```
Det   0  7  0  7  14
ChiB  7  3  0  6  16
Det  D11 R26/71  P(16-10-0) 96
ChiB D17 R41/175 P(25-14-0) 156
```
```
Cle  10  3  0 10  23
Atl   7  0  0  0   7
Cle  D17 R34/113 P(24-14-1) 217
Atl  D18 R22/71  P(38-23-2) 139
Cle-Green 121R
```
```
Min   0  7  0 14  21
Den  21 14  7  0  42
Min  D19 R21/67  P(41-23-3) 247
Den  D22 R36/206 P(23-18-0) 229
Den-Watson 123C, Elway 218P
```
```
LARm  3  3  0  0   6
GB    0 14 10  7  31
LARm D16 R31/166 P(35-16-3) 131
GB   D18 R29/122 P(27-15-2) 192
LARm-Dickerson 132R;
GB-Lofton 129C
```
```
NYJ  10  3  0  7  20
Hou   0 10 14  7  31
NYJ  D20 R33/138 P(36-19-1) 203
Hou  D20 R32/187 P(29-21-0) 215
Hou-Moriarty 138R
```
```
KC    0  0  0  7   7
LARd  7  7  0  3  17
KC   D14 R16/20  P(37-19-1) 162
LARd D20 R49/219 P(21-12-1) 80
LARd-Dickerson 132R
```
```
NE   16 10  7 17  50
Ind   0 10  0  7  17
NE   D26 R27/117 P(43-30-0) 260
Ind  D17 R28/137 P(32-16-1) 129
NE-Ramsey 104C, Eason 291P
```
```
SL    0  7  0  3  10
NYG   0  0  9  7  16
SL   D20 R34/133 P(38-19-4) 203
NYG  D14 R32/102 P(30-12-1) 165
SL-Anderson 111R, Anderson 112C
```
```
Was   0  7  3  0  10
Phi   3  3  4  6  16
Was  D16 R31/117 P(38-21-3) 144
Phi  D13 R27/64  P(28-14-1) 101
```
```
Mia   0 21  7  0   0  28
SD    7  7  0 14   6  34
Mia  D24 R22/96  P(41-28-1) 338
SD   D34 R36/166 P(56-37-1) 371
Mia-Marino 338P;
SD-Jackson 124R, Sievers 119C,
Fouts 380P
```
```
TB    0 10  0  7  17
SF    0 14  7  3  24
TB   D23 R20/89  P(41-26-2) 308
SF   D25 R38/190 P(23-19-0) 238
TB-Carter 166C, DeBerg 316P
```
```
Sea   7 10  0  9  26
Cin   0  3  0  3   6
Sea  D15 R34/120 P(16-10-1) 104
Cin  D20 R32/162 P(28-15-2) 115
Cin-Kinnebrew 119R
```

MONDAY, NOVEMBER 19
```
Pit   0 14  0 10  24
NO    3 10  0 14  27
Pit  D19 R32/115 P(28-16-2) 217
NO   D16 R32/89  P(31-18-2) 176
```

THURSDAY, NOVEMBER 22
```
NE    3  0  0 14  17
Dal   7  3  7  3  20
NE   D19 R25/150 P(38-19-1) 147
Dal  D18 R30/67  P(41-21-1) 275
NE-James 112R; Dal-Hill 125C
```
```
GB   14  7  0  7  28
Det   0 17  7  9  33
GB   D14 R16/109 P(24-13-2) 197
Det  D33 R46/186 P(34-25-1) 353
Det-Nichols 108C, Danielson 305P
```

SUNDAY, NOVEMBER 25
```
ChiB  7 10 17  0  34
Min   3  0  0  3   6
ChiB D20 R42/229 P(25-16-0) 170
Min  D9  R19/90  P(31-12-2) 71
ChiB-Payton 117R
```
```
Atl   0  0 14  0  14
Cin  14  7  7  7  35
Atl  D19 R28/117 P(34-17-2) 197
Cin  D26 R35/121 P(25-22-1) 271
Cin-Collinsworth 134C
```
```
Hou   7  0  0  3  10
Cle   7 13  0  7  27
Hou  D11 R25/109 P(20-9-2) 38
Cle  D18 R38/120 P(26-16-1) 142
Cle-Newsome 102C
```
```
Ind   0  7  0  0   7
LARd  7  7  0  7  21
Ind  D10 R29/77  P(27-10-1) 81
LARd D21 R42/177 P(23-13-2) 106
LARd-Allen 110R, Dickerson 191R
```
```
LARm  0 10  7 17  34
TB    9  7 10  7  33
LARm D19 R43/299 P(10-7-0) 68
TB   D28 R22/84  P(44-27-1) 322
LARm-Dickerson 191R;
TB-DeBerg 322P
```
```
KC    0 17  0 10  27
NYG   0  7  7 14  28
KC   D15 R22/64  P(36-18-1) 276
NYG  D29 R38/147 P(41-24-3) 324
KC-Carson 153C;
NYG-Mowatt 126C, Simms 343P
```
```
SD    0 10  7  7  24
Pit   3 21 21  7  52
SD   D23 R15/31  P(51-32-4) 391
Pit  D28 R46/202 P(22-18-0) 243
SD-Chandler 105C;
Pit-Abercrombie 109R, Lipps 118C,
Stallworth 116C, Malone 253P
```
```
Phi   0  6  0 10  16
SL    7  0  7  3  17
Phi  D17 R30/95  P(39-24-0) 196
SL   D12 R26/119 P(34-16-1) 100
Phi-Quick 107C
```
```
SF    0  7 14 14  35
NO    0  3  0  0   3
SF   D22 R33/219 P(32-15-0) 188
NO   D12 R28/131 P(26-14-1) 70
SF-Tyler 117R
```
```
Sea   7  3  7 10  27
Den   3  7  7  2  19
Sea  D20 R25/60  P(44-30-0) 406
Den  D18 R21/93  P(27-15-1) 258
Sea-Largent 191C, Krieg 406P
```
```
Buf   0  7  0  7  14
Was   7 10  7  7  31
Buf  D13 R20/85  P(34-14-2) 86
Was  D27 R39/116 P(33-26-1) 305
Was-Monk 104C, Theismann 311P
```

MONDAY, NOVEMBER 26
```
NYJ   7  3  7  0  17
Mia  14 14  0  0  28
NYJ  D26 R38/166 P(39-21-1) 235
Mia  D25 R24/154 P(32-19-1) 183
NYJ-McNeil 116R; Mia-Marino 192P
```

THURSDAY, NOVEMBER 29
```
Was  17 14  0  0  31
Min   0  0 10  7  17
Was  D19 R29/129 P(24-19-0) 213
Min  D21 R29/170 P(39-19-2) 200
Was-Muhammad 115C;
Min-Lewis 130C
```

SUNDAY, DECEMBER 2
```
Ind   0  9  3  3  15
Buf  21  0  0  0  21
Ind  D13 R31/116 P(28-11-1) 125
Buf  D15 R41/104 P(22-11-1) 155
```
```
Cin   7  0 10  0   3  20
Cle   0 10  0  7   0  17
Cin  D21 R33/119 P(41-28-1) 229
Cle  D20 R32/96  P(24-18-0) 183
```
```
Dal   7  0 16  3  26
Phi   0  3  0  7  10
Dal  D16 R39/190 P(26-8-5) 96
Phi  D13 R19/38  P(45-23-2) 135
Dal-Dorsett 110R;
Phi-Spagnola 114C
```
```
TB    0  7  0  7  14
GB    0  0  7 20  27
TB   D19 R30/100 P(39-23-2) 175
GB   D20 R33/106 P(32-18-3) 205
TB-House 105C
```
```
Pit   3  0 10  7  20
Hou   3 10  0  7  23
Pit  D14 R30/127 P(33-16-2) 145
Hou  D22 R33/101 P(45-27-3) 303
Pit-Stallworth 113C;
Hou-Smith 108C, Moon 303P
```
```
Den   7  3  3  0  13
KC    0  9  0  6  16
Den  D17 R34/145 P(36-16-1) 164
KC   D17 R27/93  P(38-20-1) 225
KC-Carson 126C
```
```
LARd  7 10  7 21  45
Mia   7  6 14  7  34
LARd D18 R32/179 P(24-13-1) 225
Mia  D30 R24/81  P(57-35-2) 434
LARd-Allen 155R, Dickerson 149R,
Williams 122C; Mia-Clayton 177C,
Marino 470P
```
```
NO    0  7  0 14  21
LARm 14  0  3 17  34
NO   D15 R21/96  P(34-15-4) 128
LARm D17 R47/214 P(24-10-2) 127
LARm-Dickerson 149R
```
```
NYG   0 10  3  7  20
NYJ   0  0  3  7  10
NYG  D26 R40/169 P(28-18-1) 216
NYJ  D20 R20/67  P(42-29-1) 341
NYJ-Jones 103C, Shuler 127C,
O'Brien 351P
```
```
SL   14 13  0  6  33
NE    3  0  0  7  10
SL   D20 R54/220 P(15-9-0) 85
NE   D14 R15/87  P(32-16-1) 136
SL 1-Anderson 136R
```
```
SF    7 14  7  7  35
Atl   3  7  0  7  17
SF   D15 R31/143 P(24-12-2) 147
Atl  D23 R36/153 P(43-22-3) 261
Atl-Riggs 133R, Jackson 193C
```
```
Det   3 14  0  0  17
Sea   0  0 14 24  38
Det  D16 R28/108 P(25-14-2) 139
Sea  D23 R28/113 P(38-27-1) 275
Sea-Largent 104C, Krieg 294P
```

MONDAY, DECEMBER 3
```
ChiB  0  0  7  0   7
SD    0 14  0  6  20
ChiB D18 R33/164 P(37-21-1) 143
SD   D9  R21/77  P(29-12-0) 236
SD-Duckworth 179C
```

SATURDAY, DECEMBER 8
```
Buf   7 10  0  0  17
NYJ   7  0  7  7  21
Buf  D11 R24/82  P(34-14-2) 140
NYJ  D21 R39/140 P(30-17-1) 203
```
```
Min   0  7  0  0   7
SF   14 17  6 14  51
Min  D18 R24/90  P(39-21-1) 175
SF   D29 R40/184 P(35-25-0) 337
SF-Nehemiah 125C
```

SUNDAY, DECEMBER 9
```
Cin   0  3 14  7  24
NO    0  7  7  7  21
Cin  D20 R35/107 P(32-19-0) 172
NO   D23 R31/146 P(32-20-1) 274
NO-Brenner 101C, Wilson 325P
```
```
SD    6  0  0  7  13
Den   0  6  7  0  13
SD   D16 R25/87  P(35-18-0) 147
Den  D22 R38/162 P(31-18-1) 181
```
```
GB    0  7  6  7  20
ChiB  0  0  7  7  14
GB   D17 R30/110 P(31-13-2) 177
ChiB D25 R51/228 P(27-11-2) 73
ChiB-Payton 175R
```
```
Sea   0  7  0  7  14
KC    7 17  7  3  34
Sea  D18 R22/66  P(46-21-6) 307
KC   D20 R38/91  P(38-19-0) 325
KC-Marshall 166C, Kenney 312P
```
```
Hou   3 10  3  0  16
LARm 17  3  0  7  27
Hou  D23 R33/154 P(29-19-1) 184
LARm D17 R34/276 P(23-12-0) 177
Hou-Moriarty 102R;
LARm-Dickerson 215R
```
```
Mia   0  7 14 14  35
Ind   7 10  0  0  17
Mia  D20 R33/170 P(26-12-2) 90
Mia-Clayton 127C, Marino 404P
```
```
NE   10  0  0  7  17
Phi   3  7 10  7  27
NE   D21 R36/175 P(28-12-1) 162
Phi  D19 R28/136 P(29-16-1) 170
NE-Morgan 101C;
Phi-Montgomery 100R
```
```
Cle   3  0 10  7  20
Pit   7 10  3  3  23
Cle  D21 R32/140 P(33-19-4) 202
Pit  D16 R30/125 P(26-13-2) 192
Cle-Byner 103R
```
```
NYG   7  0 14  0  21
SL    0 14  7 10  31
NYG  D20 R27/148 P(31-13-2) 159
SL   D22 R31/114 P(34-24-0) 291
NYG-Morris 107R; SL-Lomax 300P
```
```
Atl   0  6  0  0   6
TB    3  3 10  7  23
Atl  D15 R19/70  P(38-22-2) 204
TB   D21 R36/143 P(29-18-0) 192
TB-Wilder 125R
```
```
Was   0  6 17  7  30
Dal   7 14  0  7  28
Was  D22 R35/151 P(31-17-0) 148
Dal  D25 R24/106 P(42-22-2) 281
Was-Riggins 111R; Dal-Hill 119C,
White 327P
```

MONDAY, DECEMBER 10
```
LARd  0  7  3 14  24
Det   0  3  0  3   6
LARd D14 R34/66  P(23-14-2) 281
Det  D10 R20/61  P(39-16-2) 196
```

FRIDAY, DECEMBER 14
```
LARm  3 10  0  3  16
SF   14  3  0  2  19
LARm D19 R37/185 P(22-11-0) 170
SF   D15 R20/89  P(31-20-0) 200
```

SATURDAY, DECEMBER 15
```
Den  10  0 14  7  31
Sea   0  7  7  0  14
Den  D15 R33/143 P(21-9-4) 148
Sea  D23 R19/79  P(51-30-2) 306
Sea-Krieg 334P
```
```
NO    7  0  3  0  10
NYG   0  3  0  0   3
NO   D15 R37/101 P(24-12-1) 137
NYG  D15 R28/113 P(26-12-2) 76
```

SUNDAY, DECEMBER 16
```
Phi   3  0  7  0  10
Atl   3 10  7  6  26
Phi  D20 R12/53  P(47-25-0) 308
Atl  D24 R38/126 P(27-15-1) 187
Phi-Quick 135C, Pisarcik 334P;
Atl-Bailey 140C
```
```
ChiB  0 14  3 13  30
Det   3  3  0  7  13
ChiB D13 R42/103 P(21-11-3) 190
Det  D13 R15/47  P(38-14-1) 149
```
```
Buf   7  0  7  7  21
Cin   7 21  3 21  52
Buf  D25 R18/64  P(58-36-3) 281
Cin  D27 R36/201 P(28-20-0) 218
```
```
Cle   7  3  7 10  27
Hou   0  7 10  3  20
Cle  D23 R36/254 P(22-14-1) 145
Hou  D18 R28/90  P(31-19-0) 306
Cle-Byner 188R; Hou-Smith 167C,
Moon 306P
```
```
GB   10 21  7  0  38
Min   0  0  7  7  14
GB   D26 R41/214 P(31-19-3) 234
Min  D16 R21/70  P(37-22-3) 171
```
```
KC   14 14 14  0  42
SD    0  0  7 14  21
KC   D23 R36/120 P(25-18-0) 279
SD   D26 R31/110 P(45-24-0) 333
SD-Luther 333P
```
```
Ind   0  0 10  0  10
NE    3 10  0  3  16
Ind  D13 R21/65  P(28-15-1) 174
NE   D19 R49/175 P(17-11-0) 60
NE-James 138R
```
```
Pit   3  0  0 10  13
LARd  0  0  0  0   0
Pit  D21 R50/197 P(23-13-1) 168
LARd D14 R20/57  P(33-14-2) 131
Pit-Abercrombie 111R
```
```
NYJ   0  7  0 14  21
TB   10  7  3 21  41
NYJ  D19 R23/91  P(34-19-2) 161
TB   D28 R32/116 P(34-26-0) 230
TB-Wilder 103R
```
```
SL    0  7 10 12  29
Was   6 17  3  3  29
SL   D23 R16/43  P(46-37-1) 444
Was  D22 R32/96  P(35-20-1) 260
SL-Anderson 124C, Green 196C,
Lomax 468P; Was-Monk 136C,
Muhammad 110C
```

MONDAY, DECEMBER 17
```
Dal   0  0  7 14  21
Mia   0  7  7 14  28
Dal  D21 R28/90  P(35-20-2) 226
Mia  D17 R26/61  P(40-23-2) 328
Dal-Hill 115C; Mia-Clayton 150C,
Marino 340P
```

1985 NFL

SUNDAY, SEPTEMBER 8
```
Ind   3  0  0  0   3
Pit   7 17  7 14  45
Ind  D9  R16/47  P(30-13-2) 112
Pit  D30 R41/163 P(31-21-1) 282
Pit-Lipps 154C, Malone 287P
```
```
Mia  10  3  7  3  23
Hou   0  9  3 14  26
Mia  D17 R25/69  P(31-19-2) 291
Hou  D41 R41/165 P(17-12-1) 229
Hou-Woolfolk 120C
```
```
Phi   0  0  0  0   0
NYG  14  0  0  7  21
Phi  D11 R16/80  P(32-13-1) 88
NYG  D21 R46/192 P(21-8-1) 125
```
```
NYJ   7 14  7  3  31
LARd  7 14  7  3  31
NYJ  D19 R24/62  P(29-16-2) 131
LARd D19 R35/122 P(22-15-0) 234
LARd-Williams 131C
```

```
SD     7   7   0   0   14
Buf    3   6   0   0    9
SD  D17 R32/100  P(29-16-1)  208
Buf D19 R25/84   P(46-31-2)  371
Buf-Butler 140C, Ferragamo 377P

Sea    7  14   0   7   28
Cin    0  10  14   0   24
Sea D20 R27/91   P(25-16-0)  206
Cin D27 R38/151  P(23-13-0)  193
Cin-Kinnebrew 101R,
Collinsworth 101C

TB    14  14   0   0   28
ChiB   7  10  14   7   38
TB  D17 R29/166  P(21-13-2)  141
ChiB D27 R34/185 P(34-23-1)  251
TB-Wilder 166R; ChiB-Payton 120R

SL     7   0   3  14   3   27
Cle    0   3   0  21   0   24
SL  D15 R34/100  P(23-12-0)  186
Cle D19 R37/176  P(25-17-1)  181

Det    0  14  14   0   28
Atl   14   7   0   6   27
Det D16 R33/130  P(23-9-2)   156
Atl D21 R40/160  P(23-16-0)  140
Atl-Riggs 131R

KC    10  16   7  14   47
NO     0   3   0  24   27
KC  D22 R29/109  P(35-22-1)  395
NO  D19 R27/136  P(48-14-4)  168
KC-Carson 173C, Kenney 397P

Den    0  16   0   0   16
LARm   3   7   0  10   20
Den D13 R18/63   P(39-18-1)  214
LARm D19 R37/147 P(29-16-2)  138

SF     7   0  14  14   35
Min    0   0   7  21   28
SF  D29 R39/217  P(44-25-2)  272
Min D15 R32/86   P(25-12-0)  182
SF-Tyler 125R

GB     0   0   6  14   20
NE     7  12   0   7   26
GB  D16 R19/59   P(29-14-1)  146
NE  D26 R41/208  P(28-21-1)  202

MONDAY, SEPTEMBER 9
Was    0   7   0   7   14
Dal    3  14  13  14   44
Was D24 R33/120  P(43-19-6)  249
Dal D19 R33/113  P(33-14-0)  206

THURSDAY, SEPTEMBER 12
LARd   7   7   0   6   20
KC     3   9  17   7   36
LARd D22 R23/67  P(48-34-2)  273
KC  D18 R29/84   P(38-18-0)  241
LARd-Christensen 116C,
Plunkett 303P; KC-Carson 118C

SUNDAY, SEPTEMBER 15
Sea    7   7  28   7   49
SD    10  13   6   6   35
Sea D30 R40/196  P(33-22-0)  293
SD  D32 R19/63   P(49-34-1)  494
Sea-Warner 169R, Turner 121C,
Krieg 307P; SD-Chandler 243C,
Fouts 440P

LARm  10   0   0   7   17
Phi    3   3   0   0    6
LARm D16 R43/173 P(26-11-1)  161
Phi D16 R26/120  P(34-14-4)  180
LARm-White 144R

Hou    0  10   3   0   13
Was   13   3   0   0   16
Hou D11 R24/81   P(28-12-0)  107
Was D20 R43/240  P(22-15-1)   93

Min    7  10   7   7   31
TB     7   3   6   0   16
Min D18 R31/79   P(28-18-2)  183
TB  D22 R23/115  P(38-26-2)  234
TB-Wilder 113R

Ind    0   7   0   6   13
Mia    3  10   3  14   30
Ind D17 R23/96   P(32-16-1)  202
Mia D33 R31/157  P(48-29-0)  329
Mia-Clayton 106C, Marino 329P
```

```
Buf    3   0   0   0    3
NYJ    0  21  14   7   42
Buf D16 R14/82   P(43-21-4)  188
NYJ D27 R42/288  P(30-20-0)  244
NYJ-McNeil 192R

Cin    7   7   3  10   27
SL     7  10  10  14   41
Cin D20 R29/116  P(41-22-0)  254
SL  D27 R38/210  P(31-17-1)  237
Cin-Brown 106C

NYG    0   6   7   7   20
GB    10   7   0   6   23
NYG D17 R21/76   P(40-21-0)  239
GB  D20 R41/126  P(27-15-1)  164
NYG-Manuel 105C

Dal    0   0   0  21   21
Det   10   3  13   0   26
Dal D33 R25/102  P(62-40-3)  452
Det D13 R26/72   P(24-10-1)  128
Dal-Cosbie 159C, Hill 181C

Atl    7   3   3   3   16
SF     0  14  21   0   35
Atl D18 R30/123  P(38-23-0)  130
SF  D23 R30/196  P(26-19-1)  184
SF-Craig 107R

NO     0   6  10   7   23
Den    7  17   7   3   34
NO  D17 R27/107  P(30-18-0)  235
Den D22 R24/105  P(44-28-1)  327
Den-Elway 353P

NE     0   0   0   7    7
ChiB   7   3  10   0   20
NE  D10 R16/27   P(35-15-3)  179
ChiB D18 R44/160 P(23-13-1)  209

MONDAY, SEPTEMBER 16
Pit    0   0   0   7    7
Cle    0   7   3   7   17
Pit D15 R19/54   P(45-18-2)  162
Cle D21 R36/145  P(30-18-1)  148

THURSDAY, SEPTEMBER 19
ChiB   3   3  24   3   33
Min    3   7   7   7   24
ChiB D21 R30/127 P(33-21-1)  353
Min D23 R15/34   P(55-28-3)  411
ChiB-Gault 146C, McKinnon 133C;
Min-Carter 102C, Kramer 436P

SUNDAY, SEPTEMBER 22
Cle    0   0   0   7    7
Dal    3   7   3   7   20
Cle D15 R31/128  P(26-14-2)  169
Dal D20 R33/131  P(34-22-1)  212

NE     3   7   7   0   17
Buf    7   0   7   0   14
NE  D14 R40/122  P(22-13-1)  105
Buf D16 R20/55   P(39-23-1)  251

Den    7  14   6  17   44
Atl    7   7  14   0   28
Den D27 R39/148  P(38-19-2)  280
Atl D16 R27/108  P(32-19-1)  233
Atl-Johnson 110C

NYJ    7   0  10   7   24
GB     3   0   0   0    3
NYJ D15 R39/106  P(27-14-0)  120
GB  D10 R25/71   P(33-14-2)  122

Phi    3   3   3  10   19
Was    0   6   0   0    6
Phi D15 R44/175  P(16-9-1)   152
Was D15 R26/140  P(34-15-1)  117

KC     0   0   0   0    0
Mia    0   0  14  17   31
KC  D15 R25/97   P(38-19-2)  187
Mia D27 R29/133  P(35-23-1)  258

SD     3  17  14  10   44
Cin    7   6  21   7   41
SD  D26 R25/173  P(43-25-2)  344
Cin D32 R28/152  P(44-26-2)  296
SD-James 127R, James 118C,
Fouts 344P; Cin-Collinsworth 161C,
Esiason 320P

SF    10   3  14   7   34
LARd   3   0   0   7   10
SF  D17 R30/115  P(26-15-0)  237
LARd D20 R23/83  P(40-24-2)  197
```

```
Hou    0   0   0   0    0
Pit   14   3   3   0   20
Hou D8 R22/50    P(21-12-1)   84
Pit D22 R46/233  P(19-9-0)   102

Det    0   3   3   0    6
Ind    7   0   0   7   14
Det D10 R26/105  P(26-12-1)   99
Ind D24 R40/228  P(32-14-2)  127
Ind-Wonsley 170R

SL     7   3   0   7   17
NYG    7   3  10   7   27
SL  D18 R20/83   P(34-18-2)  206
NYG D19 R43/155  P(23-10-1)  163

TB     0   6   0   7   13
NO     7  10   3   0   20
TB  D20 R26/114  P(44-22-2)  220
NO  D18 R38/112  P(25-16-0)  226
TB-Wilder 114R

MONDAY, SEPTEMBER 23
LARm   7   0  14  14   35
Sea    0   7   3  14   24
LARm D19 R37/170 P(24-12-3)  187
Sea D17 R15/44   P(51-28-2)  270
LARm-Dickerson 150R

SUNDAY, SEPTEMBER 29
Mia    7  13   7   3   30
Den    7  10   6   3   26
Mia D19 R22/53   P(43-25-0)  365
Den D23 R31/169  P(38-18-1)  226
Mia-Moore 109C, Nathan 120C,
Marino 390P; Den-Winder 103R

Ind    0  10   7   3   20
NYJ    6  12   7   0   25
Ind D17 R29/103  P(30-17-1)  217
NYJ D23 R40/165  P(30-20-0)  227
Ind-Butler 113C; NYJ-McNeil 115R,
Sohn 112C

Atl    0   3   3   0    6
LARm   0  10   7   0   17
Atl D18 R29/104  P(34-18-1)  154
LARm D14 R29/106 P(20-16-0)  177
LARm-Ellard 123C

Dal    7   0   3   7   17
Hou    0   0  10   0   10
Dal D16 R31/156  P(32-16-0)  183
Hou D13 R29/81   P(26-11-4)  133
Dal-Dorsett 159R

NYG    0   0  10   0   6   16
Phi    0   0   3   7   10
NYG D21 R43/140  P(28-14-1)  198
Phi D11 R33/114  P(22-9-1)    54

LARd  14   0   7  14   35
NE    14  10   0   0   24
LARd D15 R38/144 P(27-10-1)  152
NE  D13 R32/97   P(36-13-3)  190
LARd-Ellard 123C

TB     3   3   3   0    9
Det    0  10   6  14   30
TB  D19 R30/119  P(31-19-1)  158
Det D24 R24/94   P(31-19-0)  221
TB-Wilder 104R

NO     0  10   3   7   20
SF     0   0   7   7   17
NO  D19 R41/175  P(30-15-2)  179
SF  D15 R27/150  P(26-12-2)   81
NO-Wilson 108R

Was    7   3   0   0   10
ChiB   0  31   7   7   45
Was D19 R35/192  P(39-21-2)  184
ChiB D16 R22/91  P(21-14-1)  159

GB     0   0   7  21   28
SL     0  19  14  10   43
GB  D24 R25/216  P(38-22-2)  238
SL  D24 R32/164  P(38-20-0)  233
GB-Clark 112C; SL-Anderson 104R

Cle    0   7   7   7   21
SD     7   0   0   7   14
Cle D23 R40/275  P(24-16-0)  165
SD  D16 R20/56   P(31-21-2)  219
Cle-Mack 130R

Sea    0   0   7   0    7
KC    14   7   7   0   28
Sea D21 R23/68   P(61-27-5)  301
KC  D10 R33/77   P(22-8-3)    88
```

```
Min    7  13   0   7   27
Buf    0   3  10   7   20
Min D19 R34/171  P(23-15-1)  167
Buf D20 R31/115  P(33-18-2)  162

MONDAY, SEPTEMBER 30
Cin    0  14   7  16   37
Pit    3   0   7  14   24
Cin D23 R38/222  P(28-19-1)  144
Pit D27 R27/113  P(44-26-2)  340
Cin-Brooks 133R; Pit-Lipps 100C,
Stallworth 151C, Malone 374P

SUNDAY, OCTOBER 6
ChiB   0   3  10  14   27
TB     0  12   0   7   19
ChiB D22 R32/147 P(34-22-2)  286
TB  D19 R20/27   P(43-23-2)  346
ChiB-Moorehead 114C;
TB-Giles 112C, House 100C,
DeBerg 346P

SF     7   3   7  21   38
Atl    0   3   3  11   17
SF  D30 R19/79   P(57-37-0)  420
Atl D22 R18/115  P(45-31-0)  271
SF-Craig 167C, Montana 429P

Dal    7   7   7   9   30
NYG    3   3  20   3   29
Dal D27 R34/106  P(46-31-4)  317
NYG D19 R26/70   P(36-18-2)  403
Dal-Hill 100C, Renfro 141C,
White 342P; NYG-Johnson 104C,
Manuel 129C, Simms 432P

SD     0   7   0  14   21
Sea    0   7   3  13   26
SD  D20 R21/40   P(35-26-3)  305
Sea D17 R39/108  P(26-16-0)  145
SD-Chandler 150C, Herrmann 344P

Det    3   0   0   7   10
GB     7  13  23   0   43
Det D19 R16/56   P(40-27-2)  317
GB  D30 R47/285  P(28-17-0)  227
Det-Chadwick 112C;
GB-Lofton 151C

NYJ    7   7  12   3   29
Cin    6   7   0   7   20
NYJ D21 R30/77   P(28-19-1)  178
Cin D25 R26/89   P(34-18-1)  212

Hou    0   3  10   7   20
Den   10   7  14   0   31
Hou D18 R28/120  P(32-19-0)  201
Den D31 R37/121  P(35-17-3)  241
Hou-Woolfolk 124C

Buf    7   3   0   7   17
Ind    7  21  14   7   49
Buf D15 R19/68   P(35-14-2)  184
Ind D28 R49/281  P(25-14-1)  183
Ind-Bentley 100R, McMillan 112R

Pit    0  17   0   3   20
Mia    7   7   3   7   24
Pit D15 R30/137  P(33-14-1)  145
Mia D24 R29/122  P(45-27-3)  277

NE     0  13   7   0   20
Cle    7   0   7   0   14
NE  D18 R25/109  P(38-20-1)  291
Cle D28 R41/146  P(35-21-2)  301
NE-Morgan 140C, Eason 304P;
Cle-Mack 115R, Brennan 104C

Min    0   0   7   3   10
LARm   0   6   7   0   13
Min D25 R29/134  P(36-21-0)  172
LARm D14 R28/58  P(20-14-0)  130

KC     3   0   0   7   10
LARd   0  10   3   6   19
KC  D14 R22/81   P(28-14-1)  181
LARd D17 R34/141 P(29-18-0)  220
LARd-Allen 126R

Phi    0   7   0  14   21
NO    10  10   0   3   23
Phi D24 R25/107  P(47-25-4)  256
NO  D12 R24/71   P(24-15-1)  146
Phi-Spagnola 124C
```

```
MONDAY, OCTOBER 7
SL     0   3   0   7   10
Was   10   7   3   7   27
SL  D17 R15/95   P(38-20-5)  215
Was D17 R48/238  P(20-11-0)   67
Was-Riggins 103R, Rogers 104R

SUNDAY, OCTOBER 13
NYG    0   3  17  10   30
Cin   14   7   7   7   35
NYG D34 R15/27   P(62-40-2)  443
Cin D16 R27/42   P(25-15-0)  157
NYG-Bavaro 176C, Manuel 111C,
Simms 513P

ChiB  13   3   0  10   26
SF     0  10   0   0   10
ChiB D22 R39/189 P(31-18-1)  183
SF  D11 R12/67   P(29-17-0)  116
ChiB-Payton 132R

SL     0   0   0   7    7
Phi    7   3   0   7   17
SL  D12 R19/81   P(37-17-2)  187
Phi D18 R37/111  P(28-18-0)  243
Phi-Jackson 103C, Hunter 120C

LARm   0  14  10   7   31
TB     3   0   7  17   27
LARm D14 R35/134 P(23-16-1)  148
TB  D15 R25/59   P(34-14-4)  151

Atl    0   6   3  17   26
Sea    7   0   7  16   30
Atl D20 R35/163  P(27-14-1)  187
Sea D22 R16/63   P(51-33-1)  358
Atl-Riggs 139R; Sea-Largent 103C,
Krieg 405P

Pit    0   3   0  10   13
Dal    0  10  10   7   27
Pit D14 R27/84   P(40-13-3)  231
Dal D18 R29/133  P(36-25-1)  241
Dal-Dorsett 113R

NO     0   7   3   3   13
LARd   7   7   0   9   23
NO  D15 R32/114  P(32-15-2)  163
LARd D16 R33/113 P(32-15-0)  165
LARd-Allen 107R

KC     3  14   3   0   20
SD     0  14   3  14   31
KC  D14 R15/48   P(40-25-2)  277
SD  D22 R31/63   P(36-26-0)  287
KC-Kenney 304P; SD-Joiner 118C,
Herrmann 320P

Min    0   7   7   7   21
GB     0   7   7   6   20
Min D18 R28/62   P(37-20-2)  223
GB  D18 R32/135  P(31-15-2)  145

Buf    0   0   3   0    3
NE     0   0   7   7   14
Buf D13 R23/72   P(31-12-2)   90
NE  D18 R25/82   P(35-23-2)  318
NE-Fryar 132C

Den    6   3   3   3   15
Ind    0   3   0   7   10
Den D20 R36/128  P(36-17-1)  223
Ind D12 R28/120  P(30-14-1)  117

Cle    0   0  14   7   21
Hou    3   0   0   3    6
Cle D13 R39/152  P(19-8-1)   208
Hou D14 R34/123  P(27-15-2)   67
Cle-Weathers 146C

Det    0   0   0   3    3
Was    3  14   7   0   24
Det D8 R12/28    P(29-13-2)  198
Was D23 R44/168  P(26-18-0)  123
Was-Riggins 114R

MONDAY, OCTOBER 14
Mia    0   0   7   0    7
NYJ    0   6  10   7   23
Mia D13 R20/74   P(23-13-1)  126
NYJ D27 R45/245  P(28-18-0)  231
NYJ-McNeil 173R
```

SUNDAY, OCTOBER 20

Cin 0 13 0 14 27
Hou 7 10 10 17 44
Cin D24 R15/106 P(52-30-3) 352
Hou D26 R43/135 P(31-20-0) 266
Cin-Brown 124C, Esiason 381P

SF 14 0 0 7 21
Det 7 13 3 0 23
SF D21 R37/208 P(29-16-1) 96
Det D15 R40/162 P(20-10-0) 130
SF-Tyler 107R; Det-Jones 116R

SD 0 3 7 7 17
Min 0 7 0 14 21
SD D23 R28/132 P(36-19-4) 163
Min D27 R22/62 P(46-31-2) 298
Min-Kramer 311P

SL 3 0 0 7 10
Pit 14 3 6 0 23
SL D22 R24/126 P(41-24-1) 160
Pit D15 R35/142 P(28-15-1) 184

Sea 0 0 7 3 10
Den 7 0 3 3 13
Sea D17 R37/172 P(32-9-3) 77
Den D14 R33/98 P(44-22-0) 148
Sea-Warner 136R

Was 0 0 0 3 3
NYG 0 7 7 3 17
Was D16 R19/69 P(38-22-3) 207
NYG D21 R41/144 P(26-17-3) 185
Was-Clark 193C

LARd 7 7 0 7 21
Cle 7 0 6 7 20
LARd D20 R30/120 P(36-15-1) 199
Cle D18 R39/109 P(22-10-0) 123

LARm 0 13 3 0 16
KC 0 0 0 0 0
LARm D12 R38/130 P(20-9-0) 54
KC D15 R30/102 P(32-14-6) 143

TB 0 14 7 17 38
Mia 14 10 14 3 41
TB D24 R25/111 P(32-19-1) 365
Mia D30 R31/144 P(39-27-1) 302
TB-Giles 116C, House 111C,
DeBerg 365P; Mia-Marino 302P

Dal 7 0 7 0 14
Phi 0 3 3 10 16
Dal D22 R31/147 P(25-15-2) 163
Phi D22 R25/55 P(35-22-0) 347
Dal-Dorsett 100R;
Phi-Jackson 134C, Jaworski 380P

NYJ 0 3 3 7 13
NE 0 3 0 14 20
NYJ D13 R24/83 P(31-15-1) 220
NE D20 R40/129 P(32-11-1) 155
NYJ-Walker 140C

NO 0 10 0 14 24
Atl 7 7 7 10 31
NO D18 R18/78 P(45-19-4) 287
Atl D23 R36/129 P(30-20-3) 248
NO-Brenner 111C, Wilson 300P;
Atl-Johnson 153C

Ind 3 3 3 0 9
Buf 7 7 0 7 21
Ind D14 R38/126 P(22-7-2) 65
Buf D13 R35/121 P(20-8-1) 61

MONDAY, OCTOBER 21

GB 7 0 0 0 7
ChiB 0 21 0 2 23
GB D16 R26/96 P(31-14-4) 223
ChiB D24 R41/175 P(32-15-0) 167
GB-Lofton 103C; ChiB-Payton 112R

SUNDAY, OCTOBER 27

Min 0 7 0 2 9
ChiB 10 3 7 7 27
Min D16 R14/30 P(46-21-5) 206
ChiB D24 R39/202 P(34-19-1) 211
ChiB-Payton 118R

GB 7 3 0 0 10
Ind 14 6 7 10 37
GB D17 R16/74 P(47-20-4) 203
Ind D24 R41/230 P(31-20-0) 266
Ind-McMillan 126R, Bouza 109C,
Capers 104C

Was 14 0 0 0 14
Cle 0 0 7 0 7
Was D19 R43/142 P(23-16-1) 142
Cle D17 R26/97 P(32-16-2) 167
Was-Riggins 112R

Hou 0 6 0 14 20
SL 10 0 0 0 10
Hou D13 R27/58 P(30-14-2) 171
SL D22 R30/187 P(40-21-0) 240
Hou-Hill 132C; SL 1-Mitchell 148R

Sea 0 14 0 0 14
NYJ 0 0 7 10 17
Sea D14 R34/138 P(21-9-2) 114
NYJ D22 R37/212 P(25-13-1) 123
NYJ-McNeil 151R

SF 14 14 0 0 28
LARm 0 0 7 7 14
SF D23 R31/139 P(36-23-0) 290
LARm D25 R17/82 P(51-35-3) 319
SF-Craig 132C, Montana 306P;
LARm-Ellard 120C, Brock 344P

NYG 0 7 0 14 21
NO 3 0 0 10 13
NYG D27 R49/234 P(28-18-0) 154
NO D12 R27/131 P(28-13-2) 101
NYG-Morris 104R

Mia 0 14 7 0 21
Det 10 14 0 7 31
Mia D20 R17/102 P(44-23-2) 239
Det D21 R49/152 P(21-14-0) 203
Det-Jones 114R, Thompson 133C

NE 0 13 3 16 32
TB 14 0 0 0 14
NE D18 R38/197 P(22-15-0) 223
TB D14 R26/79 P(26-13-2) 130
NE-Collins 109C

Den 10 17 0 3 30
KC 0 0 14 0 14
Den D25 R47/206 P(21-14-0) 118
KC D13 R21/77 P(28-14-0) 180

Buf 7 3 0 7 17
Phi 0 0 0 21 21
Buf D17 R29/128 P(36-22-2) 211
Phi D16 R15/38 P(42-21-0) 237
Phi-Quick 117C

Pit 0 7 0 14 21
Cin 3 14 9 0 26
Pit D14 R27/87 P(26-15-3) 169
Cin D20 R37/85 P(29-18-1) 221

Atl 7 3 0 0 10
Dal 0 17 0 7 24
Atl D18 R33/162 P(27-12-4) 91
Dal D28 R22/109 P(47-27-3) 352
Atl-Riggs 127R; Dal-Hill 161C,
White 362P

MONDAY, OCTOBER 28

SD 0 7 7 7 21
LARd 10 14 7 3 34
SD D22 R14/50 P(50-23-1) 274
LARd D22 R42/156 P(31-15-2) 252
SD-Fouts 315P; LARd-Allen 111R,
Christensen 134C

SUNDAY, NOVEMBER 3

LARd 0 0 3 0 3
Sea 3 23 7 0 33
LARd D18 R25/151 P(38-17-4) 131
Sea D15 R36/101 P(21-9-0) 133
LARd-Allen 101R, Dickerson 108R,
Hunter 113C

KC 0 3 3 14 20
Hou 0 6 14 3 23
KC D26 R35/153 P(33-18-1) 236
Hou D24 R31/136 P(35-24-1) 241
Hou-Woolfolk 101R

TB 3 10 0 7 20
NYG 3 3 10 6 22
TB D20 R26/88 P(42-21-1) 228
NYG D23 R38/175 P(31-18-0) 167
NYG-Morris 132R

Den 3 0 7 0 10
SD 7 10 7 6 30
Den D17 R15/64 P(39-21-2) 231
SD D24 R36/145 P(34-23-2) 285
SD-Anderson 116R, Fouts 302P

NYJ 14 14 0 7 35
Ind 0 3 7 7 17
NYJ D19 R39/201 P(25-16-0) 148
Ind D15 R18/53 P(38-19-2) 205
NYJ-McNeil 149R

Cle 0 6 0 3 9
Pit 0 0 7 3 10
Cle D9 R31/66 P(19-13-0) 87
Pit D17 R38/155 P(17-9-0) 83

Was 3 28 3 10 44
Atl 3 0 7 0 10
Was D24 R37/307 P(24-13-0) 154
Atl D14 R30/169 P(29-13-1) 123
Was-Griffin 164R, Rogers 124R,
Monk 106C; Atl-Riggs 127R

Cin 0 6 7 10 23
Buf 3 7 0 7 17
Cin D21 R53/207 P(22-12-1) 182
Buf D16 R20/95 P(34-12-2) 173
Cin-Kinnebrew 128R

Mia 7 3 0 3 13
NE 0 3 0 14 17
Mia D19 R29/91 P(33-15-2) 145
NE D22 R40/203 P(31-14-3) 177
Mia-Clayton 122C; NE-James 119R

ChiB 0 7 0 9 16
GB 3 0 7 0 10
ChiB D16 R37/188 P(20-9-0) 65
GB D15 R28/87 P(26-11-1) 155
ChiB-Payton 192R

Det 0 0 7 3 13
Min 0 6 7 3 16
Det D11 R29/69 P(13-9-0) 84
Min D20 R36/163 P(23-16-1) 138
Min-Nelson 122R

Phi 3 0 10 0 13
SF 7 7 10 0 24
Phi D20 R16/61 P(48-24-3) 366
SF D24 R34/137 P(32-20-1) 227
Phi-Quick 146C, Jaworski 394P

NO 0 0 3 0 3
LARm 7 7 7 7 28
NO D13 R17/65 P(41-23-3) 122
LARm D20 R32/130 P(30-15-0) 213
LARm-Dickerson 108R,
Hunter 113C

MONDAY, NOVEMBER 4

Dal 0 10 0 0 10
SL 0 0 14 7 21
Dal D18 R24/89 P(36-21-1) 159
SL D19 R32/49 P(32-17-0) 237
SL-Tilley 113C

SUNDAY, NOVEMBER 10

GB 3 3 0 21 27
Min 7 0 3 7 17
GB D20 R30/175 P(24-14-0) 195
Min D19 R34/177 P(26-12-2) 134
GB-Ivery 111R, Epps 118C;
Min-Nelson 146R

LARm 7 6 3 3 19
NYG 0 7 10 7 24
LARm D14 R34/158 P(25-10-1) 103
NYG D21 R35/109 P(30-16-2) 224
LARm-Dickerson 101R

Sea 0 7 0 20 27
NO 3 0 0 0 3
Sea D17 R30/90 P(29-21-1) 256
NO D21 R21/87 P(22-13-1) 96
Sea-Largent 110C

LARd 7 6 14 7 34
SD 7 3 16 14 40
LARd D26 R37/165 P(32-18-2) 289
SD D29 R36/167 P(41-26-1) 426
LARd-Allen 119R, Dickerson 101R,
Christensen 112C; SD-James 168C,
Fouts 436P

NYJ 3 3 7 4 17
Mia 0 7 7 7 21
NYJ D27 R30/120 P(43-26-0) 371
Mia D19 R19/53 P(37-21-3) 347
NYJ-McNeil 107R, Toon 156C,
O'Brien 393P; Mia-Duper 217C,
Marino 362P

Atl 0 0 17 0 0 17
Phi 0 14 3 0 6 23
Atl D20 R41/216 P(25-12-2) 94
Phi D15 R26/95 P(30-11-2) 235
Atl-Riggs 129R; Phi-Quick 145C

Pit 10 17 3 6 36
KC 7 7 0 14 28
Pit D17 R45/145 P(25-13-1) 251
KC D15 R14/36 P(39-22-1) 259
Pit-Stallworth 126C

Ind 0 6 0 9 15
NE 0 7 17 10 34
Ind D16 R24/103 P(36-20-2) 179
NE D17 R36/141 P(22-13-0) 156
NE-Morgan 120C

Cle 0 7 3 0 10
Cin 7 7 3 10 27
Cle D13 R17/112 P(32-16-2) 213
Cin D23 R36/118 P(33-23-0) 252
Cin-Collinsworth 135C

Det 0 0 3 0 3
ChiB 7 7 7 3 24
Det D8 R22/68 P(17-8-2) 38
ChiB D26 R55/250 P(13-7-0) 110
ChiB-Payton 107R, Suhey 102R

SL 0 0 0 0 0
TB 3 7 0 6 16
SL D17 R25/95 P(33-21-2) 184
TB D16 R31/124 P(27-11-1) 182
TB-Wilder 120R, Giles 134C

Dal 0 3 10 0 13
Was 0 0 0 7 7
Dal D14 R29/119 P(29-16-0) 219
Was D15 R25/124 P(31-14-3) 143
Dal-Hill 136C; Was-Monk 103C

Hou 0 0 0 3 3
Buf 10 0 10 0 20
Hou D7 R25/111 P(21-6-3) 31
Buf D18 R43/147 P(22-11-0) 60

MONDAY, NOVEMBER 11

SF 0 3 10 3 16
Den 7 7 0 3 17
SF D16 R29/138 P(41-17-0) 203
Den D18 R35/121 P(42-20-1) 215
SF-Craig 117R

SUNDAY, NOVEMBER 17

Pit 3 7 13 7 30
Hou 0 0 7 0 7
Pit D24 R51/248 P(20-12-1) 130
Hou D10 R16/106 P(27-16-1) 56
Pit-Abercrombie 107R, Pollard 123R

LARm 0 0 0 14 14
Atl 10 10 3 7 30
LARm D9 R13/45 P(25-11-2) 132
Atl D22 R53/158 P(30-15-0) 132
Atl-Riggs 123R

Buf 7 0 0 0 7
Cle 3 0 7 7 17
Buf D13 R22/55 P(30-15-2) 162
Cle D17 R37/201 P(25-12-0) 93
Cle-Byner 109R

Cin 0 0 0 0 0
LARd 3 3 0 7 13
Cin D13 R21/94 P(31-14-0) 146
LARd D19 R36/152 P(31-16-1) 132
LARd-Allen 135R

NE 0 7 0 13 20
Sea 0 3 10 0 13
NE D14 R32/87 P(27-15-1) 198
Sea D19 R30/135 P(43-19-3) 189
Sea-Warner 105R, Largent 138C

TB 14 7 7 0 28
NYJ 17 24 14 7 62
TB D15 R16/22 P(32-16-0) 190
NYJ D35 R52/202 P(33-25-1) 379
NYJ-Toon 133C, O'Brien 367P

NO 0 0 7 7 14
GB 7 14 7 10 38
NO D12 R16/75 P(37-19-0) 132
GB D26 R37/137 P(36-23-2) 296
GB-Dickey 302P

Min 0 7 7 7 21
Det 17 14 7 3 41
Min D16 R15/63 P(34-20-3) 248
Det D24 R44/148 P(29-19-1) 217
Min-Carter 102C

KC 3 6 0 0 9
SF 3 14 7 7 31
KC D12 R19/75 P(46-22-0) 125
SF D24 R35/163 P(36-24-0) 254
SF-Tyler 111R

Mia 3 10 14 7 34
Ind 10 3 7 0 20
Mia D25 R37/135 P(37-22-0) 323
Ind D17 R25/142 P(33-14-2) 210
Mia-Marino 330P

SD 7 7 0 10 24
Den 7 0 17 6 30
SD D22 R35/95 P(45-23-2) 245
Den D21 R25/91 P(50-28-2) 240

ChiB 7 17 3 17 44
Dal 0 0 0 0 0
ChiB D18 R40/216 P(19-11-0) 162
Dal D12 R16/52 P(39-15-4) 119
ChiB-Payton 132R

Phi 14 0 0 10 24
SL 0 0 0 14 14
Phi D21 R42/176 P(18-11-1) 107
SL D20 R31/237 P(22-12-0) 147
Phi-Jackson 162R;
SL-Mitchell 179R

MONDAY, NOVEMBER 18

NYG 7 0 14 0 21
Was 0 7 9 7 23
NYG D12 R24/152 P(18-9-1) 101
Was D22 R41/98 P(31-21-0) 258
NYG-Morris 118R; Was-Monk 130C

SUNDAY, NOVEMBER 24

Atl 0 0 0 0 0
ChiB 0 20 7 9 36
Atl D10 R37/141 P(17-3-2) -22
ChiB D24 R43/196 P(24-12-0) 183
Atl-Riggs 110R; ChiB-Payton 102R

NO 14 6 3 7 30
Min 7 3 3 10 23
NO D19 R50/234 P(14-10-1) 137
Min D17 R13/59 P(45-19-3) 225
NO-Campbell 160R

Was 14 6 7 3 30
Pit 3 14 0 6 23
Was D16 R38/83 P(28-15-0) 176
Pit D20 R32/102 P(35-15-3) 206
Pit-Lipps 121C

NE 0 3 10 0 0 13
NYJ 6 0 7 0 3 16
NE D21 R32/174 P(38-26-0) 225
NYJ D20 R40/110 P(32-20-0) 291
NE-James 108C; NYJ-Walker 168C,
O'Brien 311P

Mia 7 7 3 6 23
Buf 0 7 0 7 14
Mia D28 R41/172 P(31-22-2) 216
Buf D12 R19/94 P(28-15-0) 161

Det 0 7 6 3 16
TB 3 3 10 3 19
Det D16 R25/73 P(39-22-1) 200
TB D23 R40/169 P(27-16-0) 119

Den 7 14 0 7 28
LARd 7 14 7 3 31
Den D25 R37/153 P(32-19-0) 138
LARd D21 R32/201 P(34-16-3) 223
LARd-Allen 173R, Dickerson 150R

NYG 0 10 10 14 34
SL 3 0 0 0 3
NYG D20 R40/161 P(26-16-0) 152
SL D13 R12/40 P(46-23-3) 181
NYG-Adams 113R

GB 0 10 0 7 17
LARm 7 7 7 13 34
GB D20 R18/78 P(36-20-1) 203
LARm D20 R42/187 P(19-15-0) 142
LARm-Dickerson 150R

```
SD    0   7  14  14  35
Hou  14   3   3  17  37
SD  D29 R28/116 P(36-24-2) 323
Hou D26 R29/137 P(42-24-1) 278
SD-Winslow 107C, Fouts 343P

Phi  10   0   0   7  17
Dal   7  14   0  13  34
Phi D20 R20/125 P(42-23-3) 277
Dal D28 R46/143 P(29-20-1) 234

Ind   0   0   0   7   7
KC    7  10   3   0  20
Ind D11 R23/125 P(24-10-1)  86
KC  D21 R39/127 P(31-16-1) 231

Cin   0   3   0   6   9
Cle   3   7  14   0  24
Cin D14 R30/136 P(19-13-1)  90
Cle D14 R36/181 P(9-5-0)   102
Cle-Mack 117R
```

MONDAY, NOVEMBER 25
```
Sea   0   0   0   6   6
SF    0  12   0   7  19
Sea D15 R26/76 P(41-17-2) 177
SF  D21 R36/146 P(34-17-3) 230
```

THURSDAY, NOVEMBER 28
```
NYJ   0   3   7  10  20
Det   3  14   7   7  31
NYJ D23 R25/118 P(35-23-0) 239
Det D18 R32/66  P(29-19-1) 264
NYJ-Hector 114R;
Det-Thompson 115C, Hipple 269P

SL    7  10   0   0  17
Dal   7  14  14   0  35
SL  D24 R26/84  P(43-28-0) 281
Dal D23 R31/116 P(27-15-1) 277
SL-Tilley 115C, Lomax 319P;
Dal-Cosbie 111C, White 235P
```

SUNDAY, DECEMBER 1
```
TB    0   0   0   0   0
GB    0   7   7   7  21
TB  D5  R19/54  P(17-8-1)   11
GB  D31 R36/232 P(36-22-2) 280
GB-Ellis 101R, Ivery 109R,
Lofton 106C

KC    3   0   3   0   6
Sea   3  14   7   0  24
KC  D11 R20/52  P(30-16-3) 149
Sea D22 R31/94  P(34-21-1) 243
Sea-Largent 101C

LARm  0   3   0   0   3
NO    6   3   0  20  29
LARm D13 R26/105 P(18-10-1)  59
NO  D14 R34/84  P(22-13-0) 196

SF    7  14   7   7  35
Was   3   5   0   0   8
SF  D15 R32/107 P(25-13-0) 117
Was D21 R22/87  P(58-30-2) 311
Was-Clark 116C, Monk 150C,
Schroeder 348P

NE    7  17   0  14  38
Ind   7  10   0  14  31
NE  D24 R43/136 P(28-20-1) 276
Ind D23 R29/130 P(29-16-2) 170

Hou   0  10   3  14  27
Cin  21   7  14   3  45
Hou D22 R18/73  P(39-22-0) 272
Cin D28 R39/231 P(25-19-0) 324
Hou-Hill 129C, Woolfolk 130C;
Cin-Esiason 320P

Den   0  10   0  21  31
Pit   7   0   7   7  21
Den D20 R26/93 P(42-24-1) 238
Pit D22 R26/77 P(40-19-4) 250
Pit-Sweeney 119C

Buf   0   7   0   0   7
SD    7  17  10   6  40
Buf D21 R28/109 P(36-18-4) 238
SD  D21 R30/96  P(39-23-2) 269
Buf-Reed 103C

Cle   7  14   0  14  35
NYG   7  13   3  10  33
Cle D17 R31/109 P(33-14-1) 205
NYG D28 R33/229 P(37-23-2) 267
NYG-Morris 131R
```


```
LARd  7   6   7  14  34
Atl  10   7   0   7  24
LARd D20 R39/177 P(27-13-1) 211
Atl D16 R33/130 P(28-11-2) 235
LARd-Allen 156R,
Christensen 109C;
Atl-Johnson 136C

Min   0   0   0  28  28
Phi  10  10   3   0  23
Min D13 R18/67  P(37-14-0) 172
Phi D24 R39/137 P(42-23-1) 306
Min-Carter 124C; Phi-Quick 127C,
Jaworski 320P
```

MONDAY, DECEMBER 2
```
ChiB  7   3  14   0  24
Mia  10  21   7   0  38
ChiB D23 R37/167 P(28-14-3) 176
Mia D17 R24/90  P(27-14-1) 245
ChiB-Payton 121R; Mia-Duper 107C
```

SUNDAY, DECEMBER 8
```
Det   3   0   3   0   6
NE    7  10   0   6  23
Det D15 R21/105 P(38-16-1) 141
NE  D23 R45/216 P(22-14-1) 136
NE-James 115R

Ind   0   3   0   7  10
ChiB  0   3   7   7  17
Ind D10 R21/99  P(24-10-0) 133
ChiB D22 R44/191 P(23-11-0) 157
ChiB-Payton 111R

Was   0   3   7   7  17
Phi   0   5   0   7  12
Was D19 R41/166 P(29-16-1) 144
Phi D14 R18/37  P(38-17-2) 165
Was-Rogers 150R, Monk 109C

NYJ   0  21   0   6  27
Buf   0   0   7   0   7
NYJ D24 R36/118 P(40-25-1) 367
Buf D22 R23/86  P(40-23-2) 350
NYJ-Walker 129C, O'Brien 370P;
Buf-Burkett 127C, Mathison 357P

Dal   0   3   7  14  24
Cin  22   0  21   7  50
Dal D20 R20/64  P(33-22-1) 196
Cin D31 R42/274 P(33-19-0) 296
Cin-Brooks 109R, Collinsworth 123C

Pit   7  13  14  10  44
SD   21  13   7  13  54
Pit D28 R38/152 P(35-24-2) 275
SD  D23 R26/84  P(33-21-3) 364
SD-Chandler 154C, Joiner 110C,
Fouts 372P

LARd  0   0  14   0   3  17
Den   7   7   0   0   0  14
LARd D20 R37/181 P(28-13-4)  93
Den D17 R29/87  P(36-18-3) 120
LARd-Allen 135R

TB    0   0   0   7   0   7
Min   6  10   3   7   0  26
TB  D17 R34/151 P(32-13-3) 176
Min D23 R38/165 P(36-21-2) 309
Min-Jones 104C, Kramer 309P

Atl   0  10   0   0  10
KC   14  10  14   0  38
Atl D21 R32/261 P(28-16-3)  93
KC  D21 R37/164 P(19-11-1) 205
Atl-Riggs 197R; KC-Pruitt 102R

NYG  14  21   0   0  35
Hou   0  14   0   0  14
NYG D25 R46/198 P(24-13-1) 234
Hou D28 R7/22   P(48-26-2) 298
NYG-Morris 129R; Hou-Hill 103R,
Smith 120C, Moon 330P

NO    0   6   0  10  16
SL    7  14   0   7  28
NO  D21 R22/71  P(40-20-2) 216
SL  D24 R38/186 P(20-14-0) 197
SL-Mitchell 158R

Cle   3   0   3   7  13
Sea   3  14   7   7  31
Cle D16 R23/92  P(31-18-0) 214
Sea D21 R34/92  P(34-24-0) 246
Sea-Krieg 268P
```


```
Mia   6   0  14  14  34
GB    3   0  14   7  24
Mia D24 R22/63  P(44-30-1) 345
GB  D20 R29/125 P(35-20-2) 241
Mia-Marino 345P
```

MONDAY, DECEMBER 9
```
LARm  0   3   7  17  27
SF    7   7   6   0  20
LARm D12 R24/114 P(22-16-0) 150
SF  D22 R31/110 P(36-26-2) 300
SF-Rice 241C, Montana 328P
```

SATURDAY, DECEMBER 14
```
KC    3   0   3   7  13
Den   0   0   7   7  14
KC  D14 R29/106 P(29-15-1) 156
Den D20 R34/110 P(38-22-5) 301
Den-Johnson 116C, Elway 301P

ChiB  3   7   3   6  19
NYJ   3   0   3   0   6
ChiB D20 R40/116 P(31-15-1) 203
NYJ D11 R23/70  P(26-12-0)  89
```

SUNDAY, DECEMBER 15
```
Phi   7   0   0   7  14
SD    0   3  14   3  20
Phi D22 R16/75  P(48-29-3) 307
SD  D22 R29/94  P(37-19-1) 323
Phi-Jaworski 334P;
SD-Chandler 124C

SL    7   0   7   0  14
LARm 13  23   7   3  46
SL  D14 R22/82  P(28-14-2) 131
LARm D22 R41/208 P(23-14-0) 217
LARm-Dickerson 124R, Brock 216P

Sea   3   0   0   0   3
LARd  0   6   0   7  13
Sea D12 R20/51  P(33-16-2) 150
LARd D16 R37/104 P(22-11-0) 195
LARd-Allen 109R, Dickerson 124R,
Brock 216P

SF    0   7  10  14  31
NO    0   9   3   7  19
SF  D27 R33/151 P(38-25-1) 349
NO  D14 R23/75  P(34-20-0) 214
SF-Montana 354P;
NO-Goodlow 135C

NYG   0  14   0   7  21
Dal   7  14   0   7  28
NYG D25 R28/100 P(51-24-3) 296
Dal D13 R28/101 P(29-16-1) 172
NYG-McConkey 128C, Simms 329P;
Dal-Renfro 123C

Hou   0   7   0  14  21
Cle   7   7  14   0  28
Hou D21 R28/96  P(48-22-2) 303
Cle D19 R39/158 P(28-14-0) 156
Hou-Smith 125C, Moon 339P

Cin  21   3   0   0  24
Was   7  10   3   7  27
Cin D18 R23/69  P(40-23-2) 330
Was D21 R36/128 P(35-18-1) 255
Cin-Esiason 357P; Was-Monk 230C

Ind   7   0   0  14  21
TB    7  10   0   6  23
Ind D23 R40/257 P(28-17-1) 127
TB  D23 R31/157 P(25-12-2) 230
Ind-McMillan 108R; TB-House 131C

GB    0   6   7  13  26
Det  14   3   0   6  23
GB  D17 R31/173 P(23-10-1) 133
Det D25 R28/72  P(36-23-4) 289
Det-Jones 104R, Bland 109C

Buf   7  14   0   3  24
Pit   0  14   6  10  30
Buf D14 R35/189 P(20-10-2) 134
Pit D25 R36/170 P(45-20-2) 264
Buf-Bell 123R; Pit-Lipps 116C

Min   0   0   7   6  13
Atl   0   7   0   7  14
Min D23 R22/91  P(43-22-2) 286
Atl D15 R36/84  P(22-14-0) 190
Min-Carter 144C, Kramer 315P
```


MONDAY, DECEMBER 16
```
NE    7   0   3  17  27
Mia   7  10   3  10  30
NE  D19 R34/122 P(26-14-3) 199
Mia D22 R32/92  P(33-17-1) 177
```

FRIDAY, DECEMBER 20
```
Den   0  10   0  17  27
Sea   7  10   0   7  24
Den D26 R31/94  P(43-24-0) 385
Sea D20 R24/126 P(40-17-1) 205
Den-Elway 432P
```

SATURDAY, DECEMBER 21
```
Pit   0   3   7   0  10
NYG   7  21   0   0  28
Pit D10 R23/115 P(29-11-1)  99
NYG D23 R53/289 P(16-10-1)  82
NYG-Morris 202R

Was   0  13   7   7  27
SL    9   0   0   7  16
Was D8  R40/221 P(31-16-0) 192
SL  D13 R19/155 P(28-18-0)  90
Was-Rogers 206R, Clark 118C;
SL-Mitchell 129R
```

SUNDAY, DECEMBER 22
```
SD    3   3   7  21  34
KC    7  28   3   0  38
SD  D32 R30/191 P(58-37-3) 341
KC  D19 R31/98  P(23-13-0) 338
SD-Herrmann 362P; KC-Paige 309C

GB    7   3   7   3  20
TB    3   7   0   7  17
GB  D18 R30/139 P(33-16-2) 192
TB  D22 R33/89  P(37-21-2) 241

Buf   0   7   0   7  14
Mia   7   0   7  14  28
Buf D11 R26/111 P(24-10-3) 188
Mia D24 R36/179 P(26-16-1) 129

Atl   3  10   0   3  16
NO    0   0   0  10  10
Atl D22 R50/243 P(27-17-0) 189
NO  D15 R14/68  P(36-17-1) 178
Atl-Riggs 158R

Cin   3   3   7  10  23
NE   10   0  10  14  34
Cin D17 R26/91  P(39-18-1) 268
NE  D17 R46/281 P(15-8-1)  138
Cin-Brown 129C; NE-James 142R,
Morgan 121C

Phi   7  17   7   6  37
Min   7   7  21   0  35
Phi D23 R30/124 P(45-21-2) 266
Min D25 R25/73  P(36-21-1) 281
Phi-Jackson 106R; Min-Carter 132C,
Kramer 321P

ChiB  3   3  10  21  37
Det   3   0   7   7  17
ChiB D20 R33/161 P(26-14-3) 221
Det D22 R21/73  P(47-24-3) 253
Det-Mandley 127C, Thompson 101C

Cle   3   0   0   7  10
NYJ  10   7  10  10  37
Cle D12 R30/138 P(24-10-1) 104
NYJ D23 R38/135 P(34-21-1) 226
Cle-Byner 101R

Hou   0   9   0   7  16
Ind   7  13   7   7  34
Hou D18 R26/76  P(40-22-2) 345
Ind D22 R41/299 P(24-14-0) 168
Hou-Hill 210C, Moon 364P

Dal   7   9   0   0  16
SF    0   7  14  10  31
Dal D25 R30/60  P(50-29-2) 359
SF  D22 R22/109 P(35-25-1) 312
Dal-Powe 127C, Renfro 164C,
Hogeboom 389P; SF-Rice 111C,
Montana 322P
```

MONDAY, DECEMBER 23
```
LARd  0   6   0  10  16
LARm  3   3   0   0   6
LARd D13 R31/135 P(29-19-1) 180
LARm D15 R27/110 P(28-14-0) 110
LARd-Allen 123R
```


1986 NFL

SUNDAY, SEPTEMBER 7
```
Atl   7   7   7  10  31
NO    0   3   0   7  10
Atl D28 R55/245 P(19-14-1) 197
NO  D14 R20/75  P(33-13-2) 101
Atl-Austin 104R, Brown 119C

Cin   0   7   0   7  14
KC    7   0  14   3  24
Cin D17 R21/60  P(41-22-1) 223
KC  D21 R36/180 P(28-13-1) 145

Cle   7   7   7  10  31
ChiB 21   3   7  10  41
Cle D21 R24/69  P(40-23-1) 280
ChiB D26 R37/193 P(27-13-0) 174
ChiB-Payton 113R

Det   0   7   3   3  13
Min   3   0   0   7  10
Det D19 R52/224 P(15-8-1)   79
Min D14 R17/62  P(38-21-1) 213
Det-Jones 174R

Hou   7   7  10   7  31
GB    3   0   0   0   3
Hou D23 R54/157 P(21-14-1) 218
GB  D9  R24/77  P(23-10-1) 147

Ind   0   0   0   3   3
NE    3   7  10  13  33
Ind D15 R26/91  P(32-15-0) 193
NE  D20 R39/122 P(29-18-0) 251
NE-Morgan 116C, Starring 102C

LARd 16   6  14   0  36
Den   7  14   7  10  38
LARd D22 R29/116 P(33-20-0) 315
Den D20 R26/55  P(36-22-0) 235
LARd-Allen 102R, Dickerson 193R,
Allen 102C, Wilson 346P

LARm  0   6   0  10  16
SL    0   3   0   7  10
LARm D17 R45/199 P(21-5-0)   70
SL  D22 R22/70  P(34-19-1) 177
LARm-Dickerson 193R

Mia   0   7   7  14  28
SD   17   9  14  10  50
Mia D20 R9/45   P(42-26-0) 294
SD  D31 R45/224 P(36-23-0) 276
Mia-Clayton 143C

NYJ   7   7   0  14  28
Buf   7   3   0  14  24
NYJ D19 R32/103 P(25-18-0) 287
Buf D19 R28/79  P(33-20-0) 289
NYJ-Toon 119C, O'Brien 318P

Phi   7   7   0   0  14
Was   3  14   7  17  41
Phi D16 R18/66  P(43-24-1) 201
Was D21 R33/159 P(38-19-1) 274
Was-Rogers 104R, Clark 100C

Pit   0   0   0   0   0
Sea   0   6  10  14  30
Pit D9  R30/85  P(29-9-3)   61
Sea D20 R33/202 P(33-21-2) 172
Sea-Warner 114R

SF   14   0   7  10  31
TB    0   0   7   0   7
SF  D28 R30/108 P(48-33-1) 345
TB  D17 R20/91  P(40-18-7) 195
SF-Clark 100C, Montana 356P
```

MONDAY, SEPTEMBER 8
```
NYG   0  14   7   7  28
Dal  17   0  14   0  31
NYG D24 R28/116 P(45-22-1) 261
Dal D22 R23/113 P(40-23-0) 265
NYG-Johnson 105C, Simms 300P;
Dal-Hill 107C
```

THURSDAY, SEPTEMBER 11
```
NE    7   0  10   3  20
NYJ   0   6   0   0   6
NE  D21 R44/127 P(24-15-0) 138
NYJ D14 R25/70  P(30-16-2) 151
NE-Morgan 104C
```

SUNDAY, SEPTEMBER 14

Buf 3 6 17 7 0 33
Cin 7 14 0 12 3 36
Buf D20 R36/171 P(22-13-2) 207
Cin D22 R34/165 P(29-17-1) 240

Cle 0 3 6 14 23
Hou 7 0 0 13 20
Cle D9 R28/87 P(26-11-0) 156
Hou D20 R40/140 P(31-22-3) 264
Cle-Langhorne 115C

Dal 0 17 0 14 31
Det 0 0 0 7 7
Dal D24 R36/197 P(32-21-2) 191
Det D12 R23/80 P(28-14-0) 104
Dal-Dorsett 117R

GB 0 3 7 0 10
NO 17 7 0 0 24
GB D20 R18/63 P(59-28-7) 295
NO D13 R38/98 P(14-9-2) 191
GB-Lofton 100C; NO-Martin 164C

Ind 7 3 0 0 10
Mia 7 13 10 0 30
Ind D15 R25/75 P(30-18-1) 178
Mia D21 R28/134 P(29-17-1) 254

KC 3 0 7 7 17
Sea 0 13 10 0 23
KC D13 R21/98 P(29-15-2) 167
Sea D19 R36/128 P(35-21-1) 203

LARd 3 0 3 0 6
Was 3 0 0 7 10
LARd D18 R28/138 P(39-20-3) 128
Was D14 R30/96 P(19-12-1) 175
LARd-Allen 104R

Min 10 7 0 6 23
TB 3 7 0 0 10
Min D17 R35/122 P(22-9-0) 120
TB D21 R30/83 P(28-18-2) 156

Phi 3 0 0 7 10
ChiB 0 0 10 3 13
Phi D17 R34/101 P(36-20-4) 146
ChiB D21 R44/244 P(22-10-3) 100
ChiB-Payton 177R

SL 0 13 0 0 13
Atl 3 14 0 16 33
SL D15 R26/106 P(26-12-1) 159
Atl D23 R43/190 P(24-10-0) 152
Atl-Riggs 108R

SD 0 7 0 0 7
NYG 3 7 0 10 20
SD D18 R13/41 P(43-19-5) 221
NYG D25 R45/134 P(38-18-1) 257
NYG-Simms 300P

SF 0 7 3 3 13
LARm 3 7 3 3 16
SF D13 R28/78 P(24-19-2) 247
LARm D14 R27/103 P(24-13-0) 89
SF-Rice 157C

MONDAY, SEPTEMBER 15

Den 0 7 7 7 21
Pit 0 0 3 7 10
Den D20 R28/91 P(39-21-0) 235
Pit D17 R15/30 P(48-22-2) 206

THURSDAY, SEPTEMBER 18

Cin 3 10 7 10 30
Cle 0 7 3 3 13
Cin D20 R42/257 P(21-12-1) 142
Cle D24 R24/83 P(40-28-0) 255
Cin-Brooks 118R

SUNDAY, SEPTEMBER 21

Atl 3 10 14 10 37
Dal 0 21 7 7 35
Atl D26 R38/187 P(29-15-0) 233
Dal D22 R25/152 P(30-23-1) 263
Atl-Riggs 109R; Dal-Hill 104C, White 280P

Den 12 14 7 0 33
Phi 0 0 7 0 7
Den D19 R36/203 P(23-14-1) 125
Phi D16 R21/77 P(39-19-1) 196
Den-Winder 104R; Phi-Jackson 127C

Hou 0 0 7 6 13
KC 3 10 14 0 27
Hou D16 R29/97 P(40-18-2) 187
KC D12 R33/106 P(23-6-0) 117

LARm 14 7 0 3 24
Ind 7 0 0 0 7
LARm D21 R40/154 P(26-18-0) 162
Ind D14 R20/55 P(32-17-1) 122
LARm-Dickerson 121R

Mia 7 14 10 14 0 45
NYJ 3 28 0 14 6 51
Mia D27 R17/50 P(50-30-2) 435
NYJ D32 R34/132 P(43-29-1) 449
Mia-Clayton 174C, Duper 154C, Marino 448P; NYJ-Toon 111C, Walker 194C, O'Brien 479P

NO 3 7 7 0 17
SF 10 3 7 6 26
NO D10 R17/119 P(21-10-0) 110
SF D30 R42/136 P(44-29-1) 325
SF-Clark 100C, Rice 120C, Kemp 332P

NYG 0 0 7 7 14
LARd 6 0 3 0 9
NYG D18 R25/129 P(30-18-2) 205
LARd D14 R22/58 P(41-21-0) 260
NYG-Morris 110R, Bavaro 106C; LARd-Dickerson 121R

Pit 7 0 0 0 7
Min 14 3 7 7 31
Pit D13 R23/81 P(31-13-3) 154
Min D22 R31/162 P(28-20-0) 250
Min-Jones 140C

SL 0 0 3 7 10
Buf 0 10 0 7 17
SL D25 R26/122 P(47-27-0) 259
Buf D10 R28/94 P(10-6-0) 82

Sea 0 7 24 0 31
NE 7 10 0 14 31
Sea D12 R32/120 P(20-9-0) 183
NE D24 R33/120 P(45-22-0) 386
Sea-Butler 128C; NE-Fryar 110C, Morgan 161C, Eason 414P

TB 0 14 10 0 24
Det 3 0 3 14 20
TB D14 R41/229 P(15-6-0) 24
Det D26 R24/93 P(46-31-2) 286
TB-Wonsley 138R; Det-Chadwick 106C, Hipple 318P

Was 3 7 13 7 30
SD 14 7 3 3 27
Was D19 R30/92 P(36-16-0) 333
SD D26 R32/147 P(45-26-3) 204
Was-Clark 144C, Monk 174C, Schroeder 341P

MONDAY, SEPTEMBER 22

ChiB 3 7 0 15 25
GB 3 6 3 0 12
ChiB D18 R31/113 P(27-17-1) 183
GB D16 R19/47 P(44-23-1) 231

SUNDAY, SEPTEMBER 28

Atl 7 0 7 6 3 23
TB 3 17 0 0 0 20
Atl D28 R47/249 P(36-19-0) 241
TB D18 R36/175 P(21-12-1) 147
Atl-Riggs 129R, Brown 110C

ChiB 21 3 14 6 44
Cin 0 7 0 0 7
ChiB D23 R35/222 P(26-15-1) 254
Cin D16 R18/60 P(45-22-5) 278
ChiB-Gault 174C; Cin-Collinsworth 115C

Det 0 7 0 14 21
Cle 0 7 7 10 24
Det D25 R30/105 P(48-33-0) 228
Cle D15 R22/84 P(28-18-0) 170

GB 0 7 0 0 7
Min 28 7 7 0 42
GB D15 R25/82 P(28-12-2) 138
Min D25 R32/86 P(30-19-1) 297
Min-Jones 106C, Jordan 112C, Kramer 241P

KC 3 7 0 10 20
Buf 7 0 7 3 17
KC D20 R31/126 P(29-17-1) 201
Buf D24 R20/97 P(39-24-3) 269

LARm 0 0 6 14 20
Phi 10 17 7 0 34
LARm D18 R26/113 P(40-20-2) 207
Phi D20 R38/136 P(33-19-1) 259

NE 0 13 0 7 20
Den 3 0 14 10 27
NE D16 R22/40 P(38-23-1) 184
Den D22 R29/156 P(34-18-1) 182

NO 14 3 0 0 17
NYG 3 7 3 7 20
NO D10 R25/65 P(20-12-0) 131
NYG D26 R33/114 P(41-24-3) 274
NYG-Bavaro 110C

NYJ 3 10 0 13 26
Ind 0 0 0 7 7
NYJ D17 R35/85 P(34-19-2) 166
Ind D16 R24/52 P(53-21-1) 230

Pit 3 0 13 0 6 22
Hou 3 7 0 6 0 16
Pit D22 R48/214 P(31-10-1) 161
Hou D19 R31/81 P(42-22-1) 200

SD 6 7 0 0 13
LARd 0 7 7 3 17
SD D16 R24/56 P(46-21-3) 200
LARd D21 R33/101 P(28-19-2) 276
LARd-Christensen 105C, Williams 143C, Wilson 314P

SF 7 10 0 14 31
Mia 0 9 0 7 16
SF D16 R34/146 P(29-14-1) 168
Mia D24 R15/72 P(58-35-4) 365
Mia-Duper 102C, Nathan 101C, Marino 301P

Sea 7 0 0 7 14
Was 6 3 7 3 19
Sea D17 R27/148 P(32-19-2) 213
Was D20 R41/162 P(26-14-0) 195
Sea-Warner 106R; Was-Rogers 115R, Monk 103C

MONDAY, SEPTEMBER 29

Dal 7 3 7 14 31
SL 0 0 7 0 7
Dal D18 R30/107 P(29-16-2) 180
SL D13 R26/133 P(34-14-4) 92

SUNDAY, OCTOBER 5

Buf 0 7 3 3 13
NYJ 0 7 0 7 14
Buf D16 R28/126 P(35-18-1) 194
NYJ D20 R25/110 P(39-29-1) 272
NYJ-Hector 117R, Hector 100C

Cin 0 27 0 7 34
GB 7 0 7 14 28
Cin D26 R47/195 P(24-15-0) 183
GB D24 R25/75 P(31-19-1) 253
GB-Lofton 109C

Cle 10 7 3 7 27
Pit 0 14 7 3 24
Cle D16 R32/108 P(23-14-0) 162
Pit D19 R40/176 P(23-15-1) 132
Cle-Langhorne 108C

Dal 0 0 7 7 14
Den 0 22 0 7 29
Dal D19 R21/41 P(44-24-3) 225
Den D19 R37/121 P(25-12-0) 198

Hou 3 10 0 0 13
Det 0 21 0 3 24
Hou D16 R24/56 P(38-21-3) 398
Det D17 R47/158 P(14-7-0) 76
Hou-Givins 155C, Moon 398P

Ind 0 14 0 0 14
SF 7 7 14 7 35
Ind D17 R29/95 P(39-18-3) 228
SF D16 R25/110 P(28-18-0) 248
SF-Rice 172C

LARd 0 7 14 3 24
KC 10 7 0 0 17
LARd D18 R32/102 P(26-17-1) 168
KC D15 R26/97 P(29-12-1) 84
LARd-Dickerson 207R

Mia 0 0 0 7 7
NE 10 17 0 7 34
Mia D13 R22/99 P(23-13-3) 152
NE D25 R41/167 P(26-18-0) 262
Mia-Duper 102C; NE-Morgan 125C

Min 0 0 0 0 0
ChiB 0 10 3 10 23
Min D11 R20/45 P(30-11-2) 114
ChiB D18 R47/171 P(21-13-1) 199
ChiB-Payton 108C, Ortego 157C

NYG 0 6 0 7 13
SL 3 0 3 0 6
NYG D8 R25/61 P(24-8-0) 83
SL D12 R32/83 P(30-17-1) 159

Phi 0 10 0 6 16
Atl 0 0 0 0 0
Phi D15 R36/97 P(26-14-0) 212
Atl D23 R35/55 P(38-15-1) 173
Atl-Dixon 146C

TB 0 10 7 3 20
LARm 14 3 0 3 6 26
TB D14 R37/174 P(20-8-0) 60
LARm D20 R43/251 P(22-11-0) 106
TB-Wonsley 108R; LARm-Dickerson 207R

Was 7 7 0 0 14
NO 3 3 0 0 6
Was D22 R38/130 P(27-14-0) 169
NO D18 R22/108 P(30-16-1) 129
Was-Rogers 110R

MONDAY, OCTOBER 6

SD 7 0 0 0 7
Sea 0 6 17 10 33
SD D15 R21/49 P(32-20-3) 222
Sea D29 R45/218 P(36-22-2) 294
Sea-Warner 142R, Franklin 118C

SUNDAY, OCTOBER 12

Buf 7 0 0 7 14
Mia 3 7 10 7 27
Buf D18 R28/108 P(28-20-2) 197
Mia D27 R29/119 P(41-24-1) 328
Mia-Marino 337P

ChiB 0 7 7 6 20
Hou 0 0 0 0 0
ChiB D23 R36/157 P(33-13-1) 203
Hou D19 R29/128 P(29-12-1) 155

Den 7 3 7 14 31
SD 7 0 0 7 14
Den D25 R37/156 P(35-21-1) 247
SD D19 R10/42 P(40-26-2) 316
SD-Fouts 352P

Det 0 14 0 7 21
GB 7 0 0 7 14
Det D25 R52/236 P(19-15-1) 102
GB D16 R15/44 P(42-25-1) 235
Det-James 140R

KC 0 7 0 0 7
Cle 0 7 10 3 20
KC D10 R21/43 P(26-11-1) 83
Cle D20 R28/71 P(35-22-1) 285

LARm 0 7 0 7 14
Atl 3 7 10 6 26
LARm D19 R24/106 P(29-14-1) 184
Atl D14 R46/167 P(20-9-2) 108
Atl-Riggs 141R

Min 14 3 3 7 27
SF 7 10 7 0 24
Min D21 R30/34 P(41-26-2) 317
SF D21 R28/65 P(29-13-1) 348
Min-Kramer 326P; SF-Rice 144C, Kemp 359P

NO 0 0 10 7 17
Ind 0 7 0 7 14
NO D19 R34/161 P(28-12-3) 144
Ind D22 R26/95 P(44-24-1) 287
NO-Mayes 108R; Ind-Trudeau 315P

NYJ 7 17 0 7 31
NE 0 0 17 7 24
NYJ D24 R50/177 P(25-14-0) 145
NE D19 R10/17 P(42-23-0) 383
NYJ-Hector 143R; NE-Fryar 126C, Morgan 162C, Grogan 401P

Phi 0 3 0 0 3
NYG 0 14 14 7 35
Phi D9 R17/59 P(28-9-1) 58
NYG D24 R46/178 P(30-21-0) 216

SL 0 9 7 14 30
TB 0 7 0 12 19
SL D23 R38/218 P(28-17-0) 213
TB D19 R31/90 P(30-16-0) 257
SL-Mitchell 126R

Sea 0 3 7 0 10
LARd 7 7 0 0 14
Sea D12 R24/91 P(26-17-0) 120
LARd D18 R35/138 P(26-15-1) 185

Was 0 0 0 6 6
Dal 7 9 0 14 30
Was D14 R18/71 P(29-12-1) 113
Dal D25 R41/106 P(30-19-1) 318
Was-Schroeder 352P; Dal-Walker 155C, Pelluer 323P

MONDAY, OCTOBER 13

Pit 7 2 10 3 22
Cin 7 7 0 10 24
Pit D15 R37/108 P(33-12-0) 180
Cin D16 R30/148 P(31-15-1) 211

SUNDAY, OCTOBER 19

ChiB 0 0 0 7 7
Min 13 3 0 7 23
ChiB D10 R18/53 P(24-13-1) 137
Min D19 R45/157 P(18-12-0) 219

Dal 7 0 7 3 17
Phi 7 0 0 0 7
Dal D17 R24/136 P(36-20-2) 253
Phi D19 R30/217 P(25-11-0) 100

Det 0 0 0 10 10
LARm 14 0 0 0 14
Det D21 R26/69 P(50-31-2) 303
LARm D10 R37/178 P(12-6-0) 22
Det-Hipple 316P; LARm-Dickerson 130R

GB 0 3 14 0 17
Cle 7 7 0 0 14
GB D19 R29/96 P(27-21-0) 264
Cle D14 R22/32 P(37-29-1) 233

Hou 7 7 0 14 28
Cin 7 14 3 7 31
Hou D16 R29/78 P(24-14-2) 155
Cin D22 R40/224 P(25-13-0) 188
Cin-Brooks 133R

Ind 3 7 0 3 13
Buf 7 10 7 0 24
Ind D20 R28/130 P(41-19-1) 167
Buf D25 R21/121 P(31-20-2) 243

LARd 6 17 0 7 30
Mia 0 7 7 14 28
LARd D19 R43/214 P(19-11-0) 101
Mia D17 R13/57 P(32-20-2) 273
LARd-Dickerson 130R; Mia-Clayton 109C, Duper 101C

NE 10 14 7 3 34
Pit 0 0 0 0 0
NE D16 R31/74 P(29-19-1) 243
Pit D11 R35/114 P(27-9-2) 54

NYG 0 9 0 3 12
Sea 3 0 7 7 17
NYG D22 R38/162 P(25-14-4) 145
Sea D13 R27/72 P(22-15-1) 146
NYG-Morris 116R

SL 0 7 7 7 21
Was 7 14 7 0 28
SL D20 R29/118 P(30-17-0) 124
Was D21 R32/122 P(23-13-1) 232
Was-Rogers 118R

SD 7 17 7 10 41
KC 7 21 7 7 42
SD D35 R30/131 P(65-37-4) 381
KC D13 R24/64 P(24-12-1) 158

SF 7 3 0 0 10
Atl 3 0 0 7 10
SF D17 R32/115 P(30-13-2) 139
Atl D21 R52/217 P(35-16-3) 139

TB 0 0 0 7 7
NO 10 7 7 14 38
TB D16 R22/60 P(26-15-2) 160
NO D28 R50/265 P(23-14-1) 185
NO-Mayes 172R

MONDAY, OCTOBER 20

Den 0 0 3 7 10
NYJ 10 12 0 0 **22**
Den D19 R12/47 P(42-23-2) 232
NYJ D20 R44/137 P(22-14-0) 74

SUNDAY, OCTOBER 26

Atl 0 0 7 0 7
LARm 0 14 0 0 **14**
Atl D8 R24/96 P(25-13-2) 55
LARm D18 R50/234 P(17-8-2) 101
LARm-Dickerson 170R

Cin 0 3 3 3 9
Pit 3 14 6 7 **30**
Cin D23 R24/122 P(33-19-1) 249
Pit D22 R45/238 P(20-12-0) 94
Pit-Abercrombie 109R, Jackson 132R

Cle 3 0 7 13 **23**
Min 3 14 3 0 20
Cle D14 R31/149 P(18-9-1) 50
Min D20 R35/158 P(35-18-1) 238
Cle-Dickey 106R; Min-Nelson 118R

Det 0 0 7 0 7
ChiB 7 3 0 3 **13**
Det D11 R22/76 P(27-12-2) 138
ChiB D19 R38/124 P(26-18-2) 128

LARd 7 14 7 0 **28**
Hou 0 7 10 0 17
LARd D21 R39/134 P(34-16-1) 218
Hou D18 R14/82 P(46-18-4) 253
LARd-Dickerson 170R, Wilson 230P; Hou-Hill 138C, Moon 304P

Mia 7 10 0 0 **17**
Ind 7 3 0 3 13
Mia D21 R29/97 P(42-23-0) 243
Ind D17 R36/182 P(24-14-1) 121

NE 7 10 3 3 **23**
Buf 0 0 3 0 3
NE D20 R39/125 P(26-17-0) 173
Buf D16 R23/77 P(34-15-4) 147

NO 6 0 0 17 23
NYJ 7 14 7 0 **28**
NO D21 R26/61 P(37-22-2) 243
NYJ D20 R34/55 P(32-20-0) 226
NYJ-Toon 101C

SL 0 6 0 0 6
Dal 6 21 10 0 **37**
SL D11 R14/48 P(34-17-0) 152
Dal D30 R45/177 P(32-22-0) 268
Dal-Walker 120R, Sherrard 111C

SD 0 0 0 7 7
Phi 3 3 3 14 **23**
SD D14 R20/72 P(45-16-1) 187
Phi D15 R39/127 P(27-15-1) 124

SF 0 7 7 17 **31**
GB 7 7 0 3 17
SF D16 R24/92 P(29-17-1) 130
GB D29 R35/152 P(57-32-3) 312
GB-Wright 328P

Sea 0 3 3 7 13
Den 10 3 0 7 **20**
Sea D13 R30/164 P(21-10-0) 50
Den D24 R33/118 P(33-19-1) 332
Sea-Warner 139R; Den-Elway 321P

TB 3 10 0 7 20
KC 7 3 10 7 **27**
TB D16 R32/130 P(20-11-1) 86
KC D20 R32/133 P(29-15-1) 222
TB-Wilder 110R

MONDAY, OCTOBER 27

Was 0 3 14 3 20
NYG 3 10 7 7 **27**
Was D17 R18/32 P(40-22-2) 378
NYG D24 R37/202 P(30-20-0) 195
Was-Clark 241C, Schroeder 420P; NYG-Morris 181R

SUNDAY, NOVEMBER 2

Atl 3 7 0 7 17
NE 3 6 10 6 **25**
Atl D21 R39/218 P(27-16-0) 148
NE D16 R24/86 P(31-15-1) 263

Buf 0 0 14 14 28
TB 10 10 0 14 **34**
Buf D23 R19/79 P(39-29-0) 324
TB D20 R32/135 P(24-14-0) 171
Buf-Metzelaars 113C, Kelly 342P

Cin 0 10 7 7 **24**
Det 7 0 3 7 17
Cin D26 R40/222 P(27-13-1) 167
Det D21 R26/97 P(33-23-2) 268
Cin-Brooks 120R; Det-Chadwick 100C

Cle 14 0 10 0 **24**
Ind 0 3 0 6 9
Cle D15 R26/46 P(25-15-0) 213
Ind D20 R25/105 P(42-20-0) 159

Dal 0 7 0 7 14
NYG 3 7 0 7 **17**
Dal D25 R25/102 P(41-29-0) 306
NYG D14 R37/199 P(18-6-1) 46
Dal-Walker 148C, Pelluer 339P; NYG-Morris 181R

Den 0 7 7 7 **21**
LARd 3 0 0 7 10
Den D11 R29/114 P(12-11-0) 132
LARd D25 R27/81 P(47-25-4) 326
LARd-Christensen 158C, Wilson 367P

GB 0 3 0 0 3
Pit 10 3 7 7 **27**
GB D11 R24/61 P(36-18-2) 179
Pit D19 R37/126 P(32-20-0) 195

Hou 0 0 0 7 7
Mia 0 21 7 0 **28**
Hou D18 R37/164 P(27-14-2) 137
Mia D17 R29/128 P(29-12-2) 217
Mia-Duper 110C, Marino 220P

KC 0 0 7 17 **24**
SD 2 14 0 7 23
KC D16 R23/49 P(32-21-0) 233
SD D14 R49/191 P(17-4-4) 34
SD-Anderson 100R

Min 14 3 14 7 0 38
Was 10 6 10 12 6 **44**
Min D21 R27/55 P(35-20-1) 471
Was D20 R25/109 P(47-24-1) 378
Min-Jordan 179C, Lewis 159C, Kramer 490P; Was-Clark 123C, Monk 102C, Schroeder 378P

NYJ 3 21 7 7 **38**
Sea 7 0 0 0 7
NYJ D22 R38/126 P(33-27-0) 427
Sea D16 R15/51 P(44-25-2) 271
NYJ-Toon 195C, Walker 161C, O'Brien 431P; Sea-Largent 108C

Phi 7 0 3 0 10
SL 0 0 0 13 **13**
Phi D17 R30/95 P(32-16-0) 133
SL D14 R23/122 P(26-14-1) 68

SF 3 7 0 0 10
NO 14 0 3 6 **23**
SF D18 R20/52 P(40-23-2) 297
NO D14 R38/154 P(17-12-1) 137
SF-Moroski 332P; NO-Mayes 128R

MONDAY, NOVEMBER 3

LARm 0 0 17 3 **20**
ChiB 3 0 14 0 17
LARm D14 R40/141 P(25-6-1) 137
ChiB D14 R37/146 P(28-11-2) 123
LARm-Dickerson 111R

SUNDAY, NOVEMBER 9

ChiB 14 3 0 6 **23**
TB 3 0 0 0 3
ChiB D20 R37/176 P(25-11-1) 258
TB D14 R20/84 P(43-22-1) 188
ChiB-Payton 139R, Gault 116C

Cin 0 0 14 14 28
Hou 10 9 10 3 **32**
Cin D22 R23/46 P(39-24-2) 358
Hou D26 R31/61 P(44-25-0) 297
Cin-Brown 132C; Hou-Hill 185C, Moon 310P

LARd 0 3 7 7 **17**
Dal 3 7 3 0 13
LARd D15 R30/130 P(26-11-3) 116
Dal D20 R32/166 P(30-14-5) 147
LARd-Williams 107C; Dal-Dorsett 101R

LARm 0 0 0 0 0
NO 0 0 3 3 **6**
LARm D10 R28/53 P(35-17-1) 123
NO D9 R33/102 P(20-9-3) 134

Min 10 0 7 7 **24**
Det 0 0 10 0 10
Min D22 R31/162 P(39-24-2) 270
Det D15 R23/81 P(37-22-1) 201
Min-Carter 111C

NE 3 3 14 10 **30**
Ind 7 7 0 7 21
NE D27 R42/114 P(33-19-1) 222
Ind D17 R26/85 P(36-19-4) 212

NYG 0 10 7 0 **17**
Phi 0 0 0 14 14
NYG D15 R40/153 P(18-8-2) 112
Phi D17 R18/78 P(36-18-2) 159
NYG-Morris 111R

NYJ 0 21 7 0 **28**
Atl 0 0 7 7 14
NYJ D22 R37/104 P(33-26-0) 322
Atl D23 R20/88 P(36-21-1) 305
NYJ-O'Brien 322P; Atl-Brown 112C, Cox 108C, Archer 350P

Pit 0 0 12 0 12
Buf 6 7 0 3 **16**
Pit D11 R18/53 P(36-18-1) 132
Buf D18 R42/172 P(22-11-0) 76
Buf-Riddick 108R

SL 3 7 0 7 17
SF 10 13 7 13 **43**
SL D22 R27/95 P(40-23-3) 269
SF D23 R33/164 P(22-16-1) 296
SL-Smith 154C; SF-Cribbs 105R, Rice 156C

SD 3 3 0 3 **9**
Den 0 3 0 0 3
SD D14 R39/78 P(23-17-1) 147
Den D12 R17/61 P(31-13-3) 184

Sea 0 0 0 7 7
KC 0 17 7 3 **27**
Sea D8 R17/25 P(38-15-1) 108
KC D24 R37/127 P(41-22-3) 248

Was 6 0 7 3 **16**
GB 7 0 0 0 7
Was D17 R34/87 P(23-13-0) 167
GB D18 R34/140 P(28-18-1) 141

MONDAY, NOVEMBER 10

Mia 0 10 0 6 16
Cle 6 10 7 3 **26**
Mia D20 R17/58 P(39-22-1) 295
Cle D29 R28/168 P(51-32-1) 390
Cle-Kosar 401P

SUNDAY, NOVEMBER 16

ChiB 0 3 10 0 **13**
Atl 3 7 0 0 10
ChiB D15 R39/165 P(22-9-2) 203
Atl D11 R28/118 P(24-10-3) 41

Cle 0 7 7 0 14
LARd 10 7 0 10 **27**
Cle D8 R20/72 P(34-15-2) 145
LARd D16 R37/121 P(26-14-0) 202
LARd-Dickerson 102R, Ellard 129C, Williams 113C

Dal 10 0 0 14 **24**
SD 0 7 7 7 21
Dal D20 R29/101 P(33-18-0) 153
SD D19 R27/65 P(41-22-0) 242
Dal-Sherrard 115C

Det 7 0 0 6 **13**
Phi 0 5 0 6 11
Det D12 R16/40 P(33-10-1) 146
Phi D20 R37/226 P(31-17-3) 68
Det-Chadwick 139C; Phi-Cunningham 110R

Hou 7 3 0 0 10
Pit 14 7 0 0 **21**
Hou D19 R23/71 P(41-22-2) 220
Pit D20 R38/171 P(21-11-0) 116
Hou-Givins 156C

Ind 7 2 0 7 16
NYJ 7 7 3 14 **31**
Ind D23 R23/58 P(57-27-4) 350
NYJ D19 R32/142 P(35-20-2) 218
Ind-Brooks 177C, Trudeau 359P; NYJ-McNeil 104R, Walker 110C

KC 0 7 10 0 17
Den 21 10 7 0 **38**
KC D16 R20/77 P(54-23-1) 220
Den D18 R32/67 P(31-16-0) 198

NE 6 10 0 14 **30**
LARm 0 14 7 7 28
NE D23 R15/49 P(52-36-2) 341
LARm D18 R35/149 P(24-15-0) 220
NE-Morgan 118C, Eason 375P; LARm-Dickerson 102R, Ellard 129C

Mia 0 10 10 14 **34**
Buf 7 14 3 0 24
Mia D29 R24/85 P(54-39-0) 389
Buf D14 R17/80 P(33-17-0) 181
Mia-Duper 109C, Marino 404P

NYG 3 6 3 10 **22**
Min 3 3 7 7 20
NYG D23 R25/90 P(38-25-2) 293
Min D21 R25/109 P(31-20-0) 244
NYG-Simms 310P

NO 0 10 0 6 **16**
SL 0 0 7 0 7
NO D15 R36/182 P(16-7-0) 76
SL D21 R29/114 P(35-19-3) 168
NO-Mayes 131R; SL-Smith 106C

Sea 0 0 7 0 7
Cin 7 3 7 17 **34**
Sea D22 R36/179 P(30-18-2) 127
Cin D23 R28/105 P(33-22-1) 320
Sea-Largent 102C; Cin-Esiason 334P

TB 0 0 0 7 7
GB 14 7 10 0 **31**
TB D16 R21/63 P(35-20-2) 200
GB D24 R36/154 P(33-20-3) 283
TB-Carter 143C

MONDAY, NOVEMBER 17

SF 0 3 3 0 6
Was 7 0 7 0 **14**
SF D24 R18/83 P(60-33-3) 418
Was D20 R34/136 P(40-17-2) 130
SF-Rice 204C, Montana 441P; Was-Rogers 104R

THURSDAY, NOVEMBER 20

LARd 14 7 10 0 6 **37**
SD 0 10 7 14 0 31
LARd D25 R32/139 P(40-23-1) 327
SD D30 R37/129 P(40-21-3) 263
LARd-Christensen 173C, Plunkett 348P; SD-Anderson 113C

SUNDAY, NOVEMBER 23

Atl 0 0 0 0 0
SF 7 13 0 0 **20**
Atl D12 R18/75 P(38-22-1) 154
SF D21 R36/155 P(34-23-0) 210
SF-Craig 101R

Buf 0 3 3 13 19
NE 9 6 0 7 **22**
Buf D13 R20/49 P(32-22-2) 192
NE D17 R30/68 P(34-24-1) 193

Dal 0 0 7 7 14
Was 14 20 7 0 **41**
Dal D16 R19/54 P(35-17-1) 197
Was D23 R39/167 P(32-16-1) 316
Was-Clark 152C, Schroeder 325P

Den 3 3 3 7 16
NYG 0 10 3 6 **19**
Den D26 R22/80 P(48-29-2) 325
NYG D14 R36/143 P(20-11-0) 119
Den-Elway 336P; NYG-Morris 106R

Det 7 7 14 10 **38**
TB 3 0 7 7 17
Det D22 R32/129 P(22-15-1) 264
TB D26 R33/187 P(32-23-2) 193
TB-Wilder 130R

GB 0 0 3 7 10
ChiB 2 7 0 3 **12**
GB D11 R25/89 P(29-10-2) 106
ChiB D15 R38/198 P(38-15-3) 102
GB-West 103C

Ind 3 0 0 14 17
Hou 3 7 21 0 **31**
Ind D13 R22/64 P(36-16-1) 178
Hou D28 R37/173 P(37-23-2) 298
Ind-Brooks 105C; Hou-Givins 102C

KC 0 0 0 14 14
SL 6 3 7 7 **23**
KC D20 R25/82 P(43-24-2) 209
SL D17 R31/92 P(29-17-1) 162

Min 10 10 0 0 20
Cin 21 0 0 3 **24**
Min D22 R29/120 P(33-16-1) 164
Cin D24 R37/165 P(26-17-2) 248

NO 0 6 0 7 13
LARm 7 3 13 3 **26**
NO D23 R25/89 P(43-24-4) 223
LARm D18 R47/189 P(20-7-2) 50
LARm-Dickerson 116R

Phi 3 3 7 7 20
Sea 7 14 0 3 **24**
Phi D24 R30/142 P(37-22-0) 182
Sea D14 R27/80 P(26-14-0) 260

Pit 7 7 7 10 0 31
Cle 0 21 7 3 6 **37**
Pit D20 R33/142 P(28-17-1) 197
Cle D35 R34/122 P(46-28-1) 414
Cle-Mack 106R, Slaughter 134C, Kosar 414P

MONDAY, NOVEMBER 24

NYJ 0 0 3 0 3
Mia 7 14 10 14 **45**
NYJ D17 R19/89 P(28-14-2) 191
Mia D31 R36/189 P(39-32-0) 325
Mia-Hampton 148R, Marino 288P

THURSDAY, NOVEMBER 27

GB 13 10 7 14 **44**
Det 10 10 17 3 40
GB D18 R26/95 P(26-18-1) 272
Det D22 R35/104 P(37-19-2) 234
GB-Stanley 124C; Det-Chadwick 121C

Sea 7 17 0 7 **31**
Dal 7 0 7 0 14
Sea D24 R38/201 P(24-16-1) 214
Dal D22 R26/127 P(36-22-0) 201
Sea-Warner 122R

SUNDAY, NOVEMBER 30

Atl 10 0 0 10 **20**
Mia 0 0 7 7 14
Atl D13 R45/219 P(13-8-0) 143
Mia D16 R18/72 P(41-20-4) 303
Atl-Riggs 172R; Mia-Duper 115C, Marino 303P

Buf 0 10 7 0 **17**
KC 7 0 0 7 14
Buf D25 R39/164 P(34-17-1) 172
KC D26 R21/73 P(50-25-3) 273
Buf-Riddick 118R; KC-Paige 119C

Cin 7 7 0 14 28
Den 3 21 10 0 **34**
Cin D22 R21/124 P(30-21-1) 302
Den D27 R44/182 P(35-22-0) 219
Cin-Collinsworth 138C, Esiason 306P

Hou 0 0 3 7 0 10
Cle 0 0 0 10 3 **13**
Hou D18 R33/128 P(38-17-6) 162
Cle D18 R42/175 P(41-16-3) 170
Cle-Mack 121R

LARm 0 10 0 7 **17**
NYJ 0 0 0 3 3
LARm D14 R40/138 P(17-9-2) 155
NYJ D19 R24/89 P(47-28-2) 261
LARm-Dickerson 107R

```
NE    0   0   7  14  21
NO    0   0  10  10  20
NE    D14 R18/2   P(38-22-1) 229
NO    D25 R42/178 P(33-20-0) 247
NO-Mayes 157R

Phi  13   0   7   7   6  33
LARd  7   3  14   3   0  27
Phi   D22 R31/106 P(39-22-1) 241
LARd  D16 R26/61  P(42-16-2) 318
Phi-Quick 145C;
LARd-Dickerson 107R, Hester 193R,
Plunkett 366P

Pit   0   3   7   0  10
ChiB  3   0   7   3  13
Pit   D18 R35/132 P(30-14-2) 159
ChiB  D25 R46/171 P(30-19-2) 235

SD   10   0   0   7  17
Ind   0   0   3   0   3
SD    D21 R37/101 P(31-24-2) 290
Ind   D11 R17/55  P(28-15-1) 122
SD-Chandler 110C

TB    0   6   0   7  13
Min   7   7   7  24  45
TB    D20 R25/101 P(29-19-1) 166
Min   D25 R27/121 P(34-23-0) 342
Min-Wilson 339P

Was   7  10   0   3  20
SL    3   7   0   7  17
Was   D23 R31/97  P(44-23-1) 256
SL    D13 R24/148 P(16-10-0) 123
```

MONDAY, DECEMBER 1
```
NYG   0   0  21   0  21
SF    3  14   0   0  17
NYG   D20 R19/13  P(38-27-2) 384
SF    D26 R27/116 P(52-32-1) 251
NYG-Robinson 116C, Simms 388P
```

SUNDAY, DECEMBER 7
```
Cin   0   7  10  14  31
NE    0   0   7   0   7
Cin   D22 R42/300 P(31-17-0) 284
NE    D18 R20/76  P(40-22-2) 215
Cin-Brooks 163R, Wilson 120R,
Brooks 101C; NE-Morgan 107C

Cle   7   7   7   0  21
Buf   0   3   7   7  17
Cle   D21 R37/141 P(33-18-0) 230
Buf   D17 R22/83  P(39-20-0) 308
Buf-Burkett 122C, Kelly 315P

Den   3   7   0   0  10
KC    3   7   7  20  37
Den   D16 R21/81  P(47-25-5) 242
KC    D12 R29/76  P(29-14-0)  93

Det   0  10   7   0  17
Pit   3   7  14   3  27
Det   D13 R16/103 P(39-23-3) 178
Pit   D23 R46/203 P(32-18-2) 218
Pit-Jackson 147R, Lipps 150C

Hou   0   0   0   0   0
SD    0  17   3   7  27
Hou   D9  R17/79  P(26-10-2)  55
SD    D23 R40/124 P(35-25-0) 285

Ind   7   0   7  14  28
Atl  14   3   3   3  23
Ind   D14 R19/74  P(29-15-3) 151
Atl   D25 R44/219 P(28-17-0) 189
Atl-Riggs 136R

Mia  14  17   0   0  31
NO    7   3  10   7  27
Mia   D25 R25/111 P(41-27-0) 241
NO    D26 R36/257 P(34-19-1) 269
NO-Mayes 203R, Jones 119C

Min  13   0   9  10  32
GB    3   3   0   0   6
Min   D20 R35/157 P(25-13-1) 146
GB    D19 R34/144 P(38-18-0) 223

NYG   0  14  10   0  24
Was   0   7   0   7  14
NYG   D17 R32/74  P(29-15-2) 259
Was   D22 R17/73  P(51-28-6) 276
NYG-Bavaro 111C;
Was-Bryant 130C, Schroeder 309P

NYJ   0   0   7   3  10
SF    0  14   7   3  24
NYJ   D16 R13/38  P(44-20-3) 161
SF    D27 R41/198 P(37-23-1) 234
```

```
SL    0   3   0   7  10
Phi   3   0   0   7  10
SL    D23 R26/105 P(48-30-1) 356
Phi   D25 R46/230 P(31-15-1) 124
SL-Green 100C, Smith 131C,
Lomax 390P; hi-Byars 127R,
Quick 127C

TB    0   0   0  14  14
ChiB  7  21  14   6  48
TB    D13 R22/50  P(32-16-2) 221
ChiB  D23 R46/245 P(18-9-1)  187
TB-Magee 143C

Dal   7   3   0   0  10
LARm  7  13   2   7  29
Dal   D14 R21/84  P(29-18-2) 140
LARm  D21 R43/206 P(25-14-1) 212
LARm-Dickerson 106R, Brown 100C
```

MONDAY, DECEMBER 8
```
LARd  0   0   0   0   0
Sea  14  10   6   7  37
LARd  D10 R13/40  P(29-13-3)  98
Sea   D21 R45/183 P(21-14-0) 224
Sea-Warner 116R
```

SATURDAY, DECEMBER 13
```
Pit   0  17   0  28  45
NYJ   0  14   3   7  24
Pit   D25 R44/175 P(27-16-1) 189
NYJ   D22 R25/146 P(40-27-3) 223
Pit-Jackson 101R; NYJ-McNeil 137R

Was   6   7   0  17  30
Den   0   7  14  10  31
Was   D19 R31/127 P(33-15-2) 285
Den   D23 R31/71  P(35-20-0) 259
Was-Monk 129C
```

SUNDAY, DECEMBER 14
```
Buf   7   7   0   0  14
Ind   0   7   7  10  24
Buf   D18 R23/94  P(29-18-1) 264
Ind   D21 R30/79  P(33-23-0) 296
Buf-Burkett 145C;
Ind-Hogeboom 318P

Cle  14   3  14   3  34
Cin   3   0   0   0   3
Cle   D19 R38/126 P(29-13-0) 246
Cin   D15 R32/135 P(32-15-2) 148

GB    0   7   7   7  21
TB    0   0   0   7   7
GB    D20 R36/176 P(28-14-0) 173
TB    D14 R20/125 P(30-14-2) 117

KC   10  10   0   0  20
LARd  0  10   7   0  17
KC    D18 R32/99  P(31-15-0) 164
LARd  D19 R28/128 P(29-15-4) 137
LARd-Dickerson 124R, Ellard 121C

Mia   0  21  13   3  37
LARm  0   7  14  10  31
Mia   D23 R21/107 P(46-29-1) 399
LARm  D25 R31/142 P(31-14-0) 230
Mia-Duper 145C, Marino 403P;
LARm-Dickerson 124R, Ellard 121C

Min   0   0   7   3  10
Hou   3  10   0  14  27
Min   D18 R22/110 P(41-14-3) 191
Hou   D18 R33/118 P(38-22-0) 259
Hou-Givins 108C

NO    7   0   0   7  14
Atl   0   0   6   3   9
NO    D14 R38/80  P(23-13-1) 161
Atl   D18 R21/62  P(36-24-2) 185

Phi   3   3   7  10  23
Dal   7   0   7   7  21
Phi   D15 R34/98  P(27-15-1) 225
Dal   D15 R25/196 P(33-15-2) 248
Dal-Walker 122R, Walker 170C

SL    0   0   0   7   7
NYG   7  10   3   7  27
SL    D15 R20/84  P(28-21-1) 100
NYG   D20 R47/251 P(21-5-0)   62
NYG-Morris 179R

SF    7   9   0  13  29
NE   10   0   7   7  24
SF    D23 R47/198 P(26-14-1) 202
NE    D16 R20/60  P(37-22-2) 207
SF-Cribbs 107R; NE-Morgan 121C
```

```
Sea  10   7   3  14  34
SD    0  17   0   7  24
Sea   D24 R44/140 P(21-15-0) 286
SD    D22 R26/85  P(38-21-1) 220
Sea-Krieg 305P; SD-Winslow 105C
```

MONDAY, DECEMBER 15
```
ChiB  0   3   0  13  16
Det   3   3   0   7  13
ChiB  D18 R39/161 P(26-13-1) 112
Det   D14 R21/56  P(24-12-1) 104
```

FRIDAY, DECEMBER 19
```
LARm  0   7   0   7  14
SF   10   7   7   0  24
LARm  D12 R22/101 P(35-13-3) 128
SF    D27 R45/170 P(36-23-1) 238
```

SATURDAY, DECEMBER 20
```
Den   0  10   3   3  16
Sea   3  17   7  14  41
Den   D18 R21/75  P(43-20-0) 193
Sea   D27 R37/298 P(24-17-0) 238
Sea-Warner 192R, Largent 101C

GB    0  17   0   7  24
NYG  21   3  14  17  55
GB    D17 R19/119 P(36-19-2) 195
NYG   D30 R45/226 P(27-18-2) 222
NYG-Morris 115R
```

SUNDAY, DECEMBER 21
```
Atl   7   7   3   3  20
Det   0   0   6   0   6
Atl   D17 R37/119 P(24-17-1) 119
Det   D12 R25/120 P(28-11-1)  73

Buf   0   0   0   7   7
Hou   7   3   3   3  16
Buf   D19 R21/60  P(39-24-1) 218
Hou   D16 R29/87  P(29-14-0) 191
Hou-Hill 114C

ChiB  7  14   3   0  24
Dal   0   0   0  10  10
ChiB  D17 R38/161 P(22-9-3)  161
Dal   D16 R25/110 P(37-18-3) 150

Ind   3   3  17   7  30
LARd 17   0   0   7  24
Ind   D23 R31/196 P(30-19-2) 215
LARd  D25 R21/89  P(45-25-0) 334
Ind-Bentley 162R;
LARd-Barksdale 179C,
Christensen 104C

KC    7  17   0   0  24
Pit   0   6   7   6  19
KC    D8  R21/38  P(24-12-1) 133
Pit   D28 R40/175 P(43-22-1) 340
Pit-Malone 351P

NO    0   3   0  14  17
Min   9  21   0   3  33
NO    D16 R25/80  P(33-20-4) 187
Min   D23 R30/78  P(39-24-0) 317
Min-Jones 100C, Wilson 361P

NYJ   7  14   0   0  21
Cin   7  10  21  14  52
NYJ   D16 R23/126 P(27-13-3)  73
Cin   D32 R42/205 P(30-23-1) 416
NYJ-McNeil 106R;
Cin-Holman 129C, Esiason 425P

SD    0  10   7   0  17
Cle   7  13  17  10  47
SD    D17 R21/41  P(36-21-1) 292
Cle   D24 R34/117 P(32-24-0) 345
SD-Chandler 113C;
Cle-Brennan 176C

TB    0   7  10   0  17
SL    0  21   0   0  21
TB    D15 R33/86  P(34-13-2) 157
SL    D15 R26/129 P(31-19-2) 136

Was   0   0  21   0  21
Phi  14   0   0   0  14
Was   D20 R23/72  P(34-18-3) 192
Phi   D20 R40/147 P(24-12-0) 112
```

MONDAY, DECEMBER 22
```
NE    7   6   7  14  34
Mia   0  10  10   7  27
NE    D22 R41/126 P(33-21-1) 264
Mia   D20 R17/122 P(39-23-2) 266
NE-Morgan 148C;
Mia-Hampton 109R
```

1987 NFL

SUNDAY, SEPTEMBER 13
```
Det   6  10   3   0  19
Min   0  10  21   3  34
Det   D17 R26/83  P(38-24-2) 189
Min   D21 R32/113 P(22-12-3) 240

SF    0   3   7   7  17
Pit   7  10   3  10  30
SF    D24 R20/47  P(49-34-3) 309
Pit   D21 R41/183 P(33-9-0)   83
SF-Rice 106C, Montana 316P;
Pit-Jackson 103R

Dal   0   6   0   7  13
SL    3   0   0  21  24
Dal   D19 R32/125 P(32-20-0) 197
SL    D20 R27/108 P(33-17-0) 252

Phi   0  10  14   0  24
Was   0  14   7  13  34
Phi   D24 R30/112 P(36-21-2) 239
Was   D19 R27/110 P(30-17-0) 264
Was-Clark 102C

Sea  14   3   0   0  17
Den   7  13  14   6  40
Sea   D15 R20/108 P(28-14-3) 169
Den   D25 R41/166 P(32-22-1) 338
Den-Elway 338P

NYJ   0  14   3  14  31
Buf   7   7  14   0  28
NYJ   D26 R44/133 P(35-24-1) 261
Buf   D23 R16/67  P(42-25-1) 292
Buf-Kelly 305P

Mia   0  14   0   7  21
NE    7   7  14   0  28
Mia   D20 R25/64  P(43-24-2) 221
NE    D18 R39/159 P(21-14-2) 150
Mia-Duper 123C

Cle   0   7   7   7  21
NO    7   0  14   7  28
Cle   D25 R23/93  P(39-28-1) 294
NO    D21 R34/191 P(22-13-0) 147
Cle-Kosar 314P; NO-Mayes 147R

LARd  0   7   7   6  20
GB    0   0   0   0   0
LARd  D21 R48/193 P(23-11-0) 100
GB    D9  R17/66  P(28-10-3)  81
LARd-Allen 136R, Dickerson 149R

Atl   0   3   0   7  10
TB   14  13   7  14  48
Atl   D13 R16/63  P(33-14-2) 134
TB    D30 R41/127 P(34-24-1) 333
TB-DeBerg 333P

LARm  6   7   0   7  20
Hou   0   3   0  17  20
LARm  D14 R30/147 P(26-9-2)   97
Hou   D22 R27/113 P(43-21-2) 287
LARm-Dickerson 149R;
Hou-Givins 117C, Moon 310P

Cin  13   0   0  10  23
Ind   7   0   7   7  21
Cin   D25 R42/187 P(26-17-0) 216
Ind   D15 R27/85  P(23-13-3) 206
Ind-Brooks 146C

SD    0   0   3  10  13
KC    0   7   0   3  13
SD    D19 R23/84  P(40-21-3) 258
KC    D15 R40/174 P(15-6-1)   58
SD-James 100C; KC-Okoye 105R
```

MONDAY, SEPTEMBER 14
```
NYG   7   0   6   6  19
ChiB  3   7  14  10  34
NYG   D14 R20/81  P(30-15-0) 122
ChiB  D17 R39/124 P(34-20-2) 292
```

SUNDAY, SEPTEMBER 20
```
Min   7   7   0   7  21
LARm  9   7   0   0  16
LARm  D17 R25/96  P(38-17-0) 257
Min   D15 R35/122 P(25-15-1)  88
Min-Carter 117C

Dal   3   7   3   3  16
NYG   7   0   7   0  14
Dal   D21 R38/114 P(38-23-4) 242
NYG   D14 R20/60  P(37-17-4) 205

Was   7   0   6   7  20
Atl   7   7   0   7  21
Was   D21 R32/145 P(30-18-2) 190
Atl   D18 R29/125 P(34-17-1) 269
Atl-Riggs 120R, Dixon 105C

SF    0   7  13   7  27
Cin  10  10   0   6  26
SF    D16 R20/56  P(37-21-0) 205
Cin   D19 R50/128 P(29-14-1) 164
SF-Wilson 104C

KC    0   0   7   7  14
Sea   3  14  20   6  43
KC    D12 R20/75  P(26-14-1) 107
Sea   D23 R45/223 P(22-16-0) 137
Sea-Williams 112R

Den   0   3   7   7  17
GB    7   7   0   3  17
Den   D29 R45/197 P(49-30-3) 281
GB    D14 R41/134 P(21-10-0) 100

NO    0  10   0   7  17
Phi   0  17   3   7  27
NO    D14 R18/32  P(39-18-3) 188
Phi   D19 R43/161 P(34-19-1) 175

Hou   3  14   3  10  30
Buf   3  10   0  21  34
Hou   D19 R37/197 P(27-13-1) 130
Buf   D30 R31/135 P(25-20-2) 248
Hou-Rozier 150R; Buf-Burkett 115C

Mia   7   9   7   0  23
Ind   0   7   3   0  10
Mia   D20 R34/130 P(32-23-0) 245
Ind   D20 R23/84  P(43-27-1) 258

TB    0   3   0   0   3
ChiB  7   7   0   6  20
TB    D18 R25/89  P(40-19-2) 173
ChiB  D18 R36/168 P(27-15-2) 133
ChiB-Anderson 117R

SL    0   0  10  14  24
SD   14   0  14   0  28
SL    D24 R20/59  P(61-32-1) 412
SD    D17 R37/130 P(19-13-1) 152
SL-Green 139C, Novacek 101C,
Lomax 457P

Pit   0   3   7   0  10
Cle   0  10   7  17  34
Pit   D17 R23/58  P(41-13-6) 127
Cle   D18 R35/124 P(30-18-1) 180

Det   0   7   0   0   7
LARd  6   0   7  14  27
Det   D16 R15/47  P(35-21-2) 244
LARd  D25 R41/171 P(40-20-1) 234
Det-Mandley 110C
```

MONDAY, SEPTEMBER 21
```
NE    0   3   7  14  24
NYJ   6   0  21  16  43
NE    D17 R20/48  P(34-18-1) 145
NYJ   D21 R42/127 P(27-20-0) 281
NYJ-O'Brien 313P
```

SUNDAY, OCTOBER 4
```
LARm  0   0   3   7  10
NO    0   7   9  21  37
LARm  D12 R22/72  P(30-11-1) 135
NO    D19 R43/154 P(21-16-1) 195

Hou   7  10  10  13  40
Den   0   7   7   2  16
Hou   D20 R42/154 P(25-15-0) 260
Den   D14 R16/38  P(45-22-3) 182

GB    7  13   0   3  23
Min   0   7   7   2  16
GB    D16 R40/147 P(21-12-0) 153
Min   D17 R25/96  P(26-15-1) 219
Min-Brim 144C
```

```
SL      0   7   7   7   21
Was     7   7  14   0   28
SL  D27 R44/167 P(35-16-0) 231
Was D18 R33/118 P(24-14-1) 334
SL-Smith 116C; Was-Allen 255C,
  Rubbert 334P

ChiB    7  28   0   0   35
Phi     0   3   0   0    3
ChiB D22 R35/134 P(33-17-1) 184
Phi  D14 R29/105 P(36-14-0) 65

Ind     7  21  19   0   47
Buf     0   0   0   6    6
Ind D28 R41/166 P(30-20-0) 297
Buf D14 R28/81  P(35-12-3) 82
Ind-Murray 161C, Hogeboom 259P

TB      0  21  10   0   31
Det    17   7   0   3   27
TB  D12 R39/113 P(23-8-0) 106
Det D12 R32/101 P(26-10-3) 161

KC      0   0  14   3   17
LARd   14   7   7   7   35
KC   D22 R35/131 P(25-14-0) 137
LARd D21 R39/252 P(18-10-0) 248

SD      0   0   0  10   10
Cin     7   2   0   0    9
SD  D15 R34/92  P(28-17-1) 169
Cin D11 R50/219 P(13-5-0) -13

Dal     7  17  14   0   38
NYJ     7   7   7   3   24
Dal D14 R37/114 P(15-6-1) 132
NYJ D22 R30/82  P(35-18-2) 159

Mia     7   0   6   7   20
Sea     7   3   0  14   24
Mia D19 R35/164 P(30-18-1) 160
Sea D20 R25/76  P(42-20-3) 326
Sea-Teal 137C, Mathison 326P

Pit     0  14   0  14   28
Atl     3   0   2   7   12
Pit D19 R41/142 P(26-14-1) 219
Atl D13 R21/67  P(34-18-1) 141
Pit-Jackson 104R, Clinkscales 150C

Cle     0   0   6  14   20
NE      0  10   0   0   10
Cle D22 R54/217 P(30-10-0) 131
NE  D10 R27/31  P(26-10-0) 110
Cle-Mason 133R
```

MONDAY, OCTOBER 5
```
SF      3  14  10  14   41
NYG     0   7   0  14   21
SF  D28 R49/242 P(23-14-0) 191
NYG D14 R22/77  P(21-9-1) 154
```

SUNDAY, OCTOBER 11
```
Det     3   0   3  10   3  19
GB      0   6   0  10   0  16
Det D21 R42/122 P(39-19-0) 220
GB  D16 R36/151 P(30-17-1) 122

NYJ     0   0   0   0    0
Ind     0   3   3   0    6
NYJ D16 R28/66  P(35-17-3) 145
Ind D14 R32/174 P(31-15-1) 96
Ind-Banks 159R

Phi     3   7   6   6   22
Dal    21   6  14   0   41
Phi D24 R30/72  P(45-29-0) 362
Dal D19 R31/160 P(25-15-0) 240
Phi-Bowman 123C, Tinsley 338P;
  Dal-Burbage 110C, Edwards 100C

Pit     7   7   0   7   21
LARm   14   7   7   3   31
Pit D16 R28/149 P(32-13-1) 191
LARm D15 R38/172 P(19-13-1) 141
LARm-White 166R

NO      0   6   6   7   19
SL     10   7   0   7   24
NO D30 R48/213 P(36-17-1) 155
SL D9 R31/139   P(10-3-1) 4
NO-Beverly 139R, Martin 101C

Buf     0   0   0   7    7
NE      7   0   7   0   14
Buf D14 R37/107 P(21-9-2) 61
NE  D15 R55/213 P(13-4-1) 43
NE-LeBlanc 146R
```

```
KC      0   0   0   0    0
Mia     7   7  21   7   42
KC  D8  R30/90  P(18-10-2) 42
Mia D25 R35/202 P(31-17-0) 142

Was     3  21   7   7   38
NYG     3   0   9   0   12
Was D24 R48/200 P(23-11-0) 176
NYG D13 R19/47  P(41-14-1) 124
Was-Vital 128R

Cin     0  17   0   0   17
Sea     0   0   3   7   10
Cin D22 R61/270 P(11-6-0) 97
Sea D17 R21/90  P(32-15-2) 126
Cin-Logan 103R

Hou     0   7   6   2   15
Cle     3   0   0   7   10
Hou D17 R46/174 P(25-13-2) 143
Cle D9 R18/50   P(27-13-3) 119
Hou-Hunter 121R, Harris 104C

SD      0   0  10   7   17
TB      7   3   0   3   13
SD D22 R33/125 P(33-23-0) 260
TB D7 R29/131   P(17-6-1) 70
SD-Williams 110C

Min     0   0   0   7    7
ChiB    0   7  10  10   27
Min D15 R22/43  P(32-15-1) 108
ChiB D26 R41/185 P(31-16-0) 159

SF      6  14   0   5   25
Atl     0   0  10   7   17
SF D20 R43/239 P(18-9-1) 122
Atl D20 R20/50 P(46-18-2) 188
```

MONDAY, OCTOBER 12
```
LARd    0  14   0   0   14
Den    14   3   6   7   30
LARd D16 R29/102 P(34-18-3) 168
Den D24 R43/204 P(26-11-0) 142
Den-Dudek 128R
```

SUNDAY, OCTOBER 18
```
Min     3   0   7   0   10
TB      3   0  14   3   20
Min D16 R17/23 P(37-20-4) 152
TB D15 R29/75  P(36-20-2) 193
TB-Holloway 107C

Ind     0   7   0   0    7
Pit     7   0   0  14   21
Ind D15 R22/75 P(30-17-3) 195
Pit D23 R47/252 P(23-11-1) 126
Pit-Jackson 134R

Sea    21   9   7   0   37
Det     7   0   7   0   14
Sea D24 R34/80 P(30-21-1) 324
Det D15 R22/93 P(27-14-2) 104
Sea-Largent 261R, Kemp 344P

SD      7   0   0  16   23
LARd    0  14   0   3   17
SD D14 R30/97 P(27-17-0) 147
LARd D19 R30/138 P(31-11-1) 176
LARd-White 155R

LARm    7  10   3   0   20
Atl     0   0   7  17   24
LARm D21 R36/186 P(29-14-1) 164
Atl D22 R19/46  P(46-27-2) 296
LARm-White 155R;
  Atl-Barney 109C, Kramer 335P

Cle     3  17   7   7   34
Cin     0   0   0   0    0
Cle D29 R42/123 P(32-26-0) 287
Cin D6 R25/65  P(11-4-1) 30
Cle-Brennan 139C, Danielson 281P

NO      0  10   3   6   19
ChiB   10   0   7   0   17
NO D18 R40/112 P(35-16-1) 179
ChiB D11 R25/67 P(29-9-4) 66

NE     14   7   0   0   21
Hou     7   0   0   0    7
NE D17 R30/114 P(25-15-0) 196
Hou D17 R26/113 P(49-21-2) 221
Hou-Williams 124C

Mia    10   0  14   0   7  31
NYJ     0  17   0  14   6  37
Mia D30 R35/128 P(55-26-5) 286
NYJ D24 R40/183 P(49-30-2) 294
NYJ-Ryan 301P
```

```
Den     9  10   0   7   26
KC      3   7   7   0   17
Den D23 R35/98  P(39-25-2) 275
KC  D16 R31/122 P(29-17-1) 125
Den-Micho 105C

SL      7  14   7   0   28
SF      0  14   7  13   34
SL  D18 R36/160 P(17-10-2) 164
SF  D28 R32/121 P(39-31-2) 327
SL-McAdoo 111R;
  SF-Montana 334P

NYG     0   0   0   3   0    3
Buf     0   0   0   3   3    6
NYG D19 R36/128 P(46-17-2) 180
Buf D22 R40/167 P(39-20-3) 164
NYG-Willhite 100R, Morris 132C;
  Buf-Byrum 139R

Phi     7   0   0   3   10
GB      0   3   7   6   16
Phi D17 R30/141 P(31-17-4) 224
GB  D20 R39/175 P(28-17-2) 224
Phi-Grant 135C; GB-Willhite 100R,
  Morris 132C
```

MONDAY, OCTOBER 19
```
Was     3   0   7   3   13
Dal     0   0   7   0    7
Was D19 R42/186 P(20-12-2) 153
Dal D18 R22/93  P(23-12-1)
Was-Vital 136R, McEwen 108C;
  Dal-Edwards 104C
```

SUNDAY, OCTOBER 25
```
NE      3   0   6   7   16
Ind     0  10  13   7   30
NE  D18 R27/79 P(43-22-1) 225
Ind D17 R25/87 P(28-17-0) 213
NE-Morgan 102C

Buf     0   3  14  14   3  34
Mia    14   7   0  10   0  31
Buf D29 R39/144 P(39-29-0) 330
Mia D21 R20/70  P(36-24-0) 296
Buf-Burkett 130C, Kelly 359P;
  Mia-Marino 303P

ChiB    0  14   0  13   27
TB     20   3   0   3   26
ChiB D19 R14/91 P(34-23-1) 209
TB D20 R26/101  P(38-23-0) 184

SF      7  10   0   7   24
NO      3   3   6  10   22
SF D23 R26/75 P(32-18-0) 228
NO D20 R43/177 P(27-14-1) 202
NO-Mayes 144R

Sea     7  21   0   7   35
LARd    0   0   7   6   13
Sea D21 R44/144 P(20-14-1) 149
LARd D18 R13/44 P(40-20-3) 206
Sea-Warner 112R;
  LARd-Christensen 124C

KC      0  14   7   0   21
SD     14  21   0   7   42
KC D21 R15/66 P(38-23-1) 305
SD D30 R39/114 P(34-24-0) 277
KC-Carson 197C, Kenney 328P

Dal     3   7   3   7   20
Phi     3  10   7  17   37
Dal D18 R26/97 P(36-22-0) 197
Phi D18 R34/141 P(24-10-0) 96

NYJ     0   3  10   3   16
Was     0   0   0  17   17
NYJ D14 R25/74 P(27-18-1) 126
Was D16 R26/103 P(38-15-1) 275

Cin     7   7   6   0   20
Pit     7   0   3  13   23
Cin D17 R27/141 P(32-20-2) 292
Pit D17 R33/78  P(30-18-0) 204
Cin-Esiason 303P;
  Pit-Stallworth 100C

Atl     3  10  14   6   33
Hou     3  10   7  17   37
Atl D14 R26/121 P(26-14-1) 183
Hou D24 R43/205 P(36-15-2) 234
Atl-Riggs 113R; Hou-Rozier 144R
```

```
GB     21  10   0   3   34
Det     0  16   3  14   33
GB  D23 R38/172 P(29-19-1) 293
Det D23 R12/17  P(47-33-0) 336
GB-Davis 129R, Stanley 150C,
  Majkowski 323P; Det-Long 362P

LARm    0   7  10   0   17
Cle     3  20   0   7   30
LARm D22 R24/101 P(50-21-3) 227
Cle D15 R23/65   P(30-19-1) 202
```

MONDAY, OCTOBER 26
```
Den     7  10   0  10   27
Min     7   7  13   7   34
Den D21 R27/123 P(39-22-1) 206
Min D27 R36/197 P(23-13-5) 196
```

SUNDAY, NOVEMBER 1
```
Pit    14   7   3   0   24
Mia     0   7  14  14   35
Pit D22 R30/116 P(36-18-1) 199
Mia D26 R31/146 P(31-25-2) 332
Mia-Stradford 110R, Duper 100C,
  Marino 332P

Was     3  14  10   0   27
Buf     0   0   0   7    7
Was D24 R53/299 P(18-11-0) 107
Buf D14 R10/21  P(43-25-3) 259
Was-Rogers 125R; Buf-Reed 108C

Det     0   0   0   0    0
Den    17   7   0  10   34
Det D14 R17/63 P(34-16-1) 128
Den D28 R39/212 P(33-19-0) 248

NO     14   7   3  14   38
Atl     0   0   0   0    0
NO D29 R42/244 P(26-16-0) 166
Atl D12 R16/55 P(29-14-5) 128
NO-Mayes 112R

SF      7  17   0   7   31
LARm    0   0   0   0    0
SF D23 R36/149 P(30-21-1) 286
LARm D19 R24/62 P(35-20-0) 218
SF-Craig 104R

TB      0   3  17   3   23
GB      0   0   3  14   17
TB D20 R41/89 P(30-17-1) 190
GB D22 R24/89 P(33-17-0) 190

Cle     7   7  10   0   24
SD     14   0   0  13   27
Cle D19 R21/72 P(42-24-2) 267
SD D22 R27/128 P(42-25-1) 286
SD-Fouts 315P

Ind     3   7   3   6   19
NYJ     0   7   0   7   14
Ind D21 R45/186 P(23-14-0) 191
NYJ D15 R20/101 P(30-16-1) 129
Ind-Bentley 145R

Phi     0   7   7  14   28
SL      6   0   7  10   23
Phi D14 R21/62 P(33-17-1) 266
SL D27 R31/177 P(50-29-3) 232
SL-Smith 112C

Hou     7   0   7  17   31
Cin     3   6   7  13   29
Hou D19 R20/82 P(29-18-1) 145
Cin D25 R33/121 P(41-26-2) 383
Cin-Brooks 103C,
  Collinsworth 121C, Esiason 387P

KC     14   7   7   0   28
ChiB    7   7   3  14   31
KC D20 R34/111 P(28-15-1) 256
ChiB D20 R30/80 P(34-23-1) 263
KC-Carson 117C, Paige 121C,
  Kenney 270P

Min     3   7   0   7   17
Sea     7   7   7   7   28
Min D23 R26/143 P(39-23-1) 252
Sea D19 R34/123 P(21-14-1) 195
```

MONDAY, NOVEMBER 2
```
NYG     0  10   7   7   24
Dal     7   7   0  19   33
NYG D16 R24/55 P(27-20-2) 242
Dal D15 R24/26 P(33-24-1) 214
NYG-Manuel 151C
```

SUNDAY, NOVEMBER 8
```
Den     0   0   7   7   14
Buf     0  18   0   3   21
Den D12 R22/76 P(30-13-0) 139
Buf D25 R58/258 P(24-15-1) 170

SD      0   0   6  10   16
Ind     3  10   0   0   13
SD D15 R26/82 P(30-16-3) 214
Ind D18 R45/191 P(18-12-0) 112
Ind-Dickerson 138R

Pit     0   7   7   3   17
KC      7   3   0   6   16
Pit D25 R48/250 P(31-14-2) 141
KC D15 R28/101 P(29-14-4) 123
Pit-Jackson 125R

Dal     0  10   7   0   17
Det    10   0   7  10   27
Dal D20 R29/123 P(38-17-4) 167
Det D20 R30/76 P(28-15-2) 217

LARd    3   0  10   7   20
Min     0  14  10   7   31
LARd D19 R30/157 P(39-18-4) 219
Min D13 R38/116 P(18-7-0) 84
LARd-Lofton 128C

ChiB    7   6   0  13   26
GB     14   7   0   3   24
ChiB D22 R33/104 P(42-21-2) 247
GB D17 R24/42 P(42-20-0) 298
ChiB-Anderson 102C;
  GB-Epps 139C

NE      0   0   7   3   10
NYG     0  14   3   0   17
NE D11 R22/73 P(36-18-3) 159
NYG D24 R44/130 P(33-21-2) 217

Mia     0   7   6   7   20
Cin     7   0   0   7   14
Mia D22 R24/98 P(41-26-0) 235
Cin D23 R27/156 P(37-18-1) 202
Cin-Brown 105C

Was     7  14   0   6   27
Phi     7  10   0  14   31
Was D23 R28/129 P(46-16-2) 231
Phi D23 R41/195 P(31-18-3) 232
Was-Clark 119C

TB      7   7  14   0   28
SL      7   3   0  21   31
TB D26 R33/83 P(37-23-0) 294
SL D26 R31/137 P(36-25-1) 278
TB-DeBerg 303P; SL-Awalt 124C,
  Lomax 314P

NO     10   7   7   7   31
LARm    0   7   0   7   14
NO D20 R44/232 P(21-13-1) 211
LARm D18 R22/102 P(34-17-2) 202

Atl     0   0   0   0    0
Cle     0  14  21   3   38
Atl D13 R23/117 P(22-15-1) 126
Cle D24 R40/173 P(24-13-0) 192

Hou     7   0   7   6   20
SF      7   7   7   6   27
Hou D15 R19/48 P(38-18-3) 221
SF D33 R34/163 P(46-32-2) 280
Hou-Hill 101C
```

MONDAY, NOVEMBER 9
```
Sea     0   0  14   0   14
NYJ     0  10  10  10   30
Sea D17 R28/111 P(29-12-2) 164
NYJ D23 R37/132 P(30-23-0) 210
```

SUNDAY, NOVEMBER 15
```
NYG     7   3   7   3   20
Phi    10   0   7   0   17
NYG D17 R28/116 P(30-16-2) 268
Phi D22 R39/191 P(34-17-1) 146
NYG-Bavaro 102C, Manuel 105C
```

NYJ 3 0 3 10 **16**
KC 0 3 6 0 9
NYJ D19 R38/227 P(23-14-0) 102
KC D18 R22/104 P(24-13-3) 195
NYJ-McNeil 184R; KC-Hayes 105C

TB 0 7 3 7 17
Min 0 6 10 7 **23**
TB D14 R9/15 P(37-22-1) 244
Min D23 R47/224 P(28-12-1) 106
Min-Nelson 103R

Dal 7 7 0 3 6 **23**
NE 0 7 0 10 0 17
Dal D24 R30/181 P(44-25-2) 257
NE D15 R33/88 P(28-14-1) 177
Dal-Walker 173R

LARm 14 0 10 3 **27**
SL 3 14 7 0 24
LARm D21 R44/239 P(26-14-1) 144
SL D19 R24/124 P(29-19-0) 156
LARm-White 213R

Det 3 0 10 0 13
Was 0 17 3 0 **20**
Det D23 R28/103 P(37-23-4) 238
Was D18 R34/135 P(28-16-0) 174

Cin 3 0 0 13 **16**
Atl 0 0 7 3 10
Cin D27 R50/270 P(30-13-2) 146
Atl D13 R25/119 P(22-13-0) 147
Cin-Kinnebrew 100R; Atl-Riggs 112R

Hou 0 3 14 6 **23**
Pit 3 0 0 0 3
Hou D21 R43/152 P(22-16-0) 221
Pit D8 R20/86 P(29-10-3) 84
Hou-Rozier 112R, Hill 107C

GB 3 10 0 0 13
Sea 0 21 0 3 **24**
GB D13 R25/100 P(35-14-2) 198
Sea D16 R42/193 P(15-9-3) 88
Sea-Warner 123R

NO 3 6 14 3 **26**
SF 7 0 7 10 24
NO D16 R31/105 P(27-10-1) 156
SF D20 R29/144 P(36-22-2) 258
SF-Rice 108C

Buf 7 0 0 14 21
Cle 3 14 7 3 **27**
Buf D17 R20/61 P(35-22-0) 206
Cle D24 R31/84 P(34-24-1) 337
Cle-Kosar 346P

LARd 0 0 0 14 14
SD 0 9 0 7 **16**
LARd D12 R23/150 P(32-15-1) 215
SD D16 R41/114 P(32-15-1) 134
LARd-White 213R

Ind 7 13 3 17 **40**
Mia 0 0 0 21 21
Ind D32 R44/239 P(37-22-0) 218
Mia D22 R23/77 P(38-16-2) 209
Ind-Dickerson 154R

MONDAY, NOVEMBER 16

ChiB 14 0 15 0 29
Den 0 21 0 10 **31**
ChiB D24 R30/146 P(36-23-1) 300
Den D26 R27/98 P(41-21-2) 341
ChiB-Gault 133C, McMahon 311P; Den-Elway 341P

SUNDAY, NOVEMBER 22

Buf 0 7 10 0 **17**
NYJ 0 7 0 7 14
Buf D15 R31/127 P(33-21-1) 204
NYJ D21 R30/126 P(40-18-1) 192
NYJ-McNeil 103R

SL 7 24 0 0 **31**
Phi 0 0 7 12 19
SL D18 R38/92 P(30-18-2) 232
Phi D17 R20/60 P(51-26-2) 240

SD 0 3 0 0 3
Sea 3 14 10 7 **34**
SD D6 R12/17 P(25-14-2) 139
Sea D34 R54/277 P(28-19-0) 219
Sea-Warner 119R

Det 0 10 0 0 10
ChiB 14 13 0 3 **30**
Det D10 R12/30 P(31-14-2) 149
ChiB D29 R39/178 P(32-20-1) 205

Mia 7 3 3 7 **20**
Dal 7 3 0 7 14
Mia D21 R26/182 P(39-22-1) 258
Dal D16 R34/185 P(18-12-2) 134
Mia-Stradford 169R

Atl 0 7 6 0 13
Min 0 10 7 7 **24**
Atl D16 R25/96 P(35-19-1) 194
Min D18 R35/133 P(33-14-1) 169

SF 7 10 0 7 **24**
TB 0 10 0 0 10
SF D28 R34/137 P(45-29-1) 295
TB D14 R20/60 P(35-19-1) 196
SF-Rice 103C, Montana 304P

Ind 0 0 0 0 0
NE 0 10 14 0 **24**
Ind D18 R31/126 P(38-17-4) 198
NE D15 R38/139 P(26-12-0) 174
Ind-Dickerson 117R; NE-Morgan 102C

Den 10 10 0 3 **23**
LARd 0 14 3 0 17
Den D20 R38/127 P(29-16-0) 276
LARd D17 R26/149 P(21-15-0) 122
Den-Johnson 115C

NYG 0 7 7 0 14
NO 3 10 0 10 **23**
NYG D16 R17/75 P(36-20-5) 223
NO D16 R37/103 P(27-17-1) 175
NYG-Baker 100C

Cle 9 17 14 0 **40**
Hou 0 0 0 7 7
Cle D27 R51/200 P(28-15-0) 257
Hou D11 R14/43 P(34-11-4) 204
Cle-Mack 114R; Hou-Givins 126C

Pit 3 10 7 10 **30**
Cin 3 3 3 7 16
Pit D14 R31/134 P(28-15-2) 194
Cin D28 R25/75 P(53-30-3) 373
Cin-McGee 139C, Esiason 409P

GB 7 0 13 3 **23**
KC 0 0 3 0 3
GB D14 R37/108 P(26-9-0) 165
KC D10 R24/116 P(34-14-1) 85

MONDAY, NOVEMBER 23

LARm 14 9 7 0 **30**
Was 9 7 3 7 26
LARm D14 R44/138 P(13-7-1) 96
Was D20 R22/66 P(47-24-1) 277
LARm-White 112R; Was-Williams 308P

THURSDAY, NOVEMBER 26

Min 14 7 10 7 6 **44**
Dal 0 14 10 14 0 38
Min D27 R40/188 P(36-18-2) 288
Dal D23 R34/112 P(41-25-3) 291
Min-Nelson 118R, Carter 184C; Dal-Renfro 100C, White 341P

KC 7 17 3 0 **27**
Det 0 10 3 7 20
KC D22 R34/162 P(26-18-1) 246
Det D22 R26/151 P(41-21-0) 206

SUNDAY, NOVEMBER 29

NO 3 0 7 10 **20**
Pit 0 14 0 2 16
NO D15 R38/114 P(24-14-1) 144
Pit D17 R32/112 P(31-16-3) 172

Cle 7 10 0 7 24
SF 7 14 3 14 **38**
Cle D18 R20/92 P(37-26-1) 268
SF D23 R34/119 P(32-23-1) 336
SF-Rice 126C, Montana 342P

SL 14 14 0 6 **34**
Atl 7 7 0 7 21
SL D24 R33/113 P(42-25-1) 363
Atl D18 R27/120 P(39-11-1) 147
SL 1-White 137R, Smith 109C, Lomax 369P; tl-Matthews 115C

NYG 10 6 3 0 **19**
Was 0 9 0 14 **23**
NYG D16 R37/119 P(29-12-1) 200
Was D20 R25/82 P(46-28-2) 275
Was-Clark 112C, Schroeder 331P

Hou 0 10 7 10 27
Ind 7 21 3 20 **51**
Hou D26 R32/136 P(44-24-2) 318
Ind D18 R38/211 P(19-10-0) 148
Hou-Rozier 122R, Hill 134C, Moon 327P; Ind-Dickerson 136R

GB 7 3 0 0 **10**
ChiB 0 10 3 10 23
GB D20 R30/111 P(36-18-2) 289
ChiB D20 R35/127 P(27-16-1) 192

TB 0 0 3 0 3
LARm 7 14 7 7 **35**
TB D11 R14/79 P(34-17-1) 122
LARm D27 R50/213 P(21-16-0) 212
LARm-White 137R

Den 7 10 14 0 **31**
SD 3 7 0 7 17
Den D31 R47/175 P(32-21-1) 347
SD D18 R10/66 P(40-23-2) 312
Den-Nattiel 118C, Elway 347P; SD-Fouts 322P

Cin 0 10 7 3 20
NYJ 7 10 0 10 **27**
Cin D21 R29/106 P(34-16-2) 233
NYJ D20 R38/123 P(33-19-2) 205

Mia 0 0 0 0 0
Buf 0 21 3 3 **27**
Mia D13 R16/23 P(42-20-3) 206
Buf D21 R47/229 P(21-15-0) 217
Buf-Harmon 119R

Phi 3 14 7 7 **34**
NE 0 10 0 21 0 31
Phi D23 R47/184 P(31-18-1) 287
NE D11 R23/89 P(53-32-1) 356
Phi-Toney 123R, Quick 121C, Cunningham 314P; NE-Collins 100C, Ramsey 402P

MONDAY, NOVEMBER 30

LARd 7 20 10 0 **37**
Sea 0 0 7 7 14
LARd D24 R50/356 P(18-11-0) 151
Sea D14 R16/37 P(31-17-2) 130
LARd-Jackson 221R

SUNDAY, DECEMBER 6

KC 0 3 14 10 0 27
Cin 10 7 3 3 7 **30**
KC D21 R25/113 P(39-19-0) 209
Cin D31 R39/144 P(44-28-0) 359
Cin-Esiason 368P

TB 7 3 10 14 34
NO 14 14 0 16 **44**
TB D27 R22/97 P(47-22-2) 352
NO D19 R37/117 P(24-16-0) 248
TB-Carrier 212C, Testaverde 369P; NO-Martin 101C

Atl 14 0 7 0 **21**
Dal 3 0 7 0 10
Atl D18 R32/111 P(30-17-2) 253
Dal D24 R27/91 P(43-26-1) 263
Atl-Riggs 119R

Sea 3 6 0 0 9
Pit 3 3 0 7 **13**
Sea D16 R38/135 P(15-9-1) 80
Pit D18 R44/209 P(18-11-0) 99
Pit-Pollard 106R

ChiB 3 10 7 10 **30**
Min 3 7 7 7 24
ChiB D26 R32/159 P(34-17-1) 264
Min D18 R27/75 P(39-22-1) 281
Min-Carter 106C

Buf 0 14 7 0 21
LARd 10 3 14 7 **34**
Buf D19 R21/84 P(36-22-0) 303
LARd D29 R40/144 P(33-22-0) 350
Buf-Reed 153C, Kelly 315P; LARd-White 102R, Ellard 171C, Lofton 132C, Everett 324P, Wilson 337P

SF 7 9 0 7 **23**
GB 0 6 6 0 12
SF D22 R38/143 P(35-26-1) 296
GB D18 R30/188 P(32-19-3) 127
SF-Montana 308P

Phi 0 6 0 14 20
NYG 7 0 6 7 3 **23**
Phi D15 R29/95 P(43-20-0) 164
NYG D15 R39/78 P(34-16-1) 221
NYG-Bavaro 133C

SD 0 5 6 7 18
Hou 10 0 10 7 6 **33**
SD D19 R12/43 P(48-28-0) 289
Hou D21 R45/146 P(25-13-1) 184
SD-Chandler 140C

LARm 3 7 10 17 **37**
Det 3 0 10 3 16
LARm D22 R36/110 P(26-20-1) 313
Det D19 R17/57 P(48-26-2) 271
LARm-White 102R, Ellard 171C, Everett 324P

Ind 0 9 0 0 **9**
Cle 0 0 0 7 7
Ind D18 R30/114 P(34-20-0) 183
Cle D15 R26/87 P(35-16-0) 160

Was 10 0 21 3 **34**
SL 0 3 0 14 17
Was D18 R41/180 P(25-13-1) 231
SL D21 R26/128 P(39-21-0) 195
Was-Rogers 133R, Clark 130C; SL-Mitchell 101R

NE 7 10 3 0 20
Den 0 3 14 14 **31**
NE D20 R35/211 P(39-17-4) 158
Den D21 R32/112 P(37-17-1) 259

MONDAY, DECEMBER 7

NYJ 0 0 14 14 28
Mia 14 13 3 7 **37**
NYJ D13 R12/40 P(25-18-1) 216
Mia D30 R41/139 P(40-29-0) 293
NYJ-Toon 100C; Mia-Stradford 120R

SUNDAY, DECEMBER 13

Mia 0 14 14 0 **28**
Phi 0 0 10 0 10
Mia D23 R30/119 P(39-25-1) 357
Phi D15 R25/155 P(38-22-0) 155
Mia-Clayton 104C, Marino 376P

NYG 3 7 7 7 24
SL 14 13 0 0 **27**
NYG D23 R16/62 P(48-30-1) 335
SL D23 R38/158 P(30-17-0) 164
NYG-Bavaro 137C, Simms 359P; SL 1-Mitchell 111R

Atl 0 0 0 0 0
LARm 9 17 0 7 **33**
Atl D13 R15/59 P(33-17-2) 210
LARm D28 R46/238 P(29-18-0) 256
LARm-White 159R

Hou 0 3 0 7 10
NO 0 7 14 3 **24**
Hou D20 R26/110 P(36-16-0) 244
NO D21 R39/151 P(27-15-0) 240
Hou-Hill 102C; NO-Martin 130C

Min 7 0 0 3 10
GB 0 7 3 6 **16**
Min D14 R31/127 P(21-14-0) 179
GB D19 R33/121 P(31-18-1) 179

LARd 0 3 0 7 10
KC 0 7 3 6 **16**
LARd D26 R32/88 P(38-22-3) 312
KC D28 R12/112 P(27-10-1) 164
LARd-White 159R, Lofton 112C, Wilson 339P; KC-Carson 142C

Buf 7 6 0 14 **27**
Ind 0 0 0 3 3
Buf D25 R49/218 P(35-18-0) 303
Ind D9 R17/33 P(27-14-4) 97

Dal 3 0 10 7 20
Was 3 7 0 14 **24**
Dal D25 R25/87 P(49-27-1) 341
Was D15 R31/68 P(26-13-1) 249
Dal-White 359P; Was-Clark 187C

Pit 0 7 10 3 **20**
SD 9 0 0 7 16
Pit D14 R31/104 P(26-13-0) 150
SD D27 R29/114 P(52-29-1) 321
SD-Chandler 116C, Fouts 334P

Den 0 0 14 7 21
Sea 0 14 7 7 **28**
Den D20 R18/72 P(43-21-2) 308
Sea D24 R37/141 P(34-23-2) 226
Den-Elway 335P; Sea-Butler 107C

Cin 3 0 7 14 24
Cle 0 28 7 3 **38**
Cin D24 R28/65 P(39-22-2) 352
Cle D19 R29/153 P(26-17-0) 237
Cin-McGee 117C, Esiason 361P; Cle-Mack 133R, Slaughter 119C, Kosar 241P

NYJ 3 3 0 14 20
NE 14 21 7 0 **42**
NYJ D24 R29/111 P(43-22-1) 197
NE D19 R36/129 P(18-11-0) 171
NYJ-Hector 104R, Toon 110C; NE-Grogan 180P

Det 3 7 3 7 **20**
TB 0 3 0 7 10
Det D22 R50/190 P(23-12-0) 108
TB D20 R14/47 P(39-20-1) 216

MONDAY, DECEMBER 14

ChiB 0 0 0 0 0
SF 10 10 14 7 **41**
ChiB D16 R25/109 P(36-19-4) 154
SF D20 R41/198 P(27-13-0) 133
SF-Young 100P

SATURDAY, DECEMBER 19

KC 0 3 7 7 17
Den 7 10 3 0 **20**
KC D20 R21/123 P(39-26-0) 254
Den D22 R40/143 P(31-18-0) 226

GB 0 0 3 7 10
NYG 3 0 7 0 **10**
GB D10 R22/74 P(34-20-1) 105
NYG D21 R36/111 P(26-21-0) 215

SUNDAY, DECEMBER 20

Ind 7 6 0 7 **20**
SD 7 0 0 0 7
Ind D19 R32/146 P(39-20-0) 194
SD D17 R22/59 P(37-22-3) 214
Ind-Dickerson 115R

NE 7 6 0 0 **13**
Buf 0 0 7 0 7
NE D15 R47/150 P(15-9-2) 85
Buf D12 R24/84 P(31-13-1) 64

Phi 10 14 14 0 **38**
NYJ 3 17 0 7 27
Phi D22 R39/143 P(32-19-0) 265
NYJ D21 R21/78 P(49-25-0) 276
Phi-Quick 148C; NYJ-Toon 168C, O'Brien 301P

Pit 3 3 7 3 16
Hou 0 10 7 7 **24**
Pit D22 R42/176 P(27-12-3) 172
Hou D17 R30/62 P(25-12-1) 221
Hou-Hill 109C

Cle 7 10 7 0 **24**
LARd 3 0 0 14 17
Cle D24 R31/127 P(32-21-1) 294
LARd D20 R20/71 P(36-23-0) 228
Cle-Slaughter 115C

Atl 0 0 0 7 7
SF 0 7 14 14 **35**
Atl D13 R17/51 P(36-13-4) 165
SF D26 R48/255 P(30-13-0) 206

Sea 0 20 7 7 **34**
ChiB 0 7 7 7 21
Sea D17 R29/116 P(26-17-0) 184
ChiB D31 R36/161 P(36-21-2) 276
Sea-Williams 117C

SL 0 14 10 7 **31**
TB 7 0 0 7 14
SL D24 R34/134 P(30-22-1) 217
TB D19 R31/163 P(38-16-2) 207
SL-Mitchell 101R; TB-Carter 116C

NO 3 7 14 17 **41**
Cin 14 10 0 0 24
NO D24 R36/101 P(31-16-0) 220
Cin D24 R26/125 P(37-17-2) 112

Min 0 10 0 7 **17**
Det 0 7 0 7 14
Min D20 R37/205 P(27-16-0) 135
Det D17 R26/129 P(31-16-4) 235
Min-Dickerson 115R

Was 0 7 7 7 21
Mia 0 9 0 14 **23**
Was D28 R39/204 P(38-19-1) 268
Mia D22 R17/66 P(50-22-1) 393
Mia-Duper 170C, Marino 393P

MONDAY, DECEMBER 21

Dal 10 6 10 3 **29**
LARm 7 0 7 7 21
Dal D20 R42/194 P(30-15-0) 171
LARm D19 R30/74 P(39-19-3) 237
Dal-Walker 108R

SATURDAY, DECEMBER 26

Cle 3 6 3 7 **19**
Pit 0 3 0 10 13
Cle D22 R30/85 P(36-21-1) 230
Pit D10 R26/95 P(18-11-2) 126

Was 0 7 7 10 3 **27**
Min 7 0 0 17 0 24
Was D18 R19/77 P(39-20-4) 291
Min D24 R44/204 P(27-14-3) 177
Was-Sanders 164C

SUNDAY, DECEMBER 27

GB 14 3 7 0 24
NO 9 3 14 7 **33**
GB D17 R28/123 P(29-14-1) 207
NO D22 R39/144 P(24-16-1) 148
GB-Stanley 109C

TB 3 0 0 3 6
Ind 7 3 7 7 **24**
TB D10 R21/96 P(32-8-1) 136
Ind D23 R45/226 P(27-17-0) 246
Ind-Dickerson 196R

NYJ 7 0 0 0 7
NYG 0 17 3 0 **20**
NYJ D13 R24/68 P(36-20-0) 166
NYG D23 R39/156 P(40-20-0) 264
NYG-Morris 132R, Bavaro 109C

Cin 7 0 7 3 17
Hou 7 14 0 0 **21**
Cin D16 R26/92 P(38-19-2) 267
Hou D25 R36/194 P(25-14-2) 267
Cin-Collinsworth 119C;
Hou-Rozier 103R, Hill 109C

SL 3 7 0 6 16
Dal 0 14 0 7 **21**
SL D26 R30/126 P(55-28-1) 296
Dal D17 R34/163 P(22-10-0) 122
SL-Green 112C, Smith 102C,
Lomax 314P; Dal-Walker 137R

SD 0 0 0 0 0
Den 14 0 0 10 **24**
SD D7 R21/43 P(29-16-5) 108
Den D15 R40/129 P(24-7-3) 86

LARm 0 0 0 0 0
SF 13 14 7 14 **48**
LARm D9 R31/121 P(18-6-1) 24
SF D23 R40/149 P(22-16-0) 278

ChiB 0 3 0 3 **6**
LARd 3 0 0 0 3
ChiB D18 R35/121 P(28-12-1) 146
LARd D14 R26/101 P(26-13-1) 92

Buf 0 0 0 7 7
Phi 0 10 7 0 **17**
Buf D14 R14/57 P(39-20-2) 134
Phi D22 R52/210 P(21-16-1) 134
Phi-Byars 102R

Sea 7 13 0 0 20
KC 17 10 7 7 **41**
Sea D24 R29/169 P(32-17-0) 195
KC D28 R32/199 P(35-23-0) 313
KC-Heard 107R, Carson 120C,
Paige 110C, Kenney 320P

Det 7 3 10 10 **30**
Atl 0 13 0 0 13
Det D19 R43/173 P(24-11-2) 150
Atl D14 R22/98 P(36-16-4) 180

MONDAY, DECEMBER 28

NE 14 10 0 0 **24**
Mia 3 0 0 7 10
NE D25 R44/138 P(32-21-0) 238
Mia D17 R16/54 P(37-21-2) 243

1988 NFL

SUNDAY, SEPTEMBER 4

Dal 7 0 7 7 21
Pit 10 0 7 7 **24**
Dal D25 R31/134 P(37-24-2) 280
Pit D17 R29/142 P(27-13-0) 214

Hou 7 7 0 0 3 **17**
Ind 7 7 0 0 0 14
Hou D18 R44/173 P(21-14-0) 174
Ind D16 R27/111 P(21-15-1) 170
Hou-Rozier 100R;
Ind-Dickerson 109R

Phi 21 13 7 0 **41**
TB 0 0 14 0 14
Phi D18 R42/141 P(26-13-2) 248
TB D19 R15/43 P(45-21-5) 319
TB-Hill 157C, Testaverde 324P

Phx 0 7 7 0 14
Cin 0 7 7 7 **21**
Phx D23 R33/167 P(31-21-2) 207
Cin D21 R27/152 P(26-17-1) 251
Phx-Mitchell 110R; Cin-Brown 143C

NYJ 3 0 0 0 3
NE 3 3 10 12 **28**
NYJ D16 R25/87 P(30-15-0) 92
NE D20 R38/94 P(31-16-1) 249

LARm 7 14 10 3 **34**
GB 0 0 0 7 7
LARm D18 R36/114 P(28-19-0) 176
GB D12 R17/78 P(34-16-3) 131

Atl 3 0 0 14 17
Det 0 10 14 7 **31**
Atl D26 R29/172 P(38-25-1) 187
Det D19 R34/142 P(19-13-1) 88

SF 7 3 21 3 **34**
NO 7 10 0 16 33
SF D21 R32/124 P(26-14-1) 165
NO D23 R31/147 P(31-22-2) 197
NO-Hebert 245P

SD 0 3 3 7 13
LARd 0 14 0 10 **24**
SD D15 R27/111 P(29-17-1) 152
LARd D18 R32/94 P(31-14-0) 183

Sea 0 7 14 0 **21**
Den 0 7 0 7 14
Sea D19 R42/178 P(30-14-0) 152
Den D19 R18/76 P(45-21-2) 226

Min 0 3 0 7 10
Buf 10 0 0 3 **13**
Min D21 R32/130 P(33-19-1) 170
Buf D18 R27/114 P(31-17-1) 196

Cle 0 3 0 3 **6**
KC 0 3 0 0 3
Cle D20 R36/142 P(37-21-1) 195
KC D9 R20/60 P(29-11-2) 89

Mia 7 0 0 0 7
ChiB 14 14 0 6 **34**
Mia D10 R10/45 P(25-10-0) 118
ChiB D28 R54/262 P(23-14-0) 165
ChiB-Anderson 123R

MONDAY, SEPTEMBER 5

Was 6 7 0 7 20
NYG 0 3 10 14 **27**
Was D20 R24/117 P(50-24-0) 269
NYG D16 R21/56 P(37-19-0) 162
Was-Smith 100R

SUNDAY, SEPTEMBER 11

ChiB 7 3 0 7 **17**
Ind 0 6 0 7 13
ChiB D23 R39/154 P(32-19-1) 172
Ind D11 R28/108 P(15-4-2) 65

NO 3 9 10 7 **29**
Atl 7 7 7 0 21
NO D25 R46/212 P(27-20-0) 222
Atl D19 R27/161 P(29-15-1) 146
Atl-Settle 102R

Mia 3 0 3 0 6
Buf 0 3 0 6 **9**
Mia D16 R30/115 P(34-22-0) 219
Buf D15 R30/104 P(24-15-1) 215
Buf-Reed 122C

TB 0 10 0 3 **13**
GB 10 0 0 0 10
TB D18 R37/148 P(24-11-0) 118
GB D13 R25/59 P(27-22-0) 181

Det 3 7 0 0 10
LARm 0 7 10 0 **17**
Det D16 R24/76 P(37-15-1) 134
LARm D23 R42/191 P(27-17-1) 124
LARm-Bell 139R

Pit 3 10 6 10 29
Was 7 3 7 13 **30**
Pit D14 R27/83 P(28-12-0) 258
Was D25 R30/93 P(52-30-1) 422
Was-Sanders 145C, Williams 430P

NYJ 3 3 3 14 **23**
Cle 3 0 0 0 3
NYJ D22 R43/154 P(30-19-0) 248
Cle D12 R16/36 P(37-20-1) 186

KC 3 0 0 7 10
Sea 3 28 0 0 **31**
KC D19 R16/50 P(53-29-4) 236
Sea D19 R39/156 P(23-14-1) 107
KC-Palmer 105C

NE 3 3 0 0 6
Min 10 14 2 10 **36**
NE D12 R22/103 P(29-10-4) 111
Min D24 R42/150 P(32-17-1) 265

SD 0 3 0 0 3
Den 10 14 7 3 **34**
SD D13 R24/133 P(30-13-2) 111
Den D24 R41/184 P(28-17-0) 259
Den-Dorsett 113R

Cin 7 7 0 14 **28**
Phi 14 0 3 7 24
Cin D20 R26/78 P(32-20-1) 353
Phi D28 R39/190 P(37-25-1) 225
Cin-McGee 114C, Esiason 363P

LARd 7 21 0 7 35
Hou 7 14 3 14 **38**
LARd D17 R28/74 P(24-10-1) 84
Hou D29 R39/156 P(34-21-1) 250
LARd-Bell 139R; Hou-Givins 108C

SF 0 10 3 7 **20**
NYG 7 3 0 7 17
SF D25 R33/181 P(37-21-0) 249
NYG D17 R29/112 P(37-21-0) 197
SF-Craig 110R, Rice 109C

MONDAY, SEPTEMBER 12

Dal 3 7 0 7 **17**
Phx 0 7 0 7 14
Dal D18 R39/190 P(24-12-1) 162
Phx D22 R28/130 P(34-20-0) 237
Dal-Walker 149R

SUNDAY, SEPTEMBER 18

Den 3 7 0 3 13
KC 3 7 7 3 **20**
Den D17 R22/70 P(32-15-2) 213
KC D22 R35/130 P(35-21-0) 250

NYG 5 0 7 0 **12**
Dal 3 0 7 0 10
NYG D21 R37/128 P(25-13-2) 150
Dal D22 R24/91 P(36-20-2) 275
NYG-Morris 107R, Manuel 142C

Phx 13 7 3 7 **30**
TB 0 3 7 14 24
Phx D24 R38/181 P(32-19-0) 294
TB D15 R21/114 P(28-16-2) 184
Phx-Mitchell 110R, Novacek 102C,
Smith 103C

Phi 0 3 0 7 10
Was 14 0 3 0 **17**
Phi D13 R20/90 P(37-16-0) 209
Was D16 R39/150 P(23-12-2) 135
Phi-Quick 105C; Was-Smith 107R

LARm 7 3 2 10 **22**
LARd 0 3 7 7 17
LARm D16 R31/140 P(27-16-0) 173
LARd D18 R22/103 P(38-19-1) 305
LARm-Bell 109R;
LARd-Lofton 130C, Beuerlein 375P

Hou 3 0 0 0 3
NYJ 14 14 3 14 **45**
Hou D15 R28/135 P(30-11-3) 102
NYJ D28 R32/93 P(31-22-0) 302
NYJ-Walker 129C

Atl 0 21 3 10 **34**
SF 3 0 7 7 17
Atl D19 R41/196 P(24-12-2) 171
SF D22 R19/104 P(49-32-4) 322
Atl-Riggs 115R; SF-Rice 163C,
Montana 343P

NO 0 7 12 3 **22**
Det 7 7 0 0 14
NO D22 R35/119 P(32-23-1) 282
Det D18 R18/40 P(35-20-2) 232

Sea 0 3 0 3 6
SD 7 3 0 7 **17**
Sea D20 R29/105 P(32-16-4) 194
SD D14 R32/159 P(23-11-1) 78
SD-Anderson 120R

Cin 0 7 3 7 **17**
Pit 2 0 7 3 12
Cin D20 R36/116 P(27-15-1) 190
Pit D19 R35/124 P(30-15-2) 195

GB 0 14 3 0 17
Mia 17 7 0 0 **24**
GB D22 R25/78 P(43-29-0) 260
Mia D17 R19/98 P(33-22-2) 256

Buf 0 3 3 10 **16**
NE 0 14 0 0 14
Buf D18 R29/105 P(33-21-2) 149
NE D14 R32/105 P(20-14-2) 159

Min 7 10 14 0 **31**
ChiB 7 0 0 0 7
Min D20 R35/127 P(27-15-1) 249
ChiB D14 R18/70 P(36-16-3) 165

MONDAY, SEPTEMBER 19

Ind 3 7 0 7 17
Cle 7 10 3 3 **23**
Ind D15 R25/128 P(27-13-2) 154
Cle D22 R36/101 P(38-23-1) 255
Ind-Dickerson 117R

SUNDAY, SEPTEMBER 25

Pit 0 14 0 14 28
Buf 10 6 14 6 **36**
Pit D25 R24/94 P(36-22-3) 314
Buf D22 R37/116 P(32-20-1) 282
Pit-Thompson 118C, Brister 330P

ChiB 0 17 0 7 **24**
GB 6 0 0 0 6
ChiB D22 R51/242 P(20-11-2) 116
GB D16 R16/34 P(41-19-2) 199
ChiB-Anderson 105R;
GB-Sharpe 137C

TB 0 6 0 3 9
NO 10 3 0 0 **13**
TB D19 R23/92 P(33-14-1) 204
NO D18 R34/117 P(28-16-1) 151

NE 6 0 0 0 6
Hou 7 7 7 10 **31**
NE D13 R22/51 P(39-19-5) 133
Hou D17 R45/172 P(17-8-2) 156

LARm 7 21 7 10 **45**
NYG 0 10 14 7 31
LARm D21 R42/137 P(24-14-1) 232
NYG D24 R19/79 P(49-29-1) 284
LARm-Bell 112R, Everett 236P;
NYG-Simms 309P

Phi 0 14 0 7 21
Min 10 0 7 6 **23**
Phi D12 R24/70 P(24-13-1) 135
Min D21 R40/105 P(37-19-1) 287
Min-Carter 113C

NYJ 3 7 0 7 **17**
Det 3 0 7 0 10
NYJ D19 R29/86 P(38-27-1) 230
Det D12 R28/86 P(21-10-1) 97

SD 14 0 0 10 **24**
KC 0 14 9 0 23
SD D19 R33/165 P(25-13-1) 138
KC D20 R24/94 P(38-20-1) 237
SD-Anderson 131R;
KC-Palmer 122C

Was 7 7 0 7 21
Phx 2 7 7 14 **30**
Was D20 R19/53 P(41-26-1) 282
Phx D18 R42/185 P(17-8-1) 138
Was-Rypien 303P; Phx-Ferrell 108R

Atl 7 10 3 0 20
Dal 14 0 2 10 **26**
Atl D15 R24/107 P(31-13-1) 207
Dal D17 R33/113 P(26-17-1) 210
Atl-Bailey 169C; Dal-Alexander 107C

Mia 7 0 0 6 13
Ind 3 9 0 3 **15**
Mia D18 R18/71 P(36-22-1) 252
Ind D18 R44/213 P(18-10-1) 91
Ind-Dickerson 125R

Cle 3 7 0 7 17
Cin 7 17 0 0 **24**
Cle D20 R21/68 P(48-24-0) 254
Cin D22 R44/213 P(23-8-0) 180
Cin-Brown 127C

SF 7 10 14 7 **38**
Sea 0 0 7 0 7
SF D27 R48/239 P(35-24-1) 341
Sea D8 R12/29 P(27-12-4) 125
SF-Craig 107R, Rice 163C,
Montana 302P

MONDAY, SEPTEMBER 26

LARd 0 0 14 13 3 **30**
Den 7 17 0 3 0 27
LARd D20 R36/128 P(35-13-1) 235
Den D23 R45/189 P(28-14-4) 209
LARd-Smith 122C;
Den-Dorsett 119R, Johnson 134C

SUNDAY, OCTOBER 2

Buf 3 0 0 0 3
ChiB 7 17 0 0 **24**
Buf D13 R10/0 P(37-20-1) 217
ChiB D22 R37/163 P(27-20-1) 260

GB 3 7 7 7 24
TB 0 10 0 17 **27**
GB D22 R22/72 P(52-29-2) 354
TB D17 R24/85 P(37-20-4) 283
GB-Stanley 107C, Wright 321P;
TB-Testaverde 300P

KC 0 0 3 14 0 17
NYJ 3 7 0 7 0 17
KC D17 R36/124 P(34-17-2) 261
NYJ D31 R46/272 P(48-27-1) 270
KC-Carson 162C, DeBerg 312P;
NYJ-McNeil 154R, Shuler 152C

Cin 3 21 14 7 **45**
LARd 0 7 0 14 21
Cin D28 R40/164 P(28-21-0) 332
LARd D20 R19/96 P(44-17-4) 309
Cin-Esiason 332P;
LARd-Fernandez 104C, Gault 102C,
Everett 300P, Schroeder 324P

NYG 10 7 7 0 **24**
Was 6 3 7 7 23
NYG D20 R34/74 P(31-17-1) 190
Was D19 R24/93 P(27-16-1) 251
NYG-Turner 103C;
Was-Sanders 141C

Phx 10 14 3 14 **41**
LARm 7 7 6 7 27
Phx D30 R32/187 P(43-28-1) 332
LARm D23 R22/85 P(33-25-0) 268
Phx-Lomax 342P;
LARm-Everett 300P

Cle 0 7 6 10 **23**
Pit 6 3 0 0 9
Cle D15 R45/168 P(26-15-1) 131
Pit D13 R26/89 P(38-11-4) 94

Sea 7 10 7 7 **31**
Atl 3 0 10 7 20
Sea D22 R39/168 P(21-11-0) 149
Atl D18 R30/140 P(32-18-2) 245
Sea-Warner 110R; Atl-Settle 115R

Den 6 0 3 3 **12**
SD 0 0 0 0 **0**
Den D22 R42/129 P(29-17-1) 162
SD D11 R13/20 P(35-18-1) 170

Min 0 0 0 7 **7**
Mia 0 17 7 0 **24**
Min D17 R19/58 P(48-20-4) 295
Mia D20 R31/78 P(37-20-3) 264

Det 0 3 3 7 **13**
SF 0 10 7 3 **20**
Det D18 R21/49 P(37-21-0) 248
SF D19 R35/176 P(30-19-0) 163
Det-Mandley 116C

Hou 16 0 0 7 **23**
Phi 0 20 9 3 **32**
Hou D14 R18/55 P(28-10-1) 147
Phi D26 R35/190 P(38-24-0) 265

Ind 0 7 0 10 **17**
NE 0 7 0 14 **21**
Ind D15 R32/103 P(26-14-1) 164
NE D19 R33/105 P(35-20-2) 193
Ind-Dickerson 118R

MONDAY, OCTOBER 3
Dal 0 7 7 3 **17**
NO 7 7 3 3 **20**
Dal D28 R35/186 P(35-23-1) 271
NO D17 R25/65 P(37-17-1) 268
Dal-Walker 124R

SUNDAY, OCTOBER 9
Sea 7 6 0 3 **16**
Cle 0 3 0 7 **10**
Sea D14 R37/126 P(17-9-0) 101
Cle D21 R30/160 P(28-14-2) 174

KC 3 3 0 0 **6**
Hou 0 0 0 7 **7**
KC D11 R18/65 P(30-15-2) 119
Hou D16 R48/206 P(16-4-3) 24
Hou-Rozier 141R

NO 0 13 7 3 **23**
SD 3 14 0 3 **17**
NO D24 R39/134 P(36-22-0) 231
SD D12 R21/93 P(22-8-1) 113

ChiB 7 10 0 7 **24**
Det 0 0 0 7 **7**
ChiB D20 R28/101 P(36-22-0) 222
Det D18 R13/42 P(57-19-1) 220

Den 0 3 7 3 **16**
SF 3 7 3 0 **13**
Den D24 R31/147 P(39-21-2) 167
SF D21 R48/246 P(28-12-3) 171
Den-Winder 100R; SF-Craig 143R

Pit 7 0 0 7 **14**
Phx 7 17 7 0 **31**
Pit D10 R20/78 P(31-11-0) 125
Phx D21 R38/103 P(28-19-1) 285
Phx-Green 119C

NE 3 0 0 0 **3**
GB 0 17 7 21 **45**
NE D14 R19/76 P(40-19-5) 191
GB D23 R38/207 P(26-18-0) 192
GB-Fullwood 118R

TB 0 10 0 3 **13**
Min 7 0 7 0 **14**
TB D18 R39/177 P(25-12-2) 154
Min D15 R20/69 P(30-19-1) 207

Was 7 21 0 7 **35**
Dal 7 3 0 7 **17**
Was D19 R40/180 P(21-13-0) 170
Dal D18 R20/60 P(40-19-4) 301
Was-Bryant 118R

Ind 10 7 3 7 **17**
Buf 0 7 14 13 **34**
Ind D25 R22/67 P(43-22-2) 241
Buf D25 R35/141 P(39-21-1) 315
Buf-Reed 124C, Kelly 315P

LARm 10 17 6 0 **33**
Atl 0 0 0 0 **0**
LARm D27 R45/252 P(26-16-1) 249
Atl D12 R20/73 P(28-14-1) 77
LARm-Bell 155R, Ellard 134C

Mia 0 24 0 0 **24**
LARd 0 0 7 7 **14**
Mia D19 R28/91 P(37-14-1) 175
LARd D19 R21/78 P(37-21-4) 266
LARd-Bell 155R, Ellard 134C, Lofton 113C

MONDAY, OCTOBER 10
NYG 9 3 7 0 **19**
Cin 6 13 7 10 **36**
NYJ D16 R28/109 P(38-18-0) 117
Cin D23 R37/206 P(20-10-0) 196
Cin-Woods 139R, Brown 103C

NYG 3 0 3 7 **13**
Phi 0 14 3 7 **24**
NYG D23 R24/100 P(45-23-1) 336
Phi D23 R26/109 P(41-31-0) 343
NYG-Bavaro 148C, Simms 324P; Phi-Carter 162C, Cunningham 369P

SUNDAY, OCTOBER 16
GB 9 7 8 10 **34**
Min 0 7 0 7 **14**
GB D22 R45/125 P(32-19-1) 230
Min D20 R15/67 P(38-20-1) 257
GB-Stanley 101C

Det 0 10 0 0 **10**
NYG 0 7 16 7 **30**
Det D10 R23/48 P(28-9-1) 65
NYG D23 R38/122 P(32-23-0) 280
NYG-Simms 320P

Dal 0 0 0 7 **7**
ChiB 0 17 0 0 **17**
Dal D18 R24/96 P(35-24-2) 195
ChiB D24 R26/124 P(39-22-0) 261

Hou 6 12 7 9 **34**
Pit 0 7 0 7 **14**
Hou D18 R42/124 P(20-12-0) 185
Pit D23 R24/93 P(42-21-2) 251
Hou-Givins 104C; Pit-Lipps 109C

Phx 7 3 0 7 **17**
Was 9 14 7 3 **33**
Phx D23 R25/76 P(44-26-1) 305
Was D16 R30/97 P(29-15-1) 289
Phx-Lomax 332P; Was-Rypien 303P

LARd 7 7 0 13 **27**
KC 0 7 0 10 **17**
LARd D20 R46/114 P(24-11-0) 119
KC D16 R22/93 P(30-16-2) 241
KC-Palmer 103C

NO 0 10 7 3 **20**
Sea 3 3 6 7 **19**
NO D20 R33/141 P(22-16-1) 177
Sea D23 R28/93 P(46-27-1) 341
Sea-Blades 145C, Stouffer 370P

Cin 0 0 14 7 **21**
NE 7 7 6 7 **27**
Cin D23 R30/140 P(28-18-5) 225
NE D22 R43/158 P(14-10-0) 153

SF 7 10 0 7 **24**
LARm 7 0 14 0 **21**
SF D24 R40/245 P(33-21-1) 184
LARm D14 R17/42 P(33-20-2) 194
SF-Craig 190R

Phi 0 3 0 0 **3**
Cle 0 3 6 10 **19**
Phi D12 R19/71 P(27-15-2) 48
Cle D17 R44/182 P(18-11-1) 179
Cle-Mack 100R

TB 0 10 0 21 **31**
Ind 7 14 14 0 **35**
TB D24 R15/39 P(42-25-2) 444
Ind D25 R35/103 P(33-20-2) 246
TB-Hall 121C, Hill 162C, Testaverde 469P; Ind-Brooks 139C

SD 7 14 7 0 **28**
Mia 7 3 7 14 **31**
SD D23 R25/113 P(38-25-2) 283
Mia D25 R25/46 P(45-26-0) 329
Mia-Duper 118C, Marino 329P

Atl 0 7 0 7 **14**
Den 0 7 10 13 **30**
Atl D20 R34/174 P(34-19-2) 137
Den D21 R32/104 P(36-20-0) 302
Atl-Settle 125R

MONDAY, OCTOBER 17
Buf 17 14 3 3 **37**
NYJ 0 7 0 7 **14**
Buf D24 R45/135 P(27-16-1) 292
NYJ D10 R13/45 P(30-18-1) 154
Buf-Reed 132C, Kelly 302P

SUNDAY, OCTOBER 23
Min 7 21 7 14 **49**
TB 10 0 3 7 **20**
Min D25 R42/128 P(30-22-0) 305
TB D18 R16/28 P(45-19-6) 215
Min-Carter 123C, Wilson 335P

Sea 0 3 0 7 **10**
LARm 10 14 7 0 **31**
Sea D21 R30/153 P(32-21-4) 143
LARm D24 R37/154 P(27-20-0) 311
LARm-Ellard 101C, Everett 311P

Den 0 0 7 14 **21**
Pit 14 13 3 9 **39**
Den D15 R20/45 P(39-21-3) 278
Pit D18 R47/256 P(18-10-1) 130
Den-Nattiel 102C; Pit-Carter 105R

Det 0 7 0 0 **7**
KC 0 3 3 0 **6**
Det D14 R40/127 P(18-8-2) 88
KC D12 R19/61 P(29-17-1) 110

Cle 7 10 3 9 **29**
Phx 0 14 0 7 **21**
Cle D21 R21/68 P(43-25-3) 301
Phx D27 R32/169 P(32-17-3) 161
Cle-Kosar 314P; Phx-Ferrell 110R

Ind 3 3 3 7 **16**
SD 0 0 0 0 **0**
Ind D28 R42/198 P(36-20-3) 255
SD D14 R20/118 P(30-13-0) 121
Ind-Dickerson 169R

NYG 0 3 3 17 **23**
Atl 3 7 3 3 **16**
NYG D22 R30/121 P(27-17-3) 225
Atl D23 R36/152 P(39-19-2) 216
NYG-Baker 104C

NYJ 6 24 7 7 **44**
Mia 7 3 13 7 **30**
NYJ D24 R36/159 P(37-18-1) 174
Mia D29 R17/63 P(60-35-5) 521
Mia-Clayton 153C, Duper 132C, Marino 521P

Dal 17 3 3 0 **23**
Phi 0 7 3 14 **24**
Dal D25 R31/105 P(46-32-1) 332
Phi D23 R15/65 P(53-26-1) 274
Dal-Alexander 112C, Pelluer 342P

Was 10 0 3 7 **20**
GB 7 3 0 7 **17**
Was D22 R35/160 P(42-25-1) 225
GB D10 R17/82 P(26-8-0) 123
Was-Bryant 140R

Hou 0 7 14 0 **21**
Cin 28 0 7 9 **44**
Hou D18 R24/104 P(32-13-2) 101
Cin D25 R46/222 P(20-11-2) 131
Cin-Brooks 102R

NE 7 6 0 7 **20**
Buf 7 6 7 7 **27**
NE D20 R42/176 P(16-5-0) 47
Buf D18 R36/190 P(18-12-1) 149
NE-Stephens 134R; Buf-Johnson 132C

LARd 0 6 0 0 **6**
NO 3 0 14 3 **20**
LARd D16 R28/185 P(31-10-2) 182
NO D20 R40/190 P(24-11-0) 127
LARd-Allen 102R, Ellard 101C, Fernandez 155C, Everett 311P; NO-Heyward 109R

MONDAY, OCTOBER 24
SF 7 0 2 0 **9**
ChiB 0 10 0 0 **10**
SF D12 R21/78 P(30-14-1) 135
ChiB D14 R41/122 P(22-10-1) 115

SUNDAY, OCTOBER 30
KC 0 7 0 3 **10**
LARd 7 7 0 3 **17**
KC D17 R31/145 P(22-11-0) 63
LARd D23 R42/156 P(29-18-1) 248

NYG 0 3 7 3 **13**
Det 0 7 0 3 **10**
NYG D20 R29/76 P(36-22-0) 196
Det D11 R20/48 P(29-14-1) 98

Cin 0 0 10 3 **16**
Cle 3 7 10 3 **23**
Cin D18 R31/128 P(25-12-0) 153
Cle D17 R28/99 P(28-18-2) 203
Cle-Weathers 140C

Atl 0 7 13 7 **27**
Phi 3 7 0 14 **24**
Atl D11 R27/92 P(23-10-0) 202
Phi D25 R31/155 P(49-21-2) 269

ChiB 7 0 0 0 **7**
NE 6 14 3 7 **30**
ChiB D11 R25/134 P(24-7-1) 74
NE D19 R54/185 P(18-6-0) 165
NE-Stephens 124R, Fryar 122C, Flutie 165P

Min 0 7 7 7 **21**
SF 0 3 14 7 **24**
Min D15 R31/92 P(30-18-2) 229
SF D16 R28/130 P(25-14-0) 209

LARm 3 3 3 3 **12**
NO 0 0 0 7 **7**
LARm D16 R32/96 P(34-21-0) 236
NO D14 R18/33 P(37-19-1) 209
NO-Martin 132C

GB 0 0 0 0 **0**
Buf 7 7 7 7 **28**
GB D10 R20/77 P(29-11-1) 54
Buf D18 R49/195 P(14-10-2) 166
Buf-Thomas 116R

Pit 10 0 0 10 **20**
NYJ 0 10 7 7 **24**
Pit D15 R30/143 P(25-11-2) 209
NYJ D15 R33/84 P(33-14-0) 112

Mia 0 0 17 0 **17**
TB 0 0 0 14 **14**
Mia D20 R23/43 P(46-27-0) 266
TB D21 R27/79 P(36-26-1) 283
TB-Carrier 142C

Phx 0 0 3 13 **16**
Dal 0 0 0 10 **10**
Phx D15 R36/160 P(32-13-0) 135
Dal D11 R26/125 P(31-9-2) 103
Phx-Ferrell 110R

SD 0 0 0 14 **14**
Sea 3 7 0 7 **17**
SD D18 R28/130 P(32-20-1) 169
Sea D16 R35/126 P(28-14-0) 149

Was 0 3 7 7 **17**
Hou 0 7 10 24 **41**
Was D16 R14/29 P(43-23-1) 221
Hou D21 R32/152 P(30-16-1) 184
Hou-Hill 148C

MONDAY, OCTOBER 31
Den 0 10 0 13 **23**
Ind 21 24 3 7 **55**
Den D22 R20/131 P(44-27-0) 266
Ind D23 R46/244 P(15-11-0) 220
Ind-Dickerson 159R, Brooks 108C

SUNDAY, NOVEMBER 6
SF 3 13 7 0 **23**
Phx 0 0 17 7 **24**
SF D22 R38/240 P(27-14-0) 117
Phx D21 R19/67 P(41-25-0) 288
SF-Craig 162R; Phx-Lomax 323P

NYJ 0 14 0 0 **14**
Ind 7 3 21 7 **38**
NYJ D20 R25/91 P(37-24-2) 182
Ind D22 R35/140 P(23-15-1) 196
NYJ-Toon 106C

Mia 0 3 7 0 **10**
NE 0 0 7 14 **21**
Mia D23 R17/78 P(51-29-2) 359
NE D18 R44/203 P(14-7-1) 74
Mia-Jensen 110C, Marino 359P; NE-Stephens 104R

LARm 3 7 0 14 **24**
Phi 0 10 10 10 **30**
LARm D22 R23/69 P(45-24-4) 358
Phi D21 R33/123 P(40-22-0) 313
LARm-Ellard 166C, Everett 377P; Phi-Cunningham 323P

KC 2 3 3 3 **11**
Den 0 14 0 3 **17**
KC D16 R26/90 P(27-16-1) 183
Den D23 R37/131 P(29-14-2) 177

NO 7 7 10 0 **24**
Was 0 14 3 10 **27**
NO D20 R15/50 P(32-19-0) 272
Was D21 R39/113 P(28-20-1) 299
NO-Martin 146C

GB 0 0 0 0 **0**
Atl 7 10 0 3 **20**
GB D13 R22/101 P(38-17-4) 183
Atl D18 R38/164 P(25-15-2) 177

LARd 0 3 0 10 **13**
SD 3 0 0 0 **3**
LARd D18 R38/136 P(28-13-1) 170
SD D12 R20/63 P(30-14-2) 153
LARd-Ellard 166C, Everett 377P

Pit 0 0 0 0 **0**
Cin 14 14 7 7 **42**
Pit D15 R30/101 P(29-11-0) 97
Cin D28 R36/221 P(26-18-2) 338
Cin-Woods 110R, Brown 216C, Esiason 318P

TB 3 7 0 0 **10**
ChiB 0 14 14 0 **28**
TB D25 R27/84 P(52-22-2) 273
ChiB D19 R25/69 P(26-18-1) 269
TB-Testaverde 305P

Det 0 0 0 17 **17**
Min 7 6 10 21 **44**
Det D8 R15/68 P(22-8-1) 21
Min D33 R39/198 P(35-28-1) 355
Min-Carter 188C, Wilson 391P

Buf 3 7 0 3 **13**
Sea 0 3 0 0 **3**
Buf D18 R37/142 P(26-17-1) 194
Sea D10 R20/72 P(23-10-1) 73

Dal 0 0 7 14 **21**
NYG 10 16 0 3 **29**
Dal D21 R23/103 P(55-29-0) 262
NYG D15 R37/111 P(25-11-1) 151
Dal-Alexander 103C; NYG-Manuel 106C

MONDAY, NOVEMBER 7
Cle 3 0 7 7 **17**
Hou 0 7 14 3 **24**
Cle D15 R16/44 P(33-16-0) 209
Hou D18 R43/148 P(17-11-0) 182

SUNDAY, NOVEMBER 13
Min 17 0 17 9 **43**
Dal 0 3 0 0 **3**
Min D18 R29/103 P(30-13-1) 222
Dal D12 R28/110 P(28-10-4) 49
Min-Jones 132C

Phi 0 14 3 10 **27**
Pit 10 6 7 3 **26**
Phi D27 R33/106 P(41-25-2) 252
Pit D19 R31/164 P(26-12-1) 197
Pit-Hoge 102R, Lipps 171C

NYG 0 0 7 10 **17**
Phx 14 0 0 10 **24**
NYG D21 R18/92 P(45-20-0) 188
Phx D24 R36/144 P(38-25-1) 351
Phx-Green 176C, Lomax 353P

Hou 7 3 7 7 **24**
Sea 7 0 13 7 **27**
Hou D22 R35/237 P(22-13-1) 182
Sea D22 R32/177 P(26-14-1) 188
Hou-Hill 139C; Sea-Williams 102R

LARd 0 0 6 3 **9**
SF 0 7 7 7 **21**
LARd D17 R45/159 P(22-8-0) 92
SF D15 R26/83 P(31-16-0) 136

SD 0 3 0 7 **10**
Atl 0 0 0 0 **0**
SD D15 R34/185 P(32-16-2) 170
Atl D13 R22/57 P(38-18-1) 188
SD-Anderson 145R; Atl-Settle 106C

```
Cle    0   0   7   0    7
Den   10  20   0   0   30
Cle   D15 R17/87   P(30-19-1) 140
Den   D27 R40/120  P(32-22-0) 215

NE     0   0   7   7   14
NYJ    0   3   3   7   13
NE    D13 R45/177  P(20-6-2)   78
NYJ   D17 R34/189  P(30-11-1) 109

ChiB   7  13   0  14   34
Was    0   0   0   7    7
ChiB  D20 R36/145  P(27-16-0) 273
Was   D22 R13/28   P(52-20-5) 295
ChiB-Gentry 116C;
Was-McEwen 120C

TB     7   3   0  13   23
Det   10   0   0  10   20
TB    D17 R38/225  P(13-9-2)   79
Det   D21 R26/75   P(41-20-2) 203
TB-Tate 106R

Cin    7   7  14   0   28
KC     6   3  10  12   31
Cin   D19 R29/150  P(22-11-1) 157
KC    D24 R37/142  P(37-22-0) 276
KC-Okoye 102R

Ind    0  13   7   0   20
GB     3   0   0  10   13
Ind   D14 R37/136  P(18-10-0) 111
GB    D22 R22/98   P(41-24-0) 199

NO     0   7   7   0   14
LARm   7   3   0   7   10
NO    D19 R29/88   P(37-22-2) 249
LARm  D15 R22/60   P(35-18-2) 196
```

MONDAY, NOVEMBER 14

```
Buf    7   3  14   7   31
Mia    0   6   0   0    6
Buf   D29 R45/205  P(26-18-0) 211
Mia   D15 R13/33   P(30-19-3) 224
```

SUNDAY, NOVEMBER 20

```
SD    14   3   7  14   38
LARm   7   7   0  10   24
SD    D17 R32/101  P(26-13-1) 196
LARm  D20 R27/151  P(34-17-1) 212

Pit    0   7   0   0    7
Cle    3  14   7   3   27
Pit   D18 R33/118  P(36-16-2) 167
Cle   D11 R27/70   P(25-12-0) 192

Det    3   6   0  10   19
GB     0   0   3   6    9
Det   D15 R37/156  P(20-10-0) 114
GB    D24 R16/52   P(45-30-1) 304
GB-Sharpe 124C, Majkowski 327P

NE     0   3   3   0    6
Mia    0   3   0   0    3
NE    D17 R39/170  P(13-9-0)   66
Mia   D15 R24/124  P(29-19-0) 169

Sea    0   7   7  10   24
KC     7   3  10   7   27
Sea   D20 R29/105  P(30-20-1) 208
KC    D23 R39/162  P(26-16-2) 203
KC-Paige 106C

Cin    7  17   7   7   38
Dal    3   0   7  14   24
Cin   D23 R32/214  P(29-16-0) 196
Dal   D23 R34/179  P(36-20-2) 176
Cin-Brooks 148R; Dal-Walker 131R

Ind    0   0   0   3    3
Min    0   6   3   3   12
Ind   D17 R27/103  P(27-13-2) 110
Min   D13 R28/83   P(29-17-0) 192

NYJ    0   3   0   3    6
Buf    0   0   3   3    9
NYJ   D16 R31/140  P(23-10-0) 119
Buf   D20 R44/229  P(19-9-1)  112
Buf-Riddick 103R

Den    0   0   0   0    0
NO    14   7  14   7   42
Den   D17 R15/52   P(44-24-1) 206
NO    D28 R43/196  P(23-20-0) 189
NO-Mayes 115R, Martin 111C

ChiB  14   7   0   6   27
TB     3   3   0   9   15
ChiB  D16 R37/139  P(25-10-2) 200
TB    D18 R38/168  P(32-12-2) 153
```

```
Phi    7   3   0   7   6   23
NYG    0  14   3   0   0   17
Phi   D18 R30/107  P(36-14-1) 176
NYG   D21 R35/78   P(41-24-3) 316

Atl    0   3   3   6   12
LARd   0   0   3   6    9
Atl   D17 R39/130  P(29-18-0) 150
LARd  D9  R20/65   P(31-11-1) 147

Phx    0   7   7   6   20
Hou    7  17   7   7   38
Phx   D17 R16/60   P(32-21-2) 254
Hou   D23 R41/124  P(32-17-0) 261
Phx-Smith 114C; Hou-Givins 118C,
Hill 100C
```

MONDAY, NOVEMBER 21

```
Was    7   0   7   7   21
SF     7  16   0  14   37
Was   D20 R25/56   P(42-27-2) 271
SF    D18 R30/112  P(25-15-2) 208
SF-Rice 105C
```

THURSDAY, NOVEMBER 24

```
Min    0  20   3   0   23
Det    0   0   0   0    0
Min   D24 R51/181  P(21-16-0) 172
Det   D3  R11/18   P(20-6-2)   42

Hou    0  10   3  12   25
Dal    7   3   7   0   17
Hou   D19 R32/145  P(29-15-0) 210
Dal   D17 R26/79   P(32-17-1) 203
Hou-Hill 113C
```

SUNDAY, NOVEMBER 27

```
SF     7  17  14  10   48
SD     0   7   3   0   10
SF    D24 R36/203  P(25-16-0) 272
SD    D21 R23/136  P(45-23-2) 176
SF-Rice 171C

NE     7   7   0   7   21
Ind    0   7   7   0   14
NE    D18 R34/105  P(24-15-1) 180
Ind   D16 R27/81   P(24-12-2) 160

Cle    0   3   0  14   17
Was    0   0  10   3   13
Cle   D25 R31/158  P(36-23-1) 166
Was   D11 R23/103  P(24-11-2) 124
Cle-Mack 116R

Mia    7   7  20   0   34
NYJ    7  17   0  14   38
Mia   D20 R18/87   P(35-17-0) 353
NYJ   D39 R35/171  P(52-33-1) 426
Mia-Clayton 116C, Edmunds 117C;
Marino 353P; NYJ-Toon 181C,
Ryan 341P

Phx    7   7   0   7   21
Phi    0   7  17   7   31
Phx   D25 R35/167  P(43-24-4) 202
Phi   D17 R22/91   P(36-18-2) 201

TB     0   0  10   0   10
Atl    3   7   7   0   17
TB    D16 R26/127  P(29-12-3) 186
Atl   D16 R36/181  P(24-14-1) 108

GB     0   0   0   0    0
ChiB   0   7   7   2   16
GB    D9  R11/22   P(30-14-2) 167
ChiB  D22 R41/213  P(36-18-0) 159
ChiB-Anderson 139R

KC     0   7   0   3   10
Pit    6   7   3   0   16
KC    D19 R22/88   P(42-23-1) 278
Pit   D19 R43/214  P(27-13-1) 122

NYG    0   7   0   6   13
NO     3   0   7   0   10
NYG   D8  R17/14   P(27-16-1) 205
NO    D16 R37/155  P(33-15-3) 100
NYG-Baker 134C

Buf    0   0   7   7   21
Cin    7  14   7   7   35
Buf   D21 R18/110  P(35-24-2) 243
Cin   D34 R52/232  P(25-18-0) 223
Cin-Woods 129R
```

```
LARm   7   3   7   7   24
Den    0  14  21   0   35
LARm  D28 R27/132  P(47-25-1) 352
Den   D19 R28/98   P(37-22-1) 270
LARm-Bell 112R, Ellard 167C,
Everett 365P; Den-Jackson 140C
```

MONDAY, NOVEMBER 28

```
LARd  14   6   7   0   27
Sea    7  14   0  14   35
LARd  D15 R23/113  P(30-8-2)  144
Sea   D25 R51/247  P(28-16-2) 212
LARd-Brown 114C;
Sea-Warner 130R, Williams 105R,
Krieg 220P
```

SUNDAY, DECEMBER 4

```
Sea    0   0   7   0    7
NE     0   0   0  13   13
Sea   D2  R19/20   P(20-9-0)   45
NE    D16 R55/171  P(10-5-1)   41
NE-Stephens 121R

Pit    3  14   7  13   37
Hou    0  13  14   7   34
Pit   D23 R29/94   P(37-18-0) 332
Hou   D23 R31/134  P(39-19-3) 269
Pit-Lipps 166C, Brister 311P

Buf    0   0   2   3    5
TB     0  10   0   0   10
Buf   D16 R19/39   P(40-23-2) 234
TB    D19 R35/110  P(29-12-0) 143

Phx    0   7   0   0    7
NYG   10   7   7  20   44
Phx   D7  R16/67   P(32-12-2)  91
NYG   D25 R53/170  P(20-11-0) 131
NYG-Morris 122R

GB     0   0   0  14   14
Det   10  17   0   3   30
GB    D21 R16/92   P(52-29-3) 268
Det   D15 R30/94   P(25-11-0) 126

SD     3   0   7   0   10
Cin   13   0   7   7   27
SD    D14 R24/88   P(37-14-3) 123
Cin   D21 R36/207  P(20-10-0) 145
Cin-Woods 141R

Was    7   0   3  10   20
Phi    3  13   3   0   19
Was   D22 R21/81   P(50-28-3) 329
Phi   D21 R31/163  P(32-16-2) 147
Was-Sanders 128C

Ind    0  21   0   3   31
Mia    7   0   7  14   28
Ind   D23 R47/221  P(15-12-0) 101
Mia   D21 R17/58   P(32-26-1) 304
Ind-Dickerson 169R;
Mia-Marino 304P

Den    0   0   3   7   20
LARd   0   0  14   7   21
Den   D20 R16/50   P(49-29-3) 297
LARd  D14 R36/129  P(19-10-1) 167
Den-Jackson 145C, Elway 324P

NO     0   0   3   0    3
Min   10  21  14   0   45
NO    D13 R29/126  P(37-10-2) 107
Min   D20 R38/209  P(24-15-1) 217

NYJ   10  10   7   7   34
KC    14   7   0  17   38
NYJ   D21 R35/179  P(25-13-0) 192
KC    D26 R41/163  P(25-16-1) 267
NYJ-Toon 102C; KC-Paige 113C

SF     0   0   0   6   13
Atl    0   0   0   3    3
SF    D20 R37/164  P(35-21-0) 238
Atl   D8  R21/43   P(27-13-1) 134
SF-Craig 103R
```

MONDAY, DECEMBER 5

```
ChiB   0   3   0   0    3
LARm   3   3   7  10   23
ChiB  D13 R27/114  P(30-11-2)  99
LARm  D24 R38/132  P(31-17-3) 232
LARm-Ellard 132C
```

SATURDAY, DECEMBER 10

```
Ind    6   7   3   0   16
NYJ   10   0  21   3   34
Ind   D18 R26/109  P(36-17-3) 220
NYJ   D22 R42/173  P(30-14-3) 158
NYJ-McNeil 100R, Toon 103C

Phi   21   0   0   2   23
Phx    0   7   7   3   17
Phi   D16 R34/141  P(26-10-1) 142
Phx   D23 R27/46   P(50-29-1) 353
Phx-Jones 166C, Lomax 384P
```

SUNDAY, DECEMBER 11

```
Pit    0   0   0  14   14
SD     0  14   0   6   20
Pit   D20 R24/130  P(33-17-2) 172
SD    D17 R37/180  P(24-17-0) 144
SD-Anderson 170R

TB     0   0   0   7    7
NE     0   0   7   3   10
TB    D14 R36/131  P(19-10-1) 131
NE    D11 R33/76   P(27-16-2) 147
TB-Howard 101R

Den    0   0   0   7   14
Sea    7  21  14   0   42
Den   D25 R20/101  P(41-26-0) 301
Sea   D30 R45/230  P(22-19-0) 220
Den-Jackson 137C;
Sea-Warner 126R, Williams 109R

Cin    0   3   3   0    6
Hou    7  17   3  14   41
Cin   D10 R33/132  P(22-10-1)  94
Hou   D19 R33/147  P(26-14-1) 249
Hou-Rozier 126R

NO     3   7   7   0   17
SF     7  21   3   6   30
NO    D15 R24/70   P(35-20-1) 182
SF    D20 R35/152  P(29-18-1) 221
SF-Craig 115R

Atl    0   0   0   7    7
LARm   3  16   3   0   22
Atl   D9  R22/65   P(33-13-2) 128
LARm  D21 R36/127  P(33-24-1) 291
LARm-Holohan 126C, Everett 303P

Min    0   0   0   3    6
GB     7   3   6   2   18
Min   D15 R19/44   P(41-20-1) 211
GB    D37 R37/97   P(30-16-3) 201
GB-Kemp 108C

Dal    3   7   7   7   24
Was    3   0  14   0   17
Dal   D21 R33/124  P(36-21-1) 320
Was   D15 R14/24   P(46-20-3) 348
Dal-Irvin 149C, Pelluer 333P;
Was-Monk 103C, Orr 104C

Det    0   3   7   0   13
ChiB   0   3   7   3   13
Det   D14 R30/115  P(28-13-0) 195
ChiB  D14 R32/82   P(26-18-0) 168

LARd   0   0   7   7   21
Buf    7  13   7  10   37
LARd  D17 R29/111  P(24-14-0) 207
Buf   D24 R48/255  P(24-11-0) 112
LARd-Holohan 126C, Everett 303P;
Buf-Thomas 106R

KC     0   3   9   0   12
NYG    7   0   7  14   28
KC    D16 R33/107  P(35-15-0) 151
NYG   D17 R39/159  P(15-6-1)   85
NYG-Morris 140R
```

MONDAY, DECEMBER 12

```
Cle    0  10   7  14   31
Mia    0  17   7  14   38
Cle   D22 R19/87   P(41-28-0) 266
Mia   D35 R27/93   P(50-30-3) 404
Mia-Banks 118C, Clayton 108C,
Marino 404P
```

SATURDAY, DECEMBER 17

```
NE     7   3   0   0   10
Den    7   7   0   7   21
NE    D18 R33/165  P(39-22-2) 186
Den   D20 R37/188  P(29-14-1) 143
NE-Stephens 130R
```

```
Was    3   7   7   0   0   17
Cin    0  10   0   7   3   20
Was   D23 R47/166  P(22-17-1) 206
Cin   D16 R28/135  P(19-10-0) 183
Was-Morris 152R, Sanders 120C;
Cin-Woods 115R, Brown 115C
```

SUNDAY, DECEMBER 18

```
Det    0   0  10   0   10
TB     7   7   0   7   21
Det   D14 R21/59   P(40-16-3) 191
TB    D17 R35/103  P(23-12-3) 139

Buf    0   7   0   7   14
Ind    3   0   0  14   17
Buf   D14 R19/53   P(29-17-0) 195
Ind   D25 R45/184  P(26-14-0) 117
Ind-Dickerson 166R

LARm   0  21  10   7   38
SF     3  10   0   3   16
LARm  D23 R30/121  P(38-19-1) 201
SF    D20 R21/70   P(37-22-0) 246
LARm-Everett 201P

Sea   14   9   6  14   43
LARd   7  10  10  10   37
Sea   D30 R30/101  P(32-19-1) 389
LARd  D22 R28/111  P(49-22-1) 331
Sea-Blades 123C, Williams 180C,
Krieg 410P; LARd-Fernandez 113C,
Gault 108C, Everett 201P, Schroeder

NYG    0   7   7   7   21
NYJ   10   3   7   7   27
NYG   D24 R33/197  P(33-18-0) 170
NYJ   D15 R27/100  P(26-16-0) 198

Phi    0  10   7   6   23
Dal    7   0   0   0    7
Phi   D18 R30/133  P(38-20-0) 238
Dal   D13 R30/137  P(26-10-3) 102

Hou   10   6   7   0   23
Cle    0   7   7  14   28
Hou   D18 R23/37   P(35-20-0) 280
Cle   D25 R33/78   P(42-25-3) 310
Hou-Givins 119C;
Cle-Slaughter 136C, Strock 326P

Atl    0   3   3   3    9
NO     0   0   7   3   10
Atl   D13 R32/109  P(27-14-0)  93
NO    D18 R34/203  P(26-13-1) 122
NO-Hilliard 127R

KC    13   0   0   0   13
SD    10   0   7   0   24
KC    D22 R29/139  P(36-17-2) 167
SD    D20 R45/246  P(10-6-0)   91
SD-Anderson 217R

GB    13   7   6   0   26
Phx    7  10   0   0   17
GB    D22 R36/105  P(36-18-2) 239
Phx   D16 R27/118  P(33-15-0) 147

Mia   10   7   0   0   17
Pit    7  13   7  13   40
Mia   D18 R18/82   P(41-25-2) 303
Pit   D24 R47/305  P(26-13-0)  99
Mia-Schwedes 110C;
Pit-Williams 117R
```

MONDAY, DECEMBER 19

```
ChiB   0   3  14  10   27
Min    7  14   0   7   28
ChiB  D21 R38/185  P(32-16-1) 280
Min   D17 R21/62   P(35-16-2) 156
ChiB-Anderson 122R,
McKinnon 106C
```

1989 NFL

SUNDAY, SEPTEMBER 10

```
LARm   3  14   7   7   31
Atl    7  14   0   6   27
LARm  D21 R36/168  P(25-14-0) 195
Atl   D16 R15/43   P(37-23-0) 271
LARm-Bell 128R

NE     7  14   0   6   27
NYJ    0   0  17   7   24
NE    D26 R48/154  P(23-15-2) 273
NYJ   D14 R16/49   P(31-18-1) 255
NE-Jones 148C
```

```
Sea    7  0  0  0   7
Phi    7 10  7  7  31
Sea D17 R19/77  P(41-18-3) 193
Phi D18 R37/131 P(27-13-0) 234
  Phi-Quick 140C

KC     0 10  3  7  20
Den   17  0  7 10  34
KC  D14 R20/45  P(34-21-2) 242
Den D14 R32/100 P(28-16-2) 150

Hou    7  0  0  0   7
Min   14 10  7  7  38
Hou D11 R23/70  P(24-10-1) 34
Min D29 R36/155 P(25-16-0) 188
  Min-Carter 123C

Buf    3  0 10 14  27
Mia    0 10  7  7  24
Buf D27 R27/141 P(40-25-0) 226
Mia D20 R23/68  P(38-25-2) 255

Cle   17 13 14  7  51
Pit    0  0  0  0   0
Cle D19 R44/152 P(25-16-0) 205
Pit D5  R17/36  P(22-10-3) 17

Dal    0  0  0  0   0
NO     7 14  0  7  28
Dal D10 R10/20  P(36-18-2) 154
NO  D26 R45/199 P(19-16-0) 145

TB     0 20  3  0  23
GB     7  0  7  7  21
TB  D26 R40/142 P(27-22-0) 205
GB  D17 R17/103 P(27-17-3) 218

SD     7  0  7  0  14
LARd   7 14  7 12  40
SD  D16 R25/171 P(29-12-1) 134
LARd D23 R40/160 P(25-17-0) 258
  LARd-Bell 128R, Gault 131C

Phx    0  6  0 10  16
Det    3  0  7  3  13
Phx D19 R25/65  P(35-21-1) 264
Det D13 R27/159 P(20-7-0) 99
  Phx-Smith 121C

SF     3 10  7  7  30
Ind    3  7  0 14  24
SF  D24 R37/200 P(26-15-0) 204
Ind D22 R27/154 P(32-14-1) 190
  SF-Craig 131R, Rice 163C;
  Ind-Dickerson 106R

Cin    7  0  7  0  14
ChiB   0  7  3  7  17
Cin D23 R41/179 P(36-18-0) 151
ChiB D19 R38/212 P(24-10-2) 153
  ChiB-Anderson 146R
```

MONDAY, SEPTEMBER 11

```
NYG    7  7  0 13  27
Was    7  3 14  4  24
NYG D19 R37/159 P(19-11-2) 231
Was D19 R25/112 P(32-22-1) 345
  Was-Riggs 111R, Clark 101C,
  Sanders 143C, Rypien 349P
```

SUNDAY, SEPTEMBER 17

```
Phx   13  0  7 14  34
Sea    0  7  7 10  31
Phx D25 R42/171 P(24-18-1) 298
Sea D23 R20/77  P(43-25-1) 269
  Phx-Green 166C, Smith 104C,
  Hogeboom 298P; Sea-Blades 146C

Pit    3  0  7  0  10
Cin    3 17  7 14  41
Pit D18 R25/86  P(35-19-0) 188
Cin D31 R37/192 P(27-16-0) 328
  Pit-Lipps 122C; Cin-Brooks 113R,
  McGee 100C, Esiason 328P

NYJ    0  7 10  7  24
Cle    0 14 14 10  38
NYJ D21 R31/136 P(43-24-4) 246
Cle D18 R23/85  P(30-15-0) 192

SF     0  6  0 14  20
TB     3  0  6  7  16
SF  D22 R30/63  P(39-25-2) 244
TB  D13 R26/91  P(35-14-2) 126
  SF-Rice 122C

Mia   17  7  0  0  24
NE     0  0  3  7  10
Mia D18 R30/103 P(28-17-3) 226
NE  D19 R13/43  P(51-25-1) 282
  NE-Eason 341P
```

```
Ind    3 14  0  0  17
LARm  10  7  7  7  31
Ind D20 R22/120 P(33-20-1) 266
LARm D26 R28/97  P(35-28-1) 352
  Ind-Dickerson 116R;
  LARm-Ellard 230C, Everett 368P

Dal   14  0  0  0  14
Atl    7  3 10  7  27
Dal D18 R30/108 P(23-13-2) 241
Atl D23 R30/90  P(29-21-0) 243
  Dal-Ellard 230C, Irvin 115C,
  Everett 368P

Hou    3 17 14  0  34
SD     7  7  0 13  27
Hou D26 R35/132 P(35-21-0) 235
SD  D24 R17/41  P(45-27-3) 372
  SD-Miller 162C, McMahon 389P

LARd   6 10  3  0  19
KC     7 10  0  7  24
LARd D18 R29/115 P(21-14-1) 153
KC  D23 R42/152 P(18-12-1) 171
  LARd-Ellard 230C, Everett 368P

Phi    7  7  7 21  42
Was   20 10  0  7  37
Phi D32 R28/65  P(46-34-1) 409
Was D20 R22/220 P(23-12-2) 272
  Phi-Byars 130C, Jackson 126C,
  Cunningham 447P;
  Was-Riggs 221R, Clark 153C,
  Rypien 288P

Det    0  7  7  0  14
NYG    3  0 14  7  24
Det D19 R19/95  P(31-21-3) 315
NYG D21 R39/129 P(26-20-0) 216
  Det-Johnson 172C, Gagliano 344P

Min    0  0  0  0   7
ChiB   7  3  0 28  38
Min D18 R21/67  P(42-24-1) 253
ChiB D20 R39/164 P(26-10-1) 142

NO    14 10  0 10  34
GB     0  7 14 14  35
NO  D21 R24/85  P(32-23-1) 282
GB  D29 R27/149 P(32-25-1) 341
  GB-Fullwood 125R, Sharpe 107C,
  Majkowski 354P
```

MONDAY, SEPTEMBER 18

```
Den    5 13  3  7  28
Buf    0  0  7  7  14
Den D26 R43/201 P(29-15-2) 181
Buf D28 R22/94  P(46-28-3) 319
  Buf-Reed 157C
```

SUNDAY, SEPTEMBER 24

```
KC     3  3  0  0   6
SD     0  7  7  7  21
KC  D13 R22/118 P(28-16-5) 154
SD  D18 R37/200 P(18-11-0) 96
  KC-Okoye 112R

Min    7  7  0  0  14
Pit    7 14  0  6  27
Min D17 R25/112 P(30-15-2) 146
Pit D23 R42/159 P(22-16-0) 119

Sea    0 21  3  0  24
NE     3  0  0  0   3
Sea D20 R37/157 P(24-14-0) 159
NE  D13 R23/91  P(33-17-1) 128

Atl    3  3  3  0   9
Ind    0  0  6  7  13
Atl D11 R24/105 P(28-13-1) 103
Ind D15 R39/130 P(21-7-1) 84

NO     7  3  0  0  10
TB     0 10  7  3  20
NO  D25 R28/114 P(35-20-2) 211
TB  D20 R29/118 P(26-15-1) 218
  TB-Carrier 120C

Was   14  3  3 10  30
Dal    0  0  0  7   7
Was D20 R40/165 P(37-15-0) 208
Dal D10 R15/34  P(39-15-4) 156
  Was-Morris 100R, Monk 114C

NYJ    3  9  7 21  40
Mia    7 13 10  3  33
NYJ D25 R25/102 P(37-27-1) 309
Mia D30 R20/78  P(56-34-2) 446
  NYJ-Toon 159C, O'Brien 329P;
  Mia-Duper 113C, Marino 427P
```

```
ChiB  10 10 13 14  47
Det    0 13  7  7  27
ChiB D23 R37/219 P(26-18-0) 323
Det D20 R29/198 P(19-9-3) 107
  ChiB-Anderson 116R,
  Tomczak 302P; Det-Sanders 126R

Buf   10 10  7 14  6  47
Hou    7  3 14 17  0  41
Buf D22 R24/112 P(29-17-1) 337
Hou D33 R39/128 P(42-28-2) 311
  Buf-Reed 135C, Kelly 363P;
  Hou-Moon 338P

SF     7  3  0 28  38
Phi    3  9  6 10  28
SF  D19 R19/59  P(34-25-1) 385
Phi D22 R37/154 P(38-19-1) 161
  SF-Rice 164C, Taylor 136C,
  Montana 428P

Phx    0  0  0  7   7
NYG   14  6  5 10  35
Phx D16 R25/65  P(32-19-4) 183
NYG D16 R38/162 P(22-12-0) 204

LARd   0  0  7 14  21
Den   21  7  0  3  31
LARd D15 R22/90  P(28-15-3) 270
Den D16 R41/170 P(23-11-1) 113
  LARd-Bell 221R, Fernandez 124C

GB     0  7 21 10  38
LARm  10 28  0  3  41
GB  D29 R23/116 P(43-25-3) 326
LARm D20 R33/217 P(31-19-2) 223
  GB-Sharpe 164C, Majkowski 335P;
  LARm-Bell 221R
```

MONDAY, SEPTEMBER 25

```
Cle    0 14  0  0  14
Cin    0 14  7  0  21
Cle D16 R21/92  P(23-15-0) 175
Cin D21 R40/187 P(20-14-1) 184
```

SUNDAY, OCTOBER 1

```
Den    0  3  3  7  13
Cle    7  3  3  3  16
Den D10 R25/80  P(19-6-1) 161
Cle D16 R26/95  P(38-25-1) 201
  Den-Johnson 145C

SD     0  0  7 17  24
Phx    0  3 10  0  13
SD  D13 R31/103 P(23-15-0) 165
Phx D17 R22/69  P(43-22-2) 232
  Phx-Smith 123C

NYG    3 17  7  3  30
Dal    0  6  7  3  16
NYG D20 R36/137 P(19-14-3) 205
Dal D12 R31/87  P(30-14-2) 201

NE     3  0  7  0  10
Buf    7 17  0  7  31
NE  D17 R30/124 P(41-15-1) 155
Buf D16 R31/115 P(17-12-0) 256
  Buf-Thomas 105R, Reed 114C

Was    3  0 10  3  16
NO     0  0  0 14  14
Was D13 R33/92  P(28-15-1) 216
NO  D20 R28/136 P(25-16-1) 245

Ind    0  0  7 10  17
NYJ    7  3  0  0  10
Ind D17 R32/74  P(31-17-1) 242
NYJ D18 R23/63  P(32-20-1) 182
  Ind-Brooks 159C

Atl    7  7  7  0  21
GB     0  6  0 17  23
Atl D17 R23/75  P(29-20-1) 258
GB  D27 R35/153 P(35-19-2) 295
  Atl-Collins 126C

LARm   3  7  0  3  13
SF     6  3  0  3  12
LARm D11 R20/37  P(25-16-0) 250
SF  D22 R33/152 P(35-25-0) 215
  LARm-Anderson 112C

Mia    0  0  0  7   7
Hou    2 17  6 14  39
Mia D9  R11/43  P(32-12-2) 117
Hou D23 R41/197 P(25-20-1) 251
```

```
Cin    0 14  0  7  21
KC     0 14  0  0  14
Cin D14 R39/163 P(16-6-1) 114
KC  D16 R34/139 P(28-14-4) 153
  KC-Okoye 101R

Sea    7  0  0 17  24
LARd   0 10  7  3  20
Sea D25 R40/160 P(31-22-0) 194
LARd D16 R18/114 P(30-16-1) 197
  Sea-Warner 102R, Blades 113C;
  LARd-Anderson 112C,
  Fernandez 113C

Pit    0 10  7  6  23
Det    0  3  0  0   3
Pit D20 R38/102 P(27-21-0) 213
Det D13 R10/18  P(46-19-2) 222
  Pit-Lipps 126C; Det-Clark 124C

TB     0  3  0  0   3
Min    0 10  7  0  17
TB  D7  R25/94  P(23-6-0) 64
Min D23 R41/162 P(35-21-2) 203
```

MONDAY, OCTOBER 2

```
Phi    0  0  3 10  13
ChiB   0 13  7  7  27
Phi D23 R15/67  P(62-32-4) 368
ChiB D22 R34/113 P(38-24-1) 261
  Phi-Carter 113C, Cunningham 401P
```

SUNDAY, OCTOBER 8

```
Buf    0  0  7  7  14
Ind   14  6  3 14  37
Buf D25 R17/71  P(51-31-4) 353
Ind D20 R39/153 P(24-13-1) 177
  Ind-Brooks 111C

Hou    0  3  0 10  13
NE     0  0  3 10  23
Hou D14 R24/105 P(29-14-2) 202
NE  D19 R43/144 P(18-9-0) 138
  Hou-Givins 128C

Dal    6  0  7  0  13
GB     0 10  7 14  31
Dal D12 R13/45  P(29-18-1) 168
GB  D28 R45/189 P(32-21-0) 313
  GB-Fullwood 119R, Sharpe 132C,
  Majkowski 313P

Cin    0 13  0 13  26
Pit    7  3  3  3  16
Cin D21 R28/190 P(32-17-0) 192
Pit D25 R36/172 P(36-21-0) 168
  Cin-Brooks 127R

Atl    7  0  7  0  14
LARm  10 10  0  6  26
Atl D19 R15/38  P(39-28-1) 315
LARm D21 R33/165 P(28-16-1) 273
  Atl-Miller 340P; LARm-Ellard 165C

SD     3  0  7  0  10
Den    0  0  0 16  16
SD  D12 R26/118 P(19-10-1) 93
Den D24 R35/156 P(35-19-1) 179
  Den-Humphrey 102R

Det    7  3  0  7  17
Min    0 24  0  0  24
Det D20 R34/153 P(27-11-3) 84
Min D14 R32/91  P(18-11-0) 138

ChiB   0 14  7 14  35
TB    14 14  0 14  42
ChiB D22 R26/136 P(37-22-1) 214
TB  D27 R30/147 P(36-22-2) 268
  TB-Tate 112R, Carrier 105C,
  Hill 107C

NYG    0  0  6 13  19
Phi    0  7  0 14  21
NYG D20 R25/84  P(40-22-1) 239
Phi D18 R36/158 P(24-10-0) 85

Phx    7  7  7  7  28
Was   10  3  0 17  30
Phx D19 R20/90  P(36-20-4) 291
Was D28 R42/175 P(42-23-1) 333
  Phx-Smith 114C; Was-Byner 100R,
  Monk 102C, Rypien 333P

SF     0  3  7 14  24
NO     0  7  0 13  20
SF  D18 R23/76  P(29-21-0) 282
NO  D18 R16/35  P(49-31-0) 299
  SF-Rice 149C; NO-Hebert 308P
```

```
Cle    0  3  7  0  10
Mia    3  7  0  3  13
Cle D19 R27/141 P(35-22-2) 189
Mia D18 R29/70  P(33-19-1) 234

KC     3  0  7 10  20
Sea    7  9  0  0  16
KC  D17 R40/199 P(18-12-0) 104
Sea D16 R19/52  P(36-20-2) 236
  KC-Okoye 156R
```

MONDAY, OCTOBER 9

```
LARd   0  0  7  7  14
NYJ    0  0  7  0   7
LARd D14 R27/130 P(24-11-1) 185
NYJ D20 R26/90  P(48-24-2) 302
  NYJ-O'Brien 338P
```

SUNDAY, OCTOBER 15

```
Mia    0  3  7 10  20
Cin   10  3  0  0  13
Mia D19 R34/109 P(33-16-1) 266
Cin D14 R32/146 P(24-16-0) 168
  Mia-Duper 129C

KC     7  0  0  7  14
LARd   3  7  3  7  20
KC  D17 R28/78  P(33-23-1) 227
LARd D13 R35/157 P(21-6-2) 89

Pit    3  7  0  7  17
Cle    0  0  0  7   7
Pit D16 R35/93  P(29-10-1) 193
Cle D17 R23/107 P(41-15-4) 153
  Cle-Slaughter 106C

Hou    0 10  9 14  33
ChiB   0 14  7  7  28
Hou D20 R32/140 P(26-16-2) 317
ChiB D22 R36/93  P(29-20-4) 239
  Hou-Hill 128C, Moon 317P;
  ChiB-Gentry 110C

SF     0  7  7 17  31
Dal    0  7  7  0  14
SF  D17 R31/146 P(18-13-1) 172
Dal D19 R20/60  P(36-23-2) 270

Det    3  0  7  7  17
TB     0 10  3  0  13
Det D20 R27/139 P(31-17-2) 237
TB  D14 R30/88  P(29-16-1) 103

NYJ    0  7  0  7  14
NO     6  7  7  9  29
NYJ D15 R21/52  P(34-21-1) 199
NO  D20 R36/152 P(29-18-1) 266
  NO-Martin 131C

Was    3  7  7  0  17
NYG    3  0  3 14  20
Was D18 R23/122 P(30-19-0) 194
NYG D19 R38/133 P(32-16-1) 173
  NYG-Anderson 101R

GB     7  0  7  0  14
Min    0 17  9  0  26
GB  D11 R18/68  P(24-9-2) 151
Min D21 R43/238 P(24-14-1) 160
  Min-Walker 148R

Phi    0  0 14  3  17
Phx    5  0  0  0   5
Phi D18 R39/167 P(29-16-3) 186
Phx D20 R30/114 P(41-16-6) 223
  Phx-Jones 144C

Sea   10  0  7  0  17
SD     7  3  0  6  16
Sea D15 R27/85  P(24-14-2) 139
SD  D26 R30/99  P(39-25-2) 263
  SD-Miller 116C

NE     6  9  0  0  15
Atl    3 10  0  3  16
NE  D13 R33/93  P(30-12-3) 148
Atl D14 R21/72  P(34-19-1) 240

Ind    3  0  0  0   3
Den    0  7  0  7  14
Ind D7  R17/44  P(28-12-1) 84
Den D20 R43/169 P(25-13-1) 150
```

MONDAY, OCTOBER 16

```
LARm   7  0  3 10  20
Buf    0  0 17  6  23
LARm D15 R30/59  P(36-15-1) 207
Buf D17 R31/134 P(37-21-1) 214
  Buf-Thomas 105R, Reed 106C
```

SUNDAY, OCTOBER 22

Den 0 0 7 14 3 **24**
Sea 7 7 0 7 0 21
Den D15 R23/55 P(35-18-0) 316
Sea D23 R43/139 P(38-22-2) 224
Den-Young 137C, Elway 344P

GB 3 3 0 14 20
Mia 7 3 7 6 **23**
GB D21 R21/81 P(42-26-0) 215
Mia D24 R28/105 P(37-24-2) 333
Mia-Marino 333P

LARd 0 0 0 7 7
Phi 0 0 10 0 **10**
LARd D20 R35/126 P(30-12-2) 142
Phi D13 R32/132 P(20-8-0) 63

Min 3 10 7 0 **20**
Det 0 0 0 7 7
Min D13 R32/117 P(24-17-0) 147
Det D21 R23/84 P(36-19-2) 198
Min-Dickerson 152R

Dal 7 7 0 14 28
KC 14 13 9 0 **36**
Dal D14 R17/116 P(29-14-0) 166
KC D26 R43/202 P(25-17-0) 221
KC-Okoye 170R

NYG 3 3 7 7 **20**
SD 0 3 3 7 13
NYG D24 R38/109 P(33-22-1) 218
SD D9 R19/51 P(27-12-1) 128

NE 0 10 7 3 20
SF 0 17 7 13 **37**
NE D19 R28/94 P(29-15-2) 231
SF D28 R31/141 P(34-27-0) 353
NE-Fryar 102C; SF-Rathman 103C, Rice 112C

TB 7 0 0 21 28
Was 0 12 17 3 **32**
TB D13 R10/1 P(38-19-2) 296
Was D24 R41/179 P(36-24-1) 209
TB-Carrier 106C, Testaverde 311P

NYJ 0 0 3 0 3
Buf 3 8 7 14 **34**
NYJ D9 R12/39 P(31-13-1) 115
Buf D22 R52/204 P(20-13-0) 139

Atl 0 6 7 7 20
Phx 14 7 3 10 **34**
Atl D22 R20/111 P(44-24-0) 240
Phx D21 R37/125 P(25-17-1) 174

Ind 0 3 6 14 **23**
Cin 6 3 0 3 12
Ind D18 R36/168 P(27-14-1) 168
Cin D15 R28/95 P(31-14-2) 123
Ind-Dickerson 152R

Pit 0 0 0 0 0
Hou 0 7 17 3 0 **27**
Pit D10 R17/32 P(27-11-2) 100
Hou D22 R41/132 P(30-17-0) 229

NO 10 9 14 7 **40**
LARm 0 7 7 7 21
NO D16 R31/106 P(22-15-1) 267
LARm D22 R18/53 P(46-27-3) 260
NO-Martin 116C

MONDAY, OCTOBER 23

ChiB 0 0 0 7 0
Cle 7 0 10 10 **27**
ChiB D16 R31/149 P(30-13-1) 152
Cle D17 R24/53 P(29-22-0) 273
Cle-Slaughter 186C

SUNDAY, OCTOBER 29

Phx 6 0 7 6 **19**
Dal 0 3 0 7 10
Phx D17 R44/158 P(31-17-0) 142
Dal D18 R15/45 P(49-21-2) 264

KC 0 3 14 0 17
Pit 10 6 7 0 **23**
KC D23 R28/120 P(36-24-2) 318
Pit D19 R31/80 P(27-17-0) 232
KC-Okoye 101R, Paige 163C, DeBerg 338P; Pit-Lipps 130C

LARm 0 3 0 7 10
ChiB 0 3 7 10 **20**
LARm D17 R24/84 P(35-13-2) 168
ChiB D19 R39/148 P(29-14-0) 170
LARm-Ellard 100C

Phi 14 0 7 7 28
Den 0 7 10 7 24
Phi D17 R45/215 P(21-11-1) 98
Den D22 R20/104 P(39-19-0) 216
Den-Johnson 148C

Mia 3 0 7 7 17
Buf 0 21 0 10 **31**
Mia D19 R18/65 P(47-26-3) 348
Buf D18 R51/280 P(9-6-0) 114
Mia-Brown 105C, Clayton 122C; Buf-Kinnebrew 121R, Thomas 148C

NE 3 0 7 10 3 **23**
Ind 10 0 0 10 0 20
NE D30 R39/120 P(46-28-2) 328
Ind D19 R27/130 P(33-16-0) 227
NE-Sievers 113C, Grogan 355P; Ind-Rison 129C

TB 7 9 0 7 23
Cin 7 14 21 14 **56**
TB D21 R27/139 P(39-23-3) 336
Cin D30 R33/188 P(34-22-0) 294
TB-Carrier 100C, Hill 125C, Testaverde 336P; Cin-Brooks 131R, McGee 127C, Esiason 197P

Det 7 3 0 10 0 20
GB 3 7 10 3 0 **23**
Det D21 R34/210 P(28-14-1) 192
GB D24 R20/76 P(45-29-1) 345
Det-Sanders 184R; GB-Sharpe 105C, Majkowski 367P

SD 0 0 0 7 7
Sea 3 0 0 7 **10**
SD D11 R17/92 P(29-15-1) 103
Sea D23 R27/70 P(49-27-2) 269
Sea-Blades 117C, Krieg 311P

Atl 0 0 3 0 3
NO 7 3 3 7 **20**
Atl D11 R19/57 P(32-15-0) 91
NO D17 R34/131 P(30-18-1) 261

Hou 3 0 7 0 10
Cle 0 0 21 7 **28**
Hou D17 R25/89 P(25-15-0) 210
Cle D18 R31/103 P(20-15-2) 280
Cle-Slaughter 184C

SF 7 13 0 3 **23**
NYJ 0 7 3 0 10
SF D20 R35/159 P(25-17-0) 340
NYJ D19 R22/130 P(36-25-0) 121

Was 7 3 7 7 24
LARd 14 3 20 0 **37**
Was D22 R14/21 P(63-32-4) 420
LARd D18 R38/187 P(31-12-2) 155
Was-Clark 145C, Sanders 158C, Rypien 364P; LARd-Jackson 144R, Ellard 100C

MONDAY, OCTOBER 30

Min 7 0 0 7 14
NYG 0 0 17 7 **24**
Min D20 R24/110 P(34-18-2) 140
NYG D13 R42/119 P(14-6-0) 55

SUNDAY, NOVEMBER 5

Sea 7 3 0 0 10
KC 7 10 0 3 **20**
Sea D10 R14/39 P(32-14-0) 90
KC D18 R57/246 P(13-7-0) 69
KC-Okoye 126R

ChiB 3 0 10 0 13
GB 7 0 0 7 **14**
ChiB D19 R34/133 P(30-16-0) 188
GB D19 R15/69 P(40-23-1) 270

Pit 0 7 0 0 7
Den 10 3 7 14 **34**
Pit D7 R25/93 P(26-11-0) 77
Den D22 R44/153 P(23-16-2) 261
Den-Humphrey 105R

Phi 0 7 0 10 **17**
SD 0 7 0 3 10
Phi D24 R33/178 P(29-19-1) 195
SD D17 R26/104 P(29-14-1) 254
SD-Miller 129C

NYG 3 7 0 10 **20**
Phx 3 0 7 3 13
NYG D22 R48/210 P(24-12-2) 174
Phx D14 R17/75 P(31-13-1) 111

Cin 0 0 0 7 7
LARd 14 7 0 7 **28**
Cin D20 R30/154 P(40-17-1) 196
LARd D12 R28/206 P(17-8-1) 223
LARd-Jackson 159R, Gault 147C

LARm 7 0 14 0 21
Min 3 9 6 5 **23**
LARm D14 R27/119 P(30-18-1) 185
Min D23 R33/100 P(39-20-1) 276

Buf 7 0 14 7 28
Atl 3 0 17 10 **30**
Buf D19 R31/118 P(22-17-1) 211
Atl D20 R37/127 P(23-10-0) 213
Buf-Reed 100C

Det 3 7 14 7 31
Hou 7 7 14 7 **35**
Det D19 R20/94 P(29-18-1) 257
Hou D30 R38/110 P(38-30-1) 345
Det-Clark 141C; Hou-Hill 101C, Moon 345P

Ind 3 0 0 10 13
Mia 3 9 7 0 **19**
Ind D17 R23/85 P(41-21-2) 214
Mia D19 R37/159 P(26-14-0) 149
Mia-Smith 123R

NYJ 7 7 3 10 **27**
NE 3 0 17 6 26
NYJ D19 R33/112 P(29-22-0) 374
NE D27 R29/135 P(44-25-1) 318
NYJ-O'Brien 386P; NE-Jones 127C

Cle 7 28 0 7 **42**
TB 3 10 7 7 27
Cle D18 R29/114 P(22-18-0) 157
TB D24 R16/49 P(50-27-4) 349
TB-Wilder 107C, Testaverde 370P

Dal 0 3 7 3 **13**
Was 0 0 3 0 3
Dal D17 R29/148 P(30-10-0) 114
Was D20 R21/50 P(52-28-2) 296
Dal-Palmer 110R

MONDAY, NOVEMBER 6

NO 7 3 3 0 13
SF 7 14 3 7 **31**
NO D16 R20/83 P(33-20-2) 160
SF D21 R30/95 P(31-22-0) 302
SF-Montana 302P

SUNDAY, NOVEMBER 12

GB 0 3 14 5 22
Det 3 7 0 21 **31**
GB D30 R27/104 P(60-35-2) 328
Det D8 R23/74 P(15-7-1) 54
GB-Majkowski 357P

LARd 3 6 3 0 12
SD 0 0 7 7 **14**
LARd D15 R33/134 P(25-12-3) 161
SD D12 R27/136 P(20-9-1) 66
LARd-Jackson 103R

Dal 3 10 0 7 20
Phx 0 7 0 17 **24**
Dal D21 R25/77 P(40-21-2) 367
Phx D15 R24/69 P(35-21-0) 316
Dal-Dixon 203C, Aikman 379P; Phx-Awalt 105C, Jones 139C

Atl 0 3 0 0 3
SF 7 21 10 7 **45**
Atl D11 R17/73 P(32-17-0) 119
SF D30 R47/235 P(20-17-0) 280
SF-Craig 109R

ChiB 7 13 0 0 **20**
Pit 0 0 3 0 3
ChiB D20 R44/203 P(28-14-1) 134
Pit D10 R16/54 P(26-14-3) 162
Pit-Lipps 112C

Cle 0 7 7 3 **17**
Sea 7 0 0 0 7
Cle D20 R34/139 P(27-16-0) 138
Sea D14 R22/46 P(30-17-3) 134

Was 3 7 0 0 **10**
Phi 0 0 0 10 10
Was D14 R43/99 P(24-14-0) 155
Phi D12 R17/47 P(39-17-1) 157

Mia 0 10 21 0 **31**
NYJ 3 17 0 3 23
Mia D19 R27/103 P(34-19-2) 344
NYJ D23 R32/136 P(35-22-3) 274
Mia-Clayton 125C, Schwedes 107C, Marino 359P

Den 3 3 7 3 **16**
KC 0 6 0 7 13
Den D12 R29/101 P(22-11-1) 112
KC D20 R35/141 P(27-17-0) 171

Min 17 0 0 7 **24**
TB 0 3 0 7 10
Min D18 R39/158 P(21-13-0) 145
TB D13 R27/90 P(30-18-1) 111

Ind 0 0 0 7 7
Buf 13 14 0 3 **30**
Ind D13 R20/86 P(27-12-0) 103
Buf D26 R51/232 P(30-14-0) 161
Buf-Thomas 127R

NO 7 21 0 0 **28**
NE 0 10 0 14 24
NO D14 R39/129 P(17-9-1) 82
NE D28 R23/82 P(59-27-1) 272
NO-Hilliard 106R; NE-Dykes 105C

NYG 0 3 0 7 10
LARm 10 14 0 7 **31**
NYG D13 R10/6 P(38-25-1) 201
LARm D28 R40/150 P(33-23-2) 295

MONDAY, NOVEMBER 13

Cin 0 14 0 10 24
Hou 0 7 6 13 **26**
Cin D16 R31/162 P(19-11-0) 175
Hou D20 R32/136 P(33-17-1) 175
Cin-Brooks 141R

SUNDAY, NOVEMBER 19

Phx 0 0 7 7 14
LARm 14 10 3 10 **37**
Phx D13 R21/76 P(36-20-4) 216
LARm D16 R35/135 P(24-15-0) 301
LARm-Ellard 163C, Everett 308P

KC 0 0 7 3 **10**
Cle 0 3 7 0 10
KC D17 R33/119 P(45-19-3) 188
Cle D17 R37/78 P(42-21-1) 183

Buf 7 3 0 14 24
NE 0 6 7 20 **33**
Buf D24 R28/84 P(41-21-2) 340
NE D19 R38/192 P(26-12-3) 167
Buf-Reed 107C, Kelly 356P; NE-Stephens 126R

Mia 0 10 0 7 **17**
Dal 7 7 0 0 14
Mia D18 R19/65 P(36-21-0) 238
Dal D28 R35/167 P(33-25-1) 261

NYJ 0 3 0 7 10
Ind 3 17 0 7 **27**
NYJ D22 R22/124 P(43-27-3) 244
Ind D23 R40/185 P(28-17-0) 239
Ind-Dickerson 131R, Rison 108C

SD 0 0 0 17 17
Pit 3 3 7 7 **20**
SD D20 R29/134 P(36-19-1) 225
Pit D14 R30/88 P(27-12-0) 103
SD-Miller 104C

Sea 0 0 0 3 3
NYG 7 0 0 8 **15**
Sea D12 R20/63 P(29-16-2) 132
NYG D21 R45/162 P(26-17-0) 187

TB 10 3 0 19 **32**
ChiB 7 7 0 7 21
TB D21 R31/127 P(41-19-0) 263
ChiB D14 R24/111 P(31-18-3) 266
TB-Carrier 164C; ChiB-Anderson 100R

NO 3 0 9 14 **26**
Atl 3 7 0 7 17
NO D21 R41/206 P(24-13-4) 190
Atl D15 R16/77 P(38-18-1) 190
NO-Hilliard 158C

LARd 7 0 0 0 7
Hou 7 10 3 3 **23**
LARd D12 R15/74 P(27-13-2) 169
Hou D23 R41/170 P(30-20-1) 249
LARd-Ellard 163C, Fernandez 102C, Everett 308P

Min 6 0 3 0 9
Phi 3 0 0 7 **10**
Min D18 R25/83 P(34-14-2) 136
Phi D22 R34/91 P(43-26-0) 179

GB 7 7 0 7 **21**
SF 0 3 0 14 17
GB D21 R31/109 P(30-18-0) 139
SF D22 R16/71 P(42-30-1) 289
SF-Rice 106C, Montana 325P

Det 7 0 0 0 7
Cin 0 28 7 7 **42**
Det D10 R28/122 P(27-13-2) 156
Cin D27 R31/99 P(45-33-2) 447
Det-Sanders 114R; Cin-McGee 194C, Esiason 399P

MONDAY, NOVEMBER 20

Den 7 7 0 0 **14**
Was 7 0 3 0 10
Den D19 R44/126 P(27-13-1) 106
Was D14 R25/77 P(29-15-0) 146
Den-Humphrey 110R

THURSDAY, NOVEMBER 23

Phi 0 10 14 3 **27**
Dal 0 0 0 0 0
Phi D22 R34/138 P(35-22-0) 243
Dal D10 R19/123 P(25-9-3) 68

Cle 0 10 0 0 10
Det 0 0 3 10 **13**
Cle D14 R18/70 P(39-28-1) 289
Det D15 R29/146 P(19-9-0) 125
Det-Sanders 145R

SUNDAY, NOVEMBER 26

Hou 0 0 0 0 0
KC 10 10 7 7 **34**
Hou D12 R27/103 P(31-13-1) 170
KC D20 R32/84 P(27-16-1) 229
KC-Paige 114C

Pit 0 17 17 0 **34**
Mia 14 0 0 0 14
Pit D13 R44/131 P(18-8-0) 161
Mia D15 R28/80 P(35-15-2) 222

SD 0 3 0 3 6
Ind 0 3 0 7 **10**
SD D14 R33/177 P(33-18-0) 137
Ind D11 R24/59 P(30-16-1) 205
Ind-Brooks 101C

Atl 0 0 7 0 7
NYJ 3 14 10 0 **27**
Atl D12 R18/66 P(41-13-1) 147
NYJ D24 R43/180 P(34-20-0) 138

Min 3 3 10 3 19
GB 3 7 7 3 **20**
Min D22 R27/76 P(38-23-2) 301
GB D16 R23/84 P(35-26-1) 248
Min-Carter 103C, Wilson 309P; GB-Sharpe 157C

Cin 0 0 0 7 7
Buf 3 7 7 7 **24**
Cin D16 R30/165 P(26-11-1) 133
Buf D18 R47/228 P(15-10-0) 117
Cin-Brooks 105R; Buf-Thomas 100R

TB 0 0 7 7 **14**
Phx 0 10 3 0 13
TB D23 R35/121 P(42-19-1) 139
Phx D12 R22/43 P(38-17-0) 194

NE 0 14 0 7 21
LARd 7 7 7 3 **24**
NE D13 R37/132 P(25-15-0) 136
LARd D19 R37/132 P(25-15-0) 136
LARd-Anderson 336C, Everett 454P

Sea 0 0 0 7 7
Den 14 24 0 3 **41**
Sea D21 R21/133 P(46-22-2) 192
Den D18 R37/137 P(24-11-0) 216
Sea-Blades 122C; Den-Johnson 154C, Elway 217P

ChiB 0 14 0 0 14
Was 14 14 10 14 **38**
ChiB D13 R19/59 P(24-13-2) 132
Was D35 R37/102 P(47-30-1) 390
Was-Clark 124C, Monk 152C, Rypien 401P

(continued)

```
LARm  0  3  0 14  3  20
NO    7  3  7  0  0  17
LARm D23 R22/57  P(51-29-2) 415
NO   D14 R31/138 P(27-13-1) 163
LARm-Anderson 336C,
Everett 454P; NO-Hilliard 112R,
Martin 107C
```

MONDAY, NOVEMBER 27
```
NYG  7  3  7  7  24
SF  14 10  0 10  34
NYG D23 R14/52 P(48-25-3) 290
SF  D24 R32/96 P(34-27-0) 285
NYG-Simms 326P; SF-Rice 117C
```

SUNDAY, DECEMBER 3
```
Mia  0  0  7 14  21
KC  13  3  3  7  26
Mia D15 R19/73  P(37-18-1) 218
KC  D25 R42/199 P(25-15-1) 239
Mia-Clayton 128C; KC-Okoye 148R,
Paige 133C

Cin  0  7 14  0  21
Cle  0  0  0  0   0
Cin D16 R34/101 P(32-14-2) 197
Cle D15 R23/88  P(43-19-2) 176

NYJ  7  0  0 13  20
SD   0  7  3  7  17
NYJ D19 R37/181 P(31-12-3) 68
SD  D14 R15/71  P(51-24-2) 187
NYJ-Hector 106R

Was  3  7 14  5  29
Phx 10  0  0  0  10
Was D23 R37/135 P(28-18-1) 168
Phx D15 R16/29  P(32-18-3) 234
Phx-Green 116C

LARm 14  0  7 14  35
Dal   0  7 14  0  31
LARm D20 R28/78  P(37-27-1) 325
Dal  D20 R31/138 P(34-19-1) 165
LARm-Cox 103C, Everett 341P;
Dal-Aikman 179P

Den  0 10  0  3  0  13
LARd 3  0  3  7  3  16
Den D26 R38/156 P(37-23-2) 176
LARd D11 R21/79 P(23-9-0) 178
Den-Humphrey 125R;
LARd-Cox 103C, Dyal 134C,
Everett 341P

SF   6  0  7 10  23
Atl  0 10  0  0  10
SF  D23 R33/129 P(25-20-1) 296
Atl D13 R14/37  P(34-18-2) 226
SF-Taylor 162C

GB   7  0  0 10  17
TB   0  3  3 10  16
GB  D19 R20/61 P(53-25-2) 315
TB  D18 R27/88 P(39-19-5) 170
GB-Sharpe 169C, Majkowski 331P;
TB-Carrier 104C

NO  0 14  0  0  14
Det 7  7  7  0  21
NO  D11 R24/70 P(29-18-1) 99
Det D17 R26/85 P(31-14-1) 316
Det-Johnson 248C

Hou  0 14  2  7  23
Pit  3  7  3  3  16
Hou D19 R34/140 P(20-12-0) 144
Pit D15 R36/169 P(21-9-1) 43
Hou-White 115R; Pit-Worley 103R

Phi 14  3  0  7  24
NYG  0 10  0  7  17
Phi D13 R45/149 P(16-9-1) 130
NYG D17 R25/58 P(37-11-2) 239
NYG-Manuel 126C

Ind  0  3  7  6  16
NE   6  0  3 13  22
Ind D14 R29/88  P(30-12-3) 207
NE  D23 R41/187 P(32-17-1) 239
NE-Stephens 124R, Dykes 114C

ChiB 3  0  7  6  16
Min  7 10  7  3  27
ChiB D18 R34/137 P(33-13-2) 178
Min  D35 R35/136 P(26-15-1) 251
```

MONDAY, DECEMBER 4
```
Buf  0 10  6  0  16
Sea 10  0  0  7  17
Buf D11 R29/97 P(23-10-1) 135
Sea D22 R29/78 P(40-20-2) 277
```

SUNDAY, DECEMBER 10
```
Cle  0 10  7  0  17
Ind  7  0  3  7  6  23
Cle D24 R33/123 P(40-26-2) 347
Ind D19 R30/145 P(44-23-1) 251
Cle-Slaughter 152C, Kosar 353P;
Ind-Dickerson 137R, Rison 135C

NYG  0 14  0  0  14
Den  0  0  0  7   7
NYG D16 R37/113 P(22-13-0) 148
Den D18 R24/83  P(47-23-0) 284

KC  0 21  0  0  21
GB  0  3  0  0   3
KC  D21 R48/178 P(19-15-0) 203
GB  D11 R17/110 P(34-14-1) 98
KC-Okoye 131R

NO  13  3  3  3  22
Buf  0 12  0  7  19
NO  D21 R40/150 P(27-15-1) 286
Buf D16 R25/75  P(35-17-3) 204
NO-Martin 100C, Fourcade 302P

Pit  7  0  0  6  13
NYJ  0  0  0  0   0
Pit D17 R32/157 P(30-15-1) 160
NYJ D19 R23/70  P(42-27-2) 243

Det  0 17  7  3  27
ChiB 3  7  0  7  17
Det D17 R31/127 P(23-13-1) 168
ChiB D21 R27/130 P(37-25-1) 172
Det-Sanders 120R

Sea  0  7 10  7  24
Cin  7  3  0  7  17
Sea D15 R25/109 P(33-22-1) 252
Cin D23 R29/150 P(42-21-0) 215
Sea-Blades 107C; Cin-McGee 109C

TB   0  0  7  7  17
Hou  3 17  0  0  20
TB  D23 R19/66  P(48-31-1) 287
Hou D15 R30/135 P(21-14-0) 149
TB-Carrier 135C, Testaverde 328P

Atl  3  7  7  0  17
Min  7 13 17  6  43
Atl D15 R19/67  P(28-15-1) 188
Min D23 R37/220 P(26-15-1) 237

Phx  0  7  0  7  14
LARd 0  6  3  7  16
Phx D18 R30/122 P(24-12-0) 126
LARd D19 R34/154 P(30-13-0) 230
LARd-Jackson 114R,
Fernandez 119C

Dal  0  3  7  0  10
Phi  0 17  3  0  20
Dal D14 R23/87  P(30-17-0) 107
Phi D19 R35/122 P(32-18-0) 158

SD  14  0  0  7  21
Was  0  7  9 10  26
SD  D21 R27/77 P(39-24-0) 350
Was D20 R24/87 P(39-23-1) 302
SD-Miller 152C, Walker 105C,
Tolliver 350P; Was-Rypien 302P

NE   3  0  0  7  10
Mia  7 14  0 10  31
NE  D17 R19/66  P(37-17-1) 231
Mia D24 R41/108 P(32-21-1) 300
NE-Sievers 117C; Mia-Banks 119C,
Clayton 102C, Marino 300P
```

MONDAY, DECEMBER 11
```
SF   0 10  0 20  30
LARm 17  0  7  3  27
SF  D25 R25/63  P(42-30-2) 439
LARm D24 R31/106 P(31-18-0) 231
SF-Taylor 286C, Montana 458P
```

SATURDAY, DECEMBER 16
```
Den  7 13 14  3  37
Phx  0  0  0  0   0
Den D28 R47/204 P(34-25-2) 271
Phx D7 R12/22   P(31-15-1) 79
Den-Humphrey 128R
```

```
Dal  0  0  0  0   0
NYG  6  3  6  0  15
Dal D7 R18/41   P(22-11-1) 67
NYG D14 R46/140 P(19-9-0) 133
```

SUNDAY, DECEMBER 17
```
Buf  3  0  0  7  10
SF   0  0  7 14  21
Buf D17 R18/46  P(42-26-3) 255
SF  D18 R42/151 P(19-9-2) 241
Buf-Reed 115C; SF-Craig 105R

NE   3  0  0  7  10
Pit  7  7  7  7  28
NE  D26 R35/121 P(56-27-2) 282
Pit D18 R39/219 P(16-9-0) 128
NE-Dykes 130C; Pit-Worley 104R

Min  0  3  7  7  17
Cle  0  0 14  3  23
Min D19 R30/122 P(48-17-1) 194
Cle D16 R29/64  P(39-18-0) 256
Cle-Langhorne 140C

GB  14 10  6 10  40
ChiB 7  7 14  0  28
GB  D24 R36/217 P(36-21-1) 239
ChiB D19 R23/158 P(28-20-3) 197
GB-Woodside 116R;
ChiB-Anderson 119R

NYJ  7  0  0  7  14
LARm 7 21  0 10  38
NYJ D14 R20/92  P(32-20-1) 199
LARm D21 R35/150 P(27-17-0) 272

Mia 10  3  0  0  13
Ind  7  7 14 14  42
Mia D16 R17/41  P(50-23-2) 201
Ind D25 R29/121 P(35-23-1) 184
Ind-Dickerson 107R, Trudeau 195P

TB   0  0  7  0   7
Det 14 10  3  6  33
TB  D6 R15/62   P(26-11-4) 163
Det D24 R35/170 P(38-21-1) 212
TB-Carrier 131C; Det-Sanders 104R,
Phillips 115C

SD   0  7  3 10  20
KC   0 13  0  0  13
SD  D22 R44/217 P(30-13-1) 159
KC  D11 R23/90  P(33-14-2) 124
SD-Butts 176R

Hou  0  0  0  7   7
Cin 21 10 21  9  61
Hou D14 R14/39  P(34-16-3) 155
Cin D35 R43/192 P(35-17-0) 392
Cin-Brown 107C, McGee 147C,
Esiason 326P

Was  3  7 21  0  31
Atl  3 24  3  0  30
Was D26 R37/131 P(39-24-1) 376
Atl D15 R9/28   P(44-21-2) 346
Was-Monk 131C, Sanders 167C;
Atl-Haynes 190C, Miller 310P

LARd  3  0 14  0  17
Sea   7  6  3  3  23
LARd D15 R19/98 P(23-13-1) 175
Sea D23 R32/82  P(34-25-0) 268
Sea-Williams 129C
```

MONDAY, DECEMBER 18
```
Phi  0 10 10  0  20
NO   7  9  0 14  30
Phi D22 R27/127 P(40-20-2) 281
NO  D21 R31/86  P(35-18-1) 205
Phi-Byars 109C, Cunningham 306P;
NO-Martin 120C
```

SATURDAY, DECEMBER 23
```
Cle 10  7  0  7  24
Hou  0  3  7 10  20
Cle D21 R26/105 P(36-18-0) 219
Hou D28 R19/102 P(51-32-1) 381
Hou-Hill 141C, Moon 414P

Buf  3  7 20  7  37
NYJ  0  0  0  0   0
Buf D28 R48/233 P(21-13-1) 208
NYJ D11 R14/54  P(32-16-1) 146
```

```
Was 10  3 16  0  29
Sea
Was D26 R40/137 P(32-23-1) 319
Sea D12 R9/25   P(29-18-1) 176
Was-Clark 149C
```

SUNDAY, DECEMBER 24
```
Den  0  7  3  6  16
SD   0  6  3 10  19
Den D16 R29/97  P(27-17-1) 109
SD  D18 R29/82  P(48-22-4) 305
SD-Tolliver 305P

GB   3  7  7  3  20
Dal  0  3  0  7  10
GB  D16 R22/43  P(32-21-0) 207
Dal D16 R24/113 P(28-18-4) 116

Det  7  7 10  7  31
Atl  0  0 10 14  24
Det D17 R26/179 P(30-17-1) 197
Atl D27 R21/89  P(66-37-1) 324
Det-Sanders 158R, Johnson 135C;
Atl-Miller 334P

Pit  7 17  7  0  31
TB   7  3  3  9  22
Pit D14 R37/147 P(15-7-2) 169
TB  D19 R25/84  P(41-21-1) 237
Pit-Lipps 137C; TB-Carrier 101C

Phx  0  7  0  7  14
Phi  7 14  3  7  31
Phx D14 R20/68  P(29-13-2) 197
Phi D26 R46/267 P(37-20-1) 165

ChiB 0  0  0  0   0
SF   3 13  3  7  26
ChiB D15 R31/122 P(34-17-3) 167
SF  D19 R29/130 P(30-16-1) 184
SF-Rice 101C

LARm 0  3  7  7  24
NE   0  7 10  0  20
LARm D22 R32/234 P(29-13-2) 181
NE  D26 R24/73  P(54-27-3) 321
LARm-Bell 210R, Ellard 111C;
NE-Dykes 108C, Grogan 313P

Ind  0  6  0  0   6
NO   3  7  7 24  41
Ind D13 R24/111 P(29-16-2) 119
NO  D23 R34/128 P(28-21-1) 261

KC   0 21  3  3  27
Mia  7  0  0 10  24
KC  D23 R32/117 P(26-17-1) 225
Mia D27 R19/62  P(47-28-1) 319
Mia-Clayton 102C, Marino 339P

LARd  7 10  0  0  17
NYG   7 10 10  7  34
LARd D19 R23/82 P(34-16-2) 230
NYG D20 R38/116 P(25-13-0) 164
LARd-Bell 210R, Ellard 111C,
Fernandez 125C
```

MONDAY, DECEMBER 25
```
Cin  0  7  7  7  21
Min  6 16  0  7  29
Cin D26 R23/120 P(54-31-3) 309
Min D24 R34/119 P(35-19-0) 274
Cin-Brown 109C, Esiason 367P;
Min-Carter 118C, Wilson 303P
```

1990 NFL

SUNDAY, SEPTEMBER 9
```
Den  3  3  0  3   9
LARd 0  0 14  0  14
Den D13 R20/39  P(35-17-2) 157
LARd D12 R31/123 P(18-9-1) 71
Den-Jackson 121C;
LARd-Anderson 128C, Ellard 106C,
Everett 340P

Mia  3 10  7  7  27
NE   7  0  7  0  14
Mia D23 R29/177 P(34-22-3) 255
NE  D13 R26/82  P(29-17-0) 183
Mia-Smith 159R

Hou  0  0  7 20  27
Atl 21  6  7 13  47
Hou D28 R12/29  P(52-31-2) 389
Atl D19 R27/95  P(30-19-1) 206
Hou-Givins 109C, Moon 397P
```

```
NYJ  0 10  7  3  20
Cin  0  3  7 15  25
NYJ D21 R21/72  P(49-27-1) 270
Cin D18 R29/111 P(30-17-2) 192
NYJ-Toon 118C, O'Brien 300P

Ind  3  0  0  7  10
Buf  3 13  0 10  26
Ind D15 R17/56  P(35-19-1) 173
Buf D24 R28/100 P(37-28-0) 283

Pit  0  3  0  0   3
Cle  0  0 10  3  13
Pit D14 R26/49  P(32-17-2) 161
Cle D11 R26/80  P(30-13-0) 78

Phi  3  0  7 10  20
NYG  6  0 14  7  27
Phi D23 R23/81  P(43-26-3) 214
NYG D11 R24/79  P(27-15-1) 148

Sea  0  0  0  0   0
ChiB 3  7  0  7  17
Sea D6 R14/58   P(27-12-3) 74
ChiB D21 R36/171 P(29-21-1) 195
ChiB-Anderson 101R

LARm 7  7  3  7  24
GB   0 17  3 16  36
LARm D18 R24/87 P(40-24-2) 321
GB  D18 R29/95  P(32-20-0) 238
LARm-Anderson 128C, Ellard 106C,
Everett 340P

Min  7  7  0  7  21
KC  14  3  0  7  24
Min D20 R27/138 P(36-18-1) 224
KC  D18 R37/114 P(28-16-0) 190

SD   0  0  0 14  14
Dal  7  0  0 10  17
SD  D12 R23/85  P(34-18-1) 127
Dal D14 R29/88  P(29-13-1) 161

Phx  0  0  0  0   0
Was  7  7 14  3  31
Phx D20 R24/88  P(39-20-4) 206
Was D19 R31/118 P(31-17-0) 229

TB   7 14  7 10  38
Det 14  0  7  0  21
TB  D20 R43/138 P(21-16-1) 237
Det D18 R18/90  P(31-14-3) 168
Det-Clark 117C
```

MONDAY, SEPTEMBER 10
```
SF   3  0  7  3  13
NO   3  6  0  3  12
SF  D17 R19/53  P(43-26-1) 184
NO  D11 R27/88  P(34-12-3) 180
```

SUNDAY, SEPTEMBER 16
```
Buf  0  0  0  7   7
Mia  0 16  7  7  30
Buf D12 R15/44  P(35-19-1) 161
Mia D19 R38/128 P(26-18-0) 177

Cin  0 14  0  7  21
SD  13  3  0  0  16
Cin D18 R24/79  P(34-20-3) 223
SD  D17 R27/139 P(38-20-1) 278
Cin-Brown 178C; SD-Butts 103R,
Miller 137C

LARd  3  0  0 14  17
Sea   0  3  7  3  13
LARd D16 R25/91 P(17-10-0) 235
Sea D23 R36/122 P(24-19-1) 222
LARd-Everett 269P

Hou  0  7  2  0   9
Pit  7  3  0 10  20
Hou D20 R16/51  P(48-24-4) 258
Pit D10 R27/68  P(23-9-0) 55

Cle  0  0  0  0   0
NYJ 14 10  0  0  24
Cle D13 R15/44  P(41-24-0) 215
NYJ D21 R40/170 P(21-13-0) 192

NE   0  7  3  6  16
Ind  7  0  0  7  14
NE  D16 R39/123 P(24-16-1) 187
Ind D14 R22/64  P(24-12-4) 143

Atl  0  0  0  0   0
Det  7 14  0  0  21
Atl D14 R27/122 P(31-18-0) 173
Det D17 R27/83  P(29-14-2) 181
```

```
NYG   0  14   7   7   28
Dal   0   7   0   0    7
NYG  D23 R51/161 P(21-16-0) 208
Dal  D9 R11/20 P(27-14-2) 136

NO    0   3   0   0    3
Min   3  15  14   0   32
NO   D11 R30/118 P(26-10-4) 135
Min  D17 R33/119 P(26-16-0) 191
Min-Jones 103C

Phx   0   7   7   9   23
Phi  14   0   7   0   21
Phx  D14 R31/145 P(19-11-1) 89
Phi  D17 R27/104 P(24-17-2) 223

Was   0  10   3   0   13
SF    3  17   3   3   26
Was  D16 R20/87 P(37-17-0) 241
SF   D22 R29/97 P(44-29-1) 390
Was-Clark 106C; SF-Taylor 160C,
Montana 390P

ChiB  0  17   7   7   31
GB    7   3   3   0   13
ChiB D18 R41/146 P(16-11-1) 157
GB   D17 R15/81 P(40-22-2) 189

LARm 14  14   7   0   35
TB    0   7   0   7   14
LARm D22 R35/136 P(25-18-0) 253
TB   D13 R18/61 P(31-16-1) 194
LARm-Everett 269P
```

MONDAY, SEPTEMBER 17

```
KC    3   6   0  14   23
Den   7   7   3   7   24
KC   D22 R22/78 P(45-26-0) 363
Den  D18 R28/149 P(30-14-0) 250
KC-Paige 206C, DeBerg 395P;
Den-Humphrey 132R,
Johnson 150C
```

SUNDAY, SEPTEMBER 23

```
KC    0   7   0  10   17
GB    0   3   0   0    3
KC   D14 R34/153 P(21-9-0) 118
GB   D17 R26/121 P(31-19-2) 136
KC-Okoye 122R

Mia   0   0   3   0    3
NYG   3   7   0  10   20
Mia  D7 R11/39 P(33-16-2) 119
NYG  D17 R45/131 P(25-13-0) 179

NE    0   7   0   0    7
Cin  17  14   3   7   41
NE   D18 R17/52 P(47-27-2) 250
Cin  D18 R32/110 P(28-16-2) 236
Cin-McGee 163C

Pit   3   0   0   0    3
LARd  0   3  14   3   20
Pit  D18 R27/90 P(28-19-1) 118
LARd D16 R34/125 P(20-9-1) 148
LARd-Ellard 145C, Fernandez 130C

SD    3   7   7   7   24
Cle   0   7   7   0   14
SD   D16 R36/137 P(29-12-2) 129
Cle  D14 R19/44 P(36-17-3) 218

Sea   7   7  10   7   31
Den  14  14   0   3   34
Sea  D24 R38/184 P(28-20-0) 185
Den  D30 R32/141 P(40-30-0) 281
Sea-Fenner 144R;
Den-Humphrey 129R,
Johnson 120C

Ind   0   0  10   0   10
Hou   0  14   3   7   24
Ind  D18 R18/57 P(38-20-2) 195
Hou  D22 R20/69 P(39-29-1) 303
Hou-Hill 123C, Moon 308P

Phx   0   0   7   0    7
NO    0   7   7  14   28
Phx  D15 R30/111 P(26-14-1) 186
NO   D21 R35/151 P(23-11-1) 146

Atl   3   0   7   3   13
SF    0   5  14   0   19
Atl  D18 R18/49 P(41-25-2) 320
SF   D17 R29/66 P(35-24-0) 379
Atl-Rison 128C, Miller 337P;
SF-Jones 125C, Rice 171C,
Montana 398P
```

```
Dal   0   3   3   9   15
Was   3   3   6   7   19
Dal  D19 R26/91 P(43-23-2) 143
Was  D11 R22/79 P(30-13-0) 135

Det   0   3   0   7   20
TB    0   6   3  14   23
Det  D18 R26/155 P(26-17-0) 152
TB   D19 R39/152 P(22-13-0) 171

Min   0   6   3   7   16
ChiB  3  10   3   3   19
Min  D15 R37/173 P(28-13-2) 152
ChiB D15 R43/215 P(16-5-1) 40

Phi   3  14   3   7   27
LARm  7   7   0   7   21
Phi  D15 R37/171 P(29-18-1) 234
LARm D15 R15/35 P(35-17-1) 246
Phi-Toney 103R; LARm-Ellard 145C
```

MONDAY, SEPTEMBER 24

```
Buf   7  13   3   7   30
NYJ   7   0   0   7    7
Buf  D23 R35/292 P(26-16-1) 159
NYJ  D21 R29/124 P(30-15-0) 125
Buf-Thomas 214R
```

SUNDAY, SEPTEMBER 30

```
Cle   0   0   0   0    0
KC    7  17  10   0   34
Cle  D13 R21/68 P(44-22-1) 202
KC   D14 R30/77 P(22-12-0) 182

Den   7   7   7   7   28
Buf   0   3   6  20   29
Den  D28 R46/208 P(28-15-2) 202
Buf  D15 R24/64 P(34-18-1) 133
Den-Humphrey 177R

Hou   7   7   0   3   17
SD    0   7   0   0    7
Hou  D29 R21/92 P(46-27-1) 329
SD   D14 R21/131 P(25-14-2) 167
Hou-Moon 355P

Dal   0   3   7   7   17
NYG   7  10   0  14   31
Dal  D20 R20/51 P(26-21-1) 233
NYG  D21 R33/136 P(24-18-0) 198
Was-Clark 162C

Was   0   7  10  21   38
Phx   3   7   0   0   10
Was  D26 R39/179 P(25-20-0) 257
Phx  D13 R21/112 P(23-11-1) 80

NYJ   7  17  10   3   37
NE    3   3   0   7   13
NYJ  D25 R42/224 P(29-19-1) 175
NE   D18 R17/89 P(42-19-4) 169
NYJ-Thomas 100R, Moore 175C

GB    0  10   0  14   24
Det   7   7   0   0   14
GB   D24 R21/143 P(46-28-0) 269
Det  D21 R26/144 P(34-17-0) 194

Mia   7  14   0   7   28
Pit   0   3   0   6    9
Mia  D20 R42/122 P(29-18-1) 202
Pit  D8 R14/41 P(25-12-3) 119

TB    7   3   3   7   3   23
Min   0   3  14   7   0   24
TB   D15 R38/186 P(19-11-0) 150
Min  D24 R38/170 P(37-19-2) 244
TB-Anderson 108R, Hill 104C;
Min-Jones 101C

ChiB  0   7   3   0   10
LARd 10   7   0   7   24
ChiB D11 R20/101 P(21-10-0) 128
LARd D18 R36/156 P(15-8-0) 170
LARd-Gault 103C

Ind   3   7   7   7   24
Phi   3  14   3   3   23
Ind  D17 R14/52 P(40-19-1) 305
Phi  D21 R38/143 P(34-22-0) 266
Ind-Bentley 104C, Trudeau 329P;
Phi-Byars 133C
```

MONDAY, OCTOBER 1

```
Cin   0   6   3   7   16
Sea   3   7   7  14   31
Cin  D16 R21/69 P(31-16-1) 161
Sea  D20 R31/151 P(24-17-1) 201
```

SUNDAY, OCTOBER 7

```
Cin  14   7   7   6   34
LARm  0   7  14  10   0   31
Cin  D27 R28/99 P(45-31-0) 483
LARm D26 R26/113 P(46-25-0) 364
Cin-Brooks 109C, Holman 161C,
McGee 142C, Esiason 490P;
LARm-Anderson 144C, Ellard 100C,
Everett 372

KC   10   6   3   0   19
Ind   0   0  10  13   23
KC   D13 R26/78 P(36-16-3) 177
Ind  D15 R21/88 P(28-18-2) 143

LARd  7   3   7   7   24
Buf   0   7   7  24   38
LARd D22 R37/122 P(29-17-1) 225
Buf  D14 R22/98 P(22-13-2) 182
LARd-Anderson 144C, Ellard 100C,
Fernandez 134C, Everett 372P

NYJ   3  10   3   0   16
Mia   0   0  13   7   20
NYJ  D22 R34/114 P(33-20-0) 228
Mia  D21 R19/72 P(39-20-0) 262
Mia-Duper 125C

SD    0   0   0   0   14
Pit   3  14   7  12   36
SD   D14 R16/92 P(29-11-3) 96
Pit  D25 R41/183 P(25-18-0) 191

NO    7  10   7   3   27
Atl   7   7   7   7   28
NO   D15 R26/75 P(17-10-0) 218
Atl  D25 R32/91 P(44-23-1) 366
Atl-Rison 154C, Miller 366P

SF    0   7   7  10   24
Hou  14   0   7   0   21
SF   D17 R25/83 P(33-21-0) 300
Hou  D17 R20/86 P(33-18-0) 170
SF-Taylor 132C, Montana 318P

GB    3   3   0   7   13
ChiB  7   3   7  10   27
GB   D10 R15/32 P(39-12-2) 205
ChiB D21 R42/202 P(28-15-1) 151
GB-Sharpe 129C;
ChiB-Anderson 141R

Det   3   7  17   7   34
Min   6  14   0   7   27
Det  D24 R26/104 P(31-16-2) 279
Min  D22 R28/141 P(35-23-1) 199

Sea  13   6   0  14   33
NE    3   7   3   0   13
Sea  D21 R35/111 P(25-17-1) 227
NE   D16 R19/61 P(33-20-2) 213
NE-Dykes 103C

TB    0   3   7   0   10
Dal   7   0   0   7   14
TB   D12 R25/107 P(21-13-0) 164
Dal  D19 R33/154 P(24-17-1) 149
Dal-Smith 121R
```

MONDAY, OCTOBER 8

```
Cle   6   7   7  10   30
Den   7  12   0  10   29
Cle  D23 R31/97 P(38-24-2) 318
Den  D19 R27/141 P(33-16-2) 175
Cle-Slaughter 123C, Kosar 318P;
Den-Humphrey 106R
```

SUNDAY, OCTOBER 14

```
Cin   7   3   7   0   17
Hou   7  24   7  10   48
Cin  D17 R31/116 P(24-13-3) 135
Hou  D27 R21/113 P(40-24-1) 401
Hou-Givins 101C, Moon 369P

Cle   0   6   0  14   20
NO    3   6   7   9   25
Cle  D20 R22/81 P(36-18-0) 157
NO   D19 R29/89 P(31-18-1) 259
NO-Martin 153C

Pit   0  14   7  13   34
Den  10   7   0   0   17
Pit  D25 R30/108 P(28-21-0) 343
Den  D16 R20/66 P(36-17-0) 178
Pit-Lipps 141C, Brister 353P
```

```
SD    2  20  10   7   39
NYJ   0   0   0   3    3
SD   D22 R44/224 P(21-14-0) 188
NYJ  D9 R23/95 P(20-7-1) 53
SD-Butts 121R, Miller 100C

Sea   0  14   3   0   17
LARd  7  14   0   3   24
Sea  D19 R19/77 P(36-22-0) 265
LARd D19 R30/78 P(26-19-0) 227

Dal   0   0   3   0    3
Phx   0   0  10   0   10
Dal  D9 R19/66 P(25-9-2) 34
Phx  D23 R41/223 P(28-20-0) 191
Phx-Johnson 120R

Det  14   0   0  10   24
KC    3  14  12  14   43
Det  D20 R22/136 P(24-12-1) 192
KC   D25 R43/310 P(26-15-0) 256
Det-Sanders 135C; KC-Word 200R

GB    0   0   0  14   14
TB    3  13  10   0   26
GB   D22 R13/36 P(42-25-5) 345
TB   D15 R28/100 P(29-17-0) 256
GB-Sharpe 139C; TB-Majkowski 355P

LARm  0   0   6   3    9
ChiB 14  14   3   7   38
LARm D15 R19/88 P(36-15-1) 179
ChiB D22 R35/154 P(26-18-0) 248

NYG   0   7  14   3   24
Was   3   0  10   7   20
NYG  D13 R25/57 P(22-13-0) 275
Was  D37 R37/162 P(28-15-3) 166
NYG-Baker 109C

SF   14  17   7   7   45
Atl   7  14   0  14   35
SF   D30 R24/57 P(49-32-2) 442
Atl  D21 R14/29 P(47-27-0) 365
SF-Rice 225C, Montana 476P;
Atl-Rison 172C
```

MONDAY, OCTOBER 15

```
Min   7  14   0   3   24
Phi   9   0   6  17   32
Min  D12 R20/34 P(34-17-1) 239
Phi  D16 R34/128 P(34-17-1) 219
Min-Carter 151C; Phi-Barnett 114C
```

THURSDAY, OCTOBER 18

```
NE    0   3   0   7   10
Mia   0  10   0   7   17
NE   D13 R24/49 P(38-18-0) 148
Mia  D15 R27/50 P(34-20-1) 229
```

SUNDAY, OCTOBER 21

```
Den   7  10   0  10   27
Ind   3   7   0   7   17
Den  D23 R34/151 P(30-21-0) 293
Ind  D23 R14/59 P(39-24-1) 304
Den-Jackson 127C, Elway 317P;
Ind-Hester 152C, Trudeau 312P

KC    0   0   0   7    7
Sea   0   3   3  13   19
KC   D15 R19/69 P(34-23-0) 179
Sea  D16 R34/136 P(35-13-4) 124

Pit   7   0   0   0    7
SF    0  10  10   7   27
Pit  D14 R23/97 P(22-13-1) 103
SF   D22 R37/150 P(30-20-2) 154

Dal   0   0   3  14   17
TB    3   7   0   3   13
Dal  D14 R24/78 P(29-13-1) 145
TB   D22 R24/90 P(35-22-3) 241
TB-Carrier 113C

NO    0   0   0   7   10
Hou   0  10  10   3   23
NO   D19 R16/61 P(39-21-0) 259
Hou  D21 R28/103 P(37-23-0) 202

Phi   0   0   0   7    7
Was   0   7   0   6   13
Phi  D16 R18/94 P(42-21-0) 176
Was  D20 R36/121 P(31-14-0) 200

Phx   3   3   6   7   19
NYG   7   3   0  10   20
Phx  D14 R35/125 P(20-11-0) 96
NYG  D18 R31/157 P(25-13-1) 164
Phx-Johnson 108R
```

```
LARd  0  10   7   7   24
SD    3   3   3   0    9
LARd D17 R30/116 P(20-11-1) 173
SD   D16 R31/139 P(28-14-0) 150
LARd-Gary 102R, Ellard 109C,
Everett 302P

NYJ   7  14   3   3   27
Buf   0  17   7   6   30
NYJ  D23 R40/150 P(28-14-1) 192
Buf  D24 R22/129 P(32-19-1) 276
Buf-Reed 116C, Kelly 297P

Atl  10   0   7   7   24
LARm  0  20  14  10   44
Atl  D12 R16/79 P(33-18-1) 236
LARm D26 R32/129 P(43-30-0) 302
Atl-Rison 161C; LARm-Gary 102R,
Ellard 109C, Everett 302P
```

MONDAY, OCTOBER 22

```
Cin   7  10   3  14   34
Cle   3  10   0   0   13
Cin  D15 R37/233 P(17-7-1) 79
Cle  D17 R28/96 P(34-17-2) 157
```

SUNDAY, OCTOBER 28

```
Cin   0   7   3   7   17
Atl  10   7  14   7   38
Cin  D21 R29/84 P(40-22-2) 225
Atl  D17 R28/175 P(18-13-0) 124

Cle   0   0   3  14   17
SF    0  14   3   3   20
Cle  D18 R18/38 P(39-22-2) 236
SF   D20 R28/117 P(37-17-2) 177

Mia  10   3   7   7   27
Ind   0   7   0   0    7
Mia  D23 R37/206 P(29-21-0) 150
Ind  D7 R12/31 P(26-13-3) 101

TB    0   7   3   0   10
SD    7  10   7  17   41
TB   D8 R18/38 P(26-13-4) 119
SD   D17 R42/157 P(27-11-0) 157

ChiB  7  21   0   3   31
Phx   0   7   7   7   21
ChiB D20 R41/223 P(14-9-1) 159
Phx  D19 R19/108 P(31-18-1) 223

Buf   7   7  13   0   27
NE    0   3   0   7   10
Buf  D19 R35/161 P(20-14-0) 192
NE   D17 R24/108 P(31-15-2) 154
Buf-Thomas 136R

Min   0   7   0   0    7
GB    3   7   7   7   24
Min  D16 R21/97 P(41-19-5) 219
GB   D14 R29/126 P(22-11-0) 166
Min-Carter 141C

Phi   7   0   0  14   21
Dal   0   3   3  14   20
Phi  D23 R29/144 P(30-17-0) 160
Dal  D23 R24/130 P(41-22-1) 215
Dal-Novacek 105C

NYJ   0   0  10   7   17
Hou   3   3   6   0   12
NYJ  D13 R21/87 P(23-11-1) 142
Hou  D28 R20/82 P(43-30-0) 343
NYJ-Toon 119C; Hou-Moon 381P

Det   0   7  10  10   27
NO    7   3   0   0   10
Det  D12 R15/48 P(25-16-0) 214
NO   D15 R29/131 P(36-23-4) 138
Det-Clark 127C

Was   0   3   7   0   10
NYG   0  14   0   7   21
Was  D16 R21/64 P(35-23-3) 149
NYG  D16 R34/122 P(25-15-0) 141
```

MONDAY, OCTOBER 29

```
LARm  7   3   0   0   10
Pit  14   3  10  14   41
LARm D13 R23/44 P(35-15-2) 173
Pit  D18 R34/189 P(24-15-1) 156
Pit-Brister 161P
```

SUNDAY, NOVEMBER 4

Buf 7 7 7 21 42
Cle 0 0 0 0 0
Buf D24 R38/102 P(20-15-0) 208
Cle D10 R20/43 P(38-16-2) 191
Buf-Reed 122C

Den 6 10 6 0 22
Min 0 7 10 10 27
Den D19 R34/146 P(25-14-3) 141
Min D15 R32/145 P(13-6-1) 111
Min-Carter 146C

Hou 10 0 0 3 13
LARm 3 14 0 0 17
Hou D20 R12/33 P(43-26-2) 333
LARm D23 R31/118 P(27-19-1) 198
Hou-Moon 343P

LARd 0 0 0 7 7
KC 6 0 0 3 9
LARd D12 R26/96 P(31-10-1) 138
KC D11 R36/124 P(21-10-0) 45

NE 3 7 3 7 20
Phi 6 14 7 21 48
NE D16 R15/41 P(34-14-1) 247
Phi D28 R43/304 P(24-15-0) 210
NE-Fryar 115C;
Phi-Cunningham 124R,
Sherman 113R, Cunningham 240P

SD 7 7 17 0 31
Sea 0 0 7 7 14
SD D15 R40/144 P(24-11-0) 145
Sea D17 R16/65 P(31-15-1) 129

Atl 6 3 0 0 9
Pit 0 0 7 14 21
Atl D21 R32/93 P(38-23-3) 239
Pit D10 R22/119 P(17-11-0) 214

SF 0 7 3 14 24
GB 3 7 0 10 20
SF D17 R20/34 P(40-25-0) 411
GB D17 R23/70 P(33-22-0) 251
SF-Rice 187C, Montana 411P

Was 7 7 7 17 3 41
Det 7 21 10 0 0 38
Was D39 R41/194 P(63-43-3) 482
Det D12 R17/164 P(28-13-0) 187
Was-Clark 132C, Monk 168C,
Sanders 132C, Rutledge 363P;
Det-Sanders 104R

ChiB 0 17 9 0 26
TB 0 0 0 6 6
ChiB D21 R38/187 P(26-15-0) 191
TB D9 R19/92 P(24-10-5) 113

Dal 3 3 0 3 9
NYJ 0 7 3 14 24
Dal D28 R25/95 P(40-25-2) 226
NYJ D15 R23/116 P(25-8-0) 71

Phx 0 3 0 0 3
Mia 3 10 10 0 23
Phx D11 R19/74 P(25-13-1) 131
Mia D20 R38/145 P(25-18-0) 205

NO 7 7 0 7 21
Cin 0 7 0 0 7
NO D21 R52/249 P(17-8-0) 101
Cin D13 R20/136 P(32-15-0) 125
NO-Heyward 122R, Mayes 115R

MONDAY, NOVEMBER 5

NYG 3 14 0 7 24
Ind 0 0 7 0 7
NYG D17 R30/116 P(21-17-1) 158
Ind D11 R17/55 P(37-23-0) 126

SUNDAY, NOVEMBER 11

Atl 3 0 7 14 24
ChiB 0 17 7 6 30
Atl D17 R18/49 P(49-28-4) 227
ChiB D19 R35/100 P(33-14-1) 187
ChiB-Davis 105C

Den 7 0 0 0 7
SD 0 9 3 7 19
Den D15 R24/62 P(30-17-2) 149
SD D17 R32/181 P(27-16-0) 159
SD-Butts 114R

Ind 3 0 3 7 13
NE 7 3 0 0 10
Ind D5 R25/54 P(24-6-0) 101
NE D14 R43/175 P(23-8-0) 72

Mia 3 0 7 7 17
NYJ 0 3 0 0 3
Mia D24 R35/128 P(36-21-1) 192
NYJ D11 R23/88 P(25-12-2) 66

Sea 0 3 7 7 17
KC 0 6 10 0 16
Sea D13 R19/61 P(23-16-0) 236
KC D16 R29/114 P(30-16-0) 115
Sea-Krieg 306P

GB 3 13 3 10 29
LARd 13 3 0 0 16
GB D20 R35/101 P(26-16-1) 155
LARd D12 R18/53 P(23-11-3) 112

Min 0 7 3 7 17
Det 0 0 0 7 7
Min D15 R43/144 P(17-12-1) 156
Det D14 R20/110 P(24-13-4) 127

NYG 3 7 7 14 31
LARm 0 0 7 0 7
NYG D20 R33/115 P(26-19-0) 185
LARm D14 R19/100 P(36-17-3) 174

TB 0 7 0 0 7
NO 0 14 14 7 35
TB D15 R27/89 P(26-16-2) 110
NO D17 R39/211 P(13-7-1) 84
NO-Heyward 155R

Phx 7 0 7 0 14
Buf 0 21 0 24 45
Phx D11 R29/81 P(10-5-1) 46
Buf D20 R52/206 P(16-11-1) 154
Buf-Thomas 112R, Kelly 165P

SF 0 17 0 7 24
Dal 3 3 0 0 6
SF D25 R35/107 P(37-27-1) 281
Dal D9 R15/78 P(24-9-1) 80
SF-Rice 147C

MONDAY, NOVEMBER 12

Was 0 7 0 7 14
Phi 7 0 21 0 28
Was D13 R20/50 P(36-15-2) 150
Phi D16 R41/165 P(22-12-1) 97
Phi-Sherman 124R

SUNDAY, NOVEMBER 18

Hou 7 7 0 21 35
Cle 6 7 3 7 23
Hou D21 R19/94 P(32-24-0) 284
Cle D21 R22/98 P(35-25-2) 263
Hou-Duncan 130C, Moon 322P;
Cle-Slaughter 104C

NE 0 0 0 0 0
Buf 7 0 0 7 14
NE D18 R32/90 P(33-21-2) 196
Buf D14 R30/209 P(15-5-0) 67
Buf-Thomas 165R

NYJ 3 5 6 0 14
Ind 0 0 7 10 17
NYJ D22 R29/121 P(42-27-0) 304
Ind D15 R24/88 P(22-14-1) 225
NYJ-Toon 100C

Pit 0 0 0 3 3
Cin 7 3 14 3 27
Pit D11 R18/94 P(27-14-0) 112
Cin D20 R40/178 P(16-10-1) 134
Cin-Brooks 105R

SD 3 0 7 0 10
KC 10 7 3 7 27
SD D21 R24/99 P(41-21-3) 187
KC D16 R36/132 P(24-11-0) 165

ChiB 0 3 10 0 3 16
Den 3 3 0 7 0 13
ChiB D21 R45/202 P(29-13-0) 139
Den D21 R27/108 P(41-24-1) 222
ChiB-Anderson 110R

Dal 7 14 0 3 24
LARm 7 7 0 7 21
Dal D17 R28/64 P(32-17-1) 295
LARm D18 R31/168 P(25-14-0) 124
Dal-Smith 117C, Aikman 303P;
LARm-Gary 103R

Det 0 0 0 0 0
NYG 7 13 0 0 20
Det D15 R16/75 P(32-20-1) 133
NYG D15 R38/144 P(19-13-0) 170

GB 7 3 0 14 24
Phx 0 7 7 7 21
GB D21 R25/125 P(34-20-2) 250
Phx D21 R27/161 P(30-17-1) 280
GB-Sharpe 157C;
Phx-Johnson 103R, Green 102C,
Jones 117C

Min 7 7 0 10 24
Sea 7 7 0 7 21
Min D14 R24/141 P(33-19-0) 161
Sea D17 R32/101 P(28-13-1) 132

NO 7 3 0 7 17
Was 3 14 14 0 31
NO D24 R24/93 P(39-23-3) 274
Was D24 R29/112 P(39-26-0) 311
NO-Martin 131C; Was-Byner 116R,
Clark 131C, Rypien 311P

TB 0 0 7 0 7
SF 7 10 7 7 31
TB D13 R22/102 P(29-13-1) 78
SF D22 R29/152 P(36-24-1) 241

Phi 0 7 0 17 24
Atl 0 10 0 13 23
Phi D16 R22/88 P(27-16-0) 191
Atl D16 R26/59 P(41-19-0) 256

MONDAY, NOVEMBER 19

LARd 0 10 3 0 13
Mia 0 7 0 3 10
LARd D18 R42/177 P(19-10-0) 116
Mia D16 R12/14 P(36-20-0) 199

THURSDAY, NOVEMBER 22

Den 7 10 3 7 27
Det 21 6 7 6 40
Den D19 R24/73 P(36-24-1) 211
Det D22 R30/173 P(30-18-1) 248
Det-Sanders 147R

Was 0 7 10 0 17
Dal 10 0 7 10 27
Was D20 R15/36 P(54-26-1) 261
Dal D18 R30/162 P(31-20-2) 208
Dal-Smith 132R

SUNDAY, NOVEMBER 25

Ind 7 10 14 3 34
Cin 6 0 14 0 20
Ind D21 R35/182 P(31-21-0) 237
Cin D20 R22/145 P(35-20-1) 236
Ind-Dickerson 143R

KC 0 10 10 7 27
LARd 0 10 7 7 24
KC D16 R31/97 P(21-12-0) 142
LARd D20 R30/155 P(19-10-0) 211
LARd-Anderson 149C

Mia 14 13 3 0 30
Cle 0 3 3 7 13
Mia D20 R33/111 P(29-16-0) 245
Cle D20 R20/109 P(37-17-2) 185

NE 7 7 0 0 14
Phx 7 7 10 10 34
NE D16 R20/114 P(29-17-0) 142
Phx D25 R38/201 P(26-15-0) 162
Phx-Thompson 136R

Pit 0 7 3 14 24
NYJ 0 7 0 0 7
Pit D22 R37/158 P(24-18-2) 175
NYJ D8 R20/73 P(22-10-2) 100

Sea 0 3 0 7 13
SD 0 3 7 0 10
Sea D13 R26/58 P(26-18-0) 175
SD D16 R34/164 P(22-15-2) 140
Sea-Williams 110C; SD-Butts 128R

Atl 0 0 0 7 7
NO 0 3 0 7 10
Atl D9 R17/59 P(31-18-0) 167
NO D19 R33/85 P(37-22-1) 173

LARm 7 14 0 7 28
SF 0 7 10 0 17
LARm D19 R37/111 P(28-17-1) 239
SF D16 R19/66 P(38-23-3) 225
LARm-Anderson 149C

NYG 7 6 0 0 13
Phi 7 3 14 7 31
NYG D16 R14/108 P(40-17-2) 219
Phi D22 R41/176 P(31-17-0) 229
Phi-Byars 128C

TB 0 3 7 0 10
GB 0 7 10 3 20
TB D19 R18/61 P(49-25-0) 261
GB D16 R31/144 P(22-13-0) 187

ChiB 0 3 3 7 13
Min 13 21 7 0 41
ChiB D19 R27/107 P(31-20-0) 159
Min D20 R32/101 P(19-12-0) 145

MONDAY, NOVEMBER 26

Buf 7 7 3 7 24
Hou 7 6 7 7 27
Buf D24 R24/79 P(34-23-1) 210
Hou D21 R28/128 P(22-16-0) 283
Hou-White 125R, Hill 102C,
Moon 300P

SUNDAY, DECEMBER 2

Cin 7 9 0 0 16
Pit 6 0 3 3 12
Cin D17 R42/165 P(14-8-2) 154
Pit D16 R20/79 P(40-18-1) 226

Hou 0 3 0 0 0 3
Sea 0 7 3 0 3 13
Hou D19 R16/56 P(38-24-1) 220
Sea D20 R39/123 P(27-16-1) 158

Mia 0 3 3 14 20
Was 7 14 14 7 42
Mia D13 R10/34 P(37-18-2) 218
Was D29 R47/222 P(28-21-1) 245
Was-Byner 157R

NYJ 3 7 0 7 17
SD 7 10 7 14 38
NYJ D21 R31/145 P(37-19-2) 207
SD D20 R32/189 P(27-14-1) 220
SD-Butts 159R

Ind 10 0 7 0 17
Phx 0 6 0 14 20
Ind D14 R25/109 P(28-13-1) 142
Phx D17 R34/132 P(26-12-0) 144

KC 13 10 7 7 37
NE 0 0 7 0 7
KC D20 R38/150 P(21-15-0) 321
NE D12 R13/64 P(39-20-2) 167
KC-Word 112R, Paige 151R,
DeBerg 331P

LARd 0 7 7 9 23
Den 3 7 0 10 20
LARd D17 R29/148 P(23-16-0) 145
Den D20 R28/141 P(31-20-1) 216
LARd-Jackson 117R, Everett 261P

GB 0 0 0 7 7
Min 3 3 17 0 23
GB D11 R16/59 P(29-16-3) 131
Min D16 R39/137 P(21-11-0) 149

LARm 3 14 14 7 38
Cle 0 0 14 9 23
LARm D27 R36/150 P(29-22-0) 261
Cle D18 R12/37 P(39-23-0) 266
LARm-Everett 261P

NO 3 7 0 3 13
Dal 0 0 7 10 17
NO D14 R27/113 P(27-18-0) 170
Dal D17 R29/113 P(21-15-0) 161

Phi 0 16 0 7 23
Buf 24 0 3 3 30
Phi D19 R31/176 P(25-15-1) 181
Buf D31 R25/59 P(32-19-1) 334
Phi-Barnett 112C; Buf-Lofton 174C,
Kelly 334P

Atl 7 0 0 10 17
TB 0 13 0 10 23
Atl D22 R43/222 P(22-11-3) 152
TB D16 R11/42 P(33-17-1) 331
Atl-Rozier 115R; TB-Drewery 119C,
Testaverde 351P

Det 7 3 0 7 17
ChiB 0 14 0 3 6 23
Det D17 R27/92 P(37-18-1) 204
ChiB D21 R34/164 P(39-23-0) 197

MONDAY, DECEMBER 3

NYG 0 3 0 0 3
SF 0 0 0 7 7
NYG D15 R29/75 P(32-14-0) 146
SF D11 R28/88 P(29-12-0) 152

SUNDAY, DECEMBER 9

Den 0 13 0 7 20
KC 7 3 7 14 31
Den D26 R24/74 P(36-24-1) 300
KC D19 R30/111 P(27-18-0) 254
Den-Elway 328P

Buf 14 3 7 7 31
Ind 0 0 0 7 7
Buf D23 R35/161 P(26-18-0) 247
Ind D12 R22/75 P(25-13-3) 52

Cle 0 7 7 0 14
Hou 14 31 7 6 58
Cle D12 R15/57 P(26-13-2) 138
Hou D34 R34/206 P(38-28-0) 271
Hou-White 116R

Min 5 7 3 0 15
NYG 0 3 7 13 23
Min D18 R33/134 P(29-13-0) 135
NYG D14 R38/115 P(19-8-0) 113

NO 0 3 7 14 24
LARm 0 0 7 0 7
NO D9 R16/108 P(26-13-2) 110
LARm D24 R25/103 P(50-31-2) 341
NO-Fenerty 104R;
LARm-Anderson 123C, Ellard 107C,
Everett 365P

NE 0 3 0 0 3
Pit 3 7 7 7 24
NE D9 R23/56 P(27-14-1) 126
Pit D21 R45/251 P(20-10-1) 166
Pit-Hoge 117R

Sea 7 10 3 0 20
GB 0 0 14 0 14
Sea D14 R37/158 P(18-11-1) 133
GB D19 R10/13 P(53-29-1) 239
Sea-Fenner 112R

Phx 0 10 7 7 24
Atl 3 7 0 3 13
Phx D20 R38/145 P(29-15-1) 216
Atl D15 R21/96 P(31-14-3) 222
Phx-Proehl 102C

Phi 0 10 3 7 20
Mia 10 0 0 10 3 23
Phi D21 R47/257 P(29-18-1) 177
Mia D26 R15/54 P(54-27-0) 351
Mia-Marino 365P

SF 7 7 3 3 20
Cin 3 7 7 0 17
SF D25 R42/202 P(26-19-1) 170
Cin D14 R23/113 P(20-12-1) 102
SF-Rice 101C

ChiB 3 6 0 0 9
Was 0 0 3 7 10
ChiB D17 R27/107 P(33-17-2) 181
Was D15 R31/151 P(25-12-5) 137
Was-Byner 121R

MONDAY, DECEMBER 10

LARd 14 7 14 3 38
Det 21 3 0 7 31
LARd D16 R30/164 P(19-12-2) 186
Det D19 R31/197 P(24-11-1) 171
LARd-Jackson 129R, Gault 101C;
Det-Sanders 176R

SATURDAY, DECEMBER 15

Buf 7 7 0 3 17
NYG 7 3 3 0 13
Buf D13 R24/65 P(26-15-0) 199
NYG D20 R42/157 P(26-15-0) 156
NYG-Hampton 105R

Was 9 10 0 6 25
NE 0 0 7 3 10
Was D13 R45/158 P(11-5-1) 100
NE D13 R22/63 P(24-13-1) 183
Was-Byner 149R

SUNDAY, DECEMBER 16

Cin 7 0 0 0 7
LARd 7 10 7 0 24
Cin D11 R35/109 P(22-9-2) 142
LARd D12 R32/185 P(20-10-0) 163
LARd-Jackson 117R

```
Pit    0   3   0   6    9
NO     0   0   3   3    6
Pit  D14 R31/78  P(25-15-1) 154
NO   D12 R26/100 P(26-8-0)   95

SD     0   3   0   7   10
Den    0   7   7   6   20
SD   D24 R26/92  P(51-26-1) 298
Den  D11 R24/89  P(29-18-0) 233
SD-Harmon 116C, Tolliver 308P

Hou    7   3   7  10   27
KC     0   7   3   0   10
Hou  D22 R17/58  P(45-27-0) 505
KC   D17 R21/101 P(34-17-2) 249
Hou-Jeffires 245C, Moon 527P

Min    0   0  13   0   13
TB     7  16   3   0   26
Min  D20 R16/56  P(49-26-5) 377
TB   D13 R37/199 P(31-13-2) 146
Min-Carter 106C, Jones 162C,
Wilson 374P; TB-Testaverde 105R

Phx    3   0   0   7   10
Dal   13   7   7  14   41
Phx  D9  R21/49  P(35-14-3) 151
Dal  D25 R43/188 P(22-13-1) 166
Dal-Smith 103R

Ind    3   7  13   6   29
NYJ    7   7   0   7   21
Ind  D18 R34/156 P(28-18-0) 217
NYJ  D21 R22/154 P(27-14-0) 146
Ind-Dickerson 117R

Atl    0   3   0   7   10
Cle    0  13   0   0   13
Atl  D16 R20/81  P(36-14-0) 179
Cle  D20 R27/142 P(37-22-1) 206
Atl-Rison 100C

Sea    3   7   0   7   17
Mia    3  14   7   0   24
Sea  D21 R22/83  P(37-21-3) 261
Mia  D20 R31/105 P(29-17-1) 242
Sea-Kane 162C

ChiB   7   0   7   7   21
Det    0  21   7  10   38
ChiB D19 R30/137 P(28-15-1)  88
Det  D20 R24/101 P(27-18-2) 310
ChiB-Anderson 100R; Det-Peete 316P

GB     0   0   0   0    0
Phi    7  10   0  14   31
GB   D14 R17/55  P(33-14-1) 103
Phi  D23 R36/173 P(29-15-0) 249
Phi-Barnett 108C
```

MONDAY, DECEMBER 17
```
SF     3  13   3   7   26
LARm   0   7   3   0   10
SF   D21 R36/173 P(30-15-0) 215
LARm D17 R19/53  P(35-17-2) 213
SF-Carter 124R, Rice 104C
```

SATURDAY, DECEMBER 22
```
LARd  14   0   7   7   28
Min    0  10   0  14   24
LARd D15 R35/125 P(15-10-0) 234
Min  SD  R21/87  P(40-23-1) 314
LARd-Gault 117C, Schroeder 234P;
Min-Carter 127C

Det    7   0   3  14   24
GB     0  10   0   7   17
Det  D17 R24/168 P(28-13-1) 184
GB   D24 R29/80  P(36-20-1) 234
Det-Sanders 133R; GB-West 103C

Was    7   6   5  10   28
Ind    0  14   0  21   35
Was  D28 R45/223 P(37-18-2) 244
Ind  D20 R11/33  P(33-18-0) 216
Was-Byner 154R
```

SUNDAY, DECEMBER 23
```
Den    3   7   2   0   12
Sea    3   7   7   0   17
Den  R6  R30/101 P(35-18-2) 145
Sea  D13 R26/110 P(26-14-1) 103

Cle    0   0   0   0    0
Pit   21  14   0   0   35
Cle  D10 R16/25  P(31-14-1) 133
Pit  D20 R42/197 P(22-12-1) 132
Pit-Foster 100R, Brister 139P
```

```
Hou    0  13   7   0   20
Cin    0  13  14  13   40
Hou  D19 R11/22  P(54-26-2) 282
Cin  D18 R35/222 P(21-11-0) 165
Cin-Brooks 201R

KC     7  14   0   3   24
SD     0   7   7   7   21
KC   D21 R31/117 P(27-19-0) 251
SD   D17 R21/104 P(27-18-2) 151
KC-Word 106R, McNair 111C

NE     0   7   0   0    7
NYJ   14  14   7   7   42
NE   D18 R18/91  P(38-23-1) 210
NYJ  D29 R42/239 P(16-15-0) 226

Dal    0   0   3   0    3
Phi    7   3   0   7   17
Dal  D11 R17/74  P(37-13-4) 125
Phi  D17 R36/178 P(29-17-2)  98

Mia    0   0   7   7   14
Buf    0   7  10   7   24
Mia  D20 R12/35  P(43-24-1) 274
Buf  D25 R47/206 P(21-15-0) 223
Buf-Thomas 154R

LARm   7   3   3   0   13
Atl   10  10   0   0   20
LARm D18 R26/73  P(40-13-2) 155
Atl  D16 R35/111 P(21-13-0) 170
Atl-Rozier 102R

NO     7   3   0   3   13
SF     7   0   3   0   10
NO   D12 R25/84  P(30-10-2) 110
SF   D20 R29/159 P(37-22-0) 175
SF-Young 102R

NYG    3   7   7   7   24
Phx    0   7   7   7   21
NYG  D20 R37/163 P(23-13-0) 185
Phx  D20 R21/84  P(41-23-2) 368
Phx-Green 147C, Jones 130C,
Rosenbach 381P

TB     7   0   0   7   14
ChiB   0  14  10   3   27
TB   D13 R26/99  P(25-11-2) 110
ChiB D24 R35/119 P(38-18-3) 249
```

SATURDAY, DECEMBER 29
```
KC     6   6   6   3   21
ChiB   3   7   0   0   10
KC   D23 R41/123 P(32-25-0) 260
ChiB D6  R20/101 P(23-5-0)   75

Phi    7   6   7   3   23
Phx    0   0  14   7   21
Phi  D24 R37/174 P(27-18-1) 220
Phx  D18 R24/73  P(31-19-1) 264
Phx-Proehl 132C, Rosenbach 301P
```

SUNDAY, DECEMBER 30
```
Buf    0   0   7   7   14
Was    3   6   3  17   29
Buf  D15 R23/105 P(29-15-2) 168
Was  D16 R36/127 P(26-16-1) 172

Cle    0   0  14   0   14
Cin    0  14   0   7   21
Cle  D19 R33/161 P(32-14-3) 184
Cin  D14 R36/151 P(16-10-2) 151
Cle-Slaughter 115C

SD     3   6   0   3   12
LARd   0   7   0  10   17
SD   D14 R35/180 P(22-11-1)  91
LARd D15 R31/114 P(22-11-0) 134
SD-Bernstine 114R

Dal    0   0   0   7    7
Atl    0   7   9  10   26
Dal  D8  R20/47  P(24-10-2) 104
Atl  D15 R46/184 P(15-10-0)  59
Atl-Rozier 155R

Det    0  10   0   0   10
Sea    7   3  10  10   30
Det  D12 R17/87  P(30-12-1) 106
Sea  D27 R33/151 P(33-21-2) 209

GB     3   7   0   3   13
Den    3   3  14   2   22
GB   D14 R16/88  P(23-15-1) 208
Den  D24 R40/185 P(32-16-1) 188
```

```
NYG   10   0   0   3   13
NE     0  10   0   0   10
NYG  D17 R37/213 P(23-12-0) 111
NE   D31 R21/140 P(23-12-1) 118

SF     0   0   3  17   20
Min    3   7   0   7   17
SF   D22 R25/121 P(44-25-1) 281
Min  D20 R20/98  P(38-17-1) 181
SF-Rice 118C

NYJ    0  13   3   0   16
TB     0   7   7   0   14
NYJ  D17 R36/155 P(24-15-0) 162
TB   D16 R17/70  P(27-19-2) 168

Pit    0   0   7   7   14
Hou    7  17   7   3   34
Pit  D17 R19/79  P(26-15-1) 220
Hou  D28 R33/195 P(29-22-1) 232
Pit-Green 105C

Ind    7   7   0   3   17
Mia    7   9   0   7   23
Ind  D20 R24/123 P(30-18-2) 193
Mia  D16 R31/115 P(26-14-0) 192
Ind-Dickerson 110R;
Mia-Smith 108R
```

MONDAY, DECEMBER 31
```
LARm   0   3   0  14   17
NO     7   7   0   6   20
LARm D16 R24/104 P(36-22-0) 275
NO   D14 R30/94  P(26-11-0) 174
LARm-Ellard 130C
```

1991 NFL
SUNDAY, SEPTEMBER 1
```
Phi    0  13   0   7   20
GB     0   0   3   0    3
Phi  D13 R31/70  P(29-18-2) 248
GB   D14 R13/44  P(42-16-3) 184
Phi-Byars 111C

Mia    7   7   3  14   31
Buf    0   7  14  14   35
Mia  D23 R30/146 P(28-17-0) 250
Buf  D33 R33/185 P(41-31-1) 397
Mia-Higgs 146R, Clayton 138C;
Buf-Thomas 165R, Reed 154C,
Thomas 103C, Kelly 381P

SD     0   3   0  17   20
Pit    3   7   6  10   26
SD   D20 R23/95  P(42-20-1) 186
Pit  D16 R31/124 P(25-14-2) 266
Pit-Stone 124C

TB     3   3   0   7   13
NYJ    7   3   0   6   16
TB   D15 R21/87  P(28-12-1) 190
NYJ  D19 R39/119 P(25-16-0) 152

Det    0   0   0   0    0
Was   21  14   7   3   45
Det  D9  R20/93  P(22-8-3)   61
Was  D23 R42/191 P(21-16-1) 201
Was-Clark 107C

Cin    0   7   0   7   14
Den    7  21   7  10   45
Cin  D10 R23/53  P(22-11-3) 193
Den  D25 R43/185 P(29-19-0) 286
Cin-George 301P; Den-Green 116R

Phx   14   3   0   7   24
LARm   0   7   0   7   14
Phx  D10 R34/69  P(18-10-0) 124
LARm D25 R21/99  P(35-25-2) 276
LARm-Delpino 113C, Ellard 116C

Sea    0  17   0   7   24
NO     0   0   7  20   27
Sea  D19 R15/46  P(41-30-2) 302
NO   D13 R20/43  P(29-18-2) 201
Sea-Blades 160C

Dal    3  17   0   6   26
Cle    0   0   7   0    7
Dal  D25 R36/130 P(37-24-0) 265
Cle  D15 R14/32  P(31-22-0) 243
Dal-Smith 112R, Irvin 123C

Min    3   0   3   0    6
ChiB   0   7   0   3   10
Min  D14 R20/86  P(37-21-3) 245
ChiB D17 R33/90  P(24-17-0) 186
```

```
NE     7   3   3   3   16
Ind    7   0   0   0    7
NE   D14 R31/81  P(18-13-0) 125
Ind  D19 R17/66  P(42-27-2) 271
Ind-George 301P

LARd   0   3   7   7   17
Hou    6  10  21  10   47
LARd D11 R17/62  P(31-14-2) 224
Hou  D25 R36/219 P(36-20-0) 240
LARd-Delpino 113C, Ellard 116C,
Graddy 102C; Hou-Pinkett 144R

Atl    3   0   0   0    3
KC     0   0   7   7   14
Atl  D13 R29/141 P(21-9-4) 102
KC   D17 R33/152 P(24-13-0) 139
KC-Okoye 143R
```

MONDAY, SEPTEMBER 2
```
SF     7   0   0   7   14
NYG    3  10   0   3   16
SF   D14 R24/106 P(22-12-1) 152
NYG  D17 R31/130 P(31-17-0) 201
```

SUNDAY, SEPTEMBER 8
```
Hou    0   6   7  17   30
Cin    0   0   7   0    7
Hou  D21 R23/110 P(37-22-1) 315
Cin  D19 R26/131 P(31-20-1) 218
Hou-Pinkett 101R, Moon 315P;
Cin-Brooks 101R

Min    7   0   7   6   20
Atl    3   7   0   9   19
Min  D17 R30/133 P(18-13-1) 157
Atl  D23 R27/159 P(41-27-1) 280
Min-Walker 125R; Atl-Thomas 128C,
Miller 300P

Cle    0   7   3  10   20
NE     0   0   0   0    0
Cle  D16 R37/113 P(22-15-0) 166
NE   D8  R18/72  P(26-12-2)  71

GB     7   0   0   7   14
Det    7   3  10   3   23
GB   D20 R22/76  P(28-20-1) 177
Det  D21 R26/76  P(38-25-0) 271
Det-Clark 143C

LARm   0  10   3   6   19
NYG    0   6   0   7   13
LARm D10 R38/143 P(16-7-0)   74
NYG  D18 R28/116 P(32-17-1) 177
LARm-Delpino 116R

ChiB   7   7   7   0   21
TB    10   3   0   7   20
ChiB D20 R31/100 P(20-13-1) 147
TB   D16 R21/132 P(32-19-0) 125

Ind    0   3   0   3    6
Mia    3   0   7   7   17
Ind  D11 R21/69  P(31-17-0)  81
Mia  D20 R38/148 P(25-14-1) 129
Mia-Higgs 111R

Pit    0  10  17   7   34
Buf   10  14   7  21   52
Pit  D14 R23/152 P(29-15-1) 113
Buf  D31 R40/194 P(43-31-2) 343
Pit-Foster 121R; Buf-Thomas 107R,
Beebe 112C, Reed 118C, Kelly 363P

Phx   13   3   3   7   26
Phi    0  10   0   0   10
Phx  D10 R33/80  P(19-6-1) 217
Phi  D17 R25/78  P(43-25-1) 229

Den    3   3   0   7   13
LARd   0   3   7   6   16
Den  D12 R17/33  P(29-15-0) 214
LARd D16 R38/133 P(19-12-0) 140
LARd-Delpino 116R

SD     7   7   0   0   14
SF     3  14  13   4   34
SD   D19 R27/156 P(34-14-1) 170
SF   D24 R29/114 P(36-26-0) 344
SF-Rice 150C, Young 348P

NO    10   7   0   0   17
KC     0   3   0   7   10
NO   D15 R25/72  P(27-19-0) 187
KC   D17 R21/67  P(43-23-2) 205

NYJ    0   3   0  10   13
Sea    3   0  17   0   20
NYJ  D18 R29/158 P(34-15-3) 158
Sea  D18 R30/97  P(29-18-2) 193
```

MONDAY, SEPTEMBER 9
```
Was    7  13   3  10   33
Dal   14   7   3   7   31
Was  D20 R33/140 P(26-14-1) 192
Dal  D19 R18/125 P(28-20-0) 224
Was-Byner 101R; Dal-Smith 112R
```

SUNDAY, SEPTEMBER 15
```
NYG    0   0  10   7   17
ChiB   0  13   0   7   20
NYG  D21 R33/132 P(36-25-1) 205
ChiB D10 R17/101 P(25-15-1) 206

Phx    0   0   0   0    0
Was    7   7  14   6   34
Phx  D10 R16/55  P(31-16-3) 110
Was  D22 R41/169 P(23-15-0) 181
Was-Byner 109R

Atl    7   3   3   0   13
SD     0   0   7   3   10
Atl  D18 R27/122 P(33-16-1) 195
SD   D13 R27/184 P(22-13-0) 129
Atl-Broussard 101R

NE     0   6   0   0    6
Pit    3   3   0  14   20
NE   D12 R29/82  P(25-11-2)  92
Pit  D16 R21/43  P(29-22-0) 247

TB     0   5   0  10   15
GB     0   5   0  10   15
TB   D17 R21/74  P(30-19-1) 231
GB   D21 R25/97  P(39-20-1) 243

Cin    0   0   0   0    0 
Cle    0   5   6   3   14
Cin  D16 R34/134 P(26-15-0) 134
Cle  D17 R28/84  P(41-20-0) 179
Cin-Brooks 111R;
Cle-Slaughter 107C

Buf    0  10   6   7   23
NYJ    0  10   0   3   20
Buf  D22 R15/64  P(37-27-1) 240
NYJ  D25 R37/168 P(36-22-1) 220
Buf-Thomas 112C

Sea    0   0   0  10   10
Den    0  10   3   3   16
Sea  D17 R16/50  P(50-21-2) 312
Den  D16 R30/99  P(32-19-0) 246
Sea-Blades 107C, Kane 122C,
Kemp 322P

Mia    3   7   0   3   13
Det    3   7   7   0   17
Mia  D17 R20/72  P(34-16-0) 154
Det  D24 R40/189 P(24-13-1) 164
Det-Sanders 143R

Ind    0   0   0   0    0
LARd   0  13   0   3   16
Ind  D16 R22/73  P(32-21-0) 193
LARd D15 R32/115 P(22-13-0) 153

Phi    7  10   0   7   24
Dal    0   0   0   0    0
Phi  D16 R29/55  P(29-18-0) 207
Dal  D8  R14/45  P(25-11-3)  45
Phi-Barnett 111C

LARm   0   0   7   0    7
NO     0   7  10   7   24
LARm D6  R20/77  P(17-6-1)   43
NO   D18 R36/153 P(28-14-1) 181

SF     7   0   0   7   14
Min    0  17   0   0   17
SF   D20 R24/90  P(27-19-1) 265
Min  D17 R30/120 P(24-17-1) 179
```

MONDAY, SEPTEMBER 16
```
KC     0   7   0   0    7
Hou    7   0   7   3   17
KC   D15 R35/145 P(14-9-1)   85
Hou  D22 R20/48  P(38-29-0) 227
```

SUNDAY, SEPTEMBER 22
```
Dal   14   0   0   3   17
Phx    0   6   0   3    9
Dal  D11 R25/181 P(20-12-0) 139
Phx  D20 R31/102 P(38-24-0) 220
Dal-Smith 182R
```

Det 0 7 16 10 **33**
Ind 10 0 0 14 24
Det D25 R39/208 P(25-19-2) 194
Ind D20 R14/4 P(40-29-1) 324
Det-Sanders 179R;
Ind-Johnson 105C, George 348P

Was 3 21 3 7 **34**
Cin 7 3 14 3 27
Was D20 R32/132 P(23-15-1) 212
Cin D21 R25/136 P(37-18-1) 186

LARm 0 10 0 0 10
SF 3 7 3 14 **27**
LARm D15 R21/64 P(37-17-1) 208
SF D20 R26/149 P(31-21-0) 273

GB 0 13 0 0 13
Mia 6 0 0 10 **16**
GB D13 R15/44 P(36-19-1) 219
Mia D11 R25/37 P(32-19-1) 195

Buf 7 0 3 7 **17**
TB 0 0 7 3 10
Buf D19 R25/120 P(35-20-1) 301
TB D22 R42/138 P(37-18-1) 165
Buf-Kelly 322P

Hou 3 3 0 14 20
NE 3 14 0 7 **24**
Hou D18 R16/85 P(44-20-2) 268
NE D23 R30/109 P(34-23-3) 234

Pit 14 0 0 0 14
Phi 7 6 7 3 **23**
Pit D11 R17/66 P(25-12-1) 160
Phi D20 R36/95 P(31-22-1) 279
Pit-Green 158C; Phi-Green 114C

Min 0 0 0 0 0
NO 0 13 0 13 **26**
Min D6 R16/43 P(25-12-2) 108
NO D16 R42/196 P(26-12-1) 147
NO-Fenerty 106R

SD 3 3 3 10 19
Den 3 3 7 14 **27**
SD D17 R32/171 P(29-13-1) 126
Den D18 R29/144 P(28-17-1) 216
SD-Bernstine 103R;
Den-Green 127R

LARd 0 7 7 3 17
Atl 7 0 7 7 **21**
LARd D12 R26/72 P(32-10-2) 87
Atl D16 R26/80 P(31-17-3) 240

Sea 0 0 3 10 13
KC 0 10 0 10 **20**
Sea D24 R34/170 P(30-18-2) 208
KC D16 R25/98 P(32-21-0) 214

Cle 0 0 3 7 10
NYG 3 10 0 0 **13**
Cle D10 R25/78 P(22-13-0) 67
NYG D12 R34/212 P(15-9-0) 52
NYG-Hampton 104R

MONDAY, SEPTEMBER 23

NYJ 3 3 7 0 0 13
ChiB 3 0 0 10 6 **19**
NYJ D24 R40/169 P(30-16-0) 177
ChiB D26 R31/104 P(42-28-0) 289
NYJ-Thomas 125R;
ChiB-Waddle 102C, Harbaugh 303P

SUNDAY, SEPTEMBER 29

KC 7 7 0 0 **14**
SD 7 0 3 3 13
KC D12 R31/86 P(20-11-1) 96
SD D17 R37/156 P(25-10-0) 155
SD-Bernstine 112R

Mia 3 10 3 7 23
NYJ 7 14 3 17 **41**
Mia D19 R13/46 P(40-22-1) 278
NYJ D20 R37/206 P(25-18-0) 221
Mia-Clayton 100C

TB 0 3 0 0 3
Det 14 7 0 10 **31**
TB D16 R20/81 P(39-17-2) 106
Det D21 R40/212 P(22-12-1) 147
Det-Sanders 160R

ChiB 0 6 0 14 20
Buf 0 7 14 14 **35**
ChiB D20 R28/84 P(42-22-1) 269
Buf D22 R34/142 P(29-19-0) 280
Buf-Thomas 117R, Lofton 122C,
Kelly 303P

SF 3 0 0 3 6
LARd 0 6 3 3 **12**
SF D17 R18/126 P(35-18-2) 213
LARd D18 R32/93 P(25-14-0) 127

GB 0 7 0 14 21
LARm 3 17 3 0 **23**
GB D17 R22/88 P(23-14-1) 172
LARm D18 R31/77 P(29-18-1) 233

Den 0 3 7 3 **13**
Min 3 0 3 0 6
Den D17 R33/179 P(22-8-0) 63
Min D15 R26/203 P(28-14-3) 121
Den-Green 158R; Min-Walker 103R

NO 3 7 10 7 **27**
Atl 0 6 0 0 6
NO D17 R38/170 P(29-18-0) 197
Atl D8 R14/33 P(30-14-0) 129

Ind 0 3 0 0 3
Sea 7 10 7 7 **31**
Ind D9 R13/42 P(34-18-2) 95
Sea D16 R44/168 P(17-10-1) 83

NE 0 7 0 3 10
Phx 0 14 0 10 **24**
NE D12 R21/115 P(21-12-0) 99
Phx D24 R39/135 P(29-17-1) 300
Phx-Jones 145C, Proehl 107C,
Tupa 312P

NYG 0 3 3 10 16
Dal 0 7 7 7 **21**
NYG D26 R26/119 P(34-28-1) 368
Dal D20 R22/58 P(27-20-0) 269
NYG-Ingram 142C, Hostetler 368P

MONDAY, SEPTEMBER 30

Phi 0 0 0 0 0
Was 0 10 3 10 **23**
Phi D4 R15/54 P(22-9-3) 35
Was D17 R41/173 P(23-13-2) 184

SUNDAY, OCTOBER 6

Mia 0 17 0 3 **20**
NE 7 0 0 3 10
Mia D19 R24/56 P(38-25-0) 314
NE D14 R24/55 P(31-17-2) 140
Mia-Marino 321P

Dal 0 14 3 3 **20**
GB 0 3 7 7 17
Dal D25 R35/124 P(41-31-0) 287
GB D15 R14/60 P(35-18-2) 199
Dal-Smith 122R, Novacek 121C

Sea 7 0 6 0 **13**
Cin 0 7 0 0 7
Sea D15 R27/103 P(31-16-3) 202
Cin D20 R33/124 P(38-18-2) 240
Cin-Brown 117C

SD 0 14 0 7 **21**
LARd 3 7 3 0 13
SD D17 R36/158 P(22-12-0) 100
LARd D16 R22/99 P(23-15-2) 178

Den 0 0 7 7 14
Hou 7 28 0 7 **42**
Den D23 R23/91 P(47-27-1) 272
Hou D17 R20/51 P(31-19-1) 327
Den-Jackson 111C, Elway 301P;
Hou-Givins 151C, Moon 334P

NYJ 0 14 0 3 **17**
Cle 0 0 14 0 14
NYJ D18 R28/76 P(24-20-0) 211
Cle D14 R23/106 P(25-16-0) 131

Was 0 10 0 10 **20**
ChiB 0 0 7 0 7
Was D12 R26/75 P(31-18-1) 168
ChiB D19 R28/120 P(41-17-3) 199
ChiB-Morris 106C

Phi 0 0 13 0 13
TB 0 0 0 14 **14**
Phi D12 R41/117 P(20-9-2) 54
TB D12 R22/60 P(29-12-3) 133

Pit 0 0 7 14 **21**
Ind 0 3 0 0 3
Pit D17 R28/120 P(17-14-2) 172
Ind D15 R24/42 P(28-22-0) 147

Min 7 7 3 3 20
Det 0 3 0 21 **24**
Min D15 R29/97 P(23-10-0) 105
Det D25 R27/124 P(38-24-1) 276
Det-Sanders 116R

Phx 3 0 6 0 9
NYG 14 3 0 3 **20**
Phx D21 R19/93 P(40-23-2) 214
NYG D19 R36/168 P(18-14-0) 200
NYG-Hampton 137R

MONDAY, OCTOBER 7

Buf 0 6 0 0 6
KC 3 10 17 3 **33**
Buf D11 R14/65 P(23-17-0) 146
KC D26 R54/239 P(23-16-0) 150
KC-Okoye 122R, Williams 103R

SUNDAY, OCTOBER 13

SD 7 7 7 3 24
LARm 0 16 7 7 **30**
SD D17 R21/89 P(33-21-1) 298
LARm D21 R27/80 P(25-19-0) 204
SD-Miller 149C, Friesz 306P

Atl 14 6 13 6 **39**
SF 0 14 13 7 34
Atl D19 R27/160 P(28-16-0) 208
SF D24 R25/94 P(38-22-3) 343
Atl-Broussard 104R; SF-Rice 138C,
Young 348P

LARd 0 0 7 13 3 **23**
Sea 3 14 0 3 0 20
LARd D25 R27/146 P(52-28-2) 274
Sea D12 R31/119 P(25-10-3) 145

Phx 0 0 0 7 7
Min 7 13 7 7 **34**
Phx D17 R16/50 P(36-21-0) 204
Min D25 R34/131 P(31-23-0) 254
Min-Carter 118C

Cin 10 0 13 0 23
Dal 0 21 0 14 **35**
Cin D17 R30/174 P(31-17-2) 178
Dal D19 R30/112 P(22-14-2) 264
Cin-Green 124R; Dal-Irvin 148C

Ind 0 6 0 0 6
Buf 14 14 7 7 **42**
Ind D20 R29/66 P(37-23-2) 174
Buf D23 R38/276 P(12-9-1) 120
Buf-Davis 108R, Thomas 117R

Hou 0 13 0 10 **23**
NYJ 10 0 3 7 20
Hou D25 R15/27 P(50-35-2) 409
NYJ D21 R21/43 P(42-24-1) 236
Hou-Jeffires 186C, Moon 423P

Cle 7 0 10 0 17
Was 7 14 7 14 **42**
Cle D17 R22/88 P(37-26-1) 301
Was D23 R36/208 P(22-16-0) 190
Was-Ervins 133R, Monk 106C

Mia 0 0 0 7 7
KC 14 14 14 0 **42**
Mia D19 R20/92 P(36-18-1) 253
KC D25 R43/221 P(18-14-0) 231
Mia-Martin 104C; KC-Okoye 153R

NO 0 3 7 3 **13**
Phi 0 6 0 0 6
NO D10 R30/64 P(25-10-2) 98
Phi D11 R17/53 P(35-18-5) 151

MONDAY, OCTOBER 14

NYG 7 6 7 3 **23**
Pit 0 0 3 17 20
NYG D17 R38/197 P(25-14-0) 114
Pit D20 R18/148 P(37-17-1) 229

THURSDAY, OCTOBER 17

ChiB 0 7 0 3 **10**
GB 0 0 0 0 0
ChiB D18 R41/161 P(29-18-1) 137
GB D5 R19/91 P(25-7-1) 50

SUNDAY, OCTOBER 20

Cle 0 3 7 14 6 **30**
SD 3 0 14 7 0 24
Cle D17 R21/70 P(42-26-0) 294
SD D29 R30/132 P(54-33-2) 305
SD-Friesz 321P

Atl 7 3 0 0 10
Phx 3 0 10 3 **16**
Atl D15 R18/107 P(35-13-4) 211
Phx D16 R40/168 P(23-9-1) 98

Hou 0 7 3 7 **17**
Mia 3 7 3 0 13
Hou D23 R31/120 P(35-21-3) 162
Mia D16 R17/57 P(40-19-3) 218

Det 0 3 0 0 3
SF 0 21 14 0 **35**
Det D10 R8/24 P(27-14-1) 183
SF D29 R54/233 P(23-21-0) 272
SF-Henderson 104R

TB 0 0 7 0 7
NO 7 9 0 7 **23**
TB D12 R16/46 P(31-17-2) 173
NO D17 R32/79 P(31-19-2) 205

Sea 3 14 3 7 **27**
Pit 0 0 7 0 7
Sea D18 R30/65 P(31-25-0) 259
Pit D12 R15/78 P(22-14-1) 162
Sea-Kane 102C

LARm 7 3 7 0 17
LARd 7 0 3 10 **20**
LARm D21 R21/53 P(35-22-2) 294
LARd D18 R24/84 P(26-15-1) 255
LARm-Delpino 118C, Everett 300P

KC 3 3 3 7 16
Den 0 13 3 3 **19**
KC D22 R29/119 P(36-21-0) 209
Den D14 R24/95 P(27-14-0) 229

Min 0 10 3 10 0 23
NE 7 7 0 9 3 **26**
Min D29 R27/141 P(63-35-0) 303
NE D20 R37/97 P(32-22-1) 302
Min-Carter 114C, Gannon 317P;
NE-Fryar 161C, Millen 326P

NYJ 7 7 3 0 **17**
Ind 0 6 0 0 6
NYJ D19 R41/138 P(19-14-1) 193
Ind D11 R17/91 P(22-14-0) 79

MONDAY, OCTOBER 21

Cin 3 0 10 3 16
Buf 0 14 14 7 **35**
Cin D24 R37/187 P(35-23-1) 224
Buf D19 R27/95 P(27-18-3) 392
Cin-Green 141R; Buf-Lofton 220C,
Kelly 392P

SUNDAY, OCTOBER 27

SF 7 7 3 6 **23**
Phi 0 7 0 0 7
SF D14 R40/137 P(15-10-0) 85
Phi D16 R14/29 P(33-21-2) 206

Pit 0 7 0 7 14
Cle 3 7 7 0 **17**
Pit D18 R23/75 P(35-19-2) 207
Cle D19 R27/83 P(29-21-0) 179

Cin 0 3 0 0 3
Hou 13 10 6 6 **35**
Cin D8 R17/37 P(33-15-2) 146
Hou D26 R24/110 P(44-28-2) 376
Hou-Hill 129C

Dal 0 10 0 0 10
Det 3 7 10 14 **34**
Dal D22 R20/74 P(47-31-2) 341
Det D13 R28/72 P(19-12-0) 136
Dal-Irvin 143C, Novacek 131C,
Aikman 331P

Was 0 0 7 10 **17**
NYG 10 3 0 0 13
Was D16 R32/95 P(26-12-1) 159
NYG D15 R33/134 P(21-14-1) 137

Den 3 3 0 3 **9**
NE 0 3 0 3 6
Den D14 R30/102 P(27-15-0) 141
NE D15 R29/141 P(25-17-0) 146

SD 0 6 3 0 9
Sea 7 3 0 10 **20**
SD D19 R31/128 P(41-27-0) 192
Sea D15 R25/75 P(21-13-2) 127

ChiB 0 6 7 7 **20**
NO 7 3 7 0 17
ChiB D11 R31/142 P(22-5-2) 36
NO D13 R23/51 P(39-27-1) 262
NO-Turner 179C

Min 0 7 7 14 **28**
Phx 0 0 0 0 0
Min D23 R41/212 P(26-17-1) 142
Phx D7 R13/36 P(35-15-2) 122

LARm 0 0 0 14 14
Atl 7 14 10 0 **31**
LARm D13 R18/100 P(29-10-1) 109
Atl D16 R35/121 P(24-19-0) 278
Atl-Haynes 110C

GB 10 3 7 7 **27**
TB 0 0 0 0 0
GB D13 R27/59 P(28-19-1) 185
TB D12 R15/35 P(38-14-5) 135

MONDAY, OCTOBER 28

LARd 11 7 3 0 21
KC 0 7 3 14 **24**
LARd D15 R25/73 P(27-13-3) 249
KC D19 R32/119 P(30-19-1) 148
LARd-Fernandez 107C

SUNDAY, NOVEMBER 3

Pit 3 7 0 3 13
Den 0 17 3 0 **20**
Pit D19 R31/146 P(33-18-1) 163
Den D17 R31/144 P(23-10-1) 130
Den-Lewis 111R

Hou 0 6 0 7 0 13
Was 0 3 3 7 3 **16**
Hou D16 R16/25 P(44-25-2) 242
Was D19 R35/154 P(34-21-1) 195
Was-Byner 112R

NE 0 3 7 7 17
Buf 3 3 7 9 **22**
NE D17 R31/122 P(30-14-1) 143
Buf D20 R41/153 P(28-14-2) 235
NE-Russell 106R;
Buf-Thomas 126R, Reed 121C

GB 3 3 7 3 0 16
NYJ 3 10 0 3 3 **19**
GB D15 R31/91 P(30-18-1) 171
NYJ D17 R31/121 P(29-16-0) 172
NYJ-Toon 109C

Mia 10 0 0 0 **10**
Ind 0 3 3 0 6
Mia D15 R27/67 P(37-21-0) 231
Ind D15 R24/95 P(34-18-1) 183

NO 10 7 0 7 **24**
LARm 3 7 0 7 17
NO D19 R30/90 P(33-17-1) 269
LARm D16 R23/55 P(31-18-3) 326
LARm-Everett 346P

TB 0 3 3 7 13
Min 0 0 14 14 **28**
TB D16 R32/126 P(22-10-3) 105
Min D18 R30/162 P(28-19-0) 153
Min-Allen 127R

Phx 0 7 0 0 7
Dal 10 0 7 10 **27**
Phx D16 R24/109 P(34-15-2) 130
Dal D22 R35/121 P(23-17-2) 165

SF 0 7 0 7 14
Atl 0 0 0 17 **17**
SF D19 R29/129 P(35-20-2) 267
Atl D11 R30/75 P(31-12-1) 127
SF-Taylor 127C

Det 0 10 0 0 10
ChiB 3 0 10 7 **20**
Det D16 R19/72 P(40-19-2) 203
ChiB D16 R33/104 P(31-17-0) 187

Cle 0 14 7 0 21
Cin 3 10 7 3 **23**
Cle D22 R29/83 P(31-19-0) 280
Cin D19 R33/162 P(30-18-1) 185
Cle-Slaughter 107C; Cin-Green 135R

MONDAY, NOVEMBER 4

NYG 0 0 7 0 7
Phi 0 13 7 10 **30**
NYG D9 R21/53 P(19-10-0) 134
Phi D19 R37/137 P(26-16-0) 222

SUNDAY, NOVEMBER 10

NE 3 3 7 7 20
Mia 7 10 3 10 **30**
NE D18 R28/84 P(26-20-1) 239
Mia D20 R24/69 P(29-19-1) 255

Det 7 0 7 7 21
TB 7 16 7 0 **30**
Det D18 R24/119 P(30-20-2) 226
TB D19 R34/181 P(22-12-0) 165
Det-Sanders 118R, Perriman 127C;
TB-Cobb 139R

Sea 0 0 0 14 14
SD 7 7 0 3 **17**
Sea D18 R13/37 P(39-29-1) 350
SD D16 R28/102 P(25-17-0) 213
Sea-Blades 131C, Krieg 379P;
SD-Miller 124C

SF 3 0 0 0 3
NO 0 7 3 0 **10**
SF D15 R24/114 P(32-15-0) 102
NO D10 R32/82 P(25-10-1) 109

Buf 0 14 10 10 **34**
GB 7 3 7 7 24
Buf D27 R37/147 P(36-17-0) 223
GB D23 R23/84 P(38-23-2) 297
Buf-Thomas 106R, Lofton 114C;
GB-Sharpe 133C, Tomczak 317P

Ind 0 7 21 0 **28**
NYJ 7 7 7 7 27
Ind D16 R22/43 P(26-16-2) 239
NYJ D24 R32/118 P(36-23-0) 318
Ind-Hester 100C; NYJ-O'Brien 329P

Atl 3 0 14 0 17
Was 7 21 7 21 **56**
Atl D12 R18/62 P(36-14-3) 209
Was D20 R36/108 P(32-17-0) 451
Atl-Haynes 105C; Was-Clark 203C,
Monk 164C, Rypien 442P

Pit 0 6 7 14 **33**
Cin 10 7 0 10 27
Pit D18 R22/58 P(39-24-0) 223
Cin D25 R24/70 P(43-32-1) 336
Pit-O'Donnell 309P;
Cin-McGee 101C, Esiason 361P

NYG 7 7 7 0 **21**
Phx 0 7 0 7 14
NYG D17 R38/180 P(21-12-0) 110
Phx D14 R20/55 P(28-17-2) 189

Dal 10 3 3 7 23
Hou 0 10 3 10 **26**
Dal D21 R13/50 P(39-24-0) 241
Hou D33 R28/158 P(56-41-0) 425
Hou-Moon 432P

KC 7 7 6 7 **27**
LARm 0 14 0 6 20
KC D22 R30/164 P(26-17-0) 190
LARm D20 R26/111 P(37-26-1) 319
LARm-Ellard 160C, Everett 329P

LARd 0 0 10 7 **17**
Den 3 7 0 6 16
LARd D13 R28/118 P(20-13-0) 183
Den D23 R39/200 P(31-13-2) 183
LARd-Ellard 160C, Everett 329P;
Den-Green 103R

Phi 0 17 6 9 **32**
Cle 16 14 0 0 30
Phi D24 R28/97 P(43-26-1) 321
Cle D16 R11/25 P(33-14-1) 233
Phi-Barnett 146C, McMahon 341P

MONDAY, NOVEMBER 11
ChiB 0 17 3 14 **34**
Min 3 0 7 0 10
ChiB D28 R43/178 P(27-18-1) 180
Min D15 R20/87 P(30-19-1) 168

SUNDAY, NOVEMBER 17
ChiB 7 3 14 7 **31**
Ind 7 3 0 7 17
ChiB D25 R32/175 P(32-18-1) 273
Ind D14 R19/111 P(33-16-0) 140
ChiB-Muster 101R;
Ind-Brooks 106C

Was 7 10 10 14 **41**
Pit 0 0 0 14 14
Was D23 R37/97 P(29-22-0) 365
Pit D16 R14/41 P(36-23-1) 241
Was-Monk 130C, Rypien 325P

Phx 0 7 0 3 10
SF 0 7 0 7 **14**
Phx D13 R19/64 P(26-14-0) 112
SF D22 R29/88 P(35-20-0) 169

NO 7 14 0 0 21
SD 7 7 0 10 **24**
NO D17 R27/92 P(34-21-1) 193
SD D15 R23/146 P(30-16-1) 159

Min 7 7 7 14 **35**
GB 14 7 0 0 21
Min D32 R47/231 P(30-19-0) 212
GB D18 R14/29 P(40-20-2) 271

Sea 0 7 0 0 7
LARd 3 21 0 7 **31**
Sea D13 R7/23 P(38-24-0) 162
LARd D20 R34/116 P(20-16-0) 223
LARd-Horton 123C, Everett 308P

Den 3 7 14 0 **24**
KC 0 10 3 7 20
Den D14 R35/172 P(20-9-0) 102
KC D21 R28/125 P(38-20-4) 292
Den-Green 133R

TB 0 0 0 7 7
Atl 0 33 3 7 **43**
TB D15 R16/42 P(31-17-2) 207
Atl D20 R31/132 P(25-15-0) 226
TB-Carrier 104C

Dal 0 3 6 0 9
NYG 6 10 6 0 **22**
Dal D14 R19/101 P(25-16-0) 142
NYG D21 R41/138 P(22-14-0) 177

LARm 3 0 7 0 10
Det 0 7 0 14 **21**
LARm D18 R19/26 P(45-26-1) 308
Det D16 R32/68 P(25-15-0) 181
LARm-Everett 308P

Cin 0 7 0 3 10
Phi 0 7 0 10 **17**
Cin D17 R25/74 P(28-17-3) 124
Phi D17 R30/70 P(33-18-1) 195
Phi-Barnett 108C

NYJ 7 7 7 7 **28**
NE 0 0 0 21 21
NYJ D25 R29/113 P(41-26-0) 309
NE D24 R23/75 P(44-30-1) 351
NYJ-Toon 127C, O'Brien 309P;
NE-Fryar 143C, Millen 372P

Cle 7 7 3 7 24
Hou 0 7 14 14 **35**
Cle D17 R24/49 P(34-21-1) 262
Hou D25 R15/45 P(44-31-1) 395
Cle-Hoard 107C; Hou-Hill 144C,
Moon 399P

MONDAY, NOVEMBER 18
Buf 10 10 14 7 **41**
Mia 3 10 7 7 27
Buf D27 R50/262 P(28-20-0) 171
Mia D25 R17/75 P(42-23-2) 317
Buf-Thomas 135R;
Mia-Marino 326P

SUNDAY, NOVEMBER 24
Mia 0 3 0 10 3 **16**
ChiB 7 3 3 0 0 13
Mia D17 R26/103 P(30-16-2) 172
ChiB D23 R36/124 P(40-25-0) 204

Det 7 3 14 10 **34**
Min 0 7 0 7 14
Det D20 R38/267 P(26-13-0) 116
Min D20 R21/90 P(31-20-3) 230
Det-Sanders 220R; Min-Carter 111C

Ind 0 3 0 7 10
GB 7 0 7 0 **14**
Ind D16 R28/72 P(40-21-1) 117
GB D11 R30/164 P(17-5-1) 28

Dal 0 14 0 10 **24**
Was 7 0 0 14 21
Dal D23 R38/122 P(32-20-1) 277
Was D15 R17/50 P(33-17-1) 212
Dal-Smith 132R, Harper 101C,
Irvin 130C

Den 0 0 10 0 0 10
Sea 3 3 0 0 7 **13**
Den D12 R32/98 P(23-13-2) 112
Sea D11 R30/146 P(19-9-2) 53
Sea-Williams 109R

Atl 0 3 7 10 3 **23**
NO 0 7 6 7 0 20
Atl D12 R28/91 P(31-15-3) 240
NO D20 R43/164 P(35-16-1) 255
Atl-Haynes 187C; NO-McAfee 138R,
Turner 115C

Hou 7 0 0 7 14
Pit 6 10 7 3 **26**
Hou D21 R17/24 P(48-24-5) 307
Pit D16 R39/139 P(29-12-1) 155
Hou-Jeffires 122C, Moon 324P

NYG 7 0 7 7 **21**
TB 0 7 0 7 14
NYG D15 R22/78 P(28-16-0) 158
TB D13 R30/139 P(27-16-2) 88
TB-Cobb 110R

SD 0 3 0 0 3
NYJ 14 0 3 7 **24**
SD D18 R28/186 P(31-16-2) 105
NYJ D21 R32/138 P(32-17-1) 176

KC 0 0 3 12 15
Cle 0 10 10 0 **20**
KC D21 R24/78 P(50-30-2) 311
Cle D9 R19/123 P(24-12-1) 114
KC-Harry 159C, DeBerg 319P

Buf 3 7 3 0 13
NE 0 9 0 7 **16**
Buf D20 R29/140 P(44-26-4) 168
NE D18 R30/82 P(40-21-2) 230
NE-Fryar 134C

Phi 20 0 7 7 **34**
Phx 7 7 0 0 14
Phi D16 R38/135 P(25-10-3) 154
Phx D14 R18/68 P(40-19-4) 168

LARd 7 21 7 3 **38**
Cin 0 7 0 7 14
LARd D14 R34/157 P(10-4-0) 19
Cin D21 R33/165 P(31-17-3) 114

MONDAY, NOVEMBER 25
SF 16 14 0 3 **33**
LARm 0 3 7 0 10
SF D23 R30/81 P(33-18-1) 306
LARm D18 R20/35 P(35-22-0) 285
SF-Taylor 121C, Bono 306P

THURSDAY, NOVEMBER 28
Pit 0 0 3 7 10
Dal 7 3 0 10 **20**
Pit D17 R21/65 P(36-17-0) 134
Dal D20 R35/116 P(25-14-0) 181
Dal-Smith 109R, Irvin 157C

ChiB 0 6 0 0 6
Det 10 0 3 3 **16**
ChiB D18 R21/88 P(48-27-4) 231
Det D11 R26/100 P(27-9-1) 108

SUNDAY, DECEMBER 1
NYG 7 7 3 7 24
Cin 3 7 7 10 **27**
NYG D22 R24/69 P(44-26-0) 278
Cin D15 R24/47 P(30-17-0) 204
NYG-Ingram 116C

NO 0 10 14 0 24
SF 0 14 3 21 **38**
NO D22 R26/98 P(42-25-0) 317
SF D22 R18/40 P(41-27-0) 343
NO-Turner 132C, Walsh 317P;
SF-Rice 154C, Bono 347P

NYJ 7 3 3 0 13
Buf 7 3 7 7 **24**
NYJ D21 R26/124 P(31-16-2) 172
Buf D24 R31/152 P(39-22-2) 242
Buf-Thomas 124R, Lofton 109C

TB 7 0 0 7 14
Mia 6 24 6 3 **33**
TB D19 R16/59 P(39-21-1) 199
Mia D25 R36/171 P(32-20-0) 297
TB-Dawsey 100C; Mia-Higgs 131C,
Martin 106C, Marino 307P

NE 0 0 3 0 3
Den 10 0 7 3 **20**
NE D14 R16/50 P(36-19-2) 202
Den D19 R37/116 P(25-18-0) 209

LARd 3 6 0 0 **9**
SD 0 0 7 0 7
LARd D14 R34/161 P(29-12-3) 122
SD D12 R28/75 P(27-12-1) 124

KC 3 6 3 7 **19**
Sea 0 3 0 3 6
KC D21 R43/157 P(26-17-0) 154
Sea D13 R15/47 P(25-16-1) 226

Was 7 0 14 6 **27**
LARm 3 3 0 0 6
Was D15 R27/84 P(24-15-1) 269
LARm D16 R26/97 P(40-19-0) 181

Cle 3 28 0 0 **31**
Ind 0 0 0 0 0
Cle D19 R31/138 P(23-18-0) 177
Ind D11 R22/143 P(21-10-2) 28
Ind-Dickerson 117R

GB 7 14 0 10 31
Atl 7 0 7 21 **35**
GB D22 R30/132 P(35-22-0) 261
Atl D23 R20/79 P(37-20-1) 181
Atl-Rison 124C

MONDAY, DECEMBER 2
Phi 0 0 0 10 3 **13**
Hou 0 3 3 0 0 6
Phi D14 R26/94 P(37-22-1) 146
Hou D15 R11/21 P(46-24-0) 226

SUNDAY, DECEMBER 8
Ind 0 14 3 0 0 17
NE 0 0 14 6 3 **23**
Ind D13 R33/55 P(24-15-0) 147
NE D22 R32/123 P(40-21-2) 277
NE-McMurtry 119C, Millen 330P

Pit 0 3 3 0 6
Hou 7 3 7 14 **31**
Pit D14 R23/85 P(30-16-1) 147
Hou D23 R22/117 P(38-24-1) 233

SD 0 14 0 3 0 17
KC 0 0 10 7 3 **20**
SD D23 R40/158 P(37-19-1) 208
KC D21 R23/104 P(41-24-2) 245

Den 0 7 0 10 **17**
Cle 7 0 0 0 7
Den D17 R35/90 P(29-16-1) 200
Cle D9 R19/101 P(24-12-1) 80

Buf 7 7 0 13 3 **30**
LARd 10 10 7 0 0 27
Buf D25 R21/79 P(52-33-1) 330
LARd D18 R45/136 P(21-11-2) 250
Buf-Reed 107C, Kelly 347P;
LARd-Brown 106C

Atl 10 14 7 0 **31**
LARm 0 7 0 7 14
Atl D21 R29/84 P(31-20-1) 275
LARm D15 R30/109 P(26-12-1) 165
Atl-Haynes 112C

Was 0 0 14 6 **20**
Phx 0 14 0 0 14
Was D21 R33/135 P(34-22-0) 249
Phx D11 R22/66 P(27-14-2) 128
Was-Byner 116R

Min 10 10 3 3 **26**
TB 3 7 7 7 24
Min D22 R40/296 P(24-12-0) 140
TB D20 R16/45 P(41-23-0) 328
Min-Walker 126R; TB-Carrier 110C,
Testaverde 330P

GB 3 10 0 0 13
ChiB 3 14 6 4 **27**
GB D17 R22/62 P(39-22-1) 199
ChiB D22 R24/101 P(25-16-1) 195

NO 0 7 7 0 14
Dal 7 3 3 10 **23**
NO D22 R19/99 P(40-26-1) 229
Dal D22 R31/117 P(29-17-0) 184
Dal-Smith 112R, Irvin 101C

Phi 0 6 6 7 **19**
NYG 7 7 0 0 14
Phi D20 R35/151 P(30-16-2) 173
NYG D10 R22/67 P(24-7-2) 84

NYJ 14 0 7 0 21
Det 14 10 10 0 **34**
NYJ D19 R28/132 P(37-20-2) 154
Det D15 R28/101 P(31-18-1) 235
Det-Sanders 114R

SF 0 10 7 7 **24**
Sea 6 3 7 6 22
SF D17 R36/150 P(44-25-2) 261
Sea D17 R36/150 P(28-16-0) 128
SF-Taylor 113C

MONDAY, DECEMBER 9
Cin 0 6 0 7 13
Mia 7 10 3 17 **37**
Cin D19 R30/159 P(28-16-0) 196
Mia D21 R25/92 P(33-24-0) 266
Mia-Duper 134C

SATURDAY, DECEMBER 14
TB 0 0 0 0 0
ChiB 6 7 7 7 **27**
TB D7 R17/52 P(18-8-3) 54
ChiB D23 R49/182 P(14-7-0) 72

KC 0 0 7 7 14
SF 7 7 7 7 **28**
KC D17 R22/137 P(38-15-1) 173
SF D24 R30/177 P(38-26-0) 231
KC-Word 115R

SUNDAY, DECEMBER 15
Phx 0 3 10 6 19
Den 7 3 7 7 **24**
Phx D13 R25/73 P(32-15-0) 158
Den D22 R30/122 P(33-19-3) 243

NE 3 0 3 0 **6**
NYJ 3 0 0 0 3
NE D14 R34/126 P(20-11-1) 100
NYJ D18 R27/109 P(38-19-0) 159
NE-Russell 112R

Dal 5 0 3 17 **25**
Phi 0 10 0 3 13
Dal D11 R29/72 P(31-9-0) 138
Phi D16 R27/111 P(37-18-2) 129

Cin 0 7 3 0 10
Pit 10 0 0 7 **17**
Cin D13 R26/75 P(26-14-2) 120
Pit D18 R36/149 P(28-15-2) 177

Hou 0 10 0 7 **17**
Cle 7 0 0 0 7
Hou D20 R19/83 P(40-26-1) 247
Cle D22 R21/101 P(40-28-1) 239

NYG 3 7 7 0 17
Was 3 17 7 7 **34**
NYG D20 R20/78 P(41-23-2) 259
Was D18 R36/151 P(23-12-0) 264
Was-Clark 129C

Sea 0 0 0 13 13
Atl 2 10 7 7 **26**
Sea D14 R12/33 P(37-22-3) 202
Atl D14 R33/131 P(27-14-0) 140

Buf 21 7 0 7 **35**
Ind 0 0 0 7 7
Buf D22 R37/156 P(17-13-0) 159
Ind D18 R29/133 P(31-18-3) 195

Mia 3 7 13 7 30
SD 10 0 28 0 **38**
Mia D23 R20/75 P(41-26-1) 273
SD D20 R32/198 P(25-17-0) 170
Mia-Duper 106C;
SD-Bernstine 104R

LARm 7 0 0 7 14
Min 0 10 3 7 **20**
LARm D21 R21/63 P(43-26-4) 254
Min D20 R36/122 P(20-13-0) 141
LARm-Anderson 103C

Det 7 0 0 14 **21**
GB 3 7 0 7 17
Det D14 R28/94 P(29-14-0) 112
GB D19 R34/160 P(40-18-1) 207

MONDAY, DECEMBER 16
LARd 0 0 0 0 0
NO 3 0 7 17 **27**
LARd D6 R15/71 P(17-7-1) 46
NO D26 R32/161 P(39-28-0) 314
NO-Early 127C, Hebert 320P

SATURDAY, DECEMBER 21

```
GB    10   0  10   7   27
Min    0   0   0   7    7
GB  D16 R40/108 P(19-11-0) 80
Min D12 R17/47  P(39-20-1) 225
Min-Carter 112C

Hou    0   0   6  14   20
NYG    7  10   7   0   24
Hou D23 R18/123 P(36-22-0) 222
NYG D21 R40/193 P(17-15-0) 190
NYG-Hampton 140R
```

SUNDAY, DECEMBER 22

```
Was    3  10   6   3   22
Phi    7   0   0  17   24
Was D18 R36/87 P(43-16-1) 200
Phi D14 R17/50 P(40-19-1) 157

KC     7  10   0  10   27
LARd   7   0   0  14   21
KC   D30 R48/206 P(20-14-0) 262
LARd D17 R13/70  P(40-23-0) 243
KC-Word 152R, Birden 188C

Det    0   0  14   3   17
Buf    0   7   0   7   14
Det D22 R31/111 P(36-17-2) 245
Buf D14 R33/151 P(25-15-1) 124
Det-Sanders 108R; Buf-Davis 118R

LARm   3   6   0   0    9
Sea    0   7  16   0   23
LARm D12 R26/96 P(38-16-2) 131
Sea  D13 R29/97 P(27-13-2) 156

NO     0  13   7   7   27
Phx    3   0   0   0    3
NO  D12 R28/95 P(24-12-1) 95
Phx D18 R22/72 P(36-19-5) 173

Atl   14   3  10   0   27
Dal   21   3   0   7   31
Atl D17 R18/87  P(39-19-0) 316
Dal D24 R33/163 P(35-18-2) 228
Atl-Haynes 148C, Miller 325P;
Dal-Smith 160R, Irvin 169C

Den    3   7   0   7   17
SD     0   7   0   7   14
Den D21 R39/145 P(34-14-1) 166
SD  D13 R21/114 P(34-12-3) 107

Ind    0   3   0   0    3
TB     0   7   7   3   17
Ind D12 R20/64  P(37-20-0) 166
TB  D18 R32/132 P(31-15-3) 168

NYJ    7   0   7   6   3  23
Mia    0   7   3  10   0  20
NYJ D23 R39/231 P(24-13-1) 128
Mia D22 R17/46  P(46-28-1) 287
NYJ-Hector 132R

Cle    0   3   0   7   10
Pit    3   0   7   7   17
Cle D26 R27/86  P(49-28-3) 315
Pit D12 R32/138 P(26-7-0) 87
Cle-Slaughter 138C, Kosar 335P

NE     7   0   0   0    7
Cin    7  14   0   8   29
NE  D14 R20/53 P(33-21-2) 255
Cin D22 R29/83 P(42-22-0) 360
NE-Timpson 150C;
Cin-Esiason 333P
```

MONDAY, DECEMBER 23

```
ChiB   0   0   7   7   14
SF     7  17   0  28   52
ChiB D21 R24/95  P(35-23-1) 309
SF   D30 R24/115 P(37-25-0) 371
ChiB-Davis 136C; SF-Rice 125C,
Young 338P
```

1992 NFL

SUNDAY, SEPTEMBER 6

```
Pit    7   9   6   7   29
Hou   14  10   0   0   24
Pit D19 R34/136 P(24-15-0) 245
Hou D24 R14/104 P(45-29-5) 330
Pit-Foster 107R; Hou-White 100R,
Jeffires 117C, Moon 330P
```

```
NYJ    0  10   7   0   17
Atl   17   3   0   0   20
NYJ D21 R18/68  P(37-21-0) 343
Atl D17 R26/117 P(30-21-0) 189
NYJ-Carpenter 109C, Nagle 366P

NO     3   3   0   7   13
Phi    6   3   0   6   15
NO  D8 R16/55   P(30-12-2) 147
Phi D21 R40/184 P(25-18-0) 136
Phi-Walker 112R

Min    0  10   3   7   3  23
GB     7   3   0  10   0  20
Min D18 R24/177 P(44-21-1) 248
GB  D18 R33/116 P(38-27-1) 155
Min-Allen 140R

Det    0   0   0  14   24
ChiB   7   3   0  17   27
Det  D17 R23/121 P(26-18-1) 232
ChiB D21 R29/140 P(30-19-0) 227
Det-Sanders 109R, Green 114C

Cin    0   7   0  14   21
Sea    3   0   0   0    3
Cin D18 R36/167 P(29-18-1) 102
Sea D18 R27/92  P(33-15-0) 110
Cin-Green 123R

Buf   14  13   7   6   40
LARm   0   0   0   7    7
LARm D15 R22/66  P(38-19-4) 149
Buf  D23 R33/207 P(30-19-1) 156
Buf-Thomas 103R

Cle    0   0   3   0    3
Ind    0   7   0   7   14
Cle D13 R16/42 P(26-15-2) 103
Ind D15 R33/64 P(24-15-1) 172

Phx    0   7   0   0    7
TB     3   7  10   3   23
Phx D14 R22/61  P(40-22-2) 140
TB  D17 R33/128 P(25-14-0) 140

KC     7   3   7   7   24
SD     3   0   0   7   10
KC D14 R28/61 P(25-15-1) 127
SD D13 R24/88 P(30-14-3) 67

SF     7  10   7   7   31
NYG    0   7   7   0   14
SF  D27 R35/172 P(28-19-0) 212
NYG D21 R22/119 P(37-20-1) 196
SF-Watters 100R

LARd   0  10   3   0   13
Den    0   0   3   0   17
LARd D20 R45/152 P(24-7-2) 161
Den  D12 R22/47  P(24-10-1) 153
```

MONDAY, SEPTEMBER 7

```
Was    0   0   3  10   13
Dal    9   7   7   0   23
Was D17 R22/75  P(38-20-0) 185
Dal D23 R36/175 P(31-18-2) 216
Dal-Smith 140R
```

SUNDAY, SEPTEMBER 13

```
ChiB   0   6   0   0    6
NO     0   0   7  21   28
ChiB D19 R27/141 P(45-25-2) 240
NO   D15 R24/94  P(25-13-0) 251

NE     0   0   0   0    0
LARm   0   0   7   7   14
NE   D14 R26/118 P(32-18-4) 109
LARm D13 R27/121 P(22-10-0) 119

Buf    3  10  14   7   34
SF     7   7   7   0   31
Buf D25 R33/107 P(33-22-1) 381
SF  D26 R30/159 P(37-26-1) 439
Buf-Metzelaars 113C, Reed 144C,
Kelly 403P; SF-Sherrard 159C,
Taylor 112C, Young 449P

Min    0   3   0  14   17
Det    7  10  14   0   31
Min D20 R26/95 P(36-20-3) 175
Det D12 R29/73 P(15-10-1) 96

Phi    3  14   7   7   31
Phx    0  14   0   0   14
Phi D21 R34/130 P(22-17-0) 235
Phx D14 R17/54  P(34-19-0) 185
Phi-Walker 115R, Barnett 193C;
Phx-Hill 109C
```

```
SD     0  10   3   0   13
Den    7   0  14   0   21
SD  D27 R30/168 P(45-23-2) 187
Den D12 R21/64  P(24-14-1) 162

Hou    7   3   7   3   20
Ind    0   3   0   7   10
Hou D23 R21/69 P(39-29-0) 350
Ind D14 R21/56 P(25-14-1) 106
Hou-White 106C, Moon 361P

NYJ    3   0   0   7   10
Pit    0  10   0  17   27
NYJ D12 R22/110 P(33-10-4) 129
Pit D17 R45/215 P(22-11-2) 155
Pit-Foster 190R, Graham 146C

Sea    0   7   0   0    7
KC     7   6   7   6   26
Sea D11 R26/91  P(31-13-2) 98
KC  D16 R34/115 P(19-13-0) 206

Dal   17  10   7   0   34
NYG    0   0  14  14   28
Dal D20 R26/98 P(35-22-0) 229
NYG D22 R18/67 P(42-25-1) 264

GB     0   0   3   0    3
TB    14   3   7   7   31
GB D16 R22/109 P(29-18-2) 106
TB D21 R24/62  P(26-22-0) 333
TB-Carrier 115C, Dawsey 107C,
Testaverde 363P

LARd   0   7   7   0   7  21
Cin    7   7   7   0   3  24
LARd D22 R22/87  P(40-25-1) 367
Cin  D19 R40/178 P(27-16-0) 154
LARd-Brown 104C, Schroeder 380P

Atl    0  14   0   3   17
Was    0  21   3   0   24
Atl D7 R12/34  P(25-11-1) 232
Was D24 R42/174 P(28-18-1) 169
```

MONDAY, SEPTEMBER 14

```
Mia   14   0   3  10   27
Cle    0   0   3  20   23
Mia D24 R28/101 P(35-25-0) 300
Cle D17 R24/111 P(28-19-0) 211
Mia-Marino 322P
```

SUNDAY, SEPTEMBER 20

```
Den    0   0   0   0    0
Phi    3  14  10   3   30
Den D4 R17/52   P(19-8-1) 30
Phi D20 R39/130 P(26-18-0) 258
Phi-Barnett 102C, Williams 108C

Cin    0  10   7   6   23
GB     0   3   0  21   24
Cin D18 R37/164 P(24-12-2) 137
GB  D22 R26/93  P(41-23-0) 252
Cin-Green 101R; GB-Sharpe 109C

SF     7  17   7   0   31
NYJ    0   0  14   0   14
SF  D19 R30/131 P(28-18-1) 204
NYJ D15 R18/66  P(43-23-1) 245
NYJ-Mathis 111C

NO     0   0   0   3   10
Atl    0   7   0   0    7
NO  D13 R25/121 P(19-9-0) 108
Atl D19 R27/97  P(35-21-1) 181

LARm   0   0   7   3   10
Mia   17   0   3   6   26
LARm D15 R19/84  P(32-17-2) 214
Mia  D24 R37/158 P(37-21-1) 223
Mia-Higgs 111R

Phx    7   3   3   7   20
Dal   14   7   3   7   31
Phx D24 R17/67  P(43-28-0) 371
Dal D21 R38/150 P(21-14-0) 263
Phx-Chandler 383P;
Dal-Smith 112R, Irvin 210C

Det    0   3   0   7   10
Was    7   3   0   3   13
Det D8 R17/37   P(26-14-1) 169
Was D17 R41/147 P(24-14-3) 128
Was-Byner 120R

KC     3  10   0   7   20
Hou    3   3   0  14   3  23
KC  D21 R36/187 P(30-17-0) 158
Hou D18 R18/77  P(28-19-2) 265
KC-Word 114R
```

```
Cle   14   0   7   7   28
LARd   0   3  10   3   16
Cle  D7 R22/31   P(20-10-0) 200
LARd D27 R23/110 P(59-33-3) 354
Cle-Metcalf 177C;
LARd-Graddy 114C,
Marinovich 395P

Pit    7   0   0  16   23
SD     3   3   0   0    6
Pit D15 R33/67  P(24-17-1) 205
SD  D15 R24/109 P(36-16-3) 221

Sea    0   0   0   3   10
NE     0   0   6   0    6
Sea D14 R35/140 P(28-14-0) 110
NE  D16 R22/99  P(27-17-1) 146
Sea-Warren 122R; NE-Fryar 101C

TB     3  10   0   7   20
Min    7   0  14   5   26
TB  D18 R23/102 P(38-23-1) 231
Min D20 R40/129 P(28-15-1) 190

Ind    0   0   0   0    0
Buf    7   3  14  14   38
Ind D9 R24/37   P(26-13-3) 103
Buf D24 R41/169 P(27-17-0) 211
```

MONDAY, SEPTEMBER 21

```
NYJ    7   7  10   3   27
ChiB   7   0   7   0   14
NYJ  D26 R43/174 P(29-19-0) 212
ChiB D16 R17/99  P(30-17-2) 175
NYJ-Baker 109C
```

SUNDAY, SEPTEMBER 27

```
Atl    0   7  14  10   31
ChiB  17   0   7   7  10  41
Atl  D19 R10/24  P(48-30-1) 324
ChiB D23 R36/217 P(24-18-0) 272
Atl-Rison 177C, Miller 351P

Buf    3   3  21  14   41
NE     0   0   0   0    0
Buf D23 R40/182 P(20-15-0) 308
NE  D16 R25/69  P(33-24-1) 196
Buf-Thomas 120R, Lofton 113C,
Reed 168C, Kelly 308P

TB     3   0  17   7   27
Det    0   3  13   7   23
TB  D17 R36/147 P(30-17-3) 248
Det D18 R20/70  P(31-20-0) 298
TB-Cobb 107R; Det-Perriman 117C,
Peete 323P

NYJ    3   7   0   0   10
LARm   0   5   7   6   18
NYJ  D21 R26/149 P(39-19-2) 181
LARm D15 R27/118 P(25-13-1) 151

Pit    3   0   0   0    3
GB     0  10   0   7   17
Pit D16 R18/145 P(41-16-0) 208
GB  D16 R38/99  P(19-14-0) 195
Pit-Foster 117R, Stone 101C

SD     0   0   0   0    0
Hou   10   0   7  10   27
SD  D15 R23/52  P(38-22-3) 210
Hou D21 R24/106 P(35-20-1) 197

Den    3   0   3   6   12
Cle    0   0   0   0    0
Den D15 R41/188 P(17-10-1) 112
Cle D10 R30/141 P(20-9-3) 75

Min   14  14   7   7   42
Cin    0   0   0   7    7
Min D28 R31/106 P(38-28-0) 317
Cin D14 R28/113 P(25-12-4) 65
Min-Carter 124C, Gannon 318P

Mia    3   3   3  10   19
Sea    0  10   0   7   17
Mia D18 R26/59 P(40-24-3) 255
Sea D14 R24/86 P(28-16-1) 135

SF     7   3   0   6   16
NO     7   3   0   0   10
SF D19 R32/154 P(26-17-0) 179
NO D19 R20/77  P(40-25-3) 259
```

MONDAY, SEPTEMBER 28

```
LARd   0   7   0   0    7
KC     0  10   0  17   27
LARd D13 R23/90  P(26-12-2) 128
KC   D17 R39/180 P(18-9-1) 61
KC-Word 125R
```

SUNDAY, OCTOBER 4

```
Mia    3  14  17   3   37
Buf    3   7   0   0   10
Mia D20 R26/80 P(33-21-1) 282
Buf D26 R22/63 P(58-31-4) 337
Buf-Kelly 306P

NO     0   3   7   3   13
Det    0   7   0   0    7
NO  D19 R40/133 P(21-16-0) 152
Det D12 R11/42  P(30-15-0) 145

ChiB   3  10   7   0   20
Min    0   0   0  21   21
ChiB D19 R28/86  P(34-20-2) 189
Min  D18 R27/127 P(26-21-2) 205

GB     0   0   7   3   10
Atl   14   0   3   7   24
GB  D21 R19/77  P(43-33-1) 261
Atl D17 R24/102 P(26-16-0) 166
GB-Sharpe 107C

Ind    7   0  10   7   24
TB     7   0   0   0    7
Ind D15 R22/69  P(33-15-3) 224
TB  D28 R34/116 P(48-24-2) 243

KC     0  10   3   6   19
Den    0   3  14   0   20
KC  D20 R27/90 P(31-22-0) 279
Den D20 R20/68 P(38-23-0) 279
KC-Davis 127C, Krieg 301P;
Den-Sharpe 118C, Elway 311P

NYG    0   0   0   0   10
LARd   0   0  10   3   13
NYG  D20 R29/105 P(29-19-1) 173
LARd D14 R23/81  P(25-15-0) 219
LARd-Gary 110R

Was   14   3   7   0   24
Phx    0   0   6  21   27
Was D19 R34/107 P(28-12-3) 258
Phx D21 R20/103 P(31-21-2) 163
Was-Clark 106C

LARm   0   0  17   0   24
SF     7   3   7   0   27
LARm D15 R24/123 P(24-20-1) 224
SF   D20 R27/174 P(29-20-1) 238
LARm-Gary 110R

Sea    0   3   3   0    6
SD    10   7   0   0   17
Sea D11 R19/110 P(28-15-3) 70
SD  D17 R32/107 P(28-15-0) 195
SD-Miller 142C

NE     0   0   7  14   21
NYJ    3  14   0  13   30
NE  D14 R15/75  P(33-23-2) 207
NYJ D20 R32/117 P(33-20-1) 195
NE-Fryar 165C
```

MONDAY, OCTOBER 5

```
Dal    7   0   0   0    7
Phi    0  10   7  14   31
Dal D17 R22/80  P(38-19-3) 231
Phi D21 R36/160 P(19-11-0) 106
Dal-Irvin 105C
```

SUNDAY, OCTOBER 11

```
SF     0  10   0  14   24
NE     0   3   9   0   12
SF D24 R29/183 P(28-19-1) 228
NE D17 R27/70  P(34-20-2) 157
SF-Watters 104R

Phi    0   3   0  14   17
KC     7   3   7   7   24
Phi D18 R34/184 P(28-16-2) 129
KC  D11 R19/62  P(26-12-1) 254
KC-Davis 167C

Phx    7   7   0   7   21
NYG    7  14  10   0   31
Phx D22 R26/113 P(30-16-1) 193
NYG D20 R40/260 P(17-9-0) 139
Phx-Jones 125C;
NYG-Hampton 167R

Sea    0   0   0   0    0
Dal    7  13   7   0   27
Sea D6 R22/38   P(19-8-1) 24
Dal D30 R30/116 P(28-17-2) 197
Dal-Irvin 113C
```

Pit 3 3 0 3 9
Cle 0 3 7 7 17
Pit D20 R31/120 P(32-25-0) 228
Cle D12 R27/85 P(17-10-0) 168

Atl 0 10 7 0 17
Mia 7 0 7 7 21
Atl D19 R16/69 P(41-26-1) 254
Mia D22 R22/98 P(40-20-0) 248
Atl-Rison 101C

Hou 10 14 14 0 38
Cin 0 10 7 7 24
Hou D28 R34/202 P(32-21-2) 216
Cin D15 R16/69 P(37-20-2) 205
Hou-White 149R, Moon 216P

Buf 0 3 0 0 3
LARd 7 10 3 0 20
Buf D22 R29/92 P(45-26-1) 258
LARd D16 R31/92 P(21-11-1) 156
Buf-Kelly 302P

LARm 0 3 7 0 10
NO 7 3 0 3 13
LARm D13 R23/53 P(20-11-1) 143
NO D19 R33/135 P(24-15-1) 166
NO-Martin 103C

NYJ 0 0 0 3 0 3
Ind 0 3 0 0 3 6
NYJ D8 R23/74 P(16-6-0) 73
Ind D22 R27/99 P(40-20-1) 183

MONDAY, OCTOBER 12

Den 3 0 0 3
Was 17 7 7 3 34
Den D7 R17/26 P(40-17-3) 102
Was D17 R38/117 P(26-16-0) 245

THURSDAY, OCTOBER 15

Det 0 7 0 7 14
Min 21 3 0 7 31
Det D17 R18/67 P(29-18-2) 226
Min D23 R32/102 P(34-21-0) 291
Det-Perriman 124C;
Min-Carter 109C

SUNDAY, OCTOBER 18

GB 0 0 3 3 6
Cle 3 0 7 7 17
GB D16 R21/72 P(33-20-0) 208
Cle D20 R35/142 P(21-13-0) 158

NE 10 0 0 7 17
Mia 0 17 21 0 38
NE D15 R18/18 P(43-25-0) 255
Mia D20 R29/98 P(32-21-2) 289
Mia-Marino 294P

SD 14 0 3 17 34
Ind 7 0 7 0 14
SD D26 R38/212 P(17-12-1) 180
Ind D22 R17/37 P(41-28-2) 293
SD-Bernstine 150R;
Ind-Hester 105C, George 318P

Phi 0 3 0 9 12
Was 3 3 3 7 16
Phi D19 R18/115 P(40-22-1) 171
Was D16 R40/98 P(24-14-1) 222

KC 3 7 0 0 10
Dal 7 7 3 0 17
KC D18 R25/91 P(31-16-1) 139
Dal D17 R24/95 P(29-21-2) 183
KC-Davis 100C

LARd 0 12 0 7 19
Sea 0 0 0 0 0
LARd D11 R36/179 P(22-9-0) 69
Sea D14 R19/41 P(41-17-1) 196
LARd-Gary 126R

Hou 7 0 7 7 21
Den 7 0 0 10 17
Hou D21 R19/109 P(39-23-1) 298
Den D14 R22/170 P(21-13-0) 152
Hou-Duncan 133C, Moon 321P

NYG 0 10 0 7 17
LARm 7 7 10 14 38
NYG D18 R22/124 P(36-20-2) 172
LARm D22 R35/130 P(21-18-0) 226
LARm-Gary 126R

NO 0 10 13 7 30
Phx 7 7 0 7 21
NO D20 R25/50 P(26-19-1) 349
Phx D15 R18/60 P(30-19-0) 194
NO-Martin 151C, Hebert 355P

Atl 7 3 0 7 17
SF 21 21 14 0 56
Atl D18 R15/47 P(43-23-2) 250
SF D29 R34/191 P(31-18-1) 399
SF-Rice 183C, Young 399P

ChiB 7 7 7 10 31
TB D18 R30/126 P(35-18-2) 172
ChiB D18 R35/93 P(26-13-1) 298
TB-Cobb 109R, Hawkins 102C;
ChiB-Waddle 114C, Harbaugh 304P

MONDAY, OCTOBER 19

Cin 0 0 0 0 0
Pit 3 7 0 10 20
Cin D6 R19/48 P(24-11-0) 70
Pit D26 R37/173 P(37-23-0) 251
Pit-Foster 108R, Graham 115C

SUNDAY, OCTOBER 25

Sea 0 3 7 0 10
NYG 0 6 14 3 23
Sea D12 R22/78 P(32-22-1) 108
NYG D13 R41/176 P(9-5-0) 85

Ind 0 7 7 17 31
Mia 0 7 7 6 20
Ind D20 R31/109 P(34-18-1) 153
Mia D24 R20/65 P(45-25-3) 348
Mia-Marino 355P

ChiB 3 17 3 7 30
GB 0 10 0 0 10
ChiB D26 R39/130 P(24-17-0) 226
GB D14 R16/60 P(37-20-1) 188
GB-Sharpe 144C

Dal 7 0 7 14 28
LARd 6 0 7 0 13
Dal D23 R39/162 P(25-16-0) 207
LARd D12 R20/71 P(26-8-0) 94
Dal-Smith 152R

Den 0 7 0 14 21
SD 7 0 14 3 24
Den D18 R21/91 P(39-21-3) 260
SD D20 R33/101 P(27-20-1) 340
Den-Jackson 113C; SD-Miller 129C,
Walker 104C, Humphries 355P

Was 3 9 0 3 15
Min 0 0 3 10 13
Was D15 R30/116 P(32-18-1) 136
Min D12 R24/75 P(29-16-1) 143

Cin 0 10 0 0 10
Hou 7 3 7 9 26
Cin D11 R20/88 P(19-13-1) 113
Hou D26 R24/93 P(40-27-1) 332
Hou-Givins 100C, Moon 342P

Det 14 10 7 7 38
TB 0 7 0 0 7
Det D21 R32/164 P(24-14-1) 236
TB D15 R23/88 P(34-17-1) 148
Det-Sanders 122R, Moore 108C

Cle 6 3 0 10 19
NE 0 7 10 0 17
Cle D18 R36/123 P(29-14-0) 165
NE D14 R18/77 P(33-17-0) 176

Phx 0 0 3 0 3
Phi 0 0 0 7 7
Phx D13 R31/95 P(29-14-1) 158
Phi D11 R31/163 P(20-9-1) 84
Phi-Walker 112R

Pit 7 6 7 7 27
KC 0 3 0 0 3
Pit D18 R40/154 P(22-13-0) 109
KC D13 R26/121 P(27-9-3) 58
Pit-Foster 105R

MONDAY, OCTOBER 26

Buf 0 14 3 7 24
NYJ 3 3 7 7 20
Buf D21 R28/165 P(29-15-1) 208
NYJ D22 R33/142 P(37-22-2) 184
Buf-Thomas 142R, Beebe 106C

SUNDAY, NOVEMBER 1

Mia 0 0 7 7 14
NYJ 9 14 0 3 26
Mia D11 R19/83 P(26-14-0) 213
NYJ D21 R39/160 P(30-21-1) 203
NYJ-Baxter 103R

TB 0 7 7 7 21
NO 3 10 3 7 23
TB D10 R24/84 P(25-13-1) 70
NO D18 R34/145 P(27-14-3) 164

LARm 0 14 14 0 28
Atl 7 3 13 7 30
LARm D19 R20/147 P(33-22-0) 212
Atl D19 R28/136 P(33-19-0) 214
LARm-Gary 144R, Everett 253P

Cle 3 0 0 7 10
Cin 7 7 10 6 30
Cle D16 R28/58 P(31-18-0) 270
Cin D20 R32/105 P(26-14-0) 195

SF 0 0 7 7 14
Phx 0 10 14 0 24
SF D19 R14/63 P(32-23-1) 267
Phx D21 R33/145 P(33-19-1) 197
Phx-Johnson 102R

GB 7 10 3 7 27
Det 3 0 10 0 13
GB D24 R34/145 P(37-22-0) 202
Det D9 R12/38 P(33-17-1) 152
GB-Workman 101R

NE 0 7 0 0 7
Buf 0 0 9 7 16
NE D14 R26/69 P(26-17-1) 127
Buf D20 R34/89 P(33-22-2) 199

Hou 3 3 14 0 20
Pit 0 7 0 14 21
Hou D21 R15/55 P(42-28-0) 228
Pit D25 R33/119 P(22-14-1) 183
Pit-Foster 118R

Phi 0 0 10 0 10
Dal 0 3 7 10 20
Phi D10 R21/73 P(27-13-2) 117
Dal D22 R35/175 P(33-19-1) 214
Dal-Smith 163R

NYG 7 14 0 3 24
Was 7 0 0 0 7
NYG D24 R42/241 P(29-15-0) 148
Was D12 R17/61 P(31-14-0) 178
NYG-Hampton 138R

Ind 0 0 0 0 0
SD 3 0 7 16 26
Ind D8 R12/30 P(29-12-1) 113
SD D26 R38/151 P(33-22-2) 247
SD-Butts 118R, Miller 105C

MONDAY, NOVEMBER 2

Min 7 7 10 14 38
ChiB 0 3 0 7 10
Min D18 R40/164 P(16-8-0) 148
ChiB D16 R22/128 P(32-20-3) 165

SUNDAY, NOVEMBER 8

NO 14 7 7 3 31
NE 0 7 0 7 14
NO D17 R39/118 P(26-14-1) 198
NE D6 R18/84 P(31-13-2) 38

Mia 14 0 7 7 28
Ind 0 0 0 0 0
Mia D28 R40/212 P(28-22-0) 241
Ind D11 R19/84 P(31-17-2) 125
Mia-Higgs 107R

GB 0 0 0 7 7
NYG 6 7 0 14 27
GB D20 R23/88 P(45-27-3) 273
NYG D9 R22/58 P(16-9-0) 119
GB-Sharpe 160C

Min 14 14 0 7 35
TB 0 0 0 7 7
Min D22 R29/125 P(24-18-2) 171
TB D24 R24/73 P(48-33-2) 278

LARd 0 0 3 7 10
Phi 3 14 7 7 31
LARd D14 R23/90 P(37-14-4) 125
Phi D16 R38/128 P(24-12-1) 139

Dal 14 6 14 3 37
Det 0 3 0 0 3
Dal D26 R37/158 P(27-18-1) 240
Det D10 R22/124 P(17-9-3) 77
Dal-Irvin 114C; Det-Sanders 108R

Cle 3 7 7 7 24
Hou 0 0 0 14 14
Cle D17 R30/86 P(27-17-0) 205
Hou D13 R18/92 P(36-21-1) 181

SD 0 0 7 7 14
KC 0 3 3 10 16
SD D17 R24/57 P(35-20-1) 238
KC D11 R31/107 P(28-10-0) 104

NYJ 0 6 7 3 16
Den 3 14 3 7 27
NYJ D15 R20/159 P(30-16-1) 182
Den D19 R32/114 P(33-18-2) 261
Den-Marshall 134C

Pit 0 6 14 0 20
Buf 7 14 7 0 28
Pit D17 R25/87 P(25-15-0) 146
Buf D31 R44/174 P(33-26-0) 284
Buf-Thomas 155R, Beebe 101C

Cin 7 3 14 7 31
ChiB 7 14 7 0 28
Cin D17 R37/147 P(29-16-1) 140
ChiB D15 R35/152 P(28-11-2) 149
Cin-Green 117R

Phx 0 3 10 7 20
LARm 0 7 0 7 14
Phx D18 R29/108 P(30-21-0) 216
LARm D19 R18/54 P(32-21-1) 248
Phx-Proehl 126C

Was 0 3 6 7 16
Sea 3 0 0 0 3
Was D15 R31/88 P(30-21-1) 242
Sea D9 R26/124 P(24-9-2) 59
Sea-Warren 103R

MONDAY, NOVEMBER 9

SF 7 7 13 14 41
Atl 0 3 0 0 3
SF D16 R39/152 P(19-13-0) 151
Atl D20 R14/59 P(41-25-3) 245

SUNDAY, NOVEMBER 15

NE 14 7 0 13 3 37
Ind 14 7 3 0 10 34
NE D18 R33/144 P(29-20-1) 226
Ind D26 R27/87 P(35-18-3) 330
Ind-Johnson 163C, George 330P

Det 0 7 0 7 14
Pit 7 3 0 7 17
Det D20 R23/90 P(37-20-2) 286
Pit D18 R30/152 P(35-19-1) 164
Det-Green 115C, Kramer 304P;
Pit-Foster 106R

Cin 0 0 0 14 14
NYJ 0 0 10 7 17
Cin D16 R27/148 P(33-11-2) 79
NYJ D17 R45/173 P(24-8-2) 98

Phi 3 0 14 7 24
GB 0 14 0 13 27
Phi D17 R23/119 P(23-14-0) 153
GB D24 R25/144 P(33-23-2) 266
GB-Sharpe 116C

Was 0 0 13 3 16
KC 7 21 0 7 35
Was D15 R20/81 P(41-23-1) 204
KC D20 R30/98 P(29-19-1) 287
KC-Barnett 148C, Krieg 302P

Phx 7 0 10 0 17
Atl 0 10 0 10 20
Phx D15 R18/32 P(34-19-2) 239
Atl D19 R27/114 P(27-19-1) 223

Hou 0 10 0 7 17
Min 0 0 3 10 13
Hou D27 R25/127 P(40-30-1) 215
Min D10 R22/74 P(28-9-0) 96

SD 7 0 0 7 14
Cle 0 0 3 10 13
SD D16 R27/88 P(32-19-1) 224
Cle D19 R28/87 P(32-18-2) 298
SD-Miller 110C; Cle-Tillman 148C,
Tomczak 322P

Sea 0 0 0 3 3
LARd 0 6 7 7 20
Sea D10 R29/113 P(23-11-1) 46
LARd D12 R30/100 P(23-10-1) 88
LARd-Gary 110R

ChiB 0 0 3 14 17
TB 10 0 0 0 20
ChiB D19 R25/113 P(33-17-0) 202
TB D14 R33/127 P(21-12-1) 172
TB-Cobb 114R

NO 3 7 10 0 20
SF 0 7 0 14 21
NO D16 R15/43 P(35-22-0) 293
SF D24 R30/176 P(37-24-1) 191
NO-Hebert 301P; SF-Watters 115R

NYG 0 6 0 7 13
Den 14 0 3 10 27
NYG D10 R29/120 P(14-8-0) 39
Den D18 R37/149 P(22-15-1) 230
Den-Jackson 108C

LARm 7 14 0 6 27
Dal 3 10 10 0 23
LARm D24 R32/123 P(37-22-0) 244
Dal D19 R19/80 P(37-22-0) 269
LARm-Gary 110R; Dal-Irvin 168C

MONDAY, NOVEMBER 16

Buf 3 10 13 0 26
Mia 3 10 3 0 20
Buf D26 R36/111 P(32-19-0) 212
Mia D19 R18/54 P(33-26-1) 286
Mia-Duper 100C, Marino 321P

SUNDAY, NOVEMBER 22

Phi 0 20 20 7 47
NYG 10 10 7 7 34
Phi D17 R33/184 P(21-10-3) 181
NYG D23 R20/94 P(54-22-2) 251
Phi-Sherman 109R

Cle 10 3 0 0 13
Min 0 0 3 14 17
Cle D14 R33/95 P(31-18-3) 180
Min D10 R32/89 P(25-9-2) 52

Hou 10 3 0 3 16
Mia 0 10 3 6 19
Hou D16 R23/96 P(35-22-2) 201
Mia D18 R17/72 P(40-19-1) 221

GB 0 7 7 3 17
ChiB 3 0 0 0 3
GB D18 R34/130 P(24-16-0) 204
ChiB D15 R13/54 P(41-24-2) 251
GB-Bennett 107R; ChiB-Davis 106C

Atl 0 0 7 7 14
Buf 28 10 0 3 41
Atl D11 R19/46 P(36-17-1) 128
Buf D19 R44/315 P(17-8-1) 97
Buf-Davis 181R, Thomas 103R

Det 0 9 0 10 19
Cin 3 3 0 7 13
Det D17 R33/161 P(25-12-3) 163
Cin D10 R23/52 P(25-12-2) 43
Det-Sanders 151R

Ind 0 0 7 7 14
Pit 7 6 14 3 30
Ind D16 R21/71 P(42-19-3) 258
Pit D20 R44/253 P(22-10-1) 109
Pit-Foster 168R

TB 0 7 0 7 14
SD 12 10 0 7 29
TB D18 R25/113 P(35-22-0) 174
SD D17 R33/181 P(28-13-0) 126
SD-Butts 104R

SF 7 3 3 14 27
LARm 0 7 3 0 10
SF D21 R37/213 P(26-14-0) 153
LARm D14 R23/96 P(29-13-0) 149
SF-Watters 163R

Dal 0 10 6 0 16
Phx 3 0 0 7 10
Dal D18 R30/97 P(36-25-1) 237
Phx D9 R18/46 P(24-15-0) 103

Den 7 0 0 7 14
LARd 3 14 0 7 24
Den D15 R20/85 P(26-18-2) 182
LARd D20 R31/167 P(30-16-0) 150
LARd-Dickerson 107R

NYJ 0 3 0 0 3
NE 10 14 0 0 24
NYJ D11 R19/77 P(33-13-2) 89
NE D17 R41/164 P(16-7-0) 96
NE-Vaughn 110R

KC 10 7 7 0 24
Sea 0 7 7 0 14
KC D11 R31/117 P(15-11-0) 73
Sea D20 R26/181 P(30-13-4) 129
Sea-Warren 154R

MONDAY, NOVEMBER 23

Was 3 0 0 0 3
NO 0 14 3 3 20
Was D14 R20/58 P(39-21-1) 169
NO D12 R26/82 P(18-14-0) 142

THURSDAY, NOVEMBER 26

Hou 0 3 7 14 24
Det 0 7 7 7 21
Hou D21 R19/51 P(33-24-2) 332
Det D14 R25/73 P(21-12-2) 141
Hou-Givins 100C, Carlson 338P

NYG 0 3 0 0 3
Dal 3 6 14 7 30
NYG D12 R22/80 P(31-14-0) 127
Dal D17 R30/157 P(29-19-1) 142
NYG-McCaffrey 105C;
Dal-Smith 120R

SUNDAY, NOVEMBER 29

KC 3 3 14 3 23
NYJ 0 0 0 7 7
KC D21 R36/93 P(21-17-0) 203
NYJ D15 R19/62 P(33-17-0) 189

Mia 0 7 3 3 13
NO 7 0 10 7 24
Mia D17 R18/58 P(43-26-1) 223
NO D15 R32/127 P(22-11-0) 125

Phx 3 0 0 0 3
Was 14 6 7 14 41
Phx D14 R19/53 P(36-19-5) 255
Was D22 R34/143 P(27-16-2) 191
Phx-Proehl 104C

Pit 7 7 7 0 21
Cin 0 6 0 3 9
Pit D17 R33/99 P(18-10-1) 141
Cin D15 R25/160 P(34-16-0) 68
Pit-Foster 102R; Cin-Green 116R

NE 0 0 0 0 0
Atl 14 10 7 3 34
NE D8 R22/90 P(16-9-2) 15
Atl D17 R38/141 P(19-10-0) 112

Phi 0 0 7 7 14
SF 7 3 3 7 20
Phi D18 R16/46 P(42-28-0) 234
SF D18 R28/96 P(35-24-0) 329
SF-Rice 133C, Young 342P

Min 7 10 14 0 31
LARm 7 3 0 7 17
Min D24 R35/134 P(35-24-1) 274
LARm D22 R22/90 P(40-19-3) 247
Min-Allen 110C

TB 7 0 7 0 14
GB 3 6 3 7 19
TB D14 R27/129 P(22-12-3) 152
GB D17 R25/65 P(41-26-0) 218

Buf 0 3 7 3 0 13
Ind 0 3 0 10 3 16
Buf D16 R29/136 P(33-11-2) 176
Ind D22 R33/107 P(41-26-1) 305
Buf-Thomas 102R, Beebe 110C;
Ind-Arbuckle 106C, Trudeau 337P

LARd 0 3 0 0 3
SD 7 14 0 6 27
LARd D15 R26/154 P(24-16-1) 170
SD D20 R34/169 P(26-13-1) 164
LARd-Dickerson 103R

ChiB 0 7 7 0 14
Cle 7 6 7 7 27
ChiB D16 R19/73 P(28-19-2) 247
Cle D12 R35/131 P(17-8-0) 47
ChiB-Waddle 100C

MONDAY, NOVEMBER 30

Den 10 0 3 0 0 13
Sea 0 3 0 10 3 16
Den D10 R34/84 P(26-11-2) 112
Sea D15 R27/74 P(42-24-2) 234

THURSDAY, DECEMBER 3

Atl 0 0 7 7 14
NO 3 6 0 13 22
Atl D10 R13/76 P(21-11-2) 92
NO D22 R40/144 P(29-20-1) 244

SUNDAY, DECEMBER 6

Ind 3 3 0 0 6
NE 0 0 0 0 0
Ind D13 R34/65 P(35-23-1) 200
NE D9 R21/71 P(31-11-0) 23

NYJ 3 0 14 7 24
Buf 3 7 0 7 17
NYJ D17 R34/124 P(22-14-1) 151
Buf D21 R29/147 P(36-20-2) 204
Buf-Thomas 116R

Cin 0 7 7 7 21
Cle 10 3 21 3 37
Cin D15 R18/62 P(33-17-0) 165
Cle D17 R31/149 P(23-19-0) 232

Sea 0 7 7 0 14
Pit 7 3 0 10 20
Sea D10 R22/67 P(28-13-1) 153
Pit D16 R37/138 P(29-16-5) 168
Pit-Foster 125R

Min 3 7 0 7 17
Phi 7 7 7 7 28
Min D15 R26/138 P(23-12-1) 81
Phi D26 R44/225 P(23-16-0) 135
Phi-Cunningham 121R

Det 0 10 0 0 10
GB 14 21 0 3 38
Det D17 R26/156 P(29-15-1) 148
GB D21 R35/166 P(19-15-0) 208
Det-Sanders 114R, Moore 114C;
GB-Sharpe 107C

Dal 14 3 7 7 31
Den 7 6 7 7 27
Dal D22 R32/82 P(35-25-0) 222
Den D15 R19/93 P(31-18-4) 261

SD 0 10 7 10 27
Phx 14 0 7 0 21
SD D14 R20/29 P(32-20-1) 267
Phx D20 R25/96 P(35-20-2) 227
Phx-Proehl 112C

Was 7 7 7 7 28
NYG 0 3 7 0 10
Was D22 R40/177 P(18-15-0) 216
NYG D10 R24/105 P(16-8-0) 60
Was-Byner 100R

KC 0 7 0 0 7
LARd 14 7 7 0 28
KC D12 R14/17 P(33-18-1) 248
LARd D15 R39/151 P(18-12-2) 79
LARd-Everett 342P

Mia 0 0 3 0 3
SF 0 13 7 7 27
Mia D15 R15/40 P(36-20-0) 199
SF D20 R34/136 P(28-19-1) 220

LARm 0 3 21 7 31
TB 6 21 0 0 27
LARm D21 R24/63 P(38-25-0) 342
TB D16 R33/150 P(22-12-2) 163
LARm-Everett 342P; TB-Cobb 100R

MONDAY, DECEMBER 7

ChiB 0 0 0 7 7
Hou 0 10 7 7 24
ChiB D14 R24/99 P(25-11-2) 158
Hou D21 R29/175 P(27-18-0) 164
Hou-White 116R

SATURDAY, DECEMBER 12

NYG 0 0 0 0 0
Phx 0 9 3 7 19
NYG D8 R19/70 P(25-9-2) 61
Phx D18 R43/179 P(18-12-0) 101
Phx-Johnson 156R

Den 0 0 7 10 17
Buf 0 21 3 3 27
Den D24 R30/98 P(48-23-3) 222
Buf D17 R37/151 P(23-13-2) 210
Den-Sharpe 109C;
Buf-Thomas 120R, Beebe 104C

SUNDAY, DECEMBER 13

Phi 3 7 0 7 3 20
Sea 3 7 0 7 0 17
Phi D25 R41/190 P(44-27-1) 276
Sea D11 R24/63 P(31-9-2) 24
Phi-Walker 111R, Barnett 161C,
Cunningham 365P

Ind 0 0 3 7 10
NYJ 0 6 0 0 6
Ind D15 R23/64 P(38-20-2) 220
NYJ D15 R26/104 P(33-13-3) 142
Ind-Cash 104C; NYJ-Burkett 110C

Dal 3 14 0 0 17
Was 0 7 3 10 20
Dal D22 R29/121 P(35-23-1) 221
Was D14 R25/68 P(30-13-1) 178
Dal-Irvin 105C

NO 6 17 7 7 37
LARm 0 0 0 14 14
NO D25 R33/161 P(27-16-0) 238
LARm D18 R20/102 P(42-24-3) 226

Atl 7 7 14 7 35
TB 0 7 0 0 7
Atl D20 R25/86 P(30-22-0) 327
TB D17 R21/104 P(30-20-1) 150
Atl-Haynes 113C, Wilson 324P

Cle 0 0 0 14 14
Det 7 0 14 3 24
Cle D14 R16/61 P(28-20-2) 260
Det D19 R35/155 P(14-10-0) 121

NE 13 0 0 7 20
KC 3 3 7 14 27
NE D10 R33/109 P(18-8-1) 101
KC D14 R31/85 P(21-10-0) 185

Cin 7 3 0 0 10
SD 3 7 14 3 27
Cin D15 R18/67 P(26-13-2) 156
SD D22 R39/161 P(28-19-2) 209

SF 3 14 3 0 20
Min 7 0 3 7 17
SF D21 R35/135 P(26-20-1) 152
Min D10 R23/114 P(21-9-1) 71
SF-Lee 134R

Pit 0 3 0 3 6
ChiB 3 10 7 10 30
Pit D10 R15/35 P(31-14-2) 105
ChiB D20 R44/212 P(21-11-0) 71

GB 0 3 6 7 16
Hou 0 0 7 7 14
GB D16 R24/61 P(30-19-1) 154
Hou D21 R18/59 P(36-25-2) 328
Hou-Duncan 100C, Carlson 330P

MONDAY, DECEMBER 14

LARd 0 0 0 7 7
Mia 0 10 7 3 20
LARd D9 R17/73 P(30-13-1) 78
Mia D20 R37/132 P(26-16-1) 228

SATURDAY, DECEMBER 19

TB 7 0 0 7 14
SF 7 0 7 7 21
TB D18 R29/127 P(31-16-0) 181
SF D19 R28/82 P(31-18-0) 255
SF-Rice 118C

KC 0 7 7 7 21
NYG 14 7 14 0 35
KC D14 R17/48 P(34-18-2) 250
NYG D22 R44/217 P(16-10-0) 131

SUNDAY, DECEMBER 20

SD 3 20 3 10 36
LARd 0 0 7 7 14
SD D19 R41/104 P(32-17-0) 228
LARd D14 R13/49 P(33-13-3) 118

ChiB 0 0 3 0 3
Det 3 10 0 3 16
ChiB D16 R19/106 P(35-15-3) 136
Det D15 R28/134 P(20-12-2) 265
Det-Sanders 113R, Moore 108C

Phx 7 3 0 3 13
Ind 0 3 7 6 16
Phx D18 R34/159 P(25-11-3) 131
Ind D21 R20/47 P(41-25-1) 319
Phx-Johnson 146R;
Ind-George 328P

Sea 0 3 3 0 6
Den 0 0 7 3 10
Sea D16 R30/142 P(25-14-0) 80
Den D15 R23/89 P(30-20-3) 204

Min 0 0 0 6 6
Pit 0 3 0 0 3
Min D18 R44/216 P(18-7-0) 125
Pit D17 R31/158 P(22-13-0) 130
Min-Allen 172R; Pit-Foster 118R

NE 7 0 0 3 10
Cin 14 0 3 3 20
NE D10 R30/116 P(20-7-2) 60
Cin D21 R41/211 P(26-14-0) 154
Cin-Green 190R

Hou 0 3 0 14 17
Cle 7 0 7 0 14
Hou D21 R23/104 P(34-19-2) 214
Cle D19 R33/145 P(26-17-3) 140
Hou-White 105C

Buf 3 0 7 10 20
NO 6 7 3 0 16
Buf D19 R40/181 P(28-13-1) 126
NO D12 R21/48 P(32-17-1) 157
Buf-Thomas 115R

LARm 7 3 3 0 13
GB 0 28 0 0 28
LARm D17 R22/121 P(44-24-3) 216
GB D15 R32/101 P(23-14-1) 158
GB-Sharpe 110C

Was 0 13 0 0 13
Phi 0 7 7 3 17
Was D19 R23/118 P(38-22-2) 246
Phi D16 R34/159 P(24-13-1) 140
Was-Sanders 114C

NYJ 0 0 14 3 17
Mia 7 0 0 12 19
NYJ D12 R30/112 P(18-12-2) 158
Mia D14 R24/91 P(30-15-2) 203

MONDAY, DECEMBER 21

Dal 3 17 14 7 41
Atl 7 3 0 7 17
Dal D19 R29/196 P(21-18-0) 239
Atl D18 R11/40 P(46-34-0) 333
Dal-Smith 174R; Atl-Haynes 100C,
Pritchard 105C, Wilson 340P

SATURDAY, DECEMBER 26

LARd 0 0 7 14 21
Was 0 3 7 10 20
LARd D25 R32/148 P(33-19-2) 234
Was D18 R26/99 P(31-15-0) 196

NO 7 3 7 3 20
NYJ 0 0 0 0 0
NO D17 R31/95 P(25-14-3) 185
NYJ D10 R20/55 P(34-16-2) 117

SUNDAY, DECEMBER 27

SD 0 6 7 18 31
Sea 7 0 7 0 14
SD D18 R29/98 P(29-17-0) 243
Sea D17 R24/156 P(33-17-2) 202
Sea-Blades 103C

Mia 3 0 3 7 3 16
NE 7 6 0 0 0 13
Mia D21 R30/114 P(39-21-1) 216
NE D17 R44/177 P(22-8-0) 102
NE-Lockwood 123R

Den 7 0 3 10 20
KC 0 14 7 21 42
Den D16 R27/82 P(35-19-2) 208
KC D13 R22/60 P(25-14-1) 160

Cle 0 3 7 3 13
Pit 7 10 3 3 23
Cle D17 R27/120 P(22-13-1) 173
Pit D20 R30/105 P(25-18-0) 203
Pit-Foster 103R

GB 7 0 0 0 7
Min 7 13 7 0 27
GB D13 R13/29 P(35-23-3) 182
Min D22 R42/165 P(33-20-0) 282
Min-Allen 100R

Atl 0 20 0 7 27
LARm 14 0 3 21 38
Atl D23 R17/82 P(47-31-2) 363
LARm D16 R35/168 P(18-11-1) 108
Atl-Hill 107C, Wilson 374P

Buf 3 0 0 0 3
Hou 10 10 0 7 27
Buf D17 R30/147 P(32-16-3) 90
Hou D17 R29/107 P(32-18-1) 178

Ind 0 0 7 14 21
Cin 3 14 0 0 17
Ind D18 R15/92 P(31-22-0) 206
Cin D18 R37/197 P(18-12-0) 97

NYG 0 0 3 7 10
Phi 7 10 0 3 20
NYG D13 R21/67 P(33-20-1) 168
Phi D16 R34/198 P(21-11-0) 98
Phi-Walker 104R

ChiB 0 0 0 14 14
Dal 0 3 24 0 27
ChiB D9 R15/28 P(23-9-3) 64
Dal D22 R44/179 P(31-18-1) 175
Dal-Smith 131R

TB 0 7 0 0 7
Phx 3 0 0 0 3
TB D12 R19/30 P(41-24-1) 210
Phx D21 R25/120 P(45-23-5) 233

MONDAY, DECEMBER 28

Det 3 3 0 0 6
SF 0 7 0 17 24
Det D15 R24/139 P(29-15-1) 88
SF D22 R20/98 P(39-27-0) 263
Det-Sanders 104R

1993 NFL

SUNDAY, SEPTEMBER 5

SF 10 7 0 7 24
Pit 0 3 10 0 13
SF D21 R32/86 P(36-24-3) 240
Pit D12 R24/102 P(27-13-2) 109

NE 0 7 7 0 14
Buf 0 17 0 21 38
NE D15 R37/133 P(30-14-1) 135
Buf D20 R42/177 P(22-13-1) 157
Buf-Thomas 114R, Reed 110C,
Kelly 167P

Den 6 7 13 0 26
NYJ 0 6 0 14 20
Den D18 R32/99 P(29-20-0) 254
NYJ D20 R19/71 P(40-29-1) 351
NYJ-Moore 140C, Esiason 371P

Mia 7 3 7 7 24
Ind 7 0 3 10 20
Mia D19 R28/119 P(40-22-1) 236
Ind D16 R21/42 P(43-23-1) 232

Cin 14 0 0 0 14
Cle 0 14 6 7 27
Cin D12 R20/55 P(28-20-2) 172
Cle D18 R30/96 P(30-18-0) 167

NYG 3 6 7 10 26
ChiB 0 7 10 3 20
NYG D21 R28/105 P(34-24-0) 256
ChiB D17 R25/103 P(28-16-1) 166

Hou 7 0 0 14 21
NO 3 10 6 14 33
Hou D21 R18/70 P(45-27-1) 335
NO D21 R30/142 P(25-16-0) 204
NO-Martin 111C

Min 0 0 0 7 7
LARd 7 14 0 3 24
Min D18 R18/58 P(27-15-2) 147
LARd D19 R35/98 P(27-23-1) 214

LARm 3 3 0 0 6
GB 9 10 14 3 36
LARm D14 R19/53 P(41-17-2) 175
GB D22 R36/138 P(29-19-1) 243
GB-Sharpe 120C

```
Sea    7   3   0   2   12
SD     6   6   0   6   18
Sea  D15 R21/89   P(27-20-1) 141
SD   D19 R38/160  P(30-13-2) 109

KC     0  17   7   0   27
TB     3   0   0   0    3
KC   D20 R31/122  P(26-18-0) 278
TB   D15 R20/25   P(35-20-1) 132

Atl    0   3   7   3   13
Det   14  10   3   3   30
Atl  D12 R8/21    P(50-26-2) 216
Det  D12 R35/96   P(20-11-0) 166
Atl-Rison 106C; Det-Moore 113C

Phx    0   3   7   7   17
Phi    7   7   2   7   23
Phx  D14 R19/48   P(39-15-1) 183
Phi  D22 R38/167  P(29-18-1) 192
```

MONDAY, SEPTEMBER 6

```
Dal    6   0   7   3   16
Was    0  14  14   7   35
Dal  D16 R21/91   P(33-19-0) 254
Was  D23 R35/171  P(34-22-0) 161
Dal-Harper 140C;
Was-Mitchell 116R
```

SUNDAY, SEPTEMBER 12

```
NO    10  14   7   3   34
Atl    0  10   0  21   31
NO   D24 R31/227  P(34-22-1) 293
Atl  D20 R20/78   P(33-20-1) 297
NO-Wilson 341P; Atl-Haynes 182C

NYJ    0  14   3   7   24
Mia    7   7   0   0   14
NYJ  D22 R38/106  P(33-22-1) 323
Mia  D14 R14/27   P(29-19-0) 267
NYJ-Moore 124C, Esiason 323P

ChiB   7   0   0   0    7
Min    0   3   0   7   10
ChiB D7 R22/88    P(20-11-1) 52
Min  D15 R37/121  P(29-23-0) 155

Pit    0   0   0   0    0
LARm   0  14   3  10   27
Pit  D11 R19/55   P(33-17-1) 120
LARm D20 R33/99   P(34-21-2) 215
LARm-Ellard 127C

KC     0   0   0   0    0
Hou    0   7   6  17   30
KC   D10 R18/46   P(30-16-2) 160
Hou  D17 R28/57   P(35-22-1) 190

Buf    7   3   0   3   13
Dal    0   3   0   7   10
Buf  D16 R38/100  P(27-16-1) 129
Dal  D23 R28/103  P(45-28-2) 290
Dal-Irvin 115C, Novacek 106C

Phx   10   7   0   0   17
Was    0   0   7   3   10
Phx  D17 R39/152  P(27-17-2) 151
Was  D14 R17/58   P(35-18-1) 175

TB     0   7   0   0    7
NYG    7  10   3   3   23
TB   D12 R19/45   P(28-16-1) 154
NYG  D21 R41/181  P(26-12-1) 200
NYG-Hampton 134R

LARd   7  10   0   0   17
Sea    0  10   0   3   13
LARd D16 R28/83   P(33-18-1) 181
Sea  D14 R29/112  P(22-14-2) 120
LARd-Ellard 127C

Phi    0   7   0  13   20
GB     7   3   7   0   17
Phi  D23 R39/161  P(29-23-1) 191
GB   D10 R20/52   P(24-12-2) 107

SD     0   0  14   3   17
Den    0  17   7  10   34
SD   D26 R24/68   P(55-31-1) 322
Den  D17 R29/128  P(34-24-1) 284
SD-Lewis 119C

Det    7   0   3   6   19
NE     6   3   0   7   16
Det  D21 R44/186  P(25-16-3) 154
NE   D21 R23/61   P(49-28-1) 231
Det-Sanders 148R
```

```
Ind    0   3   3   3    9
Cin    3   0   3   0    6
Ind  D17 R29/120  P(36-17-2) 212
Cin  D16 R26/128  P(37-16-1) 141
```

MONDAY, SEPTEMBER 13

```
SF     6   7   0   0   13
Cle    3  17   3   0   23
SF   D22 R26/130  P(33-19-3) 266
Cle  D18 R33/128  P(32-17-0) 176
Cle-Jackson 105C
```

SUNDAY, SEPTEMBER 19

```
Sea    7   0  10   0   17
NE     0   0   0  14   14
Sea  D23 R43/209  P(21-15-2) 125
NE   D19 R17/51   P(44-20-2) 223
Sea-Warren 174R

LARm   0   3   0   7   10
NYG    7   6   7   0   20
LARm D8 R12/45    P(28-11-2) 126
NYG  D23 R47/146  P(27-21-0) 184
NYG-Hampton 134R

Hou    0  14   0   3   17
SD     3   6   3   6   18
Hou  D17 R17/71   P(43-23-4) 224
SD   D19 R29/111  P(41-15-1) 173

Det    0   3   0   0    3
NO     0   7   0   7   14
Det  D9 R21/84    P(22-15-0) 86
NO   D16 R35/172  P(22-11-0) 86
NO-Brown 125R

Cle    0   0   0  19   19
LARd  10   3   0   3   16
Cle  D20 R27/113  P(39-18-4) 203
LARd D11 R25/71   P(27-13-0) 85
Cle-Vardell 104R

Dal    7   3   7   0   17
Phx    3   7   0   0   10
Dal  D23 R33/130  P(27-21-0) 280
Phx  D14 R19/68   P(27-20-1) 205
Dal-Harper 136C

Was    0  14   7  10   31
Phi    3   7   7  17   34
Was  D19 R31/167  P(36-17-2) 210
Phi  D20 R22/93   P(39-25-2) 345
Was-Brooks 154R;
Phi-Williams 181C;
Cunningham 360P

Cin    0   7   0   0    7
Pit    0  10   7  17   34
Cin  D11 R19/44   P(26-18-1) 126
Pit  D23 R36/223  P(25-21-0) 181
Pit-Foster 103R

Atl    3  10   7  10   30
SF     3   6  14  14   37
Atl  D24 R29/194  P(38-23-0) 187
SF   D23 R33/268  P(22-18-1) 210
Atl-Pegram 192R; SF-Watters 112R
```

MONDAY, SEPTEMBER 20

```
Den    0   0   0   7    7
KC     6   6   0   3   15
Den  D17 R14/35   P(45-28-1) 300
KC   D21 R31/160  P(36-21-0) 254
Den-Russell 104C, Elway 300P;
KC-Davis 139C
```

SUNDAY, SEPTEMBER 26

```
LARm   7   7   7   7   28
Hou    0   3  10   0   13
LARm D22 R32/58   P(28-19-0) 316
Hou  D18 R20/82   P(42-19-2) 288
LARm-Ellard 132C, Everett 316P;
Hou-Givins 107C, Moon 310P

GB     7   3   0   3   13
Min    3   3   6   3   15
GB   D15 R23/106  P(31-20-2) 150
Min  D17 R29/107  P(35-18-0) 210

Cle    0   0   7   0    7
Ind    0   6   3  14   23
Cle  D13 R24/100  P(24-13-1) 153
Ind  D21 R32/97   P(38-22-0) 260
Ind-Hester 110C
```

```
Mia   16   3   0   3   22
Buf    0   6   0   7   13
Mia  D23 R43/137  P(32-20-1) 275
Buf  D16 R22/106  P(39-20-2) 176
Mia-Fryar 103C

NE     0   0   0   7    7
NYJ   14  21   0  10   45
NE   D15 R13/31   P(42-19-2) 180
NYJ  D21 R41/167  P(22-18-0) 221

SF     0   3   7   3   13
NO     0   7   3   3   13
SF   D19 R32/176  P(30-22-1) 163
NO   D17 R24/103  P(32-18-0) 161
SF-Watters 135R

Sea    0   6   3  10   19
Cin    0   0   0  10   10
Sea  D17 R35/139  P(30-18-0) 166
Cin  D19 R17/30   P(45-25-1) 324
Cin-McGee 102C

Phx    0  17   0   3   20
Det    6  10   7   3   26
Phx  D20 R25/79   P(31-23-0) 264
Det  D11 R26/147  P(24-11-0) 183
Det-Green 102C

TB     0   0   0   7    7
ChiB   0  28   3  16   47
TB   D17 R18/36   P(41-20-4) 292
ChiB D18 R38/126  P(23-18-0) 206
TB-Dawsey 101C;
ChiB-Anderson 104R
```

MONDAY, SEPTEMBER 27

```
Pit    7  17   7  14   45
Atl   14   3   0   0   17
Pit  D22 R34/109  P(25-19-0) 259
Atl  D16 R17/44   P(38-17-4) 176
```

SUNDAY, OCTOBER 3

```
Ind    0  10   3   0   13
Den   21   7   7   0   35
Ind  D16 R22/111  P(33-15-2) 160
Den  D26 R37/196  P(31-21-0) 258

NYG    0  14   0   0   14
Buf   10   0   0   7   17
NYG  D19 R43/146  P(28-12-3) 153
Buf  D17 R35/139  P(25-14-1) 112
Buf-Thomas 122R

NO    10   3   3  21   37
LARm   3   0   3   0    6
NO   D17 R32/154  P(25-15-0) 205
LARm D17 R30/127  P(34-13-2) 129
LARm-Bettis 102R

Min    7   2   3   7   19
SF     7  14   3  14   38
Min  D15 R15/52   P(49-27-1) 219
SF   D17 R26/50   P(24-17-1) 204

Phi    0  14   7  14   35
NYJ   14   7   7   2   30
Phi  D18 R31/112  P(30-21-1) 191
NYJ  D19 R30/115  P(22-19-2) 297
NYJ-Burkett 103C, Mitchell 146C,
Esiason 297P

SD     7   0   0   7   14
Sea    7  10   7   7   31
SD   D19 R20/94   P(41-21-2) 221
Sea  D24 R31/57   P(42-26-0) 287
SD-Miller 123C; Sea-Blades 132C

GB     7   0   7   0   14
Dal   10   6  13   7   36
GB   D18 R18/36   P(42-24-0) 178
Dal  D20 R30/98   P(24-18-0) 297
Dal-Irvin 155C, Aikman 317P

Atl    0   0   0   0    0
ChiB   0   3   3   0    6
Atl  D16 R23/87   P(35-23-2) 184
ChiB D14 R31/106  P(23-16-0) 114

LARd   0   0   6   3    9
KC    14   7   3   0   24
LARd D15 R20/76   P(26-15-0) 146
KC   D26 R43/115  P(18-12-0) 127
LARd-Bettis 102R

Det    7   0   0   3   10
TB     0   3  21   3   27
Det  D17 R26/144  P(38-16-2) 167
TB   D17 R31/128  P(25-12-1) 196
Det-Sanders 130R; TB-Cobb 113R
```

MONDAY, OCTOBER 4

```
Was    0   3   0   7   10
Mia   14   0   0   3   17
Was  D20 R23/84   P(34-18-1) 148
Mia  D17 R27/106  P(30-16-1) 248
Mia-Martin 110C
```

SUNDAY, OCTOBER 10

```
NYG    7  20   0  14   41
Was    0   7   0   0    7
NYG  D26 R47/199  P(19-15-0) 216
Was  D16 R12/65   P(43-26-3) 239
NYG-Tillman 104R, Sherrard 124C

TB     0   0   0   0    0
Min    0  12   0   3   15
TB   D11 R20/59   P(29-12-4) 110
Min  D18 R33/124  P(28-17-1) 144

Cin    3   9   0   3   15
KC     0   7   7   3   17
Cin  D17 R34/115  P(31-16-1) 162
KC   D14 R28/94   P(20-10-0) 109

SD     0   0   0   3    3
Pit    3   3   7   3   16
SD   D12 R20/19   P(31-17-1) 119
Pit  D15 R36/148  P(25-16-0) 156
Pit-Foster 110R

Dal   14   0   7   6   27
Ind    0   3   0   0    3
Dal  D24 R35/143  P(30-21-0) 231
Ind  D19 R25/126  P(39-22-4) 235
Dal-Smith 104R, Irvin 112C;
Ind-Potts 113R, Dawkins 144C

Mia    0  10  14   0   24
Cle    7   7   0   0   14
Mia  D20 R31/70   P(35-24-1) 268
Cle  D16 R16/90   P(33-22-1) 112

NYJ    0  17   0   7   24
LARd   0   7  10   7   24
NYJ  D21 R29/96   P(41-21-1) 190
LARd D22 R30/105  P(34-18-3) 309

ChiB  10   7   0   0   17
Phi    0   0   7  10   17
ChiB D15 R41/102  P(27-14-1) 159
Phi  D14 R23/110  P(33-18-2) 166

NE     0  13   0   7   23
Phx    0  14   0   7   21
NE   D25 R41/151  P(37-20-1) 281
Phx  D13 R18/124  P(28-14-2) 187
NE-Russell 116R

Den    0   7  14   6   27
GB    17  13   0   0   30
Den  D26 R19/55   P(59-33-1) 333
GB   D15 R29/64   P(32-20-3) 235
Den-Johnson 148C, Elway 367P;
GB-Harris 128C
```

MONDAY, OCTOBER 11

```
Hou    7   0   0   0    7
Buf    7  21   0   7   35
Hou  D18 R17/84   P(40-25-4) 245
Buf  D23 R46/141  P(25-15-0) 241
```

SUNDAY, OCTOBER 17

```
KC     7   3   0   7   17
SD     0   7   0   7   14
KC   D20 R22/83   P(39-21-1) 264
SD   D18 R26/79   P(35-18-1) 190
SD-Miller 105C

Phi    0   0   0   7    7
NYG    0  14   0   7   21
Phi  D19 R26/90   P(35-21-1) 209
NYG  D18 R31/210  P(22-11-2) 137
NYG-Tillman 169R

Hou    0  14   7  14   28
NE     0   0   7   0    7
Hou  D15 R25/104  P(30-22-0) 142
NE   D19 R19/54   P(40-23-3) 261

Cle    0  14   7   7   28
Cin    7   0   7   3   17
Cle  D17 R42/183  P(24-11-1) 110
Cin  D14 R14/34   P(46-22-0) 160

Was    7   0   3   0   10
Phx    0  13   7  16   36
Was  D16 R26/138  P(29-17-1) 108
Phx  D18 R34/156  P(25-12-1) 224
Phx-Proehl 115C
```

```
SF    10   0   7   0   17
Dal    3  13   7   3   26
SF   D25 R24/156  P(33-24-0) 249
Dal  D24 R35/123  P(35-21-0) 230
Dal-Irvin 168C

Sea    7   0   3   0   10
Det    0   7   0   3   10
Sea  D16 R20/66   P(39-23-3) 166
Det  D20 R32/141  P(26-14-1) 151
Det-Sanders 101R

NO     0   0   0  14   14
Pit   14  10   6   7   37
NO   D11 R17/49   P(34-16-3) 215
Pit  D22 R47/201  P(29-15-1) 192
Pit-Thompson 101R

LARm  10   7   0   7   24
Atl    3   7   7  13   30
LARm D22 R29/167  P(35-17-2) 283
Atl  D16 R28/103  P(34-18-1) 208
```

MONDAY, OCTOBER 18

```
LARd  10   3   0  10   23
Den    0   0   3  17   20
LARd D12 R23/53   P(25-15-1) 255
Den  D18 R32/132  P(30-16-1) 121
LARd-Brown 116C;
Den-Bernstine 101R, Russell 111C
```

SUNDAY, OCTOBER 24

```
GB     7  17   6   7   37
TB     0   0   7   7   14
GB   D18 R34/162  P(36-21-1) 259
TB   D13 R20/84   P(31-12-3) 162
GB-Thompson 105R, Sharpe 147C,
Favre 268P

Cin    0   9   3   0   12
Hou    7   0   7  14   28
Cin  D20 R22/97   P(37-21-0) 241
Hou  D24 R25/125  P(34-24-1) 244
Cin-Pickens 127C

Buf    0   6   7   6   19
NYJ    7   0   0   0    7
Buf  D27 R45/197  P(35-22-2) 216
NYJ  D15 R21/78   P(25-14-2) 159
Buf-Thomas 117R

Phx    0   0   0  14   14
SF     0   0  14   0   28
Phx  D25 R24/107  P(50-26-3) 322
SF   D26 R30/148  P(34-22-0) 280
Phx-Edwards 112C, Beuerlein 334P;
SF-Rice 155C

NE     0   0   3   6    9
Sea    0   3   0   7   10
NE   D16 R36/166  P(33-15-2) 194
Sea  D15 R26/67   P(43-22-2) 194

Det    0   3   3  10   16
LARm   0   0   0  13   13
Det  D18 R34/134  P(25-15-1) 229
LARm D23 R30/150  P(26-14-1) 141
Det-Moore 120C; LARm-Bettis 113R

Pit    0  14   6   3   23
Cle    0  14   0   7   21
Pit  D23 R33/92   P(39-25-1) 348
Cle  D12 R22/98   P(16-10-0) 147
Pit-Green 108C, O'Donnell 355P;
Cle-Jackson 106C

Atl    0  17   3   6   26
NO     3   3   2   7   15
Atl  D17 R39/123  P(18-13-0) 156
NO   D16 R12/47   P(45-27-2) 274
Atl-Pegram 123R

Ind    0   6   7  14   27
Mia   17   3  14   7   41
Ind  D24 R25/88   P(44-27-3) 234
Mia  D18 R33/171  P(20-13-0) 195
Mia-Higgs 114R
```

MONDAY, OCTOBER 25

```
Min   10   3   6   0   19
ChiB   3   6   0   3   12
Min  D14 R34/165  P(27-14-1) 87
ChiB D12 R22/91   P(32-20-2) 159
```

SUNDAY, OCTOBER 31

```
Dal   3   7   3  10  23
Phi   0   7   0   3  10
Dal  D19 R39/271 P(19-9-0)   85
Phi  D16 R30/139 P(24-11-0)  89
Dal-Smith 237R

Sea   7   0   3   7  17
Den   0  21   7   0  28
Sea  D19 R26/103 P(30-16-2) 184
Den  D25 R31/87  P(36-23-1) 239

Det   7   6   0  17  30
Min   7  10  10   0  27
Det  D13 R23/78  P(28-20-2) 260
Min  D25 R30/116 P(42-29-1) 262
Det-Moore 113C; Min-Smith 115R

ChiB  0   3   0   0   3
GB    3   7   0   7  17
ChiB D15 R34/118 P(22-15-1) 112
GB   D16 R27/135 P(24-15-1) 126

NYJ   0   3   7   0  10
NYG   3   3   0   0   6
NYJ  D17 R37/127 P(17-12-0) 129
NYG  D17 R32/124 P(30-20-1) 141

TB    7  10  14   0  31
Atl   0  10  14   0  24
TB   D16 R34/98  P(28-18-2) 307
Atl  D16 R15/68  P(47-25-1) 269
TB-Copeland 104C, Erickson 318P;
Atl-Rison 147C

SD    7   3  14   6  30
LARd 10   0   7   6  23
SD   D17 R31/177 P(25-13-0) 159
LARd D20 R22/65  P(32-20-0) 402
LARd-Brown 156C, Hostetler 424P

LARm  3   0   7   7  17
SF    6  17   7  10  40
LARm D16 R26/110 P(26-15-2) 119
SF   D24 R33/129 P(34-22-0) 245

NO    7   0   3  10  20
Phx  10   7   0   0  17
NO   D18 R32/96  P(27-16-1) 176
Phx  D10 R25/89  P(26-14-1)  54

KC    0   3   0  10  13
Mia   6   7  14   3  30
KC   D18 R20/99  P(36-22-0) 206
Mia  D26 R40/139 P(33-22-0) 344
Mia-Ingram 103C, Mitchell 344P

NE    0   0   0   3   6
Ind   3   0   0   6   9
NE   D23 R25/87  P(37-23-2) 276
Ind  D14 R29/89  P(26-18-0) 179
NE-Coates 108C
```

MONDAY, NOVEMBER 1

```
Was   7   3   0   0  10
Buf  14   0   7   3  24
Was  D21 R29/140 P(42-15-4) 169
Buf  D22 R42/164 P(24-18-1) 238
Was-Brooks 117R;
Buf-Thomas 129R, Reed 159C
```

SUNDAY, NOVEMBER 7

```
Den   0  16   7   6  29
Cle   7   0   0   7  14
Den  D21 R42/160 P(23-17-0) 233
Cle  D14 R14/75  P(30-16-0) 191

Buf   0   0  10   3  13
NE    0   0   7   3  10
Buf  D25 R37/134 P(46-29-0) 298
NE   D17 R48/187 P(23-10-1)  91
Buf-Thomas 111R, Kelly 317P

SD    7   3   6  14  30
Min   0   3  14   0  17
SD   D24 R36/148 P(32-20-0) 263
Min  D21 R13/20  P(47-29-1) 326
SD-Means 105R, Miller 142C;
Min-Carter 164C, Salisbury 347P

Ind   0  10   0  14  24
Was   0  14   6  10  30
Ind  D21 R17/49  P(59-37-1) 356
Was  D16 R28/109 P(28-17-0) 166
Ind-Langhorne 203C, George 376P;
Was-Brooks 105R
```

```
Phi   3   0   0   0   3
Phx   3  13   0   0  16
Phi  D12 R15/65  P(32-14-1) 136
Phx  D21 R46/243 P(20-10-0) 116
Phx-Moore 160R

LARd  3  10   0   3  16
ChiB  0   0   7   7  14
LARd D20 R39/179 P(23-11-0)  95
ChiB D19 R36/124 P(24-12-1) 137

NYG   0   6   0   3   9
Dal  10   7   0  14  31
NYG  D18 R28/118 P(36-18-0) 177
Dal  D17 R32/139 P(20-17-0) 230
Dal-Smith 117R

Mia   0   3   7   0  10
NYJ  10   7   3   7  27
Mia  D15 R18/48  P(44-23-1) 289
NYJ  D24 R36/100 P(32-23-0) 256
Mia-Fryar 103C

Sea   7   0   0   7  14
Hou  13   9   2   0  24
Sea  D14 R21/84  P(23-14-1) 168
Hou  D26 R26/111 P(55-36-2) 347
Hou-Slaughter 135C, Moon 369P

Pit   0  14   0  10  24
Cin   3  13   0   0  16
Pit  D21 R33/146 P(34-14-1) 244
Cin  D14 R30/103 P(29-13-1)  96
Pit-Foster 120R

TB    0   0   0   0   0
Det   3   3   7  10  23
TB   D6  R14/44  P(26-13-1) 102
Det  D20 R43/241 P(22-16-0) 125
Det-Sanders 187R
```

MONDAY, NOVEMBER 8

```
GB    3   6   0   7  16
KC    3   0  10  10  23
GB   D20 R24/99  P(34-20-3) 188
KC   D15 R26/100 P(30-17-0) 153
```

SUNDAY, NOVEMBER 14

```
Mia   6   7   3   3  19
Phi   0  14   0   0  14
Mia  D13 R38/120 P(23-11-1) 178
Phi  D19 R27/103 P(37-23-0) 157

GB    3   7   3   6  19
NO    0  14   0   3  17
GB   D13 R21/69  P(32-18-0) 125
NO   D19 R35/157 P(29-20-2) 172
NO-Brown 106R

SF   10  21   7   7  45
TB    0  14   7   0  21
SF   D27 R32/124 P(34-25-0) 324
TB   D18 R21/94  P(33-19-1) 228
SF-Rice 172C, Young 311P

Atl   3   3   7   0  13
LARm  0   0   0   0   0
Atl  D15 R34/137 P(21-12-1) 182
LARm D14 R20/95  P(41-20-0) 165
Atl-Pegram 128R, Rison 120C

Hou   7  21  10   0  38
Cin   0   0   3   0   3
Hou  D32 R37/240 P(37-23-2) 222
Cin  D9  R22/102 P(28-8-0)   63
Hou-Brown 166R, Moon 225P

NYJ   7  10   7   7  31
Ind   3   7   7   0  17
NYJ  D27 R38/202 P(31-21-1) 256
Ind  D15 R19/92  P(27-14-0) 123
NYJ-Johnson 141R;
Ind-Langhorne 112C

Min   3  14   3   6  26
Den   6  14   0   3  23
Min  D18 R27/70  P(37-19-1) 357
Den  D25 R22/92  P(40-30-1) 250
Min-Carter 111C, Carter 134C,
Langhorne 112C, Salisbury 366P;
Den-Sharpe 104C

Cle   2   3   0   0   5
Sea   7   0   7   8  22
Cle  D13 R38/175 P(20-9-2)   57
Sea  D12 R33/119 P(27-11-0) 104
Sea-Warren 112R
```

```
ChiB  0   6  10   0  16
SD    3   7   0   3  13
ChiB D14 R26/84  P(24-13-1) 140
SD   D19 R32/104 P(38-19-0) 152

KC    0   7  14  10  31
LARd  7  10   0   3  20
KC   D14 R34/164 P(27-12-0) 174
LARd D22 R25/102 P(35-16-1) 178
KC-Davis 115C

Phx   0   0  10   5  15
Dal   3  10   3   4  20
Phx  D15 R20/51  P(46-27-1) 214
Dal  D15 R34/87  P(27-15-0) 224
Dal-Smith 102C

Was   0   0   3   3   6
NYG   7   7   3   3  20
Was  D20 R25/95  P(49-22-1) 230
NYG  D16 R38/152 P(16-9-1)  110
```

MONDAY, NOVEMBER 15

```
Buf   0   0   0   0   0
Pit   3   7  10   3  23
Buf  D9  R14/47  P(28-11-0) 110
Pit  D26 R50/227 P(27-16-0) 173
Pit-Thompson 108R
```

SUNDAY, NOVEMBER 21

```
Hou   0  14   3  10  27
Cle   3   7   0  10  20
Hou  D25 R39/202 P(40-19-2) 182
Cle  D20 R16/49  P(47-22-4) 300
Hou-Brown 194R; Cle-Carrier 123C,
Philcox 316P

Was   3   0   3   0   6
LARm  0   0   0  10  10
Was  D16 R28/114 P(39-24-1) 159
LARm D12 R22/89  P(26-17-0) 193

Pit   0   0   6   7  13
Den  10  10  14   3  37
Pit  D19 R22/101 P(38-23-1) 248
Den  D23 R34/107 P(25-18-0) 257

NYG   0   0   0   7   7
Phi   0   0   3   0   3
NYG  D14 R33/127 P(22-13-1) 165
Phi  D13 R29/129 P(32-13-1)  99
NYG-Hampton 101R

LARd  3   3   3   3  12
SD    0   0   0   7   7
LARd D24 R45/158 P(31-19-1) 270
SD   D13 R18/59  P(20-11-1)  95
LARd-Jett 138C

ChiB  0   6   6   7  19
KC    0   0  14   3  17
ChiB D18 R43/185 P(20-13-2)  96
KC   D19 R29/133 P(28-14-1) 119

Ind   3   3   0   3   9
Buf   0  16   7   0  23
Ind  D21 R29/113 P(41-21-1) 252
Buf  D18 R38/135 P(27-19-1) 268
Buf-Thomas 116R

Cin   0   9   0   3  12
NYJ   0  14   0   3  17
Cin  D14 R14/50  P(31-22-2) 176
NYJ  D21 R39/111 P(26-17-0) 177

Dal   0   7   0   7  14
Atl   3  10   7   7  27
Dal  D13 R13/48  P(39-22-0) 182
Atl  D22 R34/85  P(32-24-0) 315
Atl-Hebert 315P

NE    0   3   0   7  13
Mia   0   0   3  14  17
NE   D23 R24/88  P(42-23-1) 261
Mia  D15 R24/111 P(37-16-0) 233
Mia-Higgs 108R

Min   0   7   3   0  10
TB    3   3  10   7  23
Min  D12 R18/82  P(34-15-2) 153
TB   D18 R34/100 P(32-19-0) 200
Min-Carter 104C

Det   0  10   7   0  17
GB   10   3   3  10  26
Det  D12 R25/116 P(25-13-1)  89
GB   D25 R41/153 P(33-24-2) 251
```

MONDAY, NOVEMBER 22

```
NO    0   0   0   7   7
SF    7  21  14   0  42
NO   D17 R23/119 P(30-16-4) 142
SF   D25 R38/219 P(25-17-0) 236
SF-Watters 116R
```

THURSDAY, NOVEMBER 25

```
Mia   7   0   3   6  16
Dal   0  14   0   0  14
Mia  D15 R20/108 P(41-24-2) 274
Dal  D19 R28/112 P(43-28-1) 181

ChiB  0  10   0   0  10
Det   0   3   0   3   6
ChiB D11 R34/112 P(16-9-1)  113
Det  D14 R23/84  P(34-22-2) 146
```

SUNDAY, NOVEMBER 28

```
Den   0   7   3   7  17
Sea   0   0   2   9  11
Den  D19 R35/101 P(37-20-1) 206
Sea  D13 R26/127 P(37-17-1) 161

Phx   0   0   0  17  17
NYG   3   3   7   6  19
Phx  D19 R32/127 P(33-19-1) 176
NYG  D17 R17/46  P(41-22-0) 328
NYG-Jackson 113C, Simms 337P

Pit   0   3   0   0   3
Hou   0  10   0  13  23
Pit  D18 R17/65  P(39-21-2) 169
Hou  D20 R30/125 P(34-21-1) 266
Pit-Graham 102C; Hou-Jeffires 139C

NYJ   3   3   0   0   6
NE    0   0   0   0   0
NYJ  D14 R35/120 P(30-15-0) 174
NE   D14 R34/155 P(18-10-1) 134
NE-Russell 147R

TB    0   0   3   7  10
GB    0   3   3   7  13
TB   D11 R22/92  P(25-12-0) 115
GB   D14 R30/107 P(36-23-0) 152

Cle   0   0   7   7  14
Atl  10   7   0   0  17
Cle  D16 R29/115 P(26-14-0) 191
Atl  D13 R24/67  P(30-21-0) 194

LARd  0   0   0  10  10
Cin   3   7   3   3  16
LARd D16 R16/81  P(32-12-1) 202
Cin  D14 R43/131 P(25-14-0) 133
LARd-Bettis 133R, Jett 117C

Buf   7   0   0   0   7
KC    7   3   3  10  23
Buf  D17 R18/43  P(42-28-3) 213
KC   D19 R35/106 P(32-18-1) 208

NO    0   7   0   7  17
Min   7   0   0   7  14
NO   D15 R32/154 P(25-15-0) 100
Min  D16 R32/106 P(26-16-1) 182

SF    7  14   7   7  35
LARm  3   0   0   7  10
SF   D25 R25/64  P(35-21-0) 475
LARm D17 R27/161 P(28-13-1) 139
SF-Rice 166C, Taylor 150C,
Young 462P; LARm-Bettis 133R

Phi   3   7   0   7  17
Was   0   0   0  14  14
Phi  D19 R29/104 P(31-19-0) 164
Was  D19 R21/97  P(32-20-3) 252
Phi-Walker 103C
```

MONDAY, NOVEMBER 29

```
SD    0  14   3  14  31
Ind   0   0   0   0   0
SD   D31 R44/247 P(26-17-0) 227
Ind  D16 R20/55  P(34-19-1) 207
```

SUNDAY, DECEMBER 5

```
KC   10   7  14   0  31
Sea   3   3   3   3  16
KC   D23 R30/106 P(30-20-0) 231
Sea  D16 R24/90  P(30-18-2) 275
Sea-Blades 134C

Den   3   3   0   0  10
SD    0   0   3  10  13
Den  D14 R23/86  P(33-15-1) 138
SD   D20 R27/95  P(39-22-0) 203
```

```
Cin   2   6   0   0   8
SF    7   7   7   0  21
Cin  D19 R33/144 P(44-23-1) 195
SF   D19 R26/111 P(25-13-2) 173

Atl   0   7   7   3  17
Hou   3  14   3  13  33
Atl  D25 R12/37  P(52-30-6) 296
Hou  D18 R22/52  P(42-24-0) 336
Atl-Hebert 317P;
Hou-Slaughter 108C, Moon 342P

Ind   0   3   0   6   9
NYJ   3   3   0   0   6
Ind  D7  R28/67  P(24-11-0) 102
NYJ  D15 R39/122 P(30-12-1) 145

NYG   7   7   3   2  19
Mia   7   0   7   0  14
NYG  D19 R29/110 P(24-17-0) 241
Mia  D20 R20/51  P(43-27-2) 357
Mia-DeBerg 365P

LARm  7   0   0   3  10
Phx   7   7  14  10  38
LARm D16 R26/152 P(29-12-1) 151
Phx  D22 R35/134 P(25-14-0) 245
LARm-Bettis 115R;
Phx-Moore 126R, Clark 159C

LARd  3   7   6   9  25
Buf   3   7   3   7  24
LARd D25 R37/138 P(31-18-0) 261
Buf  D19 R24/91  P(30-20-1) 276
LARd-Bettis 115R, Brown 183C;
Buf-Beebe 115C

Was   7   3  13   0  23
TB    0   0  10   7  17
Was  D10 R36/175 P(16-9-1)   63
TB   D18 R31/144 P(34-15-3) 163
Was-Brooks 128R;
TB-Hawkins 112C

NO    7   0   3   3  13
Cle   0  10   0   7  17
NO   D12 R24/79  P(29-15-0)  48
Cle  D15 R28/131 P(35-16-2) 183

Min   3   3   0   7  13
Det   0   0   0   0   0
Min  D14 R26/101 P(32-15-0) 133
Det  D16 R27/108 P(32-19-5) 111

GB    7   0  10   0  17
ChiB  3   3  10  14  30
GB   D29 R28/79  P(54-36-3) 387
ChiB D10 R23/69  P(20-10-1) 141
GB-Sharpe 114C, Favre 402P

NE   14   0   0   0  14
Pit   0  17   0   0  17
NE   D20 R24/53  P(48-18-5) 296
Pit  D14 R32/125 P(32-17-0)  92
```

MONDAY, DECEMBER 6

```
Phi   0   3   7   7  17
Dal   7   9   0   7  23
Phi  D21 R18/59  P(45-27-1) 248
Dal  D17 R29/182 P(24-17-0) 165
Dal-Smith 172R
```

SATURDAY, DECEMBER 11

```
SF    7  10   7   0  24
Atl   7   0   0  20  27
SF   D22 R19/79  P(39-24-2) 251
Atl  D20 R25/92  P(39-24-0) 270
SF-Rice 105C; Atl-Rison 107C

NYJ   3   0   0   0   3
Was   0   0   0   0   0
NYJ  D17 R50/210 P(22-12-0)  98
Was  D7  R15/39  P(24-10-0) 111
NYJ-Johnson 155R
```

SUNDAY, DECEMBER 12

```
KC    7   7   7   0  21
Den   3   7   7  10  27
KC   D17 R21/77  P(30-17-1) 234
Den  D23 R38/136 P(30-20-2) 204

Dal   3  17   7  10  37
Min   6   0   7   7  20
Dal  D25 R35/148 P(29-19-0) 208
Min  D20 R24/97  P(25-20-1) 173
Dal-Smith 104R, Irvin 125C
```

Sea 0 9 0 14 23
LARd 3 7 17 0 27
Sea D21 R32/134 P(36-20-1) 169
LARd D18 R23/59 P(30-21-1) 303
LARd-Bettis 212R

ChiB 0 3 7 0 10
TB 3 7 3 0 13
ChiB D18 R28/119 P(36-22-0) 167
TB D13 R29/103 P(21-12-1) 112

Det 0 7 7 7 21
Phx 0 7 7 0 14
Det D13 R23/105 P(25-19-0) 235
Phx D19 R25/96 P(35-23-3) 191
Det-Moore 107R

GB 7 6 7 0 20
SD 3 3 7 0 13
GB D17 R39/103 P(23-13-1) 124
SD D17 R17/57 P(51-27-3) 225
SD-Miller 103C

LARm 10 0 13 0 23
NO 7 6 0 7 20
LARm D16 R42/266 P(13-5-0) 40
NO D24 R24/97 P(43-25-1) 267
LARm-Bettis 212R

Cle 10 0 7 0 17
Hou 3 13 0 3 19
Cle D19 R27/105 P(38-19-2) 305
Hou D18 R28/128 P(28-13-1) 129
Cle-Metcalf 101C, Testaverde 319P;
Hou-Brown 109R

Ind 0 6 0 0 6
NYG 7 6 0 7 20
Ind D14 R15/55 P(38-22-0) 250
NYG D19 R43/205 P(15-9-0) 85
NYG-Hampton 173R

Buf 0 0 0 10 10
Phi 0 0 7 0 7
Buf D19 R29/101 P(37-23-2) 234
Phi D21 R23/70 P(48-28-0) 298
Phi-Walker 109C

Cin 0 0 0 2 2
NE 0 7 0 0 7
Cin D11 R34/102 P(25-9-1) 63
NE D16 R44/118 P(22-11-0) 106

MONDAY, DECEMBER 13

Pit 0 7 7 7 21
Mia 3 3 0 14 20
Pit D19 R38/120 P(28-16-0) 145
Mia D21 R17/49 P(44-27-2) 299
Mia-Kirby 107C, DeBerg 344P

SATURDAY, DECEMBER 18

Den 0 10 3 0 13
ChiB 3 0 0 0 3
Den D15 R33/129 P(24-14-0) 105
ChiB D14 R26/84 P(29-14-3) 101
Den-Bernstine 103R

Dal 0 7 14 7 28
NYJ 0 0 0 7 7
Dal D19 R30/129 P(27-21-3) 235
NYJ D23 R27/81 P(46-24-1) 214

SUNDAY, DECEMBER 19

Phx 7 0 7 13 3 30
Sea 10 10 0 7 0 27
Phx D26 R29/71 P(53-34-2) 405
Sea D19 R36/212 P(31-15-0) 153
Phx-Clark 152C, Beuerlein 431P;
Sea-Warren 168R

SD 10 7 0 7 24
KC 0 14 7 7 28
SD D20 R28/94 P(39-20-2) 174
KC D20 R29/104 P(36-22-1) 217

Phi 10 0 7 3 20
Ind 3 0 0 7 10
Phi D23 R39/151 P(39-21-1) 189
Ind D16 R12/31 P(39-21-0) 230
Phi-Williams 105C

TB 0 10 0 10 20
LARd 14 3 0 10 27
TB D24 R30/101 P(34-21-0) 265
LARd D17 R23/17 P(30-19-0) 248
LARd-Bettis 124R, Wright 104C

SF 14 17 14 10 55
Det 0 10 0 7 17
SF D26 R37/172 P(28-20-0) 393
Det D16 R18/81 P(29-19-0) 207
SF-Rice 132C, Taylor 115C,
Young 354P

NE 0 10 3 7 20
Cle 7 7 0 3 17
NE D23 R27/120 P(47-19-1) 203
Cle D18 R27/80 P(31-21-2) 297

Hou 14 6 3 3 26
Pit 0 3 7 7 17
Hou D20 R25/117 P(38-19-0) 266
Pit D21 R18/38 P(57-24-2) 347
Hou-Brown 100R; Pit-Graham 192C

LARm 0 3 0 0 3
Cin 3 6 3 3 15
LARm D14 R32/166 P(24-11-0) 107
Cin D20 R37/170 P(30-16-0) 223
LARm-Bettis 124R

Atl 7 0 7 3 17
Was 0 16 0 14 30
Atl D22 R35/182 P(43-24-4) 196
Was D8 R19/38 P(23-13-1) 129
Atl-Broussard 162R

Min 0 7 7 7 21
GB 3 7 0 7 17
Min D21 R38/154 P(31-22-0) 207
GB D16 R19/67 P(33-20-1) 253
Min-Graham 139R, Carter 106C;
GB-Sharpe 106C

Buf 9 17 21 0 47
Mia 7 13 7 7 34
Buf D28 R44/129 P(31-20-1) 245
Mia D24 R11/23 P(59-32-3) 400
Mia-Kirby 148C

MONDAY, DECEMBER 20

NYG 7 7 3 7 24
NO 0 7 0 7 14
NYG D20 R42/133 P(23-15-0) 144
NO D15 R12/11 P(41-23-2) 293

SATURDAY, DECEMBER 25

Hou 0 10 0 0 10
SF 0 0 0 7 7
Hou D16 R23/116 P(29-14-3) 195
SF D20 R23/90 P(42-26-2) 247
Hou-Brown 114R

SUNDAY, DECEMBER 26

Cle 7 7 7 21 42
LARm 7 0 0 7 14
Cle D23 R32/102 P(23-21-0) 213
LARm D20 R21/95 P(32-24-2) 287
LARm-Ellard 114C

Det 0 10 3 7 20
ChiB 7 0 0 7 14
Det D20 R26/84 P(31-23-1) 223
ChiB D14 R32/77 P(23-14-0) 103

KC 0 3 0 7 10
Min 3 7 10 10 30
KC D12 R16/37 P(33-23-2) 183
Min D23 R46/205 P(25-17-1) 219
Min-Graham 166R

Was 3 0 0 0 3
Dal 7 14 14 3 38
Was D16 R28/126 P(33-15-2) 72
Dal D27 R32/175 P(23-17-0) 205
Dal-Smith 153R

NYG 3 3 0 0 6
Phx 0 0 10 7 17
NYG D16 R26/78 P(36-23-0) 215
Phx D20 R28/144 P(24-15-2) 189
Phx-Moore 135R

TB 0 10 7 0 17
Den 7 0 3 0 10
TB D13 R36/65 P(30-14-1) 171
Den D18 R23/110 P(41-26-0) 225
TB-Hawkins 105C

Pit 0 3 0 3 6
Sea 7 3 3 3 16
Pit D18 R20/116 P(43-20-1) 264
Sea D25 R45/267 P(30-12-1) 101
Pit-Green 119C, Stone 100C;
Sea-Vaughn 131R

NYJ 7 0 7 0 14
Buf 7 6 0 3 16
NYJ D19 R25/120 P(31-22-0) 232
Buf D19 R36/90 P(31-20-2) 256

Ind 0 0 0 0 0
NE 7 10 14 7 38
Ind D7 R18/37 P(25-13-0) 99
NE D24 R58/257 P(11-9-0) 143
NE-Russell 138R

Atl 7 0 3 7 17
Cin 7 7 0 7 21
Atl D22 R39/191 P(31-16-1) 185
Cin D16 R24/122 P(30-16-0) 162
Atl-Pegram 180R

LARd 0 0 0 0 0
GB 0 7 7 14 28
LARd D11 R18/46 P(38-18-2) 136
GB D17 R37/148 P(28-14-0) 181
LARd-Ellard 114C;
GB-Thompson 101R, Sharpe 119C

NO 9 3 7 7 26
Phi 0 18 6 13 37
NO D7 R21/83 P(18-6-2) 75
Phi D20 R44/134 P(30-20-0) 180

MONDAY, DECEMBER 27

Mia 3 10 7 0 20
SD 10 14 14 7 45
Mia D23 R25/61 P(40-24-3) 260
SD D25 R37/220 P(30-19-0) 239
SD-Means 118R, Miller 110C

FRIDAY, DECEMBER 31

Min 0 7 7 0 14
Was 0 3 3 3 9
Min D16 R27/46 P(32-19-1) 226
Was D14 R23/112 P(36-24-0) 153
Min-Carter 113C

SUNDAY, JANUARY 2

Den 10 17 3 0 30
LARd 0 13 7 10 33
Den D22 R31/110 P(36-25-0) 361
LARd D24 R24/94 P(41-25-0) 304
Den-Sharpe 115C, Elway 361P;
LARd-Bettis 146R, Brown 173C,
Hostetler 310P

Sea 3 7 0 14 24
KC 10 17 0 7 34
Sea D16 R25/140 P(30-19-0) 140
KC D26 R32/109 P(39-24-1) 263
Sea-Williams 102R

ChiB 0 3 0 3 6
LARm 3 3 0 14 20
ChiB D10 R16/89 P(21-13-1) 74
LARm D27 R47/181 P(28-18-0) 213
LARm-Bettis 146R

Buf 3 7 6 14 30
Ind 0 3 0 7 10
Buf D19 R40/149 P(28-16-0) 148
Ind D25 R24/116 P(48-30-0) 286
Buf-Thomas 110R; Ind-Potts 100R,
George 330P

GB 7 3 10 0 20
Det 0 10 6 14 30
GB D17 R22/101 P(37-23-4) 172
Det D16 R30/115 P(29-15-1) 182
Det-Lynch 115R

Dal 3 10 0 0 3 16
NYG 0 0 10 3 0 13
Dal D21 R36/182 P(30-24-0) 157
NYG D16 R35/130 P(25-16-0) 183
Dal-Smith 168R;
NYG-Hampton 114R

SD 10 3 3 16 32
TB 3 0 7 7 17
SD D16 R28/92 P(30-18-0) 272
TB D22 R23/72 P(46-25-3) 312
SD-Miller 119C; TB-Copeland 101C

Phx 7 10 3 7 27
Atl 3 0 7 0 10
Phx D22 R34/117 P(33-27-0) 278
Atl D16 R13/81 P(32-18-2) 189
Phx-Clark 121C

Mia 0 7 3 17 0 27
NE 3 7 7 10 6 33
Mia D23 R30/119 P(41-22-0) 230
NE D25 R32/68 P(43-27-1) 329
NE-Bledsoe 329P

NYJ 0 0 0 0 0
Hou 7 7 3 7 24
NYJ D9 R17/54 P(30-13-1) 110
Hou D25 R29/108 P(42-26-1) 255
Hou-Wellman 106C

Cin 0 3 0 10 13
NO 0 6 7 7 20
Cin D13 R34/84 P(23-13-0) 104
NO D15 R30/76 P(27-15-1) 193
NO-Martin 120C

Cle 0 9 0 0 9
Pit 0 3 3 10 16
Cle D12 R20/61 P(30-15-0) 234
Pit D20 R32/135 P(39-22-0) 185
Cle-Carrier 118C

MONDAY, JANUARY 3

Phi 10 14 10 0 3 37
SF 3 7 14 10 0 34
Phi D23 R23/74 P(43-26-1) 307
SF D31 R27/131 P(48-33-1) 346
Phi-Joseph 109C, Brister 350P

1994 NFL

SUNDAY, SEPTEMBER 4

Hou 0 0 0 21 21
Ind 7 28 7 3 45
Hou D26 R14/79 P(57-30-1) 295
Ind D19 R37/182 P(13-10-1) 106
Ind-Faulk 143R

Atl 0 7 7 14 0 28
Det 7 0 7 14 3 31
Atl D22 R28/118 P(37-29-0) 271
Det D21 R31/149 P(31-16-1) 203
Atl-Rison 193C; Det-Sanders 120R

Arz 0 6 6 0 12
LARm 7 0 7 0 14
Arz D23 R32/106 P(40-18-2) 128
LARm D9 R22/50 P(16-6-1) 102

Dal 3 13 0 10 26
Pit 0 3 0 6 9
Dal D26 R41/197 P(32-21-1) 245
Pit D14 R17/55 P(26-13-0) 71
Dal-Smith 171R, Irvin 139C

Cle 11 14 0 3 28
Cin 0 10 3 7 20
Cle D16 R27/107 P(24-14-2) 149
Cin D23 R30/118 P(43-27-2) 213

TB 0 3 6 0 9
ChiB 7 7 0 7 21
TB D17 R30/123 P(32-18-0) 181
ChiB D17 R25/66 P(25-18-0) 204

Phi 0 10 3 10 23
NYG 14 7 7 0 28
Phi D20 R25/78 P(39-20-0) 317
NYG D15 R34/141 P(20-10-1) 149
Phi-Cunningham 344P

SD 6 21 3 7 37
Den 17 7 3 7 34
SD D19 R34/138 P(22-12-0) 232
Den D30 R18/129 P(46-36-2) 341
Den-Pritchard 119C, Elway 371P

NYJ 0 17 3 3 23
Buf 3 0 0 0 3
NYJ D17 R41/116 P(28-14-1) 214
Buf D13 R13/43 P(37-22-1) 166

KC 7 10 3 10 30
NO 0 3 7 7 17
KC D28 R43/152 P(33-24-0) 308
NO D22 R11/37 P(37-26-2) 312
KC-Davis 109C, Montana 315P;
NO-Early 101C, Everett 326P

Sea 7 14 7 0 28
Was 7 0 0 0 7
Sea D23 R38/184 P(28-17-0) 176
Was D17 R21/34 P(40-20-2) 224
Sea-Warren 100R; Was-Ellard 105C

Min 0 0 3 7 10
GB 3 10 0 3 16
Min D12 R17/48 P(37-20-3) 146
GB D15 R26/94 P(36-22-0) 170

NE 7 7 14 7 35
Mia 0 10 15 14 39
NE D25 R24/54 P(51-32-2) 418
Mia D21 R23/69 P(42-23-1) 456
NE-Coates 161C, Bledsoe 421P;
Mia-Fryar 211C, Marino 473P

MONDAY, SEPTEMBER 5

LARd 0 14 0 0 14
SF 14 9 0 21 44
LARd D12 R20/34 P(33-19-1) 147
SF D24 R36/156 P(32-19-1) 292
SF-Rice 169C, Young 308P

SUNDAY, SEPTEMBER 11

Mia 3 14 7 0 24
GB 0 0 0 14 14
Mia D20 R34/146 P(25-17-0) 162
GB D23 R7/38 P(51-31-1) 345
GB-Favre 362P

NYG 6 14 0 0 20
Arz 3 7 0 7 17
NYG D19 R41/118 P(17-11-1) 88
Arz D11 R16/39 P(27-14-2) 135

Sea 7 3 14 14 38
LARd 3 0 0 6 9
Sea D22 R38/97 P(26-19-0) 235
LARd D20 R14/99 P(43-21-3) 198
LARd-Bettis 102R, Anderson 154C

Ind 0 3 7 0 10
TB 7 3 7 7 24
Ind D20 R39/163 P(24-19-1) 201
TB D13 R24/54 P(24-19-0) 313
Ind-Faulk 104R; TB-Erickson 313P

Buf 14 14 0 10 38
NE 7 7 7 14 35
Buf D25 R38/144 P(41-25-3) 322
NE D26 R25/96 P(42-26-2) 371
Buf-Thomas 106R, Reed 142C,
Kelly 328P; NE-Coates 124C,
Timpson 101C, Bledsoe 380P

LARm 0 7 0 6 13
Atl 14 3 7 7 31
LARm D20 R29/140 P(37-19-3) 281
Atl D24 R24/124 P(42-30-1) 304
LARm-Bettis 102R, Anderson 154C;
Atl-Rison 123C

Pit 0 14 0 3 17
Cle 7 3 0 0 10
Pit D17 R38/116 P(25-15-0) 199
Cle D18 R19/81 P(38-19-4) 197

Den 0 13 6 3 0 22
NYJ 7 7 0 8 3 25
Den D22 R24/85 P(42-29-1) 316
NYJ D19 R21/79 P(37-26-2) 287
Den-Miller 105C, Pritchard 100C,
Elway 319P; NYJ-Moore 147C

Cin 3 0 0 7 10
SD 3 10 7 7 27
Cin D17 R22/113 P(34-21-1) 167
SD D21 R35/166 P(29-18-0) 299
SD-Means 107R, Seay 119C

Was 14 0 14 10 38
NO 3 0 6 15 24
Was D22 R46/153 P(22-15-0) 190
NO D27 R15/28 P(49-33-1) 380
Was-Friesz 195P; NO-Everett 376P

Det 0 0 0 3 3
Min 3 7 0 0 10
Det D13 R15/37 P(41-18-1) 175
Min D14 R30/86 P(35-22-1) 203

SF 0 14 0 3 17
KC 7 2 15 0 24
SF D23 R26/110 P(34-24-2) 271
KC D18 R32/98 P(31-19-0) 194

Hou 3 7 0 7 17
Dal 7 6 7 0 20
Hou D20 R28/137 P(42-20-2) 202
Dal D18 R34/115 P(25-14-1) 225
Hou-Jeffires 103C; Dal-Harper 109C

MONDAY, SEPTEMBER 12

```
ChiB   0    0    0   22   22
Phi    7   17    6    0   30
ChiB D13 R11/37  P(31-18-1) 275
Phi  D24 R39/105 P(36-24-0) 311
  ChiB-Conway 148C;
  Phi-Barnett 102C,
  Cunningham 311P
```

SUNDAY, SEPTEMBER 18

```
KC     7    3    7   13   30
Atl    0    0    3    7   10
KC  D22 R23/66  P(39-28-2) 361
Atl D21 R19/100 P(45-29-2) 284
  KC-Montana 361P; Atl-Mathis 123C

SF    10    7    3   14   34
LARm   7    3    0    9   19
SF   D28 R30/105 P(39-31-0) 349
LARm D22 R24/115 P(34-17-0) 163
  SF-Rice 147C, Taylor 103C,
  Young 355P; LARm-Bettis 104R

Was    3   17    0    3   23
NYG   10    7    7    7   31
Was D24 R21/80  P(50-32-2) 376
NYG D20 R34/106 P(20-15-0) 231
  Was-Ellard 197C, Friesz 381P

NE     7    6   12    6   31
Cin    6    7    8    7   28
NE  D28 R36/82  P(50-30-2) 365
Cin D21 R20/99  P(29-21-0) 219
  NE-Coates 108C, Timpson 125C,
  Bledsoe 365P

SD     0   10   14    0   24
Sea    0    3    0    7   10
SD  D18 R33/95  P(30-19-1) 251
Sea D23 R24/59  P(36-20-1) 128
  SD-Martin 152C

NYJ    0    0    7    7   14
Mia   14    0    7    7   28
NYJ D18 R17/59  P(37-22-4) 284
Mia D26 R36/155 P(31-23-1) 289
  Mia-Kirby 100R, Jackson 100C

Buf    0    9    3    3   15
Hou    0    0    0    7    7
Buf D17 R34/115 P(28-18-1) 183
Hou D13 R27/97  P(24-11-1) 159
  Buf-Thomas 112R;
  Hou-Slaughter 110C

Min    0   10   18   14   42
ChiB   0    0    0   14   14
Min  D28 R36/212 P(32-25-1) 252
ChiB D19 R14/60  P(35-27-1) 244
  Min-Allen 159R

LARd  21    7   10   10   48
Den    0    3    0   13   16
LARd D20 R30/102 P(34-21-0) 322
Den  D21 R17/69  P(50-25-1) 223
  LARd-Bettis 104R, Brown 136C,
  Hostetler 338P

GB     7    0    0    0    7
Phi    0    3   10    0   13
GB  D13 R14/37  P(45-24-2) 238
Phi D20 R28/91  P(43-20-1) 182
  GB-Sharpe 108C

Arz    0    0    0    0    0
Cle    0    3   15   14   32
Arz D21 R17/63  P(58-26-3) 255
Cle D17 R27/79  P(27-17-1) 243
  Cle-Alexander 136C

Ind    7    7    7    0   21
Pit    0   17    0   14   31
Ind D10 R19/73  P(19-9-0)  102
Pit D32 R45/261 P(35-22-1) 239
  Pit-Foster 179R

NO     6    3    0    0    9
TB     0    7    0    0    7
NO D12 R23/57  P(31-19-0) 176
TB D16 R26/85  P(32-17-0) 147
```

MONDAY, SEPTEMBER 19

```
Det    3    7    7    3   20
Dal    3    7    0    7   17
Det D22 R47/206 P(27-13-0) 173
Dal D25 R34/162 P(39-26-0) 206
  Det-Sanders 194R; Dal-Smith 143R
```

SUNDAY, SEPTEMBER 25

```
Mia    0    6   15   14   35
Min   14   14    0   10   38
Mia D27 R19/47  P(54-29-3) 426
Min D24 R31/147 P(37-26-0) 311
  Mia-Fryar 160C, Marino 431P;
  Min-Allen 113R, Reed 127C,
  Moon 326P

Cin    0    0    3   10   13
Hou    7   10    3    0   20
Cin D13 R22/102 P(30-10-3) 74
Hou D19 R42/148 P(34-12-2) 193
  Hou-Coleman 112C

ChiB   0   10    3    6   19
NYJ    7    0    0    0    7
ChiB D17 R40/104 P(24-14-0) 122
NYJ  D17 R18/164 P(32-16-1) 161
  NYJ-Johnson 126R

Pit    3    3    0    7   13
Sea    7   13    0   10   30
Pit D29 R30/131 P(46-24-4) 321
Sea D20 R35/145 P(24-14-1) 152
  Sea-Warren 126R

NE     3   14    3    3   23
Det    0    7    3    7   17
NE  D21 R37/108 P(33-21-0) 245
Det D15 R22/159 P(29-14-2) 183
  Det-Sanders 131R

Atl    7    0   17    3   27
Was    0   13    0    7   20
Atl D19 R28/71  P(35-22-1) 238
Was D18 R14/44  P(45-27-4) 310
  Was-Ellard 162C

NO     3   10    0    0   13
SF     3    7    7    7   24
NO D17 R19/49  P(55-31-2) 291
SF D18 R19/74  P(39-25-2) 224

SD    10   10    3    3   26
LARd   3   14    7    2   24
SD   D17 R31/84  P(26-18-2) 179
LARd D15 R20/59  P(26-15-0) 220
  LARd-Bettis 132R

TB     0    0    3    0    3
GB     0   13   10    7   30
TB D15 R16/54  P(30-12-1) 177
GB D24 R34/95  P(39-30-0) 306
  GB-Favre 306P

Cle    7    7    0    7   21
Ind    7    0    7    0   14
Cle D17 R31/119 P(28-16-1) 257
Ind D18 R33/146 P(26-16-1) 189

LARm  13    0    3    0   16
KC     0    0    0    0    0
LARm D17 R42/155 P(21-13-0) 202
KC   D21 R17/76  P(37-18-3) 166
  LARm-Bettis 132R
```

MONDAY, SEPTEMBER 26

```
Den    0    7   10    3   20
Buf    3   14    7    3   27
Den D21 R23/77  P(46-26-1) 260
Buf D19 R35/149 P(26-16-1) 166
  Buf-Thomas 103R
```

SUNDAY, OCTOBER 2

```
Phi   14   16    3    7   40
SF     0    8    0    0    8
Phi D26 R41/191 P(29-20-0) 246
SF  D11 R18/60  P(31-15-2) 129
  Phi-Garner 111R, Williams 122C

Mia    0   10    7    6   23
Cin    7    0    0    0    7
Mia D21 R37/141 P(35-26-0) 204
Cin D14 R17/62  P(30-16-3) 184

Dal    7   24    3    0   34
Was    0    0    7    0    7
Dal D26 R46/142 P(28-20-1) 181
Was D12 R18/28  P(30-11-1) 82

Det    0   14    0    0   14
TB    10    7    7    0   24
Det D17 R24/196 P(30-13-0) 125
TB  D16 R38/119 P(20-10-0) 115
  Det-Sanders 166R
```


```
Min    0    7    0    0    7
Arz    7    0    0   10   17
Min D19 R13/18  P(47-29-2) 340
Arz D21 R30/109 P(37-26-0) 200
  Min-Carter 167C, Moon 355P

Sea    5    3    0    7   15
Ind   10    0    7    0   17
Sea D17 R25/102 P(38-20-1) 174
Ind D14 R34/119 P(27-15-0) 168
  Sea-Martin 104C

NYJ    0    0    0    7    7
Cle    7   17    3    0   27
NYJ D19 R19/72  P(46-28-2) 274
Cle D18 R26/117 P(36-21-0) 246
  Cle-Alexander 105C

NYG    3   10    0    9   22
NO     3   14    3    7   27
NYG D11 R21/50  P(35-20-2) 152
NO  D15 R28/67  P(30-20-1) 247

Atl    0    0    0    8    8
LARm   0    0    3    2    5
Atl  D23 R22/81  P(39-26-1) 285
LARm D16 R32/126 P(25-13-2) 120
  LARm-Bettis 117R

GB     3    7    0    6   16
NE     0    0    7   10   17
GB D20 R27/100 P(47-25-2) 264
NE D21 R17/48  P(53-29-1) 312
  GB-Sharpe 132C; NE-Brisby 117C,
  Bledsoe 334P

Buf    3    3    7    0   13
ChiB   0    7    3   10   20
Buf  D17 R22/105 P(33-19-2) 99
ChiB D17 R42/111 P(28-19-1) 150
```

MONDAY, OCTOBER 3

```
Hou    0    0    0   14   14
Pit   20    3    0    7   30
Hou D14 R19/69  P(32-17-0) 221
Pit D21 R44/215 P(18-10-0) 164
  Pit-Foster 115R
```

SUNDAY, OCTOBER 9

```
LARd   0   14    7    0   21
NE     0   17    0    0   17
LARd D14 R27/86  P(31-17-3) 242
NE   D25 R29/54  P(55-23-3) 305
  NE-Coates 123C, Bledsoe 321P

Was    0    6   11    0   17
Phi    7    0    7    7   21
Was D12 R16/55  P(27-10-1) 171
Phi D26 R44/193 P(39-22-2) 238
  Phi-Garner 122R

NO     0    7    0    0    7
ChiB   0    0   10    7   17
NO   D17 R25/107 P(40-22-1) 209
ChiB D16 R32/131 P(26-16-0) 174
  ChiB-Tillman 100R

TB     0    3    0   10   13
Atl   14   10    3    7   34
TB  D19 R16/32  P(47-30-3) 288
Atl D20 R23/85  P(36-24-2) 271

Den    3    7    6    0   16
Sea    0    3    3    3    9
Den D19 R44/150 P(29-15-0) 128
Sea D16 R20/94  P(39-19-2) 244
  Den-Russell 103R

Arz    0    0    3    0    3
Dal   21    7   10    0   38
Arz D10 R18/53  P(35-16-5) 168
Dal D22 R36/78  P(28-19-0) 273
  Dal-Irvin 136C

KC     0    3    0    3    6
SD     3   10    0    7   20
KC D20 R18/64  P(55-37-1) 297
SD D18 R30/151 P(25-16-0) 171
  KC-Montana 310P; SD-Means 125R

LARm   7   10    0    0   17
GB     3    0   14    7   24
LARm D13 R24/64  P(29-18-1) 147
GB   D21 R29/84  P(41-25-1) 208

Mia    3    0    0    8   11
Buf    0    7    7    7   21
Mia D19 R19/114 P(43-20-0) 212
Buf D25 R48/214 P(22-13-1) 130
  Buf-Thomas 125R
```


```
SF     0   14    7    6   27
Det    7    7    0    7   21
SF  D20 R32/90  P(26-19-0) 143
Det D21 R25/98  P(27-18-1) 242

Ind    3    0    0    3    6
NYJ    0    6    0   10   16
Ind D10 R29/141 P(21-12-0) 90
NYJ D14 R41/150 P(29-13-1) 100
```

MONDAY, OCTOBER 10

```
Min    3    7   14    3   27
NYG    0    0   10    0   10
Min D25 R36/103 P(34-23-1) 292
NYG D16 R18/37  P(36-19-3) 203
  Min-Ismail 117C
```

THURSDAY, OCTOBER 13

```
Cle    0   11    0    0   11
Hou    0    0    0    8    8
Cle D12 R24/64  P(25-15-2) 196
Hou D20 R24/106 P(40-22-1) 199
```

SUNDAY, OCTOBER 16

```
SF    14   14   14    0   42
Atl    0    3    0    0    3
SF  D16 R35/101 P(19-16-0) 180
Atl D17 R18/62  P(37-25-4) 192
  SF-Young 143P

NE     0    7    0   10   17
NYJ    7   14    0    3   24
NE  D19 R30/104 P(41-22-1) 220
NYJ D17 R37/172 P(17-12-0) 70
  NYJ-Johnson 122R

Ind    3    7    7   10   27
Buf    7    3    0    7   17
Ind D20 R37/94  P(24-20-0) 231
Buf D22 R22/79  P(34-25-0) 250
  Ind-Dawkins 105C

Phi    7    0    0    6   13
Dal    0   14    7    3   24
Phi D18 R24/124 P(34-17-4) 170
Dal D19 R35/113 P(23-12-1) 153
  Dal-Smith 106R

Arz    0    3    0   13   19
Was    0   14    0    2   16
Arz D19 R48/151 P(34-16-3) 173
Was D11 R29/85  P(32-11-5) 149
  Arz-Moore 118R

NYG    3    0    0    0    3
LARm  14    3    0    0   17
NYG  D14 R31/121 P(27-15-2) 161
LARm D17 R36/105 P(26-13-1) 169
  NYG-Hampton 112R

Cin    0    0    0    3   10
Pit    0   14    0    0   14
Cin D11 R33/106 P(31-17-1) 135
Pit D16 R30/114 P(22-15-0) 129

SD    14   13    0    9   36
NO     0    7    7    8   22
SD D25 R40/198 P(29-17-0) 180
NO D24 R18/104 P(35-24-0) 188
  SD-Means 120R

LARd  10    0    7    0   17
Mia    0    7    3   10   20
LARd D21 R33/106 P(27-9-0)  86
Mia  D19 R38/169 P(37-17-1) 175
  Mia-Parmalee 150R
```

MONDAY, OCTOBER 17

```
KC     0   14    7   10   31
Den    0   14    7    7   28
KC  D26 R24/90  P(54-34-1) 393
Den D21 R27/97  P(29-18-0) 233
  KC-Montana 393P
```

THURSDAY, OCTOBER 20

```
GB     0   10    0    0   10
Min    7    0    3    3   13
GB  D12 R26/71  P(34-17-1) 87
Min D16 R19/22  P(50-31-2) 230
```

SUNDAY, OCTOBER 23

```
Sea    0    0    7   16   23
KC     0   13    8   17   38
Sea D16 R29/167 P(30-15-0) 96
KC  D24 R37/172 P(33-23-0) 305
  Sea-Warren 117R
```


```
Cin   10    3    0    0   13
Cle    3    7   17   10   37
Cin D15 R30/75  P(37-18-0) 146
Cle D13 R24/120 P(29-11-1) 120

Was    3   10   14   14   41
Ind    3   14    0   10   27
Was D20 R33/100 P(32-17-0) 226
Ind D20 R30/109 P(30-18-3) 272
  Was-Ellard 108C; Ind-Faulk 127C

Atl   10    0    0    7   17
LARd   0   14   10    6   30
Atl  D15 R21/70  P(30-16-2) 185
LARd D21 R31/116 P(30-21-0) 197
  LARd-Williams 107R, Brown 130C

Pit    0    3    0    7   10
NYG    3    0    0    0    6
Pit D16 R36/175 P(29-16-1) 121
NYG D8  R24/53  P(25-13-2) 162
  Pit-Morris 146R

ChiB   0    7    9    0   16
Det    0   14    7    0   21
ChiB D22 R28/117 P(48-29-3) 285
Det  D8  R31/183 P(17-6-1)  49
  ChiB-Graham 136C, Kramer 309P;
  Det-Sanders 167R

Den    0    7    7    6   20
SD     6    6    0    3   15
Den D16 R36/69  P(31-22-1) 225
SD  D18 R25/166 P(39-19-3) 155
  Den-Sharpe 121C; SD-Means 100R

TB     0    0    0   16   16
SF     7   10   17    7   41
TB D17 R25/110 P(31-13-1) 125
SF D28 R35/181 P(29-23-0) 270
  SF-Watters 103R

Dal    7    7    0   14   28
Arz    0   14    0    7   21
Dal D14 R26/75  P(24-15-0) 237
Arz D22 R37/107 P(31-18-0) 208
  Dal-Irvin 115C

LARm   0   17    3   14   34
NO    14   13   10    0   37
LARm D13 R21/85  P(28-14-3) 157
NO   D18 R38/118 P(26-17-0) 196
```

MONDAY, OCTOBER 24

```
Hou    3    3    0    0    6
Phi    0    7    7    7   21
Hou D15 R29/68  P(33-16-1) 214
Phi D14 R30/85  P(24-13-1) 287
  Phi-Barnett 187C,
  Cunningham 310P
```

SUNDAY, OCTOBER 30

```
KC     7    0    3    0   10
Buf   14   17    3   10   44
KC  D16 R27/87  P(35-18-2) 179
Buf D17 R39/177 P(22-14-0) 180
  Buf-Reed 106C, Kelly 184P

Min   10   13   10    3   36
TB     0    7    0    6   13
Min D19 R32/149 P(38-24-1) 212
TB  D14 R14/49  P(31-17-3) 185
  Min-Allen 113R

Sea    0    0    8    7   15
SD     0   14    7   14   35
Sea D14 R24/112 P(30-15-0) 171
SD  D25 R41/161 P(31-18-1) 187
  SD-Means 104R

NYJ    0   10    8    7   25
Ind   14    0    7    7   28
NYJ D14 R21/57  P(41-22-1) 199
Ind D22 R39/179 P(22-14-2) 151
  Ind-Faulk 110R

Cle    0    6    0    8   14
Den    7    7    6    6   26
Cle D17 R17/41  P(45-23-0) 276
Den D29 R37/114 P(41-30-0) 343
  Den-Elway 349P

Mia    0   13    7    3   23
NE     0    0    0    0    0
Mia D20 R34/140 P(36-21-2) 198
NE  D11 R20/46  P(41-21-3) 142
  Mia-Parmalee 123R
```

```
Det    2  6 10  7  3 28
NYG    0 10  0 15  0 25
Det   D24 R29/149 P(30-16-3) 180
NYG   D23 R45/195 P(25-19-1) 149
Det-Sanders 146R, Moore 106C;
NYG-Hampton 138R

Pit    0 14  0  3  0 17
Arz    7 10  0  0  3 20
Pit   D12 R20/85 P(31-18-1) 232
Arz   D16 R37/99 P(27-13-0) 236

Hou    0  7  0  7 14
LARd   7  0  3  7 17
Hou   D21 R25/99 P(43-19-0) 203
LARd  D16 R33/134 P(30-15-2) 144
LARd-Williams 128R

Phi    0  7  7 17 31
Was    7 10  3  9 29
Phi   D19 R32/131 P(31-18-0) 165
Was   D20 R32/168 P(30-13-2) 181

Dal    0 14  6  3 23
Cin    7 10  3  0 20
Dal   D20 R32/96 P(33-20-1) 272
Cin   D13 R23/77 P(32-14-0) 243
Dal-Harper 125C; Cin-Scott 155C
```

MONDAY, OCTOBER 31
```
GB     0 14  7 12 33
ChiB   0  0  0  6  6
GB    D17 R45/223 P(15-6-0) 82
ChiB  D12 R28/94 P(35-21-3) 159
GB-Bennett 105R
```

SUNDAY, NOVEMBER 6
```
NO     0  0  7 13 20
Min    0  7  7  7 21
NO    D17 R21/72 P(36-24-1) 141
Min   D28 R20/84 P(57-33-1) 410
Min-Carter 151C, Reed 157C, Moon 420P

Cin    5  3  3  6  3 20
Sea    7  0  3  7  0 17
Cin   D23 R34/119 P(43-31-1) 377
Sea   D21 R29/148 P(32-13-0) 170
Cin-Scott 157C, Blake 387P

Buf    0 14  0  3 17
NYJ    3  7  6  6 22
Buf   D18 R26/95 P(31-19-1) 187
NYJ   D17 R35/94 P(26-17-1) 174

Arz    0  0  0  7  7
Phi    0  3 14  0 17
Arz   D21 R24/73 P(30-19-0) 181
Phi   D18 R31/150 P(24-15-0) 172
Phi-Barnett 173C

LARd   0  0  0  3  3
KC     0  7  3  3 13
LARd  D15 R25/100 P(33-17-2) 148
KC    D11 R31/93 P(28-17-0) 159

ChiB   3  3  7  7 20
TB     0  3  0  3  6
ChiB  D23 R45/178 P(32-19-1) 205
TB    D9 R14/38 P(28-14-1) 150

Pit    0  6  0  3  3 12
Hou    3  3  0  3  0 9
Pit   D17 R34/111 P(29-17-0) 155
Hou   D17 R25/84 P(48-22-0) 160

Ind    7  0  7  7 21
Mia    3  0  3 16 22
Ind   D17 R24/105 P(21-11-1) 108
Mia   D25 R32/118 P(41-30-2) 254
Mia-McDuffie 108C

SF    10  4 14  7 37
Was    0  3  3 16 22
SF    D17 R28/117 P(28-18-1) 304
Was   D20 R26/76 P(44-23-2) 206

SD     7  0  7  3  3 20
Atl    7  0  0  3 10
SD    D20 R29/117 P(38-22-0) 179
Atl   D11 R17/43 P(31-19-2) 176
SD-Means 102R

Den    0  3  3 15 21
LARm   7 10  7  3 27
Den   D24 R14/48 P(45-24-0) 236
LARm  D23 R38/141 P(29-22-1) 244
```


```
NE     0  0  3  3  6
Cle    0  3  0 10 13
NE    D20 R36/118 P(43-20-4) 159
Cle   D16 R32/148 P(28-14-1) 160
Cle-Hoard 123R

Det    0  7  7 16 30
GB    10 21  7  0 38
Det   D20 R19/49 P(48-28-2) 317
GB    D21 R28/117 P(36-24-1) 230
Det-Moore 151C
```

MONDAY, NOVEMBER 7
```
NYG    0  3  0  7 10
Dal    0 14 21  3 38
NYG   D11 R22/55 P(31-13-1) 133
Dal   D27 R45/209 P(25-19-0) 241
Dal-Smith 163R, Irvin 118C
```

SUNDAY, NOVEMBER 13
```
SD     0  0  7  7 14
KC     0 13  0  0 13
SD    D13 R26/48 P(36-21-1) 187
KC    D15 R27/84 P(46-20-2) 165

Hou    0 14  7  7 28
Cin    3 14  0 17 34
Hou   D24 R31/155 P(34-20-0) 129
Cin   D17 R19/39 P(33-23-0) 348
Cin-Pickens 188C, Blake 354P

Min   10 10  0  0 20
NE     0  3  7 10  6 26
Min   D22 R31/101 P(42-26-0) 339
NE    D27 R12/42 P(70-45-0) 426
Min-Moon 349P; NE-Timpson 113C, Bledsoe 426P

Atl   17  6  0  9 32
NO     7 10  0 16 33
Atl   D21 R16/72 P(49-29-1) 317
NO    D30 R26/153 P(36-28-3) 276
Atl-Mathis 125C, Rison 118C, George 328P; NO-Bates 141R

Sea    0  0  3  7 10
Den    0  7  3  7 17
Sea   D14 R28/158 P(30-10-0) 131
Den   D21 R38/169 P(33-17-2) 128
Sea-Warren 122R; Den-Russell 109R

LARd   7  7  0  6 20
LARm   7  0  0 10 17
LARd  D18 R36/95 P(26-17-1) 208
LARm  D20 R11/22 P(37-23-1) 268
LARd-Anderson 105C

NYJ    0 10  0  0 10
GB     7  0  7  3 17
NYJ   D16 R23/116 P(43-24-1) 199
GB    D14 R23/62 P(28-20-0) 172

TB     3  0  3  3  9
Det    0  0 14  0 14
TB    D18 R32/125 P(23-16-0) 218
Det   D16 R33/243 P(13-5-0) 99
TB-Rhett 112R; Det-Sanders 237R

Dal    7  0  0  7 14
SF     0  7  7  7 21
Dal   D19 R29/87 P(42-23-3) 321
SF    D19 R32/147 P(21-12-0) 161
Dal-Harper 136C, Aikman 339P

ChiB   7  0  0 10 17
Mia    3  3  0  8 14
ChiB  D18 R30/62 P(28-19-0) 211
Mia   D18 R32/66 P(38-24-1) 275
Mia-Fryar 112C

Cle   10  3  6  7 26
Phi    0  7  0  0  7
Cle   D18 R40/140 P(30-12-1) 158
Phi   D15 R21/112 P(38-22-1) 176

Arz    0  0  3  7 10
NYG    7  2  0  0  9
Arz   D18 R28/66 P(33-17-1) 173
NYG   D17 R33/150 P(26-9-1) 81
```

MONDAY, NOVEMBER 14
```
Buf    0  3  7  0 10
Pit   10  6  7  0 23
Buf   D24 R31/128 P(53-27-2) 198
Pit   D10 R26/86 P(27-14-1) 140
```


SUNDAY, NOVEMBER 20
```
Phi    0  3  0  3  6
Arz    3  3  3  3 12
Phi   D14 R14/75 P(44-17-1) 110
Arz   D16 R39/158 P(23-12-0) 123

Cle    0  6  7  0 13
KC     0  7  3 10 20
Cle   D15 R27/94 P(37-14-1) 145
KC    D23 R37/134 P(33-19-0) 153

Atl    0 14  7  7 28
Den   10  0  7 15 32
Atl   D16 R17/76 P(43-19-0) 254
Den   D25 R29/89 P(42-27-1) 336
Atl-Mathis 163C, George 254P; Den-Miller 102C, Tillman 175C, Elway 382P

Det    0 10  0  0 10
ChiB   0 10  3  7 20
Det   D11 R12/52 P(21-11-0) 128
ChiB  D23 R43/161 P(31-25-1) 177
Det-Perriman 120C; ChiB-Tillman 126R

SD     0  0 10  7 17
NE     7  3  3 10 23
SD    D19 R28/72 P(37-20-3) 169
NE    D21 R36/101 P(36-21-2) 217

NO     0  0  7 12 19
LARd   7  3  7  7 24
NO    D16 R11/16 P(44-28-1) 230
LARd  D22 R34/121 P(28-22-2) 307
LARd-Brown 132C, Hostetler 310P

NYJ   10  7  7  7 31
Min    7  7  0  7 21
NYJ   D17 R26/62 P(29-22-0) 220
Min   D26 R18/87 P(51-33-4) 374
NYJ-Mitchell 120C; Min-Carter 100C, Cooper 101C, Reed 121C, Moon 400P

Was    0  0  0  0  7
Dal   17  7  7  0 31
Was   D20 R27/84 P(51-22-4) 229
Dal   D15 R38/130 P(23-11-0) 111
Was-Howard 107C

GB     0  6 14  0 20
Buf   14 13  0  2 29
GB    D18 R12/61 P(40-22-1) 205
Buf   D27 R40/108 P(44-32-1) 347
Buf-Reed 191C, Kelly 365P

LARm   3 13  3  8 27
SF    14  7  3  7 31
LARm  D17 R18/86 P(37-19-0) 272
SF    D32 R37/134 P(44-30-0) 325
SF-Rice 165C, Young 325P

TB     0  3  7 11 21
Sea    7  8  0  7 22
TB    D23 R32/120 P(32-22-1) 212
Sea   D18 R34/177 P(25-13-1) 117
TB-Rhett 111R; Sea-Warren 116R

Ind    7  0  0 10 17
Cin    3  3  7  0 13
Ind   D15 R32/72 P(24-14-0) 165
Cin   D16 R25/103 P(38-22-1) 250
Cin-Pickens 103C

Mia    3  7  3  0 13
Pit    3  3  0  7  3 16
Mia   D20 R19/40 P(45-31-1) 283
Pit   D21 R31/88 P(42-26-0) 335
Mia-Fryar 113C, Marino 312P; Pit-Tomczak 343P
```

MONDAY, NOVEMBER 21
```
NYG    0  0  7  6 13
Hou    0  0  7  3 10
NYG   D18 R43/163 P(21-10-0) 124
Hou   D13 R29/166 P(15-10-0) 112
NYG-Hampton 122R, Sherrard 109C; Hou-White 156R
```

THURSDAY, NOVEMBER 24
```
Buf    0  7  7  7 21
Det    7 14  0 14 35
Buf   D25 R29/121 P(35-29-2) 246
Det   D20 R21/47 P(25-20-0) 341
Det-Moore 169C, Krieg 351P
```


```
GB     7 10  7  7 31
Dal    0  6 19 17 42
GB    D17 R18/29 P(40-27-0) 248
Dal   D21 R37/138 P(26-15-1) 298
GB-Sharpe 122C, Favre 257P; Dal-Smith 133R, Garrett 311P
```

SUNDAY, NOVEMBER 27
```
Cin    0  6  0  7 13
Den    6  9  0  0 15
Cin   D16 R30/130 P(34-16-1) 198
Den   D12 R22/50 P(38-21-0) 206
Cin-Pickens 132C; Den-Miller 116C

LARm   0 14  0  3 17
SD     0  6 15 10 31
LARm  D17 R13/48 P(47-26-4) 278
SD    D16 R30/114 P(33-17-1) 129

KC     3  3  0  3  9
Sea    0  0  7  3 10
KC    D18 R29/115 P(47-26-0) 197
Sea   D12 R26/59 P(35-18-0) 207
Sea-Blades 141C

ChiB   7  3  6  0  3 19
Arz    3  3 10  0 16
ChiB  D20 R40/132 P(28-15-2) 186
Arz   D15 R17/67 P(43-23-1) 177
ChiB-Graham 154C

NYG    7  7  0  7 21
Was    3  6  3  9 21
NYG   D20 R45/131 P(17-10-0) 160
Was   D14 R24/152 P(28-11-1) 161
NYG-Hampton 106R

NE     3  0  3  6 12
Ind    0  7  0  3 10
NE    D19 R35/79 P(36-26-1) 257
Ind   D15 R19/132 P(27-16-0) 158
NE-Coates 119C

Hou    0  0  0 10 10
Cle    3 14  0 17 34
Hou   D11 R19/80 P(33-16-0) 102
Cle   D23 R38/144 P(29-15-1) 199
Cle-Hoard 103R

TB     7  7  0  3  3 20
Min    0  9  0  8  0 17
TB    D20 R31/72 P(38-20-1) 254
Min   D19 R22/85 P(46-24-1) 246
Min-Ismail 101C

Mia    0  0 14 14 28
NYJ    3  7 14  0 24
Mia   D22 R11/38 P(44-31-2) 359
NYJ   D25 R28/76 P(41-26-2) 365
Mia-Fryar 103C, Ingram 117C, Marino 359P; NYJ-Monk 108C, Moore 124C, Esiason 382P

Pit    7  0  0 14 21
LARd   0  3  0  0  3
Pit   D19 R39/175 P(27-12-0) 131
LARd  D14 R25/57 P(28-15-0) 122

Phi    0  7  7  7 21
Atl    7  6  8  7 28
Phi   D14 R14/115 P(36-19-1) 203
Atl   D24 R24/64 P(46-26-3) 354
Atl-Mathis 124C, George 364P
```

MONDAY, NOVEMBER 28
```
SF    10 10  8  7 35
NO     0 14  0  0 14
SF    D28 R42/191 P(30-24-0) 270
NO    D13 R17/83 P(25-13-1) 139
SF-Watters 105R, Young 281P
```

THURSDAY, DECEMBER 1
```
ChiB   7  0 17  3 27
Min    7  6  3 11  6 33
ChiB  D15 R32/80 P(33-24-1) 232
Min   D21 R27/100 P(48-27-1) 285
Min-Carter 124C, Moon 306P
```

SUNDAY, DECEMBER 4
```
Was    7 14  0  0 21
TB     3 14  0  9 26
Was   D7 R12/10 P(25-13-1) 258
TB    D28 R48/213 P(35-18-2) 251
Was-Howard 130C; TB-Rhett 192R
```


```
NYG    7  0  3  6 16
Cle    3  3  0  7 13
NYG   D18 R33/96 P(33-17-1) 202
Cle   D16 R32/148 P(38-20-2) 229
NYG-Sherrard 101C; Cle-Alexander 171C

NO     7 21  3  0 31
LARm   0  7  0  8 15
NO    D20 R38/137 P(27-17-1) 191
LARm  D20 R21/75 P(37-26-0) 258
LARm-Bailey 116C

Pit    7  7  7 17 38
Cin    7  0  0  8 15
Pit   D23 R47/185 P(24-17-0) 123
Cin   D13 R20/76 P(20-8-2) 119
Pit-Morris 108R; Cin-Pickens 105C

NYJ    0 10  3  0 13
NE     3  7  7  7 24
NYJ   D13 R19/64 P(40-16-1) 155
NE    D20 R39/135 P(34-19-1) 191

Arz    0 10  0 20 30
Hou    9  0  0  3 12
Arz   D18 R45/161 P(20-12-1) 171
Hou   D16 R16/37 P(34-11-5) 161
Arz-Clark 120C

Buf    0  7 21 14 42
Mia    0 17  0 14 31
Buf   D19 R28/76 P(29-19-1) 322
Mia   D25 R19/73 P(54-32-4) 387
Buf-Reed 106C, Kelly 299P; Mia-Fryar 110C, Marino 311P

Atl    7  7  0  0 14
SF     3 24  7 16 50
Atl   D12 R12/43 P(40-19-3) 205
SF    D28 R39/161 P(38-25-1) 315
Atl-Mathis 128C

Dal    7  7 10  7 31
Phi    0  6  7  6 19
Dal   D15 R32/104 P(17-10-1) 160
Phi   D25 R26/108 P(46-29-1) 285
Dal-Irvin 117C; Phi-Cunningham 327P

Ind    7  7  7 10 31
Sea   10  3  0  6 19
Ind   D14 R39/183 P(19-10-2) 105
Sea   D15 R27/107 P(37-20-2) 131
Ind-Faulk 129R

Den    7  0  7  3  3 20
KC     0  3  6  0  8 17
Den   D26 R43/123 P(36-24-0) 270
KC    D17 R25/78 P(37-18-0) 323
Den-Miller 153C; KC-Birden 101C, Davis 107C, Bono 323P

GB    14  7 10  0 31
Det    3 21  3  7 34
GB    D23 R23/58 P(43-29-2) 359
Det   D21 R27/199 P(26-15-1) 188
GB-Morgan 103C, Sharpe 115C, Favre 366P; Det-Sanders 188R
```

MONDAY, DECEMBER 5
```
LARd   7  7  0 10 24
SD     7  7  0  3 17
LARd  D22 R29/88 P(31-24-1) 322
SD    D18 R22/47 P(37-20-0) 214
LARd-Hostetler 319P
```

SATURDAY, DECEMBER 10
```
Cle    7  3  0  9 19
Dal    7  0  0  7 14
Cle   D16 R38/134 P(25-15-1) 110
Dal   D27 R7/112 P(36-21-2) 177
Dal-Smith 112R

Det    3  6  3  6 18
NYJ    0  7  0  0  7
Det   D19 R31/137 P(24-18-1) 189
NYJ   D14 R26/120 P(30-17-0) 141
Det-Sanders 127R
```

SUNDAY, DECEMBER 11
```
ChiB   3  0  0  0  3
GB     7 17 10  6 40
ChiB  D9 R14/27 P(35-15-2) 149
GB    D28 R46/257 P(34-20-1) 259
GB-Bennett 106R, Brooks 105C
```

```
Ind    0  10   0   3  13
NE     0   7  14   7  28
Ind  D13 R27/74  P(32-12-2) 138
NE   D24 R37/84  P(45-25-4) 277

NO     3  10   3  13  29
Atl    0  14   3   3  20
NO   D19 R32/138 P(31-18-0) 264
Atl  D23 R20/92  P(42-25-1) 284
NO-Haynes 103C

SF     7  14   3  14  38
SD     0   3   6   6  15
SF   D27 R33/119 P(32-25-0) 298
SD   D20 R22/56  P(43-25-2) 322
SF-Rice 144C, Young 304P;
SD-Martin 172C, Humphries 337P

Cin    0   7   3  10  20
NYG    0  17   3   7  27
Cin  D20 R37/121 P(38-18-0) 205
NYG  D18 R30/89  P(26-16-2) 215

Sea    3   7   6   0  16
Hou    0  14   0   0  14
Sea  D21 R50/266 P(17-8-0) 64
Hou  D14 R20/63  P(29-16-1) 145
Sea-Warren 185R

Was    3   3   0   9  15
Arz    7   0   0  10  17
Was  D19 R28/123 P(27-16-1) 283
Arz  D14 R28/84  P(25-16-0) 194
Was-Ellard 191C

Min    3   6   3   9  21
Buf    7   3   7   0  17
Min  D20 R32/116 P(34-21-0) 261
Buf  D19 R27/85  P(32-19-1) 183
Min-Carter 111C

Phi    0   0   0   3   3
Pit    0   0   0  14  14
Phi  D9 R23/71   P(27-9-1) 34
Pit  D20 R39/124 P(35-19-1) 145

Den    0   3   3  14  ..
LARd   0   6   3  14  23
Den  D16 R21/63  P(33-20-0) 228
LARd D16 R32/128 P(31-16-0) 177

LARm   0   7   0   7  14
TB     0  17   0   7  24
LARm D19 R26/63  P(34-18-0) 198
TB   D17 R35/125 P(22-10-0) 230
TB-Rhett 119R, Wilson 176C
```

MONDAY, DECEMBER 12

```
KC     7   7   7   7  28
Mia    0  14  21  10  45
KC   D26 R16/84  P(55-33-3) 314
Mia  D23 R31/144 P(30-21-0) 241
KC-Birden 131C, Bono 314P;
Mia-Parmalee 127R
```

SATURDAY, DECEMBER 17

```
Min    3  10   6   0  19
Det   10  10  14   7  41
Min  D18 R23/64  P(51-29-1) 273
Det  D17 R25/124 P(20-15-0) 160
Det-Sanders 110R

Den    0   6  13   0  19
SF    14  14  14   0  42
Den  D20 R15/48  P(41-29-1) 286
SF   D25 R30/102 P(33-23-1) 386
Den-Miller 118C; SF-Rice 121C,
Watters 106C, Young 350P
```

SUNDAY, DECEMBER 18

```
SD     0   7   7   7  21
NYJ    3   3   0   0   6
SD   D24 R38/152 P(26-19-0) 251
NYJ  D14 R21/76  P(32-20-0) 167
SD-Martin 116C

NYG    0   3   3  10  16
Phi    0   3   0  10  13
NYG  D20 R34/122 P(27-18-1) 230
Phi  D12 R16/51  P(39-25-1) 171

LARd   0  10   0   7  17
Sea    0  10   3   3  16
LARd D16 R27/116 P(29-17-0) 206
Sea  D15 R30/125 P(34-14-0) 155
LARd-Brown 107C;
Sea-Warren 122R
```


```
Cle    0   7   0   0   7
Pit   14   0   0   3  17
Cle  D21 R24/86  P(42-21-2) 245
Pit  D18 R41/123 P(18-10-0) 153
Pit-Foster 106R

Cin    0   0   7   0   7
Arz   14   7   0   7  28
Cin  D12 R14/64  P(28-10-1) 125
Arz  D24 R39/152 P(34-21-0) 212

Hou    3   0   0   6   9
KC     7   0  14  10  31
Hou  D16 R29/119 P(26-15-1) 98
KC   D23 R28/152 P(27-16-0) 228
KC-Dawson 101C

LARm   7   3   0   3  13
ChiB   3  14   3   7  27
LARm D13 R19/37  P(35-17-0) 206
ChiB D19 R42/163 P(25-12-0) 135

Mia    3   0   3   0   6
Ind    7   0   0   3  10
Mia  D17 R26/97  P(37-21-0) 214
Ind  D12 R30/143 P(19-9-0) 69

Atl    3   6   8   0  17
GB    14   0   0   7  21
Atl  D22 R22/97  P(45-21-1) 236
GB   D23 R21/74  P(44-29-1) 310
GB-Bennett 101C, Favre 321P

NE     3  14  14  10  41
Buf   10   7   0   0  17
NE   D22 R34/101 P(31-22-0) 276
Buf  D16 R26/135 P(29-19-2) 191
Buf-Reed 112C

TB     0  10   0   7  17
Was    0   0   0  14  14
TB   D20 R33/108 P(34-19-2) 267
Was  D14 R23/73  P(35-17-0) 194
TB-Dawsey 116C
```

MONDAY, DECEMBER 19

```
Dal    7   3   7   7  24
NO     0   6   3   7  16
Dal  D23 R34/105 P(28-21-2) 175
NO   D19 R25/90  P(32-18-3) 147
```

SATURDAY, DECEMBER 24

```
NYJ    0   7   3   0  10
Hou    7   6   8   3  24
NYJ  D14 R23/89  P(31-15-1) 127
Hou  D25 R40/175 P(30-17-2) 206
Hou-Slaughter 123C

Pit    0  13   6  15  34
SD     3  14   7  13  37
Pit  D22 R29/136 P(29-18-0) 306
SD   D21 R27/87  P(41-24-0) 263
Pit-Johnson 165C

Dal    3   0   7   0  10
NYG    0  10   2   3  15
Dal  D11 R24/90  P(19-15-0) 93
NYG  D15 R37/127 P(19-11-0) 122

Buf    0   6   0   3   9
Ind    0   0  10   0  10
Buf  D20 R25/57  P(46-26-2) 243
Ind  D13 R27/145 P(28-12-1) 100
Buf-Beebe 111C

Arz    0   3   0   3   6
Atl    7   0   3   0  10
Arz  D18 R25/72  P(42-26-0) 313
Atl  D12 R19/51  P(32-15-1) 256
Arz-Schroeder 317P;
Atl-Emanuel 136C

Sea    0   0   3   6   9
Cle    7  14   7   7  35
Sea  D18 R23/84  P(37-18-1) 217
Cle  D23 R38/106 P(26-19-1) 245

Was    0  17   7   0  24
LARm   7  14   0   0  21
Was  D19 R37/150 P(28-13-1) 138
LARm D18 R21/77  P(40-27-1) 293
LARm-Miller 304P

NO     0  17   0  13  30
Den    0   6   8  14  28
NO   D22 R26/80  P(35-28-0) 367
Den  D23 R23/90  P(44-25-3) 258
NO-Small 200C, Everett 343P
```


```
Phi    3  17   7   3  30
Cin    7   3  10  13  33
Phi  D19 R24/81  P(37-26-0) 297
Cin  D23 R28/152 P(42-17-3) 233
Phi-Williams 122C, Brister 325P;
Cin-Pickens 135C

NE     3   3   0   7  13
ChiB   3   0   0   0   3
NE   D19 R31/80  P(38-23-1) 263
ChiB D14 R21/65  P(38-17-0) 183
NE-Brisby 115C

GB    14  14   6   0  34
TB     0   6   6   7  19
GB   D25 R38/143 P(36-24-1) 290
TB   D14 R16/62  P(32-16-1) 152
GB-Bennett 100R, Sharpe 132C

KC     7   7   3   2  19
LARd   0   3   0   6   9
KC   D24 R44/204 P(25-16-0) 218
LARd D14 R16/53  P(28-15-1) 221
KC-Allen 132R; LARd-Miller 304P
```

SUNDAY, DECEMBER 25

```
Det    3   7   3   7  20
Mia    7  20   0   0  27
Det  D15 R14/52  P(46-21-2) 170
Mia  D21 R35/98  P(35-26-0) 285
```

MONDAY, DECEMBER 26

```
SF     0   7   0   7  14
Min    7   3  11   0  21
SF   D18 R19/49  P(36-30-1) 246
Min  D14 R32/102 P(34-16-1) 150
```

1995 NFL

SUNDAY, SEPTEMBER 3

```
TB     7   0   0  14  21
Phi    6   0   0   0   6
TB   D15 R29/83  P(19-11-1) 202
Phi  D20 R27/111 P(36-25-1) 162
TB-Copeland 155C

SF     0  17   7   0  24
NO     0   9   6   7  22
SF   D26 R35/154 P(35-26-1) 282
NO   D15 R13/26  P(28-23-1) 252

Det    0  10   0  10  20
Pit    3   3   7  10  23
Det  D16 R22/122 P(32-18-1) 180
Pit  D26 R33/150 P(35-22-4) 204
Det-Sanders 108R, Moore 131C

Cle    7   7   0   0  14
NE     6   0   0  11  17
Cle  D13 R16/60  P(29-20-1) 241
NE   D27 R28/125 P(47-30-0) 302
Cle-Jackson 157C; NE-Martin 102R,
Coates 106C, Bledsoe 302P

Car   13   0   0   7   0  20
Atl    3  10   7   0   3  23
Car  D17 R20/51  P(44-23-0) 261
Atl  D20 R26/117 P(46-27-1) 274
Car-Green 121C, Reich 329P

Cin    3  10   8   3  24
Ind    7   3   0  11   0  21
Cin  D18 R23/87  P(34-19-0) 249
Ind  D24 R31/144 P(44-28-3) 246
Cin-McGee 118C

Slr    0   7   7   3  17
GB     0   0   7   7  14
Slr  D11 R23/54  P(30-19-0) 133
GB   D21 R18/53  P(51-29-3) 262

Min    7   0   0   7  14
ChiB   7   7  14   3  31
Min  D21 R25/118 P(37-26-1) 202
ChiB D20 R28/143 P(28-19-1) 254
ChiB-Conway 110C, Graham 107C

Arz    0   7   0   0   7
Was    0  10   7   7  24
Arz  D10 R25/109 P(23-10-4) 88
Was  D20 R40/259 P(27-14-1) 197
Was-Allen 131R

Hou    7   0   3   0  10
Jax    0   0   0   3   3
Hou  D14 R41/160 P(23-13-0) 80
Jax  D10 R22/101 P(26-10-1) 45
Hou-Brown 101R
```


```
SD     0   7   0   0   7
Oak    0   7  10   0  17
SD   D20 R20/77  P(47-23-1) 294
Oak  D19 R33/139 P(26-14-0) 108
SD-Jefferson 120C,
Humphries 305P

Buf    7   0   0   0   7
Den    3   9   0  10  22
Buf  D14 R20/60  P(32-15-0) 174
Den  D24 R37/140 P(41-22-1) 299
Den-Sharpe 180C, Elway 317P

KC     7  13  14   0  34
Sea    3   0   0   7  10
KC   D17 R33/141 P(23-18-0) 278
Sea  D20 R18/78  P(46-24-1) 264
KC-Hill 109R, Davis 155C;
Sea-Blades 107C

NYJ    0  14   0   0  14
Mia    0  21  21  10  52
NYJ  D16 R16/64  P(44-24-4) 195
Mia  D22 R36/111 P(29-17-2) 251
Mia-Fryar 110C
```

MONDAY, SEPTEMBER 4

```
Dal    7  14   7   0  35
NYG    0   0   0   0   0
Dal  D26 R35/232 P(21-16-0) 229
NYG  D19 R20/65  P(34-20-1) 146
Dal-Smith 163R, Irvin 109C
```

SUNDAY, SEPTEMBER 10

```
NO     3   0   7   3  13
Slr    7  10   0   0  17
NO   D19 R15/97  P(40-24-1) 211
Slr  D19 R32/151 P(32-12-0) 171

Pit   14   3   7  10  34
Hou    0   0   7   7  14
Pit  D19 R36/127 P(22-13-0) 123
Hou  D19 R24/38  P(35-19-2) 178

NYG    7   3   0   7  17
KC     3   0  14   3  20
NYG  D12 R34/102 P(14-10-0) 136
KC   D28 R35/155 P(47-29-1) 178
NYG-Calloway 100C

TB     0   0   0   6   6
Cle    0  19   0   3  22
TB   D24 R26/101 P(36-20-2) 210
Cle  D19 R31/70  P(27-17-0) 253

Mia   10   7   0   3  20
NE     0   3   0   0   3
Mia  D21 R35/182 P(21-15-1) 224
NE   D19 R21/39  P(51-25-2) 253
Mia-Fryar 113C; NE-Moore 112C

Atl    3   0   7   0  10
SF    17   3   7  10  41
Atl  D15 R11/25  P(48-27-3) 242
SF   D28 R31/158 P(51-29-1) 331
SF-Rice 167C, Young 331P

Den    0   0   7   0   7
Dal    0  14   7  10  31
Den  D17 R21/89  P(35-17-1) 198
Dal  D27 R38/162 P(31-18-1) 196
Den-Miller 108C; Dal-Smith 114R

Sea    0   7   3   0  10
SD     7   0   0   7  14
Sea  D15 R22/82  P(29-13-2) 127
SD   D25 R36/146 P(35-23-1) 251
SD-Means 115R, Martin 163C

Jax    7   0   3   7  17
Cin    3   7   7   7  24
Jax  D14 R29/119 P(30-12-1) 140
Cin  D17 R30/118 P(30-20-0) 228
Cin-Pickens 102C

Ind    0   3   7  14   3  27
NYJ   14   3   7   0   0  24
Ind  D25 R31/122 P(34-23-1) 239
NYJ  D21 R32/146 P(30-19-0) 198

Oak    0   3  10   7  20
Was    0   3   3   2   8
Oak  D25 R36/153 P(29-22-0) 205
Was  D15 R24/98  P(34-20-1) 260

Car    0   6   0   6  12
Buf    0   3   0  28  31
Car  D6 R32/101  P(23-6-1) 12
Buf  D16 R43/172 P(21-4-3) 176
Buf-Copeland 112C
```


```
Det   10   0   0   0  10
Min    7   3   3   7  20
Det  D19 R15/54  P(48-27-1) 272
Min  D19 R29/155 P(29-19-0) 225
Min-Smith 111R

Phi    0  10   7  14  31
Arz    0   3   3  13  19
Phi  D19 R34/168 P(21-11-1) 170
Arz  D17 R23/30  P(30-19-2) 244
Arz-Sanders 102C
```

MONDAY, SEPTEMBER 11

```
GB    14  10   3   0  27
ChiB   0   7  10   7  24
GB   D23 R36/125 P(38-21-1) 306
ChiB D17 R24/92  P(25-15-1) 151
GB-Brooks 161C, Favre 312P
```

SUNDAY, SEPTEMBER 17

```
Cle    0   7   0   7  14
Hou    0   0   0   7   7
Cle  D14 R30/132 P(23-10-0) 138
Hou  D20 R29/71  P(41-22-4) 256

SD     0  17   0  10  27
Phi    7   7   0   7  21
SD   D11 R30/131 P(23-10-0) 139
Phi  D18 R33/138 P(39-23-1) 181
SD-Means 122R

Arz    0   6   0  14  20
Det    3   7   7   0  17
Arz  D18 R27/121 P(25-15-0) 109
Det  D19 R29/160 P(26-17-0) 198
Arz-Hearst 121R;
Det-Sanders 147R, Perriman 114C

Ind    7   7   0   0  14
Buf    7   3   3   7  20
Ind  D17 R28/91  P(33-19-0) 205
Buf  D17 R29/60  P(35-19-0) 201

Oak    0  14   3   0   0  17
KC     0   0  10   6   7  23
Oak  D21 R36/151 P(30-19-2) 193
KC   D14 R29/121 P(28-19-0) 141

NYG    0   3   0   3   6
GB     7   7   0   0  14
NYG  D17 R24/116 P(50-23-1) 187
GB   D16 R25/85  P(25-14-0) 113

Atl    3  10   3   8   3  27
NO    10   0   7   0   0  24
Atl  D24 R31/124 P(39-27-1) 337
NO   D18 R22/50  P(44-30-0) 360
Atl-Heyward 102R, Emanuel 104C,
Metcalf 155C, George 386P;
NO-Everett 370P

Was    0  14  10   7  31
Den    0  24   0  14  38
Was  D20 R20/129 P(26-16-1) 225
Den  D28 R33/158 P(47-30-0) 318
Was-Means 122R; Den-Elway 327P

Cin    7   0   0  14  21
Sea    7  10   0   7  24
Cin  D18 R23/110 P(43-23-1) 291
Sea  D24 R36/143 P(30-21-0) 263
Sea-Warren 109R

ChiB   3   6  13   3  25
TB     0   0   7   7  14
ChiB D20 R35/128 P(38-18-0) 207
TB   D15 R22/74  P(34-15-4) 165

Jax    0   3   0   7  10
NYJ    7   6  14   0  27
Jax  D20 R35/146 P(33-15-1) 105
NYJ  D23 R26/79  P(43-27-1) 296

NE     0   3   0   0   3
SF     0   7  14   7  28
NE   D18 R28/76  P(52-22-3) 292
SF   D21 R23/90  P(42-29-1) 273

Slr    0  14  10   7  31
Car    3   0   7   0  10
Slr  D14 R29/116 P(27-16-0) 202
Car  D21 R20/89  P(47-26-5) 205
Slr-Bruce 100C

Dal    6   3   0   8   6  23
Min    3   7   0   7   0  17
Dal  D20 R23/154 P(38-24-0) 233
Min  D17 R27/92  P(38-22-0) 160
Dal-Smith 150R, Irvin 107C;
Min-Reed 107C
```

MONDAY, SEPTEMBER 18
Pit 0 3 0 7 10
Mia 3 14 3 3 23
Pit D21 R23/93 P(52-28-3) 273
Mia D16 R20/46 P(33-21-0) 210

SUNDAY, SEPTEMBER 24
NO 7 10 0 12 29
NYG 7 17 14 7 45
NO D18 R18/87 P(32-19-2) 235
NYG D31 R48/218 P(27-19-1) 256
NYG-Hampton 149R

ChiB 0 21 0 7 28
Slr 10 7 14 3 34
ChiB D20 R20/47 P(38-27-0) 317
Slr D22 R33/106 P(33-23-0) 233
ChiB-Graham 145C, Kramer 317P;
Slr-Drayton 106C

Was 3 3 0 0 6
TB 0 0 7 7 14
Was D23 R24/95 P(40-21-1) 216
TB D15 R30/113 P(18-13-0) 123
TB-Rhett 104R

Min 0 13 24 7 44
Pit 0 6 0 18 24
Min D20 R30/134 P(31-18-2) 244
Pit D22 R25/70 P(49-29-6) 335
Min-Smith 115R; Pit-Thigpen 141C

Hou 14 14 10 0 38
Cin 0 14 7 7 28
Hou D24 R36/137 P(26-23-0) 350
Cin D20 R15/60 P(46-24-0) 347
Hou-Sanders 104C, Chandler 352P;
Cin-McGee 109C, Scott 125C,
Blake 356P

Arz 0 10 3 7 20
Dal 14 10 3 7 34
Arz D22 R17/52 P(34-25-3) 329
Dal D26 R36/189 P(30-19-0) 251
Arz-Moore 154C, Krieg 324P;
Dal-Smith 116R, Irvin 105C

Den 0 3 0 3 6
SD 7 0 10 0 17
Den D12 R15/65 P(34-19-0) 181
SD D23 R39/158 P(32-18-1) 176
SD-Means 115R

KC 0 3 0 14 17
Cle 7 0 7 21 35
KC D14 R16/59 P(49-29-2) 263
Cle D23 R32/124 P(37-22-0) 221
KC-Cash 111C

NYJ 3 0 0 0 3
Atl 3 7 3 0 13
NYJ D16 R21/94 P(37-20-3) 176
Atl D24 R28/148 P(35-22-1) 200
Atl-Heyward 120R

GB 0 10 7 7 24
Jax 0 0 0 14 14
GB D16 R29/129 P(30-20-1) 193
Jax D13 R23/76 P(29-16-0) 125

Phi 17 0 0 0 17
Oak 0 17 10 21 48
Phi D17 R22/107 P(34-17-2) 129
Oak D28 R32/108 P(36-25-2) 331
Oak-Hobbs 135C

MONDAY, SEPTEMBER 25
SF 0 10 7 7 24
Det 3 10 3 11 27
SF D23 R20/78 P(44-27-1) 338
Det D23 R22/30 P(42-28-0) 286
SF-Rice 181C, Young 348P;
Det-Perriman 115C

SUNDAY, OCTOBER 1
Slr 7 3 0 8 18
Ind 7 7 7 0 21
Slr D16 R16/37 P(45-26-2) 305
Ind D16 R36/235 P(19-11-1) 146
Slr-Bruce 181C, Miller 326P;
Ind-Faulk 177R

Dal 10 0 3 10 23
Was 3 17 7 0 27
Dal D19 R26/118 P(32-23-1) 238
Was D19 R34/136 P(24-13-1) 183
Dal-Irvin 105C; Was-Allen 121R

Phi 3 3 6 3 15
NO 0 0 7 0 10
Phi D20 R43/155 P(28-18-0) 147
NO D9 R16/119 P(28-12-1) 81

NE 7 7 3 0 17
Atl 3 14 0 13 30
NE D17 R26/108 P(45-24-0) 224
Atl D19 R22/87 P(38-26-1) 288
NE-Brisby 161C

Mia 3 10 3 10 26
Cin 0 10 7 6 23
Mia D27 R20/48 P(48-33-1) 442
Cin D23 R24/144 P(35-18-0) 198
Mia-Marino 450P; Cin-Pickens 117C

Jax 10 0 0 7 17
Hou 0 6 7 3 16
Jax D16 R20/68 P(27-15-1) 151
Hou D19 R28/91 P(47-27-1) 206

Den 0 0 3 7 10
Sea 0 0 10 17 27
Den D18 R19/75 P(45-23-0) 243
Sea D26 R41/230 P(24-16-0) 192
Sea-Warren 115R

NYG 3 3 0 0 6
SF 3 14 3 0 20
NYG D17 R18/33 P(43-22-1) 204
SF D22 R27/109 P(40-26-0) 202

TB 7 6 0 7 20
Car 0 7 6 0 13
TB D16 R26/58 P(33-13-0) 252
Car D20 R33/159 P(32-18-1) 234
TB-Harris 108C; Car-Moore 123R

SD 0 6 3 7 16
Pit 21 10 0 0 31
SD D20 R20/95 P(41-22-4) 232
Pit D21 R39/120 P(21-12-1) 141

Oak 14 17 9 7 47
NYJ 0 3 7 0 10
Oak D25 R42/220 P(23-14-0) 237
NYJ D15 R20/94 P(34-16-0) 147
Oak-Brown 156C, Hostetler 261P

KC 0 14 10 0 24
Arz 0 0 0 3 3
KC D17 R37/221 P(17-7-1) 72
Arz D16 R20/56 P(41-25-1) 240
Arz-Krieg 308P

MONDAY, OCTOBER 2
Buf 10 0 3 9 22
Cle 7 3 6 3 19
Buf D23 R36/160 P(34-27-1) 246
Cle D16 R20/90 P(35-18-1) 204
Cle-Rison 126C

SUNDAY, OCTOBER 8
GB 0 3 7 14 24
Dal 0 17 7 10 34
GB D20 R19/74 P(41-21-1) 295
Dal D25 R34/136 P(31-24-0) 312
GB-Brooks 124C; Dal-Smith 106R,
Irvin 150C, Aikman 316P

NYJ 0 3 7 0 10
Buf 3 13 3 10 29
NYJ D14 R21/51 P(32-17-2) 122
Buf D22 R45/220 P(22-9-1) 98
Buf-Thomas 133R

Cin 3 3 3 7 16
TB 3 7 3 6 19
Cin D13 R23/108 P(31-16-3) 204
TB D20 R35/117 P(33-15-0) 182
TB-Harper 117C

Hou 3 3 8 3 17
Min 0 17 0 6 23
Hou D15 R25/75 P(32-20-2) 281
Min D21 R28/107 P(43-28-2) 281
Min-Carter 115C

Pit 3 3 3 7 16
Jax 7 10 3 0 20
Pit D16 R23/68 P(35-19-0) 282
Jax D17 R29/96 P(30-17-0) 171
Pit-Thigpen 160C

Car 0 0 13 14 27
ChiB 7 7 3 14 31
Car D10 R26/69 P(28-14-1) 228
ChiB D27 R38/141 P(41-23-0) 249
Car-Carrier 114C;
ChiB-Salaam 105R

Was 10 7 7 10 0 34
Phi 10 14 7 3 3 37
Was D19 R26/65 P(45-22-1) 226
Phi D30 R38/272 P(45-30-1) 252
Was-Ellard 110C; Phi-Garner 120R,
Watters 139R

Ind 0 3 7 14 3 27
Mia 14 10 0 0 0 24
Ind D22 R26/109 P(33-25-0) 310
Mia D26 R37/148 P(31-20-0) 195
Ind-Harbaugh 319P

Arz 3 7 11 0 21
NYG 7 0 7 6 20
Arz D29 R30/140 P(38-23-1) 291
NYG D23 R35/186 P(35-14-2) 158
Arz-Hearst 122R, Sanders 108C,
Krieg 305P

Cle 3 0 7 10 20
Det 14 10 7 7 38
Cle D15 R25/59 P(40-22-0) 196
Det D22 R22/161 P(38-24-1) 268
Det-Sanders 157R, Moore 125C

Den 14 9 14 0 37
NE 3 0 0 0 3
Den D23 R35/121 P(34-21-1) 282
NE D22 R19/81 P(59-27-0) 248

Sea 0 0 7 7 14
Oak 3 10 14 7 34
Sea D19 R27/116 P(33-15-2) 227
Oak D24 R33/195 P(34-21-0) 335
Oak-Williams 160R, Brown 143C,
Hostetler 333P

MONDAY, OCTOBER 9
SD 3 10 0 10 0 23
KC 0 13 0 10 6 29
SD D25 R31/51 P(42-28-1) 318
KC D21 R25/62 P(42-28-1) 318
SD-Humphries 315P; KC-Bono 329P

THURSDAY, OCTOBER 12
Atl 0 10 6 3 19
Slr 7 14 0 0 21
Atl D10 R14/44 P(30-16-0) 148
Slr D24 R29/133 P(38-27-1) 318
Slr-Bruce 191C, Miller 328P

SUNDAY, OCTOBER 15
Min 3 3 0 11 0 17
TB 7 7 3 0 3 20
Min D23 R26/62 P(48-33-2) 332
TB D19 R23/44 P(37-24-0) 219
Min-Moon 332P

Sea 0 7 7 7 21
Buf 0 10 14 3 27
Sea D16 R30/78 P(34-15-3) 190
Buf D23 R38/113 P(36-21-0) 259
Sea-Galloway 102C;
Buf-Brooks 109C

Det 0 0 14 7 21
GB 3 17 7 3 30
Det D18 R20/129 P(41-17-1) 205
GB D26 R37/109 P(34-23-0) 327
Det-Sanders 124R; GB-Favre 342P

Phi 0 14 0 3 17
NYG 0 6 0 8 14
Phi D14 R45/153 P(16-7-1) 66
NYG D15 R23/84 P(41-15-3) 112
Phi-Watters 122R

ChiB 3 7 10 10 30
Jax 7 3 0 17 27
ChiB D23 R33/135 P(29-17-0) 245
Jax D26 R23/121 P(48-30-1) 288
Jax-Brunell 302P

Was 7 6 7 0 20
Arz 3 7 7 7 24
Was D13 R18/42 P(29-15-1) 217
Arz D20 R29/113 P(33-22-1) 198

SF 0 7 7 3 17
Ind 3 3 9 3 18
SF D21 R20/62 P(41-28-1) 207
Ind D14 R34/88 P(18-12-1) 169
Ind-Dilger 125C

Mia 0 10 7 13 30
NO 7 6 13 7 33
Mia D23 R18/28 P(43-29-2) 353
NO D18 R31/80 P(33-21-0) 255
Mia-Kosar 368P; NO-Everett 242P

Dal 7 7 6 3 23
SD 2 0 7 0 9
Dal D22 R34/105 P(30-21-0) 215
SD D20 R29/159 P(32-20-3) 174
Dal-Irvin 103C

NE 7 3 9 7 26
KC 3 21 0 7 31
NE D23 R27/108 P(47-25-1) 213
KC D17 R33/150 P(40-16-0) 203

NYJ 0 12 0 3 15
Car 3 10 7 6 26
NYJ D7 R12/25 P(41-17-3) 113
Car D15 R36/133 P(26-14-2) 132

MONDAY, OCTOBER 16
Oak 0 0 0 0 0
Den 3 11 10 3 27
Oak D10 R13/21 P(45-19-2) 148
Den D24 R33/124 P(49-26-0) 351
Den-Miller 149C, Elway 324P

THURSDAY, OCTOBER 19
Cin 0 10 14 3 27
Pit 0 3 3 3 9
Cin D18 R29/93 P(22-18-0) 275
Pit D24 R22/121 P(52-30-1) 347
Cin-Pickens 108C;
Pit-O'Donnell 359P

SUNDAY, OCTOBER 22
SF 14 10 20 0 44
Slr 3 0 0 7 10
SF D17 R29/113 P(22-15-0) 144
Slr D16 R26/71 P(44-21-4) 284
Slr-Bruce 173C

Atl 0 14 7 3 24
TB 7 7 0 7 21
Atl D23 R27/121 P(37-24-1) 268
TB D16 R24/89 P(28-14-0) 169
Atl-Emanuel 121C, Metcalf 106C

NO 0 3 0 0 3
Car 0 3 14 3 20
NO D17 R28/64 P(48-27-4) 238
Car D10 R34/126 P(21-8-0) 29

Mia 3 6 7 0 16
NYJ 0 0 10 7 17
Mia D21 R27/146 P(42-27-3) 174
NYJ D12 R22/57 P(26-15-1) 143
Mia-Parmalee 120R

Jax 13 7 0 3 23
Cle 0 12 3 0 15
Jax D23 R45/159 P(28-16-1) 156
Cle D24 R28/89 P(34-20-2) 298
Cle-Smith 106C

Det 3 10 7 10 0 30
Was 6 7 7 10 6 36
Det D17 R23/99 P(50-30-1) 322
Was D26 R32/166 P(39-21-0) 239
Det-Moore 102C, Perriman 115C,
Mitchell 327P; Was-Allen 110R,
Ellard 112C

Hou 0 15 10 7 32
ChiB 15 13 0 7 35
Hou D15 R15/46 P(38-24-0) 281
ChiB D26 R38/131 P(41-24-2) 349
ChiB-Salaam 109R, Conway 111C,
Graham 137C, Kramer 349P

SD 6 19 0 10 35
Sea 3 3 6 13 25
SD D15 R36/153 P(26-14-1) 146
Sea D24 R25/150 P(31-19-3) 233
Sea-Warren 112C

Min 7 7 0 7 21
GB 7 7 7 17 38
Min D17 R23/93 P(52-26-3) 170
GB D22 R23/69 P(43-22-0) 277
GB-Chmura 101C, Favre 295P

KC 7 7 7 0 21
Den 7 0 0 0 7
KC D21 R41/171 P(28-15-0) 161
Den D19 R26/85 P(40-21-2) 200
KC-Allen 121R

Ind 3 7 7 0 17
Oak 7 3 7 13 30
Ind D13 R21/91 P(26-17-0) 163
Oak D18 R25/74 P(35-23-1) 322
Oak-Ismail 125C, Evans 335P

MONDAY, OCTOBER 23
Buf 6 8 0 0 14
NE 7 14 3 3 27
Buf D14 R20/115 P(31-20-0) 186
NE D24 R48/161 P(40-23-0) 262
NE-Martin 127R

SUNDAY, OCTOBER 29
Dal 0 14 7 7 28
Atl 7 3 3 0 13
Dal D23 R33/186 P(25-19-1) 194
Atl D16 R23/100 P(30-18-0) 158
Dal-Smith 167R, Irvin 135C

NYJ 3 0 0 7 10
Ind 3 14 0 0 17
NYJ D19 R33/101 P(31-19-1) 140
Ind D10 R23/52 P(16-9-0) 62

Slr 0 3 0 6 9
Phi 0 10 10 0 20
Slr D24 R26/104 P(43-26-2) 224
Phi D15 R24/114 P(34-15-1) 160
Slr-Bruce 105C

Jax 0 0 7 0 7
Pit 7 14 0 3 24
Jax D14 R20/84 P(33-18-0) 145
Pit D20 R33/138 P(25-17-0) 178

Car 0 0 17 0 3 20
NE 0 4 10 0 3 17
Car D23 R40/143 P(46-25-1) 291
NE D23 R31/98 P(44-22-0) 228
Car-Moore 119R, Collins 309P

Cle 3 6 3 14 3 29
Cin 6 3 7 10 0 26
Cle D26 R35/179 P(46-26-1) 301
Cin D27 R21/92 P(46-25-2) 292
Cle-Rison 173C, Zeier 310P

NO 0 3 8 0 11
SF 0 7 0 0 7
NO D17 R32/108 P(26-12-0) 144
SF D19 R23/55 P(42-29-2) 231
NO-Bates 106R; SF-Rice 108C

GB 6 0 10 0 16
Det 7 14 0 3 24
GB D28 R27/145 P(43-26-3) 298
Det D18 R25/98 P(23-15-0) 238
GB-Bennett 121R, Brooks 127C,
Favre 304P; Det-Sanders 167R,
Moore 147C

TB 0 3 3 0 6
Hou 6 3 7 3 19
TB D10 R17/94 P(23-10-3) 61
Hou D22 R42/119 P(29-19-0) 156

Buf 0 3 0 6 ...
Buf 0 3 0 6
Mia 3 3 7 10 23
Buf D11 R17/47 P(37-18-0) 139
Mia D21 R34/148 P(35-20-0) 214

Sea 0 7 0 7 14
Arz 14 0 0 6 20
Sea D17 R37/230 P(34-17-4) 198
Arz D20 R33/115 P(45-23-2) 190
Sea-Warren 127R

NYG 9 7 0 8 24
Was 3 3 6 3 15
NYG D13 R30/114 P(22-11-0) 129
Was D20 R28/103 P(44-22-4) 306
Was-Ellard 111C, Shepherd 135C,
Frerotte 345P

MONDAY, OCTOBER 30
ChiB 0 14 0 0 14
Min 0 3 0 3 6
ChiB D19 R30/180 P(25-18-0) 231
Min D19 R22/70 P(42-28-0) 227

SUNDAY, NOVEMBER 5
GB 7 9 0 8 24
Min 10 0 14 3 27
GB D23 R23/83 P(51-29-4) 261
Min D17 R23/94 P(39-21-0) 225
GB-Brooks 120C

```
Det    0   7   6   9   22
Atl   10  17   7   0   34
Det  D19 R16/61   P(50-23-2) 314
Atl  D30 R23/85   P(40-31-0) 349
Det-Moore 176C, Mitchell 321P;
Atl-Emanuel 104C, George 362P

Oak    7  10   0   3   20
Cin    0   3   0  14   17
Oak  D16 R34/184  P(30-17-1) 168
Cin  D14 R26/119  P(31-16-2) 121
Oak-Williams 134R

Hou    3  14  10  10   37
Cle    7   0   3   0   10
Hou  D16 R27/136  P(22-17-1) 141
Cle  D25 R23/102  P(54-28-3) 265
Hou-Thomas 108R

Was    0   3   0   0    3
KC     7  10   0   7   24
Was  D13 R18/79   P(39-12-2) 122
KC   D21 R38/178  P(37-21-1) 190

NE     3  10   7   0   20
NYJ    0   0   0   7    7
NE   D18 R37/172  P(27-13-0) 173
NYJ  D26 R26/132  P(37-19-1) 123
NE-Martin 166R

Car   10   3   0   0   13
SF     0   0   0   7    7
Car  D13 R29/72   P(30-17-1) 132
SF   D19 R19/65   P(42-27-2) 339
SF-Rice 111C, Grbac 327P

Arz    3   3   0   0    6
Den   14  10   7   7   38
Arz  D18 R21/74   P(32-19-0) 203
Den  D24 R30/148  P(22-17-0) 258
Den-Davis 135R

Buf   10   6   0   0   16
Ind    0   3   0   0    3
Buf  D12 R27/80   P(24-15-0) 244
Ind  D16 R31/100  P(28-16-1) 219

Pit    0  17   3  14   37
ChiB   3   7  14  10   34
Pit  D27 R32/85   P(52-34-2) 298
ChiB D20 R29/120  P(28-15-3) 223
Pit-Thigpen 108C, O'Donnell 341P;
ChiB-Graham 111C

Slr    7   0   3   0   10
NO     0  10   3   6   19
Slr  D12 R19/80   P(24-12-1) 144
NO   D24 R41/153  P(25-17-0) 168
Slr-Bruce 135C; NO-Bates 106R

Mia    7   0   7   0   24
SD     3   0  11   0   14
Mia  D24 R29/126  P(39-25-1) 291
SD   D17 R24/70   P(28-19-1) 229
Mia-Parmalee 103R;
SD-Martin 121C

NYG    3  19   0   6   28
Sea   21   0   3   6   30
NYG  D26 R31/117  P(41-20-0) 286
Sea  D24 R32/138  P(31-17-1) 248
NYG-Sherrard 128C;
Sea-Blades 153C
```

MONDAY, NOVEMBER 6

```
Phi    3   3   6   0   12
Dal   10   7   7  10   34
Phi  D14 R29/110  P(26-11-2) 120
Dal  D22 R34/164  P(24-17-1) 202
Dal-Smith 158R, Irvin 115C
```

SUNDAY, NOVEMBER 12

```
Ind    0   7   0   7   14
NO     0   7   3   7   17
Ind  D15 R26/120  P(20-15-0) 180
NO   D18 R24/69   P(37-27-1) 225

Atl    7   3   7   0   17
Buf    7   7   6   3   23
Atl  D18 R16/67   P(34-17-1) 252
Buf  D27 R48/154  P(36-22-1) 261
Atl-Emanuel 100C;
Buf-Holmes 100R, Brooks 101C

NE     0  10  14  10   34
Mia    0  10   7   0   17
NE   D22 R35/147  P(25-14-0) 205
Mia  D27 R23/75   P(46-34-2) 373
NE-Martin 142R, Brisby 118C;
Mia-Marino 333P
```

```
ChiB   7  14   7   0   28
GB    14   7   7   7   35
ChiB D26 R33/140  P(38-23-1) 304
GB   D18 R17/43   P(33-25-0) 313
ChiB-Conway 126C, Graham 108C,
Kramer 318P; GB-Brooks 138C,
Favre 336P

Oak    3   7   0   7   17
NYG    0   3  10   0   13
Oak  D20 R37/153  P(19-13-1) 146
NYG  D15 R26/76   P(31-18-0) 191

TB     7  10   0   7   24
Det    7   7   3  10   27
TB   D26 R33/190  P(29-17-2) 221
Det  D23 R22/102  P(34-21-0) 254
TB-Rhett 144R; Det-Moore 104C,
Perriman 125C

Cin   10   6   9   7   32
Hou   10   3   0  12   25
Cin  D16 R31/80   P(34-21-1) 220
Hou  D19 R22/107  P(44-20-1) 180
Cin-Pickens 108C

Sea   14   7   7  19   47
Jax    7  20   0   3   30
Sea  D26 R40/246  P(31-18-1) 235
Jax  D20 R28/161  P(20-13-1) 105
Sea-Warren 121R, Galloway 114C

Car    0   7   3   7   17
Slr    0  14   0  14   28
Car  D17 R21/77   P(36-17-4) 246
Slr  D18 R34/124  P(32-19-1) 191
Car-Green 157C; Slr-Bruce 110C

SF    17  14   0   7   38
Dal    0   7   6   7   20
SF   D21 R32/86   P(30-20-0) 300
Dal  D21 R21/108  P(37-23-3) 188
SF-Rice 161C, Grbac 305P;
Dal-Smith 100R

Min    3  14   0   7   6  30
Arz    0  10   6   8   0  24
Min  D22 R30/89   P(43-24-0) 302
Arz  D20 R24/118  P(38-19-1) 204
Min-Carter 157C, Moon 342P;
Arz-Hearst 103R

KC     7   6   6   3   22
SD     0   0   0   7    7
KC   D19 R40/166  P(27-17-1) 120
SD   D17 R19/70   P(42-21-0) 213

Den    7   3   3   0   13
Phi   14   7   0  10   31
Den  D15 R20/132  P(32-22-0) 148
Phi  D25 R32/125  P(37-25-0) 256
Phi-Barnett 105C
```

MONDAY, NOVEMBER 13

```
Cle    0   3   0   0    3
Pit    0   7   6   7   20
Cle  D7 R17/77    P(19-7-1)  43
Pit  D22 R41/153  P(32-18-0) 157
Pit-Pegram 112R
```

SUNDAY, NOVEMBER 19

```
Det    7   3   7   7   24
ChiB   0   3   7   7   17
Det  D24 R33/143  P(31-24-1) 279
ChiB D20 R28/80   P(26-17-1) 231
Det-Sanders 120R, Perriman 142C;
ChiB-Graham 109C

Sea    3   7   7  10   27
Was    3   7   0  10   20
Sea  D21 R39/167  P(32-18-2) 173
Was  D20 R22/67   P(44-24-4) 281
Sea-Warren 136R

Slr    0   6   0   0    6
Atl    7   7  10   7   31
Slr  D19 R16/71   P(50-33-2) 180
Atl  D22 R23/115  P(34-20-0) 325
Atl-Heyward 117R, Mathis 184C,
George 352P

Jax    0   0   3  13   16
TB     3   7   0   7   17
Jax  D19 R23/87   P(33-24-1) 263
TB   D17 R33/145  P(20-9-1)  101
Jax-Mitchell 161C; TB-Rhett 100R
```

```
GB     7  14   3   7   31
Cle    3   0   3  14   20
GB   D20 R32/82   P(28-23-0) 203
Cle  D32 R21/77   P(32-21-1) 240
Cle-McCardell 102C

Arz    0   7   0   0    7
Car    0  14   6   7   27
Arz  D7 R12/34    P(26-14-1)  62
Car  D23 R45/188  P(23-15-0) 182

Ind    0  17   0   7   24
NE     3   0   7   0   10
Ind  D18 R39/138  P(27-20-1) 232
NE   D14 R19/51   P(39-20-0) 151
Ind-Dawkins 101C

Pit    3  10  15  21   49
Cin   14  10   0   7   31
Pit  D28 R33/191  P(31-24-0) 365
Cin  D19 R21/57   P(31-21-1) 208
Pit-Morris 101R, O'Donnell 377P;
Cin-Pickens 129C

NYG    7   0   3   9   19
Phi   14   7   0   7   28
NYG  D15 R28/105  P(25-13-2) 118
Phi  D30 R38/151  P(27-18-1) 179
NYG-Lewis 126C

NO     0   7   3  14   24
Min   14  16   6   7   43
NO   D20 R14/68   P(37-25-0) 319
Min  D32 R33/146  P(39-30-0) 398
NO-Early 150C, Everett 335P;
Min-Carter 137C, Ismail 142C,
Moon 338P

SD     7   3   3  14   27
Den   21   6   0   3   30
SD   D20 R26/70   P(28-17-0) 199
Den  D19 R31/173  P(34-19-2) 290
Den-Davis 176R, Sharpe 137C

Dal    7  10   3  14   34
Oak    0   7   7   7   21
Dal  D25 R32/113  P(24-19-0) 223
Oak  D32 R30/140  P(55-27-3) 309
Dal-Smith 110R, Irvin 109C;
Oak-Brown 161C

Buf    7  14   0   7   28
NYJ    3   0  10  13   26
Buf  D20 R36/88   P(37-22-0) 285
NYJ  D17 R22/74   P(43-24-2) 277
Buf-Brooks 107C, Kelly 316P;
NYJ-Esiason 312P

Hou    0   6   0   7   13
KC     3   7   0  10   20
Hou  D16 R31/105  P(38-19-3) 189
KC   D11 R26/66   P(30-13-1) 115
```

MONDAY, NOVEMBER 20

```
SF     7  17  14   6   44
Mia    0  13   0   0   13
SF   D27 R27/121  P(41-31-0) 376
Mia  D20 R14/52   P(42-26-1) 256
SF-Rice 149C, Grbac 382P
```

THURSDAY, NOVEMBER 23

```
Min    7  21   3   7   38
Det   14  10  10  10   44
Min  D22 R15/34   P(47-30-2) 351
Det  D27 R25/139  P(45-30-1) 395
Min-Reed 149C, Moon 384P;
Det-Sanders 138R, Moore 127C,
Morton 102C, Perriman 153C;
Mitchell 410P

KC     0   6   6   0   12
Dal   14   0   7   3   24
KC   D19 R19/73   P(36-20-0) 261
Dal  D23 R35/118  P(29-21-0) 175
Dal-Irvin 121C
```

SUNDAY, NOVEMBER 26

```
Phi    6   0   0   8   14
Was    0   0   0   7    7
Phi  D19 R39/179  P(26-16-1) 137
Was  D15 R32/147  P(27-12-1) 153
Phi-Watters 124R

TB     0   0   3  10   13
GB     7  14   7   7   35
TB   D22 R19/42   P(48-27-0) 283
GB   D22 R25/108  P(24-16-0) 261
TB-Harris 122C, Dilfer 312P;
GB-Brooks 114C
```

```
NE     3   7   3  22   35
Buf    3  16   6   0   25
NE   D26 R32/173  P(45-21-3) 257
Buf  D31 R31/132  P(32-17-2) 202
NE-Martin 148R, Brisby 101C

ChiB   7   3  10   7   27
NYG    7   7   3   7   24
ChiB D26 R30/143  P(39-25-0) 266
NYG  D23 R34/121  P(33-17-0) 217

NYJ    7   6   0   3   16
Sea    0   0  10   0   10
NYJ  D17 R32/112  P(34-19-1) 143
Sea  D14 R23/74   P(34-17-1) 118
NYJ-Murrell 116R

Den   10   7   7   9   33
Hou   14  14   7   7   42
Den  D22 R24/140  P(41-27-2) 332
Hou  D23 R32/168  P(26-18-0) 280
Den-Davis 110R, Miller 152C,
Elway 332P; Hou-Thomas 104R,
Sanders 147C

Pit    7  10   0   3   20
Cle    0  10   7   0   17
Pit  D19 R32/60   P(32-23-0) 258
Cle  D19 R25/75   P(33-20-2) 178
Pit-Thigpen 106C

Slr    7   0   6   0   13
SF     7  21   7   6   41
Slr  D13 R20/81   P(40-18-4) 148
SF   D23 R31/79   P(40-26-2) 269

Atl    0  20   7  10   37
Arz    6  14   7  10   40
Atl  D15 R15/34   P(34-15-1) 260
Arz  D28 R35/121  P(43-27-2) 392
Arz-Centers 101C, Moore 121C,
Krieg 413P

Mia    0   6   8  14   28
Ind   14  10   2  10   36
Mia  D24 R23/107  P(36-23-1) 231
Ind  D21 R37/193  P(18-12-0) 159
Mia-Parmalee 102R, Marino 254P

Car    3   8   7   8   26
NO     7  10  10   7   34
Car  D17 R20/80   P(46-17-4) 329
NO   D24 R43/180  P(29-15-1) 172
Car-Carrier 132C, Green 105C,
Collins 335P

Cin    0   7   0  10   17
Jax    0   0   3   0    3
Cin  D20 R27/113  P(39-19-3) 210
Jax  D18 R20/78   P(34-18-1) 213
```

MONDAY, NOVEMBER 27

```
Oak    3   0   0   3    6
SD     0   6   3   3   12
Oak  D16 R26/120  P(32-17-3) 164
SD   D17 R31/78   P(34-24-0) 204
Oak-Williams 101R
```

THURSDAY, NOVEMBER 30

```
NYG    0   3   7   0   10
Arz    0   6   0   0    6
NYG  D14 R25/66   P(27-17-0) 133
Arz  D17 R24/92   P(39-23-2) 250
```

SUNDAY, DECEMBER 3

```
Was    0   0   7  10   24
Dal    0  10   0   7   17
Was  D18 R39/140  P(24-11-0) 152
Dal  D24 R25/96   P(47-29-1) 285
Was-Hayden 127R, Martin 132C;
Dal-Irvin 101C

KC     6   6  10   7   29
Oak    7   3   0  13   23
KC   D16 R36/187  P(25-16-1) 121
Oak  D20 R11/8    P(48-28-2) 325
KC-Allen 124R; Oak-Brown 150C

Atl    7   7   0   7   21
Mia    3   6   0  12   21
Atl  D18 R24/92   P(23-17-0) 204
Mia  D29 R22/85   P(50-35-2) 343
Mia-Marino 343P

Cin    0  10   0   0   10
GB     7   7   3   7   24
Cin  D12 R13/31   P(36-19-2) 186
GB   D23 R30/95   P(43-31-1) 339
GB-Chmura 109C, Favre 339P
```

```
Cle    0   3   7   3   13
SD     7  10   0  14   31
Cle  D19 R16/26   P(41-28-1) 287
SD   D25 R43/186  P(25-18-0) 230
Cle-Testaverde 303P;
SD-Hayden 127R, Martin 132C

Hou    0   7   0   0    7
Pit    7   7   0   7   21
Hou  D11 R27/75   P(33-17-1) 174
Pit  D17 R30/153  P(40-15-2) 205
Pit-Morris 102R

Ind   10   0   0   0   10
Car    0  10   0   3   13
Ind  D12 R25/65   P(29-14-2) 135
Car  D12 R27/85   P(35-14-1) 170

TB     0   0   7   7   17
Min    3  14  14   0   31
TB   D17 R22/90   P(31-15-1) 166
Min  D22 R32/190  P(32-20-2) 261
Min-Carter 136C

NO    14   3   0  14   31
NE     7   7   0   3   17
NO   D17 R22/139  P(26-17-1) 293
NE   D21 R39/140  P(32-18-2) 191
NO-Bates 123R; NE-Martin 112R

Phi    0   7   0   7   14
Sea    7  10   3   6   26
Phi  D17 R21/69   P(36-19-1) 200
Sea  D20 R38/167  P(30-17-0) 149

Buf    3   7   0   7   17
SF     7   3   7  10   27
Buf  D15 R24/84   P(43-19-3) 191
SF   D18 R27/102  P(44-28-1) 221

Jax    3   7   6   7   23
Den    7  14   7   3   31
Jax  D13 R21/69   P(28-15-1) 191
Den  D23 R30/111  P(34-22-1) 286
Den-Elway 286P

Slr    0   7   9   7   23
NYJ    0   7   3  10   20
Slr  D13 R27/76   P(38-17-4) 134
NYJ  D13 R22/61   P(35-20-1) 188
```

MONDAY, DECEMBER 4

```
ChiB   0   0   7   0    7
Det   14   7   3   3   27
ChiB D13 R18/77   P(33-21-0) 108
Det  D27 R25/109  P(39-26-0) 310
Det-Moore 183C, Mitchell 320P
```

SATURDAY, DECEMBER 9

```
Cle    0   3   0   8   11
Min    3  10   7   7   27
Cle  D10 R13/29   P(28-15-4) 172
Min  D26 R39/111  P(40-29-2) 325
Min-Carter 124C

Arz    0  14   3   8   25
SD     0  14  14   0   28
Arz  D13 R15/32   P(40-24-0) 250
SD   D20 R33/92   P(41-26-4) 288
Arz-Moore 104C; SD-Seay 114C
```

SUNDAY, DECEMBER 10

```
Det    7  10   0   7   24
Hou    0   7   3   7   17
Det  D15 R23/59   P(36-16-2) 263
Hou  D26 R26/93   P(49-31-3) 312
Det-Moore 105C, Perriman 128C

Dal    7  10   0   0   17
Phi    3   3   8   6   20
Dal  D15 R29/109  P(28-11-0)  87
Phi  D19 R40/149  P(29-20-1) 162
Dal-Smith 108R; Phi-Watters 112R

SF     7  14   7   3   31
Car    0   3   0   7   10
SF   D26 R29/79   P(47-31-1) 322
Car  D12 R23/76   P(29-12-1) 119
SF-Rice 121C, Young 336P

NYJ    0   7  14   7   28
NE     0   7   7  17   31
NYJ  D23 R28/92   P(42-27-1) 254
NE   D18 R35/160  P(36-11-1) 167
NYJ-Mitchell 108C,
Yarborough 105C, Esiason 296P;
NE-Martin 148R
```

ChiB 0 3 0 7 10
Cin 3 3 10 0 **16**
ChiB D17 R26/119 P(36-18-0) 183
Cin D19 R26/91 P(41-30-0) 246
ChiB-Salaam 105R

Ind 14 10 3 14 **41**
Jax 0 7 3 21 31
Ind D15 R35/91 P(16-9-0) 128
Jax D27 R25/126 P(39-26-1) 298
Jax-Jackson 113C, Brunell 312P

Pit 7 13 3 6 **29**
Oak 0 7 3 0 10
Pit D21 R44/144 P(31-15-1) 211
Oak D9 R15/28 P(37-20-4) 162
Pit-Pegram 122R

Sea 0 3 7 21 **31**
Den 10 10 0 7 27
Sea D19 R27/134 P(34-16-2) 192
Den D25 R37/240 P(29-16-3) 148
Sea-Warren 101R, Blades 127C;
Den-Milburn 131R

NO 0 0 0 14 14
Atl 6 3 7 3 **19**
NO D21 R18/55 P(47-31-1) 287
Atl D18 R22/91 P(39-20-0) 242

Was 0 3 0 10 13
NYG 3 10 0 7 **20**
Was D21 R40/161 P(32-17-1) 145
NYG D9 R24/88 P(12-10-0) 72
Was-Allen 120R

Buf 7 14 14 10 **45**
Slr 10 3 3 11 27
Buf D28 R38/222 P(25-19-1) 232
Slr D27 R22/73 P(61-34-0) 377
Buf-Thomas 129R, Kelly 237P;
Slr-Bruce 136C, Rypien 372P

GB 0 3 0 7 0 10
TB 0 0 7 3 3 **13**
GB D20 R20/61 P(46-27-1) 285
TB D19 R25/127 P(42-23-2) 218
GB-Brooks 122C; TB-Rhett 118R,
Copeland 122C

MONDAY, DECEMBER 11

KC 0 0 0 6 6
Mia 6 7 0 0 **13**
KC D17 R24/153 P(37-15-1) 180
Mia D15 R33/102 P(34-18-1) 146

SATURDAY, DECEMBER 16

NE 3 3 6 15 27
Pit 0 17 7 17 **41**
NE D28 R23/117 P(60-39-1) 322
Pit D14 R24/95 P(28-16-1) 226
NE-Martin 120R, Bledsoe 336P

GB 14 14 6 0 **34**
NO 7 7 0 9 23
GB D22 R30/103 P(30-21-0) 294
NO D26 R19/55 P(45-29-1) 349
GB-Brooks 118C, Favre 308P;
NO-Early 117C, Everett 364P

SUNDAY, DECEMBER 17

TB 7 3 0 0 10
ChiB 7 7 10 7 **31**
TB D15 R18/76 P(37-22-3) 213
ChiB D23 R35/173 P(28-20-0) 256
ChiB-Salaam 134R, Graham 102C

NYJ 0 0 0 6 6
Hou 10 3 0 10 **23**
NYJ D10 R16/30 P(34-19-0) 134
Hou D21 R38/108 P(27-13-0) 166

Arz 6 11 3 0 20
Phi 0 7 7 7 **21**
Arz D18 R33/93 P(38-21-2) 231
Phi D11 R25/76 P(31-14-3) 198
Phi-Williams 105C

Atl 14 3 0 0 17
Car 0 7 7 7 **21**
Atl D25 R17/87 P(56-31-2) 332
Car D15 R24/45 P(28-18-1) 283
Atl-Mathis 102C, George 310P;
Car-Green 147C

Was 7 7 14 7 **35**
Slr 10 0 0 13 23
Was D18 R34/118 P(23-15-1) 140
Slr D23 R24/96 P(50-34-1) 345
Slr-Wright 132C, Rypien 347P

Jax 0 0 0 0 0
Det 10 17 10 7 **44**
Jax D15 R20/109 P(28-13-4) 126
Det D28 R41/156 P(28-19-0) 230

Cin 0 3 0 7 10
Cle 0 17 6 3 **26**
Cin D16 R16/65 P(46-22-1) 247
Cle D23 R41/159 P(32-22-0) 241
Cle-Byner 121R

NYG 0 14 0 6 20
Dal 3 3 6 9 **21**
NYG D21 R44/244 P(20-10-1) 103
Dal D21 R26/110 P(34-16-1) 222
NYG-Hampton 187R;
Dal-Smith 103R

Den 0 7 3 7 17
KC 7 7 0 6 **20**
Den D18 R16/64 P(36-24-0) 204
KC D22 R33/145 P(37-23-0) 219

Oak 3 0 0 7 10
Sea 17 10 14 3 **44**
Oak D15 R32/140 P(34-18-0) 182
Sea D18 R25/119 P(25-16-0) 220
Oak-Brown 102C; Sea-Warren 105R,
Galloway 108C

SD 7 0 7 13 **27**
Ind 3 7 0 14 24
SD D26 R32/114 P(40-21-1) 265
Ind D24 R24/89 P(43-20-1) 276
SD-Martin 168C; Ind-Dawkins 123C

Mia 0 3 10 7 20
Buf 3 10 7 3 **23**
Mia D12 R18/42 P(28-18-1) 227
Buf D24 R48/208 P(28-16-1) 134
Buf-Thomas 148R

MONDAY, DECEMBER 18

Min 0 20 7 3 30
SF 21 6 3 7 **37**
Min D17 R18/75 P(39-22-0) 189
SF D21 R23/42 P(49-30-2) 425
SF-Rice 289C, Young 425P

SATURDAY, DECEMBER 23

SD 0 3 7 17 **27**
NYG 3 14 0 0 17
SD D13 R30/97 P(24-14-0) 108
NYG D21 R34/98 P(36-21-1) 202

Det 14 3 10 10 **37**
TB 0 3 0 7 10
Det D24 R24/60 P(42-27-1) 346
TB D17 R16/144 P(39-19-2) 170
Det-Moore 105C, Perriman 135C,
Mitchell 352P

NE 0 7 0 0 7
Ind 0 0 7 3 **10**
NE D15 R26/110 P(37-17-3) 169
Ind D19 R31/127 P(30-20-0) 195
NE-Martin 103R

SUNDAY, DECEMBER 24

Sea 0 3 0 0 3
KC 13 7 3 3 **26**
Sea D8 R17/26 P(33-12-0) 63
KC D21 R42/174 P(29-15-1) 201
KC-Hill 113R

Hou 0 8 13 7 **28**
Buf 0 0 3 14 17
Hou D15 R35/135 P(26-12-0) 164
Buf D15 R21/76 P(33-16-1) 96

Cle 0 7 7 7 21
Jax 10 3 0 11 **24**
Cle D26 R28/134 P(45-28-3) 316
Jax D18 R27/105 P(29-17-0) 268
Cle-Jackson 130C, Testaverde 325P

SF 14 7 0 6 27
Atl 3 13 6 6 **28**
SF D23 R19/86 P(45-32-1) 348
Atl D20 R15/56 P(40-26-0) 307
SF-Rice 153C, Stokes 106C,
Young 316P

NO 3 0 3 6 **12**
NYJ 0 0 0 0 0
NO D13 R27/40 P(38-20-0) 199
NYJ D11 R16/67 P(46-28-3) 139

Min 3 21 0 0 24
Cin 3 0 14 10 **27**
Min D27 R33/163 P(43-26-0) 285
Cin D18 R16/71 P(41-23-2) 231
Min-Graham 115R, Reed 111C

Phi 0 7 0 7 14
ChiB 7 10 0 3 **20**
Phi D12 R18/44 P(31-15-2) 167
ChiB D23 R47/181 P(30-15-1) 169
ChiB-Salaam 122R

Car 3 7 0 7 17
Was 7 3 7 3 **20**
Car D19 R24/79 P(43-19-2) 193
Was D17 R38/151 P(24-10-0) 166
Car-Carrier 101C

Den 0 17 0 14 **31**
Oak 7 7 14 0 28
Den D30 R30/130 P(41-24-1) 307
Oak D19 R28/98 P(30-20-0) 238
Den-Craver 108R, Elway 320P;
Oak-Brown 127C

Mia 10 17 0 14 **41**
Slr 3 9 7 3 22
Mia D17 R24/60 P(35-23-2) 280
Slr D21 R16/58 P(45-29-1) 316
Slr-Bruce 210C, Rypien 320P

Pit 0 10 3 6 19
GB 0 14 7 3 **24**
Pit D27 R24/84 P(55-33-0) 314
GB D19 R19/64 P(33-24-0) 295
Pit-O'Donnell 318P;
GB-Brooks 137C, Favre 301P

MONDAY, DECEMBER 25

Dal 17 7 3 10 **37**
Arz 0 3 10 0 13
Dal D27 R34/101 P(33-22-1) 373
Arz D12 R19/63 P(35-18-2) 222
Dal-Williams 203C, Aikman 350P;
Arz-Centers 172C

1996 NFL

SUNDAY, SEPTEMBER 1

Atl 3 3 0 0 6
Car 7 13 3 6 **29**
Atl D12 R19/119 P(35-16-0) 162
Car D23 R37/129 P(31-17-0) 186
Atl-Anderson 108R, Mathis 123C

Pit 3 3 3 0 9
Jax 7 7 0 10 **24**
Pit D13 R25/101 P(23-12-1) 86
Jax D22 R36/119 P(31-20-2) 194

Oak 0 14 0 0 14
Bal 7 0 6 6 **19**
Oak D13 R21/60 P(26-17-2) 178
Bal D21 R30/95 P(33-19-0) 219

Phi 7 10 0 0 **17**
Was 7 0 7 0 14
Phi D23 R37/144 P(34-20-1) 258
Was D11 R24/127 P(25-12-0) 93
Was-Allen 111R

Det 0 10 0 3 13
Min 7 0 0 10 **17**
Det D27 R29/191 P(42-21-4) 244
Min D16 R27/128 P(37-21-0) 183
Det-Sanders 163R, Moore 157C;
Min-Smith 113R

NYJ 0 0 0 6 6
Den 7 24 0 0 **31**
NYJ D12 R25/116 P(25-11-1) 72
Den D21 R37/200 P(34-16-2) 167

Sea 0 7 0 0 7
SD 7 6 3 13 **29**
Sea D16 R19/106 P(41-24-2) 251
SD D27 R38/186 P(39-21-0) 191

Arz 3 3 0 7 13
Ind 0 10 0 10 **20**
Arz D20 R24/84 P(38-25-0) 226
Ind D19 R21/74 P(33-21-1) 238
Arz-Centers 108C

GB 10 14 10 0 **34**
TB 0 3 0 0 3
GB D24 R35/139 P(28-21-0) 267
TB D15 R23/59 P(30-13-4) 117
GB-Favre 247P

NE 0 3 7 0 10
Mia 10 7 7 0 **24**
NE D16 R14/29 P(38-19-2) 200
Mia D19 R39/146 P(22-16-1) 176
Mia-Abdul-Jabbar 115R

NO 0 0 3 8 11
SF 14 10 0 3 **27**
NO D14 R18/56 P(41-16-1) 175
SF D23 R38/157 P(31-18-0) 181

Cin 3 6 7 0 16
Slr 7 0 3 16 **26**
Cin D14 R22/37 P(40-23-2) 205
Slr D18 R35/70 P(35-13-1) 139

KC 7 10 0 3 **20**
Hou 10 6 0 3 19
KC D17 R24/79 P(37-21-0) 169
Hou D16 R26/72 P(29-16-1) 191

Buf 0 7 10 3 3 **23**
NYG 3 14 3 0 0 20
Buf D25 R43/153 P(41-24-1) 257
NYG D12 R31/93 P(27-11-0) 138
Buf-Reed 138C, Kelly 313P

MONDAY, SEPTEMBER 2

Dal 3 0 0 3 6
ChiB 0 10 0 12 **22**
Dal D18 R25/83 P(37-21-1) 173
ChiB D14 R32/91 P(29-14-1) 213
ChiB-Harris 103C

SUNDAY, SEPTEMBER 8

ChiB 3 0 0 0 3
Was 0 3 7 0 **10**
ChiB D19 R33/148 P(37-20-1) 156
Was D13 R24/81 P(29-18-0) 168
ChiB-Green 106R

Mia 7 17 7 7 **38**
Arz 0 0 10 0 10
Mia D26 R32/128 P(27-18-0) 203
Arz D13 R19/27 P(37-21-3) 176

Slr 0 0 0 0 0
SF 0 14 3 17 **34**
Slr D6 R17/36 P(27-11-1) 69
SF D23 R42/130 P(30-21-0) 222

Oak 0 0 0 3 3
KC 0 7 7 5 **19**
Oak D22 R26/136 P(40-19-1) 160
KC D16 R31/125 P(19-11-0) 121

Cin 0 7 0 7 14
SD 7 7 3 10 **27**
Cin D14 R22/62 P(36-17-1) 187
SD D25 R34/114 P(42-27-2) 269

Hou 10 14 7 3 **34**
Jax 10 3 7 7 27
Hou D21 R31/181 P(22-14-0) 220
Jax D26 R21/72 P(38-27-2) 298
Hou-George 143R;
Jax-McCardell 100C, Brunell 302P

Den 3 10 7 10 **30**
Sea 3 3 7 7 20
Den D22 R40/180 P(28-18-0) 194
Sea D10 R19/39 P(30-18-1) 172
Den-Davis 111R

NYG 0 0 0 0 0
Dal 14 7 3 3 **27**
NYG D7 R24/63 P(19-10-1) 42
Dal D21 R40/140 P(27-19-0) 228

Ind 7 7 0 7 **21**
NYJ 0 7 0 0 7
Ind D17 R30/66 P(20-15-0) 225
NYJ D21 R24/69 P(46-26-1) 290
Ind-Dilger 156C;
NYJ-O'Donnell 319P

TB 3 3 0 0 6
Det 0 14 7 0 **21**
TB D13 R29/74 P(41-19-2) 200
Det D12 R26/120 P(27-14-0) 114
TB-Hawkins 111C;
Det-Sanders 125R

Min 3 7 0 13 **23**
Atl 3 0 14 0 17
Min D18 R33/99 P(26-15-1) 266
Atl D21 R19/79 P(41-24-1) 245
Min-Reed 148C; Atl-Emanuel 116C

NE 3 0 7 0 10
Buf 3 7 0 7 **17**
NE D23 R35/114 P(47-21-0) 179
Buf D15 R35/77 P(27-14-3) 154
Buf-Early 119C

Car 7 6 3 6 **22**
NO 7 7 3 3 20
Car D15 R34/83 P(21-13-1) 142
NO D14 R20/94 P(32-22-0) 244

Bal 7 10 0 0 17
Pit 14 14 3 0 **31**
Bal D17 R25/97 P(24-13-1) 154
Pit D26 R42/206 P(25-18-1) 191
Pit-Bettis 116R

MONDAY, SEPTEMBER 9

Phi 0 7 0 6 13
GB 10 20 7 2 **39**
Phi D14 R17/59 P(36-16-3) 200
GB D23 R38/171 P(32-17-0) 261
GB-Brooks 130C

SUNDAY, SEPTEMBER 15

Bal 0 7 0 6 13
Hou 14 3 9 3 **29**
Bal D19 R22/73 P(40-25-3) 208
Hou D19 R32/140 P(28-17-0) 172

TB 3 10 7 3 23
Den 7 3 10 7 **27**
TB D15 R22/121 P(30-12-1) 186
Den D20 R39/194 P(34-25-2) 180
TB-Brooks 114R; Den-Davis 137R

Det 0 3 7 7 17
Phi 7 3 7 7 **24**
Det D17 R19/60 P(26-14-1) 173
Phi D25 R39/175 P(30-25-0) 271
Phi-Watters 153R, Jones 121C

Jax 0 0 0 3 3
Oak 0 10 0 7 **17**
Jax D14 R21/69 P(37-18-2) 201
Oak D18 R30/134 P(27-18-2) 197

Arz 0 0 0 0 0
NE 7 13 8 3 **31**
Arz D9 R16/46 P(31-13-3) 124
NE D26 R43/163 P(37-22-0) 221

Was 3 14 0 14 **31**
NYG 0 7 3 0 10
Was D26 R44/235 P(23-15-1) 192
NYG D19 R20/104 P(31-17-4) 182
Was-Allen 146R

KC 14 7 7 7 **35**
Sea 0 10 0 7 17
KC D24 R30/157 P(27-18-0) 166
Sea D17 R32/97 P(31-15-1) 141

NYJ 0 14 0 13 27
Mia 0 14 12 10 **36**
NYJ D20 R19/74 P(44-25-3) 304
Mia D20 R40/194 P(23-13-1) 251
NYJ-Graham 136C, O'Donnell 325P;
Mia-Abdul-Jabbar 124R

Ind 3 6 13 3 **25**
Dal 7 14 0 3 24
Ind D18 R28/103 P(28-19-1) 218
Dal D18 R30/111 P(27-17-0) 184
Dal-Smith 101R

NO 3 3 6 3 15
Cin 3 14 3 10 **30**
NO D15 R15/27 P(39-21-3) 287
Cin D24 R37/101 P(39-22-0) 218
NO-Haynes 156C

SD 3 0 0 7 10
GB 7 14 7 14 **42**
SD D11 R13/33 P(35-18-2) 108
GB D23 R36/132 P(33-22-1) 204
GB-Brooks 108C

Min 0 14 0 6 **20**
ChiB 7 7 0 0 14
Min D21 R34/138 P(44-22-1) 239
ChiB D17 R23/108 P(40-18-3) 191

MONDAY, SEPTEMBER 16

Buf 3 0 3 0 6
Pit 7 17 0 0 24
Buf D11 R23/86 P(31-15-4) 99
Pit D22 R49/222 P(21-14-0) 160
Pit-Bettis 133R

SUNDAY, SEPTEMBER 22

Phi 3 10 10 10 33
Atl 0 10 0 8 18
Phi D14 R31/123 P(29-16-0) 195
Atl D18 R11/40 P(49-33-5) 351
Phi-Watters 121R

Sea 0 3 0 14 17
TB 3 7 0 3 13
Sea D22 R26/124 P(37-20-1) 198
TB D14 R33/111 P(26-15-1) 106

SD 21 6 0 13 40
Oak 0 14 7 13 34
SD D20 R30/103 P(25-18-0) 218
Oak D28 R22/182 P(57-34-2) 371
SD-Martin 138C, Humphries 226P; Oak-Kaufman 116R, Brown 120C

Jax 0 7 15 3 25
NE 9 13 3 3 28
Jax D12 R11/29 P(39-23-1) 413
NE D26 R31/123 P(44-27-1) 230
Jax-Jackson 101C, Rison 115C, Brunell 432P

GB 7 0 14 0 21
Min 7 7 3 13 30
GB D8 R15/60 P(27-14-1) 157
Min D18 R33/88 P(41-24-2) 263
Min-Reed 129C

ChiB 0 16 0 0 16
Det 0 21 7 7 35
ChiB D19 R24/70 P(46-23-1) 248
Det D19 R29/85 P(34-24-1) 309
ChiB-Conway 126C; Det-Morton 174C, Mitchell 336P

Dal 0 0 0 7 7
Buf 7 0 3 0 10
Dal D12 R18/32 P(34-16-3) 160
Buf D14 R43/135 P(22-13-1) 89

SF 0 0 7 0 7
Car 10 7 3 3 23
SF D15 R13/48 P(40-24-1) 252
Car D21 R29/117 P(31-22-1) 272
SF-Rice 127C

Was 7 3 7 0 17
Slr 0 0 3 7 10
Was D16 R32/106 P(23-12-2) 151
Slr D17 R28/112 P(36-18-3) 173
Slr-Bruce 136C

Arz 3 8 14 3 28
NO 0 0 7 0 7
Arz D20 R45/267 P(25-11-0) 165
NO D15 R27/76 P(33-18-1) 142
Arz-Johnson 214R

Den 7 7 0 0 14
KC 0 7 7 7 17
Den D17 R27/161 P(30-14-2) 138
KC D20 R29/75 P(35-20-1) 231
Den-Davis 141R, Sharpe 131C

NYG 0 7 0 6 13
NYJ 3 0 3 0 6
NYG D12 R38/91 P(13-9-0) 110
NYJ D13 R21/78 P(38-22-1) 130

MONDAY, SEPTEMBER 23

Mia 3 3 0 0 6
Ind 0 7 0 3 10
Mia D12 R15/28 P(30-20-0) 162
Ind D20 R32/171 P(26-19-0) 106

SUNDAY, SEPTEMBER 29

NYJ 0 13 3 0 16
Was 0 10 7 14 31
NYJ D27 R37/156 P(40-27-1) 287
Was D18 R26/139 P(22-15-0) 293
NYJ-Murrell 134R; Was-Allen 101R

Slr 7 14 7 0 0 28
Arz 0 14 0 14 3 31
Slr D10 R22/60 P(17-10-1) 162
Arz D27 R27/150 P(58-37-0) 348
Slr-Bruce 117C; Arz-Moore 143C, Graham 366P

Car 0 0 6 8 14
Jax 14 3 0 7 24
Car D21 R21/57 P(37-17-0) 215
Jax D22 R38/179 P(27-15-1) 199
Car-Carrier 124C

Den 7 0 7 0 14
Cin 3 7 0 0 10
Den D22 R27/114 P(38-23-1) 288
Cin D17 R24/106 P(29-15-1) 147
Den-Davis 112R, Miller 131C, Elway 335P

KC 0 9 7 3 19
SD 6 0 10 6 22
KC D19 R19/58 P(54-25-2) 257
SD D18 R29/75 P(41-19-0) 238

Hou 0 0 14 2 16
Pit 17 3 0 10 30
Hou D16 R20/80 P(42-24-2) 193
Pit D15 R35/112 P(28-15-1) 197
Pit-Bettis 115R

NO 3 0 0 7 10
Bal 7 3 0 7 17
NO D18 R29/96 P(30-23-0) 202
Bal D16 R33/165 P(20-11-0) 178
Bal-Byner 149R

Atl 3 0 7 7 17
SF 6 21 9 3 39
Atl D18 R24/126 P(32-17-3) 191
SF D16 R22/150 P(37-23-0) 246

Min 0 7 0 3 10
NYG 3 3 6 3 15
Min D10 R20/88 P(25-13-1) 140
NYG D21 R40/145 P(29-18-0) 146

GB 10 7 7 7 31
Sea 0 7 3 0 10
GB D23 R35/142 P(34-20-0) 202
Sea D19 R26/159 P(34-11-4) 170
GB-Freeman 108C, Favre 209P; Sea-Warren 103R

Oak 0 10 7 0 17
ChiB 0 3 7 9 19
Oak D17 R25/117 P(35-19-4) 166
ChiB D15 R33/108 P(30-16-0) 188

Det 7 10 0 10 27
TB 0 0 0 0 0
Det D20 R27/129 P(33-22-0) 221
TB D13 R26/70 P(31-16-3) 156
Det-Moore 104C

MONDAY, SEPTEMBER 30

Dal 7 13 3 0 23
Phi 10 0 7 2 19
Dal D15 R34/108 P(22-13-0) 131
Phi D14 R27/85 P(30-16-2) 174

SUNDAY, OCTOBER 6

Sea 7 7 0 8 22
Mia 3 6 6 0 15
Sea D12 R27/59 P(32-18-1) 299
Mia D17 R32/85 P(28-16-1) 214
Sea-Galloway 137C

Jax 0 7 3 3 13
NO 10 0 0 7 17
Jax D22 R34/141 P(35-28-0) 241
NO D11 R19/36 P(28-15-1) 161

Hou 3 7 7 13 30
Cin 3 7 10 7 27
Hou D18 R29/160 P(32-18-1) 175
Cin D22 R36/163 P(37-18-0) 152
Hou-George 152R

Oak 0 13 0 21 34
NYJ 3 3 7 0 13
Oak D26 R43/222 P(28-17-1) 182
NYJ D20 R24/111 P(38-18-2) 171
Oak-Aska 136R; NYJ-Murrell 102R

SF 7 14 0 7 28
Slr 0 0 3 8 11
SF D23 R37/154 P(36-22-2) 235
Slr D15 R20/65 P(33-18-2) 137
SF-Rice 108C

Ind 0 0 3 10 0 13
Buf 0 7 3 3 3 16
Ind D16 R30/86 P(42-17-0) 163
Buf D20 R34/113 P(44-23-0) 299
Buf-Thomas 111R, Collins 309P

SD 3 14 0 0 17
Den 0 7 14 7 28
SD D14 R16/35 P(36-24-0) 210
Den D23 R26/94 P(41-32-1) 312
Den-Sharpe 153C, Elway 323P

NE 3 17 15 11 46
Bal 0 14 0 24 38
NE D26 R23/54 P(39-25-0) 310
Bal D28 R28/133 P(45-29-1) 330
NE-Bledsoe 310P; Bal-Alexander 123C, Jackson 128C, Testaverde 353P

Car 0 0 9 3 12
Min 0 7 0 7 14
Car D15 R28/101 P(30-15-4) 155
Min D16 R30/101 P(34-19-1) 192
Car-Johnson 102R; Min-Smith 102R

Atl 0 7 14 3 24
Det 7 21 0 0 28
Atl D19 R22/116 P(36-18-1) 165
Det D23 R32/95 P(37-20-0) 262
Atl-Anderson 103R; Det-Moore 107C

GB 0 20 14 3 37
ChiB 0 3 3 0 6
GB D21 R29/100 P(28-19-1) 243
ChiB D15 R27/53 P(32-19-3) 190
GB-Freeman 146C, Favre 246P; ChiB-Conway 101C

MONDAY, OCTOBER 7

Pit 0 6 8 3 17
KC 0 7 0 0 7
Pit D21 R32/98 P(32-20-1) 338
KC D17 R31/130 P(29-18-2) 170
Pit-Bettis 103R, Johnson 125C, Tomczak 338P

SUNDAY, OCTOBER 13

Bal 0 7 7 7 21
Ind 3 10 7 6 26
Bal D20 R23/112 P(30-17-1) 213
Ind D15 R38/123 P(15-9-0) 132

Arz 0 0 0 3 3
Dal 0 3 7 7 17
Arz D13 R22/58 P(31-16-1) 120
Dal D22 R29/125 P(37-23-1) 199
Dal-Smith 112R

Det 0 0 21 0 21
Oak 7 13 14 3 37
Det D23 R13/63 P(50-31-2) 333
Oak D20 R29/124 P(38-27-0) 295
Det-Moore 109C, Morton 109C, Mitchell 343P; Oak-Jett 112C, Hostetler 295P

NYJ 7 7 0 3 17
Jax 3 11 7 0 21
NYJ D23 R30/91 P(44-23-2) 276
Jax D10 R23/72 P(23-14-0) 217
NYJ-Chrebet 162C; Jax-Smith 135C

Phi 0 3 3 13 19
NYG 3 7 0 0 10
Phi D17 R35/140 P(33-18-0) 164
NYG D9 R23/87 P(25-11-1) 63
Phi-Watters 110R

Cin 0 0 3 7 10
Pit 3 0 7 10 20
Cin D20 R23/94 P(30-23-1) 158
Pit D17 R32/124 P(28-14-2) 182
Pit-Bettis 109R

Was 3 7 14 3 27
NE 6 10 0 6 22
Was D22 R32/108 P(34-18-0) 276
NE D23 R23/177 P(33-23-0) 205
Was-Ellard 152C; NE-Martin 164R

Min 7 0 3 3 13
TB 0 0 7 17 24
Min D17 R21/139 P(34-22-1) 255
TB D20 R31/76 P(35-22-0) 218
Min-Smith 133R

ChiB 3 14 7 0 24
NO 0 7 10 10 27
ChiB D18 R28/105 P(34-18-0) 218
NO D23 R34/205 P(31-22-1) 218
ChiB-Conway 111C; NO-Zellars 174R

Mia 0 7 7 7 21
Buf 0 0 7 0 7
Mia D15 R32/63 P(29-14-0) 176
Buf D17 R25/105 P(32-21-3) 191
Buf-Reed 134C

Slr 0 13 0 0 13
Car 14 14 10 7 45
Slr D15 R20/78 P(36-19-2) 141
Car D21 R42/184 P(18-11-1) 177
Car-Johnson 126R

Hou 7 3 7 6 23
Atl 0 0 0 13 13
Hou D16 R27/121 P(23-14-0) 199
Atl D20 R16/55 P(46-31-2) 268
Hou-George 109R, Sanders 100C

MONDAY, OCTOBER 14

SF 0 17 0 3 0 20
GB 6 0 8 6 3 23
SF D14 R28/74 P(39-21-2) 179
GB D24 R26/68 P(61-28-2) 378
GB-Beebe 220C, Favre 395P

THURSDAY, OCTOBER 17

Sea 0 3 7 6 16
KC 10 10 7 7 34
Sea D18 R20/110 P(34-20-1) 213
KC D27 R39/146 P(26-17-0) 194

SUNDAY, OCTOBER 20

NE 0 10 14 3 27
Ind 3 3 0 3 9
NE D15 R31/80 P(24-14-0) 142
Ind D27 R18/45 P(55-36-0) 319

NO 0 0 7 0 7
Car 3 3 10 3 19
NO D10 R20/71 P(29-14-1) 103
Car D21 R42/159 P(30-14-0) 155
Car-Johnson 123R

NYG 0 0 14 7 21
Was 7 21 0 3 31
NYG D24 R28/107 P(43-26-2) 287
Was D20 R34/123 P(24-18-1) 207
Was-Ellard 119C

Atl 3 15 7 3 28
Dal 7 10 8 7 32
Atl D22 R31/113 P(40-25-0) 256
Dal D17 R16/56 P(24-17-0) 250
Atl-Mathis 101C; Dal-Irvin 119C

Mia 3 8 0 17 28
Phi 14 7 7 7 35
Mia D18 R24/93 P(37-23-1) 254
Phi D21 R30/196 P(24-18-1) 223
Mia-McDuffie 121C; Phi-Watters 173R, Fryar 116C, Detmer 226P

Buf 3 3 3 16 25
NYJ 7 0 8 7 22
Buf D23 R43/138 P(36-19-0) 195
NYJ D19 R22/64 P(36-21-2) 253

TB 0 0 3 6 9
Arz 3 7 3 0 13
TB D19 R26/95 P(35-22-0) 218
Arz D21 R32/104 P(26-17-0) 133

Jax 0 7 7 0 14
Slr 7 7 0 3 17
Jax D36 R33/118 P(52-37-5) 420
Slr D8 R20/83 P(17-9-1) 121
Jax-Stewart 112R, McCardell 232C, Brunell 421P

Cin 14 7 0 0 21
SF 0 7 14 7 28
Cin D18 R36/149 P(34-15-1) 196
SF D20 R23/80 P(42-27-4) 338
SF-Popson 116C

Pit 7 3 0 3 13
Hou 3 6 0 14 23
Pit D12 R23/83 P(30-13-0) 192
Hou D23 R30/91 P(38-23-1) 237
Pit-Johnson 155C

Bal 0 13 21 0 34
Den 14 14 3 14 45
Bal D23 R18/75 P(45-27-1) 317
Den D26 R34/222 P(39-25-1) 326
Bal-Alexander 126C, Testaverde 338P; Den-Davis 194R, Sharpe 161C, Elway 326P

MONDAY, OCTOBER 21

Oak 7 3 10 3 23
SD 7 0 0 7 14
Oak D22 R34/131 P(33-20-1) 179
SD D16 R20/29 P(40-23-1) 253

SUNDAY, OCTOBER 27

Pit 3 0 14 3 20
Atl 7 3 0 7 17
Pit D20 R29/127 P(29-23-0) 184
Atl D19 R16/67 P(36-24-1) 234
Pit-Bettis 126R, Johnson 110C

SF 3 0 0 7 10
Hou 0 6 3 0 9
SF D12 R28/63 P(32-20-0) 175
Hou D12 R27/107 P(27-12-1) 77

Ind 0 13 0 3 16
Was 10 7 7 7 31
Ind D18 R24/100 P(33-17-0) 198
Was D25 R37/215 P(25-18-1) 173
Was-Allen 124R

Slr 7 6 7 11 31
Bal 6 11 14 6 37
Slr D26 R47/162 P(40-26-2) 324
Bal D25 R17/74 P(51-31-2) 404
Slr-Bruce 229C, Banks 353P; Bal-Jackson 113C, Turner 108C, Testaverde 429P

Jax 0 7 7 7 21
Cin 0 0 21 7 28
Jax D19 R28/149 P(31-18-2) 189
Cin D18 R31/60 P(31-20-0) 207

TB 0 0 0 7 7
GB 3 10 0 0 13
TB D14 R26/57 P(29-15-2) 139
GB D24 R37/129 P(31-19-1) 169

SD 3 3 0 7 13
Sea 3 17 3 9 32
SD D15 R21/69 P(43-21-4) 253
Sea D18 R34/208 P(33-16-0) 196
Sea-Warren 146R

KC 7 0 0 0 7
Den 17 7 7 3 34
KC D10 R12/24 P(49-21-2) 208
Den D26 R43/213 P(32-16-2) 286

Dal 3 6 13 7 29
Mia 0 0 0 10 10
Dal D27 R36/123 P(41-33-0) 359
Mia D10 R13/48 P(27-12-1) 173
Dal-Irvin 186C, Aikman 363P

NYJ 3 14 0 14 31
Arz 0 0 14 7 21
NYJ D27 R38/208 P(31-22-2) 246
Arz D19 R21/107 P(32-17-1) 246
NYJ-Murrell 199R; Arz-Moore 143C

Car 0 3 6 0 9
Phi 7 7 3 3 20
Car D10 R26/61 P(34-16-0) 239
Phi D16 R27/30 P(38-22-0) 239
Phi-Fryar 143C, Detmer 342P

NYG 2 23 0 10 35
Det 7 0 0 0 7
NYG D18 R39/100 P(28-16-1) 235
Det D14 R20/67 P(47-20-5) 185

Buf 0 0 10 15 25
NE 7 6 2 13 28
Buf D18 R32/141 P(32-15-1) 196
NE D23 R28/59 P(45-32-0) 358
Buf-Thomas 119R, Reed 121C; NE-Bledsoe 373P

MONDAY, OCTOBER 28

ChiB 2 13 0 0 15
Min 3 0 10 0 13
ChiB D21 R29/96 P(35-23-2) 180
Min D16 R14/11 P(41-25-1) 268
Min-Reed 153C

SUNDAY, NOVEMBER 3

```
Phi   7   7   7  10  31
Dal   7   3   3   8  21
Phi  D22 R30/130 P(33-19-0) 217
Dal  D22 R31/117 P(33-21-2) 179
Phi-Watters 116R, Fryar 120C;
Dal-Smith 113R

Det   3   7   0   8  18
GB    7   7  14   0  28
Det  D18 R26/166 P(32-15-0) 127
GB   D23 R24/101 P(35-24-1) 254
Det-Sanders 152R; GB-Beebe 106C,
Favre 281P

Arz   0   0   0   8   8
NYG   3   0   3  10  16
Arz  D14 R18/29  P(43-22-2) 216
NYG  D17 R39/135 P(30-16-0) 144

Car   3   7   0   7  17
Atl  10   3   0   7  20
Car  D17 R21/104 P(36-21-0) 243
Atl  D16 R27/124 P(32-19-1) 189
Car-Ismail 108C; Atl-Anderson 109R

Cin   0   3   7  14  24
Bal   7  14   0   0  21
Cin  D33 R39/168 P(40-23-1) 265
Bal  D23 R24/92  P(43-20-4) 279
Bal-Turner 104C

Slr   0   3   0   3   6
Pit  14   7  14   7  42
Slr  D18 R27/64  P(35-16-2) 137
Pit  D20 R41/248 P(15-10-0) 100
Slr-Bruce 108C; Pit-Bettis 129R

SD    7   9   3   7  26
Ind   0   6   6   7  19
SD   D14 R25/75  P(31-19-0) 237
Ind  D22 R28/91  P(44-18-4) 173
SD-Martin 128C

TB    0  10   0   0  10
ChiB  3   3   7   4  17
TB   D14 R23/67  P(32-15-1) 178
ChiB D18 R38/185 P(25-11-1)  84
ChiB-Harris 118R

KC    0   7   0  14  21
Min   0   0   0   6   6
KC   D23 R43/202 P(33-19-1) 157
Min  D13 R14/48  P(42-22-2) 210
KC-Hill 100R

Hou   0   3  10   3  16
Sea   3   3   3  14  23
Hou  D13 R33/128 P(18-12-1) 225
Sea  D19 R21/32  P(38-24-1) 310
Sea-Friesz 323P

Mia   3   7   3   6  23
NE    7   7   7  21  42
Mia  D22 R33/115 P(42-24-1) 315
NE   D28 R21/59  P(41-30-2) 409
Mia-Abdul-Jabbar 104R;
NE-Coates 135C, Glenn 112C,
Bledsoe 419P

Was   7   0   0   6  13
Buf   0  17  14   7  38
Was  D16 R24/75  P(28-13-0) 159
Buf  D31 R56/266 P(24-20-0) 210
Buf-Holmes 122R, Thomas 107R

SF    3  11   3   7  24
NO    0   0  10   7  17
SF   D17 R32/191 P(23-12-0) 115
NO   D18 R28/64  P(40-20-2) 229
NO-Haynes 121C
```

MONDAY, NOVEMBER 4

```
Den   7   6   0   9  22
Oak   7   0   0  14  21
Den  D18 R31/152 P(33-16-1) 160
Oak  D17 R16/105 P(34-22-0) 216
Oak-Brown 126C
```

SUNDAY, NOVEMBER 10

```
NE    0   7  10  14  31
NYJ   7  14   3   3  27
NE   D21 R17/68  P(34-24-2) 275
NYJ  D28 R36/142 P(44-22-1) 280
NYJ-Murrell 128R
```

```
GB    3   3   7   7  20
KC    3  17   7   0  27
GB   D24 R20/75  P(49-27-1) 289
KC   D19 R40/182 P(22-9-0)  201
GB-Favre 314P

Buf   7  10   7   0  24
Phi  10   0   0   7  17
Buf  D18 R37/140 P(22-11-1) 112
Phi  D25 R29/111 P(44-26-1) 274
Phi-Detmer 315P

Ind   3   3   0   7  13
Mia   7  14  16   0  37
Ind  D15 R15/33  P(41-23-2) 260
Mia  D19 R34/114 P(15-17-0) 193
Mia-McDuffie 106C

Oak   0  10   7   0   0  17
TB    7   3   0   7   3  20
Oak  D17 R22/89  P(23-16-1) 182
TB   D27 R49/162 P(29-20-1) 177

Pit   0  17   7   0  24
Cin   3  14   7  10  34
Pit  D18 R28/137 P(28-13-3) 180
Cin  D25 R32/112 P(39-24-3) 260
Pit-Bettis 111R; Cin-Pickens 103C

Atl   0   7   9   0  16
Slr  14  17   7  21  59
Atl  D15 R16/44  P(38-22-2) 248
Slr  D29 R38/279 P(24-15-0) 185
Atl-Emanuel 109C; Slr-Green 106R,
Phillips 106R

Bal   7  10   3   7  27
Jax   0   3  10  17  30
Bal  D24 R36/152 P(27-17-0) 235
Jax  D22 R20/86  P(37-24-1) 332
Bal-Morris 109R; Jax-Brunell 354P

Dal   0   7   0  13  20
SF   10   0   0   7  17
Dal  D20 R31/94  P(39-24-1) 222
SF   D16 R26/111 P(30-17-2) 156

ChiB  3   3   0   6  12
Den   7   7   0   3  17
ChiB D24 R39/174 P(35-17-2) 172
Den  D17 R26/92  P(32-19-0) 192
ChiB-Harris 112R

Min   0   7   0  16  23
Sea  10  18   7   7  42
Min  D16 R12/15  P(42-22-2) 300
Sea  D26 R37/199 P(34-23-0) 253
Min-Carter 142C

Hou  14   7   7   3  31
NO    3   3   0   8  14
Hou  D20 R37/148 P(21-13-1) 161
NO   D14 R21/73  P(33-16-0) 154
Hou-Harmon 108C

Arz   3  10   0  21   3  37
Was   3  10  14   7   0  34
Arz  D32 R33/108 P(59-35-4) 507
Was  D25 R39/204 P(36-18-1) 212
Arz-Esiason 522P; Was-Allen 124R

NYG  14   0   3   0  17
Car   7   3  10   7  27
NYG  D14 R20/74  P(31-15-3) 215
Car  D23 R40/142 P(34-20-1) 208
```

MONDAY, NOVEMBER 11

```
Det   7   7   0   7  21
SD    7  10   7   3  27
Det  D19 R19/82  P(27-15-0) 140
SD   D27 R40/127 P(32-24-0) 279
SD-Martin 113C, Humphries 311P
```

SUNDAY, NOVEMBER 17

```
NO    0   3   3   9  15
Atl  10   7   0   0  17
NO   D15 R17/35  P(33-23-2) 235
Atl  D18 R22/74  P(39-26-1) 219

Was   3  10  10   3  26
Phi   0   7   7   7  21
Was  D19 R31/95  P(33-18-1) 205
Phi  D27 R30/129 P(33-21-1) 235
Phi-Jones 103C

Den  14  10   7   3  34
NE    0   0   8   0   8
Den  D26 R45/198 P(27-16-1) 224
NE   D12 R9/17   P(42-22-1) 201
Den-Davis 154R
```

```
ChiB  0   0   0  10  10
KC    7   7   0   0  14
ChiB D14 R19/35  P(36-21-1) 221
KC   D20 R40/149 P(25-15-1) 151

Sea   7   3   3   3  16
Det   0   7   7   3  17
Sea  D24 R41/184 P(25-13-1) 194
Det  D17 R21/144 P(23-18-1) 141
Sea-Smith 148C; Det-Sanders 134R

Jax   3   0   0   0   3
Pit   0  14  14   0  28
Jax  D20 R18/78  P(47-28-2) 161
Pit  D15 R32/108 P(25-7-1)   90

NYG   0   6   7  10  23
Arz  14   7   7   3  31
NYG  D24 R28/91  P(41-22-2) 240
Arz  D20 R34/97  P(27-18-1) 250

TB    3  10   0  12  25
SD   14   0   3   0  17
TB   D23 R34/99  P(40-30-1) 324
SD   D11 R19/94  P(33-15-3) 183
TB-Dilfer 327P

Bal   7   6   7   0  20
SF   10   7   7  14  38
Bal  D16 R28/109 P(30-14-1) 159
SF   D22 R31/110 P(31-26-2) 262

Mia   0  10   3  10  23
Hou  14   0   3   3  20
Mia  D17 R26/94  P(28-21-0) 209
Hou  D17 R23/97  P(27-15-1) 164

NYJ   3  12   6   8  29
Ind   3   7  16   8  34
NYJ  D21 R27/87  P(42-20-4) 332
Ind  D14 R31/152 P(30-15-0) 151
NYJ-Graham 189C, Reich 352P

Cin   0   0  10   7  17
Buf   7  17   7   0  31
Cin  D19 R21/114 P(31-11-3) 105
Buf  D23 R51/134 P(25-14-2) 174
Buf-Reed 105C

Car   0   3  14   3  20
Slr  10   0   0   0  10
Car  D22 R33/147 P(28-13-1) 108
Slr  D15 R28/122 P(33-14-1) 121
Car-Johnson 123R

Min  10   0   0   3   3  16
Oak   0   0   7   3   0  10
Min  D20 R44/182 P(33-20-2) 263
Oak  D13 R32/125 P(27-14-1) 112
Min-Hoard 108R, Reed 134C
```

MONDAY, NOVEMBER 18

```
GB    0   0   0   6   6
Dal   3   6   9   3  21
GB   D15 R21/90  P(37-21-0) 164
Dal  D15 R28/112 P(35-24-0) 205
```

SUNDAY, NOVEMBER 24

```
Den   7   7   0   7  21
Min   0  10   7   0  17
Den  D22 R23/79  P(36-27-1) 309
Min  D20 R28/50  P(35-24-2) 246
Den-Elway 334P

Atl   0  10   7  14  31
Cin  17   3   7  14  41
Atl  D21 R20/112 P(42-24-3) 305
Cin  D24 R35/121 P(36-21-0) 342
Atl-Metcalf 122C, Hebert 304P;
Cin-Pickens 176C, Blake 349P

NO    0   0   0   7   7
TB    3   3   7   0  13
NO   D14 R19/58  P(31-20-3) 184
TB   D15 R31/130 P(34-20-0) 251

Car   0  10   7  14  31
Hou   0   3   0   3   6
Car  D12 R30/94  P(18-11-0) 160
Hou  D17 R25/85  P(39-23-2) 186

SD    7  14   0   7  28
KC    0   0   0  14  14
SD   D20 R39/128 P(26-13-0) 252
KC   D26 R16/102 P(54-32-2) 332
SD-Martin 148C
```

```
Phi   7   3   3  17  30
Arz   3  10   3  20  36
Phi  D22 R26/67  P(38-21-1) 292
Arz  D27 R29/107 P(43-24-0) 340
Phi-Fryar 131C, Detmer 322P;
Arz-Moore 156C, Esiason 367P

Oak   0  14   3  10  27
Sea   7   3   3   3  16
Oak  D19 R43/200 P(23-13-0) 149
Sea  D17 R28/130 P(25-16-0) 166
Oak-Kaufman 104R

NYJ   3   0   0   7  10
Buf   7  14   7   7  35
NYJ  D22 R24/112 P(50-25-3) 229
Buf  D17 R36/81  P(24-16-1) 267
NYJ-Murrell 103R, Graham 124C;
Buf-Tasker 160C

SF    3   3  10   3  19
Was   0   6   3   7  16
SF   D17 R25/114 P(41-33-0) 275
Was  D15 R25/78  P(26-18-0) 282
Was-Westbrook 126C

Dal   3   0   0   3   6
NYG   0  13   0   7  20
Dal  D15 R16/33  P(39-28-2) 272
NYG  D14 R38/111 P(18-12-1) 104

Det  14   0   0   0  14
ChiB 14  10   7   0  31
Det  D17 R25/114 P(35-18-3) 203
ChiB D22 R37/139 P(28-18-0) 219
Det-Sanders 107R;
ChiB-Harris 122R

Jax   0  10   0  15   3  28
Bal   7   9   9   0   0  25
Jax  D23 R27/82  P(46-28-2) 292
Bal  D29 R30/104 P(30-19-0) 356
Jax-McCardell 107C, Smith 131C,
Brunell 306P; Bal-Jackson 150C,
Testaverde 366P

Ind   0   0   3   7  13
NE   10   7   3   7  27
Ind  D15 R13/44  P(40-22-1) 247
NE   D25 R44/195 P(30-21-0) 234
NE-Martin 141R

GB    0   3  14   7  24
Slr   0   9   0   0   9
GB   D15 R27/58  P(38-25-2) 185
Slr  D15 R23/65  P(37-17-1) 165
```

MONDAY, NOVEMBER 25

```
Pit   3   7   7   7  24
Mia   7   7   3   0  17
Pit  D23 R36/142 P(29-16-1) 239
Mia  D15 R20/75  P(37-22-0) 237
Pit-Bettis 119R
```

THURSDAY, NOVEMBER 28

```
KC    7   7   0  14  28
Det   0  14   7   3  24
KC   D26 R45/243 P(18-15-0)  95
Det  D21 R24/81  P(30-18-3) 237
KC-Hill 103R; Det-Perriman 131C

Was   0   3   7   0  10
Dal   7   0   7   7  21
Was  D13 R16/46  P(33-17-2) 163
Dal  D19 R48/201 P(19-9-1)   46
Dal-Smith 155R
```

SUNDAY, DECEMBER 1

```
Arz   0   3   0  14  17
Min   3  10  14  14  41
Arz  D18 R12/35  P(40-26-2) 245
Min  D29 R45/149 P(29-21-0) 263
Min-Johnson 238P

Buf   0  10   0   0   0  10
Ind   7   0   0   3   3  13
Buf  D11 R38/124 P(17-9-2)  183
Ind  D18 R32/85  P(40-22-0) 203
Buf-Early 113C

TB    0   0   0   0   0
Car   3   7   7   7  24
TB   D17 R23/78  P(41-23-2) 206
Car  D13 R30/132 P(24-14-0)  83
Car-Johnson 111R
```

```
Pit   7   3   7   0  17
Bal   7  17   0   7  31
Pit  D18 R30/119 P(36-18-1) 214
Bal  D16 R30/86  P(24-17-1) 250
Pit-Bettis 105R, Johnson 117C;
Bal-Morris 100R, Alexander 198C

ChiB  0   7   3   7  17
GB    7   7  14   0  28
ChiB D21 R26/88  P(44-28-1) 204
GB   D20 R26/126 P(27-19-0) 216
GB-Freeman 156C

Hou  14   7   0  14  35
NYJ   0  10   0   0  10
Hou  D18 R48/243 P(17-6-0)  142
NYJ  D15 R21/79  P(39-19-1) 185
Hou-George 141R, Sanders 102C

Sea   7   0   0   0   7
Den  14  13   7   0  34
Sea  D13 R19/105 P(28-13-2) 172
Den  D31 R45/205 P(34-23-0) 236
Sea-Galloway 108C;
Den-Davis 106R

Slr   3  10  10   3  26
NO    7   0   0   0   7
Slr  D15 R35/92  P(23-11-1) 220
NO   D14 R24/86  P(31-15-0) 142
Slr-Bruce 112C

Cin   7  10   3   7  27
Jax   3   7   3  17  30
Cin  D27 R31/172 P(39-23-2) 313
Jax  D19 R23/66  P(34-21-0) 356
Cin-Pickens 109C, Blake 313P;
Jax-Smith 162C, Brunell 356P

Mia   0   0   7   0   7
Oak   0  14   0   3  17
Mia  D21 R20/34  P(39-22-3) 281
Oak  D20 R34/156 P(29-21-0) 158

NYG   0   0   0   0   0
Phi  10  14   0   0  24
NYG  D9  R21/84  P(24-7-2)   37
Phi  D24 R43/139 P(33-25-1) 271
Phi-Watters 104R

NE   14  17  14   0  45
SD    0   0   0   0   0
NE   D15 R36/84  P(29-19-0) 229
SD   D15 R15/32  P(51-22-4) 204
NE-Bledsoe 232P
```

MONDAY, DECEMBER 2

```
SF    6  19   7   2  34
Atl   3   0   0   7  10
SF   D25 R38/202 P(38-26-1) 264
Atl  D9  R15/61  P(30-12-2) 117
SF-Kirby 105R
```

THURSDAY, DECEMBER 5

```
Phi   3   0   0   7  10
Ind   7  16   7   7  37
Phi  D18 R15/76  P(47-27-3) 254
Ind  D19 R34/151 P(29-21-0) 172
Ind-Faulk 101R, Harrison 106C
```

SUNDAY, DECEMBER 8

```
Atl   7   7   7  10  31
NO    3   0   6   6  15
Atl  D19 R25/122 P(29-20-2) 182
NO   D14 R21/83  P(36-21-1) 168

NYG   7   7   3   0  17
Mia   7   0   0   0   7
NYG  D21 R41/131 P(28-21-0) 149
Mia  D15 R20/103 P(30-16-2) 191
Mia-Barnett 139C

Was   0   3   0   7  10
TB   10   3  11   0  24
Was  D17 R16/41  P(39-20-1) 206
TB   D18 R45/209 P(15-8-0)   92

Den   3   0   3   0   6
GB    3  10   7  21  41
Den  D9  R24/93  P(24-13-0)  83
GB   D22 R29/103 P(29-20-0) 276
GB-Freeman 175C, Favre 280P

Bal   0   7   0   7  14
Cin   0  10   0  11  21
Bal  D21 R25/123 P(39-21-1) 199
Cin  D25 R31/93  P(42-26-0) 267
Bal-Morris 117R; Cin-Scott 103C
```

```
Slr    0  3  0  6    9
ChiB   7  0  14 14  35
Slr    D17 R19/94   P(42-24-1) 229
ChiB   D22 R37/162  P(25-17-1) 222
Slr-Kennison 102C;
ChiB-Salaam 115R, Timpson 111C

Buf    0  8  0  10  18
Sea    10 6  3  7   26
Buf    D21 R24/79   P(48-28-3) 312
Sea    D10 R35/170  P(23-9-0)  132
Buf-Kelly 324P; Sea-Warren 116R

NYJ    0  3  7  0   10
NE     7  13 7  7   34
NYJ    D16 R14/42   P(45-22-2) 202
NE     D27 R33/119  P(43-24-1) 248

SD     0  0  3  0    3
Pit    6  7  0  3   16
SD     D8  R23/65   P(29-10-1) 93
Pit    D21 R37/167  P(33-16-3) 160

Car    10 17 3  0   30
SF     0  17 0  7   24
Car    D22 R33/58   P(37-22-0) 324
SF     D23 R13/75   P(41-27-2) 375
Car-Green 157C, Collins 327P;
SF-Owens 110C, Rice 129C,
Young 393P

Dal    0  0  7  3   10
Arz    3  3  0  0    6
Dal    D15 R35/80   P(24-15-0) 254
Arz    D20 R26/134  P(36-18-2) 213
Dal-Irvin 198C

Jax    7  3  7  6   23
Hou    0  7  0  13  20
Jax    D19 R35/114  P(25-15-0) 165
Hou    D21 R20/74   P(37-24-1) 287
Hou-Sanders 127C, McNair 308P

Min    3  14 0  7   24
Det    0  10 3  9   22
Min    D21 R31/116  P(29-19-0) 173
Det    D23 R23/145  P(31-21-0) 235
Det-Sanders 134R, Moore 126C
```

MONDAY, DECEMBER 9
```
KC     0  0  0  7    7
Oak    10 0  16 0   26
KC     D13 R23/98   P(33-12-1) 71
Oak    D15 R37/170  P(27-13-0) 145
Oak-Kaufman 109R
```

SATURDAY, DECEMBER 14
```
Phi    0  0  7  14  21
NYJ    7  3  10 0   20
Phi    D15 R33/151  P(34-17-2) 172
NYJ    D14 R23/71   P(26-16-4) 173

SD     7  7  0  0   14
ChiB   14 0  6  7   27
SD     D17 R23/66   P(38-23-1) 217
ChiB   D19 R28/91   P(38-24-0) 203
```

SUNDAY, DECEMBER 15
```
TB     7  0  3  0   10
Min    0  7  7  7   21
TB     D8  R20/92   P(32-13-2) 77
Min    D21 R32/145  P(35-25-2) 194
Min-Hoard 101R

NE     6  0  0  0    6
Dal    3  3  6  0   12
NE     D16 R21/101  P(40-20-3) 178
Dal    D16 R35/107  P(28-16-2) 144

SF     16 6  0  3   25
Pit    0  0  8  7   15
SF     D21 R24/56   P(36-24-0) 232
Pit    D23 R28/120  P(43-23-2) 248
Pit-Pegram 103R

GB     3  7  6  15  31
Det    0  0  3  0    3
GB     D20 R26/111  P(25-16-1) 253
Det    D19 R23/79   P(40-23-1) 186

NO     0  0  0  10  17
NYG    0  0  3  0    3
NO     D11 R41/155  P(22-12-1) 106
NYG    D19 R23/90   P(38-13-3) 48
NO-Bates 129R

Bal    7  6  0  3   16
Car    3  7  10 7   27
Bal    D17 R25/99   P(37-20-2) 220
Car    D21 R28/82   P(39-26-2) 268
```

```
Oak    3  0  9  7   19
Den    7  17 0  0   24
Oak    D18 R13/105  P(39-19-3) 150
Den    D23 R37/99   P(31-19-1) 186

Was    3  13 7  3   26
Arz    7  7  3  10  27
Was    D19 R24/80   P(40-22-0) 249
Arz    D20 R27/78   P(46-20-1) 221

Slr    7  17 3  7   34
Atl    3  7  10 7   27
Slr    D17 R44/174  P(17-12-1) 306
Atl    D24 R15/63   P(49-28-6) 360
Slr-Phillips 112R, Kennison 226C,
Banks 304P; Atl-Emanuel 173C,
Hebert 363P

Ind    14 0  0  10  24
KC     0  7  0  9   19
Ind    D19 R27/89   P(28-16-0) 222
KC     D20 R27/120  P(41-23-0) 237

Cin    0  0  14 7   21
Hou    3  3  0  7   13
Cin    D12 R21/79   P(23-13-0) 126
Hou    D22 R31/106  P(39-22-3) 235

Sea    0  10 3  0   13
Jax    7  0  0  13  20
Sea    D19 R29/159  P(31-16-1) 147
Jax    D18 R31/133  P(26-19-0) 218
Jax-Smith 124C
```

MONDAY, DECEMBER 16
```
Buf    0  7  0  7   14
Mia    3  3  3  7   16
Buf    D15 R17/51   P(29-17-1) 223
Mia    D22 R40/145  P(37-26-0) 249
Buf-Reed 127C
```

SATURDAY, DECEMBER 21
```
NE     0  0  3  20  23
NYG    2  20 0  0   22
NE     D17 R18/26   P(47-31-2) 282
NYG    D17 R32/97   P(34-14-1) 199
NE-Glenn 124C, Bledsoe 301P

NO     10 0  0  3   13
Slr    7  7  0  0   14
NO     D12 R33/93   P(26-17-0) 148
Slr    D14 R25/51   P(29-16-3) 136
```

SUNDAY, DECEMBER 22
```
Hou    10 7  7  0   24
Bal    7  0  0  14  21
Hou    D18 R36/117  P(24-19-0) 234
Bal    D20 R17/120  P(32-23-2) 257
Bal-Jackson 117C, Testaverde 307P

Min    7  3  0  0   10
GB     3  18 14 3   38
Min    D12 R17/49   P(34-17-1) 203
GB     D29 R41/233  P(25-16-0) 207
GB-Bennett 109R

ChiB   7  0  0  12  19
TB     7  24 0  3   34
ChiB   D25 R19/67   P(43-30-1) 272
TB     D15 R31/89   P(14-11-0) 92
ChiB-Conway 120C

Arz    0  3  3  13  19
Phi    13 10 3  3   29
Arz    D15 R16/71   P(41-16-1) 158
Phi    D22 R40/127  P(32-20-1) 216

Ind    7  3  7  7   24
Cin    7  3  7  14  31
Ind    D16 R19/35   P(34-23-2) 231
Cin    D26 R31/157  P(37-22-1) 284

Atl    0  3  7  7   17
Jax    7  6  3  3   19
Atl    D21 R31/146  P(26-17-0) 163
Jax    D21 R32/143  P(29-18-0) 214
Jax-Means 110R

KC     3  3  3  0    9
Buf    0  3  14 0   17
KC     D15 R39/119  P(28-14-2) 130
Buf    D15 R26/78   P(29-20-1) 257

Dal    0  7  0  0    7
Was    3  13 7  14  37
Dal    D14 R23/119  P(21-11-1) 116
Was    D32 R39/157  P(31-22-1) 326
Was-Ellard 155C, Frerotte 346P
```

```
Sea    0  13 15 0   28
Oak    8  6  7  0   21
Sea    D8  R29/116  P(18-5-1)  13
Oak    D21 R29/118  P(47-22-1) 238

Pit    0  14 0  0   14
Car    7  2  6  3   18
Pit    D12 R26/185  P(31-14-2) 80
Car    D15 R28/79   P(39-21-0) 148
Pit-Stewart 102R

Mia    0  7  17 7   31
NYJ    14 0  7  7   28
Mia    D26 R40/157  P(43-20-0) 259
NYJ    D21 R22/83   P(41-20-0) 195
Mia-Abdul-Jabbar 152R

Den    10 0  0  0   10
SD     7  3  6  0   16
Den    D13 R21/66   P(43-25-2) 148
SD     D14 R27/81   P(36-17-3) 163
```

MONDAY, DECEMBER 23
```
Det    7  0  7  0   14
SF     7  7  7  3   24
Det    D18 R33/189  P(27-15-0) 88
SF     D18 R31/129  P(23-17-0) 152
Det-Sanders 175R
```

1997 NFL
SUNDAY, AUGUST 31
```
Arz    7  7  7  0   21
Cin    0  3  0  21  24
Arz    D18 R30/75   P(36-20-1) 248
Cin    D21 R25/87   P(35-24-1) 230
Arz-Sanders 105C

Atl    3  7  0  7   17
Det    0  14 0  14  28
Atl    D13 R29/55   P(37-20-3) 268
Det    D10 R23/46   P(30-12-1) 175
Det-Moore 115C

Dal    0  17 17 3   37
Pit    0  0  0  7    7
Dal    D21 R34/85   P(31-19-0) 295
Pit    D15 R23/85   P(28-13-1) 89
Dal-Irvin 153C, Aikman 295P

Ind    7  0  0  3   10
Mia    3  3  7  3   16
Ind    D18 R26/130  P(42-22-2) 168
Mia    D11 R28/97   P(26-10-1) 105

Jax    14 7  0  7   28
Bal    0  17 3  7   27
Jax    D19 R31/108  P(29-23-0) 303
Bal    D22 R17/72   P(41-24-3) 301
Jax-Smith 106C; Bal-Jackson 143C,
Testaverde 322P

KC     0  0  3  0    3
Den    3  6  0  10  19
KC     D12 R19/133  P(25-14-1) 108
Den    D20 R35/146  P(28-17-0) 232
Den-Davis 101R, Smith 122C

Min    0  10 3  21  34
Buf    0  7  0  6   13
Min    D17 R28/185  P(30-17-1) 200
Buf    D22 R24/147  P(25-20-2) 279
Min-Smith 169R, Carter 121C;
Buf-Reed 142C

NO     6  11 0  7   24
Slr    0  14 21 3   38
NO     D13 R19/82   P(33-12-3) 159
Slr    D20 R43/189  P(21-13-1) 214
Slr-Phillips 125R

NYJ    17 10 14 0   41
Sea    0  3  0  0    3
NYJ    D28 R40/164  P(26-18-0) 270
Sea    D16 R19/84   P(42-17-1) 163
NYJ-Murrell 131R, Graham 100C,
O'Donnell 270P

Oak    0  0  7  14  0   21
Ten    10 0  3  8  3   24
Oak    D17 R17/45   P(38-21-0) 287
Ten    D20 R42/255  P(25-13-1) 164
Oak-Brown 158C; Ten-George 216R

Phi    3  0  7  7   17
NYG    7  10 7  7   31
Phi    D24 R26/120  P(48-26-1) 327
NYG    D12 R27/101  P(27-13-0) 189
Phi-Timpson 125C
```

```
SD     0  0  7  0    7
NE     14 17 0  10  41
SD     D14 R20/85   P(38-18-1) 142
NE     D22 R26/84   P(39-26-0) 340
NE-Bledsoe 340P

SF     3  3  0  0    6
TB     0  0  3  10  13
SF     D12 R27/100  P(21-14-1) 91
TB     D15 R27/115  P(26-14-1) 156

Was    0  10 0  14  24
Car    3  0  0  7   10
Was    D23 R40/198  P(29-11-0) 125
Car    D16 R29/158  P(26-12-2) 104
Was-Allen 141R; Car-Johnson 134R
```

MONDAY, SEPTEMBER 1
```
ChiB   0  11 0  13  24
GB     3  15 6  14  38
ChiB   D19 R30/164  P(41-17-2) 172
GB     D18 R31/107  P(22-15-1) 208
ChiB-Harris 122R
```

SUNDAY, SEPTEMBER 7
```
Buf    0  14 7  7   28
NYJ    3  10 6  3   22
Buf    D15 R33/76   P(22-15-2) 193
NYJ    D12 R21/39   P(37-16-2) 163
Buf-Tindale 105C

Car    0  0  0  9    9
Atl    0  3  6  0    9
Car    D21 R28/93   P(35-21-0) 228
Atl    D8  R27/48   P(23-11-0) 162
Car-Walls 147C

Cin    0  0  0  10  10
Bal    0  3  10 10  23
Cin    D18 R14/56   P(45-25-2) 283
Bal    D24 R35/146  P(36-12-1) 266
Cin-Blake 317P; Bal-Alexander 104C

Dal    6  13 0  3   22
Arz    7  7  8  3   25
Dal    D15 R29/180  P(40-21-0) 147
Arz    D21 R25/66   P(47-26-0) 210
Dal-Smith 132R; Arz-Moore 108C

Den    10 3  15 7   35
Sea    0  14 0  0   14
Den    D22 R30/143  P(26-18-0) 188
Sea    D16 R24/69   P(33-20-1) 220
Den-Davis 107R

GB     0  6  3  0    9
Phi    0  0  7  3   10
GB     D21 R28/107  P(41-19-1) 273
Phi    D16 R30/100  P(32-19-0) 158
Phi-Fryar 125C

Min    3  0  10 14  27
ChiB   0  10 7  7   24
Min    D23 R25/117  P(44-33-1) 261
ChiB   D16 R23/147  P(36-21-0) 158
Min-Carter 107C, Reed 118C

NE     7  7  7  10  31
Ind    3  0  0  7   10
NE     D15 R26/122  P(25-15-0) 260
Ind    D19 R21/41   P(38-30-0) 214
NE-Martin 121R, Bledsoe 267P

NYG    0  0  6  7   13
Jax    0  20 3  17  40
NYG    D13 R16/39   P(35-16-1) 167
Jax    D22 R39/123  P(35-23-0) 252
Jax-Smith 117C

SD     3  3  7  7   20
NO     3  0  3  0    6
SD     D11 R30/93   P(29-17-1) 171
NO     D14 R23/65   P(38-20-3) 178

SF     0  0  0  15  15
Slr    3  6  3  0   12
SF     D12 R34/135  P(28-10-3) 93
Slr    D11 R34/99   P(25-9-0)  104

TB     7  7  10 0   24
Det    0  3  7  7   17
TB     D20 R41/173  P(24-12-0) 99
Det    D13 R12/24   P(50-29-1) 178
TB-Dunn 130R; Det-Morton 102C,
Sanders 102C, Mitchell 331P
```

```
Ten    0  10 3  0   13
Mia    0  3  3  7   16
Ten    D13 R40/185  P(14-7-1)  109
Mia    D21 R25/54   P(43-24-0) 300
Ten-George 106R;
Mia-McDuffie 135C, Marino 324P

Was    0  0  0  13  13
Pit    7  0  0  7   14
Was    D19 R21/69   P(37-21-3) 285
Pit    D23 R39/222  P(17-8-1)  73
Pit-Bettis 134R
```

MONDAY, SEPTEMBER 8
```
KC     3  10 9  6   28
Oak    7  3  17 0   27
KC     D21 R26/128  P(35-21-0) 300
Oak    D20 R30/108  P(39-19-2) 281
KC-Rison 162C, Grbac 312P;
Oak-Brown 155C
```

SUNDAY, SEPTEMBER 14
```
Arz    7  0  3  3   13
Was    3  7  3  6   19
Arz    D14 R34/118  P(40-17-0) 116
Was    D17 R30/76   P(36-19-1) 252

Bal    7  7  0  10  24
NYG    0  12 8  3   23
Bal    D19 R21/63   P(35-22-1) 210
NYG    D29 R37/121  P(46-28-0) 269

Buf    7  7  0  2   16
KC     6  6  0  13  22
Buf    D17 R23/50   P(43-22-1) 275
KC     D15 R27/107  P(37-20-0) 160
Buf-Reed 113C

Car    10 3  3  10  26
SD     7  0  0  0    7
Car    D21 R41/141  P(36-17-1) 138
SD     D17 R21/96   P(34-17-0) 155

Det    3  10 10 9   32
ChiB   7  0  0  0    7
Det    D27 R35/202  P(25-16-0) 202
ChiB   D19 R28/94   P(40-21-1) 190
Det-Sanders 161R

Mia    6  3  3  6   18
GB     3  7  3  10  23
Mia    D20 R22/59   P(47-21-1) 240
GB     D22 R29/142  P(37-24-0) 250
Mia-Jordan 100C; GB-Levens 121R

NO     0  0  0  7    7
SF     13 10 10 0   33
NO     D12 R25/84   P(26-12-6) 176
SF     D17 R33/91   P(27-22-0) 213

NYJ    7  3  7  7   24
NE     14 3  7  3   27
NYJ    D22 R21/130  P(50-30-0) 225
NE     D23 R46/213  P(34-16-2) 162
NYJ-Murrell 110R; NE-Martin 199R

Oak    7  3  21 5   36
Atl    7  10 7  7   31
Oak    D11 R20/149  P(22-12-0) 265
Atl    D24 R26/116  P(42-26-0) 250
Oak-Kaufman 140R

Sea    7  10 0  14  31
Ind    3  0  0  0    3
Sea    D27 R25/153  P(38-24-1) 270
Ind    D11 R25/95   P(17-11-0) 23

Slr    7  0  0  7   14
Den    7  7  7  14  35
Slr    D18 R23/130  P(33-18-2) 184
Den    D34 R34/144  P(28-16-1) 233
Den-Davis 103R, Smith 126C,
Elway 247P

TB     0  14 7  7   28
Min    3  8  0  3   14
TB     D17 R37/191  P(20-15-0) 185
Min    D20 R15/72   P(44-29-0) 310
TB-Dunn 101R; Min-Reed 131C,
Johnson 334P
```

MONDAY, SEPTEMBER 15
```
Phi    10 7  0  3   20
Dal    3  3  3  12  21
Phi    D16 R29/157  P(30-18-0) 176
Dal    D18 R28/92   P(36-17-0) 187
Phi-Watters 106R
```

SUNDAY, SEPTEMBER 21

```
Atl   0   0   7   0    7
SF    3  21   7   3   34
Atl  D15 R29/57  P(36-20-1) 154
SF   D18 R20/71  P(31-19-0) 353
SF-Young 336P

Bal   3  17   3  13   36
Ten   7   3   0   0   10
Bal  D21 R28/89  P(37-23-0) 309
Ten  D18 R18/97  P(35-22-1) 188
Bal-Lewis 124C, Testaverde 318P

ChiB  0   0   3   0    3
NE    7   7   0  17   31
ChiB D9  R24/79  P(25-17-2) 120
NE   D23 R21/87  P(40-27-1) 315
NE-Brown 124C, Bledsoe 301P

Cin   7   0  10   3   20
Den   0  14   7  17   38
Cin  D22 R25/195 P(30-20-0) 194
Den  D23 R29/222 P(26-14-1) 150
Cin-Carter 104R, Pickens 125C;
Den-Davis 215R

Det   0   7   0  10   17
NO    0  21   7   7   35
Det  D22 R19/118 P(43-24-3) 237
NO   D21 R36/172 P(22-16-0) 213
Det-Sanders 113R, Moore 111C;
NO-Bates 162R

Ind  14  12   0   9   35
Buf   0  10   6  21   37
Ind  D17 R30/124 P(39-19-1) 198
Buf  D25 R23/163 P(38-23-1) 230
Buf-Smith 129R

KC    7   7   7  14   35
Car   0   7   0   7   14
KC   D18 R34/117 P(29-16-1) 154
Car  D24 R24/86  P(47-24-4) 278
Car-Carruth 110C, Collins 328P

Mia   0   7   0  14   21
TB    7   7  10   7   31
Mia  D21 R17/48  P(37-24-0) 235
TB   D24 R32/109 P(24-18-1) 248
TB-Dunn 106C, Dilfer 248P

Min   7   0  15  10   32
GB    7  24   7   0   38
Min  D22 R37/185 P(34-19-2) 208
GB   D24 R22/93  P(31-18-2) 257
Min-Smith 132R, Reed 119C;
GB-Freeman 122C, Favre 266P

NYG   0   0   0   3    3
Slr   0   6   0   7   13
NYG  D11 R24/47  P(33-16-1) 147
Slr  D15 R32/92  P(35-15-0) 133

Oak   6  16   0   0   22
NYJ   3   7   6   7   23
Oak  D26 R28/129 P(38-26-0) 339
NYJ  D16 R21/83  P(33-18-0) 205
Oak-Kaufman 126R, Brown 153C,
Jett 148C, George 374P

SD    0  16   0   6   22
Sea   3  10   0  13   26
SD   D20 R26/79  P(46-25-3) 230
Sea  D21 R27/92  P(34-17-2) 251
Sea-Galloway 106C
```

MONDAY, SEPTEMBER 22

```
Pit   7   0   7   7   21
Jax   7  10   3  10   30
Pit  D19 R30/153 P(16-11-1) 153
Jax  D23 R26/40  P(43-25-0) 303
Pit-Bettis 114R; Jax-Smith 164C,
Brunell 306P
```

SUNDAY, SEPTEMBER 28

```
Arz   0   7  11   0   18
TB    6   6   0   7   19
Arz  D23 R25/70  P(52-31-2) 294
TB   D6  R20/54  P(25-13-1) 113
Arz-Moore 147C, Graham 339P

Bal   3   3  11   0   17
SD    7   7   7   0   21
Bal  D18 R25/111 P(42-18-2) 217
SD   D15 R28/88  P(26-17-2) 352
SD-Martin 155C, Humphries 358P
```

```
ChiB  3   0   0   0    3
Dal   0   7  17   3   27
ChiB D17 R33/141 P(37-18-2) 102
Dal  D13 R21/56  P(27-12-1) 124
ChiB-Harris 120R; Dal-Irvin 105C

Den  15   8   6   0   29
Atl   0   7   7   7   21
Den  D16 R27/101 P(33-18-1) 228
Atl  D17 R21/112 P(31-18-1) 196
Den-Sharpe 119C

GB    6   3   6   0   15
Det   0  17   3   6   26
GB   D23 R18/107 P(43-22-3) 289
Det  D18 R36/173 P(31-18-1) 196
GB-Levens 107R, Brooks 164C;
Det-Sanders 139R, Moore 105C

Jax   6   3   3   0   12
Was   0  14   0  10   24
Jax  D11 R22/70  P(31-16-2) 134
Was  D20 R42/113 P(24-16-1) 223
Was-Allen 122R

NO    7   3   0   9   19
NYG   7   7   0   0   14
NO   D14 R24/73  P(31-16-1) 193
NYG  D18 R33/105 P(25-16-1) 159

NYJ   7  17   0   7   31
Cin   7   0   0   7   14
NYJ  D28 R48/190 P(34-20-0) 212
Cin  D10 R16/66  P(21-10-1) 149
NYJ-Murrell 156R

Phi   3  10   6   0   19
Min   7   7   7   7   28
Phi  D25 R21/100 P(45-28-2) 272
Min  D17 R29/144 P(32-17-1) 221
Phi-Fryar 120C; Min-Smith 125R,
Reed 134C

Sea   7   3   7   0   17
KC    0   7   3  10   20
Sea  D16 R26/156 P(26-19-1) 220
KC   D29 R47/203 P(38-24-3) 263

Slr   0  14   0   3   17
Oak   0  13  15   7   35
Slr  D20 R28/119 P(49-24-3) 255
Oak  D20 R33/170 P(30-17-1) 213
Slr-Lee 109C; Oak-Kaufman 162R,
Dudley 106C, George 219P

Ten   0   6   3  15   24
Pit  10  21   3   3   37
Ten  D20 R15/58  P(43-22-2) 226
Pit  D19 R40/137 P(26-18-0) 262
```

MONDAY, SEPTEMBER 29

```
SF    7  13   7   7   34
Car   0   7   0  14   21
SF   D27 R49/219 P(24-16-0) 149
Car  D16 R17/44  P(35-20-3) 210
SF-Hearst 141R
```

SUNDAY, OCTOBER 5

```
Cin   0   7   6   0   13
Jax   7   0   7   7   21
Cin  D17 R29/148 P(27-16-0) 200
Jax  D21 R33/160 P(27-14-0) 148

Dal   3   3   3   8   17
NYG   0   3  10   7   20
Dal  D27 R28/118 P(52-34-2) 310
NYG  D13 R21/57  P(24-12-0) 109
Dal-Aikman 317P

Det   0   3   3   7   13
Buf   3  10   0   9   22
Det  D17 R28/120 P(38-20-1) 189
Buf  D10 R30/164 P(18-11-0) 102
Det-Dunn 125R, Sanders 107R,
Moore 116C

KC    0  14   0   0   14
Mia   7   7   0   3   17
KC   D14 R26/96  P(30-23-0) 163
Mia  D19 R27/83  P(31-19-0) 254

Min   3   3   7   7   20
Arz   3  10   3   3   19
Min  D20 R23/81  P(39-25-2) 272
Arz  D22 R26/108 P(38-22-0) 277
Arz-Moore 108C
```

```
NO    0   3  10   7   20
ChiB  3   0   0  14   17
NO   D11 R30/137 P(23-9-1)  185
ChiB D19 R33/101 P(36-19-0) 165
NO-Hill 121C

NYJ   7   6   0   3   16
Ind   0   0   9   3   12
NYJ  D13 R34/78  P(28-15-1) 128
Ind  D20 R19/45  P(45-24-3) 265

Pit   0   7  14  21   42
Bal  14  10   0  10   34
Pit  D22 R40/214 P(28-18-3) 217
Bal  D20 R18/52  P(47-28-2) 280
Pit-Bettis 137R, Dunn 125R,
Thigpen 162C

SD    6   3  10   6   25
Oak   0   3   7   0   10
SD   D23 R45/180 P(33-18-0) 218
Oak  D11 R13/13  P(42-19-0) 228
SD-Brown 181R;
Oak-Kaufman 100C

TB    3   0   7   6   16
GB    0  21   0   0   21
TB   D23 R36/217 P(29-16-1) 155
GB   D13 R18/64  P(31-21-0) 170
TB-Dunn 125R

Ten   3   7   0   3   13
Sea   0   0  10   6   16
Ten  D18 R35/156 P(28-12-2)  97
Sea  D20 R19/167 P(40-27-0) 238
Ten-George 116R;
Sea-Broussard 138R

Was   0   3   7   0   10
Phi   0   7   0  17   24
Was  D12 R12/30  P(37-16-1) 198
Phi  D26 R50/203 P(27-17-0) 246
Phi-Watters 104R
```

MONDAY, OCTOBER 6

```
NE    0  13   0   0   13
Den  14   0  17   3   34
NE   D13 R19/51  P(41-20-1) 211
Den  D25 R38/192 P(27-13-2) 188
Den-Davis 171R, Smith 130C
```

SUNDAY, OCTOBER 12

```
Atl  10   6   7   0   23
NO    0   3   0  14   17
Atl  D14 R31/89  P(22-10-0)  77
NO   D13 R28/80  P(22-14-2)  99

Buf   0   0   0   6    6
NE   10   6  17   0   33
Buf  D13 R18/94  P(41-21-4) 148
NE   D19 R39/139 P(27-14-1) 171

Car   0   0   7   7   14
Min   3   7   0  14   24
Car  D15 R20/80  P(35-19-0) 197
Min  D17 R29/158 P(34-17-1) 203
Car-Carruth 107C; Min-Smith 120R

Cin   0   0   0   7    7
Ten   7   7   6  10   30
Cin  D14 R18/65  P(34-18-0) 137
Ten  D26 R41/198 P(30-16-0) 193
Ten-George 106R

Det   7   3   7  10   27
TB    9   0   0   0    9
Det  D17 R33/259 P(20-16-0) 188
TB   D13 R25/72  P(31-17-2) 217
Det-Sanders 215R, Moore 120C;
TB-Copeland 105C

GB    0  14   7   3   24
ChiB 10   0   7   6   23
GB   D22 R25/100 P(35-19-1) 177
ChiB D26 R34/121 P(35-22-2) 232
ChiB-Harris 101R

Ind  10   0   3   9   22
Pit   0  17   7   0   24
Ind  D18 R29/79  P(36-19-1) 191
Pit  D17 R35/185 P(22-11-2) 142
Pit-Bettis 164R

Mia   0  17   0  14   31
NYJ   7   3   3   7   20
Mia  D25 R30/93  P(38-27-0) 372
NYJ  D20 R20/81  P(37-24-0) 288
Mia-Marino 372P;
NYJ-Chrebet 104C, O'Donnell 319P
```

```
NYG   3   3   7  14   27
Arz   0   6   0   7   13
NYG  D23 R46/239 P(28-13-1) 187
Arz  D19 R14/27  P(47-22-4) 208
NYG-Wheatley 103R

Phi   0   0  14   7   21
Jax  21   0   7  10   38
Phi  D23 R27/90  P(42-27-1) 303
Jax  D21 R24/149 P(20-15-0) 157
Phi-Fryar 124C; Jax-Stewart 102R
```

MONDAY, OCTOBER 13

```
Dal   3   0   6   7   16
Was   7   7   0   7   21
Dal  D16 R28/115 P(31-17-0) 175
Was  D16 R32/116 P(23-12-0) 139
```

THURSDAY, OCTOBER 16

```
SD    0   0   3   0    3
KC    7  10   7   7   31
SD   D12 R18/69  P(43-14-2) 189
KC   D25 R33/89  P(40-20-0) 224
```

SUNDAY, OCTOBER 19

```
Arz   0   0   3   7   10
Phi   0   7   0   3   13
Arz  D15 R28/92  P(31-16-0) 143
Phi  D25 R32/130 P(36-23-2) 277
Arz-Moore 101C

Car  10   0   0   3   13
NO    0   0   0   0    0
Car  D15 R29/73  P(31-23-1)  96
NO   D15 R26/111 P(32-13-2)  89

Den   7   3   7   8   25
Oak   7   7   7   7   28
Den  D25 R29/147 P(46-26-0) 294
Oak  D12 R32/243 P(12-9-1)   81
Den-Elway 309P;
Oak-Kaufman 227R

Jax   7   0   7   8   22
Dal   3  10   6   7   26
Jax  D15 R18/42  P(31-21-1) 229
Dal  D24 R33/99  P(32-21-0) 238
Jax-McCardell 120C

Mia  14   7   0   3   24
Bal   3   0   3   7   13
Mia  D24 R41/148 P(27-19-0) 189
Bal  D20 R16/54  P(47-32-0) 331
Mia-Abdul-Jabbar 108R;
Bal-Lewis 105C, Testaverde 331P

NE    0   5  14   0   19
NYJ   3   0  14   7   24
NE   D19 R25/105 P(38-24-1) 192
NYJ  D22 R22/76  P(38-23-0) 254
NE-Brown 125C

NYG   7   3   7   3   6   26
Det   0   0   3   7   0   10
NYG  D15 R29/121 P(31-17-1) 210
Det  D20 R30/111 P(32-19-0) 226
NYG-Calloway 145C;
Det-Sanders 105R

Pit   0  13   7   6   26
Cin   7   0   3   0   10
Pit  D24 R45/166 P(33-16-2) 246
Cin  D13 R21/71  P(29-15-2) 165
Pit-Bettis 135R, Thigpen 120C

Sea   0   3   7   7   17
Slr   0   3   3   3    9
Sea  D27 R30/106 P(36-24-2) 251
Slr  D10 R17/37  P(31-17-1) 155

SF    7  14   7   7   35
Atl   7   7   7   7   28
SF   D24 R35/197 P(25-16-1) 241
Atl  D19 R16/39  P(44-22-0) 253
SF-Hearst 105R

Was   0   0  14   0   14
Ten   0  14   7   7   28
Was  D18 R18/92  P(31-16-3) 120
Ten  D23 R46/204 P(21-13-0) 185
Ten-George 125R
```

MONDAY, OCTOBER 20

```
Buf   3   3   0   3    9
Ind   0   0   3   3    6
Buf  D16 R27/90  P(22-17-0) 156
Ind  D15 R25/94  P(18-14-0) 144
```

SUNDAY, OCTOBER 26

```
Atl   0   3   3   6   12
Car  14   0   0   7   21
Atl  D17 R23/68  P(46-21-2) 233
Car  D14 R36/137 P(25-12-1)  91
Atl-Mathis 107C;
Car-Biakabutuka 104R

Bal   3   7   3   7   20
Was   7   0   7   3   17
Bal  D20 R44/199 P(21-10-0) 133
Was  D16 R21/67  P(33-17-1) 182
Bal-Morris 176R

Cin   7  14   0   6   27
NYG   3   7   6  13   29
Cin  D22 R27/98  P(34-17-1) 225
NYG  D28 R43/109 P(31-18-0) 214
NYG-Alexander 100C

Dal   3   6   0   3   12
Phi   0   0   3  10   13
Dal  D14 R31/151 P(22-13-0)  93
Phi  D17 R33/154 P(22-13-0) 120
Dal-Smith 126R

Den   0  10  10   0   3   23
Buf   0   3   7  10   0   20
Den  D17 R46/225 P(30-16-2) 116
Buf  D19 R29/155 P(42-19-3) 160
Den-Davis 207R

Ind   0   0   6  13   19
SD    3   9  14   9   35
Ind  D14 R16/31  P(39-20-2) 219
SD   D24 R38/202 P(34-21-0) 222
SD-Brown 169R

Jax   0  10   0   7   17
Pit   0   0   7  10   6   23
Jax  D16 R23/73  P(31-15-1) 194
Pit  D26 R37/141 P(42-25-1) 298
Pit-Thigpen 196C, Stewart 317P

KC    6  11  11   0   28
Slr   0   7   7   6   20
KC   D19 R26/87  P(37-20-0) 168
Slr  D20 R28/99  P(31-18-1) 261

Min   0   0   0  10   10
TB    0   0   0   6    6
Min  D16 R35/94  P(29-20-0) 214
TB   D11 R18/52  P(29-15-0) 177

Oak  14  11   9   0   34
Sea   3  15  14  13   45
Oak  D19 R21/119 P(29-18-0) 235
Sea  D26 R27/145 P(46-22-0) 409
Oak-Kaufman 112R, Brown 107C;
Sea-Galloway 117C, McKnight 100C,
Moon 409P

SF    7   6   3   0   7   23
NO    0   0   0   0   0    0
SF   D21 R37/137 P(32-20-0) 210
NO   D6  R18/55  P(25-12-1)  87

Ten   3  17  14   7   41
Arz   0   0   7   7   14
Ten  D15 R35/148 P(19-10-0) 135
Arz  D22 R24/106 P(40-21-4) 157
```

MONDAY, OCTOBER 27

```
ChiB  7   8   3  15   3   36
Mia   7   6   6  14   0   33
ChiB D26 R37/128 P(50-32-0) 336
Mia  D18 R16/119 P(39-18-1) 246
ChiB-Harris 106R, Conway 100C,
Kramer 343P; Mia-McDuffie 137C

GB    7   7   7   7   28
NE    0  10   0   0   10
GB   D27 R39/144 P(34-23-0) 227
NE   D18 R20/69  P(36-20-3) 255
GB-Levens 100R; NE-Glenn 163C
```

SUNDAY, NOVEMBER 2

```
Bal   6   3   0   7   0   16
NYJ   7   3   3   3   3   19
Bal  D23 R35/159 P(46-25-1) 288
NYJ  D15 R30/65  P(33-18-0) 160
Bal-Morris 130R
```

Dal 7 0 3 0 10
SF 0 0 7 10 17
Dal D16 R25/87 P(36-22-2) 184
SF D18 R33/128 P(23-15-1) 173
SF-Hearst 104R

Det 0 0 0 0 10
GB 0 14 3 3 20
Det D18 R28/125 P(47-21-4) 131
GB D11 R25/81 P(28-15-1) 163
Det-Sanders 105R

Jax 17 7 3 3 30
Ten 3 7 7 7 24
Jax D17 R31/135 P(31-17-1) 155
Ten D15 R27/107 P(22-13-1) 195

Mia 0 3 0 3 6
Buf 3 3 0 3 9
Mia D13 R23/54 P(33-13-2) 176
Buf D17 R41/179 P(22-13-0) 86

NE 0 0 0 15 18
Min 10 3 3 7 23
NE D21 R24/117 P(42-27-1) 293
Min D18 R29/66 P(31-18-0) 222
NE-Martin 104R, Jefferson 108C,
Bledsoe 313P; Min-Carter 116C

Oak 0 7 7 0 14
Car 14 14 3 7 38
Oak D20 R16/38 P(45-28-2) 319
Car D27 R41/216 P(32-18-0) 192
Oak-Brown 163C, George 304P;
Car-Lane 147R

Phi 7 0 14 0 21
Arz 7 3 7 14 31
Phi D18 R28/95 P(40-18-3) 265
Arz D17 R33/90 P(27-12-1) 141

SD 7 10 0 14 31
Cin 0 24 7 7 38
SD D14 R21/67 P(41-20-1) 168
Cin D18 R37/174 P(33-19-0) 162
Cin-Dillon 123R

Sea 3 7 10 7 27
Den 0 10 14 3 30
Sea D22 R18/104 P(46-28-0) 245
Den D19 R31/140 P(30-19-0) 245
Den-Davis 101R, Smith 114C

Slr 3 21 0 7 31
Atl 0 17 14 3 34
Slr D24 R29/108 P(34-23-1) 399
Atl D28 R26/197 P(32-19-1) 265
Slr-Bruce 233C, Banks 401P;
Atl-Anderson 162R, Emanuel 108C

TB 7 14 0 10 31
Ind 3 7 11 7 28
TB D18 R25/84 P(25-16-0) 150
Ind D23 R34/147 P(33-20-1) 212

Was 14 10 7 0 31
ChiB 0 0 0 8 8
Was D24 R42/203 P(20-14-0) 185
ChiB D16 R16/62 P(42-25-2) 274
Was-Allen 125R

MONDAY, NOVEMBER 3
Pit 10 0 0 0 10
KC 0 13 0 0 13
Pit D12 R23/142 P(21-11-1) 93
KC D24 R42/183 P(35-22-1) 209
Pit-Bettis 103R

SUNDAY, NOVEMBER 9
Arz 3 0 3 0 6
Dal 0 10 14 0 24
Arz D18 R26/101 P(36-18-0) 173
Dal D19 R35/125 P(22-15-1) 204

Bal 0 0 0 0 0
Pit 7 10 14 6 37
Bal D11 R21/60 P(39-15-4) 112
Pit D19 R39/143 P(29-15-0) 198
Pit-Bettis 114R, Thigpen 130C

Car 0 0 0 0 0
Den 14 3 10 7 34
Car D7 R14/34 P(29-13-3) 113
Den D20 R42/160 P(24-15-0) 233
Den-Davis 104R, Sharpe 174C

ChiB 7 3 9 3 22
Min 7 14 0 8 29
ChiB D20 R29/90 P(35-23-1) 251
Min D19 R27/109 P(33-22-2) 193
ChiB-Proehl 132C

Cin 0 7 14 7 28
Ind 0 7 3 3 13
Cin D17 R33/144 P(25-16-0) 129
Ind D22 R30/150 P(32-19-3) 191
Ind-Faulk 110R

Det 0 0 7 0 7
Was 3 10 7 10 30
Det D11 R15/105 P(43-15-3) 163
Was D25 R44/141 P(41-20-0) 247
Det-Sanders 105R

KC 0 0 7 0 7
Jax 7 17 0 0 24
KC D22 R29/148 P(50-29-2) 265
Jax D16 R27/150 P(21-9-1) 182
KC-Gannon 314P; Jax-Smith 112C

NE 7 10 7 7 31
Buf 3 0 7 0 10
NE D17 R32/103 P(22-15-0) 164
Buf D14 R27/122 P(33-15-4) 119

NO 0 3 0 10 13
Oak 0 0 7 0 7
NO D17 R35/59 P(34-21-1) 154
Oak D12 R20/32 P(39-17-1) 189
Oak-Dudley 116C

NYG 0 3 3 0 6
Ten 3 7 0 0 10
NYG D10 R20/107 P(28-15-1) 111
Ten D19 R40/153 P(23-13-1) 173
Ten-George 122R

NYJ 0 10 0 7 17
Mia 7 7 7 3 24
NYJ D20 R18/79 P(48-25-1) 303
Mia D21 R36/120 P(29-18-0) 176
NYJ-Ward 108C, Foley 322P;
Mia-Abdul-Jabbar 103R

Sea 0 10 14 13 37
SD 14 3 7 7 31
Sea D24 R27/92 P(45-24-1) 281
SD D13 R25/81 P(29-17-1) 179
SD-Martin 100C

Slr 0 0 7 0 7
GB 3 7 7 0 17
Slr D16 R25/66 P(41-18-1) 203
GB D18 R25/96 P(37-18-2) 291
Slr-Lee 104C; GB-Freeman 160C,
Favre 306P

TB 7 10 7 7 31
Atl 0 7 3 0 10
TB D20 R38/199 P(20-12-0) 150
Atl D18 R24/102 P(27-19-0) 173

MONDAY, NOVEMBER 10
SF 7 17 0 0 24
Phi 3 3 0 6 12
SF D13 R38/117 P(23-13-1) 96
Phi D18 R20/69 P(45-21-1) 188
Phi-Fryar 138C

SUNDAY, NOVEMBER 16
Arz 0 0 10 0 10
NYG 0 0 10 9 19
Arz D21 R23/49 P(33-22-2) 350
NYG D21 R40/201 P(21-14-0) 172
Arz-Moore 139C, Sanders 188C,
Plummer 388P; NYG-Way 114R

Atl 7 3 7 10 27
Slr 0 7 14 0 21
Atl D22 R29/100 P(30-20-1) 214
Slr D22 R25/88 P(38-21-0) 242

Car 0 6 13 0 19
SF 3 14 7 3 27
Car D18 R23/85 P(33-18-3) 169
SF D20 R35/99 P(22-17-0) 221

Cin 0 0 3 0 3
Pit 3 3 7 7 20
Cin D16 R30/116 P(21-15-0) 128
Pit D20 R40/186 P(22-11-0) 123
Pit-Bettis 101R, Thigpen 101C

Den 3 10 3 6 22
KC 0 14 7 3 24
Den D26 R40/135 P(31-18-0) 194
KC D30 R30/106 P(21-11-1) 96
Den-Davis 127R, Smith 114C

GB 14 14 0 10 38
Ind 9 18 3 11 41
GB D20 R16/107 P(25-18-2) 334
Ind D26 R34/147 P(30-24-0) 320
GB-Levens 103R, Mayes 119C,
Favre 363P; Ind-Faulk 116R,
Justin 340P

Min 0 7 0 8 15
Det 3 21 14 0 38
Min D18 R28/126 P(37-19-1) 174
Det D27 R32/211 P(30-21-0) 266
Min-Faulk 116R, Justin 340P;
Det-Sanders 108R, Moore 130C

NE 0 0 0 7 7
TB 7 3 7 10 27
NE D10 R16/75 P(31-16-2) 93
TB D21 R41/146 P(29-21-0) 202

NYJ 10 13 0 0 23
ChiB 0 0 7 8 15
NYJ D11 R32/77 P(25-12-0) 116
ChiB D27 R20/49 P(65-33-4) 307
ChiB-Proehl 118C, Kramer 354P

Oak 7 14 14 3 38
SD 7 6 0 0 13
Oak D22 R34/140 P(34-16-2) 257
SD D11 R25/91 P(26-14-0) 157
Oak-Kaufman 109R

Phi 0 0 3 7 10
Bal 7 0 3 0 10
Phi D18 R23/63 P(38-26-0) 210
Bal D19 R44/204 P(32-19-2) 125
Bal-Graham 154R

Sea 0 10 0 7 0 17
NO 0 7 0 10 3 20
Sea D19 R29/111 P(46-23-2) 229
NO D14 R30/75 P(18-10-2) 102

Ten 0 3 0 6 9
Jax 0 7 7 3 17
Ten D17 R33/136 P(23-9-2) 184
Jax D21 R36/103 P(30-22-0) 249
Jax-Smith 158C

Was 0 0 7 7 14
Dal 0 6 0 11 17
Was D16 R28/104 P(31-16-0) 155
Dal D20 R25/105 P(45-25-0) 207

MONDAY, NOVEMBER 17
Buf 0 0 10 3 13
Mia 3 10 3 14 30
Buf D15 R29/92 P(37-19-1) 131
Mia D16 R31/96 P(24-18-1) 218

SUNDAY, NOVEMBER 23
Arz 3 0 3 10 16
Bal 0 3 7 3 13
Arz D15 R24/71 P(34-19-2) 202
Bal D17 R28/129 P(37-21-0) 185
Arz-Moore 112C

Buf 0 0 7 7 14
Ten 14 7 3 7 31
Buf D21 R42/163 P(40-25-1) 286
Ten D21 R42/163 P(24-15-0) 159
Buf-Early 103C

Car 0 10 3 3 16
Slr 0 3 0 7 10
Car D17 R27/48 P(30-23-0) 254
Slr D12 R22/81 P(32-16-1) 187
Car-Walls 106C

Dal 3 7 0 7 17
GB 3 14 21 7 45
Dal D11 R20/93 P(25-12-0) 120
GB D29 R41/220 P(35-22-1) 189
GB-Levens 190R, Favre 203P

Ind 7 3 0 0 10
Det 9 9 7 7 32
Ind D12 R19/53 P(28-18-1) 120
Det D21 R36/249 P(28-16-0) 142
Det-Sanders 216R

Jax 7 3 13 3 26
Cin 21 7 3 0 31
Jax D20 R24/135 P(33-20-1) 280
Cin D24 R36/124 P(36-22-0) 203
Jax-McCardell 109C, Smith 106C

KC 7 3 7 2 19
Sea 7 7 0 0 14
KC D22 R34/120 P(29-16-0) 204
Sea D18 R23/68 P(37-20-1) 223

Mia 0 3 7 14 24
NE 3 21 3 0 27
Mia D33 R22/36 P(60-38-3) 370
NE D15 R24/84 P(27-16-0) 234
Mia-McDuffie 110C, Marino 389P

Min 0 7 0 14 21
NYJ 7 13 3 0 23
Min D19 R27/74 P(35-24-0) 312
NYJ D22 R32/130 P(34-23-0) 227
Min-Carter 105C, Reed 150C,
Johnson 312P; NYJ-Johnson 104C

NO 0 3 0 0 3
Atl 3 3 7 7 20
NO D11 R20/55 P(29-14-4) 118
Atl D16 R32/92 P(27-17-0) 177

NYG 0 0 7 0 7
Was 0 0 7 0 7
NYG D18 R37/157 P(37-20-1) 105
Was D23 R31/83 P(60-28-3) 291
Was-Westbrook 125C

Pit 3 3 7 7 20
Phi 7 3 3 10 23
Pit D22 R25/111 P(43-20-3) 272
Phi D19 R35/97 P(31-15-0) 229
Pit-Johnson 106C; Phi-Fryar 116C

SD 0 0 0 10 10
SF 3 7 7 0 17
SD D8 R23/92 P(28-10-3) 111
SF D19 R34/111 P(30-20-0) 228

TB 0 0 7 0 7
ChiB 10 3 0 0 13
TB D14 R18/35 P(33-19-0) 237
ChiB D17 R42/169 P(28-15-0) 110
ChiB-Harris 116R

MONDAY, NOVEMBER 24
Oak 0 3 0 0 3
Den 0 7 3 21 31
Oak D14 R21/110 P(41-22-0) 150
Den D23 R30/110 P(33-21-0) 260
Den-Sharpe 142C

THURSDAY, NOVEMBER 27
ChiB 14 6 0 0 20
Det 3 14 17 21 55
ChiB D16 R32/71 P(30-16-0) 262
Det D25 R29/222 P(31-20-1) 274
ChiB-Proehl 164C;
Det-Sanders 167R, Morton 120C

Ten 14 10 0 3 27
Dal 0 7 0 7 14
Ten D14 R49/164 P(17-9-0) 81
Dal D16 R13/46 P(42-27-3) 340
Ten-George 110R; Dal-Irvin 118C,
Aikman 356P

SUNDAY, NOVEMBER 30
Atl 7 10 7 0 24
Sea 0 7 7 3 17
Atl D14 R25/72 P(23-15-0) 201
Sea D19 R25/123 P(38-24-1) 228

Bal 7 7 0 13 27
Jax 3 13 10 3 29
Bal D17 R22/58 P(29-18-0) 163
Jax D23 R31/91 P(40-25-1) 313
Jax-Brunell 317P

Cin 14 0 7 21 42
Phi 7 17 10 10 44
Cin D29 R27/124 P(47-27-1) 373
Phi D27 R35/196 P(42-26-1) 311
Cin-Dillon 114R, Hundon 118C,
Esiason 378P; Phi-Fryar 122C,
Hoying 313P

Den 7 21 7 3 38
SD 0 7 7 14 28
Den D28 R29/198 P(33-20-0) 240
SD D22 R21/47 P(51-23-2) 222
Den-Davis 178R, McCaffrey 111C

Ind 3 0 7 7 17
NE 7 6 0 7 20
Ind D23 R26/118 P(41-22-0) 285
NE D17 R25/71 P(33-20-0) 187
Ind-Dawkins 120C, Harbaugh 310P

Mia 3 14 14 3 34
Oak 0 3 7 6 16
Mia D23 R38/137 P(34-19-1) 241
Oak D18 R19/114 P(34-17-1) 212
Mia-Jordan 106C; Oak-Brown 125C

NO 0 13 0 3 16
Car 0 3 0 13 16
NO D18 R32/136 P(30-14-1) 190
Car D21 R23/186 P(42-24-3) 241
Car-Lane 112R, Ismail 102C

NYJ 0 3 0 7 10
Buf 7 3 0 10 20
NYJ D16 R15/30 P(47-25-1) 264
Buf D19 R34/197 P(31-12-1) 139
Buf-Thomas 104R

Pit 7 3 7 3 6 26
Arz 0 3 14 3 0 20
Pit D25 R44/179 P(35-18-0) 165
Arz D18 R17/48 P(27-16-0) 243
Pit-Bettis 142R; Arz-Moore 188C

SF 3 3 3 0 9
KC 7 21 0 16 44
SF D13 R21/127 P(24-17-2) 152
KC D22 R42/153 P(22-13-1) 187
KC-Rison 117C

Slr 0 10 7 6 23
Was 7 3 0 10 20
Slr D19 R30/114 P(38-19-0) 284
Was D19 R22/61 P(45-20-2) 240
Slr-Lee 128C

TB 0 7 7 6 20
NYG 0 3 3 2 8
TB D21 R41/147 P(22-12-3) 152
NYG D13 R21/99 P(31-14-2) 103
TB-Dunn 120R

MONDAY, DECEMBER 1
GB 3 7 7 10 27
Min 0 3 0 8 11
GB D17 R36/139 P(29-15-0) 187
Min D17 R24/99 P(42-21-1) 154
GB-Levens 108R

THURSDAY, DECEMBER 4
Ten 0 0 0 14 14
Cin 14 14 10 3 41
Ten D12 R12/44 P(25-14-0) 131
Cin D34 R54/276 P(28-20-0) 239
Cin-Dillon 246R

SUNDAY, DECEMBER 7
Atl 0 7 7 0 14
SD 0 0 0 3 3
Atl D13 R28/96 P(23-10-1) 108
SD D16 R17/47 P(41-22-3) 221
SD-Metcalf 109C

Buf 0 3 0 0 3
ChiB 0 13 0 7 20
Buf D10 R16/55 P(32-13-0) 105
ChiB D23 R43/120 P(36-24-2) 272
ChiB-Conway 115C

Den 14 7 3 0 24
Pit 7 14 7 7 35
Den D18 R24/89 P(42-17-1) 231
Pit D22 R36/186 P(29-18-1) 290
Den-Smith 115C; Pit-Bettis 125R,
Thigpen 175C, Stewart 303P

Det 3 7 6 14 30
Mia 14 6 3 10 33
Det D24 R33/145 P(29-19-2) 279
Mia D19 R27/81 P(39-24-1) 310
Det-Sanders 137R, Morton 171C;
Mia-Marino 310P

GB 7 0 7 3 17
TB 3 3 0 0 6
GB D20 R31/82 P(33-25-1) 280
TB D8 R22/67 P(26-10-1) 94

Ind 0 12 3 7 22
NYJ 0 0 0 14 14
Ind D19 R46/193 P(24-15-0) 173
NYJ D12 R11/33 P(32-14-1) 93
Ind-Faulk 133R

Min 7 7 3 0 17
SF 14 7 7 0 28
Min D20 R26/137 P(31-16-1) 161
SF D24 R37/98 P(25-20-0) 270

```
NE    13   7   3   3   26
Jax    0   7  13   0   20
NE  D16 R20/55  P(35-26-0) 227
Jax D23 R27/107 P(42-25-0) 234
   Jax-McCardell 152C

NYG    7  14   0  10   31
Phi    0   7   7   7   21
NYG D18 R46/208 P(27-14-1) 137
Phi D15 R20/70  P(35-16-3) 186
   NYG-Barber 114R

Oak    0   0   0   0    0
KC    10  10   0  10   30
Oak D5  R15/36  P(18-8-0)   57
KC  D27 R48/214 P(21-15-0) 204

Sea    7  10   7   0   24
Bal    3  14   7   7   31
Sea D14 R27/103 P(34-17-4) 170
Bal D15 R28/88  P(28-17-0) 286
   Bal-Alexander 150C, Zeier 302P

Slr    0  13   0  21   34
NO    10   3   7   7   27
Slr D23 R35/114 P(42-22-1) 229
NO  D16 R12/44  P(37-23-2) 240
   Slr-Bruce 144C; NO-Hastings 120C

Was    7  10   7  14   38
Arz    0  14   7   7   28
Was D17 R35/139 P(34-18-1) 223
Arz D14 R20/57  P(38-19-2) 301
   Arz-Moore 114C, Plummer 337P
```

MONDAY, DECEMBER 8
```
Car    3   7   6   7   23
Dal    0   6   0   7   13
Car D22 R45/155 P(30-17-0) 169
Dal D9  R21/78  P(27-14-0) 138
   Car-Lane 138R
```

SATURDAY, DECEMBER 13
```
Pit    0   7   3  11   3   24
NE     0  14   0   7   0   21
Pit D22 R40/138 P(48-26-2) 266
NE  D15 R18/42  P(36-21-2) 211

Was    0   3   7   0   10
NYG   17   3   0  10   30
Was D18 R15/45  P(42-23-4) 275
NYG D14 R37/130 P(25-13-2) 110
```

SUNDAY, DECEMBER 14
```
Arz    7   3   0   0   10
NO     0   3   7  17   27
Arz D18 R28/111 P(37-17-2) 154
NO  D17 R34/130 P(24-14-1) 252
   NO-Hill 124C

ChiB   0   7   0   6   13
Slr    7   0   0  14   21
ChiB D13 R39/120 P(30-15-2) 189
Slr D11 R20/49  P(28-13-3) 116
   ChiB-Conway 109C

Dal   10   0   0  14   24
Cin    0  17  14   0   31
Dal D29 R31/128 P(53-28-2) 274
Cin D17 R31/157 P(25-13-1) 262
   Dal-Irvin 117C; Cin-Dillon 127R, Scott 112C

Det    0   7   0   7   14
Min    7   6   0   0   13
Det D21 R27/148 P(39-24-1) 242
Min D13 R37/214 P(18-9-0)  43
   Det-Sanders 138R; Min-Smith 101R

GB    14   3   7   7   31
Car    0   7   0   3   10
GB  D26 R41/218 P(34-18-1) 240
Car D9  R24/140 P(26-7-0)  32
   GB-Freeman 166C; Car-Lane 119R

Jax    7   7   3   3   20
Buf    0   0   0  14   14
Jax D20 R31/91  P(32-24-1) 297
Buf D24 R33/143 P(41-19-1) 192
   Jax-Brunell 317P

KC     7   7   8   7   29
SD     0   7   0   0    7
KC  D14 R27/131 P(25-8-0)  108
SD  D22 R28/63  P(38-23-1) 219
```

```
Mia    0   0   0   0    0
Ind    3  31   0   7   41
Mia D10 R26/76  P(25-12-0) 107
Ind D23 R36/148 P(26-20-0) 253
   Ind-Dilger 100C, Harbaugh 255P

Phi    7   0   0  10   17
Atl    0   0   7   6   20
Phi D15 R20/106 P(34-16-1) 171
Atl D21 R36/211 P(21-12-0) 175

Sea    0   3   9  10   22
Oak   14   7   0   0   21
Sea D22 R33/103 P(37-23-2) 278
Oak D15 R17/34  P(31-21-0) 241

TB     0   0   0   0    0
NYJ    3  14   7  10   34
TB  D6  R25/90  P(22-3-2)  21
NYJ D14 R43/122 P(22-14-1) 112

Ten    3   3   6   7   19
Bal    7   7   0   7   21
Ten D23 R37/190 P(45-22-1) 200
Bal D11 R21/54  P(28-13-0) 192
   Ten-George 129R, Sanders 100C
```

MONDAY, DECEMBER 15
```
Den   10   0   7   0   17
SF     0  14  10  10   34
Den D15 R23/96  P(41-16-2) 141
SF  D18 R26/58  P(34-22-0) 265
```

SATURDAY, DECEMBER 20
```
Buf    0   0   8  13   21
GB    14   7   3   7   31
Buf D21 R21/51  P(45-24-3) 274
GB  D14 R34/102 P(28-17-0) 170
   Buf-Early 120C

Slr   10   6   7   7   30
Car    0   0   8  10   18
Slr D23 R39/148 P(25-16-0) 149
Car D21 R20/94  P(42-21-3) 233
   Slr-Moore 113R
```

SUNDAY, DECEMBER 21
```
Atl   14   3   6   3   26
Arz    7   0  15   7   29
Atl D22 R40/189 P(20-13-1) 167
Arz D20 R18/66  P(39-19-2) 231
   Atl-Anderson 152R

Bal    7   0   7   0   14
Cin    7   0   3   6   16
Bal D15 R17/51  P(41-28-0) 304
Cin D18 R29/65  P(34-21-0) 237
   Bal-Alexander 111C, Zeier 349P; Cin-Scott 129C

ChiB   0   7   0   8   15
TB    14   7  10   0   31
ChiB D15 R27/90  P(29-18-2) 104
TB  D12 R33/183 P(19-11-0) 86
   TB-Dunn 119R

Ind    7   3   8  10   28
Min    7  22   3   7   39
Ind D21 R34/132 P(35-20-3) 166
Min D17 R30/180 P(27-13-2) 165
   Ind-Faulk 102R; Min-Smith 160R, Cunningham 174P

Jax   14   0   0   6   20
Oak    0   3   6   0    9
Jax D20 R31/143 P(28-19-0) 274
Oak D19 R24/108 P(37-24-0) 192
   Jax-McCardell 116C; Oak-Brown 164C

NO     0   0   0   7    7
KC     3   9   0  13   25
NO  D17 R25/103 P(29-13-3) 149
KC  D14 R41/156 P(19-9-0)  20

NYG   10  10   0   0   20
Dal    0   0   0   7    7
NYG D17 R44/147 P(25-10-0) 136
Dal D11 R21/79  P(32-17-1) 105

NYJ   10   0   0   0   10
Det    0   3   3   7   13
NYJ D20 R23/108 P(40-24-3) 207
Det D13 R31/206 P(28-15-0) 95
   Det-Sanders 184R
```

```
Phi    7   7   3  15   32
Was   14  14   0   7   35
Phi D24 R36/193 P(31-21-1) 208
Was D17 R20/78  P(24-16-2) 143
   Phi-Garner 115R

Pit    0   0   0   3    6
Ten    3  10   0   3   16
Pit D19 R36/93  P(27-14-1) 176
Ten D14 R29/156 P(26-10-1) 85

SD     3   0   0   0    3
Den    0  24   7   7   38
SD  D9  R23/70  P(28-15-1) 133
Den D24 R33/130 P(35-23-1) 321
   Den-Sharpe 162C, Elway 273P

SF     6   0   3   0    9
Sea    7  14   7  10   38
SF  D17 R24/125 P(33-18-1) 199
Sea D24 R25/124 P(33-24-0) 283
   Sea-Galloway 101C, Moon 232P
```

MONDAY, DECEMBER 22
```
NE     0   0   7   7   14
Mia    3   3   0   6   12
NE  D10 R17/47  P(26-18-1) 160
Mia D17 R21/42  P(44-28-1) 253
```

1998 NFL
SUNDAY, SEPTEMBER 6
```
Pit    3   0  10   7   20
Bal    0   0   0  13   13
Pit D14 R30/114 P(27-14-2) 157
Bal D17 R28/112 P(34-20-0) 264

Oak    0   0   8   0    8
KC     7  11   3   7   28
Oak D18 R20/52  P(32-19-0) 212
KC  D18 R36/143 P(35-16-0) 157
   KC-Bennett 115R

TB     0   7   0   0    7
Min   14   7   0  10   31
TB  D17 R23/68  P(37-23-1) 251
Min D19 R27/117 P(25-15-1) 181
   Min-Johnson 189P

NYJ    3  14   7   6   0   30
SF     7   7   9   7   6   36
NYJ D25 R24/59  P(58-30-1) 406
SF  D26 R24/207 P(46-26-1) 350
   NYJ-Chrebet 125C, Johnson 126C,
   Foley 415P; SF-Hearst 187R,
   Stokes 111C, Young 363P

Mia    3  14   0   7   24
Ind    0   3   0  12   15
Mia D15 R30/137 P(24-13-0) 135
Ind D24 R26/64  P(37-21-3) 273
   Mia-Abdul-Jabbar 108R;
   Ind-Harrison 102C, Manning 302P

Arz    0   0  10   0   10
Dal    0  14   7  17   38
Arz D13 R17/45  P(31-14-0) 160
Dal D30 R43/188 P(32-22-2) 256
   Dal-Smith 124R, Irvin 119C

Buf    0   0   7   7   14
SD     3   0  10   7   20
Buf D20 R28/90  P(34-20-2) 160
SD  D14 R20/67  P(31-16-2) 187
   SD-Still 128C

Atl    0   7   9   3   19
Car    0   7   0   7   14
Atl D19 R31/93  P(32-17-1) 230
Car D16 R20/54  P(37-21-1) 263
   Car-Ismail 119C

NO    14  10   0   0   24
Slr    7   0   7   3   17
NO  D15 R24/35  P(30-15-1) 197
Slr D23 R24/47  P(44-29-1) 267
   Slr-Bruce 131C

Sea   14   0  17   7   38
Phi    0   0   0   0    0
Sea D18 R34/188 P(22-14-0) 218
Phi D17 R32/162 P(23-9-1)  95
   Sea-Green 100R, Galloway 142C

Det    3   3  13   0   19
GB    10   7   7  14   38
Det D20 R22/85  P(44-23-0) 236
GB  D21 R30/75  P(32-24-0) 267
   Det-Moore 100C; GB-Freeman 110C
```

```
Jax    0   7   7  10   24
ChiB   0  10   0  10   20
Jax D21 R33/160 P(35-22-0) 207
ChiB D16 R34/132 P(27-16-0) 189
   Jax-Stewart 115R

Was    7   3   7   7   24
NYG    0  10   0  21   31
Was D21 R23/73  P(37-25-2) 258
NYG D15 R30/82  P(28-15-1) 153

Ten    3   7   7   6   23
Cin    7   0   7   0   14
Ten D19 R29/89  P(34-17-0) 264
Cin D16 R23/100 P(32-24-1) 192
```

MONDAY, SEPTEMBER 7
```
NE     0   7   7   7   21
Den   10   7   3   7   27
NE  D17 R24/81  P(32-20-0) 258
Den D20 R30/91  P(34-22-0) 248
```

SUNDAY, SEPTEMBER 13
```
Ind    0   0   0   6    6
NE    10   6   6   7   29
Ind D20 R32/136 P(33-21-3) 173
NE  D15 R33/103 P(29-15-0) 218
   Ind-Faulk 127R

Cin    7   7   7   6   7   34
Det    7   7   7   7   0   28
Cin D18 R21/100 P(36-25-0) 284
Det D22 R34/224 P(31-15-2) 188
   Cin-Faulk 127R, Scott 130C,
   O'Donnell 303P; Det-Sanders 185R

SD     3   3   7   0   13
Ten    0   0   7   0    7
SD  D18 R34/141 P(24-13-0) 179
Ten D18 R19/63  P(35-21-0) 187

Arz    0   0   7   7   14
Sea    3   3  17  10   33
Arz D17 R26/111 P(36-23-3) 163
Sea D16 R32/123 P(23-14-0) 121
   Sea-Watters 105R

Dal    7  10   3   3   23
Den   21  14   0   7   42
Dal D18 R30/169 P(31-19-0) 201
Den D21 R31/209 P(23-17-0) 306
   Den-Davis 191R, McCaffrey 117C

ChiB   0   9   0   3   12
Pit    0   7  10   0   17
ChiB D19 R33/130 P(33-18-1) 190
Pit D17 R27/142 P(30-17-1) 109
   Pit-Bettis 131R

Min   14  10   7   7   38
Slr    0  10  14   7   31
Min D23 R31/194 P(37-21-2) 227
Slr D20 R24/95  P(31-15-2) 275
   Min-Smith 179R; Slr-Bruce 192C

Bal    7   7   3   7   24
NYJ    0   3   0   7   10
Bal D16 R34/122 P(30-18-0) 209
NYJ D18 R24/52  P(32-22-3) 224

KC     0   6   3   7   16
Jax    7   7   0   7   21
KC  D23 R25/111 P(37-23-0) 253
Jax D19 R38/145 P(18-11-0) 111
   Jax-Stewart 103R

Car    0  14   0   0   14
NO     3   3   7   6   19
Car D20 R25/137 P(35-15-2) 238
NO  D18 R38/207 P(18-13-0) 104
   Car-Lane 100R, Muhammad 192C;
   NO-Dawkins 110C

Buf    0   7   0   7   14
Mia    0   7   3   3   13
Buf D12 R28/110 P(18-10-1) 143
Mia D12 R27/116 P(26-14-0) 143

TB     0   0   0  15   15
GB    10   6   0   7   23
TB  D17 R19/50  P(40-22-1) 161
GB  D15 R25/37  P(33-22-0) 223

Phi    6   3   0   3   12
Atl    0   0  14   3   17
Phi D19 R25/63  P(35-24-0) 221
Atl D17 R25/78  P(26-14-0) 167
```

```
NYG    7   0  10   0   17
Oak    7   3  10   0   20
NYG D15 R23/71  P(33-23-1) 162
Oak D21 R26/162 P(44-25-0) 252
   Oak-Kaufman 139R, Brown 127C,
   George 303P
```

MONDAY, SEPTEMBER 14
```
SF     7  14   7  17   45
Was    7   3   0   0   10
SF  D28 R34/210 P(32-21-0) 294
Was D17 R27/140 P(25-14-1) 182
   SF-Hearst 138R, Young 303P;
   Was-Westbrook 109C
```

SUNDAY, SEPTEMBER 20
```
Phi    0   0   0   3    3
Arz    0   0   0  17   17
Phi D20 R27/91  P(46-26-1) 226
Arz D16 R26/153 P(35-21-0) 129
   Arz-Murrell 145R

Was    0   7   0   7   14
Sea    7   3  14   0   24
Was D27 R21/96  P(54-27-2) 369
Sea D16 R32/163 P(33-16-0) 136
   Was-Westbrook 132C, Green 383P;
   Sea-Watters 136R

Den    7  10   7  10   34
Oak    0  10   7   0   17
Den D25 R36/145 P(27-16-1) 193
Oak D13 R20/94  P(29-17-3) 164
   Den-Davis 104R; Oak-Jett 116C

Bal    3   7   0   0   10
Jax    7   3  14   0   24
Bal D11 R25/81  P(34-17-1) 232
Jax D21 R32/154 P(34-25-0) 365
   Bal-Lewis 117C; Jax-Taylor 128R,
   McCardell 108C, Smith 116C,
   Brunell 376P

ChiB  10   5   0   0   15
TB     0   0  13  14   27
ChiB D13 R25/85  P(32-19-0) 169
TB  D20 R38/220 P(18-12-0) 144
   TB-Alstott 103R

Ind    3   0   3   0    6
NYJ    7  20   7  10   44
Ind D21 R27/120 P(44-20-2) 190
NYJ D28 R44/302 P(22-12-1) 203
   NYJ-Martin 144R, Testaverde 203P

Det    3   3   0   0    6
Min    0   6  13  10   29
Det D19 R31/137 P(40-20-2) 142
Min D17 R24/76  P(35-20-0) 211

Ten    3   3   7   3   16
NE     3   3   7  14   27
Ten D18 R26/112 P(38-28-2) 194
NE  D13 R18/94  P(30-18-0) 228
   Ten-George 100R; NE-Glenn 102C

Pit    0   0   0   0    0
Mia    0  14   0   7   21
Pit D13 R24/122 P(35-11-3) 78
Mia D11 R38/110 P(22-14-0) 143
   Mia-Abdul-Jabbar 108R

SD     0   0   0   7    7
KC     6  10   0   7   23
SD  D6  R28/171 P(15-1-2)  -19
KC  D16 R44/122 P(29-10-0) 129
   SD-Means 165R

GB     7   3   0   3   13
Cin    3   0   3   0    6
GB  D22 R30/86  P(35-23-1) 242
Cin D7  R17/28  P(30-16-0) 132

Slr    0  10  10  14   34
Buf    7   7  14   5   33
Slr D21 R25/181 P(27-13-2) 225
Buf D23 R35/215 P(30-18-1) 192
   Slr-Hill 158R; Buf-Smith 118R
```

MONDAY, SEPTEMBER 21
```
Dal    0  17   7   7   31
NYG    0   7   0   0    7
Dal D11 R30/78  P(27-11-0) 224
NYG D16 R18/56  P(53-26-2) 196
```

SUNDAY, SEPTEMBER 27

Min 7 3 14 7 **31**
ChiB 7 14 0 7 **28**
Min D17 R27/93 P(25-16-0) 258
ChiB D23 R26/91 P(39-25-1) 361
Min-Cunningham 275P;
ChiB-Engram 123C, Kramer 372P

GB 6 14 10 7 **37**
Car 10 10 0 10 30
GB D26 R33/109 P(45-27-3) 378
Car D13 R16/60 P(53-20-1) 170
GB-Favre 388P

Arz 0 17 0 3 **20**
Slr 7 3 0 7 17
Arz D22 R35/78 P(31-21-1) 203
Slr D17 R27/120 P(26-15-0) 144

Atl 7 0 0 13 20
SF 14 17 0 0 **31**
Atl D19 R20/147 P(38-16-3) 222
SF D23 R31/161 P(39-28-1) 377
Atl-Anderson 123R, Mathis 130C;
SF-Hearst 105C, Rice 162C,
Young 387P

Sea 0 7 3 0 10
Pit 3 7 3 0 **13**
Sea D14 R21/61 P(27-14-1) 169
Pit D16 R45/185 P(25-16-0) 100
Sea-Galloway 139C; Pit-Bettis 138R

Den 7 14 7 10 **38**
Was 7 3 6 0 16
Den D18 R35/185 P(24-16-0) 180
Was D18 R25/152 P(31-19-2) 235
Den-Davis 119R;
Was-Westbrook 104C

Oak 3 7 0 3 **13**
Dal 0 3 0 9 12
Oak D13 R37/129 P(20-12-0) 159
Dal D16 R25/68 P(33-18-2) 207
Oak-Kaufman 116R

NYG 14 7 7 6 **34**
SD 0 6 10 0 16
NYG D19 R40/105 P(33-17-1) 208
SD D17 R21/89 P(49-21-4) 266
SD-Still 104C

Jax 7 7 7 6 **27**
Ten 10 9 3 0 22
Jax D19 R37/148 P(28-17-2) 149
Ten D15 R20/40 P(33-17-2) 179
Jax-Taylor 116R; Ten-Thigpen 102C

Cin 0 10 7 7 24
Bal 14 7 7 3 **31**
Cin D19 R29/132 P(25-16-0) 143
Bal D21 R35/181 P(20-15-0) 227
Cin-Dillon 116R, Pickens 120C;
Bal-Holmes 173R, Lewis 122C

NO 0 3 3 7 13
Ind 3 3 0 7 13
NO D14 R32/183 P(28-12-1) 137
Ind D16 R31/65 P(32-19-3) 292
NO-Smith 157R; Ind-Faulk 128C,
Manning 309P

KC 0 7 0 17 **24**
Phi 7 0 7 0 21
KC D24 R33/131 P(25-17-0) 262
Phi D24 R27/111 P(36-21-1) 250

MONDAY, SEPTEMBER 28

TB 0 3 0 3 6
Det 0 6 14 7 **27**
TB D6 R17/55 P(32-12-2) 78
Det D17 R41/156 P(25-15-0) 124
Det-Sanders 131R

SUNDAY, OCTOBER 4

Car 3 0 6 14 23
Atl 14 3 21 13 **51**
Car D16 R17/57 P(38-20-2) 289
Atl D18 R42/130 P(23-14-2) 193
Car-Muhammad 104C, Collins 302P;
Atl-Anderson 117R

Dal 3 14 7 7 **31**
Was 0 3 0 7 10
Dal D21 R43/224 P(17-14-0) 163
Was D14 R22/92 P(29-13-1) 164
Dal-Smith 120R, Warren 104R

NE 3 14 10 3 **30**
NO 0 14 3 10 27
NE D20 R25/97 P(35-21-3) 291
NO D19 R18/39 P(47-25-2) 237
NE-Glenn 105C, Bledsoe 317P

NYG 0 0 0 3 3
TB 10 0 0 10 **20**
NYG D8 R21/64 P(28-10-3) 71
TB D16 R43/174 P(20-12-1) 60

Mia 3 0 0 6 9
NYJ 0 10 7 3 **20**
Mia D11 R15/34 P(34-15-3) 119
NYJ D22 R38/117 P(32-19-0) 172
NYJ-Martin 108R

Oak 6 17 0 0 **23**
Arz 7 0 0 6 20
Oak D14 R34/112 P(32-16-1) 110
Arz D16 R21/49 P(39-23-3) 187
Arz-Sanders 118C

Det 10 0 17 0 27
ChiB 0 10 0 21 **31**
Det D15 R26/94 P(31-16-0) 246
ChiB D23 R37/125 P(38-27-0) 280
Det-Morton 138C; ChiB-Penn 106C

Phi 0 2 0 14 16
Den 28 7 6 0 **41**
Phi D12 R19/57 P(33-14-1) 100
Den D22 R39/231 P(32-17-2) 192
Den-Davis 168R, Brister 203P

SD 0 6 0 6 12
Ind 11 0 0 6 **17**
SD D17 R34/152 P(23-12-1) 143
Ind D11 R29/55 P(23-12-1) 137
SD-Means 130R

SF 0 0 0 21 21
Buf 10 10 3 3 **26**
SF D23 R18/65 P(38-23-1) 312
Buf D21 R38/115 P(27-19-0) 237
SF-Young 329P

Sea 3 0 0 3 6
KC 3 7 7 0 **17**
Sea D10 R26/73 P(33-11-2) 94
KC D12 R42/131 P(19-12-0) 120

MONDAY, OCTOBER 5

Min 3 21 3 10 **37**
GB 0 10 0 14 24
Min D22 R34/103 P(32-20-0) 442
GB D21 R20/102 P(39-23-3) 204
Min-Carter 119C, Moss 190C,
Cunningham 442P

SUNDAY, OCTOBER 11

Car 7 7 0 6 20
Dal 3 7 14 3 **27**
Car D16 R21/37 P(32-22-1) 267
Dal D22 R36/151 P(22-14-0) 277
Car-Ismail 117C; Dal-Smith 112R,
Irvin 146C, Mills 110C

Buf 0 7 17 7 **31**
Ind 6 6 0 12 24
Buf D24 R40/176 P(28-23-0) 205
Ind D21 R22/106 P(41-20-2) 235
Buf-Smith 130R

Ten 6 3 3 0 **12**
Bal 2 0 3 3 8
Ten D16 R35/166 P(29-17-1) 178
Bal D13 R18/36 P(44-25-1) 227
Ten-George 121R

Pit 0 10 7 3 **20**
Cin 0 0 3 10 13
Pit D20 R39/257 P(22-13-0) 129
Cin D17 R27/108 P(26-20-0) 281
Pit-Stewart 103R; Cin-Pickens 204C

SD 0 3 0 3 6
Oak 0 0 0 7 **7**
SD D9 R43/117 P(24-10-4) 78
Oak D6 R18/18 P(42-13-1) 141
SD-Means 101R

KC 0 0 7 3 10
NE 7 20 10 3 **40**
KC D9 R11/14 P(29-14-1) 120
NE D31 R54/206 P(28-18-0) 232
NE-Edwards 104R

SF 7 14 10 0 **31**
NO 0 0 0 0 0
SF D30 R38/140 P(41-22-0) 319
NO D10 R13/32 P(30-15-1) 135
SF-Young 309P

Den 14 0 0 7 **21**
Sea 0 7 3 6 16
Den D17 R34/202 P(27-13-2) 171
Sea D16 R24/77 P(40-21-1) 242
Den-Davis 208R, Smith 136C

Was 0 3 3 6 12
Phi 7 3 0 7 **17**
Was D17 R25/128 P(37-19-1) 150
Phi D14 R32/115 P(28-15-1) 83

NYJ 3 0 0 7 10
Slr 7 10 6 7 **30**
NYJ D14 R15/54 P(33-14-2) 123
Slr D18 R42/141 P(25-19-0) 178

Atl 7 7 10 10 **34**
NYG 6 0 7 7 20
Atl D20 R34/128 P(27-14-0) 253
NYG D17 R25/110 P(37-22-0) 156
Atl-Anderson 110R

ChiB 0 0 0 7 7
Arz 3 14 0 3 **20**
ChiB D12 R22/66 P(28-16-4) 223
Arz D12 R46/138 P(25-18-2) 150
ChiB-Engram 142C

MONDAY, OCTOBER 12

Mia 0 7 14 0 21
Jax 7 7 0 14 **28**
Mia D25 R28/67 P(49-30-1) 307
Jax D12 R23/186 P(18-12-1) 199
Mia-Marino 323P

THURSDAY, OCTOBER 15

GB 10 0 3 7 20
Det 0 10 0 17 **27**
GB D23 R21/93 P(43-22-3) 275
Det D16 R32/186 P(19-16-0) 199
GB-Freeman 126C, Favre 300P;
Det-Sanders 155R

SUNDAY, OCTOBER 18

Jax 7 3 6 0 16
Buf 0 7 3 7 **17**
Jax D16 R34/134 P(28-16-0) 104
Buf D22 R23/110 P(39-18-0) 227

Was 7 0 0 0 7
Min 14 7 3 17 **41**
Was D9 R22/82 P(26-10-1) 95
Min D25 R38/147 P(38-22-0) 288
Min-Smith 103R, Carter 109C

Arz 0 3 0 7 10
NYG 7 10 10 7 **34**
Arz D15 R20/62 P(26-14-2) 132
NYG D26 R37/141 P(36-22-0) 249
NYG-Brown 108R

Cin 0 0 7 7 14
Ten 7 13 17 7 **44**
Cin D19 R29/84 P(25-20-0) 184
Ten D24 R39/171 P(25-20-0) 344
Cin-Dillon 124R; Ten-George 107R,
Sanders 101C

Bal 3 3 0 0 6
Pit 3 0 7 6 **16**
Bal D16 R29/96 P(32-17-3) 134
Pit D13 R30/79 P(27-12-1) 162

Phi 0 3 0 7 10
SD 3 0 7 3 **13**
Phi D21 R24/51 P(39-22-2) 210
SD D11 R28/140 P(19-9-0) 28
SD-Means 112R

NO 0 14 2 7 23
Atl 3 0 14 14 **31**
NO D15 R26/67 P(29-14-1) 255
Atl D19 R30/134 P(21-14-0) 163
NO-Poole 154C; Atl-Anderson 132R,
Martin 116C

Car 0 3 10 0 13
TB 0 0 3 13 **16**
Car D17 R23/67 P(31-22-0) 223
TB D21 R28/136 P(31-21-1) 213

Slr 0 0 0 0 0
Mia 0 0 7 7 **14**
Slr D15 R24/76 P(29-14-1) 128
Mia D16 R32/141 P(26-14-1) 104

Dal 3 3 6 0 12
ChiB 0 0 7 6 **13**
Dal D13 R26/108 P(26-14-1) 128
ChiB D18 R31/79 P(30-18-1) 220

Ind 14 7 10 0 31
SF 0 0 17 17 **34**
Ind D15 R20/105 P(30-18-0) 231
SF D36 R25/127 P(51-33-0) 321
Ind-Faulk 103R; SF-Stokes 110C,
Young 331P

MONDAY, OCTOBER 19

NYJ 7 3 0 14 **24**
NE 7 7 0 0 14
NYJ D25 R33/121 P(32-22-0) 271
NE D19 R24/110 P(30-18-1) 181
NYJ-Martin 107R;
NE-Edwards 104R

SUNDAY, OCTOBER 25

Min 0 0 17 17 **34**
Det 3 10 0 0 13
Min D23 R27/159 P(30-17-2) 170
Det D17 R28/137 P(37-20-1) 214
Min-Smith 134R; Det-Sanders 127R

Atl 0 0 3 0 3
NYJ 7 7 14 0 **28**
Atl D13 R21/55 P(34-16-2) 152
NYJ D21 R34/119 P(29-16-0) 192
NYJ-Martin 101R

SF 14 0 7 7 **28**
Slr 0 3 0 7 10
SF D16 R30/93 P(24-13-2) 210
Slr D15 R24/79 P(35-15-3) 89
SF-Owens 120C

Bal 0 0 3 7 10
GB 0 14 0 14 **28**
Bal D11 R17/56 P(39-17-2) 177
GB D20 R33/76 P(41-22-2) 252
GB-Freeman 103C

TB 0 0 3 0 3
NO 0 3 3 9 15
TB D11 R18/58 P(44-20-2) 180
NO D12 R27/56 P(32-20-0) 210

Jax 3 7 7 7 24
Den 3 24 0 10 **37**
Jax D24 R16/66 P(46-28-0) 282
Den D24 R36/170 P(35-21-0) 295
Jax-McCardell 113C, Smith 121C,
Brunell 353P; Den-Davis 136R

ChiB 7 3 10 3 **23**
Ten 0 10 0 10 20
ChiB D20 R41/148 P(24-13-0) 138
Ten D25 R28/180 P(29-18-1) 176
Ten-George 137R

Sea 7 10 3 7 **27**
SD 0 10 7 3 20
Sea D14 R22/40 P(21-14-0) 234
SD D27 R32/111 P(52-25-0) 280
Sea-Galloway 130C

Buf 10 7 10 3 **30**
Car 0 7 0 7 14
Buf D18 R34/144 P(22-18-1) 282
Car D21 R22/81 P(40-22-2) 279
Buf-Moulds 145C; Car-Carrier 100C

NE 0 0 3 6 9
Mia 3 0 6 3 **12**
NE D13 R22/26 P(33-13-1) 225
Mia D18 R29/70 P(42-23-3) 263
NE-Jefferson 116C

Cin 0 7 3 0 10
Oak 7 14 3 3 **27**
Cin D14 R16/62 P(30-17-1) 108
Oak D23 R53/251 P(21-9-0) 160
Oak-Kaufman 143R

MONDAY, OCTOBER 26

Pit 7 3 3 7 **20**
KC 3 3 7 0 13
Pit D20 R43/182 P(23-12-0) 90
KC D16 R19/72 P(36-15-2) 218
Pit-Bettis 119R

SUNDAY, NOVEMBER 1

Mia 7 7 7 3 24
Buf 0 14 0 16 **30**
Mia D15 R33/128 P(27-15-0) 168
Buf D16 R30/116 P(26-15-1) 197

Ten 3 14 10 14 **41**
Pit 0 0 24 7 31
Ten D19 R38/169 P(21-13-0) 152
Pit D26 R20/54 P(49-38-3) 347
Ten-George 153R;
Pit-Hawkins 147C, Johnson 115C

Slr 0 7 0 8 15
Atl 17 10 7 3 **37**
Slr D16 R14/40 P(37-23-0) 207
Atl D25 R37/199 P(28-13-1) 235
Atl-Anderson 172R

NO 0 3 0 14 17
Car 7 10 7 7 **31**
NO D21 R15/53 P(48-24-2) 301
Car D16 R38/106 P(17-13-1) 110
NO-Dawkins 102C, Tolliver 325P;
Car-Lane 101R

Min 7 10 7 0 24
TB 0 18 9 0 **27**
Min D18 R19/70 P(25-21-1) 270
TB D22 R41/246 P(22-11-0) 132
Min-Reed 117C; TB-Alstott 128R,
Dunn 115R

NE 7 7 0 7 **21**
Ind 7 3 0 6 16
NE D20 R27/77 P(35-22-1) 293
Ind D18 R14/32 P(52-30-2) 278
NE-Coates 109C, Simmons 109C,
Bledsoe 306P; Ind-Faulk 119C

NYG 7 0 7 0 14
Was 7 7 7 0 **21**
NYG D10 R22/86 P(32-17-0) 143
Was D21 R38/124 P(31-21-0) 196

Den 3 3 7 20 **33**
Cin 3 9 0 14 26
Den D20 R29/150 P(26-15-1) 202
Cin D25 R39/127 P(37-20-0) 245
Den-Davis 149R, McCaffrey 133C;
Cin-Dillon 110R

Arz 0 7 7 3 **17**
Det 0 6 3 6 15
Arz D11 R25/37 P(25-15-1) 172
Det D18 R29/113 P(32-20-3) 167
Arz-Moore 107C; Det-Sanders 107R,
Morton 115C

Jax 14 28 0 3 **45**
Bal 7 6 0 6 19
Jax D20 R32/111 P(22-15-1) 253
Bal D22 R23/126 P(34-27-1) 231

SF 6 7 9 0 22
GB 16 3 0 17 **36**
SF D19 R28/134 P(39-24-1) 132
GB D15 R25/98 P(28-15-3) 274
GB-Freeman 193C

NYJ 0 10 10 0 **20**
KC 7 0 3 7 17
NYJ D17 R32/53 P(34-20-1) 253
KC D13 R29/92 P(28-13-3) 112
NYJ-Chrebet 101C

Oak 0 3 0 7 10
Sea 3 7 8 0 **18**
Oak D14 R31/73 P(23-13-1) 220
Sea D22 R28/80 P(39-29-1) 253

MONDAY, NOVEMBER 2

Dal 10 7 10 7 **34**
Phi 0 0 0 0 0
Dal D20 R36/121 P(27-15-0) 173
Phi D15 R18/96 P(42-13-2) 104
Dal-Smith 101R

SUNDAY, NOVEMBER 8

NYG 3 3 0 0 6
Dal 3 3 3 7 **16**
NYG D15 R28/159 P(24-12-0) 127
Dal D16 R33/162 P(26-17-0) 165
NYG-Brown 119R; Dal-Smith 163R

Oak 0 3 0 7 10
Bal 0 3 0 10 **13**
Oak D20 R28/111 P(29-18-2) 245
Bal D15 R34/126 P(17-10-1) 87
Oak-Dudley 105C

```
Slr    0  14   3   3  20
ChiB   7   0   3   2  12
Slr   D20 R29/64  P(31-24-0) 202
ChiB  D15 R24/129 P(26-15-1) 122

Cin    0   0   3   8  11
Jax   10  14   0   0  24
Cin   D19 R27/118 P(40-24-1) 200
Jax   D14 R32/137 P(21-9-0)  135
Jax-Taylor 118R

Ind    0   0   0  14  14
Mia    7  13   0   7  27
Ind   D21 R26/114 P(42-22-2) 140
Mia   D20 R33/152 P(27-18-1) 207
Mia-McDuffie 132C

NO     0   7  10   7  24
Min    7  10   7   7  31
NO    D11 R21/52  P(16-11-0) 138
Min   D23 R32/162 P(40-28-2) 303
Min-Smith 137R, Johnson 316P

Atl   14  14   3  10  41
NE     3   0   7   0  10
Atl   D22 R39/117 P(25-16-2) 249
NE    D15 R14/18  P(44-22-2) 205
Atl-Anderson 104R, Mathis 117C

Det    0   3   3   3   9
Phi    0   7   0   3  10
Det   D9  R22/146 P(27-14-0) 111
Phi   D16 R36/216 P(21-15-0)  73
Det-Sanders 140R; Phi-Garner 129R

Was    3  14   0  10  27
Arz    0   7   7  15  29
Was   D18 R26/89  P(33-17-0) 167
Arz   D23 R37/187 P(30-22-0) 164
Arz-Murrell 107R

SD     0   0   0  10  10
Den    7  13   7   0  27
SD    D13 R21/77  P(38-17-1) 136
Den   D19 R24/72  P(36-21-1) 217
Den-McCaffrey 133C

Buf    3   6   3   0  12
NYJ    7   6   7  14  34
Buf   D11 R18/48  P(30-12-2) 134
NYJ   D23 R37/121 P(32-23-1) 277

Car    3  13   0   7  23
SF     0   7  15   3  25
Car   D16 R24/50  P(41-25-0) 237
SF    D22 R25/105 P(36-22-3) 261

Ten    3   0  14  14  31
TB     8  13   0   6  22
Ten   D20 R36/236 P(16-9-0)  117
TB    D19 R26/103 P(38-20-1) 294
Ten-George 134R; TB-Emanuel 106C

KC     3   3   0   6  12
Sea   14  10   0   0  24
KC    D24 R19/97  P(50-32-3) 260
Sea   D16 R32/108 P(20-12-2)  94
Sea-Watters 105R
```

MONDAY, NOVEMBER 9

```
GB     0   0   3  17  20
Pit   14  10   3   0  27
GB    D17 R19/39  P(39-22-1) 217
Pit   D19 R41/142 P(22-15-0) 218
Pit-Bettis 100R
```

SUNDAY, NOVEMBER 15

```
NE     0   3   0   7  10
Buf    3   3   7   0  13
NE    D11 R16/48  P(31-12-0) 158
Buf   D23 R46/213 P(26-14-2) 178

Pit    0  14   0   0  14
Ten    3  10   0  10  23
Pit   D16 R24/79  P(28-22-0) 231
Ten   D18 R33/108 P(31-19-1) 230

NYJ    3  20   0   0  23
Ind    0   0   7   7  24
NYJ   D20 R33/157 P(28-12-1) 212
Ind   D23 R24/90  P(44-26-2) 267
NYJ-Martin 134R, Chrebet 112C,
Johnson 107C; Ind-Harrison 128C

Sea    7   3   0   7  17
Oak    0   7   0  13  20
Sea   D15 R29/101 P(33-17-3) 192
Oak   D21 R33/131 P(31-20-2) 249
```

```
SF     0   3   3  13  19
Atl    0   7   3  21  31
SF    D18 R20/76  P(40-21-1) 307
Atl   D19 R36/114 P(21-12-0) 184
SF-Rice 169C, Young 342P;
Atl-Anderson 100R

Mia    7   3   0   3  13
Car    3   3   0   3   9
Mia   D15 R40/184 P(21-14-1) 131
Car   D12 R18/62  P(30-17-2) 148
Mia-Abdul-Jabbar 127R

Cin    3   0   0   0   3
Min    7   0   7  10  24
Cin   D15 R34/103 P(27-16-1)  91
Min   D16 R29/125 P(22-14-3) 224

Slr    3   0   0   0   3
NO    14  10   0   0  24
Slr   D17 R19/55  P(37-24-2) 179
NO    D13 R31/102 P(26-13-0) 135

Phi    0   0   0   0   0
Was    7   7   7   7  28
Phi   D9  R29/105 P(36-17-3) 110
Was   D16 R35/151 P(33-14-0) 138

TB     3  14   0   7  24
Jax    7   7   6   9  29
TB    D13 R33/157 P(24-10-2) 186
Jax   D18 R28/144 P(37-22-0) 230
TB-Dunn 107R, Anthony 126C;
Jax-Taylor 128R

GB     7  13  10   7  37
NYG    0   3   0   0   3
GB    D24 R46/169 P(34-21-0) 264
NYG   D9  R19/65  P(25-10-2)  62
GB-Holmes 111R

ChiB   0   3   0   0   3
Det    7  10   6   3  26
ChiB  D14 R21/105 P(27-14-0) 147
Det   D24 R34/145 P(21-16-0) 246
Det-Sanders 114R, Morton 109C

Bal    0   3   7   3  13
SD     0   0   7   0   7
Bal   D8  R15/40  P(34-12-2) 121
SD    D19 R32/57  P(42-15-0) 146

Dal   14  14   7   0  35
Arz    0   7  14   7  28
Dal   D23 R35/146 P(18-14-0) 208
Arz   D28 R21/32  P(56-31-1) 448
Dal-Smith 118R; Arz-Sanders 190C,
Plummer 465P
```

MONDAY, NOVEMBER 16

```
Den   14   6   3   7  30
KC     0   7   0   0   7
Den   D26 R35/205 P(23-13-0) 174
KC    D15 R19/31  P(39-26-1) 190
Den-Davis 111R
```

SUNDAY, NOVEMBER 22

```
GB     0   7   0   7  14
Min   10  10   0   8  28
GB    D22 R18/53  P(39-31-1) 277
Min   D15 R21/92  P(30-20-0) 248
GB-Favre 303P; Min-Moss 153C

ChiB   0   3  10   0  13
Atl    0   3   7  10  20
ChiB  D10 R27/106 P(19-7-2)  104
Atl   D21 R28/95  P(30-20-0) 263
Atl-Martin 100C

Det   14   7   0   7  28
TB     0  14   3   8  25
Det   D19 R27/112 P(23-14-0) 188
TB    D22 R35/145 P(30-16-2) 283

Ind    3   0   0   8  11
Buf    0  24   7   3  34
Ind   D14 R22/86  P(29-14-2) 164
Buf   D25 R38/187 P(30-20-0) 215
Ind-Faulk 102C; Buf-Smith 107R,
Reed 108C

Phi    0   0   0   0   0
NYG    3   0   7  10  20
Phi   D16 R26/117 P(28-14-2)  97
NYG   D15 R40/123 P(21-10-1) 138

Jax    0   0   7   8  15
Pit    7   6   3  14  30
Jax   D17 R26/97  P(42-18-3) 204
Pit   D18 R34/121 P(36-25-0) 208
```

```
Arz   17  14   7   7  45
Was    0   6  21  15  42
Arz   D25 R40/188 P(28-17-1) 248
Was   D31 R17/68  P(49-30-1) 353
Was-Shepherd 107C,
Westbrook 135C, Green 382P

Bal    7  10   0   3  20
Cin    0   3  10   0  13
Bal   D18 R41/247 P(18-9-1)   91
Cin   D16 R23/58  P(33-19-2) 184
Bal-Holmes 227R

Car    7  10   0   7  24
Slr    0   7   7   6  20
Car   D17 R30/73  P(26-21-1) 184
Slr   D17 R19/42  P(36-18-0) 239

Sea    0  14   0   8  22
Dal   10   6   0  14  30
Sea   D17 R17/66  P(28-15-1) 183
Dal   D29 R36/173 P(42-28-1) 292

KC     7   7  13  10  37
SD     7  10   0  21  38
KC    D21 R26/69  P(25-11-1) 297
SD    D25 R28/95  P(37-19-1) 271
KC-Alexander 173C, Gannon 304P

Oak    0   7   7   0  14
Den    3  14   0  23  40
Oak   D15 R19/49  P(35-20-3) 245
Den   D28 R41/196 P(26-18-0) 201
Den-Davis 162R

NYJ    0   3   7  14  24
Ten    0   0   3   0   3
NYJ   D22 R33/130 P(33-21-0) 231
Ten   D12 R24/94  P(26-14-0) 129
NYJ-Martin 123R, Johnson 112C

NO    10   3   0   7  20
SF     0  14  17   0  31
NO    D23 R17/90  P(44-22-2) 311
SF    D23 R34/154 P(31-22-1) 289
NO-Dawkins 148C, Collins 328P;
SF-Hearst 103C, Young 290P
```

MONDAY, NOVEMBER 23

```
Mia    7   7   3   6  23
NE     7   3   6  10  26
Mia   D17 R19/33  P(38-24-1) 289
NE    D21 R19/41  P(54-28-2) 414
NE-Jefferson 131C, Bledsoe 423P
```

THURSDAY, NOVEMBER 26

```
Pit    0   6   7   3  16
Det    0   3   3  10  19
Pit   D22 R34/85  P(36-21-1) 208
Det   D13 R23/70  P(27-17-0) 213
Det-Moore 148C

Min   21   3  15   7  46
Dal    6   6  10  14  36
Min   D21 R19/118 P(35-17-1) 353
Dal   D32 R24/58  P(57-34-0) 455
Min-Carter 135C, Moss 163C,
Cunningham 359P; Dal-Irvin 137C,
Aikman 455P
```

SUNDAY, NOVEMBER 29

```
Car    7   0   7   7  21
NYJ   10  12  19   7  48
Car   D15 R23/82  P(23-13-1) 134
NYJ   D21 R39/201 P(21-16-0) 255
NYJ-Martin 110R, Chrebet 107C

Arz    0  10   7   7  24
KC     7   7  10  10  34
Arz   D22 R23/124 P(37-20-2) 214
KC    D20 R30/128 P(29-22-1) 248
Arz-Sanders 100C;
KC-Alexander 116C

Ind   17   7   7   0  31
Bal    3  10   8  17  38
Ind   D26 R23/196 P(42-27-1) 344
Bal   D18 R27/116 P(25-16-0) 198
Ind-Faulk 192R, Small 153C,
Manning 357P; Bal-Holmes 103R

Atl    3   0  11   7  21
Slr    0   0   7   3  10
Atl   D20 R35/204 P(31-13-1) 170
Slr   D12 R20/40  P(34-16-0) 129
Atl-Anderson 188R
```

```
TB     7  14  10   0  31
ChiB   0  14   0   3  17
TB    D13 R39/114 P(22-13-1) 153
ChiB  D13 R24/69  P(42-19-0) 155

Ten    3   3   0  12  18
Sea    0   3   7  10  20
Ten   D23 R30/164 P(35-18-0) 179
Sea   D20 R19/82  P(39-24-1) 296

Jax    7  10  10   7  34
Cin    0  10   7   0  17
Jax   D16 R29/79  P(35-19-0) 243
Cin   D20 R24/131 P(43-24-2) 224
Jax-Smith 110C, Brunell 244P;
Cin-Dillon 107R

NO     3   0   0   7  10
Mia    0  13   3  14  30
NO    D11 R17/87  P(24-9-3)   70
Mia   D24 R38/120 P(40-22-1) 255
Mia-McDuffie 102C

Buf    0   6   9   6  21
NE     0  10   3   8  21
Buf   D23 R31/99  P(39-21-0) 329
NE    D24 R14/44  P(43-28-1) 215
Buf-Moulds 177C, Flutie 339P;
NE-Glenn 104C

Was    7  10   2  10  29
Oak    7   0   0  12  19
Was   D17 R31/94  P(31-16-0) 209
Oak   D23 R26/187 P(44-23-2) 189
Was-Davis 110C;
Oak-Kaufman 152R

Phi    0   6   7   3  16
GB    10   0   7   7  24
Phi   D15 R19/65  P(36-22-0) 167
GB    D26 R39/178 P(33-20-2) 321
GB-Holmes 163R, Schroeder 128C,
Favre 321P

Den   14   7   3   7  31
SD    10   0   0   6  16
Den   D18 R30/96  P(34-19-3) 226
SD    D21 R17/65  P(53-30-5) 302
Den-Smith 101C, Elway 239P;
SD-Whelihan 304P
```

MONDAY, NOVEMBER 30

```
NYG    7   0   0   0   7
SF     7   7   7  10  31
NYG   D18 R25/120 P(41-21-1) 224
SF    D23 R34/237 P(33-19-0) 229
NYG-Hilliard 141C; SF-Hearst 166R,
Owens 140C
```

THURSDAY, DECEMBER 3

```
Slr    0   6   0   8  14
Phi    0   0   0  17  17
Slr   D17 R26/82  P(37-22-1) 248
Phi   D16 R30/130 P(33-17-1) 169
```

SUNDAY, DECEMBER 6

```
SF     7  14   7   3  31
Car    7   0   7  14  28
SF    D22 R35/236 P(32-20-1) 238
Car   D22 R34/203 P(33-18-1) 226
SF-Hearst 139C

NE     3  10   0  10  23
Pit    0   6   3   0   9
NE    D19 R34/73  P(34-21-3) 304
Pit   D13 R13/54  P(45-21-2) 195
NE-Glenn 193C, Bledsoe 327P

SD     3  11   3   3  20
Was    0   7   0  15  22
SD    D21 R38/127 P(38-21-1) 217
Was   D17 R16/66  P(38-19-1) 212
SD-Fletcher 122R

Dal    3   0   0   0   3
NO     2  17   3   0  22
Dal   D10 R18/8   P(32-16-0) 174
NO    D17 R36/113 P(28-16-1) 215
NO-Hastings 122C

Ind    0  14   7   0  21
Atl    7  14   7   0  28
Ind   D17 R21/85  P(27-19-2) 159
Atl   D27 R35/137 P(28-20-1) 257
Atl-Anderson 122R, Martin 140C
```

```
Sea   14   7  10   0  31
NYJ    7   6   6  13  32
Sea   D13 R22/106 P(24-17-2) 271
NYJ   D31 R23/70  P(63-42-1) 418
Sea-Galloway 127C;
NYJ-Johnson 114C,
Testaverde 418P

Buf   10  10   6   7  33
Cin    0   0   3  10  13
Buf   D21 R34/139 P(30-18-3) 309
Cin   D15 R17/58  P(36-22-1) 176
Buf-Moulds 196C, Flutie 319P

KC    21   0   7   3  31
Den    7  14   0  14  35
KC    D20 R17/44  P(43-27-0) 222
Den   D23 R29/93  P(32-22-1) 383
Den-McCaffrey 103C, Smith 165C,
Elway 400P

NYG    7   3  10   3  23
Arz   14   0   3   2  19
NYG   D15 R42/200 P(23-8-2)  144
Arz   D17 R26/75  P(40-18-2) 253
NYG-Brown 124R

Det    3  10   3   6  22
Jax   14  10   3  10  37
Det   D16 R22/120 P(33-14-0) 212
Jax   D24 R43/205 P(24-15-0) 221
Det-Sanders 102R, Moore 116C;
Jax-Taylor 183R, Smith 112C

Mia   17   7   0   3  27
Oak    0   3   7   7  17
Mia   D9  R31/90  P(33-22-0) 170
Oak   D23 R23/107 P(44-21-6) 207
Oak-Brown 104C

ChiB   0   0  14   8  22
Min   14  13   7  14  48
ChiB  D19 R24/67  P(25-17-0) 272
Min   D23 R27/109 P(31-21-1) 349
ChiB-Engram 140C,
Stenstrom 303P; Min-Moss 106C,
Cunningham 349P

Bal    0   0   7   7  14
Ten   10   3   0   3  16
Bal   D10 R14/58  P(28-15-1) 163
Ten   D19 R33/78  P(43-25-1) 213
Bal-Turner 108C
```

MONDAY, DECEMBER 7

```
GB     3   3   3  13  22
TB     7   7   7   3  24
GB    D23 R22/105 P(41-29-0) 228
TB    D12 R30/105 P(23-9-1)  178
```

SUNDAY, DECEMBER 13

```
Cin    3   3   6  14  26
Ind   10  14   7   8  39
Cin   D22 R29/155 P(33-19-0) 223
Ind   D21 R31/128 P(26-17-0) 210
Ind-Faulk 115R

Pit    3   0   0   0   3
TB     3   3   7   3  16
Pit   D10 R27/88  P(23-10-4) 147
TB    D14 R45/144 P(18-9-0)  109

Was   14   7   7   0  28
Car    0   8  10   7  25
Was   D27 R32/160 P(42-23-0) 249
Car   D16 R24/124 P(25-16-2) 241
Was-Connell 116C;
Car-Biakabutuka 103R,
Muhammad 118C

Oak    0   7   7   7  21
Buf    7   7  14   7  44
Oak   D13 R22/91  P(26-16-2) 182
Buf   D18 R39/134 P(26-17-0) 182
ChiB   7   0   6   7  20
GB    10   0   0  16  26
ChiB  D12 R20/94  P(28-16-0)  98
GB    D24 R27/119 P(42-26-2) 274
GB-Levens 105R, Freeman 103C

NE     3  12   3   0  18
Slr   10   7  15   0  32
NE    D14 R28/200 P(37-11-1) 119
Slr   D18 R31/116 P(35-18-1) 162
NE-Edwards 196R
```

```
Den    3  3  3  7  16
NYG    3  7  0 10  20
Den  D21R33/170  P(36-19-1) 159
NYG  D18R25/138  P(33-21-0) 254
Den-Davis 147R; NYG-Brown 112R

Atl   14  3  0 10  27
NO     0  7  7  3  17
Atl  D25R37/182  P(28-19-2) 322
NO   D15R18/52   P(38-18-3) 164
Atl-Anderson 148R, Martin 109C,
Mathis 198C, Chandler 345P

Arz   10  0  3  7  20
Phi    0 10  0  7  17
Arz  D25R43/204  P(26-18-1) 220
Phi  D21R33/148  P(28-16-1) 219
Arz-Murrell 174R, Moore 109C;
Phi-Staley 141R

SD     7  7  0  3  17
Sea   14  7  7 10  38
SD   D16R25/66   P(42-17-7) 211
Sea  D18R34/108  P(31-16-3) 130

Ten    0 10  0  6  16
Jax   10  0  0  3  13
Ten  D20R27/131  P(39-22-1) 223
Jax  D15R23/69   P(29-18-1) 172
Jax-Smith 103C

Min   12 13 10  3  38
Bal   14  0  0 14  28
Min  D26R33/88   P(56-32-1) 332
Bal  D26R19/55   P(26-16-1) 212
Min-Cunningham 345P;
Bal-Turner 147C

Dal    0  3  0 14  17
KC     3  0  3 14  20
Dal  D14R16/51   P(35-18-1) 196
KC   D23R38/183  P(41-19-0) 200
KC-Morris 137R

NYJ    7  0  7  7  21
Mia    3  0  0 13  16
NYJ  D16R23/82   P(29-17-1) 232
Mia  D22R18/79   P(57-30-1) 278
NYJ-Chrebet 105C;
Mia-McDuffie 105C, Marino 321P
```

MONDAY, DECEMBER 14

```
Det    0  0  0 13  13
SF     7 14  7  7  35
Det  D25R19/69   P(44-21-2) 311
SF   D29R46/328  P(18-12-1) 81
SF-Hearst 198R
```

SATURDAY, DECEMBER 19

```
NYJ    7  0 10  0  17
Buf    0  7  3  0  10
NYJ  D14R27/92   P(23-14-0) 177
Buf  D21R35/149  P(38-14-1) 217
Buf-Moulds 107C

TB     7  6  3  0  16
Was    7  0  0 13  20
TB   D17R37/150  P(34-14-2) 87
Was  D11R20/90   P(33-16-1) 136
```

SUNDAY, DECEMBER 20

```
Slr    3  7  3  0  13
Car    0  7  3 10  20
Slr  D16R26/110  P(37-20-2) 151
Car  D11R27/82   P(25-15-0) 164

Bal    0  0  3  0  3
ChiB   3  0  7  0  24
Bal  D12R17/24   P(34-20-1) 154
ChiB D20R34/189  P(28-19-0) 202
ChiB-Allen 163R

Ten    0  7  7  8  22
GB    14  7  3  6  30
Ten  D22R24/79   P(49-29-1) 262
GB   D16R32/117  P(25-15-0) 245
GB-Freeman 186C

SF     0 21  0  0  21
NE     7  7  0 10  24
SF   D21R34/151  P(24-19-2) 259
NE   D20R31/132  P(30-14-2) 200
SF-Hearst 107R, Rice 115C;
NE-Edwards 101R
```


```
KC     0  0  7  0  7
NYG    7  7  0 14  28
KC   D15R19/61   P(36-18-4) 218
NYG  D25R36/160  P(34-16-0) 149
NYG-Brown 103R

Cin    3 13  6  3  25
Pit    0  7 14  3  24
Cin  D23R33/124  P(41-21-1) 359
Pit  D11R23/125  P(24-10-1) 86
Cin-Bennett 119C, Scott 152C,
Blake 367P; Pit-Bettis 104R

Atl    7  3  0 14  24
Det    7  7  3  0  17
Atl  D20R35/145  P(19-11-0) 123
Det  D17R30/117  P(26-15-2) 141
Atl-Anderson 147R

Oak    0 14  3  0  17
SD     3  0  7  0  10
Oak  D14R35/120  P(25-14-2) 167
SD   D16R23/79   P(39-19-2) 236
Oak-Jett 106C

Ind    7  3 10  3  23
Sea    7  3  0 17  27
Ind  D18R18/32   P(39-23-1) 330
Sea  D23R41/226  P(29-16-0) 150
Ind-Small 120C, Manning 335P;
Sea-Watters 178R

NO     0 10  0  7  17
Arz    3  3  7  6  19
NO   D18R22/82   P(43-25-0) 238
Arz  D28R26/119  P(44-32-1) 394
Arz-Sanders 138C, Plummer 394P

Jax    0  3  0  7  10
Min    3  9 14 24  50
Jax  D15R28/138  P(27-12-2) 169
Min  D25R33/180  P(37-20-0) 237
Jax-Taylor 105R; Min-Smith 101R

Phi    3  0  3  3  9
Dal    7  0  6  0  13
Phi  D15R26/125  P(43-24-1) 231
Dal  D11R34/153  P(23-10-1) 95
Dal-Smith 110R
```

MONDAY, DECEMBER 21

```
Den    3 10  0  8  21
Mia    0 14  0 14  31
Den  D14R23/58   P(40-15-2) 161
Mia  D19R28/36   P(38-23-1) 355
Mia-Thomas 136C, Marino 355P
```

SATURDAY, DECEMBER 26

```
Min    2  6 15  3  26
Ten    3 10  3  0  16
Min  D22R29/103  P(35-23-1) 235
Ten  D20R21/90   P(36-18-0) 264

KC     0  7 17  7  31
Oak   14  0  3  7  24
KC   D20R26/119  P(32-20-2) 197
Oak  D25R24/40   P(42-26-0) 281
Oak-Brown 140C
```

SUNDAY, DECEMBER 27

```
TB    14 14  0  7  35
Cin    0  0  0  0  0
TB   D22R51/223  P(16-10-1) 97
Cin  D11R23/87   P(27-11-2) 159

Car    3  3 14  7  27
Ind    3 13  0  3  19
Car  D17R43/183  P(21-12-1) 149
Ind  D12R18/72   P(35-17-2) 207
Car-Biakabutuka 109R, Ismail 109C,
Sanders 106C

GB     7  0  6  3  16
ChiB   3  0  7  0  13
GB   D14R27/70   P(26-19-2) 169
ChiB D17R31/98   P(31-17-2) 183

Mia    0  6 10  0  16
Atl   21  3 14  0  38
Mia  D20R19/38   P(42-25-2) 362
Atl  D15R31/143  P(13-8-0) 203
Mia-Gadsden 153C, Marino 320P;
Atl-Anderson 103R, Martin 105C

NE     0  3  0  7  10
NYJ    3 14  7  7  31
NE   D9R20/130   P(31-14-0) 119
NYJ  D21R41/149  P(31-18-1) 190
NYJ-Martin 102R, Testaverde 179P
```


```
Det    0  3  0  7  10
Bal    9  7  0  3  19
Det  D11R21/44   P(29-18-0) 192
Bal  D19R35/153  P(28-18-0) 142
Det-Moore 120C; Bal-Holmes 132R

Buf   21  7  3 14  45
NO     0 14  7 12  33
Buf  D21R34/116  P(18-12-0) 192
NO   D26R19/75   P(54-26-2) 291
NO-Bech 113C, Cleeland 112C

Sea    7  0  0 14  21
Den    0 14  0 14  28
Sea  D19R13/24   P(38-23-1) 217
Den  D40R40/195  P(36-26-0) 316
Den-Davis 178R, Smith 158C,
Elway 338P

SD     0  3  0 10  13
Arz    7  3  3  3  16
SD   D22R36/174  P(40-16-4) 203
Arz  D16R18/25   P(41-20-0) 245
SD-Fletcher 127R;
Arz-Sanders 106C

NYG    3  3  7  7  20
Phi    0 10  0  0  10
NYG  D22R43/209  P(26-15-0) 130
Phi  D12R24/123  P(27-13-1) 141
NYG-Brown 112R

Was    7  0  0  0  7
Dal    3 17  0  3  23
Was  D14R21/80   P(36-21-1) 212
Dal  D22R34/156  P(26-15-0) 222
Was-Fletcher 127R

Slr    0  7  0 12  19
SF     3  7 18 10  38
Slr  D17R18/57   P(41-19-1) 264
SF   D22R35/120  P(32-22-0) 277
Slr-Proehl 100C

Det    3 22  0  3  28
Sea    0  7  7  6  20
Det  D19R36/167  P(26-16-1) 202
Sea  D16R16/31   P(30-20-0) 174
Det-Crowell 141C
```

MONDAY, DECEMBER 28

```
Pit    0  3  0  0  3
Jax    0 14  7  0  21
Pit  D20R36/205  P(37-17-2) 156
Jax  D16R33/129  P(19-10-0) 168
Pit-Bettis 139R
```

1999 NFL

SUNDAY, SEPTEMBER 12

```
Cin    7 14  8  6  35
Ten   14 12  0 10  36
Cin  D28R42/201  P(34-20-2) 197
Ten  D22R18/69   P(32-21-1) 334
Ten-Dyson 162C, McNair 341P

Pit    7 13  6 17  43
Cle    0  0  0  0  0
Pit  D33R57/217  P(32-24-0) 247
Cle  D2R9/9      P(16-6-2) 31

Arz    0  6  6 13  25
Phi    3  3  0  0  6
Arz  D23R36/78   P(48-25-3) 266
Phi  D13R26/138  P(26-12-2) 67
Phi-Staley 111R

Min    0 17  0  0  17
Atl    0  0  7  7  14
Min  D19R32/115  P(33-22-0) 184
Atl  D22R23/81   P(31-18-0) 278

KC     3  0  7  7  17
ChiB   7 13  0  0  20
KC   D17R17/71   P(42-20-1) 278
ChiB D22R28/81   P(47-31-0) 307
KC-Alexander 154C

NYG    7  0  7  3  17
TB     0 10  3  0  13
NYG  D4R25/28    P(24-12-0) 79
TB   D15R27/77   P(42-18-4) 177

NE     3  7 17  3  30
NYJ    7  9  6  6  28
NE   D16R27/70   P(30-21-1) 326
NYJ  D19R24/106  P(36-20-3) 257
NE-Glenn 113C, Bledsoe 340P;
NYJ-Johnson 194C
```


```
Buf    0  6  8  0  14
Ind    7  7 10  7  31
Buf  D19R15/47   P(42-22-2) 274
Ind  D20R29/109  P(33-21-2) 284
Buf-Moulds 147C, Flutie 300P;
Ind-James 112R, Green 124C,
Harrison 121C

Car    0 10  0  0  10
NO     7  3  0  9  19
Car  D12R16/85   P(32-16-1) 161
NO   D13R41/147  P(22-11-0) 108

SF     3  0  0  0  3
Jax    3  3 18 17  41
SF   D11R20/94   P(35-14-3) 109
Jax  D18R34/97   P(31-22-0) 247
Jax-Smith 139C

Oak    3  7  7  7  24
GB     7  7  0 14  28
Oak  D20R32/153  P(31-16-1) 210
GB   D25R20/91   P(47-28-3) 318
GB-Freeman 111C, Favre 333P

Dal    7  7  0 21  6  41
Was    3 10 22  0  0  35
Dal  D30R34/186  P(49-28-3) 355
Was  D25R30/135  P(34-20-0) 369
Dal-Smith 109R, Irvin 201C,
Ismail 149C, Aikman 362P;
Was-Davis 109R, Connell 137C,
Westbrook 159C

Bal    0  3  0  7  10
Slr    3 14  0 10  27
Bal  D13R15/60   P(40-17-2) 163
Slr  D23R25/59   P(44-28-2) 284
Slr-Warner 309P

Det    3 22  0  3  28
Sea    0  7  7  6  20
Det  D19R36/167  P(26-16-1) 202
Sea  D16R16/31   P(30-20-0) 174
Det-Crowell 141C
```

MONDAY, SEPTEMBER 13

```
Mia    0 17  7 14  38
Den    7  0  7  7  21
Mia  D22R33/111  P(23-15-0) 215
Den  D25R26/113  P(40-24-0) 240
Mia-Martin 101C;
Den-McCaffrey 105C
```

SUNDAY, SEPTEMBER 19

```
Den    0  3  0  7  10
KC     0  6 10 10  26
Den  D20R26/88   P(31-20-2) 156
KC   D17R41/188  P(20-15-1) 177
KC-Anders 142R, Alexander 117C

Cle    0  0  0  0  0
Ten    2 14  3  7  26
Cle  D12R16/83   P(24-12-0) 90
Ten  D24R34/102  P(40-31-0) 310
Ten-O'Donnell 310P

Sea    0  0  0 14  14
ChiB   0  3  0 10  13
Sea  D19R28/100  P(30-18-0) 249
ChiB D20R30/115  P(44-23-0) 196
Sea-Mayes 137C

NYJ    0  0  3  0  3
Buf    0  7  3  7  17
NYJ  D11R18/74   P(28-13-0) 116
Buf  D23R47/224  P(25-15-0) 160
Buf-Smith 113R

NO     0 14  7  0  21
SF     7  7  0 14  28
NO   D17R30/101  P(37-20-2) 223
SF   D21R23/88   P(35-23-1) 223

Oak    0  6 16  0  22
Min    7  3  0  7  17
Oak  D22R33/162  P(33-21-0) 240
Min  D19R15/34   P(39-23-2) 320
Min-Reed 100C, Cunningham 364P

Pit    7  7  3  6  23
Bal    7  0 10  0  17
Pit  D19R36/149  P(27-18-0) 121
Bal  D16R29/125  P(31-14-2) 167
Bal-Rhett 101R
```


```
Was   21 12 10  7  50
NYG    0 14  0  7  21
Was  D28R41/164  P(28-20-0) 231
NYG  D18R17/83   P(38-23-2) 290
Was-Davis 126R; NYG-Hilliard 114C,
Toomer 105C

Arz    0 13  3  0  16
Mia    3 10  6  0  19
Arz  D13R28/64   P(28-12-4) 120
Mia  D14R31/83   P(35-21-2) 221

TB     7  6  6  0  19
Phi    5  0  0  0  5
TB   D16R44/156  P(14-7-2) 64
Phi  D9R20/84    P(30-16-1) 66

SD    13 15  3  3  34
Cin    7  0  0  0  7
SD   D14R35/91   P(31-18-0) 175
Cin  D10R17/47   P(33-17-1) 133

GB     3  3  0  9  15
Det    0 14  0  9  23
GB   D21R31/154  P(41-20-1) 283
Det  D9R32/82    P(16-9-2) 196
GB-Levens 153R; Det-Morton 118C

Jax    3  3  6 10  22
Car    0 14  0  8  22
Jax  D27R46/214  P(32-20-0) 200
Car  D16R18/87   P(26-11-0) 196
Jax-Stewart 124R, Smith 115C;
Car-Muhammad 103C

Ind   14 14  0  0  28
NE     0  7  7 17  31
Ind  D23R33/121  P(30-18-2) 223
NE   D26R27/108  P(45-27-0) 292
Ind-James 118R, Harrison 105C;
NE-Glenn 122C, Bledsoe 299P
```

MONDAY, SEPTEMBER 20

```
Atl    0  0  0  7  7
Dal   10  0  7  7  24
Atl  D13R24/85   P(38-16-3) 239
Dal  D17R37/134  P(22-10-2) 98
Dal-Smith 109R
```

SUNDAY, SEPTEMBER 26

```
Ind   10  0  3 14  27
SD     0  3  0 16  19
Ind  D26R22/64   P(54-29-1) 404
SD   D16R25/95   P(37-15-1) 179
Ind-Harrison 196C, Manning 404P

NYG    7  0  0  7  14
NE     0  7  6  3  16
NYG  D19R26/57   P(36-23-0) 201
NE   D17R29/67   P(28-20-0) 223

ChiB   7  3  7  0  17
Oak    7  7  0 10  24
ChiB D11R16/34   P(35-23-1) 198
Oak  D22R26/109  P(35-26-0) 283
Oak-Brown 121C

Ten    0  0  7 13  20
Jax    3  0 14  2  19
Ten  D15R26/51   P(32-17-1) 191
Jax  D22R33/137  P(42-22-3) 232
Jax-Smith 129C

Det    0  7  6  8  21
KC     7 10  7  7  31
Det  D18R22/118  P(34-16-2) 193
KC   D21R35/155  P(29-20-0) 228

Min    7  3  3  7  20
GB     0 10  3 10  23
Min  D21R29/97   P(32-18-2) 231
GB   D22R27/71   P(39-24-0) 289
Min-Reed 108C; GB-Favre 304P

Sea   17  9  0  3  29
Pit    0  0  0 10  10
Sea  D16R34/90   P(29-18-0) 251
Pit  D15R19/65   P(41-21-5) 207
Sea-Dawkins 105C

Cle    0  0  3  7  10
Bal    3  7  7  0  17
Cle  D11R24/100  P(32-13-1) 89
Bal  D16R37/184  P(25-12-3) 150
Bal-Rhett 113R

Den    7  0  0  3  10
TB     0  7  0  6  13
Den  D8R20/53    P(29-14-1) 120
TB   D17R42/165  P(19-15-0) 78
TB-Alstott 131R
```

Atl 0 0 7 0 **7**
Slr 7 21 7 0 **35**
Atl D12 R22/68 P(31-19-1) 165
Slr D19 R34/167 P(25-17-0) 275
Slr-Faulk 105R

Cin 0 0 3 0 **3**
Car 10 3 7 7 **27**
Cin D20 R28/129 P(43-24-1) 243
Car D13 R18/146 P(23-17-0) 197
Cin-Dillon 113R;
Car-Biakabutuka 132R,
Muhammad 117C

Phi 0 0 0 0 **0**
Buf 9 10 7 0 **26**
Phi D11 R12/22 P(37-20-0) 147
Buf D25 R40/191 P(29-20-1) 186

Was 0 10 3 14 **27**
NYJ 7 0 7 6 **20**
Was D21 R29/96 P(28-17-0) 237
NYJ D19 R31/142 P(31-17-1) 195

MONDAY, SEPTEMBER 27

SF 14 3 0 7 **24**
Arz 0 0 0 10 **10**
SF D18 R36/210 P(29-18-1) 112
Arz D20 R29/101 P(31-16-2) 149
SF-Phillips 102R

SUNDAY, OCTOBER 3

NE 0 6 7 6 **19**
Cle 7 0 0 0 **7**
NE D23 R35/90 P(43-29-0) 361
Cle D12 R20/70 P(28-13-0) 180
NE-Glenn 214C, Bledsoe 393P;
Cle-Johnson 131C

Slr 7 14 14 3 **38**
Cin 3 0 0 7 **10**
Slr D18 R28/73 P(22-18-0) 326
Cin D18 R26/92 P(41-19-1) 165
Slr-Bruce 152C, Warner 310P

Oak 7 7 0 7 **21**
Sea 3 6 10 3 **22**
Oak D21 R32/166 P(34-19-1) 217
Sea D15 R26/75 P(30-15-1) 201
Oak-Wheatley 100R

Ten 7 3 3 9 **22**
SF 0 14 0 10 **24**
Ten D17 R21/55 P(40-20-1) 337
SF D17 R26/86 P(33-21-0) 243
Ten-Thigpen 143C, O'Donnell 355P

NO 0 7 0 3 **10**
ChiB 0 0 0 14 **14**
NO D17 R35/137 P(28-15-0) 132
ChiB D20 R28/112 P(43-25-2) 212
ChiB-Conway 103C

KC 14 0 0 0 **14**
SD 0 7 0 14 **21**
KC D19 R38/121 P(40-19-4) 193
SD D8 R17/40 P(29-14-2) 92

Car 21 3 3 9 **36**
Was 0 28 7 3 **38**
Car D23 R19/155 P(47-23-1) 308
Was D22 R31/110 P(33-20-0) 308
Car-Biakabutuka 142R,
Muhammad 151C, Beuerlein 334P;
Was-Connell 134C, Westbrook 140C,
Johnson 337P

NYJ 7 0 0 14 **21**
Den 10 3 0 0 **13**
NYJ D23 R35/110 P(28-17-2) 224
Den D17 R29/108 P(36-18-5) 218

Arz 0 7 0 0 **7**
Dal 14 7 7 7 **35**
Arz D12 R21/71 P(39-20-4) 137
Dal D17 R39/114 P(21-15-0) 192
Dal-Ismail 101C

TB 0 7 0 7 **14**
Min 21 0 0 0 **21**
TB D22 R24/84 P(39-25-1) 286
Min D20 R23/68 P(35-26-1) 296
TB-Dilfer 301P; Min-Moss 120C

Bal 0 3 7 9 **19**
Atl 0 6 7 0 **13**
Bal D17 R34/144 P(27-13-0) 163
Atl D20 R26/52 P(46-24-0) 246
Bal-Rhett 136R

Phi 9 0 3 3 **15**
NYG 7 3 3 3 **16**
Phi D10 R26/84 P(22-9-2) 90
NYG D24 R38/128 P(41-21-3) 233
NYG-Toomer 123C

Jax 0 7 3 7 **17**
Pit 0 3 0 0 **3**
Jax D13 R35/124 P(25-10-1) 80
Pit D14 R31/117 P(32-15-1) 99

MONDAY, OCTOBER 4

Buf 3 10 0 10 **23**
Mia 6 3 0 9 **18**
Buf D11 R27/73 P(25-12-0) 177
Mia D18 R24/59 P(44-22-2) 233

SUNDAY, OCTOBER 10

Pit 7 7 0 7 **21**
Buf 3 7 10 4 **24**
Pit D17 R23/48 P(29-21-1) 207
Buf D24 R33/111 P(32-21-0) 254
Buf-Moulds 122C

NE 7 0 0 7 **14**
KC 3 3 4 6 **16**
NE D19 R19/62 P(45-23-2) 316
KC D20 R42/140 P(26-18-1) 189
NE-Simmons 107C, Bledsoe 334P

SF 3 14 3 0 **20**
Slr 21 7 7 7 **42**
SF D21 R21/72 P(36-22-3) 233
Slr D20 R28/109 P(23-20-1) 314
Slr-Bruce 134C, Warner 323P

Mia 3 6 0 25 **34**
Ind 3 7 7 14 **31**
Mia D19 R28/76 P(38-25-0) 393
Ind D18 R24/68 P(24-17-1) 264
Mia-Gadsden 123C, Martin 166C,
Marino 393P

Dal 3 7 0 0 **10**
Phi 0 0 0 13 **13**
Dal D19 R32/130 P(39-21-2) 170
Phi D12 R27/105 P(30-11-1) 139
Dal-Smith 114R; Phi-Staley 110R

Atl 7 0 7 6 **20**
NO 0 17 0 0 **17**
Atl D12 R33/104 P(20-11-0) 147
NO D18 R24/71 P(40-22-2) 319
NO-Kennison 138C

ChiB 7 7 7 3 **24**
Min 3 9 3 7 **22**
ChiB D23 R33/101 P(42-28-0) 278
Min D26 R20/166 P(47-25-3) 279
Min-Smith 107R, Moss 122C,
Cunningham 309P

NYG 0 0 0 3 **3**
Arz 0 14 0 0 **14**
NYG D15 R28/107 P(38-24-1) 178
Arz D13 R27/31 P(27-17-0) 175
Arz-Boston 101C

Den 3 10 0 3 **16**
Oak 0 0 10 3 **13**
Den D16 R28/81 P(30-17-1) 221
Oak D17 R24/55 P(36-25-2) 210
Den-Kennison 138C

Bal 3 3 5 0 **11**
Ten 7 0 7 0 **14**
Bal D16 R26/68 P(37-15-0) 178
Ten D16 R24/56 P(35-24-0) 216

SD 0 10 3 7 **20**
Det 0 7 0 3 **10**
SD D15 R24/64 P(34-20-1) 192
Det D14 R24/37 P(38-21-1) 192

Cin 6 6 0 6 **18**
Cle 0 14 0 3 **17**
Cin D25 R36/215 P(42-25-0) 204
Cle D13 R23/80 P(27-15-1) 144
Cin-Dillon 168R, Scott 110C

TB 0 13 0 10 **23**
GB 10 3 3 10 **26**
TB D21 R32/173 P(26-16-3) 100
GB D18 R23/98 P(40-22-0) 352
GB-Freeman 152C, Schroeder 158C,
Favre 390P

MONDAY, OCTOBER 11

Jax 7 3 3 3 **16**
NYJ 0 3 0 3 **6**
Jax D16 R34/125 P(35-21-0) 197
NYJ D13 R24/89 P(38-19-2) 141

SUNDAY, OCTOBER 17

Mia 3 16 0 12 **31**
NE 14 10 3 3 **30**
Mia D22 R32/122 P(45-25-2) 195
NE D14 R14/46 P(36-17-1) 213
Mia-Martin 118C

Ind 0 7 3 6 **16**
NYJ 6 7 0 0 **13**
Ind D19 R28/108 P(35-21-1) 210
NYJ D16 R29/156 P(30-16-1) 125
Ind-James 111R; NYJ-Martin 128R

Oak 10 3 7 0 **20**
Buf 7 0 0 7 **14**
Oak D23 R48/195 P(22-15-0) 148
Buf D14 R13/109 P(41-19-3) 201

Cle 0 7 0 0 **7**
Jax 3 3 8 10 **24**
Cle D16 R28/113 P(23-18-0) 130
Jax D21 R33/103 P(33-24-0) 222

Phi 7 13 0 0 **20**
ChiB 7 3 10 3 **23**
Phi D19 R26/99 P(39-22-0) 217
ChiB D17 R29/113 P(33-17-2) 239
Phi-Staley 101R;
ChiB-Robinson 136C

Pit 7 0 7 3 **17**
Cin 3 0 0 0 **3**
Pit D18 R37/130 P(29-17-0) 125
Cin D14 R20/84 P(38-19-2) 177
Pit-Bettis 111R

GB 3 0 0 7 **10**
Den 3 0 21 7 **31**
GB D5 R11/21 P(23-7-3) 112
Den D28 R51/151 P(31-19-1) 363
Den-Gary 124R, Chamberlain 123C,
McCaffrey 116C, Griese 363P

Ten 0 0 7 17 **24**
NO 3 7 3 8 **21**
Ten D15 R35/165 P(25-12-2) 113
NO D22 R21/55 P(45-28-2) 354
Ten-George 155R; NO-Tolliver 354P

Slr 14 14 6 7 **41**
Atl 0 10 0 3 **13**
Slr D17 R28/189 P(20-13-0) 94
Atl D16 R19/46 P(36-20-2) 270
Slr-Faulk 181R

Car 0 24 7 0 **31**
SF 6 10 0 13 **29**
Car D18 R27/101 P(36-23-3) 282
SF D23 R24/124 P(45-22-0) 209
Car-Beuerlein 300P

Min 0 0 14 9 **23**
Det 10 9 0 6 **25**
Min D17 R19/60 P(27-20-2) 267
Det D19 R25/110 P(40-24-0) 189
Min-James 111R, Moss 125C

Sea 0 3 7 0 **10**
SD 0 0 7 6 **13**
Sea D15 R27/61 P(29-17-1) 140
SD D19 R21/49 P(45-27-4) 281

Was 0 10 7 7 **24**
Arz 3 0 7 0 **10**
Was D24 R34/167 P(40-24-2) 243
Arz D15 R20/67 P(43-20-3) 207
Was-Connell 110C

MONDAY, OCTOBER 18

Dal 3 0 0 7 **10**
NYG 0 3 0 10 **13**
Dal D14 R25/24 P(33-20-1) 195
NYG D13 R30/75 P(21-15-0) 153

THURSDAY, OCTOBER 21

KC 0 7 7 21 **35**
Bal 0 0 0 8 **8**
KC D12 R35/112 P(16-9-0) 106
Bal D18 R27/105 P(51-23-3) 172

SUNDAY, OCTOBER 24

Was 0 10 10 0 **20**
Dal 10 7 7 14 **38**
Was D14 R16/61 P(35-23-0) 211
Dal D23 R34/108 P(32-20-0) 244

Cin 0 3 0 7 **10**
Ind 7 17 0 7 **31**
Cin D12 R26/105 P(31-17-0) 149
Ind D18 R28/57 P(33-17-1) 278
Ind-Harrison 156C

SF 3 10 3 0 **16**
Min 7 17 7 9 **40**
SF D14 R21/82 P(35-18-2) 178
Min D25 R31/155 P(28-15-1) 240
Min-Hoard 105R

Den 10 0 3 10 **23**
NE 10 7 7 0 **24**
Den D23 R27/133 P(38-25-0) 309
NE D15 R28/130 P(22-13-0) 192
Den-McCaffrey 111C, Griese 316P;
NE-Allen 106R

Det 0 10 14 0 **24**
Car 3 3 0 3 **9**
Det D20 R27/90 P(27-16-1) 210
Car D22 R21/61 P(47-26-1) 259

NO 3 0 0 0 **3**
NYG 7 7 10 7 **31**
NO D12 R27/107 P(35-14-3) 163
NYG D19 R37/106 P(29-19-1) 215
NO-Williams 111R

ChiB 0 0 0 3 **3**
TB 3 3 0 0 **6**
ChiB D15 R24/86 P(45-19-2) 189
TB D11 R28/124 P(27-16-0) 101

Phi 0 3 7 3 **13**
Mia 10 3 0 3 **16**
Phi D11 R22/93 P(25-13-1) 89
Mia D15 R39/149 P(21-15-1) 134

Cle 3 0 0 0 **3**
Slr 14 7 3 10 **34**
Cle D13 R15/94 P(40-22-2) 178
Slr D27 R29/211 P(34-27-0) 225
Slr-Faulk 133R

GB 7 7 14 3 **31**
SD 3 0 0 0 **3**
GB D19 R28/129 P(25-12-1) 166
SD D21 R27/76 P(54-25-6) 227

NYJ 0 10 10 3 **23**
Oak 3 0 7 14 **24**
NYJ D14 R34/177 P(22-13-2) 147
Oak D24 R23/117 P(51-26-1) 344
NYJ-Martin 123R; Oak-Brown 190C,
Gannon 352P

Buf 0 3 6 7 **16**
Sea 13 10 0 3 **26**
Buf D25 R25/98 P(50-24-2) 254
Sea D18 R32/110 P(30-17-0) 275
Buf-Price 106C; Sea-Mayes 105C

MONDAY, OCTOBER 25

Atl 0 0 0 9 **9**
Pit 7 6 0 0 **13**
Atl D20 R25/49 P(34-20-1) 187
Pit D14 R33/111 P(21-13-0) 115
Atl-Mathis 166C

SUNDAY, OCTOBER 31

Car 3 3 7 7 **20**
Atl 7 6 7 7 **27**
Car D19 R18/63 P(35-21-3) 227
Atl D20 R32/107 P(21-14-0) 176

Slr 0 0 14 7 **21**
Ten 21 0 3 0 **24**
Slr D23 R19/128 P(46-29-0) 287
Ten D17 R31/103 P(29-13-0) 178
Slr-Warner 328P

Buf 0 3 0 10 **13**
Bal 10 0 0 0 **10**
Buf D19 R29/111 P(40-18-3) 138
Bal D22 R27/82 P(34-13-1) 118

ChiB 0 14 14 0 **28**
Was 14 17 14 3 **48**
ChiB D22 R26/74 P(63-36-4) 371
Was D18 R24/164 P(33-17-1) 212
ChiB-Robinson 161C;
Was-Davis 143R

SD 0 0 0 0 **0**
KC 10 10 14 0 **34**
SD D10 R20/72 P(37-20-2) 141
KC D11 R39/97 P(15-11-0) 186
KC-Alexander 113C

Jax 14 13 7 7 **41**
Cin 0 3 0 6 **9**
Jax D23 R34/183 P(28-17-0) 194
Cin D14 R23/93 P(36-20-2) 207
Jax-Taylor 128R

Mia 3 3 7 3 **16**
Oak 0 3 6 0 **9**
Mia D19 R42/141 P(32-16-0) 184
Oak D13 R19/80 P(31-9-1) 107
Oak-Brown 113C

Min 0 13 0 10 **23**
Den 0 8 20 0 **28**
Min D15 R24/97 P(29-17-0) 205
Den D24 R30/135 P(40-24-1) 256
Min-James 117R, Carter 144C,
Manning 313P; Den-Smith 117C

Dal 3 10 7 0 **24**
Ind 3 3 15 13 **34**
Dal D18 R26/103 P(25-19-0) 129
Ind D18 R23/119 P(34-22-0) 300
Ind-James 117R, Manning 313P

NYG 3 0 14 6 **23**
Phi 3 14 0 0 **17**
NYG D20 R25/92 P(41-26-0) 207
Phi D15 R31/112 P(30-19-2) 248
Phi-Small 119C

Cle 0 7 7 7 **21**
NO 7 3 3 3 **16**
Cle D9 R21/62 P(19-11-0) 181
NO D25 R50/231 P(29-13-2) 120
NO-Williams 179R

NE 14 6 0 7 **27**
Arz 0 0 0 3 **3**
NE D17 R43/142 P(22-14-0) 244
Arz D8 R19/76 P(39-13-2) 90
NE-Jefferson 113C, Bledsoe 276P

TB 0 3 0 0 **3**
Det 0 10 7 3 **20**
TB D18 R22/72 P(44-29-0) 220
Det D13 R24/147 P(19-10-0) 109
Det-Hill 123R

MONDAY, NOVEMBER 1

Sea 7 7 7 6 **27**
GB 0 7 0 0 **7**
Sea D12 R36/132 P(19-12-0) 90
GB D17 R29/125 P(41-16-4) 182
Sea-Watters 125R; GB-Levens 104R,
Bradford 106C

SUNDAY, NOVEMBER 7

Arz 0 7 0 0 **7**
NYJ 3 0 3 6 **12**
Arz D10 R18/55 P(26-16-0) 151
NYJ D15 R46/184 P(18-12-0) 111
NYJ-Martin 131R

KC 3 7 7 0 **17**
Ind 3 10 3 9 **25**
KC D19 R29/108 P(34-19-0) 211
Ind D22 R23/119 P(33-21-0) 256
Ind-James 109R

Jax 7 10 7 10 **30**
Atl 0 7 0 0 **7**
Jax D20 R34/152 P(34-19-0) 215
Atl D10 R11/42 P(30-17-3) 140
Jax-Taylor 124R

Slr 2 0 10 15 **27**
Det 0 10 11 10 **31**
Slr D20 R16/57 P(43-25-2) 275
Det D17 R20/21 P(36-22-0) 311
Slr-Warner 305P; Det-Crowell 163C

Phi 0 0 0 7 **7**
Car 0 23 3 7 **33**
Phi D17 R23/168 P(29-11-1) 81
Car D24 R38/111 P(35-21-0) 270
Phi-Staley 140R

Buf 3 14 14 3 **34**
Was 3 0 7 7 **17**
Buf D24 R49/204 P(22-16-0) 209
Was D16 R13/57 P(37-19-1) 222

THE GAMES

Bal 7 10 7 17 **41**
Cle 3 0 0 6 9
Bal D20 R38/203 P(25-14-0) 112
Cle D10 R20/56 P(36-16-2) 114
Bal-Rhett 117R

ChiB 7 0 7 0 **14**
GB 3 7 0 3 13
ChiB D19 R29/160 P(34-18-3) 151
GB D21 R29/85 P(40-27-1) 254

TB 7 10 7 7 **31**
NO 3 3 0 10 16
TB D18 R40/156 P(20-15-0) 225
NO D23 R23/98 P(37-18-2) 205
TB-Alstott 117R

Ten 0 0 0 0 0
Mia 0 14 0 3 **17**
Ten D14 R23/103 P(42-22-3) 190
Mia D14 R27/52 P(25-15-0) 185

Den 3 10 7 13 **33**
SD 0 3 7 7 17
Den D17 R31/114 P(24-14-0) 127
SD D19 R19/59 P(39-25-2) 214
Den-Gary 108R

Pit 14 3 3 7 **27**
SF 3 3 0 0 6
Pit D14 R31/141 P(26-15-0) 130
SF D16 R34/223 P(33-12-1) 90
SF-Garner 166R

Cin 10 0 3 7 20
Sea 14 14 3 6 **37**
Cin D19 R23/103 P(38-20-2) 190
Sea D26 R37/173 P(24-14-2) 187
Cin-Pickens 104C;
Sea-Watters 133R

MONDAY, NOVEMBER 8

Dal 0 17 0 0 17
Min 0 7 6 14 **27**
Dal D14 R24/205 P(35-17-1) 123
Min D17 R32/118 P(30-17-1) 190
Dal-Smith 140R; Min-Carter 116C

SUNDAY, NOVEMBER 14

Car 7 3 0 0 10
Slr 14 7 7 7 **35**
Car D18 R23/117 P(39-24-2) 260
Slr D16 R20/79 P(29-19-1) 284
Car-Muhammad 125C

Ind 7 0 17 3 **27**
NYG 0 6 0 13 19
Ind D13 R19/105 P(35-20-1) 237
NYG D26 R24/147 P(50-27-2) 237
Ind-James 108R, Harrison 109C

Mia 0 3 0 0 3
Buf 9 7 7 0 **23**
Mia D6 R19/60 P(25-9-1) 41
Buf D18 R48/177 P(20-10-0) 157
Buf-Smith 126R

Min 7 7 3 7 3 **27**
ChiB 14 3 0 7 0 24
Min D23 R28/110 P(44-25-1) 349
ChiB D21 R22/49 P(48-34-1) 407
Min-Carter 141C, Moss 204C,
George 374P; ChiB-Booker 134C,
Robinson 148C, Miller 422P

SF 3 3 0 0 6
NO 7 7 7 3 **24**
SF D16 R19/94 P(32-18-1) 140
NO D20 R39/143 P(15-12-0) 222

Cle 7 0 0 9 **16**
Pit 3 0 9 3 15
Cle D14 R21/74 P(28-18-1) 161
Pit D17 R37/168 P(32-15-2) 130

KC 3 0 0 7 10
TB 0 10 7 0 **17**
KC D11 R22/87 P(38-23-1) 184
TB D14 R37/100 P(27-17-1) 270
TB-Green 164C

SD 0 0 3 6 9
Oak 14 0 7 7 **28**
SD D12 R16/33 P(32-18-0) 192
Oak D25 R43/173 P(28-14-0) 244
Oak-Brown 117C, Gannon 254P

Det 7 0 6 6 19
Arz 3 13 7 0 **23**
Det D17 R14/42 P(39-24-0) 331
Arz D17 R32/159 P(30-16-0) 184
Det-Crowell 142C, Morton 110C,
Frerotte 375P; Arz-Pittman 133R

Bal 0 3 0 0 3
Jax 0 3 3 0 **6**
Bal D13 R24/88 P(33-17-0) 154
Jax D9 R26/47 P(29-20-0) 85

Ten 14 0 10 0 **24**
Cin 0 0 7 7 14
Ten D16 R37/149 P(25-12-0) 98
Cin D15 R19/67 P(32-18-0) 197
Ten-George 123R

Was 14 7 0 7 28
Phi 10 3 11 11 **35**
Was D22 R27/130 P(33-18-3) 294
Phi D16 R42/198 P(21-8-0) 38
Was-Davis 122R, Westbrook 152C,
Johnson 313P; Phi-Staley 122R

Den 0 0 0 17 17
Sea 3 7 0 10 **20**
Den D18 R31/87 P(30-20-1) 236
Sea D14 R21/41 P(31-16-1) 230
Den-McCaffrey 125C

GB 0 3 0 10 13
Dal 7 3 7 10 **27**
GB D20 R17/40 P(50-26-2) 244
Dal D19 R34/149 P(23-13-0) 190
GB-Freeman 110C

MONDAY, NOVEMBER 15

NYJ 0 21 0 3 **24**
NE 0 3 0 14 17
NYJ D19 R43/188 P(31-18-2) 153
NE D16 R20/79 P(36-15-3) 150
NYJ-Martin 149R

SUNDAY, NOVEMBER 21

Atl 0 0 0 0 0
TB 0 6 0 13 **19**
Atl D9 R24/76 P(25-14-2) 92
TB D12 R27/119 P(31-15-1) 120

Pit 7 0 0 3 10
Ten 14 0 2 0 **16**
Pit D14 R20/106 P(30-18-1) 161
Ten D17 R32/112 P(26-14-1) 149

Sea 0 14 10 7 **31**
KC 3 0 0 6 19
Sea D20 R32/133 P(33-14-1) 235
KC D22 R25/76 P(49-30-1) 295
Sea-Watters 107R, Dawkins 114C;
KC-Alexander 101C, Grbac 320P

Det 7 10 0 0 17
GB 0 12 11 3 **26**
Det D20 R23/110 P(33-22-1) 201
GB D24 R27/64 P(40-26-0) 307
Det-Crowell 112C; GB-Favre 309P

Car 3 14 7 7 **31**
Cle 0 3 0 14 17
Car D22 R31/129 P(30-23-0) 201
Cle D22 R19/49 P(46-29-2) 257

NE 7 3 7 0 17
Mia 3 7 14 3 **27**
NE D14 R19/102 P(34-15-5) 168
Mia D19 R36/117 P(34-18-0) 110
Mia-Johnson 106R

Dal 7 0 0 2 9
Arz 0 3 7 3 **13**
Dal D15 R34/156 P(29-16-0) 102
Arz D13 R30/102 P(29-13-2) 105
Dal-Smith 127R

Buf 0 0 7 0 7
NYJ 0 14 3 0 **17**
Buf D14 R17/68 P(40-22-2) 205
NYJ D14 R35/95 P(21-16-0) 113

ChiB 0 3 14 3 3 **23**
SD 7 3 0 10 0 20
ChiB D19 R28/75 P(39-25-0) 355
SD D20 R27/84 P(46-29-1) 264
ChiB-Engram 121C, Robinson 163C,
Miller 357P

Slr 3 10 10 0 **23**
SF 0 7 0 0 7
Slr D21 R30/164 P(40-22-1) 181
SF D14 R25/106 P(27-15-3) 145
Slr-Faulk 126R; SF-Owens 120C

NYG 0 6 0 7 13
Was 7 3 3 10 **23**
NYG D21 R24/72 P(31-16-3) 229
Was D24 R40/206 P(29-17-1) 157
NYG-Hilliard 101C; Was-Davis 183R

Ind 17 13 14 0 **44**
Phi 0 3 0 14 17
Ind D22 R36/200 P(31-20-1) 255
Phi D13 R20/94 P(39-20-2) 118
Ind-James 152R, Wilkins 111C

Bal 0 10 21 3 **34**
Cin 14 0 7 10 31
Bal D19 R26/56 P(40-24-1) 225
Cin D20 R23/102 P(39-20-2) 246

NO 7 10 0 6 23
Jax 14 3 14 10 **41**
NO D21 R29/106 P(27-18-1) 233
Jax D30 R27/139 P(32-21-1) 355
Jax-Smith 220C, Brunell 351P

MONDAY, NOVEMBER 22

Oak 0 7 11 3 21
Den 10 5 0 6 6 **27**
Oak D16 R29/79 P(34-17-1) 205
Den D17 R30/120 P(41-18-0) 171

THURSDAY, NOVEMBER 25

Mia 0 0 0 0 0
Dal 0 0 7 13 **20**
Mia D16 R20/69 P(41-19-5) 206
Dal D15 R34/101 P(29-16-0) 223
Dal-Smith 103R, Ismail 125C

ChiB 0 7 3 7 17
Det 7 14 0 0 **21**
ChiB D12 R12/52 P(39-25-1) 184
Det D20 R29/84 P(42-29-0) 293
Det-Frerotte 309P

SUNDAY, NOVEMBER 28

SD 7 0 17 3 27
Min 0 28 0 7 **35**
SD D19 R20/62 P(39-25-1) 396
Min D27 R29/129 P(43-28-2) 356
SD-Graham 141C, Harbaugh 404P;
Min-Smith 104R, Carter 136C,
Moss 127C, George 363P

NO 3 9 0 0 12
Slr 7 8 7 21 **43**
NO D28 R28/102 P(47-25-2) 263
Slr D24 R27/129 P(27-15-0) 195
NO-Hastings 113C; Slr-Faulk 102R

NE 0 0 0 7 7
Buf 3 7 7 0 **17**
NE D17 R25/93 P(34-18-1) 174
Buf D13 R35/92 P(16-9-0) 207

Cin 14 10 3 0 **27**
Pit 3 10 7 0 20
Cin D18 R35/180 P(28-15-1) 235
Pit D20 R31/111 P(46-24-2) 280
Cin-Dillon 120R, Scott 123C

NYJ 6 0 0 0 6
Ind 7 0 3 3 **13**
NYJ D14 R26/126 P(23-12-0) 88
Ind D23 R27/100 P(31-23-2) 187

Jax 0 7 0 23 **30**
Bal 10 3 3 7 23
Jax D24 R25/60 P(47-27-2) 328
Bal D22 R22/81 P(34-17-1) 199
Jax-McCardell 102C, Smith 132C,
Brunell 338P

Phi 0 3 0 14 0 17
Was 3 7 7 0 3 **20**
Phi D16 R28/143 P(28-16-0) 156
Was D23 R32/94 P(36-25-1) 218

TB 0 6 0 10 **16**
Sea 3 0 0 0 3
TB D9 R37/105 P(18-8-0) 51
Sea D15 R22/89 P(44-19-5) 170

Ten 7 6 13 7 **33**
Cle 0 14 0 7 21
Ten D22 R33/158 P(36-18-0) 179
Cle D18 R24/81 P(35-19-0) 228
Ten-George 113R

Arz 3 3 7 21 **34**
NYG 0 10 0 14 24
Arz D23 R34/69 P(35-23-0) 222
NYG D20 R20/52 P(45-22-3) 282
Arz-Moore 102C

KC 0 10 10 17 **37**
Oak 3 10 21 0 34
KC D16 R28/98 P(27-18-2) 195
Oak D18 R25/108 P(29-19-2) 207

Atl 0 0 14 20 34
Car 3 17 7 7 **34**
Atl D22 R15/64 P(42-24-0) 279
Car D25 R38/126 P(27-16-0) 254
Atl-Dwight 102C, Chandler 315P;
Car-Hayes 133C

MONDAY, NOVEMBER 29

GB 0 10 7 3 **20**
SF 0 3 0 0 3
GB D19 R22/79 P(35-24-0) 229
SF D14 R23/137 P(35-19-1) 185

THURSDAY, DECEMBER 2

Pit 3 0 3 0 6
Jax 0 6 7 7 **20**
Pit D15 R15/63 P(39-19-0) 172
Jax D24 R34/168 P(37-25-0) 298
Jax-Stewart 145R, McCardell 113C,
Smith 124C, Brunell 308P

SUNDAY, DECEMBER 5

NYJ 0 7 0 21 28
NYG 17 10 7 7 **41**
NYJ D18 R12/15 P(48-31-0) 276
NYG D25 R45/152 P(29-17-0) 338
NYJ-Lucas 284P;
NYG-Montgomery 111R,
Hilliard 121C, Toomer 181C,
Collins 341P

Slr 14 7 0 13 **34**
Car 0 7 7 7 21
Slr D22 R33/122 P(32-23-2) 358
Car D14 R16/55 P(42-21-2) 252
Slr-Faulk 118R, Bruce 111C,
Hakim 122C, Warner 351P;
Car-Jeffers 107C

Phi 0 14 3 0 17
Arz 7 0 0 14 **21**
Phi D18 R37/146 P(31-19-1) 148
Arz D16 R19/54 P(38-20-1) 173

Sea 0 7 7 7 21
Oak 3 14 7 6 **30**
Sea D20 R19/90 P(39-22-2) 234
Oak D24 R41/162 P(24-19-1) 253

Was 3 7 7 0 17
Det 0 20 0 13 **33**
Was D16 R21/116 P(43-26-2) 217
Det D22 R32/121 P(32-21-0) 261
Was-Westbrook 108C;
Det-Crowell 122C

Cle 3 7 0 0 10
SD 3 10 7 3 **23**
Cle D13 R16/55 P(30-18-2) 147
SD D20 R44/145 P(23-16-0) 132

SF 0 10 14 6 **30**
Cin 14 0 7 6 27
SF D29 R23/105 P(49-33-1) 437
Cin D27 R28/151 P(30-21-0) 325
SF-Owens 145C, Rice 157C,
Garcia 437P; Cin-Dillon 133R,
Pickens 107C, Blake 334P

NO 3 0 3 6 12
Atl 7 14 14 0 **35**
NO D21 R26/149 P(37-17-2) 91
Atl D21 R28/128 P(25-15-3) 233

Ind 17 7 7 6 **37**
Mia 3 7 14 10 34
Ind D21 R25/129 P(29-23-2) 241
Mia D22 R22/69 P(38-24-1) 299
Ind-James 130R, Harrison 125C;
Mia-Gadsden 103C, Martin 109C,
Marino 313P

Ten 3 11 0 0 14
Bal 7 10 7 17 **41**
Ten D21 R14/65 P(53-31-2) 288
Bal D17 R22/116 P(31-18-0) 332
Bal-Holmes 100R, Ismail 113C,
Banks 332P

KC 0 10 0 6 **16**
Den 3 7 0 0 10
KC D17 R38/177 P(34-20-1) 175
Den D14 R18/83 P(36-20-1) 208
Den-Smith 106C

GB 0 21 0 14 **35**
ChiB 6 6 0 7 19
GB D19 R35/188 P(24-17-2) 139
ChiB D17 R24/91 P(39-21-1) 206
GB-Parker 113R

Dal 3 0 0 3 6
NE 0 7 0 6 **13**
Dal D12 R23/63 P(30-20-0) 140
NE D18 R36/108 P(25-14-2) 176

MONDAY, DECEMBER 6

Min 0 14 0 3 17
TB 7 3 7 7 **24**
Min D21 R24/93 P(45-26-2) 246
TB D13 R27/103 P(19-11-1) 87

THURSDAY, DECEMBER 9

Oak 0 0 7 7 14
Ten 0 0 7 14 **21**
Oak D21 R22/111 P(28-20-1) 253
Ten D17 R33/204 P(20-12-1) 103
Ten-George 199R

SUNDAY, DECEMBER 12

Cle 7 8 6 7 28
Cin 10 20 14 0 **44**
Cle D19 R11/11 P(41-22-2) 312
Cin D25 R53/279 P(23-12-0) 180
Cle-Johnson 135C; Cin-Dillon 192R

Car 3 7 14 9 **33**
GB 7 7 7 10 31
Car D21 R13/13 P(42-29-0) 368
GB D26 R24/79 P(38-26-1) 283
Car-Jeffers 147C, Beuerlein 373P;
GB-Favre 302P

NE 3 3 3 6 15
Ind 7 7 6 0 **20**
NE D23 R20/57 P(44-31-1) 344
Ind D15 R25/109 P(27-15-0) 178
NE-Glenn 148C, Bledsoe 379P;
Ind-James 101R, Harrison 118C

NYG 3 10 3 3 **19**
Buf 3 7 0 7 17
NYG D20 R28/94 P(44-23-1) 240
Buf D13 R28/76 P(32-15-1) 161
NYG-Favre 302P

Phi 0 0 0 10 10
Dal 7 6 7 0 **20**
Phi D14 R24/95 P(29-15-1) 143
Dal D22 R31/112 P(40-22-0) 225

Arz 0 0 0 0 0
Was 7 14 0 7 **28**
Arz D10 R14/53 P(32-15-3) 120
Was D25 R46/226 P(31-17-2) 180
Was-Davis 189R

Slr 7 17 3 3 **30**
NO 6 0 8 0 14
Slr D23 R34/156 P(31-21-1) 336
NO D13 R18/66 P(28-12-3) 144
Slr-Faulk 154R, Bruce 102C,
Holt 113C, Warner 346P

Bal 7 3 21 0 **31**
Pit 10 0 7 7 24
Bal D12 R25/132 P(26-8-0) 242
Pit D21 R22/109 P(43-24-0) 243
Bal-Holmes 130R, Ismail 258C

SD 10 3 0 6 **19**
Sea 3 6 7 0 16
SD D22 R39/107 P(35-20-1) 222
Sea D20 R21/76 P(40-25-1) 271
SD-Graham 114C

Mia 6 0 7 7 20
NYJ 0 6 0 22 **28**
Mia D20 R19/73 P(47-25-2) 246
NYJ D18 R28/95 P(38-22-0) 225
NYJ-Johnson 144C

Det 10 0 3 3 16
TB 0 7 2 14 **23**
Det D16 R20/55 P(44-23-1) 210
TB D17 R19/41 P(37-23-1) 271
Det-Morton 107C; TB-Dunn 115C

Atl 0 0 7 0 7
SF 7 12 0 7 **26**
Atl D7 R12/38 P(27-9-1) 67
SF D21 R44/181 P(26-17-0) 153
SF-Garner 107R

Min 0 14 7 7 28
KC 14 7 0 10 **31**
Min D21 R35/175 P(23-13-0) 151
KC D22 R40/173 P(29-19-0) 207
Min-Smith 118R

MONDAY, DECEMBER 13

Den 7 7 3 7 24
Jax 0 17 0 10 **27**
Den D18 R27/90 P(33-21-2) 268
Jax D18 R32/161 P(25-11-0) 104

SATURDAY, DECEMBER 18

Pit 10 3 0 6 19
KC 7 14 7 7 **35**
Pit D21 R28/107 P(46-23-4) 269
KC D16 R32/218 P(22-12-0) 145

SF 10 0 7 7 24
Car 17 7 10 7 **41**
SF D18 R18/100 P(46-29-1) 297
Car D25 R26/90 P(38-27-0) 362
SF-Garcia 303P; Car-Jeffers 138C,
Muhammad 126C, Beuerlein 368P

SUNDAY, DECEMBER 19

Jax 0 14 3 7 **24**
Cle 0 7 7 0 14
Jax D20 R33/181 P(33-21-1) 261
Cle D19 R20/72 P(41-24-0) 197
Jax-Taylor 136R, Smith 134C;
Cle-Chiaverini 108C

Atl 7 7 3 0 17
Ten 14 6 0 10 **30**
Atl D23 R19/56 P(43-24-3) 291
Ten D14 R28/131 P(30-16-0) 268
Ten-Sanders 100C

NO 0 0 0 8 8
Bal 3 14 0 14 **31**
NO D8 R16/11 P(49-21-4) 237
Bal D15 R24/61 P(39-24-4) 274
Bal-Ismail 115C

NYG 0 0 3 7 10
Slr 3 7 7 14 **31**
NYG D20 R19/67 P(37-21-2) 261
Slr D19 R27/100 P(32-18-0) 319
NYG-Toomer 162C; Slr-Warner 319P

SD 0 3 0 6 9
Mia 3 3 0 6 **12**
SD D13 R21/26 P(40-20-0) 160
Mia D11 R23/53 P(36-22-0) 231

Sea 7 7 3 13 30
Den 14 3 6 7 **36**
Sea D19 R17/114 P(42-22-0) 250
Den D26 R33/260 P(39-20-2) 170
Sea-Watters 115R; Den-Gary 183R

NYJ 6 7 6 3 **22**
Dal 0 14 7 0 21
NYJ D19 R35/126 P(35-20-1) 229
Dal D16 R31/195 P(28-13-1) 152
NYJ-Martin 113R, Chrebet 108C;
Dal-Smith 110R

Det 3 0 0 7 10
ChiB 0 14 7 14 **35**
Det D19 R19/103 P(40-23-3) 236
ChiB D27 R32/104 P(36-27-2) 292
Det-Morton 100C;
ChiB-Robinson 170C,
McNown 301P

Was 3 10 0 8 21
Ind 7 3 0 14 **24**
Was D21 R32/151 P(30-16-0) 208
Ind D24 R23/88 P(37-23-1) 291
Ind-Harrison 117C

NE 0 6 3 0 9
Phi 10 7 7 0 **24**
NE D20 R27/62 P(49-23-4) 288
Phi D11 R37/114 P(29-10-2) 181
NE-Brown 105C, Bledsoe 331P

TB 0 0 0 0 0
Oak 10 7 21 7 **45**
TB D9 R19/34 P(29-17-1) 103
Oak D21 R37/262 P(28-15-0) 138
Oak-Kaufman 122R, Wheatley 111R

Buf 14 0 3 14 **31**
Arz 0 14 0 7 21
Buf D25 R41/159 P(32-21-2) 217
Arz D14 R21/70 P(30-11-1) 108

MONDAY, DECEMBER 20

GB 0 13 0 7 20
Min 0 10 7 7 **24**
GB D20 R28/107 P(40-23-2) 212
Min D15 R26/76 P(29-16-0) 229
Min-Moss 131C

FRIDAY, DECEMBER 24

Dal 0 7 17 0 24
NO 0 0 17 14 **31**
Dal D24 R26/122 P(39-23-2) 246
NO D18 R29/61 P(28-16-1) 249
Dal-Smith 110R, Tucker 128C

SATURDAY, DECEMBER 25

Den 0 0 10 7 **17**
Det 0 0 0 7 7
Den D22 R36/204 P(30-22-1) 165
Det D16 R12/32 P(40-21-0) 242
Den-Gary 185R

SUNDAY, DECEMBER 26

Arz 0 14 0 0 14
Atl 7 13 7 10 **37**
Arz D17 R24/77 P(26-15-2) 212
Atl D22 R39/163 P(23-14-0) 230
Arz-Sanders 106C;
Atl-Hanspard 102R

Min 0 14 7 13 **34**
NYG 3 3 3 8 17
Min D18 R25/174 P(22-11-2) 204
NYG D25 R27/76 P(51-31-1) 268
Min-Smith 146R, Carter 131C

Jax 0 7 0 7 14
Ten 7 17 14 3 **41**
Jax D16 R18/65 P(33-12-3) 172
Ten D26 R37/148 P(29-26-0) 328
Jax-Smith 104C; Ten-George 102R,
McNair 291P

Cin 0 0 0 0 0
Bal 7 9 0 6 **22**
Cin D15 R25/93 P(37-20-2) 148
Bal D18 R32/130 P(33-15-1) 181

Oak 10 0 10 0 20
SD 0 13 0 10 **23**
Oak D18 R24/46 P(33-16-1) 248
SD D17 R21/49 P(36-23-1) 293
Oak-Brown 109C; SD-Graham 113C,
Harbaugh 325P

GB 0 10 0 0 10
TB 3 6 7 13 **29**
GB D14 R12/12 P(48-25-2) 231
TB D17 R37/124 P(31-18-1) 150

KC 0 7 0 7 14
Sea 10 7 6 0 **23**
KC D17 R22/72 P(42-22-3) 230
Sea D17 R28/60 P(30-18-0) 207

Buf 3 0 7 3 **13**
NE 0 3 0 7 10
Buf D23 R41/168 P(35-22-0) 206
NE D14 R34/158 P(21-10-0) 67
NE-Allen 126R

Car 7 13 0 0 20
Pit 10 13 0 7 **30**
Car D17 R20/119 P(35-18-1) 256
Pit D21 R44/211 P(23-13-1) 82
Car-Jeffers 160C; Pit-Bettis 137R

Ind 0 13 6 10 **29**
Cle 7 7 14 0 28
Ind D28 R30/120 P(43-22-0) 276
Cle D17 R26/141 P(26-15-0) 173
Ind-James 103R, Harrison 138C

ChiB 0 0 6 6 12
Slr 0 17 14 3 **34**
ChiB D24 R17/69 P(55-32-2) 365
Slr D23 R27/115 P(42-27-1) 361
ChiB-Engram 143C; Slr-Faulk 204C,
Warner 334P

Was 0 7 3 10 6 **26**
SF 7 6 7 0 0 20
Was D24 R37/250 P(30-17-1) 168
SF D21 R37/262 P(28-15-0) 153
Was-Connell 106C, Westbrook 125C,
Johnson 471P; SF-Garner 129R

MONDAY, DECEMBER 27

NYJ 10 7 7 14 **38**
Mia 7 0 7 17 31
NYJ D16 R25/101 P(23-11-0) 189
Mia D25 R24/100 P(52-29-3) 322
Mia-Martin 102C, Marino 322P

SUNDAY, JANUARY 2

Sea 6 0 3 0 9
NYJ 3 10 3 3 **19**
Sea D14 R12/33 P(45-21-2) 233
NYJ D20 R41/177 P(26-15-2) 202
NYJ-Martin 158R

Det 7 3 0 7 17
Min 7 10 0 7 **24**
Det D20 R14/16 P(46-31-1) 286
Min D20 R30/137 P(24-14-2) 242
Det-Crowell 120C, Morton 128C;
Min-Moss 155C

Ind 3 3 0 0 6
Buf 7 14 0 10 **31**
Ind D13 R19/44 P(37-21-1) 182
Buf D23 R31/132 P(32-24-0) 287
Buf-Moulds 110C

Arz 0 3 7 14 24
GB 7 7 14 21 **49**
Arz D20 R24/80 P(57-35-3) 384
GB D26 R28/176 P(34-21-1) 299
Arz-Moore 120C, Sanders 118C,
Plummer 396P; GB-Levens 146R,
Favre 311P

Bal 0 3 0 0 3
NE 0 13 0 7 **20**
Bal D23 R23/119 P(40-26-2) 194
NE D12 R22/49 P(26-15-1) 102
Bal-Johnson 114C

Oak 7 21 3 7 3 **41**
KC 17 7 7 7 0 38
Oak D20 R30/106 P(47-25-2) 302
KC D25 R38/189 P(39-20-0) 240
Oak-Brown 122C, Gannon 324P

TB 0 10 3 7 **20**
ChiB 0 0 3 6 9
TB D16 R40/143 P(24-18-0) 175
ChiB D13 R18/71 P(42-20-1) 186
TB-Green 113C

Slr 7 10 7 7 31
Phi 3 14 7 14 **38**
Slr D20 R26/201 P(40-21-4) 239
Phi D13 R23/51 P(32-15-2) 156
Slr-Holt 122C

Cin 7 0 0 7 14
Jax 7 10 0 7 **24**
Cin D13 R18/110 P(23-13-2) 126
Jax D30 R36/135 P(39-28-0) 305
Jax-McCardell 108C, Smith 165C,
Fiedler 317P

SD 0 12 0 0 **12**
Den 0 0 3 0 3
SD D17 R34/194 P(26-17-2) 183
Den D15 R22/44 P(46-23-0) 191
SD-Fazande 183R, Graham 102C;
Den-Smith 106C

Ten 7 24 9 7 **47**
Pit 0 7 22 7 36
Ten D21 R33/140 P(23-15-1) 203
Pit D22 R29/138 P(39-21-1) 295
Pit-Shaw 131C, Tomczak 309P

NYG 0 0 3 15 18
Dal 6 10 3 7 **26**
NYG D19 R18/72 P(47-30-1) 308
Dal D20 R29/149 P(33-23-0) 288
NYG-Barber 100C, Collins 316P;
Dal-Smith 122R, Tucker 122C

NO 0 0 0 13 13
Car 10 7 14 14 **45**
NO D22 R25/105 P(49-26-4) 230
Car D18 R14/67 P(41-22-0) 288
NO-Poole 104C; Car-Jeffers 165C,
Beuerlein 322P

Mia 3 0 0 7 10
Was 0 7 7 7 **21**
Mia D25 R26/119 P(53-29-2) 270
Was D18 R30/105 P(20-13-0) 165
Mia-Gadsden 114C

MONDAY, JANUARY 3

SF 0 7 8 14 29
Atl 7 10 14 3 **34**
SF D23 R24/143 P(34-26-0) 363
Atl D24 R21/37 P(37-19-0) 306
SF-Rice 143C, Stokes 130C,
Garcia 373P; Atl-Dwight 162C,
Chandler 306P

2000 NFL

SUNDAY, SEPTEMBER 3

Ten 0 6 0 7 13
Buf 0 7 3 6 **16**
Ten D9 R20/53 P(31-17-1) 119
Buf D17 R35/129 P(26-13-0) 137

NYJ 0 7 3 10 **20**
GB 7 3 3 3 16
NYJ D24 R34/118 P(44-23-1) 261
GB D13 R16/62 P(34-14-1) 149
NYJ-Martin 110R, Ward 104C

Phi 14 10 3 14 **41**
Dal 0 6 3 8 14
Phi D27 R46/306 P(29-16-3) 119
Dal D10 R13/67 P(31-13-2) 100
Phi-Staley 201R

Arz 0 0 3 13 16
NYG 7 7 0 7 **21**
Arz D19 R20/43 P(49-28-3) 312
NYG D20 R41/223 P(25-17-1) 172
Arz-Boston 128C, Plummer 318P;
NYG-Barber 144R

Bal 10 3 0 0 **13**
Pit 0 0 0 0 0
Bal D18 R36/140 P(32-18-0) 196
Pit D21 R18/30 P(35-20-0) 193
Bal-Holmes 119R, Ismail 102C

SD 0 3 0 0 3
Oak 0 0 2 7 **9**
SD D17 R28/76 P(42-19-3) 179
Oak D13 R25/67 P(35-20-0) 166

Car 7 0 3 10 20
Was 7 0 3 10 **20**
Car D12 R20/112 P(26-17-0) 124
Was D23 R31/162 P(36-25-0) 234
Was-Davis 133R

Ind 0 7 7 13 **27**
KC 0 7 0 7 14
Ind D20 R32/119 P(32-22-1) 267
KC D17 R24/74 P(37-16-1) 206
Ind-James 124R, Harrison 115C

Sea 0 0 0 0 0
Mia 0 7 0 16 **23**
Sea D8 R19/71 P(24-10-4) 172
Mia D16 R41/181 P(24-15-0) 127
Mia-Smith 145R

Det 0 6 8 0 **14**
NO 0 0 0 0 0
Det D10 R32/98 P(25-13-1) 89
NO D13 R25/106 P(34-18-1) 146

ChiB 7 6 7 7 27
Min 6 3 7 14 **30**
ChiB D23 R25/153 P(41-27-0) 272
Min D17 R30/186 P(23-13-1) 188
Min-Smith 109R

Jax 0 10 10 7 **27**
Cle 0 7 0 0 7
Jax D28 R40/119 P(34-24-0) 279
Cle D9 R16/96 P(27-19-0) 153
Jax-McCardell 115C, Brunell 301P

SF 0 7 7 0 14
Atl 6 16 14 0 **36**
SF D23 R24/92 P(36-23-1) 247
Atl D22 R32/95 P(31-16-0) 264
Atl-Jefferson 148C

TB 0 14 0 7 **21**
NE 3 7 0 6 16
TB D17 R38/140 P(24-12-0) 156
NE D14 R21/88 P(39-26-0) 190

MONDAY, SEPTEMBER 4

Den 7 10 10 9 36
Slr 7 14 14 6 **41**
Den D25 R28/150 P(29-19-0) 274
Slr D23 R18/80 P(35-25-3) 433
Den-McCaffrey 115C, Griese 307P;
Slr-Faulk 100C, Hakim 116C,
Holt 103C, Warner 441P

SUNDAY, SEPTEMBER 10

Dal 7 14 3 7 31
Arz 3 10 10 9 **32**
Dal D17 R22/90 P(34-24-0) 240
Arz D21 R33/98 P(24-18-0) 224
Arz-Boston 102C

NO 7 6 6 9 **28**
SD 3 21 0 3 27
NO D23 R31/64 P(46-33-2) 259
SD D15 R20/72 P(26-13-2) 116
NO-Horn 116C

Oak 0 7 24 7 **38**
Ind 14 0 0 7 21
Oak D21 R38/152 P(22-15-0) 207
Ind D28 R20/111 P(48-33-2) 351
Ind-Harrison 141C, Manning 367P

Atl 0 7 7 0 14
Den 3 21 8 10 **42**
Atl D12 R13/47 P(29-12-0) 139
Den D29 R39/152 P(33-20-0) 255
Den-Anderson 131R, Smith 117C

KC 0 7 0 7 14
Ten 0 7 7 3 **17**
KC D14 R33/62 P(21-13-0) 127
Ten D23 R29/121 P(36-23-2) 232
Ten-Dyson 104C

Slr 3 10 7 17 **37**
Sea 3 7 10 14 34
Slr D28 R22/97 P(47-35-1) 379
Sea D24 R24/101 P(31-20-2) 237
Slr-Holt 101C, Warner 386P

Car 14 14 10 0 **38**
SF 0 0 7 15 22
Car D27 R34/98 P(32-24-1) 352
SF D21 R22/90 P(40-22-1) 301
Car-Hayes 115C, Muhammad 108C,
Beuerlein 364P

Was 0 7 3 0 10
Det 3 3 3 6 **15**
Was D20 R23/104 P(35-23-4) 229
Det D15 R24/62 P(31-16-2) 182

Mia 0 0 0 7 7
Min 0 0 0 13 **13**
Mia D10 R16/49 P(31-12-1) 160
Min D24 R28/125 P(37-23-3) 343
Mia-Martin 120C; Min-Carter 168C,
Culpepper 355P

NYG 3 17 7 6 **33**
Phi 3 0 9 6 18
NYG D24 R39/167 P(29-21-0) 220
Phi D13 R12/56 P(33-19-0) 181

ChiB 0 0 0 0 0
TB 0 20 14 7 **41**
ChiB D9 R22/116 P(29-15-2) 49
TB D16 R35/156 P(24-13-0) 171
TB-Green 104C

Cle 7 7 3 7 **24**
Cin 0 7 0 0 7
Cle D17 R33/105 P(31-19-1) 249
Cin D17 R19/111 P(43-15-2) 207

GB 8 10 0 0 18
Buf 0 10 10 7 **27**
GB D14 R16/40 P(35-25-0) 234
Buf D20 R34/89 P(26-18-1) 220
Buf-Moulds 103C

Jax 17 6 3 10 36
Bal 0 7 15 17 **39**
Jax D22 R21/46 P(50-28-2) 375
Bal D17 R18/89 P(40-23-2) 242
Jax-Smith 291C, Brunell 386P;
Bal-Banks 262P

MONDAY, SEPTEMBER 11
```
NE     3   9   0   7   19
NYJ    7   0   0  13   20
NE   D21 R34/100  P(43-25-0)  193
NYJ  D18 R17/59   P(37-16-1)  271
NYJ-Ward 100C
```

SUNDAY, SEPTEMBER 17
```
Bal    0   0   3   3    6
Mia    3   3   7   6   19
Bal  D18 R18/118  P(31-19-1)  144
Mia  D15 R34/106  P(16-11-1)  152

Cin    0   0   0   0    0
Jax   10   0   0   3   13
Cin  D14 R23/71   P(41-18-2)  162
Jax  D15 R29/84   P(32-20-1)  157
Jax-McCardell 108C

NO     7   3   0   0   10
Sea    7   0   3  10   20
NO   D13 R26/116  P(24-14-0)  147
Sea  D22 R31/126  P(29-22-1)  169
NO-Williams 107R;
Sea-Watters 105R

Atl    3   7   0   5   15
Car    0  10   0   0   10
Atl  D10 R30/108  P(27-21-0)  154
Car  D17 R16/59   P(38-21-2)  225

SD    10   0   0   0   10
KC     0  14  14  14   42
SD   D10 R14/49   P(35-17-1)  138
KC   D25 R34/117  P(33-20-1)  232
KC-Morris 112C, Grbac 235P

Pit    0  10   0  10   20
Cle   14   0   3   6   23
Pit  D19 R31/170  P(29-14-1)  166
Cle  D14 R23/61   P(31-23-0)  316
Pit-Bettis 133R; Cle-Couch 316P

TB    14   7   3   7   31
Det    3   7   0   0   10
TB   D22 R39/120  P(30-18-0)  211
Det  D13 R10/17   P(36-26-2)  226

Min    7  14   0   0   21
NE     0   7   0   6   13
Min  D23 R43/154  P(28-19-1)  161
NE   D18 R18/103  P(35-21-1)  164

Den   17   7   3   6   33
Oak    7  10   0   0   17
Den  D25 R39/180  P(31-21-0)  207
Oak  D16 R19/123  P(21-13-2)  140
Den-Anderson 187R, Williams 107R

NYG    7   0   7   0   14
ChiB   0   7   0   0    7
NYG  D23 R41/172  P(33-24-0)  237
ChiB D13 R17/48   P(36-23-0)  180

Buf    7   7   0   0   14
NYJ    7  14   3   3   27
Buf  D16 R23/80   P(36-21-1)  274
NYJ  D15 R36/91   P(32-16-1)  188

SF     7  10   0   7   24
Slr    3  14   7  17   41
SF   D16 R21/111  P(34-21-2)  290
Slr  D32 R28/140  P(34-23-2)  389
SF-Owens 108C; Slr-Faulk 134R,
Bruce 188C, Warner 394P

Phi    0   3   0   0    3
GB     0   0   3   3    6
Phi  D12 R22/85   P(31-15-1)   86
GB   D19 R29/79   P(33-18-3)  157
```

MONDAY, SEPTEMBER 18
```
Dal    7   7   3  10   27
Was    7   0   7   7   21
Dal  D15 R31/153  P(23-10-1)  179
Was  D24 R29/107  P(49-30-1)  224
```

SUNDAY, SEPTEMBER 24
```
Cin    0   0   0   0    0
Bal   10   3  14  10   37
Cin  D7  R16/4    P(24-15-2)   90
Bal  D27 R38/176  P(39-22-0)  215
Bal-Lewis 116R

Phi    0  14   7   0   21
NO     0   0   0   7    7
Phi  D14 R25/67   P(32-20-0)  201
NO   D17 R25/146  P(38-18-2)  141
NO-Williams 103R
```

```
Slr    3  14  10  14   41
Atl    7   6   0   7   20
Slr  D14 R25/74   P(19-12-1)  321
Atl  D18 R21/68   P(38-22-2)  218
Slr-Holt 189C, Warner 336P

Det    7   7   0   7   21
ChiB   0   0  14   0   14
Det  D15 R29/80   P(37-20-1)  194
ChiB D16 R31/147  P(35-21-3)  254

SF     3  14  10  14   41
Dal    0  10   0  14   24
SF   D27 R47/261  P(27-16-0)  178
Dal  D18 R14/76   P(31-18-1)  222
SF-Garner 201R, Garcia 178P;
Dal-McKnight 129C

Ten   10   0   3  10   23
Pit    3  14   0   3   20
Ten  D15 R31/85   P(30-16-3)  287
Pit  D20 R25/115  P(37-19-0)  249
Ten-Pickens 105C

NE     0   3   0   0    3
Mia    0  10   0   0   10
NE   D12 R29/56   P(33-16-1)  154
Mia  D12 R33/99   P(24-12-2)  143

KC     7   0   7   9   23
Den    3   9  10   0   22
KC   D21 R27/49   P(33-21-2)  245
Den  D21 R30/145  P(31-18-1)  197
KC-Gonzalez 127C; Den-Smith 134C

Cle    7   0   3   0   10
Oak    7  21   0   8   36
Cle  D14 R21/89   P(34-18-2)  141
Oak  D18 R36/113  P(25-14-0)  179

Sea   10   3   7   0   20
SD     6   6   0   0   12
Sea  D15 R25/108  P(21-11-0)  161
SD   D15 R24/91   P(40-24-2)  212

GB     7  10   6   6   29
Arz    0   3   0   0    3
GB   D23 R36/176  P(32-18-0)  279
Arz  D12 R13/28   P(43-21-4)  181

NYJ    3   3   0  15   21
TB     3   7   7   0   17
NYJ  D16 R24/98   P(44-24-3)  198
TB   D12 R32/119  P(19-7-2)   120

Was    0  10   6   0   16
NYG    0   0   0   6    6
Was  D17 R39/110  P(20-14-0)  284
NYG  D21 R22/93   P(44-21-1)  168
Was-Connell 122C
```

MONDAY, SEPTEMBER 25
```
Jax    0  14   0   0   14
Ind    7  14   5  17   43
Jax  D18 R24/97   P(36-21-2)  189
Ind  D21 R28/93   P(36-23-0)  440
Jax-Smith 132C; Ind-Harrison 103C,
Wilkins 148C, Manning 440P
```

SUNDAY, OCTOBER 1
```
Bal    3   6   3   0   12
Cle    0   0   0   0    0
Bal  D22 R37/188  P(34-18-1)  160
Cle  D11 R13/23   P(36-21-3)  207
Cle-Patten 113C

Dal    0  10   3   3   16
Car    0  10   0   3   13
Dal  D20 R38/173  P(23-15-2)  118
Car  D13 R29/119  P(29-17-0)  153
Dal-Smith 132R

Ind    0   7   0  11   18
Buf    3   6   0   7   16
Ind  D14 R24/81   P(27-16-1)  184
Buf  D21 R33/170  P(32-21-0)  215
Buf-Moulds 112C

Min    7   3   7  14   31
Det    3   0  14   0   24
Min  D19 R29/178  P(29-17-0)  261
Det  D27 R25/129  P(44-25-1)  226
Min-Smith 134R, Moss 168C;
Det-Stewart 123R
```

```
SD     3   7   7  14   31
Slr   17  13  17  10   57
SD   D23 R15/48   P(40-27-1)  333
Slr  D29 R26/163  P(34-27-0)  451
SD-Graham 107C, Harbaugh 348P;
Slr-Watson 102R, Bruce 167C,
Faulk 116C, Hakim 104C,
Warner 390P

Pit    7  10   7   0   24
Jax    3   3   0   7   13
Pit  D22 R44/209  P(16-10-1)  123
Jax  D17 R16/26   P(45-23-1)  180
Jax-McCardell 137C

NYG    0   0   7   7   14
Ten    7  14   0   7   28
NYG  D14 R12/24   P(36-17-1)  191
Ten  D28 R43/152  P(35-24-0)  284
Ten-George 125R, Mason 103C

TB     7   0   0  10   17
Was    0   7   7   6   20
TB   D16 R28/72   P(38-19-1)  183
Was  D14 R32/145  P(32-20-0)  185
Was-Davis 141R

NE    14   7   7   0   28
Den    0   3   8   8   19
NE   D19 R27/54   P(27-18-1)  260
Den  D26 R21/79   P(50-31-1)  326
NE-Brown 108C, Bledsoe 271P;
Den-Smith 160C, Griese 361P

Mia    0  10  14   7   31
Cin   10   3   0   3   16
Mia  D18 R29/159  P(21-14-1)  143
Cin  D24 R35/191  P(38-20-0)  159
Cin-Dillon 110R

ChiB  10   7   7   3   27
GB     0   3   7  14   24
ChiB D13 R36/178  P(20-11-0)  192
GB   D22 R14/44   P(48-31-1)  320
ChiB-Robinson 126C;
GB-Schroeder 108C, Favre 333P

Atl    0   0   7   3   10
Phi    3   3  11  21   38
Atl  D13 R22/61   P(35-15-1)  139
Phi  D22 R21/195  P(45-30-2)  307
Phi-Mitchell 105R, Small 122C,
McNabb 311P

Arz    0  10   0  10   20
SF     7  10   7   3   27
Arz  D16 R24/126  P(41-24-0)  239
SF   D18 R32/130  P(33-22-0)  215
```

MONDAY, OCTOBER 2
```
Sea    7   7   3   0   17
KC     0   7   7  10   24
Sea  D20 R34/186  P(28-17-1)  103
KC   D18 R26/136  P(27-16-0)  242
KC-Alexander 153C
```

SUNDAY, OCTOBER 8
```
Ten    3   7  10   3   23
Cin    0  14   0   0   14
Ten  D21 R44/203  P(31-19-1)  214
Cin  D7  R20/129  P(23-10-0)   84
Ten-George 181R

Pit    3   7   0  10   20
NYJ    0   3   0   0    3
Pit  D21 R41/193  P(26-17-0)  137
NYJ  D12 R21/112  P(26-13-2)   94
Pit-Bettis 107R

NO     0  17   7   7   31
ChiB   7   0   0   3   10
NO   D24 R49/186  P(25-18-1)  217
ChiB D13 R15/72   P(37-18-3)  273
NO-Williams 128R

GB     0   6  11   7   24
Det   10  14   7   0   31
GB   D19 R22/69   P(43-27-0)  270
Det  D11 R24/74   P(26-13-1)  179

Cle    7   7   0   7   21
Arz    0  16  10   3   29
Cle  D12 R31/104  P(22-16-0)  136
Arz  D20 R31/146  P(30-17-0)  169
Arz-Pittman 107R

Buf    3   0   0  10   13
Mia    3  10   2   7   22
Buf  D15 R21/76   P(32-14-1)  134
Mia  D15 R37/120  P(24-14-1)  134
```

```
Was    7   0   0  10   17
Phi    0   7   0   7   14
Was  D23 R31/141  P(36-25-1)  266
Phi  D16 R18/75   P(35-18-2)  199

Den    7   0   7   7   21
SD     0   7   0   0    7
Den  D18 R30/96   P(40-27-0)  208
SD   D17 R20/65   P(43-18-3)  212
SD-Jones 101C

Ind    0  10   3   3   16
NE     3   7   0  14   24
Ind  D27 R26/84   P(54-31-3)  324
NE   D19 R29/118  P(25-17-0)  183
Ind-Harrison 159C, Manning 334P

NYG   10   3   0   0   13
Atl    0   3   3   0    6
NYG  D14 R33/104  P(25-14-2)  151
Atl  D17 R14/13   P(47-23-2)  225

Sea    0   0   3   0    3
Car    7  13   3   3   26
Sea  D10 R11/63   P(34-19-0)  146
Car  D26 R33/125  P(39-27-1)  322
Car-Biakabutuka 103C, Walls 102C,
Beuerlein 332P

Oak    3   3  15   7   6   34
SF     0  14   0  14   0   28
Oak  D31 R33/164  P(43-21-1)  307
SF   D28 R34/136  P(41-28-0)  336
Oak-Brown 172C, Gannon 310P;
SF-Garner 109R, Owens 176C,
Garcia 336P

Bal    3   3   3   6   15
Jax    3   0   0   7   10
Bal  D10 R25/56   P(39-17-0)  138
Jax  D22 R27/95   P(43-29-3)  253
```

MONDAY, OCTOBER 9
```
TB     7   3   6   7   23
Min    7  10   3  10   30
TB   D22 R20/63   P(41-26-0)  283
Min  D17 R30/115  P(19-15-1)  207
TB-Green 131C; Min-Moss 118C
```

SUNDAY, OCTOBER 15
```
NYJ   14  10   7   3   34
NE     3   7   0   7   17
NYJ  D20 R43/164  P(23-15-0)  130
NE   D16 R14/51   P(41-18-4)  198
NYJ-Martin 143R

Oak    0   7   3  10   20
KC     0  17   0   0   17
Oak  D23 R33/161  P(33-28-0)  230
KC   D20 R19/58   P(40-23-0)  288
KC-Gonzalez 100C

Cin    0   0   0   0    0
Pit    7   3   3   2   15
Cin  D12 R26/120  P(36-14-2)  112
Pit  D13 R32/103  P(33-13-0)  171
Pit-Bettis 101R

Phi    7  10   7   9   33
Arz    0   7   0   7   14
Phi  D28 R38/172  P(35-24-0)  219
Arz  D17 R14/98   P(30-18-2)  207
Arz-Boston 123C

SF     0   7   7  14   28
GB     3   7   7  14   31
SF   D23 R19/95   P(42-27-0)  319
GB   D22 R31/132  P(27-20-0)  246
SF-Garcia 336P; GB-Freeman 116C

SD     3   7  14   0   24
Buf    0  14   0  13   27
SD   D15 R27/52   P(34-21-2)  251
Buf  D25 R28/95   P(50-31-1)  329
SD-Conway 143C, Graham 113C;
Buf-Moulds 170C, Johnson 321P

Car    0   6   0   0    6
NO     0  10   0  14   24
Car  D8  R12/10   P(31-15-1)  131
NO   D21 R47/215  P(24-12-0)  182
NO-Williams 144R

Atl   14   7   0   8   29
Slr    7  22   0  16   45
Atl  D21 R16/61   P(30-18-1)  198
Slr  D29 R31/227  P(40-24-1)  302
Slr-Faulk 208R, Warner 313P
```

```
Dal    0   0  14   0   14
NYG    0   7   6   6   19
Dal  D23 R27/76   P(42-22-5)  193
NYG  D17 R33/203  P(25-14-0)  108
NYG-Dayne 108R

Ind    7  13  14   3   37
Sea    0  17   0   7   24
Ind  D28 R39/219  P(30-20-0)  280
Sea  D21 R16/65   P(32-24-1)  252
Ind-James 219R, Harrison 134C;
Sea-Dawkins 118C

Cle    3   0   7   0   10
Den    0  14   0  30   44
Cle  D12 R9/38    P(45-26-3)  240
Den  D24 R31/146  P(40-22-0)  353
Den-Anderson 103R,
McCaffrey 129C, Smith 111C,
Griese 336P

Bal    0   3   0   0    3
Was    0   3   0   7   10
Bal  D15 R25/91   P(27-16-1)  108
Was  D15 R29/101  P(27-18-1)  145

Min    0  14   0  14   28
ChiB   6   3   0   7   16
Min  D17 R29/191  P(26-15-0)  177
ChiB D17 R26/98   P(33-19-0)  196
Min-Smith 170R, Carter 111C
```

MONDAY, OCTOBER 16
```
Jax    3   0   0  10   13
Ten    7  10   7   3   27
Jax  D13 R26/143  P(27-18-0)  161
Ten  D18 R38/175  P(21-13-0)  234
Jax-Taylor 112R; Ten-George 167R
```

THURSDAY, OCTOBER 19
```
Det    0  11   3  14   28
TB     6   5   0   3   14
Det  D21 R37/170  P(31-13-0)  107
TB   D12 R19/109  P(34-17-3)  149
Det-Stewart 116R
```

SUNDAY, OCTOBER 22
```
Arz    0   0   0   7    7
Dal   14  13  14   7   48
Arz  D15 R24/109  P(31-20-3)  167
Dal  D23 R40/200  P(15-9-0)   147
Dal-Smith 112R

SF     0  13   3   0   16
Car    7  17   7   3   34
SF   D20 R18/128  P(39-25-1)  283
Car  D26 R25/98   P(44-28-0)  292
SF-Garner 112C, Garcia 307P;
Car-Muhammad 127C,
Beuerlein 309P

Buf    7   7   3  10   27
Min    3   3   7  18   31
Buf  D21 R28/120  P(43-28-0)  286
Min  D17 R22/97   P(29-17-1)  251
Buf-Moulds 135C; Min-Carter 107C,
Moss 110C

Ten    0   7   7   0   14
Bal    3   3   0   6   12
Ten  D7  R26/90   P(21-11-1)  101
Bal  D24 R29/113  P(46-25-4)  255
Bal-Sharpe 104C

ChiB   0   0   0   9    9
Phi    3   7   3   0   13
ChiB D14 R25/114  P(43-20-1)  160
Phi  D17 R27/97   P(35-22-1)  201

Den    7   7   0   7   21
Cin    3   7   7  14   31
Den  D32 R32/142  P(45-30-1)  358
Cin  D15 R37/407  P(14-2-0)    14
Den-McCaffrey 136C, Smith 110C,
Griese 365P; Cin-Dillon 278R

Slr    0  14  16   4   34
KC    20   7  13  14   54
Slr  D24 R20/66   P(46-30-3)  362
KC   D21 R22/106  P(34-22-0)  362
Slr-Bruce 129C; KC-Anders 102R,
Alexander 117C, Gonzalez 117C

NO     7   0   7   7   21
Atl    3  10   0   6   19
NO   D25 R38/196  P(31-19-1)  206
Atl  D13 R17/75   P(20-15-0)  203
NO-Williams 156R
```

```
NE    7  6 10  0     23
Ind   7  7 16  0     30
NE  D24 R42/155 P(34-23-0) 231
Ind D20 R21/130 P(20-16-0) 268
Ind-James 124R, Harrison 156C

Was   7 14  7  7     35
Jax   3 13  0  0     16
Was D18 R30/130 P(24-16-1) 269
Jax D21 R26/146 P(42-21-2) 239
Was-Davis 114R, Connell 211C;
Jax-Taylor 124R, Brady 111C

Sea   3  0  0  0      3
Oak   7 14  0 10     31
Sea D17 R32/137 P(30-15-1) 146
Oak D17 R27/206 P(22-15-1) 174
Oak-Wheatley 156R

Cle   0  0  0  0      0
Pit   3 10  3  6     22
Cle D5 R19/49 P(23-10-3) 55
Pit D17 R45/143 P(25-10-0) 105
Pit-Bettis 105R
```

MONDAY, OCTOBER 23
```
Mia  17  6  7  7  0  37
NYJ   0  7  0 30  3  40
Mia D20 R38/198 P(35-16-3) 235
NYJ D31 R22/79 P(59-36-3) 376
Mia-Smith 155R, Gadsden 119C;
NYJ-Anderson 109C, Chrebet 104C,
Testaverde 378P
```

SUNDAY, OCTOBER 29
```
Pit   0  0  9  0      9
Bal   0  6  0  0      6
Pit D14 R34/120 P(18-9-0) 111
Bal D14 R27/135 P(25-12-1) 139
Pit-Johnson 121C, King 267P

Cin   0  7  3  2     12
Cle   0  0  3  0      3
Cin D18 R51/192 P(20-7-1) 61
Cle D10 R20/54 P(32-13-1) 128
Cin-Dillon 137R; Cle-Johnson 102C

Car   3  3  3  3     12
Atl   3  0  0 10     13
Car D16 R20/30 P(41-21-3) 179
Atl D16 R27/97 P(29-19-2) 184

Min   3 10  0  0     13
TB   14 17  3  7     41
Min D25 R17/99 P(53-29-2) 302
TB  D23 R25/152 P(23-16-0) 261
Min-Carter 115C, Culpepper 313P;
TB-Johnson 121C, King 267P

GB   10  7  0  3     20
Mia   0  7 21  0     28
GB  D21 R24/133 P(34-21-1) 186
Mia D17 R30/140 P(25-16-0) 156

Det   0  0 11  7     18
Ind   7 16  0  7     30
Det D18 R23/154 P(39-18-2) 174
Ind D24 R31/139 P(33-22-2) 281
Ind-James 139R, Harrison 109C

NYJ   7  0 10  3     20
Buf   7 10  0  6     23
NYJ D19 R20/51 P(38-28-2) 286
Buf D18 R29/86 P(35-18-0) 252
NYJ-Coles 131C; Buf-Moulds 137C

Jax   0 17  0  0  6  23
Dal   7  0  3  7  0  17
Jax D18 R38/161 P(24-20-0) 231
Dal D22 R32/118 P(25-17-1) 207
Jax-Taylor 107R, Brady 138C;
Dal-Smith 102R, McKnight 113C

KC    7 14  0  3     24
Sea   3  7  0  9     19
KC  D17 R26/76 P(35-22-3) 334
Sea D22 R25/143 P(42-26-3) 208
KC-Alexander 137C, Gonzalez 101C,
Grbac 342P

Slr   7  7 10 10     34
SF    7 10  7  0     24
Slr D22 R30/149 P(39-22-1) 298
SF  D15 R18/92 P(44-26-0) 233
Slr-Bruce 129C, Green 310P;
SF-Owens 115C
```

```
Phi   0  0  0  7      7
NYG   7  7 10  0     24
Phi D8 R11/72 P(31-10-1) 120
NYG D25 R44/152 P(37-22-0) 232
NYG-Toomer 108C

NO    7  0  7  7     21
Arz   7  3  0  0     10
NO  D17 R29/89 P(26-16-1) 158
Arz D24 R27/125 P(47-26-2) 269

Oak   9  0  0  3     15
SD    0  0  7  6     13
Oak D19 R28/83 P(35-16-1) 145
SD  D18 R20/29 P(35-25-1) 195
SD-Jones 111C
```

MONDAY, OCTOBER 30
```
Ten   0 20  0  7     27
Was   7  0  7  7     21
Ten D13 R27/96 P(18-14-0) 93
Was D21 R24/90 P(40-21-3) 176
```

SUNDAY, NOVEMBER 5
```
Ind   0  0  8 16     24
ChiB 10 10  7  0     27
Ind  D20 R20/90 P(39-26-1) 281
ChiB D20 R35/143 P(36-25-0) 227
Ind-Manning 302P

Bal   3 21  0  3     27
Cin   0  0  7  0      7
Bal D19 R31/142 P(34-23-0) 236
Cin D11 R26/44 P(27-15-0) 130
Bal-Lewis 109R

Mia  14  3  6  0     23
Det   0  0  0  8      8
Mia D15 R37/189 P(18-13-0) 104
Det D14 R22/99 P(27-15-1) 154
Mia-Smith 125R

Pit   0  0  0  7      7
Ten   0  3  0  6      9
Pit D10 R20/74 P(22-7-1) 93
Ten D21 R40/148 P(31-20-1) 216

Buf   3  7  0  3  3  16
NE    0  0  0 13      13
Buf D20 R31/141 P(37-18-0) 174
NE  D14 R34/89 P(27-14-2) 100

NYG   0 10  7  7     24
Cle   0  0  0  3      3
NYG D24 R44/149 P(31-19-0) 221
Cle D11 R16/41 P(29-17-1) 152
NYG-Toomer 100C

Dal   0  7  3  0  3  13
Phi   0  0  0 13  3  16
Dal D16 R46/204 P(22-14-1) 91
Phi D23 R31/129 P(42-23-2) 228
Dal-Smith 134R

Den  10 10  3  7     30
NYJ   0 10 10  3     23
Den D23 R39/130 P(35-22-1) 317
NYJ D22 R17/88 P(42-21-2) 293
Den-Davis 115R, Smith 134C,
Griese 327P

TB    7  7  3 10     27
Atl   0  0  7  7     14
TB  D15 R36/126 P(26-12-1) 141
Atl D22 R15/59 P(50-30-4) 224

SF    0  0  7  8     15
NO    7 21  3  0     31
SF  D19 R20/84 P(36-22-2) 262
NO  D25 R38/111 P(27-21-0) 249
NO-Horn 180C

Was   3  9  3  0     15
Arz  10  0  6  0     16
Was D27 R37/164 P(39-20-2) 258
Arz D11 R24/45 P(19-12-1) 133
Was-Davis 124R, Thrash 102C

SD    0  3  9  3     15
Sea   0  3  0  7     17
SD  D22 R33/116 P(37-26-1) 282
Sea D9 R25/50 P(19-11-1) 78

KC    0 10  7 14     31
Oak  14 14  7 14     49
KC  D31 R9/39 P(53-39-2) 474
Oak D31 R42/231 P(31-20-0) 242
KC-Alexander 139C, Gonzalez 134C,
Morris 102C, Grbac 504P;
Oak-Wheatley 112R, Gannon 242P
```

```
Car   6  7  3 11     27
Slr   7  3 14  0     24
Car D18 R24/90 P(25-15-1) 178
Slr D20 R16/31 P(42-29-0) 395
Slr-Hakim 147C, Holt 130C,
Green 431P
```

MONDAY, NOVEMBER 6
```
Min   3 10  7  0  0  20
GB    0 10 10  0  6  26
Min D22 R33/157 P(35-17-4) 250
GB  D19 R26/81 P(36-17-0) 217
Min-Smith 122R, Moss 130C;
GB-Freeman 118C
```

SUNDAY, NOVEMBER 12
```
Atl   0  7  3  0     10
Det   7  0  0  6     13
Atl D17 R29/114 P(34-14-2) 104
Det D12 R33/107 P(27-12-1) 115
Atl-Anderson 119R

Bal   7 10  0  7     24
Ten   0 14  0  9     23
Bal D19 R29/103 P(36-23-1) 258
Ten D17 R16/62 P(34-21-0) 224

NO    0  7  7  6     20
Car   0  3  0  7     10
NO  D16 R31/157 P(23-14-1) 165
Car D21 R17/53 P(42-24-2) 258

Arz   7  0  0  7     14
Min   7  3  7 14     31
Arz D14 R18/51 P(28-19-0) 198
Min D29 R32/158 P(34-26-1) 302
Min-Smith 117R, Carter 119C,
Moss 104C, Culpepper 302P

Phi   3  7  3 10  3  26
Pit   0  6  7 10     23
Phi D21 R22/88 P(55-26-0) 202
Pit D21 R37/182 P(31-14-1) 140
Pit-Bettis 134R

ChiB  0  3  0  0      3
Buf   0  6  7  7     20
ChiB D12 R21/99 P(37-20-3) 135
Buf  D14 R35/105 P(29-18-1) 194

Cin   0  6  0  0      6
Dal   0  7 13  3     23
Cin D15 R32/139 P(25-10-1) 56
Dal D22 R32/97 P(37-24-0) 308
Cin-James 131R;
Dal-McKnight 164C, Aikman 308P

NE    3  0  0  8     11
Cle   3 10  3  3     19
NE  D18 R22/102 P(35-21-1) 184
Cle D18 R35/139 P(37-20-0) 133

GB    0  3  6  6     15
TB    0 14  0  6     20
GB  D16 R19/97 P(43-23-0) 205
TB  D14 R30/108 P(27-16-1) 164

Sea   0 14  7  7     28
Jax   7 14  0  0     21
Sea D22 R32/96 P(33-22-0) 230
Jax D24 R26/122 P(34-24-0) 315
Jax-Taylor 103R, McCardell 156C,
Smith 117C, Brunell 340P

Slr  14 14 10  0     38
NYG   0  7  0  7     14
Slr D28 R28/141 P(45-27-1) 256
NYG D14 R19/135 P(34-17-2) 213
Slr-Green 272P; NYG-Hilliard 110C

NYJ   0  0  7  8     15
Ind   0 10  3  3     16
NYJ D22 R22/96 P(38-20-2) 271
Ind D25 R38/148 P(35-21-0) 210
NYJ-Chrebet 140C; Ind-James 131R

KC    0  0  0  7      7
SF    0 21  0  0     21
KC  D20 R15/49 P(40-22-1) 245
SF  D25 R37/149 P(25-20-0) 240
SF-Garner 102R

Mia   7  7  3  0     17
SD    0  0  0  7      7
Mia D15 R41/84 P(20-13-0) 160
SD  D19 R16/82 P(47-20-4) 156
```

MONDAY, NOVEMBER 13
```
Oak   3  7  0 14     24
Den   7  0 10 10     27
Oak D25 R18/38 P(53-30-2) 373
Den D18 R23/71 P(39-26-1) 258
Oak-Brown 122C, Rison 117C,
Gannon 382P
```

SUNDAY, NOVEMBER 19
```
TB    0  3  7  0     10
ChiB  3  7  0  3     13
TB   D14 R33/165 P(19-12-2) 60
ChiB D15 R28/83 P(34-20-1) 160

Cle   0  0 10  0     10
Ten   0  7  0 17     24
Cle D5 R18/45 P(20-13-1) 80
Ten D23 R47/182 P(25-16-4) 192
Ten-George 134R

Dal   0  0  0  0      0
Bal   7  0 14  6     27
Dal D9 R14/55 P(33-19-3) 137
Bal D22 R44/250 P(24-18-2) 229
Bal-Lewis 187R, Sharpe 101C

Oak   3 14  0 14     31
NO    0  7  6  2     15
Oak D19 R36/159 P(21-14-0) 134
NO  D19 R30/133 P(27-16-1) 200

Cin   0 10  3  0     13
NE    7  3  0  6     16
Cin D25 R37/137 P(38-20-1) 228
NE  D17 R22/39 P(36-22-1) 252
NE-Brown 110C, Glenn 129C

Car   7  0  3  7     17
Min  14 10  7  0     31
Car D23 R26/78 P(44-26-2) 252
Min D19 R26/117 P(29-22-0) 329
Min-Smith 103R, Carter 138C,
Moss 106C, Culpepper 357P

Buf   7  0  0 14     21
KC    3  7  7  0     17
Buf D21 R26/75 P(37-22-0) 252
KC  D24 R19/103 P(48-28-1) 275
KC-Alexander 146C, Grbac 341P

Arz   3  0  0  6      9
Phi   0  7 10 17     34
Arz D12 R17/54 P(28-19-1) 156
Phi D21 R31/134 P(34-25-1) 204

Ind   0  0  3 21     24
GB    5 14  0  7     26
Ind D25 R17/71 P(44-25-1) 207
GB  D25 R28/145 P(37-23-1) 287
GB-Green 153R, Schroeder 155C,
Favre 301P

Det   0 21  7  3     31
NYG   0  0 14  7     21
Det D22 R35/95 P(32-20-1) 219
NYG D25 R15/53 P(39-23-2) 249
NYG-Toomer 108C, Collins 350P

Jax   0 17 17  0     34
Pit   7  3  0 14     24
Jax D20 R36/240 P(31-17-1) 177
Pit D15 R24/147 P(27-13-2) 155
Jax-Taylor 234R

NYJ   3  3  0 14     20
Mia   0  7  0  3     10
NYJ D18 R32/133 P(29-14-2) 106
Mia D10 R22/83 P(29-16-3) 117

Atl   0  3  0  3      6
SF    3  3  7  3     16
Atl D11 R20/93 P(33-16-1) 118
SF  D17 R32/127 P(31-16-0) 210

SD    3 21 10  3     37
Den   0 10  7 21     38
SD  D14 R27/86 P(27-13-1) 209
Den D34 R22/93 P(58-36-4) 443
SD-Conway 118C, Graham 144C,
Leaf 311P; Den-McCaffrey 148C,
Smith 187C, Frerotte 462P
```

MONDAY, NOVEMBER 20
```
Was   3 10 12  8     33
Slr  10  3  7  0     20
Was D21 R32/138 P(34-24-1) 262
Slr D18 R14/50 P(38-23-1) 344
Slr-Holt 125C, Green 366P
```

THURSDAY, NOVEMBER 23
```
NE    6  0  3  0      9
Det   3  3  7 21     34
NE  D15 R20/66 P(35-18-2) 149
Det D17 R28/110 P(25-17-0) 189

Min   0 10 17  0     27
Dal   3  6  0  6     15
Min D18 R30/168 P(22-15-0) 192
Dal D22 R24/128 P(43-30-1) 276
Min-Smith 148R, Moss 144C;
Dal-Smith 100R
```

SUNDAY, NOVEMBER 26
```
Cle   7  0  0  0      7
Bal   7 24  6  7     44
Cle D5 R17/28 P(25-13-1) 84
Bal D25 R51/247 P(26-14-1) 214
Bal-Lewis 170R

Buf   0  7  0 10     17
TB    3  7  0 21     31
Buf D25 R27/139 P(49-28-0) 294
TB  D13 R25/114 P(18-10-0) 66
Buf-Moulds 102C; TB-Dunn 106R

Phi   7  3  7  6     23
Was   7  3  3  7     20
Phi D14 R26/171 P(31-19-1) 118
Was D20 R19/44 P(43-25-0) 282
Phi-McNabb 125R;
Was-Thrash 121C

Pit  14 10 21  3     48
Cin   7  7  7  7     28
Pit D21 R38/185 P(22-12-0) 187
Cin D23 R41/209 P(20-10-0) 100
Cin-Dillon 128R

NO    7 14  3  7     31
Slr   7  3  7  7     24
NO  D22 R44/147 P(29-17-2) 185
Slr D21 R10/28 P(41-20-1) 251

Ten   7  3  0  3     13
Jax  10  0  3  3     16
Ten D17 R31/117 P(24-13-0) 217
Jax D16 R28/111 P(25-15-2) 223
Ten-George 109C; Jax-Taylor 104R

ChiB  0  0  3  7     10
NYJ   0 10  0  7     17
ChiB D13 R30/135 P(32-13-0) 98
NYJ D17 R32/59 P(35-21-1) 218
ChiB-Allen 122R

KC    3  3 10  0     16
SD    7  7  0  3     17
KC  D10 R31/77 P(31-12-1) 84
SD  D14 R22/52 P(30-17-2) 149

Den   0 10  7 21     38
Sea   0 14 10  7     31
Den D25 R41/301 P(31-15-2) 237
Sea D17 R21/85 P(48-23-2) 269
Den-Anderson 195R;
Sea-Watters 126C

Mia   0  3  7  7     17
Ind   7  0  0  7     14
Mia D17 R24/82 P(33-22-0) 171
Ind D19 R31/144 P(34-16-1) 209
Ind-James 118R

Atl   7  0  0  7     14
Oak   3 21 14  3     41
Atl D15 R13/31 P(29-18-1) 150
Oak D24 R38/270 P(22-15-0) 222
Atl-Jefferson 109C

NYG   7  7  7 10     31
Arz   0  7  0  0      7
NYG D25 R40/146 P(30-20-0) 225
Arz D14 R16/88 P(39-20-1) 179
```

MONDAY, NOVEMBER 27
```
GB    0 14  0  0     14
Car  14  3  7  7     31
GB  D20 R14/87 P(51-31-3) 209
Car D24 R31/133 P(37-22-1) 223
Car-Hoover 117R, Muhammad 131C
```

THURSDAY, NOVEMBER 30
```
Det   0  3  0 14     17
Min   7 10  0  7     24
Det D20 R25/139 P(36-25-1) 213
Min D19 R25/145 P(32-19-2) 160
Det-Foster 106C; Min-Smith 115R
```

THE GAMES

SUNDAY, DECEMBER 3

Sea 17 7 6 0 **30**
Atl 0 3 0 7 10
Sea D17 R25/83 P(34-25-0) 252
Atl D20 R24/97 P(33-17-2) 204

Arz 0 0 7 6 13
Cin 7 7 7 3 **24**
Arz D15 R19/72 P(44-22-1) 268
Cin D27 R54/292 P(23-11-1) 106
Arz-Boston 184C; Cin-Dillon 216R

Oak 0 17 0 3 20
Pit 7 0 7 7 **21**
Oak D20 R28/117 P(40-21-0) 273
Pit D19 R32/199 P(26-15-1) 112
Pit-Bettis 128R

Den 7 21 3 7 **38**
NO 0 7 6 3 7
Den D24 R49/283 P(16-11-0) 200
NO D19 R9/21 P(48-30-2) 425
Den-Anderson 251R;
NO-Horn 170C, Wilson 122C, Brooks 441P

Slr 3 0 0 0 3
Car 0 0 7 9 **16**
Slr D15 R16/99 P(36-18-4) 179
Car D20 R33/68 P(30-20-2) 169

NYG 0 6 3 0 **9**
Was 0 0 0 7 7
NYG D13 R36/141 P(29-18-1) 164
Was D15 R13/29 P(47-24-2) 261

Mia 7 17 6 3 **33**
Buf 0 0 0 6 6
Mia D15 R37/133 P(21-13-0) 200
Buf D14 R26/160 P(27-8-3) 36
Mia-Smith 100R

SF 0 17 10 18 **45**
SD 7 3 0 7 17
SF D19 R28/73 P(33-19-0) 312
SD D18 R13/49 P(47-24-4) 254
SF-Garcia 323P

Dal 0 0 7 0 7
TB 17 3 0 7 **27**
Dal D19 R28/113 P(33-17-1) 153
TB D17 R36/250 P(15-9-0) 51
TB-Dunn 210R

GB 0 14 7 7 **28**
ChiB 0 3 0 3 6
GB D17 R28/81 P(31-19-0) 223
ChiB D17 R23/104 P(44-22-2) 226
GB-Schroeder 119C

Cle 0 0 0 0 0
Jax 3 17 21 7 **48**
Cle D2 R18/62 P(18-7-0) -9
Jax D28 R47/244 P(33-16-0) 205
Jax-Taylor 181R, Smith 104C

Ten 0 6 3 6 **15**
Phi 3 3 0 7 13
Ten D24 R36/118 P(39-24-0) 213
Phi D14 R17/56 P(31-18-0) 261
Ten-George 101R

Ind 0 0 10 7 17
NYJ 14 6 0 7 **27**
Ind D21 R12/49 P(51-27-2) 326
NYJ D26 R39/211 P(41-26-1) 280
Ind-Wilkins 109C, Manning 339P;
NYJ-Martin 203R

MONDAY, DECEMBER 4

KC 3 7 0 14 24
NE 10 10 7 3 **30**
KC D18 R19/68 P(46-25-1) 350
NE D24 R31/105 P(48-33-0) 263
KC-Alexander 116C, Gonzalez 147C,
Grbac 350P; NE-Brown 119C

SUNDAY, DECEMBER 10

NE 0 10 0 7 17
ChiB 3 7 7 7 **24**
NE D15 R12/38 P(46-25-0) 207
ChiB D21 R39/102 P(27-22-0) 237
ChiB-Kennison 100C

Phi 7 14 14 0 **35**
Cle 0 14 0 10 24
Phi D23 R15/41 P(36-23-0) 350
Cle D25 R30/101 P(43-30-3) 317
Phi-Lewis 100C, McNabb 390P;
Cle-Patten 103C, Pederson 309P

Arz 0 3 0 7 10
Jax 10 17 10 7 **44**
Arz D11 R19/40 P(26-15-1) 149
Jax D25 R45/214 P(21-15-0) 255
Jax-Taylor 137R, Smith 147C

Pit 0 3 0 7 10
NYG 3 10 7 10 **30**
Pit D17 R20/47 P(24-21-0) 217
NYG D20 R26/68 P(35-24-0) 326
NYG-Toomer 136C, Collins 333P

Cin 0 3 0 3 6
Ten 14 7 7 7 **35**
Cin D9 R25/60 P(26-12-0) 111
Ten D21 R36/112 P(33-23-0) 331

Min 0 7 14 8 29
Slr 14 6 13 7 **40**
Min D23 R19/104 P(33-21-0) 208
Slr D32 R34/162 P(32-27-0) 346
Slr-Faulk 135R, Holt 172C,
Warner 346P

Was 0 7 0 6 13
Dal 6 6 10 10 **32**
Was D17 R22/79 P(33-19-1) 191
Dal D19 R43/242 P(8-5-0) 72
Dal-Smith 150R

Car 0 7 0 7 14
KC 0 3 3 9 **15**
Car D21 R16/23 P(31-23-1) 234
KC D26 R26/138 P(44-31-2) 315
Car-Muhammad 102C;
KC-Grbac 315P

SD 0 0 3 0 3
Bal 3 7 14 0 **24**
SD D9 R26/64 P(23-9-1) 64
Bal D19 R40/110 P(24-16-2) 166

Sea 3 0 7 14 24
Den 3 7 0 21 **31**
Sea D22 R26/107 P(41-26-3) 298
Den D20 R36/131 P(25-14-1) 182
Den-Anderson 131R,
McCaffrey 112C

NO 3 0 11 17 **31**
SF 7 7 0 13 27
NO D21 R38/216 P(29-12-0) 172
SF D21 R21/110 P(38-25-2) 288
NO-Brooks 108R, Horn 105C;
SF-Owens 129C, Garcia 305P

TB 0 10 0 6 **16**
Mia 0 0 0 10 10
TB D14 R38/100 P(15-11-1) 121
Mia D17 R27/84 P(28-13-4) 170

Det 0 0 3 10 13
GB 6 0 3 17 **26**
Det D15 R31/103 P(33-17-3) 190
GB D16 R32/128 P(36-15-1) 203
GB-Green 118R

NYJ 0 0 0 7 7
Oak 0 21 0 10 **31**
NYJ D14 R20/10 P(44-22-4) 290
Oak D17 R38/180 P(23-11-1) 150
NYJ-Anderson 103C

MONDAY, DECEMBER 11

Buf 3 3 6 8 20
Ind 3 6 14 21 **44**
Buf D16 R22/66 P(34-18-2) 228
Ind D20 R32/121 P(24-13-0) 116
Ind-James 111R

SATURDAY, DECEMBER 16

Was 3 0 0 0 3
Pit 0 17 0 7 **24**
Was D14 R21/64 P(32-18-2) 207
Pit D21 R45/200 P(21-11-0) 174
Pit-Bettis 104R

Oak 7 3 7 7 24
Sea 3 0 7 14 24
Oak D15 R42/227 P(17-5-3) 134
Sea D18 R31/173 P(32-19-1) 153
Oak-Wheatley 146R;
Sea-Watters 168R

SUNDAY, DECEMBER 17

GB 10 10 3 10 **33**
Min 7 7 7 7 28
GB D28 R31/154 P(38-26-0) 280
Min D19 R17/68 P(38-23-1) 332
GB-Green 161R; Min-Moss 136C,
Culpepper 335P

Jax 0 7 7 0 14
Cin 0 0 7 10 **17**
Jax D17 R34/114 P(28-19-0) 162
Cin D27 R27/106 P(22-10-1) 157
Jax-Taylor 110R, Cin-Farmer 102C

Den 0 0 7 0 7
KC 3 0 7 10 **20**
Den D11 R14/53 P(35-22-0) 225
KC D24 R41/264 P(28-14-0) 160
Den-Smith 101C;
KC-Richardson 156R

Atl 0 0 7 0 7
NO 0 13 7 3 **23**
Atl D9 R21/64 P(20-9-2) 99
NO D19 R30/92 P(35-24-0) 281
NO-Horn 116C

Ten 10 7 0 7 **24**
Cle 0 0 0 0 0
Ten D19 R47/212 P(20-12-1) 93
Cle D6 R17/50 P(30-13-0) 63
Ten-George 176R

ChiB 0 0 0 0 0
SF 7 3 7 0 **17**
ChiB D8 R18/39 P(29-9-1) 65
SF D26 R28/77 P(44-36-0) 379
SF-Owens 283C, Garcia 402P

SD 2 14 6 0 22
Car 7 0 13 10 **30**
SD D19 R34/100 P(43-23-1) 258
Car D13 R15/11 P(40-18-1) 158

Bal 3 0 10 0 **13**
Arz 0 0 7 0 7
Bal D14 R37/177 P(22-12-1) 37
Arz D18 R23/51 P(43-23-2) 258
Bal-Lewis 126R

Det 0 0 3 7 **10**
NYJ 7 0 0 0 7
Det D16 R44/210 P(18-8-1) 78
NYJ D12 R18/51 P(36-21-1) 189
Det-Stewart 164R

Ind 7 10 3 0 **20**
Mia 0 3 7 3 13
Ind D20 R35/132 P(26-12-0) 195
Mia D14 R26/140 P(26-12-1) 132
Ind-James 112R

NYG 0 0 7 10 **17**
Dal 7 6 0 0 13
NYG D12 R31/99 P(26-12-1) 126
Dal D15 R30/75 P(25-13-1) 70

MONDAY, DECEMBER 18

Slr 7 7 7 14 35
TB 10 14 7 7 **38**
Slr D19 R23/90 P(32-20-3) 298
TB D27 R32/205 P(38-18-2) 241
Slr-Holt 165C, Warner 316P;
TB-Dunn 145R, Johnson 116C

SATURDAY, DECEMBER 23

SF 0 0 0 9 9
Den 0 17 21 0 **38**
SF D16 R15/46 P(40-18-1) 146
Den D28 R42/159 P(31-20-0) 203

Jax 3 3 15 4 25
NYG 7 0 0 21 **28**
Jax D14 R18/70 P(41-23-1) 257
NYG D19 R31/80 P(39-22-1) 293
Jax-McCardell 131C;
NYG-Toomer 193C, Collins 321P

Buf 21 7 7 7 **42**
Sea 7 7 3 6 23
Buf D27 R37/213 P(25-20-0) 366
Sea D17 R26/126 P(29-18-1) 186
Buf-Smith 147R, Moulds 101C,
Price 132C, Flutie 366P

SUNDAY, DECEMBER 24

Slr 7 3 9 7 **26**
NO 0 7 0 14 21
Slr D26 R42/246 P(27-18-1) 228
NO D12 R15/73 P(31-16-1) 196
Slr-Faulk 220R, Holt 121C

NYJ 14 0 3 3 20
Bal 0 20 7 7 **34**
NYJ D22 R21/51 P(69-36-3) 473
Bal D5 R26/64 P(25-11-2) 78
NYJ-Anderson 139C, Ward 147C,
Testaverde 481P

Cin 0 0 0 7 7
Phi 10 3 0 3 **16**
Cin D15 R26/102 P(34-18-1) 169
Phi D22 R35/138 P(40-23-1) 183

KC 7 0 0 6 13
Atl 7 6 6 10 **29**
KC D15 R12/49 P(32-18-0) 210
Atl D20 R36/131 P(29-20-0) 157
Atl-Anderson 107R

Arz 0 3 0 0 3
Was 14 6 0 0 **20**
Arz D14 R21/104 P(32-14-3) 141
Was D19 R33/140 P(34-21-2) 175
Was-Davis 120R

ChiB 0 6 7 10 **23**
Det 10 0 0 10 20
ChiB D15 R26/105 P(29-19-0) 181
Det D18 R26/100 P(36-19-1) 140

Mia 3 14 0 10 **27**
NE 7 14 0 3 24
Mia D25 R24/47 P(46-31-0) 263
NE D18 R21/37 P(35-18-2) 311
NE-Brown 102C, Bledsoe 312P

Min 7 3 0 0 10
Ind 3 14 7 7 **31**
Min D11 R21/67 P(28-16-1) 169
Ind D25 R29/128 P(36-25-1) 283
Ind-James 128R, Harrison 109C,
Manning 283P

GB 0 0 3 11 14
TB 7 7 0 3 **17**
TB D16 R23/67 P(42-21-0) 205
GB D21 R38/135 P(42-20-2) 184

Car 3 6 0 0 9
Oak 7 17 14 14 **52**
Car D19 R12/79 P(37-22-1) 218
Oak D26 R39/179 P(32-26-0) 230
Car-Muhammad 114C;
Oak-Gannon 230P

Pit 7 17 0 10 **34**
SD 14 0 7 0 21
Pit D21 R41/131 P(33-16-2) 185
SD D6 R12/31 P(29-15-1) 140
SD-Graham 113C

MONDAY, DECEMBER 25

Dal 0 0 0 0 0
Ten 7 0 24 0 **31**
Dal D6 R29/86 P(20-5-2) 9
Ten D23 R36/158 P(33-20-2) 216

2001 NFL
SUNDAY, SEPTEMBER 9

Oak 6 0 8 13 **27**
KC 7 7 3 7 24
Oak D23 R28/100 P(46-31-1) 327
KC D16 R17/35 P(37-16-1) 219
Oak-Brown 133C, Gannon 341P

Was 0 0 0 3 3
SD 10 10 0 10 **30**
Was D8 R19/44 P(32-15-2) 117
SD D19 R46/133 P(18-10-2) 122
SD-Tomlinson 113R

Atl 7 3 3 0 13
SF 3 0 10 3 **16**
Atl D13 R31/134 P(22-11-0) 107
SF D20 R28/105 P(40-26-1) 324
SF-Garcia 335P

Ind 3 28 7 7 **45**
NYJ 3 0 7 14 24
Ind D22 R30/154 P(22-22-2) 222
NYJ D17 R29/138 P(31-18-0) 192
Ind-James 135R

NE 0 10 0 7 17
Cin 0 10 13 0 **23**
NE D16 R21/68 P(38-22-0) 224
Cin D18 R33/157 P(27-18-0) 196
NE-Brown 106C; Cin-Dillon 104R,
Scott 104C

Slr 7 3 10 0 **20**
Phi 3 0 0 14 17
Slr D22 R23/82 P(42-28-2) 282
Phi D19 R18/57 P(48-32-1) 277
Slr-Warner 308P; Phi-McNabb 312P

Sea 0 3 0 6 **9**
Cle 0 3 0 3 6
Sea D16 R27/101 P(34-20-2) 150
Cle D13 R25/90 P(33-17-1) 149

Det 3 3 0 0 6
GB 21 0 7 0 **28**
Det D14 R20/56 P(39-20-2) 232
GB D20 R29/179 P(48-22-0) 245
Det-Morton 111C; GB-Green 157R,
Schroeder 104C

NO 0 0 17 7 **24**
Buf 3 3 0 0 6
NO D17 R26/109 P(30-18-0) 192
Buf D12 R28/125 P(28-16-3) 126

TB 3 0 0 7 **10**
Dal 3 0 0 0 3
TB D19 R33/71 P(34-25-1) 192
Dal D8 R23/99 P(19-9-2) 28

Mia 10 7 7 7 **31**
Ten 0 7 7 9 23
Mia D11 R33/82 P(20-12-0) 225
Ten D19 R25/105 P(40-16-3) 210

Pit 0 3 0 0 3
Jax 0 0 0 21 **21**
Pit D15 R28/120 P(37-21-2) 161
Jax D16 R29/101 P(26-15-0) 198
Jax-Smith 126C

Car 7 3 7 7 **24**
Min 0 0 13 0 13
Car D15 R38/91 P(22-13-1) 200
Min D19 R26/109 P(38-22-3) 234

ChiB 3 0 3 0 6
Bal 0 7 3 7 **17**
ChiB D16 R28/56 P(39-24-2) 133
Bal D19 R30/54 P(30-24-0) 262

MONDAY, SEPTEMBER 10

NYG 0 7 7 6 20
Den 7 7 10 7 **31**
NYG D17 R19/63 P(34-19-0) 245
Den D25 R36/143 P(29-21-0) 330
Den-Davis 101R, Smith 115C,
Griese 330P

SUNDAY, SEPTEMBER 23

Oak 3 3 3 6 15
Mia 0 3 12 3 **18**
Oak D12 R26/96 P(25-14-0) 120
Mia D19 R34/144 P(34-16-2) 215

Min 3 0 7 0 10
ChiB 0 0 3 14 **17**
Min D19 R25/104 P(37-24-0) 215
ChiB D15 R19/47 P(38-23-1) 237

Phi 3 14 0 10 **27**
Sea 0 3 0 0 3
Phi D18 R31/102 P(37-24-0) 242
Sea D9 R26/126 P(24-9-0) 21
Phi-Thrash 165C

Det 0 0 7 7 14
Cle 7 7 0 7 **21**
Det D18 R20/82 P(42-22-7) 189
Cle D17 R37/139 P(20-12-2) 118
Det-Morton 100C; Cle-Jackson 124R

Slr 9 3 10 8 **30**
SF 0 16 0 10 26
Slr D20 R25/115 P(35-24-1) 310
SF D14 R25/116 P(34-19-1) 116
Slr-Faulk 105R, Bruce 144C,
Warner 321P

Buf 7 10 3 6 26
Ind 14 21 7 0 **42**
Buf D19 R22/145 P(37-24-1) 229
Ind D28 R30/137 P(29-23-2) 418
Ind-James 111R, Harrison 146C,
Pathon 168C, Manning 421P

Den 0 17 14 7 **38**
Arz 3 7 0 7 17
Den D27 R37/147 P(31-22-0) 234
Arz D14 R18/84 P(28-16-1) 224
Den-Smith 162C; Arz-Boston 145C

Ten 3 3 0 0 6
Jax 3 7 3 0 **13**
Ten D13 R22/87 P(36-21-0) 177
Jax D16 R30/119 P(27-17-0) 210

SD 14 6 6 6 **32**
Dal 0 14 0 7 21
SD D26 R38/130 P(38-23-0) 345
Dal D14 R26/101 P(25-12-3) 188
SD-Flutie 348P

Car 3 7 3 3 16
Atl 7 3 7 7 **21**
Car D18 R21/89 P(41-27-0) 270
Atl D16 R28/121 P(16-13-1) 256
Car-Muhammad 132C

NYJ 0 3 7 0 **10**
NE 3 0 0 0 3
NYJ D14 R27/111 P(28-16-0) 127
NE D15 R26/107 P(38-23-2) 201
NYJ-Martin 106R

Bal 3 0 0 7 10
Cin 0 0 14 7 **21**
Bal D24 R20/64 P(64-34-3) 318
Cin D13 R23/67 P(30-19-0) 136
Bal-Grbac 326P

NYG 3 10 0 0 **13**
KC 0 0 3 0 3
NYG D20 R31/98 P(34-20-3) 201
KC D11 R20/88 P(34-17-1) 178

MONDAY, SEPTEMBER 24
Was 0 0 0 0 0
GB 7 3 10 17 **37**
Was D8 R15/71 P(24-15-1) 66
GB D23 R40/160 P(31-20-1) 226
GB-Green 116R

SUNDAY, SEPTEMBER 30
TB 3 3 3 7 16
Min 7 3 3 7 **20**
TB D20 R16/108 P(34-20-1) 223
Min D25 R24/90 P(44-30-2) 312
Min-Culpepper 322P

GB 0 6 15 7 **28**
Car 0 7 0 0 7
GB D22 R31/75 P(39-25-2) 308
Car D9 R17/36 P(30-18-1) 133
GB-Favre 308P

Bal 3 3 7 7 **20**
Den 10 0 3 0 13
Bal D16 R34/112 P(30-17-1) 221
Den D13 R24/61 P(33-17-2) 167

Pit 7 3 0 10 **20**
Buf 0 3 0 0 3
Pit D16 R31/170 P(22-15-0) 100
Buf D14 R22/52 P(27-16-1) 120
Pit-Bettis 114R

Ind 0 0 7 6 13
NE 7 13 3 21 **44**
Ind D20 R24/82 P(43-25-3) 240
NE D19 R39/177 P(23-13-0) 159

Sea 0 0 7 7 14
Oak 7 17 14 0 **38**
Sea D21 R16/42 P(47-25-1) 306
Oak D17 R25/93 P(32-22-0) 251
Sea-Jackson 125C

Cin 0 0 7 0 7
SD 0 7 14 7 **28**
Cin D17 R26/111 P(32-18-3) 126
SD D16 R35/133 P(19-12-0) 112
SD-Tomlinson 107R

Mia 7 3 0 0 10
Slr 7 14 7 14 **42**
Mia D15 R25/64 P(27-19-2) 189
Slr D27 R27/123 P(31-24-0) 318
Slr-Holt 111C, Warner 328P

Dal 6 0 0 12 18
Phi 7 26 7 0 **40**
Dal D11 R30/181 P(30-11-1) 61
Phi D14 R30/131 P(28-14-0) 145
Dal-Hambrick 107R

Atl 10 3 7 14 **34**
Arz 0 0 7 7 14
Atl D21 R34/111 P(28-20-0) 268
Arz D21 R15/90 P(35-23-3) 245
Atl-Smith 108C

Cle 3 10 0 10 **23**
Jax 0 0 14 0 14
Cle D19 R36/95 P(34-24-1) 226
Jax D14 R19/98 P(37-19-2) 161

KC 0 28 7 10 **45**
Was 3 7 3 0 13
KC D29 R38/200 P(30-24-0) 346
Was D11 R20/111 P(27-11-1) 107
KC-Holmes 147R, Green 307P

NO 0 3 0 10 13
NYG 0 14 0 7 **21**
NO D20 R22/74 P(54-28-1) 256
NYG D13 R28/153 P(18-9-0) 100
NO-Jackson 105C; NYG-Dayne 111R

MONDAY, OCTOBER 1
SF 0 13 3 3 **19**
NYJ 7 0 3 7 17
SF D21 R43/233 P(20-16-0) 126
NYJ D16 R23/82 P(25-12-0) 186

SUNDAY, OCTOBER 7
Was 3 3 3 0 9
NYG 3 6 0 14 **23**
Was D9 R17/57 P(31-13-2) 124
NYG D21 R46/142 P(29-15-2) 167

Min 7 0 8 0 15
NO 6 9 10 3 **28**
Min D16 R11/34 P(34-23-1) 306
NO D20 R37/160 P(30-15-1) 210
Min-Culpepper 332P; NO-Williams 136R

KC 0 6 0 0 6
Den 7 3 3 7 **20**
KC D16 R17/42 P(40-25-4) 255
Den D15 R39/197 P(20-11-1) 103
KC-Gonzalez 129C; Den-Anderson 155R, Smith 110C

Jax 3 9 3 0 15
Sea 14 7 0 3 **24**
Jax D18 R21/57 P(39-21-0) 199
Sea D21 R36/185 P(23-15-1) 210
Sea-Alexander 176R

GB 0 7 3 0 10
TB 0 7 0 7 **14**
GB D15 R22/69 P(35-20-3) 253
TB D12 R19/99 P(29-23-0) 154
GB-Schroeder 119C

NYJ 21 7 14 0 **42**
Buf 6 9 14 7 36
NYJ D21 R32/162 P(25-15-0) 173
Buf D26 R32/162 P(45-26-2) 311
NYJ-Martin 135R; Buf-Henry 113R, Moulds 107C, Price 103C

Dal 0 7 7 7 21
Oak 7 14 7 0 **28**
Dal D17 R30/108 P(27-15-0) 123
Oak D23 R34/101 P(28-21-0) 207
Oak-Brown 114C

Cin 0 0 0 7 7
Pit 0 10 0 6 **16**
Cin D15 R21/65 P(34-19-1) 149
Pit D19 R40/275 P(24-15-0) 138
Pit-Bettis 153R

Car 0 7 7 0 14
SF 0 10 14 0 **24**
Car D17 R16/61 P(47-29-3) 275
SF D21 R35/150 P(31-17-1) 203
SF-Owens 118C

SD 3 0 7 6 16
Cle 0 10 0 10 **20**
SD D15 R26/126 P(37-17-0) 143
Cle D16 R31/97 P(27-14-0) 181
SD-Tomlinson 102R

Ten 0 0 7 0 7
Bal 3 8 8 7 **26**
Ten D9 R17/47 P(33-17-2) 138
Bal D23 R40/207 P(31-15-0) 253
Bal-Allen 108R

NE 7 3 0 0 10
Mia 7 10 10 3 **30**
NE D12 R23/80 P(24-12-0) 69
Mia D19 R44/209 P(21-11-1) 87
Mia-Smith 144R

ChiB 0 10 0 21 **31**
Atl 0 0 0 3 3
ChiB D15 R24/79 P(27-18-2) 221
Atl D19 R25/103 P(30-19-3) 232
ChiB-Robinson 114C

Arz 14 0 0 7 **21**
Phi 7 10 0 3 20
Arz D19 R28/97 P(32-18-1) 232
Phi D19 R30/179 P(29-19-1) 261
Arz-Jenkins 119C; Phi-Buckhalter 134R

MONDAY, OCTOBER 8
Slr 7 14 0 14 **35**
Det 7 0 0 0 7
Slr D23 R21/94 P(37-29-0) 284
Det D14 R18/105 P(34-26-2) 229

SUNDAY, OCTOBER 14
Arz 0 6 0 7 13
ChiB 3 10 7 0 **20**
Arz D16 R25/82 P(37-20-0) 206
ChiB D13 R32/137 P(21-15-2) 116

SD 3 3 7 13 26
NE 3 6 7 10 3 **29**
SD D20 R28/85 P(32-20-0) 258
NE D30 R24/29 P(54-33-0) 345
SD-Conway 117C; NE-Brown 117C, Glenn 110C, Brady 364P

NO 10 7 3 7 **27**
Car 0 6 6 13 25
NO D21 R39/198 P(40-14-1) 160
Car D13 R20/34 P(39-21-1) 184
NO-Williams 147R

Cle 7 0 0 7 14
Cin 3 0 10 11 **24**
Cle D15 R19/40 P(28-14-0) 171
Cin D23 R42/199 P(38-20-0) 258
Cle-Johnson 153C; Cin-Dillon 140R

Mia 7 0 0 10 17
NYJ 0 0 14 7 **21**
Mia D19 R29/115 P(35-24-2) 229
NYJ D19 R25/128 P(22-15-0) 140
NYJ-Martin 120R

Den 0 14 0 7 21
Sea 10 14 7 3 **34**
Den D20 R20/92 P(36-24-3) 189
Sea D21 R40/161 P(18-12-0) 93
Sea-Alexander 142R

Oak 3 10 7 3 **23**
Ind 0 9 6 3 18
Oak D18 R30/101 P(32-18-0) 216
Ind D26 R27/118 P(41-26-2) 234
Oak-Brown 145C; Ind-James 116R

Det 3 3 7 13 26
Min 7 17 7 0 **31**
Det D28 R20/129 P(41-31-0) 328
Min D23 R27/145 P(27-20-1) 198
Det-Stewart 108R, Crowell 125C, Batch 345P; Min-Carter 111C

NYG 7 0 0 7 14
Slr 6 3 0 6 **15**
NYG D16 R24/97 P(32-17-2) 227
Slr D19 R16/41 P(46-28-1) 274
Slr-Warner 316P

Bal 7 0 3 13 23
GB 0 7 7 17 **31**
Bal D22 R34/158 P(31-16-2) 199
GB D23 R24/60 P(34-27-0) 331
GB-Freeman 138C, Favre 337P

SF 0 7 10 14 6 **37**
Atl 14 6 0 11 0 31
SF D27 R35/187 P(41-27-0) 330
Atl D21 R24/88 P(36-19-1) 254
SF-Owens 183C, Garcia 332P

TB 7 0 7 14 0 28
Ten 7 10 0 11 3 **31**
TB D22 R17/24 P(50-24-1) 282
Ten D21 R41/142 P(26-18-1) 223
TB-Johnson 140C

Pit 0 6 14 0 **20**
KC 0 2 0 15 17
Pit D16 R35/203 P(25-15-0) 113
KC D19 R24/165 P(33-16-1) 106
Pit-Bettis 112R; KC-Holmes 150R

MONDAY, OCTOBER 15
Was 0 0 0 7 7
Dal 0 3 0 6 **9**
Was D10 R26/103 P(18-10-0) 123
Dal D23 R45/211 P(28-15-1) 175
Dal-Smith 107R

THURSDAY, OCTOBER 18
Buf 0 3 7 3 **13**
Jax 0 0 7 3 10
Buf D19 R35/98 P(30-23-0) 219
Jax D14 R21/115 P(26-16-2) 132

SUNDAY, OCTOBER 21
ChiB 3 7 7 7 **24**
Cin 0 0 0 0 0
ChiB D21 R32/203 P(30-23-0) 232
Cin D16 R21/35 P(46-19-1) 229
ChiB-Thomas 188R

Pit 0 7 10 0 **17**
TB 0 3 0 7 10
Pit D17 R35/220 P(17-11-2) 124
TB D19 R19/64 P(40-24-1) 214
Pit-Bettis 143R; TB-Johnson 159C

Car 7 0 0 7 14
Was 0 0 14 3 **17**
Car D19 R25/124 P(35-24-4) 218
Was D19 R28/98 P(30-17-1) 345
Car-Biakabutuka 121R; Was-Gardner 208C, Banks 346P

Den 0 7 0 3 10
SD 7 6 7 7 **27**
Den D19 R21/81 P(41-26-2) 182
SD D22 R32/107 P(32-21-1) 272
SD-Graham 107C

Bal 0 6 0 8 14
Cle 7 3 14 0 **24**
Bal D21 R27/113 P(45-27-2) 208
Cle D10 R29/88 P(18-11-0) 131

GB 0 0 7 6 13
Min 0 20 0 15 **35**
GB D10 R15/74 P(35-21-1) 160
Min D23 R36/200 P(27-18-0) 177

Ten 3 6 8 10 **27**
Det 0 14 0 10 24
Ten D18 R33/102 P(36-16-2) 227
Det D18 R19/41 P(42-25-1) 322
Ten-Wycheck 100C; Det-Morton 113C, Batch 338P

NE 7 21 7 3 **38**
Ind 3 3 11 0 17
NE D19 R30/123 P(21-17-0) 262
Ind D28 R34/179 P(34-22-0) 305
NE-Brown 120C, Patten 117C; Ind-James 143R, Harrison 157C, Manning 335P

Slr 0 21 0 13 **34**
NYJ 0 7 0 7 14
Slr D22 R34/234 P(28-19-0) 214
NYJ D17 R24/132 P(27-18-1) 134
Slr-Canidate 195R

Atl 10 0 0 10 **20**
NO 0 10 0 3 13
Atl D12 R30/124 P(21-15-1) 173
NO D16 R24/63 P(39-23-1) 213

KC 3 6 0 7 16
Arz 0 3 7 14 **24**
KC D20 R20/119 P(44-21-2) 340
Arz D20 R37/135 P(25-16-0) 228
KC-Green 352P; Arz-Boston 131C

MONDAY, OCTOBER 22
Phi 0 0 3 7 **10**
NYG 3 6 0 0 9
Phi D13 R20/91 P(26-15-1) 124
NYG D16 R31/96 P(33-21-0) 142

THURSDAY, OCTOBER 25
Ind 0 7 10 18 **35**
KC 0 3 11 14 28
Ind D17 R33/194 P(30-19-0) 179
KC D25 R23/101 P(43-22-3) 314
Ind-James 102R; KC-Green 324P

SUNDAY, OCTOBER 28
Cin 7 14 3 7 **31**
Det 3 10 14 0 27
Cin D21 R37/224 P(27-17-2) 188
Det D17 R21/61 P(35-20-2) 215
Cin-Dillon 184R

Oak 7 3 7 3 **20**
Phi 0 3 0 7 10
Oak D22 R47/202 P(26-17-0) 152
Phi D11 R16/78 P(27-12-0) 117

Jax 3 7 7 0 17
Bal 0 3 3 12 **18**
Jax D19 R15/81 P(37-25-0) 284
Bal D23 R32/114 P(31-23-1) 191
Jax-McCardell 118C, Smith 119C, Brunell 306P

NYG 0 14 0 7 21
Was 3 10 8 14 **35**
NYG D25 R19/42 P(52-32-1) 346
Was D17 R35/157 P(20-12-0) 196
NYG-Toomer 109C, Collins 346P; Was-Davis 107R

NYJ 0 3 3 7 **13**
Car 6 3 3 0 12
NYJ D17 R34/186 P(34-21-3) 172
Car D7 R21/92 P(34-12-1) 70
NYJ-Martin 159R

SF 14 0 14 3 0 31
ChiB 0 9 7 15 6 **37**
SF D20 R28/83 P(29-21-2) 267
ChiB D29 R30/135 P(47-30-2) 229
SF-Hearst 105C; ChiB-Thomas 127R

Min 0 0 0 8 6 14
TB 7 21 13 0 0 **41**
Min D11 R18/65 P(26-14-1) 130
TB D26 R43/177 P(28-20-0) 269
TB-Alstott 129R

NO 3 3 25 3 **34**
Slr 14 10 0 7 31
NO D15 R26/82 P(31-20-0) 238
Slr D25 R16/48 P(48-30-4) 426
NO-Horn 121C; Slr-Bruce 179C, Canidate 107C, Warner 385P

NE 10 0 3 7 20
Den 7 3 14 7 **31**
NE D21 R24/117 P(39-25-5) 183
Den D18 R29/86 P(30-19-2) 269
Den-Smith 159C

Mia 0 10 7 7 **24**
Sea 3 3 7 7 20
Mia D15 R34/76 P(21-15-2) 213
Sea D18 R30/96 P(28-16-0) 206
Sea-Jackson 121C

Buf 0 10 0 14 24
SD 0 13 0 14 **27**
Buf D22 R25/105 P(39-26-1) 291
SD D17 R20/95 P(33-21-0) 243
Buf-Price 151C, Johnson 310P; SD-Conway 120C

Arz 0 0 0 3 3
Dal 0 3 14 0 **17**
Arz D17 R22/75 P(41-25-2) 217
Dal D34 R34/145 P(19-9-1) 80
Arz-Boston 108C

MONDAY, OCTOBER 29
Ten 0 0 0 7 7
Pit 7 10 10 7 **34**
Ten D15 R24/57 P(23-14-2) 157
Pit D24 R39/133 P(24-14-0) 272
Pit-Burress 151C

SUNDAY, NOVEMBER 4
Cle 7 0 14 0 21
ChiB 0 7 0 14 6 **27**
Cle D12 R23/70 P(23-14-1) 191
ChiB D29 R32/99 P(50-30-3) 314
ChiB-Matthews 357P

```
Jax   0  17   0   7  24
Ten   7   0   7  14  28
Jax  D20 R17/70  P(32-21-1) 239
Ten  D27 R33/146 P(34-27-0) 216
Jax-Smith 120C

Ind   0  17   7   6  30
Buf   0   7   0   7  14
Ind  D17 R37/144 P(27-17-0) 161
Buf  D14 R21/84  P(33-17-0) 148
Ind-Rhodes 100R

Det   7   3   3   0  13
SF    0   7   7   7  21
Det  D12 R21/58  P(25-10-0)  73
SF   D27 R35/145 P(35-26-2) 282
SF-Owens 125C

TB    0  10   7   3  20
GB    7   0   7   7  21
TB   D15 R24/61  P(30-18-0) 133
GB   D16 R29/184 P(27-16-2) 168
GB-Green 169R

Car   3   3   0   0   6
Mia   3  10   0  10  23
Car  D12 R20/103 P(33-15-1) 178
Mia  D19 R29/59  P(33-20-1) 278
Mia-Gadsden 102C

NE    0  17   0   7  24
Atl   7   0   0   3  10
NE   D21 R34/135 P(31-21-0) 236
Atl  D11 R19/140 P(29-10-1) 104
NE-Smith 117R

NYJ   6   7   0   3  16
NO    0   0   9   0   9
NYJ  D12 R34/142 P(22-13-1) 130
NO   D13 R27/108 P(29-12-2) 138

Dal  10  14   0   0  24
NYG   0   7  10   0  27
Dal  D17 R32/86  P(31-17-4) 289
NYG  D19 R26/93  P(34-24-2) 265
Dal-Ismail 107C

Sea   7   0   7   0  14
Was   0   7   7   7  21
Sea  D12 R14/60  P(30-14-3) 215
Was  D21 R46/226 P(23-15-1) 139
Was-Davis 142R

Phi   7  14   0   0  21
Arz   0   7   0   0   7
Phi  D13 R22/113 P(33-19-1) 219
Arz  D20 R24/57  P(41-24-1) 270
Arz-Boston 138C

KC    9  10   0   6  25
SD    0   0  10  10  20
KC   D21 R39/208 P(26-14-1) 170
SD   D22 R20/66  P(43-21-1) 259
KC-Holmes 181R

Bal   7   0   0   6  13
Pit   3   7   0   0  10
Bal  D10 R26/41  P(22-14-1) 142
Pit  D21 R35/123 P(37-22-0) 225
```

MONDAY, NOVEMBER 5

```
Den   3   3   6  16  28
Oak   7  14   7  10  38
Den  D26 R23/119 P(38-26-2) 247
Oak  D27 R30/114 P(34-25-0) 242
```

SUNDAY, NOVEMBER 11

```
Cin   0  13   0   0  13
Jax   7   0  21   2  30
Cin  D18 R23/73  P(48-28-1) 279
Jax  D21 R25/97  P(32-20-0) 164
Cin-Kitna 303P

NO    3  11  10   3  27
SF    0   7   7  14  28
NO   D24 R32/152 P(37-22-0) 336
SF   D21 R26/164 P(34-21-0) 251
NO-Williams 121R, Jackson 167C,
Brooks 347P; SF-Hearst 145R,
Owens 100C, Garcia 252P

Mia   7  10   0  10  27
Ind   3   7  14   0  24
Mia  D14 R28/134 P(30-17-2) 241
Ind  D19 R25/65  P(33-20-2) 224
Mia-Chambers 113C;
Ind-Harrison 174C
```

```
Min   0  10   0   7  17
Phi   7  24   7  10  48
Min  D16 R21/56  P(35-21-1) 245
Phi  D33 R35/272 P(29-19-0) 215
Phi-Staley 146R

NYG   7   7   0   3  17
Arz   0   7   3   0  10
NYG  D20 R41/186 P(24-15-1) 148
Arz  D12 R25/78  P(26-13-1) 135
NYG-Barber 118R; Arz-Boston 137C

GB    0  10   7   3  20
ChiB  6   3   3   0  12
GB   D17 R23/100 P(32-19-1) 268
ChiB D17 R24/47  P(48-29-0) 215
GB-Schroeder 100C

Pit   3   3   3   3  15
Cle   9   0   3   0  12
Pit  D20 R41/247 P(32-18-0) 181
Cle  D16 R23/74  P(33-18-0) 113
Pit-Bettis 163R

Buf   3   0   0   8  11
NE    7   0   7   7  21
Buf  D15 R21/69  P(33-16-2) 173
NE   D15 R31/134 P(21-15-1)  71
NE-Smith 100R

TB    0  10   7   3  20
Det   0   0  10   7  17
TB   D16 R25/99  P(37-20-0) 175
Det  D19 R23/52  P(40-21-2) 218

Dal   3  10   0   0  13
Atl   7   0   3  10  20
Dal  D15 R33/207 P(33-17-0)  96
Atl  D12 R33/155 P(16-7-0)   46
Dal-Hambrick 127R; Atl-Smith 148R

Car   0   7   0   7  14
Slr   7  14  14  13  48
Car  D8  R19/31  P(25-15-2) 115
Slr  D20 R41/337 P(22-16-3) 156
Slr-Canidate 145R, Faulk 183R

KC    0   0   0   7   7
NYJ   0  14  13   0  27
KC   D16 R26/100 P(31-16-3) 124
NYJ  D22 R37/174 P(28-18-1) 179
NYJ-Martin 113R

Oak   3   7  10   7  27
Sea   6   7  14   7  34
Oak  D20 R18/88  P(38-24-0) 250
Sea  D26 R42/319 P(23-15-0) 178
Sea-Alexander 266R, Jackson 102C

SD    0   0   3  13  16
Den   3  17   6   0  26
SD   D9  R17/96  P(31-12-4) 147
Den  D19 R42/117 P(31-21-0) 221
SD-Conway 111C
```

MONDAY, NOVEMBER 12

```
Bal   0   0  10   6  16
Ten   0   0  10   0  10
Bal  D12 R24/77  P(28-16-1) 161
Ten  D20 R28/90  P(49-27-1) 228
Bal-Ismail 129C
```

SUNDAY, NOVEMBER 18

```
NYJ   7   7   7   3  24
Mia   0   0   0   0   0
NYJ  D11 R28/86  P(21-10-0)  76
Mia  D15 R30/78  P(36-24-3) 176

Ind  14   3   0   3  20
NO    0  17   7  10  34
Ind  D18 R23/77  P(28-18-1) 262
NO   D25 R37/157 P(22-19-0) 221
Ind-Pollard 126C;
NO-Williams 120R, Horn 148C

SF    0   7   7  11  25
Car   7   0   3   9  22
SF   D26 R26/121 P(54-34-2) 296
Car  D14 R16/103 P(41-22-0) 177
SF-Garcia 305P

Cle   3  17   0   7  27
Bal   0   7  10   0  17
Cle  D17 R30/95  P(30-19-3) 137
Bal  D19 R27/108 P(44-23-4) 242
```

```
Phi   0  20   6  10  36
Dal   0   0   0   3   3
Phi  D17 R35/98  P(32-16-1) 129
Dal  D11 R23/132 P(26-11-2)  81
Phi-Staley 102R

Jax   0   0   7   0   7
Pit   3   7   7   3  20
Jax  D14 R16/48  P(31-17-0) 186
Pit  D20 R34/145 P(33-21-0) 257
Pit-Ward 112C

Slr   7   7   3   7  24
NE    0   7   0  10  17
Slr  D26 R28/86  P(42-30-2) 396
NE   D13 R20/51  P(27-19-2) 179
Slr-Bruce 130C, Warner 401P

Atl   6  10   0   7  23
GB    3   7   3   7  20
Atl  D25 R25/82  P(50-29-2) 335
GB   D14 R19/70  P(29-16-3) 243
Atl-Chandler 352P;
GB-Bradford 117C

Det   0  14  17   7  38
Arz   7   7   7  24  45
Det  D30 R22/49  P(62-36-3) 429
Arz  D23 R26/89  P(33-21-1) 328
Det-Morton 153C, Batch 436P;
Arz-Sanders 127C, Plummer 334P

ChiB  0   7  17   3  27
TB    3   6   0  15  24
ChiB D13 R29/68  P(25-14-1) 206
TB   D26 R15/19  P(57-41-2) 395
ChiB-Booker 165C; TB-Dunn 138C,
Johnson 399P

Ten  10   0   7   3  20
Cin   7   0   0   0   7
Ten  D13 R31/129 P(25-16-1) 164
Cin  D17 R21/40  P(41-23-2) 224

Sea   3   7   7   6  23
Buf   0  10   3   7  20
Sea  D16 R32/112 P(23-16-0) 134
Buf  D25 R22/69  P(42-28-0) 303
Buf-Price 138C, Van Pelt 316P

SD    7   0  10   7  24
Oak  14   0   3  17  34
SD   D12 R29/152 P(27-12-1)  98
Oak  D21 R28/88  P(38-25-1) 293
Oak-Rice 131C, Gannon 311P

Was   0   3   0  14  17
Den   0  10   0   0  10
Was  D18 R32/118 P(31-16-0) 127
Den  D10 R27/88  P(31-11-0)  98
Was-Westbrook 104C
```

MONDAY, NOVEMBER 19

```
NYG  10   3   3   0  16
Min   7   7   0  14  28
NYG  D18 R15/61  P(37-21-2) 297
Min  D24 R28/96  P(38-26-2) 263
NYG-Hilliard 106C, Collins 321P;
Min-Moss 171C, Culpepper 277P
```

THURSDAY, NOVEMBER 22

```
Den   3  14   6   3  26
Dal   3   0   0  21  24
Den  D19 R39/119 P(29-17-1) 160
Dal  D16 R16/27  P(33-17-0) 164
Den-Anderson 118R

GB    7  10   7   5  29
Det   3  10   0  14  27
GB   D23 R27/104 P(26-18-0) 235
Det  D19 R25/167 P(31-17-1) 193
GB-Green 102R; Det-Stewart 102R
```

SUNDAY, NOVEMBER 25

```
Cin   0   0   0   0   0
Cle   3   9   0   6  18
Cin  D12 R24/84  P(33-13-5) 107
Cle  D14 R39/78  P(27-16-2) 171
Cle-Johnson 113C

NO    0   0   0   7  17
NE    7  13   0  14  34
NO   D23 R22/121 P(39-16-2) 307
NE   D26 R38/191 P(26-19-0) 241
NO-Brooks 307P; NE-Smith 111C,
Brady 258P
```

```
Bal   3   7   7   7  24
Jax   0   0  14   7  21
Bal  D24 R42/115 P(30-21-1) 220
Jax  D19 R19/75  P(38-23-0) 230

Oak   7  14   0   7  28
NYG   3   0   7   0  10
Oak  D15 R32/119 P(20-13-0) 220
NYG  D18 R27/153 P(38-19-0) 160
Oak-Brown 117C; NYG-Barber 124R

ChiB  0  10   0   3  13
Min   0   7   0   0   7
ChiB D11 R30/142 P(21-10-0)  93
Min  D15 R23/124 P(46-26-1) 192
ChiB-Allen 107R

Sea   0   7   0   0   7
KC    3   7   0   9  19
Sea  D11 R17/65  P(26-16-0) 139
KC   D23 R44/188 P(26-16-0) 245
KC-Holmes 120R

Mia   7   3   0  24  34
Buf   7   7   7   6  27
Mia  D19 R30/101 P(32-19-0) 261
Buf  D21 R26/127 P(34-21-1) 295
Mia-Chambers 101C,
Gadsden 116C; Buf-Moulds 196C,
Van Pelt 309P

Atl   3   7   0   0  10
Car   0   0   0   7   7
Atl  D13 R33/145 P(27-14-0)  94
Car  D14 R28/96  P(31-17-2) 151

Arz   0   7   3  10  20
SD    0   0  14   7  21
Arz  D18 R24/71  P(31-19-2) 227
SD   D20 R23/84  P(44-33-0) 308
Arz-Boston 121C; SD-Flutie 308P

SF    3  17   7  13  40
Ind   7   7   7   0  21
SF   D16 R23/171 P(22-14-1) 169
Ind  D30 R32/127 P(51-31-4) 364
SF-Hearst 106C, Owens 103C;
Ind-Rhodes 104R, Harrison 128C,
Manning 370P

Was   0  10   0   3  13
Phi   0   0   0   3   3
Was  D16 R45/155 P(18-12-0)  85
Phi  D7  R22/94  P(27-15-0)  92

Pit   3   7  14  10  34
Ten   7   7   3   7  24
Pit  D20 R31/130 P(32-19-0) 247
Ten  D21 R21/81  P(37-23-2) 324
Pit-Burress 114C; Ten-Dyson 112C,
Mason 114C, McNair 334P
```

MONDAY, NOVEMBER 26

```
TB    0  10   7   7  24
Slr   3   6   8   0  17
TB   D18 R31/91  P(34-21-1) 173
Slr  D19 R19/76  P(39-19-2) 269
Slr-Holt 139C
```

THURSDAY, NOVEMBER 29

```
Phi   3  10   7   3  23
KC    0   7   0   0   7
Phi  D19 R36/127 P(26-18-1) 251
KC   D18 R20/83  P(35-21-1) 208
KC-Holmes 100C
```

SUNDAY, DECEMBER 2

```
Min   3   0   0  13  16
Pit   0  14   0   7  21
Min  D12 R16/45  P(32-23-2) 340
Pit  D21 R46/207 P(19-13-1) 157
Min-Moss 144C

Arz   7  13   0  11   3  34
Oak   7   0   7  17   0  31
Arz  D24 R34/145 P(38-22-0) 245
Oak  D26 R32/135 P(45-29-2) 301
Arz-Boston 106C; Oak-Gannon 302P

Ind   3  17   0   0  20
Bal   3  13  10  13  39
Ind  D16 R17/51  P(48-27-1) 263
Bal  D20 R31/130 P(39-23-1) 268
Ind-Manning 310P;
Bal-Williams 111R
```

```
Buf   0   0   0   0   0
SF    0  14   7  14  35
Buf  D11 R11/29  P(38-21-4) 162
SF   D26 R43/230 P(27-19-0) 179
SF-Hearst 124R

Car   0   7   3  13  23
NO    0  14   3  10  27
Car  D11 R19/49  P(21-11-1) 101
NO   D25 R34/125 P(40-26-1) 307
NO-Williams 102R, Horn 150C,
Brooks 330P

Ten  14   3  14   0  31
Cle   0   7   0   8  15
Ten  D14 R39/111 P(19-13-0) 272
Cle  D16 R17/65  P(38-24-1) 217
Ten-Dyson 110C, Mason 122C

Det   7   0   3   0  10
ChiB  0   3   0  10  13
Det  D17 R23/67  P(37-22-0) 228
ChiB D18 R34/108 P(34-17-1) 124

NE    0  14   0   3  17
NYJ  10   3   3   0  16
NE   D14 R23/73  P(28-20-0) 191
NYJ  D18 R28/131 P(32-18-2) 157

Dal   7   0   0  13  20
Was   0   0   7   7  14
Dal  D19 R45/215 P(14-7-1)  122
Was  D15 R22/81  P(32-17-1) 196
Dal-Smith 102R

Slr  14   0  14   7  35
Atl   3   3   0   0   6
Slr  D19 R20/89  P(23-17-0) 333
Atl  D20 R30/128 P(37-21-1) 192
Slr-Faulk 128C, Warner 342P

Den   0   0   3   7  10
Mia   0   0   0  21  21
Den  D19 R32/147 P(33-18-1) 126
Mia  D12 R22/42  P(28-18-0) 176

TB    0   7   3   3   3  16
Cin   3   0   0  10   0  13
TB   D19 R30/65  P(33-26-0) 199
Cin  D17 R24/86  P(38-19-1) 115

SD    0   3   7   0   0  10
Sea   7   0   3   0   3  13
SD   D19 R27/107 P(33-19-2) 185
Sea  D18 R36/117 P(35-19-0) 192
```

MONDAY, DECEMBER 3

```
GB    0   7  14   7  28
Jax   3  10   8   0  21
GB   D20 R21/37  P(42-24-0) 352
Jax  D20 R23/62  P(45-26-2) 286
GB-Freeman 104C, Schroeder 106C,
Favre 362P; Jax-Smith 116C,
Brunell 311P
```

SUNDAY, DECEMBER 9

```
Ten  10   0   0  14  24
Min   0  14  14  14  42
Ten  D24 R29/182 P(36-25-0) 271
Min  D24 R25/148 P(31-21-1) 348
Ten-McNair 302P;
Min-Bennett 113R, Moss 158C,
Bouman 348P

Cle  10   0   3   3  16
NE    3  17   0   7  27
Cle  D17 R19/50  P(39-20-3) 227
NE   D18 R33/81  P(28-19-2) 209

Jax   7   0   0   7  14
Cin   0   7   3   0  10
Jax  D17 R25/62  P(32-23-1) 193
Cin  D12 R27/60  P(30-16-1) 140
Jax-Smith 119C

SD    7   7   0   0  14
Phi  14   7   0   3  24
SD   D18 R27/96  P(44-20-2) 297
Phi  D14 R24/63  P(45-22-1) 210
SD-Graham 110C, Flutie 307P

ChiB  0   0   7   0   7
GB    0   3   7   7  17
ChiB D11 R19/50  P(33-18-1) 139
GB   D17 R36/167 P(27-15-1) 185
GB-Green 125R
```

KC 10 7 3 6 26
Oak 7 14 7 0 28
KC D23 R36/204 P(32-15-1) 243
Oak D16 R26/79 P(24-18-1) 185
KC-Holmes 168R, Holmes 109C

Was 0 10 0 10 20
Arz 0 3 0 7 10
Was D17 R35/130 P(26-19-0) 201
Arz D17 R22/80 P(34-20-1) 246
Was-Davis 110R; Arz-Boston 132C

SF 0 7 0 7 14
Slr 14 7 3 3 27
SF D16 R23/76 P(36-13-2) 144
Slr D23 R30/115 P(42-26-1) 270
Slr-Proehl 109C

Det 0 3 6 3 12
TB 0 7 0 8 15
Det D14 R24/102 P(25-11-0) 151
TB D24 R22/81 P(54-31-2) 275
TB-Johnson 101C, Johnson 305P

Car 3 21 0 0 24
Buf 3 10 6 6 25
Car D17 R27/78 P(30-15-1) 153
Buf D18 R35/102 P(29-20-1) 267
Car-Muhammad 104C;
Buf-Henry 101R

NYG 6 7 0 0 13
Dal 3 3 7 7 20
NYG D12 R24/125 P(26-13-1) 120
Dal D14 R36/104 P(26-17-0) 185
NYG-Barber 110R; Dal-Ismail 118C

NYJ 0 7 0 0 7
Pit 3 9 0 6 18
NYJ D14 R19/61 P(27-16-0) 159
Pit D23 R39/134 P(36-20-0) 211
Pit-Ward 124C

NO 14 0 0 14 28
Atl 7 3 0 0 10
NO D19 R21/114 P(31-21-0) 265
Atl D20 R21/50 P(32-18-1) 180
NO-Horn 138C

Sea 0 7 0 0 7
Den 7 3 10 0 20
Sea D15 R21/70 P(37-17-2) 207
Den D20 R28/165 P(37-21-1) 144
Sea-Jackson 104C; Den-Davis 109R

MONDAY, DECEMBER 10

Ind 0 3 3 0 6
Mia 7 13 0 21 41
Ind D16 R18/84 P(32-19-3) 170
Mia D24 R38/183 P(26-18-0) 183
Mia-Smith 107R

SATURDAY, DECEMBER 15

Arz 3 3 0 7 13
NYG 7 0 0 10 17
Arz D19 R30/88 P(45-27-0) 197
NYG D15 R25/105 P(32-14-0) 139

Oak 3 0 7 3 13
SD 0 3 0 3 6
Oak D15 R27/91 P(28-20-1) 208
SD D14 R22/68 P(37-19-3) 206

SUNDAY, DECEMBER 16

Jax 9 0 0 6 15
Cle 0 0 7 3 10
Jax D19 R33/128 P(35-20-2) 154
Cle D11 R15/47 P(30-21-1) 173
Jax-Mack 115R

Den 0 10 7 6 0 23
KC 10 3 7 3 3 26
Den D22 R34/94 P(34-23-0) 241
KC D22 R33/137 P(21-17-1) 259
Den-Smith 100C; KC-Holmes 121R

Dal 0 3 0 0 3
Sea 10 0 2 17 29
Dal D10 R21/102 P(33-14-1) 116
Sea D22 R44/173 P(26-13-0) 139
Sea-Watters 104R

Pit 3 10 0 13 26
Bal 0 7 0 14 21
Pit D22 R39/158 P(31-20-0) 318
Bal D15 R13/58 P(38-20-1) 149
Pit-Burress 164C, Johnson 119C,
Shaw 100C, Stewart 333P

NE 3 3 0 3 3 12
Buf 0 0 3 6 0 9
NE D17 R27/129 P(35-19-1) 206
Buf D19 R28/98 P(44-22-1) 212

GB 10 3 0 7 20
Ten 2 13 3 8 26
GB D14 R15/31 P(38-20-1) 192
Ten D23 R34/167 P(36-25-0) 256
Ten-Hicks 142R, Mason 107C

Phi 0 10 7 3 20
Was 3 3 0 0 6
Phi D11 R23/63 P(34-16-3) 224
Was D16 R29/157 P(36-17-2) 205
Was-Davis 111R

Atl 0 14 3 10 27
Ind 7 21 0 13 41
Atl D21 R19/66 P(40-24-0) 250
Ind D29 R33/187 P(35-23-1) 325
Ind-Rhodes 177R, Pollard 101C,
Manning 325P

Mia 0 0 0 0 0
SF 14 0 7 0 21
Mia D12 R15/67 P(28-16-3) 107
SF D21 R50/152 P(20-14-0) 133
SF-Hearst 103R

Min 7 0 17 0 24
Det 14 6 0 7 27
Min D16 R17/80 P(38-18-2) 234
Det D19 R35/167 P(28-15-0) 202
Min-Rhodes 177R, Moss 144C,
Pollard 101C, Manning 325P

TB 0 3 0 0 3
ChiB 3 10 7 7 27
TB D10 R18/61 P(40-18-2) 177
ChiB D21 R40/207 P(29-14-1) 172
TB-Johnson 119C;
ChiB-Thomas 173R

Cin 7 0 7 0 14
NYJ 0 3 0 12 15
Cin D17 R33/120 P(23-14-3) 128
NYJ D17 R29/113 P(28-17-0) 196

MONDAY, DECEMBER 17

Slr 7 14 7 6 34
NO 7 7 7 0 21
Slr D21 R25/56 P(32-23-0) 309
NO D17 R19/68 P(40-23-2) 242
Slr-Warner 338P; NO-Jackson 156C

SATURDAY, DECEMBER 22

Ten 0 0 10 3 13
Oak 0 10 0 0 10
Ten D14 R33/103 P(27-15-2) 159
Oak D20 R21/77 P(50-29-1) 234

Phi 0 3 0 0 3
SF 0 3 3 7 13
Phi D12 R22/79 P(34-23-1) 213
SF D14 R30/117 P(24-14-0) 127
Phi-Staley 103C

Mia 0 3 0 10 13
NE 0 20 0 0 20
Mia D19 R19/58 P(37-21-0) 310
NE D20 R44/196 P(20-12-0) 117
Mia-Chambers 124C, Fiedler 320P;
NE-Smith 156R

SUNDAY, DECEMBER 23

Jax 10 6 7 10 33
Min 0 3 0 0 3
Jax D23 R37/214 P(24-17-0) 209
Min D16 R14/28 P(42-24-1) 186
Jax-Mack 111R

Dal 3 7 0 0 10
Arz 0 17 0 0 17
Dal D21 R40/174 P(29-16-2) 169
Arz D11 R20/75 P(31-17-0) 134
Dal-Smith 128R

NO 0 0 14 7 21
TB 17 13 3 15 48
NO D16 R13/41 P(38-21-4) 230
TB D23 R39/157 P(31-16-0) 207
TB-Alstott 101R

Det 7 7 0 0 14
Pit 14 13 10 10 47
Det D11 R18/74 P(28-12-1) 77
Pit D25 R43/215 P(26-17-0) 214
Pit-Faumatu-Ma'afala 126R

Buf 7 7 6 10 30
Atl 10 3 10 10 33
Buf D15 R21/190 P(31-17-0) 208
Atl D22 R29/67 P(40-28-2) 422
Buf-Bryson 130R;
Atl-Chandler 431P

Slr 7 14 10 7 38
Car 7 6 10 9 32
Slr D21 R33/215 P(24-18-2) 197
Car D24 R21/97 P(51-24-0) 305
Slr-Faulk 202R; Car-Weinke 312P

Sea 7 10 7 0 24
NYG 7 10 0 10 27
Sea D14 R30/98 P(26-15-1) 161
NYG D22 R21/88 P(47-30-0) 332
NYG-Hilliard 105C, Toomer 124C,
Collins 338P

NYJ 3 10 6 10 29
Ind 0 10 7 11 28
NYJ D26 R31/166 P(48-28-2) 285
Ind D18 R18/133 P(36-26-0) 260
NYJ-Martin 122R, Chrebet 118C;
Ind-Rhodes 126R, Harrison 127C

ChiB 3 7 0 10 20
Was 7 3 3 2 15
ChiB D14 R32/112 P(27-14-0) 125
Was D18 R28/89 P(43-23-0) 204

Cle 0 7 0 0 7
GB 13 10 0 7 30
Cle D16 R26/168 P(33-22-3) 169
GB D17 R33/222 P(28-18-0) 139
Cle-White 131R; GB-Green 150R

SD 7 0 7 3 17
KC 7 0 3 10 20
SD D20 R29/165 P(27-15-0) 164
KC D24 R32/120 P(28-19-2) 203
SD-Tomlinson 145R

Cin 0 0 0 0 0
Bal 3 10 0 3 16
Cin D21 R30/150 P(39-16-3) 131
Bal D20 R35/157 P(30-16-0) 148
Cin-Dillon 127R

SATURDAY, DECEMBER 29

Bal 0 7 0 3 10
TB 3 13 0 6 22
Bal D15 R26/90 P(37-21-2) 167
TB D13 R31/123 P(29-13-0) 90

SUNDAY, DECEMBER 30

Cle 14 10 0 17 41
Ten 14 10 7 7 38
Cle D18 R29/87 P(27-20-1) 322
Ten D21 R35/188 P(26-16-1) 264
Cle-Couch 336P; Ten-George 130R

ChiB 14 3 0 7 24
Det 0 0 0 0 0
ChiB D15 R30/83 P(30-17-0) 243
Det D19 R14/64 P(52-31-3) 268
ChiB-Bates 107C, Booker 115C;
Det-Detmer 303P

SF 0 14 0 7 21
Dal 0 10 14 3 27
SF D16 R18/56 P(36-21-0) 229
Dal D24 R44/186 P(25-15-0) 234
Dal-Smith 126R, Galloway 146C

Arz 7 20 3 0 30
Car 0 7 0 0 7
Arz D16 R33/158 P(24-12-0) 173
Car D20 R20/95 P(63-36-1) 223
Arz-Boston 127C

Min 0 3 3 7 13
GB 0 7 0 17 24
Min D19 R44/199 P(30-11-3) 103
GB D13 R20/56 P(29-18-0) 157
Min-Bennett 104R

KC 7 10 10 3 30
Jax 7 10 0 9 26
KC D23 R31/92 P(35-26-2) 273
Jax D22 R26/182 P(37-22-1) 249
KC-Kennison 121C; Jax-Mack 125R,
McCardell 132C, Smith 122C

Sea 0 14 8 3 25
SD 10 3 3 6 22
Sea D14 R25/61 P(23-14-0) 246
SD D21 R16/52 P(53-34-2) 346
Sea-Jackson 114C, Williams 101C;
SD-Conway 156C, Flutie 377P

Buf 0 7 7 0 14
NYJ 3 3 0 3 9
Buf D19 R40/192 P(27-16-0) 176
NYJ D19 R23/148 P(37-19-2) 227
Buf-Bryson 107R; NYJ-Martin 123R

Oak 3 7 7 0 17
Den 3 10 0 10 23
Oak D24 R16/51 P(49-35-2) 283
Den D15 R25/106 P(26-19-0) 125
Oak-Rice 108C, Gannon 313P

Ind 7 7 3 0 17
Slr 7 28 0 7 42
Ind D17 R22/83 P(28-15-1) 178
Slr D27 R29/124 P(30-23-1) 359
Slr-Faulk 118R, Holt 203C,
Warner 359P

Atl 7 0 0 7 14
Mia 7 14 0 0 21
Atl D21 R37/152 P(31-18-3) 236
Mia D12 R20/50 P(29-16-1) 176

Was 0 13 17 10 40
NO 10 0 0 0 10
Was D19 R44/173 P(15-9-1) 90
NO D12 R23/100 P(28-14-3) 113
Was-Davis 111R

NYG 0 0 10 11 21
Phi 7 0 0 17 24
NYG D18 R26/129 P(39-22-0) 291
Phi D21 R23/120 P(39-21-1) 241
NYG-Collins 303P; Phi-Thrash 143C

Pit 14 3 6 0 0 23
Cin 0 10 0 13 3 26
Pit D16 R28/73 P(35-19-4) 240
Cin D32 R29/141 P(68-35-1) 403
Pit-Burress 102C; Cin-Scott 113C,
Warrick 109C, Kitna 411P

SUNDAY, JANUARY 6

GB 14 3 17 0 34
NYG 7 3 0 15 25
GB D18 R26/105 P(30-15-0) 308
NYG D25 R21/146 P(59-36-2) 378
GB-Green 101R, Bradford 111C,
Schroeder 102C, Favre 315P;
NYG-Collins 386P

Dal 0 7 0 3 10
Det 0 6 3 6 15
Dal D12 R27/106 P(26-11-1) 158
Det D20 R28/124 P(40-24-0) 242

Den 0 7 3 0 10
Ind 9 10 3 7 29
Den D17 R25/115 P(32-16-4) 104
Ind D22 R35/151 P(30-16-1) 184
Ind-Rhodes 141R, Harrison 128C

SF 14 7 3 14 38
NO 0 0 0 0 0
SF D22 R41/138 P(23-16-0) 269
NO D11 R17/40 P(34-21-4) 86
SF-Owens 116C, Garcia 263P

KC 0 0 10 8 18
Sea 0 14 7 0 21
KC D18 R28/126 P(33-15-1) 182
Sea D20 R33/150 P(39-22-2) 239
KC-Holmes 117R;
Sea-Alexander 127R

Phi 0 3 0 14 17
TB 3 10 0 0 13
Phi D15 R25/111 P(28-15-2) 185
TB D16 R25/71 P(32-22-1) 165

NE 10 0 14 14 38
Car 0 3 3 0 6
NE D16 R36/102 P(29-17-2) 196
Car D18 R26/193 P(36-15-3) 129
Car-Huntley 168R

Jax 0 0 6 7 13
ChiB 3 10 10 10 33
Jax D17 R16/91 P(36-19-3) 146
ChiB D19 R40/169 P(29-19-0) 153
ChiB-Thomas 160R

Buf 0 0 7 0 7
Mia 3 10 0 21 34
Buf D16 R17/39 P(40-18-3) 211
Mia D21 R43/202 P(16-9-0) 87
Mia-Smith 158R

Atl 0 6 7 0 13
Slr 10 7 14 0 31
Atl D13 R21/96 P(30-12-1) 159
Slr D23 R29/192 P(30-25-3) 266
Slr-Faulk 168R

Cle 7 0 0 0 7
Pit 0 7 14 7 28
Cle D12 R19/68 P(26-13-2) 105
Pit D19 R36/221 P(24-14-3) 155

Cin 0 14 6 3 23
Ten 7 7 7 0 21
Cin D25 R27/100 P(48-28-2) 336
Ten D16 R23/57 P(32-18-0) 272
Cin-Scott 152C, Kitna 340P;
Ten-Mason 186C

NYJ 7 7 7 3 24
Oak 3 13 3 3 22
NYJ D14 R22/94 P(29-18-2) 208
Oak D17 R30/119 P(38-23-0) 218
NYJ-Coles 111C

Arz 7 10 0 0 17
Was 0 6 6 8 20
Arz D10 R17/45 P(25-11-1) 142
Was D22 R49/178 P(26-14-1) 162
Was-Davis 148R

MONDAY, JANUARY 7

Min 3 0 0 0 3
Bal 0 9 3 7 19
Min D10 R21/86 P(30-14-2) 93
Bal D16 R42/212 P(27-10-0) 139
Bal-Allen 133R

2002 NFL

THURSDAY, SEPTEMBER 5

SF 3 0 7 6 16
NYG 3 3 0 7 13
SF D13 R25/113 P(26-16-1) 166
NYG D21 R22/43 P(45-28-3) 318
NYG-Toomer 134C, Collins 342P

SUNDAY, SEPTEMBER 8

Arz 10 3 3 7 23
Was 3 7 14 7 31
Arz D14 R20/70 P(36-14-1) 187
Was D21 R32/122 P(40-28-1) 320
Arz-Boston 138C; Was-Davis 104R,
Gardner 131C, Matthews 327P

Atl 0 21 3 10 0 34
GB 3 10 14 7 3 37
Atl D22 R30/180 P(23-15-0) 194
GB D29 R38/211 P(36-25-0) 273
GB-Green 155R

Bal 7 0 0 0 7
Car 7 3 0 0 10
Bal D15 R19/77 P(34-20-1) 212
Car D15 R36/145 P(19-12-0) 120

Dal 0 3 7 0 10
Hot 7 3 0 9 19
Dal D11 R24/155 P(30-13-1) 112
Hot D13 R35/87 P(22-10-1) 123

Det 0 7 7 7 21
Mia 7 21 14 7 49
Det D15 R19/51 P(36-17-1) 206
Mia D27 R41/182 P(27-18-0) 207
Mia-Williams 111R

Ind 7 7 7 7 28
Jax 0 7 10 8 25
Ind D18 R28/104 P(31-19-0) 203
Jax D19 R32/118 P(36-22-1) 225
Jax-Smith 104C

KC 7 7 3 23 40
Cle 6 14 7 12 39
KC D24 R30/194 P(29-20-1) 276
Cle D24 R20/59 P(40-28-0) 352
KC-Holmes 122R, Kennison 120C;
Cle-Morgan 151C, Holcomb 326P

Min 3 17 0 3 23
ChiB 7 3 3 14 **27**
Min D19 R33/140 P(28-16-2) 228
ChiB D20 R26/80 P(33-20-1) 288
ChiB-Booker 198C

NO 6 7 7 0 6 **26**
TB 0 3 7 10 0 20
NO D21 R34/118 P(42-24-1) 250
TB D19 R21/72 P(53-28-1) 261
NO-McAllister 109R, Horn 108C

NYJ 0 17 3 11 6 **37**
Buf 3 14 7 7 0 31
NYJ D18 R14/73 P(30-24-0) 193
Buf D26 R32/142 P(39-26-2) 242
Buf-Henry 149R, Moulds 112C

Phi 14 10 0 0 24
Ten 7 3 3 14 **27**
Phi D17 R22/80 P(36-18-2) 181
Ten D22 R25/61 P(34-24-1) 267
Ten-Mason 109C

SD 10 10 7 7 **34**
Cin 0 0 3 3 6
SD D27 R45/241 P(19-15-0) 160
Cin D13 R13/36 P(31-18-1) 167
SD-Tomlinson 114R

Sea 7 0 0 10 17
Oak 7 21 3 0 **31**
Sea D14 R16/43 P(32-23-0) 143
Oak D27 R40/221 P(28-19-1) 202
Oak-Garner 127R

Slr 0 6 7 3 16
Den 7 9 0 7 **23**
Slr D15 R13/32 P(41-32-1) 295
Den D18 R26/104 P(27-18-2) 187
Slr-Warner 315P

MONDAY, SEPTEMBER 9

Pit 7 0 0 7 14
NE 7 3 17 3 **30**
Pit D20 R24/74 P(38-25-3) 209
NE D20 R18/63 P(43-29-0) 280

SUNDAY, SEPTEMBER 15

Arz 3 0 7 14 **24**
Sea 3 7 0 3 13
Arz D19 R35/249 P(22-10-1) 98
Sea D26 R29/81 P(47-29-0) 345
Arz-Jones 173R; Sea-Jackson 174C, Dilfer 352P

Buf 6 7 10 16 6 **45**
Min 3 10 13 13 0 39
Buf D26 R14/31 P(49-35-0) 437
Min D31 R39/213 P(46-25-0) 236
Buf-Price 185C, Reed 110C, Bledsoe 463P; Min-Williams 102R, Moss 111C

ChiB 0 7 7 0 **14**
Atl 0 10 3 0 13
ChiB D13 R31/106 P(24-12-1) 136
Atl D19 R30/122 P(28-17-0) 135

Cin 0 0 0 7 7
Cle 3 14 0 3 **20**
Cin D28 R31/156 P(47-26-3) 201
Cle D15 R27/75 P(30-17-0) 190
Cin-Dillon 108R

Den 0 3 7 14 **24**
SF 0 7 0 7 14
Den D21 R35/201 P(19-14-0) 98
SF D18 R20/71 P(36-27-1) 190

Det 0 0 7 0 7
Car 0 10 14 7 **31**
Det D12 R22/73 P(30-12-2) 49
Car D20 R30/75 P(33-21-0) 310
Car-Muhammad 107C, Peete 310P

GB 0 10 7 3 20
NO 7 14 7 7 **35**
GB D18 R21/95 P(44-29-1) 262
NO D16 R28/146 P(28-16-2) 211
NO-McAllister 123R, Horn 120C

Hot 0 3 0 0 3
SD 14 3 0 7 **24**
Hot D7 R25/89 P(25-6-2) 29
SD D16 R35/124 P(28-15-1) 143
SD-Conway 113C

Jax 0 9 0 14 **23**
KC 3 3 0 10 16
Jax D19 R29/130 P(36-25-0) 320
KC D18 R28/140 P(32-16-2) 196
Jax-Taylor 114R, Brunell 320P

Mia 14 7 0 0 **21**
Ind 0 3 0 10 13
Mia D17 R34/163 P(18-13-1) 179
Ind D29 R31/143 P(45-26-3) 289
Mia-Williams 132R; Ind-James 138R, Harrison 144C

NE 0 10 17 17 **44**
NYJ 0 0 7 0 7
NE D24 R40/163 P(35-25-1) 269
NYJ D9 R9/32 P(33-18-1) 168

NYG 3 14 3 6 **26**
Slr 0 7 7 7 21
NYG D16 R38/103 P(26-22-1) 291
Slr D18 R17/92 P(39-26-2) 260
NYG-Collins 307P

Oak 10 7 3 10 **30**
Pit 7 3 7 0 17
Oak D27 R17/95 P(65-43-2) 369
Pit D14 R18/72 P(34-18-1) 201
Oak-Gannon 403P

TB 10 3 5 7 **25**
Bal 0 0 0 0 0
TB D17 R30/74 P(31-24-0) 205
Bal D12 R20/55 P(38-16-1) 118

Ten 7 3 0 3 13
Dal 0 7 7 7 **21**
Ten D19 R26/98 P(43-23-1) 235
Dal D14 R26/67 P(24-14-0) 230
Ten-Mason 118C

MONDAY, SEPTEMBER 16

Phi 14 9 7 7 **37**
Was 0 7 0 0 7
Phi D22 R28/168 P(38-26-0) 283
Was D11 R18/89 P(31-16-2) 90
Phi-Thrash 107C

SUNDAY, SEPTEMBER 22

Buf 0 7 3 13 23
Den 7 7 7 7 **28**
Buf D17 R14/39 P(41-27-0) 252
Den D22 R32/163 P(31-19-0) 179
Den-Portis 103R

Car 0 0 7 14 **21**
Min 0 7 0 7 14
Car D20 R33/164 P(30-20-2) 206
Min D13 R18/73 P(30-19-4) 177
Car-Smith 154R

Cin 0 3 0 0 3
Atl 13 7 7 3 **30**
Cin D11 R20/66 P(42-18-2) 125
Atl D18 R36/143 P(26-16-0) 163

Cle 7 0 7 14 3 **31**
Ten 7 14 0 7 0 28
Cle D26 R20/92 P(50-36-1) 311
Ten D13 R34/86 P(23-15-0) 101
Cle-Couch 326P

Dal 10 0 3 0 13
Phi 3 17 14 10 **44**
Dal D18 R27/121 P(35-21-1) 183
Phi D26 R26/153 P(40-26-0) 294
Phi-Freeman 118C

GB 7 10 14 6 **37**
Det 7 10 0 14 31
GB D22 R31/95 P(47-31-1) 347
Det D14 R21/95 P(35-15-4) 176
GB-Favre 357P

Ind 7 6 0 10 **23**
Hot 0 0 3 0 3
Ind D16 R27/88 P(28-21-0) 251
Hot D10 R30/126 P(22-12-1) 78
Ind-Harrison 110C

KC 3 7 7 21 0 38
NE 0 9 8 21 3 **41**
KC D21 R34/221 P(25-16-2) 128
NE D27 R20/97 P(55-39-1) 399
KC-Holmes 180R; NE-Brown 176C, Patten 108C, Brady 410P

NO 0 14 7 8 **29**
ChiB 10 10 0 3 23
NO D18 R24/73 P(34-22-1) 229
ChiB D21 R30/125 P(40-26-1) 228
ChiB-Thomas 111R

NYJ 0 3 0 0 3
Mia 10 3 0 17 **30**
NYJ D13 R22/58 P(28-16-3) 131
Mia D21 R35/211 P(30-16-0) 183
Mia-Williams 151R

SD 0 14 0 9 **23**
Arz 7 0 0 8 15
SD D19 R34/125 P(31-17-1) 164
Arz D15 R21/97 P(36-16-2) 200

Sea 3 3 0 0 6
NYG 0 0 3 6 **9**
Sea D7 R18/40 P(25-16-1) 105
NYG D21 R35/94 P(38-23-0) 257
NYG-Toomer 100C

Was 0 10 0 0 10
SF 7 10 3 0 **20**
Was D12 R16/57 P(30-18-1) 160
SF D22 R41/252 P(28-15-1) 114

MONDAY, SEPTEMBER 23

Slr 7 0 0 7 14
TB 3 10 0 13 **26**
Slr D21 R20/89 P(45-30-4) 269
TB D14 R16/63 P(32-23-0) 189
Slr-Holt 139C, Warner 301P

SUNDAY, SEPTEMBER 29

Car 7 0 0 7 14
GB 3 7 0 7 **17**
Car D18 R35/139 P(24-10-0) 193
GB D17 R22/99 P(33-19-1) 199
Car-Smith 116C

ChiB 7 7 3 10 0 27
Buf 7 10 3 7 6 **33**
ChiB D15 R26/52 P(31-19-0) 188
Buf D26 R25/103 P(36-28-0) 307
Buf-Moulds 124C, Bledsoe 328P

Cle 3 3 0 7 0 13
Pit 0 6 0 7 3 **16**
Cle D13 R24/123 P(29-16-2) 122
Pit D21 R34/93 P(39-26-2) 265
Cle-White 105R; Pit-Ward 104C

Dal 7 0 0 6 **13**
Slr 0 7 3 0 10
Dal D17 R27/122 P(36-26-1) 193
Slr D19 R21/93 P(40-25-2) 273
Slr-Holt 106C

Hot 7 0 10 0 17
Phi 3 17 8 7 **35**
Hot D12 R24/91 P(29-16-2) 151
Phi D21 R29/102 P(44-25-1) 289

Mia 7 9 7 7 30
KC 10 14 7 17 **48**
Mia D28 R19/105 P(45-29-4) 294
KC D25 R33/122 P(34-24-0) 328
Mia-Chambers 102C, Fiedler 310P; KC-Gonzalez 140C, Green 328P

Min 7 3 7 6 23
Sea 14 31 0 3 **48**
Min D28 R32/194 P(53-29-2) 249
Sea D18 R31/159 P(28-13-0) 222
Sea-Alexander 139R

NE 7 7 0 0 14
SD 7 7 7 0 **21**
NE D25 R23/87 P(53-36-2) 353
SD D14 R34/238 P(18-10-0) 104
NE-Branch 128C, Brady 353P; SD-Tomlinson 217R

NO 0 7 8 6 21
Det 13 7 3 3 **26**
NO D24 R16/110 P(48-27-2) 247
Det D16 R30/85 P(35-20-0) 267

NYG 7 0 0 0 7
Arz 0 7 0 14 **21**
NYG D14 R17/67 P(36-19-2) 196
Arz D18 R36/102 P(32-23-0) 161

NYJ 0 3 0 0 3
Jax 7 7 14 0 **28**
NYJ D18 R22/78 P(39-21-2) 267
Jax D20 R40/223 P(15-10-0) 160
Jax-Taylor 142R

TB 0 21 7 7 **35**
Cin 7 0 0 0 7
TB D17 R28/101 P(30-19-2) 262
Cin D11 R29/74 P(33-12-1) 94
TB-McCardell 108C

Ten 7 0 12 6 25
Oak 21 10 7 14 **52**
Ten D23 R16/43 P(46-32-4) 387
Oak D24 R21/90 P(39-29-0) 374
Ten-McNair 398P; Oak-Rice 144C, Gannon 381P

MONDAY, SEPTEMBER 30

Den 3 0 13 7 23
Bal 0 31 3 0 **34**
Den D30 R21/97 P(54-35-3) 306
Bal D14 R30/84 P(24-13-0) 146
Den-Griese 328P

SUNDAY, OCTOBER 6

Arz 0 6 0 10 **16**
Car 0 7 6 0 13
Arz D18 R29/91 P(40-18-1) 221
Car D12 R24/58 P(34-20-2) 186

Bal 0 13 10 3 **26**
Cle 0 0 0 21 21
Bal D18 R34/201 P(30-19-0) 208
Cle D21 R17/62 P(49-29-4) 371
Bal-Lewis 187R; Cle-Northcutt 165C

Cin 0 7 7 7 21
Ind 7 14 0 7 **28**
Cin D23 R24/173 P(43-31-3) 237
Ind D19 R25/87 P(34-21-1) 224
Cin-Dillon 164R; Ind-Harrison 145C

KC 3 9 3 14 **29**
NYJ 7 8 0 10 25
KC D24 R28/215 P(33-23-1) 289
NYJ D23 R27/147 P(29-22-1) 212
KC-Holmes 152R; NYJ-Martin 119R, Coles 116C

NE 0 0 6 7 13
Mia 6 10 7 3 **26**
NE D16 R17/37 P(31-17-2) 208
Mia D21 R44/137 P(27-17-0) 182
NE-Patten 102C; Mia-Williams 105R

NYG 0 14 0 7 **21**
Dal 0 10 0 7 17
NYG D16 R28/104 P(27-18-1) 212
Dal D20 R24/95 P(42-23-0) 245
Dal-Galloway 109C

Oak 7 14 7 21 **49**
Buf 0 21 10 0 31
Oak D24 R27/142 P(38-23-0) 353
Buf D29 R18/80 P(53-32-3) 399
Oak-Porter 117C, Gannon 357P; Buf-Moulds 112C, Price 126C, Bledsoe 417P

Phi 0 7 3 15 25
Jax 3 11 0 14 **28**
Phi D28 R30/199 P(48-28-0) 207
Jax D16 R27/70 P(23-13-0) 197
Phi-McNabb 100R

Pit 0 14 7 8 29
NO 10 9 10 3 **32**
Pit D23 R26/120 P(38-22-1) 244
NO D17 R28/121 P(23-13-0) 194
NO-McAllister 123R

SD 0 0 3 6 9
Den 7 12 0 7 **26**
SD D16 R18/79 P(42-26-2) 235
Den D20 R31/117 P(35-26-1) 300
Den-Portis 102R, McCaffrey 113C, Griese 316P

Slr 3 0 3 7 13
SF 10 17 0 10 **37**
Slr D19 R24/88 P(40-23-2) 225
SF D21 R27/179 P(27-18-0) 207
SF-Hearst 116R

TB 0 3 7 10 **20**
Atl 3 0 3 0 6
TB D15 R26/74 P(31-17-1) 253
Atl D14 R22/70 P(38-17-4) 173
TB-Johnson 131C

Was 3 7 14 7 **31**
Ten 0 14 0 0 14
Was D25 R30/156 P(38-22-0) 286
Ten D17 R15/59 P(39-24-3) 230

MONDAY, OCTOBER 7

GB 14 10 7 3 **34**
ChiB 7 7 0 7 21
GB D20 R30/124 P(33-22-0) 333
ChiB D20 R16/45 P(50-27-3) 335
GB-Green 107R, Driver 120C, Glenn 154C, Favre 359P; ChiB-Booker 141C, Miller 353P

SUNDAY, OCTOBER 13

Atl 0 10 0 7 **17**
NYG 0 3 7 0 10
Atl D15 R24/67 P(25-19-0) 246
NYG D18 R27/113 P(31-20-1) 190

Bal 6 0 7 7 20
Ind 7 6 0 9 **22**
Bal D15 R26/105 P(28-15-1) 139
Ind D19 R19/60 P(40-30-1) 257
Ind-Harrison 150C

Buf 3 7 7 14 **31**
Hot 3 14 0 7 24
Buf D25 R33/173 P(33-19-0) 230
Hot D18 R29/141 P(24-13-0) 197
Buf-Henry 159R, Price 121C; Hot-Bradford 126C

Car 7 0 3 3 13
Dal 0 0 0 14 **14**
Car D14 R34/110 P(27-16-0) 198
Dal D17 R24/137 P(32-15-1) 174
Dal-Galloway 104C

Cle 0 0 0 3 3
TB 7 3 0 7 **17**
Cle D11 R18/60 P(40-20-1) 134
TB D22 R38/186 P(32-15-1) 194
TB-Alstott 126R

Det 14 7 3 0 24
Min 3 7 7 14 **31**
Det D17 R17/53 P(41-25-1) 301
Min D22 R25/111 P(36-27-1) 291
Det-Harrington 309P

GB 0 14 7 7 **28**
NE 0 3 0 7 10
GB D20 R36/158 P(27-17-0) 143
NE D20 R22/123 P(44-24-3) 166
GB-Green 136R

Jax 0 7 7 0 14
Ten 7 9 0 7 **23**
Jax D13 R26/130 P(13-7-2) 68
Ten D25 R40/152 P(36-26-0) 218
Ten-George 113R

KC 10 7 7 10 34
SD 7 0 7 21 **35**
KC D17 R29/88 P(29-17-2) 231
SD D27 R28/153 P(41-28-2) 312
SD-Conway 129C, Brees 319P

Mia 0 7 0 17 **24**
Den 6 3 3 10 22
Mia D16 R23/58 P(29-19-1) 201
Den D27 R26/111 P(46-27-2) 299
Den-Griese 335P

NO 13 16 7 7 **43**
Was 0 21 0 6 27
NO D16 R34/119 P(23-12-1) 192
Was D20 R17/54 P(43-21-4) 264
NO-McAllister 121R; Was-Ramsey 320P

Oak 0 3 3 7 13
Slr 7 7 0 14 **28**
Oak D20 R17/65 P(45-30-2) 302
Slr D19 R32/158 P(21-14-0) 164
Oak-Rice 133C, Gannon 332P; Slr-Faulk 158R

Pit 7 17 7 3 **34**
Cin 0 0 7 0 7
Pit D21 R35/211 P(25-16-2) 197
Cin D18 R24/78 P(35-23-3) 190
Pit-Bettis 109R, Burress 149C

MONDAY, OCTOBER 14

SF 10 3 7 8 **28**
Sea 7 7 7 0 21
SF D24 R31/161 P(29-16-0) 190
Sea D24 R30/123 P(31-21-2) 211

SUNDAY, OCTOBER 20

```
Buf    3  14   3        23
Mia    7   3   0   0    10
Buf D15 R27/132 P(31-15-0) 162
Mia D17 R34/132 P(33-13-4) 155
Buf-Henry 132R

Car    0   0   0   0     0
Atl    3   7  14   6    30
Car D12 R21/101 P(26-9-1) 104
Atl D25 R39/187 P(27-20-0) 206

ChiB   0  10  10   0    20
Det    0  14   3   3  3 23
ChiB D17 R31/89 P(25-16-1) 135
Det D23 R39/192 P(29-16-0) 170
Det-Stewart 172R

Dal    0   0   6   0  0  6
Arz    3   3   0   0  3  9
Dal D14 R36/148 P(22-13-4) 194
Arz D22 R38/152 P(46-23-0) 228
Arz-Boston 110C

Den    3   3  14  14  3 37
KC     7   6  14   7  0 34
Den D22 R27/141 P(50-30-0) 366
KC D24 R31/162 P(33-20-0) 143
Den-Sharpe 214C; Griese 376P;
KC-Holmes 113R

Hot    0   7  10   0    17
Cle    0   7  17  10    34
Hot D17 R22/89 P(37-23-0) 265
Cle D14 R24/89 P(31-21-0) 141

Jax    0   7   0   3    10
Bal    0   7  10   0    17
Jax D22 R30/173 P(46-24-3) 224
Bal D16 R32/118 P(28-14-0) 143
Jax-Taylor 151R; Bal-Lewis 119R

Min    0   0   0   7     7
NYJ    3   7   7   3    20
Min D21 R23/101 P(39-26-3) 288
NYJ D21 R29/91 P(29-24-0) 316
NYJ-Moss 111C, Pennington 324P

SD     0   7   7   7  6 27
Oak    0  14   0   7  0 21
SD D24 R42/172 P(25-16-0) 161
Oak D26 R12/37 P(45-35-1) 353
SD-Tomlinson 153R;
Oak-Gannon 361P

Sea    0  14   0   3    17
Slr    7   6  10  14    37
Sea D13 R16/50 P(30-10-2) 240
Slr D28 R42/218 P(40-22-1) 260
Sea-Robinson 166C; Slr-Faulk 183R

SF     7  10   7   3    27
NO     7   3   3  22    35
SF D26 R25/143 P(39-23-1) 275
NO D27 R27/179 P(35-23-0) 243
NO-McAllister 139R, Horn 109C

TB     7   0   0   3    10
Phi    3   7   3   7    20
TB D15 R21/81 P(38-23-1) 126
Phi D14 R34/159 P(25-12-1) 110
Phi-Staley 152R

Was    3   3   3   0     9
GB     7  10   0  13    30
Was D19 R34/146 P(24-10-0) 92
GB D19 R25/88 P(29-20-0) 155
```

MONDAY, OCTOBER 21

```
Ind    0   3   7   0    10
Pit   14   7   7   0    28
Ind D23 R21/72 P(48-32-3) 295
Pit D22 R33/182 P(23-15-1) 182
Ind-Manning 304P
```

SUNDAY, OCTOBER 27

```
Arz    0   7  14   7    28
SF    17  14   0   7    38
Arz D23 R27/151 P(36-24-3) 269
SF D18 R29/105 P(28-18-0) 252
SF-Owens 132C, Garcia 252P

Atl    0  14  10  13    37
NO    10  10   0  15    35
Atl D28 R38/260 P(25-16-0) 186
NO D22 R24/159 P(35-16-2) 192
Atl-Dunn 142R; NO-McAllister 115R
```

```
ChiB   0   0   0   7     7
Min    0  13  12   0    25
ChiB D12 R12/44 P(31-16-2) 174
Min D24 R44/148 P(30-22-0) 216
Min-Bennett 106R, Moss 119C

Cle    3   3  15   3    24
NYJ   14   7   0   0    21
Cle D18 R21/55 P(48-32-0) 279
NYJ D14 R20/66 P(27-19-1) 175

Den    7  14   0   3    24
NE     0   7   3   6    16
Den D23 R40/136 P(23-18-1) 215
NE D16 R19/69 P(29-15-0) 110
Den-Portis 111R, McCaffrey 116C

Det    0  14   0   3    17
Buf    7   7   0  10    24
Det D16 R24/83 P(42-20-1) 199
Buf D23 R24/74 P(36-21-0) 269
Buf-Moulds 123C, Price 101C,
Bledsoe 302P

Hot    0   7   3  11    21
Jax    0   9   3   7    19
Hot D12 R31/81 P(18-11-0) 161
Jax D18 R32/126 P(34-16-0) 164

Ind    0   7   0  14    21
Was   10  13   0   3    26
Ind D18 R19/63 P(32-21-2) 195
Was D23 R37/165 P(36-17-0) 205

Oak    7   0   0   3    10
KC     3   3   7   7    20
Oak D26 R17/83 P(55-35-1) 334
KC D22 R30/133 P(30-14-0) 190
Oak-Brown 144C, Gannon 334P

Pit   14  14   0   3    31
Bal    0   3   8   7    18
Pit D16 R30/104 P(25-19-1) 179
Bal D26 R21/67 P(51-29-3) 293

Sea    0   7   0  10    17
Dal    0   0   7   7    14
Sea D18 R34/97 P(31-19-2) 170
Dal D17 R28/105 P(24-12-0) 132
Dal-Smith 109R

TB     3   0   0   9    12
Car    3   6   0       24
TB D14 R27/71 P(34-23-1) 155
Car D9 R31/110 P(18-5-3) 20

Ten    0   6  14  10    30
Cin    7   7   3   7    24
Ten D20 R27/134 P(27-16-0) 208
Cin D22 R40/191 P(23-17-0) 193
Ten-George 106R; Cin-Dillon 138R
```

MONDAY, OCTOBER 28

```
NYG    0   3   0   0     3
Phi    3   6   0   8    17
NYG D18 R23/103 P(34-20-0) 245
Phi D21 R40/295 P(30-20-1) 127
Phi-McNabb 107R, Staley 126R
```

SUNDAY, NOVEMBER 3

```
Bal    3   7   7   0    17
Atl    3  14   3   0    20
Bal D15 R24/153 P(28-14-1) 187
Atl D14 R34/126 P(24-12-1) 115
Bal-Taylor 127C

Cin   10  14   0  14    38
Hot    3   0   0   0     3
Cin D25 R35/127 P(27-22-0) 263
Hot D22 R25/82 P(32-18-2) 186
Cin-Kitna 263P

Dal    0   0   0   7     7
Det    0   0   6   3     9
Dal D17 R27/71 P(39-22-0) 150
Det D8 R23/52 P(33-14-2) 96

Jax    0   0   3  14    17
NYG    7   7  10   0    24
Jax D16 R20/126 P(38-23-0) 203
NYG D26 R35/177 P(28-20-0) 217
Jax-Smith 123C; NYG-Barber 101R

Min    0   0   7        24
TB    14  10   7   7    38
Min D22 R23/173 P(29-18-2) 214
TB D27 R30/133 P(31-24-0) 313
Min-Bennett 114R;
TB-Johnson 133C, Johnson 313P
```

MONDAY, NOVEMBER 4

```
Mia    0   0   0  10    10
GB     0  14  10   0    24
Mia D25 R30/143 P(42-22-2) 163
GB D16 R23/104 P(27-17-1) 166
```

SUNDAY, NOVEMBER 10

```
Atl    0   7  10  17  0 34
Pit    3  14  14   3  0 34
Atl D21 R31/168 P(46-24-0) 279
Pit D30 R42/182 P(41-28-1) 463
Atl-Dunn 129R, Jefferson 131C;
Pit-Zereoue 123R, Burress 253C,
Ward 139C, Maddox 473P

Cin    7   7   3  10    27
Bal    7  17   7   7    38
Cin D20 R28/123 P(41-28-3) 249
Bal D32 R32/162 P(24-16-0) 163
Cin-Dillon 102R, Johnson 110C;
Bal-Lewis 135R

Det    7   0   0   7    14
GB     3  27  10   0    40
Det D13 R17/126 P(44-20-0) 236
GB D24 R34/150 P(42-29-0) 353
Det-Stewart 122R, Hakim 143C;
GB-Driver 130C, Favre 351P

Hot    0   3   0   7    10
Ten    7   3   7   0    17
Hot D13 R24/68 P(34-19-2) 165
Ten D15 R39/142 P(21-10-2) 109

Ind   14   0  14   7    35
Phi    3   3   0   7    13
Ind D18 R35/127 P(23-18-0) 319
Phi D21 R22/105 P(48-27-0) 269
Ind-Mungro 114R, Harrison 137C,
Wayne 121C, Manning 319P

KC     3   7   0   3    13
SF     3  14   0   0    17
KC D14 R16/80 P(27-15-0) 176
SF D22 R35/155 P(35-25-1) 168
KC-Kennison 134C

Mia    0   3   7   0    10
NYJ    7   3   0   3    13
Mia D15 R23/69 P(28-19-0) 210
NYJ D19 R31/97 P(27-17-0) 167
```

```
NE     0   6  10  17    33
ChiB   0   6  21   3    30
NE D19 R19/82 P(55-36-1) 315
ChiB D14 R28/125 P(30-16-1) 174
NE-Faulk 109C, Brady 328P

NO     6   7   7  14    34
Car    0   7   0   7    14
NO D17 R25/97 P(38-20-0) 248
Car D21 R27/100 P(40-23-1) 296
NO-Horn 101C;
Car-Muhammad 112C, Peete 310P

NYG    7   6   6   8    27
Min    3   3  14   0    20
NYG D26 R35/169 P(35-25-1) 291
Min D17 R26/224 P(26-12-0) 132
NYG-Barber 127R, Dixon 107C,
Collins 300P; Min-Bennett 167R

SD     7  10   7   0    24
Slr    7   7   0  14    28
SD D15 R29/126 P(20-12-2) 130
Slr D25 R16/71 P(48-36-0) 453
SD-Tomlinson 120R;
Slr-Bruce 163C, Holt 118C,
Bulger 453P

Sea   10  17   0   0    27
Arz    3   3   0   0     6
Sea D27 R36/151 P(31-23-0) 255
Arz D19 R29/111 P(29-17-2) 226
Arz-McAddley 113C

Was    7   0   0   0     7
Jax    3  10   3  10    26
Was D23 R16/68 P(51-27-3) 239
Jax D18 R32/142 P(29-19-0) 167
Was-Gardner 100C
```

MONDAY, NOVEMBER 11

```
Oak   10  11   6   7    34
Den    0   7   0   3    10
Oak D20 R14/27 P(38-34-0) 347
Den D27 R22/77 P(47-34-1) 265
Oak-Rice 103C, Gannon 352P
```

SUNDAY, NOVEMBER 17

```
Arz    7   7   0   0    14
Phi    7  21   3   7    38
Arz D15 R20/124 P(35-20-1) 124
Phi D26 R43/212 P(25-20-1) 250
Phi-Staley 135R, McNabb 255P

Bal    0   7   0   0     7
Mia    7  10   3   6    26
Bal D10 R22/66 P(28-14-1) 91
Mia D17 R39/116 P(26-18-0) 221
Mia-Williams 102R

Buf    0  13   3   0    16
KC     7   3   0   7    17
Buf D21 R26/133 P(36-24-1) 211
KC D22 R37/128 P(20-12-0) 192
Buf-Henry 126R; KC-Holmes 104R

Car    7   3   0   0    10
TB     0  10   7   6    23
Car D14 R19/63 P(38-22-3) 168
TB D19 R29/67 P(40-22-0) 247

Cle   14   3   7   3    27
Cin    7   7   3   0    17
Cle D22 R35/140 P(36-22-1) 242
Cin D14 R22/102 P(30-17-0) 248
Cin-Johnson 103C

Dal    0   3   0   0     3
Ind    0   3   0  17    20
Dal D11 R18/84 P(23-11-0) 94
Ind D20 R34/110 P(38-29-1) 252
Ind-James 106R, Harrison 138C

Den    0   3   7  21    31
Sea    0   0   6   3     9
Den D22 R34/202 P(29-19-1) 199
Sea D13 R16/51 P(36-22-2) 153
Den-Portis 136R

GB     0   7   7   7    21
Min   14   0   7  10    31
GB D18 R18/71 P(43-24-3) 296
Min D24 R37/218 P(26-13-2) 207
GB-Driver 121C; Min-Bennett 130R,
Moss 115C

Jax    7  10   7   0    24
Hot    0   7   7   7    21
Jax D16 R28/122 P(25-15-1) 199
Hot D18 R28/78 P(30-22-1) 194
```

```
NE     3   3   7   7    20
Oak    3  14   7   3    27
NE D12 R17/48 P(30-18-0) 147
Oak D22 R31/97 P(38-26-1) 289

NO     0   0   3  14    17
Atl    0   7   7  10    24
NO D16 R21/80 P(31-20-1) 264
Atl D22 R37/155 P(23-11-1) 137
NO-Horn 134C; Atl-Gaylor 100C

NYJ    7   6   8  10    31
Det    0   7   0   7    14
NYJ D26 R39/189 P(26-21-1) 219
Det D13 R20/108 P(30-15-1) 171
NYJ-Martin 112R, Coles 114C,
Pennington 229P

Pit    7   0   0  16    23
Ten    7   7  14   3    31
Pit D20 R15/45 P(45-27-3) 312
Ten D22 R40/121 P(33-18-0) 257
Pit-Ward 168C

SF     0   7  10   0    17
SD     7   0   0  10  3 20
SF D21 R31/136 P(43-25-1) 331
SD D26 R28/105 P(50-29-1) 336
SF-Owens 171C, Garcia 337P;
SD-Conway 152C, Brees 336P

Was    0  10   7   0    17
NYG    3   7   6   3    19
Was D12 R21/60 P(35-15-1) 106
NYG D21 R38/88 P(46-22-2) 211
NYG-Shockey 111C
```

MONDAY, NOVEMBER 18

```
ChiB   0   6   7   3    16
Slr    7   7   0   7    21
ChiB D16 R22/103 P(35-20-0) 117
Slr D21 R20/61 P(37-22-1) 327
Slr-Bruce 141C, Bulger 347P
```

SUNDAY, NOVEMBER 24

```
Atl   14  14  13   0    41
Car    0   0   0   0     0
Atl D23 R47/149 P(25-20-0) 277
Car D10 R14/71 P(26-13-4) 51
Atl-Finneran 104C

Buf    3   0  10   0    13
NYJ    7   7   3  14    31
Buf D17 R20/88 P(35-23-2) 170
NYJ D22 R37/155 P(24-15-0) 170
NYJ-Martin 120R

Cin    0  14   0   7    21
Pit   14   3   3   9    29
Cin D17 R21/54 P(39-22-0) 298
Pit D21 R35/156 P(26-22-0) 235
Cin-Johnson 152C; Pit-Ward 125C

Cle    7   7   3   7    24
NO     3   6   3   3    15
Cle D17 R37/163 P(22-12-2) 176
NO D21 R71/74 P(40-23-3) 309
Cle-Green 114R; NO-Lewis 114C,
Brooks 318P

Det    0   3  14   0    17
ChiB   3  10   3   0    20
Det D19 R29/102 P(40-21-1) 199
ChiB D21 R25/75 P(51-31-0) 347
ChiB-Booker 157C, White 106C

GB     7   0   0   0     7
TB     3   8  11   7    29
GB D15 R23/96 P(38-20-4) 171
TB D14 R25/93 P(30-18-1) 153

Ind    3   0  14   3    23
Den    0   7   0   7    20
Ind D26 R39/128 P(44-27-1) 216
Den D15 R22/113 P(24-15-2) 172
Ind-Harrison 107C

Jax    0   5   0  14    19
Dal    0   7   7   7    21
Jax D19 R26/132 P(40-22-1) 194
Dal D21 R31/118 P(24-16-2) 287
Jax-Taylor 100R; Dal-Galloway 144C,
Hutchinson 301P
```

```
KC    10   7   0  15   32
Sea    0  21   7  11   39
KC   D32 R26/217  P(34-26-1) 335
Sea  D32 R30/180  P(36-25-0) 354
KC-Holmes 197R, Holmes 110C,
Green 343P; Sea-Alexander 145R,
Robinson 168C, Hasselbeck 362P

Min    0   7   7   3   17
NE     7  14   0   3   24
Min  D26 R25/153  P(49-24-0) 264
NE   D20 R33/80   P(34-21-0) 219

NYG    0   7   0   7   14
Hot    0   5   8   3   16
NYG  D19 R26/168  P(41-18-2) 201
Hot  D12 R35/123  P(23-10-0) 89
NYG-Barber 147R, Toomer 113C

Oak   14   7  17   3   41
Arz    0  14   0   6   20
Oak  D28 R37/187  P(45-27-1) 333
Arz  D15 R20/132  P(34-16-2) 131
Oak-Garner 100R, Rice 110C,
Gannon 340P; Arz-Shipp 135R

SD     3   0   0   0    3
Mia    7   3   0   3   30
SD   D12 R20/64   P(22-15-1) 80
Mia  D24 R44/222  P(23-14-0) 191
Mia-Williams 143R, McKnight 111C

Slr    7   3   0   7   17
Was    0   7  13   0   20
Slr  D25 R17/84   P(49-34-1) 280
Was  D21 R39/127  P(24-16-0) 235
Slr-Warner 301P

Ten    0   6   0   6   12
Bal   10   0   3   0   13
Ten  D19 R30/121  P(44-22-3) 281
Bal  D12 R27/112  P(24-11-1) 87
```

MONDAY, NOVEMBER 25

```
Phi    0  21  14   3   38
SF     0   7  10   0   17
Phi  D19 R31/107  P(29-21-0) 236
SF   D24 R18/104  P(63-36-0) 305
SF-Owens 166C
```

THURSDAY, NOVEMBER 28

```
NE    10   7   0   3   20
Det    3   3   3   3   12
NE   D23 R38/139  P(30-18-1) 210
Det  D14 R15/82   P(44-22-3) 210
NE-Brown 111C

Was    0  14   6   0   20
Dal    0  10   7  10   27
Was  D16 R25/83   P(37-21-4) 232
Dal  D19 R36/211  P(25-12-0) 117
Dal-Smith 144R
```

SUNDAY, DECEMBER 1

```
Arz    0   0   0   0    0
KC    14  21   7  14   49
Arz  D10 R15/26   P(43-18-4) 96
KC   D27 R38/216  P(25-18-0) 261
KC-Holmes 113R

Atl    0  14   7   3   6  30
Min    7   7   3   7      24
Atl  D19 R29/227  P(28-11-1) 152
Min  D21 R32/139  P(43-23-3) 230
Atl-Vick 173R, Finneran 114C;
Min-Moss 134C

Bal    0  14   0  13   27
Cin    6  10   7   0   23
Bal  D15 R31/148  P(19-10-0) 99
Cin  D25 R29/78   P(46-30-1) 303
Bal-Lewis 121R; Cin-Kitna 308P

Car    7   0   0   6   13
Cle    3   0   3   0    6
Car  D11 R38/145  P(19-8-2) 89
Cle  D14 R28/140  P(27-12-3) 118
Car-Brown 122R

ChiB   7   7   0   6   20
GB     3   3  10  14   30
ChiB D19 R17/74   P(38-27-1) 210
GB   D26 R32/181  P(42-24-1) 215
```

```
Den   10   7   3   7   27
SD     0  24   0   3   3  30
Den  D20 R27/156  P(39-22-2) 261
SD   D32 R38/220  P(41-27-0) 214
Den-Portis 159R, McCaffrey 126C;
SD-Tomlinson 220R

Hot    0   0   0   3    3
Ind   10   3   0   6   19
Hot  D10 R20/65   P(35-20-0) 100
Ind  D13 R32/88   P(28-15-0) 190
Ind-Harrison 101C

Mia   14   0   7   0   21
Buf    3  14  14   7   38
Mia  D14 R34/270  P(20-11-1) 30
Buf  D21 R37/161  P(27-15-0) 270
Mia-Williams 228R;
Buf-Henry 151R, Moulds 130C,
Bledsoe 306P

Pit    6  10   3   6   25
Jax    7   3   0  13   23
Pit  D23 R40/219  P(27-17-1) 184
Jax  D13 R21/102  P(23-12-0) 124

Sea    0   3   7  14   24
SF     0  17   7   7   31
Sea  D25 R19/80   P(55-30-2) 427
SF   D21 R38/142  P(29-16-2) 157
Sea-Jackson 114C,
Hasselbeck 427P; SF-Hearst 124R

Slr    0   3   0   0    3
Phi    7   3   0   0   10
Slr  D13 R20/76   P(42-20-2) 174
Phi  D12 R31/108  P(30-14-0) 157

TB     2   7   3   8   20
NO     0   6  14   3   23
TB   D17 R16/34   P(44-28-1) 249
NO   D14 R31/102  P(26-10-0) 136
TB-McCardell 107C; NO-Horn 106C
```

MONDAY, DECEMBER 2

```
NYJ    0  10   0  10   20
Oak    3   3  14   6   26
NYJ  D18 R14/32   P(34-22-1) 242
Oak  D25 R26/98   P(42-31-0) 313
NYJ-Coles 158C; Oak-Gannon 342P
```

SUNDAY, DECEMBER 8

```
Atl    0   3   0   7   10
TB     0  21   6   7   34
Atl  D10 R23/62   P(25-12-1) 119
TB   D22 R29/150  P(31-23-0) 271
TB-Jurevicius 100C, Johnson 276P

Buf    0   0  10   7   17
NE    17   3   0   7   27
Buf  D24 R18/78   P(51-32-4) 312
NE   D14 R26/92   P(27-15-0) 183
Buf-Price 105C, Bledsoe 328P

Cin    7  10  14   0   31
Car    9   7  21  15   52
Cin  D25 R29/83   P(37-25-0) 257
Car  D23 R29/82   P(29-21-1) 319
Cin-Johnson 114C;
Car-Muhammad 106C, Smith 144C,
Peete 319P

Cle    0   0  14   7   21
Jax    7   7   0   6   20
Cle  D21 R33/173  P(35-21-2) 244
Jax  D13 R31/157  P(14-10-0) 54
Cle-Green 119R, Morgan 118C;
Jax-Taylor 145R

Den    3  10   0   0   13
NYJ    0   6   3  10   19
Den  D21 R29/111  P(37-28-1) 258
NYJ  D18 R22/64   P(30-19-0) 217
Den-Portis 103R, Sharpe 100C;
NYJ-Coles 126C

Det   14   3   3   0   20
Arz    3   3   3   7   23
Det  D15 R15/51   P(39-20-0) 152
Arz  D21 R31/133  P(43-24-1) 180
```

```
Hot   14   0  10   0   24
Pit    0   3   3   0    6
Hot  D3 R26/37    P(10-3-0) 10
Pit  D24 R31/128  P(58-31-2) 294
Pit-Maddox 325P

Ind   10   0   0   7   17
Ten    7  14   0   6   27
Ind  D22 R24/92   P(42-26-3) 297
Ten  D18 R33/119  P(23-19-0) 229
Ind-Wayne 103C

Min   10   3   9   0   22
GB     0   6   7  13   26
Min  D15 R25/191  P(28-15-1) 125
GB   D20 R28/124  P(32-22-1) 204
Min-Bennett 120R;
GB-Ferguson 105C

NO    10  10   7  10   37
Bal    7   0   7  11   25
NO   D22 R41/150  P(33-16-0) 209
Bal  D19 R24/114  P(39-18-2) 296
NO-McAllister 127R;
Bal-Lewis 108C, Blake 316P

NYG    3  14   7   3   27
Was    0   3  11   7   21
NYG  D16 R29/111  P(31-17-0) 205
Was  D23 R20/132  P(46-25-1) 315
Was-Thompson 122C

Oak   10   3   7   7   27
SD     0   0   0   7    7
Oak  D22 R25/67   P(41-26-0) 326
SD   D19 R25/65   P(41-22-3) 226
Oak-Jolley 104C, Rice 113C,
Gannon 328P

Phi    7  13   0   7   27
Sea    6   0   7   7   20
Phi  D20 R31/126  P(36-21-1) 190
Sea  D24 R25/172  P(45-24-3) 195
Phi-Staley 100R;
Sea-Alexander 123R

SF     0   7   3  21   31
Dal    6   0   7   4   17
SF   D26 R29/125  P(55-36-0) 276
Dal  D10 R27/110  P(28-11-2) 147
SF-Owens 123C

Slr   10   0   0   0   10
KC    14  21   0  14   49
Slr  D16 R17/33   P(35-24-2) 169
KC   D21 R37/180  P(16-11-0) 113
KC-Holmes 132R
```

MONDAY, DECEMBER 9

```
ChiB   0   0   3   6    9
Mia    7   7   7   6   27
ChiB D12 R24/107  P(32-11-3) 88
Mia  D22 R43/248  P(29-15-1) 188
Mia-Williams 216R
```

SUNDAY, DECEMBER 15

```
Arz    0   7  14   7   28
Slr    3  21   0   6   30
Arz  D20 R31/129  P(27-17-1) 249
Slr  D20 R19/66   P(40-24-2) 300
Slr-Holt 141C, Bulger 319P

Bal    3  10   7   3   23
Hot    7   5   7   0   19
Bal  D16 R33/70   P(30-18-0) 228
Hot  D15 R24/95   P(34-19-2) 182

Car    7   0   0   7   14
Pit    7   7   6  10   30
Car  D11 R16/50   P(34-17-1) 81
Pit  D19 R38/129  P(34-21-1) 203
Pit-Burress 120C

Dal    0   0   0   7    7
NYG   21   3   3  10   37
Dal  D14 R27/104  P(40-16-2) 137
NYG  D20 R33/157  P(31-16-0) 220

GB     3   0  14   3   20
SF     0   6   8   0   14
GB   D21 R33/104  P(33-25-0) 198
SF   D16 R23/107  P(34-19-1) 156

Ind    0   0  14  14   28
Cle   13   3   0   7   23
Ind  D20 R33/143  P(34-20-1) 274
Cle  D18 R28/96   P(35-21-0) 253
Ind-Harrison 172C
```

```
Jax    7   7   8   7   29
Cin    3   9   3   0   15
Jax  D20 R30/109  P(28-19-0) 212
Cin  D19 R24/65   P(42-22-1) 235

KC     0   0  14  10   24
Den   14   0  14   3   31
KC   D22 R26/185  P(42-18-0) 309
Den  D24 R35/197  P(26-18-1) 285
KC-Holmes 161R, Hall 143C,
Green 310P; Den-Portis 130R

Min   14  10   0   8   32
NO     0  10   3   8   31
Min  D22 R25/146  P(36-26-0) 293
NO   D18 R22/78   P(33-21-0) 221
Min-Moss 113C, Culpepper 312P

NYJ    0   0  10   3   13
ChiB   0  10   7   3   20
NYJ  D19 R24/134  P(33-22-0) 200
ChiB D20 R26/105  P(27-22-0) 161
NYJ-Martin 127R

Oak    3   3   3   8   17
Mia   10   7   3   3   23
Oak  D14 R12/56   P(31-17-1) 162
Mia  D21 R33/121  P(32-21-0) 213
Mia-Williams 101R, Chambers 138C

SD     3   7   0   3   13
Buf    7   6   0   7   20
SD   D14 R30/116  P(35-16-0) 192
Buf  D17 R25/155  P(33-11-0) 101
SD-Tomlinson 110R;
Buf-Henry 144R

Sea    7   0  14   3   6  30
Atl   14   3   0   7      24
Sea  D25 R37/166  P(31-22-0) 298
Atl  D21 R35/150  P(38-21-2) 223
Sea-Alexander 127R,
Robinson 143C; Atl-Dunn 101R

TB     3  10   0  10   23
Det    0  10   3   7   20
TB   D22 R28/123  P(41-24-0) 253
Det  D15 R26/144  P(22-10-1) 148

Was    0   0  14   7   21
Phi    7  10  14   3   34
Was  D16 R25/86   P(35-23-0) 206
Phi  D15 R30/110  P(28-16-1) 210
```

MONDAY, DECEMBER 16

```
NE     0   0   7   0    7
Ten    0  14   7   3   24
NE   D11 R13/56   P(31-15-1) 120
Ten  D20 R48/238  P(24-11-1) 127
Ten-George 101R
```

SATURDAY, DECEMBER 21

```
Mia    7   0   7   3   17
Min    0   3   7  10   20
Mia  D13 R17/69   P(21-15-1) 170
Min  D21 R32/129  P(30-21-2) 239
Min-Moss 110C

Phi    7  10   0  10   27
Dal    0   0   3   0    3
Phi  D17 R32/114  P(33-19-2) 245
Dal  D9 R19/68    P(24-15-1) 78

SF     7   3   0   7   17
Arz    0   7   7   0   14
SF   D21 R33/106  P(39-23-1) 252
Arz  D14 R24/108  P(26-16-1) 76
```

SUNDAY, DECEMBER 22

```
Buf    0   0   0   0    0
GB     0   3   0   7   10
Buf  D17 R24/43   P(36-18-2) 142
GB   D14 R30/119  P(33-15-2) 104
GB-Green 116R

ChiB   7   0   0   7   14
Car    0  21   0   3   24
ChiB D8 R22/55    P(30-15-0) 131
Car  D15 R39/88   P(35-18-0) 165

Cle    7   0   0   7   14
Bal    3   7   3   0   13
Cle  D19 R26/63   P(31-22-1) 193
Bal  D16 R29/146  P(28-16-1) 129
Bal-Lewis 100R
```

```
Den    0   3   7   6   16
Oak   14   7   0   7   28
Den  D21 R18/81   P(43-20-3) 243
Oak  D21 R37/136  P(27-18-0) 186
Den-Lelie 106C, Stallworth 111C

Det    0   0   0  15   15
Atl    3  10   6  17   36
Det  D12 R21/87   P(33-11-3) 121
Atl  D27 R41/197  P(38-20-1) 336
Atl-Dunn 132R, McCord 182C,
Vick 337P

Hot    0   3   0   7   10
Was    7   9   0  10   26
Hot  D10 R24/67   P(31-12-1) 99
Was  D27 R46/247  P(31-14-0) 190
Was-Betts 116R, Watson 110R

NO     3   3   0  13   13
Cin    7   0   0  13   20
NO   D11 R20/33   P(38-16-0) 177
Cin  D25 R39/240  P(40-20-2) 183
NO-Stallworth 111C;
Cin-Dillon 126R

NYG    3   7  20  14   44
Ind    3   3  21     27
NYG  D24 R36/103  P(29-23-0) 366
Ind  D20 R19/50   P(46-30-2) 349
NYG-Shockey 116C, Toomer 204C,
Collins 366P; Ind-Harrison 128C,
Wayne 104C, Manning 365P

NYJ   14  10   0      30
NE     7   3   7   0   17
NYJ  D19 R31/108  P(34-23-0) 285
NE   D14 R23/97   P(37-19-1) 119
NYJ-Martin 106R

SD     3   3   9   7   22
KC     7   7   7   3   24
SD   D20 R26/148  P(40-26-0) 235
KC   D19 R24/53   P(36-23-1) 323
SD-Tomlinson 131R;
KC-Boerigter 144C, Green 337P

Slr    0   3   7   0   10
Sea    3  10  10   7   30
Slr  D17 R15/17   P(49-32-3) 254
Sea  D26 R34/100  P(32-20-0) 292
Sea-Hasselbeck 303P

Ten    7   7   7   7   28
Jax    0   3   0   7   10
Ten  D20 R40/175  P(22-14-0) 123
Jax  D13 R18/75   P(36-18-1) 139
```

MONDAY, DECEMBER 23

```
Pit   17   0   0   0   17
TB     0   0   0   0    0
Pit  D19 R35/94   P(24-18-0) 233
TB   D18 R14/74   P(44-21-1) 203
Pit-Burress 127C; TB-Johnson 132C
```

SATURDAY, DECEMBER 28

```
KC     0   0   0   0    0
Oak    0  14   3   7   24
KC   D11 R15/44   P(32-15-1) 132
Oak  D26 R60/280  P(14-7-0) 74
Oak-Garner 135R

Phi    7   0   0   0    7
NYG    0   0   7   3   10
Phi  D9 R23/65    P(25-13-1) 144
NYG  D23 R39/213  P(35-25-1) 248
NYG-Barber 203R
```

SUNDAY, DECEMBER 29

```
Arz    0   7   0   0    7
Den    3   6   7  21   37
Arz  D18 R19/84   P(33-16-1) 123
Den  D24 R32/259  P(24-16-0) 191
Den-Portis 228R, McCaffrey 112C

Atl    0   7   9   0   16
Cle    3   0  14   7   24
Atl  D16 R27/105  P(40-17-1) 226
Cle  D17 R34/189  P(25-14-3) 189
Cle-Green 178R

Bal    7   7  10   7   31
Pit    7  13   0  14   34
Bal  D21 R23/114  P(26-19-2) 308
Pit  D25 R37/175  P(30-20-2) 176
Bal-Heap 146C, Blake 336P;
Pit-Zereoue 104R
```

Car 0 7 3 0 **10**
NO 3 0 3 0 6
Car D13 R26/85 P(32-20-2) 188
NO D13 R30/125 P(31-12-2) 119
NO-McAllister 117R

Cin 0 3 0 6 9
Buf 6 14 7 0 **27**
Cin D19 R18/84 P(35-19-2) 233
Buf D23 R38/99 P(31-23-0) 225
Cin-Johnson 123C

Dal 0 7 0 7 14
Was 0 7 10 3 **20**
Dal D8 R22/38 P(23-12-1) 148
Was D18 R37/151 P(31-17-2) 201
Dal-Bryant 170C

GB 0 0 0 7 17
NYJ 0 14 14 14 **42**
GB D19 R27/114 P(41-22-1) 208
NYJ D22 R29/129 P(25-18-0) 208
NYJ-Pennington 196P

Jax 3 7 0 3 13
Ind 0 10 0 10 **20**
Jax D20 R33/154 P(26-13-0) 112
Ind D18 R29/126 P(28-20-0) 146
Jax-Johnson 123C

Mia 7 14 0 3 0 24
NE 0 10 3 11 3 **27**
Mia D37 R37/256 P(25-11-0) 103
NE D20 R31/116 P(45-25-1) 216
Mia-Williams 185R

Min 14 14 7 3 **38**
Det 14 3 7 12 36
Min D24 R34/154 P(29-21-1) 296
Det D20 R20/93 P(44-19-3) 293
Min-Moss 109C, Culpepper 312P;
Det-Schroeder 132C

Sea 7 0 0 21 3 **31**
SD 0 10 10 8 0 28
Sea D34 R34/163 P(53-36-2) 428
SD D24 R20/88 P(50-28-1) 326
Sea-Mili 119C, Robinson 103C,
Hasselbeck 449P;
SD-Alexander 129C, Brees 332P

TB 0 6 0 9 **15**
ChiB 0 0 0 0 0
TB D15 R36/161 P(25-16-0) 111
ChiB D14 R22/85 P(29-13-4) 133

Ten 3 3 0 7 **13**
Hot 0 0 3 0 3
Ten D15 R35/140 P(23-8-0) 137
Hot D16 R22/28 P(41-21-1) 196
Ten-George 102R

MONDAY, DECEMBER 30

SF 3 14 0 3 20
Slr 0 0 3 28 **31**
SF D19 R36/193 P(24-16-0) 136
Slr D16 R14/35 P(40-24-2) 228

2003 NFL
THURSDAY, SEPTEMBER 4

NYJ 7 0 3 3 13
Was 3 10 0 3 **16**
NYJ D11 R22/57 P(24-15-0) 101
Was D17 R34/160 P(23-17-1) 167
Was-Coles 106C

SUNDAY, SEPTEMBER 7

Arz 7 7 10 0 24
Det 3 7 7 10 **27**
Arz D21 R20/95 P(46-28-1) 339
Det D16 R23/66 P(30-17-0) 195
Arz-Boldin 217C, Blake 358P;
Det-Harrington 195P

Atl 3 0 14 10 **27**
Dal 7 0 0 6 13
Atl D17 R30/98 P(27-16-1) 220
Dal D16 R24/149 P(32-15-1) 254
Dal-Galloway 139C

Bal 0 0 7 8 15
Pit 6 7 14 7 **34**
Bal D17 R23/88 P(43-22-1) 143
Pit D21 R34/88 P(29-21-0) 251
Pit-Burress 116C

ChiB 0 7 0 0 7
SF 10 23 6 10 **49**
ChiB D8 R20/55 P(34-14-3) 72
SF D23 R42/162 P(35-19-1) 229
SF-Owens 112C

Den 3 17 7 3 **30**
Cin 0 0 3 7 10
Den D19 R40/184 P(25-12-3) 109
Cin D15 R22/51 P(37-20-2) 243
Den-Portis 120R

Hot 3 3 9 6 **21**
Mia 0 14 0 6 20
Hot D16 R34/127 P(32-17-0) 266
Mia D14 R22/86 P(32-17-2) 215
Mia-Chambers 118C

Ind 0 3 3 3
Cle 3 0 0 3 6
Ind D18 R15/67 P(43-27-2) 204
Cle D18 R26/98 P(29-20-2) 182

Jax 0 14 3 6 23
Car 0 0 7 17 **24**
Jax D17 R28/75 P(27-23-0) 256
Car D17 R26/122 P(30-16-2) 120
Car-Davis 111R

Min 10 10 7 3 **30**
GB 0 3 8 14 25
Min D21 R36/154 P(30-15-0) 183
GB D22 R19/62 P(41-25-4) 242
Min-Moss 150C

NE 0 0 0 0 0
Buf 7 14 0 10 **31**
NE D16 R21/105 P(35-17-4) 134
Buf D23 R33/107 P(28-17-1) 215

NO 3 0 0 7 10
Sea 0 21 3 3 **27**
NO D20 R26/96 P(47-29-1) 263
Sea D17 R33/151 P(23-12-0) 119
NO-Stallworth 101C;
Sea-Alexander 108R

Oak 3 7 0 10 20
Ten 6 6 3 10 **25**
Oak D13 R10/34 P(39-24-0) 246
Ten D20 R28/76 P(38-25-1) 258
Oak-Garner 112C

SD 0 0 7 7 14
KC 14 10 3 0 **27**
SD D13 R18/64 P(33-18-2) 168
KC D19 R32/131 P(32-21-1) 259

Slr 3 0 7 3 13
NYG 7 3 13 0 **23**
Slr D18 R13/40 P(55-35-1) 315
NYG D15 R27/149 P(26-14-0) 187
Slr-Bruce 120C, Holt 111C,
Warner 342P; NYG-Barber 146R

MONDAY, SEPTEMBER 8

TB 0 3 7 7 **17**
Phi 0 0 0 0 0
TB D19 R31/90 P(36-27-1) 238
Phi D13 R16/121 P(37-19-1) 124

SUNDAY, SEPTEMBER 14

Buf 14 7 14 3 **38**
Jax 0 7 3 7 7
Buf D20 R32/43 P(27-20-0) 328
Jax D20 R22/95 P(40-26-0) 192
Buf-Moulds 133C, Bledsoe 314P

Car 3 3 3 3 **12**
TB 0 0 3 6 9
Car D14 R40/171 P(23-9-2) 87
TB D25 R22/60 P(61-34-1) 337
Car-Davis 142R; TB-Johnson 102C,
Johnson 339P

ChiB 3 7 3 0 13
Min 7 10 0 7 **24**
ChiB D10 R17/80 P(23-14-1) 128
Min D25 R39/202 P(26-20-0) 198
Min-Williams 108R

Cin 3 7 3 7 20
Oak 10 0 3 10 **23**
Cin D27 R39/129 P(41-25-2) 287
Oak D12 R20/134 P(28-13-0) 103
Cin-Horn 111C, Johnson 131C,
Warrick 109C, Kitna 303P

Cle 0 3 10 0 13
Bal 10 6 0 17 **33**
Cle D9 R20/60 P(37-17-2) 115
Bal D14 R41/343 P(18-7-1) 50
Bal-Lewis 295R

Den 14 10 10 3 **37**
SD 0 3 3 7 13
Den D24 R33/197 P(29-16-0) 185
SD D19 R18/121 P(41-20-1) 182
Den-Portis 129R

Det 0 6 0 0 6
GB 14 3 7 7 **31**
Det D14 R17/56 P(55-26-3) 237
GB D17 R35/200 P(28-15-1) 132
GB-Green 160R

Hot 0 10 0 0 10
NO 7 0 10 14 **31**
Hot D16 R24/75 P(36-17-2) 183
NO D28 R35/105 P(27-18-0) 182
NO-Horn 111C

Mia 7 14 0 0 **21**
NYJ 3 0 0 7 10
Mia D23 R44/187 P(19-14-0) 189
NYJ D17 R11/21 P(45-29-1) 366
Mia-Williams 125R;
NYJ-Moss 142C, Testaverde 373P

NE 3 14 7 7 **31**
Phi 0 7 0 3 10
NE D17 R30/62 P(44-30-0) 247
Phi D23 R16/100 P(48-20-2) 168

Pit 17 3 0 0 20
KC 7 20 7 7 **41**
Pit D16 R16/60 P(47-28-3) 320
KC D19 R35/159 P(21-15-2) 123
Pit-Burress 115C, Ward 146C,
Maddox 336P; KC-Holmes 122R

Sea 7 17 0 7 **38**
Arz 0 0 0 0 0
Sea D16 R30/130 P(21-10-0) 193
Arz D18 R24/93 P(46-25-4) 193
Sea-Jackson 133C

SF 7 3 7 7 24
Slr 7 0 7 10 3 **27**
SF D20 R26/148 P(38-21-1) 242
Slr D21 R24/88 P(36-25-0) 190

Ten 0 7 0 0 7
Ind 3 14 3 13 **33**
Ten D14 R19/53 P(34-22-1) 183
Ind D20 R34/127 P(21-14-0) 164
Ind-James 120R

MONDAY, SEPTEMBER 15

Was 0 17 9 7 **33**
Atl 3 0 7 21 31
Was D23 R31/125 P(39-25-0) 310
Atl D17 R22/99 P(36-16-2) 184
Was-Coles 180C, Gardner 118C,
Ramsey 356P

SUNDAY, SEPTEMBER 21

Bal 7 3 14 0 **24**
SD 3 0 0 7 10
Bal D16 R32/152 P(21-12-1) 97
SD D25 R30/132 P(45-28-3) 257
Bal-Lewis 132R;
SD-Tomlinson 105R

Buf 0 0 0 7 7
Mia 0 7 3 7 **17**
Buf D8 R14/41 P(26-10-3) 77
Mia D23 R44/166 P(28-16-2) 147
Mia-Williams 153R

Cle 0 0 0 13 **13**
SF 3 3 0 3 12
Cle D20 R19/51 P(38-25-1) 200
SF D15 R24/75 P(35-21-1) 190
Cle-Johnson 109C

GB 0 10 0 3 13
Arz 7 3 3 7 **20**
GB D18 R23/66 P(33-23-1) 245
Arz D21 R31/81 P(31-20-1) 273

THURSDAY, SEPTEMBER 4

Jax 0 3 0 10 13
Ind 0 0 17 6 **23**
Jax D15 R25/152 P(28-16-0) 114
Ind D17 R30/73 P(33-21-1) 216
Jax-Taylor 126R; Ind-Wayne 141C

KC 7 7 14 14 **42**
Hot 0 0 7 7 14
KC D27 R35/168 P(28-16-2) 258
Hot D20 R26/107 P(38-24-2) 209
Hot-Johnson 102C

Min 0 16 0 7 **23**
Det 10 0 0 3 13
Min D14 R22/127 P(32-15-1) 287
Det D22 R26/77 P(42-24-3) 225
Min-Wayne 141C

NO 2 0 3 7 12
Ten 10 3 7 7 **27**
NO D11 R15/23 P(23-15-0) 165
Ten D28 R35/105 P(35-24-0) 280
Ten-George 100R, Bennett 105C

NYG 7 14 0 3 **24**
Was 3 0 7 11 21
NYG D25 R31/129 P(39-24-0) 270
Was D25 R22/124 P(45-23-1) 332
NYG-Barber 126R; Was-Coles 105C,
Ramsey 348P

NYJ 3 3 3 7 16
NE 3 3 0 17 **23**
NYJ D16 R17/65 P(44-25-1) 264
NE D19 R36/147 P(26-15-0) 147

Pit 0 0 7 3 **17**
Cin 0 0 3 7 10
Pit D22 R38/138 P(34-21-1) 238
Cin D11 R16/57 P(24-16-1) 125

Slr 7 10 6 0 23
Sea 7 3 0 14 **24**
Slr D19 R28/82 P(34-21-2) 226
Sea D20 R22/96 P(39-22-1) 220

TB 3 14 14 0 **31**
Atl 0 3 7 0 10
TB D18 R37/132 P(24-16-0) 184
Atl D13 R19/29 P(31-18-4) 107

MONDAY, SEPTEMBER 22

Oak 0 0 7 3 10
Den 21 3 7 0 **31**
Oak D11 R16/39 P(35-17-1) 156
Den D20 R39/190 P(21-14-0) 193
Den-Lelie 108C

SUNDAY, SEPTEMBER 28

Arz 0 7 6 0 13
Slr 14 6 3 14 **37**
Arz D7 R14/36 P(21-13-0) 125
Slr D34 R41/133 P(42-28-1) 268
Slr-Holt 133C

Atl 0 0 0 3 3
Car 7 10 0 6 **23**
Atl D11 R23/144 P(23-14-1) 123
Car D19 R39/193 P(27-17-0) 168
Atl-Duckett 100R; Car-Davis 153R

Cin 7 7 0 7 **21**
Cle 7 0 0 7 14
Cin D17 R29/80 P(31-23-0) 215
Cle D18 R22/69 P(36-23-1) 270

Dal 0 14 0 3 **17**
NYJ 3 0 3 0 6
Dal D18 R41/202 P(23-11-1) 158
NYJ D15 R26/66 P(29-21-0) 219
Dal-Hambrick 127R, Galloway 100C

Det 7 3 0 6 16
Den 7 7 3 3 **20**
Det D16 R24/144 P(33-15-0) 141
Den D20 R23/79 P(34-25-0) 253

Ind 14 10 24 7 **55**
NO 3 0 0 7 10
Ind D20 R28/100 P(27-21-0) 318
NO D20 R25/155 P(36-21-2) 208
Ind-Harrison 158C, Manning 314P;
NO-McAllister 101R

Jax 3 7 10 0 20
Hot 7 7 3 7 **24**
Jax D15 R22/79 P(37-18-3) 263
Hot D21 R37/110 P(37-23-2) 229
Jax-Edwards 111C

KC 0 3 7 7 **17**
Bal 0 0 3 7 10
KC D15 R28/129 P(28-17-0) 136
Bal D22 R36/202 P(26-15-3) 124
Bal-Lewis 115R

NE 3 0 7 7 17
Was 3 0 14 3 **20**
NE D23 R30/106 P(38-25-3) 281
Was D15 R29/119 P(22-10-0) 134

Phi 10 3 3 7 **23**
Buf 0 0 13 0 13
Phi D19 R34/176 P(29-18-0) 159
Buf D15 R12/21 P(43-27-0) 287
Buf-Moulds 114C

SD 7 14 3 7 31
Oak 7 7 0 17 3 **34**
SD D22 R39/222 P(32-22-1) 208
Oak D23 R24/120 P(43-26-1) 328
SD-Tomlinson 187R;
Oak-Brown 110C, Rice 126C,
Gannon 348P

SF 0 0 0 7 7
Min 10 7 6 12 **35**
SF D18 R25/145 P(41-23-3) 227
Min D19 R30/102 P(21-16-0) 252
Min-Moss 172C, Frerotte 267P

Ten 0 16 7 7 **30**
Pit 3 0 0 0 3
Ten D9 R22/40 P(16-15-0) 158
Pit D25 R25/69 P(47-31-2) 307
Pit-Maddox 332P

MONDAY, SEPTEMBER 29

GB 17 7 0 14 **38**
ChiB 0 6 3 14 23
GB D20 R25/187 P(30-22-1) 193
ChiB D23 R28/181 P(44-25-2) 180
GB-Green 176R; ChiB-Thomas 110R

SUNDAY, OCTOBER 5

Arz 7 0 0 0 7
Dal 7 10 7 0 **24**
Arz D9 R18/32 P(28-14-2) 119
Dal D18 R36/97 P(31-20-1) 268
Dal-Glenn 104C

Cin 0 6 0 10 16
Buf 3 0 13 6 **22**
Cin D18 R27/67 P(44-26-1) 212
Buf D17 R27/80 P(35-19-0) 177

Cle 10 13 7 3 **33**
Pit 0 0 13 0 13
Cle D22 R40/124 P(25-20-1) 200
Pit D11 R18/60 P(30-14-2) 149
Cle-Green 115R

Den 7 6 7 3 23
KC 7 3 7 7 **24**
Den D22 R31/176 P(39-21-0) 292
KC D13 R24/133 P(29-15-1) 129
Den-Portis 141R, Smith 130C

SF 10 7 7 0 **24**
Det 0 10 0 7 17
SF D15 R20/84 P(36-20-2) 221
Det D20 R39/142 P(27-15-1) 183

Mia 0 13 0 10 **23**
NYG 10 0 0 0 10
Mia D15 R30/134 P(26-14-0) 151
NYG D25 R23/77 P(43-31-3) 273
NYG-Shockey 110C

Min 0 12 15 12 **39**
Atl 6 14 0 6 26
Min D16 R38/166 P(24-14-1) 233
Atl D17 R17/104 P(41-28-2) 336
Atl-Price 168C, Johnson 352P

NO 3 0 7 3 13
Car 3 7 6 3 **19**
NO D17 R29/155 P(31-16-1) 189
Car D21 R40/185 P(23-15-0) 124
NO-McAllister 124R;
Car-Davis 159R

Oak 6 12 0 6 24
ChiB 0 3 3 18 **24**
Oak D18 R26/119 P(35-17-2) 182
ChiB D18 R35/200 P(24-13-2) 144
ChiB-Thomas 123R

THE GAMES


```
SD     0   7   0  14   21
Jax    7   3  10   7   27
SD  D21 R13/69  P(41-24-0) 277
Jax D21 R37/123 P(28-19-0) 313
SD-Boston 181C; Jax-Smith 137C,
Leftwich 336P

Sea    7   6   0   0   13
GB     7  14  14   0   35
Sea D23 R23/128 P(39-23-1) 215
GB  D27 R35/159 P(25-19-0) 177
Sea-Alexander 102R;
GB-Green 118R

Ten    6   7   3  14   30
NE     7   0  14  17   38
Ten D27 R27/70  P(45-23-1) 341
NE  D21 R27/161 P(31-17-0) 193
Ten-McNair 360P

Was    0  10   3  12   25
Phi    3  10   7   7   27
Was D20 R21/49  P(50-25-2) 258
Phi D18 R30/127 P(30-16-2) 140
```

MONDAY, OCTOBER 6
```
Ind    0   3   7  28   38
TB    14   7   7   7   35
Ind D24 R22/74  P(47-34-1) 381
TB  D25 R33/139 P(39-26-1) 318
Ind-Harrison 176C, Manning 386P;
TB-Pittman 106R, McCardell 106C,
Johnson 318P
```

SUNDAY, OCTOBER 12
```
Bal    3  13   7   3   26
Arz    3   0   8   7   18
Bal D13 R38/213 P(18-9-0) 72
Arz D16 R20/90 P(36-22-3) 230
Bal-Lewis 131R

Buf    3   0   0   0    3
NYJ    0  13  14   3   30
Buf D15 R19/53  P(41-24-2) 140
NYJ D13 R33/118 P(17-11-0) 115

Car    3   0  14   6   23
Ind    0  13   0   7   20
Car D17 R41/189 P(20-12-1) 152
Ind D20 R27/76  P(34-23-1) 293
Car-Smith 103C; Ind-Harrison 119C

ChiB   0   3   0  10   13
NO     3   3   7   7   20
ChiB D16 R32/140 P(21-10-0) 131
NO   D18 R34/130 P(29-14-0) 153
NO-McAllister 116R

Hot    0   3   7   7   17
Ten   14   7   3  14   38
Hot D24 R16/91  P(42-25-3) 367
Ten D22 R33/114 P(27-18-0) 421
Hot-Bradford 127C, Carr 371P;
Ten-Mason 177C, McNair 421P

KC     7   7   0  20   6  40
GB    14  10   3   0   7  34
KC D22 R26/82  P(45-27-0) 400
GB D24 R35/183 P(36-25-1) 257
KC-Gonzalez 121C, Morton 109C,
Green 400P; GB-Green 139R

Mia   10   0   0  14   24
Jax    0   3   7   0   10
Mia D16 R24/91 P(27-14-1) 143
Jax D22 R30/88 P(42-24-3) 244

NYG    3   0   3   0    6
NE     7   0  10   0   17
NYG D26 R24/76  P(59-35-4) 306
NE  D12 R31/129 P(21-8-0) 91
NYG-Collins 314P

Oak    7   0   0   0    7
Cle    0   3   7   3   13
Oak D12 R21/90 P(33-21-0) 164
Cle D20 R32/171 P(26-16-0) 113
Oak-Gonzalez 121C, Morton 109C,
Green 400P; Cle-Green 145R

Phi    0   7   7   7   21
Dal    7   3   7   6   23
Phi D14 R32/117 P(26-11-0) 115
Dal D15 R36/119 P(26-15-1) 173

Pit    3   3   0   8   14
Den    0   7   0  10   17
Pit D17 R30/85  P(31-20-0) 130
Den D15 R18/77  P(28-17-2) 165
```


```
SF     0   3  13   3   19
Sea    7  10   0   3   20
SF  D19 R29/111 P(27-16-0) 150
Sea D21 R34/147 P(27-17-1) 186

TB     0   7   7  21   35
Was    3   7   3   0   13
TB  D25 R25/111 P(30-22-0) 268
Was D19 R23/68  P(36-25-2) 207
TB-Johnson 258P
```

MONDAY, OCTOBER 13
```
Atl    0   0   0   0    0
Slr    3   7   9  17   36
Atl D9  R21/73  P(28-12-2) 136
Slr D26 R31/119 P(35-24-2) 377
Slr-Holt 161C, Bulger 352P
```

SUNDAY, OCTOBER 19
```
Bal    7   0   3  16   26
Cin   14  10   3   7   34
Bal D21 R29/120 P(27-15-1) 281
Cin D17 R28/59  P(27-16-0) 244
Bal-Lewis 101R, Heap 129C,
Taylor 138C, Boller 302P;
Cin-Johnson 130C

ChiB   3   3   0  11   17
Sea    0  14   3   7   24
ChiB D19 R28/87 P(34-19-2) 124
Sea  D22 R28/124 P(27-19-1) 211
Sea-Alexander 101R

Dal    7  21   3   7   38
Det    7   0   0   0    7
Dal D25 R43/134 P(27-19-0) 197
Det D9  R21/83  P(33-10-3) 74

Den    0   7   3  10   20
Min    7   7  14   0   28
Den D27 R27/138 P(37-21-3) 183
Min D14 R22/72  P(29-19-0) 268
Den-Portis 117R; Min-Moss 151C

GB     3   7   7   7   24
Slr   14   7   7   6   34
GB  D22 R26/116 P(32-23-1) 256
Slr D22 R27/134 P(34-22-2) 239
Slr-Bruce 129C

NE     3   3   7   0   6  19
Mia    0  10   3   0   0  13
NE  D16 R29/59  P(34-24-0) 273
Mia D20 R29/97  P(35-20-2) 229
NE-Brown 131C;
Mia-McMichael 102C

NO    14  21   3   7   45
Atl   14   0   3   0   17
NO  D27 R36/164 P(31-23-0) 342
Atl D11 R22/130 P(29-9-1) 108
NO-McAllister 116R, Horn 133C,
Brooks 352P

NYJ    0   7   3   9   19
Hot    7   7   0   0   14
NYJ D18 R27/140 P(29-15-0) 160
Hot D17 R36/169 P(23-15-0) 156
NYJ-Moss 111C; Hot-Davis 129R

Phi    7   0   0   7   14
NYG    0   3   7   0   10
Phi D9  R23/87  P(23-9-1) 47
NYG D25 R41/180 P(36-22-0) 159

SD     6   7  10   3   26
Cle    0   3  14   0   17
SD  D15 R36/228 P(19-9-1) 61
Cle D20 R22/101 P(44-24-2) 176
SD-Tomlinson 200R

TB     7   0   0   0    7
SF     7  14   0   3   24
TB  D14 R14/68  P(41-25-3) 258
SF  D22 R41/212 P(29-15-1) 246
TB-McCardell 119C;
SF-Hearst 117R, Owens 152C

Ten   17  10   0  10   37
Car    0   3   0  14   17
Ten D15 R36/134 P(25-13-0) 187
Car D19 R17/44  P(49-31-0) 339
Car-Smith 151C, Delhomme 362P

Was    0   0   7   0    7
Buf    3   7   7   7   24
Was D8  R23/59  P(28-9-0) 110
Buf D25 R39/196 P(26-19-1) 236
Buf-Henry 167R, Reed 109C
```


MONDAY, OCTOBER 20
```
KC     7   3   0   7   17
Oak    0   0   0  10   10
KC  D16 R31/125 P(22-11-1) 194
Oak D25 R25/100 P(47-26-2) 257
KC-Holmes 123R
```

SUNDAY, OCTOBER 26
```
Buf    2   3   0   0    5
KC     7  21   0  10   38
Buf D15 R26/133 P(38-25-5) 133
KC  D22 R24/100 P(37-21-0) 275
Buf-Henry 124R; KC-Hall 107C

Car    3   7   3   7   23
NO     0  17   0   3   20
Car D20 R39/223 P(27-12-0) 145
NO  D19 R29/104 P(34-21-1) 190
Car-Davis 178R, Smith 100C;
NO-McAllister 101R

Cle    0   3   0   0    3
NE     3   0   3   3    9
Cle D13 R19/84  P(36-22-1) 119
NE  D19 R30/94  P(33-20-0) 253
NE-Graham 110C

Dal    0   0   0   0    0
TB     0  10   6   0   16
Dal D9  R22/60  P(25-15-2) 118
TB  D14 R35/128 P(26-13-0) 133
TB-Pittman 113R

Den    0   3   3   0    6
Bal    0   9   0  17   26
Den D12 R27/104 P(31-16-2) 90
Bal D22 R37/151 P(27-15-0) 126
Bal-Lewis 134R

Det    0   0   8   8   16
ChiB   0  10  14   0   24
Det D16 R24/80 P(40-23-2) 180
ChiB D14 R26/68 P(31-20-0) 193

Hot    0  14   0   7   21
Ind    3  14  10   3   30
Hot D18 R28/131 P(26-20-1) 139
Ind D23 R27/122 P(30-22-0) 269
Hot-Davis 109R; Ind-James 104R,
Harrison 100C

NYG    7   6   3  13   29
Min    3   7   7   0   17
NYG D26 R28/83  P(39-23-1) 367
Min D22 R28/137 P(31-18-2) 222
NYG-Hilliard 100C, Collins 375P;
Min-Moss 125C

NYJ   10   0   7   0   17
Phi    7   7   0  10   24
NYJ D22 R24/125 P(35-21-1) 252
Phi D23 R32/194 P(23-17-1) 112
NYJ-Martin 110R;
Phi-Buckhalter 100R

Sea    7  10   0   7   24
Cin    7   0  13   7   27
Sea D24 R24/121 P(43-26-3) 338
Cin D19 R34/194 P(30-18-0) 218
Sea-Hasselbeck 344P;
Cin-Johnson 101R

SF     6   0   0   7   0  13
Arz    7   3   3   0   3  16
SF  D15 R27/106 P(28-15-0) 149
Arz D18 R44/221 P(25-14-1) 93
Arz-Shipp 165R

Slr    7  10  10   6   33
Pit    7   0   7   0   14
Slr D26 R37/89  P(37-22-0) 359
Pit D11 R18/94  P(28-12-3) 151
Slr-Holt 174C, Bulger 375P

Ten   10  10   3   7   30
Jax    0  10   0   7   17
Ten D23 R38/133 P(27-21-1) 187
Jax D15 R11/54  P(39-24-2) 239
```

MONDAY, OCTOBER 27
```
Mia   10  14   0   2   26
SD     3   0   0   7   10
Mia D14 R27/81  P(29-20-0) 183
SD  D18 R31/104 P(30-19-3) 146
```


SUNDAY, NOVEMBER 2
```
Car    7   0   3   0   10
Hot    0   0   7   7   14
Car D17 R35/174 P(23-13-1) 193
Hot D14 R30/118 P(19-13-0) 149
Car-Davis 153R

Cin    7   7   0   0   14
Arz    7   3   7   0   17
Cin D17 R18/48  P(28-21-1) 215
Arz D20 R37/161 P(28-18-0) 143
Arz-Shipp 141R

GB     6  14   0  10   30
Min    7   7   6   7   27
GB  D24 R34/261 P(28-18-1) 190
Min D20 R25/125 P(34-21-0) 198
GB-Green 137R

Ind    0   9   7   7   23
Mia    3   7   0   7   17
Ind D23 R35/115 P(37-23-1) 241
Mia D12 R14/47  P(29-18-0) 192

Jax    0   3   7   7   17
Bal    7   0   6  11   24
Jax D20 R33/134 P(34-22-1) 186
Bal D9  R30/103 P(23-10-1) 156

NO     0   7   7   3   17
TB     0   0  14   0   14
NO  D10 R28/124 P(30-13-1) 133
TB  D21 R18/56  P(46-27-2) 296
NO-McAllister 110R;
TB-Johnson 123C, Johnson 323P

NYG    0  13   7   8   3  31
NYJ    7   0  14   0   28
NYG D23 R33/115 P(40-24-0) 298
NYJ D28 R38/132 P(45-27-2) 260
NYG-Toomer 127C, Collins 303P;
NYJ-Martin 108R, Moss 121C,
Pennington 281P

Oak    0   3   7   3   13
Det   10   0   7   6   23
Oak D18 R26/94  P(39-21-3) 171
Det D14 R33/112 P(21-13-1) 117

Phi   10   0   3  10   23
Atl    0  13   0   3   16
Phi D24 R28/128 P(33-21-0) 302
Atl D17 R28/131 P(28-16-1) 147
Phi-McNabb 312P

Pit    3   3  10   0   16
Sea    3   3   3  14   23
Pit D19 R30/105 P(35-21-0) 215
Sea D19 R25/98  P(31-18-0) 191

SD     3   0   0   7   10
ChiB   3   7   3   7   20
SD  D11 R19/80  P(26-15-1) 119
ChiB D19 R33/125 P(30-21-1) 216
ChiB-Thomas 111R

Slr    3   0   0   7   10
SF    14  10   6   0   30
Slr D18 R8/9    P(42-26-2) 331
SF  D24 R35/165 P(29-19-1) 224
Slr-Holt 200C, Bulger 378P

Was    6   0   0   8   14
Dal    0   7   7   7   21
Was D13 R16/89  P(33-18-0) 124
Dal D24 R40/208 P(33-17-2) 192
Dal-Hambrick 100R
```

MONDAY, NOVEMBER 3
```
NE     7   6   7  10   30
Den    7  10   7   2   26
NE  D17 R26/69  P(35-20-1) 350
Den D18 R29/114 P(35-16-1) 163
NE-Branch 107C, Brady 350P;
Den-Portis 111R
```

SUNDAY, NOVEMBER 9
```
Arz    0   3   6   6   15
Pit    0   7  21   0   28
Arz D19 R28/96  P(43-23-0) 283
Pit D11 R27/87  P(24-12-0) 159
Arz-Boldin 118C, Blake 307P

Atl    7   0  13   7   27
NYG    0   0   0   0    0
Atl D20 R37/216 P(23-9-0) 58
NYG D18 R19/124 P(44-27-2) 196
Atl-Dunn 178R; NYG-Barber 120R
```


```
Bal    3  16   3   0   22
Slr   14   7   0  12   33
Bal D16 R38/145 P(33-17-3) 122
Slr D7  R21/47  P(26-13-2) 74
Bal-Lewis 111R

Buf    0   6   0   0    6
Dal    7   0   3   0   10
Buf D15 R25/100 P(34-17-0) 85
Dal D14 R35/122 P(33-15-0) 114

ChiB   0   3   7   0   10
Det    3   3   3   3   12
ChiB D11 R24/66 P(28-16-1) 133
Det D10 R20/17  P(39-24-0) 231

Cle    3  14   0   3   20
KC    14  13   7   7   41
Cle D16 R21/80 P(27-19-1) 119
KC  D30 R26/95 P(42-29-0) 348
KC-Kennison 115C, Green 368P

Hot    3  14  10   0   27
Cin   10   7  10   7   34
Hot D13 R19/140 P(25-11-1) 129
Cin D27 R57/240 P(26-18-1) 182
Hot-Davis 104R; Cin-Johnson 182R

Ind    7  13   0   3   23
Jax    7   0   7  14   28
Ind D20 R21/47  P(45-28-2) 347
Jax D20 R38/174 P(24-12-1) 179
Ind-Manning 347P; Jax-Taylor 152R

Ten    0   0   0   7    7
Mia   14   7   7   3   31
Ten D17 R38/101 P(26-19-0) 223
Mia D12 R16/59  P(33-19-3) 165

Min    7   7   0  14   28
SD    14  14   7   7   42
Min D27 R23/110 P(44-32-1) 350
SD  D26 R26/211 P(29-21-0) 247
Min-Moss 120C, Williams 126C,
Culpepper 370P;
SD-Tomlinson 162R

NYJ    7   3   0  14   3  27
Oak    7  14   0   3   0  24
NYJ D16 R30/155 P(27-18-0) 269
Oak D24 R52/169 P(25-18-0) 186
NYJ-Moss 146C

Sea   14   3   0   3   20
Was    3  14   3   7   27
Sea D21 R28/125 P(29-19-1) 221
Was D19 R32/137 P(33-18-2) 242
Was-Coles 125C

TB     0   0  17   7   24
Car   10   0  10   7   27
TB  D18 R19/89  P(43-24-1) 258
Car D18 R31/78  P(32-20-2) 263
TB-McCardell 118C;
Car-Proehl 133C
```

MONDAY, NOVEMBER 10
```
Phi    0   0   3  14   17
GB     0   0   7   7   14
Phi D15 R30/92  P(31-15-0) 190
GB  D17 R37/241 P(22-14-1) 114
GB-Green 192R
```

SUNDAY, NOVEMBER 16
```
Arz    0   3   0   3    6
Cle   10  10  14  10   44
Arz D10 R13/41  P(32-13-3) 146
Cle D27 R33/89  P(35-29-0) 392
Cle-Davis 117C, Morgan 116C,
Holcomb 392P

Atl   10  10   0   0   20
NO     0   3  10   3   23
Atl D11 R28/168 P(27-8-2) 76
NO  D23 R36/210 P(38-21-2) 193
Atl-Dunn 162R; NO-McAllister 173R

Bal    0   3   0   3    6
Mia    0   3   3   0   3   9
Bal D13 R33/114 P(25-14-2) 109
Mia D19 R42/141 P(32-13-1) 126
Mia-Williams 105R

Dal    0   0   3   0    3
NE     3   6   0   3   12
Dal D17 R28/84  P(36-20-3) 207
NE  D14 R25/65  P(34-15-0) 203
```

```
Det    7   7   0   0   14
Sea   14  21   0   0   35
Det  D20 R17/81  P(48-26-2) 276
Sea  D22 R33/159 P(29-21-0) 207
Sea-Alexander 110R

GB     7   6   0   7   20
TB     0   6   7   0   13
GB   D15 R38/190 P(28-13-1) 92
TB   D10 R18/154 P(28-17-2) 131
GB-Green 109R; TB-Jones 134R

Hot    0   6   3   3   12
Buf    2   3   3   2   10
Hot  D12 R28/34  P(20-13-1) 211
Buf  D17 R28/182 P(26-15-0) 153
Hot-Jones 134R, Johnson 122C;
Buf-Henry 149R

Jax    0   0   0   3    3
Ten    3   7   0   0   10
Jax  D16 R30/126 P(31-15-2) 145
Ten  D13 R32/96  P(26-13-1) 150

KC     0   3  13   3   19
Cin    0   3   7  14   24
KC   D20 R17/67  P(42-28-0) 304
Cin  D21 R33/200 P(32-19-0) 222
KC-Green 313P; Cin-Johnson 165R,
Warrick 114C

Min    0   3   7   8   18
Oak    7   7   7   7   28
Min  D24 R22/94  P(49-27-3) 373
Oak  D19 R43/191 P(13-9-0) 184
Min-McAllister 173R,
Campbell 115C, Culpepper 396P;
Oak-Wheatley 109R

NYG    3   0   0   7   10
Phi    7   7   7   7   28
NYG  D20 R24/109 P(44-25-1) 252
Phi  D20 R21/62  P(30-24-0) 314
NYG-Barber 111R, Tyree 106C;
Phi-McNabb 314P

NYJ    7   3  21   0   31
Ind   10  14  14   0   38
NYJ  D12 R17/132 P(14-11-0) 192
Ind  D30 R40/145 P(36-27-0) 393
NYJ-Martin 105R; Ind-James 126R,
Clark 100C, Wayne 141C,
Manning 401P

SD     0   0   0   8    8
Den   10  17   7   3   37
SD   D5  R13/40  P(25-9-1) 56
Den  D26 R49/201 P(35-23-2) 247
Den-Portis 106R, Sharpe 101C

Slr    3   0   7  13   23
ChiB   0  14   0   7   21
Slr  D22 R25/112 P(46-29-2) 208
ChiB D13 R26/95  P(32-16-2) 146
Slr-Faulk 103R, Holt 124C

Was    0   3   0  14   17
Car    0   3   7  10   20
Was  D13 R22/54  P(35-16-1) 127
Car  D17 R35/110 P(30-20-2) 317
Car-Muhammad 189C,
Delhomme 317P
```

MONDAY, NOVEMBER 17
```
Pit    0   0   7   7   14
SF     7   3  14   6   30
Pit  D21 R20/44  P(45-26-1) 305
SF   D17 R32/169 P(27-21-0) 254
Pit-Maddox 327P; SF-Owens 155C
```

SUNDAY, NOVEMBER 23
```
Car    3   7   7   3   20
Dal   10   0  14   0   24
Car  D15 R28/75  P(25-9-1) 169
Dal  D19 R25/65  P(43-29-1) 254

ChiB   3   6   0  10   19
Den    7   0   3   0   10
ChiB D19 R33/106 P(33-15-0) 111
Den  D18 R21/200 P(36-19-0) 165
Den-Portis 165R

Cin   14  14   3   3   34
SD     0   0   7   0    7
Cin  D33 R47/210 P(38-24-0) 234
SD   D17 R20/118 P(33-15-0) 207
Cin-Dillon 108R, Johnson 107C,
Kitna 243P; SD-Boston 139C
```

```
Det    0   0   7   7   14
Min    7   0   0  17   24
Det  D16 R19/74  P(41-21-4) 167
Min  D18 R28/121 P(30-20-1) 186

Ind    0   3   0  14   17
Buf    0   7   0   7   14
Ind  D21 R30/103 P(42-26-0) 223
Buf  D16 R27/110 P(28-15-1) 118
Ind-James 108R

Jax    0   3   0   7   10
NYJ    3   0  10   0   13
Jax  D20 R37/158 P(33-17-1) 172
NYJ  D17 R21/61  P(39-25-1) 221
Jax-Taylor 119R

NE     0  10   0  10   3  23
Hot    3   0   7  10   0  20
NE   D29 R41/128 P(47-29-2) 344
Hot  D11 R30/89  P(25-10-1) 80
NE-Faulk 108C, Brady 368P

NO     0   7   7   6   20
Phi   10  10   3  10   33
NO   D27 R24/199 P(39-24-0) 267
Phi  D22 R32/201 P(35-16-0) 247
NO-McAllister 184R, Williams 110C

Oak    0   7  10   7   24
KC    14   7   3   3   27
Oak  D20 R35/166 P(31-19-0) 213
KC   D22 R25/142 P(33-23-0) 242
KC-Holmes 100C

Pit    0  10   0   3   13
Cle    3   0   0   3    6
Pit  D11 R31/109 P(24-9-0) 59
Cle  D19 R28/90  P(44-25-2) 213

Sea    0  17  17   7   0  41
Bal    0   3  21  17   3  44
Sea  D24 R32/133 P(42-23-0) 293
Bal  D20 R35/150 P(37-20-0) 276
Sea-Jackson 146C,
Hasselbeck 333P; Bal-Lewis 117R,
Robinson 131C, Wright 319P

SF     3   7   0  10   20
GB     7  10   0   3   20
SF   D13 R21/73  P(30-14-1) 119
GB   D18 R48/243 P(15-10-3) 136
GB-Green 154R

Slr   14   3   7   3   3  30
Arz    0  10   7   0  10  27
Slr  D26 R26/117 P(44-28-4) 298
Arz  D15 R30/166 P(28-15-2) 192
Slr-Faulk 100R, Holt 145C,
Bulger 329P; Arz-Boldin 123C

Ten    0  14  14  10   38
Atl   21   0   3   7   31
Ten  D20 R35/144 P(26-18-0) 203
Atl  D16 R20/25  P(32-19-1) 257
Ten-George 115R; Atl-Dunn 129C

Was    6  14   3   0   23
Mia    7   3   0  14   24
Was  D21 R32/129 P(34-16-1) 148
Mia  D16 R32/144 P(23-13-2) 173
Mia-Williams 107R
```

MONDAY, NOVEMBER 24
```
NYG    0   3   3   7   13
TB     0  14   3   2   19
NYG  D12 R17/79  P(34-18-2) 133
TB   D21 R38/93  P(32-22-1) 265
```

THURSDAY, NOVEMBER 27
```
GB     0   7   7   0   14
Det    0   9   0  13   22
GB   D18 R16/52  P(37-23-3) 268
Det  D17 R34/94  P(32-21-1) 172

Mia    7  16  14   3   40
Dal    0  14   0   7   21
Mia  D22 R45/126 P(20-16-0) 239
Dal  D21 R16/91  P(40-24-3) 263
Mia-Williams 104R
```

SUNDAY, NOVEMBER 30
```
Arz    3   0   0   0    3
ChiB   7   0   0  21   28
Arz  D9  R18/46  P(32-20-2) 151
ChiB D25 R36/154 P(37-22-0) 268
ChiB-Forsey 134R, Gage 100C
```

```
Atl    0   7   0   6   13
Hot    0   3  14   0   17
Atl  D16 R24/69  P(39-20-1) 174
Hot  D17 R31/135 P(19-10-1) 101
Hot-Davis 101R

Buf    0  17   7   0   24
NYG    0   7   0   0    7
Buf  D23 R36/151 P(34-21-0) 252
NYG  D10 R13/24  P(35-17-0) 198
Buf-Henry 113R; NYG-Toomer 110C

Cin    7   7   0  10   24
Pit    0   3   7  10   20
Cin  D18 R25/113 P(32-18-0) 266
Pit  D23 R25/85  P(44-29-1) 299
Cin-Johnson 117C;
Pit-Burress 112C, Ward 149C,
Maddox 313P

Cle    0   0   0   7    7
Sea    7  10  10   7   34
Cle  D11 R16/47  P(34-23-1) 167
Sea  D26 R36/157 P(36-26-1) 306
Sea-Alexander 127R, Jackson 102C,
Robinson 122C, Hasselbeck 328P

Den    0  14   0   8   22
Oak    5   3   0   0    8
Den  D20 R46/193 P(20-11-1) 94
Oak  D12 R23/120 P(30-13-0) 142
Den-McAllister 165R, Portis 170R

KC     7  14   0   7   28
SD     0   3  10   7   20
KC   D23 R39/194 P(30-17-2) 141
SD   D17 R28/159 P(34-16-2) 211
KC-Holmes 162R;
SD-Tomlinson 106R

NE    10  14   7   7   38
Ind    0  10  10  14   34
NE   D21 R23/56  P(35-26-2) 226
Ind  D26 R29/98  P(48-29-1) 272
Ind-Manning 278P

NO     0  10   7   7   24
Was    0  14   3   3   20
NO   D23 R37/189 P(30-14-0) 121
Was  D20 R26/161 P(42-22-1) 231
NO-McAllister 165R;
Was-Candidate 115R

Phi    7   3   3  12   25
Car    3   0   7   6   16
Phi  D17 R28/124 P(26-18-1) 159
Car  D19 R29/136 P(29-18-0) 200
Car-Davis 115R

SF     3   3   0   0    6
Bal    7  17   0  20   44
SF   D10 R30/106 P(36-17-4) 158
Bal  D15 R29/117 P(25-14-1) 165

TB     0  10   0   0   10
Jax    0  10   0   7   17
TB   D16 R19/77  P(38-21-1) 144
Jax  D21 R35/135 P(34-20-0) 224
Jax-Taylor 118R, Smith 136C
```

MONDAY, DECEMBER 1
```
Ten    7   7   3   0   17
NYJ    7   3   7   7   24
Ten  D19 R23/84  P(35-21-2) 263
NYJ  D19 R30/97  P(23-18-2) 146
Ten-Mason 133C
```

SUNDAY, DECEMBER 7
```
Arz    0   0   7   7   14
SF    14  20   9   7   50
Arz  D18 R22/59  P(40-19-1) 151
SF   D30 R36/232 P(29-20-0) 264
Arz-Boldin 123C; SF-Barlow 154R,
Garcia 252P

Car    0   7   0   7   14
Atl    0   7   7   6   20
Car  D13 R33/90  P(25-13-2) 141
Atl  D24 R37/224 P(34-16-1) 156
Atl-Vick 141R
```

```
ChiB  14   0   0   7   21
GB     0  13   6  15   34
ChiB D13 R20/44  P(40-17-3) 231
GB   D17 R38/97  P(33-22-1) 210
ChiB-Booker 115C

Cin    3   7   3   0   13
Bal    7  10   7   7   31
Cin  D15 R21/100 P(31-23-2) 168
Bal  D21 R45/223 P(19-8-2) 130
Bal-Lewis 180R

Dal    3   7   0   0   10
Phi    0  10   9  17   36
Dal  D13 R34/150 P(24-15-2) 75
Phi  D20 R23/175 P(34-18-0) 228
Phi-Buckhalter 115R

Hot    0   0   3   0    3
Jax    7  10   0  10   27
Hot  D7  R23/70  P(23-11-1) 54
Jax  D23 R40/208 P(29-18-0) 182
Jax-Taylor 163R

Ind    3   9  17   0   29
Ten   10   0   3  14   27
Ind  D21 R34/116 P(34-22-0) 224
Ten  D23 R19/93  P(38-22-0) 234
Ind-Harrison 124C

KC     7  14   0   6   27
Den    7  10  14  14   45
KC   D28 R19/63  P(47-34-0) 381
Den  D26 R32/270 P(29-20-0) 238
KC-Hall 124C, Green 397P;
Den-Portis 218R

Mia    0   0   6   0    6
NE     3   0   0   9   12
Mia  D7  R25/68  P(31-13-2) 66
NE   D13 R34/78  P(31-16-0) 150

NYJ    0   3   0   6    9
Buf    0   7   7   3   17
NYJ  D14 R26/88  P(29-15-1) 127
Buf  D19 R41/203 P(15-9-1) 53
Buf-Henry 169R

Oak    0   0   0   7    7
Pit    0  17   7   3   27
Oak  D9  R23/122 P(25-10-2) 39
Pit  D21 R40/133 P(28-19-1) 266
Pit-Bettis 106R

SD     7   0   0   7   14
Det    0   0   0   7    7
SD   D17 R35/131 P(25-17-1) 244
Det  D14 R18/68  P(47-26-0) 208
SD-Tomlinson 148C

Sea    0   0   0   7    7
Min    0  13   7  14   34
Sea  D13 R16/56  P(34-17-2) 202
Min  D22 R44/193 P(33-21-0) 272
Min-Bennett 103R, Moss 133C

TB     0  14   0   0   14
NO     0   0   0   7    7
TB   D16 R29/107 P(34-20-1) 207
NO   D16 R24/90  P(30-20-0) 202
NO-Horn 118C

Was    3   7   7   3   20
NYG    7   0   0   0    7
Was  D20 R48/150 P(19-13-0) 138
NYG  D15 R23/120 P(25-12-1) 100
```

MONDAY, DECEMBER 8
```
Slr    3  20   3   0   26
Cle    7   0   6   7   20
Slr  D18 R31/118 P(36-22-1) 210
Cle  D18 R24/162 P(26-16-2) 147
Slr-Faulk 102R; Cle-White 101R
```

SUNDAY, DECEMBER 14
```
Atl    0   0   0   7    7
Ind   14  10  14   0   38
Atl  D12 R26/125 P(25-9-1) 29
Ind  D27 R31/178 P(31-26-0) 287
Ind-James 126R, Harrison 117C,
Manning 290P

Bal    3   3   6   0   12
Oak   10   7   0   3   20
Bal  D14 R31/149 P(27-12-1) 170
Oak  D15 R31/79  P(35-16-0) 186
Bal-Lewis 125R
```

```
Buf    0  10   7   9   26
Ten    3   3   8  14   28
Buf  D13 R20/89  P(30-17-0) 152
Ten  D23 R32/86  P(41-26-0) 263
Ten-Mason 137C

Car    7   0   3  10   20
Arz    7   7   0   3   17
Car  D17 R18/67  P(32-20-1) 231
Arz  D23 R39/171 P(25-14-1) 146

Cle    0  10   0  10   20
Den    0   0  10   3   23
Cle  D12 R26/102 P(21-8-1) 173
Den  D28 R40/165 P(36-22-1) 252
Cle-Northcutt 115C;
Den-Portis 139R

Dal    7   7   3  10   27
Was    0   0   0   0    0
Dal  R45/222 P(24-10-0) 104
Was  D8  R26/106 P(27-7-4) 55
Dal-Hambrick 189R

Det    0  10   7   0   17
KC    14  14   7  10   45
Det  D22 R30/137 P(36-20-1) 197
KC   D28 R28/149 P(32-25-0) 372
Det-Bryson 105R;
KC-Blaylock 106C, Green 341P

GB     7  10   0  21   38
SD     3   0   3  15   21
GB   D17 R27/83  P(33-23-1) 278
SD   D17 R27/88  P(48-28-1) 336
GB-Driver 112C, Favre 278P;
SD-Gates 117C, Tomlinson 144C,
Brees 363P

Hot    0   3   0   0    3
TB     7   6   3   0   16
Hot  D7  R19/65  P(17-9-0) 42
TB   D24 R42/161 P(28-17-0) 237
TB-Jones 134R

Jax    3   3   0   7   13
NE     7   6   0  14   27
Jax  D17 R20/72  P(40-21-2) 282
NE   D18 R32/84  P(34-22-0) 212

Min    0   0   7   0    7
ChiB   3   7   0   3   13
Min  D22 R38/178 P(34-24-1) 215
ChiB D15 R23/87  P(30-13-0) 145
Min-Smith 148R

NYG    7   0   0   0    7
NO    10  14  14   7   45
NYG  D16 R26/111 P(26-15-0) 130
NO   D26 R29/208 P(39-28-0) 308
NO-Horn 133C, Brooks 296P

Pit    0   0   0   6    6
NYJ    3   3   0   0    6
Pit  D16 R24/94  P(38-16-0) 137
NYJ  D15 R36/175 P(25-15-0) 144
NYJ-Martin 174R

Sea    2  10   3   7   22
Slr   14   7   0   6   27
Sea  D22 R27/135 P(37-21-1) 231
Slr  D21 R30/86  P(32-20-1) 230
Sea-Alexander 126R; Slr-Holt 100C

SF     0  17   0  21   38
Cin    0  10  10  21   41
SF   D31 R27/171 P(33-26-0) 331
Cin  D23 R37/225 P(25-18-0) 168
SF-Owens 127C, Garcia 344P;
Cin-Johnson 174R
```

MONDAY, DECEMBER 15
```
Phi   14  10   0  10   34
Mia    3  10   7   7   27
Phi  D23 R28/140 P(28-16-1) 261
Mia  D22 R29/177 P(40-21-2) 221
Mia-Williams 107R
```

SATURDAY, DECEMBER 20
```
Atl   10  17   3   0   30
TB     0   0   7  21   28
Atl  D16 R42/148 P(15-8-0) 119
TB   D25 R22/94  P(48-34-4) 346
TB-McCardell 122C, Johnson 346P

KC     0   0   7  13   20
Min    7  17   7  14   45
KC   D21 R23/105 P(38-18-2) 224
Min  D27 R39/223 P(30-20-1) 246
Min-Smith 146R, Moss 111C
```

```
NE    7   7   7   0   21
NYJ   7   3   0   6   16
NE   D13 R24/133  P(26-15-1) 138
NYJ  D22 R26/109  P(43-24-5) 212
NE-Smith 121R
```

SUNDAY, DECEMBER 21
```
Arz   0   3   0   7   10
Sea  14   0   7   7   28
Arz  D17 R26/79   P(40-25-0) 220
Sea  D23 R30/160  P(27-19-2) 180
Arz-Boldin 122C;
Sea-Alexander 135R

Bal   0   7   7  21   35
Cle   0   0   0   0    0
Bal  D18 R41/276  P(19-11-1) 83
Cle  D14 R24/78   P(33-17-1) 133
Bal-Lewis 205R

Cin   0  10   0   0   10
Slr   7  10   3   7   27
Cin  D14 R23/99   P(29-16-3) 187
Slr  D17 R26/77   P(38-24-1) 228
Cin-Johnson 115C; Slr-Faulk 121R,
Holt 124C

Den  14  14   0   3   31
Ind   0   0   7  10   17
Den  D26 R54/227  P(17-14-1) 238
Ind  D11 R12/47   P(23-12-0) 136
Den-Griffin 136R, Lelie 115C

Det   0   0   0  14   14
Car   7  10   3   0   20
Det  D8 R21/53    P(19-7-1) 53
Car  D22 R36/124  P(35-29-1) 260

Mia  10   3   7   0   20
Buf   0   0   3   3    6
Mia  D11 R38/132  P(17-8-1) 37
Buf  D11 R28/73   P(28-15-1) 104
Mia-Williams 111R

NO    3   7   3   6   19
Jax   0  17   3   0   20
NO   D20 R25/61   P(38-22-0) 289
Jax  D22 R45/243  P(17-9-2) 131
Jax-Taylor 194R

NYG   3   0   0   0    3
Dal  10   3   3   3   19
NYG  D10 R22/54   P(32-18-0) 159
Dal  D16 R31/104  P(26-17-0) 222

SD    0  10   7   7   24
Pit  14   7   7  12   40
SD   D21 R27/116  P(36-21-2) 228
Pit  D21 R43/181  P(19-12-0) 161
SD-Osgood 102C; Pit-Bettis 115R

SF    7   7   3  14   31
Phi   0  14   7   7   28
SF   D22 R43/203  P(29-15-0) 211
Phi  D18 R19/88   P(27-17-2) 205
SF-Barlow 154R; Phi-Pinkston 121C

Ten   0  10   7  10   27
Hot   0   3  14   7   24
Ten  D21 R35/182  P(26-17-1) 268
Hot  D14 R18/91   P(34-17-2) 235
Hot-Johnson 108C

Was  10   7   0   7   24
ChiB 10   0  14   3   27
Was  D15 R18/44   P(27-17-0) 242
ChiB D25 R40/191  P(32-19-1) 238
ChiB-Thomas 141R
```

MONDAY, DECEMBER 22
```
GB   14  17   3   7   41
Oak   7   0   0   0    7
GB   D23 R37/156  P(30-22-0) 194
Oak  D18 R16/104  P(41-22-2) 194
GB-Green 127R, Walker 124C,
Favre 399P; Oak-Rice 159C
```

SATURDAY, DECEMBER 27
```
Buf   0   0   0   0    0
NE   14  14   0   3   31
Buf  D16 R20/82   P(43-23-2) 174
NE   D26 R34/131  P(33-21-0) 190
NE-Brady 204P

Phi   7  14   7   3   31
Was   0   0   0   7    7
Phi  D24 R25/83   P(34-24-1) 249
Was  D16 R18/79   P(34-22-1) 181
```

```
Sea   0  14   7   3   24
SF    0   3   0   0    3
Sea  D25 R32/89   P(37-24-2) 305
SF   D14 R22/59   P(38-22-1) 231
Sea-Hasselbeck 315P
```

SUNDAY, DECEMBER 28
```
Car  17  13   7   0   37
NYG   0  10   7   7   24
Car  D15 R35/110  P(30-16-1) 141
NYG  D14 R19/76   P(43-18-4) 99

ChiB  0   0   3   0    3
KC    0  14   7  10   31
ChiB D16 R22/84   P(42-17-2) 157
KC   D23 R34/87   P(30-22-1) 195

Cle   3  10   3   6   22
Cin   7   0   0   7   14
Cle  D19 R40/264  P(18-9-0) 115
Cin  D21 R25/115  P(35-23-1) 156
Cle-Suggs 186R

Dal   0   7   0   0    7
NO    3   7   3   0   13
Dal  D21 R23/85   P(47-27-3) 267
NO   D13 R24/58   P(33-15-0) 233
NO-Stallworth 114C

Den   0   0   0   3    3
GB    7   3  14   7   31
Den  D17 R34/114  P(27-13-2) 102
GB   D16 R34/262  P(22-13-1) 104
GB-Green 218R

Ind   0   3   0  17   20
Hot   0  10   7   0   17
Ind  D27 R38/207  P(38-26-1) 211
Hot  D10 R22/99   P(23-13-1) 105
Ind-James 171R

Jax   7   0   0   7   14
Atl  14   7   0   0   21
Jax  D21 R28/157  P(32-19-0) 163
Atl  D21 R39/166  P(22-12-1) 178
Jax-Taylor 121R

Min   0   0   7  10   17
Arz   3   3   0  12   18
Min  D20 R33/150  P(28-18-1) 192
Arz  D15 R19/64   P(33-20-1) 155

NYJ   0  10   5   6   21
Mia   3  17   0   3   23
NYJ  D19 R25/94   P(28-22-0) 191
Mia  D20 R26/81   P(29-21-1) 316
Mia-Chambers 153C, Fiedler 328P

Oak   0  14   0   0   14
SD    7   7   0   7   21
Oak  D9 R32/141   P(22-6-1) 0
SD   D20 R37/263  P(28-15-0) 74
SD-Tomlinson 243R

Pit   0   0  10   0   10
Bal   3   7   0   3   13
Pit  D9 R27/56    P(29-15-3) 158
Bal  D14 R34/128  P(27-16-1) 151
Bal-Lewis 114R, Robinson 102C

Slr   0  20   0   0   20
Det   3   7  13   7   30
Slr  D13 R13/41   P(42-22-1) 153
Det  D21 R29/112  P(36-26-1) 230

TB    3   0   3   7   13
Ten   3  10  13   7   33
TB   D16 R19/89   P(38-24-4) 185
Ten  D20 R34/112  P(27-18-1) 232
```

2004 NFL
THURSDAY, SEPTEMBER 9
```
Ind   0  17   0   7   24
NE    3  10  14   0   27
Ind  D28 R42/202  P(29-16-1) 244
NE   D22 R17/82   P(38-26-1) 320
Ind-James 142R; NE-Brady 335P
```

SATURDAY, SEPTEMBER 11
```
Ten   0   7   7   3   17
Mia   3   0   0   0    3
Ten  D15 R36/182  P(14-9-0) 61
Mia  D14 R20/65   P(44-26-3) 198
Ten-Brown 100R
```

SUNDAY, SEPTEMBER 12
```
Jax   0   3   3   7   13
Buf   7   0   0   3   10
Jax  D14 R23/83   P(36-18-2) 142
Buf  D16 R36/95   P(26-17-0) 147

Det   0   3  10   7   20
ChiB  7   0   0   9   16
Det  D13 R29/77   P(26-14-1) 185
ChiB D18 R32/128  P(35-16-2) 214
ChiB-Terrell 126C

Bal   0   0   3   0    3
Cle   0   3   7  10   20
Bal  D16 R26/88   P(38-22-2) 166
Cle  D10 R29/85   P(24-15-0) 165

KC    7   0  17   0   24
Den   3  14   7  10   34
KC   D15 R28/167  P(32-16-1) 151
Den  D24 R36/192  P(29-18-2) 221
KC-Holmes 151R, Kennison 101C;
Den-Griffin 156R

SD    3   7  10   7   27
Hot   3  10   7   0   20
SD   D17 R32/122  P(24-17-0) 202
Hot  D20 R29/110  P(25-19-2) 226
SD-Tomlinson 121R, Gates 123C

Dal   3   7   0   7   17
Min   0  14  14   7   35
Dal  D27 R21/71   P(51-29-0) 352
Min  D23 R28/136  P(24-18-0) 279
Dal-Bryant 112C,
Johnson 111C, Testaverde 355P;
Min-Culpepper 242P

Sea   0  14   7   0   21
NO    0   7   0   0    7
Sea  D21 R43/169  P(29-19-1) 246
NO   D12 R19/74   P(37-18-1) 207
Sea-Alexander 135R; NO-Horn 110C

Cin   7   3   7   7   24
NYJ  14   0  10   7   31
Cin  D19 R28/113  P(27-18-1) 238
NYJ  D24 R34/219  P(27-20-0) 219
NYJ-Martin 196R

NYG   7   3   0   7   17
Phi  14  10   7   0   31
NYG  D19 R23/170  P(37-19-0) 243
Phi  D21 R27/141  P(36-20-0) 313
NYG-Barber 125R;
Phi-Westbrook 119R, McNabb 330P

Oak   0   7   3  11   21
Pit   7   7   7   3   24
Oak  D18 R22/61   P(37-20-2) 297
Pit  D17 R33/107  P(22-13-0) 130
Oak-Gannon 305P

Atl   7   7   0   7   21
SF    0   3   3  13   19
Atl  D14 R28/95   P(22-13-1) 132
SF   D21 R23/93   P(46-27-1) 266

Arz   0   3   0   7   10
Slr   0   6   3   8   17
Arz  D14 R23/103  P(29-18-0) 157
Slr  D27 R30/176  P(34-23-1) 277
Slr-Faulk 128R, Bruce 112C

TB    0   7   0   3   10
Was   7   3   0   6   16
TB   D10 R15/30   P(37-24-1) 139
Was  D13 R39/166  P(24-13-0) 125
Was-Portis 148R
```

MONDAY, SEPTEMBER 13
```
GB    3   7  14   0   24
Car   0   7   0   7   14
GB   D22 R47/152  P(22-15-0) 127
Car  D17 R13/38   P(40-23-1) 262
GB-Green 119R
```

SUNDAY, SEPTEMBER 19
```
NE    7   7   3   6   23
Arz   0   6   6   0   12
NE   D24 R42/172  P(26-15-2) 207
Arz  D14 R16/50   P(29-13-2) 117
NE-Dillon 158R, Givens 120C
```

```
Slr   0   7  10   0   17
Atl   7  10   0  17   34
Slr  D14 R15/30   P(31-24-1) 250
Atl  D22 R38/242  P(19-14-0) 174
Slr-Bruce 102C, Holt 121C;
Atl-Vick 109R

Pit   0   0   0  13   13
Bal   7   6   7  10   30
Pit  D16 R25/93   P(33-16-2) 217
Bal  D16 R41/172  P(18-10-0) 87
Pit-Ward 151C

Mia   0   0   3  10   13
Cin   0   0  13   3   16
Mia  D11 R20/25   P(39-21-2) 201
Cin  D12 R29/94   P(38-21-1) 116

Cle   0   9   0   3   12
Dal   7   3   7   2   19
Cle  D12 R26/136  P(28-8-3) 66
Dal  D20 R28/126  P(35-23-3) 315
Dal-Testaverde 322P

Hot   0   3   7   6   16
Det   0   7  14   7   28
Hot  D24 R32/112  P(34-23-1) 274
Det  D18 R23/94   P(25-18-1) 172
Hot-Carr 313P

ChiB  0  14   7   0   21
GB    3   0   0  10   13
ChiB D18 R35/182  P(18-10-1) 125
GB   D23 R31/152  P(42-24-2) 252
ChiB-Jones 152R; GB-Green 128R,
Walker 102C

Den   0   6   0   0    6
Jax   0   7   0   0    7
Den  D20 R35/106  P(39-23-0) 250
Jax  D8 R22/67    P(16-8-0) 109

Car   0   7   0  14   21
KC    3   7   7   7   24
Car  D23 R39/183  P(29-16-2) 175
KC   D17 R23/109  P(34-17-1) 172
Car-Foster 174R

SF    3  14   3   7   27
NO   10  10   3   7   30
SF   D22 R34/180  P(25-18-1) 190
NO   D17 R24/46   P(34-25-0) 256
SF-Barlow 114R, Conway 112C;
NO-Stallworth 113C

Was   7   0   0   7   14
NYG   0  20   0   0   20
Was  D20 R28/108  P(36-19-4) 214
NYG  D15 R28/62   P(33-22-0) 215
Was-Coles 100C

Buf   0   3   0   7   10
Oak   0   3   3   7   13
Buf  D14 R24/67   P(25-14-1) 176
Oak  D12 R26/73   P(27-19-0) 200

NYJ  14   3  10   7   34
SD    0   7  14   7   28
NYJ  D22 R35/122  P(29-22-0) 258
SD   D21 R25/111  P(35-15-2) 216
NYJ-Martin 119R

Sea   3   7   0   0   10
TB    0   3   0   3    6
Sea  D9 R22/58    P(26-12-1) 124
TB   D17 R24/92   P(39-25-2) 179

Ind   3   0   7  21   31
Ten   7   3   7   0   17
Ind  D27 R23/129  P(33-24-0) 244
Ten  D25 R30/153  P(14-9-0) 236
Ind-James 124R, Wayne 119C;
Ten-Brown 152R, Mason 104C
```

MONDAY, SEPTEMBER 20
```
Min   3   3   3   7   16
Phi   7   3   7  10   27
Min  D25 R19/78   P(47-37-1) 332
Phi  D19 R17/91   P(28-19-0) 226
Min-Culpepper 343P
```

SUNDAY, SEPTEMBER 26
```
Arz   0   0   0   3    3
Atl   3   3   0   0    6
Arz  D13 R26/61   P(32-25-0) 179
Atl  D15 R29/194  P(20-10-1) 89
Atl-Dunn 117R
```

```
Bal  10   7   0   6   23
Cin   0   3   3   3    9
Bal  D14 R34/254  P(18-11-0) 126
Cin  D26 R26/109  P(52-25-3) 289
Bal-Lewis 186R;
Cin-Houshmandzadeh 116C,
Palmer 316P

SD    0   3   7   3   13
Den   7   6   7   3   23
SD   D16 R30/85   P(30-15-0) 123
Den  D18 R21/37   P(36-25-0) 291

Phi  14   7   6   3   30
Det   0   7   0   6   13
Phi  D19 R19/59   P(42-29-0) 343
Det  D15 R18/77   P(39-21-0) 179
Phi-Owens 107C, McNabb 356P;
Det-Williams 135C

GB    3  14   7   7   31
Ind  21  14   0  10   45
GB   D24 R19/74   P(50-34-1) 385
Ind  D26 R24/60   P(40-28-0) 393
GB-Walker 200C, Favre 360P;
Ind-Stokley 110C, Wayne 184C,
Manning 393P

Hot   0   6   8  10   24
KC    7   7  14   7   35
Hot  D18 R26/76   P(25-13-1) 220
KC   D25 R36/168  P(30-21-1) 198
KC-Holmes 134R, Gonzalez 106C

Pit   3   0   3   7   13
Mia   0   0   0   3    3
Pit  D15 R38/153  P(22-12-1) 161
Mia  D13 R29/52   P(27-13-2) 117
Pit-Staley 101R

ChiB  3   3   0  16   22
Min   0  10   7  10   27
ChiB D24 R28/146  P(34-21-0) 239
Min  D24 R23/93   P(31-19-0) 350
ChiB-Jones 110R; Min-Moss 119C,
Smith 104C, Culpepper 360P

Cle   0   0   0  10   10
NYG   7   3   7  10   27
Cle  D18 R23/124  P(31-21-1) 161
NYG  D25 R32/116  P(27-19-0) 274
NYG-Barber 106R, Toomer 126C

TB    3   3   0  14   20
Oak   3  10  17   0   30
TB   D19 R22/92   P(36-22-1) 297
Oak  D23 R31/173  P(31-18-1) 226
TB-Schroeder 126C, Johnson 309P;
Oak-Wheatley 102R

SF    0   0   0   0    0
Sea  17   0  10   7   34
SF   D9 R18/48    P(32-19-2) 127
Sea  D24 R37/117  P(32-22-0) 257

NO    0  13   3   9   28
Slr   7   3  15   0   25
NO   D27 R32/146  P(41-24-0) 316
Slr  D25 R15/74   P(49-32-0) 325
NO-Stecker 106R, Brooks 316P;
Slr-Bruce 134C, Bulger 358P

Jax   0   0   7   8   15
Ten   0   6   0   6   12
Jax  D15 R29/136  P(20-14-0) 117
Ten  D13 R26/119  P(27-16-1) 130
Ten-Brown 101R
```

MONDAY, SEPTEMBER 27
```
Dal   7   0   7   7   21
Was   0   3   8   7   18
Dal  D14 R21/50   P(30-15-0) 237
Was  D21 R24/94   P(43-25-0) 290
Was-Gardner 167C, Brunell 325P
```

SUNDAY, OCTOBER 3
```
NO    0   3   7   0   10
Arz   7   7   3  17   34
NO   D14 R14/41   P(40-24-0) 238
Arz  D19 R40/211  P(19-13-0) 162
Arz-Smith 127R

NE   10   7   0  14   31
Buf   7   0   7   0   14
NE   D21 R26/99   P(30-17-0) 298
Buf  D18 R27/123  P(30-18-1) 214
NE-Patten 113C; Buf-Moulds 126C
```

Atl 10 3 0 14 **27**
Car 7 3 0 0 10
Atl D20 R40/165 P(18-10-0) 148
Car D19 R21/67 P(38-23-2) 293
Car-Muhammad 114C, Delhomme 308P

Phi 3 13 3 0 **19**
ChiB 0 3 0 6 9
Phi D24 R32/158 P(38-24-1) 218
ChiB D14 R13/32 P(43-26-0) 192
Phi-Westbrook 119R, Owens 110C; ChiB-Terrell 116C

Was 3 7 0 3 13
Cle 3 0 7 7 **17**
Was D13 R25/73 P(32-17-0) 192
Cle D14 R32/96 P(21-14-0) 184
Was-Coles 122C

NYG 0 0 7 7 **14**
GB 0 0 7 0 7
NYG D21 R35/245 P(26-20-1) 158
GB D15 R19/81 P(36-20-2) 220
NYG-Barber 182R

Oak 3 14 0 0 17
Hot 3 14 3 10 **30**
Oak D18 R20/151 P(38-21-3) 224
Hot D20 R41/158 P(24-14-0) 228
Oak-Zereoue 117R; Hot-Wells 105R, Johnson 115C

Ind 7 3 7 7 **24**
Jax 0 3 3 11 17
Ind D23 R27/117 P(29-20-1) 220
Jax D23 R31/97 P(41-29-0) 311
Jax-Leftwich 318P

NYJ 7 3 7 0 **17**
Mia 0 9 0 0 9
NYJ D16 R31/110 P(24-14-1) 125
Mia D13 R21/97 P(33-18-2) 196
NYJ-Martin 110R

Cin 7 3 7 0 17
Pit 7 7 0 14 **28**
Cin D22 R27/137 P(37-20-2) 156
Pit D23 R40/165 P(25-17-0) 168
Cin-Johnson 123R; Pit-Staley 123R

Ten 0 7 0 10 17
SD 7 14 3 14 **38**
Ten D21 R18/72 P(58-39-0) 258
SD D16 R24/195 P(20-16-0) 198
Ten-Bennett 109C; SD-Tomlinson 147R, Caldwell 110C

Slr 14 10 0 0 **24**
SF 0 0 6 8 14
Slr D24 R36/174 P(25-17-0) 186
SF D26 R19/58 P(47-31-1) 274
Slr-Faulk 121R, Bruce 100C; SF-Johnson 113C

Den 7 6 0 3 **16**
TB 0 10 3 0 13
Den D19 R35/111 P(30-13-0) 138
TB D12 R24/110 P(24-15-0) 159

MONDAY, OCTOBER 4

KC 10 7 3 7 **27**
Bal 3 14 0 7 24
KC D25 R46/178 P(31-21-0) 220
Bal D13 R20/80 P(17-10-0) 127
KC-Holmes 125R

SUNDAY, OCTOBER 10

Det 0 14 3 0 **17**
Atl 0 7 0 3 10
Det D15 R33/101 P(24-16-0) 126
Atl D17 R27/94 P(31-20-1) 185

NYG 3 3 7 13 **26**
Dal 0 10 0 0 10
NYG D19 R26/125 P(33-18-0) 211
Dal D16 R30/166 P(25-15-1) 112
NYG-Barber 122R

Car 0 10 7 0 17
Den 6 7 0 7 **20**
Car D12 R26/64 P(20-13-0) 163
Den D23 R37/210 P(29-17-2) 224
Car-Colbert 115C; Den-Droughns 193R

Min 0 14 7 7 6 **34**
Hot 0 0 7 21 0 28
Min D27 R26/122 P(50-36-0) 388
Hot D19 R17/52 P(42-27-0) 358
Min-Robinson 150C, Culpepper 396P; Hot-Armstrong 101C, Johnson 170C, Carr 372P

Oak 0 7 0 7 14
Ind 7 14 0 14 **35**
Oak D18 R13/53 P(44-28-3) 216
Ind D25 R40/150 P(26-16-1) 188
Ind-James 136R

Mia 0 7 3 0 10
NE 7 10 7 0 **24**
Mia D18 R26/67 P(43-21-1) 228
NE D14 R38/135 P(19-7-1) 69
Mia-Booker 123C

TB 3 10 7 0 **20**
NO 0 7 7 3 17
TB D16 R26/81 P(27-21-0) 238
NO D16 R29/145 P(23-11-1) 106
NO-McAllister 102R

Buf 0 0 0 14 14
NYJ 0 10 3 3 **16**
Buf D17 R22/80 P(29-16-1) 172
NYJ D24 R23/85 P(42-31-1) 298
NYJ-Pennington 304P

Cle 10 3 3 7 23
Pit 14 13 7 0 **34**
Cle D17 R21/98 P(34-16-0) 207
Pit D21 R43/170 P(21-16-1) 231
Cle-Davis 101C; Pit-Staley 117R, Burress 136C

Jax 0 7 0 14 21
SD 14 7 6 7 **34**
Jax D28 R18/80 P(54-36-2) 349
SD D18 R35/176 P(26-17-0) 210
Jax-Smith 113C, Leftwich 357P; SD-Chatman 103R

Slr 0 7 3 17 6 **33**
Sea 7 17 0 3 0 27
Slr D21 R24/124 P(42-24-3) 317
Sea D20 R30/187 P(35-20-0) 204
Slr-Bulger 325P; Sea-Alexander 150R

Arz 0 14 0 14 0 28
SF 0 6 6 16 3 **31**
Arz D19 R29/103 P(34-19-1) 217
SF D28 R19/57 P(57-38-0) 391
SF-Johnson 162C, Rattay 417P

Bal 0 0 14 3 **17**
Was 0 10 0 0 10
Bal D15 R43/156 P(18-9-3) 76
Was D9 R26/52 P(29-13-1) 55
Bal-Lewis 116R

MONDAY, OCTOBER 11

Ten 17 10 7 14 **48**
GB 3 10 0 14 27
Ten D23 R44/224 P(27-16-0) 232
GB D22 R11/35 P(52-31-3) 402
Ten-Brown 148R; GB-Driver 150C, Walker 159C, Favre 338P

SUNDAY, OCTOBER 17

SD 0 14 3 3 20
Atl 0 7 0 14 **21**
SD D18 R31/95 P(31-23-1) 223
Atl D15 R25/93 P(21-12-1) 206

Mia 0 10 0 3 13
Buf 7 0 10 3 **20**
Mia D14 R25/111 P(23-12-1) 101
Buf D18 R31/137 P(28-15-0) 204
Buf-McGahee 111R

Was 3 7 0 3 **13**
ChiB 0 7 0 3 10
Was D18 R47/218 P(22-8-1) 93
ChiB D9 R28/126 P(22-10-1) 34
Was-Portis 171R

Cin 0 17 0 0 17
Cle 7 14 3 10 **34**
Cin D11 R18/58 P(36-20-1) 131
Cle D21 R46/139 P(23-16-2) 310
Cle-Green 115R, Suggs 100C, Garcia 310P

Pit 7 3 0 14 **24**
Dal 7 3 10 0 20
Pit D21 R29/125 P(25-21-0) 172
Dal D20 R21/100 P(36-23-0) 248
Dal-Glenn 140C

GB 7 10 14 7 **38**
Det 7 3 0 0 10
GB D28 R39/157 P(39-26-0) 277
Det D5 R16/33 P(23-12-1) 92
GB-Driver 110C

KC 3 0 7 6 16
Jax 7 7 0 8 **22**
KC D19 R21/77 P(33-23-1) 273
Jax D19 R23/101 P(36-24-0) 277
KC-Morton 111C, Green 315P

Sea 0 6 3 11 20
NE 10 10 0 10 **30**
Sea D23 R21/102 P(50-27-2) 341
NE D20 R33/138 P(30-19-1) 224
Sea-Robinson 150C, Hasselbeck 349P; NE-Dillon 105R

Min 7 14 10 7 **38**
NO 0 14 7 10 31
Min D29 R28/188 P(38-26-2) 417
NO D25 R23/159 P(38-22-1) 226
Min-Moore 109R, Burleson 134C, Culpepper 425P

SF 7 7 0 0 14
NYJ 0 3 6 13 **22**
SF D19 R27/99 P(28-18-1) 272
NYJ D22 R32/152 P(30-20-0) 222
NYJ-Martin 111R

Den 7 14 10 0 **31**
Oak 3 0 0 0 3
Den D25 R51/254 P(20-11-1) 190
Oak D9 R16/31 P(31-15-1) 114
Den-Droughns 176R

Car 0 0 0 8 8
Phi 10 3 10 7 **30**
Car D21 R31/158 P(42-24-4) 186
Phi D10 R20/81 P(26-14-1) 202
Phi-Owens 123C

Hot 3 10 0 7 **20**
Ten 0 10 0 0 10
Hot D19 R37/98 P(26-16-1) 247
Ten D19 R22/101 P(41-19-4) 204

MONDAY, OCTOBER 18

TB 7 7 7 0 21
Slr 7 7 7 7 **28**
TB D17 R22/55 P(40-27-1) 277
Slr D14 R30/94 P(30-18-1) 230
TB-Clayton 142C; Slr-Holt 124C

SUNDAY, OCTOBER 24

Sea 0 3 7 7 17
Arz 7 6 3 9 **25**
Sea D12 R14/77 P(41-14-4) 180
Arz D16 R37/127 P(36-22-1) 189
Sea-Jackson 109C; Arz-Smith 106R

Buf 3 0 3 0 6
Bal 10 7 0 3 **20**
Buf D15 R23/85 P(37-20-4) 185
Bal D12 R33/100 P(19-10-0) 60

SD 0 0 10 7 **17**
Car 6 0 0 0 6
SD D19 R27/114 P(32-21-0) 188
Car D20 R30/116 P(36-17-1) 147

Phi 14 7 0 10 3 **34**
Cle 7 10 7 7 0 31
Phi D23 R23/121 P(43-28-1) 367
Cle D27 R34/165 P(32-21-1) 229
Phi-Owens 109C, Pinkston 100C, McNabb 376P

Dal 6 0 7 7 20
GB 3 17 21 0 **41**
Dal D18 R16/66 P(36-23-0) 296
GB D23 R31/220 P(30-24-0) 260
Dal-Witten 112C, Testaverde 308P; GB-Green 163R, Walker 129C

Jax 0 10 3 14 **27**
Ind 0 14 0 10 24
Jax D20 R27/128 P(30-23-1) 286
Ind D23 R18/87 P(40-27-0) 359
Jax-Taylor 107R, Smith 113C, Leftwich 300P; Ind-Stokley 112C, Manning 368P

Atl 3 0 7 0 10
KC 14 21 7 14 **56**
Atl D9 R21/119 P(25-9-2) 103
KC D36 R49/271 P(28-20-0) 269
KC-Holmes 139R

Slr 0 7 0 7 14
Mia 7 7 0 17 **31**
Slr D20 R19/103 P(40-23-1) 269
Mia D19 R34/117 P(18-14-0) 206
Mia-Chambers 128C

Ten 3 0 0 0 3
Min 3 14 0 3 **20**
Ten D16 R14/55 P(42-20-3) 188
Min D20 R27/152 P(30-24-0) 161
Min-Moore 138R

NYJ 0 7 0 0 7
NE 3 10 0 0 **13**
NYJ D15 R27/106 P(30-19-0) 162
NE D21 R29/133 P(29-20-0) 210
NE-Dillon 115R, Givens 107C

Det 7 0 7 14 **28**
NYG 7 3 0 3 13
Det D22 R29/115 P(22-18-0) 210
NYG D22 R26/75 P(34-23-1) 250
NYG-Barber 102C

NO 0 7 14 10 **31**
Oak 6 3 0 17 26
NO D20 R28/42 P(39-23-0) 280
Oak D20 R24/82 P(45-26-1) 350
NO-Horn 123C; Oak-Porter 113C, Collins 350P

ChiB 0 0 7 0 7
TB 0 10 3 6 **19**
ChiB D11 R20/76 P(28-14-1) 91
TB D17 R37/138 P(23-15-0) 155
TB-Pittman 109R

MONDAY, OCTOBER 25

Den 0 7 3 0 10
Cin 7 6 7 3 **23**
Den D22 R26/123 P(40-23-2) 195
Cin D13 R33/133 P(21-12-1) 188
Den-Droughns 110R; Cin-Johnson 119R, Johnson 149C

SUNDAY, OCTOBER 31

Arz 0 7 0 7 14
Buf 10 7 0 21 **38**
Arz D14 R38/128 P(24-9-0) 85
Buf D11 R38/128 P(17-8-0) 81
Buf-McGahee 102R

SF 10 3 0 0 13
ChiB 7 6 0 10 **23**
SF D10 R23/62 P(36-16-1) 100
ChiB D14 R33/120 P(25-13-1) 134

Det 7 7 0 7 21
Dal 7 7 7 10 **31**
Det D15 R14/39 P(32-19-1) 245
Dal D22 R41/127 P(24-19-3) 230

Atl 3 17 7 14 **41**
Den 14 0 0 14 28
Atl D22 R36/195 P(25-19-0) 272
Den D27 R19/68 P(55-31-3) 499
Atl-Vick 115R; Den-Smith 208C, Plummer 499P

Jax 0 3 0 3 6
Hot 7 3 0 10 **20**
Jax D14 R12/39 P(42-27-2) 248
Hot D24 R32/93 P(35-26-0) 276
Jax-Smith 117C

Ind 7 7 14 7 35
KC 7 24 0 14 **45**
Ind D23 R12/33 P(44-25-1) 472
KC D33 R42/203 P(34-27-0) 387
Ind-Harrison 119C, Wayne 119C, Manning 472P; KC-Holmes 143R, Gonzalez 125C, Green 389P

NYG 10 10 7 7 **34**
Min 0 0 0 13 13
NYG D22 R39/168 P(21-13-0) 115
Min D15 R20/93 P(41-24-2) 231
NYG-Barber 101R

Bal 3 0 0 7 10
Phi 3 3 0 9 **15**
Bal D19 R27/113 P(38-24-1) 214
Phi D19 R23/98 P(34-18-0) 200
Phi-Owens 101C

NE 3 7 3 7 20
Pit 21 3 10 0 **34**
NE D19 R6/5 P(43-25-2) 243
Pit D25 R49/221 P(24-18-0) 196
NE-Givens 101C; Pit-Staley 125R

Oak 0 7 7 0 14
SD 14 14 14 0 **42**
Oak D15 R11/22 P(39-24-2) 259
SD D33 R38/175 P(25-22-0) 273
SD-Brees 281P

Car 0 7 3 7 17
Sea 7 7 3 6 **23**
Car D16 R20/94 P(36-19-1) 248
Sea D24 R43/237 P(30-21-1) 196
Car-Colbert 100C, Muhammad 106C; Sea-Alexander 195R

Cin 3 0 10 7 20
Ten 0 13 14 0 **27**
Cin D16 R17/57 P(36-20-1) 217
Ten D22 R37/163 P(32-21-1) 195
Ten-Brown 147R

GB 3 14 3 8 **28**
Was 0 7 0 7 14
GB D20 R28/88 P(32-20-3) 273
Was D20 R19/81 P(45-25-2) 191

MONDAY, NOVEMBER 1

Mia 0 7 0 7 14
NYJ 7 10 14 10 **41**
Mia D16 R16/78 P(41-20-2) 181
NYJ D22 R41/275 P(20-12-0) 197
NYJ-Jordan 115R, Martin 115R

SUNDAY, NOVEMBER 7

Cle 10 0 0 3 13
Bal 3 9 0 15 **27**
Cle D13 R28/91 P(26-15-1) 126
Bal D15 R28/106 P(30-17-0) 134

NYJ 0 10 0 7 17
Buf 7 3 7 5 **22**
NYJ D12 R25/88 P(18-9-1) 194
Buf D19 R46/157 P(30-18-0) 184
NYJ-Moss 157C; Buf-McGahee 132R

Oak 3 14 0 10 **27**
Car 0 7 7 10 24
Oak D21 R28/69 P(32-20-1) 228
Car D24 R18/37 P(45-25-0) 267
Oak-Gonzalez 123C, Kennison 104C, Green 369P

Dal 0 3 0 0 3
Cin 3 6 7 10 **26**
Dal D13 R27/109 P(30-18-3) 202
Cin D15 R31/116 P(32-21-0) 212

Hot 0 7 0 6 13
Den 7 17 7 0 **31**
Hot D22 R27/103 P(41-22-0) 228
Den D21 R36/139 P(24-16-0) 225
Den-Droughns 120R, Plummer 234P

Was 0 3 14 0 **17**
Det 0 3 0 7 10
Was D15 R40/156 P(18-7-0) 73
Det D21 R24/64 P(52-26-1) 258
Was-Portis 147R, Brees 257P; Det-Hakim 120C

Arz 3 0 7 14 **24**
Mia 9 3 0 11 23
Arz D17 R27/121 P(31-18-0) 149
Mia D22 R31/168 P(36-18-1) 235
Mia-Chambers 104C

ChiB 0 20 0 8 **28**
NYG 14 0 0 7 21
ChiB D13 R34/122 P(21-8-0) 109
NYG D15 R25/91 P(36-18-2) 167
ChiB-Thomas 110R

Phi 0 3 0 0 3
Pit 14 7 3 3 **27**
Phi D7 R9/23 P(24-15-1) 90
Pit D25 R56/252 P(18-11-1) 168
Pit-Bettis 149R

NO 0 7 0 10 17
SD 14 6 16 7 **43**
NO D18 R18/55 P(29-16-1) 165
SD D28 R35/152 P(37-22-0) 250
SD-Brees 257P

Sea 7 14 14 7 **42**
SF 14 3 7 3 **27**
Sea D26 R37/184 P(28-17-0) 269
SF D19 R21/74 P(35-23-1) 243
Sea-Alexander 160R, Jackson 114C

NE 6 13 14 7 **40**
Slr 0 14 0 8 22
NE D22 R32/147 P(32-19-0) 229
Slr D21 R19/81 P(33-23-1) 259
NE-Dillon 112R, Givens 100C; Slr-Holt 111C

KC 7 17 7 0 31
TB 7 14 7 6 **34**
KC D27 R30/105 P(42-32-2) 354
TB D23 R20/130 P(34-22-0) 288
KC-Gonzalez 123C, Kennison 104C, Green 369P; TB-Pittman 128R

MONDAY, NOVEMBER 8

Min 0 6 8 14 28
Ind 7 7 7 10 **31**
Min D15 R24/138 P(19-16-0) 154
Ind D26 R31/144 P(29-23-0) 264
Ind-James 123R, Manning 268P

SUNDAY, NOVEMBER 14

NYG 7 7 0 0 14
Arz 0 10 7 0 **17**
NYG D19 R28/147 P(31-19-0) 161
Arz D18 R32/104 P(24-12-0) 74
NYG-Barber 108R, Toomer 100C

TB 0 7 7 0 14
Atl 10 7 0 7 **24**
TB D14 R23/68 P(26-19-1) 125
Atl D18 R39/205 P(16-8-1) 120
Atl-Crumpler 118C

Pit 7 7 0 10 **24**
Cle 3 0 0 7 10
Pit D18 R47/180 P(16-10-1) 120
Cle D12 R22/68 P(25-12-2) 160
Pit-Bettis 103R

Min 7 3 7 14 31
GB 7 17 0 10 **34**
Min D22 R16/71 P(44-27-0) 345
GB D24 R35/206 P(29-20-0) 236
Min-Burleson 141C, Culpepper 363P; GB-Green 145R, Favre 236P

Hot 0 0 7 7 14
Ind 7 14 21 7 **49**
Hot D20 R37/132 P(41-22-0) 312
Ind D17 R20/86 P(27-18-2) 312
Ind-Clark 102C, Stokley 132C, Manning 320P

Det 0 0 0 17 17
Jax 7 3 7 0 6 **23**
Det D10 R19/81 P(33-11-1) 109
Jax D22 R50/239 P(36-19-0) 176
Jax-Taylor 144R, Smith 109C

Buf 0 0 6 0 6
NE 3 17 3 6 **29**
Buf D8 R17/50 P(21-9-4) 75
NE D25 R45/208 P(35-19-1) 220
NE-Dillon 151R

KC 10 3 0 7 20
NO 0 14 3 10 **27**
KC D28 R36/200 P(33-22-2) 297
NO D20 R23/134 P(27-15-1) 240
KC-Blaylock 186R, Kennison 121C, Green 311P; NO-McAllister 127R, Horn 167C

Bal 0 7 3 7 3 **20**
NYJ 0 14 0 3 0 17
Bal D18 R32/76 P(33-19-0) 186
NYJ D16 R36/156 P(23-13-1) 149
NYJ-Martin 119R

Car 0 3 17 17 **37**
SF 10 7 3 7 27
Car D17 R18/57 P(34-19-0) 170
SF D23 R33/110 P(37-22-4) 247
Car-Muhammad 123C, Delhomme 303P; SF-Wilson 101C

Sea 0 6 6 0 12
Slr 14 3 3 3 **23**
Sea D20 R29/200 P(36-15-1) 172
Slr D24 R31/202 P(34-23-0) 260
Sea-Alexander 176R; Slr-Faulk 139R, Bruce 104C

ChiB 0 7 7 3 2 **19**
Ten 7 0 0 10 0 17
ChiB D10 R34/101 P(28-10-2) 75
Ten D14 R24/72 P(44-27-1) 318
Ten-Bennett 148C, Volek 334P

Cin 7 10 0 0 **17**
Was 0 0 0 10 10
Cin D19 R34/99 P(39-24-2) 217
Was D17 R20/87 P(46-19-3) 181
Cin-Johnson 102R

MONDAY, NOVEMBER 15

Phi 7 28 7 7 **49**
Dal 0 14 7 0 21
Phi D20 R33/149 P(27-15-0) 336
Dal D14 R24/71 P(30-21-1) 246
Phi-Owens 134C, McNabb 345P; Dal-Witten 133C

SUNDAY, NOVEMBER 21

Dal 3 0 0 7 10
Bal 0 0 14 16 **30**
Dal D16 R35/94 P(28-15-2) 128
Bal D15 R21/59 P(35-23-0) 228

Slr 10 7 0 0 17
Buf 0 17 20 0 **37**
Slr D19 R20/35 P(45-27-3) 235
Buf D16 R26/119 P(24-15-1) 175
Buf-McGahee 100R

Arz 0 0 10 0 10
Car 14 14 0 7 **35**
Arz D23 R28/85 P(52-28-3) 314
Car D17 R21/168 P(27-13-1) 160
Arz-King 343P; Car-Goings 121R, Muhammad 118C

Ind 7 20 14 0 **41**
ChiB 3 0 0 7 10
Ind D31 R39/275 P(28-17-1) 211
ChiB D14 R26/79 P(24-14-2) 145
Ind-James 204R, Wayne 106C, Manning 211P

Pit 3 7 7 2 **19**
Cin 7 7 0 0 14
Pit D21 R40/151 P(21-15-0) 84
Cin D10 R16/62 P(25-13-1) 147
Pit-Bettis 129R

NYJ 0 0 3 7 **10**
Cle 0 7 0 0 7
NYJ D17 R39/157 P(20-11-1) 78
Cle D13 R27/99 P(27-14-0) 117

GB 0 3 0 13 **16**
Hot 0 13 0 0 13
GB D22 R21/90 P(50-33-2) 383
Hot D13 R27/107 P(27-13-0) 144
GB-Driver 148C, Favre 383P; Hot-Johnson 107C

Ten 3 7 0 8 **18**
Jax 0 6 7 2 15
Ten D14 R27/103 P(30-18-2) 192
Jax D18 R32/151 P(27-13-1) 123
Jax-Taylor 103R

Det 14 3 2 0 19
Min 7 0 0 15 **22**
Det D13 R27/146 P(19-12-1) 67
Min D22 R34/107 P(32-22-1) 212
Det-Jones 100R

Den 20 7 0 7 **34**
NO 0 13 0 0 13
Den D18 R31/165 P(29-19-0) 224
NO D20 R14/49 P(60-34-3) 362
Den-Droughns 166R; NO-Stallworth 122C, Brooks 377P

Atl 7 7 0 0 **14**
NYG 0 0 7 3 10
Atl D16 R34/201 P(20-12-0) 97
NYG D20 R26/119 P(37-17-2) 158
Atl-Vick 104R; NYG-Barber 107R

SD 6 7 3 7 **23**
Oak 0 7 7 3 17
SD D26 R44/176 P(35-18-0) 226
Oak D14 R14/53 P(31-18-0) 220
SD-Tomlinson 164R, Gates 101C

Was 3 3 0 0 6
Phi 7 0 7 14 **28**
Was D15 R23/51 P(34-21-1) 162
Phi D20 R30/125 P(27-18-1) 208
Phi-Pinkston 106C, McNabb 222P

Mia 7 0 7 3 **17**
Sea 10 7 0 0 17
Mia D19 R23/69 P(46-24-2) 219
Sea D17 R38/116 P(28-14-2) 177
Mia-Chambers 103C

SF 0 0 3 0 3
TB 7 14 7 7 **35**
SF D13 R23/72 P(31-15-1) 125
TB D19 R35/159 P(21-15-2) 193
TB-Pittman 106R

MONDAY, NOVEMBER 22

NE 7 10 7 3 **27**
KC 0 10 6 3 19
NE D21 R32/98 P(26-17-0) 309
KC D20 R20/64 P(42-27-1) 353
NE-Branch 105C, Brady 315P; KC-Morton 107C, Green 381P

THURSDAY, NOVEMBER 25

ChiB 0 7 0 0 7
Dal 7 0 0 14 **21**
ChiB D10 R20/49 P(31-15-2) 91
Dal D18 R40/154 P(26-13-2) 113
Dal-Jones 150R

Ind 13 14 14 0 **41**
Det 6 3 0 0 9
Ind D24 R29/113 P(31-24-0) 243
Det D19 R21/168 P(38-25-1) 218
Ind-James 105R, Harrison 127C, Manning 236P

SUNDAY, NOVEMBER 28

NYJ 0 3 10 0 **13**
Arz 0 3 0 0 3
NYJ D16 R38/146 P(21-13-0) 179
Arz D17 R24/71 P(36-19-3) 174
NYJ-Moss 109C

NO 0 6 8 7 21
Atl 7 10 0 7 **24**
NO D19 R28/141 P(34-19-2) 165
Atl D21 R33/186 P(29-16-1) 210
NO-McAllister 100R, Horn 101C; Atl-Crumpler 103C

TB 0 7 0 7 14
Car 7 0 7 7 **21**
TB D20 R28/62 P(39-27-1) 336
Car D15 R25/112 P(21-14-1) 188
TB-Pittman 134C, Griese 347P; Car-Goings 106R

Cle 10 3 21 14 48
Cin 14 13 14 17 **58**
Cle D23 R17/76 P(39-30-2) 386
Cin D26 R32/253 P(29-22-3) 251
Cle-Bryant 131C, Holcomb 413P; Cin-Johnson 202C, Johnson 117C, Palmer 251P

Oak 0 7 6 12 **25**
Den 0 10 0 14 24
Oak D19 R18/61 P(45-26-2) 334
Den D16 R34/122 P(23-14-1) 245
Oak-Curry 110C, Porter 135C, Collins 339P; Den-Droughns 102R

Ten 14 7 0 0 21
Hot 3 7 14 7 **31**
Ten D23 R25/134 P(34-25-1) 221
Hot D19 R21/149 P(30-21-1) 179
Hot-Davis 129R

SD 7 7 3 17 **34**
KC 7 10 0 14 31
SD D25 R31/127 P(37-28-0) 371
KC D20 R20/110 P(34-21-1) 200
SD-Brees 378P; KC-Gonzalez 105C

Jax 0 13 0 3 16
Min 3 10 7 7 **27**
Jax D18 R27/154 P(34-19-0) 225
Min D24 R30/112 P(27-19-1) 218
Jax-Taylor 147R

Bal 0 3 0 0 3
NE 0 3 6 15 **24**
Bal D8 R20/77 P(35-15-1) 47
NE D18 R41/144 P(30-15-0) 170
NE-Dillon 123R

Phi 0 7 13 7 **27**
NYG 3 3 0 0 6
Phi D22 R38/152 P(27-18-0) 238
NYG D12 R26/161 P(21-6-2) 111
NYG-Barber 110R, Taylor 102C

Was 0 0 7 0 7
Pit 3 10 0 3 **16**
Was D10 R14/51 P(35-19-1) 105
Pit D15 R38/107 P(20-9-0) 100
Pit-Bettis 100R

Buf 7 10 7 14 **38**
Sea 0 3 0 6 9
Buf D25 R37/148 P(38-26-3) 286
Sea D17 R17/55 P(38-19-1) 175
Buf-McGahee 116R

Mia 7 0 0 17 **24**
SF 0 3 0 14 17
Mia D15 R26/49 P(33-17-1) 151
SF D16 R24/77 P(38-23-0) 197

MONDAY, NOVEMBER 29

Slr 0 10 0 7 17
GB 7 14 7 17 **45**
Slr D25 R17/47 P(53-35-1) 405
GB D22 R28/231 P(27-18-0) 215
Slr-Bruce 170C, Bulger 448P; GB-Davenport 178R

SUNDAY, DECEMBER 5

Cin 0 3 0 24 **27**
Bal 3 3 14 6 26
Cin D23 R24/98 P(36-29-1) 355
Bal D21 R31/192 P(33-19-1) 164
Cin-Houshmandzadeh 171C, Johnson 161C, Palmer 382P; Bal-Taylor 139R

Min 7 7 0 0 14
ChiB 7 10 0 7 **24**
Min D24 R22/146 P(33-23-3) 245
ChiB D21 R35/144 P(30-18-0) 174

NE 14 7 21 0 **42**
Cle 0 0 7 8 15
NE D27 R50/225 P(26-14-1) 187
Cle D15 R17/46 P(35-20-2) 241
NE-Dillon 100R; Cle-Bryant 115C

Arz 3 9 0 0 12
Det 7 7 6 6 **26**
Arz D15 R26/94 P(40-18-4) 160
Det D16 R32/215 P(27-15-1) 183
Det-Jones 196R

Ten 24 0 0 0 24
Ind 17 14 10 10 **51**
Ten D17 R25/115 P(36-21-2) 225
Ind D29 R28/150 P(27-19-2) 417
Ten-Brown 104R, Bennett 124C; Ind-James 105R, Harrison 106C, Stokley 153C, Manning 425P

Pit 7 7 0 3 **17**
Jax 7 0 6 3 16
Pit D15 R25/120 P(17-14-0) 196
Jax D20 R34/100 P(27-16-0) 259

Buf 14 7 7 14 **42**
Mia 21 0 8 3 32
Buf D16 R28/105 P(30-19-0) 257
Mia D25 R26/106 P(51-25-5) 297
Buf-Evans 110C, Bledsoe 277P; Mia-Feeley 303P

Car 13 13 0 6 **32**
NO 0 0 7 7 14
Car D25 R42/132 P(29-22-0) 269
NO D15 R11/30 P(40-20-2) 250
Car-Goings 122R, Muhammad 179C; NO-Horn 160C

Hot 0 7 0 0 7
NYJ 3 3 7 16 **29**
Hot D13 R25/83 P(25-12-2) 147
NYJ D26 R30/210 P(27-20-1) 150
Hot-Johnson 125C; NYJ-Martin 134R

KC 7 3 14 10 **34**
Oak 6 14 0 7 27
KC D29 R36/160 P(35-23-1) 340
Oak D16 R9/31 P(41-27-0) 333
KC-Johnson 118R, Kennison 149C, Green 340P; Oak-Curry 141C, Collins 343P

GB 0 3 0 14 17
Phi 7 28 9 3 **47**
GB D20 R18/50 P(40-22-2) 199
Phi D29 R21/93 P(45-32-0) 449
Phi-Owens 161C, Westbrook 156C, McNabb 464P

Den 0 7 0 10 17
SD 7 10 3 0 **20**
Den D21 R24/74 P(40-16-4) 263
SD D14 R35/122 P(27-14-1) 86
Den-Lelie 105C; SD-Tomlinson 113R

SF 3 0 3 0 6
Slr 3 10 0 3 **16**
SF D7 R27/63 P(21-10-1) 97
Slr D19 R31/136 P(31-21-1) 214
Slr-Jackson 119R, Holt 160C

Atl 0 0 0 0 0
TB 7 6 7 7 **27**
Atl D13 R28/163 P(30-13-3) 92
TB D15 R31/132 P(21-13-1) 115

NYG 0 0 7 0 7
Was 7 14 3 7 **31**
NYG D7 R15/38 P(25-12-0) 107
Was D27 R45/211 P(22-19-0) 168
Was-Portis 148R

MONDAY, DECEMBER 6

Dal 3 16 10 14 **43**
Sea 14 0 3 22 39
Dal D24 R31/198 P(34-18-2) 207
Sea D25 R27/109 P(40-28-0) 398
Dal-Jones 198R, Johnson 116C; Sea-Jackson 113C, Rice 145C, Hasselbeck 414P

SUNDAY, DECEMBER 12

SF 7 14 7 0 3 **31**
Arz 0 3 7 18 0 28
SF D23 R41/168 P(34-18-0) 184
Arz D25 R25/75 P(44-26-1) 299
SF-Hicks 139R; Arz-Boldin 109C, McCown 307P

Oak 0 0 3 7 10
Atl 0 21 7 7 **35**
Oak D18 R23/131 P(28-14-1) 165
Atl D23 R46/219 P(21-13-0) 154
Atl-Dunn 103R

NYG 0 7 0 7 14
Bal 10 7 10 10 **37**
NYG D11 R21/51 P(27-10-2) 145
Bal D23 R44/169 P(34-18-0) 184
Bal-Taylor 104R, Boller 219P

Cle 7 0 0 0 7
Buf 3 14 3 17 **37**
Cle D6 R18/29 P(21-9-2) -3
Buf D22 R42/215 P(30-13-1) 106
Buf-McGahee 105R

Slr 7 0 6 7 20
Car 14 6 0 0 **20**
Slr D11 R21/66 P(29-16-6) 226
Car D18 R38/119 P(30-16-1) 189
Slr-Holt 151C; Car-Goings 108R

NO 0 10 3 14 **27**
Dal 10 0 3 0 13
NO D21 R37/105 P(31-18-2) 239
Dal D18 R27/121 P(36-14-2) 148
NO-Stallworth 113C

Mia 3 7 0 7 17
Den 0 14 3 3 **20**
Mia D13 R22/70 P(35-17-1) 144
Den D24 R40/196 P(30-16-2) 219
Den-Bell 123R

```
Det   3  10   0   0  13
GB    0   0  10   6  16
Det  D17 R39/193  P(22-5-0)  35
GB   D20 R29/116  P(36-19-0)  185
Det-Jones 156R

Ind  14   0   3   6  23
Hot   0   7   7   0  14
Ind  D22 R30/101  P(33-26-0)  281
Hot  D17 R28/148  P(21-16-1)  125
Ind-James 104R; Hot-Davis 128R

ChiB  0   3   0   0   3
Jax   7   3   9      22
ChiB D10 R14/31  P(33-17-1)  179
Jax  D22 R28/90  P(45-25-1)  242

Sea   7  14   3   3  27
Min  10  10   3   0  23
Sea  D26 R31/138  P(34-23-2)  317
Min  D22 R25/113  P(34-21-1)  261
Sea-Alexander 112R, Jackson 135C,
Hasselbeck 334P; Min-Moss 104C

Cin   0  14   7   7  28
NE    7  21   7   0  35
Cin  D26 R31/150  P(37-27-2)  328
NE   D22 R29/94  P(26-18-0)  257
Cin-Houshmandzadeh 145C;
NE-Patten 107C

NYJ   0   0   3   3   6
Pit   3   0  14   0  17
NYJ  D15 R32/107  P(31-17-3)  189
Pit  D15 R31/120  P(20-10-2)  142

TB    0   7   7  10  24
SD    0  14   7  10  31
TB   D21 R18/63  P(50-36-3)  373
SD   D18 R30/130  P(23-17-2)  206
TB-Clayton 145C, Griese 392P;
SD-Tomlinson 131R, Parker 118C

Phi   7   0  10   0  17
Was   7   0   0   7  14
Phi  D15 R17/67  P(38-21-1)  245
Was  D19 R25/88  P(46-29-1)  224
Was-Coles 100C
```

MONDAY, DECEMBER 13
```
KC    0  14  14  21  49
Ten   7  14   7  10  38
KC   D24 R24/146  P(32-18-1)  237
Ten  D30 R33/163  P(43-29-0)  379
KC-Johnson 104R;
Ten-Bennett 233C, Volek 426P
```

SATURDAY, DECEMBER 18
```
Car   0  10   0  21   0  31
Atl   7   3  14   7   3  34
Car  D22 R25/61  P(35-24-1)  314
Atl  D22 R38/204  P(28-11-2)  125
Car-Muhammad 135C,
Delhomme 340P; Atl-Dunn 134R

Pit  10  10   3  10  33
NYG  14   0  10   6  30
Pit  D27 R39/160  P(29-19-2)  309
NYG  D18 R21/96  P(23-16-1)  182
Pit-Bettis 140R, Randle El 149C,
Ward 134C, Roethlisberger 316P

Was   7  16   3   0  26
SF   14   0   0   2  16
Was  D17 R40/128  P(27-18-0)  209
SF   D18 R18/55  P(38-20-4)  199
Was-Portis 110R, Gardner 111C
```

SUNDAY, DECEMBER 19
```
Slr   0   7   0   0   7
Arz  10   7   7   7  31
Slr  D12 R10/22  P(36-17-1)  163
Arz  D26 R40/131  P(34-22-0)  271

Hot   7   0   7  10  24
ChiB  0   0   2   3   5
Hot  D15 R34/106  P(29-13-0)  208
ChiB D11 R26/54  P(35-17-2)  149
Hot-Gaffney 109C

Buf  14  13   0   6  33
Cin   7   3   0   7  17
Buf  D13 R29/43  P(30-15-0)  169
Cin  D16 R31/149  P(36-16-2)  126
Buf-Evans 101C; Cin-Johnson 130R
```

```
SD    7   7   7   0  21
Cle   0   0   0   0   0
SD   D16 R50/174  P(6-4-0)  83
Cle  D11 R29/126  P(28-11-1)  105
SD-Tomlinson 111R;
Cle-Suggs 105R

Min   7   7   7   7  28
Det   3  10   0  14  27
Min  D21 R23/91  P(35-25-1)  370
Det  D24 R25/113  P(44-25-2)  350
Min-Burleson 134C, Moss 102C,
Culpepper 404P; Det-Hakim 108C,
Williams 104C, Harrington 361P

Jax   7   7   7   7  28
GB    0  10   7   8  25
Jax  D19 R36/197  P(20-9-0)  115
GB   D26 R21/94  P(44-30-3)  350
Jax-Taylor 165R; GB-Walker 152C,
Favre 367P

Bal   0   0   0   7  10
Ind   3   3  14   0  20
Bal  D19 R29/160  P(40-19-2)  194
Ind  D17 R24/67  P(33-20-0)  249
Bal-Lewis 130R

Den   3   0   7   7  17
KC   14  14   7  10  45
Den  D24 R21/129  P(41-23-2)  273
KC   D22 R36/162  P(23-17-0)  248
KC-Johnson 151R, Kennison 101C

Sea   7   7   0   0  14
NYJ   3  21   6   7  37
Sea  D19 R22/88  P(32-22-1)  187
NYJ  D27 R41/229  P(24-18-0)  253
NYJ-Martin 134R

Ten   7  14   0  14  35
Oak  14   7  14   5  40
Ten  D31 R19/61  P(61-40-1)  466
Oak  D20 R22/57  P(37-21-1)  358
Ten-Bennett 160C, Mason 121C,
Volek 492P; Oak-Porter 148C,
Collins 371P

Dal   0   7   0   0   7
Phi   0   6   6   0  12
Dal  D14 R26/80  P(28-16-2)  157
Phi  D24 R28/120  P(35-20-2)  208

NO    7   0   0  14  21
TB    7   0   7   3  17
NO   D15 R29/115  P(21-14-0)  132
TB   D17 R34/169  P(22-13-1)  114
TB-Pittman 131R
```

MONDAY, DECEMBER 20
```
NE    7   7   7   7  28
Mia   7   3   7  12  29
NE   D24 R38/166  P(29-18-4)  156
Mia  D18 R20/52  P(35-22-0)  179
NE-Dillon 121R
```

FRIDAY, DECEMBER 24
```
GB    0  17   7  10  34
Min   0  21   0  10  31
GB   D26 R34/102  P(43-30-1)  358
Min  D17 R24/131  P(23-16-0)  285
GB-Driver 162C, Favre 365P;
Min-Burleson 110C
```

SATURDAY, DECEMBER 25
```
Oak   7  14   3   6  30
KC    7  14   0  10  31
Oak  D18 R22/100  P(37-18-1)  200
KC   D32 R29/99  P(45-32-1)  334
KC-Gonzalez 124C, Green 358P

Den  17   7   3  10  37
Ten  10   6   0   0  16
Den  D26 R46/193  P(26-21-1)  303
Ten  D10 R14/59  P(27-12-2)  94
Den-Plummer 303P
```

SUNDAY, DECEMBER 26
```
NYG   0  13   3   6  22
Cin   7   3   7   6  23
NYG  D18 R28/142  P(37-19-1)  184
Cin  D16 R25/63  P(32-20-1)  170
NYG-Barber 109R
```

```
Was   3   0   0   7  10
Dal   0   6   0   7  13
Was  D15 R25/84  P(29-19-2)  149
Dal  D21 R30/89  P(39-23-1)  217
Was-Parker 103C

ChiB  0   0   6   7  13
Det   3  13   0   3  19
ChiB D16 R25/124  P(35-20-0)  105
Det  D17 R32/158  P(30-15-1)  156
ChiB-Jones 109R; Det-Jones 123R

SD    7  10   7   7  31
Ind   3   7  13  11  34
SD   D22 R29/93  P(31-21-1)  281
Ind  D30 R25/104  P(44-27-1)  360
SD-Parker 103C; Ind-Harrison 111C,
Stokley 123C, Manning 383P

Hot   7   7   0   7  21
Jax   0   0   0   0   0
Hot  D19 R44/219  P(19-13-2)  114
Jax  D6 R20/95  P(21-10-1)  31
Hot-Davis 158R

Cle   7   0   0   0   7
Mia   7   0   0   3  10
Cle  D14 R40/142  P(16-9-2)  143
Mia  D19 R25/116  P(44-25-0)  164
Cle-Suggs 143R, Northcutt 114C

Atl   0   6   0   7  13
NO    5   7  14   0  26
Atl  D5 R24/93  P(41-17-2)  174
NO   D17 R40/160  P(24-12-2)  209
NO-McAllister 128R

NE    0  13   0  10  23
NYJ   0   0   0   7   7
NE   D21 R38/114  P(32-21-0)  258
NYJ  D17 R18/46  P(36-22-2)  233

Bal   7   0   0   0   7
Pit   7   3   7   3  20
Bal  D16 R21/71  P(32-18-1)  177
Pit  D20 R42/183  P(20-15-1)  221
Pit-Bettis 117R

Arz   7   0   0  14  21
Sea   0  10   7   7  24
Arz  D18 R30/97  P(33-21-2)  220
Sea  D16 R36/175  P(26-10-1)  126
Arz-Boldin 107C;
Sea-Alexander 154R, Jackson 101C

Buf   0  17  10  14  41
SF    0   0   0   7   7
Buf  D27 R36/226  P(36-23-0)  215
SF   D12 R28/98  P(20-9-3)  91
Buf-McGahee 102R

Car   7  10   7  13  37
TB    7   6   0   7  20
Car  D22 R36/141  P(24-19-0)  207
TB   D22 R13/46  P(41-30-2)  299
Car-Goings 127R,
Muhammad 115C, Delhomme 214P;
TB-Griese 321P
```

MONDAY, DECEMBER 27
```
Phi   7   0   0   0   7
Slr   7   3   7   3  20
Phi  D11 R23/81  P(23-8-0)  74
Slr  D22 R44/209  P(28-20-0)  210
Slr-Jackson 148R
```

SUNDAY, JANUARY 2
```
TB    0   0   7   0   7
Arz   3   3   0   6  12
TB   D11 R21/62  P(32-16-2)  187
Arz  D12 R34/107  P(36-16-1)  115

Mia   7   0  14   2  23
Bal   7  13  10   0  30
Mia  D18 R20/97  P(38-16-3)  248
Bal  D21 R41/190  P(27-14-0)  142
Mia-Chambers 146C;
Bal-Lewis 167R

Pit  10   6   0  13  29
Buf   7   3   7   7  24
Pit  D21 R43/157  P(25-12-2)  105
Buf  D16 R21/96  P(30-16-1)  171
Pit-Parker 102R

NO    7   7   0   7  21
Car   3   8          18
NO   D15 R37/164  P(24-14-0)  196
Car  D21 R13/46  P(50-24-0)  274
```

```
NO-McAllister 140R;
Car-Delhomme 307P

GB    7  21   3   0  31
ChiB  0   7   0   0   7
GB   D17 R30/60  P(26-16-0)  327
ChiB D17 R27/110  P(29-20-1)  136
ChiB-Jones 108R

Ind   7   7   0   0  14
Den   7  13  10   3  33
Ind  D8 R15/34  P(27-17-0)  166
Den  D23 R42/214  P(30-17-0)  239

Cle   3   6   7   6  22
Hot   7   0   7   0  14
Cle  D18 R32/137  P(29-20-2)  227
Hot  D18 R24/136  P(27-16-0)  102
Cle-Suggs 131R; Hot-Davis 103R

SF    7   0   0   0   7
NE    0   7   7   7  21
SF   D15 R35/135  P(29-18-0)  183
NE   D6 R28/174  P(34-23-1)  231
SF-Barlow 103R; NE-Dillon 116R

Dal   3   6   7   8  24
NYG   0   7   0  21  28
Dal  D21 R31/147  P(31-23-1)  220
NYG  D18 R25/98  P(27-18-1)  133
Dal-Jones 149R

Jax   0   3  10   0  13
Oak   3   0   0   6   9
Jax  D13 R34/93  P(28-15-1)  193
Oak  D16 R28/147  P(39-15-3)  134
Oak-Crockett 134R

Cin   0  17  14   7  38
Phi   0   3   0   7  10
Cin  D16 R35/148  P(27-16-0)  160
Phi  D18 R16/80  P(54-31-3)  262

KC    0   3   0  14  17
SD    3  14   0   7  24
KC   D26 R20/70  P(53-33-4)  373
SD   D21 R29/138  P(31-18-1)  215
KC-Gonzalez 144C, Johnson 115C,
Green 373P

Atl   7  10   0   9  26
Sea   7   7   7   7  28
Atl  D22 R38/204  P(29-20-1)  150
Sea  D21 R21/83  P(27-21-1)  170
Atl-Dunn 132R

NYJ   3   3  16   3  29
Slr   0  14   7   8   32
NYJ  D22 R39/180  P(36-21-0)  144
Slr  D21 R19/47  P(40-29-2)  432
NYJ-Martin 153R; Slr-Holt 116C,
Bulger 450P

Det   3   7   3   6  19
Ten   7   7   7   3  24
Det  D23 R26/103  P(49-33-1)  331
Ten  D15 R26/95  P(33-18-0)  217
Det-Harrington 346P

Min   0   3   7   8  18
Was   7   7   0   7  21
Min  D21 R18/52  P(44-27-0)  268
Was  D20 R31/117  P(26-17-1)  201
Was-Betts 118R
```

2005 NFL
TUESDAY, SEPTEMBER 8
```
Oak   7   0   7   6  20
NE   10   7   6   7  30
Oak  D19 R22/92  P(39-18-0)  246
NE   D22 R31/73  P(25-21-0)  306
Oak-Moss 130C; NE-Brady 306P
```

SUNDAY, SEPTEMBER 11
```
Arz   0  13   6   0  19
NYG   7   0  21  14  42
Arz  D20 R21/31  P(56-32-2)  287
NYG  D14 R25/121  P(23-10-2)  154
Arz-Fitzgerald 155C

ChiB  0   0   0   7   7
Was   0   6   0   3   9
ChiB D11 R18/41  P(28-15-1)  125
Was  D18 R40/164  P(25-14-1)  159
Was-Portis 121R
```

```
Cin   0  17  10   0  27
Cle   3   7   0   3  13
Cin  D26 R32/148  P(34-26-1)  272
Cle  D16 R18/95  P(43-26-2)  278
Cin-Johnson 126R;
Cle-Jackson 128C

Dal   0  14   7   7  28
SD    7   7  10   0  24
Dal  D23 R33/109  P(24-18-0)  192
SD   D19 R26/103  P(35-18-2)  188
SD-McCardell 123C

Den   0   0   3   7  10
Mia   3   3   7  21  34
Den  D19 R20/70  P(48-22-0)  242
Mia  D21 R33/151  P(36-24-1)  275
Mia-Booker 104C

GB    0   0   0   3   3
Det   7   0   3   7  17
GB   D13 R17/46  P(44-27-2)  170
Det  D18 R31/102  P(28-15-0)  152

Hot   7   0   0   0   7
Buf   6  13   0   3  22
Hot  D12 R23/95  P(21-9-3)  25
Buf  D20 R36/152  P(28-17-0)  164
Hot-Williams 148R;
Buf-McGahee 117R

Ind   0   3  14   7  24
Bal   0   0   0   0   0
Ind  D19 R26/86  P(36-21-0)  254
Bal  D22 R21/77  P(54-34-3)  324

NO    7   7   3   6  23
Car   0   7   7   0  14
NO   D21 R33/101  P(24-18-0)  190
Car  D20 R25/141  P(31-19-2)  209
Car-Smith 138C

NYJ   0   0   0   7   7
KC   14   3   3   7  27
NYJ  D19 R23/57  P(44-27-1)  333
KC   D23 R34/198  P(26-15-1)  191
NYJ-Baker 124C; KC-Johnson 110R

Sea   0  14   0   0  14
Jax   6   7   7   6  26
Sea  D20 R19/97  P(36-21-2)  225
Jax  D18 R31/119  P(32-18-0)  243
Jax-Smith 130C

Slr   6   3  13      25
SF    0  21   7   0  28
Slr  D26 R26/89  P(56-34-1)  316
SF   D21 R34  P(18-13-0)  183
Slr-Holt 125C, Bulger 362P

TB    0  17   0   7  24
Min   7   0   3   3  13
TB   D12 R31/146  P(29-18-2)  199
Min  D15 R15/33  P(33-22-3)  215
TB-Williams 148R

Ten   7   0   0   0   7
Pit   7  13  14   0  34
Ten  D16 R23/97  P(27-18-2)  206
Pit  D18 R41/206  P(11-9-0)  218
Pit-Parker 161R
```

MONDAY, SEPTEMBER 12
```
Phi   0   7   0   3  10
Atl  14   0   0   0  14
Phi  D18 R14/51  P(45-24-1)  250
Atl  D18 R40/200  P(23-12-1)  119
Phi-Owens 112C; Atl-Dunn 117R
```

SUNDAY, SEPTEMBER 18
```
Atl   0   0  10   8  18
Sea   0  21   0   0  21
Atl  D14 R28/115  P(20-11-0)  108
Sea  D24 R34/163  P(31-20-0)  265
Sea-Alexander 144R, Jackson 131C

Bal   0   0   3   7  10
Ten   7   6   3   9  25
Bal  D12 R13/14  P(41-25-1)  168
Ten  D16 R29/97  P(37-19-0)  193

Buf   0   3   0   0   3
TB    0   9   7   3  19
Buf  D8 R17/47  P(31-13-0)  100
TB   D16 R40/191  P(22-16-0)  127
TB-Williams 128R
```

```
Cle    7   6   6   7   26
GB     7   0   0  17   24
Cle  D19 R23/55  P(32-21-0) 336
GB   D27 R30/116 P(44-32-2) 336
Cle-Edwards 107C, Heiden 104C,
Dilfer 336P; GB-Driver 105C,
Favre 342P

Det    6   0   0   0    6
ChiB  10  21   0   7   38
Det  D14 R17/29  P(43-21-5) 205
ChiB D18 R37/187 P(22-15-0) 149
ChiB-Jones 139R

Jax    0   0   3   0    3
Ind    0   0   0  10   10
Jax  D12 R24/128 P(29-16-0) 175
Ind  D18 R38/146 P(28-13-1) 122
Jax-Johnson 139C, Palmer 337P;
Ind-James 128R

KC     7  10   3   3   23
Oak    0  10   7   0   17
KC   D17 R36/125 P(28-18-0) 255
Oak  D16 R18/72  P(35-21-0) 255
Oak-Moss 127C

Mia    0   0   0   7    7
NYJ    7   3   0   7   17
Mia  D15 R18/66  P(43-20-1) 169
NYJ  D20 R34/98  P(30-19-0) 173

Min    0   0   0   8    8
Cin   14  13   7   3   37
Min  D21 R14/77  P(37-21-5) 227
Cin  D26 R39/167 P(40-27-1) 337
Cin-Johnson 139C, Palmer 337P

NE     7   0  10   0   17
Car    7  10   3   7   27
NE   D14 R16/39  P(44-23-1) 249
Car  D17 R36/104 P(26-11-1) 146

Pit   10  10   7   0   27
Hot    0   0   7   0    7
Pit  D18 R32/135 P(21-14-0) 253
Hot  D16 R25/114 P(26-16-0) 108
Pit-Parker 111R

SD     0  14   0   3   17
Den    3   0   7  10   20
SD   D15 R24/79  P(23-15-1) 134
Den  D21 R26/98  P(37-23-1) 233

SF     0   0   3   0    3
Phi   14  14   7   7   42
SF   D8  R17/58  P(27-13-3)  84
Phi  D30 R30/140 P(39-33-0) 443
Phi-Owens 143C, Smith 119C,
McNabb 342P

Slr    7   3   7   0   17
Arz    3   3   3   3   12
Slr  D16 R22/108 P(29-18-1) 189
Arz  D18 R16/82  P(42-29-1) 297
Arz-Boldin 119C, Warner 327P
```

MONDAY, SEPTEMBER 19

```
NYG   14   7   3   3   27
NO     0   0  10   0   10
NYG  D15 R29/92  P(24-13-0) 165
NO   D23 R22/72  P(45-27-3) 350
NO-Horn 143C, Stallworth 141C,
Brooks 375P

Was    0   0   0  14   14
Dal    0   3   7   3   13
Was  D14 R25/104 P(34-20-1) 242
Dal  D14 R29/90  P(36-21-0) 261
Was-Moss 159C; Dal-Glenn 157C
```

SUNDAY, SEPTEMBER 25

```
Arz    3   6   3   0   12
Sea    7   3  14  13   37
Arz  D15 R21/90  P(36-18-1) 176
Sea  D29 R37/163 P(32-21-0) 284
Sea-Alexander 140R, Jackson 125C

Atl    7  10   0   7   24
Buf    3  10   3   0   16
Atl  D24 R36/236 P(27-15-1) 167
Buf  D18 R35/172 P(23-10-1)  36
Buf-McGahee 140R

Car    3   0   0  24   24
Mia   14   7   0   6   27
Car  D23 R26/61  P(35-14-1) 238
Mia  D16 R30/144 P(33-14-1) 171
Car-Smith 170C; Mia-Brown 132R
```

```
Cin   10   0   7   7   24
ChiB   0   0   0   7    7
Cin  D11 R34/83  P(23-16-0) 161
ChiB D16 R28/106 P(39-17-5) 149
ChiB-Jones 106R

Cle    0   3   0   3    6
Ind    7   3   3   0   13
Cle  D14 R23/75  P(29-22-0) 188
Ind  D20 R33/111 P(23-19-1) 228
Ind-James 108R

Dal    0  12   7  15   34
SF     7  17   7   0   31
Dal  D26 R32/95  P(38-24-2) 348
SF   D19 R25/124 P(34-21-2) 266
Dal-Glenn 137C, Bledsoe 363P;
SF-Lloyd 142C

Jax    3   7   3   6   26
NYJ    0   7   6   0   20
Jax  D16 R47/139 P(24-16-1) 169
NYJ  D12 R25/89  P(22-11-2)  79

NE     7   0   3  13   23
Pit   10   0   3   7   20
NE   D24 R30/80  P(41-31-1) 346
Pit  D14 R23/79  P(28-12-0) 190
NE-Givens 130C, Brady 372P;
Pit-Ward 110C

NO     0   6   3   7   16
Min   17   7   0   9   33
NO   D15 R20/114 P(32-12-2) 182
Min  D21 R39/146 P(29-21-0) 274
Min-Moore 101R, Culpepper 300P

NYG    3  17   0   3   23
SD     7  14  14  10   45
NYG  D23 R23/86  P(41-24-0) 338
SD   D25 R33/268 P(23-20-0) 217
NYG-Shockey 101C, Manning 352P;
SD-Tomlinson 192R

Oak    7   3   0  10   20
Phi    0   6  14   3   23
Oak  D18 R22/21  P(42-24-0) 344
Phi  D26 R18/83  P(52-30-1) 365
Oak-Anderson 100C, Collins 345P;
Phi-Westbrook 140C, McNabb 365P

TB     7  10   0   0   17
GB     6   7   0   3   16
TB   D19 R41/161 P(26-17-1) 132
GB   D15 R25/75  P(24-14-3) 185
TB-Williams 158R

Ten   10   0  14   3   27
Slr    0  17   7   7   31
Ten  D18 R24/87  P(39-24-2) 248
Slr  D22 R21/101 P(28-21-1) 259
Slr-Holt 163C
```

MONDAY, SEPTEMBER 26

```
KC     0   3   0   7   10
Den   17   3   7   3   30
KC   D18 R22/74  P(44-23-0) 211
Den  D24 R37/221 P(18-13-0) 137
KC-Kennison 112C
```

SUNDAY, OCTOBER 2

```
Buf    7   0   0   0    7
NO     0  13   0   6   19
Buf  D13 R23/141 P(21-10-0)  67
NO   D23 R41/167 P(26-15-0) 166
NO-McAllister 130R,
Stallworth 129C

Dal    0   3   3   7   13
Oak   10   0   3   6   19
Dal  D16 R32/116 P(27-11-1) 187
Oak  D16 R30/129 P(23-13-0) 204
Oak-Jordan 126R, Moss 123C

Den    0  14   0   6   20
Jax    0   0   7   0    7
Den  D24 R44/188 P(26-19-0) 118
Jax  D13 R11/12  P(34-20-2) 229
Den-Anderson 115R;
Jax-Smith 109C

Det    0  10   3   0   13
TB     3   7   7   0   17
Det  D11 R25/91  P(27-15-0) 135
TB   D17 R22/69  P(39-22-3) 284
TB-Galloway 166C, Griese 302P
```

```
Hot    0   3   7   0   10
Cin    3   7   0   6   16
Hot  D18 R25/126 P(26-17-0) 128
Cin  D22 R25/98  P(34-25-0) 273
Cin-Houshmandzadeh 105C

Ind    7  10   7   7   31
Ten    7   3   3   0   13
Ind  D22 R26/100 P(27-20-0) 264
Ten  D18 R19/109 P(37-28-1) 204
Ind-Harrison 109C, Manning 264P

Min    0   0   0  10   10
Atl    7  17   3   3   30
Min  D17 R16/63  P(34-23-2) 198
Atl  D22 R41/285 P(22-11-0)  83
Atl-Dunn 126R

NYJ    0   0   3   0    3
Bal    3   3   7   0   13
NYJ  D8  R15/28  P(28-14-0) 124
Bal  D17 R45/115 P(21-15-1) 144

Phi    0  13  11  13   37
KC    10  14   0   7   31
Phi  D25 R17/28  P(48-33-1) 368
KC   D19 R27/144 P(30-19-2) 209
Phi-Owens 171C, McNabb 369P;
KC-Kennison 109C

SD     3  14  14  10   41
NE     7  10   0   0   17
SD   D26 R40/183 P(24-19-0) 248
NE   D18 R18/72  P(36-21-2) 231
SD-Tomlinson 134R, Gates 108C

Sea    3   0   7   7   17
Was    0   7  10   3   20
Sea  D21 R23/119 P(38-26-0) 235
Was  D26 R39/141 P(36-20-1) 211
Sea-Engram 106C

SF    14   0   0   0   14
Arz    0   6  13   9   28
SF   D8  R14/51  P(31-17-1) 117
Arz  D24 R34/97  P(46-32-0) 366
SF-Lloyd 102C; Arz-Boldin 116C,
Fitzgerald 102C, McCown 385P

Slr    7  10   0   7   24
NYG   17  10   7  10   44
Slr  D27 R15/42  P(62-40-3) 434
NYG  D24 R29/164 P(35-19-0) 292
Slr-McDonald 121C, Bulger 442P;
NYG-Barber 128R, Burress 204C,
Manning 296P
```

MONDAY, OCTOBER 3

```
GB     7   0   6  16   29
Car    7  16   3   6   32
GB   D22 R19/58  P(47-28-1) 294
Car  D17 R33/90  P(24-17-0) 196
GB-Favre 303P
```

SUNDAY, OCTOBER 9

```
Bal    0  10   0   7   17
Det   14   0   7  14   35
Bal  D26 R30/159 P(37-20-2) 228
Det  D22 R37/169 P(23-10-2)  97

Car    3   0   7  14   24
Arz    0  17   3   0   20
Car  D15 R27/87  P(29-18-1) 243
Arz  D19 R27/72  P(46-29-3) 396
Car-Smith 119C; Arz-Boldin 162C,
Fitzgerald 136C, McCown 398P

ChiB   0   0   3   7   10
Cle    3   3   0  14   20
ChiB D16 R34/176 P(26-16-0)  90
Cle  D15 R22/76  P(34-23-2) 202
ChiB-Jones 137R

Cin    3   7   0   7   20
Jax   10   3   7   3   23
Cin  D20 R26/132 P(33-22-0) 232
Jax  D19 R37/181 P(24-10-0) 161
Jax-Taylor 132R

Ind    7   7   0  14   28
SF     0   0   3   0    3
Ind  D22 R28/120 P(34-23-2) 245
SF   D12 R28/133 P(23-9-4)   44
Ind-James 105R

Mia    0   0   7   7   14
Buf    0   3   3  14   20
Mia  D16 R20/113 P(33-21-3) 210
Buf  D21 R36/99  P(26-20-0) 137
```

```
NE    14   0  14   3   31
Atl    0  13   0  15   28
NE   D20 R30/141 P(27-22-1) 342
Atl  D22 R26/116 P(34-18-0) 284
NE-Dillon 106R, Branch 107C,
Graham 119C, Brady 350P;
Atl-Finneran 103C

NO     3   0   0   0    3
GB    14  21  10   7   52
NO   D14 R26/95  P(35-14-3) 159
GB   D21 R28/84  P(28-20-0) 215
NO-Hakim 108C

Phi    0   3   7   0   10
Dal   17  10   3   3   33
Phi  D6  R19/91  P(30-16-0) 110
Dal  D28 R46/167 P(35-24-0) 289
Dal-Glenn 118C

Sea   14  10  10   3   37
Slr    7  14   7   3   31
Sea  D26 R30/134 P(38-27-0) 299
Slr  D20 R17/77  P(40-26-1) 309
Sea-Alexander 119R,
Jurevicius 137C, Hasselbeck 316P;
Slr-Holt 126C, Bulger 336P

TB     3   6   3   0   12
NYJ    0   7   0   7   14
TB   D20 R26/84  P(42-27-1) 201
NYJ  D15 R27/62  P(19-13-1) 150

Ten    7   3  14  10   34
Hot    0   6   3  11   20
Ten  D22 R31/90  P(31-22-0) 220
Hot  D14 R28/161 P(27-18-1)  96
Hot-Davis 130R

Was    7   3   0   9   19
Den    7   7   0   7   21
Was  D28 R26/125 P(53-30-0) 322
Den  D11 R28/165 P(26-10-0)  92
Was-Portis 103R, Moss 116C,
Brunell 322P; Den-Bell 127R
```

MONDAY, OCTOBER 10

```
Pit    0  14   0  10   24
SD     0   7   6   9   22
Pit  D25 R32/104 P(26-17-0) 207
SD   D20 R21/66  P(35-20-1) 213
```

SUNDAY, OCTOBER 16

```
Atl    3  14   0  17   34
NO     7   3   7  14   31
Atl  D21 R33/160 P(23-11-1) 106
NO   D32 R32/211 P(33-22-1) 245
Atl-Dunn 100R

Cin    0   7  10  14   31
Ten    7   0   0  16   23
Cin  D24 R28/119 P(33-27-0) 268
Ten  D21 R24/118 P(41-26-2) 259
Cin-Johnson 135C

Cle    0   0   3   0    3
Bal   14   0   0   2   16
Cle  D12 R18/70  P(29-16-1) 116
Bal  D16 R33/150 P(31-23-1) 201

Hot    0   3   7   0   10
Sea   14   7  14   7   42
Hot  D14 R22/67  P(33-19-0) 160
Sea  D31 R42/320 P(20-14-1) 139
Sea-Alexander 141R, Morris 104R

Jax    7   3   7   6   23
Pit    0  14   0   3   17
Jax  D17 R35/93  P(35-19-1) 153
Pit  D16 R30/73  P(28-11-3) 145

Mia    0   0   3   7   13
TB    10   0  17   0   27
Mia  D13 R18/64  P(43-21-0) 243
TB   D15 R34/180 P(26-18-0) 162
TB-Pittman 127R

Min    0   0   3   0    3
ChiB   0   0   7  14   28
Min  D16 R19/80  P(49-26-2) 203
ChiB D16 R30/95  P(25-16-1)  97
```

```
NE     3   0   3  14   20
Den    0  21   7   0   28
NE   D20 R30/89  P(46-24-0) 299
Den  D20 R34/178 P(24-17-0) 254
Den-Bell 114R, Smith 123C

NYG    3   3   0   7   13
Dal    0   7   0   6   3   16
NYG  D11 R19/91  P(29-14-1) 179
Dal  D25 R38/92  P(37-26-1) 293
NYG-Shockey 129C;
Dal-Johnson 120C, Bledsoe 312P

NYJ    0  10   7   0   17
Buf    7  10   7   3   27
NYJ  D17 R21/149 P(26-12-2) 126
Buf  D24 R39/177 P(26-18-2) 164
NYJ-Martin 148R, McCareins 116C;
Buf-McGahee 143R

SD    14  10   3   0   27
Oak    7   0   7   0   14
SD   D22 R41/190 P(21-15-0) 255
Oak  D19 R13/39  P(48-24-1) 271
SD-Tomlinson 140R

Was    0   7  14   0   21
KC     3   3  15   7   28
Was  D26 R28/101 P(41-25-0) 297
KC   D18 R32/96  P(25-15-0) 178
Was-Moss 173C, Brunell 331P;
KC-Holmes 100C
```

MONDAY, OCTOBER 17

```
Slr   17   3   0   8   28
Ind    0  14  10  21   45
Slr  D20 R21/105 P(29-23-3) 244
Ind  D31 R38/176 P(32-22-0) 187
Ind-James 143R
```

FRIDAY, OCTOBER 21

```
KC     7   7  10   6   30
Mia    0   6   7   0   13
KC   D24 R45/185 P(34-20-0) 277
Mia  D9  R14/94  P(31-12-1) 192
```

SUNDAY, OCTOBER 23

```
Bal    0   6   0   0    6
ChiB   7   0   3   0   10
Bal  D12 R22/66  P(32-18-0) 133
ChiB D17 R29/143 P(29-15-0) 133
ChiB-Jones 139R

Buf    7   3   0   7   17
Oak    0  17   7  14   38
Buf  D15 R23/84  P(27-19-0) 126
Oak  D26 R37/162 P(27-19-0) 254
Oak-Jordan 122R, Gabriel 101C

Dal    7   0   0   3   10
Sea    0   0   0  13   13
Dal  D16 R39/164 P(24-13-2) 111
Sea  D20 R22/72  P(42-23-2) 217

Den    6   7   7   3   23
NYG    7   3   0  14   24
Den  D20 R33/191 P(29-18-0) 194
NYG  D22 R20/97  P(42-23-1) 214
Den-Anderson 120R

Det    0   7   3   3   13
Cle    0   0   3   0    3
Det  D19 R37/119 P(34-22-0) 210
Cle  D11 R22/118 P(19-10-3)  56
Cle-Droughns 100R

Min    0   0  10  13   23
GB     0   7   3   7   17
GB   D19 R23/45  P(37-29-0) 329
Min  D24 R26/108 P(31-23-0) 255
GB-Driver 114C, Favre 315P

Ind    7   7  10  14   38
Hot    0  14   0   6   20
Ind  D30 R34/205 P(27-21-1) 232
Hot  D13 R33/133 P(9-6-1)     6
Ind-James 139R

NO    14   0   0   3   17
Slr    0   7   0  21   28
NO   D24 R32/119 P(39-18-1) 213
Slr  D16 R27/109 P(29-18-0) 189
NO-Hakim 100C

Pit    0   7  17   3   27
Cin    3   0   3   7   13
Pit  D20 R47/221 P(14-9-1)   83
Cin  D20 R19/91  P(36-21-2) 211
Pit-Parker 131R
```

```
SD      0   0   7  10  17
Phi     0   7   3  10  20
SD   D15 R20/21   P(40-23-2) 270
Phi  D22 R14/24   P(54-35-2) 262

SF      7   0   0  10  17
Was    14  21  10   7  52
SF   D9 R26/140   P(16-8-1)   54
Was  D24 R39/204  P(21-14-0) 253
Was-Portis 101R, Moss 112C

Ten    10   0   0   0  10
Arz     0  10   3   7  20
Ten  D16 R28/90   P(45-26-1) 258
Arz  D9 R22/55    P(28-12-1) 118
```

MONDAY, OCTOBER 24

```
NYJ     0   7   0   7  14
Atl    10  10   7   0  27
NYJ  D16 R18/37   P(38-23-1) 194
Atl  D19 R38/205  P(26-11-3) 105
Atl-Dunn 155R
```

SUNDAY, OCTOBER 30

```
Arz     3   7   3   0  13
Dal    10  14   3   7  34
Arz  D12 R24/71   P(34-16-2) 142
Dal  D21 R32/146  P(24-19-0) 202
Dal-Barber 127R

Buf     0   3   7   6  16
NE      0   0   7  14  21
Buf  D24 R39/147  P(33-20-1) 247
NE   D18 R22/93   P(21-14-0) 180
Buf-McGahee 136R, Moulds 125C

ChiB    0  13   0   0   6  19
Det     3   0   7   3   0  13
ChiB D14 R29/115  P(31-17-0) 218
Det  D17 R29/93   P(35-23-1) 185

Cle    10   0   3   3  16
Hot     7   3   3   6  19
Cle  D16 R33/156  P(25-12-0) 169
Hot  D11 R37/117  P(20-10-1) 120

GB      0   7   0   7  14
Cin     7   7   0   7  21
GB   D23 R22/76   P(39-26-5) 277
Cin  D21 R27/95   P(34-22-1) 222

Jax     7   7   0   7  21
Slr    14   3   0   7  24
Jax  D16 R28/221  P(31-18-1) 206
Slr  D15 R33/200  P(21-13-3) 186
Jax-Taylor 165R, Wilford 145C;
Slr-Jackson 179R, Curtis 105C

KC      0   3   7  10  20
SD      7  14   0   7  28
KC   D21 R21/95   P(43-31-0) 323
SD   D22 R22/83   P(44-26-1) 341
KC-Kennison 115C, Green 347P;
SD-Gates 145C, Brees 324P

Mia     3   6   2  10  21
NO      3   0   3   0   6
Mia  D20 R47/188  P(28-16-1) 154
NO   D14 R17/90   P(31-14-1) 100
Mia-Brown 106R

Min     0   0   7   6  13
Car    10  14   7   7  38
Min  D14 R18/82   P(32-16-0) 171
Car  D27 R39/111  P(31-21-0) 338
Car-Smith 201C, Delhomme 341P

Oak    17   7   7   3  34
Ten     0   0   3   3   6
Oak  D17 R23/92   P(29-17-1) 232
Ten  D19 R25/140  P(40-26-0) 186
Oak-Porter 123C

Phi     0   7  14   0  21
Den    14   0  14  21  49
Phi  D12 R19/79   P(34-12-2) 272
Den  D28 R36/255  P(35-22-0) 309
Phi-Owens 154C;
Den-Anderson 126R, Bell 107R,
Plummer 309P

TB      0   3   0   7  10
SF      0   0   0   0   0
TB   D13 R20/43   P(34-21-2) 232
SF   D9 R39/158   P(19-8-0)   50
TB-Galloway 149C; SF-Barlow 101R
```

```
Was     0   0   0   0   0
NYG     6  13  17   0  36
Was  D7 R13/381   P(34-14-1)  87
NYG  D19 R45/262  P(31-12-1) 124
NYG-Barber 206R
```

MONDAY, OCTOBER 31

```
Bal     7   3   0   9  19
Pit     7   3   7   3  20
Bal  D20 R27/72   P(44-25-2) 246
Pit  D19 R28/101  P(31-18-1) 160
```

SUNDAY, NOVEMBER 6

```
Atl     7   7   3   0  17
Mia     0  10   0   0  10
Atl  D27 R41/162  P(31-22-0) 220
Mia  D11 R25/105  P(22-13-1) 103

Car    10   7  10   7  34
TB      0   7   0   7  14
Car  D15 R32/77   P(18-11-0) 210
TB   D18 R17/44   P(42-25-2) 226
Car-Smith 106C

ChiB    3   7   3   7  20
NO      3   7   0   7  17
ChiB D15 R32/183  P(26-12-2) 131
NO   D15 R33/133  P(26-16-2) 150
NO-Smith 110R

Cin     0  14   0   7  21
Bal     3   3   0   3   9
Cin  D25 R35/95   P(26-19-0) 234
Bal  D17 R25/118  P(31-19-0) 122

Det     0   7   0   7  14
Min     3  21   0   3  27
Det  D20 R20/58   P(48-28-2) 231
Min  D19 R35/164  P(22-17-0) 150
Det-Vines 109C; Min-Bennett 106R

Hot     0   7   7   0  14
Jax     0   0   7  14  21
Hot  D17 R23/88   P(30-22-0) 191
Jax  D18 R27/98   P(25-19-0) 214

NYG     3   7   0  14  24
SF      0   0   6   0   6
NYG  D23 R32/93   P(33-18-0) 251
SF   D9 R22/52    P(21-12-1)  86

Oak     0   3   6  14  23
KC      0   6   7  14  27
Oak  D22 R26/101  P(40-21-1) 162
KC   D18 R24/114  P(35-22-0) 207
KC-Johnson 107R

Phi     7   0   3   0  10
Was     0  10   7   0  17
Phi  D17 R23/45   P(35-22-1) 291
Was  D17 R29/78   P(29-21-0) 215
Phi-McNabb 304P

Pit     6   7   0   7  20
GB      3   0   7   0  10
Pit  D13 R33/154  P(16-9-1)   59
GB   D16 R29/65   P(35-20-1) 203

SD     14   7   7   3  31
NYJ     0  10   3  13  26
SD   D27 R35/133  P(27-20-1) 262
NYJ  D19 R25/89   P(31-17-0) 180
SD-Tomlinson 107R, Gates 132C

Sea     3  14  10   6  33
Arz     3   3  10   3  19
Sea  D22 R33/208  P(20-13-0) 162
Arz  D23 R20/71   P(48-29-3) 307
Sea-Alexander 173R;
Arz-Fitzgerald 102C, Warner 334P

Ten     0   7   0   7  14
Cle     7   0  10   3  20
Ten  D19 R24/98   P(42-18-1) 225
Cle  D16 R32/169  P(34-18-1) 272
Cle-Droughns 116R
```

MONDAY, NOVEMBER 7

```
Ind     7  14  10   9  40
NE      7   0   7   7  21
Ind  D28 R38/132  P(37-28-1) 321
NE   D17 R14/34   P(22-15-2) 254
Ind-James 104R, Harrison 128C,
Wayne 124C, Manning 321P
```

SUNDAY, NOVEMBER 13

```
Arz     0   3   8  10  21
Det     9  10   7   3  29
Arz  D21 R16/38   P(45-29-0) 359
Det  D22 R32/157  P(31-21-0) 226
Arz-Fitzgerald 141C, Warner 359P;
Det-Williams 117C

Bal     3   0   0   0   3
Jax     0  10   7  13  30
Bal  D8 R17/53    P(33-19-3) 110
Jax  D20 R35/133  P(30-16-0) 205
Jax-Jones 106R, Jones 117C

Cle     7   0   0  14  21
Pit     0  17   7  10  34
Cle  D16 R19/61   P(34-17-1) 242
Pit  D25 R41/159  P(27-18-0) 223
Pit-Ward 124C

Den     0  13  10   8  31
Oak     0   0   0  17  17
Den  D18 R38/121  P(22-16-0) 205
Oak  D20 R17/60   P(50-26-3) 275
Oak-Collins 310P

GB     14   3   6  10  33
Atl     0  14  11   0  25
GB   D25 R29/107  P(40-27-1) 244
Atl  D19 R29/129  P(30-20-0) 192
GB-Gado 103R, Driver 114C

Hot     0   7  10   0  17
Ind     7  14   7   3  31
Hot  D11 R24/83   P(25-16-0) 126
Ind  D26 R29/126  P(35-26-0) 293
Ind-James 122R, Harrison 108C

KC      3   0   0   0   3
Buf     0   7   7   0  14
KC   D22 R32/150  P(40-23-3) 166
Buf  D9 R28/61    P(22-13-0) 148
KC-Johnson 132R

Min     0   7  14   3  24
NYG     0   6   7   8  21
Min  D11 R21/12   P(31-18-0) 125
NYG  D25 R29/124  P(48-23-4) 281
NYG-Barber 111C

NE      0   3   9  11  23
Mia     0   7   0   9  16
NE   D19 R25/91   P(36-21-2) 274
Mia  D22 R25/77   P(40-25-0) 360
Mia-Booker 102C, Frerotte 360P

NYJ     0   3   0   0   3
Car     7   3   0  20  30
NYJ  D15 R32/33   P(21-11-4)  77
Car  D15 R36/101  P(30-10-2) 119

SF      0   9   0   0   9
ChiB    0   7   0  10  17
SF   D9 R46/133   P(13-1-1)   28
ChiB D12 R40/172  P(14-8-1)   67
ChiB-Peterson 120R

Slr     3   0   6   7  16
Sea     3  14   7   7  31
Slr  D22 R21/75   P(40-28-1) 278
Sea  D21 R36/174  P(29-17-2) 243
Slr-Bulger 304P;
Sea-Alexander 165R

Was     3  10  15   7  35
TB      7  14   7   8  36
Was  D23 R33/185  P(35-23-2) 204
TB   D19 R27/61   P(29-15-0) 279
Was-Portis 144R; TB-Galloway 131C
```

MONDAY, NOVEMBER 14

```
Dal     7   0   0  14  21
Phi     7   3   3   7  20
Dal  D13 R24/58   P(24-17-1) 183
Phi  D21 R36/181  P(39-21-1) 178
```

SUNDAY, NOVEMBER 20

```
Arz     3  10   3  22  38
Slr     3   7  11   7  28
Arz  D27 R26/94   P(39-27-0) 278
Slr  D19 R12/6    P(43-33-0) 351
Arz-Boldin 105C, Fitzgerald 104C;
Slr-Holt 129C

Buf     3   7   0   0  10
SD     14  21   3  10  48
Buf  D12 R13/65   P(36-20-1) 137
SD   D28 R34/141  P(33-28-0) 337
SD-Brees 339P
```

```
Car     0   0   0   3   3
ChiB   10   3   0   0  13
Car  D13 R16/55   P(39-22-2) 183
ChiB D15 R31/122  P(26-15-1) 136
Car-Smith 169C

Det     0   7   0   0   7
Dal     7   6   7   0  20
Det  D11 R19/57   P(25-17-0) 169
Dal  D26 R42/149  P(23-12-0) 104

Ind    14  21   7   3  45
Cin    10  14   0  13  37
Ind  D28 R30/92   P(40-24-1) 359
Cin  D23 R26/164  P(38-25-1) 328
Ind-Clark 125C, Wayne 117C,
Manning 365P; Cin-Johnson 189C,
Palmer 335P

Jax     0   7  14  10  31
Ten     7  14   7   0  28
Jax  D22 R30/49   P(38-22-0) 246
Ten  D16 R21/63   P(30-20-1) 191

KC     10  21   0  14  45
Hot     7   0  10   0  17
KC   D28 R42/226  P(29-19-1) 220
Hot  D14 R19/78   P(36-19-1) 181
KC-Johnson 211R

Mia     0   0   0   0   0
Cle     9   3  10   0  22
Mia  D12 R25/139  P(28-9-2)   55
Cle  D19 R39/181  P(29-17-1) 195
Cle-Droughns 166R

NO      0   0   7  10  17
NE      7   7   7   3  24
NO   D23 R21/87   P(50-27-1) 338
NE   D20 R30/132  P(29-15-0) 194
NO-Brooks 343P

NYJ     0   0   0   0   0
Den     7  10   0  10  27
NYJ  D10 R8/19    P(32-20-2) 176
Den  D28 R48/191  P(26-18-0) 213
Den-Anderson 113R

Oak     3   0   7   6  16
Was     7   6   0   0  13
Oak  D16 R29/50   P(36-19-1) 286
Was  D13 R27/108  P(32-14-0) 138
Oak-Porter 142C

Phi     0   0  10   7  17
NYG     0  10   3  14  27
Phi  D20 R30/106  P(39-18-1) 298
NYG  D17 R29/115  P(26-17-0) 200
NYG-Barber 112R, Burress 113C

Pit     0   6   0   7   0  13
Bal     0   3   0   3  10  16
Pit  D17 R25/70   P(38-21-1) 212
Bal  D18 R38/104  P(36-21-1) 137
Pit-Williams 116R

Sea     3  14  10   0  27
SF      3   6   3  13  25
Sea  D21 R34/145  P(31-19-0) 228
SF   D17 R26/110  P(29-18-0) 226
Sea-Alexander 115R; SF-Lloyd 119C

TB     10   3   7  10  30
Atl     0  10   7  10  27
TB   D15 R27/140  P(19-11-1) 118
Atl  D26 R36/150  P(38-21-0) 293
TB-Williams 116R; Atl-White 108C,
Vick 306P
```

MONDAY, NOVEMBER 21

```
Min     0   7   7   6  20
GB      7   7   0   3  17
Min  D22 R37/160  P(30-18-1) 171
GB   D19 R14/21   P(33-20-2) 215
Min-Moore 122R
```

TUESDAY, NOVEMBER 24

```
Atl    10   7  10   0  27
Det     0   0   7   0   7
Atl  D22 R45/256  P(22-12-1) 146
Det  D20 R13/75   P(48-25-2) 229
Atl-Dunn 116R, Crumpler 104C

Den     7   7   7   3  24
Dal     7   0   7   7  21
Den  D13 R20/144  P(24-15-1) 149
Dal  D23 R32/85   P(44-29-2) 229
```

SUNDAY, NOVEMBER 27

```
Bal     0   0  14  15  29
Cin     3  14  17   8  42
Bal  D23 R33/133  P(32-18-2) 189
Cin  D23 R32/135  P(30-22-1) 302
Bal-Lewis 113R; Cin-Johnson 114R,
Houshmandzadeh 147C,
Palmer 302P

Car     0   3   3   7  13
Buf     0   6   0   3   9
Car  D19 R33/113  P(27-20-0) 182
Buf  D14 R23/55   P(29-16-1) 161

ChiB    0   3   3   7  13
TB      3   0   0   7  10
ChiB D15 R33/118  P(28-14-1) 121
TB   D15 R25/107  P(30-19-0) 168
TB-Galloway 138C

Cle     0   3   6   3  12
Min     3   7   7   7  24
Cle  D20 R20/78   P(36-23-3) 184
Min  D18 R31/81   P(28-19-1) 200

GB      7   7   0   0  14
Phi    10   0   3   6  19
GB   D18 R30/128  P(33-15-2) 164
Phi  D15 R35/176  P(28-12-0)  88
GB-Gado 111R;
Phi-Westbrook 120R

Jax     7   3   7   0  17
Arz     0   3   0  14  17
Jax  D19 R33/162  P(28-14-0) 133
Arz  D23 R16/67   P(46-29-1) 301
Arz-Boldin 115C, Warner 315P

Mia     7   7   9  10  33
Oak     0   7   7   7  21
Mia  D21 R32/145  P(31-18-1) 249
Oak  D24 R25/129  P(37-21-2) 185
Mia-Chambers 101C

NE      0   3   7   6  16
KC      7  12   7   0  26
NE   D20 R18/74   P(40-22-4) 232
KC   D24 R37/112  P(26-19-0) 308
KC-Johnson 119R, Green 323P

NO      0  14   0   7  21
NYJ     3   6   7   3  19
NO   D18 R25/97   P(23-17-0) 172
NYJ  D19 R35/118  P(28-19-0) 242

NYG     0  10   3   8  21
Sea     7   0   7  10  24
NYG  D25 R28/166  P(53-29-1) 324
Sea  D17 R34/127  P(37-21-1) 228
NYG-Barber 151R, Burress 109C,
Shockey 127C, Manning 344P;
Sea-Alexander 110R,
Jurevicius 137C

SD      0   7  10   6  23
Was     3   7   0   0  10
SD   D24 R28/202  P(45-22-3) 195
Was  D15 R33/91   P(27-17-0) 191
SD-Tomlinson 184R

SF      0  14   0   8  22
Ten     3   6  21   3  33
SF   D15 R22/74   P(43-23-2) 187
Ten  D15 R27/118  P(41-23-1) 343
Ten-Brown 105C, McNair 343P

Slr     0   3   7  17   6  33
Hot     7  17   0   7   0  31
Slr  D22 R29/138  P(33-21-1) 291
Hot  D26 R31/124  P(35-25-1) 288
Slr-Jackson 110R, Holt 130C,
Fitzpatrick 310P; Hot-Johnson 159C,
Carr 393P
```

MONDAY, NOVEMBER 28

```
Pit     7   0   0   0   7
Ind    10   6   7   3  26
Pit  D10 R25/86   P(26-17-2) 111
Ind  D17 R32/127  P(25-15-1) 239
Ind-James 124R, Harrison 128C
```

SUNDAY, DECEMBER 4

```
Arz     3   0   6   8  17
SF      0   7   3   0  10
Arz  D18 R23/65   P(45-29-2) 339
SF   D11 R20/51   P(24-16-3) 169
Arz-Boldin 156C, Fitzgerald 129C,
Warner 354P
```

```
Atl    3   3   0   0    6
Car    7   7   0  10   24
Atl   D14 R24/111  P(35-17-2) 148
Car   D14 R34/142  P(27-17-1) 164
Car-Foster 131R

Buf   21   0   2       23
Mia    0   3  21       24
Buf   D16 R33/92  P(27-14-1) 202
Mia   D26 R22/73  P(65-34-1) 361
Buf-Evans 117C;
Mia-Chambers 238C

Cin    7  14  10   7   38
Pit   14   3   7   7   31
Cin   D21 R25/102  P(38-22-0) 222
Pit   D28 R28/95   P(41-29-3) 379
Pit-Ward 135C, Roethlisberger 386P

Dal    0   0  10   0   10
NYG    0  10   7   0   17
Dal   D16 R27/81  P(39-15-2) 125
NYG   D17 R34/127 P(31-12-2) 150
NYG-Barber 115R

Den    7  14   3   3   27
KC     7  14   3   7   31
Den   D19 R29/131 P(29-18-2) 257
KC    D24 R37/168 P(23-16-2) 253
KC-Johnson 140R, Kennison 108C

GB     0   7   0   0    7
ChiB   0  10   0   9   19
GB    D26 R24/100 P(58-31-2) 258
ChiB  D10 R31/141 P(17-6-1) 49

Hot    3   3   0   9   15
Bal    0   7   0   9   16
Hot   D16 R34/165 P(37-17-1) 133
Bal   D15 R23/73  P(33-17-0) 165
Hot-Davis 155R

Jax    3   0  17   0   20
Cle    0  14   0   0   14
Jax   D17 R38/122 P(20-11-1) 115
Cle   D15 R32/98  P(20-13-0) 205
Jax-Jones 103R

Min    7   7   7   0   21
Det    3   3   3   7   16
Min   D20 R32/103 P(23-17-0) 242
Det   D19 R23/105 P(35-17-1) 118
Min-James 107R, Robinson 148C

NYJ    0   3   0   0    3
NE     0   6   7   3   16
NYJ   D12 R16/41  P(37-15-1) 123
NE    D24 R35/146 P(37-27-0) 251

Oak    3   0   0       10
SD     3  14   7  10   34
Oak   D16 R17/81  P(40-22-1) 210
SD    D19 R37/130 P(22-17-0) 144

TB     0   7   0   3   10
NO     0   3   0   0    3
TB    D14 R30/133 P(21-12-0) 115
NO    D16 R27/65  P(34-18-4) 214

Ten    0   0   0   3    3
Ind    7   7  14   7   35
Ten   D17 R19/53  P(39-26-0) 207
Ind   D21 R31/105 P(17-13-0) 187
Ind-James 107R

Was    7   3   0  14   24
Slr    0   7   0   2    9
Was   D19 R40/257 P(22-14-0) 150
Slr   D13 R17/49  P(36-21-1) 142
Was-Cartwright 118R, Portis 136R
```

MONDAY, DECEMBER 5

```
Sea   14  21   7   0   42
Phi    0   0   0   0    0
Sea   D14 R42/96  P(17-8-0) 98
Phi   D11 R25/61  P(39-17-4) 129
```

SUNDAY, DECEMBER 11

```
Bal    3   0   0   7   10
Den    3   0   6   3   12
Bal   D20 R23/72  P(40-23-2) 251
Den   D17 R32/96  P(33-19-0) 222
Bal-Clayton 105C

ChiB   3   0   0   6    9
Pit    7   7   7   0   21
ChiB  D15 R18/83  P(35-17-0) 185
Pit   D20 R46/190 P(20-13-0) 173
Pit-Bettis 101R
```

```
Cle    7   7   3   3   20
Cin    7   6   7   3   23
Cle   D15 R26/84  P(24-16-1) 124
Cin   D18 R34/185 P(27-13-1) 93
Cin-Johnson 169R

Det   13   0   0   0   0  13
GB     3   7   0   3   16
Det   D11 R31/129 P(24-13-0) 112
GB    D19 R35/181 P(32-21-1) 149
GB-Gado 171R

Hot    3   7   0   0   10
Ten    0   3   7   3   13
Hot   D12 R26/152 P(26-17-0) 82
Ten   D15 R30/93  P(30-18-0) 208
Hot-Davis 139R

Ind    7  10   6   3   26
Jax    0   3   0  15   18
Ind   D25 R34/99  P(37-24-0) 300
Jax   D18 R23/74  P(35-26-0) 250
Ind-Harrison 137C, Manning 324P;
Jax-Smith 102C

KC     7   7   7   7   28
Dal    0  17   0  14   31
KC    D25 R28/161 P(32-20-0) 332
Dal   D21 R28/129 P(34-22-0) 316
KC-Johnson 143R, Green 340P;
Dal-Glenn 138C, Bledsoe 332P

Mia    0   3  17   3   23
SD     7   0   0  14   21
Mia   D14 R26/71  P(22-14-0) 229
SD    D27 R27/96  P(52-35-1) 245
Mia-Chambers 121C;
SD-Gates 123C

NE     7   7   7  14   35
Buf    8  12  14         17
NE    D32 R41/159 P(40-30-2) 335
Buf   D8  R12/14  P(27-10-3) 169
NE-Dillon 102R, Brady 329P

NYG    7  10   3   3   3  26
Phi    7  10   0   6   0  23
NYG   D28 R40/138 P(44-28-3) 299
Phi   D17 R25/175 P(32-14-0) 162
NYG-Barber 124R, Shockey 107C,
Manning 312P; Phi-Moats 114R

Oak    0   3   0   7   10
NYJ    3   3   6  14   26
Oak   D14 R17/95  P(26-14-2) 84
NYJ   D23 R43/184 P(26-14-0) 110

SF     0   0   0   0    0
Sea    7  17  14   3   41
SF    D8  R21/62  P(22-9-1) 51
Sea   D31 R40/185 P(30-24-1) 253
Sea-Alexander 108R,
Hasselbeck 226P,

Slr    0   6   0   7   13
Min    6   7  14   0   27
Slr   D20 R29/108 P(45-26-5) 229
Min   D16 R29/113 P(25-16-0) 146

TB     7   3   3   7   20
Car    0   0   3   7   10
TB    D17 R36/114 P(27-20-0) 133
Car   D14 R20/82  P(33-21-1) 194
TB-Williams 112R; Car-Smith 103C

Was    0   3  14   0   17
Arz    0  10   3   0   13
Was   D16 R34/109 P(28-18-3) 122
Arz   D17 R18/62  P(41-25-1) 240
Was-Portis 105R; Arz-Boldin 114C
```

MONDAY, DECEMBER 12

```
NO     3  14   0   0   17
Atl    7  14   9   6   36
NO    D22 R24/125 P(46-27-0) 207
Atl   D19 R32/127 P(25-13-1) 279
```

SATURDAY, DECEMBER 17

```
Den    0   7  14   7   28
Buf    7   0   3   7   17
Den   D27 R37/178 P(37-20-0) 259
Buf   D17 R16/75  P(35-22-0) 197
Den-Smith 137R; Buf-Moulds 110C
```

```
KC     0   3   7   7   17
NYG    0  10   3  14   27
KC    D22 R34/188 P(28-15-1) 174
NYG   D22 R34/223 P(32-17-1) 183
KC-Johnson 167R;
NYG-Barber 220R

TB     0   0   0   0    0
NE     7  14   0   7   28
TB    D12 R18/30  P(34-21-0) 108
NE    D22 R32/83  P(31-20-0) 253
NE-Givens 137C
```

SUNDAY, DECEMBER 18

```
Arz    3   7   0   9   19
Hot    0  24   3   3   30
Arz   D16 R13/39  P(38-25-2) 262
Hot   D18 R35/119 P(33-22-1) 134
Arz-Boldin 134C

Atl    0   3   0   0    3
ChiB   0   6  10   0   16
Atl   D12 R31/114 P(32-13-2) 117
ChiB  D14 R32/128 P(26-11-1) 98

Car    2  10   7   3   27
NO     7   0   0   3   10
Car   D19 R43/161 P(21-13-1) 165
NO    D15 R22/94  P(34-17-4) 183
NO-Stallworth 102C

Cin   17   7   7  10   41
Det    0   7   3   7   17
Cin   D29 R32/155 P(42-30-2) 271
Det   D13 R17/59  P(28-19-3) 211
Cin-Johnson 117R, Harrison 135C,
Manning 336P

Cle    0   3   3   3    9
Oak    0   0   0   7    7
Cle   D13 R26/70  P(32-21-1) 185
Oak   D16 R31/143 P(30-14-1) 113
Oak-Jordan 132R

Dal    0   0   0   7    7
Was    7  21   7   0   35
Dal   D13 R24/109 P(29-16-3) 107
Was   D19 R40/171 P(20-12-0) 163
Was-Portis 112R, Brunell 163P

NYJ    0  10   7   3   20
Mia    7   0   3  14   24
NYJ   D24 R25/99  P(42-28-0) 298
Mia   D14 R31/128 P(29-14-1) 169
NYJ-Jolley 102C, Bollinger 327P

Phi    0   7   3   7   17
Slr    3  10   3   0   16
Phi   D13 R28/125 P(28-15-3) 76
Slr   D16 R36/178 P(35-18-1) 127

Pit    3   7   6   2   18
Min    3   0   0   0    3
Pit   D14 R39/142 P(15-10-0) 133
Min   D11 R17/54  P(30-16-2) 131

SD    10   3   3  10   26
Ind    0   0  17   0   17
SD    D18 R37/206 P(33-22-2) 247
Ind   D21 R15/24  P(45-26-2) 314
SD-Turner 113R; Ind-Harrison 135C,
Manning 336P

Sea   14   0   7   7   28
Ten    0  14  10   0   24
Sea   D26 R33/183 P(27-21-0) 276
Ten   D25 R26/81  P(39-24-0) 336
Sea-Alexander 172R;
Ten-Troupe 116C, McNair 310P

SF     3   3   0   3    9
Jax    0   7   0   3   10
SF    D11 R25/110 P(24-8-1) 107
Jax   D21 R35/134 P(40-21-0) 202
```

MONDAY, DECEMBER 19

```
GB     3   0   0   0    3
Bal   14  10  10  14   48
GB    D16 R19/107 P(44-22-3) 181
Bal   D25 R38/182 P(27-19-0) 253
Bal-Lewis 105R, Heap 110C
```

SATURDAY, DECEMBER 24

```
Atl    7  10   0   7   0  24
TB     7   7   0  10   3  27
Atl   D19 R36/154 P(26-16-0) 127
TB    D30 R37/174 P(42-29-2) 270
TB-Williams 150R
```

```
Buf    6   7   7  17   37
Cin    0  14  10   3   27
Buf   D19 R25/67  P(31-24-1) 288
Cin   D23 R23/104 P(38-27-2) 270
Buf-Evans 107C, Holcomb 308P;
Cin-Johnson 117C

Dal    7   3   7   7   24
Car   10   3   0   7   20
Dal   D22 R41/214 P(23-15-1) 180
Car   D13 R24/71  P(31-14-1) 247
Dal-Jones 194R; Car-Proehl 104C

Det    0   7   0   6   13
NO     0   3   6   3   12
Det   D14 R24/71  P(30-17-1) 208
NO    D19 R25/47  P(38-21-0) 226
Det-Williams 111C

Ind    3   3   0   7   13
Sea    7   7   7   7   28
Ind   D20 R23/43  P(43-31-0) 344
Sea   D21 R30/173 P(21-17-0) 159
Ind-Stokley 122C; Sea-Alexander 139R

Jax    7   3   7  21   38
Hot    3  10   0   7   20
Jax   D30 R33/172 P(31-18-0) 276
Hot   D18 R29/107 P(29-19-1) 263
Jax-Taylor 101R, Wilford 118C;
Hot-Bradford 101C, Johnson 119C

NYG    0   3   0   0   3  20
Was   14   7   7   7      35
NYG   D18 R19/99  P(42-23-1) 233
Was   D22 R43/156 P(19-13-1) 224
Was-Portis 108R, Moss 160C

Oak    0   0   0   3    3
Den    6   6   0   6   22
Oak   D15 R17/87  P(41-17-1) 161
Den   D24 R40/155 P(29-19-1) 259
Den-Lelie 110C

Phi    0   7   0  14   21
Arz    6   7   7   7   27
Phi   D11 R17/43  P(36-14-1) 146
Arz   D19 R32/75  P(38-27-1) 285

Pit   14   6  14   7   41
Cle    0   0   0   0    0
Pit   D20 R35/209 P(21-14-0) 248
Cle   D12 R19/63  P(39-20-0) 123
Pit-Parker 130R, Ward 105C

SD     7   0   0   0    7
KC     7  13   0   0   20
SD    D15 R20/80  P(33-18-1) 153
KC    D20 R37/144 P(35-19-0) 197
KC-Johnson 131R

SF     7  10   0   7   24
Slr    7  17   0   0   20
SF    D15 R29/217 P(16-12-0) 104
Slr   D20 R21/44  P(41-33-2) 345
SF-Hicks 109R; Slr-Holt 163C,
Martin 354P

Ten    3   0   0   7   10
Mia    0  17   0   7   24
Ten   D11 R25/92  P(37-19-2) 142
Mia   D19 R38/192 P(30-14-1) 130
Mia-Williams 172R
```

SUNDAY, DECEMBER 25

```
ChiB   7   7  10   0   24
GB     0   7   0  10   17
ChiB  D16 R33/135 P(23-11-1) 197
GB    D24 R21/65  P(51-30-4) 300
ChiB-Jones 105R; GB-Driver 107C,
Favre 317P

Min    7   7   6   3   23
Bal    7   3   7  13   30
Min   D18 R14/42  P(36-25-0) 220
Bal   D23 R32/88  P(34-24-1) 279
Bal-Mason 103C
```

MONDAY, DECEMBER 26

```
NE     7  14   7   3   31
NYJ    7   0   0  14   21
NE    D26 R50/151 P(30-19-1) 170
NYJ   D10 R10/40  P(26-14-1) 131
```

SATURDAY, DECEMBER 31

```
Den    0  14   2   7   23
SD     0   7   0   0    7
Den   D17 R40/157 P(22-10-0) 84
SD    D15 R20/91  P(36-20-1) 145

NYG    7  13   7   3   30
Oak    7   7   7   0   21
NYG   D13 R34/211 P(24-12-0) 191
Oak   D21 R17/25  P(48-26-0) 300
NYG-Barber 203R, Burress 128C;
Oak-Gabriel 100C, Moss 116C,
Collins 331P
```

SUNDAY, JANUARY 1

```
Arz    0   3   7   3   13
Ind    0   0  10   7   17
Arz   D23 R31/129 P(42-31-1) 284
Ind   D15 R10/11  P(32-21-1) 207

Bal    0  13   3   0   16
Cle    0   6  14   0   20
Bal   D12 R32/129 P(36-15-2) 138
Cle   D12 R23/54  P(38-22-1) 172
Cle-Bryant 123C

Buf    3  10  10   3   26
NYJ    3  14   3  10   30
Buf   D21 R30/159 P(37-23-4) 172
NYJ   D12 R27/81  P(20-11-0) 126
Buf-McGahee 113R

Car   14  13  10   7   44
Atl    3   0   0   8   11
Car   D23 R38/229 P(25-16-0) 174
Atl   D15 R15/26  P(25-7-1) 185
Car-Foster 165R, Smith 131C

ChiB   0   0   7   0    7
Min    0  17   7  10   34
ChiB  D13 R33/154 P(23-14-0) 97
Min   D22 R18/149 P(40-27-0) 247

Cin    0   0   0   3    3
KC     3  17  10   7   37
Cin   D10 R22/37  P(32-18-2) 124
KC    D24 R32/202 P(29-21-0) 335
KC-Johnson 201R, Kennison 151C,
Green 344P

Det   14   0   7   0   21
Pit   14   7  14   0   35
Det   D16 R25/105 P(33-17-0) 203
Pit   D20 R44/199 P(16-7-2) 132
Pit-Parker 135R

Hot   10   0   7   0   17
SF     0   7  10   0   3  20
Hot   D13 R25/88  P(36-18-2) 196
SF    D19 R47/182 P(29-16-1) 142
SF-Gore 108R

Mia    6   6   5  10   28
NE     7   3   3  13   26
Mia   D25 R40/148 P(35-22-0) 230
NE    D16 R28/55  P(28-14-1) 204
Mia-Williams 108R

NO     0   0   0   3   13
TB     7  10   0  10   27
NO    D18 R23/71  P(37-25-2) 235
TB    D14 R26/149 P(25-12-0) 136

Sea    0   7  10   0      
GB     6   7   7   3   23
Sea   D17 R30/98  P(25-15-1) 147
GB    D21 R33/68  P(37-24-1) 246
GB-Driver 118C

Slr    0  10   0  10   20
Dal    7   3   0   0   10
Slr   D20 R33/106 P(32-19-0) 147
Dal   D15 R22/57  P(39-18-2) 214

Ten    0   0   0  13   13
Jax   17  10  13   0   40
Ten   D15 R22/99  P(39-21-1) 171
Jax   D25 R35/122 P(31-19-0) 213
Jax-Toefield 102R

Was    7   3   7  14   31
Phi   10   7   3   0   20
Was   D14 R36/151 P(25-9-1) 128
Phi   D18 R25/96  P(42-21-2) 239
Was-Portis 112R
```

A HISTORY OF *MONDAY NIGHT FOOTBALL*

From the moment Pete Rozelle became National Football League commissioner in 1960, he was relentless in his efforts to expand the relationship between pro football and television. He saw how putting games on the air could not just bring in money, but could also dramatically expand the league's popularity by bringing games to new audiences.

During his first three years as commissioner, Rozelle's efforts had resulted in a tenfold increase in broadcasting revenue. Despite increasing competition from the rival American Football League, the NFL had become a staple on Sunday afternoon television. The ratings were soaring, but Rozelle knew that even larger audiences could be found in prime time.

The idea was greeted with skepticism from all quarters. The networks doubted that pro football games could draw ratings equal to regular nighttime programming. Team owners worried whether they could draw crowds on a weekday night. NCAA president Walter Byers feared that pro football games on Friday or Saturday would overshadow college and high school games.

Rozelle set his sites on Monday nights, a concept that wasn't completely new. It had first been tried 30 years earlier. On October 22, 1934, the Detroit Lions hosted the Brooklyn Dodgers under the lights at Titan Stadium. Only 10,000 fans showed up, but that didn't discourage the Lions from scheduling another Monday night game two years later. In their 1946 inaugural season, the Miami Seahawks of the All-America Football Conference scheduled four Monday night games late in the season as an attempt to boost flagging attendance. While the concept didn't help save the Seahawks from folding at season's end, other owners embraced the novelty with various degrees of success. In all, there were 24 Monday night games played between 1934 and 1952. As entertainment programming became a more important part of networks' schedules, the idea of devoting three hours to a football game became less appealing to them.

Rozelle believed that times had changed. He argued that the popularity of both television and pro football had grown tremendously in the intervening years, and that the two were perfectly suited for each other. Two Monday night games were scheduled for 1964, and while they weren't nationally televised, they definitely proved Rozelle's point. A record crowd turned out in Detroit on September 28, and more than 60,000 fans packed Baltimore's Memorial Stadium two weeks later.

Over the next three years, the St. Louis Cardinals hosted one Monday night game each season. By 1967 Rozelle had convinced CBS to broadcast the game nationally. It worked well enough that the league scheduled two Monday night games in each of the next two seasons, and the AFL played one in 1968 and again in 1969. By then, it was clear to everybody that football in prime time was a winning idea.

With the AFL and NFL merging in 1970, both CBS and NBC networks had contracts to televise games on Sunday. Neither network seemed too interested in adding a Monday night game to their regular schedule, but Rozelle found a willing partner in ABC. In a three-network world, ABC's ratings were usually the lowest, but their fresh approach to sports coverage was not going unnoticed. They had a young producer named Roone Arledge who was changing the way sports were being broadcast.

Football games (and other sporting events) had been televised as if they were news events. The networks typically used a stationary camera for most of the shots, with an announcer who reported the facts as they were unfolding. Arledge recognized that the medium of television offered the opportunity to make the viewer feel closer to the action. He used that approach to create the popular program *Wide World of Sports*. Arledge took track meets and other less popular sporting events and highlighted the human drama of athletic competition. The famous tagline captured the philosophy and spirit behind the program: "The thrill of victory and the agony of defeat."

Arledge brought this same approach to his production of *Monday Night Football*, firm in his belief that the idea wasn't simply putting NFL games on in prime time, but turning Monday nights into an event. Some of this was accomplished with the groundbreaking technical advances of director Chet Forte. He doubled the number of cameras used for each game. Some were mounted on carts that could be moved up and down the sideline. Others were handheld cameras at field level, offering sidelined shots and reverse angle views of the plays. A separate crew was dedicated to running instant replay equipment and another to generating on-screen graphics.

The first episode of *Monday Night Football* aired on September 21, 1970, a game between the New York Jets and Cleveland Browns. It was an instant success. Thirty-five percent of the American viewing audience tuned in, and while the game wasn't particularly well played, critics raved about the quality of the presentation. It wasn't just the viewers who were excited.

Mayors and governors saw that hosting a Monday night game was a great way to showcase their communities. Aerial coverage and shots of an illuminated skyline painted an indelible portrait of a big league city. Politicians and movie stars stopped by the booth to talk about what they were doing and to show that they were on the scene. Halftime shows attracted the biggest names in entertainment. From the very beginning, *Monday Night Football* was not just a game, it was a cultural event.

LEGENDS IN THE BOOTH

Arledge's biggest innovation, however, was the introduction of the three-man commentator booth. Rather than using just one man to provide color commentary, Arledge opted for two, and the pair he picked would be legendary. Don Meredith, the former Cowboys quarterback, had a jovial light-hearted style, a self-described "good old boy." He was paired with Howard Cosell, a broadcasting veteran who brought an intellectual approach to his duties. In an era when many sportscasters avoided controversial issues and shied away from criticizing the athletes that they covered, Cosell seemed to be at his best when discussing these issues. "I'm just telling it like it is," he said.

Meredith and Cosell often sparred during the game, trading barbs or disagreeing over their analysis of what was happening on the field. Audiences loved the exchanges. In a *TV Guide* poll, viewers named Cosell as both the most loved sportscaster and the most hated sportscaster. Meredith won an Emmy for his work that first season. Frank Gifford joined the crew in its second season, replacing Keith Jackson. Gifford brought both the experience from his Hall of Fame playing career and the steadying presence needed to keep Cosell and Meredith in check. Even those who could not stand Cosell looked forward to his halftime highlights of the Sunday games. The clips were prepared by NFL Films and usually done in one take by Cosell before Monday's game. At a time when footage of out-of-town games was rarely seen, it was must-see TV for football fans. And it was a way for even the least desirable teams to be recognized by the most-watched show in sports.

The names in the booth changed over the years, but the quality of their work never diminished. Cosell left the show at the end of the 1983 season and Meredith left a year later. When Al Michaels came on board in 1986, Gifford shifted from doing play-by-play to doing color commentary.

John Madden joined the show in 2002. He had won 13 Emmys for his work as an analyst for football telecasts on CBS and Fox. He would win two more in his four years with *Monday Night Football*. In all, *Monday Night Football* announcers have won a total of eight individual Emmys for their work on the show. In 1975 the show itself received the first Emmy Award for Outstanding Live Sports Series, and would win the award eight more times (1978, 1987, 1989, 1993, 1994, 1997, 2004, and 2005). Cosell, Gifford, and Arledge would all receive an Emmy for Lifetime Achievement. The show that became the longest-running prime time sports series in television history broadcast its final game on ABC during the 2005 season. *Monday Night Football* moves to ESPN in fall 2006 with new announcers Mike Tirico, Joe Theismann, and Tony Kornheiser.

Monday Night Football Broadcasters

Play-by-Play
Keith Jackson, 1970
Frank Gifford, 1971–85
Al Michaels, 1986–05
Mike Tirico, 2006

Color Commentators
Howard Cosell, 1970–83
Don Meredith, 1970–73, 1977–84
Alex Karras, 1974–76
Fran Tarkenton, 1979–82
O. J. Simpson, 1983–85
Joe Namath, 1985
Frank Gifford, 1986–97
Dan Dierdorf, 1987–98
Boomer Esiason, 1998–99
Dan Fouts, 2000–01
Dennis Miller, 2000–01
John Madden, 2002–05
Tony Kornheiser, 2006
Joe Theismann, 2006

Sideline Reporters
Lynn Swann, 1994–97
Lesley Visser, 1998–99
Eric Dickerson, 2000–01
Melissa Stark, 2000–02
Lisa Guerrero, 2003
Michele Tafoya, 2004–06
Sam Ryan, 2005
Suzy Kolber, 2006

Others
Gary Bender, 1987, play-by-play (second game)
Lynn Swann, 1987, color commentator (second game)
Mike Patrick, 1997, 2005, play-by-play (second game)
Joe Theismann, 1997, 2005, color commentator (second game)
Paul Maguire, 1997, 2005, color commentator (second game)

Twenty Memorable Monday Night Games

September 21, 1970: Cleveland Browns 31, New York Jets 21.
Monday Night Football debuted in Cleveland before a record crowd of 85,703 at Municipal Stadium. The New York Jets, perhaps the most popular of the AFL teams, were making their NFL debut in the week after the long-awaited merger of the once rival leagues. Quarterback Joe Namath was sharp, and the Jets had 455 yards in total offense compared to just 221 for the Browns. Mistakes doomed the Jets, however. New York committed 4 turnovers and was flagged for a team record 161 penalty yards. It was the third night game of the opening week. Games were played in Los Angeles Friday night and New York Saturday night, the only night games other than Monday all year.

December 3, 1973: Miami Dolphins 30, Pittsburgh Steelers 26.
With Steelers quarterback Terry Bradshaw recovering from a broken collarbone, backup Jim Gilliam made his first NFL start in his place. It was a disastrous debut. Gilliam's first 3 passes were intercepted, and 2 were returned for touchdowns. Miami's No-Name Defense was relentless, and the Dolphins jumped to a 30–3 first-half lead. Miami safety Dick Anderson had 4 of his team's 6 interceptions, returning 2 for touchdowns. A late rally made the score sound close.

September 16, 1974: Buffalo Bills 21, Oakland Raiders 20.
For the first 58 minutes, this game was a low scoring affair. The Raiders were nursing a 13–7 lead, but the game got wild at the finish. With 1:56 left to play, quarterback Joe Ferguson connected with Ahmad Rashad for a 9-yard touchdown pass that gave Buffalo a 14-13 lead. The Raiders retook the lead with a touchdown 5 plays later, and the Bills responded with an 8-play, 72-yard drive, capped by another touchdown catch by Rashad. Oakland made a last ditch effort to

swing the score back in their favor, but kicker George Blanda—one day shy of his 47th birthday—missed a 50-yard field goal with six seconds left.

September 18, 1978: Baltimore Colts 34, New England Patriots 27. Baltimore running back Joe Washington turned in one of the most remarkable individual performances in *Monday Night Football* history. His Colts had been outscored 80–0 in their first two games of the season, but they exploded for 27 points in the fourth quarter to upset the Patriots. Washington accounted for 3 touchdowns in the final period, starting with a 54-yard pass to Roger Carr on a halfback option play. He caught a 23-yard touchdown pass on Baltimore's next possession, and then he scored the game-winner on a 90-yard kickoff return.

November 20, 1978: Houston Oilers 35, Miami Dolphins 30. The irresistible force of rookie running back Earl Campbell met the immovable object that was Miami's vaunted defense. At the end of the day, there was no doubt who had prevailed. With his team trailing, 23—21, in the fourth quarter, Campbell put Houston ahead with a 12-yard touchdown run. Minutes later, he sealed the victory with an 80-yard run down the right sideline that mesmerized the crowd and left the Dolphins defenders speechless. Campbell finished with 199 yards and 4 touchdowns on the night, en route to both Rookie of the Year and Most Valuable Player honors.

January 3, 1983: Minnesota Vikings 31, Dallas Cowboys 27. It was the last game of the season and the first *Monday Night Football* broadcast in a new calendar year. Both teams were heading for the playoffs and not much was going right this night for the Cowboys, but it still had one of the show's most memorable moments. Trailing 24–13, Dallas return man Timmy Newsome fumbled a kickoff out of bounds at the 1-yard line, and on the ensuing play, the Cowboys offense only had 10 men on the field. Tony Dorsett, who had been held in check by the Minnesota defense all night, made the most of a bad situation. He took a handoff up the middle, cut to the right sideline, and ran 99 yards for a touchdown. It was the longest run in NFL history, and although it wasn't enough to give the Cowboys a win, it remains one of pro football's most memorable plays.

September 5, 1983: Dallas Cowboys 31, Washington Redskins 30. The 1983 season began with a contest between bitter division rivals, a rematch of the 1982 NFC Championship Game. The Redskins seemed to still be invincible, jumping to a 23–3 halftime lead. Dallas quarterback Danny White completed just 1 of 9 pass attempts for 10 yards in the first half, but came to life after intermission. He ran for a touchdown and threw three more, including scoring passes of 51 and 75 yards to Tony Hill. Dallas took the lead for good with two minutes left, capping a remarkable comeback.

October 17, 1983: Green Bay Packers 48, Washington Redskins 47. The defending champion Redskins lost just twice in 1983. Both were Monday night thrillers and both were by a single point. Green Bay and Washington each scored on a fumble recovery in the first quarter, but the defenses seemed to disappear after that. The Packers moved the ball at will, taking a 31–20 lead early in the third quarter. Washington's offense battled back, with the lead changing five times in the fourth quarter. A 20-yard field goal by kicker Jan Stenerud gave Green Bay a one point lead with 54 seconds remaining. The Redskins moved quickly, but Mark Moseley's 39-yard field-goal attempt sailed wide right as time expired. The two teams combined for 1,125 yards of total offense in the highest scoring game in *Monday Night Football* history.

November 18, 1985: Washington Redskins 23, New York Giants 21. This game is remembered less for the final score than for the gruesome injury that ended the career of Redskins quarterback Joe Theismann. With the game tied in the second quarter, Washington tried a flea-flicker play that didn't fool any of the Giants defenders. Linebacker Lawrence Taylor grabbed Theismann in the backfield and dragged him down, falling awkwardly on the quarterback's right leg. Taylor immediately leapt to his feet, signaling frantically for medical attention. Both the tibia and fibula were broken, and the

36-year old quarterback was carried from the field on a stretcher. The Redskins would rally to win the game, but that was the last thought in anybody's mind. Theismann would never play again.

December 2, 1985: Miami Dolphins 38, Chicago Bears 24.
Chicago's revolutionary 46 Defense baffled opponents who couldn't figure out how to withstand the relentless pressure. The Bears started the season at 12–0 and were threatening to become the first NFL team to go undefeated since the 1972 Dolphins. With members of that legendary squad watching on the sidelines, Dan Marino found the solution. The normally immobile quarterback spent most of the night rolling out, with fullback Woody Bennett serving as an extra blocker in pass protection. The Dolphins scored on their first 5 possessions to take a 31–10 halftime lead and coasted the rest of the way. It was Chicago's only loss of the season and Don Shula, coach of the undefeated 1972 Dolphins, helped keep the Bears from perfection.

October 6, 1986: Seattle Seahawks 33, San Diego Chargers 7.
Two of the game's greatest receivers set significant records in an otherwise lopsided game. When Seattle's Steve Largent caught a 17-yard pass in the second quarter, it marked the 128th consecutive game in which he'd caught a pass, breaking the record held by Harold Carmichael. Largent's remarkable streak would extend to 177 games by the time he retired. On the other side of the field, San Diego's Charlie Joiner became the all-time leader in receiving yards. He passed Don Maynard's record of 11,834.

November 30, 1987: Los Angeles Raiders 37, Seattle Seahawks 14.
After Bo Jackson won the Heisman Trophy in 1985, he passed up a pro football career—and the woeful Tampa Bay Buccaneers who drafted him—to play left field for the Kansas City Royals. When the baseball season ended in 1987, he joined the Raiders, who'd taken a chance and drafted Jackson in the seventh round. Jackson stepped up to the national stage in his fifth NFL game. Jackson took a handoff on a third-and-six play in the second quarter. Safety Eugene Robinson tried in vain to beat the ball carrier to the outside, and Jackson seemed to hit a higher gear as he turned upfield. He sprinted 91 yards down the sideline, through the end zone, down the tunnel, and out of sight. Stunned commentator Dan Dierdorf called out, "He might not stop 'til Tacoma." Jackson was not done. He pounded the Seahawks defense for a *Monday Night Football*-record 221 yards, capping his night by carrying braggadocio Brian Bosworth across the goal line on a 2-yard touchdown run.

December 11, 1989: San Francisco 49ers 30, Los Angeles Rams 27.
San Francisco's prolific passing game was at its peak, and the 49ers needed every bit of it to hold off their NFC West rivals. Joe Montana connected with receiver John Taylor for touchdown passes of 92 and 95 yards, and both players set new team records with their performances. Montana finished with 458 passing yards, while Taylor caught 11 passes for 286 yards. San Francisco overcame a 17-point deficit to win the game and clinch the division title.

September 5, 1994: San Francisco 49ers 44, Los Angeles Raiders 14.
The largest crowd in San Francisco history turned out to watch the first Monday night game of the season. Jerry Rice was 2 touchdowns shy of Jim Brown's career record, and he wasted no time in staking his claim. On San Francisco's first possession, Rice scored on a 69-yard bomb. He tied Brown's mark in the fourth quarter, running 23 yards on a reverse. The record breaker came with four minutes left to play, as Rice leapt over cornerback Albert Lewis in the end zone to grab a 38-yard catch. It was his 127th career touchdown, and Rice served notice that he had plenty of gas left in his tank, finishing with 7 catches for 169 yards in a rout of the Raiders.

October 17, 1994: Kansas City Chiefs 31, Denver Broncos 28.
The Chiefs and Broncos had long been bitter rivals, but the main focus for this game was the head-to-head matchup of two of the game's great quarterbacks. Denver's John Elway and Kansas City's Joe Montana each threw a first half touchdown pass, but like a great chess match, the two masters saved their best moves for the end. With the game tied, 21–21, in the fourth quarter, Montana led the Chiefs on a long drive, capped by a 19-yard field goal with 4:08 left on the clock. Elway responded by leading a dramatic drive, scampering into the end zone from 4 yards out to retake the lead. It was a perfect ending, except for one thing. Kansas City got the ball back with 89 seconds remaining, more than enough time for Montana to conjure some magic of his own. He moved the Chiefs down the field, throwing a game-winning touchdown pass with just eight seconds to go.

December 18, 1995: San Francisco 49ers 37, Minnesota Vikings 30.
Pro football's greatest receiver had the best game of his career, despite battling a flu bug that left him coughing throughout the night. Jerry Rice dissected the Vikings secondary, using his speed to outrun defenders, showing his shifty moves to juke defenders off their feet, and when necessary, simply running over the man between him and his destination. He caught 14 passes for a career best 289 yards and three touchdowns.

December 25, 1995: Dallas Cowboys 37, Arizona Cardinals 13.
The Cowboys entered the game needing a win to clinch the division title, but what was on everybody's mind was getting Emmitt Smith a touchdown for Christmas. The Dallas running back had scored 24 in his first 15 games, tying John Riggins's record. From the outset, it was the Dallas passing game setting the tone. With receiver Michael Irvin facing double coverage on every play, quarterback Troy Aikman kept tossing the ball to Kevin Williams. The strategy was effective, as Dallas jumped out to a 24–0 lead in the second quarter. Then the Cardinals defense stiffened, and it didn't look as if Smith would get a chance to break the record. Finally in the fourth quarter, the Cowboys mounted a drive, and Smith carried the ball in from the 3-yard line for his 25th touchdown.

October 23, 2000: New York Jets 40, Miami Dolphins 37 (OT).
When ABC asked its viewers to name the best game in the history of *Monday Night Football*, they selected this one. The Dolphins dominated the Jets for three quarters, and fans at the Meadowlands were streaming towards the exits with their team trailing, 30–7. Quarterback Vinny Testaverde played like a man possessed in the fourth quarter. He completed 18 of 26 passes for 235 yards in the final period, leading the Jets to scores on 4 straight possessions and tying the game at 30. After Miami regained the lead, Testaverde came right back, tossing a 3-yard touchdown pass to tackle-eligible Jumbo Elliott to tie the game with 42 seconds left. Jets kicker John Hall booted a 40-yard field goal in overtime, capping one of the most remarkable comebacks in NFL history.

October 6, 2003: Indianapolis Colts 38, Tampa Bay Buccaneers 35 (OT).
With 5:09 left in the game, Tampa Bay cornerback Ronde Barber returned an interception 29 yards for a touchdown, giving the Buccaneers a 35–14 lead. The Colts never surrendered, scoring 21 points in a span of four and a half minutes to tie the game and send it to overtime. Kicker Mike Vanderjagt missed a 40-yard field goal attempt, but Tampa Bay's Simeon Rice was penalized for leaping, a rule which only the officials seemed to be aware of. Given another chance, Vanderjagt bounced the kick off the right upright and through for the victory. The Colts became the first NFL team to win after trailing by 21 points with less than four minutes to play.

December 22, 2003: Green Bay Packers 41, Oakland Raiders 7.
A day after the sudden death of his father, Green Bay's Brett Favre told his teammates he had no intentions of missing their game that night in Oakland. It was his 205th consecutive game, and it became one of the greatest performances of his storied career. Favre came out throwing, connecting with four different receivers for gains of more than 30 yards. By halftime, he had thrown for 311 yards and 4 touchdowns. On top of that, he passed Fran Tarkenton and moved into second place in career touchdown passes. Favre left the game in the fourth quarter with his Packers leading by 34 points. He finished with 399 yards, 3 yards shy of his career high. Nobody would have thought twice if he had asked for a day off to grieve, but his ability to be brilliant despite his personal burden inspired his teammates and added to his legendary aura.

RESULTS BY FRANCHISE

TEAM	G	W	L	T	PF	PA
Arizona / Phoenix / St. Louis Cardinals	16	5	10	1	280	319
Atlanta Falcons	27	9	18	0	433	660
Baltimore Ravens	6	4	2	0	160	86
Buffalo Bills	37	17	20	0	732	797
Carolina Panthers	5	3	2	0	121	114
Chicago Beards	48	16	32	0	780	1139
Cincinnati Bengals	24	8	16	0	449	621
Cleveland Browns (1946–95)	24	13	11	0	502	506
Cleveland Browns (1999–)	1	0	1	0	20	26
Dallas Cowboys	67	39	28	0	1544	1319
Denver Broncos	53	23	29	1	1110	1196
Detroit Lions	25	11	13	1	479	507
Green Bay Packers	48	24	23	1	1052	972
Houston Texans	0	0	0	0	0	0
Indianapolis / Baltimore Colts	27	17	10	0	592	568
Jacksonville Jaguars	8	5	3	0	170	173
Kansas City Chiefs	35	20	15	0	791	760
Miami Dolphins	71	39	32	0	1641	1415
Minnesota Vikings	44	22	22	0	855	887
New England Patriots	33	12	21	0	714	797
New Orleans Saints	21	6	15	0	365	535
New York Giants	46	16	29	1	751	1048
New York Jets	37	16	21	0	741	840
Oakland / Los Angeles Raiders	57	35	21	1	1306	1213
Philadelphia Eagles	42	22	20	0	808	822
Pittsburgh Steelers	54	33	21	0	1196	935
San Diego Padres	28	14	14	0	648	582
Seattle Seahawks	21	13	8	0	536	393
San Francisco 49ers	59	37	22	0	1516	1037
St. Louis / Los Angeles Rams	52	26	26	0	1182	1053
Tampa Bay Buccaneers	15	8	7	0	296	310
Tennessee Titans/Houston Oilers	31	16	15	0	585	681
Washington Redskins	53	25	28	0	1040	1084

MOST WINS BY COACH

NAME	G	W	L	T
Allen, George	14	10	4	0
Belichick, Bill	13	6	7	0
Coryell, Don	19	9	10	0
Cowher, Bill	25	18	7	0
Ditka, Mike	20	8	12	0
Dungy, Tony	12	9	3	0
Fisher, Jeff	10	5	5	0
Flores, Tom	19	15	4	0
Gibbs, Joe	24	10	14	0
Grant, Bud	19	9	10	0
Green, Dennis	15	9	6	0
Holmgren, Mike	17	9	8	0
Johnson, Jimmy	18	7	11	0
Knox, Chuck	22	12	10	0
Landry, Tom	35	19	16	0
Levy, Marv	23	13	10	0
Madden, John	13	11	1	1
Mariucci, Steve	13	9	4	0
Martz, Mike	14	9	5	0
Mora, Jim	14	7	7	0
Noll, Chuck	29	15	14	0
Parcells, Bill	29	15	13	1
Pardee, Jack	14	6	8	0
Phillips, Bum	10	7	3	0
Reeves, Dan	25	12	13	0
Reid, Andy	13	8	5	0
Robinson, John	17	7	10	0
Schottenheimer, Marty	27	13	14	0
Seifert, George	24	18	6	0
Shanahan, Mike	23	12	11	0
Shell, Art	10	5	5	0
Sherman, Mike	15	9	6	0
Shula, Don	51	31	20	0
Switzer, Barry	12	8	4	0
Vermeil, Dick	11	6	5	0
Walsh, Bill	12	7	5	0
Walton, Joe	11	6	5	0
Wannstedt, Dave	17	7	10	0
Wyche, Sam	10	4	6	0

MONDAY NIGHT FOOTBALL GAME LIST

DATE	VIS	HOME
9/21/1970	NYJ (21)	CLE (31)
9/28/1970	KC (44)	BAL (24)
10/5/1970	CHI (14)	DET (28)
10/12/1970	GB (22)	SD (20)
10/19/1970	WAS (20)	OAK (34)
10/26/1970	LA (3)	MIN (13)
11/2/1970	CIN (10)	PIT (21)
11/9/1970	BAL (13)	GB (10)
11/16/1970	STL (38)	DAL (0)
11/23/1970	NYG (20)	PHI (23)
11/30/1970	MIA (20)	ATL (7)
12/7/1970	CLE (21)	HOU (10)
12/14/1970	DET (28)	LA (23)
9/20/1971	MIN (16)	DET (13)
9/27/1971	NYJ (10)	STL (17)
10/4/1971	OAK (34)	CLE (20)
10/11/1971	NYG (13)	DAL (20)
10/18/1971	PIT (16)	KC (38)
10/25/1971	BAL (3)	MIN (10)
11/1/1971	DET (14)	GB (14)
11/8/1971	LA (17)	BAL (24)
11/15/1971	STL (17)	SD (20)
11/22/1971	GB (21)	ATL (28)
11/29/1971	CHI (3)	MIA (34)
12/6/1971	KC (26)	SF (17)
12/13/1971	WAS (38)	LA (24)
9/18/1972	WAS (24)	MIN (21)
9/25/1972	KC (20)	NO (17)
10/2/1972	NYG (27)	PHI (12)
10/9/1972	OAK (34)	HOU (0)
10/16/1972	GB (24)	DET (23)
10/23/1972	MIN (10)	CHI (13)
10/30/1972	DET (24)	DAL (28)
11/6/1972	BAL (24)	NE (17)
11/13/1972	CLE (21)	SD (17)
11/20/1972	ATL (13)	WAS (24)
11/27/1972	STL (10)	MIA (31)
12/4/1972	LA (26)	SF (16)
12/11/1972	NYJ (16)	OAK (24)
9/17/1973	NYJ (7)	GB (23)
9/24/1973	NO (3)	DAL (40)
10/1/1973	ATL (6)	DET (31)
10/8/1973	DAL (7)	LA (37)
10/15/1973	MIA (17)	CLE (9)
10/22/1973	OAK (23)	DEN (23)
10/29/1973	KC (14)	BUF (23)
11/5/1973	WAS (16)	PIT (21)
11/12/1973	CHI (7)	KC (19)
11/19/1973	MIN (14)	ATL (20)

DATE	VIS	HOME
11/26/1973	GB (6)	SF (20)
12/3/1973	PIT (26)	MIA (30)
12/10/1973	NYG (6)	LA (40)
9/16/1974	OAK (20)	BUF (21)
9/23/1974	DAL (10)	PHI (13)
9/30/1974	DEN (3)	WAS (30)
10/7/1974	NYJ (21)	MIA (21)
10/14/1974	SF (13)	DET (17)
10/21/1974	GB (9)	CHI (10)
10/28/1974	ATL (7)	PIT (24)
11/4/1974	LA (15)	SF (13)
11/11/1974	MIN (28)	STL (24)
11/18/1974	KC (42)	DEN (34)
11/25/1974	PIT (28)	NO (7)
12/2/1974	CIN (3)	MIA (24)
12/9/1974	WAS (23)	LA (17)
9/22/1975	OAK (31)	MIA (21)
9/29/1975	GB (13)	DEN (23)
10/6/1975	DAL (36)	DET (10)
10/13/1975	STL (17)	WAS (27)
10/20/1975	NYG (17)	BUF (14)
10/27/1975	MIN (13)	CHI (9)
11/3/1975	LA (42)	PHI (3)
11/10/1975	KC (34)	DAL (31)
11/17/1975	BUF (24)	CIN (33)
11/24/1975	PIT (32)	HOU (9)
12/1/1975	NE (7)	MIA (20)
12/8/1975	DEN (10)	OAK (17)
12/15/1975	NYJ (16)	SD (24)
9/13/1976	MIA (30)	BUF (21)
9/20/1976	OAK (24)	KC (21)
9/27/1976 OT	WAS (20)	PHI (17)
10/4/1976	PIT (6)	MIN (17)
10/11/1976	SF (16)	LA (0)
10/18/1976	NYJ (7)	NE (41)
10/25/1976	STL (10)	WAS (20)
11/1/1976	HOU (14)	BAL (38)
11/8/1976	LA (12)	CIN (20)
11/15/1976	BUF (10)	DAL (17)
11/22/1976	BAL (17)	MIA (16)
11/29/1976	MIN (16)	SF (20)
12/6/1976	CIN (20)	OAK (35)
9/19/1977	SF (0)	PIT (27)
9/26/1977 OT	NE (27)	CLE (30)
10/3/1977	OAK (37)	KC (28)
10/10/1977	LA (23)	CHI (24)
10/17/1977	CIN (14)	PIT (20)
10/24/1977	MIN (3)	LA (35)
10/31/1977	NYG (0)	STL (28)

DATE	VIS	HOME
11/7/1977	WAS (3)	BAL (10)
11/14/1977	STL (24)	DAL (17)
11/21/1977	GB (9)	WAS (10)
11/28/1977	BUF (13)	OAK (34)
12/5/1977	BAL (6)	MIA (17)
12/12/1977	DAL (42)	SF (35)
9/4/1978	BAL (0)	DAL (38)
9/11/1978 OT	DEN (9)	MIN (12)
9/18/1978	BAL (34)	NE (27)
9/25/1978	MIN (20)	CHI (24)
10/2/1978	DAL (5)	WAS (9)
10/9/1978	CIN (0)	MIA (21)
10/16/1978	CHI (7)	DEN (16)
10/23/1978	HOU (24)	PIT (17)
10/30/1978	LA (7)	ATL (15)
11/6/1978	WAS (17)	BAL (21)
11/13/1978	OAK (34)	CIN (21)
11/20/1978	MIA (30)	HOU (35)
11/27/1978	PIT (24)	SF (7)
12/4/1978	CHI (7)	SD (40)
12/11/1978	CIN (20)	LA (19)
12/18/1978	NE (3)	MIA (23)
9/3/1979 OT	PIT (16)	NE (13)
9/10/1979	ATL (14)	PHI (10)
9/17/1979	NYG (0)	WAS (27)
9/24/1979	DAL (7)	CLE (26)
10/1/1979	NE (14)	GB (27)
10/8/1979	MIA (3)	OAK (13)
10/15/1979	MIN (7)	NYJ (14)
10/22/1979	DEN (7)	PIT (42)
10/29/1979	SEA (31)	ATL (28)
11/5/1979	HOU (9)	MIA (6)
11/12/1979	PHI (31)	DAL (21)
11/19/1979	ATL (14)	LA (20)
11/26/1979	NYJ (7)	SEA (30)
12/3/1979	OAK (42)	NO (35)
12/10/1979	PIT (7)	HOU (20)
12/17/1979	DEN (7)	SD (17)
9/8/1980	DAL (17)	WAS (3)
9/15/1980	HOU (16)	CLE (7)
9/22/1980	NYG (35)	PHI (35)
9/29/1980	DEN (14)	NE (23)
10/6/1980	TB (0)	CHI (23)
10/13/1980	WAS (17)	DEN (20)
10/20/1980	OAK (45)	PIT (34)
10/27/1980	MIA (14)	NYJ (17)
11/3/1980	CHI (21)	CLE (27)
11/10/1980	NE (34)	HOU (38)
11/17/1980	OAK (19)	SEA (17)

DATE	VIS	HOME
11/24/1980	LA (27)	NO (7)
12/1/1980	DEN (3)	OAK (9)
12/8/1980 OT	NE (13)	MIA (16)
12/15/1980	DAL (14)	LA (38)
12/22/1980	PIT (17)	SD (26)
9/7/1981	SD (44)	CLE (14)
9/14/1981	OAK (36)	MIN (10)
9/21/1981	DAL (35)	NE (21)
9/28/1981	LA (24)	CHI (7)
10/5/1981	ATL (13)	PHI (16)
10/12/1981	MIA (21)	BUF (31)
10/19/1981	CHI (17)	DET (48)
10/26/1981	HOU (13)	PIT (26)
11/2/1981	MIN (7)	DEN (19)
11/9/1981	BUF (14)	DAL (27)
11/16/1981	SD (23)	SEA (44)
11/23/1981	MIN (30)	ATL (31)
11/30/1981	PHI (10)	MIA (13)
12/7/1981	PIT (27)	OAK (30)
12/14/1981	ATL (16)	LA (21)
12/21/1981	OAK (10)	SD (23)
9/13/1982	PIT (36)	DAL (28)
9/20/1982	GB (27)	NYG (19)
11/22/1982	SD (24)	LAO (28)
11/29/1982	MIA (17)	TB (23)
12/6/1982	NYJ (28)	DET (13)
12/13/1982	DAL (37)	HOU (7)
12/20/1982	CIN (34)	SD (50)
12/27/1982	BUF (10)	MIA (2)
1/3/1983	DAL (27)	MIN (31)
9/5/1983	DAL (31)	WAS (30)
9/12/1983	SD (17)	KC (14)
9/19/1983	MIA (14)	LAO (27)
9/26/1983	GB (3)	NYG (27)
10/3/1983	NYJ (34)	BUF (10)
10/10/1983	PIT (24)	CIN (14)
10/17/1983	WAS (47)	GB (48)
10/24/1983 OT	NYG (20)	STL (20)
10/31/1983	WAS (27)	SD (24)
11/7/1983	NYG (9)	DET (15)
11/14/1983	LA (36)	ATL (13)
11/21/1983	NYJ (31)	NO (28)
11/28/1983	CIN (14)	MIA (38)
12/5/1983	MIN (2)	DET (13)
12/12/1983 OT	GB (12)	TB (9)
12/19/1983	DAL (17)	SF (42)
9/3/1984	DAL (20)	LA (13)
9/10/1984	WAS (31)	SF (37)
9/17/1984	MIA (21)	BUF (17)

Monday Night Football Game List (cont.)

DATE	VIS	HOME
9/24/1984	SD (30)	LAO (33)
10/1/1984	CIN (17)	PIT (38)
10/8/1984	SF (31)	NYG (10)
10/15/1984	GB (14)	DEN (17)
10/22/1984	LA (24)	ATL (10)
10/29/1984	SEA (24)	SD (0)
11/5/1984	ATL (14)	WAS (27)
11/12/1984	LAO (14)	SEA (17)
11/19/1984	PIT (24)	NO (27)
11/26/1984	NYJ (17)	MIA (28)
12/3/1984	CHI (7)	SD (20)
12/10/1984	LAO (24)	DET (3)
12/17/1984	DAL (21)	MIA (28)
9/9/1985	WAS (14)	DAL (44)
9/16/1985	PIT (7)	CLE (17)
9/23/1985	LA (35)	SEA (24)
9/30/1985	CIN (37)	PIT (24)
10/7/1985	STL (10)	WAS (27)
10/14/1985	MIA (7)	NYJ (23)
10/21/1985	GB (7)	CHI (23)
10/28/1985	SD (21)	LAO (34)
11/4/1985	DAL (10)	STL (21)
11/11/1985	SF (16)	DEN (17)
11/18/1985	NYG (21)	WAS (23)
11/25/1985	SEA (6)	SF (19)
12/2/1985	CHI (24)	MIA (38)
12/9/1985	LA (27)	SF (20)
12/16/1985	NE (27)	MIA (30)
12/23/1985	LAO (16)	LA (6)
9/8/1986	NYG (28)	DAL (31)
9/15/1986	DEN (21)	PIT (10)
9/22/1986	CHI (25)	GB (12)
9/29/1986	DAL (31)	STL (7)
10/6/1986	SD (7)	SEA (33)
10/13/1986	PIT (22)	CIN (24)
10/20/1986	DEN (10)	NYJ (22)
10/27/1986	WAS (20)	NYG (27)
11/3/1986	LA (20)	CHI (17)
11/10/1986	MIA (16)	CLE (26)
11/17/1986	SF (6)	WAS (14)
11/24/1986	NYJ (3)	MIA (45)
12/1/1986	NYG (21)	SF (17)
12/8/1986	LAO (0)	SEA (37)
12/15/1986	CHI (16)	DET (13)
12/22/1986	NE (34)	MIA (27)
9/14/1987	NYG (19)	CHI (34)
9/21/1987	NE (24)	NYJ (43)
10/5/1987	SF (41)	NYG (21)
10/12/1987	LAO (14)	DEN (30)
10/19/1987	WAS (13)	DAL (7)
10/26/1987	LA (17)	CLE (30)
10/26/1987	DEN (27)	MIN (34)
11/2/1987	NYG (24)	DAL (33)
11/9/1987	SEA (14)	NYJ (30)
11/16/1987	CHI (29)	DEN (31)
11/23/1987	LA (30)	WAS (26)
11/30/1987	LAO (37)	SEA (14)
12/7/1987	NYJ (28)	MIA (37)
12/14/1987	CHI (0)	SF (41)
12/21/1987	DAL (29)	LA (21)
12/28/1987	NE (24)	MIA (10)
9/5/1988	WAS (20)	NYG (27)
9/12/1988	DAL (17)	PHO (14)
9/19/1988	IND (17)	CLE (23)
9/26/1988 OT	LAO (30)	DEN (27)
10/3/1988	DAL (17)	NO (20)
10/10/1988	NYG (13)	PHI (24)
10/17/1988	BUF (37)	NYJ (14)
10/24/1988	SF (9)	CHI (10)
10/31/1988	DEN (23)	IND (55)
11/7/1988	CLE (17)	HOU (24)
11/14/1988	BUF (31)	MIA (6)
11/21/1988	WAS (21)	SF (37)
11/28/1988	LAO (27)	SEA (35)
12/5/1988	CHI (3)	LA (23)
12/12/1988	CLE (31)	MIA (38)
12/19/1988	CHI (27)	MIN (28)
9/11/1989	NYG (27)	WAS (24)
9/18/1989	DEN (28)	BUF (14)
9/25/1989	CLE (14)	CIN (21)
10/2/1989	PHI (13)	CHI (27)
10/9/1989	LAO (14)	NYJ (7)
10/16/1989	LA (20)	BUF (23)
10/23/1989	CHI (7)	CLE (27)
10/30/1989	MIN (14)	NYG (24)
11/6/1989	NO (13)	SF (31)
11/13/1989	CIN (24)	HOU (26)
11/20/1989	DEN (14)	WAS (10)
11/27/1989	NYG (24)	SF (34)
12/4/1989	BUF (16)	SEA (17)
12/11/1989	SF (30)	LA (27)
12/18/1989	PHI (20)	NO (30)
12/25/1989	CIN (21)	MIN (29)
9/10/1990	SF (13)	NO (12)
9/17/1990	KC (23)	DEN (24)
9/24/1990	BUF (30)	NYJ (7)
10/1/1990	CIN (16)	SEA (31)
10/8/1990	CLE (30)	DEN (29)
10/15/1990	MIN (24)	PHI (32)
10/22/1990	CIN (34)	CLE (13)
10/29/1990	LA (10)	PIT (41)
11/5/1990	NYG (24)	IND (7)
11/12/1990	WAS (14)	PHI (28)
11/19/1990	LAO (13)	MIA (10)
11/26/1990	BUF (24)	HOU (27)
12/3/1990	NYG (3)	SF (7)
12/10/1990	LAO (38)	DET (31)
12/17/1990	SF (26)	LA (10)
12/31/1990	LA (17)	NO (20)
9/2/1991	SF (14)	NYG (16)
9/9/1991	WAS (33)	DAL (31)
9/16/1991	KC (7)	HOU (17)
9/23/1991 OT	NYJ (13)	CHI (19)
9/30/1991	PHI (0)	WAS (23)
10/7/1991	BUF (6)	KC (33)
10/14/1991	NYG (23)	PIT (20)
10/21/1991	CIN (16)	BUF (35)
10/28/1991	LAO (21)	KC (24)
11/4/1991	NYG (7)	PHI (30)
11/11/1991	CHI (34)	MIN (17)
11/18/1991	BUF (41)	MIA (27)
11/25/1991	SF (33)	LA (10)
12/2/1991	PHI (13)	HOU (6)
12/9/1991	CIN (13)	MIA (37)
12/16/1991	LAO (0)	NO (27)
12/23/1991	CHI (14)	SF (52)
9/7/1992	WAS (10)	DAL (23)
9/14/1992	MIA (27)	CLE (23)
9/21/1992	NYG (27)	CHI (14)
9/28/1992	LAO (7)	KC (27)
10/5/1992	DAL (7)	PHI (31)
10/12/1992	DEN (3)	WAS (34)
10/19/1992	CIN (0)	PIT (20)
10/26/1992	BUF (24)	NYJ (20)
11/2/1992	MIN (38)	CHI (10)
11/9/1992	SF (41)	ATL (3)
11/16/1992	BUF (26)	MIA (20)
11/23/1992	WAS (3)	NO (20)
11/30/1992 OT	DEN (13)	SEA (16)
12/7/1992	CHI (7)	HOU (24)
12/14/1992	LAO (7)	MIA (20)
12/21/1992	DAL (41)	ATL (17)
12/28/1992	DET (6)	SF (24)
9/6/1993	DAL (16)	WAS (35)
9/13/1993	SF (13)	CLE (23)
9/20/1993	DEN (7)	KC (15)
9/27/1993	PIT (45)	ATL (17)
10/4/1993	WAS (10)	MIA (17)
10/11/1993	HOU (7)	BUF (35)
10/18/1993	LAO (23)	DEN (20)
10/25/1993	MIN (19)	CHI (12)
11/1/1993	WAS (10)	BUF (24)
11/8/1993	GB (16)	KC (23)
11/15/1993	BUF (0)	PIT (23)
11/22/1993	NO (7)	SF (42)
11/29/1993	SD (31)	IND (0)
12/6/1993	PHI (17)	DAL (23)
12/13/1993	PIT (21)	MIA (20)
12/20/1993	NYG (24)	NO (14)
12/27/1993	MIA (20)	SD (45)
1/3/1994 OT	PHI (37)	SF (34)
9/5/1994	LAO (14)	SF (44)
9/12/1994	CHI (22)	PHI (30)
9/19/1994 OT	DET (20)	DAL (17)
9/26/1994	DEN (20)	BUF (27)
10/3/1994	HOU (14)	PIT (30)
10/10/1994	MIN (27)	NYG (10)
10/17/1994	KC (31)	DEN (28)
10/24/1994	HOU (6)	PHI (21)
10/31/1994	GB (33)	CHI (6)
11/7/1994	NYG (10)	DAL (38)
11/14/1994	BUF (10)	PIT (23)
11/21/1994	NYG (13)	HOU (10)
11/28/1994	SF (35)	NO (14)
12/5/1994	LAO (24)	SD (17)
12/12/1994	KC (28)	MIA (45)
12/19/1994	DAL (24)	NO (16)
12/26/1994	SF (14)	MIN (21)
9/4/1995	DAL (35)	NYG (0)
9/11/1995	GB (27)	CHI (24)
9/18/1995	PIT (10)	MIA (23)
9/25/1995	SF (24)	DET (27)
10/2/1995	BUF (22)	CLE (19)
10/9/1995 OT	SD (23)	KC (29)
10/16/1995	OAK (0)	DEN (27)
10/23/1995	BUF (14)	NE (27)
10/30/1995	CHI (14)	MIN (6)
11/6/1995	PHI (12)	DAL (34)
11/13/1995	CLE (3)	PIT (20)
11/20/1995	SF (44)	MIA (20)
11/27/1995	OAK (6)	SD (12)
12/4/1995	CHI (7)	DET (27)
12/11/1995	KC (6)	MIA (13)
12/18/1995	MIN (30)	SF (37)
12/25/1995	DAL (37)	ARI (13)
9/2/1996	DAL (6)	CHI (22)
9/9/1996	PHI (13)	GB (39)
9/16/1996	BUF (6)	PIT (24)
9/23/1996	MIA (6)	IND (10)
9/30/1996	DAL (23)	PHI (19)
10/7/1996	PIT (17)	KC (7)
10/14/1996 OT	SF (20)	GB (23)
10/21/1996	OAK (23)	SD (14)
10/28/1996	CHI (15)	MIN (13)
11/4/1996	DEN (22)	OAK (21)
11/11/1996	DET (21)	SD (27)
11/18/1996	GB (6)	DAL (21)
11/25/1996	PIT (24)	MIA (17)
12/2/1996	SF (34)	ATL (10)
12/9/1996	KC (7)	OAK (26)
12/16/1996	BUF (14)	MIA (16)
12/23/1996	DET (14)	SF (24)
9/1/1997	CHI (24)	GB (38)
9/8/1997	KC (28)	OAK (27)
9/15/1997	PHI (20)	DAL (21)
9/22/1997	PIT (21)	JAC (30)
9/29/1997	SF (34)	CAR (21)
10/6/1997	NE (13)	DEN (34)
10/13/1997	DAL (16)	WAS (21)
10/20/1997	BUF (9)	IND (6)
10/27/1997 OT	CHI (36)	MIA (33)
10/27/1997	GB (28)	NE (10)
11/3/1997	PIT (10)	KC (13)
11/10/1997	SF (24)	PHI (12)
11/17/1997	BUF (13)	MIA (30)
11/24/1997	OAK (3)	DEN (31)
12/1/1997	GB (27)	MIN (11)
12/8/1997	CAR (23)	DAL (13)
12/15/1997	DEN (17)	SF (34)
12/22/1997	NE (14)	MIA (12)
9/7/1998	NE (21)	DEN (27)
9/14/1998	SF (45)	WAS (10)
9/21/1998	DAL (31)	NYG (7)
9/28/1998	TB (6)	DET (27)
10/5/1998	MIN (37)	GB (24)
10/12/1998	MIA (21)	JAC (28)
10/19/1998	NYJ (24)	NE (14)
10/26/1998	PIT (20)	KC (13)
11/2/1998	DAL (34)	PHI (0)
11/9/1998	GB (20)	PIT (27)
11/16/1998	DEN (30)	KC (7)
11/23/1998	MIA (23)	NE (26)
11/30/1998	NYG (7)	SF (31)
12/7/1998	GB (22)	TB (24)
12/14/1998	DET (13)	SF (35)
12/21/1998	DEN (21)	MIA (31)
12/28/1998	PIT (3)	JAC (21)
9/13/1999	MIA (38)	DEN (21)
9/20/1999	ATL (7)	DAL (24)
9/27/1999	SF (24)	ARI (10)
10/4/1999	BUF (23)	MIA (18)
10/11/1999	JAC (16)	NYJ (6)
10/18/1999	DAL (10)	NYG (13)
10/25/1999	ATL (9)	PIT (13)
11/1/1999	SEA (27)	GB (7)
11/8/1999	DAL (17)	MIN (27)
11/15/1999	NYJ (24)	NE (17)
11/22/1999 OT	OAK (21)	DEN (27)
11/29/1999	GB (20)	SF (3)
12/6/1999	MIN (17)	TB (24)
12/13/1999	DEN (24)	JAC (27)
12/20/1999	GB (20)	MIN (24)
12/27/1999	NYJ (38)	MIA (31)
1/3/2000	SF (29)	ATL (34)
9/4/2000	DEN (36)	SLR (41)
9/11/2000	NE (19)	NYJ (20)
9/18/2000	DAL (27)	WAS (21)
9/25/2000	JAC (14)	IND (43)
10/2/2000	SEA (17)	KC (24)
10/9/2000	TB (23)	MIN (30)
10/16/2000	JAC (13)	TEN (27)
10/23/2000 OT	MIA (37)	NYJ (40)
10/30/2000	TEN (27)	WAS (21)
11/6/2000 OT	MIN (20)	GB (26)
11/13/2000	OAK (24)	DEN (27)
11/20/2000	WAS (33)	SLR (20)
11/27/2000	GB (14)	CAR (31)
12/4/2000	KC (24)	NE (30)
12/11/2000	BUF (20)	IND (44)
12/18/2000	SLR (35)	TB (38)
12/25/2000	DAL (0)	TEN (31)
9/10/2001	NYG (20)	DEN (31)
9/24/2001	WAS (0)	GB (37)
10/1/2001	SF (19)	NYJ (17)
10/8/2001	SLR (35)	DET (0)
10/15/2001	WAS (7)	DAL (9)
10/22/2001	PHI (10)	NYG (9)
10/29/2001	TEN (7)	PIT (34)
11/5/2001	DEN (28)	OAK (38)
11/12/2001	BAR (16)	TEN (10)
11/19/2001	NYG (16)	MIN (28)
11/26/2001	TB (24)	SLR (17)
12/3/2001	GB (28)	JAC (21)
12/10/2001	IND (6)	MIA (41)
12/17/2001	SLR (34)	NO (21)
1/7/2002	MIN (3)	BAR (19)
9/9/2002	PIT (14)	NE (30)
9/16/2002	PHI (37)	WAS (7)
9/23/2002	SLR (14)	TB (26)
9/30/2002	DEN (23)	BAR (34)
10/7/2002	GB (34)	CHI (21)
10/14/2002	SF (28)	SEA (21)
10/21/2002	IND (10)	PIT (28)
10/28/2002	NYG (3)	PHI (17)
11/4/2002	MIA (10)	GB (24)
11/11/2002	OAK (34)	DEN (10)
11/18/2002	CHI (16)	SLR (21)
11/25/2002	PHI (38)	SF (17)
12/2/2002	NYJ (20)	OAK (26)
12/9/2002	CHI (9)	MIA (27)
12/16/2002	NE (7)	TEN (24)
12/23/2002	PIT (17)	TB (7)
12/30/2002	SF (20)	SLR (31)
9/8/2003	TB (17)	PHI (0)
9/15/2003 OT	DAL (35)	NYG (32)
9/22/2003	OAK (10)	DEN (31)
9/29/2003	GB (38)	CHI (23)
10/6/2003 OT	IND (38)	TB (35)
10/13/2003	ATL (0)	SLR (36)
10/20/2003	KC (17)	OAK (10)
10/27/2003 at ARI	MIA (26)	SD (10)
11/3/2003	NE (30)	DEN (26)
11/10/2003	PHI (17)	GB (14)
11/17/2003	PIT (14)	SF (30)
11/24/2003	NYG (13)	TB (19)
12/1/2003	TEN (17)	NYJ (24)
12/8/2003	SLR (26)	CLB (20)
12/15/2003	PHI (34)	MIA (27)
12/22/2003	GB (41)	OAK (7)
9/13/2004	GB (24)	CAR (14)
9/20/2004	MIN (16)	PHI (27)
9/27/2004	DAL (21)	WAS (18)
10/4/2004	KC (27)	BAR (24)
10/11/2004	TEN (48)	GB (27)
10/18/2004	TB (21)	SLR (28)
10/25/2004	DEN (10)	CIN (23)
11/1/2004	MIA (14)	NYJ (41)
11/8/2004	MIN (28)	IND (31)
11/15/2004	PHI (49)	DAL (21)
11/22/2004	NE (27)	KC (19)
11/29/2004	SLR (17)	GB (45)
12/6/2004	DAL (43)	SEA (39)
12/13/2004	KC (49)	TEN (38)
12/20/2004	NE (28)	MIA (29)
12/27/2004	PHI (7)	SLR (20)
9/12/2005	PHI (10)	ATL (14)
9/19/2005 at NYG	NYG (27)	NO (10)
9/19/2005	WAS (14)	DAL (13)
9/26/2005	KC (10)	DEN (30)
10/3/2005	GB (29)	CAR (32)
10/10/2005	PIT (24)	SD (22)
10/17/2005	SLR (28)	IND (45)
10/24/2005	NYJ (14)	ATL (27)
10/31/2005	BAR (19)	PIT (20)
11/7/2005	IND (40)	NE (21)
11/14/2005	DAL (21)	PHI (20)
11/21/2005	MIN (20)	GB (17)
11/28/2005	PIT (7)	IND (26)
12/5/2005	SEA (42)	PHI (0)
12/12/2005	NO (17)	ATL (36)
12/19/2005	GB (3)	BAR (48)
12/26/2005	NE (31)	NYJ (21)

RUSHING

ATTEMPTS
40	Barry Sanders, Det vs Dal, Sept. 19, 1994 (OT)	
39	O.J. Simpson, Buf vs KC, Oct. 29, 1973	
36	Curtis Martin, NE vs Buf, Oct. 23, 1995	
36	Ron Johnson, NYG vs Phl, Oct. 2, 1972	
35	Emmitt Smith, Dal vs NYG, Nov. 7, 1994	
35	Heath Sherman, Phl vs Was, Nov. 12, 1990	
35	Charles White, LARm vs Was, Nov. 23, 1987	

YARDS
221	Bo Jackson, LARd vs Sea, Nov. 30, 1987
216	Ricky Williams, Mia vs ChiB, Dec. 9, 2002
214	Thurman Thomas, Buf vs NYJ, Sept. 24, 1990
199	Earl Campbell, Hou vs Mia, Nov. 20, 1978
198	Julius Jones, Dal vs Sea, Dec. 6, 2004
198	Garrison Hearst, SF vs Det, Dec. 14, 1998

TOUCHDOWNS
4	Emmitt Smith, Dal vs NYG, Sept. 4, 1995
4	Eric Dickerson, Ind vs Den, Oct. 31, 1988
4	Earl Campbell, Hou vs Mia, Nov. 20, 1978
3	17 players tied, most recently:
	Edgerrin James, Ind vs SL, Oct. 17, 2005

PASSING

ATTEMPTS
62	Randall Cunningham, Phl vs ChiB, Oct. 2, 1989
61	Brett Favre, GB vs SF, Oct. 14, 1996 (OT)
60	Joe Montana, SF vs Was, Nov. 17, 1986
59	Vinny Testaverde, NYJ vs Mia, Oct. 23, 2000 (OT)
57	Brian Sipe, Cle vs SD, Sept. 7, 1981

COMPLETIONS
40	Ken Anderson, Cin vs SD, Dec. 20, 1982
37	Daunte Culpepper, Min vs Phl, Sept. 20, 2004
36	Vinny Testaverde, NYJ vs Mia, Oct. 23, 2000 (OT)
35	Marc Bulger, SL vs GB, Nov. 29, 2004
35	Brian Griese, Den vs Bal, Sept. 30, 2002

GROSS YARDS
458	Joe Montana, SF vs LARm, Dec. 11, 1989
448	Marc Bulger, SL vs GB, Nov. 29, 2004
447	Ken Anderson, Cin vs Buf, Nov. 17, 1975
445	Charley Johnson, Den vs KC, Nov. 18, 1974
442	Randall Cunningham, Min vs GB, Oct. 5, 1998

TOUCHDOWNS
5	Vinny Testaverde, NYJ vs Mia, Oct. 23, 2000 (OT)
5	Jim Kelly, Buf vs Cin, Oct. 21, 1991
5	Dave Krieg, Sea vs LARd, Nov. 28, 1988
4	seventeen players tied, most recently
	Brett Favre, GB vs Car, Oct. 3, 2005

INTERCEPTIONS
6	Ed Luther, SD vs Was, Oct. 31, 1983
5	Wade Wilson, Min vs Den, Oct. 26, 1987
5	Joe Theismann, Was vs Dal, Sept. 9, 1985
5	Scott Bull, SF vs Pit, Nov. 27, 1978
5	Mike Boryla, Phl vs Was, Sept. 27, 1976 (OT)

PASSER RATING (MIN. 14 ATTEMPTS)
157.1	Dan Fouts, SD vs Cle, Sept. 7, 1981
154.9	Brett Favre, GB vs Oak, Dec. 22, 2003
153.7	Troy Aikman, Dal vs Atl, Dec. 21, 1992
151.3	Roger Staubach, Dal vs SF, Dec. 12, 1977
146.8	Danny White, Dal vs Hou, Dec. 13, 1982

RECEIVING

RECEPTIONS
14	Jerry Rice, SF vs Min, Dec. 18, 1995
14	Herman Moore, Det vs ChiB, Dec. 4, 1995
13	Terrell Owens, SF vs Phl, Nov. 25, 2002
13	Andre Reed, Buf vs Den, Sept. 18, 1989
12	thirteen players tied, most recently
	Drew Bennett, Ten vs KC, Dec. 13, 2004

YARDS
289	Jerry Rice, SF vs Min, Dec. 18, 1995
286	John Taylor, SF vs LARm, Dec. 11, 1989
260	Wes Chandler, SD vs Cin, Dec. 20, 1982
241	Gary Clark, Was vs NYG, Oct. 27, 1986
241	Jerry Rice, SF vs LARm, Dec. 9, 1985

TOUCHDOWNS
3	12 players tied, most recently
	Drew Bennett, Ten vs KC, Dec. 13, 2004
	Terrell Owens, Phl vs Dal, Nov. 15, 2004
	Isaac Bruce, SL vs NO, Dec. 17, 2001
	Randy Moss, Min vs NYG, Nov. 19, 2001
	Ed McCaffrey, Den vs Mia, Sept. 13, 1999

PLAYER TOTALS

TOTAL TOUCHDOWNS
4	Marshall Faulk, SL vs TB, Dec. 18, 2000
4	Emmitt Smith, Dal vs NYG, Sept. 4, 1995
4	Eric Dickerson, Ind vs Den, Oct. 31, 1988
4	Marcus Allen, LARd vs SD, Sept. 24, 1984
4	Earl Campbell, Hou vs Mia, Nov. 20, 1978
4	Ron Johnson, NYG vs Phl, Oct. 2, 1972

SPECIAL TEAMS

FIELD GOALS
7	Billy Cundiff, Dal vs NYG, Sept. 15, 2003 (OT)
7	Chris Boniol, Dal vs GB, Nov. 18, 1996
5	Richie Cunningham, Dal vs Phi, Sept. 15, 1997
5	Chris Jacke, GB vs SF, Oct. 14, 1996 (OT)
5	Nick Lowery, KC vs Den, Sept. 20, 1993
5	Rich Karlis, Min vs Cin, Dec. 25, 1989
5	Roger Ruzek, Dal vs LARm, Dec. 21, 1987
5	Tim Mazzetti, Atl vs LARm, Oct. 30, 1978

POINTS (KICKERS)
23	Billy Cundiff, Dal vs NYG, Sept. 15, 2003 (OT)
21	Chris Boniol, Dal vs GB, Nov. 18, 1996
17	Rich Karlis, Min vs Cin, Dec. 25, 1989
17	Roger Ruzek, Dal vs LARm, Dec. 21, 1987
17	Mark Moseley, Was vs GB, Oct. 17, 1983

PUNT RETURN YARDS
152	Cleo Montgomery, LARd vs Det, Dec. 10, 1984
134	Dennis McKinnon, Chi vs NYG, Sept. 14, 1987
131	Andre Hastings, Pit vs Cle, Nov. 13, 1995
128	Louis Lipps, Pit vs NO, Nov. 19, 1984
128	Kirk Springs, NYJ vs NO, Nov. 21, 1983

PUNT RETURN AVERAGE (MIN. 3 RETURNS)
42.7	Kirk Springs, NYJ vs NO, Nov. 21, 1983
34.7	Henry Ellard, LARm vs Atl, Oct. 22, 1984
33.0	Brian Mitchell, Phi vs SF, Nov. 25, 2002
32.0	Louis Lipps, Pit vs NO, Nov. 19, 1984
31.7	JoJo Townsell, NYJ vs Sea, Nov. 9, 1987

KICKOFF RETURN YARDS
256	Roell Preston, GB vs Min, Oct. 5, 1998
251	Jon Vaughn, KC vs Mia, Dec. 12, 1994
249	Tony Smith, Atl vs Pit, Sept. 27, 1993
208	Harlan Huckleby, GB vs Was, Oct. 17, 1983
194	Brian Mitchell, NYG vs Dal, Sept. 15, 2003 (OT)

KICKOFF RETURN AVERAGE (MIN. 3 RETURNS)
53.0	Harold Hart, Oak vs Mia, Sept. 22, 1975
44.7	Ron J. Brown, LARm vs SF, Dec. 9, 1985
42.8	Eddie Payton, Min vs Oak, Sept. 14, 1981
42.7	Cannonball Butler, Atl vs GB, Nov. 22, 1971
42.5	Kevin Faulk, NE vs NYJ, Nov. 15, 1999

DEFENSE

INTERCEPTIONS
4	Dick Anderson, Mia vs Pit, Dec. 3, 1973
3	Marcus Coleman, NYJ vs Mia, Oct. 23, 2000 (OT)
3	Dwayne Harper, SD vs Oak, Nov. 27, 1995
3	Kenny Easley, Sea vs SD, Oct. 29, 1984
3	Mark Murphy, Was vs SD, Oct. 31, 1983
3	Charlie Phillips, Oak vs Den, Dec. 8, 1975
3	Charlie Babb, Mia vs Oak, Sept. 22, 1975
3	Johnny Robinson, KC vs Bal, Sept. 28, 1970

INTERCEPTION RETURN YARDS
121	Dick Anderson, Mia vs Pit, Dec. 3, 1973
108	Felix Wright, Cle vs LARm, Oct. 26, 1987
102	Eddie Anderson, LARd vs Mia, Dec. 14, 1992
101	Lito Sheppard, Phi vs Dal, Nov. 15, 2004
98	Rod Woodson, Oak vs Den, Nov. 11, 2002
98	Marcus Coleman, NYJ vs Mia, Dec. 27, 1999

SACKS (1982–PRESENT)
4.0	Peter Boulware, Bal vs Min, Jan. 7, 2002
4.0	Dana Stubblefield, SF vs Phi, Nov. 10, 1997
4.0	Derrick Thomas, KC vs Buf, Oct. 7, 1991
4.0	Pierce Holt, SF vs NYG, Nov. 27, 1989
4.0	Chris Doleman, Min vs Cin, Dec. 25, 1989
4.0	Too Tall Jones, Dal vs NYG, Nov. 2, 1987

LONG PLAYS

RUSHING
99	Tony Dorsett, Dal, Jan. 3, 1983
91	Bo Jackson, LARd, Nov. 30, 1987
83	James Lofton, GB, Sept. 20, 1982
81	Earl Campbell, Hou, Nov. 20, 1978
78	Kevan Barlow, SF, Nov. 17, 2003
77	Leroy Harris, Mia, Dec. 5, 1977
77	Fred Taylor, Jax, Oct. 12, 1998
77	Dominic Rhodes, Ind, Oct. 22, 2001
75	Tony Dorsett, Dal, Sept. 21, 1981
75	Emmitt Smith, Dal, Sept. 9, 1991

PASSING
99	Robert Brooks from Brett Favre, GB, Sept. 11, 1995
97	Webster Slaughter from Bernie Kosar, Cle, Oct. 23, 1989
95	John Taylor from Joe Montana, SF, Dec. 11, 1989
94	Leonard Thompson from Eric Hipple, Det, Oct. 19, 1981
92	John Taylor from Joe Montana, SF, Dec. 11, 1989
91	Tony Dorsett from Roger Staubach, Dal, Sept. 4, 1978
89	Rich Caster from Joe Namath, NYJ, Oct. 7, 1974
88	Bobby Duckworth from Ed Luther, SD, Dec. 3, 1984
85	Marcus Anderson from Vince Evans, ChiB, Oct. 19, 1981
85	Curtis Conway from Jeff George, ChiB, Sept. 12, 1994
85	Donald Driver from Brett Favre, GB, Oct. 7, 2002

KICKOFF RETURNS
105	Terry Fair, Det, Sept. 28, 1998
102	Harold Hart, Oak, Sept. 22, 1975
101	Roell Preston, GB, Oct. 5, 1998
99	Gaston Green, LARm, Oct. 29, 1990
99	Eddie Payton, Min, Sept. 14, 1981
97	Tony Smith, Atl, Sept. 27, 1993
95	Ron Brown, LARm, Nov. 23, 1987
95	Vaughn Hebron, Den, Dec. 21, 1998
95	Kevin Faulk, NE, Nov. 15, 1999 (no td)
94	Homer Jones, Cle, Sept. 21, 1970
93	Terry Metcalf, StL, Oct. 13, 1975

PUNT RETURNS
95	John Taylor, SF, Nov. 21, 1988
94	Dennis McKinnon, ChiB, Sept. 14, 1987
91	Jo-Jo Townsell, NYJ, Nov. 9, 1987
91	Nate Burleson, Min, Nov. 8, 2004
90	Jacquez Green, Was, Sept. 16, 2002
86	Tamarick Vanover, KC, Oct. 9, 1995
86	Az-Zahir Hakim, SL, Sept. 4, 2000
85	Tiki Barber, NYG, Oct. 18, 1999
83	Dana McLemore, SF, Dec. 14, 1987
80	Ken Ellis, GB, Oct. 16, 1972

INTERCEPTION RETURNS
102	Eddie Anderson, LARd, Dec. 14, 1992
101	Lito Sheppard, Phi, Nov. 15, 2004
98	Marcus Coleman, NYJ, Dec. 27, 1999
98	Rod Woodson, Oak, Nov. 11, 2002
94	Walker Lee Ashley, Min, Dec. 19, 1988
94	Nolan Cromwell, LARm, Dec. 14, 1981 (no td)
93	Dre' Bly, SL, Oct. 8, 2001
90	Mel Renfro, Dal, Oct. 4, 1965
89	Darren Sharper, GB, Nov. 4, 2002
87	Eddie Anderson, LARd, Oct. 29, 1989
87	Greg Ellis, Dal, Sept. 20, 1999

FUMBLE RETURNS
99	Don Griffin, SF, Dec. 13, 1991
96	Joe Lavender, Phi-Dal, Sept. 23, 1974
93	Adam Archuleta, StL-TB, Oct. 18, 2004
88	Keith McKenzie, GB-Pit, Nov. 9, 1998

PUNTS
90	Rodney Williams, NYG, Sept. 10, 2001
83	Bryan Barker, Jac, Oct. 11, 1999
74	Craig Colquitt, Pit, Dec. 7, 1981

FIELD GOALS
59	Tony Franklin, Phi, Nov. 12, 1979
57	Fred Steinfort, Den, Oct. 13, 1980
56	Ali Haji-Sheikh, NYG, Nov. 7, 1983
56	Ali Haji-Sheikh, NYG, Sept. 26, 1983
55	Kevin Butler, Chi, Oct. 25, 1993

OFFENSE

POINTS SCORED
55	Ind vs Den, Oct. 31, 1988
52	SF vs ChiB, Dec. 23, 1991
50	SD vs Cin, Dec. 20, 1982
49	KC vs Ten, Dec. 13, 2004
49	Phl vs Dal, Nov. 15, 2004

TOTAL NET YARDS
661	SD vs Cin, Dec. 20, 1982
583	Dal vs Bal, Sept. 4, 1978
558	Cle vs Mia, Nov. 10, 1986
553	Cin vs Buf, Nov. 17, 1975
552	Was vs GB, Oct. 17, 1983

RUSHING YARDS
356	LARd vs Sea, Nov. 30, 1987
330	NE vs NYJ, Oct. 18, 1976
328	SF vs Det, Dec. 14, 1998
317	SF vs Min, Nov. 29, 1976
307	Oak vs Buf, Nov. 28, 1977

NET PASSING YARDS
486	SD vs Cin, Dec. 20, 1982
459	Den vs KC, Nov. 18, 1974
442	Min vs GB, Oct. 5, 1998
441	Cin vs Buf, Nov. 17, 1975
440	Ind vs Jax, Sept. 25, 2000

FIRST DOWNS
35	Mia vs Cle, Dec. 12, 1988
34	SD vs Cin, Dec. 20, 1982
34	Cin vs Buf, Nov. 17, 1975
34	Den vs KC, Nov. 18, 1974
33	Was vs GB, Oct. 17, 1983

TURNOVERS
10	SL vs Was, Oct. 25, 1976
8	SD vs Was, Oct. 31, 1983
7	seven teams, most recently GB vs Sea, Nov. 1, 1999

DEFENSE

POINTS ALLOWED
55	Den vs Ind, Oct. 31, 1988
52	ChiB vs SF, Dec. 23, 1991
50	Cin vs SD, Dec. 20, 1982
49	Ten vs KC, Dec. 13, 2004
49	Dal vs Phl, Nov. 15, 2004

NET YARDS ALLOWED
89	Was vs Phl, Sept. 30, 1991
89	Oak vs Hou, Oct. 9, 1972
95	Ten vs Dal, Dec. 25, 2000
96	LARm vs NO, Nov. 24, 1980
100	Min vs LARm, Oct. 26, 1970

FIRST DOWNS ALLOWED
4	Was vs Phl, Sept. 30, 1991
5	Dal vs Phl, Sept. 23, 1974
5	Min vs LARm, Oct. 26, 1970
6	Ten vs Dal, Dec. 25, 2000
6	Det vs TB, Sept. 28, 1998
6	Pit vs Cin, Oct. 19, 1992
6	NO vs LARd, Dec. 16, 1991

RUSHING YARDS ALLOWED
11	ChiB vs Min, Oct. 28, 1996
11	NYG vs NO, Dec. 20, 1993
13	SF vs NYG, Dec. 1, 1986
14	LARd vs Mia, Nov. 19, 1990
21	Min vs GB, Nov. 21, 2005
21	Den vs Oak, Oct. 16, 1995
21	Phl vs Hou, Dec. 2, 1991

NET PASSING YARDS ALLOWED
-1	Oak vs Hou, Oct. 9, 1972
0	Det vs GB, Nov. 1, 1971
9	Ten vs Dal, Dec. 25, 2000
11	Mia vs Hou, Nov. 5, 1979
14	Min vs SF, Nov. 29, 1976

SACKS
11	Sea vs LARd, Dec. 8, 1986
11	Dal vs Det, Oct. 6, 1975
10	SF vs LARm, Oct. 11, 1976
10	Oak vs Den, Dec. 8, 1975
9	four teams, most recently Ind vs Buf, Dec. 11, 2000

INTERCEPTIONS
6	Dal vs Was, Sept. 9, 1985
6	Was vs SD, Oct. 31, 1983
6	Mia vs Pit, Dec. 3, 1973
5	ten teams, most recently Den vs Min, Oct. 26, 1987

INTERCEPTION RETURN YARDS
154	Dal vs Atl, Sept. 20, 1999
148	Sea vs Phl, Dec. 5, 2005
142	KC vs LARd, Oct. 28, 1991
140	Mia vs Pit, Dec. 3, 1973
120	TB vs SL, Sept. 23, 2002

SACKS (1982–PRESENT)
11.0	Sea vs LARd, Dec. 8, 1986
9.0	Ind vs Buf, Dec. 11, 2000
9.0	Min vs Chi, Oct. 25, 1993
9.0	Chi vs NYG, Sept. 14, 1987
9.0	Pit vs Cin, Oct. 10, 1983

PENALTIES

PENALTIES
17	LARd vs SD, Dec. 5, 1994
16	NO vs SL, Dec. 17, 2001
16	SF vs Atl, Jan. 3, 2000
16	ChiB vs Den, Oct. 16, 1978
15	four teams, most recently NYG vs Min, Nov. 19, 2001

PENALTY YARDS
161	NYJ vs Cle, Sept. 21, 1970
150	NYG vs Min, Nov. 19, 2001
147	ChiB vs Den, Oct. 16, 1978
146	LARd vs SD, Dec. 5, 1994
145	SF vs LARm, Dec. 11, 1989

COMBINED POINTS
95	Was vs GB, Oct. 17, 1983
87	KC vs Ten, Dec. 13, 2004
84	Cin vs SD, Dec. 20, 1982
82	Dal vs Sea, Dec. 6, 2004
79	Oak vs Pit, Oct. 20, 1980

FEWEST POINTS/BOTH TEAMS
10	NYG vs SF, Dec. 3, 1990
12	Den vs Oak, Dec. 1, 1980
13	Was vs Bal, Nov. 7, 1977
13	Bal vs Min, Oct. 25, 1971
14	Dal vs Was, Oct. 2, 1978

COACHING

COACHING WINS

31	Don Shula
19	Tom Landry
18	George Seifert
18	Bill Cowher
15	Bill Parcells
15	Chuck Noll
15	Tom Flores
13	Marty Schottenheimer
13	Marv Levy
12	Mike Shanahan
12	Dan Reeves
12	Chuck Knox

RUSHING

ATTEMPTS

520	Emmitt Smith
421	Tony Dorsett
381	Marcus Allen
375	Thurman Thomas
336	Walter Payton
336	Jerome Bettis
322	Franco Harris
293	John Riggins
279	Curtis Martin
266	Roger Craig

YARDS

2434	Emmitt Smith
1897	Tony Dorsett
1769	Thurman Thomas
1486	Marcus Allen
1435	Franco Harris
1391	Walter Payton
1330	Jerome Bettis
1326	Eric Dickerson
1138	Ahman Green
1112	Garrison Hearst

TOUCHDOWNS

23	Emmitt Smith
17	Marcus Allen
14	Eric Dickerson
13	John Riggins
10	Chuck Muncie
10	Terrell Davis
9	Steve Young
9	Joe Morris
9	Franco Harris
9	Ahman Green
9	Jerome Bettis
9	Ottis Anderson
9	James Brooks
9	Earl Campbell
9	Tony Dorsett

100-YARD GAMES

12	Emmitt Smith
8	Jerome Bettis
7	Franco Harris
7	Eric Dickerson
6	Thurman Thomas
6	Ahman Green
6	Tony Dorsett
5	Barry Sanders
5	Walter Payton
5	Edgerrin James
5	Chuck Muncie
5	Earl Campbell
5	Larry Csonka

PASSING

ATTEMPTS

1303	Dan Marino
1013	Brett Favre
784	John Elway
690	Joe Montana
644	Troy Aikman
585	Steve Young
581	Jim Kelly
523	Phil Simms
495	Danny White
451	Dan Fouts

COMPLETIONS

798	Dan Marino
596	Brett Favre
412	Joe Montana
409	John Elway
399	Troy Aikman
377	Steve Young
355	Jim Kelly
293	Phil Simms
290	Danny White
266	Dan Fouts

GROSS YARDS

9654	Dan Marino
7076	Brett Favre
5148	Joe Montana
5012	John Elway
4614	Troy Aikman
4608	Steve Young
4348	Jim Kelly
3760	Phil Simms
3721	Dan Fouts
3693	Danny White

TOUCHDOWNS

74	Dan Marino
54	Brett Favre
42	Steve Young
36	Joe Montana
31	Jim Kelly
27	Danny White
27	Ken Stabler
25	John Elway
23	Troy Aikman
22	Dave Krieg

INTERCEPTIONS

74	Dan Marino
54	Brett Favre
42	Steve Young
36	Joe Montana
31	Jim Kelly
27	Danny White
27	Ken Stabler
25	John Elway
23	Troy Aikman
22	Dave Krieg

PASSER RATING (MIN. 100 ATTEMPTS)

95.9	Lynn Dickey
90.1	Daunte Culpepper
89.8	Kurt Warner
89.2	Marc Bulger
86.5	Peyton Manning
85.4	Stan Humphries
85.4	Ken Stabler
84.3	Bob Griese
83.9	Brian Griese
83.3	Jeff Garcia

300-YARD GAMES

8	Dan Marino
7	Brett Favre
6	Joe Montana
6	Randall Cunningham
5	Steve Young
5	Dan Fouts
4	Kurt Warner
4	Phil Simms
4	Joe Theismann
4	Peyton Manning
4	Ken Anderson

RECEIVING

RECEPTIONS

254	Jerry Rice
124	Andre Reed
123	Cris Carter
121	Tim Brown
114	Art Monk
102	Rod Smith
96	Torry Holt
96	Michael Irvin
93	Shannon Sharpe
93	Ed McCaffrey

YARDS

4029	Jerry Rice
1783	Andre Reed
1537	Art Monk
1512	Michael Irvin
1480	Tony Hill
1479	Tim Brown
1443	Torry Holt
1431	Cris Carter
1339	Mark Clayton
1333	Rod Smith

TOUCHDOWNS

34	Jerry Rice
15	Terrell Owens
15	Mark Clayton
13	Andre Reed
12	Tony Hill
11	Randy Moss
10	Brent Jones
10	Cris Carter
9	Rod Smith
9	John Taylor
9	Nat Moore
9	Cliff Branch

100-YARD GAMES

14	Jerry Rice
7	Torry Holt
6	Tony Hill
5	Terrell Owens
5	Andre Reed
5	Kellen Winslow
5	Randy Moss
5	Tim Brown
5	Cris Carter
4	Drew Pearson
4	Marvin Harrison
4	Tony Martin
4	Michael Irvin
4	Art Monk
4	James Lofton
4	Terry Glenn

PLAYER TOTALS

TOTAL YARDS

4116	Jerry Rice
2836	Emmitt Smith
2567	Tony Dorsett
2317	Thurman Thomas
2164	Marcus Allen
1888	Walter Payton
1862	Andre Reed
1718	Franco Harris
1593	Roger Craig
1566	Art Monk

TOTAL TOUCHDOWNS

36	Jerry Rice
24	Emmitt Smith
19	Marcus Allen
16	Mark Clayton
15	Terrell Owens
14	John Riggins
14	Ahman Green
14	Eric Dickerson
13	Andre Reed
13	Tony Dorsett

SPECIAL TEAMS

FIELD GOALS MADE

51	Anderson, Gary
41	Elam, Jason
34	Andersen, Morten
33	Moseley, Mark
32	Longwell, Ryan
31	Stoyanovich, Pete
30	Bahr, Matt
29	Johnson, Norm
28	Wilkins, Jeff
27	Christie, Steve
27	Septien, Rafael
27	Stenerud, Jan

POINTS (KICKERS)

247	Anderson, Gary
176	Elam, Jason
161	Longwell, Ryan
145	Moseley, Mark
144	Andersen, Morten
143	Septien, Rafael
142	Wilkins, Jeff
138	Johnson, Norm
136	Bahr, Matt
134	Stoyanovich, Pete

PUNT RETURN AVERAGE (MIN. 10 RETURNS)

17.3	Lipps, Louis
16.5	Podolak, Ed
16.1	McLemore, Dana
15.4	Sanders, Deion
15.4	O'Neal, Deltha
15.2	Barber, Tiki
15.1	Mason, Derrick
15.1	Lewis, Leo
14.8	Vanover, Tamarick
13.0	Swann, Lynn

KICKOFF RETURN AVERAGE (MIN. 10 RETURNS)

31.6	Davis, Clarence
28.9	Tate, Robert
28.9	Payton, Eddie
27.7	Faulk, Kevin
27.5	Marion, Brock
27.4	Johnson, Marshall
27.2	Brown, Eddie
26.9	Washington, Vic
26.5	Woodson, Rod
26.3	Avery, John

DEFENSE

SACKS (1982-DATE)

24.5	Smith, Bruce
20.0	Dent, Richard
18.0	Greene, Kevin
16.5	White, Reggie
16.5	Doleman, Chris
16.0	Haley, Charles
15.5	Taylor, Lawrence
14.5	Gbaja-Biamila, Kabeer
14.0	Randle, John
14.0	Townsend, Greg

INTERCEPTIONS

11	Walls, Everson
9	Hanks, Merton
8	Thomas, Emmitt
7	Buckley, Terrell
7	Downs, Michael
7	Anderson, Dick
6	eighteen players tied

INTERCEPTION RETURN AVERAGE (MIN. 5 RETURNS)

36.7	Woodson, Rod
36.2	Wright, Felix
33.0	Robertson, Isiah
30.5	Tatum, Jack
28.6	Cromwell, Nolan
27.1	Anderson, Dick
26.8	Sanders, Deion
22.8	Hanks, Merton
22.5	Vincent, Troy
22.0	Marion, Brock

THE HISTORICAL RECORD

The National Football League season seems too long in arriving and way too quick in leaving. Through the NFL draft, minicamps, training camps, preseason games, season openers, bye weeks, playoff pushes, wild-card games, championship games, and the Super Bowl, it seems that one day the Hall of Fame Game is on TV in August, and then six flips of the calendar pass by quicker than a couple of three-and-outs. Soon it's February and all that's left are the fleeting moments of the Pro Bowl and six long months before the next game in Canton.

But while the season is in session, the knowledge of the years that preceded it seemingly gets compressed to process the new season. Which year was it that the Rams were good and which was the one where they fell off the map? And which came first? Did the Giants make the playoffs and wasn't their season in doubt in November? When was it that Al Davis struck fear in the league by bringing in a bunch of chewed-up veterans and mixing them with a few hot-shot rookies, and when was the year the same recipe made mud? If it's your team, a gang of futuristic memory-erasers couldn't blot out the image of the long-awaited celebration amid the blizzard of confetti at the Super Bowl, but if your team wasn't so hot that year, do you remember everything that happened? The passage of time plays tricks on the mind, especially concerning a 32-team league with a high turnover rate. This doesn't just happen to those games of childhood where Denver's jerseys seemed so orange or the Cowboys seemed to take on the posture and purpose of their coach, but it even enters the modern NFL, where every game can be watched on television, and barring a satellite dish, can at least be dissected well on into Tuesday. When it's all said and done, the league is always looking forward, but the past is what gives the game perspective. The present and the future aren't worth as much without knowing what made the old days so good.

That is this book's and this section's purpose: to fill in the holes of the season, whether it's finding out who was the league's first champion (the Akron Pros) or who was the last NFC team to win consecutive Super Bowls (the Dallas Cowboys). The Historical Record highlights the numbers that went beyond the pale and then analyzes what went on beyond the numbers. A team is judged by its record and a player by his stats, but how did the 2005 Steelers go from barely over .500 on December 4 to clutching the Vince Lombardi Trophy just two months later?

The Historical Record section covers everything that goes into a football season … that can fit on a single page. There are 135 seasons depicted, including the first two years when the league was known as the American Professional Football Association, the four years of the All-America Football League of the 1960s, and the decade of the American Football League that became the linchpin of the game we know today.

The top of each page features the standings for each season, alongside with points scored and allowed, plus detailed team running and passing information. Below the standings and team statistics are the individual league (1920–69) or conference (1970–present) leaders in as many as 35 categories. Every season of the AAFC (1946–49) and AFL (1960–69) is listed as well.

NFL record keeping has improved as time has worn on, but the early days provided scant information on much beyond who scored. Because of this lack of information, the first decade of the NFL has two seasons per page. From 1930 forward, however, there is one season per page as the leaders eventually expand to 35 statistical categories.

While many great players are included in this section, many thousands more are not. For most ball carriers, passers, receivers, and the like, it is because they were unable to accrue enough yardage, score enough points, or perform at a high enough rate to make the top five in their league or conference in any year. Defensive players and special teams performers have even fewer categories in which to shine. Many other names will never appear among the annual leaders in the Historical Record not because of their skill, but because they have no measurable statistics. These men are often simply labeled in the category of linemen.

That generic term refers to men who played on either offense or defense or, in the heady days of the two-way men before the 1950s, those who played both. While the defensive tackles and ends can accrue statistics like interceptions and sacks, their foes on the other side of the line must content themselves with the knowledge that their strength or weakness on a given play at the line of scrimmage makes the difference between a play that gains yardage and one that doesn't. Infrequently, offensive linemen have been included in publicity campaigns. There was the Seven Blocks of Granite at Fordham in the 1940s, featuring future Hall of Famers Alex Wojciechowicz and Vince Lombardi (although Lombardi was inducted as a coach, Wojciechowicz, a great two-way player for two teams, proved to be as hard for defensive lineman to get around as it was for everyone else to spell his name). Later there was the Electric Company that opened holes for O.J. Simpson and "turned on the Juice." The most famous offensive line of all, thought, was the Hogs in Washington, who became better known than some of the ball-handling teammates in the 1980s. There was a television commercial that decade where Dan Marino, shattering passing records left and right, bought his linemen a certain brand of dress gloves for Christmas. (The commercial didn't point out that his well-gloved, never-on-camera protectors all resided in the Miami area). Two decades later an ad campaign featured New England quarterback Tom Brady bringing his linemen—in full uniform—to the set of a TV commercial where they argued over the merits of a credit card's security provisions. Not exactly the Purple People Eaters or Joe Greene scarfing a soda, but it's rock star status for the O-line, whose vast majority remain anonymous except to diehard fans and grateful ball carriers and quarterbacks bearing gloves and credit card statements. While these integral blockers have our undying gratitude and respect, it is the men who handle the ball—plus those who try to prevent it from being handled efficiently—that are the subject of the leaders in the middle of every page in this section.

At the bottom of each page is a brief essay that gives a snapshot of what it was like to follow pro football in a given year. The section deals with how the teams got through the regular season, innovations that may have helped them, tragedies that may have befallen them and their triumphs over a field of worthy pursuers. Sometimes the most memorable events in a season happen to the worst teams. In almost every season in pro football history a good team has been done in by bad luck; these developments will also be explored. Off-field events that brought change to the game, such as wars, strikes, outside competition, and league-altering television contracts are also discussed. The debuts and exits of great players are noted periodically, as are deaths that can make even that greatest feeling in pro football, a winning Sunday, feel like a blue Monday.

KEY TO THE HISTORICAL RECORD

The lists below show all abbreviations used in the Historical Record section. Those that have not been defined elsewhere are explained here. A dash indicates that the numbers are both for and against; the team in question's total always comes first, followed by the dash and the opponent's total.

W Wins
L Losses
T Ties
PCT Winning Percentage
POST Postseason Performance. **#** is used for a tie-breaker, and each letter indicates a playoff game. * shows the final playoff game was won (league championship for 1933–65, Super Bowl for 1966–present). Intermediate games are **P** for playoff round (1949 AAFC, 1969 AFL and 1982 NFL), **W** for wild card (NFL 1970–present), **D** for division round, **C** for conference championship, **L** for league championship, and **S** for Super Bowl. The letter **E** is used for the divisional champ who played in the wild card round (NFL 1990-date). If the game was won, then another letter appears for the next round.
PTS Points
RA Rushing Attempts
RY Rushing Yards
RY/A Rushing Yards Average
RTD Rushing Touchdowns
FL Fumbles Lost
PA Pass Attempts

PC   Passes Completed
GPY   Gross Passing Yards
PTD   Passing Touchdowns
PI   Passes Intercepted
PSY   Passing Sack Yards
PRat   Passer Rating. The passer's efficiency rating is based on the NFL passer rating system, which ranks passers on a scale using a formula derived from their completion percentage, yards gained per attempt, touchdown percentage, and interception percentage.

SECONDARY TEAM TOTALS

More information on these and other statistical formulas and theory can be found in the Guide to Football Statistics section.

1D   First Downs
PENY   Penalty Yards
PNT   Punting Average
FGM/A   Field Goals Made/Attempted
RTNY   Return Yards. Includes punts and interceptions but not kickoff returns (kickoffs are not included because kickoff yards are correlated to touchdowns allowed).
RTNTD   Returns for Touchdowns. Includes all non-scrimmage touchdowns: punt, kickoff, interception, fumble, blocked punts, blocked field goals, and field goal returns (usually occurring on long-distance missed field goals).
OFFY/DEFY   Offensive Yardage /Defensive Yardage. Rushing yardage plus passing yardage minus sack yardage/same for opponent.
NETY   Net Yardage. Same as above, only offensive yardage minus defensive yardage.
NETTO   Net Turnovers. Turnovers gained minus turnovers lost.
NP   Net Points. Points scored minus points allowed.
PNP   Predicted Net Points. Net yards/12 plus net turnovers/4.
DELP   Delta Net Points. Net points minus predicted net points.
PW   Predicted Wins. Games/2 plus net points/40.
DELW   Delta Wins. Net wins minus predicted net wins.

PRT   Improved Passer Rating. The improved rating is derived as yards plus 10 times touchdowns minus 45 times interceptions/attempts, or $YDs \times 10 \times TD - 45 \times INT/ATT$.
DR   Drives. Derived as games plus safeties plus opponent punts plus fumbles lost plus passes intercepted plus extra points plus field goals. This is available since 1941, the first year opponent punts were kept.
YPD   Yards Per Drive. Derived as net yards/drives.
DELY   Delta Yards. Delta yards per drive/offensive yards minus defensive yards.

LEADERS IN THE HISTORICAL RECORD

These are derived cumulatively for most categories, except those that require percentages, averages, or ratings. Keep the following guidelines in mind.

Minimum requirements. Passing Percentage, Average Gain, Rating: 14 attempts/game, 1985–present; 10 attempts/game, 1960–84; 100 attempts, 1950–59; 6 attempts/game, 1940–49; 5 attempts per game, 1932–39.

Averages   Rushing average gain: 5 attempts/game.

Receiving Average Gain   2 receptions/game: 1.25 receptions/game for 1932–37.

Punting Average   2 per game.

Field-Goal Percentage   1 per game; 1/2 per game before 1950.

Punt or Kickoff Return Average   1 per game.

Overall Rank   This final category is based on the total number of adjusted yards accrued by a player. It's a metric that counts not just the raw yards a player gained, but the value of other events such as kick returns or interceptions.

1920 APFA

TEAM	W-L-T	PCT	PTS	TEAM	W-L-T	PCT	PTS
Akron Pros	8-0-3	**1.000**	151-7	Detroit Heralds	2-3-3	.400	53-82
Decatur Staleys	10-1-2	.909	164-21	Cleveland Tigers	2-4-2	.333	28-46
Buffalo All-Americans	9-1-1	.900	**258**-32	Chicago Tigers	2-5-1	.286	49-63
Chicago Cardinals	6-2-2	.750	115-43	Hammond Pros	2-5	.286	41-154
Rock Island Independents	6-2-2	.750	201-49	Columbus Panhandles	2-6-2	.250	41-121
Dayton Triangles	5-2-2	.714	150-54	Muncie Flyers	0-1	.000	0-45
Rochester Jeffersons	6-3-2	.667	156-57	Aver	9	—	115
Canton Bulldogs	7-4-2	.636	208-57				

ALL IN FAVOR OF A CHAMPION, SAY AYE

Owners of the leading professional football teams met in Canton, Ohio, on September 17 to form the American Professional Football Association. Fourteen teams banded together in an effort to keep salaries down and stop players from jumping from club to club. The first matchup between two league teams took place on October 3 with a game between the Dayton Triangles and Columbus Panhandles. Lou Partlow scored the league's first touchdown on a 7-yard run in the third quarter, and Dayton went on to win the historic game, 14–0.

Dayton was one of five teams in the APFA from Ohio, and the Triangles boasted the most prolific offense in the league's inaugural year. Most observers figured that the best teams would be the Canton Bulldogs or the Cleveland Tigers, but the Akron Pros beat them both in October to emerge as the frontrunner. Halfback Fritz Pollard, one of two African Americans in the new league, along with wingback Frank McCormack and fullback Rip King provided Akron's balanced offensive attack.

Illinois boasted four teams in the new league and probably its most powerful figure: George Halas. His Decatur Staleys shut out six of eight opponents in league games. Their lone loss was a 7–6 defeat to the rival Chicago Cardinals, who started the year named the Racine Cardinals because of the street where their field was located. The Rock Island Independents, a strong pro football team before the league formed, played the first game by a league team, a 48–0 rout of the independent and inept St. Paul Ideals on September 26. The Chicago Tigers were the lone APFA team from the first season not to make it to second.

The league's founding fathers had decided that a cup would be awarded to the yearly champion, but they hadn't bothered to figure out exactly how the championship would be decided. Several teams had claims to the title. Akron was undefeated, while the Staleys and Buffalo All-Americans each had just one loss to blemish their record. At the league meeting in April 1921, held in Akron, APFA owners settled the matter by voting the Pros the league champions for 1920.

1921 APFA

TEAM	W-L-T	PCT	PTS	TEAM	W-L-T	PCT	PTS
Chicago Staleys	9-1-1	**.900**	128-53	Washington Senators	1-2	.333	21-43
Buffalo All-Americans	9-1-2	**.900**	**211**-29	Hammond Pros	1-3-1	.250	17-45
Akron Pros	8-3-1	.727	148-31	Minneapolis Marines	1-3	.250	37-41
Canton Bulldogs	5-2-3	.714	106-55	Cincinnati Celts	1-3	.250	14-117
Rock Island Independents	4-2-1	.667	65-30	Detroit Tigers	1-5-1	.167	19-109
Green Bay Packers	3-2-1	.600	70-55	Columbus Panhandles	1-8	.111	47-222
Evansville Crimson Giants	3-2	.600	89-46	Tonawanda Kardex	0-1	.000	0-45
Dayton Triangles	4-4-1	.500	96-67	Louisville Brecks	0-2	.000	0-**27**
Chicago Cardinals	3-3-2	.500	54-53	Muncie Flyers	0-2	.000	0-28
Rochester Jeffersons	2-3	.400	85-76	New York Brickley Giants	0-2	.000	0-72
Cleveland Indians	3-5	.375	95-58	Aver	6	—	62

Rushing TDs		TD Passes		Receiving TDs		Total TDs		Field Goals		Extra Points		Total Points	
F.Pollard-Akr	6	E.Oliphant-Buf	7	H.Miller-Buf	3	F.Pollard-Akr	7	D.Sternaman-ChiS	5	E.Oliphant-Buf	26	E.Oliphant-Buf	47
F.Bacon-Day	5	F.Nesser-Col	3	G.Halas-ChiS	3	O.Anderson-Buf	7	E.Oliphant-Buf	5	R.Hathaway-Day	12	F.Pollard-Akr	42
O.Anderson-Buf	5	R.King-Akr	3			F.Bacon-Day	6	R.Hathaway-Day	4	J.Guyon-Cle	10	O.Anderson-Buf	42
		C.Harley-ChiS	3			J.Scott-Buf	5	C.Lambeau-GB	3	C.Copley-Akr	10	D.Sternaman-ChiS	36
		B.Boynton-Roc	3			C.Cramer-Akr	5			D.Sternaman-ChiS	9	F.Bacon-Day	36

REACHING MORE PLACES BY CARR

Buoyed by the success of their inaugural season, the AFPA made several significant changes in 1921. Most significant was the selection of Joe Carr, founder of the Columbus Panhandles, to be the league's president. He moved the league office to Columbus, drafted a league constitution, restricted player movement, and established membership criteria. With many unaffiliated professional clubs clamoring to be included, the AFPA expanded from 14 to 21 teams. These new entrants stretched the league's geographical reach to Washington in the east, Minneapolis in the west, and Louisville in the south.

While most of these new members struggled both financially and on the field, one notable exception was the Green Bay Packers, owned by the Acme Packing Company. Green Bay native Curley Lambeau, the team's coach and star player, garnered major attention for the Packers with a 43–6 win against the Evansville Crimson Giants on November 6.

The Akron Pros set out to defend their disputed 1920 championship, and started 7–0, shutting out each opponent. After

a scoreless tie against Buffalo, the Pros stumbled, dropping three straight games by a combined score of 31–0. That left an opening for enterprising George Halas, who moved his Decatur team to Chicago in midseason when Decatur starch magnate A.E. Staley turned over ownership of the franchise to him. The club, still called the Staleys, drew much larger crowds in Cubs Park, and their improving finances mirrored their strong play on the field.

To avoid the confusion over awarding a championship, the league decided to keep official standings, and the team with the best record would be declared champion. The Buffalo All-Americans defeated the Staleys on Thanksgiving Day, 7–6, seemingly wrapping up the APFA championship. But Halas recognized that the league had no fixed schedule and no declared end date, so he kept playing. Halas scheduled Buffalo on December 4—a game the All-Americans viewed as a mere postseason exhibition—and the Staleys won, followed by victories against two weaker opponents. In the end, the Staley's 9–1–1 record stood slightly better than Buffalo's 9–1–2 mark, and Halas laid claim to the championship.

1922 NFL

TEAM	W-L-T	PCT	PTS	TEAM	W-L-T	PCT	PTS
Canton Bulldogs	**10-0-2**	**1.000**	**184-15**	Oorang Indians	3-6	.333	69-190
Chicago Bears	9-3	.750	123-44	Milwaukee Badgers	2-4-3	.333	51-71
Chicago Cardinals	8-3	.727	96-50	Minneapolis Marines	1-3	.250	19-40
Toledo Maroons	5-2-2	.714	94-59	Louisville Brecks	1-3	.250	13-140
Rock Island Independents	4-2-1	.667	154-27	Evansville Crimson Giants	0-3	.000	6-88
Racine Legion	6-4-1	.600	122-56	Rochester Jeffersons	0-4-1	.000	13-76
Dayton Triangles	4-3-1	.571	80-62	Hammond Pros	0-5-1	.000	0-69
Green Bay Packers	4-3-3	.571	70-54	Columbus Panhandles	0-8	.000	24-174
Buffalo All-Americans	5-4-1	.556	87-41	Aver	8	—	75
Akron Pros	3-5-2	.375	146-95				

Rushing TDs	TD Passes	Receiving TDs	Total TDs	Field Goals	Extra Points	Total Points
J.Conzelman-RI 7	R.Watson-Tol 2	C.Mathys-GB 2	J.Conzelman-RI 7	P.Driscoll-ChiC.............8	R.Hathaway-Day...........9	H.Gillo-Rac 52
C.Cramer-Akr..............6	C.Lambeau-GB...........2	P.Driscoll-ChiC.............2	M.Casteel-Can...........7	D.Sternaman-ChiB......6	P.Sheeks-Akr 8	J.Conzelman-RI 48
H.Gillo-Rac 5	R.King-Akr 2	S.Bierce-Akr 2	C.Cramer-Akr...........6	H.Gillo-Rac 6	E.Shaw-Can 8	M.Casteel-Can...........42
B.Gavin-RI 5	T.Hughitt-Buf 2	D.Annan-Tol 2		P.Sheeks-Akr 3	F.Morrissey-Buf...........8	D.Sternaman-ChiB......41
	J.Conzelman-RI 2			R.Horween-ChiC 3		P.Driscoll-ChiC...........40

THE CHICAGO BEARS AND THE NFL

The 1922 season marked two significant name changes. In practice, the APFA had become more of a league than a loose association of clubs, and so the owners changed their name to the National Football League. George Halas changed his team's name from the Staleys to the Bears. The other owners viewed the Bears and Staleys as two different franchises and ruled that everyone who had played with the Staleys in 1921 was now a free agent. Halas lost some of his best players from a team that was the league's defending champion. Tarzan Taylor joined the Canton Bulldogs, while Chic Harley and Pete Stinchcomb signed contracts with the new Toledo club.

The defection that hurt the most was Guy Chamberlin, regarded by many as the best end in football. He was lured to Canton as both end and head coach. With quarterback Harry Robb and fullback Doc Elliott, the Bulldogs had the league's most prolific offense. Tackles Pete Henry and Link Lyman led a stellar defense, which held their opponents to just 15 points in 12 games. Canton won 10 games without a loss and twice played scoreless ties. For the first time in the league's brief history, a season concluded with no dispute regarding its champion.

Despite having his team gutted, Halas still put together the league's second-best record. He lured Stinchcomb back to Chicago by naming him as an assistant coach. Halas signed Hunk Anderson, an All-American guard from the nearby University of Notre Dame, and Laurie Walquist, a back from the University of Illinois.

The Bears were the money-makers in a struggling league and Halas flexed his muscles often, especially in regard to the Packers. After the 1921 season, he'd gotten Green Bay's franchise revoked because Curly Lambeau had used college players Halas had wanted to hire illegally for the Bears. Lambeau borrowed money to start up again in 1922, but Halas canceled a Thanksgiving Day game in Green Bay because the Packers couldn't guarantee a large enough gate. The Bears played—and lost to—the crosstown Cardinals instead.

1923 NFL

TEAM	W-L-T	PCT	PTS	TEAM	W-L-T	PCT	PTS
Canton Bulldogs	**11-0-1**	**1.000**	**246-19**	Rock Island Independents	2-3-3	.400	84-62
Chicago Bears	9-2-1	.818	123-35	Minneapolis Marines	2-5-2	.286	48-81
Green Bay Packers	7-2-1	.778	85-34	St. Louis All-Stars	1-4-2	.200	14-39
Milwaukee Badgers	7-2-3	.778	100-49	Hammond Pros	1-5-1	.167	14-59
Cleveland Indians	3-1-3	.750	52-49	Akron Pros	1-6	.143	25-74
Chicago Cardinals	8-4	.667	161-56	Dayton Triangles	1-6-1	.143	16-95
Duluth Kelleys	4-3	.571	35-33	Oorang Indians	1-10	.091	50-257
Columbus Tigers	5-4-1	.556	119-35	Louisville Brecks	0-3	.000	0-90
Buffalo All-Americans	5-4-3	.556	94-43	Rochester Jeffersons	0-4	.000	6-141
Racine Legion	4-4-2	.500	86-76	Aver	9	—	70
Toledo Maroons	3-3-2	.500	35-66				

Rushing TDs	TD Passes	Receiving TDs	Total TDs	Field Goals	Extra Points	Total Points
L.Smyth-Can..............7	L.Smyth-Can...............6	B.Rapp-Col 3	L.Smyth-Can...............7	P.Driscoll-ChiC...........10	P.Henry-Can 25	P.Driscoll-ChiC...........78
B.Jones-Can 6	S.Winters-Col 5		P.Driscoll-ChiC............7	P.Henry-Can 9	B.Winkelman-Mil..........8	P.Henry-Can 58
D.Elliott-Can...............6	S.Barr-Rac..................5		B.Jones-Can 6	F.Morrissey-Buf...........8	H.Sies-RI 8	D.Sternaman-ChiB......51
P.Driscoll-ChiC............6			D.Elliott-Can................6	H.Gillo-Rac 8	H.Gillo-Rac 8	B.Winkelman-Mil.........44
						H.Gillo-Rac 44

BULLDOGS, BADGERS, AND THE FIRST PACKER BACKERS

The league was only four years old, but by the end of the 1923 season, the NFL's first dynasty had been born. Under the leadership of coach Guy Chamberlin, the Canton Bulldogs posted their second consecutive undefeated season. They dominated opponents with a balanced yet seemingly unstoppable offensive attack. The power running of Doc Elliott and Lou Smyth was complimented by the speed of Tex Grigg and Harry Robb. Canton's defense, led by tackle Pete Henry, held opponents to 19 points in 12 games.

Once again, the biggest challenger for the NFL championship was the Chicago Bears. A stout defense kept the club in contention while the offense struggled early in the season. Without halfback Pete Stinchcomb, who left for Columbus, Chicago didn't score a touchdown until their fifth game in 1923. But late in the season against the Oorang Indians, George Halas scooped up a Jim Thorpe fumble and raced 98 yards for a touchdown—a mark that would stand for five decades, or slightly longer than Papa Bear's coaching tenure.

The Green Bay Packers were rescued from financial ruin when local backers proposed making the team a non-profit corporation. Five dollars bought a share in the hometown team, plus admission to every home game. This move raised more than $5,000, and the Packers went from the brink of bankruptcy to one of the league's most solvent teams. Freed of the pressures of keeping the franchise afloat, Curley Lambeau could focus on the game. He led the league's best passing offense and coached the team to third place. Another Wisconsin team emerged as a contender. The Milwaukee Badgers, unimpressive in their 1922 debut, flourished with Jimmy Conzelman as head coach and top player. Their only losses were to the rival Packers.

The Columbus Panhandles had managed just one league win in three seasons, but the club reorganized in 1923, dumping most of their veteran players in favor of youth. The name was changed to the Tigers and Stinchcomb was hired as head coach and backfield star. Columbus posted a winning record and scored more points than in the previous three seasons combined.

1924 NFL

TEAM	W-L-T	PCT	PTS	TEAM	W-L-T	PCT	PTS
Cleveland Bulldogs	7-1-1	.875	229-60	Hammond Pros	2-2-1	.500	18-45
Chicago Bears	6-1-4	.857	136-55	Milwaukee Badgers	5-8	.385	142-188
Frankford Yellow Jackets	11-2-1	.846	326-109	Akron Pros	2-6	.250	59-132
Duluth Kelleys	5-1	.833	56-16	Dayton Triangles	2-6	.250	45-148
Rock Island Independents	5-2-2	.714	88-38	Kansas City Blues	2-7	.222	46-124
Green Bay Packers	7-4	.636	108-38	Kenosha Maroons	0-4-1	.000	12-117
Racine Legion	4-3-3	.571	69-47	Minneapolis Marines	0-6	.000	14-108
Chicago Cardinals	5-4-1	.556	90-67	Rochester Jeffersons	0-7	.000	7-156
Buffalo Bisons	6-5	.545	120-140	Aver	9	—	92
Columbus Tigers	4-4	.500	91-68				

Rushing TDs	TD Passes	Receiving TDs	Total TDs	Field Goals	Extra Points	Total Points
T.Hamer-Fra.............12	H.Workman-Cle.............9	T.Voss-GB..............5	T.Hamer-Fra.............12	J.Sternaman-ChiB.........9	J.Welsh-Fra.............17	J.Sternaman-ChiB.....75
J.Storer-Fra.............7	S.Winters-Col.............8	B.Rapp-Col..............5	J.Storer-Fra.............8	H.Gillo-Rac.............8	H.Workman-Cle.............16	T.Hamer-Fra.............72
B.Gavin-RI.............7	C.Lambeau-GB.............8		B.Gavin-RI.............7	J.Welsh-Fra.............7	R.Dunn-Mil.............14	B.Boynton-Buf.............59
D.Elliott-Cle.............6	R.Dunn-Mil.............6			R.Dunn-Mil.............7	J.Sternaman-ChiB.............12	J.Storer-Fra.............48
G.Sullivan-Fra.............5	B.Boynton-Buf.............6			P.Driscoll-ChiC.............7	R.Stein-Fra.............12	H.Gillo-Rac.............48

BULLDOGS ON THE MARCH

At their annual meeting in January, NFL owners voted to split the league into two divisions—east and west—to promote geographical rivalries and set up a championship game. Everyone agreed the idea made sense, but none of the owners could agree on how to implement the plan. When all was said and done, the owners reverted to the old format. They named a fixed start and end date, but scheduling was otherwise left up to the individual clubs.

The Canton Bulldogs were two-time defending champs, but neither those titles nor their collection of star players could overcome the economic realities of playing professional sports in a small town. The Bulldogs were the NFL's biggest draw on the road, but the home crowds weren't big enough to cover expenses. Mired in debt, the ownership group sold the franchise's assets to Cleveland businessman Sam Deutsch. The deal caused an uproar in Canton. Locals tried to raise enough money to keep their team, but their wallets didn't match their outrage. The franchise was declared inactive and the team's best players, including star end and head coach Guy Chamberlin, moved 50 miles north to Cleveland. The existing Indians changed their name to Bulldogs.

The Frankford Yellow Jackets, arguably the best independent pro team, were finally convinced to join the NFL. Led by Tex Hamer, the Yellow Jackets made an immediate splash. Their dominating rushing attack helped them average 23 points per game. Only the Cleveland Bulldogs averaged more. Eager to compete, the Yellow Jackets played two games per weekend, but the heavy schedule didn't slow them down. The team went 8–0 in the month of November and finished with 11 wins—plus a tie—in 14 league games.

It was a tight three-team race for the championship, between Frankford, the Bulldogs, and the Chicago Bears. Frankford's eight-game win streak couldn't help them overcome two losses in October. The Bears made a valiant effort, but lost their head-to-head matchup with Cleveland. The Bears again finished second, as they had every year since they'd taken the disputed title away from Buffalo in 1921.

1925 NFL

TEAM	W-L-T	PCT	PTS	TEAM	W-L-T	PCT	PTS
Chicago Cardinals	11-2-1	.846	230-65	Cleveland Bulldogs	5-8-1	.385	75-135
Pottsville Maroons	10-2	.833	270-45	Kansas City Cowboys	2-5-1	.286	65-97
Detroit Panthers	8-2-2	.800	129-39	Hammond Pros	1-4	.200	23-87
New York Giants	8-4	.667	122-67	Buffalo Bisons	1-6-2	.143	33-113
Akron Pros	4-2-2	.667	65-51	Duluth Kelleys	0-3	.000	6-25
Frankford Yellow Jackets	13-7	.650	190-169	Rochester Jeffersons	0-6-1	.000	26-111
Chicago Bears	9-5-3	.643	158-96	Milwaukee Badgers	0-6	.000	7-191
Rock Island Independents	5-3-3	.625	99-58	Dayton Triangles	0-7-1	.000	3-84
Green Bay Packers	8-5	.615	151-110	Columbus Tigers	0-9	.000	28-124
Providence Steam Roller	6-5-1	.545	111-101	Aver	10	—	92
Canton Bulldogs	4-4	.500	50-73				

Rushing TDs	TD Passes	Receiving TDs	Total TDs	Field Goals	Extra Points	Total Points
T.Latone-Pot.............7	R.Dunn-ChiC.............9	M.Norton-GB.............4	T.Latone-Pot.............8	P.Driscoll-ChiC.............11	C.Berry-Pot.............29	C.Berry-Pot.............74
	J.Ernst-Pot.............8	H.Erickson-ChiC.........4	T.Hamer-Fra.............7	L.Smyth-Det.............5	J.Sternaman-ChiB.............17	P.Driscoll-ChiC.............67
	D.Vick-Det.............7	C.Berry-Pot.............4	H.Flanagan-Pot.............7	B.Behman-Fra.............5	L.Smyth-Det.............12	J.Sternaman-ChiB.....62
	H.Stockton-Fra.............7		H.Erickson-ChiC.........7		B.Behman-Fra.............12	T.Latone-Pot.............48
						T.Hamer-Fra.............45

THE GALLOPING GHOST SAVES THE DAY

Professional football changed forever on Thanksgiving Day when the nation's best college player opted to turn pro. Red Grange, the 22-year-old star from the University of Illinois, ranked with slugger Babe Ruth and boxer Jack Dempsey as one of the most popular athletes of the era. The day after his last college game, Grange signed a contract with the Chicago Bears. The spotlight followed Grange and the attention thrust pro football onto the national stage for the first time.

Bears owner George Halas and C.C. Pyle, Grange's manager, arranged to capitalize on the attention by playing 10 games in 18 days. Despite a raging snowstorm, 32,000 fans turned out for Grange's NFL debut at Wrigley Field on Thanksgiving. A similar crowd assembled three days later. Then Grange and his barnstorming teammates hit the road and set an attendance record in Philadelphia. Almost 70,000 crammed the Polo Grounds to see Grange face the Giants. The Bears won, 19–7, but for the first-year Giants, the league's second try for a team in New York, the attention was unbelievable. A month earlier the club had drawn just 4,000.

While the Bears soared at the box office, the grueling schedule limited Grange's impact on the field. The team went 3–3–1 after adding the Galloping Ghost and dropped to seventh place, their worst finish ever. Grange and the Bears continued their barnstorming after the season ended, playing games across the South, in California, and in the Pacific Northwest until the end of January.

The best team on the field was probably the Pottsville Maroons, a newcomer to the league but well established as a powerhouse among the eastern independents. Despite their strong showing, a controversy in December kept them from claiming the championship. It started with protests over a game the Maroons played against a team of college all-stars in Philadelphia, and ended with the club being fined and stripped of its claim to the league championship. That left the Chicago Cardinals atop the standings. Led by triple-threat Paddy Driscoll, the Cards claimed their first NFL title after five seasons of relative mediocrity.

1926 NFL

TEAM	W-L-T	PCT	PTS	TEAM	W-L-T	PCT	PTS
Frankford Yellow Jackets	14-1-2	.933	236-49	Hartford Blues	3-7	.300	57-99
Chicago Bears	12-1-3	.923	216-63	Brooklyn Lions	3-8	.273	60-150
Pottsville Maroons	10-2-2	.833	155-29	Milwaukee Badgers	2-7	.222	41-66
Kansas City Cowboys	8-3	.727	76-53	Akron Indians	1-4-3	.200	23-89
Green Bay Packers	7-3-3	.700	151-61	Dayton Triangles	1-4-1	.200	15-82
New York Giants	8-4-1	.667	147-51	Racine Tornadoes	1-4	.200	8-92
Los Angeles Buccaneers	6-3-1	.667	67-57	Columbus Tigers	1-6	.143	26-93
Duluth Eskimos	6-5-3	.545	113-81	Canton Bulldogs	1-9-3	.100	46-161
Buffalo Rangers	4-4-2	.500	53-62	Hammond Pros	0-4	.000	3-56
Chicago Cardinals	5-6-1	.455	74-98	Louisville Colonels	0-4	.000	0-108
Providence Steam Roller	5-7-1	.417	89-103	Aver	11	—	80
Detroit Panthers	4-6-2	.400	107-60				

Rushing TDs	TD Passes	Receiving TDs	Total TDs	Field Goals	Extra Points	Total Points
B.Wentz-Pot............10	E.Scharer-Det............6	D.Hanny-ChiB............4	B.Wentz-Pot............10	P.Driscoll-ChiB............12	J.Welsh-Pot............15	P.Driscoll-ChiB............86
E.Nevers-Dul.............8	P.Driscoll-ChiB............6	V.Lewellen-GB............3	C.Oden-Pro............10	G.Snell-Det............9	J.McBride-NYG............15	E.Nevers-Dul............71
B.Senn-ChiB.............7	H.Stockton-Fra............5		B.Jones-Fra............9	A.Bloodgood-KC............8	P.Purdy-GB............14	B.Wentz-Pot............60
B.Jones-Fra.............7	J.Kendrick-Buf............5		E.Nevers-Dul............8	J.Budd-Fra............6	P.Driscoll-ChiB............14	C.Oden-Pro............60
C.Oden-Pro.............6				J.Welsh-Pot............5	J.Budd-Fra............12	B.Jones-Fra............54

GHOST IN THE MACHINE

The NFL's biggest drawing card in 1925 became its biggest nemesis a year later. Anxious to capitalize on the big crowds coming to see him play, Red Grange asked the league to let him field his own team in New York. He signed a five-year lease at Yankee Stadium that promised to generate tremendous revenues not only for himself, but also for the visiting clubs. Tim Mara, owner of the New York Giants, objected strenuously. His team played less than a mile away in the Polo Grounds. Putting a new team so close would hurt attendance, and he pointed out that his franchise agreement promised him exclusivity in New York City.

Other owners saw a larger problem developing: a challenge to their control of the game by star players. Determined not to let this become a players' league and fearful of setting a precedent, they refused to let Grange launch a team in New York or anywhere else. Undaunted, Grange started his own pro circuit. His American Football League went head to head with the NFL not only in New York, but also in Philadelphia, Cleveland, and Chicago. Grange's AFL even enticed the Rock Island Independents to jump leagues.

The NFL countered by expanding, and heavily recruiting college players, especially the previously overlooked talent from the West Coast. Stanford's star halfback Ernie Nevers surprised everybody by signing with the relatively unsuccessful Duluth Eskimos. Suddenly, the Eskimos were the league's biggest draw, and they played all but one of their 14 games on the road. It was a one-man show, with Nevers running, passing, and kicking the ball from a double-wing formation. Nevers played in all but 29 minutes of Duluth's season, which also included 15 exhibition games.

Three teams battled for the championship, with the Frankford Yellow Jackets eventually finishing on top thanks to a 7–6 win over Chicago on December 4. It was coach Guy Chamberlin's fourth title in five years.

Despite generating a lot of attention, Grange's league struggled and folded at the end of the year. Even though the popularity of pro football was growing, there wasn't enough interest—or talent—to sustain two leagues.

1927 NFL

TEAM	W-L-T	PCT	PTS	TEAM	W-L-T	PCT	PTS
New York Giants	11-1-1	.917	197-20	Pottsville Maroons	5-8	.385	80-163
Green Bay Packers	7-2-1	.778	113-43	Chicago Cardinals	3-7-1	.300	69-134
Chicago Bears	9-3-2	.750	149-98	Dayton Triangles	1-6-1	.143	15-57
Cleveland Bulldogs	8-4-1	.667	209-107	Duluth Eskimos	1-8	.111	68-134
Providence Steam Roller	8-5-1	.615	105-88	Buffalo Bisons	0-5	.000	8-123
New York Yankees	7-8-1	.467	142-174	Aver	12	—	109
Frankford Yellow Jackets	6-9-3	.400	152-166				

Rushing TDs	TD Passes	Receiving TDs	Total TDs	Field Goals	Extra Points	Total Points
J.McBride-NYG............6	B.Friedman-Cle............11	H.Haines-NYG............4	Many............6	K.Mercer-Fra............5	J.McBride-NYG............15	J.McBride-NYG............57
J.Simmons-Cle............5	J.McBride-NYG............7	R.Flaherty-NYY............4		J.Simmons-Pro............3	B.Friedman-Cle............11	A.Bloodgood-Cle............45
B.Senn-ChiB............5	E.Nevers-Dul............5	J.Rooney-Dul............3		H.Moran-Fra............3	E.Tryon-NYY............8	E.Tryon-NYY............44
V.Lewellen-GB............5	W.Kelly-NYY............5	J.Conzelman-Pro............3				P.Driscoll-ChiB............43
P.Driscoll-ChiB............5		C.Bacchus-Cle............3				K.Mercer-Fra............39

GIANTS IN THEIR MIDST

Buoyed by the success of teams in big cities and the growing influx of college stars, the National Football League got lean and mean in 1927. Even the healthiest teams had lost money competing against Red Grange's rival league in 1926, and while the NFL's expansion strategy had helped them survive, the lesser teams threatened to pull everybody else down. A modest crowd at Chicago's Wrigley Field or at the Polo Grounds in New York generated much more revenue than a sellout in small towns like Canton, Ohio, or Hammond, Indiana. The NFL turned its back on towns and teams that had been instrumental in founding the league just a few years earlier. The 12 remaining franchises, though, were now stronger financially, and all had rosters improved by the best players from the disbanded teams.

It was another college star who made the biggest impact of 1927. Benny Friedman, from the University of Michigan, brought his aggressive passing attack to the Cleveland Bulldogs. He led the league with 11 touchdown passes at a time when the rules discouraged throwing the ball. Guy Chamberlin concluded his remarkable playing

and head coaching career with a poor Cardinals club. Across town, Ed Healey called it quits with the Bears.

Despite the trouble Red Grange's rival league had given the NFL in 1926, he was still good business. The NFL allowed his New York Yankees to join the league, playing mostly on the road and operating under the Brooklyn Lions franchise (with Giants owner Tim Mara holding title in lieu of payment). Grange refused surgery after injuring his knee in October, limiting him for the rest of the season and his career. Even with outstanding end Red Badgro, the Yankees went winless their last six games.

With Grange sidelined and Ernie Nevers toiling for the hapless Duluth Eskimos, the league's most productive runner was Joe Guyon of the Giants. The 35-year-old journeyman had the best season of his career, but it was the defense that propelled the Giants to a championship. The club had 10 shutouts, outscoring their opponents, 197–20. New York's line featured three future Hall of Famers: Pete Henry, Steve Owen, and Cal Hubbard.

1928 NFL

TEAM	W-L-T	PCT	PTS	TEAM	W-L-T	PCT	PTS
Providence Steam Roller	8-1-2	.889	128-42	New York Yankees	4-8-1	.333	103-179
Frankford Yellow Jackets	11-3-2	.786	175-84	Pottsville Maroons	2-8	.200	74-134
Detroit Wolverines	7-2-1	.778	189-76	Chicago Cardinals	1-5	.167	7-107
Green Bay Packers	6-4-3	.600	120-92	Dayton Triangles	0-7	.000	9-131
Chicago Bears	7-5-1	.583	182-85	Aver	11	—	107
New York Giants	4-7-2	.364	79-136				

Rushing TDs	TD Passes	Receiving TDs	Total TDs	Field Goals	Extra Points	Total Points
V.Lewellen-GB 6	B.Friedman-Det 9	G.Welch-NYY 6	V.Lewellen-GB 9	H.O'Boyle-GB 3	B.Friedman-Det 19	B.Friedman-Det 55
B.Friedman-Det 6	W.Kelly-NYY 7	B.Senn-ChiB..............4	G.Welch-NYY 8	R.Smith-Pro 1	H.O'Boyle-GB 8	V.Lewellen-GB 54
T.Feather-Det 6	W.Wilson-Pro 5	C.Bacchus-Det 4	T.Feather-Det 7	J.Roepke-Fra 1	P.Driscoll-ChiB 8	G.Welch-NYY 48
W.Wilson-Pro............5	K.Mercer-Fra 5	C.Oden-Pro 3		B.Caldwell-NYG 1	R.Smith-Pro 7	T.Feather-Det 42
K.Mercer-Fra............5	R.Dunn-GB 4	V.Lewellen-GB 3		F.Abbott-Day 1	J.Sternaman-ChiB 6	K.Mercer-Fra............38

STEAM ROLLING TO A TITLE

Right from the start, the New York Giants struggled to defend their NFL championship. Joe Guyon retired, fullback Frank McBride was injured, and the dominating defense of the previous season suddenly couldn't stop anybody. The Giants suffered some decisive defeats early and lost their last five games to finish with a losing record for the first time in their history.

When the Cleveland Bulldogs folded after the 1927 season, quarterback Benny Friedman returned to Michigan to lead the team that replaced the Bulldogs: the Detroit Wolverines. End Carl Bacchus and backs Tiny Feather and Len Sedbrook gave Friedman an assortment of offensive weapons. Detroit's only defeats came on a weekend road trip to play the Frankford Yellow Jackets on Saturday and the Providence Steam Roller on Sunday. Those weekend doubleheaders were popular with the Yellow Jackets, who played nine games in five weeks during November. Back-to-back losses in a weekend doubleheader with Providence cost Frankford a chance to win the season championship.

Early in the season, Providence quarterback Jimmy Conzelman suffered a knee injury that would sideline him for the remainder of the season. He remained on the sidelines to coach a Steam Roller team that dominated the opposition. A pair of professional wrestlers, Gus Sonnenberg and Jack Spellman, anchored the defense. Providence didn't allow any opponent to score more than 10 points. A 7–7 tie with the Packers in the season finale broke their streak of five straight shutouts, but that didn't keep the Steam Roller from finishing as champions of the 1928 season.

Jim Thorpe played his final game in 1928, taking the field one last time for a game with the Chicago Cardinals at age 41. Thorpe was the league's first president. It was in name only, but that name carried more clout than any one else who suited up in 1920. The name George Halas came to carry plenty of weight itself. He played his final game at age 43, but Halas would remain on the sidelines as coach for 32 more seasons, controlling the Bears until his death in 1983. Halas and Thorpe would fittingly be among the first men enshrined in the Pro Football Hall of Fame.

1929 NFL

TEAM	W-L-T	PCT	PTS	TEAM	W-L-T	PCT	PTS
Green Bay Packers	12-0-1	1.000	198-22	Providence Steam Roller	4-6-2	.400	107-117
New York Giants	13-1-1	.929	312-86	Chicago Bears	4-9-2	.308	119-227
Frankford Yellow Jackets	9-4-5	.692	129-128	Buffalo Bisons	1-7-1	.125	48-142
Boston Bulldogs	4-4	.500	98-73	Minneapolis Red Jackets	1-9	.100	48-185
Chicago Cardinals	6-6-1	.500	154-83	Dayton Triangles	0-6	.000	7-136
Staten Island Stapletons	3-4-3	.429	89-65	Aver	12	—	112
Orange Tornadoes	3-4-4	.429	35-80				

Rushing TDs	TD Passes	Receiving TDs	Total TDs	Field Goals	Extra Points	Total Points
E.Nevers-ChiC...........12	B.Friedman-NYG 20	R.Flaherty-NYG..........8	E.Nevers-ChiC...........12	C.Weimer-Buf 3	B.Friedman-NYG 20	E.Nevers-ChiC...........85
T.Latone-Bos 9	E.Nevers-ChiC 6	H.Moran-NYG.............5	L.Sedbrook-NYG 11	T.Plansky-NYG 2	R.Dunn-GB 11	L.Sedbrook-NYG 66
T.Plansky-NYG 8	W.Holmer-ChiB 5	G.Welch-Pro 4	T.Plansky-NYG 9	K.Mercer-Fra...............2	E.Nevers-ChiC 10	T.Plansky-NYG 62
	R.Dunn-GB 5		T.Latone-Bos 9	R.Dunn-GB 2	K.Strong-SI 9	T.Latone-Bos 54
					J.Sternaman-ChiB 8	R.Flaherty-NYG..........49

PACKERS OUT FOR BLOOD

Two teams dominated the season, beneficiaries of some offseason player acquisitions that made them tough to beat. The Green Bay Packers signed Johnny Blood, a speedy back and great pass catcher. They also added Cal Hubbard and Mike Michalske to solidify the line and give them the league's most formidable defense. These players joined a roster that already included stars like tailback Verne Lewellen, end Lavie Dilweg, and punter and passer Red Dunn.

Giants owner Tim Mara purchased the failing Detroit Wolverines, primarily so that he could bring their offensive stars to New York. The brightest of these was quarterback Benny Friedman, who led the most prolific scoring attack that professional football had ever seen. His 20 touchdown passes would stand as a record until 1942. Friedman's favorite target was end Ray Flaherty, acquired when the crosstown Yankees had folded during the offseason. The Giants didn't have a dominating defense, but they scored so many points they usually overwhelmed their opponents.

The Packers and Giants were both undefeated when they met in late November at the Polo Grounds. Green Bay's stifling defense produced a 20–6 win, and that was all that separated the two teams in the final standings. It was Green Bay's first NFL championship.

Other perennial contenders struggled. The Bears had a miserable season. Paddy Driscoll had slowed down in what was his final season and Red Grange couldn't regain his previous form after sitting out a year to recover from a knee injury. The Chicago Cardinals made a late-season surge, prompted by the acquisition of Ernie Nevers. The big fullback spent his summers pitching for the St. Louis Browns, but his athletic glory came on the gridiron. Nevers was still a virtual one-man team. He ran for 6 touchdowns—a feat that has never been surpassed—and scored all of his team's points in a 40–6 victory over the Bears on Thanksgiving.

Football's first night game took place in Providence on November 6 when temporary floodlights were used to illuminate the field. The visiting Cardinals won, 16–0, six years before major league baseball's first game after dark.

1930 NFL

TEAM	W-L-T	PCT	PTS	TEAM	W-L-T	PCT	PTS
Green Bay Packers	10-3-1	.769	234-111	Chicago Cardinals	5-6-2	.455	128-132
New York Giants	13-4	.765	308-98	Portsmouth Spartans	5-6-3	.455	176-161
Chicago Bears	9-4-1	.692	169-71	Frankford Yellow Jackets	4-13-1	.235	113-321
Brooklyn Dodgers	7-4-1	.636	154-59	Minneapolis Red Jackets	1-7-1	.125	27-165
Providence Steam Roller	6-4-1	.600	90-125	Newark Tornadoes	1-10-1	.091	51-190
Staten Island Stapletons	5-5-2	.500	95-112	Aver	13	—	140

Rushing TDs	TD Passes	Receiving TDs	Total TDs	Field Goals	Extra Points	Total Points
J.McBride-Bkn 8	B.Friedman-NYG 13	R.Thomas-Bkn............5	V.Lewellen-GB 9	F.Peters-Pro.................2	R.Dunn-GB 14	J.McBride-Bkn 56
V.Lewellen-GB 8	R.Dunn-GB 11	K.Strong-SI................5	L.Sedbrook-NYG 8	K.Strong-SI.................5	T.Lewis-Por 10	V.Lewellen-GB 54
E.Nevers-ChiC............6	W.Kelly-Bkn 7	J.Blood-GB 5	J.McBride-Bkn 8	E.Nevers-ChiC.............1	B.Friedman-NYG 10	K.Strong-SI................53
R.Grange-ChiB 6	D.Wycoff-SI.................5	L.Johnsos-ChiB 4	R.Grange-ChiB 8	B.Meeker-Pro...............1	E.Nevers-ChiC............9	R.Grange-ChiB 49
B.Friedman-NYG 6	E.Nevers-ChiC............5			B.Friedman-NYG 1		B.Friedman-NYG 49

PAPA BEAR MOVES OVER

Unable to shake his team out of their doldrums, Chicago Bears owner George Halas tabbed Ralph Jones to take over his coaching duties. The move seemed to work, as Jones cut loose some popular but aging players and re-invigorated the team with youth. Bronko Nagurski, the hard-charging All-American fullback-tackle from the University of Minnesota, joined a restored Red Grange in the backfield and generated a fearsome power running game in Jones's new T-formation. Once again, however, it was a two-team race for the NFL championship—and neither of those teams called Chicago home.

The Green Bay Packers returned all of the key players from their undefeated 1929 campaign, and the addition of a local gridiron star helped give their offense a new element. Quarterback Arnie Herber couldn't throw the ball as accurately as the Giants' Benny Friedman, but he had the ability and the willingness to throw it deep. Herber's favorite target was Johnny Blood, who caught 5 touchdown passes.

Friedman's passing attack was equally explosive for New York. Although end Ray Flaherty took the year off to coach Gonzaga, his alma mater, the Giants added another standout receiver to pair with their star quarterback. Red Badgro, who had quit football a few years earlier to play right field for baseball's St. Louis Browns, stepped in and New York's high-scoring offense didn't miss a beat.

The Packers and Giants met twice in head-to-head competition during the regular season. The Packers took the first game at Green Bay by a score of 14–7 in early October. When the two teams met for a rematch at the Polo Grounds in late November, the Giants prevailed by a score of 13–6. The Packers were fading, going 2–3–1 to end their season. Faced with a chance to take over first place, the Giants dropped three of four games, allowing Green Bay to claim its second consecutive championship. Coach Curly Lambeau, who'd ended his career as a player a year earlier, now had more titles than his hated and now retired rival, Halas, whose Bears finished third.

1931 NFL

TEAM	W-L-T	PCT	PTS	TEAM	W-L-T	PCT	PTS
Green Bay Packers	12-2	.857	291-87	Staten Island Stapletons	4-6-1	.400	79-118
Portsmouth Spartans	11-3	.786	175-77	Cleveland Indians	2-8	.200	45-137
Chicago Bears	8-5	.615	145-92	Brooklyn Dodgers	2-12	.143	64-199
Chicago Cardinals	5-4	.556	120-128	Frankford Yellow Jackets	1-6-1	.143	13-99
New York Giants	7-6-1	.538	154-100	Aver	12	—	116
Providence Steam Roller	4-4-3	.500	78-127				

Rushing TDs	TD Passes	Receiving TDs	Total TDs	Field Goals	Extra Points	Total Points
D.Clark-Por 9	R.Dunn-GB 8	J.Blood-GB 11	J.Blood-GB 14	K.Strong-SI.................2	E.Nevers-ChiC 15	J.Blood-GB 84
E.Nevers-ChiC............8	E.Nevers-ChiC............6	B.McKalip-Por.............4	D.Clark-Por 9	G.Presnell-Por.............1	R.Dunn-GB 15	E.Nevers-ChiC...........66
K.Strong-SI.................6	G.Presnell-Por............5	L.Dilweg-GB 4	E.Nevers-ChiC............8	E.Nevers-ChiC.............1	G.Presnell-Por 8	D.Clark-Por 60
V.Lewellen-GB 6	B.Molenda-GB 4		K.Strong-SI.................7	H.Moran-NYG..............1	H.Moran-NYG 8	K.Strong-SI................53
R.Grange-ChiB 5			R.Grange-ChiB 7	L.Johnsos-ChiB 1	D.Clark-Por 6	R.Grange-ChiB 42

THE GOING GETS TOUGH

The world was in the throes of the Great Depression, and the economic stresses that had devastated so many Americans really started taking a toll on the NFL. The Dayton Triangles, the last of the NFL's original franchises to keep its same name from day one, moved to Brooklyn, and were renamed the Dodgers. Franchises disbanded in Newark and Minneapolis over the summer. In mid-November the 1926 league champion Frankford Yellow Jackets called it quits, unable to complete the schedule. Two more teams, the Cleveland Indians and the Providence Steam Roller, the 1928 NFL champs, dropped out of the league at season's end.

Steve Owen took over coaching duties for the Giants, who bolstered their line with the addition of center Mel Hein. A powerful and durable blocker, Hein had been a two-way star at the University of Washington. Despite the improvements up front, New York's offense slumped. Quarterback Benny Friedman was much less productive than in recent seasons, due both to a knee injury and his moonlighting as an assistant coach for Yale.

Once again, the Packers were the team to beat. Curley Lambeau's squad featured the highest scoring offense in the league. With Red Dunn's passing and the backfield tandem of Johnny Blood and Verne Lewellen, the Packers ripped through opponents. At the end of October, the Packers were undefeated, and late losses to the Bears and Cardinals were the only blemishes on their record.

Their biggest challenger was the Portsmouth Spartans, a second-year town team located near Cincinnati. Potsy Clark took over as coach of a club that most observes felt had underachieved in its inaugural season. Two rookies helped key the turnaround. One was guard George Christensen, who brought a measure of toughness to the line. The other was Dutch Clark, a triple-threat back who helped give the Spartans a dangerous offense.

The Spartans and Packers did not meet head-to-head, the first time that the NFL's top two contenders avoided playing each other during the regular season. Green Bay won its third straight title in the standings, but it was the last time an NFL champion would be crowned without deciding matters on the field.

1932 NFL

TEAM	W-L-T	PCT	POST	PTS	RA	RY	RY/A	RTD	FL	PA	PC	GPY	GPY/A	PTD	PI	PSY	PRAT
ChiB	7-1-6	.875	—	160-44	513	1620	3.2	13	—	148	67	982	6.6	8	7	—	65.8
GB	10-3-1	.769	—	152-63	434	1333	3.1	7	—	134	48	798	6.0	9	14	—	39.6
Por	6-2-4	.750	—	116-71	373	1230	3.3	9	—	113	43	623	5.5	6	12	—	34.9
Bos	4-4-2	.500	—	55-79	304	1249	4.1	4	—	92	17	216	2.3	1	15	—	3.6
NYG	4-6-2	.400	—	93-113	423	1311	3.1	3	—	164	82	949	5.8	9	14	—	50.6
Bkn	3-9	.250	—	63-131	391	1109	2.8	4	—	136	42	586	4.3	5	16	—	18.4
ChiC	2-6-2	.250	—	72-114	310	917	3.0	6	—	126	40	628	5.0	2	4	—	41.4
SI	2-7-3	.222	—	77-173	490	1780	3.6	9	—	131	33	518	4.0	2	16	—	9.1
Aver	12			99	405	1319	3.3	7	—	131	47	663	5.1	5	12	—	27.2

TEAM	1D	PENY	PNT	FGM/A	RTNY	RTNTD	OFFY/DEFY	NETY	NETTO	NP	PNP	DELP	PW	DELW	PRT	DR	YPD	DEL
ChiB	—	—	—	1-0	—	2	2602	—	—	116	—	—	9.9	0.1	5.0	—	—	—
GB	—	—	—	0-3	—	6	2131	—	—	89	—	—	9.2	1.3	1.9	—	—	—
Por	—	—	—	3-0	—	1	1853	—	—	45	—	—	7.1	0.9	1.3	—	—	—
Bos	—	—	—	0-1	—	3	1465	—	—	-24	—	—	4.4	0.6	-4.9	—	—	—
NYG	—	—	—	0-0	—	2	2260	—	—	-20	—	—	5.5	-0.5	2.5	—	—	—
Bkn	—	—	—	1-1	—	0	1695	—	—	-68	—	—	4.3	-1.3	-0.6	—	—	—
ChiC	—	—	—	0-1	—	2	1545	—	—	-42	—	—	4.0	-1.0	3.7	—	—	—
SI	—	—	—	1-0	—	0	2298	—	—	-96	—	—	3.6	-0.1	-1.4	—	—	—
Aver	—	—	—	1	—	2	1981	—	—	—	—	—	—	—	1.3	—	—	—

Rushing Attempts
C.Battles-Bos 148
D.Clark-Por 137
D.Wycoff-SI 135
J.Grossman-Bkn 129
B.Nagurski-ChiB 121

Rushing Yards
C.Battles-Bos 576
B.Nagurski-ChiB 533
B.Campiglio-SI 504
D.Clark-Por 461
D.Wycoff-SI 454

Rushing Average
B.Campiglio-SI 4.85
B.Nagurski-ChiB 4.40
A.Gutowsky-Por 3.92
K.Strong-SI 3.91
C.Battles-Bos 3.89

Rushing TDs
B.Nagurski-ChiB 4

Rushing Rank
C.Battles-Bos 606
B.Nagurski-ChiB 573
B.Campiglio-SI 524
D.Clark-Por 491
D.Wycoff-SI 464

Passing Yards
A.Herber-GB 639
W.Holmer-ChiC 449
J.McBride-NYG 363
B.Molenda-ChiB 346
B.Friedman-Bkn 319

Passing Average
A.Herber-GB 6.33
W.Holmer-ChiC 5.76
B.Molenda-ChiB 5.41
D.Clark-Por 5.23
J.McBride-NYG 4.91

Completion Percent
J.McBride-NYG 48.6
B.Molenda-ChiB 39.1
A.Herber-GB 36.6
D.Clark-Por 32.7
W.Holmer-ChiC 32.1

TD Passes
A.Herber-GB 9
J.McBride-NYG 6
B.Friedman-Bkn 5
B.Nagurski-ChiB 3
B.Molenda-ChiB 3

TD Percent
A.Herber-GB 8.9
J.McBride-NYG 8.1
A.Herber-GB 6.8
B.Molenda-ChiB 4.7
D.Clark-Por 3.8

INT Percent
W.Holmer-ChiC 1.3
B.Molenda-ChiB 6.3
A.Herber-GB 8.9
J.McBride-NYG 12.2
B.Friedman-Bkn 13.5

Passer Rating
W.Holmer-ChiC 56.0
A.Herber-GB 51.5
J.McBride-NYG 50.5
B.Molenda-ChiB 46.7
B.Friedman-Bkn 28.9

Passing Rank
W.Holmer-ChiC 195
J.Doehring-ChiB 72
B.Campiglio-SI 55
R.Grange-ChiB 48
H.Moran-NYG 46

Receptions
R.Flaherty-NYG 21
L.Johnsos-ChiB 19
H.Ebding-Por 14
J.Blood-GB 14

Receiving Yards
R.Flaherty-NYG 350
L.Johnsos-ChiB 321
H.Ebding-Por 171
R.Grange-ChiB 168
J.Blood-GB 168

Receiving Average
L.Johnsos-ChiB 16.89
R.Flaherty-NYG 16.67
H.Ebding-Por 12.21
J.Blood-GB 12.00

Receiving TDs
R.Flaherty-NYG 5
R.Grange-ChiB 4

Receiving Rank
R.Flaherty-NYG 200
L.Johnsos-ChiB 171
R.Grange-ChiB 104
J.Blood-GB 99
H.Ebding-Por 91

Combined Net Yards
C.Battles-Bos 636
B.Nagurski-ChiB 600
D.Clark-Por 568
B.Campiglio-SI 563
D.Wycoff-SI 454

Total TDs
R.Grange-ChiB 7
D.Clark-Por 6
J.Grossman-Bkn 5
R.Flaherty-NYG 5

Total Points
D.Clark-Por 55
R.Grange-ChiB 42
J.Grossman-Bkn 30
R.Flaherty-NYG 30
L.Johnsos-ChiB 26

Punt Average
Not kept

Field Goals
D.Clark-Por 3
S.Wilson-SI 1
B.Friedman-Bkn 1
T.Edwards-ChiB 1

Field Goal Percent
Not kept

Kickoff Returns
Not kept

Kickoff Return Average
Not kept

Punt Returns
Not kept

Punt Return Average
Not kept

Punt/Kick Return Yards
Not kept

Punt/Kick Return TDs
O.Pape-Bos 1
C.Cagle-NYG 1

Interceptions
Not kept

Interception Return Yards
Not kept

Interception Return TDs
Many 1

Sacks
Not kept

Overall Rank
B.Nagurski-ChiB 617
B.Campiglio-SI 613
C.Battles-Bos.........582
D.Wycoff-SI 454
W.Holmer-ChiC........435

CIRCUS MAXIMUS, CHAMPIONSHIP SPECTACLE

Although the NFL dropped to just eight teams, its lowest number ever, the NFL welcomed a new team and a powerful and charismatic figure: George Preston Marshall. The Boston Braves owner had a knack for publicity and promotion, using things like a marching band and a rally song to recreate the atmosphere of college football. It didn't hurt that he also had some very talented players such as Turk Edwards, a dominating tackle, plus halfback Cliff Battles, the league's first official rushing champion now that the NFL kept track of such things.

After winning three straight titles, the Green Bay Packers rolled to a 10–1–1 mark through November. But the Pack fell flat and dropped out of contention following shutout losses to the Portsmouth Spartans and the Chicago Bears.

The race came down to two teams. The Bears had started the season with three scoreless ties and then lost to the Packers, 2–0. Rookie end Bill Hewitt, bruising fullback Bronko Nagurski, and lineman George Trafton, in his final season, helped Chicago rebound from a disappointing start. The Bears did not lose another game,

although they endured six ties. Two of those came against Portsmouth, making another strong showing after 11 wins in 1931. Quarterback Dutch Clark guided Portsmouth to a 6–1 finish, leaving the Spartans and Bears with the fewest losses and 10 ties between them. There was no clear champion.

To avoid past championship controversies, a playoff game was hastily arranged for the following Sunday. A blizzard made it impossible to play at Wrigley Field, so the two teams moved indoors to nearby Chicago Stadium, where a circus had just concluded its run. The arena floor was covered with dirt, but it was only 80 yards long and too narrow for a regulation field. The sidelines ran right along the edge of the bleachers and the goal posts were moved from the end line to the goal line. The Bears triumphed in a close game decided by Nagurski's controversial touchdown pass. But beyond determining a champion for 1932, this game—deemed an extension of the regular season in the record books—set the stage for several dramatic changes in the NFL.

1933 NFL

TEAM	W-L-T	PCT	POST	PTS	RA	RY	RY/A	RTD	FL	PA	PC	GPY	GPY/A	PTD	PI	PSY	PRAT
Eastern Division																	
NYG	11-3	.786	L	244-101	476-493	1624-1777	3.4-3.6	15-7	—	178-202	74-62	1348-809	7.6-4.0	15-6	19-40	—	56.8-14.7
Bkn	5-4-1	.556	—	93-54	356-339	1112-964	3.1-2.8	4-3	—	170-161	79-55	1129-813	6.6-5.0	7-2	21-22	—	42.6-16.1
Bos	5-5-2	.500	—	103-97	467-329	2260-1159	4.8-3.5	11-6	—	106-162	33-72	514-1312	4.8-8.1	1-7	25-24	—	11.8-47.7
Phi	3-5-1	.375	—	77-158	354-308	1103-1083	3.1-3.5	6-11	—	149-176	40-63	657-1223	4.4-6.9	4-8	34-19	—	14.8-36.4
Pit	3-6-2	.333	—	67-208	338-441	914-1805	2.7-4.1	4-16	—	196-142	60-57	1029-930	5.3-6.5	3-8	40-19	—	15.0-42.0
Western Division																	
ChiB	10-2-1	.833	L*	133-82	496-514	1734-1625	3.5-3.2	3-4	—	212-187	74-63	1229-691	5.8-3.7	11-4	29-32	—	33.0-13.1
Por	6-5	.545	—	128-87	456-413	1720-1422	3.8-3.4	9-5	—	170-107	65-32	959-558	5.6-5.2	7-5	18-22	—	31.6-24.8
GB	5-7-1	.417	—	170-107	487-442	1513-1210	3.1-2.7	13-4	—	209-179	89-48	1186-711	5.7-4.0	6-7	18-30	—	34.9-17.1
Cin	3-6-1	.333	—	38-110	320-417	795-1361	2.5-3.3	2-7	—	102-162	25-66	357-980	3.5-6.0	0-6	15-22	—	2.1-34.0
ChiC	1-9-1	.100	—	52-101	368-422	1017-1386	2.8-3.3	2-6	—	139-153	37-58	470-851	3.4-5.6	3-4	30-19	—	8.8-26.0
Aver	11	—		111	412	1379	3.3	7	—	163	58	888	5.4	6	25	—	26.3

TEAM	1D	PENY	PNT	FGM/A	RTNY	RTNTD	OFFY/DEFY	NETY	NETTO	NP	PNP	DELP	PW	DELW	PRT	DR	YPD	DEL
Eastern Division																		
NYG	—	—	—	6-3	—	3-0	2972-2586	386	21	143	116	27	10.6	0.4	3.6/-4.6	—	—	—
Bkn	—	—	—	2-4	—	2-1	2241-1777	464	1	39	43	-4	6.0	-0.5	1.5/-1.0	—	—	—
Bos	—	—	—	2-3	—	2-0	2774-2471	303	-1	6	21	-15	6.2	-0.2	-5.7/1.9	—	—	—
Phi	—	—	—	1-5	—	1-2	1760-2306	-546	-15	-81	-106	25	2.5	1.0	-5.6/2.5	—	—	—
Pit	—	—	—	4-3	—	1-6	1943-2735	-792	-21	-141	-150	9	2.0	2.0	-3.8/1.1	—	—	—
Western Division																		
ChiB	—	—	—	6-5	—	2-2	2963-2316	647	3	51	66	-15	7.8	2.7	0.2/-3.8	—	—	—
Por	—	—	—	6-4	—	0-1	2679-1980	699	4	41	74	-33	6.5	-0.5	1.3/-3.6	—	—	—
GB	—	—	—	2-3	—	5-3	2699-1921	778	12	63	113	-50	8.1	-2.6	2.1/-3.2	—	—	—
Cin	—	—	—	5-2	—	1-2	1152-2341	-1189	7	-72	-71	-1	3.2	0.3	-3.1/0.3	—	—	—
ChiC	—	—	—	2-4	—	2-2	1487-2237	-750	-11	-49	-107	58	4.3	-2.8	-6.1/0.2	—	—	—
Aver	—	—	—	4	—	2	2267	—	—	—	—	—	—	—	-1.1	—	—	—

Leaders

Rushing Attempts		Rushing Yards		Rushing Average		Rushing TDs		Rushing Rank		Passing Yards		Passing Average	
J.Musick-Bos	173	J.Musick-Bos	809	C.Battles-Bos	5.42	G.Presnell-Por	6	J.Musick-Bos	859	H.Newman-NYG	973	B.Molenda-ChiB	8.66
C.Hinkle-GB	139	C.Battles-Bos	737	J.Musick-Bos	4.68	J.Musick-Bos	5	C.Battles-Bos	767	G.Presnell-Por	774	T.Holm-Pit	7.81
C.Battles-Bos	136	B.Nagurski-ChiB	533	G.Presnell-Por	4.42	K.Richards-NYG	4	G.Presnell-Por	582	A.Herber-GB	656	A.Herber-GB	7.43
S.Hanson-Phi	133	G.Presnell-Por	522	J.Sisk-ChiB	4.21	C.Hinkle-GB	4	B.Nagurski-ChiB	543	B.Friedman-Bkn	594	H.Newman-NYG	7.15
H.Newman-NYG	130	S.Hanson-Phi	475	B.Nagurski-ChiB	4.16	B.Friedman	4	S.Hanson-Phi	505	C.Cagle-Bkn	457	G.Presnell-Por	6.19

Completion Percent		TD Passes		TD Percent		INT Percent		Passer Rating		Passing Rank		Receptions	
B.Friedman-Bkn	52.5	H.Newman-NYG	11	H.Newman-NYG	8.1	B.Molenda-ChiB	8.0	B.Molenda-ChiB	63.2	K.Strong-NYG	107	S.Kelly-Bkn	22
C.Cagle-Bkn	41.9	G.Presnell-Por	6	B.Molenda-ChiB	8.0	B.Friedman-Bkn	8.8	B.Friedman-Bkn	61.1	B.Molenda-ChiB	77	R.Grove-GB	17
A.Herber-GB	40.3	B.Friedman-Bkn	5	B.Friedman-Bkn	6.3	G.Presnell-Por	9.6	H.Newman-NYG	51.7	B.Monnett-GB	58	R.Tesser-Pit	14
G.Presnell-Por	40.0	B.Molenda-ChiB	4	G.Presnell-Por	4.8	A.Herber-GB	9.7	G.Presnell-Por	37.6	S.Hokuf-Bos	53	B.Hewitt-ChiB	14
H.Newman-NYG	39.0			T.Holm-Pit	3.8	H.Newman-NYG	12.5	T.Holm-Pit	35.1	B.Hewitt-ChiB	45		

Receiving Yards		Receiving Average		Receiving TDs		Receiving Rank		Combined Net Yards		Total TDs		Total Points	
P.Moss-Pit	283	P.Moss-Pit	21.77	Many	3	P.Moss-Pit	152	C.Battles-Bos	922	K.Richards-NYG	7	K.Strong-NYG	64
R.Tesser-Pit	282	R.Tesser-Pit	20.14			B.Hewitt-ChiB	147	J.Musick-Bos	887	S.Kelly-Bkn	7	G.Presnell-Por	64
B.Hewitt-ChiB	273	B.Hewitt-ChiB	19.50			R.Tesser-Pit	141	S.Hanson-Phi	661	B.Friedman-GB	7	J.Musick-Bos	45
S.Kelly-Bkn	246	L.Dilweg-GB	17.31			S.Kelly-Bkn	138	H.Newman-NYG	573	K.Strong-NYG	6	K.Richards-NYG	43
L.Dilweg-GB	225	L.Peterson-Bkn	13.08			J.Blood-GB	123	B.Nagurski-ChiB	556	G.Presnell-Por	6	S.Kelly-Bkn	43

Punt Average	Field Goals		Field Goal Percent	Kickoff Returns	Kickoff Return Average	Punt Returns	Punt Return Average
Not kept	J.Manders-ChiB	6	Not kept	Not kept	Not kept	Not kept	Not kept
	K.Strong-NYG	5					
	G.Presnell-Por	5					
	A.Clark-Cin	4					
	M.Kelsch-Pit	3					

Punt/Kick Return Yards	Punt/Kick Return TDs		Interceptions	Interception Return Yards	Interception Return TDs		Sacks	Overall Rank	
Not kept	B.Monnett-GB	1	Not kept	Not kept	Many	1	Not kept	C.Battles-Bos	782
	J.Lillard-ChiC	1						B.Nagurski-ChiB	551
	G.LeFebvre-Cin	1						B.Monnett-GB	533
	S.Kelly-Bkn	1						G.Presnell-Por	531
	C.Battles-Bos	1						K.Strong-NYG	502

TWO STEPS FORWARD, ONE STEP BACK

The success of the 1932 playoff game prompted the owners to implement several significant changes for the new season. They split the league into two five-team divisions with the winners meeting for a championship game at the end of the regular season. The addition of two Pennsylvania teams gave the league geographical balance, not to mention influential owners Bert Bell in Philadelphia and Art Rooney in Pittsburgh.

While they had previously chosen to use the same rulebook as college football, the owners realized that they could make their brand of football more exciting by adopting some of the temporary rules from the 1932 Chicago Stadium game, such as implementing hashmarks to spot the ball after an out of bounds play and moving the goal posts from the end line to the goal line. The owners also changed the rule requiring a forward pass to be thrown from at least five yards behind the line of scrimmage—a major bone of contention in the 1932 indoor game—to encourage throwing the ball.

These rules represented a transformation, but the league also regressed. For the first time since its inception, no African American players appeared on the rosters of any NFL team. While the owners denied that they had imposed an official ban, the NFL remained segregated until 1946. Some historians have suggested that the driving force behind this move was George Preston Marshall, who, while changing his team's name to Redskins, kept the franchise all-white until 1961.

On the field, two teams dominated from the outset. The New York Giants started slowly but won their last seven games to clinch the Eastern Division title. The addition of veteran halfback Ken Strong gave the Giants an overpowering ground game to go with their already potent passing attack. In the West Division, the Bears didn't lose to a divisional foe all season. When the Bears and Giants met for the championship game at Wrigley Field, each team featured six future Hall of Famers, including head coaches Steve Owen and George Halas. Chicago's exciting victory in that game gave the Bears their second consecutive NFL championship.

1934 NFL

TEAM	W-L-T	PCT	POST	PTS	RA	RY	RY/A	RTD	FL	PA	PC	GPY	GPY/A	PTD	PI	PSY	PRAT
Eastern Division																	
NYG	8-5	.615	L*	147-107	567-465	1935-1634	3.4-3.5	12-7	—	149-184	64-54	796-744	5.3-4.0	5-5	17-22	—	31.7-13.4
Bos	6-6	.500	—	107-94	415-418	1668-1715	4.0-4.1	10-5	—	138-159	35-45	459-682	3.3-4.3	4-4	22-18	—	11.0-13.8
Bkn	4-7	.364	—	61-153	309-496	980-2153	3.2-4.3	1-16	—	161-123	42-41	577-595	3.6-4.8	5-6	26-17	—	12.8-26.7
Phi	4-7	.364	—	127-85	460-411	1876-1658	4.1-4.0	11-9	—	163-135	48-41	576-545	3.5-4.0	7-1	23-22	—	16.5-7.1
Pit	2-10	.167	—	51-206	418-517	1527-2569	3.7-5.0	2-15	—	186-133	58-45	952-610	5.1-4.6	4-10	23-20	—	17.0-34.9
Western Division																	
ChiB	**13-0**	**1.000**	L	**286**-86	567-429	2847-1407	5.0-3.3	20-9	—	192-226	57-73	955-806	5.0-3.6	16-2	24-27	—	36.0- 7.2
Det	10-3	.769	—	238-**59**	**632**-437	2740-1231	4.3-2.8	27-2	—	142-200	46-53	747-678	5.3-3.4	3-5	15-33	—	18.5-10.0
GB	7-6	.538	—	156-112	456-517	1183-1564	2.6-3.0	8-9	—	197-172	74-56	1165-686	5.9-4.0	10-3	19-25	—	35.4-12.1
ChiC	5-6	.455	—	80-84	316-360	1141-954	3.6-2.7	7-5	—	132-106	34-37	302-585	2.3-5.5	1-5	13-14	—	2.5-30.3
Cin	0-8	.000	—	10-243	197-255	731-1631	3.7-6.4	1-19	—	88-116	26-46	248-877	2.8-7.6	0-11	14-5	—	0.0-80.3
SL	1-2	.333	—	27-61	104-**136**	339-451	3.3-3.3	2-5	—	58-52	21-14	340-309	5.9-5.9	1-4	10-3	—	22.8-53.4
Aver	12	—	—	129	444	1697	3.8	10	—	161	51	712	4.4	6	21	—	18.8

TEAM	1D	PENY	PNT	FGM/A	RTNY	RTNTD	OFFY/DEFY	NETY	NETTO	NP	PNP	DELP	PW	DELW	PRT	DR	YPD	DEL
Eastern Division																		
NYG	—	—	—	7-5	—	1-2	2731-2378	353	5	40	49	-9	7.5	0.5	0.5/-1.1	—	—	—
Bos	—	—	—	1-8	—	2-1	2127-2397	-270	-4	13	-39	52	6.3	-0.3	-3.6/-0.6	—	—	—
Bkn	—	—	—	4-1	—	1-0	1557-2748	-1191	-9	-92	-135	43	3.2	0.8	-3.4/-0.9	—	—	—
Phi	—	—	—	1-6	—	1-0	2452-2203	249	-1	42	17	25	6.6	-2.6	-2.4/-3.2	—	—	—
Pit	—	—	—	4-5	—	0-3	2479-3179	-700	-3	-155	-70	-85	2.1	-0.1	-0.2/-1.4	—	—	—
Western Division																		
ChiB	—	—	—	10-3	—	1-0	3802-2213	1589	3	200	144	56	11.5	1.5	0.2/-1.7	—	—	—
Det	—	—	—	8-4	—	2-0	3487-1909	1578	18	179	204	-25	11.0	-1.0	0.7/-3.8	—	—	—
GB	—	—	—	8-6	—	1-2	2348-2250	98	6	44	32	12	7.6	-0.6	2.1/-2.4	—	—	—
ChiC	—	—	—	3-5	—	3-0	1443-1539	-96	1	-4	-4	0	5.4	-0.4	-2.1/ 0.0	—	—	—
Cin	—	—	—	1-6	—	0-4	979-2508	-1529	-9	-233	-163	-70	-1.8	1.8	-4.3/ 6.6	—	—	—
SL	—	—	—	2-0	—	0-0	679- 760	-81	-7	-34	-35	1	0.6	0.4	-1.7/ 4.1	—	—	—
Aver	—	—	—	5	—	1	2408	—	—	—	—	—	—	—	-1.0	—	—	—

Rushing Attempts	Rushing Yards	Rushing Average	Rushing TDs	Rushing Rank	Passing Yards	Passing Average
S.Hanson-Phi 146	B.Feathers-ChiB 1004	B.Feathers-ChiB 8.44	B.Feathers-ChiB 8	B.Feathers-ChiB 1084	A.Herber-GB 799	D.Clark-Det 7.66
A.Gutowsky-Det...... 146	S.Hanson-Phi 805	D.Clark-Det 6.20	D.Clark-Det 8	S.Hanson-Phi 875	W.Heller-Pit 511	A.Herber-GB 6.95
C.Hinkle-GB 144	D.Clark-Det 763	G.Ronzani-ChiB 5.77	G.Presnell-Det 7	D.Clark-Det 843	H.Newman-NYG 391	E.Matesic-Phi 4.63
H.Newman-NYG 141	B.Nagurski-ChiB 586	S.Hanson-Phi 5.51	B.Nagurski-ChiB 7	B.Nagurski-ChiB 656	D.Clark-Det 383	W.Heller-Pit 4.56
K.Strong-NYG 138		D.Russell-ChiC 5.43	S.Hanson-Phi 7	E.Caddel-Det 568	E.Matesic-Phi 278	H.Newman-NYG 4.20

Completion Percent	TD Passes	TD Percent	INT Percent	Passer Rating	Passing Rank	Receptions
D.Clark-Det 46.0	A.Herber-GB 8	A.Herber-GB 7.0	D.Clark-Det 6.0	D.Clark-Det 47.3	D.Clark-Det 72	J.Carter-Phi 16
H.Newman-NYG 37.6	G.Ronzani-ChiB 3	S.Hokuf-Bos 5.9	E.Matesic-Phi 6.3	A.Herber-GB 45.1	H.McPhail-Bos 48	R.Badgro-NYG 16
A.Herber-GB 36.5	G.Molenda-ChiB 3	C.Cagle-Bkn 5.0	A.Herber-GB 10.4	E.Matesic-Phi 25.6	C.Brumbaugh-ChiB ... 46	B.Smith-Pit 14
E.Matesic-Phi 33.3	S.Hokuf-Bos 3	G.Presnell-Det 3.5	C.Cagle-Bkn 11.7	S.Hokuf-Bos 23.7	R.Weiner-Phi 30	
W.Heller-Pit 27.7	C.Cagle-Bkn 3	E.Matesic-Phi 3.3	H.Newman-NYG 12.9	C.Cagle-Bkn 19.7	J.Doehring-ChiB 29	

Receiving Yards	Receiving Average	Receiving TDs	Receiving Rank	Combined Net Yards	Total TDs	Total Points
H.Ebding-Det 264	B.Smith-Pit 15.57	B.Hewitt-ChiB 5	H.Ebding-Det 142	B.Feathers-ChiB 1178	B.Feathers-ChiB 9	J.Manders-ChiB 76
J.Carter-Phi 238	J.Carter-Phi 14.88	J.Carter-Phi 4	J.Carter-Phi 139	D.Clark-Det 835	S.Hanson-Phi 8	D.Clark-Det 73
J.Skladany-Pit 222	R.Badgro-NYG 12.88	G.Ronzani-ChiB 3	J.Skladany-Pit 121	S.Hanson-Phi 827	D.Clark-Det 8	G.Presnell-Det 63
B.Smith-Pit 218		R.Kercheval-Bkn 3	B.Smith-Pit 109	E.Caddel-Det 655		K.Strong-NYG 56
R.Badgro-NYG 206		R.Grove-GB 3	R.Badgro-NYG 108	W.Heller-Pit 624		B.Feathers-ChiB 55

Punt Average	Field Goals	Field Goal Percent	Kickoff Returns	Kickoff Return Average	Punt Returns	Punt Return Average
Not kept	J.Manders-ChiB 10	Not kept	Not kept	Not kept	Not kept	Not kept

Punt/Kick Return Yards	Punt/Kick Return TDs	Interceptions	Interception Return Yards	Interception Return TDs	Sacks	Overall Rank
Not kept	D.Russell-ChiC 1	Not kept	Not kept	J.Manders-ChiB 1	Not kept	B.Feathers-ChiB 1127
	H.Newman-NYG 1			F.Lumpkin-Det 1		D.Clark-Det 951
	J.Grossman-Bkn 1			S.Hanson-Phi 1		S.Hanson-Phi 830
	H.Griffith-ChiC 1			E.Caddel-Det 1		B.Nagurski-ChiB 666
				H.Bruder-GB 1		E.Caddel-Det 665

MAKING A GO WITH NO OHIO

The league's effort to maintain a foothold in Ohio continued to be unsuccessful. A strong finish in the Cincinnati Reds' inaugural season buoyed the hopes of fans, but the 1934 squad was completely overmatched. After going 0–8 and being outscored, 243–10, the Reds folded. To fill their spot on the schedule, the league turned to the semi-pro St. Louis Gunners. Although they were expected to do no more than keep games from being cancelled, the Gunners managed a shutout victory against Pittsburgh.

The league's other Ohio Valley team, the Portsmouth Spartans, moved north to Detroit. Re-christened the Detroit Lions, they started the season looking like they were unbeatable. Tackle George Christiansen helped quarterback Dutch Clark, back from a year off as a college coach, become an offensive juggernaut. Defensively, the Lions shut out their first seven opponents and were 10–0 by mid-November. On the Sunday before Thanksgiving, they were upended by the Packers, 3–0. Detroit went on to lose twice to the Bears to fall from contention.

The Bears improved an already overpowering backfield with the addition of Beattie Feathers. The rookie became the first 1,000-yard rusher in a season, and he combined with Bronko Nagurski for 15 touchdowns. Chicago's offense overwhelmed opponents, although it took a fourth-quarter rally to squeak past the Giants, 10–9.

The Giants were the class of the East once again. After starting 0–2, coach Steve Owen's club beat up on the weaker teams in their division. New York finished with an 8–5 record and advanced to the championship game with the 13–0 Bears, the first team to go without a loss or a tie during the regular season. This time the fourth-quarter comeback belonged to the Giants.

Three extraordinary players appeared for the last time in 1934: revolutionary lineman Link Lyman; the league's first great passer, Benny Friedman; and Red Grange, whose mere presence brought national attention to the fledgling pro game. The first Chicago College All-Star Game was held in August at Soldier Field before 79,432. Although the Bears and college stars finished in a scoreless tie, the 1934 NFL season became the first without a single regular-season tie.

1935 NFL

TEAM	W-L-T	PCT	POST	PTS	RA	RY	RY/A	RTD	FL	PA	PC	GPY	GPY/A	PTD	PI	PSY	PRAT
Eastern Division																	
NYG	9-3	**.750**	L	180-96	497-436	1453-1089	2.9-2.5	9-4	**18-18**	154-205	69-66	947-962	6.1-4.7	10-5	**19-26**	—	**47.1**-17.0
Bkn	5-6-1	.455	—	90-141	367-531	1108-1810	3.0-3.4	6-8	29-38	178-163	52-55	718-997	4.0-6.1	5-7	23-26	—	13.7-30.4
Pit	4-8	.333	—	100-209	327-543	508-1957	1.6-3.6	4-12	28-27	**234**-209	67-68	996-1208	4.3-5.8	5-13	40-21	—	12.4-34.4
Bos	2-8-1	.200	—	65-123	448-**404**	1265-998	2.8-2.5	5-5	28-19	175-167	48-68	767-928	4.4-5.6	3-8	35-29	—	11.5-35.6
Phi	2-9	.182	—	60-179	411-443	1054-1697	2.6-3.8	2-15	26-30	169-168	46-59	823-871	4.9-5.2	6-6	30-23	—	19.6-25.3
Western Division																	
Det	7-3-2	.700	L*	191-111	532-443	1773-1039	3.3-2.3	**15-3**	19-27	142-181	57-58	920-931	**6.5**-5.1	9-8	20-25	—	44.1-25.4
GB	8-4	.667	—	181-**96**	448-448	1562-1219	3.5-2.7	7-6	27-21	230-190	**93**-61	**1449**-837	6.3-4.4	11-6	27-27	—	38.4-18.1
ChiC	6-4-2	.600	—	99-97	**547**-420	1521-1261	2.8-3.0	6-8	25-23	127-153	47-58	612-793	4.8-5.2	2-4	23-24	—	18.7-24.4
ChiB	6-4-2	.600	—	**192**-106	539-448	**2096**-1270	**3.9**-2.8	13-6	33-30	221-194	73-59	1221-926	5.5-4.8	**13**-7	21-37	—	32.7-19.8
Aver	12	—		129	457	1371	3.0	7	26	181	61	939	5.2	7	26		25.4

TEAM	1D	PENY	PNT	FGM/A	RTNY	RTNTD	OFFY/DEFY	NETY	NETTO	NP	PNP	DELP	PW	DELW	PRT	DR	YPD	DEL
Eastern Division																		
NYG	112	175	42	7-1	—	4-5	2414-2051	363	7	84	58	26	**8.1**	**0.9**	1.2/-0.8	—	—	—
Bkn	90	179	**43**	5-7	—	0-2	1876-2807	-931	12	-51	-30	-21	4.7	0.8	-1.5/-0.6	—	—	—
Pit	64	201	41	6-4	—	3-4	1557-3165	-1608	-20	-109	-214	**105**	3.3	0.7	-3.2/1.9	—	—	—
Bos	95	**166**	38	0-9	—	2-1	2103-1926	177	-15	-58	-45	-13	4.1	-1.5	-4.4/-1.8	—	—	—
Phi	82	330	35	2-6	—	0-3	2003-2568	-565	-3	-119	-59	-60	2.5	-0.5	-2.8/-0.6	—	—	—
Western Division																		
Det	121	195	36	5-7	—	1-2	2756-1970	786	**13**	80	118	-38	8.0	0.0	0.8/-0.6	—	—	—
GB	125	295	37	**8-3**	—	**5-1**	3021-2056	965	-6	85	56	29	8.1	-0.1	1.5/-1.7	—	—	—
ChiC	107	255	36	7-3	—	4-1	2233-2054	179	-1	2	11	-9	6.1	**0.9**	-3.2/-1.6	—	—	—
ChiB	**140**	354	37	3-3	—	1-1	**3454**-2196	**1258**	13	86	**157**	-71	8.1	-1.2	**1.8**/-3.4	—	—	—
Aver	104	239	0.0	5	—	2	2380	—	—	—	—	—	—	—	-1.0	—	—	—

Rushing Attempts	Rushing Yards	Rushing Average	Rushing TDs	Rushing Rank	Passing Yards	Passing Average
K.Richards-NYG......153	D.Russell-ChiC........499	E.Caddel-Det...........5.17	E.Caddel-Det................6	E.Caddel-Det............510	E.Danowski-NYG......794	E.Danowski-NYG....7.03
D.Russell-ChiC........140	E.Caddel-Det..........450	K.Richards-NYG......4.94	D.Russell-ChiC............4	D.Russell-ChiC.........499	A.Herber-GB.............729	A.Herber-GB...........6.69
E.Danowski-NYG......130	K.Richards-NYG........449	G.Ronzani-ChiB.......4.51	A.Nichelini-ChiC..........4	K.Richards-NYG........489	J.Gildea-Pit.............529	P.Sarboe-ChiC........5.49
D.Clark-Det..............120	D.Clark-Det..............427	S.Kostka-Bkn..........3.95	B.Molenda-ChiB...........4	D.Clark-Det...............467	B.Masterson-ChiB.....446	B.Monnett-GB..........5.45
A.Gutowsky-Det.......102	G.Ronzani-ChiB........356	G.Sauer-GB.............3.75	D.Clark-Det...............4	G.Ronzani-ChiB.........366	E.Storm-Phi..............372	J.Gildea-Pit............5.04

Completion Percent	TD Passes	TD Percent	INT Percent	Passer Rating	Passing Rank	Receptions
E.Danowski-NYG....50.4	E.Danowski-NYG......10	E.Danowski-NYG....8.8	B.Monnett-GB............7.7	E.Danowski-NYG...69.7	B.Masterson-ChiB......93	T.Goodwin-NYG........26
B.Monnett-GB........47.7	A.Herber-GB...............8	A.Herber-GB...........7.3	E.Danowski-NYG.......8.0	A.Herber-GB...........45.4	E.Danowski-NYG........87	J.Blood-GB................25
P.Sarboe-ChiC........46.3	B.Masterson-ChiB.......6	E.Matesic-Phi...........3.1	A.Herber-GB.............12.8	B.Monnett-GB..........42.7	R.Kercheval-Bkn........67	B.Smith-ChiC.............24
A.Herber-GB..........36.7	E.Storm-Phi...............4	B.Monnett-GB..........3.1	P.Sarboe-ChiC..........14.9	P.Sarboe-ChiC..........23.9	B.Shepherd-Det.........55	C.Malone-Bos............22
J.Gildea-Pit.............26.7	B.Molenda-ChiB.........3	J.Gildea-Pit.............1.9	J.Gildea-Pit..............19.0	E.Matesic-Phi............16.4	E.Caddel-Det............55	L.Johnsos-ChiB.........19

Receiving Yards	Receiving Average	Receiving TDs	Receiving Rank	Combined Net Yards	Total TDs	Total Points
C.Malone-Bos..........433	D.Hutson-GB.........23.33	B.Karr-ChiB...............6	D.Hutson-GB............240	E.Caddel-Det............621	D.Hutson-GB.............7	D.Clark-Det..............55
T.Goodwin-NYG........432	C.Malone-Bos........19.68	D.Hutson-GB..............6	T.Goodwin-NYG.........236	D.Clark-Det...............551	B.Karr-ChiB...............6	D.Hutson-GB.............43
D.Hutson-GB...........420	T.Goodwin-NYG......16.62		C.Malone-Bos...........227	D.Russell-ChiC.........532	D.Clark-Det...............6	B.Karr-ChiB...............36
J.Blood-GB..............404	J.Blood-GB............16.16		J.Blood-GB...............217	J.Blood-GB................519	E.Caddel-Det............6	E.Caddel-Det............36
B.Smith-ChiC...........318	L.Johnsos-ChiB......15.68			K.Richards-NYG........490	D.Burnett-NYG.........6	D.Burnett-NYG.........36

Punt Average	Field Goals	Field Goal Percent	Kickoff Returns	Kickoff Return Average	Punt Returns	Punt Return Average
Not kept	B.Smith-ChiC..............6	Not kept	Not kept	Not kept	Not kept	Not kept
	A.Niccolai-Pit.............6					
	R.Kercheval-Bkn.........5					

Punt/Kick Return Yards	Punt/Kick Return TDs	Interceptions	Interception Return Yards	Interception Return TDs	Sacks	Overall Rank
Not kept	P.Sarboe-ChiC..............1	Not kept	Not kept	Many...........................1	Not kept	E.Caddel-Det..........650
	P.Rentner-Bos.............1					K.Richards-NYG.....510
	G.Presnell-Det.............1					D.Clark-Det............456
	C.Battles-Bos..............1					E.Danowski-NYG.....442
						B.Molenda-ChiB......438

FLEET FEET AND TRADITION IN DETROIT

The defending champion New York Giants had a decidedly different look as they sought to defend their title. Ed Danowski and Kink Richards replaced Harry Newman and Ken Strong in the backfield, and rookie Tod Goodwin relegated ends Red Badgro and Ray Flaherty to supporting roles. Despite these changes—or perhaps because of them—the Giants continued their three-year reign as the best team in the East. They won every game against division opponents, all with losing records.

The West was a study in contrasts. The Packers were already a team that loved to throw the ball, but the arrival of rookie Don Hutson propelled Green Bay to a whole new level. With the lanky young Hutson lined up on one side and the elusive Johnny Blood on the other, opponents struggled to stop Green Bay's passing game. Existing defenses couldn't account for the speed of these two men, and passer Arnie Herber took advantage of the opportunities to throw the ball down the field. The only defense that seemed to have an answer for the new aerial attack was the Chicago Cardinals. They held the Packers to a total of 13 points while going 3–0 in head-to-head matchups.

The Lions, on the other hand, attacked their opponents with the league's most dominating running game. At the end of the season, three of the league's top five rushers came from Detroit. Dutch Clark continued to be a threat as both a passer and a runner, but the emergence of wingback Ernie Caddel and the midseason acquisition of fullback Bill Sheppard from the Boston Redskins gave opponents more trouble than they could handle, including the Giants, whom the Lions defeated for their first NFL title.

Detroit, with three failed NFL franchises in the 1920s, was establishing traditions in the 1930s. After a sellout crowd of 25,000 packed Titan Stadium for the Thanksgiving Day game in 1934 and again in 1935, the game became an annual holiday tradition in the Motor City. They have continued to host a Thanksgiving Day every year, except for a gap during World War II.

1936 NFL

TEAM	W-L-T	PCT	POST	PTS	RA	RY	RY/A	RTD	FL	PA	PC	GPY	GPY/A	PTD	PI	PSY	PRAT
Eastern Division																	
Bos	7-5	.583	L.	149-110	435-**434**	1454-1148	3.3-2.6	8-3	27-32	214-198	77-62	1102-954	5.1-4.8	5-7	23-22	—	21.7-20.5
Pit	6-6	.500	—	98-187	472-543	1100-2150	2.3-4.0	4-11	30-26	198-164	81-52	1078-907	5.4-5.5	5-13	28-25	—	27.7-38.4
NYG	5-6-1	.455	—	115-163	517-488	1837-1781	3.6-3.6	4-12	32-24	179-149	69-60	887-997	5.0-6.7	10-7	**17**-19	—	33.9-39.6
Bkn	3-8-1	.273	—	92-161	364-579	1300-1868	3.6-3.2	9-11	22-27	141-174	43-65	621-905	4.4-5.2	2-7	23-23	—	11.0-28.7
Phi	1-11	.083	—	51-206	473-468	1415-1973	3.0-4.2	2-12	29-29	170-147	39-61	603-853	3.5-5.8	3-10	36-15	—	8.2-43.9
Western Division																	
GB	10-1-1	**.909**	L*	**248**-118	490-478	1664-1494	3.4-3.1	11-5	20-19	**255**-227	**108**-81	**1629**-1170	6.4-5.2	**17**-7	19-31	—	**55.2**-24.0
ChiB	9-3	.750	—	222-**94**	552-510	2206-1822	4.0-3.6	12-9	21-24	170-227	58-86	1099-1174	**6.5**-5.2	16-3	21-35	—	49.2-20.0
Det	8-4	.667	—	235-102	**591**-446	2885-1427	**4.9**-3.2	**22**-3	**18**-13	146-194	61-70	818-1027	5.6-5.3	6-6	23-22	—	34.4-24.9
ChiC	3-8-1	.273	—	74-143	559-507	1509-1707	2.7-3.4	5-11	30-35	183-176	68-67	1123-973	6.1-5.5	3-7	26-24	—	24.5-30.5
Aver	12	—	—	143	495	1708	3.5	9	25	184	67	996	5.4	7	24	—	28.9

TEAM	1D	PENY	PNT	FGM/A	RTNY	RTNTD	OFFY/DEFY	NETY	NETTO	NP	PNP	DELP	PW	DELW	PRT	DR	YPD	DEL
Eastern Division																		
Bos	113	275	40	6-7	—	6-3	2622-2102	520	4	39	59	-20	7.0	0.0	0.5/0.2	—	—	—
Pit	117	336	42	9-1	—	1-3	2225-3057	-832	-7	-89	-97	8	3.8	**2.2**	-0.7/-0.5	—	—	—
NYG	146	205	41	1-6	—	2-2	2764-2778	-14	-6	-48	-25	-23	4.8	0.7	1.2/1.4	—	—	—
Bkn	90	210	**45**	5-5	—	1-3	1932-2773	-841	5	-69	-50	-19	4.3	-0.8	-2.8/-0.3	—	—	—
Phi	99	**159**	35	3-10	—	1-4	2068-2826	-758	-21	-155	-147	-8	2.1	-1.1	-5.8/ 1.9	—	—	—
Western Division																		
GB	148	478	38	**10**-6	—	3-2	3323-2664	659	11	130	99	31	**9.3**	1.3	**3.7**/-0.7	—	—	—
ChiB	145	435	40	7-3	—	2-0	3416-2996	420	**17**	128	**103**	25	9.2	-0.2	1.8/-1.6	—	—	—
Det	**170**	290	38	5-7	—	4-3	**3703**-2454	**1249**	-6	**133**	80	**53**	**9.3**	-1.3	-1.1/0.5	—	—	—
ChiC	138	415	35	2-3	—	2-2	2654-2680	-26	3	-69	10	-79	4.3	-0.8	-0.1/-0.2	—	—	—
Aver	130	311	0.0	5	—	2	2745	—	—	—	—	—	—	—	-0.1	—	—	—

Rushing Attempts		Rushing Yards		Rushing Average		Rushing TDs		Rushing Rank		Passing Yards		Passing Average	
T.Leemans-NYG	206	T.Leemans-NYG	830	E.Caddel-Det	6.37	D.Clark-Det	7	A.Gutowsky-Det	887	A.Herber-GB	1239	A.Herber-GB	7.16
A.Gutowsky-Det	191	A.Gutowsky-Det	827	D.Clark-Det	5.11	A.Gutowsky-Det	6	T.Leemans-NYG	850	E.Matesic-Pit	850	P.Vaughan-ChiC	6.91
C.Battles-Bos	176	D.Clark-Det	628	B.Wilson-Bkn	4.86	C.Hinkle-GB	5	D.Clark-Det	698	P.Vaughan-ChiC	546	D.Clark-Det	6.58
G.Grosvenor-ChiC	169	C.Battles-Bos	614	C.Hinkle-GB	4.76	C.Battles-Bos	5	C.Battles-Bos	664	E.Danowski-NYG	515	P.Sarboe-ChiC	6.42
D.Clark-Det	123	G.Grosvenor-ChiC	609	R.Nolting-ChiB	4.63			G.Grosvenor-ChiC	649	D.Clark-Det	467	E.Matesic-Pit	6.16

Completion Percent		TD Passes		TD Percent		INT Percent		Passer Rating		Passing Rank		Receptions	
D.Clark-Det	53.5	A.Herber-GB	11	A.Herber-GB	6.4	A.Herber-GB	7.5	A.Herber-GB	58.9	A.Herber-GB	155	D.Hutson-GB	34
E.Matesic-Pit	46.4	E.Danowski-NYG	5	D.Clark-Det	5.6	D.Clark-Det	8.5	D.Clark-Det	57.7	B.Monnett-GB	80	B.Smith-ChiC	20
E.Danowski-NYG	45.2			E.Danowski-NYG	4.8	D.Smukler-Phi	8.8	E.Danowski-NYG	36.8	J.Doehring-ChiB	78	E.Caddel-Det	19
A.Herber-GB	44.5			D.Smukler-Phi	4.4	E.Danowski-NYG	9.6	E.Matesic-Pit	36.5	J.Manders-ChiB	26	W.Millner-Bos	18
P.Sarboe-ChiC	40.3			E.Matesic-Pit	2.9	E.Matesic-Pit	11.6	P.Vaughan-ChiC	31.4	D.Crayne-Bkn	26	E.Manske-Phi	17

Receiving Yards		Receiving Average		Receiving TDs		Receiving Rank		Combined Net Yards		Total TDs		Total Points	
D.Hutson-GB	536	B.Hewitt-ChiB	23.87	D.Hutson-GB	8	D.Hutson-GB	308	A.Gutowsky-Det	857	D.Hutson-GB	9	D.Clark-Det	73
B.Smith-ChiC	414	B.Smith-ChiC	20.70	B.Hewitt-ChiB	6	B.Smith-ChiC	212	T.Leemans-NYG	852	B.Hewitt-ChiB	7	J.Manders-ChiB	62
B.Hewitt-ChiB	358	E.Manske-Phi	19.12	W.Heller-Pit	3	B.Hewitt-ChiB	209	E.Caddel-Det	730	D.Clark-Det	7	D.Hutson-GB	54
E.Manske-Phi	325	D.Hutson-GB	15.76	H.Ebding-Det	3	E.Manske-Bos	163	C.Battles-Bos	717	C.Battles-Bos	7	B.Hewitt-ChiB	42
J.Barrett-Bkn	268	D.Burnett-NYG	15.38	D.Burnett-NYG	3	J.Barrett-Bkn	139	D.Clark-Det	633	A.Gutowsky-Det	6	C.Battles-Bos	42

Punt Average	Field Goals		Field Goal Percent	Kickoff Returns	Kickoff Return Average	Punt Returns	Punt Return Average
Not kept	A.Niccolai-Pit	7	Not kept	Not kept	Not kept	Not kept	Not kept
	J.Manders-ChiB	7					
	R.Kercheval-Bkn	5					
	S.Ellstrom-GB	5					

Punt/Kick Return Yards	Punt/Kick Return TDs		Interceptions	Interception Return Yards	Interception Return TDs		Sacks	Overall Rank	
Not kept	G.Grosvenor-ChiC	1	Not kept -	Not kept	P.Rentner-Bos	2	Not kept	T.Leemans-NYG	765
	C.Battles-Bos	1						A.Gutowsky-Det	753
								D.Clark-Det	714
								E.Caddel-Det	635
								C.Battles-Bos	617

1936: Drafting a New Plan

After three seasons in the National Football League and very little measurable success, Philadelphia Eagles owner Bert Bell was tired of being outbid for talent by wealthier owners like Chicago's George Halas and New York's Tim Mara. Bell was particularly frustrated by his inability to lure young college stars to his team, and he knew he wasn't alone. Bell made a passionate argument that a draft of college players would help restore competitive balance, and the other owners agreed.

Bell's Eagles owned the top pick by virtue of their 2–9 record the previous season. He used the pick to select Jay Berwanger, the University of Chicago halfback who had won the first Heisman Trophy. But Berwanger had no intention of playing pro football, preferring to go into business. Berwanger, whose rights were traded to the Bears (and he wouldn't play there, either), was one of many college prospects who spurned the NFL. Just 24 of the 81 players selected in the first draft signed contracts. Some played in a rival pro league—the short-lived American Football League—but most simply followed Berwanger's path and steered clear of professional football.

Ironically, the biggest beneficiaries of the NFL's first draft seemed to be the two wealthiest teams. The Giants signed three of their picks, most notably workhorse fullback Tuffy Leemans. The Bears found a pair of future Hall of Famers to bolster their offensive line: tackle Joe Stydahar and guard Dan Fortmann, the third-from last overall pick in the inaugural draft. None of Bell's picks signed with the Eagles and the team went 1–11 to secure the first pick in 1937.

The Boston Redskins didn't land any superstars, but four of their draft picks played significant roles for new coach Ray Flaherty. Back-to-back shutouts of the Pirates and Giants to end the season clinched the division with a 7–5 record; the franchise's first—and last—in Boston.

Green Bay's aerial attack became even more potent in Don Hutson's second season, and his 8 touchdown led the NFL. The steady play of running back Clarke Hinkle gave the Packers balance. Green Bay lost just once en route to its fourth NFL championship.

1937 NFL

TEAM	W-L-T	PCT	POST	PTS	RA	RY	RY/A	RTD	FL	PA	PC	GPY	GPY/A	PTD	PI	PSY	PRAT
Eastern Division																	
Was	8-3	.727	L*	195-120	450-**352**	1604-1149	3.6-3.3	11-3	26-24	**222**-171	99-66	1316-946	5.9-5.5	11-12	20-17	—	42.9-41.1
NYG	6-3-2	.667	—	128-109	476-390	1519-1216	3.2-3.1	4-6	17-14	203-182	83-71	1024-929	5.0-5.1	10-5	**11**-30	—	51.0-25.4
Pit	4-7	.364	—	122-145	**493**-405	1419-1311	2.9-3.2	5-7	22-23	164-185	57-60	918-902	5.6-4.9	9-9	27-17	—	33.1-27.4
Bkn	3-7-1	.300	—	82-174	357-474	982-1764	2.8-3.7	5-10	19-16	179-165	64-74	995-990	5.6-6.0	4-10	25-21	—	22.9-45.1
Phi	2-8-1	.200	—	86-177	285-502	884-1812	3.1-3.6	2-6	**12**-17	207-196	63-79	849-1315	4.1-6.7	8-15	24-19	—	17.8-49.6
Western Division																	
ChiB	9-1-1	**.900**	L	201-**100**	479-412	1612-933	3.4-2.3	5-5	18-21	147-195	56-78	1014-1292	**6.9**-6.6	**17**-6	13-17	—	**64.3**-37.0
GB	7-4	.636	—	**220**-122	483-400	1786-1184	3.7-3.0	10-8	**12**-11	216-197	95-70	**1398**-1115	6.5-5.7	16-7	26-22	—	50.8-27.5
Det	7-4	.636	—	180-105	484-387	**2074**-1329	**4.3**-3.4	**12**-8	12-17	120-165	44-59	631-804	5.3-4.9	4-4	18-24	—	26.1-20.7
ChiC	5-5-1	.500	—	135-165	385-475	1149-1457	3.0-3.1	7-6	21-21	189-204	77-73	1243-1051	6.6-5.2	8-13	21-24	—	38.0-35.0
Cle	1-10	.091	—	75-207	370-465	930-1804	2.5-3.9	6-8	19-15	168-155	59-67	839-883	5.0-5.7	3-9	21-15	—	18.5-41.6
Aver	11	—	—	142	426	1396	3.3	7	18	182	70	1023	5.6	9	21	—	34.5

TEAM	1D	PENY	PNT	FGM/A	RTNY	RTNTD	OFFY/DEFY	NETY	NETTO	NP	PNP	DELP	PW	DELW	PRT	DR	YPD	DEL
Eastern Division																		
Was	**149**	338	38	5-3	—	4-1	2923-2095	828	-5	75	49	26	7.4	0.6	2.4/ 1.8	—	—	—
NYG	127	275	37	8-6	—	1-2	2613-2145	468	**16**	19	**103**	-84	6.0	1.0	3.1/-2.0	—	—	—
Pit	105	358	**42**	4-3	—	2-4	2388-2213	175	-9	-23	-21	-2	4.9	-0.9	-1.3/ 1.2	—	—	—
Bkn	88	190	38	5-5	—	1-3	2005-2754	-749	-2	-92	-90	-2	3.2	0.3	-0.5/ 0.9	—	—	—
Phi	68	146	40	1-5	—	2-3	1766-3127	-1361	0	-91	-113	22	3.2	-0.7	-0.7/ 3.1	—	—	—
Western Division																		
ChiB	114	505	41	8-2	—	4-2	2641-2225	416	7	**101**	63	38	**8.0**	1.5	4.1/ 3.0	—	—	—
GB	140	291	**42**	4-2	—	4-2	**3201**-2299	**902**	-5	98	55	**43**	7.9	-1.0	1.8/ 1.0	—	—	—
Det	120	**139**	37	8-3	—	7-2	2707-2133	574	11	75	92	-17	7.4	-0.4	-1.2/-1.4	—	—	—
ChiC	99	305	38	2-7	—	4-2	2450-2508	-58	3	-30	7	-37	4.8	0.8	2.0/ 0.5	—	—	—
Cle	88	228	36	1-10	—	1-9	1794-2687	-893	-10	-132	-114	-18	2.2	-1.2	-0.5/ 1.9	—	—	—
Aver	110	278	0.0	5	—	3	2449	—	—	—	—	—	—	1.0	—	—	—	—

Rushing Attempts		Rushing Yards		Rushing Average		Rushing TDs		Rushing Rank		Passing Yards		Passing Average	
C.Battles-Was	216	C.Battles-Was	874	E.Caddel-Det	5.64	C.Hinkle-GB	5	C.Battles-Was	924	S.Baugh-Was	1127	B.Masterson-ChiB	8.54
T.Leemans-NYG	144	C.Hinkle-GB	552	E.Jankowski-GB	5.31	D.Clark-Det	5	C.Hinkle-GB	602	P.Coffee-ChiC	824	A.Parker-Bkn	8.43
G.Grosvenor-ChiC	143	B.Karcis-Pit	513	D.Clark-Det	4.88	C.Battles-Was	5	B.Karcis-Pit	543	E.Danowski-NYG	814	B.Monnett-GB	7.95
C.Hinkle-GB	129	D.Clark-Det	468	J.Maniaci-Bkn	4.71			D.Clark-Det	518	A.Herber-GB	684	P.Coffee-ChiC	6.92
A.Gutowsky-Det	128	G.Grosvenor-ChiC	461	B.Nagurski-ChiB	4.70			G.Grosvenor-ChiC	481	B.Masterson-ChiB	615	S.Baugh-Was	6.59

Completion Percent		TD Passes		TD Percent		INT Percent		Passer Rating		Passing Rank		Receptions	
B.Monnett-GB	50.7	B.Masterson-ChiB	9	B.Masterson-ChiB	12.5	E.Danowski-NYG	3.7	B.Monnett-GB	74.4	E.Danowski-NYG	247	D.Hutson-GB	41
E.Danowski-NYG	49.3	B.Monnett-GB	8	B.Monnett-GB	11.0	S.Baugh-Was	8.2	E.Danowski-NYG	72.8	B.Masterson-ChiB	73	G.Tinsley-ChiC	36
S.Baugh-Was	47.4	E.Danowski-NYG	8	A.Herber-GB	6.7	B.Snyder-Cle	9.1	B.Masterson-ChiB	67.8	R.Buivid-ChiB	53	C.Malone-Was	28
A.Parker-Bkn	45.9	S.Baugh-Was	8	E.Danowski-NYG	6.7	P.Coffee-ChiC	9.2	S.Baugh-Was	50.5	R.Keen-Phi	48	J.Barrett-Bkn	20
A.Herber-GB	45.2	A.Herber-GB	7	S.Baugh-Was	4.7	A.Herber-GB	9.6	A.Herber-GB	50.0	S.Baugh-Was	44	B.Hewitt-Phi	16

Receiving Yards		Receiving Average		Receiving TDs		Receiving Rank		Combined Net Yards		Total TDs		Total Points	
G.Tinsley-ChiC	675	J.Barrett-Bkn	23.05	D.Hutson-GB	7	G.Tinsley-ChiC	363	C.Battles-Was	955	D.Hutson-GB	7	J.Manders-ChiB	69
D.Hutson-GB	552	J.Carter-Phi	18.80	G.Tinsley-ChiC	5	D.Hutson-GB	311	G.Tinsley-ChiC	677	C.Hinkle-GB	7	C.Hinkle-GB	57
J.Barrett-Bkn	461	G.Tinsley-ChiC	18.75	B.Hewitt-Phi	5	J.Barrett-Bkn	246	J.Barrett-Bkn	668	C.Battles-Was	7	R.Smith-Was	55
C.Malone-Was	419	W.Millner-Was	15.43			C.Malone-Was	230	T.Leemans-NYG	586	G.Tinsley-ChiC	6	D.Clark-Det	45
J.Carter-Phi	282	C.Malone-Was	14.96			J.Carter-Phi	156	D.Hutson-GB	578	D.Clark-Det	6		

Punt Average		Field Goals		Field Goal Percent		Kickoff Returns		Kickoff Return Average		Punt Returns		Punt Return Average	
Not kept		J.Manders-ChiB	8	Not kept		Not kept		Not kept		Not kept		Not kept	
		R.Smith-Was	5										
		R.Monahan-Det	5										
		T.Manton-NYG	5										
		A.Niccolai-Pit	4										

Punt/Kick Return Yards		Punt/Kick Return TDs		Interceptions		Interception Return Yards		Interception Return TDs		Sacks		Overall Rank	
Not kept		D.Russell-ChiC	1	Not kept		Not kept		Many	1	Not kept		C.Battles-Was	931
		A.Parker-Bkn	1									C.Hinkle-GB	692
		J.Blood-Pit	1									D.Clark-Det	526
												B.Karcis-Pit	518
												T.Leemans-NYG	510

RAMS AND REDSKINS ON THE MOVE

Once again, the NFL tried to re-establish a presence in Ohio by granting a Cleveland franchise to Homer Marshman, a local attorney. Marshman had run a successful franchise in the American Football League in 1936 (that league folded in '37), and the other NFL owners saw a chance to capitalize by expanding. None of the players carried over, but Marshman kept the same name: the Cleveland Rams. Playing in cavernous Cleveland Stadium, the new team went just 1–10 in its inaugural NFL season.

That wasn't the biggest change in the league. Redskins owner George Preston Marshall had grown frustrated by the lack of fan support in Boston. When fewer than 5,000 fans showed up at Fenway Park to watch his team clinch its first division title in 1936, he'd had enough. First he moved the NFL Championship Game home field from Boston to New York. Then he moved the franchise. Washington, D.C. immediately embraced the Redskins. Attendance soared, and when the team needed a win in the season finale to claim the East division title again, more than 8,000 fans traveled with the team to

New York. Buoyed by the support, the Redskins scored 49 points and claimed the crown.

Running back Cliff Battles had been the star of the Redskins offense for several years, but it was the addition of a brash young player that vaulted the team to the top. Sammy Baugh, a prolific college passer, was unlike anything the league had seen. He had a great arm and threw with tremendous accuracy. Coach Ray Flaherty ran the pass-friendly double wing formation that Baugh had mastered at Texas Christian University, and it was a great success. Baugh led the league in passing, Battles led the league in rushing, and the Redskins won their first NFL championship.

George Halas's Bears were the only team running the T-formation. It was the first offense to feature a direct snap to the quarterback under center, which let the play get started more quickly. With their dominating offensive line and bruising fullback Bronko Nagurski, Chicago's running game was nearly unstoppable. The Bears won the West division for the third time in five years.

1938 NFL

TEAM	W-L-T	PCT	POST	PTS	RA	RY	RY/A	RTD	FL	PA	PC	GPY	GPY/A	PTD	PI	PSY	PRAT
Eastern Division																	
NYG	**8-2-1**	**.800**	L*	194-**79**	466-373	1550-1114	3.3-3.0	**12-3**	10-14	186-226	91-77	1142-914	6.1-**4.0**	10-**5**	19-**34**	—	46.8-**15.1**
Was	6-3-2	.667	—	148-154	388-427	1424-1231	3.7-**2.9**	10-8	20-9	**248**-195	**114-69**	**1536**-943	6.2-4.8	9-9	28-19	—	38.7-27.5
Bkn	4-4-3	.500	—	131-161	381-410	1212-1509	3.2-3.7	9-6	11-9	171-246	69-105	992-1414	5.8-5.7	6-13	**9**-28	—	49.6-39.6
Phi	5-6	.455	—	154-164	346-463	1011-1855	2.9-4.0	2-12	**6-17**	191-197	64-97	917-1396	4.8-7.1	15-7	19-16	—	36.6-50.6
Pit	2-9	.182	—	79-169	457-425	1414-1368	3.1-3.2	5-7	**6**-8	194-185	72-74	916-1213	4.7-6.6	5-13	32-14	—	21.7-54.6
Western Division																	
GB	**8-3**	.727	L	**223**-118	454-372	1571-1206	3.5-3.2	9-8	8-12	210-232	91-92	1466-1343	**7.0**-5.8	**20**-5	20-22	—	**59.4**-26.9
Det	7-4	.636	—	119-108	**472-338**	**1893-1081**	**4.0**-3.2	11-6	8-13	148-205	49-77	747-1105	5.0-5.4	3-9	16-23	—	17.9-30.9
ChiB	6-5	.545	—	194-148	461-382	1686-1236	3.7-3.2	11-8	25-14	197-190	72-76	1222-**897**	6.2-4.7	12-9	18-24	—	40.6-31.3
Cle	4-7	.364	—	131-215	336-500	798-1745	2.4-3.5	5-15	10-16	245-**172**	88-77	1363-1248	5.6-7.3	9-12	34-23	—	27.9-53.3
ChiC	2-9	.182	—	111-168	382-453	1149-1363	3.0-3.0	9-10	15-10	240-182	**114**-80	1340-1168	5.6-6.4	4-11	26-18	—	30.9-46.0
Aver	11	—	—	148	414	1371	3.3	8	12	203	82	1164	5.7	9	22	—	35.5

TEAM	1D	PENY	PNT	FGM/A	RTNY	RTNTD	OFFY/DEFY	NETY	NETTO	NP	PNP	DELP	PW	DELW	PRT	DR	YPD	DEL
Eastern Division																		
NYG	132	233	41	5/11-**1**	—	4-3	2692-**2028**	664	**19**	**115**	**131**	-16	**8.4**	0.1	2.1/-2.5	—	—	—
Was	**147**	410	41	5/12-8	—	1-2	2986-2174	812	-20	-6	-12	6	5.3	**1.6**	1.5/ 0.9	—	—	—
Bkn	96	332	**46**	**7**/15-5	—	1-2	2231-2923	-692	17	-30	10	-40	4.8	0.8	**3.8**/ 1.2	—	—	—
Phi	86	220	40	1/9-4	—	**5**-3	1927-3251	-1324	8	-10	-78	68	5.3	-0.3	1.1/ 3.8	—	—	—
Pit	103	225	39	1/6-5	—	1-3	2358-2581	-223	-16	-90	-83	-7	3.3	-1.3	-2.4/ 3.9	—	—	—
Western Division																		
GB	134	250	42	5/14-4	—	1-2	**3037**-2549	488	6	105	65	40	8.1	-0.1	3.6/ 1.7	—	—	—
Det	129	345	39	**7**/10-**1**	—	0-0	2640-2186	454	12	11	86	-75	5.8	1.2	0.4/ 0.8	—	—	—
ChiB	141	350	40	4/12-4	—	3-3	2979-2133	**846**	-5	46	51	-5	6.7	-0.6	2.7/-0.5	—	—	—
Cle	101	**195**	44	3/4-5	—	4-2	2253-2993	-740	-5	-84	-82	-2	3.4	0.6	-0.3/ 1.9	—	—	—
ChiC	121	286	40	3/8-4	—	2-2	2512-2531	-19	-13	-57	-54	-3	4.1	-2.1	0.9/ 2.6	—	—	—
Aver	119	285	0.0	4/10	—	2	2562							1.3				

Rushing Attempts		Rushing Yards		Rushing Average		Rushing TDs		Rushing Rank		Passing Yards		Passing Average	
W.White-Pit	152	W.White-Pit	567	C.Isbell-GB	5.24	A.Farkas-Was	6	W.White-Pit	607	A.Parker-Bkn	865	B.Monnett-GB	8.16
A.Gutowsky-Det	131	T.Leemans-NYG	463	W.White-Pit	4.71	W.White-Pit	4	T.Leemans-NYG	503	S.Baugh-Was	853	B.Masterson-ChiB	7.57
H.Soar-NYG	122	B.Shepherd-Det	455	B.Shepherd-Det	4.55	T.Leemans-NYG	4	B.Shepherd-Det	485	B.Masterson-ChiB	848	B.Snyder-Cle	7.25
T.Leemans-NYG	121	C.Isbell-GB	445	J.Laws-GB	4.22	B.Karcis-NYG	4	C.Isbell-GB	465	E.Danowski-NYG	848	B.Hartman-Was	7.25
C.Hinkle-GB	114	A.Gutowsky-Det	444	A.Farkas-Was	4.20	L.Cardwell-Det	4	A.Gutowsky-Det	464	C.Isbell-GB	659	C.Isbell-GB	7.24

Completion Percent		TD Passes		TD Percent		INT Percent		Passer Rating		Passing Rank		Receptions	
B.Monnett-GB	54.4	B.Monnett-GB	9	B.Monnett-GB	15.8	A.Parker-Bkn	4.7	B.Monnett-GB	91.8	A.Parker-Bkn	178	G.Tinsley-ChiC	41
E.Danowski-NYG	54.3	C.Isbell-GB	8	E.Mortell-Phi	10.5	E.Danowski-NYG	6.2	E.Danowski-NYG	66.9	E.Danowski-NYG	139	D.Hutson-GB	32
J.Robbins-ChiC	53.6	B.Snyder-Cle	7	C.Isbell-GB	8.8	B.Monnett-GB	7.0	C.Isbell-GB	55.9	B.Monnett-GB	118	J.Carter-Phi	27
B.Hartman-Was	49.4	D.Smukler-Phi	7	B.Snyder-Cle	8.0	A.Herber-GB	7.3	B.Snyder-Cle	54.0	R.Buivid-ChiB	93	C.Malone-Was	24
S.Baugh-Was	49.2	E.Danowski-NYG	7	D.Smukler-Phi	6.9	D.Smukler-Phi	7.8	A.Parker-Bkn	53.5	B.Masterson-ChiB	89	J.Benton-Cle	21

Receiving Yards		Receiving Average		Receiving TDs		Receiving Rank		Combined Net Yards		Total TDs		Total Points	
D.Hutson-GB	548	D.Hutson-GB	17.13	D.Hutson-GB	9	D.Hutson-GB	319	W.White-Pit	655	D.Hutson-GB	9	C.Hinkle-GB	58
G.Tinsley-ChiC	516	J.Carter-Phi	14.30	J.Carter-Phi	7	G.Tinsley-ChiC	263	H.Soar-NYG	565	J.Carter-Phi	8	D.Hutson-GB	57
J.Benton-Cle	418	G.Tinsley-ChiC	12.59	J.Benton-Cle	5	J.Benton-Cle	234	C.Isbell-GB	549	C.Hinkle-GB	7	J.Carter-Phi	48
J.Carter-Phi	386	C.Malone-Was	10.71			J.Carter-Phi	228	D.Hutson-GB	547	A.Farkas-Was	6	W.Cuff-NYG	45
B.Smith-ChiC	338					B.Smith-ChiC	174	G.Tinsley-ChiC	542	J.Benton-Cle	6		

Punt Average		Field Goals		Field Goal Percent		Kickoff Returns		Kickoff Return Average		Punt Returns		Punt Return Average	
Not kept		R.Kercheval-Bkn	5	W.Cuff-NYG	55.6	Not kept		Not kept		Not kept		Not kept	
		W.Cuff-NYG	5	R.Kercheval-Bkn	38.5								
		R.Monahan-Det	4	J.Manders-ChiB	33.3								
		J.Manders-ChiB	3	C.Hinkle-GB	33.3								
		C.Hinkle-GB	3	H.Reese-Phi	16.7								

Punt/Kick Return Yards		Punt/Kick Return TDs		Interceptions		Interception Return Yards		Interception Return TDs		Sacks		Overall Rank	
Not kept		D.Smukler-Phi	1	Not kept		Not kept		Many	1	Not kept		A.Gutowsky-Det	497
												C.Isbell-GB	487
												A.Parker-Bkn	475
												T.Leemans-NYG	437
												L.Cardwell-Det	426

BATTLES LOST AND WON

After five years in the league, the Pittsburgh Pirates still hadn't finished a season with a winning record. They tried to gain respectability by signing veterans Johnny Blood and Walt Kiesling, but the club's fortune seemed poised to change in 1938 after drafting Colorado's Byron "Whizzer" White, one of college football's biggest stars. White chose to delay his Rhodes scholarship to play pro football, and he led the league in rushing as a rookie. Despite his contributions, Pittsburgh limped to the finish at 2–9. White left at the end of the season to study at Oxford. While he would eventually be named a Justice on the United States Supreme Court, he never played for Pittsburgh again—although he did spend two years with the Lions.

Buoyed by the addition of rookie passer Cecil Isbell, Green Bay triumphed in the West. The Packers led the league in scoring, but Don Hutson's knee injury in November led to consecutive losses to the Giants.

Washington's hopes of defending its title appeared dashed early in the season. Running back Cliff Battles retired when Redskins owner George Preston Marshall refused to pay him more than $3,000. Battles left to take a $1,000 raise as an assistant at Columbia University. Quarterback Sammy Baugh then separated his shoulder in the season opener. The team rallied after Baugh returned in November, and for the third consecutive year, the Redskins went into their finale with a chance to clinch the division by beating the New York Giants. This time, though, the Giants beat Washington, 36–0, and went on to win the NFL title.

For the first time, the league decided to give an award for the Most Valuable Player, and it went to Giants center Mel Hein. He was a dominating blocker who never missed a down, and was also one of the league's best pass defenders. Hein's team lost two close games early in the season, but New York held seven of their last eight opponents to a touchdown or less. The Giants continued winning after the season, beating a team of collected NFL and independent stars in the first Pro All-Star Game in Los Angeles.

1939 NFL

TEAM	W-L-T	PCT	POST	PTS	RA	RY	RY/A	RTD	FL	PA	PC	GPY	GPY/A	PTD	PI	PSY	PRAT
Eastern Division																	
NYG	9-1-1	.900	L	168-85	448-406	1281-1216	2.9-3.0	9-5	9-10	177-222	75-89	971-1283	5.5-5.8	8-3	11-35	—	49.4-24.5
Was	8-2-1	.800	—	242-94	410-412	1693-999	4.1-2.4	12-5	14-12	201-243	117-90	1795-1116	8.9-4.6	18-6	18-24	—	80.3-20.7
Bkn	4-6-1	.400	—	108-219	407-427	1327-1488	3.3-3.5	7-13	13-6	176-195	77-92	1024-1599	5.8-8.2	4-13	16-22	—	32.5-58.2
Phi	1-9-1	.100	—	105-200	329-455	631-1661	1.9-3.7	5-11	12-13	267-210	119-98	1516-1290	5.7-6.1	7-11	22-17	—	37.3-50.3
Pit	1-9-1	.100	—	114-216	428-440	1138-1701	2.7-3.9	7-18	10-11	221-193	70-88	1084-1368	4.9-7.1	8-10	34-11	—	21.4-63.1
Western Division																	
GB	9-2	.818	L*	233-153	500-333	1574-1165	3.1-3.5	13-12	7-9	248-239	101-106	1871-1602	7.5-6.7	14-9	15-26	—	61.1-39.9
ChiB	8-3	.727	•	298-157	439-353	2043-812	4.7-2.3	21-9	14-17	221-319	89-133	1965-1768	8.9-5.5	16-9	19-25	—	61.0-36.7
Det	6-5	.545	—	145-150	406-375	1487-1203	3.7-3.2	10-5	11-12	227-217	92-92	1357-1400	6.0-6.5	7-13	20-14	—	34.3-57.4
Cle	5-5-1	.500	—	195-164	387-431	1260-1499	3.3-3.5	14-11	12-14	253-199	127-78	1415-1249	5.6-6.3	12-9	21-23	—	48.4-36.4
ChiC	1-10	.091	—	84-254	321-443	835-1525	2.6-3.4	4-13	14-10	247-201	85-86	1170-1493	4.7-7.4	5-16	33-12	—	17.7-70.3
Aver	11	—	—	169	408	1327	3.3	10	11	224	95	1417	6.3	10	21	—	39.7

TEAM	1D	PENY	PNT	FGM/A	RTNY	RTNTD	OFFY/DEFY	NETY	NETTO	NP	PNP	DELP	PW	DELW	PRT	DR	YPD	DEL
Eastern Division																		
NYG	109	267	38	**14/32**-8	—	1-1	2257-2499	-242	**25**	83	80	3	7.6	**1.9**	3.1/-1.2	—	—	—
Was	125	332	40	2/13-4	—	5-1	3490-**2115**	1375	4	**148**	131	17	**9.2**	**5.8**/0.4	2.0/3.8	—	—	—
Bkn	113	**210**	38	8/20-**2**	—	1-5	2347-3087	-740	-1	-111	-66	-45	2.7	1.8	2.0/3.8	—	—	—
Phi	97	237	**41**	4/8-9	—	2-3	2165-2951	-786	-4	-95	-82	-13	3.1	-1.6	2.2/3.0	—	—	—
Pit	113	279	38	3/8-7	—	0-1	2237-3069	-832	-22	-102	-157	**55**	3.0	-1.5	-1.7/5.0	—	—	—
Western Division																		
GB	**149**	259	40	5/18-4	—	4-0	3445-2767	678	13	80	109	-29	7.5	1.5	5.4/2.2	—	—	—
ChiB	148	416	40	5/11-4	—	5-3	**3988**-2580	**1408**	9	141	**153**	-12	9.0	-1.0	5.7/2.3	—	—	—
Det	133	304	40	7/12-5	—	1-1	2905-2603	302	-5	-5	5	-10	5.4	0.6	2.3/4.1	—	—	—
Cle	131	220	40	1/2-4	—	2-2	2683-2748	-65	4	31	11	20	6.3	-0.8	2.3/1.5	—	—	—
ChiC	101	238	40	3/10-5	—	2-6	2027-3018	-991	-25	-170	-183	13	4.3	-0.3	-1.1/5.5	—	—	—
Aver	122	276	0.0	5/13	—	2	2754	—	—	—	—	—	—	—	2.6	—	—	—

Rushing Attempts	Rushing Yards	Rushing Average	Rushing TDs	Rushing Rank	Passing Yards	Passing Average
A.Farkas-Was 139	B.Osmanski-ChiB 699	J.Maniaci-ChiB 7.06	J.Drake-Cle 9	B.Osmanski-ChiB 769	D.O'Brien-Phi.........1324	F.Filchock-Was......12.29
C.Hinkle-GB 135	A.Farkas-Was 547	B.Osmanski-ChiB ...5.78	B.Osmanski-ChiB 7	A.Farkas-Was 597	P.Hall-Cle 1227	B.Masterson-ChiB 8.09
C.Isbell-GB 132	J.Maniaci-ChiB 544	D.Todd-Was 4.67	J.Maniaci-ChiB 5	J.Maniaci-ChiB 584	A.Herber-GB 1107	A.Herber-GB 7.96
T.Leemans-NYG 128	P.Manders-Bkn 482	P.Manders-Bkn 4.23	C.Hinkle-GB 5	J.Drake-Cle 543	F.Filchock-Was.......1094	C.Isbell-GB 7.27
B.Osmanski-ChiB 121	P.Hall-Cle 458	J.Pingel-Det 4.07	A.Farkas-Was 5	P.Manders-Bkn 502	A.Parker-Bkn 977	D.O'Brien-Phi......6.59

Completion Percent	TD Passes	TD Percent	INT Percent	Passer Rating	Passing Rank	Receptions
F.Filchock-Was......61.8	F.Filchock-Was...... 11	F.Filchock-Was......12.4	D.Sloan-Det 2.9	F.Filchock-Was......111.7	F.Filchock-Was......322	D.Hutson-GB 34
S.Baugh-Was......55.2	P.Hall-Cle 9	B.Masterson-ChiB ...5.78	C.Isbell-GB 4.9	C.Isbell-GB 66.4	A.Herber-GB 234	P.Schwartz-Bkn.......33
P.Hall-Cle 51.0	B.Masterson-ChiB ... 8	S.Baugh-Was 6.3	E.Danowski-NYG 5.9	A.Herber-GB 61.6	D.Sloan-Det 219	F.Souchak-Cle 32
D.O'Brien-Phi......49.3	A.Herber-GB 8	C.Isbell-GB 5.8	P.Hall-Cle 6.3	D.Sloan-Det 60.0	C.Isbell-GB 205	R.Ramsey-Phi 31
A.Parker-Bkn 45.9		A.Herber-GB 5.8	A.Herber-GB 6.5	B.Masterson-ChiB ..58.6	S.Luckman-ChiB......183	J.Benton-Cle 27

Receiving Yards	Receiving Average	Receiving TDs	Receiving Rank	Combined Net Yards	Total TDs	Total Points
D.Hutson-GB 846	D.Hutson-GB 24.88	J.Benton-Cle 7	D.Hutson-GB 453	A.Farkas-Was 984	A.Farkas-Was 11	A.Farkas-Was 68
P.Schwartz-Bkn....550	P.Schwartz-Bkn...16.67	D.Hutson-GB 6	P.Schwartz-Bkn......290	D.Hutson-GB 872	J.Drake-Cle 9	J.Drake-Cle 54
A.Farkas-Was 437	J.Benton-Cle 14.37	A.Farkas-Was 5	A.Farkas-Was 244	B.Osmanski-ChiB 764	B.Osmanski-ChiB 8	J.Manders-ChiB 50
S.Boyd-Pit 423	J.Carter-Phi 12.17	B.Smith-ChiC 4	J.Benton-Cle 229	T.Leemans-NYG 614	J.Benton-Cle 8	B.Osmanski-ChiB 48
D.Plasman-ChiB 403	R.Ramsey-Phi 11.58	W.Millner-Was 4	S.Boyd-Pit 222	B.Shepherd-Det.......563		J.Benton-Cle 48

Punt Average	Field Goals	Field Goal Percent	Kickoff Returns	Kickoff Return Average	Punt Returns	Punt Return Average
S.Luckman-ChiB......44.4	W.Cuff-NYG.........7	K.Strong-NYG.........50.0	Not kept	Not kept	Not kept	Not kept
G.Faust-ChiC......44.0	R.Kercheval-Bkn 6	E.Manske-Det 50.0				
J.Pingel-Det 42.8	K.Strong-NYG 4	D.Ellis-GB 50.0				
A.Parker-Bkn 42.0	C.Hanneman-Det......4	R.Kercheval-Bkn.....46.2				
P.Hall-Cle 40.8	D.Ellis-GB 4	W.Cuff-NYG 43.8				

Punt/Kick Return Yards	Punt/Kick Return TDs	Interceptions	Interception Return Yards	Interception Return TDs	Sacks	Overall Rank
Not kept	D.Todd-Was 1	Not kept	Not kept	Many...........................1	Not kept	A.Farkas-Was 851
	J.Laws-GB 1					B.Osmanski-ChiB 807
	A.Farkas-Was 1					F.Filchock-Was.........745
						C.Isbell-GB 667
						P.Hall-Cle.............609

WATCHING FROM THE STANDS AND FROM HOME

The league lost one of its most important figures in May, when NFL president Joe Carr died. He was instrumental in helping professional football gain legitimacy in the 1920s, and his efforts to get teams in big cities enabled the league to survive during the economic woes of the early 1930s. Carl Storck, former owner of the Dayton Triangles and long-time league secretary, took over Carr's duties.

The NFL surpassed one million in attendance for the first time. The league also got its first glimpse of television. NBC televised a contest from Ebbets Field on October 22. There were only about 1,000 television sets in the city, but those who had one watched the Brooklyn Dodgers beat the Philadelphia Eagles, 23–14. A few miles away at the Polo Grounds, the Giants weren't on TV, but they were beating the Bears in front of 45,000 more people than in Brooklyn. New York dominated the East and held opponents to just 85 points in 11 games. Their staunch seven-man line was tough to run against, and throwing the ball wasn't much better. The Giants led the league with 35 interceptions.

Dutch Clark called it quits as player–coach in Detroit in 1938, joining the Cleveland Rams as coach in 1939. Although Cleveland started the year losing four of five games, rookie tailback Parker Hall emerged as a playmaker. With Hall leading the team in both rushing and passing, Cleveland lost just once the rest of the way—a 7–6 squeaker against the Packers. Despite a fourth-place finish in the competitive West, Hall was named the league's Most Valuable Player.

Chicago Bears rookie Sid Luckman was a halfback at Columbia University, but Bears coach George Halas gradually converted him to quarterback during his first pro season. It was a great success, and Luckman's aerial feats helped the Bears lead the league in scoring.

The late-season turnarounds in Chicago and Cleveland weren't enough as Green Bay claimed the West division crown for the second straight season. The formula remained the same, with the relentless passing attack of Arnie Herber, Don Hutson, and Cecil Isbell overwhelming most opponents, including the Giants in the championship game.

1940 NFL

TEAM	W-L-T	PCT	POST	PTS	RA	RY	RY/A	RTD	FL	PA	PC	GPY	GPY/A	PTD	PI	PSY	PRAT
Eastern Division																	
Was	9-2	**.818**	L	**245**-142	400-**362**	1402-1075	3.5-3.0	15-**5**	20-9	244-287	144-125	**1887**-1782	7.7-6.2	**18**-11	22-18	—	**70.5**-50.9
Bkn	8-3	.727	—	186-**120**	414-429	1546-1391	**3.7**-3.2	9-7	12-14	191-259	80-113	1267-1445	6.6-5.6	14-8	**13**-18	—	60.7-43.0
NYG	6-4-1	.600	—	131-133	454-413	1476-**977**	3.3-**2.4**	6-8	14-11	174-234	78-91	1036-1242	6.0-**5.3**	9-7	15-23	—	45.6-**27.0**
Pit	2-7-2	.222	—	60-178	403-438	1102-1491	2.7-3.4	2-12	13-15	189-192	58-83	875-1231	4.6-6.4	4-9	27-8	—	14.4-63.1
Phi	1-10	.091	—	111-211	317-460	298-1778	0.9-3.9	8-18	**7**-13	362-151	152-80	1855-**1012**	5.1-6.7	6-9	20-12	—	40.9-60.9
Western Division																	
ChiB	8-3	.727	L*	238-152	**494**-372	**1818**-1003	3.7-2.7	**16**-7	18-11	171-269	68-133	1401-1747	**8.2**-6.5	10-14	15-27	—	52.3-48.1
GB	6-4-1	.600	—	238-155	463-387	1604-1040	3.5-2.7	10-9	11-7	283-252	118-98	1796-1492	6.3-5.9	**18**-9	26-**40**	—	46.2-31.5
Det	5-5-1	.500	—	138-153	427-381	1457-1323	3.4-3.5	12-13	14-**20**	195-177	86-77	1177-1034	6.0-5.8	3-6	27-29	—	29.5-34.4
Cle	4-6-1	.400	—	171-191	364-467	1142-1612	3.1-3.5	11-9	13-14	247-247	109-99	1582-1490	6.4-6.0	12-13	25-25	—	42.2-38.6
ChiC	2-7-2	.222	—	139-222	400-427	1315-1470	3.3-3.4	11-12	12-19	198-186	75-**69**	912-1313	4.6-7.1	6-14	33-23	—	23.4-47.9
Aver	11	—		166	414	1316	3.2	10	13	225	97	1379	6.1	10	22	—	38.6

TEAM	1D	PENY	PNT	FGM/A	RTNY	RTNTD	OFF/DEFY	NETY	NETTO	NP	PNP	DELP	PW	DELW	PRT	DR	YPD	DEL
Eastern Division																		
Was	147	427	**45**	2/5-5	—	2-2	3289-2857	432	-15	**103**	-24	**127**	8.1	0.9	4.4/3.8	—	—	—
Bkn	115	285	40	4/12-6	—	2-**0**	2813-2836	-23	7	66	26	40	7.2	0.9	4.3/2.8	—	—	—
NYG	127	349	40	6/13-3	—	1-3	2512-**2219**	293	5	-2	44	-46	**1.0**	1.0	2.6/1.2	—	—	—
Pit	97	336	39	6/14-6	—	0-2	1977-2722	-745	-17	-118	-130	12	2.6	0.5	-1.6/5.0	—	—	—
Phi	122	**215**	37	3/11-6	—	1-1	2153-2790	-637	-2	-100	-61	-39	3.0	-2.0	2.8/3.7	—	—	—
Western Division																		
ChiB	141	605	40	6/10-**2**	—	**6-0**	3219-2750	469	5	86	59	27	7.7	0.3	**4.8**/2.5	—	—	—
GB	**154**	295	38	10/20-**2**	—	2-4	**3400**-2532	**868**	10	83	-29	**112**	7.6	-1.1	2.8/-0.9	—	—	—
Det	133	259	41	2/6-3	—	4-2	2634-2357	277	8	-15	55	-70	5.1	0.4	-0.0/-1.2	—	—	—
Cle	113	260	42	1/7-7	—	2-3	2724-3102	-378	1	-20	-28	8	5.0	-0.5	2.3/2.0	—	—	—
ChiC	112	331	37	2/8-**2**	—	2-5	2227-2783	-556	-3	-83	-58	-25	3.4	-0.4	-2.6/2.2	—	—	—
Aver	126	336	40.0	4/11	—	2	2695								2.1			

Rushing Attempts		Rushing Yards		Rushing Average		Rushing TDs		Rushing Rank		Passing Yards		Passing Average	
W.White-Det	146	W.White-Det	514	D.Todd-Was	5.37	J.Drake-Cle	9	J.Drake-Cle	570	S.Baugh-Was	1367	S.Luckman-ChiB	8.96
J.Drake-Cle	134	J.Drake-Cle	480	B.McChesney-ChiC	4.88	W.White-Det	5	W.White-Det	564	D.O'Brien-Phi	1290	S.Baugh-Was	7.72
T.Leemans-NYG	132	T.Leemans-NYG	474	B.McFadden-Bkn	4.84	P.Manders-Bkn	5	T.Leemans-NYG	448	P.Hall-Cle	1108	A.Parker-Bkn	7.36
C.Hinkle-GB	109	B.McFadden-Bkn	411	R.Nolting-ChiB	4.78			D.Todd-Was	448	C.Isbell-GB	1037	E.Miller-NYG	6.92
D.O'Brien-Phi	100	D.Todd-Was	408	H.Clarke-ChiB	4.61			B.McFadden-Bkn	421	S.Luckman-ChiB	941	C.Isbell-GB	6.91

Completion Percent		TD Passes		TD Percent		INT Percent		Passer Rating		Passing Rank		Receptions	
S.Baugh-Was	62.7	S.Baugh-Was	12	A.Parker-Bkn	9.0	F.Watkins-Phi	3.5	S.Baugh-Was	85.6	S.Baugh-Was	344	D.Looney-Phi	58
C.Price-Det	50.0	A.Parker-Bkn	10	S.Baugh-Was	6.8	S.Baugh-Was	5.6	A.Parker-Bkn	73.3	A.Parker-Bkn	179	D.Hutson-GB	45
E.Miller-NYG	47.9	C.Isbell-GB	8	A.Herber-GB	6.7	D.O'Brien-Phi	6.1	S.Luckman-ChiB	54.5	F.Watkins-Phi	168	J.Johnston-Was	29
S.Luckman-ChiB	45.7	P.Hall-Cle	7	E.Miller-NYG	5.5	A.Parker-Bkn	6.3	A.Herber-GB	53.6	S.Luckman-ChiB	131		
C.Isbell-GB	45.3			C.Isbell-GB	5.3	A.Herber-GB	7.9	C.Isbell-GB	53.1	C.Isbell-GB	79		

Receiving Yards		Receiving Average		Receiving TDs		Receiving Rank		Combined Net Yards		Total TDs		Total Points	
D.Looney-Phi	707	J.Benton-Cle	15.95	D.Hutson-GB	7	D.Looney-Phi	374	D.Todd-Was	813	D.Todd-Was	9	D.Hutson-GB	57
D.Hutson-GB	664	D.Hutson-GB	14.76	B.Morse-GB	6	D.Hutson-GB	367	D.Looney-Phi	703	J.Drake-Cle	9	J.Drake-Cle	56
D.Todd-Was	402	B.Sortet-Cle	12.55	D.Todd-Was	4	D.Todd-Was	221	D.Hutson-GB	688	B.Morse-GB	7	D.Todd-Was	54
P.Schwartz-Bkn	370	D.Looney-Phi	12.19	B.Masterson-Was	4	P.Schwartz-Bkn	200	J.Johnston-Was	671	J.Johnston-Was	7	A.Parker-Bkn	49
J.Benton-Cle	351	J.Johnston-Was	12.07	D.Looney-Phi	4	J.Benton-Cle	191	W.White-Det	606	D.Hutson-GB	7	C.Hinkle-GB	48

Punt Average		Field Goals		Field Goal Percent		Kickoff Returns		Kickoff Return Average		Punt Returns		Punt Return Average	
S.Baugh-Was	51.4	C.Hinkle-GB	9	C.Hinkle-GB	64.3	Not kept		Not kept		Not kept		Not kept	
P.Hall-Cle	43.7	B.Morse-GB	6	W.Cuff-NYG	62.5								
S.Luckman-ChiB	42.5	W.Cuff-NYG	5	A.Niccolai-Pit	42.9								
W.White-Det	41.0	R.Kercheval-Bkn	4	R.Kercheval-Bkn	36.4								
B.McChesney-ChiC	40.5			G.Somers-Phi	22.2								

Punt/Kick Return Yards		Punt/Kick Return TDs		Interceptions		Interception Return Yards		Interception Return TDs		Sacks		Overall Rank	
Not kept		D.Todd-Was	1	K.Ryan-Det	6	A.Parker-Bkn	146	Many	1	Not kept		A.Parker-Bkn	710
		R.Nolting-ChiB	1	A.Parker-Bkn	6	L.Brock-GB	116					D.Todd-Was	676
		R.McLean-ChiB	1	D.Hutson-GB	6	D.O'Brien-Phi	92					J.Drake-Cle	626
		G.McAfee-ChiB	1			S.Baugh-Was	84					J.Johnston-Was	546
		B.Leckonby-Bkn	1			B.Sortet-Cle	83					B.McFadden-Bkn	526

CRYBABIES 73, REDSKINS 0

While many mediocre teams tried to improve their fortunes by pursuing star players from the college ranks, the Brooklyn Dodgers went after one of the top college coaches. John "Jock" Sutherland was a protégé of the legendary Pop Warner, compiling a college record of 144–28–14 at Lafayette and the University of Pittsburgh while earning successive national championships in 1936 and 1937. Sutherland left Pitt after a dispute with the school's chancellor, and a year later took the helm in Brooklyn. It was the first time that such a prestigious college coach was lured to the National Football League, but it would certainly not be the last.

Sutherland brought his potent Single-Wing formation to Brooklyn, and it was a system in which tailback Ace Parker flourished. The triple-threat back won the league's Most Valuable Player award, and the Dodgers finished with the best record in franchise history. A loss to the Redskins in their opener was all that kept them from winning the Eastern Division.

Washington's Sammy Baugh led the league in passing, and the club's high-powered offense overwhelmed most opponents. A late-season game against the Bears was a preview of the championship game, and although Washington triumphed, postgame quotes by owner George Marshall stoked a feud. After the Bears protested an official's call on a controversial play in the fourth quarter, Marshall questioned their toughness. "The Bears are front-runners ... quitters," he said. "They are not a second-half team, just a bunch of crybabies."

Those words stung the Chicago players, who had dominated their division with a power running game and a ferocious defense. Rookie lineman Bulldog Turner was a devastating blocker and tackler, joining a line already stacked with All-Pros. The Bears were determined to respond to Marshall's attack when they met the Redskins three weeks later for the NFL championship. They jumped to a 21–0 lead in the first quarter, then proved what kind of a second-half team they were by adding 45 points after halftime. The 73–0 record rout was first game broadcast nationally on radio, beaming out to 120 stations and bringing in $2,500 to the league.

1941 NFL

TEAM	W-L-T	PCT	POST	PTS	RA	RY	RY/A	RTD	FL	PA	PC	GPY	GPY/A	PTD	PI	PSY	PRAT
Eastern Division																	
NYG	8-3	.727	L	238-114	433-408	1296-1166	3.0-2.9	16-9	14-13	156-218	68-103	1088-1212	7.0-5.6	11-6	12-29	—	58.9-34.2
Bkn	7-4	.636	—	158-127	444-376	1667-1210	3.8-3.2	14-6	10-8	202-189	90-86	1131-1169	5.6-6.2	5-6	18-20	—	33.7-36.8
Was	6-5	.545	—	176-174	406-410	1097-1110	2.7-2.7	7-9	11-12	262-229	134-103	1563-1338	6.0-5.8	11-14	30-23	—	44.0-44.7
Phi	2-8-1	.200	—	119-218	360-432	849-1518	2.4-3.5	6-14	15-10	249-238	115-100	1363-1369	5.5-5.8	10-13	27-21	—	37.2-42.5
Pit	1-9-1	.100	—	103-276	381-426	1213-1556	3.2-3.7	9-17	15-8	168-189	42-84	654-1168	3.9-6.2	5-10	34-19	—	13.6-42.9
Western Division																	
ChiB	10-1	.909	DL*	396-147	495-373	2156-1076	4.4-2.9	30-6	19-14	196-265	98-106	2002-1463	10.2-5.5	19-9	11-34	—	95.2-30.2
GB	10-1	.909	D	258-120	467-356	1550-1221	3.3-3.4	13-10	11-23	253-233	133-104	1731-1343	6.8-5.8	17-8	13-25	—	75.4-35.2
Det	4-6-1	.400	—	121-195	361-475	975-1416	2.7-3.0	7-8	11-12	187-247	58-112	854-1605	4.6-6.5	5-8	20-18	—	16.3-47.4
ChiC	3-7-1	.300	—	127-197	386-384	1086-1334	2.8-3.5	8-13	12-15	252-196	117-90	1659-1305	6.6-6.7	6-12	20-16	—	43.1-54.5
Cle	2-9	.182	—	116-244	343-436	951-1553	2.8-3.6	4-23	8-11	285-206	123-90	1352-1425	4.7-6.9	10-14	35-15	—	29.9-59.6
Aver	11	—		181	408	1284	3.2	11	13	221	98	1340	6.1	10	22	—	39.6

TEAM	1D	PENY	PNT	FGM/A	RTNY	RTNTD	OFFY/DEFY	NETY	NETTO	NP	PNP	DELP	PW	DELW	PRT	DR	YPD	DEL
Eastern Division																		
NYG	110-116	323-371	41.5-40.3	10/20-4/11	1286-574	3-0	2378-2378	0	16	124	64	60	8.6	-0.6	4.2/-0.2	154-151	15.4-15.7	-0.3
Bkn	132-110	371-370	41.6-40.1	4/14-4/10	571-724	2-5	2886-2379	507	0	31	42	-11	6.3	0.7	1.8/1.7	137-134	21.1-17.8	3.3
Was	135-129	402-269	45.9-41.6	6/14-5/13	966-660	5-0	2675-2448	227	-6	2	-5	7	5.6	0.4	1.2/1.9	147-144	18.2-17.0	1.2
Phi	128-126	407-455	41.0-38.4	3/8-8/14	423-1011	0-1	2313-2887	-574	-11	-99	-92	-7	3.0	-0.5	1.0/2.3	150-144	15.4-20.0	-4.6
Pit	75-116	363-495	37.4-40.6	2/6-4/12	558-1012	0-11	1871-2724	-853	-22	-173	-159	-14	1.2	0.3	-4.9/2.2	153-168	12.2-16.2	-4.0
Western Division																		
ChiB	181-143	677-448	38.7-39.5	5/11-3/7	1102-554	7-5	4265-2539	1726	18	249	216	33	11.7	-1.7	8.7/0.1	142-140	30.0-18.1	11.9
GB	166-124	509-539	42.1-40.5	10/20-4/10	942-602	3-2	3296-2564	732	24	138	157	-19	8.9	1.0	5.2/1.3	146-141	22.6-18.2	4.4
Det	86-160	455-415	39.7-42.8	1/9-9/18	829-761	5-8	1843-3021	-1178	-1	-74	-102	28	3.7	0.9	0.0/3.5	150-147	12.3-20.6	-8.3
ChiC	138-110	446-437	39.3-43.3	4/12-2/6	456-892	3-3	2756-2639	117	-1	-70	6	-76	3.8	-0.3	3.3/3.6	138-149	20.0-17.7	2.3
Cle	121-138	265-419	40.4-40.1	2/4-4/15	484-827	2-3	2320-2978	-658	-17	-128	-123	-5	2.3	-0.3	-0.4/4.3	154-152	15.1-19.6	-4.5
Aver	127	422	40.6	5/12	762	3	2660	—	—	—	—	—	—	—	2.0	147	18.1	—

Rushing Attempts
C.Hinkle-GB 129
M.Goldberg-ChiC 117
F.Filchock-Was 115
P.Manders-Bkn 111
D.Riffle-Pit 109

Rushing Yards
P.Manders-Bkn 486
G.McAfee-ChiB 474
M.Goldberg-ChiC 427
N.Standlee-ChiB 414
C.Hinkle-GB 393

Rushing Average
G.McAfee-ChiB 7.29
B.Osmanski-ChiB 5.30
N.Standlee-ChiB 5.11
C.Isbell-GB 4.40
P.Manders-Bkn 4.38

Rushing TDs
T.Furst-ChiB 8
N.Standlee-ChiB 5
G.McAfee-ChiB 5
P.Manders-Bkn 5
C.Hinkle-GB 5

Rushing Rank
P.Manders-Bkn 536
G.McAfee-ChiB 524
N.Standlee-ChiB 464
M.Goldberg-ChiC 457
C.Hinkle-GB 443

Passing Yards
C.Isbell-GB 1479
S.Baugh-Was 1236
S.Luckman-ChiB 1181
T.Thompson-Phi 959
P.Hall-Cle 863

Passing Average
S.Luckman-ChiB 9.92
R.Mallouf-ChiC 7.55
T.Leemans-NYG 7.20
C.Isbell-GB 7.18
J.Clement-ChiC 6.90

Completion Percent
S.Luckman-ChiB 57.1
C.Isbell-GB 56.8
S.Baugh-Was 54.9
T.Thompson-Phi 53.1

TD Passes
C.Isbell-GB 15
S.Baugh-Was 10
S.Luckman-ChiB 9
T.Thompson-Phi 8
P.Hall-Cle 7

TD Percent
S.Luckman-ChiB 7.6
S.Luckman-ChiB 7.3
T.Leemans-NYG 6.1
S.Baugh-Was 5.2
T.Thompson-Phi 4.9

INT Percent
R.Mallouf-ChiC 4.2
S.Luckman-ChiB 5.0
C.Isbell-GB 5.3
J.Clement-ChiC 7.0
T.Leemans-NYG 7.0

Passer Rating
S.Luckman-ChiB 95.3
C.Isbell-GB 81.4
R.Mallouf-ChiC 64.8
T.Leemans-NYG 59.8
S.Baugh-Was 52.2

Passing Rank
S.Luckman-ChiB 396
C.Isbell-GB 375
R.Mallouf-ChiC 213
B.Snyder-ChiB 112
M.Pugh-NYG 86

Receptions
D.Hutson-GB 58
D.Humbert-Phi 29
B.Dewell-ChiC 27
P.Schwartz-Bkn 25
L.Brock-GB 22

Receiving Yards
D.Hutson-GB 738
P.Schwartz-Bkn 362
B.Dewell-ChiC 362
D.Humbert-Phi 332
W.Cuff-NYG 317

Receiving Average
P.Schwartz-Bkn 14.48
L.Brock-GB 13.95
B.Dewell-ChiC 13.41
C.Hinkle-GB 12.72
D.Humbert-Phi 11.45

Receiving TDs
D.Hutson-GB 10
K.Kavanaugh-ChiB 6
R.Hickey-Cle 4

Receiving Rank
D.Hutson-GB 419
P.Schwartz-Bkn 191
K.Kavanaugh-ChiB 187
B.Dewell-ChiC 186
D.Humbert-Phi 181

Combined Net Yards
G.McAfee-ChiB 1236
G.McAfee-ChiB 1077
W.White-Det 1027
D.Hutson-GB 800
D.Riffle-Pit 780

Total TDs
G.McAfee-ChiB 12
D.Hutson-GB 12
T.Furst-ChiB 11
P.Manders-Bkn 7

Total Points
D.Hutson-GB 95
G.McAfee-ChiB 72
T.Furst-ChiB 66
C.Hinkle-GB 56
W.Cuff-NYG 46

Punt Average
S.Baugh-Was 48.7
C.Hinkle-GB 44.5
L.Barnum-Phi 43.6
W.White-Det 41.6
R.Mallouf-ChiC 41.1

Field Goals
C.Hinkle-GB 6
W.Cuff-NYG 5
C.Hinkle-GB 4
A.Daddio-ChiC 4
B.Masterson-Was 3

Field Goal Percent
B.Masterson-Was 50.0
B.Daddio-ChiC 50.0
C.Hinkle-GB 42.9
W.Cuff-NYG 38.5
L.Barnum-Phi 33.3

Kickoff Returns
M.Goldberg-ChiC 12
W.White-Det 11
B.Brumbaugh-Pit 11
D.Riffle-Pit 9
N.Mathews-Det 9

Kickoff Return Average
W.White-Det 25.9
B.Brumbaugh-Pit 24.6
M.Goldberg-ChiC 24.2

Punt Returns
W.White-Det 19
A.Parker-Bkn 16
B.Leckonby-Bkn 15
L.Brock-GB 15

Punt Return Average
P.Todd-Was 17.0
A.Jones-Pit 16.6
G.Franck-NYG 14.9
W.White-Det 13.8
M.Goldberg-ChiC 12.7

Punt/Kick Return Yards
W.White-Det 547
M.Goldberg-ChiC 442
G.McAfee-ChiB 381
A.Jones-Pit 354
B.Brumbaugh-Pit 331

Punt/Kick Return TDs
G.McAfee-ChiB 2

Interceptions
A.Jones-Pit 7
M.Goldberg-ChiC 7
D.Riffle-Pit 6
G.McAfee-ChiB 6
N.Mathews-Det 5

Interception Return Yards
W.Cuff-NYG 152
N.Mathews-Det 128
H.Van Every-GB 104
G.Franck-NYG 94
D.Riffle-Pit 93

Interception Return TDs
Many 1

Sacks
Not kept

Overall Rank
G.McAfee-ChiB 967
M.Goldberg-ChiC 820
C.Isbell-GB 702
W.White-Det 697
P.Manders-Bkn 656

REALITY INVADES THE ARENA

Carl Storck stepped down after serving two years as league president. The owners recruited Notre Dame head coach Elmer Layden to take his place, and he became the first man to hold the title of "commissioner." Three teams also saw changes at the top, with Dan Reeves purchasing the Cleveland Rams and a peculiar arrangement that led to new owners in Pittsburgh and Philadelphia.

Tired of losing both games and money, Art Rooney sold the Pittsburgh club to 28-year-old Boston businessman Alexis Thompson. Rooney used the proceeds to buy half interest in Bert Bell's Philadelphia Eagles. During the summer, both Thompson and Rooney had second thoughts, and they agreed to swap franchises. Rooney moved back to Pittsburgh with Bell while Thompson took control of the Eagles. About 30 players also changed teams. It was one of the most convoluted deals in NFL history, and to add to the confusion, Rooney changed the name of his re-claimed club from the Pirates to the Steelers. After all that, Pittsburgh still finished last.

The NFL's best teams were in the West. The Bears had the league's stingiest run defense and led the league in interceptions. With Sid Luckman leading the aerial attack and the elusive George McAfee in the backfield, Chicago also scored the most points. Green Bay got a little of everything from feisty rookie Tony Canadeo and a solid final season from reliable Clarke Hinkle. When the two teams met in November, the only loss on either slate was Green Bay's September defeat by the Bears. The Packers pulled off a 16–14 upset in the rematch. Both teams finished 10–1, forcing the first divisional playoff.

Three games were slated for the last Sunday of the season, December 7. During the first half, servicemen at the Polo Grounds and Comiskey Park were told to report to their units. Government and military personnel in Washington's Griffith Stadium were similarly summoned, and by halftime, fans in attendance learned about the Japanese attacks at Pearl Harbor. War was declared the next day. The world was about to change, and football wouldn't be the same.

1942 NFL

TEAM	W-L-T	PCT	POST	PTS	RA	RY	RY/A	RTD	FL	PA	PC	GPY	GPY/A	PTD	PI	PSY	PRAT
Eastern Division																	
Was	10-1	.909	L*	227-102	413-367	1521-848	3.7-2.3	9-5	13-7	257-216	137-81	1600-1093	6.2-5.1	16-5	17-19	—	65.6-25.5
Pit	7-4	.636	—	167-119	490-366	1851-1205	3.8-3.3	15-6	10-7	161-211	51-100	686-1183	4.3-5.6	2-9	11-21	—	21.9-39.6
NYG	5-5-1	.500	—	155-139	401-466	1203-1465	3.0-3.1	10-13	7-19	148-228	67-114	957-1401	6.5-6.1	10-4	14-15	—	49.9-47.8
Bkn	3-8	.273	—	100-168	431-426	1465-1600	3.4-3.8	9-13	10-12	159-199	56-89	714-1175	4.5-5.9	3-9	24-14	—	16.9-49.7
Phi	2-9	.182	—	134-239	407-464	1089-1717	2.7-3.7	8-20	11-10	213-178	96-79	1416-1241	6.6-7.0	8-12	17-18	—	46.6-51.0
Western Division																	
ChiB	11-0	1.000	L	376-84	470-294	1881-519	4.0-1.8	23-3	15-18	194-280	94-111	1974-1179	10.2-4.2	21-7	29-33	—	81.4-21.4
GB	8-2-1	.800	—	300-215	422-376	1374-1549	3.3-4.1	10-17	8-15	330-242	172-100	2407-1471	7.3-6.1	28-8	18-33	—	81.5-33.3
Cle	5-6	.455	—	150-207	310-463	875-1744	2.8-3.8	5-11	8-10	249-262	109-125	1537-1740	6.2-6.6	13-17	27-23	—	42.1-54.6
ChiC	3-8	.273	—	98-209	366-390	1021-1470	2.8-3.8	4-11	11-8	316-214	131-84	1432-1502	4.5-7.0	6-15	29-25	—	23.6-47.8
Det	0-11	.000	—	38-263	342-440	1261-1423	3.7-3.2	4-13	23-10	222-219	73-103	885-1623	4.0-7.4	1-22	33-18	—	8.0-71.4
Aver	11	—		175	405	1354	3.3	10	12	225	99	1361	6.1	11	22	—	40.3

TEAM	1D	PENY	PNT	FGM/A	RTNY	RTNTD	OFFY/DEFY	NETY	NETTO	NP	PNP	DELP	PW	DELW	PRT	DR	YPD	DEL
Eastern Division																		
Was	149-111	610-340	44.3-38.1	3/9-4/8	769-694	6-3	3121-1950	1171	-4	125	82	43	8.6	1.4	3.9/ 1.3	143-144	21.8-13.5	8.3
Pit	130-114	383-512	36.6-41.3	3/16-5/17	1082-543	6-0	2606-2388	218	7	48	46	2	6.7	0.3	1.3/ 1.6	142-146	18.4-16.4	2.0
NYG	105-159	437-290	38.5-37.6	3/16-3/8	662-715	1-2	2160-2877	-717	13	16	-8	24	5.9	-0.4	2.9/ 3.4	136-134	15.9-21.5	-5.6
Bkn	109-131	288-485	40.6-40.0	3/6-3/13	538-724	1-1	2219-2794	-575	-8	-68	-80	12	3.8	-0.8	-2.1/ 3.2	135-137	16.4-20.4	-4.0
Phi	124-131	392-452	37.2-40.5	3/8-3/9	775-670	2-1	2535-3016	-481	0	-105	-40	-65	2.9	-0.9	3.4/ 3.1	146-137	17.4-22.0	-4.7
Western Division																		
ChiB	155-98	905-324	38.9-38.2	4/6-0/2	861-580	9-2	3900-1703	2197	7	292	211	81	12.8	-1.8	4.5/-0.8	152-163	25.7-10.4	15.2
GB	176-147	312-539	37.4-37.0	5/10-6/9	676-677	3-3	3790-3076	714	22	85	-63	148	7.6	0.9	5.7/ 0.3	152-146	24.9-21.1	3.9
Cle	103-165	315-387	40.3-40.6	3/6-4/9	562-814	2-0	2413-3543	-1130	-2	-57	-102	45	4.1	0.9	1.8/ 3.3	138-150	17.5-23.6	-6.1
ChiC	132-114	400-636	39.5-40.2	5/10-3/9	627-922	2-3	2453-2972	-519	-7	-111	-71	-40	2.7	0.3	0.6/ 2.5	157-146	15.6-20.4	-4.7
Det	115-128	364-441	40.6-41.0	1/6-2/9	566-779	0-2	2206-3083	-877	-28	-225	-185	-40	-0.1	0.1	-2.7/ 4.7	153-150	14.4-20.6	-6.1
Aver	130	441	39.4	3/ 9	712	3	2740	-877	—	—	—	—	—	—	2.1	145	18.8	—

Rushing Attempts		Rushing Yards		Rushing Average		Rushing TDs		Rushing Rank		Passing Yards		Passing Average	
B.Dudley-Pit	162	B.Dudley-Pit	696	D.Magnani-Cle	5.83	M.Evans-ChiB	8	B.Dudley-Pit	746	C.Isbell-GB	2021	C.O'Rourke-ChiB	10.81
M.Condit-Bkn	129	M.Condit-Bkn	647	M.Condit-Bkn	5.02	P.Manders-Bkn	6	M.Condit-Bkn	667	S.Baugh-Was	1524	S.Luckman-ChiB	9.75
A.Farkas-Was	125	M.Evans-ChiB	503	H.Clarke-ChiB	4.71	B.Dudley-Pit	5	M.Evans-ChiB	583	T.Thompson-Phi	1410	T.Leemans-NYG	8.04
M.Evans-ChiB	118	A.Farkas-Was	468	C.Sample-GB	4.47			D.Riffle-Pit	507	B.Schwenk-ChiC	1360	C.Isbell-GB	7.54
M.Goldberg-ChiC	116	D.Riffle-Pit	467	T.Fritsch-GB	4.36			A.Farkas-Was	498	S.Luckman-ChiB	1024	T.Thompson-Phi	6.95

Completion Percent		TD Passes		TD Percent		INT Percent		Passer Rating		Passing Rank		Receptions	
S.Baugh-Was	58.7	C.Isbell-GB	24	C.O'Rourke-ChiB	12.5	S.Baugh-Was	4.9	T.Leemans-NYG	87.5	C.Isbell-GB	571	D.Hutson-GB	74
C.Isbell-GB	54.5	S.Baugh-Was	16	T.Leemans-NYG	10.1	C.Isbell-GB	5.2	C.Isbell-GB	87.0	S.Baugh-Was	402	P.Ivy-ChiC	27
S.Luckman-ChiB	54.3	C.O'Rourke-ChiB	11	S.Luckman-ChiB	9.5	B.Dudley-Pit	5.3	S.Baugh-Was	82.5	T.Leemans-NYG	153	D.Magnani-Cle	24
T.Leemans-NYG	50.7	S.Luckman-ChiB	10	C.Isbell-GB	9.0	T.Leemans-NYG	5.8	C.O'Rourke-ChiB	82.2	J.Jacobs-Cle	110	D.Todd-Was	23
T.Thompson-Phi	46.8	T.Thompson-Phi	8	S.Baugh-Was	7.1	J.Jacobs-Cle	6.5	S.Luckman-ChiB	80.1	T.Thompson-Phi	105	J.Benton-Cle	23

Receiving Yards		Receiving Average		Receiving TDs		Receiving Rank		Combined Net Yards		Total TDs		Total Points	
D.Hutson-GB	1211	D.Hutson-GB	16.36	D.Hutson-GB	17	D.Hutson-GB	691	B.Dudley-Pit	1349	D.Hutson-GB	17	D.Hutson-GB	138
R.McLean-ChiB	571	J.Benton-Cle	15.00	R.McLean-ChiB	8	R.McLean-ChiB	326	D.Hutson-GB	1286	R.McLean-ChiB	9	R.McLean-ChiB	54
A.Uram-GB	420	D.Todd-Was	14.26	H.Pool-ChiB	5	A.Uram-GB	230	M.Condit-Bkn	1257	M.Evans-ChiB	8	M.Evans-ChiB	48
J.Benton-Cle	345	J.Martin-ChiC	14.18			H.Pool-ChiB	186	A.Farkas-Was	1062	T.Fritsch-ChiB	7	F.Maznicki-ChiB	45
D.Todd-Was	328	B.Masterson-Was	14.00			D.Todd-Was	184	M.Goldberg-ChiC	969			T.Fritsch-ChiB	42

Punt Average		Field Goals		Field Goal Percent		Kickoff Returns		Kickoff Return Average		Punt Returns		Punt Return Average	
S.Baugh-Was	48.2	B.Daddio-ChiC	5	B.Daddio-ChiC	50.0	M.Goldberg-ChiC	15	B.Dudley-Pit	27.1	M.Condit-Bkn	21	A.Tomasic-Pit	16.6
J.Jacobs-Cle	42.3	F.Maznicki-ChiB	4	M.Condit-Bkn	50.0	D.Magnani-Cle	11	M.Goldberg-ChiC	26.2	B.Dudley-Pit	20	M.Hapes-NYG	15.5
L.Barnum-Phi	42.1	T.Fritsch-GB	4	C.Adams-Cle	50.0	B.Dudley-Pit	11	D.Magnani-Cle	22.7	A.Farkas-Was	16	A.Farkas-Was	13.7
D.McAdams-Bkn	41.5			L.Barnum-Phi	42.9	P.Hall-Cle	10			D.Todd-Was	13	B.Dudley-Pit	13.6
				W.Cuff-NYG	27.3					S.Lach-ChiC	13	P.Hall-Cle	12.3

Punt/Kick Return Yards		Punt/Kick Return TDs		Interceptions		Interception Return Yards		Interception Return TDs		Sacks		Overall Rank	
B.Dudley-Pit	569	Many	1	B.Turner-ChiB	8	M.Condit-Bkn	117	Many	1	Not kept		B.Dudley-Pit	1146
M.Goldberg-ChiC	453			D.Hutson-GB	7	B.Turner-ChiB	96					M.Condit-Bkn	910
A.Farkas-Was	425					S.Luckman-ChiB	96					A.Farkas-Was	886
M.Hapes-NYG	385					C.Sandig-Pit	94					D.Hutson-GB	731
M.Condit-Bkn	382					S.Baugh-Was	77					C.Isbell-GB	693

PLAYERS BECOME SCARCE

By the time the season started, more than 200 players who had been on NFL rosters were serving in the armed services now that the United States was engaged in World War II. The teams they left behind were struggling.

One of the teams hit hardest by enlistment was the New York Giants. The club lost 27 players, including quarterback Ed Danowski and All-Pro guard Doug Oldershaw. After winning the division a year earlier, the Giants slumped to 5–5–1. The Chicago Bears also lost some key people, including their three leading rushers, tackle Joe Stydahar, and coach George Halas, who left midseason to join the Navy. Luke Johnsos and Hunk Anderson served as co-coaches until Halas returned from the war. The Monsters of the Midway marched through the regular season undefeated like nothing had happened.

The new ownership arrangement in Pittsburgh paid dividends, as the Steelers finished with a winning record for the first time since joining the league in 1933. Rookie tailback Bill Dudley was a threat both running and throwing the ball. He led the league in rushing yards, and the Steelers finished in second place.

Green Bay's Don Hutson continued to revolutionize the game with his receiving accomplishments. He set new records for pass receptions (74), receiving yards (1,211), touchdowns (17), and points (138). Hutson became the first player to surpass 1,000 receiving yards, and his mark for touchdown catches would stand for more than 40 years. The man throwing him the ball, Cecil Isbell, also set new single-season records for passing yards and touchdowns. Hutson was named the league's Most Valuable Player for the second consecutive year. Isbell, however, never played again. He left Green Bay before the 1943 to coach at his alma mater, Purdue University.

A strong defense helped Washington win the Eastern Division. They lost just once and allowed only 19 points in their last five games, including the NFL Championship Game. Despite the loss of some key players to military service, the Redskins found enough players to keep the offense going. Fullback Andy Farkas handled the running duties, while end Bob Masterson and wingback Dick Todd caught passes from Sammy Baugh.

1943 NFL

TEAM	W-L-T	PCT	POST	PTS	RA	RY	RY/A	RTD	FL	PA	PC	GPY	GPY/A	PTD	PI	PSY	PRAT
Eastern Division																	
Was	6-3-1	.667	DL	229-**137**	320-406	1085-1330	3.4-3.3	7-**8**	11-8	**254-193**	139-77	1837-1026	7.2-5.3	24-9	20-26	—	76.5-33.4
NYG	6-3-1	.667	D	197-170	386-366	1420-1006	3.7-2.7	14-**8**	**5**-10	149-229	63-119	760-1724	5.1-7.5	8-16	**9**-18	—	51.3-67.3
P-P	5-4-1	.556	—	225-230	**459-312**	**1730-793**	3.8-**2.5**	18-15	15-8	175-221	65-102	1138-1393	6.5-6.3	11-15	20-22	—	41.5-49.8
Bkn	2-8	.200	—	65-234	333-404	610-1562	1.8-3.9	4-14	9-9	205-219	90-86	969-1552	4.7-7.1	5-15	21-15	—	26.9-58.6
Western Division																	
ChiB	8-1-1	**.889**	L*	**303**-157	422-332	1651-1282	**3.9**-3.9	14-13	18-6	229-203	117-**64**	**2310-980**	10.1-4.8	28-8	17-24	—	**95.4-22.0**
GB	7-2-1	.778	—	264-172	397-350	1442-1112	3.6-3.2	13-9	6-9	253-242	114-111	1909-1420	7.5-5.9	21-16	19-**42**	—	67.4-47.2
Det	3-6-1	.333	—	178-218	294-381	817-1223	2.8-3.2	10-13	**5**-12	248-227	93-109	1290-1606	5.2-7.1	11-16	37-19	—	30.2-60.2
ChiC	0-10	.000	—	95-238	334-394	709-1166	2.1-3.0	5-11	**5**-12	219-198	88-101	1095-1607	5.0-8.1	6-21	39-16	—	26.0-80.1
Aver	10	—	—	195	368	1183	3.2	11	9	217	96	1414	6.5	14	23	—	48.6

TEAM	1D	PENY	PNT	FGM/A	RTNY	RTNTD	OFFY/DEFY	NETY	NETTO	NP	PNP	DELP	PW	DELW	PRT	DR	YPD	DEL
Eastern Division																		
Was	112-110	499-349	**43.1**-37.0	1/7-2/6	689-**498**	2-2	2925-2358	567	3	92	59	33	7.3	-0.8	4.6/-0.3	145-146	20.2-16.2	4.0
NYG	102-118	293-329	39.5-37.2	3/10-1/7	671-526	**5**-0	2180-2738	-558	14	27	10	17	5.7	0.8	2.9/ 4.7	145-130	15.0-21.1	-6.0
P-P	138-**96**	484-466	34.4-39.9	1/6-1/11	639-606	3-3	2878-2301	577	-5	-5	28	-33	4.9	0.6	2.0/ 2.5	144-145	20.0-15.9	4.1
Bkn	80-128	**292**-435	36.2-37.3	1/6-7/14	431-623	0-2	1629-3122	-1493	-6	-169	-148	-21	0.8	**1.2**	0.4/ 4.7	139-144	11.7-21.7	-10.0
Western Division																		
ChiB	**161**-100	748-475	37.2-38.9	2/7-1/10	578-740	1-1	**4042-2262**	**1780**	-5	**146**	128	18	**8.6**	-0.2	**8.0**/-0.1	134-143	**30.2-15.8**	**14.3**
GB	134-122	403-391	36.0-**36.6**	**4/15-0/3**	**977**-520	2-0	3351-2707	644	**26**	92	**158**	-66	7.3	0.2	5.0/-1.3	144-138	23.3-19.6	3.7
Det	106-130	472-501	41.4-41.9	2/12-3/10	740-727	4-1	2408-2837	-429	-11	-40	-80	**40**	4.0	-0.5	-1.1/ 4.0	**147**-154	16.4-18.4	-2.0
ChiC	102-131	389-**634**	38.7-37.2	2/5-1/7	406-891	2-2	1854-2933	-1079	-16	-143	-154	11	1.4	-1.4	-2.7/ 5.5	130-**128**	14.3-22.9	-8.7
Aver	117	448	38.3	2/ 9	641	2	2658	—	—	—	—	—	—	—	2.5	141	18.9	—

Rushing Attempts		Rushing Yards		Rushing Average		Rushing TDs		Rushing Rank		Passing Yards		Passing Average	
B.Paschal-NYG	147	B.Paschal-NYG	572	W.Cuff-NYG	6.54	B.Paschal-NYG	10	B.Paschal-NYG	672	S.Luckman-ChiB	2194	S.Luckman-ChiB	10.86
H.Clarke-ChiB	120	J.Hinkle-P-P	571	D.Magnani-ChiB	6.08	B.Thurbon-P-P	5	J.Hinkle-P-P	601	S.Baugh-Was	1754	S.Baugh-Was	7.34
J.Hinkle-P-P	116	H.Clarke-ChiB	556	T.Canadeo-GB	5.20	A.Farkas-Was	5	H.Clarke-ChiB	576	T.Canadeo-GB	875	I.Comp-GB	7.20
A.Farkas-Was	110	W.Cuff-NYG	523	J.Hinkle-P-P	4.92	E.Steele-P-P	4	W.Cuff-NYG	553	R.Zimmerman-P-P	846	R.Zimmerman-P-P	6.82
J.Grigas-ChiC	105	T.Canadeo-GB	489	E.Steele-P-P	4.81	T.Fritsch-GB	4	T.Canadeo-GB	519	F.Sinkwich-Det	699	T.Canadeo-GB	6.78

Completion Percent		TD Passes		TD Percent		INT Percent		Passer Rating		Passing Rank		Receptions	
S.Baugh-Was	55.6	S.Luckman-ChiB	28	S.Luckman-ChiB	13.9	I.Comp-GB	4.3	S.Luckman-ChiB	107.6	S.Luckman-ChiB	757	D.Hutson-GB	47
S.Luckman-ChiB	54.5	S.Baugh-Was	23	S.Baugh-Was	9.6	T.Leemans-NYG	5.7	I.Comp-GB	81.0	S.Baugh-Was	232	J.Aguirre-Was	37
I.Comp-GB	50.0	R.Zimmerman-P-P	9	I.Comp-GB	7.6	S.Luckman-ChiB	5.9	S.Baugh-Was	78.0	I.Comp-GB	206	W.Moore-Was	30
D.McAdams-Bkn	49.3	T.Canadeo-GB	9	R.Zimmerman-P-P	7.3	S.Baugh-Was	7.9	T.Canadeo-GB	51.0	L.Brock-GB	112	E.Rucinski-ChiC	26
R.Cahill-ChiC	45.9			T.Canadeo-GB	7.0	T.Canadeo-GB	9.3	T.Leemans-NYG	50.0	E.Nix-NYG	93	H.Jacunski-GB	24

Receiving Yards		Receiving Average		Receiving TDs		Receiving Rank		Combined Net Yards		Total TDs		Total Points	
D.Hutson-GB	776	H.Clarke-ChiB	23.26	D.Hutson-GB	11	D.Hutson-GB	443	H.Clarke-ChiB	1607	B.Paschal-NYG	12	D.Hutson-GB	117
W.Moore-Was	537	H.Jacunski-GB	22.00	W.Moore-Was	7	W.Moore-Was	304	D.Hutson-GB	1014	D.Hutson-GB	12	B.Paschal-NYG	72
H.Clarke-ChiB	535	W.Moore-Was	17.90	H.Clarke-ChiB	7	H.Clarke-ChiB	303	A.Farkas-Was	976	H.Clarke-ChiB	10	H.Clarke-ChiB	60
H.Jacunski-GB	528	D.Hutson-GB	16.51	J.Aguirre-Was	7	H.Jacunski-GB	279	E.Steele-P-P	965				
R.McLean-ChiB	435	E.Rucinski-ChiC	15.31			J.Aguirre-Was	245	J.Hinkle-P-P	934				

Punt Average		Field Goals		Field Goal Percent		Kickoff Returns		Kickoff Return Average		Punt Returns		Punt Return Average	
S.Baugh-Was	45.9	D.Hutson-GB	3	D.Hutson-GB	60.0	K.Heineman-Bkn	16	K.Heineman-Bkn	27.8	A.Farkas-Was	15	F.Sinkwich-Det	20.7
L.Younce-NYG	42.6	W.Cuff-NYG	3	W.Cuff-NYG	33.3	H.Clarke-ChiB	13	H.Clarke-ChiB	25.1	B.Seymour-Was	13	H.Clarke-ChiB	15.8
C.Kinscherf-NYG	40.7	B.Snyder-ChiB	2	B.Snyder-ChiB	28.6	E.Steele-P-P	11	T.Canadeo-GB	24.2	J.Butler-P-P	13	B.Seymour-Was	13.3
J.Martin-ChiC	39.6	A.Lio-Det	2	B.Masterson-Was	20.0	J.Hinkle-P-P	11	E.Steele-P-P	21.5	E.Steele-P-P	12	E.Steele-P-P	12.7
H.Hopp-Det	39.1			A.Lio-Det	18.2	C.Fenenbock-Det	11	C.Fenenbock-Det	20.4	F.Sinkwich-Det	11	A.Farkas-Was	11.2

Punt/Kick Return Yards		Punt/Kick Return TDs		Interceptions		Interception Return Yards		Interception Return TDs		Sacks		Overall Rank	
K.Heineman-Bkn	522	N.Mathews-Det	1	S.Baugh-Was	11	D.Hutson-GB	197	Many	1	Not kept		H.Clarke-ChiB	1085
H.Clarke-ChiB	484	D.Magnani-ChiB	1	I.Comp-GB	10	I.Comp-GB	149					B.Paschal-NYG	844
A.Farkas-Was	447	E.Hackney-Det	1	D.Hutson-GB	8	B.Kish-P-P	114					S.Luckman-ChiB	810
E.Steele-P-P	388			J.Laws-GB	7	S.Baugh-Was	112					J.Hinkle-P-P	758
F.Sinkwich-Det	356			D.Brown-NYG	6	J.Hinkle-P-P	98					A.Farkas-Was	735

HELMETS ON, RAMS OUT, STEAGLES IN

Helmets became a mandatory piece of equipment in 1943, though virtually every player had been wearing one since 1940. As the start of the season approached, however, the owners were concerned with protecting more than their players' heads.

By the summer of 1943, more than 350 NFL players were serving in the military, and most teams were struggling to assemble a roster of quality players. With owner Dan Reeves among those serving overseas, the Cleveland Rams suspended operations for the season. In Pennsylvania, the Steelers and Eagles merged their operations. Splitting home dates between Pittsburgh and Philadelphia, the hybrid was called the "Steagles" by fans. This mixed squad finished with a winning record, something the Eagles had never managed to do on their own.

A free substitution rule allowed players to come on and of the field as never before. The problem was the people doing the subbing. The declining quality of play was evident in a November 7 game in which neither the Lions nor the Giants scored a point. It was the last scoreless tie in NFL history.

Player losses forced the Bears to abandon their once powerful running game and throw the ball with reckless abandon. In a game against the Giants, quarterback Sid Luckman threw 7 touchdown passes—an NFL record that has not been surpassed. Bronko Nagurski was one of several retired players lured back to the gridiron. Injuries had slowed the once dominating fullback, who spent the season playing tackle. The Bears needed a win in the season finale to clinch the division, and they trailed the Cardinals by a touchdown at the end of the third quarter. Coach Hunk Anderson moved Nagurski to fullback, and he helped lead the team to the win.

The Redskins had a 6-1-1 record at the end of November, but back-to-back losses against the Giants left the two teams tied for first place at the end of the regular season. That forced a divisional playoff game a week later. The Redskins won the third matchup and earned the right to return to the NFL Championship Game. Bronko and the Bears were there waiting for them.

1944 NFL

TEAM	W-L-T	PCT	POST	PTS	RA	RY	RY/A	RTD	FL	PA	PC	GPY	GPY/A	PTD	PI	PSY	PRAT
Eastern Division																	
NYG	8-1-1	.889	L	206-75	416-374	1532-1000	3.7-2.7	12-5	7-11	125-258	47-114	857-1290	6.9-5.0	9-3	17-34	—	46.4-24.0
Phi	7-1-2	.875	—	267-131	424-321	1663-558	3.9-1.7	23-6	20-4	136-231	55-105	941-1379	6.9-6.0	9-12	12-33	—	49.9-42.6
Was	6-3-1	.667	—	169-180	342-409	904-1492	2.6-3.6	6-12	12-9	299-188	170-84	2021-1166	6.8-6.2	17-9	17-19	—	72.9-41.5
Bos	2-8	.200	—	82-233	324-446	471-1575	1.5-3.5	5-17	8-11	198-166	85-76	1030-1131	5.2-6.8	6-11	22-16	—	30.1-51.1
Bkn	0-10	.000	—	69-166	367-362	960-1181	2.6-3.3	6-13	8-9	213-181	76-78	996-1227	4.7-6.8	3-9	29-10	—	16.4-59.8
Western Division																	
GB	8-2	.800	L*	238-141	395-357	1517-1130	3.8-3.2	16-9	7-12	253-227	105-89	1471-1229	5.8-5.4	15-10	24-29	—	41.1-32.4
ChiB	6-3-1	.667	—	258-172	412-298	1551-954	3.8-3.2	14-10	14-10	217-208	107-69	1616-1052	7.4-5.1	21-10	18-24	—	71.9-27.2
Det	6-3-1	.667	—	216-151	326-403	1141-1216	3.5-3.0	14-7	8-16	207-246	89-106	1475-1442	7.1-5.9	16-15	28-26	—	53.8-43.2
Cle	4-6	.400	—	188-224	358-387	1141-1412	3.2-3.6	13-15	15-17	208-206	85-87	1261-1434	6.1-7.0	13-16	26-27	—	42.6-52.6
C-P	0-10	.000	—	108-328	360-366	1019-1381	2.8-3.8	7-23	12-12	258-204	87-98	1257-1575	4.9-7.7	8-22	41-16	—	21.2-77.6
Aver	10	—	—	180	372	1190	3.2	12	11	211	91	1293	6.1	12	23	—	42.1

TEAM	1D	PENY	PNT	FGM/A	RTNY	RTNTD	OFFY/DEFY	NETY	NETTO	NP	PNP	DELP	PW	DELW	PRT	DR	YPD	DEL
Eastern Division																		
NYG	99-137	502-412	38.6-37.2	7/16-4/10	948-520	5-1	2389-2318	71	21	131	90	41	8.3	0.2	1.5/-0.8	136-136	17.6-17.0	0.5
Phi	110-86	523-570	39.9-39.8	4/8-1/5	1107-425	5-1	2623-1943	680	5	136	77	59	8.4	-0.4	3.6/0.1	142-142	18.5-13.7	4.8
Was	133-123	545-421	39.0-36.6	4/8-5/13	446-728	0-3	2930-2695	235	-1	-11	16	-27	4.7	1.8	4.8/2.1	130-129	22.5-20.9	1.6
Bos	87-126	228-561	35.0-35.8	2/9-5/7	693-785	0-3	1506-2723	-1217	-3	-151	-113	-38	1.2	0.8	0.5/3.1	137-133	11.0-20.5	-9.5
Bkn	110-95	639-539	38.0-38.6	0/6-3/13	435-733	1-1	2017-2410	-393	-18	-97	-105	8	2.6	-2.6	-1.3/4.8	136-137	14.8-17.6	-2.8
Western Division																		
GB	147-114	558-700	36.9-36.8	0/5-1/2	695-537	3-1	3024-2417	607	10	97	91	6	7.4	0.6	2.1/0.1	131-128	23.1-18.9	4.2
ChiB	140-110	1025-489	36.6-38.4	0/0-2/6	650-676	0-3	3239-2006	1233	2	86	111	-25	7.2	-0.7	4.7/0.3	132-136	24.5-14.8	9.8
Det	106-129	417-405	40.5-35.8	2/8-0/3	747-603	1-0	2655-2673	-18	6	65	23	42	6.6	-0.1	1.8/1.7	134-139	19.8-19.2	0.6
Cle	104-116	441-627	38.4-38.5	4/7-1/3	636-579	0-3	2411-2887	-476	3	-36	-28	-8	4.1	-0.1	1.1/1.8	144-142	16.7-20.3	-3.6
C-P	109-109	479-633	32.7-37.2	0/2-1/7	305-1076	1-2	2282-3004	-722	-25	-220	-160	-60	-0.5	0.5	-2.0/5.3	142-142	16.1-21.2	-5.1
Aver	115	536	37.5	2/7	666	2	2508	—	—	—	—	—	—	—	1.7	136	18.4	—

Rushing Attempts		Rushing Yards		Rushing Average		Rushing TDs		Rushing Rank		Passing Yards		Passing Average	
B.Paschal-NYG	196	B.Paschal-NYG	737	A.Grygo-ChiB	6.08	B.Paschal-NYG	9	B.Paschal-NYG	827	I.Comp-GB	1159	F.Filchock-Was	7.75
J.Grigas-C-P	185	J.Grigas-C-P	610	W.Cuff-NYG	5.59	F.Sinkwich-Det	5	J.Grigas-C-P	640	F.Filchock-Was	1139	A.Herber-NYG	7.57
F.Sinkwich-Det	150	F.Sinkwich-Det	563	S.Van Buren-Phi	5.55	S.Van Buren-Phi	5	F.Sinkwich-Det	623	F.Sinkwich-Det	1060	R.Zimmerman-Phi	7.48
P.Manders-Bkn	127	B.Margarita-ChiB	463	B.Margarita-ChiB	5.26	E.Steele-Phi	5	B.Margarita-ChiB	503	S.Luckman-ChiB	1018	F.Sinkwich-Det	7.16
B.Davis-Bos	95	S.Van Buren-Phi	444	M.Bleeker-Phi	5.25	P.Manders-Bkn	5	S.Van Buren-Phi	494	S.Baugh-Was	849	S.Luckman-ChiB	7.12

Completion Percent		TD Passes		TD Percent		INT Percent		Passer Rating		Passing Rank		Receptions	
F.Filchock-Was	57.1	F.Filchock-Was	13	F.Filchock-Was	8.8	S.Baugh-Was	5.5	F.Filchock-Was	86.0	F.Filchock-Was	275	D.Hutson-GB	58
S.Baugh-Was	56.2	F.Sinkwich-Det	12	F.Sinkwich-Det	8.1	F.Filchock-Was	6.1	S.Luckman-ChiB	63.8	S.Baugh-Was	125	J.Benton-Cle	39
S.Luckman-ChiB	49.7	I.Comp-GB	12	S.Luckman-ChiB	7.7	S.Luckman-ChiB	8.4	S.Baugh-Was	59.4	S.Luckman-ChiB	84	J.Aguirre-Was	34
G.Cafego-Bos	47.9	S.Luckman-ChiB	11	R.Zimmerman-Phi	7.6	A.Reisz-Cle	8.8	A.Reisz-Cle	53.6	G.Ronzani-ChiB	69	W.Moore-Was	33
I.Comp-GB	45.2	G.Ronzani-ChiB	9	A.Reisz-Cle	7.1	A.Herber-NYG	9.3	A.Herber-NYG	53.0	L.Brock-GB	57		

Receiving Yards		Receiving Average		Receiving TDs		Receiving Rank		Combined Net Yards		Total TDs		Total Points	
D.Hutson-GB	866	C.Berry-ChiB	18.00	D.Hutson-GB	9	D.Hutson-GB	478	J.Grigas-C-P	1156	B.Paschal-NYG	9	D.Hutson-GB	85
J.Benton-Cle	505	J.Matheson-Det	15.70	C.Berry-ChiB	6	J.Benton-Cle	283	B.Paschal-NYG	1099	D.Hutson-GB	9	F.Sinkwich-Det	66
D.Diehl-Det	426	D.Hutson-GB	14.93	J.Benton-Cle	6	W.Moore-Was	237	D.Hutson-GB	1003	M.Bleeker-Phi	8	R.Zimmerman-Phi	62
W.Moore-Was	424	J.Benton-Cle	12.95			D.Diehl-Det	233	S.Van Buren-Phi	987			B.Paschal-NYG	54
R.McLean-ChiB	414	E.Rucinski-C-P	12.91			R.McLean-ChiB	232	B.Davis-Bos	931			J.Aguirre-Was	51

Punt Average		Field Goals		Field Goal Percent		Kickoff Returns		Kickoff Return Average		Punt Returns		Punt Return Average	
C.Johnson-Bkn	42.7	K.Strong-NYG	6	L.Zontini-Cle	50.0	J.Grigas-C-P	23	T.Fritsch-GB	26.2	B.Davis-Bos	22	E.Steele-Phi	16.5
F.Sinkwich-Det	41.0	R.Zimmerman-Phi	4	R.Zimmerman-Phi	50.0	B.Thurbon-C-P	12	B.Thurbon-C-P	24.3	S.Van Buren-Phi	15	S.Van Buren-Phi	15.3
S.Baugh-Was	40.6	J.Aguirre-Was	4	K.Strong-NYG	50.0	A.Reisz-Cle	12	T.Colella-Cle	24.1	J.Laws-GB	15	F.Sinkwich-Det	13.5
L.Younce-NYG	40.4	L.Zontini-Cle	3	J.Aguirre-Was	50.0	B.Margarita-ChiB	12	A.Reisz-Cle	23.8			F.Seno-Was	12.9
A.Reisz-Cle	40.0							B.Margarita-ChiB	23.3			B.Davis-Bos	12.3

Punt/Kick Return Yards		Punt/Kick Return TDs		Interceptions		Interception Return Yards		Interception Return TDs		Sacks		Overall Rank	
J.Grigas-C-P	511	S.Van Buren-Phi	2	A.Lio-NYG	9	A.Lio-NYG	172	B.Petrilas-NYG	2	Not kept		B.Paschal-NYG	955
S.Van Buren-Phi	496	A.Van Tone-Det	1	Wojciechowicz-Det	7	B.Petrilas-NYG	144	D.Perkins-GB	2			S.Van Buren-Phi	837
B.Davis-Bos	423	R.Ugucioni-Bkn	1	E.Steele-Phi	6	D.Perkins-GB	123					B.Margarita-ChiB	670
B.Paschal-NYG	362	E.Schultz-C-P	1	T.Fritsch-GB	6	T.Fritsch-GB	115					B.Davis-Bos	627
A.Reisz-Cle	353	V.Carroll-NYG	1	I.Comp-GB	6	E.Steele-Phi	115					W.Cuff-NYG	617

TIGERS DON'T WALK ON CARPETS

Although the war was making it difficult for teams to find quality players, NFL owners decided to expand in 1944. Recording executive Ted Collins wanted a team at Yankee Stadium, but Giants owner Tim Mara insisted he had exclusive rights for New York. Collins settled for a team in Boston and called them the Yanks.

The league's ranks also grew when the Cleveland Rams returned from a year's hiatus. They reclaimed a handful of veterans who had played elsewhere during the team's year off, but the roster was stocked mostly with rookies and castoffs. After a surprising 3–0 start, Cleveland's defensive weaknesses became glaring; the reborn Rams finished 4–6.

The Brooklyn Dodgers changed their name to the Tigers, but they couldn't hide how bad the team was on the field. The hapless club went through three head coaches in what would prove to be the last season of NFL football in Brooklyn. Art Rooney still needed help to keep his Steelers afloat, and he joined efforts with the Chicago Cardinals for the year. The result was Card–Pitt. People called them "Carpets" because—as the joke went—"everyone walked all over them." The schedule did not have the Carpets and Lions play each other, so neither team won a game all season.

There were some bright spots. The Philadelphia Eagles, back on their own, continued to improve under second-year coach Greasy Neale. Rookie Steve Van Buren emerged as a powerful runner. A loss to the Giants kept them out of the playoffs, but the Eagles posted the best finish in club history.

New York's offense found a spark with running back Bill Paschal, who led the league in rushing. Arnie Herber, 34, came out of retirement to quarterback the Giants. He was helped by a defense registered 5 shutouts in 10 games.

The Packers ended their four-year playoff drought by beating up on weaker opponents. Coach Curley Lambeau hadn't been able to put much of a team around Don Hutson, but the legendary end was so good that it didn't really matter. Green Bay and New York won their divisions, the best teams in a diluted field.

1945 NFL

TEAM	W-L-T	PCT	POST	PTS	RA	RY	RY/A	RTD	FL	PA	PC	GPY	GPY/A	PTD	PI	PSY	PRAT
Eastern Division																	
Was	8-2	.800	L	209-121	394-337	1708-1003	4.3-3.0	15-8	9-6	228-209	146-95	1838-1121	8.1-5.4	12-9	11-16	—	86.5-44.8
Phi	7-3	.700	—	272-133	381-318	1638-817	4.3-2.6	26-8	10-7	187-205	98-89	1321-1243	7.1-6.1	11-10	14-19	—	63.6-41.2
NYG	3-6-1	.333	—	179-198	317-395	769-1643	2.4-4.2	7-17	9-14	201-186	92-99	1534-1410	7.6-7.6	16-6	16-13	—	65.4-59.7
Bos	3-6-1	.333	—	123-211	345-387	846-1364	2.5-3.5	10-15	15-8	160-227	66-104	1000-1427	6.3-6.3	6-10	21-30	—	35.4-41.6
Pit	2-8	.200	—	79-220	358-363	961-1374	2.7-3.8	9-16	8-14	165-187	61-103	652-1617	4.0-8.6	0-14	21-13	—	9.8-80.0
Western Division																	
Cle	9-1	.900	L*	244-136	372-349	1714-1026	4.6-2.9	19-10	18-16	199-253	99-99	1767-1463	8.9-5.8	16-9	20-28	—	67.8-31.1
Det	7-3	.700	—	195-194	317-356	857-912	2.7-2.6	10-7	10-10	238-227	87-89	1544-1615	6.5-7.1	15-17	36-23	—	41.0-49.8
GB	6-4	.600	—	258-173	377-388	1325-1349	3.5-3.5	16-16	7-17	218-231	81-111	1536-1708	7.0-7.4	14-9	24-24	—	44.2-46.3
ChiB	3-7	.300	—	192-235	423-343	1515-1464	3.6-4.3	13-20	10-6	244-195	132-83	1857-1283	7.6-6.6	14-10	12-15	—	77.5-50.0
ChiC	1-9	.100	—	98-228	334-382	939-1320	2.8-3.5	9-17	13-11	267-187	99-87	1328-1490	5.0-8.0	5-15	18-12	—	31.9-74.1
Aver	10	—		185	362	1227	3.4	13	11	211	96	1438	6.8	11	19	—	47.6

TEAM	1D	PENY	PNT	FGM/A	RTNY	RTNTD	OFFY/DEFY	NETY	NETTO	NP	PNP	DELP	PW	DELW	PRT	DR	YPD	DEL
Eastern Division																		
Was	154-111	672-411	43.3-40.1	7/13-1/5	623-394	0-0	3549-2208	1341	2	88	120	-32	7.2	0.8	6.4/2.3	100-103	35.5-21.4	14.1
Phi	131-104	529-422	37.8-37.5	4/8-3/6	709-415	1-0	3007-2073	934	2	139	86	53	8.5	-1.5	4.3/2.4	123-127	24.4-16.3	8.1
NYG	98-140	492-472	38.4-40.0	6/13-6/14	393-641	0-3	2344-3083	-739	2	-19	-54	35	4.5	-1.0	4.8/4.8	121-121	19.4-25.5	-6.1
Bos	83-133	533-811	36.4-38.9	4/6-8/16	497-713	0-2	1897-2857	-960	2	-88	-72	-16	2.8	0.7	0.7/0.8	134-134	14.2-21.3	-7.2
Pit	96-116	436-600	39.3-38.2	4/5-5/8	573-665	1-0	1719-3043	-1324	-2	-141	-118	-23	1.5	0.5	-1.8/6.3	123-119	14.0-25.6	-11.6
Western Division																		
Cle	137-129	593-391	40.1-36.4	1/3-1/4	751-686	0-0	3546-2510	1036	6	108	110	-2	7.7	1.3	5.2/1.2	129-133	27.5-18.9	8.6
Det	102-105	673-568	38.0-35.5	2/7-4/5	987-648	2-2	2485-2548	-63	-13	1	-57	58	5.0	2.0	0.3/3.3	139-145	17.9-17.6	0.3
GB	131-137	723-701	39.9-37.2	5/13-0/2	774-659	5-0	2869-3116	-247	10	85	19	66	7.1	-1.1	2.7/3.1	138-135	20.8-23.1	-2.3
ChiB	164-126	666-581	35.7-39.7	1/3-3/7	266-589	0-2	3400-2756	644	-1	-43	50	-93	3.9	-0.9	6.0/3.6	112-107	30.4-25.8	4.6
ChiC	115-110	389-749	36.7-41.6	0/4-3/8	409-573	0-0	2269-2891	-622	-8	-130	-84	-46	1.8	-0.8	2.1/5.9	126-121	18.0-23.9	-5.9
Aver	121	571	38.3	3/8	598	1	2709	—	—	—	—	—			3.2	125	21.8	

Rushing Attempts	Rushing Yards	Rushing Average	Rushing TDs	Rushing Rank	Passing Yards	Passing Average
F.Akins-Was 147	S.Van Buren-Phi 832	F.Gehrke-Cle 6.31	S.Van Buren-Phi 15	S.Van Buren-Phi 982	S.Luckman-ChiB 1727	B.Warren-Cle 9.41
S.Van Buren-Phi 143	F.Akins-Was 797	J.Gillette-Cle 6.19	F.Gehrke-Cle 7	F.Akins-Was 857	S.Baugh-Was 1669	S.Baugh-Was 9.17
B.Margarita-ChiB 112	B.Margarita-ChiB 497	S.Van Buren-Phi 5.82	T.Fritsch-GB 7	F.Gehrke-Cle 537	B.Warren-Cle 1609	I.Comp-GB 8.16
D.Greenwood-Cle 101	F.Gehrke-Cle 467	F.Akins-Was 5.42		B.Margarita-ChiB 527	P.Christman-ChiC 1147	A.Herber-NYG 8.01
B.Warren-Pit 95	J.Gillette-Cle 390	B.Margarita-ChiB 4.44		D.Greenwood-Cle 416	R.Zimmerman-Phi 991	S.Luckman-ChiB 7.96

Completion Percent	TD Passes	TD Percent	INT Percent	Passer Rating	Passing Rank	Receptions
S.Baugh-Was 70.3	B.Warren-Cle 14	A.Herber-NYG 11.3	S.Baugh-Was 2.2	S.Baugh-Was 109.9	S.Baugh-Was 730	D.Hutson-GB 47
S.Luckman-ChiB 53.9	S.Luckman-ChiB 14	B.Warren-Cle 8.2	S.Luckman-ChiB 4.6	S.Luckman-ChiB 82.5	S.Luckman-ChiB 534	J.Benton-Cle 45
R.Zimmerman-Phi 52.8	S.Baugh-Was 11	R.Zimmerman-Phi 7.1	P.Christman-ChiC 5.5	R.Zimmerman-Phi 75.9	R.Zimmerman-Phi 221	S.Bagarus-Was 34
B.Warren-Cle 52.0	R.Zimmerman-Phi 9	I.Comp-GB 6.6	R.Zimmerman-Phi 6.3	B.Warren-Cle 72.4	B.Warren-Cle 195	G.Wilson-ChiB 28
A.Herber-NYG 43.8	A.Herber-NYG 9	S.Luckman-ChiB 6.5	B.Warren-Cle 9.9	A.Herber-NYG 69.8	P.Christman-ChiC 119	

Receiving Yards	Receiving Average	Receiving TDs	Receiving Rank	Combined Net Yards	Total TDs	Total Points
J.Benton-Cle 1067	F.Liebel-NYG 26.95	F.Liebel-NYG 10	J.Benton-Cle 574	S.Van Buren-Phi 1478	S.Van Buren-Phi 18	S.Van Buren-Phi 110
D.Hutson-GB 834	J.Benton-Cle 23.71	D.Hutson-GB 9	D.Hutson-GB 462	S.Bagarus-Was 1360	F.Liebel-NYG 10	D.Hutson-GB 97
S.Bagarus-Was 617	J.Ferrante-Phi 22.10	J.Benton-Cle 8	F.Liebel-NYG 347	B.Margarita-ChiB 1176	D.Hutson-GB 10	B.Warren-Cle 64
F.Liebel-NYG 593	K.Kavanaugh-ChiB 21.72	J.Ferrante-Phi 7	S.Bagarus-Was 334	J.Benton-Cle 1083	B.Westfall-Det 9	F.Liebel-NYG 60
J.Greene-Det 550	J.Greene-Det 21.15	K.Kavanaugh-ChiB 6	K.Kavanaugh-ChiB 302	F.Seno-ChiC 1002		T.Fritsch-GB 57

Punt Average	Field Goals	Field Goal Percent	Kickoff Returns	Kickoff Return Average	Punt Returns	Punt Return Average
S.Baugh-Was 43.3	J.Aguirre-Was 7	A.Lio-Bos 80.0	F.Seno-ChiC 19	S.Van Buren-Phi 28.7	S.Bagarus-Was 21	D.Ryan-Det 14.7
R.McKay-GB 41.2	K.Strong-NYG 6	J.Aguirre-Was 53.8	S.Van Buren-Phi 13	S.Bagarus-Was 27.1	D.Ryan-Det 15	B.Warren-Pit 12.9
B.Warren-Cle 40.6	R.Zimmerman-Phi 4	R.Zimmerman-Phi 50.0	J.Martin-Bos 13	J.Martin-Bos 23.2	S.Van Buren-Phi 14	W.Cuff-NYG 12.4
S.Tinsley-Pit 40.5	A.Lio-Bos 4	K.Strong-NYG 46.2	S.Bagarus-Was 12	F.Seno-ChiC 21.5	B.Warren-Pit 13	S.Bagarus-Was 12.0
	B.Agajanian-Pit 4	T.Fritsch-GB 37.5	B.Davis-Was 11	B.Davis-Was 19.1	P.Lipscomb-NYG 13	S.Van Buren-Phi 11.0

Punt/Kick Return Yards	Punt/Kick Return TDs	Interceptions	Interception Return Yards	Interception Return TDs	Sacks	Overall Rank
S.Bagarus-Was 576	S.Van Buren-Phi 1	R.Zimmerman-Phi 7	C.Brock-GB 122	C.Brock-GB 2	Not kept	S.Van Buren-Phi 1323
S.Van Buren-Phi 527	C.DeShane-Det 1	B.Warren-Cle 6	B.Warren-Cle 114			F.Akins-Was 892
F.Seno-ChiC 511		B.Margarita-ChiB 6	B.Warren-Cle 92			B.Margarita-ChiB 809
D.Ryan-Det 358		B.Davis-Bos 6	R.Zimmerman-Phi 90			S.Bagarus-Was 789
J.Martin-Bos 309		L.Cantor-ChiC 5	D.Ryan-Det 90			S.Baugh-Was 753

WAR OVER; BACK TO BUSINESS

With the fighting in Europe ending in May and the Japanese surrender in August, the country was beginning to return to the way it had been before the war. But the cost of World War II could not be forgotten. Among those Americans called to military duty were 638 men with NFL playing experience. Twenty-one of those players were killed, including Gus Sonnenberg, one of the great linemen of the late 1920s, and former all-pros Al Blozis, Chuck Braidwood, Eddie Kahn, and Jim Mooney. Jack Chevigny, the one-time head coach of the Chicago Cardinals, was killed at Iwo Jima in February.

The number of teams remained at 10, although there were some changes. For the first time since 1942, the Pittsburgh Steelers did not need to join forces with another club. The same could not be said of the Brooklyn Tigers, who merged with the Boston Yanks.

Despite suffering a shoulder injury early in the season, Philadelphia's Steve Van Buren led the league in rushing and established an NFL mark with 15 touchdown runs. Quarterback Tommy Thompson returned from the Army late in the season, but that wasn't enough to get the Eagles out of second place. The return of others meant legends like Don Hutson, Arnie Herber, and Mel Hein could retire with the knowledge that their teams wouldn't be shorthanded.

Sammy Baugh flourished in Washington's new T-formation offense. Baugh completed more than 70 percent of his pass attempts to lead the league's most prolific passing offense. The backfield featured Frank Akins, a big bruising fullback, and Steve Bagarus, who used his speed to run outside and to catch passes down the field.

The biggest star of the season was Cleveland's Bob Waterfield, a rookie out of UCLA who was married to film star Jane Russell. The young quarterback was an aggressive passer and a fiery leader. In the first Thanksgiving Day game in Detroit since 1938, the Rams needed a win against the Lions to clinch the division. Waterfield connected with end Jim Benton on 10 passes for an NFL record 303 yards in a 28–21, win. Waterfield earned league Most Valuable Player honors for the league champs.

1946 NFL

TEAM	W-L-T	PCT	POST	PTS	RA	RY	RY/A	RTD	FL	PA	PC	GPY	GPY/A	PTD	PI	PSY	PRAT
Eastern Division																	
NYG	7-3-1	.700	L	236-162	414-394	1464-1289	3.5-3.3	17-9	16-26	194-258	100-128	1450-1823	7.5-7.1	14-9	25-19	—	60.7-53.8
Phi	6-5	.545	—	231-220	423-418	1263-1123	3.0-2.7	13-17	27-18	217-220	115-95	1641-1360	7.6-6.2	14-11	20-26	—	60.9-40.9
Was	5-5-1	.500	—	171-191	438-407	1497-1103	3.4-2.7	11-12	22-10	221-216	112-101	1613-1342	7.3-6.2	10-10	22-24	—	50.2-42.8
Pit	5-5-1	.500	—	136-**117**	414-466	1307-1754	3.2-3.8	14-**9**	15-17	161-**162**	58-**64**	970-**939**	6.0-**5.8**	**4**-6	**13**-14	—	31.8-35.5
Bos	2-8-1	.200	*	189-273	365-452	1110-1852	3.0-4.1	11-22	18-14	239-227	103-106	1566-1642	6.6-7.2	15-15	19-17	—	53.1-62.0
Western Division																	
ChiB	**8**-2-1	**.800**	L*	**289**-193	496-**334**	1719-**1044**	3.5-3.1	**21**-12	16-22	253-257	120-108	1950-1610	**7.7**-6.3	18-14	18-**27**	—	**67.8**-41.8
LA	6-4-1	.600	—	277-257	404-402	1683-1325	**4.2**-3.3	16-13	20-15	**326**-265	**153**-112	**2080**-2154	6.4-8.1	**19**-21	24-23	—	56.5-61.4
GB	6-5	.545	—	148-158	**560**-367	**1765**-1372	3.2-3.7	13-14	**11**-28	178-214	54-94	841-1288	4.7-6.0	**4**-6	18-24	—	15.0-**33.5**
ChiC	6-5	.545	—	260-198	371-438	1529-1249	4.1-2.9	17-12	29-20	266-273	115-118	1951-1603	7.3-5.9	17-14	20-25	—	58.6-41.5
Det	1-10	.091	—	142-310	274-481	472-1698	1.7-3.5	8-21	12-16	286-249	119-123	1674-1975	5.9-7.9	11-20	33-13	—	34.4-81.3
Aver	11	—	—	208	416	1381	3.3	14	19	234	105	1574	6.7	13	21		47.6

TEAM	1D	PENY	PNT	FGM/A	RTNY	RTNTD	OFFY/DEFY	NETY	NETTO	NP	PNP	DELP	PW	DELW	PRT	DR	YPD	DEL
Eastern Division																		
NYG	163-161	785-837	40.3-38.9	4/9-5/9	673-496	1-3	2927-3134	-207	4	74	-1	**75**	7.3	0.1	2.4/4.1	144-143	20.3-21.9	-1.6
Phi	156-146	769-817	38.2-40.3	8/15-4/10	**917**-736	2-2	2917-2490	427	-3	11	24	-13	5.8	0.2	4.1/1.4	**161**-160	18.1-**15.6**	2.6
Was	161-147	842-552	44.1-41.0	6/**18**-3/13	807-863	1-4	3132-**2451**	681	-10	-20	17	-37	5.0	0.5	3.3/1.7	142-141	22.1-17.4	4.7
Pit	120-147	**534**-707	39.7-42.2	2/9-4/10	793-**378**	1-0	2313-2719	-406	3	19	-22	41	6.0	-0.5	2.6/2.3	135-**137**	17.1-19.8	-2.7
Bos	147-182	691-870	40.3-**38.7**	0/2-5/14	599-1051	2-0	2699-3586	-887	-6	-84	-98	-14	3.4	-0.9	3.6/4.5	145-151	18.6-23.7	-5.1
Western Division																		
ChiB	211-**137**	940-716	38.1-44.6	4/11-4/11	801-556	1-0	3695-2689	**1006**	15	**96**	144	-48	**7.9**	0.6	**5.2**/2.1	156-154	23.7-17.5	**6.2**
LA	**214**-170	764-702	**44.4**-40.4	6/11-5/11	671-736	2-1	**3793**-3525	268	-6	20	-2	22	6.0	0.8	3.7/5.0	146-149	**26.0**-23.7	2.3
GB	160-158	693-628	42.9-41.9	**9**/17-**4/7**	683-689	0-1	2618-2661	-43	**23**	-10	88	-98	5.3	**0.8**	0.4/**1.3**	153-139	17.1-19.1	-2.0
ChiC	175-176	761-673	39.7-41.4	5/12-5/10	517-754	1-0	3572-2882	690	-4	62	42	20	7.1	-1.0	4.6/2.3	150-158	23.8-18.2	5.6
Det	120-203	635-**912**	43.4-40.3	3/6-8/15	562-764	0-0	2169-3698	-1529	-16	-168	-191	23	1.3	-0.3	1.0/6.4	149-149	14.6-24.8	-10.3
Aver	163	741	41.0	5/11	702	1	2984	—	—	—	—	—	—	—	3.2	148	20.1	—

Rushing Attempts		Rushing Yards		Rushing Average		Rushing TDs		Rushing Rank		Passing Yards		Passing Average	
B.Dudley-Pit	146	B.Dudley-Pit	604	F.Gehrke-LA	5.23	T.Fritsch-GB	9	B.Dudley-Pit	624	S.Luckman-ChiB	1826	S.Luckman-ChiB	7.97
T.Fritsch-GB	128	P.Harder-ChiC	545	P.Harder-ChiC	5.14	J.Gaffney-ChiB	6	P.Harder-ChiC	585	R.Zimmerman-Phi	1747	R.Zimmerman-Phi	7.56
T.Canadeo-GB	122	S.Van Buren-Phi	529	J.Grigas-Bos	5.07			S.Van Buren-Phi	579	P.Christman-ChiC	1656	F.Filchock-NYG	7.47
B.Paschal-NYG	117	J.Gaffney-ChiB	476	S.Van Buren-Phi	4.56			J.Gaffney-ChiB	536	P.Governali-Bos	1293	T.Thompson-Phi	7.23
S.Van Buren-Phi	116	T.Canadeo-GB	476	B.Osmanski-ChiB	4.40			T.Fritsch-GB	534	F.Filchock-NYG	1262	P.Christman-ChiC	7.23

Completion Percent		TD Passes		TD Percent		INT Percent		Passer Rating		Passing Rank		Receptions	
T.Thompson-Phi	55.3	B.Ward-LA	17	S.Luckman-ChiB	7.4	P.Governali-Bos	5.2	S.Luckman-ChiB	71.0	S.Luckman-ChiB	358	J.Benton-LA	63
S.Baugh-Was	54.0	S.Luckman-ChiB	17	F.Filchock-NYG	7.1	B.Ward-LA	6.8	B.Ward-LA	67.6	P.Governali-Bos	312	H.Crisler-Bos	32
R.Zimmerman-Phi	51.9	P.Governali-Bos	13	B.Ward-LA	6.8	S.Luckman-ChiB	7.0	P.Governali-Bos	67.0	B.Ward-LA	279	S.Bagarus-Was	31
F.Filchock-NYG	51.5	P.Christman-ChiC	13	P.Governali-Bos	6.8	P.Christman-ChiC	7.9	T.Thompson-Phi	61.3	P.Christman-ChiC	173	J.Ferrante-Phi	28
B.Ward-LA	50.6	F.Filchock-NYG	12	T.Thompson-Phi	5.8	I.Comp-GB	8.5	F.Filchock-NYG	60.2	E.Nix-NYG	88		

Receiving Yards		Receiving Average		Receiving TDs		Receiving Rank		Combined Net Yards		Total TDs		Total Points	
J.Benton-LA	981	B.Dewell-ChiC	23.81	B.Dewell-ChiC	7	J.Benton-LA	521	B.Dudley-Pit	1650	T.Fritsch-GB	10	T.Fritsch-GB	100
B.Dewell-ChiC	643	M.Kutner-ChiC	23.48	J.Benton-LA	6	B.Dewell-ChiC	357	S.Bagarus-Was	1212	J.Gaffney-ChiB	7	B.Ward-LA	61
M.Kutner-ChiC	634	J.Ferrante-Phi	16.11	M.Kutner-ChiC	5	M.Kutner-ChiC	342	S.Van Buren-Phi	1012	B.Dewell-ChiC	7	W.Cuff-ChiC	55
J.Ferrante-Phi	451	J.Benton-LA	15.57	K.Kavanaugh-ChiB	5	J.Ferrante-Phi	246	J.Benton-LA	981			A.Lio-Phi	51
S.Bagarus-Was	438	S.Bagarus-Was	14.13	H.Crisler-Bos	5	S.Bagarus-Was	234	F.Seno-ChiC	932				

Punt Average		Field Goals		Field Goal Percent		Kickoff Returns		Kickoff Return Average		Punt Returns		Punt Return Average	
B.Cifers-Det	45.6	T.Fritsch-GB	9	B.Ward-LA	66.7	A.Karnofsky-Bos	21	F.Seno-ChiC	31.4	B.Dudley-Pit	27	B.Dudley-Pit	14.3
S.Baugh-Was	45.1	B.Ward-LA	6	A.Lio-Phi	54.5	D.Ryan-Det	16	S.Van Buren-Phi	29.0	S.Bagarus-Was	18	B.Pritchard-Phi	13.8
B.Ward-LA	44.7	D.Poillon-Was	6*	F.Seno-ChiC	52.9	B.Dudley-Pit	14	A.Karnofsky-Bos	28.5	J.Youel-Was	13	J.Youel-Was	11.5
R.McKay-GB	42.7	A.Lio-Phi	6	K.Strong-NYG	44.4	F.Seno-ChiC	13	S.Bagarus-Was	25.5	B.Davis-Bos	13	S.Bagarus-Was	10.7
B.Blackburn-ChiC	41.9	W.Cuff-ChiC	5	F.Maznicki-ChiB	44.4	S.Bagarus-Was	13	E.Saenz-Was	24.0			F.Seno-ChiC	10.4

Punt/Kick Return Yards		Punt/Kick Return TDs		Interceptions		Interception Return Yards		Interception Return TDs		Sacks		Overall Rank	
B.Dudley-Pit	665	S.Van Buren-Phi	1	B.Dudley-Pit	10	B.Dudley-Pit	242	Many	1	Not kept		B.Dudley-Pit	1082
A.Karnofsky-Bos	637	B.Shaw-LA	1	B.Davis-Bos	7	H.Rohrig-GB	134					S.Van Buren-Phi	862
F.Seno-ChiC	584	F.Seno-ChiC	1	G.Steinke-Phi	6	B.Davis-Bos	129					J.Gaffney-ChiB	723
S.Bagarus-Was	524	A.Karnofsky-Bos	1			F.Liebel-NYG	117					S.Bagarus-Was	687
S.Van Buren-Phi	408											P.Harder-ChiC	676

CALIFORNIA, HERE WE COME

Bert Bell was selected to replace ineffective Elmer Layden as commissioner in January. In more than two decades as a team owner, Bell had a reputation as someone dedicated to making the NFL stronger. Now he faced several significant challenges. A new league had announced plans to begin play in the fall. Unlike previous rivals, the All-America Football Conference had owners with enough money to get the league off the ground and had locked up big stadiums in big cities, including two teams in California.

The AAFC had teams in Chicago, New York, and Cleveland, and the latter caused great distress for Rams owner Dan Reeves. Three weeks after winning the 1945 NFL title, he announced plans to move his team from Cleveland to Los Angeles. After some initial hesitation—of small concern was an AAFC team in LA—the other NFL owners approved the move. The team also helped to end 13 years of racial segregation in the NFL by signing two African American players from UCLA, Kenny Washington and Woody Strode.

Another former UCLA star, Jackie Robinson, did not integrate major league baseball until 1947.

Now that players were returning from the war, free substitution was withdrawn. Substitutions were limited to no more than three men at a time. A player like Pittsburgh's Bill Dudley made it seem like the fewer changes the better. In his first full season after returning from the Army, "Bullet Bill" led the league in rushing, punt returns, and interceptions.

The influx of talented young players returning from the service helped the Giants rebuild their defense quickly. The Bears had George Halas back from the Navy, and Sid Luckman led the NFL in passing yards for a second straight season for the league's most dominant team.

On the eve of the championship game between the Giants and Bears, a scandal erupted when the commissioner learned that two Giants players had been offered money by gamblers to throw the game. Fullback Merle Hapes was suspended immediately, while quarterback Frank Filchock was allowed to play. Despite suffering a broken nose, Filchock threw 2 touchdowns. The Giants, 10-point underdogs, were 24–14 losers.

1946 AAFC

TEAM	W-L-T	PCT	POST	PTS	RA	RY	RY/A	RTD	FL	PA	PC	GPY	GPY/A	PTD	PI	PSY	PRAT
Eastern Division																	
NYY	10-3-1	.769	L	270-192	514-449	1845-1055	3.6-2.3	17-9	24-18	274-**252**	129-123	1645-1564	6.0-6.2	13-13	21-16	—	50.2-59.4
Bkn	3-10-1	.231	—	226-339	374-575	1017-2458	2.7-4.3	9-24	17-26	**327**-255	162-132	2258-2077	6.9-8.1	17-19	23-12	—	60.2-84.4
Buf	3-10-1	.231	—	249-370	501-497	2046-2075	**4.1**-4.2	13-21	35-**29**	238-295	96-146	1367-2370	5.7-8.0	16-23	23-22	—	42.5-71.7
Mia	3-11	.214	—	167-378	408-528	848-2248	2.1-4.3	13-24	23-20	295-**252**	131-123	1725-1876	5.8-7.4	10-19	33-24	—	35.2-59.3
Western Division																	
Cle	**12-2**	**.857**	L*	**423-137**	496-546	1978-1616	4.0-3.0	**27-8**	30-23	237-299	123-125	**2266-1317**	9.6-4.4	**22-8**	**7-41**	—	**103.8-24.6**
SF	9-5	.643	—	307-189	**592-425**	**2175-873**	3.7-**2.1**	22-**7**	21-26	252-359	130-185	1721-2150	6.8-6.0	18-15	21-21	—	62.6-59.5
LAD	7-5-2	.583	—	305-290	549-451	1949-1356	3.6-3.0	17-19	**13-17**	322-284	**176**-138	2193-2101	6.8-7.4	19-17	30-20	—	56.9-64.0
ChiR	5-6-3	.455	—	263-315	512-475	1541-1718	3.0-3.6	10-16	18-22	310-259	144-**119**	1898-1618	6.1-6.2	18-19	29-31	—	46.7-51.3
Aver	14	—	—	276	493	1675	3.4	16	23	282	136	1884	6.7	17	23		55.4

TEAM	1D	PENY	PNT	FGM/A	RTNY	RTNTD	OFFY/DEFY	NETY	NETTO	NP	PNP	DELP	PW	DELW	PRT	DR	YPD	DEL
Eastern Division																		
NYY	158-**119**	558-449	36.0-42.3	6/9-8/16	1044-824	**6-2**	3490-**2619**	871	-11	78	29	49	8.9	**1.5**	3.0/3.9	176-184	19.8-**14.2**	5.6
Bkn	135-192	453-395	**46.5**-40.6	5/11-5/16	598-973	4-3	3275-4535	-1260	-2	-113	-113	0	4.2	-0.7	4.3/6.8	189-188	17.3-24.1	-6.8
Buf	147-170	**296**-588	35.6-41.5	4/8-**3/9**	831-1018	5-8	3413-4445	-1032	-7	-121	-114	-7	4.0	-0.5	2.1/5.5	193-202	17.7-22.0	-4.3
Mia	121-155	402-**625**	40.6-42.0	2/7-13/16	580-1154	0-6	2573-4124	-1551	-12	-211	-177	-34	1.7	1.3	1.2/3.9	174-180	14.8-22.9	-8.1
Western Division																		
Cle	146-160	600-326	39.2-41.6	**13/29-4/9**	1126-**626**	**6-2**	4244-2933	**1311**	27	286	217	69	14.1	-2.2	**9.2/-1.5**	177-193	**24.0**-15.2	**8.8**
SF	170-140	440-377	40.6-38.8	4/8-**3/9**	1031-725	3-4	3896-3023	873	5	118	93	25	9.9	-1.0	3.8/3.8	184-174	21.2-17.4	3.8
LAD	**183**-144	379-329	44.2-**38.7**	6/17-7/12	1017-917	5-3	4142-3457	685	-6	15	33	-18	7.4	0.6	3.2/4.8	188-**172**	22.0-20.1	1.9
ChiR	149-129	514-553	41.9-40.0	9/12-6/14	**1168**-1158	**6-7**	3439-3336	103	6	-52	33	-85	5.7	0.8	2.5/1.6	**212**-200	16.2-16.7	-0.5
Aver	151	455	40.6	6/13	924	4	3559	—	—	—	—	—	—	—	3.5	187	19.1	—

Rushing Attempts		Rushing Yards		Rushing Average		Rushing TDs		Rushing Rank		Passing Yards		Passing Average	
S.Sanders-NYY	140	S.Sanders-NYY	709	M.Motley-Cle	8.23	S.Sanders-NYY	9	S.Sanders-NYY	769	G.Dobbs-Bkn	1886	O.Graham-Cle	10.54
N.Standlee-SF	134	N.Standlee-SF	651	E.Jones-Cle	7.00	J.Kimbrough-LAD	6	N.Standlee-SF	671	O.Graham-Cle	1834	A.Bertelli-LAD	7.22
J.Kimbrough-LAD	122	V.Kulbitski-Buf	605	S.Juzwik-Buf	6.41	D.Greenwood-Cle	6	M.Motley-Cle	651	F.Albert-SF	1404	F.Albert-SF	7.13
Hoernschemeyer-ChiR	111	M.Motley-Cle	601	V.Kulbitski-Buf	6.24	L.Eshmont-SF	6	V.Kulbitski-Buf	625	Hoernschemeyer-ChiR	1266	G.Dobbs-Bkn	7.01
V.Kulbitski-Buf	97	E.Jones-Cle	539	S.Sanders-NYY	5.06			E.Jones-Cle	579	C.O'Rourke-LAD	1250	C.O'Rourke-LAD	6.87

Completion Percent		TD Passes		TD Percent		INT Percent		Passer Rating		Passing Rank		Receptions	
C.O'Rourke-LAD	57.7	O.Graham-Cle	17	O.Graham-Cle	9.8	A.Parker-NYY	2.6	O.Graham-Cle	112.1	O.Graham-Cle	802	D.Lavelli-Cle	40
O.Graham-Cle	54.6	Hoernschemeyer-ChiR	14	Hoernschemeyer-ChiR	7.3	O.Graham-Cle	2.9	A.Parker-NYY	87.0	G.Dobbs-Bkn	408	A.Beals-SF	40
A.Parker-NYY	53.9	F.Albert-SF	14	F.Albert-SF	7.1	G.Dobbs-Bkn	5.6	F.Albert-SF	69.8	A.Parker-NYY	302	S.Judd-Bkn	34
F.Albert-SF	52.8	G.Dobbs-Bkn	13	A.Parker-NYY	7.0	F.Albert-SF	7.1	C.O'Rourke-LAD	68.7	F.Albert-SF	212	F.King-Buf	30
A.Bertelli-LAD	52.8	C.O'Rourke-LAD	12	C.O'Rourke-LAD	6.6	Hoernschemeyer-ChiR	7.3	G.Dobbs-Bkn	66.0	B.Schwenk-Cle	158	E.Hirsch-ChiR	27

Receiving Yards		Receiving Average		Receiving TDs		Receiving Rank		Combined Net Yards		Total TDs		Total Points	
D.Lavelli-Cle	843	D.Lavelli-Cle	21.08	A.Beals-SF	10	D.Lavelli-Cle	462	S.Sanders-NYY	1691	S.Sanders-NYY	12	L.Groza-Cle	84
A.Beals-SF	586	F.King-Buf	15.53	D.Lavelli-Cle	8	A.Beals-SF	343	S.Juzwik-Buf	1507	A.Beals-SF	10	S.Sanders-NYY	72
M.Speedie-Cle	564	A.Beals-SF	14.65	M.Speedie-Cle	7	M.Speedie-Cle	317	E.Hirsch-ChiR	1289	L.Eshmont-SF	8	A.Beals-SF	61
F.King-Buf	466	S.Judd-Bkn	13.03	F.King-Buf	6	F.King-Buf	263	C.Fenenbock-LAD	1265	D.Lavelli-Cle	8	S.Nemeth-ChiR	59
S.Judd-Bkn	443					S.Judd-Bkn	242	E.Jones-Cle	1055	R.Heywood-ChiR	8	J.Aguirre-LAD	55

Punt Average		Field Goals		Field Goal Percent		Kickoff Returns		Kickoff Return Average		Punt Returns		Punt Return Average	
G.Dobbs-Bkn	47.8	L.Groza-Cle	13	S.Nemeth-ChiR	75.0	S.Juzwik-Buf	21	C.Fenenbock-LAD	28.2	B.Seymour-LAD	18	C.Fenenbock-LAD	18.7
B.Reinhard-LAD	45.4	S.Nemeth-ChiR	9	H.Johnson-NYY	75.0	C.Fenenbock-LAD	15	E.Hirsch-ChiR	27.4	K.Casanega-SF	18	S.Sanders-NYY	15.1
E.Lewis-ChiR	41.7	H.Johnson-NYY	6	J.Vetrano-SF	57.1	E.Elsey-LAD	15	E.Elsey-LAD	22.3	S.Sanders-NYY	17	E.Hirsch-ChiR	13.8
K.Eakin-Mia	41.4	A.Marefos-Bkn	5	L.Zontini-Buf	50.0	E.Hirsch-ChiR	14	S.Juzwik-Buf	21.5	E.Hirsch-ChiR	17	K.Casanega-SF	13.8
F.Albert-SF	41.0			A.Marefos-Bkn	50.0	S.Sanders-NYY	13			C.Fenenbock-LAD	16	B.Perina-NYY	13.7

Punt/Kick Return Yards		Punt/Kick Return TDs		Interceptions		Interception Return Yards		Interception Return TDs		Sacks		Overall Rank	
C.Fenenbock-LAD	778	S.Sanders-NYY	2	T.Colella-Cle	10	W.Williams-ChiR	148	Many	1	Not kept		S.Sanders-NYY	1242
S.Sanders-NYY	652	E.Hirsch-ChiR	2	K.Casanega-SF	8	K.Casanega-SF	146					S.Juzwik-Buf	989
E.Hirsch-ChiR	619	R.Heywood-ChiR	2	E.Hirsch-ChiR	6	T.Colella-Cle	110					C.Fenenbock-LAD	937
S.Juzwik-Buf	587			W.Clay-ChiR	6	S.Juzwik-Buf	108					O.Graham-Cle	843
E.Elsey-LAD	482					O.Graham-Cle	102					G.Dobbs-Bkn	843

AAFC: ALL ABOUT FOOTBALL IN CLEVELAND

As professional football's popularity was growing, prospective owners stepped forward in big cities, eager to get in on the action. Commissioner Elmer Layden had consistently rebuffed overtures from prominent businessmen and celebrities in cities such as Los Angeles, San Francisco, Baltimore, and Buffalo. Chicago sportswriter Arch Ward helped these spurned suitors form their own league, which they dubbed the All-America Football Conference. After two years of planning, the league announced plans for its inaugural season in 1946. A publicity campaign promised colorful uniforms and a variety of innovative offensive styles.

The new league put together teams in New York and Chicago, NFL strongholds, and tapped hungry markets in Buffalo, Los Angeles, Miami, and San Francisco. The AAFC even persuaded an existing NFL team to switch leagues. Brooklyn owner Dan Topping moved his team to Yankee Stadium and re-christened them the New York Yankees.

The AAFC also went after the NFL's players. About 100 veteran players opted to switch leagues, as did a number of college stars whose pro careers had been delayed by military service. Players like Glenn Dobbs, Frankie Albert, and 1943 Heisman Trophy winner Angelo Bertelli gave the league instant credibility.

The AAFC also landed some high-profile coaches. Ray Flaherty, who had won two NFL titles with the Redskins, was tabbed as the head coach for the Yankees. Cleveland hired Paul Brown, who had coached Ohio State to its first national championship in 1942. His popularity in Ohio was instrumental in a fan vote to name the franchise. Coach Brown assembled a roster that included six rookies who would eventually be inducted into the Hall of Fame: Frank Gatski, Lou Groza, Otto Graham, Dante Lavelli, Marion Motley, and Bill Willis. Motley and Willis were African Americans, ensuring that the AAFC would be integrated right from the start. Half of Cleveland's 12 wins came by 20 points or more.

The Yankees dominated in the East, finishing with 10 wins; the other three teams combined for nine victories. Veteran Ace Parker and rookie Spec Sanders proved to be a formidable backfield combination, and two of the Yankees' three losses came in games against the eventual champion Browns.

1947 NFL

TEAM	W-L-T	PCT	POST	PTS	RA	RY	RY/A	RTD	FL	PA	PC	GPY	GPY/A	PTD	PI	PSY	PRAT
Eastern Division																	
Phi	8-4	.667	DL	308-242	474-**380**	1971-**1329**	4.2-3.5	**21**-13	14-13	223-334	116-151	1761-2410	7.9-7.2	18-19	19-23	—	69.7-60.1
Pit	8-4	.667	D	240-259	496-403	1948-1622	3.9-4.0	15-11	16-14	209-**244**	85-**98**	1410-1847	6.7-7.6	10-20	19-18	—	42.2-63.7
Bos	4-7-1	.364	—	168-256	343-493	973-2020	2.8-4.1	5-18	**8**-17	238-303	95-158	1661-2042	7.0-6.7	15-17	27-28	—	45.9-53.8
Was	4-8	.333	—	295-367	384-409	1343-1564	3.5-3.8	11-18	21-8	**416**-282	**231**-146	**3336**-2422	8.0-8.6	28-26	**18**-21	—	**86.2**-80.7
NYG	2-8-2	.200	—	190-309	366-457	1195-1836	3.3-4.0	7-18	16-12	293-276	123-121	1999-2015	6.8-7.3	17-19	26-27	—	47.9-52.4
Western Division																	
ChiC	9-3	**.750**	L*	306-231	468-400	1735-1759	3.7-4.4	20-10	16-18	340-314	160-148	2580-2206	7.6-7.0	18-18	25-27	—	59.9-53.9
ChiB	8-4	.667		**363**-241	448-392	1959-1423	4.4-3.6	**21**-6	23-20	378-345	194-161	3093-2449	**8.2**-7.1	**29**-20	35-27	—	65.9-57.3
GB	6-5-1	.545		274-**210**	**510**-433	2149-1606	4.2-3.7	14-13	13-21	253-277	112-122	1724-**1790**	6.8-**6.5**	17-**14**	19-**30**	—	58.5-**43.0**
LA	6-6	.500		259-214	459-453	**2171**-1544	**4.7**-3.4	15-12	20-**24**	293-306	123-145	1660-2059	5.7-6.7	**13**-14	28-24	—	35.9-52.2
Det	3-9	.250		231-305	333-461	1234-1975	3.7-4.3	6-18	18-18	348-310	167-156	2446-2430	7.0-7.8	23-21	34-25	—	53.8-65.7
Aver	12	—		263	428	1668	3.9	14	17	299	141	2167	7.2	19	25	—	57.6

TEAM	1D	PENY	PNT	FGM/A	RTNY	RTNTD	OFFY/DEFY	NETY	NETTO	NP	PNP	DELP	PW	DELW	PRT	DR	YPD	DEL
Eastern Division																		
Phi	203-188	848-1017	42.4-**38.4**	4/20-2/10	**1003**-586	4-2	3760-3769	-9	3	66	11	55	7.7	0.4	4.9/ 4.7	162-171	23.2-22.0	1.2
Pit	176-**170**	**527**-622	41.1-42.5	6/14-5/7	980-617	**6**-4	3358-3488	-130	-3	-19	-23	4	5.5	**2.5**	3.1/ 5.1	159-160	21.1-21.8	-0.7
Bos	117-219	855-1030	40.6-41.8	3/4-3/11	714-1149	3-**1**	2719-4064	-1345	10	-88	-72	-16	3.8	0.7	2.5/ 3.1	165-168	16.5-24.2	-7.7
Was	242-196	860-745	40.3-40.8	4/7-8/17	617-940	2-5	4679-4033	646	-10	-72	-14	-86	4.2	-0.2	**6.7**/ 6.2	167-**152**	28.0-26.5	1.5
NYG	149-190	945-861	42.3-41.8	3/6-8/17	806-1069	2-4	3201-3908	-707	-3	-119	-71	-48	3.0	-0.0	3.4/ 3.6	**179**-163	17.9-24.0	-6.1
Western Division																		
ChiC	241-201	688-852	40.8-41.2	7/10-5/14	808-668	3-3	4351-3971	380	4	75	48	27	7.9	1.1	4.8/ 3.7	160-160	27.2-24.8	2.4
ChiB	**263**-206	1020-580	41.5-42.4	0/1-8/15	986-841	3-5	**5053**-3879	**1174**	-11	**122**	54	**68**	**9.1**	-1.0	4.8/ 4.2	169-163	**29.9**-23.8	**6.1**
GB	206-193	1019-759	**43.6**-43.5	**13/29**-5/11	991-**776**	2-1	3873-**3396**	477	**19**	64	**116**	-52	7.6	-1.1	4.1/**2.1**	169-172	22.9-**19.7**	3.2
LA	206-209	800-761	40.1-41.1	8/17-4/**6**	928-839	6-3	3831-3659	172	0	45	14	31	7.1	-1.1	1.8/ 3.7	171-184	22.4-19.9	2.5
Det	189-220	704-**1039**	43.0-42.2	5/11-5/15	678-1026	2-3	3771-4429	-658	-9	-74	-91	17	4.2	-1.1	3.3/ 4.9	167-171	22.6-25.9	-3.3
Aver	199	827	41.6	5/12	851	3	3860								4.1	167	23.1	

Rushing Attempts		Rushing Yards		Rushing Average		Rushing TDs		Rushing Rank		Passing Yards		Passing Average	
S.Van Buren-Phi	217	S.Van Buren-Phi	1008	B.Ward-LA	7.40	S.Van Buren-Phi	13	S.Van Buren-Phi	1138	S.Baugh-Was	2938	S.Luckman-ChiB	8.40
J.Clement-Pit	129	J.Clement-Pit	670	J.Clement-Pit	5.19	S.Lach-Pit	8	J.Clement-Pit	710	S.Luckman-ChiB	2712	T.Thompson-Phi	8.36
S.Lach-Pit	120	T.Canadeo-GB	464	J.Osmanski-ChiB	5.13	P.Harder-ChiC	7	B.Ward-LA	494	P.Christman-ChiC	2191	S.Baugh-Was	8.30
J.Sanchez-GB	115	B.Ward-LA	444	T.Harmon-LA	5.10	E.Angsman-ChiC	7	T.Canadeo-GB	484	T.Thompson-Phi	1680	J.Clement-Pit	8.16
P.Harder-ChiC	113	J.Sanchez-GB	439	C.Trippi-ChiC	4.83			E.Angsman-ChiC	482	J.Jacobs-GB	1615	C.LeForce-Det	7.91

Completion Percent		TD Passes		TD Percent		INT Percent		Passer Rating		Passing Rank		Receptions	
S.Baugh-Was	59.3	S.Baugh-Was	25	T.Thompson-Phi	8.0	S.Baugh-Was	4.2	S.Baugh-Was	92.0	S.Baugh-Was	994	J.Keane-ChiB	64
S.Luckman-ChiB	54.5	S.Luckman-ChiB	24	S.Luckman-ChiB	7.4	R.Zimmerman-Det	6.5	T.Thompson-Phi	76.3	T.Thompson-Phi	320	J.Niles-Was	47
C.LeForce-Det	53.7	P.Christman-ChiC	17	C.LeForce-Det	7.4	J.Jacobs-GB	7.0	S.Luckman-ChiB	67.7	P.Christman-ChiC	301	K.Kavanaugh-ChiB	43
T.Thompson-Phi	52.7	T.Thompson-Phi	16	P.Governali-NYG	7.1	P.Christman-ChiC	7.3	C.LeForce-Det	65.0	S.Luckman-ChiB	236	N.Luhn-GB	42
P.Christman-ChiC	45.8	J.Jacobs-GB	16	S.Baugh-Was	7.1	J.Clement-Pit	7.3	J.Jacobs-GB	59.8	J.Jacobs-GB	208	B.Dewell-ChiC	42

Receiving Yards		Receiving Average		Receiving TDs		Receiving Rank		Combined Net Yards		Total TDs		Total Points	
M.Kutner-ChiC	944	D.Currivan-Bos	32.58	K.Kavanaugh-ChiB	13	M.Kutner-ChiC	507	E.Saenz-Was	1846	S.Van Buren-Phi	14	P.Harder-ChiC	102
J.Keane-ChiB	910	K.Kavanaugh-ChiB	25.56	J.Keane-ChiB	10	J.Keane-ChiB	505	S.Van Buren-Phi	1465	K.Kavanaugh-ChiB	13	D.Poillon-Was	85
K.Kavanaugh-ChiB	818	M.Kutner-ChiC	21.95	D.Currivan-Bos	9	K.Kavanaugh-ChiB	474	B.Dudley-Det	1322	B.Dudley-Det	11	S.Van Buren-Phi	84
D.Currivan-Bos	782	H.Taylor-Was	19.65			D.Currivan-Bos	436	F.Seno-Bos	1300	J.Keane-ChiB	10	K.Kavanaugh-ChiB	78
N.Luhn-GB	696	E.Saenz-Was	17.59			N.Luhn-GB	383	C.Trippi-ChiC	1162	D.Currivan-Bos	10	B.Dudley-Det	66

Punt Average		Field Goals		Field Goal Percent		Kickoff Returns		Kickoff Return Average		Punt Returns		Punt Return Average	
S.Baugh-Was	43.7	B.Ward-LA	7	P.Harder-ChiC	70.0	E.Saenz-Was	29	S.Van Buren-Phi	29.4	W.Slater-Pit	28	F.Seno-Bos	17.8
J.Muha-Phi	43.5	P.Harder-ChiC	7	D.Poillon-Was	66.7	F.Seno-Bos	27	E.Saenz-Was	27.5	F.Reagan-NYG	27	W.Slater-Pit	15.5
J.Jacobs-GB	43.5	W.Cuff-GB	7	T.Fritsch-GB	46.2	W.Slater-Pit	22	B.Dudley-Det	23.9	T.Harmon-LA	27	T.Harmon-LA	14.5
F.Reagan-NYG	42.8	J.Glamp-Pit	6	R.Zimmerman-Det	45.5			F.Seno-Bos	23.6	E.Saenz-Was	24	G.McAfee-ChiB	14.5
		T.Fritsch-GB	6					W.Slater-Pit	21.8	B.Pritchard-Phi	24	E.Saenz-Was	12.8

Punt/Kick Return Yards		Punt/Kick Return TDs		Interceptions		Interception Return Yards		Interception Return TDs		Sacks		Overall Rank	
E.Saenz-Was	1105	E.Saenz-Was	2	F.Seno-Bos	10	F.Reagan-NYG	203	T.Compagno-Pit	2	Not kept		S.Van Buren-Phi	1370
W.Slater-Pit	915			F.Reagan-NYG	10	T.Compagno-Pit	163					S.Baugh-Was	1061
F.Seno-Bos	849			B.Forte-GB	9	B.Forte-GB	140					E.Saenz-Was	1032
T.Harmon-LA	600			T.Harmon-LA	8	T.Harmon-LA	136					B.Dudley-Det	927
B.Dudley-Det	541			R.Cochran-ChiC	8	R.Cochran-ChiC	122					J.Clement-Pit	899

CARDINALS—YES, CARDINALS—ARE CHAMPIONS

Since the adoption of a two-division alignment in 1933, two teams had dominated the East. Between them, the Giants and the Redskins had accounted for every division title for 14 seasons. In 1947 the old order was upended, and perennial cellar dwellers staked their claim to the top of the standings.

Hopes weren't high at the start of the season in Pittsburgh. The Steelers were forced to trade their best player during the offseason. Bill Dudley was the reigning MVP, but he didn't get along with head coach Jock Sutherland, so the Steelers traded him to Detroit. Pittsburgh's fortunes actually improved. Tailback Johnny Clement emerged as a dangerous weapon, leading the team in passing and rushing. After a slow start, the Steelers rallied to finish 8–4, the best season they had yet enjoyed.

For a couple of seasons, the Eagles had been assembling the pieces of a pretty good team, and in 1947 it all came together. Steve Van Buren went over the 1,000-yard mark and led the league in rushing. The addition of rookie end Pete Pihos gave veteran passer Tommy Thompson a star receiver, and gave the Eagles offense a new dimension. Pittsburgh and Philadelphia split a pair of regular-season games and finished with identical records, forcing a divisional playoff game.

Cardinals owner Charlie Bidwell died in April, but not before opening his wallet to assemble what everyone was calling "the Dream Backfield." Since 1939 running back Marshall Goldberg had been the club's only star, but Bidwell added quarterback Paul Christman in 1945, fullback Pat Harder in 1946, and much-heralded University of Georgia halfback Charley Trippi in 1947. All four had been college All-Americans, and along with halfback Elmer Angsman, the Cards had an offense that seemed unstoppable. Head coach Jimmy Conzleman spread the ball around to keep defenses from finding a way to slow the Cardinals. They scored 45 points in their opening game and were 7–1 by mid-November. In their final regular season game, the Cards defeated the rival Bears, 30–21, to win their first division title. The Cardinals beat the Eagles for their first, and counting, only championship game victory.

1947 AAFC

TEAM	W-L-T	PCT	POST	PTS	RA	RY	RY/A	RTD	FL	PA	PC	GPY	GPY/A	PTD	PI	PSY	PRAT
Eastern Division																	
NYY	11-2-1	.846	L	378-239	534-371	2930-1237	5.5-3.3	27-13	17-12	216-304	111-144	1795-1910	8.3-6.3	16-17	18-17	—	69.5-63.1
Buf	8-4-2	.667	—	320-288	496-507	2217-2218	4.5-4.4	18-22	17-14	267-260	129-133	1891-1929	7.1-7.4	24-14	23-18	—	65.9-64.7
Bkn	3-10-1	.231	—	181-340	495-514	1936-2516	3.9-4.9	21-16	13-20	232-265	92-124	1060-2130	4.6-8.0	4-21	17-16	—	29.4-75.8
Bal	2-11-1	.154	—	167-377	417-571	1161-2665	2.8-4.7	7-29	23-25	352-239	177-124	2337-1791	6.6-7.5	13-17	24-14	—	55.6-75.8
Western Division																	
Cle	12-1-1	.923	L*	410-185	479-503	2557-2181	5.3-4.3	24-12	16-19	296-303	174-129	2990-1707	10.1-5.6	26-11	12-32	—	105.5-33.6
SF	8-4-2	.667	—	327-264	587-405	2767-1631	4.7-4.0	22-10	18-21	297-332	147-177	1993-2502	6.7-7.5	22-23	19-24	—	69.3-70.9
LAD	7-7	.500	—	328-256	487-461	1780-1668	3.7-3.6	17-9	14-13	300-310	141-157	2127-2376	7.1-7.7	19-24	25-24	—	57.2-69.8
ChiR	1-13	.071	—	263-425	401-564	1520-2752	3.8-4.9	9-34	26-20	341-288	157-140	2358-2206	6.9-7.7	23-20	26-19	—	60.0-70.2
Aver	14	—	—	297	487	2109	4.3	18	18	288	141	2069	7.2	18	21	—	64.5

TEAM	1D	PENY	PNT	FGM/A	RTNY	RTNTD	OFF/DEFY	NETY	NETTO	NP	PNP	DELP	PW	DELW	PRT	DR	YPD	DEL
Eastern Division																		
NYY	187-140	522-382	40.0-41.4	7/8-7/15	831-710	8-2	4725-3147	1578	-6	139	108	31	10.5	1.0	5.3/4.3	169-163	28.0-19.3	8.7
Buf	175-182	390-456	37.0-42.8	2/4-4/10	949-639	4-3	4108-4147	-39	-8	32	-35	67	7.8	1.2	4.1/4.8	159-164	25.8-25.3	0.5
Bkn	138-178	374-261	42.8-40.0	3/20-12/18	582-963	0-7	2996-4646	-1650	6	-159	-114	-45	3.0	0.5	1.4/6.1	167-173	17.9-26.9	-8.9
Bal	161-183	360-488	36.2-40.0	4/10-3/12	759-1044	2-7	3498-4456	-958	-8	-210	-112	-98	1.8	0.8	3.9/5.4	175-171	20.0-26.1	-6.1
Western Division																		
Cle	214-188	650-385	43.6-43.0	8/20-4/11	977-714	23	5547-3888	1659	-5	225	230		12.6	-0.1	9.2/1.2	159-170	34.9-22.9	12.0
SF	218-178	472-416	43.5-37.1	4/12-4/10	906-680	2-3	4760-4133	627	8	63	84	-21	8.6	0.4	4.6/5.0	167-160	28.5-25.8	2.7
LAD	161-160	478-507	45.0-40.9	15/24-6/13	928-789	4-2	3907-4044	-137	-2	72	-19	91	8.8	-1.8	4.0/5.0	176-176	22.2-23.0	-0.8
ChiR	155-200	264-610	39.1-39.7	4/9-7/18	689-1082	4-4	3878-4958	-1080	-13	-162	-142	-20	2.9	-1.9	4.2/5.4	183-178	21.2-27.9	-6.7
Aver	176	439	40.7	6/13	828	4	4177	—	—	—	—	—	—	—	4.6	169	24.7	—

Rushing Attempts	Rushing Yards	Rushing Average	Rushing TDs	Rushing Rank	Passing Yards	Passing Average
S.Sanders-NYY 231	S.Sanders-NYY 1432	B.Steuber-SF 6.34	S.Sanders-NYY 18	S.Sanders-NYY 1612	O.Graham-Cle 2753	O.Graham-Cle 10.23
M.Colmer-Bkn 152	B.Steuber-SF 906	C.Mutryn-Buf 6.20	C.Mutryn-Buf 9	M.Motley-Cle 969	B.Schwenk-Bal 2236	S.Sanders-NYY 8.43
Hoernschemeyer-Bkn 147	M.Motley-Cle 889	S.Sanders-NYY 6.20	M.Colmer-Bkn 9	C.Mutryn-Buf 958	G.Ratterman-Buf 1840	C.O'Rourke-LAD 8.14
M.Motley-Cle 146	C.Mutryn-Buf 868	R.Ramsey-ChiR 6.19		B.Steuber-SF 956	F.Albert-SF 1692	G.Ratterman-Buf 7.54
N.Standlee-SF 145	B.Young-NYY 712	B.Young-NYY 6.14		Hoernschemeyer-Bkn 752	S.Vacanti-ChiR 1571	F.Albert-SF 6.99

Completion Percent	TD Passes	TD Percent	INT Percent	Passer Rating	Passing Rank	Receptions
O.Graham-Cle 60.6	O.Graham-Cle 25	O.Graham-Cle 9.3	O.Graham-Cle 4.1	O.Graham-Cle 109.2	O.Graham-Cle 1062	M.Speedie-Cle 67
S.Sanders-NYY 54.4	G.Ratterman-Buf 22	G.Ratterman-Buf 9.0	B.Schwenk-Bal 6.1	F.Albert-SF 74.3	B.Schwenk-Bal 383	D.Lavelli-Cle 49
F.Albert-SF 52.9	F.Albert-SF 18	S.Sanders-NYY 8.2	F.Albert-SF 6.2	G.Ratterman-Buf 71.8	F.Albert-SF 336	A.Beals-SF 47
B.Schwenk-Bal 51.4	S.Vacanti-ChiR 16	F.Albert-SF 7.4	G.Dobbs-LAD 6.4	S.Sanders-NYY 70.2	G.Ratterman-Buf 230	L.Davis-Bal 46
G.Ratterman-Buf 50.8	S.Sanders-NYY 14	C.O'Rourke-LAD 7.3	S.Vacanti-ChiR 7.1	C.O'Rourke-LAD 64.6	S.Vacanti-ChiR 226	B.Hein-Bal 39

Receiving Yards	Receiving Average	Receiving TDs	Receiving Rank	Combined Net Yards	Total TDs	Total Points
M.Speedie-Cle 1146	R.Ramsey-ChiR 21.94	A.Beals-SF 10	M.Speedie-Cle 603	S.Sanders-NYY 2265	S.Sanders-NYY 19	S.Sanders-NYY 114
D.Lavelli-Cle 799	B.Hein-Bal 18.00	D.Lavelli-Cle 9	D.Lavelli-Cle 445	C.Mutryn-Buf 1933	C.Mutryn-Buf 12	B.Agajanian-LAD 84
R.Ramsey-ChiR 768	M.Speedie-Cle 17.10	R.Ramsey-ChiR 8	R.Ramsey-ChiR 424	R.Ramsey-ChiR 1804	J.Kimbrough-LAD 11	C.Mutryn-Buf 73
B.Hein-Bal 702	D.Lavelli-Cle 16.31	B.Hein-Bal 7	B.Hein-Bal 386	B.Hein-Bal 1621		H.Johnson-NYY 70
A.Beals-SF 655	A.Beals-SF 13.94	A.Baldwin-SF 7	A.Beals-SF 378	B.Young-NYY 1474		J.Kimbrough-LAD 66

Punt Average	Field Goals	Field Goal Percent	Kickoff Returns	Kickoff Return Average	Punt Returns	Punt Return Average
B.Reinhard-LAD 45.7	B.Agajanian-LAD 15	H.Johnson-NYY 87.5	S.Sanders-NYY 22	C.Mutryn-Buf 32.9	G.Dobbs-LAD 19	C.Fenenbock-LAD 12.4
M.Colmer-Bkn 44.7	H.Johnson-NYY 7	B.Agajanian-LAD 62.5	C.Mutryn-Buf 21	S.Sanders-NYY 27.0	C.Fenenbock-LAD 17	G.Dobbs-LAD 11.3
H.Gillom-Cle 44.6	L.Groza-Cle 7	J.Rokisky-ChiR 50.0	M.Gafford-Bkn 21	M.Gafford-Bkn 26.9	D.Jones-Bkn 14	D.Jones-Bkn 11.2
G.Dobbs-LAD 44.3	J.Vetrano-SF 4	A.Lio-Bal 37.5	B.Hein-Bal 18	B.Hein-Bal 25.9	C.Mutryn-Buf 13	
F.Albert-SF 44.0	J.Rokisky-ChiR 4	L.Groza-Cle 36.8	C.Fenenbock-LAD 18	R.Ramsey-ChiR 25.4	B.Hein-Bal 13	

Punt/Kick Return Yards	Punt/Kick Return TDs	Interceptions	Interception Return Yards	Interception Return TDs	Sacks	Overall Rank
C.Mutryn-Buf 878	B.Young-NYY 2	B.Kellagher-ChiR 6	N.Mathews-SF 149	B.Schroeder-ChiR 2	Not kept	S.Sanders-NYY 2185
S.Sanders-NYY 757	B.Alford-NYY 2	L.Eshmont-SF 6	B.Schroeder-ChiR 148			C.Mutryn-Buf 1570
M.Gafford-Bkn 751		T.Colella-Cle 6	T.Colella-Cle 130			O.Graham-Cle 1210
B.Hein-Bal 702			W.Heap-LAD 107			B.Steuber-SF 1198
C.Fenenbock-LAD 662			B.Bass-ChiR 104			M.Motley-Cle 1191

PLENTY OF POINTS TO GO AROUND

One thing could be said for the AAFC: the games were exciting. Wide-open offenses allowed players to set statistical marks that eclipsed their NFL brethren. Los Angeles Dons kicker Ben Agaijanian booted 15 field goals. Spec Sanders rushed for 1,432 yards—424 more than the NFL record—and 18 touchdowns. Otto Graham was redefining the quarterback position with Cleveland's dynamic passing offense. San Francisco's Frankie Albert was inventing the concept of a bootlegging quarterback.

But for all of the highlights on the field, the AAFC was struggling with the economic realities of competing against the NFL for the attention of pro football fans. The Miami Seahawks had folded at the end of the 1946 season, leaving an ocean of red ink for the rest of the league to handle. A new franchise in Baltimore took their place, but the Colts inherited Miami's mediocre roster.

The Rockets had a tough time getting off the ground in Chicago. Playing in the same city as the Cardinals (the 1947 NFL champs) and the Bears (winners of four championships in eight years), the Rockets couldn't draw fans. Things were so bad that AAFC commissioner Jim Crowley stepped down to take over the Rockets. Their offense was stocked with players who had been college All-Americans, but their porous defense made that irrelevant by giving up 30 points per game.

The AAFC reached its high-water mark in attendance at 1.8 million. Los Angeles became the only team in AAFC history besides Cleveland to draw 300,000. Meanwhile, the 1947 combined attendance of Chicago and Brooklyn barely reached 200,000. The Yankees repeated as Eastern Division champions, and once again they were the only team in the division with a winning record. Sanders had the top performance in a season of high-octane offense: a 250-yard performance against Chicago in late October.

With bruising fullback Marion Motley running the ball and Graham throwing to ends Mac Speedie and Dante Lavelli, the Browns scored more points than any other team. The addition rookie linebacker Tony Adamle made Cleveland's already formidable defense even stronger. The Browns rolled through the schedule, suffering just one loss and winning their second straight AAFC championship.

1948 NFL

TEAM	W-L-T	PCT	POST	PTS	RA	RY	RY/A	RTD	FL	PA	PC	GPY	GPY/A	PTD	PI	PSY	PRAT
Eastern Division																	
Phi	9-2-1	.818	L*	376-156	528-**376**	2378-**1209**	4.5-**3.2**	21-**5**	18-16	301-338	159-139	2241-1951	7.4-5.8	27-14	16-23	—	**84.9**-45.9
Was	7-5	.583	—	291-287	434-482	1603-1958	3.7-4.1	11-17	17-18	360-289	**202**-135	**2861**-1953	**7.9**-6.8	24-20	26-24	—	74.1-57.6
NYG	4-8	.333	—	297-388	362-481	1219-2168	3.4-4.5	15-26	20-11	363-311	191-157	2504-2406	6.9-7.7	24-25	16-**39**	—	78.3-63.6
Pit	4-8	.333	—	200-243	510-434	1934-1648	3.8-3.8	17-7	17-18	266-279	108-149	1529-1987	5.7-7.1	8-18	29-13	—	30.3-78.4
Bos	3-9	.250	—	174-372	365-511	1170-2320	3.2-4.5	4-19	20-**24**	261-356	101-161	1308-2463	5.0-6.9	13-27	34-18	—	32.2-72.8
Western Division																	
ChiC	**11**-1	**.917**	L	**395**-226	531-408	**2560**-1516	**4.8**-3.7	**25**-8	**16-24**	285-336	134-159	2134-2520	7.5-7.5	22-22	**12**-23	—	80.7-66.1
ChiB	10-2	.833	—	375-**151**	**557**-384	2452-1254	4.4-3.3	**25**-8	21-16	287-336	142-139	1894-1646	6.6-**4.9**	22-**12**	19-30	—	68.8-**31.7**
LA	6-5-1	.545	—	327-269	427-441	1743-1570	4.1-3.6	15-13	17-**24**	**395**-309	201-164	2748-2143	7.0-6.9	**28**-20	25-19	—	70.7-71.2
GB	3-9	.250	—	154-290	446-537	1759-2153	3.9-4.0	11-21	19-15	274-**260**	109-**134**	1364-**1626**	5.0-6.3	8-13	29-29	—	26.1-48.2
Det	2-10	.167	—	200-407	389-495	1360-2382	3.5-4.8	7-27	20-19	324-302	151-161	2288-2176	7.1-7.2	20-25	26-14	—	57.5-84.8
Aver	12	—	—	279	455	1818	4.0	15	19	312	150	2087	6.7	20	23	—	60.0

TEAM	1D	PENY	PNT	FGM/A	RTNY	RTNTD	OFFY/DEFY	NETY	NETTO	NP	PNP	DELP	PW	DELW	PRT	DR	YPD	DEL
Eastern Division																		
Phi	241-**158**	773-860	**45.9-38.8**	**8**/17-**1/5**	782-668	2-3	4651-3169	**1482**	5	220	144	76	11.5	-2.0	6.0/ 3.1	167-175	27.9-18.1	9.7
Was	236-233	1100-771	42.2-43.8	5/7-3/10	852-772	5-3	4479-3933	546	-1	4	42	-38	6.1	0.9	5.4/ 3.7	157-**153**	**28.5**-25.7	2.8
NYG	212-227	815-880	38.6-39.5	1/8-4/8	773-1028	3-3	3847-4673	-826	14	-91	-13	-78	3.7	0.3	5.6/ 2.9	182-176	21.1-26.6	-5.4
Pit	210-188	616-927	39.0-42.8	4/10-7/16	673-752	2-7	3478-3707	-229	-15	-43	-79	36	4.9	-0.9	1.1/ 5.7	158-158	22.0-23.5	-1.4
Bos	121-244	813-**929**	42.0-40.2	3/7-6/11	881-976	**7**-5	2522-4858	-2336	-12	-198	-243	45	1.1	**1.9**	-0.4/ 5.4	**185**-189	13.6-25.7	-12.1
Western Division																		
ChiC	233-190	749-743	39.7-39.2	**8/21**-2/11	1019-647	6-2	**4705**-4058	647	**19**	169	130	39	10.2	0.8	**6.4**/ 5.1	174-180	27.0-22.5	4.5
ChiB	**242**-174	1066-633	42.8-39.5	2/7-4/8	**1169-638**	6-**0**	4405-**2931**	1474	6	**224**	**147**	**77**	**11.6**	-1.6	4.4/**1.2**	168-182	26.2-**16.1**	**10.1**
LA	239-204	859-719	41.8-41.0	6/11-6/11	737-756	2-3	4576-3794	782	1	58	69	-11	7.4	-1.0	4.8/ 4.8	179-174	25.6-21.8	3.8
GB	172-222	941-771	40.3-43.3	6/16-6/14	932-930	1-5	3135-3848	-713	-4	-136	-75	-61	2.6	0.4	0.5/ 1.7	179-174	17.5-22.1	-4.6
Det	187-253	**395**-894	35.4-40.5	2/6-6/16	380-1031	1-4	3735-4562	-827	-13	-207	-121	-86	0.8	1.2	4.1/ 5.9	173-160	21.6-28.5	-6.9
Aver	209	813	40.7	5/11	820	4	3953	—	—	—	—	—	—	—	4.0	172	23.0	—

Rushing Attempts	Rushing Yards	Rushing Average	Rushing TDs	Rushing Rank	Passing Yards	Passing Average
S.Van Buren-Phi......201	S.Van Buren-Phi......945	G.Papach-Pit..........5.40	S.Van Buren-Phi........10	S.Van Buren-Phi....1045	S.Baugh-Was.........2599	C.LeForce-Det........9.03
C.Wilson-Det..........157	C.Trippi-ChiC..........690	C.Trippi-ChiC..........5.39	J.Shipkey-Pit..............8	C.Trippi-ChiC..........750	C.Conerly-NYG......2175	S.Baugh-Was..........8.25
G.Roberts-NYG.......145	E.Angsman-ChiC.....638	F.Enke-Det.............4.93	E.Angsman-ChiC.........8	E.Angsman-ChiC.....718	T.Thompson-Phi....1965	R.Mallouf-ChiC.......8.11
E.Angsman-ChiC.....131	C.Wilson-Det..........612	E.Angsman-ChiC....4.87	C.Trippi-ChiC..............6	C.Wilson-Det..........632	J.Hardy-LA.............1390	T.Thompson-Phi.....7.99
C.Trippi-ChiC..........128	T.Canadeo-GB........589	T.Canadeo-GB........4.79	P.Harder-ChiC.............6	T.Canadeo-GB........629	P.Walker-LA..........1354	P.Walker-LA...........7.52

Completion Percent	TD Passes	TD Percent	INT Percent	Passer Rating	Passing Rank	Receptions
S.Baugh-Was..........58.7	T.Thompson-Phi........25	T.Thompson-Phi.....10.2	J.Hardy-LA...............3.3	T.Thompson-Phi.....98.4	C.Conerly-NYG........678	T.Fears-LA................51
T.Thompson-Phi.....57.3	C.Conerly-NYG..........22	R.Mallouf-ChiC.........9.1	P.Christman-ChiC.....3.5	R.Mallouf-ChiC.......91.2	T.Thompson-Phi......668	P.Pihos-Phi...............46
S.Luckman-ChiB.....54.6	S.Baugh-Was............22	C.LeForce-Det..........8.9	R.Mallouf-ChiC.........4.2	C.Conerly-NYG.......84.0	S.Baugh-Was...........490	M.Kutner-ChiC...........41
C.Conerly-NYG.......54.2	P.Walker-LA...............14	S.Luckman-ChiB.......8.0	C.Conerly-NYG.........4.3	J.Hardy-LA.............82.1	J.Hardy-LA...............485	B.Swiacki-NYG..........39
J.Hardy-LA.............53.1	J.Hardy-LA.................14	P.Walker-LA.............7.8	T.Thompson-Phi.......4.5	S.Baugh-Was.........78.3	R.Mallouf-ChiC........405	V.Jansante-Pit...........39

Receiving Yards	Receiving Average	Receiving TDs	Receiving Rank	Combined Net Yards	Total TDs	Total Points
M.Kutner-ChiC.........943	J.Greene-Det........23.80	M.Kutner-ChiC...........14	M.Kutner-ChiC.........542	C.Trippi-ChiC.........1485	M.Kutner-ChiC...........15	P.Harder-ChiC..........110
P.Pihos-Phi..............766	M.Kutner-ChiC......23.00	P.Pihos-Phi................11	P.Pihos-Phi.............438	S.Van Buren-Phi....1365	P.Pihos-Phi................11	M.Kutner-ChiC...........90
T.Fears-LA...............698	H.Crisler-Was.......18.15	B.Swiacki-NYG..........10	T.Fears-LA...............369	D.Sandifer-Was......1340	S.Van Buren-Phi........10	C.Patton-Phi.............74
V.Jansante-Pit..........623	B.Mann-Det..........16.97	R.Hickey-LA.................7	H.Crisler-Was..........330	B.Pritchard-Phi......1318	C.Trippi-ChiC.............10	D.Poillon-Was............66
H.Crisler-Was..........599	R.Hickey-LA.........16.97	J.Ferrante-Phi..............7	V.Jansante-Pit.........327	F.Gehrke-LA..........1129	B.Swiacki-NYG..........10	P.Pihos-Phi...............66

Punt Average	Field Goals	Field Goal Percent	Kickoff Returns	Kickoff Return Average	Punt Returns	Punt Return Average
J.Muha-Phi.............47.3	C.Patton-Phi................8	D.Poillon-Was.........71.4	D.Sandifer-Was..........26	F.Minini-ChiB...........30.8	G.McAfee-ChiB..........30	J.Davis-ChiC...........20.9
G.Gulyanics-ChiB...44.2	P.Harder-ChiC..............7	C.Patton-Phi...........66.7	B.Paschal-Bos...........24	J.Davis-ChiC...........29.1	B.Pritchard-Phi..........24	L.Horvath-LA..........15.6
R.Zimmerman-Bos.....43.4	P.Walker-LA.................6	P.Walker-LA...........54.5	J.Scott-NYG...............20	J.Scott-NYG............28.5	D.Sandifer-Was..........20	G.McAfee-ChiB.......13.9
P.Walker-LA............42.6	T.Fritsch-GB.................6	P.Harder-ChiC.........41.2	F.Gehrke-LA...............17	F.Gehrke-LA............27.3	F.Gehrke-LA...............19	P.McHugh-Phi.........12.2
D.Poillon-Was.........42.2	D.Poillon-Was..............5	J.Glamp-Pit............40.0	C.Trippi-ChiC.............16	E.Smith-GB.............23.9		D.Sandifer-Was.......11.8

Punt/Kick Return Yards	Punt/Kick Return TDs	Interceptions	Interception Return Yards	Interception Return TDs	Sacks	Overall Rank
D.Sandifer-Was........830	C.Trippi-ChiC...............2	D.Sandifer-Was.........13	D.Sandifer-Was........258	D.Sandifer-Was............2	Not kept	C.Trippi-ChiC.........1230
J.Davis-ChiC............771	J.Davis-ChiC................2	F.Reagan-NYG...........9	J.Golding-Bos..........205	J.Golding-Bos.............2		S.Van Buren-Phi....1197
F.Gehrke-LA............681		J.Lujack-ChiB..............8	T.Compagno-Pit.......179	B.Blackburn-ChiC........2		B.Pritchard-Phi........979
J.Scott-NYG.............594			F.Reagan-NYG........145			C.Conerly-NYG........900
B.Paschal-Bos.........577			G.Cheverko-NYG.....144			G.McAfee-ChiB........878

A Survivor's League

The sudden death of Jock Sutherland in April rocked the Pittsburgh Steelers. Doctors discovered a brain tumor after the coach collapsed during a scouting trip. He died a few days later. Sutherland's absence and a season-ending injury to tailback Johnny Clement sent the Steelers into a tailspin. A year after finishing 8–4 and playing in a divisional playoff game, Pittsburgh fell to 4–8.

Death also visited the Chicago Cardinals. Spirits were high when the Cards opened their title defense with a win against the Eagles, but tackle Stan Mauldin collapsed after the game and died in the locker room. Coroners later determined that the 27-year-old had died of a heart attack. The distracted Cards lost their next game to the Chicago Bears, but regrouped after that and played like one of the league's best teams. Going into the final weekend of the season, the Bears and Cardinals were tied for the Western Division lead with identical 10–1 records. The two Chicago teams met in the season finale, with the Bears heavily favored because of their league-leading defense. With a 21–10 fourth-quarter lead, that defense crumbled. The Cardinals scored 2 late touchdowns to repeat as division champions.

Washington quarterback Sammy Baugh, 34, was still the league's best passer and the Redskins looked like contenders early in the season. It didn't take long for the rest of the league to figure out that Washington's pass defense was porous. Opponents threw so often that rookie Dan Sandifer bagged a record 13 interceptions. Washington gave up more than 40 points in three straight games to fade from contention.

After narrowly losing the NFL Championship Game in 1947, the Eagles remained the strongest team in the East. Steve Van Buren led the league in rushing, but it was head coach Greasy Neale's defense that made the biggest difference. To counter the growing emergence of the passing game, Neale used his linebackers to slow opposing receivers in what would come to be known as the "Eagles Defense." The innovation—and a Philadelphia snowstorm—helped lead the Eagles to their first NFL championship.

1948 AAFC

TEAM	W-L-T	PCT	POST	PTS	RA	RY	RY/A	RTD	FL	PA	PC	GPY	GPY/A	PTD	PI	PSY	PRAT
Eastern Division																	
Buf	7-7	.500	DL	360-358	539-463	2738-1983	5.1-4.3	29-25	13-**26**	360-414	177-211	2683-2829	7.5-6.8	17-23	26-14	—	59.8-77.5
Bal	7-7	.500	D	333-327	532-504	2166-2522	4.1-5.0	22-21	21-14	340-364	185-177	**2899**-2438	**8.5**-6.7	19-18	**13**-22	—	85.6-61.8
NYY	6-8	.429	—	265-301	464-467	1977-2015	4.3-4.3	20-18	15-16	316-341	139-160	1966-2767	6.2-8.1	15-19	24-27	—	48.8-60.6
Bkn	2-12	.143	—	253-387	409-585	1787-3146	4.4-5.4	12-30	15-17	**410**-296	188-160	2524-**1985**	6.2-6.7	20-23	32-25	—	49.7-65.8
Western Division																	
Cle	**14-0**	**1.000**	L*	389-**190**	544-**436**	2557-**1519**	4.7-**3.5**	25-**10**	**11**-16	344-354	178-159	2809-2097	8.2-**5.9**	26-**14**	16-24	—	85.0-**49.1**
SF	12-2	.857	—	**495**-248	603-468	**3663**-1906	**6.1**-4.1	**35**-11	21-20	288-374	162-184	2104-2615	7.3-7.0	**30**-23	14-**32**	—	**93.9**-57.1
LAD	7-7	.500	—	258-305	400-514	1554-2456	3.9-4.8	11-14	16-16	406-344	195-164	2497-2473	6.2-7.2	21-24	24-24	—	60.3-66.0
ChiR	1-13	.071	—	202-439	484-538	1719-2614	3.6-4.9	8-33	27-14	341-318	146-**155**	2290-2568	6.7-8.1	19-23	38-19	—	44.7-75.6
Aver	14	—	—	319	497	2270	4.6	20	17	351	171	2472	7.0	21	23		64.2

TEAM	TD	PENY	PNT	FGM/A	RTNY	RTNTD	OFFY/DEFY	NETY	NETTO	NP	PNP	DELP	PW	DELW	PRT	DR	YPD	DEL
Eastern Division																		
Buf	223-207	644-616	38.7-43.5	1/3-5/11	851-1067	6-1	5421-4812	609	1	2	55	-53	7.1	-0.1	4.7/ 5.9	**182**-171	29.8-28.1	1.6
Bal	218-224	743-556	38.6-43.4	10/18-2/11	859-526	2-7	5065-4960	105	2	6	17	-11	7.2	-0.2	**7.4/** 4.5	166-176	30.5-28.2	2.3
NYY	178-192	690-733	40.4-41.3	2/7-6/12	976-907	2-4	3943-4782	-839	4	-36	-54	18	6.1	-0.1	3.3/ 5.1	174-174	22.7-27.5	-4.8
Bkn	194-226	**410**-775	42.8-39.8	2/8-7/12	752-1020	4-0	4311-5131	-820	-5	-134	-88	-46	3.7	-1.7	3.1/ 3.7	172-**168**	25.1-30.5	-5.5
Western Division																		
Cle	**243-171**	761-657	35.0-**39.7**	8/**19**-3/8	668-715	1-2	5366-**3616**	**1750**	9	199	198	1	12.0	**2.0**	6.8/**3.3**	162-168	**33.1-21.5**	**11.6**
SF	227-203	794-567	42.6-40.5	5/8-2/5	**1033-433**	4-1	**5767**-4521	1246	**17**	**247**	172	**75**	**13.2**	-1.2	6.2/ 3.8	175-170	33.0-26.6	6.4
LAD	186-209	715-**805**	**47.2**-40.7	5/15-7/12	1025-850	3-2	4051-4929	-878	0	-47	-73	26	5.8	1.2	4.0/ 4.7	173-183	23.4-26.9	-3.5
ChiR	180-217	659-707	44.7-42.3	2/4-3/11	595-1241	1-6	4009-5182	-1173	-32	-237	-226	-11	1.1	-0.1	2.3/ 6.1	177-171	22.6-30.3	-7.7
Aver	206	677	41.4	4/10	845	3	4742	—	—	—	—	—	—	—	4.6	173	27.5	—

Rushing Attempts
S.Sanders-NYY 169
M.Colmer-Bkn 164
M.Motley-Cle 157
B.Mertes-Bal 155
C.Mutryn-Buf 147

Rushing Yards
M.Motley-Cle 964
J.Still-SF 915
C.Mutryn-Buf 823
S.Sanders-NYY 759
L.Tomasetti-Buf........716

Rushing Average
J.Perry-SF 7.30
C.Mutryn-Buf 6.49
M.Motley-Cle 6.14
P.Layden-NYY 6.06
G.Dobbs-LAD 5.92

Rushing TDs
J.Perry-SF 10
C.Mutryn-Buf 10
S.Sanders-NYY 9
F.Albert-SF 8

Rushing Rank
M.Motley-Cle 1014
J.Still-SF 955
C.Mutryn-Buf 923
S.Sanders-NYY 849
L.Tomasetti-Buf........786

Passing Yards
O.Graham-Cle 2713
G.Ratterman-Buf 2577
Y.Tittle-Bal 2522
G.Dobbs-LAD 2403
F.Albert-SF 1990

Passing Average
Y.Tittle-Bal 8.73
J.Freitas-ChiR 8.53
O.Graham-Cle 8.15
P.Layden-NYY 7.77
G.Ratterman-Buf 7.69

Completion Percent
F.Albert-SF 58.3
Y.Tittle-Bal 55.7
O.Graham-Cle 52.0
J.Freitas-ChiR 50.3
G.Ratterman-Buf 50.1

TD Passes
F.Albert-SF 29
O.Graham-Cle 25
G.Dobbs-LAD 21
Y.Tittle-Bal 16
G.Ratterman-Buf 16

TD Percent
F.Albert-SF 11.0
P.Layden-NYY 8.6
J.Freitas-ChiR 8.4
O.Graham-Cle 7.5
G.Dobbs-LAD 5.7

INT Percent
Y.Tittle-Bal 3.1
F.Albert-SF 3.8
O.Graham-Cle 4.5
G.Dobbs-LAD 5.4
S.Sanders-NYY 6.5

Passer Rating
F.Albert-SF 102.9
Y.Tittle-Bal 90.3
O.Graham-Cle 85.6
J.Freitas-ChiR 67.9
G.Dobbs-LAD 67.4

Passing Rank
Y.Tittle-Bal 981
O.Graham-Cle 882
F.Albert-SF 740
G.Dobbs-LAD 507
G.Ratterman-Buf 489

Receptions
M.Speedie-Cle 58
A.Baldwin-Buf 54
F.King-ChiR 50
W.Heap-Bal 50
A.Beals-SF 46

Receiving Yards
W.Heap-Bal 970
A.Baldwin-Buf...........916
M.Speedie-Cle 816
C.Mutryn-Buf 794
L.Davis-Bal 765

Receiving Average
C.Mutryn-Buf 20.36
W.Heap-Bal 19.40
L.Ford-LAD 19.29
L.Davis-Bal 18.66
B.Alford-NYY 18.06

Receiving TDs
A.Beals-SF 14
J.Aguirre-LAD 9
A.Baldwin-Buf 8

Receiving Rank
W.Heap-Bal 515
A.Baldwin-Buf...........498
M.Speedie-Cle 428
C.Mutryn-Buf 422
L.Davis-Bal 418

Combined Net Yards
C.Mutryn-Buf 2288
W.Heap-Bal 2067
J.Still-SF 1807
M.Motley-Cle 1493
M.Colmer-Bkn 1239

Total TDs
C.Mutryn-Buf 16
A.Beals-SF 14
W.Heap-Bal 13
J.Perry-SF 12
J.Still-SF 11

Total Points
C.Mutryn-Buf 96
A.Beals-SF 84
J.Vetrano-SF 83
W.Heap-Bal 78
L.Groza-Cle 75

Punt Average
G.Dobbs-LAD 49.1
F.Albert-SF...............44.8
E.Lewis-ChiR 44.7
M.Colmer-Bkn 42.5
S.Sanders-NYY 40.6

Field Goals
R.Grossman-Bal 10
L.Groza-Cle 8
J.Vetrano-SF 5
B.Agajanian-LAD 5

Field Goal Percent
J.Vetrano-SF 62.5
R.Grossman-Bal 55.6
L.Groza-Cle 42.1
B.Agajanian-LAD 33.3

Kickoff Returns
M.Gafford-Bkn 23
C.Mutryn-Buf 19
B.Pfohl-Bal 17
W.Heap-Bal 16
E.Prokop-ChiR 15

Kickoff Return Average
C.Mutryn-Buf 26.3
M.Gafford-Bkn 24.3
M.Motley-Cle 24.1
W.Heap-Bal 22.3
C.Fenenbock-ChiR 22.2

Punt Returns
C.Lewis-Cle 26
H.Wedemeyer-LAD...23
J.Cason-SF 22
W.Heap-Bal 18
C.Fenenbock-ChiR 17

Punt Return Average
B.Bryant-Buf 21.0
B.Reinhard-LAD 17.3
H.Wedemeyer-LAD..16.0
J.Cason-SF 14.0
W.Heap-Bal 12.8

Punt/Kick Return Yards
M.Gafford-Bkn 689
C.Mutryn-Buf 671
H.Wedemeyer-LAD...608
W.Heap-Bal 587
J.Cason-SF 521

Punt/Kick Return TDs
B.Bryant-Buf 2

Interceptions
Schnellbacher-NYY 11
C.Lewis-Cle 9
R.Ramsey-Bkn 7
E.Carr-SF 7
B.Perina-ChiR.............6

Interception Return Yards
Schnellbacher-NYY 239
E.Carr-SF 144
R.Ramsey-Bkn 124
L.Davis-Bal 110
C.Lewis-Cle 103

Interception Return TDs
Many 1

Sacks
Not kept

Overall Rank
C.Mutryn-Buf 1702
J.Still-SF 1425
W.Heap-Bal 1352
M.Motley-Cle 1247
Y.Tittle-Bal 1178

GIVE TO THE POOR (TEAMS)

With the novelty of the new league wearing off and the NFL rejecting talk of a merger, the AAFC hit hard times. Ownership changes in several cities illustrated the strangling effect of tight finances. The bidding war for veteran players and college prospects was taking its toll on both NFL and AAFC teams, but the younger league was fighting a battle it couldn't win.

Competitive balance was one of the biggest problems. While the Browns once again dominated the league, none of the teams in the Eastern Division managed a winning record. In order to shore up some of the weaker teams, the league asked its stronger clubs to charitably send them any good players they could spare. The Baltimore Colts got 14 men, including former All-Pro linemen Dick Barwegan and Lee Artoe. The biggest catch was rookie Y.A. Tittle, a standout quarterback at LSU. He was Cleveland's first-round draft choice, but with Otto Graham entrenched at quarterback, the Browns were encouraged to share the wealth. Paul Brown reluctantly complied.

Despite a 6–7 record, the rejuvenated Colts had a chance to tie for the Eastern Division title with a win over the Bills in the season finale. Buffalo had rebounded from a rocky start, thanks to a potent offense featuring quarterback George Ratterman and halfback Chet Mutryn. The Colts trounced the Bills, 35–17, forcing a divisional playoff game for the right to face the Cleveland Browns in the championship game.

For the third straight season, the 49ers played bridesmaid to the Browns. Rookie running back Joe Perry scored 12 touchdowns, part of an overpowering rushing attack that was arguably the best in pro football history. San Francisco's offense averaged 262 rushing yards and 35 points per game. Quarterback Frankie Albert also led the league with 29 touchdown passes, but two narrow losses to the Browns kept the Niners stuck in second place. Browns fullback Marion Motley led the league in rushing. The Cleveland defense held 10 opponents to 14 points or less, and after finishing the regular season unbeaten and untied, the Browns trounced the Bills in to win their third AAFC championship.

1949 NFL

TEAM	W-L-T	PCT	POST	PTS	RA	RY	RY/A	RTD	FL	PA	PC	GPY	GPY/A	PTD	PI	PSY	PRAT
Eastern Division																	
Phi	11-1	.917	L*	364-134	632-353	2607-1217	4.1-3.4	25-5	12-14	251-303	130-121	1909-1607	7.6-5.3	18-11	14-29	85-359	77.6-30.0
Pit	6-5-1	.545	—	224-214	535-463	2209-1862	4.1-4.0	20-17	9-9	209-337	81-161	1310-2043	6.3-6.1	10-9	18-22	107-152	40.6-48.9
NYG	6-6	.500	—	287-298	419-465	1404-1664	3.4-3.6	15-20	10-18	322-374	155-193	2157-2460	6.7-6.6	17-16	23-22	233-213	57.9-62.2
Was	4-7-1	.364	—	268-339	407-487	1579-2316	3.9-4.8	14-23	13-13	394-316	197-148	2816-2409	7.1-7.6	22-24	29-18	285-218	61.5-74.5
NYB	1-10-1	.091	—	153-368	353-535	1184-2360	3.4-4.4	10-20	22-14	343-303	172-147	2025-2132	5.9-7.0	10-25	23-14	378-77	50.2-80.1
Western Division																	
LA	8-2-2	.800	L	360-239	445-472	1732-1679	3.9-3.6	19-14	18-18	366-335	192-144	2819-2084	7.7-6.2	23-16	27-30	145-273	68.1-42.4
ChiB	9-3	.750	—	332-218	483-428	1785-1196	3.7-2.8	18-6	18-16	385-320	193-152	3055-2147	7.9-6.7	24-20	30-27	125-168	65.2-55.3
ChiC	6-5-1	.545	—	360-301	467-446	2130-1874	4.6-4.2	21-19	16-21	307-383	138-174	1763-2617	5.7-6.8	21-18	26-33	184-203	51.0-48.2
Det	4-8	.333	—	237-259	397-491	1381-1827	3.5-3.7	9-15	21-17	399-312	178-149	2291-1814	5.7-5.8	18-14	28-32	337-206	49.0-41.5
GB	2-10	.167	—	114-329	503-501	2061-2077	4.1-4.1	8-20	16-15	299-292	91-138	1291-2123	4.3-7.3	5-15	29-20	233-244	11.4-60.3
Aver	12	—	—	270	464	1807	3.9	16	16	328	153	2144	6.5	17	25	211	53.9

TEAM	1D	PENY	PNT	FGM/A	RTNY	RTNTD	OFFY/DEFY	NETY	NETTO	NP	PNP	DELP	PW	DELW	PRT	DR	YPD	DEL
Eastern Division																		
Phi	243-148	729-533	40.8-38.6	9/19-5/8	986-625	5-1	4448-2472	1976	17	230	233	-3	11.8	-0.8	5.2/0.2	162-158	27.5-15.6	11.8
Pit	189-210	460-862	40.9-40.7	2/7-7/14	759-707	1-2	3437-3759	-322	4	10	-11	21	6.3	0.3	2.2/2.8	152-154	22.6-24.4	-1.8
NYG	177-232	800-559	36.9-38.6	8/13-6/12	793-824	6-4	3373-3928	-555	7	-11	-18	7	5.7	0.3	3.0/3.5	169-167	20.0-23.5	-3.6
Was	217-233	675-676	40.4-40.7	4/7-5/15	600-819	1-0	4110-4533	-423	-11	-71	-79	8	4.2	0.3	3.4/4.7	163-166	25.2-27.3	-2.1
NYB	183-238	420-766	41.2-39.7	3/10-7/12	422-1016	1-5	2878-4430	-1552	-17	-215	-197	-18	0.6	0.9	1.8/5.4	165-165	17.4-26.8	-9.4
Western Division																		
LA	245-213	795-676	44.4-44.2	9/17-5/13	983-444	6-2	4415-3549	866	3	121	84	37	9.0	-0.0	4.4/1.7	173-175	25.5-20.3	5.2
ChiB	248-170	901-521	43.3-41.4	8/16-5/7	840-858	2-3	4748-3196	1552	-5	114	109	5	8.9	0.2	4.5/2.8	170-172	27.9-18.6	9.3
ChiC	207-231	590-625	40.9-38.4	8/11-6/14	1032-762	6-4	3747-4296	-549	12	59	2	57	7.5	-1.0	1.9/2.7	181-178	20.7-24.1	-3.4
Det	206-204	662-700	37.9-43.5	5/14-5/15	1213-732	5-6	3350-3462	-112	0	-22	-9	-13	5.4	-1.5	2.0/0.9	170-170	19.7-20.4	-0.7
GB	182-218	722-836	40.2-39.8	6/22-11/26	497-1338	1-7	3119-3999	-880	-10	-215	-113	-102	0.6	1.4	-0.6/3.5	182-182	17.1-22.0	-4.8
Aver	210	675	40.5	6/14	813	3	3763	—	—	—	—	—	—	—	3.0	169	22.3	—

Rushing Attempts	Rushing Yards	Rushing Average	Rushing TDs	Rushing Rank	Passing Yards	Passing Average
S.Van Buren-Phi 263	S.Van Buren-Phi ...1146	B.Pritchard-Phi 6.02	S.Van Buren-Phi 11	S.Van Buren-Phi ...1256	J.Lujack-ChiB 2658	J.Lujack-ChiB 8.52
T.Canadeo-GB 208	T.Canadeo-GB 1052	E.Angsman-ChiC 5.39	G.Roberts-NYG 9	T.Canadeo-GB 1092	J.Wade-LA 2168	T.Thompson-Phi 8.07
D.Hoerner-LA 155	E.Angsman-ChiC 674	T.Canadeo-GB 5.06	P.Harder-ChiC 7	E.Angsman-ChiC 734	C.Conerly-NYG 2138	S.Baugh-Was 7.46
G.Roberts-NYG 152	G.Roberts-NYG 634	C.Trippi-ChiC 4.94		G.Roberts-NYG 724	S.Baugh-Was 1903	J.Wade-LA 7.32
J.Nuzum-Pit 139	J.Nuzum-Pit 611	G.Gulyanics-ChiB 4.43		J.Nuzum-Pit 661	B.Layne-NYB 1796	J.Geri-Pit 7.19

Completion Percent	TD Passes	TD Percent	INT Percent	Passer Rating	Passing Rank	Receptions
S.Baugh-Was 56.9	J.Lujack-ChiB 23	T.Thompson-Phi 7.5	F.Enke-Det 3.5	T.Thompson-Phi 84.4	J.Lujack-ChiB 564	T.Fears-LA 77
T.Thompson-Phi 54.2	S.Baugh-Was 18	J.Lujack-ChiB 7.4	T.Thompson-Phi 5.1	S.Baugh-Was 81.2	T.Thompson-Phi 504	B.Mann-Det 66
J.Wade-LA 52.0	J.Wade-LA 17	P.Christman-ChiC 7.3	S.Baugh-Was 5.5	J.Lujack-ChiB 76.0	S.Baugh-Was 482	B.Chipley-NYB 57
J.Lujack-ChiB 51.9	C.Conerly-NYG 17	S.Baugh-Was 7.1	B.Layne-NYB 6.0	C.Conerly-NYG 64.1	C.Conerly-NYG 354	B.Swiacki-NYG 47
B.Layne-NYB 51.8	T.Thompson-Phi 16	J.Hardy-ChiC 6.7	J.Geri-Pit 6.5	F.Enke-Det 61.7	Van Brocklin-LA 251	J.Keane-ChiB 47

Receiving Yards	Receiving Average	Receiving TDs	Receiving Rank	Combined Net Yards	Total TDs	Total Points
B.Mann-Det 1014	E.Nickel-Pit 24.35	H.Taylor-Was 9	T.Fears-LA 552	C.Trippi-ChiC 1552	G.Roberts-NYG 17	G.Roberts-NYG 102
T.Fears-LA 1013	K.Kavanaugh-ChiB 22.59	K.Kavanaugh-ChiB 9	B.Mann-Det 527	S.Van Buren-Phi 1522	S.Van Buren-Phi 12	P.Harder-ChiC 102
H.Taylor-Was 781	G.Roberts-NYG 20.31	T.Fears-LA 9	H.Taylor-Was 436	G.Roberts-NYG 1361		B.Dudley-Det 81
G.Roberts-NYG 711	B.Shaw-LA 18.45	G.Roberts-NYG 8	G.Roberts-NYG 396	D.Sandifer-Was 1161		J.Wade-LA 76
J.Keane-ChiB 696	T.Cook-GB 17.68	J.Greene-Det 7	J.Keane-ChiB 378	E.Saenz-Was 1076		S.Van Buren-Phi 72

Punt Average	Field Goals	Field Goal Percent	Kickoff Returns	Kickoff Return Average	Punt Returns	Punt Return Average
G.Gulyanics-ChiB 47.2	J.Wade-LA 9	V.Yablonski-ChiC 83.3	D.Sandifer-Was 24	E.Saenz-NYG 31.6	V.Smith-LA 27	R.Cochran-ChiC 20.9
J.Wade-LA 44.4	C.Patton-Phi 9	B.Agajanian-NYG 61.5	E.Saenz-Was 24	W.Dreyer-ChiB 26.0	E.Tunnell-NYG 26	B.Gage-Pit 15.9
M.Boyda-NYB 44.2	B.Agajanian-NYG 8	D.Poillon-Was 57.1	D.Doll-Det 21	D.Doll-Det 25.5	G.McAfee-ChiB 24	V.Smith-LA 15.8
J.Geri-Pit 43.2	B.Agajanian-NYG 7	J.Wade-LA 56.3	R.Cochran-ChiC 20	F.Minini-Pit 24.4	W.Triplett-Det 21	W.Triplett-Det 13.4
R.Cochran-ChiC 42.0	G.Blanda-ChiB 7	C.Patton-Phi 50.0		S.Van Buren-Phi 24.0	F.Reagan-Phi 21	F.Reagan-Phi 12.7

Punt/Kick Return Yards	Punt/Kick Return TDs	Interceptions	Interception Return Yards	Interception Return TDs	Sacks	Overall Rank
R.Cochran-ChiC 724	R.Cochran-ChiC 2	J.Nolan-ChiC 12	D.Doll-Det 301	E.Tunnell-NYG 2	Not kept	S.Van Buren-Phi 1413
D.Sandifer-Was 717		D.Doll-Det 11	E.Tunnell-NYG 251			C.Trippi-ChiC 1086
V.Smith-LA 662		E.Tunnell-NYG 10	B.Smith-Det 218			T.Canadeo-GB 1081
E.Saenz-Was 643		B.Smith-Det 9	J.Nolan-ChiC 157			G.Roberts-NYG 1081
D.Doll-Det 588		G.Sims-LA 9	F.Reagan-Phi 146			E.Angsman-ChiC 754

LAMBEAU FORCED TO LEAP

A second straight losing season was a first in Green Bay and Curley Lambeau's head was fitted for a noose. With the club facing financial difficulties, his power struggle with the team's board of directors made him a convenient scapegoat. Lambeau, who had founded the team, been its first star player, and served as coach for every one of its 29 NFL seasons, was forced to resign after the season ended.

Boston Yanks owner Ted Collins finally got his wish by moving his football team to New York. With an AAFC team inhabiting Yankee Stadium (and bearing the name New York Yankees), Collins was forced to share the Polo Grounds with the New York Giants. Fans were indifferent to the transplanted team, which Collins dubbed the New York Bulldogs. A trade for Bears quarterback Bobby Layne gave them a good young player as a cornerstone, but with a porous line and nobody for him to throw to, the Bulldogs weren't competitive.

With veteran quarterback Sid Luckman sidelined by illness, the Bears turned to former Heisman Trophy winner Johnny Lujack, and the results couldn't have been better. The 24-year-old quarterback led the league in passing yards and touchdowns, including 468 yards and 6 touchdown passes in the season finale against the Cardinals. His backup was rookie George Blanda, who would play in the NFL for four decades.

Offensive guru Clark Shaughnessy continued to improve the T-formation in Los Angeles. Shaughnessy moved halfback Elroy Hirsch to a flanker position, creating a new variation of his offense with three ends and making "Crazy Legs" a star. Tom Fears set an NFL record with 77 receptions, and the Rams won the division by percentage points over the Bears.

Despite his team's success on the field, Philadelphia Eagles owner Alexis Thompson continued to lose money. Before the season started, he sold the team to a group of local businessmen. The change at the top didn't change a thing on the field. With Steve van Buren leading the league in rushing for the third straight season and coach Greasy Neale's "Eagle Defense" grounding enemy passing attacks, Philadelphia rolled to its second straight NFL title.

1949 AAFC

TEAM	W-L-T	PCT	POST	PTS	RA	RY	RY/A	RTD	FL	PA	PC	GPY	GPY/A	PTD	PI	PSY	PRAT
Cle	9-1-2	.900	PL*	339-171	403-437	1682-1905	4.2-4.4	24-13	21-13	296-304	166-120	2929-1677	9.9-5.5	21-9	12-29	—	96.8-28.2
SF	9-3	.750	PL	416-227	506-401	2798-1364	5.5-3.4	26-12	22-15	287-318	139-137	1995-1949	7.0-6.1	28-15	20-32	—	74.9-39.7
NYY	8-4	.667	P	196-206	510-360	2143-1134	4.2-3.2	16-8	20-17	199-316	66-159	1032-2189	5.2-6.9	5-13	22-24	—	20.1-54.9
Buf	5-5-2	.500	P	236-256	492-385	2047-1616	4.2-4.2	16-13	18-22	273-282	156-132	1873-2109	6.9-7.5	15-18	16-9	—	72.2-80.2
ChiH	4-8	.333	—	179-268	342-467	1080-2309	3.2-4.9	9-24	19-37	297-197	129-107	2009-1732	6.8-8.8	12-9	28-15	—	40.6-67.5
LAD	4-8	.333	—	253-322	430-484	1838-2148	4.3-4.4	19-20	17-17	286-290	114-148	1728-2414	6.0-8.3	9-22	23-21	—	37.5-74.4
Bal	1-11	.083	—	172-341	362-511	1284-2396	3.5-4.7	8-28	21-17	325-256	160-127	2355-1851	7.2-7.2	14-18	22-13	—	59.5-75.8
Aver	12	—	—	256	435	1839	4.2	17	20	280	133	1989	7.1	15	20	—	58.4

TEAM	1D	PENY	PNT	FGM/A	RTNY	RTNTD	OFFY/DEFY	NETY	NETTO	NP	PNP	DELP	PW	DELW	PRT	DR	YPD	DEL
Cle	176-156	617-359	36.8-39.6	2/11-3/10	608-467	3-1	4611-3582	1029	9	168	122	46	10.2	-0.2	8.8/1.5	150-163	30.7-22.0	8.8
SF	175-150	595-374	45.5-39.3	3/7-6/10	1187-546	4-3	4793-3313	1480	5	189	143	46	10.7	-1.7	4.8/2.1	175-163	27.4-20.3	7.1
NYY	135-129	358-414	43.8-41.8	7/15-6/9	883-834	4-6	3175-3323	-148	-1	-10	-16	6	5.8	2.3	0.5/3.9	167-165	19.0-20.1	-1.1
Buf	184-139	454-419	36.1-42.4	4/11-3/16	484-593	1-4	3920-3725	195	-3	-20	-24		5.5	0.5	4.8/6.7	152-150	25.8-24.8	1.0
ChiH	122-163	426-521	42.2-37.6	6/13-3/10	563-918	2-4	3089-4041	-952	5	-89	-59	-30	3.8	0.2	2.9/5.8	166-166	18.6-24.3	-5.7
LAD	157-174	536-678	39.9-40.0	3/6-6/12	746-666	7-2	3566-4562	-996	-2	-69	-91	22	4.3	-0.3	2.7/5.8	158-159	22.6-28.7	-6.1
Bal	151-189	369-590	37.9-40.7	6/13-4/9	478-925	0-1	3639-4247	-608	-13	-169	-103	-66	1.8	-0.8	4.6/5.6	150-152	24.3-27.9	-3.7
Aver	157	479	40.3	4/11	707	3	3828	—	—	—	—	—	—	—	4.3	160	24.0	—

Rushing Attempts	Rushing Yards	Rushing Average	Rushing TDs	Rushing Rank	Passing Yards	Passing Average
Hoernschemeyer-ChiH ..133	J.Perry-SF..............783	J.Perry-SF...............6.81	J.Perry-SF...................8	J.Perry-SF..............863	O.Graham-Cle 2785	O.Graham-Cle 9.77
H.Rodgers-LAD .131	C.Mutryn-Buf 696	B.Young-NYY 6.51	M.Motley-Cle 8	C.Mutryn-Buf 746	Y.Tittle-Bal 2209	J.Clement-ChiH 7.95
C.Mutryn-Buf 131	M.Motley-Cle 570	S.Cathcart-SF 5.97		M.Motley-Cle 650	F.Albert-SF......1862	Y.Tittle-Bal 7.64
O.Cline-Buf 125	O.Cline-Buf 518	C.Mutryn-Buf 5.31		O.Cline-Buf 548	G.Ratterman-Buf 1777	F.Albert-SF...........7.16
B.Kennedy-NYY 118	B.Young-NYY 495	B.Grimes-LAD 5.17		B.Young-NYY 545	Hoernschemeyer-ChiH 1063	G.Ratterman-Buf 7.05

Completion Percent	TD Passes	TD Percent	INT Percent	Passer Rating	Passing Rank	Receptions
G.Ratterman-Buf 57.9	F.Albert-SF............27	F.Albert-SF............10.4	O.Graham-Cle 3.5	O.Graham-Cle 97.5	O.Graham-Cle 1088	M.Speedie-Cle..........62
O.Graham-Cle 56.5	O.Graham-Cle 19	O.Graham-Cle 6.7	G.Ratterman-Buf 5.2	F.Albert-SF............82.2	Y.Tittle-Bal 455	A.Baldwin-Buf 53
Y.Tittle-Bal 51.2	Y.Tittle-Bal 14	G.Ratterman-Buf 5.6	G.Dobbs-LAD 5.9	G.Ratterman-Buf 76.8	G.Ratterman-Buf 439	A.Beals-SF 44
J.Clement-ChiH 50.9	G.Ratterman-Buf 14	J.Clement-ChiH 5.3	F.Albert-SF............6.2	Y.Tittle-Bal 66.8	F.Albert-SF............426	C.Edwards-ChiH 42
F.Albert-SF.............49.6		Y.Tittle-Bal 4.8	Y.Tittle-Bal 6.2	J.Clement-ChiH 55.6	Hoernschemeyer-ChiH 122	L.Davis-Bal 38

Receiving Yards	Receiving Average	Receiving TDs	Receiving Rank	Combined Net Yards	Total TDs	Total Points
M.Speedie-Cle.......1028	M.Speedie-Cle......20.03	A.Beals-SF 12	M.Speedie-Cle......549	C.Mutryn-Buf 1330	A.Beals-SF 12	A.Beals-SF 73
A.Baldwin-Buf 719	J.North-Bal 19.60	M.Speedie-Cle......7	A.Beals-SF 399	J.Perry-SF 1266	J.Perry-SF 11	J.Perry-SF..............66
A.Beals-SF 678	D.Wilkins-LAD 18.41	D.Lavelli-Cle......7	A.Baldwin-Buf 395	H.Wedemeyer-Bal .1226	B.Young-NYY 8	J.Vetrano-SF 65
B.Stone-Bal 621	D.Lavelli-Cle 16.96	A.Baldwin-Buf 7	B.Stone-Bal 341	B.Young-NYY 1153	B.Stone-Bal 8	
D.Wilkins-LAD.........589	M.Speedie-Cle 16.58	B.Stone-Bal 6	D.Wilkins-LAD......310	B.Grimes-LAD 1096	M.Motley-Cle 8	

Punt Average	Field Goals	Field Goal Percent	Kickoff Returns	Kickoff Return Average	Punt Returns	Punt Return Average
F.Albert-SF 48.2	H.Johnson-NYY 7	R.Grossman-Bal 54.5	H.Wedemeyer-Bal 30	R.Ramsey-ChiH.......29.1	P.Layden-NYY 29	S.Cathcart-SF 17.0
T.Landry-NYY 44.1	J.McCarthy-ChiH 6	R.Nelson-LAD 50.0	B.Grimes-LAD 16	Hoernschemeyer-ChiH 26.6	J.Cason-SF 21	J.Cason-SF 16.7
G.Dobbs-LAD 42.3	R.Grossman-Bal 6	H.Johnson-NYY 46.7	R.Ramsey-ChiH 14	B.Grimes-LAD 25.7	C.Lewis-Cle 20	H.Wedemeyer-Bal ..13.8
R.Collins-ChiH 42.1	C.Adams-Buf 4	J.McCarthy-ChiH 46.2	J.Perry-SF 14	B.Sweiger-LAD 24.1	S.Cathcart-SF 18	P.Layden-NYY 9.9
C.O'Rourke-Bal 39.2		J.Vetrano-SF 42.9	Hoernschemeyer-ChiH ..14	J.Perry-SF 24.1	H.Wedemeyer-Bal 16	C.Lewis-Cle 8.7

Punt/Kick Return Yards	Punt/Kick Return TDs	Interceptions	Interception Return Yards	Interception Return TDs	Sacks	Overall Rank
H.Wedemeyer-Bal ..823	B.Young-NYY 1	J.Cason-SF 9	J.Cason-SF 152	Many.........................1	Not kept	O.Graham-Cle 1225
J.Cason-SF 598	B.Sweiger-LAD 1	P.Layden-NYY 7	P.Layden-NYY 137			J.Perry-SF..............1078
B.Young-NYY 487	E.Lewis-Buf 1	E.Carr-SF 7	L.Wagner-SF 121			C.Mutryn-Buf 1029
B.Grimes-LAD 478	D.Edwards-ChiH 1	L.Wagner-SF 6	P.Patterson-ChiH 104			B.Young-NYY 928
R.Ramsey-ChiH 471		C.Lewis-Cle 6	E.Carr-SF 87			B.Grimes-LAD 844

THE REST OF YOU CAN ALL GO HOME

The AAFC was collapsing. Unable to compete with the NFL's New York Giants, plus the relocated New York Bulldogs, the AAFC's Brooklyn Dodgers and New York Yankees merged in 1949. The combined team—called the Yankees—had a good offensive line, diminutive halfback Buddy Young, and a rookie back and punter named Tom Landry.

The Chicago Rockets had an equally hard time competing against two NFL teams in the same town. Their strategy was to change the nickname to Hornets and adopt black-and-yellow striped jerseys. The players looked like bees and played like dogs. In fairness, they brought in legendary coach Ray Flaherty, but the club's scarcity of talent meant there was little any coach could do.

With the New York merger leaving the league with just seven clubs, the AAFC abandoned the division format in favor of having the top four finishers meet in a playoff pool. If nothing else, it allowed the 49ers, the league's second-best team to finally go to the postseason after sitting behind the unbeatable Browns in the Western Division. San Francisco

halted Cleveland's remarkable 29-game unbeaten streak (including playoffs) with a 56–28 thrashing on October 9. The game came three days shy of the two-year anniversary of Cleveland's last loss.

Talks between the AAFC and NFL were on and off throughout the year. Just three AAFC teams were invited to join the NFL: the Browns, the 49ers, and the Baltimore Colts. The first two teams were AAFC powerhouses, and Baltimore was a city where the NFL desperately wanted a presence. The other teams disbanded and their players were dispersed. In the end, the resolution was more of a surrender than a merger.

The Browns had an unprecedented stockpile of talent and finished their AAFC run with a regular-season record of 47–4–3. The agreement between the leagues was announced just days before the final AAFC game, the championship between Cleveland and San Francisco. That game was won by … the Browns, of course. Cleveland's supremacy may have helped kill the AAFC, but the Browns would show their new friends that they could dominate any opponent from any league.

1950 NFL

TEAM	W-L-T	PCT	POST	PTS	RA	RY	RY/A	RTD	FL	PA	PC	GPY	GPY/A	PTD	PI	PSY	PRAT
American Conference																	
Cle	10-2	.833	CL*	310-144	457-451	2089-1573	4.6-3.5	20-10	12-24	260-292	139-121	1984-1581	7.6-5.4	15-8	21-31	305-191	64.0-28.7
NYG	10-2	.833	C	268-150	515-473	2336-1387	4.5-2.9	21-8	20-27	187-295	81-145	1338-1848	7.2-6.3	12-11	10-27	267-266	67.1-43.4
Phi	6-6	.500	—	254-141	581-391	2328-1603	4.0-4.1	13-5	15-17	285-277	121-102	1836-1621	6.4-5.9	15-10	28-31	150-175	42.3-29.6
Pit	6-6	.500	—	180-195	477-460	1659-1889	3.5-4.1	12-12	29-16	255-300	100-146	1729-1801	6.8-6.0	10-10	29-22	83-369	36.5-48.2
ChiC	5-7	.417	—	233-287	386-525	1604-2132	4.2-4.1	8-21	14-24	368-269	165-130	2375-2075	6.5-7.7	21-14	31-22	391-167	50.3-57.8
Was	3-9	.250	—	232-326	410-462	1773-1944	4.3-4.2	10-17	22-12	314-328	154-145	2093-2276	6.7-6.9	18-19	25-19	108-216	56.7-63.0
Northern Conference																	
LA	9-3	.750	CL	466-309	404-431	1711-1882	4.2-4.4	28-12	17-15	453-385	253-165	3709-2576	8.2-6.7	31-26	27-31	180-297	80.7-54.6
ChiB	9-3	.750	C	279-207	574-388	2308-1449	4.0-3.7	25-14	17-16	296-354	135-169	1927-2265	6.5-6.4	5-11	24-16	140-357	39.1-60.1
NYY	7-5	.583	—	366-367	397-434	1832-2445	4.6-5.6	16-28	13-14	355-396	174-189	2894-2775	8.2-7.0	29-17	26-30	241-252	73.6-53.8
Det	6-6	.500	—	321-285	389-399	1626-1367	4.2-3.5	14-13	18-24	403-381	176-191	2772-2580	6.9-6.8	22-23	29-31	368-270	55.4-58.3
GB	3-9	.250	—	244-406	398-422	1706-1885	4.3-4.5	15-23	20-15	367-379	140-185	1831-2818	5.0-7.4	14-24	37-27	327-230	27.8-65.2
SF	3-9	.250	—	213-300	460-443	1955-1662	4.3-3.8	14-17	21-21	326-347	164-164	1875-2289	5.8-6.6	14-16	25-22	324-248	50.3-57.9
Bal	1-11	.083	—	213-462	345-514	1148-2857	3.3-5.6	12-28	21-14	438-304	206-156	2687-2545	6.1-8.4	14-31	31-34	309-156	48.0-74.1
Aver	12	—	—	275	446	1852	4.2	16	18	331	154	2235	6.7	17	26	246	52.9

TEAM	ID	PENY	PNT	FGM/A	RTNY	RTNTD	OFFY/DEFY	NETY	NETTO	NP	PNP	DELP	PW	DELW	PRT	DR	YPD	DEL
American Conference																		
Cle	199-184	968-554	43.2-41.5	14/21-4/11	731-472	3-1	3768-2963	805	22	166	155	11	10.1	-0.2	3.0/0.2	167-170	22.6-17.4	5.1
NYG	173-176	562-553	37.1-41.2	6/12-6/11	818-540	3-0	3407-2969	438	24	118	133	-15	8.9	1.0	3.4/1.5	175-167	19.5-17.8	1.7
Phi	231-141	612-590	41.4-38.9	8/22-8/18	802-681	5-2	4014-3049	965	5	113	100	13	8.8	-2.8	1.9/0.5	172-166	23.3-18.4	5.0
Pit	177-198	477-733	41.3-40.8	8/14-5/12	682-748	0-3	3305-3321	-16	-20	-15	-81	66	5.6	0.4	1.7/1.6	158-170	20.9-19.5	1.4
ChiC	194-216	609-876	40.6-43.3	6/12-8/18	528-810	2-3	3588-4040	-452	1	-54	-34	-20	4.7	0.4	1.9/3.6	171-176	21.0-23.0	-2.0
Was	187-217	829-638	40.6-40.3	5/10-8/18	628-792	3-7	3758-4004	-246	-16	-94	-85	-9	3.7	-0.7	3.2/3.9	164-165	22.9-24.3	-1.4
Northern Conference																		
LA	278-217	1038-859	40.5-39.3	7/14-3/13	905-688	5-5	5240-4161	1079	2	157	98	59	9.9	-0.9	5.5/2.7	187-196	28.0-21.2	6.8
ChiB	236-178	738-671	41.7-39.7	9/20-5/12	884-699	6-3	4095-3357	738	-9	72	26	46	7.8	1.2	2.4/3.3	171-174	23.9-19.3	4.7
NYY	210-249	762-824	42.2-38.8	2/9-9/17	743-1042	6-4	4485-4968	-483	-9	-1	-20	19	6.0	1.0	4.6/3.1	183-183	24.5-27.1	-2.6
Det	209-200	804-803	40.2-42.7	8/18-4/11	869-901	7-3	4030-3677	353	8	36	61	-25	6.9	-0.9	2.9/2.8	190-189	21.2-19.5	1.8
GB	174-220	757-919	38.1-40.2	3/17-6/13	1066-947	5-9	3210-4473	-1263		-162	-165	3	1.9	1.1	-0.1/4.0	194-195	16.5-22.9	-6.4
SF	201-204	851-599	38.7-39.4	4/8-7/14	710-842	1-7	3505-3703	-198	-3	-87	-29	-58	3.0	-0.8	1.5/3.2	160-170	20.6-23.1	-2.5
Bal	188-257	579-967	40.2-39.1	0/4-7/13	949-1153	5-4	3526-5246	-1720	-4	-249	-159	-90	-0.2	1.2	2.4/3.6	192-183	18.4-28.7	-10.3
Aver	204	737	40.4	6/14	793	4	3841	—	—	—	—	—	—	—	2.9	176	21.8	—

Rushing Attempts	Rushing Yards	Rushing Average	Rushing TDs	Rushing Rank	Passing Yards	Passing Average
S.Van Buren-Phi....188	M.Motley-Cle....810	J.Lujack-ChiB....6.30	J.Lujack-ChiB....11	M.Motley-Cle....840	B.Layne-Det....2323	Van Brocklin-LA....8.85
J.Geri-Pit....188	F.Ziegler-Phi....733	M.Motley-Cle....5.79	D.Hoerner-LA....10	F.Ziegler-Phi....743	G.Ratterman-NYY....2251	O.Graham-Cle....7.68
F.Ziegler-Phi....172	J.Geri-Pit....705	B.Grimes-GB....5.71	J.Rykovich-ChiB....7	E.Price-NYG....743	Van Brocklin-LA....2061	J.Geri-Pit....7.66
G.Gulyanics-ChiB....146	E.Price-NYG....703	Hoernschemeyer-Det....5.61	J.Parmer-Phi....7	J.Geri-Pit....725	O.Graham-Cle....1943	G.Ratterman-NYY....7.66
M.Motley-Cle....140	J.Perry-SF....647	E.Price-NYG....5.58		J.Perry-SF....697	Y.Tittle-Bal....1884	C.Conerly-NYG....7.58

Completion Percent	TD Passes	TD Percent	INT Percent	Passer Rating	Passing Rank	Receptions
B.Walsh-LA....57.3	G.Ratterman-NYY....22	Van Brocklin-LA....7.7	C.Conerly-NYG....5.3	Van Brocklin-LA....85.1	Van Brocklin-LA....561	T.Fears-LA....84
Van Brocklin-LA....54.5	Van Brocklin-LA....18	G.Ratterman-NYY....7.5	B.Layne-Det....5.4	B.Walsh-LA....71.7	B.Layne-Det....522	D.Edwards-NYY....52
S.Baugh-Was....54.2	J.Hardy-ChiC....17	J.Hardy-ChiC....6.6	P.Christman-GB....5.6	S.Baugh-Was....68.1	B.Walsh-LA....305	C.Box-Det....50
O.Graham-Cle....54.2	B.Layne-Det....16	C.Conerly-NYG....6.1	Van Brocklin-LA....6.0	C.Conerly-NYG....67.1	G.Ratterman-NYY....276	B.Shaw-ChiC....48
Y.Tittle-Bal....51.1		S.Baugh-Was....6.0	Y.Tittle-Bal....6.0	O.Graham-Cle....64.7	C.Conerly-NYG....260	P.Salata-Bal....45

Receiving Yards	Receiving Average	Receiving TDs	Receiving Rank	Combined Net Yards	Total TDs	Total Points
T.Fears-LA....1116	H.Taylor-Was....21.36	B.Shaw-ChiC....12	T.Fears-LA....593	B.Grimes-GB....1896	B.Shaw-ChiC....12	D.Walker-Det....128
C.Box-Det....1009	A.Weiner-NYY....20.63	C.Box-Det....11	C.Box-Det....560	V.Smith-LA....1489		J.Lujack-ChiB....109
B.Shaw-ChiC....971	B.Shaw-ChiC....20.23	H.Taylor-Was....9	B.Shaw-ChiC....546	W.Szot-LA....1312		B.Walsh-LA....81
H.Taylor-Was....833	C.Box-Det....20.18	E.Hirsch-LA....7	H.Taylor-Was....462	D.Walker-Det....1262		L.Groza-Cle....74
D.Edwards-NYY....775	A.Baldwin-GB....19.82	T.Fears-LA....7	D.Edwards-NYY....418	B.Young-NYY....1218		B.Shaw-ChiC....72

Punt Average	Field Goals	Field Goal Percent	Kickoff Returns	Kickoff Return Average	Punt Returns	Punt Return Average
F.Morrison-ChiB....43.3	L.Groza-Cle....13	L.Groza-Cle....68.4	D.Paul-ChiC....28	V.Smith-LA....33.7	G.McAfee-ChiB....33	H.Rich-Bal....23.0
H.Gillom-Cle....43.2	D.Walker-Det....8	J.Geri-Pit....57.1	B.Grimes-GB....26	L.Chandnois-Pit....29.3	E.Tunnell-NYG....31	B.Grimes-GB....19.1
S.Sanders-NYY....42.3	C.Patton-Phi....8	B.Walsh-LA....50.0	W.Szot-NYY....25	E.Saenz-Was....28.9	B.Grimes-GB....29	B.Dudley-Was....15.4
F.Reagan-Phi....42.0	J.Geri-Pit....8	C.Patton-Phi....47.1	V.Smith-LA....22	C.Hunsinger-ChiB....28.6	V.Smith-LA....22	B.Gage-Pit....13.7
B.Smith-Det....40.9	B.Walsh-LA....7	D.Walker-Det....44.4	B.Young-NYY....20	T.Kalmanir-LA....27.5	R.Craft-Phi....19	D.Phelps-Det....13.4

Punt/Kick Return Yards	Punt/Kick Return TDs	Interceptions	Interception Return Yards	Interception Return TDs	Sacks	Overall Rank
B.Grimes-GB....1155	V.Smith-LA....3	S.Sanders-NYY....13	W.Lewis-LA....275	B.Weatherly-ChiB....2	Not kept	B.Grimes-GB....1306
V.Smith-LA....960	B.Grimes-GB....2	W.Lewis-LA....12	S.Sanders-NYY....199	W.Lahr-Cle....2		V.Smith-LA....975
D.Paul-ChiC....887		D.Doll-Det....12	R.Steiner-GB....190			M.Motley-Cle....921
H.Rich-Bal....710		T.James-Cle....9	E.Tunnell-NYG....167			F.Ziegler-Phi....920
W.Szot-NYY....602		J.Davis-ChiC....9	C.Maggioli-Bal....165			D.Walker-Det....898

BROWN BULL'S EYE ON THE NFL

Major changes swept through the league in 1950. Free substitution, a wartime trial, was restored, effectively ending the two-way era. The new rule allowed for different platoons to be used for running and passing plays, and enabled the development of defensive specialization. But a more noticeable change was the addition of three new teams. The New York Bulldogs inherited many of the players from the AAFC's defunct New York Yankees and also took their name, shortening it to Yanks. The Giants got their fair share of ex-Yankees as well. The other AAFC players worth having were scattered to the NFL through a dispersal draft. Even with five extra picks, the brutal Colts lasted just one year in the NFL.

The season opened with a much-anticipated matchup between pro football's two premier teams. The Eagles had won back-to-back NFL titles, while the Browns were four-time champions of the AAFC. Cleveland quarterback Otto Graham threw 3 touchdowns, shredding the "Eagle Defense" and Alex Wojciechowicz in his final season. The 35–10 victory quieted those who questioned Cleveland's legitimacy.

For those who thought it was all because of the pass, the Browns eliminated Philadelphia from postseason contention in December without putting a single ball in the air.

The Browns were as relentless in the NFL as they'd been in the AAFC. Marion Motley led the league in rushing, Otto Graham was named Most Valuable Player, and Cleveland won its fifth straight championship. Philadelphia, on the other hand, endured a season-long feud between coach Greasy Neale and owner James Clark. After a decade with the Eagles, Neale was fired after the last game and never coached in the league again.

With former Bears tackle Joe Stydahar taking over the coaching duties from deposed Clark Shaughnessy, Los Angeles scored an NFL record 466 points. The platoon of Norm Van Brocklin and Bob Waterfield at quarterback was overwhelmingly successful, and end Tom Fears set a new record with 84 receptions. Everyone watched from home. The Rams were the first to televise all their home games, but a 50 percent drop in attendance meant an end to future TV broadcasts by home teams.

1951 NFL

TEAM	W-L-T	PCT	POST	PTS	RA	RY	RY/A	RTD	FL	PA	PC	GPY	GPY/A	PTD	PI	PSY	PRAT
American Conference																	
Cle	11-1	.917	L	331-152	415-428	1708-1454	4.1-3.4	20-8	19-29	271-330	151-151	2273-1978	8.4-6.0	18-10	17-22	371-430	79.5-47.5
NYG	9-2-1	.818	—	254-161	491-392	1713-913	3.5-2.3	10-8	13-12	210-377	101-162	1432-2337	6.8-6.2	11-11	26-41	245-276	48.5-33.9
Was	5-7	.417	—	183-296	547-464	2151-2093	3.9-4.5	14-20	18-15	226-295	99-140	1508-2104	6.7-7.1	8-16	25-18	104-147	38.6-64.0
Pit	4-7-1	.364	—	183-235	425-499	1428-1859	3.4-3.7	9-13	17-16	330-266	130-136	1842-1687	5.6-6.3	10-12	26-30	318-201	35.4-46.6
Phi	4-8	.333	—	234-264	509-462	1562-1816	3.1-3.9	13-12	18-19	284-287	120-119	1713-1748	6.0-6.1	17-17	29-18	223-270	42.8-55.6
ChiC	3-9	.250	—	210-287	440-476	1963-1977	4.5-4.2	14-15	20-16	334-265	161-123	2244-1973	6.7-7.4	13-18	24-27	360-197	53.3-54.8
Northern Conference																	
LA	8-4	.667	L*	392-261	426-478	2210-2206	5.2-4.6	22-17	15-10	373-329	189-140	3296-1992	8.8-6.1	26-13	22-19	97-319	79.8-51.9
Det	7-4-1	.636	—	336-259	410-454	1841-1509	4.5-3.3	11-13	9-16	351-374	158-181	2500-2608	7.1-7.0	29-11	24-15	153-253	68.3-70.8
SF	7-4-1	.636	—	255-205	523-417	2366-1549	4.5-3.7	18-9	20-9	281-353	154-158	1955-2313	7.0-6.6	14-15	19-33	308-212	65.2-41.9
ChiB	7-5	.583	—	286-282	539-372	2408-1958	4.5-5.3	24-15	15-21	315-337	143-160	2239-2431	7.1-7.2	12-21	20-21	283-343	55.8-66.5
GB	3-9	.250	—	254-375	313-496	1196-2152	3.8-4.3	8-22	15-13	478-313	231-157	2846-2535	6.0-8.1	12-25	26-25	289-217	60.0-75.0
NYY	1-9-2	.100	—	241-382	364-464	1337-2397	3.7-5.2	12-23	9-12	428-355	172-182	2634-2776	6.2-7.8	16-24	27-22	296-182	47.4-74.1
Aver	12	—	—	263	450	1824	4.1	15	16	323	151	2207	6.8	17	24	254	55.6

TEAM	1D	PENY	PNT	FGM/A	RTNY	RTNTD	OFFY/DEFY	NETY	NETTO	NP	PNP	DELP	PW	DELW	PRT	DR	YPD	DEL
American Conference																		
Cle	203-201	1017-505	45.5-39.8	10/23-4/14	465-435	5-2	3610-3002	608	15	179	111	68	10.5	0.5	4.2/1.7	166-188	21.7-16.0	5.8
NYG	151-174	569-506	40.2-40.2	12/16-7/15	1217-679	10-1	2900-2974	-74	14	93	50	43	8.3	1.2	0.5/0.8	187-185	15.5-16.1	-0.6
Was	199-241	560-630	38.7-40.8	10/13-6/13	499-610	0-4	3555-4050	-495	-10	-113	-81	-32	3.2	1.8	1.5/4.2	153-149	23.2-27.2	-3.9
Pit	172-188	430-725	38.6-40.7	7/14-7/12	925-867	4-6	2952-3345	-393	3	-52	-31	-31	4.7	-0.2	1.2/0.9	178-172	16.6-19.4	-2.9
Phi	200-183	428-458	39.1-44.4	6/11-13/21	638-736	1-3	3052-3294	-242	-10	-30	-60	30	5.3	-1.3	1.1/2.6	173-179	17.6-18.4	-0.8
ChiC	224-212	729-711	39.8-40.9	7/13-7/17	582-1019	0-5	3847-3753	94	-1	-77	4	-81	4.1	-1.1	2.5/2.6	172-166	22.4-22.6	-0.2
Northern Conference																		
LA	272-231	813-1028	41.5-40.9	13/24-6/12	537-678	3-5	5409-3879	1530	-8	131	96	35	9.3	-1.3	6.4/2.6	163-176	33.2-22.0	11.1
Det	231-235	746-656	41.3-41.7	9/17-12/22	718-663	4-1	4188-3264	924	-2	-77	19	58	7.9	-0.4	4.2/4.6	154-164	23.2-23.6	3.6
SF	237-188	694-526	43.6-40.4	6/18-13/24	905-363	2-0	4013-3650	363	3	50	42	8	7.3	0.9	2.9/2.0	173-156	23.2-23.4	-0.2
ChiB	256-228	1107-1022	38.5-37.7	7/19-3/5	590-572	2-3	4364-4046	318	7	4	55	-51	6.1	0.9	3.4/3.6	164-167	26.6-24.2	2.4
GB	218-236	790-924	41.0-37.6	5/8-8/17	505-951	1-3	3753-4470	-717	-9	-121	-96	-25	3.0	0.0	2.9/4.4	176-161	21.3-27.8	-6.4
NYY	211-257	605-797	38.3-39.9	6/14-12/18	614-632	4-3	3675-4991	-1316	-2	-141	-118	-23	2.5	-0.5	2.8/4.9	179-175	20.5-28.5	-8.0
Aver	215	707	40.4	8/16	683	3	3777	—	—	—	—	—	—	—	3.2	170	22.2	—

Rushing Attempts		Rushing Yards		Rushing Average		Rushing TDs		Rushing Rank		Passing Yards		Passing Average	
E.Price-NYG	271	E.Price-NYG	971	T.Rote-GB	6.88	R.Goode-Was	9	E.Price-NYG	1041	B.Layne-Det	2403	B.Walston-LA	8.90
R.Goode-Was	208	R.Goode-Was	951	D.Towler-LA	6.78	E.Price-NYG	7	R.Goode-Was	1041	O.Graham-Cle	2205	Van Brocklin-LA	8.89
J.Perry-SF	136	D.Towler-LA	854	C.Trippi-ChiC	6.42	J.Lujack-ChiB	7	D.Towler-LA	914	B.Celeri-NYY	1797	O.Graham-Cle	8.32
Hoernschemeyer-Det	132	Hoernschemeyer-Det	678	D.Hoerner-LA	6.05	D.Jones-Cle	7	J.Perry-SF	707	Van Brocklin-LA	1725	S.Romanik-ChiB	7.83
J.Dottley-ChiB	127	J.Perry-SF	677	W.Lewis-SF	5.93			J.Dottley-ChiB	700	B.Walston-LA	1566	B.Celeri-NYY	7.55

Completion Percent		TD Passes		TD Percent		INT Percent		Passer Rating		Passing Rank		Receptions	
B.Thomason-GB	56.6	B.Layne-Det	26	B.Layne-Det	7.8	B.Thomason-GB	4.1	B.Walston-LA	81.8	O.Graham-Cle	548	E.Hirsch-LA	66
O.Graham-Cle	55.5	O.Graham-Cle	17	B.Walston-LA	7.4	J.Lujack-ChiB	4.5	Van Brocklin-LA	80.8	Van Brocklin-LA	488	G.Soltau-SF	59
Y.Tittle-SF	55.3	T.Rote-GB	15	Y.Tittle-SF	7.0	Van Brocklin-LA	5.7	O.Graham-Cle	79.2	B.Walston-LA	448	F.Polsfoot-ChiC	57
F.Albert-SF	54.2	A.Burk-Phi	14	Van Brocklin-LA	6.7	B.Walston-LA	5.7	B.Thomason-GB	73.5	B.Layne-Det	412	B.Mann-GB	50
Van Brocklin-LA	51.5			A.Burk-Phi	6.4	F.Albert-SF	6.0	J.Lujack-ChiB	69.2	J.Lujack-ChiB	368	D.Lavelli-Cle	43

Receiving Yards		Receiving Average		Receiving TDs		Receiving Rank		Combined Net Yards		Total TDs		Total Points	
E.Hirsch-LA	1495	E.Hirsch-LA	22.65	E.Hirsch-LA	17	E.Hirsch-LA	833	E.Hirsch-LA	1501	E.Hirsch-LA	17	E.Hirsch-LA	102
G.Soltau-SF	826	D.Dibble-Det	20.43	L.Hart-Det	12	G.Soltau-SF	448	B.Young-NYY	1331	D.Jones-Cle	12	B.Walston-LA	98
F.Polsfoot-ChiC	796	G.Schroeder-ChiB	19.21	B.Walston-Phi	8	F.Polsfoot-ChiC	418	A.Tait-NYY	1324	L.Hart-Det	12	D.Walker-Det	97
B.Mann-GB	696	D.Jones-Cle	19.00	B.Mann-GB	8	B.Mann-GB	388	D.Walker-Det	1270	R.Goode-Was	9	B.Walston-Phi	94
D.Dibble-Det	613	M.Speedie-Cle	17.32	G.Soltau-SF	7	D.Dibble-Det	337	D.Paul-ChiC	1264			G.Soltau-SF	90

Punt Average		Field Goals		Field Goal Percent		Kickoff Returns		Kickoff Return Average		Punt Returns		Punt Return Average	
H.Gillom-Cle	45.5	B.Walston-LA	13	B.Dudley-Was	76.9	A.Tait-NYY	27	L.Chandnois-Pit	32.5	E.Tunnell-NYG	34	B.Young-NYY	19.3
F.Albert-SF	44.3	R.Poole-NYG	12	R.Poole-NYG	75.0	B.Grimes-GB	23	B.Young-NYY	30.5	B.Dudley-Was	22	R.Mathews-Pit	15.4
B.Smith-Det	42.5	L.Groza-Cle	10	B.Walston-LA	56.5	J.Arenas-SF	21	D.Paul-ChiC	28.3	J.Arenas-SF	21	E.Tunnell-NYG	14.4
Van Brocklin-LA	41.5	B.Dudley-Was	10	D.Walker-Det	50.0	D.Moselle-GB	20	D.Moselle-GB	27.4	D.Paul-ChiC	19	J.Arenas-SF	13.0
F.Polsfoot-ChiC	40.7			J.Geri-Pit	50.0	E.Sitko-ChiC	17	D.Walker-Det	27.2				

Punt/Kick Return Yards		Punt/Kick Return TDs		Interceptions		Interception Return Yards		Interception Return TDs		Sacks		Overall Rank	
J.Arenas-SF	814	E.Tunnell-NYG	4	Schnellbacher-NYG	11	Schnellbacher-NYG	194	Schnellbacher-NYG	2	Not kept		R.Goode-Was	1064
E.Tunnell-NYG	716	Christiansen-Det	4	H.Hartley-Pit	10	J.Cason-SF	147	T.Landry-NYG	2			E.Price-NYG	1051
A.Tait-NYY	690	B.Young-NYY	2	L.Wagner-SF	9	J.Butler-Pit	142	W.Lahr-Cle	2			D.Towler-LA	1038
B.Grimes-GB	682			E.Tunnell-NYG	9	T.Landry-NYG	121					Hoernschemeyer-Det	917
B.Young-NYY	658					L.Wagner-SF	115					D.Jones-Cle	872

GOING FOR BROKE

After just one season in the NFL, the AAFC refugee Baltimore Colts folded. Owner Abraham Watner turned the franchise over to the league, and the players were made available in the annual draft. Four of them were selected in the first round. San Francisco grabbed quarterback Y.A. Tittle and Philadelphia took halfback Chet Mutryn.

The Lions were steadily improving under head coach Buddy Parker, posting their first winning record since 1945. Quarterback Bobby Layne led the league in passing yards for the second consecutive season. After a slow start the team rallied back into title contention, and a win against the Rams left them tied for first place with one week to go. Detroit's loss to the Niners in the season finale left them in second place in the final standings.

It was business as usual in Cleveland, where the Browns finished with the league's best record once again. Rumors that coach Paul Brown might leave Cleveland to return to Ohio State turned out to be false, and the Browns won 11 straight after dropping the season opener. The highlight of the season came November 25, when Dub Jones tied a 1929 record by scoring 6 touchdowns against the Bears.

There were fireworks in Los Angeles right from the start. Quarterback Norm Van Brocklin threw for 554 yards in the season opener against the New York Yankees. That broke the existing single game record by nearly 100 yards, and set a record that has never been matched. It also gave a clear signal that LA's aerial attack was better than ever. Elroy Hirsch set a record with 1,495 receiving yards for the season, and Crazy Legs tied Don Hutson's record with 17 touchdown catches. The prolific passing game helped the Rams overcome a fourth-quarter deficit in the championship game. A 73-yard pass from Van Brocklin to Tom Fears gave Los Angeles the victory, ending Cleveland's streak of five straight titles.

The Pro Bowl, initiated for the first time a year earlier, pitted all-star teams from each conference against each other. Even with three Rams in the National Conference's backfield, the game still drew just 19,400 in Los Angeles.

1952 NFL

TEAM	W-L-T	PCT	POST	PTS	RA	RY	RY/A	RTD	FL	PA	PC	GPY	GPY/A	PTD	PI	PSY	PRAT
American Conference																	
Cle	8-4	.667	L	310-213	394-411	1786-1386	4.5-3.4	12-11	11-14	374-348	184-141	2839-2028	7.6-5.8	22-17	26-22	273-339	65.4-50.1
NYG	7-5	.583	—	234-231	442-404	1636-1303	3.7-3.2	11-8	14-17	280-337	121-162	1713-2514	6.1-7.5	16-18	22-28	321-336	49.9-56.4
Phi	7-5	.583	—	252-271	434-408	1370-1396	3.2-3.4	10-12	22-19	361-343	154-157	2272-2164	6.3-6.3	13-19	19-20	307-410	53.9-60.7
Pit	5-7	.417	—	300-273	384-460	1204-1744	3.1-3.8	12-8	14-13	365-369	167-167	2504-2765	6.9-7.5	21-24	23-27	313-220	61.7-62.2
ChiC	4-8	.333	—	172-221	477-455	1748-1588	3.7-3.5	10-8	23-18	289-307	124-149	1512-1942	5.2-6.3	10-16	22-25	301-177	39.5-52.3
Was	4-8	.333	—	240-287	467-426	1655-1817	3.5-4.3	10-19	17-16	286-275	147-121	2127-1817	7.4-6.6	20-12	21-18	387-237	68.6-53.6
Northern Conference																	
Det	9-3	.750	CL*	344-192	442-353	1780-1145	4.0-3.2	14-8	10-25	362-382	171-182	2495-2421	6.9-6.3	24-15	28-32	287-321	60.0-46.4
LA	9-3	.750	C	349-234	411-441	1811-1613	4.4-3.7	17-10	17-18	329-360	167-161	2438-2252	7.4-6.3	17-18	31-38	146-369	53.2-42.5
SF	7-5	.583	—	285-221	421-412	1905-1566	4.5-3.8	16-10	13-18	342-342	171-158	2371-1929	6.9-5.6	19-15	23-17	396-291	64.6-55.6
GB	6-6	.500	—	295-312	405-415	1485-1507	3.7-3.6	11-16	31-19	337-340	161-162	2688-2205	8.0-6.5	26-17	25-22	314-443	69.9-58.5
ChiB	5-7	.417	—	245-326	411-463	1543-1921	3.8-4.1	11-20	24-26	347-311	141-160	2015-2350	5.8-7.6	18-16	27-20	280-259	45.0-66.8
Aver	12	—		275	426	1629	3.8	12	18	334	156	2270	6.8	19	24	302	57.7

TEAM	1D	PENY	PNT	FGM/A	RTNY	RTNTD	OFFY/DEFY	NETY	NETTO	NP	PNP	DELP	PW	DELW	PRT	DR	YPD	DEL
American Conference																		
Cle	228-186	744-425	45.7-40.6	19/33-4/11	660-696	2-1	4352-3075	1277	-1	97	102	-5	8.4	-0.4	4.0/2.2	172-180	25.3-17.1	8.2
NYG	155-189	626-518	41.0-40.5	10/17-8/19	873-654	2-4	3028-3481	-453	9	3	-2	5	6.1	0.9	1.8/2.9	192-177	15.8-19.7	-3.9
Phi	181-187	747-699	40.2-41.3	11/20-4/14	736-758	8-7	3335-3150	185	-2	-19	7	-26	5.5	1.5	3.1/2.6	192-188	17.4-16.8	0.6
Pit	187-224	520-623	43.0-42.4	4/11-8/18	966-909	9-3	3395-4289	-894	3	27	-63	90	6.7	-1.7	3.4/4.0	179-186	19.0-23.1	-4.1
ChiC	176-176	743-883	37.3-42.1	2/18-8/20	682-840	4-4	2959-3353	-394	-2	-49	-41	-8	4.8	-0.8	1.0/2.4	173-178	17.1-18.8	-1.7
Was	206-189	669-817	41.3-41.2	4/10-10/23	753-813	3-6	3395-3397	-2	-4	-47	-16	-31	4.8	-0.8	3.0/2.9	164-161	20.7-21.1	-0.4
Northern Conference																		
Det	219-195	799-596	44.1-40.6	14/28-7/15	997-669	5-2	3988-3245	743	19	152	138	14	9.8	-0.8	3.0/1.9	184-188	21.7-17.3	4.4
LA	205-212	891-746	42.8-42.8	11/19-6/16	1239-696	11-3	4103-3496	607	8	115	83	32	8.9	0.1	3.1/0.9	182-184	22.5-19.0	3.5
SF	213-167	628-530	42.6-41.3	6/12-10/21	688-658	3-2	3880-3204	676	-1	64	52	12	7.6	-0.6	2.9/2.7	176-167	22.0-19.2	2.9
GB	197-202	739-752	40.7-39.0	6/21-11/20	624-620	3-7	3859-3269	590	-15	-17	-11	-6	5.6	0.4	4.0/2.4	186-195	20.7-16.8	4.0
ChiB	194-209	583-795	41.4-41.5	8/28-8/20	504-935	2-7	3278-4012	-734	-5	-81	-81	0	4.0	1.0	1.8/3.9	191-191	17.2-21.0	-3.8
Aver	196	699	41.8	9/20	793	5	3597	—	—	—	—	—	—	—	3.2	181	19.9	—

Rushing Attempts		Rushing Yards		Rushing Average		Rushing TDs		Rushing Rank		Passing Yards		Passing Average	
E.Price-NYG	183	D.Towler-LA	894	H.McElhenny-SF	6.98	D.Towler-LA	10	D.Towler-LA	994	O.Graham-Cle	2816	Van Brocklin-LA	8.47
J.Perry-SF	158	E.Price-NYG	748	D.Towler-LA	5.73	J.Perry-SF	8	J.Perry-SF	805	J.Finks-Pit	2307	T.Rote-GB	8.08
D.Towler-LA	156	J.Perry-SF	725	K.Carpenter-Cle	5.67	H.McElhenny-SF	6	E.Price-NYG	798	B.Layne-Det	1999	B.Parilli-GB	8.00
Hoernschemeyer-Det	106	H.McElhenny-Det	684	T.Younger-LA	5.25	E.Price-NYG	5	H.McElhenny-SF	744	Van Brocklin-LA	1736	O.Graham-Cle	7.74
J.Huzvar-Phi	105	Hoernschemeyer-Det	457	B.Cross-ChiC	4.89	J.Finks-Pit	5	Hoernschemeyer-Det	497	E.LeBaron-Was	1420	F.Albert-SF	7.47

Completion Percent		TD Passes		TD Percent		INT Percent		Passer Rating		Passing Rank		Receptions	
Van Brocklin-LA	55.1	O.Graham-Cle	20	T.Rote-GB	8.3	B.Thomason-Phi	4.2	O.Graham-Cle	85.6	O.Graham-Cle	548	M.Speedie-Cle	62
F.Albert-SF	55.0	J.Finks-Pit	20	C.Conerly-NYG	7.7	T.Rote-GB	5.1	Van Brocklin-LA	71.5	J.Finks-Pit	494	B.Grant-Phi	56
T.Rote-GB	52.2	B.Layne-Det	19	B.Parilli-GB	7.3	J.Finks-Pit	5.7	C.Conerly-NYG	70.4	T.Rote-GB	379	G.Soltau-SF	55
Y.Tittle-SF	51.0	Van Brocklin-LA	14	E.LeBaron-Was	7.2	Y.Tittle-SF	5.8	F.Albert-SF	67.5	B.Thomason-Phi	347	E.Nickel-Pit	55
O.Graham-Cle	49.7	E.LeBaron-Was	14	Van Brocklin-LA	6.8	C.Conerly-NYG	5.9	O.Graham-Cle	66.6	B.Layne-Det	295	B.Stone-ChiC	54

Receiving Yards		Receiving Average		Receiving TDs		Receiving Rank		Combined Net Yards		Total TDs		Total Points	
B.Howton-GB	1231	E.Hirsch-LA	23.60	T.Rote-GB	15	B.Howton-GB	681	H.McElhenny-SF	1731	C.Box-Det	15	G.Soltau-SF	94
B.Grant-Phi	997	H.Taylor-Was	23.44	B.Howton-GB	13	H.Taylor-Was	541	R.Mathews-Pit	1622	B.Howton-GB	13	C.Box-Det	90
H.Taylor-Was	961	B.Howton-GB	23.23	B.Box-Det	12	C.Box-Det	537	L.Chandnois-Pit	1378	H.Taylor-Was	12	L.Groza-Cle	89
C.Box-Det	924	C.Box-Det	22.00	E.Nickel-Pit	9	B.Grant-Phi	534	O.Matson-ChiC	1326	D.Towler-LA	10	P.Harder-Det	85
M.Speedie-Cle	911	J.Boone-SF	18.44			E.Nickel-Pit	487	H.McElhenny-SF	1231	H.McElhenny-SF	10	B.Walston-Phi	83

Punt Average		Field Goals		Field Goal Percent		Kickoff Returns		Kickoff Return Average		Punt Returns		Punt Return Average	
H.Gillom-Cle	45.7	L.Groza-Cle	19	B.Walston-LA	61.1	B.Young-DalT	23	L.Chandnois-Pit	35.2	B.Bawel-Phi	34	Christiansen-Det	21.5
B.Smith-Det	44.7	B.Walston-LA	11	R.Poole-NYG	58.8	B.Baggett-DalT	23	O.Matson-ChiC	31.2	E.Tunnell-NYG	30	W.Lewis-LA	18.5
P.Brady-Pit	43.2	B.Walston-Phi	11	L.Groza-Cle	57.6	A.Pollard-Phi	21	B.Young-DalT	28.0	R.Mathews-Pit	26	R.Mathews-Pit	15.3
Van Brocklin-LA	43.1	P.Harder-Det	11	B.Walston-Phi	55.0	J.Williams-Was	20	D.Stevens-Phi	27.1	J.Williams-Was	24	J.Williams-Was	15.3
F.Albert-SF	42.6	R.Poole-NYG	10	G.Soltau-SF	50.0	O.Matson-ChiC	20	R.Mathews-Pit	26.2	W.White-ChiB	23	H.McElhenny-SF	14.2

Punt/Kick Return Yards		Punt/Kick Return TDs		Interceptions		Interception Return Yards		Interception Return TDs		Sacks		Overall Rank	
J.Williams-Was	852	Many	2	N.Lane-LA	14	N.Lane-LA	298	N.Lane-LA	2	Not kept		H.McElhenny-SF	1263
E.Tunnell-NYG	775			T.Keane-DalT	10	H.Rich-LA	201					R.Mathews-Pit	1068
R.Mathews-Pit	764			B.Smith-Det	9	B.Smith-Det	184					D.Towler-LA	1017
Christiansen-Det	731					J.Butler-Pit	168					O.Matson-ChiC	909
						E.Tunnell-NYG	149					L.Chandnois-Pit	893

DEEP IN THE HEART OF AKRON

After a dismal 1–9–2 record in 1951, New York Yankees owner Ted Collins called it quits, turning his franchise over to the league. A group of Dallas businessmen purchased the club in January. The Dallas Texans drew sparse crowds and the new owners bailed out midseason. The league took over the team and moved their practices to Hershey, Pennsylvania. They became a road club. The Texans' lone win came on Thanksgiving at "home" in Akron, Ohio. The Texans disbanded at season's end. They were the second club in as many years to fold, but it was the last time that happened in the NFL.

Detroit had the league's best defense and ranked second in scoring. Bobby Layne emerged as a leader, and the team surged after Doak Walker returned from a preseason injury. Detroit's secondary smothered opponents and the club finished at 9–3. The Lions beat the Rams in a playoff en route to their first NFL championship in 17 years.

Giants fans were unhappy that rookie Frank Gifford and second-year back Kyle Rote languished in coach Steve Owen's A-formation offense, but New York had a share of first place. So did Philadelphia, with first year head coach Jim Trimble rebuilding the defense. By Thanksgiving the Giants, Eagles, and Browns were tied for first place in the American Conference, but New York and Philadelphia dropped two of their last three games. Cleveland finished on top, but injuries to end Mac Speedie, back Dub Jones, and tackle John Kissell in the season finale left the Browns undermanned in the championship game.

An unusually strong crop of rookies debuted in 1952: Cardinals fullback Ollie Matson, 49ers running back Hugh McElhenny, Bears linebacker Bill George, Texans defensive end Gino Marchetti, and Rams rookie Dick "Night Train" Lane, who set an NFL record with 14 interceptions. It was the end of the line for some of the game's biggest stars. Injuries forced Philadelphia's Steve Van Buren to quit during training camp. He retired as the all-time leader in rushing attempts, yards, and touchdowns. Washington's Sammy Baugh, no longer a starter, retired at the end of the season holding every NFL career passing record.

1953 NFL

TEAM	W-L-T	PCT	POST	PTS	RA	RY	RY/A	RTD	FL	PA	PC	GPY	GPY/A	PTD	PI	PSY	PRAT
Eastern Conference																	
Cle	11-1	.917	L	348-**162**	379-374	1577-1560	4.2-4.2	20-11	15-16	303-389	191-164	3059-2271	**10.1**-5.8	16-10	**9**-25	245-256	**101.9**-43.3
Phi	7-4-1	.636	—	352-215	410-**331**	1722-**1117**	4.2-3.4	22-**6**	15-17	438-374	**224**-167	**3357**-2289	7.7-6.1	**25**-17	31-24	268-**408**	66.2-53.2
Was	6-5-1	.545	—	208-215	413-455	1726-1886	4.2-4.1	10-15	18-17	278-350	107-171	1736-**1950**	6.2-**5.6**	12-8	29-27	228-198	35.0-41.5
Pit	6-6	.500	—	211-263	432-366	1549-1125	3.6-**3.1**	13-9	14-14	416-372	189-193	2014-2413	4.8-6.5	10-22	21-21	164-157	47.1-68.5
NYG	3-9	.250	—	179-277	398-385	1049-1360	2.6-3.5	6-12	**9**-14	345-368	158-173	1985-2558	5.8-7.0	16-20	34-23	274-177	40.1-62.3
ChiC	1-10-1	.091	—	190-337	322-440	1179-1662	3.7-3.8	7-24	21-12	408-341	181-176	2191-2619	5.4-7.7	14-17	27-24	328-255	45.3-64.4
Western Conference																	
Det	10-2	.833	L*	271-205	427-404	1812-1580	4.2-3.9	12-10	15-15	316-354	144-159	2309-2162	7.3-6.1	18-13	27-**38**	163-197	53.9-**37.6**
SF	9-3	.750	—	**372**-237	443-398	**2230**-1548	**5.0**-3.9	**26**-12	19-17	322-356	174-173	2407-2100	7.5-5.9	22-17	19-23	239-223	76.4-56.2
LA	8-3-1	.727	—	366-236	426-375	2148-1570	5.0-4.2	23-10	22-13	324-366	173-161	2672-2181	8.2-6.0	19-15	18-30	**107**-299	77.3-43.1
ChiB	3-8-1	.273	—	218-262	367-437	1129-1776	3.1-4.1	9-15	21-23	**446**-364	206-174	2637-2530	5.9-7.0	15-14	30-14	138-154	48.4-67.7
Bal	3-9	.250	—	182-350	376-445	1459-2315	3.9-5.2	7-21	21-**7**	319-321	126-165	1625-2411	5.1-7.5	13-21	27-29	368-240	34.5-60.4
GB	2-9-1	.182	—	200-338	424-407	1665-1746	3.9-4.3	14-24	14-19	352-**312**	147-**144**	1833-2341	5.2-7.5	9-15	34-28	278-236	27.5-50.3
Aver	12	—	—	258	401	1604	4.0	14	17	356	168	2319	6.5	16	26	233	53.6

TEAM	1D	PENY	PNT	FGM/A	RTNY	RTNTD	OFFY/DEFY	NETY	NETO	NP	PNP	DELP	PW	DELW	PRT	DR	YPD	DEL
Eastern Conference																		
Cle	213-206	680-335	43.8-40.8	23/26-2/13	421-**250**	4-1	4391-3575	816	**17**	**186**	**136**	50	**10.6**	0.3	**7.7**/2.4	160-167	27.4-21.4	6.0
Phi	**256**-186	779-606	42.4-42.5	4/15-9/18	465-608	2-4	**4811**-2998	1813	-5	137	131	6	9.4	-1.9	4.1/2.3	177-175	27.2-**17.1**	**10.0**
Was	181-210	**408**-596	38.5-41.7	11/22-12/23	553-626	3-2	3234-3638	-404	-3	-7	-46	39	5.8	0.7	1.1/1.6	158-176	20.5-20.7	-0.2
Pit	206-**184**	546-603	**46.9**-42.5	4/12-11/19	542-776	5-2	3399-3381	18	0	-52	2	-54	4.7	1.3	2.3/3.9	184-167	18.5-20.2	-1.8
NYG	166-189	411-625	39.2-43.0	3/12-9/20	746-1047	2-4	2760-3741	-981	-6	-98	-106	8	3.6	-0.5	0.9/4.0	178-177	15.5-21.1	-5.6
ChiC	184-216	611-615	41.6-42.0	9/24-8/**13**	788-270	2-4	3042-4026	-984	-12	-147	-130	-17	2.3	-0.8	1.8/3.9	181-183	16.8-22.0	-5.2
Western Conference																		
Det	206-194	427-463	40.6-40.4	14/23-6/19	**896**-701	3-4	3958-3545	413	11	66	78	-12	7.7	**2.3**	3.3/**1.0**	172-179	23.0-19.8	3.2
SF	243-206	772-615	40.6-41.0	10/18-9/16	638-313	1-1	4398-3425	973	2	135	89	46	9.4	-0.4	4.4/2.6	158-**159**	27.8-21.5	6.3
LA	214-194	597-465	42.2-40.5	11/25-11/23	743-729	6-4	4713-3452	1261	3	130	117	13	9.3	-0.8	5.8/1.7	182-186	25.9-18.6	7.3
ChiB	214-213	530-711	42.6-**36.5**	7/21-11/30	435-683	4-4	3628-4152	-524	-14	-44	-100	56	4.9	-1.4	2.8/4.9	186-177	19.5-23.5	-4.0
Bal	157-232	623-**757**	38.4-40.3	7/18-9/16	492-776	3-4	2716-4486	-1770	8	-168	-116	-52	1.8	1.2	0.5/3.1	186-185	14.6-24.2	-9.6
GB	189-199	624-617	37.6-41.7	5/16-11/22	699-639	4-5	3220-3851	-631	-1	-138	-57	-81	2.6	-0.0	0.3/2.9	**190**-181	16.9-21.3	-4.3
Aver	202	584	41.1	9/19	618	3	3689								3.1	176	21.0	

Rushing Attempts		Rushing Yards		Rushing Average		Rushing TDs		Rushing Rank		Passing Yards		Passing Average	
J.Perry-SF	192	J.Perry-SF	1018	S.Quinlan-LA	7.27	J.Perry-SF	10	J.Perry-SF	1118	O.Graham-Cle	2722	O.Graham-Cle	10.55
D.Towler-LA	152	D.Towler-LA	879	R.Renfro-Cle	5.87	T.Younger-LA	8	D.Towler-LA	949	B.Thomason-Phi	2462	Van Brocklin-LA	8.37
F.Rogel-Pit	137	S.Quinlan-LA	705	D.Towler-LA	5.78	D.Towler-LA	7	S.Quinlan-LA	745	Van Brocklin-LA	2393	Y.Tittle-SF	8.19
L.Chandnois-Pit	123	C.Justice-Was	616	J.Williams-Phi	5.66	Hoernschemeyer-Det	7	C.Justice-Was	636	G.Blanda-ChiB	2164	B.Thomason-Phi	8.10
J.Huzvar-Bal	119	F.Rogel-Pit	527	C.Justice-Was	5.36			J.Huzvar-Bal	555	Y.Tittle-SF	2121	B.Layne-Det	7.65

Completion Percent		TD Passes		TD Percent		INT Percent		Passer Rating		Passing Rank		Receptions	
O.Graham-Cle	64.7	B.Thomason-Phi	21	Y.Tittle-SF	7.7	O.Graham-Cle	3.5	O.Graham-Cle	99.7	O.Graham-Cle	1056	P.Pihos-Phi	63
Y.Tittle-SF	57.5	Y.Tittle-SF	20	J.Scarbath-Was	7.0	J.Finks-Pit	4.8	Van Brocklin-LA	84.1	Van Brocklin-LA	732	E.Nickel-Pit	62
Van Brocklin-LA	54.5	Van Brocklin-LA	19	B.Thomason-Phi	6.9	J.Root-ChiC	4.9	Y.Tittle-SF	84.1	B.Thomason-Phi	536	E.Hirsch-LA	61
B.Thomason-Phi	53.3	B.Layne-Det	16	Van Brocklin-LA	6.6	O.Graham-Cle	5.7	B.Thomason-Phi	75.8	Y.Tittle-SF	521	B.Stone-ChiC	56
C.Conerly-NYG	47.2	G.Blanda-ChiB	14	B.Layne-Det	5.9	Y.Tittle-SF	6.2	B.Layne-Det	59.6	B.Layne-Det	284	J.Dooley-ChiB	53

Receiving Yards		Receiving Average		Receiving TDs		Receiving Rank		Combined Net Yards		Total TDs		Total Points	
P.Pihos-Phi	1049	B.Boyd-LA	22.83	B.Wilson-SF	10	P.Pihos-Phi	575	L.Chandnois-Pit	1593	J.Perry-SF	13	G.Soltau-SF	114
E.Hirsch-LA	941	H.Taylor-Was	20.09	P.Pihos-Phi	10	E.Hirsch-LA	491	H.McElhenny-SF	1449	B.Wilson-SF	10	L.Groza-Cle	108
J.Dooley-ChiB	841	P.Brewster-Cle	19.75	H.Taylor-Was	8	B.Wilson-SF	470	J.Perry-SF	1230	P.Pihos-Phi	10	D.Walker-Det	93
B.Wilson-SF	840	L.Hart-Det	18.88	L.Hart-Det	7	J.Dooley-ChiB	441	J.Szafaryn-Bal	1187			B.Walston-Phi	87
D.Lavelli-Cle	783	B.Howton-GB	18.52			D.Lavelli-Cle	422	W.Lewis-LA	1186			J.Perry-SF	78

Punt Average		Field Goals		Field Goal Percent		Kickoff Returns		Kickoff Return Average		Punt Returns		Punt Return Average	
P.Brady-Pit	46.9	L.Groza-Cle	23	L.Groza-Cle	88.5	W.Lewis-LA	32	J.Arenas-SF	34.4	E.Tunnell-NYG	38	C.Trippi-ChiC	11.4
H.Gillom-Cle	43.8	D.Walker-Det	12	G.Soltau-SF	66.7	J.Cannady-GB	26	L.Chandnois-Pit	29.0	W.Lewis-LA	35	J.Cannady-GB	9.9
A.Burk-Phi	43.0	B.Dudley-Was	11	D.Walker-Det	63.2	L.Chandnois-Pit	21	E.Macon-ChiB	28.7	L.Chandnois-Pit	26	J.Williams-Was	9.6
C.Trippi-ChiC	42.9	G.Soltau-SF	10	B.Dudley-Was	50.0	L.Campbell-ChiB	19	E.Tunnell-NYG	28.2	C.Trippi-ChiC	21	Y.Lary-Det	8.8
F.Morrison-ChiB	42.6	B.Agajanian-LA	10	B.Agajanian-LA	41.7	E.Tunnell-NYG	17	W.Lewis-LA	25.9			R.Mathews-Pit	8.0

Punt/Kick Return Yards		Punt/Kick Return TDs		Interceptions		Interception Return Yards		Interception Return TDs		Sacks		Overall Rank	
W.Lewis-LA	1097	Many	1	Christiansen-Det	12	Christiansen-Det	238	Many	1	Not kept		O.Graham-Cle	1259
J.Cannady-GB	840			T.Keane-Bal	11	R.Ramsey-ChiC	237					J.Perry-SF	1227
L.Chandnois-Pit	711			R.Ramsey-ChiC	10	D.Kindt-ChiB	172					D.Towler-LA	1017
E.Tunnell-NYG	702			D.Doll-Was	10	J.Butler-Pit	147					L.Chandnois-Pit	988
J.Arenas-SF	644					R.Berry-SF	142					H.McElhenny-SF	964

THE PROUD FIRST FACE OF THE LEAGUE

Jim Thorpe, the league's first president and one of its early stars, died in March. Thorpe often said that football was his favorite sport, but he also played major league baseball for six seasons. He set Olympic records in the pentathlon and decathlon, although those marks were expunged and his medals taken back because of a discrepancy regarding his amateur status. Regardless, a 1950 poll of sportswriters had dubbed Thorpe the greatest athlete of the first half of the 20th century.

After eight division titles and two NFL championships, Giants coach Steve Owen retired after a disappointing season. In his 23rd season, Owen still helped draft and develop rookie tackle Rosey Brown. Center Jim Ringo quit the Packers in training camp only to return and embark on a Hall of Fame career.

Pro football came back to Baltimore after a two-year absence. A new franchise was granted to Carroll Rosenbloom to replace the defunct Dallas Texans. The second incarnation of the Baltimore Colts inherited the Texans players, including future Hall of Famers Art Donovan and Gino Marchetti. They also restocked with a trade that sent five players to Cleveland in exchange for ten. Despite a good foundation, the overmatched Colts allowed a league-worst 350 points and finished at 3–9.

Mickey McBride, founder of the Cleveland Browns, sold the club to a group of local investors in June. Along with coach Paul Brown, McBride had been the architect of one of the most successful teams in pro football history. After the NFL and AAFC merged, however, McBride's interest waned. Brown's didn't. With Otto Graham leading the league in passing for the second straight season, and Lou Groza setting a record by kicking 23 field goals, Cleveland seemed headed for an undefeated season. It ended harshly with a trouncing by the Eagles, 42–27.

A pair of narrow wins over San Francisco gave Detroit the Eastern Division title. Rookie linebacker Joe Schmidt and defensive backs Yale Lary and Jack Christiansen helped form one of the league's best defenses. Free-spirited quarterback Bobby Layne engineered a touchdown drive in the closing minutes of the title game to give the Lions their second straight championship.

1954 NFL

TEAM	W-L-T	PCT	POST	PTS	RA	RY	RY/A	RTD	FL	PA	PC	GPY	GPY/A	PTD	PI	PSY	PRAT
Eastern Conference																	
Cle	9-3	.750	L*	336-162	476-372	1793-1050	3.8-2.8	23-4	17-19	295-300	174-126	2557-1784	8.7-5.9	14-15	22-23	226-176	72.1-46.6
Phi	7-4-1	.636	—	284-230	401-354	1196-1063	3.0-3.0	4-8	22-22	401-345	206-143	2982-2030	7.4-5.9	33-13	30-28	375-346	72.1-39.9
NYG	7-5	.583	—	293-184	380-415	1482-1332	3.9-3.2	8-9	15-22	334-352	163-164	2467-2322	7.4-6.6	27-11	22-33	141-306	73.0-39.7
Pit	5-7	.417	—	219-263	368-466	1282-2193	3.5-4.7	10-14	17-20	386-295	189-167	2321-2458	6.0-8.3	15-18	26-30	148-281	52.8-64.7
Was	3-9	.250	—	207-432	427-400	1626-1888	3.8-4.7	9-20	23-18	257-387	116-217	1813-3060	7.1-7.9	15-33	32-19	319-155	49.0-90.8
ChiC	2-10	.167	—	183-347	418-400	1612-1532	3.9-3.8	10-13	23-19	349-356	184-193	1903-3006	5.5-8.4	8-29	30-24	241-212	32.0-81.5
Western Conference																	
Det	9-2-1	.818	L	337-189	393-397	1608-1520	4.1-3.8	11-13	11-12	395-357	215-150	2972-2390	7.5-6.7	25-10	21-30	147-164	77.7-39.3
ChiB	8-4	.667	—	301-279	353-427	1142-1917	3.2-4.5	8-15	15-18	429-369	208-177	3299-2432	7.7-6.6	26-13	35-27	195-244	60.7-50.8
SF	7-4-1	.636	—	313-251	442-348	2498-1371	5.7-3.9	28-8	13-18	340-374	187-193	2444-3015	7.2-8.1	10-24	12-19	238-366	73.0-78.9
LA	6-5-1	.545	—	314-285	432-368	2140-1615	5.0-4.4	24-14	18-6	321-393	171-219	3180-2697	9.9-6.9	15-16	23-23	133-130	73.5-66.3
GB	4-8	.333	—	234-251	321-403	1328-1871	4.1-4.6	13-13	12-14	412-374	195-208	2454-2690	6.0-7.2	14-17	19-19	295-211	58.5-72.4
Bal	3-9	.250	—	131-279	364-425	1275-1630	3.5-3.8	4-21	12-10	313-330	163-178	1995-2503	6.4-7.6	9-12	22-20	336-203	52.3-65.5
Aver	12	—		263	398	1582	4.0	13	17	353	178	2532	7.2	18	25	233	61.7

TEAM	1D	PENY	PNT	FGM/A	RTNY	RTNTD	OFFY/DEFY	NETY	NETTO	NP	PNP	DELP	PW	DELW	PRT	DR	YPD	DEL
Eastern Conference																		
Cle	238-147	796-608	42.9-40.1	16/24-3/9	693-496	4-3	4124-2658	1466	3	174	134	40	10.4	-1.3	4.6/2.2	170-168	24.3-15.8	8.4
Phi	221-171	874-589	40.0-42.3	4/10-13/28	599-780	2-6	3803-2747	1056	-2	54	80	-26	7.3	0.1	3.5/1.4	189-188	20.1-14.6	5.5
NYG	197-195	502-562	42.5-40.2	13/25-8/15	675-504	1-3	3808-3348	460	18	109	110	-1	8.7	-1.7	4.6/1.6	177-175	21.5-19.1	2.4
Pit	205-221	471-823	43.2-39.9	8/13-8/17	679-634	3-2	3455-4370	-915	7	-44	-48	4	4.9	0.1	2.8/3.1	168-163	20.6-26.8	-6.2
Was	188-282	455-739	40.2-39.6	5/10-12/16	254-728	3-4	3120-4793	-1673	-19	-225	-215	-10	0.4	2.6	0.7/6.0	167-166	18.7-28.9	-10.2
ChiC	184-226	819-716	39.2-41.7	8/19-11/16	502-452	5-3	3274-4326	-1052	-10	-164	-128	-36	1.9	0.1	1.0/5.2	170-171	19.3-25.3	-6.0
Western Conference																		
Det	236-199	689-489	41.0-39.3	12/23-10/18	736-254	7-0	4433-3746	687	10	148	97	51	9.7	-0.2	5.2/2.6	160-173	27.7-21.7	6.1
ChiB	219-221	592-696	40.1-39.4	12/22-13/25	644-827	4-6	4246-4105	141	-5	-22	-8	30	6.6	1.5	3.9/2.8	181-181	23.5-22.7	0.8
SF	252-207	614-426	37.0-41.0	12/21-9/19	487-436	2-0	4704-4020	684	12	62	105	-43	7.6	-0.0	4.8/4.8	159-158	29.6-25.4	4.1
LA	255-240	757-605	42.6-43.0	9/16-16/26	475-666	2-4	5187-4182	1005	-12	29	36	-7	6.7	-0.2	6.4/4.1	159-154	32.6-27.2	5.5
GB	207-228	522-666	41.7-40.1	9/16-7/14	679-670	3-3	3487-4350	-863	-9	-17	-64	47	5.6	-1.6	3.2/4.5	156-160	22.4-27.2	-4.8
Bal	169-234	662-834	37.2-39.8	11/23-9/19	334-382	1-3	2934-3930	-996	-4	-148	-99	-49	2.3	0.7	2.1/4.3	155-154	18.9-25.5	-6.6
Aver	214	646	40.5	10/19	563	3	3881	—	—	—	—	—	—	—	3.9	168	23.2	

Rushing Attempts		Rushing Yards		Rushing Average		Rushing TDs		Rushing Rank		Passing Yards		Passing Average	
J.Perry-SF	173	J.Perry-SF	1049	H.McElhenny-SF	8.05	D.Towler-LA	11	J.Perry-SF	1129	Van Brocklin-LA	2637	Van Brocklin-LA	10.14
C.Jagade-ChiB	157	J.Johnson-SF	681	T.Younger-LA	6.70	J.Johnson-SF	9	J.Johnson-SF	771	T.Rote-GB	2311	O.Graham-Cle	8.72
D.Towler-LA	149	T.Younger-LA	610	J.Perry-SF	6.06			D.Towler-LA	709	Y.Tittle-SF	2205	J.Brandt-ChiB	8.36
M.Bassett-Cle	144	D.Towler-LA	599	S.Quinlan-LA	5.98			T.Younger-LA	690	O.Graham-Cle	2092	T.Dublinski-Det	7.78
E.Price-NYG	135	M.Bassett-Cle	588	F.Gifford-NYG	5.58			M.Bassett-Cle	648	J.Finks-Pit	2003	G.Cifelli-NYG	7.73

Completion Percent		TD Passes		TD Percent		INT Percent		Passer Rating		Passing Rank		Receptions	
O.Graham-Cle	59.2	A.Burk-Phi	23	A.Burk-Phi	10.0	Y.Tittle-SF	3.1	A.Burk-Phi	80.4	Y.Tittle-SF	788	B.Wilson-SF	60
Y.Tittle-SF	57.6	C.Conerly-NYG	17	C.Conerly-NYG	8.1	T.Rote-GB	4.7	T.Dublinski-Det	79.2	Van Brocklin-LA	544	P.Pihos-Phi	60
T.Dublinski-SF	55.8	G.Blanda-ChiB	15	J.Scarbath-Was	6.4	B.Layne-Det	4.9	Y.Tittle-SF	78.7	T.Rote-GB	506	B.Boyd-LA	53
B.Layne-Det	54.9			J.Brandt-ChiB	6.2	T.Dublinski-Det	5.1	B.Layne-Det	77.3	B.Layne-Det	499	B.Howton-GB	52
G.Kerkorian-Bal	53.9			G.Cifelli-NYG	5.9	C.Conerly-NYG	5.2	C.Conerly-NYG	76.7	O.Graham-Cle	421	D.Lavelli-Cle	47

Receiving Yards		Receiving Average		Receiving TDs		Receiving Rank		Combined Net Yards		Total TDs		Total Points	
B.Boyd-LA	1212	H.Hill-ChiB	24.98	H.Hill-ChiB	12	B.Boyd-LA	636	O.Matson-ChiC	1666	H.Hill-ChiB	12	B.Walston-Phi	114
H.Hill-ChiB	1124	B.Boyd-LA	22.87	B.Walston-Phi	11	H.Hill-ChiB	622	J.Perry-SF	1252	B.Walston-Phi	11	D.Walker-Det	106
P.Pihos-Phi	872	E.Hirsch-LA	20.57	P.Pihos-Phi	10	P.Pihos-Phi	486	B.Boyd-LA	1212	P.Pihos-Phi	10	L.Groza-Cle	85
B.Wilson-SF	830	J.Dooley-ChiB	19.35	M.McGee-GB	9	B.Wilson-SF	440	B.Wells-Was	1154			G.Soltau-SF	76
D.Lavelli-Cle	802	K.Rote-NYG	19.00			D.Lavelli-Cle	436	H.Hill-ChiB	1124			B.Agajanian-NYG	74

Punt Average		Field Goals		Field Goal Percent		Kickoff Returns		Kickoff Return Average		Punt Returns		Punt Return Average	
P.Brady-Pit	43.2	L.Groza-Cle	16	L.Groza-Cle	66.7	W.Lewis-LA	34	B.Reynolds-Cle	29.5	C.Hanulak-Cle	27	V.Switzer-GB	12.8
H.Gillom-Cle	42.9	B.Agajanian-NYG	13	D.Walker-Det	64.7	L.Goble-ChiC	27	L.Goble-ChiC	27.7	B.Reynolds-Cle	25	H.Johnson-NYG	10.3
Van Brocklin-LA	42.6	D.Walker-Det	11	G.Soltau-SF	61.1	D.Atkeson-Was	24	B.Carey-GB	26.5	V.Switzer-GB	24	Christiansen-Det	9.8
T.Landry-NYG	42.5	G.Soltau-SF	11	F.Cone-GB	56.3	V.Switzer-GB	20	O.Matson-ChiC	26.4			J.Williams-Phi	6.7
M.McGee-GB	41.7	F.Cone-GB	9	L.Richter-LA	53.3	B.Carey-GB	20	D.Atkeson-Was	26.0			B.Reynolds-GB	5.5

Punt/Kick Return Yards		Punt/Kick Return TDs		Interceptions		Interception Return Yards		Interception Return TDs		Sacks		Overall Rank	
W.Lewis-LA	918	O.Matson-ChiC	2	N.Lane-ChiC	10	N.Lane-ChiC	181	K.Konz-Cle	2	Not kept		J.Perry-SF	1248
V.Switzer-GB	806	L.Goble-ChiC	2	D.Alban-Was	9	K.Konz-Cle	133	J.Butler-Pit	2			O.Matson-ChiC	1121
L.Goble-ChiC	800					R.Craft-Pit	120					Y.Tittle-SF	896
D.Atkeson-Was	652					P.Cameron-Pit	118					T.Rote-GB	887
B.Carey-GB	574											J.Johnson-SF	868

SAN FRANCISCO'S GOLDEN RUSHERS

San Francisco's ground attack was overwhelming. The 49ers averaged more than 200 yards a game, with leading rusher Hugh McElhenny gaining a phenomenal 8.0 yards per carry midway through the season. McElhenny separated his shoulder on October 31, and the 49ers lost their first game and their biggest star. Their running game was still formidable, but without McElhenny's explosiveness, the offense was inconsistent and the Niners lost three of their final six games. Still, halfback Joe Perry led the league in rushing while rookie fullback John Henry Johnson finished second. Perry became the first player to surpass 1,000 yards rushing in consecutive seasons. All three backs would eventually be inducted into the Hall of Fame.

A prolific passing game helped the Eagles to a 4-0 start. Quarterback Adrian Burk threw 7 touchdown passes in a lopsided win against the Redskins, but then the offense suddenly went flat. Philadelphia lost four of its next five games, including a tough 6-0 loss to the first-place Browns that kept Philadelphia from challenging for the division title.

A new era began in New York when Jim Lee Howell was named head coach of the Giants. He recruited Vince Lombardi to run the offense and picked All-Pro defensive back Tom Landry to run the defense as a player-coach. Lombardi breathed new life into a stagnant offense, while Landry's innovative strategies helped the Giants nab a league-high 33 interceptions.

When the Browns were routed in two of their first three games, many began to suspect that the Cleveland dynasty might be over. Quarterback Otto Graham rallied the offense with wins by scores of 35-3 and 62-3, and a re-energized defense allowed just 58 points during an eight-game winning streak.

Detroit coach Buddy Parker kept his team on track, despite the loss of several players to military service and injuries to quarterback Bobby Layne. A big factor in that success was a stellar defense. Les Bingaman was one of the league's toughest linemen, and Jack Christiansen led a secondary that came to be known as "Chris's Crew." For the third straight season, the Lions and Browns met in the title game.

1955 NFL

TEAM	W-L-T	PCT	POST	PTS	RA	RY	RY/A	RTD	FL	PA	PC	GPY	GPY/A	PTD	PI	PSY	PRAT
Eastern Conference																	
Cle	9-2-1	.818	L*	349-218	536-351	2020-1189	3.8-3.4	20-11	18-15	234-323	130-126	2225-1775	9.5-5.5	21-15	11-25	275-123	98.3-40.7
Was	8-4	.667	—	246-222	478-391	2000-1275	4.2-3.3	17-8	21-24	257-340	101-165	1549-2189	6.0-6.4	11-17	21-19	201-274	40.2-62.7
NYG	6-5-1	.545	—	267-223	414-418	1693-1441	4.1-3.4	12-10	16-16	292-373	137-181	1865-2543	6.4-6.8	17-16	15-23	105-176	65.8-59.5
ChiC	4-7-1	.364	—	224-252	438-465	1626-1902	3.7-4.1	10-11	20-18	280-371	106-154	1520-2146	5.4-5.8	14-16	25-29	175-138	35.7-42.6
Phi	4-7-1	.364	—	248-231	392-455	1317-1637	3.4-3.6	9-12	21-20	400-272	198-124	2696-1810	6.7-6.7	19-12	24-16	224-216	62.3-58.0
Pit	4-8	.333	—	195-285	420-494	1284-1814	3.1-3.7	13-11	17-19	390-242	189-123	2550-1530	6.5-6.3	12-19	30-10	163-235	47.9-79.7
Western Conference																	
LA	8-3-1	.727	L	260-231	451-423	1943-1624	4.3-3.8	17-10	10-15	344-351	175-193	2206-2518	6.4-7.2	9-18	18-31	145-209	58.1-58.1
ChiB	8-4	.667	—	294-251	487-398	2388-2100	4.9-5.3	19-17	18-15	306-354	145-177	2108-2369	6.9-6.7	17-14	23-19	180-312	57.5-62.5
GB	6-6	.500	—	258-276	433-475	1883-2174	4.3-4.6	11-18	25-18	159-118	109-154	2004-1768	5.8-6.8	17-13	19-31	225-80	57.7-45.6
Bal	5-6-1	.455	—	214-239	456-448	1833-2035	4.0-4.5	15-18	8-14	266-320	134-158	1795-2288	6.7-7.2	11-12	22-19	164-201	51.5-60.8
SF	4-8	.333	—	216-298	408-538	1713-2135	4.2-4.0	12-24	18-13	303-311	151-147	2225-2045	7.3-6.6	17-10	28-21	287-172	54.4-51.5
Det	3-9	.250	—	230-275	392-449	1477-1851	3.8-4.1	11-16	19-24	400-304	204-163	2542-2304	6.4-7.6	15-18	22-15	182-140	60.6-77.5
Aver	12	—	—	250	442	1765	4.0	14	18	318	152	2107	6.6	15	22	190	57.1

TEAM	1D	PENY	PNT	FGM/A	RTNY	RTNTD	OFFY/DEFY	NETY	NETTO	NP	PNP	DELP	PW	DELW	PRT	DR	YPD	DEL
Eastern Conference																		
Cle	224-171	603-560	41.2-39.1	11/22-7/15	624-367	4-3	3970-2841	1129	11	131	138	-7	9.3	0.2	6.2/2.0	167-166	23.8-17.1	6.7
Was	193-189	648-694	41.6-41.2	6/21-9/19	622-496	5-3	3348-3190	158	1	24	17	7	6.6	1.4	1.8/3.3	167-170	20.0-18.8	1.3
NYG	189-209	458-439	40.3-41.6	10/15-5/20	480-375	5-4	3453-3808	-355	8	44	2	42	7.1	-0.6	4.1/3.8	165-168	20.9-22.7	-1.7
ChiC	150-224	695-677	40.3-40.6	9/21-11/29	776-549	5-4	2971-3910	-939	2	-28	-70	42	5.3	-0.8	1.2/2.2	180-183	16.5-21.4	-4.9
Phi	219-174	542-463	42.9-39.1	11/26-12/23	397-434	3-4	3789-3231	558	-9	17	11	6	6.4	-1.9	3.7/3.3	173-175	21.9-18.5	3.4
Pit	211-176	604-657	38.4-42.1	4/18-12/25	173-798	2-6	3671-3109	562	-18	-90	-25	-65	3.8	0.3	2.8/3.8	182-175	20.2-17.8	2.4
Western Conference																		
LA	233-245	612-430	44.6-42.4	14/32-10/17	582-602	5-1	4004-3933	71	18	29	78	-49	6.7	1.8	3.7/2.9	161-163	24.9-24.1	0.7
ChiB	235-216	498-530	39.9-40.2	11/16-11/24	446-448	1-1	4316-4157	159	-7	43	-15	58	7.1	0.9	3.2/3.4	168-163	25.7-25.5	0.2
GB	213-196	401-490	43.2-41.8	16/24-8/17	680-491	2-5	3662-3862	-200	5	-18	3	-21	5.6	0.4	2.9/1.6	166-166	22.1-23.3	-1.2
Bal	206-234	565-681	39.3-39.9	11/26-10/14	438-340	0-0	3464-4122	-658	3	-25	-43	18	5.4	0.1	2.6/3.9	145-149	23.9-27.7	-3.8
SF	204-250	541-528	40.6-42.6	3/12-12/24	360-468	1-3	3651-4008	-357	-12	-82	-78	-4	4.0	0.0	2.5/3.1	164-165	22.3-24.3	-2.0
Det	224-217	526-544	39.7-40.6	9/17-8/23	448-458	3-2	3887-4015	-128	-2	-45	-19	-26	4.9	-1.9	3.8/5.2	171-166	22.7-24.2	-1.5
Aver	208	558	41.0	10/21	502	3	3682								3.5	167	22.0	—

Rushing Attempts	Rushing Yards	Rushing Average	Rushing TDs	Rushing Rank	Passing Yards	Passing Average
A.Ameche-Bal..........213	A.Ameche-Bal......961	R.Casares-ChiB......5.38	A.Ameche-Bal............9	A.Ameche-Bal.......1051	J.Finks-Pit.............2270	O.Graham-Cle.........9.30
H.Ferguson-GB 192	H.Ferguson-GB....859	B.Watkins-ChiB......5.28	B.Watkins-ChiB........8	H.Ferguson-GB.......899	Y.Tittle-SF.............2185	E.Brown-ChiB.........7.97
P.Miller-Cle.........185	F.Morrison-Cle....824	B.Watkins-ChiB......5.03	R.Waller-LA.............7	F.Morrison-Cle.......854	T.Rote-GB.............1977	B.Thomason-Phi......7.82
F.Rogel-Pit.........168	R.Waller-LA........716	A.Webster-NYG.....4.95		R.Waller-LA...........786	Van Brocklin-LA......1890	Y.Tittle-SF..............7.61
	J.Perry-SF.........701	J.Hoffman-ChiB......4.83		J.Perry-SF............721	B.Layne-Det...........1830	E.LeBaron-Was.......7.13
Completion Percent	**TD Passes**	**TD Percent**	**INT Percent**	**Passer Rating**	**Passing Rank**	**Receptions**
O.Graham-Cle....53.0	Y.Tittle-SF...........17	O.Graham-Cle........8.1	H.Gilmer-Det.........3.3	O.Graham-Cle........94.0	O.Graham-Cle.......616	P.Pihos-Phi...........62
B.Layne-Det.....53.0	T.Rote-GB............17	C.Conerly-NYG.......6.4	B.Thomason-Phi.....4.1	B.Thomason-Phi.....80.0	B.Thomason-Phi.....439	B.Wilson-SF..........53
Van Brocklin-LA..52.9	O.Graham-Cle.......15	Y.Tittle-SF.............5.9	O.Graham-Cle........4.3	E.Brown-ChiB........71.4	Van Brocklin-LA......385	
E.Brown-ChiB....51.8	C.Conerly-NYG......13	B.Thomason-Phi......5.8	Van Brocklin-LA.....5.5	C.Conerly-NYG........64.2	T.Rote-GB............314	
B.Thomason-Phi...51.5		E.Brown-ChiB........5.5	T.Rote-GB.............5.6	Van Brocklin-LA......62.0	E.Brown-ChiB.........299	
Receiving Yards	**Receiving Average**	**Receiving TDs**	**Receiving Rank**	**Combined Net Yards**	**Total TDs**	**Total Points**
P.Pihos-Phi..........864	R.Renfro-Cle......20.79	H.Hill-ChiB...............9	P.Pihos-Phi...........467	R.Waller-LA..........1465	H.Hill-ChiB...............9	D.Walker-Det..........96
B.Wilson-SF.........831	H.Hill-ChiB.........18.79	K.Rote-NYG............8	B.Wilson-SF...........451	O.Matson-ChiC.......1325	A.Ameche-Bal...........9	V.Janowicz-Was......88
H.Hill-ChiB...........789	K.Rote-NYG........18.71	R.Renfro-Cle...........8	H.Hill-ChiB............440	A.Ameche-Bal........1162		G.Blanda-ChiB........82
R.Mathews-Pit.......762	E.Hirsch-LA........18.40	G.Knafelc-GB...........8	R.Mathews-Pit........411	B.Zagers-Was........1106		F.Cone-GB.............78
B.Howton-GB........697	P.Brewster-Cle....18.29		B.Howton-GB..........374	B.George-Phi.........1061		L.Groza-GB............77
Punt Average	**Field Goals**	**Field Goal Percent**	**Kickoff Returns**	**Kickoff Return Average**	**Punt Returns**	**Punt Return Average**
Van Brocklin-LA.....44.6	F.Cone-GB.............16	G.Blanda-ChiB......68.8	S.Watson-Pit............27	A.Carapella-GB......29.9	B.Rechichar-Bal........30	O.Matson-ChiC........18.8
D.Deschaine-GB....43.2	L.Richter-LA...........13	F.Cone-GB...........66.7	J.Scudero-Was.........25	J.Scudero-Was........28.0	W.Lewis-LA.............29	J.Scudero-Was.........9.6
A.Burk-Phi.........42.9	L.Groza-Cle...........11	B.Agajanian-NYG.....66.7	D.Doyle-ChiB...........25	R.Waller-LA...........27.1	E.Tunnell-NYG..........25	F.Bernardi-ChiC........8.6
E.LeBaron-Was.....41.6	G.Blanda-ChiB........11	D.Walker-Det.......56.3	J.Arenas-SF............24	S.Watson-Pit..........26.5	J.Scudero-Was..........25	K.Konz-Cle...........8.1
J.Girard-Det.......41.3		L.Richter-LA........54.2	W.Lewis-LA.............20	V.Switzer-GB..........26.2	V.Switzer-GB...........24	D.Paul-Cle.............7.8
Punt/Kick Return Yards	**Punt/Kick Return TDs**	**Interceptions**	**Interception Return Yards**	**Interception Return TDs**	**Sacks**	**Overall Rank**
J.Scudero-Was 940	J.Scudero-Was 2	W.Sherman-LA........11	B.Bawel-Phi............168	B.Bawel-Phi................2	Not kept	A.Ameche-Bal.........1122
S.Watson-Pit.........731	J.Patton-NYG.............2	B.Dillon-GB.............9	C.Sumner-ChiB.........162			R.Waller-LA............1101
D.Doyle-ChiB........691	O.Matson-ChiC............2	D.Burroughs-LA.........9	B.Dillon-GB.............153			H.Ferguson-GB 981
J.Arenas-SF.........649		B.Bawel-Phi.............9	B.Rechichar-Bal........109			O.Matson-ChiC........978
O.Matson-ChiC.......613			K.Gorgal-ChiB..........107			F.Morrison-Cle........947

GRAHAM ENDS LIKE HE STARTED

Three straight trips to the NFL Championship Game had the Lions flying high, but it all came crashing down in 1955. The retirement of Les Bingaman left a hole in the middle of defense that couldn't be filled. Making matters worse, quarterback Bobby Layne injured his shoulder in a horse-riding accident during the offseason. Their fiery leader suited up, but he was largely ineffective. The Lions dropped their first six games and finished last.

For the third time in his career, George Halas announced that he would step down as Chicago's coach. After losing their first three games, the Bears rallied and won six straight. Halas built an effective running game around rookie backs Rick Casares and Bobby Watkins. In late November the Bears were thrashed by the rival Cardinals, 53–14. The Bears fell percentage points behind the Rams.

The Redskins welcomed old friends and new respectability. Quarterback Eddie LeBaron and defensive end Gene Brito had spent the previous season playing in Canada, and their homecoming sparked Washington to a second-place finish. Running back Vic Janowicz, the former Ohio State star who had spent two years playing major league baseball, scored 88 points.

Sid Gillman took over as coach of the Rams and restored some balance to an offense that had grown pass-happy. Rookie Ron Waller gave the team a breakaway runner to compliment hard-charging Tank Younger. Los Angeles now threw less but won more. Three straight victories at the end of the season helped them to surge pass the Bears and claim the division title.

Otto Graham retired at the end of the 1954 season, and Cleveland felt prepared for life without him. But when rookie quarterback Bobby Freeman jumped to Canada and backup George Ratterman struggled during the preseason, head coach Paul Brown lured Graham back to action. With just three weeks of practice, the 33-year old passer was rusty and the Browns lost their opening game. It didn't take Graham too long to get back on track. The Browns won their next six games and cruised to their 10th straight division title. Graham finished his remarkable career with his seventh career championship.

1956 NFL

TEAM	W-L-T	PCT	POST	PTS	RA	RY	RY/A	RTD	FL	PA	PC	GPY	GPY/A	PTD	PI	PSY	PRAT
Eastern Conference																	
NYG	8-3-1	.727	L*	264-197	499-415	2129-1443	4.3-3.5	18-10	13-16	275-297	133-149	1601-1890	5.8-6.4	17-12	14-17	34-252	66.0-60.0
ChiC	7-5	.583	—	240-182	527-478	2053-2075	3.9-4.3	14-14	21-12	214-287	100-129	1492-1670	7.0-5.8	13-8	14-33	123-146	63.1-33.5
Was	6-6	.500	—	183-225	501-446	1743-1570	3.5-3.5	5-15	17-16	215-240	104-120	1335-1739	6.2-7.2	11-11	18-18	117-110	50.4-58.0
Cle	5-7	.417	—	167-177	480-463	1845-2032	3.8-4.4	8-13	12-8	202-226	105-107	1358-1215	6.7-5.4	8-7	18-18	183-112	49.5-41.1
Pit	5-7	.417	—	217-250	413-468	1350-1743	3.3-3.7	14-14	10-22	318-234	136-128	1793-1646	5.6-7.0	14-14	24-18	127-203	44.4-64.9
Phi	3-8-1	.273	—	143-215	418-513	1377-1893	3.3-3.7	11-10	11-11	249-243	122-114	1556-1506	6.2-6.2	6-15	27-16	279-173	37.4-60.1
Western Conference																	
ChiB	9-2-1	.818	L	363-246	536-384	2468-1483	4.6-3.9	22-14	10-15	250-332	135-159	2193-2413	8.8-7.3	19-16	19-23	124-220	77.3-59.5
Det	9-3	.750	—	300-188	507-373	2011-1503	4.0-4.0	21-9	11-12	301-297	160-138	2250-2045	7.5-6.9	13-11	23-28	55-140	60.1-42.6
SF	5-6-1	.455	—	233-284	419-481	1836-2192	4.4-4.6	17-23	12-17	297-279	162-147	2262-2115	7.6-7.6	8-12	19-17	285-145	61.6-66.5
Bal	5-7	.417	—	270-322	432-447	2202-1916	5.1-4.3	21-16	14-15	279-297	158-165	2210-2463	7.9-8.3	14-12	18-13	289-203	72.1-89.4
GB	4-8	.333	—	264-342	337-512	1421-2619	4.2-5.1	13-20	11-8	353-260	171-144	2591-2166	7.3-8.3	21-17	18-21	193-75	71.6-71.1
LA	4-8	.333	—	291-307	384-473	1978-1944	5.2-4.1	15-21	18-8	329-290	170-156	2601-2374	7.9-8.2	18-17	28-18	182-212	60.9-74.7
Aver	12	—		245	454	1868	4.1	15	13	274	138	1937	7.1	14	20	166	59.6

TEAM	1D	PENY	PNT	FGM/A	RTNY	RTNTD	OFFY/DEFY	NETY	NETTO	NP	PNP	DELP	PW	DELW	PRT	DR	YPD	DEL
Eastern Conference																		
NYG	223-188	474-495	41.8-36.5	6/15-7/16	360-572	0-3	3696-3081	615	6	67	75	-8	7.7	0.8	4.0/3.0	149-150	24.8-20.5	4.3
ChiC	191-211	626-543	37.8-39.2	10/22-7/16	756-305	3-1	3422-3599	-177	10	58	25	33	7.4	-0.5	3.8/0.4	148-155	23.1-23.2	-0.1
Was	176-188	383-548	42.4-40.7	17/25-8/15	421-449	3-3	2961-3199	-238	-1	-42	-24	-18	4.9	1.0	2.3/3.7	152-155	19.5-20.6	-1.2
Cle	173-188	457-529	41.9-40.7	11/20-10/17	591-416	3-1	3020-3135	-115	-4	-10	-26	16	5.8	-0.8	2.0/1.5	136-131	22.2-23.9	-1.7
Pit	184-167	614-606	38.2-41.6	5/9-7/16	611-815	1-5	3016-3186	-170	6	-33	10	-43	5.2	-0.2	2.2/3.0	167-161	18.1-19.8	-1.7
Phi	160-200	542-686	41.8-41.0	6/14-14/21	487-648	1-0	2654-3226	-572	-11	-72	-92	20	4.2	-0.7	0.4/2.9	153-150	17.3-21.5	-4.2
Western Conference																		
ChiB	244-207	553-624	39.3-40.0	12/28-3/18	615-586	6-4	4537-3676	861	9	117	108	9	8.9	0.6	5.3/3.7	166-160	27.3-23.0	4.4
Det	247-181	668-519	41.3-39.4	16/25-11/20	593-440	2-2	4206-3408	798	6	112	91	21	8.8	0.2	4.2/2.4	153-160	27.5-21.3	6.2
SF	221-236	562-321	38.4-40.7	13/20-14/25	286-453	3-0	3813-4162	-349	3	-51	-17	-34	4.7	0.8	3.6/4.5	147-150	25.9-27.7	-1.8
Bal	216-238	507-486	38.4-44.4	3/16-8/19	431-428	3-5	4123-4176	-53	-4	-52	-20	-32	4.7	0.3	4.0/5.9	158-156	26.1-26.8	-0.7
GB	212-246	393-493	42.7-40.8	5/8-12/18	645-592	2-7	3819-4710	-891	-9	-78	-74	-4	4.1	-0.0	4.8/4.9	153-146	25.0-32.3	-7.3
LA	227-224	583-512	43.1-42.0	9/19-12/20	581-673	5-1	4397-4106	291	-20	-16	-56	40	5.6	-1.6	3.8/4.8	155-163	28.4-25.2	3.2
Aver	206	530	40.5	9/18	531	3	3639	—	—	—	—	—			3.7	153	23.8	

Rushing Attempts	Rushing Yards	Rushing Average	Rushing TDs	Rushing Rank	Passing Yards	Passing Average
R.Casares-ChiB......234	R.Casares-ChiB.....1126	L.Moore-Bal......7.55	R.Casares-ChiB......12	R.Casares-ChiB......1246	T.Rote-GB......2203	E.Brown-ChiB......9.92
O.Matson-ChiC......192	O.Matson-ChiC.....924	T.Wilson-LA......7.34	T.Rote-GB......11	H.McElhenny-SF......996	B.Layne-Det......1909	B.Wade-LA......8.21
P.Carpenter-Cle......188	H.McElhenny-SF.....916	R.Waller-LA......6.54	L.Moore-Bal......8	O.Matson-ChiC......974	E.Brown-ChiB......1667	B.Layne-Det......7.82
H.McElhenny-SF......185	A.Ameche-Bal.....858	P.Jeter-ChiB......5.27	H.McElhenny-SF......8	A.Ameche-Bal......938	Y.Tittle-SF......1641	Van Brocklin-LA......7.79
	F.Gifford-NYG.....819	F.Gifford-NYG......5.15	A.Ameche-Bal......8	F.Gifford-NYG......869	G.Marchetti-Pit......1585	L.McHan-ChiC......7.63

Completion Percent	TD Passes	TD Percent	INT Percent	Passer Rating	Passing Rank	Receptions
E.Brown-ChiB......57.1	T.Rote-GB......18	A.Dorow-Was......7.1	C.Conerly-NYG......4.0	E.Brown-ChiB......83.1	T.Rote-GB......592	B.Wilson-SF......60
Y.Tittle-SF......56.9	G.Marchetti-Pit......12	L.McHan-ChiC......6.6	T.Rote-GB......4.9	C.Conerly-NYG......75.0	E.Brown-ChiB......409	B.Howton-GB......55
J.Unitas-Bal......55.6	E.Brown-ChiB......11	E.Brown-ChiB......6.5	J.Unitas-Bal......5.1	J.Unitas-Bal......74.0	J.Unitas-Bal......394	F.Gifford-NYG......51
Van Brocklin-LA......54.8		T.Rote-GB......5.8	L.McHan-ChiC......5.3	L.McHan-ChiC......73.3	Y.Tittle-SF......376	H.Hill-ChiB......47
B.Layne-Det......52.9		C.Conerly-NYG......5.7	Y.Tittle-SF......5.3	T.Rote-GB......70.6	C.Conerly-NYG......342	F.Morrison-Bal......44

Receiving Yards	Receiving Average	Receiving TDs	Receiving Rank	Combined Net Yards	Total TDs	Total Points
B.Howton-GB......1188	H.Hill-ChiB......24.00	B.Howton-GB......12	B.Howton-GB......654	O.Matson-ChiC......1524	R.Casares-ChiB......14	B.Layne-Det......99
H.Hill-ChiB......1128	B.Howton-GB......21.60	H.Hill-ChiB......11	H.Hill-ChiB......619	H.Carl-GB......1471	B.Howton-GB......12	R.Casares-ChiB......84
B.Wilson-SF......889	B.Boyd-LA......19.53	B.Boyd-LA......7	B.Wilson-SF......470	H.McElhenny-SF......1447	T.Rote-GB......11	G.Blanda-ChiB......81
F.Morrison-Bal......715	D.Dibble-Det......18.66		F.Morrison-Bal......388	R.Casares-ChiB......1424	H.Hill-ChiB......11	B.Howton-GB......72
L.Clarke-LA......650	L.Clarke-LA......18.06		L.Clarke-LA......345	F.Gifford-NYG......1422	A.Webster-NYG......10	F.Cone-GB......72

Punt Average	Field Goals	Field Goal Percent	Kickoff Returns	Kickoff Return Average	Punt Returns	Punt Return Average
Van Brocklin-LA......43.1	S.Baker-Was......17	B.Layne-Det......80.0	H.Carl-GB......33	T.Wilson-LA......31.8	C.Taseff-Bal......26	K.Konz-Cle......14.4
D.Deschaine-GB......42.7	G.Soltau-SF......13	S.Baker-Was......68.0	J.Arenas-SF......27	J.Arenas-SF......29.7	H.Ford-Pit......25	F.Bernardi-ChiC......12.1
S.Baker-Was......42.5	B.Layne-Det......12	G.Soltau-SF......65.0	J.Filipski-NYG......19	H.Carl-GB......28.1	E.Tunnell-NYG......22	K.Keller-Phi......9.7
D.Chandler-NYG......41.9	G.Blanda-ChiB......12	L.Groza-Cle......55.0	T.Runnels-Was......17	O.Matson-ChiC......27.8	Y.Lary-Det......22	C.Taseff-Bal......8.6
A.Burk-Phi......41.8	L.Groza-Cle......11	L.Richter-LA......53.3	D.Bingham-ChiB......17	D.Bingham-ChiB......26.1	H.Carl-GB......21	W.Sherman-LA......8.3

Punt/Kick Return Yards	Punt/Kick Return TDs	Interceptions	Interception Return Yards	Interception Return TDs	Sacks	Overall Rank
H.Carl-GB......1092	J.Arenas-SF......2	L.Crow-ChiC......11	B.Dillon-GB......244	J.Caroline-ChiB......2	Not kept	R.Casares-ChiB......1368
J.Arenas-SF......918		Y.Lary-Det......8	N.Lane-ChiC......206			O.Matson-ChiC......1275
K.Keller-Phi......499		N.Hecker-Was......8	D.Paul-Cle......190			F.Gifford-NYG......1178
T.Wilson-LA......477		Christiansen-Det......8	Y.Lary-Det......182			H.McElhenny-SF......1121
T.Runnels-Was......466			J.Caroline-ChiB......182			T.Rote-GB......1100

HIGH TV RATINGS, BUT LOW MORALE

The television era began as CBS began national broadcasts of regular-season NFL games across the country. Different matchups were televised in different regions, and fans got their first chance to see games that didn't involve the hometown team. The league's television contract brought a cash windfall for owners, and attendance continued to skyrocket.

For fans in Baltimore, the 1956 season began like a bad show they couldn't turn off. The Colts lost two of their first three and then quarterback George Shaw broke his leg in the fourth game. Onto the field trotted unheralded rookie Johnny Unitas to take his place. Released by the Steelers at the end of training camp a year earlier, he'd spent 1955 playing semi-pro ball for $6 a game. His debut was unspectacular, but Unitas won his first two starts, and when the Colts upset the Rams, 56–21, people really began to take notice. Two other rookies, Bart Starr and Earl Morrall, also took their first NFL snaps.

Early losses in Cleveland torpedoed the morale of a team that was unaccustomed to defeat. Each of the Browns' 10 seasons had ended with a trip to the championship game in either the AAFC or the NFL. For the first time the Browns had plenty of time to go Christmas shopping. The retirement of Otto Graham and a slew of injuries had left the dynasty in deterioration. The team rebounded from a 1–4 start to finish 5–7, but for Dante Lavelli, in his final year, it was a disappointing December.

Morale was also low in Washington. During training camp, halfback Vic Janowicz was seriously injured in an automobile accident. The former Heisman Trophy winner suffered a brain injury that left him partially paralyzed, ending a promising career. Washington owner George Preston Marshall dropped Janowicz from the payroll because the injury occurred in an off-the-field incident. His teammates started a fund to help defray medical costs, but players throughout the league were outraged at how easily a star player was abandoned. This was just one of several grievances that led the players to form a union in December.

1957 NFL

TEAM	W-L-T	PCT	POST	PTS	RA	RY	RY/A	RTD	FL	PA	PC	GPY	GPY/A	PTD	PI	PSY	PRAT
Eastern Conference																	
Cle	9-2-1	.818	L	269-172	501-396	1958-1502	3.9-3.8	19-11	10-12	195-242	108-105	1873-1511	9.6-6.2	12-8	14-19	161-211	78.9-42.6
NYG	7-5	.583	—	254-211	441-442	1649-1777	3.7-4.0	13-12	20-14	269-226	147-104	2158-1596	8.0-7.1	15-10	12-18	58-202	81.0-51.4
Pit	6-6	.500	—	161-178	390-412	1174-1425	3.0-3.5	7-7	18-23	312-234	149-112	2013-1523	6.5-6.5	11-12	14-19	297-157	61.8-52.4
Was	5-6-1	.455	—	251-230	500-394	1873-1567	3.7-4.0	17-11	17-12	201-262	109-135	1741-2193	8.7-8.4	11-18	13-16	120-165	74.7-77.4
Phi	4-8	.333	—	173-230	424-451	1582-1714	3.7-3.8	9-15	16-19	204-257	99-133	1379-2083	6.8-8.1	10-10	23-17	224-114	47.4-64.4
ChiC	3-9	.250	—	200-299	365-521	1442-2201	4.0-4.2	12-9	15-13	271-233	111-117	1969-2027	7.3-8.7	12-17	22-12	194-120	47.4-83.0
Western Conference																	
Det	8-4	.667	CL*	251-231	409-406	1811-1521	4.4-3.7	12-13	13-18	361-290	163-163	2239-2099	6.2-7.2	17-15	22-25	210-255	55.9-60.4
SF	8-4	.667	C	260-264	377-434	1622-1847	4.3-4.6	15-18	14-16	305-332	191-182	2407-2582	7.9-7.8	17-13	18-18	371-181	81.1-70.6
Bal	7-5	.583	—	303-235	434-375	1735-1174	4.0-3.1	12-10	12-12	314-342	177-175	2608-2548	8.3-7.5	25-19	19-28	220-316	85.0-60.2
LA	6-6	.500	—	307-278	474-440	2142-1845	4.5-4.2	15-15	14-11	296-301	144-153	2256-2186	7.6-7.3	21-15	23-14	255-306	65.7-71.9
ChiB	5-7	.417	—	203-211	457-419	1686-1383	3.7-3.3	15-10	15-15	286-306	130-153	1945-2212	6.8-7.2	7-15	28-15	177-479	36.9-69.8
GB	3-9	.250	—	218-311	380-462	1441-2159	3.8-4.7	13-18	18-17	325-314	157-153	2157-2185	6.6-7.0	12-18	23-30	366-147	52.8-51.2
Aver	12	—	—	238	429	1676	3.9	13	15	278	140	2062	7.4	14	19	221	63.2

TEAM	1D	PENY	PNT	FGM/A	RTNY	RTNTD	OFFY/DEFY	NETY	NETTO	NP	PNP	DELP	PW	DELW	PRT	DR	YPD	DEL
Eastern Conference																		
Cle	180-164	597-412	39.3-41.8	15/22-7/14	454-456	1-3	3670-2802	868	7	97	100	-3	8.4	1.1	5.6/2.0	151-151	24.3-18.6	5.7
NYG	216-174	597-423	44.6-38.8	10/18-12/17	456-515	4-3	3749-3171	578	0	43	48	-5	7.1	-0.1	6.2/2.7	146-154	25.7-20.6	5.1
Pit	159-156	405-370	40.1-42.7	8/26-10/19	471-554	2-2	2890-2791	99	10	-17	48	-65	5.6	0.4	3.4/2.5	157-161	18.4-17.3	1.1
Was	197-174	321-599	42.8-39.6	14/23-7/14	663-260	2-1	3494-3595	-101	-2	21	-16	37	6.5	-1.0	5.3/5.3	143-145	24.4-24.8	-0.4
Phi	149-199	654-642	41.1-42.8	9/14-14/29	641-691	2-2	2737-3683	-946	-3	-57	-91	34	4.6	-0.6	0.9/4.8	162-154	16.9-23.9	-7.0
ChiC	174-208	468-726	42.5-39.7	6/17-14/23	441-606	2-1	3217-4108	-891	-12	-99	-122	23	3.5	-0.5	3.1/6.2	158-151	20.4-27.2	-6.8
Western Conference																		
Det	221-198	673-577	39.9-40.9	13/25-10/17	511-346	1-1	3840-3365	475	8	20	72	-52	6.5	1.5	3.1/2.7	157-156	24.5-21.6	2.9
SF	223-239	629-502	44.7-40.3	9/15-13/24	386-541	1-1	3658-4248	-590	2	-4	-41	37	5.9	2.1	4.0/4.8	150-150	24.4-28.3	-3.9
Bal	222-204	712-546	34.5-42.5	7/19-10/21	482-289	4-0	4123-3406	717	9	68	96	-28	7.7	-0.7	5.2/3.0	158-159	26.1-21.4	4.7
LA	235-216	580-516	44.4-40.2	11/19-15/26	434-610	3-3	4143-3725	418	-12	29	-13	42	6.7	-0.7	3.6/4.1	158-164	26.2-22.7	3.5
ChiB	188-185	614-744	38.8-42.0	14/26-4/19	331-818	1-4	3454-3612	338	-13	-8	-24	16	5.8	-0.8	1.9/3.3	166-167	20.8-18.7	2.1
GB	179-226	516-709	42.0-43.0	12/21-12/22	817-401	1-3	3232-4197	-965	6	-93	-56	-37	3.7	-0.7	2.4/2.6	170-164	19.0-25.6	-6.6
Aver	195	564	41.2	11/20	507	2	3517	—	—	—	—	—	—	—	4.0	156	22.5	—

Rushing Attempts	Rushing Yards	Rushing Average	Rushing TDs	Rushing Rank	Passing Yards	Passing Average
R.Casares-ChiB 204	J.Brown-Cle 942	P.Hornung-GB 5.32	J.Brown-Cle 9	J.Brown-Cle 1032	J.Unitas-Bal 2550	T.O'Connell-Cle 11.17
J.Brown-Cle 202	R.Casares-ChiB 700	T.Rote-Det 5.23	D.Bosseler-Was 7	R.Casares-ChiB 760	Y.Tittle-SF 2157	E.LeBaron-Was 9.03
D.Bosseler-Was 167	D.Bosseler-Was 673	L.Moore-Bal 4.98	Y.Tittle-SF 6	D.Bosseler-Was 743	Van Brocklin-LA 2105	J.Unitas-Bal 8.47
B.Wells-Pit 154	J.Johnson-Det 621	T.Wilson-LA 4.85	O.Matson-ChiC 6	J.Johnson-Det 671	E.Morrall-Pit 1900	Van Brocklin-LA 7.94
A.Ameche-Bal 144	T.Wilson-LA 616	J.Johnson-Det 4.81	R.Casares-ChiB 6	T.Wilson-LA 646	C.Conerly-NYG 1712	L.McHan-ChiC 7.84

Completion Percent	TD Passes	TD Percent	INT Percent	Passer Rating	Passing Rank	Receptions
Y.Tittle-SF 63.1	J.Unitas-Bal 24	T.O'Connell-Cle 8.2	E.Morrall-Pit 4.2	T.O'Connell-Cle 93.3	J.Unitas-Bal 715	B.Wilson-SF 52
E.LeBaron-Was 59.3	Van Brocklin-LA 20	Van Brocklin-LA 7.5	B.Starr-GB 4.7	J.Unitas-Bal 88.0	Y.Tittle-SF 544	R.Berry-Bal 47
T.O'Connell-Cle 57.3	Y.Tittle-SF 13	E.LeBaron-Was 6.6	C.Conerly-NYG 4.7	E.LeBaron-Was 86.1	E.Morrall-Pit 525	J.McClairen-Pit 46
J.Unitas-Bal 57.1		T.Rote-Det 6.6	Y.Tittle-SF 5.4	Y.Tittle-SF 80.0	Van Brocklin-LA 471	F.Gifford-NYG 41
C.Conerly-NYG 55.2			J.Unitas-Bal 5.6	C.Conerly-NYG 74.9	E.LeBaron-Was 409	L.Moore-Bal 40

Receiving Yards	Receiving Average	Receiving TDs	Receiving Rank	Combined Net Yards	Total TDs	Total Points
R.Berry-Bal 800	J.Podoley-Was 20.52	L.Morris-Bal 8	R.Berry-Bal 430	W.Lewis-ChiC 1315	L.Moore-Bal 11	L.Groza-Cle 77
B.Wilson-SF 757	P.Brewster-Cle 20.47	L.Moore-Bal 7	B.Wilson-SF 409	L.Moore-Bal 1267	J.Brown-Cle 10	S.Baker-Was 77
B.Howton-GB 727	B.Howton-GB 19.13		B.Howton-GB 389	J.Arnett-LA 1258	O.Matson-ChiC 9	F.Cone-GB 74
L.Moore-Bal 687	J.Doran-Det 18.91		L.Moore-Bal 379	O.Matson-ChiC 1236	F.Gifford-NYG 9	P.Cothren-LA 71
J.McClairen-Pit 630	B.Boyd-LA 18.41		J.Doran-Det 337	S.Campbell-GB 1182	L.Morris-Bal 8	G.Blanda-ChiB 71

Punt Average	Field Goals	Field Goal Percent	Kickoff Returns	Kickoff Return Average	Punt Returns	Punt Return Average
D.Chandler-NYG 44.6	L.Groza-Cle 15	B.Walston-Phi 75.0	S.Campbell-GB 31	J.Arnett-LA 28.0	T.McDonald-Phi 26	B.Zagers-Was 15.5
Van Brocklin-LA 44.3	G.Blanda-ChiB 14	F.Cone-GB 70.6	W.Lewis-ChiC 26	J.Arenas-SF 27.4	Y.Lary-Det 25	S.Campbell-GB 7.6
B.Jessup-SF 43.6	S.Baker-Was 14	L.Groza-Cle 68.2	G.Filipski-NYG 26	J.Smith-SF 26.3	S.Campbell-GB 25	W.Lewis-ChiC 7.3
S.Baker-Was 42.8	F.Cone-GB 12	S.Baker-Was 60.9	J.Arenas-SF 24	W.Lewis-ChiC 26.2	J.Arenas-SF 25	B.Wells-Pit 6.8
D.Mann-ChiC 42.5	P.Cothren-LA 11	G.Soltau-SF 60.0	J.Arnett-LA 18	D.McIlhenny-GB 25.9		J.Arnett-LA 6.1

Punt/Kick Return Yards	Punt/Kick Return TDs	Interceptions	Interception Return Yards	Interception Return TDs	Sacks	Overall Rank
S.Campbell-GB 880	B.Zagers-Was 2	M.Davis-Bal 10	M.Davis-Bal 219	M.Davis-Bal 2	Not kept	J.Brown-Cle 1111
W.Lewis-ChiC 857	B.Wells-Pit 1	Christiansen-Det 10	J.Symank-GB 198			L.Moore-Bal 989
J.Arenas-SF 737	L.Moore-Bal 1	J.Butler-Pit 10	B.Dillon-GB 180			F.Gifford-NYG 974
G.Filipski-NYG 704	J.Arnett-LA 1	J.Symank-GB 9	J.Norton-Phi 155			O.Matson-ChiC 960
J.Arnett-LA 589		B.Dillon-GB 9	Christiansen-Det 137			J.Unitas-Bal 896

DOUBLING UP ON BROWN IN CLEVELAND

The draft yielded a bumper crop of talent. Eight future Hall of Famers were selected, along with more than a dozen other players who made a significant impact in the league. Cleveland was one of the teams to benefit most, though it didn't seem that way on draft day. With the fifth overall pick, the Browns hoped to land a quarterback to replace the retired Otto Graham. After Green Bay took Paul Hornung (a quarterback at Notre Dame), San Francisco grabbed John Brodie, and the Steelers picked Len Dawson. The Browns settled for a running back: Jim Brown of Syracuse. The move settled the Eastern Division in Cleveland's favor.

Brown was a ferocious runner with the speed to elude most defensive backs and the power to knock most linebackers off their feet. Coach Paul Brown tailored the offense around his rookie back, and the results were amazing. Brown led the league in rushing yards and touchdowns while setting a new single-game record by running for 237 yards against the Rams on November 24.

While an influx of young players transformed some teams, a trio of 30-year old players sparked the 49ers. Quarterback Y.A. Tittle, running back Joe Perry, and receiver Billy Wilson formed the backbone of one of the league's best offenses. Tittle perfected an alley-oop pass with rookie end R.C. Owens, a former college basketball star. He'd float a soft pass up high and Owens would out-jump defenders to catch it. A strong finish left San Francisco tied with Detroit for the division lead.

The Lions were one of the few teams that didn't reap significant benefits from the talent-laden draft. Weeks before the season started, head coach Buddy Parker suddenly resigned, expressing his disgust at the state of the team. Assistant George Wilson took over, and while the players grumbled about some of the changes he made, it was hard to argue with the results. The Lions shored up the offense by acquiring fullback John Henry Johnson from San Francisco and quarterback Tobin Rote from Green Bay. Rote shared playing time with Bobby Layne and proved remarkably successful when Layne broke his leg late in the season.

1958 NFL

TEAM	W-L-T	PCT	POST	PTS	RA	RY	RY/A	RTD	FL	PA	PC	GPY	GPY/A	PTD	PI	PSY	PRAT
Eastern Conference																	
NYG	9-3	.750	CL	246-183	450-399	1725-1440	3.8-3.6	14-7	14-19	266-311	119-142	1718-2130	6.5-6.8	15-11	12-21	113-152	66.3-52.3
Cle	9-3	.750	C	302-217	475-369	2526-1448	5.3-3.9	24-6	8-18	206-312	110-162	1758-2387	8.5-7.7	12-20	14-16	177-175	73.2-77.2
Pit	7-4-1	.636	—	261-230	394-403	1521-1491	3.9-3.7	14-14	21-18	336-334	156-173	2895-2136	8.6-6.4	16-11	21-24	143-244	66.5-52.9
Was	4-7-1	.364	—	214-268	480-396	1977-1734	4.1-4.4	11-13	16-22	251-300	121-153	1989-2782	7.9-9.3	14-21	17-16	293-114	65.6-84.3
ChiC	2-9-1	.182	—	261-356	366-449	1456-2133	4.0-4.8	9-26	22-16	407-337	198-171	2735-2793	6.7-8.3	23-18	27-15	161-166	61.8-78.2
Phi	2-9-1	.182	—	235-306	334-488	1093-1929	3.3-4.0	13-15	22-12	402-289	214-138	2772-2244	6.9-7.8	18-22	21-15	75-126	68.3-78.0
Western Conference																	
Bal	9-3	.750	L*	381-203	456-331	2127-1440	4.7-3.9	24-13	11-17	354-363	178-168	2537-2248	7.2-6.2	26-9	11-35	125-255	85.4-35.1
ChiB	8-4	.667	—	298-230	437-351	1770-1297	4.1-3.7	15-12	19-18	321-327	146-153	2021-2142	4.3-6.6	18-14	24-22	210-373	53.8-54.6
LA	8-4	.667	—	344-278	345-405	1734-1777	5.0-4.4	18-12	23-13	358-381	186-188	2909-2303	8.1-6.0	19-21	26-28	237-252	66.7-56.1
SF	6-6	.500	—	257-324	359-380	1628-2038	4.5-5.4	18-15	11-15	383-341	223-163	2691-2218	7.0-6.5	15-25	29-16	208-246	61.4-73.9
Det	4-7-1	.364	—	261-276	364-407	1360-1720	3.7-4.2	9-19	19-16	319-320	141-167	2148-2255	6.7-7.0	20-15	14-22	279-138	69.6-61.9
GB	1-10-1	.091	—	193-382	345-427	1421-2040	4.1-4.8	7-24	17-19	348-336	161-175	2118-2653	6.1-7.9	15-24	27-13	298-78	48.0-86.1
Aver	12	—		271	400	1695	4.2	15	17	329	163	2358	7.2	18	20	193	65.3

TEAM	1D	PENY	PNT	FGM/A	RTNY	RTNTD	OFFY/DEFY	NETY	NETTO	NP	PNP	DELP	PW	DELW	PRT	DR	YPD	DEL
Eastern Conference																		
NYG	191-170	379-451	44.0-41.7	12/23-10/19	462-499	1-4	3330-3418	-88	14	63	49	14	7.6	1.4	4.3/ 3.5	150-156	22.2-21.9	0.3
Cle	206-201	554-347	41.2-42.7	8/19-11/23	603-229	4-0	4107-3660	447	12	85	85	0	8.1	0.9	4.7/ 5.1	150-145	27.4-25.2	2.1
Pit	202-209	875-585	39.7-42.0	14/28-12/20	549-563	1-3	4273-3383	890	0	31	74	-43	6.8	0.7	5.6/ 2.5	165-164	25.9-20.6	5.3
Was	213-215	365-642	45.4-36.8	13/26-8/21	334-505	0-1	3673-4402	-729	5	-54	-41	-13	4.7	-0.1	3.7/ 6.9	148-144	24.8-30.6	-5.8
ChiC	219-253	615-696	37.8-41.2	6/17-12/25	380-364	3-2	4030-4760	-730	-18	-95	-133	38	3.6	-1.1	3.7/ 6.0	168-170	24.0-28.0	-4.0
Phi	222-225	570-722	41.2-43.1	6/14-11/23	539-605	0-2	3790-4047	-257	-16	-71	-85	14	4.2	-1.7	4.7/ 5.5	154-154	24.6-26.3	-1.7
Western Conference																		
Bal	253-188	518-555	36.7-44.1	5/14-6/17	751-345	3-5	4539-3284	1255	30	178	225	-47	10.4	-1.4	5.9/1.3	169-162	26.9-20.3	6.6
ChiB	202-168	742-832	39.4-37.5	11/23-12/24	377-756	5-2	3581-3066	515	-3	68	31	37	7.7	0.3	2.6/ 2.5	177-175	20.2-17.5	2.7
LA	209-235	636-476	40.9-37.9	14/25-7/21	729-459	6-4	4406-3828	578	-8	66	16	50	7.7	0.4	4.4/ 2.4	177-174	24.9-21.4	3.5
SF	237-227	619-510	38.3-40.7	8/21-10/17	260-580	1-2	4111-4010	101	-9	-67	-28	-39	4.3	1.7	3.2/ 4.0	150-155	27.4-25.9	1.5
Det	195-199	513-458	42.5-40.2	11/23-8/19	551-344	4-2	3229-3837	-608	-12	-15	-31	16	5.6	-1.1	4.1/ 3.8	159-161	20.3-23.8	-3.5
GB	177-236	545-657	42.3-41.6	11/21-12/25	353-639	1-2	3241-4615	-1374	-12	-189	-163	-26	1.3	0.2	2.0/ 6.4	160-162	20.3-28.5	-8.2
Aver	211	578	40.8	10/21	491	2	3859								4.3	161	24.0	

Rushing Attempts		Rushing Yards		Rushing Average		Rushing TDs		Rushing Rank		Passing Yards		Passing Average	
J.Brown-Cle	257	J.Brown-Cle	1527	L.Moore-Bal	7.29	J.Brown-Cle	17	J.Brown-Cle	1697	B.Wade-LA	2875	E.LeBaron-Was	9.41
R.Casares-ChiB	176	A.Ameche-Bal	791	T.Wilson-LA	6.51	T.Wilson-LA	9	A.Ameche-Bal	871	Van Brocklin-Phi	2409	B.Layne-Pit	8.73
A.Ameche-Bal	171	J.Perry-SF	758	B.Mitchell-Cle	6.25	F.Gifford-NYG	8	J.Perry-SF	798	B.Layne-Pit	2339	M.Plum-ChiC	8.57
T.Tracy-Pit	169	T.Tracy-Pit	714	J.Perry-SF	6.06	W.Galimore-ChiB	8	T.Tracy-Pit	764	J.Unitas-Bal	2007	B.Wade-LA	8.43
B.Barnes-Phi	156	J.Arnett-LA	683	J.Brown-Cle	5.94	A.Ameche-Bal	8	J.Arnett-LA	743	T.Rote-Det	1678	J.Unitas-Bal	7.63

Completion Percent		TD Passes		TD Percent		INT Percent		Passer Rating		Passing Rank		Receptions	
J.Brodie-SF	59.9	J.Unitas-Bal	19	E.LeBaron-Was	7.6	J.Unitas-Bal	2.7	J.Unitas-Bal	90.0	B.Layne-Pit	835	P.Retzlaff-Phi	56
Y.Tittle-SF	57.7	B.Wade-LA	18	J.Unitas-Bal	7.2	B.Layne-Pit	3.7	E.LeBaron-Was	83.3	J.Unitas-Bal	819	R.Berry-Bal	56
E.LeBaron-Was	54.5	Van Brocklin-Phi	15	B.Parilli-GB	6.4	T.Rote-Det	3.9	B.Layne-Pit	80.4	B.Wade-LA	648	D.Shofner-LA	51
M.Plum-Cle	54.0	T.Rote-Det	14	L.McHan-ChiC	6.1	C.Conerly-NYG	4.9	M.Plum-Cle	77.9	T.Rote-Det	509	L.Moore-Bal	50
M.Reynolds-ChiC	53.8	B.Layne-Pit	13	M.Plum-Cle	5.8	Van Brocklin-Phi	5.3	M.Reynolds-ChiC	72.6	Van Brocklin-Phi	480	C.Conner-SF	49

Receiving Yards		Receiving Average		Receiving TDs		Receiving Rank		Combined Net Yards		Total TDs		Total Points	
D.Shofner-LA	1097	J.Orr-Pit	27.58	T.McDonald-Phi	9	D.Shofner-LA	589	J.Brown-Cle	1739	J.Brown-Cle	18	J.Brown-Cle	108
L.Moore-Bal	938	R.Renfro-Cle	23.88	R.Berry-Bal	9	L.Moore-Bal	504	J.Arnett-LA	1731	L.Moore-Bal	14	L.Moore-Bal	84
J.Orr-Pit	910	D.Shofner-LA	21.51	D.Shofner-LA	8	J.Orr-Pit	490	L.Moore-Bal	1638	W.Galimore-ChiB	12	P.Cothren-LA	84
R.Berry-Bal	794	R.Mathews-Pit	21.00	B.McColl-ChiB	8	R.Berry-Bal	442	O.Matson-ChiC	1467			T.Miner-Pit	73
P.Retzlaff-Phi	766	T.McDonald-Phi	20.79			P.Retzlaff-Phi	393	B.Mitchell-Cle	1250			W.Galimore-ChiB	72

Punt Average		Field Goals		Field Goal Percent		Kickoff Returns		Kickoff Return Average		Punt Returns		Punt Return Average	
S.Baker-Was	45.4	T.Miner-Pit	14	P.Cothren-LA	56.0	J.Sears-ChiC	32	O.Matson-ChiC	35.5	C.Taseff-Bal	29	J.Arnett-LA	12.4
D.Chandler-NYG	44.0	P.Cothren-LA	14	P.Hornung-GB	52.4	B.Carey-GB	30	L.Bolden-Cle	25.9	Y.Lary-Det	27	B.Mitchell-Cle	11.8
Y.Lary-Det	42.8	S.Baker-Was	13	P.Summerall-NYG	52.2	S.Watson-Was	19	B.Mitchell-Cle	25.2	B.Reynolds-Phi	25	D.Christy-Pit	9.0
M.McGee-GB	42.3	P.Summerall-NYG	13	T.Miner-Pit	50.0	B.Mitchell-Cle	18	J.Morris-ChiB	24.9	H.McElhenny-SF	24	B.Wells-Phi	8.3
E.Brown-ChiB	42.2			S.Baker-Was	50.0			B.Carey-GB	24.1	D.Maynard-NYG	24	K.Konz-Cle	7.9

Punt/Kick Return Yards		Punt/Kick Return TDs		Interceptions		Interception Return Yards		Interception Return TDs		Sacks		Overall Rank	
J.Sears-ChiC	850	B.Mitchell-Cle	2	J.Patton-NYG	11	A.Nelson-Bal	199	W.Sherman-LA	2	Not kept		J.Brown-Cle	1800
B.Carey-GB	767	O.Matson-ChiC	2	J.Butler-Pit	9	J.Patton-NYG	183					J.Arnett-LA	1219
B.Mitchell-Cle	619	L.Lyles-Bal	2	A.Nelson-Bal	8	W.Sherman-LA	171					L.Moore-Bal	1204
J.Arnett-LA	554			W.Sherman-LA	8	J.Morris-LA	152					T.Tracy-Pit	1117
D.Christy-Pit	537			R.Brown-Bal	8	R.Brown-Bal	149					O.Matson-ChiC	1112

PAPA BEAR WON'T REST

George Halas, 63, came out of retirement for the third time to resume coaching the Chicago Bears. The old master helped the team improve from 5–7 to 8–4, and the Bears stayed in contention for the division crown until a loss to Baltimore late in the year.

Weeb Ewbank's young Colts featured a trio of dangerous weapons: halfback Alan Ameche, end Ray Berry, and double-threat back Lenny Moore. Quarterback Johnny Unitas missed three weeks with broken ribs and a punctured lung, but when he returned, Unitas helped overcome a 27–7 halftime deficit against San Francisco to win Baltimore's first division title.

There was a changing of the guard in Los Angeles as head coach Sid Gillman shook up the offense. Veteran passer Norm Van Brocklin was traded to the Eagles so Billy Wade could take over at quarterback. Gillman also shifted Del Shofner from defensive back to receiver to replace the retired Elroy Hirsch. Wade led the league in passing yards, and the Rams posted a winning record for the first time since 1955.

In the second week of the season, Joe Perry became the NFL's all-time leading rusher. He was not the only back breaking records. Cleveland's Jim Brown set a new mark with 17 rushing touchdowns in 12 games and ran for 1,527 yards, shattering Steve Van Buren's single-season record of 1,146. Quarterback Milt Plum and rookie Bobby Mitchell adeptly kept defenses from focusing solely on Brown.

A stingy defense was New York's calling card, particularly a run defense that held opponents to a league-low 3.6 yards per carry. The Giants entered the last weekend of the regular season needing a win against the Browns to tie for first place and force a divisional playoff game. After Jim Brown ran 65 yards for a touchdown on the first play of the game, the Giants held him in check. A light snowfall turned into a raging snowstorm, and a late field goal by Pat Summerall gave the Giants a victory. New York held Brown to 8 rushing yards in a 10–0 win the next week to set the stage for the greatest game in NFL history.

1959 NFL

TEAM	W-L-T	PCT	POST	PTS	RA	RY	RY/A	RTD	FL	PA	PC	GPY	GPY/A	PTD	PI	PSY	PRAT
Eastern Conference																	
NYG	**10**-2	**.833**	L	284-**170**	433-379	1646-**1261**	3.8-**3.3**	11-**6**	20-16	302-304	165-137	2633-**1811**	**8.7-6.0**	18-**11**	13-22	106-229	85.9-46.4
Cle	7-5	.583	—	270-214	**457**-360	**2149**-1422	4.7-4.0	**20**-9	**5**-12	276-319	159-168	2033-2457	7.4-7.7	14-17	**9**-18	167-115	84.1-72.3
Phi	7-5	.583	—	268-278	391-429	1315-2068	3.4-4.8	13-15	8-20	352-292	194-144	2644-2074	7.5-7.1	17-17	16-20	**72**-204	76.5-63.6
Pit	6-5-1	.545	—	257-216	406-405	1543-1500	3.8-3.7	10-10	10-12	319-285	150-**128**	2298-2014	7.2-7.1	21-12	23-22	246-172	63.2-50.8
Was	3-9	.250	—	185-350	422-404	1964-2214	4.7-5.5	9-19	17-14	284-319	121-185	1824-2606	6.4-8.2	13-26	23-13	301-176	45.9-94.6
ChiC	2-10	.167	—	234-324	367-477	1613-1874	4.4-3.9	10-15	36-15	280-**266**	125-138	1766-2359	6.3-8.9	14-22	19-15	207-218	54.0-86.3
Western Conference																	
Bal	9-3	.750	L*	**374**-251	435-**325**	1705-1557	3.9-4.8	13-16	9-9	**375**-351	**196**-171	**2938**-2497	7.8-7.1	**33**-13	14-**40**	185-155	**92.1-45.1**
ChiB	8-4	.667	—	252-196	392-429	1438-1783	3.7-4.2	14-11	16-17	310-333	156-144	2284-2147	7.4-6.4	15-14	16-22	211-**254**	69.3-51.5
GB	7-5	.583	—	248-246	421-430	1907-1770	4.5-4.1	15-14	16-15	268-329	128-169	1963-2030	7.3-6.2	16-14	17-14	131-248	65.9-67.1
SF	7-5	.583	—	255-237	407-433	1839-1974	4.5-4.6	16-16	10-**22**	264-341	132-176	1685-2272	6.4-6.7	12-15	22-14	136-228	50.8-70.4
Det	3-8-1	.273	—	203-275	399-403	1792-1562	4.5-3.9	13-13	19-19	328-288	136-147	2131-2340	6.5-8.1	10-19	27-14	467-246	39.6-80.2
LA	2-10	.167	—	242-315	371-427	1778-1704	**4.8**-4.0	15-15	19-14	356-287	**196**-151	2723-2315	7.6-8.1	14-17	22-7	241-225	67.2-89.1
Aver	12	—	—	256	408	1724	4.2	13	15	310	155	2244	7.2	16	18	206	66.9

TEAM	1D	PENY	PNT	FGM/A	RTNY	RTNTD	OFFY/DEFY	NETY	NETTO	NP	PNP	DELP	PW	DELW	PRT	DR	YPD	DEL
Eastern Conference																		
NYG	198-**167**	480-324	**46.6**-42.7	**20/30**-6/16	452-700	3-5	4173-**2843**	**1330**	5	114	131	-17	8.9	1.2	**6.7**/ 2.1	160-162	26.1-**17.5**	**8.5**
Cle	234-205	**329**-285	37.1-42.4	5/16-6/**13**	453-**178**	3-2	4015-3764	251	16	56	85	-29	7.4	-0.4	5.4/ 5.1	133-**129**	**30.2**-29.2	1.0
Phi	211-220	501-457	42.7-41.1	8/24-9/20	406-672	5-4	3887-3938	-51	16	-10	60	-70	5.8	**1.3**	5.6/ 3.6	156-149	24.9-26.4	-1.5
Pit	207-179	532-483	40.4-46.5	11/18-12/32	515-705	1-4	3595-3342	253	1	41	25	16	7.0	-0.5	3.5/ 3.2	163-166	22.1-20.1	1.9
Was	193-252	453-570	45.5-**40.8**	10/22-10/19	266-412	0-**1**	3487-4644	-1157	-13	-165	-148	-17	1.9	1.1	1.9/ 6.2	147-145	23.7-32.0	-8.3
ChiC	179-212	431-528	44.6-41.3	6/9-12/22	**849**-339	**7**-4	3172-4015	-843	-25	-90	-170	**80**	3.8	-1.8	2.8/ 5.8	**172**-170	18.4-23.6	-5.2
Western Conference																		
Bal	**267**-195	634-**610**	42.1-44.7	6/18-12/22	810-319	5-2	**4458**-3899	559	**26**	**123**	**151**	-28	**9.1**	-0.1	6.2/**1.8**	164-157	27.2-24.8	2.3
ChiB	190-208	597-553	41.3-42.3	10/19-**4**/17	442-456	3-**1**	3511-3676	-165	7	56	14	42	7.4	0.6	4.5/ 2.9	156-164	22.5-22.4	0.1
GB	212-215	435-450	42.4-44.3	7/17-12/22	547-518	1-2	3739-3552	187	-4	2	0	2	6.1	0.9	4.3/ 3.6	151-159	24.8-22.3	2.4
SF	182-238	489-417	45.7-41.6	12/26-5/**13**	458-458	3-**1**	3388-4018	-630	4	18	-37	55	6.4	0.6	2.4/ 4.2	150-161	22.6-25.0	-2.4
Det	198-196	496-603	46.5-43.7	10/23-11/21	413-600	2-2	3456-3656	-200	-13	-72	-69	-3	4.2	-0.7	1.4/ 5.2	169-164	20.4-22.3	-1.8
LA	232-216	465-562	41.7-44.1	11/26-17/31	256-510	1-6	4260-3794	466	-20	-73	-41	-32	4.2	-2.2	4.2/ 6.2	163-158	26.1-24.0	2.1
Aver	209	487	43.0	10/21	489	3	3762	—	—	—	—	—	—	—	4.4	157	24.0	—

Rushing Attempts	Rushing Yards	Rushing Average	Rushing TDs	Rushing Rank	Passing Yards	Passing Average
J.Brown-Cle 290	J.Brown-Cle 1329	J.Olszewski-Was 6.65	J.Brown-Cle 14	J.Brown-Cle 1469	J.Unitas-Bal 2899	C.Conerly-NYG 8.79
J.Smith-SF 207	J.Smith-SF 1036	R.Phillips-Det 5.88	J.Smith-SF 10	J.Smith-SF 1136	Van Brocklin-Phi 2617	E.Morrall-Det 8.04
T.Tracy-Pit 199	O.Matson-LA 863	B.Mitchell-Cle 5.67	R.Casares-ChiB 10	O.Matson-LA 923	B.Wade-LA 2001	J.Unitas-Bal 7.90
B.Barnes-Phi 181	T.Tracy-Pit 794	D.Bosseler-Was 5.41		T.Tracy-Pit 824	M.Plum-Cle 1992	Van Brocklin-Phi 7.70
A.Ameche-Bal 178	B.Mitchell-Cle 743	L.Carpenter-GB 5.37		R.Casares-ChiB 799	B.Layne-Pit 1986	B.Wade-LA 7.67

Completion Percent	TD Passes	TD Percent	INT Percent	Passer Rating	Passing Rank	Receptions
M.Plum-Cle 58.6	J.Unitas-Bal 32	J.Unitas-Bal 8.7	C.Conerly-NYG 2.1	C.Conerly-NYG 102.7	J.Unitas-Bal 1050	R.Berry-Bal 66
B.Wade-LA 58.6	B.Layne-Pit 20	L.McHan-GB 7.4	M.Plum-Cle 3.0	J.Unitas-Bal 92.0	Van Brocklin-Phi 829	D.Shofner-LA 47
C.Conerly-NYG 58.2	Van Brocklin-Phi 16	C.Conerly-NYG 7.2	J.Unitas-Bal 3.8	M.Plum-Cle 87.2	C.Conerly-NYG 763	L.Moore-Bal 47
Van Brocklin-Phi 56.2	M.Plum-Cle 14	B.Layne-Pit 6.7	E.Brown-ChiB 4.0	Van Brocklin-Phi 79.5	M.Plum-Cle 746	T.McDonald-Phi 47
J.Unitas-Bal 52.6	C.Conerly-NYG 14		Van Brocklin-Phi 4.1	E.Brown-ChiB 76.7	E.Brown-ChiB 606	

Receiving Yards	Receiving Average	Receiving TDs	Receiving Rank	Combined Net Yards	Total TDs	Total Points
R.Berry-Bal 959	M.McGee-GB 23.17	R.Berry-Bal 14	R.Berry-Bal 550	J.Brown-Cle 1607	J.Brown-Cle 14	P.Hornung-GB 94
D.Shofner-LA 936	B.Anderson-Was 20.97	T.McDonald-Phi 10	D.Shofner-LA 503	B.Mitchell-Cle 1507	R.Berry-Bal 14	P.Summerall-NYG 90
L.Moore-Bal 846	D.Shofner-LA 19.91	F.Morze-Bal 8	T.McDonald-Phi 473	O.Matson-LA 1421	R.Casares-ChiB 12	B.Conrad-ChiC 84
T.McDonald-Phi 846	B.Schnelker-NYG 19.30	D.Shofner-LA 7	L.Moore-Bal 453	T.McDonald-Phi 1395	J.Smith-SF 11	J.Brown-Cle 84
F.Gifford-NYG 768	F.Gifford-NYG 18.29		F.Gifford-NYG 404	F.Gifford-NYG 1308	T.McDonald-Phi 11	R.Berry-Bal 84

Punt Average	Field Goals	Field Goal Percent	Kickoff Returns	Kickoff Return Average	Punt Returns	Punt Return Average
Y.Lary-Det 47.1	P.Summerall-NYG 20	P.Summerall-NYG 69.0	L.Lyles-SF 25	A.Woodson-SF 29.4	B.Stacy-ChiC 29	J.Morris-ChiB 12.2
D.Chandler-NYG 46.6	T.Davis-SF 12	B.Layne-Pit 64.7	T.McDonald-Phi 24	A.Powell-Phi 27.1	J.Sample-Bal 22	L.Carpenter-GB 11.5
T.Davis-SF 45.7	B.Layne-Pit 11	J.Aveni-ChiB 52.6	D.James-Was 23	J.Sample-Bal 26.9	E.Dove-SF 22	J.Arnett-LA 10.8
S.Baker-Was 45.5	S.Baker-Was 10	L.Michaels-LA 47.1	B.Butler-GB 21	J.Morris-ChiB 25.8		B.Mitchell-Cle 10.4
J.Norton-ChiC 44.9	J.Aveni-ChiB 10	T.Davis-SF 46.2	B.Conrad-ChiC 18	J.Symank-GB 24.1		B.Stacy-ChiC 9.7

Punt/Kick Return Yards	Punt/Kick Return TDs	Interceptions	Interception Return Yards	Interception Return TDs	Sacks	Overall Rank
B.Butler-GB 635	B.Stacy-ChiC 2	D.Shinnick-Bal 7	G.Lowe-Det 130	Many 1	Not kept	J.Brown-Cle 1592
J.Morris-ChiB 609		D.Derby-Pit 7	D.Derby-Pit 127			J.Unitas-Bal 1215
D.James-Was 598		M.Davis-Bal 7	N.Lane-ChiC 125			J.Smith-SF 1208
J.Sample-Bal 586		A.Nelson-Bal 6	M.Davis-Bal 119			B.Mitchell-Cle 1162
L.Lyles-SF 565		D.Alban-Pit 6	D.Alban-Pit 119			O.Matson-LA 1066

Eras Shift and New Legends Emerge

Two of the league's key figures died in 1959. Giants owner Tim Mara passed away in February after a long illness. He founded the team, survived financial hardships and challenges from rival leagues, and helped turn the Giants into a perennial powerhouse. Commissioner Bert Bell died of a heart attack while watching the Eagles beat the Steelers in Philadelphia on October 11. As the owner of the Eagles, Bell had introduced important innovations such as the annual college draft. He served as commissioner for 14 years, leading the NFL through battles with both the AAFC and the Canadian Football League, campaigning for anti-gambling legislation, and successfully ushering in the television era. Bell's sudden death left a power vacuum just as the league prepared to face off with a new rival, the American Football League.

The Packers hadn't posted a winning record since 1947, and four different coaches had failed in their attempts to succeed the legendary Curley Lambeau. Green Bay turned to Vince Lombardi, the architect of the New York Giants' power running game. He built the Packers' offense around versatile halfback Paul Hornung. Midway through the season Lombardi installed Bart Starr as the starting quarterback. Starr found a favorite target in rookie Boyd Dowler and Green Bay improved from 1–10–1 to 7–5 in the first year of the Lombardi era.

Lombardi's departure from New York didn't derail the Giants. Frank Gifford continued to be a double threat out of the backfield, leading the team in rushing and receiving. Quarterback Charlie Connerly, 35, had the best season of his career, while the Giants still had the league's stingiest defense.

Baltimore's defense had its weak spots, but the Colts were scoring points so rapidly that opponents were hard pressed to keep pace. They never scored fewer than 21 points and topped 30 in seven games. This forced opponents to throw the ball, and Baltimore's secondary responded with a league-high 40 interceptions. Johnny Unitas threw for 2,899 yards and became the first quarterback to throw more than 30 touchdown passes in a season. Head coach Weeb Ewbank led the Colts to their second straight NFL title.

1960 NFL

TEAM	W-L-T	PCT	POST	PTS	RA	RY	RY/A	RTD	FL	PA	PC	GPY	GPY/A	PTD	PI	PSY	PRAT
Eastern Conference																	
Phi	**10-2**	**.833**	L*	321-246	351-449	1134-2200	3.2-4.9	9-14	10-15	331-**283**	177-**139**	2957-1984	**8.9**-7.0	**29**-14	20-30	141-157	87.9-49.1
Cle	8-3-1	.727	—	**362**-217	383-405	1930-1643	**5.0**-4.1	18-10	12-14	264-319	160-163	2343-2370	**8.9**-7.4	22-15	**5-31**	299-207	**109.5**-51.7
NYG	6-4-2	.600	—	271-261	406-396	1440-1267	3.5-**3.2**	10-8	26-12	322-297	156-142	2385-2010	7.4-6.8	20-19	23-22	131-177	64.3-60.6
SL	6-5-1	.545	—	288-230	**484-344**	**2356-1212**	4.9-3.5	13-8	22-**23**	285-300	126-156	1990-2147	7.0-7.2	20-20	25-21	179-330	54.9-68.3
Pit	5-6-1	.455	—	240-275	411-414	1623-1493	3.9-3.6	9-13	14-13	285-361	139-184	2511-3075	8.8-8.5	20-20	21-16	**89**-284	72.1-80.0
Was	1-9-2	.100	—	178-309	415-362	1313-1502	3.2-4.1	9-9	15-19	274-321	147-169	1816-2768	6.6-8.6	9-24	23-15	385-204	50.4-87.3
Western Conference																	
GB	8-4	.667	L	332-209	463-350	2150-1285	4.6-3.7	**29-7**	12-15	279-365	137-192	1993-2432	7.1-6.7	9-19	13-22	118-275	64.1-65.9
Det	7-5	.583	—	239-212	392-360	1714-1348	4.4-3.7	19-9	9-11	333-354	166-175	2022-2275	6.1-6.4	17-21	19-24	344-226	48.7-63.7
SF	7-5	.583	—	208-**205**	413-363	1681-1587	4.1-4.4	9-13	**4**-8	336-293	174-140	1866-2001	5.6-6.8	11-11	12-20	287-183	64.4-54.4
Bal	6-6	.500	—	288-234	345-379	1289-1591	3.7-4.2	10-17	12-9	**392**-298	**196**-144	**3164**-2068	8.1-6.9	26-**8**	24-30	208-342	74.0-**40.6**
ChiB	5-6-1	.455	—	194-299	373-403	1639-1679	4.4-4.2	11-17	10-9	324-291	146-146	2130-**1808**	6.6-**6.2**	13-14	32-10	304-**420**	60.8-71.5
LA	4-7-1	.364	—	265-297	343-419	1449-1718	4.2-4.1	9-16	9-13	335-339	177-168	2188-2510	6.5-7.4	19-18	22-23	366-155	64.9-63.7
Dal	0-11-1	.000	—	177-369	312-447	1049-2242	3.4-5.0	6-20	17-11	354-293	163-146	2388-2305	6.7-7.9	17-22	33-15	284-175	45.7-80.1
Aver	12	—	—	259	392	1597	4.1	12	13	316	159	2289	7.2	17	21	241	64.2

TEAM	1D	PENY	PNT	FGM/A	RTNY	RTNTD	OFFY/DEFY	NETY	NETTO	NP	PNP	DELP	PW	DELW	PRT	DR	YPD	DEL
Eastern Conference																		
Phi	190-205	544-597	43.1-43.6	14/20-16/28	460-443	2-1	3950-4027	-77	15	75	54	21	7.9	**2.1**	6.3/ 2.0	160-162	24.7-24.9	-0.2
Cle	219-208	534-526	42.0-45.5	12/20-12/21	**832-226**	**7-1**	3974-3806	168	**28**	**145**	**126**	19	**9.6**	-1.1	**6.8**/ 2.7	150-**150**	26.5-25.4	1.1
NYG	202-183	460-532	39.2-40.8	13/26-12/23	503-353	3-5	3694-3100	594	-15	10	-11	21	6.3	0.8	4.2/ 3.2	**168**-169	22.0-**18.3**	3.6
SL	229-**158**	**456**-500	**44.9**-44.3	15/25-7/16	410-581	1-2	4167-**3029**	1138	-3	58	83	-25	7.4	-1.0	2.9/ 3.1	**168**-162	24.8-18.7	**6.1**
Pit	198-224	606-565	44.2-43.4	11/19-14/21	313-363	1-**0**	4045-4284	-239	-6	-35	-44	9	5.1	0.4	5.7/ 5.7	149-159	**27.1**-26.9	0.2
Was	166-223	713-654	42.1-39.5	15/23-21/32	254-452	1-2	2744-4066	-1322	-4	-131	-126	-5	2.7	-0.7	1.5/ 6.1	162-153	16.9-26.6	-9.6
Western Conference																		
GB	**237**-199	578-636	41.2-39.4	15/28-9/13	530-329	3-**0**	4025-3442	583	12	123	97	26	9.1	-1.1	4.7/ 3.4	153-156	26.3-22.1	4.2
Det	192-204	726-637	43.8-**39.0**	13/24-**5/12**	592-610	3-2	3392-3397	-5	0	27	0	**27**	6.7	0.3	2.1/ 3.6	154-159	22.0-21.4	0.7
SF	201-180	604-580	44.3-41.2	**19/35**-10/20	358-341	1-1	3260-3405	-145	12	3	36	-33	6.1	0.9	3.1/ 3.3	149-**150**	21.9-22.7	-0.8
Bal	227-195	504-538	38.5-46.4	9/19-15/30	424-320	1-2	**4245**-3317	928	3	54	89	-35	7.3	-1.4	5.1/**1.3**	164-156	25.9-21.3	4.6
ChiB	183-202	707-**704**	39.7-41.3	7/16-8/20	293-876	1-8	3465-3067	398	-23	-105	-59	-46	3.4	**2.1**	1.4/ 3.1	161-161	21.5-19.0	2.5
LA	194-221	625-517	42.3-43.8	14/22-17/29	491-381	4-1	3271-4073	-802	5	-32	-47	15	5.2	-0.7	2.7/ 4.2	162-161	20.2-25.3	-5.1
Dal	180-216	600-671	42.0-42.1	6/13-17/25	272-457	0-3	3153-4372	-1219	-24	-192	-198	6	1.2	-0.7	2.0/ 5.3	158-160	20.0-27.3	-7.4
Aver	201	589	42.2	13/22	441	2	3645	—	—	—	—	—	—	—	4.0	158	23.0	—

Rushing Attempts		Rushing Yards		Rushing Average		Rushing TDs		Rushing Rank		Passing Yards		Passing Average	
J.Taylor-GB	230	J.Brown-Cle	1257	J.Crow-SL	5.85	P.Hornung-GB	13	J.Brown-Cle	1347	J.Unitas-Bal	3099	M.Plum-Cle	9.19
J.Brown-Cle	215	J.Taylor-GB	1101	J.Brown-Cle	5.85	J.Taylor-GB	11	J.Taylor-GB	1211	Van Brocklin-Phi	2471	Van Brocklin-Phi	8.70
T.Tracy-Pit	192	J.Crow-SL	1071	J.Morris-Chi	5.71	J.Brown-Cle	9	J.Crow-SL	1131	M.Plum-Cle	2297	B.Layne-Pit	8.68
J.Crow-SL	183	R.Phillips-Det	872	R.Phillips-Det	5.42	R.Phillips-Det	8	R.Phillips-Det	952	B.Layne-Pit	1814	J.Unitas-Bal	8.20
J.Smith-SF	174	J.Smith-SF	780	C.Peaks-Phi	5.41	J.Crow-SL	6	J.Smith-SF	830	E.LeBaron-Dal	1736	G.Shaw-NYG	8.15

Completion Percent		TD Passes		TD Percent		INT Percent		Passer Rating		Passing Rank		Receptions	
M.Plum-Cle	60.4	J.Unitas-Bal	25	J.Roach-SL	9.0	M.Plum-Cle	2.0	M.Plum-Cle	110.4	M.Plum-Cle	1054	R.Berry-Bal	74
B.Wade-LA	58.2	Van Brocklin-Phi	24	Van Brocklin-Phi	8.5	J.Brodie-SF	4.3	Van Brocklin-Phi	86.5	J.Unitas-Bal	715	S.Randle-SL	62
B.Starr-GB	57.0	M.Plum-Cle	21	M.Plum-Cle	8.4	B.Starr-GB	4.7	B.Wade-LA	77.0	Van Brocklin-Phi	676	R.Phillips-LA	52
R.Guglielmi-Was	56.1	J.Roach-SL	17	G.Shaw-NYG	7.1	Van Brocklin-Phi	6.0	J.Unitas-Bal	73.7	B.Starr-GB	379	J.Gibbons-Det	51
Van Brocklin-Phi	53.9	B.Layne-Pit	13	J.Unitas-Bal	6.6	B.Wade-LA	6.0	B.Starr-GB	70.8	B.Layne-Pit	292	P.Retzlaff-Phi	46

Receiving Yards		Receiving Average		Receiving TDs		Receiving Rank		Combined Net Yards		Total TDs		Total Points	
R.Berry-Bal	1298	B.Dial-Pit	24.30	S.Randle-SL	15	R.Berry-Bal	699	J.Brown-Cle	1761	S.Randle-SL	15	P.Hornung-GB	176
B.Dial-Pit	972	L.Moore-Bal	20.80	T.McDonald-Phi	13	B.Dial-Pit	531	B.Mitchell-Cle	1651	P.Hornung-GB	15	B.Walston-Phi	105
L.Moore-Bal	936	M.McGee-GB	20.71	K.Rote-NYG	10	S.Randle-SL	522	J.Crow-SL	1533	L.Moore-Bal	13	S.Randle-SL	90
S.Randle-SL	893	T.McDonald-Phi	20.54	R.Berry-Bal	10	L.Moore-Bal	513	L.Moore-Bal	1333	T.McDonald-Cle	13	S.Baker-Cle	80
R.Phillips-LA	883	B.Walston-Phi	18.77			R.Phillips-LA	482	R.Berry-Bal	1298	B.Mitchell-Cle	12		

Punt Average		Field Goals		Field Goal Percent		Kickoff Returns		Kickoff Return Average		Punt Returns		Punt Return Average	
J.Norton-SL	45.6	T.Davis-SF	19	B.Walston-Phi	70.0	Franckhauser-Dal	26	L.Lyles-SF	30.9	B.Stits-NYG	18	B.Stits-NYG	9.2
B.Green-Pit	44.2	B.Khayat-Was	15	B.Khayat-Was	65.2	T.Dean-Phi	26	A.Woodson-SF	29.3	W.Wood-GB	16	T.Barr-Det	7.4
T.Davis-SF	44.1	P.Hornung-GB	15	G.Perry-SL	65.0	S.Horner-Was	24	J.Sample-Bal	28.8	T.Dean-Phi	16	J.Sample-Bal	7.2
Y.Lary-Det	43.8	B.Walston-Phi	14	E.Vereb-LA	63.2	B.Stits-NYG	20	B.Mitchell-Cle	25.4			W.Wood-GB	6.6
Van Brocklin-Phi	43.1			S.Baker-Cle	60.0	B.Butler-Dal	20	J.Arnett-LA	24.5			J.Steffen-Det	5.9

Punt/Kick Return Yards		Punt/Kick Return TDs		Interceptions		Interception Return Yards		Interception Return TDs		Sacks		Overall Rank	
A.Woodson-SF	672	J.Sample-Bal	1	J.Norton-SL	10	B.Parrish-Cle	238	B.Franklin-Cle	2	Not kept		J.Brown-Cle	1549
B.Stits-NYG	652	B.Mitchell-Cle	1	D.Baker-SF	10	B.Boyd-Bal	132					J.Crow-SL	1471
J.Sample-Bal	620	L.Lyles-SF	1	D.Burroughs-Phi	9	B.Franklin-Cle	131					J.Taylor-GB	1272
T.Dean-Phi	598	J.LoVetere-LA	1	J.Shofner-Cle	8	D.Burroughs-Phi	124					B.Mitchell-Cle	1152
				B.Franklin-Cle	8	C.Britt-LA	117					T.Tracy-Pit	1081

New Beginnings

With direct competition came innovation and change, and as a result, 1960 was a season marked by several historic developments in the league. New commissioner Pete Rozelle was elevated to replace the late Bert Bell. With the fledgling AFL mounting its initial challenge, Rozelle and the NFL responded by expanding for the first time since its merger with the AAFC in 1949.

In addition to letting the Cardinals move to St. Louis, the league wooed away the prospective owners of the AFL's Minneapolis franchise, even though the city would not be ready to field a team until 1961. That left the league in the awkward position of only moving up to 13 teams, with the newly-created Cowboys going toe-to-toe against the AFL's reinvention of the Texans in the Dallas market. With Giants defensive coordinator Tom Landry getting the opportunity as head coach, the Cowboys posted the league's first winless season since 1944.

Other beginnings yielded happier results. Green Bay's halfback–kicker Paul Hornung set the all-time single-season scoring record, shattering legendary Packer Don Hutson's 1942 mark of 138 points. Hornung, teamed in the backfield with bruising Jim Taylor, helped secure Vince Lombardi's first division title with the Packers. The launch of Green Bay's dynasty would be no sure thing. With two games to go, the Pack was tied up with both San Francisco and defending league champion Baltimore at 6–4. Lombardi's crew beat the 49ers and the Rams to clinch, while the Colts fell apart. Despite the collapse, Johnny Unitas led the league for the fourth straight year in touchdowns passes.

In the Eastern Division, the Eagles beat out a Browns team that led the league in scoring and had Jim Brown, who won his fourth consecutive rushing title. After an opening loss to Cleveland, the Eagles ran off nine straight wins, relying on Norm Van Brocklin in his final season. "The Dutchman" was the consensus Player of the Year and the league's All-Pro QB. Philadelphia also featured Chuck Bednarik in his last season as a full-time double-duty player, snapping on offense and playing linebacker on defense.

1960 AFL

TEAM	W-l-T	PCT	POST	PTS	RA	RY	RY/A	RTD	FL	PA	PC	GPY	GPY/A	PTD	PI	PSY	PRAT
Eastern Division																	
Hou	10-4	.714	L*	379-285	452-397	1733-1384	3.8-**3.5**	15-6	17-**26**	456-557	218-271	**3371**-3874	**7.4**-7.0	31-28	28-25	**168**-357	69.8-69.7
NYT	7-7	.500	—	**382**-399	445-393	1817-1914	4.1-4.9	14-24	20-16	474-450	236-216	3334-2919	7.0-6.5	**32**-27	28-24	357-164	**70.8**-66.9
Buf	5-8-1	.385	—	296-303	417-438	1544-1724	3.7-3.9	15-15	**15**-16	447-429	184-**185**	2689-**2461**	6.0-**5.7**	19-**19**	29-**33**	333-331	48.6-**44.6**
Bos	5-9	.357	—	286-349	365-449	1479-1729	4.1-3.9	11-20	22-20	475-429	223-210	2865-2958	6.0-6.9	25-**19**	23-25	261-216	63.7-62.1
Western Division																	
LAC	10-4	.714	L	373-336	397-414	1900-1672	**4.8**-4.0	23-20	16-17	441-467	229-227	3177-2851	7.2-6.1	21-21	29-28	364-294	63.8-58.0
DalT	8-6	.571	—	362-**253**	**463**-381	2007-**1329**	4.3-**3.5**	**24**-14	18-16	435-503	209-261	2831-3002	6.5-6.0	16-**19**	**19**-32	193-349	63.3-56.3
Oak	6-8	.429	—	319-388	444-413	**2056**-1845	4.6-4.5	23-17	18-15	463-477	235-234	2923-3385	6.3-7.1	18-28	28-25	271-247	58.4-70.3
Den	4-9-1	.308	—	309-393	408-506	1467-2406	3.6-4.8	10-19	17-17	**508**-387	**259**-189	3247-2987	6.4-7.7	24-25	35-27	272-261	58.2-67.4
Aver	14	—	—	338	424	1750	4.1	17	18	462	224	3055	6.6	23	27	277	62.1

TEAM	1D	PENY	PNT	FGM/A	RTNY	RTNTD	OFFY/DEFY	NETY	NETTO	NP	PNP	DELP	PW	DELW	PRT	DR	YPD	DEL
Eastern Division																		
Hou	262-282	750-664	35.8-**37.1**	15/34-12/27	398-574	2-2	**4936**-4901	35	6	94	27	**67**	9.4	0.7	**4.7**/4.5	192-213	**25.7**-23.0	2.7
NYT	**286**-252	672-**911**	37.8-37.3	9/21-10/25	306-546	5-2	4794-4669	125	-8	-17	-22	5	6.6	0.4	4.0/4.1	196-195	24.5-23.9	0.5
Buf	211-**225**	615-608	39.0-37.6	12/26-14/27	517-654	4-3	3900-**3854**	46	5	-7	24	-31	6.8	-1.3	2.5/**1.8**	204-209	19.1-**18.4**	0.7
Bos	234-237	730-825	36.1-37.7	8/23-10/27	506-693	1-7	4083-4471	-388	0	-63	-32	-31	5.4	-0.4	3.6/4.0	207-192	19.7-23.3	-3.6
Western Division																		
LAC	263-259	648-569	**39.7**-40.2	13/24-14/28	614-481	4-1	4713-4229	484	0	37	40	-3	7.9	**2.1**	3.6/3.0	187-**190**	25.2-22.3	**2.9**
DalT	272-253	753-579	39.3-37.3	14/**34**-4/23	**906**-328	6-2	4645-3982	**663**	11	**109**	99	10	**9.7**	-1.7	4.3/2.6	195-190	23.8-21.0	**2.9**
Oak	254-268	718-598	38.9-37.5	6/25-14/30	429-610	2-5	4708-4983	-275	-6	-69	-47	-22	5.3	0.7	3.2/4.5	**208**-200	22.6-24.9	-2.3
Den	248-254	**501**-633	37.3-39.0	**18**/28-17/28	678-468	3-5	4442-5132	-690	-8	-84	-90	6	4.9	-0.4	3.0/4.2	200-200	22.2-25.7	-3.5
Aver	254	673	37.9	12/27	544	3	4528	—	—	—	—	—	—	—	3.8	199	22.8	—

Rushing Attempts	Rushing Yards	Rushing Average	Rushing TDs	Rushing Rank	Passing Yards	Passing Average
A.Haynes-DalT 156	A.Haynes-DalT 875	P.Lowe-LAC 6.29	A.Haynes-DalT 9	A.Haynes-DalT 965	F.Tripucka-Den........3038	J.Kemp-LAC 7.43
D.Smith-Hou 154	P.Lowe-LAC 855	A.Haynes-DalT 5.61	P.Lowe-LAC 8	P.Lowe-LAC 935	J.Kemp-LAC 3018	T.O'Connell-Buf 7.12
B.Cannon-Hou 152	B.Cannon-Hou 644	B.Lott-Oak 5.25	J.Kemp-LAC 8	D.Smith-Hou 693	A.Dorow-NYT 2748	A.Dorow-NYT 6.94
T.Teresa-Oak 139	D.Smith-Hou 643	A.Dorow-NYT 5.03	A.Dorow-NYT 7	T.Teresa-Oak 668	B.Songin-Bos 2476	T.Flores-Oak 6.90
W.Carlton-Buf 137	T.Teresa-Oak 608	J.Robinson-DalT 4.67	W.Carlton-Buf 7	B.Cannon-Hou 654	C.Davidson-DalT 2474	G.Blanda-Hou 6.65

Completion Percent	TD Passes	TD Percent	INT Percent	Passer Rating	Passing Rank	Receptions
T.Flores-Oak 54.0	A.Dorow-NYT 26	G.Blanda-Hou 6.6	B.Songin-Bos..........3.8	T.Flores-Oak 71.8	B.Songin-Bos..........748	L.Taylor-Den 92
J.Kemp-LAC 52.0	F.Tripucka-Den 24	A.Dorow-NYT 6.6	C.Davidson-DalT 4.2	B.Songin-Bos..........70.9	C.Davidson-DalT 672	D.Maynard-NYT 72
F.Tripucka-Den 51.9	G.Blanda-Hou 24	B.Songin-Bos..........5.6	J.Green-Buf 4.4	A.Dorow-NYT 67.8	J.Kemp-LAC 609	B.Groman-Hou 72
A.Dorow-NYT 50.8	B.Songin-Bos..........22	F.Tripucka-Den 5.0	T.Flores-Oak 4.8	J.Kemp-LAC 67.1	A.Dorow-NYT 464	A.Powell-NYT 69
B.Songin-Bos..........47.7	J.Kemp-LAC 20	J.Kemp-LAC 4.9	B.Parilli-Oak 5.9	G.Blanda-Hou..........65.4	T.Flores-Oak 449	A.Haynes-DalT 55

Receiving Yards	Receiving Average	Receiving TDs	Receiving Rank	Combined Net Yards	Total TDs	Total Points
B.Groman-Hou 1473	B.Groman-Hou 20.46	A.Powell-NYT 14	B.Groman-Hou 797	A.Haynes-DalT 2100	A.Powell-NYT 14	G.Mingo-Den 123
D.Maynard-NYT 1265	W.Carlton-Den 19.25	L.Taylor-Den 12	L.Taylor-Den 678	P.Lowe-LAC 1843	L.Taylor-Den 12	G.Blanda-Hou..........115
L.Taylor-Den 1235	E.Dubenion-Buf 17.90	B.Groman-Hou 12	D.Maynard-NYT 663	J.Larscheid-Oak 1542	A.Haynes-DalT 12	J.Spikes-DalT 104
A.Powell-NYT 1167	D.Maynard-NYT 17.57	J.Colclough-Bos 9	A.Powell-NYT 654	W.Carlton-Den 1509	B.Groman-Hou 12	B.Shockley-NYT 86
C.Burford-DalT 789	C.Burford-DalT 17.15	E.Dubenion-Buf 7	C.Burford-DalT 420	B.Groman-Hou 1473	W.Carlton-Buf 11	B.Agajanian-LAC 85

Punt Average	Field Goals	Field Goal Percent	Kickoff Returns	Kickoff Return Average	Punt Returns	Punt Return Average
P.Maguire-LAC 40.5	G.Mingo-Den 18	G.Mingo-Den 64.3	J.Larscheid-Oak 30	K.Hall-Hou 31.3	W.Carlton-Den 15	A.Haynes-DalT 15.4
C.Davidson-DalT 39.4	G.Blanda-Hou 15	B.Agajanian-LAC 54.2	L.Burton-NYT 30	L.Burton-NYT 28.7	J.Robinson-DalT 14	J.Robinson-DalT 14.8
B.Atkins-Buf 39.0	J.Spikes-DalT 13	G.Blanda-Hou 45.5	P.Lowe-LAC 28	J.Larscheid-Oak 28.4	A.Haynes-DalT 14	W.Carlton-Den 6.7
W.Crow-Oak 38.9	B.Agajanian-LAC 13	B.Shockley-NYT 42.9	D.Christy-Bos 24	J.Smith-Oak 26.6	D.Harris-LAC 13	
G.Herring-Den 37.3	B.Shockley-NYT 9	J.Spikes-DalT 41.9	W.Carlton-Den 22	W.Carlton-Den 26.4		

Punt/Kick Return Yards	Punt/Kick Return TDs	Interceptions	Interception Return Yards	Interception Return TDs	Sacks	Overall Rank
J.Larscheid-Oak 958	L.Burton-NYT 2	G.Gonsoulin-Den 11	D.Webster-DalT 156	D.Webster-DalT 2	Not kept	A.Haynes-DalT 1562
L.Burton-NYT 955		E.Macon-Oak..........9	A.Matsos-Buf 142			P.Lowe-LAC 1332
D.Christy-Bos 690		A.Matsos-Buf 8	E.Macon-Oak 105			B.Cannon-Hou 1005
W.Carlton-Den 682			C.Shonta-Bos 101			A.Dorow-NYT 987
K.Hall-Hou 666			G.Gonsoulin-Den 98			J.Robinson-DalT 940

LOADS OF OFFENSE AND AMBITION

Born of Lamar Hunt's ambition, and guaranteed an extended trial through its national television contract with ABC, the American Football League was designed to mount a serious challenge to the National Football League. Taking advantage of the multitude of talent cranked out by colleges, the league leaned west by launching franchises in Denver and Houston, while also moving into open eastern markets in Boston and Buffalo. The new league challenged the NFL directly in California, New York, and Dallas, where Hunt had his own franchise. Not all of this was by design. The Raiders were born out of a desperate need for an eighth team to replace the Minneapolis ownership group that quickly defected to the NFL.

Neither a longer 14-game schedule nor the AFL's brand of pass-happy offense could elevate attendance beyond sparse. The absence of competitive races didn't help as both the Houston Oilers and the Los Angeles Chargers handily won their divisions. Each team relied heavily on journeyman quarterbacks. Former Bears reserve George Blanda took snaps and made kicks for the Oilers, while Jack Kemp made a name for himself as a gunslinger in a league that didn't seem to have any other kind of quarterback.

The Dallas Texans, under University of Miami assistant Hank Stram, had the AFL's best defense. Dallas, the only team to allow fewer than 20 points per game, won its last three games by a combined score of 82–7. Rookie Abner Hayes led the league in rushing en route to the league's first Player of the Year award.

The AFL relied on NFL rejects and reserves. Talented wideouts like Denver's Lionel Taylor and New York's Don Maynard caught passes from castoffs Frank Tripucka and Al Dorow, respectively. The AFL coaxed Heisman Trophy winner Billy Cannon to sign with the Oilers and also debuted Raiders center Jim Otto, Chargers halfback Paul Lowe, and offensive tackle Ron Mix. The league was filled with two-way players. Besides Blanda, there was Patriots kicker–defensive back (and eventual wideout) Gino Cappelletti, Chargers linebacker–punter Paul Maguire, and the new league's first scoring leader, Gene Mingo, who ran, caught, kicked, and even returned kicks for the Broncos.

1961 NFL

TEAM	W-L-T	PCT	POST	PTS	RA	RY	RY/A	RTD	FL	PA	PC	GPY	GPY/A	PTD	PI	PSY	PRAT
Eastern Conference																	
NYG	10-3-1	.769	L	368-**220**	464-419	1857-1761	4.0-4.2	13-**6**	20-21	416-386	215-176	3035-2600	7.3-6.7	27-21	23-**33**	295-399	74.1-**50.7**
Phi	10-4	.714	—	361-297	373-474	1507-2007	4.0-4.2	10-12	14-16	429-383	**241**-224	**3824**-3183	**8.9**-8.3	**34**-23	26-17	219-263	**87.2**-87.0
Cle	8-5-1	.615	—	319-270	476-411	2163-1605	4.5-3.9	15-16	20-18	320-358	185-200	2538-2831	7.9-7.9	20-16	**13**-20	164-305	**87.2**-73.2
SL	7-7	.500	—	279-267	386-477	1405-1676	3.6-**3.5**	8-9	18-20	351-389	168-187	2434-2644	6.9-6.8	21-18	23-24	461-334	63.5-60.2
Pit	6-8	.429	—	295-287	**543-396**	1761-**1463**	3.2-3.7	10-11	22-20	334-420	176-201	2622-2780	7.9-6.6	23-22	34-25	290-334	62.1-62.2
Dal	4-9-1	.308	—	236-380	416-454	1819-2161	4.4-4.8	6-20	21-18	422-**326**	215-168	2918-2635	6.9-8.1	23-21	27-25	257-204	64.9-68.2
Was	1-12-1	.077	—	174-392	361-412	1072-1550	3.0-3.8	9-10	12-15	420-409	189-238	2566-3493	6.1-8.5	12-37	28-26	391-218	46.8-89.8
Western Conference																	
GB	**11**-3	**.786**	L*	**391**-223	474-412	**2350**-1694	**5.0**-4.1	**27**-12	**10**-17	306-414	177-218	2502-2630	8.2-**6.4**	18-13	16-29	**138**-273	82.2-53.7
Det	8-5-1	.615	—	270-258	439-412	1868-1520	4.3-3.7	16-14	15-12	398-385	186-203	2830-2744	7.1-7.1	14-**11**	27-29	286-326	54.1-53.9
Bal	8-6	.571	—	302-307	456-418	2119-1869	4.6-4.5	17-17	13-8	**438**-351	232-**161**	3018-**2320**	6.9-6.6	17-18	29-16	215-**407**	60.3-65.9
ChiB	8-6	.571	—	326-302	436-401	1890-1652	4.3-4.1	16-10	14-13	349-398	186-209	3011-3164	8.6-7.9	26-27	24-24	339-367	78.6-76.5
SF	7-6-1	.538	—	346-272	448-419	2100-1701	4.7-4.1	**27**-13	17-12	346-380	187-196	3057-2874	8.8-7.6	15-18	19-19	253-394	75.5-71.5
LA	4-10	.286	—	263-333	415-508	1958-2440	4.7-4.8	17-26	11-16	386-328	199-184	2709-2642	7.0-8.1	13-19	21-23	372-269	62.8-72.5
Min	3-11	.214	—	285-407	419-493	1897-2667	4.5-5.4	14-29	22-**23**	377-365	203-194	2527-3051	6.7-8.4	22-21	22-22	538-125	70.0-75.3
Aver	14	—	—	301	436	1840	4.2	15	16	378	197	2828	7.5	20	24	301	68.5

TEAM	1D	PENY	PNT	FGM/A	RTNY	RTNTD	OFFY/DEFY	NETY	NETTO	NP	PNP	DELP	PW	DELW	PRT	DR	YPD	DEL
Eastern Conference																		
NYG	**275-212**	629-677	43.9-42.4	14/34-**5/20**	815-493	6-2	4597-3962	635	11	148	97	51	10.7	-0.2	4.4/**2.1**	202-206	22.8-19.2	3.5
Phi	252-267	500-684	43.7-41.8	14/25-11/24	592-529	2-3	**5112**-4927	185	-7	64	-13	**77**	8.6	**1.4**	**6.1**/ 5.7	173-180	29.5-27.4	2.2
Cle	246-243	455-367	43.3-42.9	16/23-11/28	443-515	4-2	4537-4131	406	5	49	54	-5	8.2	0.3	5.8/ 4.5	168-**162**	27.0-25.5	1.5
SL	202-215	535-546	44.7-42.0	7/17-19/38	695-756	**8**-3	3378-3986	-608	3	12	-39	51	7.3	-0.3	2.8/ 3.3	194-194	17.4-20.5	-3.1
Pit	239-218	486-533	47.0-43.8	15/28-10/26	**945**-761	3-4	4093-3909	184	-11	8	-29	37	7.2	-1.2	2.8/ 3.3	**208**-207	19.7-**18.9**	0.8
Dal	239-254	427-362	36.7-45.5	11/24-14/28	477-782	0-8	4480-4592	-112	-5	-144	-29	-115	3.4	1.1	3.7/ 4.3	177-176	25.3-26.1	-0.8
Was	193-261	651-603	38.1-44.2	5/28-13/24	522-757	2-3	3247-4825	-1578	1	-218	-128	-90	1.6	-0.1	2.2/ 5.7	187-177	17.4-27.3	-9.9
Western Conference																		
GB	274-245	647-609	43.0-**37.8**	16/24-13/21	801-551	4-1	4714-4051	663	**20**	**168**	**135**	33	**11.2**	-0.2	5.6/ 2.6	156-165	**30.2**-24.6	5.7
Det	233-222	678-381	**47.6**-43.0	15/33-20/34	669-587	2-3	4412-3938	474	-1	12	36	-24	7.3	1.2	3.4/ 2.9	185-178	23.8-22.1	1.7
Bal	274-232	589-548	43.0-41.4	**21/39**-16/26	392-654	0-2	4922-**3782**	**1140**	-18	-5	23	-28	6.9	1.1	3.6/ 3.4	166-171	29.7-22.1	**7.5**
ChiB	239-223	720-**860**	41.7-42.7	11/27-10/27	541-648	0-2	4562-4449	113	-1	24	5	19	7.6	0.4	4.7/ 4.5	183-182	24.9-24.4	0.5
SF	258-234	635-456	44.6-44.0	12/22-16/29	554-518	2-1	4904-4181	723	-5	74	40	34	8.9	-1.4	5.6/ 4.2	169-175	29.0-23.9	5.1
LA	236-279	599-662	40.1-43.3	13/27-6/21	461-664	2-**0**	4295-4813	-518	7	-70	-15	-55	5.3	-1.3	3.5/ 4.2	170-169	25.3-28.5	-3.2
Min	236-291	**375**-638	39.0-41.4	9/21-15/26	665-**357**	1-2	3886-5593	-1707	1	-122	-138	16	4.0	-1.0	2.7/ 5.6	183-179	21.2-31.2	-10.0
Aver	243	566	42.6	13/27	612	3	4367	—	—	—	—	—	—	—	4.4	180	24.3	—

Rushing Attempts	Rushing Yards	Rushing Average	Rushing TDs	Rushing Rank	Passing Yards	Passing Average
J.Brown-Cle 305	J.Brown-Cle 1408	L.Moore-Bal 7.04	J.Taylor-GB 15	J.Brown-Cle 1488	S.Jurgensen-Phi 3723	J.Brodie-SF 9.14
J.Taylor-GB 243	J.Taylor-GB 1307	D.Bass-LA 6.20	B.Kilmer-SF 10	J.Taylor-GB 1457	J.Unitas-Bal 2990	B.Wade-Chi 9.03
J.Johnson-Pit 213	A.Webster-NYG 928	B.Mitchell-Cle 5.43		A.Webster-NYG 948	J.Brodie-SF 2588	S.Jurgensen-Phi 8.95
R.Phillips-Det 201	R.Phillips-Det 841	J.Taylor-GB 5.38		J.Smith-SF 903	B.Starr-GB 2418	B.Starr-GB 8.20
D.Perkins-Dal 200	J.Smith-SF 823	C.Roberts-SF 5.37		R.Phillips-Det 891	M.Plum-Cle 2416	B.Layne-Pit 8.09

Completion Percent	TD Passes	TD Percent	INT Percent	Passer Rating	Passing Rank	Receptions
M.Plum-Cle 58.6	S.Jurgensen-Phi 32	B.Wade-Chi 8.8	M.Plum-Cle 3.3	B.Wade-Chi 93.7	S.Jurgensen-Phi 1062	R.Phillips-LA 78
B.Starr-GB 58.3	B.Wade-Chi 22	S.Jurgensen-Phi 7.7	Y.Tittle-NYG 4.2	M.Plum-Cle 90.3	M.Plum-Cle 898	R.Berry-Bal 75
Y.Tittle-NYG 57.2	F.Tarkenton-Min 18	B.Layne-Pit 7.4	J.Brodie-SF 4.2	S.Jurgensen-Phi 88.1	J.Brodie-SF 884	D.Shofner-NYG 68
R.Bukich-Pit 57.1	M.Plum-Cle 18	L.Dupre-SL 7.1	F.Ryan-LA 4.9	Y.Tittle-NYG 85.3	Y.Tittle-NYG 741	T.McDonald-Phi 64
S.Jurgensen-Phi 56.5	Y.Tittle-NYG 17	R.Bukich-Pit 7.1	B.Wade-Chi 5.2	J.Brodie-SF 84.7	B.Wade-Chi 719	

Receiving Yards	Receiving Average	Receiving TDs	Receiving Rank	Combined Net Yards	Total TDs	Total Points
T.McDonald-Phi 1144	F.Clarke-Dal 22.41	T.McDonald-Phi 13	T.McDonald-Phi 637	J.Brown-Cle 1917	J.Taylor-GB 16	P.Hornung-GB 146
D.Shofner-NYG 1125	G.Cogdill-Det 21.24	M.Ditka-Chi 12	D.Shofner-NYG 618	D.Perkins-Dal 1588	L.Moore-Bal 15	B.Walston-Phi 97
R.Phillips-LA 1092	B.Dial-Pit 19.75	B.Dial-Pit 12	M.Ditka-Chi 598	D.Bass-LA 1560	T.McDonald-Phi 13	J.Taylor-GB 96
M.Ditka-Chi 1076	M.Ditka-Chi 19.21	D.Shofner-NYG 11	B.Dial-Pit 584	T.Brown-Phi 1538	M.Ditka-Chi 12	S.Myhra-Bal 96
B.Dial-Pit 1047	R.Owens-SF 18.76	J.Reichow-Min 11	R.Phillips-LA 571	J.Arnett-LA 1531	B.Dial-Pit 12	L.Moore-Bal 90

Punt Average	Field Goals	Field Goal Percent	Kickoff Returns	Kickoff Return Average	Punt Returns	Punt Return Average
Y.Lary-Det 48.4	S.Myhra-Bal 21	L.Groza-Cle 69.6	T.Brown-Phi 29	D.Bass-LA 30.3	J.Sample-Pit 26	W.Wood-GB 16.1
B.Green-Pit 47.0	L.Groza-Cle 16	P.Hornung-GB 68.2	L.Lyles-Bal 28	D.James-Was 29.4	J.Morris-Chi 23	B.Mitchell-Cle 11.7
T.Davis-SF 45.4	L.Michaels-Pit 15	L.Michaels-Pit 57.7	A.Woodson-SF 27	A.Woodson-SF 29.0	T.Dean-Phi 18	J.Sample-Pit 10.9
J.Norton-SL 44.7	J.Martin-Det 15	B.Walston-Phi 56.0	A.Marsh-Dal 26	P.Studstill-Det 28.0	B.Boyd-Bal 18	A.Woodson-SF 10.8
B.Dowler-GB 44.1	P.Hornung-GB 15	T.Davis-SF 54.5		T.Brown-Phi 28.0		T.Mason-Min 10.4

Punt/Kick Return Yards	Punt/Kick Return TDs	Interceptions	Interception Return Yards	Interception Return TDs	Sacks	Overall Rank
A.Woodson-SF 954	A.Woodson-SF 2	D.Lynch-NYG 9	E.Barnes-NYG 195	B.Stacy-SL 2	Not kept	J.Brown-Cle 1771
T.Brown-Phi 936	W.Wood-GB 2	J.Sample-Pit 8	D.Bishop-Dal 172	J.Norton-SL 2		J.Taylor-GB 1550
J.Sample-Pit 815	B.Mitchell-Cle 2	J.Patton-NYG 8	J.Patton-NYG 163	D.Hackbart-Was 2		D.Bass-LA 1173
D.Bass-LA 807	T.Brown-Phi 2	D.Bishop-Dal 8	J.Sample-Pit 141	E.Barnes-NYG 2		D.Perkins-Dal 1125
T.Mason-Min 749			J.Norton-SL 136			A.Webster-NYG 1120

14 Games for 14 Teams

In its continued response to the new league, the NFL launched its 14th franchise. Minnesota was lured to the NFL days after the ownership group had taken part in the first AFL draft. Although just 3–11 in the first year of the 14-game NFL schedule, the inaugural Vikings launched the career of scrambling quarterback Fran Tarkenton. The Cowboys, who followed a winless first season by winning three of their first four in 1961, moved to the Eastern Division—geography be damned—while launching generations of rivalries to come with Washington, Philadelphia, and New York.

In response to the AFL's air circus, the NFL boasted a number of its own pass-driven offenses. Sonny Jurgensen took over for Norm Van Brocklin in Philadelphia, throwing an NFL record-tying 32 touchdowns. Y.A. Tittle, abandoned on San Francisco's bench, crossed the country to take snaps for the Giants in a late-career renaissance. Chicago's George Halas effectively reinvented the tight end position with his reliance on rookie Mike Ditka. The rookie finished among the league's leaders in receptions, touchdown catches, and receiving yardage.

None of these developments could slow Green Bay's growing superiority. Between a crushing defense—reinforced by rookie Herb Adderley—and an equally crunching running game built around an incomparable offensive line, the Lombardi way seemed to be settling into a formula for success. But even in Green Bay, passing was becoming part of the program. Bart Starr set the club mark for passing yards as the Packers easily won the Western Conference. The retirement standout defensive lineman Art Donovan marked Baltimore's continuing decline.

In the Eastern Conference, things were more interesting. A tight race between the Eagles and the Giants came down to a showdown on the next-to-last weekend. Although the Eagles basically outgunned opponents with Sonny Jurgensen's air game, the Giants made their biggest improvements on defense. New York surrendered almost a touchdown less per game than in 1960, in no small part because an outstanding defensive backfields. Tied at 9–3 in the standings, the Giants won a 28–24 upset in Philadelphia, and then tied the Browns in the season finale to finish a half-game up on the Eagles.

1961 AFL

TEAM	W-L-T	PCT	POST	PTS	RA	RY	RY/A	RTD	FL	PA	PC	GPY	GPY/A	PTD	PI	PSY	PRAT
Eastern Division																	
Hou	10-3-1	.769	L*	**513**-242	**452**-365	1896-1634	4.2-4.5	15-17	10-15	498-493	254-212	**4568**-2750	**9.2**-5.6	**48**-13	29-33	176-359	**90.7**-42.1
Bos	9-4-1	.692	—	413-313	389-350	1675-**1041**	4.3-**3.0**	14-9	**9**-20	420-479	206-241	2795-3490	6.7-7.3	29-27	**21**-22	256-**408**	72.9-74.0
NYT	7-7	.500	—	301-390	426-414	1678-1880	3.9-4.5	17-20	20-**21**	460-462	204-211	2733-3044	5.9-6.6	20-26	32-25	346-247	49.3-63.8
Buf	6-8	.429	—	294-342	438-**349**	1606-1377	3.7-3.9	18-9	17-15	439-430	194-206	2786-3237	6.3-7.5	15-28	25-29	442-350	53.0-67.0
Western Division																	
SD	**12**-2	**.857**	L	396-**219**	391-401	1466-1357	3.7-3.4	**24**-7	19-17	423-485	190-224	3121-**2736**	7.4-5.6	17-16	25-**49**	274-373	59.0-**35.5**
DalT	6-8	.429	—	334-343	439-410	**2183**-1525	**5.0**-3.7	23-17	18-18	399-439	177-219	2815-3077	7.1-7.0	18-20	27-24	239-300	55.3-65.3
Den	3-11	.214	—	251-442	333-435	1091-1633	3.3-3.8	11-17	23-14	**568**-433	**265**-194	3004-3060	5.3-7.1	14-30	45-26	284-275	40.6-66.9
Oak	2-12	.143	—	237-458	350-494	1234-2382	3.5-4.8	10-36	16-12	423-**409**	209-**192**	2514-2942	5.9-7.2	17-22	28-24	463-168	53.8-64.7
Aver	14	—	—	342	402	1604	4.0	17	17	454	212	3042	6.7	23	29	310	59.1

TEAM	1D	PENY	PNT	FGM/A	RTNY	RTNTD	OFFY/DEFY	NETY	NETTO	NP	PNP	DELP	PW	DELW	PRT	DR	YPD	DEL
Eastern Division																		
Hou	**293**-235	889-588	39.1-40.7	16/26-**6**/24	646-678	3-3	**6288**-4025	**2263**	9	**271**	**225**	**46**	**13.8**	-3.3	**7.0**/ 1.9	195-201	**32.2**-20.0	**12.2**
Bos	238-243	659-661	37.6-40.7	**17/32**-9/23	571-**396**	9-5	4214-4123	91	12	100	56	44	9.5	0.0	4.2/ 4.5	190-190	22.2-21.7	0.5
NYT	247-242	585-**870**	41.8-42.4	8/23-14/27	778-954	3-4	4065-4677	-612	-6	-89	-75	-14	4.8	**2.2**	2.3/ 3.9	205-202	19.8-23.2	-3.3
Buf	243-**200**	549-693	**44.5**-**38.7**	9/26-13/28	498-689	5-6	3950-4264	-314	2	-48	-18	-30	5.8	0.2	2.7/ 4.0	204-199	19.4-21.4	-2.1
Western Division																		
SD	208-224	682-501	41.5-39.5	13/27-10/**23**	**1347**-444	**11**-4	4313-**3720**	593	**22**	177	137	40	11.4	0.6	4.2/**0.6**	200-199	21.6-**18.7**	2.9
DalT	247-238	875-619	40.0-41.0	7/24-12/31	625-595	4-7	4759-4302	457	-3	-9	26	-35	6.8	-0.8	3.6/ 4.0	189-186	25.2-23.1	2.1
Den	219-233	560-799	39.4-40.8	8/25-13/26	679-1186	3-9	3811-4418	-607	-28	-181	-163	-18	2.5	0.5	1.5/ 4.1	**213**-216	17.9-20.5	-2.6
Oak	200-280	**456**-524	39.0-40.4	11/26-12/27	402-604	2-**2**	3285-5156	-1871	-8	-221	-188	-33	1.5	0.5	2.1/ 4.5	182-**185**	18.0-27.9	-9.8
Aver	237	657	40.5	11/26	693	5	4336	—	—	—	—	—	—	—	3.6	197	22.0	—

Rushing Attempts	Rushing Yards	Rushing Average	Rushing TDs	Rushing Rank	Passing Yards	Passing Average
B.Mathis-NYT 202	B.Cannon-Hou.......948	B.Cannon-Hou........4.74	P.Lowe-SD 9	B.Cannon-Hou......1008	G.Blanda-Hou.......3330	G.Blanda-Hou......9.20
B.Cannon-Hou.........200	B.Mathis-NYT 846	A.Haynes-DalT 4.70	A.Haynes-DalT 9	A.Haynes-DalT 931	J.Kemp-SD 2686	C.Davidson-DalT ... 7.41
A.Haynes-DalT 179	A.Haynes-DalT 841	B.Lott-Bos 4.61	B.Mathis-NYT 7	B.Mathis-NYT 916	A.Dorow-NYT ...2651	J.Kemp-SD 7.38
P.Lowe-SD 175	P.Lowe-SD 767	P.Lowe-SD 4.38	J.Kemp-SD 6	P.Lowe-SD 857	C.Davidson-DalT ...2445	B.Songin-Bos.......6.74
C.Tolar-Hou............157	C.Tolar-Hou...........577	B.Mathis-NYT 4.19	B.Cannon-Hou.........6	C.Tolar-Hou.......617	T.Flores-Oak 2176	B.Parilli-Bos.......6.64

Completion Percent	TD Passes	TD Percent	INT Percent	Passer Rating	Passing Rank	Receptions
B.Parilli-Bos 52.5	G.Blanda-Hou 36	G.Blanda-Hou.....9.9	B.Songin-Bos 4.2	G.Blanda-Hou.....91.3	G.Blanda-Hou......965	L.Taylor-Den 100
T.Flores-Oak 51.9	A.Dorow-NYT 19	B.Songin-Bos 6.6	B.Parilli-Bos 4.5	B.Parilli-Bos 76.5	J.Kemp-SD 538	C.Hennigan-Hou....82
G.Blanda-Hou......51.7	C.Davidson-DalT ...17	B.Parilli-Bos 6.6	T.Flores-Oak 5.2	B.Songin-Bos 73.0	B.Songin-Bos 425	A.Powell-NYT 71
F.Tripucka-Den....48.5	J.Kemp-SD 15	C.Davidson-DalT ...5.2	J.Kemp-SD 6.0	T.Flores-Oak 62.1	J.Lee-Hou 423	D.Kocourek-SD 55
B.Songin-Bos.......46.2	T.Flores-Oak 15	A.Dorow-NYT 4.3	G.Blanda-Hou........6.1	C.Davidson-DalT ...59.2	T.Flores-Oak 403	C.Burford-SD 51

Receiving Yards	Receiving Average	Receiving TDs	Receiving Rank	Combined Net Yards	Total TDs	Total Points
C.Hennigan-Hou 1746	B.Groman-Hou 23.50	B.Groman-Hou 17	C.Hennigan-Hou 933	B.Cannon-Hou 2043	B.Groman-Hou 18	B.Cannon-Bos 147
L.Taylor-Den 1176	C.Hennigan-Hou 21.29	C.Hennigan-Hou 12	B.Groman-Hou 673	A.Haynes-DalT 1865	B.Cannon-Hou 15	G.Blanda-Hou 112
B.Groman-Hou 1175	D.Kocourek-SD 19.18	J.Colclough-Bos 9	L.Taylor-Den 608	C.Hennigan-Hou 1746	A.Haynes-DalT 13	B.Groman-Hou 108
D.Kocourek-SD 1055	J.Colclough-Bos 18.02	B.Cannon-Hou.........9	D.Kocourek-SD 548	A.Frazier-Den 1644	C.Hennigan-Hou 12	B.Cannon-Hou 90
A.Powell-NYT 881	D.Christy-NYT 17.97		A.Powell-NYT 466	D.Christy-NYT 1444	B.Lott-Bos 11	G.Blair-SD 81

Punt Average	Field Goals	Field Goal Percent	Kickoff Returns	Kickoff Return Average	Punt Returns	Punt Return Average
B.Atkins-Buf 44.5	B.Cannon-Bos 17	G.Blanda-Hou........61.5	G.Fleming-Oak 29	D.Grayson-DalT 28.3	F.Bruney-Bos 23	D.Christy-NYT.......21.3
C.Johnson-NYT 42.7	G.Blanda-Hou 16	B.Cannon-Bos 53.1	F.Jackson-DalT 24	A.Frazier-Den 28.0	A.Haynes-DalT 19	C.Gibson-SD 14.9
P.Maguire-SD 41.5	G.Blair-SD 13	G.Blair-SD 48.1	A.Frazier-Den 18	L.Garron-Bos 27.4	A.Frazier-Den 18	A.Frazier-Den 12.8
W.Crow-Oak 41.5	G.Fleming-Oak 11	J.Hergert-Buf 42.9	B.Cannon-Hou 18	F.Jackson-DalT 26.9	D.Christy-NYT......18	A.Haynes-DalT 10.3
J.Norton-Hou 40.7	J.Hergert-Buf 6	G.Fleming-Oak 42.3		R.Burton-Bos 26.7	C.Gibson-SD 14	F.Bruney-Bos 4.7

Punt/Kick Return Yards	Punt/Kick Return TDs	Interceptions	Interception Return Yards	Interception Return TDs	Sacks	Overall Rank
D.Christy-NYT.........743	A.Frazier-Den 2	B.Atkins-Buf 10	C.McNeil-SD 349	D.Harris-SD 3	Not kept	B.Cannon-Hou 1500
A.Frazier-Den 735	D.Christy-NYT..........2	J.Norton-Hou 9	B.Atkins-Buf 158	D.Webb-Bos.............2		A.Haynes-DalT 1486
F.Jackson-DalT 647		C.McNeil-SD 9	D.Webb-Bos 153	C.McNeil-SD 2		P.Lowe-SD 1029
G.Fleming-Oak 612		B.Zeman-SD 8	B.Laraba-SD 151	B.Laraba-SD 2		G.Blanda-Hou 969
R.Burton-Bos 529		T.Banfield-Hou 8	J.Norton-Hou 150	S.Headrick-DalT 2		B.Mathis-NYT 942

DOWN THE COAST AND DOWN THE FIELD

Unlike the three failed American Football Leagues that preceded it, this AFL was not going away. The league made adjustments on the go. It was for the AFL's long-term good that owner Barron Hilton moved the Chargers out of Los Angeles and away from the cavernous Coliseum. In San Diego the club had the league's best regular-season record and nearly doubled attendance. Five AFL cities saw attendance declines, but increases in Houston, San Diego, and Buffalo pushed overall attendance up by 72,000 in year two.

The league wasn't forced to scramble as it had the year before in inventing the Raiders, and might have looked forward to a more settled set-up. That didn't last. Owners stirred things up by firing coaches. The Raiders axed Eddie Erdelatz after two losses, the Patriots dumped Lou Saban for a 2–3 record, and even more surprisingly, the defending champion Oilers whacked Lou Rymkus for a 1–3–1 start.

But on-field hijinks easily overshadowed those events. The Oilers put on an unparalleled offensive show, scoring an incredible 513 points—more than 36 per game. George Blanda repeated his grand old man act by slinging 36 touchdowns, not to mention 464 yards passing against Buffalo on October 29 (both marks stood as the most in AFL history). The Oilers weren't just a one-man show. Billy Cannon broke out in his second season, leading the league in rushing and scoring 15 touchdowns, while wideouts Bill Groman and Charley Hennigan caught 17 and 12, respectively. The Oilers went 9–0 under new coach Wally Lamm, a streak they needed because the post-Saban Pats were 7–1–1 under Mike Holovak; both the loss and the tie came at Houston's hands.

The West remained the province of the Sid Gillman Chargers juggernaut, although this was in no small part aided by having the league's weakest pair of teams—Denver and Oakland—in their division. Although Gillman's fame as a coach was a product of his high-flying offenses with the Rams and now the Chargers, this year's team was more reliant on a defense with five consensus All-AFL players.

1962 NFL

TEAM	W-L-T	PCT	POST	PTS	RA	RY	RY/A	RTD	FL	PA	PC	GPY	GPY/A	PTD	PI	PSY	PRAT
Eastern Conference																	
NYG	12-2	.857	L	398-283	430-413	1698-1677	3.9-4.1	11-13	14-13	411-450	215-223	3446-3238	8.4-7.2	**35**-21	22-26	**139**-369	86.7-64.8
Pit	9-5	.643	—	312-363	**572**-363	2333-1419	4.1-3.9	17-13	**13**-10	319-438	160-223	2419-3490	7.6-8.0	14-34	23-28	350-284	60.1-77.0
Cle	7-6-1	.538	—	291-257	414-466	1772-1940	4.3-4.2	18-17	17-13	370-341	200-189	2747-2277	7.4-6.7	17-15	16-24	213-293	75.4-61.4
Was	5-7-2	.417	—	305-376	371-411	1088-1636	2.9-4.0	10-12	17-20	428-412	223-247	3532-3860	8.3-9.4	27-35	27-28	309-258	74.6-91.1
Dal	5-8-1	.385	—	398-402	434-387	2040-1510	**4.7**-3.9	16-17	19-16	380-437	200-233	3115-3904	8.2-8.9	31-33	17-20	243-230	**88.7**-89.8
SL	4-9-1	.308	—	287-361	416-452	1698-1724	4.1-3.8	20-18	21-15	**434**-377	220-196	3388-3302	7.8-8.8	18-21	30-16	288-315	61.9-82.8
Phi	3-10-1	.231	—	282-356	324-526	1155-2126	3.6-4.0	13-23	**13**-13	428-363	228-198	**3632**-3023	**8.5**-8.3	23-16	31-26	247-103	69.6-67.1
Western Conference																	
GB	**13**-1	**.929**	L*	**415-148**	518-404	**2460**-1531	**4.7**-3.8	**36-4**	15-19	311-355	187-187	2621-**2084**	8.4-**5.9**	14-**10**	**13-31**	290-338	84.9-**43.4**
Det	11-3	.786	—	315-177	489-**353**	1922-**1231**	3.9-**3.5**	14-6	18-23	379-367	211-187	2827-2441	7.5-6.7	19-11	24-24	246-**455**	69.9-55.0
ChiB	9-5	.643	—	321-287	386-438	1489-2073	3.9-4.7	17-17	16-**24**	430-363	229-170	3286-2460	7.6-6.8	20-14	28-23	226-386	66.7-55.8
Bal	7-7	.500	—	293-288	448-423	1601-1504	3.6-3.6	9-17	19-19	423-381	**237**-206	3330-2975	7.9-7.8	27-19	25-23	265-356	78.2-71.1
SF	6-8	.429	—	282-331	460-464	1873-2241	4.1-4.8	15-22	14-14	323-**296**	185-**164**	2491-2494	7.7-8.4	19-17	19-12	423-186	77.0-85.6
Min	2-11-1	.154	—	254-410	426-463	1864-1978	4.4-4.3	7-20	23-18	348-397	170-214	2699-3365	7.8-8.5	22-29	31-25	483-242	59.1-80.4
LA	1-12-1	.077	—	220-334	376-501	1689-2092	4.5-4.2	10-14	16-18	372-379	189-217	2524-3144	6.8-8.3	14-25	19-19	348-255	64.0-85.5
Aver	14	—	—	312	433	1763	4.1	15	17	383	204	3004	7.9	21	23	291	72.6

TEAM	1D	PENY	PNT	FGM/A	RTNY	RTNTD	OFFY/DEFY	NETY	NETTO	NP	PNP	DELP	PW	DELW	PRT	DR	YPD	DEL
Eastern Conference																		
NYG	267-256	601-636	40.6-38.8	19/28-13/27	390-320	3-**1**	**5005**-4546	459	3	115	50	**65**	9.9	2.1	**6.2**/ 3.8	180-182	27.8-25.0	2.8
Pit	261-250	**427**-581	40.0-40.7	**26/42**-9/19	487-376	2-**1**	4402-4625	-223	2	-51	-11	-40	5.7	**3.3**	3.2/ 4.8	183-185	24.1-25.0	-0.9
Cle	252-263	600-547	42.8-40.6	14/31-**7/14**	463-**282**	1-2	4306-3924	382	4	34	48	-14	7.8	-0.4	5.0/ 2.8	155-159	27.8-24.7	3.1
Was	241-280	663-**863**	34.5-42.4	11/25-12/26	469-326	2-2	4311-5238	-927	4	-71	-61	-10	5.2	0.8	4.9/ 6.1	186-185	23.2-28.3	-5.1
Dal	246-274	639-569	45.4-40.6	14/27-13/25	447-453	4-2	4912-5184	-272	0	-4	-23	19	6.9	-1.4	5.9/ 6.7	190-186	25.9-27.9	-2.0
SL	268-251	655-584	38.3-40.6	5/14-18/33	363-511	1-5	4798-4711	87	-20	-74	-73	-1	5.2	-0.6	4.1/ 6.0	183-177	26.2-26.6	-0.4
Phi	235-275	619-479	42.9-**38.2**	6/19-19/37	384-729	2-4	4540-5046	-506	-5	-74	-62	-12	5.2	-1.6	4.8/ 5.1	175-179	25.9-28.2	-2.2
Western Conference																		
GB	**281**-191	617-611	40.9-43.2	15/21-9/22	742-305	3-3	4791-3277	**1514**	**22**	**267**	**214**	53	**13.7**	-0.7	5.4/**1.1**	161-167	**29.8**-19.6	**10.1**
Det	243-**180**	624-527	45.3-44.1	14/34-14/25	**771**-678	**5**-2	4503-**3217**	1286	5	138	127	11	10.4	0.5	4.1/ 2.4	179-182	25.2-**17.7**	7.5
ChiB	228-228	776-643	43.7-41.8	13/27-16/31	749-636	4-3	4549-4147	402	3	34	46	-12	7.8	1.1	4.4/ 2.9	**197**-197	23.1-21.1	2.0
Bal	251-226	675-792	41.5-42.7	12/28-9/22	603-568	1-**1**	4666-4123	543	-2	5	37	-32	7.1	-0.1	4.8/ 4.2	184-183	25.4-22.5	2.8
SF	239-240	636-626	**45.6**-44.6	10/23-12/20	334-619	2-3	3941-4549	-608	-7	-49	-79	30	5.8	0.2	3.7/ 6.1	163-**156**	24.2-29.2	-5.0
Min	223-266	447-633	40.3-43.3	11/25-15/30	654-706	2-3	4080-5101	-1021	-11	-156	-129	-27	3.1	-0.6	2.6/ 5.4	193-190	21.1-26.8	-5.7
LA	201-256	704-592	45.5-45.5	10/20-14/33	513-860	3-3	3865-4981	-1116	2	-114	-85	-29	4.2	-2.7	3.5/ 5.6	183-184	21.1-27.1	-6.0
Aver	245	620	42.0	13/26	526	3	4476	—	—	—	—	—	—	—	4.9	179	24.9	—

Rushing Attempts	Rushing Yards	Rushing Average	Rushing TDs	Rushing Rank	Passing Yards	Passing Average
J.Taylor-GB 272	J.Taylor-GB 1474	A.Marsh-Dal 5.57	J.Taylor-GB 19	J.Taylor-GB 1664	S.Jurgensen-Phi 3261	S.Jurgensen-Phi 8.91
J.Smith-SF 258	J.Johnson-Pit 1141	J.Taylor-GB 5.42	J.Crow-SL 14	J.Johnson-Pit 1211	Y.Tittle-NYG 3224	E.LeBaron-Dal 8.65
J.Johnson-Pit 251	D.Bass-LA 1033	D.Bass-LA 5.27	J.Brown-Cle 13	J.Brown-Cle 1126	B.Wade-Chi 3172	Y.Tittle-NYG 8.60
J.Brown-Cle 230	J.Brown-Cle 996	B.Kilmer-SF 5.14		D.Bass-LA 1093	J.Unitas-Bal 2967	B.Starr-GB 8.55
D.Perkins-Dal 222	D.Perkins-Dal 945	J.Marconi-Chi 4.56		D.Perkins-Dal 1015	N.Snead-Was 2926	N.Snead-Was 8.27

Completion Percent	TD Passes	TD Percent	INT Percent	Passer Rating	Passing Rank	Receptions
B.Starr-GB 62.5	Y.Tittle-NYG 33	E.LeBaron-Dal 9.6	B.Starr-GB 3.2	E.LeBaron-Dal 95.4	Y.Tittle-NYG 977	B.Mitchell-Was 72
F.Ryan-Cle 57.7	J.Unitas-Bal 23	Y.Tittle-NYG 8.8	F.Ryan-Cle 3.6	B.Starr-GB 90.7	B.Starr-GB 919	S.Randle-SL 63
J.Brodie-SF 57.6	F.Tarkenton-Min 22	D.Meredith-Dal 7.1	D.Meredith-Dal 3.8	Y.Tittle-NYG 89.5	B.Wade-Chi 716	B.Conrad-SL 62
E.LeBaron-Dal 57.2	N.Snead-Was 22	F.Tarkenton-Min 6.7	J.Ninowski-Cle 4.6	F.Ryan-Cle 85.4	S.Jurgensen-Phi 701	R.Phillips-LA 60
J.Unitas-Bal 57.1	S.Jurgensen-Phi 22	N.Snead-Was 6.2	J.Brodie-SF 5.3	D.Meredith-Dal 84.2	N.Snead-Was 693	

Receiving Yards	Receiving Average	Receiving TDs	Receiving Rank	Combined Net Yards	Total TDs	Total Points
B.Mitchell-Was 1384	F.Clarke-Dal 22.19	F.Clarke-Dal 14	B.Mitchell-Was 747	T.Brown-Phi 2306	J.Taylor-GB 19	J.Taylor-GB 114
S.Randle-SL 1158	D.Shofner-NYG 21.38	D.Shofner-NYG 12	D.Shofner-NYG 627	A.Marsh-Dal 1998	J.Brown-Cle 18	L.Michaels-Pit 110
T.McDonald-Phi 1146	R.Renfro-Cle 20.58	J.Orr-Bal 11	T.McDonald-Phi 623	D.Bass-LA 1822	J.Crow-SL 17	J.Brown-Cle 108
D.Shofner-NYG 1133	F.Gifford-NYG 20.41	B.Mitchell-Was 11	S.Randle-SL 614	B.Mitchell-Was 1794	F.Clarke-Dal 14	D.Chandler-NYG 104
F.Clarke-Dal 1043	C.Dale-LA 20.14	T.McDonald-Phi 10	F.Clarke-Dal 592	T.Mason-Min 1696	T.Brown-Phi 13	J.Crow-SL 102

Punt Average	Field Goals	Field Goal Percent	Kickoff Returns	Kickoff Return Average	Punt Returns	Punt Return Average
T.Davis-SF 45.6	L.Michaels-Pit 26	D.Chandler-NYG 67.9	A.Woodson-SF 37	A.Woodson-SF 31.3	P.Studstill-Det 29	P.Studstill-Det 15.8
J.Unitas-LA 45.5	D.Chandler-NYG 19	L.Michaels-Pit 61.9	D.James-Was 32	J.Counts-NYG 30.2	W.Wood-GB 23	W.Wood-GB 11.9
S.Baker-Dal 45.4	L.Groza-Cle 14	Christopherson-Min 55.0	T.Brown-Phi 30	H.Adderley-GB 27.9	J.Morris-Chi 20	J.Morris-Chi 10.4
Y.Lary-Det 45.3	S.Baker-Dal 14	S.Baker-Dal 51.9	A.Marsh-Dal 29	D.James-Was 27.8	A.Woodson-SF 19	A.Woodson-SF 9.4
B.Green-Chi 43.7	R.LeClerc-Chi 13	J.Unitas-LA 50.0		T.Brown-Phi 27.7	D.James-Was 19	D.James-Was 7.6

Punt/Kick Return Yards	Punt/Kick Return TDs	Interceptions	Interception Return Yards	Interception Return TDs	Sacks	Overall Rank
A.Woodson-SF 1336	Many 1	W.Wood-GB 9	R.Petitbon-Chi 212	Many 1	Not kept	J.Taylor-GB 1717
D.James-Was 1034		Y.Lary-Det 8	B.Boyd-Bal 163			T.Brown-Phi 1492
P.Studstill-Det 968			M.Gaechter-Dal 136			D.Bass-LA 1457
T.Brown-Phi 912			D.Bishop-Dal 134			J.Brown-Cle 1424
J.Counts-NYG 817						A.Marsh-Dal 1395

A League Colored Green and Yellow

If there was one thing that Vince Lombardi's brand of football relished, it was the ability to repeat anything they did. Building on that reputation, the Packers did it again, running off a 10–0 start en route to a 13–1 season. Finishing first in points scored and fewest points allowed, the Packers were the beneficiaries of Jim Taylor's best season yet. The fullback led the NFL in rushing and scored a league-record 19 touchdowns, breaking Jim Brown's 1958 tally. Green Bay's lone loss came on Thanksgiving Day to a Detroit team that won 11 games.

Y.A. Tittle continued his late-career renaissance in his second year with the Giants. The 36-year-old quarterback threw a league-leading 33 touchdowns, a new NFL record, and the Giants took advantage of the relatively mediocre Eastern Conference and won their last nine games. The Cowboys gave up the most points in the conference, but they were breaking in two rookies on that side of the ball, defensive end George Andrie and cornerback Cornell Green, along with inexperienced linebacker Chuck Howley and second-year defensive tackle Bob Lilly. The Browns finished a distant third and lost their namesake when owner Art Modell fired Paul Brown.

After a three-year run as a contender in the Eastern Conference, Philadelphia finished last in Chuck Bednarik's final season. The continued struggles of the once mighty Rams proved equally disappointing. Things were slowly changing, though. The Rams took Roman Gabriel and Merlin Olsen with the second and third picks in the draft. Gabriel would re-invigorate the stagnant offense, while Olsen joined Deacon Jones, a 14th-round pick the previous year, to lay the foundation for one of the game's all-time great defensive lines.

The league's surprise was the Steelers, who won nine games for the first time in franchise history behind an aging backfield, including two future Hall of Famers: Bobby Layne under center for his final season, and 33-year-old running back John Henry Johnson, who cranked out 1,141 yards. Pittsburgh's prickly defensive tackle, Gene "Big Daddy" Lipscomb, had an outstanding season and was named top lineman in the Pro Bowl. He died a few months later from a heroin overdose.

1962 AFL

TEAM	W-L-T	PCT	POST	PTS	RA	RY	RY/A	RTD	FL	PA	PC	GPY	GPY/A	PTD	PI	PSY	PRAT
Eastern Division																	
Hou	11-3	.786	L	387-270	457-362	1742-1569	3.8-4.3	15-10	9-17	475-486	227-213	3323-2865	7.0-5.9	32-18	48-35	94-304	53.9-45.5
Bos	9-4-1	.692	—	346-295	432-393	1970-1426	4.6-3.6	11-14	20-10	382-450	195-216	2930-3435	7.7-7.6	25-19	13-25	164-327	84.2-64.8
Buf	7-6-1	.538	—	309-272	501-373	2480-1687	5.0-4.5	20-10	12-14	351-440	150-215	2181-2996	6.2-6.8	15-24	26-36	197-254	47.0-55.3
NYT	5-9	.357	—	278-423	317-452	1213-2006	3.8-4.4	9-19	20-16	505-417	242-194	3161-2929	6.3-7.0	20-28	35-29	419-323	52.4-63.5
Western Division																	
DalT	11-3	.786	L*	389-233	479-351	2407-1250	5.0-3.6	21-14	14-16	322-467	195-239	2824-2953	8.8-6.3	29-13	17-32	369-252	97.1-51.8
Den	7-7	.500	—	353-334	322-439	1298-1868	4.0-4.4	12-11	14-19	559-423	292-202	3739-2894	6.7-6.8	21-24	40-27	335-224	56.2-62.7
SD	4-10	.286	—	314-392	410-437	1647-1903	4.0-4.4	13-16	14-13	416-402	168-196	2686-2926	6.5-7.3	23-29	34-29	252-311	47.0-67.0
Oak	1-13	.071	—	213-370	367-478	1392-2440	3.8-5.1	14-21	20-18	446-371	175-169	2671-2517	6.0-6.8	11-21	29-29	376-211	40.9-54.6
Aver	14	—		324	411	1769	4.3	14	15	432	206	2939	6.8	22	30	276	57.9

TEAM	TD	PENY	PNT	FGM/A	RTNY	RTNTD	OFFY/DEFY	NETY	NETTO	NP	PNP	DELP	PW	DELW	PRT	DR	YPD	DEL
Eastern Division																		
Hou	266-217	633-559	41.0-38.9	11/26-14/31	535-973	3-5	4971-4130	841	-5	117	50	67	9.9	1.1	2.9/2.3	203-202	24.5-20.4	4.0
Bos	230-220	456-554	38.5-38.5	20/37-15/26	503-109	5-3	4736-4534	202	2	51	25	26	8.3	1.2	6.0/4.5	187-193	25.3-23.5	1.8
Buf	238-229	797-786	38.8-38.1	9/23-10/20	692-501	6-1	4464-4429	35	12	37	51	-14	7.9	-0.4	2.6/2.9	187-191	23.9-23.2	0.7
NYT	206-253	771-711	41.0-37.9	13/27-21/31	653-839	5-5	3955-4612	-657	-10	-145	-95	-50	3.4	1.6	2.4/3.5	212-206	18.7-22.4	-3.7
Western Division																		
DalT	259-239	644-660	35.8-41.2	14/27-11/28	631-329	0-2	4862-3951	911	17	156	144	12	10.9	0.1	5.5/2.8	180-175	27.0-22.6	4.4
Den	270-234	613-678	42.9-41.5	27/39-16/27	611-645	6-6	4702-4538	164	-8	19	-18	37	7.5	-0.5	3.1/3.8	192-204	24.5-22.2	2.2
SD	217-248	768-709	41.6-40.7	17/20-17/31	618-737	2-3	4081-4518	-437	-6	-78	-60	-18	5.1	-1.0	2.6/3.6	199-198	20.5-22.8	-2.3
Oak	187-233	695-720	37.4-40.9	9/27-16/32	647-757	2-4	3687-4746	-1059	-2	-157	-96	-61	3.1	-2.1	2.2/3.1	206-197	17.9-24.1	-6.2
Aver	234	672	39.6	15/28	611	4	4432	—	—	—	—	—	—	—	3.5	196	22.6	—

Rushing Attempts
C.Tolar-Hou.....244
A.Haynes-DalT.....221
C.Gilchrist-Buf.....214
C.Daniels-Oak.....161
B.Cannon-Hou.....147

Rushing Yards
C.Gilchrist-Buf.....1096
A.Haynes-DalT.....1049
C.Tolar-Hou.....1012
C.Daniels-Oak.....766
C.McClinton-DalT.....604

Rushing Average
W.Carlton-Buf.....5.64
C.McClinton-Buf.....5.44
W.Crow-Buf.....5.35
C.Gilchrist-Buf.....5.12
K.Lincoln-SD.....4.91

Rushing TDs
A.Haynes-DalT.....13
C.Gilchrist-Buf.....13
C.Tolar-Hou.....7
C.Daniels-Oak.....7
B.Cannon-Hou.....7

Rushing Rank
C.Gilchrist-Buf.....1226
A.Haynes-DalT.....1179
C.Tolar-Hou.....1082
C.Daniels-Oak.....836
C.McClinton-DalT.....624

Passing Yards
F.Tripucka-Den.....2917
G.Blanda-Hou.....2810
L.Dawson-DalT.....2759
B.Parilli-Bos.....1988
C.Davidson-Oak.....1977

Passing Average
L.Dawson-DalT.....8.90
B.Parilli-Bos.....7.86
W.Rabb-Buf.....6.76
J.Green-NYT.....6.75
G.Blanda-Hou.....6.72

Completion Percent
L.Dawson-DalT.....61.0
B.Parilli-Bos.....55.3
F.Tripucka-Den.....54.5
J.Green-NYT.....49.6
G.Blanda-Hou.....47.1

TD Passes
L.Dawson-DalT.....29
G.Blanda-Hou.....27
B.Parilli-Bos.....18
F.Tripucka-Den.....17
J.Hadl-SD.....15

TD Percent
L.Dawson-DalT.....9.4
B.Parilli-Bos.....7.1
G.Blanda-Hou.....6.5
J.Hadl-SD.....5.8
W.Rabb-Buf.....5.6

INT Percent
B.Parilli-Bos.....3.2
L.Dawson-DalT.....5.5
F.Tripucka-Den.....5.7
J.Green-NYT.....7.0
C.Davidson-Oak.....7.2

Passer Rating
L.Dawson-DalT.....98.3
B.Parilli-Bos.....91.5
F.Tripucka-Den.....64.4
J.Green-NYT.....55.4
G.Blanda-Hou.....51.3

Passing Rank
L.Dawson-DalT.....845
B.Parilli-Bos.....764
F.Tripucka-Den.....544
T.Yewcic-Bos.....287
J.Green-NYT.....201

Receptions
L.Taylor-Den.....77
A.Powell-NYT.....64
D.Christy-NYT.....62
B.Dickinson-Den.....60
D.Maynard-NYT.....56

Receiving Yards
A.Powell-NYT.....1130
D.Maynard-NYT.....1041
L.Taylor-Den.....908
J.Colclough-Bos.....868
C.Hennigan-Hou.....867

Receiving Average
J.Colclough-Bos.....21.70
B.Roberson-Oak.....20.10
B.Scarpitto-Den.....19.06
D.Maynard-NYT.....18.59
T.Romeo-Bos.....17.88

Receiving TDs
C.Burford-DalT.....12
J.Colclough-Bos.....10
A.Powell-NYT.....8
D.Maynard-NYT.....8
C.Hennigan-Hou.....8

Receiving Rank
A.Powell-NYT.....605
D.Maynard-NYT.....561
J.Colclough-Bos.....484
L.Taylor-Den.....474
C.Hennigan-Hou.....474

Combined Net Yards
D.Christy-NYT.....2147
A.Haynes-DalT.....1768
C.Daniels-Oak.....1614
B.Roberson-Oak.....1601
C.Gilchrist-Buf.....1565

Total TDs
A.Haynes-DalT.....19
C.Gilchrist-Buf.....15
B.Cannon-Hou.....13
C.Burford-DalT.....12
J.Colclough-Bos.....10

Total Points
G.Mingo-Den.....137
C.Gilchrist-Buf.....128
B.Cannon-Bos.....128
A.Haynes-DalT.....114
T.Brooker-DalT.....87

Punt Average
J.Fraser-Den.....43.6
P.Maguire-SD.....41.6
J.Norton-Hou.....41.0
C.Johnson-NYT.....40.0
W.Crow-Buf.....38.8

Field Goals
G.Mingo-Den.....27
B.Cannon-Bos.....20
G.Blair-SD.....17
B.Shockley-NYT.....13
T.Brooker-DalT.....12

Field Goal Percent
G.Blair-SD.....85.0
G.Mingo-Den.....69.2
T.Brooker-DalT.....54.5
B.Cannon-Bos.....54.1
B.Shockley-NYT.....50.0

Kickoff Returns
D.Christy-NYT.....38
J.Robinson-SD.....32
B.Roberson-Oak.....27

Kickoff Return Average
B.Jancik-Hou.....30.3
D.Grayson-DalT.....29.7
L.Garron-Bos.....28.6
K.Lincoln-SD.....28.4
B.Roberson-Oak.....27.7

Punt Returns
R.Burton-Bos.....21
B.Garner-Oak.....20
W.West-Buf.....15
L.Garron-Bos.....15
D.Christy-NYT.....15

Punt Return Average
D.Christy-NYT.....16.7
B.Jancik-Hou.....8.3
W.West-Buf.....8.3
B.Garner-Oak.....8.1
A.Haynes-DalT.....7.9

Punt/Kick Return Yards
D.Christy-NYT.....1074
B.Jancik-Hou.....842
J.Robinson-SD.....748
B.Roberson-Oak.....748
L.Garron-Bos.....686

Punt/Kick Return TDs
D.Christy-NYT.....2

Interceptions
L.Riley-DalT.....11
T.Morrow-Oak.....10

Interception Return Yards
B.Whitehead-Oak.....151
W.Fontes-NYT.....145
B.Ply-DalT.....144
T.Morrow-Oak.....141
B.Zeman-Den.....133

Interception Return TDs
Many.....1

Sacks
Not kept

Overall Rank
A.Haynes-DalT.....1552
C.Gilchrist-Buf.....1441
D.Christy-NYT.....1298
C.Daniels-Oak.....1170
C.Tolar-Hou.....1161

OPPORTUNITIES MADE AND LOST

Lamar Hunt may have been the biggest mover and shaker behind the launch of the AFL, but he hadn't really gotten to enjoy much on-field success. His Texans played second fiddle to Sid Gillman's Chargers in the Western Division, and seemed to be falling behind the NFL's Cowboys in the hearts of Dallas fans. That changed in 1962. San Diego was completely derailed by the loss of quarterback Jack Kemp. First, he went down with a finger injury in the second game, and then he was gone for good on an unexpected waiver claim by the Bills. Left with rookie John Hadl running Gillman's complicated offense, the Chargers endured a lost season, the only highlight being the largely unnoticed arrival of rookie wide receiver Lance Alworth.

The Texans, by contrast, solved their problems at quarterback when Cleveland's Paul Brown reluctantly acquiesced to backup Len Dawson's request for his release. When no NFL team claimed him, Dawson slipped away to the AFL. In his first opportunity to really play as a pro, Dawson became the league's best field general. His accuracy and touch meshed nicely with coach Hank Stram's ball-control offense that centered around feature back Abner Hayes. Dallas fans didn't have long to relish their first championship team.

The Eastern Division was even wilder because of a Bills team that was suddenly much more dangerous with the acquisition of CFL star Cookie Gilchrist. Having belatedly taken up pro football in Canada after first playing rugby, the colorful Gilchrist was an unlikely AFL rushing leader, but he provided Buffalo with a power running game and a perfect compliment to newfound Kemp.

The Oilers were vulnerable, particularly as George Blanda tossed a mind-boggling 42 interceptions, more than competitors Boston and Buffalo combined. Going into the season's final week, the Patriots were only a half-game behind Houston, and matched up against the winless Raiders. The Oilers, however, played the hapless Titans one day before Boston's game in Oakland. The Patriots watched Houston trounce New York to clinch the title. Their hopes crushed, Boston suffered the additional indignity of being shut out by Oakland to break a 19-game losing streak.

1963 NFL

TEAM	W-L-T	PCT	POST	PTS	RA	RY	RY/A	RTD	FL	PA	PC	GPY	GPY/A	PTD	PI	PSY	PRAT
Eastern Conference																	
NYG	**11**-3	.786	L	**448**-280	453-411	1777-1669	3.9-4.1	12-14	13-16	426-368	243-176	3558-2588	**8.4**-7.0	**39**-22	21-34	311-**499**	**94.4**-52.7
Cle	10-4	.714	—	343-262	460-423	**2639**-1651	**5.7**-3.9	15-10	17-10	322-408	164-208	2449-2718	7.6-6.7	27-16	20-22	232-243	78.3-62.9
SL	9-5	.643	—	341-283	423-461	1839-1802	4.3-3.9	10-19	18-19	**438**-370	228-180	3403-2519	7.8-6.8	30-13	21-18	372-367	80.7-62.4
Pit	7-4-3	.636	—	321-295	**578**-419	2136-1728	3.7-4.1	14-14	13-19	368-384	170-191	3028-3400	8.2-8.9	21-21	20-25	251-299	71.2-71.5
Dal	4-10	.286	—	305-378	420-455	1795-2094	4.3-4.6	18-12	15-11	375-403	200-202	2799-3392	7.5-8.4	20-31	21-26	331-161	72.1-77.7
Was	3-11	.214	—	279-398	344-469	1289-1863	3.7-4.0	15-12	19-10	430-417	204-230	3525-3484	8.2-8.4	17-33	34-21	391-270	56.0-88.3
Phi	2-10-2	.167	—	242-381	376-466	1438-1985	3.8-4.3	8-17	16-15	380-375	193-211	2666-3106	7.0-8.3	22-28	31-15	252-270	58.9-91.7
Western Conference																	
ChiB	**11**-1-2	**.917**	L*	301-**144**	487-412	1679-**1442**	3.4-**3.5**	15-**7**	11-18	404-353	221-**164**	2670-**2045**	6.6-**5.8**	18-10	14-**36**	**177**-311	75.6-**34.8**
GB	**11**-2-1	.846	—	369-206	504-428	2248-1586	4.5-3.7	**22**-11	20-21	345-378	179-180	2711-2340	7.9-6.2	22-**9**	21-22	178-327	74.0-51.2
Bal	8-6	.571	—	316-285	396-434	1642-1794	4.1-4.1	11-16	25-17	433-**348**	**248**-181	**3605**-2589	8.3-7.4	20-19	**12**-15	309-347	88.4-76.7
Det	5-8-1	.385	—	326-265	415-**405**	1601-1564	3.9-3.9	11-12	14-11	406-378	202-183	2997-2597	7.4-6.9	26-17	26-24	274-400	69.0-59.6
Min	5-8-1	.385	—	309-390	445-410	1842-1733	4.1-4.2	17-12	18-**31**	355-404	197-233	2687-3362	7.6-8.3	16-31	17-11	518-364	74.9-99.1
LA	5-9	.357	—	210-350	405-431	1393-1785	3.4-4.1	14-14	17-13	384-379	186-208	2558-3025	6.7-8.0	11-25	22-19	481-272	55.9-82.2
SF	2-12	.143	—	198-391	406-488	1454-2076	3.6-4.3	8-20	**8**-13	349-450	156-244	2090-3581	6.0-8.0	13-27	22-14	263-210	50.4-87.5
Aver	14	—	—	308	437	1769	4.1	14	16	387	199	2910	7.5	22	22	310	71.7

TEAM	1D	PENY	PNT	FGM/A	RTNY	RTNTD	OFFY/DEFY	NETY	NETTO	NP	PNP	DELP	PW	DELW	PRT	DR	YPD	DEL
Eastern Conference																		
NYG	**278**-213	755-617	44.9-40.4	18/29-**3/14**	910-662	**6**-3	**5024**-3758	**1266**	16	**168**	170	-2	**11.2**	-0.2	5.8/ 1.8	188-193	26.7-19.5	7.3
Cle	252-242	609-592	40.0-43.7	15/23-17/35	628-533	1-4	4856-4126	730	-5	81	41	40	9.0	1.0	4.6/ 3.8	168-**172**	**28.9**-24.0	4.9
SL	254-235	692-577	40.7-40.1	11/21-15/26	549-578	4-2	4870-3954	916	-2	58	68	-10	8.4	0.5	5.0/ 3.6	185-183	26.3-21.6	4.7
Pit	272-244	495-780	39.4-44.5	21/**41**-15/22	611-603	2-**1**	4913-4829	84	11	26	51	-25	7.7	0.9	5.2/ 5.2	183-184	26.8-26.2	0.6
Dal	248-266	627-479	44.2-43.2	9/20-15/33	726-613	2-5	4263-5325	-1062	1	-73	-85	12	5.2	-1.2	4.1/ 5.6	182-181	23.4-29.4	-6.0
Was	244-285	736-**917**	41.7-44.5	12/26-17/33	748-839	3-5	4423-5077	-654	-22	-119	-143	24	4.0	-1.0	3.8/ 5.8	185-181	23.9-28.0	-4.1
Phi	203-266	558-598	43.1-**39.1**	7/15-19/31	436-967	2-2	3852-4821	-969	-17	-139	-149	10	3.5	-0.5	3.0/ 6.0	179-177	21.5-27.2	-5.7
Western Conference																		
ChiB	257-196	804-718	**46.5**-43.2	14/33-6/17	814-493	4-**1**	4172-**3176**	996	**29**	157	**199**	-42	10.9	1.1	4.8/**0.6**	177-173	23.6-**18.4**	5.2
GB	258-**193**	517-568	44.7-43.4	16/34-15/33	541-517	2-3	4781-3599	1182	2	163	107	**56**	11.1	0.4	5.0/ 2.7	173-186	27.6-19.3	**8.3**
Bal	257-228	823-685	41.0-43.5	**24**/39-12/27	659-**280**	4-**1**	4938-4036	902	-5	31	55	-24	7.8	0.2	**6.2**/ 4.5	182-181	27.1-22.3	4.8
Det	230-194	531-624	44.6-45.5	10/26-13/24	**1105**-712	5-3	4324-3761	563	-5	61	27	34	8.5	-3.0	4.1/ 3.0	**189**-190	22.9-19.8	3.1
Min	223-258	627-621	38.7-43.9	12/24-13/22	605-323	**6**-7	4011-4731	-720	7	-81	-32	-49	5.0	0.5	3.9/ 6.3	188-183	21.3-25.9	-4.5
LA	209-244	788-558	44.7-42.5	9/17-17/35	388-1050	1-4	3470-4538	-1068	-7	-140	-117	-23	3.5	**1.5**	2.7/ 5.3	186-182	18.7-24.9	-6.3
SF	183-304	**439**-667	45.4-43.1	10/31-11/27	320-870	3-4	3281-5447	-2166	-3	-193	-193	0	2.2	-0.2	2.5/ 6.3	174-173	18.9-31.5	-12.6
Aver	241	643	42.9	13/27	646	3	4370	—	—	—	—	—	—	—	4.8	181	24.1	—

Rushing Attempts	Rushing Yards	Rushing Average	Rushing TDs	Rushing Rank	Passing Yards	Passing Average
J.Brown-Cle 291	J.Brown-Cle 1863	J.Brown-Cle 6.40	J.Brown-Cle 12	J.Brown-Cle 1983	J.Unitas-Bal 3481	Y.Tittle-NYG 8.57
J.Taylor-GB 248	J.Taylor-GB 1018	E.Green-Cle 6.05	J.Taylor-GB 9	J.Taylor-GB 1108	C.Johnson-SL 3280	J.Unitas-Bal 8.49
D.Hoak-Pit 216	T.Brown-Phi 841	T.Moore-GB 4.98	D.Perkins-Dal 7	T.Brown-Phi 901	Y.Tittle-NYG 3145	N.Snead-Was 8.38
T.Brown-Phi 192	J.Johnson-Pit 773	A.Marsh-Dal 4.88	T.Mason-Min 7	T.Mason-Min 833	N.Snead-Was 3043	E.Brown-Pit 8.24
J.Johnson-Pit 186	T.Mason-Min 763	B.Triplett-SL 4.87		J.Johnson-Pit 813	E.Brown-Pit 2982	E.Morrall-Det 7.99
Completion Percent	**TD Passes**	**TD Percent**	**INT Percent**	**Passer Rating**	**Passing Rank**	**Receptions**
Y.Tittle-NYG 60.2	Y.Tittle-NYG 36	Y.Tittle-NYG 9.8	J.Unitas-Bal 2.9	Y.Tittle-NYG 104.8	J.Unitas-Bal 1361	B.Conrad-SL 73
J.Unitas-Bal 57.8	C.Johnson-SL 28	F.Ryan-Cle 9.8	B.Wade-Chi 3.4	F.Ryan-Cle 90.4	Y.Tittle-NYG 1193	B.Mitchell-Was 69
F.Tarkenton-Min 57.2	F.Ryan-Cle 25	E.Morrall-Det 7.3	Y.Tittle-NYG 3.8	J.Unitas-Bal 89.7	C.Johnson-SL 940	T.Barr-Det 66
B.Starr-GB 54.1	E.Morrall-Det 24	C.Johnson-SL 6.6	R.Gabriel-LA 3.9	E.Morrall-Det 86.2	E.Morrall-Det 871	D.Shofner-NYG 64
B.Wade-Chi 53.9	E.Brown-Pit 21	B.Starr-GB 6.1	B.Starr-GB 4.1	B.Starr-GB 82.3	E.Brown-Pit 796	B.Dial-Pit 60
Receiving Yards	**Receiving Average**	**Receiving TDs**	**Receiving Rank**	**Combined Net Yards**	**Total TDs**	**Total Points**
B.Mitchell-Was 1436	B.Dial-Pit 21.58	G.Collins-Cle 13	B.Mitchell-Was 753	T.Brown-Phi 2428	J.Brown-Cle 15	D.Chandler-NYG 106
B.Dial-Pit 1295	B.Mitchell-Was 20.81	T.Barr-Det 13	B.Dial-Pit 693	J.Brown-Cle 2131	G.Collins-Cle 13	J.Martin-Bal 104
D.Shofner-NYG 1181	J.Mackey-Bal 20.74	S.Randle-SL 12	D.Shofner-NYG 636	B.Mitchell-Was 1852	T.Barr-Det 13	L.Michaels-Pit 95
T.Barr-Det 1086	S.Randle-SL 19.88		T.Barr-Det 608	D.James-Was 1751	S.Randle-SL 12	J.Kramer-GB 91
S.Randle-SL 1014	G.Cogdill-Det 19.69		S.Randle-SL 567	T.Watkins-Det 1437	T.Brown-Phi 11	J.Brown-Cle 90
Punt Average	**Field Goals**	**Field Goal Percent**	**Kickoff Returns**	**Kickoff Return Average**	**Punt Returns**	**Punt Return Average**
Y.Lary-Det 48.9	J.Martin-Bal 24	L.Groza-Cle 65.2	B.Butler-Min 33	A.Woodson-SF 32.2	T.Watkins-Det 32	D.James-Was 13.4
B.Green-Chi 46.5	L.Michaels-Pit 21	D.Chandler-NYG 62.1	T.Brown-Phi 33	G.Ballman-Pit 31.7	J.Logan-Bal 28	T.Watkins-Det 12.5
L.Vargo-LA 45.4	D.Chandler-NYG 18	J.Martin-Bal 61.5	D.James-Was 30	H.Adderley-GB 29.9	B.Butler-Min 21	E.Dove-NYG 11.6
T.Davis-SF 45.4	J.Kramer-GB 16	R.LeClerc-Chi 56.5	A.Woodson-SF 29	C.Shannon-LA 29.4	W.Wood-GB 19	B.Butler-Min 10.5
D.Chandler-NYG 44.9	L.Groza-Cle 15	L.Vargo-LA 52.9	C.Shannon-LA 28	T.Brown-Phi 28.6		J.Morris-Chi 10.3
Punt/Kick Return Yards	**Punt/Kick Return TDs**	**Interceptions**	**Interception Return Yards**	**Interception Return TDs**	**Sacks**	**Overall Rank**
T.Brown-Phi 1097	A.Woodson-SF 3	R.Taylor-Chi 9	D.Lynch-NYG 251	D.Lynch-NYG 3	Not kept	J.Brown-Cle 2132
D.James-Was 1044		D.Lynch-NYG 9	C.Green-Dal 211			T.Brown-Phi 1667
A.Woodson-SF 1030		C.Thomas-Pit 8	R.Taylor-Chi 172			J.Unitas-Bal 1585
C.Shannon-LA 955		R.Petitbon-Chi 8	P.Fischer-SL 169			Y.Tittle-NYG 1312
B.Butler-Min 933		P.Fischer-SL 8	R.Petitbon-Chi 161			J.Taylor-GB 1147

Suspensions, Inductions, and No Sunday Mourning

The Packers and the Lions both came into the season knowing that they'd have to cope with the full-season suspensions of a star player apiece—Green Bay's Paul Hornung, and Detroit's tremendous defensive tackle, Alex Karras. Both had been implicated in a gambling scandal, and while neither was found to have bet against his own team, commissioner Pete Rozelle held a firm line, while also fining a number of other Lions players.

The Lions tumbled, but Lombardi's Packers rose to the occasion again. Green Bay beat, or at least tied, every team they met, with one exception: the Bears. George Halas's club beat Green Bay twice, propelling Chicago to a surprising conference championship, even though the Bears lost to the league's worst team (San Francisco), and had back-to-back ties against Pittsburgh and Minnesota near the end of the season. The first of those ties came just two days after the assassination of President John F. Kennedy. The AFL postponed its game the weekend of the tragedy. Rozelle would always regret not having done the same thing.

Spectacular individual performances drove both the Browns and the Giants in the Eastern Conference. Jim Brown had never done anything other than excel in his previous six seasons, but he enjoyed his best year yet in his seventh. He set a new rushing record with 1,863 yards, outpacing runner-up Jim Taylor by more than 800 yards. But the ageless Y.A. Tittle also had his best season yet, setting another record for passing touchdowns, and guiding the Giants to an overwhelming 448 points (or 32 per game). Knotted up in a three-way tie with the Browns and the surprising Cardinals, Tittle's Giants swept a trio of weaker opponents to finish with the conference title.

For the first time, NFL players had a place to aim for when the last play was made: Canton, Ohio. The town where the league was formed in 1920 was selected to house the Pro Football Hall of Fame. Halas led a first induction class of 17 and would eventually be followed by Lombardi, Allen, Brown, Tittle, Taylor, Rozelle, and even the castigated Hornung, along with some 200 more.

1963 AFL

TEAM	W-L-T	PCT	POST	PTS	RA	RY	RY/A	RTD	FL	PA	PC	GPY	GPY/A	PTD	PI	PSY	PRAT
Eastern Division																	
Bos	7-6-1	.538	DL	327-257	433-312	1618-**1108**	3.7-**3.6**	16-12	**12**-13	410-477	184-230	2816-3253	6.9-6.8	17-21	29-29	259-**626**	52.4-60.0
Buf	7-6-1	.538	D	304-291	**453**-301	1851-1235	4.1-4.1	**21**-13	16-12	457-472	227-218	3382-3237	7.4-6.9	16-24	24-21	329-397	64.1-67.6
Hou	6-8	.429	—	302-372	341-446	1209-1981	3.5-4.4	11-12	24-14	**501**-424	**261-190**	**3478-2896**	6.9-6.8	26-24	33-**36**	268-296	64.3-**51.4**
NYJ	5-8-1	.385	—	249-399	306-459	978-2129	3.2-4.6	8-25	15-15	480-417	209-223	2830-3218	5.9-7.7	21-25	29-21	298-180	52.3-77.8
Western Division																	
SD	**11-3**	.786	L*	399-255	395-378	2201-1468	5.6-3.9	20-10	**12**-16	357-472	202-231	3138-2976	8.8-6.3	28-17	24-29	194-297	84.0-55.5
Oak	10-4	.714	—	363-282	357-369	1613-1488	4.5-4.0	11-10	15-17	442-440	191-208	3387-3011	7.7-6.8	**31**-23	23-35	487-454	71.7-54.3
KC	5-7-2	.417	—	347-263	400-386	1697-1546	4.2-4.0	12-12	16-19	439-429	231-218	2983-2929	6.8-6.8	30-18	**22**-26	332-302	76.1-61.6
Den	2-11-1	.154	—	301-473	381-414	1496-1709	3.9-4.1	10-15	16-**20**	453-408	217-204	3072-3566	6.8-8.7	23-40	28-15	585-200	61.4-97.5
Aver	14	—	—	324	383	1583	4.1	14	16	442	215	3136	7.1	24	27	344	65.3

TEAM	1D	PENY	PNT	FGM/A	RTNY	RTNTD	OFFY/DEFY	NETY	NETTO	NP	PNP	DELP	PW	DELW	PRT	DR	YPD	DEL
Eastern Division																		
Bos	227-**222**	614-583	38.9-**39.9**	22/38-4/21	1018-663	4-2	4175-**3735**	440	1	70	41	29	8.8	-1.3	3.2/2.8	**202**-203	20.7-**18.4**	2.3
Buf	**272**-224	**532**-508	40.5-40.1	10/23-10/26	463-**316**	2-0	4904-4075	829	-7	13	41	-28	7.3	0.2	4.3/4.2	190-**177**	25.8-23.0	2.8
Hou	254-256	565-704	43.0-42.6	9/22-14/23	769-1075	2-11	4419-4581	-162	-7	-70	-42	-28	5.3	0.8	3.8/2.6	**202**-198	21.9-23.1	-1.3
NYJ	200-280	650-**953**	42.1-42.2	9/24-11/23	486-712	3-2	3510-5167	-1657	-8	-150	-170	20	3.3	**2.3**	2.8/5.3	180-185	19.5-27.9	-8.4
Western Division																		
SD	250-239	773-784	38.6-43.7	17/27-20/37	577-561	2-1	**5145**-4147	**998**	9	**144**	**119**	25	**10.6**	0.4	**5.7**/3.1	174-185	**29.6**-22.4	**7.2**
Oak	244-224	857-743	40.1-40.5	8/19-15/24	785-456	**6**-1	4513-4045	468	**14**	81	95	-14	9.0	1.0	4.3/**2.4**	201-194	22.5-20.9	1.6
KC	250-238	611-411	40.1-40.1	8/28-10/24	645-649	4-3	4348-4753	175	7	84	43	**41**	9.1	-3.1	4.1/3.5	184-188	23.6-22.2	1.4
Den	230-254	648-564	**44.4**-43.7	16/29-15/32	525-836	3-6	3983-5075	-1092	-9	-172	-127	-45	2.7	-0.2	2.8/7.2	**202**-205	19.7-24.8	-5.0
Aver	241	656	41.4	12/26	659	3	4375	—	—	—	—	—	—	—	4.2	192	22.8	—

Rushing Attempts		Rushing Yards		Rushing Average		Rushing TDs		Rushing Rank		Passing Yards		Passing Average	
C.Gilchrist-Buf	232	C.Daniels-Oak	1099	K.Lincoln-SD	6.45	C.Gilchrist-Buf	12	C.Daniels-Oak	1129	G.Blanda-Hou	3003	T.Rote-SD	8.78
C.Daniels-Oak	215	P.Lowe-SD	1010	P.Lowe-SD	5.71	P.Lowe-SD	8	C.Gilchrist-Buf	1099	J.Kemp-Buf	2910	T.Flores-Oak	8.51
C.Tolar-Hou	194	C.Gilchrist-Buf	979	C.Gilchrist-Buf	5.11	J.Kemp-Buf	8	P.Lowe-SD	1090	T.Rote-SD	2510	J.Kemp-Buf	7.58
P.Lowe-SD	177	K.Lincoln-SD	826	L.Garron-Bos	4.29			K.Lincoln-SD	876	L.Dawson-KC	2389	M.Slaughter-Den	7.57
L.Garron-Bos	175	L.Garron-Bos	750	C.Gilchrist-Buf	4.22			L.Garron-Bos	770	B.Parilli-Bos	2345	G.Blanda-Hou	7.10

Completion Percent		TD Passes		TD Percent		INT Percent		Passer Rating		Passing Rank		Receptions	
T.Rote-SD	59.4	L.Dawson-KC	26	T.Flores-Oak	8.1	C.Davidson-Oak	5.2	T.Rote-SD	86.7	J.Kemp-Buf	720	L.Taylor-Den	78
L.Dawson-KC	54.0	G.Blanda-Hou	24	L.Dawson-KC	7.4	J.Kemp-Buf	5.2	T.Flores-Oak	80.7	T.Rote-SD	675	A.Powell-Oak	73
G.Blanda-Hou	53.0	T.Rote-SD	20	T.Rote-SD	7.0	T.Flores-Oak	5.3	L.Dawson-KC	77.5	T.Flores-Oak	631	B.Turner-NYJ	71
J.Kemp-Buf	50.3	T.Flores-Oak	20	G.Blanda-Hou	5.7	D.Wood-NYJ	5.4	G.Blanda-Hou	70.1	G.Blanda-Hou	622	B.Miller-Buf	69
M.Slaughter-Den	50.2	D.Wood-NYJ	18	C.Davidson-Oak	5.7	L.Dawson-KC	5.4	M.Slaughter-Den	65.4	L.Dawson-KC	565	C.Burford-KC	68

Receiving Yards		Receiving Average		Receiving TDs		Receiving Rank		Combined Net Yards		Total TDs		Total Points	
A.Powell-Oak	1304	C.Daniels-Oak	22.83	A.Powell-Oak	16	A.Powell-Oak	732	L.Garron-Bos	1884	A.Powell-Oak	16	B.Cannon-Bos	113
L.Alworth-SD	1205	D.Maynard-NYJ	20.53	L.Alworth-SD	11	L.Alworth-SD	658	C.Daniels-Oak	1784	C.Gilchrist-Buf	14	A.Powell-Oak	96
L.Taylor-Den	1101	L.Alworth-SD	19.75	L.Taylor-Den	10	L.Taylor-Den	601	K.Lincoln-SD	1688	L.Alworth-SD	11	G.Blair-SD	95
C.Hennigan-Hou	1051	E.Dubenion-Buf	18.09	C.Hennigan-Hou	10	C.Hennigan-Hou	576	L.Alworth-SD	1555			C.Gilchrist-Buf	84
B.Turner-NYJ	1009	A.Powell-Oak	17.86			B.Turner-NYJ	535	B.Jancik-Hou	1493			G.Mingo-Den	83

Punt Average		Field Goals		Field Goal Percent		Kickoff Returns		Kickoff Return Average		Punt Returns		Punt Return Average	
J.Fraser-Den	44.4	G.Cannon-Bos	22	G.Blair-SD	60.7	B.Jancik-Hou	45	B.Jancik-Hou	29.3	C.Gibson-Oak	26	C.Gibson-Oak	11.8
J.Wilson-KC	43.1	G.Blair-SD	17	B.Cannon-Bos	57.9	B.Roberson-Oak	38	D.Grayson-KC	28.2	B.Suci-Bos	25	B.Suci-Bos	9.3
J.Norton-Hou	43.0	G.Mingo-Den	16	G.Mingo-Den	55.2	C.Mitchell-Den	37	K.Lincoln-SD	25.8	F.Glick-Hou	19	F.Glick-Hou	9.0
C.Johnson-NYJ	42.1	M.Yoho-Buf	10	T.Brooker-KC	42.9	L.Garron-Bos	28	C.Mitchell-Den	25.8	R.Abruzzese-Buf	17	R.Abruzzese-Buf	8.9
				M.Mercer-Oak	42.1	D.Christy-NYJ	24	L.Garron-Bos	24.8	T.Stephens-Bos	14	T.Stephens-Bos	8.4

Punt/Kick Return Yards		Punt/Kick Return TDs		Interceptions		Interception Return Yards		Interception Return TDs		Sacks		Overall Rank	
B.Jancik-Hou	1462	C.Gibson-Oak	2	F.Glick-Hou	12	B.Suci-Bos	277	B.Suci-Bos	2	Not kept		C.Daniels-Oak	1502
C.Mitchell-Den	1095	C.Mitchell-Den	1	T.Morrow-Oak	9	B.Hunt-KC	228					K.Lincoln-SD	1301
B.Roberson-Oak	843	D.Grayson-KC	1	D.Harris-SD	8	F.Glick-Hou	180					L.Garron-Bos	1280
L.Garron-Bos	716	B.Baird-NYJ	1	B.Suci-Bos	7	D.Paulson-NYJ	114					P.Lowe-SD	1268
D.Christy-NYJ	631			T.Banfield-Hou	7	T.Morrow-Oak	104					C.Gilchrist-Buf	1232

OAKLAND MAKEOVER, KANSAS CITY TAKEOVER

The Texans might have been defending champs, but Lamar Hunt gave up on competing against the Cowboys in Dallas. Pocketing money from the Cowboys for his practice facilities as well as for leaving town, Hunt moved the Texans to Kansas City. The Chiefs' first season in Missouri was immediately overshadowed by the fatal injury of rookie Stone Johnson in the final preseason game. The division was further shaken up by the defection of a young Chargers assistant, Al Davis, to take over as general manager and head coach in Oakland, which had three wins in two years. Changing the roster and the uniform, Davis invented the silver-and-black while importing the vertical offense. Suddenly, Raiders football was worth watching, with halfback Clem Daniels producing a league-leading 1,784 yards from scrimmage.

Regardless of the changes in Oakland, the Western Division still belonged to San Diego. Sid Gillman imported former Lions quarterback Tobin Rote from the CFL to run his high-powered offense. The Chargers pummeled opponents with the one–two backfield punch of Paul Lowe and Keith Lincoln, and then speared them with bombs to Lance Alworth, who blossomed into one of the game's great deep threats in his second season.

The Eastern Conference was more of a slugfest, as the Patriots and Oilers both faltered, the Oilers falling entirely out of the picture with a season-ending four-game losing streak. This created the opportunity for the Bills to slip into the running, as a scheduling oddity gave them a home-and-away matchup against New York, re-christened the Jets by new owner Sonny Werblin. By beating New York twice, the Bills forced the league's first playoff. The Pats crushed the upstarts, pushing on to their first championship game.

The wide-open passing attracted national attention, but the AFL didn't ignore defense. Raiders cornerback Fred "the Hammer" Williamson and linebackers Larry Grantham (Jets) and E.J. Holub (Chiefs) were already settled in, while Broncos cornerback Willie Brown and linebacker Bobby Bell and defensive tackle Buck Buchanan of the Chiefs made their debuts. The league even welcomed an NFL championship coach aboard. Fired Colts coach Weeb Ewbank took over the Jets and brought them from laughingstock to just bad.

1964 NFL

TEAM	W-L-T	PCT	POST	PTS	RA	RY	RY/A	RTD	FL	PA	PC	GPY	GPY/A	PTD	PI	PSY	PRAT
Eastern Conference																	
Cle	10-3-1	.769	L*	415-293	435-465	2163-2012	**5.0**-4.3	14-18	**7**-21	344-401	181-230	2542-2932	7.4-7.3	**28**-18	19-19	219-222	80.8-75.6
SL	9-3-2	.750	—	357-331	456-414	1770-1800	3.9-4.3	12-13	16-14	422-389	223-193	3045-2848	7.2-7.3	21-21	24-25	298-356	69.1-65.2
Phi	6-8	.429	—	312-313	430-445	1922-1746	4.5-3.9	16-15	22-12	397-406	199-202	2746-2950	6.9-7.3	19-18	18-17	268-379	69.7-71.2
Was	6-8	.429	—	307-305	366-440	1237-1813	3.4-4.1	11-20	17-21	415-406	214-193	**3071**-2600	7.4-6.4	25-16	16-**34**	350-353	79.9-**46.6**
Dal	5-8-1	.385	—	250-289	421-439	1691-1504	4.0-**3.4**	15-**6**	19-20	404-377	192-**172**	2516-2571	6.2-6.8	10-22	24-18	503-325	51.1-68.1
Pit	5-9	.357	—	253-315	516-454	2102-1994	4.1-4.4	14-15	17-14	323-378	141-185	2308-2582	7.1-6.8	14-16	24-12	450-345	51.7-72.2
NYG	2-10-2	.167	—	241-399	435-468	1404-1919	3.2-4.1	12-15	23-18	431-361	217-188	2848-2799	6.6-7.8	16-28	26-15	373-355	58.8-86.3
Western Conference																	
Bal	**12**-2	**.857**	L	**428-225**	456-422	2007-1798	4.4-4.3	**29**-13	10-18	345-385	176-217	3045-2621	**8.8**-6.8	22-14	9-23	273-**489**	**91.8**-64.6
GB	8-5-1	.615	—	342-245	495-417	**2276**-1532	4.6-3.7	23-15	17-**25**	321-**318**	186-173	2474-**1980**	7.7-**6.2**	16-**11**	**6**-16	369-333	91.3-63.9
Min	8-5-1	.615	—	355-296	**519-389**	2183-1616	4.2-4.2	14-10	18-16	326-375	179-182	2614-2993	8.0-8.0	23-23	12-19	491-269	89.4-75.1
Det	7-5-2	.583	—	280-260	412-429	1414-1638	3.4-3.8	7-10	13-8	386-406	206-226	2890-2906	7.5-7.2	23-14	21-22	332-482	74.9-67.2
LA	5-7-2	.417	—	283-339	400-419	1629-**1501**	4.1-3.6	11-14	19-13	368-435	173-213	2769-3094	7.5-7.1	18-27	20-17	490-400	66.3-76.9
ChiB	5-9	.357	—	260-379	356-436	1166-1863	3.3-4.3	5-19	12-20	**494**-366	**282**-188	3056-2897	6.2-7.9	25-27	21-10	**215**-275	74.6-91.1
SF	4-10	.286	—	236-330	383-443	1332-1560	3.5-3.5	11-11	24-14	461-434	225-232	2990-3141	6.5-7.2	18-23	22-15	249-297	62.9-80.0
Aver	14	—	—	309	434	1735	4.0	14	17	388	200	2780	7.2	20	19	349	71.7

TEAM	1D	PENY	PNT	FGM/A	RTNY	RTNTD	OFFY/DEFY	NETY	NETTO	NP	PNP	DELP	PW	DELW	PRT	DR	YPD	DEL
Eastern Conference																		
Cle	255-275	611-643	41.9-39.7	22/33-15/**23**	747-337	**8-0**	4486-4722	-236	14	122	36	**86**	10.1	0.5	4.7/ 4.7	170-**172**	26.4-27.5	-1.1
SL	**275**-235	579-695	40.9-43.5	**25**/38-27/34	639-453	7-2	4517-4292	225	-1	26	15	11	7.7	**2.3**	4.1/ 3.7	191-188	23.6-22.8	0.8
Phi	243-234	**450**-748	41.7-40.5	16/26-11/26	473-606	3-7	4400-4317	83	-11	-1	-37	36	7.0	-1.0	4.3/ 4.4	189-191	23.3-22.6	0.7
Was	193-243	825-624	41.2-42.1	12/28-11/27	547-683	3-3	3958-4060	-102	**22**	2	80	-78	7.1	-1.0	4.9/**2.0**	**203**-206	19.5-19.7	-0.2
Dal	230-211	952-781	38.9-43.5	14/29-17/29	775-422	5-6	3704-3750	-46	-5	-39	-24	-15	6.0	-0.5	2.2/ 3.9	195-195	19.0-19.2	-0.2
Pit	233-253	615-706	43.2-**39.5**	13/25-15/25	334-637	3-8	3960-4231	-271	-15	-62	-83	21	5.4	-0.5	2.5/ 4.4	171-173	23.2-24.5	-1.3
NYG	240-247	532-674	45.4-42.2	9/20-19/39	372-891	3-6	3879-4363	-484	-16	-158	-104	-54	3.1	-0.0	3.1/ 5.1	194-188	20.0-23.2	-3.2
Western Conference																		
Bal	245-242	785-641	41.8-44.0	17/35-**10**/24	**819-294**	3-1	**4779**-3930	849	**22**	**203**	159	44	**12.1**	-0.1	**6.7**/ 2.8	180-181	**26.5**-21.7	4.8
GB	250-**197**	576-521	42.2-43.5	12/**39**-12/**23**	706-455	5-4	4381-**3179**	**1202**	18	97	**172**	-75	9.4	-0.9	5.4/ 2.9	180-176	24.3-**18.1**	**6.3**
Min	258-216	787-708	**46.4**-43.8	21/33-13/28	530-396	5-4	4306-4340	-34	5	59	17	42	8.5	0.0	4.8/ 5.1	184-192	23.4-22.6	0.8
Det	221-241	674-**805**	45.7-44.0	14/25-19/38	678-490	4-5	3972-4062	-90	-4	20	-24	44	7.5	0.5	4.4/ 3.5	178-175	22.3-23.2	-0.9
LA	208-235	803-675	44.1-45.1	18/24-11/27	668-812	4-3	3908-4195	-287	-9	-56	-60	4	5.6	0.4	3.6/ 4.5	188-192	20.8-21.8	-1.1
ChiB	248-248	817-743	44.5-46.6	13/23-17/26	477-696	2-1	4007-4485	-478	-3	-119	-52	-67	4.0	1.0	4.1/ 6.2	179-173	22.4-25.9	-3.5
SF	233-255	741-783	45.6-45.8	8/25-17/34	477-1070	1-6	4073-4404	-331	-17	-94	-96	2	4.7	-0.7	4.0/ 5.0	194-194	21.0-22.7	-1.7
Aver	238	696	43.2	15/29	589	4	4166	—	—	—	—	—	—	—	4.6	185	22.5	—

Rushing Attempts	Rushing Yards	Rushing Average	Rushing TDs	Rushing Rank	Passing Yards	Passing Average
J.Brown-Cle 280	J.Brown-Cle 1446	J.Brown-Cle 5.16	L.Moore-Bal 16	J.Brown-Cle 1516	C.Johnson-SL 3045	J.Unitas-Bal 9.26
J.Taylor-GB 235	J.Taylor-GB 1169	T.Lorick-Bal 5.13	J.Taylor-GB 12	J.Taylor-GB 1289	S.Jurgensen-Was 2934	R.Gabriel-LA 8.64
J.Johnson-Pit 235	J.Johnson-Pit 1048	J.Taylor-GB 4.97		J.Johnson-Pit 1118	J.Unitas-Bal 2824	F.Tarkenton-Min 8.19
B.Brown-Min 226	B.Brown-Min 866	E.Gros-Phi 4.86		B.Brown-Min 936	F.Tarkenton-Min 2506	B.Starr-GB 7.88
C.Taylor-Was 199	D.Perkins-Dal 768	D.Bass-LA 4.75		D.Perkins-Dal 828	J.Brodie-SF 2498	M.Plum-Det 7.81

Completion Percent	TD Passes	TD Percent	INT Percent	Passer Rating	Passing Rank	Receptions
R.Bukich-Chi 61.9	F.Ryan-Cle 25	R.Bukich-Chi 7.5	B.Starr-GB 1.5	B.Starr-GB 97.1	J.Unitas-Bal 1267	J.Morris-Chi 93
B.Starr-GB 59.9	S.Jurgensen-Was 24	F.Ryan-Cle 7.5	J.Unitas-Bal 2.0	J.Unitas-Bal 96.4	S.Jurgensen-Was 1067	M.Ditka-Chi 75
F.Tarkenton-Min 55.9	F.Tarkenton-Min 22	F.Tarkenton-Min 7.2	G.Wood-NYG 2.1	F.Tarkenton-Min 91.8	B.Starr-GB 987	F.Clarke-Dal 65
B.Wade-Chi 55.7	C.Johnson-SL 21	R.Gabriel-LA 6.3	S.Jurgensen-Was 3.4	R.Bukich-Chi 89.0	F.Tarkenton-Min 923	B.Conrad-SL 61
S.Jurgensen-Was 53.8	J.Unitas-Bal 19	M.Plum-Det 6.3	R.Gabriel-LA 3.5	S.Jurgensen-Was 85.4	J.Brodie-SF 679	B.Mitchell-Was 60

Receiving Yards	Receiving Average	Receiving TDs	Receiving Rank	Combined Net Yards	Total TDs	Total Points
J.Morris-Chi 1200	J.Orr-Bal 21.67	B.Pope-LA 10	J.Morris-Chi 650	J.Brown-Cle 1786	L.Moore-Bal 20	L.Moore-Bal 120
T.Barr-Det 1030	G.Ballman-Pit 19.89	J.Morris-Chi 10	T.Barr-Det 560	B.Brown-Min 1637	B.Brown-Min 16	L.Groza-Cle 115
F.Clarke-Dal 973	D.Parks-SF 19.53	B.Mitchell-Was 10	F.Clarke-Dal 512	C.Taylor-Was 1589	J.Taylor-GB 15	J.Bakken-SL 115
G.Ballman-Pit 935	M.McGee-GB 19.10		P.Warfield-Cle 505	M.Renfro-Dal 1545		P.Hornung-GB 107
P.Warfield-Cle 920	T.Barr-Det 18.07		G.Ballman-Pit 503	J.Taylor-GB 1523		L.Michaels-Bal 104

Punt Average	Field Goals	Field Goal Percent	Kickoff Returns	Kickoff Return Average	Punt Returns	Punt Return Average
B.Walden-Min 46.4	J.Bakken-SL 25	B.Gossett-LA 75.0	M.Renfro-Dal 40	C.Childs-NYG 29.0	M.Renfro-Dal 32	T.Watkins-Det 14.9
Y.Lary-Det 46.3	L.Groza-Cle 22	L.Groza-Cle 66.7	C.Childs-NYG 34	G.Ballman-Pit 27.6	A.Woodson-SF 22	W.Wood-GB 13.3
T.Davis-SF 45.6	F.Cox-Min 21	J.Bakken-SL 65.8	A.Woodson-SF 32	W.Roberts-Cle 27.5	B.Butler-Min 22	M.Renfro-Dal 13.1
D.Chandler-NYG 45.6	B.Gossett-LA 18	F.Cox-Min 63.6	T.Brown-Phi 30	A.Woodson-SF 27.5	D.James-NYG 21	E.Pitts-GB 12.7
B.Green-Chi 44.5	L.Michaels-Bal 17	R.LeClerc-Chi 62.5	P.Studstill-Det 29	T.Moore-GB 26.9	K.Alexander-SF 21	W.Harris-Bal 12.6

Punt/Kick Return Yards	Punt/Kick Return TDs	Interceptions	Interception Return Yards	Interception Return TDs	Sacks	Overall Rank
M.Renfro-Dal 1435	T.Watkins-Det 2	P.Krause-Was 12	B.Boyd-Bal 185	R.Hawkins-Min 2	Not kept	J.Brown-Cle 1708
C.Childs-NYG 1027		P.Fischer-SL 10	P.Fischer-SL 164	P.Fischer-SL 2		J.Taylor-GB 1481
A.Woodson-SF 1013		B.Boyd-Bal 9	P.Retzlaff-LA 146			J.Unitas-Bal 1449
P.Studstill-Det 845		M.Renfro-Dal 7	P.Krause-Was 140			B.Brown-Min 1326
W.Roberts-Cle 793			J.Ridlon-Dal 121			F.Tarkenton-Min 1273

New Coach Brings Out Old Fire in Colts

After helping pro football reach previously unimagined levels to end the 1950s, the Colts had slowly returned to the pack. Young Don Shula had been brought in as coach in 1963 and his offensive scheme changed things for the better in his second year in Baltimore. Johnny Unitas pushed the ball downfield while spreading the running game's workload among four different backs. Baltimore still counted on veterans Raymond Berry to go deep and Lenny Moore to finish drives with a quick dive over the goal line. Combined with the league's best defense, Baltimore had a formula for success, even without a feature running back racking up yards.

The Colts handily won the Western Conference, although they were pursued by one of the most promising teams in the league: the Vikings. With homegrown stars like the light-footed Fran Tarkenton improvising plays at quarterback, Mick Tingelhoff snapping, and rookie defensive lineman Carl Eller attacking offensive lines, pro football's newest franchise was clearly a team on the rise.

Change also came in the Eastern Conference. The Giants had been one of the league's best teams for almost a decade, but it was not a young team, and what finally came was perhaps predictable. Linebacker Sam Huff was traded to the Redskins. Y.A. Tittle had little left in what would be his final season, and he was joined in retirement by his frequent target, Frank Gifford, as well as defensive lineman Andy Robustelli. New York also lost Steve Owen, who coached the Giants to two championship over 27 seasons. He died in May.

Riding Jim Brown's league-leading rushing yet again, and introducing rookie deep threat Paul Warfield to their offensive scheme, the Browns were back on top. More surprising was the situation in Washington, where the long-dormant Redskins were finally improving themselves. Picking up veterans like Huff from the Giants and quarterback Sonny Jurgensen from the Eagles provided Washington with identifiable stars. Safety Paul Krause debuted with 12 interceptions. Rookie of the Year Charley Taylor gave them a running back with the hands and speed who could also line up wide. The Redskins still went just 6–8, but they had the league's top passing attack.

1964 AFL

TEAM	W-L-T	PCT	POST	PTS	RA	RY	RY/A	RTD	FL	PA	PC	GPY	GPY/A	PTD	PI	PSY	PRAT
Eastern Division																	
Buf	**12-2**	.857	L*	400-242	492-300	2040-913	4.1-3.0	25-4	18-15	397-517	174-241	3422-3361	8.6-6.5	19-24	34-28	256-396	54.8-60.9
Bos	10-3-1	.769	—	365-297	381-356	1361-1143	3.6-3.2	9-10	12-17	476-530	229-261	3467-3645	7.3-6.9	31-23	27-31	301-428	70.6-61.9
NYJ	5-8-1	.385	—	278-315	384-410	1457-1675	3.8-4.1	11-14	7-10	451-473	201-228	2694-3472	6.0-7.3	19-22	33-34	262-231	47.7-58.4
Hou	4-10	.286	—	310-355	327-438	1347-1961	4.1-4.5	14-18	15-8	592-433	299-229	3734-3469	6.3-8.0	19-24	29-30	207-189	60.7-69.1
Western Division																	
SD	8-5-1	.615	L	341-300	392-399	1522-1522	3.9-3.8	14-10	16-15	445-484	224-240	3363-2926	7.6-6.0	28-22	30-30	221-408	68.4-57.9
KC	7-7	.500	—	366-306	415-390	1825-1315	4.4-3.4	14-9	20-18	412-440	228-218	3321-2910	8.1-6.6	32-25	21-28	446-279	86.4-63.4
Oak	5-7-2	.417	—	303-350	331-396	1480-1750	4.5-4.4	9-20	18-10	521-433	253-206	3886-3292	7.5-7.6	28-21	33-26	464-299	65.2-64.6
Den	2-11-1	.154	—	240-438	391-424	1311-2064	3.4-4.9	10-21	8-21	456-440	230-215	2541-3353	5.6-7.6	14-29	32-32	520-447	48.3-66.2
Aver	14	—		325	389	1543	4.0	13	14	469	230	3304	7.0	24	30	335	62.6

TEAM	1D	PENY	PNT	FGM/A	RTNY	RTNTD	OFFY/DEFY	NETY	NETTO	NP	PNP	DELP	PW	DELW	PRT	DR	YPD	DEL
Eastern Division																		
Buf	255-206	511-577	42.7-41.9	19/29-14/27	891-656	4-1	5206-3878	1328	-9	158	75	83	10.9	1.0	4.2/ 3.4	197-206	26.4-18.8	7.6
Bos	226-243	447-734	38.0-41.5	25/39-15/30	703-670	1-3	4527-4360	167	9	68	50	18	8.7	1.8	4.5/ 3.6	208-206	21.8-21.2	0.6
NYJ	209-245	477-951	41.3-40.5	13/27-15/27	760-874	4-3	3889-4916	-1027	4	-37	-70	33	6.1	-0.6	2.4/ 3.9	195-193	19.9-25.5	-5.5
Hou	284-276	683-496	41.2-39.1	13/29-14/30	689-791	6-3	4874-5241	-367	-6	-45	-55	10	5.9	-1.9	3.9/ 4.7	181-180	26.9-29.1	-2.2
Western Division																		
SD	254-248	709-528	39.3-43.0	12/26-14/32	770-794	2-4	4664-4040	624	-1	41	48	-7	8.0	0.5	4.4/2.7	186-194	25.1-20.8	4.3
KC	250-211	604-451	42.5-40.7	8/17-14/20	808-479	3-4	4700-3946	754	5	60	83	-23	8.5	-1.5	4.9/ 3.5	194-197	24.2-20.0	4.2
Oak	270-255	752-647	41.5-41.7	15/24-11/34	877-985	0-4	4902-4713	159	-15	-47	-47	0	5.8	0.2	3.8/ 4.3	194-183	25.3-25.9	-0.6
Den	207-271	774-573	43.4-41.4	14/34-22/25	718-967	4-2	3332-4970	-1638	13	-198	-85	-113	2.1	0.4	1.4/ 3.6	204-200	16.3-24.9	-8.5
Aver	244	620	41.3	15/28	777	3	4512	—	—	—	—	—	—	—	4.0	195	23.2	—

Rushing Attempts		Rushing Yards		Rushing Average		Rushing TDs		Rushing Rank		Passing Yards		Passing Average	
C.Gilchrist-Buf	230	C.Gilchrist-Buf	981	M.Hill-KC	5.49	D.Lamonica-Buf	6	C.Gilchrist-Buf	1041	B.Parilli-Bos	3465	J.Kemp-Buf	8.49
M.Snell-NYJ	215	M.Snell-NYJ	948	S.Blanks-Hou	5.21	C.Gilchrist-Buf	6	M.Snell-NYJ	998	G.Blanda-Hou	3287	L.Dawson-KC	8.13
L.Garron-Bos	183	C.Daniels-Oak	824	A.Haynes-KC	5.01	S.Blanks-Hou	6	C.Daniels-Oak	844	L.Dawson-KC	2879	J.Hadl-SD	7.87
C.Mitchell-Den	177	S.Blanks-Hou	756	C.Daniels-Oak	4.76			S.Blanks-Hou	816	C.Davidson-Oak	2497	C.Davidson-Oak	7.80
C.Daniels-Oak	173	A.Haynes-KC	697	M.Snell-NYJ	4.41			A.Haynes-KC	737	D.Wood-NYJ	2298	B.Parilli-Bos	7.33

Completion Percent		TD Passes		TD Percent		INT Percent		Passer Rating		Passing Rank		Receptions	
L.Dawson-KC	56.2	B.Parilli-Bos	31	L.Dawson-KC	8.5	L.Dawson-KC	5.1	L.Dawson-KC	89.9	L.Dawson-KC	870	C.Hennigan-Hou	101
J.Hadl-SD	53.6	L.Dawson-KC	30	G.Blanda-Hou	5.3	G.Blanda-Hou	5.3	J.Hadl-SD	78.7	B.Parilli-Bos	808	L.Taylor-Den	76
G.Blanda-Hou	51.9	C.Davidson-Oak	21	J.Hadl-SD	6.6	J.Hadl-SD	5.5	C.Davidson-Oak	72.1	G.Blanda-Hou	649	A.Powell-Oak	76
M.Slaughter-Den	51.3	J.Hadl-SD	18	B.Parilli-Bos	6.6	B.Parilli-Bos	5.7	B.Parilli-Bos	70.8	C.Davidson-Oak	594	F.Jackson-KC	62
J.Lee-Den	50.2			T.Rote-NYJ	5.5	M.Slaughter-Den	5.8	G.Blanda-Hou	61.4	J.Hadl-SD	569	L.Alworth-SD	61

Receiving Yards		Receiving Average		Receiving TDs		Receiving Rank		Combined Net Yards		Total TDs		Total Points	
C.Hennigan-Hou	1546	E.Dubenion-Buf	27.12	L.Alworth-SD	13	C.Hennigan-Hou	813	B.Roberson-Oak	1615	L.Alworth-SD	15	B.Cannon-Bos	155
A.Powell-Oak	1361	G.Bass-Buf	20.86	A.Powell-Oak	11	A.Powell-Oak	736	C.Daniels-Oak	1552	A.Powell-Oak	11	P.Gogolak-Buf	102
L.Alworth-SD	1235	J.Colclough-Bos	20.53	E.Dubenion-Buf	10	L.Alworth-SD	683	A.Haynes-KC	1548	E.Dubenion-Buf	10	L.Alworth-SD	90
E.Dubenion-Buf	1139	L.Alworth-SD	20.25	L.Taylor-NYJ	9	E.Dubenion-Buf	620	C.Hennigan-Hou	1546			M.Mercer-Oak	79
B.Turner-NYJ	974	F.Arbanas-KC	20.18	F.Jackson-KC	9	B.Turner-NYJ	532	M.Snell-NYJ	1499			G.Blanda-Hou	76

Punt Average		Field Goals		Field Goal Percent		Kickoff Returns		Kickoff Return Average		Punt Returns		Punt Return Average	
J.Fraser-Den	44.2	B.Cannon-Bos	25	P.Gogolak-Buf	65.5	O.Barry-Den	47	B.Roberson-Oak	27.1	H.Clarke-Buf	33	C.Gibson-Oak	14.4
P.Maguire-Buf	42.7	P.Gogolak-Buf	19	B.Cannon-Bos	64.1	B.Roberson-Oak	36	O.Barry-Den	26.5	C.Gibson-Oak	29	L.Alworth-SD	10.5
J.Wilson-KC	42.6	M.Mercer-Oak	15	M.Mercer-Oak	62.5	J.Garrett-Bos	32	O.Burrell-Hou	26.4	D.Cloutier-Bos	20	H.Clarke-Buf	9.6
M.Mercer-Oak	41.5	J.Turner-NYJ	13	J.Turner-NYJ	48.1	D.Grayson-KC	30	D.Cannon-Oak	24.7			B.Baird-NYJ	9.4
C.Johnson-NYJ	41.3	G.Blanda-Hou	13	T.Brooker-KC	47.1			E.Rutkowski-Buf	23.7			O.Barry-Den	9.3

Punt/Kick Return Yards		Punt/Kick Return TDs		Interceptions		Interception Return Yards		Interception Return TDs		Sacks		Overall Rank	
O.Barry-Den	1394	B.Jancik-Hou	1	D.Paulson-NYJ	12	D.Grayson-KC	187	Many	1	Not kept		C.Daniels-Oak	1239
B.Roberson-Oak	995	H.Clarke-Buf	1	R.Hall-Bos	11	B.Byrd-Buf	178					C.Gilchrist-Buf	1214
J.Garrett-Bos	777	O.Burrell-Hou	1	W.Brown-Den	9	D.Paulson-NYJ	157					M.Snell-NYJ	1213
B.Jancik-Hou	708	O.Barry-Den	1	P.Jaquess-Hou	8	R.Hall-Bos	148					S.Blanks-Hou	1151
D.Grayson-KC	679			B.Baird-NYJ	8	P.Jaquess-Hou	141					A.Haynes-KC	1137

IT'S TELEVISION TO THE RESCUE

The AFL was finishing the fifth year of its national television contract with ABC, and if the league had earned respect, it needed more than that. The AFL's ability to bid with the older league on college talent was in serious danger after NFL commissioner Pete Rozelle had secured massive national broadcasting deals with CBS in 1962 and again in 1964. In cooperation with Jets owner Sonny Werblin, AFL commissioner Joe Foss managed to get ABC and NBC into competitive bidding, finally wangling a $36 million deal with NBC that guaranteed the league's future.

Teams started spending that money quickly. Bidding wars on highly-regarded college players like Scott Appleton, Pete Beathard, and Jack Concannon sprung up. The Chiefs fruitlessly pursued Navy star quarterback Roger Staubach, losing out to the Cowboys, who would still have to wait until his military commitment was up in 1969. The AFL's biggest success was New York's inking top pick Matt Snell to provide them with the feature back the team had always lacked. Snell would be the league's Rookie of the Year, while finishing second in rushing.

Leading the league was Buffalo's Cookie Gilchrist, although he wasn't the same back he'd been two years before. He was not Buffalo's only star, however. Revolutionizing the art of place-kicking was rookie Pete Gogolak, a Hungarian immigrant who introduced soccer-style kicking to professional football. Gogolak success would help teams recognize that they could reliably score points from further out than ever before, encouraging even more specialization in kicking roles. Gogolak still finished a distant second in scoring to league MVP Gino Cappelletti of the Patriots, a wideout who doubled as Boston's kicker. But Bills coach Lou Saban had built a balanced team that was easily the league's best, relying on a big, rugged defensive unit and strong offensive line play.

Although the AFL still boasted its share of gunslinging, often inaccurate quarterbacks, passers like Boston's Babe Parilli or Kansas City's Len Dawson showed more than mere arm strength in exceeding 30 touchdowns passes apiece. Lance Alworth in San Diego and Art Powell in Oakland ranked as the league's top deep threats.

1965 NFL

TEAM	W-L-T	PCT	POST	PTS	RA	RY	RY/A	RTD	FL	PA	PC	GPY	GPY/A	PTD	PI	PSY	PRAT
Eastern Conference																	
Cle	**11**-3	**.786**	L	363-325	476-412	**2331**-1866	**4.9**-4.5	19-11	9-8	329-419	160-204	2339-3153	7.1-7.5	23-31	16-24	272-307	75.3-74.8
Dal	7-7	.500	—	325-280	416-422	1608-1444	3.9-**3.4**	8-13	17-20	362-426	168-205	2756-3063	7.6-7.2	25-17	18-18	369-315	74.8-67.8
NYG	7-7	.500	—	270-338	423-447	1651-1956	3.9-4.4	12-20	14-20	342-393	171-208	2685-3251	7.9-8.3	23-18	16-16	255-294	79.4-79.0
Was	6-8	.429	—	257-301	354-486	1037-1753	2.9-3.6	7-18	21-15	427-**318**	220-**161**	2908-2539	6.8-8.0	20-15	20-**27**	337-**422**	69.5-57.9
Phi	5-9	.357	—	363-359	404-419	1824-1582	4.5-3.8	21-11	10-11	434-393	223-215	3442-3123	7.9-7.9	22-28	26-25	254-287	69.9-78.0
SL	5-9	.357	—	296-309	431-433	1619-1813	3.8-4.2	10-11	**7**-15	448-380	221-184	3222-2826	7.2-7.4	20-24	25-17	279-342	64.8-75.8
Pit	2-12	.143	—	202-397	407-483	1378-2080	3.4-4.3	10-19	22-15	354-353	161-173	2503-2703	7.1-7.7	10-25	35-12	527-253	39.3-84.3
Western Conference																	
GB	10-3-1	.769	CL*	316-**224**	432-480	1488-1988	3.4-4.1	14-10	12-23	306-383	166-187	2508-**2316**	8.2-**6.0**	19-**11**	14-**27**	395-335	83.1-**48.2**
Bal	10-3-1	.769	C	389-284	445-410	1593-1483	3.6-3.6	13-11	19-14	399-400	222-213	3330-2903	8.3-7.3	31-22	17-22	325-341	91.4-72.1
ChiB	9-5	.643	—	409-275	479-**400**	2131-1530	4.4-3.8	**27**-11	16-**24**	361-444	201-217	3020-3086	**8.4**-7.0	22-18	**12**-20	254-348	89.8-66.5
SF	7-6-1	.538	—	**421**-402	428-405	1783-1535	4.2-3.8	13-20	19-17	**454**-448	**272**-225	**3633**-3302	8.0-7.4	**35**-24	21-13	**146**-197	**91.8**-80.4
Min	7-7	.500	—	383-403	**505**-408	2278-1755	4.5-4.3	19-17	25-11	372-357	189-187	2861-2692	7.7-7.5	21-31	**12**-19	315-199	81.8-83.9
Det	6-7-1	.462	—	257-295	453-409	1469-1460	3.2-3.6	16-**9**	15-20	374-344	170-190	2083-2508	5.6-7.3	14-21	26-26	249-411	46.7-67.3
LA	4-10	.286	—	269-328	378-417	1464-**1409**	3.9-**3.4**	8-16	22-15	445-349	230-205	3059-2884	6.9-8.3	22-22	19-11	344-270	72.5-93.3
Aver	14	—	—	323	431	1690	3.9	14	16	386	198	2882	7.5	22	20	309	73.5

TEAM	1D	PENY	PNT	FGM/A	RTNY	RTNTD	OFFY/DEFY	NETY	NETTO	NP	PNP	DELP	PW	DELW	PRT	DR	YPD	DEL
Eastern Conference																		
Cle	257-265	976-586	45.7-41.1	16/25-**9/18**	776-534	3-**1**	4398-4712	-314	7	38	2	36	7.9	**3.1**	4.4/ 4.5	176-178	25.0-26.5	-1.5
Dal	211-240	710-483	41.3-42.9	16/27-17/30	510-407	**7**-3	3995-4192	-197	3	45	-4	49	8.1	-1.1	4.4/ 4.5	186-190	21.5-22.1	-0.6
NYG	230-266	618-**848**	41.6-42.7	4/25-16/29	284-**319**	2-3	4081-4913	-832	6	-68	-45	-23	5.3	1.7	5.2/ 5.6	166-**169**	24.6-29.1	-4.5
Was	210-237	692-738	42.1-43.4	10/22-12/22	**950**-329	6-5	3608-3870	-262	1	-44	-18	-26	5.9	0.1	4.0/ 2.9	185-180	19.5-21.5	-2.0
Phi	267-243	686-653	42.2-41.8	10/25-11/26	496-739	5-8	5012-4418	594	0	4	50	-46	7.1	-2.1	4.8/ 4.6	177-179	28.3-24.7	3.6
SL	251-238	458-750	40.4-43.3	21/31-17/32	355-732	3-2	4562-4297	265	0	-13	22	-35	6.7	-1.7	4.2/ 4.7	181-177	25.2-24.3	0.9
Pit	194-243	**326**-615	45.1-42.2	11/19-10/26	541-1083	5-9	3354-4530	-1176	-30	-195	-218	23	2.1	-0.1	1.2/ 5.6	**196**-193	17.1-23.5	-6.4
Western Conference																		
GB	201-240	529-677	42.9-42.1	17/26-22/33	626-499	5-**1**	3601-3969	-368	**24**	92	65	27	9.3	1.2	4.8/**2.1**	179-180	20.1-22.0	-1.9
Bal	266-233	616-786	39.6-43.9	17/28-13/23	739-539	4-2	4598-4045	553	0	105	46	**59**	9.6	0.9	5.8/ 4.1	180-182	25.5-22.2	3.3
ChiB	257-244	826-611	42.7-42.3	11/26-15/24	596-342	5-4	4897-4268	629	16	**134**	**116**	18	**10.4**	-1.3	**6.3**/ 4.2	180-181	27.2-23.6	3.6
SF	**292**-259	785-727	**45.8**-41.9	17/27-14/27	380-640	5-8	**5270**-4640	**630**	-10	19	13	6	7.5	0.0	6.1/ 5.8	185-188	**28.5**-24.7	**3.8**
Min	277-242	771-643	42.1-**38.4**	**23/35**-11/20	401-476	4-5	4824-4248	576	-7	-20	20	-40	6.5	0.5	5.4/ 5.1	184-181	26.2-23.5	2.7
Det	204-210	767-637	42.8-42.9	8/22-13/22	701-833	3-6	3303-**3557**	-254	5	-38	-1	-37	6.1	0.4	2.0/ 2.9	193-190	17.1-**18.7**	-1.6
LA	251-**208**	560-566	39.7-45.4	15/26-16/32	449-332	2-2	4179-4023	156	-15	-59	-47	-12	5.5	-1.5	4.2/ 6.1	179-179	23.3-22.5	0.9
Aver	241	666	42.5	14/26	557	4	4263	—	—	—	—	—	—	—	4.9	182	23.4	—

Rushing Attempts	**Rushing Yards**	**Rushing Average**	**Rushing TDs**	**Rushing Rank**	**Passing Yards**	**Passing Average**
J.Brown-Cle 289	J.Brown-Cle 1544	T.Brown-Phi 5.45	J.Brown-Cle 17	J.Brown-Cle 1714	J.Brodie-SF...........3112	J.Unitas-Bal 8.97
J.Taylor-GB 207	G.Sayers-Chi 867	J.Brown-Cle 5.34	G.Sayers-Chi 14	G.Sayers-Chi 1007	R.Bukich-Chi..........2641	R.Bukich-Chi...........8.46
Frederickson-NYG 195	T.Brown-Phi 861	G.Sayers-Chi 5.22	T.Mason-Min 10	T.Brown-Phi 921	F.Tarkenton-Min 2609	B.Starr-GB 8.19
K.Willard-SF 189	K.Willard-SF 778	P.King-Min..............4.94	E.Gros-Phi 7	K.Willard-SF 828	J.Unitas-Bal 2530	N.Snead-Phi 8.15
D.Perkins-Dal..........177	J.Taylor-GB 734	R.Bull-Chi 4.58		J.Taylor-GB 774	E.Morrall-NYG 2446	E.Morrall-NYG 8.10
Completion Percent	**TD Passes**	**TD Percent**	**INT Percent**	**Passer Rating**	**Passing Rank**	**Receptions**
J.Brodie-SF............61.9	J.Brodie-SF...............30	J.Unitas-Bal 8.2	R.Bukich-Chi.............2.9	J.Unitas-Bal 97.4	J.Brodie-SF...........1066	D.Parks-SF 80
J.Unitas-Bal 58.2	J.Unitas-Bal 23	J.Brodie-SF...............7.7	R.Gabriel-LA.............2.9	J.Brodie-SF.............95.3	R.Bukich-Chi..........1061	T.McDonald-LA..........67
R.Bukich-Chi...........56.4	E.Morrall-NYG 22	F.Ryan-Cle 7.4	F.Tarkenton-Min 3.3	R.Bukich-Chi...........93.7	F.Tarkenton-Min 960	P.Retzlaff-Phi 66
B.Starr-GB 55.8	D.Meredith-Dal...........22	E.Morrall-NYG 7.3	B.Starr-GB 3.6	B.Starr-GB 89.0	J.Unitas-Bal 900	B.Mitchell-Was..........60
B.Munson-LA...........53.9	R.Bukich-Chi.............20	D.Meredith-Dal.........7.2	E.Morrall-NYG 4.0	E.Morrall-NYG 86.3	E.Morrall-NYG 853	B.Casey-SF 59
Receiving Yards	**Receiving Average**	**Receiving TDs**	**Receiving Rank**	**Combined Net Yards**	**Total TDs**	**Total Points**
D.Parks-SF 1344	B.Hayes-Dal.........21.80	D.Parks-SF 12	D.Parks-SF 732	G.Sayers-Chi 2272	G.Sayers-Chi 22	G.Sayers-Chi 132
P.Retzlaff-Phi 1190	G.Ballman-Pit 21.48	B.Hayes-Dal...............12	P.Retzlaff-Phi 645	J.Brown-Cle 1872	J.Brown-Cle 21	J.Brown-Cle 126
T.McDonald-LA......1036	J.Mackey-Bal 20.35	P.Retzlaff-Phi 10	T.McDonald-LA........563	T.Brown-Phi 1602	B.Hayes-Dal...............13	F.Cox-Min.................113
B.Hayes-Dal...........1003	R.Poage-Phi 19.74	J.Orr-Bal 10	B.Hayes-Dal.............562	B.Hayes-Dal...........1598	D.Parks-SF 12	T.Davis-SF 103
B.Conrad-SL...........909	J.Orr-Bal 18.82	G.Collins-Cle 10	G.Collins-Cle 492	D.Parks-SF 1344	T.Mason-Min 11	L.Michaels-Bal 101
Punt Average	**Field Goals**	**Field Goal Percent**	**Kickoff Returns**	**Kickoff Return Average**	**Punt Returns**	**Punt Return Average**
G.Collins-Cle 46.7	F.Cox-Min...................23	J.Bakken-SL 67.7	K.Alexander-SF 32	T.Watkins-Det 34.4	A.Haymond-Bal 41	L.Kelly-Cle 15.6
T.Davis-SF 45.8	J.Bakken-SL 21	F.Cox-Min...............65.7	C.Childs-NYG 29	G.Sayers-Chi 31.4	K.Alexander-SF 35	G.Sayers-Chi 14.9
F.Lambert-Pit 45.1	L.Michaels-Bal 17	D.Chandler-GB 65.4	A.Woodson-SL 27	A.Haymond-Bal 30.7	R.Harris-Was 31	R.Harris-Was 12.2
P.Richter-Was 43.8	T.Davis-SF 17	L.Groza-Cle 64.0	A.Nelson-Phi.............26	M.Renfro-Dal 30.0	M.Renfro-Dal 24	T.Watkins-Det 10.2
D.Chandler-GB 42.9	D.Chandler-GB 17	T.Davis-SF 63.0		W.Roberts-Cle 27.4	T.Watkins-Det 23	A.Haymond-Bal 9.8
Punt/Kick Return Yards	**Punt/Kick Return TDs**	**Interceptions**	**Interception Return Yards**	**Interception Return TDs**	**Sacks**	**Overall Rank**
A.Haymond-Bal 1017	G.Sayers-Chi 2	B.Boyd-Bal...................9	H.Adderley-GB 175	H.Adderley-GB 3	Not kept	J.Brown-Cle 1923
K.Alexander-SF 1003	L.Kelly-Cle 2	D.LeBeau-Det.............7	L.Wilson-SL 153	W.Rasmussen-Det.......2		G.Sayers-Chi 1805
G.Sayers-Chi 898			D.Robinson-GB.......141	J.Logan-Bal 2		F.Tarkenton-Min 1326
L.Kelly-Cle 886			W.Rasmussen-Det...122			T.Brown-Phi 1271
T.Watkins-Det 818			L.Sanders-Was........121			J.Brodie-SF...........1136

Six Ways to Sunday

With past contenders like the Bears, Lions, or Giants all no longer mounting bids, the list of the league's powers had really been whittled down to two teams: the Colts in the Western Conference, and the Browns in the Eastern Conference. After coming up just short in 1963, and then finishing nowhere close in 1964 (not even Paul Hornung's return from exile had helped), were the Packers about to join the list of formerly great teams? Now playing in the stadium renamed after recently departed Green Bay legend Curly Lambeau, Vince Lombardi was about to take the decade for his own.

Even if Jim Taylor and Hornung had each lost a step, the Packers' ability to execute remained incomparable. They benefited from a late Baltimore collapse, as the Colts couldn't convert after an 8–1 start. First, the Colts lost Johnny Unitas and then Gary Cuozzo before winning in the season's final week with converted running back Tom Matte taking snaps. The ensuing playoff with Green Bay ended up being considerably tighter than expected, as Bart Starr went down with an injury. The Packers took a 13–10 overtime win in what was the last significant game of this rivalry.

In the Eastern Conference the Browns rolled yet again behind the power running game of Jim Brown. Brown not only wound up the league's lone 1,000-yard rusher, he scored a career-high 21 touchdowns. But that figure was only good enough for second in the NFL, thanks to Bears rookie Gale Sayers. The lightning-fast Sayers scored 6 touchdowns at muddy Wrigley Field on December 16. George Halas, on the losing side of the first two 6-touchdown games, kept him on the bench while Chicago scored twice more. Like Sayers, Bears rookie linebacker Dick Butkus established himself among the best at his position.

There were rookies outside Chicago, too. The Cowboys introduced the blazing speed of wide receiver Bob Hayes and Washington brought out linebacker Chris Hanburger. Symbolic of the passing of those great Giants and Lions teams into the league's past, New York lineman Rosey Brown hung up his spikes, as did Lions defensive stalwarts Night Train Lane and Joe Schmidt.

1965 AFL

TEAM	W-L-T	PCT	POST	PTS	RA	RY	RY/A	RTD	FL	PA	PC	GPY	GPY/A	PTD	PI	PSY	PRAT
Eastern Division
Buf	**10**-3-1	.769	L*	313-**226**	392-360	1288-1114	3.3-**3.1**	**16-4**	14-**25**	461-502	208-227	2744-3416	6.0-6.8	13-19	24-**32**	283-246	52.2-54.2
NYJ	5-8-1	.385	—	285-303	367-432	1476-1551	4.0-3.6	11-10	18-12	459-472	209-220	2751-2900	6.0-6.1	21-22	22-26	**162**-238	60.3-59.1
Bos	4-8-2	.333	—	244-302	373-425	1117-1531	3.0-3.6	8-10	12-9	473-431	193-206	2854-2891	6.0-6.7	19-**17**	29-21	347-291	49.1-62.7
Hou	4-10	.286	—	298-429	324-507	1175-2683	3.6-5.3	10-17	11-13	**550**-416	224-177	3070-2643	5.6-6.4	**25**-20	35-27	257-173	47.9-53.0
Western Division
SD	9-2-3	**.818**	L	**340**-227	**486-306**	**1998-1094**	4.1-3.6	12-7	13-13	401-474	203-206	**3379-2480**	**8.4-5.2**	23-**17**	26-28	276-312	71.5-**47.4**
Oak	8-5-1	.615	—	298-239	390-407	1538-1487	3.9-3.7	8-10	**9**-14	431-466	195-206	2713-2947	6.3-6.3	22-27	**17**-24	253-246	66.6-61.9
KC	7-5-2	.583	—	322-285	418-382	1752-1376	**4.2**-3.6	15-12	20-13	395-451	199-216	2894-2711	7.3-6.0	22-18	20-20	351-**326**	**72.1**-61.9
Den	4-10	.286	—	303-392	453-384	1829-1337	4.0-3.5	14-24	16-14	482-440	222-202	2848-3265	5.9-7.4	18-23	30-25	208-305	51.6-65.0
Aver	14	—	—	300	400	1522	3.8	12	14	440	207	2907	6.4	20	25	267	58.0

TEAM	1D	PENY	PNT	FGM/A	RTNY	RTNTD	OFFY/DEFY	NETY	NETTO	NP	PNP	DELP	PW	DELW	PRT	DR	YPD	DEL
Eastern Division
Buf	206-226	685-832	43.0-40.2	**28/46**-15/30	782-689	4-2	3749-4284	-535	**19**	87	31	**56**	9.2	**1.3**	3.1/3.6	198-210	18.9-20.4	-1.5
NYJ	213-235	684-**865**	**45.3-39.8**	20/34-20/34	401-691	0-3	4065-4213	-148	-2	-18	-20	2	6.6	-1.0	3.8/3.5	197-191	20.6-22.1	-1.4
Bos	214-232	**537**-658	40.1-42.1	17/27-22/40	385-597	0-7	3624-4131	-507	-11	-58	-86	28	5.6	-0.5	2.7/4.0	192-191	18.9-21.6	-2.8
Hou	227-271	856-701	43.7-42.5	12/23-25/43	605-965	2-13	3988-5153	-1165	-6	-131	-121	-10	3.7	0.3	2.6/3.3	**205**-203	19.5-25.4	-5.9
Western Division
SD	**268-190**	929-665	40.0-43.4	18/30-16/34	**885**-693	6-1	**5101-3262**	**1839**	2	113	161	-48	**9.8**	0.7	**5.1/2.1**	194-195	**26.3-16.7**	**9.6**
Oak	225-235	661-666	41.1-42.1	17/34-**10/20**	847-**443**	5-7	3998-4188	-190	12	59	32	27	8.5	0.0	4.1/3.8	179-**184**	22.3-22.8	-0.4
KC	232-207	744-623	44.6-44.1	13/30-16/28	761-639	3-4	4295-3761	534	-7	37	17	20	7.9	0.1	4.3/3.4	191-193	22.5-19.5	3.0
Den	255-244	750-836	43.2-45.9	13/29-14/24	820-769	6-3	4469-4297	172	-7	-89	-14	-75	4.8	-0.8	2.9/4.4	200-189	22.3-22.7	-0.4
Aver	230	731	42.5	17/32	686	3	4161	—	—	—	—	—	—	—	3.7	195	21.4	—

Rushing Attempts		Rushing Yards		Rushing Average		Rushing TDs		Rushing Rank		Passing Yards		Passing Average	
C.Gilchrist-Den	252	P.Lowe-SD	1121	P.Lowe-SD	5.05	C.McClinton-KC	6	P.Lowe-SD	1181	J.Hadl-SD	2798	J.Hadl-SD	8.04
P.Lowe-SD	222	C.Gilchrist-Den	954	M.Hill-KC	5.02	P.Lowe-SD	6	C.Gilchrist-Den	1014	B.Parilli-Bos	2597	L.Dawson-KC	7.42
C.Daniels-Oak	219	C.Daniels-Oak	884	M.Snell-NYJ	4.51	C.Gilchrist-Den	6	C.Daniels-Oak	934	G.Blanda-Hou	2542	J.Namath-NYJ	6.53
C.McClinton-KC	175	M.Snell-NYJ	763	B.Mathis-NYJ	4.11	W.Carlton-Buf	6	M.Snell-NYJ	803	J.Kemp-Buf	2368	D.Wood-Oak	6.39
M.Snell-NYJ	169	C.McClinton-KC	661	K.Lincoln-SD	4.08			C.McClinton-KC	721	L.Dawson-KC	2262	B.Parilli-Bos	6.10

Completion Percent		TD Passes		TD Percent		INT Percent		Passer Rating		Passing Rank		Receptions	
L.Dawson-KC	53.4	L.Dawson-KC	21	L.Dawson-KC	6.9	D.Wood-Oak	3.8	L.Dawson-KC	81.3	L.Dawson-KC	676	L.Taylor-Den	85
M.Slaughter-Den	51.0	J.Hadl-SD	20	J.Hadl-SD	5.3	T.Flores-Oak	4.1	J.Hadl-SD	71.3	J.Hadl-SD	659	L.Alworth-SD	69
J.Hadl-SD	50.0	G.Blanda-Hou	20	J.Namath-NYJ	5.3	J.Namath-NYJ	4.4	J.Namath-NYJ	68.8	J.Namath-NYJ	600	D.Maynard-NYJ	68
J.Namath-NYJ	48.2	B.Parilli-Bos	18	T.Flores-Oak	5.2	L.Dawson-KC	4.6	D.Wood-Oak	66.4	J.Kemp-Buf	514	O.Burrell-Hou	55
J.Kemp-Buf	45.8	J.Namath-NYJ	18	D.Wood-Oak	5.1	J.Kemp-Buf	4.6	T.Flores-Oak	64.9	T.Flores-Oak	427	A.Powell-Oak	52

Receiving Yards		Receiving Average		Receiving TDs		Receiving Rank		Combined Net Yards		Total TDs		Total Points	
L.Alworth-SD	1602	L.Alworth-SD	23.22	D.Maynard-NYJ	14	L.Alworth-SD	871	L.Alworth-SD	1590	D.Maynard-NYJ	14	B.Cannon-Bos	132
D.Maynard-NYJ	1218	C.Frazier-Hou	18.87	L.Alworth-SD	14	D.Maynard-NYJ	679	C.Daniels-Oak	1452	L.Alworth-SD	14	P.Gogolak-Buf	115
L.Taylor-Den	1131	B.Cannon-Bos	18.38	A.Powell-Oak	12	L.Taylor-Den	596	O.Burrell-Hou	1419	A.Powell-Oak	12	H.Travenio-SD	94
A.Powell-Oak	800	B.Scarpitto-Den	18.28	B.Cannon-Bos	9	A.Powell-Oak	460	A.Haynes-Den	1404	C.Daniels-Oak	12	J.Turner-NYJ	91
C.Frazier-Hou	717	D.Maynard-NYJ	17.91	W.Frazier-Hou	8	C.Frazier-Hou	389	C.McClinton-KC	1251				

Punt Average		Field Goals		Field Goal Percent		Kickoff Returns		Kickoff Return Average		Punt Returns		Punt Return Average	
J.Wilson-SD	45.4	P.Gogolak-Buf	28	B.Cannon-Bos	63.0	A.Haynes-Den	34	A.Haynes-Den	26.5	C.Gibson-Oak	31	S.Duncan-SD	15.5
C.Johnson-NYJ	45.3	J.Turner-NYJ	20	P.Gogolak-Buf	60.9	C.Warner-Buf	32	C.Warner-Buf	25.8	S.Duncan-SD	30	W.Mitchell-KC	12.7
J.Norton-Hou	43.7	H.Travenio-SD	18	H.Travenio-SD	60.0	S.Duncan-SD	26	B.Coan-SD	25.2	B.Byrd-Buf	22	C.Gibson-Oak	11.5
P.Maguire-Buf	43.0	B.Cannon-Bos	17	M.Mercer-Oak	60.0	O.Barry-Den	26	B.Jancik-Hou	23.9	O.Barry-Den	21	B.Byrd-Buf	10.0
B.Scarpitto-Den	42.3			J.Turner-NYJ	58.8	L.Todd-Oak	20	S.Duncan-SD	23.5	W.Mitchell-KC	19	O.Barry-Den	10.0

Punt/Kick Return Yards		Punt/Kick Return TDs		Interceptions		Interception Return Yards		Interception Return TDs		Sacks		Overall Rank	
S.Duncan-SD	1076	C.Warner-Buf	2	W.Hicks-Hou	9	W.Hicks-Hou	156	G.Otto-Oak	2	Not kept		C.Daniels-Oak	1301
A.Haynes-Den	1022	S.Duncan-SD	2	B.Whitehead-SD	7	D.Grayson-Oak	145	D.Grayson-Oak	2			P.Lowe-SD	1290
C.Warner-Buf	841	W.Mitchell-KC	1	D.Paulson-NYJ	7	G.Otto-Oak	131					C.Gilchrist-Den	1096
O.Barry-Den	821	A.Haynes-Den	1	J.Norton-Hou	7	B.Whitehead-SD	127					C.McClinton-KC	1031
C.Gibson-Oak	543	C.Gibson-Oak	1	H.Clarke-Buf	7	B.Byrd-Buf	119					O.Burrell-Hou	1009

NO AVERAGE JOE

If the AFL had a hole in its ability to sell itself to a curious nation, it may well have been the absence of a strong New York franchise. Neither the arrival of coach Weeb Ewbank nor that of running back Matt Snell had significantly improved the franchise's fortunes since the team's changeover from the Titans after the 1962 season. Attendance had improved with the move into Shea Stadium in 1964, but how long would people pay to see a loser?

Armed with television money and frustration, the Jets drafted and signed Alabama quarterback Joe Namath for the unheard-of price of $427,000. Not only did the signing help create enough buzz around the Jets that they became the first team to average 50,000 per game in attendance, it was a clear sign that intra-league warfare would only grow more expensive. A merger would be good business for everybody.

Even with Namath making football interesting in the Big Apple, the team finished no differently than it had in the two previous

seasons. The Eastern Division remained Buffalo's property. The Bills again rolled over their competition on the strength of a strong defense, sturdy line play on both sides of the ball, and Pete Gogolak's kicking. (The mercurial Cookie Gilchrist had been shipped off to Denver.)

This was symptomatic of what had changed from the early AFL. Scoring was down and the quality of play was becoming much more even—the Chargers led the league in scoring with 340 points, a total that would have only rated fifth the year before. Buffalo's only real rival within the league was Sid Gillman's Chargers, who, after beating the Raiders in both head-to-head matchups, had nothing to worry about in the West. In their two in-season games, San Diego had beaten and tied the Bills, setting up the best possible confrontation in the championship game. Quarterback John Hadl had started to develop with Gillman's offense, Paul Lowe was easily the league's best back, and the Chargers could always try to get the ball to Lance Alworth downfield to break a game wide open. That much hadn't changed.

1966 NFL

TEAM	W-L-T	PCT	POST	PTS	RA	RY	RY/A	RTD	FL	PA	PC	GPY	GPY/A	PTD	PI	PSY	PRAT
Eastern Conference																	
Dal	10-3-1	.769	L	**445**-239	471-**356**	2122-**1176**	4.5-3.3	**24-6**	**10**-14	413-457	214-212	**3331**-2802	8.1-6.1	27-17	14-17	308-420	86.5-63.2
Cle	9-5	.643	—	403-259	415-450	**2166**-1894	**5.2**-4.2	18-12	**10**-19	402-406	212-221	3142-2650	7.8-6.5	**33**-14	15-**30**	237-278	90.4-55.3
Phi	9-5	.643	—	326-340	478-390	1859-1693	3.9-4.3	19-13	17-15	378-446	179-226	2159-2964	5.7-6.6	14-23	22-20	259-287	53.4-70.5
SL	8-5-1	.615	—	264-265	458-377	1601-1192	3.5-**3.2**	10-11	18-10	386-443	180-197	2292-2733	5.9-6.2	13-15	19-21	352-**433**	56.4-56.4
Was	7-7	.500	—	351-355	356-438	1377-1831	3.9-4.2	9-19	15-20	443-411	255-224	3230-3237	7.3-7.9	28-21	20-23	**216**-376	82.7-74.0
Pit	5-8-1	.385	—	316-347	375-468	1092-1786	2.9-3.8	13-11	17-16	401-397	188-192	2877-2849	7.2-7.2	18-27	22-24	523-344	63.1-69.8
Atl	3-11	.214	—	204-437	405-472	1519-2172	3.8-4.6	11-20	17-13	381-396	175-227	2362-3376	6.2-8.5	14-26	27-19	345-276	48.9-87.3
NYG	1-12-1	.077	—	263-501	380-480	1457-2053	3.8-4.3	7-23	13-7	424-**357**	208-194	2999-3086	7.1-8.6	20-36	31-17	524-194	57.7-97.2
Western Conference																	
GB	**12**-2	**.857**	LS*	335-**163**	475-446	1673-1644	3.5-3.7	18-9	19-14	318-390	193-202	2831-**2316**	**8.9-5.9**	18-**7**	**5**-28	229-357	**102.1-46.1**
Bal	9-5	.643	—	314-226	418-460	1556-1733	3.7-3.8	7-7	12-18	401-425	221-240	3172-2759	7.9-6.5	26-14	27-22	242-401	74.5-65.6
LA	8-6	.571	—	289-212	448-401	1742-1302	3.9-**3.2**	12-10	12-20	450-406	249-**190**	2891-2830	6.4-7.0	12-13	17-26	351-361	68.1-54.1
SF	6-6-2	.500	—	320-325	422-414	1790-1629	4.2-3.9	12-15	12-11	**500**-414	**261**-206	3239-2895	6.5-7.0	21-22	26-18	247-345	64.9-72.3
ChiB	5-7-2	.417	—	234-272	463-466	1927-1604	4.2-3.4	12-13	12-**23**	338-406	159-202	2016-2600	6.0-6.4	10-13	23-15	244-233	47.6-65.5
Det	4-9-1	.308	—	206-317	394-479	1429-2006	3.6-4.2	13-16	21-11	456-363	239-210	2752-2702	6.0-7.4	8-19	28-24	328-294	51.2-71.2
Min	4-9-1	.308	—	292-304	**551**-412	2091-1686	3.8-4.1	15-15	14-8	417-391	216-206	2932-2426	7.0-6.2	18-13	22-14	384-190	67.0-68.0
Aver	14	—	—	304	434	1693	3.9	13	15	407	210	2815	6.9	19	21	319	67.4

TEAM	1D	PENY	PNT	FGM/A	RTNY	RTNTD	OFFY/DEFY	NETY	NETTO	NP	PNP	DELP	PW	DELW	PRT	DR	YPD	DEL
Eastern Conference																		
Dal	**287**-221	824-778	39.2-42.4	17/31-12/31	561-382	5-6	**5145**-3558	**1587**	7	**206**	160	46	**12.1**	-1.7	5.9/ 3.5	185-190	27.8-18.7	**9.1**
Cle	278-255	747-563	39.0-39.7	9/23-19/28	554-**179**	3-3	5071-4266	805	**24**	144	**163**	-19	10.6	-1.6	5.9/ 2.6	176-173	**28.8**-24.7	4.2
Phi	231-249	666-703	39.8-39.9	18/25-20/30	507-680	6-4	3759-4370	-611	-4	-14	-67	**53**	6.7	**2.3**	2.5/ 4.2	179-182	21.0-24.0	-3.0
SL	212-209	586-761	35.6-40.7	23/40-23/41	646-395	5-2	3541-**3492**	49	-6	-1	-20	19	7.0	1.5	2.9/ 3.0	**199**-200	17.8-**17.5**	0.3
Was	225-261	591-626	42.4-38.4	22/34-21/31	570-499	4-2	4391-4692	-301	8	-4	7	-11	6.9	0.1	5.1/ 4.5	191-192	23.0-24.4	-1.4
Pit	207-238	768-835	42.1-**37.8**	21/32-19/33	323-561	5-4	3446-4291	-845	1	-31	-66	35	6.2	-0.7	3.3/ 3.9	194-199	17.8-21.6	-3.8
Atl	211-295	753-588	40.7-38.6	9/19-25/41	277-582	1-6	3536-5272	-1736	-12	-233	-193	-40	1.2	1.8	2.2/ 5.8	177-177	20.0-29.8	-9.8
NYG	236-273	602-788	38.9-39.8	16/28-13/23	337-683	4-7	3932-4945	-1013	-20	-238	-164	-74	1.1	0.4	2.6/ 6.5	185-**171**	21.3-28.9	-7.7
Western Conference																		
GB	231-211	**544**-745	41.0-41.3	12/28-15/27	**762**-246	**7-1**	4275-3603	672	18	172	128	44	11.3	0.7	**7.3/1.8**	169-**171**	25.3-21.1	4.2
Bal	237-245	617-704	**45.6**-40.6	21/39-17/33	624-568	3-4	4486-4091	395	1	88	37	51	9.2	-0.2	4.6/ 3.2	183-177	24.5-23.1	1.4
LA	255-**196**	651-704	42.8-43.8	**28/49-10/22**	703-607	5-3	4282-3771	511	17	77	111	-34	8.9	-0.9	3.8/ 3.2	182-192	23.5-19.6	3.9
SF	282-238	819-**938**	40.6-41.2	16/31-16/31	617-702	6-3	4782-4179	603	-9	-5	14	-19	6.9	0.1	3.8/ 4.3	190-192	25.2-21.8	3.4
ChiB	196-239	714-636	42.0-42.4	18/30-12/29	252-676	4-8	3699-3971	-272	3	-38	-11	-27	6.1	-0.1	2.3/ 4.2	186-185	19.9-21.5	-1.6
Det	216-240	931-564	41.1-41.1	15/30-17/31	**762**-507	2-3	3853-4414	-561	-14	-111	-103	-8	4.2	0.3	2.5/ 3.8	189-188	20.4-23.5	-3.1
Min	279-213	787-667	41.1-40.6	18/33-24/41	359-587	1-5	4639-3922	717	-14	-12	4	-16	6.7	-2.2	3.8/ 4.2	182-178	25.5-22.0	3.5
Aver	239	707	40.7	18/31	524	4	4189	—	—	—	—	—	—	—	4.2	184	22.7	—

Rushing Attempts	Rushing Yards	Rushing Average	Rushing TDs	Rushing Rank	Passing Yards	Passing Average
B.Brown-Min 251	G.Sayers-Chi 1231	L.Kelly-Cle 5.46	L.Kelly-Cle 15	G.Sayers-Chi 1311	S.Jurgensen-Was 3209	B.Starr-GB 8.99
D.Bass-LA 248	L.Kelly-Cle 1141	G.Sayers-Chi 5.38	G.Sayers-Chi 8	L.Kelly-Cle 1291	F.Ryan-Cle 2974	D.Meredith-Dal 8.15
G.Sayers-Chi 229	D.Bass-LA 1090	E.Green-Cle 5.21	D.Reeves-Dal 8	D.Bass-LA 1170	J.Brodie-SF 2810	J.Unitas-Bal 7.90
L.Kelly-Cle 209	B.Brown-Min 829	A.Whitfield-Was 5.08	D.Perkins-Dal 8	B.Brown-Min 889	D.Meredith-Dal 2805	F.Ryan-Cle 7.79
J.Taylor-GB 204	K.Willard-SF 763	T.Matte-Bal 4.43	D.Bass-LA 8	D.Reeves-Dal 837	J.Unitas-Bal 2748	S.Jurgensen-Was 7.36

Completion Percent	TD Passes	TD Percent	INT Percent	Passer Rating	Passing Rank	Receptions
B.Starr-GB 62.2	F.Ryan-Cle 29	F.Ryan-Cle 7.6	B.Starr-GB 1.2	B.Starr-GB 105.0	B.Starr-GB 1079	C.Taylor-Was 72
S.Jurgensen-Was 58.3	S.Jurgensen-Was 28	D.Meredith-Dal 7.0	D.Meredith-Dal 3.5	F.Ryan-Cle 88.2	F.Ryan-Cle 1072	P.Studstill-Det 67
M.Plum-Det 56.2	D.Meredith-Dal 24	S.Jurgensen-Was 6.4	F.Ryan-Cle 3.7	D.Meredith-Dal 87.7	D.Meredith-Dal 1043	D.Parks-SF 66
J.Unitas-Bal 56.0	J.Unitas-Bal 22	J.Unitas-Bal 6.3	R.Gabriel-LA 4.0	S.Jurgensen-Was 84.5	S.Jurgensen-Was 985	B.Hayes-Dal 64
R.Gabriel-LA 54.7	F.Tarkenton-Min 17	B.Starr-GB 5.6	S.Jurgensen-Was 4.4	J.Unitas-Bal 74.0	F.Tarkenton-Min 726	T.Moore-LA 60

Receiving Yards	Receiving Average	Receiving TDs	Receiving Rank	Combined Net Yards	Total TDs	Total Points
P.Studstill-Det 1266	R.Jefferson-Pit 24.13	B.Hayes-Dal 13	B.Hayes-Dal 681	G.Sayers-Chi 2440	D.Reeves-Dal 16	B.Gossett-LA 113
B.Hayes-Dal 1232	C.Dale-GB 23.68	C.Taylor-Was 12	P.Studstill-Det 658	L.Kelly-Cle 2014	L.Kelly-Cle 16	T.Vaughn-Dal 107
C.Taylor-Was 1119	H.Jones-NYG 21.75	G.Collins-Cle 12	C.Taylor-Was 620	C.Taylor-Was 1542	C.Taylor-Was 15	C.Gogolak-Was 105
H.Jones-NYG 1044	P.Warfield-Cle 20.58	B.Mitchell-Was 9	H.Jones-NYG 562	T.Brown-Phi 1481	B.Hayes-Dal 13	L.Michaels-Bal 98
D.Parks-SF 974	B.Hayes-Dal 19.25	J.Mackey-Bal 9	G.Collins-Cle 533	J.Roland-SL 1476		M.Clark-Pit 97

Punt Average	Field Goals	Field Goal Percent	Kickoff Returns	Kickoff Return Average	Punt Returns	Punt Return Average
D.Lee-Bal 45.6	B.Gossett-LA 28	S.Baker-Phi 72.0	R.Smith-Atl 43	G.Sayers-Chi 31.2	A.Haymond-Bal 40	J.Roland-SL 11.1
J.Kilgore-LA 42.8	J.Bakken-SL 23	M.Clark-Pit 65.6	K.Alexander-SF 37	R.Shivers-SL 28.2	J.Stiger-LA 33	T.Vaughn-Det 9.9
P.Richter-Was 42.4	C.Gogolak-Was 22	C.Gogolak-Was 64.7	C.Childs-NYG 34	T.Brown-Phi 28.1	K.Alexander-SF 30	A.Haymond-Bal 8.7
F.Lambert-Pit 42.1	L.Michaels-Bal 21	R.LeClerc-Chi 60.0	R.Shivers-SL 27	C.Williams-LA 28.0	W.Wood-GB 22	J.Stiger-LA 7.8
B.Green-Chi 42.0	M.Clark-Pit 21	G.Yepremian-Det 59.1	O.Matson-Phi 26	D.Gordon-Chi 27.4	M.Renfro-Dal 21	S.Lockhart-NYG 6.6

Punt/Kick Return Yards	Punt/Kick Return TDs	Interceptions	Interception Return Yards	Interception Return TDs	Sacks	Overall Rank
K.Alexander-SF 1182	G.Sayers-Chi 2	L.Wilson-SL 10	J.Scarpati-Phi 182	L.Wilson-SL 2	Not kept	G.Sayers-Chi 1941
R.Smith-Atl 1093	T.Brown-Phi 2	C.Williams-LA 8	L.Wilson-SL 180	B.Jeter-GB 2		L.Kelly-Cle 1636
C.Childs-NYG 855		J.Scarpati-Phi 8	B.Owens-Was 165			D.Meredith-Dal 1335
R.Shivers-SL 811		M.Howell-Cle 8	R.Fichtner-Cle 152			D.Bass-LA 1307
T.Vaughn-Det 774		R.Fichtner-Cle 8	B.Jeter-GB 142			F.Ryan-Cle 1228

A Summer of Surprises, a Fall of Change

Before the season even started, pro football was crackling with activity. Whether it was the AFL's achieving a new television contract, the improved quality of play, or concern of the bidding wars that had created events like Joe Namath's signing with the Jets, merger talk took on a new seriousness in the spring before the season. It wasn't all love and kisses, but the two leagues finalized a plan to merge entirely in 1970, hold a combined amateur draft in the future, and to play an interleague championship game, beginning with the season to come. Congress later ratified the merger and excluded it from antitrust action.

If that hadn't set NFL fans entirely on the heads, the news that came the following month was certain to: Jim Brown retired. The owner of football's career and single-season rushing records walked away when owner Art Modell demanded that he show up in camp and abandon the set of the movie *The Dirty Dozen*, in which Brown had a supporting role. Fans also had to get used to the NFL's latest addition: the Atlanta Falcons. The odd number of teams produced an in-season scheduled off-week for all teams.

The new season promised change in the Eastern Conference, because the traditional powerhouses weren't in great shape. The Brown-less Browns had to prove they'd hold up, and the Giants were a ruin. Although the Browns replaced Jim Brown pretty nicely with Leroy Kelly (second in the league in rushing yardage and tied for the league lead in touchdowns), the surprise teams were the Cowboys and the Cardinals. Tied at 8–2–1, the two clashed in Dallas, but Tom Landry's charges whipped St. Louis, 31–17, en route to the franchise's first conference title and playoff appearance.

By contrast, the Western Conference was another classic Packers finish. Lombardi's veterans again fended off an early Colts challenge. The teams were tied at 7–2 before Baltimore went into what seemed like their traditional late fade. Green Bay simply got comfortable as the weather got colder, winning their final five to walk into the NFL championship game, beat Dallas, and fulfilling their seeming destiny as the first Super Bowl champs.

1966 AFL

TEAM	W-L-T	PCT	POST	PTS	RA	RY	RY/A	RTD	FL	PA	PC	GPY	GPY/A	PTD	PI	PSY	PRAT
Eastern Division																	
Buf	9-4-1	.692	L	358-255	455-344	1892-1051	4.2-3.1	19-6	15-9	473-466	199-205	3000-3307	6.3-7.1	15-22	21-29	144-249	55.6-58.1
Bos	8-4-2	.667	—	315-283	471-369	1963-1135	4.2-3.1	17-7	13-15	393-509	186-247	2784-3565	7.1-7.0	20-26	21-22	211-209	65.7-70.7
NYJ	6-6-2	.500	—	322-312	376-388	1442-1524	3.8-3.9	15-14	9-8	514-467	251-212	3556-3064	6.9-6.6	21-19	29-21	92-310	61.7-62.1
Hou	3-11	.214	—	335-396	413-422	1515-1833	3.7-4.3	11-10	12-13	485-438	226-209	3168-3390	6.5-7.7	29-35	28-18	271-228	64.0-83.6
Mia	3-11	.214	—	213-362	394-416	1410-1510	3.6-3.6	5-15	10-15	454-425	179-198	2374-3281	5.2-7.7	16-25	32-31	326-180	39.1-62.3
Western Division																	
KC	11-2-1	.846	LS	448-276	439-353	2274-1356	5.2-3.8	19-10	16-8	377-494	199-226	3123-2876	8.3-5.8	31-18	15-33	283-262	91.4-48.8
Oak	8-5-1	.615	—	315-288	363-418	1427-1792	3.9-4.3	13-16	12-17	450-405	212-183	3425-2440	7.6-6.0	26-15	26-23	281-322	68.2-53.5
SD	7-6-1	.538	—	335-284	361-497	1537-2403	4.3-4.8	9-19	7-8	434-382	224-170	3347-2386	7.7-6.2	29-13	15-27	331-231	85.1-47.1
Den	4-10	.286	—	196-381	376-441	1173-2029	3.1-4.6	6-17	17-18	402-396	166-192	2351-2819	5.8-7.1	12-26	30-13	356-304	39.7-80.4
Aver	14			315	405	1626	4.0	13	12	442	205	3014	6.8	22	24	255	63.0

TEAM	1D	PENY	PNT	FGM/A	RTNY	RTNTD	OFFY/DEFY	NETY	NETTO	NP	PNP	DELP	PW	DELW	PRT	DR	YPD	DEL
Eastern Division																		
Buf	255-192	637-546	41.2-39.6	19/38-13/22	883-604	9-3	4748-4109	639	2	103	61	42	9.6	-0.1	4.2/ 4.0	187-199	25.4-20.6	4.7
Bos	243-243	601-757	36.5-38.5	16/32-11/26	491-310	1-3	4536-4491	45	3	32	16	16	7.8	1.2	4.4/ 4.9	199-192	22.8-23.4	-0.6
NYJ	254-231	652-913	42.5-40.4	18/35-18/28	478-418	2-4	4906-4278	628	-9	10	16	-6	7.3	-0.3	4.5/ 4.0	189-184	26.0-23.3	2.7
Hou	246-244	682-725	42.2-40.0	16/30-15/30	418-717	1-5	4412-4995	-583	-9	-61	-85	24	5.5	-2.5	3.8/ 5.9	193-193	22.9-25.9	-3.0
Mia	200-237	660-852	39.4-43.9	10/22-18/36	726-782	5-4	3458-4611	-1153	4	-149	-80	-69	3.3	-0.3	1.6/ 4.4	202-185	17.1-24.9	-7.8
Western Division																		
KC	266-222	680-592	43.8-41.3	22/28-18/28	663-584	5-4	5114-3970	1144	10	172	135	37	11.3	0.2	6.1/2.5	180-187	28.4-21.2	7.2
Oak	226-211	752-614	41.6-41.3	12/30-16/30	747-748	1-3	4571-3910	661	2	27	63	-36	7.7	0.8	4.6/ 2.8	188-197	24.3-19.8	4.5
SD	230-260	667-527	41.0-41.3	16/31-17/31	616-362	3-1	4553-4558	-5	13	51	52	-1	8.3	-0.8	5.6/ 2.6	165-174	27.6-26.2	1.4
Den	171-251	771-576	45.2-42.7	14/25-17/40	344-841	4-4	3168-4544	-1376	-16	-185	-179	-6	2.4	1.6	1.7/ 5.1	191-183	16.6-24.8	-8.2
Aver	232	678	41.0	16/30	596	3	4385								4.3	188	23.3	

Rushing Attempts		Rushing Yards		Rushing Average		Rushing TDs		Rushing Rank		Passing Yards		Passing Average	
J.Nance-Bos	299	J.Nance-Bos	1458	M.Garrett-KC	5.45	J.Nance-Bos	11	J.Nance-Bos	1568	J.Namath-NYJ	3379	L.Dawson-KC	8.90
C.Daniels-Oak	204	M.Garrett-KC	801	B.Coan-KC	5.43	D.Trull-Hou	7	C.Daniels-Oak	871	J.Hadl-SD	2846	T.Flores-Oak	8.62
B.Burnett-Buf	187	C.Daniels-Oak	801	J.Nance-Bos	4.88	C.Daniels-Oak	7	M.Garrett-KC	861	B.Parilli-Bos	2721	J.Hadl-SD	7.59
M.Snell-NYJ	178	B.Burnett-Buf	766	E.Boozer-NYJ	4.69	B.Coan-KC	7	B.Burnett-Buf	806	T.Flores-Oak	2638	J.Namath-NYJ	7.17
W.Carlton-Buf	156	W.Carlton-Buf	696	W.Carlton-Buf	4.46			W.Carlton-Buf	756	L.Dawson-KC	2527	B.Parilli-Bos	7.12
Completion Percent		**TD Passes**		**TD Percent**		**INT Percent**		**Passer Rating**		**Passing Rank**		**Receptions**	
L.Dawson-KC	56.0	L.Dawson-KC	26	L.Dawson-KC	9.2	D.Trull-Hou	2.9	L.Dawson-KC	101.7	L.Dawson-KC	994	L.Alworth-SD	73
J.Hadl-SD	53.3	T.Flores-Oak	24	T.Flores-Oak	7.8	L.Dawson-KC	3.5	T.Flores-Oak	86.2	J.Hadl-SD	978	G.Sauer-NYJ	63
M.Choboian-Den	50.3	J.Hadl-SD	23	G.Blanda-Hou	6.3	J.Hadl-SD	3.7	J.Hadl-SD	83.0	T.Flores-Oak	879	O.Taylor-KC	58
T.Flores-Oak	49.3	B.Parilli-Bos	20	J.Hadl-SD	6.1	J.Kemp-Buf	4.1	D.Trull-Hou	79.1	J.Namath-NYJ	705	C.Burford-KC	58
J.Namath-NYJ	49.3	J.Namath-NYJ	19	D.Trull-Hou	5.8	T.Flores-Oak	4.6	B.Parilli-Bos	66.9	B.Parilli-Bos	661	C.Frazier-Hou	57
Receiving Yards		**Receiving Average**		**Receiving TDs**		**Receiving Rank**		**Combined Net Yards**		**Total TDs**		**Total Points**	
L.Alworth-SD	1383	O.Taylor-KC	22.36	L.Alworth-SD	13	L.Alworth-SD	757	J.Nance-Bos	1561	L.Alworth-SD	13	B.Cappadona-Bos	119
O.Taylor-KC	1297	A.Denson-Den	20.14	C.Frazier-Hou	12	O.Taylor-KC	689	J.Auer-Mia	1476	C.Frazier-Hou	12	B.Lusteg-Buf	98
C.Frazier-Hou	1129	C.Frazier-Hou	19.81	A.Powell-Oak	11	C.Frazier-Hou	625	C.Daniels-Oak	1453	A.Powell-Oak	11	M.Mercer-KC	93
G.Sauer-NYJ	1079	A.Powell-Oak	19.36	O.Taylor-KC	8	A.Powell-Oak	568	M.Garrett-KC	1438	J.Nance-Bos	11	J.Turner-NYJ	88
A.Powell-Oak	1026	L.Alworth-SD	18.95	C.Burford-KC	8	G.Sauer-NYJ	565	L.Alworth-SD	1393	C.Daniels-Oak	10		
Punt Average		**Field Goals**		**Field Goal Percent**		**Kickoff Returns**		**Kickoff Return Average**		**Punt Returns**		**Punt Return Average**	
B.Scarpitto-Den	45.2	M.Mercer-KC	20	M.Mercer-KC	76.9	B.Jancik-Hou	34	G.Sellers-Den	28.5	R.Bird-Oak	37	S.Duncan-SD	13.2
J.Wilson-KC	43.8	B.Lusteg-Buf	19	G.Kroner-Den	56.0	C.Warner-Buf	33	B.Jancik-Hou	25.7	B.Byrd-Buf	23	E.Rutkowski-Buf	11.6
C.Johnson-NYJ	42.5	J.Turner-NYJ	18	G.Blanda-Hou	53.3	E.Thomas-KC	29	S.Duncan-SD	25.7	E.Rutkowski-Buf	18	R.Bird-Oak	8.7
G.Wilson-Mia	42.2			Van Raaphorst-SD	51.6	P.Atkins-Oak	29	C.Warner-Buf	25.6	S.Duncan-SD	18	M.Garrett-KC	8.2
J.Norton-Hou	42.1			J.Turner-NYJ	51.4	J.Auer-Mia	28	E.Boozer-NYJ	25.3	M.Garrett-KC	17	B.Byrd-Buf	8.1
Punt/Kick Return Yards		**Punt/Kick Return TDs**		**Interceptions**		**Interception Return Yards**		**Interception Return TDs**		**Sacks**		**Overall Rank**	
B.Jancik-Hou	937	G.Sellers-Den	2	J.Robinson-KC	10	J.Warren-Mia	198	T.Janik-Buf	2	Not kept		J.Nance-Bos	1620
S.Duncan-SD	880			B.Hunt-KC	10	R.Hall-Bos	159					C.Daniels-Oak	1172
C.Warner-Buf	846			W.West-Mia	8	J.Robinson-KC	136					L.Dawson-KC	1161
J.Auer-Mia	797			T.Janik-Buf	8	T.Janik-Buf	136					M.Garrett-KC	1131
E.Thomas-KC	729			S.Duncan-SD	7	J.Norton-Hou	125					J.Hadl-SD	1087

WARTIME CONSIGLIERI OUTGUNNED BY PEACE

The AFL had arrived and had nothing left to apologize for. Any doubts they were on a par with the NFL were moot once furtive merger talks between the Chiefs' Lamar Hunt and the Cowboys' Tex Schramm started up early in 1966. Unfortunately, the negotiations were almost derailed when Giants owner Wellington Mara signed kicker Pete Gogolak away from the Bills, leading the AFL to suddenly declare war. There was no better way to try and win an interleague war than tabbing Al Davis from the Raiders to replace Joe Foss as commissioner.

As determined to win in the boardroom as on the field, Davis pursued and signed leading NFL stars like quarterbacks Roman Gabriel and John Brodie, and tight end Mike Ditka. With the penalty of open warfare spelled out so bluntly, peace was quickly achieved. The signings after Gogolak's defection were politely voided, and the AFL agreed to fully merge into the NFL as the core of a realigned American Football Conference in 1970. NFL commissioner Pete Rozelle would reign over both leagues. Davis, disgusted by the speedy settlement, resigned his post and returned the Raiders as general manager and managing partner, having come and gone from Oakland in the space of a single offseason.

Like the NFL, the AFL expanded towards the South, launching the Miami Dolphins. Deposited into the Eastern Division, they had little impact on a race that was a simple showdown between the Bills and Patriots. After years of reliance on an offense that depended on Babe Parilli hitting Gino Cappelletti or Jim Colclough early and often, the 1966 Pats had Jim Nance leading the league in rushing yardage and rushing touchdowns. The Patriots needed to beat or tie the Jets in the final weekend to win the division title, but Boston lost in New York on the final Saturday, and had to watch as Buffalo beat the Oilers on Sunday to pull ahead and into the playoffs.

The Western Division wasn't nearly as interesting. The Chiefs enjoyed the benefits of alternating between having Len Dawson steadily guide a ball-control offense and putting one of the league's most punishing defenses on the field.

1967 NFL

TEAM	W-L-T	PCT	POST	PTS	RA	RY	RY/A	RTD	FL	PA	PC	GPY	GPY/A	PTD	PI	PSY	PRAT
Capitol Conference																	
Dal	9-5	.643	CL	342-268	477-**339**	1900-**1081**	4.0-3.2	13-11	14-**19**	417-482	210-260	3093-3167	7.4-6.6	28-21	28-29	294-377	69.4-63.9
Phi	6-7-1	.462	—	351-409	328-434	1250-1741	3.8-4.0	12-16	16-14	445-480	244-255	3463-3382	7.8-7.0	30-29	24-21	369-151	80.2-77.6
Was	5-6-3	.455	—	347-353	345-431	1247-1852	3.6-4.3	13-19	14-14	**527**-468	**301**-261	**3887**-3713	7.4-7.9	31-25	17-20	**157**-310	86.6-81.6
NO	3-11	.214	—	233-379	334-469	1192-2092	3.6-4.5	9-22	14-10	478-410	237-207	2989-3035	6.3-7.4	13-25	23-22	391-199	58.5-73.0
Century Conference																	
Cle	9-5	.643	C	334-297	444-459	**2139**-1767	**4.8**-3.8	15-15	17-14	333-454	160-250	2314-3231	6.9-7.1	22-19	18-22	372-332	70.6-71.4
NYG	7-7	.500	—	369-379	436-416	1864-1799	4.3-4.3	16-20	10-15	406-389	221-195	3382-2731	**8.3**-7.0	**33**-25	20-17	342-246	**88.7**-76.3
SL	6-7-1	.462	—	333-356	472-410	1839-1502	3.9-3.7	15-13	11-13	431-360	204-169	3170-3023	7.4-8.4	20-26	35-19	229-340	53.8-78.3
Pit	4-9-1	.308	—	281-320	431-418	1397-1377	3.2-3.3	13-12	16-13	442-397	214-201	2781-2854	6.3-7.2	19-22	29-26	270-276	55.6-65.4
Coastal Conference																	
LA	**11**-1-2	**.917**	DC	**398-196**	**490**-361	1906-1119	3.9-**3.1**	16-6	13-13	390-445	206-212	2947-2694	7.6-6.1	28-14	**16-32**	213-287	84.4-47.5
Bal	**11**-1-2	**.917**	D	394-198	443-387	1645-1411	3.7-3.6	**21-5**	**8**-8	457-395	265-221	3561-2678	7.8-6.8	22-13	17-**32**	198-246	83.4-54.2
SF	7-7	.500	—	273-337	434-407	1764-1698	4.1-4.2	16-17	10-13	469-403	228-212	2862-2755	6.1-6.8	16-19	26-16	208-**409**	56.3-73.6
Atl	1-12-1	.077	—	175-422	344-504	1303-2139	3.8-4.2	6-18	14-10	370-421	179-238	2144-3588	5.8-8.5	13-31	25-17	434-196	50.1-92.4
Central Conference																	
GB	9-4-1	.692	CLS*	332-209	474-443	1915-1923	4.0-4.3	18-7	10-14	331-337	182-155	2758-**1644**	**8.3-4.9**	15-13	27-26	394-267	63.7-**41.5**
ChiB	7-6-1	.538	—	239-218	489-419	1852-1531	3.8-3.7	12-11	14-16	268-384	131-164	1673-2146	6.2-5.6	9-14	18-28	232-271	52.0-42.7
Det	5-7-2	.417	—	260-259	473-471	1907-1795	4.0-3.8	14-15	21-10	351-**312**	160-**143**	1826-2089	5.2-6.7	14-**11**	19-23	195-356	52.5-49.2
Min	3-8-3	.273	—	233-294	454-500	1811-2104	4.0-4.2	10-12	13-**19**	336-314	150-149	1951-2071	5.8-6.6	11-17	24-16	284-319	44.6-65.9
Aver	14	—	—	306	429	1683	3.9	14	13	403	206	2800	6.9	20	23	286	66.6

TEAM	1D	PENY	PNT	FGM/A	RTNY	RTNTD	OFFY/DEFY	NETY	NETTO	NP	PNP	DELP	PW	DELW	PRT	DR	YPD	DEL
Capitol Conference																		
Dal	261-236	785-717	40.4-42.5	9/23-**8**/23	651-619	4-3	4699-3871	828	6	74	93	-19	8.9	0.1	4.0/ 3.2	194-191	24.2-20.3	4.0
Phi	239-286	830-715	38.3-**38.8**	12/19-15/32	432-559	3-7	4344-4972	-628	-5	-58	-72	14	5.6	1.0	4.7/ 5.1	183-179	23.7-27.8	-4.0
Was	280-274	588-882	41.3-40.1	7/26-10/24	386-485	3-2	4977-5255	-278	3	-6	-11	5	6.8	-0.3	**6.0**/ 5.4	191-191	26.1-27.5	-1.5
NO	220-276	785-824	42.9-39.9	14/32-15/29	412-564	5-**1**	3790-4928	-1138	-5	-146	-115	-31	3.3	-0.3	3.2/ 4.8	187-184	20.3-26.8	-6.5
Century Conference																		
Cle	238-281	773-655	37.1-39.9	11/23-13/25	732-**360**	6-3	4081-4666	-585	1	37	-45	**82**	7.9	1.1	3.6/ 4.2	174-182	23.5-25.6	-2.2
NYG	274-261	842-774	36.0-39.7	10/21-14/21	311-430	0-3	4904-4284	620	2	-10	60	-70	6.8	0.3	5.6/ 4.7	171-**170**	28.7-25.2	3.5
SL	248-216	720-782	40.8-39.0	**27**/39-12/**19**	403-548	1-7	4780-4185	595	-14	-23	-6	-17	6.4	0.1	3.4/ 5.3	192-198	24.9-21.1	3.8
Pit	252-228	759-833	38.1-38.9	12/22-16/30	407-645	3-5	3908-3955	-47	-6	-39	-28	-11	6.0	-1.5	3.0/ 3.8	192-189	20.4-20.9	-0.6
Coastal Conference																		
LA	262-200	854-912	42.2-40.8	20/**43**-12/26	**804**-426	4-3	4640-3526	1114	**16**	**202**	**157**	45	**12.1**	-0.1	5.5/ 2.3	**195**-202	23.8-**17.5**	6.3
Bal	**289**-208	**458-927**	42.3-39.4	20/37-17/28	776-416	5-3	**5008**-3843	**1165**	15	196	**157**	39	11.9	0.1	5.8/ 2.6	172-173	**29.1**-22.2	**6.9**
SF	242-237	931-596	37.6-43.8	14/33-17/35	512-467	1-5	4418-4044	374	-7	-64	3	-67	5.4	**1.6**	3.3/ 4.0	189-189	23.4-21.4	2.0
Atl	180-294	866-853	**43.7**-39.9	7/18-16/39	437-734	3-4	3013-5531	-2518	-12	-247	-258	11	0.8	0.7	1.7/ 6.6	182-182	16.6-30.4	-13.8
Central Conference																		
GB	243-**183**	531-482	36.5-41.6	19/29-14/28	441-392	6-4	4279-**3300**	979	3	123	94	29	10.1	-0.6	3.5/**0.9**	182-185	23.5-17.8	5.7
ChiB	175-215	953-782	42.9-41.3	13/26-10/26	528-414	**8**-2	3293-3406	-113	12	21	39	-18	7.5	-0.0	2.4/ 1.8	188-180	17.5-18.9	-1.4
Det	215-205	712-822	40.5-39.3	7/21-12/29	440-558	6-6	3538-3528	10	-7	1	-27	28	7.0	-1.0	2.4/ 2.3	188-192	18.8-18.4	0.4
Min	199-217	1075-906	41.6-38.9	17/33-18/31	423-478	5-5	3478-3856	-378	-2	-61	-40	-21	5.5	-1.0	1.9/ 3.4	193-186	18.0-20.7	-2.7
Aver	239	779	40.3	14/28	506	4	4197	—	—	—	—	—	—	—	4.2	186	22.6	—

Rushing Attempts	Rushing Yards	Rushing Average	Rushing TDs	Rushing Rank	Passing Yards	Passing Average
L.Kelly-Cle 235	L.Kelly-Cle 1205	L.Kelly-Cle 5.13	L.Kelly-Cle 11	L.Kelly-Cle 1315	S.Jurgensen-Was 3747	B.Starr-GB 8.68
J.Roland-SL 234	D.Osborn-Min 972	E.Green-Cle 4.90	J.Roland-SL 10	D.Osborn-Min 992	J.Unitas-Bal 3428	F.Tarkenton-NYG 8.19
D.Osborn-Min 215	G.Sayers-Chi 880	E.Koy-NYG 4.82	T.Matte-Bal 9	J.Roland-SL 976	N.Snead-Phi 3399	J.Unitas-Bal 7.86
M.Farr-Det 206	J.Roland-SL 876	G.Sayers-Chi 4.73	G.Sayers-Chi 7	G.Sayers-Chi 950	F.Tarkenton-NYG 3088	N.Snead-Phi 7.83
D.Perkins-Dal 201	M.Farr-Det 860	D.Osborn-Min 4.52		M.Farr-Det 890	J.Hart-SL 3008	J.Hart-SL 7.58
Completion Percent	**TD Passes**	**TD Percent**	**INT Percent**	**Passer Rating**	**Passing Rank**	**Receptions**
J.Unitas-Bal 58.5	S.Jurgensen-Was 31	F.Tarkenton-NYG 7.7	S.Jurgensen-Was 3.1	S.Jurgensen-Was 87.3	S.Jurgensen-Was 1389	C.Taylor-Was 70
S.Jurgensen-Was 56.7	F.Tarkenton-NYG 29	F.Ryan-Cle 7.1	R.Gabriel-LA 3.5	F.Tarkenton-NYG 85.9	J.Unitas-Bal 1174	J.Smith-Was 67
N.Snead-Phi 55.3	N.Snead-Phi 29	R.Gabriel-LA 6.7	J.Unitas-Bal 3.7	R.Gabriel-LA 85.2	R.Gabriel-LA 995	J.Rhome-Bal 63
B.Starr-GB 54.8	R.Gabriel-LA 25	N.Snead-Phi 6.7	J.Brodie-SF 4.6	J.Unitas-Bal 83.6	F.Tarkenton-NYG 929	B.Mitchell-Was 60
F.Tarkenton-NYG 54.1		D.Meredith-Dal 6.3	G.Cuozzo-NO 4.6	N.Snead-Phi 80.0	N.Snead-Phi 885	B.Hawkins-Phi 59
Receiving Yards	**Receiving Average**	**Receiving TDs**	**Receiving Rank**	**Combined Net Yards**	**Total TDs**	**Total Points**
B.Hawkins-Phi 1265	J.Snow-LA 26.25	H.Jones-NYG 13	B.Hawkins-Phi 683	G.Sayers-Chi 1689	H.Jones-NYG 14	J.Bakken-SL 117
H.Jones-NYG 1209	H.Jones-NYG 24.67	J.Smith-Was 12	H.Jones-NYG 670	L.Kelly-Cle 1677	L.Kelly-Cle 13	B.Gossett-LA 108
J.Smith-SL 1205	P.Warfield-Cle 21.94	B.Hayes-Dal 10	J.Smith-SL 648	B.Hawkins-Phi 1515	J.Smith-Was 12	L.Michaels-Bal 106
B.Hayes-Dal 998	J.Smith-SL 21.52	B.Hawkins-Phi 10	B.Hayes-Dal 549	T.Crutcher-SF 1408	G.Sayers-Chi 12	D.Chandler-GB 96
L.Rentzel-Dal 996	B.Hawkins-Phi 21.44		C.Taylor-Was 540	R.Smith-Atl 1337	T.Matte-Bal 12	H.Jones-NYG 84
Punt Average	**Field Goals**	**Field Goal Percent**	**Kickoff Returns**	**Kickoff Return Average**	**Punt Returns**	**Punt Return Average**
P.Studstill-Det 44.5	J.Bakken-SL 27	J.Bakken-SL 69.2	R.Smith-Atl 39	T.Williams-GB 41.1	T.Crutcher-SF 27	B.Davis-Cle 12.7
B.Lothridge-Atl 43.7	L.Michaels-Bal 20	D.Chandler-GB 65.5	T.Crutcher-SF 31	G.Sayers-Chi 37.7	A.Haymond-Bal 26	B.Hayes-Dal 11.5
T.McNeill-NO 42.9	B.Gossett-LA 20	S.Baker-Phi 63.2	C.Childs-NYG 29	J.Gilliam-NO 30.1	B.Grim-Min 25	T.Crutcher-SF 9.2
B.Green-Chi 42.9	D.Chandler-GB 19	M.Clark-Pit 54.5	W.Roberts-NO 28	T.Vaughn-Det 27.9	B.Hayes-Dal 24	R.Harris-Was 9.0
D.Lee-Bal 42.3	F.Cox-Min 17	L.Michaels-Bal 54.1	B.Davis-Cle 27	T.Crutcher-SF 26.6	R.Harris-Was 23	P.Spiller-SL 8.3
Punt/Kick Return Yards	**Punt/Kick Return TDs**	**Interceptions**	**Interception Return Yards**	**Interception Return TDs**	**Sacks**	**Overall Rank**
T.Crutcher-SF 1075	T.Williams-GB 4	D.Whitsell-NO 10	L.Barney-Det 232	L.Barney-Det 3	Not kept	L.Kelly-Cle 1536
R.Smith-Atl 1068	G.Sayers-Chi 4	L.Barney-Det 10	D.Whitsell-NO 178			G.Sayers-Chi 1486
B.Davis-Cle 937		E.Meador-LA 8	K.Reaves-Atl 153			S.Jurgensen-Was 1455
R.Harris-Was 788		P.Krause-Was 8	R.Volk-Bal 145			J.Unitas-Bal 1263
W.Roberts-NO 787		B.Jeter-GB 8	B.Boyd-Bal 145			F.Tarkenton-NYG 1255

1967 NFL: Addition by Division

With the league expanding by one more team—the New Orleans Saints were now in the fold—the NFL divided its Eastern and Western Conferences into two four-team divisions. The Century and Capital Divisions would play in the Eastern Conference, and the Central and Coastal Divisions in the Western. Although there was some of the NFL's murky geography involved—Atlanta is on a coast?—the realignment did create the first formal linking of the Bears, Packers, Lions, and Vikings into a single group. Hard-hitting rookies Lem Barney in Detroit and Alan Page in Minnesota punctuated the new black 'n' blue division.

The new alignment produced an upset. Baltimore did not win their division or even get to the playoffs despite matching Los Angeles for the league's best record. The new tiebreaker system determined that the Rams were the Coastal Division champs, on the basis of head-to-head results. It was a bittersweet year for the Colts. Baltimore grabbed Bubba Smith with the first selection in the first merged draft (finagling the precious pick from the Saints), but greats Lenny Moore and Raymond Berry played their final seasons.

This also marked the end for a few great Packers of the era. After being drafted by the Saints in the expansion draft, Paul Hornung discovered he'd suffered irreparable damage to his neck and back, and retired before a game was played. Jim Taylor shut down his career after the indignity of also finishing his career a Saint, and Jim Ringo made his last snap. And in the end, after winning the already legendary "Ice Bowl" and Super Bowl II, Vince Lombardi made his own decision to retire.

The war in Vietnam caused change everywhere, even in the NFL. Former Cleveland Browns defensive end Don Steinbrunner was killed when his plane was shot down in Vietnam in July. (Bob Kalsu, a Buffalo Bill, would be the only other player killed in action in Vietnam.) St. Louis quarterback Jim Hart, undrafted by either league in 1966, got a chance to play in '67 when Charley Johnson was called to active military duty. Hart started every game for the Cardinals and threw for 3,008 yards.

1967 AFL

TEAM	W-L-T	PCT	POST	PTS	RA	RY	RY/A	RTD	FL	PA	PC	GPY	GPY/A	PTD	PI	PSY	PRAT
Eastern Division																	
Hou	9-4-1	.692	L	258-199	476-424	2122-1637	4.5-3.9	12-7	7-13	332-461	143-228	1532-2619	4.6-5.7	11-10	20-26	151-201	43.1-50.7
NYJ	8-5-1	.615	—	371-329	389-386	1307-1633	3.4-4.2	17-14	8-6	515-424	271-195	4128-2489	8.0-5.9	27-20	29-27	283-347	73.3-54.1
Buf	4-10	.286	—	237-285	371-437	1271-1622	3.4-3.7	9-11	13-9	434-377	183-162	2763-2191	6.4-5.8	14-17	34-27	446-366	41.9-47.3
Mia	4-10	.286	—	219-407	326-466	1323-2145	4.1-4.6	10-18	16-8	480-349	229-188	2741-3082	5.7-8.8	16-31	28-28	405-247	52.4-79.9
Bos	3-10-1	.231	—	280-389	391-417	1604-1350	4.1-3.2	10-12	22-17	434-423	191-211	2784-3123	6.4-7.4	20-28	32-17	361-267	50.1-79.7
Western Division																	
Oak	13-1	.929	LS	468-233	458-352	1928-1129	4.2-3.2	19-9	13-15	464-459	236-189	3541-2831	7.6-6.2	33-18	23-30	353-666	79.3-47.9
KC	9-5	.643	—	408-254	462-343	2018-1408	4.4-4.1	18-10	8-18	382-462	213-229	2773-2890	7.3-6.3	26-13	19-31	301-354	80.8-50.9
SD	8-5-1	.615	—	360-352	417-441	1715-1553	4.1-3.5	14-17	10-10	463-464	230-230	3517-3455	7.6-7.4	26-26	24-13	107-303	72.3-81.4
Den	3-11	.214	—	256-409	420-444	1265-2076	3.0-4.7	10-21	12-13	374-459	150-214	2190-3289	5.9-7.2	17-27	18-25	508-164	55.0-65.0
Aver	14	—		317	412	1617	3.9	13	12	431	205	2885	6.7	21	25	324	61.6

TEAM	1D	PENY	PNT	FGM/A	RTNY	RTNTD	OFFY/DEFY	NETY	NETTO	NP	PNP	DELP	PW	DELW	PRT	DR	YPD	DEL
Eastern Division																		
Hou	207-233	698-614	42.6-41.0	14/28-23/42	931-539	8-1	3503-4055	-552	12	59	2	57	8.5	1.0	1.7/2.8	172-171	20.4-23.7	-3.3
NYJ	282-203	691-717	42.1-43.2	17/32-14/26	648-1022	2-7	5152-3775	1377	-4	42	99	-57	8.1	0.5	5.2/2.4	192-188	26.8-20.1	6.8
Buf	203-201	828-507	43.1-41.0	16/27-17/38	600-855	4-5	3588-3447	141	-11	-48	-32	-16	5.8	-1.8	1.9/1.9	195-193	18.4-17.9	0.5
Mia	212-269	490-691	41.6-41.1	8/18-14/26	530-663	2-4	3659-4980	-1321	-8	-188	-142	-46	2.3	1.7	2.4/5.0	178-174	20.6-28.6	-8.1
Bos	219-219	520-722	40.5-41.9	16/31-19/31	669-892	3-8	4027-4206	-179	-20	-109	-95	-14	4.3	-0.8	2.5/5.2	200-195	20.1-21.6	-1.4
Western Division																		
Oak	250-182	768-702	44.3-41.9	20/30-9/14	1046-459	6-2	5116-3294	1822	9	235	188	47	12.9	0.1	4.9/1.9	212-214	24.1-15.4	8.7
KC	251-221	680-757	41.3-43.0	21/36-14/25	823-802	5-7	4490-3944	546	22	154	134	20	10.9	-1.8	4.5/2.5	181-184	24.8-21.4	3.4
SD	259-251	817-666	37.5-45.2	15/30-14/27	754-553	5-1	5125-4705	420	-11	8	17		7.2	1.3	5.5/5.7	180-187	28.5-25.2	3.3
Den	172-276	512-628	44.9-41.5	12/28-15/31	764-980	4-4	2947-5201	-2254	11	-153	-144	-9	3.2	-0.2	2.4/4.5	203-207	14.5-25.1	-10.6
Aver	228	667	42.2	15/29	752	4	4179	—	—	—	—	—	—	—	3.8	190	22.0	—

Rushing Attempts		Rushing Yards		Rushing Average		Rushing TDs		Rushing Rank		Passing Yards		Passing Average	
J.Nance-Bos	269	J.Nance-Bos	1216	B.Hubbert-SD	5.54	E.Boozer-NYJ	10	J.Nance-Bos	1286	J.Namath-NYJ	4007	J.Namath-NYJ	8.16
H.Granger-Hou	236	H.Granger-Hou	1194	H.Granger-Hou	5.06	M.Garrett-KC	9	H.Granger-Hou	1254	J.Hadl-SD	3365	J.Hadl-SD	7.88
M.Garrett-KC	236	M.Garrett-KC	1087	W.Campbell-Hou	4.65	D.Post-SD	7	M.Garrett-KC	1177	D.Lamonica-Oak	3228	D.Lamonica-Oak	7.60
D.Post-SD	161	D.Post-SD	663	M.Garrett-KC	4.61	J.Nance-Bos	7	D.Post-SD	733	L.Dawson-KC	2651	L.Dawson-KC	7.43
K.Lincoln-Buf	159	B.Hubbert-SD	643	J.Nance-Bos	4.52	H.Granger-Hou	6	B.Hubbert-SD	663	J.Kemp-Buf	2503	J.Kemp-Buf	6.78

Completion Percent		TD Passes		TD Percent		INT Percent		Passer Rating		Passing Rank		Receptions	
L.Dawson-KC	57.7	D.Lamonica-Oak	30	D.Lamonica-Oak	7.1	D.Lamonica-Oak	4.7	L.Dawson-KC	83.7	J.Namath-NYJ	1014	G.Sauer-NYJ	75
J.Namath-NYJ	52.5	J.Namath-NYJ	26	L.Dawson-KC	6.7	L.Dawson-KC	4.8	D.Lamonica-Oak	80.8	D.Lamonica-Oak	964	D.Maynard-NYJ	71
D.Lamonica-Oak	51.8	J.Hadl-SD	24	J.Hadl-SD	5.6	J.Hadl-SD	5.2	J.Hadl-SD	74.5	J.Hadl-SD	923	J.Clancy-Mia	67
J.Hadl-SD	50.8	L.Dawson-KC	24	B.Parilli-Bos	5.5	S.Tensi-Den	5.2	J.Namath-NYJ	73.8	L.Dawson-KC	766	O.Taylor-KC	59
B.Griese-Mia	50.2	B.Parilli-Bos	19	J.Namath-NYJ	5.3	B.Griese-Mia	5.4	B.Griese-Mia	61.6			H.Dixon-Oak	59

Receiving Yards		Receiving Average		Receiving TDs		Receiving Rank		Combined Net Yards		Total TDs		Total Points	
D.Maynard-NYJ	1434	V.Biggs-Oak	21.90	O.Taylor-KC	11	D.Maynard-NYJ	767	F.Little-Den	1626	E.Boozer-NYJ	13	G.Blanda-Oak	116
G.Sauer-NYJ	1189	D.Maynard-NYJ	20.20	A.Denson-Den	11	G.Sauer-NYJ	625	H.Granger-Hou	1494	O.Taylor-KC	12	J.Stenerud-KC	108
L.Alworth-SD	1010	B.Cannon-Oak	19.66	D.Maynard-NYJ	10	L.Alworth-SD	550	D.Maynard-NYJ	1452	A.Denson-Den	11	B.Cappadona-Bos	95
O.Taylor-KC	958	A.Denson-Den	19.54	W.Frazier-SD	10	O.Taylor-KC	534	J.Nance-Bos	1412			Van Raaphorst-SD	90
W.Frazier-SD	922	L.Alworth-SD	19.42	B.Cannon-Oak	10	W.Frazier-SD	511	N.Smith-KC	1400			J.Turner-NYJ	87

Punt Average		Field Goals		Field Goal Percent		Kickoff Returns		Kickoff Return Average		Punt Returns		Punt Return Average	
B.Scarpitto-Den	44.9	J.Stenerud-KC	21	G.Blanda-Oak	66.7	N.Smith-KC	41	Z.Moore-Hou	28.9	R.Bird-Oak	46	F.Little-Den	16.9
M.Eischeid-Oak	44.3	G.Blanda-Oak	20	M.Mercer-Buf	59.3	N.Smith-KC	35	N.Smith-KC	28.0	S.Duncan-SD	36	R.Bird-Oak	13.3
P.Maguire-Buf	43.1	J.Turner-NYJ	17	J.Stenerud-KC	58.3	E.Crabtree-Bos	30	F.Little-Den	26.9	B.Byrd-Buf	30	S.Duncan-SD	12.1
J.Norton-Hou	42.6	M.Mercer-Buf	16	J.Turner-NYJ	53.1	D.Post-SD	30	D.Post-SD	24.7	N.Smith-KC	26	B.Baird-NYJ	8.8
J.Wilson-KC	42.4	B.Cappadona-Bos	16	B.Cappadona-Bos	51.6	A.Haynes-Mia	22	J.Tolbert-SD	24.5	B.Baird-NYJ	25	J.Bellino-Bos	8.6

Punt/Kick Return Yards		Punt/Kick Return TDs		Interceptions		Interception Return Yards		Interception Return TDs		Sacks		Overall Rank	
N.Smith-KC	1360	N.Smith-KC	1	Westmoreland-Mia	10	M.Farr-Hou	264	M.Farr-Hou	3	Not kept		H.Granger-Hou	1419
F.Little-Den	1212	Z.Moore-Hou	1	T.Janik-Buf	10	T.Janik-Buf	222	N.Wilson-Den	2			J.Nance-Bos	1389
R.Bird-Oak	755	F.Little-Den	1	M.Farr-Hou	10	W.Powers-Oak	154	W.Powers-Oak	2			M.Garrett-KC	1328
E.Crabtree-Bos	732			G.Sellers-Den	7	N.Wilson-Den	153	T.Janik-Buf	2			D.Lamonica-Oak	1114
S.Duncan-SD	665			W.Brown-Oak	7	K.Houston-Hou	151	K.Houston-Hou	2			J.Hadl-SD	1060

OAKLAND UPSETS AFL HOPES

Upsets wound up defining the season. The Chiefs' hopes of avenging their Super Bowl loss and the league's fervent wish that the Jets would finally win a division title both came to naught.

The real surprise was that the Jets didn't finally do it. Despite injuries to both of their best running backs, Matt Snell and Emerson Boozer, they were in first place in the Eastern Division after 10 games. Even with Joe Namath becoming the first pro quarterback to pass for 4,000 yards in a season, the Jets still lost three straight games—at home to Denver and Kansas City, and then on the road in Oakland—to provide an opening for the Oilers.

After starting off as the league's marquee team, Houston had been moribund since 1962. The Oilers no longer featured the famous air show, having finally discarded George Blanda before the season. Instead, Houston was a young team, with linebacker George Webster winning the league's Rookie of the Year award, and fellow rookie Ken Houston beginning a Hall of Fame career as a safety. Allowing a league-low 18 touchdowns, the Oilers kept things close. Rather than bombing their way to fame, glory, and turnovers, the new-look Oilers relied on second-year running back Hoyle Granger to bang out yardage and provide the margin for victory. It might not have been as much fun from the stands, but it beat finishing in the basement for the fourth straight season.

The class of the AFL was again in the Western Division, but it wouldn't be the defending champion Chiefs. Perhaps all Daryle Lamonica needed to fully blossom into his Mad Bomber reputation was a chance to play instead of watching Jack Kemp as Buffalo's backup. Perhaps he was overdue for an introduction to Vertical Offense. Maybe it was getting protection from an incomparable rookie guard, Gene Upshaw. Whatever it was, the confidence of a young assistant named Ron Wolf had scored another surprising find for Al Davis. After liberating Lamonica from the Bills' bench, the quarterback flung a league-leading 30 touchdowns to help lead the Raiders to an outstanding 13–1 record and their first AFL title.

1968 NFL

TEAM	W-L-T	PCT	POST	PTS	RA	RY	RY/A	RTD	FL	PA	PC	GPY	GPY/A	PTD	PI	PSY	PRAT
Capitol Conference																	
Dal	12-2	.857	C	**431**-186	480-**369**	2091-**1195**	4.4-**3.2**	**22-2**	15-15	399-428	217-220	**3295**-2838	8.3-6.6	25-20	18-26	269-**400**	83.9-62.8
NYG	7-7	.500	—	294-325	474-425	1882-2001	4.0-4.7	13-22	13-14	366-364	195-191	2715-2498	7.4-6.9	21-18	17-26	273-158	77.2-61.1
Was	5-9	.357	—	249-358	360-497	1164-2194	3.2-4.4	6-18	19-14	408-359	227-202	2824-2662	6.9-7.4	23-16	18-21	340-173	77.7-70.4
Phi	2-12	.143	—	202-351	369-515	1411-2141	3.8-4.2	3-18	13-7	380-327	194-182	2357-2557	6.2-7.8	16-20	29-13	207-184	52.7-84.9
Century Conference																	
Cle	10-4	.714	CL	394-273	447-423	2031-1842	4.5-4.4	20-11	14-14	363-439	184-213	3039-2447	8.4-**5.6**	27-19	16-**32**	**181**-199	85.6-49.8
SL	9-4-1	.692	—	325-289	463-423	1996-1558	4.3-3.7	**22**-10	**11**-8	385-399	169-210	2389-3261	6.2-8.2	16-23	20-13	202-**400**	56.7-85.6
NO	4-9-1	.308	—	246-327	409-439	1527-2105	3.7-4.8	7-13	**11-26**	439-366	210-**153**	2549-2483	5.8-6.8	17-25	29-16	213-297	51.5-69.7
Pit	2-11-1	.154	—	244-397	399-441	1721-1624	4.3-3.7	7-14	14-9	**451**-413	211-220	2764-3360	6.1-8.1	22-29	26-17	285-199	58.8-86.6
Coastal Conference																	
Bal	**13**-1	**.929**	CLS	402-**144**	463-375	1809-1339	3.9-3.6	16-6	12-12	359-432	196-224	3094-2405	**8.6-5.6**	**28-9**	22-29	222-367	84.0-47.5
LA	10-3-1	.769	—	312-200	**503**-397	1932-1305	3.8-3.3	14-9	12-19	384-353	189-158	2413-2196	6.3-6.2	20-12	17-25	241-383	68.2-**47.1**
SF	7-6-1	.538	—	303-310	443-445	1784-1776	4.0-4.0	11-12	14-11	417-416	**239**-201	3107-2548	7.5-6.1	24-19	23-20	182-304	77.1-63.1
Atl	2-12	.143	—	170-389	366-518	1305-2235	3.6-4.3	9-17	15-16	326-389	158-248	2386-3306	7.3-8.5	9-30	24-14	527-221	51.5-101.3
Central Conference																	
Min	8-6	.571	C	282-242	500-432	1921-1903	3.8-4.4	19-8	14-22	282-**315**	154-185	1995-2162	7.1-6.9	11-16	17-16	310-307	65.0-75.4
ChiB	7-7	.500	—	250-333	500-427	**2377**-1704	**4.8**-4.0	14-17	16-12	343-333	158-172	1868-2893	5.4-8.7	10-25	21-18	187-226	47.4-83.8
GB	6-7-1	.462	—	281-227	450-476	1749-1800	3.9-3.8	12-11	18-17	318-327	188-157	2651-**2031**	8.3-6.2	21-14	**15**-17	376-235	**88.4**-60.6
Det	4-8-2	.333	—	207-241	433-457	1702-1680	3.9-3.7	6-13	17-12	377-337	204-157	2649-2448	7.0-7.3	17-12	**15**-24	329-291	74.9-53.4
Aver	14	—	—	287	441	1775	4.0	13	14	375	193	2631	7.0	19	20	272	68.7

TEAM	1D	PENY	PNT	FGM/A	RTNY	RTNTD	OFFY/DEFY	NETY	NETTO	NP	PNP	DELP	PW	DELW	PRT	DR	YPD	DEL
Capitol Conference																		
Dal	**297**-202	751-657	40.9-40.4	17/29-**9**/22	680-458	**7**-1	**5117**-3633	**1484**	8	245	**156**	89	13.1	-1.1	5.7/ 3.1	178-189	**28.7**-19.2	**9.5**
NYG	256-263	608-579	36.0-40.0	14/24-10/23	491-294	2-3	4324-4341	-17	10	-31	39	-70	6.2	0.8	4.8/ 3.5	167-**161**	25.9-27.0	-1.1
Was	223-259	643-879	43.3-39.6	9/19-23/32	419-677	3-7	3648-4683	-1035	-2	-109	-94	-15	4.3	0.7	4.3/ 4.5	179-179	20.4-26.2	-5.8
Phi	197-256	666-843	41.3-38.9	19/30-24/35	315-678	2-2	3561-4514	-953	-22	-149	-167	18	3.3	-1.3	2.5/ 5.7	165-167	21.6-27.0	-5.4
Century Conference																		
Cle	248-259	841-620	37.3-39.9	18/24-14/26	482-272	2-3	4889-4090	799	**16**	121	131	-10	10.0	-0.0	**6.3**/ 2.1	179-180	27.3-22.7	4.6
SL	245-238	708-728	41.6-**38.1**	15/24-15/33	421-439	2-2	4183-4419	-236	-10	36	-60	96	7.9	1.6	3.5/ 5.7	173-174	24.2-25.4	-1.2
NO	224-228	843-757	37.6-40.8	19/**37**-12/27	415-614	3-4	3863-4291	-428	2	-81	-28	-53	5.0	-0.5	2.5/ 4.3	**194**-194	19.9-22.1	-2.2
Pit	245-244	**479**-844	40.4-40.0	8/21-16/26	459-695	3-7	4200-4785	-585	-14	-153	-105	-48	3.2	-0.7	3.1/ 6.1	182-175	23.1-27.3	-4.3
Coastal Conference																		
Bal	258-207	655-799	39.5-40.8	18/28-11/19	**833**-254	6-1	4681-3377	1304	7	**258**	137	**121**	**13.4**	-0.4	5.6/**1.7**	168-175	27.9-19.3	8.6
LA	245-**190**	760-806	39.6-40.0	17/31-**9/17**	527-492	3-4	4104-**3118**	986	15	112	142	-30	9.8	0.7	3.9/ 2.0	189-192	21.7-**16.2**	5.5
SF	260-250	794-646	39.0-40.9	11/24-22/32	487-628	4-4	4709-4020	689	-6	-7	33	-40	6.8	0.7	4.8/ 3.4	180-182	26.2-22.1	4.1
Atl	174-302	659-628	**44.3**-41.5	11/21-16/30	396-612	2-2	3164-5320	-2156	-9	-219	-216	-3	1.5	0.5	2.2/ 6.6	168-169	18.8-31.5	-12.6
Central Conference																		
Min	223-210	692-875	39.3-38.4	19/29-18/27	517-564	2-3	3606-3758	-152	7	40	15	25	8.0	0.0	3.2/ 3.6	171-167	21.1-22.5	-1.4
ChiB	219-240	1194-**896**	38.0-40.1	**25**/36-11/31	307-380	1-1	4058-4371	-313	-7	-83	-54	-29	4.9	**2.1**	2.3/ 5.8	184-179	22.1-24.4	-2.4
GB	240-213	653-541	40.0-39.6	13/29-17/26	482-**216**	2-**0**	4024-3596	428	1	54	40	14	8.4	-1.9	5.0/ 3.3	176-171	22.9-21.0	1.8
Det	221-214	810-658	40.4-40.7	9/29-15/29	331-289	3-3	4022-3837	185	4	-34	31	-65	6.2	-1.1	4.3/ 3.2	173-172	23.2-22.3	0.9
Aver	236	735	40.0	15/27	473	3	4135	—	—	—	—	—	—	—	4.4	177	23.4	—

Rushing Attempts	Rushing Yards	Rushing Average	Rushing TDs	Rushing Rank	Passing Yards	Passing Average
L.Kelly-Cle 248	L.Kelly-Cle 1239	G.Sayers-Chi 6.20	L.Kelly-Cle 16	L.Kelly-Cle 1399	J.Brodie-SF 3020	B.Starr-GB 9.46
K.Willard-SF 227	K.Willard-SF 967	L.Kelly-Cle 5.00	B.Brown-Min 11	K.Willard-SF 1037	E.Morrall-Bal 2909	B.Berry-Atl 9.37
B.Brown-Min 222	W.Wood-Phi 947	D.Hoak-Pit 4.90	T.Matte-Bal 9	W.Wood-Phi 977	F.Tarkenton-NYG 2555	E.Morrall-Bal 9.18
W.Wood-Phi 217	D.Hoak-Pit 858	M.Farr-Det 4.66	K.Willard-SF 7	B.Brown-Min 915	D.Meredith-Dal 2500	D.Meredith-Dal 8.09
W.Crenshaw-SL 203	G.Sayers-Chi 856	D.Anderson-GB 4.48		D.Hoak-Pit 888	B.Nelsen-Cle 2366	B.Nelsen-Cle 8.08

Completion Percent	TD Passes	TD Percent	INT Percent	Passer Rating	Passing Rank	Receptions
B.Starr-GB 63.7	E.Morrall-Bal 26	B.Starr-GB 8.8	B.Munson-Det 2.4	B.Starr-GB 104.3	B.Munson-Det 911	C.McNeil-SF 71
J.Brodie-SF 57.9	J.Brodie-SF 22	E.Morrall-Bal 8.2	B.Nelsen-Cle 3.4	E.Morrall-Bal 93.2	E.Morrall-Bal 905	R.Jefferson-Pit 58
E.Morrall-Bal 57.4	F.Tarkenton-NYG 21	D.Meredith-Dal 6.8	F.Tarkenton-NYG 3.6	D.Meredith-Dal 88.4	F.Tarkenton-NYG 903	L.Rentzel-Dal 54
S.Jurgensen-Was 57.2	D.Meredith-Dal 21	B.Nelsen-Cle 6.5	S.Jurgensen-Was 3.8	B.Nelsen-Cle 86.4	B.Nelsen-Cle 878	L.Wright-NO 54
D.Meredith-Dal 55.3		F.Tarkenton-NYG 6.2	D.Meredith-Dal 3.9	F.Tarkenton-NYG 84.6	D.Meredith-Dal 875	B.Hayes-Dal 53

Receiving Yards	Receiving Average	Receiving TDs	Receiving Rank	Combined Net Yards	Total TDs	Total Points
R.Jefferson-Pit 1074	J.Orr-Bal 25.62	P.Warfield-Cle 12	P.Warfield-Cle 594	P.Larson-SL 1597	L.Kelly-Cle 20	L.Kelly-Cle 120
P.Warfield-Cle 1067	H.Jones-NYG 23.49	R.Jefferson-Pit 11	R.Jefferson-Pit 592	L.Kelly-Cle 1556	B.Brown-Min 14	M.Clark-Dal 105
H.Jones-NYG 1057	P.Warfield-Cle 21.34	B.Hayes-Dal 10	H.Jones-NYG 564	G.Sayers-Chi 1463	P.Warfield-Cle 12	L.Michaels-Bal 102
L.Rentzel-Dal 1009	B.Casey-LA 19.48	P.Richter-Was 9	L.Rentzel-Dal 535	C.Baynham-Dal 1408	R.Jefferson-Pit 12	M.Percival-Chi 100
C.McNeil-SF 994	C.Dale-GB 19.48		C.McNeil-SF 532	R.Jefferson-Pit 1405	B.Hayes-Dal 12	D.Cockroft-Cle 100

Punt Average	Field Goals	Field Goal Percent	Kickoff Returns	Kickoff Return Average	Punt Returns	Punt Return Average
B.Lothridge-Atl 44.3	M.Percival-Chi 25	D.Cockroft-Cle 75.0	P.Larson-SL 46	P.Pearson-Bal 35.1	P.Larson-SL 28	B.Hayes-Dal 20.8
M.Bragg-Was 43.3	C.Durkee-NO 19	M.Percival-Chi 69.4	C.Butler-Atl 37	R.Smith-LA 27.6	R.Jefferson-Pit 28	A.Haymond-Phi 13.4
P.Larson-SL 41.6	F.Cox-Min 19	F.Cox-Min 65.5	R.Blye-NYG 35	G.Sayers-Chi 27.1	R.Smith-LA 27	P.Larson-SL 12.3
T.McNeill-NO 41.0	S.Baker-Phi 19	L.Michaels-Bal 64.3	J.Henderson-Pit 29	P.Larson-SL 26.9	W.Wood-GB 26	C.West-Min 10.1
K.Hill-Min 41.0		S.Baker-Phi 63.3		L.Barney-Det 26.8	R.Volk-Bal 25	R.Jefferson-Pit 9.8

Punt/Kick Return Yards	Punt/Kick Return TDs	Interceptions	Interception Return Yards	Interception Return TDs	Sacks	Overall Rank
P.Larson-SL 1582	P.Pearson-Bal 2	W.Williams-NYG 10	B.Davis-Cle 162	J.Pardee-LA 2	Not kept	L.Kelly-Cle 1589
R.Smith-LA 889	A.Haymond-Phi 2	K.Alexander-SF 9	B.Boyd-Bal 160	S.Lockhart-NYG 2		F.Tarkenton-NYG 1234
A.Haymond-Phi 878	B.Hayes-Dal 2		K.Alexander-SF 155			G.Sayers-Chi 1160
C.Butler-Atl 799			R.Volk-Bal 154			K.Willard-SF 1153
C.West-Min 777			S.Lockhart-NYG 130			W.Wood-Phi 1141

Looking for the Next Star

After winning the first two Super Bowls, the reigning champion Packers really weren't the same team. Many of the famous names were gone, creating the league-wide question about which team might possibly take the Packers' place.

One potential claimant to the abandoned throne was the Browns. Leroy Kelly led the league in rushing and scoring as they rolled through the Century Division, The Cowboys? Tom Landry's squad led the NFL in scoring and had its second-best ground game. Dallas had the league's strongest team against the run, allowing the least yardage and only 2 rushing touchdowns. There were also the Rams, whose inconsistencies in the backfield put more pressure on quarterback Roman Gabriel, but the team boasted an all-time great defensive line now that rookie Coy Bacon had been added to Deacon Jones and Merlin Olsen. The Bears treaded water with George Halas retired as coach for the fourth—and final—time. Chicago went 7–7 under Jim Dooley, missing the division title by a game to Minnesota.

None of those teams had the chip on their collective shoulders that the Colts did. After being so frequently disappointed in their attempts to build on their greatness in the previous decade, one had to wonder when coach Don Shula would finally try to shake things up. Shula got the opportunity when veteran quarterback Earl Morrall replaced injured Johnny Unitas. The results were electric. Morrall wound up winning the league's MVP, leading the NFL in touchdown passes. The defense was simply brilliant. With fearsome second-year lineman Bubba Smith at the fore, there was no real weak spot in the unit. The Colts tore through the competition and just needed to beat a seemingly inferior AFL team to be crowned world champion.

Three decades before the reality TV boom, the NFL hit the big screen with set-up truth. The film of the 1964 book, *Paper Lion*, starred Alan Alda as author George Plimpton, who had been in training camp with the 1963 Lions despite not possessing any of the prerequisite talent. The movie featured Busch Stadium, one of several new multipurpose stadiums popping up in professional sports.

1968 AFL

TEAM	W-L-T	PCT	POST	PTS	RA	RY	RY/A	RTD	FL	PA	PC	GPY	GPY/A	PTD	PI	PSY	PRAT
Eastern Division																	
NYJ	11-3	.786	LS*	419-280	467-368	1608-**1195**	3.4-**3.2**	**22**-9	9-15	436-403	217-187	3574-2567	8.2-6.4	20-17	19-28	**135**-399	74.8-52.4
Hou	7-7	.500	—	303-248	462-462	1804-1704	3.9-3.7	16-9	13-10	414-359	191-158	2864-**2003**	6.9-**5.6**	17-**13**	25-20	316-332	57.9-50.9
Mia	5-8-1	.385	—	276-355	417-445	1704-2172	4.1-4.9	12-19	**8-18**	423-342	216-179	2843-2904	6.7-8.5	21-23	22-22	441-192	67.5-76.7
Bos	4-10	.286	—	229-406	421-479	1362-1825	3.2-3.8	8-22	20-17	409-416	160-200	2121-2826	5.2-6.8	16-20	33-23	356-236	35.7-63.4
Buf	1-12-1	.077	—	199-367	400-505	1527-2021	3.8-4.0	9-15	14-13	405-**340**	168-**143**	1714-2477	4.2-7.3	7-19	28-22	371-273	31.2-59.2
Western Division																	
Oak	12-2	**.857**	DL	**453**-233	471-442	2168-1804	**4.6**-4.1	16-12	21-15	468-446	**237**-189	3771-2657	8.1-6.0	**31**-13	18-25	243-400	83.9-48.6
KC	12-2	**.857**	D	371-**170**	537-365	2227-1266	4.1-3.5	16-**4**	16-12	270-461	156-214	2492-3262	**9.2**-7.1	20-14	**11-37**	216-**439**	**96.4-46.9**
SD	9-5	.643	—	382-310	428-439	1765-1641	4.1-3.7	12-13	12-15	**472**-430	225-217	3813-2896	8.1-6.7	29-20	33-20	190-204	66.8-68.3
Den	5-9	.357	—	255-404	411-457	1614-1861	3.9-4.1	11-20	13-12	427-429	179-217	2826-3419	6.6-8.0	20-25	27-20	469-256	53.9-77.4
Cin	3-11	.214	—	215-329	421-473	1807-2097	4.3-4.4	14-13	10-9	313-411	167-212	1896-2903	6.1-7.1	8-25	**11**-10	277-283	65.7-84.6
Aver	14	—	—	310	444	1759	4.0	14	14	404	192	2791	6.9	19	23	301	62.6

TEAM	TD	PENY	PNT	FGM/A	RTNY	RTNTD	OFFY/DEFY	NETY	NETTO	NP	PNP	DELP	PW	DELW	PRT	DR	YPD	DEL
Eastern Division																		
NYJ	249-**178**	742-695	43.8-**38.4**	**34/46**-9/17	742-986	3-10	5047-**3363**	**1684**	15	139	**200**	-61	10.5	0.5	6.1/2.4	207-199	24.4-**16.9**	7.5
Hou	240-198	644-526	41.2-44.1	12/29-21/30	839-705	5-4	4352-3375	977	-8	55	49	6	8.4	-1.4	3.6/2.3	188-193	23.1-17.5	5.7
Mia	247-240	**485**-655	40.6-43.4	8/19-12/24	591-682	3-3	4106-4884	-778	10	-79	-25	-54	5.0	0.5	3.4/5.4	177-176	23.2-27.8	-4.6
Bos	181-237	682-874	39.9-40.5	15/27-21/31	417-1012	2-7	3127-4415	-1288	-13	-177	-159	-18	2.6	1.4	1.0/4.0	**216**-216	14.5-20.4	-6.0
Buf	159-210	687-540	41.8-39.7	14/28-27/48	776-993	6-7	2870-4225	-1355	-7	-168	-141	-27	2.8	-1.3	0.3/3.8	214-203	13.4-20.8	-7.4
Western Division																		
Oak	**287**-215	958-**932**	43.6-42.3	21/34-17/28	**1090**-366	8-1	**5696**-4061	1635	1	**220**	140	80	12.5	-0.5	6.1/2.5	201-206	28.3-19.7	**8.6**
KC	223-215	650-564	**45.3**-42.8	30/40-14/27	919-339	4-0	4503-4089	414	**22**	201	123	78	12.0	-0.0	**6.7**/2.6	182-187	24.7-21.9	2.9
SD	270-225	654-692	40.7-42.3	22/32-19/31	567-754	4-3	5388-4333	1055	-10	72	48	24	8.8	0.2	5.0/4.4	190-191	**28.4**-22.7	5.7
Den	217-251	772-750	42.7-43.0	10/23-21/34	497-610	1-3	3971-5024	-1053	-9	-8	-149	-120	-29	3.3	1.7	2.8/5.5	204-207	19.5-24.3	-4.8
Cin	171-275	586-632	40.9-44.2	13/27-18/35	340-**331**	3-1	3426-4717	-1291	-2	-114	-116	2	4.2	-1.2	3.4/5.5	171-**172**	20.0-27.4	-7.4
Aver	224	686	41.9	18/31	678	4	4249	—	—	—	—	—	—	—	4.1	195	21.8	—

Rushing Attempts		Rushing Yards		Rushing Average		Rushing TDs		Rushing Rank		Passing Yards		Passing Average	
P.Robinson-Cin	238	P.Robinson-Cin	1023	C.Smith-Oak	5.31	P.Robinson-Cin	8	P.Robinson-Cin	1103	J.Hadl-SD	3473	L.Dawson-KC	9.42
H.Dixon-Oak	206	R.Holmes-KC	866	D.Post-SD	5.02	R.Holmes-KC	7	R.Holmes-KC	936	D.Lamonica-Oak	3245	J.Namath-NYJ	8.28
H.Granger-Hou	202	H.Dixon-Oak	865	R.Holmes-KC	4.98	H.Granger-Hou	7	H.Granger-Hou	918	J.Namath-NYJ	3147	J.Hadl-SD	7.89
M.Snell-NYJ	179	H.Granger-Hou	848	R.Smith-SD	4.84			H.Dixon-Oak	885	B.Griese-Mia	2473	D.Lamonica-Oak	7.80
J.Nance-Bos	177	D.Post-SD	758	P.Robinson-Cin	4.30			M.Snell-NYJ	807	L.Dawson-KC	2109	M.Briscoe-Den	7.09

Completion Percent		TD Passes		TD Percent		INT Percent		Passer Rating		Passing Rank		Receptions	
L.Dawson-KC	58.5	J.Hadl-SD	27	L.Dawson-KC	7.6	J.Stofa-Cin	2.8	L.Dawson-KC	98.6	D.Lamonica-Oak	1148	L.Alworth-SD	68
B.Griese-Mia	52.4	D.Lamonica-Oak	25	M.Briscoe-Den	6.3	D.Lamonica-Oak	3.6	D.Lamonica-Oak	80.9	J.Namath-NYJ	969	G.Sauer-NYJ	66
D.Lamonica-Oak	49.5	B.Griese-Mia	21	J.Hadl-SD	6.1	L.Dawson-KC	4.0	B.Griese-Mia	75.7	L.Dawson-KC	780	R.Beverly-Oak	61
J.Namath-NYJ	49.2	L.Dawson-KC	17	D.Lamonica-Oak	6.0	J.Namath-NYJ	4.5	J.Namath-NYJ	72.1	B.Griese-Mia	702	K.Noonan-Mia	58
J.Stofa-Cin	48.0	J.Namath-NYJ	15	B.Griese-Mia	4.5	B.Griese-Mia	4.5	J.Hadl-SD	64.5	J.Hadl-SD	592	D.Maynard-NYJ	57

Receiving Yards		Receiving Average		Receiving TDs		Receiving Rank		Combined Net Yards		Total TDs		Total Points	
L.Alworth-SD	1312	D.Maynard-NYJ	22.75	W.Wells-Oak	11	L.Alworth-SD	706	F.Little-Den	1825	W.Wells-Oak	12	J.Turner-NYJ	145
D.Maynard-NYJ	1297	F.Pitts-KC	21.83	K.Noonan-Mia	11	D.Maynard-NYJ	699	M.Anderson-Buf	1636	K.Noonan-Mia	11	J.Stenerud-KC	129
G.Sauer-NYJ	1141	W.Wells-Oak	21.45	D.Maynard-NYJ	10	W.Wells-Oak	624	G.Atkinson-Oak	1358	D.Maynard-NYJ	10	G.Blanda-Oak	117
W.Wells-Oak	1137	G.Garrison-SD	21.21	G.Garrison-SD	10	G.Garrison-SD	602	L.Alworth-SD	1330	G.Garrison-SD	10	D.Partee-SD	106
G.Garrison-SD	1103	J.MacKinnon-SD	19.58	L.Alworth-SD	10	G.Sauer-NYJ	586	D.Maynard-NYJ	1297	L.Alworth-SD	10	B.Cappadona-Bos	83

Punt Average		Field Goals		Field Goal Percent		Kickoff Returns		Kickoff Return Average		Punt Returns		Punt Return Average	
J.Wilson-KC	45.1	J.Turner-NYJ	34	J.Stenerud-KC	75.0	M.Anderson-Buf	39	G.Atkinson-Oak	25.1	G.Atkinson-Oak	36	N.Smith-KC	15.0
J.Urbanek-Den	43.8	J.Stenerud-KC	30	J.Turner-NYJ	73.9	W.Porter-Bos	36	F.Little-Den	25.0	H.Clarke-Buf	29	G.Atkinson-Oak	13.6
C.Johnson-NYJ	43.8	D.Partee-SD	22	D.Partee-SD	68.8	Z.Moore-Hou	32	M.Anderson-Buf	24.9	I.Carwell-Hou	27	S.Duncan-SD	11.4
M.Eischeid-Oak	43.6	G.Blanda-Oak	21	G.Blanda-Oak	61.8	G.Atkinson-Oak	32	Z.Moore-Hou	24.6	F.Little-Den	24	F.Little-Den	10.9
L.Little-Cin	43.4	B.Cappadona-Bos	15	B.Alford-Buf	58.3	F.Little-Den	26	E.Christy-NYJ	24.0			L.Carwell-Hou	8.4

Punt/Kick Return Yards		Punt/Kick Return TDs		Interceptions		Interception Return Yards		Interception Return TDs		Sacks		Overall Rank	
G.Atkinson-Oak	1292	G.Atkinson-Oak	2	D.Grayson-Oak	10	D.Anderson-Mia	230	K.Houston-Hou	2	Not kept		D.Lamonica-Oak	1256
M.Anderson-Buf	971			D.Anderson-Mia	8	D.Grayson-Oak	195	M.Farr-Hou	2			F.Little-Den	1195
W.Porter-Bos	947			J.Sample-NYJ	7	K.Houston-Hou	160	B.Edgerson-Buf	2			P.Robinson-Cin	1181
F.Little-Den	910			L.Mitchell-Bos	7	T.Janik-Buf	137	J.Beauchamp-SD	2			H.Granger-Hou	1099
N.Smith-KC	819					R.Beverly-NYJ	135					H.Dixon-Oak	1075

A BROWN IN EVERY LEAGUE

The AFL balanced itself out with its final expansion, creating the Cincinnati Bengals as a home for legend Paul Brown. From the NCAA to the AAFC to the NFL to the AFL (and later the AFC), Brown would see it all. And in this go-round, he'd get to see the basement. The Bengals were quickly consigned to last place in what was becoming an increasingly stratified AFL, with clear divisions between good teams and bad.

After two one-sided defeats in the Super Bowl, the AFL had to ask itself at this point whether the Chiefs or the Raiders could go toe-to-toe with the NFL's best after each team had lost decisively to the Packers in the Super Bowl. The two Western Division foes still seemed to be the strongest teams in the league. Or would some other team take a shot? Houston had the novelty of indoor football at the Astrodome and Miami had a stellar rookie class with Larry Csonka, Jim Kiick and Manny Fernandez at the Orange Bowl, but those were Eastern sidebars in a Western-dominated regular season.

The Chiefs and the Raiders both finished 12–2, forcing a playoff. There, the league's best offensive team dismantled the Chiefs. The Raiders had improved an already good offensive line by adding rookie offensive tackle Art Shell, and made their defense all the more fearsome with the addition of safety George Atkinson.

The Jets, meanwhile, finally lived up to their billing. Although the team's running game never really got on a roll, and while Joe Namath didn't have his best season, they were more than good enough to wrap up the East with a 7–1 division mark. What the Jets could do was get the ball down the field with Namath hitting Don Maynard and George Sauer routinely, and then finishing off opponents with the run. On defense, they could contain a good running game and cover a short passing game effectively. It might not have seemed the stuff of greatness, but it was at least goodness, and that was enough to give the Jets their first divisional title and put Namath on the big stage, where he shone the brightest.

1969 NFL

TEAM	W-L-T	PCT	POST	PTS	RA	RY	RY/A	RTD	FL	PA	PC	GPY	GPY/A	PTD	PI	PSY	PRAT
Capitol Conference																	
Dal	11-2-1	.846	C	369-223	**532-313**	**2276-1050**	4.3-3.4	**17-3**	12-11	355-458	189-235	3212-3109	**9.0**-6.8	24-23	18-24	366-**452**	85.6-68.0
Was	7-5-2	.583	—	307-319	377-511	1532-2299	4.1-4.5	11-26	**10**-10	444-369	275-192	3106-2316	7.0-6.3	22-11	16-16	322-139	84.3-63.5
NO	5-9	.357	—	311-393	399-419	1705-1835	4.3-4.4	12-15	12-10	453-382	245-200	3215-3382	7.1-8.9	22-32	20-12	241-199	74.5-97.4
Phi	4-9-1	.308	—	279-377	395-467	1563-1909	4.0-4.1	10-15	11-14	458-444	216-243	3022-3250	6.6-7.3	20-23	28-15	240-181	58.0-81.4
Century Conference																	
Cle	10-3-1	.769	CL	351-300	447-417	1788-1990	4.0-4.8	**17**-18	14-22	378-387	199-202	2830-2787	7.5-7.2	24-19	21-19	190-323	75.2-71.5
NYG	6-8	.429	—	264-298	397-466	1593-2053	4.0-4.4	8-14	15-14	435-340	234-171	3076-2430	7.1-7.1	24-18	8-19	301-275	**87.1**-68.1
SL	4-9-1	.308	—	314-389	382-438	1446-1644	3.8-3.8	**17**-10	**10**-12	430-465	216-260	2940-3752	6.8-8.1	19-38	25-15	201-220	62.9-96.1
Pit	1-13	.071	—	218-404	400-455	1542-1732	3.9-3.8	8-17	20-16	391-410	176-227	2458-2973	6.3-7.3	17-27	29-25	374-304	49.4-75.0
Coastal Conference																	
LA	11-3	.786	C	320-243	382-415	1413-1475	3.7-3.6	8-8	11-12	416-430	222-202	2650-2919	6.4-6.8	**25**-18	**7**-26	**129**-393	86.1-58.3
Bal	8-5-1	.615	—	279-268	417-399	1490-1400	3.6-3.5	16-8	12-10	429-459	225-271	3143-3499	7.3-7.6	17-20	27-15	156-250	63.3-84.0
Atl	6-8	.429	—	276-268	455-475	2058-2032	**4.5**-4.3	9-14	19-**27**	282-383	149-225	2230-2536	7.9-6.6	20-13	12-19	477-251	85.0-69.3
SF	4-8-2	.333	—	277-319	391-422	1536-1704	3.9-4.0	13-14	12-11	**496**-402	**278**-205	**3379**-2726	6.8-6.8	22-22	26-20	221-255	70.1-70.3
Central Conference																	
Min	**12**-2	**.857**	CLS	**379-133**	489-337	1850-1089	3.8-**3.2**	15-4	12-12	346-410	176-213	2498-**2035**	7.2-**5.0**	24-**8**	18-**30**	252-404	76.0-**42.1**
Det	9-4-1	.692	—	259-188	474-372	1755-1223	3.7-3.3	11-7	12-21	329-350	165-167	1958-2238	6.0-6.4	12-15	18-21	358-377	58.0-57.8
GB	8-6	.571	—	269-221	432-485	1692-1982	3.9-4.1	11-7	21-7	319-360	182-177	2678-2133	8.4-5.9	20-13	17-19	302-288	83.3-57.8
ChiB	1-13	.071	—	210-339	462-440	2078-1900	**4.5**-4.3	14-17	17-11	384-**296**	193-**150**	1929-2239	5.0-7.6	11-23	21-16	439-258	51.7-79.2
Aver	14	—	—	293	427	1707	4.0	12	14	397	209	2770	7.0	20	19	286	71.6

TEAM	1D	PENY	PNT	FGM/A	RTNY	RTNTD	OFFY/DEFY	NETY	NETTO	NP	PNP	DELP	PW	DELW	PRT	DR	YPD	DEL
Capitol Conference																		
Dal	275-203	840-680	43.3-42.2	20/36-9/25	612-472	3-2	**5122**-3707	**1415**	5	146	138	8	10.6	0.8	**5.7**/ 3.5	185-187	**27.7**-19.8	**7.9**
Was	256-277	756-904	42.2-40.7	16/27-17/27	436-512	4-1	4316-4476	-160	0	-12	-13	1	6.7	1.3	4.7/ 4.0	168-175	25.7-25.6	0.1
NO	**282**-242	943-773	41.4-41.6	22/**41**-16/29	290-441	1-2	4679-5018	-339	-10	-82	-68	-14	4.9	0.0	4.8/ 7.4	173-173	27.0-29.0	-2.0
Phi	231-268	843-**950**	39.8-40.9	16/30-23/37	398-436	3-6	4345-4978	-633	-10	-98	-93	-5	4.6	-0.0	3.5/ 5.6	194-190	22.4-26.2	-3.8
Century Conference																		
Cle	250-257	603-746	37.5-40.5	12/23-12/22	400-347	4-1	4428-4454	-26	6	51	22	29	8.3	**2.2**	4.9/ 4.2	179-177	24.7-25.2	-0.4
NYG	235-243	777-601	37.6-38.9	11/21-18/29	271-527	1-3	4368-4208	160	10	-34	53	-87	6.2	-0.1	5.6/ 4.0	164-**165**	26.6-25.5	1.1
SL	224-289	765-773	37.6-40.4	12/24-18/31	446-360	4-**0**	4185-5176	-991	-8	-75	-115	40	5.1	-0.6	4.0/ 6.5	187-186	22.4-27.8	-5.4
Pit	210-260	659-793	42.3-40.1	12/26-17/26	422-931	1-6	3626-4401	-775	-8	-186	-97	-89	2.3	-1.3	2.1/ 4.1	**196**-194	18.5-22.7	-4.2
Coastal Conference																		
LA	209-242	994-709	40.7-41.0	22/34-20/26	**980-221**	3-**0**	3934-4001	-67	**20**	77	74	3	8.9	2.1	**5.7**/ 3.2	182-183	21.6-21.9	-0.2
Bal	255-256	**561**-848	**45.3**-38.4	14/31-15/34	298-576	1-4	4477-4649	-172	-14	11	-70	81	7.3	1.2	4.3/ 5.6	174-175	25.7-26.6	-0.8
Atl	209-254	601-762	41.2-38.8	15/30-14/27	282-404	4-5	3811-4317	-506	15	8	18	-10	7.2	-1.2	4.1/ 3.8	175-178	21.8-24.3	-2.5
SF	253-242	845-671	40.5-40.4	6/21-15/36	257-597	2-3	4694-4175	519	-7	-42	15	-57	5.9	-1.0	4.2/ 4.1	186-182	25.2-22.9	2.3
Central Conference																		
Min	239-**158**	744-795	40.0-**36.8**	**26**/37-**7/18**	725-445	4-4	4096-**2720**	1376	12	**246**	**163**	**83**	**13.1**	-1.2	4.4/**0.8**	190-191	21.6-**14.2**	7.3
Det	198-182	734-857	33.9-40.0	25/37-9/29	437-301	3-1	3355-3084	271	12	71	71	0	8.8	0.7	2.5/ 2.7	179-181	18.7-17.0	1.7
GB	242-224	602-733	40.1-39.7	6/22-20/34	715-318	**5**-3	4068-3827	241	-12	48	-28	76	8.2	-0.2	5.1/ 2.8	169-169	24.1-22.6	1.4
ChiB	237-208	940-612	39.0-41.4	8/21-13/31	296-377	1-3	3568-3881	-313	-11	-129	-70	-59	3.8	-2.8	1.5/ 4.5	180-175	19.8-22.2	-2.4
Aver	238	763	40.0	15/29	454	3	4192	—	—	—	—	—	—	—	4.6	180	23.3	—

Rushing Attempts	Rushing Yards	Rushing Average	Rushing TDs	Rushing Rank	Passing Yards	Passing Average
G.Sayers-Chi 236	G.Sayers-Chi 1032	H.Wages-Atl 5.21	T.Matte-Bal 11	G.Sayers-Chi 1112	S.Jurgensen-Was 3102	D.Horn-GB 8.96
T.Matte-Bal 235	C.Hill-Dal 942	T.Baker-NO 4.79	L.Kelly-Cle 9	C.Hill-Dal 1022	F.Tarkenton-NYG 2918	C.Morton-Dal 8.67
C.Hill-Dal 204	T.Matte-Bal 909	O.Reed-Min 4.73	G.Sayers-Chi 8	T.Matte-Bal 1019	N.Snead-Phi 2768	B.Starr-GB 7.84
L.Brown-Was 202	L.Brown-Was 888	C.Edwards-SL 4.71	C.Hill-Dal 8	L.Brown-Was 928	B.Nelsen-Cle 2743	B.Nelsen-Cle 7.79
L.Kelly-Cle 196	W.Wood-Phi 831	W.Garrison-Dal 4.65		L.Kelly-Cle 907	C.Morton-Dal 2619	N.Snead-Phi 7.30
Completion Percent	**TD Passes**	**TD Percent**	**INT Percent**	**Passer Rating**	**Passing Rank**	**Receptions**
B.Starr-GB 62.2	R.Gabriel-LA 24	J.Kapp-Min 8.0	R.Gabriel-LA 1.8	B.Starr-GB 89.9	F.Tarkenton-NYG 1254	B.Young-NO 73
S.Jurgensen-Was 62.0	F.Tarkenton-NYG 23	C.Morton-Dal 7.0	F.Tarkenton-NYG 2.0	F.Tarkenton-NYG 87.2	R.Gabriel-LA 1115	C.Taylor-Was 71
J.Brodie-SF 55.9	B.Nelsen-Cle 23	D.Horn-GB 6.5	S.Jurgensen-Was 3.4	R.Gabriel-LA 86.8	S.Jurgensen-Was 1061	R.Jefferson-Pit 67
S.Spurrier-SF 55.5	S.Jurgensen-Was 22	B.Nelsen-Cle 6.5	B.Starr-GB 4.1	S.Jurgensen-Was 85.4	C.Morton-Dal 815	H.Jackson-Phi 65
J.Unitas-Bal 54.4	C.Morton-Dal 21	B.Starr-GB 6.1	J.Brodie-SF 4.3	C.Morton-Dal 85.4	B.Nelsen-Cle 727	D.Williams-SL 56
Receiving Yards	**Receiving Average**	**Receiving TDs**	**Receiving Rank**	**Combined Net Yards**	**Total TDs**	**Total Points**
H.Jackson-Phi 1116	L.Rentzel-Dal 22.33	L.Rentzel-Dal 12	H.Jackson-Phi 603	T.Williams-GB 1517	L.Rentzel-Dal 13	F.Cox-Min 121
R.Jefferson-Pit 1079	P.Warfield-Cle 21.10	G.Collins-Cle 11	R.Jefferson-Pit 585	G.Sayers-Chi 1487	T.Matte-Bal 13	M.Clark-Dal 103
B.Young-NO 1015	L.Warwick-Min 21.05	P.Warfield-Cle 10	J.Gilliam-SL 544	T.Matte-Bal 1422	J.Morrison-NYG 11	B.Gossett-LA 102
J.Gilliam-SL 997	C.Dale-GB 19.53		B.Young-NO 543	C.Butler-Atl 1357	G.Collins-Cle 11	E.Mann-Det 101
L.Rentzel-Dal 960	J.Gilliam-SL 19.17		L.Rentzel-Dal 540	J.Gilliam-SL 1332		T.Dempsey-NO 99
Punt Average	**Field Goals**	**Field Goal Percent**	**Kickoff Returns**	**Kickoff Return Average**	**Punt Returns**	**Punt Return Average**
D.Lee-Bal 45.3	F.Cox-Min 26	F.Cox-Min 70.3	P.Pearson-Bal 31	B.Williams-Det 33.1	C.West-Min 39	A.Haymond-LA 13.2
R.Widby-Dal 43.3	E.Mann-Det 25	E.Mann-Det 67.6	R.Smith-LA 27	J.Duncan-Bal 29.5	A.Haymond-LA 33	R.Harris-Was 11.3
B.Walden-Pit 42.3	B.Gossett-LA 22	B.Gossett-LA 64.7	B.Campbell-Pit 26	B.Scott-Cle 28.9	B.Campbell-Pit 28	B.Hayes-Dal 9.9
M.Bragg-Was 42.2	T.Dempsey-NO 22	C.Knight-Was 59.3	B.Scott-Cle 25	D.Shy-NO 27.9	B.Bradley-Phi 28	A.Dodd-NO 7.1
B.Lothridge-Atl 41.2	M.Clark-Dal 20	M.Clark-Dal 55.6	D.Hampton-GB 22	D.Hampton-GB 26.5	R.Smith-LA 23	B.Bradley-Phi 6.5
Punt/Kick Return Yards	**Punt/Kick Return TDs**	**Interceptions**	**Interception Return Yards**	**Interception Return TDs**	**Sacks**	**Overall Rank**
A.Haymond-LA 810	T.Williams-GB 2	M.Renfro-Dal 10	H.Adderley-GB 169	E.Meador-LA 2	Not kept	F.Tarkenton-NYG 1426
P.Pearson-Bal 743		B.Bryant-Min 8	D.Hart-GB 156			R.Gabriel-LA 1321
B.Scott-Cle 722		L.Barney-Det 8	L.Barney-Det 126			T.Matte-Bal 1309
R.Smith-LA 707			M.Renfro-Dal 118			G.Sayers-Chi 1299
T.Williams-GB 706			B.Maher-NYG 112			C.Hill-Dal 1282

Farewell to Old Friends and Old Ways

The final season before the league merger was also the 50th anniversary season of the NFL—as noted on every player's jersey—and it proved to be a heart-warming year tinged with sadness. Chicago running back Gale Sayers returned from a career-altering knee injury he'd suffered in 1968. Although he no longer had the breakaway speed that made him the Offensive Rookie of the Year in 1965, and despite playing for a particularly miserable Bears team, Sayers nevertheless managed to lead the league in rushing. His friend and blocking back, Brian Piccolo, was diagnosed with cancer during the season and died the next summer.

Vince Lombardi reappeared as part owner, executive vice president, and head coach of the Redskins. He gave Washington its first winning club in 14 years, but the game's great teacher died of cancer before the 1970 season. The man who brought the Redskins to Washington, George Preston Marshall, also died.

A new power arose to replace the Packers in the Central Division. Minnesota had been turned over to local sports legend and former CFL coach Bud Grant in 1967. He'd steered the Vikings to their first division title and playoff appearance in 1968, but that was only the start for a new perennial contender. The Vikings had the game's most suffocating defense, combining an all-time great defensive line with one of the league's best defensive backfields.

Another key development was in Pittsburgh. Although the Steelers finished just 1–13, the future held promise with the arrival of new head coach Chuck Noll. Noll had coached under Sid Gillman in San Diego and Don Shula in Baltimore after playing for Paul Brown in Cleveland. Noll oversaw the drafting of two outstanding defensive linemen: Joe Greene and L.C. Greenwood. Baltimore rookie Ted Hendricks began a career that would make him one of the greatest outside linebackers of all time. Another rookie certain to make some noise someday was Roger Staubach, finally debuting in the NFL after four years of active military service. Craig Morton had waited four years to inherit Dandy Don Meredith's job in Dallas, but he would not have long before the former Navy star got his shot.

1969 AFL

TEAM	W-L-T	PCT	POST	PTS	RA	RY	RY/A	RTD	FL	PA	PC	GPY	GPY/A	PTD	PI	PSY	PRAT
Eastern Division																	
NYJ	10-4	.714	P	353-269	469-343	1782-1326	3.8-3.9	14-7	13-16	394-437	203-232	2939-3086	7.5-7.1	21-22	20-29	138-330	72.7-64.9
Hou	6-6-2	.500	P	278-279	440-430	1706-1556	3.9-3.6	12-10	17-17	**489**-371	**239**-167	3147-2495	6.4-6.7	15-18	31-23	322-278	53.4-58.0
Bos	4-10	.286	—	266-316	367-528	1489-2359	4.1-4.5	11-18	10-14	338-**348**	162-203	2191-2610	6.5-7.5	19-18	18-20	261-159	65.6-75.2
Buf	4-10	.286	—	230-359	384-454	1522-1858	4.0-4.1	7-17	21-**18**	442-368	215-175	2716-2772	6.1-7.5	17-21	30-19	371-296	52.8-70.6
Mia	3-10-1	.231	—	233-332	401-422	1513-1489	3.8-**3.5**	12-9	13-13	424-404	201-196	2558-2845	6.0-7.0	12-25	29-18	481-208	47.7-73.9
Western Division																	
Oak	**12**-1-1	**.923**	PL	**377**-242	459-438	1765-1661	3.8-3.8	4-13	**7**-16	439-422	227-**164**	**3375**-2511	7.7-6.0	**36**-15	26-26	**104**-402	79.9-45.4
KC	11-3	.786	PLS*	359-**177**	**522**-314	**2220**-1091	4.3-**3.5**	**19**-6	19-15	351-426	196-200	2638-**2491**	7.5-**5.8**	16-**10**	20-**32**	251-**419**	71.4-**42.1**
SD	8-6	.571	—	288-276	455-366	1985-1442	**4.4**-3.9	18-11	13-6	444-423	208-241	2927-3075	6.6-7.3	13-22	21-31	301-280	58.6-66.7
Den	5-8-1	.385	—	297-344	394-436	1637-1709	4.2-3.9	12-15	8-14	403-437	192-223	2835-3295	7.0-7.3	23-19	23-14	311-363	66.3-77.2
Cin	4-9-1	.308	—	280-367	363-523	1523-2651	4.2-5.1	10-13	23-15	308-396	163-205	2720-2866	**8.8**-7.2	22-24	**15**-21	375-180	**86.5**-73.5
Aver	14	—	—	296	425	1714	4.0	12	14	403	201	2805	7.0	19	23	292	64.5

TEAM	TD	PENY	PNT	FGM/A	RTNY	RTNTD	OFFY/DEFY	NETY	NETTO	NP	PNP	DELP	PW	DELW	PRT	DR	YPD	DEL
Eastern Division																		
NYJ	252-229	725-788	44.3-39.8	**32/47**-15/27	604-660	2-3	4583-4082	501	**12**	84	90	-6	9.1	0.9	5.1/3.5	183-183	25.0-22.3	2.7
Hou	256-183	730-592	38.9-43.1	19/40-16/30	726-637	4-5	4531-3773	758	-8	-1	31	-32	7.0		3.0/3.4	**203**-201	22.3-18.8	3.5
Bos	166-278	837-810	41.5-**38.6**	14/34-17/28	538-**339**	2-2	3419-4810	-1391	6	-50	-92	42	5.8	-1.8	3.6/4.7	171-**175**	20.0-27.5	-7.5
Buf	224-236	632-719	44.5-42.7	17/26-26/41	438-915	2-2	3867-4334	-467	-14	-129	-95	-34	3.8	0.2	2.4/4.6	194-194	19.9-22.3	-2.4
Mia	224-206	631-840	40.6-44.1	13/22-24/36	583-726	4-3	3590-4126	-536	-11	-99	-89	-10	4.5	-1.0	1.9/4.8	194-192	18.5-21.5	-3.0
Western Division																		
Oak	261-232	1274-**918**	42.7-41.8	20/37-14/30	709-500	**5**-1	**5036**-3770	1266	9	135	142	-7	10.4	**2.1**	**5.5**/2.3	201-198	**25.1**-19.0	6.0
KC	258-**181**	757-443	44.4-43.0	27/35-15/27	**846**-827	**5**-3	4607-**3163**	**1444**	8	**182**	152	30	**11.6**	-0.6	4.4/**1.5**	189-195	24.4-**16.2**	**8.2**
SD	**275**-232	731-791	**44.6**-40.3	15/28-**13/25**	744-556	4-1	4611-4237	374	3	12	43	-31	7.3	0.7	3.8/3.5	185-181	24.3-24.0	1.5
Den	243-276	753-901	40.1-43.1	13/29-22/32	678-667	2-6	4161-4641	-480	-3	-47	-52	5	5.8	-0.3	3.8/5.2	183-183	22.7-25.4	-2.6
Cin	172-278	**556**-824	38.8-41.4	16/24-24/46	497-536	1-5	3868-5337	-1469	-2	-87	-130	**43**	4.8	-0.3	5.2/4.8	194-195	19.9-27.4	-7.4
Aver	233	763	41.9	19/32	636	3	4227	—	—	—	—	—	—	—	4.1	190	22.3	—

Rushing Attempts		Rushing Yards		Rushing Average		Rushing TDs		Rushing Rank		Passing Yards		Passing Average	
J.Nance-Bos	193	D.Post-SD	873	C.Garrett-Bos	5.04	J.Kiick-Mia	9	D.Post-SD	933	D.Lamonica-Oak	3302	G.Cook-Cin	9.41
M.Snell-NYJ	191	J.Nance-Bos	750	F.Little-Den	4.99	W.McVea-KC	7	J.Nance-Bos	810	J.Namath-NYJ	2734	L.Dawson-KC	7.97
H.Granger-Hou	186	H.Granger-Hou	740	J.Phillips-Cin	4.90			M.Garrett-KC	792	P.Beathard-Hou	2455	D.Lamonica-Oak	7.75
D.Post-SD	182	M.Garrett-KC	732	D.Post-SD	4.80			F.Little-Den	789	J.Hadl-SD	2253	J.Namath-NYJ	7.57
O.Simpson-Buf	181	F.Little-Den	729	W.McVea-KC	4.72			H.Granger-Hou	770	T.Swanson-Bos	2160	F.Little-KC	6.98

Completion Percent		TD Passes		TD Percent		INT Percent		Passer Rating		Passing Rank		Receptions	
L.Dawson-KC	59.0	D.Lamonica-Oak	34	D.Lamonica-Oak	8.0	J.Hadl-SD	3.4	G.Cook-Cin	88.3	D.Lamonica-Oak	821	L.Alworth-SD	64
G.Cook-Cin	53.8	T.Swanson-Bos	19	G.Cook-Cin	7.6	F.Little-KC	3.7	D.Lamonica-Oak	79.8	J.Namath-NYJ	782	V.Biggs-Oak	54
F.Little-KC	52.2	J.Namath-NYJ	19	T.Swanson-Bos	5.7	S.Tensi-Den	4.2	J.Namath-NYJ	74.3	J.Hadl-SD	737	A.Denson-Den	53
D.Lamonica-Oak	51.9	L.Dawson-KC	15	L.Dawson-KC	5.4	J.Namath-NYJ	4.7	L.Dawson-KC	69.9	S.Tensi-Den	585	A.Reed-Hou	51
J.Namath-NYJ	51.2	S.Tensi-Den	14	J.Namath-NYJ	5.3	T.Swanson-Bos	5.4	S.Tensi-Den	68.1	G.Cook-Cin	562		

Receiving Yards		Receiving Average		Receiving TDs		Receiving Rank		Combined Net Yards		Total TDs		Total Points	
W.Wells-Oak	1260	W.Wells-Oak	26.81	W.Wells-Oak	14	W.Wells-Oak	700	J.LeVias-Hou	1946	W.Wells-Oak	14	J.Turner-NYJ	129
L.Alworth-SD	1003	B.Trumpy-Cin	22.57	V.Biggs-Oak	12	L.Alworth-SD	522	C.Garrett-Bos	1909	V.Biggs-Oak	12	J.Stenerud-KC	119
D.Maynard-NYJ	938	E.Crabtree-Cin	21.38	A.Denson-Den	10	D.Maynard-NYJ	499	O.Simpson-Buf	1569	A.Denson-Den	10	G.Blanda-Oak	105
E.Crabtree-Cin	855	G.Garrison-SD	20.10	B.Trumpy-Cin	9	V.Biggs-Oak	479	M.Morris-Mia	1483	B.Trumpy-Cin	9	R.Gerela-Hou	86
V.Biggs-Oak	837	D.Maynard-NYJ	19.96	G.Sauer-NYJ	8			W.Wells-Oak	1284			W.Wells-Oak	84

Punt Average		Field Goals		Field Goal Percent		Kickoff Returns		Kickoff Return Average		Punt Returns		Punt Return Average	
D.Partee-SD	44.6	J.Turner-NYJ	32	J.Stenerud-KC	77.1	M.Morris-Mia	43	B.Thompson-Den	28.5	J.LeVias-Hou	35	B.Thompson-Den	11.5
P.Maguire-SD	44.5	J.Stenerud-KC	27	J.Turner-NYJ	68.1	J.LeVias-Hou	38	C.Garrett-Bos	28.3	M.Battle-NYJ	34	S.Duncan-SD	10.4
J.Wilson-KC	44.4	G.Blanda-Oak	20	H.Muhlmann-Cin	66.7	M.Battle-NYJ	31	S.Duncan-SD	28.0	S.Duncan-SD	27	J.LeVias-Hou	8.3
S.O'Neal-NYJ	44.3	R.Gerela-Hou	19	B.Alford-Buf	65.4	B.Thornton-Buf	30	M.Morris-Mia	26.4			M.Anderson-Buf	7.5
M.Eischeid-Oak	42.7	B.Alford-Buf	17	K.Kremser-Mia	59.1	C.Garrett-Bos	28	O.Simpson-Buf	25.2			M.Battle-NYJ	6.9

Punt/Kick Return Yards		Punt/Kick Return TDs		Interceptions		Interception Return Yards		Interception Return TDs		Sacks		Overall Rank	
M.Morris-Mia	1308	M.Morris-Mia	1	E.Thomas-KC	9	J.Robinson-KC	158	B.Stanfill-Mia	2	Not kept		C.Garrett-Bos	1356
J.LeVias-Hou	1232	B.Bell-KC	1	J.Robinson-KC	8	E.Thomas-KC	146	K.Graham-SD	2			O.Simpson-Buf	1118
M.Battle-NYJ	985			D.Grayson-Oak	8	J.Kearney-KC	143					D.Post-SD	1067
C.Garrett-Bos	951			J.Hill-SD	7	D.Grayson-Oak	132					M.Garrett-KC	1006
S.Duncan-SD	867			B.Byrd-Buf	7	S.Duncan-SD	118					F.Little-Den	979

LEAVING NO CARDS ON THE TABLE

This was the league's 10th and final season, achieving more than anyone could have hoped for a decade earlier. The AFL had built a worthy contender to the NFL, creating a brand of football that caught people's attention. The rivalry between the leagues had generated tremendous expansion over the previous decade. Professional football had spread into almost every corner of the country, and was now a national television staple. While the competition between the two leagues had been resolved with the merger, the creative dynamic between the two had helped make football the nation's most popular sport.

The Jets' victory in Super Bowl III certified that achievement. But as the league's time drew short, the decline and departure of many of the league's original stars symbolized the changing times. This would be the final year that Jack Kemp, Tom Flores, and Babe Parilli would take a snap, and names like Tobin Rote or Cotton Davidson already belonged to history. The gunslingers of the past were fading into memory.

In their place was a more accomplished brand of quarterback play. Joe Namath and Daryle Lamonica were in their primes, and were the league's obvious marquee players. Where Namath was the personality who'd said he'd win and did, Oakland's Lamonica was the ultimate example of the strong-armed, downfield passer, football's most daring downfield virtuoso since George Blanda or Y.A. Tittle.

Everyone anticipated a postseason showdown between the Jets and the Raiders. That wasn't a foregone conclusion. Since the league had only two divisions where the NFL had four, the AFL decided to introduce an extra playoff round, both to make money and to make sure their teams didn't have a week off while the NFL played its conference championship. The "inter-divisional playoff" matched the second-place finisher in each division against the division winners. Where the Chiefs would have normally been eliminated after a season in which Len Dawson had suffered a badly injured knee in the second week, the team with the league's best defense and a healthy (or at least healthy enough) starting quarterback would have a new lease on life. And the AFL had one last thing to prove.

1970 NFC

TEAM	W-L-T	PCT	POST	PTS	RA	RY	RY/A	RTD	FL	PA	PC	GPY	GPY/A	PTD	PI	PSY	PRAT
Eastern Division																	
Dal	10-4	.714	DCS	299-221	**522**-415	**2300**-1656	4.4-4.0	16-10	**12**-15	297-399	149-193	2445-2226	**8.2**-5.6	18-10	16-24	296-313	75.9-48.9
NYG	9-5	.643	—	301-270	465-419	1799-1692	3.9-4.0	11-11	14-13	403-364	**230**-186	2892-2650	7.2-7.3	19-19	12-17	258-279	82.9-72.9
SL	8-5-1	.615	—	325-228	429-472	1998-1762	**4.7**-3.7	**18**-10	14-14	390-382	178-183	2689-2416	6.9-6.3	16-16	19-21	216-309	62.2-59.4
Was	6-8	.429	—	297-314	444-468	2021-2068	4.6-4.4	11-19	14-13	342-374	203-205	2357-2434	6.9-6.5	23-14	**10**-15	249-169	90.5-70.6
Phi	3-10-1	.231	—	241-332	450-457	1539-2064	3.4-4.5	11-16	16-18	410-**313**	218-**161**	2651-2176	6.5-7.0	16-16	23-10	200-287	63.0-77.6
Central Division																	
Min	**12**-2	**.857**	D	335-**143**	508-398	1634-1365	3.2-3.4	16-**4**	16-16	344-367	173-195	2378-**1798**	6.9-**4.9**	12-6	15-**28**	197-360	66.3-**40.4**
Det	10-4	.714	W	347-202	514-**362**	2127-**1152**	4.1-**3.2**	16-7	15-16	294-371	167-194	2121-2491	7.2-6.7	19-14	12-**28**	264-195	84.0-54.8
ChiB	6-8	.429	—	256-261	353-459	1092-1471	3.1-**3.2**	3-11	13-14	422-394	210-233	2431-2925	5.8-7.4	21-18	22-17	258-329	62.4-79.5
GB	6-8	.429	—	196-293	453-453	1595-1829	3.5-4.0	8-14	17-17	351-369	177-177	2196-2496	6.3-6.8	11-13	24-20	382-270	52.1-59.4
Western Division																	
SF	10-3-1	.769	DC	352-267	471-425	1580-1799	3.4-4.2	13-12	15-**20**	383-384	226-185	**2990**-2434	7.8-6.3	25-19	**10**-22	67-261	94.7-61.3
LA	9-4-1	.692	—	325-202	430-395	1763-1359	4.1-3.4	17-16	15-16	**426**-376	218-196	2658-2615	6.2-6.9	17-15	13-19	150-**426**	71.3-66.4
Atl	4-8-2	.333	—	206-264	431-479	1600-1722	3.7-3.6	4-14	17-16	342-348	197-191	2262-2397	6.6-6.9	18-11	21-19	431-243	69.6-64.3
NO	2-11-1	.154	—	172-347	371-469	1215-1891	3.3-4.0	4-15	18-16	415-430	213-238	2690-3197	6.5-7.4	11-19	22-22	232-136	58.6-72.6
Aver	14	—		270	440	1685	3.8	11	14	377	193	2535	6.7	16	20	275	65.6

TEAM	1D	PENY	PNT	FGM/A	RTNY	RTNTD	OFFY/DEFY	NETY	NETTO	NP	PNP	DELP	PW	DELW	PRT	DR	YPD	DEL
Eastern Division																		
Dal	229-205	934-732	41.3-41.1	18/27-17/26	544-540	1-4	4449-3569	880	11	78	117	-39	8.9	1.0	4.8/ 2.1	177-174	25.1-20.5	4.6
NYG	**257**-223	641-675	38.3-39.7	25/41-16/29	416-**233**	2-2	4433-4063	370	4	31	47	-16	7.8	1.2	5.2/ 4.5	168-167	**26.4**-24.3	2.1
SL	226-242	896-659	40.9-40.0	20/32-**13**/26	570-366	4-1	4471-3869	602	2	97	58	39	9.4	-0.9	4.3/ 3.1	182-182	24.6-21.3	3.3
Was	249-266	**613**-930	40.9-39.3	20/27-18/26	285-440	0-4	4129-4333	-204	-4	-17	-1	-16	6.6	-0.6	5.1/ 4.3	161-**161**	25.6-26.9	-1.3
Phi	229-213	799-**991**	36.6-39.1	14/25-27/39	202-624	2-4	3990-3953	37	-11	-91	-41	-50	4.7	-1.2	3.6/ 4.6	179-178	22.3-22.2	0.1
Central Division																		
Min	225-**168**	631-586	37.9-**37.5**	30/46-15/27	628-497	7-4	3815-**2803**	1012	13	**192**	136	56	**11.8**	0.2	4.4/**0.6**	183-187	20.8-**15.0**	**5.9**
Det	243-186	659-805	40.9-39.1	20/29-16/26	723-287	6-1	3984-3448	536	**17**	145	113	32	10.6	-0.6	4.6/ 3.0	176-173	22.6-19.9	2.7
ChiB	179-234	853-826	40.8-37.6	20/34-16/29	375-519	4-2	3265-4067	-802	-4	-5	-83	78	6.9	-0.9	4.1/ 3.6	192-195	17.0-20.9	-3.9
GB	194-202	691-686	40.2-40.1	15/28-28/42	496-759	3-3	3409-4055	-646	-4	-97	-70	-27	4.6	1.4	2.1/ 3.6	194-192	17.6-21.1	-3.5
Western Division																		
SF	237-213	997-965	38.4-40.4	21/31-15/24	**858**-275	3-1	4503-3972	531	**17**	85	112	-27	9.1	1.4	**7.0**/ 3.3	**196**-186	23.0-21.4	1.6
LA	224-195	959-825	39.1-37.8	29/45-16/25	698-273	5-1	4271-3548	723	5	123	80	43	10.1	-0.6	4.7/ 3.4	184-190	23.2-18.7	4.5
Atl	199-211	807-897	38.7-41.2	9/25-20/40	547-550	4-4	3431-3876	-445	-3	-55	-49	-6	5.6	-0.6	2.7/ 3.7	178-179	19.3-21.7	-2.4
NO	183-263	1029-875	42.5-40.4	18/34-23/34	474-690	2-6	3673-4952	-1279	-2	-175	-115	-60	2.6	-0.1	3.6/ 5.1	182-182	20.2-27.2	-7.0
Aver	221	839	41.0	18/31	539	3	3945	—	—	—	—	—	4.1			183	21.5	

Rushing Attempts		Rushing Yards		Rushing Average		Rushing TDs		Rushing Rank		Passing Yards		Passing Average	
R.Johnson-NYG	263	L.Brown-Was	1125	D.Thomas-Dal	5.32	M.Lane-SL	11	L.Brown-Was	1175	J.Brodie-SF	2941	C.Morton-Dal	8.79
L.Brown-Was	237	R.Johnson-NYG	1027	C.Edwards-SL	5.00	C.Jones-Min	9	R.Johnson-NYG	1107	F.Tarkenton-NYG	2777	J.Brodie-SF	7.78
K.Willard-SF	236	M.Lane-SL	977	L.Brown-Was	4.75	M.Farr-Det	9	M.Lane-SL	1087	J.Hart-SL	2575	F.Tarkenton-NYG	7.14
D.Anderson-GB	222	D.Anderson-GB	853	M.Lane-SL	4.74	R.Johnson-NYG	8	D.Anderson-GB	903	R.Gabriel-LA	2552	S.Jurgensen-Was	6.99
D.Osborn-Min	207	D.Thomas-Dal	803	L.Smith-LA	4.39	K.Willard-SF	7	K.Willard-SF	859	S.Jurgensen-Was	2354	N.Snead-Phi	6.93

Completion Percent		TD Passes		TD Percent		INT Percent		Passer Rating		Passing Rank		Receptions	
S.Jurgensen-Was	59.9	J.Brodie-SF	24	C.Morton-Dal	7.2	J.Brodie-SF	2.6	J.Brodie-SF	93.8	J.Brodie-SF	1191	D.Gordon-Chi	71
J.Brodie-SF	59.0	S.Jurgensen-Was	23	S.Jurgensen-Was	6.8	E.Hargett-NO	2.9	S.Jurgensen-Was	91.5	F.Tarkenton-NYG	1004	S.Wyche-NO	55
B.Berry-Atl	58.0	F.Tarkenton-NYG	19	J.Brodie-SF	6.3	R.Gabriel-LA	2.9	C.Morton-Dal	89.8	S.Jurgensen-Was	892	L.Warwick-SF	53
B.Kilmer-NO	57.0			B.Munson-Det	6.3	S.Jurgensen-Was	3.0	F.Tarkenton-NYG	82.2	R.Gabriel-LA	876	J.Snow-LA	51
F.Tarkenton-NYG	56.3			B.Berry-Atl	5.9	F.Tarkenton-NYG	3.1	B.Berry-Atl	78.1	C.Morton-Dal	705		

Receiving Yards		Receiving Average		Receiving TDs		Receiving Rank		Combined Net Yards		Total TDs		Total Points	
L.Warwick-SF	1100	B.Hayes-Dal	26.15	D.Gordon-Chi	13	L.Warwick-SF	610	R.Johnson-NYG	1654	M.Lane-SL	13	F.Cox-Min	125
D.Gordon-Chi	1026	J.Gilliam-SL	21.16	L.Warwick-SF	12	D.Gordon-Chi	578	L.Brown-Was	1466	D.Gordon-Chi	13	D.Ray-LA	121
J.Gilliam-SL	952	L.Warwick-SF	20.75	B.Hayes-Dal	10	J.Gilliam-SL	501	A.Haymond-LA	1398	L.Warwick-SF	12	P.Gogolak-NYG	107
S.Wyche-NO	906	B.Hawkins-Phi	20.40	J.Smith-Was	9	B.Hayes-Dal	495	M.Lane-SL	1342	R.Johnson-NYG	12	B.Gossett-SF	102
B.Hayes-Dal	889	L.Rentzel-Dal	19.86	C.Taylor-Was	8	S.Wyche-NO	478	D.Thomas-Dal	1292			E.Mann-Det	101

Punt Average		Field Goals		Field Goal Percent		Kickoff Returns		Kickoff Return Average		Punt Returns		Punt Return Average	
J.Fagan-NO	42.5	F.Cox-Min	30	C.Knight-Was	74.1	A.Haymond-LA	35	C.Turner-Chi	32.7	A.Haymond-LA	53	B.Taylor-SF	12.0
R.Widby-NO	41.3	D.Ray-LA	29	E.Mann-Det	72.4	B.Walik-Phi	32	A.Haymond-LA	29.2	B.Taylor-SF	43	J.Mallory-Atl	11.9
G.Larson-SL	40.9	P.Gogolak-NYG	25	B.Gossett-SF	67.7	T.Vactor-Was	28	L.Krause-GB	28.5	R.Smith-Chi	33	L.Barney-Det	10.4
B.Green-Chi	40.9	B.Gossett-SF	21	M.Clark-Dal	66.7	R.Smith-Chi	28	L.Shy-NYG	25.9	G.Larson-SL	30	T.McCauley-Atl	9.9
M.Bragg-Was	40.9			F.Cox-Min	65.2			B.Walik-Phi	25.2	C.West-Min	29	A.Dodd-NO	9.2

Punt/Kick Return Yards		Punt/Kick Return TDs		Interceptions		Interception Return Yards		Interception Return TDs		Sacks		Overall Rank	
A.Haymond-LA	1398	C.Turner-Chi	4	D.LeBeau-Det	9	L.Barney-Det	168	L.Barney-Det	2	Not kept		R.Johnson-NYG	1436
B.Walik-Phi	883			W.Wood-GB	7	J.Seymour-Min	132					L.Brown-Was	1356
R.Smith-Chi	777			J.Seymour-Min	7	W.Williams-NYG	114					M.Lane-SL	1280
C.Turner-Chi	752			L.Barney-Det	7	D.Hart-GB	114					F.Tarkenton-NYG	1260
T.Vactor-Was	707					W.Wood-GB	110					J.Brodie-SF	1240

And It Is ... Good!

With merging came realignment into two 13-team conferences, each then subdivided into a three divisions. This in turn meant the formal creation of a wild-card slot for the playoffs. Rules were consolidated so that teams could only score one point after touchdowns. Names were placed on the back of jerseys. Amid much gnashing of teeth, Baltimore, Cleveland, and Pittsburgh each took a $3 million payment and joined the American Football Conference. Two men who were instrumental in founding the now merged leagues, George Halas and Lamar Hunt, were named the first presidents of the NFC and AFC, respectively.

Although the Cowboys again won the Eastern Division (the NFC's only five-team division), and the Vikings continued to dominate in the Central, two surprise teams wound up completing the NFC playoff picture. The 49ers were more than overdue for some good news, and they rode the coattails of John Brodie's career year. Driving a ball-control offense with masterful aplomb, the 35-year-old steered the Niners to their first playoff appearance since his rookie

season in 1957. Brodie won the league MVP while helping his team hold off the Rams for the NFC West title.

Perhaps an even greater surprise was the Lions becoming the NFC's first wild card. Detroit, 12 years removed from the postseason, used a veteran defense to put together a 5–0 stretch run that included wins against four winning teams. The December 14 victory over the Rams gave the Lions—and beneficiary San Francisco—the edge in the standings. It was also the final episode of ABC's new Monday night hit. It didn't take long for football in prime time to gain an audience, or for announcer Howard Cosell to become the most controversial man in the game.

One of the season's most memorable moments was a Detroit loss. Tom Dempsey's record 63-yard field goal on the final play on November 8 gave the Saints one of their two victories. Dempsey was already noted for playing despite being born without toes on his right (kicking) foot, requiring a special flat-fronted shoe. After his record-setting kick, the NFL passed a rule stating that all players wear "normal" shoes.

1970 AFC

TEAM	W-L-T	PCT	POST	PTS	RA	RY	RY/A	RTD	FL	PA	PC	GPY	GPY/A	PTD	PI	PSY	PRAT
Eastern Division																	
Bal	**11**-2-1	.846	DCS*	321-234	411-390	1336-1439	3.3-3.7	9-6	14-9	416-452	219-238	**3087**-2780	7.4-6.2	23-16	22-25	289-374	73.3-60.3
Mia	10-4	.714	W	297-**228**	**492**-387	**2082**-1453	4.2-3.8	14-8	11-15	299-403	159-234	2284-2708	**7.6**-6.7	15-17	19-23	327-157	68.5-68.8
NYJ	4-10	.286	—	255-286	463-408	1653-**1283**	3.6-**3.1**	11-7	11-11	386-383	193-165	2592-2680	6.7-7.0	14-20	22-23	285-308	60.1-59.5
Buf	3-10-1	.231	—	204-337	367-484	1465-1718	4.0-3.5	8-16	26-15	402-338	213-**157**	2916-2334	7.3-6.9	13-15	26-11	486-246	60.3-70.8
Bos	2-12	.143	—	149-361	334-503	1040-2074	3.1-4.1	11-20	13-**17**	392-**334**	176-177	1975-2430	5.0-7.3	7-19	28-8	389-243	36.7-85.5
Central Division																	
Cin	8-6	.571	D	312-255	461-418	2057-1543	**4.5**-3.7	16-11	12-16	339-428	172-209	2097-2885	6.2-6.7	12-18	**11**-23	227-250	68.4-62.5
Cle	7-7	.500	—	286-265	462-451	1579-2006	3.4-4.4	14-10	14-12	392-357	190-186	2752-2528	7.0-7.1	17-16	24-19	170-290	60.7-67.8
Pit	5-9	.357	—	210-272	432-487	1715-1679	4.0-3.4	13-8	16-15	384-393	150-191	2312-2555	6.0-6.5	12-21	32-23	275-238	35.4-63.1
Hou	3-10-1	.231	—	217-352	419-466	1556-1793	3.7-3.8	10-16	15-8	**470**-344	**238**-164	2768-2851	5.9-8.3	12-25	23-18	262-246	56.9-78.8
Western Division																	
Oak	8-4-2	.667	DC	300-293	471-460	1964-2027	4.2-4.4	7-10	9-8	418-339	210-157	3029-2386	7.2-7.0	**28**-22	21-19	**164**-297	**75.5**-68.3
KC	7-5-2	.583	—	272-244	448-418	1858-1657	4.1-4.0	14-10	15-12	289-408	154-195	2038-**2280**	7.1-**5.6**	13-15	16-**31**	319-270	67.8-**45.8**
SD	5-6-3	.455	—	282-278	395-480	1450-1967	3.7-4.1	9-15	**6**-15	387-365	192-207	2936-2422	**7.6**-6.6	24-**13**	19-9	433-207	75.3-78.6
Den	5-8-1	.385	—	253-264	436-409	1802-1351	4.1-3.3	**17**-7	13-16	403-379	183-191	2358-2810	5.9-7.4	11-20	28-16	333-**456**	44.5-75.0
Aver	14	—	—	270	440	1685	3.8	11	14	377	193	2535	6.7	16	20	275	65.6

TEAM	1D	PENY	PNT	FGM/A	RTNY	RTNTD	OFFY/DEFY	NETY	NETTO	NP	PNP	DELP	PW	DELW	PRT	DR	YPD	DEL
Eastern Division																		
Bal	242-214	708-1032	44.7-**38.4**	19/34-19/37	759-648	**6**-3	4134-3845	289	-2	**87**	16	71	**9.2**	**2.3**	4.5/ 2.9	188-186	22.0-20.7	1.3
Mia	228-226	834-704	41.2-41.7	22/30-**11/22**	709-499	4-3	4039-4004	35	8	69	35	34	8.7	1.3	3.7/ 4.0	165-**165**	24.5-24.3	0.2
NYJ	230-216	1022-655	40.1-38.9	19/35-18/32	431-777	3-6	3960-**3655**	305	1	-31	29	-60	6.2	-2.2	3.5/ 3.7	182-184	21.8-19.9	1.9
Buf	203-213	1108-814	38.9-44.0	10/19-30/46	477-625	4-4	3895-3806	89	-26	-133	-97	-36	3.7	-0.2	3.1/ 4.7	197-194	19.8-19.6	0.2
Bos	184-242	849-1096	39.1-43.8	8/22-17/28	489-605	0-5	2626-4261	-1635	-16	-212	-200	-12	1.7	0.3	0.9/ 5.6	174-182	15.1-23.4	-8.3
Central Division																		
Cin	210-236	831-784	**46.2**-43.8	25/37-12/24	507-542	6-2	3927-4178	-251	**16**	57	43	14	8.4	-1.3	4.0/ 3.9	188-188	20.9-22.2	-1.3
Cle	239-236	**634**-871	42.6-42.4	12/22-14/26	560-**482**	4-6	4161-4244	-83	-7	21	-35	56	7.5	-0.5	4.1/ 3.9	172-180	24.2-23.6	0.6
Pit	206-225	835-790	44.2-41.9	10/28-15/32	547-622	1-3	3752-3996	-244	-10	-62	-60	-2	5.4	-0.5	1.7/ 3.6	**201**-197	18.7-20.3	-1.6
Hou	232-227	833-833	42.4-44.4	18/32-14/30	499-775	1-3	4062-4398	-336	-12	-135	-76	-59	3.6	-0.1	3.2/ 5.5	192-192	21.2-22.9	-1.8
Western Division																		
Oak	**270**-223	1021-**1148**	39.5-41.6	16/29-21/31	420-606	1-1	**4829**-4116	713	-3	7	**47**	-40	7.2	1.8	**5.0**/ 3.8	185-188	**26.1**-21.9	**4.2**
KC	183-226	888-817	44.9-43.4	**30/42**-21/28	766-609	2-1	3577-3667	-90	12	28	41	-13	7.7	0.3	3.5/**1.7**	190-189	18.8-19.4	-0.6
SD	231-245	852-998	42.8-44.1	12/19-23/40	263-547	2-2	3953-4182	-229	-1	4	-23	27	7.1	-0.6	4.3/ 4.9	173-167	22.3-20.0	-2.2
Den	217-**199**	887-817	42.9-44.9	18/32-23/36	**776**-629	0-1	3827-3705	122	-9	-11	-26	15	6.7	-1.2	2.0/ 4.3	**201**-202	19.0-**18.3**	0.7
Aver	221	839	41.0	18/31	539	1	3945	—	—	—	—	—			4.1	93	21.1	—

Rushing Attempts		Rushing Yards		Rushing Average		Rushing TDs		Rushing Rank		Passing Yards		Passing Average	
F.Little-Den	209	F.Little-Den	901	J.Fuqua-Pit	5.01	B.Scott-Cle	7	L.Csonka-Mia	934	D.Lamonica-Oak	2516	B.Griese-Mia	8.24
L.Kelly-Cle	206	L.Csonka-Mia	874	L.Csonka-Mia	4.53	J.Nance-Bos	7	F.Little-Den	931	D.Shaw-Buf	2507	D.Shaw-Buf	7.81
H.Dixon-Oak	197	H.Dixon-Oak	861	E.Podolak-KC	4.46	J.Fuqua-Pit	7	H.Dixon-Oak	871	J.Hadl-SD	2388	J.Hadl-SD	7.30
L.Csonka-Mia	193	E.Podolak-KC	749	B.Anderson-Den	4.43			E.Podolak-KC	779	J.Unitas-Bal	2213	L.Dawson-KC	7.16
J.Kiick-Mia	191	J.Fuqua-Pit	691	H.Dixon-Oak	4.37			J.Fuqua-Pit	761	B.Nelsen-Cle	2156	D.Lamonica-Oak	7.07

Completion Percent		TD Passes		TD Percent		INT Percent		Passer Rating		Passing Rank		Receptions	
B.Griese-Mia	58.0	D.Lamonica-Oak	22	J.Hadl-SD	6.7	V.Carter-Cin	3.2	J.Hadl-SD	77.1	D.Lamonica-Oak	768	M.Briscoe-Buf	57
D.Shaw-Buf	55.5	J.Hadl-SD	22	D.Lamonica-Oak	6.2	D.Lamonica-Oak	4.2	D.Lamonica-Oak	76.5	J.Hadl-SD	704	A.Reed-Hou	47
L.Dawson-KC	53.8	B.Nelsen-Cle	16	B.Nelsen-Cle	5.1	C.Johnson-Hou	4.3	B.Griese-Mia	72.1	B.Nelsen-Cle	518	E.Hinton-Bal	47
J.Rhome-Hou	52.4	J.Unitas-Bal	14	L.Dawson-KC	5.0	J.Hadl-SD	4.6	L.Dawson-KC	71.0	V.Carter-Cin	509	A.Denson-Den	47
J.Unitas-Bal	51.7	L.Dawson-KC	13	B.Griese-Mia	4.9	P.Liske-Den	4.6	B.Nelsen-Cle	68.9	D.Shaw-Buf	504	V.Biggs-Oak	45

Receiving Yards		Receiving Average		Receiving TDs		Receiving Rank		Combined Net Yards		Total TDs		Total Points	
M.Briscoe-Buf	1036	P.Warfield-Mia	25.11	G.Garrison-SD	12	G.Garrison-SD	563	E.Podolak-KC	1715	G.Garrison-SD	12	J.Stenerud-KC	116
G.Garrison-SD	1006	R.Shanklin-Pit	23.03	W.Wells-Oak	11	M.Briscoe-Buf	558	J.LeVias-Hou	1377	W.Wells-Oak	11	H.Muhlmann-Cin	108
W.Wells-Oak	935	G.Garrison-SD	22.86	M.Briscoe-Buf	8	W.Wells-Oak	523	F.Little-Den	1375	B.Scott-Cle	11	G.Yepremian-Mia	97
V.Biggs-Oak	768	W.Wells-Oak	21.74			V.Biggs-Oak	419	M.Morris-Mia	1369	J.Fuqua-Pit	9	J.O'Brien-Bal	93
R.Jefferson-Bal	749	H.Moses-Den	18.62			R.Jefferson-Bal	410	C.Garrett-Bos	1167			J.Turner-NYJ	85

Punt Average		Field Goals		Field Goal Percent		Kickoff Returns		Kickoff Return Average		Punt Returns		Punt Return Average	
D.Lewis-Cin	46.2	J.Stenerud-KC	30	G.Yepremian-Mia	75.9	M.Battle-NYJ	40	J.Duncan-Bal	35.3	H.Bryant-Pit	37	E.Podolak-KC	13.5
B.Walden-Pit	45.2	H.Muhlmann-Cin	25	J.Stenerud-KC	71.4	H.Jones-Cle	29	L.Parrish-Oak	30.1	R.Gardin-Bal	28	R.Gardin-Bal	11.8
J.Wilson-KC	44.9	G.Yepremian-Mia	22	H.Muhlmann-Cin	67.6	M.Morris-Mia	26	M.Blount-Pit	29.7	J.Scott-Mia	28	J.Scott-Mia	10.7
D.Lee-Bal	44.7	J.Turner-NYJ	19	M.Mercer-SD	63.2	J.LeVias-Hou	26	M.Morris-Mia	29.0	A.Wyatt-Oak	25	B.Thompson-Den	10.1
D.Partee-SD	43.9	J.O'Brien-Bal	19			O.Lawson-Bos	25	R.Holmes-KC	28.2	J.LeVias-Hou	25	C.Garrett-Bos	9.9

Punt/Kick Return Yards		Punt/Kick Return TDs		Interceptions		Interception Return Yards		Interception Return TDs		Sacks		Overall Rank	
M.Battle-NYJ	1008	L.Parrish-Cin	2	J.Robinson-KC	10	D.Anderson-Mia	191	J.Logan-Bal	2	Not kept		E.Podolak-KC	1247
M.Morris-Mia	811			W.Hicks-NYJ	8	J.Robinson-KC	155					F.Little-Den	1125
J.LeVias-Hou	811			D.Anderson-Mia	8	J.Scott-Mia	112					L.Csonka-Mia	981
H.Jones-Cle	739			L.Calland-Pit	7	P.Martha-Den	99					H.Dixon-Oak	980
J.Duncan-Bal	707					W.Hicks-NYJ	99					J.Kiick-Mia	979

OLD CLUBS, NEW RIVALRIES

Don Shula defected to Miami before the season. Shula might have had the benefit of making a well-timed jump to a team loaded with young talent, but his veteran former club got him back. Baltimore was one of three teams agreeing to join the American Football Conference to even out the number of clubs in each conference. The Colts made themselves at home in their new division, rattling off a 6–1–1 record in the AFC East, steering toward the Super Bowl they so desperately wanted another shot at.

This was to be Johnny Unitas's last effective season. He could still lead an offense capably enough to outperform expectations, and perhaps please Colts fans with a couple of easy wins over their new division rivals, the Jets, as vengeance for Super Bowl III. Miami handed Baltimore one of its two losses. The Dolphins finished with the AFC's second-best record and handed the Colts one of their two defeats. Miami matched a stellar defense with an offense that already boasted an incomparable trio of talented running backs in Mercury

Morris, Larry Csonka, and Jim Kiick, plus young quarterback Bob Griese. The Dolphins were clearly the team of the very near future.

Realignment didn't similarly reward the Browns. Cleveland was deposited into the same division as Paul Brown's Bengals, and Cincinnati followed a six-game losing streak with a seven-game winning streak to claim the new Central Division. In getting his new team into the playoffs after just three years of existence, Brown had cultivated many of same qualities of his old club: a bend-but-not-break defense and a mistake-free, ball-control offense. Cincinnati also passed Pittsburgh, another old NFL club in a new conference. The top pick in the 1970 draft brought in strong-armed Terry Bradshaw out of Louisiana Tech. Thrown into the fire, Bradshaw clearly wasn't ready, and neither were the Steelers.

At age 43, Oakland's George Blanda had a remarkable five-week run in which he led fourth-quarter rallies with either his foot or his arm (or both). His last-second 48-yard kick to tie the Chiefs in November wound up making the difference in a tight AFC West race.

1971 NFC

TEAM	W-L-T	PCT	POST	PTS	RA	RY	RY/A	RTD	FL	PA	PC	GPY	GPY/A	PTD	PI	PSY	PRAT
Eastern Division																	
Dal	**11**-3	**.786**	DCS*	**406**-222	512-**353**	2249-**1144**	4.4-**3.2**	**25**-8	21-**25**	361-421	206-209	3037-2660	8.4-6.3	**22**-15	14-26	251-**336**	**88.8**-55.9
Was	9-4-1	.692	W	276-190	477-408	1757-1396	3.7-3.4	8-7	20-12	334-411	182-191	2391-2448	7.2-6.0	13-11	15-**29**	118-321	71.6-**45.1**
Phi	6-7-1	.462	—	221-302	407-450	1248-1962	3.1-4.4	6-16	15-**25**	390-407	200-220	2552-2971	6.5-7.3	13-16	20-22	229-311	61.8-68.1
SL	4-9-1	.308	—	231-279	417-486	1530-1985	3.7-4.1	8-10	20-16	385-375	170-212	2656-2546	6.9-6.8	14-12	26-17	185-166	51.6-69.3
NYG	4-10	.286	—	228-362	394-449	1461-2059	3.7-4.6	11-12	20-15	**462**-333	**268**-173	**3062**-2458	6.6-7.4	14-25	25-15	348-151	65.6-82.4
Central Division																	
Min	**11**-3	**.786**	D	245-**139**	484-447	1695-1600	3.5-3.6	14-**2**	12-18	334-405	157-206	1910-2022	5.7-**5.0**	9-10	18-27	255-216	51.6-45.7
Det	7-6-1	.538	—	341-286	**532**-432	**2376**-1842	4.5-4.3	15-15	19-11	299-**306**	157-163	2453-2163	8.2-7.1	17-17	14-22	252-146	79.5-64.5
ChiB	6-8	.429	—	185-276	365-509	1434-2116	3.9-4.2	6-14	18-23	443-362	186-192	2294-2607	5.2-7.2	12-12	28-22	392-203	41.3-62.0
GB	4-8-2	.333	—	274-298	500-489	2229-1707	4.5-3.5	18-7	20-16	254-353	121-186	1842-2469	7.3-7.0	12-21	24-16	157-168	48.4-76.1
Western Division																	
SF	9-5	.643	DC	300-216	498-408	2129-1668	4.3-4.1	12-4	18-16	391-341	209-**152**	2688-2309	6.9-6.8	18-17	24-14	**111**-298	65.0-67.0
LA	8-5-1	.615	—	313-260	460-455	2139-1658	**4.7**-3.6	15-11	18-7	370-387	185-200	2304-2693	6.2-7.0	18-15	**11**-27	210-314	73.5-58.0
Atl	7-6-1	.538	—	274-277	494-500	1703-2149	3.4-4.3	12-19	15-18	285-343	167-164	2495-**1895**	**8.8**-5.5	16-**9**	21-20	239-257	75.4-49.4
NO	4-8-2	.333	—	266-347	452-495	1711-2200	3.8-4.4	18-18	**11-25**	387-333	182-175	2355-2472	6.1-7.4	12-20	14-20	400-234	61.9-71.8
Aver	14	—	—	271	453	1822	4.0	13	16	362	184	2433	6.7	15	21	253	62.2

TEAM	1D	PENY	PNT	FGM/A	RTNY	RTNTD	OFFY/DEFY	NETY	NETTO	NP	PNP	DELP	PW	DELW	PRT	DR	YPD	DEL
Eastern Division																		
Dal	**288**-200	952-647	41.6-41.5	18/33-16/25	650-535	3-**2**	**5035**-3468	**1567**	16	**184**	**195**	-11	**11.6**	-0.6	**6.0**/ 2.8	181-188	**27.8**-18.4	**9.4**
Was	212-213	801-720	40.5-41.2	**29/49**-17/33	**907**-371	6-**2**	4030-3523	507	6	86	66	20	9.1	0.3	4.9/ 2.1	185-183	21.8-19.3	2.5
Phi	201-251	838-908	**41.9**-40.5	18/37-17/33	546-731	5-4	3571-4622	-1051	12	-81	-40	-41	5.0	**1.5**	3.7/ 4.2	187-185	19.1-25.0	-5.9
SL	212-244	643-831	38.8-40.4	21/32-25/39	425-518	2-7	4001-4365	-364	-13	-48	-82	34	5.8	-1.3	3.6/ 4.4	173-178	23.1-24.5	-1.4
NYG	236-228	640-730	40.6-39.8	6/17-22/32	349-696	5-5	4175-4366	-191	-15	-134	-76	-58	3.7	0.3	3.4/ 5.4	179-173	23.3-25.2	-1.9
Central Division																		
Min	198-**194**	661-615	39.5-40.0	22/32-14/32	736-540	2-**2**	3350-**3406**	-56	15	106	55	**51**	9.6	1.3	2.6/**1.6**	185-190	18.1-**17.9**	0.2
Det	269-210	738-942	41.7-40.2	22/37-**13**/25	489-318	**7**-3	4577-3859	718	0	55	60	-5	8.4	-0.9	5.3/ 3.7	166-166	27.6-23.2	4.3
ChiB	189-234	746-819	40.2-40.2	15/33-24/41	529-637	2-3	3336-4520	-1184	-1	-91	-103	12	4.7	1.3	1.5/ 3.9	**196**-191	17.0-23.7	-6.6
GB	208-230	**568**-514	40.0-40.1	14/26-20/37	382-618	3-6	3914-4008	-94	-12	-24	-56	32	6.4	-1.4	2.7/ 4.8	179-174	21.9-23.0	-1.2
Western Division																		
SF	257-199	961-610	38.7-39.7	23/36-19/33	454-429	3-**2**	4706-3679	1027	-12	84	38	46	9.1	-0.1	4.2/ 4.1	173-176	27.2-20.9	6.3
LA	234-239	642-665	41.4-**39.4**	18/29-17/32	624-**150**	4-4	4233-4037	196	5	53	36	17	8.3	0.2	4.5/ 3.1	176-179	24.1-22.6	1.5
Atl	221-237	723-614	36.9-41.4	13/21-20/**23**	354-359	6-3	3959-3787	172	2	-3	22	-25	6.9	0.6	4.7/ 2.2	170-**165**	23.3-23.0	0.3
NO	242-260	869-**967**	41.4-41.2	17/28-**13**/26	442-422	1-6	3666-4438	-772	**20**	-81	16	-97	5.0	0.0	3.3/ 4.3	179-175	20.5-25.4	-4.9
Aver	227	751	40.8	18/31	533	3	4002	—	—	—	—	—	—	—	3.8	180	22.3	—

Rushing Attempts	Rushing Yards	Rushing Average	Rushing TDs	Rushing Rank	Passing Yards	Passing Average
L.Brown-Was 253	G.Brezina-GB 1105	G.Landry-Det 6.97	D.Thomas-Dal 11	G.Brezina-GB 1145	J.Brodie-SF 2642	R.Staubach-Dal 8.92
S.Owens-Det 246	S.Owens-Det 1035	G.Brezina-GB 5.12	S.Owens-Det 8	S.Owens-Det 1115	F.Tarkenton-NYG 2567	B.Berry-Atl 8.87
K.Willard-SF 216	W.Ellison-LA 1000	W.Ellison-LA 4.74	C.Hill-Dal 8	W.Ellison-LA 1040	R.Gabriel-LA 2238	G.Landry-Det 8.57
G.Brezina-GB 216	L.Brown-Was 948	L.Josephson-LA 4.54	A.Malone-Atl 6	L.Brown-Was 988	G.Landry-Det 2237	C.Morton-Dal 7.91
W.Ellison-LA 211	K.Willard-SF 855	D.Thomas-Dal 4.53	B.Gresham-NO 6	D.Thomas-Dal 903	B.Kilmer-Was 2221	S.Hunter-GB 7.42
Completion Percent	**TD Passes**	**TD Percent**	**INT Percent**	**Passer Rating**	**Passing Rank**	**Receptions**
B.Berry-Atl 60.2	J.Brodie-SF 18	R.Staubach-Dal 7.1	R.Staubach-Dal 1.9	R.Staubach-Dal 104.8	R.Staubach-Dal 856	B.Tucker-NYG 59
R.Staubach-Dal 59.7	R.Gabriel-LA 17	G.Landry-Det 6.1	E.Hargett-NO 2.4	G.Landry-Det 80.9	R.Gabriel-LA 804	T.Kwalick-SF 52
F.Tarkenton-NYG 58.5	G.Landry-Det 16	C.Morton-Dal 4.9	R.Gabriel-LA 2.8	B.Berry-Atl 75.9	G.Landry-Det 679	R.Jefferson-Was 47
C.Morton-Dal 54.5	R.Staubach-Dal 15	B.Berry-Atl 4.9	B.Kilmer-Was 4.2	R.Gabriel-LA 75.4	B.Kilmer-Was 656	H.Jackson-Phi 47
B.Kilmer-Was 54.2	B.Kilmer-Was 13	R.Gabriel-LA 4.8	G.Cuozzo-Min 4.8	B.Kilmer-Was 74.0	F.Tarkenton-NYG 499	
Receiving Yards	**Receiving Average**	**Receiving TDs**	**Receiving Rank**	**Combined Net Yards**	**Total TDs**	**Total Points**
J.Ward-SF 884	B.Hayes-Dal 24.00	B.Hayes-Dal 8	J.Ward-SF 462	J.Ward-SF 1986	D.Thomas-Dal 13	C.Knight-Was 114
B.Hayes-Dal 840	K.Burrow-Atl 22.45	B.Grim-Min 7	B.Hayes-Dal 460	D.Hampton-GB 1658	C.Hill-Dal 11	E.Mann-Det 103
J.Gilliam-SL 837	J.Gilliam-SL 19.93	K.Burrow-Atl 6	J.Gilliam-SL 434	S.Owens-Det 1385	S.Owens-Det 10	B.Gossett-SF 101
B.Tucker-NYG 791	C.Dale-GB 19.29		B.Tucker-NYG 416	M.Gray-SL 1330	A.Malone-Atl 8	D.Ray-LA 91
K.Burrow-Atl 741	J.Ward-SF 19.22		K.Burrow-Atl 401	W.Ellison-LA 1238	B.Hayes-Dal 8	F.Cox-Min 91
Punt Average	**Field Goals**	**Field Goal Percent**	**Kickoff Returns**	**Kickoff Return Average**	**Punt Returns**	**Punt Return Average**
T.McNeill-Phi 42.0	C.Knight-Was 29	T.Dempsey-Phi 70.6	D.Hampton-GB 46	T.Williams-LA 29.7	B.Taylor-SF 34	S.Duncan-Was 10.6
H.Weaver-Det 41.7	B.Gossett-SF 23	C.Durkee-NO 69.6	R.Thompson-NYG 36	R.Jessie-Det 29.4	W.Belton-Atl 30	L.Barney-Det 8.7
R.Widby-Dal 41.6	E.Mann-Det 22	F.Cox-Min 68.8	J.Ward-SF 33	D.Hampton-GB 28.6	R.Smith-Chi 26	T.Vactor-Was 8.4
P.Studstill-LA 41.4	F.Cox-Min 22	J.Bakken-SL 65.6	C.Turner-Chi 31	C.Harris-Dal 28.4	A.Haymond-LA 24	C.Harris-Dal 7.6
J.Fagan-NO 41.4	J.Bakken-SL 21	B.Gossett-SF 63.9	M.Gray-SL 30	S.Duncan-Was 26.8	T.Vactor-Was 23	R.Smith-Chi 7.5
Punt/Kick Return Yards	**Punt/Kick Return TDs**	**Interceptions**	**Interception Return Yards**	**Interception Return TDs**	**Sacks**	**Overall Rank**
D.Hampton-GB 1314	I.Thomas-Dal 2	B.Bradley-Phi 11	B.Bradley-Phi 248	M.Lucci-Det 2	Not kept	J.Ward-SF 1383
S.Duncan-Was 957	R.Jessie-Det 2	M.Bass-Was 8	C.West-Min 236			S.Owens-Det 1300
C.Harris-Dal 952		C.West-Min 7	H.Adderley-Dal 182			G.Landry-Det 1239
R.Thompson-NYG 947			C.Howley-Dal 122			R.Staubach-Dal 1219
W.Belton-Atl 869			K.Alexander-LA 122			G.Brezina-GB 1199

At Long Last, Staubach Starts

The anticipation of what would happen once Roger Staubach took over in Dallas turned out to be well worth it. Eight years removed from the Heisman Trophy that had brought him to national attention, with his Navy service fulfilled, and beginning his third season on the Cowboys' bench, Staubach finally got his opportunity to replace Craig Morton after Dallas stumbled to a 4–3 start. Staubach helped Dallas win seven straight games and a division title.

Even as Staubach worked his magic in Dallas, the rising power of defense in pro football was increasingly obvious. The Lions fell short of the playoffs despite the league's second-best offense—their backfield boasted fleet quarterback Greg Landry and Heisman Trophy running back Steve Owens, plus a stellar offensive line—but Detroit's defense didn't have the stopping power of the four playoff-bound teams.

The Redskins and 49ers both relied heavily on their tough defenses and on conservative offenses guided by veteran quarterbacks—Billy Kilmer and John Brodie, respectively—supplemented by quality running back tandems. The Vikings couldn't boast even that much firepower on offense, but they had the Purple People Eaters on defense. Led by league MVP and Defensive Player of the Year Alan Page, Minnesota allowed fewer than 10 points per game. The Dallas defense didn't instill that level of fear, but the opportunistic Cowboys picked up a league-leading 51 turnovers.

Although the Packers had rookie John Brockington winning the NFC rushing title, nothing could hide the fact that the team's proud past was fading away. Bart Starr, Forrest Gregg (finishing his career a Cowboy), Boyd Dowler (as a Redskin), and Willie Wood all retired. Future greats came into the conference, notably Rams defensive end Jack Youngblood and gargantuan receiver Harold Carmichael in Philadelphia. Tackle Dan Dierdorf and center Tom Banks both took their places on the St. Louis line, while rookie Mel Gray went deep for the Cardinals.

Two greats from the 1920, Joe Guyon and George Trafton, died in 1971. Sadder still was the death of Detroit's Chuck Hughes, 28, on the field at Tiger Stadium. He had a fatal heart attack while running a pass route on October 24.

1971 AFC

TEAM	W-L-T	PCT	POST	PTS	RA	RY	RY/A	RTD	FL	PA	PC	GPY	GPY/A	PTD	PI	PSY	PRAT
Eastern Division																	
Mia	**10-3-1**	.769	DCS	315-174	486-403	**2429**-1661	**5.0**-4.1	11-10	13-14	293-363	156-206	2248-2293	7.7-6.3	20-10	**10**-17	265-293	**87.0**-65.4
Bal	**10-4**	.714	WC	313-**140**	**512**-352	2149-**1113**	4.2-**3.2**	**23**-8	11-13	344-361	176-185	2152-**2027**	6.3-**5.6**	10-9	21-**28**	230-288	55.0-**44.2**
NE	6-8	.429	—	238-325	419-481	1669-1918	4.0-4.0	7-14	16-14	330-350	159-170	2206-2403	6.7-6.9	19-16	16-15	319-249	69.1-68.5
NYJ	6-8	.429	—	212-299	485-472	1888-2302	3.9-4.9	12-18	**10**-14	278-342	119-163	1556-2285	5.6-6.7	15-17	16-13	177-230	55.1-70.4
Buf	1-13	.071	—	184-394	320-562	1337-2496	4.2-4.4	6-21	16-11	401-**303**	202-157	2410-2333	6.0-7.7	12-20	32-11	421-225	45.8-84.2
Central Division																	
Cle	9-5	.643	D	285-273	461-484	1558-2227	3.4-4.6	19-14	18-16	376-339	188-156	2521-2170	6.7-6.4	14-12	27-24	222-203	54.2-49.4
Pit	6-8	.429	—	246-292	416-440	1758-1482	4.2-3.4	10-13	16-18	414-408	214-235	2446-3060	5.9-7.5	15-16	26-17	322-294	55.7-77.0
Hou	4-9-1	.308	—	251-330	361-489	1106-1723	3.1-3.5	10-22	14-14	423-354	194-180	2643-2416	6.2-6.8	12-11	37-23	234-344	39.3-56.2
Cin	4-10	.286	—	284-265	462-446	2142-1778	4.6-4.0	14-11	12-12	365-335	214-157	2427-2382	6.6-7.1	15-19	11-27	303-254	79.8-56.1
Western Division																	
KC	**10-3-1**	.769	D	302-208	487-367	1843-1300	3.8-3.5	14-9	13-6	337-418	183-209	2694-2703	**8.0**-6.5	15-11	13-27	347-235	79.4-52.6
Oak	8-4-2	.667	—	**344**-278	473-480	2130-1751	4.5-3.6	19-14	13-17	348-359	174-184	2363-2609	6.8-7.3	21-15	26-23	235-223	61.0-62.3
SD	6-8	.429	—	311-341	390-493	1604-2296	4.1-4.7	11-25	15-10	**450**-347	**244**-193	**3305**-2439	7.3-7.0	**23**-15	28-22	**171**-177	69.0-65.7
Den	4-9-1	.308	—	203-275	**512**-426	2093-1834	4.1-4.3	9-11	12-**20**	358-356	175-**150**	2243-2420	6.3-6.8	8-18	27-20	178-**435**	44.9-59.0
Aver	14	—	—	271	453	1822	4.0	13	16	362	184	2433	6.7	15	21	253	62.2

TEAM	1D	PENY	PNT	FGM/A	RTNY	RTNTD	OFF/DEFY	NETY	NETTO	NP	PNP	DELP	PW	DELW	PRT	DR	YPD	DEL
Eastern Division																		
Mia	232-214	632-569	40.1-40.7	**28**/40-9/21	575-**272**	2-1	4412-3661	751	8	141	95	46	10.5	-0.0	**5.4**/3.4	159-**162**	27.7-22.6	5.1
Bal	242-166	**529**-687	41.0-38.9	20/29-**5/18**	**718**-487	3-1	4071-**2852**	**1219**	9	**173**	138	35	**11.3**	-1.3	2.9/**1.4**	180-173	22.6-**16.5**	**6.1**
NE	190-237	657-559	37.3-38.8	12/21-27/36	410-436	3-5	3556-4072	-516	-3	-87	-55	-32	4.8	1.2	3.7/4.4	180-183	19.8-22.3	-2.5
NYJ	202-235	672-814	38.8-**38.1**	8/19-14/25	291-638	0-2	3267-4357	-1090	1	-87	-87	0	4.8	1.2	2.7/4.4	168-164	19.4-26.6	-7.1
Buf	185-250	691-883	40.9-39.0	12/25-25/38	436-864	3-4	3326-4604	-1278	-26	-210	-211	1	1.8	-0.8	1.5/5.4	186-185	17.9-24.9	-7.0
Central Division																		
Cle	231-232	612-772	39.9-42.4	15/28-21/31	642-680	1-4	3857-4194	-337	-5	12	-48	**60**	7.3	**1.7**	3.1/2.8	182-188	21.2-22.3	-1.1
Pit	226-225	898-784	43.7-41.5	17/27-22/35	510-669	3-3	3882-4248	-366	-7	-46	-59	13	5.8	0.1	2.4/4.9	193-192	20.1-22.1	-2.0
Hou	201-237	856-**916**	40.6-40.9	17/28-24/35	654-809	**7**-4	3515-3795	-280	-14	-79	-79	0	5.0	-0.5	1.9/2.9	**199**-197	17.7-19.3	-1.6
Cin	236-213	921-722	44.7-40.9	20/36-14/22	418-523	3-2	4266-3906	360	16	19	94	-75	7.5	-3.5	4.4/3.0	180-178	23.7-21.9	1.8
Western Division																		
KC	240-223	734-751	**44.8**-40.7	26/**45**-20/32	553-453	3-1	4190-3768	422	7	94	63	31	9.4	1.2	5.1/3.1	167-182	25.1-20.7	4.4
Oak	258-242	869-832	39.9-41.7	15/22-22/34	635-435	3-1	4258-4137	121	1	66	14	52	8.6	0.4	3.1/3.8	177-181	24.1-22.9	1.2
SD	**264**-272	895-887	43.5-43.7	17/29-11/24	532-379	3-4	**4738**-4558	180	-11	-30	-29	-1	6.3	-0.3	4.5/3.9	182-178	26.0-25.6	0.4
Den	217-206	781-771	41.8-45.7	25/38-17/35	608-900	1-3	4158-3819	339	1	-72	-104		5.2	-0.7	2.4/3.2	189-185	22.0-20.6	1.4
Aver	227	751	40.8	18/31	533	1	4002	—	—	—	—		3.8	—		90	22.0	—

Rushing Attempts		Rushing Yards		Rushing Average		Rushing TDs		Rushing Rank		Passing Yards		Passing Average	
F.Little-Den	284	F.Little-Den	1133	E.Johnson-Cin	6.14	L.Kelly-Cle	10	F.Little-Den	1193	J.Hadl-SD	3075	L.Dawson-KC	8.32
L.Kelly-Cle	234	L.Csonka-Mia	1051	L.Csonka-Mia	5.39	B.Scott-SD	9	L.Csonka-Mia	1121	L.Dawson-KC	2504	B.Griese-Mia	7.94
L.Csonka-Mia	195	M.Hubbard-Oak	867	N.Bulaich-Bal	4.88	E.Podolak-KC	9	L.Kelly-Cle	965	B.Nelsen-Cle	2319	V.Carter-Cin	7.32
E.Boozer-NYJ	188	L.Kelly-Cle	865	M.Hubbard-Oak	4.79			M.Hubbard-Oak	917	T.Bradshaw-Pit	2259	E.Morrall-Bal	7.25
E.Podolak-KC	184	C.Garrett-NE	784	P.Pearson-Pit	4.62			N.Bulaich-Bal	821	J.Plunkett-NE	2158	B.Nelsen-Cle	7.14

Completion Percent		TD Passes		TD Percent		INT Percent		Passer Rating		Passing Rank		Receptions	
V.Carter-Cin	62.2	J.Hadl-SD	21	B.Griese-Mia	7.2	V.Carter-Cin	3.2	B.Griese-Mia	90.9	L.Dawson-KC	807	R.Beverly-Oak	61
L.Dawson-KC	55.5	J.Plunkett-NE	19	D.Lamonica-Oak	6.6	B.Griese-Mia	3.4	V.Carter-Cin	86.2	B.Griese-Mia	780	O.Taylor-KC	57
B.Griese-Mia	55.1	B.Griese-Mia	19	J.Plunkett-NE	5.8	L.Dawson-KC	4.3	L.Dawson-KC	81.6	J.Hadl-SD	643	R.Vataha-NE	51
T.Bradshaw-Pit	54.4	D.Lamonica-Oak	16	L.Dawson-KC	5.0	J.Plunkett-NE	4.9	J.Hadl-SD	68.9	V.Carter-Cin	582	R.Shanklin-Pit	49
J.Hadl-SD	54.1	L.Dawson-KC	15	J.Hadl-SD	4.9	J.Unitas-Bal	5.1	J.Plunkett-NE	68.6	J.Plunkett-NE	534	J.Fuqua-Pit	49

Receiving Yards		Receiving Average		Receiving TDs		Receiving Rank		Combined Net Yards		Total TDs		Total Points	
O.Taylor-KC	1110	P.Warfield-Mia	23.16	P.Warfield-Mia	11	O.Taylor-KC	590	C.Garrett-NE	1711	L.Kelly-Cle	12	G.Yepremian-Mia	117
P.Warfield-Mia	996	C.Joiner-Hou	21.97	R.Vataha-NE	9	P.Warfield-Mia	553	F.Little-Den	1587	P.Warfield-Mia	11	J.Stenerud-KC	110
R.Beverly-Oak	929	G.Garrison-SD	21.17	R.Beverly-Oak	9	R.Beverly-Oak	510	L.Kelly-Cle	1420	B.Scott-SD	10	J.O'Brien-Bal	95
G.Garrison-SD	889	O.Taylor-KC	19.47			R.Vataha-NE	481	L.Csonka-Mia	1164	N.Bulaich-Bal	10	J.Turner-Den	93
R.Vataha-NE	872	R.Vataha-NE	17.10			G.Garrison-SD	475	C.Davis-Oak	1152			H.Muhlmann-Cin	91

Punt Average		Field Goals		Field Goal Percent		Kickoff Returns		Kickoff Return Average		Punt Returns		Punt Return Average	
J.Wilson-KC	44.8	G.Yepremian-Mia	28	G.Yepremian-Mia	70.0	L.Cole-Hou	32	M.Morris-Mia	28.2	J.Scott-Mia	33	L.Kelly-Cle	9.7
D.Lewis-Cle	44.8	J.Stenerud-KC	26	J.O'Brien-Bal	69.0	A.Wyatt-Buf	30	C.Davis-Oak	27.2	J.Staggers-Pit	31	J.Scott-Mia	9.6
B.Walden-Pit	43.7	J.Turner-Den	25	G.Blanda-Oak	68.2	C.Davis-Oak	27	L.Cole-Hou	26.1	L.Kelly-Cle	30	I.Hill-Buf	9.5
D.Partee-SD	43.5	J.O'Brien-Bal	20	J.Turner-Den	65.8	Farasopoulos-NYJ	25	A.Wyatt-Buf	25.4	B.Thompson-Den	29	B.Thompson-Den	9.4
J.Unitas-Den	41.8	H.Muhlmann-Cin	20	R.Gerela-Pit	63.0			C.Pittman-Bal	23.6	A.Wyatt-Buf	23	J.Staggers-Pit	8.5

Punt/Kick Return Yards		Punt/Kick Return TDs		Interceptions		Interception Return Yards		Interception Return TDs		Sacks		Overall Rank	
A.Wyatt-Buf	950	A.Wyatt-Buf	1	K.Houston-Hou	9	K.Houston-Hou	220	K.Houston-Hou	4	Not kept		F.Little-Den	1415
L.Cole-Hou	941	J.Staggers-Pit	1	E.Thomas-KC	8	E.Thomas-KC	145	J.Warren-Oak	2			L.Kelly-Cle	1251
C.Davis-Oak	734	M.Morris-Mia	1	C.Stukes-Bal	8	J.Tatum-Oak	136					C.Garrett-NE	1194
J.LeVias-SD	704	I.Hill-Buf	1	J.Scott-Mia	7	J.Warren-Oak	114					L.Csonka-Mia	1183
Farasopoulos-NYJ	700			L.Parrish-Cin	7	L.Parrish-Cin	105					M.Hubbard-Oak	1007

QUARTERBACKS INTO THE FIRE

The NFL draft generated considerable attention because of the quarterbacks available, particularly Heisman Trophy winner Jim Plunkett (Stanford), and Archie Manning (Mississippi), who was seen by some as the better pro prospect. With the first choice, the Patriots picked Plunkett, the Saints took Manning, and the Oilers followed by selecting Dan Pastorini with the third pick in the draft. (Just to be sure, Houston took quarterback Lynn Dickey with its next pick.) Plunkett, Manning, and Pastorini would all be thrown onto the field by their equally desperate clubs. Draft day was not yet a televised, over-analyzed event, but the attention given to the quarterback class of 1971 was symptomatic of the growing interest in all things football.

In-season, the AFC wound up being a true test of the staying power of some of the newly-configured conference's veteran squads against the rising power of Don Shula's Dolphins. On the strength of the AFC's best defense, the aging Colts made it a race with Miami, only falling behind the Dolphins in the final week because of an upset loss to the Patriots. That they got even that far—and won the wild card—was a credit to the old club, because the Dolphins featured the league's best running game, the conference's most effective passing attack now that Bob Griese had come into his own, and a defense second only to Baltimore's in the AFC.

If the Browns had been surprised to fall short of the Bengals in their first year in the AFC, they won five out of six games within their division to pass a slumping Steelers squad that lost three of four to end the year. Still, two more defensive building blocks came to Pittsburgh with the debuts of defensive end Dwight White and outside linebacker Jack Ham.

In the Western Division, Kansas City managed an upset. Relying heavily on Len Dawson hitting wideout Otis Taylor (for an NFL-best 1,110 receiving yards), the Chiefs put the Raiders away in the season's next-to-last game, winning at home on a late Jan Stenerud field goal, 16–14. It would the Chiefs' last division title for 22 years.

1972 NFC

TEAM	W-L-T	PCT	POST	PTS	RA	RY	RY/A	RTD	FL	PA	PC	GPY	GPY/A	PTD	PI	PSY	PRAT
Eastern Division																	
Was	**11-3**	.786	DCS	336-218	513-427	2082-1733	4.1-4.1	17-12	11-15	284-367	159-186	2281-2130	**8.0**-5.8	21-10	15-17	88-268	**84.8**-58.3
Dal	10-4	.714	WC	319-240	499-428	2124-**1515**	4.3-3.5	17-**7**	15-17	367-382	196-187	2580-2508	7.0-6.6	16-18	23-16	238-268	64.3-68.5
NYG	8-6	.571	—	331-247	524-**402**	2022-1855	3.9-4.6	16-9	14-15	344-333	206-182	2537-2571	7.4-7.7	20-19	15-23	**76**-232	83.9-70.0
SL	4-9-1	.321	—	193-303	361-548	1229-2189	3.4-4.0	9-11	16-16	363-365	171-221	2259-2733	6.2-7.5	11-15	23-11	221-183	51.0-84.9
Phi	2-11-1	.179	—	145-352	398-544	1393-2266	3.5-4.2	2-22	18-8	375-318	184-175	2527-2615	6.7-8.2	10-20	20-19	457-143	57.7-78.3
Central Division																	
GB	10-4	.714	D	304-226	**544**-443	2127-1517	3.9-**3.4**	17-14	10-**19**	237-340	101-174	1536-2209	6.5-6.5	7-**7**	**9**-17	124-252	58.6-57.8
Det	8-5-1	.607	—	339-290	473-491	2021-2204	4.3-4.5	20-14	7-15	305-312	155-171	2283-2146	7.5-6.9	19-18	12-18	149-142	71.8-79.6
Min	7-7	.500	—	301-252	472-454	1740-2002	3.7-4.4	11-13	19-14	385-331	218-169	2726-**1791**	7.1-**5.4**	19-13	13-**26**	203-92	81.2-**47.5**
ChiB	4-9-1	.321	—	225-275	536-476	**2360**-1751	4.4-3.7	15-11	22-14	205-342	78-180	1283-2345	6.3-6.9	9-16	13-21	175-173	48.1-64.5
Western Division																	
SF	8-5-1	.607	D	**353**-249	445-446	1616-1847	3.6-4.1	11-12	13-17	380-366	217-169	**2888**-2582	7.6-7.1	**27**-14	24-19	153-**403**	78.7-61.1
Atl	7-7	.500	—	269-274	500-504	2092-2063	4.2-4.1	16-16	19-15	296-**301**	157-**137**	2202-1911	7.4-6.3	13-15	15-18	283-207	70.8-55.9
LA	6-7-1	.464	—	291-286	472-438	2209-1762	**4.7**-4.0	17-9	9-11	371-363	184-181	2282-2472	6.2-6.8	13-20	22-16	136-327	56.0-72.0
NO	2-11-1	.179	—	215-361	337-482	1230-2089	3.6-4.3	5-15	16-13	**449**-367	230-213	2781-2596	6.2-7.1	18-21	21-14	347-194	64.5-83.1
Aver	14	—	—	284	471	1951	4.1	14	14	347	179	2363	6.8	16	18	233	66.3

TEAM	1D	PENY	PNT	FGM/A	RTNY	RTNTD	OFFY/DEFY	NETY	NETTO	NP	PNP	DELP	PW	DELW	PRT	DR	YPD	DEL
Eastern Division																		
Was	235-223	721-568	38.5-40.1	14/30-19/33	446-**199**	4-1	4275-3595	680	6	**118**	81	37	9.9	1.0	**5.9**/3.0	172-171	24.9-21.0	3.8
Dal	256-217	841-586	38.2-40.6	21/36-**15**/34	347-343	3-0	4466-3755	711	-5	79	39	40	9.0	1.0	3.7/4.1	176-175	25.4-21.5	**3.9**
NYG	**265**-218	512-641	42.7-**38.1**	21/31-18/29	330-363	3-0	**4483**-4194	289	9	84	60	24	9.1	-1.1	5.6/4.0	156-160	**28.7**-26.2	2.5
SL	181-276	582-645	39.4-39.4	14/22-28/47	179-433	2-5	3267-4739	-1472	-12	-110	-171	61	4.3	0.3	2.8/5.7	167-171	19.6-27.7	-8.2
Phi	203-268	690-637	40.3-40.5	20/35-16/**25**	343-335	0-1	3463-4738	-1275	-11	-207	-150	-57	1.8	0.7	3.0/5.4	164-164	21.1-28.9	-7.8
Central Division																		
GB	195-209	610-446	41.8-41.4	**33**/48-**15**/27	587-294	**5**-5	3539-**3474**	65	**17**	78	73	5	8.9	1.0	4.2/3.4	170-175	20.8-**19.9**	1.0
Det	240-239	**417**-703	40.3-38.8	20/29-18/34	284-615	1-2	4155-4208	-53	2	49	4	45	8.2	0.3	4.6/4.9	155-**151**	26.8-27.9	-1.1
Min	235-**200**	440-490	42.8-41.5	21/33-22/35	524-433	4-1	4263-3701	562	8	49	79	-30	8.2	-1.2	5.2/**1.9**	178-175	23.9-21.1	2.8
ChiB	190-224	574-644	41.2-43.0	12/24-19/27	371-230	3-4	3468-3923	-455	0	-50	-38	-12	5.8	-1.3	2.6/3.8	169-168	20.5-23.4	-2.8
Western Division																		
SF	234-221	664-677	39.7-43.4	18/29-17/29	519-310	**5**-2	4351-4026	325	-1	104	23	**81**	9.6	-1.1	4.8/3.6	**179**-188	24.3-21.4	2.9
Atl	231-221	650-555	42.8-41.8	16/30-17/31	399-445	2-3	4011-3767	244	-1	-5	16	-21	6.9	0.1	4.1/3.2	168-170	23.9-22.2	1.7
LA	238-235	648-553	**44.2**-41.2	24/41-16/30	**598**-493	1-5	4355-3907	448	-4	5	21	-16	7.1	-0.6	3.3/4.0	177-171	24.6-22.8	1.8
NO	226-251	585-**711**	40.8-39.3	11/25-31/43	184-630	1-2	3664-4491	-827	-10	-146	-109	-37	3.3	-0.8	3.4/5.1	175-174	20.9-25.8	-4.9
Aver	235	663	40.9	19/31	446	3	4080								4.2	173	23.6	—

Rushing Attempts		Rushing Yards		Rushing Average		Rushing TDs		Rushing Rank		Passing Yards		Passing Average	
R.Johnson-NYG	298	L.Brown-Was	1216	B.Douglass-Chi	6.87	G.Landry-Det	9	L.Brown-Was	1296	A.Manning-NO	2781	B.Berry-Atl	7.79
L.Brown-Was	285	R.Johnson-NYG	1182	G.Landry-Det	6.47	R.Johnson-NYG	9	R.Johnson-NYG	1272	F.Tarkenton-Min	2651	G.Landry-Det	7.71
G.Brezina-GB	274	C.Hill-Dal	1036	B.Thomas-LA	5.62			G.Brezina-GB	1107	C.Morton-Dal	2396	S.Spurrier-SF	7.37
C.Hill-Dal	245	G.Brezina-GB	1027	J.Bertelsen-LA	4.72			C.Hill-Dal	1096	N.Snead-NYG	2307	B.Kilmer-Was	7.32
D.Hampton-Atl	230	D.Hampton-Atl	995	W.Garrison-Dal	4.69			D.Hampton-Atl	1055	B.Berry-Atl	2158	N.Snead-NYG	7.10

Completion Percent		TD Passes		TD Percent		INT Percent		Passer Rating		Passing Rank		Receptions	
N.Snead-NYG	60.3	B.Kilmer-Was	19	B.Kilmer-Was	8.4	F.Tarkenton-Min	3.4	B.Kilmer-Was	84.8	F.Tarkenton-Min	896	H.Jackson-Phi	62
F.Tarkenton-Min	56.9	F.Tarkenton-Min	18	G.Landry-Det	6.7	N.Snead-NYG	3.7	N.Snead-NYG	84.0	N.Snead-NYG	759	B.Tucker-NYG	55
B.Berry-Atl	55.6	S.Spurrier-SF	18	S.Spurrier-SF	6.7	B.Berry-Atl	4.3	F.Tarkenton-Min	80.2	B.Berry-Atl	664	A.Malone-Atl	50
S.Spurrier-SF	54.6	A.Manning-NO	18	A.Manning-NO	5.2	S.Hunter-GB	4.5	B.Berry-Atl	78.5	A.Manning-NO	641	C.Taylor-Was	49
C.Morton-Dal	54.6	G.Landry-Det	18	F.Tarkenton-Min	4.8	R.Gabriel-LA	4.6	S.Spurrier-SF	75.9	B.Kilmer-Was	479		

Receiving Yards		Receiving Average		Receiving TDs		Receiving Rank		Combined Net Yards		Total TDs		Total Points	
H.Jackson-Phi	1048	J.Gilliam-Min	22.02	L.Warwick-SF	12	J.Gilliam-Min	553	D.Hampton-Atl	1780	R.Johnson-NYG	14	C.Marcol-GB	128
J.Gilliam-Min	1035	R.Sellers-Dal	21.06	T.Kwalick-SF	9	H.Jackson-Phi	544	L.Brown-Was	1689	L.Warwick-SF	12	D.Ray-LA	103
L.Warwick-SF	918	L.Warwick-SF	19.96			L.Warwick-SF	519	R.Johnson-NYG	1633	L.Brown-Was	12	T.Fritsch-Dal	99
B.Tucker-NYG	764	J.Snow-LA	19.67			T.Kwalick-SF	421	L.Warwick-SF	1632	A.Malone-Atl	10	E.Mann-Det	98
T.Kwalick-SF	751	T.Kwalick-SF	18.77			B.Tucker-NYG	402	J.Gilliam-Min	1431	W.Garrison-Dal	10		

Punt Average		Field Goals		Field Goal Percent		Kickoff Returns		Kickoff Return Average		Punt Returns		Punt Return Average	
D.Chapple-LA	44.2	C.Marcol-GB	33	E.Mann-Det	69.0	M.Adkins-NO	43	R.Smith-Chi	30.8	R.Smith-Chi	26	K.Ellis-GB	15.4
J.James-Atl	42.8	D.Ray-LA	24	C.Marcol-GB	68.8	R.Smith-Chi	30	A.Nelson-Phi	29.1	R.McGill-SF	22	J.Bertelsen-LA	14.5
M.Eischeid-Min	42.8	P.Gogolak-NYG	21	P.Gogolak-NYG	67.7	R.Thompson-NYG	29	L.Warwick-SF	28.6	B.Bradley-Phi	22	R.McGill-SF	10.0
T.Blanchard-NYG	42.7	T.Fritsch-Dal	21	F.Cox-Min	63.6	L.Warwick-SF	27	R.Thompson-NYG	28.3	B.Taylor-SF	21	L.Barney-Det	7.2
R.Widby-GB	41.8	F.Cox-Min	21	J.Bakken-SL	63.6			I.Thomas-GB	27.2	C.Harris-Dal	19	B.Bradley-Phi	7.0

Punt/Kick Return Yards		Punt/Kick Return TDs		Interceptions		Interception Return Yards		Interception Return TDs		Sacks		Overall Rank	
R.Smith-Chi	1087	Many	1	B.Bradley-Phi	9	J.Nettles-LA	168	J.Van Note-SF	2	Not kept		L.Brown-Was	1553
M.Adkins-NO	1020			C.Ford-Chi	7	C.Waters-Dal	132					R.Johnson-NYG	1523
R.Thompson-NYG	821			C.Waters-Dal	6	P.Krause-Min	109					D.Hampton-Atl	1342
L.Warwick-SF	771			J.Nettles-LA	6	K.Ellis-GB	106					C.Hill-Dal	1326
A.Nelson-Phi	728			P.Krause-Min	6	C.Ford-Chi	104					B.Douglass-Chi	1204

RUNNING WILD

Despite a record 10 rushers surpassing 1,000 yards, NFL football wasn't getting more offensive. The widespread adoption of zone pass defenses had in many ways reduced quarterbacking to the fine art of handing off. It even contributed to a reversion to run-first quarterback play with the particularly quixotic example of Chicago's Bobby Douglass, who barely missed the 1,000-yard rushing plateau.

The Vikings decided to fix their problems on offense by reacquiring quarterback Fran Tarkenton from the Giants, but whatever ambitions Minnesota had were spoiled by injuries to their vaunted defense. Injuries also affected the outcome of the season in Dallas, where the defending Super Bowl champion Cowboys lost Rogers Staubach for most of the season when he suffered a separated shoulder. Still, the offense was good enough under veteran Craig Morton's direction to still capture the wild card. Things were changing in Dallas, though. Defenders Herb Adderley and George Andrie, pass-catchers Lance Alworth and Mike Ditka, and running back and assistant coach Dan Reeves all played their last games as Cowboys. A new all-female pep squad in hot pants cheered them all on.

While the 49ers won their third straight Western Division title despite injuries in the defensive line and quarterback John Brodie, two other teams swooped in to fill the sudden openings in the otherwise formulaic NFC playoff picture. In the Eastern Division, coach George Allen's Over the Hill Gang had been cobbled together through a crazy quilt of trades and late-career resurrections. Relying on backup quarterback Billy Kilmer and conference rushing leader Larry Brown, the Redskins ran off to a surprising 11–1 start. In the Central Division, Green Bay staged an equally surprising comeback. Relying on the NFC's best rushing tandem (John Brockington and newly-acquired fullback MacArthur Lane) and a top-notch run defense, the new Packers were representative of the most reliable way to win games at this time.

The season's final week saw a particularly odd event in Atlanta. When Falcons running back Dave Hampton gained his 1,000th yard, the game was stopped so that he could be given the ball; on the next play, he lost 5 yards. He finished the season with 995.

1972 AFC

TEAM	W-L-T	PCT	POST	PTS	RA	RY	RY/A	RTD	FL	PA	PC	GPY	GPY/A	PTD	PI	PSY	PRAT
Eastern Division																	
Mia	**14**-0	**1.000**	DCS*	**385-171**	**613-389**	**2960-1548**	4.8-4.0	**26**-8	16-**20**	259-348	144-178	2235-2029	**8.6-5.8**	17-10	12-26	159-280	**86.9**-47.4
NYJ	7-7	.500	—	367-324	461-476	2010-2072	4.4-4.4	18-16	**9**-12	347-363	172-186	**2930**-2888	8.4-8.0	21-18	22-19	**153**-251	72.3-72.7
Bal	5-9	.357	—	235-252	462-515	1894-1989	4.1-3.9	10-15	22-13	381-313	203-178	2503-2555	6.6-8.2	15-15	12-23	210-232	73.9-68.8
Buf	4-9-1	.321	—	257-377	512-532	2132-2241	4.2-4.2	11-26	15-8	316-**308**	164-**131**	2012-2148	6.4-7.0	16-19	24-23	411-197	57.1-56.0
NE	3-11	.214	—	192-446	386-548	1532-2717	4.0-5.0	13-27	10-14	**412**-326	198-175	2579-2634	6.3-8.1	10-24	28-10	452-101	48.0-92.2
Central Division																	
Pit	11-3	.786	DC	343-175	497-445	2520-1715	**5.1**-3.9	22-**6**	14-**20**	324-411	156-206	1958-2393	6.0-**5.8**	12-**9**	12-**28**	247-337	64.3-**47.0**
Cle	10-4	.714	W	268-249	453-520	1793-2333	4.0-4.5	13-13	**9**-16	337-310	158-160	2135-**1994**	6.3-6.4	13-14	19-13	219-258	56.9-69.5
Cin	8-6	.571	—	299-229	491-406	1996-1815	4.1-4.5	16-11	18-9	384-350	**219**-167	2513-2033	6.5-**5.8**	10-11	**11**-20	192-296	73.6-52.7
Hou	1-13	.071	—	164-380	397-546	1518-2591	3.8-4.7	7-23	10-18	375-324	181-174	2045-2315	5.5-7.1	10-12	23-6	372-172	48.4-81.2
Western Division																	
Oak	10-3-1	.750	D	365-248	521-469	2376-1764	4.6-**3.8**	20-9	17-12	370-348	198-166	2599-2363	7.0-6.8	**23**-14	15-25	230-211	79.8-53.6
KC	8-6	.571	—	287-254	476-453	1915-1805	4.0-4.0	6-12	12-19	384-368	217-186	2335-2483	6.1-6.7	20-17	20-24	297-261	70.2-60.5
Den	5-9	.357	—	325-350	409-439	1838-1668	4.5-**3.8**	17-15	11-12	384-397	201-206	2900-2540	7.6-6.4	19-19	23-10	266-**357**	68.7-77.4
SD	4-9-1	.321	—	264-344	504-435	1995-1673	4.0-**3.8**	12-18	20-10	377-358	192-201	2516-2441	6.7-6.8	15-18	28-24	212-233	54.6-66.1
Aver	14	—	—	284	471	1951	4.1	14	14	347	179	2363	6.8	16	18	233	66.3

TEAM	1D	PENY	PNT	FGM/A	RTNY	RTNTD	OFFY/DEFY	NETY	NETTO	NP	PNP	DELP	PW	DELW	PRT	DR	YPD	DEL
Eastern Division																		
Mia	291-**186**	714-659	39.4-41.1	24/37-**9/19**	615-316	2-3	**5036-3297**	**1739**	18	**214**	**217**	-3	**12.4**	1.7	**6.1/1.8**	168-**168**	**30.0-19.6**	**10.4**
NYJ	250-255	719-856	39.3-39.4	27/37-22/33	524-510	2-3	4787-4709	78	0	43	7	36	8.1	-1.1	5.5/ 5.0	171-174	28.0-27.1	0.9
Bal	251-233	605-826	42.1-39.0	13/39-15/24	679-373	3-**0**	4187-4312	-125	2	-17	-2	-15	6.6	-1.6	4.7/ 4.3	175-172	23.9-25.1	-1.1
Buf	221-249	900-685	38.8-39.5	16/24-16/27	533-634	3-2	3733-4192	-459	-8	-120	-70	-50	4.0	0.5	1.9/ 3.4	**184**-187	20.3-22.4	-2.1
NE	236-288	761-**862**	38.1-40.4	8/16-22/36	260-856	1-3	3659-5250	-1591	-14	-254	-189	-65	0.7	2.3	2.1/ 6.8	176-**168**	20.8-31.3	-10.5
Central Division																		
Pit	228-228	728-712	43.6-40.3	**28/41**-16/27	657-364	3-3	4231-3771	460	**22**	168	126	42	11.2	-0.2	3.6/ 2.0	182-185	23.2-20.4	2.9
Cle	215-240	**536**-557	43.2-40.9	22/27-20/29	365-502	3-**0**	3709-4069	-360	1	19	-26	**45**	7.5	**2.5**	3.3/ 3.7	173-179	21.4-22.7	-1.3
Cin	255-207	738-581	42.1-42.4	27/40-20/29	**763-222**	5-2	4317-3552	765	0	70	64	6	8.8	-0.8	4.7/ 2.4	181-181	23.9-**19.6**	4.2
Hou	183-263	581-741	41.0-42.1	13/21-33/40	256-618	1-5	3191-4734	-1543	-9	-216	-165	-51	1.6	-0.6	1.8/ 5.7	179-172	17.8-27.5	-9.7
Western Division																		
Oak	**297**-227	757-801	36.9-42.5	17/26-20/37	394-393	2-4	4745-3916	829	5	117	89	28	9.9	0.6	4.9/ 3.1	171-172	27.7-22.8	5.0
KC	245-227	653-643	**44.8**-40.3	21/36-15/31	522-606	**6**-1	3953-4027	-74	11	33	38	-5	7.8	0.2	3.2/ 3.3	179-180	22.1-22.4	-0.3
Den	237-251	827-784	40.1-45.2	20/29-21/33	419-690	2-7	4472-3851	621	-12	-25	4	-29	6.4	-1.4	4.2/ 4.4	176-176	25.4-21.9	3.5
SD	262-244	789-679	40.3-**38.4**	18/31-19/28	495-386	3-5	4299-3881	418	-14	-80	-21	-59	5.0	-0.5	3.0/ 3.4	174-**168**	24.7-23.1	1.6
Aver	235	663	40.9	19/31	446	1	4080	—	—	—	—	—	—	—	4.2	88	23.7	—

Rushing Attempts	Rushing Yards	Rushing Average	Rushing TDs	Rushing Rank	Passing Yards	Passing Average
O.Simpson-Buf........292	O.Simpson-Buf......1251	F.Harris-Pit..............5.61	M.Morris-Mia.............12	O.Simpson-Buf......1311	J.Namath-NYJ.......2816	E.Morrall-Mia..........9.07
M.Garrett-SD...........272	L.Csonka-Mia........1117	M.Morris-Mia...........5.26	E.Boozer-NYJ............11	L.Csonka-Mia........1177	J.Hadl-SD..............2449	J.Namath-NYJ.........8.69
L.Kelly-Cle..............224	M.Hubbard-Oak......1100	L.Csonka-Mia..........5.24	F.Harris-Pit................10	F.Harris-Pit............1155	J.Plunkett-NE.........2196	C.Johnson-Den.......7.49
M.Hubbard-Oak.......219	F.Harris-Pit............1055	C.Davis-Oak...........5.11	F.Little-Den....................9	M.Hubbard-Oak.....1140	D.Lamonica-Oak....1998	D.Lamonica-Oak.....7.11
F.Little-Den..............216	M.Garrett-SD.........1031	M.Hubbard-Oak......5.02	C.Smith-Oak.................8	M.Morris-Mia..........1120	M.Phipps-Cle.........1994	J.Unitas-Bal............7.08
Completion Percent	**TD Passes**	**TD Percent**	**INT Percent**	**Passer Rating**	**Passing Rank**	**Receptions**
L.Dawson-KC.........57.4	J.Namath-NYJ...........19	E.Morrall-Mia............7.3	K.Anderson-Cin........2.3	E.Morrall-Mia..........91.0	K.Anderson-Cin.......714	E.Bethea-Oak............58
K.Anderson-Cin......56.8	D.Lamonica-Oak........18	D.Lamonica-Oak.......6.4	M.Domres-Bal...........2.7	D.Lamonica-Oak.....79.5	J.Namath-NYJ.........663	O.Taylor-KC..............57
J.Unitas-Bal............56.1	J.Hadl-SD..................15	C.Johnson-Den.........5.9	J.Unitas-Bal..............3.8	M.Domres-Bal.........76.6	D.Lamonica-Oak......609	C.Myers-Cin...............57
C.Johnson-Den.......55.5	D.Shaw-Buf................14	J.Namath-NYJ..........5.9	T.Bradshaw-Pit..........3.9	C.Johnson-Den.......74.6	T.Bradshaw-Pit.........524	J.Hill-Buf....................52
E.Morrall-Mia..........55.3	C.Johnson-Den..........14	D.Shaw-Buf..............5.4	L.Dawson-KC............3.9	K.Anderson-Cin......74.0	M.Domres-Bal.........511	G.Garrison-SD...........52
Receiving Yards	**Receiving Average**	**Receiving TDs**	**Receiving Rank**	**Combined Net Yards**	**Total TDs**	**Total Points**
R.Caster-NYJ..........833	R.Caster-NYJ.......21.36	R.Caster-NYJ............10	R.Caster-NYJ..........467	M.Morris-Mia..........1502	E.Boozer-NYJ............14	B.Howfield-NYJ........121
O.Taylor-KC.............821	P.Warfield-Mia.......20.90	F.Pitts-Cle....................8	O.Taylor-KC.............441	O.Simpson-Buf......1470	F.Little-Den.................13	R.Gerela-Pit.............119
E.Bethea-Oak..........802	M.Morin-Cle.........18.00	R.Chester-Oak............8	E.Bethea-Oak..........436	F.Harris-Pit............1413	M.Morris-Mia.............12	G.Yepremian-Mia.....115
C.Myers-Cin.............792	E.Bell-NYJ............17.97	G.Garrison-SD............7	C.Myers-Cin.............411	C.Garrett-NE..........1344	F.Harris-Pit.................11	H.Muhlmann-Cin......111
J.Hill-Buf..................754	M.Siani-Oak..........17.71	E.Bethea-Oak.............7	G.Garrison-SD.........407	F.Little-Den............1332		J.Turner-Den.............97
Punt Average	**Field Goals**	**Field Goal Percent**	**Kickoff Returns**	**Kickoff Return Average**	**Punt Returns**	**Punt Return Average**
J.Wilson-KC...........44.8	R.Gerela-Pit...............28	D.Cockroft-Cle........81.5	J.Taylor-SD...............31	B.Laird-Bal..............29.1	B.Laird-Bal.................34	Farasopoulos-NYJ......10.5
B.Walden-Pit..........43.8	H.Muhlmann-Cin........27	B.Howfield-NYJ.......73.0	T.Mitchell-Den............29	L.Marshall-KC.........28.3	T.Casanova-Cin.........30	T.Casanova-Cin........9.6
D.Cockroft-Cle........43.2	B.Howfield-NYJ..........27	J.Turner-Den...........69.0	B.Laird-Bal.................29	T.Mitchell-Den.........26.1	K.Houston-Hou..........25	C.Leigh-Mia.............9.5
D.Lewis-Cin............42.1	G.Yepremian-Mia.......24	R.Gerela-Pit...........68.3	Farasopoulos-NYJ.........26	L.Cole-Buf...............25.9	C.Leigh-Mia...............22	L.Dunlap-SD.............9.4
D.Lee-Bal................42.1	D.Cockroft-Cle...........22	H.Muhlmann-Cin.....67.5	L.Marshall-KC............23	C.Davis-Oak...........25.8	G.Edwards-Pit...........22	L.Parrish-Cin............9.4
Punt/Kick Return Yards	**Punt/Kick Return TDs**	**Interceptions**	**Interception Return Yards**	**Interception Return TDs**	**Sacks**	**Overall Rank**
B.Laird-Bal............1146	Many..........................1	A.Selfridge-KC............8	J.Kearney-KC..........192	J.Kearney-KC.............4	Not kept	O.Simpson-Buf......1478
Farasopoulos-NYJ.......806		S.Tannen-NYJ.............7	K.Lee-Buf.................155	L.Parrish-Cin...............2		M.Morris-Mia..........1328
T.Mitchell-Den..........756		B.Salter-SD.................7	H.Jackson-NE..........133			F.Harris-Pit............1313
L.Marshall-KC..........754		J.Ham-Pit....................7	S.Tannen-NYJ.........125			M.Garrett-SD.........1219
J.Taylor-SD.............676			B.Salter-SD.............111			F.Little-Den............1206

Perfect in Every Way

It didn't seem like a perfect season when Miami quarterback Bob Griese broke his leg in the fifth game. But while their league-leading defense earned the moniker, a No-Name offensive line might have been the key, generating the gaps that let the Dolphins gain almost 3,000 yards on the ground (Larry Csonka and Mercury Morris became football's first 1,000-yard teammates). All five starting linemen had once been released by other clubs, and center Jim Langer and guard Larry Little were both bound for the Hall of Fame. Earl Morrall—at 38, quite experienced at these situations—was the league's top-rated passer. With complete command of both sides of the scrimmage line, the Dolphins rolled to a perfect 14–0 record. And then they ran the table in the postseason.

As one dynasty took flight, another was in the offing in Pittsburgh. With their Steel Curtain defense almost completely in place, the Steelers won their first title of any sort, forcing Cleveland to settle for the wild card. The Raiders reasserted themselves in the West by integrating young talent into their defense while modulating their offense to be more possession oriented.

From among the also-rans, the Bills were a feel-good story as well-traveled coach Lou Saban returned to the team he'd led to the 1965 AFL title. Despite an injury-depleted offensive line, Saban decided to simply set the club's offense on O.J. Simpson's shoulders. The 1968 Heisman Trophy winner had gone through three seasons as nondescript as those of the Bills, but now as the team's star, the Juice cranked out a league-leading 1,251 yards.

There was also off-field mayhem, as Colts owner Carroll Rosenbloom traded his team for the Rams, who had only just been bought from Dan Reeves's estate by Bob Irsay. Irsay immediately installed a new GM, Joe Thomas, who fired coach Don McCafferty for a 1–4 start, forced the benching of Johnny Unitas, and shortly thereafter began dismantling the beloved club. The Patriots moved just a few miles away to Foxboro, but it was far enough to change the title from Boston to New England. The Pats still managed their sixth straight losing season.

1973 NFC

TEAM	W-L-T	PCT	POST	PTS	RA	RY	RY/A	RTD	FL	PA	PC	GPY	GPY/A	PTD	PI	PSY	PRAT
Eastern Division																	
Dal	10-4	.714	#DC	382-203	542-435	2418-1471	**4.5**-3.4	17-**5**	12-**23**	321-352	192-187	2602-2301	**8.1**-6.5	**26**-15	16-18	269-306	**91.9**-66.5
Was	10-4	.714	#W	325-198	459-480	1439-1603	3.1-**3.3**	9-8	18-18	372-406	209-203	2560-2531	6.9-6.2	20-12	14-**26**	202-**355**	79.8-52.9
Phi	5-8-1	.393	—	310-393	417-512	1791-2423	4.3-4.7	9-22	15-15	**479**-370	**275**-219	**3236**-2789	6.8-7.5	23-22	13-15	238-150	82.8-85.7
SL	4-9-1	.321	—	286-365	416-504	1671-2120	4.0-4.2	13-16	14-17	394-417	210-252	2592-3226	6.6-7.7	16-23	15-10	209-197	71.6-93.1
NYG	2-11-1	.179	—	226-362	456-497	1478-2174	3.2-4.4	11-21	**9**-12	412-**275**	230-161	2762-2252	6.7-8.2	14-17	30-20	201-267	57.5-75.3
Central Division																	
Min	**12**-2	**.857**	DCS	296-**168**	538-450	2275-1974	4.2-4.4	14-**5**	17-15	298-377	179-198	2234-2124	7.5-5.6	16-**8**	**9**-21	278-230	88.7-53.2
Det	6-7-1	.464	—	271-247	496-501	2133-2117	4.3-4.2	17-10	14-11	327-332	171-173	2105-2058	6.4-6.2	12-15	19-22	192-270	60.5-58.8
GB	5-7-2	.429	—	202-259	527-506	1973-1999	3.7-4.0	10-13	12-18	255-327	119-180	1503-2050	5.9-6.3	7-14	17-15	220-228	46.9-69.2
ChiB	3-11	.214	—	195-334	496-563	1907-2509	3.8-4.5	11-19	26-19	303-303	136-156	1617-1978	5.3-6.5	8-17	16-14	395-304	48.5-71.6
Western Division																	
LA	**12**-2	**.857**	D	**388**-178	**659-366**	**2925-1270**	4.4-3.5	**18-5**	**9**-18	271-328	144-179	2107-2023	7.8-6.2	22-10	11-20	**126**-342	88.9-58.0
Atl	9-5	.643	—	318-224	518-520	2037-2129	3.9-4.1	**18**-12	21-15	320-324	168-**151**	2362-**1619**	7.4-**5.0**	14-11	12-22	361-189	75.5-**44.8**
NO	5-9	.357	—	163-312	497-556	1842-2402	3.7-4.3	5-17	17-14	338-337	163-176	1901-2333	5.6-6.9	11-15	17-16	242-155	55.6-69.5
SF	5-9	.357	—	262-319	422-513	1743-1963	4.1-3.8	15-11	14-15	466-383	233-194	2645-2591	5.7-6.8	9-19	25-17	164-225	51.5-70.5
Aver	14	—	—	272	498	2021	4.1	13	16	340	177	2231	6.6	15	18	258	64.9

TEAM	1D	PENY	PNT	FGM/A	RTNY	RTNTD	OFFY/DEFY	NETY	NETTO	NP	PNP	DELP	PW	DELW	PRT	DR	YPD	DEL
Eastern Division																		
Dal	281-208	762-516	41.5-39.4	19/30-**14**/30	474-303	3-3	4751-3466	1285	13	179	159	20	11.5	-1.5	5.1/ 3.4	180-177	26.4-19.6	6.8
Was	232-233	771-708	40.3-**38.4**	22/42-17/29	929-277	**8-1**	3797-3779	18	12	127	50	**77**	10.2	-0.2	4.8/ 2.5	189-189	20.1-20.0	0.1
Phi	267-286	566-692	40.9-39.9	24/40-22/40	236-663	2-3	4789-5062	-273	2	-83	-15	-68	4.9	0.6	5.2/ 5.6	180-180	26.6-28.1	-1.5
SL	238-307	594-**892**	37.5-41.4	23/32-24/34	263-453	2-3	4054-5149	-1095	-2	-79	-99	20	5.0	-0.5	4.4/ 6.3	171-172	23.7-29.9	-6.2
NYG	239-240	586-484	38.8-40.9	17/28-22/30	374-905	0-4	4039-4159	-120	-7	-136	-38	-98	3.6	-1.1	3.1/ 4.0	170-175	23.8-23.8	-0.0
Central Division																		
Min	246-220	**482**-633	39.8-41.0	21/35-21/38	403-359	3-2	4231-3868	363	10	128	70	58	10.2	**1.8**	5.2/ 2.5	161-174	26.3-22.2	4.0
Det	237-245	584-606	43.2-41.5	21/33-22/31	811-337	1-**1**	4046-3905	141	0	24	12	12	7.6	-1.1	3.3/ 2.6	169-**164**	23.9-23.8	0.1
GB	187-230	653-483	41.0-38.9	21/35-19/**27**	357-556	3-**1**	3256-3821	-565	4	-57	-31	-26	5.6	0.4	2.1/ 3.7	169-169	19.3-22.6	-3.3
ChiB	193-247	817-672	39.8-40.5	14/24-25/38	380-629	3-**1**	3129-4183	-1054	-9	-139	-124	-15	3.5	-0.5	1.7/ 3.6	188-189	16.6-22.1	-5.5
Western Division																		
LA	**294-173**	606-566	40.8-40.8	**30/47**-20/**27**	778-364	2-2	**4906-2951**	**1955**	**18**	**210**	**235**	-25	**12.3**	-0.3	**5.9**/ 2.4	180-174	**27.3-17.0**	**10.3**
Atl	240-212	598-562	42.6-42.1	26/38-19/28	**957-268**	2-**1**	4038-3559	479	4	94	56	38	9.4	-0.3	4.4/**1.6**	184-182	21.9-19.6	2.4
NO	207-271	516-751	41.7-44.5	17/36-19/34	344-867	0-4	3501-4580	-1079	-4	-149	-106	-43	3.3	1.7	2.7/ 4.5	177-183	19.8-25.0	-5.2
SF	251-242	903-754	**43.7**-41.3	26/33-31/45	527-746	2-2	4224-4329	-105	-7	-57	-37	-20	5.6	-0.6	2.9/ 4.3	**196**-192	21.6-22.5	-1.0
Aver	232	664	41.0	21/33	544	3	3994	—	—	—	—	—	—	—	3.8	180	22.2	—

Rushing Attempts	Rushing Yards	Rushing Average	Rushing TDs	Rushing Rank	Passing Yards	Passing Average
C.Hill-Dal 273	G.Brezina-GB 1144	B.Douglass-Chi....5.59	D.Anderson-SL 10	C.Hill-Dal 1202	R.Gabriel-Phi 3219	R.Staubach-Dal 8.49
L.Brown-Was 273	C.Hill-Dal 1142	M.McCoy-LA....5.22	E.Ray-Atl 9	G.Brezina-GB 1174	R.Staubach-Dal 2428	J.Hadl-LA....7.78
G.Brezina-GB 265	M.McCoy-LA....1097	R.Newhouse-Dal 5.19	L.Warwick-SF 8	M.McCoy-LA....1117	J.Hart-SL 2223	B.Lee-Atl....7.77
D.Hampton-Atl 263	D.Hampton-Atl 997	E.Ray-Atl 4.52	L.Brown-Was 8	D.Hampton-Atl 1037	F.Tarkenton-Min 2113	F.Tarkenton-Min 7.71
R.Johnson-NYG 260	T.Sullivan-Phi....968	T.Sullivan-Phi....4.46	T.Baker-LA....7	T.Sullivan-Phi....1008	J.Hadl-LA....2008	B.Kilmer-Was....7.30
Completion Percent	**TD Passes**	**TD Percent**	**INT Percent**	**Passer Rating**	**Passing Rank**	**Receptions**
R.Staubach-Dal 62.6	R.Staubach-Dal 23	J.Hadl-LA....8.5	F.Tarkenton-Min 2.6	R.Staubach-Dal 94.6	R.Gabriel-Phi....1245	B.Cappleman-Phi 67
F.Tarkenton-Min 61.7	R.Gabriel-Phi....23	R.Staubach-Dal 8.0	R.Gabriel-Phi....2.6	F.Tarkenton-Min 93.2	F.Tarkenton-Min 852	C.Taylor-Was 59
S.Jurgensen-Was ...60.0	J.Hadl-LA....22	B.Kilmer-Was....6.2	J.Hart-SL 3.1	J.Hadl-LA....88.8	J.Hart-SL 787	C.Young-Phi....55
R.Gabriel-Phi....58.7	F.Tarkenton-Min 15	F.Tarkenton-Min 5.5	S.Jurgensen-Was 3.4	R.Gabriel-Phi....86.0	R.Staubach-Dal 729	B.Tucker-NYG....50
R.Johnson-NYG 55.9	J.Hart-SL 15	R.Gabriel-Phi....5.0	B.Lee-Atl....3.5	B.Kilmer-Was....81.3	J.Hadl-LA....674	T.Sullivan-Phi....50
Receiving Yards	**Receiving Average**	**Receiving TDs**	**Receiving Rank**	**Combined Net Yards**	**Total TDs**	**Total Points**
B.Cappleman-Phi ..1116	H.Jackson-LA 21.85	H.Jackson-LA 13	B.Cappleman-Phi 603	T.Sullivan-Phi....1570	L.Brown-Was 14	D.Ray-LA 130
J.Gilliam-Min....907	J.Gilliam-Min....21.60	B.Cappleman-Phi 9	H.Jackson-LA 502	D.Hampton-Atl 1528	H.Jackson-LA 13	L.Mialik-Atl 112
H.Jackson-LA 874	K.Burrow-Atl 18.29	J.Gilliam-Min....8	J.Gilliam-Min....494	C.Garrett-Chi 1433	D.Anderson-SL 13	T.Dempsey-Phi 106
C.Young-Phi....854	M.Gray-SL 17.69		C.Young-Phi....457	C.Hill-Dal 1432	E.Ray-Atl 11	B.Gossett-SF 104
C.Taylor-Was 801	B.Newland-NO....16.86		C.Taylor-Was 436	J.Bertelsen-LA....1395		C.Knight-Was....103
Punt Average	**Field Goals**	**Field Goal Percent**	**Kickoff Returns**	**Kickoff Return Average**	**Punt Returns**	**Punt Return Average**
T.Wittum-SF....43.7	D.Ray-LA 30	B.Gossett-SF 78.8	H.Mul-Key-Was....36	C.Garrett-Chi 30.4	R.Brown-Atl 40	B.Taylor-SF 13.8
H.Weaver-Det....43.2	L.Mialik-Atl....26	J.Bakken-SL 71.9	I.Hill-Chi....27	H.Mul-Key-Was....28.1	I.Hill-Chi....36	H.Stevens-NO....10.1
R.Widby-GB....43.1	B.Gossett-SF 26	L.Mialik-Atl....68.4	H.Stevens-NO....26	D.Shy-SL....27.8	S.Duncan-Was....28	J.Bertelsen-LA....10.0
J.James-Atl....42.6	T.Dempsey-Phi 24	E.Mann-Det 68.4	L.Warwick-SF 24	P.James-Phi....25.8	L.Barney-Det 27	R.Brown-Atl 9.0
T.Blanchard-NYG....41.9	J.Bakken-SL 23	T.Fritsch-Dal....64.3	I.Thomas-GB 23	J.McCann-Min 25.6	J.Bertelsen-LA....26	L.Barney-Det 8.6
Punt/Kick Return Yards	**Punt/Kick Return TDs**	**Interceptions**	**Interception Return Yards**	**Interception Return TDs**	**Sacks**	**Overall Rank**
H.Mul-Key-Was....1114	I.Hill-Chi....2	B.Bryant-Min....7	D.Jauron-Det 208	T.Hayes-Atl 2	Not kept	C.Hill-Dal 1347
I.Hill-Chi....841	D.Shy-SL....1	B.Taylor-SF 6	M.Bass-Was 161			T.Sullivan-Phi....1274
H.Stevens-NO....761	H.Mul-Key-Was....1	L.Jordan-Dal....6	T.Hayes-Atl 142			D.Hampton-Atl 1272
R.McGill-SF 560	C.Bryant-LA....1	K.Houston-Was....6	L.Barney-Det 130			M.McCoy-LA....1268
L.Warwick-SF 549		R.Brown-Atl 6	B.Owens-Was....123			R.Gabriel-Phi....1265

The Spinning of the Spectacle

The Eastern Division remained a duel between the almost mechanical efficiency of Dallas, Roger Staubach's on-field brio notwithstanding, and the hand-to-mouth existence of Washington, where George Allen constantly dealt away draft picks to add a little more veteran help. With a healthy Staubach finally playing every game, the Cowboys had the league's best passing attack, and finished just ahead of the defending conference champs for the division title.

Misery continued in New York, where the renovation of Yankee Stadium forced the Giants to play all but one of their home games at the Yale Bowl in Connecticut. In the Central Division, the Vikings came back from the previous season's injuries, easily winning the title by regaining their status as the NFC's best defense. Minnesota also enjoyed rookie running back Chuck Foreman, who finally gave the Vikings the needed balance in a run-first league.

The Rams had managed to disappoint fans in each of the last three seasons, failing to earn a title since winning the 1969 Coastal Division. As the man who had given both Weeb Ewbank and Don Shula their first head coaching jobs, it wasn't surprising that new Rams owner Carroll Rosenbloom made a canny choice in giving Chuck Knox his first opportunity in the top job. Second-year backs Lawrence McCutcheon and Jim Bertelsen helped forge the nickname Ground Chuck. Knox's Rams had the league's best offense—and, not surprisingly, the most rushing yards—on the way to their first Western Division title. The Falcons mounted a plausible challenge, but losses to the Bills and Cardinals kept Atlanta just short of the wild card.

And each week NFL Films brought the heartbeat of pro football into American homes. This venture, begun in 1962 by Ed Sabol, and filmed with enough reverence and technology to make an incomplete pass seem as significant as D-Day, elevated the game from sport to living history. Howard Cosell's Monday night highlights recap—prepared by NFL Films—and the extended syndicated films, featuring the incomparable voice of John Facenda, illustrated the significance of every NFL game. Stylized, mythic, and overblown, it was like a painting of a favorite image that constantly changed.

1973 AFC

TEAM	W-L-T	PCT	POST	PTS	RA	RY	RY/A	RTD	FL	PA	PC	GPY	GPY/A	PTD	PI	PSY	PRAT
Eastern Division																	
Mia	**12**-2	**.857**	DCS*	343-**150**	507-511	2521-1991	5.0-3.9	16-10	16-8	256-322	133-151	1675-1604	6.5-**5.0**	17-**5**	**12**-21	**93**-314	75.2-39.9
Buf	9-5	.643	—	259-230	**605**-455	**3088**-1797	**5.1**-3.9	**20**-11	13-19	213-368	96-166	1236-2394	5.8-6.5	4-12	14-14	239-276	42.7-61.8
NE	5-9	.357	—	258-300	454-560	1612-2850	3.6-5.1	15-16	25-18	380-**240**	195-**134**	2581-**1600**	6.8-6.7	13-11	17-13	350-262	65.9-69.1
Bal	4-10	.286	—	226-341	536-491	2031-2089	3.8-4.3	9-15	13-**22**	300-331	137-199	1746-2599	5.8-7.9	14-16	25-15	271-200	45.2-82.1
NYJ	4-10	.286	—	240-306	453-538	1864-2228	4.1-4.1	7-12	17-19	373-296	181-150	2353-2148	6.3-7.3	16-18	22-19	297-198	58.5-68.1
Central Division																	
Cin	10-4	.714	#D	286-231	515-459	2236-1807	4.3-3.9	13-15	14-16	332-338	180-182	2439-2240	7.3-6.6	18-9	**12**-18	163-**342**	**80.9**-61.3
Pit	10-4	.714	#W	347-210	555-488	2143-1652	3.9-**3.4**	12-8	14-18	309-359	140-164	2157-1923	7.0-5.4	20-11	26-**37**	230-251	55.4-**33.1**
Cle	7-5-2	.571	—	234-255	506-513	1968-2091	3.9-4.1	12-7	17-9	308-312	152-144	1741-1984	5.7-6.4	10-16	20-12	368-248	50.5-68.1
Hou	1-13	.071	—	199-447	386-576	1388-2410	3.6-4.2	9-19	25-10	**411**-326	**225**-178	2370-2466	5.8-7.6	11-26	27-17	451-229	53.3-84.0
Western Division																	
Oak	9-4-1	.679	DC	292-175	547-**435**	2510-**1470**	4.6-**3.4**	14-**5**	16-16	353-370	205-170	2611-1995	**7.4**-5.4	16-12	18-17	348-305	75.2-54.5
Den	7-5-2	.571	—	**354**-296	487-455	1954-1795	4.0-3.9	16-14	**9**-15	378-387	196-202	**2706**-2766	7.2-7.1	**22**-15	20-14	187-326	72.5-73.2
KC	7-5-2	.571	—	231-192	511-493	1793-1956	3.5-4.0	11-11	18-18	313-324	173-157	2039-1942	6.5-6.0	10-11	13-21	296-323	68.6-51.7
SD	2-11-1	.179	—	188-386	431-559	1814-2264	4.2-4.1	9-23	21-18	363-341	161-177	2129-2473	5.9-7.3	9-18	30-16	321-219	37.3-73.6
Aver	14	—	—	272	498	2021	4.1	13	16	340	177	2231	6.6	15	18	258	64.9

TEAM	1D	PENY	PNT	FGM/A	RTNY	RTNTD	OFFY/DEFY	NETY	NETTO	NP	PNP	DELP	PW	DELW	PRT	DR	YPD	DEL
Eastern Division																		
Mia	215-195	**416**-616	42.3-38.5	25/37-15/27	717-372	**5-0**	4103-3281	822	1	**193**	73	**120**	**11.8**	0.2	4.5/ 1.1	162-166	25.3-19.8	5.6
Buf	219-231	744-485	40.3-39.8	21/30-19/34	503-461	4-2	4085-3915	170	6	29	38	-9	7.7	1.3	1.7/ 4.0	169-**165**	24.2-23.7	0.4
NE	237-215	550-693	37.7-40.5	15/29-26/32	429-437	3-5	3843-4188	-345	-11	-42	-73	31	5.9	-1.0	3.8/ 3.2	172-177	22.3-23.7	-1.3
Bal	218-243	483-684	38.7-**37.4**	16/28-23/33	245-616	3-8	3506-4488	-982	-1	-115	-86	-29	4.1	-0.1	1.5/ 5.3	170-168	20.6-26.7	-6.1
NYJ	222-226	575-783	37.1-40.9	17/24-23/34	453-707	4-4	3920-4178	-258	-1	-66	-26	-40	5.3	-1.4	3.0/ 4.0	187-178	21.0-23.5	-2.5
Central Division																		
Cin	252-219	799-710	41.0-41.7	21/31-14/**23**	499-**321**	1-3	4512-3705	807	8	55	99	-44	8.4	**1.6**	**5.4**/ 3.1	175-171	**25.8**-21.7	4.1
Pit	217-210	817-757	41.1-42.4	**29/43**-19/29	**1089**-820	**5**-3	4070-3324	746	**15**	137	122	15	10.4	-0.4	2.8/**0.3**	196-196	20.8-**17.0**	3.8
Cle	200-196	620-738	40.5-40.4	22/31-29/46	510-541	2-1	3341-3827	-486	-16	-21	-105	84	6.5	1.5	1.6/ 4.0	183-188	18.3-20.4	-2.1
Hou	193-274	900-811	38.8-39.6	15/24-25/42	525-700	2-8	3307-4647	-1340	-25	-248	-212	-36	0.8	0.2	1.8/ 4.9	**198**-198	16.7-23.5	-6.8
Western Division																		
Oak	**288-194**	759-623	45.3-43.1	23/33-14/30	506-477	2-2	**4773-3160**	**1613**	-1	117	**130**	-13	9.9	-0.4	4.1/ 2.5	186-182	25.7-17.4	**8.3**
Den	253-239	745-**824**	45.1-43.3	22/33-26/35	624-588	3-2	4473-4235	238	0	58	20	38	8.4	-0.5	4.5/ 4.6	179-187	25.0-22.6	2.3
KC	208-209	797-649	**45.5**-42.9	24/38-**13**/27	607-597	2-**0**	3536-3575	-39	8	39	29	10	8.0	0.0	3.6/ 2.2	186-186	19.0-19.2	-0.2
SD	198-267	628-579	41.1-43.1	12/27-22/38	613-789	4-5	3622-4518	-896	-17	-198	-143	-55	2.1	0.4	1.4/ 4.7	192-187	18.9-24.2	-5.3
Aver	232	664	41.0	21/33	544	2	3994	—	—	—	—	—	—	—	3.8	91	21.7	—

Rushing Attempts	Rushing Yards	Rushing Average	Rushing TDs	Rushing Rank	Passing Yards	Passing Average
O.Simpson-Buf........332	O.Simpson-Buf......2003	M.Morris-Mia...........6.40	O.Simpson-Buf..........12	O.Simpson-Buf......2123	J.Plunkett-NE.........2550	K.Stabler-Oak.........7.68
F.Little-Den..............256	L.Csonka-Mia........1003	O.Simpson-Buf.......6.03	F.Little-Den...............12	F.Little-Den............1099	C.Johnson-Den......2465	K.Anderson-Cin......7.38
B.Clark-Cin..............254	E.Johnson-Cin.........997	C.Davis-Oak...........5.25	M.Morris-Mia.............10	B.Clark-Cin............1068	K.Anderson-Cin.....2428	C.Johnson-Den.......7.12
L.Mitchell-Bal...........253	B.Clark-Cin.............988	E.Johnson-Cin..........5.11	B.Clark-Cin..................8	M.Morris-Mia..........1054	K.Stabler-Oak........1997	J.Plunkett-NE..........6.78
L.Csonka-Mia..........219	F.Little-Den..............979	M.Hubbard-Oak......4.68	R.Holmes-SD...............7	L.Csonka-Mia........1053	M.Phipps-Cle..........1719	T.Bradshaw-Pit.......6.57
Completion Percent	**TD Passes**	**TD Percent**	**INT Percent**	**Passer Rating**	**Passing Rank**	**Receptions**
K.Stabler-Oak.........62.7	C.Johnson-Den..........20	B.Griese-Mia.............7.8	K.Anderson-Cin........3.6	K.Stabler-Oak.........88.3	K.Anderson-Cin.......824	F.Willis-Hou................57
K.Anderson-Cin......54.4	K.Anderson-Cin.........18	C.Johnson-Den.........5.8	B.Griese-Mia.............3.7	B.Griese-Mia...........84.3	K.Stabler-Oak..........669	E.Podolak-KC............55
B.Griese-Mia...........53.2	B.Griese-Mia..............17	T.Bradshaw-Pit..........5.6	K.Stabler-Oak............3.8	K.Anderson-Cin......81.2	J.Plunkett-NE............660	R.Rucker-NE...............53
C.Johnson-Den.......53.2	K.Stabler-Oak............14	K.Anderson-Cin........5.5	A.Woodall-NYJ..........4.0	C.Johnson-Den.......74.9	C.Johnson-Den........653	E.Bethea-Oak............48
D.Pastorini-Hou.......53.1	J.Plunkett-NE.............13	K.Stabler-Oak...........5.4	J.Plunkett-NE............4.5	A.Woodall-NYJ.......67.8	B.Griese-Mia............476	
Receiving Yards	**Receiving Average**	**Receiving TDs**	**Receiving Rank**	**Combined Net Yards**	**Total TDs**	**Total Points**
I.Curtis-Cin..............843	R.Shanklin-Pit.......23.70	P.Warfield-Mia............11	I.Curtis-Cin..............467	O.Simpson-Buf......2073	F.Little-Den................13	R.Gerela-Pit.............123
J.Barkum-NYJ.........810	I.Curtis-Cin...........18.73	R.Shanklin-Pit............10	J.Barkum-NYJ.........435	M.Herron-NE.........1839	O.Simpson-Buf..........12	G.Yepremian-Mia.....113
R.Rucker-NE............743	H.Moses-Den........18.50	I.Curtis-Cin...................9	R.Shanklin-Pit..........406	F.Little-Den............1409	P.Warfield-Mia............11	J.Turner-Den............106
M.Siani-Oak.............742	J.Barkum-NYJ......18.41	H.Moses-Den...............8	R.Rucker-NE............387	B.Gresham-Hou.....1367	R.Shanklin-Pit............10	G.Blanda-Oak..........100
R.Shanklin-Pit..........711	J.LeVias-SD..........17.87	R.Odoms-Den..............7	M.Siani-Oak.............386	E.Johnson-Cin.......1361	M.Morris-Mia..............10	H.Muhlmann-Cin.......94
Punt Average	**Field Goals**	**Field Goal Percent**	**Kickoff Returns**	**Kickoff Return Average**	**Punt Returns**	**Punt Return Average**
J.Wilson-KC............45.5	R.Gerela-Pit..............29	D.Cockroft-Cle........71.0	M.Herron-NE.............41	W.Francis-Buf.........29.9	G.Atkinson-Oak.........41	R.Smith-SD.............13.0
R.Guy-Oak..............45.3	G.Yepremian-Mia.......25	B.Howfield-NYJ.......70.8	R.Smith-SD.................36	C.Speyrer-Bal.........29.2	G.Edwards-Pit...........34	B.Thompson-Den...12.2
B.Van Dyke-Den.....45.1	J.Stenerud-KC...........24	J.Leypoldt-Buf.........70.0	M.Adkins-NYJ.............31	G.Pruitt-Cle.............28.3	B.Thompson-Den......30	J.Scott-Mia..............12.1
L.Seiple-Mia............42.3	G.Blanda-Oak............23	G.Blanda-Oak.........69.7	A.Haymond-Hou........28	L.Marshall-KC.........27.9	L.Marshall-KC...........29	G.Pruitt-Cle.............11.3
		H.Muhlmann-Cin.....67.7	B.Gresham-Hou.........27	S.Davis-Pit..............26.9		M.Herron-NE..........10.4
Punt/Kick Return Yards	**Punt/Kick Return TDs**	**Interceptions**	**Interception Return Yards**	**Interception Return TDs**	**Sacks**	**Overall Rank**
M.Herron-NE.........1374	R.Smith-SD..................2	M.Wagner-Pit..............8	G.Edwards-Pit.........186	D.Anderson-Mia..........2	Not kept	O.Simpson-Buf......2157
R.Smith-SD...........1299	W.Francis-Buf.............2	D.Anderson-Mia...........8	D.Anderson-Mia.......163			F.Little-Den.............1318
A.Haymond-Hou......804		J.Rowser-Pit................6	M.Wagner-Pit...........134			B.Clark-Cin.............1242
B.Gresham-Hou.......723		G.Edwards-Pit.............6	J.Rowser-Pit............131			E.Johnson-Cin.......1230
W.Francis-Buf..........687		R.Bolton-NE................6	J.Blahak-Hou...........120			M.Morris-Mia.........1157

Turning It On

Perfection wasn't an option in Miami this time around. The Dolphins had to live with a tough 12–7 loss to the Raiders in week two, their first loss since December 11, 1971. But this year's edition of the Dolphins featured an even better defense. The Dolphins allowed the fewest points in football. Safety Dick Anderson won Defensive Player of the Year, and with players like linebacker Nick Buoniconti and end Bill Stanfill steadily providing great work, the Dolphins' D was No Name in name only.

Finishing a surprising second in the Eastern Division was Buffalo. Carrying the Bills even that far was O.J. Simpson, clearly the league MVP, but the offensive line—featuring rookie guard Joe DeLamielleure—earned its share of credit. Buffalo's public relations department came up with the nickname, the Electric Company, because "they turn on the Juice." A reach? Maybe, but Simpson became the first player in history to rush for 2,000 yards.

Franco Harris, Terry Bradshaw, and even backup quarterback Terry Hanratty lost chunks of the season to injury in Pittsburgh. It took the Steel Curtain's pressure on the pocket and a secondary led by Mel Blount and Mike Wagner to generate a league-leading 37 interceptions and 55 turnovers. The Steelers reached the playoffs, albeit as a wild card. That's because the Bengals made another surprise entry into the playoff picture, as gray eminence Paul Brown guided third-year pro Ken Anderson and a quartet of talented rookies: running backs Boobie Clark, Essex Johnson, and Lenville Elliott, and wideout Isaac Curtis.

The Western Division was also tight. After 10 games, the Chiefs led at 6–3–1, trailed by the Broncos at 5–3–2 and the Raiders 5–4–1. Oakland finished by beating both clubs—plus sad sacks San Diego and Houston—to clinch the title. Ken Stabler, a backup his first three seasons, took over for Daryle Lamonica after the old AFL bomber failed to put up a touchdown in the first three weeks. Another quarterbacking changing of the guard was in San Diego, where rookie Dan Fouts had the benefit of playing with Johnny Unitas in his final season; both men were bound for the Hall of Fame.

1974 NFC

TEAM	W-L-T	PCT	POST	PTS	RA	RY	RY/A	RTD	FL	PA	PC	GPY	GPY/A	PTD	PI	PSY	PRAT
Eastern Division																	
SL	**10**-4	**.714**	#D	285-218	466-461	1956-1888	4.2-4.1	12-15	**9**-9	391-413	201-230	2492-2581	6.4-6.2	20-11	**8**-16	134-218	80.0-67.3
Was	**10**-4	**.714**	#W	**320**-196	470-414	1443-1439	3.1-3.5	11-7	**9**-15	413-399	254-197	**2978**-2102	7.2-**5.3**	**22**-13	11-**25**	176-256	**90.0-49.9**
Dal	8-6	.571	—	297-235	542-417	**2454**-1344	**4.5-3.2**	**22**-8	16-13	385-349	206-178	2856-2451	**7.4**-7.0	14-17	15-13	327-332	73.5-74.6
Phi	7-7	.500	—	242-217	415-460	1385-1797	3.3-3.9	13-14	12-16	**461**-434	**258**-230	2531-2684	5.5-6.2	14-9	17-18	319-211	66.4-61.6
NYG	2-12	.143	—	195-299	441-521	1496-1916	3.4-3.7	11-15	10-10	393-415	207-245	2349-2688	6.0-6.5	12-22	26-15	156-147	53.5-80.9
Central Division																	
Min	**10**-4	**.714**	DCS	310-195	488-437	1856-1605	3.8-3.7	17-12	**9**-11	400-396	234-214	2909-2569	7.3-6.5	**22-8**	13-22	154-267	85.9-57.7
Det	7-7	.500	—	256-270	397-486	1433-2102	3.6-4.3	13-17	14-13	377-405	216-219	2475-2423	6.6-6.0	11-13	11-17	255-187	74.8-65.3
GB	6-8	.429	—	210-206	482-465	1571-1641	3.3-3.5	10-10	16-12	385-383	187-188	2162-2254	5.6-5.9	5-10	21-23	**126**-254	47.6-51.2
ChiB	4-10	.286	—	152-279	434-519	1480-1739	3.4-3.4	10-17	15-14	396-329	185-174	2079-2250	5.3-6.8	8-12	22-18	359-171	46.5-64.0
Western Division																	
LA	**10**-4	**.714**	DC	263-**181**	**566-381**	2125-**1302**	3.8-3.4	16-**4**	14-3	338-381	169-194	2368-2465	7.0-6.5	16-16	13-22	161-**363**	72.7-61.4
SF	6-8	.429	—	226-236	477-503	1981-2033	4.2-4.0	10-13	14-**20**	361-339	170-178	2281-2178	6.3-6.4	15-14	28-20	274-247	49.2-61.8
NO	5-9	.357	—	166-263	503-447	1983-1758	3.9-3.9	9-11	12-19	389-369	185-193	2037-2330	5.2-6.3	10-17	21-16	276-291	49.6-69.3
Atl	3-11	.214	—	111-271	400-627	1493-2564	3.7-4.1	6-19	24-12	356-**302**	160-**136**	1781-**1847**	5.0-6.1	4-13	31-17	474-275	27.8-56.0
Aver	14	—	—	255	481	1866	3.9	14	13	370	194	2400	6.5	14	19	254	64.2

TEAM	1D	PENY	PNT	FGM/A	RTNY	RTNTD	OFFY/DEFY	NETY	NETTO	NP	PNP	DELP	PW	DELW	PRT	DR	YPD	DEL
Eastern Division																		
SL	247-249	645-654	38.7-39.2	13/22-**10/14**	**884**-593	4-1	4314-4251	63	8	67	37	30	8.7	**1.3**	5.4/ 3.9	165-170	26.1-25.0	1.1
Was	249-210	621-529	38.1-38.4	19/31-**10**/15	781-533	**5**-4	4245-**3285**	960	**20**	**124**	**160**	-36	**10.1**	-0.1	**5.8/2.0**	173-177	24.5-**18.6**	6.0
Dal	**295**-199	703-657	38.5-39.9	10/21-13/21	683-436	2-3	**4983**-3463	**1520**	-5	62	107	-45	8.6	-0.5	4.6/ 4.4	183-177	27.2-19.6	**7.7**
Phi	244-248	722-722	36.0-39.1	10/16-12/26	515-614	4-3	3597-4270	-673	5	25	-36	**61**	7.6	-0.6	3.2/ 3.8	173-174	20.8-24.5	-3.7
NYG	215-291	567-616	40.1-**36.2**	10/19-11/24	499-850	1-2	3689-4457	-768	-11	-104	-108	4	4.4	-2.4	2.8/ 4.7	166-**162**	22.2-27.5	-5.3
Central Division																		
Min	264-230	**501**-660	36.1-37.1	12/20-17/24	602-530	1-1	4611-3907	704	11	115	103	12	9.9	0.1	5.7/ 3.3	168-169	**27.4**-23.1	4.3
Det	211-270	719-566	38.2-37.2	23/32-20/32	695-**424**	3-**0**	3653-4338	-685	5	-14	-37	23	6.7	0.3	4.5/ 3.7	169-172	21.6-25.2	-3.6
GB	214-218	536-715	38.4-36.6	**25/39**-17/26	694-645	4-3	3607-3641	-34	-2	4	-11	15	7.1	-1.1	2.8/ 2.6	183-178	19.7-20.5	-0.7
ChiB	203-231	679-601	37.7-38.5	9/13-16/23	541-858	0-4	3200-3818	-618	-5	-127	-72	-55	3.8	0.2	1.9/ 3.9	179-175	17.9-21.8	-3.9
Western Division																		
LA	265-**186**	550-772	36.4-41.2	9/16-**10/14**	847-545	3-2	4332-3404	928	-2	82	69	13	9.1	1.0	5.0/ 3.0	170-167	25.5-20.4	5.1
SF	227-232	606-**830**	40.8-39.5	11/24-12/19	645-900	3-2	3988-3964	24	-2	-10	-6	-4	6.8	-0.8	2.3/ 3.2	176-178	22.7-22.3	0.4
NO	233-226	598-690	**41.8**-42.5	9/16-**10**/17	594-1164	1-6	3744-3797	-53	2	-97	4	-101	4.6	0.4	2.2/ 3.7	177-174	21.2-21.8	-0.7
Atl	174-238	636-449	40.5-38.3	9/16-12/28	845-1109	2-2	2800-4136	-1336	-26	-160	-215	55	3.0	0.0	-0.1/ 2.8	**189**-193	14.8-21.4	-6.6
Aver	239	659	39.0	13/21	723	3	4012	—	—	—	—	—	—	—	3.9	176	22.8	—

Rushing Attempts	Rushing Yards	Rushing Average	Rushing TDs	Rushing Rank	Passing Yards	Passing Average
G.Brezina-GB..........266	S.McCullum-LA......1109	T.Metcalf-SL...........4.72	T.Sullivan-Phi............11	S.McCullum-LA......1139	F.Tarkenton-Min.....2598	J.Harris-LA.............7.80
T.Sullivan-Phi..........244	G.Brezina-GB..........883	S.McCullum-LA.......4.70	C.Foreman-Min............9	G.Brezina-GB..........933	R.Staubach-Dal.....2552	F.Tarkenton-Min......7.40
S.McCullum-LA........236	C.Hill-Dal................844	C.Hill-Dal................4.56	C.Hill-Dal....................7	C.Hill-Dal.................914	J.Hart-SL..............2411	T.Owen-SF.............7.21
C.Foreman-Min........199	C.Foreman-Min........777	A.Maxson-NO.........4.33	T.Metcalf-SL................6	T.Sullivan-Phi...........870	B.Munson-Det........1874	S.Jurgensen-Was...7.10
C.Hill-Dal................185	T.Sullivan-Phi..........760	J.Otis-SL................4.20		C.Foreman-Min........867	R.Gabriel-Phi.........1867	R.Staubach-Dal......7.09
Completion Percent	**TD Passes**	**TD Percent**	**INT Percent**	**Passer Rating**	**Passing Rank**	**Receptions**
S.Jurgensen-Was...64.1	J.Hart-SL..................20	S.Jurgensen-Was.....6.6	J.Hart-SL.................2.1	S.Jurgensen-Was...94.5	J.Hart-SL.................986	C.Young-Phi..............63
B.Kilmer-Was..........58.5	F.Tarkenton-Min.........17	J.Harris-LA................5.6	B.Munson-Det...........2.4	J.Harris-LA.............85.1	F.Tarkenton-Min.......904	D.Pearson-Dal...........62
R.Gabriel-Phi..........57.1	R.Staubach-Dal.........11	T.Owen-SF...............5.4	B.Kilmer-Was...........2.6	B.Kilmer-Was..........83.5	R.Staubach-Dal.......731	C.Capria-Phi..............56
B.Munson-Det.........56.8	S.Jurgensen-Was......11	J.Hart-SL.................5.2	S.Jurgensen-Was.....3.0	F.Tarkenton-Min......82.1	B.Munson-Det..........697	C.Taylor-Was.............54
F.Tarkenton-Min......56.7	J.Harris-LA................11	F.Tarkenton-Min........4.8	J.Harris-LA...............3.0	J.Hart-SL................79.5	B.Kilmer-Was..........626	R.Jessie-Det..............54
Receiving Yards	**Receiving Average**	**Receiving TDs**	**Receiving Rank**	**Combined Net Yards**	**Total TDs**	**Total Points**
D.Pearson-Dal.......1087	L.Walton-SF..........21.21	C.Capria-Phi...............8	D.Pearson-Dal.........554	T.Metcalf-SL..........2058	C.Foreman-Min..........15	C.Marcol-GB..............94
M.Gray-SL...............770	M.Gray-SL...........19.74	L.Walton-SF................6	M.Gray-SL...............415	S.McCullum-LA......1517	T.Sullivan-Phi............12	E.Mann-Det...............92
R.Jessie-Det............761	J.Lash-Min...........19.72	M.Gray-SL..................6	R.Jessie-Det...........396	H.Stevens-NO........1396	T.Metcalf-SL................8	C.Foreman-Min..........90
C.Taylor-Was...........738	D.Pearson-Dal......17.53	C.Foreman-Min............6	C.Taylor-Was..........394	C.Foreman-Min......1393	C.Capria-Phi................8	M.Moseley-Was.........81
C.Young-Phi............696	C.Wade-Chi..........17.51		C.Capria-Phi...........365	L.Gotshalk-Chi.......1255		T.Sullivan-Phi............72
Punt Average	**Field Goals**	**Field Goal Percent**	**Kickoff Returns**	**Kickoff Return Average**	**Punt Returns**	**Punt Return Average**
T.Blanchard-NO......42.1	C.Marcol-GB..............25	E.Mann-Det............71.9	J.Jones-Det..............38	T.Metcalf-SL...........31.1	H.Stevens-NO...........37	D.Jauron-Det..........16.8
T.Wittum-SF...........41.2	E.Mann-Det...............23	C.Marcol-GB...........64.1	D.Morgan-Dal...........35	L.Jones-Was...........29.2	I.Hill-Chi......................33	D.Morgan-Dal.........15.1
J.James-Atl............40.5	M.Moseley-Was.........18	T.Dempsey-Phi.......62.5	H.Stevens-NO...........33	L.McQuay-NYG......27.6	A.Dodd-Atl..................27	G.Tinker-Atl...........13.9
D.Jennings-NYG.....39.8	J.Bakken-SL.............13	M.Moseley-Was......60.0	S.Odom-GB..............31	C.Bryant-LA............26.8	T.Metcalf-SL...............26	T.Metcalf-SL..........13.1
D.Carrell-Dal..........39.8	F.Cox-Min...................12	F.Cox-Min...............60.0	G.Tinker-Atl..............29	L.Gotshalk-Chi........25.8	C.Harris-Dal...............26	A.Dodd-Atl.............12.7
Punt/Kick Return Yards	**Punt/Kick Return TDs**	**Interceptions**	**Interception Return Yards**	**Interception Return TDs**	**Sacks**	**Overall Rank**
H.Stevens-NO........1125	Many............................1	R.Brown-Atl................8	N.Thompson-SL......190	L.Johnson-Det.............2	Not kept	T.Metcalf-SL..........1515
D.Morgan-Dal........1110		C.Stukes-LA.................7	D.Elmendorf-LA.......186	D.Elmendorf-LA...........2		S.McCullum-LA......1353
T.Metcalf-SL............963		D.Elmendorf-LA...........7	R.Brown-Atl............164			C.Foreman-Min......1205
J.Jones-Det.............927		N.Wright-Min................6	L.Johnson-Det.........139			G.Brezina-GB........1090
S.Odom-GB.............904		N.Thompson-SL..........6	K.Stone-Was.............95			R.Staubach-Dal.....1075

A Different Way of Getting There

Even against a backdrop of player unrest and a rival league, it seemed like the NFC would settle into the same sort of season with the same sorts of contenders as in recent years. But this was a season of surprises and setbacks, starting with the shocking death of Lions coach Don McCafferty in July. Only 53, McCafferty had guided the Colts to victory in Super Bowl V. He was just entering his fifth season as a head coach.

Although not as tragic, the Cowboys were doomed to misfortune. An early four-game losing streak put them in danger from the start, and Roger Staubach struggled through his worst season as a regular. He was sacked a career-high 45 times, and the Cowboys, in Bob Lilly's last season, wound up watching the playoffs for the first time in nine years.

St. Louis proved ready to take the Cowboys' place. The Cardiac Cardinals won nine times in the final two minutes to steal their first division title since 1948. It was the first of many high-flying offenses designed by coach Don Coryell. The Redskins ran off a 6–1 stretch drive, pushing past Dallas for the wild card despite a Thanksgiving Day loss engineered by Dallas backup quarterback Clint Longley. With the league's fourth-worst rushing attack, Washington relied on 40-year-old legend Sonny Jurgensen. In what would be his final campaign, Jurgensen provided a reminder of the arm that had once produced passing records. His backup was Joe Theismann, 25, who'd spent three years in the CFL and now returned punts in Washington.

Minnesota still reigned supreme in the Central. The Vikings dashed to their second straight conference title with Chuck Foreman scoring a league-leading 15 touchdowns. In the Western Division, although heavy favorites, the Rams traded veteran John Hadl to give James Harris an opportunity. Much was made about an African American as a starting NFL quarterback. Harris gave the Rams a play-caller with better mobility than Hadl, providing a needed change of pace. His arm, running back Lawrence McCutcheon's legs, and the league's most choking run defense enabled the Rams to fulfill expectations.

1974 AFC

TEAM	W-L-T	PCT	POST	PTS	RA	RY	RY/A	RTD	FL	PA	PC	GPY	GPY/A	PTD	PI	PSY	PRAT
Eastern Division																	
Mia	11-3	.786	D	327-216	**570-404**	2191-1624	3.8-4.0	**25-7**	13-17	283-372	171-200	2313-2452	**8.2**-6.6	18-14	18-16	229-270	81.2-69.0
Buf	9-5	.643	W	264-244	545-489	2094-1878	3.8-3.8	11-19	14-11	251-311	128-146	1728-1898	6.9-6.1	14-**11**	15-20	236-287	67.0-51.6
NE	7-7	.500	—	348-289	520-467	2134-**1587**	4.1-**3.4**	21-16	15-14	359-374	177-210	2514-2774	7.0-7.4	19-17	23-24	**174**-294	63.3-68.2
NYJ	7-7	.500	—	279-300	444-539	1625-2240	3.7-4.2	12-20	**8**-9	369-347	194-186	2631-2249	7.1-6.5	20-14	24-17	195-192	66.6-66.8
Bal	2-12	.143	—	190-329	450-516	1818-1961	4.0-3.8	13-20	13-14	**425**-312	221-180	2424-2348	5.7-7.5	9-16	24-10	399-183	52.7-85.3
Central Division																	
Pit	10-3-1	.750	DCS*	305-**189**	546-472	**2417**-1608	**4.4-3.4**	19-**7**	19-**22**	386-339	166-147	2154-**1872**	5.6-**5.5**	12-14	21-25	196-**406**	48.9-**44.3**
Cin	7-7	.500	—	283-259	445-497	1978-2152	**4.4**-4.3	14-16	18-11	353-359	**224**-186	**2804**-2110	7.9-5.9	18-13	**13**-9	293-320	**89.7**-71.4
Hou	7-7	.500	—	236-282	421-474	1361-2050	3.2-4.3	16-15	14-15	363-405	203-231	2275-2724	6.3-6.7	12-19	19-21	298-349	64.0-71.7
Cle	4-10	.286	—	251-344	461-555	1924-2415	4.2-4.4	14-17	15-16	367-**308**	179-**139**	2129-2259	5.8-7.3	12-22	24-24	402-234	50.6-61.6
Western Division																	
Oak	**12**-2	**.857**	DC	**355**-228	561-459	2334-2108	4.2-4.6	15-12	10-14	335-367	186-175	2561-2425	7.6-6.6	**28**-12	18-27	177-314	85.7-49.6
Den	7-6-1	.536	—	302-294	486-487	2157-1808	**4.4**-3.7	20-17	13-11	329-426	184-237	2660-2805	8.1-6.6	18-14	17-22	332-222	79.1-65.3
KC	5-9	.357	—	233-293	469-502	1720-1801	3.7-3.6	10-16	13-16	395-408	211-206	2421-2838	6.1-7.0	11-22	25-**28**	313-175	55.0-62.5
SD	5-9	.357	—	212-285	508-508	2111-2160	4.2-4.3	15-21	11-13	349-367	165-222	2479-2815	7.1-7.7	12-13	22-15	175-145	56.3-79.2
Aver	14	—	—	255	481	1866	3.9	14	13	370	194	2400	6.5	14	19	254	64.2

TEAM	1D	PENY	PNT	FGM/A	RTNY	RTNTD	OFFY/DEFY	NETY	NETTO	NP	PNP	DELP	PW	DELW	PRT	DR	YPD	DEL
Eastern Division																		
Mia	272-208	556-525	38.6-39.2	8/15-14/21	659-579	0-4	4275-3806	469	2	111	47	**64**	9.8	1.2	4.6/ 4.0	164-168	26.1-22.7	3.4
Buf	220-219	706-597	40.6-**37.1**	19/**33**-8/15	873-599	**5**-2	3586-3489	97	2	20	16	4	7.5	1.5	3.4/ 2.4	170-175	21.1-19.9	1.2
NE	255-240	843-642	36.2-38.4	16/22-11/18	827-645	3-4	4474-4067	407	0	59	34	25	8.5	-1.5	3.9/ 3.8	182-189	24.6-21.5	3.1
NYJ	234-267	600-684	35.9-37.2	12/18-12/24	703-804	4-4	4061-4297	-236	-6	-21	-44	23	6.5	0.5	4.0/ 3.8	173-174	23.5-24.7	-1.2
Bal	244-237	587-737	37.1-38.4	12/20-17/27	340-797	0-4	3843-4126	-283	-13	-139	-76	-63	3.5	-1.5	2.2/ 5.6	172-**164**	22.3-25.2	-2.8
Central Division																		
Pit	251-**200**	978-575	39.0-41.2	**20**/29-12/17	**1094**-635	4-1	4375-**3074**	**1301**	7	116	**136**	-20	9.9	0.6	2.8/**1.2**	192-196	22.8-**15.7**	**7.1**
Cin	260-256	653-640	40.9-37.8	11/18-17/22	742-597	4-1	4489-3942	547	-11	24	2	22	7.6	-0.6	**5.4**/ 3.8	168-165	26.7-23.9	2.8
Hou	200-268	749-**872**	39.2-39.1	9/19-16/23	808-738	2-**0**	3338-4425	-1087	3	-46	-79	33	5.8	1.1	3.1/ 3.6	177-175	18.9-25.3	-6.4
Cle	223-247	767-731	40.5-38.0	14/16-14/23	859-1128	4-4	3651-4440	-789	1	-93	-62	-31	4.7	-0.7	1.8/ 3.5	**196**-192	18.6-23.1	-4.5
Western Division																		
Oak	**284**-237	845-502	**42.2**-39.9	11/17-13/22	895-**559**	3-3	**4718**-4219	499	**13**	**127**	94	33	**10.2**	**1.8**	5.2/ 2.5	178-180	26.5-23.4	3.1
Den	258-265	632-595	40.3-42.6	11/21-16/24	785-833	1-4	4485-4391	94	3	8	20	-12	7.2	0.3	4.6/ 3.8	176-180	25.5-24.4	1.1
KC	224-267	**515**-811	41.7-40.1	17/24-**6/14**	827-970	**5**-2	3828-4464	-636	6	-60	-29	-31	5.5	-0.5	2.5/ 3.7	193-186	19.8-24.0	-4.2
SD	245-272	609-751	40.0-40.6	6/16-9/20	560-712	1-3	4415-4830	-415	-5	-73	-55	-18	5.2	-0.2	3.9/ 5.5	165-167	**26.8**-28.9	-2.2
Aver	239	659	39.0	13/21	723	1	4012	—	—	—	—	—	—	—	3.9	89	23.2	—

Rushing Attempts	Rushing Yards	Rushing Average	Rushing TDs	Rushing Rank	Passing Yards	Passing Average
O.Simpson-Buf........270	O.Armstrong-Den..1407	O.Armstrong-Den...5.35	J.Keyworth-Den.........10	O.Armstrong-Den..1497	K.Anderson-Cin.....2667	K.Anderson-Cin......8.13
O.Armstrong-Den....263	D.Woods-SD..........1162	C.Davis-Cin............5.21	L.Csonka-NE...............9	D.Woods-SD..........1232	J.Namath-NYJ.......2616	C.Johnson-Den.......8.07
M.Herron-NE...........231	O.Simpson-Buf......1125	D.Woods-SD...........5.12	L.Csonka-Mia.............9	O.Simpson-Buf......1155	K.Stabler-Oak........2469	K.Stabler-Oak.........7.96
D.Woods-SD............227	F.Harris-Pit............1006	L.Csonka-NE..........4.89	O.Armstrong-Den........9	F.Harris-Pit............1056	J.Plunkett-NE.........2457	B.Griese-Mia..........7.78
L.Mitchell-Bal...........214	M.Hubbard-Oak.......865	F.Harris-Pit.............4.84	E.Newman-Mia............8	M.Hubbard-Oak.......905	C.Johnson-Den......1969	D.Fouts-SD............7.31
Completion Percent	**TD Passes**	**TD Percent**	**INT Percent**	**Passer Rating**	**Passing Rank**	**Receptions**
K.Anderson-Cin......64.9	K.Stabler-Oak............26	K.Stabler-Oak...........8.4	K.Anderson-Cin........3.0	K.Anderson-Cin......95.7	K.Anderson-Cin.....1024	L.Mitchell-Bal............72
B.Griese-Mia...........60.1	J.Namath-NYJ...........20	B.Griese-Mia.............6.3	C.Johnson-Den.........3.7	K.Stabler-Oak.........94.9	K.Stabler-Oak..........885	C.Branch-Oak............60
L.Dawson-KC.........58.7	J.Plunkett-NE............19	J.Namath-NYJ..........5.5	J.Gilliam-Pit.............3.8	C.Johnson-Den.......84.5	C.Johnson-Den........690	E.Podolak-KC...........43
K.Stabler-Oak.........57.4	K.Anderson-Cin.........18	K.Anderson-Cin........5.5	K.Stabler-Oak...........3.9	B.Griese-Mia...........80.9	J.Namath-NYJ.........528	R.Odoms-Den...........42
D.Pastorini-Hou.......56.7	B.Griese-Mia.............16	J.Plunkett-NE...........5.4	D.Pastorini-Hou.........4.0	D.Pastorini-Hou.......72.4	B.Griese-Mia...........464	D.Beverly-Oak...........42
Receiving Yards	**Receiving Average**	**Receiving TDs**	**Receiving Rank**	**Combined Net Yards**	**Total TDs**	**Total Points**
C.Branch-Oak........1092	I.Curtis-Cin...........21.10	C.Branch-Oak............13	C.Branch-Oak..........611	M.Herron-NE.........2444	C.Branch-Oak............13	R.Gerela-Pit...............93
G.Garrison-SD.........785	R.Caster-NYJ.......19.61	I.Curtis-Cin...............10	G.Garrison-SD.........418	O.Armstrong-Den..2198	M.Herron-NE............12	J.Smith-NE................90
R.Caster-NYJ..........745	G.Garrison-SD......19.15	R.Caster-NYJ.............7	R.Caster-NYJ.........408	G.Pruitt-Cle............1769	O.Armstrong-Den......12	J.Leypoldt-Buf...........82
R.Odoms-Den..........639	C.Branch-Oak.......18.20	D.Beverly-Oak.............7	I.Curtis-Cin.............367	B.Johnson-Hou......1664	L.Csonka-NE............11	C.Branch-Oak...........78
I.Curtis-Cin.............633	J.Hill-Buf...............17.88		R.Odoms-Den..........350	D.Woods-SD.........1572		G.Blanda-Oak...........77
Punt Average	**Field Goals**	**Field Goal Percent**	**Kickoff Returns**	**Kickoff Return Average**	**Punt Returns**	**Punt Return Average**
M.Bateman-Buf.......43.9	R.Gerela-Pit...............20	D.Cockroft-Cle........87.5	L.Piccone-NYJ...........39	G.Pruitt-Cle.............27.5	D.Walker-Buf.............43	L.Parrish-Cin...........18.8
R.Guy-Oak..............42.2	J.Leypoldt-Buf............19	J.Smith-NE.............72.7	W.Francis-Buf...........37	B.Johnson-Hou.......27.1	L.Swann-Pit..............41	M.Herron-NE..........14.8
J.Wilson-KC............41.7	J.Stenerud-KC...........17	J.Stenerud-KC........70.8	B.Johnson-Hou..........29	N.Moore-Mia...........26.7	R.Smith-Oak..............41	L.Swann-Pit...........14.1
D.Green-Cin............40.9	J.Smith-NE................16	R.Gerela-Pit............69.0	B.Jackson-Cin............29	B.Laird-Bal.............26.3	R.Word-NYJ.............38	B.Johnson-Hou.......13.6
D.Cockroft-Cle........40.5	D.Cockroft-Cle...........14	G.Blanda-Oak.........64.7	M.Herron-NE.............28	H.Hart-Oak.............25.9	M.Herron-NE............35	B.Thompson-Den...13.5
Punt/Kick Return Yards	**Punt/Kick Return TDs**	**Interceptions**	**Interception Return Yards**	**Interception Return TDs**	**Sacks**	**Overall Rank**
B.Johnson-Hou......1194	L.Parrish-Cin................2	E.Thomas-KC............12	E.Thomas-KC..........214	E.Thomas-KC.............2	Not kept	O.Armstrong-Den..1861
M.Herron-NE.........1146	L.Swann-Pit.................1	T.Greene-Buf..............9	T.Greene-Buf...........157			M.Herron-NE.........1707
L.Piccone-NYJ.......1036	G.Pruitt-Cle..................1	J.Scott-Mia..................8	G.Edwards-Pit.........153			D.Woods-SD.........1417
G.Pruitt-Cle.............955		T.Darden-Cle...............8	B.Thompson-Den....105			K.Anderson-Cin.....1358
W.Francis-Buf..........947		R.Bolton-NE................7	T.Darden-Cle...........105			G.Pruitt-Cle...........1280

Steel Away

The creation of the rival World Football League and a simmering strike by the Player's Association threatened the NFL's stability. Although both challenges were addressed quickly enough—the strike ended before the season, and the WFL was quickly mired by its financial shortcomings—the NFL was affected in different ways. A number of star players defected, signing future contracts with the WFL that would start after their current NFL contracts expired. The three-time defending AFC champion Dolphins endured a season knowing Larry Csonka, Jim Kiick, Paul Warfield, and Bob Kuechenberg would defect at its conclusion. Before enjoying a breakthrough season, Raiders quarterback Ken Stabler had inked a future deal as well.

A more lasting effect came with the NFL's decision to mimic some of the offense-minded rules changes that the WFL introduced: moving the goal post back to the end line, lowering the penalty for offensive holding from 15 to 10 yards, tougher pass interference rules with the introduction of "illegal contact," and re-spotting the ball at the line of scrimmage with a change of possession after a missed field goal (previously, this was a touchback). The NFL also added a feature to the regular season that was already an element of the playoffs: a sudden-death overtime period.

Within the season, despite the distractions of their eventual defections, both the Dolphins and the Raiders dominated their divisions. Stabler was the signature player in an offense that led the league in scoring and touchdown passes, and placed third in rushing yardage. Stabler's center, Jim Otto, concluded a career in which he played every game of Oakland's existence.

Pittsburgh won back the Central Division despite a quarterback controversy. Joe Gilliam held the job in the early going, with Terry Bradshaw on the bench. Bradshaw was there at the end, though, as were five sensational rookies: linebacker Jack Lambert, defensive back Donnie Shell, center Mike Webster, and the receiving duo of Lynn Swann and John Stallworth. These players, plus the cache of talent already on the roster, enabled Pittsburgh to give owner Art Rooney the one thing he had never come across in five decades in the NFL: a championship trophy.

1975 NFC

TEAM	W-L-T	PCT	POST	PTS	RA	RY	RY/A	RTD	FL	PA	PC	GPY	GPY/A	PTD	PI	PSY	PRAT
Eastern Division																	
SL	11-3	.786	D	356-276	555-487	2402-1925	4.3-4.0	19-16	19-15	355-446	187-233	2619-2862	7.4-6.4	20-16	20-22	66-192	72.0-63.8
Dal	10-4	.714	WCS	350-268	571-474	2432-1699	4.3-3.6	17-13	18-19	376-373	207-162	2835-2328	7.5-6.2	19-19	17-25	242-288	77.4-53.3
Was	8-6	.571	—	325-276	444-525	1752-2047	3.9-3.9	9-11	17-19	448-389	229-217	3092-2712	6.9-7.0	28-17	29-18	175-276	67.3-72.9
NYG	5-9	.357	—	216-306	482-555	1627-2422	3.4-4.4	17-16	19-8	379-365	193-196	2457-2539	6.5-7.0	11-20	18-16	355-172	62.3-57.3
Phi	4-10	.286	—	225-302	461-529	1702-2233	3.7-4.2	3-20	12-18	458-424	238-226	2640-2658	5.8-6.3	19-13	23-26	200-120	62.3-57.3
Central Division																	
Min	12-2	.857	D	377-180	556-383	2094-1532	3.8-4.0	18-7	12-14	446-360	281-175	3121-1994	7.0-5.5	27-14	14-28	260-373	90.8-46.2
Det	7-7	.500	—	245-262	532-480	2147-1929	4.0-4.0	10-12	18-17	362-360	183-181	2240-2377	6.2-6.6	15-16	12-20	323-306	70.0-63.2
ChiB	4-10	.286	—	191-379	441-547	1653-2070	3.7-3.8	11-25	17-14	356-399	191-180	2169-2825	6.1-7.1	9-22	23-13	330-319	53.7-79.8
GB	4-10	.286	—	226-285	431-580	1547-2339	3.6-4.0	14-14	16-27	394-369	212-192	2400-2474	6.1-6.7	11-13	22-14	328-302	58.3-69.3
Western Division																	
LA	12-2	.857	DC	312-135	585-423	2371-1533	4.1-3.6	18-4	8-18	334-387	181-187	2450-2126	7.3-5.5	14-11	17-22	255-337	70.6-51.0
SF	5-9	.357	—	255-286	422-518	1598-1829	3.8-3.5	12-14	25-16	450-411	234-228	2806-2521	6.2-6.1	15-15	19-11	246-324	64.9-74.9
Atl	4-10	.286	—	240-289	465-571	1794-2277	3.9-4.0	12-13	19-12	388-437	165-227	2361-2810	6.1-6.4	18-16	29-25	294-275	47.2-60.5
NO	2-12	.143	—	165-360	463-507	1642-1930	3.5-3.8	9-15	16-23	392-354	181-206	1961-2587	5.0-7.3	8-25	24-16	416-200	42.7-85.7
Aver	14	—	—	288	508	2037	4.0	16	16	384	201	2561	6.7	17	21	282	65.8

TEAM	1D	PENY	PNT	FGM/A	RTNY	RTNTD	OFFY/DEFY	NETY	NETTO	NP	PNP	DELP	PW	DELW	PRT	DR	YPD	DEL
Eastern Division																		
SL	276-284	730-679	37.7-40.1	19/24-15/26	659-545	4-2	4955-4595	360	-2	80	22	58	9.0	2.0	5.1/3.9	177-184	28.0-25.0	3.0
Dal	288-234	715-639	39.4-39.6	22/35-13/18	659-464	5-1	5025-3739	1286	9	82	143	-61	9.1	1.0	4.9/2.7	190-192	26.4-19.5	7.0
Was	272-255	723-773	40.6-38.9	16/25-17/30	799-709	3-5	4669-4483	186	-9	49	-21	70	8.2	-0.2	4.0/4.2	201-196	23.2-22.9	0.4
NYG	229-264	440-755	39.0-37.6	6/11-11/21	467-578	1-3	3729-4789	-1060	-13	-90	-140	50	4.8	0.3	3.3/4.7	180-178	20.7-26.9	-6.2
Phi	237-275	744-784	38.9-37.0	20/29-18/27	643-941	2-3	4142-4771	-629	9	-77	-16	-61	5.1	-1.1	3.3/3.4	186-185	22.3-25.8	-3.5
Central Division																		
Min	314-190	708-781	41.1-39.6	13/17-9/13	572-654	3-1	4955-3153	1802	16	197	214	-17	11.9	0.1	5.3/1.2	181-179	27.4-17.6	9.8
Det	241-235	838-784	41.9-37.0	14/21-16/23	643-606	4-3	4064-4000	64	7	-17	-33	-50	6.6	0.4	3.8/3.3	187-176	21.7-22.7	-1.0
ChiB	190-282	881-723	39.0-41.4	13/23-14/18	753-537	2-1	3492-4576	-1084	-13	-188	-142	-46	2.3	1.7	2.3/4.9	194-194	18.0-23.6	-5.6
GB	211-260	606-544	35.8-39.7	12/17-21/31	364-609	2-5	3619-4511	-892	3	-59	-62	3	5.5	-1.5	2.7/4.2	191-191	18.9-23.6	-4.7
Western Division																		
LA	273-204	746-626	39.4-39.7	21/26-10/19	889-610	4-0	4566-3322	1244	15	177	164	13	11.4	0.6	4.3/2.1	178-175	25.7-19.0	6.7
SF	240-253	693-730	41.9-39.7	14/28-17/22	754-702	4-5	4158-4026	132	-17	-31	-57	26	6.2	-1.2	3.8/4.1	181-184	23.0-21.9	1.1
Atl	225-288	635-716	41.5-41.1	4/10-25/38	590-991	3-2	3861-4812	-951	-11	-49	-123	74	5.8	-1.8	2.2/3.3	191-194	20.2-24.8	-4.6
NO	215-251	527-726	41.0-42.7	11/21-8/12	675-1042	2-8	3187-4317	-1130	-1	-195	-98	-97	2.1	-0.1	1.2/5.0	188-188	17.0-23.0	-6.0
Aver	257	728	39.6	14/22	682	3	4316	—	—	—	—	—	—	—	4.0	184	23.4	

Rushing Attempts		Rushing Yards		Rushing Average		Rushing TDs		Rushing Rank		Passing Yards		Passing Average	
C.Foreman-Min	280	J.Otis-SL	1076	D.Williams-SF	5.39	C.Foreman-Min	13	C.Foreman-Min	1200	F.Tarkenton-Min	2994	R.Staubach-Dal	7.66
J.Otis-SL	269	C.Foreman-Min	1070	T.Metcalf-SL	4.95	T.Metcalf-SL	9	J.Otis-SL	1126	R.Staubach-Dal	2666	J.Harris-LA	7.54
D.Hampton-Atl	250	D.Hampton-Atl	1002	R.Harper-Chi	4.53	W.Payton-Chi	7	D.Hampton-Atl	1052	J.Hart-SL	2507	J.Hart-SL	7.27
M.Thomas-Was	235	R.Newhouse-Dal	930	R.Newhouse-Dal	4.45	D.Dennison-Dal	7	M.Thomas-Was	959	B.Kilmer-Was	2440	N.Snead-SF	7.07
S.McCullum-LA	213	M.Thomas-Was	919	D.Bussey-Det	4.43	M.Briscoe-GB	7	R.Newhouse-Dal	950	C.Morton-NYG	2359	B.Kilmer-Was	7.05

Completion Percent		TD Passes		TD Percent		INT Percent		Passer Rating		Passing Rank		Receptions	
F.Tarkenton-Min	64.2	F.Tarkenton-Min	25	B.Kilmer-Was	6.6	F.Tarkenton-Min	3.1	F.Tarkenton-Min	91.8	F.Tarkenton-Min	1102	C.Foreman-Min	73
N.Snead-SF	57.1	B.Kilmer-Was	23	F.Tarkenton-Min	5.9	S.Spurrier-SF	3.4	R.Staubach-Dal	78.5	R.Staubach-Dal	778	K.Payne-GB	58
R.Staubach-Dal	56.9	J.Hart-SL	19	J.Hart-SL	5.5	R.Gabriel-Phi	3.8	B.Kilmer-Was	77.2	B.Kilmer-Was	695	E.Marinaro-Min	54
G.Huff-Chi	55.6	R.Staubach-Dal	17	L.Barney-Atl	5.1	G.Huff-Chi	4.4	J.Harris-LA	73.8	C.Morton-NYG	595	C.Taylor-Was	53
J.Harris-LA	55.1	J.Harris-LA	14	J.Harris-LA	4.9	C.Morton-NYG	4.4	N.Snead-SF	73.0	J.Hart-SL	589	J.Gilliam-Min	50

Receiving Yards		Receiving Average		Receiving TDs		Receiving Rank		Combined Net Yards		Total TDs		Total Points	
M.Gray-SL	926	A.Jenkins-Atl	20.18	M.Gray-SL	11	M.Gray-SL	518	T.Metcalf-SL	2462	C.Foreman-Min	22	C.Foreman-Min	132
D.Pearson-Dal	822	M.Gray-SL	19.29	S.Walters-SF	9	D.Pearson-Dal	451	C.Foreman-Min	1765	T.Metcalf-SL	13	T.Fritsch-Dal	104
H.Jackson-LA	786	F.Grant-Was	18.93	C.Foreman-Min	9	H.Jackson-LA	428	L.Jones-Was	1526	M.Gray-SL	11	J.Bakken-SL	97
J.Gilliam-Min	777	H.Jackson-LA	18.28	D.Pearson-Dal	8	F.Grant-Was	428	M.Thomas-Was	1402	S.Walters-SF	9	T.Dempsey-LA	94
F.Grant-Was	776	D.Pearson-Dal	17.87	F.Grant-Was	8	J.Gilliam-Min	424	S.Odom-GB	1388				

Punt Average		Field Goals		Field Goal Percent		Kickoff Returns		Kickoff Return Average		Punt Returns		Punt Return Average	
H.Weaver-Det	42.0	T.Fritsch-Dal	22	T.Dempsey-LA	80.8	L.Jones-Was	47	W.Payton-Chi	31.7	L.Jones-Was	53	T.Metcalf-SL	12.4
T.Wittum-SF	41.9	T.Dempsey-LA	21	J.Bakken-SL	79.2	S.Odom-GB	42	T.Metcalf-SL	27.4	V.Livers-Chi	42	G.Chapman-NO	12.2
J.James-Atl	41.5	H.Muhlmann-Phi	20	F.Cox-Min	76.5	T.Metcalf-SL	35	B.Thompson-Det	25.7	R.McGill-SF	31	V.Livers-Chi	10.9
N.Clabo-Min	41.1	J.Bakken-SL	19	H.Muhlmann-Phi	69.0	G.Chapman-NO	28	L.Marshall-Phi	25.3	G.Richards-Dal	28	B.Taylor-SF	10.4
T.Blanchard-NO	41.0	M.Moseley-Was	16	J.Danelo-GB	68.8			M.Moore-SF	25.0	R.Colbert-NYG	27	G.Richards-Dal	10.3

Punt/Kick Return Yards		Punt/Kick Return TDs		Interceptions		Interception Return Yards		Interception Return TDs		Sacks		Overall Rank	
L.Jones-Was	1493	T.Metcalf-SL	2	P.Krause-Min	10	P.Krause-Min	201	Many	1	Not kept		T.Metcalf-SL	1761
T.Metcalf-SL	1245			R.Lawrence-Atl	9	R.Lawrence-Atl	163					C.Foreman-Min	1580
S.Odom-GB	1034			N.Thompson-SL	7	N.Thompson-SL	141					F.Tarkenton-Min	1230
V.Livers-Chi	985					F.LeMaster-Phi	133					M.Thomas-Was	1216
G.Chapman-NO	821					R.Brown-Atl	119					J.Otis-SL	1166

THUNDER AND LIGHTNING ON FIELD AND IN COURT

The start of the season was again marred by labor woes. Preseason player strikes aimed at bringing free agency to football caused the cancellation of several exhibition games. After agreeing to take the field for the regular season, the players would win a significant victory in court, as federal judge Earl Larson ruled that the league was guilty of illegal monopolistic practices. However, the league would successfully defend the amateur draft in court, and continued to appeal to avoid letting player value become market-driven.

The Vikings handily won the Central Division again. Chuck Foreman led the conference with 22 touchdowns and Fran Tarkenton, the league MVP, moved past Johnny Unitas for most career touchdown passes. Minnesota's defense remained one of the game's best, with linemen Alan Page and Carl Eller creating pressure while safety Paul Krause, nearing the end of a fantastic career, reaped the benefit with 10 picks.

Although the Bears were largely irrelevant once more, they liked what they saw in their top draft choice, Jackson State's Walter Payton.

The NFC went indoors as the Lions moved to the Pontiac Silverdome and the Saints entered the Superdome.

In something of an upset, the Cardinals successfully defended their title in the Eastern Division. Quarterback Jim Hart had plenty of options, targeting flanker Mel Gray for a league-leading 11 scores when not relying on a thunder and lighting running game. Terry Metcalf provided speed and a great target out of the backfield, while journeyman fullback Jim Otis pounded the ground between the tackles, leading the NFC with 1,076 rushing yards. All of it was made possible by an offensive line anchored by Pro Bowl tackle Dan Dierdorf and a guard known for devious tactics, Conrad Dobler. St. Louis allowed just 8 sacks all season.

The Cowboys returned to the postseason. Tom Landry's retooled roster boasted young defensive linemen Too Tall Jones, Harvey Martin, and Randy White. The Rams won the West for the third straight year. This time it had more about a league-best defense than an increasingly predictable offense. When quarterback James Harris went down with shoulder injury, young Ron Jaworski took over and won his playoff debut.

1975 AFC

TEAM	W-L-T	PCT	POST	PTS	RA	RY	RY/A	RTD	FL	PA	PC	GPY	GPY/A	PTD	PI	PSY	PRAT
Eastern Division																	
Bal	10-4	.714	#D	395-269	536-453	2217-1821	4.1-4.0	**28**-17	10-12	354-393	211-193	2606-2848	7.4-7.2	19-17	**8**-29	325-**496**	**90.9**-56.9
Mia	10-4	.714	#	357-222	594-443	2500-1768	4.2-4.0	26-14	9-9	279-375	170-200	2196-2335	7.9-6.2	19-**9**	17-21	187-314	83.0-57.1
Buf	8-6	.571	—	**420**-355	588-480	**2974**-1993	**5.1**-4.2	26-21	15-20	354-431	182-237	2661-3355	7.5-7.8	**28**-25	19-25	**168**-275	80.2-75.5
NE	3-11	.214	—	258-358	472-555	1845-2220	3.9-4.0	14-20	22-16	401-368	193-213	2768-2515	6.9-6.8	16-18	28-13	330-271	55.2-80.4
NYJ	3-11	.214	—	258-433	501-574	2079-2737	4.1-4.8	15-25	**8**-13	384-**316**	174-180	2468-2860	6.4-9.1	16-26	33-15	317-141	44.7-94.9
Central Division																	
Pit	**12**-2	**.857**	DCS*	373-**162**	581-**431**	2633-1825	4.5-4.2	22-**8**	20-10	337-396	191-183	2544-2194	7.5-5.5	21-**9**	12-27	290-358	86.7-42.8
Cin	11-3	.786	W	340-246	499-473	1819-2194	3.6-4.6	20-15	20-**22**	433-389	**255**-175	**3497-2001**	**8.1-5.1**	23-11	14-22	256-272	89.0-46.9
Hou	10-4	.714	—	293-226	526-498	2068-**1680**	3.9-**3.4**	14-13	17-19	347-409	165-235	2099-2800	6.0-6.8	14-14	17-24	230-343	59.9-65.4
Cle	3-11	.214	—	218-372	440-544	1850-2032	4.2-3.7	14-21	14-16	**437**-361	220-202	2297-2889	5.3-8.0	7-25	23-10	340-298	49.3-93.6
Western Division																	
Oak	11-3	.786	DC	375-255	**643**-475	2573-1785	4.0-3.8	**28**-15	20-6	350-398	196-**171**	2625-2318	7.5-5.8	19-14	28-**35**	234-474	64.8-**37.2**
Den	6-8	.429	—	254-307	490-526	1993-1974	4.1-3.8	9-19	14-16	427-348	210-181	2900-2245	6.8-6.5	15-14	34-16	359-213	49.9-66.6
KC	5-9	.357	—	282-341	487-562	1847-2724	3.8-4.8	14-24	18-**22**	395-325	217-186	2785-2703	7.1-8.3	15-18	16-20	425-191	73.0-77.3
SD	2-12	.143	—	189-345	434-606	1801-2442	4.1-4.0	14-21	12-14	337-390	165-237	1998-2719	5.9-7.0	7-16	17-20	388-209	53.5-74.1
Aver	14	—	—	288	508	2037	4.0	16	16	384	201	2561	6.7	17	21	282	65.8

TEAM	1D	PENY	PNT	FGM/A	RTNY	RTNTD	OFFY/DEFY	NETY	NETTO	NP	PNP	DELP	PW	DELW	PRT	DR	YPD	DEL
Eastern Division																		
Bal	266-242	760-700	39.6-38.6	10/18-**6/10**	932-624	5-2	4498-4173	325	**23**	126	119	7	10.1	-0.2	5.4/ 2.7	185-188	24.3-22.2	2.1
Mia	266-224	**575**-709	38.6-40.5	13/16-11/20	692-587	1-4	4509-3789	720	4	135	76	59	10.4	-0.4	4.7/ 2.8	164-168	27.5-22.6	4.9
Buf	**318**-300	748-651	41.6-40.5	9/16-9/16	654-441	3-1	**5467**-5073	394	11	65	77	-12	8.6	-0.6	5.1/ 4.8	181-182	**30.2**-27.9	2.3
NE	253-254	719-759	38.8-39.5	9/17-23/35	427-901	3-4	4283-4464	-181	-21	-100	-99	-1	4.5	-1.5	3.0/ 4.6	**197**-197	21.7-22.7	-0.9
NYJ	266-308	799-800	36.5-**33.7**	13/21-12/16	214-746	1-6	4230-5456	-1226	-13	-175	-154	-21	2.6	0.4	2.0/ 6.9	171-**167**	24.7-32.7	-7.9
Central Division																		
Pit	288-**214**	756-701	39.4-40.1	17/21-11/18	969-**246**	3-2	4887-3661	1226	5	**211**	122	**89**	**12.3**	-0.3	5.2/ 1.6	179-182	27.3-20.1	**7.2**
Cin	295-241	783-824	39.0-40.9	10/21-12/14	677-630	2-4	5060-3923	1137	10	94	**135**	-41	9.4	**1.7**	**6.1**/ 2.0	179-184	28.3-21.3	6.9
Hou	234-264	849-871	39.3-41.0	18/30-13/23	1045-542	**6-0**	3937-4137	-200	9	67	19	48	8.7	1.3	3.3/ 3.3	182-188	21.6-22.0	-0.4
Cle	247-274	851-750	40.5-38.5	17/23-13/21	401-809	3-2	3807-4623	-816	-11	-154	-112	-42	3.2	-0.2	2.1/ 6.1	183-180	20.8-25.7	-4.9
Western Division																		
Oak	315-242	951-527	**43.8**-38.7	13/21-11/20	**1138**-814	1-3	4964-**3629**	**1335**	-7	120	83	37	10.0	1.0	3.5/**0.9**	195-199	25.5-**18.2**	**7.2**
Den	268-247	790-786	39.9-42.1	21/28-21/28	763-981	4-2	4534-4006	528	-16	-53	-20	-33	5.7	0.3	2.4/ 3.9	185-181	24.5-22.1	2.4
KC	261-289	658-**934**	39.3-40.7	**22/32**-11/22	691-682	2-2	4207-5236	-1029	8	-59	-54	-5	5.5	-0.5	4.0/ 5.1	183-185	23.0-28.3	-5.3
SD	198-312	705-686	36.8-39.8	12/24-22/34	665-744	1-3	3411-4952	-1541	5	-156	-108	-48	3.1	-1.1	2.4/ 4.3	178-170	19.2-29.1	-10.0
Aver	257	728	39.6	14/22	682	1	4316	—	—	—	—	—	—	—	4.0	91	24.5	—

Rushing Attempts	Rushing Yards	Rushing Average	Rushing TDs	Rushing Rank	Passing Yards	Passing Average
O.Simpson-Buf........329	O.Simpson-Buf......1817	O.Simpson-Buf.......5.52	O.Simpson-Buf..........16	O.Simpson-Buf......1977	K.Anderson-Cin.....3169	B.Griese-Mia..........8.86
L.Mitchell-Bal..........289	F.Harris-Pit............1246	G.Pruitt-Cle............4.92	P.Banaszak-Oak..........16	F.Harris-Pit............1346	B.Jones-Bal.............2483	K.Anderson-Cin.........8.41
F.Harris-Pit...............262	L.Mitchell-Bal.........1193	F.Harris-Pit..............4.76	J.Nicholson-Mia.........12	L.Mitchell-Bal.........1303	J.Ferguson-Buf......2426	K.Stabler-Oak..........7.84
J.Riggins-NYJ...........238	G.Pruitt-Cle............1067	C.Garrett-NYJ..........4.64	L.Mitchell-Bal.............11	G.Pruitt-Cle............1147	K.Stabler-Oak.........2296	L.Dawson-KC...........7.82
M.Morris-Mia............219	J.Riggins-NYJ.........1005	R.Coleman-Hou.......4.51		J.Riggins-NYJ........1085	J.Namath-NYJ........2286	J.Ferguson-Buf.........7.56
Completion Percent	**TD Passes**	**TD Percent**	**INT Percent**	**Passer Rating**	**Passing Rank**	**Receptions**
L.Dawson-KC.........66.4	J.Ferguson-Buf..........25	J.Ferguson-Buf..........7.8	B.Jones-Bal.............2.3	K.Anderson-Cin......93.9	K.Anderson-Cin.....1250	R.Rucker-Cle.............60
B.Griese-Mia.............61.8	K.Anderson-Cin..........21	B.Griese-Mia..............7.3	L.Dawson-KC............2.9	L.Dawson-KC..........90.0	B.Jones-Bal............1012	L.Mitchell-Bal............60
K.Anderson-Cin.......60.5	B.Jones-Bal...............18	T.Bradshaw-Pit..........6.3	K.Anderson-Cin.........2.9	B.Jones-Bal..............89.1	T.Bradshaw-Pit.........758	B.Chandler-Buf...........55
B.Jones-Bal..............59.0	T.Bradshaw-Pit..........18	K.Anderson-Cin.........5.6	T.Bradshaw-Pit..........3.1	T.Bradshaw-Pit.........88.0	J.Ferguson-Buf.........658	K.Burrough-Hou..........53
K.Stabler-Oak..........58.4	K.Stabler-Oak............16	K.Stabler-Oak............5.5	L.Little-KC..................3.4	B.Griese-Mia............86.6	D.Pastorini-Hou........457	C.Branch-Oak.............51
Receiving Yards	**Receiving Average**	**Receiving TDs**	**Receiving Rank**	**Combined Net Yards**	**Total TDs**	**Total Points**
K.Burrough-Hou.....1063	I.Curtis-Cin............21.23	L.Swann-Pit...............11	K.Burrough-Hou.......572	O.Simpson-Buf......2243	O.Simpson-Buf..........23	O.Simpson-Buf........138
I.Curtis-Cin...............934	K.Burrough-Hou....20.06	C.Branch-Oak..............9	I.Curtis-Cin...............502	R.Upchurch-Den.....1929	P.Banaszak-Oak.........16	J.Stenerud-KC...........96
C.Branch-Oak...........893	C.Joiner-Cin..........19.62	K.Burrough-Hou...........8	C.Branch-Oak............492	B.Johnson-Hou......1820	L.Mitchell-Bal.............15	P.Banaszak-Oak.........96
R.Caster-NYJ...........820	J.Hill-Buf...............18.53		L.Swann-Pit...............446	G.Pruitt-Cle...........1798	J.Braxton-Buf.............13	R.Gerela-Pit...............95
L.Swann-Pit..............781	R.Francis-NE..........18.17		R.Caster-NYJ............430	L.Mitchell-Bal.........1737	J.Nicholson-Mia.........12	L.Mitchell-Bal.............90
Punt Average	**Field Goals**	**Field Goal Percent**	**Kickoff Returns**	**Kickoff Return Average**	**Punt Returns**	**Punt Return Average**
R.Guy-Oak..............43.8	J.Stenerud-KC...........22	G.Yepremian-Mia....81.3	R.Upchurch-Den........40	H.Hart-Oak..............30.5	N.Colzie-Oak.............48	B.Johnson-Hou.......15.3
M.Bateman-Buf.......41.6	J.Turner-Den..............21	R.Gerela-Pit..............81.0	J.Wallace-Buf............35	A.Carter-NE..............27.5	B.Johnson-Hou...........40	N.Colzie-Oak.............13.6
J.Wilson-KC............41.4	S.Butler-Hou..............18	J.Turner-Den.............75.0	B.Johnson-Hou...........33	R.Upchurch-Den......27.1	H.Stevens-Bal.............36	F.Solomon-Mia..........12.3
D.Cockroft-Cle.........40.5	R.Gerela-Pit...............17	D.Cockroft-Cle.........73.9	A.Carter-NE...............32	J.Wallace-Buf...........26.4	M.Fuller-SD...............36	R.Upchurch-Den.....11.6
R.Upchurch-Den.....39.9	D.Cockroft-Cle...........17	J.Stenerud-KC..........68.8		B.Laird-Bal..............25.8	R.Upchurch-Den.........27	M.Fuller-SD..............11.4
Punt/Kick Return Yards	**Punt/Kick Return TDs**	**Interceptions**	**Interception Return Yards**	**Interception Return TDs**	**Sacks**	**Overall Rank**
B.Johnson-Hou......1410	B.Johnson-Hou............4	M.Blount-Pit...............11	Z.Moore-Hou............137	J.Wallace-Bal..............2	Not kept	O.Simpson-Buf.......2225
R.Upchurch-Den....1396		S.White-Bal..................8	S.White-Bal...............135			L.Mitchell-Bal.........1595
M.Fuller-SD............1135		D.Harrison-Buf.............8	B.Atkins-Hou.............133			F.Harris-Pit..............1470
J.Wallace-Buf...........923			J.Wallace-Bal............126			G.Pruitt-Cle.............1459
A.Carter-NE.............879			L.Seiple-KC...............123			K.Anderson-Cin......1458

Another League Bites the Dust

The WFL, hemorrhaging money from the outset, collapsed in midseason of its second year. Amid the rubble, 380 players were left jobless. Many would find work in the NFL in 1976, including Danny White and future Philadelphia folk hero Vince Papale, who went from touch football to the pros. But as for 1975, it was a lost year for the Dolphins.

Shorn by defections to the WFL, Miami missed the playoffs for the first time since the merger. Buffalo was even more disappointed. The Bills led the NFL in scoring, had the league's top rusher and scorer in O.J. Simpson, and quarterback Joe Ferguson led the NFL with 25 scoring strikes, but injuries to the secondary made the Bills as likely to give up points as score them.

The Colts moved the ball with confidence behind quarterback Bert Jones and running back Lydell Mitchell. Baltimore claimed the East by beating the Dolphins twice in the midst of a season-ending nine-game win streak. The Colts put pressure on opposing quarterbacks and rolled up 59 sacks.

In the Central, the defending champion Steelers had Terry Bradshaw developing one of the game's all-time great connections with second-year receiver Lynn Swann. Although Pittsburgh's defense had long been famous for its ferocious front line, linebackers Jack Ham, Jack Lambert, and Andy Russell were consensus All-Pros, and corner Mel Blount won Defensive Player of the Year with a league-leading 11 interceptions. The Steelers needed every weapon to fend off Cincinnati in Paul Brown's final season as a head coach. The Bengals, with the NFL's best passing attack, took the wild card at 11–3.

The Raiders dominated the Western Division again. The addition of linebacker Ted Hendricks meant that teams couldn't even throw underneath coverage to avoid Oakland's ferocious defensive backfield; the Raiders picked off a league-leading 35 passes. After losing fullback Marv Hubbard, the Raiders made reserve Pete Banaszak a temporary star by putting him over the goal line 16 times. Two of the old AFL's leading lights packed it in after the season: Oakland's George Blanda and Kansas City's Len Dawson both headed into retirement and eventual enshrinement in the Hall of Fame.

1976 NFC

TEAM	W-L-T	PCT	POST	PTS	RA	RY	RY/A	RTD	FL	PA	PC	GPY	GPY/A	PTD	PI	PSY	PRAT
Eastern Division																	
Dal	**11**-3	.786	D	296-194	538-484	2147-1821	4.0-3.8	16-12	16-12	390-391	222-187	2967-2236	7.6-**5.7**	17-12	13-16	230-327	81.9-58.9
Was	10-4	.714	#W	291-217	548-555	2111-2205	3.9-4.0	10-12	23-21	370-354	187-146	2288-2241	6.2-6.3	**20**-11	20-26	303-324	65.5-**42.6**
SL	10-4	.714	#	309-267	580-491	2301-1979	4.0-4.0	17-19	24-20	392-342	220-176	2967-2358	7.6-6.9	18-13	13-19	**132**-248	81.9-63.2
Phi	4-10	.286	—	165-286	505-532	2080-2053	4.1-3.9	8-16	14-15	369-404	182-237	1844-2688	5.0-6.7	11-17	18-9	352-138	53.6-83.4
NYG	3-11	.214	—	170-250	530-560	1904-2203	3.6-3.9	11-14	**12**-15	326-330	175-189	2104-2230	6.5-6.8	9-11	24-12	312-242	52.2-73.9
Central Division																	
Min	**11**-2-1	**.821**	DCS	305-**176**	540-487	2003-2096	3.7-4.3	18-14	19-13	442-323	**270**-158	**3117-1897**	7.1-5.9	17-**8**	**10**-19	262-322	**85.8**-51.1
ChiB	7-7	.500	—	253-216	578-522	2363-1984	4.1-3.8	20-**10**	13-23	278-401	123-200	1705-2612	6.1-6.5	9-15	15-24	225-395	52.8-58.3
Det	6-8	.429	—	262-220	516-496	2213-1901	**4.3**-3.8	9-13	21-15	356-**313**	201-**137**	2630-1904	7.4-6.1	**20**-11	12-24	490-218	84.6-43.7
GB	5-9	.357	—	218-299	485-546	1722-2288	3.6-4.2	15-17	23-15	357-354	164-196	2105-2192	5.9-6.2	10-13	22-11	375-357	48.6-73.3
Western Division																	
LA	10-3-1	.750	DC	**351**-190	**613-429**	**2528-1564**	4.1-**3.6**	**23**-11	21-16	315-397	171-199	2629-2487	**8.3**-6.3	17-11	15-**32**	288-395	80.2-45.6
SF	8-6	.571	—	270-190	576-487	2447-1786	4.2-3.7	14-**10**	**12**-16	306-374	155-180	1963-2349	6.4-6.3	15-13	21-9	325-**573**	58.8-69.9
Atl	4-10	.286	—	172-312	470-574	1689-2577	3.6-4.5	10-22	17-20	354-340	157-184	1809-2276	5.1-6.7	10-14	24-18	395-275	41.5-66.7
NO	4-10	.286	—	253-346	431-554	1775-2289	4.1-4.1	16-22	18-**27**	403-367	206-200	2353-2514	5.8-6.9	8-18	14-12	369-312	61.2-78.8
Sea	2-12	.143	—	229-429	374-614	1416-2876	3.8-4.7	14-20	18-11	**480**-367	229-223	2874-2770	6.0-7.5	13-27	30-15	225-246	49.8-91.7
Aver	14	—	—	268	516	2109	4.1	15	17	366	191	2428	6.6	15	18	300	67.0

TEAM	1D	PENY	PNT	FGM/A	RTNY	RTNTD	OFFY/DEFY	NETY	NETTO	NP	PNP	DELP	PW	DELW	PRT	DR	YPD	DEL
Eastern Division																		
Dal	269-246	761-643	37.0-38.7	18/23-7/**12**	622-407	1-1	4884-3730	1154	-1	102	92	10	9.6	1.5	5.5/ 3.0	176-174	27.8-21.4	6.3
Was	255-215	868-818	38.9-38.9	**22/34**-19/30	**878**-472	2-**0**	4096-4122	-26	4	74	14	60	8.9	1.1	3.1/ 2.2	**208**-213	19.7-19.4	0.3
SL	**307**-239	683-708	35.3-38.8	20/27-10/20	593-438	1-2	**5136**-4089	1047	2	42	95	-53	8.1	**2.0**	**5.9**/ 3.7	178-181	**28.9**-22.6	6.3
Phi	220-262	722-907	35.5-37.9	11/16-13/24	620-594	0-2	3572-4603	-1031	-8	-121	-118	-3	4.0	0.0	1.9/ 5.5	183-180	19.5-25.6	-6.1
NYG	216-251	734-835	39.7-37.0	8/21-20/31	259-749	1-2	3696-4191	-495	-9	-80	-77	-3	5.0	-2.0	2.2/ 4.3	177-**170**	20.9-24.7	-3.8
Central Division																		
Min	294-207	**615**-653	38.8-37.1	19/31-10/25	484-471	1-**0**	4858-3671	1187	3	129	111	18	10.2	1.3	5.4/ 2.2	172-179	28.2-20.5	**7.7**
ChiB	201-250	984-699	37.3-36.3	12/25-13/25	484-559	2-**0**	3843-4201	-358	**19**	37	46	-9	7.9	-0.9	3.0/ 2.9	198-199	19.4-21.1	-1.7
Det	259-**191**	819-696	38.8-40.1	14/24-15/28	652-**399**	3-1	4353-3587	766	6	42	88	-46	8.1	-2.1	4.3/ 2.1	190-188	22.9-19.1	3.8
GB	210-262	791-914	36.6-38.5	10/19-22/33	497-630	2-4	3452-4123	-671	-19	-81	-132	51	5.0	0.0	2.1/ 3.7	185-189	18.7-21.8	-3.2
Western Division																		
LA	265-213	764-747	38.1-41.2	17/26-12/20	852-492	4-**0**	4869-3656	**1213**	12	**161**	**149**	12	**11.0**	-0.5	5.3/**1.7**	199-200	24.5-18.3	6.2
SF	242-218	848-906	39.9-40.1	16/28-**6**/21	650-604	3-2	4085-**3562**	523	-8	80	12	**68**	9.0	-1.0	2.5/ 3.5	194-199	21.1-**17.9**	3.2
Atl	191-257	714-868	**42.1**-38.5	10/21-12/17	592-829	0-4	3103-4578	-1475	-3	-140	-135	-5	3.5	0.5	1.1/ 3.5	197-199	15.8-23.0	-7.3
NO	226-275	901-883	39.3-39.4	18/23-14/17	587-882	**5**-4	3759-4491	-732	7	-93	-33	-60	4.7	-0.7	3.2/ 4.5	202-201	18.6-22.3	-3.7
Sea	239-323	684-**926**	37.4-**35.0**	9/16-20/30	464-925	2-6	4065-5400	-1335	-22	-200	-199	-1	2.0	0.0	2.8/ 5.4	189-189	21.5-28.6	-7.1
Aver	247	790	38.6	14/24	638	2	4238	—	—	—	—	—	—	—	4.0	187	22.6	—

Rushing Attempts	Rushing Yards	Rushing Average	Rushing TDs	Rushing Rank	Passing Yards	Passing Average
W.Payton-Chi..........311	W.Payton-Chi.........1390	D.Williams-SF.........4.85	W.Payton-Chi............13	W.Payton-Chi.........1520	F.Tarkenton-Min.....2961	J.Harris-LA.............9.24
S.McCullum-LA........291	D.Williams-SF........1203	M.Hogan-Phi...........4.56	C.Foreman-Min.........13	C.Foreman-Min......1285	J.Hart-SL..............2946	J.Hart-SL...............7.59
C.Foreman-Min........278	S.McCullum-LA......1168	S.Smith-Sea...........4.51	S.McCullum-LA...........9	D.Williams-SF........1273	R.Staubach-Dal.....2715	G.Landry-Det..........7.53
M.Thomas-Was.......254	C.Foreman-Min......1155	S.Laidlaw-Dal.........4.51	S.Jones-SL.................8	S.McCullum-LA......1258	J.Zorn-Sea............2571	R.Staubach-Dal......7.36
D.Williams-SF..........248	M.Thomas-Was.....1101	W.Payton-Chi..........4.47		M.Thomas-Was.....1151	G.Landry-Det.........2191	F.Tarkenton-Min......7.19
Completion Percent	**TD Passes**	**TD Percent**	**INT Percent**	**Passer Rating**	**Passing Rank**	**Receptions**
F.Tarkenton-Min......61.9	J.Hart-SL..................18	G.Landry-Det...........5.8	F.Tarkenton-Min........1.9	J.Harris-LA.............89.6	F.Tarkenton-Min.....1246	D.Pearson-Dal..........58
G.Landry-Det..........57.7	F.Tarkenton-Min.........17	B.Kilmer-Was............5.8	G.Landry-Det...........2.7	G.Landry-Det..........89.6	J.Hart-SL..............1043	C.Foreman-Min..........55
J.Harris-LA.............57.6	G.Landry-Det............17	J.Plunkett-SF...........5.3	R.Staubach-Dal........3.0	F.Tarkenton-Min......89.3	R.Staubach-Dal.......988	S.Largent-Sea..........54
R.Staubach-Dal......56.4	R.Staubach-Dal.........14	J.Harris-LA...............5.1	B.Scott-NO...............3.2	J.Hart-SL................82.0	G.Landry-Det..........861	T.Galbreath-NO........54
J.Hart-SL................56.2	J.Plunkett-SF.............13	J.Theismann-Was.....4.9	J.Hart-SL.................3.4	R.Staubach-Dal......79.9	J.Harris-LA..............530	A.Rashad-Min...........53
Receiving Yards	**Receiving Average**	**Receiving TDs**	**Receiving Rank**	**Combined Net Yards**	**Total TDs**	**Total Points**
S.White-Min.............906	R.Jessie-LA..........22.91	S.White-Min..............10	S.White-Min.............503	C.Foreman-Min......1723	C.Foreman-Min.........14	M.Moseley-Was.........97
R.Jarvis-Det.............822	R.Jarvis-Det..........21.08		R.Jarvis-Det.............436	W.Payton-Chi.........1539	W.Payton-Chi............13	J.Bakken-SL..............93
F.Grant-Was.............818	H.Jackson-LA.......19.26		F.Grant-Was.............434	D.Williams-SF........1486	S.McCullum-LA.........11	F.Cox-Min...................89
D.Pearson-Dal.........806	M.Gray-SL...........19.06		D.Pearson-Dal.........433	S.McCullum-LA......1473	S.White-Min...............10	E.Herrera-Dal...........88
I.Harris-SL...............782	S.White-Min..........17.76		R.Jessie-LA.............420	T.Metcalf-SL..........1438		T.Dempsey-LA...........87
Punt Average	**Field Goals**	**Field Goal Percent**	**Kickoff Returns**	**Kickoff Return Average**	**Punt Returns**	**Punt Return Average**
J.James-Atl............42.1	M.Moseley-Was.........22	R.Szaro-NO............78.3	O.Ross-Sea...............30	C.Bryant-LA............28.7	R.Lawrence-Atl..........54	E.Brown-Was..........13.5
D.Jennings-NYG.....41.3	J.Bakken-SL..............20	E.Herrera-Dal.........78.3	L.Marshall-Phi............30	J.Hunter-Det...........26.8	E.Brown-Was.............48	C.Bryant-LA............11.1
T.Wittum-SF............40.8	F.Cox-Min...................19	J.Bakken-SL...........74.1	E.Brown-Was.............30	L.Barney-Chi...........26.0	B.Johnson-Dal...........45	T.Metcalf-SL............11.1
H.Weaver-Det.........39.5	R.Szaro-NO...............18	B.Ricardo-Det.........71.4	S.Odom-GB...............29	M.McCoy-GB..........25.4	J.Gray-GB..................37	B.Johnson-Dal........10.9
T.Blanchard-NO......39.3	E.Herrera-Dal............18	H.Muhlmann-Phi.....68.8	L.Barney-Chi.............29	R.Lawrence-Atl.......24.8		L.Marshall-Phi.........10.7
Punt/Kick Return Yards	**Punt/Kick Return TDs**	**Interceptions**	**Interception Return Yards**	**Interception Return TDs**	**Sacks**	**Overall Rank**
E.Brown-Was.........1384	R.McGill-SF.................1	M.Jackson-LA...........10	L.Johnson-Det.........206	M.Jackson-LA.............3	Not kept	W.Payton-Chi.........1580
B.Johnson-Dal.......1182	T.Leonard-SF..............1	R.Perry-LA...................8	M.Jackson-LA..........173	J.Merlo-NO.................2		C.Foreman-Min......1574
L.Marshall-Phi..........941	C.Bryant-LA.................1	J.Lavender-Was..........8	J.Merlo-NO.............142			D.Williams-SF........1434
R.Lawrence-Atl........893	E.Brown-Was...............1		J.Hunter-Det...........120			S.McCullum-LA......1421
T.Leonard-SF...........846			J.Gray-GB...............101			M.Thomas-Was.....1316

Vikings Left at the Party, Again

The Vikings were the NFC's most prolific passing team. With rookie Sammy White and newcomer Ahmad Rashad for Fran Tarkenton to throw to, and Chuck Foreman enjoying the best rushing season of his career and also catching 55 balls, the Vikings had the highest winning percentage in the NFL. Minnesota lost just twice—by a total of five points—and avenged an earlier tie with Los Angeles by beating the Rams for the NFC title. The Vikings became the first team to reach the Super Bowl four times and the first to go 0–4.

The NFL expanded in 1976, with the Tampa Bay Buccaneers in the AFC and the Seattle Seahawks in the NFC. The Seahawks went just 2–12, with their first win a 13–10 decision against the brutal Buccaneers. But Seattle had a solid passing game behind rookie quarterback Jim Zorn, who threw more passes—and interceptions—than any other quarterback in the league. And why not? He had a great first-year receiver in Steve Largent and an obligation to score as often as possible to make up for the NFL's worst defense. Other debuts included Harry Carson, Randy Cross, and Jackie Slater, who began the first of 20 seasons with the Rams, the longest continuous tenure with one franchise in league history.

The NFL adopted the use of the 30-second clock, giving teams that much time to get off a play or be penalized. Three of the league's premiere defenders retired: Lee Roy Jordan, Jimmy Johnson, and Merlin Olsen.

Ernie Nevers died in 1976. On November 28, 1929, Nevers became the first man to score 6 touchdowns in a game, that same day establishing a still-standing record by scoring all 40 points for the Cardinals against the Bears. Jake Mintun, an original Decatur Staley, forerunner of the Bears in the league's first season in 1920, died at age 81. The death of Paul Robeson was felt far beyond the football arena. Robeson, one of the earliest African American players in the NFL in 1921–22, gained international prominence as a singer, actor, and activist.

1976 AFC

TEAM	W-L-T	PCT	POST	PTS	RA	RY	RY/A	RTD	FL	PA	PC	GPY	GPY/A	PTD	PI	PSY	PRAT
Eastern Division																	
Bal	11-3	.786	#D	**417**-246	565-**438**	2303-1844	4.1-4.2	26-11	18-21	361-372	215-192	3221-2804	**8.9**-7.5	24-16	**10**-15	288-**461**	99.5-74.0
NE	11-3	.786	#W	376-236	591-462	2948-1847	**5.0**-4.0	24-12	16-**27**	309-437	146-229	1910-2604	6.2-6.0	18-16	20-23	164-429	59.7-60.9
Mia	6-8	.429	—	263-264	491-525	2118-2411	4.3-4.6	15-14	**8**-18	346-347	193-195	2604-2863	7.5-8.3	15-20	15-11	336-193	76.3-89.3
NYJ	3-11	.214	—	169-383	438-582	1924-2592	4.4-4.5	10-14	25-21	393-374	180-204	1989-2468	5.1-6.6	7-25	28-11	383-144	37.6-85.1
Buf	2-12	.143	—	245-363	548-533	2566-2465	4.7-4.6	11-19	26-23	383-337	156-163	2084-2475	5.4-7.3	16-18	17-19	246-210	54.1-67.3
Central Division																	
Pit	10-4	.714	#DC	342-**138**	**653**-452	**2971**-**1457**	4.5-**3.2**	**33**-**5**	19-24	277-373	143-**158**	1935-**2179**	7.0-**5.8**	10-9	12-22	269-313	68.2-**45.2**
Cin	10-4	.714	#	335-210	481-520	2109-1912	4.4-3.7	15-11	20-15	360-364	187-177	2443-2202	6.8-6.0	21-13	15-**26**	252-444	75.7-50.0
Cle	9-5	.643	—	267-287	533-445	2295-1761	4.3-4.0	9-15	22-11	373-392	209-225	2399-2353	6.4-6.0	21-18	15-21	**152**-321	77.6-67.9
Hou	5-9	.357	—	222-273	416-540	1498-2072	3.6-3.8	6-13	14-17	**423**-345	227-173	2429-2259	5.7-6.5	17-17	19-11	357-344	65.4-74.3
Western Division																	
Oak	**13**-1	**.929**	DCS*	350-237	557-478	2285-1903	4.1-4.0	14-17	11-9	361-389	**232**-197	3195-2846	**8.9**-7.3	**33**-13	18-16	290-370	**102.2**-68.8
Den	9-5	.643	—	315-206	500-496	1932-1709	3.9-3.4	14-14	12-13	353-391	168-214	2510-2265	7.1-**5.8**	15-**8**	22-24	306-240	59.6-53.1
SD	6-8	.429	—	248-285	473-516	2040-2048	4.3-4.0	13-10	13-11	388-386	223-219	2687-2822	6.9-7.3	17-21	18-20	271-194	74.1-76.4
KC	5-9	.357	—	290-376	498-555	1873-2861	3.8-5.2	18-24	16-20	419-375	229-215	**3303**-2684	7.9-7.2	15-25	17-23	374-188	75.5-76.3
TB	0-14	.000	—	125-412	433-588	1503-2560	3.5-4.4	5-23	17-19	376-**321**	181-178	1926-2412	5.1-7.5	9-19	20-9	423-171	49.4-87.6
Aver	14	—	—	268	516	2109	4.1	15	17	366	191	2428	6.6	15	18	300	67.0

TEAM	1D	PENY	PNT	FGM/A	RTNY	RTNTD	OFFY/DEFY	NETY	NETTO	NP	PNP	DELP	PW	DELW	PRT	DR	YPD	DEL
Eastern Division																		
Bal	301-229	786-770	39.7-**36.9**	20/27-15/20	526-377	1-2	**5236**-4187	1049	8	171	119	52	11.3	-0.3	**7.0**/ 4.3	179-179	29.3-23.4	5.9
NE	260-258	914-715	40.1-38.8	15/25-12/**17**	**1133**-668	6-1	4694-4022	672	14	140	112	28	10.5	0.5	3.1/ 2.7	185-190	25.4-21.2	4.2
Mia	267-268	582-716	38.2-41.2	16/23-10/21	559-400	1-**0**	4386-5081	-695	6	-1	-34	33	7.0	-1.0	4.6/ 6.5	161-**153**	27.2-33.2	-6.0
NYJ	220-277	627-796	39.7-40.5	11/16-23/29	435-888	3-6	3530-4916	-1386	-21	-214	-200	-14	1.7	1.3	0.9/ 5.3	186-185	19.0-26.6	-7.6
Buf	250-262	797-704	**42.3**-38.5	13/24-26/30	513-1124	3-4	4404-4730	-326	-1	-118	-31	-87	4.1	-2.1	3.0/ 4.4	**199**-198	22.1-23.9	-1.8
Central Division																		
Pit	271-**182**	836-630	39.2-37.5	14/26-14/24	898-**312**	0-**0**	4637-**3323**	**1314**	**15**	**204**	**170**	34	**12.1**	-2.1	4.0/ 2.3	193-190	24.0-**17.5**	**6.5**
Cin	238-234	700-768	39.5-38.2	14/27-12/22	673-425	6-1	4300-3670	630	6	125	77	48	10.1	-0.1	4.3/**1.8**	189-194	22.8-18.9	3.8
Cle	260-244	1037-711	37.4-37.4	15/28-11/19	603-640	2-4	4542-3793	749	-5	-20	42	-62	6.5	2.5	4.5/ 3.0	174-180	26.1-21.1	5.0
Hou	199-226	776-**963**	35.3-38.7	16/27-18/29	680-856	2-1	3570-3987	-417	-5	-51	-55	4	5.7	-0.7	3.0/ 4.0	198-201	18.0-19.8	-1.8
Western Division																		
Oak	**303**-261	957-918	41.6-38.9	8/19-**8/17**	681-449	0-1	5190-4379	811	-4	113	52	61	9.8	**3.2**	6.2/ 4.3	175-176	**29.7**-24.9	4.8
Den	239-222	986-715	35.1-37.3	15/21-12/28	1092-632	**10**-3	4136-3734	402	3	109	46	**63**	9.7	-0.7	3.4/ 2.4	195-192	21.2-19.4	1.8
SD	256-259	**579**-823	38.7-41.2	10/20-17/34	789-786	2-3	4456-4676	-220	0	-37	-18	-19	6.1	-0.1	4.1/ 4.7	179-178	24.9-26.3	-1.4
KC	275-309	789-762	41.1-39.1	**21/38**-9/18	590-619	0-2	4802-5357	-555	10	-86	-6	-80	4.8	0.2	5.0/ 4.3	191-186	25.1-28.8	-3.7
TB	191-284	875-935	39.3-39.3	8/17-20/31	465-1244	1-8	3006-4801	-1795	-9	-287	-186	-101	-0.2	0.2	1.6/ 5.9	188-177	16.0-27.1	-11.1
Aver	247	790	38.6	14/24	638	1	4238	—	—	—	—	—	—	—	4.0	93	23.5	—

Rushing Attempts	Rushing Yards	Rushing Average	Rushing TDs	Rushing Rank	Passing Yards	Passing Average
O.Simpson-Buf 290	O.Simpson-Buf 1503	D.Calhoun-NE.........5.59	F.Harris-Pit..................14	O.Simpson-Buf 1583	B.Jones-Bal 3104	K.Stabler-Oak 9.41
L.Mitchell-Bal...........289	L.Mitchell-Bal 1200	O.Simpson-Buf 5.18	S.Grogan-NE 12	F.Harris-Pit.............1268	K.Stabler-Oak 2737	B.Jones-Bal 9.05
F.Harris-Pit...............289	F.Harris-Pit.............1128	R.Young-SD.............4.95	D.McCauley-Bal...........9	L.Mitchell-Bal 1250	L.Little-KC..............2682	L.Little-KC...............7.93
O.Armstrong-Den 247	R.Bleier-Pit 1036	C.Culp-NE 4.79	O.Simpson-Buf 8	R.Bleier-Pit 1086	D.Fouts-SD 2535	B.Griese-Mia...........7.71
R.Upchurch-Oak......233	R.Upchurch-Oak....1012	G.Pruitt-Cle.............4.78		O.Armstrong-Den ..1058	K.Anderson-Cin 2367	J.Ferguson-Buf 7.19
Completion Percent	**TD Passes**	**TD Percent**	**INT Percent**	**Passer Rating**	**Passing Rank**	**Receptions**
K.Stabler-Oak 66.7	K.Stabler-Oak............27	K.Stabler-Oak 9.3	J.Ferguson-Buf 0.7	K.Stabler-Oak 103.4	B.Jones-Bal 1312	M.Lane-KC 66
B.Jones-Bal 60.3	B.Jones-Bal 24	B.Jones-Bal 7.0	B.Jones-Bal 2.6	B.Jones-Bal 102.5	L.Little-KC................881	B.Chandler-Buf 61
B.Griese-Mia...........59.6	K.Anderson-Cin 19	S.Grogan-NE 6.0	D.Pastorini-Hou.........3.2	J.Ferguson-Buf 90.0	K.Stabler-Oak 824	L.Mitchell-Bal 60
D.Fouts-SD 57.9	S.Grogan-NE.............18	J.Ferguson-Buf 6.0	L.Little-KC.................3.8	B.Griese-Mia...........78.9	D.Fouts-SD 738	D.Casper-Oak............53
B.Sipe-Cle 57.1	B.Sipe-Cle 17	K.Anderson-Cin 5.6	S.Spurrier-TB............3.9	L.Little-KC..............77.6	K.Anderson-Cin 719	K.Burrough-Hou.........51
Receiving Yards	**Receiving Average**	**Receiving TDs**	**Receiving Rank**	**Combined Net Yards**	**Total TDs**	**Total Points**
R.Carr-Bal..............1112	R.Carr-Bal.............25.86	C.Branch-Oak............12	C.Branch-Oak..........616	O.Simpson-Buf 1762	F.Harris-Pit.................14	T.Linhart-Bal 109
C.Branch-Oak........1111	C.Branch-Oak.......24.15	R.Carr-Bal..................11	R.Carr-Bal................611	L.Mitchell-Bal 1755	S.Grogan-NE.............13	J.Stenerud-KC 90
C.Joiner-SD 1056	C.Joiner-SD 21.12	B.Chandler-Buf..........10	C.Joiner-SD 563	B.Johnson-Hou......1483	C.Branch-Oak............12	J.Smith-NE 87
K.Burrough-Hou.......932	L.Brunson-KC.......19.88	D.Casper-Oak............10	K.Burrough-Hou.......501	O.Armstrong-Den ..1465	D.McCauley-Bal.........11	F.Harris-Pit.................84
B.Chandler-Buf........824	N.Moore-Mia.........18.94	R.Rucker-Cle 8	B.Chandler-Buf 462	R.Upchurch-Den....1461	R.Carr-Bal..................11	R.Gerela-Pit...............82
Punt Average	**Field Goals**	**Field Goal Percent**	**Kickoff Returns**	**Kickoff Return Average**	**Punt Returns**	**Punt Return Average**
M.Bateman-Buf.......42.8	J.Stenerud-KC 21	T.Linhart-Bal 74.1	L.Piccone-NYJ...........31	D.Harris-Mia............32.9	M.Haynes-NE 45	R.Upchurch-Den.....13.7
J.Wilson-KC............42.0	T.Linhart-Bal 20	J.Turner-Den............71.4	H.Stevens-Bal............30	J.Phillips-NE 28.4	N.Colzie-Oak 41	M.Haynes-NE 13.5
R.Guy-Oak..............41.6	G.Yepremian-Mia.......16	G.Jakowenko-Buf ...70.6	W.Shelby-Cin.............30	L.Perrin-Den 27.9	R.Upchurch-Den........39	M.Fuller-SD 13.2
J.West-SD...............40.7	S.Butler-Hou 16	G.Yepremian-Mia....69.6		L.Williams-KC.........27.5	H.Stevens-Bal............39	L.Brunson-KC.........12.5
M.Patrick-NE...........40.1		P.Leahy-NYJ 68.8		R.Jennings-Oak......26.1	T.Bell-Pit 39	N.Colzie-Oak 10.9
Punt/Kick Return Yards	**Punt/Kick Return TDs**	**Interceptions**	**Interception Return Yards**	**Interception Return TDs**	**Sacks**	**Overall Rank**
R.Upchurch-Den....1050	R.Upchurch-Den..........4	K.Riley-Cin...................9	P.McCray-NE 182	J.Rowser-Den..............2	Not kept	O.Simpson-Buf 1718
H.Stevens-Bal........1025	M.Haynes-NE 2	M.Haynes-NE 8	K.Riley-Cin...............141	P.McCray-NE 2		B.Jones-Bal 1546
B.Johnson-Hou.......982		T.Jackson-Den.............7	T.Jackson-Den.........136	T.Casanova-Cin...........2		L.Mitchell-Bal 1543
W.Shelby-Cin..........923		T.Darden-Cle 7	T.Greene-Buf 135			F.Harris-Pit.............1344
L.Piccone-NYJ........872			T.Casanova-Cin 109			O.Armstrong-Den ..1292

Buc, Buc, Goose Egg

The expansion Tampa Bay Buccaneers debuted in the only division with room available: the AFC West. Despite outstanding rookie defensive end Lee Roy Selmon, Tampa Bay was completely out of place. The Bucs were shut out five times and allowed 40 or more points four times. After absorbing a terrific pounding for the first NFL team to go through an NFL season with no wins or ties since1944, Bucs quarterback and former Heisman Trophy winner Steve Spurrier retired. Going out more gracefully were Earl Morrall, Bubba Smith, and Mercury Morris. Bill Stanfill, and Nick Buoniconti, two key names in Miami's No-Name Defense, also played their last games. Patriots cornerback Mike Haynes was the league's top rookie defender.

The Oakland Raiders dominated the AFC in the regular season, winning every game except for a 48–17 blowout loss in New England. A rematch in the playoffs in Oakland was tarnished by several controversial penalties called against the Patriots that led to the winning score in the closing seconds. The Steelers, the best defensive team in football, mauled the NFL's best offensive team, the Colts, to set up the fifth consecutive postseason meeting between Pittsburgh and Oakland. The Raiders beat the Steelers and then became the fifth straight AFC team to win the Super Bowl.

The 43rd and last College All-Star Games was held in July. Devised in 1934 by the *Chicago Tribune*'s Arch Ward, founder of baseball's All-Star Game, it pitted the best pro team against the best players in college football from the previous year. There were great moments through the years, but it transformed into a pro-dominated affair. The final game was a 24–0 Steelers' rout at Soldier Field when a rainstorm forced the teams off the field in the third quarter. The paltry crowd turned fierce and tore down the goalposts. Commissioner Pete Rozelle discontinued both the game and the series.

On the other side of the world, the first NFL game outside of North America was played in August, an exhibition between the Chargers and Cardinals at Korakuen Stadium in Tokyo. St. Louis won in front of 38,000 thoroughly confused fans.

1977 NFC

TEAM	W-L-T	PCT	POST	PTS	RA	RY	RY/A	RTD	FL	PA	PC	GPY	GPY/A	PTD	PI	PSY	PRAT
Eastern Division																	
Dal	12-2	.857	DCS*	345-212	564-**457**	2369-**1651**	4.2-3.6	**21**-9	14-10	372-370	215-154	2689-1991	**7.2**-5.4	18-14	**10**-21	246-**429**	**85.3**-48.2
Was	9-5	.643	#	196-189	502-537	1752-2039	3.5-3.8	4-8	14-12	383-380	183-167	2284-2430	6.0-6.4	15-12	16-21	421-359	62.4-52.9
SL	7-7	.500	—	272-287	507-514	2042-2237	4.0-4.4	19-11	16-12	366-375	195-198	2608-2476	7.1-6.6	14-22	21-19	**109**-209	65.0-72.0
Phi	5-9	.357	—	220-207	484-521	1722-1917	3.6-3.7	10-10	17-13	349-358	167-183	2198-2192	6.3-6.1	18-14	21-21	342-316	60.3-58.8
NYG	5-9	.357	—	181-265	548-519	1897-1773	3.5-**3.4**	11-16	12-20	311-328	134-185	1762-2399	5.7-7.3	6-12	22-12	375-302	38.6-76.5
Central Division																	
Min	9-5	.643	#DC	231-227	510-548	1821-2218	3.6-4.0	9-11	24-13	**388**-312	228-149	**2692**-1835	6.9-5.9	**19**-15	22-16	324-254	72.7-61.0
ChiB	9-5	.643	#	255-253	599-544	**2811**-2158	**4.7**-4.0	18-14	17-13	305-377	161-182	2070-2334	6.8-6.2	11-**7**	18-18	226-207	61.8-54.4
Det	6-8	.429	—	183-252	479-521	1706-1905	3.6-3.7	11-13	14-16	384-302	191-161	1959-2123	5.1-7.0	7-14	16-19	441-256	53.5-65.0
GB	4-10	.286	—	134-219	469-582	1464-2314	3.1-4.0	5-16	9-11	327-319	164-186	2013-2042	6.2-6.4	6-10	21-13	265-323	48.9-70.8
TB	2-12	.143	—	103-223	465-581	1424-2031	3.1-3.5	4-13	16-18	321-338	131-191	1714-2149	5.3-6.4	3-10	30-23	445-246	22.5-57.2
Western Division																	
LA	10-4	.714	D	302-146	**621**-462	2575-1698	4.1-3.7	19-7	17-16	393-370	182-180	2253-2236	6.6-6.0	16-11	11-25	237-359	76.7-49.6
Atl	7-7	.500	—	179-**129**	582-504	1890-1858	3.2-3.7	9-5	9-**22**	297-320	140-141	1740-**1775**	5.9-5.5	8-9	16-**26**	289-360	52.3-**37.4**
SF	5-9	.357	—	220-260	564-551	2086-1869	3.7-**3.4**	16-16	8-10	277-**270**	136-**139**	1797-1948	6.5-7.2	9-14	17-8	289-360	55.3-80.0
NO	3-11	.214	—	232-336	484-623	2024-2729	4.2-4.4	14-21	11-15	321-290	166-154	1933-2127	6.0-7.3	13-15	21-10	360-234	56.5-79.8
Aver	14	—		240	523	2014	3.8	13	16	350	179	2271	6.5	14	20	285	61.2

TEAM	1D	PENY	PNT	FGM/A	RTNY	RTNTD	OFFY/DEFY	NETY	NETTO	NP	PNP	DELP	PW	DELW	PRT	DR	YPD	DEL
Eastern Division																		
Dal	**272**-205	865-731	38.7-37.1	18/29-10/**15**	774-464	3-3	**4812**-3213	1599	7	133	**161**	-28	10.3	1.7	**5.4**/1.8	189-191	25.5-16.8	**8.6**
Was	227-234	802-857	38.5-36.6	**21**/37-14/29	640-524	0-1	3615-4110	-495	3	7	-29	36	7.2	1.8	3.0/2.9	192-191	18.8-21.5	-2.7
SL	247-258	835-817	36.2-39.5	7/16-17/26	567-340	3-1	4541-4504	37	-6	-15	-21	6	6.6	0.4	4.4/4.1	177-175	**25.7**-25.7	-0.1
Phi	211-216	642-698	36.5-38.7	7/15-11/26	818-500	1-1	3578-3793	-215	-4	13	-34	**47**	7.3	-2.3	2.8/2.6	190-191	18.8-19.9	-1.0
NYG	201-226	880-886	39.9-38.9	14/23-12/22	625-1010	3-5	3284-3870	-586	-2	-84	-57	-27	4.9	0.1	1.3/4.6	189-191	17.4-20.3	-2.9
Central Division																		
Min	245-212	**556**-688	39.8-38.2	8/17-**7**/17	455-694	2-4	4189-3799	390	-17	4	-36	40	7.1	1.9	3.7/3.0	182-189	23.0-20.1	2.9
ChiB	247-241	852-731	39.4-39.1	14/27-21/29	609-387	2-6	4655-4285	370	-4	2	15	-13	7.1	**2.0**	3.5/3.4	193-190	24.1-22.6	1.6
Det	218-206	692-770	36.2-39.5	8/19-12/24	664-742	**5**-4	3224-3772	-548	5	-69	-26	-43	5.3	0.7	2.0/3.4	192-188	16.8-20.1	-3.3
GB	195-261	690-799	39.4-36.5	13/21-11/23	410-660	4-3	3212-4033	-821	-6	-85	-92	7	4.9	-0.9	2.4/3.5	164-166	19.6-24.3	-4.7
TB	168-241	717-714	39.9-39.9	9/17-14/27	727-898	4-3	2693-3934	-1241	-5	-120	-123	3	4.0		-0.1/2.6	192-188	14.0-20.9	-6.9
Western Division																		
LA	270-203	869-825	35.2-38.7	18/30-**7**/18	832-**252**	1-**0**	4591-3575	1016	13	**156**	137	19	**10.9**		4.6/2.1	180-181	25.5-19.8	5.8
Atl	198-**192**	898-860	**41.2-36.3**	13/30-9/16	**864**-714	1-0	3246-3242	4	**23**	50	92	-42	8.3	-1.3	2.1/**0.8**	**194**-195	16.7-**16.6**	0.1
SF	219-221	830-820	35.0-37.5	11/19-13/22	425-742	2-2	3594-3457	137	-7	-40	-17	-23	6.0	-1.0	2.7/4.4	172-**165**	20.9-21.0	-0.1
NO	223-272	794-**972**	41.0-38.8	5/12-15/24	364-996	4-6	3597-4622	-1025	-7	-104	-113	9	4.4	-1.4	2.1/5.0	181-176	19.9-26.3	-6.4
Aver	236	778	38.4	13/22	675	3	4001	—	—	—	—	—	—	—	3.5	182	22.0	—

Rushing Attempts	Rushing Yards	Rushing Average	Rushing TDs	Rushing Rank	Passing Yards	Passing Average
W.Payton-Chi....339	W.Payton-Chi....1852	W.Payton-Chi....5.46	W.Payton-Chi....14	W.Payton-Chi....1992	R.Staubach-Dal....2620	R.Staubach-Dal....7.26
G.McCrary-LA....294	G.McCrary-LA....1238	T.Metcalf-SL....4.96	T.Dorsett-Dal....12	G.McCrary-LA....1308	J.Hart-SL....2542	P.Haden-LA....7.18
C.Foreman-Min....270	C.Foreman-Min....1112	T.Dorsett-Dal....4.84	W.Morris-SL....8	C.Foreman-Min....1172	R.Jaworski-Phi....2183	J.Hart-SL....7.16
D.Williams-SF....268	T.Dorsett-Dal....1007	W.Jackson-SF....4.36		T.Dorsett-Dal....1127	B.Avellini-Chi....2004	B.Avellini-Chi....6.84
H.Stanback-Atl....247	D.Williams-SF....931	G.McCrary-LA....4.21		D.Williams-SF....1001	F.Tarkenton-Min....1734	J.Plunkett-SF....6.83

Completion Percent	TD Passes	TD Percent	INT Percent	Passer Rating	Passing Rank	Receptions
F.Tarkenton-Min....60.1	R.Staubach-Dal....18	R.Jaworski-Phi....5.2	S.Hunter-Atl....2.0	R.Staubach-Dal....87.0	R.Staubach-Dal....1040	A.Rashad-Min....51
R.Staubach-Dal....58.2	R.Jaworski-Phi....18	P.Haden-LA....5.1	R.Staubach-Dal....2.5	P.Haden-LA....84.5	P.Haden-LA....591	J.Scott-Chi....50
P.Haden-LA....56.5	J.Hart-SL....13	R.Staubach-Dal....5.0	P.Haden-LA....2.8	F.Tarkenton-Min....69.2	J.Hart-SL....536	D.Pearson-Dal....48
G.Landry-Det....56.3	P.Haden-LA....11	B.Kilmer-Was....5.0	G.Landry-Det....2.9	A.Manning-NO....66.8	G.Landry-Det....430	H.Jackson-LA....48
A.Manning-NO....55.1	B.Avellini-Chi....11	A.Manning-NO....3.9	B.Kilmer-Was....3.5	G.Landry-Det....68.7	B.Kilmer-Was....354	

Receiving Yards	Receiving Average	Receiving TDs	Receiving Rank	Combined Net Yards	Total TDs	Total Points
D.Pearson-Dal....870	M.Gray-SL....20.58	S.White-Min....9	D.Pearson-Dal....445	W.Payton-Chi....2216	W.Payton-Chi....16	W.Payton-Chi....96
J.Scott-Chi....809	Walterscheid-SF....19.94	H.Childs-NO....9	S.White-Min....425	T.Metcalf-SL....2022	T.Dorsett-Dal....13	E.Herrera-Dal....93
M.Gray-SL....782	M.Owens-TB....19.26	J.Campbell-Phi....7	J.Scott-Chi....420	G.McCrary-LA....1512		R.Septien-LA....86
S.White-Min....760	W.Jackson-SF....18.54	H.Jackson-LA....6	M.Gray-SL....416	B.Hammond-NYG....1466		M.Moseley-Was....82
A.Rashad-SF....681	D.Pearson-Dal....18.13		J.Campbell-Phi....368	C.Foreman-Min....1423		T.Dorsett-Dal....78

Punt Average	Field Goals	Field Goal Percent	Kickoff Returns	Kickoff Return Average	Punt Returns	Punt Return Average
T.Blanchard-NO....42.4	M.Moseley-Was....21	E.Herrera-Dal....62.1	P.Hofer-SF....36	T.Mitchell-Phi....26.9	E.Brown-Was....57	L.Marshall-Phi....10.6
J.James-Atl....41.4	R.Septien-LA....18	C.Marcol-GB....61.9	E.Brown-Was....34	C.Chapman-NO....25.7	R.Lawrence-Atl....51	B.Hammond-NYG....10.4
B.Parsons-Chi....40.4	E.Herrera-Dal....18	J.Danelo-NYG....60.9	T.Metcalf-SL....32	E.Payton-Det....25.4	B.Johnson-Dal....50	E.Payton-Det....10.1
D.Green-TB....40.3	B.Thomas-GB....14	R.Septien-LA....60.0	R.Mauti-NO....27	E.Brown-Was....25.1	M.Moore-Min....47	S.Schubert-Chi....9.4
	J.Danelo-NYG....14	R.Wersching-SF....58.8		B.Johnson-Dal....24.4	L.Marshall-Phi....46	W.Harrell-GB....9.0

Punt/Kick Return Yards	Punt/Kick Return TDs	Interceptions	Interception Return Yards	Interception Return TDs	Sacks	Overall Rank
E.Brown-Was....1304	E.Payton-Det....2	R.Lawrence-Atl....7	B.Simpson-LA....157	Many....1	Not kept	W.Payton-Chi....2202
B.Johnson-Dal....959			R.Lawrence-Atl....138			G.McCrary-LA....1455
L.Marshall-Phi....944			R.Logan-Phi....124			C.Foreman-Min....1341
R.Mauti-NO....890			J.Sanders-Phi....122			T.Metcalf-SL....1299
T.Metcalf-SL....880			R.Byas-Atl....122			T.Dorsett-Dal....1286

SWEETNESS FOLLOWS THE JUICE

The last 14-game season brought a rare sense of urgency concerning NFL records. With a 16-game schedule on tap for 1978, the 1977 season was the last chance to break records without the benefit of two extra games. Although no one surpassed 3,000 yards passing or 1,000 yards receiving, nine running backs rushed for 1,000 yards. Walter Payton led NFL rushers by almost 600 yards, accumulating the third-highest total in history and the best since O.J. Simpson's 2,003 yards on the ground in 1973.

Although Payton fell short of Simpson's mark, Sweetness did what the Juice couldn't in '73: get his team to the playoffs. The Bears, without a winning record since George Halas retired as coach a decade earlier and out of the postseason since 1963, stood at 3–5 following a 47–0 pasting by the Oilers. The Bears suddenly became unstoppable. Payton ran for a record 275 yards (on 40 carries) against Minnesota—2 yards better than Simpson's mark of a year earlier. A sleet storm in the season finale at Giants Stadium kept Payton from the rushing mark, but the Bears won in overtime to reach the playoffs.

After trading for the second overall pick in the draft, the Cowboys watched the Buccaneers take Ricky Bell and then selected Tony Dorsett. Dallas went on to win the Super Bowl, but Tampa Bay, now shifted to the NFC Central, finally won after 26 tries. The Bucs beat the Saints and then the Cardinals to end the year. Both coaches, Hank Stram and Don Coryell, were subsequently fired.

Charley Taylor, Mel Renfro, Lem Barney, Charlie Sanders, and Roman Gabriel all retired. Fred Cox kicked the last of his 1,365 points for the NFC Central champion Vikings. Three Hall of Famers died in 1976: Giants and Packers legend Cal Hubbard, a former major league umpire and the only man enshrined in both the Pro Football and Baseball Halls of Fame; Joe Stydahar, who dominated the line for Chicago's Monsters of the Midway; and Green Bay defensive lineman Henry Jordan, who played in six NFL Championship Games under Vince Lombardi.

1977 AFC

TEAM	W-L-T	PCT	POST	PTS	RA	RY	RY/A	RTD	FL	PA	PC	GPY	GPY/A	PTD	PI	PSY	PRAT
Eastern Division																	
Bal	10-4	.714	#D	295-221	566-423	2123-1798	3.8-4.3	17-11	14-17	395-382	**224**-181	2686-2549	6.8-6.7	17-**10**	**12**-30	221-359	79.4-45.4
Mia	10-4	.714	#	313-197	519-467	2366-1749	**4.6**-3.7	18-12	13-18	311-414	182-226	2264-2393	7.3-**5.8**	22-**10**	14-15	303-160	**86.0**-64.6
NE	9-5	.643	—	278-217	603-452	2303-1605	3.8-3.6	13-8	15-10	305-356	160-188	2162-2504	7.1-7.0	17-16	21-19	155-**471**	65.2-68.1
NYJ	3-11	.214	—	191-300	437-575	1618-2245	3.7-3.9	6-14	14-17	360-377	170-215	2286-2587	6.3-6.9	14-23	26-11	284-184	50.8-86.4
Buf	3-11	.214	—	160-313	450-589	1861-2405	4.1-4.1	3-21	20-12	**458-316**	221-**155**	**2803**-2213	6.1-7.0	12-17	24-21	273-165	54.7-62.4
Central Division																	
Pit	9-5	.643	D	283-243	581-493	2258-1723	3.9-3.5	**20**-9	28-13	341-357	173-157	2632-2254	**7.7**-6.3	17-16	21-**31**	245-285	67.5-**43.8**
Hou	8-6	.571	—	299-230	509-522	1989-1815	3.9-3.5	15-11	17-**28**	347-379	181-192	2107-2431	6.1-6.4	14-12	21-26	232-289	59.1-53.0
Cin	8-6	.571	—	238-235	488-525	1861-1897	3.8-3.6	10-15	16-23	385-351	192-196	2550-2453	6.6-7.0	12-14	16-16	217-226	64.3-72.0
Cle	6-8	.429	—	269-267	510-524	2200-2098	4.3-4.0	9-14	22-16	377-340	208-184	2374-2298	6.3-6.8	19-15	31-23	199-281	56.8-61.9
Western Division																	
Den	**12**-2	**.857**	DCS	274-**148**	523-470	2043-**1531**	3.9-**3.3**	16-**5**	15-14	313-426	163-235	2265-2556	7.2-6.0	15-11	**12**-25	402-312	75.6-57.2
Oak	11-3	.786	WC	**351**-230	**681-408**	**2627**-1754	3.9-4.3	**20**-7	16-21	324-367	184-177	2338-2503	7.2-6.8	21-17	24-26	229-281	70.2-56.6
SD	7-7	.500	—	222-205	488-508	1761-1927	3.6-3.8	10-11	**11**-10	369-330	206-172	2442-**2088**	6.6-6.3	11-14	20-21	198-363	63.5-59.5
Sea	5-9	.357	—	282-373	461-596	1964-2485	4.3-4.2	12-21	14-11	387-349	175-199	2459-2464	6.4-7.1	**23**-19	32-25	**131**-131	51.6-67.3
KC	2-12	.143	—	225-349	456-634	1843-2971	4.0-4.7	13-23	21-23	374-333	190-175	2514-2244	6.7-6.7	11-15	26-21	421-222	53.3-62.7
Aver	14	—	—	240	523	2014	3.8	13	16	350	179	2271	6.5	14	20	285	61.2

TEAM	1D	PENY	PNT	FGM/A	RTNY	RTNTD	OFFY/DEFY	NETY	NETTO	NP	PNP	DELP	PW	DELW	PRT	DR	YPD	DEL
Eastern Division																		
Bal	269-210	620-618	37.4-36.2	17/26-11/21	757-779	1-6	4588-3988	600	**21**	74	**134**	-60	8.9	1.1	**5.0**/ 2.2	191-186	24.0-21.4	2.6
Mia	267-227	**432**-644	36.9-38.5	10/22-12/20	439-505	1-1	4327-3982	345	6	116	53	63	9.9	0.1	4.5/ 3.8	157-**163**	**27.6**-24.4	3.1
NE	247-215	931-610	34.6-39.1	15/21-13/21	623-549	3-2	4310-**3638**	672	-7	61	28	33	8.5	0.5	3.9/ 3.2	169-172	25.5-21.2	4.4
NYJ	195-283	508-788	37.6-38.2	15/25-10/21	633-868	1-2	3620-4648	-1028	-12	-109	-134	25	4.3	-1.3	2.5/ 5.3	176-177	20.6-26.3	-5.7
Buf	246-260	866-638	38.9-36.2	9/17-14/21	709-930	4-1	4391-4453	-62	-11	-153	-49	-104	3.2	-0.2	3.2/ 3.8	181-177	24.3-25.2	-0.9
Central Division																		
Pit	266-228	973-784	36.3-40.3	9/14-14/21	763-679	0-4	4645-3692	**953**	-5	40	59	-19	8.0	1.0	4.4/**1.9**	187-187	24.8-**19.7**	**5.1**
Hou	228-247	835-791	38.4-40.8	16/25-16/22	968-593	**7**-3	3864-3957	-93	16	69	56	13	8.7	-0.7	2.9/ 2.7	**196**-193	19.7-20.5	-0.8
Cin	248-253	859-788	41.3-37.6	19/27-11/18	566-**452**	4-**0**	4194-4124	70	7	3	34	-31	7.1	0.9	4.2/ 4.4	175-170	24.0-24.3	-0.3
Cle	271-261	1046-**979**	39.0-37.7	17/23-16/22	752-909	3-3	4375-4115	260	-14	2	-34	36	7.1	-1.0	2.4/ 3.1	178-183	24.6-22.5	2.1
Western Division																		
Den	223-217	883-718	39.2-40.7	13/19-**8**/22	**1203**-569	3-2	3906-3775	131	12	**126**	59	**67**	**10.1**	**1.8**	4.1/ 2.7	188-185	20.8-20.4	0.4
Oak	**305-204**	747-717	**43.3**-37.6	**20/28**-11/19	725-590	1-5	**4736**-3976	760	7	121	91	30	10.0	1.0	3.6/ 3.0	183-183	25.9-21.7	4.2
SD	235-228	813-831	37.1-40.6	17/23-**8/13**	838-487	4-1	4005-3652	353	0	17	29	-12	7.4	-0.4	3.7/ 2.5	160-166	25.0-22.0	3.0
Sea	251-295	656-794	38.0-**36.0**	9/18-23/31	573-981	2-3	4292-4818	-526	-10	-91	-84	-7	4.7	0.3	2.7/ 3.8	178-181	24.1-26.6	-2.5
KC	228-304	706-929	39.4-41.0	8/18-20/28	584-1093	5-4	3936-4993	-1057	-3	-124	-100	-24	3.9	-1.9	2.4/ 3.4	191-197	20.6-25.3	-4.7
Aver	236	778	38.4	13/22	675	1	4001	—	—	—	—	—	—	—	3.5	90	23.6	—

Rushing Attempts	Rushing Yards	Rushing Average	Rushing TDs	Rushing Rank	Passing Yards	Passing Average
R.Upchurch-Oak......324	R.Upchurch-Oak....1273	B.Malone-Mia 4.77	F.Harris-Pit................11	R.Upchurch-Oak....1343	J.Ferguson-Buf......2803	T.Bradshaw-Pit........8.04
L.Mitchell-Bal...........301	F.Harris-Pit............1162	S.Smith-Sea 4.68	R.Upchurch-Oak..........7	F.Harris-Pit............1272	B.Jones-Bal 2686	C.Morton-Den.........7.59
F.Harris-Pit..............300	L.Mitchell-Bal.........1159	C.Miller-Cle............4.64	D.McCauley-Bal..........6	L.Mitchell-Bal.........1189	T.Bradshaw-Pit......2523	K.Stabler-Oak.........7.40
C.Culp-NE 270	G.Pruitt-Cle............1086	G.Pruitt-Cle............4.60		G.Pruitt-Cle............1116	B.Griese-Mia.........2252	B.Griese-Mia..........7.34
G.Pruitt-Cle.............236	C.Culp-NE 1015	L.Harris-Mia...........4.58		C.Culp-NE 1055	K.Stabler-Oak........2176	S.Grogan-NE..........7.09
Completion Percent	**TD Passes**	**TD Percent**	**INT Percent**	**Passer Rating**	**Passing Rank**	**Receptions**
B.Griese-Mia..........58.6	B.Griese-Mia.............22	B.Griese-Mia............7.2	B.Jones-Bal 2.8	B.Griese-Mia..........87.8	B.Jones-Bal 988	L.Mitchell-Bal............71
K.Stabler-Oak.........57.5	K.Stabler-Oak...........20	K.Stabler-Oak..........6.8	C.Morton-Den...........3.1	C.Morton-Den.........82.0	B.Griese-Mia...........716	B.Chandler-Buf..........60
B.Sipe-Cle 57.4	B.Jones-Bal 17	J.Zorn-Sea...............6.4	K.Anderson-Cin 3.4	B.Jones-Bal 80.8	C.Morton-Den..........715	C.Gaines-NYJ............55
B.Jones-Bal 57.0	S.Grogan-NE.............17	S.Grogan-NE...........5.6	B.Griese-Mia............4.2	K.Stabler-Oak.........75.2	K.Anderson-Cin 688	N.Moore-Mia.............52
D.Pastorini-Hou.......53.0	T.Bradshaw-Pit..........17	C.Morton-Den..........5.5	J.Harris-SD..............5.2	T.Bradshaw-Pit........71.4	T.Bradshaw-Pit.........587	D.McCauley-Bal.........51
Receiving Yards	**Receiving Average**	**Receiving TDs**	**Receiving Rank**	**Combined Net Yards**	**Total TDs**	**Total Points**
K.Burrough-Hou.......816	W.Walker-NYJ 21.14	N.Moore-Mia.............12	K.Burrough-Hou.......448	B.Harper-NYJ 1867	N.Moore-Mia.............13	E.Mann-Oak 99
L.Swann-Pit 789	B.Brooks-Cin 19.79	S.Largent-Sea 10	N.Moore-Mia...........443	L.Mitchell-Bal.........1779	F.Harris-Pit................11	T.Linhart-Bal 83
K.Stabler-Pit 784	S.Largent-Sea 19.48	K.Burrough-Hou...........8	L.Swann-Pit 430	B.Johnson-Hou......1683	S.Largent-Sea 10	C.Bahr-Cin................82
B.Brooks-Cin 772	K.Burrough-Hou....18.98	L.Swann-Pit 7	K.Stabler-Pit 427	G.Pruitt-Cle...........1557		D.Cockroft-Cle 81
N.Moore-Mia...........765	R.Chester-Bal.......17.94	K.Stabler-Pit 7	B.Brooks-Cin 406	R.Upchurch-Oak....1408		
Punt Average	**Field Goals**	**Field Goal Percent**	**Kickoff Returns**	**Kickoff Return Average**	**Punt Returns**	**Punt Return Average**
R.Guy-Oak.............43.3	E.Mann-Oak 20	T.Fritsch-Hou 75.0	B.Harper-NYJ 42	R.Clayborn-NE 31.0	R.Upchurch-Den........51	B.Johnson-Hou.......15.4
P.McInally-Cin.........41.8	C.Bahr-Cin.................19	D.Cockroft-Cle 73.9	A.Hunter-Sea.............36	G.Davis-Mia............29.6	J.Smith-Pit 36	S.Morgan-NE.........13.8
J.Wilson-KC............39.9	T.Linhart-Bal 17	T.Beeson-SD 73.9	K.Moody-Buf..............30	B.Johnson-Hou.......25.2	B.Johnson-Hou..........35	K.Moody-Buf..........13.1
M.Bateman-Buf.......39.9	D.Cockroft-Cle 17	J.Smith-NE 71.4	R.Clayborn-NE 28	B.Harper-NYJ 24.6	H.Stevens-Bal...........34	M.Fuller-SD 12.9
H.Weaver-Sea 39.5	T.Beeson-SD 17	E.Mann-Oak 71.4	B.Johnson-Hou 25	J.Smith-Pit 23.8	B.Harper-NYJ 34	R.Upchurch-Den.....12.8
Punt/Kick Return Yards	**Punt/Kick Return TDs**	**Interceptions**	**Interception Return Yards**	**Interception Return TDs**	**Sacks**	**Overall Rank**
B.Harper-NYJ 1460	B.Johnson-Hou...........3	L.Blackwood-Bal.......10	G.Barbaro-KC.........165	Many..........................1	Not kept	L.Mitchell-Bal.........1519
B.Johnson-Hou......1169	R.Clayborn-NE 3	T.Greene-Buf 9	L.Blackwood-Bal.....163			R.Upchurch-Oak....1411
R.Upchurch-Den....1109		G.Barbaro-KC..............8	E.McMillan-Sea 157			G.Pruitt-Cle...........1386
R.Clayborn-NE 869		S.White-Bal.................7	M.Clark-Buf.............151			F.Harris-Pit............1303
K.Moody-Buf...........832		M.Clark-Buf..................7	J.Tatum-Oak 146			C.Culp-NE 1245

Orange Crushes Silver and Black

The Denver Broncos had never made the playoffs in 16 years of existence, neither in the AFL nor the NFL. Their ferocious 3–4 Orange Crush defense and a revitalized Craig Morton at quarterback suddenly turned them into an AFC powerhouse. Denver won 12 of its first 13 games, the only loss coming to defending Super Bowl champion Oakland. With home-field advantage secured by both teams, Dallas beat Denver in the season finale, but it turned out to be far from meaningless.

The Raiders won a remarkable playoff game in two overtimes against the Colts, who had beaten out the Dolphins for the AFC East title on a tiebreaker. A final Oakland–Denver showdown in the AFC Championship Game turned on a second-quarter Broncos fumble at the goal line. The play was blown dead and Denver scored on the next play. A late Oakland rally fell short and the Broncos were bound for New Orleans and the first indoor Super Bowl. Dallas turned out the lights on the Broncos as Cowboys running back Robert Newhouse passed for nearly as many yards as two Denver quarterbacks facing the Doomsday Defense.

Rosters were increased to 43 players. The NFL approved rules changes to open up the passing game and cut down on injuries. The league outlawed the head slap, also known as the "Deacon Jones rule" after the former defensive end's favorite move. Defenders could now make contact with eligible receivers only once.

The Seattle Seahawks switched from the NFC to the AFC West. Seattle recorded the most points scored in a game in 1977 (56). Although they still had the league's worst defense, the Seahawks managed the first shutout in franchise history.

A new wave of outstanding defenders debuted in the AFC: Joe Klecko, A.J. Duhe, Raymond Clayborn, and Lester Hayes. They would be needed to help contain speedy rookie receivers Stanley Morgan and Wesley Walker. Willie Lanier, Paul Warfield, Dick Anderson, John Hadl, and eight-time Pro Bowl lineman Winston Hill retired. And even though worn-out Joe Namath called it quits out in Los Angeles, many fans still felt a shudder back in New York.

1978 NFC

TEAM	W-L-T	PCT	POST	PTS	RA	RY	RY/A	RTD	FL	PA	PC	GPY	GPY/A	PTD	PI	PSY	PRAT
Eastern Division																	
Dal	**12**-4	**.750**	DCS	**384-208**	625-**477**	**2783-1721**	**4.5**-3.6	**22**-13	18-13	449-432	251-202	3405-2730	**7.6**-6.3	**25**-11	17-23	229-442	**83.1**-53.7
Phi	9-7	.563	W	270-250	587-505	2456-1862	4.2-3.7	16-11	22-20	401-443	207-228	2485-2986	6.2-6.7	16-17	**16**-28	288-213	67.6-59.5
Was	8-8	.500	—	273-283	537-625	2082-2536	3.9-4.1	10-15	16-10	438-409	212-197	2978-2701	6.8-6.6	17-11	21-22	413-323	63.7-56.3
SL	6-10	.375	—	248-296	554-588	1954-2396	3.5-4.1	14-15	14-16	508-428	252-212	3357-2641	6.6-6.2	16-19	21-26	**186**-290	64.2-58.6
NYG	6-10	.375	—	264-298	580-640	2304-2656	4.0-4.2	12-25	12-18	382-443	176-210	2428-2637	6.4-**6.0**	13-**10**	27-21	283-251	48.9-54.2
Central Division																	
Min	8-7-1	.531	#D	294-306	505-559	1536-2116	3.0-3.8	10-20	17-21	**592**-442	**352**-240	**3528**-2917	6.0-6.6	**25**-15	34-22	285-227	66.6-65.4
GB	8-7-1	.531	#	249-269	550-620	2023-2439	3.7-3.9	16-19	24-20	357-463	180-254	2358-2910	6.6-6.3	11-16	18-27	274-386	60.9-61.2
Det	7-9	.438	—	290-300	525-565	2163-2184	4.1-3.9	12-18	15-19	429-**350**	247-191	2746-2781	6.4-7.9	19-19	18-22	444-**482**	74.0-72.6
ChiB	7-9	.438	—	253-274	**634**-568	2526-2174	4.0-3.8	19-15	**8**-16	352-436	186-239	2221-2857	6.3-6.6	7-16	28-17	288-351	45.9-71.1
TB	5-11	.313	—	241-259	549-595	2098-2049	3.8-**3.4**	16-12	20-14	361-419	151-241	2171-2535	6.0-6.1	12-13	18-**29**	468-256	52.3-56.7
Western Division																	
LA	**12**-4	**.750**	DC	316-245	609-505	2308-1845	3.8-3.7	12-11	22-15	466-399	236-**188**	3109-**2449**	6.7-6.1	13-15	22-28	235-401	61.7-**50.2**
Atl	9-7	.563	WD	240-290	533-578	1660-2067	3.1-3.6	13-21	18-25	449-444	221-215	2883-2789	6.4-6.3	11-11	23-12	481-425	56.7-65.6
NO	7-9	.438	—	281-298	512-574	1845-2420	3.6-4.2	17-**9**	15-20	479-418	294-215	3452-2700	7.2-6.5	17-21	**16**-21	301-236	81.2-67.7
SF	2-14	.125	—	219-350	585-649	2091-2365	3.6-3.6	14-17	27-**27**	435-413	190-219	2306-2948	5.3-7.1	9-20	36-18	350-289	33.0-74.0
Aver	16	—	—	293	574	2269	4.0	16	18	422	224	2841	6.7	17	23	300	65.0

TEAM	1D	PENY	PNT	FGM/A	RTNY	RTNTD	OFFY/DEFY	NETY	NETTO	NP	PNP	DELP	PW	DELW	PRT	DR	YPD	DEL
Eastern Division																		
Dal	**342**-232	816-783	39.9-39.4	16/26-11/22	818-487	1-**1**	**5959**-4009	**1950**	1	**176**	**167**	9	**12.4**	-0.4	**5.5**/ 2.8	208-203	**28.6**-19.7	**8.9**
Phi	271-248	805-884	36.8-39.1	8/17-14/26	687-**485**	4-2	4653-4635	18	**10**	20	42	-22	8.5	0.5	3.7/ 3.6	203-199	22.9-23.3	-0.4
Was	261-283	978-830	39.0-37.0	19/30-24/34	716-808	4-4	4647-4914	-267	-5	-10	-42	**32**	7.8	0.3	3.7/ 3.4	217-219	21.4-22.4	-1.0
SL	281-286	890-809	37.4-38.9	11/22-13/18	644-878	1-3	5125-4747	378	7	-48	60	-108	6.8	-0.8	4.5/ 2.9	208-206	24.6-23.0	1.6
NYG	246-316	1016-862	**42.1**-37.1	21/29-12/26	712-1000	4-3	4449-5042	-593	0	-34	-49	15	7.2	-1.1	2.5/ 3.3	209-209	21.3-24.1	-2.8
Central Division																		
Min	308-278	817-1013	36.4-36.2	12/19-13/19	431-965	2-4	4779-4806	-27	-8	-12	-34	22	7.7	0.8	3.2/ 3.9	209-208	22.9-23.1	-0.2
GB	226-302	**776**-949	35.5-37.9	11/19-**5**/18	737-548	4-**1**	4107-4963	-856	5	-20	-51	31	7.5	1.0	3.5/ 2.9	207-215	19.8-23.1	-3.2
Det	269-276	1003-1043	42.0-40.2	20/28-8/**13**	722-542	2-2	4465-4483	-18	8	-10	31	-41	7.8	-0.8	3.5/ 3.7	196-199	22.8-22.5	0.3
ChiB	262-282	958-801	37.0-**35.8**	17/22-16/19	502-607	3-2	4459-4680	-221	-3	-21	-30	9	7.5	-0.5	1.9/ 4.0	197-199	22.6-23.5	-0.9
TB	238-256	860-963	40.1-40.4	14/24-24/32	824-682	1-2	3801-4328	-527	5	-18	-24	6	7.6	-2.6	2.5/ 2.4	215-210	17.7-20.6	-2.9
Western Division																		
LA	301-**229**	1169-755	36.1-38.0	**29/43**-17/26	**1138**-492	**8**-2	5182-**3893**	1289	-1	71	103	-32	9.8	2.2	4.0/**2.1**	217-221	23.9-**17.6**	6.3
Atl	253-267	1083-1010	38.4-36.6	16/26-13/23	504-557	3-4	4062-4431	-369	-4	-50	-47	-3	6.8	**2.3**	2.9/ 3.9	222-220	18.3-20.1	-1.8
NO	295-286	1044-929	41.1-40.2	12/25-22/33	561-737	1-3	4996-4884	112	**10**	-17	49	-66	7.6	-0.6	5.0/ 3.8	195-**194**	25.6-25.2	0.4
SF	257-298	930-**1301**	36.9-40.2	15/23-23/38	606-964	2-3	4047-5024	-977	-18	-131	-153	22	4.7	-2.7	0.9/ 4.6	**226**-225	17.9-22.3	-4.4
Aver	282	924	38.6	15/24	697	3	4811	—	—	—	—	—	—	—	4.0	205	23.5	—

Rushing Attempts	Rushing Yards	Rushing Average	Rushing TDs	Rushing Rank	Passing Yards	Passing Average
W.Payton-Chi..........333	W.Payton-Chi.........1395	J.Mitchell-Phi..........4.71	W.Payton-Chi............11	W.Payton-Chi.........1505	F.Tarkenton-Min.....3468	R.Staubach-Dal......7.72
T.Dorsett-Dal...........290	T.Dorsett-Dal.........1325	T.Dorsett-Dal..........4.57	T.Middleton-GB.........11	T.Dorsett-Dal.........1395	A.Manning-NO.......3416	A.Manning-NO........7.25
T.Middleton-GB........284	J.Mitchell-Phi.........1220	H.King-Det.............4.26	J.Mitchell-Phi..............9	J.Mitchell-Phi.........1310	R.Staubach-Dal.....3190	J.Pisarcik-NYG.......6.96
J.Mitchell-Phi..........259	T.Middleton-GB......1116	B.Hammond-NYG...4.23	J.Otis-SL....................8	T.Middleton-GB......1226	J.Hart-SL...............3121	P.Haden-LA............6.75
J.Riggins-Was..........248	J.Riggins-Was........1014	D.Kotar-NYG..........4.19	R.Newhouse-Dal.........8	J.Riggins-Was........1064	P.Haden-LA............2995	L.Barnes-Atl...........6.75
Completion Percent	**TD Passes**	**TD Percent**	**INT Percent**	**Passer Rating**	**Passing Rank**	**Receptions**
A.Manning-NO........61.8	F.Tarkenton-Min.........25	R.Staubach-Dal........6.1	A.Manning-NO..........3.4	R.Staubach-Dal......84.9	A.Manning-NO.......1153	R.Young-Min.............88
F.Tarkenton-Min......60.3	R.Staubach-Dal.........25	G.Danielson-Det.......5.1	J.Hart-SL.................3.8	A.Manning-NO........81.7	R.Staubach-Dal.....1080	T.Galbreath-NO.........74
G.Danielson-Det.....56.7	G.Danielson-Det........18	F.Tarkenton-Min........4.4	R.Staubach-Dal........3.9	G.Danielson-Det.....73.5	J.Hart-SL................921	A.Rashad-Min...........66
R.Staubach-Dal......55.9	A.Manning-NO...........17	R.Jaworski-Phi..........4.0	R.Jaworski-Phi..........4.0	F.Tarkenton-Min......68.9	P.Haden-LA.............803	P.Tilley-SL.................62
B.Avellini-Chi..........53.4		J.Pisarcik-NYG.........4.0	D.Williams-TB...........4.1	R.Jaworski-Phi........67.9	R.Jaworski-Phi.........684	C.Foreman-Min..........61
Receiving Yards	**Receiving Average**	**Receiving TDs**	**Receiving Rank**	**Combined Net Yards**	**Total TDs**	**Total Points**
B.Campfield-Phi.....1072	M.Owens-TB.........20.00	S.White-Min................9	B.Campfield-Phi.......576	W.Payton-Chi.........1875	T.Middleton-GB..........12	F.Corral-LA..............118
P.Tilley-SL...............900	M.Gray-SL............19.80	B.DuPree-Dal..............9	P.Tilley-SL...............465	T.Dorsett-Dal..........1757	W.Payton-Chi.............11	R.Septien-Dal............94
M.Gray-SL...............871	B.Campfield-Phi....19.49	A.Rashad-Min.............8	H.Childs-NO............455	J.Mitchell-Phi.........1569	R.Newhouse-Dal.......10	B.Ricardo-Det............92
H.Childs-NO............869	J.Robinson-NYG...19.38	B.Campfield-Phi...........8	T.Hill-Dal.................442	T.Green-Was..........1484	J.Mitchell-Phi.............10	J.Danelo-NYG..........90
T.Hill-Dal.................823	J.Scott-Chi............18.07	J.Fugett-Was..............7	M.Gray-SL..............441	W.Chandler-NO.....1475	T.Dorsett-Dal.............10	M.Moseley-Was.........87
Punt Average	**Field Goals**	**Field Goal Percent**	**Kickoff Returns**	**Kickoff Return Average**	**Punt Returns**	**Punt Return Average**
T.Skladany-Det.......42.5	F.Corral-LA.................29	T.Mazzetti-Atl..........81.3	K.Miller-Min...............40	S.Odom-GB............27.1	J.Wallace-LA.............52	J.Wallace-LA...........11.9
D.Jennings-NYG.....42.1	J.Danelo-NYG...........21	B.Thomas-Chi.........77.3	D.Williams-SF............34	D.Pearson-Atl..........26.5	B.Johnson-Dal...........51	T.Green-Was...........10.5
T.Blanchard-NO......42.0	B.Ricardo-Det............20	J.Danelo-NYG.........72.4	T.Green-Was..............34	T.Green-Was...........25.6	K.Miller-Min...............48	J.Thompson-Det.....10.1
D.Green-TB............40.9	M.Moseley-Was.........19	B.Ricardo-Det.........71.4	W.Chandler-NO.........32	W.Chandler-NO......23.8	D.Reece-TB...............44	W.Harrell-SL.............9.3
D.White-Dal............40.5	B.Thomas-Chi............17	F.Corral-LA.............67.4	B.Johnson-Dal...........29	G.Ragsdale-TB.......23.1	T.Green-Was..............42	S.Odom-GB.............9.0
Punt/Kick Return Yards	**Punt/Kick Return TDs**	**Interceptions**	**Interception Return Yards**	**Interception Return TDs**	**Sacks**	**Overall Rank**
T.Green-Was..........1313	T.Green-Was................2	K.Stone-SL..................9	T.Myers-NO............167	R.Perry-LA..................3	Not kept	W.Payton-Chi.........1745
K.Miller-Min............1093		W.Buchanon-GB..........9	C.Crist-SF...............159			T.Dorsett-Dal..........1594
B.Johnson-Dal.......1004		P.Thomas-LA..............8	K.Stone-SL.............139			J.Mitchell-Phi.........1477
W.Chandler-NO.......993		R.Perry-LA..................8	R.Perry-LA..............117			T.Middleton-GB......1404
S.Odom-GB.............975			T.Jackson-NYG........115			A.Manning-NO.......1365

Miracle Zone, No Kneeling

November 19, 1978 was the day that football teams at every level in America began taking a knee to run out the clock in close games. The Miracle at the Meadowlands converted them all. With the Eagles trailing, 17–12, and just one play needed to run out the clock, Giants quarterback Joe Pisarcik bobbled a handoff to fullback Larry Csonka. Philadelphia's Herman Edwards scooped up the ball and ran 26 yards for the touchdown and an inconceivable change of events. Offensive coordinator Bob Gibson, responsible for the play call, was fired the next day. The game led to a bloodless and brief Giants fan revolt and sparked the Eagles to their first playoff berth since 1960.

The Falcons used last-play magic at the Superdome. With the clock reaching zero, Steve Bartkowski heaved a desperation pass that found Alfred Jackson emerging from a crowd 57 yards away. The expanded 16-game schedule and two Wild Cards worked for Atlanta, which hosted Philadelphia despite a 9–7 record. Two Bartkowski scoring passes late in the fourth quarter helped beat the Eagles in the first Wild Card game.

The Cowboys and Steelers were involved in the first Super Bowl rematch. It was even played at the same location as three years earlier—although the Orange Bowl was now back to a grass surface—and Pittsburgh won by the same four-point margin. The lasting image of the game, however, came at the expense of Jackie Smith. Concluding an excellent career by playing in his first Super Bowl, the tight end dropped a sure touchdown pass that could have changed the outcome. Minnesota lost both its center and quarterback with the retirement of Mick Tingelhoff and Fran Tarkenton, who left the NFL as its all-time leading passer.

James Lofton, Wes Chandler, Doug Williams, Steve DeBerg, and Tom Mack all debuted. Deaths included Hall of Famers Dutch Clark, Lions signal-caller and the last of the great drop kickers, and Ed Healey, the first player ever sold in the NFL (cost: $100 for the 1922 Bears), and considered by George Halas to be "the most versatile tackle in history."

1978 AFC

TEAM	W-L-T	PCT	POST	PTS	RA	RY	RY/A	RTD	FL	PA	PC	GPY	GPY/A	PTD	PI	PSY	PRAT
Eastern Division																	
NE	11-5	.688	#D	358-286	**671**-511	**3165**-1852	**4.7**-3.6	**30**-14	21-**21**	390-425	196-235	3006-3059	7.7-7.2	15-21	25-22	206-296	62.2-73.1
Mia	11-5	.688	#W	**372**-254	548-543	2366-2261	4.3-4.2	18-15	12-**21**	379-437	226-256	2707-3251	7.1-7.4	24-15	18-**32**	238-343	**82.9**-62.8
NYJ	8-8	.500	—	359-364	562-600	2250-2701	4.0-4.5	21-20	**9**-17	388-447	193-260	2957-3052	7.6-6.8	19-21	28-23	350-229	61.5-73.2
Buf	5-11	.313	—	302-354	556-677	2381-3228	4.3-4.8	15-23	17-16	388-**317**	203-**167**	2503-**2156**	6.5-6.8	21-20	17-14	254-196	72.3-77.0
Bal	5-11	.313	—	239-421	532-662	2044-3010	3.8-4.5	9-21	17-20	383-357	202-191	2543-3125	6.6-8.8	17-29	30-17	480-224	55.9-90.4
Central Division																	
Pit	**14**-2	**.875**	DCS*	356-**195**	641-513	2297-**1774**	3.6-**3.5**	16-**11**	17-**21**	380-442	212-221	2961-2755	**7.8-6.2**	**28**-10	22-27	262-361	81.5-**51.8**
Hou	10-6	.625	WDC	283-298	603-556	2476-2072	4.1-3.7	19-14	21-17	373-428	201-240	2473-3125	6.6-7.3	16-17	17-17	**135**-283	69.9-75.9
Cle	8-8	.500	—	334-356	559-563	2488-2149	4.5-3.8	17-19	29-18	442-489	236-265	3137-3435	7.1-7.0	22-20	21-27	278-232	72.9-67.1
Cin	4-12	.250	—	252-284	526-607	2131-2396	4.1-3.9	10-16	19-17	470-396	250-193	3039-2520	6.5-6.4	14-14	30-20	298-284	56.7-60.0
Western Division																	
Den	10-6	.625	D	282-198	601-549	2451-1979	4.1-3.6	15-12	17-13	391-438	217-246	2710-2712	6.9-**6.2**	17-**9**	17-31	332-242	73.6-52.0
Oak	9-7	.563	—	311-283	577-583	2186-2183	3.8-3.7	18-15	12-15	433-448	251-234	3095-2916	7.1-6.5	16-17	31-28	368-205	62.7-59.3
Sea	9-7	.563	—	345-358	561-551	2394-2513	4.3-4.6	28-20	19-17	467-460	261-263	3401-3225	7.3-7.0	15-21	22-22	284-220	70.1-74.2
SD	9-7	.563	—	355-309	590-**510**	2096-2208	3.6-4.3	16-12	21-16	**477**-441	**271**-237	**3566**-2825	7.5-6.4	26-23	30-22	191-**474**	72.5-70.2
KC	4-12	.250	—	243-327	663-602	2986-2384	4.5-4.0	19-21	18-14	370-365	204-219	2032-2820	5.5-7.7	7-17	**16**-21	198-238	59.2-75.8
Aver	16	—	—	293	574	2269	4.0	16	18	422	224	2841	6.7	17	23	300	65.0

TEAM	1D	PENY	PNT	FGM/A	RTNY	RTNTD	OFFY/DEFY	NETY	NETTO	NP	PNP	DELP	PW	DELW	PRT	DR	YPD	DEL
Eastern Division																		
NE	322-258	852-683	35.0-39.5	12/24-**9**/19	878-524	1-3	**5965**-4615	**1350**	-3	72	101	-29	9.8	1.2	4.4/ 4.3	196-193	**30.4**-23.9	**6.5**
Mia	270-298	**603**-865	40.3-37.0	19/23-14/21	799-527	3-**0**	4835-5169	-334	**23**	118	64	54	10.9	0.0	4.7/ 3.4	196-197	24.7-26.2	-1.6
NYJ	277-324	854-855	40.1-37.4	**22/30**-18/24	802-1079	2-4	4857-5524	-667	3	-5	-44	39	7.9	0.1	3.6/ 4.3	195-199	24.9-27.8	-2.9
Buf	274-305	1103-941	37.9-36.5	10/13-11/21	665-661	3-3	4630-5188	-558	-4	-52	-63	11	6.7	-1.7	4.1/ 4.5	185-192	25.0-27.0	-2.0
Bal	249-291	771-1006	37.4-**35.7**	8/17-14/24	468-989	5-4	4107-5911	-1804	-10	-182	-190	8	3.4	1.6	2.0/ 6.3	212-206	19.4-28.7	-9.3
Central Division																		
Pit	316-265	948-987	40.0-39.4	12/26-14/26	740-451	2-1	4996-**4168**	828	9	**161**	**105**	**56**	**12.0**	2.0	**4.9**/ 2.6	194-192	25.8-21.7	4.0
Hou	276-292	833-940	38.5-42.7	14/18-19/32	615-691	0-3	4814-4914	-100	-4	-15	-24	9	7.6	**2.4**	4.4/ 4.8	197-201	24.4-24.4	-0.0
Cle	293-329	1170-**1110**	39.1-38.4	19/28-22/29	670-709	1-3	5347-5352	-5	-5	-22	-20	-2	7.4	0.6	4.5/ 4.2	213-214	25.1-25.0	0.1
Cin	271-269	956-1074	**42.4**-41.6	16/**30**-16/23	583-775	5-4	4872-4632	240	-12	-32	-28	-4	7.2	-3.2	3.0/ 3.4	**220**-220	22.1-**21.1**	1.1
Western Division																		
Den	294-**251**	1092-894	36.4-39.9	11/22-17/27	**889-421**	4-**0**	4829-4449	380	10	84	72	12	10.1	-0.1	4.1/**2.5**	197-203	24.5-21.9	2.6
Oak	309-299	948-793	41.7-39.5	12/20-14/**17**	717-683	**6**-3	4913-4894	19	0	28	2	26	8.7	0.3	3.2/ 3.4	202-201	24.3-24.3	-0.0
Sea	**345**-331	789-997	36.4-37.4	13/21-19/27	535-671	1-2	5511-5518	-7	-2	-13	-9	-4	7.7	1.3	4.5/ 4.6	193-192	28.6-28.7	-0.2
SD	315-273	748-862	36.3-38.5	18/22-11/22	781-826	2-5	5471-4559	912	-13	46	24	22	9.1	-0.1	4.5/ 3.2	215-207	25.4-22.0	3.4
KC	287-284	1048-921	40.6-39.9	20/**30**-14/18	762-747	0-4	4820-4966	-146	1	-84	-8	-76	5.9	-1.9	3.0/ 4.6	186-**186**	25.9-26.7	-0.8
Aver	282	924	38.6	15/24	697	1	4811	—	—	—	—	—	—	—	4.0	100	25.0	—

Rushing Attempts	Rushing Yards	Rushing Average	Rushing TDs	Rushing Rank	Passing Yards	Passing Average
F.Harris-Pit....310	E.Campbell-Hou....1450	S.Grogan-NE....6.65	D.Sims-Sea....14	E.Campbell-Hou....1580	J.Zorn-Sea....3283	T.Bradshaw-Pit....7.92
E.Campbell-Hou....302	D.Williams-Mia....1258	T.McKnight-KC....6.03	E.Campbell-Hou....13	D.Williams-Mia....1338	D.Fouts-SD....2999	D.Fouts-SD....7.87
D.Williams-Mia....272	F.Harris-Pit....1082	G.Pruitt-Cle....5.45	H.Ivory-NE....11	B.Van Duyne-Oak..1170	K.Stabler-Oak....2944	S.Grogan-NE....7.80
B.Van Duyne-Oak....270	B.Van Duyne-Oak..1080	T.Reed-KC....5.11	K.Long-NYJ....10	F.Harris-Pit....1162	T.Bradshaw-Pit....2915	B.Griese-Mia....7.62
L.Walton-Bal....240	T.Miller-Buf....1060	H.Ivory-NE....4.91	B.Van Duyne-Oak....9	T.Miller-Buf....1130	B.Sipe-Cle....2906	M.Robinson-NYJ....7.53

Completion Percent	TD Passes	TD Percent	INT Percent	Passer Rating	Passing Rank	Receptions
B.Griese-Mia....63.0	T.Bradshaw-Pit....28	T.Bradshaw-Pit....7.6	C.Morton-Den....3.0	T.Bradshaw-Pit....84.7	B.Sipe-Cle....958	S.Largent-Sea....71
D.Fouts-SD....58.8	D.Fouts-SD....24	D.Fouts-SD....6.3	B.Sipe-Cle....3.8	D.Fouts-SD....83.0	J.Zorn-Sea....917	D.Casper-Oak....62
K.Stabler-Oak....58.4	B.Sipe-Cle....21	B.Sipe-Cle....5.3	T.Linhart-KC....4.5	B.Griese-Mia....82.4	D.Fouts-SD....820	L.Swann-Pit....61
T.Bradshaw-Pit....56.3		M.Robinson-NYJ....4.9	J.Zorn-Sea....4.5	B.Sipe-Cle....80.7	T.Bradshaw-Pit....798	L.Mitchell-SD....57
J.Zorn-Sea....56.0		J.Ferguson-Buf....4.8	J.Ferguson-Buf....4.5	C.Morton-Den....77.0	D.Pastorini-Hou....637	J.Jefferson-SD....56

Receiving Yards	Receiving Average	Receiving TDs	Receiving Rank	Combined Net Yards	Total TDs	Total Points
W.Walker-NYJ....1169	W.Walker-NYJ....24.35	J.Jefferson-SD....13	W.Walker-NYJ....625	B.Harper-NYJ....2157	D.Sims-Sea....15	P.Leahy-NYJ....107
S.Largent-Sea....1168	S.Morgan-NE....24.12	L.Swann-Pit....11	S.Largent-Sea....624	L.Walton-Bal....1869	J.Jefferson-SD....13	G.Yepremian-Mia....98
J.Jefferson-SD....1001	R.Rucker-Cle....20.77	N.Moore-Mia....10	J.Jefferson-SD....566	T.Reed-KC....1536	E.Campbell-Hou....13	D.Cockroft-Cle....94
R.Rucker-Cle....893	H.Moses-Den....20.11	K.Stabler-Pit....9	L.Swann-Pit....495	E.Campbell-Hou....1498	L.Swann-Pit....11	H.Belton-SD....91
L.Swann-Pit....880	H.Jackson-NE....20.08	D.Casper-Oak....9	R.Rucker-Cle....487	D.Williams-Mia....1450	H.Ivory-NE....11	D.Sims-Sea....90

Punt Average	Field Goals	Field Goal Percent	Kickoff Returns	Kickoff Return Average	Punt Returns	Punt Return Average
P.McInally-Cin....43.1	P.Leahy-NYJ....22	G.Yepremian-Mia....82.6	B.Harper-NYJ....55	K.Wright-Cle....26.3	N.Colzie-Oak....47	R.Upchurch-Den....13.7
R.Guy-Oak....42.7	J.Stenerud-KC....20	H.Belton-SD....81.8	M.Johnson-Bal....41	L.Walton-Bal....26.3	M.Fuller-SD....39	K.Moody-Buf....12.6
T.Anderson-KC....41.1	G.Yepremian-Mia....19	T.Fritsch-Hou....77.8	R.Griffin-Cin....37	A.Owens-SD....26.2	K.Wright-Cle....37	B.Harper-NYJ....12.6
G.Roberts-Mia....40.3	D.Cockroft-Cle....19	P.Leahy-NYJ....73.3	L.Anderson-Pit....37	E.Payton-KC....25.8	R.Upchurch-Den....36	E.Payton-KC....11.4
C.Ramsey-NYJ....40.1	H.Belton-SD....18	D.Cockroft-Cle....67.9	R.Crawford-Sea....35	C.Brown-Buf....25.2	R.Crawford-Sea....34	M.Fuller-SD....11.2

Punt/Kick Return Yards	Punt/Kick Return TDs	Interceptions	Interception Return Yards	Interception Return TDs	Sacks	Overall Rank
B.Harper-NYJ....1658	Many....1	T.Darden-Cle....10	T.Darden-Cle....200	S.Perry-Cin....2	Not kept	E.Campbell-Hou....1604
E.Payton-KC....1139			G.Small-Mia....157	L.Blackwood-Bal....2		D.Williams-Mia....1434
R.Crawford-Sea....1113			B.Owens-NYJ....156			L.Walton-Bal....1426
K.Wright-Cle....1077			L.Blackwood-Bal....146			T.Reed-KC....1350
M.Johnson-Bal....1070			B.Jackson-Den....128			B.Van Duyne-Oak..1316

The Bizarre and the Tragic

The league added two games to the schedule, two wild cards per conference, and several rules to keep the action going. Defenders now could contact receivers only within 5 yards of the line of scrimmage. Pass blockers could extend their arms and open their hands. A seventh official was added to better enforce the rules of the past two years.

No rule changes, however, could have foreseen the Holy Roller. On the final play of a close game in San Diego, the Raiders fumbled intentionally and kept batting the ball forward until Dave Casper fell on it in the end zone and Oakland won the game. A rule was added after the season to prevent a repeat performance. The season marked the end of an era in Oakland as Fred Biletnikoff, Willie Brown, Otis Sistrunk, Pete Banaszak, Errol Mann, and head coach John Madden all retired.

Earl Campbell turned pro and immediately became the NFL's top running back, leading the league in rushing, yards per carry, and most defenders injured while trying to tackle. As Air Coryell moved from St. Louis to San Diego, Chargers rookie John Jefferson immediately became Dan Fouts's favorite target. Cleveland introduced two players who would help transform their offense: Ozzie Newsome and Clay Matthews. Nick Lowery, who would one day set the NFL record for career field goals, made none in his debut as New England's fill-in.

What should have been a great year for the Patriots began and ended terribly. Wide receiver Darryl Stingley was paralyzed from the chest down following a vicious hit by Jack Tatum in a preseason game in Oakland. New England began the season in a daze but took an 11–4 record into the final game. The Patriots owners suspended Chuck Fairbanks, rumored to be leaving for the University of Colorado, before the final game in Miami. Hank Bullough and Ron Erhardt served as co-coaches in a 23–3 loss. Fairbanks returned to Foxboro for a playoff game two weeks later, but the Oilers pounded the Pats amid chants of "Goodbye, Chuckie." Fairbanks wound up in court with the owners on his way to Boulder.

1979 NFC

TEAM	W-L-T	PCT	POST	PTS	RA	RY	RY/A	RTD	FL	PA	PC	GPY	GPY/A	PTD	PI	PSY	PRAT
Eastern Division																	
Dal	**11**-5	**.688**	#D	**371**-313	578-**500**	2375-2115	4.1-4.2	15-15	21-10	503-435	287-**207**	**3883**-2833	**7.7**-6.5	**29**-21	**13**-13	290-362	**90.2**-72.5
Phi	**11**-5	**.688**	#WD	339-282	567-515	2421-2271	4.3-4.4	17-16	16-11	410-459	209-243	2882-2798	7.0-6.1	21-18	**13**-22	272-324	77.7-64.7
Was	10-6	.625	#	348-295	609-541	2328-2154	3.8-4.0	17-21	**10**-21	401-470	235-234	2839-3339	7.1-7.1	20-18	15-26	263-347	81.5-62.9
NYG	6-10	.375	—	237-323	498-618	1820-2452	3.7-4.0	12-14	18-17	401-463	190-253	2419-3154	6.0-6.8	15-22	22-21	465-228	56.3-72.9
SL	5-11	.313	—	307-358	566-567	**2582**-2204	**4.6**-3.9	24-18	21-19	492-478	248-258	2870-3067	5.8-6.4	12-22	24-18	268-194	56.2-73.4
Central Division																	
TB	10-6	.625	#DC	273-**237**	609-539	2437-**1873**	4.0-**3.5**	13-13	15-**24**	434-436	183-250	2700-**2405**	6.2-**5.5**	19-**14**	26-14	**88**-329	52.8-70.2
ChiB	10-6	.625	#W	306-249	**627**-519	2486-1978	4.0-3.8	17-**9**	13-14	373-458	195-222	2429-2908	6.5-6.3	16-21	16-**29**	278-380	69.2-**57.8**
Min	7-9	.438	—	259-337	487-583	1764-2526	3.6-4.3	9-24	17-11	566-424	315-229	3397-2965	6.0-7.0	23-**14**	24-22	258-268	69.3-65.6
GB	5-11	.313	—	246-316	483-639	1861-2885	3.9-4.5	14-14	22-14	444-440	240-249	3057-3041	6.9-6.9	15-21	22-18	376-279	66.4-76.9
Det	2-14	.125	—	219-365	441-638	1677-2515	3.8-3.9	11-22	19-12	452-**402**	218-220	2775-2787	6.1-6.9	14-15	27-14	439-345	53.3-74.5
Western Division																	
LA	9-7	.563	DCS	323-309	592-548	2460-1997	4.2-3.6	16-13	20-16	456-454	242-220	3032-3007	6.6-6.6	19-24	29-25	359-**451**	61.4-64.7
NO	8-8	.500	—	370-360	551-521	2476-2469	4.5-4.7	**28**-22	14-16	428-488	257-265	3291-3457	**7.7**-7.1	16-24	22-26	140-391	75.2-71.0
Atl	6-10	.375	—	300-388	500-555	2200-2163	4.4-3.9	15-27	20-21	479-487	251-268	3127-3799	6.5-7.8	19-17	23-15	398-203	66.2-79.2
SF	2-14	.125	—	308-416	480-544	1932-2213	4.0-4.1	17-24	18-19	**602**-441	**361**-262	3760-3407	6.2-7.7	18-25	21-15	119-227	73.5-88.5
Aver	16	—	—	321	542	2169	4.0	17	17	464	251	3185	6.9	19	21	299	70.4

TEAM	1D	PENY	PNT	FGM/A	RTNY	RTNTD	OFFY/DEFY	NETY	NETTO	NP	PNP	DELP	PW	DELW	PRT	DR	YPD	DEL
Eastern Division																		
Dal	**339**-259	845-704	41.7-40.8	19/29-17/27	527-366	1-2	**5968**-4586	**1382**	-11	**58**	71	-13	**9.4**	1.5	**6.1**/ 4.4	202-200	**29.5**-22.9	**6.6**
Phi	292-274	**680**-681	38.9-39.8	23/31-15/23	**810**-332	1-**0**	5031-4745	286	4	57	40	17	**9.4**	**1.6**	5.0/ 3.3	191-191	26.3-24.8	1.5
Was	298-320	749-617	38.4-40.7	**25/33**-**8/17**	521-**217**	2-**0**	4904-5146	-242	**22**	53	68	-15	9.3	0.7	4.8/ 3.9	189-191	25.9-26.9	-1.0
NYG	223-322	1047-800	**42.7**-**36.7**	9/20-18/35	274-896	3-3	3774-5378	-1604	-2	-86	-142	56	5.8	0.2	2.4/ 4.4	209-210	18.1-25.6	-7.6
SL	305-302	954-744	37.8-39.2	12/26-19/31	656-679	4-3	5184-5077	107	-8	-51	-23	-28	6.7	-1.7	3.1/ 4.5	217-209	23.9-24.3	-0.4
Central Division																		
TB	267-**247**	905-870	38.7-41.1	11/19-14/24	676-594	3-1	5049-**3949**	1100	-3	36	**80**	-44	8.9	1.1	3.7/ 3.3	210-207	24.0-**19.1**	5.0
ChiB	262-272	816-864	37.5-37.8	16/27-12/20	736-644	4-1	4637-4506	131	14	57	67	-10	**9.4**	0.6	3.9/**2.8**	201-202	23.1-22.3	0.8
Min	311-297	787-786	39.0-39.7	13/22-15/24	639-662	0-5	4903-5223	-320	-8	-78	-59	-19	6.1	1.0	3.8/ 4.1	208-202	23.6-25.9	-2.3
GB	279-327	681-912	40.4-39.3	12/20-20/33	384-552	2-2	4542-5647	-1105	-12	-70	-140	**70**	6.3	-1.3	3.7/ 4.6	181-**181**	25.1-31.2	-6.1
Det	227-311	897-972	40.1-40.0	10/18-24/36	445-836	2-5	4013-4957	-944	-20	-146	-159	13	4.3	-2.3	2.5/ 4.4	204-205	19.7-24.2	-4.5
Western Division																		
LA	299-266	743-**993**	39.3-40.3	13/25-14/21	685-792	**6**-1	5133-4553	580	-8	14	16	-2	8.4	0.6	3.1/ 3.3	**225**-227	22.8-20.1	2.8
NO	315-334	812-871	39.5-38.4	16/21-11/**17**	582-422	2-1	5627-5535	92	6	10	32	-22	8.3	-0.3	5.2/ 4.0	193-188	29.2-29.4	-0.3
Atl	303-311	1026-815	39.2-37.3	13/25-20/29	412-621	4-3	4929-5759	-830	-7	-88	-97	9	5.8	0.2	3.5/ 6.0	202-206	24.4-28.0	-3.6
SF	336-326	853-858	36.5-38.1	20/24-14/**17**	485-617	1-5	5573-5393	180	-5	-108	-5	-103	5.3	-3.3	4.6/ 5.9	195-189	28.6-28.5	0.0
Aver	295	871	39.3	16/26	630	3	5055	—	—	—	—	—	—	—	4.6	203	24.9	—

Rushing Attempts	Rushing Yards	Rushing Average	Rushing TDs	Rushing Rank	Passing Yards	Passing Average
W.Payton-Chi...369	W.Payton-Chi...1610	W.Tyler-LA...5.09	W.Payton-Chi...14	W.Payton-Chi...1750	S.DeBerg-SF...3652	R.Staubach-Dal...7.78
J.Montana-Phi...338	O.Anderson-SL...1605	C.Muncie-NO...5.03	C.Muncie-NO...11	O.Anderson-SL...1685	R.Staubach-Dal...3586	A.Manning-NO...7.55
O.Anderson-SL...331	J.Montana-Phi...1512	P.Hofer-SF...5.00		J.Montana-Phi...1602	T.Kramer-Min...3397	R.Jaworski-Phi...7.14
R.Bell-TB...283	R.Bell-TB...1263	O.Anderson-SL...4.85		R.Bell-TB...1333	A.Manning-NO...3169	J.Theismann-Was...7.08
J.Riggins-Was...260	C.Muncie-NO...1198	L.Harris-Phi...4.71		C.Muncie-NO...1308	J.Theismann-Was..2797	S.White-GB...6.98

Completion Percent	TD Passes	TD Percent	INT Percent	Passer Rating	Passing Rank	Receptions
S.DeBerg-SF...60.0	R.Staubach-Dal...27	R.Staubach-Dal...5.9	R.Staubach-Dal...2.4	R.Staubach-Dal...92.3	R.Staubach-Dal...1488	A.Rashad-Min...80
A.Manning-NO...60.0	T.Kramer-Min...23	J.Theismann-Was...5.1	M.Phipps-Chi...3.1	J.Theismann-Was...83.9	S.DeBerg-SF...1071	W.Francis-Atl...74
J.Theismann-Was...59.0	J.Theismann-Was...20	P.Simms-NYG...4.9	R.Jaworski-Phi...3.2	R.Jaworski-Phi...76.8	J.Theismann-Was...979	R.Young-Min...72
R.Staubach-Dal...57.9	D.Williams-TB...18	R.Jaworski-Phi...4.8	J.Theismann-Was...3.3	A.Manning-NO...75.6	R.Jaworski-Phi...945	W.Chandler-NO...65
P.Haden-LA...56.2	R.Jaworski-Phi...18	D.Williams-TB...4.5	S.DeBerg-SF...3.6	S.DeBerg-SF...73.1	A.Manning-NO...860	F.Scott-Det...62

Receiving Yards	Receiving Average	Receiving TDs	Receiving Rank	Combined Net Yards	Total TDs	Total Points
A.Rashad-Min...1156	D.Pearson-Dal...18.65	B.Campfield-Phi...11	A.Rashad-Min...623	J.Montana-Phi...2012	W.Payton-Chi...16	M.Moseley-Was...114
W.Chandler-NO...1069	K.Krepfle-Phi...18.54	T.Hill-Dal...10	T.Hill-Dal...581	W.Payton-Chi...1923	J.Montana-Phi...14	T.Franklin-Phi...105
T.Hill-Dal...1062	J.Lofton-GB...17.93	A.Rashad-Min...9	W.Chandler-NO...565	O.Anderson-SL...1913	J.Riggins-Was...12	R.Septien-Dal...97
D.Pearson-Dal...1026	P.Dennard-LA...17.81	D.Pearson-Dal...8	D.Pearson-Dal...553	R.Bell-TB...1511		W.Payton-Chi...96
W.Francis-Atl...1013	I.Hagins-TB...17.74	W.Francis-Atl...8	W.Francis-Atl...547	C.Muncie-NO...1506		R.Wersching-SF...92

Punt Average	Field Goals	Field Goal Percent	Kickoff Returns	Kickoff Return Average	Punt Returns	Punt Return Average
D.Jennings-NYG...42.7	M.Moseley-Was...25	R.Wersching-SF...83.3	J.Edwards-Min...44	J.Edwards-Min...25.1	D.Reece-TB...70	J.Sciarra-Phi...11.4
D.White-Dal...41.7	T.Franklin-Phi...23	M.Moseley-Was...75.8	J.Owens-SF...41	R.Green-SL...24.5	E.Brown-LA...56	S.Schubert-Chi...9.5
R.Partridge-NO...40.9	R.Wersching-SF...20	G.Yepremian-NO...75.0	R.Green-SL...41	J.Owens-SF...24.4	S.Wilson-Dal...35	W.Henry-Phi...9.1
D.Beverly-GB...40.4	R.Septien-Dal...19	T.Franklin-Phi...74.2	D.Hill-LA...40	W.Henry-Phi...23.9	W.Henry-Phi...35	J.Arnold-Det...8.6
K.Clark-LA...40.1	B.Thomas-Chi...16	R.Septien-Dal...65.5	R.Springs-Dal...38	J.Arnold-Det...23.4	J.Edwards-Min...33	B.Hardeman-Was...8.6

Punt/Kick Return Yards	Punt/Kick Return TDs	Interceptions	Interception Return Yards	Interception Return TDs	Sacks	Overall Rank
J.Edwards-Min...1289	Many...1	L.Parrish-Was...9	T.Myers-NO...127	R.Young-LA...2	Not kept	W.Payton-Chi...1949
R.Green-SL...1047		T.Myers-NO...7	C.Allen-SL...126			J.Montana-Phi...1865
R.Mauti-NO...1019			R.Lawrence-Atl...120			O.Anderson-SL...1849
J.Owens-SF...1002			N.Cromwell-LA...109			R.Staubach-Dal...1660
W.Henry-Phi...988			R.Hughes-Dal...91			C.Muncie-NO...1487

The Bucs Stop (Losing) Here

After three years of existence and a franchise record of 7–37, the Buccaneers went 10–6 in year four and advanced to the playoffs. Running back Ricky Bell gave Tampa Bay a potent ground game and second-year quarterback Doug Williams emerged as a leader. It was the defense, however, that resuscitated the Buccaneers. Defensive end Lee Roy Selmon and his linebacker brother, Dewey, led an aggressive young defense that allowed the fewest points and yards in the NFL

Dallas quarterback Roger Staubach, in his last season, led a prolific passing attack. Cowboys receivers Tony Hill and Drew Pearson each topped 1,000 yards as the Cowboys won the NFC East. The Eagles earned a wild-card berth, with Wilbert Montgomery combining for 2,006 yards from scrimmage. Philadelphia rookie Tony Franklin, the NFL's first barefoot kicker, booted a 59-yarder against Dallas, the second-longest field goal in history.

Despite being known as a strong swimmer, 72-year-old Rams owner Carroll Rosenbloom drowned outside his oceanfront home in April. Rumors of foul play swirled, with suggestions that his alleged underworld connections might have been a factor. Ultimately, the death was ruled an accidental drowning. Rosenbloom's wife Georgia assumed control of the club.

Los Angeles, preseason favorites in the NFC, stumbled early. When quarterback Pat Haden broke his hand in November, the Rams were just 4–5. Backup Vince Ferragamo completed fewer than 50 percent of his passes and threw twice as many interceptions (10) as touchdowns (5), but the Rams started winning. Victories in four of their last five games gave them a 9–7 record, good enough for first place in the weak NFC West.

The 49ers and the Giants were bad, but they debuted exceptional quarterbacks: Joe Montana and Phil Simms, respectively. Explosive Cardinals rookie Ottis Anderson finished just 5 yards behind NFC rushing leader Walter Payton of wild card Chicago. Beattie Feathers, the Bears runner who 45 years earlier became the first man to surpass 1,000 yards, died in 1979. His 8.44 yards per carry in 1934 remains unsurpassed for backs with more than 100 attempts. Two other great runners of that era, Hall of Famers Tuffy Leemans and Ken Strong, also died.

1979 AFC

TEAM	W-L-T	PCT	POST	PTS	RA	RY	RY/A	RTD	FL	PA	PC	GPY	GPY/A	PTD	PI	PSY	PRAT
Eastern Division																	
Mia	10-6	.625	D	341-257	561-484	2187-1702	3.9-3.5	19-9	15-15	416-418	235-230	3018-3051	7.3-7.3	20-17	22-23	255-314	73.4-69.0
NE	9-7	.563	—	411-326	604-495	2252-1770	3.7-3.6	16-22	16-23	475-467	237-246	3600-3065	7.6-6.6	**30**-13	23-20	382-**512**	76.1-64.8
NYJ	8-8	.500	—	337-383	**634**-502	**2646**-1706	4.2-**3.4**	23-13	13-19	369-570	190-339	2864-4288	7.8-7.5	16-31	25-21	266-173	63.6-85.8
Buf	7-9	.438	—	268-279	474-617	1621-2481	3.4-4.0	11-18	19-17	465-**382**	241-**193**	3603-**2713**	7.7-7.1	14-14	**15**-24	387-183	74.2-59.8
Bal	5-11	.313	—	271-351	515-559	1674-2306	3.3-4.1	12-15	21-16	**550**-411	313-203	3575-3080	6.5-7.5	18-23	19-23	403-312	73.1-69.8
Central Division																	
Pit	**12**-4	**.750**	DCS*	**416**-262	561-506	2603-1709	**4.6-3.4**	**25**-9	26-15	492-480	272-226	3877-2912	**7.9-6.1**	26-19	26-27	222-351	76.6-**56.4**
Hou	11-5	.688	WDC	362-331	616-522	2571-2225	4.2-4.3	24-19	11-16	386-465	195-242	2494-3186	6.5-6.9	17-18	21-**34**	238-421	63.1-**56.4**
Cle	9-7	.563	—	359-352	504-577	2281-2604	4.5-4.5	16-25	17-16	545-468	289-271	3838-3289	7.0-7.0	28-14	27-16	347-243	72.1-75.3
Cin	4-12	.250	—	337-421	560-528	2329-2219	4.2-4.2	23-22	14-**24**	426-492	228-275	2821-3908	6.6-7.9	17-27	**15**-20	511-216	72.9-83.1
Western Division																	
SD	**12**-4	**.750**	D	411-**246**	481-**475**	1668-1907	3.5-4.0	**25**-19	**10**-18	541-472	**338**-261	**4138**-2881	7.6-**6.1**	24-**11**	25-28	223-332	**81.6**-56.6
Den	10-6	.625	W	289-262	525-502	2036-**1693**	3.9-**3.4**	13-16	17-18	476-512	260-296	3433-3321	7.2-6.5	18-**11**	23-19	327-162	70.1-69.0
Sea	9-7	.563	—	378-372	500-533	1967-2375	3.9-4.5	24-23	18-16	523-508	292-317	3791-3739	7.2-7.4	20-21	18-17	**201**-280	77.2-84.6
Oak	9-7	.563	—	365-337	491-534	1763-2374	3.6-4.4	13-17	15-22	513-471	311-247	3704-3366	7.2-7.1	27-21	23-24	293-254	**81.6**-69.2
KC	7-9	.438	—	238-262	569-522	2316-1847	4.1-3.5	18-**8**	18-14	361-528	190-296	1953-3404	5.4-6.4	7-22	18-23	293-280	54.2-71.4
Aver	16	—	—	321	542	2169	4.0	17	17	464	251	3185	6.9	19	21	299	70.4

TEAM	1D	PENY	PNT	FGM/A	RTNY	RTNTD	OFFY/DEFY	NETY	NETTO	NP	PNP	DELP	PW	DELW	PRT	DR	YPD	DEL
Eastern Division																		
Mia	297-**238**	**651**-834	39.5-37.9	21/29-15/26	622-513	1-5	4950-4439	511	1	84	47	37	10.1	-0.1	4.4/ 4.1	188-193	26.3-23.0	3.3
NE	318-283	864-902	36.2-38.7	**23/33**-18/26	663-734	3-4	5470-4323	1147	4	85	112	-27	10.1	-1.1	4.7/ 3.4	219-222	25.0-**19.5**	5.5
NYJ	299-331	876-888	40.8-**36.6**	16/30-22/29	553-674	3-**2**	5244-5821	-577	2	-46	-40	-6	6.8	1.1	4.1/ 5.9	201-200	26.1-29.1	-3.0
Buf	252-273	887-788	38.2-38.2	21/**33**-16/31	688-716	**5-2**	4837-5011	-174	7	-11	14	-25	7.7	-0.7	5.3/ 3.9	214-209	22.6-24.0	-1.4
Bal	291-265	1239-1014	36.2-40.0	14/28-20/28	773-617	3-4	4846-5074	-228	-1	-80	-23	-57	6.0	-1.0	4.1/ 4.4	**220**-219	22.0-23.2	-1.1
Central Division																		
Pit	337-260	866-732	40.2-40.0	18/30-16/26	723-677	1-3	**6258-4270**	**1988**	-10	154	126	28	11.9	0.2	5.3/ 2.9	215-218	29.1-19.6	**9.5**
Hou	268-304	947-920	40.6-41.0	21/25-18/28	839-1016	2-3	4827-4990	-163	**18**	31	58	-27	8.8	**2.2**	3.5/**2.7**	207-209	23.3-23.9	-0.6
Cle	**350**-307	709-1018	40.1-41.4	17/29-22/35	623-690	1-3	5772-5650	122	-12	7	-38	45	8.2	0.8	4.3/ 4.9	205-204	28.2-27.7	0.5
Cin	289-334	744-871	40.4-39.6	13/23-20/27	576-630	3-3	4639-5911	-1272	15	-84	-46	-38	5.9	-1.9	3.7/ 5.8	210-202	22.1-29.3	-7.2
Western Division																		
SD	330-268	908-812	36.5-40.7	16/26-**8/12**	**1050**-483	3-**2**	5583-4456	1127	11	**165**	**138**	27	**12.1**	-0.1	5.3/**2.7**	191-205	**29.2**-21.7	7.5
Den	306-273	996-1033	39.9-42.1	13/21-15/26	590-771	**5**-4	5142-4852	290	-3	27	12	15	8.7	1.3	4.3/ 4.5	199-202	25.8-24.0	1.8
Sea	315-350	903-**1045**	38.4-37.9	19/23-18/29	565-**474**	2-**2**	5557-5834	-277	-3	6	-35	41	8.1	0.9	**5.5**/ 5.3	194-**191**	28.6-30.5	-1.9
Oak	321-319	1024-1018	42.0-37.7	18/27-12/22	492-889	**5**-5	5174-5486	-312	8	28	6	22	8.7	0.3	4.8/ 4.4	190-198	27.2-27.7	-0.5
KC	241-297	971-1018	**43.1**-38.8	12/23-13/21	1049-524	4-**2**	3976-4971	-995	1	-24	-79	**55**	7.4	-0.4	2.3/ 4.1	194-194	20.5-25.6	-5.1
Aver	295	871	39.3	16/26	630	1	5055	—	—	—	—	—	—	—	4.6	102	25.4	—

Rushing Attempts	Rushing Yards	Rushing Average	Rushing TDs	Rushing Rank	Passing Yards	Passing Average
E.Campbell-Hou 368	E.Campbell-Hou 1697	S.Thornton-Pit 4.96	E.Campbell-Hou 19	E.Campbell-Hou 1887	D.Fouts-SD 4082	R.Todd-NYJ 7.96
F.Harris-Pit...............267	M.Pruitt-Cle............1294	T.McKnight-KC........4.93	P.Johnson-Cin............14	M.Pruitt-Cle............1384	B.Sipe-Cle 3793	T.Bradshaw-Pit........7.89
M.Pruitt-Cle...............264	F.Harris-Pit.............1186	A.Griffin-Cin 4.91	C.Williams-SD 12	F.Harris-Pit.............1296	T.Bradshaw-Pit.......3724	J.Ferguson-Buf 7.80
P.Johnson-Cin..........243	C.Gaines-NYJ..........905	M.Pruitt-Cle.............4.90	L.Csonka-Mia 12	P.Johnson-Cin........1005	J.Zorn-Sea.............3661	S.Grogan-NE 7.77
W.Walker-Bal 242	W.Walker-Bal 884	C.Gaines-NYJ.........4.87		L.Csonka-Mia 957	K.Stabler-Oak 3615	D.Fouts-SD 7.70
Completion Percent	**TD Passes**	**TD Percent**	**INT Percent**	**Passer Rating**	**Passing Rank**	**Receptions**
D.Fouts-SD 62.6	B.Sipe-Cle 28	S.Grogan-NE 6.6	K.Anderson-Cin 2.9	D.Fouts-SD 82.6	J.Ferguson-Buf 1256	W.Walker-Bal 82
K.Stabler-Oak.........61.0	S.Grogan-NE 28	T.Bradshaw-Pit..........5.5	J.Ferguson-Buf 3.3	K.Stabler-Oak 82.2	J.Zorn-Sea.............1211	C.Joiner-SD 72
G.Landry-Bal 59.1	K.Stabler-Oak............26	B.Sipe-Cle 5.2	G.Landry-Bal 3.3	K.Anderson-Cin 80.7	D.Fouts-SD 1201	K.Stabler-Pit 70
B.Griese-Mia...........56.8	T.Bradshaw-Pit...........26	K.Stabler-Oak...........5.2	J.Zorn-Sea................3.6	J.Zorn-Sea..............77.7	K.Stabler-Oak 1058	S.Largent-Sea 66
J.Zorn-Sea..............56.4	D.Fouts-SD 24	R.Todd-NYJ 4.8	K.Stabler-Oak 4.4	S.Grogan-NE 77.4	B.Sipe-Cle 997	R.Upchurch-Den........64
Receiving Yards	**Receiving Average**	**Receiving TDs**	**Receiving Rank**	**Combined Net Yards**	**Total TDs**	**Total Points**
S.Largent-Sea 1237	S.Morgan-NE........22.77	S.Morgan-NE.............12	S.Largent-Sea 664	B.Harper-NYJ 1980	E.Campbell-Hou 19	J.Smith-NE 115
K.Stabler-Pit 1183	H.Jackson-NE.......22.51	J.Jefferson-SD...........10	K.Stabler-Pit 632	E.Campbell-Hou 1790	S.Smith-Sea 15	E.Campbell-Hou 114
J.Jefferson-SD 1090	F.Lewis-Buf 20.04	O.Newsome-Cle 9	J.Jefferson-SD 595	M.Pruitt-Cle............1666	P.Johnson-Cin............15	T.Fritsch-Hou 104
F.Lewis-Buf 1082	L.Swann-Pit 19.71	S.Largent-Sea 9	S.Morgan-NE...........561	W.Walker-Bal 1639	S.Morgan-NE.............13	M.Bahr-Pit................104
H.Jackson-NE........1013	D.Harris-Mia..........19.00		F.Lewis-Buf 551	T.Nathan-Mia 1603	L.Csonka-Mia 13	E.Herrera-Sea 100
Punt Average	**Field Goals**	**Field Goal Percent**	**Kickoff Returns**	**Kickoff Return Average**	**Punt Returns**	**Punt Return Average**
B.Grupp-KC 43.6	J.Smith-NE 23	T.Fritsch-Hou 84.0	D.Turner-Cin 55	L.Brunson-Oak 25.9	J.Smith-KC 58	T.Nathan-Mia 10.9
R.Guy-Oak..............42.6	von Schamann-Mia 21	E.Herrera-Sea 82.6	B.Harper-NYJ 55	I.Matthews-Oak 24.9	M.Fuller-SD 46	J.Smith-KC 10.6
P.McInally-Cin.........41.3	T.Fritsch-Hou 21	von Schamann-Mia 72.4	D.Hall-Cle 50	A.Owens-SD............22.6	T.Bell-Pit 45	D.Hall-Cle 10.2
J.Evans-Cle 41.2	M.Merrill-Buf 20	J.Smith-NE 69.7	N.Glasgow-Bal............50	T.Nathan-Mia 22.6	N.Glasgow-Bal...........44	R.Upchurch-Den.....10.1
C.Ramsey-NYJ 40.8	E.Herrera-Sea 19	M.Merrill-Buf 69.0	T.Nathan-Mia 45	N.Glasgow-Bal........22.5	K.Moody-Buf..............38	S.Morgan-NE.........10.0
Punt/Kick Return Yards	**Punt/Kick Return TDs**	**Interceptions**	**Interception Return Yards**	**Interception Return TDs**	**Sacks**	**Overall Rank**
N.Glasgow-Bal.......1478	J.Smith-KC 2	M.Reinfeldt-Hou.........12	M.Reinfeldt-Hou.......205	W.Lowe-SD..................2	Not kept	E.Campbell-Hou 1934
B.Harper-NYJ 1448	T.Nathan-Mia 1	L.Hayes-Oak...............7	R.Griffin-Cin.............167	L.Hayes-Oak...............2		M.Pruitt-Cle...........1580
T.Nathan-Mia 1322	S.Morgan-NE...............1	G.Barbaro-KC.............7	W.Lowe-SD..............150			J.Zorn-Sea............1510
D.Hall-Cle 1309	I.Matthews-Oak 1		G.Green-KC.............148			F.Harris-Pit............1447
D.Turner-Cin 1149	N.Glasgow-Bal.............1		G.Barbaro-KC..........142			S.Grogan-NE 1371

Offense Heats Up the AFC

Linebacker Tom Cousineau was the first player selected in the draft, but he spurned Buffalo to play in Canada. Despite his absence, the Bills defense improved from 24th to eighth in yards allowed. The team progressed in its second season under coach Chuck Knox, but the absence of a quality runner kept the Bills from contending. O.J. Simpson was in San Francisco—his last year as a player—and Buffalo's running game was the worst in the NFL.

The ground game definitely wasn't a problem in Houston. Earl Campbell continued to redefine the concept of power running. The second-year back set a new single-season AFC record with 19 rushing touchdowns, and he led the league with 1,697 yards. An improving defense helped the Oilers win six of their last eight games and advance to the AFC Championship Game for the second year in a row.

In his first full season at the helm, coach Don Coryell implemented an aggressive passing attack for 12–4 San Diego. Strong-armed quarterback Dan Fouts threw for 4,082 yards. Rookie tight end Kellen Winslow played a major role in the wide-open offense, catching 25 passes before suffering a season-ending knee injury in week seven. Receivers Charlie Joiner and John Jefferson each topped 1,000 yards.

A strong defense propelled Miami to the Eastern Division title. The Dolphins integrated younger players like Kim Bokamper and Bob Baumhower with a veteran unit. Nine of Miami's first 11 opponents were held to 16 points or less. The aging offense sputtered, however. Quarterback Bob Griese and running back Larry Csonka, both in their last full seasons, played well below their previous levels.

Pittsburgh was perfect at home but suffered two close defeats and two blowouts on the road: a 34–10 drubbing in Cincinnati and a 35–7 pounding in San Diego. The Steelers doled out the punishment the rest of the season, winning six times by at least 20 points. Individually, no Steeler led the league in a significant statistical category. That was a testament to their balance on offense, equally dangerous running the ball or throwing it. The defense was good enough to order another Lombardi Trophy.

1980 NFC

TEAM	W-L-T	PCT	POST	PTS	RA	RY	RY/A	RTD	FL	PA	PC	GPY	GPY/A	PTD	PI	PSY	PRAT
Eastern Division																	
Phi	12-4	.750	#DCS	384-222	527-445	1995-1618	3.8-3.6	19-8	16-10	477-543	275-265	3771-3180	7.9-5.9	28-16	12-25	247-355	92.2-57.8
Dal	12-4	.750	#WDC	454-311	595-469	2378-2069	4.0-4.4	26-15	14-20	449-484	265-231	3356-3568	7.5-7.4	30-21	25-27	252-358	81.5-63.8
Was	6-10	.375	—	261-293	517-585	2016-2524	3.9-4.3	12-16	18-12	486-392	284-187	3171-2504	6.5-6.4	17-17	18-33	333-333	74.2-47.8
SL	5-11	.313	—	299-350	519-547	2183-2059	4.2-3.8	19-17	13-14	470-531	239-287	3063-3616	6.5-6.8	16-23	24-20	387-291	61.7-74.2
NYG	4-12	.250	—	249-425	483-584	1730-2507	3.6-4.3	10-31	18-23	514-448	245-255	2931-3469	5.7-7.7	19-22	25-18	322-224	57.6-81.4
Central Division																	
Min	9-7	.563	#D	317-308	433-531	1642-2456	3.8-4.6	14-15	3-14	574-499	331-283	3934-3644	6.9-7.3	22-24	23-24	246-244	74.8-75.8
Det	9-7	.563	#	334-272	572-449	2599-1599	4.5-3.6	21-9	19-11	423-462	248-302	3287-3234	7.8-7.0	13-14	12-23	346-300	81.7-66.8
ChiB	7-9	.438	—	304-264	579-506	2440-2015	4.2-4.0	22-10	14-14	404-451	209-238	2669-3271	6.6-7.3	13-20	25-17	274-379	57.7-75.4
TB	5-10-1	.344	—	271-341	477-548	1839-2101	3.9-3.8	9-20	21-13	530-516	256-328	3414-3477	6.4-6.7	20-17	17-15	194-173	68.4-82.0
GB	5-10-1	.344	—	231-371	493-565	1806-2399	3.7-4.2	13-19	12-14	511-460	289-259	3615-3617	7.1-7.9	15-19	29-13	360-234	65.1-83.8
Western Division																	
Atl	12-4	.750	D	405-272	559-441	2405-1670		15-8	9-16	467-564	259-333	3568-3990	7.6-7.1	31-24	17-26	324-396	87.1-75.7
LA	11-5	.688	W	424-289	615-445	2799-1945	4.6-4.4	17-13	13-17	451-510	261-245	3441-3097	7.6-6.1	31-23	23-25	234-496	83.8-62.0
SF	6-10	.375	—	320-415	415-556	1743-2218	4.2-4.0	10-20	14-17	597-495	363-327	3799-3958	6.4-8.0	27-29	26-17	222-207	76.2-95.7
NO	1-15	.063	—	291-487	348-630	1362-3106	3.9-4.9	9-28	13-12	566-445	334-255	4010-3341	7.1-7.5	26-31	22-12	362-229	79.9-93.1
Aver	16	—	—	328	514	2041	4.0	15	15	489	275	3426	7.0	22	22	291	73.7

TEAM	1D	PENY	PNT	FGM/A	RTNY	RTNTD	OFFY/DEFY	NETY	NETTO	NP	PNP	DELP	PW	DELW	PRT	DR	YPD	DEL
Eastern Division																		
Phi	326-270	809-789	38.8-41.3	16/31-14/26	730-444	1-2	5519-4443	1076	7	162	118	44	12.1	-0.1	6.4/3.2	192-199	28.7-22.3	6.4
Dal	337-286	908-989	40.9-43.5	11/17-15/28	1079-394	4-2	5482-5279	203	8	94			11.6	0.4	4.7/4.2	206-203	26.6-26.0	0.6
Was	279-298	1008-766	39.2-40.7	18/33-13/17	806-570	1-3	4854-4695	159	9	-32	49	-81	7.2	-1.2	4.2/2.0	198-201	24.5-23.4	1.2
SL	281-311	922-919	41.1-40.1	14/23-17/33	726-891	2-3	4859-5384	-525	-3	-51	-56	5	6.7	-1.7	3.4/4.7	214-213	22.7-25.3	-2.6
NYG	261-336	962-862	44.8-40.3	16/24-14/24	415-882	0-2	4339-5752	-1413	-2	-176	-126	-50	3.6	0.4	3.0/5.6	206-207	21.1-27.8	-6.7
Central Division																		
Min	324-330	717-914	38.8-39.3	16/26-12/20	547-446	3-1	5330-5856	-526	12	9	4	5	8.2	0.8	4.7/4.8	186-188	28.7-31.1	-2.5
Det	308-265	844-815	41.6-41.6	27/42-16/21	631-473	2-9	5540-4533	1007	3	62	96	-34	9.6	-0.5	5.4/4.0	196-199	28.3-22.8	5.5
ChiB	286-285	842-1109	40.6-39.0	13/18-14/27	439-576	3-2	4835-4907	-72	-8	40	-38	78	9.0	-2.0	3.2/4.7	188-189	25.7-26.0	-0.2
TB	281-313	840-1077	41.8-42.0	16/23-20/33	492-714	3-3	5059-5405	-346	-10	-70	-69	-1	6.3	-0.8	4.8/5.2	206-199	24.6-27.2	-2.6
GB	307-316	697-872	38.2-39.1	11/20-25/27	389-825	1-5	5097-5782	-685	-14	-140	-113	-27	4.5	1.0	3.9/6.0	196-193	26.0-30.0	-4.0
Western Division																		
Atl	336-298	861-919	39.1-41.3	19/27-16/25	849-383	4-0	5649-5264	385	16	133	96	37	11.3	0.7	5.6/4.4	201-198	28.1-26.6	1.5
LA	316-291	973-778	39.0-42.0	16/30-9/20	861-660	6-2	6006-4546	1460	6	135	146	-17	11.4	-0.4	5.2/3.0	206-213	29.2-21.3	7.8
SF	298-341	933-826	40.9-38.3	15/19-17/26	595-849	3-3	5320-5969	-649	-6	-95	-78	-17	5.6	0.4	4.3/6.2	196-193	27.1-30.9	-3.8
NO	285-360	837-690	39.3-38.5	12/22-23/31	372-707	2-1	5010-6218	-1208	-11	-196	-145	-51	3.1	-2.1	4.8/6.1	195-200	25.7-31.1	-5.4
Aver	305	851	40.2	17/27	634	3	5176	—	—	—	—	—	—	—	4.8	198	26.2	—

Statistical Leaders

Rushing Attempts
- W.Payton-Chi 317
- B.Sims-Det 313
- O.Anderson-SL 301
- T.Dorsett-Dal 278
- W.Andrews-Atl 265

Rushing Yards
- W.Payton-Chi 1460
- O.Anderson-SL 1352
- W.Andrews-Atl 1308
- B.Sims-Det 1303
- T.Dorsett-Dal 1185

Rushing Average
- D.Bussey-Det 4.97
- W.Andrews-Atl 4.94
- E.Peacock-LA 4.74
- W.Payton-Chi 4.61
- J.Rogers-NO 4.57

Rushing TDs
- B.Sims-Det 13
- T.Dorsett-Dal 11
- O.Anderson-SL 9

Rushing Rank
- W.Payton-Chi 1520
- O.Anderson-SL 1442
- B.Sims-Det 1433
- W.Andrews-Atl 1348
- T.Dorsett-Dal 1295

Passing Yards
- A.Manning-NO 3716
- T.Kramer-Min 3582
- B.Barnes-Atl 3544
- R.Jaworski-Phi 3529
- L.Dickey-GB 3529

Passing Average
- V.Ferragamo-LA 7.92
- R.Jaworski-Phi 7.82
- G.Danielson-Det 7.73
- B.Barnes-Atl 7.65
- D.White-Dal 7.54

Completion Percent
- J.Montana-SF 64.5
- A.Manning-NO 60.7
- D.White-Dal 59.6
- V.Ferragamo-LA 59.4
- G.Danielson-Det 58.5

TD Passes
- B.Barnes-Atl 31
- V.Ferragamo-LA 30
- D.White-Dal 28
- R.Jaworski-Phi 27
- A.Manning-NO 23

TD Percent
- V.Ferragamo-LA 7.4
- B.Barnes-Atl 6.7
- D.White-Dal 6.4
- R.Jaworski-Phi 6.0
- J.Montana-SF 5.5

INT Percent
- G.Danielson-Det 2.6
- R.Jaworski-Phi 2.7
- D.Williams-TB 3.1
- J.Montana-SF 3.3
- B.Barnes-Atl 3.3

Passer Rating
- R.Jaworski-Phi 91.0
- V.Ferragamo-LA 89.7
- B.Barnes-Atl 88.2
- J.Montana-SF 87.8
- G.Danielson-Det 82.4

Passing Rank
- R.Jaworski-Phi 1420
- B.Barnes-Atl 1287
- G.Danielson-Det 1237
- A.Manning-NO 1173
- D.Williams-TB 1158

Receptions
- E.Cooper-SF 83
- D.Clark-SF 82
- J.Lofton-GB 71
- A.Rashad-Min 69
- P.Tilley-SL 68

Receiving Yards
- J.Lofton-GB 1226
- A.Rashad-Min 1095
- T.Hill-Dal 1055
- A.Jenkins-Atl 1035
- D.Clark-SF 991

Receiving Average
- J.Scott-Chi 19.33
- I.Harris-NO 18.70
- J.Giles-TB 18.24
- A.Jenkins-Atl 17.84
- M.Gray-SL 17.73

Receiving TDs
- E.Gray-NYG 10
- J.Miller-Atl 9
- H.Carmichael-Phi 9

Receiving Rank
- J.Lofton-GB 633
- A.Rashad-Min 573
- T.Hill-Dal 568
- A.Jenkins-Atl 548
- D.Clark-SF 536

Combined Net Yards
- B.Sims-Det 1907
- W.Payton-Chi 1827
- W.Andrews-Atl 1764
- O.Anderson-SL 1660
- J.Rogers-NO 1563

Total TDs
- B.Sims-Det 16
- T.Dorsett-Dal 11

Total Points
- E.Murray-Det 116
- T.Mazzetti-Atl 103
- F.Corral-LA 99
- B.Sims-Det 96
- T.Franklin-Phi 96

Punt Average
- D.Jennings-NYG 44.8
- T.Blanchard-TB 42.3
- T.Skladany-Det 42.2
- L.Swider-SL 41.5

Field Goals
- E.Murray-Det 27
- T.Mazzetti-Atl 19
- M.Moseley-Was 18

Field Goal Percent
- R.Wersching-SF 78.9
- B.Thomas-Chi 72.2
- T.Mazzetti-Atl 70.4
- G.Yepremian-TB 69.6
- J.Danelo-NYG 66.7

Kickoff Returns
- E.Payton-Min 53
- G.Davis-TB 44
- D.Hill-LA 43
- J.Rogers-NO 41
- M.Nelms-Was 38

Kickoff Return Average
- R.Mauti-NO 25.7
- D.Williams-Chi 24.7
- J.Owens-SF 23.4
- R.Green-SL 23.3
- J.Rogers-NO 22.7

Punt Returns
- D.Reece-TB 57
- J.Jones-Dal 54
- M.Nelms-Was 48
- L.Irvin-LA 42
- J.Sciarra-Phi 36

Punt Return Average
- K.Johnson-Atl 12.2
- F.Solomon-SF 11.0
- R.Green-SL 10.5
- J.Jones-Dal 10.1
- M.Nelms-Was 10.1

Punt/Kick Return Yards
- E.Payton-Min 1435
- M.Nelms-Was 1297
- J.Jones-Dal 1268
- G.Davis-TB 951
- J.Rogers-NO 930

Punt/Kick Return TDs
- F.Solomon-SF 2

Interceptions
- N.Cromwell-LA 8
- B.Ricardo-Atl 7
- L.Parrish-Was 7

Interception Return Yards
- N.Cromwell-LA 140
- B.Ricardo-Atl 139
- R.Perry-LA 115
- D.Thurman-Dal 114
- C.Allen-SL 104

Interception Return TDs
- Many 1

Sacks
- Not kept

Overall Rank
- B.Sims-Det 1759
- W.Payton-Chi 1709
- O.Anderson-SL 1596
- W.Andrews-Atl 1581
- D.Williams-TB 1568

SHIFTING REAL ESTATE VALUES IN CALIFORNIA

Following their first Super Bowl appearance, the Rams moved to newly-expanded Anaheim Stadium in Orange County. Playing in the 100,000-seat Los Angeles Memorial Coliseum made sellouts a rarity, and the television blackout rule meant few home games were televised. This made it harder for the team to maintain its fan base, and the suburb 35 miles to the south offered a better market.

The move was just the first of many distractions the Rams suffered during the preseason. Running back Wendell Tyler suffered a hip injury in an automobile accident. Four key veterans staged a preseason holdout, and while they all returned before the season opener, there was dissension in the new locker room. A quarterback controversy pitted veteran Pat Haden against Vince Ferragamo, the backup who won the NFC title. Haden won the battle but suffered a season-ending injury in the opener. Ferragamo again rallied the offense, but the Rams couldn't repeat their postseason magic.

Atlanta's Steve Bartkowski led the NFL with 31 touchdown passes, and the backfield tandem of William Andrews (1,308 rushing yards) and Lynn Cain (914 rushing yards) gave the Falcons one of the league's most balanced attacks. A nine-game winning streak helped Atlanta claim its first division title. Two of those wins came against San Francisco, which faded after a 3–0 start under second-year coach Bill Walsh.

The retirement of quarterback Roger Staubach did nothing to slow Dallas. The Cowboys led the league in scoring, twice putting up more than 50 points. Tony Dorsett rushed for 1,185 yards while fullbacks Robert Newhouse and Ron Springs each scored 6 touchdowns.

The Eagles crushed their first three opponents by a combined score of 104–16. After a loss to the Cardinals, Philadelphia won eight straight. The smothering defense allowed a league-low 222 points and just 8 rushing touchdowns. Harold Carmichael's record streak of 127 straight games with a catch came to an end, but he snared 9 touchdowns. (Rookie Art Monk, who would break Carmichael's record, caught 58 passes for Washington.) Eagles running back Wilbert Montgomery returned from injury to run for 194 yards against the Cowboys in Philadelphia's first championship game since 1960.

1980 AFC

TEAM	W-L-T	PCT	POST	PTS	RA	RY	RY/A	RTD	FL	PA	PC	GPY	GPY/A	PTD	PI	PSY	PRAT
Eastern Division																	
Buf	**11**-5	**.688**	D	320-260	**603**-486	2222-1819	3.7-3.7	17-14	22-20	461-**433**	262-**240**	2936-**2561**	6.4-**5.9**	20-**15**	19-24	**186**-279	73.3-**61.4**
NE	10-6	.625	—	**441**-325	588-482	2240-1876	3.8-3.9	19-12	9-10	413-458	240-266	3395-3232	**8.2**-7.1	27-28	27-24	200-346	79.3-78.4
Mia	8-8	.500	—	266-305	492-530	1876-2018	3.8-3.8	9-13	16-17	492-505	267-290	2953-3439	6.0-6.8	21-21	26-28	265-233	64.5-69.1
Bal	7-9	.438	—	355-387	527-574	2078-2210	3.9-3.9	**20**-20	13-17	493-476	272-260	3409-3576	6.9-7.5	25-21	24-17	281-240	73.5-78.7
NYJ	4-12	.250	—	302-395	470-508	1873-1951	4.0-3.8	17-20	11-9	481-544	265-337	3335-3899	6.9-7.2	17-27	30-23	326-235	62.7-82.5
Central Division																	
Cle	**11**-5	**.688**	#D	357-310	436-485	1673-1761	3.8-3.6	15-12	14-10	554-536	337-336	4132-4089	7.5-7.6	**30**-23	**14**-22	217-224	**91.4**-83.3
Hou	**11**-5	**.688**	#W	295-**251**	573-**444**	**2635**-1811	**4.6**-4.1	18-**8**	19-13	463-454	296-246	3271-3053	7.1-6.7	15-16	28-26	264-252	70.4-63.1
Pit	9-7	.563	—	352-313	512-486	1986-1762	3.9-3.6	15-9	18-14	484-532	250-280	3832-3517	7.9-6.6	26-25	24-26	264-145	75.4-68.8
Cin	6-10	.375	—	244-312	513-469	2069-**1680**	4.0-3.6	9-13	**8-22**	510-491	281-284	3102-3426	6.1-7.0	17-22	25-20	287-302	64.0-77.3
Western Division																	
SD	**11**-5	**.688**	#DC	418-327	509-478	1879-1842	3.7-3.9	18-18	22-18	**594**-519	**350**-300	**4741**-3324	8.0-6.4	**30**-18	26-20	210-**475**	83.0-72.4
Oak	**11**-5	**.688**	#WDCS*	364-306	541-501	2146-1726	4.0-**3.4**	14-19	20-17	456-524	235-296	3294-3731	7.2-7.1	23-17	24-**35**	395-419	70.0-61.8
KC	8-8	.500	—	319-336	552-536	1873-2206	3.4-4.1	15-17	16-15	401-523	237-278	2869-3393	7.2-6.5	15-25	**14**-28	421-284	79.1-67.0
Den	8-8	.500	—	310-323	480-554	1865-2120	3.9-3.8	16-10	12-12	467-448	262-270	3107-3449	6.7-7.7	14-20	25-16	330-324	64.2-84.4
Sea	4-12	.250	—	291-408	456-550	1783-2067	3.9-3.8	13-17	15-11	517-462	287-267	3494-3280	6.8-7.1	18-28	23-23	398-170	69.6-79.3
Aver	16	—	—	328	514	2041	4.0	15	15	489	275	3426	7.0	22	22	291	73.7

TEAM	1D	PENY	PNT	FGM/A	RTNY	RTNTD	OFFY/DEFY	NETY	NETTO	NP	PNP	DELP	PW	DELW	PRT	DR	YPD	DEL
Eastern Division																		
Buf	317-**251**	731-805	38.2-39.3	13/23-15/**20**	593-**397**	3-2	4972-**4101**	871	3	60	85	-25	9.5	1.5	4.4/**2.9**	195-194	25.5-**21.1**	4.4
NE	319-270	696-833	38.0-40.9	**26**/34-14/**20**	801-606	6-**0**	5435-4762	673	-2	**116**	48	68	**10.9**	-0.9	5.1/ 4.2	202-203	26.9-23.5	3.4
Mia	284-309	**567-923**	41.5-**37.3**	14/23-18/25	411-725	2-2	4564-5224	-660	3	-39	-43	4	7.0	1.0	3.3/ 4.1	194-193	23.5-27.1	-3.5
Bal	327-338	914-775	38.1-39.7	12/23-20/30	498-735	1-6	5206-5546	-340	-3	-32	-40	8	7.2	-0.2	4.3/ 5.5	199-206	26.2-26.9	-0.8
NYJ	289-348	767-872	41.8-39.9	14/22-**13**/24	562-777	3-4	4882-5615	-733	-9	-93	-97	4	5.7	-1.7	3.5/ 5.1	187-190	26.1-29.6	-3.4
Central Division																		
Cle	336-340	1042-766	38.3-37.4	16/26-18/29	436-515	0-2	5588-5626	-38	4	47	13	34	9.2	1.8	**6.2**/ 5.5	177-**182**	**31.6**-30.9	0.7
Hou	329-259	838-763	40.7-40.9	20/25-21/29	697-818	1-3	5642-4612	1030	-8	44	54	-10	9.1	**1.9**	3.9/ 3.7	189-189	29.9-24.4	5.4
Pit	308-302	933-806	40.2-40.7	19/28-19/29	651-443	1-3	5554-5134	420	-2	39	27	12	9.0	0.0	5.3/ 4.5	197-194	28.2-26.5	1.7
Cin	283-286	949-809	39.7-38.5	15/29-16/27	507-829	2-3	4884-4804	80	9	-68	43	-111	6.3	-0.3	3.4/ 4.6	197-193	24.8-24.9	-0.1
Western Division																		
SD	**372**-284	912-880	38.5-40.4	24/36-16/34	605-778	2-4	**6410**-4691	**1719**	-10	91	**103**	-12	10.3	0.7	5.8/ 3.7	214-210	30.0-22.3	**7.6**
Oak	281-319	929-922	43.6-38.9	19/**37**-14/24	922-421	**7**-2	5045-5038	7	8	58	33	25	9.4	1.5	4.1/ 3.3	**217**-212	23.2-23.8	-0.5
KC	270-328	591-617	39.0-42.2	20/26-15/30	**945**-419	**7-0**	4321-5315	-994	**13**	-17	-31	14	7.6	0.4	4.3/ 3.7	197-194	21.9-27.4	-5.5
Den	286-303	899-850	**43.9**-41.6	**26**/34-29/40	751-831	3-4	4642-5245	-603	-9	-13	-86	**73**	7.7	0.3	3.5/ 5.3	189-190	24.6-27.6	-3.0
Sea	302-301	901-876	40.4-40.2	20/31-25/33	444-646	2-2	4879-5177	-298	-4	-117	-41	-76	5.1	-1.1	3.9/ 4.8	196-191	24.9-27.1	-2.2
Aver	305	851	40.2	17/27	634	1	5176	—	—	—	—	—	—	—	4.8	98	26.2	—

Rushing Attempts	Rushing Yards	Rushing Average	Rushing TDs	Rushing Rank	Passing Yards	Passing Average
E.Campbell-Hou......373	E.Campbell-Hou....1934	E.Campbell-Hou.....5.18	E.Campbell-Hou........13	E.Campbell-Hou....2064	D.Fouts-SD............4715	S.Grogan-NE..........8.09
J.Cribbs-Buf............306	J.Cribbs-Buf..........1185	C.Muncie-SD.........4.88	C.Dickey-Bal..............11	J.Cribbs-Buf..........1295	B.Sipe-Cle............4132	D.Fouts-SD.............8.01
M.Pruitt-Cle.............249	M.Pruitt-Cle...........1034	J.Jensen-Den.........4.71	J.Cribbs-Buf...............11	M.Pruitt-Cle...........1094	J.Zorn-Sea............3346	T.Bradshaw-Pit........7.88
Z.Valentine-Oak.......222	Z.Valentine-Oak.......838	C.Dickey-Bal..........4.55	D.Calhoun-NE.............9	C.Dickey-Bal............910	T.Bradshaw-Pit.......3339	B.Sipe-Cle..............7.46
V.Ferguson-NE........211	V.Ferguson-NE........818	O.Armstrong-Den...4.43		Z.Valentine-Oak.......888	R.Todd-NYJ...........3329	J.Plunkett-Oak........7.18

Completion Percent	TD Passes	TD Percent	INT Percent	Passer Rating	Passing Rank	Receptions
K.Stabler-Hou.........64.1	B.Sipe-Cle.................30	S.Grogan-NE............5.9	B.Sipe-Cle................2.5	B.Sipe-Cle.............91.4	B.Sipe-Cle.............1656	K.Winslow-SD...........89
B.Sipe-Cle..............60.8	D.Fouts-SD................30	T.Bradshaw-Pit..........5.7	S.Fuller-KC...............3.8	D.Fouts-SD.............84.7	D.Fouts-SD.............1548	J.Jefferson-SD..........82
C.Morton-Den.........60.8	T.Bradshaw-Pit...........24	J.Plunkett-Oak..........5.6	D.Fouts-SD...............4.1	C.Morton-Den.........77.8	J.Zorn-Sea...............958	C.Joiner-SD..............71
K.Anderson-Cin......60.4	B.Jones-Bal...............23	B.Sipe-Cle...............5.4	J.Zorn-Sea................4.1	S.Fuller-KC............76.4	T.Bradshaw-Pit.........910	S.Largent-Sea...........66
S.Fuller-KC.............60.3	J.Ferguson-Buf..........20	B.Jones-Bal.............5.2	J.Ferguson-Buf.........4.1	B.Jones-Bal............75.3	B.Jones-Bal.............842	M.Pruitt-Cle..............63

Receiving Yards	Receiving Average	Receiving TDs	Receiving Rank	Combined Net Yards	Total TDs	Total Points
J.Jefferson-SD.......1340	S.Morgan-NE........22.02	J.Jefferson-SD...........13	J.Jefferson-SD.........735	B.Harper-NYJ........2072	J.Jefferson-SD...........13	J.Smith-NE.............129
K.Winslow-SD........1290	H.Jackson-NE.......21.06	B.Chandler-Oak.........10	K.Winslow-SD..........690	E.Campbell-Hou....1981	C.Dickey-Bal.............13	H.Belton-SD............118
C.Joiner-SD..........1132	C.Branch-Oak.......19.50	K.Winslow-SD..............9	C.Joiner-SD.............586	J.Cribbs-Buf..........1786	E.Campbell-Hou........13	F.Steinfort-Den.........110
S.Largent-Sea.......1064	J.Smith-Pit............19.22	J.Smith-Pit....................9	S.Largent-Sea.........562	M.Pruitt-Cle...........1505	J.Cribbs-Buf...............12	C.Bahr-Oak................98
S.Morgan-NE...........991	H.Moses-Den........17.74	R.Francis-NE................8	S.Morgan-NE..........526	J.Jefferson-SD.......1356	B.Chandler-Oak.........10	N.Lowery-KC.............97

Punt Average	Field Goals	Field Goal Percent	Kickoff Returns	Kickoff Return Average	Punt Returns	Punt Return Average
R.Preston-Den........43.9	F.Steinfort-Den...........26	T.Fritsch-Hou..........79.2	B.Harper-NYJ............49	H.Ivory-NE.............27.6	I.Matthews-Oak.........48	J.Smith-KC.............14.5
R.Guy-Oak.............43.6	J.Smith-NE.................26	N.Lowery-KC..........76.9	J.Mohring-Cin............44	W.Lewis-Sea...........23.4	C.Roaches-Hou.........47	R.James-NE...........10.0
G.Roberts-Mia........42.6	H.Belton-SD...............24	F.Steinfort-Den........76.5	C.Carson-KC.............40	L.Brunson-Den.......23.1	W.Lewis-Sea.............41	T.Bell-Pit...............10.0
C.Ramsey-NYJ........42.4	N.Lowery-KC.............20	J.Smith-NE............76.5	L.Brunson-Den..........40	K.Wright-Cle...........23.0	J.Smith-KC...............40	M.Fuller-SD.............9.9
H.Weaver-Sea........41.8	E.Herrera-Sea............20	M.Bahr-Pit..............67.9	W.Bennett-Mia...........40	C.Carson-KC..........22.9	R.Upchurch-Den........37	R.Upchurch-Den.......9.5

Punt/Kick Return Yards	Punt/Kick Return TDs	Interceptions	Interception Return Yards	Interception Return TDs	Sacks	Overall Rank
B.Harper-NYJ.......1312	J.Smith-KC..................2	L.Hayes-Oak.............13	L.Hayes-Oak...........273	R.Griffin-Cin................2	Not kept	E.Campbell-Hou....2121
C.Roaches-Hou.......1130		G.Barbaro-KC............10	G.Barbaro-KC.........163			B.Sipe-Cle............1721
J.Mohring-Cin........1066		K.Schroy-NYJ..............8	D.Shell-Pit...............135			D.Fouts-SD............1583
I.Matthews-Oak.....1006			D.Ray-NYJ...............132			J.Cribbs-Buf...........1532
H.Ivory-NE..............992			G.Edwards-SD.........122			M.Pruitt-Cle...........1330

The Steel Curtain Drops

As the 1970s came to an end, so too did a dynasty. Pittsburgh's streak of eight consecutive division titles was broken when the Steelers finished with a lackluster 9–7 record. Injuries were the primary cause of their downfall. John Stallworth's broken foot knocked him out of action after just three games. Injuries also kept Franco Harris, Lynn Swann, and Jack Lambert sidelined for parts of the season. Rocky Bleier retired.

Free of Pittsburgh's shadow, Houston's path to a division title was suddenly blocked by resurgent Cleveland and league MVP Brian Sipe at quarterback. While Earl Campbell continued to be the game's most dominating rusher, opponents knew Houston had no other offensive weapons. During the offseason, Houston had traded quarterback Dan Pastorini to Oakland for passer Ken Stabler. The Oilers hoped the 35-year-old Stabler could inject some life into their moribund passing game, but he threw 28 interceptions against just 13 touchdowns.

The deal didn't work out too well for the Raiders, either. Pastorini struggled early and then broke his leg in a loss to the Chiefs on October 12. Jim Plunkett, who'd thrown just 1 touchdown since 1977, took over and gave Oakland a much-needed spark. The Raiders averaged 30 points over the next six games, winning them all. Rookie linebacker Matt Millen helped bolster an already solid defense. Cornerback Lester Hayes intercepted 13 passes, the second-highest total in NFL history.

Even as the Raiders were bringing a championship to Oakland, they were looking for an exit. The Raiders joined with the Los Angeles Memorial Coliseum to bring an antitrust lawsuit against the NFL. Owner Al Davis took the action after his proposed move south was blocked. It was the most contentious of the many legal battles between Davis and the league.

Air Coryell continued to reach greater heights in San Diego. Quarterback Dan Fouts set new single-season records for pass attempts (589), completions (348), and yards (4,715). Tight end Kellen Winslow led the NFL with 89 receptions, John Jefferson led the league with 13 touchdown catches, and Charlie Joiner also kept busy as the trio finished 1–2–3 in the AFC in both catches and receiving yards.

1981 NFC

TEAM	W-L-T	PCT	POST	PTS	RA	RY	RY/A	RTD	FL	PA	PC	GPY	GPY/A	PTD	PI	PSY	PRAT
Eastern Division																	
Dal	12-4	.750	DC	367-277	**630**-468	2711-2049	4.3-4.4	15-16	20-16	439-511	241-236	3414-3717	7.8-7.3	24-17	15-**37**	245-347	84.2-**51.8**
Phi	10-6	.625	W	368-**221**	559-476	2509-1751	4.5-3.7	17-11	17-21	476-507	258-248	3249-**3050**	6.8-**6.0**	25-12	22-26	205-354	73.9-54.4
NYG	9-7	.563	WD	295-257	481-553	1685-1891	3.5-**3.4**	11-**10**	16-17	506-544	251-294	3009-3318	5.9-6.1	16-14	20-17	368-**384**	62.3-68.1
Was	8-8	.500	—	347-349	532-532	2157-2161	4.1-4.1	19-17	19-15	525-452	307-214	3743-3310	7.1-7.3	19-21	22-24	277-265	75.1-65.4
SL	7-9	.438	—	315-408	519-509	2213-2428	4.3-4.8	20-20	20-17	477-495	253-282	3269-3547	6.9-7.2	15-29	24-21	405-252	64.4-81.3
Central Division																	
TB	9-7	.563	D	315-268	458-551	1731-2172	3.8-3.9	13-16	14-14	473-541	239-317	3565-3297	7.5-6.1	20-**10**	14-32	**136**-157	77.4-57.8
Det	8-8	.500	—	397-322	596-469	**2795-1623**	**4.7**-3.5	**26**-14	20-15	436-475	228-261	3475-3596	**8.0**-7.6	18-22	23-24	337-373	70.7-73.8
GB	8-8	.500	—	324-361	478-546	1670-2098	3.5-3.8	11-21	17-**24**	514-505	286-284	3576-3353	7.0-6.6	24-18	24-30	387-266	73.5-63.7
Min	7-9	.438	—	325-369	391-540	1512-2045	3.9-3.8	8-15	21-19	**709**-481	**382**-265	**4567**-3599	6.4-7.5	27-26	29-16	234-271	69.5-83.3
ChiB	6-10	.375	—	253-324	608-521	2171-2146	3.6-4.1	13-13	17-22	489-525	222-233	2728-3527	5.6-6.7	14-23	23-18	266-279	53.1-67.4
Western Division																	
SF	**13**-3	**.813**	DCS*	357-250	560-464	1941-1918	3.5-4.1	17-**10**	**12**-21	517-514	328-273	3766-3135	7.3-6.1	20-16	**13**-27	223-290	**87.7**-60.2
Atl	7-9	.438	—	**426**-355	495-**459**	1965-1666	4.0-3.6	15-**10**	17-21	563-565	311-322	3986-3927	7.1-7.0	**30**-30	24-25	287-239	77.6-77.8
LA	6-10	.375	—	303-351	559-585	2236-2397	4.0-4.1	17-19	15-16	477-**439**	235-**204**	3008-3057	6.3-7.0	15-17	32-17	451-330	51.9-66.6
NO	4-12	.250	—	207-378	546-504	2286-1916	4.2-3.8	16-17	20-17	441-471	238-287	2778-3578	6.3-7.6	8-26	27-17	359-241	53.8-87.9
Aver	16	—	—	331	518	2082	4.0	16	18	506	277	3561	7.0	21	22	292	72.9

TEAM	1D	PENY	PNT	FGM/A	RTNY	RTNTD	OFFY/DEFY	NETY	NETTO	NP	PNP	DELP	PW	DELW	PRT	DR	YPD	DEL
Eastern Division																		
Dal	321-286	839-837	40.5-41.2	**27**/35-14/29	717-**355**	1-**1**	5880-5419	461	18	90	110	-20	10.3	1.8	5.8/ 3.4	215-207	27.3-26.2	1.2
Phi	332-**266**	855-813	40.3-40.7	20/31-14/28	688-603	2-3	5553-**4447**	**1106**	8	**147**	124	23	**11.7**	-1.7	4.6/**3.0**	194-194	28.6-22.9	5.7
NYG	253-291	897-876	43.3-**39.6**	24/**38**-22/33	724-813	5-3	4326-4825	-499	-2	38	-50	**88**	8.9	0.1	3.4/ 3.9	215-220	20.1-**21.9**	-1.8
Was	334-310	940-921	40.0-41.7	19/30-17/24	756-779	4-5	5623-5206	417	-2	-2	27	-29	7.9	0.1	4.8/ 4.5	202-203	27.8-25.6	2.2
SL	300-328	877-845	41.8-41.3	19/32-20/26	734-588	2-**1**	5077-5723	-646	-6	-93	-78	-15	5.7	1.3	3.7/ 5.0	199-198	25.5-28.9	-3.4
Central Division																		
TB	269-320	779-650	41.2-41.2	17/28-25/33	892-847	5-**1**	5160-5312	-152	18	47	59	-12	9.2	-0.2	**6.1**/ 3.2	195-194	26.5-27.4	-0.9
Det	340-279	990-872	**43.5**-42.9	25/35-19/**22**	736-573	2-2	**5933**-4846	1087	-4	75	75	0	9.9	-1.9	4.8/ 4.5	196-204	**30.3**-23.8	**6.5**
GB	308-326	**687**-907	39.6-39.7	22/24-16/24	801-986	2-6	4859-5185	-326	13	-37	25	-62	7.1	0.9	4.2/ 3.5	208-202	23.4-25.7	-2.3
Min	**343**-299	865-991	41.4-40.7	21/25-17/27	423-783	2-5	5845-5373	472	-15	-44	-21	-23	6.9	0.1	4.5/ 5.6	211-216	27.7-24.9	2.8
ChiB	278-290	996-961	39.7-40.7	12/23-17/29	863-979	4-3	4633-5394	-761	0	-71	-63	-8	6.2	-0.2	3.0/ 4.8	223-225	20.8-24.0	-3.2
Western Division																		
SF	317-280	752-866	41.5-41.4	19/29-**13**/23	792-961	6-4	5484-4763	721	**23**	107	**152**	-45	10.7	**2.3**	5.8/ 3.3	200-207	27.4-23.0	4.4
Atl	318-303	940-804	40.3-42.2	21/33-18/29	877-878	**7**-3	5664-5354	310	5	71	46	25	9.8	-2.8	4.9/ 4.8	**230**-231	24.6-23.2	1.4
LA	305-285	916-1018	42.0-41.0	17/26-26/33	**913**-842	4-3	4793-5124	-331	-14	-48	-84	36	6.8	-0.8	2.4/ 4.4	215-215	22.3-23.8	-1.5
NO	280-303	899-**1089**	40.5-44.1	13/25-19/25	640-761	0-3	4705-5253	-548	-13	-171	-98	-73	3.7	0.3	2.7/ 5.7	190-**178**	24.8-29.5	-4.7
Aver	310	868	41.0	19/28	690	3	5352	—	—	—	—	—	—	—	4.9	204	26.2	—

Rushing Attempts	Rushing Yards	Rushing Average	Rushing TDs	Rushing Rank	Passing Yards	Passing Average
G.Rogers-NO...........378	G.Rogers-NO.........1674	J.Montana-Phi 4.90	B.Sims-Det 13	G.Rogers-NO.........1804	T.Kramer-Min..........3912	E.Hipple-Det 8.45
T.Dorsett-Dal............342	T.Dorsett-Dal..........1646	B.Sims-Det 4.85	G.Rogers-NO.............13	T.Dorsett-Dal..........1686	B.Barnes-Atl 3829	D.White-Dal 7.92
W.Payton-Chi............339	B.Sims-Det 1437	T.Dorsett-Dal...........4.81	J.Riggins-Was............13	B.Sims-Det 1567	J.Theismann-Was..3568	D.Williams-TB 7.56
O.Anderson-SL........328	J.Montana-Phi 1402	W.Andrews-Atl 4.50	W.Tyler-LA 12	J.Montana-Phi 1482	J.Montana-SF 3565	L.Dickey-GB............7.32
B.Sims-Det 296	O.Anderson-SL......1376	J.Owens-TB............4.46		O.Anderson-SL......1466	D.Williams-TB 3563	J.Montana-SF 7.31
Completion Percent	**TD Passes**	**TD Percent**	**INT Percent**	**Passer Rating**	**Passing Rank**	**Receptions**
J.Montana-SF 63.7	B.Barnes-Atl 30	B.Barnes-Atl 5.6	J.Montana-SF 2.5	J.Montana-SF 88.4	J.Montana-SF 1398	D.Clark-SF 85
J.Theismann-Was...59.1	T.Kramer-Min 26	D.White-Dal 5.6	P.Simms-NYG...........2.8	D.White-Dal 87.5	D.Williams-TB 1317	T.Brown-Min...............83
A.Manning-NO........57.8	R.Jaworski-Phi...........23	E.Hipple-Det 5.0	D.Williams-TB 3.0	B.Barnes-Atl 79.2	B.Barnes-Atl 1145	W.Andrews-Atl 81
L.Dickey-GB.............57.6	D.White-Dal 22	R.Jaworski-Phi..........5.0	D.White-Dal 3.3	L.Dickey-GB............79.0	D.White-Dal 1139	J.Senser-Min 79
D.White-Dal 57.0		L.Dickey-GB..............4.8	J.Theismann-Was.....4.0	J.Theismann-Was...77.3	T.Kramer-Min 1126	J.Lofton-GB 71
Receiving Yards	**Receiving Average**	**Receiving TDs**	**Receiving Rank**	**Combined Net Yards**	**Total TDs**	**Total Points**
A.Jenkins-Atl..........1358	R.Green-SL 21.45	A.Jenkins-Atl.............13	A.Jenkins-Atl............744	W.Andrews-Atl 2036	W.Tyler-LA 17	R.Septien-Dal 121
J.Lofton-GB 1294	K.House-TB 21.00	K.House-TB.................9	J.Lofton-GB 687	T.Dorsett-Dal..........1971	B.Sims-Det 15	E.Murray-Det 121
K.House-TB...........1176	T.Hill-Dal 20.72	F.Solomon-SF.............8	K.House-TB 633	S.Mitchell-SL 1947	G.Rogers-NO............13	M.Luckhurst-Atl........114
D.Clark-SF 1105	A.Jenkins-Atl.........19.40	J.Senser-Min 8	D.Clark-SF 573	J.Montana-Phi 1923	J.Riggins-Was...........13	J.Danelo-NYG 103
P.Tilley-SL..............1040	F.Scott-Det...........19.28	J.Lofton-GB 8	G.Carano-Phi...........544	B.Sims-Det 1888	A.Jenkins-Atl.............13	W.Tyler-LA 102
Punt Average	**Field Goals**	**Field Goal Percent**	**Kickoff Returns**	**Kickoff Return Average**	**Punt Returns**	**Punt Return Average**
T.Skladany-Det 43.5	R.Septien-Dal 27	J.Stenerud-GB........91.7	D.Hill-LA.....................60	M.Nelms-Was 29.7	W.Henry-Phi 54	L.Irvin-LA 13.4
D.Jennings-NYG.....43.3	E.Murray-Det 25	R.Danmeier-Min 84.0	S.Mitchell-SL 55	A.Lawrence-SF.......25.7	R.Martin-Det..............52	J.Fisher-Chi 11.8
L.Swider-TB............42.7	J.Danelo-NYG 24	R.Septien-Dal 77.1	R.Smith-Atl 47	R.Smith-Atl 24.3	L.Bright-NYG 52	J.Groth-NO 11.8
F.Corral-LA..............42.0	J.Stenerud-GB...........22	R.Wersching-SF 73.9	E.Payton-Min 39	S.Mitchell-SL 23.5	L.Irvin-LA...................46	M.Nelms-Was 10.9
C.Birdsong-SL 41.8		E.Murray-Det 71.4	M.Nelms-Was 37	W.Wilson-NO 23.3	M.Nelms-Was 45	S.Mitchell-SL 10.6
Punt/Kick Return Yards	**Punt/Kick Return TDs**	**Interceptions**	**Interception Return Yards**	**Interception Return TDs**	**Sacks**	**Overall Rank**
S.Mitchell-SL 1737	L.Irvin-LA.....................3	E.Walls-Dal...............11	D.Hicks-SF...............239	R.Lott-SF 3	Not kept	G.Rogers-NO........1867
M.Nelms-Was 1591	M.Nelms-Was 2	D.Thurman-Dal 9	T.Pridemore-Atl........221	C.Brown-TB 2		T.Dorsett-Dal.........1859
R.Smith-Atl 1242		D.Hicks-SF...................9	M.Harvey-GB...........217			B.Sims-Det 1803
E.Payton-Min 1201		C.Brown-TB 9	C.Brown-TB 215			W.Andrews-Atl 1779
D.Hill-LA................1192		J.Allen-Det 9	D.Thurman-Dal 187			J.Montana-Phi 1753

L.T. Powers Turnover

New Orleans running back George Rogers led the NFL in rushing and was named Rookie of the Year. The Heisman Trophy winner injected some life into a team that had finished the previous season as the "Aints." The 1 15 team had been so bad that some fans hid their identities beneath paper bags. The arrival of coach Bum Phillips from Houston and the promise of a brighter future gave fans reason to show their faces despite again having the NFC's worst record.

While standout linebacker Mike Singletary debuted in Chicago and defensive back Ronnie Lott in San Francisco, New York had the rookie with the biggest impact in 1981. Linebacker Lawrence Taylor helped the Giants reach the playoffs for the first time in 18 years. The club's defense moved from 27th place to third place. Taylor's speed and athleticism made him extremely disruptive as a pass rusher, forcing opposing offenses to find new ways to try to contain him.

The Buccaneers won their division for the second time in three years. A solid defense and the strong play of quarterback Doug Williams gave Tampa Bay the edge in a very tight NFC Central. The lack of a competent running game, however, kept the team from putting up much of a fight against Dallas in the playoffs. For the Cowboys, a playoff team for the 15th time in 16 seasons, the formula for success remained largely the same: a solid defense and a dominating running game. Linemen Randy White and Too Tall Jones led the defense, and Tony Dorsett rushed for a career-high 1,646 yards.

They weren't quite as accustomed to winning in San Francisco. It had been 10 seasons since the 49ers made the playoffs. Coach Bill Walsh had groomed quarterback Joe Montana, polishing his skills for an attacking offense based on the short passing game. That work came to fruition in 1981. After losing two of their first three games, San Francisco was nearly unstoppable. They won 12 of their remaining 13 games, including a 45–14 thrashing of the Cowboys that made everybody realize San Francisco was for real and set up a highly-anticipated playoff rematch.

1981 AFC

TEAM	W-L-T	PCT	POST	PTS	RA	RY	RY/A	RTD	FL	PA	PC	GPY	GPY/A	PTD	PI	PSY	PRAT
Eastern Division																	
Mia	11-4-1	.719	D	345-**275**	535-492	2173-2032	4.1-4.1	18-10	**10**-15	498-509	271-297	3385-3645	6.8-7.2	18-23	21-18	236-314	70.2-80.9
NYJ	10-5-1	.656	W	355-287	571-**465**	2341-1867	4.1-4.0	11-19	17-15	507-505	283-275	3279-3522	6.5-7.0	26-15	14-21	224-**518**	81.1-69.1
Buf	10-6	.625	#WD	311-276	524-516	2125-2075	4.1-4.0	13-**7**	18-17	503-474	253-267	3661-3243	7.3-6.8	25-21	20-19	146-373	74.3-75.6
Bal	2-14	.125	—	259-533	441-607	1850-2665	4.2-4.4	11-30	14-14	479-491	265-301	3379-4228	7.1-8.6	21-37	23-16	321-100	72.2-100.6
NE	2-14	.125	—	322-370	499-644	2040-2950	4.1-4.6	23-20	16-17	482-**439**	254-**243**	3904-**3052**	8.1-7.0	17-18	34-16	321-175	62.1-75.7
Central Division																	
Cin	**12**-4	**.750**	DCS	421-304	493-**465**	1973-1881	4.0-4.0	19-12	12-18	550-548	332-316	4200-3757	7.6-6.9	30-24	**12**-19	205-349	**93.3**-78.9
Pit	8-8	.500	—	356-297	554-500	2372-1869	**4.3**-3.7	21-10	22-16	461-544	247-302	3457-4108	7.5-7.6	25-22	19-**30**	231-325	78.9-70.3
Hou	7-9	.438	—	281-355	466-549	1734-2411	3.7-4.4	11-16	21-13	441-502	258-295	3119-3554	7.1-7.1	21-22	23-18	342-239	74.4-80.2
Cle	5-11	.313	—	276-375	474-516	1929-2078	4.1-4.0	11-14	26-20	624-469	348-275	4339-3512	7.0-7.5	21-28	27-15	353-223	70.7-88.7
Western Division																	
SD	10-6	.625	#DC	**478**-390	481-491	2005-1825	4.2-3.7	**26**-25	22-18	**629**-571	**368**-313	**4873**-4695	7.7-8.2	**34**-22	18-23	**134**-384	89.2-78.1
Den	10-6	.625	#	321-289	515-467	1895-2005	3.7-4.3	12-17	18-23	485-497	289-267	3992-3168	**8.2-6.4**	27-**13**	21-23	461-295	86.6-**62.8**
KC	9-7	.563	—	343-290	**610**-507	**2633-1747**	**4.3-3.4**	22-17	24-21	410-567	224-291	2917-3821	7.1-6.7	12-16	22-26	277-195	64.7-63.2
Oak	7-9	.438	—	273-343	493-524	2058-1832	4.2-3.5	11-15	20-19	545-537	267-289	3356-4011	6.2-7.5	18-24	28-13	437-370	58.2-82.9
Sea	6-10	.375	—	322-388	440-588	1594-2806	3.6-4.8	14-20	23-**27**	524-502	307-294	3727-3394	7.1-6.8	21-25	15-21	300-260	82.0-78.2
Aver	16	—	—	331	518	2082	4.0	16	18	506	277	3561	7.0	21	22	292	72.9

TEAM	1D	PENY	PNT	FGM/A	RTNY	RTNTD	OFFY/DEFY	NETY	NETTO	NP	PNP	DELP	PW	DELW	PRT	DR	YPD	DEL
Eastern Division																		
Mia	306-296	**541**-886	40.8-41.0	24/31-14/21	712-574	3-**0**	5322-5363	-41	2	70	5	65	9.8	**1.8**	4.5/ 5.0	191-201	27.9-26.7	1.2
NYJ	318-291	936-935	40.6-40.4	25/**36-12/20**	769-**361**	3-2	5396-**4871**	525	5	68	64	4	9.7	0.8	5.0/ 3.9	203-205	26.6-23.8	2.8
Buf	315-298	1001-690	39.7-42.0	14/24-22/26	644-553	0-2	5640-4945	**695**	-2	35	50	-15	8.9	1.1	5.5/ 4.3	187-196	30.2-25.2	**4.9**
Bal	274-406	913-776	39.4-**37.9**	10/18-20/31	266-683	1-1	4908-6793	-1885	-7	-274	-185	-89	1.2	0.8	4.3/ 7.5	194-**182**	25.3-37.3	-12.0
NE	306-328	742-763	39.3-38.8	15/24-25/39	394-875	0-4	5623-5827	-204	-17	-48	-85	37	6.8	-4.8	4.2/ 5.1	203-207	27.7-28.1	-0.5
Central Division																		
Cin	361-324	896-787	**44.8**-40.3	22/32-**12**/21	523-559	2-2	5968-5289	679	**13**	**117**	**109**	8	**10.9**	1.1	6.4/ 4.7	193-197	30.9-26.8	4.1
Pit	318-323	840-**960**	43.3-42.1	12/17-18/33	788-584	1-3	5598-5652	-54	5	59	16	43	9.5	-1.5	5.4/ 4.5	208-204	26.9-27.7	-0.8
Hou	241-325	825-838	39.7-41.9	15/22-27/42	655-649	2-1	4511-5726	-1215	-13	-74	-153	**79**	6.2	0.9	4.1/ 5.1	198-196	22.8-29.2	-6.4
Cle	364-299	971-870	41.2-40.7	17/33-21/34	534-600	0-3	5915-5367	548	-18	-99	-26	-73	5.5	-0.5	4.5/ 5.8	209-205	28.3-26.2	2.1
Western Division																		
SD	**379**-365	947-877	40.3-40.3	19/26-19/26	602-545	1-1	**6744**-6136	608	1	88	55	33	10.2	-0.2	**6.6**/ 5.7	203-206	**33.2**-29.8	3.4
Den	306-**268**	833-949	40.4-43.1	17/30-15/27	783-793	0-5	5426-4878	548	7	32	74	-42	8.8	1.2	5.2/**3.7**	212-210	25.6-**23.2**	2.4
KC	315-316	924-740	38.5-38.9	**26/36**-19/27	**934**-540	4-1	5273-5373	-100	1	53	-4	57	9.3	-0.3	4.0/ 4.4	204-206	25.8-26.1	-0.2
Oak	296-316	867-826	43.2-38.9	14/24-17/30	477-853	4-3	4977-5473	-496	-16	-70	-105	35	6.3	0.8	3.1/ 5.6	**224**-220	22.2-24.9	-2.7
Sea	295-371	823-944	39.0-42.5	15/24-23/29	690-410	**5**-1	5021-5940	-919	10	-66	-37	-29	6.3	-0.4	5.3/ 4.5	194-187	25.9-31.8	-5.9
Aver	310	868	41.0	19/28	690	1	5352	—	—	—	—	—	—	—	4.9	101	27.0	—

Rushing Attempts	Rushing Yards	Rushing Average	Rushing TDs	Rushing Rank	Passing Yards	Passing Average
E.Campbell-Hou 361	E.Campbell-Hou 1376	T.Nathan-Mia 5.32	C.Muncie-SD 19	E.Campbell-Hou 1476	D.Fouts-SD 4802	S.Grogan-NE 8.61
P.Johnson-Cin 274	C.Muncie-SD 1144	K.King-Oak 4.87	P.Johnson-Cin 12	C.Muncie-SD 1334	B.Sipe-Cle 3876	C.Morton-Den 8.50
J.Cribbs-Buf 257	J.Delaney-KC 1121	B.Harper-NYJ 4.85	B.Jackson-KC 10	P.Johnson-Cin 1197	K.Anderson-Cin 3754	D.Fouts-SD 7.89
C.Muncie-SD 251	M.Pruitt-Cle 1103	J.Brooks-SD 4.82	E.Campbell-Hou 10	M.Pruitt-Cle 1173	J.Ferguson-Buf 3652	K.Anderson-Cin 7.84
M.Pruitt-Cle 247	J.Cribbs-Buf 1097	J.Delaney-KC 4.79	F.Harris-Pit 8	J.Delaney-KC 1151	R.Todd-NYJ 3231	T.Bradshaw-Pit 7.80
Completion Percent	**TD Passes**	**TD Percent**	**INT Percent**	**Passer Rating**	**Passing Rank**	**Receptions**
K.Anderson-Cin 62.6	D.Fouts-SD 33	K.Anderson-Cin 6.1	K.Anderson-Cin 2.1	K.Anderson-Cin 98.4	D.Fouts-SD 1886	K.Winslow-SD 88
C.Morton-Den 59.8	K.Anderson-Cin 29	T.Bradshaw-Pit 5.9	J.Zorn-Sea 2.3	D.Fouts-SD 90.6	K.Anderson-Cin 1622	S.Largent-Sea 75
J.Zorn-Sea 59.4	R.Todd-NYJ 25	C.Morton-Den 5.6	R.Todd-NYJ 2.6	C.Morton-Den 90.5	R.Todd-NYJ 1221	D.Ross-Cin 71
D.Fouts-SD 59.1	J.Ferguson-Buf 24	D.Fouts-SD 5.4	D.Fouts-SD 2.8	T.Bradshaw-Pit 83.9	J.Ferguson-Buf 1146	F.Lewis-Buf 70
K.Stabler-Hou 57.9	T.Bradshaw-Pit 22	R.Todd-NYJ 5.0	D.Woodley-Mia 3.6	J.Zorn-Sea 82.4	C.Morton-Den 1143	C.Joiner-SD 70
Receiving Yards	**Receiving Average**	**Receiving TDs**	**Receiving Rank**	**Combined Net Yards**	**Total TDs**	**Total Points**
S.Watson-Den 1244	S.Morgan-NE 23.39	S.Watson-Den 13	S.Watson-Den 687	J.Brooks-SD 2093	C.Muncie-SD 19	N.Lowery-KC 115
F.Lewis-Buf 1244	S.Watson-Den 20.73	K.Winslow-SD 10	S.Largent-Sea 657	T.Collins-NE 1893	P.Johnson-Cin 16	J.Breech-Cin 115
S.Largent-Sea 1224	R.Butler-Bal 18.09	W.Walker-NYJ 9	F.Lewis-Buf 642	J.Cribbs-Buf 1700	S.Watson-Den 13	C.Muncie-SD 114
C.Joiner-SD 1188	F.Lewis-Buf 17.77	S.Largent-Sea 9	C.Joiner-SD 629	B.Harper-NYJ 1597	B.Jackson-KC 11	P.Leahy-NYJ 113
K.Stabler-Pit 1098	J.Haslett-NE 17.57	R.Butler-Bal 9	K.Winslow-SD 588	M.Pruitt-Cle 1545		M.Bell-SD 112
Punt Average	**Field Goals**	**Field Goal Percent**	**Kickoff Returns**	**Kickoff Return Average**	**Punt Returns**	**Punt Return Average**
P.McInally-Cin 45.4	N.Lowery-KC 26	von Schamann-Mia 77.4	J.Brooks-SD 40	C.Roaches-Hou 27.5	J.Smith-KC 50	J.Brooks-SD 13.2
R.Guy-Oak 43.7	P.Leahy-NYJ 25	M.Bell-SD 73.1	T.Collins-NE 39	F.Walker-Mia 24.5	W.Manning-Den 41	P.Johns-Sea 11.1
C.Colquitt-Pit 43.3	von Schamann-Mia 24	N.Lowery-KC 72.2	F.Walker-Mia 38	W.Tullis-Hou 24.3	C.Roaches-Hou 39	J.Smith-KC 10.6
S.Cox-Cle 42.4	J.Breech-Cin 22	D.Trout-Pit 70.6	L.Anderson-Pit 37	D.Verser-Cin 23.8	T.Vigorito-Mia 36	T.Vigorito-Mia 10.5
R.Camarillo-NE 41.7	M.Bell-SD 19	E.Herrera-Sea 70.6		J.Brooks-SD 23.7		L.Anderson-Pit 10.4
Punt/Kick Return Yards	**Punt/Kick Return TDs**	**Interceptions**	**Interception Return Yards**	**Interception Return TDs**	**Sacks**	**Overall Rank**
J.Brooks-SD 1239	T.Watts-Oak 1	J.Harris-Sea 10	D.Ray-NYJ 227	D.Ray-NYJ 2	Not kept	K.Anderson-Cin 1952
C.Roaches-Hou 1065	F.Walker-Mia 1	D.Ray-NYJ 7	J.Harris-Sea 155	J.Harris-Sea 2		D.Fouts-SD 1942
D.Hall-Cle 1061	T.Vigorito-Mia 1	E.Harris-KC 7	K.Easley-Sea 155			E.Campbell-Hou 1554
L.Anderson-Pit 1033	W.Tullis-Hou 1	J.Lambert-Pit 6	L.Breeden-Cin 145			C.Muncie-SD 1522
F.Walker-Mia 982	C.Roaches-Hou 1	M.Blount-Pit 6	M.Clark-Buf 142			J.Cribbs-Buf 1473

A Bengal *Can* Change Its Stripes

Even the loss of their best receiver couldn't slow down San Diego's aerial attack. John Jefferson refused to report to training camp because of a contract dispute. After leading the league in receiving yards and touchdowns in 1980, the fourth-year player wanted to renegotiate his deal. Whatever leverage he might have had vanished when the Chargers averaged 38 points per game during a 3–0 start. Seeing that the San Diego offense would be just fine without him, owner Gene Klein traded the disgruntled receiver to Green Bay for a package of draft picks

Quarterback Dan Fouts not only survived the loss, he got better, setting new records for pass attempts (609), completions (360), and yards (4,802). Running back Chuck Muncie, healthy for the first time in three years, exploited opposing defenses that were keyed to stopping the pass. He ran for 19 touchdowns, tying the single-season record. The Chargers offense set a new record for total yards gained, but the defense also set a record for most passing yards allowed.

For the first time since the playoffs were expanded, both AFC wild cards came from the same division. The second-place Jets and third-place Bills of the AFC East had better records than the runners up in the West or Central. This included Pittsburgh, which finished without a winning record for the first time since 1971. Joe Greene and L.C Greenwood, who'd debuted together, ended their careers together.

After three straight last-place finishes, the Bengals surprised everyone by finishing with the AFC's best record. Cincinnati sported new tiger-striped uniforms, but the most substantive change was the stern leadership of head coach Forrest Gregg. A Hall of Fame tackle under Vince Lombardi in Green Bay, Gregg brought the same fiery discipline to a team that many critics had accused of being soft. The Bengals purred behind the deadly accurate passing of quarterback Ken Anderson. Rookie Cris Collinsworth and veteran Isaac Curtis were both well suited to the short passing attack that Anderson loved, and this helped soften defenses for bruising fullback Pete Johnson. Cincinnati's young offensive line, with Anthony Munoz, Max Montoya, and Blair Bush, was among the league's best.

1982 NFC

TEAM	W-L-T	PCT	POST	PTS	RA	RY	RY/A	RTD	FL	PA	PC	GPY	GPY/A	PTD	PI	PSY	PRAT
Was	8-1	.889	PDCS*	190-128	315-247	1140-946	3.6-3.8	5-8	7-13	253-275	162-146	2068-1870	8.2-6.8	13-8	9-11	223-256	91.8-67.7
Dal	6-3	.667	PC	226-145	296-260	1313-1011	4.4-3.9	10-5	12-10	258-289	160-152	2150-2002	8.3-6.9	16-10	14-15	264-260	86.5-64.7
GB	5-3-1	.611	PD	226-169	283-275	1081-932	3.8-3.4	12-9	11-11	267-327	143-177	2068-1950	7.7-6.0	12-9	15-12	239-175	70.6-65.9
Min	5-4	.556	PD	187-198	245-260	912-1020	3.7-3.9	6-8	5-9	334-292	187-157	2105-2106	6.3-7.2	15-11	12-12	138-231	75.0-72.4
Atl	5-4	.556	P	183-199	310-253	1181-1044	3.8-4.1	12-13	10-15	275-280	176-157	1992-1945	7.2-6.9	9-12	11-10	210-141	79.8-77.2
SL	5-4	.556	P	135-170	307-256	1209-995	3.9-3.9	10-5	10-9	240-291	129-174	1576-2035	6.6-7.0	6-16	6-6	243-182	72.2-90.8
TB	5-4	.556	P	158-178	268-285	952-1058	3.6-3.7	6-9	12-10	308-254	144-145	2071-1608	6.7-6.3	9-10	11-11	128-224	69.3-71.1
Det	4-5	.444	#P	181-176	283-271	1140-854	3.6-3.2	5-6	8-8	285-288	136-155	1754-2098	6.2-7.3	12-11	18-18	242-230	55.2-64.0
NO	4-5	.444	#	129-160	331-255	1257-974	3.8-3.8	8-8	10-13	248-245	137-149	1571-1864	6.3-7.6	8-11	14-9	173-231	61.7-84.1
NYG	4-5	.444	#	164-160	244-301	842-1118	3.5-3.7	7-7	10-6	298-244	161-148	2017-1810	6.8-7.4	10-10	9-12	130-244	73.9-76.7
SF	3-6	.333	—	209-206	219-303	740-1199	3.4-4.0	6-9	10-4	348-278	215-158	2668-1949	7.7-7.0	17-14	11-9	166-113	88.6-82.0
ChiB	3-6	.333	—	141-174	276-261	988-902	3.6-3.5	5-4	8-7	262-294	141-164	1749-2189	6.7-7.4	10-14	11-13	244-240	70.0-77.0
Phi	3-6	.333	—	191-195	211-299	829-1031	3.9-3.4	11-5	10-7	288-285	163-148	2100-2136	7.3-7.5	12-14	13-15	244-235	76.2-76.9
LARm	2-7	.222	—	200-250	251-307	1025-1202	4.1-3.9	13-13	10-7	297-281	166-175	2136-2290	7.2-8.1	11-16	14-11	137-159	71.3-90.6
Aver	9	—	—	181	277	1060	3.8	8	9	283	160	1988	7.0	11	12	193	73.4

TEAM	1D	PENY	PNT	FGM/A	RTNY	RTNTD	OFFY/DEFY	NETY	NETTO	NP	PNP	DELP	PW	DELW	PRT	DR	YPD	DEL
Was	165-151	404-419	37.3-40.1	20/21-6/9	380-174	1-0	2985-2560	425	8	62	67	-5	6.1	2.0	5.5/3.9	114-117	26.2-21.9	4.3
Dal	180-162	304-431	41.7-42.5	10/14-9/15	405-243	2-2	3199-2753	446	-1	81	33	48	6.5	-0.5	5.0/3.6	115-114	27.8-24.1	3.7
GB	175-164	343-629	40.1-41.8	13/18-12/18	372-432	3-1	2910-2707	203	-3	57	5	52	5.9	-0.4	4.3/3.8	115-123	25.3-22.0	3.3
Min	167-159	496-399	41.1-41.9	8/14-11/19	287-513	2-5	2879-2895	-16	4	-11	15	-26	4.2	0.8	4.4/4.5	124-121	23.2-23.9	-0.7
Atl	190-170	655-549	39.3-41.7	10/14-6/12	363-255	1-1	2963-2848	115	4	-16	26	-42	4.1	0.9	4.6/4.9	110-109	26.9-26.1	0.8
SL	162-163	528-420	43.8-41.2	8/13-8/18	244-325	0-0	2542-2848	-306	-1	-35	-30	-5	3.6	1.4	4.1/5.6	114-108	22.3-26.4	-4.1
TB	163-160	297-325	40.5-43.4	18/23-12/17	282-306	0-2	2895-2442	453	-2	-20	30	-50	4.0	1.0	4.8/3.5	110-110	26.3-22.2	4.1
Det	160-162	548-605	40.9-39.8	16/17-12/21	429-485	2-3	2534-2722	-188	0	5	-16	21	4.6	-0.6	2.6/3.7	122-119	20.8-22.9	-2.1
NO	173-151	514-459	43.0-41.1	6/13-9/12	252-318	0-0	2655-2607	48	-2	-31	-4	-27	3.7	0.3	3.1/4.8	113-108	23.5-24.1	-0.6
NYG	153-149	369-417	42.8-41.0	12/21-12/13	578-354	1-1	2729-2684	45	-1	4	0	4	4.6	-0.6	5.0/4.1	118-116	23.1-23.1	-0.0
SF	183-170	451-542	37.2-42.7	12/17-13/19	482-354	2-1	3242-3035	207	-8	3	-15	18	4.6	-1.6	5.9/5.4	115-117	28.2-25.9	2.3
ChiB	153-166	422-451	41.6-41.6	9/20-12/17	241-509	1-2	2493-2851	-358	1	-33	-26	-7	3.7	-0.7	3.8/4.6	116-123	21.5-23.2	-1.7
Phi	157-177	253-341	40.5-36.8	6/9-20/22	150-434	2-0	2685-2938	-253	4	-4	-5	1	4.4	-1.4	4.4/4.4	115-111	23.3-26.5	-3.1
LARm	163-193	550-531	42.6-38.1	9/15-14/19	348-499	1-1	3024-3333	-309	-6	-50	-50	0	3.3	-1.3	4.7/6.0	118-119	25.6-28.0	-2.4
Aver	170	462	40.6	11/16	345	2	2855	—	—	—	—	—	—	—	4.8	113	25.2	—

Rushing Attempts
J.Riggins-Was...177
T.Dorsett-Dal...177
B.Sims-Det...172
W.Payton-Chi...148
O.Anderson-SL...145

Rushing Yards
T.Dorsett-Dal...745
B.Sims-Det...639
W.Payton-Chi...596
O.Anderson-SL...587
W.Andrews-Atl...573

Rushing Average
J.Montana-Phi...4.52
G.Rogers-NO...4.39
T.Brown-Min...4.29
T.Dorsett-Dal...4.21
W.Harrell-Phi...4.13

Rushing TDs
W.Tyler-LARm...9
E.Ivery-GB...9
J.Montana-Phi...7

Rushing Rank
T.Dorsett-Dal...795
B.Sims-Det...679
W.Tyler-LARm...654
W.Andrews-Atl...623
O.Anderson-SL...617

Passing Yards
J.Montana-SF...2613
D.White-Dal...2079
R.Jaworski-Phi...2076
D.Williams-TB...2071
T.Kramer-Min...2037

Passing Average
D.White-Dal...8.42
L.Dickey-GB...8.21
J.Theismann-Was...8.07
V.Ferragamo-LARm...7.70
J.Montana-SF...7.55

Completion Percent
J.Theismann-Was...63.9
R.Barnes-Atl...63.4
D.White-Dal...63.2
K.Stabler-NO...61.9
J.Montana-SF...61.6

TD Passes
J.Montana-SF...17
D.White-Dal...16
T.Kramer-Min...15
J.Theismann-Was...13

TD Percent
D.White-Dal...6.5
L.Dickey-GB...5.5
J.Theismann-Was...5.5
G.Danielson-Det...5.1
J.Montana-SF...4.9

INT Percent
N.Lomax-SL...2.9
S.Brunner-NYG...3.0
J.Montana-SF...3.2
J.McMahon-Chi...3.3
J.Theismann-Was...3.6

Passer Rating
J.Theismann-Was...91.3
D.White-Dal...91.1
J.Montana-SF...88.0
J.McMahon-Chi...79.9
R.Barnes-Atl...77.9

Passing Rank
J.Montana-SF...952
J.Theismann-Was...722
S.Brunner-NYG...699
D.Williams-TB...641
D.White-Dal...640

Receptions
D.Clark-SF...60
J.Wilder-TB...53
W.Andrews-Atl...42
W.Tyler-LARm...38
J.Moore-SF...37

Receiving Yards
D.Clark-SF...913
J.Lofton-GB...696
C.Brown-Was...690
B.Capece-Phi...540
T.Hill-Dal...526

Receiving Average
C.Brown-Was...21.56
J.Lofton-GB...19.89
J.Giles-TB...17.82
S.White-Min...17.34
E.Gray-NYG...17.04

Receiving TDs
C.Brown-Was...8
S.White-Min...5
E.Moorehead-Chi...5
D.Clark-SF...5

Receiving Rank
D.Clark-SF...482
C.Brown-Was...385
J.Lofton-GB...368
B.Capece-Phi...290
S.White-Min...277

Combined Net Yards
B.Woolfolk-NYG...1091
W.Andrews-Atl...1076
B.Sims-Det...981
W.Tyler-LARm...939
T.Dorsett-Dal...924

Total TDs
W.Tyler-LARm...10
E.Ivery-GB...9
J.Montana-Phi...9
J.Moore-SF...8
C.Brown-Was...8

Total Points
W.Tyler-LARm...78
M.Moseley-Was...76
B.Capece-TB...68
J.Stenerud-GB...64
E.Ivery-GB...60

Punt Average
C.Birdsong-SL...43.8
J.Misko-LARm...43.6
R.Erxleben-NO...43.0
D.Jennings-NYG...42.8
D.White-Dal...41.7

Field Goals
M.Moseley-Was...20
B.Capece-TB...18
J.Stenerud-GB...13
R.Wersching-SF...12
J.Danelo-NYG...12

Field Goal Percent
M.Moseley-Was...95.2
E.Murray-Det...91.7
B.Capece-TB...78.3
J.Stenerud-GB...72.2

Kickoff Returns
W.Henry-Phi...24
R.Brown-Atl...24
M.Nelms-Was...23
B.Redden-LARm...22
M.Morton-TB...21

Kickoff Return Average
A.Hall-Det...26.6
M.Nelms-Was...24.2
J.Redwine-Min...23.8
R.Watts-Chi...23.6
B.Redden-LARm...22.8

Punt Returns
L.Bright-NYG...37
M.Nelms-Was...32
S.Mitchell-SL...27
R.Martin-Det...26
R.Fellows-Dal...25

Punt Return Average
B.Johnson-Atl...11.4
L.Irvin-LARm...11.0
R.Martin-Det...10.6
F.Solomon-SF...9.4
L.Bright-NYG...8.8

Punt/Kick Return Yards
M.Nelms-Was...809
W.Henry-Phi...644
R.Fellows-Dal...548
R.Martin-Det...543
S.Mitchell-SL...529

Punt/Kick Return TDs
D.McLemore-SF...1
L.Irvin-LARm...1
A.Hall-Det...1

Interceptions
E.Walls-Dal...7
B.Watkins-Det...5
H.Edwards-Phi...5

Interception Return Yards
L.Taylor-NYG...97
R.Lott-SF...95
D.Thurman-Dal...75
T.Jackson-NYG...75
N.Colzie-TB...64

Interception Return TDs
Many...1

Sacks
D.Martin-Min...11.5
D.Harrison-Phi...10.5
D.Hampton-Chi...9.0
A.Baker-Det...8.5
H.Martin-Dal...8.0

Overall Rank
J.Montana-SF...1080
T.Dorsett-Dal...885
W.Andrews-Atl...885
J.Theismann-Was...872
W.Tyler-LARm...862

AN OCTOBER WITHOUT THE NFL

The season opened under the storm clouds of a brewing labor war. The NFLPA wanted the league to set aside 55 percent of gross revenues to pay player salaries, which would be determined through a combination of service time and performance; management was comfortable with the status quo. The situation grew yet more acrimonious as a few preseason roster cuts seemed to single out union representatives. Players knew that the following spring would bring the alternative of jumping to the United States Football League.

Despite some movement towards compromise in the season's first two weeks, the players voted to strike, and pro football was virtually absent from the nation's entertainment menu. The two sides reached an agreement in mid-November. The strike whittled the season to nine games, but the playoffs were expanded to include the top eight teams from each conference, temporarily erasing divisions.

Only two teams, Washington and Dallas, rose above the conference parity. The Redskins provided an antidote to the season's glum proceedings—even if they did provide the first full-time kicker,

Mark Mosley, to be named MVP—as ageless John Riggins ground out yardage behind what would become football's most famous offensive line, the Hogs. The Redskins also gained notoriety for the choreographed end zone celebrations of the Fun Bunch. All of this was anathema to Tom Landry's Cowboys, who seemed comparatively bland despite the conference's best offense and a talented defense. Otherwise, the short season gave fans the odd experience of seeing sad sacks like the Packers and Cardinals reaching—and playing against each other in—the playoffs. The 4–5 Lions, along with the Browns in the AFC, became the first below-.500 teams ever in the NFL playoffs. Somehow missing from the expanded postseason were the defending champion 49ers.

There weren't many new names of note, except in Chicago, where first-year head coach Mike Ditka was joined by rookie quarterback Jim McMahon, but at 3–6, the Bears weren't making news. Something that did generate immediate attention was dubbing the sack an official statistic. The NFL's first official league leader in sacks was Vikings end Doug Martin, with 11 ½ in the shortened schedule.

1982 AFC

TEAM	W-L-T	PCT	POST	PTS	RA	RY	RY/A	RTD	FL	PA	PC	GPY	GPY/A	PTD	PI	PSY	PRAT
LARd	**8**-1	**.889**	PD	260-200	292-234	1080-778	3.7-3.3	**15**-12	9-11	267-375	154-193	2086-2617	7.8-7.0	14-11	15-18	211-**329**	76.8-63.8
Mia	7-2	.778	PDCS	198-**131**	**333**-293	1344-1285	4.0-4.4	11-7	10-8	238-**226**	129-119	1401-**1281**	5.9-5.7	8-7	13-**19**	**87**-254	60.2-**44.9**
Cin	7-2	.778	P	232-177	269-**223**	949-850	3.5-3.8	13-8	7-6	310-306	**219**-187	2501-2250	8.1-7.4	12-12	9-14	162-207	**95.4**-77.7
Pit	6-3	.667	P	204-146	289-236	1187-**762**	4.1-**3.2**	7-**5**	9-8	275-329	141-176	1922-2385	7.0-7.2	17-12	16-17	139-273	70.3-67.5
SD	6-3	.667	PD	**288**-221	267-230	1121-961	4.2-4.2	**15**-10	8-12	**338**-342	208-233	**3021**-2437	**8.9**-7.1	**19**-10	12-13	94-145	94.6-82.5
NYJ	6-3	.667	PDC	245-166	304-269	1317-983	**4.3**-3.7	13-**5**	9-9	279-298	165-159	2107-1817	7.6-6.1	16-10	9-17	206-171	88.5-59.4
NE	5-4	.556	P	143-157	324-315	1347-1289	4.2-4.1	3-9	8-11	187-267	93-142	1420-1691	7.6-6.3	12-9	9-12	134-172	76.5-65.3
Cle	4-5	.444	#P	140-182	256-306	873-1292	3.4-4.2	7-13	8-11	334-266	174-144	2057-1967	6.2-7.4	9-9	16-17	212-145	60.2-62.7
Buf	4-5	.444	#	150-154	319-268	**1371**-1034	**4.3**-3.9	9-6	9-8	273-256	149-**114**	1671-1382	6.1-**5.4**	8-8	17-13	115-82	56.9-50.9
Sea	4-5	.444	#	127-147	227-337	795-1461	3.5-4.3	4-12	11-9	326-246	176-138	2068-1468	6.3-6.0	9-**4**	13-13	269-135	66.1-57.1
KC	3-6	.333	—	176-184	269-280	943-1065	3.5-3.8	3-7	**4**-10	264-262	145-155	1864-1787	7.1-6.8	10-12	**8**-12	309-120	77.3-76.0
Den	2-7	.222	—	148-226	257-293	1018-935	4.0-**3.2**	6-8	17-7	311-307	181-172	2019-2350	6.5-7.7	8-14	19-12	200-116	60.8-79.6
Hou	1-8	.111	—	136-245	225-298	799-1225	3.6-4.1	5-10	11-**14**	287-284	153-179	1882-2453	6.6-8.6	12-18	15-3	308-240	66.0-107.3
Bal	0-8-1	.056	—	113-236	293-348	1044-1473	3.6-4.2	4-10	11-6	283-246	142-138	1613-1920	5.7-7.8	6-18	10-5	174-97	60.0-97.3
Aver	9	—	—	181	277	1060	3.8	8	9	283	160	1988	7.0	11	12	193	73.4

TEAM	1D	PENY	PNT	FGM/A	RTNY	RTNTD	OFFY/DEFY	NETY	NETTO	NP	PNP	DELP	PW	DELW	PRT	DR	YPD	DEL
LARd	175-206	840-588	39.1-38.3	10/16-11/14	**565**-251	**4**-1	2955-3066	-111	5	60	11	49	6.0	**2.0**	4.6/ 3.8	**125**-129	23.6-23.8	-0.1
Mia	165-**147**	**240**-461	38.7-40.1	15/20-9/15	475-173	3-1	2658-**2312**	346	4	67	45	22	6.2	0.8	3.2/**0.9**	106-109	25.1-**21.2**	3.9
Cin	207-170	475-551	38.7-40.1	14/18-10/12	335-161	2-1	3288-2893	395	4	55	49	6	5.9	1.1	6.1/ 4.7	99-102	33.2-28.4	4.8
Pit	171-174	459-355	40.4-**38.1**	10/12-9/14	444-350	1-**0**	2970-2874	96	0	58	8	**50**	5.9	0.0	4.2/ 4.0	119-119	25.0-24.2	0.8
SD	**233**-196	530-**612**	37.7-44.9	16/22-16/19	286-348	0-5	**4048**-3253	**795**	5	67	**86**	-19	6.2	-0.2	**7.4**/ 5.0	106-108	**38.2**-30.1	**8.1**
NYJ	193-160	533-345	37.4-42.1	11/17-9/15	445-305	2-5	3218-2629	589	8	**79**	81	-2	**6.5**	-0.5	5.5/ 3.1	112-111	28.7-23.7	5.0
NE	146-185	412-290	43.7-39.7	8/13-10/15	315-291	2-**0**	2633-2808	-175	6	-14	9	-23	4.2	0.9	5.0/ 3.7	109-106	24.2-26.5	-2.3
Cle	176-189	461-436	38.3-38.8	7/16-7/**11**	236-380	1-1	2718-3114	-396	4	-42	-17	-25	3.5	0.5	3.4/ 4.0	111-116	24.5-26.8	-2.4
Buf	180-151	582-395	37.9-39.3	9/18-16/20	241-298	1-1	2927-2334	593	-5	-4	29	-33	4.4	-0.4	3.1/ 3.0	109-107	26.9-21.8	5.0
Sea	159-167	523-406	38.6-40.6	10/14-**6**/15	388-**157**	1-2	2594-2794	-200	-2	-20	-25	5	4.0	0.0	3.6/ 3.0	114-112	22.8-24.9	-2.2
KC	163-170	372-486	40.5-39.7	**19/24**-10/14	337-520	**4**-3	2498-2732	-234	**10**	-8	21	-29	4.3	-1.3	4.3/ 4.5	104-**101**	24.0-27.0	-3.0
Den	170-176	516-571	**45.0**-39.4	11/13-17/24	411-658	2-3	2837-3169	-332	-17	-78	-96	18	2.6	-0.5	3.1/ 5.7	121-119	23.4-26.6	-3.2
Hou	138-187	424-454	39.7-43.0	4/6-11/18	151-340	1-2	2373-3438	-1065	-9	-109	-125	16	1.8	-0.8	3.1/ 7.2	112-115	21.2-29.9	-8.7
Bal	152-197	433-466	44.4-39.9	10/18-14/19	228-355	2-**0**	2483-3296	-813	-10	-123	-108	-15	1.4	-0.9	3.5/ 6.9	108-105	23.0-31.4	-8.4
Aver	170	462	40.6	11/16	345	1	2855	—	—	—	—	—	—	—	4.8	56	25.9	—

Rushing Attempts	Rushing Yards	Rushing Average	Rushing TDs	Rushing Rank	Passing Yards	Passing Average
A.Franklin-Mia..........177	F.McNeil-NYJ...........786	F.McNeil-NYJ..........5.21	M.Allen-LARd 11	F.McNeil-NYJ...........846	D.Fouts-SD............2883	D.Fouts-SD.............8.74
T.Collins-NE............164	A.Franklin-Mia..........701	G.Willhite-Den 4.96	C.Muncie-SD 8	M.Allen-LARd 807	K.Anderson-Cin 2495	K.Anderson-Cin 8.07
M.Allen-LARd 160	M.Allen-LARd 697	J.Brooks-SD 4.94	P.Johnson-Cin.............7	A.Franklin-Mia..........771	J.Plunkett-LARd.....2035	J.Plunkett-LARd......7.80
E.Campbell-Hou 157	J.Cribbs-Buf.............633	J.Cribbs-Buf............4.72	A.Franklin-Mia.............7	P.Johnson-Cin..........692	R.Todd-NYJ 1961	S.Grogan-NE.........7.62
P.Johnson-Cin..........156	T.Collins-NE.............632	R.Upchurch-NE 4.71		J.Cribbs-Buf.............663	T.Bradshaw-Pit.......1768	R.Todd-NYJ 7.51
Completion Percent	**TD Passes**	**TD Percent**	**INT Percent**	**Passer Rating**	**Passing Rank**	**Receptions**
K.Anderson-Cin 70.6	D.Fouts-SD 17	T.Bradshaw-Pit..........7.1	S.Fuller-KC 2.2	K.Anderson-Cin 95.3	D.Fouts-SD 1087	K.Winslow-SD...........54
D.Fouts-SD 61.8	T.Bradshaw-Pit...........17	S.Grogan-NE 5.7	K.Anderson-Cin 2.9	D.Fouts-SD 93.3	K.Anderson-Cin 948	O.Newsome-Cle 49
S.DeBerg-Den 58.7	R.Todd-NYJ 14	R.Todd-NYJ 5.4	R.Todd-NYJ 3.1	R.Todd-NYJ 87.3	R.Todd-NYJ 731	Collinsworth-Cin 49
R.Todd-NYJ 58.6	J.Plunkett-LARd.........14	J.Plunkett-LARd........5.4	M.Pagel-Bal 3.2	S.Grogan-NE 84.4	T.Bradshaw-Pit.........529	W.Chandler-SD.........49
J.Plunkett-LARd......58.2	K.Anderson-Cin 12	D.Fouts-SD 5.2	S.Grogan-NE 3.3	T.Bradshaw-Pit........81.4	J.Plunkett-LARd.......488	D.Ross-Cin 47
Receiving Yards	**Receiving Average**	**Receiving TDs**	**Receiving Rank**	**Combined Net Yards**	**Total TDs**	**Total Points**
W.Chandler-SD......1032	W.Chandler-SD.....21.06	W.Chandler-SD............9	W.Chandler-SD........561	J.Brooks-SD 1383	M.Allen-LARd 14	M.Allen-LARd 84
K.Winslow-SD..........721	S.Morgan-NE........20.86	J.Squirek-Pit 7	K.Winslow-SD..........391	M.Allen-LARd 1098	C.Muncie-SD 9	R.Bell-SD...................80
Collinsworth-Cin 700	C.Branch-LARd.....19.17	K.Winslow-SD.............6	Collinsworth-Cin 355	W.Chandler-SD......1064	W.Chandler-SD...........9	N.Lowery-KC 74
O.Newsome-Cle 633	C.Carson-KC 18.30	W.Walker-NYJ 6	W.Walker-NYJ 340	G.Willhite-Den 974		J.Breech-Cin.............67
W.Walker-NYJ 620	M.Barnwell-LARd..16.83	D.Casper-Hou.............6	O.Newsome-Cle 332	F.McNeil-NYJ...........973		von Schamann-Mia 66
Punt Average	**Field Goals**	**Field Goal Percent**	**Kickoff Returns**	**Kickoff Return Average**	**Punt Returns**	**Punt Return Average**
R.Preston-Den........45.0	N.Lowery-KC 19	R.Karlis-Den 84.6	J.Brooks-SD 33	M.Mosley-Buf..........27.1	G.Pruitt-LARd 27	R.Upchurch-Den.....16.1
R.Stark-Bal 44.4	R.Bell-SD...................16	G.Anderson-Pit.......83.3	A.Hancock-KC...........27	G.Pruitt-LARd 26.5	B.Harper-NYJ 23	J.Brooks-SD 11.5
R.Camarillo-NE.......43.7	von Schamann-Mia 15	N.Lowery-KC 79.2	L.Anderson-Bal..........27	R.Smith-NE.............23.6	W.Sydnor-Pit..............22	P.Johns-Sea...........11.1
J.Gossett-KC 41.4	J.Breech-Cin..............14	J.Breech-Cin...........77.8	R.Smith-NE................24	F.Bohannon-Pit.......23.5	T.Vigorito-Mia.............20	R.Woods-Pit 10.9
M.Buford-SD...........41.3		von Schamann-Mia 75.0	D.Hall-Cle 22	W.Manning-Den......23.1		T.Vigorito-Mia............9.6
Punt/Kick Return Yards	**Punt/Kick Return TDs**	**Interceptions**	**Interception Return Yards**	**Interception Return TDs**	**Sacks**	**Overall Rank**
J.Brooks-SD 887	R.Upchurch-Den..........2	D.Woodruff-Pit 5	J.Davis-LARd...........107	Many............................1	J.Baker-Hou..............7.5	D.Fouts-SD 1105
A.Hancock-KC 712	T.Vigorito-Mia...............1	D.Shell-Pit....................5	R.Sanford-NE 105		T.Hendricks-LARd.....7.0	K.Anderson-Cin 1073
R.Smith-NE.............706	R.Smith-NE.................1	K.Riley-Cin...................5	T.Fox-SD.................103		L.Alzado-LARd 7.0	M.Allen-LARd 1046
G.Pruitt-LARd 580		B.Jackson-NYJ 5	J.Burroughs-Bal.........94		R.Brazile-Hou 6.5	F.McNeil-NYJ..........945
L.Anderson-Bal........571			D.Ray-NYJ.................91			J.Brooks-SD 855

Stormy Weather

As if the league's labor woes weren't enough of a distraction, the issue of franchise relocation became a major issue when Raiders owner Al Davis moved his team to the empty Los Angeles Coliseum (the Rams went to Anaheim two years earlier) for the 1982 season. The league's rules required the approval of 21 teams for a move like this, but Davis won the first of many court battles with the NFL, as the rule was declared a violation of federal antitrust law.

The Raiders didn't just win in court, for that matter. The revamped offense that relied on a healthy Jim Plunkett taking snaps, the discovery of tight end Todd Christensen, and Heisman Trophy winner Marcus Allen, who brought legions of his USC fans with him to the Coliseum to see the 8–1 Raiders. The Chargers likewise relied on offensive firepower provided by quarterback Dan Fouts and his incomparable collection of targets, tight end Kellen Winslow and wideouts Charlie Joiner and Wes Chandler. Missing from both teams were defenses to match, but in the season's confusion, weak defenses weren't crippling.

The defending conference champion Bengals might have had the best balance. Quarterback Ken Anderson completed a record 70.6 percent of his passes to go along with the power running of Pete Johnson. The Jets might not have had the benefit of a fully-functioning New York Sack Exchange—Joe Klecko missed much of the season with a knee injury—but New York could move the ball with Richard Todd excelling at quarterback and running back Freeman McNeil's sophomore season explosion as the NFL's rushing leader.

The Dolphins relied less on their Woodstrock combination at quarterback—the fleet David Woodley combined with strong-armed veteran Don Strock—but Don Shula settled on a ball-control offense to give him leads, and a tremendous defensive backfield to hold them. One lead the Dolphins never got was on December 12. In the closing minutes of a snowstorm at Foxboro, New England coach Ron Meyer ordered a convict on a work release program to clear the path for John Smith's field goal attempt. Smith's kick iced the Snowplow Game, 3–0.

1983 NFC

TEAM	W-L-T	PCT	POST	PTS	RA	RY	RY/A	RTD	FL	PA	PC	GPY	GPY/A	PTD	PI	PSY	PRAT
Eastern Division																	
Was	**14**-2	**.875**	DCS	**541**-332	**629-349**	2625-**1289**	4.2-3.7	**30-9**	**7-27**	463-570	278-301	3765-4377	8.1-7.7	29-28	11-**34**	251-402	**97.0**-69.6
Dal	12-4	.750	W	479-360	519-410	2117-1499	4.1-3.7	21-12	14-21	554-558	**346**-299	4156-4365	7.5-7.8	31-27	25-27	314-437	85.2-75.3
SL	8-7-1	.531	—	374-428	525-443	2277-1838	4.3-4.1	15-23	27-20	460-519	267-290	3309-3635	7.2-7.0	29-24	21-28	441-**468**	82.4-70.8
Phi	5-11	.313	—	233-322	402-633	1417-2655	3.5-4.2	5-14	18-15	486-**430**	252-**247**	3532-**3048**	7.3-7.1	22-20	18-8	415-256	75.2-87.2
NYG	3-12-1	.219	—	267-347	506-502	1794-1733	3.5-**3.5**	9-10	27-13	**575**-493	284-283	3854-3584	6.7-7.3	12-26	31-23	363-323	55.7-78.4
Central Division																	
Det	9-7	.563	D	347-**286**	513-503	2181-2104	4.3-4.2	18-11	16-15	503-515	263-297	3297-3401	6.6-6.6	19-21	23-22	342-289	66.5-73.5
GB	8-8	.500	—	429-439	439-597	1807-2641	4.1-4.4	15-28	18-12	526-518	311-300	**4688**-4033	**8.9**-7.8	**33**-20	32-19	323-271	84.1-80.4
ChiB	8-8	.500	—	311-301	583-482	**2727**-2000	**4.7**-4.1	14-20	14-17	447-490	255-249	3461-3516	7.7-7.2	21-**15**	22-21	358-384	77.0-**66.7**
Min	8-8	.500	—	316-348	470-579	1808-2584	3.8-4.5	17-16	10-23	555-478	310-263	3514-3229	6.3-6.8	15-23	22-25	303-326	67.5-70.3
TB	2-14	.125	—	241-380	428-561	1353-2082	3.2-3.7	9-19	13-18	528-490	300-300	3490-3624	6.6-7.4	18-**15**	24-23	366-309	69.4-74.6
Western Division																	
SF	10-6	.625	DC	432-293	511-449	2257-1936	4.4-4.3	17-10	19-18	528-526	339-322	4021-3701	7.6-7.0	27-23	12-24	224-448	94.9-78.0
LARm	9-7	.563	WD	361-344	511-489	2253-1781	4.4-3.6	20-21	24-20	489-556	286-319	3411-3869	7.0-7.0	23-18	23-24	**190**-258	76.0-71.7
NO	8-8	.500	—	319-337	595-472	2461-2000	4.1-4.2	19-11	22-16	425-496	243-271	2782-3128	6.5-**6.3**	14-20	25-23	305-437	63.5-68.0
Atl	7-9	.438	—	370-389	492-499	2224-2309	4.5-4.6	17-20	19-15	507-493	321-313	3793-3734	7.5-7.6	24-28	**10**-15	389-217	93.6-92.8
Aver	16	—	—	349	508	2076	4.1	16	18	502	285	3604	7.2	22	22	330	75.9

TEAM	1D	PENY	PNT	FGM/A	RTNY	RTNTD	OFFY/DEFY	NETY	NETTO	NP	PNP	DELP	PW	DELW	PRT	DR	YPD	DEL
Eastern Division																		
Was	**353**-290	776-710	38.8-41.6	33/**47**-20/28	824-497	4-2	6139-5264	**875**	**43**	**209**	**245**	-36	**13.2**	0.8	**6.6**/ 4.4	211-216	29.1-24.4	**4.7**
Dal	342-**286**	847-873	39.4-41.8	22/27-22/30	928-946	**7**-3	5959-5427	532	9	119	80	39	11.0	1.0	5.1/ 4.9	221-224	27.0-24.2	2.7
SL	296-**286**	770-819	41.5-40.3	15/28-**12/15**	727-692	3-9	5145-5005	140	0	-54	12	-66	6.7	**1.9**	4.3/ 3.7	**224**-225	23.0-**22.2**	0.7
Phi	253-310	**637**-755	40.9-**37.8**	15/26-28/37	338-666	0-**0**	4534-5447	-913	-13	-89	-128	39	5.8	-0.8	4.7/ 5.6	191-191	23.7-28.5	-4.8
NYG	296-289	1020-927	39.8-39.2	**35**/42-22/32	587-719	2-4	5285-4994	291	-22	-80	-64	-16	6.0	-2.5	3.6/ 4.6	**224**-225	23.6-**22.2**	1.4
Central Division																		
Det	315-324	988-**1062**	40.4-40.1	25/32-18/26	707-543	1-1	5136-5216	-80	-2	61	-15	76	9.5	-0.5	3.9/ 4.2	194-198	26.5-26.3	0.1
GB	340-366	648-965	41.0-39.1	21/26-19/29	556-721	4-7	**6172**-6403	-231	-19	-10	-95	**85**	7.8	0.3	5.7/ 5.6	209-215	29.5-29.8	-0.3
ChiB	308-**286**	869-687	36.2-38.6	14/25-17/23	662-613	4-1	5830-5132	698	2	10	66	-56	8.3	-0.3	4.6/ 4.3	212-210	27.5-24.4	3.1
Min	303-318	748-759	41.5-39.3	25/33-18/27	378-605	2-3	5019-5487	-468	16	-32	25	-57	7.2	0.8	4.0/ 3.8	212-207	23.7-26.5	-2.8
TB	249-320	832-799	**41.8**-40.7	10/24-28/34	666-919	4-8	4477-5397	-920	4	-139	-61	-78	4.5	-2.5	3.9/ 4.6	212-206	21.1-26.2	-5.1
Western Division																		
SF	344-302	695-793	38.7-40.4	25/30-17/27	802-446	**7**-2	6054-5189	865	11	139	116	23	11.5	-1.5	6.3/ 4.1	194-194	**31.2**-26.7	4.5
LARm	316-311	748-804	39.8-41.7	11/20-17/28	**1053**-554	4-3	5474-5392	82	-3	17	-5	22	8.4	0.6	4.7/ 4.6	215-214	25.5-25.2	0.3
NO	286-289	802-814	40.7-41.8	18/24-20/34	687-997	5-8	4938-**4691**	247	-8	-18	-11	-7	7.6	0.4	3.2/**3.4**	211-206	23.4-22.8	0.6
Atl	325-342	806-710	39.8-42.0	17/22-17/26	701-**273**	5-1	5628-5826	-198	1	-19	-13	-6	7.5	-0.5	5.7/ 6.0	188-**183**	29.9-31.8	-1.9
Aver	311	847	40.8	20/28	678	4	5350	—	—	—	—	—	—	—	5.0	206	26.0	—

Rushing Attempts	Rushing Yards	Rushing Average	Rushing TDs	Rushing Rank	Passing Yards	Passing Average
E.Dickerson-LARm..390	E.Dickerson-LARm 1808	J.Warren-Was.........5.32	J.Riggins-Was...........24	E.Dickerson-LARm....1988	L.Dickey-GB..........4458	L.Dickey-GB............9.21
J.Riggins-Was..........375	W.Andrews-Atl.......1567	H.Gajan-NO...........5.12	E.Dickerson-LARm....18	W.Andrews-Atl.......1637	D.White-Dal...........3980	J.Theismann-Was...8.09
W.Andrews-Atl.........331	W.Payton-Chi.........1421	G.Ellis-GB..............4.94	T.Brown-Min..............10	J.Riggins-Was........1587	J.Montana-SF........3910	J.Montana-SF.........7.59
W.Payton-Chi...........314	J.Riggins-Was........1347	W.Tyler-SF.............4.86	W.Wilson-NO..............9	W.Payton-Chi.........1481	J.Theismann-Was..3714	D.White-Dal...........7.47
O.Anderson-SL........296	T.Dorsett-Dal.........1321	W.Andrews-Atl........4.73		T.Dorsett-Dal.........1401	R.Jaworski-Phi.......3315	N.Lomax-SL...........7.45
Completion Percent	**TD Passes**	**TD Percent**	**INT Percent**	**Passer Rating**	**Passing Rank**	**Receptions**
J.Montana-SF.........64.5	L.Dickey-GB..............32	N.Lomax-SL.............6.8	D.Barnett-Atl............1.2	D.Barnett-Atl...........97.6	J.Montana-SF.......1605	R.Green-SL..............78
D.Barnett-Atl...........63.4	D.White-Dal...............29	L.Dickey-GB.............6.6	J.Montana-SF...........2.3	J.Theismann-Was...97.0	J.Theismann-Was..1562	E.Gray-NYG..............78
D.White-Dal............62.7	J.Theismann-Was......29	J.Theismann-Was.....6.3	J.Theismann-Was.....2.4	J.Montana-SF.........94.6	D.Barnett-Atl.........1494	C.Brown-Was............78
J.Theismann-Was...60.1	J.Montana-SF............26	D.White-Dal.............5.4	N.Lomax-SL..............3.1	N.Lomax-SL............92.0	L.Dickey-GB..........1229	R.Springs-Dal...........73
L.Dickey-GB............59.7	N.Lomax-SL..............24	D.Barnett-Atl............5.1	S.Dils-Min................3.6	L.Dickey-GB............87.3	D.White-Dal..........1215	D.Clark-SF...............70
Receiving Yards	**Receiving Average**	**Receiving TDs**	**Receiving Rank**	**Combined Net Yards**	**Total TDs**	**Total Points**
M.Quick-Phi...........1409	J.Lofton-GB..........22.41	R.Green-SL..............14	M.Quick-Phi............770	E.Dickerson-LARm....2212	J.Riggins-Was...........24	M.Moseley-Was.......161
J.Lofton-GB...........1300	W.Gault-Chi..........20.90	M.Quick-Phi..............13	J.Lofton-GB............690	W.Andrews-Atl.......2176	E.Dickerson-LARm....20	J.Riggins-Was..........144
R.Green-SL...........1227	M.Quick-Phi..........20.42	P.Coffman-GB...........11	R.Green-SL............684	W.Payton-Chi.........2028	R.Green-SL..............14	C.Hairston-NYG.......127
C.Brown-Was.........1225	L.Thompson-Det...18.34		C.Brown-Was..........653	O.Anderson-SL......1729	M.Quick-Phi..............13	R.Wersching-SF......126
E.Gray-NYG..........1139	K.House-TB..........16.36		E.Gray-NYG............595	D.Nelson-Min.........1705	R.Craig-SF................12	R.Septien-Dal.........123
Punt Average	**Field Goals**	**Field Goal Percent**	**Kickoff Returns**	**Kickoff Return Average**	**Punt Returns**	**Punt Return Average**
F.Garcia-TB............42.2	C.Hairston-NYG.........35	R.Wersching-SF.....83.3	R.Fellows-Dal...........43	D.Nelson-Min..........24.7	B.Johnson-Atl...........46	H.Ellard-LARm........13.6
M.Runager-Phi.......41.7	M.Moseley-Was.........33	C.Hairston-NYG......83.3	H.Huckleby-GB..........41	M.Morton-TB..........23.0	J.Groth-NO................39	D.McLemore-SF.....10.7
B.Scribner-GB........41.6	R.Wersching-SF........25	R.Septien-Dal.........81.5	J.Redwine-Min...........38	M.Nelms-Was.........22.9	M.Nelms-Was............38	B.Johnson-Atl.........10.6
G.Coleman-Min......41.5	B.Ricardo-Min............25	J.Stenerud-GB........80.8	S.Mitchell-SL............36	L.Bright-NYG..........22.6	S.Mitchell-SL............38	K.Jenkins-Det.........10.0
C.Birdsong-SL........41.5	E.Murray-Det.............25	E.Murray-Det..........78.1	M.Nelms-Was............35	J.Redwine-Min........22.1	P.Epps-GB................36	D.McKinnon-Chi........9.3
Punt/Kick Return Yards	**Punt/Kick Return TDs**	**Interceptions**	**Interception Return Yards**	**Interception Return TDs**	**Sacks**	**Overall Rank**
S.Mitchell-SL.........1115	Many............................1	M.Murphy-Was............9	E.Wright-SF............164	E.Wright-SF.................2	F.Dean-SF..............17.5	E.Dickerson-LARm....2200
M.Nelms-Was.........1091		J.Warren-SL................8	J.Poe-NO.................146	K.Johnson-Atl..............2	C.Greer-SL............16.0	W.Andrews-Atl.......1962
R.Fellows-Dal..........930			R.Fellows-Dal..........139	J.Johnson-LARm.........2	E.Johnson-GB........14.5	J.Montana-SF........1909
D.McLemore-SF......907			L.Frazier-Chi............135	D.Hicks-SF..................2	W.Gay-Det.............13.5	J.Theismann-Was..1806
J.Redwine-Min.........838			M.Murphy-Was........127	H.Green-TB.................2		W.Payton-Chi.........1777

Living High on the Hogs

If the strike-shortened 1982 season saw the Redskin–Cowboy rivalry return to its former prominence, the full-length '83 season would be defined by it. Washington lost a squeaker to Dallas, 31–30, in an opening week Monday night matchup. Three months later, tied at 12–2, the Redskins clinched the division with a 31–10 victory in Dallas.

Washington relied on the combination of running backs John Riggins between the tackles and Joe Washington outside them, while the Cowboys had the electricity of Tony Dorsett and Ron Springs. The Redskins had the edge in nimble quarterback Joe Theismann, the protection he received from his immortal offensive line, the Hogs, and an equally dominating defensive line that featured an ageless Dave Butz and three great youngsters: Dexter Manley, Darryl Grant, and rookie Charles Mann. With rookie Darrell Green at corner, the Redskins had a stifling defense to match their overpowering offense. Riggins rushed for a then-record 24 touchdowns, and Mark Moseley, the league's last straight-ahead kicker, scored the most points (161) since Paul Hornung's all-time record of 176 in 1960. The record for successful field goals was also set, but by the Giants' Ali Haji-Sheikh, with 35.

Legend George Halas died on Halloween in Chicago. The Bears beat the team Halas loved to hate, the Packers, in the final week of the season to go 8–8, but the Lions won that same day against the hapless Buccaneers to keep the division title from going to a .500 team. Although the Vikings started out 6–2, a 2–6 swoon drove coach Bud Grant into a brief retirement.

In the Western Division, the 49ers and Rams both returned to the playoff picture, in no small part through revived running games. The Rams relied on Eric Dickerson, who rushed for a rookie-record 1,808 yards, while the 49ers alternated rookie Roger Craig with ex-Ram Wendell Tyler (traded to San Francisco upon Dickerson's arrival). Bill Walsh's club took the title with a three-game win streak, while the Rams nabbed the wild-card slot on the last weekend with a last-second win in New Orleans, denying the luckless Saints their first winning season and playoff appearance.

1983 AFC

TEAM	W-L-T	PCT	POST	PTS	RA	RY	RY/A	RTD	FL	PA	PC	GPY	GPY/A	PTD	PI	PSY	PRAT
Eastern Division																	
Mia	**12**-4	**.750**	D	389-**250**	568-460	2150-2037	3.8-4.4	16-11	16-17	442-480	254-277	3235-3365	7.3-7.0	28-19	**11**-26	**190**-363	**91.2**-70.0
NE	8-8	.500	—	274-289	538-549	2605-2281	**4.8**-4.2	19-**9**	20-19	412-514	220-277	3040-3565	7.4-6.9	16-19	18-17	334-270	72.1-74.4
Buf	8-8	.500	—	283-351	415-566	1736-2503	4.2-4.4	4-14	12-18	571-480	317-286	3438-3553	6.0-7.4	30-22	28-13	351-247	70.5-86.6
Bal	7-9	.438	—	264-354	601-516	**2695**-2118	4.5-4.1	10-13	11-16	377-488	188-281	2663-3832	7.1-7.9	12-31	22-20	340-310	59.4-86.9
NYJ	7-9	.438	—	313-331	474-547	2068-2378	4.4-4.3	11-13	19-14	559-463	330-269	3742-3301	6.7-7.1	21-22	28-22	317-378	70.8-76.2
Central Division																	
Pit	10-6	.625	D	355-303	**614**-509	2610-1833	4.3-3.6	17-14	20-17	409-447	211-**238**	2754-3260	6.7-7.3	15-19	23-28	350-361	61.9-64.9
Cle	9-7	.563	#	356-342	465-528	1922-2065	4.1-3.9	13-15	**10**-10	567-469	324-280	3932-3316	6.9-7.1	27-22	28-22	271-239	73.9-77.4
Cin	7-9	.438	—	346-302	542-**430**	2104-**1499**	3.9-**3.5**	**24**-16	15-16	454-502	290-288	3492-3163	7.7-**6.3**	14-**17**	18-23	309-335	81.1-68.3
Hou	2-14	.125	—	288-460	502-576	1998-2787	4.0-4.8	16-23	18-15	482-**424**	260-252	3286-**3095**	6.8-7.3	16-26	29-14	384-250	61.4-88.7
Western Division																	
LARd	**12**-4	**.750**	DCS*	**442**-338	542-436	2240-1586	4.1-3.6	18-13	25-16	504-531	301-282	3910-3646	**7.8**-6.9	**31**-20	24-20	464-**484**	84.8-71.8
Sea	9-7	.563	#WDC	403-397	546-511	2119-2198	3.9-4.3	19-14	20-**28**	449-521	251-311	3316-4182	7.4-8.0	25-33	18-26	343-351	81.3-85.6
Den	9-7	.563	#W	302-327	471-509	1784-1938	3.8-3.8	15-14	19-20	499-552	254-307	3466-3988	6.9-7.2	17-18	22-27	439-317	66.4-69.0
SD	6-10	.375	—	358-462	423-552	1536-2173	3.6-3.9	16-26	22-17	635-544	**369**-330	**4891**-4051	7.7-7.4	27-28	33-16	230-269	75.1-88.6
KC	6-10	.375	—	386-367	387-554	1254-2275	3.2-4.1	13-18	19-21	**641**-500	**369**-261	4684-3361	7.3-6.7	29-21	19-**30**	343-250	83.2-**62.6**
Aver	16	—	—	349	508	2076	4.1	16	18	502	285	3604	7.2	22	22	330	75.9

TEAM	1D	PENY	PNT	FGM/A	RTNY	RTNTD	OFFY/DEFY	NETY	NETTO	NP	PNP	DELP	PW	DELW	PRT	DR	YPD	DEL
Eastern Division																		
Mia	314-288	**567**-837	42.5-40.8	18/27-**9/15**	**926-432**	4-2	5195-5039	156	**16**	**139**	77	62	**11.5**	0.5	**6.1**/ 3.8	197-193	26.4-26.1	0.3
NE	284-326	815-674	44.6-42.0	9/22-24/31	601-753	1-3	5311-5576	-265	-2	-15	-30	15	7.6	0.4	4.5/ 4.9	191-194	27.8-28.7	-0.9
Buf	309-332	1094-**1298**	39.7-42.9	11/26-26/39	395-733	2-3	4823-5809	-986	-9	-68	-118	50	6.3	**1.7**	3.5/ 5.7	203-207	23.8-28.1	-4.3
Bal	272-321	986-666	**45.3**-41.6	**30/35**-14/23	608-759	3-**1**	5018-5640	-622	3	-90	-40	-50	5.8	1.3	3.4/ 5.5	201-199	25.0-28.3	-3.4
NYJ	313-298	1059-784	39.2-41.1	16/24-20/28	762-739	6-4	5493-5301	192	-11	-18	-28	10	7.6	-0.6	3.9/ 4.2	204-208	26.9-25.5	1.4
Central Division																		
Pit	312-278	836-782	41.9-41.1	27/31-15/20	856-670	**7**-4	5014-4732	282	2	52	32	20	9.3	0.7	3.3/ 3.7	207-209	24.2-22.6	1.6
Cle	327-309	991-940	40.8-40.5	22/25-16/22	606-817	2-5	5583-5142	441	-6	14	13	1	8.4	0.6	4.5/ 4.6	185-190	30.2-27.1	3.1
Cin	327-**276**	837-871	40.6-42.3	16/23-17/22	779-608	5-3	5287-**4327**	**960**	6	44	**104**	-60	9.1	-2.1	5.1/**3.6**	189-**184**	28.0-23.5	4.5
Hou	295-332	784-825	39.2-**39.5**	17/21-29/36	294-746	2-5	4900-5632	-732	-18	-172	-133	-39	3.7	-1.7	3.3/ 5.4	199-198	24.6-28.4	-3.8
Western Division																		
LARd	356-285	992-947	42.8-40.6	21/27-19/25	904-715	5-7	5686-4748	938	-13	104	26	**78**	10.6	1.4	4.8/ 4.2	219-225	26.0-**21.1**	**4.9**
Sea	300-351	890-725	39.5-40.5	18/25-20/26	729-464	6-**1**	5092-6029	-937	**16**	6	-14	20	8.1	0.9	4.9/ 5.3	212-211	24.0-28.6	-4.6
Den	292-321	804-1097	41.6-44.2	21/25-25/33	775-805	2-4	4811-5609	-798	6	-25	-43	18	7.4	1.6	4.0/ 4.5	210-204	22.9-27.5	-4.6
SD	**361**-347	961-953	43.9-39.7	15/24-22/29	366-676	2-3	**6197**-5955	242	-22	-104	-68	-36	5.4	0.6	5.2/ 5.8	204-203	**30.4**-29.3	1.0
KC	314-319	911-837	39.9-41.2	24/30-20/26	773-882	3-5	5595-5386	209	13	19	69	-50	8.5	-2.5	5.5/ 3.7	**222**-222	25.2-24.3	0.9
Aver	311	847	40.8	20/28	678	2	5350	—	—	—	—	—	—	—	5.0	102	26.0	—

Rushing Attempts	Rushing Yards	Rushing Average	Rushing TDs	Rushing Rank	Passing Yards	Passing Average
C.Warner-Sea 335	C.Warner-Sea 1449	M.Tatupu-NE 5.45	P.Johnson-Cin 14	C.Warner-Sea 1579	B.Kenney-KC 4348	D.Krieg-Sea 8.80
E.Campbell-Hou 322	E.Campbell-Hou 1301	T.Collins-NE 4.79	C.Warner-Sea 13	E.Campbell-Hou 1421	B.Sipe-Cle 3566	D.Fouts-SD 8.75
M.Pruitt-Cle 293	M.Pruitt-Cle 1184	F.Hawkins-LARd 4.78	C.Muncie-SD 12	M.Pruitt-Cle 1284	R.Todd-NYJ 3478	S.Grogan-NE 7.96
F.Harris-Pit 279	J.Cribbs-Buf 1131	B.Green-Cle 4.78	E.Campbell-Hou 12	C.Dickey-Bal 1162	J.Ferguson-Buf 2995	K.Anderson-Cin 7.86
M.Allen-LARd 266	C.Dickey-Bal 1122	R.Odoms-Mia 4.61		J.Cribbs-Buf 1161	D.Fouts-SD 2975	J.Plunkett-LARd 7.74
Completion Percent	**TD Passes**	**TD Percent**	**INT Percent**	**Passer Rating**	**Passing Rank**	**Receptions**
K.Anderson-Cin 66.7	B.Sipe-Cle 26	D.Krieg-Sea 7.4	D.Marino-Mia 2.0	D.Marino-Mia 96.0	B.Kenney-KC 1574	D.Cherry-LARd 92
D.Fouts-SD 63.2	J.Ferguson-Buf 26	D.Marino-Mia 6.8	B.Kenney-KC 3.0	D.Krieg-Sea 95.0	B.Sipe-Cle 993	O.Newsome-Cle 89
J.Plunkett-LARd 60.7	B.Kenney-KC 24	D.Fouts-SD 5.9	S.DeBerg-Den 3.3	D.Fouts-SD 92.5	D.Fouts-SD 988	K.Winslow-SD 88
D.Krieg-Sea 60.5		J.Plunkett-LARd 5.3	J.Zorn-Sea 3.4	K.Anderson-Cin 85.6	D.Marino-Mia 965	T.Smith-Hou 83
R.Todd-NYJ 59.5		B.Sipe-Cle 5.2	S.Grogan-NE 4.0	J.Plunkett-LARd 82.7	J.Plunkett-LARd 848	C.Carson-KC 80
Receiving Yards	**Receiving Average**	**Receiving TDs**	**Receiving Rank**	**Combined Net Yards**	**Total TDs**	**Total Points**
C.Carson-KC 1351	M.Duper-Mia 19.67	D.Cherry-LARd 12	C.Carson-KC 711	C.Warner-Sea 1774	C.Warner-Sea 14	G.Anderson-Pit 119
D.Cherry-LARd 1247	S.Watson-Den 19.20	S.Largent-Sea 11	D.Cherry-LARd 684	J.Cribbs-Buf 1655	P.Johnson-Cin 14	N.Lowery-KC 116
T.Smith-Hou 1176	C.Branch-LARd 17.85	M.Duper-Mia 10	K.Winslow-SD 626	C.Dickey-Bal 1605	C.Muncie-SD 13	C.Bahr-LARd 114
K.Winslow-SD 1172	Collinsworth-Cin 17.12	K.Winslow-SD 8	T.Smith-Hou 618	M.Allen-LARd 1604		R.Allegre-Bal 112
S.Watson-Den 1133	L.Jones-NYJ 17.07		S.Largent-Sea 592	E.Campbell-Hou 1517		N.Johnson-Sea 103
Punt Average	**Field Goals**	**Field Goal Percent**	**Kickoff Returns**	**Kickoff Return Average**	**Punt Returns**	**Punt Return Average**
R.Stark-Bal 45.3	R.Allegre-Bal 30	M.Bahr-Cle 87.5	Z.Dixon-Sea 49	F.Walker-Mia 26.7	G.Pruitt-LARd 58	K.Springs-NYJ 12.5
R.Camarillo-NE 44.6	G.Anderson-Pit 27	G.Anderson-Pit 87.1	R.Smith-NE 42	S.Brown-Hou 25.6	P.Skansi-Pit 43	G.Pruitt-LARd 11.5
M.Buford-SD 43.9	N.Lowery-KC 24	R.Allegre-Bal 85.7	H.Odom-Pit 39	K.Williams-Bal 24.5	R.Riddick-Buf 42	P.Johns-Sea 11.3
R.Roby-Mia 43.1		R.Karlis-Den 84.0	F.Walker-Mia 36	Z.Dixon-Sea 23.4	M.Clayton-Mia 41	Z.Thomas-Den 11.2
R.Guy-LARd 42.8		F.Kempf-Hou 81.0	C.Roaches-Hou 34	K.Springs-NYJ 22.8	D.Hall-Cle 39	R.Smith-NE 10.5
Punt/Kick Return Yards	**Punt/Kick Return TDs**	**Interceptions**	**Interception Return Yards**	**Interception Return TDs**	**Sacks**	**Overall Rank**
R.Smith-NE 1314	Many 1	K.Riley-Cin 8	M.Harden-Den 127	K.Riley-Cin 2	M.Gastineau-NYJ 19.0	C.Warner-Sea 1747
G.Pruitt-LARd 1270		V.McElroy-LARd 8	R.Horton-Cin 121	R.Martin-LARd 2	J.Green-Sea 16.0	B.Kenney-KC 1663
Z.Dixon-Sea 1148			D.Roquemore-KC 117	M.Kozlowski-Mia 2	D.Betters-Mia 16.0	E.Campbell-Hou 1529
F.Walker-Mia 1048			J.Holmes-NYJ 107		K.Willis-Pit 14.0	M.Allen-LARd 1480
Z.Thomas-Den 941			K.Easley-Sea 106			J.Cribbs-Buf 1460

Hope and Heroes

The preseason opened with misfortune. Chiefs running back Joe Delaney, 24, drowned while attempting to save three boys; one was rescued but Delaney and the other two were not. President Ronald Reagan posthumously awarded Delaney the Presidential Citizens Medal.

Hope for the future came in the form of one of the most heralded draft classes of all time, with six quarterbacks selected in the first round. Even there, expectations went amiss from the start. Buffalo's pick, Jim Kelly, elected to sign with the Houston Gamblers of the USFL. Kelly would not be the only defector to the new league—stars like running back Joe Cribbs and quarterback Brian Sipe were also outward bound. Of the other five new QBs, most struggled or watched, including first overall choice John Elway, who refused to go to the moribund Colts and forced a trade to Denver. The last of the half-dozen selected, Dan Marino, made an immediate impact on the defending conference champion Dolphins. Don Shula finally lost confidence in the Woodstrock quarterback tandem and turned to the rookie in the sixth week. Miami went on a 9–2 run that won the AFC East.

The Central Division was marked by confusion. The Bengals struggled with drug suspensions and USFL defections. In their stead, a veteran Steelers squad rose to the occasion one more time. Despite the absence of Terry Bradshaw for all but a single half in his final season, the Steelers took the division by outmuscling and overpowering opponents through heavy doses of rushing and defense.

The Raiders were especially strong in the West. The season was already off on the right foot after trading for Patriots Pro Bowl corner Mike Haynes to complement Lester Hayes. The defense was impregnable now with youngsters Matt Millen and Howie Long alongside veteran greats Rod Martin, Lyle Alzado, and Ted Hendricks. Behind the Raiders, a rebuilt Seahawks squad made its first playoff appearance. Chuck Knox's club relied on youngsters like ballhawking safety Ken Easley and rookie running back Curt Warner. Canny veteran lineman pickups like guard Reggie McKenzie and center Blair Bush gave new starting quarterback Dave Krieg plenty of time to throw.

1984 NFC

TEAM	W-L-T	PCT	POST	PTS	RA	RY	RY/A	RTD	FL	PA	PC	GPY	GPY/A	PTD	PI	PSY	PRAT
Eastern Division																	
Was	11-5	.688	D	426-310	588-390	2274-1589	3.9-4.1	20-13	15-**22**	485-575	286-318	3417-4301	7.0-7.5	24-25	13-21	341-529	85.9-78.6
NYG	9-7	.563	#WD	299-301	493-474	1660-1818	3.4-3.8	12-10	9-16	535-529	288-288	4066-3736	7.6-7.1	22-20	18-19	434-361	78.3-74.5
SL	9-7	.563	#	423-345	488-442	2088-1923	4.3-4.4	21-11	20-12	566-494	**347**-251	**4634**-3574	**8.2**-7.2	28-26	16-21	377-403	92.0-74.4
Dal	9-7	.563	#	308-308	469-510	1714-2226	3.7-4.4	12-**8**	17-16	604-527	322-250	3995-3200	6.6-**6.1**	19-23	26-**28**	389-390	66.6-**59.3**
Phi	6-9-1	.406	—	278-320	381-556	1338-2189	3.5-3.9	6-12	16-11	**606**-492	331-262	3823-3506	6.3-7.1	19-22	17-20	463-456	72.6-74.1
Central Division																	
ChiB	10-6	.625	DC	325-248	**674-378**	**2974-1377**	4.4-3.6	**22**-10	16-13	390-435	226-**198**	2695-3069	6.9-7.1	14-**14**	15-21	232-**583**	75.1-60.0
GB	8-8	.500	—	390-309	461-545	2019-2145	4.4-3.9	18-14	**7**-15	506-551	281-315	3740-3470	7.4-6.3	30-16	30-27	310-324	74.2-65.2
TB	6-10	.375	—	335-380	483-511	1776-2233	3.7-4.4	17-27	20-14	563-490	334-286	3907-3480	6.9-7.1	22-20	23-18	362-239	76.4-78.6
Det	4-11-1	.281	—	283-408	446-519	2017-1808	4.5-**3.5**	13-17	14-11	531-466	298-288	3787-3782	7.1-8.1	19-27	22-14	486-271	73.2-94.2
Min	3-13	.188	—	276-484	444-547	1844-2573	4.2-4.7	10-20	16-18	533-490	281-319	3337-3954	6.3-8.1	18-35	25-11	465-175	63.8-104.4
Western Division																	
SF	**15**-1	**.938**	DCS*	**475-227**	534-432	2465-1795	4.6-4.2	21-10	12-13	496-546	312-298	4079-3744	**8.2**-6.9	**32-14**	**10**-25	**178**-363	**101.9**-65.6
LARm	10-6	.625	W	346-316	541-449	2864-1600	**5.3**-3.6	16-15	18-**22**	358-566	176-346	2382-3964	6.7-7.0	16-18	17-17	240-298	65.9-80.3
NO	7-9	.438	—	298-361	523-549	2171-2461	4.2-4.5	9-13	13-10	476-**422**	246-239	3198-**2873**	6.7-6.8	21-23	28-13	361-420	63.3-83.0
Atl	4-12	.250	—	281-382	489-538	1994-2153	4.1-4.0	16-16	21-20	478-443	294-262	3546-3413	7.4-7.7	14-27	20-12	496-287	76.6-92.5
Aver	16	—	—	339	493	1982	4.0	15	15	512	288	3651	7.1	22	21	357	76.1

TEAM	1D	PENY	PNT	FGM/A	RTNY	RTNTD	OFFY/DEFY	NETY	NETTO	NP	PNP	DELP	PW	DELW	PRT	DR	YPD	DEL
Eastern Division																		
Was	339-307	723-803	38.8-39.9	24/31-**13/20**	865-346	**7**-1	5350-5361	-11	15	116	59	57	10.9	0.1	5.1/ 4.8	196-199	27.3-26.9	0.4
NYG	310-296	703-699	38.3-40.0	17/33-17/26	550-701	2-5	5292-5193	99	8	-2	40	-42	7.9	1.0	5.2/ 4.7	204-209	25.9-24.8	1.1
SL	345-292	904-578	38.1-**39.0**	23/35-25/38	562-458	2-2	6345-5094	1251	-3	78	92	-14	9.9	-1.0	6.2/ 4.5	207-206	30.7-24.7	5.9
Dal	323-283	947-868	38.2-42.8	23/29-19/28	743-602	3-5	5320-5036	284	1	0	28	-28	8.0	1.0	4.0/**3.0**	**224**-230	23.8-21.9	1.9
Phi	280-307	**632**-904	42.2-39.3	**30/37**-22/35	537-697	2-2	4698-5239	-541	-2	-42	-53	11	6.9	-0.5	4.2/ 4.3	207-206	22.7-25.4	-2.7
Central Division																		
ChiB	297-**216**	851-698	39.2-41.6	22/28-16/22	848-490	1-5	5437-**3863**	**1574**	3	77	143	-66	9.9	0.1	4.5/ 3.3	202-197	26.9-**19.6**	7.3
GB	315-323	915-**1129**	42.3-40.9	12/21-24/31	689-685	3-4	5449-5291	158	5	81	33	48	10.0	-2.0	4.3/ 3.5	212-210	25.7-25.2	0.5
TB	344-311	875-1078	41.9-41.0	19/26-18/27	515-559	1-**0**	5321-5474	-153	-11	-45	-57	12	6.9	-0.9	4.5/ 5.0	189-193	28.2-28.4	-0.2
Det	306-328	1165-978	41.6-40.0	20/27-24/29	328-767	0-4	5318-5319	-1	-11	-125	-44	-81	4.9	-0.4	4.2/ 6.3	191-186	27.8-28.6	-0.8
Min	289-342	762-1047	42.4-40.8	20/23-24/28	337-779	3-4	4716-6352	-1636	-12	-208	-184	-24	2.8	0.2	3.2/ 7.1	200-193	23.6-32.9	-9.3
Western Division																		
SF	**356**-302	884-723	40.9-40.5	25/35-19/25	866-**345**	4-**0**	**6366**-5176	1190	**16**	**248**	**163**	**85**	**14.2**	0.8	**7.2**/ 4.0	184-193	**34.6**-26.8	**7.8**
LARm	258-309	830-871	38.7-41.5	25/33-22/31	**888**-436	6-3	5006-5266	-260	4	30	-6	36	8.8	**1.3**	3.9/ 5.1	196-197	25.5-26.7	-1.2
NO	298-298	849-1025	**43.1**-41.6	20/27-24/33	481-970	4-5	5008-4914	94	-18	-63	-64	1	6.4	0.6	3.4/ 4.4	197-189	25.4-26.0	-0.6
Atl	292-317	1011-820	40.8-41.6	20/27-16/30	411-754	1-5	5044-5279	-235	-9	-101	-56	-45	5.5	-1.5	4.2/ 5.9	188-**185**	26.8-28.5	-1.7
Aver	309	859	41.0	20/28	676	3	5276	—	—	—	—	—	—	—	5.0	201	26.2	—

Rushing Attempts	Rushing Yards	Rushing Average	Rushing TDs	Rushing Rank	Passing Yards	Passing Average
J.Wilder-TB...407	E.Dickerson-LARm 2105	H.Gajan-NO...6.03	J.Riggins-Was...14	E.Dickerson-LARm...2245	N.Lomax-SL...4614	J.Montana-SF...8.40
W.Payton-Chi...381	W.Payton-Chi...1684	E.Ivery-GB...5.58	E.Dickerson-LARm...14	W.Payton-Chi...1794	P.Simms-NYG...4044	N.Lomax-SL...8.24
E.Dickerson-LARm..379	J.Wilder-TB...1544	E.Dickerson-LARm..5.55	J.Wilder-TB...13	J.Wilder-TB...1674	J.Montana-SF...3630	M.Barber-Atl...8.02
G.Riggs-Atl...353	G.Riggs-Atl...1486	S.Mitchell-SL...5.36	G.Riggs-Atl...13	G.Riggs-Atl...1616	S.DeBerg-TB...3554	L.Dickey-GB...7.97
J.Riggins-Was...327	W.Tyler-SF...1262	B.Sims-Det...5.28	W.Payton-Chi...11	J.Riggins-Was...1379	J.Theismann-Was..3391	P.Simms-NYG...7.59

Completion Percent	TD Passes	TD Percent	INT Percent	Passer Rating	Passing Rank	Receptions
M.Barber-Atl...67.3	J.Montana-SF...28	J.Montana-SF...6.5	J.Pisarcik-Phi...1.7	J.Montana-SF...102.9	N.Lomax-SL...1807	A.Monk-Was...106
J.Montana-SF...64.6	N.Lomax-SL...28	L.Dickey-GB...6.2	J.Montana-SF...2.3	N.Lomax-SL...92.5	J.Montana-SF...1555	J.Wilder-TB...85
N.Lomax-SL...61.6	L.Dickey-GB...25	J.Theismann-Was...5.0	J.Kemp-LARm...2.5	M.Barber-Atl...89.7	P.Simms-NYG...1412	R.Green-SL...78
G.Danielson-Det...61.5	J.Theismann-Was...24	N.Lomax-SL...5.0	J.Theismann-Was...2.7	J.Theismann-Was...86.6	J.Theismann-Was..1296	J.Jones-Det...77
S.DeBerg-TB...60.5	P.Simms-NYG...22	D.White-Dal...4.7	N.Lomax-SL...2.9	L.Dickey-GB...85.6	S.DeBerg-TB...1152	K.House-TB...76

Receiving Yards	Receiving Average	Receiving TDs	Receiving Rank	Combined Net Yards	Total TDs	Total Points
R.Green-SL...1555	J.Lofton-GB...21.95	R.Green-SL...12	R.Green-SL...838	E.Dickerson-LARm 2259	J.Riggins-Was...14	R.Wersching-SF...131
A.Monk-Was...1372	M.Nichols-Det...21.88	F.Solomon-SF...10	A.Monk-Was...721	J.Wilder-TB...2229	E.Dickerson-LARm...14	M.Moseley-Was...120
J.Lofton-GB...1361	R.Green-SL...19.94	M.Quick-Phi...9	J.Lofton-GB...716	W.Payton-Chi...2052	J.Wilder-TB...13	N.Noga-SL...117
S.Bailey-Atl...1138	L.Manuel-NYG...18.76	P.Coffman-GB...9	S.Bailey-Atl...599	S.Mitchell-SL...1889	G.Riggs-Atl...13	P.McFadden-Phi...116
M.Quick-Phi...1052	F.Solomon-SF...18.42		M.Quick-Phi...571	O.Anderson-SL...1785	R.Green-SL...12	M.Lansford-LARm...112

Punt Average	Field Goals	Field Goal Percent	Kickoff Returns	Kickoff Return Average	Punt Returns	Punt Return Average
B.Hansen-NO...43.8	P.McFadden-Phi...30	J.Stenerud-Min...87.0	M.Nelms-Was...42	S.Stamps-Atl...23.8	J.Fisher-Chi...57	H.Ellard-LARm...13.4
G.Coleman-Min...42.4	R.Wersching-SF...25	P.McFadden-Phi...81.1	D.Rodgers-GB...39	B.Redden-LARm...23.0	G.Allen-Dal...54	D.McLemore-SF...11.6
B.Scribner-GB...42.3	M.Lansford-LARm...25	R.Septien-Dal...79.3	D.Nelson-Min...39	S.Mitchell-SL...23.0	M.Nelms-Was...49	S.Mitchell-SL...8.8
M.Horan-Phi...42.2	M.Moseley-Was...24	B.Thomas-Chi...78.6	M.Morton-TB...38	D.Nelson-Min...22.8	P.McConkey-NYG...46	J.Fields-NO...8.7
D.Gentry-Atl...42.0		M.Moseley-Was...77.4	S.Mitchell-SL...35	T.Anthony-NO...22.3	D.McLemore-SF...45	M.Nelms-Was...8.7

Punt/Kick Return Yards	Punt/Kick Return TDs	Interceptions	Interception Return Yards	Interception Return TDs	Sacks	Overall Rank
M.Nelms-Was...1288	H.Ellard-LARm...2	T.Flynn-GB...9	L.Irvin-LARm...166	D.Winston-NO...2	R.Dent-Chi...17.5	E.Dickerson-LARm 2275
S.Mitchell-SL...1137	A.Waters-Phi...1		T.Lewis-GB...151	L.Irvin-LARm...2	G.Brown-Phi...16.0	J.Wilder-TB...2030
G.Allen-Dal...1112	D.Rodgers-GB...1		M.Downs-Dal...126	V.Dean-Was...2	C.Greer-SL...14.0	N.Lomax-SL...2021
D.Nelson-Min...1071	D.McLemore-SF...1		M.Cotney-TB...123		D.Manley-Was...13.5	W.Payton-Chi...1972
P.McConkey-NYG...847	M.Guman-LARm...1		R.Ellis-Phi...119		R.White-Dal...12.5	G.Riggs-Atl...1755

Niners Are First to Unearth 15 Wins

San Francisco bashed the NFC into submission. Between an offensive line that gelled under the direction of legendary assistant Bobb McKittrick and a defense armed with unprecedented depth, the 49ers averaged twice as many points as they allowed. Joe Montana, enjoying his best season yet, was the perfect interpreter of head coach Bill Walsh's offensive scheme. San Francisco became the first 15-win team in NFL history, losing only to the Steelers in week seven.

The Rams had to settle for a wild card and continued improvement under John Robinson. His famous reliance on the running game as head coach at USC found its professional expression in Eric Dickerson's 2,105 yards, the NFL's new mark for a season. Rams Jack and Jim Youngblood weren't related, but they called it quits after 12 seasons together heading the Rams defense.

In the East, Washington proved it had plenty left in the tank. The Skins pulverized opponents with the inside running of John Riggins while Joe Theismann hit wideout Art Monk for a league-record 106 receptions. Second-year Giants coach Bill Parcells relied on brilliant defensive play, particularly from linebackers Lawrence Taylor and Harry Carson. Parcells also stabilized the offense when he ended a long quarterback controversy by choosing Phil Simms and sticking with him. Division rivals New York, Dallas, and St. Louis all finished 9–7, but the Giants won out because the Cardinals missed a field goal on their final play of the season and the Cowboys lost on Monday night.

A new power arose on the Midway. Mike Ditka's Bears started taking shape around a ferocious 46 defense designed by defensive coordinator Buddy Ryan, balanced against a ball-control offense that relied, as ever, on Walter Payton. Dreams of glory beyond a division title faded behind a rash of injuries at quarterback, forcing Greg Landry to start the final game of his long career and backup Steve Fuller to become a playoff quarterback. With defensive stars like Dan Hampton, Mike Singletary, Otis Wilson, Richard Dent, and Gary Fencik terrorizing opponents, the Bears allowed almost 1,000 fewer yards than any other team. If Chicago could build a reliable offense, greatness was in the offing.

1984 AFC

TEAM	W-L-T	PCT	POST	PTS	RA	RY	RY/A	RTD	FL	PA	PC	GPY	GPY/A	PTD	PI	PSY	PRAT
Eastern Division																	
Mia	**14**-2	**.875**	DCS	**513**-298	484-458	1918-2155	4.0-4.7	18-16	**10**-12	572-551	367-310	**5146**-3604	**9.0**-6.5	**49**-22	18-24	**128**-339	**108.5**-71.4
NE	9-7	.563	—	362-352	482-498	2032-1886	4.2-3.8	15-11	15-8	500-513	292-283	3685-3666	7.4-7.1	26-25	**14**-17	454-452	87.1-80.3
NYJ	7-9	.438	—	332-364	504-497	**2189**-2064	**4.3**-4.2	17-16	13-18	488-511	272-312	3341-3862	6.8-7.6	20-24	21-15	382-360	72.8-87.9
Ind	4-12	.250	—	239-414	510-559	2025-2007	4.0-**3.6**	13-16	16-13	411-515	206-298	2543-3890	6.2-7.6	13-31	22-18	436-320	57.9-87.3
Buf	2-14	.125	—	250-454	398-531	1643-2106	4.1-4.0	9-19	14-21	588-495	298-300	3252-3667	5.5-7.4	18-32	30-16	554-191	56.3-91.5
Central Division																	
Pit	9-7	.563	DC	387-310	**574**-454	2179-**1617**	3.8-**3.6**	13-12	15-11	443-515	240-299	3519-3689	7.9-7.2	25-19	25-31	278-390	75.6-67.5
Cin	8-8	.500	—	339-339	540-477	2179-1868	4.0-3.9	18-21	17-15	496-517	306-302	3659-3689	7.4-7.1	17-**15**	22-25	358-298	77.2-70.0
Cle	5-11	.313	—	250-297	489-494	1696-1945	3.5-3.9	10-**10**	16-15	495-458	273-261	3490-**3049**	7.1-6.7	14-**15**	23-20	358-353	67.5-70.0
Hou	3-13	.188	—	240-437	433-596	1656-2789	3.8-4.7	13-27	16-11	487-**447**	282-271	3610-3446	7.4-7.7	14-23	15-13	382-267	78.0-89.8
Western Division																	
Den	13-3	.813	D	353-**241**	508-**435**	2076-1664	4.1-3.8	12-**10**	17-24	475-631	263-346	3116-4453	6.6-7.1	22-16	17-31	257-430	76.1-65.2
Sea	12-4	.750	WD	418-282	495-475	1645-1789	3.3-3.8	10-11	13-**25**	497-521	283-265	3751-3572	7.5-6.9	32-18	26-**38**	328-398	80.6-**54.2**
LARd	11-5	.688	W	368-278	516-517	1886-1892	3.7-3.7	**19**-12	20-14	491-508	266-**254**	3718-3268	7.6-**6.4**	21-19	28-20	360-**516**	69.3-66.6
KC	8-8	.500	—	314-324	408-523	1527-1980	3.7-3.8	12-**10**	15-11	593-586	305-332	3869-4009	6.5-6.8	21-19	22-30	301-364	68.5-67.3
SD	7-9	.438	—	394-413	456-457	1654-1851	3.6-4.1	18-23	17-17	**662**-531	**401**-323	4928-4303	7.4-8.1	25-27	21-19	285-218	82.9-88.6
Aver	16	—	—	339	493	1982	4.0	15	15	512	288	3651	7.1	22	21	357	76.1

TEAM	1D	PENY	PNT	FGM/A	RTNY	RTNTD	OFFY/DEFY	NETY	NETTO	NP	PNP	DELP	PW	DELW	PRT	DR	YPD	DEL
Eastern Division																		
Mia	**387**-314	**527**-772	44.7-41.9	9/19-**9/17**	843-515	3-1	**6936**-5420	**1516**	8	**215**	**158**	57	**13.4**	0.6	**8.0**/ 4.1	190-184	**36.5**-29.5	**7.0**
NE	315-311	674-773	42.4-40.3	22/28-21/31	640-679	1-6	5263-5100	163	-4	10	-2	12	8.3	0.8	5.1/ 4.8	198-207	26.6-24.6	1.9
NYJ	310-341	779-723	39.1-42.6	17/24-26/37	476-**449**	3-1	5148-5566	-418	-1	-32	-39	7	7.2	-0.2	4.1/ 5.5	195-189	26.4-29.4	-3.0
Ind	254-343	798-813	44.7-42.0	14/23-21/23	468-1023	2-3	4132-5577	-1445	-7	-175	-148	-27	3.6	0.4	2.7/ 5.5	201-205	20.6-27.2	-6.6
Buf	263-345	997-734	41.1-**39.1**	11/21-20/28	530-1013	4-5	4341-5582	-1241	-7	-204	-131	-73	2.9	-0.9	2.4/ 5.9	209-203	20.8-27.5	-6.7
Central Division																		
Pit	302-282	948-945	41.2-42.4	24/32-22/28	1129-722	7-4	5420-4916	504	2	77	50	27	9.9	-0.9	4.9/ 3.7	211-203	25.7-24.2	1.5
Cin	339-322	693-743	42.3-41.4	22/31-22/27	841-674	4-3	5480-5259	221	1	0	22	-22	8.0	0.0	4.6/ 4.3	190-193	28.8-27.2	1.6
Cle	295-**270**	928-765	42.3-40.6	**25/35**-29/33	558-1007	1-5	4828-**4641**	187	-4	-47	0	-47	6.8	-1.8	4.1/ 3.9	191-191	25.3-24.3	1.0
Hou	284-345	813-876	39.6-42.2	15/19-22/30	291-832	1-3	4884-5968	-1084	-7	-197	-118	-79	3.1	-0.1	5.0/ 5.9	187-**183**	26.1-32.6	-6.5
Western Division																		
Den	299-311	636-891	40.1-41.5	21/28-19/33	828-524	8-**0**	4935-5687	-752	21	112	21	91	10.8	**2.2**	4.5/ 4.1	211-217	23.4-26.2	-2.8
Sea	287-288	1179-883	37.5-40.3	20/24-14/22	**1181**-538	**9**-5	5068-4963	105	**24**	136	105	31	11.4	0.6	4.8/**2.9**	219-226	23.1-22.0	1.2
LARd	301-297	1209-**1061**	41.9-43.3	20/27-17/21	1006-645	4-2	5244-4644	600	-14	90	-6	**96**	10.3	0.8	4.2/ 3.6	**223**-226	23.5-**20.5**	3.0
KC	295-335	801-951	**44.9**-40.0	23/33-19/27	811-1144	2-9	5095-5625	-530	4	-10	-28	18	7.8	0.3	4.5/ 3.9	213-220	23.9-25.6	-1.6
SD	374-322	1023-905	42.0-39.6	20/29-19/25	711-579	5-1	6297-5936	361	-2	-19	22	-41	7.5	-0.5	5.7/ 6.2	201-196	31.3-30.3	1.0
Aver	309	859	41.0	20/28	676	2	5276	—	—	—	—	—	—	—	5.0	101	25.7	—

Rushing Attempts	Rushing Yards	Rushing Average	Rushing TDs	Rushing Rank	Passing Yards	Passing Average
S.Winder-Den..........296	E.Jackson-SD........1179	J.Carter-Mia............4.95	M.Allen-LARd 13	M.Allen-LARd 1298	D.Marino-Mia 5084	D.Marino-Mia 9.01
E.Jackson-SD..........296	M.Allen-LARd 1168	C.James-NE 4.94	L.Kinnebrew-Cin 9	E.Jackson-SD........1259	D.Fouts-SD 3740	M.Malone-Pit 7.86
M.Allen-LARd 275	S.Winder-Den........1153	T.Nathan-Mia 4.73	P.Johnson-Mia 9	S.Winder-Den........1193	D.Krieg-Sea 3671	K.Anderson-Cin 7.66
G.Bell-Buf 262	G.Bell-Buf 1100	F.McNeil-NYJ 4.67	E.Jackson-SD..............8	G.Bell-Buf 1170	P.McDonald-Cle 3472	D.Krieg-Sea 7.65
F.McNeil-NYJ...........229	F.McNeil-NYJ.........1070	R.McMillan-Ind........4.33		F.McNeil-NYJ.........1120	W.Moon-Hou..........3338	M.Wilson-LARd.......7.63

Completion Percent	TD Passes	TD Percent	INT Percent	Passer Rating	Passing Rank	Receptions
D.Marino-Mia 64.2	D.Marino-Mia 48	D.Marino-Mia 8.5	T.Eason-NE 1.9	D.Marino-Mia 108.9	D.Marino-Mia 2102	O.Newsome-Cle 89
K.Anderson-Cin 63.6	D.Krieg-Sea 32	D.Krieg-Sea 6.7	D.Marino-Mia 3.0	T.Eason-NE 93.4	T.Eason-NE 1409	J.Squirek-Pit 80
D.Fouts-SD 62.5	T.Eason-NE 23	M.Malone-Pit 5.9	W.Moon-Hou.............3.1	D.Fouts-SD 83.4	D.Fouts-SD 1285	D.Cherry-LARd 80
T.Eason-NE 60.1	D.Fouts-SD 19	T.Eason-NE 5.3	D.Fouts-SD 3.4	D.Krieg-Sea 83.3	W.Moon-Hou..........1169	S.Largent-Sea 74
W.Moon-Hou...........57.6	J.Elway-Den...............18		K.O'Brien-NYJ 3.4	K.Anderson-Cin 81.0	D.Krieg-Sea 1036	M.Clayton-Mia 73

Receiving Yards	Receiving Average	Receiving TDs	Receiving Rank	Combined Net Yards	Total TDs	Total Points
J.Squirek-Pit 1395	D.Turner-Sea 20.43	M.Clayton-Mia 18	M.Clayton-Mia 785	M.Allen-LARd 1926	M.Clayton-Mia 18	G.Anderson-Pit........117
M.Clayton-Mia 1389	L.Lipps-Pit.............19.11	S.Largent-Sea 12	J.Squirek-Pit 753	L.Lipps-Pit.............1587	M.Allen-LARd 18	N.Johnson-Sea........110
M.Duper-Mia..........1306	M.Clayton-Mia 19.03	J.Squirek-Pit 11	M.Duper-Mia............693	M.Clayton-Mia 1518	S.Largent-Sea 12	T.Franklin-NE...........108
S.Watson-Den 1170	C.Carson-KC 18.91	D.Turner-Sea 10	S.Largent-Sea 642	L.James-SD...........1488	J.Squirek-Pit 11	M.Clayton-Mia 108
S.Largent-Sea 1164	M.Barnwell-LARd..18.91	L.Lipps-Pit....................9	S.Watson-Den 620	S.Winder-Den 1441	L.Lipps-Pit.................11	M.Allen-LARd 108

Punt Average	Field Goals	Field Goal Percent	Kickoff Returns	Kickoff Return Average	Punt Returns	Punt Return Average
J.Arnold-KC 44.9	M.Bahr-Cle 24	N.Johnson-Sea.......83.3	L.James-SD...............43	B.Humphery-NYJ....30.7	G.Pruitt-LARd 53	M.Martin-Cin...........15.7
R.Stark-Ind 44.7	G.Anderson-Pit..........24	T.Franklin-NE..........78.6	V.Williams-Buf............39	D.Williams-LARd.....25.9	L.Lipps-Pit..................53	L.Lipps-Pit...............12.4
R.Roby-Mia.............44.7	N.Lowery-KC 23	R.Karlis-Den 75.0	D.Wilson-Buf..............34	L.Anderson-Ind 23.9	J.Smith-KC 39	K.Easley-Sea...........12.1
S.Cox-Cle 43.4	T.Franklin-NE.............22	M.Bahr-Cle 75.0	P.Smith-Ind 32	K.Springs-NYJ 22.7	I.Fryar-NE 36	G.Willhite-Den 10.0
R.Pratt-NE 42.8	J.Breech-Cin..............22	G.Anderson-Pit.......75.0	C.Roaches-Hou 30	C.Roaches-Hou 22.6	D.Wilson-Buf..............33	I.Fryar-NE 9.6

Punt/Kick Return Yards	Punt/Kick Return TDs	Interceptions	Interception Return Yards	Interception Return TDs	Sacks	Overall Rank
L.James-SD...........1167	Many...........................1	K.Easley-Sea............10	M.Haynes-LARd 220	C.Warner-Pit................2	M.Gastineau-NYJ ...22.0	D.Marino-Mia 2095
D.Wilson-Buf............873		D.Brown-Sea 8	D.Brown-Sea 179	K.Simpson-Sea............2	A.Tippett-NE...........18.5	M.Allen-LARd 1721
C.Roaches-Hou 831		D.Shell-Pit....................7	G.Blackwood-Mia 169	K.Easley-Sea...............2	Merriweather-Pit........15.0	T.Eason-NE 1613
V.Williams-Buf..........820		D.Cherry-KC 7	G.Byrd-SD 157	G.Byrd-SD 2	A.Still-KC 14.5	W.Moon-Hou..........1390
F.Walker-Mia............786			D.Cherry-KC 140	D.Brown-Sea 2	J.Bryant-Sea...........14.5	E.Jackson-SD........1370

Marino Trains Dolphins, Colts Run Away

After the previous year's postseason surprise at the hands of the Seahawks, the Dolphins needed to prove they weren't about to slide back. Miami rolled to a 14–2 record on the strength of a swarming defense and Dan Marino's demonstration that sophomore slumps happen to other people. Marino set single-season NFL records for completions, touchdowns, and the league's only 5,000-yard passing season. His teammates shared in making history. By becoming Marino's top target, Mark Clayton set a new league record for touchdown receptions with 18. Kicker Uwe von Schamann benefited in the form of a record 66 PATs (in 70 tries).

The rest of the league saw a blend of old and new. The Steelers held on to repeat as division champs in the Central, although beyond veteran wideout John Stallworth's contributions, the team was a tribute to Chuck Noll's coaching more than anything else. The Broncos returned to prominence with a blend of their traditionally strong defense while coach Dan Reeves's low-key offense made for John Elway's slow development as a playcaller. Behind them in the West, both the Seahawks and Raiders had to deal major injuries. Seattle learned to get by without star running back Curt Warner, reverting to their old offensive reliance on throwing to Steve Largent early and often, and challenging opponents to try to keep up against a turnover-generating defense. Meanwhile, the Raiders sputtered after quarterback Jim Plunkett was injured, but with Marcus Allen's rushing and a tough defense, the defending champs managed to keep up, joining both Denver and Seattle in the postseason.

Major news was made with the decision of Colts owner Bob Irsay to mimic Raiders owner Al Davis. Irsay, who had traded the Rams for the Colts in 1972, traded in Baltimore, one of the birthplaces of the truly modern game. The team's belongings were packed up in the middle of the night and taken to Indianapolis and the comforts of a dome.

Less noted was the arrival of longtime CFL great Warren Moon. Helping the Edmonton Eskimos win an unprecedented five consecutive Grey Cups was enough to belatedly convince the Oilers that Moon, 27, could play quarterback in any league.

1985 NFC

TEAM	W-L-T	PCT	POST	PTS	RA	RY	RY/A	RTD	FL	PA	PC	GPY	GPY/A	PTD	PI	PSY	PRAT
Eastern Division																	
Dal	10-6	.625	#D	357-333	462-465	1741-1853	3.8-4.0	11-18	16-15	**587**-549	**344**-279	**4236**-4214	7.2-7.7	27-20	25-33	375-459	78.6-63.5
NYG	10-6	.625	#WD	399-283	581-419	2451-1482	4.2-**3.5**	24-9	18-13	497-535	275-278	3829-3377	**7.7-6.3**	22-20	20-24	396-**539**	78.3-65.5
Was	10-6	.625	#	297-312	571-424	2523-1734	4.4-4.1	20-11	19-11	512-465	280-**239**	3243-**3124**	6.3-6.7	13-19	21-23	428-378	65.4-65.9
Phi	7-9	.438	—	286-310	428-526	1630-2205	3.8-4.2	8-17	12-14	567-478	290-251	4036-3289	7.1-6.9	19-18	28-18	450-359	65.0-71.4
SL	5-11	.313	—	278-414	417-552	1974-2378	**4.7**-4.3	14-11	16-14	534-**461**	296-253	3581-3257	6.7-7.1	19-34	18-13	469-254	74.0-90.1
Central Division																	
ChiB	**15**-1	**.938**	DCS*	**456-198**	**610-359**	**2761-1319**	4.5-3.7	**27-6**	15-20	432-522	237-249	3303-3299	7.6-**6.3**	17-16	16-**34**	**227**-483	77.3-**51.2**
GB	8-8	.500	—	337-355	470-494	2208-2047	**4.7**-4.1	16-17	18-**25**	513-509	267-295	3552-3509	6.9-6.9	21-22	27-15	389-383	66.0-81.2
Min	7-9	.438	—	346-359	406-542	1516-2223	3.7-4.1	19-16	18-22	576-490	311-280	3931-3464	6.8-7.1	22-20	29-22	296-223	67.3-74.1
Det	7-9	.438	—	307-366	452-560	1538-2685	3.4-4.8	13-19	20-18	462-478	254-283	3316-3242	7.2-6.8	19-16	21-18	378-336	72.6-75.1
TB	2-14	.125	—	294-448	434-547	1644-2430	3.8-4.4	11-28	22-22	508-505	269-318	3423-3955	6.7-7.8	22-18	26-18	301-277	67.4-84.2
Western Division																	
LARm	11-5	.688	DC	340-277	503-444	2057-1586	4.1-3.6	15-9	21-17	403-548	234-296	2872-3483	7.1-6.4	16-19	**14**-29	409-421	78.9-63.1
SF	10-6	.625	#W	411-263	477-435	2232-1683	**4.7**-3.9	20-10	20-17	550-621	331-346	3987-3965	7.2-6.4	**28-11**	**14**-18	299-457	**88.8**-68.9
NO	5-11	.313	—	294-401	431-508	1683-2162	3.9-4.3	4-19	13-16	508-529	260-306	3257-3975	6.4-7.5	20-26	23-21	461-322	65.7-81.4
Atl	4-12	.250	—	282-452	560-437	2466-2052	4.4-4.7	14-24	**10**-12	462-535	254-289	3025-4129	6.5-7.7	13-32	20-22	531-331	66.5-82.1
Aver	16	—	—	344	487	1999	4.1	16	17	515	283	3626	7.0	21	22	353	73.5

TEAM	1D	PENY	PNT	FGM/A	RTNY	RTNTD	OFFY/DEFY	NETY	NETTO	NP	PNP	DELP	PW	DELW	PRT	DR	YPD	DEL
Eastern Division																		
Dal	336-312	759-990	41.4-41.3	19/28-18/27	500-605	5-2	5602-5608	-6	7	24	28	-4	8.6	1.4	4.8/ 4.0	209-212	26.8-26.5	0.4
NYG	**356**-258	781-821	**42.9**-40.8	22/33-18/21	781-532	2-4	5884-4320	1564	-1	116	126	-10	10.9	-0.9	5.0/ 3.2	**214**-215	27.5-**20.1**	7.4
Was	319-244	**596**-699	40.7-43.8	22/35-22/28	728-500	0-5	5338-4480	858	-6	-15	48	-63	7.6	**2.4**	3.5/ 3.7	199-198	26.8-22.6	4.2
Phi	292-307	736-834	41.5-42.6	25/30-13/29	518-936	3-4	5216-5135	81	-8	-24	-25	1	7.4	-0.4	4.0/ 4.3	208-206	25.1-24.9	0.1
SL	301-314	816-742	40.7-40.9	13/28-28/38	633-701	1-2	5086-5381	-295	-7	-136	-53	-83	4.6	0.4	4.2/ 5.6	204-200	24.9-26.9	-2.0
Central Division																		
ChiB	343-**236**	912-944	41.6-40.4	**31/37-12/19**	**1015-302**	7-**1**	5837-**4135**	**1702**	**23**	**258**	**234**	24	**14.4**	0.6	5.3/**2.5**	205-205	28.5-20.2	**8.3**
GB	318-310	798-797	39.8-42.7	19/26-16/31	632-737	3-4	5371-5173	198	-5	-18	-4	-14	7.6	0.4	3.8/ 4.8	208-213	25.8-24.3	1.5
Min	317-324	690-**1000**	42.8-41.4	15/26-29/37	533-639	2-3	5151-5464	-313	-3	-13	-38	25	7.7	-0.7	4.1/ 4.7	202-199	25.5-27.5	-2.0
Det	259-359	741-729	41.8-40.2	26/31-28/36	539-667	1-5	4476-5591	-1115	-5	-59	-113	54	6.5	0.5	4.2/ 4.3	192-**195**	23.3-28.7	-5.4
TB	291-351	751-945	40.9-44.4	22/32-32/43	375-887	0-4	4766-6108	-1342	-8	-154	-144	-10	4.2	-2.2	4.0/ 5.6	208-209	22.9-29.2	-6.3
Western Division																		
LARm	258-281	730-529	42.7-42.0	22/29-23/29	860-435	**8**-2	4520-4648	-128	11	63	33	30	9.6	1.4	4.3/ 3.2	211-207	21.4-22.5	-1.0
SF	340-293	868-778	39.3-**39.6**	13/21-27/35	568-374	5-5	**5920**-5191	729	1	148	65	**83**	11.7	-1.7	**5.6**/ 4.1	205-212	**28.9**-24.5	4.4
NO	250-335	805-837	42.3-42.2	**31**/35-21/28	527-648	5-3	4479-5815	-1336	1	-107	-107	0	5.3	-0.3	3.5/ 5.2	210-206	21.3-28.2	-6.9
Atl	296-329	1149-738	42.2-42.0	24/31-17/23	470-589	3-**1**	4960-5850	-890	4	-170	-58	-112	3.8	0.3	3.2/ 5.4	198-198	25.1-29.5	-4.5
Aver	307	807	41.4	21/30	639	3	5271	—	—	—	—	—	—	—	4.9	206	25.6	—

Rushing Attempts	Rushing Yards	Rushing Average	Rushing TDs	Rushing Rank	Passing Yards	Passing Average
G.Riggs-Atl 397	G.Riggs-Atl 1719	S.Mitchell-SL 5.50	J.Morris-NYG 21	G.Riggs-Atl 1819	P.Simms-NYG 3829	P.Simms-NYG 7.74
J.Wilder-TB 365	W.Payton-Chi 1551	G.Ellis-GB 5.49	E.Dickerson-LARm 12	W.Payton-Chi 1641	J.Montana-SF 3653	J.McMahon-Chi 7.64
W.Payton-Chi 324	J.Morris-NYG 1336	W.Tyler-SF 5.07	J.Wilder-TB 10	J.Morris-NYG 1546	T.Kramer-Min 3522	J.Montana-SF 7.39
T.Dorsett-Dal 305	T.Dorsett-Dal 1307	R.Craig-SF 4.91	G.Riggs-Atl 10	J.Wilder-TB 1400	R.Jaworski-Phi 3450	D.Brock-LARm 7.28
J.Morris-NYG 294	J.Wilder-TB 1300	E.Ivery-GB 4.82		T.Dorsett-Dal 1377	N.Lomax-SL 3214	E.Hipple-Det 7.27
Completion Percent	**TD Passes**	**TD Percent**	**INT Percent**	**Passer Rating**	**Passing Rank**	**Receptions**
J.Montana-SF 61.3	J.Montana-SF 27	J.Montana-SF 5.5	N.Lomax-SL 2.5	J.Montana-SF 91.3	J.Montana-SF 1442	R.Craig-SF 92
D.Brock-LARm 59.7	P.Simms-NYG 22	S.DeBerg-TB 5.1	J.Montana-SF 2.6	J.McMahon-Chi 82.6	P.Simms-NYG 1225	A.Monk-Was 91
D.White-Dal 59.3	D.White-Dal 21	J.McMahon-Chi 4.8	J.McMahon-Chi 3.5	D.Brock-LARm 82.0	N.Lomax-SL 1217	T.Hill-Dal 74
J.McMahon-Chi 56.9	T.Kramer-Min 19	L.Dickey-GB 4.8	D.Brock-LARm 3.6	D.White-Dal 80.6	R.Jaworski-Phi 1010	M.Quick-Phi 73
N.Lomax-SL 56.3	S.DeBerg-TB 19	D.White-Dal 4.7	D.White-Dal 3.8	N.Lomax-SL 79.5	D.White-Dal 1004	G.Clark-Was 72
Receiving Yards	**Receiving Average**	**Receiving TDs**	**Receiving Rank**	**Combined Net Yards**	**Total TDs**	**Total Points**
M.Quick-Phi 1247	W.Gault-Chi 21.33	M.Quick-Phi 11	M.Quick-Phi 679	R.Craig-SF 2066	J.Morris-NYG 21	K.Butler-Chi 144
A.Monk-Was 1226	A.Carter-Min 19.09	D.Clark-SF 10	A.Monk-Was 623	W.Payton-Chi 2034	R.Craig-SF 15	J.Morris-NYG 126
J.Lofton-GB 1153	J.Rice-SF 18.92		J.Lofton-GB 597	G.Riggs-Atl 1986	E.Dickerson-LARm 12	M.Andersen-NO 120
T.Hill-Dal 1113	E.Goodlow-NO 18.84		T.Hill-Dal 592	S.Mitchell-SL 1950	M.Quick-Phi 11	E.Murray-Det 109
R.Craig-SF 1016	K.House-TB 18.25		R.Craig-SF 538	T.Dorsett-Dal 1756	W.Payton-Chi 11	
Punt Average	**Field Goals**	**Field Goal Percent**	**Kickoff Returns**	**Kickoff Return Average**	**Punt Returns**	**Punt Return Average**
R.Donnelly-Atl 43.6	K.Butler-Chi 31	M.Andersen-NO 88.6	B.Rhymes-Min 53	R.Brown-LARm 32.8	P.McConkey-NYG 53	H.Ellard-LARm 13.5
D.Hatcher-LARm 43.2	M.Andersen-NO 31	E.Murray-Det 83.9	H.Hunter-Phi 48	W.Gault-Chi 26.2	E.Cooper-Phi 43	D.Green-Was 13.4
S.Landeta-NYG 42.9	E.Murray-Det 26	K.Butler-Chi 83.8	P.Freeman-TB 48	D.Gentry-Chi 25.9	D.McLemore-SF 38	J.Smith-SL 10.9
G.Coleman-Min 42.8	P.McFadden-Phi 25	P.McFadden-Phi 83.3	K.Jenkins-Was 41	C.Monroe-SF 25.6	P.Mandley-Det 38	P.Mandley-Det 10.6
B.Hansen-NO 42.3	M.Luckhurst-Atl 24	M.Luckhurst-Atl 77.4		B.Rhymes-Min 25.4	H.Ellard-LARm 37	K.Jenkins-Was 10.5
Punt/Kick Return Yards	**Punt/Kick Return TDs**	**Interceptions**	**Interception Return Yards**	**Interception Return TDs**	**Sacks**	**Overall Rank**
B.Rhymes-Min 1345	R.Brown-LARm 3	E.Walls-Dal 9	J.Rice-Chi 174	Many 1	R.Dent-Chi 17.0	G.Riggs-Atl 1953
K.Jenkins-Was 1290		J.Castille-TB 7	P.Williams-SF 137		L.Marshall-NYG 15.5	W.Payton-Chi 1946
P.Freeman-TB 1085			M.Douglass-GB 126		D.Manley-Was 15.0	R.Craig-SF 1678
H.Hunter-Phi 1053			L.Frazier-Chi 119		C.Mann-Was 14.5	J.Morris-NYG 1647
R.Brown-LARm 918			E.Junior-SL 109			J.Montana-SF 1625

One Night Shy of Perfection

The Bears had only recently returned to competitiveness, but the combination of talent and genius made for one of the greatest single-season teams of all time. The talent had already been drafted for the most part by former general manager Jim Finks, and defensive coordinator Buddy Ryan designed the most dominating defense in league history. Armed with that combination, head coach Mike Ditka's Bears were a force unlike anything seen since the Lombardi Packers of old … or the 1972 Dolphins.

It was the Dolphins who finally ended Chicago's 12–0 start. The Bears had allowed a total of just three points over three games coming into Monday night in Miami, but Dan Marino put up 38 points on the 46 Defense. The Bears still finished 15–1, scoring 258 more points than they allowed.

The Rams overcame a two-game holdout by Eric Dickerson with a season-opening, seven-game winning streak that proved to be enough to keep them ahead of San Francisco. Bill Walsh's team was retooling, however, with rookie wideout Jerry Rice giving the West Coast offense a vertical dimension, while running back Roger Craig posted the first double-thousand season: 1,000 yards rushing *and* receiving. With the abrupt conclusion of Joe Theismann's career on a gruesome (but legal) sack by Giant Lawrence Taylor, and John Riggins's running out of steam in his final year, the Redskins fell just short of the playoffs.

Giants coach Bill Parcells had solved his team's quarterback controversy the year before, and he found the power running back he needed in mighty mite Joe Morris, who rushed for 21 touchdowns. New York had to settle for tying the Cowboys in the standings—Dallas won on tiebreakers—but the Giants still reached the playoffs for the second straight year, something that hadn't happened since 1963. The Cowboys were leaky defensively and the offense leaned heavily on the talents of two aging Tonys: Dorsett had his eighth and final 1,000-yard rushing season and Hill reached the 1,000-yard receiving mark for the last time, too. Two Packers greats of the 1930s passed on in Cecil Isbell and Johnny McNally, better known by his Hall of Fame pseudonym, Johnny Blood.

1985 AFC

TEAM	W-L-T	PCT	POST	PTS	RA	RY	RY/A	RTD	FL	PA	PC	GPY	GPY/A	PTD	PI	PSY	PRAT
Eastern Division																	
Mia	**12**-4	**.750**	DC	428-320	444-509	1729-2256	3.9-4.4	19-15	20-18	576-487	343-257	4278-3789	7.4-7.8	31-21	21-23	**164**-278	85.4-73.2
NYJ	11-5	.688	#W	393-**264**	564-**433**	2312-**1516**	4.1-**3.5**	18-10	21-20	497-507	303-267	3983-3626	8.0-7.2	25-17	**8**-22	399-370	**96.3**-68.9
NE	11-5	.688	#WDCS	362-290	**565**-466	2331-1655	4.1-3.6	15-15	20-**24**	457-525	255-262	3483-3393	7.6-6.5	20-**14**	22-23	315-334	74.9-**61.2**
Ind	5-11	.313	—	320-386	485-539	**2439**-2145	**5.0**-4.0	**22**-20	14-17	468-504	235-275	2811-3721	6.0-7.4	15-24	20-16	244-267	61.8-81.0
Buf	2-14	.125	—	200-381	412-569	1611-2462	3.9-4.3	13-20	21-15	517-477	263-265	3331-3301	6.4-6.9	9-24	31-20	347-223	52.1-76.5
Central Division																	
Cle	8-8	.500	D	287-294	533-497	2285-1851	4.3-3.7	16-14	23-9	414-509	222-289	2885-3460	7.0-6.8	17-18	13-18	249-353	76.4-74.8
Cin	7-9	.438	—	441-437	503-461	2183-1999	4.3-4.3	20-23	16-19	518-518	302-297	4082-3998	7.9-7.7	31-26	13-19	365-334	93.0-83.5
Pit	7-9	.438	—	379-355	541-470	2177-1876	4.0-4.0	14-19	9-14	512-484	254-287	3397-**3088**	6.6-**6.4**	23-18	27-20	224-305	64.1-73.3
Hou	5-11	.313	—	284-412	428-588	1570-2814	3.7-4.8	13-21	15-20	512-**462**	277-260	3523-3654	6.9-7.9	18-29	22-15	441-313	69.7-89.3
Western Division																	
LARd	**12**-4	**.750**	D	354-308	532-461	2262-1605	4.3-**3.5**	18-**7**	14-13	506-511	269-**251**	3481-3486	6.9-6.8	20-22	24-17	335-**488**	68.5-71.9
Den	11-5	.688	#	380-329	497-475	1851-1973	3.7-4.2	20-10	**8**-12	617-547	329-277	3952-3584	6.4-6.6	23-22	23-24	307-378	70.1-66.7
Sea	8-8	.500	—	349-303	462-473	1644-1837	3.6-3.9	9-12	18-20	575-496	304-273	3820-3787	6.6-7.6	28-22	23-24	457-464	73.4-74.4
SD	8-8	.500	—	**467**-435	440-470	1665-1972	3.8-4.2	20-25	19-16	**632**-595	**386**-357	**5175**-4597	**8.2**-7.7	**37**-28	30-26	305-304	86.8-81.8
KC	6-10	.375	—	317-360	428-513	1486-2169	3.5-4.2	10-18	11-14	511-576	267-332	3726-3752	7.3-6.5	23-22	23-**27**	335-263	72.3-70.5
Aver	16	—	—	344	487	1999	4.1	16	17	515	283	3626	7.0	21	22	353	73.5

TEAM	1D	PENY	PNT	FGM/A	RTNY	RTNTD	OFFY/DEFY	NETY	NETTO	NP	PNP	DELP	PW	DELW	PRT	DR	YPD	DEL
Eastern Division																		
Mia	361-314	**637**-854	43.7-40.7	22/27-19/28	584-471	2-2	5843-5767	76	0	108	6	**102**	10.7	1.3	5.8/ 5.1	196-195	29.8-29.6	0.2
NYJ	344-276	907-868	40.2-41.8	26/34-18/25	513-**420**	2-3	5896-4772	**1124**	**13**	**129**	**146**	-17	**11.2**	-0.2	**6.2**/ 4.4	202-198	29.2-24.1	**5.1**
NE	294-284	842-699	43.0-40.5	24/30-22/25	957-841	6-3	5499-4714	785	5	72	85	-13	9.8	1.2	4.8/**3.8**	219-222	25.1-**21.2**	3.9
Ind	282-330	678-699	**44.8**-41.4	16/26-25/31	524-804	2-**1**	5006-5599	-593	-1	-66	-53	-13	6.3	-1.4	3.6/ 5.5	198-195	25.3-28.7	-3.4
Buf	256-320	965-870	41.5-40.5	13/17-**12/15**	518-856	1-6	4595-5540	-945	-17	-181	-147	-34	3.5	-1.5	3.0/ 4.8	197-200	23.3-27.7	-4.4
Central Division																		
Cle	271-297	753-773	40.3-42.2	14/18-19/29	625-521	2-2	4921-4958	-37	-9	-7	-39	32	7.8	0.2	4.9/ 4.5	197-**186**	25.0-26.7	-1.7
Cin	344-337	795-731	40.7-41.3	24/33-26/34	551-753	2-2	5900-5663	237	9	4	56	-52	8.1	-1.1	**6.2**/ 5.5	200-195	29.5-29.0	0.5
Pit	315-**273**	665-679	39.1-40.9	**33/42**-19/25	694-789	3-6	5350-4659	691	-2	24	50	-26	8.6	-1.6	4.0/ 4.0	204-213	26.2-21.9	4.4
Hou	270-356	1150-908	41.5-39.4	21/27-19/34	394-612	1-**1**	4652-6155	-1503	-2	-128	-133	5	4.8	0.2	4.0/ 5.9	204-196	22.8-31.4	-8.6
Western Division																		
LARd	304-**273**	962-856	40.8-41.9	20/32-24/35	**1020**-524	4-5	5408-**4603**	805	-8	46	35	11	9.1	**2.8**	4.1/ 4.3	219-217	24.7-**21.2**	3.5
Den	339-290	677-**953**	40.0-41.1	23/38-26/33	719-657	2-4	5496-5179	317	5	51	46	5	9.3	1.7	4.3/ 3.9	215-223	25.6-23.2	2.3
Sea	299-290	827-840	40.3-42.1	14/25-20/28	755-763	**7-1**	5007-5160	-153	3	46	-1	47	9.1	-1.1	4.2/ 4.4	**221**-218	22.7-23.7	-1.0
SD	**380**-364	937-703	42.4-**38.8**	18/28-18/30	674-542	3-2	**6535**-6265	270	-7	32	-6	38	8.8	-0.8	5.8/ 5.4	212-220	**30.8**-28.5	2.3
KC	258-336	666-777	40.3-41.2	24/27-25/30	679-781	2-**1**	4877-5658	-781	7	-43	-37	-6	6.9	-0.9	4.7/ 4.1	203-207	24.0-27.3	-3.3
Aver	307	807	41.4	21/30	639	1	5271	—	—	—	—	—	—	—	4.9	103	26.0	—

Rushing Attempts	Rushing Yards	Rushing Average	Rushing TDs	Rushing Rank	Passing Yards	Passing Average
M.Allen-LARd 380	M.Allen-LARd 1759	G.Wonsley-Ind 5.19	R.Davenport-Mia 11	M.Allen-LARd 1869	D.Marino-Mia 4137	D.Fouts-SD 8.46
F.McNeil-NYJ 294	F.McNeil-NYJ 1331	K.Mack-Cle 4.97	M.Allen-LARd 11	F.McNeil-NYJ 1361	J.Elway-Den 3891	B.Esiason-Cin 7.99
C.Warner-Sea 291	C.James-NE 1227	L.James-SD 4.91	T.Spencer-SD 10	C.James-NE 1277	K.O'Brien-NYJ 3888	K.O'Brien-NYJ 7.97
C.James-NE 263	K.Mack-Cle 1104	J.Brooks-Cin 4.84	L.Kinnebrew-Cin 9	C.Warner-Sea 1174	D.Fouts-SD 3638	B.Kenney-KC 7.50
E.Byner-Cle 244	C.Warner-Sea 1094	C.James-NE 4.67		K.Mack-Cle 1174	D.Krieg-Sea 3602	D.Marino-Mia 7.30
Completion Percent	**TD Passes**	**TD Percent**	**INT Percent**	**Passer Rating**	**Passing Rank**	**Receptions**
K.O'Brien-NYJ 60.9	D.Marino-Mia 30	D.Fouts-SD 6.3	K.O'Brien-NYJ 1.6	K.O'Brien-NYJ 96.2	K.O'Brien-NYJ 1749	L.James-SD 86
D.Marino-Mia 59.3	D.Krieg-Sea 27	B.Esiason-Cin 6.3	B.Kenney-KC 2.7	B.Esiason-Cin 93.2	D.Marino-Mia 1379	R.Childress-LARd 82
D.Fouts-SD 59.1	D.Fouts-SD 27	M.Malone-Pit 5.6	B.Esiason-Cin 2.8	D.Fouts-SD 88.1	B.Esiason-Cin 1377	B.Woolfolk-Hou 80
B.Esiason-Cin 58.2	B.Esiason-Cin 27	D.Marino-Mia 5.3	B.Kosar-Cle 2.8	D.Marino-Mia 84.1	D.Fouts-SD 1154	S.Largent-Sea 79
T.Eason-NE 56.2	K.O'Brien-NYJ 25	K.O'Brien-NYJ 5.1	M.Malone-Pit 3.0	B.Kenney-KC 83.6	D.Krieg-Sea 1136	M.Shuler-NYJ 76
Receiving Yards	**Receiving Average**	**Receiving TDs**	**Receiving Rank**	**Combined Net Yards**	**Total TDs**	**Total Points**
S.Largent-Sea 1287	S.Paige-KC 21.93	D.Turner-Sea 13	S.Largent-Sea 674	L.James-SD 2535	L.Lipps-Pit 15	G.Anderson-Pit 139
W.Chandler-SD 1199	W.Walker-NYJ 21.32	L.Lipps-Pit 12	W.Chandler-SD 650	M.Allen-LARd 2308	M.Allen-LARd 14	P.Leahy-NYJ 121
D.Hill-Hou 1169	J.Hester-LARd 20.78	S.Paige-KC 10	D.Hill-Hou 630	L.Lipps-Pit 1827	D.Turner-Sea 13	J.Breech-Cin 120
L.Lipps-Pit 1134	D.Turner-Sea 19.71	W.Chandler-SD 10	L.Lipps-Pit 627	F.McNeil-NYJ 1758	R.Davenport-Mia 13	F.Reveiz-Mia 116
Collinsworth-Cin 1125	S.Morgan-NE 19.49	D.Hill-Hou 9	Collinsworth-Cin 588	V.Johnson-Den 1757	J.Brooks-Cin 12	T.Franklin-NE 112
Punt Average	**Field Goals**	**Field Goal Percent**	**Kickoff Returns**	**Kickoff Return Average**	**Punt Returns**	**Punt Return Average**
R.Stark-Ind 45.9	G.Anderson-Pit 33	N.Lowery-KC 88.9	S.Starring-NE 48	S.Tasker-Hou 26.3	F.Walker-LARd 62	I.Fryar-NE 14.1
R.Roby-Mia 43.7	P.Leahy-NYJ 26	F.Reveiz-Mia 81.5	M.Martin-Cin 48	G.Young-Cle 25.7	G.Lane-KC 43	L.Lipps-Pit 12.1
R.Camarillo-NE 43.0	N.Lowery-KC 24	T.Franklin-NE 80.0	L.Hampton-Mia 45	A.Bentley-Ind 25.0	R.Martin-Ind 40	F.Walker-LARd 11.2
T.Moffett-SD 42.4	T.Franklin-NE 24	G.Anderson-Pit 78.6	L.James-SD 36	W.Drewrey-Hou 24.7	I.Fryar-NE 37	R.Martin-Ind 11.1
P.McInally-Cin 42.3	J.Breech-Cin 24		G.Young-Cle 35	V.Johnson-Den 24.7	L.Lipps-Pit 36	G.Willhite-Den 10.6
Punt/Kick Return Yards	**Punt/Kick Return TDs**	**Interceptions**	**Interception Return Yards**	**Interception Return TDs**	**Sacks**	**Overall Rank**
M.Martin-Cin 1372	L.Lipps-Pit 2	A.Lewis-KC 8	F.Marion-NE 189	Many 1	A.Tippett-NE 16.5	M.Allen-LARd 2170
F.Walker-LARd 1159	I.Fryar-NE 2	E.Daniel-Ind 8	J.Hendy-SD 139		J.Green-Sea 13.5	K.O'Brien-NYJ 1807
R.Martin-Ind 1081	R.Martin-Ind 1		J.Griffin-Cin 116		M.Gastineau-NYJ 13.5	F.McNeil-NYJ 1585
L.Hampton-Mia 1020	B.Brennan-Cle 1		A.Gross-Cle 109		J.Meads-Den 13.0	C.James-NE 1470
S.Starring-NE 1012	G.Anderson-SD 1				B.Pickel-LARd 12.5	B.Esiason-Cin 1466

Young Arms Are Strong Arms

The AFC had two solid divisions, and then there was the Central. The Browns might not have had the offensive firepower the Bengals, or the fading fame of the Steelers, but under Marty Schottenheimer, Cleveland focused on the basics. That was enough to win a division title with only a .500 record. Schottenheimer's fundamentalism took shape in a very young backfield on offense, with rookies Bernie Kosar at quarterback and Kevin Mack at fullback joining second-year back Earnest Byner. Mack and Byner provided Cleveland with two 1,000-yard rushers and some offensive power beyond their great tight end, Ozzie Newsome. The defense was much improved with a quality cadre of linebackers and former USFL cornerback Frank Minnifield.

In the West, the Raiders relied on a strong defense and on Marcus Allen's electrifying ball-handling. They won the division by beating the Broncos twice—in overtime both times—to force the Broncos out of the playoffs despite an 11–5 record. Denver's '83 QB, John Elway, showed continuing improvement while the defense labored in relative anonymity beyond the contributions of roving linebacker–defensive end Karl Mecklenburg.

The Jets, Patriots, and Dolphins battled through the season, each guided by quarterbacks from the Class of 1983. Dan Marino remained the brightest star of the group, leading the league in completions, yards, and touchdown passes. Miami took the division and earned praise from Dolphins alumni for defending coach Don Shula's perfect season with a December win over the undefeated Bears. Jets quarterback Ken O'Brien showed remarkable accuracy while absorbing a then-record 62 sacks. With sporadic third-year quarterback Tony Eason, New England relied on USFL refugee Craig James in a ball-control offense powered by tackle Brian Holloway and guard John Hannah, playing his final season in his franchise's most successful season to that time.

Beyond New England's James and Cleveland's Minnifield, other former USFL players arriving in the NFL included QBs Steve Young (Buccaneers) and Bobby Hebert (Saints), defensive end Reggie White (Eagles), center Bart Oates (Giants), wide receiver Anthony Carter (Vikings), and running back Mike Rozier (Oilers). They were jumping off a ship, and a league, not far from sinking.

1986 NFC

TEAM	W-L-T	PCT	POST	PTS	RA	RY	RY/A	RTD	FL	PA	PC	GPY	GPY/A	PTD	PI	PSY	PRAT
Eastern Division																	
NYG	**14**-2	**.875**	DCS*	371-236	558-**350**	2245-**1284**	4.0-3.7	18-10	10-**19**	472-587	260-334	3500-3887	7.4-6.6	22-15	22-24	367-414	75.0-68.6
Was	12-4	.750	WDC	368-296	474-459	1732-1805	3.7-3.9	**23**-14	10-9	542-532	276-302	4109-3916	7.6-7.4	22-21	22-19	240-424	72.7-78.3
Dal	7-9	.438	—	346-337	447-500	1969-2200	4.4-4.4	21-17	17-18	547-464	319-226	4003-3149	7.3-6.8	21-21	24-17	498-364	75.7-70.8
Phi	5-10-1	.344	—	256-312	499-458	2002-1989	4.0-4.3	8-14	10-13	514-532	268-260	3248-3641	6.3-6.8	19-21	17-23	708-406	70.4-66.5
SL	4-11-1	.281	—	218-351	419-560	1787-2227	4.3-4.0	8-17	10-12	516-**436**	293-**215**	3140-**2992**	6.1-6.9	17-21	19-10	424-355	70.4-78.3
Central Division																	
ChiB	**14**-2	**.875**	D	352-**187**	**606**-427	**2700**-1463	**4.5**-3.4	21-**4**	22-16	415-513	208-243	2912-3170	7.0-**6.2**	12-**12**	25-31	**153-503**	57.6-**49.9**
Min	9-7	.563	—	**398**-273	461-481	1738-1796	3.8-3.7	14-10	14-18	519-494	290-276	4185-3475	**8.1**-7.0	**31**-16	**15**-24	272-259	**90.1**-68.5
Det	5-11	.313	—	277-326	470-519	1771-2349	3.8-4.5	13-15	17-**19**	500-468	286-279	3107-3090	6.2-6.6	18-14	20-22	323-290	71.0-69.7
GB	4-12	.250	—	254-418	424-565	1614-2095	3.8-3.7	8-16	18-12	565-448	305-267	3708-3142	6.6-7.0	18-31	27-20	261-222	65.1-85.4
TB	2-14	.125	—	239-473	455-558	1863-2648	4.1-4.7	12-31	17-**19**	459-484	245-289	2892-3838	6.3-7.9	13-23	25-13	394-153	59.6-89.5
Western Division																	
SF	10-5-1	.656	D	374-247	510-406	1986-1555	3.9-3.8	16-8	**9**-10	**582**-604	**353**-324	**4299**-3773	7.4-**6.2**	21-18	20-**39**	203-448	81.1-55.8
LARm	10-6	.625	W	309-267	578-460	2457-1681	4.3-3.7	16-9	22-15	403-539	194-313	2380-3482	5.9-6.5	15-17	**15**-28	184-292	63.7-66.3
Atl	7-8-1	.469	—	280-280	578-485	2524-1916	4.4-4.0	12-10	16-14	452-453	246-241	3046-3169	6.7-7.0	14-19	17-22	464-177	70.2-69.3
NO	7-9	.438	—	288-287	505-486	2074-1559	4.1-**3.2**	15-11	18-17	425-576	232-331	2893-3886	6.8-6.7	13-21	25-26	225-343	61.6-71.4
Aver	16	—	—	328	482	1899	3.9	14	15	517	286	3612	7.0	21	21	323	74.1

TEAM	1D	PENY	PNT	FGM/A	RTNY	RTNTD	OFFY/DEFY	NETY	NETTO	NP	PNP	DELP	PW	DELW	PRT	DR	YPD	DEL
Eastern Division																		
NYG	324-284	738-988	**44.8**-39.3	26/37-18/25	583-604	2-1	5378-4757	621	11	135	96	39	11.4	**2.6**	4.6/ 3.9	199-206	27.0-23.1	3.9
Was	312-316	860-**1026**	43.6-41.3	18/32-17/24	676-406	1-**0**	5601-5297	304	-4	72	9	**63**	9.8	2.2	5.4/ 4.9	198-200	28.3-26.5	1.8
Dal	325-286	936-822	40.2-41.6	15/21-16/30	435-632	1-3	5474-4985	489	-6	9	17	-8	8.2	-1.2	4.3/ 4.3	209-210	26.2-23.7	2.5
Phi	287-278	901-884	41.0-**38.7**	20/31-**13**/26	498-826	1-4	4542-5224	-682	9	-56	-21	-35	6.6	-1.1	3.2/ 4.1	**215**-213	21.1-24.5	-3.4
SL	273-304	932-682	37.1-42.3	11/24-24/32	649-567	2-2	4503-4864	-361	-7	-133	-58	-75	4.7	-0.2	3.5/ 5.0	193-189	23.3-25.7	-2.4
Central Division																		
ChiB	305-**241**	765-866	40.7-40.9	**28/41**-16/**22**	852-**225**	5-4	5459-**4130**	**1329**	0	**165**	111	54	**12.1**	1.9	4.0/**2.4**	207-212	26.4-**19.5**	**6.9**
Min	321-286	890-806	40.0-40.3	22/28-27/33	534-444	3-2	5651-5012	639	13	125	105	20	11.1	-2.1	**6.3**/ 4.3	193-194	**29.3**-25.8	3.4
Det	287-298	658-781	39.9-41.7	18/25-24/35	610-828	1-7	4555-5149	-594	4	-49	-34	-15	6.8	-1.8	3.8/ 3.8	196-196	23.2-26.3	-3.0
GB	286-313	949-657	37.7-39.6	17/27-18/25	463-644	3-5	5061-5015	46	-13	-164	-48	-116	3.9	0.1	4.0/ 4.9	195-194	26.0-25.9	0.1
TB	273-362	661-941	40.2-41.3	17/24-21/30	238-650	2-5	4361-6333	-1972	-10	-234	-204	-30	2.2	-0.2	2.9/ 6.6	195-**187**	22.4-33.9	-11.5
Western Division																		
SF	**346**-285	691-653	40.6-41.4	25/35-15/25	**975**-578	**6**-3	**6082**-4880	1202	**20**	127	**180**	-53	11.2	-0.7	5.6/ 2.7	210-208	29.0-23.5	5.5
LARm	269-272	**603**-804	38.2-41.4	17/24-24/31	819-544	**6**-2	4653-4871	-218	6	42	6	36	9.1	1.0	3.9/ 3.6	214-211	21.7-23.1	-1.3
Atl	305-268	763-834	43.3-41.4	23/36-15/26	586-675	4-5	5106-4908	198	3	0	29	-29	8.0	-0.5	3.9/ 4.6	196-194	26.1-25.3	0.8
NO	275-331	855-791	42.1-42.5	26/30-17/27	612-596	2-2	4742-5102	-360	0	1	-30	31	8.0	-1.0	3.7/ 4.1	198-201	23.9-25.4	-1.4
Aver	303	830	40.4	20/29	592	3	5188	—	—	—	—	—	—	—	5.0	202	25.6	—

Rushing Attempts	Rushing Yards	Rushing Average	Rushing TDs	Rushing Rank	Passing Yards	Passing Average
E.Dickerson-LARm 404	E.Dickerson-LARm 1821	H.Walker-Dal 4.88	G.Rogers-Was 18	E.Dickerson-LARm 1931	J.Schroeder-Was 4109	T.Kramer-Min 8.06
G.Riggs-Atl 343	J.Morris-NYG 1516	R.Mayes-NO 4.73	J.Morris-NYG 14	J.Morris-NYG 1656	P.Simms-NYG 3487	J.Schroeder-Was 7.60
J.Morris-NYG 341	R.Mayes-NO 1353	S.Mitchell-SL 4.60	H.Walker-Dal 12	R.Mayes-NO 1433	R.Wright-GB 3247	P.Simms-NYG 7.45
W.Payton-Chi 321	W.Payton-Chi 1333	K.Davis-GB 4.55	E.Dickerson-LARm 11	G.Riggs-Atl 1417	T.Kramer-Min 3000	J.Montana-SF 7.28
G.Rogers-Was 303	G.Riggs-Atl 1327	E.Dickerson-LARm 4.51	G.Riggs-Atl 9	W.Payton-Chi 1413	S.Pelluer-Dal 2727	S.Pelluer-Dal 7.21
Completion Percent	**TD Passes**	**TD Percent**	**INT Percent**	**Passer Rating**	**Passing Rank**	**Receptions**
E.Hipple-Det 63.0	T.Kramer-Min 24	T.Kramer-Min 6.5	R.Jaworski-Phi 2.4	T.Kramer-Min 92.6	J.Schroeder-Was 1285	J.Rice-SF 86
J.Montana-SF 62.2	J.Schroeder-Was 22	P.Simms-NYG 4.5	T.Kramer-Min 2.7	J.Montana-SF 80.7	T.Kramer-Min 1220	R.Craig-SF 81
N.Lomax-SL 57.0	P.Simms-NYG 21	J.Schroeder-Was 4.1	N.Lomax-SL 2.9	E.Hipple-Det 75.6	P.Simms-NYG 969	J.Smith-SL 80
S.Pelluer-Dal 56.9	R.Wright-GB 17	R.Wright-GB 3.5	J.Montana-SF 2.9	P.Simms-NYG 74.6	N.Lomax-SL 877	H.Walker-Dal 76
T.Kramer-Min 55.9	N.Lomax-SL 13	D.Archer-Atl 3.4	D.Archer-Atl 3.1	N.Lomax-SL 73.6	J.Montana-SF 798	G.Clark-Was 74
Receiving Yards	**Receiving Average**	**Receiving TDs**	**Receiving Rank**	**Combined Net Yards**	**Total TDs**	**Total Points**
J.Rice-SF 1570	W.Stanley-GB 20.66	J.Rice-SF 15	J.Rice-SF 860	E.Dickerson-LARm 2026	G.Rogers-Was 18	K.Butler-Chi 120
G.Clark-Was 1265	C.Didier-Was 20.32	M.Quick-Phi 9	G.Clark-Was 668	J.Morris-NYG 1749	J.Rice-SF 16	R.Wersching-SF 116
A.Monk-Was 1068	W.Gault-Chi 19.48	G.Clark-Was 7	A.Monk-Was 554	W.Payton-Chi 1715	J.Morris-NYG 15	C.Nelson-Min 110
J.Smith-SL 1014	J.Chadwick-Det 18.77	A.Carter-Min 7	J.Smith-SL 537	R.Mayes-NO 1662	H.Walker-Dal 14	G.Rogers-Was 108
M.Bavaro-NYG 1001	L.Lewis-Min 18.75		J.Chadwick-Det 523	J.Rice-SF 1642		M.Andersen-NO 108
Punt Average	**Field Goals**	**Field Goal Percent**	**Kickoff Returns**	**Kickoff Return Average**	**Punt Returns**	**Punt Return Average**
S.Landeta-NYG 44.8	K.Butler-Chi 28	M.Andersen-NO 86.7	H.Hunter-Det 49	D.Gentry-Chi 28.8	L.Barnes-Chi 57	V.Sikahema-SL 12.1
R.Donnelly-Atl 43.9	M.Andersen-NO 26	C.Nelson-Min 78.6	V.Sikahema-SL 37	M.Gray-NO 27.9	V.Sikahema-SL 43	G.Garrity-Phi 11.0
S.Cox-Was 43.6	R.Wersching-SF 25	R.Allegre-NYG 75.0	R.Lavette-Dal 36	V.Sikahema-SL 22.9	P.Mandley-Det 43	D.Griffin-SF 9.9
B.Hansen-NO 42.7	R.Allegre-NYG 24	E.Murray-Det 72.0	R.Brown-LARm 36	R.Bess-Min 22.7	D.Griffin-SF 38	P.Mandley-Det 9.8
J.Arnold-Det 42.6	C.Nelson-Min 22			D.Clack-Dal 22.2	W.Stanley-GB 33	K.Jenkins-Was 9.6
Punt/Kick Return Yards	**Punt/Kick Return TDs**	**Interceptions**	**Interception Return Yards**	**Interception Return TDs**	**Sacks**	**Overall Rank**
V.Sikahema-SL 1369	V.Sikahema-SL 2	R.Lott-SF 10	L.Irvin-LARm 150	T.Holmoe-SF 2	L.Taylor-NYG 20.5	E.Dickerson-LARm 2046
H.Hunter-Det 1007		D.Waymer-NO 9	T.Holmoe-SF 149		D.Manley-Was 18.5	J.Morris-NYG 1778
W.Stanley-GB 875		M.Lee-GB 9	D.Duerson-Chi 139		R.White-Phi 18.0	W.Payton-Chi 1579
R.Bess-Min 867		I.Holt-Min 8	R.Lott-SF 134		J.Jeffcoat-Dal 14.0	R.Mayes-NO 1544
M.Gray-NO 866		J.Gray-LARm 8	T.Nixon-SF 106			G.Riggs-Atl 1485

Giants in Court, and on Field

The USFL had announced a fall schedule for 1986. By the time autumn rolled around, the league was gone. The USFL won one of nine counts against the NFL in an antitrust suit in July, but counsel Paul Tagliabue got credit for the victory when trebled damages amounted to just $3. For the first time, NFL officials got a second look with the introduction of instant replay.

The Bears seemed ready to roll again, until Jim McMahon suffered a season-ending injury. Doug Flutie was forced into his first NFL and playoff action. During the regular season, though, the Bears handily captured the Central thanks to a defense that held opponents to 187 points, the lowest yet for a 16-game season, and the always-reliable Walter Payton. After coach Bud Grant retired for the second (and last) time, the Vikings shook off years of disappointment, surprising opponents with an aggressive passing game and a much-improved defense.

The Giants simply took charge of the NFC East. Tight end Mark Bavaro became the third weapon in a grinding offense, while the development of outside linebacker Carl Banks paved the way for an MVP season by Lawrence Taylor and a Super Bowl title. The Redskins couldn't beat New York, but former Saint George Rogers bashed his way to a league-leading 18 touchdowns. USFL refugees Gary Clark, Kelvin Bryant, and Jay Schroeder gave Washington a new look at the skill positions.

In the West, Joe Montana showed his mettle by coming back from a career-threatening back injury to help the 49ers stage a late-season rally for the division title. Jerry Rice posted the highest yardage total by any receiver since the old AFL, while Ronnie Lott snagged 10 interceptions. The Rams lost their last two games, including a season-ending match-up with the Niners, but coach John Robinson's team made the playoffs again on the strength of Eric Dickerson's rushing, outstanding line play, and a solid defense.

Fritz Pollard, the league's first African American coach while a star player in the 1920s, died at age 92. That was followed by the death of Bobby Layne, the cocky quarterback who helped the Lions roar to prominence in the 1950s.

1986 AFC

TEAM	W-L-T	PCT	POST	PTS	RA	RY	RY/A	RTD	FL	PA	PC	GPY	GPY/A	PTD	PI	PSY	PRAT
Eastern Division																	
NE	11-5	.688	D	412-307	469-510	1373-2203	2.9-4.3	10-19	**11**-19	557-**473**	340-255	4321-3324	7.8-7.0	29-**15**	13-21	367-346	92.9-68.4
NYJ	10-6	.625	#WD	364-386	490-450	1729-1661	3.5-3.7	16-12	16-18	537-603	334-348	4032-4567	7.5-7.6	27-35	21-20	386-178	85.7-87.3
Mia	8-8	.500	—	**430**-405	349-540	1545-2493	4.4-4.6	9-23	14-14	**645**-485	**392**-290	**4898**-3825	7.6-7.9	**46**-22	23-13	**119**-268	**93.3**-88.7
Buf	4-12	.250	—	287-348	419-465	1654-1721	3.9-3.7	9-18	20-8	499-570	294-343	3697-4069	7.4-7.1	22-21	19-10	334-267	80.9-86.9
Ind	3-13	.188	—	229-400	407-517	1491-1962	3.7-3.8	10-14	20-19	586-510	300-306	3615-3933	6.2-7.7	16-28	24-16	406-194	62.5-89.4
Central Division																	
Cle	**12**-4	**.750**	DC	391-310	470-494	1650-1981	3.5-4.0	20-12	13-19	538-518	315-291	4018-3546	7.5-6.8	18-21	**11**-18	274-258	84.6-76.5
Cin	10-6	.625	#	409-394	521-514	**2533**-2122	**4.9**-4.1	**24**-23	16-11	497-495	287-278	4160-3520	**8.4**-7.1	25-17	20-17	203-368	85.1-75.7
Pit	6-10	.375	—	307-336	**564**-471	2223-1872	3.9-4.0	18-**10**	16-13	491-536	238-311	2747-3669	5.6-6.8	16-22	20-20	159-289	59.7-77.1
Hou	5-11	.313	—	274-329	490-532	1700-2035	3.5-3.8	13-13	12-16	551-490	288-**228**	3843-**3200**	7.0-6.5	14-25	31-16	394-201	59.7-71.5
Western Division																	
Den	11-5	.688	DCS	378-327	455-**432**	1678-**1651**	3.7-3.8	17-13	13-17	549-545	306-301	3811-3755	6.9-6.9	22-21	16-18	273-459	78.7-75.9
KC	10-6	.625	#W	358-326	432-485	1468-1739	3.4-3.6	10-13	17-18	521-569	257-303	3122-3555	6.0-**6.2**	23-21	18-**31**	372-360	68.5-**62.1**
Sea	10-6	.625	#	366-**293**	513-471	2300-1759	4.5-3.7	15-12	13-14	453-535	268-301	3424-3888	7.6-7.3	24-20	14-22	315-306	87.7-74.6
LARd	8-8	.500	—	323-346	475-439	1790-1728	3.8-3.9	6-19	24-12	530-501	281-271	3973-3539	7.5-7.1	27-21	25-26	464-**463**	74.8-68.9
SD	4-12	.250	—	335-396	471-475	1576-1678	3.3-**3.5**	19-14	16-**22**	604-509	339-288	4045-4128	6.7-8.1	21-27	33-15	265-440	65.6-88.4
Aver	16	—	—	328	482	1899	3.9	14	15	517	286	3612	7.0	21	21	323	74.1

TEAM	1D	PENY	PNT	FGM/A	RTNY	RTNTD	OFFY/DEFY	NETY	NETTO	NP	PNP	DELP	PW	DELW	PRT	DR	YPD	DEL
Eastern Division																		
NE	314-286	672-866	40.7-39.8	**32/41**-21/28	708-716	6-**1**	5327-5181	146	**16**	**105**	**76**	29	**10.6**	0.4	6.1/ 4.2	210-218	25.4-23.8	1.6
NYJ	319-349	981-795	39.4-39.7	16/19-**16**/27	505-395	2-**1**	5375-6050	-675	1	-22	-52	30	7.4	**2.6**	5.1/ 6.1	205-202	26.2-30.0	-3.7
Mia	**351**-337	**609**-596	44.2-41.4	14/22-26/31	449-421	1-2	6324-6050	274	-10	25	-17	42	8.6	-0.6	**6.4**/ 6.2	184-**186**	**34.4**-32.5	1.8
Buf	291-334	878-**1098**	40.4-38.1	17/27-22/33	336-544	3-**1**	5017-5523	-506	-21	-61	-126	**65**	6.5	-2.5	5.0/ 5.9	190-193	26.4-28.6	-2.2
Ind	278-334	880-728	**44.7**-40.7	13/25-24/35	416-843	1-5	4700-5701	-1001	-9	-171	-119	-52	3.7	-0.7	3.6/ 6.2	201-193	23.4-29.5	-6.2
Central Division																		
Cle	302-302	807-754	41.2-37.9	26/33-20/29	534-403	7-3	5394-5269	125	13	81	62	19	10.0	2.0	5.9/ 4.9	198-200	27.2-26.3	0.9
Cin	348-336	847-840	33.8-39.8	17/32-22/30	381-**371**	2-7	**6490**-5274	**1216**	-8	15	69	-54	8.4	1.6	6.3/ 4.8	199-195	32.6-27.0	**5.6**
Pit	292-303	853-904	38.7-39.0	21/32-22/39	528-608	1-7	4811-5252	-441	-3	-29	-49	20	7.3	-1.3	3.6/ 4.7	209-207	23.0-25.4	-2.4
Hou	299-285	1018-674	41.1-39.5	22/27-19/29	441-628	3-**1**	5149-5034	115	-11	-55	-34	-21	6.6	-1.6	3.7/ 4.8	209-205	24.6-24.6	0.1
Western Division																		
Den	319-291	910-1034	39.3-42.9	20/28-24/32	**870**-725	6-2	5216-4947	269	6	51	46	5	9.3	1.7	5.2/ 4.5	207-206	25.2-24.0	1.2
KC	264-310	829-965	40.7-**37.0**	19/26-20/31	832-753	**10**-4	4218-4934	-716	14	32	-4	36	8.8	1.2	3.8/**3.3**	**217**-220	19.4-22.4	-3.0
Sea	291-310	813-652	38.6-40.4	22/35-19/28	673-514	4-2	5409-5341	68	9	73	42	31	9.8	0.2	5.5/ 4.8	195-200	27.7-26.7	1.0
LARd	302-**283**	951-868	40.2-42.1	21/28-**16/21**	759-639	4-3	5299-**4804**	495	-11	-23	-3	-20	7.4	0.6	4.5/ 3.8	215-219	24.6-**21.9**	2.7
SD	334-308	977-918	40.4-40.8	16/25-23/31	608-791	1-6	5356-5366	-10	-12	-61	-49	-12	6.5	-2.5	3.9/ 5.7	212-210	25.3-25.6	-0.3
Aver	303	830	40.4	20/29	592	2	5188	—	—	—	—	—	—	—	5.0	102	26.0	—

Rushing Attempts	Rushing Yards	Rushing Average	Rushing TDs	Rushing Rank	Passing Yards	Passing Average
C.Warner-Sea..........319	C.Warner-Sea........1481	J.Brooks-Cin...........5.30	C.Warner-Sea............13	C.Warner-Sea........1611	D.Marino-Mia.........4746	B.Esiason-Cin.........8.44
S.Winder-Den..........240	J.Brooks-Cin..........1087	C.Warner-Sea.........4.64	K.Mack-Cle...............10	J.Brooks-Cin..........1137	B.Esiason-Cin........3959	J.Plunkett-LARd......7.88
E.Jackson-Pit..........216	E.Jackson-Pit.............910	L.Hampton-Mia.......4.46	S.Winder-Den.............9	E.Jackson-Pit..........960	B.Kosar-Cle 3854	D.Krieg-Sea.............7.79
F.McNeil-NYJ..........214	G.Zimmerman-Pit....877	G.Willhite-Den 4.29	L.Hampton-Mia............9	G.Zimmerman-Pit.....937	K.O'Brien-NYJ.......3690	K.O'Brien-NYJ.........7.66
G.Zimmerman-Pit....214	F.McNeil-NYJ...........856	R.Riddick-Buf..........4.21		L.Hampton-Mia........920	J.Kelly-Buf..............3593	D.Marino-Mia..........7.62
Completion Percent	**TD Passes**	**TD Percent**	**INT Percent**	**Passer Rating**	**Passing Rank**	**Receptions**
K.O'Brien-NYJ........62.2	D.Marino-Mia.............44	D.Marino-Mia...........7.1	B.Kosar-Cle 1.9	D.Marino-Mia..........92.5	D.Marino-Mia.........1673	R.Childress-LARd......95
T.Eason-NE 61.6	K.O'Brien-NYJ............25	D.Krieg-Sea 5.6	T.Eason-NE 2.2	D.Krieg-Sea............91.0	B.Kosar-Cle 1612	A.Toon-NYJ 85
D.Marino-Mia 60.7	B.Esiason-Cin............24	J.Plunkett-LARd........5.6	J.Elway-Den...............2.6	T.Eason-NE 89.2	B.Esiason-Cin.........1420	S.Morgan-NE.............84
D.Krieg-Sea 60.0	J.Kelly-Buf..................22	K.O'Brien-NYJ 5.2	D.Krieg-Sea 2.9	B.Esiason-Cin..........87.7	T.Eason-NE 1359	G.Anderson-SD..........80
J.Kelly-Buf...............59.4	D.Krieg-Sea 21	B.Esiason-Cin...........5.1	J.Kelly-Buf..................3.5	K.O'Brien-NYJ 85.8	J.Elway-Den............1318	T.Collins-NE...............77
Receiving Yards	**Receiving Average**	**Receiving TDs**	**Receiving Rank**	**Combined Net Yards**	**Total TDs**	**Total Points**
S.Morgan-NE.........1491	C.Burkett-Buf..........22.88	W.Walker-NYJ 12	S.Morgan-NE...........796	G.Anderson-SD.....2022	S.Winder-Den............14	T.Franklin-NE..........140
M.Duper-Mia..........1313	W.Walker-NYJ 20.73	S.Paige-KC................11	M.Duper-Mia............712	C.Warner-Sea........1823	C.Warner-Sea............13	N.Johnson-Sea........108
A.Toon-NYJ 1176	D.Williams-LARd...19.60	M.Duper-Mia..............11	A.Toon-NYJ 628	J.Brooks-Cin..........1773	W.Walker-NYJ 12	R.Karlis-Den............104
R.Childress-LARd..1153	M.Duper-Mia............19.60		M.Clayton-Mia 625	S.Morgan-NE.........1491	L.Hampton-Mia..........12	J.Breech-Cin............101
M.Clayton-Mia 1150	M.Jackson-Den......19.42		R.Childress-LARd....617	L.Hampton-Mia......1458		N.Lowery-KC 100
Punt Average	**Field Goals**	**Field Goal Percent**	**Kickoff Returns**	**Kickoff Return Average**	**Punt Returns**	**Punt Return Average**
R.Stark-Ind 45.2	T.Franklin-NE.............32	P.Leahy-NYJ...........84.2	G.McNeil-Cle 47	L.Sanchez-Pit...........23.6	F.Walker-LARd..........49	B.Edmonds-Sea 12.3
R.Roby-Mia..............44.2	T.Zendejas-Hou 22	T.Zendejas-Hou 81.5	T.McGee-Cin..............43	T.McGee-Cin............23.4	G.Willhite-Den 42	G.Willhite-Den 11.1
R.Camarillo-NE........42.1	N.Johnson-Sea...........22	T.Franklin-NE...........78.0	S.Starring-NE 36	B.Humphery-NYJ....23.4	G.McNeil-Cle 40	R.Pitts-Buf 10.8
T.Moffett-SD............42.0	C.Bahr-LARd 21	M.Bahr-Cle 76.9	B.Edmonds-Sea 34	K.Bell-Den 23.1	K.Sohn-NYJ................35	I.Fryar-NE 10.5
	G.Anderson-Pit...........21	C.Bahr-LARd 75.0	A.Bentley-Ind 32	G.Lang-Den 22.9	I.Fryar-NE 35	G.Anderson-SD 9.1
Punt/Kick Return Yards	**Punt/Kick Return TDs**	**Interceptions**	**Interception Return Yards**	**Interception Return TDs**	**Sacks**	**Overall Rank**
G.McNeil-Cle 1345	G.McNeil-Cle 2	D.Cherry-KC 9	L.Burruss-KC............193	L.Burruss-KC..............3	S.Jones-LARd 15.5	C.Warner-Sea........1782
B.Edmonds-Sea 1183		R.Lippett-NE................8	M.Harden-Den.........179	M.Harden-Den.............2	L.Williams-SD 15.0	D.Marino-Mia 1670
T.McGee-Cin..........1028		V.McElroy-LARd...........7	J.Dale-SD 153		B.Smith-Buf 15.0	B.Kosar-Cle 1632
S.Starring-NE 820		L.Breeden-Cin 7	D.Cherry-KC 150		R.Jones-Den............13.5	J.Elway-Den...........1601
F.Walker-LARd.........808			V.McElroy-LARd.......105		L.O'Neal-SD 12.5	B.Esiason-Cin.........1576

Mediocre No More in Cleveland

If being an 8–8 playoff team the year before had caused any snickers about the Browns, that was no longer the case. Cleveland was the only division champ to repeat. Offensive coordinator Lindy Infante's influence on young quarterback Bernie Kosar took special importance because both starting running backs were injured, and Ozzie Newsome began to show his age. Head coach Marty Schottenheimer's defense was effective at bending without breaking—until the championship game.

The Patriots didn't let their Super Bowl humiliation carry over, as they unseated the Dolphins to win the East. New England passed by a Jets team that squandered a 10–1 start. The Patriots overcame the collapse of their running game, instead relying on a tag-team of quarterbacks Tony Eason and Steve Grogan to get the ball to wide receiver Stanley Morgan, and hoping that their quality defense could keep the game in reach.

Despite their late collapse, the Jets had started out remarkably hot with an effective passing game, but as the offense sputtered at the end, the defense also fell apart. The club was lucky to sneak in the playoffs as a wild card. In Miami, the complete collapse of the team's defense reduced Dan Marino to trying to will the team to wins—the Dolphins did lead the NFL in scoring—and setting an all-time record for completions plus the second-highest number of touchdown passes in a season (44).

In the West, Denver's John Elway enjoyed his best season yet, but he lacked much help. An inspired, stunting defense wore down as the season ran on, and the team lacked a consistent running game that might help keep it off of the field. Still, a 6–0 start was enough. Trying to keep up with the Broncos were the Chiefs, who could really only point to inspired special teams play for their success. Despite Kansas City's first playoff spot since 1971, head coach John Mackovic was axed after his players grumbled to owner Lamar Hunt. The slipping Raiders said goodbye to Jim Plunkett and Ray Guy; their only big moment was Todd Christensen setting the single-season record for receptions by a tight end with 95.

1987 NFC

TEAM	W-L-T	PCT	POST	PTS	RA	RY	RY/A	RTD	FL	PA	PC	GPY	GPY/A	PTD	PI	PSY	PRAT
Eastern Division																	
Was	11-4	.733	DCS*	379-285	500-441	2102-1679	4.2-3.8	18-10	19-11	478-527	247-276	3718-3767	7.8-7.1	27-19	18-23	223-424	80.7-69.3
Dal	7-8	.467	—	340-348	465-459	1865-1617	4.0-3.5	17-19	20-20	500-502	288-269	3594-3781	7.2-7.5	19-21	20-23	403-337	76.0-73.0
SL	7-8	.467	—	362-368	462-492	1873-2001	4.1-4.1	15-16	12-19	**529**-490	305-276	3850-3668	7.3-7.5	25-30	15-14	397-285	84.4-88.7
Phi	7-8	.467	—	337-380	509-428	2027-1643	4.0-3.8	12-16	19-**27**	520-561	283-305	3561-4058	6.8-7.2	26-29	16-21	511-452	79.8-79.2
NYG	6-9	.400	—	280-312	440-493	1457-1768	3.3-3.6	4-14	20-14	499-508	265-292	3645-3272	7.3-6.4	26-17	22-20	443-382	75.8-71.6
Central Division																	
ChiB	11-4	.733	D	356-282	485-412	1954-**1413**	4.0-**3.4**	13-**5**	20-11	493-507	272-255	3420-3286	6.9-6.5	23-24	24-13	330-**484**	72.2-76.1
Min	8-7	.533	WDC	336-335	482-440	1983-1724	4.1-3.9	**20**-9	**10**-11	446-498	232-278	3185-3407	7.1-6.8	21-24	23-26	359-307	69.4-71.4
GB	5-9-1	.367	—	255-300	464-521	1801-1920	3.9-3.7	13-15	18-24	455-469	234-279	2977-3200	6.5-7.1	17-18	17-18	296-197	67.6-74.0
TB	4-11	.267	—	286-360	394-500	1365-2038	3.5-4.1	7-18	14-20	517-457	264-271	3377-3255	6.5-7.1	22-23	17-16	361-306	72.3-83.4
Det	4-11	.267	—	269-384	398-504	1435-2070	3.6-4.1	9-18	11-13	509-459	275-259	3150-3558	6.2-7.8	16-23	26-19	**194**-355	62.1-80.9
Western Division																	
SF	**13-2**	**.867**	D	**459**-253	524-429	**2237**-1611	**4.3**-3.8	11-8	12-13	501-467	247-276	**3955**-2771	7.9-5.9	**44-13**	14-25	205-287	**106.2-53.8**
NO	12-3	.800	W	422-283	**569-388**	2190-1550	3.8-4.0	**20**-6	16-18	411-489	227-246	2987-3155	7.3-6.5	23-25	**12-30**	213-355	84.9-62.4
LARm	6-9	.400	—	317-361	512-419	2097-1732	4.1-4.1	15-8	15-11	420-504	220-281	2750-3693	6.5-7.3	16-31	18-16	196-304	67.9-86.4
Atl	3-12	.200	—	205-436	333-600	1298-2734	3.9-4.6	5-24	17-12	501-**453**	247-243	3108-3291	6.2-7.3	17-26	32-15	340-118	53.7-82.4
Aver	15	—		324	471	1859	3.9	13	16	482	264	3353	7.0	22	19	294	75.2

TEAM	1D	PENY	PNT	FGM/A	RTNY	RTNTD	OFFY/DEFY	NETY	NETTO	NP	PNP	DELP	PW	DELW	PRT	DR	YPD	DEL
Eastern Division																		
Was	301-296	691-801	39.1-39.2	18/29-19/28	**944**-424	2-4	5597-5022	575	-3	94	36	58	9.9	1.2	5.9/ 4.3	201-206	27.8-24.4	3.5
Dal	293-294	1091-851	39.6-40.6	25/29-19/29	561-655	2-2	5056-5061	-5	3	8	12	-20	7.3	-0.3	4.5/ 4.7	203-205	24.9-24.7	0.2
SL	325-306	797-718	38.0-41.2	14/27-**11/18**	717-716	6-2	5326-5384	-58	6	-6	19	-25	7.3	-0.3	5.2/ 5.7	188-186	28.3-28.9	-0.6
Phi	289-301	919-830	37.0-**37.1**	19/31-18/29	399-537	2-2	5077-5249	-172	13	-43	38	-81	6.4	0.6	4.4/ 4.8	**227**-223	22.4-23.5	-1.2
NYG	266-275	835-802	39.6-38.1	20/32-23/34	711-975	2-4	4659-4658	1	-8	-32	-32	0	6.7	-0.7	4.4/ 3.8	214-212	21.8-22.0	-0.2
Central Division																		
ChiB	319-261	821-**1108**	39.3-39.9	22/32-18/31	553-673	6-4	5044-4215	829	-20	74	-11	**85**	9.4	**1.6**	4.1/ 4.3	189-195	26.7-21.6	5.1
Min	293-281	814-964	38.9-39.9	14/29-24/31	723-823	1-5	4809-4824	-15	4	1	15	-14	7.5	0.5	4.0/ 4.0	196-197	24.5-24.5	0.0
GB	248-296	1103-852	39.3-40.1	21/29-27/36	465-537	0-2	4482-4923	-441	7	-45	-9	-36	6.4	-0.9	4.1/ 4.6	201-201	22.3-24.5	-2.2
TB	263-314	894-926	39.3-41.2	19/24-18/30	505-848	4-3	4381-4987	-606	5	-74	-31	-43	5.7	-1.6	4.4/ 5.0	189-191	23.2-26.1	-2.9
Det	270-314	737-907	**41.8**-37.9	26/39-28/34	593-512	2-2	4391-5273	-882	-5	-115	-94	-21	4.6	-0.6	3.6/ 5.1	190-185	23.1-28.0	-4.9
Western Division																		
SF	**357-250**	792-660	37.4-39.6	16/23-24/35	570-453	4-5	**5987-4095**	**1892**	12	206	206	0	**12.6**	0.3	**6.7/3.0**	187-191	**32.0-21.4**	10.6
NO	304-270	994-685	41.1-37.5	**33/42**-12/18	748-**372**	3-4	4964-4350	614	**20**	139	131	8	11.0	1.0	5.6/ 3.2	191-195	26.0-22.3	3.7
LARm	276-279	**677**-888	40.8-37.3	17/21-21/24	550-543	7-4	4651-5121	-470	-6	-44	-63	19	6.4	-0.4	4.3/ 5.5	193-**184**	24.1-27.8	-3.7
Atl	230-354	807-729	40.7-39.7	12/17-19/30	403-883	2-4	4066-5907	-1841	-22	-231	-241	10	1.7	1.3	2.7/ 5.9	170-211	21.7-31.1	-9.3
Aver	291	831	39.2	20/28	594	3	4918	—	—	—	—	—	—	—	5.0	193	25.4	—

Rushing Attempts
- C.White-LARm 324
- R.Mayes-NO 243
- R.Craig-SF 215
- H.Walker-Dal 209

Rushing Yards
- C.White-LARm 1374
- R.Mayes-NO 917
- H.Walker-Dal 891
- G.Riggs-Atl 875
- R.Craig-SF 815

Rushing Average
- M.Cummings-Phi 6.64
- K.Bryant-Was 5.27
- D.Nelson-Min 4.90
- J.Wilder-TB 4.60
- N.Anderson-Chi 4.54

Rushing TDs
- C.White-LARm 11
- H.Walker-Dal 7
- D.Hilliard-NO 7
- E.Ferrell-SL 7
- G.Rogers-Was 6

Rushing Rank
- C.White-LARm 1484
- R.Mayes-NO 967
- H.Walker-Dal 961
- G.Riggs-Atl 895
- R.Craig-SF 845

Passing Yards
- N.Lomax-SL 3387
- J.Montana-SF 3054
- M.Cummings-Phi 2786
- D.White-Dal 2617
- C.Long-Det 2598

Passing Average
- W.Wilson-Min 7.98
- P.Simms-NYG 7.91
- J.McMahon-Chi 7.80
- J.Montana-SF 7.67
- N.Lomax-SL 7.32

Completion Percent
- J.Montana-SF 66.8
- J.McMahon-Chi 59.5
- N.Lomax-SL 59.4
- D.White-Dal 59.4
- S.DeBerg-TB 57.8

TD Passes
- J.Montana-SF 31
- N.Lomax-SL 24
- M.Cummings-Phi 23
- P.Simms-NYG 17
- B.Hebert-NO 15

TD Percent
- J.Montana-SF 7.8
- P.Simms-NYG 6.0
- J.McMahon-Chi 5.7
- M.Cummings-Phi 5.7
- W.Wilson-Min 5.3

INT Percent
- S.DeBerg-TB 2.5
- N.Lomax-SL 2.6
- M.Cummings-Phi 3.0
- B.Hebert-NO 3.1
- P.Simms-NYG 3.2

Passer Rating
- J.Montana-SF 102.1
- P.Simms-NYG 90.0
- N.Lomax-SL 88.5
- J.McMahon-Chi 87.4
- S.DeBerg-TB 85.3

Passing Rank
- N.Lomax-SL 1334
- J.Montana-SF 1162
- M.Cummings-Phi 1028
- P.Simms-NYG 840
- B.Hebert-NO 775

Receptions
- J.Smith-SL 91
- R.Craig-SF 66
- J.Rice-SF 65
- H.Walker-Dal 60
- P.Mandley-Det 58

Receiving Yards
- J.Smith-SL 1117
- J.Rice-SF 1078
- G.Clark-Was 1066
- A.Carter-Min 922
- M.Bavaro-NYG 867

Receiving Average
- A.Carter-Min 24.26
- W.Gault-Chi 20.14
- G.Clark-Was 19.04
- L.Manuel-NYG 18.17
- W.Stanley-GB 17.68

Receiving TDs
- J.Rice-SF 22
- M.Quick-Phi 11
- J.Smith-SL 8
- M.Bavaro-NYG 8

Receiving Rank
- J.Rice-SF 649
- J.Smith-SL 599
- G.Clark-Was 568
- A.Carter-Min 496
- M.Bavaro-NYG 474

Combined Net Yards
- H.Walker-Dal 1606
- C.White-LARm 1568
- V.Sikahema-SL 1311
- R.Craig-SF 1307
- S.Mitchell-SL 1178

Total TDs
- J.Rice-SF 23
- C.White-LARm 11
- M.Quick-Phi 11

Total Points
- J.Rice-SF 138
- M.Andersen-NO 121
- R.Ruzek-Dal 92
- L.Lansford-LARm 87
- K.Butler-Chi 85

Punt Average
- R.Donnelly-Atl 44.0
- J.Arnold-Det 43.6
- S.Landeta-NYG 42.7
- D.Hatcher-LARm 41.3
- D.Bracken-GB 40.9

Field Goals
- M.Andersen-NO 28
- R.Ruzek-Dal 22
- E.Murray-Det 20
- K.Butler-Chi 19

Field Goal Percent
- R.Ruzek-Dal 88.0
- M.Zendejas-GB 84.2
- E.Murray-Det 81.0
- D.Igwebuike-TB 77.8
- M.Andersen-NO 77.8

Kickoff Returns
- N.Guggemos-Min 36
- V.Sikahema-SL 34
- G.Lee-Det 32
- B.Futrell-TB 31
- M.Gray-NO 30

Kickoff Return Average
- S.Stamps-Atl 27.5
- D.Gentry-Chi 24.8
- L.Rouson-NYG 22.6
- G.Lee-Det 22.5
- N.Guggemos-Min 22.4

Punt Returns
- V.Sikahema-SL 44
- P.McConkey-NYG 42
- D.McKinnon-Chi 40
- E.Yarber-Was 37
- W.Stanley-GB 28

Punt Return Average
- M.Gray-NO 14.7
- D.McLemore-SF 12.6
- V.Sikahema-SL 12.5
- L.Lewis-Min 12.5
- P.Mandley-Det 10.9

Punt/Kick Return Average
- V.Sikahema-SL 1311
- M.Gray-NO 988
- B.Futrell-TB 822
- N.Guggemos-Min 808
- G.Lee-Det 719

Punt/Kick Return TDs
- D.McKinnon-Chi 2

Interceptions
- B.Wilburn-Was 9
- J.Griffin-Det 6
- J.Browner-Min 6

Interception Return Yards
- T.Kinard-NYG 163
- B.Wilburn-Was 135
- J.Morris-GB 135
- J.Griffin-Det 130
- D.Waymer-NO 78

Interception Return TDs
- Many 1

Sacks
- R.White-Min 21.0
- R.Dent-Chi 12.5
- L.Taylor-NYG 12.0
- F.Nunn-SL 11.0
- C.Doleman-Min 11.0

Overall Rank
- C.White-LARm 1573
- M.Cummings-Phi 1562
- N.Lomax-SL 1441
- H.Walker-Dal 1324
- J.Montana-SF 1313

STRUCK OUT ON THE GRIDIRON

Labor issues once again tainted the season. Two weeks in, the players hit the picket lines. But instead of repeating the misfortune of multiple canceled games in 1982, team owners chose the hardball tactic of playing on. After a one-week shutdown, replacement players were brought in, much to the dismay of coaching staffs, not to mention fans. John Fourcade, with experience in the CFL, USFL, and the new indoor Arena Football League, took over as Saints quarterback and would remain on the team for four seasons.

On October 4 the turnstiles opened, the television cameras and commentators were in place, and the strike-breakers took the field. The games counted, but to the few who showed up or watched on television, it was about as exciting as a preseason game, only less so. After three weeks of this—and with several union members crossing the lines—the NFLPA threw in the towel and ordered players back to work, playing on without a collective bargaining agreement. Luckily for ESPN, the cable network's first-ever Sunday night telecast on November 8 came after the replacements went home.

The strike had corrosive effects throughout the league. Chicago coach Mike Ditka alienated his veterans with his criticism on labor issues. Though the Bears won the Central Division again, Jim McMahon wasn't getting any healthier, and the great Walter Payton was at the end of the line. In the East, veteran quarterback Doug Williams stepped in for the injured and inconsistent Jay Schroeder in Washington. The controversy over replacing Tony Dorsett with Herschel Walker festered in Dallas, while the defending champion Giants were derailed by injuries and dissension.

San Francisco's Jerry Rice hauled in a record 22 touchdown receptions—in only 12 games—but coach Bill Walsh had his eye on the future, digging quarterback Steve Young out of the mire in Tampa Bay. The Saints enjoyed their first winning season and their first playoff appearance. Former USFL coach Jim Mora won Coach of the Year, and with general manager Jim Finks doing the shopping, the Saints created an excellent linebacker quartets by adding USFL veterans Sam Mills and Vaughan Johnson with Pro Bowler Rickey Jackson and young Pat Swilling.

1987 AFC

TEAM	W-L-T	PCT	POST	PTS	RA	RY	RY/A	RTD	FL	PA	PC	GPY	GPY/A	PTD	PI	PSY	PRAT
Eastern Division																	
Ind	9-6	.600	D	300-**238**	497-463	2143-1790	4.3-3.9	14-**6**	18-**25**	447-501	255-250	3042-3073	6.8-**6.1**	16-19	16-20	190-313	75.0-65.2
NE	8-7	.533	—	320-293	513-490	1771-1778	3.5-3.6	12-13	13-21	440-520	236-273	2929-3438	6.7-6.6	22-17	18-21	246-339	74.1-67.5
Mia	8-7	.533	—	362-335	408-498	1662-2198	4.1-4.4	16-18	17-16	**584**-494	**338**-295	**3977**-3430	6.8-6.9	29-21	20-16	**101**-183	81.0-81.5
Buf	7-8	.467	—	270-305	465-541	1840-2052	4.0-3.8	9-11	24-14	516-447	292-249	3246-3121	6.3-7.0	21-25	19-17	345-267	73.7-80.4
NYJ	6-9	.400	—	334-360	458-476	1671-1835	3.6-3.9	17-15	19-11	517-488	302-260	3402-3412	6.6-7.0	18-27	15-18	443-206	77.7-78.7
Central Division																	
Cle	**10**-5	.667	DC	**390**-239	474-**401**	1745-**1433**	3.7-3.6	16-7	17-13	482-467	291-246	3625-3088	**7.5**-6.6	27-**15**	**12**-23	170-257	**92.0**-63.7
Hou	9-6	.600	WD	345-349	486-446	1923-1848	4.0-4.1	12-10	14-14	482-495	240-266	3534-3416	7.3-6.9	24-25	23-23	234-271	70.8-73.1
Pit	8-7	.533	—	285-299	517-455	2144-1610	4.1-**3.5**	11-8	**8**-17	429-481	198-290	2464-3506	5.7-7.3	13-22	25-27	198-196	50.3-74.6
Cin	4-11	.267	—	285-370	**538**-441	2164-1641	4.0-3.7	13-15	12-12	475-456	255-267	3468-3359	7.3-7.4	17-24	20-14	255-303	71.6-86.3
Western Division																	
Den	**10**-4-1	**.700**	DCS	379-288	510-454	1970-2017	3.9-4.4	**18**-16	17-19	530-456	285-261	3874-**3040**	7.3-6.7	24-**15**	19-**28**	220-244	77.5-**62.9**
Sea	9-6	.600	W	371-314	496-472	2023-2201	4.1-4.7	13-14	15-21	405-445	237-255	3028-3196	**7.5**-7.2	**31**-20	21-17	316-238	85.9-78.8
SD	8-7	.533	—	253-317	396-522	1308-2171	3.3-4.2	11-14	20-15	516-441	303-227	3602-3080	7.0-7.0	13-19	23-13	322-298	69.9-76.2
LARd	5-10	.333	—	301-289	475-469	**2197**-1637	**4.6-3.5**	13-12	13-15	457-**425**	247-**224**	3429-3088	**7.5**-7.3	19-18	18-13	359-**361**	75.8-77.7
KC	4-11	.267	—	273-388	419-535	1799-2333	4.3-4.4	7-16	24-17	432-484	236-279	2985-3473	6.9-7.2	17-25	17-11	366-167	73.1-87.8
Aver	15	—	—	324	471	1859	3.9	13	16	482	264	3353	7.0	22	19	294	75.2

TEAM	1D	PENY	PNT	FGM/A	RTNY	RTNTD	OFFY/DEFY	NETY	NETTO	NP	PNP	DELP	PW	DELW	PRT	DR	YPD	DEL
Eastern Division																		
Ind	285-276	742-689	37.7-37.2	**27/32**-15/26	422-557	1-3	4995-4550	445	**11**	62	81	-19	9.1	-0.0	4.9/ 3.8	197-190	25.4-23.9	1.4
NE	266-293	**506**-846	37.6-38.1	16/28-18/27	520-557	5-4	4454-4877	-423	**11**	27	9	18	8.2	-0.2	4.4/ 4.1	194-203	23.0-24.0	-1.1
Mia	**331**-314	634-850	38.5-38.8	12/16-**14**/22	425-439	2-3	5538-5445	93	-5	27	-12	39	8.2	-0.2	5.5/ 5.3	181-**178**	**30.6**-30.6	0.0
Buf	294-297	762-840	38.2-**36.7**	12/20-15/**20**	325-356	3-**1**	4741-4906	-165	-12	-35	-62	27	6.6	0.4	4.1/ 4.9	193-195	24.6-25.2	-0.6
NYJ	292-300	1055-881	37.1-38.4	20/26-20/29	736-372	4-**1**	4630-5041	-411	-5	-26	-54	28	6.8	-0.9	4.2/ 5.2	197-195	23.5-25.9	-2.3
Central Division																		
Cle	310-**251**	857-**1008**	36.9-37.5	21/31-17/25	853-**266**	4-4	5200-**4264**	**936**	7	**151**	106	45	**11.3**	-1.3	**6.2**/ 3.9	183-182	28.4-**23.4**	**5.0**
Hou	294-287	1029-874	39.1-39.4	26/**32**-30/36	523-679	2-2	5223-4993	230	0	-4	19	-23	7.4	1.6	4.9/ 4.5	**203**-198	25.7-25.2	0.5
Pit	263-289	801-771	40.2-39.2	22/29-20/26	580-725	**7**-4	4410-4920	-510	**11**	-14	2	-16	7.2	0.9	2.8/ 4.6	190-192	23.2-25.6	-2.4
Cin	319-286	791-669	41.0-40.2	25/**32**-23/26	480-635	0-4	5377-4697	680	-6	-85	33	-118	5.4	-1.4	4.9/ 5.4	186-182	28.9-25.8	3.1
Western Division																		
Den	**331**-277	812-785	39.9-42.1	21/29-**14**/21	**889**-786	3-4	**5624**-4813	811	**11**	91	**112**	-21	9.8	0.7	5.4/**3.5**	194-192	29.0-25.1	3.9
Sea	301-297	668-890	38.9-39.1	17/22-21/26	611-397	2-2	4735-5159	-424	2	57	-27	**84**	8.9	0.1	4.7/ 5.0	178-180	26.6-28.7	-2.1
SD	264-280	743-869	**42.0**-41.5	16/28-19/29	799-695	5-4	4588-4953	-365	-15	-64	-90	26	5.9	**2.1**	4.3/ 4.9	200-200	22.9-24.8	-1.8
LARd	300-267	1048-652	39.4-42.6	19/30-20/29	534-627	3-3	5267-4364	903	-3	12	63	-51	7.8	-2.8	4.8/ 5.0	183-182	28.8-24.0	4.8
KC	265-344	861-936	40.4-40.4	21/25-24/35	486-583	6-4	4418-5639	-1221	-13	-115	-154	39	4.6	-0.6	4.2/ 6.0	179-181	24.7-31.2	-6.5
Aver	291	831	39.2	20/28	594	2	4918	—	—	—	—	—	—	—	5.0	95	26.0	—

Rushing Attempts	Rushing Yards	Rushing Average	Rushing TDs	Rushing Rank	Passing Yards	Passing Average
C.Warner-Sea 234	E.Dickerson-Ind 1011	B.Jackson-LARd 6.84	J.Hector-NYJ 11	C.Warner-Sea 1065	B.Esiason-Cin 3321	J.Elway-Den 7.80
M.Rozier-Hou 229	C.Warner-Sea 985	H.Heard-KC 5.68	C.Warner-Sea 8	E.Dickerson-Ind 1061	D.Marino-Mia 3245	B.Kosar-Cle 7.80
E.Dickerson-Ind 223	M.Rozier-Hou 957	E.Dickerson-Ind 4.53	L.Kinnebrew-Cin 8	M.Rozier-Hou 987	J.Elway-Den 3198	M.Wilson-LARd 7.78
K.Mack-Cle 201	M.Allen-LARd 754	A.Bentley-Ind 4.44	E.Byner-Cle 8	M.Allen-LARd 804	B.Kosar-Cle 3033	B.Kenney-KC 7.72
M.Allen-LARd 200	S.Winder-Den 741	J.Williams-Sea 4.42	A.Bentley-Ind 7	S.Winder-Den 801	W.Moon-Hou 2806	W.Moon-Hou 7.63
Completion Percent	**TD Passes**	**TD Percent**	**INT Percent**	**Passer Rating**	**Passing Rank**	**Receptions**
B.Kosar-Cle 62.0	D.Marino-Mia 26	D.Krieg-Sea 7.8	K.O'Brien-NYJ 2.0	B.Kosar-Cle 95.4	B.Kosar-Cle 1267	A.Toon-NYJ 68
D.Krieg-Sea 60.5	D.Krieg-Sea 23	D.Marino-Mia 5.9	B.Kosar-Cle 2.3	D.Marino-Mia 89.2	D.Marino-Mia 1233	S.Largent-Sea 58
J.Kelly-Buf 59.7	B.Kosar-Cle 22	W.Moon-Hou 5.7	J.Trudeau-Ind 2.6	D.Krieg-Sea 87.6	J.Elway-Den 1214	A.Reed-Buf 57
K.O'Brien-NYJ 59.5	W.Moon-Hou 21	B.Kosar-Cle 5.7	J.Kelly-Buf 2.6	B.Kenney-KC 85.8	K.O'Brien-NYJ 1093	R.Harmon-Buf 56
D.Marino-Mia 59.2		B.Kenney-KC 5.5	J.Elway-Den 2.9	M.Wilson-LARd 84.6	J.Kelly-Buf 1054	C.Burkett-Buf 56
Receiving Yards	**Receiving Average**	**Receiving TDs**	**Receiving Rank**	**Combined Net Yards**	**Total TDs**	**Total Points**
C.Carson-KC 1044	J.Lofton-LARd 21.46	S.Largent-Sea 8	C.Carson-KC 557	A.Bentley-Ind 1578	J.Hector-NYJ 11	J.Breech-Cin 97
D.Hill-Hou 989	R.Nattiel-Den 20.32	M.Duper-Mia 8	D.Hill-Hou 525	T.Stradford-Mia 1334	C.Warner-Sea 10	D.Biasucci-Ind 96
A.Toon-NYJ 976	D.Hill-Hou 20.18		A.Toon-NYJ 513	G.Anderson-SD 1196	E.Byner-Cle 10	T.Zendejas-Hou 92
E.Givins-Hou 933	C.Carson-KC 18.98		E.Givins-Hou 497	M.Allen-LARd 1164	A.Bentley-Ind 9	R.Karlis-Den 91
S.Largent-Sea 912	M.Duper-Mia 18.09		S.Largent-Sea 496	C.Warner-Sea 1152		G.Anderson-Pit 87
Punt Average	**Field Goals**	**Field Goal Percent**	**Kickoff Returns**	**Kickoff Return Average**	**Punt Returns**	**Punt Return Average**
T.Moffett-SD 42.9	J.Breech-Cin 24	D.Biasucci-Ind 88.9	P.Palmer-KC 38	P.Palmer-KC 24.3	G.McNeil-Cle 34	K.Clark-Den 12.9
R.Roby-Mia 42.8	D.Biasucci-Ind 24	N.Lowery-KC 82.6	D.Stone-Pit 28	G.Young-Cle 22.9	J.Townsell-NYJ 32	B.Edmonds-Sea 12.6
H.Newsome-Pit 41.8	G.Anderson-Pit 22	P.Leahy-NYJ 81.8	C.Duncan-Hou 28	A.Bentley-Ind 22.7	L.James-SD 32	L.James-SD 12.5
S.Fulhage-Cin 41.7	T.Zendejas-Hou 20	G.Anderson-Pit 81.5	V.Mueller-LARd 27	V.Mueller-LARd 21.8	M.Martin-Cin 28	J.Townsell-NYJ 11.9
M.Horan-Den 41.1		J.Breech-Cin 80.0	B.Edmonds-Sea 27	J.Holland-SD 21.6	C.Woods-LARd 26	G.McNeil-Cle 11.4
Punt/Kick Return Yards	**Punt/Kick Return TDs**	**Interceptions**	**Interception Return Yards**	**Interception Return TDs**	**Sacks**	**Overall Rank**
P.Palmer-KC 923	P.Palmer-KC 2	M.Prior-Ind 6	V.Glenn-SD 166	R.Lippett-NE 2	A.Tippett-NE 12.5	J.Elway-Den 1558
B.Edmonds-Sea 815		M.Kelso-Buf 6	F.Wright-Cle 152		B.Smith-Buf 12.0	B.Kosar-Cle 1299
J.Townsell-NYJ 653		K.Bostic-Hou 6	K.Clark-Den 105		J.Green-Sea 9.5	D.Marino-Mia 1238
G.McNeil-Cle 591		D.Woodruff-Pit 5	R.Lippett-NE 103		F.Young-Sea 9.0	B.Esiason-Cin 1222
V.Mueller-LARd 588		B.Smith-SD 5	D.Woodruff-Pit 91			J.Kelly-Buf 1205

Boz vs. Bo: No Contest

The defending conference champs looked rough in the early going, but the Broncos handily won their division by winning six of their final seven games. John Elway was once again Denver's key weapon, but he was supported by an improving platoon of receivers and an underrated defense with few stars beyond end Rulon Jones and rover Karl Mecklenburg. The Chargers gave Denver an early scare with an 8–1 start, including a 3–0 run with their replacement players, but the last vestiges of Air Coryell—with Al Saunders instead of Don Coryell—fell short of the playoffs with a second-half swoon. Wideout Charlie Joiner had already retired, and he'd be joined by both tight end Kellen Winslow and quarterback Dan Fouts after the season.

The Raiders provided entertainment with the debut of two-sport star Bo Jackson, but he would be forced out of action after only seven games. He managed to put cocksure rookie linebacker Brian Bosworth, an exercise in hype, in his place. Bo crushed him like a tin can in a memorable display on Monday Night Football. On the same Seahawks sideline as bellicose Boz was dignified wideout Steve Largent, who passed Joiner for the career receptions mark.

If there was a surprise team in the conference, it was the Colts. Indianapolis swung a three-way deal for disgruntled running back Eric Dickerson from the Rams (only later would the decision to send linebacker Cornelius Bennett to Buffalo come back to haunt them). With Dickerson on the field for the last nine games, the Colts had just enough offense to balance an aggressive defense that was particularly effective against the pass.

The Browns continued to improve. Quarterback Bernie Kosar spread the ball around more and utilized wide receiver Webster Slaughter as a deep threat. The improved offense matched up nicely with a defense that boasted one of the league's best run-stuffing defenses and a consensus All-Pro tandem of cornerbacks: Hanford Dixon and Frank Minnifield. The Central Division boasted a surprise team of its own in the Houston Oilers. The combination of their highly-rated offensive line helped establish quarterback Warren Moon and running back Mike Rozier as stars.

1988 NFC

TEAM	W-L-T	PCT	POST	PTS	RA	RY	RY/A	RTD	FL	PA	PC	GPY	GPY/A	PTD	PI	PSY	PRAT
Eastern Division																	
Phi	10-6	.625	#D	379-319	464-466	1945-1652	4.2-3.5	17-11	**9**-12	581-578	309-309	3927-4443	6.8-7.7	25-23	17-32	442-296	76.7-68.9
NYG	10-6	.625	#	359-304	493-454	1689-1759	3.4-3.9	15-8	13-18	525-566	290-294	3716-3755	7.1-6.6	22-23	**14**-15	450-**428**	80.5-75.5
Phx	7-9	.438	—	344-398	480-467	2027-1925	4.2-4.1	15-19	16-13	562-508	322-264	4191-3539	7.5-7.0	26-30	19-16	411-295	82.2-81.0
Was	7-9	.438	—	345-387	437-442	1543-1745	3.5-3.9	8-17	21-8	**592**-497	**327**-261	**4339**-3744	7.3-7.5	**33**-24	25-14	203-305	79.6-81.6
Dal	3-13	.188	—	265-381	469-454	1995-1858	4.3-4.1	10-13	13-9	555-523	307-264	3727-3883	6.7-7.4	21-30	27-10	239-327	68.5-86.2
Central Division																	
ChiB	**12**-4	**.750**	DC	312-**215**	**555-389**	2319-**1326**	4.2-3.4	**25-5**	19-9	461-545	248-245	3173-3399	6.9-6.2	13-18	15-26	175-365	71.4-56.7
Min	11-5	.688	WD	406-233	501-435	1806-1602	3.6-3.7	22-10	12-17	520-480	294-**219**	4100-**2763**	**7.9-5.8**	20-**12**	18-**36**	311-274	80.4-**41.2**
TB	5-11	.313	—	261-350	452-478	1753-1551	3.9-**3.2**	11-21	16-12	512-527	253-304	3608-3744	7.0-7.1	16-19	36-21	300-140	53.7-75.2
Det	4-12	.250	—	220-313	391-511	1243-2037	3.2-4.0	7-16	15-**21**	477-513	213-337	2572-3672	5.4-7.2	13-17	18-15	410-393	55.1-85.5
GB	4-12	.250	—	240-315	385-514	1379-2110	3.6-4.1	14-17	26-**21**	582-**474**	319-256	3609-2949	6.2-6.2	13-**12**	24-20	324-216	63.9-63.9
Western Division																	
SF	10-6	.625	#DCS*	369-294	527-441	**2523**-1588	**4.8**-3.6	18-8	12-16	502-530	293-292	3675-3284	7.3-6.2	21-25	**14**-22	298-297	83.5-72.2
LARm	10-6	.625	#W	**407**-293	507-414	2003-1686	4.0-4.1	16-12	16-15	522-571	312-307	4002-3694	7.7-6.5	31-17	18-22	197-394	**89.3**-67.7
NO	10-6	.625	#	312-283	512-442	2046-1779	4.0-4.0	9-7	16-15	498-505	286-277	3256-3579	6.5-7.1	21-19	16-17	**171**-252	77.9-75.8
Atl	5-11	.313	—	244-315	478-518	2016-2319	4.2-4.5	11-14	18-14	481-504	250-281	2914-3584	6.1-7.1	13-17	19-24	348-211	63.2-69.6
Aver	16	—	—	324	485	1943	4.0	15	15	505	274	3487	6.9	20	20	276	72.9

TEAM	1D	PENY	PNT	FGM/A	RTNY	RTNTD	OFFY/DEFY	NETY	NETTO	NP	PNP	DELP	PW	DELW	PRT	DR	YPD	DEL
Eastern Division																		
Phi	318-311	907-897	39.7-37.8	23/32-20/29	604-491	2-3	5430-5799	-369	18	60	41	19	9.5	0.5	4.7/ 4.7	213-222	25.5-26.1	-0.6
NYG	317-291	660-902	39.9-39.8	24/30-25/33	651-**419**	4-2	4955-5086	-131	6	55	13	42	9.4	0.6	4.9/ 4.7	208-195	23.8-26.1	-2.3
Phx	**336**-301	790-770	40.3-41.1	12/21-**13/22**	551-680	3-2	5807-5169	638	-6	-54	29	-83	6.7	0.4	5.1/ 5.2	202-199	28.7-26.0	2.8
Was	307-294	817-711	38.2-39.4	19/26-22/36	570-719	0-5	5679-5184	495	-24	-42	-55	13	6.9	0.0	5.4/ 5.6	200-197	28.4-26.3	2.1
Dal	311-297	1148-772	40.9-41.6	13/25-24/29	427-553	1-**1**	5483-5414	69	-21	-116	-78	-38	5.1	-2.1	4.2/ 6.0	195-195	28.1-27.8	0.4
Central Division																		
ChiB	303-264	644-804	41.5-40.2	15/19-**13/22**	531-622	0-2	5317-4360	957	1	97	84	13	10.4	**1.6**	5.1/ 3.5	189-**188**	28.1-23.2	4.9
Min	318-**243**	998-753	39.4-42.3	20/25-21/25	**1142**-617	**7**-2	5595-**4091**	**1504**	**23**	**173**	**217**	-44	**12.3**	-1.3	5.6/**1.9**	**216**-208	25.9-**19.7**	6.2
TB	295-293	816-872	36.4-39.0	21/30-18/30	611-759	1-2	5061-5155	-94	-19	-89	-84	-5	5.8	-0.8	3.4/ 5.2	199-195	25.4-26.4	-1.0
Det	226-334	804-869	**42.4**-39.4	20/21-25/29	593-642	3-**1**	3405-5316	-1911	3	-93	-147	**54**	5.7	-1.7	2.8/ 5.0	189-191	18.0-27.8	-9.8
GB	280-281	785-903	38.2-**37.6**	13/25-25/35	432-700	2-5	4664-4843	-179	-9	-75	-51	-24	6.1	-2.1	3.7/ 3.9	204-207	22.9-23.4	-0.5
Western Division																		
SF	326-277	986-603	38.7-41.0	**27/38**-18/24	700-611	2-**1**	**5900**-4575	1325	12	75	158	-83	9.9	0.1	5.4/ 3.9	199-202	**29.6**-22.6	**7.0**
LARm	333-289	587-**937**	39.5-39.9	24/32-16/23	603-485	1-6	5808-4986	822	3	114	81	33	10.9	-0.8	**6.0**/ 4.0	205-206	28.3-24.2	4.1
NO	306-286	821-628	39.9-40.2	26/36-27/34	708-474	3-3	5131-5106	25	0	29	2	27	8.7	1.3	4.9/ 5.1	183-190	28.0-26.9	1.2
Atl	257-312	**542**-761	40.0-39.6	19/30-26/36	528-511	3-3	4582-5692	-1110	1	-71	-89	18	6.2	-1.2	3.5/ 4.6	197-209	23.3-27.2	-4.0
Aver	303	809	40.2	20/28	588	3	5153	—	—	—	—	—	—	—	5.0	195	26.4	—

Rushing Attempts	Rushing Yards	Rushing Average	Rushing TDs	Rushing Rank	Passing Yards	Passing Average
H.Walker-Dal...361	H.Walker-Dal...1514	R.Cross-Phi...6.71	G.Bell-LARm...16	R.Craig-SF...1592	J.Everett-LARm...3964	W.Wilson-Min...8.27
R.Craig-SF...310	R.Craig-SF...1502	R.Craig-SF...4.85	N.Anderson-Chi...12	H.Walker-Dal...1564	R.Cross-Phi...3808	J.Everett-LARm...7.67
J.Morris-NYG...307	G.Bell-LARm...1212	B.Fullwood-GB...4.78	R.Craig-SF...9	G.Bell-LARm...1372	N.Lomax-Phx...3395	N.Lomax-Phx...7.66
G.Bell-LARm...288	N.Anderson-Chi...1106	K.Bryant-Was...4.61	O.Anderson-NYG...8	N.Anderson-Chi...1226	P.Simms-NYG...3359	J.Montana-SF...7.51
N.Anderson-Chi...249	J.Morris-NYG...1083	E.Ferrell-Phx...4.57		J.Morris-NYG...1133	J.Teltschik-TB...3240	S.Pelluer-Dal...7.22
Completion Percent	**TD Passes**	**TD Percent**	**INT Percent**	**Passer Rating**	**Passing Rank**	**Receptions**
W.Wilson-Min...61.4	J.Everett-LARm...31	J.Everett-LARm...6.0	P.Simms-NYG...2.3	W.Wilson-Min...91.5	J.Everett-LARm...1417	H.Ellard-LARm...86
J.Montana-SF...59.9	R.Cross-Phi...24	J.Montana-SF...4.5	N.Lomax-Phx...2.5	J.Everett-LARm...89.2	R.Cross-Phi...1384	E.Martin-NO...85
J.Everett-LARm...59.6	P.Simms-NYG...21	W.Wilson-Min...4.5	J.Montana-SF...2.5	J.Montana-SF...87.9	N.Lomax-Phx...1358	J.Smith-Phx...83
B.Hebert-NO...58.6	N.Lomax-Phx...20	N.Lomax-Phx...4.5	W.Wilson-Min...2.7	N.Lomax-Phx...86.7	P.Simms-NYG...1345	K.Jackson-Phi...81
R.Wright-GB...57.8	B.Hebert-NO...20	P.Simms-NYG...4.4	R.Cross-Phi...2.9	P.Simms-NYG...82.1	J.Montana-SF...1181	R.Craig-SF...76
Receiving Yards	**Receiving Average**	**Receiving TDs**	**Receiving Rank**	**Combined Net Yards**	**Total TDs**	**Total Points**
H.Ellard-LARm...1414	M.Irvin-Dal...20.44	R.Sanders-Was...12	H.Ellard-LARm...757	R.Craig-SF...2068	G.Bell-LARm...18	M.Cofer-SF...121
J.Rice-SF...1306	J.Rice-SF...20.41	H.Ellard-LARm...10	J.Rice-SF...698	H.Walker-Dal...2019	R.Sanders-Was...12	M.Lansford-LARm...117
A.Carter-Min...1225	C.Carter-Phi...19.51	J.Rice-SF...9	A.Carter-Min...643	J.Settle-Atl...1594	N.Anderson-Chi...12	M.Andersen-NO...110
R.Sanders-Was...1148	H.Jones-Min...19.45	B.Hill-TB...9	R.Sanders-Was...634	H.Ellard-LARm...1540		C.Nelson-Min...108
R.Green-Phx...1097	B.Hill-TB...17.93		R.Green-Phx...584	R.Sanders-Was...1524		G.Bell-LARm...108
Punt Average	**Field Goals**	**Field Goal Percent**	**Kickoff Returns**	**Kickoff Return Average**	**Punt Returns**	**Punt Return Average**
J.Arnold-Det...42.4	M.Cofer-SF...27	E.Murray-Det...95.2	D.Harris-Min...39	D.Elder-TB...22.7	L.Lewis-Min...58	J.Taylor-SF...12.6
B.Wagner-Chi...41.5	M.Andersen-NO...26	C.Nelson-Min...80.0	D.Elder-TB...34	C.Burbage-Dal...22.4	J.Taylor-SF...44	M.Gray-NO...12.2
M.Buford-NYG...41.3	M.Lansford-LARm...24	L.Zendejas-Phi...79.2	S.Beals-Phi...34	D.Clack-Dal...21.6	K.Martin-Dal...44	B.Futrell-TB...10.5
M.Saxon-Dal...40.9	C.Nelson-Min...20	K.Butler-Chi...78.9		D.Gentry-Chi...21.4	P.McConkey-NYG...40	V.Sikahema-Phx...10.3
G.Horne-Phx...40.9	E.Murray-Det...20	D.Igwebuike-TB...76.0		D.Harris-Min...21.4	P.Mandley-Det...37	L.Lewis-Min...9.5
Punt/Kick Return Yards	**Punt/Kick Return TDs**	**Interceptions**	**Interception Return Yards**	**Interception Return TDs**	**Sacks**	**Overall Rank**
M.Gray-NO...975	J.Taylor-SF...2	S.Case-Atl...10	H.Hamilton-TB...123	C.Lee-Min...2	R.White-Phi...18.0	R.Cross-Phi...2068
D.Harris-Min...833	R.Pitts-GB...1	C.Lee-Min...8	C.Lee-Min...118		K.Greene-LARm...16.5	R.Craig-SF...1866
V.Sikahema-Phx...816	M.Gray-NO...1	V.Jackson-Chi...8	T.Hoage-Phi...116		L.Taylor-NYG...15.5	H.Walker-Dal...1827
J.Taylor-SF...781		T.Hoage-Phi...8	D.Mitchell-Det...107		F.Nunn-Phx...14.0	J.Everett-LARm...1521
D.Elder-TB...772		T.McKyer-SF...7	S.Joyner-Phi...96		T.Harris-GB...13.5	P.Simms-NYG...1497

Good Teams, Bad Teams

Competitive imbalance had become a bit of a problem. Seven NFC teams won 10 or more games; no one else even reached .500. The worst team in the league was Dallas, closing out the storied career of head coach Tom Landry on a particularly ignominious note. Equally disappointing were the Super Bowl champion Redskins, whose uncharacteristically pass-happy offense was never the same after the second quarter of Super Bowl XXII.

The Eagles had labored under high expectations that former Bears defensive coordinator Buddy Ryan would be able to immediately turn the team around. Instead of winning with defense, Ryan's team won in his third year because of quarterback Randall Cunningham's ability to take the ball upfield himself if he couldn't find tight end Keith Jackson or running back Keith Byars open. Giants quarterback Phil Simms enjoyed a particularly effective season, but the defense lacked its former capacity for dominance, hindered by Carl Banks's holdout, Lawrence Taylor's drug suspension, and Harry Carson's career-ending injury. The Eagles claimed the division on a tiebreaker.

The Cardinals remained in the NFC East but moved West. Owner Bill Bidwill's long-threatened move resulted in the club's third home in the NFL: Phoenix. Bidwill charged ticket prices commensurate with the league's elite, and the Cardinals finished 7–9. It would be their best season in the desert for five years.

Bill Walsh shocked observers and players alike by starting a quarterback controversy between Joe Montana with Steve Young. The Rams blew their shot at the title with a midseason fade, but their blend of running back Greg Bell (part of the swag from the previous season's Eric Dickerson deal) and quarterback Jim Everett's ability to hit Henry Ellard downfield provided the club's most balanced offense in years. The Bears won the Central with running back Neal Anderson carrying the offense. The defense remained strong around its core of Dan Hampton, Mike Singletary, and Richard Dent. The Vikings were also coming into their own, boasting an equally talented defense with lineman Keith Millard, safety Joey Browner, and corner Carl Lee. The team's only area of want was its running game, a need the Vikings would address boldly.

1988 AFC

TEAM	W-L-T	PCT	POST	PTS	RA	RY	RY/A	RTD	FL	PA	PC	GPY	GPY/A	PTD	PI	PSY	PRAT
Eastern Division																	
Buf	**12**-4	**.750**	DC	329-**237**	528-477	2133-1854	4.0-3.9	15-14	16-17	454-448	271-250	3411-3046	7.5-6.8	15-14	17-15	229-322	78.5-73.4
Ind	9-7	.563	—	354-315	545-447	2249-1694	4.1-3.8	23-14	**8-20**	403-539	222-321	2865-3803	7.1-7.1	15-21	22-15	244-201	67.3-82.5
NE	9-7	.563	—	250-284	**588**-496	2120-2099	3.6-4.2	17-20	10-15	389-436	199-234	2333-2801	6.0-6.4	12-13	28-20	160-219	50.0-64.4
NYJ	8-7-1	.531	—	372-354	514-517	2132-2124	4.1-4.1	19-15	16-16	538-476	299-244	3374-3823	6.3-8.0	20-28	**11-24**	291-314	78.4-76.9
Mia	6-10	.375	—	319-380	335-557	1205-2506	3.6-4.5	11-22	12-15	**621**-491	**363**-298	**4557**-3442	7.3-7.0	**29**-19	23-16	**41**-167	81.5-81.2
Central Division																	
Cin	**12**-4	**.750**	DCS	**448**-329	563-493	**2710**-2048	**4.8**-4.2	**27**-18	13-14	392-524	225-283	3592-3508	**9.2**-6.7	28-19	14-22	245-**374**	**97.0**-69.6
Cle	10-6	.625	W	304-288	440-498	1575-1920	3.6-3.9	10-**13**	16-11	537-474	313-245	3686-3102	6.9-6.5	19-13	17-20	250-255	77.9-64.0
Hou	10-6	.625	WD	424-365	558-**431**	2249-**1592**	4.0-3.7	26-20	17-**20**	428-512	218-281	3166-3619	7.4-7.1	21-22	18-22	210-353	74.2-73.7
Pit	5-11	.313	—	336-421	499-516	2228-1864	4.5-**3.6**	17-20	19-13	489-532	226-309	3307-4086	6.8-7.7	15-25	20-20	331-145	62.0-82.5
Western Division																	
Sea	9-7	.563	D	339-329	517-509	2086-2286	4.0-4.5	14-14	14-18	437-501	245-280	2979-3618	6.8-7.2	22-21	20-22	223-265	74.9-74.4
Den	8-8	.500	—	327-352	464-552	1815-2538	3.9-4.6	13-21	12-13	581-467	324-262	3941-3168	6.8-6.8	24-18	22-16	250-235	74.8-75.7
LARd	7-9	.438	—	325-369	493-533	1852-2208	3.8-4.1	15-17	13-17	496-483	219-265	3503-3471	7.1-7.2	21-23	20-17	394-300	65.6-79.0
SD	6-10	.375	—	231-332	438-521	2041-2133	4.7-4.1	11-15	12-10	468-517	241-274	2628-3525	5.6-6.8	11-22	20-16	240-240	58.4-75.9
KC	4-11-1	.281	—	254-320	448-609	1713-2592	3.8-4.3	8-23	12-13	528-**410**	282-**214**	3484-**2591**	6.6-**6.3**	16-**12**	21-18	353-157	67.6-**63.4**
Aver	16	—	—	324	485	1943	4.0	15	15	505	274	3487	6.9	20	20	276	72.9

TEAM	1D	PENY	PNT	FGM/A	RTNY	RTNTD	OFFY/DEFY	NETY	NETTO	NP	PNP	DELP	PW	DELW	PRT	DR	YPD	DEL
Eastern Division																		
Buf	313-299	824-713	39.5-39.7	**32/37-12**/24	396-424	3-1	5315-**4578**	737	-1	92	57	35	10.3	1.7	5.3/ 4.4	177-181	30.0-25.3	4.7
Ind	311-315	657-965	43.5-39.4	25/32-17/25	443-709	2-3	4870-5296	-426	5	39	-16	**55**	9.0	0.0	4.1/ 5.5	182-182	26.8-29.1	-2.3
NE	264-**272**	665-858	38.3-42.2	13/24-17/26	642-503	2-**0**	4293-4681	-388	-3	-34	-44	10	7.2	**1.9**	2.5/**3.9**	196-201	21.9-**23.3**	-1.4
NYJ	331-310	931-757	38.9-38.1	23/28-20/30	646-**327**	**4-0**	5215-5633	-418	**13**	18	17	1	8.4	0.1	4.8/ 5.2	202-199	25.8-28.3	-2.5
Mia	321-359	845-734	43.0-41.8	12/23-22/28	478-717	1-4	5721-5781	-60	-4	-61	-21	-40	6.5	-0.5	6.0/ 5.3	178-179	32.1-32.3	-0.2
Central Division																		
Cin	**351**-322	647-873	36.7-39.9	12/18-17/24	425-465	4-2	**6057**-5182	**875**	9	**119**	**109**	10	**11.0**	1.0	**7.1**/ 4.1	181-187	**33.5**-27.7	**5.8**
Cle	294-301	875-789	38.5-39.4	24/29-26/34	644-494	4-4	5011-4767	244	-2	16	12	4	8.4	1.6	5.0/ 4.1	181-**178**	27.7-26.8	0.9
Hou	308-304	1150-947	38.8-**37.2**	22/34-14/**18**	527-495	4-4	5205-4858	347	7	59	57	2	9.5	0.5	5.2/ 4.5	204-203	25.5-23.9	1.6
Pit	292-319	803-705	41.5-40.7	28/36-26/32	703-785	4-4	5204-5805	-601	-6	-85	-74	-11	5.9	-0.9	4.2/ 6.0	198-199	26.3-29.2	-2.9
Western Division																		
Sea	291-321	790-861	40.8-42.1	22/28-21/32	620-397	3-3	4842-5639	-797	6	10	-42	52	8.3	0.8	4.5/ 4.8	192-187	25.2-30.2	-4.9
Den	338-316	717-**966**	**43.8**-43.4	23/36-21/27	651-708	0-2	5506-5471	35	-5	-25	-17	-8	7.4	0.6	4.8/ 4.8	197-192	27.9-28.5	-0.5
LARd	283-310	762-823	41.8-41.4	18/29-27/29	**767**-616	3-1	4961-5379	-418	1	-44	-31	-13	6.9	0.1	4.5/ 5.0	**214**-209	23.2-25.7	-2.6
SD	255-335	1039-619	43.5-39.3	14/20-22/36	493-865	**5**-1	4429-5418	-989	-6	-101	-106	5	5.5	0.5	3.2/ 5.1	187-182	23.7-29.8	-6.1
KC	289-318	**636**-854	40.3-40.2	27/32-16/24	381-679	0-4	4844-5026	-182	-2	-66	-23	-43	6.3	-1.9	4.1/ 4.0	176-181	27.5-27.8	-0.2
Aver	303	809	40.2	20/28	588	1	5153	—	—	—	—	—	—	—	5.0	95	26.8	—

Rushing Attempts	Rushing Yards	Rushing Average	Rushing TDs	Rushing Rank	Passing Yards	Passing Average
E.Dickerson-Ind.......388	E.Dickerson-Ind.....1659	I.Woods-Cin...........5.25	I.Woods-Cin..............15	E.Dickerson-Ind.....1799	D.Marino-Mia.........4434	B.Esiason-Cin.........9.21
J.Stephens-NE........297	J.Stephens-NE......1168	J.Brooks-Cin...........5.12	E.Dickerson-Ind.........14	I.Woods-Cin...........1216	B.Esiason-Cin........3572	W.Moon-Hou...........7.91
C.Warner-Sea.........266	G.Anderson-SD.....1119	G.Anderson-SD......4.97	R.Riddick-Buf.............12	J.Stephens-NE.......1208	J.Kelly-Buf.............3380	D.Krieg-Sea...........7.64
M.Rozier-Hou..........251	I.Woods-Cin...........1066	A.Highsmith-Hou....4.96		G.Anderson-SD.....1149	J.Elway-Den...........3309	J.Kelly-Buf..............7.48
G.Anderson-SD.......225	C.Warner-Sea........1025	W.Williams-Pit.........4.70		C.Warner-Sea........1125	S.DeBerg-KC.........2935	D.Marino-Mia..........7.32
Completion Percent	**TD Passes**	**TD Percent**	**INT Percent**	**Passer Rating**	**Passing Rank**	**Receptions**
B.Kosar-Cle...........60.2	D.Marino-Mia............28	D.Krieg-Sea.............7.9	K.O'Brien-NYJ.........1.7	B.Esiason-Cin.........97.4	D.Marino-Mia.........1437	A.Toon-NYJ..............93
J.Kelly-Buf...............59.5	B.Esiason-Cin............28	B.Esiason-Cin...........7.2	B.Kosar-Cle..............2.7	D.Krieg-Sea............94.6	B.Esiason-Cin........1366	M.Clayton-Mia...........86
D.Krieg-Sea...........58.8	D.Krieg-Sea..............18	W.Moon-Hou.............5.8	W.Moon-Hou.............2.7	W.Moon-Hou...........88.4	J.Kelly-Buf.............1085	D.Hill-Hou..................72
D.Marino-Mia.........58.4	W.Moon-Hou...............17	J.Schroeder-LARd.....5.1	S.Beuerlein-LARd.....2.9	B.Kosar-Cle............84.3	K.O'Brien-NYJ.......1079	A.Reed-Buf................71
B.Esiason-Cin.........57.5	J.Elway-Den..............17	D.Marino-Mia............4.6	D.Krieg-Sea..............3.5	D.Marino-Mia..........80.8	J.Elway-Den............980	M.Shuler-NYJ............70
Receiving Yards	**Receiving Average**	**Receiving TDs**	**Receiving Rank**	**Combined Net Yards**	**Total TDs**	**Total Points**
E.Brown-Cin..........1273	E.Brown-Cin.........24.02	M.Clayton-Mia...........14	E.Brown-Cin............682	T.Brown-LARd.........2317	I.Woods-Cin..............15	S.Norwood-Buf........129
D.Hill-Hou..............1141	L.Lipps-Pit..............19.46	D.Hill-Hou..................10	M.Clayton-Mia.........635	E.Dickerson-Ind.....2036	E.Dickerson-Ind..........15	G.Anderson-Pit........118
M.Clayton-Mia.......1129	T.McGee-Cin..........19.06	E.Brown-Cin.................9	D.Hill-Hou................621	J.Williams-Sea.......1526	R.Riddick-Buf.............14	T.Zendejas-Hou.......114
A.Toon-NYJ...........1067	M.Jackson-Den......18.52	B.Blades-Sea................8	A.Toon-NYJ.............559	P.Palmer-KC..........1427	M.Clayton-Mia...........14	D.Biasucci-Ind.........114
E.Givins-Hou...........976	F.Edmunds-Mia.....17.42		A.Reed-Buf..............514	J.Holland-SD.........1365	J.Brooks-Cin.............14	P.Leahy-NYJ............112
Punt Average	**Field Goals**	**Field Goal Percent**	**Kickoff Returns**	**Kickoff Return Average**	**Punt Returns**	**Punt Return Average**
H.Newsome-Pit.......45.4	S.Norwood-Buf..........32	S.Norwood-Buf.......86.5	J.Cribbs-Mia..............41	T.Brown-LARd........26.8	T.Brown-LARd..........49	J.Townsell-NYJ.......11.7
O.Mobley-SD..........44.1	G.Anderson-Pit..........28	N.Lowery-KC..........84.4	T.Brown-LARd...........41	J.Holland-SD..........26.1	G.McNeil-Cle.............38	C.Verdin-Ind............10.9
M.Horan-Den..........44.0	N.Lowery-KC.............27	M.Bahr-Cle.............82.8	B.Edmonds-Sea........40	A.Miller-SD.............25.9	I.Fryar-NE..................38	I.Fryar-NE................10.5
R.Stark-Ind............43.5	D.Biasucci-Ind...........25	P.Leahy-NYJ..........82.1	A.Bentley-Ind............39	B.Humphery-NYJ.....24.3	J.Townsell-NYJ...........35	L.James-SD...............9.9
R.Roby-Mia............43.0	M.Bahr-Cle................24	N.Johnson-Sea........78.6	R.Woodson-Pit..........37	S.Martin-NE............23.7	B.Edmonds-Sea.........35	I.Hillary-Cin...............9.8
Punt/Kick Return Yards	**Punt/Kick Return TDs**	**Interceptions**	**Interception Return Yards**	**Interception Return TDs**	**Sacks**	**Overall Rank**
T.Brown-LARd.......1542	Many...........................1	E.McMillan-NYJ...........8	M.Kelso-Buf............180	E.McMillan-NYJ...........2	G.Townsend-LARd.11.5	E.Dickerson-Ind.....1993
B.Edmonds-Sea.....1240		E.Thomas-Cin..............7	E.McMillan-NYJ.......168		L.Williams-SD.........11.0	B.Esiason-Cin........1624
R.Woodson-Pit......1131		M.Kelso-Buf.................7	F.Wright-Cle.............126		B.Smith-Buf............11.0	D.Marino-Mia.........1420
J.Townsell-NYJ......1010		D.Cherry-KC................7	D.Woodruff-Pit.........109		J.Skow-Cin...............9.5	I.Woods-Cin............1316
J.Cribbs-Mia...........863		G.Byrd-SD...................7	C.Warner-Cle............104		C.Bennett-Buf...........9.5	J.Williams-Sea.......1258

Living on the Air in Cincinnati

The Central Division hadn't been the source of AFC pride for much of the decade. The 1988 season, however, would see three teams battle for supremacy, with the fourth member, the Steelers, in mourning for beloved owner Art Rooney. The Browns were perhaps used to having things their own way—until the championship game—but a rash of injuries resulted in four starting quarterbacks in the first seven weeks. A disgusted Marty Schottenheimer resigned following the season when he refused to sacrifice his offensive coordinator. A midseason injury to Warren Moon put the Oilers on par with the Browns. Passing both clubs by were the Bengals.

With an offense much like those of his mentor, Bill Walsh, Sam Wyche's Bengals handily led the league in scoring. Quarterback Boomer Esiason provided the deep passing with the highest yards per attempt figure in the AFC since 1976, while the running back tandem of veteran James Brooks and rookie Ickey Woods rushed for almost 2,000 yards. Unfortunately, the defense was not of a similar caliber. Despite their individual flaws, the Bengals, Oilers, and Browns all made the playoffs. And Wyche and Walsh would meet on the big stage.

A new conference power took shape in Buffalo. The additions of linebackers Shane Conlan (through the draft) and Cornelius Bennett and Art Still (through trades) breathed new life into a long-suffering core of linebacker Darryl Talley and linemen Bruce Smith and Fred Smerlas. The offense featured quarterback Jim Kelly and underrated rookie rusher Thurman Thomas.

In the Western Division, Denver's John Elway couldn't get the ball downfield because of a sore arm, and aging Tony Dorsett (in his final season) couldn't punch up the running game. The defense played down to the level set during the Super Bowl humiliation of the year before. A collection of famous people didn't translate into much in Los Angeles, although Tim Brown, like another rookie wide receiver in Dallas, Michael Irvin, displayed future greatness. That left plenty of room on the plate for Ground Chuck. Chuck Knox's Seahawks used a double-barreled running attack of Curt Warner and John L. Williams to keep a barely-adequate defense off the field.

1989 NFC

TEAM	W-L-T	PCT	POST	PTS	RA	RY	RY/A	RTD	FL	PA	PC	GPY	GPY/A	PTD	PI	PSY	PRAT
Eastern Division																	
NYG	12-4	.750	D	348-**252**	**556**-421	1889-1539	3.4-3.7	17-10	14-15	444-486	248-273	3355-3427	7.6-7.1	17-16	16-22	281-302	77.9-70.4
Phi	11-5	.688	W	342-274	540-426	2208-1605	4.1-3.8	14-**6**	16-**26**	538-529	294-258	3455-3713	6.4-7.0	23-26	16-**30**	343-424	76.2-**64.7**
Was	10-6	.625	—	386-308	514-384	1904-1344	3.7-**3.5**	14-9	20-15	581-530	337-277	4476-3875	7.7-7.3	24-25	17-27	**127**-304	84.1-70.6
Phx	5-11	.313	—	258-377	407-539	1361-2302	3.3-4.3	10-12	14-11	523-531	279-286	3659-3794	7.0-7.1	17-24	30-16	379-219	62.6-79.2
Dal	1-15	.063	—	204-393	355-543	1409-1991	4.0-3.7	7-17	15-10	513-488	266-301	3124-3748	6.1-7.7	14-21	27-7	239-183	57.8-93.9
Central Division																	
Min	10-6	.625	#D	351-275	514-462	2066-1683	4.0-3.6	12-14	14-18	499-488	272-**252**	3468-**3003**	6.9-**6.2**	17-18	19-18	279-**502**	72.0-67.7
GB	10-6	.625	#	362-356	397-460	1732-2008	4.4-4.4	13-15	13-15	**600**-476	**354**-302	4325-3553	7.2-7.5	27-22	20-25	277-214	82.4-79.6
Det	7-9	.438	—	312-364	421-454	2053-1621	**4.9**-3.6	**23**-18	24-16	450-570	229-370	3282-4193	7.3-7.4	11-19	24-16	343-277	60.8-86.2
ChiB	6-10	.375	—	358-377	516-446	**2287**-1897	4.4-4.3	22-21	17-12	484-554	267-307	3262-4079	6.7-7.4	21-21	25-26	174-247	69.1-72.0
TB	5-11	.313	—	320-419	412-479	1507-2023	3.7-4.2	10-18	**9**-18	570-515	302-301	3666-3659	6.4-7.1	23-29	28-21	331-222	66.0-82.2
Western Division																	
SF	**14**-2	**.875**	DCS*	**442**-253	493-**372**	1966-1383	4.0-3.7	14-9	14-16	483-564	339-316	**4584**-3568	**9.5**-6.3	**35-15**	**11**-21	282-333	**114.8**-68.5
LARm	11-5	.688	WDC	426-344	472-404	1909-1543	4.0-3.8	19-13	11-15	523-577	308-345	4369-4302	8.4-7.5	29-24	18-21	236-278	90.1-81.7
NO	9-7	.563	—	386-301	502-373	1948-**1326**	3.9-3.6	19-10	12-18	461-577	284-320	3651-4222	7.9-7.3	23-23	19-21	271-362	85.9-76.9
Atl	3-13	.188	—	279-437	318-572	1155-2471	3.6-4.3	11-26	11-12	578-**437**	312-259	3903-3737	6.8-8.6	17-19	12-20	389-183	76.4-82.5
Aver	16	—	—	330	467	1845	4.0	14	15	512	286	3659	7.1	21	20	285	75.6

TEAM	1D	PENY	PNT	FGM/A	RTNY	RTNTD	OFFY/DEFY	NETY	NETTO	NP	PNP	DELP	PW	DELW	PRT	DR	YPD	DEL
Eastern Division																		
NYG	298-**266**	675-800	43.1-40.1	29/38-14/**21**	**912**-476	3-4	4963-4664	299	7	96	53	43	10.4	1.6	5.2/ 4.4	180-191	27.6-24.4	3.2
Phi	321-281	938-956	39.0-42.0	20/33-14/26	706-**362**	3-**1**	5320-4894	426	**24**	68	132	-64	9.7	1.3	4.5/ 3.7	**217**-210	24.5-23.3	1.2
Was	338-274	881-796	42.3-40.1	29/40-14/23	510-612	4-4	6253-4915	1338	5	78	132	-54	9.9	0.0	6.4/ 4.6	198-198	31.6-24.8	6.8
Phx	262-329	856-916	**43.6**-41.5	18/26-29/40	744-698	2-5	4641-5877	-1236	-17	-119	-171	52	5.0	-0.0	3.6/ 5.5	201-199	23.1-29.5	-6.4
Dal	246-321	771-723	39.8-39.9	10/20-28/35	234-730	4-6	4294-5556	-1262	-25	-189	-205	16	3.3	-2.3	3.3/ 6.7	185-186	23.2-29.9	-6.7
Central Division																		
Min	326-**266**	974-903	39.8-40.6	**32/44-13/21**	712-438	**7**-2	5255-**4184**	1071	3	76	101	-25	9.9	0.1	4.6/**3.3**	203-201	25.9-**20.8**	5.1
GB	342-307	**666**-851	40.6-40.7	22/28-23/30	521-737	2-4	5780-5347	433	7	6	64	-58	8.1	**1.9**	5.3/ 4.8	193-186	29.9-28.7	1.2
Det	274-314	977-**993**	42.6-41.2	20/21-23/33	679-820	2-5	4992-5537	-545	-16	-52	-109	**57**	6.7	0.3	3.9/ 5.6	203-205	24.6-27.0	-2.4
ChiB	302-332	846-802	39.5-39.6	15/19-26/36	488-444	2-**1**	5375-5729	-354	-4	-19	-46	27	7.5	-1.5	4.2/ 4.8	200-194	26.9-29.5	-2.7
TB	288-317	881-869	38.5-40.3	22/28-20/24	530-732	3-4	4842-5460	-618	2	-99	-44	-55	5.5	-0.5	3.8/ 5.1	201-204	24.1-26.8	-2.7
Western Division																		
SF	**350**-283	922-581	39.8-**38.9**	29/36-23/31	691-501	2-2	**6268**-4618	**1650**	12	**189**	**186**	3	**12.7**	1.3	**7.9**/ 4.0	184-**185**	**34.1**-25.0	**9.1**
LARm	321-306	823-798	38.3-41.5	23/30-26/29	704-522	3-**1**	6042-5567	475	7	82	68	14	10.1	1.0	6.5/ 5.4	200-201	30.2-27.7	2.5
NO	304-293	676-850	39.1-39.4	20/29-19/24	654-509	4-2	5328-5186	142	8	85	44	41	10.1	-1.1	5.5/ 5.0	192-193	27.8-26.9	0.9
Atl	261-336	671-682	40.8-41.8	23/32-31/36	626-545	2-4	4669-6025	-1356	9	-158	-77	-81	4.1	-1.0	5.0/ 6.1	189-187	24.7-32.2	-7.5
Aver	300	826	40.2	21/30	583	3	5219	—	—	—	—	—	—	—	5.2	194	27.0	—

Rushing Attempts	Rushing Yards	Rushing Average	Rushing TDs	Rushing Rank	Passing Yards	Passing Average
D.Hilliard-NO ... 344	B.Sanders-Det ... 1470	H.Cross-Phi ... 5.97	G.Bell-LARm ... 15	B.Sanders-Det ... 1610	D.Majkowski-GB ... 4318	J.Montana-SF ... 9.12
O.Anderson-NYG ... 325	N.Anderson-Chi ... 1275	B.Sanders-Det ... 5.25	B.Sanders-Det ... 14	D.Hilliard-NO ... 1392	J.Everett-LARm ... 4310	J.Everett-LARm ... 8.32
B.Sanders-Det ... 280	D.Hilliard-NO ... 1262	N.Anderson-Chi ... 4.65	O.Anderson-NYG ... 14	N.Anderson-Chi ... 1385	M.Rypien-Was ... 3768	M.Rypien-Was ... 7.92
N.Anderson-Chi ... 274	G.Bell-LARm ... 1137	E.Byner-Was ... 4.33	D.Hilliard-NO ... 13	G.Bell-LARm ... 1287	J.Montana-SF ... 3521	B.Hebert-NO ... 7.61
G.Bell-LARm ... 272	R.Craig-SF ... 1054	G.Bell-LARm ... 4.18	N.Anderson-Chi ... 11	O.Anderson-NYG ... 1163	C.Miller-Atl ... 3459	P.Simms-NYG ... 7.56

Completion Percent	TD Passes	TD Percent	INT Percent	Passer Rating	Passing Rank	Receptions
J.Montana-SF ... 70.2	J.Everett-LARm ... 29	J.Montana-SF ... 6.7	C.Miller-Atl ... 1.9	J.Montana-SF ... 112.4	J.Everett-LARm ... 1620	S.Sharpe-GB ... 90
B.Hebert-NO ... 62.9	D.Majkowski-GB ... 27	J.Everett-LARm ... 5.6	J.Montana-SF ... 2.1	J.Everett-LARm ... 90.6	J.Montana-SF ... 1571	A.Monk-Was ... 86
D.Majkowski-GB ... 58.9	J.Montana-SF ... 26	M.Tomczak-Chi ... 5.2	M.Rypien-Was ... 2.7	M.Rypien-Was ... 88.1	D.Majkowski-GB ... 1494	M.Carrier-TB ... 86
M.Rypien-Was ... 58.8	M.Rypien-Was ... 22	M.Rypien-Was ... 4.6	H.Cross-Phi ... 2.8	B.Hebert-NO ... 82.7	M.Rypien-Was ... 1474	J.Rice-SF ... 82
J.Everett-LARm ... 58.7	H.Cross-Phi ... 21	D.Majkowski-GB ... 4.5	J.Everett-LARm ... 3.3	D.Majkowski-GB ... 82.3	C.Miller-Atl ... 1410	R.Sanders-Was ... 80

Receiving Yards	Receiving Average	Receiving TDs	Receiving Rank	Combined Net Yards	Total TDs	Total Points
J.Rice-SF ... 1483	F.Anderson-LARm 26.05	J.Rice-SF ... 17	J.Rice-SF ... 827	B.Sanders-Det ... 1870	D.Hilliard-NO ... 18	M.Cofer-SF ... 136
S.Sharpe-GB ... 1423	H.Ellard-LARm ... 19.74	S.Sharpe-GB ... 12	S.Sharpe-GB ... 772	D.Meggett-NYG ... 1807	J.Rice-SF ... 17	C.Lohmiller-Was ... 128
M.Carrier-TB ... 1422	E.Jones-Phx ... 18.62	C.Carter-Phi ... 11	M.Carrier-TB ... 756	D.Hilliard-NO ... 1796	G.Bell-LARm ... 15	M.Lansford-LARm ... 120
H.Ellard-LARm ... 1382	R.Clark-Det ... 18.24	J.Taylor-SF ... 10	H.Ellard-LARm ... 731	N.Anderson-Chi ... 1709	N.Anderson-Chi ... 15	R.Karlis-Min ... 120
G.Clark-Was ... 1229	J.Rice-SF ... 18.09		G.Clark-Was ... 660	V.Sikahema-Phx ... 1697		

Punt Average	Field Goals	Field Goal Percent	Kickoff Returns	Kickoff Return Average	Punt Returns	Punt Return Average
R.Camarillo-Phx ... 43.4	R.Karlis-Min ... 31	E.Murray-Det ... 95.2	J.Dixon-Dal ... 47	M.Gray-Det ... 26.7	D.Meggett-NYG ... 46	W.Stanley-Det ... 13.8
S.Landeta-NYG ... 43.1	C.Lohmiller-Was ... 29	M.Cofer-SF ... 80.6	R.Brown-LARm ... 47	J.Dixon-Dal ... 25.1	L.Lewis-Min ... 44	D.Meggett-NYG ... 12.7
J.Arnold-Det ... 43.1	M.Cofer-SF ... 29	R.Karlis-Min ... 79.5	V.Sikahema-Phx ... 43	J.Johnson-Was ... 24.9	V.Sikahema-Phx ... 37	V.Sikahema-Phx ... 11.7
C.Mohr-Was ... 43.0	M.Lansford-LARm ... 23	K.Butler-Chi ... 78.9	D.Elder-TB ... 40	D.Gentry-Chi ... 23.8	J.Taylor-SF ... 36	J.Taylor-SF ... 11.6
S.Fulhage-Atl ... 41.3			D.Sanders-Atl ... 35	D.Meggett-NYG ... 21.4	W.Stanley-Det ... 36	W.Drewrey-TB ... 11.0

Punt/Kick Return Yards	Punt/Kick Return TDs	Interceptions	Interception Return Yards	Interception Return TDs	Sacks	Overall Rank
V.Sikahema-Phx ... 1307	Many ... 1	E.Allen-Phi ... 8	T.McDonald-Phx ... 170	Many ... 1	C.Doleman-Min ... 21.0	D.Majkowski-GB ... 1902
J.Dixon-Dal ... 1181		T.McDonald-Phx ... 7	T.Kinard-NYG ... 135		T.Harris-GB ... 19.5	H.Cross-Phi ... 1866
D.Meggett-NYG ... 1159			A.Johnson-Was ... 94		K.Millard-Min ... 18.0	J.Montana-SF ... 1828
D.Sanders-Atl ... 1032			I.Holt-Min ... 90		P.Swilling-NO ... 16.5	B.Sanders-Det ... 1794
R.Brown-LARm ... 968			R.Reynolds-TB ... 87		K.Greene-LARm ... 16.5	D.Hilliard-NO ... 1702

Return Value, in Spades

The Cowboys started from scratch. In what became one of the all-time great rebuilding projects, Jimmy Johnson dealt Herschel Walker to the Vikings in a move involving 18 players, including draft picks, to reinforce top pick Troy Aikman in the years to come. Walker provided the Vikings with a desperately needed running game in the short term, although in time Minnesota would see that the passing game had lost its zip. With eight draft picks sent to Dallas, though, the Vikes would have little means by which to rebuild. The new Plan B free agency was mostly helpful in finding bargains.

Even with a front four worthy of Purple Eater-style fame—league sack leader Chris Doleman plus Keith Millard, Al Noga, and Henry Thomas—Minnesota barely stayed ahead of the surprising Packers. Green Bay coach Lindy Infante's free-wheeling offense featured quarterback Don Majkowski and wide receiver Sterling Sharpe. A decent defense coalesced around bruising linebacker Tim Harris. The Bears collapsed, losing their last six games.

In what Ronnie Lott called their "let's show Walsh" year, the 49ers rattled off 14 wins under rookie coach George Seifert. No longer challenged to win his job, quarterback Joe Montana enjoyed his finest season yet. The 49ers thrived despite the devastating Bay Area earthquake. Days after the quake, the club hastily rescheduled its October 22 game to Stanford Stadium, where the 49ers had won Super Bowl XIX.

The Rams were entertaining. Flipper Anderson joined Henry Ellard to give Los Angeles an air show that almost rivaled San Francisco's. Beyond the pass-rushing skills of linebacker Kevin Greene, though, the defense was well short of greatness.

The Eastern Division boasted the best race. Although the Giants won the division, Philadelphia beat them twice. Coach Buddy Ryan's defense finished second to the Vikings' 71 sacks with 62 of their own. New York's big offensive line crushed weaker teams and provide space for Ottis Anderson, who gained more yards than he had in the five seasons combined since he last reached 1,000 yards. The Redskins trailed both teams, and, despite their trio of 1,000-yard receivers, joined the Packers in winning 10 games yet losing out on the playoffs.

1989 AFC

TEAM	W-L-T	PCT	POST	PTS	RA	RY	RY/A	RTD	FL	PA	PC	GPY	GPY/A	PTD	PI	PSY	PRAT
Eastern Division																	
Buf	9-7	.563	D	**409**-317	532-484	2264-1840	4.3-3.8	15-15	21-13	478-508	281-255	3831-3495	**8.0**-6.9	**32**-14	20-23	242-289	89.3-62.9
Ind	8-8	.500	—	298-301	458-507	1853-2077	4.0-4.1	11-10	**10**-15	493-556	253-322	3134-3918	6.4-7.0	18-15	17-21	174-**384**	69.1-73.0
Mia	8-8	.500	—	331-379	400-493	1330-2153	3.3-4.4	10-19	16-8	601-513	331-315	**4302**-3811	7.2-7.4	26-21	25-15	**86**-268	74.9-85.7
NE	5-11	.313	—	297-391	485-495	1749-1978	3.6-4.0	12-19	12-12	**610**-449	302-259	3972-3905	6.5-8.7	17-27	27-16	265-239	61.3-91.6
NYJ	4-12	.250	—	253-411	400-517	1596-2136	4.0-4.1	11-16	17-9	570-514	338-282	3892-4035	6.8-7.9	14-31	24-15	477-177	70.6-88.5
Central Division																	
Cle	9-6-1	.594	DC	334-254	448-446	1609-1670	3.6-**3.7**	14-**8**	15-11	529-540	309-269	3625-3520	6.9-6.5	20-20	15-**27**	192-359	80.1-**62.3**
Hou	9-7	.563	W	365-412	495-437	1928-1669	3.9-3.8	16-20	17-16	496-467	295-269	3786-3819	7.6-8.2	23-28	16-21	287-277	85.5-85.4
Pit	9-7	.563	WD	265-326	500-498	1818-2008	3.6-4.0	17-16	18-21	404-548	210-290	2662-3721	6.6-6.8	10-17	**13**-21	484-180	67.7-68.8
Cin	8-8	.500	—	404-285	529-482	**2483**-2162	**4.7**-4.5	17-9	19-16	513-482	289-296	3950-3383	7.7-7.0	**32**-22	**13**-21	332-248	**91.2**-72.6
Western Division																	
Den	11-5	**.688**	DCS	362-**226**	554-**426**	2092-**1580**	3.8-3.7	15-10	12-**22**	474-504	256-268	3352-3201	7.1-6.4	21-**13**	20-21	351-374	73.7-64.1
KC	8-7-1	.531	—	318-286	**559**-445	2227-1766	4.0-4.0	**18**-9	18-18	435-471	259-**236**	3220-**2821**	7.4-**6.0**	14-16	23-15	182-294	71.2-66.8
LARd	8-8	.500	—	315-297	454-504	2038-1940	4.5-3.8	9-15	18-18	414-506	201-277	3277-3311	7.9-6.5	21-18	22-18	326-248	70.3-72.0
Sea	7-9	.438	—	241-327	405-520	1392-2118	3.4-4.1	5-11	14-13	559-**445**	316-252	3583-3332	6.4-7.5	21-23	23-9	379-235	71.3-89.3
SD	6-10	.375	—	266-290	432-479	1873-1813	4.3-3.8	13-13	17-13	515-513	270-283	3291-3311	6.4-6.5	15-15	19-25	254-360	66.7-64.4
Aver	16	—		330	467	1845	4.0	14	14	512	286	3659	7.1	21	20	285	75.6

TEAM	1D	PENY	PNT	FGM/A	RTNY	RTNTD	OFFY/DEFY	NETY	NETTO	NP	PNP	DELP	PW	DELW	PRT	DR	YPD	DEL
Eastern Division																		
Buf	334-299	831-616	38.3-38.3	23/30-26/37	570-591	2-5	5853-5046	807	-5	92	47	**45**	10.3	-1.3	5.9/4.2	198-203	29.6-24.9	4.7
Ind	273-336	704-772	**42.4**-41.6	21/27-32/43	713-903	5-4	4813-5611	-798	9	-3	-31	28	7.9	0.1	4.6/4.5	189-184	25.5-30.5	-5.0
Mia	310-337	614-831	41.7-39.0	19/26-25/33	464-591	3-3	5546-5696	-150	-18	-48	-85	37	6.8	1.2	5.5/5.6	178-**183**	31.2-31.1	0.0
NE	335-297	**509**-954	37.4-42.1	**30/40**-19/26	497-684	1-2	5456-5644	-188	-11	-94	-60	-34	5.7	-0.7	4.1/6.7	199-189	27.4-29.9	-2.4
NYJ	292-328	953-675	39.4-39.8	14/21-21/31	560-539	5-3	5011-5994	-983	-17	-158	-150	-8	4.1	-0.0	3.9/6.4	191-196	26.2-30.6	-4.3
Central Division																		
Cle	285-276	973-985	39.4-40.4	16/24-**15/28**	**796**-724	**7**-2	5042-4831	211	8	80	50	30	10.0	-0.5	5.3/3.7	**205**-207	24.6-23.3	1.3
Hou	327-314	1153-903	41.8-**37.6**	25/37-17/**21**	385-**362**	2-4	5427-5211	216	4	-47	34	-81	6.8	2.2	5.6/5.7	183-185	29.7-28.2	1.5
Pit	244-323	986-785	40.6-40.5	21/30-19/27	539-464	2-1	3996-5549	-1553	11	-61	-85	24	6.5	2.5	3.7/4.8	192-191	20.8-29.1	-8.2
Cin	**348**-280	637-**1060**	38.5-39.1	14/20-20/27	413-365	3-1	**6101**-5297	804	5	119	87	32	11.0	-3.0	**6.1**/4.7	187-186	**32.6**-28.5	4.1
Western Division																		
Den	308-**246**	594-823	39.8-41.0	27/33-17/27	662-564	4-2	5093-4407	686	11	**136**	**101**	35	**11.4**	-0.4	4.5/3.7	196-201	26.0-**21.9**	4.1
KC	304-252	878-797	40.1-39.1	24/33-21/26	464-594	3-7	5265-**4293**	**972**	-8	32	49	-17	8.8	-0.3	4.7/4.0	190-192	27.7-22.4	**5.4**
LARd	259-308	1105-867	40.5-40.3	23/34-**15/21**	740-599	2-3	4989-5003	-14	2	18	7	11	8.4	-0.4	4.7/4.5	182-186	27.4-26.9	0.5
Sea	290-293	738-809	39.4-39.2	15/25-22/32	308-582	2-3	4596-5215	-619	-15	-86	-112	26	5.8	1.2	3.9/6.1	181-184	25.4-28.3	-3.0
SD	267-295	906-741	39.5-38.6	17/25-29/41	496-630	3-1	4910-4764	146	2	-24	20	-44	7.4	-1.4	4.2/**3.5**	203-193	24.2-24.7	-0.5
Aver	300	826	40.2	21/30	583	2	5219	—	—	—	—		5.2		96		27.0	

Rushing Attempts
C.Okoye-KC ... 370
E.Dickerson-Ind ... 314
T.Thomas-Buf ... 298
B.Humphrey-Den ... 294
J.Stephens-NE ... 244

Rushing Yards
C.Okoye-KC ... 1480
E.Dickerson-Ind ... 1311
T.Thomas-Buf ... 1244
J.Brooks-Cin ... 1239
B.Humphrey-Den ... 1151

Rushing Average
J.Brooks-Cin ... 5.61
B.Jackson-LARd ... 5.49
A.Pinkett-Hou ... 4.78
F.McNeil-NYJ ... 4.40
E.Dickerson-Ind ... 4.18

Rushing TDs
C.Okoye-KC ... 12
M.Butts-SD ... 9
M.Hoge-Pit ... 8

Rushing Rank
C.Okoye-KC ... 1600
E.Dickerson-Ind ... 1381
J.Brooks-Cin ... 1309
T.Thomas-Buf ... 1304
B.Humphrey-Den ... 1221

Passing Yards
D.Marino-Mia ... 3997
W.Moon-Hou ... 3631
B.Kosar-Cle ... 3533
B.Esiason-Cin ... 3525
K.O'Brien-NYJ ... 3346

Passing Average
J.Kelly-Buf ... 8.01
W.Moon-Hou ... 7.83
S.DeBerg-KC ... 7.81
B.Esiason-Cin ... 7.75
J.Elway-Den ... 7.33

Completion Percent
S.DeBerg-KC ... 60.5
K.O'Brien-NYJ ... 60.4
W.Moon-Hou ... 60.3
B.Kosar-Cle ... 59.1
J.Kelly-Buf ... 58.3

TD Passes
B.Esiason-Cin ... 28
J.Kelly-Buf ... 25
D.Marino-Mia ... 24
W.Moon-Hou ... 23
D.Krieg-Sea ... 21

TD Percent
J.Kelly-Buf ... 6.4
B.Esiason-Cin ... 6.2
W.Moon-Hou ... 5.00
D.Marino-Mia ... 4.4
J.Elway-Den ... 4.3

Passer Rating
B.Esiason-Cin ... 92.1
W.Moon-Hou ... 88.9
J.Kelly-Buf ... 86.2
B.Kosar-Cle ... 80.3
D.Marino-Mia ... 76.9

Passing Rank
B.Esiason-Cin ... 1463
W.Moon-Hou ... 1371
J.Kelly-Buf ... 1297
D.Marino-Mia ... 1239
K.O'Brien-NYJ ... 1013

Receptions
A.Reed-Buf ... 88
B.Blades-Sea ... 77
J.Williams-Sea ... 76
V.Johnson-Den ... 76
A.Miller-SD ... 75

Receiving Yards
A.Reed-Buf ... 1312
A.Miller-SD ... 1252
W.Slaughter-Cle ... 1236
T.McGee-Cin ... 1211
V.Johnson-Den ... 1095

Receiving Average
W.Slaughter-Cle ... 19.02
L.Lipps-Pit ... 18.88
M.Fernandez-LARd ... 18.75
T.McGee-Cin ... 18.63
J.Townsell-NYJ ... 17.49

Receiving TDs
A.Miller-SD ... 10
A.Reed-Buf ... 9
R.Holman-Cin ... 9
M.Fernandez-LARd ... 9
M.Clayton-Mia ... 9

Receiving Rank
A.Reed-Buf ... 701
A.Miller-SD ... 676
W.Slaughter-Cle ... 648
T.McGee-Cin ... 646
V.Johnson-Den ... 583

Combined Net Yards
T.Thomas-Buf ... 1913
A.Miller-SD ... 1806
E.Metcalf-Cle ... 1748
J.Townsell-NYJ ... 1739
J.Brooks-Cin ... 1545

Total TDs
T.Thomas-Buf ... 12
C.Okoye-KC ... 12
A.Miller-SD ... 11
E.Metcalf-Cle ... 10

Total Points
D.Treadwell-Den ... 120
T.Zendejas-Hou ... 115
S.Norwood-Buf ... 115
N.Lowery-KC ... 106
J.Jaeger-LARd ... 103

Punt Average
O.Mobley-Hou ... 43.3
R.Stark-Ind ... 42.9
R.Roby-Mia ... 42.4
H.Newsome-Pit ... 41.1
J.Gossett-LARd ... 40.5

Field Goals
D.Treadwell-Den ... 27
T.Zendejas-Hou ... 25
N.Lowery-KC ... 24
S.Norwood-Buf ... 23
J.Jaeger-LARd ... 23

Field Goal Percent
R.Stark-NE ... 82.4
D.Treadwell-Den ... 81.8
D.Biasucci-Ind ... 77.8
S.Norwood-Buf ... 76.7
T.Stowe-Mia ... 73.1

Kickoff Returns
R.Woodson-Pit ... 36
J.Townsell-NYJ ... 34
E.Metcalf-Cle ... 31
K.Bell-Den ... 30
J.Holland-SD ... 29

Kickoff Return Average
R.Woodson-Pit ... 27.3
M.Logan-Mia ... 25.5
A.Miller-SD ... 25.4
S.Martin-NE ... 25.4
J.Jefferson-Sea ... 23.2

Punt Returns
G.McNeil-Cle ... 49
J.Townsell-NYJ ... 33
R.Woodson-Pit ... 29
M.Sutton-Buf ... 26
C.Verdin-Ind ... 23

Punt Return Average
C.Verdin-Ind ... 12.9
S.Schwedes-Mia ... 11.7
B.Edmonds-LARd ... 10.5
G.McNeil-Cle ... 10.1
D.Hollis-Sea ... 9.1

Punt/Kick Return Yards
R.Woodson-Pit ... 1189
J.Townsell-NYJ ... 952
S.Martin-NE ... 748
K.Bell-Den ... 745
E.Metcalf-Cle ... 718

Punt/Kick Return TDs
Many ... 1

Interceptions
F.Wright-Den ... 9
D.Fulcher-Cin ... 8
K.Taylor-Ind ... 7
G.Byrd-SD ... 7

Interception Return Yards
E.Anderson-LARd ... 233
K.Taylor-Ind ... 225
E.McMillan-NYJ ... 180
T.Braxton-Den ... 103
M.Kelso-Buf ... 101

Interception Return TDs
T.Gash-Cle ... 2
E.Anderson-LARd ... 2

Sacks
L.Williams-SD ... 14.0
B.Smith-Buf ... 13.0
L.O'Neal-SD ... 12.5
S.Fletcher-Den ... 12.0

Overall Rank
B.Esiason-Cin ... 1741
W.Moon-Hou ... 1679
T.Thomas-Buf ... 1669
C.Okoye-KC ... 1606
E.Dickerson-Ind ... 1492

PARITY IS SUCH A LONELY WORD

Pete Rozelle stepped down after 29 years as commissioner. Paul Tagliabue, the league's counsel during its numerous battles in the litigious 1980s, was chosen on the 12th ballot. He took over a league that lacked greatness. San Francisco was the class of a somewhat intriguing NFC, but the AFC was another story.

Only the Broncos proved to be decisively better than .500, and the Central Division champ and cellar-dweller were separated by less than two games in the standings. If fans had the entertainment of seeing 11 of the conference's teams in the playoff hunt up to the last game, commentators pontificated whether it was balance or parity. The Broncos made people wonder by going 1–3 the last month. Still, supplemental draft pick Bobby Humphrey and the overhauled defense made the Broncos the only conference team with a double-digit win total, something that hadn't happened, discounting the 1982 strike season, since the AFC was created in 1970.

In the Central Division, defending conference champion Cincinnati fell into a strange first-to-worst scenario. The Bengals finished at .500 with an offense made inconsistent by the loss of Ickey Woods in the second game. In Cincinnati's place, the Browns lurched to the title—a tie with the Chiefs gave them the edge—even with Kevin Mack's suspension for a drug arrest. Oilers coach Jerry Glanville's indecisiveness in picking a feature back and a weak defense produced losses to the Bengals and Browns in the last two weeks. Houston finished with the same record as Pittsburgh, winners of five of the last six. The Oilers and Steelers would meet in the playoffs one last time for Chuck Noll.

Buffalo backed into its second consecutive division title, struggling through a three-game losing streak before clinching the title with a shutout of the 4-12 Jets. Even with injuries to Cornelius Bennett and Shane Conlan, the offensive trinity of Jim Kelly, Thurman Thomas, and wideout Andre Reed put up enough points for the Bills to outscore their defensive mistakes. Both the Dolphins and Colts had shots at the brass ring, but both lost in the final weekend to fall out of the playoff picture.

1990 NFC

TEAM	W-L-T	PCT	POST	PTS	RA	RY	RY/A	RTD	FL	PA	PC	GPY	GPY/A	PTD	PI	PSY	PRAT
Eastern Division																	
NYG	13-3	.813	DCS*	335-**211**	541-388	2049-1459	3.8-3.8	17-9	9-11	398-496	231-278	2898-2933	7.3-**5.9**	18-**12**	**5**-23	142-186	90.6-62.2
Phi	10-6	.625	W	**396**-299	540-**337**	**2556-1169**	4.7-3.5	10-9	15-11	479-566	281-273	3582-3771	**7.5**-6.7	**34**-23	13-19	438-280	**94.5**-69.6
Was	10-6	.625	WD	381-301	515-382	2083-1587	4.0-4.2	16-8	**6**-12	536-514	301-281	3611-3483	6.7-6.8	22-21	22-21	132-**340**	73.5-72.5
Dal	7-9	.438	—	244-308	393-482	1500-1976	3.8-4.1	13-18	9-**19**	475-470	254-271	2898-2931	6.1-6.2	12-**12**	24-11	317-292	59.4-74.9
Phx	5-11	.313	—	268-396	452-521	1912-2318	4.2-4.4	13-20	14-11	439-**402**	238-233	3118-3130	7.1-7.8	16-29	18-16	285-232	71.9-90.3
Central Division																	
ChiB	11-5	.688	ED	348-280	**551**-391	2436-1572	4.4-4.0	**22**-10	14-14	430-495	229-258	2827-3220	6.6-6.5	14-19	12-**31**	283-300	73.1-**59.3**
TB	6-10	.375	—	264-367	410-496	1626-2223	4.0-4.5	7-20	19-17	448-471	245-263	3282-3460	7.3-7.3	18-22	24-25	433-204	69.3-72.7
Det	6-10	.375	—	373-413	366-532	1927-2388	**5.3**-4.5	19-22	16-18	460-507	242-319	3328-3625	7.2-7.1	24-21	20-17	278-279	75.3-84.1
GB	6-10	.375	—	271-347	350-475	1369-2059	3.9-4.3	5-16	22-14	541-479	302-256	3696-3555	6.8-7.4	20-20	21-16	390-172	73.2-77.5
Min	6-10	.375	—	351-326	455-503	1867-2074	4.1-4.1	10-12	13-11	497-422	265-**218**	3445-**2920**	6.9-6.9	25-20	24-22	278-277	72.0-68.0
Western Division																	
SF	**14**-2	**.875**	DC	353-239	454-353	1718-1258	3.8-3.6	12-**7**	14-14	**583**-522	**360**-265	**4371**-3278	**7.5**-6.3	28-17	16-17	194-263	89.4-67.8
NO	8-8	.500	W	274-275	464-410	1850-1559	4.0-3.8	14-8	16-**19**	447-534	226-316	2757-3584	6.2-6.7	15-21	23-8	**131**-265	59.7-86.2
LARm	5-11	.313	—	345-412	422-418	1612-1649	3.8-3.9	17-17	14-**19**	561-501	310-296	4016-3942	7.2-7.9	24-30	17-12	198-180	79.6-94.1
Atl	5-11	.313	—	348-365	420-413	1594-1357	3.8-**3.3**	11-11	21-18	528-537	293-297	3726-4127	7.1-7.7	21-31	18-17	265-214	76.8-86.2
Aver	16	—	—	322	444	1822	4.1	13	15	483	270	3382	7.0	21	17	266	77.3

TEAM	1D	PENY	PNT	FGM/A	RTNY	RTNTD	OFFY/DEFY	NETY	NETTO	NP	PNP	DELP	PW	DELW	PRT	DR	YPD	DEL
Eastern Division																		
NYG	273-**245**	655-569	**44.1**-41.3	21/28-**16**/22	583-**345**	4-2	4805-**4206**	599	**20**	**124**	130	-6	**11.1**	1.9	**6.3**/ 3.5	171-**173**	28.1-24.3	3.8
Phi	325-251	981-706	40.9-40.3	21/29-23/32	586-426	4-**1**	5700-4660	1040	2	97	95	2	10.4	-0.4	5.5/ 4.7	197-195	28.9-23.9	5.0
Was	**327**-267	824-712	37.5-43.3	**30/40**-18/23	659-476	3-6	5562-4730	832	5	80	89	-9	10.0	0.0	4.9/ 4.3	185-181	30.1-26.1	3.9
Dal	250-280	729-911	43.2-40.9	18/25-18/26	376-791	2-6	4081-4615	-534	-3	-64	-57	-7	6.4	0.6	3.1/ 4.5	179-181	22.8-25.5	-2.7
Phx	270-306	883-834	42.8-43.6	17/27-**16/20**	616-459	2-**1**	4745-5216	-471	-5	-128	-59	-69	4.8	0.2	4.5/ 5.6	176-**173**	27.0-30.2	-3.2
Central Division																		
ChiB	295-256	615-676	39.4-**37.9**	26/37-22/28	667-486	3-2	4980-4492	488	19	68	117	-49	9.7	1.3	4.5/**3.2**	194-195	25.7-23.0	2.6
TB	238-313	651-617	40.3-40.5	23/27-18/27	**671**-698	3-3	4475-5479	-1004	-1	-103	-88	-15	5.4	0.6	3.9/ 4.7	185-186	24.2-29.5	-5.3
Det	278-334	711-788	40.6-40.8	17/26-23/30	634-579	3-6	4977-5734	-757	-1	-40	-67	27	7.0	-1.0	4.7/ 5.1	191-188	26.1-30.5	-4.4
GB	276-286	669-854	37.4-39.1	23/30-22/34	462-559	4-4	4675-5442	-767	-13	-76	-116	40	6.1	-0.1	4.2/ 5.7	189-184	24.7-29.6	-4.8
Min	288-257	**565**-787	41.8-39.4	25/28-30/36	583-773	4-2	5034-4717	317	-4	25	10	15	8.6	-2.6	4.3/ 4.0	**198**-199	25.4-23.7	1.7
Western Division																		
SF	324-250	828-641	36.2-40.0	24/36-19/23	527-391	0-2	**5895**-4273	**1622**	1	114	**139**	-25	10.9	**3.2**	6.0/ 4.3	179-192	**32.9-22.3**	**10.7**
NO	253-279	829-655	42.1-40.9	21/27-21/35	558-585	1-**1**	4476-4878	-402	-12	-1	-82	**81**	8.0	0.0	3.7/ 5.5	183-184	24.5-26.5	-2.1
LARm	311-286	632-**968**	38.6-41.4	15/24-24/31	451-624	2-2	5430-5411	19	0	-67	2	-69	6.3	-1.3	5.6/ 6.6	193-183	28.1-29.6	-1.4
Atl	273-300	1004-811	41.6-40.2	22/33-19/28	516-682	**8**-2	5055-5270	-215	-4	-17	-34	17	7.6	-2.6	5.0/ 6.1	**198**-199	25.5-26.5	-1.0
Aver	284	764	40.4	21/28	522	3	4938	—	—	—	—	—	—	—	5.3	182	27.1	—

Rushing Attempts	Rushing Yards	Rushing Average	Rushing TDs	Rushing Rank	Passing Yards	Passing Average
E.Byner-Was 297	B.Sanders-Det 1304	H.Cross-Phi 7.98	C.Gary-LARm 14	B.Sanders-Det 1434	J.Everett-LARm 3989	P.Terrell-TB 7.72
N.Anderson-Chi 260	E.Byner-Was 1219	T.Rosenbach-Phx 5.47	B.Sanders-Det 13	E.Byner-Was 1279	J.Montana-SF 3944	J.Montana-SF 7.58
B.Sanders-Det 255	N.Anderson-Chi 1078	B.Sanders-Det 5.11	E.Smith-Dal 11	N.Anderson-Chi 1178	H.Cross-Phi 3466	H.Cross-Phi 7.45
E.Smith-Dal 241	H.Cross-Phi 942	B.Muster-Chi 4.71	O.Anderson-NYG 11	E.Smith-Dal 1047	T.Rosenbach-Phx 3098	P.Simms-NYG 7.34
J.Johnson-Phx 234	E.Smith-Dal 937	C.Heyward-NO 4.64	N.Anderson-Chi 10	H.Cross-Phi 992	P.Terrell-TB 2818	D.Majkowski-GB 7.29
Completion Percent	**TD Passes**	**TD Percent**	**INT Percent**	**Passer Rating**	**Passing Rank**	**Receptions**
J.Montana-SF 61.7	H.Cross-Phi 30	H.Cross-Phi 6.5	P.Simms-NYG 1.3	P.Simms-NYG 92.7	J.Montana-SF 1462	J.Rice-SF 100
P.Simms-NYG 59.2	J.Montana-SF 26	M.Rypien-Was 5.3	J.Harbaugh-Chi 1.9	H.Cross-Phi 91.6	J.Everett-LARm 1430	A.Rison-Atl 82
H.Cross-Phi 58.3	J.Everett-LARm 23	J.Montana-SF 5.0	H.Cross-Phi 2.8	J.Montana-SF 89.0	H.Cross-Phi 1363	K.Byars-Phi 81
J.Harbaugh-Chi 57.7	P.Terrell-TB 17	P.Simms-NYG 4.8	R.Peete-Det 3.0	J.Harbaugh-Chi 81.9	P.Simms-NYG 1057	H.Ellard-LARm 76
C.Miller-Atl 57.2	C.Miller-Atl 17	R.Peete-Det 4.8	J.Everett-LARm 3.1	R.Peete-Det 79.8	T.Rosenbach-Phx 949	G.Clark-Was 75
Receiving Yards	**Receiving Average**	**Receiving TDs**	**Receiving Rank**	**Combined Net Yards**	**Total TDs**	**Total Points**
J.Rice-SF 1502	F.Anderson-LARm 21.51	J.Rice-SF 13	J.Rice-SF 816	H.Walker-Min 2051	B.Sanders-Det 16	C.Lohmiller-Was 131
H.Ellard-LARm 1294	F.Barnett-Phi 20.03	A.Rison-Atl 10	H.Ellard-LARm 667	B.Sanders-Det 1784	C.Gary-LARm 15	K.Butler-Chi 114
A.Rison-Atl 1208	R.Clark-Det 17.58	C.Williams-Phi 9	A.Rison-Atl 654	N.Anderson-Chi 1562	J.Rice-SF 13	M.Cofer-SF 111
G.Clark-Was 1112	H.Ellard-LARm 17.03		G.Clark-Was 596	D.Meggett-NYG 1533	N.Anderson-Chi 13	R.Ruzek-Phi 108
S.Sharpe-GB 1105	E.Jones-Phx 16.84		S.Sharpe-GB 583	J.Rice-SF 1502		G.Davis-Atl 106
Punt Average	**Field Goals**	**Field Goal Percent**	**Kickoff Returns**	**Kickoff Return Average**	**Punt Returns**	**Punt Return Average**
S.Landeta-NYG 44.1	C.Lohmiller-Was 30	D.Igwebuike-Min 87.5	H.Walker-Min 44	G.Atkins-NO 24.8	D.Meggett-NYG 43	J.Bailey-Chi 11.1
M.Saxon-Dal 43.2	K.Butler-Chi 26	S.Christie-TB 85.2	M.Gray-Det 41	D.Meggett-NYG 23.4	V.Buck-NO 37	D.Meggett-NYG 10.9
R.Camarillo-Phx 42.8	M.Cofer-SF 24	M.Andersen-NO 77.8	D.Carter-SF 41	M.Gray-Det 22.9	V.Sikahema-Phx 36	M.Gray-Det 10.6
T.Barnhardt-NO 42.7	C.Jacke-GB 23	C.Jacke-GB 76.7	D.Sanders-Atl 39	C.Wilson-GB 22.8	J.Bailey-Chi 36	D.Henley-LARm 10.3
H.Newsome-Min 42.3	S.Christie-TB 23	C.Lohmiller-Was 75.0	J.Dixon-Dal 36	G.Green-LARm 22.4	M.Gray-Det 34	J.Query-GB 9.6
Punt/Kick Return Yards	**Punt/Kick Return TDs**	**Interceptions**	**Interception Return Yards**	**Interception Return TDs**	**Sacks**	**Overall Rank**
M.Gray-Det 1300	Many 1	M.Carrier-Chi 10	W.Haddix-TB 231	W.Haddix-TB 3	C.Haley-SF 16.0	H.Cross-Phi 2355
D.Sanders-Atl 1101		D.Waymer-SF 7	D.Sanders-Atl 153	M.Turner-Phx 2	R.White-Phi 14.0	B.Sanders-Det 1689
H.Walker-Min 966		M.Mayhew-Was 7	W.White-Det 120	D.Sanders-Atl 2	K.Greene-LARm 13.0	J.Montana-SF 1634
D.Meggett-NYG 959		W.Haddix-TB 7	A.Walton-Was 118		R.Dent-Chi 12.0	J.Everett-LARm 1471
V.Sikahema-Phx 850		J.Browner-Min 7	Merriweather-Min 108			T.Rosenbach-Phx 1449

The Gifts of Time and Teams

If anything, the competitive differences in quality between the teams in the conference grew worse, as the NFC was effectively reduced to a five-team conference with a sixth playoff slot to fill thanks to the league's added playoff format. To make the long season seem even longer, a bye week was added. Teams would get one week off per year—to increase to two weeks in 1992—on an arbitrary basis. The four teams that played on Thanksgiving would still have just three days to get ready for those Thursday games. Replay would be limited to a two-minute window for decisions, although it would prove difficult for referees to throw flags on themselves. Making tougher decisions were college juniors, who could now apply for the draft but first had to renounce their college eligibility. Emmitt Smith and Jeff George took immediate advantage of the new rules, but not every collegian would have such obvious choices.

The surprise teams of 1989—the division-winning Vikings and the surprising Packers—imploded entirely. They would be joined in their collapses by the Rams, creating opportunities for something old and something new in their places. The old was a Bears team rejuvenated by successfully integrating youngsters like safety Mark Carrier (who snagged a league-leading 10 interceptions), defensive end Trace Armstrong, and quarterback Jim Harbaugh. The new was New Orleans. The Saints were the default sixth team to make the postseason. Victimized by quarterback Bobby Hebert's holdout, the Saints traded for Steve Walsh, who inspired the Saints to just 8–8.

The 49ers continued to rule the roost in the West, repeating the previous season's 14–2 record despite Roger Craig's ineffective season on offense, and Ronnie Lott's increasing fragility with age on defense. Jerry Rice continued to only get better. He had his first 100-catch season while leading the league in receiving yards for the third time in five years.

The Giants rolled behind their power running and top-shelf defense. The Eagles again had Randall Cunningham beating defenses from the pocket or ranging out of it, while the Redskins finally had the running game to complement their incomparable trio of wideouts.

1990 AFC

TEAM	W-L-T	PCT	POST	PTS	RA	RY	RY/A	RTD	FL	PA	PC	GPY	GPY/A	PTD	PI	PSY	PRAT
Eastern Division																	
Buf	**13**-3	**.813**	DCS	**428**-263	479-483	2080-1808	4.3-3.7	**20**-13	**10**-17	425-455	263-254	3404-3125	8.0-6.9	28-17	11-18	208-326	**98.2**-73.2
Mia	12-4	.750	WD	336-242	420-461	1535-1831	3.7-4.0	13-11	15-8	539-462	310-257	3611-3064	6.7-6.6	21-14	12-19	**99**-348	81.6-69.0
Ind	7-9	.438	—	281-353	335-513	1282-2212	3.8-4.3	9-12	**10**-15	488-492	269-301	3297-3605	6.8-7.3	22-20	21-9	424-203	73.3-89.5
NYJ	6-10	.375	—	295-345	476-423	2127-2018	4.5-4.8	16-15	13-11	451-516	246-311	3059-3745	6.8-7.3	14-23	11-18	300-308	76.0-82.9
NE	1-15	.063	—	181-446	383-565	1398-2676	3.7-4.7	4-29	16-18	514-**374**	274-**218**	3208-3245	6.2-8.7	14-21	20-14	443-224	65.4-89.9
Central Division																	
Cin	9-7	.563	#ED	360-352	484-442	2120-2085	4.4-4.7	16-15	12-16	425-543	237-300	3152-3725	7.4-6.9	25-24	23-15	209-205	76.5-79.9
Hou	9-7	.563	#W	405-307	328-392	1417-1575	4.3-4.0	10-12	21-12	**639**-460	**399**-267	**5072**-3332	7.9-7.2	**37**-18	15-21	267-272	96.7-74.7
Pit	9-7	.563	#	292-**240**	456-446	1880-1615	4.1-**3.6**	11-13	17-18	408-460	237-236	2887-**2728**	7.1-**5.9**	20-**9**	15-**24**	242-228	81.0-**54.3**
Cle	3-13	.188	—	228-462	345-511	1220-2105	3.5-4.1	10-21	23-9	573-444	301-253	3407-3296	5.9-7.4	13-32	23-13	260-211	61.5-92.3
Western Division																	
LARd	12-4	.750	DC	337-268	496-439	2028-1716	4.1-3.9	**20-4**	14-9	336-437	183-246	2885-3032	**8.6**-6.9	19-20	10-13	197-335	89.7-80.8
KC	11-5	.688	W	369-257	**504-373**	1948-1640	3.9-4.4	11-12	14-**25**	449-512	260-267	3458-3662	7.7-7.2	23-16	**5**-20	191-**421**	94.9-69.5
Sea	9-7	.563	#	306-286	457-413	1749-1605	3.8-3.9	18-7	16-18	448-504	265-300	3194-3256	7.1-6.5	15-19	20-12	360-252	73.6-81.3
SD	6-10	.375	—	315-281	484-424	**2257-1515**	**4.7-3.6**	14-10	13-11	472-462	246-254	2840-3255	6.0-7.0	18-22	19-19	157-345	66.5-76.0
Den	5-11	.313	—	331-374	462-456	1872-1963	4.1-4.3	19-16	14-15	527-479	305-284	3671-3671	7.0-7.7	15-22	18-10	330-289	74.6-90.0
Aver	16	—	—	322	444	1822	4.1	13	15	483	270	3382	7.0	21	17	266	77.3

TEAM	1D	PENY	PNT	FGM/A	RTNY	RTNTD	OFFY/DEFY	NETY	NETTO	NP	PNP	DELP	PW	DELW	PRT	DR	YPD	DEL
Eastern Division																		
Buf	302-288	683-839	39.3-38.2	20/29-18/24	328-407	**5-0**	5276-4607	669	14	**165**	112	53	**12.1**	0.9	6.6/ 4.3	171-177	30.9-26.0	4.8
Mia	303-268	**486**-759	42.0-40.0	21/25-20/29	521-581	**5**-1	5047-4547	500	0	94	42	52	10.4	1.7	5.7/ 3.9	174-179	29.0-25.4	3.6
Ind	245-320	590-781	42.8-42.0	17/24-32/43	575-555	2-4	4155-5614	-1459	-7	-72	-150	**78**	6.2	0.8	4.0/ 6.1	177-179	23.5-31.4	-7.9
NYJ	295-318	848-876	39.3-41.4	23/26-24/32	524-455	2-1	4886-5455	-569	5	-50	-27	-23	6.8	-0.8	4.9/ 5.2	173-**161**	28.2-33.9	-5.6
NE	239-307	744-488	40.8-40.8	16/22-27/31	328-646	1-2	4163-5697	-1534	-4	-265	-144	-121	1.4	-0.4	3.5/ 6.4	187-186	22.3-30.6	-8.4
Central Division																		
Cin	277-308	627-824	42.1-41.8	17/22-22/29	401-585	3-2	5063-5605	-542	-4	8	-61	69	8.2	0.8	4.7/ 5.4	182-182	27.8-30.8	-3.0
Hou	**376**-279	1009-**1015**	**45.0**-38.7	21/32-17/21	467-423	2-7	**6222**-4635	**1587**	-3	98	120	-22	10.4	-1.5	6.6/ 4.6	170-167	**36.6**-27.8	**8.8**
Pit	263-**257**	928-719	37.2-40.9	20/25-18/28	**783-229**	2-4	4525-**4115**	410	10	52	74	-22	9.3	-0.3	4.9/**3.1**	177-174	25.6-**23.6**	1.9
Cle	259-314	922-684	36.9-38.1	14/20-**16**/27	421-847	4-6	4367-5190	-823	-24	-234	-165	-69	2.2	0.8	3.6/ 5.9	**192**-189	22.7-27.5	-4.7
Western Division																		
LARd	258-266	682-710	37.3-38.2	15/20-29/33	397-253	3-2	4716-4413	303	-2	69	17	52	9.7	**2.3**	6.7/ 4.8	161-164	29.3-26.9	2.4
KC	280-268	886-859	38.7-**37.0**	**34/37-16/20**	504-497	4-2	5215-4881	334	**26**	112	**132**	-20	10.8	0.2	**6.9**/ 4.4	184-191	28.3-25.6	2.8
Sea	284-280	746-766	40.6-41.9	23/32-20/27	519-506	1-6	4583-4609	-26	-6	20	-26	46	8.5	0.5	4.3/ 4.9	182-186	25.2-24.8	0.4
SD	272-268	886-720	39.4-41.2	21/28-**16**/21	524-441	4-1	4940-4425	515	-2	34	35	-1	8.9	-2.8	4.1/ 4.5	171-175	28.9-25.3	3.6
Den	323-306	775-819	43.5-41.4	25/34-26/33	446-328	2-5	5213-5345	-132	-7	-43	-39	-4	6.9	-1.9	4.7/ 6.1	182-178	28.6-30.0	-1.4
Aver	284	764	40.4	21/28	522	1	4938	—	—	—	—	—	—	—	5.3	89	27.5	—

Rushing Attempts	Rushing Yards	Rushing Average	Rushing TDs	Rushing Rank	Passing Yards	Passing Average
B.Humphrey-Den.....288	T.Thomas-Buf........1297	B.Jackson-LARd.....5.58	D.Fenner-Sea............14	T.Thomas-Buf........1407	W.Moon-Hou..........4689	J.Schroeder-LARd..8.53
T.Thomas-Buf..........271	M.Butts-SD............1225	J.Brooks-Cin...........5.15	M.Allen-LARd............12	M.Butts-SD............1305	D.Marino-Mia.........3563	J.Kelly-Buf...............8.18
M.Butts-SD.............265	B.Humphrey-Den...1202	B.Thomas-NYJ.......5.04	T.Thomas-Buf............11	B.Humphrey-Den...1272	J.Elway-Den..........3526	W.Moon-Hou...........8.03
C.Okoye-KC.............245	B.Word-KC.............1015	B.Word-KC..............4.98		B.Word-KC.............1055	S.DeBerg-KC.........3444	S.DeBerg-KC..........7.76
S.Smith-Mia.............226	J.Brooks-Cin..........1004	T.Thomas-Buf.........4.79		J.Brooks-Cin..........1054	D.Krieg-Sea...........3194	B.Esiason-Cin.........7.54
Completion Percent	**TD Passes**	**TD Percent**	**INT Percent**	**Passer Rating**	**Passing Rank**	**Receptions**
J.Kelly-Buf...............63.3	W.Moon-Hou.............33	J.Kelly-Buf................6.9	S.DeBerg-KC............0.9	J.Kelly-Buf............101.2	W.Moon-Hou..........1990	H.Jeffires-Hou............74
W.Moon-Hou...........62.0	J.Kelly-Buf..................24	B.Esiason-Cin...........6.0	D.Marino-Mia............2.1	W.Moon-Hou...........96.8	S.DeBerg-KC.........1677	D.Hill-Hou..................74
D.Krieg-Sea...........59.2	B.Esiason-Cin............24	J.Schroeder-LARd....5.7	W.Moon-Hou.............2.2	S.DeBerg-KC..........96.3	D.Marino-Mia.........1447	J.Williams-Sea..........73
J.Elway-Den............58.6	S.DeBerg-KC.............23	W.Moon-Hou.............5.7	K.O'Brien-NYJ..........2.4	J.Schroeder-LARd..90.8	J.Elway-Den..........1278	E.Givins-Hou.............72
S.DeBerg-KC..........58.1	D.Marino-Mia.............21	S.DeBerg-KC............5.2	J.Kelly-Buf................2.6	D.Marino-Mia..........82.6	J.Kelly-Buf.............1175	
Receiving Yards	**Receiving Average**	**Receiving TDs**	**Receiving Rank**	**Combined Net Yards**	**Total TDs**	**Total Points**
H.Jeffires-Hou........1048	J.Lofton-Buf..........20.34	E.Givins-Hou...............9	H.Jeffires-Hou..........564	T.Thomas-Buf........1829	D.Fenner-Sea............15	N.Lowery-KC...........139
S.Paige-KC............1021	W.Gault-LARd.......19.70	E.Brown-Cin................9	S.Paige-KC.............536	E.Metcalf-Cle.........1752	T.Thomas-Buf............13	S.Norwood-Buf........110
D.Hill-Hou..............1019	T.McGee-Cin.........17.14	A.Reed-Buf..................8	D.Hill-Hou................535	A.Bentley-Ind.........1442	M.Allen-LARd............13	D.Treadwell-Den......109
W.Gault-LARd..........985	J.Hester-Ind..........17.11	H.Jeffires-Hou..............8	E.Givins-Hou............535	J.Williams-Sea.......1413	L.White-Hou..............12	N.Johnson-Sea........102
E.Givins-Hou...........979	M.Jackson-Den.....16.25		A.Reed-Buf..............513	B.Humphrey-Den...1354	M.Hoge-Pit................10	P.Leahy-NYJ...........101
Punt Average	**Field Goals**	**Field Goal Percent**	**Kickoff Returns**	**Kickoff Return Average**	**Punt Returns**	**Punt Return Average**
O.Mobley-Hou.........45.0	N.Lowery-KC.............34	N.Lowery-KC..........91.9	E.Metcalf-Cle.............52	K.Clark-Den............25.3	R.Woodson-Pit..........38	C.Verdin-Ind...........12.8
M.Horan-Den..........44.4	D.Treadwell-Den........25	J.Carney-SD..........90.5	T.Mathis-NYJ.............43	D.Elder-SD..............23.8	T.Brown-LARd...........34	R.Woodson-Pit.......10.5
R.Stark-Ind.............43.4	P.Leahy-NYJ..............23	P.Leahy-NYJ...........88.5	R.Woodson-Pit..........35	E.Ball-Cin................22.9	C.Verdin-Ind...............31	C.Warren-Sea...........9.6
L.Johnson-Cin........42.3	N.Johnson-Sea..........23	T.Stowe-Mia............84.0	D.Smith-Buf...............32	N.Lewis-SD.............22.5	G.McNeil-Hou............30	J.Townsell-NYJ.........9.1
R.Roby-Mia.............42.0	T.Stowe-Mia...............21	J.Breech-Cin...........81.0	J.Holland-LARd.........32	R.Woodson-Pit.......21.8	M.Price-Cin................29	T.Brown-LARd..........8.7
Punt/Kick Return Yards	**Punt/Kick Return TDs**	**Interceptions**	**Interception Return Yards**	**Interception Return TDs**	**Sacks**	**Overall Rank**
R.Woodson-Pit......1162	E.Metcalf-Cle..............2	R.Johnson-Hou...........8	D.Woodruff-Pit.........110	Many...........................1	D.Thomas-KC.........20.0	W.Moon-Hou..........2225
E.Metcalf-Cle.........1052		G.Byrd-SD..................7	R.Johnson-Hou........100		B.Smith-Buf............19.0	T.Thomas-Buf........1683
T.Mathis-NYJ...........952			K.Ross-KC................97		L.O'Neal-SD...........13.5	S.DeBerg-KC.........1672
C.Warren-Sea..........747			R.Lippett-NE.............94		D.Byrd-NYJ.............13.0	J.Elway-Den..........1566
C.Verdin-Ind............746			E.McMillan-NYJ.........92			D.Marino-Mia.........1476

Running and Shooting; No Huddles, Please

After the laughs at the conference's expense the previous season, the AFC now had several stronger teams. Some things were consistent, like Buffalo shuffling off to a third straight division title, or that Marty Schottenheimer's way of doing things would make his team—now the Chiefs—a contender. The Central Division was again a slaughterhouse, with the Bengals, Steelers, and Oilers trading punches while the Browns cringed. But the surprise comebacks of the Dolphins and Raiders to respectability lent an element of history as well as good football.

The Central Division's wrestling match ended with three teams at 9–7. The Bengals fielded another gifted offensive team brought back to earth by a weak defense. The Oilers decision to move to a Run-and-Shoot offense—an innovation that had served the USFL's Houston Gamblers well—suited Warren Moon, a former CFL star who'd reached Pro Bowl status in the NFL. Doing things the old-fashioned way was still the rule on Chuck Noll's watch in Pittsburgh, where, beyond blossoming star cornerback Rod Woodson, a nondescript team managed to grunt and grind its way to Noll's 14th winning season. Pittsburgh fell just short of the playoffs on a loss to the Oilers to end the season.

The East featured its own innovations, with the Bills breaking out their full-time No-Huddle offense to disrupt the highly specialized role-playing on defenses. If the playbook seemed short-stacked, the offense's ability to execute was more than enough to lead the league in scoring, with or without quarterback Jim Kelly in the lineup. The Dolphins fell just short of the title, losing to the Bills in week 15, but a rebuilt defense featuring veteran imports like linebacker E.J. Junior and cornerback Tim McKyer and a solid crew of homegrown youngsters finally gave Dan Marino games he could help win.

In the West, the Raiders finally had the combination of quality running and the vertical passing attack that were their hallmarks, while Schottenheimer's Chiefs strongly resembled his Browns teams: a power-running game, an uncannily accurate quarterback (in oft-recycled Steve DeBerg), and some brilliant defensive play, most notably from linebacker Derrick Thomas and cornerback Albert Lewis.

1991 NFC

TEAM	W-L-T	PCT	POST	PTS	RA	RY	RY/A	RTD	FL	PA	PC	GPY	GPY/A	PTD	PI	PSY	PRAT
Eastern Division																	
Was	**14**-2	**.875**	DCS*	**485**-224	**540**-348	2049-1346	3.8-3.9	**21**-11	12-14	447-549	261-292	3771-3292	**8.4-6.0**	**30**-13	11-27	**79**-345	**98.0**-58.8
Dal	11-5	.688	WD	342-310	433-400	1711-1571	4.0-3.9	15-11	12-11	500-540	305-320	3663-3646	7.3-6.8	16-17	12-12	273-151	84.1-80.8
Phi	10-6	.625	#	285-244	446-383	1396-**1136**	3.1-**3.0**	8-**4**	16-**22**	513-467	285-**206**	3169-**2807**	6.2-**6.0**	17-16	27-26	263-**394**	63.2-**52.1**
NYG	8-8	.500	—	281-297	487-414	2064-1726	4.2-4.2	16-11	15-9	428-440	261-251	3025-3128	7.1-7.1	13-17	**8**-12	181-254	84.7-80.8
Phx	4-12	.250	—	196-344	391-493	1295-2136	3.3-4.3	6-27	14-21	492-447	254-268	3039-3069	6.2-6.9	10-**12**	25-17	372-153	56.4-73.8
Central Division																	
Det	12-4	.750	DC	339-295	454-444	1930-1760	4.3-4.0	19-16	13-17	459-534	252-315	2974-3523	6.5-6.6	16-16	17-19	116-237	71.0-73.9
ChiB	11-5	.688	W	299-269	502-389	1949-1580	3.9-4.1	18-9	16-13	497-513	286-286	3292-3184	6.6-6.2	16-19	17-17	172-257	74.1-72.9
Min	8-8	.500	—	301-306	464-456	**2201**-1837	**4.7**-4.0	18-17	**10**-11	477-499	284-286	3016-3396	6.3-6.8	16-16	16-17	133-217	75.2-74.7
GB	4-12	.250	—	273-313	381-457	1389-1546	3.6-3.4	12-10	17-14	514-531	272-305	3213-3573	6.3-6.7	17-20	19-15	270-307	67.9-78.8
TB	3-13	.188	—	199-365	371-512	1429-2107	3.9-4.1	9-21	18-16	495-438	250-257	2955-3130	6.0-7.1	13-15	29-11	383-258	53.4-81.7
Western Division																	
NO	11-5	.688	E	341-**211**	483-**334**	1709-1213	3.5-3.6	15-6	15-19	506-491	292-259	3419-3057	6.8-6.2	20-**12**	15-**29**	160-337	79.2-55.5
Atl	10-6	.625	#WD	361-338	410-466	1664-1953	4.1-4.2	6-13	14-16	500-481	260-252	3634-3532	7.3-7.3	**30**-28	22-19	185-237	77.4-79.3
SF	10-6	.625	#	393-239	440-399	1861-1512	4.2-3.8	19-8	19-16	**522**-499	**325**-267	**4167**-3254	8.0-6.5	29-16	12-12	170-212	96.2-74.5
LARm	3-13	.188	—	234-390	388-469	1285-1659	3.3-3.5	11-19	20-8	518-**434**	289-259	3610-3657	7.0-8.4	13-25	20-11	200-112	69.9-95.6
Aver	16	—	—	304	439	1723	3.9	13	15	498	286	3432	6.9	18	17	246	76.2

TEAM	1D	PENY	PNT	FGM/A	RTNY	RTNTD	OFFY/DEFY	NETY	NETTO	NP	PNP	DELP	PW	DELW	PRT	DR	YPD	DEL
Eastern Division																		
Was	302-242	798-767	37.6-41.7	**31**/**43**-14/**18**	**889-299**	5-2	5741-4293	**1448**	**18**	**261**	**193**	**68**	**14.5**	-0.5	**7.7**/ 3.1	186-193	30.9-22.2	**8.6**
Dal	304-299	**610**-801	42.6-**38.8**	27/39-29/39	476-475	**6**-4	5101-5066	35	-1	32	-1	33	8.8	2.2	5.6/ 5.6	172-173	29.7-29.3	0.4
Phi	249-**206**	839-881	41.4-42.7	28/33-25/33	696-863	4-4	4302-**3549**	753	5	41	83	-42	9.0	1.0	3.3/**2.7**	**207**-210	20.8-**16.9**	3.9
NYG	280-257	719-622	43.3-40.5	24/31-29/30	458-386	1-2	4908-4600	308	-2	-16	18	-34	7.6	0.4	5.6/ 5.3	171-**164**	28.7-28.0	0.7
Phx	237-301	661-734	44.7-45.2	21/30-15/23	494-712	3-4	3962-5052	-1090	-1	-148	-95	-53	4.3	-0.3	3.1/ 4.8	191-181	20.7-27.9	-7.2
Central Division																		
Det	280-305	799-704	41.2-39.2	19/28-19/28	671-569	5-2	4788-5046	-258	6	44	3	41	9.1	**2.9**	4.7/ 4.6	182-189	26.3-26.7	-0.4
ChiB	317-254	662-891	40.2-41.3	19/29-22/30	565-350	1-**1**	5069-4507	562	-3	30	35	-5	8.8	2.3	4.8/ 4.3	186-182	27.3-24.8	2.5
Min	300-301	675-709	**45.5**-42.7	17/24-20/29	467-629	2-2	5084-5016	68	2	-5	14	-19	7.9	0.1	4.6/ 4.8	175-171	29.1-29.3	-0.3
GB	259-298	834-777	40.4-42.1	18/24-23/31	630-560	2-5	4332-4812	-480	-7	-40	-68	28	7.0	-3.0	4.0/ 4.8	188-193	23.0-24.9	-1.9
TB	249-295	780-**925**	40.3-42.9	15/20-25/35	424-908	0-5	4001-4979	-978	-20	-166	-162	-4	3.8	-0.8	2.5/ 5.3	190-191	21.1-26.1	-5.0
Western Division																		
NO	267-214	801-711	43.0-42.3	25/32-17/21	799-727	3-5	4968-3933	1035	**18**	130	158	-28	11.3	-0.3	5.3/ 2.8	196-203	25.3-19.4	6.0
Atl	258-278	929-802	42.6-40.3	21/26-**13**/26	511-666	**6**-2	5113-5248	-135	-1	23	-15	38	8.6	1.4	5.2/ 5.3	202-202	25.3-26.0	-0.7
SF	**336**-260	902-782	39.2-41.0	14/28-22/25	445-321	2-**1**	**5858**-4554	1304	-3	154	97	57	11.9	-1.8	6.9/ 5.0	177-181	**33.1**-25.2	7.9
LARm	270-286	774-743	38.1-41.6	17/17-20/28	495-589	2-3	4695-5204	-509	-21	-156	-126	-30	4.1	-1.1	4.8/ 7.3	179-175	26.2-29.7	-3.5
Aver	284	775	41.4	22/30	538	3	4909	—	—	—	—	—	—	—	5.2	184	26.7	—

Rushing Attempts	Rushing Yards	Rushing Average	Rushing TDs	Rushing Rank	Passing Yards	Passing Average
E.Smith-Dal 365	E.Smith-Dal 1563	T.Allen-Min 4.69	B.Sanders-Det 16	B.Sanders-Det 1708	M.Rypien-Was 3564	S.Young-SF 9.02
B.Sanders-Det 342	B.Sanders-Det 1548	R.Ervins-Was 4.69	E.Smith-Dal 12	E.Smith-Dal 1683	J.Everett-LARm 3438	M.Rypien-Was 8.47
E.Byner-Was 274	R.Hampton-NYG 1059	B.Muster-Chi 4.58	G.Riggs-Was 11	R.Hampton-NYG 1159	J.Harbaugh-Chi 3121	T.Aikman-Dal 7.59
R.Hampton-NYG 256	E.Byner-Was 1048	S.Broussard-Atl 4.54	H.Walker-Min 10	E.Byner-Was 1098	C.Miller-Atl 3103	C.Miller-Atl 7.51
R.Delpino-LARm 214	H.Walker-Min 825	F.McAfee-NO 4.53	R.Hampton-NYG 10	H.Walker-Min 925	T.Aikman-Dal 2754	J.McMahon-Phi 7.20

Completion Percent	TD Passes	TD Percent	INT Percent	Passer Rating	Passing Rank	Receptions
T.Aikman-Dal 65.3	M.Rypien-Was 28	M.Rypien-Was 6.7	J.Hostetler-NYG 1.4	S.Young-SF 101.8	M.Rypien-Was 1482	M.Irvin-Dal 93
S.Young-SF 64.5	C.Miller-Atl 26	C.Miller-Atl 6.3	S.Bono-SF 1.7	M.Rypien-Was 97.9	T.Aikman-Dal 1032	A.Rison-Atl 81
J.Hostetler-NYG 62.8	S.Young-SF 17	S.Young-SF 6.1	R.Gannon-Min 1.7	S.Bono-SF 88.5	S.Young-SF 1024	J.Rice-SF 80
J.McMahon-Phi 60.1	J.Harbaugh-Chi 15	S.Bono-SF 4.6	S.Walsh-NO 2.4	T.Aikman-Dal 86.7	J.Harbaugh-Chi 996	C.Carter-Min 72
B.Hebert-NO 60.1		M.Tomczak-GB 4.6	M.Rypien-Was 2.6	J.Hostetler-NYG 84.1	J.Everett-LARm 974	A.Monk-Was 71

Receiving Yards	Receiving Average	Receiving TDs	Receiving Rank	Combined Net Yards	Total TDs	Total Points
M.Irvin-Dal 1523	M.Haynes-Atl 22.44	J.Rice-SF 14	M.Irvin-Dal 802	B.Sanders-Det 1855	B.Sanders-Det 17	C.Lohmiller-Was 149
G.Clark-Was 1340	G.Clark-Was 19.14	A.Rison-Atl 12	G.Clark-Was 720	E.Smith-Dal 1821	J.Rice-SF 14	K.Willis-Dal 118
J.Rice-SF 1206	Q.Early-NO 16.91	M.Haynes-Atl 11	J.Rice-SF 673	R.Hampton-NYG 1546	E.Smith-Dal 13	M.Andersen-NO 113
M.Haynes-Atl 1122	F.Anderson-LARm 16.56	G.Clark-Was 10	M.Haynes-Atl 616	M.Irvin-Dal 1523	A.Rison-Atl 12	R.Ruzek-Phi 111
H.Ellard-LARm 1052	H.Ellard-LARm 16.44	J.Taylor-SF 9	A.Monk-Was 565	D.Carter-SF 1471		B.Sanders-Det 102

Punt Average	Field Goals	Field Goal Percent	Kickoff Returns	Kickoff Return Average	Punt Returns	Punt Return Average
H.Newsome-Min 45.5	C.Lohmiller-Was 31	T.Zendejas-LARm 100.0	D.Carter-SF 37	M.Gray-Det 25.8	R.Harris-Phi 53	M.Gray-Det 15.4
R.Camarillo-Phx 45.3	R.Ruzek-Phi 28	R.Ruzek-Phi 84.8	M.Gray-Det 36	A.Wright-Dal 24.5	B.Mitchell-Was 45	B.Mitchell-Was 13.3
T.Barnhardt-NO 43.5	K.Willis-Dal 27	N.Johnson-Atl 82.6	G.Anderson-TB 34	C.Wilson-GB 22.7	W.Drewrey-TB 38	K.Martin-Dal 11.6
S.Landeta-NYG 43.3	M.Andersen-NO 25	M.Andersen-NO 78.1	D.Nelson-Min 31	D.Carter-SF 22.7	J.Bailey-Chi 36	D.Meggett-NYG 10.3
S.Fulhage-Atl 42.8	M.Bahr-NYG 22	M.Bahr-NYG 75.9	B.Mitchell-Was 29	D.Sanders-Atl 22.2		W.Drewrey-TB 9.5

Punt/Kick Return Yards	Punt/Kick Return TDs	Interceptions	Interception Return Yards	Interception Return TDs	Sacks	Overall Rank
M.Gray-Det 1314	B.Mitchell-Was 2	A.Williams-Phx 6	G.Atkins-NO 198	Many 1	P.Swilling-NO 17.0	B.Sanders-Det 1867
B.Mitchell-Was 1183		D.Sanders-Atl 6	R.Crockett-Det 141		R.White-Phi 15.0	E.Smith-Dal 1817
R.Harris-Phi 889		T.McKyer-Atl 6	D.Sanders-Atl 119		C.Simmons-Phi 13.0	M.Rypien-Was 1498
D.Carter-SF 839		R.Crockett-Det 6	N.Mustafaa-Min 104		T.Bennett-GB 13.0	S.Young-SF 1479
D.Meggett-NYG 801			J.Browner-Min 97			R.Hampton-NYG 1355

An American Revival and a Debut Abroad

This was the season in which the powers of old were back. The Redskins posted a league-best 14 wins while the Cowboys gelled into the powerhouse Jimmy Johnson intended. The Skins added a three-headed running back committee—Earnest Byner, Ricky Ervins, and Gerald Riggs—to its trio of superb wideouts and led the NFL in scoring. Johnson's Cowboys won 11 games to herald their comeback from 1–15 just two years before. Wideout Michael Irvin turned into Troy Aikman's weapon of choice, while Emmitt Smith led the league in rushing. The Eagles, with Randall Cunningham injured, were a step behind. The Giants, with Bill Parcells having ridden off into the sunset (for now), were a wheezing .500 team.

Elsewhere, the meek were finally inheriting first place. The Lions and Saints won their respective divisions: the first title for New Orleans and a franchise-high 12 wins for Detroit. The Lions became closer following a paralyzing injury at the Silverdome to inspirational offensive lineman Mike Utley. Barry Sanders scored a league-leading 16 touchdowns, illustrating that the Run-and-Shoot wasn't bad news for a running back. Shorn of an effective running game by injuries, Chicago turned to the passing game to make the playoffs.

San Francisco lost Joe Montana to a bum elbow. Steve Young shined in the first 10 games, but then he went down, too. Falcons coach Jerry Glanville fired up the Run-and-Shoot and two gifted cornerbacks—Tim McKyer and a young Deion Sanders—came through often enough to sneak Atlanta into the playoffs, beating out the 49ers on tiebreakers. Two more outstanding defensive backs debuted in 1991, Merton Hanks for the 49ers and Aeneas Williams for the Cardinals.

The NFL launched the World League of American Football, spreading pro football from Sacramento to Frankfurt. After two years the North American arm would be deemed extraneous and more European teams would be added instead. A year after Chicago legend Bronko Nagurski died, teammate Red Grange followed at age 87. The Galloping Ghost's debut tour in 1925 made George Halas even more powerful, saved New York football, and made people think about the pro game for the first time.

1991 AFC

TEAM	W-L-T	PCT	POST	PTS	RA	RY	RY/A	RTD	FL	PA	PC	GPY	GPY/A	PTD	PI	PSY	PRAT
Eastern Division																	
Buf	**13**-3	**.813**	DCS	**458**-318	505-519	**2381**-2044	4.7-3.9	16-20	16-14	516-536	332-299	4140-3660	**8.0**-6.8	**39-12**	19-**23**	269-246	**99.0**-66.6
NYJ	8-8	.500	#W	314-293	**523-379**	2160-**1442**	4.1-3.8	**17**-8	13-19	503-540	295-331	3429-3765	6.8-7.0	12-21	12-18	273-226	77.4-81.3
Mia	8-8	.500	#	343-349	379-499	1352-2301	3.6-4.6	8-17	14-9	563-485	327-300	4077-3353	7.2-6.9	26-18	14-12	188-248	85.7-84.5
NE	6-10	.375	—	211-305	433-460	1467-1579	3.4-**3.4**	9-5	20-19	481-565	284-335	3442-4035	7.2-7.1	11-25	22-12	436-183	69.7-87.1
Ind	1-15	.063	—	143-381	354-544	1169-2327	3.3-4.3	3-23	15-13	512-**388**	305-**240**	3066-**3002**	6.0-7.7	10-22	16-15	487-202	70.2-88.7
Central Division																	
Hou	11-5	.688	ED	386-251	331-407	1366-1540	4.1-3.8	16-8	19-18	**667**-532	**411**-310	**4804**-3522	7.2-6.6	24-17	21-20	183-314	82.3-73.2
Pit	7-9	.438	—	292-344	394-466	1627-1582	4.1-**3.4**	8-14	14-11	476-535	259-334	3313-3843	7.0-7.2	20-21	16-19	359-257	76.4-82.3
Cle	6-10	.375	—	293-298	389-447	1360-1875	3.5-4.2	12-12	**8**-18	503-522	312-312	3547-3445	7.1-6.6	19-20	**10**-15	243-236	87.5-80.2
Cin	3-13	.188	—	263-435	449-454	1811-1662	4.0-3.7	11-20	20-14	511-505	290-303	3413-4119	6.7-8.2	14-26	22-17	255-129	68.4-89.2
Western Division																	
Den	12-4	.750	DC	304-**235**	507-411	2015-1794	4.0-4.4	16-8	13-10	459-476	246-246	3310-3101	7.2-6.5	13-**12**	12-**23**	313-**346**	75.3-**60.6**
KC	10-6	.625	WD	322-252	521-417	2217-1770	4.3-4.2	14-8	**8**-18	479-471	284-279	3281-3532	6.8-7.5	19-17	14-15	**177**-304	81.1-81.5
LARd	9-7	.563	W	298-297	446-447	1706-1889	3.8-4.2	8-13	13-13	414-513	220-295	2977-3559	7.2-6.9	20-18	18-18	258-283	74.3-76.0
Sea	7-9	.438	—	276-261	394-435	1426-1684	3.6-3.9	11-**4**	17-**21**	488-517	290-296	3371-3288	6.9-**6.4**	15-18	26-18	263-269	68.4-73.4
SD	4-12	.250	—	274-342	464-430	2248-1666	**4.8**-3.9	16-15	12-9	511-503	272-300	2983-3628	5.8-7.2	13-22	16-19	236-183	66.2-80.7
Aver	16	—	—	304	439	1723	3.9	13	15	498	286	3432	6.9	18	17	246	76.2

TEAM	1D	PENY	PNT	FGM/A	RTNY	RTNTD	OFFY/DEFY	NETY	NETTO	NP	PNP	DELP	PW	DELW	PRT	DR	YPD	DEL
Eastern Division																		
Buf	**359**-335	865-**938**	38.6-39.1	18/29-27/35	557-373	3-2	**6252**-5458	794	2	**140**	74	**66**	**11.5**	1.5	**6.2**/ 4.4	**192**-192	32.6-28.4	4.1
NYJ	331-298	814-774	39.4-40.6	30/**43**-26/38	440-**269**	3-2	5316-4981	335	12	21	76	-55	8.5	-0.5	5.1/ 5.1	177-180	30.0-27.7	2.4
Mia	312-327	**516**-684	**44.8**-39.8	**33**/39-23/33	393-549	1-5	5241-5406	-165	-7	-6	-42	36	7.8	0.2	6.0/ 5.3	175-175	29.9-30.9	-0.9
NE	259-312	667-608	39.0-42.2	20/29-29/42	304-457	2-**1**	4473-5431	-958	-11	-94	-124	30	5.7	0.3	3.9/ 6.0	189-191	23.7-28.4	-4.8
Ind	236-305	689-645	42.6-41.4	15/26-17/**23**	373-700	1-2	3748-5127	-1379	-3	-238	-127	-111	2.1	-1.1	3.4/ 5.6	172-170	21.8-30.2	-8.4
Central Division																		
Hou	353-280	784-797	41.7-42.1	23/31-23/29	499-488	**6-1**	5987-4748	**1239**	-2	135	**95**	40	11.4	-0.4	5.7/ 4.3	183-186	**32.7**-25.5	**7.2**
Pit	254-320	933-685	39.9-41.6	23/33-26/41	**702**-392	4-3	4581-5168	-587	0	-52	-49	-3	6.7	0.3	4.7/ 5.1	190-185	24.1-27.9	-3.8
Cle	265-298	872-770	42.5-41.3	16/22-22/30	511-483	4-**1**	4664-5084	-420	**15**	-5	25	-30	7.9	-1.9	5.6/ 4.9	174-171	26.8-29.7	-2.9
Cin	286-308	845-808	43.5-42.0	24/32-22/31	449-787	2-7	4969-5652	-683	-11	-172	-101	-71	3.7	-0.7	4.2/ 6.6	188-183	26.4-30.9	-4.5
Western Division																		
Den	284-**242**	715-848	41.2-44.5	27/36-27/33	663-271	3-2	5012-**4549**	463	8	69	71	-2	9.7	**2.3**	5.1/**3.5**	183-183	27.4-24.9	2.5
KC	322-275	724-827	40.4-42.5	25/30-21/28	474-441	2-2	5321-4998	323	11	70	71	-1	9.8	0.3	5.3/ 5.3	165-**161**	32.2-31.0	1.2
LARd	248-305	1013-905	44.2-**38.7**	29/34-**16**/28	485-715	2-5	4425-5165	-740	0	1	-62	63	8.0	1.0	4.7/ 4.8	173-178	25.6-29.0	-3.4
Sea	253-262	682-845	40.6-39.1	25/31-28/32	627-623	3-3	4534-4703	-169	-4	15	-30	45	8.4	-1.4	3.9/ 4.3	191-196	23.7-**24.0**	-0.3
SD	285-292	799-718	39.8-40.3	19/29-23/29	555-450	2-2	4995-5111	-116	0	-68	-10	-58	6.3	-2.3	4.0/ 5.3	187-182	26.7-28.1	-1.4
Aver	284	775	41.4	22/30	538	1	4909	—	—	—	—	—	—	—	5.2	91	27.4	—

Rushing Attempts	Rushing Yards	Rushing Average	Rushing TDs	Rushing Rank	Passing Yards	Passing Average
T.Thomas-Buf 288	T.Thomas-Buf 1407	R.Harmon-SD 6.11	B.Baxter-NYJ 11	T.Thomas-Buf 1477	W.Moon-Hou 4690	J.Kelly-Buf 8.11
L.Russell-NE 266	G.Green-Den 1037	B.Foster-Pit 5.08	A.Pinkett-Hou 9	C.Okoye-KC 1121	D.Marino-Mia 3970	H.Millen-NE 7.51
G.Green-Den 261	C.Okoye-KC 1031	T.Thomas-Buf 4.89	C.Okoye-KC 9	G.Green-Den 1077	J.Kelly-Buf 3844	D.Krieg-Sea 7.30
M.Higgs-Mia 231	L.Russell-NE 959	K.Davis-Buf 4.84	K.Mack-Cle 8	L.Russell-NE 999	B.Kosar-Cle 3487	D.Marino-Mia 7.23
C.Okoye-KC 225	M.Higgs-Mia 905	R.Bernstine-SD 4.82	R.Bernstine-SD 8	M.Higgs-Mia 945	K.O'Brien-NYJ 3300	J.Elway-Den 7.21
Completion Percent	**TD Passes**	**TD Percent**	**INT Percent**	**Passer Rating**	**Passing Rank**	**Receptions**
D.Krieg-Sea 65.6	J.Kelly-Buf 33	J.Kelly-Buf 7.0	B.Kosar-Cle 1.8	J.Kelly-Buf 97.6	W.Moon-Hou 1620	H.Jeffires-Hou 100
J.Kelly-Buf 64.1	D.Marino-Mia 25	D.Marino-Mia 4.6	K.O'Brien-NYJ 2.2	B.Kosar-Cle 87.8	D.Marino-Mia 1590	D.Hill-Hou 90
B.Kosar-Cle 62.1	W.Moon-Hou 23	J.Schroeder-LARd 4.2	D.Marino-Mia 2.4	D.Marino-Mia 85.8	B.Kosar-Cle 1474	M.Cook-NE 82
W.Moon-Hou 61.7	B.Kosar-Cle 18	S.DeBerg-KC 3.9	N.O'Donnell-Pit 2.4	D.Krieg-Sea 82.5	J.Kelly-Buf 1407	A.Reed-Buf 81
J.George-Ind 60.2	S.DeBerg-KC 17	D.Krieg-Sea 3.9	J.George-Ind 2.5	W.Moon-Hou 81.7	K.O'Brien-NYJ 1260	A.Toon-NYJ 74
Receiving Yards	**Receiving Average**	**Receiving TDs**	**Receiving Rank**	**Combined Net Yards**	**Total TDs**	**Total Points**
H.Jeffires-Hou 1181	D.Stone-Pit 20.28	M.Clayton-Mia 12	H.Jeffires-Hou 626	T.Thomas-Buf 2038	T.Thomas-Buf 12	M.Stover-Mia 121
A.Reed-Buf 1113	J.Lofton-Buf 18.81	A.Reed-Buf 10	A.Reed-Buf 607	A.Pinkett-Hou 1456	M.Clayton-Mia 12	J.Jaeger-LARd 116
D.Hill-Hou 1109	M.Jackson-Den 18.27	L.Hoard-Cle 9	M.Clayton-Mia 587	R.Woodson-Pit 1287	L.Hoard-Cle 11	D.Treadwell-Den 112
M.Duper-Mia 1085	T.McGee-Cin 15.73	J.Lofton-Buf 8	J.Lofton-Buf 576	A.Reed-Buf 1249	B.Baxter-NYJ 11	S.Norwood-Buf 110
J.Lofton-Buf 1072	M.Duper-Mia 15.50	H.Jeffires-Hou 7	D.Hill-Hou 575	J.Williams-Sea 1240		N.Lowery-KC 110
Punt Average	**Field Goals**	**Field Goal Percent**	**Kickoff Returns**	**Kickoff Return Average**	**Punt Returns**	**Punt Return Average**
R.Roby-Mia 45.7	M.Stover-Mia 31	J.Jaeger-LARd 85.3	R.Woodson-Pit 44	N.Lewis-SD 25.1	C.Warren-Sea 32	R.Woodson-Pit 11.4
J.Gossett-LARd 44.2	J.Jaeger-LARd 29	M.Stover-Mia 83.8	C.Verdin-Ind 36	D.Loville-Sea 22.9	T.Brown-LARd 29	T.Brown-LARd 11.4
C.Mohr-Hou 43.9	D.Treadwell-Den 27	N.Lowery-KC 83.3	C.Warren-Sea 35	C.Warren-Sea 22.6	R.Woodson-Pit 28	K.Taylor-SD 9.6
L.Johnson-Cin 43.7	P.Leahy-NYJ 26	J.Kasay-Sea 80.6	J.Vaughn-NE 34	H.Williams-KC 21.8	K.Taylor-SD 28	C.Warren-Sea 9.3
R.Tuten-Sea 43.0		J.Breech-Cin 79.3	A.Craver-Mia 32	J.Vaughn-NE 21.1	S.Miller-Mia 28	S.Miller-Mia 8.9
Punt/Kick Return Yards	**Punt/Kick Return TDs**	**Interceptions**	**Interception Return Yards**	**Interception Return TDs**	**Sacks**	**Overall Rank**
R.Woodson-Pit 1200	Many 1	R.Lott-LARd 8	E.McMillan-NYJ 168	E.McMillan-NYJ 2	W.Fuller-Hou 15.0	T.Thomas-Buf 1818
C.Warren-Sea 1090		C.Dishman-Hou 6	N.Odomes-Buf 120		D.Thomas-KC 13.5	W.Moon-Hou 1708
C.Verdin-Ind 854		G.Byrd-SD 6	S.Atwater-Den 104		S.Fletcher-Den 13.5	D.Marino-Mia 1632
T.Mathis-NYJ 756			D.Harper-Sea 84		G.Townsend-LARd 13.0	B.Kosar-Cle 1548
J.Vaughn-NE 717			L.Burruss-KC 83		A.Smith-LARd 10.5	J.Elway-Den 1539

An Empty Resurgence and Collapse

The previous season's hurrahs of the Raiders, Dolphins, and even the Steelers proved short-lived, while other recent contenders, like the Bengals and Colts, collapsed entirely. Pittsburgh's season was enough to convince Chuck Noll to call it quits after 23 seasons. The Raiders still managed to make the playoffs with a team that was less than the sum of its parts despite aggressive shopping.

While so much was going amiss for so many teams, the conference was dominated by its top "trick" offenses. Buffalo relied on its talented offensive core to punish winded defenses with its No-Huddle offense, aided by wideout James Lofton in what would be the last productive season in a Hall of Fame career. The defense started showing its age, however, and defensive end Bruce Smith missed much of the season. The Oilers handily won the Central for the first time in team history. Their reliance on the Run-and-Shoot helped Warren Moon set a new record for completions, a performance made possible by great linemen like Mike Munchak and Bruce Matthews. Houston's defense also increased pressure on quarterbacks and cornerback Chris Dishman was there to clean up.

Things were more complicated in the West. The Broncos returned to prominence through two tricks that would never get old in Denver: finding its running game in the dumpster, and John Elway's ability to pull the team's fat out of the fire late in the day. Rather than self-destruct after running back Bobby Humphrey's holdout, the Broncos dug up Rams washout Gaston Green. The defense was a fierce pass-rushing unit and featured a tough pair of safeties in veteran Dennis Smith and young Steve Atwater. The Chiefs returned to the playoffs with another iteration of Marty Schottenheimer's grinding multi-back running game, plus a sound defensive squad.

One off-field controversy garnered particular attention. Former All-Pro lineman Lyle Alzado confessed to using steroids and human growth hormone to aid his play. Alzado had a year to live, his health ruined by his pursuit of excellence. His abuses highlighted questions of the validity of the NFL's testing policies, started in 1988, long after the genie was out of the bottle—or syringe.

1992 NFC

TEAM	W-L-T	PCT	POST	PTS	RA	RY	RY/A	RTD	FL	PA	PC	GPY	GPY/A	PTD	PI	PSY	PRAT
Eastern Division																	
Dal	13-3	.813	DCS*	409-243	500-**345**	2121-**1244**	4.2-**3.6**	20-11	9-14	491-484	314-263	3597-3034	7.3-6.3	23-16	15-17	**112**-347	88.8-69.9
Phi	11-5	.688	WD	354-245	**516**-387	**2388**-1481	4.6-3.8	19-**4**	15-13	429-517	255-263	3054-3316	7.1-6.4	20-20	13-24	462-**385**	84.2-**64.8**
Was	9-7	.563	#WD	300-255	483-406	1727-1696	3.6-4.2	10-11	**7**-11	485-466	272-**258**	3339-3021	6.9-6.5	15-15	17-23	176-279	73.2-65.4
NYG	6-10	.375	—	306-367	458-458	2077-2012	4.5-4.4	20-17	13-12	433-440	232-270	2628-3228	6.1-7.3	14-22	10-14	283-197	73.2-87.2
Phx	4-12	.250	—	243-332	395-436	1491-1635	3.8-3.8	11-13	18-12	517-452	298-276	3344-3687	6.5-8.2	15-24	24-16	258-196	67.4-89.9
Central Division																	
Min	11-5	.688	E	374-249	497-438	2030-1733	4.1-4.0	19-11	17-14	458-508	258-320	3162-3124	6.9-6.1	18-**12**	15-**28**	293-342	77.2-65.1
GB	9-7	.563	#	276-296	420-406	1555-1821	3.7-4.5	7-12	21-19	527-483	**340**-277	3498-3496	6.6-7.2	20-16	15-15	268-219	84.3-78.1
TB	5-11	.313	—	267-365	438-441	1706-1675	3.9-3.8	12-15	9-13	511-508	299-293	3399-3740	6.7-7.4	17-25	20-20	334-230	73.3-80.8
ChiB	5-11	.313	—	295-361	427-468	1871-1948	4.4-4.2	15-14	10-16	479-442	266-261	3334-3290	7.0-7.4	17-20	24-14	264-286	68.3-84.2
Det	5-11	.313	—	273-332	378-460	1644-1841	4.3-4.0	9-14	15-11	406-487	231-296	3150-3402	7.8-7.0	16-20	21-21	354-185	73.4-77.6
Western Division																	
SF	**14**-2	**.875**	DC	**431**-236	482-351	2315-1418	**4.8**-4.0	**22**-5	13-12	480-551	319-320	**4054**-3642	**8.4**-6.6	29-20	**9**-17	174-273	**105.0**-77.3
NO	12-4	.750	W	330-**202**	454-381	1628-1605	3.6-4.2	10-8	13-**20**	426-511	251-287	3297-**2846**	7.7-**5.6**	19-13	16-18	119-376	82.6-65.9
Atl	6-10	.375	—	327-414	322-464	1270-2294	3.9-4.9	3-20	14-12	**548-439**	336-277	3892-3496	7.1-8.0	**33**-24	15-11	259-241	91.4-95.6
LARm	6-10	.375	—	313-383	393-467	1659-2230	4.2-4.8	12-22	17-15	495-507	289-305	3422-3481	6.9-6.9	23-18	20-18	204-188	78.2-77.9
Aver	16	—	—	300	439	1768	4.0	12	14	479	275	3286	6.9	18	19	284	75.3

TEAM	1D	PENY	PNT	FGM/A	RTNY	RTNTD	OFFY/DEFY	NETY	NETTO	NP	PNP	DELP	PW	DELW	PRT	DR	YPD	DEL
Eastern Division																		
Dal	324-**241**	650-727	43.0-42.1	24/35-14/**17**	708-697	5-**2**	5606-**3931**	**1675**	7	166	**168**	-2	12.1	0.8	5.9/ 3.9	181-184	31.0-**21.4**	**9.6**
Phi	292-242	807-683	42.2-41.5	16/25-21/32	**862**-372	5-**2**	4980-4412	568	9	109	83	26	10.7	0.3	4.5/ 3.6	**197**-195	25.3-22.6	2.7
Was	276-249	741-709	39.3-42.8	**30/40**-14/21	840-650	5-4	4890-4438	452	**10**	45	78	-33	9.1	-0.1	5.0/ 3.7	174-177	28.1-25.1	3.0
NYG	271-287	647-744	40.6-**38.7**	18/23-15/21	432-738	2-7	4422-5043	-621	3	-61	-40	-21	6.5	-0.5	4.3/ 5.6	173-184	25.6-27.4	-1.8
Phx	277-281	722-826	42.8-42.8	13/26-18/28	662-420	3-3	4577-5126	-549	-14	-89	-102	13	5.8	-1.8	3.9/ 6.3	175-171	26.2-30.0	-3.8
Central Division																		
Min	288-293	809-768	**44.4**-41.9	19/25-20/25	838-503	**8**-4	4899-4515	384	**10**	125	72	**53**	11.1	-0.1	4.8/**2.9**	187-191	26.2-23.6	2.6
GB	291-277	749-830	38.4-43.3	22/29-24/27	537-428	3-4	4785-5098	-313	-2	-20	-34	14	7.5	**1.5**	4.8/ 5.3	177-179	27.0-28.5	-1.4
TB	281-296	754-563	40.7-41.3	12/22-20/30	394-328	4-3	4771-5185	-414	4	-98	-19	-79	5.6	-0.5	4.2/ 5.3	186-176	25.7-29.5	-3.8
ChiB	282-274	776-780	42.9-40.6	19/26-20/25	364-963	2-9	4941-4952	-11	-4	-66	-17	-49	6.3	-1.4	4.1/ 5.3	184-189	26.9-26.2	0.7
Det	241-308	903-**871**	43.1-41.1	21/26-22/35	445-650	5-4	4440-5058	-618	-4	-59	-68	9	6.5	-1.5	4.3/ 4.8	176-174	25.2-29.1	-3.8
Western Division																		
SF	**344**-277	636-651	39.1-41.2	18/27-16/20	561-**303**	3-**2**	**6195**-4787	1408	7	**195**	145	50	**12.9**	1.1	**7.4**/ 4.7	168-**168**	**36.9**-28.5	8.4
NO	267-246	**567**-729	44.0-41.2	29/34-**12/17**	485-498	6-3	4806-4075	731	9	128	97	31	11.2	0.8	6.0/ 3.2	184-181	26.1-22.5	3.6
Atl	273-304	656-761	40.8-41.5	18/22-19/31	331-728	3-7	4903-5549	-646	-6	-87	-78	-9	5.8	0.2	5.6/ 6.4	182-176	26.9-31.5	-4.6
LARm	278-319	592-778	41.1-42.1	15/20-28/34	628-827	3-3	4877-5523	-646	-4	-70	-70	0	6.3	-0.3	4.9/ 4.9	193-187	25.3-29.5	-4.3
Aver	277	772	42.1	20/28	604	4	4770	—	—	—	—	—	—	—	4.9	184	25.9	—

Rushing Attempts	Rushing Yards	Rushing Average	Rushing TDs	Rushing Rank	Passing Yards	Passing Average
E.Smith-Dal 373	E.Smith-Dal 1713	H.Cross-Phi 6.31	E.Smith-Dal 18	E.Smith-Dal 1893	S.Young-SF...........3465	S.Young-SF............8.62
B.Sanders-Det.........312	B.Sanders-Det.......1352	H.Sherman-Phi.......5.21	R.Hampton-NYG 14	B.Sanders-Det.......1442	T.Aikman-Dal 3445	B.Hebert-NO...........7.79
R.Cobb-TB...............310	T.Allen-Min............1201	R.Watters-SF 4.92	T.Allen-Min................13	T.Allen-Min............1331	J.Everett-LARm 3323	T.Aikman-Dal 7.28
C.Gary-LARm..........279	R.Cobb-TB.............1171	J.Bunch-NYG..........4.82		R.Hampton-NYG ...1281	B.Hebert-NO..........3287	H.Cross-Phi 7.23
H.Walker-Phi...........267	R.Hampton-NYG ...1141	E.Smith-Dal 4.59		R.Cobb-TB............1261	M.Rypien-Was 3282	D.Tennell-TB 7.13

Completion Percent	TD Passes	TD Percent	INT Percent	Passer Rating	Passing Rank	Receptions
S.Young-SF.............66.7	S.Young-SF................25	S.Young-SF..............6.2	S.Young-SF..............1.7	S.Young-SF...........107.0	S.Young-SF...........1578	S.Sharpe-GB 108
B.Favre-GB.............64.1	T.Aikman-Dal 23	C.Miller-Atl 5.9	C.Miller-Atl 2.4	C.Miller-Atl 90.7	T.Aikman-Dal 1278	A.Rison-Atl.................93
T.Aikman-Dal 63.8	J.Everett-LARm 22	H.Cross-Phi 4.9	B.Favre-GB...............2.8	T.Aikman-Dal 89.5	B.Favre-GB............1184	J.Rice-SF 84
H.Cross-Phi 60.7	B.Hebert-NO.............19	T.Aikman-Dal 4.9	H.Cross-Phi 2.9	H.Cross-Phi 87.3	B.Hebert-NO..........1099	M.Irvin-Dal 78
C.Miller-Atl 60.1	H.Cross-Phi 19	J.Everett-LARm 4.6	T.Aikman-Dal 3.0	B.Favre-GB 85.3	J.Everett-LARm 1052	M.Pritchard-Atl...........77

Receiving Yards	Receiving Average	Receiving TDs	Receiving Rank	Combined Net Yards	Total TDs	Total Points
S.Sharpe-GB 1461	H.Moore-Det.........18.94	S.Sharpe-GB 13	S.Sharpe-GB 796	E.Smith-Dal 2048	E.Smith-Dal 19	C.Lohmiller-Was 120
M.Irvin-Dal 1396	M.Irvin-Dal 17.90	A.Rison-Atl................11	M.Irvin-Dal 733	T.Allen-Min............1679	T.Allen-Min.................15	M.Andersen-NO.......120
J.Rice-SF 1201	W.Green-Det.........17.76	J.Rice-SF 10	J.Rice-SF.................651	B.Sanders-Det.......1577	R.Hampton-NYG 14	L.Elliott-Dal 119
A.Rison-Atl............1119	F.Anderson-LARm 17.29	M.Haynes-Atl 10	A.Rison-Atl...............615	J.Bailey-Phx..........1517	S.Sharpe-GB 13	E.Smith-Dal 114
F.Barnett-Phi.........1083	M.Haynes-Atl 16.83		F.Barnett-Phi...........572	S.Sharpe-GB 1469		M.Cofer-SF 107

Punt Average	Field Goals	Field Goal Percent	Kickoff Returns	Kickoff Return Average	Punt Returns	Punt Return Average
H.Newsome-Min 45.0	C.Lohmiller-Was 30	M.Andersen-NO......85.3	M.Gray-Det................42	D.Sanders-Atl 26.7	K.Martin-Dal 42	J.Bailey-Phx............13.1
T.Barnhardt-NO 44.0	M.Andersen-NO.........29	N.Johnson-Atl.........81.8	D.Sanders-Atl 40	J.Bailey-Phx............24.6	V.Sikahema-Phi 40	K.Martin-Dal 12.7
J.Arnold-Det............43.8	L.Elliott-Dal 24	J.Hanson-Det..........80.8	J.Smith-NYG..............30	M.Gray-Det 24.0	A.Parker-Min..............33	V.Sikahema-Phi 12.6
S.Landeta-NYG 43.7	C.Jacke-GB 22	M.Bahr-NYG 76.2		D.Meggett-NYG 22.8	B.Mitchell-Was...........29	A.Parker-Min...........10.2
M.Saxon-Dal...........43.0	J.Hanson-Det.............21	F.Reveiz-Min 76.0		D.Lewis-Chi 22.2	A.Grant-SF 29	T.Buckley-GB..........10.0

Punt/Kick Return Yards	Punt/Kick Return TDs	Interceptions	Interception Return Yards	Interception Return TDs	Sacks	Overall Rank
M.Gray-Det............1181	D.Sanders-Atl 2	A.McMillian-Min 8	A.McMillian-Min 157	R.Massey-Phx 3	C.Simmons-Phi.......19.0	S.Young-SF............2155
D.Sanders-Atl 1108	K.Martin-Dal 2	D.Woolford-Chi 7	B.Edwards-Was 157	A.McMillian-Min 2	T.Harris-SF 17.0	E.Smith-Dal 2066
K.Martin-Dal 1035	T.Kinchen-LARm..........2	B.Edwards-Was 6	R.Massey-Phx 147	S.Joyner-Phi 2	W.Martin-NO...........15.5	H.Cross-Phi 1642
V.Sikahema-Phi 1031	M.Gray-Det 2	T.Cook-NO...................6	D.Sanders-Atl 105		C.Doleman-Min.......14.5	T.Allen-Min.............1580
J.Bailey-Phx.............953			D.Pollard-TB 99		R.White-Phi 14.0	B.Sanders-Det.......1560

All the Way Back

Three years removed from a 1–15 season, the Cowboys put together a 13–3 record. The 49ers (14–2) were equally dominant. San Francisco's Steve Young and Cowboy Troy Aikman had nearly identical numbers and receivers Jerry Rice and Michael Irvin were two of the NFL's five 1,000-yard receivers. Emmitt Smith won his second consecutive rushing title in Dallas while Niners rookie Ricky Watters rushed for 1,000 yards on nearly 5 yards per carry. When the two clubs clashed in the NFC Championship Game, the stats were nearly even, but the score had Dallas on top.

Eyebrows were raised when new Packers general manager Ron Wolf sent a first-round pick to Atlanta for Chris Miller's backup. Falcons coach Jerry Glanville didn't like the kid quarterback—among other things, Glanville had lost a $100 bet that the brash rookie couldn't throw a ball into the stadium's upper deck—so Brett Favre became a Packer. Don Majkowski was Green Bay's starter under rookie head coach Mike Holmgren, but the veteran was injured in the third game of the year. On September 28, Favre began what would be the longest consecutive starts streak of any quarterback in NFL history.

The Saints had the stingiest defense in the NFL and made the playoffs for the fourth time in franchise history—all since Jim Mora's hiring in 1986—but New Orleans was once again knocked out in the first round. While Chicago's Mike Singletary retired, two stars who'd begun in the NFL on the same St. Louis Cardinals sideline in 1979 ended their careers on opposite sides of the field in Philadelphia: Ottis Anderson (Giants) and Roy Green (Eagles).

Eagles defensive tackle Jerome Brown of the Eagles died in a car crash. The 27-year-old had his number retired. A pair of the great two-way players also died. Mel Hein and Alex Wojciechowicz played center and linebacker and led their teams to a combined 11 championship games in the 1930s and 1940s. Instant replay, an unimaginable concept during the heyday of the two-way man, went back on the shelf in 1992. After six seasons of use, replay fell four votes shy of owner approval. It was not subject to review.

1992 AFC

TEAM	W-L-T	PCT	POST	PTS	RA	RY	RY/A	RTD	FL	PA	PC	GPY	GPY/A	PTD	PI	PSY	PRAT
Eastern Division																	
Mia	**11**-5	**.688**	#DC	340-281	407-428	1525-1600	3.7-3.7	9-9	17-14	563-512	332-294	4148-3266	7.4-**6.4**	24-16	17-18	**173**-283	83.6-72.3
Buf	**11**-5	**.688**	#WDCS	**381**-283	**549**-427	**2436-1395**	4.4-**3.3**	**18**-8	17-12	509-520	293-305	3678-3560	7.2-6.8	23-19	21-23	221-351	78.0-73.2
Ind	9-7	.563	—	216-302	379-495	1102-2174	2.9-4.4	8-16	11-15	546-470	305-260	3584-3236	6.6-6.9	13-14	26-20	318-336	64.1-69.1
NYJ	4-12	.250	—	220-315	424-460	1752-1919	4.1-4.2	8-13	15-18	495-465	251-257	2962-3201	6.0-6.9	12-19	24-21	283-240	57.2-71.6
NE	2-14	.125	—	205-363	419-521	1550-1951	3.7-3.7	6-15	26-15	444-459	244-258	2492-3211	5.6-7.0	13-22	19-14	458-114	63.2-81.3
Central Division																	
Pit	**11**-5	**.688**	D	299-**225**	518-435	2156-1841	4.2-4.2	13-6	18-**21**	431-478	249-252	3046-3065	7.1-**6.4**	15-15	14-22	296-248	77.7-**64.0**
Hou	10-6	.625	W	352-258	353-412	1626-1634	**4.6**-4.0	10-6	12-11	**573**-445	**373**-248	**4231-2898**	7.4-6.5	**27**-20	23-20	202-321	**86.1**-71.9
Cle	7-9	.438	—	272-275	451-429	1607-1605	3.6-3.7	7-**5**	12-20	398-486	238-291	3102-3467	**7.8**-7.1	18-23	16-13	217-315	82.7-86.3
Cin	5-11	.313	—	274-364	454-490	1976-2007	4.4-4.1	11-15	10-17	435-489	227-288	2284-3620	5.3-7.4	16-24	17-16	341-294	63.4-84.7
Western Division																	
SD	**11**-5	**.688**	ED	335-241	489-**365**	1875-**1395**	3.8-3.8	**18**-10	12-11	496-491	282-271	3614-3188	7.3-6.5	16-17	21-**25**	268-356	72.9-65.5
KC	10-6	.625	W	348-282	446-441	1532-1787	3.4-4.1	14-12	**9**-15	413-458	230-253	3115-2928	7.5-**6.4**	15-19	**12**-24	323-**391**	79.9-66.7
Den	8-8	.500	—	262-329	403-489	1500-1963	3.7-4.0	11-10	14-16	473-462	258-268	3312-3437	7.0-7.4	16-21	29-15	382-317	62.4-83.0
LARd	7-9	.438	—	249-281	434-478	1794-1683	4.1-3.5	7-17	15-7	471-450	233-**243**	2950-3153	6.3-7.0	20-**11**	23-12	360-320	63.2-73.3
Sea	2-14	.125	—	140-312	402-513	1596-1922	4.0-3.7	4-14	18-11	476-**428**	230-251	2323-2978	4.9-7.0	9-**11**	23-20	545-317	48.9-69.0
Aver	16	—	—	300	439	1768	4.0	12	14	479	275	3286	6.9	18	19	284	75.3

TEAM	1D	PENY	PNT	FGM/A	RTNY	RTNTD	OFFY/DEFY	NETY	NETTO	NP	PNP	DELP	PW	DELW	PRT	DR	YPD	DEL
Eastern Division																		
Mia	316-273	**656**-679	39.7-**40.1**	**30/37**-19/26	649-828	3-7	5500-4583	917	-2	59	68	-9	9.5	1.5	**5.8**/ 4.3	180-185	30.6-24.8	5.8
Buf	**350**-278	775-933	42.2-43.9	24/30-22/30	789-608	3-4	**5893**-4604	1289	-3	**98**	95	3	**10.4**	0.5	5.1/ 4.2	192-188	30.7-24.5	6.2
Ind	267-314	958-836	44.8-42.5	16/29-21/28	577-774	3-4	4368-5074	-706	-2	-86	-67	-19	5.8	**3.2**	3.8/ 4.2	184-190	23.7-26.7	-3.0
NYJ	252-276	873-808	41.0-40.9	19/30-23/31	501-536	3-3	4431-4880	-449	0	-95	-37	-58	5.6	-1.6	3.2/ 4.4	192-182	23.1-26.8	-3.7
NE	215-292	1051-673	41.0-40.6	11/17-27/41	559-731	6-3	3584-5048	-1464	-16	-158	-186	28	4.1	-2.1	2.6/ 5.6	201-207	17.8-24.4	-6.6
Central Division																		
Pit	284-266	941-814	42.1-42.0	28/36-19/28	748-543	3-3	4906-4658	248	11	74	65	9	9.9	1.1	4.8/ 3.8	185-189	26.5-24.6	1.9
Hou	339-254	824-886	**45.2**-43.2	21/27-21/26	375-622	4-2	5655-**4211**	**1444**	-4	94	**104**	-10	**10.4**	-0.3	5.4/ 3.8	170-**174**	**33.3**-24.2	**9.1**
Cle	242-281	765-764	41.1-44.5	21/29-24/29	651-447	5-**1**	4492-4757	-265	5	-3	-2	-1	7.9	-0.9	5.4/ 5.2	181-178	24.8-26.7	-1.9
Cin	248-319	755-797	42.1-41.8	19/28-18/30	490-**411**	4-5	3919-5333	-1414	6	-90	-94	4	5.8	-0.8	2.8/ 5.3	180-179	21.8-29.8	-8.0
Western Division																		
SD	302-250	813-798	42.6-44.6	26/32-**13/16**	764-485	2-2	5221-4227	994	3	94	95	-1	**10.4**	0.7	4.8/ 3.5	180-185	29.0-22.8	6.2
KC	246-256	675-**959**	42.2-43.1	23/25-15/21	**805**-490	**11**-3	4324-4324	0	**18**	66	72	-6	9.6	0.4	5.2/**3.2**	190-188	22.8-23.0	-0.2
Den	234-283	768-715	43.6-43.3	20/25-28/38	563-949	2-4	4430-5083	-653	-12	-67	-102	35	6.3	1.7	3.4/ 5.2	198-198	22.4-25.7	-3.3
LARd	259-264	832-755	42.3-42.5	15/26-19/30	741-730	2-4	4384-4516	-132	-19	-32	-87	**55**	7.2	-0.2	3.4/ 4.8	183-186	24.0-24.3	-0.3
Sea	208-**247**	918-776	44.1-41.8	14/22-29/36	607-647	1-7	3374-4583	-1209	-10	-172	-141	-31	3.7	-1.7	1.5/ 3.9	**211**-203	16.0-**22.6**	-6.6
Aver	277	772	42.1	20/28	604	2	4770	—	—	—	—	—	—	—	4.9	94	24.5	—

Rushing Attempts	Rushing Yards	Rushing Average	Rushing TDs	Rushing Rank	Passing Yards	Passing Average
B.Foster-Pit 390	B.Foster-Pit 1690	T.Thomas-Buf 4.77	B.Foster-Pit 11	B.Foster-Pit 1800	D.Marino-Mia 4116	D.Krieg-KC 7.54
T.Thomas-Buf 312	T.Thomas-Buf 1487	R.Bernstine-SD 4.71	T.Thomas-Buf 9	T.Thomas-Buf 1577	J.Kelly-Buf 3457	C.Carlson-Hou 7.53
L.White-Hou 265	L.White-Hou 1226	L.White-Hou 4.63		L.White-Hou 1296	S.Humphries-SD 3356	J.Kelly-Buf 7.48
H.Green-Cin 265	H.Green-Cin 1170	B.Humphrey-Mia 4.62		H.Green-Cin 1190	D.Krieg-KC 3115	D.Marino-Mia 7.43
M.Higgs-Mia 256	C.Warren-Sea 1017	B.Baxter-NYJ 4.59		C.Warren-Sea 1047	W.Moon-Hou 2521	S.Humphries-SD 7.39

Completion Percent	TD Passes	TD Percent	INT Percent	Passer Rating	Passing Rank	Receptions
C.Carlson-Hou 65.6	D.Marino-Mia 24	W.Moon-Hou 5.2	N.O'Donnell-Pit 2.9	W.Moon-Hou 89.3	D.Marino-Mia 1538	H.Jeffires-Hou 90
W.Moon-Hou 64.7	J.Kelly-Buf 23	J.Kelly-Buf 5.0	D.Marino-Mia 2.9	D.Marino-Mia 85.1	D.Krieg-KC 1153	C.Duncan-Hou 82
D.Marino-Mia 59.6	W.Moon-Hou 18	J.Schroeder-LARd 4.3	D.Krieg-KC 2.9	N.O'Donnell-Pit 83.6	J.Kelly-Buf 1084	R.Harmon-SD 79
N.O'Donnell-Pit 59.1	S.Humphries-SD 16	D.Marino-Mia 4.3	W.Moon-Hou 3.5	J.Kelly-Buf 81.2	S.Humphries-SD 1038	J.Williams-Sea 74
J.Kelly-Buf 58.2	D.Krieg-KC 15	N.O'Donnell-Pit 4.2	S.Humphries-SD 4.0	C.Carlson-Hou 81.2	W.Moon-Hou 871	A.Miller-SD 72

Receiving Yards	Receiving Average	Receiving TDs	Receiving Rank	Combined Net Yards	Total TDs	Total Points
A.Miller-SD 1060	W.Davis-KC 21.00	E.Givins-Hou 10	A.Miller-SD 565	T.Thomas-Buf 2113	T.Thomas-Buf 12	M.Stover-Mia 124
C.Duncan-Hou 954	M.Duper-Mia 17.32	H.Jeffires-Hou 9	H.Jeffires-Hou 502	B.Foster-Pit 2014	B.Foster-Pit 11	S.Christie-Buf 115
R.Harmon-SD 914	N.Lewis-SD 17.06	M.Jackson-Den 8	C.Duncan-Hou 482	C.Warren-Sea 1927	E.Givins-Hou 10	J.Carney-SD 113
A.Reed-Buf 913	D.Beebe-Buf 16.79		A.Reed-Buf 472	L.White-Hou 1867	H.Jeffires-Hou 9	G.Anderson-Pit 113
H.Jeffires-Hou 913	T.Martin-Mia 16.76		R.Harmon-SD 462	E.Metcalf-Cle 1501	R.Culver-Ind 9	N.Lowery-KC 105

Punt Average	Field Goals	Field Goal Percent	Kickoff Returns	Kickoff Return Average	Punt Returns	Punt Return Average
C.Mohr-Hou 46.9	M.Stover-Mia 30	N.Lowery-KC 91.7	C.Verdin-Ind 39	J.Vaughn-NE 28.2	E.Metcalf-Cle 44	C.Pickens-Cin 12.7
M.Horan-Den 45.4	G.Anderson-Pit 28	D.Treadwell-Den 83.3	R.Baldwin-Cle 30	R.Baldwin-Cle 22.5	D.Carter-KC 38	R.Woodson-Pit 11.4
R.Stark-Ind 44.8	J.Carney-SD 26	J.Carney-SD 81.3	W.Stanley-NE 29	C.Mohr-Den 22.2	T.Brown-LARd 37	C.Verdin-Ind 11.2
R.Tuten-Sea 44.1	S.Christie-Buf 24	M.Stover-Mia 81.1	C.Warren-Sea 28	N.Lewis-SD 21.2	C.Warren-Sea 34	A.Marshall-Den 10.6
B.Barker-KC 43.3	N.Lowery-KC 22	S.Christie-Buf 80.0	T.Mathis-NYJ 28	C.Verdin-Ind 20.9	A.Marshall-Den 33	D.Carter-KC 10.5

Punt/Kick Return Yards	Punt/Kick Return TDs	Interceptions	Interception Return Yards	Interception Return TDs	Sacks	Overall Rank
C.Verdin-Ind 1083	C.Verdin-Ind 2	H.Jones-Buf 8	H.Jones-Buf 263	C.Mincy-KC 2	L.O'Neal-SD 17.0	B.Foster-Pit 1972
R.Woodson-Pit 833	D.Carter-KC 2	E.Robinson-Sea 7	L.Oliver-Mia 200	H.Jones-Buf 2	S.Fletcher-Den 16.0	T.Thomas-Buf 1905
C.Warren-Sea 776		M.Kelso-Buf 7	T.McDaniel-LARd 180		D.Thomas-KC 14.5	L.White-Hou 1622
W.Stanley-NE 756		D.Carter-KC 7	R.Carpenter-SD 152		N.Smith-KC 14.5	D.Marino-Mia 1604
R.Baldwin-Cle 675			M.Brim-NYJ 139			C.Warren-Sea 1300

The Noble Comeback

Just when it seemed like Buffalo's consecutive AFC title string would end at two, the Bills experienced a comeback for the ages. Frank Reich, playing in place of injured quarterback Jim Kelly, rallied the Bills from a 35–3 playoff deficit to beat the Houston Oilers in overtime. Reich, who'd led the University of Maryland back from a 31-point hole in 1984, established an NFL mark for the largest comeback. Kelly took over for the AFC Championship Game and got the Bills to their third straight Super Bowl.

Five of the first seven picks in the NFL draft were defensive players. The Colts took the first two—Steve Emtman and Quentin Coryatt—in what turned out to be a dud of a first round. The Colts had gone 1–15 to get in this position and had traded their most recognizable player, Eric Dickerson, for more picks. Tragedy struck when second-year defensive end Shane Curry was shot to death outside a Cincinnati nightclub in a parking dispute in May. Following Ted Marchibroda's triumphant return as head coach of the franchise after 13 years, the Colts cut quarterback Mark Herrmann one day after leading the team to a season-opening victory. But what looked like another disaster in the making turned out to be a 9–7 season in Indianapolis, the team's third winning season since moving from Baltimore in 1984. The Colts missed the playoffs by just a game despite allowing 86 more points than they scored. Emtman injured his knee and was never the same.

While the Colts experienced a bounce, the Seahawks hit bottom. The club scored just 140 points during a 2–14 season, the lowest output since the 16-game schedule went into effect in 1978. Seattle's 8.8 average scoring output was the lowest since expansion partner Tampa Bay's 7.4 in '77.

Two AFL stars, Jim Nance of the Patriots and Hall of Famer Buck Buchanan of the Chiefs, died in 1992. Junius Buchanan was considered among the best defensive tackles in either league. Nance, beloved Patriots fullback among the Fenway Park faithful, once made the cover of AFL-basher *Sports Illustrated* … with a black-and-white photo.

1993 NFC

TEAM	W-L-T	PCT	POST	PTS	RA	RY	RY/A	RTD	FL	PA	PC	GPY	GPY/A	PTD	PI	PSY	PRAT
Eastern Division																	
Dal	**12**-4	**.750**	DCS*	376-229	490-423	2161-1651	4.4-3.9	20-7	16-14	475-555	317-334	3617-3347	7.6-**6.0**	18-14	**6**-14	**163**-231	96.8-75.3
NYG	11-5	.688	WD	288-**205**	**560-395**	**2210**-1547	3.9-3.9	11-7	**8**-10	424-514	257-298	3180-3354	7.5-6.5	17-13	9-18	245-238	88.4-71.4
Phi	8-8	.500	—	293-315	456-467	1761-2080	3.9-4.5	7-11	21-15	556-463	328-**251**	3463-3153	6.2-6.8	23-22	13-20	302-214	81.2-73.5
Phx	7-9	.438	—	326-269	452-433	1809-1861	4.0-4.3	12-13	11-17	522-495	310-281	3635-3511	7.0-7.1	21-14	20-9	231-205	78.0-80.8
Was	4-12	.250	—	230-345	396-513	1728-2112	4.4-4.1	11-14	10-14	533-483	287-291	2764-3584	5.2-7.4	11-24	21-17	219-197	59.0-85.1
Central Division																	
Det	10-6	.625	E	298-292	456-433	1944-1649	4.3-3.8	9-12	13-16	435-514	264-309	2943-3273	6.8-6.4	15-19	19-19	229-253	74.1-75.6
Min	9-7	.563	W	277-290	447-415	1624-**1536**	3.6-**3.7**	8-14	10-10	526-478	315-310	3381-3146	6.4-6.6	18-**11**	14-**24**	181-276	79.1-70.3
GB	9-7	.563	WD	340-282	448-424	1619-1582	3.6-**3.7**	14-**6**	10-15	528-529	322-290	3330-3201	6.3-6.1	19-16	24-18	199-301	72.2-**68.9**
ChiB	7-9	.438	—	234-230	477-476	1677-1835	3.5-3.9	10-9	14-12	388-504	230-306	2270-3105	5.9-6.2	7-12	16-18	230-287	64.7-71.4
TB	5-11	.313	—	237-376	402-479	1290-1994	3.2-4.2	6-15	11-13	508-503	262-300	3295-3384	6.5-6.7	19-22	25-9	274-132	64.1-86.9
Western Division																	
SF	10-6	.625	DC	**473**-295	463-404	2133-1800	**4.6**-4.5	**26-6**	13-11	524-564	**354**-314	**4480**-3513	**8.5**-6.2	**29**-23	17-19	178-316	**98.9**-74.0
NO	8-8	.500	—	317-343	414-513	1766-2090	4.3-4.1	10-7	13-**20**	481-**444**	274-259	3183-**2924**	6.6-6.6	18-22	21-10	242-**318**	71.4-85.3
Atl	6-10	.375	—	316-385	395-419	1590-1784	4.0-4.3	4-14	17-11	**573**-505	334-308	3787-3786	6.6-7.5	28-27	25-13	267-149	76.3-91.2
LARm	5-11	.313	—	221-367	449-480	2014-1851	4.5-3.9	8-18	11-9	473-488	247-299	3021-3763	6.4-7.7	16-17	19-11	231-203	66.8-87.5
Aver	16	—	—	299	453	1761	3.9	11	14	515	298	3446	6.7	18	17	236	76.7

TEAM	1D	PENY	PNT	FGM/A	RTNY	RTNTD	OFFY/DEFY	NETY	NETTO	NP	PNP	DELP	PW	DELW	PRT	DR	YPD	DEL
Eastern Division																		
Dal	322-297	744-653	41.8-41.3	30/37-22/27	552-**216**	3-2	5615-4767	848	6	147	95	52	11.7	0.3	6.7/ 4.5	172-**173**	32.6-27.6	5.1
NYG	300-268	596-820	41.9-40.3	26/34-**17**/23	515-422	2-2	5145-4663	482	**11**	83	84	-1	10.1	0.9	5.8/ 4.4	170-175	30.3-26.6	3.6
Phi	303-271	770-610	40.0-41.8	16/23-23/34	608-418	5-2	4922-5019	-97	1	-22	-4	-18	7.4	0.6	4.7/ 4.5	**197**-192	25.0-26.1	-1.2
Phx	295-278	644-730	43.7-42.7	21/28-26/35	508-410	4-**0**	5213-5167	46	-5	57	-16	73	9.4	-2.4	4.9/ 5.7	184-186	28.3-27.8	0.6
Was	255-304	597-782	43.9-41.1	16/28-**17/22**	486-552	4-4	4273-5499	-1226	0	-115	-102	-13	5.1	-1.1	3.0/ 5.6	185-185	23.1-29.7	-6.6
Central Division																		
Det	248-279	665-500	**44.5**-43.1	**34/43**-23/30	505-554	4-1	4658-4669	-11	3	6	11	-5	8.1	**1.9**	4.2/ 4.2	194-191	24.0-24.4	-0.4
Min	283-**259**	806-768	42.9-42.4	26/35-25/33	491-726	2-6	4824-**4406**	418	10	-13	75	-88	7.7	1.3	4.9/**3.6**	194-193	24.9-**22.8**	2.0
GB	282-261	734-712	42.9-**40.2**	31/37-31/40	659-787	2-5	4750-4482	268	-1	58	18	40	9.4	-0.5	4.0/ 3.9	196-196	24.2-22.9	1.4
ChiB	226-289	587-783	38.5-41.4	27/36-26/34	589-220	5-1	3717-4653	-936	0	4	-78	**82**	8.1	-1.1	3.2/ 3.9	180-184	20.6-25.3	-4.6
TB	241-280	765-**913**	40.1-43.3	16/22-32/35	382-674	2-3	4311-5246	-935	-14	-139	-134	-5	4.5	0.5	3.8/ 5.8	189-196	22.8-26.8	-4.0
Western Division																		
SF	**372**-297	800-743	40.9-43.9	16/26-27/30	**678**-328	**6**-1	**6435**-4997	**1438**	0	**178**	**120**	58	**12.4**	-2.4	**6.8**/ 4.2	174-177	**37.0**-28.2	**8.8**
NO	264-273	663-590	43.6-42.3	28/35-24/30	650-792	5-10	4707-4696	11	-4	-26	-15	-11	7.3	0.6	4.2/ 4.8	196-196	24.0-24.0	0.1
Atl	292-278	838-874	43.3-40.9	26/27-20/31	436-695	2-5	5110-5421	-311	-18	-69	-98	29	6.3	-0.3	4.4/ 6.2	191-193	26.8-28.1	-1.3
LARm	278-304	**526**-542	40.9-42.3	16/23-29/37	229-880	1-5	4804-5411	-607	-10	-146	-91	-55	4.3	0.7	4.2/ 6.2	171-175	28.1-30.9	-2.8
Aver	290	737	42.2	24/31	558	3	4970	—	—	—	—	—	—	—	5.1	187	26.6	—

Rushing Attempts	Rushing Yards	Rushing Average	Rushing TDs	Rushing Rank	Passing Yards	Passing Average
J.Bettis-LARm..........294	E.Smith-Dal...........1486	E.Smith-Dal............5.25	R.Watters-SF.............10	E.Smith-Dal...........1576	S.Young-SF............4023	S.Young-SF.............8.71
E.Pegram-Atl...........292	J.Bettis-LARm........1429	R.Smith-Min............4.87	E.Smith-Dal.................9	J.Bettis-LARm........1499	B.Favre-GB............3303	T.Aikman-Dal..........7.91
R.Hampton-NYG.....292	E.Pegram-Atl.........1185	J.Bettis-LARm.........4.86	R.Moore-Phx...............9	E.Pegram-Atl.........1215	S.Beuerlein-Phx.....3164	P.Simms-NYG.........7.59
E.Smith-Dal.............283	B.Sanders-Det.......1115	L.Tillman-NYG........4.83	E.Bennett-GB..............9	B.Sanders-Det.......1145	T.Aikman-Dal.........3100	S.Beuerlein-Phx......7.57
R.Moore-Phx...........263	R.Hampton-NYG...1077	R.Brooks-Was.........4.77		R.Hampton-NYG...1127	C.Erickson-TB........3054	B.Hebert-Atl............6.93

Completion Percent	TD Passes	TD Percent	INT Percent	Passer Rating	Passing Rank	Receptions
T.Aikman-Dal..........69.1	S.Young-SF................29	S.Young-SF..............6.3	T.Aikman-Dal............1.5	S.Young-SF..........101.5	S.Young-SF...........1517	S.Sharpe-GB..........112
S.Young-SF............68.0	B.Hebert-Atl...............24	B.Hebert-Atl.............5.6	B.Brister-Phi.............1.6	T.Aikman-Dal..........99.0	T.Aikman-Dal.........1385	J.Rice-SF....................98
R.Peete-Det............62.3	B.Favre-GB................19	B.Brister-Phi.............4.5	P.Simms-NYG............2.3	P.Simms-NYG.........88.3	P.Simms-NYG........1234	M.Irvin-Dal.................88
P.Simms-NYG.........61.8	C.Erickson-TB............18	S.Beuerlein-Phx........4.3	J.McMahon-Min.........2.4	B.Brister-Phi...........84.9	S.Beuerlein-Phx.......992	A.Rison-Atl.................86
S.Beuerlein-Phx......61.7	S.Beuerlein-Phx.........18	C.Erickson-TB...........3.9	M.Rypien-Was...........3.1	B.Hebert-Atl............84.0	B.Hebert-Atl............929	C.Carter-Min..............86

Receiving Yards	Receiving Average	Receiving TDs	Receiving Rank	Combined Net Yards	Total TDs	Total Points
J.Rice-SF...............1503	A.Harper-Dal........21.58	A.Rison-Atl.................15	J.Rice-SF.................827	E.Smith-Dal..........1900	J.Rice-SF...................16	J.Hanson-Det..........130
M.Irvin-Dal.............1330	J.Taylor-SF............16.79	J.Rice-SF....................15	M.Irvin-Dal...............700	J.Bettis-LARm........1673	A.Rison-Atl.................15	C.Jacke-GB.............128
S.Sharpe-GB.........1274	H.Ellard-LARm......15.49	S.Sharpe-GB.............11	A.Rison-Atl...............696	J.Rice-SF..............1572	R.Watters-SF.............11	E.Murray-Dal...........122
A.Rison-Atl............1242	J.Rice-SF.............15.34	C.Williams-Phi...........10	S.Sharpe-GB...........692	E.Pegram-Atl.........1550	S.Sharpe-GB.............11	M.Andersen-NO.......117
C.Carter-Min..........1071	H.Moore-Det.........15.33	C.Carter-Min................9	C.Carter-Min............581	H.Walker-Phi.........1540		N.Johnson-Atl.........112

Punt Average	Field Goals	Field Goal Percent	Kickoff Returns	Kickoff Return Average	Punt Returns	Punt Return Average
J.Arnold-Det............44.5	J.Hanson-Det.............34	N.Johnson-Atl.........96.3	Q.Ismail-Min..............42	C.Harris-GB............30.1	T.Hughes-NO.............37	T.Hughes-NO..........13.6
R.Roby-Was............44.2	C.Jacke-GB...............31	E.Murray-Dal..........84.8	T.Smith-Atl.................38	R.Brooks-GB..........26.6	K.Williams-Dal...........36	D.Carter-SF...........12.1
R.Camarillo-Phx.....43.7	E.Murray-Dal..............28	C.Jacke-GB............83.8	B.Mitchell-Was...........33	T.Hughes-NO..........25.1	T.Obee-Chi................35	M.Prior-GB.............11.4
T.Barnhardt-NO......43.6	M.Andersen-NO.........28	D.Treadwell-NYG....80.6	K.Williams-Dal...........31	T.Smith-Atl.............24.9	J.Bailey-Phx...............35	K.Williams-Dal........10.6
S.Landeta-LARm....43.5	K.Butler-Chi...............27	M.Andersen-NO......80.0	J.Bailey-Phx...............31	M.Gray-Det............24.6	D.Carter-SF...............34	D.Meggett-NYG......10.3

Punt/Kick Return Yards	Punt/Kick Return TDs	Interceptions	Interception Return Yards	Interception Return TDs	Sacks	Overall Rank
T.Hughes-NO.........1256	T.Hughes-NO...............3	D.Sanders-Atl..............7	E.Allen-Phi...............201	E.Allen-Phi...................4	R.White-GB............13.0	S.Young-SF...........1945
T.Smith-Atl.............1203	K.Williams-Dal.............2	K.Smith-Dal.................6	L.Butler-GB..............131		R.Turnbull-NO.........13.0	E.Smith-Dal...........1788
K.Williams-Dal.......1070		T.Carter-Was...............6	J.Lincoln-Chi............109		J.Randle-Min..........12.5	J.Bettis-LARm........1621
J.Bailey-Phx.............981		L.Butler-GB..................6	M.Hanks-SF.............104		C.Doleman-Min.......12.5	T.Aikman-Dal.........1510
D.Carter-SF.............905		E.Allen-Phi...................6	M.Carrier-Chi.............94		R.Dent-Chi.............12.5	E.Pegram-Atl.........1369

You're Now Free to Move About the League

Free agency came to the NFL in 1993. Unlike Plan B, a limited system installed in 1989 that let clubs decide who could be a free agent, several stars suddenly showed up in new places. The most significant player to move was Reggie White, whose pending court decision regarding free agency had forced the league and the Players Association to settle the issue. White bypassed seemingly more attractive locales to go to Green Bay, an outpost a decade removed from the NFL playoffs. Green Bay's come-from-behind win in the first round against Detroit could not be duplicated in the divisional playoffs in Dallas, but there was no doubt that the Pack was back.

Despite all the player movement, the Super Bowl pitted the same two teams with the same result as the previous year: a convincing Dallas win over Buffalo. The game had the largest audience in the history of television with 134 million viewers in the U.S. Dallas, the weekly NFL soap opera, made for entertaining viewing.

The season began miserably in Dallas with Emmitt Smith's contract holdout, but he went on to win the rushing title and the Cowboys rebounded to become the first team to win the Super Bowl after starting 0–2. Dallas still had the best record in the conference and the Cowboys became the fifth franchise in history to win consecutive Super Bowls. That wasn't enough for owner Jerry Jones. He pushed out his old pal Jimmy Johnson after the season and named Barry Switzer head coach.

The NFL also gave Phoenix back the Super Bowl. In 1991 the league had taken away Super Bowl XXVII and awarded it to Pasadena because Arizona was one of two states without a holiday for Martin Luther King, Jr. Arizona voters approved a holiday in 1992 and were back on the site list for 1996.

Time ticked out on several great careers in 1993. James Lofton, Eric Dickerson, Everson Walls, and Jay Hilgenberg played their final games, as did Giants legends Phil Simms and Lawrence Taylor. Rookie Michael Strahan debuted in New York and newcomer Jerome Bettis rumbled for 1,486 yards in Los Angeles.

1993 AFC

TEAM	W-L-T	PCT	POST	PTS	RA	RY	RY/A	RTD	FL	PA	PC	GPY	GPY/A	PTD	PI	PSY	PRAT
Eastern Division																	
Buf	**12**-4	**.750**	DCS	329-242	**550**-500	1943-1921	3.5-3.8	12-7	17-**24**	497-582	304-323	3535-3889	7.1-6.7	20-18	18-23	218-256	81.0-70.0
Mia	9-7	.563	#	349-351	419-460	1459-1665	3.5-3.6	10-12	16-14	581-572	342-350	**4564**-3682	**7.9-6.4**	**27**-26	18-13	211-197	86.4-85.6
NYJ	8-8	.500	—	270-247	521-420	1880-1473	3.6-3.5	**14**-8	16-18	489-497	294-296	3492-3434	7.1-6.9	16-**15**	12-19	160-195	82.6-74.6
NE	5-11	.313	—	238-286	502-505	1780-1951	3.5-3.9	9-9	10-9	566-474	289-280	3412-3087	6.0-6.5	17-20	24-13	**127**-242	62.1-81.1
Ind	4-12	.250	—	189-378	365-575	1288-2521	3.5-4.4	4-20	20-11	594-**454**	332-270	3623-3238	6.1-7.1	10-22	15-10	206-121	69.2-88.3
Central Division																	
Hou	**12**-4	**.750**	D	368-**238**	409-**369**	1792-**1273**	**4.4**-3.4	11-9	20-17	**614**-582	**357**-302	4145-3914	6.8-6.7	23-16	25-**26**	279-313	74.2-**63.9**
Pit	9-7	.563	#W	308-281	491-399	2003-1368	4.1-3.4	13-**6**	15-14	540-521	299-277	3606-3440	6.7-6.6	16-16	12-24	374-277	76.7-64.9
Cle	7-9	.438	—	304-307	425-451	1701-1654	4.0-3.7	8-9	17-9	478-541	262-306	3328-3466	7.0-**6.4**	23-19	19-13	289-**342**	76.2-77.6
Cin	3-13	.188	—	187-319	423-521	1511-2220	3.6-4.3	3-15	9-14	510-457	272-**251**	2830-**2952**	5.5-6.5	11-20	11-12	289-154	67.9-78.4
Western Division																	
KC	11-5	.688	EDC	328-291	445-453	1655-1620	3.7-3.6	**14**-11	18-17	490-525	287-312	3384-3379	6.9-**6.4**	20-18	**10**-21	204-228	84.8-73.2
LARd	10-6	.625	WD	306-326	433-494	1425-1865	3.3-3.8	10-17	11-9	495-457	281-258	3882-3141	7.8-6.9	17-17	14-14	293-283	81.7-77.4
Den	9-7	.563	#W	**373**-284	468-397	1693-1418	3.6-3.6	13-**6**	18-13	553-562	350-314	4061-3969	7.3-7.1	**27**-21	**10**-18	293-238	**94.2**-77.2
SD	8-8	.500	—	322-290	455-414	1824-1314	4.0-**3.2**	**14**-10	**5**-12	563-556	301-329	3383-3958	6.0-7.1	18-17	14-22	240-206	72.0-74.8
Sea	6-10	.375	—	280-314	473-452	**2015**-1660	4.3-3.7	13-12	13-15	498-595	280-333	2896-3897	5.8-6.5	13-16	18-22	242-244	66.8-69.6
Aver	16	—	—	299	453	1761	3.9	11	14	515	298	3446	6.7	18	17	236	76.7

TEAM	1D	PENY	PNT	FGM/A	RTNY	RTNTD	OFFY/DEFY	NETY	NETTO	NP	PNP	DELP	PW	DELW	PRT	DR	YPD	DEL
Eastern Division																		
Buf	316-331	630-681	40.4-41.8	23/32-23/35	583-421	5-**0**	5260-5554	-294	12	87	24	63	10.2	1.8	5.1/ 4.5	189-194	27.8-28.6	-0.8
Mia	309-332	663-650	39.7-41.3	24/32-**17**/27	501-688	3-5	**5812**-5150	662	-7	-2	27	-29	7.9	1.0	**6.2**/ 5.3	188-181	**30.9**-28.5	2.5
NYJ	304-**266**	555-661	38.4-43.3	17/26-21/26	489-466	1-3	5212-4712	500	9	23	78	-55	8.6	-0.6	5.8/ 4.8	172-175	30.3-26.9	3.4
NE	315-269	**468**-803	40.7-41.2	19/31-20/**24**	584-514	0-3	5065-4796	269	-12	-48	-26	-22	6.8	-1.8	4.0/ 4.8	184-183	27.5-26.2	1.3
Ind	269-334	685-610	43.3-**40.2**	26/31-21/30	289-599	2-3	4705-5638	-933	-14	-189	-134	-55	3.3	0.7	4.6/ 6.1	183-182	25.7-31.0	-5.3
Central Division																		
Hou	**330**-289	1005-791	**45.3**-43.7	29/34-19/28	687-558	**6**-1	5658-4874	**784**	-2	**130**	57	**73**	**11.3**	0.8	4.5/ 4.1	193-191	29.3-25.5	**3.8**
Pit	307-267	861-652	42.5-43.9	28/30-24/29	739-894	3-8	5235-**4531**	704	11	27	**103**	-76	8.7	0.3	4.9/**4.0**	195-194	26.8-**23.4**	3.5
Cle	264-290	842-821	43.2-42.4	16/22-31/38	**771**-684	5-2	4740-4778	-38	-14	-3	-59	56	7.9	-0.9	4.6/ 4.6	193-196	24.6-24.4	0.2
Cin	239-306	773-567	43.9-42.2	24/31-20/28	593-465	2-2	4052-5018	-966	6	-132	-57	-75	4.7	-1.7	3.8/ 5.1	184-**173**	22.0-29.0	-7.0
Western Division																		
KC	300-300	969-1015	42.1-44.6	23/29-28/32	573-463	3-1	4835-4771	64	10	37	45	-8	8.9	2.1	5.6/ 4.3	184-187	26.3-25.5	0.8
LARd	292-302	1181-801	41.8-42.1	**35/44**-21/33	664-590	2-3	5014-4723	291	-2	-20	16	-36	7.5	**2.5**	5.7/ 4.8	189-187	26.5-25.3	1.3
Den	327-280	822-**1019**	44.4-43.7	26/35-31/36	661-**416**	2-**0**	5461-5149	312	3	89	38	51	10.2	-1.2	6.1/ 5.1	192-190	28.4-27.1	1.3
SD	313-299	699-724	42.3-42.1	31/40-26/33	731-563	1-3	4967-5066	-99	**15**	32	52	-20	8.8	-0.8	4.5/ 5.0	185-183	26.8-27.7	-0.8
Sea	279-322	745-818	44.0-42.4	23/28-29/39	476-634	3-4	4669-5313	-644	6	-34	-30	-4	7.2	-1.1	3.6/ 4.5	**201**-197	23.2-27.0	-3.7
Aver	290	737	42.2	24/31	558	1	4970	—	—	—	—	—	—	—	5.1	94	26.9	—

Rushing Attempts	Rushing Yards	Rushing Average	Rushing TDs	Rushing Rank	Passing Yards	Passing Average
T.Thomas-Buf 355	T.Thomas-Buf 1315	G.Brown-Hou 5.14	M.Allen-KC 12	T.Thomas-Buf 1375	J.Elway-Den 4030	D.Terry-Cle 7.81
L.Russell-NE 300	L.Russell-NE 1088	E.Metcalf-Cle 4.74	N.Means-SD 8	L.Russell-NE 1158	W.Moon-Hou 3485	J.Hostetler-LARd 7.74
C.Warren-Sea 273	C.Warren-Sea 1072	J.Williams-Sea 4.52	B.Foster-Pit 8	C.Warren-Sea 1142	B.Esiason-NYJ 3421	S.Mitchell-Mia 7.61
R.Bernstine-Den 223	G.Brown-Hou 1002	J.Johnson-NYJ 4.15	R.Delpino-Den 8	G.Brown-Hou 1062	J.Kelly-Buf 3382	J.Elway-Den 7.31
H.Green-Cin 215	J.Johnson-NYJ 821	M.Butts-SD 4.03		M.Allen-KC 884	J.Hostetler-LARd 3242	B.Esiason-NYJ 7.23
Completion Percent	**TD Passes**	**TD Percent**	**INT Percent**	**Passer Rating**	**Passing Rank**	**Receptions**
J.Elway-Den 63.2	J.Elway-Den 25	D.Terry-Cle 6.1	N.O'Donnell-Pit 1.4	J.Elway-Den 92.8	J.Elway-Den 1740	R.Langhorne-Ind 85
J.Kelly-Buf 61.3	W.Moon-Hou 21	S.Mitchell-Mia 5.2	J.George-Ind 1.5	J.Montana-KC 87.4	N.O'Donnell-Pit 1394	A.Miller-SD 84
B.Esiason-NYJ 60.9	J.Kelly-Buf 18	J.Elway-Den 4.5	J.Friesz-SD 1.7	D.Terry-Cle 85.7	B.Esiason-NYJ 1351	S.Sharpe-Den 81
J.Montana-KC 60.7	B.Esiason-NYJ 16	J.Montana-KC 4.4	J.Elway-Den 1.8	B.Esiason-NYJ 84.5	J.Hostetler-LARd 1291	T.Brown-LARd 80
W.Moon-Hou 58.3	D.Bledsoe-NE 15	W.Moon-Hou 4.0	B.Esiason-NYJ 2.3	S.Mitchell-Mia 84.2	J.George-Ind 1063	B.Blades-Sea 80
Receiving Yards	**Receiving Average**	**Receiving TDs**	**Receiving Rank**	**Combined Net Yards**	**Total TDs**	**Total Points**
T.Brown-LARd 1180	J.Jett-LARd 23.36	S.Sharpe-Den 9	T.Brown-LARd 625	E.Metcalf-Cle 1932	M.Allen-KC 15	J.Jaeger-LARd 132
A.Miller-SD 1162	M.Jackson-Cle 18.44	M.Jackson-Cle 8	A.Miller-SD 616	T.Thomas-Buf 1702	S.Sharpe-Den 9	A.Del Greco-Hou 126
R.Langhorne-Ind 1038	W.Davis-KC 17.48	B.Coates-NE 8	S.Sharpe-Den 543	T.Brown-LARd 1652	B.Foster-Pit 9	J.Carney-SD 124
I.Fryar-Mia 1010	M.Carrier-Cle 17.35		R.Langhorne-Ind 534	J.Johnson-NYJ 1462		J.Elam-Den 119
S.Sharpe-Den 995	A.Reed-Buf 16.42		I.Fryar-Mia 530	L.Russell-NE 1355		G.Anderson-Pit 116
Punt Average	**Field Goals**	**Field Goal Percent**	**Kickoff Returns**	**Kickoff Return Average**	**Punt Returns**	**Punt Return Average**
J.Montana-Hou 45.6	J.Jaeger-LARd 35	G.Anderson-Pit 93.3	C.Verdin-Ind 50	R.Ismail-LARd 24.2	P.Robinson-Cin 43	E.Metcalf-Cle 12.9
T.Rouen-Den 45.0	J.Carney-SD 31	A.Del Greco-Hou 85.3	N.Lewis-SD 33	O.McDuffie-Mia 23.6	R.Woodson-Pit 42	D.Gordon-SD 12.7
R.Tuten-Sea 44.5	A.Del Greco-Hou 29	D.Biasucci-Ind 83.9	O.McDuffie-Mia 32	E.Ball-Cin 21.8	W.Drewrey-Hou 41	T.Brown-LARd 11.6
B.Hansen-Cle 44.3	G.Anderson-Pit 28	J.Kasay-Sea 82.1	P.Robinson-Cin 30	C.Verdin-Ind 21.0	G.Milburn-Den 40	O.McDuffie-Mia 11.3
L.Johnson-Cin 43.9		J.Jaeger-LARd 79.5	M.Bates-Sea 30	B.Cox-NE 20.8	T.Brown-LARd 40	G.Milburn-Den 10.6
Punt/Kick Return Yards	**Punt/Kick Return TDs**	**Interceptions**	**Interception Return Yards**	**Interception Return TDs**	**Sacks**	**Overall Rank**
C.Verdin-Ind 1223	E.Metcalf-Cle 2	E.Robinson-Sea 9	R.Woodson-Pit 138	Many 1	N.Smith-KC 15.0	J.Elway-Den 1893
O.McDuffie-Mia 1072	O.McDuffie-Mia 2	N.Odomes-Buf 9	M.Robertson-Hou 137		B.Smith-Buf 14.0	T.Thomas-Buf 1569
P.Robinson-Cin 872	R.Copeland-Buf 1	R.Woodson-Pit 8	C.Warren-NYJ 128		S.Fletcher-Den 13.5	J.Hostetler-LARd 1543
E.Metcalf-Cle 782	M.Carrier-Cle 1	M.Robertson-Hou 7	D.Williams-Cin 126		S.Jones-Hou 13.0	N.O'Donnell-Pit 1505
R.Copeland-Buf 710	T.Brown-LARd 1	M.Carrier-SD 7	D.Frank-SD 119			B.Esiason-NYJ 1475

Winning Is Hard, Even for the Old Pros

Miami's Don Shula became the winningest coach in NFL history by beating the Philadelphia Eagles on November 14. His 325th victory—the first 73 came with the Baltimore Colts in the 1960s—surpassed George Halas's mark set over parts of five decades with the Chicago Bears. After a 9–2 start, the Dolphins dropped their last five and missed the playoffs.

The Oilers reached the postseason for the last time in Houston, and it ended in horror for the second straight year as an opponent overcame a fourth-quarter Oilers lead. Joe Montana, quarterbacking the Chiefs after playing just once in two seasons in San Francisco due to injuries, threw 3 touchdown passes in the final period. It was Warren Moon's last game with the Oilers. The Houston franchise was never the same.

Quarterback Drew Bledsoe, the first player taken in the 1993 draft, was quickly thrown into action in New England. The Patriots lost 10 of their first 11 games under Bill Parcells, who returned to coaching after a two-year hiatus for health reasons. The coach let the rookie air it out and the Pats won four of their last five. The New York Jets sure could have used that finish. They lost four of their last five to miss the playoffs, costing rookie coach Pete Carroll his job. The Bills continued to dominate nearly every game except the last one, which ended with a loss to Dallas in the Super Bowl for the second straight year. Buffalo became the only team to appear in—and lose—four straight Super Bowls. Their continued success made them the butt of jokes by the public instead of generating the respect that should come with four straight AFC titles.

The NFL approved two new expansion teams. Jacksonville and Carolina, starting play in 1995, would be the first new teams added since 1976. The NFL also got its first collective bargaining agreement since the last one expired in 1987. The league and the Players Association brokered a deal worth more than $1 billion in pension, health, and post-career perks. It was the best benefits package in sports in the sport where it's needed most.

1994 NFC

TEAM	W-L-T	PCT	POST	PTS	RA	RY	RY/A	RTD	FL	PA	PC	GPY	GPY/A	PTD	PI	PSY	PRAT
Eastern Division																	
Dal	12-4	.750	DC	414-**248**	**550**-437	1953-1561	3.6-3.6	**26**-8	10-9	448-522	282-269	3461-**3051**	7.7-**5.8**	19-19	14-22	**93-299**	87.8-**64.0**
NYG	9-7	.563	#	279-305	525-447	1754-1728	3.3-3.9	12-11	**7-16**	405-500	226-289	2847-3391	7.0-6.8	16-16	18-16	285-169	72.5-75.8
Arz	8-8	.500	—	235-267	480-409	1560-1370	3.3-3.3	12-**7**	10-13	538-**465**	287-**234**	3284-3310	6.1-7.1	11-19	19-**23**	237-272	64.1-66.7
Phi	7-9	.438	—	308-308	432-449	1761-1616	4.1-3.6	14-11	12-14	566-490	316-251	3736-3359	6.6-6.9	18-20	14-21	372-265	76.4-69.1
Was	3-13	.188	—	320-412	407-556	1415-1975	3.5-3.6	5-24	13-6	546-496	271-300	3524-3799	6.5-7.7	25-22	27-17	146-165	65.0-84.9
Central Division																	
Min	10-6	.625	E	356-314	419-**355**	1524-**1090**	3.6-**3.1**	11-9	14-**16**	**673**-597	**409**-368	**4570**-3902	6.8-6.5	18-25	20-18	246-250	77.6-82.1
GB	9-7	.563	#WD	382-287	417-381	1543-1363	3.7-3.6	11-9	8-12	609-605	375-337	3977-3677	6.5-6.1	33-20	14-21	204-276	89.1-70.4
Det	9-7	.563	#W	357-342	406-511	**2080**-1859	**5.1**-3.6	12-15	10-11	459-547	250-370	3085-3745	6.7-6.8	24-21	14-12	163-199	80.2-90.6
ChiB	9-7	.563	#WD	271-307	487-432	1588-1922	3.3-4.4	10-10	10-10	502-522	308-295	3230-3262	6.4-6.2	19-16	16-12	139-175	79.4-75.9
TB	6-10	.375	—	251-351	430-468	1489-1964	3.5-4.2	8-13	**7**-12	491-498	271-303	3436-3486	7.0-7.0	17-25	16-9	171-114	75.2-91.2
Western Division																	
SF	**13**-3	**.813**	DCS*	**505**-296	491-375	1897-1338	3.9-3.6	23-16	13-12	511-583	359-329	4362-3756	**8.5**-6.4	**37-15**	**11-23**	199-255	**111.4**-68.1
NO	7-9	.438	—	348-407	373-458	1336-1758	3.6-3.8	11-10	14-14	569-559	366-353	4027-4007	7.1-7.2	22-28	18-17	181-196	84.9-88.6
Atl	7-9	.438	—	317-385	330-426	1249-1693	3.8-4.0	8-16	11-11	629-580	374-364	4344-4365	6.9-7.5	25-26	25-22	232-229	77.1-84.9
LARm	4-12	.250	—	286-365	397-496	1389-1781	3.5-3.6	6-12	13-6	512-541	291-320	3597-3548	7.0-6.6	23-23	18-14	239-159	79.0-82.1
Aver	16	—	—	324	448	1668	3.7	12	13	538	312	3639	6.8	21	17	221	78.4

TEAM	1D	PENY	PNT	FGM/A	RTNY	RTNTD	OFFY/DEFY	NETY	NETTO	NP	PNP	DELP	PW	DELW	PRT	DR	YPD	DEL
Eastern Division																		
Dal	322-273	895-826	41.9-43.3	22/29-20/25	701-558	5-**0**	5321-**4313**	1008	7	166	112	54	12.1	-0.2	6.3/**3.4**	180-188	29.6-22.9	6.6
NYG	263-280	818-**1122**	40.2-40.5	22/28-29/34	516-606	2-4	4316-4950	-634	7	-26	-25	-1	7.3	1.6	4.2/ 5.1	183-187	23.6-26.5	-2.9
Arz	287-**245**	1090-800	40.8-40.9	22/30-**15**/24	583-532	1-5	4607-4408	199	7	-32	45	-77	7.2	0.8	4.0/ 4.4	196-197	23.5-**22.4**	1.1
Phi	293-275	1107-844	40.5-39.7	21/25-25/26	590-492	3-2	5125-4710	415	9	0	71	-71	8.0	-1.0	4.7/ 4.4	196-192	26.1-24.5	1.6
Was	269-331	730-839	44.4-40.3	20/28-17/28	778-923	**7**-6	4793-5609	-816	-17	-92	-136	44	5.7	-2.7	4.3/ 5.9	**202**-198	23.7-28.3	-4.6
Central Division																		
Min	325-287	880-614	42.9-40.5	**34/39**-19/30	576-702	**7**-3	5848-4742	1106	0	42	92	-50	9.1	1.0	5.1/ 4.9	197-196	29.7-24.2	5.5
GB	314-281	760-675	41.4-39.7	19/26-21/25	646-465	3-3	5316-4764	552	**11**	95	90	5	10.4	-1.4	5.4/ 4.1	186-189	28.6-25.2	3.4
Det	280-326	781-1036	43.5-44.9	18/27-21/28	400-585	**7**-4	5002-5405	-403	-1	15	-38	53	8.4	0.6	5.2/ 5.6	172-171	29.1-31.6	-2.5
ChiB	274-275	**503**-645	37.8-**39.0**	21/29-30/41	345-560	1-5	4679-5009	-330	-4	-36	-44	8	7.1	**1.9**	4.9/ 4.9	177-171	26.4-29.3	-2.9
TB	276-298	805-690	38.6-42.7	23/35-23/26	325-426	1-2	4754-5336	-582	-2	-100	-57	-43	5.5	0.5	5.2/ 6.2	169-**168**	28.1-31.8	-3.6
Western Division																		
SF	**362**-285	890-912	41.4-42.5	15/20-**15/21**	**842-349**	6-4	**6060**-4839	**1221**	**11**	**209**	**146**	**63**	**13.2**	-0.2	**7.4**/ 4.2	172-178	**35.2**-27.2	**8.0**
NO	308-337	678-922	43.6-42.6	28/**39**-30/37	349-881	5-7	5182-5569	-387	-1	-59	-36	-23	6.5	0.5	5.5/ 5.6	185-186	28.0-29.9	-1.9
Atl	302-330	934-853	39.5-42.9	21/25-26/33	510-692	3-2	5361-5829	-468	-3	-68	-51	-17	6.3	0.7	4.9/ 5.6	184-189	29.1-30.8	-1.7
LARm	274-333	922-1015	**44.8**-42.0	18/23-23/29	672-850	4-7	4747-5170	-423	-11	-79	-79	0	6.0	-2.0	5.1/ 5.3	178-176	26.7-29.4	-2.7
Aver	298	837	41.7	23/29	586	3	5086	—	—	—	—	—	—	—	5.3	186	27.4	—

Rushing Attempts	Rushing Yards	Rushing Average	Rushing TDs	Rushing Rank	Passing Yards	Passing Average
E.Smith-Dal 368	B.Sanders-Det.......1883	B.Sanders-Det........5.69	E.Smith-Dal 21	B.Sanders-Det.......1953	W.Moon-Min 4264	S.Young-SF.............8.61
B.Sanders-Det.........331	E.Smith-Dal 1484	H.Walker-Phi..........4.67	T.Allen-Min..................8	E.Smith-Dal 1694	S.Young-SF...........3969	T.Aikman-Dal 7.41
R.Hampton-NYG 327	R.Hampton-NYG ...1075	C.Heyward-Atl.........4.26		R.Hampton-NYG ...1135	B.Favre-GB............3882	C.Erickson-TB.........7.32
J.Bettis-LARm..........319	T.Allen-Min.............1031	T.Allen-Min.............4.04		T.Allen-Min.............1111	J.Everett-NO..........3855	D.Brown-NYG 7.25
E.Rhett-TB..............284	J.Bettis-LARm........1025	E.Smith-Dal 4.03		E.Rhett-TB.............1081	J.George-Atl 3734	J.Everett-NO...........7.14
Completion Percent	**TD Passes**	**TD Percent**	**INT Percent**	**Passer Rating**	**Passing Rank**	**Receptions**
S.Young-SF.............70.3	S.Young-SF...............35	S.Young-SF..............7.6	S.Young-SF..............2.2	S.Young-SF..........112.8	S.Young-SF...........1760	C.Carter-Min............122
T.Aikman-Dal 64.5	B.Favre-GB...............33	B.Favre-GB..............5.7	S.Walsh-Chi.............2.3	B.Favre-GB.............90.7	B.Favre-GB...........1546	J.Rice-SF.................112
J.Everett-NO...........64.1	J.George-Atl 23	C.Miller-LARm 5.0	B.Favre-GB..............2.4	J.Everett-NO 84.9	W.Moon-Min 1462	T.Mathis-Atl.............111
B.Favre-GB.............62.4	J.Everett-NO 22	J.George-Atl 4.4	C.Erickson-TB...........2.5	T.Aikman-Dal 84.9	J.Everett-NO..........1318	S.Sharpe-GB 94
W.Moon-Min 61.7	W.Moon-Min 18	J.Everett-NO............4.1	B.Culpepper-Phi 2.7	J.George-Atl 83.3	J.George-Atl 1262	J.Reed-Min 85
Receiving Yards	**Receiving Average**	**Receiving TDs**	**Receiving Rank**	**Combined Net Yards**	**Total TDs**	**Total Points**
J.Rice-SF...............1499	A.Harper-Dal 24.88	S.Sharpe-GB 18	J.Rice-SF..................815	B.Mitchell-Was.......2477	E.Smith-Dal 22	E.Smith-Dal 132
H.Ellard-Was..........1397	F.Anderson-LARm....20.54	J.Rice-SF..................13	H.Ellard-Was............729	B.Sanders-Det.......2166	S.Sharpe-GB 18	F.Reveiz-Min 132
T.Mathis-Atl............1342	H.Ellard-Was.........18.88	H.Moore-Det.............11	T.Mathis-Atl.............726	T.Hughes-NO.........1864	J.Rice-SF..................15	M.Andersen-NO.......116
C.Carter-Min..........1256	D.Howard-Was......18.17	T.Mathis-Atl..............11	C.Carter-Min............663	E.Smith-Dal 1825		C.Boniol-Dal 114
M.Irvin-Dal.............1241	H.Moore-Det.........16.29	B.Jones-SF..................9	M.Irvin-Dal..............651	K.Williams-Dal 1698		S.Sharpe-GB 108
Punt Average	**Field Goals**	**Field Goal Percent**	**Kickoff Returns**	**Kickoff Return Average**	**Punt Returns**	**Punt Return Average**
S.Landeta-LARm....44.8	F.Reveiz-Min 34	F.Reveiz-Min 87.2	T.Hughes-NO.............63	M.Gray-Det.............28.4	P.Robinson-Arz..........41	B.Mitchell-Was........14.1
R.Roby-Was 44.4	M.Andersen-NO.........28	E.Murray-Phi...........84.0	B.Mitchell-Was...........58	H.Walker-Phi...........27.7	J.Sydner-Phi 40	D.Meggett-NYG 12.4
S.Mitchell-Det 44.2	M.Husted-TB 23	N.Johnson-Atl.........84.0	D.Carter-SF 48	K.Williams-Dal 26.7	R.Brooks-GB 40	M.Gray-Det.............11.1
T.Barnhardt-NO 43.6	C.Boniol-Dal 22	T.Zendejas-LARm...78.3	M.Gray-Det................45	R.Smith-Min............26.2	K.Williams-Dal 39	V.Turner-TB.............10.4
M.Saxon-Min 42.9		G.Davis-Arz 76.9	C.Verdin-Atl...............44	B.Mitchell-Was........25.5	D.Carter-SF 38	T.Kinchen-LARm.......9.9
Punt/Kick Return Yards	**Punt/Kick Return TDs**	**Interceptions**	**Interception Return Yards**	**Interception Return TDs**	**Sacks**	**Overall Rank**
B.Mitchell-Was.......1930	M.Gray-Det..................3	A.Williams-Arz 9	D.Sanders-SF 303	D.Sanders-SF 3	J.Randle-Min 13.5	S.Young-SF...........2123
T.Hughes-NO.........1699		M.Hanks-SF................7	A.Collins-Was 150	F.Warren-Min 2	K.Harvey-Was.........13.5	B.Sanders-Det.......2100
M.Gray-Det............1509		D.Sanders-SF 6	D.Woodson-Dal.........140	A.Parker-Min................2	C.Haley-Dal 12.5	E.Smith-Dal 1870
K.Williams-Dal 1497		G.Jackson-Phi 6	F.Warren-Min 135	A.Collins-Was 2	C.Smith-Atl 11.0	B.Favre-GB............1768
D.Carter-SF 1426			V.Clark-Atl...............119			W.Moon-Min 1517

Changing Channels

For the first time since 1956, CBS did not broadcast NFL games. In the year that the salary cap system was enacted, Fox made things even more interesting for owners by throwing $1.58 billion into the ring for the NFC rights for four years. The network also took many of the CBS announcers—and station affiliates—with them. But watching football on TV was changing. Fans across the country could now watch games from every market at home via satellite with the league's "Sunday Ticket." Nachos not included.

The Rams announced plans to make their third franchise move, to St. Louis. The Cardinals, who'd vacated Missouri six season earlier, altered their designation from Phoenix to Arizona. They changed coaches, too. Fiery Buddy Ryan brought the Cardinals their first .500 team in a decade. Four NFC Central Division teams made the playoffs, but nobody could match the 49ers out West. San Francisco led the NFL in scoring for the third straight year. Jerry Rice broke Jim Brown's career touchdown mark and caught 3 of Steve Young's record 6 touchdown passes in the Super Bowl.

With rookie Larry Allen filling out an excellent line in Dallas, Emmitt Smith scored 22 touchdowns. Sterling Shape scored 18 times in Green Bay, but those were the last touchdowns of his brilliant career. Despite injuring his neck on December 18 against Atlanta, Sharpe came back for the season finale on Christmas Eve in Tampa Bay—he never missed a regular-season game in seven seasons—and suffered the same injury in what became his final NFL appearance.

Two Hall of Famers died: Jim Finks, a Steelers quarterback who later created winning teams in Minnesota, Chicago, and New Orleans, and Ray Flaherty, a Giants end who went on to win four NFL and two AAFC division titles as a coach. Although Flaherty was 90, a study showed many future NFL vets might not be so lucky. The National Institute for Occupational Safety and Health, conducting a survey at the request of the NFL Players Association, found that offensive and defensive linemen had a 52 percent greater risk of dying from heart disease than the general population.

1994 AFC

TEAM	W-L-T	PCT	POST	PTS	RA	RY	RY/A	RTD	FL	PA	PC	GPY	GPY/A	PTD	PI	PSY	PRAT
Eastern Division																	
Mia	10-6	.625	#ED	**389**-327	433-394	1658-1430	3.8-3.6	13-14	14-9	627-577	392-334	4533-3954	7.2-6.9	**31**-23	18-**23**	113-160	**88.8**-75.6
NE	10-6	.625	#W	351-312	478-422	1332-1760	2.8-4.2	12-11	11-18	**699**-545	**405**-298	**4583**-3737	6.6-6.9	25-21	27-22	139-290	73.5-72.2
Ind	8-8	.500	—	307-320	495-463	2060-1646	4.2-3.6	15-8	17-10	376-598	217-354	2519-3897	6.7-6.5	15-24	14-18	166-218	75.9-79.4
Buf	7-9	.438	—	340-356	483-447	1831-1515	3.8-**3.4**	14-10	13-12	542-535	342-314	3714-3812	6.9-7.1	23-26	21-16	301-152	81.2-84.4
NYJ	6-10	.375	—	264-320	416-463	1566-1809	3.8-3.9	8-17	10-21	539-522	310-333	3323-3730	6.2-7.1	18-19	18-17	186-201	72.9-83.6
Central Division																	
Pit	**12**-4	**.750**	DC	316-234	**546**-421	**2180**-1452	4.0-**3.4**	**15-7**	**8**-14	463-532	266-280	3247-3256	7.0-6.1	17-**12**	**9**-17	283-**382**	83.3-**65.6**
Cle	11-5	.688	WD	340-**204**	449-465	1657-1669	3.7-3.6	12-9	14-13	507-587	266-325	3269-3425	6.4-**5.8**	20-13	21-18	**94**-268	68.6-67.1
Cin	3-13	.188	—	276-406	404-517	1556-1906	3.9-3.7	5-16	22-8	542-505	289-294	3541-3458	6.5-6.8	21-22	19-10	305-210	72.0-85.4
Hou	2-14	.125	—	226-352	417-540	1682-2120	4.0-3.9	10-17	25-12	554-**400**	274-**221**	3216-**2963**	5.8-7.4	13-18	17-14	417-168	62.5-79.4
Western Division																	
SD	11-5	.688	DCS	381-306	482-**385**	1852-**1404**	3.8-3.6	13-11	9-15	522-577	305-363	3619-3911	6.9-6.8	20-20	14-17	251-253	81.3-82.0
KC	9-7	.563	#W	319-298	464-446	1732-1734	3.7-3.9	12-11	12-**26**	615-504	366-300	4092-3500	6.7-6.9	20-23	14-12	132-234	80.8-85.9
LARd	9-7	.563	#	303-327	428-444	1512-1543	3.5-3.5	7-11	14-13	488-564	281-306	3556-3684	**7.3**-6.5	22-24	16-12	289-284	81.8-79.8
Den	7-9	.438	—	347-396	431-432	1470-1752	3.4-4.1	**19**-12	18-14	626-568	388-322	4383-4296	7.0-7.6	18-28	13-12	366-141	83.8-88.5
Sea	6-10	.375	—	287-323	480-511	2084-1952	**4.3**-3.8	16-15	19-11	498-537	253-313	2809-3603	5.6-6.7	13-15	**9**-19	241-206	69.1-73.2
Aver	16	—	—	324	448	1668	3.7	12	13	538	312	3639	6.8	21	17	221	78.4

TEAM	1D	PENY	PNT	FGM/A	RTNY	RTNTD	OFFY/DEFY	NETY	NETTO	NP	PNP	DELP	PW	DELW	PRT	DR	YPD	DEL
Eastern Division																		
Mia	344-305	747-653	40.2-41.7	24/31-**11/18**	517-514	1-5	**6078**-5224	**854**	0	62	71	-9	9.6	0.5	**6.1**/ 4.9	174-**174**	**34.9**-30.0	**4.9**
NE	**348**-280	**597**-795	41.2-40.2	27/35-20/25	592-512	2-4	5776-5207	569	2	39	55	-16	9.0	1.0	4.8/ 4.6	197-194	29.3-26.8	2.5
Ind	252-311	658-824	41.8-42.2	16/24-27/34	699-540	**7**-2	4413-5325	-912	-3	-13	-88	75	7.7	0.3	4.6/ 5.0	179-183	24.7-29.1	-4.4
Buf	319-294	631-770	41.8-42.3	24/28-26/30	518-586	1-4	5244-5175	69	-6	-16	-18	2	7.6	-0.6	4.6/ 5.7	180-183	29.1-28.3	0.9
NYJ	265-315	754-489	42.1-43.1	20/23-21/27	700-492	3-1	4703-5338	-635	10	-56	-13	-43	6.6	-0.6	4.4/ 5.4	175-178	26.9-30.0	-3.1
Central Division																		
Pit	307-**262**	974-763	39.7-42.2	24/29-24/29	664-**369**	3-4	5144-**4326**	818	**14**	82	**124**	-42	10.1	**2.0**	5.4/**3.8**	195-191	26.4-**22.6**	3.7
Cle	273-304	969-**1139**	40.1-**40.0**	26/28-17/26	685-445	5-**0**	4832-4826	6	-4	**136**	-16	**152**	**11.4**	-0.4	4.7/ 4.0	189-191	25.6-25.3	0.3
Cin	267-310	618-861	43.3-40.6	28/33-31/35	540-635	1-7	4792-5154	-362	-23	-130	-122	-8	4.8	-1.8	4.4/ 5.6	**198**-195	24.2-26.4	-2.2
Hou	278-275	959-807	42.9-42.0	16/20-30/31	523-626	2-2	4481-4915	-434	-16	-126	-100	-26	4.8	-2.8	3.5/ 5.4	191-193	23.5-25.5	-2.0
Western Division																		
SD	311-308	875-989	41.0-43.3	**34/38**-22/27	**877**-581	**7**-3	5220-5062	158	9	75	49	26	9.9	1.1	5.3/ 5.0	181-182	28.8-27.8	1.0
KC	322-289	911-925	42.1-45.0	25/30-18/23	534-723	2-1	5692-5000	692	12	21	106	-85	8.5	0.5	5.6/ 5.4	194-187	29.3-26.7	2.6
LARd	267-303	1186-823	**43.9**-40.6	22/28-21/29	674-568	5-3	4779-4943	-164	-5	-24	-34	10	7.4	1.6	5.1/ 5.1	189-183	25.3-27.0	-1.7
Den	346-303	865-1031	42.9-43.5	30/37-31/37	434-563	0-3	5487-5907	-420	-5	-49	-55	6	6.8	0.2	5.3/ 6.6	190-189	28.9-31.3	-2.4
Sea	285-318	898-773	42.9-40.9	20/24-27/33	621-636	3-4	4652-5349	-697	2	-36	-50	14	7.1	-1.1	4.3/ 4.8	186-186	25.0-28.8	-3.7
Aver	298	837	41.7	23/29	586	2	5086	—	—	—	—	—	—	—	5.3	94	27.2	—

Rushing Attempts	Rushing Yards	Rushing Average	Rushing TDs	Rushing Rank	Passing Yards	Passing Average
N.Means-SD 343	C.Warren-Sea........1545	C.Warren-Sea.........4.64	N.Means-SD..............12	C.Warren-Sea........1635	D.Bledsoe-NE........4555	J.Hostetler-LARd....7.33
C.Warren-Sea..........333	N.Means-SD..........1350	S.Broussard-Cin.....4.29	M.Faulk-Ind...............11	N.Means-SD..........1470	D.Marino-Mia.........4453	D.Marino-Mia..........7.24
M.Faulk-Ind..............314	M.Faulk-Ind............1282	L.Hoard-Cle............4.26	C.Warren-Sea..............9	M.Faulk-Ind...........1392	J.Elway-Den...........3490	S.Humphries-SD.....7.08
T.Thomas-Buf...........287	T.Thomas-Buf.........1093	B.Morris-Pit............4.22	L.Russell-Den..............9	T.Thomas-Buf.........1163	J.Hostetler-LARd....3334	J.Elway-Den...........7.06
H.Williams-LARd......282	H.Williams-LARd......983	K.Davis-Buf.............4.19	M.Butts-NE..................8	H.Williams-LARd....1023	J.Montana-KC.........3283	J.Blake-Cin.............7.04
Completion Percent	**TD Passes**	**TD Percent**	**INT Percent**	**Passer Rating**	**Passing Rank**	**Receptions**
J.Kelly-Buf..............63.6	D.Marino-Mia............30	J.Kelly-Buf.................4.9	J.Montana-KC...........1.8	D.Marino-Mia...........89.2	D.Marino-Mia.........1697	B.Coates-NE..............96
D.Marino-Mia...........62.6	D.Bledsoe-NE............25	D.Marino-Mia............4.9	R.Mirer-Sea..............1.8	J.Elway-Den............85.7	J.Elway-Den...........1425	A.Reed-Buf.................90
J.Elway-Den.............62.1	J.Kelly-Buf..................22	J.Blake-Cin...............4.6	J.Elway-Den..............2.0	J.Kelly-Buf...............84.6	J.Montana-KC.........1362	T.Brown-LARd............89
J.Montana-KC...........60.6	J.Hostetler-LARd........20	J.Hostetler-LARd.......4.4	N.O'Donnell-Pit..........2.4	J.Montana-KC...........83.6	D.Bledsoe-NE.........1323	S.Sharpe-Den..............87
S.Humphries-SD.....58.3		D.Terry-Cle................4.3	S.Humphries-SD........2.6	S.Humphries-SD.....81.6	S.Humphries-SD....1210	B.Blades-Sea...............81
Receiving Yards	**Receiving Average**	**Receiving TDs**	**Receiving Rank**	**Combined Net Yards**	**Total TDs**	**Total Points**
T.Brown-LARd........1309	D.Scott-Cin............18.83	C.Pickens-Cin............11	T.Brown-LARd.........700	G.Milburn-Den........1922	N.Means-SD..............12	J.Carney-SD.............135
A.Reed-Buf..............1303	A.Miller-Den............18.45	T.Brown-LARd.............9	A.Reed-Buf..............692	C.Warren-Sea.........1868	M.Faulk-Ind...............12	J.Elam-Den...............119
I.Fryar-Mia..............1270	T.Martin-SD............17.70	A.Reed-Buf....................8	I.Fryar-Mia..............670	M.Faulk-Ind............1804	C.Warren-Sea............11	M.Bahr-NE.................117
B.Coates-NE...........1174	I.Fryar-Mia..............17.40		B.Coates-NE............622	T.Brown-LARd.........1796	C.Pickens-Cin............11	M.Stover-Cle..............110
C.Pickens-Cin.........1127	D.Alexander-Cle....17.25		C.Pickens-Cin..........619	N.Means-SD...........1585		S.Christie-Buf...........110
Punt Average	**Field Goals**	**Field Goal Percent**	**Kickoff Returns**	**Kickoff Return Average**	**Punt Returns**	**Punt Return Average**
J.Gossett-LARd......43.9	J.Carney-SD..............34	M.Stover-Cle..........92.9	A.Coleman-SD...........49	R.Baldwin-Cle.........26.9	D.Brewer-Ind..............42	D.Gordon-SD...........13.2
L.Johnson-Cin.........43.8	J.Elam-Den.................30	J.Carney-SD...........89.5	R.Ismail-LARd............43	A.Coleman-SD.........26.4	G.Milburn-Den............41	T.Brown-LARd..........12.2
R.Tuten-Sea............42.9	D.Pelfrey-Cin..............28	N.Lowery-NYJ.........87.0	E.Ball-Cin....................42	J.Vaughn-Sea..........24.6	T.Brown-LARd............40	C.Sawyer-Cin...........11.8
T.Rouen-Den............42.9	M.Bahr-NE...................27	S.Christie-Buf.........85.7	G.Milburn-Den............37	I.Spikes-Mia............22.8	R.Woodson-Pit...........39	J.Burris-Buf.............10.4
R.Camarillo-Hou......42.9	M.Stover-Cle................26	D.Pelfrey-Cin..........84.8	O.McDuffie-Mia...........36	B.By'Not'e-Den.......22.7	C.Hicks-NYJ...............38	E.Metcalf-Cle..............9.9
Punt/Kick Return Yards	**Punt/Kick Return TDs**	**Interceptions**	**Interception Return Yards**	**Interception Return TDs**	**Sacks**	**Overall Rank**
A.Coleman-SD.......1293	E.Metcalf-Cle................2	E.Turner-Cle.................9	S.Richard-SD...........224	R.Buchanan-Ind...........3	K.Greene-Pit...........14.0	C.Warren-Sea........1807
G.Milburn-Den........1172	D.Gordon-SD.................2	R.Buchanan-Ind............8	R.Buchanan-Ind.........221	R.Woodson-Pit.............2	L.O'Neal-SD............12.5	D.Marino-Mia..........1701
O.McDuffie-Mia.........995	A.Coleman-SD...............2	D.Perry-Pit....................7	E.Turner-Cle.............199	S.Richard-SD................2	N.Smith-KC..............11.5	J.Elway-Den...........1700
R.Ismail-LARd..........923		T.McDaniel-LARd.........7	M.Turner-NYJ...........155	T.McDaniel-LARd.........2	D.Thomas-KC...........11.0	M.Faulk-Ind.............1658
E.Ball-Cin.................915		M.Hurst-NE...................7	T.Vincent-Mia...........113	M.Lewis-NYJ................2	C.Mims-SD...............11.0	N.Means-SD............1588

Throwing Back and Going for Two

While baseball endured a cataclysmic strike in 1994, the NFL thrived. The league celebrated its 75th anniversary with pomp and circumstance while naming a team of its greatest players at each position. Two members of that all-time team—quarterback Joe Montana and safety Ronnie Lott—retired in 1994. And the teams all looked different. The 75th anniversary brought out old-time versions of NFL uniforms. It reminded fans of fashion choices best left in black-and-white photo albums—striped Bears uniforms and an X across the Steelers jersey—but many of the getups proved so popular that teams continued to bring them back beyond the anniversary year.

The league wasn't afraid of new things. The two-point conversion made its NFL debut (it had been used in the AFL in the 1960s). Although the rule conceivably helped teams make large comebacks and decreased the number of blowouts, coaches who relied on cheat sheets sometimes went home disappointed as a potential win turned into a loss. Wanting yet more offense, kickoffs were now made from the 30; on missed field goals, possession went to the opponent at the spot of the kick instead of the line of scrimmage.

The Seahawks played the first three games of the season at Husky Stadium while the Kingdome underwent repairs from roof tiles that fell there during baseball season. Seattle's first-ever outdoor NFL game was won by San Diego, which started year at 6–0. Behind Stan Humphries and Natrone Means, the Chargers beat the Steelers in the finale to clinch the division title and gain a first-round bye. In the playoffs the Chargers survived a last-second missed field goal by Miami and stopped Pittsburgh again, this time with a goal-line stand, to earn the franchise's first trip to the Super Bowl.

The biggest turnaround of the year was in New England, where the Patriots doubled their win total from 1993 and reached the playoffs. The season ended for them in Cleveland, as Bill Belichick beat his mentor Bill Parcells in the playoffs. The Colts also doubled their wins, thanks to remarkable rookie running back Marshall Faulk.

1995 NFC

TEAM	W-L-T	PCT	POST	PTS	RA	RY	RY/A	RTD	FL	PA	PC	GPY	GPY/A	PTD	PI	PSY	PRAT
Eastern Division																	
Dal	**12**-4	**.750**	DCS*	435-291	495-442	**2201**-1772	4.4-4.0	**29**-13	13-6	494-523	322-293	3741-3491	7.6-6.7	18-17	**10**-19	118-219	91.7-72.3
Phi	10-6	.625	WD	318-338	**508**-466	2121-1822	4.2-3.9	19-14	17-19	496-499	284-268	2931-**3121**	5.9-6.3	11-**14**	19-19	245-305	65.9-66.4
Was	6-10	.375	—	326-359	469-483	1956-2132	4.2-4.4	15-18	10-19	521-546	265-338	3496-3403	6.7-6.2	16-20	20-16	268-135	66.7-79.6
NYG	5-11	.313	—	290-340	478-500	1833-2109	3.8-4.2	17-17	15-15	479-508	260-299	2863-3361	6.0-6.6	11-17	13-16	213-177	68.6-76.7
Arz	4-12	.250	—	275-422	387-503	1363-2249	3.5-4.5	3-14	19-**23**	560-**461**	327-**264**	3893-3655	7.0-7.9	17-33	24-19	390-200	72.0-89.5
Central Division																	
GB	11-5	.688	#EDC	404-314	410-374	1428-1515	3.5-4.1	9-12	**6**-3	593-616	372-351	4539-3915	**7.7**-6.4	**39**-25	15-13	217-275	**97.6**-80.8
Det	10-6	.625	W	436-336	387-409	1753-1795	**4.5**-4.4	16-15	13-13	605-580	362-354	4510-4121	7.5-7.1	33-17	12-22	150-**317**	92.9-76.5
ChiB	9-7	.563	#	392-360	492-405	1930-1441	3.9-3.6	15-9	16-13	523-595	315-374	3838-4240	7.3-7.1	29-27	**10**-16	**95**-239	93.4-88.1
Min	8-8	.500	—	412-385	433-352	1733-1329	4.0-3.8	10-11	13-15	642-620	402-369	4500-4416	7.0-7.1	33-29	16-25	295-294	90.2-80.1
TB	7-9	.438	—	238-335	398-449	1587-1754	4.0-3.9	19-14	14-16	507-557	267-346	3341-4098	6.6-7.4	5-19	20-14	386-140	60.3-85.4
Western Division																	
SF	11-5	.688	#D	**457-258**	415-**348**	1479-**1061**	3.6-**3.0**	19-**5**	12-8	**644**-611	**432**-330	**4779**-3577	7.4-**5.9**	29-19	16-**26**	171-240	93.6-**64.1**
Atl	9-7	.563	#W	362-349	337-404	1393-1547	4.1-3.8	8-12	9-12	603-650	364-405	4456-4751	7.4-7.3	26-28	12-18	270-210	89.3-87.3
SL	7-9	.438	—	309-418	392-410	1431-1677	3.7-4.1	5-14	16-14	632-534	366-320	4113-3699	6.5-6.9	27-27	23-22	308-258	76.5-80.6
Car	7-9	.438	—	289-325	454-450	1573-1576	3.5-3.5	10-17	16-16	537-586	263-310	3304-3716	6.2-6.3	16-15	25-21	258-265	59.1-66.2
NO	7-9	.438	—	319-348	383-469	1390-1838	3.6-3.9	11-13	11-12	573-543	349-329	4002-3998	7.0-7.4	26-23	14-17	214-275	86.9-84.3
Aver	16	—	—	344	440	1730	3.9	13	14	557	324	3769	6.8	22	17	236	79.2

TEAM	1D	PENY	PNT	FGM/A	RTNY	RTNTD	OFFY/DEFY	NETY	NETTO	NP	PNP	DELP	PW	DELW	PRT	DR	YPD	DEL
Eastern Division																		
Dal	**364**-303	695-913	40.8-42.7	27/28-22/27	516-371	4-2	5824-5044	780	2	144	73	**71**	11.6	0.4	6.5/ 4.6	162-**171**	**36.0**-29.5	6.5
Phi	290-281	838-727	42.8-41.3	22/30-28/37	532-767	6-8	4807-4638	169	2	-20	22	-42	7.5	**2.5**	3.6/ 3.8	197-202	24.4-**23.0**	1.4
Was	297-323	**563**-780	42.4-41.4	27/36-22/27	565-511	4-4	5184-5400	-216	5	-33	2	-35	7.2	-1.2	4.5/ 4.8	191-189	27.1-28.6	-1.4
NYG	288-335	772-662	42.2-42.2	20/28-28/35	487-538	5-3	4483-5293	-810	3	-50	-56	6	6.8	-1.8	4.1/ 4.9	179-173	25.0-30.6	-5.6
Arz	285-310	835-860	43.8-43.5	30/39-18/25	431-549	6-6	4866-5704	-838	-1	-147	-74	-73	4.3	-0.3	4.2/ 6.0	196-189	24.8-30.2	-5.4
Central Division																		
GB	339-303	604-738	40.9-42.6	20/28-19/**21**	768-522	1-**0**	5750-5155	595	-5	90	30	60	10.3	0.8	6.4/ 5.0	176-180	32.7-28.6	4.0
Det	349-350	1032-**1001**	40.5-42.7	28/34-28/42	459-661	1-4	**6113**-5599	514	10	100	83	17	10.5	-0.5	6.5/ 4.8	187-183	32.7-30.6	2.1
ChiB	340-316	601-821	37.4-**37.3**	23/31-24/29	325-460	2-5	5673-5442	231	3	32	31	1	8.8	0.2	**6.7**/ 5.6	177-176	32.1-30.9	1.1
Min	342-312	797-707	40.9-42.2	26/36-26/35	740-618	5-4	5938-5451	487	**11**	27	85	-58	8.7	-0.7	5.6/ 5.0	191-197	31.1-27.7	3.4
TB	283-336	882-698	42.3-40.0	19/26-31/40	430-539	2-2	4542-5712	-1170	-4	-97	-114	17	5.6	1.4	3.7/ 6.0	176-179	25.8-31.9	-6.1
Western Division																		
SF	355-**264**	711-556	40.6-41.7	20/28-27/32	697-539	**9**-2	6087-**4398**	**1689**	6	**199**	**165**	34	**13.0**	-2.0	6.2/**3.6**	170-183	35.8-24.0	**11.8**
Atl	317-340	737-688	41.2-43.3	**33/40-17**/22	687-**285**	4-3	5579-6088	-509	9	13	-6	19	8.3	0.7	6.0/ 5.9	176-175	31.7-34.8	-3.1
SL	292-301	916-681	**44.3**-43.5	17/28-21/27	**832**-890	5-10	5236-5118	118	-3	-109	-2	-107	5.3	1.7	4.5/ 4.8	207-197	25.3-26.0	-0.7
Car	250-288	683-808	41.0-40.4	26/33-19/26	819-563	4-6	4619-5027	-408	-4	-36	-50	14	7.1	-0.1	3.6/ 4.3	**211**-215	21.9-23.4	-1.5
NO	294-320	688-830	40.1-41.8	20/31-27/35	463-506	1-2	5178-5561	-383	4	-29	-16	-13	7.3	-0.3	5.7/ 5.4	179-175	28.9-31.8	-2.8
Aver	309	820	41.8	25/32	563	4	5262	—	—	—	—	—	—	—	5.4	187	28.2	—

Rushing Attempts	Rushing Yards	Rushing Average	Rushing TDs	Rushing Rank	Passing Yards	Passing Average
E.Smith-Dal 377	E.Smith-Dal 1773	C.Garner-Phi 5.44	E.Smith-Dal 25	E.Smith-Dal 2023	B.Favre-GB 4413	B.Favre-GB 7.74
T.Allen-Was 338	B.Sanders-Det 1500	R.Green-Chi 5.33	R.Watters-Phi 11	B.Sanders-Det 1610	S.Mitchell-Det 4338	T.Aikman-Dal 7.65
R.Watters-Phi 337	T.Allen-Was 1309	B.Sanders-Det 4.78	B.Sanders-Det 11	T.Allen-Was 1409	W.Moon-Min 4228	S.Mitchell-Det 7.44
E.Rhett-TB 332	R.Watters-Phi 1273	E.Smith-Dal 4.70	E.Rhett-TB 11	R.Watters-Phi 1383	J.George-Atl 4143	J.George-Atl 7.44
E.Bennett-GB 316	E.Rhett-TB 1207	C.Heyward-Atl 4.59		E.Rhett-TB 1317	J.Everett-NO 3970	E.Kramer-Chi 7.35

Completion Percent	TD Passes	TD Percent	INT Percent	Passer Rating	Passing Rank	Receptions
S.Young-SF 66.9	B.Favre-GB 38	B.Favre-GB 6.7	T.Aikman-Dal 1.6	B.Favre-GB 99.5	B.Favre-GB 1877	H.Moore-Det 123
T.Aikman-Dal 64.8	W.Moon-Min 33	E.Kramer-Chi 5.6	E.Kramer-Chi 1.9	T.Aikman-Dal 93.6	S.Mitchell-Det 1849	J.Rice-SF 122
B.Favre-GB 63.0	S.Mitchell-Det 32	S.Mitchell-Det 5.5	J.George-Atl 2.0	E.Kramer-Chi 93.5	J.George-Atl 1752	C.Carter-Min 122
W.Moon-Min 62.2	E.Kramer-Chi 29	W.Moon-Min 5.4	S.Mitchell-Det 2.1	S.Young-SF 92.3	W.Moon-Min 1719	I.Bruce-SL 119
J.Everett-NO 60.8	J.Everett-NO 26	J.Everett-NO 4.6	D.Brown-NYG 2.2	S.Mitchell-Det 92.3	E.Kramer-Chi 1664	M.Irvin-Dal 111

Receiving Yards	Receiving Average	Receiving TDs	Receiving Rank	Combined Net Yards	Total TDs	Total Points
J.Rice-SF 1848	W.Green-Car 18.77	C.Carter-Min 17	J.Rice-SF 999	B.Mitchell-Was 2348	E.Smith-Dal 25	E.Smith-Dal 150
I.Bruce-SL 1781	Q.Ismail-Min 18.66	J.Rice-SF 15	I.Bruce-SL 956	E.Smith-Dal 2148	J.Rice-SF 17	J.Hanson-Det 132
H.Moore-Det 1686	H.Ellard-Was 17.95	H.Moore-Det 14	H.Moore-Det 913	E.Metcalf-Atl 1983	C.Carter-Min 17	C.Boniol-Dal 127
M.Irvin-Dal 1603	H.Copeland-TB 17.29	I.Bruce-SL 13	M.Irvin-Dal 852	K.Williams-Dal 1940	H.Moore-Det 14	F.Reveiz-Min 122
R.Brooks-GB 1497	F.Sanders-Arz 16.98	R.Brooks-GB 13	R.Brooks-GB 814			M.Andersen-Atl 122

Punt Average	Field Goals	Field Goal Percent	Kickoff Returns	Kickoff Return Average	Punt Returns	Punt Return Average
S.Landeta-SL 44.3	M.Andersen-Atl 31	C.Boniol-Dal 96.4	T.Hughes-NO 66	B.Mitchell-Was 25.6	T.Kinchen-SL 53	D.Palmer-Min 13.2
J.Feagles-Arz 43.8	G.Davis-Arz 30	M.Andersen-Atl 83.8	B.Edmonds-TB 58	T.Winans-Phi 25.5	E.Guliford-Car 43	B.Mitchell-Was 12.6
T.Hutton-Phi 43.3	J.Hanson-Det 28	J.Hanson-Det 82.4	B.Mitchell-Was 55	J.Willis-SF 25.1	E.Metcalf-Atl 39	K.Martin-Phi 12.6
R.Roby-TB 42.8	E.Murray-Was 27	J.Kasay-Car 78.8	K.Williams-Dal 49	Q.Ismail-Min 24.7	A.Freeman-GB 37	E.Guliford-Car 11.0
M.Horan-NYG 42.5	C.Boniol-Dal 27	G.Davis-Arz 76.9		T.Hughes-NO 24.5	B.Edmonds-TB 29	C.Jordan-GB 10.1

Punt/Kick Return Yards	Punt/Kick Return TDs	Interceptions	Interception Return Yards	Interception Return TDs	Sacks	Overall Rank
T.Hughes-NO 1879	Many 1	O.Thomas-Min 9	W.Clay-Det 173	A.Williams-Arz 2	W.Martin-NO 13.0	E.Smith-Dal 2211
B.Mitchell-Was 1723		W.Clay-Det 8	T.McDonald-SF 135	K.Norton-SF 2	W.Fuller-Phi 13.0	B.Favre-GB 2088
B.Edmonds-TB 1440		W.Thomas-Phi 7	L.Brown-Dal 124	T.McDonald-SF 2	R.White-GB 12.0	S.Mitchell-Det 1993
K.Williams-Dal 1274			T.Carter-Was 116	L.Brown-Dal 2	D.Farr-SL 11.5	B.Sanders-Det 1820
T.Kinchen-SL 1159			O.Thomas-Min 108			W.Moon-Min 1801

Passing Fancy

The Eagles tried to get back on track with a tough head coach. Ray Rhodes didn't just bring a sense of discipline to Philadelphia, he brought a bunch of new players. The roster featured 33 new faces, including running back Ricky Watters, quarterback Rodney Peete, guard Guy McIntyre, and linebacker Kurt Gouveia. Rhodes took Philadelphia to the playoffs and was named Coach of the Year.

Things weren't quite as rosy for some other NFC coaches. Critics of Detroit's Wayne Fontes maligned his soft style during a 3–6 start. The players rallied around their coach, and a resurgent offense helped the Lions to win each of their last seven games. Barry Sanders rushed for 1,500 yards, Scott Mitchell threw 32 touchdown passes, and Herman Moore set a new single-season record with 123 receptions. The Lions finished with the top-ranked offense and advanced to the playoffs for the third straight season. Dallas head coach Barry Switzer endured public censure from owner Jerry Jones. After a lopsided loss to San Francisco, Jones told reporters "our team was outcoached." Switzer accepted the criticism, despite the fact that the team was 8–2 and comfortably entrenched in first place. Emmitt Smith won his fourth rushing title and set a new NFL record by running for 25 touchdowns. Switzer's approach would be validated by Super Bowl XXX.

Milestone passing and receiving marks also fell. While Dan Marino set the all-time mark for career attempts, completions, yards, and touchdowns in Miami, San Francisco's Jerry Rice became the career leader in catches and receiving yards. At age 33 Rice had the most productive season ever for a receiver. Five times he had more than 150 receiving yards (plus another with 149), and he finished with a new single-season record of 1,848 yards. The high point came in a win over the Vikings where Rice caught 14 passes for 289 yards.

The first expansion teams in the NFL in 19 years debuted in 1995. Neither the Carolina Panthers in the NFC nor the Jacksonville Jaguars in the AFC approached the atrocious seasons of past first-year franchises. The Panthers went 7–9 and had the fourth-best defense in the conference.

1995 AFC

TEAM	W-L-T	PCT	POST	PTS	RA	RY	RY/A	RTD	FL	PA	PC	GPY	GPY/A	PTD	PI	PSY	PRAT
Eastern Division																	
Buf	10-6	.625	ED	350-335	**521**-453	1993-1626	3.8-3.6	10-16	12-11	506-582	279-310	3348-3864	6.6-6.6	24-**14**	14-17	224-**362**	79.9-70.0
Ind	9-7	.563	WDC	331-316	478-418	1855-1457	3.9-3.5	14-8	11-13	434-569	270-336	3373-3739	**7.8**-6.6	20-23	11-13	309-169	**91.1**-82.6
Mia	9-7	.563	W	398-332	413-415	1506-1675	3.6-4.0	16-**7**	12-16	592-556	**384**-327	**4398**-3756	7.4-6.8	28-30	20-14	188-187	88.8-86.7
NE	6-10	.375	—	294-377	474-448	1866-1878	3.9-4.2	16-12	20-14	**686**-549	351-342	3789-4107	5.5-7.5	14-29	16-15	198-221	64.8-91.4
NYJ	3-13	.188	—	233-384	365-526	1279-2016	3.5-3.8	2-15	18-17	589-**497**	330-**263**	3129-**3055**	5.3-6.1	20-21	24-17	341-315	65.2-71.6
Central Division																	
Pit	11-5	.688	DCS	**407**-327	494-**370**	1852-**1321**	3.7-3.6	17-9	13-12	592-531	348-314	4093-3512	6.9-6.6	21-24	21-**22**	176-272	76.9-76.7
Cin	7-9	.438	—	349-374	364-483	1439-2104	4.0-4.4	7-10	14-12	586-602	334-364	3915-4512	6.7-7.5	**29**-25	18-12	162-267	81.1-89.2
Hou	7-9	.438	—	348-324	478-400	1664-1526	3.5-3.8	12-11	20-17	536-553	314-289	3512-3325	6.6-**6.0**	22-24	18-21	271-200	77.9-**69.3**
Cle	5-11	.313	—	289-356	398-480	1482-1826	3.7-3.8	5-15	11-7	555-573	324-360	3772-4013	6.8-7.0	21-23	20-17	178-191	76.6-84.6
Jax	4-12	.250	—	275-404	410-504	1705-2003	4.2-4.0	9-17	13-11	495-509	275-304	3144-3584	6.4-7.0	19-28	15-13	354-72	75.0-88.9
Western Division																	
KC	**13**-3	**.813**	D	358-**241**	507-404	**2222**-1327	4.4-**3.3**	14-**7**	11-17	531-596	300-329	3178-3569	6.0-**6.0**	21-16	**10**-16	**158**-347	79.4-70.8
SD	9-7	.563	W	321-323	479-441	1747-1691	3.6-3.8	14-15	12-10	540-543	318-321	3706-3605	6.9-6.6	17-16	18-17	240-222	76.4-75.8
Sea	8-8	.500	—	363-366	477-496	2178-2130	**4.6**-4.3	**20**-11	**9**-9	511-554	273-310	3359-3706	6.6-6.7	19-26	23-16	267-167	67.6-80.2
Den	8-8	.500	—	388-345	440-451	1995-1895	4.5-4.2	14-19	16-13	594-529	350-297	4260-3518	7.2-6.7	27-20	14-8	215-220	86.4-82.9
Oak	8-8	.500	—	348-332	463-446	1932-1794	4.2-4.0	10-15	13-**22**	543-527	317-301	3787-3642	7.0-6.9	25-**14**	21-11	214-332	79.0-78.6
Aver	16	—	—	344	440	1730	3.9	13	14	557	324	3769	6.8	22	17	236	79.2

TEAM	1D	PENY	PNT	FGM/A	RTNY	RTNTD	OFFY/DEFY	NETY	NETTO	NP	PNP	DELP	PW	DELW	PRT	DR	YPD	DEL
Eastern Division																		
Buf	300-287	**672**-890	40.4-42.8	31/40-34/43	709-411	3-3	5117-5128	-11	2	15	7	8	8.4	1.6	5.1/ 4.6	206-204	24.8-25.1	-0.3
Ind	281-304	943-935	42.6-41.0	23/33-25/38	440-592	3-3	4919-5027	-108	4	15	7	8	8.4	0.6	5.7/ 5.4	173-**169**	28.4-29.7	-1.3
Mia	**345**-309	907-739	42.7-41.0	27/34-23/31	324-475	2-**1**	5716-5244	472	-2	66	31	35	9.6	-0.6	5.8/ 5.5	169-177	33.8-29.6	4.2
NE	335-308	676-816	39.2-38.8	23/33-23/32	526-503	2-3	5457-5764	-307	-7	-83	-54	-29	5.9	0.1	4.2/ 6.0	204-191	26.8-30.2	-3.4
NYJ	254-301	1078-759	41.2-41.1	17/21-30/41	584-1157	4-6	4067-4756	-689	-8	-151	-89	-62	4.2	-1.2	3.0/**4.0**	**218**-209	18.7-**22.8**	-4.1
Central Division																		
Pit	344-272	839-931	40.1-43.3	**34/41**-23/25	835-371	6-4	5769-4561	**1208**	0	80	101	-21	10.0	1.0	5.2/ 4.3	194-189	29.7-24.1	**5.6**
Cin	288-354	835-**1143**	41.6-**38.4**	29/36-38/49	278-461	1-2	5192-6349	-1157	-8	-25	-128	**103**	7.4	-0.4	5.3/ 6.1	189-188	27.5-33.8	-6.3
Hou	295-**267**	791-962	40.3-42.4	27/31-19/24	656-553	4-3	4905-4651	254	0	24	21	3	8.6	-1.6	4.7/ 4.2	200-199	24.5-23.4	1.2
Cle	293-342	966-736	43.6-41.7	29/33-26/34	485-572	3-2	5076-5648	-572	-7	-67	-76	9	6.3	-1.3	4.9/ 5.5	169-171	30.0-33.0	-3.0
Jax	283-320	970-958	43.8-42.0	20/27-27/31	398-501	3-**1**	4495-5515	-1020	-4	-129	-101	-28	4.8	-0.8	4.2/ 6.1	177-182	25.4-30.3	-4.9
Western Division																		
KC	295-289	851-828	43.8-41.8	24/30-16/**19**	**864**-556	**7**-5	5242-**4549**	693	**12**	**117**	**106**	11	**10.9**	**2.1**	5.0/ 4.1	195-195	26.9-23.3	3.6
SD	314-313	953-951	44.7-43.4	21/26-27/32	558-593	6-4	5213-5074	139	-3	-2	0	-2	7.9	1.0	4.9/ 4.8	178-177	29.3-28.7	0.6
Sea	311-321	852-901	**45.0**-42.6	23/28-24/35	511-933	3-6	5270-5669	-399	-7	-3	-61	58	7.9	0.1	4.0/ 5.3	195-199	27.0-28.5	-1.5
Den	344-322	851-848	40.9-42.8	31/38-**13/19**	472-**240**	1-5	**6040**-5193	847	-9	43	35	8	9.1	-1.1	**5.9**/ 5.6	174-177	**34.7**-29.3	5.4
Oak	317-293	1059-730	40.6-43.5	21/27-33/41	484-638	6-4	5505-5104	401	-1	16	29	-13	8.4	-0.4	5.0/ 5.2	189-194	29.1-26.3	2.8
Aver	309	820	41.8	25/32	563	2	5262	—	—	—	—	—	—	—	5.4	94	27.6	—

Rushing Attempts	Rushing Yards	Rushing Average	Rushing TDs	Rushing Rank	Passing Yards	Passing Average
C.Martin-NE 368	C.Martin-NE 1487	T.Davis-Den 4.71	C.Warren-Sea 15	C.Martin-NE 1627	J.Elway-Den 3970	J.Harbaugh-Ind 8.20
C.Warren-Sea 310	C.Warren-Sea 1346	N.Kaufman-Oak 4.54	C.Martin-NE 14	C.Warren-Sea 1496	J.Blake-Cin 3822	D.Marino-Mia 7.61
M.Faulk-Ind 289	T.Davis-Den 1117	H.Williams-Oak 4.37	M.Faulk-Ind 11	H.Williams-Oak 1204	D.Marino-Mia 3668	D.Tate-Cle 7.35
T.Thomas-Buf 267	H.Williams-Oak 1114	C.Warren-Sea 4.34		M.Faulk-Ind 1188	D.Bledsoe-NE 3507	J.Elway-Den 7.32
H.Williams-Oak 255	M.Faulk-Ind 1078	G.Hill-KC 4.30		T.Davis-Den 1187	S.Humphries-SD 3381	N.O'Donnell-Pit 7.14

Completion Percent	TD Passes	TD Percent	INT Percent	Passer Rating	Passing Rank	Receptions
D.Marino-Mia 64.1	J.Blake-Cin 28	J.Harbaugh-Ind 5.4	J.Harbaugh-Ind 1.6	J.Harbaugh-Ind 100.7	J.Elway-Den 1555	C.Pickens-Cin 99
J.Harbaugh-Ind 63.7	J.Elway-Den 26	D.Marino-Mia 5.0	N.O'Donnell-Pit 1.7	D.Marino-Mia 90.8	J.Blake-Cin 1371	T.Martin-SD 90
C.Chandler-Hou 63.2	D.Marino-Mia 24	J.Blake-Cin 4.9	S.Bono-KC 1.9	D.Tate-Cle 87.8	D.Marino-Mia 1354	T.Brown-Oak 89
D.Tate-Cle 61.5	J.Kelly-Buf 22	J.Kelly-Buf 4.8	M.Brunell-Jax 2.0	C.Chandler-Hou 87.8	N.O'Donnell-Pit 1290	Y.Thigpen-Pit 85
J.Hostetler-Oak 60.1	S.Bono-KC 21	J.Elway-Den 4.8	D.Bledsoe-NE 2.5	N.O'Donnell-Pit 87.7	S.Bono-KC 1266	B.Coates-NE 84

Receiving Yards	Receiving Average	Receiving TDs	Receiving Rank	Combined Net Yards	Total TDs	Total Points
T.Brown-Oak 1342	C.Sanders-Hou 23.51	C.Pickens-Cin 17	T.Brown-Oak 721	G.Milburn-Den 2080	C.Pickens-Cin 17	N.Johnson-Pit 141
Y.Thigpen-Pit 1307	A.Miller-Den 18.29	A.Miller-Den 14	C.Pickens-Cin 702	E.Mills-Pit 2024	C.Warren-Sea 16	J.Elam-Den 132
C.Pickens-Cin 1234	E.Mills-Pit 17.41	B.Brooks-Buf 11	Y.Thigpen-Pit 679	D.Meggett-NE 1931	C.Martin-NE 15	S.Christie-Buf 126
T.Martin-SD 1224	M.Jackson-Cle 16.23	T.Brown-Oak 10	T.Martin-SD 642	T.Vanover-KC 1897	A.Miller-Den 14	D.Pelfrey-Cin 121
A.Miller-Den 1079	D.Hobbs-Oak 16.11		A.Miller-Den 610	A.Coleman-SD 1804	M.Faulk-Ind 14	M.Stover-Mia 118

Punt Average	Field Goals	Field Goal Percent	Kickoff Returns	Kickoff Return Average	Punt Returns	Punt Return Average
R.Tuten-Sea 45.0	N.Johnson-Pit 34	M.Stover-Cle 87.9	A.Coleman-SD 62	R.Carpenter-NYJ 27.6	T.Vanover-KC 51	S.Tasker-Buf 12.0
D.Bennett-SD 44.7	J.Elam-Den 31	A.Del Greco-Hou 87.1	E.Mills-Pit 54	G.Milburn-Den 27.0	A.Hastings-Pit 48	A.Coleman-SD 11.6
B.Barker-Jax 43.8	S.Christie-Buf 31	N.Johnson-Pit 82.9	M.Gray-Hou 53	J.Hill-Cin 26.7	D.Meggett-NE 45	J.Burris-Buf 11.4
L.Aguiar-KC 43.8	M.Stover-Cle 29	T.Peterson-Sea 82.1	D.Dunn-Cin 50	N.Kaufman-Oak 26.0	J.Galloway-Sea 36	G.Milburn-Den 11.4
T.Tupa-Cle 43.6	D.Pelfrey-Cin 29	J.Elam-Den 81.6	G.Milburn-Den 47	T.Vanover-KC 25.5	T.Brown-Oak 36	T.Vanover-KC 10.6

Punt/Kick Return Yards	Punt/Kick Return TDs	Interceptions	Interception Return Yards	Interception Return TDs	Sacks	Overall Rank
A.Coleman-SD 1737	T.Vanover-KC 3	W.Williams-Pit 7	D.Lewis-Hou 145	Many 1	B.Paup-Buf 17.5	C.Martin-NE 1763
T.Vanover-KC 1635	A.Coleman-SD 3	O.Smith-NYJ 6	E.Daniel-Ind 142		P.Swilling-Oak 13.0	J.Elway-Den 1741
G.Milburn-Den 1623		K.Schulz-Buf 6	W.Williams-Pit 122		L.O'Neal-SD 12.5	J.Blake-Cin 1700
M.Gray-Hou 1486		T.McDaniel-Oak 6	O.Smith-NYJ 101		N.Smith-KC 12.0	C.Warren-Sea 1625
D.Meggett-NE 1347		D.Lewis-Hou 6	L.Warren-KC 100		W.McGinest-NE 11.0	M.Faulk-Ind 1441

Handing Off to a Star

With quarterback Joe Montana retired, Kansas City had to find a way to keep their offense going. They did it by shifting the emphasis from passing to running, and the Chiefs backfield by committee led the league in rushing yards. Marcus Allen and Greg Hill formed an effective ground attack, while backs Todd McNair (60 catches) and Kimble Anders (55 catches) were the team's leading receivers. The defense, led by linebacker Derrick Thomas and defensive end Neil Smith, held opponents to a league low 15 points per game. Despite losing a great quarterback, Kansas City improved from 9–7 to 13–3, the best record in the NFL.

Pittsburgh started the season 3–4, but fiery head coach Bill Cowher refused to concede defeat. After a loss to Minnesota he chased the referee across the field and stuffed a picture into his pocket; proof, he later claimed, that a penalty for having 12 men on the field had been called in error. The Steelers played with passion in the second half of the season, winning eight games in a row. They mixed a potent ground game with a dominating defense. Rookie Kordell Stewart—nicknamed Slash because of his multiple roles—caught, ran, and passed for a touchdown. The Steelers won their first conference title in 16 years, but they also learned that their closest rival wouldn't be so close any more.

On November 6 Browns owner Art Modell announced plans to move from Cleveland to Baltimore, citing heavy debt and the lack of support for building a new stadium. The move had been rumored for weeks, but the actual announcement stunned and outraged fans in Cleveland. It also wrecked team morale, and the Browns lost seven of their last eight games under beleaguered coach Bill Belichick

Out West another relocated—or re-relocated—club was still stuck in a division in which all five teams were .500 or better. After 12 years away, the Raiders drew 414,556 at Oakland Coliseum, just 5,000 more than they drew at the Los Angeles Coliseum a year earlier. In one year Los Angeles went from having the Rams and Raiders to having no team at all.

1996 NFC

TEAM	W-L-T	PCT	POST	PTS	RA	RY	RY/A	RTD	FL	PA	PC	GPY	GPY/A	PTD	PI	PSY	PRAT
Eastern Division																	
Dal	10-6	.625	#ED	286-250	475-437	1641-1576	3.5-3.6	14-10	15-14	487-484	307-271	3249-3025	6.7-6.3	12-**10**	14-19	**127**-219	78.6-65.3
Phi	10-6	.625	#W	363-341	489-421	1882-1583	3.8-3.8	16-12	14-12	548-500	328-271	**3979**-3243	**7.3**-6.5	19-18	18-19	234-264	80.1-70.4
Was	9-7	.563	#	364-312	467-520	**1910**-2275	4.1-4.4	**27**-20	7-9	471-560	270-325	3453-3655	**7.3**-6.5	12-12	**11**-21	134-207	79.2-69.2
Arz	7-9	.438	—	300-397	401-514	1502-1862	3.7-3.6	8-18	14-14	**613**-520	336-311	3917-3684	6.4-7.1	23-21	21-11	229-185	72.6-86.1
NYG	6-10	.375	—	242-297	485-487	1603-1748	3.3-3.6	4-14	13-13	459-533	238-317	2663-3477	5.8-6.5	14-15	21-22	324-178	60.6-71.0
Central Division																	
GB	**13**-3	**.813**	DCS*	**456-210**	465-400	1838-**1416**	4.0-**3.5**	9-7	11-13	548-544	328-283	3938-**2942**	7.2-**5.4**	**39**-12	13-**26**	241-202	**95.7-55.4**
Min	9-7	.563	#W	298-315	435-445	1546-1966	3.6-4.4	7-15	13-13	561-537	331-314	3899-3384	7.0-6.3	24-18	19-22	241-263	80.4-71.2
ChiB	7-9	.438	—	283-305	472-427	1720-1617	3.6-3.8	9-13	9-11	551-524	318-314	3350-3476	6.1-6.6	19-21	18-17	165-209	73.4-79.5
TB	6-10	.375	—	221-293	472-438	1589-1889	3.4-4.3	8-13	14-12	494-503	274-311	2944-3132	6.0-6.2	12-17	20-17	217-207	64.4-76.7
Det	5-11	.313	—	302-368	389-510	1810-2007	**4.7**-3.9	15-12	**5**-8	541-502	309-311	3463-3577	6.4-7.1	20-28	21-11	260-233	72.5-92.9
Western Division																	
Car	12-4	.750	#DC	367-218	**502-374**	1729-1562	3.4-4.2	9-6	14-16	487-556	273-307	3333-3585	6.8-6.4	22-17	**11**-22	250-**371**	83.0-68.7
SF	12-4	.750	#WD	398-257	454-418	1847-1497	4.1-3.6	17-**4**	8-14	550-558	**358**-287	3859-3461	7.0-6.2	24-21	16-20	200-297	88.0-68.4
SL	6-10	.375	—	303-409	448-478	1607-1854	3.6-3.9	10-22	21-13	481-558	249-341	3144-3856	6.5-6.9	18-23	23-**26**	379-181	65.0-76.1
Atl	3-13	.188	—	309-461	329-473	1461-2041	4.4-4.3	9-18	11-**17**	600-485	356-302	3909-3953	6.5-8.2	26-26	30-6	254-208	72.3-100.6
NO	3-13	.188	—	229-339	386-521	1308-2076	3.4-4.0	10-11	20-10	515-**465**	295-**267**	3069-3117	6.0-6.7	13-22	17-12	171-283	69.3-82.9
Aver	16	—	—	327	453	1744	3.8	12	13	532	307	3555	6.7	21	18	236	76.9

TEAM	1D	PENY	PNT	FGM/A	RTNY	RTNTD	OFFY/DEFY	NETY	NETTO	NP	PNP	DELP	PW	DELW	PRT	DR	YPD	DEL
Eastern Division																		
Dal	286-260	832-717	42.6-46.1	32/36-28/32	562-499	1-4	4763-4382	381	4	36	48	-12	8.9	1.1	5.2/ 3.9	176-181	27.1-24.2	2.9
Phi	319-264	963-710	42.0-44.4	25/29-31/36	633-595	6-5	**5627**-4562	1065	-1	22	85	-63	8.6	**1.5**	5.3/ 4.3	190-192	**29.6**-23.8	5.9
Was	307-358	740-867	**45.1**-44.0	26/32-27/38	472-389	2-1	5229-5723	-494	12	52	7	45	9.3	-0.3	**6.0**/ 4.4	183-183	28.6-31.3	-2.7
Arz	308-337	873-841	43.2-43.8	23/31-30/37	465-589	2-5	5190-5361	-171	-10	-97	-54	-43	5.6	1.4	4.6/ 5.9	190-190	27.3-28.2	-0.9
NYG	248-285	666-781	42.0-41.3	24/27-22/26	819-657	6-4	3942-5047	-1105	1	-55	-88	33	6.6	-0.6	3.0/ 4.4	**202**-201	19.5-25.1	-5.6
Central Division																		
GB	**338-248**	714-797	42.4-43.1	21/27-25/27	**1399**-335	**8-0**	5535-**4156**	**1379**	**15**	**246**	**175**	71	**14.1**	-1.2	**6.0/2.9**	190-189	29.1-**22.0**	**7.1**
Min	284-309	835-840	40.2-42.8	22/29-20/30	506-916	2-3	5204-5087	117	3	-17	22	-39	7.6	1.4	5.1/ 4.0	198-199	26.3-25.6	0.7
ChiB	300-295	808-849	44.8-**40.1**	23/30-**16**/23	389-621	3-3	4905-4884	21	1	-22	6	-28	7.4	-0.4	4.5/ 4.9	180-177	27.3-27.6	-0.3
TB	260-296	787-810	42.5-43.4	25/32-19/27	620-574	1-4	4316-4814	-498	-5	-72	-62	-10	6.2	-0.2	3.7/ 4.3	178-172	24.2-28.0	-3.7
Det	317-324	863-938	42.9-41.2	12/17-20/25	453-832	3-4	5013-5351	-338	-7	-66	-56	-10	6.3	-1.4	4.2/ 5.9	172-**167**	29.1-32.0	-2.9
Western Division																		
Car	292-251	**638-1155**	40.5-43.8	**37/45**-17/**20**	901-**214**	5-1	4812-4776	36	13	149	55	**94**	11.7	0.3	5.4/ 3.9	195-199	24.7-24.0	0.7
SF	315-269	925-819	42.9-42.0	30/34-26/29	528-342	2-**0**	5506-4661	845	10	141	110	31	11.5	0.5	5.4/ 4.1	192-189	28.7-24.7	4.0
SL	255-329	1015-832	44.8-40.6	21/25-19/27	829-747	6-5	4372-5529	-1157	-5	-106	-116	10	5.3	0.7	3.6/ 4.6	199-196	22.0-28.2	-6.2
Atl	292-309	961-816	42.0-42.1	22/29-42/44	356-737	0-4	5116-5786	-670	-18	-152	-128	-24	4.2	-1.2	4.0/ 7.2	190-193	26.9-30.0	-3.1
NO	232-287	853-823	40.8-43.0	21/25-33/42	273-639	1-1	4206-4910	-704	-15	-110	-119	9	5.3	-2.3	4.2/ 5.0	186-183	22.6-26.8	-4.2
Aver	299	842	42.9	24/31	613	3	5062	—	—	—	—	—	—	—	5.1	188	26.9	—

Rushing Attempts	Rushing Yards	Rushing Average	Rushing TDs	Rushing Rank	Passing Yards	Passing Average
R.Watters-Phi 353	B.Sanders-Det 1553	B.Sanders-Det 5.06	T.Allen-Was 21	B.Sanders-Det 1663	B.Favre-GB 3899	S.Young-SF 7.63
T.Allen-Was 347	R.Watters-Phi 1411	D.Levens-GB 4.68	R.Watters-Phi 13	T.Allen-Was 1563	G.Frerotte-Was 3453	G.Frerotte-Was 7.35
E.Smith-Dal 327	T.Allen-Was 1353	J.Anderson-Atl 4.55	E.Smith-Dal 12	R.Watters-Phi 1541	B.Hebert-Atl 3152	B.Johnson-Min 7.26
B.Sanders-Det 307	E.Smith-Dal 1204	L.Johnson-Arz 4.50	B.Sanders-Det 11	E.Smith-Dal 1324	T.Aikman-Dal 3126	T.Detmer-Phi 7.26
A.Johnson-Car 300	A.Johnson-Car 1120	R.Smith-Min 4.27	A.Johnson-Car 6	A.Johnson-Car 1180	S.Mitchell-Det 2917	B.Favre-GB 7.18
Completion Percent	**TD Passes**	**TD Percent**	**INT Percent**	**Passer Rating**	**Passing Rank**	**Receptions**
S.Young-SF 67.7	B.Favre-GB 39	B.Favre-GB 7.2	S.Young-SF 1.9	S.Young-SF 97.2	B.Favre-GB 1625	J.Rice-SF 108
T.Aikman-Dal 63.7	B.Hebert-Atl 22	B.Johnson-Min 5.5	G.Frerotte-Was 2.3	B.Favre-GB 95.8	G.Frerotte-Was 1347	H.Moore-Det 106
B.Johnson-Min 62.7	S.Mitchell-Det 17	B.Hebert-Atl 4.5	B.Favre-GB 2.4	B.Johnson-Min 89.4	T.Aikman-Dal 1103	L.Centers-Arz 99
B.Hebert-Atl 60.2	B.Johnson-Min 17	S.Young-SF 4.4	K.Collins-Car 2.5	T.Detmer-Phi 80.8	S.Young-SF 1035	C.Carter-Min 96
D.Krieg-Chi 59.9		K.Graham-Arz 4.4	K.Graham-Arz 2.6	T.Aikman-Dal 80.1	T.Detmer-Phi 1011	B.Perriman-Det 94
Receiving Yards	**Receiving Average**	**Receiving TDs**	**Receiving Rank**	**Combined Net Yards**	**Total TDs**	**Total Points**
I.Bruce-SL 1338	H.Ellard-Was 19.50	I.Fryar-Phi 11	I.Bruce-SL 704	B.Mitchell-Was 1995	T.Allen-Was 21	J.Kasay-Car 145
J.Reed-Min 1320	J.Reed-Min 18.33	W.Walls-Car 10	J.Reed-Min 695	T.Hughes-NO 1943	E.Smith-Dal 15	J.Wilkins-SF 130
H.Moore-Det 1296	D.Beebe-GB 17.92	K.Jackson-GB 10	H.Moore-Det 693	E.Metcalf-Atl 1937	R.Watters-Phi 13	T.Allen-Was 126
J.Rice-SF 1254	M.Haynes-NO 17.86	C.Carter-Min 10	J.Rice-SF 667	G.Milburn-Det 1911		C.Boniol-Dal 120
I.Fryar-Phi 1195	R.Moore-Arz 17.52		I.Fryar-Phi 653	R.Watters-Phi 1855		S.Blanton-Was 118
Punt Average	**Field Goals**	**Field Goal Percent**	**Kickoff Returns**	**Kickoff Return Average**	**Punt Returns**	**Punt Return Average**
M.Turk-Was 45.1	J.Kasay-Car 37	B.Daluiso-NYG 88.9	T.Hughes-NO 70	M.Bates-Car 30.2	D.Howard-GB 58	A.Toomer-NYG 16.6
T.Sauerbrun-Chi 44.8	C.Boniol-Dal 32	C.Boniol-Dal 88.9	G.Milburn-Det 64	H.Walker-Dal 28.9	W.Oliver-Car 52	D.Howard-GB 15.1
S.Landeta-SL 44.8	J.Wilkins-SF 30	J.Wilkins-SF 88.2	B.Mitchell-Was 56	T.Hughes-NO 25.6	K.Martin-Dal 41	E.Kennison-SL 14.6
T.Thompson-SF 44.1	S.Blanton-Was 26	G.Anderson-Phi 86.2	L.McElroy-Arz 54	G.Milburn-Det 25.4	D.Carter-SF 36	W.Oliver-Car 11.5
			F.Winters-Phi 53	F.Winters-Phi 24.0	M.Seay-Phi 35	B.Mitchell-Was 11.2
Punt/Kick Return Yards	**Punt/Kick Return TDs**	**Interceptions**	**Interception Return Yards**	**Interception Return TDs**	**Sacks**	**Overall Rank**
T.Hughes-NO 1943	D.Howard-GB 3	K.Lyle-SL 9	K.Lyle-SL 152	A.Parker-SL 2	K.Greene-Car 14.5	B.Favre-GB 1781
G.Milburn-Det 1911	F.Winters-Phi 2	D.Woolford-Chi 6	L.Butler-GB 149		L.Lathon-Car 13.5	R.Watters-Phi 1763
B.Mitchell-Was 1516	A.Toomer-NYG 2	A.Williams-Arz 6	T.Vincent-Phi 144		W.Fuller-Phi 13.0	B.Sanders-Det 1697
D.Howard-GB 1335	E.Kennison-SL 2	E.Robinson-GB 6	A.Parker-SL 128		S.Rice-Arz 12.5	T.Allen-Was 1660
E.Metcalf-Atl 1330		M.Pope-SF 6	B.Blades-Det 112		R.Barker-SF 12.5	E.Smith-Dal 1464

The NFL's Most Important Man Passes

Pete Rozelle, whose vision took the NFL to unforeseen heights of popularity, influence, and affluence, died in 1996. Rozelle was a compromise choice as commissioner in 1960, but he procured a landmark television contract, merged the NFL and AFL, and helped shape the Super Bowl and Monday Night Football, among numerous innovations during his 29-year rule of the game. Football also lost three talented and colorful players from years past: "Chuckin' " Charlie Conerly, Arthur "Tarzan" White, and Tom "The Bomb" Tracy.

The Packers reached the Super Bowl for the first time since Vince Lombardi last took them there after the 1967 season. Mike Holmgren's Packers dominated, especially at home, winning all 10 games at Lambeau Field, including the playoffs. Carolina, which trailed only Green Bay in the conference in points scored and allowed, could not contain the Packers in a frigid NFC Championship Game. Panthers fans had traveled to another state for games during the club's first year, but they were rewarded with a state-of-the-art stadium and the quickest trip to the conference title game in NFL history—a distinction shared by Jacksonville—in year two.

San Francisco and Philadelphia each tied for the lead in their respective divisions, but tiebreakers made them wild cards—and foes in the playoffs. Defensive-minded Dallas won the NFC East despite having just the 12th-ranked offense in the conference. The Cowboys then opened the playoffs by throwing 40 points at the Vikings.

Mike Alstott, Stephen Davis, Brian Dawkins, and Defensive Rookie of the Year Simeon Rice debuted. Two receivers with plenty of flair and talent, Joe Horn and Terrell Owens, entered the league while two reliable pass catchers, Mark Ingram and Keith Jackson, retired. Longtime Brown Clay Mathews and Houston fixture Ray Childress ended their distinguished careers away from the chaos of those relocating franchises and in the relative peace of the NFC. It was the final season for Guy McIntyre, San Francisco's five-time Pro Bowl and three-time Super Bowl guard, while center Ray Donaldson ended his career with his sixth Pro Bowl. The self-proclaimed "punky QB," Jim McMahon, serving as Brett Favre's backup, got a Super Bowl ring in his last game.

1996 AFC

TEAM	W-L-T	PCT	POST	PTS	RA	RY	RY/A	RTD	FL	PA	PC	GPY	GPY/A	PTD	PI	PSY	PRAT
Eastern Division																	
NE	11-5	.688	DCS	**418**-313	427-434	1468-1502	3.4-3.5	15-14	12-11	628-596	**374**-322	4091-4055	6.5-6.8	27-17	15-23	190-252	83.2-68.9
Buf	10-6	.625	W	319-266	**563**-495	1901-1669	3.4-**3.4**	14-12	13-14	483-562	279-292	3558-3409	7.4-6.1	18-**11**	24-14	340-341	72.6-66.8
Ind	9-7	.563	#W	317-334	420-459	1448-1760	3.4-3.8	9-12	13-10	537-534	311-318	3544-3825	6.6-7.2	16-25	**11**-13	248-182	79.2-87.0
Mia	8-8	.500	—	339-325	460-411	1622-1536	3.5-3.7	14-10	13-16	504-539	300-337	3783-3888	7.5-7.2	22-29	**11**-20	240-233	**88.4**-86.7
NYJ	1-15	.063	—	279-454	407-539	1583-2200	3.9-4.1	8-19	16-15	**629-456**	339-**257**	3911-3542	6.2-7.8	22-33	30-11	286-178	64.7-95.5
Central Division																	
Pit	10-6	.625	ED	344-**257**	525-411	2299-1415	4.4-**3.4**	18-7	14-17	456-547	246-322	2990-3316	6.6-6.1	15-17	19-23	**149-369**	68.0-69.2
Jax	9-7	.563	#WDC	325-335	431-447	1650-1781	3.8-4.0	13-9	10-14	557-508	353-290	**4367**-3541	**7.8**-7.0	19-24	20-13	257-237	84.0-83.8
Cin	8-8	.500	—	372-369	478-444	1793-1643	3.8-3.7	14-15	**9**-10	563-571	316-319	3726-4028	6.6-7.1	25-22	16-**34**	294-202	79.4-**66.1**
Hou	8-8	.500	—	345-319	475-397	1950-1385	4.1-3.5	12-**5**	15-14	463-524	272-312	3296-3467	7.1-6.6	22-24	15-12	198-242	83.0-85.0
Bal	4-12	.250	—	371-441	416-508	1745-1920	4.2-3.8	10-18	13-7	570-537	335-350	4274-4115	7.5-7.7	**34**-27	20-15	296-146	87.6-93.4
Western Division																	
Den	**13**-3	**.813**	D	391-275	525-**345**	**2362-1331**	4.5-3.9	**20-5**	15-9	536-566	327-302	3662-3413	6.8-**6.0**	26-22	17-23	233-274	84.3-67.7
KC	9-7	.563	#	297-300	488-441	2009-1666	4.1-3.8	15-11	10-10	530-536	290-289	3093-3731	5.8-7.0	18-19	14-17	203-193	72.3-74.6
SD	8-8	.500	—	310-376	412-431	1312-1755	3.2-4.1	7-10	11-14	577-636	314-369	3654-3867	6.3-6.1	23-28	21-22	296-201	71.9-76.0
Oak	7-9	.438	—	340-293	456-463	2174-1676	**4.8**-3.6	7-7	12-9	533-513	311-284	3327-**3273**	6.2-6.4	28-22	19-17	249-252	79.4-75.3
Sea	7-9	.438	—	317-376	442-506	1997-2098	4.5-4.1	16-15	12-**18**	494-512	261-303	3216-3624	6.5-7.1	14-25	17-14	189-285	68.3-85.8
Aver	16	—	—	327	453	1744	3.8	12	13	532	307	3555	6.7	21	18	236	76.9

TEAM	1D	PENY	PNT	FGM/A	RTNY	RTNTD	OFFY/DEFY	NETY	NETTO	NP	PNP	DELP	PW	DELW	PRT	DR	YPD	DEL
Eastern Division																		
NE	**339**-305	716-**1189**	43.2-42.5	27/35-23/29	843-525	**6**-3	5369-5305	64	7	105	33	**72**	10.6	0.4	5.3/ 4.7	190-185	28.3-28.7	-0.4
Buf	294-283	831-607	41.5-43.2	24/29-23/36	536-744	3-5	5119-4737	382	-9	53	-4	57	9.3	0.7	4.4/ 4.2	**208**-217	24.6-**21.8**	2.8
Ind	288-305	**615**-970	45.7-43.5	**36/40**-23/28	723-546	5-1	4744-5403	-659	-1	-17	-59	42	7.6	1.4	5.1/ 5.9	183-**176**	25.9-30.7	-4.8
Mia	294-306	852-786	**46.3**-43.8	18/29-**13/17**	726-624	5-2	5165-5191	-26	12	14	46	-32	8.4	-0.3	**6.1**/ 5.3	184-183	28.1-28.4	-0.3
NYJ	319-304	819-902	44.5-42.1	17/24-23/28	304-813	3-3	5208-5564	-356	-20	-175	-110	-65	3.6	-2.6	3.7/ 6.6	197-188	26.4-29.6	-3.2
Central Division																		
Pit	296-286	665-746	40.7-43.8	23/30-21/26	585-518	**6**-3	5140-**4362**	778	7	87	93	-6	10.2	-0.2	4.5/**3.5**	194-191	26.5-22.8	3.7
Jax	325-315	1006-800	43.7-42.0	30/36-26/34	465-770	1-4	5760-5085	675	-3	-10	44	-54	7.8	1.3	5.6/ 5.4	183-178	31.5-28.6	2.9
Cin	332-317	678-768	44.3-44.4	23/28-25/30	525-674	4-5	5225-5469	-244	**19**	3	56	-53	8.1	-0.1	4.9/ 4.2	191-192	27.4-28.5	-1.1
Hou	287-271	812-672	43.7-**41.0**	32/38-25/33	441-473	1-6	5048-4610	438	-4	26	21	5	8.6	-0.6	5.3/ 5.2	184-187	27.4-24.7	2.8
Bal	338-351	818-744	43.2-42.4	19/25-28/31	504-622	1-5	5723-5889	-166	-11	-70	-58	-12	6.3	-2.3	5.6/ 6.3	178-179	32.2-32.9	-0.7
Western Division																		
Den	336-**261**	949-834	41.8-46.1	21/28-20/23	824-**432**	1-4	**5791**-4470	**1321**	0	**116**	**110**	6	**10.9**	**2.1**	5.2/ 3.8	179-187	**32.4**-23.9	**8.4**
KC	312-296	901-876	41.7-41.8	17/24-25/36	453-560	2-2	4899-5204	-305	3	-3	-13	10	7.9	1.1	4.4/ 5.2	180-187	27.2-27.8	-0.6
SD	272-321	969-991	45.6-44.3	29/36-26/33	**895**-932	2-5	4670-5421	-751	4	-66	-47	-19	6.3	1.6	4.3/ 4.4	196-202	23.8-26.8	-3.0
Oak	306-292	1266-965	40.1-41.9	24/31-25/34	756-529	3-2	5252-4697	555	-5	47	26	21	9.2	-2.2	4.3/ 4.5	189-194	27.8-24.2	3.6
Sea	268-325	879-804	43.6-42.3	28/34-31/34	608-945	3-**0**	5024-5437	-413	3	-59	-22	-37	6.5	0.5	4.5/ 5.3	193-193	26.0-28.2	-2.1
Aver	299	842	42.9	24/31	613	2	5062	—	—	—	—	—	—	—	5.1	94	27.6	—

Rushing Attempts	Rushing Yards	Rushing Average	Rushing TDs	Rushing Rank	Passing Yards	Passing Average
T.Davis-Den....345	T.Davis-Den....1538	N.Kaufman-Oak....5.83	C.Martin-NE....14	T.Davis-Den....1668	M.Brunell-Jax....4367	M.Brunell-Jax....7.84
E.George-Hou....335	J.Bettis-Pit....1431	E.Pegram-Pit....5.25	T.Davis-Den....13	J.Bettis-Pit....1541	D.Tate-Bal....4177	D.Tate-Bal....7.61
J.Bettis-Pit....320	E.George-Hou....1368	M.Brunell-Jax....4.95	J.Bettis-Pit....11	E.George-Hou....1448	D.Bledsoe-NE....4086	D.Marino-Mia....7.49
C.Martin-NE....316	A.Murrell-NYJ....1249	G.Hill-KC....4.78	Abdul-Jabbar-Mia....11	A.Murrell-NYJ....1309	J.Blake-Cin....3624	J.Kelly-Buf....7.41
Abdul-Jabbar-Mia....307	C.Martin-NE....1152	J.Bettis-Pit....4.47	M.Allen-KC....9	C.Martin-NE....1292	J.Elway-Den....3328	J.Elway-Den....7.14
Completion Percent	**TD Passes**	**TD Percent**	**INT Percent**	**Passer Rating**	**Passing Rank**	**Receptions**
M.Brunell-Jax....63.4	D.Tate-Bal....33	D.Tate-Bal....6.0	D.Bledsoe-NE....2.4	J.Elway-Den....89.2	D.Bledsoe-NE....1578	C.Pickens-Cin....100
J.Elway-Den....61.6	D.Bledsoe-NE....27	J.Hostetler-Oak....5.7	D.Marino-Mia....2.4	D.Tate-Bal....88.7	D.Tate-Bal....1494	T.Glenn-NE....90
J.Hostetler-Oak....60.2	J.Elway-Den....26	J.Elway-Den....5.6	J.Blake-Cin....2.6	D.Marino-Mia....87.8	M.Brunell-Jax....1479	T.Brown-Oak....90
D.Bledsoe-NE....59.9	J.Blake-Cin....24	C.Chandler-Hou....5.0	J.Harbaugh-Ind....2.7	M.Brunell-Jax....84.0	J.Blake-Cin....1372	K.McCardell-Jax....85
D.Marino-Mia....59.2	J.Hostetler-Oak....23	D.Marino-Mia....4.6	S.Bono-KC....3.0	D.Bledsoe-NE....83.7	J.Elway-Den....1234	T.Martin-SD....85
Receiving Yards	**Receiving Average**	**Receiving TDs**	**Receiving Rank**	**Combined Net Yards**	**Total TDs**	**Total Points**
J.Smith-Jax....1244	C.Sanders-Hou....18.38	T.Martin-SD....14	M.Jackson-Bal....671	T.Davis-Den....1848	C.Martin-NE....17	C.Blanchard-Ind....135
M.Jackson-Bal....1201	D.Alexander-Bal....17.73	M.Jackson-Bal....14	J.Smith-Jax....657	D.Meggett-NE....1783	T.Davis-Den....15	A.Del Greco-Hou....131
C.Pickens-Cin....1180	J.Galloway-Sea....17.32	C.Pickens-Cin....12	T.Martin-SD....656	A.Coleman-SD....1696	T.Martin-SD....14	A.Vinatieri-NE....120
T.Martin-SD....1171	C.Johnson-Pit....16.80	S.Sharpe-Den....10	C.Pickens-Cin....650	N.Kaufman-Oak....1565	M.Jackson-Bal....14	J.Carney-SD....118
T.Glenn-NE....1132	Q.Early-Buf....15.96		T.Brown-Oak....597	J.Bettis-Pit....1553	C.Pickens-Cin....12	M.Hollis-Jax....117
Punt Average	**Field Goals**	**Field Goal Percent**	**Kickoff Returns**	**Kickoff Return Average**	**Punt Returns**	**Punt Return Average**
J.Kidd-Mia....46.3	C.Blanchard-Ind....36	C.Blanchard-Ind....90.0	A.Coleman-SD....55	T.Vanover-KC....25.9	D.Meggett-NE....52	D.Gordon-SD....14.9
C.Gardocki-Ind....45.7	A.Del Greco-Hou....32	A.Del Greco-Hou....84.2	E.Moulds-Buf....52	E.Pegram-Pit....24.6	A.Hastings-Pit....37	R.Smith-Den....12.3
D.Bennett-SD....45.6	M.Hollis-Jax....30	M.Hollis-Jax....83.3	M.Gray-Hou....50	M.Gray-Hou....24.5	J.Lewis-Bal....36	T.Kinchen-Den....11.5
L.Johnson-Cin....45.4	J.Carney-SD....29	S.Christie-Buf....82.8	V.Hebron-Den....45	V.Hebron-Den....24.4	D.Gordon-SD....36	D.Meggett-NE....11.3
B.Hansen-NYJ....44.5	T.Peterson-Sea....28	T.Peterson-Sea....82.4		I.Spikes-Mia....24.3		C.Hudson-Jax....10.9
Punt/Kick Return Yards	**Punt/Kick Return TDs**	**Interceptions**	**Interception Return Yards**	**Interception Return TDs**	**Sacks**	**Overall Rank**
M.Gray-Hou....1429	Many....1	T.Braxton-Den....9	T.Buckley-Mia....164	A.Glenn-NYJ....2	B.Smith-Buf....13.5	M.Brunell-Jax....1905
D.Meggett-NE....1369		A.Ambrose-Cin....8	T.McDaniel-Oak....150	J.Belser-Ind....2	M.McCrary-Sea....13.5	T.Davis-Den....1833
J.Lewis-Bal....1222		R.Woodson-Pit....6	D.Williams-Sea....148			J.Blake-Cin....1709
A.Coleman-SD....1210		M.Collins-KC....6	T.Braxton-Den....128			D.Tate-Bal....1702
E.Moulds-Buf....1205		T.Buckley-Mia....6	R.Woodson-Pit....121			D.Bledsoe-NE....1605

A 50-Year-Old Franchise with No Past

Baltimore received a new team that was actually older than its previous team. The Cleveland Browns, originated in 1946 in the AAFC, came east but had to leave their history behind. The NFL decided that Cleveland would get an expansion team in 1999 while the Browns' name, colors, and records would remain in Cleveland and await a new franchise in a new stadium in 1999. Meanwhile, Browns players and management—*not* fired head coach Bill Belichick—moved to Baltimore. This team, now called the Ravens, reopened Memorial Stadium, beloved home of the departed Baltimore Colts from 1953–83. The Oilers, meanwhile, completed their final season in Houston with less uproar.

Belichick rejoined head coach Bill Parcells in New England, becoming an assistant and helping the Patriots go from 6–10 to the Super Bowl. Four talented rookies—Tedy Bruschi, Lawyer Milloy, Terry Glenn, and Adam Vinatieri—plus slightly more experienced Drew Bledsoe and Curtis Martin, pushed the Patriots past Buffalo for the division title. New England became the first AFC East team besides the Bills to win the conference championship since the Patriots last won it in 1985. Less than a month after losing Super Bowl XXXI, Parcells orchestrated his way out of New England to the New York Jets; several of his staff and players followed.

Jacksonville, along with Carolina in the NFC, reached the playoffs after just two seasons. Free agency—and giving the expansion clubs two picks per round in the 1995 draft—had enabled new teams to be on equal footing with established franchises. The Jaguars made the 1996 playoffs on Atlanta's missed chip-shot field goal in the final game before upsetting favored Buffalo—in Jim Kelly's final game—and Denver by identical 30–27 scores. The ride ended in the dark in Foxboro, with the Jaguars enduring an 11-minute blackout and 20–6 loss.

Although Eddie George, Marvin Harrison, Jonathon Ogden, Ray Lewis, Zach Thomas, and Eric Moulds all debuted, the rookie who made the biggest splash wrote his own story. Keyshawn Johnson, while playing for the 1–15 Jets, authored a book—*Just Give Me the Damn Ball*—that had few teammates seeking autographed copies.

1997 NFC

TEAM	W-L-T	PCT	POST	PTS	RA	RY	RY/A	RTD	FL	PA	PC	GPY	GPY/A	PTD	PI	PSY	PRAT
Eastern Division																	
NYG	10-5-1	.656	E	307-265	521-432	1988-1451	3.8-**3.4**	14-17	7-**17**	474-596	249-325	2763-3957	5.8-6.6	16-**10**	12-**27**	238-341	70.9-61.9
Was	8-7-1	.531	—	327-289	453-508	1615-2212	3.6-4.4	12-15	7-14	547-513	283-267	3581-3098	6.5-6.0	22-14	22-16	198-280	69.1-66.7
Phi	6-9-1	.406	—	317-372	465-476	1943-2009	4.2-4.2	11-16	16-12	587-490	330-259	**4009**-3201	6.8-6.5	22-20	16-14	362-278	78.5-75.1
Dal	6-10	.375	—	304-314	423-511	1637-1994	3.9-3.9	6-12	11-12	553-**473**	314-**253**	3454-**2717**	6.2-**5.7**	19-20	12-7	313-195	77.8-78.5
Arz	4-12	.250	—	283-379	395-524	1255-2180	3.2-4.2	9-13	20-5	**602**-491	317-279	3953-3461	6.6-7.0	19-23	22-15	495-215	68.6-81.7
Central Division																	
GB	**13**-3	**.813**	DCS	**422**-282	459-443	1909-1876	4.2-4.2	9-16	16-11	523-563	309-288	3896-3225	7.4-**5.7**	**35-10**	16-21	**191**-274	91.9-**59.0**
TB	10-6	.625	WD	299-**263**	479-420	1934-1617	4.0-3.8	15-10	11-13	404-518	224-325	2638-3342	6.5-6.5	21-13	12-13	196-331	80.4-79.2
Det	9-7	.563	W	379-306	447-471	**2464**-1833	**5.5**-3.9	**19**-15	11-8	540-507	304-281	3605-3401	6.7-6.7	19-15	17-17	271-287	75.4-72.1
Min	9-7	.563	WD	354-359	449-442	2041-1983	4.5-4.5	14-13	**6**-15	540-542	319-336	3537-3957	6.6-7.3	26-28	16-12	224-253	82.3-92.2
ChiB	4-12	.250	—	263-421	490-421	1746-1858	3.6-4.4	14-18	19-**17**	595-476	**336**-273	3501-3289	5.9-6.9	14-25	22-13	257-259	66.1-84.8
Western Division																	
SF	**13**-3	**.813**	DC	375-265	**523-386**	1969-**1366**	3.8-3.5	16-**5**	9-16	432-509	278-258	3432-3011	**7.9**-5.9	20-23	**11**-25	289-364	**93.6**-63.6
Car	7-9	.438	—	265-314	441-497	1770-1973	4.0-4.0	11-12	15-11	534-490	289-260	3156-3253	5.9-6.6	17-17	24-11	311-246	63.7-76.2
Atl	7-9	.438	—	320-361	442-409	1643-1666	3.7-4.1	8-18	13-10	484-496	273-275	3445-3794	7.1-7.6	26-24	**11**-18	372-354	87.2-81.2
NO	6-10	.375	—	237-327	417-496	1461-1764	3.5-3.6	9-11	22-15	458-518	228-293	2901-3289	6.3-6.3	13-21	33-16	317-**408**	49.4-76.3
SL	5-11	.313	—	299-359	443-440	1563-1687	3.5-3.8	15-10	15-14	526-543	271-288	3524-3675	6.7-6.8	14-26	15-25	326-296	69.9-71.3
Aver	16	—	—	332	455	1809	4.0	13	13	524	295	3510	6.7	21	16	280	77.2

TEAM	1D	PENY	PNT	FGM/A	RTNY	RTNTD	OFFY/DEFY	NETY	NETTO	NP	PNP	DELP	PW	DELW	PRT	DR	YPD	DEL
Eastern Division																		
NYG	273-310	1005-1056	40.5-42.1	22/32-19/25	**958**-608	5-3	4513-5067	-554	**25**	42	54	-12	9.1	1.5	4.2/ 3.8	202-208	22.3-24.4	-2.0
Was	300-292	**639**-849	44.6-42.5	16/24-21/25	664-499	**6**-3	4998-5030	-32	1	38	1	37	8.9	-0.4	4.5/ 4.1	194-193	25.8-26.1	-0.3
Phi	**326**-286	866-708	41.6-41.4	22/31-24/33	420-940	3-7	5590-4932	658	-6	-55	31	-86	6.6	-0.1	4.8/ 4.7	204-200	27.4-24.7	2.7
Dal	279-281	1058-757	41.8-43.6	**34/38**-20/27	642-576	4-4	4778-4516	262	-4	-10	6	-16	7.8	-1.8	4.7/ 4.7	191-187	25.0-24.1	0.9
Arz	295-298	775-981	43.8-43.9	19/29-30/35	692-730	4-6	4713-5426	-713	-22	-96	-147	51	5.6	-1.6	3.9/ 5.3	202-208	23.3-26.1	-2.8
Central Division																		
GB	325-288	718-945	45.0-42.5	24/30-24/30	844-560	**6**-4	5614-4827	787	0	**140**	66	**74**	**11.5**	1.5	**6.1**/ 3.5	186-201	**30.2**-24.0	**6.2**
TB	249-265	660-814	42.6-41.6	13/17-18/29	740-758	2-6	4376-4628	-252	3	36	-9	45	8.9	1.1	4.8/ 4.5	184-**176**	23.8-26.3	-2.5
Det	304-268	866-841	41.6-44.3	26/29-25/32	742-625	5-3	**5798**-4947	851	-3	73	59	14	9.8	-0.8	4.7/ 4.5	201-200	28.8-24.7	4.1
Min	293-325	800-668	42.1-41.9	19/27-23/30	585-732	2-**1**	5354-5687	-333	5	-5	-8	3	7.9	1.1	5.0/ 5.9	180-180	29.7-31.6	-1.9
ChiB	305-281	867-763	42.5-43.5	21/26-24/32	381-1055	0-7	4990-4888	102	-11	-158	-36	-122	4.1	-0.0	3.8/ 5.2	205-199	24.3-24.6	-0.2
Western Division																		
SF	294-**242**	979-742	40.3-41.8	29/36-16/**20**	848-476	5-3	5112-**4013**	**1099**	21	110	**176**	-66	10.8	**2.3**	6.0/**3.1**	189-190	27.0-**21.1**	5.9
Car	284-290	763-757	42.4-42.7	22/26-21/25	382-693	0-7	4615-4980	-365	-17	-49	-98	49	6.8	0.2	3.3/ 5.1	187-191	24.7-26.1	-1.4
Atl	281-274	773-872	39.3-42.6	23/27-**14/20**	597-**179**	2-3	4716-5106	-390	4	-41	-17	-24	7.0	0.0	5.3/ 5.2	193-192	24.4-26.6	-2.2
NO	229-280	811-895	**45.9-39.9**	23/27-28/36	690-1048	2-3	4045-4645	-600	-24	-90	-146	56	5.8	0.3	2.4/ 4.1	**208**-208	19.4-22.3	-2.9
SL	271-296	1065-**1064**	41.9-44.5	25/37-26/31	555-703	3-3	4761-5066	-305	9	-60	11	-71	6.5	-1.5	4.7/ 4.3	199-211	23.9-24.0	-0.1
Aver	292	862	42.7	24/30	636	4	5038	—	—	—	—	—	—	—	5.2	191	26.3	—

Rushing Attempts	Rushing Yards	Rushing Average	Rushing TDs	Rushing Rank	Passing Yards	Passing Average
B.Sanders-Det 335	B.Sanders-Det 2053	B.Sanders-Det 6.13	B.Sanders-Det 11	B.Sanders-Det 2163	B.Favre-GB 3867	S.Young-SF 8.51
D.Levens-GB 329	D.Levens-GB 1435	R.Smith-Min 5.46	R.Harris-Chi 10	D.Levens-GB 1505	S.Mitchell-Det 3484	C.Chandler-Atl 7.87
J.Anderson-Atl 290	R.Smith-Min 1266	C.Garner-Phi 4.72	L.Phillips-SL 8	R.Smith-Min 1326	T.Aikman-Dal 3283	B.Favre-GB 7.54
R.Watters-Phi 285	R.Watters-Phi 1110	C.Way-NYG 4.62		R.Watters-Phi 1180	T.Banks-SL 3254	J.Plummer-Arz 7.44
R.Harris-Chi 275	E.Smith-Dal 1074	F.Lane-Car 4.45		R.Harris-Chi 1133	B.Johnson-Min 3036	B.Hoying-Phi 6.99

Completion Percent	TD Passes	TD Percent	INT Percent	Passer Rating	Passing Rank	Receptions
S.Young-SF 67.7	B.Favre-GB 35	B.Favre-GB 6.8	S.Young-SF 1.7	S.Young-SF 104.7	B.Favre-GB 1469	H.Moore-Det 104
B.Johnson-Min 60.8	T.Dilfer-TB 21	C.Chandler-Atl 5.8	K.Graham-Arz 2.0	C.Chandler-Atl 95.1	S.Young-SF 1370	R.Moore-Arz 97
B.Favre-GB 59.3	B.Johnson-Min 20	T.Dilfer-TB 5.4	C.Chandler-Atl 2.0	B.Favre-GB 92.6	S.Mitchell-Det 1277	C.Carter-Min 89
C.Chandler-Atl 59.1	C.Chandler-Atl 20	S.Young-SF 5.3	T.Aikman-Dal 2.3	B.Johnson-Min 84.5	T.Aikman-Dal 1257	I.Fryar-Phi 86
E.Kramer-Chi 57.7		J.Plummer-Arz 5.1	T.Detmer-Phi 2.5	B.Hoying-Phi 83.8	T.Banks-SL 1177	A.Freeman-GB 81

Receiving Yards	Receiving Average	Receiving TDs	Receiving Rank	Combined Net Yards	Total TDs	Total Points
R.Moore-Arz 1584	R.Brooks-GB 16.83	C.Carter-Min 13	R.Moore-Arz 832	B.Sanders-Det 2358	B.Sanders-Det 14	B.Culpepper-Dal 126
I.Fryar-Phi 1316	J.Reed-Min 16.74	A.Freeman-GB 12	I.Fryar-Phi 688	K.Williams-Arz 2191	C.Carter-Min 13	G.Anderson-SF 125
H.Moore-Det 1293	M.Westbrook-Was 16.44	M.Irvin-Dal 9	H.Moore-Det 687	B.Mitchell-Was 2081	D.Levens-GB 12	R.Longwell-GB 120
A.Freeman-GB 1243	R.Moore-Arz 16.33	B.Emanuel-Atl 9	A.Freeman-GB 682	E.Guliford-NO 1986	A.Freeman-GB 12	J.Hanson-Det 117
M.Irvin-Dal 1180	M.Irvin-Dal 15.73		M.Irvin-Dal 635	G.Milburn-Det 1825		J.Wilkins-SL 107

Punt Average	Field Goals	Field Goal Percent	Kickoff Returns	Kickoff Return Average	Punt Returns	Punt Return Average
M.Royals-NO 45.9	B.Culpepper-Dal 34	B.Culpepper-Dal 91.9	K.Williams-Arz 59	M.Bates-Car 27.3	T.Kinchen-Atl 52	D.Palmer-Min 13.1
M.Turk-Was 45.1	G.Anderson-SF 29	J.Hanson-Det 89.7	G.Milburn-Det 55	E.Guliford-NO 26.2	A.Toomer-NYG 47	K.Williams-TB 13.0
C.Hentrich-GB 45.0	J.Hanson-Det 26	D.Brien-NO 85.2	H.Walker-Dal 50	K.Williams-Arz 24.7	G.Milburn-Det 47	D.Sanders-Dal 12.3
J.Feagles-Arz 44.3	J.Wilkins-SL 25	M.Andersen-Atl 85.2	D.Thompson-SL 49	B.Hanspard-Atl 24.7	E.Guliford-NO 47	B.Mitchell-Was 11.6
	R.Longwell-GB 24	J.Kasay-Car 84.6		M.Williams-Min 24.3	K.Williams-TB 46	K.Williams-Arz 11.6

Punt/Kick Return Yards	Punt/Kick Return TDs	Interceptions	Interception Return Yards	Interception Return TDs	Sacks	Overall Rank
K.Williams-Arz 1920	B.Mitchell-Was 2	R.McNeil-SL 9	T.Wooten-NYG 146	A.Williams-Arz 2	J.Randle-Min 15.5	B.Sanders-Det 2331
G.Milburn-Det 1748	B.Hanspard-Atl 2	K.Lyle-SL 8	R.McNeil-SL 127	D.Sharper-GB 2	Stubblefield-SF 15.0	D.Levens-GB 1715
E.Guliford-NO 1626		A.Williams-Arz 6	M.Hanks-SF 103	R.Brown-Det 2	M.Strahan-NYG 14.0	B.Favre-GB 1666
B.Mitchell-Was 1536		J.Sehorn-NYG 6	K.Lyle-SL 102		R.Porcher-Det 12.5	S.Young-SF 1599
M.Bates-Car 1289		M.Hanks-SF 6				R.Smith-Min 1430

Lion If by Land, Packer If by Air

For the first time since 1960, two players split the NFL MVP Award. Brett Favre, the leader of a balanced championship club in Green Bay, shared the award with Barry Sanders, a one-man show in Detroit. Sanders rushed for 2,000 yards in 14 games (he had just 53 yards through the first two games of the season). He became the third player to crack 2,000 yards and the first back to ever post 14 straight 100-yard games. Sanders twice ran for 200 yards, plus 184 yards in the season finale against the Jets to put the Lions in the playoffs.

Favre and Green Bay dominated, despite playing in a division in which four of the five teams had winning records and reached the playoffs. (Only the Bears were left out.) Favre threw 35 touchdowns as his Packers rolled to 13 wins and blew past Tampa Bay and San Francisco to reach their second straight Super Bowl. The ride ended abruptly in San Diego.

While the Giants cruised to a division title, the Cowboys finished under .500 and out of the playoffs for the first time since Emmitt Smith's rookie season of 1990. The running back wasn't forgotten, though. A new rule prohibited players from removing their helmet on the playing field to cut down on excessive celebrations was called the "Emmitt Smith rule" due to the running back's inclination for showing his face after scoring. Whether by coincidence or poor blocking, Smith scored just 4 touchdowns.

Don Hutson, the game's first game-breaking pass catcher, who retired from Green Bay in 1945 holding every NFL receiving record, died in 1997, as did Abe Gibron, one of Paul Brown's Messenger Guards, and Cleveland teammate Ray Renfro. Redskins owner Jack Kent Cooke died four months before the opening of a stadium named after him in Maryland. Atlanta Falcons owner and founder Rankin Smith also died. Richard Dent, Sam Mills, Mark Tuinei, Jesse Sapolu, Chris Spielman, and Herschel Walker all played their final games. The league restocked with Orlando Pace, Jake Plummer, Chad Lewis, Darren Sharper, twins Ronde and Tiki Barber, and Offensive Rookie of the Year Warrick Dunn.

1997 AFC

TEAM	W-L-T	PCT	POST	PTS	RA	RY	RY/A	RTD	FL	PA	PC	GPY	GPY/A	PTD	PI	PSY	PRAT
Eastern Division																	
NE	10-6	.625	ED	369-289	398-436	1464-1616	3.7-3.7	6-16	**7**-13	532-619	321-368	3808-3772	7.2-6.1	**31-14**	15-19	258-303	89.9-71.8
Mia	9-7	.563	#W	339-327	430-443	1343-1813	3.1-4.1	18-9	8-17	576-530	332-329	3945-3782	6.8-7.1	16-23	12-10	153-231	79.2-90.1
NYJ	9-7	.563	#	348-287	431-470	1485-1899	3.4-4.0	10-9	12-7	564-558	319-304	3555-3663	6.3-6.6	20-23	10-18	313-242	79.9-75.1
Buf	6-10	.375	—	255-367	422-493	1782-1792	4.2-3.6	12-11	17-7	546-502	293-287	3213-3405	5.9-6.8	14-17	25-15	338-344	60.8-76.8
Ind	3-13	.188	—	313-401	450-438	1727-2034	3.8-4.6	10-18	11-13	523-**453**	317-**261**	3560-**3067**	6.8-6.8	16-26	17-12	418-247	77.6-86.4
Central Division																	
Pit	11-5	.688	#DC	372-307	**572**-403	**2479-1318**	4.3-**3.3**	19-**5**	14-14	466-554	253-295	3215-3681	6.9-6.6	22-24	19-20	**152**-294	74.8-73.5
Jax	11-5	.688	#W	394-318	454-455	1720-1734	3.8-3.8	20-12	11-15	504-532	313-320	3922-3835	**7.8**-7.2	20-24	**9**-14	218-331	**92.0**-86.3
Ten	8-8	.500	—	333-310	541-414	2414-1573	4.5-3.8	17-12	13-**18**	420-543	220-321	2704-3898	6.4-7.2	15-21	13-14	199-240	71.6-83.4
Cin	7-9	.438	—	355-405	452-514	1966-2223	4.3-4.3	**23**-15	13-10	504-542	302-309	3603-3668	7.1-6.8	21-30	**9**-13	287-209	88.3-86.2
Bal	6-9-1	.406	—	326-345	420-470	1589-1690	3.8-3.6	7-17	17-11	586-556	338-332	3929-3966	6.7-7.1	25-20	16-17	227-293	80.9-80.8
Western Division																	
KC	**13**-3	**.813**	D	375-**232**	529-413	2171-1621	4.1-3.9	15-8	10-13	493-507	281-271	3129-3618	6.3-7.1	20-15	10-**21**	236-**359**	81.1-**69.0**
Den	12-4	.750	WDCS*	**472**-287	520-**381**	2378-1803	**4.6**-4.7	18-10	10-13	513-526	287-290	3704-3166	7.2-**6.0**	27-20	11-18	210-298	87.4-71.5
Sea	8-8	.500	—	365-362	404-455	1800-1731	4.5-3.8	13-10	11-16	**609**-462	**359**-276	**4187**-3356	6.9-7.3	26-19	21-13	228-238	79.7-84.1
Oak	4-12	.250	—	324-419	360-525	1588-2246	4.4-4.3	9-19	14-12	529-552	294-324	3944-4109	7.5-7.4	29-21	10-10	430-239	89.9-87.1
SD	4-12	.250	—	266-425	409-453	1416-1698	3.5-3.7	5-12	14-11	565-568	291-297	3475-3632	6.2-6.4	12-31	21-15	386-164	62.2-79.5
Aver	16	—	—	332	455	1809	4.0	13	13	524	295	3510	6.7	21	16	280	77.2

TEAM	1D	PENY	PNT	FGM/A	RTNY	RTNTD	OFFY/DEFY	NETY	NETTO	NP	PNP	DELP	PW	DELW	PRT	DR	YPD	DEL
Eastern Division																		
NE	267-322	845-763	45.2-44.4	25/29-20/29	833-650	5-3	5014-5085	-71	10	80	34	46	10.0	0.0	5.7/ 4.1	181-186	27.7-27.3	0.4
Mia	311-299	783-892	43.6-42.5	28/36-25/35	427-630	3-4	5135-5364	-229	7	12	9	3	8.3	0.7	5.7/ 5.9	173-**174**	29.7-30.8	-1.1
NYJ	291-301	**678**-832	42.8-42.0	28/**41**-18/27	**1053**-559	8-1	4727-5320	-593	3	61	-37	**98**	9.5	-0.5	4.9/ 4.8	188-192	25.1-27.7	-2.6
Buf	268-265	742-992	41.4-42.0	24/30-37/46	503-725	0-9	4657-4853	-196	-20	-112	-96	-16	5.2	0.8	3.2/ 4.7	**206**-200	22.6-**24.3**	-1.7
Ind	301-280	880-861	**45.3**-46.1	**32/41**-27/31	482-776	5-2	4869-4854	15	-3	-88	-11	-77	5.8	-2.8	4.3/ 5.2	181-**174**	26.9-27.9	-1.0
Central Division																		
Pit	326-285	861-708	42.6-42.5	22/25-29/35	475-541	3-2	5542-4705	837	1	65	74	-9	9.6	**1.4**	5.0/ 4.5	179-179	**31.0**-26.3	4.7
Jax	308-318	914-800	44.9-41.9	31/36-17/25	557-425	3-3	5424-5238	186	9	76	52	24	9.9	1.1	**6.4**/ 5.4	175-179	**31.0**-29.3	1.7
Ten	288-292	814-830	41.6-43.6	27/35-22/30	572-478	4-2	4919-5231	-312	6	23	-2	25	8.6	-0.6	4.6/ 5.6	181-183	27.2-28.6	-1.4
Cin	310-351	877-951	42.9-44.7	12/16-24/29	384-433	2-3	5282-5682	-400	1	-50	-29	-21	6.8	0.3	5.7/ 5.5	182-178	29.0-31.9	-2.9
Bal	292-306	777-828	42.7-44.0	26/34-24/34	805-578	3-2	5291-5363	-72	-5	-19	-26	7	7.5	-1.0	5.2/ 5.2	196-199	27.0-26.9	0.0
Western Division																		
KC	315-278	1035-977	42.0-41.3	26/27-24/33	815-**403**	7-**0**	5064-4880	184	**14**	143	71	72	11.6	**1.4**	5.0/ 4.4	192-182	26.4-26.8	-0.4
Den	**340-258**	1006-**1118**	43.3-43.5	28/39-**14/19**	874-428	**10**-5	**5872-4671**	**1201**	10	**185**	**140**	45	**12.6**	-0.6	6.0/**4.0**	195-186	30.1-25.1	5.0
Sea	331-286	911-820	40.3-42.0	22/28-31/34	444-835	4-9	5759-4849	910	-3	3	64	-61	8.1	-0.1	5.1/ 5.4	189-192	30.5-25.3	**5.2**
Oak	263-345	976-977	45.0-**39.4**	13/22-38/43	359-623	3-4	5102-6116	-1014	-2	-95	-93	-2	5.6	-1.6	5.7/ 6.2	196-190	26.0-32.2	-6.2
SD	251-308	1101-784	44.1-43.6	26/31-25/26	746-803	**10**-7	4505-5166	-661	-9	-159	-91	-68	4.0	-0.0	3.7/ 5.2	199-200	22.6-25.8	-3.2
Aver	292	862	42.7	24/30	636	2	5038	—	—	—	—	—	—	—	5.2	94	27.4	—

Rushing Attempts	Rushing Yards	Rushing Average	Rushing TDs	Rushing Rank	Passing Yards	Passing Average
J.Bettis-Pit 375	T.Davis-Den 1750	S.McNair-Ten 6.67	T.Davis-Den 15	T.Davis-Den 1900	J.George-Oak 3917	M.Brunell-Jax 7.54
T.Davis-Den 369	J.Bettis-Pit 1665	K.Stewart-Pit 5.41	Abdul-Jabbar-Mia 15	J.Bettis-Pit 1735	D.Marino-Mia 3780	J.George-Oak 7.52
E.George-Ten 357	E.George-Ten 1399	C.Dillon-Cin 4.85	K.Stewart-Pit 11	E.George-Ten 1459	D.Bledsoe-NE 3706	J.Elway-Den 7.24
A.Murrell-NYJ 300	N.Kaufman-Oak 1294	N.Kaufman-Oak 4.76	M.Allen-KC 11	N.Kaufman-Oak 1354	W.Moon-Sea 3678	D.Bledsoe-NE 7.10
Abdul-Jabbar-Mia 283	C.Martin-NE 1160	T.Davis-Den 4.74	C.Dillon-Cin 10	C.Dillon-Cin 1229	J.Elway-Den 3635	W.Moon-Sea 6.97

Completion Percent	TD Passes	TD Percent	INT Percent	Passer Rating	Passing Rank	Receptions
J.Harbaugh-Ind 61.2	J.George-Oak 29	J.George-Oak 5.6	J.Harbaugh-Ind 1.3	M.Brunell-Jax 91.2	J.George-Oak 1744	T.Brown-Oak 104
M.Brunell-Jax 60.7	D.Bledsoe-NE 28	J.Elway-Den 5.4	N.O'Donnell-NYJ 1.5	J.George-Oak 91.2	D.Marino-Mia 1530	K.McCardell-Jax 85
D.Bledsoe-NE 60.2	J.Elway-Den 27	D.Bledsoe-NE 5.4	M.Brunell-Jax 1.6	D.Bledsoe-NE 87.7	J.Elway-Den 1513	J.Smith-Jax 82
W.Moon-Sea 59.3	W.Moon-Sea 25	K.Stewart-Pit 4.8	J.George-Oak 1.7	J.Elway-Den 87.5	M.Brunell-Jax 1451	Y.Thigpen-Pit 79
D.Marino-Mia 58.2	K.Stewart-Pit 21	W.Moon-Sea 4.7	E.Grbac-KC 1.9	J.Harbaugh-Ind 86.2	D.Bledsoe-NE 1393	O.McDuffie-Mia 76

Receiving Yards	Receiving Average	Receiving TDs	Receiving Rank	Combined Net Yards	Total TDs	Total Points
T.Brown-Oak 1408	J.McKnight-Sea 18.74	R.Smith-Den 12	Y.Thigpen-Pit 734	T.Davis-Den 2030	Abdul-Jabbar-Mia 16	M.Hollis-Jax 134
Y.Thigpen-Pit 1398	Y.Thigpen-Pit 17.70	J.Jett-Oak 12	T.Brown-Oak 729	J.Lewis-Bal 2025	T.Davis-Den 15	J.Elam-Den 124
J.Smith-Jax 1324	J.Jett-Oak 17.48	J.Galloway-Sea 12	J.Smith-Jax 682	T.Vanover-KC 1833	R.Smith-Den 12	J.Hall-NYJ 120
R.Smith-Den 1180	R.Smith-Den 16.86	D.Alexander-Bal 9	R.Smith-Den 650	J.Bettis-Pit 1775	J.Jett-Oak 12	O.Mare-Mia 117
K.McCardell-Jax 1164	R.Dudley-Oak 16.40		K.McCardell-Jax 607	N.Kaufman-Oak 1697	J.Galloway-Sea 12	C.Blanchard-Ind 117

Punt Average	Field Goals	Field Goal Percent	Kickoff Returns	Kickoff Return Average	Punt Returns	Punt Return Average
T.Tupa-NE 45.8	C.Blanchard-Ind 32	M.Stover-KC 96.3	D.Howard-Oak 61	A.Glenn-NYJ 26.5	L.Johnson-NYJ 51	J.Lewis-Bal 15.6
C.Gardocki-Ind 45.3	M.Hollis-Jax 31	N.Johnson-Pit 88.0	A.Bailey-Ind 55	T.Vanover-KC 25.6	E.Metcalf-SD 45	D.Gordon-Den 13.6
L.Araguz-Oak 45.0	O.Mare-Mia 28	A.Vinatieri-NE 86.2	T.Vanover-KC 51	D.Dunn-Cin 25.6	D.Meggett-NE 45	L.Johnson-NYJ 12.1
B.Barker-Jax 44.9	J.Hall-NYJ 28	M.Hollis-Jax 86.1	S.Broussard-Sea 50	D.Meggett-NE 24.7	D.Gordon-Den 40	R.Barlow-Jax 11.4
D.Bennett-SD 44.6	A.Del Greco-Ten 27	S.Christie-Buf 80.0		W.Blackwell-Pit 24.7	R.Barlow-Jax 36	T.Vanover-KC 10.9

Punt/Kick Return Yards	Punt/Kick Return TDs	Interceptions	Interception Return Yards	Interception Return TDs	Sacks	Overall Rank
T.Vanover-KC 1691	E.Metcalf-SD 3	D.Williams-Sea 8	M.McMillian-KC 274	O.Smith-NYJ 3	B.Smith-Buf 14.0	T.Davis-Den 2044
D.Howard-Oak 1528	D.Gordon-Den 3	M.McMillian-KC 8	D.Williams-Sea 172	M.McMillian-KC 3	M.Sinclair-Sea 12.0	J.Bettis-Pit 1800
J.Lewis-Bal 1342	T.Vanover-KC 2	O.Smith-NYJ 6	O.Smith-NYJ 158		P.Boulware-Bal 11.5	J.George-Oak 1788
D.Meggett-NE 1283	J.Lewis-Bal 2	W.Clay-NE 6	M.Robertson-Ten 127		D.Williams-KC 10.5	J.Elway-Den 1741
A.Bailey-Ind 1225	L.Johnson-NYJ 2		J.Belser-Ind 121		D.Footman-Ind 10.5	M.Brunell-Jax 1728

Broncos Bust Out of Super Rut

The Chiefs had the conference's best record, but the high-octane Broncos outscored them by 97 points during the season. Their head-to-head divisional playoff game seemed to play to the strength of the NFL's top defense in Kansas City, but Denver won the low-scoring affair, 14 10. The Broncos then knocked off Pittsburgh to reach their first Super Bowl since a 55–10 humiliation to San Francisco after the 1989 season. A double-digit underdog against defending champion Green Bay, Denver's balanced attack resulted in the franchise's first championship after 37 years of existence and Super Bowl letdowns in which four different NFC opponents had outscored them, 163–50.

Jeff George, benched by Atlanta coach June Jones for most of 1996 after throwing a sideline tantrum, prospered in his new home in Oakland. He led the conference in passing yards and threw a career-high 29 touchdowns against just 9 interceptions. The NFL decreed the Kingdome to be the site of the NFL's 10,000th game on October 5. The host Seahawks beat the Oilers, 16–13.

The Oilers found their new home to be mostly empty. After bolting Houston for Nashville via Memphis, the club drew just 28,000 fans per game to the Liberty Bowl. The Oilers moved up plans to move to Nashville in 1998, a year ahead of schedule; they would play in cozy Vanderbilt Stadium until completion of a new NFL facility in the city. Robert Irsay, who traded franchises in 1972—the Los Angeles Rams franchise for the Baltimore Colts—and a little more than decade later surreptitiously moved the Colts to Indianapolis, died in 1997.

Marcus Allen retired as the all-time leader with 123 rushing touchdowns, as second in career rushing attempts (3,022), and sixth in rushing yards (12,243). Also calling it quits were Boomer Esiason, Gary Zimmerman, Michael Dean Perry, and Anthony Miller, plus Steve Tasker and Pete Metzelaars, key components on Buffalo's four straight AFC championship teams. Earnest Byner, haunted by a crucial fumble in the 1987 AFC Championship Game, retired with 12,866 total yards, 72 touchdowns, and 31 fumbles. Jon Kitna, Corey Dillon, Mike Vrabel, Priest Holmes, Tony Gonzalez, and Defensive Rookie of the Year Peter Boulware debuted.

1998 NFC

TEAM	W-L-T	PCT	POST	PTS	RA	RY	RY/A	RTD	FL	PA	PC	GPY	GPY/A	PTD	PI	PSY	PRAT
Eastern Division																	
Dal	10-6	.625	E	381-**275**	499-401	2014-1619	4.0-4.0	**21**-10	7-12	474-553	279-290	3546-3767	7.5-6.8	17-21	**8**-14	**110**-222	87.2-76.3
Arz	9-7	.563	WD	325-378	450-492	1627-1989	3.6-4.0	18-18	16-19	552-518	326-299	3768-3526	6.8-6.8	17-21	20-20	286-250	74.9-76.0
NYG	8-8	.500	—	287-309	474-476	1889-2004	4.0-4.2	10-13	9-7	507-521	265-282	2822-3503	5.6-6.7	18-17	15-19	256-336	68.3-**70.9**
Was	6-10	.375	—	319-421	401-531	1685-2436	4.2-4.6	15-24	15-8	565-493	304-281	3724-3112	6.6-**6.3**	24-21	14-13	399-194	78.2-79.1
Phi	3-13	.188	—	161-344	427-528	1775-2416	4.2-4.6	10-18	8-8	534-**449**	282-**249**	2730-**3001**	5.1-6.7	7-18	18-9	317-281	57.7-81.2
Central Division																	
Min	**15**-1	**.938**	D	**556**-296	450-404	1936-1614	4.3-4.0	17-12	**4**-15	533-555	327-320	4492-3699	8.4-6.7	**41**-17	16-19	164-247	**101.5**-73.8
GB	11-5	.688	W	408-319	447-390	1526-1442	3.4-3.7	7-**7**	11-10	**575**-540	**361**-296	4340-3401	7.5-**6.3**	33-23	23-13	230-336	88.3-78.2
TB	8-8	.500	—	314-295	**523**-415	2148-1583	4.1-3.8	12-12	13-14	449-473	234-274	2787-3014	6.2-6.4	21-**15**	18-12	181-252	70.3-76.9
Det	5-11	.313	—	306-378	441-487	1955-2102	4.4-4.3	12-15	12-9	489-474	274-284	3398-3276	6.9-6.9	17-23	13-12	268-261	78.2-86.4
ChiB	4-12	.250	—	276-368	454-479	1713-1875	3.8-3.9	9-12	21-14	494-456	284-292	3277-3401	6.6-7.5	16-27	13-14	224-173	77.5-93.5
Western Division																	
Atl	14-2	.875	DCS	442-289	516-**361**	2101-**1203**	4.1-**3.3**	18-**7**	9-**25**	424-551	237-311	3744-3806	**8.8**-6.9	28-22	15-19	358-275	92.7-76.8
SF	12-4	.750	WDC	479-328	491-395	**2544**-1610	**5.2**-4.1	19-13	15-12	556-566	347-294	**4510**-3992	8.1-7.1	**41**-25	15-**21**	254-259	101.2-74.0
NO	6-10	.375	—	305-359	374-467	1325-1700	3.5-3.6	6-13	14-11	535-539	278-328	3514-4256	6.6-7.9	19-24	19-**21**	376-288	69.8-84.3
Car	4-12	.250	—	336-413	405-491	1458-2133	3.6-4.3	11-14	17-14	507-501	292-298	3624-3937	7.1-7.9	25-30	18-19	302-228	81.5-88.6
SL	4-12	.250	—	285-378	395-479	1385-2049	3.5-4.3	17-11	15-7	556-475	314-256	3381-3180	6.1-6.7	12-28	18-16	294-**349**	68.2-80.5
Aver	16	—	—	341	452	1803	4.0	13	12	516	292	3536	6.8	22	17	257	78.3

TEAM	1D	PENY	PNT	FGM/A	RTNY	RTNTD	OFFY/DEFY	NETY	NETTO	NP	PNP	DELP	PW	DELW	PRT	DR	YPD	DEL
Eastern Division																		
Dal	308-276	1106-917	42.8-42.4	29/**35**-16/**19**	743-331	4-**1**	5450-5164	286	11	106	68	38	10.6	-0.7	6.6/ 5.3	177-185	30.8-27.9	2.9
Arz	315-321	758-954	41.2-43.9	23/33-24/30	530-686	1-5	5109-5265	-156	3	-53	-1	-52	6.7	**2.3**	4.6/ 4.6	203-203	25.2-25.9	-0.8
NYG	263-286	946-967	45.2-42.1	21/27-23/30	469-819	4-4	4455-5171	-716	2	-22	-52	30	7.4	0.6	3.8/**4.3**	194-201	23.0-25.7	-2.8
Was	295-303	975-824	43.5-43.1	13/23-23/28	696-430	1-5	5010-5354	-344	-8	-102	-61	-41	5.4	0.5	4.7/ 4.8	**204**-203	24.6-26.4	-1.8
Phi	259-286	852-904	41.7-42.5	14/21-24/32	443-830	0-3	4188-5136	-948	-9	-183	-115	-68	3.4	-0.4	2.8/ 5.1	188-**184**	22.3-27.9	-5.6
Central Division																		
Min	335-300	1045-**1167**	44.7-42.6	**35/35**-17/**19**	630-546	6-6	6264-5066	1198	14	**260**	**156**	**104**	**14.5**	0.5	**7.2**/ 4.7	175-185	**35.8**-27.4	**8.4**
GB	329-246	**681**-828	42.9-43.6	29/33-23/27	523-549	6-6	5636-4507	1129	-11	89	50	39	10.2	0.8	5.5/ 4.6	187-191	30.1-23.6	6.5
TB	262-**244**	840-669	41.2-42.0	21/28-26/30	771-494	3-4	4754-**4345**	409	-5	19	14	5	8.5	-0.5	4.2/ 4.7	188-187	25.3-**23.2**	2.1
Det	278-308	1019-791	42.8-42.7	29/33-25/30	344-669	3-5	5085-5117	-32	-4	-72	-19	-53	6.2	-1.2	5.1/ 5.2	189-186	26.9-27.5	-0.6
ChiB	264-300	714-852	42.6-42.8	21/26-26/31	420-495	5-3	4766-5103	-337	-6	-92	-52	-40	5.7	-1.7	5.0/ 5.9	187-**184**	25.5-27.7	-2.2
Western Division																		
Atl	319-267	841-858	40.0-42.8	23/28-**15**/20	528-336	7-6	5487-4734	753	**20**	153	143	10	11.8	2.2	6.3/ 4.9	192-195	28.6-24.3	4.3
SF	**381**-297	1156-800	41.1-42.1	18/27-19/32	584-645	1-**1**	**6800**-5343	**1457**	3	151	133	18	11.8	0.2	6.6/ 4.9	202-194	33.7-27.5	6.1
NO	258-326	928-1164	**45.4**-43.5	20/22-26/33	**874**-835	**10**-3	4463-5668	-1205	-1	-54	-104	50	6.7	-0.6	4.2/ 5.6	197-192	22.7-29.5	-6.9
Car	261-315	931-892	40.7-44.0	19/26-30/31	759-**273**	4-2	4780-5842	-1062	-2	-77	-97	20	6.1	-2.1	4.9/ 5.9	194-193	24.6-30.3	-5.6
SL	281-282	945-915	44.2-**41.6**	20/26-24/27	616-846	3-4	4472-4880	-408	-10	-93	-74	-19	5.7	-1.7	4.0/ 4.6	198-198	22.6-24.6	-2.1
Aver	291	922	43.2	24/30	625	4	5083	—	—	—	—	—	—	—	5.3	191	26.6	—

Rushing Attempts	Rushing Yards	Rushing Average	Rushing TDs	Rushing Rank	Passing Yards	Passing Average
J.Anderson-Atl 410	J.Anderson-Atl 1846	G.Hearst-SF 5.06	J.Anderson-Atl 14	J.Anderson-Atl 1986	B.Favre-GB 4212	C.Chandler-Atl 9.65
B.Sanders-Det 343	G.Hearst-SF 1570	R.Smith-Min 4.77	E.Smith-Dal 13	G.Hearst-SF 1640	S.Young-SF............4170	B.Culpepper-Min.....8.72
E.Smith-Dal 319	B.Sanders-Det.......1491	T.Allen-Was............4.73	L.Hoard-Min.................9	B.Sanders-Det.......1531	J.Plummer-Arz.......3737	S.Young-SF.............8.07
G.Hearst-SF 310	E.Smith-Dal 1332	J.Anderson-Atl 4.50		E.Smith-Dal 1462	B.Culpepper-Min....3704	B.Favre-GB 7.64
A.Murrell-Arz............274	R.Smith-Min...........1187	B.Sanders-Det 4.35		R.Smith-Min...........1247	T.Green-Was..........3441	S.Beuerlein-Car......7.62
Completion Percent	**TD Passes**	**TD Percent**	**INT Percent**	**Passer Rating**	**Passing Rank**	**Receptions**
B.Favre-GB 63.0	S.Young-SF................36	B.Culpepper-Min.......8.0	T.Aikman-Dal 1.6	B.Culpepper-Min...106.0	S.Young-SF............1785	F.Sanders-Arz............89
S.Beuerlein-Car......63.0	B.Culpepper-Min........34	C.Chandler-Atl 7.6	C.Batch-Det 2.0	S.Young-SF...........101.1	B.Culpepper-Min....1622	A.Freeman-GB...........84
S.Young-SF.............62.3	B.Favre-GB 31	S.Young-SF...............7.0	T.Green-Was.............2.2	C.Chandler-Atl 100.9	T.Green-Was..........1396	J.Rice-SF 82
B.Culpepper-Min.....60.9	C.Chandler-Atl 25	B.Favre-GB 5.6	S.Young-SF...............2.3	T.Aikman-Dal 88.5	B.Favre-GB............1341	H.Moore-Det..............82
E.Kramer-Chi..........60.4	T.Green-Was..............23	S.Beuerlein-Car........5.0	B.Culpepper-Min.......2.4	S.Beuerlein-Car......88.2	C.Chandler-Atl 1222	C.Carter-Min..............78
Receiving Yards	**Receiving Average**	**Receiving TDs**	**Receiving Rank**	**Combined Net Yards**	**Total TDs**	**Total Points**
A.Freeman-GB.......1424	R.Moss-Min 19.03	R.Moss-Min 17	A.Freeman-GB.........782	B.Mitchell-Was.......2357	R.Moss-Min 17	G.Anderson-Min 164
R.Moss-Min 1313	T.Martin-Atl 17.89	T.Owens-SF..............14	R.Moss-Min 742	J.Anderson-Atl 2165	J.Anderson-Atl 16	R.Longwell-GB 128
T.Martin-Atl 1181	T.Mathis-Atl...........17.75	A.Freeman-GB...........14	J.Rice-SF 624	G.Hearst-SF 2105	E.Smith-Dal 15	B.Culpepper-Dal 127
J.Rice-SF 1157	B.Davis-Dal...........17.72	C.Carter-Min.............12	T.Mathis-Atl..............623	R.Preston-GB 1918	T.Owens-SF...............15	M.Andersen-Atl........120
F.Sanders-Arz........1145	A.Freeman-GB......16.95	T.Mathis-Atl...............11	T.Martin-Atl 621	G.Milburn-Chi 1886	A.Freeman-GB...........14	J.Hanson-Det...........114
Punt Average	**Field Goals**	**Field Goal Percent**	**Kickoff Returns**	**Kickoff Return Average**	**Punt Returns**	**Punt Return Average**
M.Royals-NO 45.6	G.Anderson-Min 35	G.Anderson-Min ...100.0	G.Milburn-Chi 62	T.Fair-Det................28.0	J.McPhail-SF 47	D.Sanders-Dal 15.6
B.Maynard-NYG 45.2	R.Longwell-GB 29	D.Brien-NO 90.9	B.Mitchell-Was...........59	T.Dwight-Atl 27.0	R.Preston-GB 44	J.Green-TB 15.1
M.Berger-Min..........44.7	J.Hanson-Det............29	R.Longwell-GB 87.9	M.Bates-Car 59	R.Preston-GB 26.3	W.Oliver-Car..............44	A.Hastings-NO........14.0
R.Tuten-SL.............44.2	B.Culpepper-Dal 29	J.Hanson-Det..........87.9	R.Preston-GB 57	M.Bates-Car 25.1	B.Mitchell-Was...........44	G.Milburn-Chi 11.6
M.Turk-Was 44.1	M.Andersen-Atl.........23	B.Culpepper-Dal.....82.9	E.Metcalf-Arz.............57	G.Milburn-Chi 25.0	E.Metcalf-Arz.............43	B.Mitchell-Was........11.5
Punt/Kick Return Yards	**Punt/Kick Return TDs**	**Interceptions**	**Interception Return Yards**	**Interception Return TDs**	**Sacks**	**Overall Rank**
R.Preston-GB 1895	R.Preston-GB 3	K.Lassiter-Arz.............8	J.Hitchcock-Min 242	J.Hitchcock-Min 3	R.White-GB 16.0	S.Young-SF............2299
B.Mitchell-Was.......1843	G.Milburn-Chi 3	J.Hitchcock-Min 7	S.Knight-NO 171	S.Knight-NO 2	M.Strahan-NYG......15.0	J.Anderson-Atl 2156
G.Milburn-Chi 1841	D.Sanders-Dal 2	R.Buchanan-Atl 7	D.Sanders-Dal 153	P.Ellsworth-NYG 2	K.Greene-Car 15.0	G.Hearst-SF 1918
T.Fair-Det...............1617	T.Fair-Det.....................2	S.Knight-NO 6	R.Kelly-NO...............104	E.Davis-Car 2	C.Doleman-SF 15.0	B.Culpepper-Min....1763
E.Metcalf-Arz.........1513			R.Buchanan-Atl 102		H.Douglas-Phi 12.5	B.Sanders-Det.......1676

Falcons and Cardinals in Unaccustomed Perches

The perennially downtrodden Cardinals reached the playoffs for the first time since relocating to the desert a decade earlier, winning six times on field goals in the final four minutes. Chris Jacke, playing just his fourth game as a Cardinal, booted the team into the playoffs with a 46-yarder on the final play of the season. Arizona then stunned Dallas for the franchise's first playoff victory since 1947, when the Cardinals were in Chicago and the NFL had 20 fewer teams.

The 1998 season featured 15- and 14-win teams in the NFC—the Vikings and Falcons, respectively—who met in a thrilling championship game. During the season, rejuvenated quarterback Randall Cunningham and Offensive Rookie of the Year Randy Moss led the Vikings to the most points in league history. Kicker Gary Anderson set an NFL mark with 164 points and did not miss a kick all year, but he was wide left in the fourth quarter of the championship game. Chris Chandler led the Falcons to a game-tying touchdown in the final minute and Morten Andersen's overtime field goal sent Atlanta to its first Super Bowl appearance.

Falcon Jamal Anderson carried the ball more often, gained more yards, and ran for more touchdown than anyone else in the NFC. Kick returner Tim Dwight and linebacker Keith Brooking were key rookie contributors to Atlanta. The Falcons lured Steve DeBerg, retired for four years, back to the field and he spent his final game on the sidelines in his first Super Bowl, just a few days past his 45th birthday.

Steve Young reached career highs in passing yards and touchdowns, but San Francisco's run of 16 playoff appearances in 18 seasons, just like Young's career, would draw to an abrupt close. Just as sudden would be the end of Barry Sanders's career. There was much dialogue and intrigue, but the record would show that Detroit's rushing maestro played his final game at age 30, less than 1,500 yards shy of Walter Payton's NFL rushing mark. Hall of Famers Red Badgro, Bulldog Turner, Sid Luckman, Doak Walker, Emlen Tunnell, and Ray Nitschke, as well as Nitschke's teammate Elijah Pitts, who scored twice in Super Bowl I, died during the year.

1998 AFC

TEAM	W-L-T	PCT	POST	PTS	RA	RY	RY/A	RTD	FL	PA	PC	GPY	GPY/A	PTD	PI	PSY	PRAT
Eastern Division																	
NYJ	12-4	.750	DC	416-266	500-400	1879-1659	3.8-4.1	12-11	11-9	532-544	318-285	**4032**-3299	7.6-**6.1**	**33-16**	13-21	196-259	**94.0**-64.7
Mia	10-6	.625	WD	321-**265**	458-395	1535-1511	3.4-3.8	10-**6**	12-7	546-504	316-252	3582-3194	6.6-6.3	23-17	16-**29**	187-270	79.5-**57.4**
Buf	10-6	.625	W	400-333	**531**-375	2161-1493	4.1-4.0	13-11	6-13	461-532	269-294	3621-3474	**7.9**-6.5	28-27	14-18	241-276	91.0-78.2
NE	9-7	.563	W	337-329	403-447	1480-1547	3.7-3.5	9-8	7-7	556-570	295-336	4004-3857	7.2-6.8	23-26	17-24	344-222	77.4-77.1
Ind	3-13	.188	—	310-444	384-544	1486-2570	3.9-4.7	7-20	**5**-11	**576**-461	**326**-275	3739-3497	6.5-7.6	26-27	28-8	**109**-231	71.1-95.7
Central Division																	
Jax	11-5	.688	ED	392-338	487-450	2102-2000	4.3-4.4	19-9	8-17	463-577	269-325	3343-3768	7.2-6.5	24-23	12-13	231-209	87.1-80.1
Ten	8-8	.500	—	330-320	462-414	1970-1610	4.3-3.9	12-9	9-7	519-511	305-319	3482-3683	6.7-7.2	16-24	**10**-12	191-172	81.3-90.0
Pit	7-9	.438	—	263-303	490-479	2034-1642	4.2-3.4	8-8	12-13	489-482	274-268	2781-3559	5.7-7.4	13-17	20-16	229-238	64.3-77.1
Bal	6-10	.375	—	269-335	408-472	1629-1705	4.0-3.6	7-12	15-6	477-539	272-316	3152-3878	6.6-7.2	16-20	15-17	283-286	75.2-80.1
Cin	3-13	.188	—	268-452	405-558	1639-2612	4.0-4.7	7-23	10-7	521-**406**	307-**233**	3545-3350	6.8-8.3	20-23	12-13	360-199	82.7-89.8
Western Division																	
Den	**14**-2	**.875**	DCS*	**501**-309	525-**356**	**2468**-1287	**4.7**-3.6	**26**-8	6-11	491-596	290-345	3808-3983	7.8-6.7	32-28	14-19	184-**335**	93.5-80.5
Oak	8-8	.500	—	288-356	449-482	1727-1674	3.8-3.5	6-8	18-14	519-497	282-291	3534-**3134**	6.8-6.3	21-22	25-21	446-258	69.2-74.3
Sea	8-8	.500	—	372-310	426-487	1626-1999	3.8-4.1	11-13	16-18	480-597	273-343	3219-3972	6.7-6.7	21-18	18-24	219-282	76.4-71.0
KC	7-9	.438	—	327-363	433-491	1548-1869	3.6-3.8	19-22	14-**20**	543-479	305-259	3472-3253	6.4-6.8	15-17	18-13	212-268	70.9-76.0
SD	5-11	.313	—	241-342	460-422	1728-**1140**	3.8-**2.7**	11-12	17-7	566-530	261-271	3115-3314	5.5-6.3	11-21	34-20	251-246	44.9-68.2
Aver	16	—	—	341	452	1803	4.0	13	12	516	292	3536	6.8	22	17	257	78.3

TEAM	1D	PENY	PNT	FGM/A	RTNY	RTNTD	OFFY/DEFY	NETY	NETTO	NP	PNP	DELP	PW	DELW	PRT	DR	YPD	DEL
Eastern Division																		
NYJ	338-263	651-967	40.6-**42.2**	25/35-20/25	578-543	4-3	5715-4699	1016	6	150	109	41	11.8	0.3	**6.4**/ 3.9	184-186	31.1-25.3	5.8
Mia	269-257	864-875	41.9-45.3	22/27-23/32	860-704	4-5	4930-4435	495	8	56	73	-17	9.4	0.6	5.1/**3.3**	196-202	25.2-22.0	3.2
Buf	319-283	993-836	41.8-44.9	33/**41**-21/26	573-439	2-**1**	5541-4691	850	**11**	67	115	-48	9.7	0.3	6.0/ 4.6	179-187	31.0-25.1	5.9
NE	281-305	853-787	44.5-42.5	31/39-27/32	650-690	3-2	5140-5182	-42	7	8	25	-17	8.2	0.8	5.2/ 4.6	182-185	28.2-28.0	0.2
Ind	298-341	853-917	45.4-44.6	27/31-28/37	437-804	0-5	5116-5836	-720	-14	-134	-116	-18	4.7	-1.7	4.4/ 6.4	185-182	27.7-32.1	-4.4
Central Division																		
Jax	287-309	898-953	45.0-43.5	21/26-30/35	700-548	4-4	5214-5559	-345	10	54	11	43	9.4	1.6	5.6/ 5.3	189-192	27.6-29.0	-1.4
Ten	308-279	1135-704	**47.2**-43.1	**36**/40-25/30	378-**420**	4-**1**	5261-5121	140	0	10	12	-2	8.3	-0.3	5.4/ 5.9	168-174	31.3-29.4	1.9
Pit	268-266	691-854	43.5-45.8	26/32-32/41	604-479	5-5	4586-4963	-377	-3	-40	-43	3	7.0	0.0	3.4/ 5.3	186-185	24.7-26.8	-2.2
Bal	243-298	909-1013	42.9-42.5	21/28-26/30	702-432	6-5	4498-5297	-799	-7	-66	-95	29	6.3	-0.4	4.5/ 5.2	192-190	23.4-27.9	-4.5
Cin	271-310	**620**-1012	44.2-44.5	19/27-27/31	378-709	4-7	4824-5763	-939	-2	-184	-86	-98	3.4	-0.4	5.0/ 6.4	182-**167**	26.5-34.5	-8.0
Western Division																		
Den	**347**-283	1023-865	46.2-42.4	23/27-**14/20**	838-651	4-2	**6092**-4935	**1157**	10	**192**	**136**	56	**12.8**	1.2	**6.4**/ 4.8	185-191	**32.9**-25.8	**7.1**
Oak	273-273	986-921	43.4-44.8	17/27-28/37	**984**-1222	7-8	4815-4550	265	-8	-68	-10	-58	6.3	**1.7**	3.7/ 4.0	**220**-218	21.9-20.9	1.0
Sea	267-337	914-1157	44.0-43.6	19/24-23/30	883-589	**13**-4	4626-5689	-1063	8	62	-57	**119**	9.6	-1.5	4.7/ 4.3	197-196	23.5-29.0	-5.5
KC	289-321	1304-**1292**	42.3-**42.2**	27/32-18/30	503-702	1-5	4808-4854	-46	1	-36	0	-36	7.1	-0.1	4.5/ 5.0	200-191	24.0-25.4	-1.4
SD	272-**256**	1229-1005	43.9-44.1	26/30-25/34	745-1027	1-5	4592-**4208**	384	-24	-101	-64	-37	5.5	-0.5	2.4/ 4.2	218-211	21.1-**19.9**	1.1
Aver	291	922	43.2	24/30	625	2	5083	—	—	—	—	—	—	—	5.3	95	26.5	—

Rushing Attempts	Rushing Yards	Rushing Average	Rushing TDs	Rushing Rank	Passing Yards	Passing Average
T.Davis-Den 392	T.Davis-Den 2008	T.Davis-Den 5.12	T.Davis-Den 21	T.Davis-Den 2218	P.Manning-Ind........3739	J.Elway-Den...........7.88
C.Martin-NYJ 369	M.Faulk-Ind...........1319	K.Stewart-Pit..........5.01	F.Taylor-Jax...............14	M.Faulk-Ind...........1379	D.Bledsoe-NE 3633	J.Taylor-NYJ 7.73
E.George-Ten 348	E.George-Ten 1294	F.Taylor-Jax............4.63	R.Watters-Sea 9	C.Martin-NYJ 1367	D.Marino-Mia 3497	D.Flutie-Buf............7.66
M.Faulk-Ind.............324	C.Martin-NYJ 1287	P.Holmes-Bal 4.33	R.Edwards-NE............9	F.Taylor-Jax...........1363	J.Taylor-NYJ 3256	D.Bledsoe-NE 7.55
R.Watters-Sea 319	R.Watters-Sea 1239	C.Dillon-Cin 4.31		E.George-Ten 1344	S.McNair-Ten.........3228	M.Brunell-Jax.........7.35

Completion Percent	TD Passes	TD Percent	INT Percent	Passer Rating	Passing Rank	Receptions
N.O'Donnell-Cin......61.8	J.Taylor-NYJ 29	J.Taylor-NYJ 6.9	N.O'Donnell-Cin........1.2	J.Taylor-NYJ 101.6	J.Taylor-NYJ 1493	O.McDuffie-Mia..........90
J.Taylor-NYJ 61.5	P.Manning-Ind...........26	J.Elway-Den..............6.2	J.Taylor-NYJ 1.7	J.Elway-Den............93.0	D.Bledsoe-NE 1357	R.Smith-Den..............86
J.Elway-Den............59.0	D.Marino-Mia 23	D.Flutie-Buf..............5.6	R.Gannon-KC 1.7	N.O'Donnell-Cin......90.2	S.McNair-Ten.........1289	M.Faulk-Ind...............86
M.Brunell-Jax..........58.8	J.Elway-Den..............22	M.Brunell-Jax...........5.6	S.McNair-Ten............2.0	M.Brunell-Jax..........89.9	D.Marino-Mia 1264	K.Johnson-NYJ..........83
S.McNair-Ten..........58.7		P.Manning-Ind...........4.5	M.Brunell-Jax............2.5	D.Flutie-Buf............87.4	J.Elway-Den...........1113	C.Pickens-Cin 82

Receiving Yards	Receiving Average	Receiving TDs	Receiving Rank	Combined Net Yards	Total TDs	Total Points
E.Moulds-Buf.........1368	S.Jefferson-NE 22.68	S.Sharpe-Den............10	E.Moulds-Buf...........729	M.Faulk-Ind............2240	T.Davis-Den 23	S.Christie-Buf 140
R.Smith-Den..........1222	E.Moulds-Buf........20.42	E.McCaffrey-Den.......10	R.Smith-Den............641	T.Davis-Den 2225	F.Taylor-Jax...............17	T.Davis-Den 138
J.Smith-Jax............1182	J.Jett-Oak 19.60	K.Johnson-NYJ.........10	J.Smith-Jax.............631	K.Williams-Buf 1866	J.Galloway-Sea..........12	A.Del Greco-Ten......136
K.Johnson-NYJ......1131	J.Lewis-Bal 19.12	J.Galloway-Sea.........10	K.Johnson-NYJ........616	J.Avery-Mia............1655	R.Edwards-NE...........12	A.Vinatieri-NE..........127
W.Chrebet-NYJ......1083	D.Alexander-KC....18.37		W.Chrebet-NYJ........582	F.Taylor-Jax............1653	K.Johnson-NYJ..........11	J.Elam-Den..............127

Punt Average	Field Goals	Field Goal Percent	Kickoff Returns	Kickoff Return Average	Punt Returns	Punt Return Average
C.Hentrich-Ten........47.2	A.Del Greco-Ten........36	A.Del Greco-Ten.....92.3	D.Howard-Oak...........49	C.Harris-Bal............27.6	D.Howard-Oak...........45	T.Brown-NE 13.2
T.Rouen-Den 46.9	S.Christie-Buf 33	A.Van Pelt-Ind.........87.1	K.Williams-Buf...........47	S.Broussard-Sea 26.9	R.Barlow-Jax 43	R.Barlow-Jax 12.9
C.Gardocki-Ind........45.4	A.Vinatieri-NE...........31	J.Carney-SD 86.7	V.Hebron-Den 46	V.Hebron-Den 26.4	K.Williams-Buf 37	J.Lewis-Bal 12.7
B.Barker-Jax...........45.0	A.Van Pelt-Ind...........27	J.Elam-Den.............85.2	T.Mack-Cin................45	T.Mack-Cin..............25.9	D.Gordon-Den 34	T.Buckley-Mia 12.2
L.Johnson-Cin 44.7	M.Stover-KC 27	M.Stover-KC 84.4	D.Cullors-NE..............45	J.Avery-Mia.............25.2		L.Rachal-SD 12.1

Punt/Kick Return Yards	Punt/Kick Return TDs	Interceptions	Interception Return Yards	Interception Return TDs	Sacks	Overall Rank
D.Howard-Oak.......1581	J.Lewis-Bal 2	T.Law-NE.....................9	L.Warren-Pit.............178	R.Woodson-Bal 2	M.Sinclair-Sea 16.5	T.Davis-Den 2337
K.Williams-Buf.......1428	D.Howard-Oak.............2	S.Madison-Mia............8	T.Buckley-Mia 157	L.Warren-Pit................2	M.McCrary-Bal........14.5	S.McNair-Ten.........1888
R.Barlow-Jax 1302	J.Galloway-Sea............2	T.Buckley-Mia 8	S.Springs-Sea 142	Z.Thomas-Mia 2	D.Thomas-KC 12.0	M.Faulk-Ind............1853
T.Vanover-KC.........1220		S.Springs-Sea 7	T.Law-NE.................133	S.Springs-Sea 2	L.Johnstone-Oak 11.0	J.Taylor-NYJ 1607
V.Hebron-Den 1216			D.Gordon-Den 125	D.Smith-Sea 2	J.Gildon-Pit.............11.0	F.Taylor-Jax............1589

Peyton Blossoms, But Leaf Falls

A major debate evolved regarding which quarterback should be taken with the first pick in the 1998 draft. Peyton Manning or Ryan Leaf? The Colts took Manning and the Cardinals, with the second pick, made the Chargers pay dearly to move up one spot to take Leaf. Both rookies began the season as starters. Manning led the league in pass attempts and interceptions, but Leaf threw just 2 touchdowns against 15 interceptions. Debuting with less fanfare and scrutiny were Brian Griese, Fred Taylor, Mike Vanderjagt, and Hines Ward.

Terrell Davis became the fourth player to surpass 2,000 yards rushing in a season, but all eyes in Denver were on John Elway's grand ride into the sunset. As the Broncos rolled to a franchise-best 14–2 mark, Elway became the second player to reach 4,000 career completions and 50,000 yards passing. He also joined Dan Marino and Fran Tarkenton in the 300-touchdown club. The Broncos won their second straight championship with Elway cruising in his final game in Super Bowl XXXIII. Another quarterback with longevity, Dave Krieg, retired after the 1998 season.

The high-powered Jets were second only to Denver in the conference in wins and points. New York's Vinny Testaverde became the poster child for restoring the instant replay rule after his fourth-and-goal quarterback sneak was ruled a touchdown to beat Seattle, even though he clearly had been stopped. A worse call was made during an overtime coin flip on Thanksgiving Day, when the referee declared the Steelers lost the flip despite calling it correctly in the air. The Lions received the kickoff and then kicked a winning field goal. The rule was changed four days later to have players call "heads" or "tails" *before* the coin toss. Tinted visors were also outlawed, except for medical need.

The Tennessee Oilers, following a season of poor attendance in Memphis, moved to Vanderbilt Stadium in Nashville. Lou Rymkus, who, when the Oilers originated in Houston, won the first AFL championship in 1960, and Weeb Ewbank, whose game plan against his former team helped make Joe Namath's guarantee a reality for the Jets in Super Bowl III, died in 1998.

1999 NFC

TEAM	W-L-T	PCT	POST	PTS	RA	RY	RY/A	RTD	FL	PA	PC	GPY	GPY/A	PTD	PI	PSY	PRAT
Eastern Division																	
Was	10-6	.625	ED	443-377	463-439	2039-1973	4.4-4.5	**23**-16	11-13	537-589	324-328	4112-3953	7.7-6.7	26-23	14-24	186-221	89.5-72.5
Dal	8-8	.500	W	352-276	493-417	2051-1442	4.2-**3.5**	16-6	10-9	507-545	295-297	3278-3615	6.5-6.6	20-19	**13**-24	**151**-217	80.0-68.4
NYG	7-9	.438	—	299-358	431-447	1408-1560	3.3-**3.5**	11-13	12-7	602-511	350-295	4015-3593	6.7-7.0	17-20	20-17	296-172	73.9-78.7
Arz	6-10	.375	—	245-382	396-542	1207-2265	3.0-4.2	13-17	10-10	558-493	287-294	3085-3386	5.5-6.9	11-25	30-17	282-229	52.2-82.9
Phi	5-11	.313	—	272-357	424-519	1746-2001	4.1-3.9	5-12	21-18	474-568	235-322	2405-3733	5.1-6.6	18-22	18-28	321-272	61.4-69.1
Central Division																	
TB	11-5	.688	DC	270-**235**	**502**-361	1776-1407	3.5-3.9	7-8	19-10	447-573	268-302	2781-**3164**	6.2-**5.5**	18-**11**	16-21	303-291	76.5-**60.1**
Min	10-6	.625	WD	399-335	422-413	1804-1617	4.3-3.9	13-9	19-18	530-606	316-373	4318-4252	8.1-7.0	32-20	21-12	329-272	89.3-85.4
Det	8-8	.500	#W	322-323	356-393	1245-1531	3.5-3.9	8-12	**8**-16	558-574	326-359	4074-4100	7.3-7.1	22-21	14-16	388-340	83.9-84.5
GB	8-8	.500	#	357-341	386-472	1519-1804	3.9-3.8	13-16	13-15	605-538	344-304	4132-3690	6.8-6.9	23-20	23-26	232-185	74.8-70.0
ChiB	6-10	.375	—	272-341	396-438	1387-1882	3.5-4.3	4-11	15-**19**	**684**-583	**404**-354	4352-4079	6.4-7.0	25-23	22-14	216-257	76.6-85.0
Western Division																	
SL	**13**-3	**.813**	DCS*	**526**-242	431-**338**	2059-**1189**	4.8-**3.5**	13-**4**	16-7	530-596	343-319	**4580**-3867	**8.6**-6.5	**42**-19	15-**29**	227-**358**	**106.6**-64.1
Car	8-8	.500	#	421-381	356-450	1525-1898	4.3-4.2	12-13	19-14	575-557	345-327	4447-3840	7.7-6.9	36-26	15-15	286-235	94.3-84.1
Atl	5-11	.313	—	285-380	373-487	1196-2072	3.2-4.3	9-18	16-6	509-**468**	278-**274**	3691-3409	7.3-7.3	22-20	19-12	345-258	76.7-84.8
SF	4-12	.250	—	295-453	418-426	**2095**-1619	**5.0**-3.8	14-11	13-7	560-521	324-317	3526-4295	6.3-8.2	14-36	19-13	241-227	70.7- 99.8
NO	3-13	.188	—	260-434	461-432	1690-1774	3.7-4.1	9-15	9-15	553-489	288-291	3598-3821	6.5-7.8	16-34	30-19	305-277	59.6-91.2
Aver	16	—	—	333	437	1704	3.9	12	13	541	309	3653	6.8	21	18	257	77.1

TEAM	1D	PENY	PNT	FGM/A	RTNY	RTNTD	OFFY/DEFY	NETY	NETTO	NP	PNP	DELP	PW	DELW	PRT	DR	YPD	DEL
Eastern Division																		
Was	**338**-322	808-**1137**	41.2-42.7	22/32-25/30	707-**408**	5-4	5965-5705	260	**12**	66	70	-4	9.6	0.4	6.3/ 4.6	195-194	30.6-29.4	1.2
Dal	295-266	1196-862	43.2-41.2	19/31-26/33	882-559	6-3	5178-4840	338	10	76	68	8	9.9	-1.9	5.2/ 4.3	200-192	25.9-25.2	0.7
NYG	308-270	906-750	41.0-43.9	25/30-24/37	752-727	4-8	5127-4981	146	-8	-59	-20	-39	6.5	0.5	4.6/ 5.3	194-196	26.4-25.4	1.0
Arz	254-301	**481**-938	42.0-42.4	19/27-**16**/24	765-676	3-6	4010-5422	-1412	-13	-137	-170	33	4.6	1.4	2.6/ 5.0	201-204	20.0-26.6	-6.6
Phi	218-328	905-719	41.9-41.2	21/31-36/45	875-756	6-**2**	3830-5462	-1632	7	-85	-108	23	5.9	-0.9	2.8/ 4.0	**215**-221	17.8-24.7	-6.9
Central Division																		
TB	245-**228**	583-727	43.1-41.1	**27**/32-24/31	712-504	2-4	4254-**4280**	-26	-4	35	-18	53	8.9	**2.1**	4.0/**3.3**	203-199	21.0-**21.5**	-0.6
Min	324-320	955-880	**45.4**-41.4	19/30-29/42	335-548	4-6	5793-5597	196	-10	64	-24	88	9.6	0.4	5.9/ 5.6	190-194	30.5-28.9	1.6
Det	269-305	995-839	42.3-42.0	26/32-22/29	621-576	5-3	4931-5291	-360	10	-1	10	-11	8.0	0.0	5.3/ 5.2	191-188	25.8-28.1	-2.3
GB	314-304	808-993	39.1-42.8	25/30-24/31	349-671	4-3	5419-5309	110	5	16	29	-13	8.4	-0.4	4.8/ 4.5	193-200	28.1-26.5	1.5
ChiB	302-310	915-720	40.9-**38.9**	19/**34**-25/36	575-625	2-4	5523-5704	-181	-4	-69	-31	-38	6.3	-0.3	4.7/ 5.5	203-200	27.2-28.5	-1.3
Western Division																		
SL	335-263	889-1007	41.1-42.7	20/28-20/26	**1065**-421	**11**-3	**6412**-4698	**1714**	5	**284**	**163**	**121**	**15.1**	-2.1	**7.3**/ 3.7	188-199	**34.1**-23.6	**10.5**
Car	307-331	857-877	39.4-39.5	25/28-19/25	410-425	2-8	5686-5503	183	-5	40	-5	45	9.0	-1.0	6.1/ 5.4	187-190	30.4-29.0	1.4
Atl	273-293	968-980	39.5-39.9	15/21-26/35	538-484	3-5	4542-5223	-681	-17	-95	-125	30	5.6	-0.6	4.9/ 5.5	182-187	25.0-27.9	-3.0
SF	300-315	1045-760	38.4-39.3	21/23-27/32	313-685	5-6	5380-5687	-307	-12	-158	-74	-84	4.1	-0.0	4.3/ 6.9	188-**178**	28.6-31.9	-3.3
NO	288-297	877-1006	39.5-41.3	24/29-**16/23**	396-766	2-6	4983-5318	-335	-5	-174	-48	-126	3.7	-0.7	3.5/ 5.7	204-188	24.4-28.3	-3.9
Aver	290	874	41.7	24/31	630	4	5100	—	—	—	—	—	—	—	5.2	196	26.0	—

Rushing Attempts	Rushing Yards	Rushing Average	Rushing TDs	Rushing Rank	Passing Yards	Passing Average
E.Smith-Dal 329	S.Davis-Was 1405	M.Faulk-SL 5.46	S.Davis-Was 17	S.Davis-Was 1575	S.Beuerlein-Car 4436	K.Warner-SL 8.72
D.Staley-Phi 325	E.Smith-Dal 1397	S.Beuerlein-Car 5.20	E.Smith-Dal 11	E.Smith-Dal 1507	K.Warner-SL 4353	J.George-Min 8.56
S.Davis-Was 290	M.Faulk-SL 1381	C.Garner-SF 5.10	L.Hoard-Min 10	M.Faulk-SL 1451	B.Favre-GB 4091	S.Beuerlein-Car 7.77
C.Enis-Chi 287	D.Staley-Phi 1273	S.Davis-Was 4.84	D.Levens-GB 9	D.Staley-Phi 1313	B.Johnson-Was 4005	B.Johnson-Was 7.72
D.Levens-GB 279	C.Garner-SF 1229	R.Smith-Min 4.59	M.Bates-Arz 9	C.Garner-SF 1269	T.Aikman-Dal 2964	C.Chandler-Atl 7.62
Completion Percent	**TD Passes**	**TD Percent**	**INT Percent**	**Passer Rating**	**Passing Rank**	**Receptions**
K.Warner-SL 65.1	K.Warner-SL 41	K.Warner-SL 8.2	S.Matthews-Chi 2.2	K.Warner-SL 109.2	K.Warner-SL 1862	M.Muhammad-Car 96
B.Johnson-Was 60.9	S.Beuerlein-Car 36	J.George-Min 7.0	G.Frerotte-Det 2.4	S.Beuerlein-Car 94.6	S.Beuerlein-Car 1798	C.Carter-Min 90
G.Frerotte-Det 60.8	B.Johnson-Was 24	S.Beuerlein-Car 6.3	B.Johnson-Was 2.5	J.George-Min 94.2	B.Johnson-Was 1603	B.Engram-Chi 88
S.Matthews-Chi 60.7	J.George-Min 23	C.Chandler-Atl 5.2	C.Batch-Det 2.6	B.Johnson-Was 90.0	B.Favre-GB 1236	M.Faulk-SL 87
S.Beuerlein-Car 60.1	B.Favre-GB 22	C.Batch-Det 4.8	K.Warner-SL 2.6	C.Batch-Det 84.1	T.Aikman-Dal 1087	M.Robinson-Chi 84
Receiving Yards	**Receiving Average**	**Receiving TDs**	**Receiving Rank**	**Combined Net Yards**	**Total TDs**	**Total Points**
R.Moss-Min 1413	T.Dwight-Atl 20.91	C.Carter-Min 13	R.Moss-Min 762	M.Faulk-SL 2429	S.Davis-Was 17	J.Wilkins-SL 124
M.Robinson-Chi 1400	K.Poole-NO 18.95	W.Walls-Car 12	M.Robinson-Chi 745	G.Milburn-Chi 2025	E.Smith-Dal 13	B.Conway-Was 115
G.Crowell-Det 1338	A.Hakim-SL 18.81	P.Jeffers-Car 12	G.Crowell-Det 704	T.Dwight-Atl 1861	C.Carter-Min 13	R.Longwell-GB 113
M.Muhammad-Car. 1253	M.Westbrook-Was 18.32	I.Bruce-SL 12	C.Carter-Min 686	C.Garner-SF 1764		J.Hanson-Det 106
C.Carter-Min 1241	A.Connell-Was 18.26	R.Moss-Min 11	M.Muhammad-Car 667	B.Mitchell-Was 1755		M.Gramatica-TB 106
Punt Average	**Field Goals**	**Field Goal Percent**	**Kickoff Returns**	**Kickoff Return Average**	**Punt Returns**	**Punt Return Average**
M.Berger-Min 45.4	M.Gramatica-TB 27	W.Richey-SF 91.3	G.Milburn-Chi 61	T.Horne-SL 29.7	A.Hakim-SL 44	M.Cody-Arz 11.7
T.Gowin-Dal 43.2	J.Hanson-Det 26	J.Kasay-Car 88.0	A.Rossum-Phi 54	J.Tucker-Dal 27.9	T.Barber-NYG 44	G.Milburn-Chi 11.5
M.Royals-TB 43.1	R.Longwell-GB 25	C.Blanchard-NYG 85.7	D.Philyaw-NO 53	R.Carpenter-SL 25.4	B.Mitchell-Was 40	T.Barber-NYG 11.5
R.Tuten-SL 42.5	D.Brien-NO 24	M.Gramatica-TB 84.4	M.Bates-Car 52	R.Tate-Min 25.1	E.Kennison-NO 35	D.Sanders-Dal 11.5
		R.Longwell-GB 83.3	M.Bates-Arz 52	A.Rossum-Phi 24.9	E.Metcalf-Car 34	T.Dwight-Atl 11.0
Punt/Kick Return Yards	**Punt/Kick Return TDs**	**Interceptions**	**Interception Return Yards**	**Interception Return TDs**	**Sacks**	**Overall Rank**
G.Milburn-Chi 1772	T.Horne-SL 2	T.Vincent-Phi 7	A.Harris-Phi 151	G.Wistrom-SL 2	K.Carter-SL 17.0	M.Faulk-SL 2000
A.Rossum-Phi 1597	M.Bates-Car 2	D.Abraham-TB 7	G.Wistrom-SL 131	G.Teague-Dal 2	S.Rice-Arz 16.5	K.Warner-SL 1964
M.Bates-Car 1287			G.Teague-Dal 127	M.Jones-SL 2	R.Porcher-Det 15.0	S.Beuerlein-Car 1942
M.Bates-Arz 1231			L.Schulters-SF 127	D.Abraham-TB 2	W.Sapp-TB 12.5	B.Johnson-Was 1654
B.Mitchell-Was 1225			B.Dawkins-Phi 127		K.Greene-Car 12.0	S.Davis-Was 1631

Master of a Different Arena

Five different NFL quarterbacks threw for more than 4,000 yards, and none was more surprising than Rams quarterback Kurt Warner. The relatively unknown passer had spent three seasons in the Arena Football League and another playing in NFL Europe before entering the 1999 season as the third-string quarterback for the Rams. When preseason injuries thrust Warner into a starting role, nobody expected much. Four weeks into the job, he had 14 touchdown passes. People took notice. Warner wound up with 41 touchdown passes, becoming just the second quarterback to surpass 40 in a single season.

Warner was not the only new face in the suddenly explosive St. Louis offense. His two most reliable options were running back Marshall Faulk—acquired from the Colts in a draft day trade—and rookie wide receiver Tory Holt, a first-round draft pick. The Rams started 6–0, averaging 37 points per game, and the offense was dubbed the Greatest Show on Turf.

Success followed a different recipe in Tampa Bay, where the Buccaneers were winning with a smothering defense. Defensive tackle Warren Sapp, linebacker Derrick Brooks, and safety John Lynch led a unit that held half of their opponents to 10 points or less. The offense scored just enough points to get by, thanks largely to their low-risk power running attack. Starting quarterback Trent Dilfer broke his collarbone in Seattle, but rookie Shaun King led the Bucs to a division title by winning four of their last five games.

Head coach Norv Turner employed a different type of power running game in Washington, one where runs between the tackles were complimented by long throws down the field. Stephen Davis led the league with 17 rushing touchdowns, and quarterback Brad Johnson threw for more than 4,000 yards. The Redskins finished with the NFL's second-best offense and the second-worst defense.

Hall of Famer Marion Motley died of prostate cancer. Walter Payton, beloved Bear and one of the greatest running backs of all time, died of a rare liver disease. Mark Tuinei, a Pro Bowl tackle for the Cowboys who retired at 37 in 1997, died of a drug overdose.

1999 AFC

TEAM	W-L-T	PCT	POST	PTS	RA	RY	RY/A	RTD	FL	PA	PC	GPY	GPY/A	PTD	PI	PSY	PRAT
Eastern Division																	
Ind	13-3	.813	D	**423**-333	419-406	1660-1715	4.0-4.2	15-12	11-13	546-561	**338**-328	**4182**-3775	**7.7**-6.7	**26**-21	17-10	**116**-269	**88.5**-83.9
Buf	11-5	.688	W	320-229	519-407	2040-1370	3.9-3.4	12-9	11-9	513-506	290-269	3478-**2889**	6.8-5.7	21-**12**	16-12	185-214	78.1-68.2
Mia	9-7	.563	WD	326-336	445-413	1453-1476	3.3-3.6	8-**6**	13-10	**589**-484	329-256	3736-3168	6.3-6.5	20-19	21-18	251-240	71.5-71.0
NYJ	8-8	.500	—	308-309	486-430	1961-1703	4.0-4.0	7-16	**6**-11	476-574	272-319	3001-3860	6.3-6.7	22-16	16-24	210-184	77.4-68.3
NE	8-8	.500	—	299-284	425-486	1426-1795	3.4-3.7	9-**6**	12-15	540-520	305-293	3985-3281	7.4-6.3	19-23	21-16	349-268	75.4-77.3
Central Division																	
Jax	**14**-2	**.875**	DCS	396-**217**	514-**373**	**2091**-1444	4.1-3.9	**20-6**	7-11	535-521	320-291	3716-3263	6.9-6.3	16-18	**11**-19	221-**373**	82.3-71.0
Ten	13-3	.813	WDC	392-324	459-383	1811-1550	3.9-4.0	19-8	9-**24**	527-557	304-312	3622-4000	6.9-7.2	23-26	13-16	137-305	83.1-82.3
Bal	8-8	.500	—	324-277	431-392	1754-**1231**	4.1-**3.1**	9-**6**	11-10	546-599	270-328	3360-3282	6.2-**5.5**	21-20	20-21	336-291	66.5-67.1
Pit	6-10	.375	—	317-320	495-451	1991-1958	4.0-4.3	14-10	7-14	535-**463**	301-**245**	3118-3167	5.8-6.8	19-20	18-14	235-241	71.1-76.5
Cin	4-12	.250	—	283-460	442-454	2051-1699	**4.6**-3.7	11-22	14-15	548-522	300-312	3504-4027	6.4-7.7	18-28	18-12	278-229	71.6-92.3
Cle	2-14	.125	—	217-437	313-610	1150-2736	3.7-4.5	9-29	16-12	492-523	271-331	2997-3457	6.1-6.6	19-17	15-8	385-147	73.5-86.8
Western Division																	
Sea	9-7	.563	#E	338-298	408-484	1408-1934	3.5-4.0	5-9	17-6	525-582	288-320	3629-3744	6.9-6.4	25-19	16-**30**	232-252	79.8-**64.1**
KC	9-7	.563	#	390-322	**521**-415	2082-1557	4.0-3.8	14-10	9-20	502-578	295-317	3409-3768	6.8-6.5	22-24	15-25	170-286	81.5-70.8
SD	8-8	.500	—	269-316	410-432	1246-1321	3.0-**3.1**	10-8	11-12	583-549	332-315	3627-3847	6.2-7.0	12-24	24-15	284-263	65.2-82.3
Oak	8-8	.500	—	390-329	488-398	2084-1559	4.3-3.9	18-10	15-13	520-539	306-302	3850-3630	7.4-6.7	24-22	14-20	241-309	86.1-75.0
Den	6-10	.375	—	314-318	465-440	1864-1737	4.0-3.9	13-15	10-11	554-471	319-273	3646-3299	6.6-7.0	16-17	18-15	227-283	73.6-78.3
Aver	16	—	—	333	437	1704	3.9	12	13	541	309	3653	6.8	21	18	257	77.1

TEAM	1D	PENY	PNT	FGM/A	RTNY	RTNTD	OFFY/DEFY	NETY	NETTO	NP	PNP	DELP	PW	DELW	PRT	DR	YPD	DEL
Eastern Division																		
Ind	327-304	**683**-1093	41.1-41.4	34/38-26/29	675-658	5-3	**5726**-5221	505	-5	90	22	68	10.3	2.8	**6.4**/ 5.4	182-187	**31.5**-27.9	3.5
Buf	313-**244**	789-790	38.9-41.7	25/34-23/31	527-514	2-2	5333-**4045**	**1288**	-6	91	83	8	10.3	0.7	5.2/ 4.2	183-183	29.1-22.1	**7.0**
Mia	287-252	936-708	41.0-41.1	**39/46**-31/40	675-991	2-10	4938-4404	534	-6	-10	21	-31	7.8	1.3	4.4/ 4.4	205-204	24.1-21.6	2.5
NYJ	268-299	771-685	45.0-40.9	27/33-26/31	762-575	4-1	4752-5379	-627	13	-1	0	-1	8.0	0.0	4.5/ 4.6	194-**182**	24.5-29.6	-5.1
NE	280-281	812-775	41.5-41.2	26/33-25/30	605-644	4-1	5062-4808	254	-2	15	13	2	8.4	-0.4	4.8/ 4.5	199-203	25.4-23.7	1.8
Central Division																		
Jax	**331**-248	755-728	41.8-41.4	31/38-17/**18**	792-**408**	6-**0**	5586-4334	1252	12	**179**	**152**	27	**12.5**	1.5	5.5/ 3.8	185-187	30.2-23.2	**7.0**
Ten	294-300	1069-1010	42.5-42.9	21/25-**15**/22	615-562	4-5	5296-5245	51	18	68	76	-8	9.7	**3.3**	5.7/ 5.3	195-198	27.2-26.5	0.7
Bal	259-260	1010-**1118**	41.9-42.2	28/33-19/25	855-688	4-5	4778-4222	556	0	47	46	1	9.2	-1.2	3.9/**3.5**	215-216	22.2-**19.5**	2.7
Pit	295-260	945-813	45.2-40.6	25/29-20/26	526-696	2-6	4874-4884	-10	3	-3	11	-14	7.9	-1.9	4.0/ 5.0	197-190	24.7-25.7	-1.0
Cin	293-316	1027-835	38.3-44.2	18/27-29/32	510-803	4-3	5277-5497	-220	-5	-177	-38	-139	3.6	0.4	4.3/ 6.4	196-187	26.9-29.4	-2.5
Cle	220-368	714-776	43.8-40.9	8/12-33/39	214-915	0-3	3762-6046	-2284	-11	-220	-234	14	2.5	-0.5	3.9/ 5.7	182-190	20.7-31.8	-11.2
Western Division																		
Sea	276-313	883-985	40.8-42.0	34/40-30/38	755-580	4-2	4805-5426	-621	3	40	-40	**80**	9.0	0.0	5.2/ 3.8	198-206	24.3-26.3	-2.1
KC	282-281	982-787	40.9-43.5	21/28-19/25	**1084**-572	**11**-4	5321-5039	282	**21**	68	108	-40	9.7	-0.7	5.3/ 4.2	**217**-217	24.5-23.2	1.3
SD	262-279	823-909	43.9-**40.5**	31/36-26/38	413-539	3-2	4589-4905	-316	-8	-47	-58	11	6.8	1.2	3.8/ 5.3	201-199	22.8-24.6	-1.8
Oak	326-266	825-861	39.5-43.2	25/38-26/32	644-718	3-4	5693-4880	813	4	61	84	-23	9.5	-1.5	5.7/ 4.5	196-204	29.0-23.9	5.1
Den	308-267	872-1016	**46.5**-43.6	29/36-25/29	578-831	3-3	5283-4753	530	-2	-4	36	-40	7.9	-1.9	4.7/ 4.8	197-193	26.8-24.6	2.2
Aver	290	874	41.7	24/31	630	2	5100	—	—	—	—	—	—	—	5.2	101	25.8	—

Rushing Attempts	Rushing Yards	Rushing Average	Rushing TDs	Rushing Rank	Passing Yards	Passing Average
E.James-Ind 369	E.James-Ind 1553	R.Huntley-Pit 6.10	J.Stewart-Jax 13	E.James-Ind 1683	P.Manning-Ind 4135	P.Manning-Ind 7.76
C.Martin-NYJ 367	C.Martin-NYJ 1464	P.Holmes-Bal 5.69	E.James-Ind 13	C.Martin-NYJ 1514	D.Bledsoe-NE 3985	R.Gannon-Oak 7.46
R.Watters-Sea 325	E.George-Ten 1304	D.Flutie-Buf 5.41	E.George-Ten 9	E.George-Ten 1394	R.Gannon-Oak 3840	D.Bledsoe-NE 7.39
E.George-Ten 320	R.Watters-Sea 1210	N.Kaufman-Oak 5.17		R.Watters-Sea 1260	E.Grbac-KC 3389	M.Brunell-Jax 6.94
J.Bettis-Pit 299	C.Dillon-Cin 1200	E.Rhett-KC 4.61		C.Dillon-Cin 1250	J.Kitna-Sea 3346	J.Blake-Cin 6.86
Completion Percent	**TD Passes**	**TD Percent**	**INT Percent**	**Passer Rating**	**Passing Rank**	**Receptions**
P.Manning-Ind 62.1	P.Manning-Ind 26	T.Banks-Bal 5.3	M.Brunell-Jax 2.0	P.Manning-Ind 90.7	P.Manning-Ind 1598	J.Smith-Jax 116
R.Lucas-NYJ 59.2	R.Gannon-Oak 24	R.Lucas-NYJ 5.1	R.Lucas-NYJ 2.2	R.Gannon-Oak 86.5	R.Gannon-Oak 1480	M.Harrison-Ind 115
R.Gannon-Oak 59.0	J.Kitna-Sea 23	P.Manning-Ind 4.9	S.McNair-Ten 2.4	R.Lucas-NYJ 85.1	D.Bledsoe-NE 1248	T.Brown-Oak 90
E.Grbac-KC 58.9	E.Grbac-KC 22	R.Gannon-Oak 4.7	T.Banks-Bal 2.5	M.Brunell-Jax 82.0	M.Brunell-Jax 1240	K.Johnson-NYJ 89
M.Brunell-Jax 58.7		M.Tomczak-Pit 4.7	R.Gannon-Oak 2.7	E.Grbac-KC 81.7	E.Grbac-KC 1205	R.Smith-Den 79
Receiving Yards	**Receiving Average**	**Receiving TDs**	**Receiving Rank**	**Combined Net Yards**	**Total TDs**	**Total Points**
M.Harrison-Ind 1663	S.Jefferson-NE 17.45	M.Harrison-Ind 12	M.Harrison-Ind 892	E.James-Ind 2139	E.James-Ind 17	A.Van Pelt-Ind 145
J.Smith-Jax 1636	S.Dawkins-Sea 17.10	T.Gonzalez-KC 11	J.Smith-Jax 848	T.Wilkins-Ind 2089	J.Stewart-Jax 13	O.Mare-Mia 144
T.Brown-Oak 1344	Y.Thigpen-Ten 17.05	D.Mayes-Sea 10	T.Brown-Oak 702	E.George-Ten 1762	E.George-Ten 13	T.Peterson-Sea 134
K.Johnson-NYJ 1170	J.Graham-SD 16.98	R.Dudley-Oak 9	K.Johnson-NYJ 625	N.Kaufman-Oak 1726	M.Harrison-Ind 12	M.Hollis-Jax 130
T.Glenn-NE 1147	J.Horn-KC 16.74		T.Glenn-NE 594	C.Martin-NYJ 1723		
Punt Average	**Field Goals**	**Field Goal Percent**	**Kickoff Returns**	**Kickoff Return Average**	**Punt Returns**	**Punt Return Average**
T.Rouen-Den 46.5	O.Mare-Mia 39	A.Van Pelt-Ind 89.5	B.Marion-Mia 62	T.Mack-Cin 27.1	J.Lewis-Bal 57	C.Rogers-Sea 14.5
T.Tupa-NYJ 45.2	A.Van Pelt-Ind 34	K.Brown-Pit 86.2	T.Wilkins-Ind 51	C.Rogers-Sea 25.8	T.Vanover-KC 51	N.Jacquet-Mia 12.5
J.Miller-Pit 45.2	T.Peterson-Sea 34	J.Carney-SD 86.1	T.Mack-Cin 51	D.Stone-NYJ 24.6	C.Watson-Den 44	T.Vanover-KC 12.3
D.Bennett-SD 43.9	M.Hollis-Jax 31	T.Peterson-Sea 85.0	C.Watson-Den 48	B.Marion-Mia 24.6	D.Gordon-Oak 42	R.Barlow-Jax 10.9
C.Gardocki-Cle 43.8	J.Carney-SD 31	M.Stover-Bal 84.8		K.Faulk-NE 24.2	T.Wilkins-Ind 41	T.Brown-NE 10.7
Punt/Kick Return Yards	**Punt/Kick Return TDs**	**Interceptions**	**Interception Return Yards**	**Interception Return TDs**	**Sacks**	**Overall Rank**
B.Marion-Mia 1524	C.Yeast-Cin 2	R.Woodson-Bal 7	A.Beasley-Jax 200	R.Woodson-Bal 2	J.Kearse-Ten 14.5	E.James-Ind 1996
T.Wilkins-Ind 1522	T.Wilkins-Ind 2	S.Madison-Mia 7	R.Woodson-Bal 195	J.Hasty-KC 2	T.Pryce-Den 13.0	R.Gannon-Oak 1797
T.Vanover-KC 1513	T.Vanover-KC 2	J.Hasty-KC 7	M.Coleman-NYJ 165	A.Beasley-Jax 2	C.Bratzke-Ind 12.0	P.Manning-Ind 1691
C.Watson-Den 1472		M.Coleman-NYJ 6	S.Madison-Mia 164		T.Brackens-Jax 12.0	C.Martin-NYJ 1644
T.Mack-Cin 1382		A.Beasley-Jax 6	T.Blevins-Ind 115		M.McCrary-Bal 11.5	E.George-Ten 1643

Gaining Wins in New Places

The Colts made one of the most remarkable turnarounds in NFL history, posting a 13–3 record after finishing 3–13 the previous season. Second-year quarterback Peyton Manning blossomed, the beneficiary of an improved offensive line and a more balanced offensive attack. Rookie Edgerrin James led the league in rushing and caught 62 passes. Marvin Harrison led the league in receiving yards, and the Colts generated enough points to overcome their defensive deficiencies.

Everything came together for the Jacksonville Jaguars in their fifth season of existence. Linebacker Kevin Hardy and defensive end Tony Brackens led the league's stingiest defense, holding half their opponents to a touchdown or less. The backfield combination of James Stewart and Fred Taylor combined for 1,663 rushing yards and 19 touchdowns. The Jaguars' 14–2 record was the best in the NFL.

The Oilers changed their name to the more alliterative Tennessee Titans. The franchise reached new heights despite quarterback Steve McNair losing five games to injury. Backup Neil O'Donnell kept the offense on track and rookie defensive end Jevon Kearse added a disruptive element. Tennessee improved from 8–8 to 13–3. Two of those wins came against a club the Titans hadn't played before—or had they? The expansion Cleveland Browns had a roster of castoffs and a new stadium, but the team had the untouched records and history of the club that moved to Baltimore in 1996. The 2–14 Browns were the bottom portion of a six-team AFC Central.

Doug Flutie was a fan favorite in Buffalo. His critics said he was too short—and now too old—to be an NFL quarterback, but the 37-year-old injected unpredictability into the lethargic Bills offense and provided the kind of leadership that the team had sorely lacked since the retirement of Jim Kelly. Despite starting 15 games, Flutie was inexplicably benched in the AFC Wild Card Game in favor of the younger Rob Johnson. The Bills lost that game in the final seconds on Tennessee laterals during the Music City Miracle. Shortly thereafter Buffalo cut ties with three of the most important figures in team history: defensive end Bruce Smith, running back Thurman Thomas, and wide receiver Andre Reed.

2000 NFC

TEAM	W-L-T	PCT	POST	PTS	RA	RY	RY/A	RTD	FL	PA	PC	GPY	GPY/A	PTD	PI	PSY	PRAT
Eastern Division																	
NYG	**12**-4	**.750**	DCS	328-246	**507-359**	2009-**1156**	4.0-**3.2**	16-**7**	11-11	529-585	311-327	3610-3669	6.8-6.3	22-23	13-20	243-279	83.1-73.7
Phi	11-5	.688	WD	351-**245**	397-453	1882-1830	4.7-4.0	13-10	14-12	575-552	331-314	3386-3281	5.9-**5.9**	21-**11**	15-19	262-291	75.9-66.6
Was	8-8	.500	—	281-269	445-430	1748-1853	3.9-4.3	14-9	12-16	561-462	343-**254**	3892-2904	6.9-6.3	18-12	21-17	244-283	77.0-67.4
Dal	5-11	.313	—	294-361	463-538	1953-2636	4.2-4.9	15-17	18-9	445-**458**	255-277	2771-**2882**	6.2-6.3	14-20	21-16	249-189	66.6-78.7
Arz	3-13	.188	—	210-443	343-578	1278-2609	3.7-4.5	6-29	20-10	554-459	316-296	3478-3263	6.3-7.1	16-19	24-10	228-135	67.4-90.2
Central Division																	
Min	11-5	.688	DC	397-371	428-396	**2129**-1788	**5.0**-4.5	14-17	10-10	495-584	307-369	4019-4127	8.1-7.1	33-23	18-8	187-214	94.7-91.6
TB	10-6	.625	W	388-269	490-398	2066-1648	4.2-4.1	18-12	11-16	433-594	237-339	2824-3484	6.5-**5.9**	18-15	13-**25**	241-332	76.2-**65.0**
GB	9-7	.563	—	353-323	404-417	1643-1618	4.1-3.9	13-**7**	17-7	**600**-557	348-307	3916-3695	6.5-6.6	21-28	16-21	238-244	78.2-76.7
Det	9-7	.563	—	307-307	448-421	1747-1823	3.9-4.3	15-14	12-17	503-544	277-311	2992-3372	5.9-6.2	14-16	19-**25**	317-162	66.3-66.2
ChiB	5-11	.313	—	216-355	417-469	1736-1827	4.2-3.9	6-15	13-9	542-530	304-332	3005-3637	5.5-6.9	12-25	16-11	200-230	67.0-90.0
Western Division																	
NO	10-6	.625	#ED	354-305	505-395	2068-1672	4.1-4.2	14-14	11-15	497-488	298-285	3573-3449	7.2-7.1	22-17	15-20	244-**378**	84.2-74.7
SL	10-6	.625	#W	**540**-471	383-383	1843-1697	4.8-4.4	**26**-18	12-6	587-534	**380**-323	**5492**-4085	**9.4**-7.6	**37**-32	23-19	260-288	**99.7**-89.5
Car	7-9	.438	—	310-310	363-426	1186-1944	3.3-4.6	7-12	16-**21**	566-552	340-352	3850-3938	6.8-7.1	19-19	19-17	382-226	77.7-83.6
SF	6-10	.375	—	388-422	416-435	1801-1794	4.3-4.1	15-22	**9**-8	583-558	366-320	4400-4185	7.5-7.5	32-25	**10**-13	**161**-270	97.0-86.4
Atl	4-12	.250	—	252-413	350-453	1214-1983	3.5-4.4	6-16	14-10	514-515	285-306	3166-3766	6.2-7.3	14-23	20-15	386-142	66.8-84.8
Aver	16	—	—	331	441	1801	4.1	13	13	527	306	3553	6.7	20	17	243	78.1

TEAM	1D	PENY	PNT	FGM/A	RTNY	RTNTD	OFFY/DEFY	NETY	NETTO	NP	PNP	DELP	PW	DELW	PRT	DR	YPD	DEL
Eastern Division																		
NYG	310-274	839-728	40.1-41.5	19/25-**13/24**	481-525	1-**0**	5376-4546	830	7	82	**97**	-15	10.1	2.0	5.4/ 4.3	184-182	29.2-25.0	4.2
Phi	295-295	980-936	42.3-40.4	29/33-28/33	590-521	4-2	5006-4820	186	2	106	24	**82**	10.6	0.3	4.3/ 3.7	188-200	26.6-24.1	2.5
Was	308-**254**	1009-790	40.0-42.9	20/30-30/34	575-716	0-5	5396-**4474**	922	0	12	77	-65	8.3	-0.3	4.9/ 3.9	186-187	29.0-**23.9**	5.1
Dal	276-309	963-999	41.9-40.5	25/33-26/31	531-461	2-4	4475-5329	-854	-14	-67	-127	60	6.3	-1.3	3.6/ 4.5	180-183	24.9-29.1	-4.3
Arz	253-345	785-914	44.2-41.1	16/23-27/34	374-730	2-4	4528-5737	-1209	-24	-233	-197	-36	2.2	0.8	4.0/ 5.9	180-**167**	25.2-34.4	-9.2
Central Division																		
Min	319-344	908-747	**44.7**-39.9	22/23-25/29	326-491	0-3	5961-5701	260	-10	26	-18	44	8.6	**2.3**	6.3/ 6.2	166-174	35.9-32.8	3.1
TB	275-283	702-688	41.8-40.0	28/34-22/32	612-563	**7**-2	4649-4800	-151	**17**	**119**	55	64	**11.0**	-1.0	4.6/**3.4**	**204**-201	22.8-**23.9**	-1.1
GB	315-284	685-992	38.4-41.4	**33/38**-21/25	615-406	2-2	5321-5069	252	-5	30	1	29	8.8	0.3	5.0/ 4.7	200-198	26.6-25.6	1.0
Det	264-279	805-913	42.6-41.7	24/30-26/31	**812**-768	4-2	4422-5033	-611	11	0	-7	7	8.0	1.0	3.5/ 3.9	**204**-203	21.7-24.8	-3.1
ChiB	239-297	696-727	37.8-39.9	21/27-18/26	568-401	4-3	4541-5234	-693	-9	-139	-94	-45	4.5	0.5	3.8/ 5.6	194-189	23.4-27.7	-4.3
Western Division																		
NO	312-279	1024-837	41.1-40.9	23/29-18/**24**	603-619	5-5	5397-4743	654	9	49	91	-42	9.2	0.8	5.4/ 4.2	180-182	30.0-26.1	3.9
SL	**380**-321	942-747	39.5-42.2	24/27-26/31	656-518	4-6	**7075**-5494	**1581**	-10	69	92	-23	9.7	0.3	**7.2**/ 5.6	189-181	**37.4**-30.4	**7.1**
Car	304-304	**683-1073**	37.3-**39.8**	31/35-20/30	437-552	5-4	4654-5656	-1002	3	0	-72	72	8.0	-1.0	4.4/ 5.4	173-184	26.9-30.7	-3.8
SF	334-347	1135-857	39.0-42.7	15/22-26/31	498-426	2-2	6040-5709	331	2	-34	36	-70	7.2	-1.1	6.8/ 6.0	179-172	33.7-33.2	0.6
Atl	256-308	720-1010	40.6-41.9	25/31-29/31	635-**397**	5-7	3994-5607	-1613	-9	-161	-170	9	4.0	0.0	3.5/ 5.8	181-189	22.1-29.7	-7.6
Aver	295	843	41.7	24/30	594	3	5111	—	—	—	—	—	—	—	5.2	190	26.9	—

Rushing Attempts	Rushing Yards	Rushing Average	Rushing TDs	Rushing Rank	Passing Yards	Passing Average
J.Stewart-Det...........339	R.Smith-Min...........1521	D.McNabb-Phi 7.31	M.Faulk-SL 18	R.Smith-Min...........1591	J.Garcia-SF 4278	K.Warner-SL...........9.88
S.Davis-Was............332	M.Faulk-SL 1359	M.Faulk-SL 5.37	S.Davis-Was 11	M.Faulk-SL 1539	D.Culpepper-Min....3937	T.Green-SL 8.60
R.Smith-Min.............295	S.Davis-Was..........1318	D.Culpepper-Min.....5.28	J.Stewart-Det.............10	S.Davis-Was..........1428	B.Favre-GB............3812	D.Culpepper-Min.....8.31
E.Smith-Dal 294	E.Smith-Dal 1203	R.Smith-Min............5.16	A.Green-GB...............10	E.Smith-Dal 1293	S.Beuerlein-Car.....3730	J.Garcia-SF 7.63
J.Allen-Chi 290	J.Stewart-Det.........1184	T.Barber-NYG.........4.72	E.Smith-Dal 9	J.Stewart-Det.........1284	K.Collins-NYG 3610	S.Beuerlein-Car......7.00
Completion Percent	**TD Passes**	**TD Percent**	**INT Percent**	**Passer Rating**	**Passing Rank**	**Receptions**
K.Warner-SL...........67.7	D.Culpepper-Min........33	D.Culpepper-Min.......7.0	J.Garcia-SF 1.8	T.Green-SL 101.8	J.Garcia-SF 1894	M.Muhammad-Car...102
J.Garcia-SF 63.3	J.Garcia-SF 31	T.Green-SL 6.7	T.Green-SL 2.1	K.Warner-SL...........98.3	D.Culpepper-Min....1494	T.Owens-SF..............97
D.Culpepper-Min.....62.7	K.Collins-NYG 22	K.Warner-SL.............6.1	D.McNabb-Phi 2.3	D.Culpepper-Min.....98.0	K.Collins-NYG 1395	C.Carter-Min.............96
B.Johnson-Was 62.5	K.Warner-SL..............21	J.Garcia-SF 5.5	K.Collins-NYG 2.5	J.Garcia-SF 97.6	B.Favre-GB............1366	J.Horn-NO 94
J.Blake-NO 60.9	D.McNabb-Phi 21	J.Blake-NO 4.3	B.Favre-GB...............2.8	K.Collins-NYG 83.1	D.McNabb-Phi 1268	I.Bruce-SL.................87
Receiving Yards	**Receiving Average**	**Receiving TDs**	**Receiving Rank**	**Combined Net Yards**	**Total TDs**	**Total Points**
T.Holt-SL................1635	T.Holt-SL...............19.94	R.Moss-Min 15	T.Holt-SL..................848	M.Jenkins-Arz........2402	M.Faulk-SL 26	M.Faulk-SL 160
I.Bruce-SL.............1471	A.Connell-Was......19.54	T.Owens-SF 13	R.Moss-Min 794	M.Faulk-SL 2207	R.Moss-Min 15	R.Longwell-GB 131
T.Owens-SF...........1451	R.Moss-Min 18.66	A.Freeman-GB.............9	T.Owens-SF.............791	T.Barber-NYG........2085	T.Owens-SF...............13	M.Gramatica-TB 126
R.Moss-Min 1437	J.McKnight-Dal 17.81	C.Carter-Min................9	I.Bruce-SL................781	D.Howard-Det 1872	A.Green-GB...............13	D.Akers-Phi..............121
J.Horn-NO 1340	I.Bruce-SL............16.91	I.Bruce-SL...................9	J.Horn-NO 710	R.Smith-Min...........1869		G.Anderson-Min 111
Punt Average	**Field Goals**	**Field Goal Percent**	**Kickoff Returns**	**Kickoff Return Average**	**Punt Returns**	**Punt Return Average**
M.Berger-Min..........44.7	R.Longwell-GB 33	J.Wilkins-SL..........100.0	M.Jenkins-Arz............82	D.Vaughn-Atl...........27.7	T.Barber-NYG............39	A.Hakim-SL 15.3
S.Player-Arz............44.2	D.Akers-Phi................29	G.Anderson-Min 95.7	G.Milburn-Chi 63	M.Jenkins-Arz.........26.7	G.Milburn-Chi 35	D.Howard-Det.........14.7
J.Jett-Det 43.5	M.Gramatica-TB 28	J.Nedney-Car..........92.9	D.Howard-Det............57	A.Rossum-GB.........25.8	T.Dwight-Atl 33	W.McGarity-Dal 11.8
M.Knorr-Dal 42.8	J.Nedney-Car.............26	D.Akers-Phi.............87.9	T.Horne-SL 57	D.Howard-Det 24.6	B.Mitchell-Phi.............32	B.Mitchell-Phi.........10.5
S.Landeta-Phi.........42.3		R.Longwell-GB 86.8	J.Tucker-Dal..............51	T.Horne-SL 24.2	A.Hakim-SL 32	T.Dwight-Atl 9.4
Punt/Kick Return Yards	**Punt/Kick Return TDs**	**Interceptions**	**Interception Return Yards**	**Interception Return TDs**	**Sacks**	**Overall Rank**
M.Jenkins-Arz........2187	D.Vaughn-Atl................3	D.Sharper-GB.............9	A.Ambrose-Atl 139	S.Knight-NO 2	L.Glover-NO...........17.0	J.Garcia-SF 2348
D.Howard-Det 1858	B.Mitchell-Phi..............2	D.McCleon-SL 8	B.Westbrook-Det 126		W.Sapp-TB 16.5	D.Culpepper-Min....2034
G.Milburn-Chi 1768	W.McGarity-Dal 2	K.Schulz-Det...............7	J.Hitchcock-Car 116		H.Douglas-Phi 15.0	M.Faulk-SL 1997
A.Rossum-GB.........1536		D.Abraham-TB............7	R.Buchanan-Atl 114		M.Jones-TB 13.0	D.McNabb-Phi 1959
B.Mitchell-Phi.........1459			D.Sharper-GB..........109			R.Smith-Min...........1780

The Greatest Show on Turf Hits a Snag

Even as Mike Martz replaced the retired Dick Vermeil, the St. Louis Rams scored 540 points and continued to rewrite the record books. Marshall Faulk scored 26 combined touchdowns: 18 rushing and 8 receiving. Torry Holt led the league with 1,653 receiving yards and nearly 20 yards per catch. Although quarterback Kurt Warner missed five games with a broken hand, the real disappointment was a defense that seemed determined to give up points as quickly as the Rams could score them. A win in the season finale gave St. Louis a playoff berth.

New Orleans hired Jim Haslett as head coach and received an immediate payoff. The Saints improved from 3–13 to 11–5, winning the West Division title for just the second time in franchise history. Ricky Williams, for whom the now-fired Mike Ditka regime had traded all six Saints drafts picks a year before (plus two more high picks in 2000), rushed for 1,000 yards in 10 games before breaking his ankle. Joe Horn, a backup in four seasons with the Chiefs, emerged as one of the league's best receivers with 94 catches for 1,340 yards.

Daunte Culpepper tied for the NFL lead with 33 touchdown passes in his first year as a starter for the Vikings. Donovan McNabb, another second-year quarterback, turned the boos he'd heard on draft day 1999 into cheers in Philadelphia. He threw 21 touchdown passes and ran for 6 more, leading the team with 629 rushing yards.

After suffering back-to-back losses in November, Giants head coach Jim Fassel dismissed media criticism and guaranteed the team would make the playoffs. His players responded, winning the last five games and passing the Eagles for the NFC East crown. After nearly torpedoing his career, quarterback Kerry Collins returned to form and posted his best numbers to that point. The backfield combination of powerful rookie Ron Dayne and elusive Tiki Barber (dubbed Thunder and Lightning) made the Giants ground game difficult to defend. A stifling run defense held opponents to just 3.2 yards per carry. Tom Landry, who'd played for and coached the great Giants defenses of the 1950s before taking the Cowboys from expansion team to America's Team, died at 75.

2000 AFC

TEAM	W-L-T	PCT	POST	PTS	RA	RY	RY/A	RTD	FL	PA	PC	GPY	GPY/A	PTD	PI	PSY	PRAT
Eastern Division																	
Mia	11-5	.688	ED	323-226	496-417	1894-1736	3.8-4.2	16-9	9-13	421-530	243-282	2720-3170	6.5-6.0	15-13	17-**28**	153-270	72.2-**57.5**
Ind	10-6	.625	W	429-326	435-446	1859-1935	4.3-4.3	14-13	14-8	571-530	**357**-317	4413-3674	7.7-6.9	**33**-22	15-14	131-252	**94.7**-83.6
NYJ	9-7	.563	—	321-321	418-476	1471-1888	3.5-4.0	11-9	11-14	**637**-517	352-265	4023-3166	6.3-6.1	23-17	29-21	**99**-234	67.5-64.3
Buf	8-8	.500	—	315-350	475-444	1922-1559	4.0-3.5	11-13	13-13	546-480	312-283	3936-3175	7.2-6.6	20-18	**10**-16	360-308	84.3-77.4
NE	5-11	.313	—	276-338	424-495	1390-1831	3.3-3.7	9-12	10-13	565-544	328-321	3461-3694	6.1-6.8	18-23	15-10	280-172	75.5-86.0
Central Division																	
Ten	**13**-3	**.813**	D	346-191	**547**-387	2084-1390	3.8-3.6	14-7	14-13	462-466	286-**242**	3430-**2761**	7.4-**5.9**	18-**10**	16-17	164-**338**	83.2-62.0
Bal	12-4	.750	WDCS*	333-**165**	511-361	2199-**970**	4.3-**2.7**	9-**5**	**7-26**	504-528	287-295	3102-3175	6.2-6.0	20-11	19-23	287-178	72.7-62.5
Pit	9-7	.563	—	321-255	527-425	2248-1693	4.3-4.0	19-9	11-18	439-521	217-280	2738-3249	6.2-6.2	12-13	**10**-17	220-229	68.9-67.6
Jax	7-9	.438	—	367-327	481-436	2032-1685	4.2-3.9	18-14	14-18	545-**458**	333-258	3947-3407	7.2-7.4	22-23	15-12	289-247	85.2-85.8
Cin	4-12	.250	—	185-359	495-504	2314-1925	4.7-3.8	13-12	21-12	454-538	207-318	2219-3730	4.9-6.9	6-26	14-9	273-168	52.0-89.4
Cle	3-13	.188	—	161-419	336-594	1085-2505	3.2-4.2	7-26	9-13	483-486	278-262	2728-3408	5.6-7.0	9-18	19-12	283-270	63.4-78.3
Western Division																	
Oak	12-4	.750	DC	479-299	520-383	**2470**-1551	**4.8**-4.0	**23**-8	9-16	475-588	284-359	3430-3976	7.2-6.8	28-25	11-21	124-278	92.0-80.4
Den	11-5	.688	W	**485**-369	516-**344**	2311-1598	4.5-4.6	21-13	13-17	569-574	354-310	**4464**-4197	**7.8**-7.3	28-26	12-27	221-251	94.2-73.1
KC	7-9	.438	—	355-354	383-441	1465-1809	3.8-4.1	12-13	11-14	582-549	342-358	4408-3737	7.6-6.8	29-25	15-15	259-266	88.5-88.6
Sea	6-10	.375	—	320-405	403-503	1720-2454	4.3-4.9	10-20	17-12	507-489	308-309	3198-4089	6.3-8.4	21-23	21-17	238-152	75.5-90.8
SD	1-15	.063	—	269-440	351-470	1062-1422	3.0-3.0	7-10	20-6	578-552	311-326	3540-3786	6.1-6.9	19-33	30-16	302-249	61.8-87.7
Aver	16	—	—	331	441	1801	4.1	13	13	527	306	3553	6.7	20	17	243	78.1

TEAM	1D	PENY	PNT	FGM/A	RTNY	RTNTD	OFFY/DEFY	NETY	NETTO	NP	PNP	DELP	PW	DELW	PRT	DR	YPD	DEL
Eastern Division																		
Mia	251-289	920-793	42.1-40.6	28/31-22/30	829-360	3-**1**	4461-4636	-175	15	97	45	52	10.4	0.6	4.3/**3.1**	195-199	22.9-23.3	-0.4
Ind	357-310	866-820	44.7-42.7	25/27-21/28	477-569	3-2	6141-5357	784	-7	103	37	66	10.6	-0.6	**6.7**/ 5.3	183-**184**	**33.6**-29.1	4.4
NYJ	308-267	**626**-832	44.7-**40.0**	23/34-29/34	505-1205	2-7	5395-4820	575	-5	0	28	-28	8.0	1.0	4.3/ 3.9	205-206	26.3-23.4	2.9
Buf	309-252	913-905	38.1-42.0	26/35-29/33	321-656	3-6	5498-4426	1072	6	-35	113	-148	7.1	0.9	5.5/ 4.5	203-202	27.1-21.9	5.2
NE	283-326	815-897	42.2-40.4	27/33-24/32	723-592	1-3	4571-5353	-782	-2	-62	-73	11	6.4	-1.5	4.4/ 5.8	192-190	23.8-28.2	-4.4
Central Division																		
Ten	299-**215**	870-778	40.8-42.7	27/34-17/22	956-396	6-3	5350-**3813**	**1537**	0	155	128	27	11.9	1.1	5.6/ 3.4	193-194	27.7-**19.7**	**8.1**
Bal	288-216	730-535	40.2-44.5	**35/39-14/19**	**1190**-616	3-2	5014-3967	1047	**23**	168	**179**	-11	12.2	-0.2	3.9/ 3.7	190-197	26.4-20.1	6.3
Pit	283-252	667-876	43.3-43.3	25/30-29/34	653-521	4-2	4766-4713	53	14	66	60	6	9.6	-0.6	4.5/ 4.3	194-191	24.6-24.7	-0.1
Jax	318-252	703-814	41.9-42.5	29/33-17/24	478-646	0-2	5690-4845	845	1	40	74	-34	9.0	-2.0	5.3/ 5.7	196-196	29.0-24.7	4.3
Cin	254-307	878-924	40.2-41.7	12/21-26/36	464-525	2-2	4260-5487	-1227	-14	-174	-158	-16	3.7	0.3	2.7/ 6.1	194-188	22.0-29.2	-7.2
Cle	176-343	925-626	45.5-42.2	14/17-31/34	362-1021	1-2	3530-5643	-2113	-3	-258	-188	-70	1.6	**1.4**	3.2/ 5.3	187-188	18.9-30.0	-11.1
Western Division																		
Oak	337-320	940-912	45.2-41.6	23/34-19/25	680-372	7-2	5776-5249	527	17	**180**	112	68	**12.5**	-0.5	6.1/ 4.8	189-193	30.6-27.2	3.4
Den	**383**-294	792-898	39.6-43.8	26/34-19/23	707-414	**9**-6	**6554**-5544	1010	19	116	160	-44	10.9	0.1	6.6/ 4.8	200-190	32.8-29.2	3.6
KC	321-330	848-**1020**	44.6-43.1	17/24-21/30	493-854	3-4	5614-5280	334	3	1	40	-39	8.0	-1.0	6.1/ 5.1	192-188	29.2-28.1	1.2
Sea	281-331	728-694	39.5-41.5	21/26-28/33	684-**342**	6-3	4680-6391	-1711	-9	-85	-179	**94**	5.9	0.1	4.0/ 6.6	186-188	25.2-34.0	-8.8
SD	251-312	1036-851	**46.2**-41.5	18/25-30/34	585-1237	5-7	4300-4959	-659	-28	-171	-167	-4	3.7	-2.7	3.3/ 5.3	**210**-211	20.5-23.5	-3.0
Aver	295	843	41.7	24/30	594	2	5111	—	—	—	—	—	—	—	5.2	100	26.2	—

Rushing Attempts	Rushing Yards	Rushing Average	Rushing TDs	Rushing Rank	Passing Yards	Passing Average
E.George-Ten..........403	E.James-Ind..........1709	R.Gannon-Oak.......5.94	M.Anderson-Den.......15	E.James-Ind..........1839	P.Manning-Ind........4413	B.Griese-Den..........8.00
E.James-Ind..........387	E.George-Ten........1509	N.Kaufman-Oak......5.37	L.Smith-Mia..............14	E.George-Ten........1649	E.Grbac-KC..........4169	P.Manning-Ind.........7.73
J.Bettis-Pit..............355	M.Anderson-Den...1487	M.Anderson-Den....5.01	E.George-Ten...........14	M.Anderson-Den...1637	T.Taylor-NYJ..........3732	G.Frerotte-Den........7.66
C.Martin-NYJ...........316	C.Dillon-Cin...........1435	F.Taylor-Jax............4.79	E.James-Ind.............13	F.Taylor-Jax...........1519	M.Brunell-Jax.........3640	E.Grbac-KC............7.62
C.Dillon-Cin.............315	F.Taylor-Jax...........1399	E.Rhett-KC..............4.74	F.Taylor-Jax.............12	C.Dillon-Cin...........1505	R.Gannon-Oak......3430	D.Flutie-Buf............7.36

Completion Percent	TD Passes	TD Percent	INT Percent	Passer Rating	Passing Rank	Receptions
B.Griese-Den..........64.3	P.Manning-Ind...........33	R.Gannon-Oak.........5.9	B.Griese-Den............1.2	B.Griese-Den........102.9	P.Manning-Ind........1772	M.Harrison-Ind.........102
S.McNair-Ten..........62.6	E.Grbac-KC...............28	P.Manning-Ind...........5.8	D.Flutie-Buf...............1.3	P.Manning-Ind.........94.7	E.Grbac-KC...........1665	E.McCaffrey-Den.....101
P.Manning-Ind.........62.5	R.Gannon-Oak..........28	B.Griese-Den............5.7	A.Smith-Cin...............2.2	R.Gannon-Oak.......92.4	R.Gannon-Oak......1415	R.Smith-Den............100
J.Kitna-Sea.............62.0	T.Taylor-NYJ..............21	T.Dilfer-Bal................5.3	R.Johnson-Buf..........2.3	E.Grbac-KC............89.9	M.Brunell-Jax.........1360	E.Moulds-Buf.............94
M.Brunell-Jax..........60.7	M.Brunell-Jax............20	E.Grbac-KC...............5.1	R.Gannon-Oak..........2.3	D.Flutie-Buf............86.5	B.Griese-Den.........1279	K.McCardell-Jax........94

Receiving Yards	Receiving Average	Receiving TDs	Receiving Rank	Combined Net Yards	Total TDs	Total Points
R.Smith-Den..........1602	D.Alexander-KC....17.83	M.Harrison-Ind...........14	R.Smith-Den............841	D.Mason-Ten.........2690	E.James-Ind..............18	M.Stover-Bal............135
M.Harrison-Ind.......1413	B.Shaw-Pit............16.80	T.Brown-Oak..............11	M.Harrison-Ind.........777	E.James-Ind..........2303	L.Smith-Mia...............16	A.Van Pelt-Ind..........121
D.Alexander-KC.....1391	J.Graham-SD........16.49	D.Alexander-KC.........10	D.Alexander-KC.......746	C.Rogers-Sea........1992	E.George-Ten............16	A.Del Greco-Ten......118
E.Moulds-Buf.........1326	C.Sanders-Ten......16.24	E.McCaffrey-Den.........9	E.McCaffrey-Den.....704	E.George-Ten........1962	M.Anderson-Den.......15	O.Mare-Mia..............117
E.McCaffrey-Den...1317	J.McDaniel-Buf.....16.21	T.Gonzalez-KC............9	E.Moulds-Buf..........688	K.Faulk-NE............1909		T.James-Oak...........112

Punt Average	Field Goals	Field Goal Percent	Kickoff Returns	Kickoff Return Average	Punt Returns	Punt Return Average
D.Bennett-SD..........46.2	M.Stover-Bal..............35	A.Van Pelt-Ind.........92.6	R.Jenkins-SD............67	D.Mason-Ten..........27.0	D.Mason-Ten.............51	J.Ogden-Mia...........17.0
S.Lechler-Oak.........45.9	O.Mare-Mia................28	M.Hollis-Jax............92.3	C.Rogers-Sea............66	K.Williams-NYJ.......26.2	T.Brown-NE...............39	J.Lewis-Bal.............16.1
C.Gardocki-Cle.......45.5	A.Vinatieri-NE............27	O.Mare-Mia.............90.3	T.Mack-Cin................50	A.Denson-Mia.........24.8	H.Poteat-Pit...............36	C.Rogers-Sea.........14.0
T.Tupa-NYJ.............44.7	A.Del Greco-Ten........27	M.Stover-Bal...........89.7	D.O'Neal-Den............46	C.Rogers-Sea.........24.7	J.Lewis-Bal...............36	D.Mason-Ten...........13.0
H.Smith-Ind.............44.7	S.Christie-Buf...........26	R.Lindell-Sea..........88.2		D.Dunn-Oak............24.4		H.Poteat-Pit............13.0

Punt/Kick Return Yards	Punt/Kick Return TDs	Interceptions	Interception Return Yards	Interception Return TDs	Sacks	Overall Rank
C.Rogers-Sea........1992	J.Lewis-Bal..................2	B.Walker-Mia...............7	C.McAlister-Bal........165	E.Allen-Oak.................3	T.Armstrong-Mia.....16.5	E.James-Ind...........2161
D.Mason-Ten.........1794		S.Rolle-Ten..................7	E.Allen-Oak.............145	J.Spencer-Den.............2	J.Taylor-Mia............14.5	R.Gannon-Oak......1984
R.Jenkins-SD.........1531			V.Green-NYJ...........144		E.Hicks-KC.............14.0	P.Manning-Ind.......1898
D.O'Neal-Den........1456			S.Rolle-Ten.............140		J.Gildon-Pit............13.5	E.George-Ten........1886
D.Dunn-Oak...........1172			J.Bellamy-Sea..........132		T.Pryce-Den............12.0	E.Grbac-KC...........1785

The Many Sides of Adversity

Baltimore linebacker Ray Lewis was arrested outside a Georgia nightclub after a Super Bowl party ended with the murder of two men. Lewis accepted a plea deal and agreed to testify against two of his friends. By the time the season started, the conversation had turned from his off-field legal troubles to his dominating performance on the field. Lewis led a defense that set NFL records for fewest points allowed (165) and fewest yards rushing allowed (970) in a 16-game schedule. Rookie Jamal Lewis rushed for 1,364 yards, and the Ravens defense held 11 of their 16 opponents to 10 points or less.

The defending AFC champions also had an improved defense. Tennessee's smothering secondary allowed fewer passing yards than any other team and a league-low 10 touchdown passes. The offense, however, became dependent on constant doses of Eddie George. He became just the fourth player to carry the ball more than 400 times in a season, despite averaging just 3.7 yards per carry. The decrease in offensive productivity didn't stop the Titans from winning 13 games to take the AFC Central for the second consecutive season.

Veteran quarterback Rich Gannon continued to soar, his career reborn in Oakland's vertical passing game. Lacking a single standout in the backfield, the Raiders assembled a running game using four different backs. That group led the league in rushing yards and finished second in rushing touchdowns. Coach Jon Gruden's club won 12 games and secured its first playoff berth in eight years.

Several teams were forced to adapt to the loss of great players. None was more devastated than the Kansas City Chiefs, whose star linebacker Derrick Thomas died in a car accident in January. Miami struggled with Jay Fielder replacing retired Dan Marino, but the steady running of Lamar Smith and a defense featuring five Pro Bowlers propelled the Dolphins to a division title. Broncos running back Terrell Davis was sidelined by a knee injury for the second straight season. Fullback Mike Anderson, a 27-year old rookie free agent, ran for 1,487 yards and 15 touchdowns to help the Broncos finish with the NFL's second-ranked offense and a wild-card berth.

2001 NFC

TEAM	W-L-T	PCT	POST	PTS	RA	RY	RY/A	RTD	FL	PA	PC	GPY	GPY/A	PTD	PI	PSY	PRAT
Eastern Division																	
Phi	11-5	.688	EDC	343-208	412-455	1778-1837	4.3-4.0	6-**6**	10-**19**	522-517	300-288	3427-3147	6.6-6.1	27-13	14-14	282-283	83.4-71.0
Was	8-8	.500	—	256-303	490-484	1948-1869	4.0-3.9	10-10	15-11	432-473	235-**262**	2716-3116	6.3-6.6	13-19	13-23	229-139	71.1-68.8
NYG	7-9	.438	—	294-321	424-428	1777-1545	4.2-3.6	11-7	13-13	568-521	327-298	3764-3750	6.6-7.2	19-25	16-15	206-320	77.1-83.7
Arz	7-9	.438	—	295-343	400-496	1449-2087	3.6-4.2	10-10	13-7	526-556	304-337	3653-3726	6.9-6.7	18-26	14-17	204-128	79.5-83.4
Dal	5-11	.313	—	246-338	505-472	2184-1710	4.3-3.6	8-12	14-16	413-489	210-287	2408-**3019**	5.8-6.2	14-20	20-9	190-130	59.9-82.7
Central Division																	
ChiB	13-3	.813	D	338-**203**	475-373	1742-**1313**	3.7-**3.5**	12-**6**	8-17	528-602	315-355	3072-3959	5.8-6.6	20-**12**	16-20	120-294	76.0-71.4
GB	12-4	.750	WD	390-266	410-406	1693-1769	4.1-4.4	11-10	12-**19**	510-583	314-341	3921-3505	7.7-**6.0**	32-14	15-20	151-**337**	94.1-69.6
TB	9-7	.563	W	324-280	407-415	1371-1702	3.4-4.1	17-8	10-11	592-493	362-273	3621-3223	6.1-6.5	13-20	**12-28**	298-272	77.4-**65.3**
Min	5-11	.313	—	290-390	376-477	1609-2299	4.3-4.8	10-21	16-10	555-478	335-291	3854-3571	6.9-7.5	23-16	23-8	278-204	77.9-88.1
Det	2-14	.125	—	270-424	351-470	1398-1993	4.0-4.2	8-15	14-6	**609**-514	343-312	3969-3752	6.5-7.3	18-30	24-16	373-224	69.6-89.6
Western Division																	
SL	**14**-2	**.875**	DCS	**503**-273	416-**366**	2027-1374	**4.9**-3.8	**20**-11	22-13	551-541	**379**-314	**4903**-3348	**8.9**-6.2	**37**-16	22-21	240-251	**102.2**-69.9
SF	12-4	.750	W	409-282	**509**-389	**2244**-1571	4.4-4.0	16-9	**7**-10	506-567	318-332	3559-3603	7.0-6.4	32-18	**12**-24	**114**-220	95.0-70.3
NO	7-9	.438	—	333-409	419-443	1712-1715	4.1-3.9	8-15	13-15	562-**452**	313-278	3844-3678	6.8-8.1	27-30	22-15	330-323	76.7-95.5
Atl	7-9	.438	—	291-377	439-405	1762-1943	4.0-4.8	9-13	11-12	485-515	278-331	3695-4132	7.6-8.0	19-29	17-18	387-230	80.0-93.3
Car	1-15	.063	—	253-410	354-521	1372-2301	3.9-4.4	9-13	13-12	579-510	314-306	3098-3809	5.4-7.5	12-25	22-24	216-167	60.6-79.9
Aver	16	—	—	323	441	1788	4.1	12	12	522	308	3537	6.8	20	18	244	78.5

TEAM	1D	PENY	PNT	FGM/A	RTNY	RTNTD	OFFY/DEFY	NETY	NETTO	NP	PNP	DELP	PW	DELW	PRT	DR	YPD	DEL
Eastern Division																		
Phi	256-262	768-741	43.5-40.6	26/31-23/32	660-587	5-**1**	4923-4701	222	9	135	55	80	11.4	-0.4	5.0/ 4.2	202-206	24.4-**22.8**	1.6
Was	241-271	828-672	41.5-42.3	26/33-24/29	640-681	2-4	4435-4846	-411	6	-47	-10	-37	6.8	1.2	4.3/ 4.3	190-190	23.3-25.5	-2.2
NYG	295-268	905-695	42.2-41.8	23/30-23/31	505-724	2-4	5335-4975	360	-1	-27	26	-53	7.3	-0.3	5.0/ 5.3	199-201	26.8-24.8	2.1
Arz	277-319	**620-980**	41.0-43.3	21/26-23/32	766-638	5-3	4898-5685	-787	-3	-48	-78	30	6.8	0.2	5.4/ 5.4	183-188	26.8-30.2	-3.5
Dal	247-272	744-634	38.7-41.7	22/33-27/36	684-837	4-5	4402-4599	-197	-9	-92	-52	-40	5.7	-0.7	3.3/ 5.2	190-189	23.2-24.3	-1.2
Central Division																		
ChiB	277-277	622-808	42.5-40.7	26/31-**18**/28	777-514	5-3	4694-4978	-284	13	135	28	**107**	11.4	**1.6**	4.5/ 4.4	192-194	24.4-25.7	-1.2
GB	282-278	633-921	42.5-42.4	20/31-22/28	595-540	4-4	5463-4937	526	12	124	92	32	11.1	0.9	6.4/ 3.8	190-202	28.8-24.4	4.3
TB	298-262	672-742	40.7-41.5	28/35-25/29	**815-454**	4-**1**	4694-4653	41	**17**	44	71	-27	9.1	-0.1	4.6/**3.5**	187-186	25.1-25.0	0.1
Min	288-312	836-874	42.1-**40.3**	15/18-33/38	354-585	2-5	5185-5666	-481	-21	-100	-124	24	5.5	-0.5	4.6/ 6.2	183-**175**	28.3-32.4	-4.0
Det	289-321	1081-896	43.0-42.6	21/30-19/27	472-763	4-7	4994-5521	-527	-16	-154	-108	-46	4.2	-2.2	4.0/ 5.7	187-183	26.7-30.2	-3.5
Western Division																		
SL	**357-256**	847-830	42.1-42.0	23/29-20/26	769-474	5-4	**6690-4471**	**2219**	-10	**230**	**145**	85	**13.8**	0.3	**6.8**/ 3.9	182-190	**36.8**-23.5	**13.2**
SF	328-289	669-812	40.8-41.4	18/25-23/27	481-522	3-3	5689-4954	735	15	127	121	6	11.2	0.8	6.1/ 4.1	172-177	33.1-28.0	5.1
NO	294-284	1025-877	41.8-43.5	27/31-27/31	497-505	1-2	5226-5070	156	-5	-76	-7	-69	6.1	0.9	4.6/ 5.9	187-190	27.9-26.7	1.3
Atl	280-298	754-852	38.8-43.3	**29/37**-19/**24**	617-460	1-4	5070-5845	-775	2	-86	-57	-29	5.8	1.2	5.0/ 6.1	185-178	27.4-32.8	-5.4
Car	236-304	747-793	**47.0**-40.7	23/28-25/30	794-857	**6**-10	4254-5943	-1689	1	-157	-137	-20	4.1	-3.1	3.3/ 5.2	**211**-196	20.2-30.3	-10.2
Aver	288	785	41.9	24/31	614	4	5081	—	—	—	—	—	—	—	5.2	190	26.7	—

Rushing Attempts	Rushing Yards	Rushing Average	Rushing TDs	Rushing Rank	Passing Yards	Passing Average
S.Davis-Was....356	S.Davis-Was....1432	D.McNabb-Phi....5.88	M.Faulk-SL....12	M.Faulk-SL....1502	K.Warner-SL....4830	K.Warner-SL....8.85
R.Williams-NO....313	A.Green-GB....1387	M.Faulk-SL....5.32	M.Alstott-TB....10	S.Davis-Was....1482	B.Favre-GB....3921	C.Chandler-Atl....7.80
A.Green-GB....304	M.Faulk-SL....1382	T.Barber-NYG....5.21	A.Green-GB....9	A.Green-GB....1477	A.Brooks-NO....3832	B.Favre-GB....7.69
A.Thomas-Chi....278	R.Williams-NO....1245	T.Hambrick-Dal....5.12	A.Thomas-Chi....7	R.Williams-NO....1305	K.Collins-NYG....3764	D.Culpepper-Min....7.14
E.Smith-Dal....261	G.Hearst-SF....1206	J.Stewart-Det....4.79	R.Dayne-NYG....7	A.Thomas-Chi....1253	J.Plummer-Arz....3653	J.Garcia-SF....7.02
Completion Percent	**TD Passes**	**TD Percent**	**INT Percent**	**Passer Rating**	**Passing Rank**	**Receptions**
K.Warner-SL....68.7	K.Warner-SL....36	K.Warner-SL....6.6	B.Johnson-TB....2.0	K.Warner-SL....101.4	K.Warner-SL....1715	K.Johnson-TB....106
D.Culpepper-Min....64.2	J.Garcia-SF....32	J.Garcia-SF....6.3	J.Garcia-SF....2.4	J.Garcia-SF....94.8	B.Favre-GB....1521	M.Booker-Chi....100
J.Garcia-SF....62.7	B.Favre-GB....32	B.Favre-GB....6.3	D.McNabb-Phi....2.4	B.Favre-GB....94.1	J.Garcia-SF....1449	D.Boston-Arz....98
B.Favre-GB....61.6	A.Brooks-NO....26	D.McNabb-Phi....5.1	J.Miller-Chi....2.5	D.McNabb-Phi....84.3	J.Plummer-Arz....1357	T.Owens-SF....93
C.Chandler-Atl....61.1	D.McNabb-Phi....25	A.Brooks-NO....4.7	J.Plummer-Arz....2.7	C.Chandler-Atl....84.1	K.Collins-NYG....1337	
Receiving Yards	**Receiving Average**	**Receiving TDs**	**Receiving Rank**	**Combined Net Yards**	**Total TDs**	**Total Points**
D.Boston-Arz....1598	B.Schroeder-GB....17.32	T.Owens-SF....16	D.Boston-Arz....839	M.Faulk-SL....2147	M.Faulk-SL....21	M.Faulk-SL....128
T.Owens-SF....1412	I.Bruce-SL....17.28	R.Moss-Min....10	T.Owens-SF....786	S.Smith-Car....1994	T.Owens-SF....16	J.Wilkins-SL....127
T.Holt-SL....1363	T.Holt-SL....16.83		T.Holt-SL....717	A.Green-GB....1981	A.Green-GB....11	J.Feely-Atl....115
K.Johnson-TB....1266	D.Boston-Arz....16.31		J.Horn-NO....678	R.Swinton-Dal....1854	M.Alstott-TB....11	D.Akers-Phi....115
J.Horn-NO....1265	M.Jenkins-Arz....16.19		R.Moss-Min....667	D.Howard-Det....1805	R.Moss-Min....10	J.Carney-NO....113
Punt Average	**Field Goals**	**Field Goal Percent**	**Kickoff Returns**	**Kickoff Return Average**	**Punt Returns**	**Punt Return Average**
T.Sauerbrun-Car....47.5	J.Feely-Atl....29	J.Carney-NO....87.1	D.Vaughn-Atl....61	S.Smith-Car....25.6	A.Jackson-Arz....40	D.Gordon-Atl....14.1
S.Landeta-Phi....43.5	J.Carney-NO....27	P.Edinger-Chi....83.9	D.Howard-Det....57	D.Howard-Det....25.4	B.Mitchell-Phi....39	R.Swinton-Dal....13.4
M.Berger-Min....43.5	P.Edinger-Chi....26	D.Akers-Phi....83.9	R.Swinton-Dal....56	B.Mitchell-Phi....25.0	T.Barber-NYG....38	E.Metcalf-Was....12.5
J.Jett-Det....43.3	B.Conway-Was....26	G.Anderson-Min....83.3	S.Smith-Car....56	D.Vaughn-Atl....24.4	A.Hakim-SL....36	B.Mitchell-Phi....12.0
R.Williams-NYG....42.9	D.Akers-Phi....26		Stubblefield-SF....50	F.McAfee-NO....24.2	K.Williams-TB....35	A.Jackson-Arz....11.5
Punt/Kick Return Yards	**Punt/Kick Return TDs**	**Interceptions**	**Interception Return Yards**	**Interception Return TDs**	**Sacks**	**Overall Rank**
S.Smith-Car....1795	S.Smith-Car....3	R.Barber-TB....10	Z.Bronson-SF....165	A.Williams-SL....2	M.Strahan-NYG....22.5	M.Faulk-SL....1930
R.Swinton-Dal....1741		K.Lassiter-Arz....9	D.Bly-SL....150	D.Coakley-Dal....2	L.Little-SL....14.5	A.Green-GB....1784
D.Howard-Det....1647		D.Evans-Car....8	D.Evans-Car....126	M.Brown-Chi....2	Gbaja-Biamila-GB....13.5	K.Warner-SL....1775
B.Mitchell-Phi....1492		A.Plummer-SF....7	L.Arrington-Was....120	Z.Bronson-SF....2	C.Clemons-NO....13.5	D.McNabb-Phi....1764
D.Vaughn-Atl....1491		Z.Bronson-SF....7	T.Williams-GB....117	D.Bly-SL....2	P.Kerney-Atl....12.0	J.Garcia-SF....1753

Forever Young

With his broken hand fully healed, Kurt Warner continued his assault on the record books. The Rams quarterback led the league with 36 touchdown passes and threw for 4,830 yards, the second-highest total in NFL history. Running back Marshall Faulk remained the league's most dangerous double threat, running for 12 touchdowns and catching 9 more. While the Rams offense remained explosive, they finally assembled a solid defense to go along with it. Veteran defensive back Aeneas Williams, acquired from the Cardinals, keyed the turnaround. The Rams finished with the third-ranked defense.

The Eagles didn't have a 1,000-yard receiver or a 1,000-yard rusher, but the offensive ensemble had enough separate pieces to make them formidable as a whole. Quarterback Donovan McNabb threw 25 touchdown passes, and the defense allowed just 13 points per game. The Eagles won the NFC East for the first time in 13 years. Chicago's defense was the league's stingiest, which helped overcome a lackluster rushing attack and a feeble passing game. The Bears showed a knack for coming up with big plays in close games, none more remarkable than in a week eight victory against the Browns. The Bears trailed 21–7 with less than a minute to go, but scored 2 touchdowns in the game's final 32 seconds to force overtime. An interception return for a touchdown gave the Bears a win and the belief that destiny was on their side.

After an opening win, the Carolina Panthers lost 15 straight games, the longest one-season streak in NFL history. It was an ignominious end to George Seifert's coaching career. As bad as Carolina was, the XFL was far worse. The over-hyped spring football league spawned by a pro wrestling group was put to the mat after one season. A player whose name on his XFL jersey read "He Hate Me" was Rod Smart, who would be a beloved bit player in Carolina's not-too-distant renaissance.

NFL vice president and former Giants general manager George Young died on December 8. In his two decades with the team, New York won two Super Bowls, and the cantankerously affable Young was named NFL Executive of the Year a record five times.

2001 AFC

TEAM	W-L-T	PCT	POST	PTS	RA	RY	RY/A	RTD	FL	PA	PC	GPY	GPY/A	PTD	PI	PSY	PRAT
Eastern Division																	
NE	11-5	.688	#DCS*	371-272	473-429	1793-1855	3.8-4.3	15-7	13-13	482-546	306-299	3326-3731	6.9-6.8	21-15	15-22	237-234	85.3-68.6
Mia	11-5	.688	#W	344-290	473-453	1664-1779	3.5-3.9	14-9	19-11	453-467	275-**262**	3335-**3059**	7.4-6.6	20-22	19-17	178-230	80.6-76.7
NYJ	10-6	.625	W	308-295	445-481	2054-2154	4.6-4.5	11-15	**7-19**	464-516	272-313	2871-3170	6.2-6.1	17-14	14-20	**130**-171	76.4-71.1
Ind	6-10	.375	—	**413**-486	438-455	1966-2115	4.5-4.6	16-20	15-10	557-509	349-311	**4227**-3857	**7.6**-7.6	**27**-30	23-15	238-257	84.9-91.9
Buf	3-13	.188	—	265-420	406-482	1686-2133	4.2-4.4	9-20	13-8	557-**453**	327-284	3722-3378	6.7-7.5	18-23	20-11	271-219	74.7-92.2
Central Division																	
Pit	**13**-3	**.813**	DC	352-**212**	**580-339**	**2774-1195**	**4.8**-3.5	**17-5**	9-12	454-525	274-295	3295-3309	7.3-6.3	16-19	12-16	182-**367**	83.4-74.5
Bal	10-6	.625	WD	303-265	483-410	1810-1411	3.7-3.4	11-10	16-12	557-555	320-321	3595-3325	6.5-**6.0**	18-16	20-16	281-290	72.7-72.8
Cle	7-9	.438	—	285-319	417-494	1351-2208	3.2-4.5	8-11	12-9	466-552	279-309	3154-3377	6.8-6.1	18-18	21-**33**	353-288	74.3-**60.2**
Ten	7-9	.438	—	336-388	468-405	1794-1431	3.8-3.5	12-17	11-11	515-559	307-328	3867-4259	7.5-7.6	23-27	17-13	309-175	84.2-89.1
Jax	6-10	.375	—	294-286	372-469	1600-1611	4.3-3.4	11-15	13-12	534-544	321-354	3670-3757	6.9-6.9	20-**13**	14-12	430-298	82.4-83.9
Cin	6-10	.375	—	226-309	441-453	1712-1675	3.9-3.7	11-10	11-15	**602**-512	322-311	3291-3477	5.5-6.8	12-23	26-13	203-320	58.1-85.4
Western Division																	
Oak	10-6	.625	ED	399-327	450-433	1654-1988	3.7-4.6	14-17	16-7	553-528	**364**-290	3862-3287	7.0-6.2	**27**-16	**9**-17	155-204	**95.5**-70.5
Sea	9-7	.563	—	301-324	469-427	1936-1721	4.1-4.0	15-9	9-13	462-563	258-339	3164-3733	6.8-6.6	15-20	12-14	328-248	77.2-81.4
Den	8-8	.500	—	340-339	481-406	1877-1492	3.9-3.7	7-9	8-15	511-515	312-308	3208-3561	6.3-6.9	26-23	19-22	268-279	80.6-77.8
KC	6-10	.375	—	320-344	448-481	2008-2140	4.5-4.4	16-15	9-13	528-491	300-296	3863-3403	7.3-6.9	17-19	24-13	198-239	71.7-83.1
SD	5-11	.313	—	332-321	435-449	1695-1504	3.9-**3.3**	13-10	11-12	548-535	309-317	3685-3618	6.7-6.8	16-24	18-19	180-218	73.1-79.8
Aver	16	—	—	323	441	1788	4.1	12	12	522	308	3537	6.8	20	18	244	78.5

TEAM	1D	PENY	PNT	FGM/A	RTNY	RTNTD	OFFY/DEFY	NETY	NETTO	NP	PNP	DELP	PW	DELW	PRT	DR	YPD	DEL
Eastern Division																		
NE	292-303	802-839	41.1-**39.5**	24/30-30/41	862-397	**7**-4	4882-5352	-470	7	99	-11	**110**	10.5	0.5	5.0/ 4.5	187-190	26.1-28.2	-2.1
Mia	263-283	914-623	41.1-44.1	19/21-16/22	**883-390**	**7**-4	4821-4608	213	-10	54	-22	76	9.4	1.6	5.2/ 4.5	186-196	25.9-23.5	2.4
NYJ	274-284	**507**-700	39.0-40.7	24/31-22/27	713-668	6-4	4795-5153	-358	**18**	13	42	-29	8.3	**1.7**	4.7/ 4.1	187-**177**	25.6-29.1	-3.5
Ind	**343**-323	730-759	44.5-42.7	28/34-30/36	448-1031	4-7	**5955**-5715	240	-13	-73	-32	-41	6.2	-0.2	5.5/ 5.9	197-198	30.2-28.9	1.4
Buf	287-302	954-835	40.8-43.1	18/29-28/37	364-808	4-5	5137-5292	-155	-14	-155	-69	-86	4.1	-1.1	4.5/ 5.9	186-182	27.6-29.1	-1.5
Central Division																		
Pit	314-**254**	737-585	41.4-42.3	30/**44-9/20**	690-435	5-2	5887-**4137**	**1750**	7	**140**	**174**	-34	**11.5**	1.5	5.6/ 4.2	175-183	**33.6**-22.6	**11.0**
Bal	299-262	728-**903**	38.0-41.6	30/35-19/33	758-514	2-4	5124-4446	678	-8	38	25	13	8.9	1.0	4.3/ 4.1	203-199	25.2-**22.3**	2.9
Cle	238-295	825-779	42.9-43.2	22/25-25/34	746-889	5-6	4152-5297	-1145	9	-34	-59	25	7.2	-0.1	3.9/**3.0**	199-203	20.9-26.1	-5.2
Ten	288-300	1025-832	42.0-41.3	20/28-22/29	360-427	4-2	5352-5515	-163	-4	-52	-30	-22	6.7	0.3	5.4/ 6.4	196-192	27.3-28.7	-1.4
Jax	289-300	710-834	43.6-40.5	18/28-26/35	416-594	3-2	4840-5070	-230	-3	8	-31	39	8.2	-2.2	4.7/ 5.2	188-185	25.7-27.4	-1.7
Cin	294-281	870-837	39.6-41.2	17/28-22/30	482-766	2-2	4800-4832	-32	-9	-83	-39	-44	5.9	0.1	3.2/ 5.0	191-192	25.1-25.2	-0.0
Western Division																		
Oak	316-296	897-621	**45.6**-40.9	26/32-25/33	645-649	5-3	5361-5071	290	-1	72	20	52	9.8	0.2	**6.2**/ 4.4	185-191	29.0-26.5	2.4
Sea	274-300	579-805	43.4-42.3	20/32-29/36	538-498	4-5	4772-5206	-434	6	-23	-12	-11	7.4	1.6	4.8/ 5.1	187-188	25.5-27.7	-2.2
Den	304-292	917-853	44.7-47.0	**31**/36-25/29	645-773	2-6	4817-4774	43	10	1	44	-43	8.0	-0.0	4.2/ 4.6	196-192	24.6-24.9	-0.3
KC	324-296	602-761	40.5-41.0	27/35-27/34	492-584	1-3	5673-5304	369	-7	-24	3	-27	7.4	-1.4	4.9/ 5.3	191-188	29.7-28.2	1.5
SD	290-290	777-632	42.4-42.1	30/43-26/35	577-481	6-**1**	5200-4904	296	2	11	33	-22	8.3	-3.3	5.0/ 4.8	**205**-198	25.4-24.8	0.6
Aver	288	785	41.9	24/31	614	2	5081	—	—	—	—	—	—	—	5.2	99	26.7	—

Rushing Attempts	Rushing Yards	Rushing Average	Rushing TDs	Rushing Rank	Passing Yards	Passing Average
C.Dillon-Cin 340	P.Holmes-KC 1555	K.Stewart-Pit..........5.59	S.Alexander-Sea........14	P.Holmes-KC 1635	P.Manning-Ind........4131	S.McNair-Ten..........7.77
L.Tomlinson-SD 339	C.Martin-NYJ.........1513	A.Zereoue-Pit 5.19	A.Smith-NE...............12	C.Martin-NYJ.........1613	R.Gannon-Oak 3828	P.Manning-Ind.........7.55
C.Martin-NYJ...........333	S.Alexander-Sea....1318	J.Bettis-Pit 4.76	L.Tomlinson-SD 10	S.Alexander-Sea....1458	T.Green-KC............3783	J.Fiedler-Mia...........7.31
P.Holmes-KC 327	C.Dillon-Cin 1315	P.Holmes-KC 4.76	C.Martin-NYJ 10	C.Dillon-Cin 1415	D.Flutie-SD 3464	T.Green-KC..............7.23
E.George-Ten 315	L.Tomlinson-SD 1236	D.Rhodes-Ind..........4.74	C.Dillon-Cin 10	L.Tomlinson-SD 1336	S.McNair-Ten.........3350	K.Stewart-Pit...........7.03
Completion Percent	**TD Passes**	**TD Percent**	**INT Percent**	**Passer Rating**	**Passing Rank**	**Receptions**
R.Gannon-Oak 65.8	R.Gannon-Oak 27	B.Griese-Den............5.1	R.Gannon-Oak 1.6	R.Gannon-Oak 95.5	R.Gannon-Oak 1689	R.Smith-Den............113
T.Brady-NE 63.9	P.Manning-Ind............26	R.Gannon-Oak 4.9	K.Stewart-Pit.............2.5	S.McNair-Ten..........90.2	S.McNair-Ten.........1300	J.Smith-Jax.............112
P.Manning-Ind.........62.7	B.Griese-Den.............23	S.McNair-Ten............4.9	E.Hartwell-Sea 2.5	T.Brady-NE 86.5	P.Manning-Ind.......1276	M.Harrison-Ind.........109
S.McNair-Ten..........61.3	S.McNair-Ten.............21	P.Manning-Ind...........4.8	M.Brunell-Jax............2.7	P.Manning-Ind.........84.1	M.Brunell-Jax.........1230	T.Brown-NE 101
M.Brunell-Jax..........61.1	J.Fiedler-Mia..............20	J.Fiedler-Mia.............4.4	S.McNair-Ten............2.8	M.Brunell-Jax..........84.1	K.Stewart-Pit.........1185	H.Ward-Pit.................94
Receiving Yards	**Receiving Average**	**Receiving TDs**	**Receiving Rank**	**Combined Net Yards**	**Total TDs**	**Total Points**
M.Harrison-Ind.......1524	C.Chambers-Mia ..18.40	M.Harrison-Ind...........15	M.Harrison-Ind.........837	P.Holmes-KC 2169	S.Alexander-Sea........16	A.Van Pelt-Ind..........125
J.Smith-Jax............1373	P.Price-Buf............16.27	R.Smith-Den..............11	R.Smith-Den............727	D.Mason-Ten 2004	M.Harrison-Ind...........15	J.Elam-Den..............124
R.Smith-Den..........1343	C.Conway-SD 15.85		J.Smith-Jax.............727	C.Martin-NYJ.........1833	A.Smith-NE...............13	K.Brown-Pit..............124
T.Brown-NE 1199	M.Pollard-Ind 15.72		T.Brown-Oak...........628	T.Brown-NE 1716	C.Dillon-Cin 13	M.Stover-Bal............115
T.Brown-Oak..........1165	J.Graham-SD........15.60		T.Brown-NE 625	C.Chambers-Mia ...1683	R.Smith-Den..............11	A.Vinatieri-NE..........113
Punt Average	**Field Goals**	**Field Goal Percent**	**Kickoff Returns**	**Kickoff Return Average**	**Punt Returns**	**Punt Return Average**
S.Lechler-Oak.........46.2	J.Elam-Den................31	O.Mare-Mia............90.5	R.Jenkins-SD.............58	R.Jenkins-SD..........26.6	J.Lewis-Bal 42	T.Brown-NE 14.2
T.Rouen-Den 45.3	M.Stover-Bal..............30	P.Dawson-Cle 88.0	C.Rogers-Sea............50	E.Joseph-Jax..........25.2	D.Gibson-Jax.............38	D.O'Neal-Den 13.1
H.Smith-Ind............44.5	K.Brown-Pit................30	J.Elam-Den.............86.1	C.Cole-Den................48	J.Lewis-Bal 24.7	H.Poteat-Pit 36	J.Lewis-Bal 12.4
J.Feagles-Sea.........43.9	A.Van Pelt-Ind............28	M.Stover-Bal...........85.7	T.Kirby-Oak................46	C.Cole-Den.............23.5	J.Ogden-Mia..............32	J.Ogden-Mia 11.8
C.Hanson-Jax.........43.6	T.Peterson-KC 27	A.Van Pelt-Ind.........82.4	T.Wilkins-Ind 44	T.Kirby-Oak............23.2	D.Hall-KC...................32	T.Dwight-SD.............11.3
Punt/Kick Return Yards	**Punt/Kick Return TDs**	**Interceptions**	**Interception Return Yards**	**Interception Return TDs**	**Sacks**	**Overall Rank**
J.Lewis-Bal 1558	R.Jenkins-SD..............2	A.Henry-Cle..............10	B.Marion-Mia 227	Many..........................2	P.Boulware-Bal 15.0	P.Holmes-KC 1952
R.Jenkins-SD.........1541	T.Brown-NE 2	D.O'Neal-Den 9	C.Scott-Pit 204		M.Wiley-SD............13.0	R.Gannon-Oak 1940
C.Rogers-Sea........1364		R.McNeil-SD...............8	O.Smith-NE..............181		J.Miller-Cle.............13.0	C.Martin-NYJ.........1787
T.Wilkins-Ind 1226			A.Henry-Cle.............177		J.Abraham-NYJ 13.0	K.Stewart-Pit..........1772
D.Hall-KC...............1204					J.Gildon-Pit............12.0	S.McNair-Ten.........1764

It Truly Is Only a Game

On the morning after the season's opening Monday night game, America was rocked by terrorist attacks in Washington and New York. The September 11 tragedy not only shocked the nation, but also led to restricted air travel and concerns over safety at NFL stadiums. Commissioner Paul Tagliabue postponed the games scheduled for the following weekend, not only due to concerns about practicality but with the idea of playing while most of the nation was mourning.

The games originally scheduled for week two were played in the first week of January, with playoff games played immediately after that. When teams finally returned to the field on September 23, the occasion was marked with pledges of unity and patriotism in stadiums across the country.

Action on the field was as hard-hitting as ever, as Patriots quarterback Drew Bledsoe learned. A vicious sideline tackle by Jets linebacker Mo Lewis left Bledsoe with broken ribs. Untested backup Tom Brady was forced into action, and although New England lost that game, the Pats won three out of their next four. Brady improved and the Patriots claimed their first AFC East title under coach Bill Belichick. Baltimore running back Jamal Lewis's ACL tear in training camp and quarterback Trent Dilfer's release doomed the defending champions. Veteran replacements Terry Allen and Elvis Grbac didn't work out. By season's end, ineffective Elvis had left the building. He retired along with Allen and oversized personality and defensive tackle Tony Siragusa. Guard Bruce Matthews of division rival Tennessee called it quits after 14 Pro Bowls in 19 seasons.

The Steelers opened a new stadium, but their strategy was as old as the game itself: run the ball and stop your opponent from doing the same. Pittsburgh gained more yards on the ground than any other team, thanks largely to the powerful running of Jerome Bettis. The defense allowed fewer rushing yards than anyone else, and just 5 rushing touchdowns all season. San Diego, coming off a 1–15 season, started 5–2 as rookie LaDainian Tomlinson went on to rush for 1,236 yards and 10 touchdowns, but the Chargers dropped their last nine along with coach Mike Riley.

2002 NFC

TEAM	W-L-T	PCT	POST	PTS	RA	RY	RY/A	RTD	FL	PA	PC	GPY	GPY/A	PTD	PI	PSY	PRAT
Eastern Division																	
Phi	**12**-4	**.750**	DC	415-241	489-**390**	2220-1660	4.5-4.3	15-**5**	13-**23**	548-563	318-333	3606-3442	6.6-6.1	27-18	11-15	222-**348**	85.9-76.4
NYG	10-6	.625	W	320-279	486-407	1875-1830	3.9-4.5	14-12	13-14	549-541	338-311	4103-3369	**7.5**-6.2	19-17	14-11	152-250	85.4-77.9
Was	7-9	.438	—	307-365	442-435	1889-1754	4.3-4.0	10-14	20-12	559-531	300-304	3523-3283	6.3-6.2	24-19	20-14	269-250	72.5-76.5
Dal	5-11	.313	—	217-329	423-481	1754-1818	4.1-3.8	7-10	18-11	471-574	252-334	3020-3586	6.4-6.2	14-22	16-19	399-137	69.1-75.6
Northern Division																	
GB	**12**-4	**.750**	E	398-328	451-413	1933-1998	4.3-4.8	12-14	12-21	580-531	361-287	3823-3228	6.6-6.1	**29**-24	16-24	196-241	**86.6**-68.7
Min	6-10	.375	—	390-442	473-394	**2507**-1666	**5.3**-4.2	**26**-15	18-7	558-542	337-335	3951-4300	7.1-7.9	19-33	23-16	266-197	76.1-94.6
ChiB	4-12	.250	—	281-379	382-504	1344-2076	3.5-4.1	8-13	17-19	543-547	310-335	3316-3782	6.1-6.9	22-24	18-9	265-252	74.8-89.7
Det	3-13	.188	—	306-451	358-495	1477-1967	4.1-4.0	9-19	**6**-14	577-591	277-371	3168-4404	5.5-7.5	19-27	25-10	174-254	57.9-93.6
Southern Division																	
TB	**12**-4	**.750**	DCS*	346-**196**	414-410	1557-**1554**	3.8-3.8	6-8	11-7	567-510	348-**259**	3665-**2785**	6.5-**5.5**	23-**10**	**10-31**	220-295	86.3-**48.4**
Atl	9-6-1	.594	WD	402-314	**523**-441	2368-2047	4.5-4.6	23-12	15-15	479-514	268-285	3384-3585	7.1-7.0	18-23	12-24	217-298	80.2-72.8
NO	9-7	.563	—	**432**-388	426-439	1764-1991	4.1-4.5	16-18	15-18	538-593	291-343	3685-4058	6.8-6.8	27-25	15-20	244-253	80.8-78.8
Car	7-9	.438	—	258-302	452-448	1586-1653	3.5-**3.7**	11-12	18-16	464-522	255-293	2981-3329	6.4-6.4	15-18	22-17	287-336	65.7-73.4
Western Division																	
SF	10-6	.625	ED	367-351	489-394	2244-1652	4.6-4.2	16-14	7-8	571-552	354-340	3576-3701	6.3-6.7	23-23	**10**-19	**119**-195	86.0-80.9
Sea	7-9	.438	—	355-369	430-500	1740-2441	4.0-4.9	17-18	12-11	587-555	361-321	4257-3596	7.3-6.5	19-21	16-19	179-185	83.0-75.6
SL	7-9	.438	—	316-369	343-445	1405-1816	4.1-4.1	11-15	18-14	**635-461**	**408**-292	**4480**-3449	7.1-7.5	24-15	27-12	326-240	79.9-86.0
Arz	5-11	.313	—	262-417	414-490	1823-2146	4.4-4.4	10-17	13-8	548-535	291-335	3038-4005	5.5-7.5	18-29	22-17	298-131	63.7-90.3
Aver	16	—	—	347	441	1858	4.2	14	12	540	322	3631	6.7	22	17	236	80.4

TEAM	1D	PENY	PNT	FGM/A	RTNY	RTNTD	OFFY/DEFY	NETY	NETTO	NP	PNP	DELP	PW	DELW	PRT	DR	YPD	DEL
Eastern Division																		
Phi	311-272	897-969	40.5-41.0	30/34-17/**21**	760-506	4-4	5604-4754	850	14	**174**	127	47	**12.4**	-0.3	5.4/ 4.2	189-196	29.7-24.3	**5.4**
NYG	323-266	955-897	37.5-40.0	26/32-21/31	336-371	2-**1**	5826-4949	877	-2	41	65	-24	9.0	1.0	**6.1**/ 4.8	180-179	32.4-27.6	4.7
Was	303-281	968-972	39.1-39.5	16/25-31/34	623-719	3-6	5143-4787	356	-14	-58	-26	-32	6.6	0.5	4.3/ 4.5	199-188	25.8-25.5	0.4
Dal	237-291	974-919	40.4-41.4	12/19-27/38	552-889	5-3	4375-5267	-892	-4	-112	-90	-22	5.2	-0.2	3.9/ 4.7	213-209	20.5-25.2	-4.7
Northern Division																		
GB	318-294	913-945	41.7-41.3	28/34-**16**/22	707-684	4-2	5560-4985	575	**17**	70	116	-46	9.8	**2.3**	5.3/ 3.7	196-201	28.4-24.8	3.6
Min	**350**-315	1139-824	39.3-39.1	23/29-21/28	474-407	1-7	**6192**-5769	423	-18	-52	-37	-15	6.7	-0.7	4.7/ 6.5	179-193	**34.6**-29.9	4.7
ChiB	260-328	864-935	42.3-41.8	22/28-37/44	470-644	1-**1**	4395-5606	-1211	-7	-98	-129	31	5.6	-1.5	4.2/ 5.8	200-196	22.0-28.6	-6.6
Det	242-360	916-**981**	42.2-42.4	23/28-29/33	536-555	**6**-6	4471-6117	-1646	-7	-145	-165	20	4.4	-1.4	3.4/ 6.4	202-197	22.1-31.1	-8.9
Southern Division																		
TB	287-**236**	789-749	42.6-44.4	**32**/39-17/23	**924**-576	**6**-3	5002-**4044**	**958**	**17**	150	**148**	2	11.8	0.3	5.3/**2.2**	197-199	25.4-**20.3**	5.1
Atl	316-288	931-920	41.9-42.0	**32/40**-18/24	610-**291**	3-2	5535-5334	201	12	88	65	23	10.2	-0.7	5.5/ 4.3	184-193	30.1-27.6	2.4
NO	291-327	911-953	41.4-42.7	31/35-23/28	836-429	**6**-2	5205-5796	-591	8	44	-17	**61**	9.1	-0.1	5.3/ 5.0	195-188	26.7-30.8	-4.1
Car	238-271	785-782	**45.1**-41.3	15/25-24/29	748-751	4-3	4280-4646	-366	-7	-44	-59	15	6.9	0.1	3.6/ 4.2	**215**-215	19.9-21.6	-1.7
Western Division																		
SF	342-307	725-681	38.4-41.5	26/36-22/30	727-413	2-4	5701-5158	543	10	16	85	-69	8.4	1.6	5.5/ 4.9	177-173	32.2-29.8	2.4
Sea	347-356	792-816	41.7-**39.0**	23/29-22/26	501-321	5-4	5818-5852	-34	2	-14	5	-19	7.7	-0.6	5.7/ 4.7	176-**172**	33.1-34.0	-1.0
SL	315-282	919-755	41.9-41.0	19/25-26/30	454-955	2-12	5559-5025	534	-19	-53	-32	-21	6.7	0.3	4.7/ 5.6	181-195	30.7-25.8	4.9
Arz	274-335	**617**-969	43.4-42.0	15/21-22/29	407-850	3-4	4563-6020	-1457	-10	-155	-161	6	4.1	0.9	3.3/ 6.1	184-191	24.8-31.5	-6.7
Aver	304	864	40.9	23/30	578	4	5254	—	—	—	—	—	—	—	5.3	188	28.0	—

Rushing Attempts	Rushing Yards	Rushing Average	Rushing TDs	Rushing Rank	Passing Yards	Passing Average
F.McAfee-NO...........325	F.McAfee-NO.........1388	M.Vick-Atl..............6.88	S.Alexander-Sea........16	F.McAfee-NO.........1518	K.Collins-NYG.......4073	K.Collins-NYG........7.47
T.Barber-NYG..........304	T.Barber-NYG........1387	D.Culpepper-Min.....5.75	F.McAfee-NO.............13	T.Barber-NYG........1497	D.Culpepper-Min....3853	J.Harris-Sea...........7.34
S.Alexander-Sea......295	M.Bennett-Min.......1296	M.Bennett-Min........5.08	M.Williams-Min..........11	M.Bennett-Min.......1346	B.Favre-GB............3658	D.Culpepper-Min.....7.02
A.Green-GB.............286	A.Green-GB...........1240	M.Williams-Min.......4.93	T.Barber-NYG............11	S.Alexander-Sea....1335	A.Brooks-NO.........3572	M.Vick-Atl..............6.97
D.Staley-Phi............269	S.Alexander-Sea......1175	K.Barlow-SF..........4.66	D.Culpepper-Min........10	A.Green-GB...........1310	J.Garcia-SF...........3344	R.Peete-Car............6.90
Completion Percent	**TD Passes**	**TD Percent**	**INT Percent**	**Passer Rating**	**Passing Rank**	**Receptions**
J.Harris-Sea...........63.7	B.Favre-GB..............27	A.Brooks-NO...........5.1	B.Johnson-TB...........1.3	B.Johnson-TB.........92.9	K.Collins-NYG.......1572	R.Moss-Min.............106
B.Johnson-TB..........62.3	A.Brooks-NO............27	B.Favre-GB..............4.9	D.McNabb-Phi...........1.7	J.Harris-Sea...........87.8	B.Johnson-TB.........1395	T.Owens-SF.............100
J.Garcia-SF............62.1	B.Johnson-TB...........22	B.Johnson-TB..........4.9	J.Garcia-SF..............1.9	D.McNabb-Phi.........86.0	J.Garcia-SF...........1377	M.Booker-Chi.............97
B.Favre-GB.............61.9	J.Garcia-SF..............21	D.McNabb-Phi..........4.7	M.Vick-Atl................1.9	J.Garcia-SF............85.6	B.Favre-GB............1324	T.Holt-SL....................91
K.Collins-NYG.........61.5	K.Collins-NYG..........19	S.Matthews-Was.......4.6	J.Harris-Sea.............2.4	B.Favre-GB.............85.6	A.Brooks-NO.........1321	J.Horn-NO..................88
Receiving Yards	**Receiving Average**	**Receiving TDs**	**Receiving Rank**	**Combined Net Yards**	**Total TDs**	**Total Points**
R.Moss-Min...........1347	A.Bryant-Dal.........16.66	T.Owens-SF..............13	T.Owens-SF.............715	M.Lewis-NO...........2647	S.Alexander-Sea........18	J.Feely-Atl................138
A.Toomer-NYG......1343	B.Schroeder-Det....16.53	D.Driver-GB...............9	A.Toomer-NYG.........712	T.Barber-NYG........1989	F.McAfee-NO............16	D.Akers-Phi...............133
J.Horn-NO.............1312	A.Toomer-NYG.....16.38	A.Toomer-NYG............8	R.Moss-Min.............709	S.Smith-Car...........1909	T.Owens-SF..............14	J.Carney-NO..............130
T.Holt-SL...............1302	S.Smith-Car..........16.15	D.Staley-NO................8	J.Horn-NO................691	F.McAfee-NO.........1740	M.Williams-Min..........11	R.Longwell-GB........128
T.Owens-SF...........1300	D.Boston-Arz........16.00	R.Gardner-Was...........8	T.Holt-SL.................671	B.Mitchell-Phi.........1738	T.Barber-NYG............11	M.Gramatica-TB.......128
Punt Average	**Field Goals**	**Field Goal Percent**	**Kickoff Returns**	**Kickoff Return Average**	**Punt Returns**	**Punt Return Average**
T.Sauerbrun-Car.....45.5	M.Gramatica-TB........32	J.Carney-NO...........88.6	M.Lewis-NO...............70	M.Jenkins-Arz.........28.0	S.Smith-Car...............55	J.Williams-SF.........16.8
S.Player-Arz..........43.9	J.Feely-Atl.................32	D.Akers-Phi............88.2	A.Rossum-Atl.............53	B.Mitchell-Phi..........27.0	B.Mitchell-Phi.............46	M.Lewis-NO.............14.2
S.Landeta-Phi.........42.9	J.Carney-NO..............31	R.Longwell-GB........82.4	T.Wilkins-SL...............47	E.Drummond-Det....26.0	M.Lewis-NO...............44	B.Mitchell-Phi..........12.3
T.Tupa-TB..............42.8	D.Akers-Phi...............30	J.Hanson-Det..........82.1	A.Merritt-Chi..............45	M.Lewis-NO............25.8	K.Williams-TB............43	A.Rossum-Atl..........12.0
B.Maynard-Chi.........42.3	R.Longwell-GB..........28	M.Gramatica-TB......82.1	B.Mitchell-Phi.............43	A.Stecker-TB...........25.2	D.Gordon-GB.............35	B.Engram-Sea.........10.7
Punt/Kick Return Yards	**Punt/Kick Return TDs**	**Interceptions**	**Interception Return Yards**	**Interception Return TDs**	**Sacks**	**Overall Rank**
M.Lewis-NO...........2432	M.Lewis-NO.................3	B.Kelly-TB..................8	D.Sharper-GB..........233	D.Brooks-TB................3	S.Rice-TB...............15.5	M.Vick-Atl..............2093
B.Mitchell-Phi.........1729	S.Smith-Car.................2	D.Sharper-GB.............7	D.Brooks-TB............218	R.Williams-Dal.............2	H.Douglas-Phi.........12.5	D.Culpepper-Min....1806
A.Rossum-Atl.........1452		T.Parrish-SF...............7	T.Parrish-SF............204	J.Lucas-Arz.................2	A.Carter-SF............12.5	T.Barber-NYG........1796
T.Wilkins-SL..........1316			M.Minter-Car............125	M.Anderson-GB...........2		J.Garcia-SF...........1760
E.Drummond-Det...1177			R.Tongue-Sea..........118			F.McAfee-NO.........1709

Seahawks Go National, Again

Expansion made it necessary for the league to realign, something it hadn't done since the AFL–NFL merger in 1970. The league switched from three divisions in each conference to four. The Seattle Seahawks, who started in the NFC in 1976 before switching to the AFC a year later, rejoined the NFC West.

Philadelphia quarterback Donovan McNabb broke his ankle on the third play of a week 11 game, but he stayed in and threw 4 touchdown passes to lead his team to victory. Although McNabb missed the rest of the season, the Eagles won five of their last six games to win the NFC East for the second straight year. Atlanta's Michael Vick electrified fans with his strong arm and scrambling ability. Vick set an NFL record for quarterbacks by rushing for 173 yards against the Vikings, capped by a 46-yard touchdown run to win the game in overtime. The Falcons posted a winning record for the first time since 1998.

Emmitt Smith surpassed Walter Payton to become the NFL's all-time leading rusher. He finished the season with 975 yards, ended his streak of 11 consecutive 1,000-yard seasons. It would also be Smith's last season in Dallas.

Tampa Bay coach Tony Dungy was fired the morning after his team's loss in the opening round of the 2001 playoffs. He was the most successful coach in the franchise's sordid 26-year history and had led them to the playoffs for three straight seasons. The Buccaneers thought they had a deal in place with legendary coach Bill Parcells, but he changed his mind a few days after Dungy's dismissal. Suddenly in the lurch, the Bucs dealt for 38-year-old Oakland wunderkind Jon Gruden. It cost the Bucs four high draft picks and $8 million, but it paid immediate dividends.

Gruden revamped the offense by bringing in veteran free agents Keenan McCardell and Michael Pittman. He left Dungy's defense intact and the Bucs held nine opponents to 10 points or less. Gruden was able to do what Dungy never could—win in the postseason—and the Buccaneers capped their season with a decisive Super Bowl win … against the Raiders.

2002 AFC

TEAM	W-L-T	PCT	POST	PTS	RA	RY	RY/A	RTD	FL	PA	PC	GPY	GPY/A	PTD	PI	PSY	PRAT
Eastern Division																	
NYJ	9-7	.563	#ED	359-336	400-427	1618-1973	4.0-4.6	12-17	9-8	485-551	329-359	3619-3685	7.5-6.7	25-17	10-15	201-195	**98.3**-83.2
Mia	9-7	.563	#	378-**301**	**530**-407	**2502**-1554	4.7-3.8	24-9	15-9	455-520	271-294	3069-3429	6.7-6.6	18-20	15-21	179-**327**	79.3-**72.7**
NE	9-7	.563	#	381-346	395-467	1508-2198	3.8-4.7	9-17	10-11	605-531	374-314	3767-3378	6.2-6.4	**28**-23	14-18	190-199	85.3-78.2
Buf	8-8	.500	—	379-397	388-473	1596-2122	4.1-4.5	17-20	16-9	612-495	377-**281**	4364-3279	7.1-6.6	24-24	15-10	369-212	86.0-84.7
Northern Division																	
Pit	10-5-1	.656	ED	390-345	512-**359**	2120-**1375**	4.1-3.8	15-16	14-**17**	551-573	350-336	4036-3773	7.3-6.6	26-19	22-19	204-313	84.6-75.6
Cle	9-7	.563	#W	344-320	406-483	1615-2079	4.0-4.3	10-12	9-12	552-513	338-299	3665-3441	6.6-6.7	27-20	22-17	253-172	80.5-77.8
Bal	7-9	.438	—	316-354	427-471	1792-1762	4.2-**3.7**	9-17	18-6	479-573	262-360	3118-3823	6.5-6.7	20-16	14-**25**	271-232	76.5-73.4
Cin	2-14	.125	—	279-456	426-498	1730-2003	4.1-4.0	13-16	13-11	591-**454**	350-287	3732-3415	6.3-7.5	17-30	22-9	256-153	71.8- 99.9
Southern Division																	
Ten	**11**-5	**.688**	DC	367-324	511-372	1952-1424	3.8-3.8	16-**7**	10-11	500-562	306-339	3441-3753	6.9-6.7	22-27	15-18	**121**-213	83.9-82.8
Ind	10-6	.625	W	349-313	434-459	1561-1992	3.6-4.3	12-16	13-**17**	591-468	392-288	4200-**3160**	7.1-6.8	27-19	19-10	145-243	88.8-86.1
Jax	6-10	.375	—	328-315	455-487	2089-2071	4.6-4.3	19-14	6-13	462-519	268-314	3019-3488	6.5-6.7	18-19	**9**-14	257-224	82.5-81.5
Hou	4-12	.250	—	213-356	424-509	1347-2089	3.2-4.1	6-14	14-11	447-512	235-**281**	2636-3378	5.9-6.6	11-23	15-10	411-237	64.7-82.1
Western Division																	
Oak	**11**-5	**.688**	DCS	450-304	414-384	1762-1453	4.3-3.8	21-14	9-10	**619**-570	**418**-346	**4689**-3787	7.6-6.6	26-21	10-21	214-261	97.2-77.3
Den	9-7	.563	#	392-344	457-379	2266-1489	5.0-3.9	21-21	7-13	554-566	359-360	4139-3588	7.5-**6.3**	21-**15**	20-9	315-251	84.8-83.7
KC	8-8	.500	—	**467**-399	462-431	2378-2067	**5.1**-4.8	**26**-19	**2**-13	477-616	292-403	3763-4396	**7.9**-7.1	27-27	13-18	141-215	93.5-88.8
SD	8-8	.500	—	333-367	466-410	2137-1739	4.6-4.2	19-15	8-10	538-607	324-375	3368-4526	6.3-7.5	17-26	16-17	180-231	76.5-87.2
Aver	16	—	—	347	441	1858	4.2	14	12	540	322	3631	6.7	22	17	236	80.4

TEAM	1D	PENY	PNT	FGM/A	RTNY	RTNTD	OFFY/DEFY	NETY	NETTO	NP	PNP	DELP	PW	DELW	PRT	DR	YPD	DEL
Eastern Division																		
NYJ	300-313	**685**-809	40.8-40.3	24/31-26/31	671-368	4-3	5036-5463	-427	4	23	-20	43	8.6	0.4	6.2/ 5.1	167-**167**	30.2-32.7	-2.6
Mia	318-285	859-826	40.2-42.9	24/31-28/30	551-592	2-2	5392-**4656**	736	0	77	61	16	9.9	-0.9	5.0/**4.2**	183-189	29.5-**24.6**	4.8
NE	304-315	895-928	38.4-39.4	27/30-20/34	575-358	6-1	5085-5377	-292	5	35	-4	39	8.9	0.1	5.1/ 4.6	188-177	27.0-30.4	-3.3
Buf	355-303	1031-**1053**	42.4-39.9	25/33-19/26	304-568	3-5	5591-5189	402	-12	-18	-15	-3	7.6	0.4	5.3/ 5.4	178-187	31.4-27.7	3.7
Northern Division																		
Pit	343-**279**	712-927	41.0-40.3	**29/40**-20/26	641-792	2-6	5952-4835	1117	0	45	93	-48	9.1	1.4	5.3/ 4.5	193-192	30.8-25.2	5.7
Cle	279-291	845-726	41.3-**38.7**	22/28-28/37	582-700	3-2	5027-5348	-321	-2	24	-35	**59**	8.6	0.4	4.6/ 5.0	190-193	26.5-27.7	-1.3
Bal	261-316	846-874	40.5-40.8	21/26-29/33	**833**-712	**7**-5	4639-5353	-714	-1	-38	-64	26	7.1	-0.1	4.6/ 4.3	190-193	24.4-27.7	-3.3
Cin	315-315	884-867	38.2-41.8	15/18-23/31	318-1039	4-9	5206-5265	-59	-15	-177	-65	-112	3.6	-1.6	4.2/ 6.6	184-175	28.3-30.1	-1.8
Southern Division																		
Ten	312-297	891-853	41.3-41.6	25/31-**14/21**	415-569	4-6	5272-4964	308	4	43	42	1	9.1	**1.9**	5.5/ 5.0	179-174	29.5-28.5	0.9
Ind	324-**279**	730-746	39.9-41.7	23/31-21/26	452-381	1-1	5616-4909	707	-5	36	39	-3	8.9	1.1	5.7/ 5.3	177-180	31.7-27.3	4.5
Jax	275-324	**685**-717	**44.2-38.7**	19/27-23/34	504-480	1-2	4851-5335	-484	12	13	8	5	8.3	-2.3	5.0/ 5.1	176-172	27.6-31.0	-3.5
Hou	208-291	1011-955	40.7-39.7	17/24-24/34	700-605	5-3	3572-5230	-1658	-8	-143	-170	27	4.4	-0.4	3.2/ 5.3	**210**-207	17.0-25.3	-8.3
Western Division																		
Oak	**366**-319	1094-787	41.7-41.9	26/33-17/23	665-523	6-2	**6237**-4979	1258	12	**146**	**153**	-7	**11.6**	-0.7	6.5/ 4.6	172-177	**36.3**-28.1	**8.1**
Den	357-298	877-829	39.0-40.9	26/36-25/32	382-533	3-3	6090-4826	**1264**	-5	48	85	-37	9.2	-0.2	5.2/ 5.1	182-177	33.5-27.3	6.2
KC	343-367	700-827	37.3-39.1	23/27-26/32	692-**357**	4-**0**	6000-6248	-248	**16**	68	43	25	9.7	-1.7	**6.6**/ 5.6	178-177	33.7-35.3	-1.6
SD	313-326	805-854	39.8-40.1	18/26-21/31	561-573	4-2	5325-6034	-709	3	-34	-47	13	7.2	0.9	4.7/ 5.9	200-192	26.6-31.4	-4.8
Aver	304	864	40.9	23/30	578	2	5254	—	—	—	—	—	—	—	5.3	92	28.8	—

Rushing Attempts	Rushing Yards	Rushing Average	Rushing TDs	Rushing Rank	Passing Yards	Passing Average
R.Williams-Mia.........383	R.Williams-Mia.......1853	C.Portis-Den...........5.52	P.Holmes-KC.............21	R.Williams-Mia.......2013	R.Gannon-Oak......4689	T.Green-KC.............7.85
L.Tomlinson-SD........372	L.Tomlinson-SD.....1683	S.McNair-Ten..........5.37	R.Williams-Mia...........16	P.Holmes-KC.........1825	D.Bledsoe-Buf........4359	J.Peelle-NYJ...........7.82
E.George-Ten..........343	P.Holmes-KC.........1615	C.Garner-Oak.........5.29	C.Portis-Den..............15	L.Tomlinson-SD.....1823	P.Manning-Ind........4200	R.Gannon-Oak.......7.59
T.Henry-Buf.............325	C.Portis-Den..........1508	P.Holmes-KC..........5.16	L.Tomlinson-SD.........14	C.Portis-Den..........1658	T.Brady-NE............3764	T.Maddox-Pit...........7.52
C.Dillon-Cin.............314	T.Henry-Buf............1438	R.Williams-Mia........4.84	T.Henry-Buf...............13	T.Henry-Buf...........1568	T.Green-KC............3690	B.Griese-Den..........7.37
Completion Percent	**TD Passes**	**TD Percent**	**INT Percent**	**Passer Rating**	**Passing Rank**	**Receptions**
J.Peelle-NYJ...........68.9	T.Brady-NE...............28	T.Green-KC..............5.5	J.Peelle-NYJ.............1.5	J.Peelle-NYJ.........104.2	R.Gannon-Oak......2075	M.Harrison-Ind.........143
R.Gannon-Oak.......67.6	P.Manning-Ind...........27	J.Peelle-NYJ............5.5	R.Gannon-Oak..........1.6	R.Gannon-Oak.......97.3	D.Bledsoe-Buf........1700	H.Ward-Pit...............112
B.Griese-Den..........66.7	T.Green-KC...............26	T.Maddox-Pit............5.3	M.Brunell-Jax............1.7	T.Green-KC.............92.6	P.Manning-Ind........1475	E.Moulds-Buf...........100
P.Manning-Ind.........66.3	R.Gannon-Oak...........26	J.Fiedler-Mia............4.8	T.Brady-NE...............2.3	P.Manning-Ind.........88.8	T.Brady-NE............1462	T.Brown-NE...............97
J.Kitna-Cin.............62.2	D.Bledsoe-Buf...........24	T.Brady-NE...............4.7	D.Bledsoe-Buf............2.5	D.Bledsoe-Buf.........86.0	T.Green-KC............1455	P.Price-Buf.................94
Receiving Yards	**Receiving Average**	**Receiving TDs**	**Receiving Rank**	**Combined Net Yards**	**Total TDs**	**Total Points**
M.Harrison-Ind.......1722	Q.Morgan-Cle.......17.21	H.Ward-Pit................12	M.Harrison-Ind.........916	P.Holmes-KC.........2287	P.Holmes-KC.............24	P.Holmes-KC...........144
H.Ward-Pit.............1329	E.Kennison-KC......17.09	M.Harrison-Ind..........11	H.Ward-Pit...............725	R.Williams-Mia.......2216	R.Williams-Mia...........17	M.Jameson-Oak.......128
P.Burress-Pit..........1325	P.Burress-Pit.........16.99	E.Moulds-Buf.............10	P.Burress-Pit............698	L.Tomlinson-SD.....2172	C.Portis-Den..............17	J.Elam-Den...............120
E.Moulds-Buf.........1292	C.Johnson-Cin......16.90		E.Moulds-Buf...........696	D.Hall-KC..............2120	L.Tomlinson-SD.........15	A.Vinatieri-NE.........117
L.Coles-NYJ..........1264	D.Northcutt-Cle.....15.82		P.Price-Buf...............671	C.Garner-Oak.........1904		M.Andersen-KC.........117
Punt Average	**Field Goals**	**Field Goal Percent**	**Kickoff Returns**	**Kickoff Return Average**	**Punt Returns**	**Punt Return Average**
C.Hanson-Jax.........44.2	A.Vinatieri-NE............27	A.Vinatieri-NE.........90.0	C.Rogers-Buf.............64	K.Faulk-NE.............27.9	A.Randle El-Pit..........37	S.Moss-NYJ............16.5
B.Moorman-Buf......43.1	M.Jameson-Oak.........26	J.Reed-Pit................89.5	C.Morton-NYJ............58	C.Morton-NYJ.........26.0	J.Lewis-Hou...............36	D.Northcutt-Cle.......14.7
S.Lechler-Oak.........42.5	J.Elam-Den................26	M.Andersen-KC......84.6	D.Hall-KC..................57	R.Droughns-Den......25.8	T.Walters-Ind.............35	D.Hall-KC.................13.4
C.Hentrich-Ten........41.9	J.Nedney-Ten.............25	M.Stover-Bal...........84.0	T.Walters-Ind.............53	B.Bennett-Cin.........25.1	D.O'Neal-Den............30	B.Shaw-Jax.............12.4
C.Gardocki-Cle........41.8	M.Hollis-Buf...............25	N.Rackers-Cin........83.3	A.Davis-Cle................50	M.Knight-Oak..........24.3	D.Hall-KC...................29	T.Dwight-SD.............12.2
Punt/Kick Return Yards	**Punt/Kick Return TDs**	**Interceptions**	**Interception Return Yards**	**Interception Return TDs**	**Sacks**	**Overall Rank**
D.Hall-KC..............1744	D.Hall-KC.....................3	R.Woodson-Oak..........8	R.Woodson-Oak......225	R.Woodson-Oak..........2	J.Taylor-Mia............18.5	R.Gannon-Oak......2261
C.Morton-NYJ........1560			A.Glenn-Hou.............181	D.O'Neal-Den.............2	D.Freeney-Ind.........13.0	R.Williams-Mia.......2200
T.Walters-Ind.........1420			G.Wesley-KC............170	A.Glenn-Hou...............2	R.Coleman-Oak.......11.0	P.Holmes-KC.........2176
C.Rogers-Buf.........1417			E.Reed-Bal...............167	T.Bruschi-NE..............2	K.Carter-Ten...........10.0	L.Tomlinson-SD.....2073
J.Lewis-Hou...........1241			J.Porter-Pit...............153		J.Abraham-NYJ......10.0	C.Portis-Den..........1850

Texans Two-Step: Drop Back, Dropped for a Loss

For the second time in four years, the NFL expanded in order to replace a team that had moved. Six seasons after the Oilers left for Tennessee, Houston got a new team. The Texans won their first game, upsetting the cross-state rival Dallas Cowboys, 19–10. Unfortunately, it was all downhill from there. The Texans lost eight of their next nine games and finished 4–12. Rookie quarterback David Carr survived despite horrendous pass protection. He set a dubious record by being sacked 76 times.

Indianapolis receiver Marvin Harrison set a more positive record by grabbing 143 receptions, shattering Herman Moore's single-season mark of 123. Harrison also led the league with 1,722 receiving yards. New head coach Tony Dungy helped turn around the defense, which moved from next-to-last to seventh. Colts rookie defensive end Dwight Freeney helped make the unit more aggressive, and Indianapolis improved from 6–10 to 10–6.

Oakland continued to soar as offensive coordinator Bill Callahan took over as the head coach for the traded Jon Gruden. The vertical passing game thrived with an offense whose key players were well past 30. Quarterback Rich Gannon (37) and receivers Jerry Rice (40) and Tim Brown (36) formed the core of the league's top-ranked passing offense. Running back Charlie Garner (30) caught 91 passes and had 1,903 combined yards from scrimmage.

An offseason trade brought running back Ricky Williams to Miami. The workhorse back led the league with 1,853 yards rushing, notching back-to-back 200-yard games against the Bills and Bears. Williams ran for 185 yards in New England in the season finale, a game Miami needed to clinch the division. The normally stout defense got too conservative, blowing a 10-point lead in the final three minutes. The loss bounced the Dolphins from the playoffs.

Titans quarterback Steve McNair had the best year of his career. Although teams attacked Tennessee's porous secondary early in the season—scoring 114 points over a three-game stretch—head coach Jeff Fisher solved the problem during the bye week. Seven of their last 10 opponents scored 17 points or less as the Titans finished 10–1 to clinch the first AFC South title in the revamped, four-division AFC.

2003 NFC

TEAM	W-L-T	PCT	POST	PTS	RA	RY	RY/A	RTD	FL	PA	PC	GPY	GPY/A	PTD	PI	PSY	PRAT
Eastern Division																	
Phi	**12**-4	**.750**	DC	374-287	417-461	2015-2071	4.8-4.5	**23**-13	11-13	484-559	279-337	3273-3484	6.8-6.2	17-17	11-13	253-248	80.5-78.7
Dal	10-6	.625	W	289-**260**	515-413	1999-**1425**	3.9-**3.5**	11-7	8-12	510-492	294-**239**	3347-**2820**	6.6-**5.7**	17-18	21-13	185-189	71.4-**67.6**
Was	5-11	.313	—	287-372	421-504	1653-2217	3.9-4.4	8-20	12-13	527-483	283-285	3273-3354	6.2-6.9	21-23	16-17	267-159	73.3-81.4
NYG	4-12	.250	—	243-387	387-496	1559-1908	4.0-3.8	6-12	18-12	**616**-519	344-309	3642-3710	5.9-7.1	16-25	20-10	259-298	68.4-89.5
Northern Division																	
GB	10-6	.625	ED	442-307	507-413	**2558**-1701	**5.0**-4.1	18-10	11-11	473-589	310-326	3377-3600	7.1-6.1	**32**-18	21-21	137-200	90.5-69.0
Min	9-7	.563	—	416-353	493-**387**	2343-1879	4.8-4.9	15-22	11-7	520-531	333-311	4169-3722	**8.0**-7.0	**32**-17	13-**28**	218-245	**99.0**-68.8
ChiB	7-9	.438	—	283-346	443-449	1763-1865	4.0-4.2	13-13	9-5	515-525	271-326	2905-3187	5.6-6.1	12-20	20-15	288-105	61.0-79.9
Det	5-11	.313	—	270-379	376-447	1338-1782	3.6-4.0	5-14	**4**-13	588-522	319-331	2988-3760	5.1-7.2	17-26	24-15	**64**-182	61.1-89.6
Southern Division																	
Car	11-5	.688	EDCS	325-304	**522**-434	2091-1722	4.0-4.0	9-10	15-10	460-522	270-299	3238-3215	7.0-6.2	19-19	16-16	188-212	79.6-74.8
NO	8-8	.500	—	340-326	448-480	2000-2241	4.5-4.7	11-12	20-13	535-485	314-264	3641-3164	6.8-6.5	25-20	**8**-14	203-171	88.7-76.3
TB	7-9	.438	—	301-264	421-451	1648-1756	3.9-3.9	5-**6**	9-13	592-**475**	369-274	3941-2944	6.7-6.2	27-**16**	22-20	136-234	81.5-69.7
Atl	5-11	.313	—	299-422	435-499	1949-2308	4.5-4.6	17-21	10-16	460-508	230-323	2631-4005	5.7-7.9	14-28	21-15	223-205	58.7-94.0
Western Division																	
SL	**12**-4	**.750**	D	**447**-328	411-412	1496-1980	3.6-4.8	19-9	16-**22**	600-510	**377**-296	**4287**-3363	7.1-6.6	23-23	23-24	326-291	81.0-73.3
Sea	10-6	.625	W	404-327	453-456	2009-1759	4.4-3.9	17-9	13-12	521-573	317-343	3872-3728	7.4-6.5	27-24	16-16	254-248	88.2-81.4
SF	7-9	.438	—	384-337	499-420	2279-1690	4.6-4.0	16-13	10-14	511-514	299-310	3566-3544	7.0-6.9	25-25	15-23	158-**306**	84.0-78.6
Arz	4-12	.250	—	225-452	403-475	1531-1915	3.8-4.0	5-17	14-10	534-497	303-311	3265-3686	6.1-7.4	18-29	22-13	306-97	68.9-93.7
Aver	16	—	—	333	453	1886	4.2	13	12	515	303	3421	6.6	20	17	214	78.3

TEAM	1D	PENY	PNT	FGM/A	RTNY	RTNTD	OFFY/DEFY	NETY	NETTO	NP	PNP	DELP	PW	DELW	PRT	DR	YPD	DEL
Eastern Division																		
Phi	302-306	817-**1105**	40.6-38.9	24/29-22/30	536-433	3-**2**	5035-5307	-272	4	87	-7	**94**	10.2	1.8	5.1/ 4.7	179-188	28.1-28.2	-0.1
Dal	286-**228**	837-763	38.9-42.6	23/29-21/**23**	573-512	3-3	5161-**4056**	**1105**	-4	29	76	-47	8.7	1.3	4.4/ 4.2	197-201	26.2-**20.2**	**6.0**
Was	272-325	1038-835	40.2-42.2	25/33-19/31	389-571	1-**2**	4659-5412	-753	2	-85	-55	-30	5.9	-0.9	4.4/ 5.2	194-188	24.0-28.8	-4.8
NYG	300-314	1090-983	40.0-**35.6**	20/27-28/37	362-601	4-6	4942-5320	-378	-16	-144	-96	-48	4.4	-0.4	4.0/ 5.7	199-196	24.8-27.1	-2.3
Northern Division																		
GB	315-288	699-767	41.3-41.0	23/26-30/33	592-745	3-3	5798-5101	697	0	**135**	58	77	**11.4**	-1.4	5.3/ 4.2	193-196	30.0-26.0	4.0
Min	336-316	1029-720	38.5-40.3	18/25-21/26	**940**-459	4-3	**6294**-5356	938	11	63	**122**	-59	9.6	-0.6	**6.6**/ 4.2	179-**177**	**35.2**-30.3	4.9
ChiB	264-289	806-746	40.2-40.4	26/36-31/38	652-667	4-3	4380-4947	-567	-9	-63	-83	20	6.4	0.6	3.3/ 4.8	183-189	23.9-26.2	-2.2
Det	250-298	859-953	39.5-42.5	22/23-**17**/24	706-767	**7**-7	4262-5360	-1098	0	-109	-92	-17	5.3	-0.3	3.4/ 5.8	198-190	21.5-28.2	-6.7
Southern Division																		
Car	284-274	966-1011	42.8-42.0	32/38-21/32	691-627	5-6	5141-4725	416	-5	21	15	6	8.5	**2.5**	5.2/ 4.4	197-196	26.1-24.1	2.0
NO	302-298	878-1012	**43.7**-41.9	22/30-25/31	586-398	3-4	5438-5234	204	-1	14	13	1	8.4	-0.3	5.8/ 5.0	186-183	29.2-28.6	0.6
TB	307-249	1104-817	43.3-43.4	16/26-25/34	471-883	4-5	5453-4466	987	2	37	90	-53	8.9	-1.9	5.0/**3.9**	193-190	28.3-23.5	4.7
Atl	252-333	790-1001	39.9-43.4	19/27-19/25	810-611	4-**2**	4357-6108	-1751	0	-123	-146	23	4.9	0.1	3.2/ 6.3	**202**-198	21.6-30.8	-9.3
Western Division																		
SL	335-272	**667**-882	42.8-41.4	**39/42**-19/24	842-784	5-7	5457-5052	405	7	119	62	57	11.0	1.0	4.9/ 4.0	197-203	27.7-24.9	2.8
Sea	**338**-304	777-825	40.0-39.8	22/30-25/31	477-**304**	4-3	5627-5239	388	-1	77	28	49	9.9	0.1	5.6/ 4.9	187-192	30.1-27.3	2.8
SF	313-292	807-720	38.1-39.1	26/37-**17**/26	665-549	3-3	5687-4928	759	**12**	47	111	-64	9.2	-2.2	5.5/ 4.4	196-188	29.0-26.2	2.8
Arz	256-326	761-754	42.3-40.0	18/26-21/28	411-890	2-9	4490-5504	-1014	-13	-227	-137	-90	2.3	1.7	3.7/ 6.4	187-184	24.0-29.9	-5.9
Aver	293	876	41.0	24/30	607	4	5093	—	—	—	—	—	—	—	5.2	190	26.8	—

Rushing Attempts	Rushing Yards	Rushing Average	Rushing TDs	Rushing Rank	Passing Yards	Passing Average
A.Green-GB 355	A.Green-GB 1883	O.Smith-Min 5.41	A.Green-GB 15	A.Green-GB 2033	M.Bulger-SL 3845	D.Culpepper-Min 7.66
F.McAfee-NO 351	F.McAfee-NO 1641	W.Dunn-Atl 5.38	S.Alexander-Sea 14	F.McAfee-NO 1721	C.Hart-Sea 3841	C.Hart-Sea 7.49
S.Alexander-Sea 326	S.Davis-Car 1444	A.Green-GB 5.30	T.Duckett-Atl 11	S.Alexander-Sea 1575	B.Johnson-TB 3811	M.Bulger-SL 7.23
S.Davis-Car 318	S.Alexander-Sea 1435	B.Westbrook-Phi 5.24	M.Faulk-SL 10	S.Davis-Car 1524	A.Brooks-NO 3546	J.Delhomme-Car 7.17
T.Barber-NYG 278	T.Barber-NYG 1216	K.Barlow-SF 5.09		T.Barber-NYG 1236	D.Culpepper-Min 3479	B.Favre-GB 7.14
Completion Percent	**TD Passes**	**TD Percent**	**INT Percent**	**Passer Rating**	**Passing Rank**	**Receptions**
B.Favre-GB 65.4	B.Favre-GB 32	B.Favre-GB 6.8	A.Brooks-NO 1.5	D.Culpepper-Min 96.4	A.Brooks-NO 1573	T.Holt-SL 117
D.Culpepper-Min 65.0	B.Johnson-TB 26	D.Culpepper-Min 5.5	D.McNabb-Phi 2.3	B.Favre-GB 90.4	C.Hart-Sea 1451	R.Moss-Min 111
M.Bulger-SL 63.2	C.Hart-Sea 26	C.Hart-Sea 5.1	D.Culpepper-Min 2.4	A.Brooks-NO 88.8	D.Culpepper-Min 1425	A.Boldin-Arz 101
B.Johnson-TB 62.1	D.Culpepper-Min 25	A.Brooks-NO 4.6	P.Ramsey-Was 2.7	C.Hart-Sea 88.8	D.McNabb-Phi 1248	S.Smith-Car 88
C.Hart-Sea 61.0	A.Brooks-NO 24	J.Garcia-SF 4.6	C.Hart-Sea 2.9	B.Johnson-TB 81.5	B.Johnson-TB 1196	K.McCardell-TB 84
Receiving Yards	**Receiving Average**	**Receiving TDs**	**Receiving Rank**	**Combined Net Yards**	**Total TDs**	**Total Points**
T.Holt-SL 1696	J.Galloway-Dal 19.76	R.Moss-Min 17	T.Holt-SL 908	A.Green-GB 2250	A.Green-GB 20	J.Wilkins-SL 163
R.Moss-Min 1632	J.Walker-GB 17.46	T.Holt-SL 12	R.Moss-Min 901	F.McAfee-NO 2154	R.Moss-Min 17	J.Kasay-Car 125
A.Boldin-Arz 1377	A.Toomer-NYG 16.78	J.Horn-NO 10	A.Boldin-Arz 729	S.Smith-Car 1900	S.Alexander-Sea 16	R.Longwell-GB 120
L.Coles-Was 1204	D.Jackson-Sea 16.72		L.Coles-Was 632	A.Rossum-Atl 1836	B.Westbrook-Phi 13	A.Green-GB 120
K.McCardell-TB 1174	T.Pinkston-Phi 15.97		K.McCardell-TB 627	B.Westbrook-Phi 1738	T.Holt-SL 12	
Punt Average	**Field Goals**	**Field Goal Percent**	**Kickoff Returns**	**Kickoff Return Average**	**Punt Returns**	**Punt Return Average**
T.Sauerbrun-Car 44.6	J.Wilkins-SL 39	J.Hanson-Det 95.7	J.Scobey-Arz 73	N.Davenport-GB 31.6	S.Smith-Car 44	B.Westbrook-Phi 15.3
M.Berger-NO 44.3	J.Kasay-Car 32	J.Wilkins-SL 92.9	A.Rossum-Atl 62	J.Azumah-Chi 29.0	A.Rossum-Atl 39	A.Rossum-Atl 14.0
T.Tupa-TB 43.3	P.Edinger-Chi 26	R.Longwell-GB 88.5	B.Mitchell-NYG 55	D.Ross-Dal 24.1	D.McNabb-Chi 37	R.Swinton-Det 13.8
S.Player-Arz 42.8	J.Hall-Was 25	J.Kasay-Car 84.2	A.Harris-SL 51	R.Swinton-Det 24.1	J.Williams-SF 35	D.McNabb-Chi 12.2
S.Landeta-SL 42.8	D.Akers-Phi 24	D.Akers-Phi 82.8	M.Morris-Sea 47	J.Thrash-Phi 24.0	K.Howry-Min 35	B.Engram-Sea 10.3
Punt/Kick Return Yards	**Punt/Kick Return TDs**	**Interceptions**	**Interception Return Yards**	**Interception Return TDs**	**Sacks**	**Overall Rank**
A.Rossum-Atl 1836	B.Westbrook-Phi 2	B.Russell-Min 9	B.Williams-Min 205	M.Minter-Car 2	M.Strahan-NYG 18.5	A.Green-GB 2242
J.Scobey-Arz 1684	R.Swinton-Det 2	T.Parrish-SF 9	T.Fisher-SL 205	T.Fisher-SL 2	S.Rice-TB 15.0	F.McAfee-NO 1979
M.Lewis-NO 1343	J.Azumah-Chi 2	C.Chavous-Min 8	T.Parrish-SF 202		L.Little-SL 12.5	D.Culpepper-Min 1887
R.Swinton-Det 1282		D.Jackson-Arz 6	B.Russell-Min 185		M.Rucker-Car 12.0	A.Brooks-NO 1768
B.Mitchell-NYG 1271		D.Bly-Det 6	C.Chavous-Min 143		K.Williams-Min 10.5	S.Alexander-Sea 1733

Reverse of Field

The winds of fortune can change during the course of a season, as illustrated by two teams in the NFC North. Minnesota started the season 6–0 on the strength of their explosive offense. Receiver Randy Moss was an unstoppable force, and a trio of running backs combined for 1,771 yards and 11 touchdowns. Yet a porous defense grew even weaker as the season progressed. The Vikings went 3–7 to close the season and were knocked from a playoff spot on a shocking touchdown on the final play of the year in Arizona.

The opposite story was unfolding in Green Bay, where a struggling defense left the Packers 3–4 at midseason. Green Bay improved in the second half, and the offense kicked it up a notch. Brett Favre led the league with 32 touchdown passes and Ahman Green rushed for 1,883 yards. The Packers won six of their last seven to take the division crown.

Changes at two key positions didn't slow the Rams offense. Running back Marshall Faulk missed five games with a broken hand, and quarterback Kurt Warner was benched after a rocky opening game. Marc Bulger took over the offense and Torry Holt led the league with 117 catches and 1,696 yards. Coach Bill Parcells took over a Cowboys team that had suffered three straight 5–11 seasons. He doubled their win total in his first year, focusing on making the defense tougher and more aggressive. The defense improved from 16th to first and Dallas made the playoffs despite playing with a makeshift offense.

Another hard-nosed coach, John Fox, found success in Carolina. Julius Peppers and Kris Jenkins led a disruptive defensive line that harassed opposing quarterbacks and stuffed the run. Two key free agent signings solidified the offense. Former Pro Bowler Stephen Davis gave Carolina a power running game. Quarterback Jake Delhomme, who languished on the bench for four years with the Saints, emerged as an efficient passer and the type of leader the club had been sorely lacking. Two years removed from a 1–15 season, Fox's Panthers had a shot to win the Super Bowl.

2003 AFC

TEAM	W-L-T	PCT	POST	PTS	RA	RY	RY/A	RTD	FL	PA	PC	GPY	GPY/A	PTD	PI	PSY	PRAT
Eastern Division																	
NE	**14**-2	**.875**	DCS*	348-**238**	473-401	1607-1434	3.4-3.6	9-10	11-12	537-618	320-328	3651-3485	6.8-**5.6**	23-**11**	13-**29**	219-253	84.3-**56.2**
Mia	10-6	.625	#	311-261	487-441	1817-1452	3.7-3.3	14-11	15-14	450-529	257-319	3001-3588	6.7-6.8	17-12	19-22	209-253	72.5-70.8
Buf	6-10	.375	—	243-279	427-464	1664-1606	3.9-3.5	13-11	17-8	502-508	293-285	3069-**2938**	6.1-5.8	11-18	17-10	385-231	69.4-76.5
NYJ	6-10	.375	—	283-299	409-542	1635-2294	4.0-4.2	8-17	**6**-9	496-455	312-281	3524-3243	7.1-7.1	20-14	14-11	208-218	85.8-83.4
Northern Division																	
Bal	10-6	.625	E	391-281	**552**-448	**2674**-1536	4.8-3.4	18-**6**	19-**17**	415-531	217-296	2517-3158	6.1-5.9	16-19	19-24	262-**353**	64.7-66.4
Cin	8-8	.500	—	346-384	481-461	1987-2218	4.1-4.8	12-18	7-10	520-508	324-297	3591-3598	6.9-7.1	26-23	15-14	249-196	87.4-83.9
Pit	6-10	.375	—	300-327	446-449	1488-1741	3.3-3.9	10-14	11-11	532-484	306-294	3548-3245	6.7-6.7	19-20	17-14	244-203	76.4-82.4
Cle	5-11	.313	—	254-322	412-457	1670-2113	4.1-4.6	8-14	15-7	509-502	313-297	3116-3049	6.1-6.1	17-13	18-15	282-203	75.2-72.9
Southern Division																	
Ind	12-4	.750	#EDC	447-336	453-437	1695-1980	3.7-4.5	16-19	10-15	**569-445**	**381**-277	**4289**-3034	7.5-6.8	29-18	10-15	**110**-225	99.0-81.8
Ten	12-4	.750	#W	435-324	486-**342**	1623-**1295**	3.3-3.8	11-10	12-13	502-546	315-332	4031-3829	**8.0**-7.0	**30**-20	**9**-21	153-223	**100.3**-78.2
Hou	5-11	.313	—	255-380	421-533	1651-2370	3.9-4.4	14-15	9-8	439-502	248-297	2841-3835	6.5-7.6	14-22	18-14	186-123	69.7-86.2
Jax	5-11	.313	—	276-331	481-442	2073-1406	4.3-**3.2**	13-12	14-12	515-510	303-303	3421-3385	6.6-6.6	17-23	17-15	136-134	76.0-82.0
Western Division																	
KC	13-3	.813	D	**484**-332	446-453	1929-2344	4.3-5.2	**32**-18	**6**-12	536-565	339-332	4113-3614	7.7-6.4	24-19	12-25	132-251	92.4-70.5
Den	10-6	.625	#W	381-301	543-379	2629-1605	4.8-4.2	20-11	**6**-11	479-495	280-**265**	3126-3049	6.5-6.2	19-17	18-9	157-221	75.6-76.2
Oak	4-12	.250	—	270-379	423-544	1822-2510	4.3-4.6	15-21	12-11	521-467	278-286	2988-3556	5.7-7.6	9-21	14-14	237-162	65.0-87.3
SD	4-12	.250	—	313-441	417-518	2146-2218	**5.1**-4.3	16-12	12-7	525-524	297-322	3226-3575	6.1-6.8	21-36	19-13	205-200	73.1-94.3
Aver	16	—	—	333	453	1886	4.2	13	12	515	303	3421	6.6	20	17	214	78.3

TEAM	1D	PENY	PNT	FGM/A	RTNY	RTNTD	OFFY/DEFY	NETY	NETTO	NP	PNP	DELP	PW	DELW	PRT	DR	YPD	DEL
Eastern Division																		
NE	294-293	998-845	37.1-40.6	25/34-25/35	820-**362**	**7**-2	5039-4666	373	17	110	99	11	10.8	**3.3**	5.4/**3.1**	204-201	24.7-23.2	1.5
Mia	266-283	913-766	39.0-41.2	22/29-26/31	626-379	4-3	4609-4787	-178	2	50	-7	57	9.3	0.8	4.4/ 4.3	187-199	24.6-24.1	0.6
Buf	268-270	891-996	44.6-**38.2**	17/24-23/31	362-763	3-1	4348-**4313**	35	-16	-36	-61	25	7.1	-1.1	3.7/ 4.5	187-183	23.3-23.6	-0.3
NYJ	274-316	**550**-620	36.9-**38.2**	27/32-20/27	487-486	1-3	4951-5319	-368	0	-16	-31	15	7.6	-1.6	5.5/ 5.4	163-**164**	30.4-32.4	-2.1
Northern Division																		
Bal	259-248	970-935	40.8-40.1	34/**40**-28/31	**921**-623	**7**-3	4929-4341	588	3	110	61	49	10.8	-0.8	3.4/ 3.3	**220**-220	22.4-**19.7**	2.7
Cin	313-320	846-921	39.5-42.5	22/25-28/33	454-628	2-2	5329-5620	-291	2	-38	-16	-22	7.1	0.9	5.3/ 5.6	178-180	29.9-31.2	-1.3
Pit	275-270	1005-709	41.4-40.6	23/32-21/24	766-685	4-4	4792-4783	9	-3	-27	-11	-16	7.3	-1.3	4.8/ 5.0	191-194	25.1-24.7	0.4
Cle	276-283	767-**1095**	41.8-41.4	23/28-35/43	470-707	2-4	4504-4959	-455	-11	-68	-82	14	6.3	-1.3	4.0/ 4.3	188-174	24.0-28.5	-4.5
Southern Division																		
Ind	**348**-279	662-1005	41.3-42.1	**37**/37-**16/21**	484-444	3-4	5874-4789	1085	10	111	**130**	-19	10.8	1.2	6.8/ 4.9	179-183	**32.8**-26.2	6.6
Ten	310-275	887-793	43.9-42.2	32/37-26/30	741-540	**7**-5	5501-4901	600	13	111	102	9	10.8	1.2	**7.2**/ 4.9	193-190	28.5-25.8	2.7
Hou	237-336	961-767	41.5-41.7	18/22-28/35	471-614	1-5	4306-6082	-1776	-5	-125	-168	43	4.9	0.1	4.2/ 6.3	188-191	22.9-31.8	-8.9
Jax	305-276	895-881	41.3-41.0	20/33-24/27	454-618	1-2	5358-4657	701	-4	-55	42	-97	6.6	-1.6	5.0/ 5.3	179-180	29.9-25.9	4.1
Western Division																		
KC	**348**-322	698-781	39.0-40.7	16/20-19/25	852-477	**7**-2	**5910**-5707	203	**19**	**152**	93	**59**	**11.8**	1.2	6.6/ 4.0	190-195	31.1-29.3	1.8
Den	334-**241**	922-1031	42.0-43.1	28/32-25/28	481-879	3-4	5598-4433	**1165**	-4	80	81	-1	10.0	0.0	4.7/ 4.9	179-184	31.3-24.1	**7.2**
Oak	258-317	1120-981	**46.9**-39.9	22/25-28/34	772-801	5-**0**	4573-5904	-1331	-1	-109	-115	6	5.3	-1.3	3.9/ 6.0	194-192	23.6-30.8	-7.2
SD	290-326	1016-1006	41.6-42.7	15/20-23/26	548-605	1-5	5167-5593	-426	-11	-128	-80	-48	4.8	-0.8	4.3/ 5.7	189-187	27.3-29.9	-2.6
Aver	293	876	41.0	24/30	607	2	5093	—	—	—	—	—	—	—	5.2	94	26.8	—

Rushing Attempts	Rushing Yards	Rushing Average	Rushing TDs	Rushing Rank	Passing Yards	Passing Average
R.Williams-Mia 392	J.Lewis-Bal 2066	C.Portis-Den 5.49	P.Holmes-KC 27	J.Lewis-Bal 2206	P.Manning-Ind 4267	S.McNair-Ten 8.04
J.Lewis-Bal 387	L.Tomlinson-SD 1645	J.Lewis-Bal 5.34	C.Portis-Den 14	L.Tomlinson-SD 1775	T.Green-KC 4039	T.Green-KC 7.72
F.Taylor-Jax 345	C.Portis-Den 1591	L.Tomlinson-SD 5.26	J.Lewis-Bal 14	C.Portis-Den 1731	T.Brady-NE 3620	P.Manning-Ind 7.54
T.Henry-Buf 331	F.Taylor-Jax 1572	C.Garner-Oak 4.61	L.Tomlinson-SD 13	P.Holmes-KC 1690	J.Kitna-Cin 3591	J.Plummer-Den 7.23
C.Martin-NYJ 323	P.Holmes-KC 1420	F.Taylor-Jax 4.56	E.James-Ind 11	F.Taylor-Jax 1632	T.Maddox-Pit 3414	J.Peelle-NYJ 7.20

Completion Percent	TD Passes	TD Percent	INT Percent	Passer Rating	Passing Rank	Receptions
P.Manning-Ind 67.0	P.Manning-Ind 29	S.McNair-Ten 6.0	S.McNair-Ten 1.8	S.McNair-Ten 100.4	P.Manning-Ind 1879	L.Tomlinson-SD 100
K.Holcomb-Cle 63.9	J.Kitna-Cin 26	P.Manning-Ind 5.1	P.Manning-Ind 1.8	P.Manning-Ind 99.0	T.Green-KC 1660	H.Ward-Pit 95
J.Peelle-NYJ 63.6	S.McNair-Ten 24	J.Kitna-Cin 5.0	R.Gannon-Oak 1.8	T.Green-KC 92.6	S.McNair-Ten 1448	D.Mason-Ten 95
T.Green-KC 63.1	T.Green-KC 24	J.Plummer-Den 5.0	T.Brady-NE 2.3	J.Plummer-Den 91.2	T.Brady-NE 1445	M.Harrison-Ind 94
J.Plummer-Den 62.6	T.Brady-NE 23	T.Green-KC 4.6	T.Green-KC 2.3	J.Kitna-Cin 87.4	J.Kitna-Cin 1326	C.Johnson-Cin 90

Receiving Yards	Receiving Average	Receiving TDs	Receiving Rank	Combined Net Yards	Total TDs	Total Points
C.Johnson-Cin 1355	J.McCareins-Ten 17.30	C.Chambers-Mia 11	C.Johnson-Cin 728	D.Hall-KC 2446	P.Holmes-KC 27	P.Holmes-KC 162
D.Mason-Ten 1303	A.Lelie-Den 16.97		D.Mason-Ten 692	L.Tomlinson-SD 2370	L.Tomlinson-SD 17	A.Van Pelt-Ind 157
M.Harrison-Ind 1272	T.Taylor-Bal 16.21		M.Harrison-Ind 686	J.Lewis-Bal 2271	C.Portis-Den 14	M.Stover-Bal 134
H.Ward-Pit 1163	D.Bennett-Ten 15.75		H.Ward-Pit 632	P.Holmes-KC 2110	J.Lewis-Bal 14	G.Anderson-Ten 123
S.Moss-NYJ 1105	E.Kennison-KC 15.23		S.Moss-NYJ 603	F.Taylor-Jax 1942		J.Elam-Den 120

Punt Average	Field Goals	Field Goal Percent	Kickoff Returns	Kickoff Return Average	Punt Returns	Punt Return Average
S.Lechler-Oak 46.9	A.Van Pelt-Ind 37	A.Van Pelt-Ind 100.0	J.Moses-Hou 58	J.Carter-NYJ 28.7	A.Randle El-Pit 45	D.Hall-KC 16.3
B.Moorman-Buf 44.6	M.Stover-Bal 33	Q.Jammer-Oak 88.0	D.Hall-KC 57	B.Pyatt-Ind 28.6	L.Brightful-Bal 45	P.Buchanon-Oak 13.6
C.Hentrich-Ten 43.9	J.Elam-Den 27	S.Graham-Cin 88.0	B.Bennett-Cin 53	B.Johnson-NE 28.2	D.Northcutt-Cle 36	A.Randle El-Pit 12.0
M.Knorr-Den 43.2	D.Brien-NYJ 27	J.Elam-Den 87.1	L.Johnson-SD 50	M.Bates-NYJ 27.1	J.Moses-Hou 36	D.Allen-Jax 12.0
H.Smith-Ind 42.2	G.Anderson-Ten 27	G.Anderson-Ten 87.1	A.Brown-Buf 48	D.Hall-KC 25.9	P.Buchanon-Oak 36	J.McCareins-Ten 11.4

Punt/Kick Return Yards	Punt/Kick Return TDs	Interceptions	Interception Return Yards	Interception Return TDs	Sacks	Overall Rank
D.Hall-KC 1950	D.Hall-KC 4	P.Surtain-Mia 7	P.Buchanon-Oak 176	J.Woods-KC 2	A.Ogunleye-Mia 15.0	J.Lewis-Bal 2309
J.Moses-Hou 1599	A.Randle El-Pit 2	E.Reed-Bal 7	S.Rolle-Ten 141	A.Dyson-Ten 2	J.Taylor-Mia 13.0	L.Tomlinson-SD 2173
L.Johnson-SD 1335	P.Buchanon-Oak 2	M.Coleman-Hou 7	E.Reed-Bal 132	P.Buchanon-Oak 2	S.Ellis-NYJ 12.5	P.Holmes-KC 2035
A.Brown-Buf 1157			J.Woods-KC 125	T.Bruschi-NE 2	T.Suggs-Bal 12.0	P.Manning-Ind 1904
D.Allen-Jax 1155			N.Harper-Ind 121			C.Portis-Den 1888

Chiefs with the Ball, Chumps Without

For the first half of the season, the Chiefs looked unstoppable. The offense seemed capable of scoring at will, with too many weapons for opposing defenses to contain. Priest Holmes remained the league's most versatile back, rushing for 1,420 yards and catching 74 passes. His 27 rushing touchdowns set an NFL record. Return man Dante Hall scored a touchdown in four straight games (twice each on punts and kickoffs).

After starting 9–0, everything unraveled. The Bengals used a relentless running attack to control the clock, amassing 200 yards on the ground. Other teams followed suit, and Kansas City's porous run defense surrendered an average of 191 rushing yards over the next five games. The Chiefs limped into the playoffs, their deficiencies exposed.

New England returned to the top of the AFC with a blue-collar defense and an offense that spread the ball around. That the Patriots didn't have a 1,000-yard rusher or a 1,000-yard receiver seemed immaterial; quarterback Tom Brady threw touchdown passes to eight different receivers. The defense surrendered the fewest points and led the league with 29 interceptions. The Patriots won their last 12 games and, after being shut out by Buffalo to open the season, they blanked the Bills to end the year by the same 31–0 score.

Baltimore's Jamal Lewis set a new single-game mark by rushing for 295 yards in a week two victory over the Browns. He wound up with 2,066 yards for the season, just 39 yards shy of Eric Dickerson's all-time record. The Ravens couldn't get consistent play at quarterback, and the tremendous imbalance limited their success.

The Colts had a much more versatile offense. Edgerrin James returned to form with 11 rushing touchdowns and Peyton Manning led the league in passing yards. Kicker Mike Vanderjagt hit all 37 field goal attempts and broke the record for consecutive field goals without a miss. A little over a year after the great Johnny Unitas died, the league lost Otto Graham. Automatic Otto finished each of his 10 years in pro football in a championship game for the Browns, either in the AAFC or the NFL. Graham won seven times.

2004 NFC

TEAM	W-L-T	PCT	POST	PTS	RA	RY	RY/A	RTD	FL	PA	PC	GPY	GPY/A	PTD	PI	PSY	PRAT
Eastern Division																	
Phi	**13**-3	**.813**	DCS	386-**260**	376-442	1639-1903	4.4-4.3	10-13	11-11	547-550	336-334	4208-3475	7.7-**6.3**	32-**16**	**11**-17	229-263	96.4-75.8
Dal	6-10	.375	—	293-405	449-425	1769-1764	3.9-4.2	14-14	14-9	519-502	308-310	3636-3718	7.0-7.4	19-31	23-13	208-197	74.5-94.2
NYG	6-10	.375	—	303-347	424-498	1904-2157	4.5-4.3	18-13	11-14	475-467	269-292	3097-3280	6.5-7.0	12-28	13-14	279-250	73.5-90.9
Was	6-10	.375	—	240-265	471-419	1765-**1304**	3.7-**3.1**	6-**7**	10-8	514-515	288-294	2874-3222	5.6-**6.3**	18-17	17-18	242-245	70.0-72.2
Northern Division																	
GB	10-6	.625	E	**424**-380	441-**409**	1908-1878	4.3-4.6	9-12	10-7	**598**-518	**382**-314	4550-3943	7.6-7.6	36-33	19-8	**101**-280	93.8-99.1
Min	8-8	.500	#WD	405-395	387-435	1823-2006	4.7-4.6	8-15	9-11	552-544	380-338	**4754**-4130	**8.6**-7.6	**39**-30	12-11	238-234	**109.8**-95.5
Det	6-10	.375	—	296-350	407-498	1777-1887	4.4-3.8	7-10	**7**-10	505-535	285-328	3124-3736	6.2-7.0	19-29	13-14	208-222	76.7-89.4
ChiB	5-11	.313	—	231-331	430-496	1624-2050	3.8-4.1	10-9	21-12	471-515	249-287	2641-3513	5.6-6.8	9-23	16-17	449-173	61.7-78.1
Southern Division																	
Atl	11-5	.688	DC	340-337	**524**-434	**2672**-1681	**5.1**-3.9	**20**-20	14-13	395-517	217-328	2692-3838	6.8-7.4	15-19	16-19	280-**312**	72.0-82.8
NO	8-8	.500	#	348-405	406-485	1606-2253	4.0-4.6	15-16	10-**20**	542-545	309-324	3810-4095	7.0-7.5	21-24	16-13	223-207	79.5-87.7
Car	7-9	.438	—	355-339	422-474	1582-1904	3.7-4.0	10-19	11-12	536-513	311-303	3889-3703	7.3-7.2	29-18	15-**26**	246-225	87.0-**72.0**
TB	5-11	.313	—	301-304	393-480	1489-1973	3.8-4.1	9-8	18-11	512-**436**	340-**247**	3773-**2843**	7.4-6.5	24-21	18-16	299-264	89.1-77.2
Western Division																	
Sea	9-7	.563	E	371-373	468-452	2095-2031	4.5-4.5	17-17	9-12	532-559	304-340	3715-3808	7.0-6.8	23-24	18-23	176-218	79.1-78.3
SL	8-8	.500	#WD	319-392	381-480	1624-2179	4.3-4.5	11-13	17-9	580-492	372-292	4615-3415	8.0-6.9	23-24	22-6	362-241	86.1-91.6
Arz	6-10	.375	—	284-322	475-450	1668-2105	3.5-4.7	15-12	11-15	533-505	299-271	3202-3265	6.0-6.5	14-18	18-15	320-229	68.5-73.2
SF	2-14	.125	—	259-452	413-495	1449-1995	3.5-4.0	10-22	19-12	561-490	325-308	3455-3680	6.2-7.5	16-27	21-9	319-194	69.9-96.5
Aver	16	—	—	344	451	1866	4.1	13	12	511	305	3604	7.1	23	16	236	82.8

TEAM	1D	PENY	PNT	FGM/A	RTNY	RTNTD	OFFY/DEFY	NETY	NETTO	NP	PNP	DELP	PW	DELW	PRT	DR	YPD	DEL
Eastern Division																		
Phi	301-299	952-1001	42.0-42.5	**27/32**-17/24	664-361	2-1	5618-5115	503	6	**126**	**66**	60	**11.1**	1.8	6.5/ 4.4	184-185	30.5-27.6	2.9
Dal	296-297	867-879	42.3-41.8	20/26-21/23	499-936	0-4	5197-5285	-88	-15	-112	-67	-45	5.2	0.8	4.7/ 6.1	185-186	28.1-28.4	-0.3
NYG	281-310	977-1007	40.1-**38.9**	22/28-20/25	366-490	4-**0**	4722-5187	-465	4	-44	-23	-21	6.9	-0.9	4.5/ 5.3	183-178	25.8-29.1	-3.3
Was	269-**251**	1047-797	**43.7**-40.2	19/27-17/20	736-928	2-6	4397-**4281**	116	-1	-25	6	-31	7.4	-1.4	3.7/**4.2**	194-200	22.7-**21.4**	1.3
Northern Division																		
GB	**354**-307	950-942	40.1-39.2	24/28-17/25	419-467	5-2	**6357**-5541	**816**	-14	44	12	32	9.1	0.9	6.5/ 6.5	184-187	34.5-29.6	**4.9**
Min	351-350	884-974	39.3-42.2	18/22-24/27	482-376	3-1	6339-5902	437	1	10	40	-30	8.3	-0.3	**7.3**/ 6.3	167-**162**	**38.0**-36.4	1.5
Det	263-320	1000-976	40.5-43.5	24/28-17/20	636-635	6-4	4693-5401	-708	4	-54	-43	-11	6.7	-0.6	4.7/ 5.5	183-186	25.6-29.0	-3.4
ChiB	230-302	956-914	42.6-40.4	15/24-26/36	**1056**-602	**7**-4	3816-5390	-1574	-8	-100	-163	**63**	5.5	-0.5	2.9/ 5.1	**211**-210	18.1-25.7	-7.6
Southern Division																		
Atl	284-310	905-930	40.6-43.3	18/23-**16/18**	899-**335**	6-2	5084-5207	-123	2	3	-2	5	8.1	**2.9**	4.1/ 5.1	185-186	27.5-28.0	-0.5
NO	291-343	1141-965	43.6-40.8	22/27-31/35	489-570	4-4	5193-6141	-948	7	-57	-51	-6	6.6	1.4	5.3/ 6.1	198-193	26.2-31.8	-5.6
Car	308-307	1020-1078	43.1-41.1	20/25-20/28	585-624	3-3	5225-5382	-157	**12**	16	35	-19	8.4	-1.4	5.7/ 4.5	185-186	28.2-28.9	-0.7
TB	271-258	916-897	41.8-44.4	15/24-20/31	452-607	4-6	4963-4552	411	-9	-3	-2	-1	7.9	-2.9	5.2/ 4.3	196-192	25.3-23.7	1.6
Western Division																		
Sea	320-311	**669**-748	38.4-41.8	23/25-27/32	567-402	3-1	5634-5621	13	8	-2	33	-35	7.9	1.0	5.2/ 4.7	196-188	28.7-29.9	-1.2
SL	321-311	993-827	41.9-42.5	19/24-31/36	188-607	3-6	5877-5353	524	-24	-73	-52	-21	6.2	1.8	5.5/ 6.0	177-179	33.2-29.9	3.3
Arz	280-282	948-**1121**	42.7-41.9	22/29-25/26	543-749	2-5	4550-5141	-591	1	-38	-45	7	7.1	-1.0	3.9/ 4.7	200-201	22.8-25.6	-2.8
SF	280-322	859-867	41.6-40.9	18/22-25/29	432-924	3-5	4585-5481	-896	-19	-193	-151	-42	3.2	-1.2	3.8/ 6.5	198-197	23.2-27.8	-4.7
Aver	300	913	41.8	22/27	585	4	5235	—	—	—	—	—	—	—	5.6	188	27.9	—

Rushing Attempts	Rushing Yards	Rushing Average	Rushing TDs	Rushing Rank	Passing Yards	Passing Average
S.Alexander-Sea......353	S.Alexander-Sea....1696	M.Vick-Atl 7.52	S.Alexander-Sea........16	S.Alexander-Sea....1856	D.Culpepper-Min....4717	D.Culpepper-Min.....8.61
C.Portis-Was............343	T.Barber-NYG........1518	S.Jackson-SL..........5.02	T.Barber-NYG............13	T.Barber-NYG........1648	B.Favre-GB............4088	D.McNabb-Phi 8.26
T.Barber-NYG..........322	C.Portis-Was..........1315	T.Duckett-Atl 4.89	E.Smith-Arz 9	C.Portis-Was..........1365	M.Bulger-SL...........3964	M.Bulger-SL............8.17
F.McAfee-NO 269	A.Green-GB...........1163	S.Alexander-Sea.....4.80	F.McAfee-NO 9	A.Green-GB...........1233	J.Delhomme-Car ...3886	B.Griese-TB............7.83
E.Smith-Arz 267	K.Jones-Det...........1133	T.Barber-NYG.........4.71	W.Dunn-Atl 9	W.Dunn-Atl 1196	D.McNabb-Phi 3875	B.Favre-GB.............7.57
Completion Percent	**TD Passes**	**TD Percent**	**INT Percent**	**Passer Rating**	**Passing Rank**	**Receptions**
B.Griese-TB............69.3	D.Culpepper-Min........39	D.Culpepper-Min.......7.1	K.Warner-NYG 1.4	D.Culpepper-Min...110.9	D.Culpepper-Min....2114	J.Horn-NO 94
D.Culpepper-Min.....69.2	D.McNabb-Phi 31	D.McNabb-Phi 6.6	D.McNabb-Phi 1.7	D.McNabb-Phi 104.7	D.McNabb-Phi 1773	T.Holt-SL....................94
M.Bulger-SL............66.2	B.Favre-GB................30	B.Griese-TB..............6.0	D.Culpepper-Min.......2.0	B.Griese-TB............97.5	M.Bulger-SL...........1527	M.Muhammad-Car.....93
B.Favre-GB.............64.1	J.Delhomme-Car 29	B.Favre-GB...............5.6	J.McCown-Arz 2.5	M.Bulger-SL............93.7	B.Favre-GB............1514	L.Coles-Was 90
D.McNabb-Phi 64.0	W.Harris-Sea 22	J.Delhomme-Car 5.4	D.Harper-Det 2.5	B.Favre-GB.............92.4	J.Delhomme-Car ...1488	
Receiving Yards	**Receiving Average**	**Receiving TDs**	**Receiving Rank**	**Combined Net Yards**	**Total TDs**	**Total Points**
M.Muhammad-Car.1405	T.Pinkston-Phi.......18.78	M.Muhammad-Car.....16	M.Muhammad-Car...783	T.Barber-NYG........2096	S.Alexander-Sea........20	D.Akers-Phi..............122
J.Horn-NO 1399	J.Pathon-NO 17.09	T.Owens-Phi 14	J.Horn-NO 755	S.Alexander-Sea....1866	M.Muhammad-Car.....16	R.Longwell-GB 120
J.Walker-GB 1382	D.Terrell-Chi..........16.64	R.Moss-Min 13	J.Walker-GB 751	A.Rossum-Atl.........1729	T.Barber-NYG............15	S.Alexander-Sea......120
T.Holt-SL................1372	A.Crumpler-Atl......16.13	J.Walker-GB 12	T.Holt-SL.................736	M.Lewis-NO...........1724	T.Owens-Phi 14	J.Brown-Sea 109
I.Bruce-SL..............1292	K.Colbert-Car 16.04	J.Horn-NO 11	I.Bruce-SL...............676	C.Portis-Was.........1550	R.Moss-Min 13	J.Carney-NO............104
Punt Average	**Field Goals**	**Field Goal Percent**	**Kickoff Returns**	**Kickoff Return Average**	**Punt Returns**	**Punt Return Average**
T.Tupa-Was............44.1	D.Akers-Phi................27	J.Brown-Sea 92.0	A.Rossum-Atl............58	D.Ward-NYG...........27.3	D.McNabb-Chi 44	E.Drummond-Det....13.2
T.Sauerbrun-Car.....44.1	R.Longwell-GB 24	J.Kasay-Car 86.4	M.Lewis-NO..............51	W.Ponder-NYG 26.9	K.Williams-Arz 42	A.Rossum-Atl.........12.4
M.Berger-NO 43.6	J.Hanson-Det.............24	R.Longwell-GB 85.7	M.Morris-Sea 47	E.Drummond-Det....26.6	A.Rossum-Atl.............37	M.Lewis-NO...........11.2
S.Landeta-SL..........43.3	J.Brown-Sea 23	J.Hanson-Det..........85.7	A.Harris-SL 47	T.Cox-TB.................26.2	M.Lewis-NO...............34	D.Wynn-Phi............10.8
S.Player-Arz............43.2		D.Akers-Phi............84.4	J.Azumah-Chi 42	A.Stecker-NO..........26.1	M.Jones-NYG 34	D.McNabb-Chi 9.9
Punt/Kick Return Yards	**Punt/Kick Return TDs**	**Interceptions**	**Interception Return Yards**	**Interception Return TDs**	**Sacks**	**Overall Rank**
A.Rossum-Atl.........1707	E.Drummond-Det.........4	K.Lucas-Sea 6	N.Vasher-Chi 177	L.Sheppard-Phi...........2	B.Berry-Arz.............14.5	D.Culpepper-Min....2540
M.Lewis-NO...........1597		C.Gamble-Car.............6	L.Sheppard-Phi........172	D.Sharper-GB.............2	Gbaja-Biamila-GB.......13.5	D.McNabb-Phi 2023
E.Drummond-Det...1408			J.Peppers-Car.........143	K.Mathis-Atl 2	P.Kerney-Atl 13.0	S.Alexander-Sea....1961
M.Morris-Sea.........1069			M.Trufant-Sea 141		S.Rice-TB 12.0	T.Barber-NYG........1947
W.Ponder-NYG........967			J.Azumah-Chi..........128			M.Vick-Atl 1679

Eagles Soar Above Mediocre Field

In a conference filled with mediocre teams, the Philadelphia Eagles stood out. After losing the NFC Championship Game in three straight seasons, the Eagles added controversial wide receiver Terrell Owens. Owens, who spent his first eight years with San Francisco, was originally traded to Baltimore but refused to report. Owens insisted, unlike W.C. Fields, that he would rather play in Philadelphia. A standoff was resolved when the league helped broker a three-way deal making Owens an Eagle. Quarterback Donovan McNabb set franchise records for yards and touchdowns, and led the Eagles to the best record in the team's 72-year history.

None of the other NFC teams were able to distinguish themselves. For the first time ever, multiple teams made the playoffs without winning records: the Vikings, led by Daunte Culpepper, whose passing yardage and touchdown totals were the fifth-best all-time, and the Rams, like Minnesota a good offensive team with a porous defense. They confirmed the fickleness of the postseason; both .500 teams won their first-round games.

A third member of the Manning family joined the NFL's ranks. Eli, brother of Peyton and son of Archie, was the first overall pick in the 2004 draft. San Diego selected him despite warnings that he would not play for their organization. A draft day trade sent the younger Manning to the Giants. He went 1–6 as a starter as New York finished with half as many wins as the team that Manning spurned.

The NFL's all-time leading rusher, Emmitt Smith, and receiver, Jerry Rice, each played their final games. Kickers Gary Anderson and Morten Andersen called it quits as the two highest-scoring players in history. Aeneas Williams and Eddie George also retired.

Legendary receiver Elroy "Crazy Legs" Hirsch and two of the premier tackles of the 1960s, Hall of Famers Rosey Brown and Jim Parker, died. Reggie White, an unparalleled pass rusher, landmark free agent, and ordained minister, died suddenly just three years after his career ended. The most tragic death, though, was Pat Tillman. The former Cardinal turned down a lucrative contract in 2002 to join the military; he was killed in Afghanistan.

2004 AFC

TEAM	W-L-T	PCT	POST	PTS	RA	RY	RY/A	RTD	FL	PA	PC	GPY	GPY/A	PTD	PI	PSY	PRAT
Eastern Division																	
NE	14-2	.875	DCS*	437-260	524-405	2134-1572	4.1-3.9	15-9	13-16	485-538	293-315	3750-3711	7.7-6.9	29-18	14-20	162-311	92.5-75.3
NYJ	10-6	.625	WD	333-261	527-432	2388-1566	4.5-**3.6**	15-8	**5**-14	438-497	282-289	3231-3532	7.4-7.1	19-21	11-19	181-220	90.5-78.3
Buf	9-7	.563	—	395-284	483-447	1874-1604	3.9-**3.6**	15-6	12-15	461-486	262-261	3032-2943	6.6-**6.1**	21-20	17-**24**	215-319	76.7-**65.2**
Mia	4-12	.250	—	275-354	384-539	1339-2302	3.5-4.3	10-12	16-10	586-**434**	309-**244**	3391-**2815**	5.8-6.5	19-20	26-15	326-223	62.5-76.9
Northern Division																	
Pit	**15**-1	**.938**	DC	372-**251**	**618**-357	**2464-1299**	4.0-**3.6**	16-8	8-13	358-484	228-269	2970-3060	8.3-6.3	20-**14**	13-19	250-225	93.2-68.0
Bal	9-7	.563	—	317-268	491-469	2063-1681	4.2-**3.6**	11-9	12-13	465-501	258-276	2559-3386	5.5-6.8	13-**14**	11-21	247-264	70.7-68.0
Cin	8-8	.500	—	374-372	437-474	1839-2062	4.2-4.4	14-11	10-16	536-520	324-313	3520-3560	6.6-6.8	23-23	22-20	219-257	77.0-79.5
Cle	4-12	.250	—	276-390	441-532	1657-2314	3.8-4.3	6-22	19-13	439-460	251-277	3076-3091	7.0-6.7	21-17	21-15	252-190	74.9-79.0
Southern Division																	
Ind	12-4	.750	ED	**522**-351	427-440	1852-2037	4.3-4.6	10-12	7-**17**	527-557	353-364	**4732**-4232	**9.0**-7.6	**51**-26	10-19	109-**340**	**119.7**-89.5
Jax	9-7	.563	—	261-280	446-438	1850-1777	4.1-4.1	9-7	11-12	513-497	305-306	3315-3574	6.5-7.2	17-18	11-16	156-217	80.7-82.0
Hou	7-9	.438	—	309-339	481-417	1882-1843	3.9-4.4	16-**4**	11-8	471-530	286-344	3547-3776	7.5-7.1	16-32	14-22	301-161	83.0-88.7
Ten	5-11	.313	—	344-439	420-421	1871-1917	4.5-4.6	12-18	12-12	**589**-524	356-333	3933-4027	6.7-7.7	27-29	19-18	317-220	82.1-91.2
Western Division																	
SD	12-4	.750	E	446-313	525-**355**	2185-1307	4.2-3.7	24-15	10-10	450-607	288-372	3506-4195	7.8-6.9	29-19	**8**-23	149-142	102.0-76.6
Den	10-6	.625	W	381-304	534-396	2333-1512	4.4-3.8	13-16	9-8	521-484	303-272	4089-3213	7.8-6.6	27-17	20-12	**90**-266	84.5-78.0
KC	7-9	.438	—	483-435	496-397	2289-1834	**4.6**-4.6	**31**-18	10-8	561-522	**370**-312	4633-4453	8.3-8.5	27-32	17-13	227-250	94.9-97.5
Oak	5-11	.313	—	320-442	327-537	1295-2012	4.0-3.7	10-21	13-9	582-510	330-315	4019-4106	6.9-8.1	24-30	22-9	161-182	76.1-99.4
Aver	16	—	—	344	451	1866	4.1	13	12	511	305	3604	7.1	23	16	236	82.8

TEAM	1D	PENY	PNT	FGM/A	RTNY	RTNTD	OFFY/DEFY	NETY	NETTO	NP	PNP	DELP	PW	DELW	PRT	DR	YPD	DEL
Eastern Division																		
NE	344-290	822-1014	42.0-41.5	**31**/33-**15/18**	520-607	5-4	5722-4972	750	9	**177**	99	**78**	**12.4**	1.6	6.4/ 4.6	162-180	35.3-27.6	7.7
NYJ	313-282	**693**-720	38.2-**40.1**	24/29-16/19	556-553	4-**1**	5438-4878	560	17	72	115	-43	9.8	0.2	5.9/ 5.0	186-176	29.2-27.7	1.5
Buf	271-258	1047-865	43.1-40.7	24/28-27/32	824-672	**10**-3	4691-4228	463	10	111	79	32	10.8	-1.8	4.5/**3.3**	194-196	24.2-**21.6**	2.6
Mia	267-281	852-852	41.5-41.0	19/23-20/28	656-722	2-10	4404-4894	-490	-17	-79	-109	30	6.0	-2.0	3.3/ 4.5	**214**-207	20.6-23.6	-3.1
Northern Division																		
Pit	310-248	837-875	43.0-42.7	28/33-23/27	658-442	5-4	5184-**4134**	1050	11	121	**132**	-11	11.0	**4.0**	5.9/ 4.0	179-177	29.0-23.4	5.6
Bal	260-273	894-798	40.6-**40.1**	29/32-26/31	**1316**-453	9-4	4375-4803	-428	11	49	8	41	9.2	-0.2	3.9/ 4.3	199-199	22.0-24.1	-2.2
Cin	286-303	810-887	41.7-41.9	27/31-28/31	600-824	5-7	5140-5365	-225	4	2	-3	5	8.1	-0.1	4.5/ 4.7	202-205	25.4-26.2	-0.7
Cle	245-307	854-890	40.0-41.6	24/29-24/28	682-545	2-6	4481-5215	-734	-12	-114	-109	-5	5.2	-1.2	4.4/ 4.9	201-199	22.3-26.2	-3.9
Southern Division																		
Ind	379-331	801-877	45.2-42.7	20/26-25/31	423-586	5-**1**	6475-5929	546	**19**	171	122	49	12.3	-0.3	**8.7**/ 5.5	171-178	**37.9**-33.3	4.6
Jax	279-290	940-966	42.8-44.1	24/31-21/28	531-592	0-6	5009-5134	-125	6	-19	14	-33	7.5	1.5	5.2/ 5.3	176-174	28.5-29.5	-1.0
Hou	300-304	928-979	41.2-41.7	17/24-22/29	722-422	5-3	5128-5458	-330	5	-30	-8	-22	7.3	-0.3	5.3/ 5.3	181-**173**	28.3-31.5	-3.2
Ten	308-318	923-774	42.9-43.6	19/27-23/28	458-501	2-5	5487-5724	-237	-1	-95	-24	-71	5.6	-0.6	4.8/ 5.9	198-195	27.7-29.4	-1.6
Western Division																		
SD	328-320	875-940	43.1-42.4	20/25-20/27	423-**230**	2-2	5542-5360	182	15	133	75	58	11.3	0.7	7.0/ 5.0	175-183	31.7-29.3	2.4
Den	351-**235**	880-**1062**	40.5-44.7	29/**34**-21/26	575-639	2-2	6332-4459	**1873**	-9	77	120	-43	9.9	0.1	6.3/ 4.9	189-191	33.5-23.3	**10.2**
KC	**398**-327	963-957	39.5-42.2	17/23-21/27	405-545	4-3	**6695**-6037	658	-6	48	31	17	9.2	-2.2	6.6/ 7.0	179-181	37.4-33.4	4.0
Oak	275-367	1013-837	**46.7**-41.3	25/28-17/25	353-769	1-5	5153-5936	-783	-17	-122	-133	11	4.9	0.0	5.1/ 7.1	182-184	28.3-32.3	-3.9
Aver	300	913	41.8	22/27	585	2	5235	—	—	—	—	—	—	—	5.6	93	28.5	—

Rushing Attempts	Rushing Yards	Rushing Average	Rushing TDs	Rushing Rank	Passing Yards	Passing Average
C.Martin-NYJ...........371	C.Martin-NYJ.........1697	L.Jordan-NYJ..........5.15	L.Tomlinson-SD.........17	C.Martin-NYJ.........1817	T.Green-KC............4591	P.Manning-Ind.........9.17
R.Johnson-Cin.........361	C.Dillon-NE............1635	C.Brown-Ten...........4.85	P.Holmes-KC..............14	C.Dillon-NE............1755	P.Manning-Ind........4557	Roethlisberger-Pit......8.88
C.Dillon-NE..............345	E.James-Ind..........1548	L.Johnson-KC.........4.84	W.McGahee-Buf........13	E.James-Ind..........1638	J.Plummer-Den......4089	T.Green-KC.............8.26
L.Tomlinson-SD.......339	R.Johnson-Cin.......1454	C.Dillon-NE.............4.74	D.Davis-Hou..............13	R.Johnson-Cin.......1574	T.Brady-NE............3692	D.Brees-SD.............7.90
E.James-Ind............334	L.Tomlinson-SD.....1335	F.Taylor-Jax............4.71	J.Bettis-Pit.................13	L.Tomlinson-SD.....1505	D.Carr-Hou............3531	J.Plummer-Den.......7.85

Completion Percent	TD Passes	TD Percent	INT Percent	Passer Rating	Passing Rank	Receptions
P.Manning-Ind.........67.6	P.Manning-Ind...........49	P.Manning-Ind..........9.9	D.Brees-SD...............1.8	P.Manning-Ind.......121.1	P.Manning-Ind........2124	T.Gonzalez-KC........102
Roethlisberger-Pit......66.4	T.Brady-NE...............28	D.Brees-SD...............6.8	P.Manning-Ind...........2.0	D.Brees-SD...........104.8	T.Green-KC............1751	D.Mason-Ten.............96
T.Green-KC.............66.4	J.Plummer-Den.........27	T.Brady-NE...............5.9	B.Leftwich-Jax..........2.3	Roethlisberger-Pit......98.1	D.Brees-SD............1435	C.Johnson-Cin...........95
D.Brees-SD.............65.5	T.Green-KC...............27	Roethlisberger-Pit........5.8	K.Boller-Bal...............2.4	T.Green-KC.............95.2	T.Brady-NE............1426	E.Moulds-Buf.............88
J.Peelle-NYJ...........65.4	D.Brees-SD...............27	J.Plummer-Den.........5.2	J.Peelle-NYJ..............2.4	T.Brady-NE.............92.6	J.Plummer-Den......1380	M.Harrison-Ind...........86

Receiving Yards	Receiving Average	Receiving TDs	Receiving Rank	Combined Net Yards	Total TDs	Total Points
C.Johnson-Cin.......1274	A.Lelie-Den..........20.07	M.Harrison-Ind..........15	C.Johnson-Cin.........682	D.Hall-KC..............2236	L.Tomlinson-SD.........18	A.Vinatieri-NE..........141
T.Gonzalez-KC.......1258	P.Burress-Pit.........19.94	A.Gates-SD...............13	D.Bennett-Ten..........679	E.James-Ind..........2031	P.Holmes-KC.............15	J.Elam-Den..............129
D.Bennett-Ten........1247	S.Moss-NYJ..........18.62	R.Wayne-Ind.............12	R.Wayne-Ind...........665	C.Martin-NYJ.........1933	M.Harrison-Ind..........15	J.Reed-Pit...............124
R.Wayne-Ind..........1210	D.Patten-NE..........18.18	D.Bennett-Ten...........11	T.Gonzalez-KC........664	B.Sams-Bal............1847	C.Martin-NYJ.............14	S.Graham-Cin..........122
J.Smith-Jax...........1172	L.Evans-Buf..........17.56	B.Stokley-Ind.............10	M.Harrison-Ind.........632	R.Droughns-Den....1825	D.Davis-Hou..............14	L.Tynes-Ind.............119

Punt Average	Field Goals	Field Goal Percent	Kickoff Returns	Kickoff Return Average	Punt Returns	Punt Return Average
S.Lechler-Oak.........46.7	A.Vinatieri-NE............31	A.Vinatieri-NE.........93.9	D.Hall-KC....................68	T.McGee-Buf...........26.3	B.Sams-Bal...............55	K.Ratliff-Cin............12.2
H.Smith-Ind............45.2	M.Stover-Bal.............29	M.Stover-Bal...........90.6	B.Sams-Bal................59	D.Hall-KC................25.3	W.Welker-Mia............43	D.Northcutt-Cle.......12.0
B.Moorman-Buf.......43.2	J.Elam-Den...............29	Q.Jammer-Oak.......89.3	J.Moses-Hou.............59	A.Randle El-Pit.......25.1	A.Randle El-Pit.........42	W.Welker-Mia.........10.8
M.Scifres-SD..........43.1	J.Reed-Pit.................28	S.Graham-Cin.........87.1	W.Welker-Mia............57	B.Johnson-NE........24.8	D.Northcutt-Cle..........36	B.Sams-Bal.............10.5
C.Gardocki-Pit........43.0	S.Graham-Cin............27	R.Lindell-Buf...........85.7	D.Gabriel-Oak............53	D.Rhodes-Ind..........24.8	J.Moses-Hou.............36	R.Smith-Den............10.1

Punt/Kick Return Yards	Punt/Kick Return TDs	Interceptions	Interception Return Yards	Interception Return TDs	Sacks	Overall Rank
D.Hall-KC..............1950	T.McGee-Buf................3	E.Reed-Bal.................9	E.Reed-Bal..............358	T.Spikes-Buf................2	D.Freeney-Ind.........16.0	P.Manning-Ind........2162
B.Sams-Bal............1826	B.Sams-Bal.................2	T.James-Cin................8	C.Williams-Bal.........156		S.Ellis-NYJ.............11.0	C.Martin-NYJ.........1950
W.Welker-Mia........1777	D.Hall-KC....................2	D.Robinson-Hou..........6	D.Robinson-Hou......146		T.Suggs-Bal............10.5	E.James-Ind..........1880
J.Moses-Hou.........1612		A.Dyson-Ten...............6	A.Dyson-Ten............135		R.Mathis-Ind...........10.5	T.Green-KC............1836
T.McGee-Buf..........1370		N.Clements-Buf...........6	T.Spikes-Buf............122		R.Hayward-Den......10.5	C.Dillon-NE............1812

New England's Reign Continues

Enigmatic running back Ricky Williams surprised everyone by announcing his retirement just before the start of training camp. Williams, 27, had reportedly failed a drug test and said he had lost interest in playing football. The move stunned the Miami Dolphins and left a glaring hole in their backfield. While Miami suffered its first losing season in 16 years, Curtis Martin of the division rival New York Jets became the oldest player to win a rushing title. The 31-year old running back also moved into fourth place all-time in career rushing yards.

Indianapolis quarterback Peyton Manning had what was arguably the best season ever for a quarterback, throwing for 4,557 yards and breaking Dan Marino's single season record with 49 touchdown passes. Manning posted these gaudy numbers despite sitting out the fourth quarter of many lopsided wins.

The San Diego Chargers completed one of the biggest turnarounds in NFL history. After finishing with the league's worst record in 2003, a revamped defense and a rejuvenated quarterback, Comeback Player of the Year Drew Brees, helped the Chargers win the AFC West with a 12–4 record. Marty Schottenheimer earned Coach of the Year honors for leading the turnaround.

Sparked by the emergence of rookie quarterback Ben Roethlisberger, Pittsburgh became the first AFC team to win 15 games in a season. The key for the Steelers, however, was the league's top-ranked defense and running backs Duce Staley and Jerome Bettis. The running of new addition Corey Dillon brought balance to already powerful New England. Although they lost to the Steelers on Halloween, the Patriots dominated the Steelers in a rematch in the AFC Championship Game. Quarterback Tom Brady strengthened his reputation as one of the all-time great big game players by leading his team to its third Super Bowl title in four seasons.

Rich Gannon, an unheralded passer until he became a Raider, and Tim Brown, the top target for Oakland quarterbacks for 17 seasons, retired. Justin Strzelczyk, an 11th-round pick in 1990 who became an eight-year starter on Pittsburgh's offensive line, was killed during a car chase with upstate New York police when his vehicle hit a tanker truck and exploded.

2005 NFC

TEAM	W-L-T	PCT	POST	PTS	RA	RY	RY/A	RTD	FL	PA	PC	GPY	GPY/A	PTD	PI	PSY	PRAT
Eastern Division																	
NYG	11-5	.688	E	422-314	469-428	2209-1656	4.7-3.9	17-12	8-**20**	558-580	294-329	3762-3852	6.7-6.6	24-20	17-17	184-268	75.7-76.3
Was	10-6	.625	WD	359-293	525-411	2183-1686	4.2-4.1	15-15	16-12	481-535	278-291	3346-3318	7.0-6.2	**25**-15	11-16	240-237	87.0-70.1
Dal	9-7	.563	—	325-308	521-414	1861-1731	3.6-4.2	13-13	14-11	500-495	300-271	3639-3319	7.3-6.7	23-18	17-15	298-236	83.6-75.1
Phi	6-10	.375	—	310-388	365-506	1432-1883	3.9-3.7	11-15	14-10	620-503	337-297	3903-3507	6.3-7.0	21-24	20-17	226-184	71.5-82.2
Northern Division																	
ChiB	11-5	.688	D	260-**202**	488-443	2099-1637	4.3-3.7	11-9	13-10	418-550	219-313	2201-3147	5.3-**5.7**	11-**10**	15-**24**	199-275	61.5-**61.2**
Min	9-7	.563	—	306-344	381-462	1467-1841	3.9-4.0	10-14	14-11	510-533	323-319	3449-3539	6.8-6.6	18-23	16-**24**	303-207	81.7-75.2
Det	5-11	.313	—	254-345	404-488	1471-2040	3.6-4.2	10-15	12-12	520-487	297-295	3021-3305	5.8-6.8	15-19	18-19	**173**-187	69.1-77.6
GB	4-12	.250	—	298-344	398-504	1352-2010	3.4-4.0	11-10	15-11	626-430	383-252	3964-**2876**	6.3-6.7	20-22	30-10	198-196	70.1-86.2
Southern Division																	
Car	11-5	.688	#EDC	391-259	487-**408**	1679-**1465**	3.4-3.6	17-9	10-19	449-528	269-305	3485-3351	**7.8**-6.3	**25**-15	16-23	214-294	88.1-68.0
TB	11-5	.688	#W	300-274	457-438	1826-1515	4.0-**3.5**	13-10	9-13	487-476	303-275	3171-3158	6.5-6.6	17-15	14-17	281-229	80.7-73.5
Atl	8-8	.500	—	351-341	**531**-438	**2546**-2063	**4.8**-4.7	17-18	16-13	451-526	247-320	2907-3394	6.4-6.5	19-18	13-16	228-257	76.6-78.4
NO	3-13	.188	—	235-398	423-503	1688-2145	4.0-4.3	8-16	19-9	553-**418**	308-**241**	3604-3014	6.5-7.2	15-20	24-10	261-165	66.6-86.2
Western Division																	
Sea	**13**-3	**.813**	DCS	**452**-271	519-420	2457-1510	4.7-3.6	**29-5**	**7**-11	474-571	307-331	3632-3861	7.7-6.8	**25**-18	**10**-16	174-**302**	**96.8**-77.4
SL	6-10	.375	—	363-429	380-459	1535-2178	4.0-4.7	13-22	13-14	599-507	392-314	4351-3619	7.3-7.1	23-26	24-13	315-195	83.0-89.8
Arz	5-11	.313	—	311-387	360-411	1138-1632	3.2-4.0	2-22	16-11	**670**-488	**419**-301	**4723**-3314	7.0-6.8	21-17	21-15	286-217	81.0-80.6
SF	4-12	.250	—	239-428	428-486	1689-1832	3.9-3.8	9-19	14-10	389-576	204-374	2190-4620	5.6-8.0	8-28	21-16	292-193	53.6-94.2
Aver	16	—	—	330	449	1799	4.0	13	12	515	306	3491	6.8	20	16	236	80.1

TEAM	1D	PENY	PNT	FGM/A	RTNY	RTNTD	OFFY/DEFY	NETY	NETTO	NP	PNP	DELP	PW	DELW	PRT	DR	YPD	DEL
Eastern Division																		
NYG	312-302	1115-**1180**	42.1-41.5	35/42-**21**/30	807-611	4-4	5787-5240	547	12	108	94	14	10.7	0.3	5.2/ 4.9	206-199	28.1-26.3	1.8
Was	301-258	925-879	40.3-41.3	17/21-22/31	356-**372**	4-2	5289-4767	522	1	66	48	18	9.6	0.4	5.6/ 4.4	192-194	27.5-24.6	3.0
Dal	318-256	739-1015	42.4-41.0	20/28-**21**/27	471-576	2-4	5202-4814	388	-5	17	12	5	8.4	0.6	5.1/ 4.9	199-193	26.1-24.9	1.2
Phi	282-290	1130-910	40.7-41.9	22/29-22/27	643-649	3-7	5109-5206	-97	-7	-78	-36	-42	6.1	-0.0	4.5/ 5.3	**220**-212	23.2-24.6	-1.3
Northern Division																		
ChiB	233-259	850-1016	40.5-41.1	22/31-**21**/29	**941**-378	**6**-1	4101-4509	-408	6	58	-10	68	9.4	1.5	3.2/**3.2**	196-200	20.9-**22.5**	-1.6
Min	285-304	1013-990	43.3-41.8	25/34-28/33	736-715	5-**0**	4613-5173	-560	5	-38	-27	-11	7.1	2.0	4.6/ 4.4	190-193	24.3-26.8	-2.5
Det	258-308	838-953	43.5-40.3	19/24-24/30	582-791	3-5	4319-5158	-839	1	-91	-66	-25	5.7	-0.7	4.0/ 4.7	187-**182**	23.1-28.3	-5.2
GB	318-280	918-975	38.9-42.3	20/27-29/34	586-709	3-5	5118-4690	428	-24	-46	-60	14	6.8	-2.8	4.0/ 5.3	191-189	26.8-24.8	2.0
Southern Division																		
Car	278-262	**732**-1045	43.2-45.1	26/34-23/27	884-570	3-3	4950-4522	428	**16**	132	100	32	11.3	-0.3	5.9/ 3.8	186-193	26.6-23.4	3.2
TB	268-**254**	1085-830	**45.6**-43.9	22/27-26/33	715-946	3-3	4716-**4444**	272	7	26	51	-25	8.6	**2.3**	4.6/ 4.5	187-188	25.2-23.6	1.6
Atl	313-319	1043-981	42.3-43.1	24/27-25/30	529-401	3-2	5225-5200	25	0	10	2	8	8.3	-0.3	4.7/ 4.6	193-185	27.1-28.1	-1.0
NO	312-281	1130-985	43.2-45.6	25/32-31/39	502-716	0-7	5031-4994	37	-24	-163	-93	-70	3.9	-0.9	4.1/ 5.9	193-186	26.1-26.8	-0.8
Western Division																		
Sea	**361**-295	846-909	41.0-40.1	18/25-34/42	492-436	3-1	**5915**-5069	**846**	10	**181**	**111**	**70**	**12.5**	0.5	**6.5**/ 4.9	183-195	**32.3**-26.0	**6.3**
SL	314-321	941-1066	41.2-**40.0**	27/31-26/33	539-678	4-2	5571-5602	-31	-10	-66	-43	-23	6.3	-0.4	4.9/ 5.7	194-193	28.7-29.0	-0.3
Arz	304-272	1184-819	43.3-44.1	**43/45-21/24**	668-662	3-7	5575-4729	**846**	-11	-76	27	-103	6.1	-1.1	5.2/ 4.9	196-193	28.4-24.5	3.9
SF	191-335	780-961	41.2-40.1	26/29-29/36	432-736	**6**-2	3587-6259	-2672	-9	-189	-259	**70**	3.3	0.7	2.4/ 6.6	193-209	18.6-29.9	-11.4
Aver	295	931	42.4	24/30	555	3	5055	—	—	—	—	—	—	—	5.3	188	26.9	—

Rushing Attempts	Rushing Yards	Rushing Average	Rushing TDs	Rushing Rank	Passing Yards	Passing Average
S.Alexander-Sea......370	S.Alexander-Sea....1880	M.Vick-Atl 5.85	S.Alexander-Sea........27	S.Alexander-Sea....2150	B.Favre-GB...........3881	M.Bulger-SL...........8.00
T.Barber-NYG..........357	T.Barber-NYG........1860	T.Barber-NYG.........5.21	S.Davis-Car 12	T.Barber-NYG........1950	E.Manning-NYG 3762	J.Delhomme-Car 7.86
C.Portis-Was...........352	C.Portis-Was..........1516	S.Alexander-Sea.....5.08	C.Portis-Was.............11	C.Portis-Was..........1626	D.Bledsoe-Dal........3639	W.Harris-Sea 7.70
T.Jones-Chi.............314	W.Dunn-Atl 1416	W.Dunn-Atl 5.06	T.Jones-Chi.................9	W.Dunn-Atl 1446	W.Harris-Sea 3459	D.Bledsoe-Dal.........7.29
C.Williams-TB.........290	T.Jones-Chi............1335	F.Gore-SF 4.79	T.Barber-NYG.............9	T.Jones-Chi............1425	J.Delhomme-Car ...3421	K.Warner-Arz..........7.23
Completion Percent	**TD Passes**	**TD Percent**	**INT Percent**	**Passer Rating**	**Passing Rank**	**Receptions**
M.Bulger-SL............66.9	E.Manning-NYG 24	J.Delhomme-Car 5.5	B.Johnson-Min..........1.4	W.Harris-Sea 98.2	W.Harris-Sea 1490	S.Smith-Car............103
W.Harris-Sea 65.5	W.Harris-Sea 24	W.Harris-Sea 5.3	W.Harris-Sea 2.0	M.Bulger-SL............94.4	E.Manning-NYG 1321	T.Fisher-Arz 103
K.Warner-Arz..........64.5	J.Delhomme-Car 24	M.Brunell-Was..........5.1	M.Brunell-Was..........2.2	B.Johnson-Min........88.9	D.Bledsoe-Dal........1255	T.Holt-SL.................102
B.Johnson-Min........62.6	M.Brunell-Was...........23	M.Bulger-SL.............4.9	C.Simms-TB 2.2	J.Delhomme-Car 88.1	M.Brunell-Was 1240	A.Boldin-Arz............102
B.Favre-GB.............61.3	D.Bledsoe-Dal............23	D.Bledsoe-Dal..........4.6	K.Warner-Arz............2.4	M.Brunell-Was 85.9	J.Delhomme-Car ...1191	D.Driver-GB 86
Receiving Yards	**Receiving Average**	**Receiving TDs**	**Receiving Rank**	**Combined Net Yards**	**Total TDs**	**Total Points**
S.Smith-Car...........1563	T.Glenn-Dal...........18.32	S.Smith-Car..............12	S.Smith-Car.............842	T.Barber-NYG........2390	S.Alexander-Sea........28	S.Alexander-Sea......168
S.Moss-Was 1483	S.Moss-Was 17.65	W.Joseph-Sea 10	S.Moss-Was 787	S.Alexander-Sea....1958	S.Smith-Car 13	J.Feely-NYG 148
T.Fisher-Arz 1409	T.Owens-Phi 16.23	J.Galloway-TB 10	T.Fisher-Arz 755	S.Smith-Car...........1940	S.Davis-Car 12	N.Rackers-Arz 140
A.Boldin-Arz...........1402	P.Burress-NYG 15.97	T.Fisher-Arz 10	A.Boldin-Arz.............736	R.Swinton-Arz........1790	C.Portis-Was..............11	J.Kasay-Car.............121
T.Holt-SL...............1331	J.Galloway-TB 15.51		T.Holt-SL.................711	C.Portis-Was.........1732	T.Barber-NYG............11	J.Wilkins-SL.............117
Punt Average	**Field Goals**	**Field Goal Percent**	**Kickoff Returns**	**Kickoff Return Average**	**Punt Returns**	**Punt Return Average**
J.Bidwell-TB...........45.6	N.Rackers-Arz 40	N.Rackers-Arz 95.2	R.Swinton-Arz...........63	K.Robinson-Min......26.0	M.Jones-TB 51	R.Mahe-Phi............12.8
C.Kluwe-Min 44.1	J.Feely-NYG 35	J.Nedney-SF..........92.9	J.Scobey-Sea 59	L.Betts-Was............25.9	C.Morton-NYG..........47	M.Moore-Min 11.7
S.Player-Arz...........43.9	J.Wilkins-SL...............27	T.Peterson-Atl 92.0	T.Thompson-Dal 57	W.Ponder-NYG 25.9	A.Chatman-GB 45	S.Smith-Car 10.6
S.Landeta-Phi.........43.6	J.Nedney-SF..............26	J.Wilkins-SL...........87.1	E.Drummond-Det.......49	T.Thompson-Dal 24.5	R.Swinton-Arz...........42	M.Jones-TB 9.6
N.Harris-Det...........43.5	J.Kasay-Car...............26	M.Bryant-TB 84.0	K.Robinson-Min.........47	D.McNabb-Det........23.8	A.Hakim-NO 34	C.Morton-NYG..........9.6
Punt/Kick Return Yards	**Punt/Kick Return TDs**	**Interceptions**	**Interception Return Yards**	**Interception Return TDs**	**Sacks**	**Overall Rank**
R.Swinton-Arz........1790	Many..........................1	D.Sharper-Min 9	D.Sharper-Min 276	D.Sharper-Min 2	O.Umenyiora-NYG..14.5	T.Barber-NYG........2225
T.Thompson-Dal 1399		N.Vasher-Chi 8	D.Hall-Atl..................177	K.Dansby-Arz 2	S.Rice-TB 14.0	S.Alexander-Sea....2194
J.Scobey-Sea 1326		C.Gamble-Car.............7	C.Tillman-Chi...........172		M.Strahan-NYG......11.5	C.Portis-Was.........1748
E.Drummond-Det...1234			C.Gamble-Car.........157		J.Peppers-Car.........10.5	W.Harris-Sea 1624
K.Robinson-Min.....1221			N.Vasher-Chi 145		R.Coleman-Atl 10.5	W.Dunn-Atl 1561

Bring It on Home

Arizona finished 5–11, but six of their losses came by less than a touchdown. Things were clearly on the upswing in coach Dennis Green's second year at the helm. Larry Fitzgerald tied for the league lead with 103 receptions, and Anquan Boldin finished with 102. A young defense ranked eighth overall, but the Cardinals running game produced a league-low 2 touchdowns.

The Cardinals also acted as hosts for the first regular-season NFL game ever played outside the U.S. A crowd of 103,467 saw the Cardinals beat San Francisco in Estadio Azteca in Mexico City. Meanwhile, the Saints had no place to really call home. Hurricane Katrina shut down the Superdome—and much of the Gulf Coast—just before the season started. The Saints played home games in Baton Rouge, San Antonio, and, believe it or not, New Jersey.

Giants quarterback Eli Manning emerged as one of the league's top passers despite a second-half slump. Tiki Barber had the best year of his career, rushing for 1,860 yards and topping the 200-yard mark in three different games. The Bears surged into contention with the league's stingiest defense, holding half of their opponents to single digits. Five Chicago defenders were selected to the Pro Bowl and linebacker Brian Urlacher was named Defensive Player of the Year

Steve Smith returned to the Panthers after missing most of 2004 with a broken leg. He led the league with 1,563 receiving yards and tied for first in receptions (103) and touchdowns (12). Carolina's defense continued to give teams fits, and the rejuvenated Panthers advanced to the NFC title game for the second time in three seasons.

The Seahawks finished with the NFC's best record, at one point winning 11 straight games. Their greatest strength may have been having three Pro Bowlers on the offensive line: tackle Walter Jones, guard Steve Hutchinson, and center Robbie Tobeck. They cleared the way for Shaun Alexander, who ran for a league-leading 1,880 yards and set an NFL record by scoring 28 total touchdowns. Seattle's Mike Holmgren became just the fourth coach to take two different teams to the Super Bowl.

2005 AFC

TEAM	W-L-T	PCT	POST	PTS	RA	RY	RY/A	RTD	FL	PA	PC	GPY	GPY/A	PTD	PI	PSY	PRAT
Eastern Division																	
NE	10-6	.625	ED	379-338	439-437	1512-1580	3.4-3.6	16-11	9-8	564-527	352-296	**4322**-3926	7.7-7.4	28-25	15-10	202-223	91.5-87.8
Mia	9-7	.563	—	318-317	444-480	1898-1771	4.3-3.7	11-11	14-**17**	556-549	291-323	3458-3682	6.2-6.7	22-23	16-14	158-**375**	72.8-82.4
Buf	5-11	.313	—	271-367	428-489	1607-2205	3.8-4.5	6-22	10-13	459-503	269-314	2852-3560	6.2-7.1	18-19	16-17	337-269	75.4-82.1
NYJ	4-12	.250	—	240-355	384-554	1328-2185	3.5-3.9	10-19	19-7	470-**463**	268-284	2989-**2948**	6.4-6.4	11-17	15-21	347-193	70.6-73.1
Northern Division																	
Cin	11-5	.688	#E	421-350	459-429	1910-1850	4.2-4.3	15-16	**6**-13	538-519	**362**-324	3935-3749	7.3-7.2	**32**-21	14-**31**	115-180	97.6-72.8
Pit	11-5	.688	#WDCS*	389-258	**549**-402	2223-1376	4.0-**3.4**	21-10	9-15	379-549	228-315	3104-3480	**8.2**-6.3	21-**15**	14-15	178-312	89.4-74.0
Bal	6-10	.375	—	265-299	452-431	1605-1591	3.6-3.7	5-8	15-15	562-525	335-296	3381-3228	6.0-**6.1**	17-18	21-11	293-270	71.3-77.4
Cle	6-10	.375	—	232-301	395-527	1503-2202	3.8-4.2	4-11	13-8	497-471	297-**279**	3323-3009	6.7-6.4	15-19	17-15	276-142	75.5-78.2
Southern Division																	
Ind	**14**-2	**.875**	D	**439-247**	465-398	1703-1762	3.7-4.4	18-9	8-13	515-509	347-343	4191-3469	8.1-6.8	31-17	11-18	**95**-318	**103.3**-83.0
Jax	12-4	.750	W	361-269	502-434	1959-1709	3.9-3.9	18-**4**	11-9	487-482	283-285	3352-3223	6.9-6.7	21-22	**6**-19	162-277	88.4-78.0
Ten	4-12	.250	—	299-421	397-449	1525-1894	3.8-4.2	8-12	12-11	**594**-470	358-296	3797-3462	6.4-7.4	20-33	14-9	200-246	80.3-100.7
Hou	2-14	.125	—	260-431	437-506	1816-2303	4.2-4.6	9-21	11-9	449-469	270-304	2661-3727	5.9-7.9	15-24	13-7	424-206	76.0-100.0
Western Division																	
Den	13-3	.813	DC	395-258	542-**344**	**2539**-1363	**4.7**-4.0	25-10	9-16	465-613	279-344	3373-3833	7.3-6.3	18-20	7-20	146-190	88.9-**72.2**
KC	10-6	.625	—	403-325	520-383	2382-1570	4.6-4.1	**26**-11	13-15	507-559	317-325	4014-3862	7.9-6.9	17-25	10-16	204-183	90.1-82.3
SD	9-7	.563	—	418-312	465-386	2072-**1349**	4.5-3.5	22-14	12-10	526-567	338-338	3738-3888	7.1-6.9	27-20	16-10	243-289	89.7-84.7
Oak	4-12	.250	—	290-383	361-507	1369-2049	3.8-4.0	11-18	9-14	591-486	316-296	3883-3481	6.6-7.2	21-18	14-5	301-238	76.0-90.7
Aver	16	—	—	330	449	1799	4.0	13	12	515	306	3491	6.8	20	16	236	80.1

TEAM	1D	PENY	PNT	FGM/A	RTNY	RTNTD	OFFY/DEFY	NETY	NETTO	NP	PNP	DELP	PW	DELW	PRT	DR	YPD	DEL
Eastern Division																		
NE	334-306	921-**1068**	44.6-43.7	20/25-24/30	399-593	2-2	5632-5283	349	-6	41	5	36	9.0	1.0	6.3/ 6.3	179-185	31.5-28.6	2.9
Mia	274-319	1055-827	43.1-43.0	25/30-24/24	526-354	1-**1**	5198-5078	120	1	1	14	-13	8.0	1.0	4.8/ 4.9	**198**-199	26.3-25.5	0.7
Buf	259-343	897-904	**45.7**-40.2	29/**35**-19/25	512-494	2-3	4122-5496	-1374	4	-96	-99	3	5.6	-0.6	3.9/ 5.0	178-175	23.2-31.4	-8.2
NYJ	251-321	801-981	43.3-45.0	22/28-30/35	498-452	4-2	3970-4940	-970	-6	-115	-105	-10	5.1	-1.1	4.0/**4.0**	178-177	22.3-27.9	-5.6
Northern Division																		
Cin	342-321	920-985	42.5-42.1	28/32-25/28	417-507	1-2	5730-5419	311	**24**	71	122	-51	9.8	1.2	6.3/ 4.4	175-176	32.7-30.8	2.0
Pit	297-275	876-1031	41.7-43.3	24/29-24/30	649-530	3-2	5149-**4544**	605	7	131	78	53	11.3	-0.3	6.1/ 4.4	182-182	28.3-25.0	3.3
Bal	286-277	1067-844	42.8-40.5	**30/35**-29/31	622-737	3-4	4693-4549	144	-10	-34	-28	-6	7.2	-1.1	3.8/ 4.7	191-197	24.6-**23.1**	1.5
Cle	241-292	770-716	40.4-42.5	27/29-28/35	503-562	3-**1**	4550-5069	-519	-7	-69	-71	2	6.3	-0.3	4.5/ 4.8	177-176	25.7-28.8	-3.1
Southern Division																		
Ind	**363-269**	**690**-857	44.3-41.7	23/26-19/27	441-408	4-**1**	5799-4913	886	12	**192**	122	70	**12.8**	1.2	**7.3**/ 4.5	165-**165**	35.1-29.8	5.4
Jax	301-273	1006-1055	42.4-42.8	23/30-20/27	599-326	3-4	5149-4655	494	11	92	85	7	10.3	**1.7**	6.0/ 4.4	189-185	27.2-25.2	2.1
Ten	279-294	1002-718	43.2-44.1	23/29-21/27	547-437	**5**-6	5122-5110	12	-6	-122	-23	-99	4.9	-1.0	5.1/ 6.1	**198**-181	25.9-28.2	-2.4
Hou	243-348	854-846	38.8-**40.1**	26/34-28/32	269-444	2-5	4053-5824	-1771	-8	-171	-180	9	3.7	-1.7	3.5/ 6.8	174-175	23.3-33.3	-10.0
Western Division																		
Den	330-295	756-989	43.2-44.9	24/32-**14/18**	**660-309**	3-**1**	5766-5006	760	20	137	**143**	-6	11.4	1.6	6.3/ 4.6	182-181	31.7-27.7	4.0
KC	347-292	890-805	39.4-45.7	27/33-20/26	525-375	3-2	**6192**-5249	**943**	8	78	111	-33	9.9	0.0	6.5/ 5.5	175-182	**35.4**-28.8	**6.5**
SD	337-306	890-831	43.7-42.0	21/24-20/29	450-474	2-2	5567-4948	619	-8	106	20	**86**	10.6	-1.7	5.5/ 5.5	178-189	31.3-26.2	5.1
Oak	294-299	1132-825	**45.7**-41.5	20/30-35/38	244-796	1-4	4951-5292	-341	-4	-93	-44	-49	5.7	-1.7	5.0/ 6.1	186-182	26.6-29.1	-2.5
Aver	295	931	42.4	24/30	555	1	5055	—	—	—	—	—	—	—	5.3	91	28.1	—

Rushing Attempts	Rushing Yards	Rushing Average	Rushing TDs	Rushing Rank	Passing Yards	Passing Average
E.James-Ind 360	L.Johnson-KC 1750	T.Bell-Den 5.32	L.Johnson-KC 20	L.Johnson-KC 1950	T.Brady-NE 4110	Roethlisberger-Pit 8.90
L.Tomlinson-SD 339	E.James-Ind 1506	L.Johnson-KC 5.21	L.Tomlinson-SD 18	L.Tomlinson-SD 1642	T.Green-KC 4014	P.Manning-Ind 8.27
R.Johnson-Cin 337	L.Tomlinson-SD 1462	W.Parker-Pit 4.71	E.James-Ind 13	E.James-Ind 1636	C.Palmer-Cin 3836	T.Green-KC 7.92
L.Johnson-KC 336	R.Johnson-Cin 1458	R.Williams-Mia 4.42		R.Johnson-Cin 1578	K.Collins-Oak 3759	T.Brady-NE 7.75
W.McGahee-Buf 325	W.McGahee-Buf 1247	R.Brown-Mia 4.38		W.McGahee-Buf 1297	P.Manning-Ind 3747	C.Palmer-Cin 7.54
Completion Percent	**TD Passes**	**TD Percent**	**INT Percent**	**Passer Rating**	**Passing Rank**	**Receptions**
C.Palmer-Cin 67.8	C.Palmer-Cin 32	Roethlisberger-Pit 6.3	J.Plummer-Den 1.5	P.Manning-Ind 104.1	T.Green-KC 1692	C.Johnson-Cin 97
K.Holcomb-Buf 67.4	P.Manning-Ind 28	C.Palmer-Cin 6.3	B.Leftwich-Jax 1.7	C.Palmer-Cin 101.1	T.Brady-NE 1625	A.Gates-SD 89
P.Manning-Ind 67.3	T.Brady-NE 26	P.Manning-Ind 6.2	T.Green-KC 2.0	Roethlisberger-Pit 98.6	P.Manning-Ind 1614	D.Mason-Bal 86
D.Brees-SD 64.6	D.Brees-SD 24	B.Leftwich-Jax 5.0	K.Collins-Oak 2.1	T.Brady-NE 92.3	C.Palmer-Cin 1598	R.Smith-Den 85
T.Brady-NE 63.0	K.Collins-Oak 20	T.Brady-NE 4.9	P.Manning-Ind 2.2	J.Plummer-Den 90.2	K.Collins-Oak 1500	R.Wayne-Ind 83
Receiving Yards	**Receiving Average**	**Receiving TDs**	**Receiving Rank**	**Combined Net Yards**	**Total TDs**	**Total Points**
C.Johnson-Cin 1432	A.Lelie-Den 18.33	M.Harrison-Ind 12	C.Johnson-Cin 761	D.Hall-KC 2283	L.Johnson-KC 21	S.Graham-Cin 131
M.Harrison-Ind 1146	M.Booker-Mia 17.59	H.Ward-Pit 11	M.Harrison-Ind 633	W.Welker-Mia 2208	L.Tomlinson-SD 20	L.Johnson-KC 126
C.Chambers-Mia 1118	R.Moss-Oak 16.75	C.Chambers-Mia 11	C.Chambers-Mia 614	L.Johnson-KC 2093	E.James-Ind 14	L.Tynes-KC 125
R.Smith-Den 1105	E.Wilford-Jax 16.61	A.Gates-SD 10	A.Gates-SD 601	C.Carr-Oak 1937	C.Dillon-NE 13	Vanden Bosch-Ind 121
E.Kennison-KC 1102	J.McCareins-NYJ 16.58		R.Smith-Den 583	E.James-Ind 1843	M.Anderson-Den 13	L.Tomlinson-SD 120
Punt Average	**Field Goals**	**Field Goal Percent**	**Kickoff Returns**	**Kickoff Return Average**	**Punt Returns**	**Punt Return Average**
B.Moorman-Buf 45.7	M.Stover-Bal 30	P.Dawson-Cle 93.1	C.Carr-Oak 73	T.McGee-Buf 30.2	A.Pearman-Jax 49	B.Sams-Bal 12.2
S.Lechler-Oak 45.7	R.Lindell-Buf 29	Vanden Bosch-Ind 92.0	D.Hall-KC 65	J.Mathis-Hou 28.6	A.Randle El-Pit 44	D.Northcutt-Cle 10.5
J.Miller-NE 45.1	S.Graham-Cin 28	M.Stover-Bal 88.2	T.Perry-Cin 64	J.Miller-NYJ 26.3	W.Welker-Mia 43	A.Randle El-Pit 10.2
H.Smith-Ind 44.3	L.Tynes-KC 27	N.Kaeding-SD 87.5	D.Sproles-SD 63	P.Jones-Ten 26.2	D.Hall-KC 42	P.Jones-Ten 9.4
T.Sauerbrun-Den 43.8	P.Dawson-Cle 27	S.Graham-Cin 87.5	W.Welker-Mia 61	Q.Morgan-Pit 25.3	D.Northcutt-Cle 35	W.Welker-Mia 9.1
Punt/Kick Return Yards	**Punt/Kick Return TDs**	**Interceptions**	**Interception Return Yards**	**Interception Return TDs**	**Sacks**	**Overall Rank**
C.Carr-Oak 1938	A.Randle El-Pit 2	D.O'Neal-Cin 10	T.Law-NYJ 195	C.June-Ind 2	D.Burgess-Oak 16.0	L.Johnson-KC 2127
D.Hall-KC 1836	J.Mathis-Hou 2	T.Law-NYJ 10	C.Bailey-Den 139	C.Hart-SD 2	Vanden Bosch-Ten 12.5	L.Tomlinson-SD 1876
W.Welker-Mia 1769		C.Bailey-Den 8	C.June-Ind 115	C.Bailey-Den 2	J.Taylor-Mia 12.0	E.James-Ind 1810
D.Sproles-SD 1636		G.Wesley-KC 6	C.Hart-SD 110		A.Schobel-Buf 12.0	T.Green-KC 1774
J.Mathis-Hou 1610			D.Williams-Den 108		R.Mathis-Ind 11.5	T.Brady-NE 1724

SURPRISES BOTH GREAT AND TRAGIC

Indianapolis threatened to become the NFL's first undefeated team since the 1972 Dolphins. A well-balanced offense and a stingy defense helped the Colts win their first 13 games, and none of them were particularly close. Head coach Tony Dungy tried to deflect the pressure that built with each win, insisting that success in the postseason would be more important than a perfect record.

Defeat finally came in their 14th game at the hands of the Chargers; the Colts acted relieved. Five days later, Dungy's 18-year-old son was found dead. Both events seemed to shake the team's focus and eliminate the momentum built during the 13-game win streak. The Colts played poorly the last two weeks of the season and made a quick playoff exit.

For the first time in 15 seasons, the Cincinnati Bengals posted a winning record and earned a playoff berth. Head coach Marvin Lewis engineered the turnaround, building an explosive offense around receiver Chad Johnson and bruising runner Rudi Johnson. An aggressive defense led the league with 31 interceptions, and quarterback Carson Palmer led the NFL with 32 touchdown passes.

As happened in 2004, Kansas City running back Priest Holmes missed the second half of the season due to injury. Third-year backup Larry Johnson stepped in and played like a man possessed. He rushed for more than 100 yards in each of the nine games he started, finishing with 1,751 yards and 20 rushing touchdowns. Kansas City had the league's top-ranked offense, but a mediocre pass rush, ineffective secondary, and bad luck kept the Chiefs out of the playoffs.

The Steelers played smash mouth football on both sides of the ball. A tough, physical offensive line cleared the way for Pittsburgh's power running game, with Jerome Bettis a short-yardage specialist in his final season. Quarterback Ben Roethlisberger endured a series of knee injuries, eventually missing four games after mid-season surgery. A ferocious defense kept the team on track, with hard-hitting safety Troy Polamalu and relentless linebacker Joey Porter setting the tone. Coach Bill Cowher's club snagged the final playoff spot, but it turned into an old familiar ride to the Super Bowl title.

THE PLAYOFFS

Given the expanded playoffs in every sport today, it is hard to imagine a time with no postseason sports playoffs. Major league baseball had its first winner-take-all postseason series in 1884 and hockey's Stanley Cup has been carted around since 1893. Even the short-lived American Basketball League, started by NFL president Joe Carr, had playoffs beginning in 1926. By 1932 the Stanley Cup playoffs had become a four-round tournament, and, in the 29th installment of the World Series, Babe Ruth had called (or maybe not called) his home run at Wrigley Field, the same home park where the Chicago Bears were battling for first place. George Halas had coincidentally been a very part-time New York Yankees right fielder the year before Ruth arrived in New York, but since 1920 his focus was solely on pro football. He had a championship to prove it.

In 1921 Halas's club, then known as the Chicago Staleys, was declared champion of the American Professional Football Association. (The next year the league would become known as the National Football League, just as Halas's club that year would take the name Chicago Bears.) But Halas also had reason to contest the championships of 1920, 1924, and 1926. What's more, other teams had similar gripes about different seasons. Teams still played varying numbers of games; multiple ties—although not counted in winning percentage at the time—clouded the picture further.

The Bears finished the 1932 season with a 9–0 win over Green Bay. The Portsmouth Spartans, forerunners of the Detroit Lions, had finished their season the week before with a shutout of the same Packers club. By virtue of those consecutive losses, the Packers were considered eliminated from the championship picture, but what of the Bears (6–1–6) and the Spartans (6–1–4)? Earlier head-to-head competition offered no insight as to the better club; the Spartans and Bears had tied both times they met. The league decided that a game would be played between the teams to decide matters the next week at Wrigley Field.

The game became one of the more bizarre chapters in a league filled with strange stories through its first dozen years. A blizzard hit Chicago and made Wrigley Field unplayable. Rather than postponing, the game was moved indoors to Chicago Stadium. The circus had just left town and the floor was covered with dirt and straw. (Modern players would probably prefer it to artificial turf.) Because Chicago Stadium's "field" was 20 yards shorter than a regulation field, the goalposts were placed on the goal line, hashmarks added on the narrow field, and the officials adjusted the spot when teams drove past midfield. Bronko Naguski's questionable touchdown pass was debated all winter, but one fact was certainly not in doubt: The Bears won the game and were NFL champions.

The league was so pleased with the results of the 1932 contest that they decided to eliminate the five-yard buffer for throwing a forward pass that had caused all the hullabaloo, and agreed to schedule a championship game for the next December. To do this the league was split into Eastern and Western divisions, with the top teams in each conference playing one another for the NFL title. The creation of a scheduled championship game, the addition of divisions, and the easing of the restrictions on the forward pass, would create years of thrills in the NFL for many winters to come.

The first championship game in 1933—the Chicago Stadium contest the previous year had been deemed a continuation of the regular season—solidified a great rivalry. The Bears and the New York Giants played that year and again the next and would meet in six title games over the next 30 years. (Halas's club would win four times.) Other great rivalries were forged across the frigid days of late December, and as the seasons and schedules and formats changed, the games would slide into the next calendar year.

December 1941 was a turbulent time due to the Japanese bombing of Pearl Harbor and America's entry into the war, but this was the backdrop of the non-championship playoff in NFL history. The Bears and Packers were tied for first place in the West at 10–1 and a playoff was determined to break the tie. The Bears won that game, and then the NFL title a week later. The end of the war brought a new league—the All-America Football Conference—and another championship game, which would be won all four times by the Cleveland Browns. That league also introduced pro football to its

first multi-game playoff format. In 1949, the final year of the league, only seven AAFC clubs remained, so the top four teams played each other (1 vs. 4 and 2 vs. 3) with the two survivors meeting in the championship game. It would certainly not be the last time multiple playoff games were held.

Pro football and the championship grew in stature during the 1950s. The Colts–Giants 1958 NFL Championship Game, universally hailed as the Greatest Game Ever Played, was the first time sudden death was used in a regulation NFL game. Two years later, men eager to jump into pro football started another league, the American Football League, and another championship game. The league was so successful a merger with the NFL was brokered after six seasons, bringing with it even more postseason permutations, not to mention a neutral site championship game between the two leagues that came to be known as the Super Bowl.

The NFL expanded to 16 teams in 1967 and created four divisions of four teams each. That season also brought the first tiebreaker system since the league tried to solve the championship conundrum back in the NFL's early days by using more argument than formula. The Los Angeles Rams were the first club to go into the NFL playoffs based on a tiebreaker, beating out the Baltimore Colts, also at 11–1–2. The Rams essentially made the grade because they beat the Colts the final day of the season—their first meeting had ended in a tie—making it one of the fairest and easiest to understand tiebreakers in a system that would get more and more complex as the years wore on.

The actual merger of the two leagues in 1970 added the word "wild card" to the sports fan's dictionary. The formation of two 14-team conferences with three divisions apiece left an odd number of playoff teams, so a fourth team was added. This wild card could come from any division and was considered the best team not to win a division title, even though many times this team had a better record than teams that made the playoffs by winning titles in inferior division. The wild card would not host a playoff game, making it harder for them to advance to the championship game. During the first seven years of this format with one wild card per conference, the 1975 Dallas Cowboys were the only club to win a conference championship.

In 1978 two wild cards were added to the playoffs. While the division winners each got a bye, the non-division winners with the two best records battled it out in each conference. The winner then resumed the role that the previous single wild card winner had: go on the road and try to win the conference title. The 1980 Oakland Raiders became the first team to do this, as well as the first team to win a Super Bowl after winning three postseason games to get there. In 1990 a third wild card team was added to the playoffs. The division champion with the worst record would no longer get a bye. The division winner received a home game and played the qualifier with the worst record while the top two division winners in each conference watched and waited.

The 2002 addition of the NFL's 32nd team, the Houston Texans, set up a major divisional realignment. Each conference went to four divisions of four teams each. The number of wild card teams was reduced to two and there would be four division winners. Wild card teams still had to play on the road, regardless of record, and home field advantage isn't always what it's cracked up to be. In the 2005 playoffs, for example, the AFC East champion New England Patriots with a 10–6 record hosted and beat the 12–4 wild-card Jacksonville Jaguars. Lower-seeded road teams, however, won the other three games in the first round. The 2005 Pittsburgh Steelers became the first team to qualify in the sixth playoff slot and then win all three conference playoff games on the road as well as the Super Bowl.

PLAYOFF BOWL

The Playoff Bowl was a consolation game played for third place in the NFL during the 1960s. It featured the conference runners-up in a game played in Miami after the NFL Championship Game and before the Pro Bowl. The game was officially called the Bert Bell Benefit Bowl after the NFL commissioner from 1946–59. Bell died in 1959 during a game between the Philadelphia Eagles and Pittsburgh

Steelers, having served as owner of both teams at various times. In 1967, after the realignment to four divisions in the NFL, the teams sent to the Playoff Bowl were teams that had already lost in the playoffs. It was not overly popular among players, and not every coach was thrilled, either.

Green Bay head coach Vince Lombardi detested the game, calling it "a loser's bowl for losers," among other things. After his team lost the Playoff Bowl to the St. Louis Cardinals in 1965, Lombardi used the threat of playing in another Playoff Bowl as motivation for his players. The Packers never played in another Playoff Bowl. They won the NFL championship each of the next three seasons, plus the first two Super Bowls. Super Bowl II, played at the Orange Bowl, the home of every Playoff Bowl, was Lombardi's last game with Green Bay. The Playoff Bowl was ushered out with the AFL–NFL merger in 1970, the same year Lombardi died.

The NFL Western Conference won 8 of the 10 Playoff Bowls, with Detroit the only three-time winner; Cleveland lost three times. The NFL now classifies the Playoff Bowls as exhibitions and does not count them among postseason games. In the spirit of full disclosure, the results follow.

Playoff Bowl Results

January 7, 1961: Detroit Lions 17, Cleveland Browns 16
January 6, 1962: Detroit Lions 38, Philadelphia Eagles 10
January 6, 1963: Detroit Lions 17, Pittsburgh Steelers 10
January 9, 1964: Green Bay Packers 40, Cleveland Browns 23
January 8, 1965: St. Louis Cardinals 24, Green Bay Packers 17
January 9, 1966: Baltimore Colts 35, Dallas Cowboys 3
January 8, 1967: Baltimore Colts 20, Philadelphia Eagles 14
January 7, 1968: Los Angeles Rams 30, Cleveland Browns 6
January 5, 1969: Dallas Cowboys 17, Minnesota Vikings 13
January 3, 1970: Los Angeles Rams 31, Dallas Cowboys 0

KEY TO THE PLAYOFF SECTION

This section includes information on every playoff game in NFL, AAFC, and AFL history. The writeups of the playoffs include scoring for each game, leaders in various categories, as well as the date, site, and attendance. For divisional and wild-card playoff games, only the team statistical information is given. When a player exceeds 100 yards rushing or receiving or 300 yards passing, that is denoted by the player's name, followed by **R** for Rushing, **C** for receiving, or **P** for passing. Additional information is provided for the NFL Championship Games as well as the title games for the AFC and NFC.

In the Championship Game recaps, the visiting team is listed first and the home team second; the winning team is listed in bold in the quarter-by-quarter score. There are two parts to the statistics for each playoff game: team and individual. Some of the individual abbreviations appear below. Where a dash appears below, that is used to explain the numbers that appear on each side of the dash.

FD First Downs
YDS Total Yards Gained
RUSH Number of Attempts-and Rushing Yards
PASS Passing Yards
RTN Return Yards
A-C-I Attempts-Completions-Interceptions
PUNT Number of Punts-and Average
FUMB Number of Fumbles-Number Lost
PEN Number of Penalties-and Yards Assessed

In the individual categories for championship games, the leaders in various categories are listed. Because of the vast number of playoffs that are not championship games, only players who surpassed 300 yards passing, 100 yards rushing or receiving are included for those games.

Note that for the 1935 NFL Championship game, a snowstorm at the open press box at Titan Stadium kept the scorekeepers from accurately measuring the rushing statistics for individuals on the New York Giants. Keep in mind these abbreviations for the individual leaders in the Championship Games.

Rushing

ATT Rushing Attempts
YDS Yards Gained
LNG Longest Run
TD Rushing Touchdowns

Receiving and Returns

NO Number of Catches
YDS Yards Gained
LNG Longest Play
TD Touchdowns

Passing

PA Pass Attempts
PC Passes Completed
YDS Yards Passing
TD Touchdowns
IN Interceptions

Also note that many of the games played in the postseason, especially those since the adoption of the 16-game schedule in 1978, stretch into the next calendar year. The 2005 playoffs, for example, refer to games played as part of the 2005 season, even though the date of the game is January 2006.

1933 LEAGUE CHAMPIONSHIP

Sunday, December 17, 1933 at Chicago, Wrigley Field, attendance 26,000

NEW YORK GIANTS	0	7	7	7	—	21
CHICAGO BEARS	3	3	10	7	—	**23**

SCORING ChiB—FG Manders 16 yds, ChiB—FG Manders 40 yds, NYG—Badgro 29-yd pass from Newman (Strong PAT), ChiB—FG Manders 28 yds, NYG—Krause 1-yd run (Strong PAT), ChiB—Karr 8-yd pass from Nagurski (Manders PAT), NYG—Strong 8-yd pass from Newman (Strong PAT), ChiB—Karr 19-yd lateral from Hewitt after 14-yd pass from Nagurski (Brumbaugh PAT)

TEAM	FD	YDS	RUSH	PASS	RTN	A-C-I	SACKED	PUNT	FUMB	PEN
NYG	13	307	25-99	208	39	20-14-1	—	13-29	0-0	3-15
ChiB	12	311	49-161	150	44	16-7-1	—	10-40	0-0	8-40

NEW YORK GIANTS				
RUSHING	ATT	YDS	LNG	TD
Kink Richards	5	40		0
Ken Strong	8	35		0
RECEIVING	NO	YDS	LNG	TD
Dale Burnett	5	94		0
Red Badgro	2	38		1
PASSING	PA	PC	YDS	TD	IN
Harry Newman	19	13	209	2	1

CHICAGO BEARS				
RUSHING	ATT	YDS	LNG	TD
Gene Ronzani	12	73		0
Bronko Nagurski	13	64		0
RECEIVING	NO	YDS	LNG	TD
Carl Brumbaugh	3	88	67	0
Bill Karr	1	39	19	2
PASSING	PA	PC	YDS	TD	IN
George Corbett	3	2	79	0	0
Bronko Nagurski	2	2	42	2	0

The first official NFL Championship Game had seven lead changes in the heavy fog at Wrigley Field. The Giants, the highest-scoring team in the league, scored twice on touchdown passes from rookie Harry Newman, the NFL's leading passer. Newman's 8-yard completion to Ken Strong gave the Giants a 21-16 lead early in the fourth quarter. That lead evaporated when Chicago put the ball in the air twice on one decisive play. From the New York 33, Bronko Nagurski completed a jump pass to Bill Hewitt, who ran 14 yards and lateraled to Bill Karr, who took it the final 19 yards for his second touchdown catch of the day.

1934 LEAGUE CHAMPIONSHIP

Sunday, December 9, 1934 at New York, Polo Grounds, attendance 35,059

CHICAGO BEARS	0	10	3	0	—	13
NEW YORK GIANTS	3	0	0	27	—	**30**

SCORING NYG—FG Strong 38 yds, ChiB—Nagurski 1-yd run (Manders PAT), ChiB—FG Manders 17 yds, ChiB—FG Manders 24 yds, NYG—Frankian 28-yd pass from Danowski (Strong PAT), NYG—Strong 42-yd run (Strong PAT), NYG—Strong 11-yd run (PAT failed), NYG—Danowski 9-yd run (Molenda PAT)

TEAM	FD	YDS	RUSH	PASS	RTN	A-C-I	SACKED	PUNT	FUMB	PEN
ChiB	10	165	46-89	76	83	15-6-3	—	9-41	5-0	4-30
NYG	12	276	37-173	103	76	12-7-2	—	6-46	5-2	0-0

CHICAGO BEARS				
RUSHING	ATT	YDS	LNG	TD
Bronko Nagurski	24	68		1
Keith Molesworth	16	18		0
RECEIVING	NO	YDS	LNG	TD
Bill Hewitt	2	30		0
PASSING	PA	PC	YDS	TD	IN
Keith Molesworth	9	4	60	0	1

NEW YORK GIANTS				
RUSHING	ATT	YDS	LNG	TD
Ken Strong	9	94	42	2
Ed Danowski	20	59		1
RECEIVING	NO	YDS	LNG	TD
Dale Burnett	2	30		0
Ray Flaherty	2	28		0
PASSING	PA	PC	YDS	TD	IN
Ed Danowski	11	6	83	1	2

A year after the Bears scored late in the fourth quarter at foggy Wrigley Field to win the first NFL Championship Game, the Giants won the rematch at the frozen Polo Grounds, with the help of some borrowed sneakers. The Giants played the first half on the ice-covered field wearing cleats and before changing into sneakers at halftime (many of the pairs borrowed from Manhattan College). After scoring just a field goal through three quarters, the Giants adjusted and exploded for 27 fourth-quarter points. Ed Danowski threw for a score and ran for another while Ken Strong ran for 2 touchdowns against the stunned Bears in the Sneakers Game.

1935 LEAGUE CHAMPIONSHIP

Sunday, December 15, 1935 at Detroit, Titan Stadium, attendance 15,000

NEW YORK GIANTS	0	7	0	0	—	7
DETROIT LIONS	13	0	0	13	—	**26**

SCORING Det—Gutowsky 2-yd run (Presnell PAT), Det—Clark 40-yd run (PAT failed), NYG—Strong 42-yd pass from Danowski (Strong PAT), Det—Caddel 4-yd run (Clark PAT), Det—Parker 4-yd run (PAT failed)

TEAM	FD	YDS	RUSH	PASS	RTN	A-C-I	SACKED	PUNT	FUMB	PEN
NYG	9	194	44-106	88	0	13-4-2	—	6-43	3-0	1-15
Det	16	297	65-246	51	51	5-2-0	—	6-41	4-2	0-25

NEW YORK GIANTS				
RUSHING	ATT	YDS	LNG	TD
unknown	44	106		0
RECEIVING	NO	YDS	LNG	TD
Tod Goodwin	2	29	16	0
PASSING	PA	PC	YDS	TD	IN
Ed Danowski	12	4	88	1	1

DETROIT LIONS				
RUSHING	ATT	YDS	LNG	TD
Dutch Clark	0	80	40	1
Buddy Parker	0	70		1
Ernie Caddel	0	62		1
RECEIVING	NO	YDS	LNG	TD
Frank Christensen	1	26	26	0
PASSING	PA	PC	YDS	TD	IN
Glenn Presnell	1	1	26	0	0

With the University of Detroit field a muddy mess, the Lions took an early lead and ran the ball into the ground. Snow falling in the open Titan Stadium press box made it impossible for complete statistics to be kept. What is known is that four different Lions ran for touchdowns, but 2 long pass plays on the opening drive—the only completions the Lions had all game—led to Detroit's first score. Ed Danowski's botched quick kick gave the Lions the ball at New York's 26 late in the fourth quarter. Detroit scored twice in the closing minutes to seal the city's second world championship in three months—the Tigers had won their first World Series in October.

1936 LEAGUE CHAMPIONSHIP

Sunday, December 13, 1936 at New York, Polo Grounds, attendance 29,545

GREEN BAY PACKERS	7	7	0	7	—	**21**
BOSTON REDSKINS	0	6	0	0	—	6

SCORING GB—Hutson 48-yd pass from Herber (E. Smith PAT), Bos—Rentner 2-yd run (PAT failed), GB—Gantenbein 8-yd pass from Herber (E. Smith PAT), GB—Monnett 2-yd run (Engebretsen PAT)

TEAM	FD	YDS	RUSH	PASS	RTN	A-C-I	SACKED	PUNT	FUMB	PEN
GB	7	232	43-71	161	27	23-9-2	—	8-38	2-1	3-15
Bos	8	147	34-66	81	80	23-6-1	—	11-30	5-2	3-30

GREEN BAY PACKERS				
RUSHING	ATT	YDS	LNG	TD
Clarke Hinkle	19	56	12	0
Johnny Blood	2	8	6	0
RECEIVING	NO	YDS	LNG	TD
Don Hutson	5	76	48	1
Johnny Blood	2	64	52	0
PASSING	PA	PC	YDS	TD	IN
Arnie Herber	15	6	140	2	1
Bob Monnett	8	3	21	0	1

BOSTON REDSKINS				
RUSHING	ATT	YDS	LNG	TD
Don Irwin	13	37	8	0
Cliff Battles	2	18	13	0
RECEIVING	NO	YDS	LNG	TD
Wayne Millner	2	20	11	0
PASSING	PA	PC	YDS	TD	IN
Pug Rentner	6	4	60	0	0
Riley Smith	13	2	21	0	1

The last home game ever played by the Boston Redskins was played in New York. The only neutral site NFL Championship Game took place at the Polo Grounds as a result of owner Preston Marshall's contempt for Boston fans and a perceived lack of support for the three-year-old club. Green Bay's excellent passing was the key to the game as Arnie Herber threw for 2 touchdowns. The Redskins received a bad break when star halfback Cliff Battles was injured in the first quarter. A blocked punt in the fourth quarter gave Green Bay the ball at the 3 and put the game away.

1937 LEAGUE CHAMPIONSHIP

Sunday, December 12, 1937 at Chicago, Wrigley Field, attendance 15,870

WASHINGTON REDSKINS	7	0	21	0	—	**28**
CHICAGO BEARS	14	0	7	0	—	21

SCORING Was—Battles 7-yd run (R. Smith PAT), ChiB—Manders 10-yd run (Manders PAT), ChiB—Manders 37-yd pass from Masterson (Manders PAT), Was—Millner 55-yd pass from Baugh (R. Smith PAT), ChiB—Manske 4-yd pass from Masterson (Manders PAT), Was—Millner 78-yd pass from Baugh (R. Smith PAT), Was—Justice 35-yd pass from Baugh (R. Smith PAT)

TEAM	FD	YDS	RUSH	PASS	RTN	A-C-I	SACKED	PUNT	FUMB	PEN
Was	18	475	37-77	398	41	41-21-3	—	8-19	3-3	1-5
ChiB	11	332	34-125	207	47	30-8-3	—	6-50	3-1	1-15

WASHINGTON REDSKINS				
RUSHING	ATT	YDS	LNG	TD
Cliff Battles	19	45	9	1
Don Irwin	10	33	9	0
RECEIVING	NO	YDS	LNG	TD
Wayne Millner	8	181	78	2
Cliff Battles	3	82	42	0
Ed Justice	3	63	35	1
PASSING	PA	PC	YDS	TD	IN
Sammy Baugh	34	17	358	3	1
Cliff Battles	5	3	23	0	1

CHICAGO BEARS				
RUSHING	ATT	YDS	LNG	TD
Jack Manders	10	64	17	1
Bronko Nagurski	7	47	20	0
RECEIVING	NO	YDS	LNG	TD
Eggs Manske	2	55	51	1
Dick Plasman	2	44	35	0
PASSING	PA	PC	YDS	TD	IN
Bernie Masterson	17	4	131	2	2

In their first year in Washington, the Redskins won the franchise's first NFL title. As the Boston Redskins they had been burned by Green

Bay's passing in the previous year's championship game; in 1937 the Washington Redskins rode the arm of rookie Sammy Baugh for a record-setting 358 yards in the air to win in Chicago. Slingin' Sammy also had to lead the Redskins from behind. With Washington trailing in the third quarter, Baugh threw 3 touchdown passes to twice bring Washington back from deficits. The Redskins defense twice halted Chicago drives in the fourth quarter that might have tied the game.

1938 LEAGUE CHAMPIONSHIP

Sunday, December 11, 1938 at New York, Polo Grounds, attendance 48,120

GREEN BAY PACKERS	0	14	3	0	—	17
NEW YORK GIANTS	9	7	7	0	—	**23**

SCORING NYG—FG Cuff 14 yds, NYG—Leemans 6-yd run (PAT failed), GB—C. Mulleneaux 40-yd pass from Herber (Engebretsen PAT), NYG—Barnard 21-yd pass from Danowski (Cuff PAT), GB—Hinkle 1-yd run (Engebretsen PAT), GB—FG Engebretsen 15 yds, NYG—Soar 23-yd pass from Danowski (Cuff PAT)

TEAM	FD	YDS	RUSH	PASS	RTN	A-C-I	SACKED	PUNT	FUMB	PEN
GB	14	378	46-164	214	14	19-8-1	—	6-27	2-2	2-20
NYG	10	212	43-115	97	34	15-8-1	—	8-41	1-0	2-10

GREEN BAY PACKERS				
RUSHING	ATT	YDS	LNG	TD
Clarke Hinkle	18	63	16	1
Bob Monnett	4	29	33	0
RECEIVING	NO	YDS	LNG	TD
Wayland Becker	2	79	66	0
Carl Mulleneaux	2	54	40	1
PASSING	PA	PC	YDS	TD	IN
Arnie Herber	14	5	123	1	0
Cecil Isbell	5	3	91	0	1

NEW YORK GIANTS				
RUSHING	ATT	YDS	LNG	TD
Hank Soar	21	65	13	0
Tuffy Leemans	13	42	13	1
RECEIVING	NO	YDS	LNG	TD
Hank Soar	3	41	23	1
Jim Lee Howell	2	3	3	0
PASSING	PA	PC	YDS	TD	IN
Ed Danowski	11	7	77	2	0
Tuffy Leemans	2	1	20	0	1

A crowd of more than 48,000—a championship game record that stood through World War II—saw the Giants absorb a pounding from Green Bay but still come out on top. Two blocked punts in the first quarter helped New York build a 9–0 lead. The Giants maintained the lead until the Packers snuck ahead on a third-quarter field goal. New York claimed the lead for good on Hank Soar's leaping catch from Ed Danowski at the goal line. Green Bay outgained New York, 378–212, but the Giants became the first team to win multiple championship games.

1939 LEAGUE CHAMPIONSHIP

Sunday, December 10, 1939 at Milwaukee, Wisconsin State Fair Park, attendance 32,279

NEW YORK GIANTS	0	0	0	0	—	0
GREEN BAY PACKERS	7	0	10	10	—	**27**

SCORING GB—Gantenbein 7-yd pass from Herber (Engebretsen PAT), GB—FG Engebretsen 29 yds, GB—Laws 31-yd pass from Isbell (Engebretsen PAT), GB—FG Smith 42 yds, GB—Jankowski 1-yd run (Smith PAT)

TEAM	FD	YDS	RUSH	PASS	RTN	A-C-I	SACKED	PUNT	FUMB	PEN
NYG	9	164	34-70	94	52	25-8-6	—	6-40	1-0	5-21
GB	13	232	52-136	96	64	10-7-3	—	7-24	2-0	4-50

NEW YORK GIANTS				
RUSHING	ATT	YDS	LNG	TD
Tuffy Leemans	12	24	12	0
Hank Soar	4	14	5	0
RECEIVING	NO	YDS	LNG	TD
Lee Shaffer	2	16	19	0
Nello Falaschi	2	6	6	0
PASSING	PA	PC	YDS	TD	IN
Ed Danowski	12	4	48	0	3
Eddie Miller	6	3	40	0	1

GREEN BAY PACKERS				
RUSHING	ATT	YDS	LNG	TD
Andy Uram	10	38	13	0
Cecil Isbell	14	28	7	0
RECEIVING	NO	YDS	LNG	TD
Don Hutson	2	21	15	0
Larry Craig	2	6	5	0
PASSING	PA	PC	YDS	TD	IN
Arnie Herber	8	5	59	1	3
Cecil Isbell	2	2	37	1	0

The Packers avenged a galling loss the year before in the title game in New York by recording a 27–0 drubbing of the Giants for the first shutout in an NFL Championship Game. The Green Bay offense was not as dominant as in the 1938 loss to the Giants, but the defense stymied New York all day. Four Giants passers threw 6 interceptions. New York also missed 3 field goals. Five Packers recorded points while eight men carried the ball a total of 52 times for 136 yards. Green Bay rolled in the first playoff game played in Milwaukee; the next one would be played at County Stadium in 1967.

1940 LEAGUE CHAMPIONSHIP

Sunday, December 8, 1940 at Washington, Griffith Stadium, attendance 36,034

CHICAGO BEARS	21	7	26	19	—	**73**
WASHINGTON REDSKINS	0	0	0	0	—	0

SCORING ChiB—Osmanski 68-yd run (Manders PAT), ChiB—Luckman 1-yd run (Snyder PAT), ChiB—Maniaci 42-yd run (Martinovich PAT), ChiB—Kavanaugh 30-yd pass from Luckman (Snyder PAT), ChiB—Pool 15-yd interception return (Plasman PAT), ChiB—Nolting 23-yd run (PAT failed), ChiB—McAfee 34-yd interception return (Stydahar PAT), ChiB—Turner 24-yd interception return (PAT failed), ChiB—Clark 44-yd run (PAT failed), ChiB—Famiglietti 2-yd run (Maniaci pass from Sherman), ChiB—Clark 1-yd run (pass failed)

TEAM	FD	YDS	RUSH	PASS	RTN	A-C-I	SACKED	PUNT	FUMB	PEN
ChiB	17	519	53-381	138	135	10-7-0	—	2-48	2-1	3-25
Was	17	231	15-5	226	6	51-20-8	—	3-42	4-1	8-70

CHICAGO BEARS				
RUSHING	ATT	YDS	LNG	TD
Bill Osmanski	10	107	68	1
Harry Clarke	7	75	44	2
Ray Nolting	11	67	23	1
Joe Maniaci	5	62	42	1
RECEIVING	NO	YDS	LNG	TD
Joe Maniaci	2	44	24	0
Ken Kavanaugh	2	32	28	1
PASSING	PA	PC	YDS	TD	IN
Sid Luckman	6	4	102	1	0
Bob Snyder	3	3	36	0	0

WASHINGTON REDSKINS				
RUSHING	ATT	YDS	LNG	TD
Bob Seymour	4	17	16	0
Jimmy Johnston	4	14	6	0
RECEIVING	NO	YDS	LNG	TD
Wayne Millner	6	94	52	0
Bob Masterson	3	34	15	0
Charley Malone	2	51	50	0
PASSING	PA	PC	YDS	TD	IN
Frank Filchock	23	8	101	0	4
Sammy Baugh	16	9	91	0	2

Ten different Bears scored in the most lopsided game in NFL history. After the Redskins had beaten Chicago, 7–3, three weeks earlier on the same field—and called the Bears "crybabies"—owner George Halas plotted revenge. He brought in Stanford coach Clark Shaughnessy to teach his team the T formation. They learned it well enough to score on the second play of the game on Bill Osmanski's 68-yard sweep. The Bears were in full control by the end of the first quarter, but Halas never let up, and a 28–0 pasting at halftime turned into a monumental rout. Washington's ineptitude was certainly a factor. Eight Redskins passes were intercepted—three were run back for touchdowns in the third quarter alone. The whole country could follow Washington's embarrassment play by play in the first national radio broadcast of a championship game.

1941 WESTERN DIVISION CHAMPIONSHIP

Sunday, December 14, 1941 at Chicago, Wrigley Field, attendance 43,425

GREEN BAY PACKERS	7	0	7	0	—	14
CHICAGO BEARS	6	24	0	3	—	**33**

SCORING GB—Hinkle 1-yd run (Hutson PAT), ChiB—Gallarneau 81-yd punt return (PAT blocked), ChiB—FG Snyder 24 yds, ChiB—Standlee 3-yd run (Stydahar PAT), ChiB—Standlee 2-yd run (Stydahar PAT), GB—Swisher 9-yd run (Hutson PAT), GB—Van Every 10-yd pass from Isbell (Hutson PAT), ChiB—FG Snyder 26 yds

TEAM	FD	YDS	RUSH	PASS	RTN	A-C-I	SACKED	PUNT	FUMB	PEN
GB	12	255	36-33	222	0	27-11-2	—	4-29	3-2	3-46
ChiB	14	325	48-277	48	90	12-5-0	—	6-38	5-3	12-128

ChiB-George McAfee 119R

Played one week after Pearl Harbor, the first NFL divisional playoff decided which 10–1 Western Division club—the teams' only losses came against each other—would take on the Eastern champion Giants for the NFL title. The Bears trailed Green Bay in the first quarter, but Chicago scored 30 consecutive before the half to sew up the game.

1941 LEAGUE CHAMPIONSHIP

Sunday, December 21, 1941 at Chicago, Wrigley Field, attendance 13,341

NEW YORK GIANTS	6	0	3	0	—	9
CHICAGO BEARS	3	6	14	14	—	**37**

SCORING ChiB—FG Snyder 14 yds, NYG—Franck 31-yd pass from Leemans (PAT failed), ChiB—FG Snyder 39 yds, ChiB—FG Snyder 37 yds, NYG—FG Cuff 16 yds, ChiB—Standlee 2-yd run (Snyder PAT), ChiB—Standlee 7-yd run (Maniaci PAT), ChiB—McAfee 5-yd run (Artoe PAT), ChiB—Kavanaugh 42-yd fumble return (McLean PAT)

TEAM	FD	YDS	RUSH	PASS	RTN	A-C-I	SACKED	PUNT	FUMB	PEN
NYG	8	157	25-84	73	0	15-3-3	—	4-38	2-2	3-31
ChiB	20	389	56-207	182	19	19-11-0	—	2-54	3-1	9-65

NEW YORK GIANTS

RUSHING	ATT	YDS	LNG	TD
Tuffy Leemans	9	52		0
George Franck	2	30		0

RECEIVING	NO	YDS	LNG	TD
Ward Cuff	2	42	23	0

PASSING	PA	PC	YDS	TD	IN
Tuffy Leemans	9	3	73	1	3

CHICAGO BEARS

RUSHING	ATT	YDS	LNG	TD
Norm Standlee	17	89		2
George McAfee	14	81		1

RECEIVING	NO	YDS	LNG	TD
Dick Plasman	2	48	25	0
George McAfee	2	42	42	0

PASSING	PA	PC	YDS	TD	IN
Sid Luckman	12	9	160	0	0
Bob Snyder	6	1	14	0	0

The smallest crowd ever for an NFL Championship Game (13,341), witnessed a tight game for much of the first three quarters. The Giants had the ball for just 10 of the first 63 plays, but New York took the second half kickoff and marched to Chicago's 16 and kicked a game-tying field goal. The Bears responded with their first touchdown drive of the day and a New York interception was quickly converted into another Norm Standlee score. The Bears scored again in the fourth quarter against the worn-out Giants. New York tried a lateral on the final play of the game, but it ended up in the arms of Ken Kavanaugh, who ran 42 yards with the fumble for a touchdown. Roy McLean dropkicked the extra point for fun. In consecutive championship game romps, the Bears outscored their opponents, 110–9.

1942 LEAGUE CHAMPIONSHIP

Sunday, December 13, 1942 at Washington, Griffith Stadium, attendance 36,006

CHICAGO BEARS	0	6	0	0	—	6
WASHINGTON	0	7	7	0	—	14

SCORING ChiB—Artoe 50-yd fumble return (PAT failed), Was—Moore 38-yd pass from Baugh (Masterson PAT), Was—Farkas 1-yd run (Masterson PAT)

TEAM	FD	YDS	RUSH	PASS	RTN	A-C-I	SACKED	PUNT	FUMB	PEN
ChiB	10	188	41-69	119	20	18-8-3	—	6-41	2-1	7-47
Was	9	170	36-104	66	24	13-5-2	—	6-52	1-0	4-26

CHICAGO BEARS

RUSHING	ATT	YDS	LNG	TD
Bill Osmanski	13	38	14	0
Ray Nolting	8	26	18	0

RECEIVING	NO	YDS	LNG	TD
Ray McLean	3	26		0
John Siegal	2	11		0

PASSING	PA	PC	YDS	TD	IN
Charlie O'Rourke	6	4	110	0	0

WASHINGTON

RUSHING	ATT	YDS	LNG	TD
Andy Farkas	13	46	9	1
Bob Seymour	14	34	11	0

RECEIVING	NO	YDS	LNG	TD
Wilbur Moore	2	41	38	1

PASSING	PA	PC	YDS	TD	IN
Sammy Baugh	13	5	66	1	2

As was the case in the championship game two years earlier, the Bears scored first, but unlike the 73–0 onslaught that followed in 1940, this time the Redskins did not allow another point. The extra point try was no good. And Washington tied the score when Sammy Baugh hit Wilbur Moore at the goal line for a 38-yard touchdown pass. Bob Masterson's kick provided the Redskins with the lead. The Redskins dominated the second half, adding a touchdown 10 minutes into the third quarter. Revenge was on the minds of many Redskins after the record trouncing by the Bears in the title game two years before, but priorities had changed plenty since 1940. Washington coach Ray Flaherty left the next day to receive a lieutenant's commission in the U.S. Navy. Seventeen men on the Redskins roster would soon join the armed forces in World War II.

1943 EASTERN DIVISION CHAMPIONSHIP

Sunday, December 19, 1943 at New York, Polo Grounds, attendance 42,800

WASHINGTON REDSKINS	0	14	0	14	—	28
NEW YORK GIANTS	0	0	0	0	—	0

SCORING Was—Farkas 2-yd run (Masterson PAT), Was—Farkas 2-yd run (Masterson PAT), Was—Farkas 1-yd run (Masterson PAT), Was—Lapka 11-yd pass from Baugh (Masterson PAT)

TEAM	FD	YDS	RUSH	PASS	RTN	A-C-I	SACKED	PUNT	FUMB	PEN
Was	13	296	39-83	213	97	22-17-2	—	7-44	2-1	9-83
NYG	8	112	33-55	57	5	20-4-3	—	10-36	0-0	5-35

Sammy Baugh threw for 199 yards to win a divisional playoff and get the Redskins into the championship game for the third time in four years. The Giants completed just 4 of 20 passes and had only 112 total yards against the stingy Washington defense. The Redskins had been cruising through the season at 6–0–1 when they lost to the combined Steelers–Eagles club and dropped consecutive decisions to New York to end the season and force the playoff at the Polo Grounds.

1943 LEAGUE CHAMPIONSHIP

Sunday, December 26, 1943 at Chicago, Wrigley Field, attendance 34,320

WASHINGTON REDSKINS	0	7	7	7	—	21
CHICAGO BEARS	0	14	13	14	—	41

SCORING Was—Farkas 1-yd run (Masterson PAT), ChiB—Clark 31-yd pass from Luckman (Snyder PAT), ChiB—Nagurski 3-yd run (Snyder PAT), ChiB—Magnani 36-yd pass from Luckman (Snyder PAT), ChiB—Magnani 66-yd pass from Luckman (PAT failed), Was—Farkas 17-yd pass from Baugh (Masterson PAT), ChiB—Benton 26-yd pass from Luckman (Snyder PAT), ChiB—Clark 10-yd pass from Luckman (Snyder PAT), Was—Aguirre 25-yd pass from Baugh (Aguirre PAT)

TEAM	FD	YDS	RUSH	PASS	RTN	A-C-I	SACKED	PUNT	FUMB	PEN
Was	11	249	27-50	199	6	24-11-4	—	5-41	2-2	3-35
ChiB	14	455	44-169	286	134	27-15-0	—	5-32	0-0	8-81

WASHINGTON REDSKINS

RUSHING	ATT	YDS	LNG	TD
Andy Farkas	11	36		1
Frank Seno	4	17		0

RECEIVING	NO	YDS	LNG	TD
Wilbur Moore	5	108		0

PASSING	PA	PC	YDS	TD	IN
Sammy Baugh	12	8	123	2	1
George Cafego	12	3	76	0	3

CHICAGO BEARS

RUSHING	ATT	YDS	LNG	TD
Sid Luckman	8	64		0
Bronko Nagurski	11	34		1

RECEIVING	NO	YDS	LNG	TD
Dante Magnani	4	122	66	2
Harry Clarke	3	47	31	2

PASSING	PA	PC	YDS	TD	IN
Sid Luckman	26	15	286	5	0

The Bears weren't content simply to beat the Redskins, but they berated them as well. Chicago acting president Ralph Brizzolara, filling in with George Halas in the armed service, saw Redskins owner George Preston Marshall near the Chicago bench shortly before halftime. Brizzolara loudly accused Marshall—wearing a bearskin coat, no less—of trying to steal his club's signs and ordered him from the field. Whether the confrontation fired up the Bears or not is questionable, but Chicago poured it on in the second half and turned the game into a rout. Sid Luckman, headed for the Merchant Marine the next day, threw for 286 yards and 5 touchdowns. Bronko Nagurski, playing his final game, carried the ball more than any teammate and scored the go-ahead touchdown.

1944 LEAGUE CHAMPIONSHIP

Sunday, December 17, 1944 at New York, Polo Grounds, attendance 46,015

GREEN BAY PACKERS	0	14	0	0	—	14
NEW YORK GIANTS	0	0	0	7	—	7

SCORING GB—Fritsch 1-yd run (Hutson PAT), GB—Fritsch 28-yd pass from Comp (Hutson PAT), NYG—Cuff 1-yd run (Strong PAT)

TEAM	FD	YDS	RUSH	PASS	RTN	A-C-I	SACKED	PUNT	FUMB	PEN
GB	11	237	49-163	74	127	11-3-3	—	10-40	2-0	4-48
NYG	10	199	30-85	114	33	22-8-4	—	10-40	1-0	11-90

GREEN BAY PACKERS

RUSHING	ATT	YDS	LNG	TD
Joe Laws	13	72	20	0
Ted Fritsch	18	59	15	1

RECEIVING	NO	YDS	LNG	TD
Don Hutson	2	46	24	0

PASSING	PA	PC	YDS	TD	IN
Irv Comp	10	3	74	1	3

NEW YORK GIANTS

RUSHING	ATT	YDS	LNG	TD
Ward Cuff	12	76	13	1
Howie Livingston	12	22	6	0

RECEIVING	NO	YDS	LNG	TD
Frank Liebel	3	70	41	0
Ward Cuff	2	23	22	0

PASSING	PA	PC	YDS	TD	IN
Arnie Herber	22	8	114	0	4

The Giants had the league's best record—including a 24–0 trouncing of the Packers—but Green Bay owned the day. Two second-quarter touchdowns by Ted Fritch, the second on a 28-yard pass from Irv Comp, was the difference against a New York defense that had allowed just 7.5 points per game. The Giants held the Packers the rest of the day, and New York finally scored in the opening minute of the final quarter. Green Bay's defense was stingier, though, allowing just 85 rushing yards and picking off former Packer Arnie Herber 4 times. It was the sixth (and last) NFL title for coach Curly Lambeau, and his third championship game win.

1945 LEAGUE CHAMPIONSHIP

Sunday, December 16, 1945 at Cleveland, Municipal Stadium, attendance 32,178

WASHINGTON REDSKINS	0	7	7	0	—	14
CLEVELAND RAMS	2	7	6	0	—	15

SCORING Cle—Safety, Baugh's pass hit goal post, Was—Bagarus 38-yd pass from Filchock (Aguirre PAT), Cle—Benton 37-yd pass from Waterfield (Waterfield PAT), Cle—Gillette 44-yd pass from Waterfield (PAT failed), Was—Seymour 8-yd pass from Filchock (Aguirre PAT)

TEAM	FD	YDS	RUSH	PASS	RTN	A-C-I	SACKED	PUNT	FUMB	PEN
Was	8	214	34-35	179	78	20-9-2	—	7-39	1-0	4-29
Cle	14	372	44-180	192	72	27-14-2	—	8-38	1-1	6-60

WASHINGTON REDSKINS

RUSHING	ATT	YDS	LNG	TD
Merl Condit	9	18		0
Sal Rosato	6	17		0

RECEIVING	NO	YDS	LNG	TD
Steve Bagarus	3	95	38	1
Cecil Hare	2	20	13	0

PASSING	PA	PC	YDS	TD	IN
Frank Filchock	14	8	172	2	2
Sammy Baugh	6	1	7	0	0

CLEVELAND RAMS

RUSHING	ATT	YDS	LNG	TD
Jim Gillette	17	101		0
Fred Gehrke	7	29		0

RECEIVING	NO	YDS	LNG	TD
Jim Benton	9	125	37	1
Jim Gillette	2	45	44	1

PASSING	PA	PC	YDS	TD	IN
Bob Waterfield	27	14	192	2	2

The temperature in Cleveland was zero degrees at kickoff. A midweek snowstorm left the field frozen and the stands mostly empty. Cleveland Ram Bob Waterfield threw 2 long touchdown passes and made a game-saving tackle on Steve Bagarus in the closing minutes. A Washington field goal attempt that would have won the game was no good. The Rams had much better luck with the uprights. Redskin Sammy Baugh's first-quarter pass out of the end zone hit the crossbar for an automatic safety under the day's rules. Waterfield's partially-blocked PAT try bounced off the crossbar and through for what turned out to be the deciding point of the game as the Rams won their first NFL title. Less than a month later, NFL owners voted to let the Rams move to Los Angeles.

1946 NFL CHAMPIONSHIP
Sunday, December 15, 1946 at New York, Polo Grounds, attendance 58,346

CHICAGO BEARS	14	0	0	10	—	**24**
NEW YORK GIANTS	7	0	7	0	—	14

SCORING ChiB—Kavanaugh 21-yd pass from Luckman (Maznicki PAT), ChiB—Magnani 19-yd interception return (Maznicki PAT), NYG—Liebel 38-yd pass from Filchock (Strong PAT), NYG—Filipowicz 5-yd pass from Filchock (Strong PAT), ChiB—Luckman 19-yd run (Maznicki PAT), ChiB—FG Maznicki 26 yds

TEAM	FD	YDS	RUSH	PASS	RTN	A-C-I	SACKED	PUNT	FUMB	PEN
ChiB	10	245	40-101	144	97	22-9-2	—	7-42	2-1	9-112
NYG	13	248	33-120	128	10	26-9-6	—	4-33	3-2	6-70

CHICAGO BEARS

RUSHING	ATT	YDS	LNG	TD
Hugh Gallarneau	6	24		0
Bill Osmanski	9	23		0

RECEIVING	NO	YDS	LNG	TD
George McAfee	4	57		0
Ken Kavanaugh	2	53	32	1

PASSING	PA	PC	YDS	TD	IN
Sid Luckman	22	9	144	1	2

NEW YORK GIANTS

RUSHING	ATT	YDS	LNG	TD
George Franck	6	55		0
Steve Filipowicz	9	20		0

RECEIVING	NO	YDS	LNG	TD
Jim Poole	4	40		0
Steve Filipowicz	2	41	36	1

PASSING	PA	PC	YDS	TD	IN
Frank Filchock	26	9	128	2	6

With George Halas behind the bench for a full season for the first time since 1942, the Bears were again champions. Chicago beat New York in the NFL Championship Game for the third time in four tries. The Bears started quickly with a touchdown pass by Sid Luckman, followed by a Frank Filchock pass that was intercepted by Dante Magnani and returned 19 yards for a score. Filchock completed just 9 passes and threw 6 interceptions (he'd tossed 4 pickoffs against the Bears in the 1940 championship game). Filchock did toss 2 touchdown passes for the Giants as the game was tied 14–14 in the fourth quarter. Luckman snapped the tie when he faked a handoff, kept the ball, and ran 19 yards for the touchdown. A field goal by Frank Maznicki sealed the game and sent the largest crowd to date for a championship game (58,346) home unhappy.

1946 AAFC LEAGUE CHAMPIONSHIP
Sunday, December 22, 1946 at Cleveland, Municipal Stadium, attendance 41,181

NEW YORK YANKEES	3	0	6	0	—	9
CLEVELAND BROWNS	0	7	0	7	—	**14**

SCORING NYY—FG H. Johnson 21 yds, Cle—Motley 2-yd run (Groza PAT), NYY—Sanders 2-yd run (PAT blocked), Cle—Lavelli 16-yd pass from Graham (Groza PAT)

TEAM	FD	YDS	RUSH	PASS	RTN	A-C-I	SACKED	PUNT	FUMB	PEN
NYY	10	146	29-65	81	19	20-8-1	—	5-32	2-1	4-20
Cle	18	325	37-112	213	23	27-16-1	—	2-38	3-0	5-25

NEW YORK YANKEES

RUSHING	ATT	YDS	LNG	TD
Spec Sanders	14	55	23	1
Ace Parker	9	5	7	0

RECEIVING	NO	YDS	LNG	TD
Jack Russell	5	58	20	0

PASSING	PA	PC	YDS	TD	IN
Ace Parker	18	8	81	0	1
Spec Sanders	2	0	0	0	0

CLEVELAND BROWNS

RUSHING	ATT	YDS	LNG	TD
Marion Motley	13	98	50	1
Edgar Jones	10	16	7	0

RECEIVING	NO	YDS	LNG	TD
Dante Lavelli	6	87	23	1
Mac Speedie	6	71	16	0

PASSING	PA	PC	YDS	TD	IN
Otto Graham	27	16	213	1	1

The Browns would come to dominate the All-America Football Conference, but to win the league's inaugural title game they needed a fourth-quarter touchdown pass and then an interception on defense. The Browns got both from Otto Graham. Graham threw for 213 yards, including a 16-yard touchdown to Dante Lavelli with about five minutes to go. Graham picked off New York's Ace Parker on the ensuing drive to give Cleveland the first AAFC crown. Cleveland outgained the Yankees, 325–146. It was the second loss in a week by a New York team in a pro football championship game.

1947 NFL EASTERN DIVISION CHAMPIONSHIP
Sunday, December 21, 1947 at Pittsburgh, Forbes Field, attendance 35,729

PHILADELPHIA EAGLES	7	7	7	0	—	**21**
PITTSBURGH STEELERS	0	0	0	0	—	0

SCORING Phi—Van Buren 15-yd pass from Thompson (Patton PAT), Phi—Ferrante 28-yd pass from Thompson (Patton PAT), Phi—Pritchard 79-yd punt return (Patton PAT)

TEAM	FD	YDS	RUSH	PASS	RTN	A-C-I	SACKED	PUNT	FUMB	PEN
Phi	17	255	52-124	131	101	18-11-0	—	6-36	3-2	7-49
Pit	7	154	29-102	52	0	18-4-0	—	9-40	3-2	5-65

In the first postseason game for either team, the Eagles blanked the Steelers at Forbes Field. Just four years earlier these same two clubs had combined to form one team—referred to as the "Steagles"—to combat the wartime manpower shortage. In the playoff game, Tommy Thompson twice tossed touchdowns.

1947 NFL CHAMPIONSHIP
Sunday, December 28, 1947 at Chicago, Comiskey Park, attendance 30,759

PHILADELPHIA EAGLES	0	7	7	7	—	21
CHICAGO CARDINALS	7	7	7	7	—	**28**

SCORING ChiC—Trippi 44-yd run (Harder PAT), ChiC—Angsman 70-yd run (Harder PAT), Phi—McHugh 53-yd pass from Thompson (Patton PAT), ChiC—Trippi 75-yd punt return (Harder PAT), Phi—Van Buren 1-yd run (Patton PAT), ChiC—Angsman 70-yd run (Harder PAT), Phi—Craft 1-yd run (Patton PAT)

TEAM	FD	YDS	RUSH	PASS	RTN	A-C-I	SACKED	PUNT	FUMB	PEN
Phi	22	357	37-60	297	0	44-27-3	—	8-35	2-0	7-55
ChiC	11	336	39-282	54	180	14-3-2	—	8-32	2-1	10-97

PHILADELPHIA EAGLES

RUSHING	ATT	YDS	LNG	TD
Joe Muha	8	31		0
Steve Van Buren	18	26	8	1

RECEIVING	NO	YDS	LNG	TD
Jack Ferrante	8	73		0
Bosh Pritchard	3	37		0
Pat McHugh	2	55	53	1

PASSING	PA	PC	YDS	TD	IN
Tommy Thompson	44	27	297	1	3

CHICAGO CARDINALS

RUSHING	ATT	YDS	LNG	TD
Elmer Angsman	10	159	70	2
Charlie Trippi	11	84	44	1

RECEIVING	NO	YDS	LNG	TD
Billy Dewell	1	38	38	0

PASSING	PA	PC	YDS	TD	IN
Paul Christman	14	3	54	0	2

Finally, new blood! The Bears, Giants, Packers, and Redskins had taken 26 of the 28 spots available since the championship game was introduced in 1933. Now, two first-timers played for the title. The Cardinals, charter members of the league, scored on 4 long plays: Charlie Trippi scored on a 44-yard run and a 75-yard punt return and Elmer Angsman twice ran for 70-yard touchdowns. The field was slick—Trippi twice fell down on the punt return but got up both times—but the Cardinals dominated on the ground. While both teams had almost equal the number of rushing attempts, the Cardinals gained 7.2 yards per carry while the Eagles averaged 1.6. Tommy Thompson's had 297 yards passing for Philadelphia, but he also threw 3 interceptions.

1947 AAFC LEAGUE CHAMPIONSHIP

Sunday, December 14, 1947 at New York, Yankee Stadium, attendance 61,879

CLEVELAND BROWNS	7	0	7	0	—	14
NEW YORK YANKEES	0	3	0	0	—	3

SCORING Cle—Graham 1-yd run (Groza PAT), NYY—FG H.Johnson 12 yds, Cle—Jones 4-yd run (Saban PAT)

TEAM	FD	YDS	RUSH	PASS	RTN	A-C-I	SACKED	PUNT	FUMB	PEN
Cle	15	284	33-172	112	40	21-14-0	—	5-45	2-1	7-45
NYY	13	212	33-123	89	14	18-7-0	—	6-36	3-2	3-21

CLEVELAND BROWNS

RUSHING	ATT	YDS	LNG	TD
Marion Motley	13	109	51	0
Edgar Jones	10	27	9	1

RECEIVING	NO	YDS	LNG	TD
Mac Speedie	4	25	8	0
Dante Lavelli	3	37	35	0

PASSING	PA	PC	YDS	TD	IN
Otto Graham	21	14	112	0	0

NEW YORK YANKEES

RUSHING	ATT	YDS	LNG	TD
Buddy Young	16	69	14	0
Spec Sanders	12	40	23	0

RECEIVING	NO	YDS	LNG	TD
Buddy Young	2	25	13	0
Bob Sweiger	2	12	7	0

PASSING	PA	PC	YDS	TD	IN
Spec Sanders	17	7	89	0	0

The New York Yankees played in their second straight AAFC Championship Game and held the powerhouse Browns to 14 points for the second straight year, yet they once again lost. Marion Motley had the game's biggest play, a 51-yard run that set up the Cleveland's first touchdown in the opening quarter. The Yankees managed to get to the Cleveland 6 before settling for a field goal. The Browns did not let New York get that close again and their second-half touchdown tightened Cleveland's stranglehold. The crowd of 60,103 at Yankee Stadium was larger than any in the first 15 seasons of the NFL Championship Game.

1948 NFL CHAMPIONSHIP

Sunday, December 19, 1948 at Philadelphia, Shibe Park, attendance 28,864

CHICAGO CARDINALS	0	0	0	0	—	0
PHILADELPHIA EAGLES	0	0	0	7	—	7

SCORING Phi—Van Buren 5-yd run (Patton PAT)

TEAM	FD	YDS	RUSH	PASS	RTN	A-C-I	SACKED	PUNT	FUMB	PEN
ChiC	6	131	34-96	35	31	11-3-1	—	8-37	3-2	4-33
Phi	16	232	57-225	7	22	12-2-2	—	5-37	1-1	3-17

CHICAGO CARDINALS

RUSHING	ATT	YDS	LNG	TD
Elmer Angsman	10	33	18	0
Pat Harder	11	30	5	0

RECEIVING	NO	YDS	LNG	TD
Mal Kutner	2	19	11	0

PASSING	PA	PC	YDS	TD	IN
Ray Mallouf	7	3	35	0	0
Charley Eikenberg	2	0	0	0	1

PHILADELPHIA EAGLES

RUSHING	ATT	YDS	LNG	TD
Steve Van Buren	26	98	12	1
Bosh Pritchard	16	67	15	0
Tommy Thompson	11	50	17	0

RECEIVING	NO	YDS	LNG	TD
Jack Ferrante	1	7	7	0

PASSING	PA	PC	YDS	TD	IN
Tommy Thompson	12	2	7	0	2

A rematch of the 1947 NFL Championship Game was dominated by the weather. Shibe Park was covered in snow, making it impractical to use chains for measurements and making it nearly impossible to score. Elmer Angsman, who ran for 159 yards and a pair of 70-yard touchdowns in the 1947 game, managed an 18-yard run in the rematch but was held to just 10 rushes for 15 yards the rest of the day. The Eagles, who'd been completely ineffective running against the Cardinals in 1947, rushed 57 times for 225 yards. Tommy Thompson, who'd thrown for 297 yards the year before, threw for 7 yards this time. Angsman's fumble at the end of the third quarter gave Philadelphia the ball at Chicago's 17. Steve Van Buren powered across the goal line for the only score and Philadelphia's first championship.

1948 AAFC EASTERN DIVISION CHAMPIONSHIP

Sunday, December 12, 1948 at Baltimore, Memorial Stadium, attendance 27,325

BUFFALO BILLS	0	7	0	21	—	28
BALTIMORE COLTS	3	0	14	0	—	17

SCORING Bal—FG Grossman 16 yds, Buf—O'Connor 8-yd pass from Ratterman (Armstrons PAT), Bal—Mertes 8-yd run (Grossman PAT), Bal—Mertes 1-yd run (Grossman PAT), Buf—Gompers 66-yd pass from Ratterman (Armstrong PAT), Buf—Baldwin 25-yd pass from Ratterman (Armstrong PAT), Buf—Hirsch 19-yd interception return (Armstrong PAT)

TEAM	FD	YDS	RUSH	PASS	RTN	A-C-I	SACKED	PUNT	FUMB	PEN
Buf	11	297	37-162	135	62	18-10-1	—	3-40	3-2	5-25
Bal	24	393	45-176	217	14	36-17-1	—	5-42	7-2	8-80

Buffalo and Baltimore, two 7–7 clubs, slugged it out for the right to face the undefeated Browns. George Ratterman threw 3 touchdowns covering 99 combined yards—his other 7 completions went for just 36 yards—as the Bills put up 21 points in the fourth quarter to overcome a 17–7 deficit in the first postseason game at Memorial Stadium.

1948 AAFC LEAGUE CHAMPIONSHIP

Sunday, December 19, 1948 at Cleveland, Municipal Stadium, attendance 22,981

BUFFALO BILLS	0	0	7	0	—	7
CLEVELAND BROWNS	7	7	14	21	—	49

SCORING Cle—E. Jones 3-yd run (Groza PAT), Cle—Young 18-yd fumble return (Groza PAT), Cle—E. Jones 9-yd pass from Graham (Groza PAT), Cle—Motley 29-yd run (Groza PAT), Buf—A. Baldwin 10-yd pass from Still (Armstrong PAT), Cle—Motley 31-yd run (Groza PAT), Cle—Motley 5-yd run (Groza PAT), Cle—Saban 39-yd interception return (Groza PAT)

TEAM	FD	YDS	RUSH	PASS	RTN	A-C-I	SACKED	PUNT	FUMB	PEN
Buf	13	167	33-63	104	2	36-11-5	—	6-43	3-3	7-27
Cle	20	333	40-215	118	123	26-11-1	—	3-33	6-3	9-90

BUFFALO BILLS

RUSHING	ATT	YDS	LNG	TD
Rex Bumgardner	11	34		0
Lou Tomasetti	11	20		0

RECEIVING	NO	YDS	LNG	TD
Bill O'Connor	3	41		0
Chet Mutryn	2	5		0

PASSING	PA	PC	YDS	TD	IN
Jim Still	18	6	80	1	2
George Ratterman	18	5	24	0	3

CLEVELAND BROWNS

RUSHING	ATT	YDS	LNG	TD
Marion Motley	14	133		3
Edgar Jones	8	29		1

RECEIVING	NO	YDS	LNG	TD
Edgar Jones	3	39		1
Mac Speedie	2	22		0

PASSING	PA	PC	YDS	TD	IN
Otto Graham	24	11	118	1	1
Edgar Jones	2	0	0	0	0

A championship game featuring a team with half as many regular-season wins as the host club was predictable from the start. The 50,000 empty seats in Cleveland echoed the sentiment. The Browns rolled to a 28–0 lead before the Bills managed a touchdown late in the third quarter. The Browns responded with 21 points in the final quarter. Marion Motley racked up 133 yards and 3 touchdowns as the Browns won their third consecutive AAFC title. No NFL team to that time could match the Browns' feat of going undefeated through the regular season and capping it off with a victory in the championship game. Although the dominance of the Browns threatened the future of the AAFC, it made for the greatest year in Cleveland sports history: the Indians had captured the World Series just two months before on the same field.

1949 NFL CHAMPIONSHIP

Sunday, December 18, 1949 at Los Angeles, Memorial Coliseum, attendance 22,245

PHILADELPHIA EAGLES	0	7	7	0	—	14
LOS ANGELES RAMS	0	0	0	0	—	0

SCORING Phi—Pihos 31-yd pass from Thompson (Patton PAT), Phi—Skladany 2-yd run with blocked punt (Patton PAT)

TEAM	FD	YDS	RUSH	PASS	RTN	A-C-I	SACKED	PUNT	FUMB	PEN
Phi	17	342	61-274	68	0	9-5-2	0-0	6-36	4-1	6-40
LA	7	109	24-21	88	17	27-10-1	10	9-38	1-0	4-25

PHILADELPHIA EAGLES

RUSHING	ATT	YDS	LNG	TD
Steve Van Buren	31	196	49	0
Jim Parmer	15	41		0

RECEIVING	NO	YDS	LNG	TD
Jack Ferrante	2	27	16	0

PASSING	PA	PC	YDS	TD	IN
Tommy Thompson	9	5	68	1	2

LOS ANGELES RAMS

RUSHING	ATT	YDS	LNG	TD
Fred Gehrke	3	13		0
Vitamin Smith	6	11		0

RECEIVING	NO	YDS	LNG	TD
Dick Huffman	2	26		0
Bob Shaw	2	21		0

PASSING	PA	PC	YDS	TD	IN
Norm Van Brocklin	14	5	55	0	0
Bob Waterfield	13	5	43	0	1

The first NFL postseason game ever played in sunny California was a muddy mess. Three inches of rain the day before the game was the ideal mixture for Philadelphia's Steve Van Buren, whose 196 yards rushing on 31 carries through the Los Angeles muck set an NFL mark. The only offensive score of the day, though, came through the air. Tommy Thompson, leading the Eagles to their third straight championship game, hit Pete Pihos with a 31-yard scoring pass in the

second quarter. Thompson had 58 of his 68 yards passing on the day during that drive. A blocked punt accounted for the other score. The Eagles won the NFL title for the second straight year, scoring just 21 total points while allowing none. Playing on a snow-covered field one year and a quagmire the next helped, but the Eagles defense and clock-controlling ground game made it happen.

1949 AAFC FIRST ROUND PLAYOFF
Sunday, December 4, 1949 at Cleveland, Municipal Stadium, attendance 17,270

BUFFALO BILLS	0	14	7	0	—	21
CLEVELAND BROWNS	10	0	14	7	—	**31**

SCORING Cle—Lavelli 51-yd pass from Graham (Groza PAT), Cle—FG Groza 31 yds, Buf—Tomasetti 4-yd pass from Ratterman (Adams PAT), Buf—Mutryn 8-yd pass from Ratterman (Adams PAT), Cle—E. Jones 2-yd run (Groza PAT), Buf—Mutryn 30-yd pass from Ratterman (Adams PAT), Cle—D. Jones 49-yd pass from Graham (Groza PAT), Cle—Lahr 52-yd interception return (Groza PAT)

TEAM	FD	YDS	RUSH	PASS	RTN	A-C-I	SACKED	PUNT	FUMB	PEN
Buf	19	373	25-80	293	14	42-21-2	—	5-40	3-1	2-20
Cle	15	398	20-72	326	88	43-22-2	—	4-41	0-0	5-58

Cle-Mac Speedie 113C, Otto Graham 326P

A first-round playoff that was a rematch of the dud of a championship game from the year before brought out just 17,240, but the Browns and Bills twice played ties in 1949 and this third game was another back-and-forth affair. Buffalo rallied in the second and third quarter to overcome deficits, but Cleveland's Dub Jones caught a 49-yard scoring pass from Otto Graham to regain the lead. A fourth-quarter interception at midfield went for a touchdown and put the game away.

1949 AAFC FIRST ROUND PLAYOFF
Sunday, December 4, 1949 at San Francisco, Kezar Stadium, attendance 41,393

NEW YORK YANKEES	0	7	0	0	—	7
SAN FRANCISCO 49ERS	3	7	7	0	—	**17**

SCORING SF—Lillywhite 40-yd run (Vetrano PAT), NYY—Howard 1-yd run (Johnson PAT), SF—FG Vetrano 38 yds, SF—Garlin 10-yd pass from Albert (Vetrano PAT)

TEAM	FD	YDS	RUSH	PASS	RTN	A-C-I	SACKED	PUNT	FUMB	PEN
NYY	9	190	33-74	116	72	25-7-3	—	10-55	1-0	3-35
SF	10	260	33-164	96	168	17-8-2	—	9-46	4-1	2-10

The 49ers, with the AAFC's second-best record, and the Yankees, the third team in a seven-team league, put on a punting show at Kezar Stadium. New York's Tom Landry averaged 55 yards per punt, including a 75-yarder, and San Francisco's Frankie Albert twice booted balls over 60 yards. Another kick—a field goal by Joe Vetrano—gave the 49ers the lead in the second quarter and they controlled the second half.

1949 AAFC LEAGUE CHAMPIONSHIP
Sunday, December 11, 1949 at Cleveland, Municipal Stadium, attendance 22,550

SAN FRANCISCO 49ERS	0	0	0	7	—	7
CLEVELAND BROWNS	7	0	7	7	—	**21**

SCORING Cle—E. Jones 2-yd run (Groza PAT), Cle—Motley 63-yd run (Groza PAT), SF—Salata 23-yd pass from Albert (Vetrano PAT), Cle—D. Jones 4-yd run (Groza PAT)

TEAM	FD	YDS	RUSH	PASS	RTN	A-C-I	SACKED	PUNT	FUMB	PEN
SF	14	230	33-122	108	23	25-9-0	—	6-44	2-0	0-0
Cle	16	345	41-217	128	61	17-7-0	—	4-43	0-0	1-5

SAN FRANCISCO 49ERS					CLEVELAND BROWNS				
RUSHING	ATT	YDS	LNG	TD	RUSHING	ATT	YDS	LNG	TD
Frankie Albert	5	41		0	Marion Motley	8	75	63	1
Joe Perry	6	36		0	Edgar Jones	16	63		1
					Otto Graham	9	62		0
RECEIVING	NO	YDS	LNG	TD	RECEIVING	NO	YDS	LNG	TD
Paul Salata	3	37	23	1	Dante Lavelli	4	56		0
Alyn Beals	3	26		0					
PASSING	PA	PC	YDS	TD	IN	PASSING	PA	PC	YDS	TD	IN
Frankie Albert	24	9	108	1	0	Otto Graham	17	7	128	0	0

After the merger of the AAFC and NFL was announced just two days before the championship game, a lack of interest and miserable weather hung over Cleveland. The Browns, the dominant team in the league from the first day, were their usual unbeatable selves. The Browns took a 14–0 lead before San Francisco scored in the third quarter. Joe Vetrano kicked the extra point and extended his mark

of scoring in every 49ers game since they game into existence. The Browns continued their own remarkable run, going 52–4–3, including postseason, in four years and making it clear to the world that no one else had a chance in this league. The Browns would play one last time in the AAFC and lose—too late to do the league any good—in a game against a team of hungry all-stars from the other six teams (many of whom no longer had jobs) in a charity game in Houston.

1950 AMERICAN CONFERENCE CHAMPIONSHIP
Sunday, December 17, 1950 at Cleveland, Municipal Stadium, attendance 33,054

NEW YORK GIANTS	0	0	0	3	—	3
CLEVELAND BROWNS	3	0	0	5	—	**8**

SCORING Cle—FG Groza 11 yds, NYG—FG Clay 20 yds, Cle—FG Groza 28 yds, Cle—Safety, Conerly tackled in end zone by Willis

TEAM	FD	YDS	RUSH	PASS	RTN	A-C-I	SACKED	PUNT	FUMB	PEN
NYG	11	154	37-141	13	22	15-3-2	35	9-40	2-0	5-45
Cle	9	182	40-153	29	20	9-3-1	14	9-40	0-0	9-54

The conditions were brutal—10 degrees, strong wind, frozen field—and so was the offense. The teams combined for 6 pass completions and 18 punts, and the kicking carried the day. Lou Groza booted the go-ahead field goal in the fourth quarter. On the ensuing drive, Bill Willis, who'd prevented a Giants touchdown earlier in the quarter, sacked Charlie Conerly for a safety.

1950 NATIONAL CONFERENCE CHAMPIONSHIP
Sunday, December 17, 1950 at Los Angeles, Memorial Coliseum, attendance 83,501

CHICAGO BEARS	0	7	0	7	—	14
LOS ANGELES RAMS	3	14	7	0	—	**24**

SCORING LARm—FG Waterfield 43 yds, ChiB—Campana 23-yd run (Lujack PAT), LARm—FG Waterfield 43 yds, ChiB—Hoerner 43-yd run (Waterfield PAT), LARm—Fears 68-yd pass from Waterfield (Waterfield PAT), LARm—Fears 27-yd pass from Waterfield (Waterfield PAT), ChiB—Morrison 4-yd run (Lujack PAT)

TEAM	FD	YDS	RUSH	PASS	RTN	A-C-I	SACKED	PUNT	FUMB	PEN
ChiB	23	370	48-229	141	97	29-15-3	52	7-44	2-0	5-45
LA	11	371	32-74	297	78	31-16-1	0-0	10-45	1-1	8-74

LA-Tom Fears 198C

The NFL had two playoff games in one day for the first time. The Rams, who tied the Bears for first place at 9–3 in the National Conference, relied on Bob Waterfield for all their points. Waterfield, who'd missed practice all week with the flu, threw 3 touchdown passed, kicked 3 PATs, and added a field goal as the Rams won before a new NFL postseason-record crowd.

1950 LEAGUE CHAMPIONSHIP
Sunday, December 24, 1950 at Cleveland, Municipal Stadium, attendance 29,751

LOS ANGELES RAMS	14	0	14	0	—	28
CLEVELAND BROWNS	7	6	7	10	—	**30**

SCORING LARm—Davis 82-yd pass from Waterfield (Waterfield PAT), Cle—Jones 27-yd pass from Graham (Groza PAT), LARm—Hoerner 3-yd run (Waterfield PAT), Cle—Lavelli 37-yd pass from Graham (PAT failed), Cle—Lavelli 39-yd pass from Graham (Groza PAT), LARm—Hoerner 1-yd run (Waterfield PAT), LARm—Brink 6-yd fumble run (Waterfield PAT), Cle—Bumgardner 14-yd pass from Graham (Groza PAT), Cle—FG Groza 16 yds

TEAM	FD	YDS	RUSH	PASS	RTN	A-C-I	SACKED	PUNT	FUMB	PEN
LA	22	407	36-106	301	25	32-18-5	11	4-51	0-0	4-48
Cle	22	373	25-116	257	76	33-22-1	41	5-38	3-3	3-25

LOS ANGELES RAMS					CLEVELAND BROWNS				
RUSHING	ATT	YDS	LNG	TD	RUSHING	ATT	YDS	LNG	TD
Dick Hoerner	24	86	24	2	Otto Graham	12	99	21	0
Vitamin Smith	4	11	15	0	Marion Motley	6	9	10	0
RECEIVING	NO	YDS	LNG	TD	RECEIVING	NO	YDS	LNG	TD
Tom Fears	9	136	44	0	Dante Lavelli	11	128	39	2
Elroy Hirsch	4	42	23	0	Dub Jones	4	80	31	1
Glenn Davis	2	88	82	1	Rex Bumgardner	4	46	15	1
PASSING	PA	PC	YDS	TD	IN	PASSING	PA	PC	YDS	TD	IN
Bob Waterfield	31	18	312	1	4	Otto Graham	33	22	298	4	1

The Christmas Eve game was arguably the most thrilling NFL Championship Game played to this time. It pitted the Rams, who'd won a championship in this same stadium in 1945 before bolting to Los Angeles, and the team from that other league, the Browns, whose dominance had helped bring down the AAFC and force a merger. The

game started with Bob Waterfield throwing an 82-yard touchdown pass on the opening play and ended with Otto Graham's two-minute drill that set up the winning kick with 28 seconds left by Lou Groza, whose earlier miss on a PAT had Cleveland trailing, 28–27. It was the first NFL Championship Game decided by a last-minute field goal. The aerial duel between Graham and Waterfield resulted in 610 yards in the air. Waterfield threw 4 interceptions (Norm Van Brocklin added another on his only pass), while Graham threw for 4 touchdowns.

1951 LEAGUE CHAMPIONSHIP

Sunday, December 23, 1951 at Los Angeles, Memorial Coliseum, attendance 57,522

CLEVELAND BROWNS	0	10	0	7	—	17
LOS ANGELES RAMS	0	7	7	10	—	24

SCORING LARm—Hoerner 1-yd run (Waterfield PAT), Cle—FG Groza 52 yds, Cle—Jones 17-yd pass from Graham (Groza PAT), LARm—Towler 1-yd run (Waterfield PAT), LARm—FG Waterfield 17 yds, Cle—Carpenter 2-yd run (Groza PAT), LARm—Fears 73-yd pass from Van Brocklin (Waterfield PAT)

TEAM	FD	YDS	RUSH	PASS	RTN	A-C-I	SACKED	PUNT	FUMB	PEN
Cle	22	325	23-92	233	14	41-19-3	5-47	4-37	4-1	6-41
LA	20	334	43-81	253	76	30-13-2	0-0	6-36	2-1	5-25

CLEVELAND BROWNS					LOS ANGELES RAMS				
RUSHING	ATT	YDS	LNG	TD	RUSHING	ATT	YDS	LNG	TD
Otto Graham	5	43	34	0	Dan Towler	16	36	9	1
Marion Motley	5	23	12	0	Tank Younger	4	20	14	0
RECEIVING	NO	YDS	LNG	TD	RECEIVING	NO	YDS	LNG	TD
Mac Speedie	7	81	14	0	Tom Fears	4	146	73	1
Dante Lavelli	4	66	17	0	Elroy Hirsch	4	66	20	0
Dub Jones	4	62	26	1					
PASSING	PA	PC	YDS	TD	IN	PASSING	PA	PC	YDS	TD	IN
Otto Graham	40	19	280	1	3	Norm Van Brocklin	6	4	128	1	0
						Bob Waterfield	24	9	125	0	2

A rematch of the previous year's championship game had a different location and climax. The game, the first title game to be nationally broadcast on television, was tied in the second quarter when Lou Groza booted a postseason-record 52-yard field goal to give the Browns a 10–7 lead. With Bob Waterfield and Norm Van Brocklin equally splitting time at quarterback, the Rams forged ahead in the third quarter. The Browns rallied to tie the game in the fourth quarter, but just 3 plays later, Van Brocklin hit Tom Fears at midfield. He split defenders and dashed the rest of the way for a 73-yard touchdown. Los Angeles, winners as the Cleveland Rams in 1945, became the first team to win a championship game while playing in two cities.

1952 NATIONAL CONFERENCE CHAMPIONSHIP

Sunday, December 21, 1952 at Detroit, Briggs Stadium, attendance 47,645

LOS ANGELES RAMS	0	7	0	14	—	21
DETROIT LIONS	7	7	10	7	—	31

SCORING Det—Harder 12-yd run (Harder PAT), Det—Harder 4-yd run (Harder PAT), LARm—Fears 14-yd pass from Van Brocklin (Waterfield), Det—Hart 24-yd pass from Walker (Harder PAT), Det—FG Harder 43 yds, LARm—Towler 5-yd run (Waterfield PAT), LARm—Smith 56-yd punt return (Waterfield PAT), Det—Hoernschemeyer 9-yd run (Harder PAT)

TEAM	FD	YDS	RUSH	PASS	RTN	A-C-I	SACKED	PUNT	FUMB	PEN
LA	15	276	29-128	148	108	28-18-1	31	6-33	2-2	2-14
Det	18	360	39-173	187	7	23-11-4	5	5-43	0-0	5-35

The Rams started 1–3 but won eight straight games to tie the Lions atop the National Conference. Then their luck ran out. Lion Pat Harder scored 2 touchdowns and added 4 extra points and a field goal for a postseason-record 19 points in a playoff in foggy Detroit. Bobby Layne threw 4 interceptions. The only Rams interception came in the final minute and led to Detroit's coup de grace touchdown.

1952 LEAGUE CHAMPIONSHIP

Sunday, December 28, 1952 at Cleveland, Municipal Stadium, attendance 50,934

DETROIT LIONS	0	7	7	3	—	17
CLEVELAND BROWNS	0	0	7	0	—	7

SCORING Det—Layne 2-yd run (Harder PAT), Det—Walker 67-yd run (Harder PAT), Cle—Jagade 7-yd run (Groza PAT), Det—FG Harder 36 yds

TEAM	FD	YDS	RUSH	PASS	RTN	A-C-I	SACKED	PUNT	FUMB	PEN
Det	10	258	34-199	59	7	10-7-0	9	6-41	0-0	3-25
Cle	22	384	34-227	157	18	36-20-1	34	3-43	1-1	7-65

DETROIT LIONS					CLEVELAND BROWNS				
RUSHING	ATT	YDS	LNG	TD	RUSHING	ATT	YDS	LNG	TD
Doak Walker	10	97	67	1	Chick Jagade	15	104		1
Bobby Layne	9	47		1	Marion Motley	6	74	42	0
RECEIVING	NO	YDS	LNG	TD	RECEIVING	NO	YDS	LNG	TD
Pat Harder	2	18	11	0	Rex Bumgardner	4	43		0
Doak Walker	2	11		0	Dante Lavelli	4	33		0
					Ray Renfro	4	26		0
					Pete Brewster	2	53	32	0
PASSING	PA	PC	YDS	TD	IN	PASSING	PA	PC	YDS	TD	IN
Bobby Layne	9	7	68	0	0	Otto Graham	35	20	191	0	1

The Lions stopped the Browns five times inside their 25-yard line and allowed only a lone touchdown despite Cleveland's dominance in total yards, 384–258. Detroit's Doak Walker had the game's big play, running out of the grasp of Bert Rechichar for a 67-yard score in the second quarter that made it 14–0. Cleveland finally broke through for its touchdown in the third quarter, taking 11 plays to cover the same 67 yards as Walker had in 1, but Detroit's defense kept the Browns frustrated from that point and gave Detroit its first NFL title since 1935.

1953 LEAGUE CHAMPIONSHIP

Sunday, December 27, 1953 at Detroit, Briggs Stadium, attendance 54,577

CLEVELAND BROWNS	0	3	7	6	—	16
DETROIT LIONS	7	3	0	7	—	17

SCORING Det—Walker 1-yd run (Walker PAT), Cle—FG Groza 13 yds, Det—FG Walker 23 yds, Cle—Jagade 9-yd run (Groza PAT), Cle—FG Groza 15 yds, Cle—FG Groza 43 yds, Det—Doran 33-yd pass from Layne (Walker PAT)

TEAM	FD	YDS	RUSH	PASS	RTN	A-C-I	SACKED	PUNT	FUMB	PEN
Cle	11	191	36-182	9	44	16-3-2	3-29	5-43	2-2	4-30
Det	18	293	39-129	164	48	26-12-2	2-15	4-49	3-2	4-50

CLEVELAND BROWNS					DETROIT LIONS				
RUSHING	ATT	YDS	LNG	TD	RUSHING	ATT	YDS	LNG	TD
Chick Jagade	15	104	30	1	Bob Hoernschemeyer	17	47	16	0
Dub Jones	3	28	19	0	Bobby Layne	11	46	8	0
RECEIVING	NO	YDS	LNG	TD	RECEIVING	NO	YDS	LNG	TD
Chick Jagade	1	18	18	0	Jim Doran	4	95	33	1
					Cloyce Box	4	54	16	0
PASSING	PA	PC	YDS	TD	IN	PASSING	PA	PC	YDS	TD	IN
Otto Graham	15	2	20	0	2	Bobby Layne	25	12	179	1	2

Jim Doran, a defensive end filling in for the injured Leon Hart, caught 3 passes for 71 yards from Bobby Layne in Detroit's final drive of the game. Layne, ignoring the screen pass the coaching staff sent in, called for Doran to go deep and tossed a 33-yard pass that tied the game. Doak Walker's extra point gave the Lions the lead. Otto Graham, whose fumble and interception had set up Detroit's other scores, was picked off by Carl Karilivacz to cap the win. The great Graham had physical problems with his hands all day, throwing as many interceptions as completions (2). The Lions, with two returnees from Korea, six rookies, eight second-year players, and 13 players taken from other teams, were champions for the second straight season.

1954 LEAGUE CHAMPIONSHIP

Sunday, December 26, 1954 at Cleveland, Municipal Stadium, attendance 43,827

DETROIT LIONS	3	7	0	0	—	10
CLEVELAND BROWNS	14	21	14	7	—	56

SCORING Det—FG Walker 36 yds, Cle—Renfro 35-yd pass from Graham (Groza PAT), Cle—Brewster 8-yd pass from Graham (Groza PAT), Cle—Graham 1-yd run (Groza PAT), Det—Bowman 5-yd run (Walker PAT), Cle—Graham 5-yd run (Groza PAT), Cle—Renfro 31-yd pass from Graham (Groza PAT), Cle—Graham 1-yd run (Groza PAT), Cle—Morrison 12-yd run (Groza PAT), Cle—Hanulak 10-yd run (Groza PAT)

TEAM	FD	YDS	RUSH	PASS	RTN	A-C-I	SACKED	PUNT	FUMB	PEN
Det	16	331	28-152	179	14	44-19-6	1-16	6-41	3-3	5-63
Cle	17	303	45-140	163	164	12-9-2	0-0	4-43	2-2	4-40

DETROIT LIONS

RUSHING	ATT	YDS	LNG	TD
Lew Carpenter	8	64	52	0
Bill Bowman	7	61	50	1

RECEIVING	NO	YDS	LNG	TD
Lew Carpenter	6	17	9	0
Jug Girard	5	57	15	0
Dorne Dibble	4	63	18	0

PASSING	PA	PC	YDS	TD	IN
Bobby Layne	42	18	177	0	6
Tom Dublinski	2	1	18	0	0

CLEVELAND BROWNS

RUSHING	ATT	YDS	LNG	TD
Chet Hanulak	5	44	23	1
Maurice Bassett	8	27	10	0
Otto Graham	9	27	8	3

RECEIVING	NO	YDS	LNG	TD
Ray Renfro	5	94	35	2
Pete Brewster	2	53	45	1

PASSING	PA	PC	YDS	TD	IN
Otto Graham	12	9	163	3	2

CHICAGO BEARS

RUSHING	ATT	YDS	LNG	TD
Rick Casares	14	43	12	1
J.C. Caroline	7	10	5	0

RECEIVING	NO	YDS	LNG	TD
Harlon Hill	6	87	17	0
Jim Dooley	6	66	15	0
Rick Casares	4	41	19	0

PASSING	PA	PC	YDS	TD	IN
George Blanda	27	12	140	0	1
Ed Brown	20	8	97	0	1

NEW YORK GIANTS

RUSHING	ATT	YDS	LNG	TD
Mel Triplett	13	71	20	1
Frank Gifford	5	30	14	0
Alex Webster	12	27	6	2

RECEIVING	NO	YDS	LNG	TD
Alex Webster	5	76	50	0
Frank Gifford	4	131	67	1

PASSING	PA	PC	YDS	TD	IN
Charlie Conerly	10	7	195	2	0
Don Heinrich	6	3	21	0	0

Detroit had beaten Cleveland four straight times, including the last two championship games and in the last minute of the last game of the regular season. The Browns had lost three years running in the championship game and had scored just 40 points in those games, but Cleveland surpassed that point total early in the third quarter in the 1954 title game. Detroit actually outgained the Browns, 331–313, but Bobby Layne tossed 6 interceptions and Detroit had 3 fumbles. The Lions even scored the first points of the game on a field goal, but the Browns run up a 35–10 lead by halftime and cruised the rest of way. Otto Graham threw 3 touchdowns and ran for 3 more.

1955 LEAGUE CHAMPIONSHIP

Monday, December 26, 1955 at Los Angeles, Memorial Coliseum, attendance 85,693

CLEVELAND BROWNS	3	14	14	7	—	38
LOS ANGELES RAMS	0	7	0	7	—	14

SCORING Cle—FG Groza 26 yds, Cle—Paul 65-yd interception return (Groza PAT), LARm—Quinlan 67-yd pass from Van Brocklin (Richter PAT), Cle—Lavell 50-yd pass from Graham (Groza PAT), Cle—Graham 15-yd run (Groza PAT), Cle—Graham 1-yd run (Groza PAT), Cle—Renfro 35-yd pass from Graham (Groza PAT), LARm—Waller 4-yd run (Richter PAT)

TEAM	FD	YDS	RUSH	PASS	RTN	A-C-I	SACKED	PUNT	FUMB	PEN
Cle	17	371	48-169	202	130	25-14-3	1-7	3-43	0-0	5-74
LA	17	259	26-116	143	55	28-11-7	2-23	4-45	1-0	2-10

CLEVELAND BROWNS

RUSHING	ATT	YDS	LNG	TD
Ed Modzelewski	13	61	10	0
Maurice Bassett	11	49	12	0
Otto Graham	9	21	15	2

RECEIVING	NO	YDS	LNG	TD
Ed Modzelewski	5	34	14	0
Dante Lavelli	3	95	50	1

PASSING	PA	PC	YDS	TD	IN
Otto Graham	25	14	209	2	3

LOS ANGELES RAMS

RUSHING	ATT	YDS	LNG	TD
Dan Towler	14	64	15	0
Ron Waller	11	48	13	1

RECEIVING	NO	YDS	LNG	TD
Skeets Quinlan	5	116	67	1
Ron Waller	3	18	11	0

PASSING	PA	PC	YDS	TD	IN
Norm Van Brocklin	25	11	166	1	6
Billy Wade	3	0	0	0	1

Otto Graham went out a champion in his final game, throwing for 209 yards and 2 touchdowns while overcoming 3 interceptions. Automatic Otto never missed a regular-season game—or a championship game, for that matter. Graham played in the championship game of his league in each of his 10 seasons as a professional; he had 7 wins (4 in the AAFC, 3 in the NFL). In his last game, Cleveland's defense intercepted 6 Norm Van Brocklin passes, plus 1 by Billy Wade. The Browns converted Van Brocklin's misfires into 24 points. Graham also ran for 2 touchdowns as he got to enjoy going out on top in a rout in Los Angeles.

1956 LEAGUE CHAMPIONSHIP

Sunday, December 30, 1956 at New York, Yankee Stadium, attendance 56,836

CHICAGO BEARS	0	7	0	0	—	7
NEW YORK GIANTS	13	21	6	7	—	47

SCORING NYG—Triplett 17-yd run (Agajanian PAT), NYG—FG Agajanian 17 yds, NYG—FG Agajanian 43 yds, NYG—Webster 3-yd run (Agajanian PAT), ChiB—Casares 9-yd run (Blanda PAT), NYG—Webster 1-yd run (Agajanian PAT), NYG—Moore recovered blocked punt in end zone (Agajanian PAT), NYG—Rote 9-yd pass from Conerly (PAT failed), NYG—Gifford 14-yd pass from Conerly (Agajanian PAT)

TEAM	FD	YDS	RUSH	PASS	RTN	A-C-I	SACKED	PUNT	FUMB	PEN
ChiB	19	270	32-67	203	0	47-20-2	34	9-30	2-1	4-50
NYG	16	348	34-126	222	48	20-11-0	6	3-37	3-2	6-40

The Bears were 3–1 against the Giants in championship games, but the teams hadn't met with the championship at stake since 1946, and the Giants hadn't beaten them for the title since the Sneakers Game at the Polo Grounds in 1934. The Giants turned it around at their new home at Yankee Stadium, pummeling the Bears by 40 points. Don Heinrich, started at quarterback for New York, probing the defense while star Charlie Conerly observed. The Giants were already up 13–0 when Conerly came in; the lead was 34–7 at halftime. Frank Gifford caught 4 passes for 131 yards, including a 67-yard reception and a 14-yard, fourth-quarter touchdown that signaled it was time for third-stringer Bobby Clatterbuck to run out the clock on New York's fourth NFL title and its first since 1938.

1957 WESTERN CONFERENCE CHAMPIONSHIP

Sunday, December 22, 1957 at San Francisco, Kezar Stadium, attendance 60,118

DETROIT LIONS	0	7	14	10	—	31
SAN FRANCISCO 49ERS	14	10	3	0	—	27

SCORING SF—Owens 34-yd pass from Tittle (Soltau PAT), SF—McElhenny 47-yd pass from Tittle (Soltau PAT), Det—Junker 4-yd pass from Rote (Martin PAT), SF—Wilson 12-yd pass from Tittle (Soltau PAT), SF—FG Soltau 25 yds, SF—FG Soltau 10 yds, Det—Tracy 1-yd run (Martin PAT), Det—Tracy 58-yd run (Martin PAT), Det—Gedman 2-yd run (Martin PAT), Det—FG Martin 13 yds

TEAM	FD	YDS	RUSH	PASS	RTN	A-C-I	SACKED	PUNT	FUMB	PEN
Det	22	324	29-129	195	26	30-16-1	3-19	4-43	3-3	7-61
SF	20	351	33-127	224	33	31-18-3	2-24	3-34	6-2	6-70

SF—Billy Wilson 107C

The Lions, down 24–7 in the playoff, heard the raucous celebration in the home locker room at halftime and got fired up. After the third quarter started with Hugh McElhenny running 71 yards to set up a Gordy Soltau field goal that pushed the lead to 20 points, the Lions rattled off 3 touchdowns in just 4:29. Four 49ers' drives came up empty in the fourth quarter, turning the visiting locker room at Kezar Stadium into the site of the celebration.

1957 LEAGUE CHAMPIONSHIP

Sunday, December 29, 1957 at Detroit, Briggs Stadium, attendance 55,263

CLEVELAND BROWNS	0	7	7	0	—	14
DETROIT LIONS	17	14	14	14	—	59

SCORING Det—FG Martin 31 yds, Det—Rote 1-yd run (Martin PAT), Det—Gedman 1-yd run (Martin PAT), Cle—Brown 29-yd run (Groza PAT), Det—Junker 26-yd pass from Rote (Martin PAT), Cle—Barr 19-yd interception return (Martin PAT), Cle—L. Carpenter 5-yd run (Groza PAT), Det—Doran 78-yd pass from Rote (Martin PAT), Det—Junker 23-yd pass from Rote (Martin PAT), Det—Middleton 32-yd pass from Rote (Martin PAT), Det—Cassady 16-yd pass from Reichow (Martin PAT)

TEAM	FD	YDS	RUSH	PASS	RTN	A-C-I	SACKED	PUNT	FUMB	PEN
Cle	17	313	38-218	95	1	22-9-5	2-17	4-36	2-2	4-60
Det	22	438	36-142	296	51	22-13-0	0-0	4-36	3-1	7-52

CLEVELAND BROWNS

RUSHING	ATT	YDS	LNG	TD
Lew Carpenter	14	82	27	1
Jim Brown	20	69	29	1

RECEIVING	NO	YDS	LNG	TD
Preston Carpenter	4	43	18	0
Pete Brewster	3	52	19	0

PASSING	PA	PC	YDS	TD	IN
Tommy O'Connell	8	4	61	0	2
Milt Plum	13	5	51	0	2

DETROIT LIONS

RUSHING	ATT	YDS	LNG	TD
Howard Cassady	8	48	21	0
John Henry Johnson	8	40	19	0

RECEIVING	NO	YDS	LNG	TD
Steve Junker	5	109	26	2
Jim Doran	3	101	78	1

PASSING	PA	PC	YDS	TD	IN
Tobin Rote	19	12	280	4	0
Jerry Reichow	3	1	16	1	0

Quarterback Tobin Rote, a key player but considered Detroit's second-fiddle until Bobby Layne was hurt in the season's second-to-last game, threw for 280 yards and 4 touchdowns in the championship game. The Lions went up, 17–0, after the first quarter and held a 31–7 lead at the half. Learning from the previous week, when the 49er

celebrated too soon and then watched in horror as the Lions overcame a 20-point deficit, Detroit kept the pedal down and scored 28 points after intermission. The Lions came up just short of the 46-point differential that Detroit suffered against Cleveland in the 1954 NFL Championship Game, but it was close enough. Rote helped the Lions win their third championship of the decade, and their last of the century.

1958 EASTERN CONFERENCE CHAMPIONSHIP

Sunday, December 21, 1958 at New York, Yankee Stadium, attendance 61,254

CLEVELAND BROWNS	0	0	0	0	—	0
NEW YORK GIANTS	7	3	0	0	—	10

SCORING NYG—Conerly 10-yd lateral from Gifford after 8-yd run (Summerall, NYG—FG Summerall 26 yds

TEAM	FD	YDS	RUSH	PASS	RTN	A-C-I	SACKED	PUNT	FUMB	PEN
Cle	7	86	13-24	62	35	27-10-3	6-52	8-38	1-1	2-20
NYG	17	317	53-211	106	23	18-8-2	0-0	7-47	6-2	4-35

The Giants had forced the playoff a week earlier on Pat Summerall's 49-yard field goal in the final minute against the Browns. The Giants scored the only touchdown in the playoff on a reverse-lateral: Frank Gifford ran 8 yards and gave the ball back to Charlie Conerly, who took it the last 10 yards. Summerall added the game's final points in the second quarter.

1958 LEAGUE CHAMPIONSHIP

Sunday, December 28, 1958 at New York (OT), Yankee Stadium, attendance 64,185

BALTIMORE COLTS	0	14	0	3	6	—	23
NEW YORK GIANTS	3	0	7	7	0	—	17

SCORING NYG—FG Summerall 36 yds, Bal—Ameche 2-yd run (Myhra PAT), Bal—Berry 15-yd pass from Unitas (Myhra PAT), NYG—Triplett 1-yd run (Summerall PAT), NYG—Gifford 15-yd pass from Conerly (Summerall PAT), Bal—FG Myhra 20 yds, Bal—Ameche 1-yd run (no PAT)

TEAM	FD	YDS	RUSH	PASS	RTN	A-C-I	SACKED	PUNT	FUMB	PEN
Bal	27	453	38-139	314	10	40-26-1	4-35	4-51	2-2	3-15
NYG	10	266	31-88	178	32	18-12-0	3-22	6-46	6-4	2-22

BALTIMORE COLTS						NEW YORK GIANTS				
RUSHING	ATT	YDS	LNG	TD		**RUSHING**	ATT	YDS	LNG	TD
Alan Ameche	14	59	23	2		Frank Gifford	12	60	38	0
L.G. Dupre	11	30	10	0		Alex Webster	9	24	8	0
RECEIVING	NO	YDS	LNG	TD		**RECEIVING**	NO	YDS	LNG	TD
Raymond Berry	12	178	25	1		Frank Gifford	3	14	15	1
Lenny Moore	6	101	60	0		Kyle Rote	2	76	62	0
						Bob Schnelker	2	63	46	0
PASSING	PA	PC	YDS	TD	IN	**PASSING**	PA	PC	YDS	TD	IN
John Unitas	40	26	349	1	0	Charlie Conerly	14	10	187	1	0
						Don Heinrich	4	2	13	0	0

"The Greatest Game Ever Played" was the first NFL game to feature overtime—not counting a preseason exhibition that saw a fifth quarter—and it marked the anointing of Johnny Unitas, football god. If not for coolly leading the Colts to a game-saving drive, Unitas and his Colts may have been remembered for blowing an 11-point lead. The Colts, up 14–3, were stopped on fourth down at the 1 in the third quarter. The Giants rallied to take the lead on a Frank Gifford touchdown catch, but when Gifford was stopped after what he argued was a first down, the Colts stood at their own 14 with 1:56 to go. Unitas led Baltimore to a game-tying Steve Myhra field goal. After the Giants went three and out to start the historic overtime, Unitas marched the Colts to the winning score.

1959 LEAGUE CHAMPIONSHIP

Sunday, December 27, 1959 at Baltimore, Memorial Stadium, attendance 57,545

NEW YORK GIANTS	3	3	3	7	—	16
BALTIMORE COLTS	7	0	0	24	—	31

SCORING Bal—Moore 60-yd pass from Unitas (Myhra PAT), NYG—FG Summerall 23 yds, NYG—FG Summerall 37 yds, NYG—FG Summerall 22 yds, Bal—Unitas 4-yd run (Myhra PAT), Bal—Richardson 12-yd pass from Unitas (Myhra PAT), Bal—Sample 42-yd interception return (Myhra PAT), Bal—FG Myhra 25 yds, NYG—Schnelker 32-yd pass from Conerly (Summerall PAT)

TEAM	FD	YDS	RUSH	PASS	RTN	A-C-I	SACKED	PUNT	FUMB	PEN
NYG	16	326	25-118	208	5	38-17-3	45	6-48	1-0	3-23
Bal	13	281	25-73	208	127	29-18-0	57	6-36	1-0	4-20

NEW YORK GIANTS						BALTIMORE COLTS				
RUSHING	ATT	YDS	LNG	TD		**RUSHING**	ATT	YDS	LNG	TD
Frank Gifford	9	50	23	0		Alan Ameche	9	30	6	0
Mel Triplett	6	39	28	0		Mike Sommer	6	15	5	0
RECEIVING	NO	YDS	LNG	TD		**RECEIVING**	NO	YDS	LNG	TD
Bob Schnelker	9	178	48	1		Raymond Berry	5	68	28	0
Phil King	4	17	11	0		Jim Mutscheller	5	40	15	0
						Lenny Moore	3	126	59	1
PASSING	PA	PC	YDS	TD	IN	**PASSING**	PA	PC	YDS	TD	IN
Charlie Conerly	35	16	234	1	2	John Unitas	29	18	265	2	0
Frank Gifford	2	1	19	0	1						

The championship Colts–Giants rematch could not live up to the excitement of the first NFL overtime game the previous year, but the 1959 NFL Championship Game had plenty of fourth-quarter action. The Giants had a 9–7 lead early in the final quarter when the Colts stopped Alex Webster on fourth-and-inches. The Colts then erupted for 24 points. Johnny Unitas ran for a touchdown to give Baltimore the lead. A turnover set up another quick score. Johnny Sample then picked off Charlie Conerly and ran 42 yards for a touchdown. New York's third interception of the quarter set up a field goal. The Giants finally scored a touchdown in the final minute.

1960 NFL CHAMPIONSHIP

Monday, December 26, 1960 at Philadelphia, Franklin Field, attendance 67,325

GREEN BAY PACKERS	3	3	0	7	—	13
PHILADELPHIA EAGLES	0	10	0	7	—	17

SCORING GB—FG Hornung 20 yds, GB—FG Hornung 20 yds, Phi—McDonald 35-yd pass from Van Brocklin (Walston PAT), Phi—FG Walston 15 yds, GB—McGee 7-yd pass from Starr (Hornung PAT), Phi—Dean 5-yd run (Walston PAT)

TEAM	FD	YDS	RUSH	PASS	RTN	A-C-I	SACKED	PUNT	FUMB	PEN
GB	22	401	42-223	178	18	35-21-0	0-0	5-45	1-1	4-27
Phi	13	296	28-99	197	10	20-9-1	7	6-40	3-2	0-0

GREEN BAY PACKERS						PHILADELPHIA EAGLES				
RUSHING	ATT	YDS	LNG	TD		**RUSHING**	ATT	YDS	LNG	TD
Jim Taylor	24	105	16	0		Ted Dean	13	54	8	1
Paul Hornung	11	61	16	0		Billy Ray Barnes	13	42	7	0
RECEIVING	NO	YDS	LNG	TD		**RECEIVING**	NO	YDS	LNG	TD
Gary Knafelc	6	76	20	0		Tommy McDonald	3	90	35	1
Jim Taylor	6	46	15	0		Bobby Walston	3	38	25	0
Paul Hornung	4	14	8	0						
PASSING	PA	PC	YDS	TD	IN	**PASSING**	PA	PC	YDS	TD	IN
Bart Starr	34	21	178	1	0	Norm Van Brocklin	20	9	204	1	1

The Eagles played in their first championship game since they went to three straight—and won two—to end the 1940s. The Packers, who didn't exactly thrive during the 1950s either, had their chances early. Two turnovers by Philadelphia in the first quarter helped Green Bay get on the scoreboard first, but Norm Van Brocklin erased that, hitting Tommy McDonald for 22 yards and then for 35 yards and a score. The Eagles led at the half, 10–6, and held that lead until Bart Starr connected with Max McGee in the fourth quarter. Green Bay's lead did not last long. A 58-yard kickoff return by Ted Dean set up a short drive capped off by Dean's 5-yard run. Vince Lombardi lost his first championship game, his only career defeat in 10 postseason appearances.

1960 AFL CHAMPIONSHIP

Sunday, January 1, 1961 at Houston, Jeppesen Stadium, attendance 32,183

LOS ANGELES CHARGERS	6	3	7	0	—	16
HOUSTON OILERS	0	10	7	7	—	24

SCORING LAC—FG Agajanian 38 yds, LAC—FG Agajanian 22 yds, Hou—Smith 17-yd pass from Blanda (Blanda PAT), Hou—FG Blanda 18 yds, LAC—FG Agajanian 27 yds, Hou—Groman 7-yd pass from Blanda (Blanda PAT), LAC—Lowe 2-yd run (Agajanian PAT), Hou—Cannon 88-yd pass from Blanda (Blanda PAT)

TEAM	FD	YDS	RUSH	PASS	RTN	A-C-I	SACKED	PUNT	FUMB	PEN
LAC	21	333	30-190	143	42	41-21-2	3-28	4-41	2-0	3-15
Hou	17	401	40-100	301	35	32-16-0	0-0	5-34	0-0	4-54

LOS ANGELES CHARGERS				
RUSHING	**ATT**	**YDS**	**LNG**	**TD**
Paul Lowe	21	165	30	1
Jack Kemp	3	19	14	0
RECEIVING	**NO**	**YDS**	**LNG**	**TD**
Don Norton	6	55	18	0
Royce Womble	6	29	8	0
Dave Kocourek	3	57	33	0
PASSING	**PA**	**PC**	**YDS**	**TD**	**IN**
Jack Kemp	41	21	171	0	2

HOUSTON OILERS				
RUSHING	**ATT**	**YDS**	**LNG**	**TD**
Billy Cannon	18	50	6	0
Dave Smith	19	45	14	0
RECEIVING	**NO**	**YDS**	**LNG**	**TD**
Dave Smith	5	52	17	1
Charley Hennigan	4	71	38	0
Billy Cannon	3	128	88	1
PASSING	**PA**	**PC**	**YDS**	**TD**	**IN**
George Blanda	31	16	301	3	0

Chargers kicker Ben Agajanian became the first player to score in both an NFL and AFL Championship Game, but it was George Blanda, a close second, whose 301 yards passing and 3 touchdown passes crowned the Oilers the AFL's first champion. Billy Cannon took a short Blanda pass and raced 88 yards in the fourth quarter. Los Angeles, needing a touchdown and two-point conversion to tie, got to Houston's 22, but Houston's defense held the Chargers on fourth down on the final drive. The NFL had never played a championship game that went beyond the year's calendar, but the AFL did it straight off, holding its first title game on New Year's Day.

1961 NFL CHAMPIONSHIP
Sunday, December 31, 1961 at Green Bay, Lambeau Field, attendance 39,029

NEW YORK GIANTS	0	0	0	0	—	0
GREEN BAY PACKERS	0	24	10	3	—	**37**

SCORING GB—Hornung 6-yd run (Hornung PAT), GB—Dowler 13-yd pass from Starr (Hornung PAT), GB—Kramer 14-yd pass from Starr (Hornung PAT), GB—FG Hornung 17 yds, GB—FG Hornung 22 yds, GB—Kramer 13-yd pass from Starr (Hornung PAT), GB—FG Hornung 19 yds

TEAM	FD	YDS	RUSH	PASS	RTN	A-C-I	SACKED	PUNT	FUMB	PEN
NYG	6	130	14-31	99	10	29-10-4	20	5-39	5-1	4-38
GB	19	345	44-181	164	40	19-10-0	0-0	5-42	1-0	4-16

NEW YORK GIANTS				
RUSHING	**ATT**	**YDS**	**LNG**	**TD**
Alex Webster	7	19	7	0
Joel Wells	3	9	8	0
RECEIVING	**NO**	**YDS**	**LNG**	**TD**
Kyle Rote	3	54		0
Del Shofner	3	41		0
PASSING	**PA**	**PC**	**YDS**	**TD**	**IN**
Y.A. Tittle	20	6	65	0	4
Charlie Conerly	8	4	54	0	0

GREEN BAY PACKERS				
RUSHING	**ATT**	**YDS**	**LNG**	**TD**
Paul Hornung	20	89	17	1
Jim Taylor	14	69	33	0
RECEIVING	**NO**	**YDS**	**LNG**	**TD**
Ron Kramer	4	80	38	2
Paul Hornung	3	47	26	0
PASSING	**PA**	**PC**	**YDS**	**TD**	**IN**
Bart Starr	17	10	164	3	0
Paul Hornung	2	0	0	0	0

Vince Lombardi, who came to the Packers after being an assistant with the Giants, won his first title by blanking New York in Green Bay. The game was scoreless after one quarter but was over by halftime. Paul Hornung ran for a touchdown just after the period began and kicked a field goal just before it ended. Bart Starr threw 2 touchdown passes in between, and he added another to Ron Kramer in the third quarter. Green Bay outgained the Giants, 345–130, and New York had 5 turnovers. The Packers won their first title since beating the Giants in the 1944 NFL Championship Game.

1961 AFL CHAMPIONSHIP
Sunday, December 24, 1961 at San Diego, Balboa Stadium, attendance 29,556

HOUSTON OILERS	0	3	7	0	—	**10**
SAN DIEGO CHARGERS	0	0	0	3	—	3

SCORING Hou—FG Blanda 46 yds, Hou—Cannon 35-yd pass from Blanda (Blanda PAT), SD—FG Blair 12 yds

TEAM	FD	YDS	RUSH	PASS	RTN	A-C-I	SACKED	PUNT	FUMB	PEN
Hou	18	256	33-96	160	7	41-18-6	0-0	4-42	5-1	5-68
SD	15	256	20-79	177	76	32-17-4	6-49	6-33	2-2	10-106

HOUSTON OILERS				
RUSHING	**ATT**	**YDS**	**LNG**	**TD**
Charley Tolar	16	52	20	0
Billy Cannon	15	48	22	0
RECEIVING	**NO**	**YDS**	**LNG**	**TD**
Billy Cannon	5	53	35	1
Charley Hennigan	5	43	14	0
PASSING	**PA**	**PC**	**YDS**	**TD**	**IN**
George Blanda	40	18	160	1	5

SAN DIEGO CHARGERSQ				
RUSHING	**ATT**	**YDS**	**LNG**	**TD**
Bo Roberson	8	37	23	0
Paul Lowe	5	30	12	0
RECEIVING	**NO**	**YDS**	**LNG**	**TD**
Dave Kocourek	7	123	40	0
Don Norton	3	48	28	0
PASSING	**PA**	**PC**	**YDS**	**TD**	**IN**
Jack Kemp	32	17	226	0	4

A lot of things changed between the 1960 and 1961 AFL title games: Houston coach Lou Rymkus had been replaced by Wally Lemm after a 1–3–1 start, the Chargers had moved from Los Angeles to

San Diego, the Oilers had become the first pro team to score 500 points in a season, and the Chargers had transformed into the league's stingiest defense. One thing that hadn't changed: The Oilers beat the Charges for the AFL championship. The teams combined for as many turnovers as points (13) and each side had exactly 256 total yards. The game was once again close and, for the second straight year, a George Blanda to Billy Cannon touchdown pass was the difference in the final score.

1962 NFL CHAMPIONSHIP
Sunday, December 30, 1962 at New York, Yankee Stadium, attendance 64,892

GREEN BAY PACKERS	3	7	3	3	—	**16**
NEW YORK GIANTS	0	0	7	0	—	7

SCORING GB—FG J. Kramer 26 yds, GB—Taylor 7-yd run (J. Kramer PAT), NYG—Collier blocked punt recovery in end zone(Chandler PAT), GB—FG J. Kramer 29 yds, GB—FG J. Kramer 30 yds

TEAM	FD	YDS	RUSH	PASS	RTN	A-C-I	SACKED	PUNT	FUMB	PEN
GB	18	244	46-148	96	66	22-10-0	10	6-27	2-0	5-44
NYG	18	291	26-94	197	0	41-18-1	0-0	7-42	3-2	4-62

GREEN BAY PACKERS				
RUSHING	**ATT**	**YDS**	**LNG**	**TD**
Jim Taylor	31	85	14	1
Paul Hornung	8	35	11	0
RECEIVING	**NO**	**YDS**	**LNG**	**TD**
Boyd Dowler	4	48	21	0
Jim Taylor	3	20	13	0
PASSING	**PA**	**PC**	**YDS**	**TD**	**IN**
Bart Starr	21	9	85	0	0

NEW YORK GIANTS				
RUSHING	**ATT**	**YDS**	**LNG**	**TD**
Alex Webster	15	56	12	0
Phil King	11	38	8	0
RECEIVING	**NO**	**YDS**	**LNG**	**TD**
Joe Walton	5	75	25	0
Del Shofner	5	69	21	0
Frank Gifford	4	34	15	0
PASSING	**PA**	**PC**	**YDS**	**TD**	**IN**
Y.A. Tittle	41	18	197	0	1

Despite 40 mile per hour winds and a 13-degree afternoon at Yankee Stadium, Y.A. Tittle passed for 197 yards, but could not get the Giants in the end zone—the second straight year the Packers kept the Giants offense off the scoreboard in the championship game. With Green Bay holding a 10–0 lead in the third quarter, Max McGee's punt was blocked by Erich Barnes and fallen on by Jim Collier for New York's lone touchdown. Jim Taylor, tying a championship game record with 31 carries, had the game only offensive touchdown and Jerry Kramer had 3 field goals to finish off Green Bay's eighth NFL championship and second in a row. The Giants lost in the championship game for the fourth time in five years and the 10th time in 13 appearances.

1962 AFL CHAMPIONSHIP
Sunday, December 23, 1962 at Houston, Jeppesen Stadium, attendance 37,981

DALLAS TEXANS	3	14	0	0	0	3	—	**20**
HOUSTON OILERS	0	0	7	10	0	0	—	17

SCORING Dal—FG Brooker 16 yds, Dal—Haynes 28-yd pass from Dawson (Brooker PAT), Dal—Haynes 2-yd run (Brooker PAT), Hou—Dewveall 15-yd pass from Blanda (Blanda PAT), Hou—FG Blanda 31 yds, Hou—Tolar 1-yd run (Blanda PAT), Dal—FG Brooker 25 yds

TEAM	FD	YDS	RUSH	PASS	RTN	A-C-I	SACKED	PUNT	FUMB	PEN
DalT	19	237	54-199	38	136	14-9-0	6-50	8-31	2-1	6-42
Hou	21	359	30-98	261	0	46-23-5	0-0	3-39	0-0	6-50

DALLAS TEXANS				
RUSHING	**ATT**	**YDS**	**LNG**	**TD**
Jack Spikes	11	77	33	0
Curtis McClinton	24	70	8	0
RECEIVING	**NO**	**YDS**	**LNG**	**TD**
Abner Haynes	3	45	28	1
Jack Spikes	2	24	14	0
PASSING	**PA**	**PC**	**YDS**	**TD**	**IN**
Len Dawson	14	9	88	1	0

HOUSTON OILERS				
RUSHING	**ATT**	**YDS**	**LNG**	**TD**
Charley Tolar	17	58	12	1
Billy Cannon	11	37	7	0
RECEIVING	**NO**	**YDS**	**LNG**	**TD**
Willard Dewveall	6	95	24	1
Billy Cannon	6	54	21	0
Bob McLeod	5	70	21	0
PASSING	**PA**	**PC**	**YDS**	**TD**	**IN**
George Blanda	46	23	261	1	5

For the first time, the Houston Oilers did not win the AFL championship, but it took a determined cross-state rival and the longest game yet played in pro football history to beat them. Tommy Brooker's field goal at 2:54 of the second quarter of overtime ended Houston's two-year AFL reign. Houston had come back from a 17–0 halftime deficit to shut out the Texans by the same margin in the second half. While Dallas passed for just 38 yards—Len Dawson threw for 88 yards, but lost 50 yards on 6 sacks—the Texans ran the ball 54 times for 199 yards. They kept running when the game was over, right out of Texas and up to Kansas City to become the Chiefs.

1963 NFL CHAMPIONSHIP

Sunday, December 29, 1963 at Chicago, Wrigley Field, attendance 45,801

NEW YORK GIANTS	7	3	0	0	—	10
CHICAGO BEARS	7	0	7	0	—	**14**

SCORING NYG—Gifford 14-yd pass from Tittle (Chandler PAT), ChiB—Wade 2-yd run (Jencks PAT), NYG—FG Chandler 13 yds, ChiB—Wade 1-yd run (Jencks PAT)

TEAM	FD	YDS	RUSH	PASS	RTN	A-C-I	SACKED	PUNT	FUMB	PEN
NYG	17	268	38-128	140	21	30-11-5	7	4-43	2-1	3-25
Chi	14	222	31-93	129	76	28-10-0	9	7-42	2-2	5-35

NEW YORK GIANTS

RUSHING	ATT	YDS	LNG	TD
Joe Morrison	18	61	20	0
Phil King	9	39	10	0

RECEIVING	NO	YDS	LNG	TD
Frank Gifford	3	45	16	1
Joe Morrison	3	18	11	0

PASSING	PA	PC	YDS	TD	IN
Y.A. Tittle	29	11	147	1	5

CHICAGO BEARS

RUSHING	ATT	YDS	LNG	TD
Ronnie Bull	13	42	12	0
Billy Wade	8	34	12	2

RECEIVING	NO	YDS	LNG	TD
Joe Marconi	3	64	34	0
Mike Ditka	3	38	15	0

PASSING	PA	PC	YDS	TD	IN
Billy Wade	28	10	138	0	0

George Halas won his sixth and final NFL title as a coach, beating the Giants for the fourth time in the championship game. Giants quarterback Y.A. Tittle, hobbled by a knee injury suffered in the first half, threw 5 interceptions in Chicago's 10-degree cold. Two of those interceptions—both on screen passes—set up short Bears touchdowns. New York took a 7–0 lead on Frank Gifford's touchdown catch in the first quarter. New York barely missed another score, but Del Shofner's drop in the end zone resulted in no points. The Giants held the lead in the third quarter when Ed O'Bradovich's interception and return set up the second Billy Wade touchdown run of the day.

1963 AFL EASTERN DIVISION CHAMPIONSHIP

Saturday, December 28, 1963 at Buffalo, War Memorial Stadium, attendance 33,044

BOSTON PATRIOTS	10	6	0	10	—	26
BUFFALO BILLS	0	0	8	0	—	8

SCORING Bos—FG Cappelletti 28 yds, Bos—Garron 59-yd pass from Parilli (Cappelletti PAT), Bos—FG Cappelletti 12 yds, Bos—FG Cappelletti 33 yds, Buf—Dubenion 93-yd pass from Lamonica (Tracey pass from Lamonica), Bos—Garron 17-yd pass from Parilli (Cappelletti PAT), Bos—FG Cappelletti 36 yds

TEAM	FD	YDS	RUSH	PASS	RTN	A-C-I	SACKED	PUNT	FUMB	PEN
Bos	16	375	36-83	292	47	35-14-1	1-8	7-32	0-0	7-65
Buf	13	286	12-7	279	17	45-19-4	2-22	8-35	3-2	9-100

Bos-Larry Garron 120C, Gino Cappelletti 109C, Babe Parilli 300P; Buf-Elbert Dubenion 115C

The Patriots dominated the first AFL playoff game, necessitated to break a tie between the two worst teams (7–6–1) ever to qualify for the AFL postseason. The longest scoring play in AFL postseason history—93 yards from backup Daryle Lamonica to Elbert Dubenion—briefly put the Bills in the game in the third quarter, but the Patriots put Buffalo away in the fourth

1963 AFL CHAMPIONSHIP

Sunday, January 5, 1964 at San Diego, Balboa Stadium, attendance 30,127

BOSTON PATRIOTS	7	3	0	0	—	10
SAN DIEGO CHARGERS	21	10	7	13	—	**51**

SCORING SD—Rote 2-yd run (Blair PAT), SD—Lincoln 67-yd run (Blair PAT), Bos—Garron 7-yd run (Cappelletti PAT), SD—Lowe 58-yd run (Blair PAT), SD—FG Blair 11 yds, Bos—FG Cappelletti 15 yds, SD—Norton 14-yd pass from Rote (Blair PAT), SD—Alworth 48-yd pass from Rote (Blair PAT), SD—Lincoln 25-yd pass from Hadl (pass failed), SD—Hadl 1-yd run (Blair PAT)

TEAM	FD	YDS	RUSH	PASS	RTN	A-C-I	SACKED	PUNT	FUMB	PEN
Bos	14	261	16-75	186	0	37-17-2	6-42	7-47	1-0	1-18
SD	21	610	32-318	292	15	26-17-0	2-13	2-44	1-1	6-30

BOSTON PATRIOTS

RUSHING	ATT	YDS	LNG	TD
Harry Crump	7	18	6	0
Larry Garron	3	15	7	1

RECEIVING	NO	YDS	LNG	TD
Ron Burton	4	12	8	0
Jim Colclough	3	26	10	0
Gino Cappelletti	2	72	49	0
Art Graham	2	68	45	0

PASSING	PA	PC	YDS	TD	IN
Babe Parilli	29	14	189	0	1
Tom Yewcic	8	3	39	0	1

SAN DIEGO CHARGERS

RUSHING	ATT	YDS	LNG	TD
Keith Lincoln	13	206	67	1
Paul Lowe	12	94	58	1

RECEIVING	NO	YDS	LNG	TD
Keith Lincoln	7	123	32	1
Lance Alworth	4	77	48	1
Jacque MacKinnon	2	52	33	0

PASSING	PA	PC	YDS	TD	IN
Tobin Rote	15	10	173	2	0
John Hadl	10	6	112	1	0

Sid Gillman's offense put together an AFL postseason-record 610 total yards of offense in a pounding of the Patriots. Keith Lincoln was responsible for 349 of those yards: Lincoln rushed for 206 yards on just 13 carries, caught 7 passes for 123 yards, and even completed a pass for another 20. The San Diego running game averaged almost 10 yards per carry, with Lincoln running for 123 yards on consecutive carries in the first quarter. The Chargers had leads of 21–7 after one quarter and 31–10 at the half. Tobin Rote and John Hadl each passed for more than 100 yards for the Chargers. The Patriots, who would appear in no more AFL postseason games, never knew what hit them.

1964 NFL CHAMPIONSHIP

Sunday, December 27, 1964 at Cleveland, Municipal Stadium, attendance 79,544

BALTIMORE COLTS	0	0	0	0	—	0
CLEVELAND BROWNS	0	0	17	10	—	**27**

SCORING Cle—FG Groza 43 yds, Cle—Collins 18-yd pass from Ryan (Groza PAT), Cle—Collins 42-yd pass from Ryan (Groza PAT), Cle—FG Groza 10 yds, Cle—Collins 51-yd pass from Ryan (Groza PAT)

TEAM	FD	YDS	RUSH	PASS	RTN	A-C-I	SACKED	PUNT	FUMB	PEN
Bal	11	181	25-92	89	32	20-12-2	2-6	4-34	2-2	5-48
Cle	20	339	41-142	197	23	18-11-1	1-9	3-44	0-0	7-59

BALTIMORE COLTS

RUSHING	ATT	YDS	LNG	TD
Lenny Moore	9	40	15	0
Jerry Hill	9	31	8	0

RECEIVING	NO	YDS	LNG	TD
Raymond Berry	3	38	23	0
Tony Lorick	3	18	8	0

PASSING	PA	PC	YDS	TD	IN
John Unitas	20	12	95	0	2

CLEVELAND BROWNS

RUSHING	ATT	YDS	LNG	TD
Jim Brown	27	114	46	0
Ernie Green	10	29	9	0

RECEIVING	NO	YDS	LNG	TD
Gary Collins	5	130	51	3
Jim Brown	3	37	23	0

PASSING	PA	PC	YDS	TD	IN
Frank Ryan	18	11	206	3	1

After a scoreless first half, the Browns came out firing as Frank Ryan threw 3 touchdown passes to Gary Collins in the second half. Jim Brown, who rushed for 114 yards, set up the first touchdown with a 46-yard run. Lou Groza added 2 field goals. The Colts came into the game as heavy favorites after leading the NFL in both scoring and defense, but Cleveland held both Baltimore's running and passing games under control. Johnny Unitas threw for just 95 yards and 2 interceptions. Coach Blanton Collier's victory marked the only league championship ever won by the Cleveland franchise without Paul Brown at the helm.

1964 AFL CHAMPIONSHIP

Saturday, December 26, 1964 at Buffalo, War Memorial Stadium, attendance 40,242

SAN DIEGO CHARGERS	7	0	0	0	—	7
BUFFALO BILLS	3	10	0	7	—	**20**

SCORING SD—Kocourek 26-yd pass from Rote (Lincoln PAT), Buf—FG Gogolak 12 yds, Buf—Carlton 4-yd run (Gogolak PAT), Buf—FG Gogolak 17 yds, Buf—Kemp 1-yd run (Gogolak PAT)

TEAM	FD	YDS	RUSH	PASS	RTN	A-C-I	SACKED	PUNT	FUMB	PEN
SD	15	259	18-124	135	58	36-13-3	14	5-36	1-0	3-20
Buf	21	387	41-219	168	14	20-10-0	20	5-47	0-0	3-45

SAN DIEGO CHARGERS

RUSHING	ATT	YDS	LNG	TD
Keith Lincoln	3	47	38	0
Paul Lowe	7	34	16	0

RECEIVING	NO	YDS	LNG	TD
Keith Kinderman	4	52	22	0
Jacque MacKinnon	3	12	7	0
Dave Kocourek	2	52	26	1

PASSING	PA	PC	YDS	TD	IN
Tobin Rote	26	10	118	1	2

BUFFALO BILLS

RUSHING	ATT	YDS	LNG	TD
Cookie Gilchrist	16	122	39	0
Wray Carlton	18	70	13	1

RECEIVING	NO	YDS	LNG	TD
Elbert Dubenion	3	56	26	0
Glenn Bass	2	70	50	0

PASSING	PA	PC	YDS	TD	IN
Jack Kemp	20	10	188	0	0

Keith Lincoln, who'd averaged 15 yards per carry in the previous year's championship game, gained 47 yards in just 3 carries to start the 1964 AFL Championship Game. A hit by Bills linebacker Mike Stratton broke Lincoln's rib and ended his day. None of the other six Chargers who ran the ball exceeded Lincoln's yardage total. After scoring 7 touchdowns in the 1963 title game, San Diego managed just 7 points in the 1964 contest. Those points came in the first quarter on a Tobin Rote touchdown pass, set up by Lincoln's 38-yard run. San Diego later threw 3 interceptions while Jack Kemp kept the Bills moving. His 48-yard completion set up his own 1-yard quarterback sneak to put the game away in the fourth quarter.

1965 NFL WESTERN CONFERENCE CHAMPIONSHIP

Sunday, December 26, 1965 at Green Bay, Lambeau Field, attendance 50,484

BALTIMORE	7	3	0	0	0	—	10
GREEN BAY	0	0	7	3	3	—	13

SCORING Bal—Shinnick 25-yd fumble recovery return (Michaels PAT), Bal—FG Michaels 15 yds, GB—Hornung 1-yd run (Chandler PAT), GB—FG Chandler 22 yds, GB—FG Chandler 25 yds

TEAM	FD	YDS	RUSH	PASS	RTN	A-C-I	SACKED	PUNT	FUMB	PEN
Bal	9	175	47-143	32	39	12-5-0	1-8	8-41	1-1	3-39
GB	23	362	39-112	250	20	41-23-2	1-8	5-43	3-2	4-40

Baltimore played in the first two overtime postseason games in NFL; the second one did not end as memorably as the first. Unlike 1958, when Johnny Unitas and the Colts surged from behind to tie the game and force overtime, this time it was Zeke Bratkowski and the Packers doing the rallying. Both Unitas and backup Gary Cuozzo were injured coming in and Colts halfback Tom Matte took over at quarterback for the playoff. Green Bay's Bart Starr was injured on his first pass. Bratkowski led the Packers on a 15-play drive to tie it with 1:58 remaining. Don Chandler's kick in overtime won it.

1965 NFL CHAMPIONSHIP

Sunday, January 2, 1966 at Green Bay, Lambeau Field, attendance 50,777

CLEVELAND	9	3	0	0	—	12
GREEN BAY	7	6	7	3	—	23

SCORING GB—Dale 47-yd pass from Starr (Chandler PAT), Cle—Collins 17-yd pass from Ryan (PAT failed), Cle—FG Groza 24 yds, GB—FG Chandler 15 yds, GB—FG Chandler 23 yds, Cle—FG Groza 28 yds, GB—Hornung 13-yd run (Chandler PAT), GB—FG Chandler 29 yds

TEAM	FD	YDS	RUSH	PASS	RTN	A-C-I	SACKED	PUNT	FUMB	PEN
Cle	8	161	18-64	97	11	18-8-2	18	4-46	0-0	3-35
GB	21	332	47-204	128	19	19-10-1	19	3-38	0-0	2-20

CLEVELAND

RUSHING

	ATT	YDS	LNG	TD
Jim Brown	12	50	15	0
Frank Ryan	3	9	8	0

RECEIVING

	NO	YDS	LNG	TD
Jim Brown	3	44	30	0
Gary Collins	3	41	17	1

PASSING

	PA	PC	YDS	TD	IN
Frank Ryan	18	8	115	1	2

GREEN BAY

RUSHING

	ATT	YDS	LNG	TD
Paul Hornung	18	105	34	1
Jim Taylor	27	96	8	0

RECEIVING

	NO	YDS	LNG	TD
Boyd Dowler	5	59	18	0
Carroll Dale	2	60	47	1

PASSING

	PA	PC	YDS	TD	IN
Bart Starr	18	10	147	1	1

An NFL championship game stretched into a new calendar year for the first time and the reward was a quagmire in Green Bay. Freezing rain followed snow, turning the field into thick mud. The conditions would have seemed to favor Jim Brown, but the Packers controlled the ball, running 47 times. Cleveland got off just 36 plays total (18 running, 18 passing). With Bart Starr coming off an injury, Paul Hornung rushed for 105 yards and Jim Taylor ran for 96. Still, Green Bay's big play of the first half was Starr's 47-yard scoring pass to Carroll Dale. The Browns also got a first quarter touchdown pass from Frank Ryan. Don Chandler kicked 3 field goals and Taylor handled most of the heavy second-half lifting to bury the Browns.

1965 AFL CHAMPIONSHIP

Sunday, December 26, 1965 at San Diego, Balboa Stadium, attendance 30,361

BUFFALO BILLS	0	14	6	3	—	23
SAN DIEGO CHARGERS	0	0	0	0	—	0

SCORING Buf—Warlick 18-yd pass from Kemp (Gogolak PAT), Buf—Byrd 74-yd punt return (Gogolak PAT), Buf—FG Gogolak 11 yds, Buf—FG Gogolak 39 yds, Buf—FG Gogolak 32 yds

TEAM	FD	YDS	RUSH	PASS	RTN	A-C-I	SACKED	PUNT	FUMB	PEN
Buf	23	260	36-108	152	123	20-9-1	2-15	4-46	1-0	2-21
SD	12	223	27-104	119	12	25-12-2	5-45	7-41	1-0	3-41

BUFFALO BILLS

RUSHING

	ATT	YDS	LNG	TD
Wray Carlton	16	63	8	0
Billy Joe	16	35	11	0

RECEIVING

	NO	YDS	LNG	TD
Bo Roberson	3	88	49	0
Ernie Warlick	3	35	18	1

PASSING

	PA	PC	YDS	TD	IN
Jack Kemp	19	8	155	1	1

SAN DIEGO CHARGERS

RUSHING

	ATT	YDS	LNG	TD
Paul Lowe	12	57	47	0
John Hadl	8	24	8	0

RECEIVING

	NO	YDS	LNG	TD
Lance Alworth	4	82	25	0
Paul Lowe	3	2	2	0

PASSING

	PA	PC	YDS	TD	IN
John Hadl	23	11	140	0	2
Don Breaux	2	1	24	0	0

San Diego had dominated Buffalo during two regular-season wins, but the Bills used blitzes, stunts, and an unusual three-man line to thoroughly confuse San Diego for the title. The Chargers had the AFL yardage leaders in rushing, passing, and receiving, but running back Paul Lowe, quarterback John Hadl, and flanker Lance Alworth were all held in check. Buffalo took the early lead on Jack Kemp's touchdown pass to Ernie Warlick. A 74-yard return by Butch Byrd gave the Bills a 14–0 lead. Buffalo settled for 3 Pete Gogolak field goals in the second half, but that was plenty. The Chargers never got past Buffalo's 24. The Bills won their second straight AFL title, beating San Diego both times and holding them scoreless for seven consecutive quarters in championship games.

1966 NFL CHAMPIONSHIP

Sunday, January 1, 1967 at Dallas, Cotton Bowl, attendance 74,152

GREEN BAY	14	7	7	6	—	34
DALLAS	14	3	3	7	—	27

SCORING GB—Pitts 17-yd pass from Starr (Chandler PAT), GB—Grabowski 18-yd fumble return (Chandler PAT), Dal—Reeves 3-yd run (Villanueva PAT), Dal—Perkins 23-yd run (Villanueva PAT), GB—Dale 51-yd pass from Starr (Chandler PAT), Dal—FG Villanueva 11 yds, Dal—FG Villanueva 32 yds, GB—Dowler 16-yd pass from Starr (Chandler PAT), GB—McGee 28-yd pass from Starr (PAT blocked), Dal—Clarke 68-yd pass from Meredith (Villanueva PAT)

TEAM	FD	YDS	RUSH	PASS	RTN	A-C-I	SACKED	PUNT	FUMB	PEN
GB	19	367	24-102	265	0	28-19-0	5-39	4-40	1-1	2-23
Dal	23	418	40-187	231	-9	31-15-1	2-7	4-32	3-1	6-29

GREEN BAY

RUSHING

	ATT	YDS	LNG	TD
Elijah Pitts	12	66	32	0
Jim Taylor	10	37	8	0

RECEIVING

	NO	YDS	LNG	TD
Carroll Dale	5	128	51	1
Jim Taylor	5	23	16	0
Marv Fleming	3	50	24	0

PASSING

	PA	PC	YDS	TD	IN
Bart Starr	28	19	304	4	0

DALLAS

RUSHING

	ATT	YDS	LNG	TD
Don Perkins	17	108	23	1
Dan Reeves	17	47	6	1

RECEIVING

	NO	YDS	LNG	TD
Dan Reeves	4	77	40	0
Pettis Norman	4	30	12	0
Frank Clarke	3	102	68	1

PASSING

	PA	PC	YDS	TD	IN
Don Meredith	31	15	238	1	1

The first of the epic Green Bay–Dallas postseason confrontations came down to the final minute. The Packers scored quickly to open the game as Bart Starr connected with Elijah Pitts for a touchdown. Green Bay immediately got in the end zone again on a fumble on the ensuing kickoff. The Cowboys came right back and tied the score before the end of the first quarter. Three Starr touchdown passes in the second half seemed to seal the game, but a blocked extra point and Frank Clarke's 68-yard scoring catch made the lead only a touchdown. An interference call on Tom Brown gave the Cowboys the ball at the 2, but Brown atoned for the mistake by intercepting Don Meredith with 28 seconds left to send the Packers to Super Bowl I.

1966 AFL CHAMPIONSHIP

Sunday, January 1, 1967 at Buffalo, War Memorial Stadium, attendance 42,080

KANSAS CITY CHIEFS	7	10	0	14	—	31
BUFFALO BILLS	7	0	0	0	—	7

SCORING KC—Arbanas 29-yd pass from Dawson (Mercer PAT), Buf—Dubenion 69-yd pass from Kemp (Lusteg PAT), KC—Taylor 29-yd pass from Dawson (Mercer PAT), KC—FG Mercer 22 yds, KC—Garrett 1-yd run (Mercer PAT), KC—Garrett 18-yd run (Mercer PAT)

TEAM	FD	YDS	RUSH	PASS	RTN	A-C-I	SACKED	PUNT	FUMB	PEN
KC	14	277	33-113	164	135	24-16-0	9-63	6-42	1-0	4-40
Buf	9	255	13-40	215	16	27-12-2	4-38	8-39	3-2	3-23

KANSAS CITY CHIEFS

RUSHING

	ATT	YDS	LNG	TD
Mike Garrett	13	39	18	2
Curtis McClinton	11	38	10	0

RECEIVING

	NO	YDS	LNG	TD
Otis Taylor	5	78	29	1
Chris Burford	4	76	45	0
Mike Garrett	4	16	11	0

PASSING

	PA	PC	YDS	TD	IN
Len Dawson	24	16	227	2	0

BUFFALO BILLS

RUSHING

	ATT	YDS	LNG	TD
Wray Carlton	9	31	10	0
Bobby Burnett	3	6	3	0

RECEIVING

	NO	YDS	LNG	TD
Bobby Burnett	6	127	42	0
Elbert Dubenion	2	79	69	1

PASSING

	PA	PC	YDS	TD	IN
Jack Kemp	27	12	253	1	2

The two-time defending champion Bills were moving the ball, seemingly on their way to forging a tie in the second quarter in the championship game. Johnny Robinson picked off Jack Kemp in the end zone and returned the ball 72 yards to set up a field goal that put the Chiefs ahead, 17–7. The Bills never got that close to the end zone again. Mike Garrett scored twice in the fourth quarter and Len Dawson finished with 2 touchdown throws and 227 yards passing.

Nine sacks of Dawson by the Bills hardly mattered as the Chiefs controlled the ball and moved on to play in the first showdown with the NFL.

1967 NFL WESTERN CONFERENCE CHAMPIONSHIP
Saturday, December 23, 1967 at Milwaukee, County Stadium, attendance 49,861

LOS ANGELES	7	0	0	0	—	7
GREEN BAY	0	14	7	7	—	**28**

SCORING LA—Casey 29-yd pass from Gabriel (Gossett PAT), GB—Williams 46-yd run (Chandler PAT), GB—Dale 17-yd pass from Starr (Chandler PAT), GB—Mercein 6-yd run (Chandler PAT), GB—Williams 2-yd run (Chandler PAT)

TEAM	FD	YDS	RUSH	PASS	RTN	A-C-I	SACKED	PUNT	FUMB	PEN
LA	12	217	28-75	142	24	31-11-1	5-44	6-39	0-0	3-25
GB	20	374	45-163	211	64	23-17-1	1-11	5-33	3-3	7-44

GB-Carroll Dale 109C

For the first time, an NFL conference playoff was on the schedule as opposed to being held because of a tie. The Rams, with the same 11–2–1 record as the Colts, reached the playoff on a tiebreaker system instead of a game. The Rams had the early lead and momentum against the Packers, but special teams problems—starting with a blocked field goal—pushed the momentum Green Bay's way. The Packers controlled the game after the second quarter.

1967 NFL EASTERN CONFERENCE CHAMPIONSHIP
Sunday, December 24, 1967 at Dallas, Cotton Bowl, attendance 70,786

CLEVELAND	0	7	0	7	—	14
DALLAS	14	10	21	7	—	**52**

SCORING Dal—Baynham 3-yd pass from Meredith (Villanueva PAT), Dal—Perkins 4-yd run (Villanueva PAT), Dal—Hayes 86-yd pass from Meredith (Villanueva PAT), Dal—FG Villanueva 10 yds, Cle—Morin 13-yd pass from Ryan (Groza PAT), Dal—Baynham 1-yd run (Villanueva PAT), Dal—Perkins 1-yd run (Villanueva PAT), Dal—C. Green 60-yd interception return (Villanueva PAT), Dal—Baynham 1-yd run (Villanueva PAT), Cle—Warfield 75-yd pass from Ryan (Groza PAT)

TEAM	FD	YDS	RUSH	PASS	RTN	A-C-I	SACKED	PUNT	FUMB	PEN
Cle	15	322	27-159	163	11	30-14-1	5-31	7-40	0-0	2-18
Dal	22	401	46-178	223	215	15-11-1	1-2	2-45	2-1	2-10

Dal-Bob Hayes 144C

Dallas lost Dan Reeves early in the game, but his replacement, Craig Baynham scored 3 touchdowns. Don Perkins ran for 2 scores. Don Meredith completed 10 of 12 throws for 212 yards and 2 touchdowns, including an 86-yarder to Bob Hayes in the second quarter that made it 21–0 and signaled it would be a Cowboys day.

1967 AFL CHAMPIONSHIP
Sunday, December 31, 1967 at Oakland, Oakland-Alameda County Stadium, attendance 53,330

HOUSTON	0	0	0	7	—	7
OAKLAND	3	14	10	13	—	**40**

SCORING Oak—FG Blanda 37 yds, Oak—Dixon 69-yd run (Blanda PAT), Oak—Kocourek 17-yd pass from Lamonica (Blanda PAT), Oak—Lamonica 1-yd run (Blanda PAT), Oak—FG Blanda 40 yds, Oak—FG Blanda 42 yds, Hou—Frazier 5-yd pass from Beathard (Wittenborn PAT), Oak—FG Blanda 36 yds, Oak—Miller 12-yd pass from Lamonica (Blanda PAT)

TEAM	FD	YDS	RUSH	PASS	RTN	A-C-I	SACKED	PUNT	FUMB	PEN
Hou	11	146	22-38	108	0	35-15-1	3-34	11-39	4-2	7-45
Oak	18	364	48-263	101	49	26-10-0	1-10	4-44	0-0	4-69

HOUSTON				
RUSHING	ATT	YDS	LNG	TD
Hoyle Granger	14	19	11	0
Woody Campbell	6	15	6	0
RECEIVING	NO	YDS	LNG	TD
Charley Frazier	7	81	17	1
Alvin Reed	4	60	25	0
PASSING	PA	PC	YDS	TD	IN
Pete Beathard	35	15	142	1	1

OAKLAND				
RUSHING	ATT	YDS	LNG	TD
Hewritt Dixon	21	144	69	1
Pete Banaszak	15	116	23	0
RECEIVING	NO	YDS	LNG	TD
Bill Miller	3	32	12	1
Billy Cannon	2	31	21	0
PASSING	PA	PC	YDS	TD	IN
Daryle Lamonica	24	10	111	2	0
George Blanda	2	0	0	0	0

The Oilers couldn't run the ball and they couldn't stop the Raiders from running. Oakland rushed for 263 yards on the day, with the biggest gainer coming in the second quarter on a 69-yard scoring run by Hewritt Dixon. The most important plays of the game, however, came at the end of the first half and the start of the second. Daryle Lamonica found Dave Kocoureck alone in the end zone for

a touchdown with 18 seconds left in the second quarter to make it 17–0. Houston fumbled the second-half kickoff and a few plays later it was 24–0. George Blanda kicked 4 field goals to help the Raiders, whose 13–1 regular season was the best ever in the American Football League, capture their first AFL title.

1967 NFL CHAMPIONSHIP
Sunday, December 31, 1967 at Green Bay, Lambeau Field, attendance 50,861

DALLAS	0	10	0	7	—	17
GREEN BAY	7	7	0	7	—	**21**

SCORING GB—Dowler 8-yd pass from Starr (Chandler PAT), GB—Dowler 46-yd pass from Starr (Chandler PAT), Dal—Andrie 7-yd fumble return (Villanueva PAT), Dal—FG Villanueva 21 yds, Dal—Rentzel 50-yd pass from Reeves (Villanueva PAT), GB—Starr 1-yd run (Chandler PAT)

TEAM	FD	YDS	RUSH	PASS	RTN	A-C-I	SACKED	PUNT	FUMB	PEN
Dal	11	192	33-92	100	0	26-11-1	1-9	8-39	3-1	7-58
GB	18	195	32-80	115	34	24-14-0	8-76	8-29	3-2	2-10

DALLAS				
RUSHING	ATT	YDS	LNG	TD
Don Perkins	17	51	8	0
Dan Reeves	13	42	11	0
RECEIVING	NO	YDS	LNG	TD
Bob Hayes	3	16	10	0
Dan Reeves	3	11	7	0
Lance Rentzel	2	61	50	1
PASSING	PA	PC	YDS	TD	IN
Don Meredith	25	10	59	0	1
Dan Reeves	1	1	50	1	0

GREEN BAY				
RUSHING	ATT	YDS	LNG	TD
Donny Anderson	18	35	9	0
Chuck Mercein	6	20	8	0
RECEIVING	NO	YDS	LNG	TD
Boyd Dowler	4	77	43	2
Donny Anderson	4	44	17	0
PASSING	PA	PC	YDS	TD	IN
Bart Starr	24	14	191	2	0

The thermometer read 13 below zero and the wind chill was measured at minus 46 in the last game Vince Lombardi ever coached in Green Bay. The Ice Bowl started with Green Bay leading, 14–0. Bart Starr found Boyd Dowler for touchdowns in each of the first two quarters, but a vicious hit on Starr caused a fumble that Cowboy George Andrie took 7 yards for a score. Dan Reeves, who'd been knocked out of the game a week earlier, threw a 50-yard halfback option pass to Lance Rentzel to give Dallas its first lead of the game to open the fourth quarter. An epic 12-play, 68-yard drive consumed 4:37, leaving just 13 seconds, no timeouts, and third-and-goal from the 1. A field goal would have tied it, but Starr pushed across the goal line to win one of the most memorable games in history.

1968 NFL EASTERN CONFERENCE CHAMPIONSHIP
Saturday, December 21, 1968 at Cleveland, Cleveland Stadium, attendance 81,497

DALLAS	7	3	3	7	—	20
CLEVELAND	3	7	14	7	—	**31**

SCORING Cle—FG Cockroft 38 yds, Dal—Howley 44-yd fumble return (Clark PAT), Dal—FG Clark 16 yds, Cle—Kelly 45-yd pass from Nelsen (Cockroft PAT), Cle—Lindsey 27-yd interception return (Cockroft PAT), Cle—Kelly 35-yd run (Cockroft PAT), Dal—FG Clark 47 yds, Cle—Green 2-yd run (Cockroft PAT), Dal—Garrison 2-yd pass from Morton (Clark PAT)

TEAM	FD	YDS	RUSH	PASS	RTN	A-C-I	SACKED	PUNT	FUMB	PEN
Dal	13	286	30-86	200	6	32-12-4	5	5-41	1-0	4-20
Cle	12	280	30-102	178	58	25-13-1	25	7-36	1-1	6-40

The Browns used 5 turnovers by the favored Cowboys to pull off the upset. Don Meredith threw just 9 passes but 3 interceptions. One resulted in a Dale Lindsey return that broke a third quarter tie, and another pick three plays later led to Leroy Kelly's second touchdown of the day.

1968 NFL WESTERN CONFERENCE CHAMPIONSHIP
Sunday, December 22, 1968 at Baltimore, Memorial Stadium, attendance 60,238

MINNESOTA	0	0	0	14	—	14
BALTIMORE	0	14	3	7	—	**24**

SCORING Bal—Mitchell 3-yd pass from Morrall (Michaels PAT), Bal—Mackey 49-yd pass from Morrall (Michaels PAT), Bal—Curtis 60-yd fumble return (Michaels PAT), Min—Martin 1-yd pass from Kapp (Cox PAT), Bal—FG Michaels 33 yds, Min—Brown 7-yd pass from Kapp (Cox PAT)

TEAM	FD	YDS	RUSH	PASS	RTN	A-C-I	SACKED	PUNT	FUMB	PEN
Min	22	351	28-85	266	18	44-26-2	21	6-40	2-1	4-30
Bal	15	295	27-50	245	55	22-13-1	35	5-40	1-1	2-28

Bal-Willie Richardson 148C

The Vikings outgained the Colts (351–295) and Joe Kapp had more completions than Earl Morrall had attempts (26–22), but Morrall

averaged 21 yards per completion. The longest play was John Mackey's dazzling 49-yard catch and run that helped the Colts jump to a 21–0 lead in the third quarter.

1968 AFL WESTERN DIVISION CHAMPIONSHIP
Sunday, December 22, 1968 at Oakland, Oakland-Alameda County Stadium, attendance 53,605

KANSAS CITY	0	6	0	0	—	6
OAKLAND	21	7	0	13	—	**41**

SCORING Oak—Biletnikoff 24-yd pass from Lamonica (Blanda PAT), Oak—Wells 23-yd pass from Lamonica (Blanda PAT), Oak—Biletnikoff 44-yd pass from Lamonica (Blanda PAT), KC—FG Stenerud 10 yds, KC—FG Stenerud 8 yds, Oak—Biletnikoff 54-yd pass from Lamonica (Blanda PAT), Oak—Wells 35-yd pass from Lamonica (Blanda PAT), Oak—FG Blanda 41 yds, Oak—FG Blanda 40 yds

TEAM	FD	YDS	RUSH	PASS	RTN	A-C-I	SACKED	PUNT	FUMB	PEN
KC	13	312	24-70	242	-9	36-17-4	1-11	6-50	2-0	4-49
Oak	22	454	30-118	336	65	39-19-0	1-11	5-45	1-0	1-5

KC-Otis Taylor 117C; Oak-Fred Biletnikoff 180C, Daryle Lamonica 347P

Daryle Lamonica threw 5 touchdown passes, with the average scoring strike covering 31 yards in a rout of the Chiefs. Fred Biletnikoff hauled in 3 of them and Warren Wells had 2. Lamonica threw for 347 yards on just 19 completions with Biletnikoff hauling in 7 for 180 yards.

1968 NFL CHAMPIONSHIP
Sunday, December 29, 1968 at Cleveland, Municipal Stadium, attendance 78,410

BALTIMORE	0	17	7	10	—	**34**
CLEVELAND	0	0	0	0	—	0

SCORING Bal—FG Michaels 28 yds, Bal—Matte 1-yd run (Michaels PAT), Bal—Matte 12-yd run (Michaels PAT), Bal—Matte 2-yd run (Michaels PAT), Bal—FG Michaels 10 yds, Bal—Brown 4-yd run (Michaels PAT)

TEAM	FD	YDS	RUSH	PASS	RTN	A-C-I	SACKED	PUNT	FUMB	PEN
Bal	22	353	39-184	169	26	25-11-1	0-0	2-37	2-1	3-15
Cle	12	173	22-56	117	4	32-13-2	4-34	5-33	2-1	7-54

BALTIMORE RUSHING	ATT	YDS	LNG	TD
Tom Matte	17	88	12	3
Jerry Hill	11	60	13	0

RECEIVING	NO	YDS	LNG	TD
Willie Richardson	3	78	38	0
John Mackey	2	34	26	0

PASSING	PA	PC	YDS	TD	IN
Earl Morrall	25	11	169	0	1

CLEVELAND RUSHING	ATT	YDS	LNG	TD
Leroy Kelly	13	28	5	0
Charlie Harraway	6	26	8	0

RECEIVING	NO	YDS	LNG	TD
Charlie Harraway	4	40	16	0
Milt Morin	3	41	22	0

PASSING	PA	PC	YDS	TD	IN
Bill Nelsen	26	11	132	0	2
Frank Ryan	6	2	19	0	0

The Colts allowed just over 10 points per game and they surpassed that in the NFL Championship Game, sending the Browns to just the third shutout in franchise history. The Colts proved their 13–1 regular season was no fluke. Cleveland had a chance to take the early lead, but Bubba Smith blocked Don Cockcroft's field goal try in the first quarter. Instead the Colts got on the board first on a field goal by Lou Michaels. Tom Matte followed with 2 touchdown runs before halftime. The Colts continued to pound the Browns in the second half while holding Leroy Kelly, professional football's only 1,000-yard rusher in 1968, to 28 yards on 13 carries. If they did this to the mighty Browns, what would the Colts do to the Jets in Super Bowl III?

1968 AFL CHAMPIONSHIP
Sunday, December 29, 1968 at New York, Shea Stadium, attendance 62,627

OAKLAND	0	10	3	10	—	23
NY JETS	10	3	7	7	—	**27**

SCORING NYJ—Maynard 14-yd pass from Namath (J. Turner PAT), NYJ—FG J. Turner 33 yds, Oak—Biletnikoff 29-yd pass from Lamonica (Blanda PAT), NYJ—FG J. Turner 36 yds, Oak—FG Blanda 26 yds, Oak—FG Blanda 9 yds, NYJ—Lammons 20-yd pass from Namath (J. Turner PAT), Oak—FG Blanda 20 yds, Oak—Banaszak 5-yd run (Blanda PAT), NYJ—Maynard 6-yd pass from Namath (J. Turner PAT)

TEAM	FD	YDS	RUSH	PASS	RTN	A-C-I	SACKED	PUNT	FUMB	PEN
Oak	18	443	19-50	393	49	47-20-0	2-8	7-43	2-0	2-23
NYJ	25	400	34-144	256	8	49-19-1	2-10	10-42	1-1	4-26

OAKLAND RUSHING	ATT	YDS	LNG	TD
Hewritt Dixon	8	42	28	0
Pete Banaszak	3	6	5	1

RECEIVING	NO	YDS	LNG	TD
Fred Biletnikoff	7	190	57	1
Hewritt Dixon	5	48	23	0
Billy Cannon	4	69	36	0
Warren Wells	3	83	40	0

PASSING	PA	PC	YDS	TD	IN
Daryle Lamonica	47	20	401	1	0

NY JETS RUSHING	ATT	YDS	LNG	TD
Matt Snell	19	71	32	0
Emerson Boozer	11	51	15	0

RECEIVING	NO	YDS	LNG	TD
George Sauer	7	70	25	0
Don Maynard	6	118	52	2
Pete Lammons	4	52	20	1

PASSING	PA	PC	YDS	TD	IN
Joe Namath	49	19	266	3	1

Somewhere between the *Heidi* Game and Joe Namath's "guarantee," the Jets pulled out a remarkable win against the Raiders to win their only AFL title. New York's most devastating loss of the season had come in Oakland, where an improbable Raiders comeback was blocked from the airwaves by a children's movie. This time NBC stayed with the game and the Jets benefited from a late Oakland miscue. The Raiders were at the Jets 12 with two minutes left when rookie Charlie Smith missed a Daryle Lamonica lateral and New York linebacker Ralph Baker recovered it. The Jets, who had taken the lead on Namath's touchdown pass to Don Maynard with 7:47 remaining in the fourth quarter, ran out the clock. Lamonica, whose 401 yards passing put Oakland at the doorstep, accepted the blame.

1969 AFL DIVISION CHAMPIONSHIP
Saturday, December 20, 1969 at New York, Shea Stadium, attendance 62,977

KANSAS CITY	0	3	3	7	—	**13**
NY JETS	3	0	0	3	—	6

SCORING NYJ—FG J. Turner 27 yds, KC—FG Stenerud 23 yds, KC—FG Stenerud 25 yds, NYJ—FG J. Turner 7 yds, KC—Richardson 19-yd pass from Dawson (Stenerud PAT)

TEAM	FD	YDS	RUSH	PASS	RTN	A-C-I	SACKED	PUNT	FUMB	PEN
KC	14	276	30-99	177	56	27-12-0	2-24	6-34	0-0	5-63
NYJ	19	235	22-87	148	10	40-14-3	2-16	5-37	1-1	3-15

Harsh wind and cold limited two excellent aerial attacks, but passing still made the difference. Joe Namath threw 3 interceptions while Len Dawson excelled late in the fourth quarter. After the Jets tied the game, 6–6, Dawson hit Otis Taylor with a 51-yard completion. Dawson connected with Gloster Richardson on the next play for the game's only touchdown.

1969 AFL DIVISION CHAMPIONSHIP
Sunday, December 21, 1969 at Oakland, Oakland-Alameda County Stadium, attendance 53,539

HOUSTON	0	0	0	7	—	7
OAKLAND	28	7	14	7	—	**56**

SCORING Oak—Biletnikoff 13-yd pass from Lamonica (Blanda PAT), Oak—Atkinson 57-yd interception return (Blanda PAT), Oak—Sherman 24-yd pass from Lamonica (Blanda PAT), Oak—Biletnikoff 31-yd pass from Lamonica (Blanda PAT), Oak—Smith 60-yd pass from Lamonica (Blanda PAT), Oak—Sherman 23-yd pass from Lamonica (Blanda PAT), Oak—Cannon 3-yd pass from Lamonica (Blanda PAT), Hou—Reed 8-yd pass from Beathard (Gerela PAT), Oak—Hubbard 4-yd run (Blanda PAT)

TEAM	FD	YDS	RUSH	PASS	RTN	A-C-I	SACKED	PUNT	FUMB	PEN
Hou	14	197	19-28	169	4	46-18-3	6-40	11-41	3-2	5-48
Oak	17	412	37-110	302	99	22-14-3	1-7	5-42	3-1	7-63

Oak-Charlie Smith 103C

Daryle Lamonica threw 6 touchdown passes in a rout of the Oilers. Houston made it easy, throwing an interception and fumbling on the first plays of consecutive possessions. The Raiders led 28–0 in the first quarter and held a 49–0 lead before Houston finally scored.

1969 NFL WESTERN CONFERENCE CHAMPIONSHIP
Saturday, December 27, 1969 at Bloomington, MN, Metropolitan Stadium, attendance 47,900

LOS ANGELES	7	10	0	3	—	20
MINNESOTA	7	0	7	9	—	**23**

SCORING LA—Klein 3-yd pass from Gabriel (Gossett PAT), Min—Osborn 1-yd run (Cox PAT), LA—FG Gossett 20 yds, LA—Truax 2-yd pass from Gabriel (Gossett PAT), Min—Osborn 1-yd run (Cox PAT), LA—FG Gossett 27 yds, Min—Kapp 2-yd run (Cox PAT), Min—Safety, Gabriel tackled in end zone by Eller

TEAM	FD	YDS	RUSH	PASS	RTN	A-C-I	SACKED	PUNT	FUMB	PEN
LA	19	255	30-126	129	27	32-22-1	3-21	3-37	1-0	4-37
Min	18	275	29-97	178	35	19-12-2	2-18	3-39	3-1	4-36

Joe Kapp led the Vikings to a late touchdown, passing for 40 yards and running in untouched from the 2. Fred Cox's PAT broke the tie

and Carl Eller broke LA's back moments later by sacking Roman Gabriel for a safety. The Rams had taken a 17–7 lead to end the first half, but Kapp and company came right back with a touchdown to start the third quarter.

1969 NFL EASTERN CONFERENCE CHAMPIONSHIP

Sunday, December 28, 1969 at Dallas, Cotton Bowl, attendance 69,321

CLEVELAND	7	10	7	14	—	38
DALLAS	0	0	7	7	—	14

SCORING Cle—Scott 2-yd run (Cockroft PAT), Cle—Morin 6-yd pass from Nelsen (Cockroft PAT), Cle—FG Cockroft 29 yds, Cle—Scott 2-yd run (Cockroft PAT), Dal—Morton 2-yd run (M. Clark PAT), Cle—Kelly 1-yd run (Cockroft PAT), Cle—Sumner 88-yd interception return (Cockroft PAT), Dal—Rentzel 5-yd pass from Staubach (M. Clark PAT)

TEAM	FD	YDS	RUSH	PASS	RTN	A-C-I	SACKED	PUNT	FUMB	PEN
Cle	22	344	35-97	247	134	29-20-0	1-7	1-34	1-0	6-50
Dal	17	217	25-100	117	0	29-12-2	3-19	5-36	2-1	6-51

Bill Nelsen passed for 184 of his 219 yards in the first half as Cleveland built a 17–0 lead. It was 24–0 before Dallas finally scored and the Browns stopped the next two drives with interceptions of Craig Morton, the second going 88 yards the other way in the arms of Walt Summer.

1969 AFL CHAMPIONSHIP

Sunday, January 4, 1970 at Oakland, Oakland-Alameda County Stadium, attendance 53,564

KANSAS CITY	0	7	3	—	17
OAKLAND	7	0	0	—	7

SCORING Oak—Smith 3-yd run (Blanda PAT), KC—Hayes 1-yd run (Stenerud PAT), KC—Holmes 5-yd run (Stenerud PAT), KC—FG Stenerud 22 yds

TEAM	FD	YDS	RUSH	PASS	RTN	A-C-I	SACKED	PUNT	FUMB	PEN
KC	13	207	39-86	121	118	17-7-0	1-8	8-43	5-4	5-43
Oak	18	233	28-79	154	-1	45-17-4	4-37	6-49	1-0	5-45

KANSAS CITY

RUSHING	ATT	YDS	LNG	TD
Wendell Hayes	8	35	12	1
Mike Garrett	7	19	12	0

RECEIVING	NO	YDS	LNG	TD
Otis Taylor	3	62	35	0
Robert Holmes	2	16	23	0

PASSING	PA	PC	YDS	TD	IN
Len Dawson	17	7	129	0	0

OAKLAND

RUSHING	ATT	YDS	LNG	TD
Hewritt Dixon	12	36	9	0
Charlie Smith	12	31	9	1

RECEIVING	NO	YDS	LNG	TD
Charlie Smith	8	86	23	0
Rod Sherman	3	45	15	0

PASSING	PA	PC	YDS	TD	IN
Daryle Lamonica	39	15	167	0	3
George Blanda	6	2	24	0	1

The rivalry between the Chiefs and Raiders reached a fever pitch in the last game between AFL teams before the two professional leagues merged. The Raiders beat the Chiefs twice during the season—and had won eight of the previous nine meetings, including playoffs—so it wasn't surprising when Oakland took the early lead in the championship game. Kansas City came back and tied the score. Kansas City put together a 94-yard drive to break the tie in the third quarter. Dawson completed just 7 passes all day, but his 35-yard completion to Otis Taylor from his own end zone on third-and-long was the turning point of the drive. The Chiefs became the first AFL representative to go to two Super Bowls.

1969 NFL CHAMPIONSHIP

Sunday, January 4, 1970 at Bloomington, MN, Metropolitan Stadium, attendance 46,503

CLEVELAND	0	0	0	7	—	7
MINNESOTA	14	10	3	0	—	27

SCORING Min—Kapp 7-yd run (Cox PAT), Min—Washington 75-yd pass from Kapp (Cox PAT), Min—FG Cox 30 yds, Min—Osborn 20-yd run (Cox PAT), Min—FG Cox 32 yds, Cle—Collins 3-yd pass from Nelsen (Cockroft PAT)

TEAM	FD	YDS	RUSH	PASS	RTN	A-C-I	SACKED	PUNT	FUMB	PEN
Cle	14	268	21-97	171	21	33-17-2	2-10	3-33	2-1	1-5
Min	18	383	45-222	161	1	13-7-0	1-8	3-41	0-0	3-33

CLEVELAND

RUSHING	ATT	YDS	LNG	TD
Leroy Kelly	15	80	22	0
Bo Scott	6	17	5	0

RECEIVING	NO	YDS	LNG	TD
Bo Scott	5	56	35	0
Gary Collins	5	43	16	1
Paul Warfield	4	47	18	0

PASSING	PA	PC	YDS	TD	IN
Bill Nelsen	33	17	181	1	2

MINNESOTA

RUSHING	ATT	YDS	LNG	TD
Dave Osborn	18	108	20	1
Joe Kapp	8	57	19	1

RECEIVING	NO	YDS	LNG	TD
Gene Washington	3	120	75	1
John Henderson	2	17	9	0

PASSING	PA	PC	YDS	TD	IN
Joe Kapp	13	7	169	1	0

It was quintessential playoff weather at Metropolitan Stadium, slick field, snow piled high on the sidelines, game temperature of 8 degrees. The Vikings took advantage right away. Gene Washington got open when the defender slipped and Joe Kapp connected for a 33-yard play that set up the first touchdown. On the next possession, the pair teamed up again, this time for 75 yards and a 14–0 lead. Minnesota then kept the ball on the ground, churning up 222 yards on 45 carries. Dave Osborn ran for 108 yards, including a 20-yard touchdown shortly before the half. The Vikings never turned the ball over on the way to clinching their first Super Bowl berth.

1970 AFC DIVISIONAL PLAYOFF

Saturday, December 26, 1970 at Baltimore, Memorial Stadium, attendance 51,127

CINCINNATI	0	0	0	0	—	0
BALTIMORE	7	3	0	7	—	17

SCORING Bal—Jefferson 45-yd pass from Unitas (O'Brien PAT), Bal—FG O'Brien 44 yds, Bal—Hinton 53-yd pass from Unitas (O'Brien PAT)

TEAM	FD	YDS	RUSH	PASS	RTN	A-C-I	SACKED	PUNT	FUMB	PEN
Cin	7	139	22-63	76	6	21-8-1	3-17	8-39	1-0	1-5
Bal	16	299	47-170	129	28	17-6-0	2-16	6-38	0-0	6-63

Bal-Norm Bulaich 116R

Baltimore never allowed Cincinnati into field-goal range and held the club to 139 total yards. The young Bengals, playing in their first playoff game in just their third season of existence, held their own on defense. The game was 10–0 in the fourth quarter when Johnny Unitas connected with Eddie Hinton, who dodged his way to a backbreaking 53-yard score.

1970 NFC DIVISIONAL PLAYOFF

Saturday, December 26, 1970 at Dallas, Cotton Bowl, attendance 73,167

DETROIT	0	0	0	0	—	0
DALLAS	3	0	0	2	—	5

SCORING Dal—FG Clark 26 yds, Dal—Safety, Landry tackled in end zone by Andrie and Pugh

TEAM	FD	YDS	RUSH	PASS	RTN	A-C-I	SACKED	PUNT	FUMB	PEN
Det	7	156	27-76	80	52	20-7-1	3-12	8-49	3-2	0-0
Dal	14	231	50-209	22	36	18-4-1	1-16	8-45	0-0	6-47

Dal-Duane Thomas 135R

Mike Clark's field goal was the only scoring until late in the fourth quarter. Dallas, which rushed for 209 yards, methodically moved the ball to the 1. On fourth-and-goal, Duane Thomas stumbled and the ball went to Detroit. George Andrie tacked Greg Landry for a safety and Mel Renfro picked off Landry in Dallas territory to win the final Cowboys game at the Cotton Bowl.

1970 AFC DIVISIONAL PLAYOFF

Sunday, December 27, 1970 at Oakland, Oakland-Alameda County Stadium, attendance 54,401

MIAMI	0	7	0	7	—	14
OAKLAND	0	7	7	7	—	21

SCORING Mia—Warfield 16-yd pass from Griese (Yepremian PAT), Oak—Biletnikoff 22-yd pass from Lamonica (Blanda PAT), Oak—Brown 50-yd pass interception return (Blanda PAT), Oak—Sherman 82-yd pass from Lamonica (Blanda PAT), Mia—Richardson 7-yd pass from Griese (Yepremian PAT)

TEAM	FD	YDS	RUSH	PASS	RTN	A-C-I	SACKED	PUNT	FUMB	PEN
Mia	16	242	33-118	124	-5	27-13-1	3-31	5-39	2-0	0-0
Oak	12	307	36-120	187	49	16-8-0	0-0	4-32	4-2	4-30

Like Cincinnati, Miami was playing in its first playoff game. Unlike the Bengals, though, the fifth-season Dolphins took a lead and benefited from the host's mistakes. The Raiders fumbled twice at key times, but Oakland broke the tie on Willie Brown's 50-yard return of a

Bob Griese pass. An 82-yard Daryle Lamonica bomb to Rod Sherman was crucial to holding the lead.

1970 NFC DIVISIONAL PLAYOFF

Sunday, December 27, 1970 at Bloomington, MN, Metropolitan Stadium, attendance 41,050

SAN FRANCISCO	7	3	0	7	—	17
MINNESOTA	7	0	0	7	—	14

SCORING Min—Krause 22-yd fumble recovery (Cox PAT), SF—Witcher 24-yd pass from Brodie (Gossett PAT), SF—FG Gossett 40 yds, SF—Brodie 1-yd run (Gossett PAT), Min—Washington 24-yd pass from Cuozzo (Cox PAT)

TEAM	FD	YDS	RUSH	PASS	RTN	A-C-I	SACKED	PUNT	FUMB	PEN
SF	14	289	38-96	193	74	32-16-0	1-8	8-34	5-3	3-37
Min	14	241	30-117	124	0	27-9-2	3-22	7-39	3-2	1-5

Fumbles by both teams led to first-half points, but John Brodie snuck into the end zone to give San Francisco a 10-point lead with 1:20 remaining in the game. Minnesota's touchdown in the waning seconds couldn't change the outcome as the 49ers won their first NFL playoff game 20 years after joining the league.

1970 AFC CHAMPIONSHIP

Sunday, January 3, 1971 at Baltimore, Memorial Stadium, attendance 56,368

OAKLAND	0	3	7	7	—	17
BALTIMORE	3	7	10	7	—	27

SCORING Bal—FG O'Brien 16 yds, Bal—Bulaich 2-yd run (O'Brien PAT), Oak—FG Blanda 48 yds, Oak—Biletnikoff 38-yd pass from Blanda (Blanda PAT), Bal—FG O'Brien 23 yds, Bal—Bulaich 11-yd run (O'Brien PAT), Oak—Wells 15-yd pass from Blanda (Blanda PAT), Bal—Perkins 68-yd pass from Unitas (O'Brien PAT)

TEAM	FD	YDS	RUSH	PASS	RTN	A-C-I	SACKED	PUNT	FUMB	PEN
Oak	16	336	22-107	229	10	36-18-3	5-48	5-40	1-1	2-20
Bal	18	363	38-126	237	17	30-11-0	3-8	6-45	0-0	2-10

OAKLAND				
RUSHING	ATT	YDS	LNG	TD
Hewritt Dixon	10	51	14	0
Charlie Smith	9	44	20	0
RECEIVING	NO	YDS	LNG	TD
Warren Wells	5	108	37	1
Fred Biletnikoff	5	92	38	1
PASSING	PA	PC	YDS	TD	IN
George Blanda	32	17	271	2	3
Daryle Lamonica	4	1	6	0	0

BALTIMORE				
RUSHING	ATT	YDS	LNG	TD
Norm Bulaich	22	71	11	2
Tom Nowatzke	8	32	11	0
RECEIVING	NO	YDS	LNG	TD
Eddie Hinton	5	115	43	0
Roy Jefferson	3	36	13	0
Ray Perkins	2	80	68	1
PASSING	PA	PC	YDS	TD	IN
John Unitas	30	11	245	1	0

Every time the Colts tried to pull away, the Raiders made it close. The Colts took a 10–0 lead in the second quarter, but the Raiders got a 48-yard field goal from 43-year-old George Blanda before the half. Blanda, who also threw for 271 yards, connected with Fred Biletnikoff to tie the game. After the Colts regained a 10-point lead later in the third quarter, Blanda found Warren Wells for a touchdown. Two more end zone passes by Blanda were intercepted before Johnny Unitas ended the theatrics with a 68-yard scoring pass to Ray Perkins. The Colts, who moved from the NFL to the AFC after the merger, became the first team from the newly-formed conference to advance to the Super Bowl.

1970 NFC CHAMPIONSHIP

Sunday, January 3, 1971 at San Francisco, Kezar Stadium, attendance 59,625

DALLAS	0	3	14	0	—	17
SAN FRANCISCO	3	0	7	0	—	10

SCORING SF—FG Gossett 16 yds, Dal—FG Clark 21 yds, Dal—Thomas 13-yd run (Clark PAT), Dal—Garrison 5-yd pass from Morton (Clark PAT), SF—Witcher 26-yd pass from Brodie (Gossett PAT)

TEAM	FD	YDS	RUSH	PASS	RTN	A-C-I	SACKED	PUNT	FUMB	PEN
Dal	22	319	51-229	90	31	22-7-0	2-11	6-40	4-1	7-75
SF	15	307	19-61	246	5	40-19-2	2-16	5-41	1-0	5-51

DALLAS				
RUSHING	ATT	YDS	LNG	TD
Duane Thomas	27	143	21	1
Walt Garrison	17	71	17	0
RECEIVING	NO	YDS	LNG	TD
Walt Garrison	3	51	23	1
Duane Thomas	2	24	14	0
PASSING	PA	PC	YDS	TD	IN
Craig Morton	22	7	101	1	0

SAN FRANCISCO				
RUSHING	ATT	YDS	LNG	TD
Ken Willard	13	42	7	0
Doug Cunningham	5	14	6	0
RECEIVING	NO	YDS	LNG	TD
Gene Washington	6	88	42	0
Doug Cunningham	4	34	14	0
Bob Windsor	3	70	29	0
PASSING	PA	PC	YDS	TD	IN
John Brodie	40	19	262	1	2

The Cowboys, who had reached the postseason every year since 1966, finally won a championship game. Rookie Duane Thomas ran for 143 yards on 27 carries and in the third quarter scored the game's first touchdown. Walt Garrison followed, hauling in a 5-yard scoring pass from Craig Morton. John Brodie brought the 49ers within a touchdown, but the Dallas defense intercepted him twice and controlled the final quarter. The final NFL game at Kezar Stadium marked the second consecutive week that the Cowboys closed out a stadium's NFL existence with a win.

1971 AFC DIVISIONAL PLAYOFF

Saturday, December 25, 1971 at Kansas City, Municipal Stadium, attendance 45,822

MIAMI	0	10	7	7	0	3	—	27
KANSAS CITY	10	0	7	7	0	0	—	24

SCORING KC—FG Stenerud 24 yds, KC—Podolak 7-yd pass from Dawson (Stenerud PAT), Mia—Csonka 1-yd run (Yepremian PAT), Mia—FG Yepremian 14 yds, KC—Otis 1-yd run (Stenerud PAT), Mia—Kiick 1-yd run (Yepremian PAT), KC—Podolak 3-yd run (Stenerud PAT), Mia—Fleming 5-yd pass from Griese (Yepremian PAT), Mia—FG Yepremian 37 yds

TEAM	FD	YDS	RUSH	PASS	RTN	A-C-I	SACKED	PUNT	FUMB	PEN
Mia	22	407	43-144	263	31	35-20-2	0-0	6-40	1-0	5-26
KC	23	451	44-213	238	18	26-18-2	1-8	2-51	3-2	6-44

Mia-Paul Warfield 140C; KC-Wendell Hayes 100R, Ed Podolak 110C, Elmo Wright 104C

It was the Christmas Day that seemed like it would never end. The Chiefs and Dolphins traded scores all day as Miami tied it at 24–24 with 1:36 left in regulation. Usually reliable Chiefs kicker Jan Stenerud missed a field goal as time expired and then missed again in overtime. Garo Yepremian, no good on a long field goal try in the first overtime, connected midway through the second to win the longest game in NFL history.

1971 NFC DIVISIONAL PLAYOFF

Saturday, December 25, 1971 at Bloomington, MN, Metropolitan Stadium, attendance 47,307

DALLAS	3	3	14	0	—	20
MINNESOTA	0	3	0	9	—	12

SCORING Dal—FG Clark 26 yds, Min—FG Cox 27 yds, Dal—FG Clark 44 yds, Dal—Thomas 13-yd run (Clark PAT), Dal—Hayes 9-yd pass from Staubach (Clark PAT), Min—Safety, Page tackled Staubach in end zone, Min—Voigt 6-yd pass from Cuozzo (Cox PAT)

TEAM	FD	YDS	RUSH	PASS	RTN	A-C-I	SACKED	PUNT	FUMB	PEN
Dal	10	183	39-98	85	106	14-10-0	14	7-37	0-0	2-10
Min	17	311	26-101	210	6	38-19-4	0-0	4-44	1-1	2-18

The first NFL game ever on Christmas Day saw 13 Dallas points set up by Minnesota turnovers. A 24-yard punt return by Charlie Waters late in the third quarter put the Cowboys in Vikings territory again. Roger Staubach connected with Lance Alworth for 30 yards on third-and-15. Bob Hayes caught the scoring pass that made it 20–3.

1971 AFC DIVISIONAL PLAYOFF

Sunday, December 26, 1971 at Cleveland, Municipal Stadium, attendance 70,734

BALTIMORE	0	14	3	3	—	20
CLEVELAND	0	0	3	0	—	3

SCORING Bal—Nottingham 1-yd run (O'Brien PAT), Bal—Nottingham 7-yd run (O'Brien PAT), Cle—FG Cockroft 14 yds, Bal—FG O'Brien 42 yds, Bal—FG O'Brien 15 yds

TEAM	FD	YDS	RUSH	PASS	RTN	A-C-I	SACKED	PUNT	FUMB	PEN
Bal	16	271	43-128	143	106	21-13-1	0-0	6-37	2-2	5-43
Cle	11	165	24-69	96	97	27-12-3	5-35	5-41	6-2	3-16

Cleveland's first drive ended with Baltimore's Rex Kern stealing the ball from receiver Fair Hooker after a 39-yard gain. The next drive ended with a blocked field goal. The Colts followed with drives of 92

and 15 yards that each culminated with Don Nottingham touchdown runs. Cleveland had 11 first downs against 6 fumbles, 5 sacks allowed, and 3 interceptions.

1971 NFC DIVISIONAL PLAYOFF
Sunday, December 26, 1971 at San Francisco, Candlestick Park, attendance 45,327

WASHINGTON	7	3	3	7	—	20
SAN FRANCISCO	0	3	14	7	—	24

SCORING Was—Smith 5-yd pass from Kilmer (Knight PAT), SF—FG Gossett 23 yds, Was—FG Knight 40 yds, SF—G. Washington 78-yd pass from Brodie (Gossett PAT), SF—Windsor 2-yd pass from Brodie (Gossett PAT), Was—FG Knight 36 yds, SF—Hoskins recovered fumble in end zone (Gossett PAT), Was—Brown 16-yd pass from Kilmer (Knight PAT)

TEAM	FD	YDS	RUSH	PASS	RTN	A-C-I	SACKED	PUNT	FUMB	PEN
Was	13	192	39-99	93	58	27-11-1	1-13	5-46	3-2	4-55
SF	11	285	39-112	173	30	19-10-0	1-3	10-34	0-0	3-41

A blocked San Francisco punt set up the only touchdown of the first half, but a blocked Washington field goal kept the game 10–3 at the half. After the 49ers stopped the Redskins on fourth down at the San Francisco 11, Gene Washington got free for a 78-yard touchdown from John Brodie. An interception and a poor snap on a punt led to 49ers' touchdowns.

1971 AFC CHAMPIONSHIP
Sunday, January 2, 1972 at Miami, Orange Bowl, attendance 76,622

BALTIMORE	0	0	0	0	—	0
MIAMI	7	0	7	7	—	21

SCORING Mia—Warfield 75-yd pass from Griese (Yepremian PAT), Mia—Anderson 62-yd interception return (Yepremian PAT), Mia—Csonka 5-yd run (Yepremian PAT)

TEAM	FD	YDS	RUSH	PASS	RTN	A-C-I	SACKED	PUNT	FUMB	PEN
Bal	16	302	29-93	209	20	36-20-3	3-15	3-45	1-0	2-20
Mia	13	286	35-144	142	93	8-4-1	2-16	6-43	0-0	1-12

BALTIMORE				
RUSHING	ATT	YDS	LNG	TD
Don McCauley	15	50	8	0
Don Nottingham	11	33	9	0
RECEIVING	NO	YDS	LNG	TD
Eddie Hinton	6	98	27	0
Don Nottingham	4	26	25	0
PASSING	PA	PC	YDS	TD	IN
John Unitas	36	20	224	0	3

MIAMI				
RUSHING	ATT	YDS	LNG	TD
Jim Kiick	18	66	15	0
Larry Csonka	15	63	9	1
RECEIVING	NO	YDS	LNG	TD
Paul Warfield	2	125	75	1
Howard Twilley	2	33	20	0
PASSING	PA	PC	YDS	TD	IN
Bob Griese	8	4	158	1	1

The Colts were outgained by the Dolphins in total yards (320–286), but the Dolphins, hosting a playoff game for the first time in franchise history, dominated the clock and the scoreboard. Although Bob Griese threw just 8 passes (4 completions), he connected with Paul Warfield on passes of 75 and 50 yards. Miami held a 7–0 lead until the third quarter, when a Johnny Unitas pass was batted away from one defender and into the arms of another. Dick Anderson took the interception 62 yards for a 14–0 lead. Larry Csonka finished off the Colts with a 5-yard touchdown run in the fourth quarter.

1971 NFC CHAMPIONSHIP
Sunday, January 2, 1972 at Dallas, Texas Stadium, attendance 63,409

SAN FRANCISCO	0	0	3	0	—	3
DALLAS	0	7	0	7	—	14

SCORING Dal—Hill 1-yd run (Clark PAT), SF—FG Gossett 28 yds, Dal—D. Thomas 2-yd run (Clark PAT)

TEAM	FD	YDS	RUSH	PASS	RTN	A-C-I	SACKED	PUNT	FUMB	PEN
SF	9	239	16-61	178	10	30-14-3	1-6	6-38	0-0	1-12
Dal	16	244	46-172	72	36	18-9-0	6-31	6-45	2-1	2-30

SAN FRANCISCO				
RUSHING	ATT	YDS	LNG	TD
Vic Washington	10	58	15	0
Ken Willard	6	3	5	0
RECEIVING	NO	YDS	LNG	TD
Gene Washington	4	88	37	0
Ted Kwalick	4	52	24	0
PASSING	PA	PC	YDS	TD	IN
John Brodie	30	14	184	0	3

DALLAS				
RUSHING	ATT	YDS	LNG	TD
Roger Staubach	8	55	12	0
Walt Garrison	14	52	7	0
RECEIVING	NO	YDS	LNG	TD
Billy Truax	2	43	22	0
Bob Hayes	2	22	13	0
PASSING	PA	PC	YDS	TD	IN
Roger Staubach	18	9	103	0	0

The first postseason game at Texas Stadium went like the last game at Kezar Stadium the year before: a Dallas win over San Francisco

for the NFC title. This time the Cowboys allowed just 3 points and 9 first downs. An interception by George Andrie gave the Cowboys first-and-goal at the 2. Calvin Hill scored the only touchdown of the first three quarters. San Francisco kicker Bruce Gossett kicked a field goal in the third quarter to make it 7–3, but the Cowboys finished off the 49ers with a 14-play, 80-yard drive climaxed by a Duane Thomas touchdown run.

1972 AFC DIVISIONAL PLAYOFF
Saturday, December 23, 1972 at Pittsburgh, Three Rivers Stadium, attendance 50,350

OAKLAND	0	0	0	7	—	7
PITTSBURGH	0	0	3	10	—	13

SCORING Pit—FG Gerela 18 yds, Pit—FG Gerela 29 yds, Oak—Stabler 30-yd run (Blanda PAT), Pit—Harris 60-yd pass from Bradshaw (Gerela PAT)

TEAM	FD	YDS	RUSH	PASS	RTN	A-C-I	SACKED	PUNT	FUMB	PEN
Oak	13	216	31-138	78	44	30-12-2	4-24	7-45	3-2	2-15
Pit	13	252	36-108	144	39	25-11-1	3-31	6-48	0-0	1-5

In 40 seasons as a franchise, the Steelers had played one playoff game and precious little had gone right for the organization. The Immaculate Reception changed all that. Pittsburgh led 3–0 in the third quarter and upped it to 6–0 in the fourth, but Ken Stabler ran 30 yards for a touchdown and a 7–6 lead with 1:13 left. Facing fourth-and-10 at their own 40, a Terry Bradshaw pass was deflected and caught on the run by Franco Harris, who went the last 42 yards for the unbelievable ending.

1972 NFC DIVISIONAL PLAYOFF
Saturday, December 23, 1972 at San Francisco, Candlestick Park, attendance 61,214

DALLAS	3	10	0	17	—	30
SAN FRANCISCO	7	14	7	0	—	28

SCORING SF—V. Washington 97-yd kickoff return (Gossett PAT), Dal—FG Fritsch 37 yds, SF—Schreiber 1-yd run (Gossett PAT), SF—Schreiber 1-yd run (Gossett PAT), Dal—FG Fritsch 45 yds, Dal—Alworth 28-yd pass from Morton (Fritsch PAT), SF—Schreiber 1-yd run (Gossett PAT), Dal—FG Fritsch 27 yds, Dal—Parks 20-yd pass from Staubach (Fritsch PAT), Dal—Sellers 10-yd pass from Staubach (Fritsch PAT)

TEAM	FD	YDS	RUSH	PASS	RTN	A-C-I	SACKED	PUNT	FUMB	PEN
Dal	22	402	31-165	237	14	41-20-2	5-33	6-42	4-3	3-35
SF	13	255	37-105	150	-1	22-12-2	0-0	6-37	5-1	7-56

Dal-Calvin Hill 125R, Billy Parks 136C

For the third straight year the Cowboys and 49ers met in the postseason; this result was even more painful for San Francisco. After Larry Schreiber scored his third touchdown to give the 49ers a 28–13 lead, Roger Staubach came off the bench to lead the Cowboys to a field goal, a Billy Parks touchdown with two minutes left, and, after Mel Renfro recovered the onsides kick, the winning score on a pass to Ron Sellers with 52 seconds remaining.

1972 AFC DIVISIONAL PLAYOFF
Sunday, December 24, 1972 at Miami, Orange Bowl, attendance 80,010

CLEVELAND	0	0	7	7	—	14
MIAMI	0	0	10	10	—	20

SCORING Mia—Babb 5-yd run with blocked punt (Yepremian PAT), Mia—FG Yepremian 40 yds, Cle—Phipps 5-yd run (Cockroft PAT), Mia—FG Yepremian 46 yds, Cle—Hooker 27-yd pass from Phipps (Cockroft PAT), Mia—Kiick 8-yd run (Yepremian PAT)

TEAM	FD	YDS	RUSH	PASS	RTN	A-C-I	SACKED	PUNT	FUMB	PEN
Cle	15	283	32-165	118	46	23-9-5	2-13	6-35	2-0	3-25
Mia	17	272	47-198	74	63	13-6-0	4-14	5-42	2-2	3-25

Miami's perfect season nearly ended on Christmas Eve. Mike Phipps led the Browns to a go-ahead score in the fourth quarter, but Earl Morrall took the ball with 8:11 to play and drove the Dolphins 80 yards. Morrall, with only 4 completions for 38 yards to that point, found Paul Warfield for 15 and 35 yards. Jim Kiick scored the deciding touchdown, but the final hero was Doug Swift, who ended Cleveland's comeback with an interception at the Miami 20.

1972 NFC DIVISIONAL PLAYOFF

Sunday, December 24, 1972 at Washington, RFK Stadium, attendance 53,140

GREEN BAY	0	3	0	0	— 3
WASHINGTON	0	10	0	6	— 16

SCORING GB—FG Marcol 17 yds, Was—Jefferson 32-yd pass from Kilmer (Knight PAT), Was—FG Knight 42 yds, Was—FG Knight 35 yds, Was—FG Knight 46 yds

TEAM	FD	YDS	RUSH	PASS	RTN	A-C-I	SACKED	PUNT	FUMB	PEN
GB	10	211	29-78	133	33	24-12-1	2-17	8-37	0-0	6-54
Was	13	232	36-138	94	34	14-7-0	1-6	6-47	1-1	4-30

Was-Larry Brown 101R

Coach George Allen's trademark special teams helped Washington earn its first playoff victory since 1943. Curt Knight kicked 3 field goals and Mike Bragg averaged 46.5 yards per punt. Larry Brown ran for 101 yards while Billy Kilmer threw for 100 yards and the day's only touchdown.

1972 AFC CHAMPIONSHIP

Sunday, December 31, 1972 at Pittsburgh, Three Rivers Stadium, attendance 50,350

MIAMI	0	7	7	7	— 21
PITTSBURGH	7	0	3	7	— 17

SCORING Pit—Mullins fumble recovery in end zone (Gerela PAT), Mia—Csonka 9-yd pass from Morrall (Yepremian PAT), Pit—FG Gerela 14 yds, Mia—Kiick 2-yd run (Yepremian PAT), Mia—Kiick 3-yd run (Yepremian PAT), Pit—Young 12-yd pass from Bradshaw (Gerela PAT)

TEAM	FD	YDS	RUSH	PASS	RTN	A-C-I	SACKED	PUNT	FUMB	PEN
Mia	19	314	49-193	121	11	16-10-1	0-0	4-36	0-0	2-19
Pit	13	250	26-128	122	33	20-10-2	2-15	4-51	2-0	4-30

MIAMI				
RUSHING	**ATT**	**YDS**	**LNG**	**TD**
Mercury Morris	16	76	27	0
Larry Csonka	24	68	11	0
Jim Kiick	8	12	3	2
RECEIVING	**NO**	**YDS**	**LNG**	**TD**
Marv Fleming	5	50	15	0
Paul Warfield	2	63	52	0
PASSING	**PA**	**PC**	**YDS**	**TD**	**IN**
Bob Griese	5	3	70	0	0
Earl Morrall	11	7	51	1	1

PITTSBURGH				
RUSHING	**ATT**	**YDS**	**LNG**	**TD**
Franco Harris	16	76	10	0
John Fuqua	8	47	24	0
RECEIVING	**NO**	**YDS**	**LNG**	**TD**
Al Young	4	54	25	1
Ron Shanklin	2	49	25	0
PASSING	**PA**	**PC**	**YDS**	**TD**	**IN**
Terry Bradshaw	10	5	80	1	2
Terry Hanratty	10	5	57	0	0

The AFC Championship Game featured one team coming off the Immaculate Reception and another trying to continue the Perfect Season. Something had to give and it turned out to be both starting quarterbacks. Pittsburgh's Terry Bradshaw was knocked out on a play in which he fumbled and the Steelers recovered in the end zone for a touchdown. With Pittsburgh leading in the third quarter, 10–7, Miami's Earl Morrall came out for Bob Griese. Griese completed 3 of 5 passes for 70 yards while leading the Dolphins on 2 touchdown drives—converting a fourth-down play on each. Bradshaw returned to throw a touchdown, but he was intercepted twice.

1972 NFC CHAMPIONSHIP

Sunday, December 31, 1972 at Washington, RFK Stadium, attendance 53,129

DALLAS	0	3	0	0	— 3
WASHINGTON	0	10	0	16	— 26

SCORING Was—FG Knight 18 yds, Was—Taylor 15-yd pass from Kilmer (Knight PAT), Dal—FG Fritsch 35 yds, Was—Taylor 45-yd pass from Kilmer (Knight PAT), Was—FG Knight 39 yds, Was—FG Knight 46 yds, Was—FG Knight 45 yds

TEAM	FD	YDS	RUSH	PASS	RTN	A-C-I	SACKED	PUNT	FUMB	PEN
Dal	8	169	21-96	73	-5	21-9-0	3-25	7-43	1-1	4-30
Was	16	316	44-122	194	10	18-14-0	0-0	4-36	2-1	4-38

DALLAS				
RUSHING	**ATT**	**YDS**	**LNG**	**TD**
Roger Staubach	5	59	29	0
Calvin Hill	9	22	7	0
RECEIVING	**NO**	**YDS**	**LNG**	**TD**
Ron Sellers	2	29	22	0
Walt Garrison	2	18	13	0
PASSING	**PA**	**PC**	**YDS**	**TD**	**IN**
Roger Staubach	20	9	98	0	0

WASHINGTON				
RUSHING	**ATT**	**YDS**	**LNG**	**TD**
Larry Brown	30	88	11	0
Charlie Harraway	11	19	5	0
RECEIVING	**NO**	**YDS**	**LNG**	**TD**
Charley Taylor	7	146	51	2
Charlie Harraway	3	13	7	0
PASSING	**PA**	**PC**	**YDS**	**TD**	**IN**
Billy Kilmer	18	14	194	2	0

Washington's defense slowly choked off the Dallas offense, allowing the Cowboys just a field goal in the first half and not permitting Dallas past midfield in the second half. Roger Staubach was held in check. He passed for just 98 yards while the Redskins sacked him 3 times. Washington's Charley Taylor caught 7 passes for 146 yards, including a 51-yarder from Billy Kilmer in the first quarter. They teamed up for touchdowns in the first and fourth quarters. Curt Knight, who had 4 field goals, kicked 3 of them in a Redskins 16-point fourth quarter. It was Washington's first victory in a championship game since 1942.

1973 AFC DIVISIONAL PLAYOFF

Saturday, December 22, 1973 at Oakland, Oakland-Alameda County Coliseum, attendance 50,094

PITTSBURGH	0	7	0	7	— 14
OAKLAND	7	3	13	10	— 33

SCORING Oak—Hubbard 1-yd run (Blanda PAT), Oak—FG Blanda 25 yds, Pit—B. Pearson 4-yd pass from Bradshaw (Gerela PAT), Oak—FG Blanda 31 yds, Oak—FG Blanda 22 yds, Oak—Brown 54-yd interception return (Blanda PAT), Oak—FG Blanda 10 yds, Pit—Lewis 26-yd pass from Bradshaw (Gerela PAT), Oak—Hubbard 1-yd run (Blanda PAT)

TEAM	FD	YDS	RUSH	PASS	RTN	A-C-I	SACKED	PUNT	FUMB	PEN
Pit	15	223	20-65	158	20	25-12-3	1-9	5-42	1-0	4-60
Oak	24	361	55-232	129	73	17-14-0	2-13	2-39	0-0	9-75

There was no repeat of the Immaculate Reception in Oakland in 1973. The Raiders ran the ball right down Pittsburgh's throat, rushing 55 times for 232 yards and embarking on 5 scoring drives of 57 yards or more. Oakland also picked off Pittsburgh's Terry Bradshaw 3 times. Willie Brown returned a third-quarter interception 54 yards for a score.

1973 NFC DIVISIONAL PLAYOFF

Saturday, December 22, 1973 at Bloomington, MN, Metropolitan Stadium, attendance 46,065

WASHINGTON	0	7	3	10	— 20
MINNESOTA	0	3	7	17	— 27

SCORING Min—FG Cox 19 yds, Was—L. Brown 3-yd run (Knight PAT), Min—B. Brown 2-yd run (Cox PAT), Was—FG Knight 52 yds, Was—FG Knight 42 yds, Min—Gilliam 28-yd pass from Tarkenton (Cox PAT), Min—Gilliam 6-yd pass from Tarkenton (Cox PAT), Was—Jefferson 28-yd pass from Kilmer (Knight PAT), Min—FG Cox 30 yds

TEAM	FD	YDS	RUSH	PASS	RTN	A-C-I	SACKED	PUNT	FUMB	PEN
Was	18	314	42-155	159	46	24-13-1	0-0	4-37	2-1	0-0
Min	17	359	34-141	218	29	28-16-1	1-4	6-32	2-1	2-9

Was-Larry Brown 115R

After a lackluster first half, the Vikings and Redskins traded points throughout the second half. Fran Tarkenton threw 2 touchdown passes to John Gilliam in the fourth quarter as Minnesota overcame a 13–10 deficit. Oscar Reed had the day's longest running play and catch to help carry the Vikings.

1973 AFC DIVISIONAL PLAYOFF

Sunday, December 23, 1973 at Miami, Orange Bowl, attendance 74,651

CINCINNATI	3	13	0	0	— 16
MIAMI	14	7	10	3	— 34

SCORING Mia—Warfield 13-yd pass from Griese (Yepremian PAT), Cin—FG Muhlmann 24 yds, Mia—Csonka 1-yd run (Yepremian PAT), Mia—Morris 4-yd run (Yepremian PAT), Cin—Craig 45-yd interception return (Muhlmann PAT), Cin—FG Muhlmann 46 yds, Cin—FG Muhlmann 12 yds, Mia—Mandich 7-yd pass from Griese (Yepremian PAT), Mia—FG Yepremian 50 yds, Mia—FG Yepremian 46 yds

TEAM	FD	YDS	RUSH	PASS	RTN	A-C-I	SACKED	PUNT	FUMB	PEN
Cin	11	194	20-97	97	71	27-14-1	3-16	7-36	0-0	2-19
Mia	27	400	52-241	159	25	19-11-2	0-0	2-49	2-1	1-5

Mia-Mercury Morris 106R

Three long touchdown drives built a 21–3 Miami lead in the second quarter, but Cincinnati's Neal Craig picked off Bob Griese and ran 45 yards for a touchdown. Two field goals cut it to 21–16 at the half. The Dolphins blanked the Bengals in the second half and rolled up 400 yards of offense.

1973 NFC DIVISIONAL PLAYOFF

Sunday, December 23, 1973 at Dallas, Texas Stadium, attendance 62,081

LOS ANGELES	0	6	0	10	— 16
DALLAS	14	3	0	10	— 27

SCORING Dal—Hill 3-yd run (Fritsch PAT), Dal—Pearson 4-yd pass from Staubach (Fritsch PAT), Dal—FG Fritsch 39 yds, LA—FG Ray 33 yds, LA—FG Ray 37 yds, LA—FG Ray

40 yds, LA—Baker 5-yd run (Ray PAT), Dal—Pearson 83-yd pass from Staubach (Fritsch PAT), Dal—FG Fritsch 12 yds

TEAM	FD	YDS	RUSH	PASS	RTN	A-C-I	SACKED	PUNT	FUMB	PEN
LA	11	192	30-93	99	57	24-7-1	5-34	5-44	2-2	2-20
Dal	15	298	45-162	136	5	16-8-2	7-44	7-47	2-2	5-44

The Rams turned the ball over to open consecutive drives at the start the game. Dallas turned both into short touchdown drives. The Rams held onto the ball and pulled within 17–16 in the fourth quarter. On third-and-13 from his own 17, Roger Staubach went deep and found Drew Pearson for a touchdown and the Cowboys held the lead.

1973 AFC CHAMPIONSHIP
Sunday, December 30, 1973 at Miami, Orange Bowl, attendance 74,384

OAKLAND	0	0	10	0	—	10
MIAMI	7	7	3	10	—	27

SCORING Mia—Csonka 11-yd run (Yepremian PAT), Mia—Csonka 2-yd run (Yepremian PAT), Oak—FG Blanda 21 yds, Mia—FG Yepremian 42 yds, Oak—Siani 25-yd pass from Stabler (Blanda PAT), Mia—FG Yepremian 27 yds, Mia—Csonka 2-yd run (Yepremian PAT)

TEAM	FD	YDS	RUSH	PASS	RTN	A-C-I	SACKED	PUNT	FUMB	PEN
Oak	15	236	26-107	129	0	23-15-1	0-0	2-51	1-0	3-35
Mia	21	292	53-266	26	39	6-3-1	1-8	1-39	1-0	3-26

OAKLAND
RUSHING	ATT	YDS	LNG	TD
Marv Hubbard	10	54	14	0
Charlie Smith	10	35	8	0

RECEIVING	NO	YDS	LNG	TD
Charlie Smith	5	43	14	0
Mike Siani	3	45	25	1

PASSING	PA	PC	YDS	TD	IN
Ken Stabler	23	15	129	1	1

MIAMI
RUSHING	ATT	YDS	LNG	TD
Larry Csonka	29	117	14	3
Mercury Morris	14	86	16	0

RECEIVING	NO	YDS	LNG	TD
Paul Warfield	1	27	27	0

PASSING	PA	PC	YDS	TD	IN
Bob Griese	6	3	34	0	1

Miami fullback Larry Csonka bulled his way for 117 yards and 3 touchdowns, scoring twice in the first half for a 14–0 lead and ending any Oakland hopes of a comeback with a 2-yard scoring run in the fourth quarter. Bob Griese needed to throw just 6 passes as the Dolphins ran the ball 53 times for 266 yards. Griese had more yards rushing than passing (39–34) and set up Miami's first touchdown with a 27-yard scramble. The Dolphins became the first team to reach the Super Bowl three straight seasons.

1973 NFC CHAMPIONSHIP
Sunday, December 30, 1973 at Dallas, Texas Stadium, attendance 59,668

MINNESOTA	3	7	7	10	—	27
DALLAS	0	0	10	0	—	10

SCORING Min—FG Cox 44 yds, Min—Foreman 5-yd run (Cox PAT), Dal—Richards 63-yd punt return (Fritsch PAT), Min—Gilliam 54-yd pass from Tarkenton (Cox PAT), Dal—FG Fritsch 17 yds, Min—Bryant 63-yd interception return (Cox PAT), Min—FG Cox 34 yds

TEAM	FD	YDS	RUSH	PASS	RTN	A-C-I	SACKED	PUNT	FUMB	PEN
Min	20	306	47-203	103	76	21-10-1	4-30	3-43	4-3	3-33
Dal	9	153	25-90	63	64	21-10-4	3-26	4-40	2-2	2-20

MINNESOTA
RUSHING	ATT	YDS	LNG	TD
Chuck Foreman	19	76	20	1
Oscar Reed	18	75	12	0

RECEIVING	NO	YDS	LNG	TD
Chuck Foreman	4	28	12	0
John Gilliam	2	63	54	1

PASSING	PA	PC	YDS	TD	IN
Fran Tarkenton	21	10	133	1	1

DALLAS
RUSHING	ATT	YDS	LNG	TD
Robert Newhouse	14	50	19	0
Roger Staubach	5	30	9	0

RECEIVING	NO	YDS	LNG	TD
Bob Hayes	2	25	15	0
Drew Pearson	2	24	19	0

PASSING	PA	PC	YDS	TD	IN
Roger Staubach	21	10	89	0	4

Minnesota doubled Dallas's total offense (306–153), but a lot of that had to do with two missing Cowboys. Without Calvin Hill, the home club's running game wasn't up to snuff. With injured "Mr. Cowboy"—defensive tackle Bob Lilly—on the bench, the Vikings ran at will up the middle. Chuck Foreman rushed for 76 yards and Oscar Reed for 75. Fran Tarkenton connected with John Gilliam on a 54-yard touchdown just after a Golden Richards punt return had cut Minnesota's lead to 10–7. Bobby Bryant snagged 2 of Roger Staubach's 4 interceptions. Brown's 63-yard return for a score iced the NFC title.

1974 AFC DIVISIONAL PLAYOFF
Saturday, December 21, 1974 at Oakland, Oakland-Alameda County Coliseum, attendance 52,817

MIAMI	7	3	6	10	—	26
OAKLAND	0	7	7	14	—	28

SCORING Mia—N. Moore 89-yd kickoff return (Yepremian PAT), Oak—C. Smith 31-yd pass from Stabler (Blanda PAT), Mia—FG Yepremian 33 yds, Oak—Biletnikoff 13-yd pass from Stabler (Blanda PAT), Mia—Warfield 16-yd pass from Griese (PAT blocked), Mia—FG Yepremian 46 yds, Oak—Branch 72-yd pass from Stabler (Blanda PAT), Mia—Malone 23-yd run (Yepremian PAT), Oak—Davis 8-yd pass from Stabler (Blanda PAT)

TEAM	FD	YDS	RUSH	PASS	RTN	A-C-I	SACKED	PUNT	FUMB	PEN
Mia	18	294	41-213	81	19	14-7-1	2-20	6-33	0-0	3-15
Oak	19	411	32-135	276	21	30-20-1	2-17	7-43	0-0	3-59

Mia-Larry Csonka 114R; Oak-Fred Biletnikoff 122C

The Raiders ended Miami's three-year run as AFC champions, but it wasn't easy. Ken Stabler threw his fourth touchdown pass of the day, connecting under pressure with triple-teamed Clarence Davis with 26 seconds left. His Sea of Hands catch was a fitting climax to a game that started with Nat Moore running back the opening kickoff 89 yards for a touchdown.

1974 NFC DIVISIONAL PLAYOFF
Saturday, December 21, 1974 at Bloomington, MN, Metropolitan Stadium, attendance 44,626

ST. LOUIS	0	7	0	7	—	14
MINNESOTA	0	7	16	7	—	30

SCORING StL—Thomas 13-yd pass from Hart (Bakken PAT), Min—Gilliam 16-yd pass from Tarkenton (Cox PAT), Min—FG Cox 37 yds, Min—N. Wright 20-yd fumble return (Cox PAT), Min—Gilliam 38-yd pass from Tarkenton (PAT failed), Min—Foreman 4-yd run (Cox PAT), StL—Metcalf 11-yd run (Bakken PAT)

TEAM	FD	YDS	RUSH	PASS	RTN	A-C-I	SACKED	PUNT	FUMB	PEN
SL	17	284	25-100	184	35	40-18-1	2-16	7-36	2-1	1-15
Min	19	363	42-197	166	21	23-13-2	1-3	5-38	0-0	4-39

Min-Chuck Foreman 114R

The Cardinals hadn't played a postseason game since 1948 and they played like it. The Vikings scored 30 successive points, 16 in a seven-minute span of the third quarter as nothing went right—or Wright, if you will—for St. Louis. Jeff Wright had an interception and then Nate Wright scooped up a fumble and ran 20 yards for a touchdown.

1974 AFC DIVISIONAL PLAYOFF
Sunday, December 22, 1974 at Pittsburgh, Three Rivers Stadium, attendance 48,321

BUFFALO	7	0	7	0	—	14
PITTSBURGH	3	26	0	3	—	32

SCORING Pit—FG Gerela 21 yds, Buf—Seymour 22-yd pass from Ferguson (Leypoldt PAT), Pit—Bleier 27-yd pass from Bradshaw (PAT blocked), Pit—Harris 1-yd run (Gerela PAT), Pit—Harris 4-yd run (PAT blocked), Pit—Harris 1-yd run (Gerela PAT), Buf—Simpson 3-yd pass from Ferguson (Leypoldt PAT), Pit—FG Gerela 22 yds

TEAM	FD	YDS	RUSH	PASS	RTN	A-C-I	SACKED	PUNT	FUMB	PEN
Buf	15	264	21-100	164	11	26-11-0	0-0	5-39	2-1	3-15
Pit	29	438	51-235	203	25	21-12-0	0-0	3-39	2-0	2-10

Everything worked perfectly for Pittsburgh in the second quarter, except for the extra points. Trailing Buffalo 7–3, the Steelers scored 4 touchdowns: 3 touchdown runs by Franco Harris and a 27-yard scoring pass from Terry Bradshaw to Rocky Bleier. Two Roy Gerela PATs were blocked, but it was still a 29–7 halftime lead.

1974 NFC DIVISIONAL PLAYOFF
Sunday, December 22, 1974 at Los Angeles, Memorial Coliseum, attendance 80,118

WASHINGTON	3	7	0	0	—	10
LOS ANGELES	7	0	3	9	—	19

SCORING LA—Klein 10-yd pass from Harris (Ray PAT), Was—FG Bragg 35 yds, Was—Denson 1-yd run (Bragg PAT), LA—FG Ray 37 yds, LA—FG Ray 26 yds, LA—Robertson 59-yd interception return (pass failed)

TEAM	FD	YDS	RUSH	PASS	RTN	A-C-I	SACKED	PUNT	FUMB	PEN
Was	13	218	27-49	169	55	30-13-3	1-8	5-45	3-3	1-5
LA	14	226	42-131	95	87	24-8-2	0-0	5-43	2-0	5-49

A defensive struggle was decided by a defensive player's touchdown. With the Rams leading in the fourth quarter, 13–10, and the Redskins nearing field-goal range, Isiah Robertson picked off Sonny Jurgensen and returned the ball 59 yards for the score. Washington's

only touchdown of the day had been set up by an interception of James Harris.

1974 AFC CHAMPIONSHIP

Sunday, December 29, 1974 at Oakland, Oakland-Alameda County Coliseum, attendance 53,515

PITTSBURGH	0	3	0	21	—	**24**
OAKLAND	3	0	7	3	—	13

SCORING Oak—FG Blanda 40 yds, Pit—FG Gerela 23 yds, Oak—Branch 38-yd pass from Stabler (Blanda PAT), Pit—Harris 8-yd run (Gerela PAT), Pit—Swann 6-yd pass from Bradshaw (Gerela PAT), Oak—FG Blanda 24 yds, Pit—Harris 21-yd run (Gerela PAT)

TEAM	FD	YDS	RUSH	PASS	RTN	A-C-I	SACKED	PUNT	FUMB	PEN
Pit	20	319	50-224	95	101	17-8-1	0-0	4-41	3-2	4-30
Oak	15	278	21-29	249	37	36-19-3	2-22	5-43	0-0	5-60

PITTSBURGH					OAKLAND				
RUSHING	ATT	YDS	LNG	TD	**RUSHING**	ATT	YDS	LNG	TD
Franco Harris	29	111	21	2	Clarence Davis	10	16	4	0
Rocky Bleier	18	98	23	0	Pete Banaszak	3	7	3	0
RECEIVING	NO	YDS	LNG	TD	**RECEIVING**	NO	YDS	LNG	TD
Larry Brown	2	37	23	0	Cliff Branch	9	186	43	1
Rocky Bleier	2	25	16	0	Bob Moore	4	32	12	0
PASSING	PA	PC	YDS	TD	IN	**PASSING**	PA	PC	YDS	TD	IN
Terry Bradshaw	17	8	95	1	1	Ken Stabler	36	19	271	1	3

The championship game was another tight Steelers–Raiders clash through three quarters, with Oakland holding a 10–3 lead at home. Pittsburgh tied the game early in the fourth quarter on an 8-yard touchdown run by Franco Harris. Jack Ham's interception set up the Steelers again and Terry Bradshaw connected with Lynn Swann for the lead. Ken Stabler moved the Raiders through the air—they had just 29 rushing yards on 21 carries—but Oakland had to settle for a George Blanda field goal. As Pittsburgh ran down the clock, Harris scored in the final minute to give the Steelers their first conference championship and send them to their first Super Bowl.

1974 NFC CHAMPIONSHIP

Sunday, December 29, 1974 at Bloomington, MN, Metropolitan Stadium, attendance 47,404

LOS ANGELES	0	3	0	7	—	10
MINNESOTA	0	7	0	7	—	**14**

SCORING Min—Lash 29-yd pass from Tarkenton (Cox PAT), LA—FG Ray 27 yds, Min—Osborn 1-yd run (Cox PAT), LA—Jackson 44-yd pass from Harris (Ray PAT)

TEAM	FD	YDS	RUSH	PASS	RTN	A-C-I	SACKED	PUNT	FUMB	PEN
LA	15	340	33-121	219	19	23-13-2	2-29	5-44	3-3	7-70
Min	18	269	47-164	105	39	20-10-1	2-18	6-39	5-2	2-20

LOS ANGELES					MINNESOTA				
RUSHING	ATT	YDS	LNG	TD	**RUSHING**	ATT	YDS	LNG	TD
Jim Bertelsen	14	65	11	0	Chuck Foreman	22	80	18	0
Lawrence McCutcheon	12	32	6	0	Dave Osborn	20	76	11	1
RECEIVING	NO	YDS	LNG	TD	**RECEIVING**	NO	YDS	LNG	TD
Jim Bertelsen	5	53	13	0	Stu Voigt	4	43	16	0
Harold Jackson	3	139	73	1	Jim Lash	2	40	29	1
PASSING	PA	PC	YDS	TD	IN	**PASSING**	PA	PC	YDS	TD	IN
James Harris	23	13	248	1	2	Fran Tarkenton	20	10	123	1	1

The first of four 1970s playoff clashes between the Rams and Vikings was a defensive battle. Minnesota held a 7–3 lead in the third quarter, but it looked like the Rams would take the lead when James Harris connected with a streaking Harold Jackson. Nate Wright forced the receiver out of bounds after 73 yards at the 2. Wally Hilgenberg intercepted Harris in the end zone on third down. Minnesota embarked on a 15-play drive that resulted in a 14–3 lead. After Harris and Jackson connected for a touchdown with 5:37 left, the Vikings maintained possession to gain their third trip to the Super Bowl.

1975 AFC DIVISIONAL PLAYOFF

Saturday, December 27, 1975 at Pittsburgh, Three Rivers Stadium, attendance 49,557

BALTIMORE	0	7	3	0	—	10
PITTSBURGH	7	0	7	14	—	**28**

SCORING Pit—Harris 8-yd run (Gerela PAT), Bal—Doughty 5-yd pass from Domres (Linhart PAT), Bal—FG Linhart 21 yds, Pit—Bleier 7-yd run (Gerela PAT), Pit—Bradshaw 2-yd run (Gerela PAT), Pit—Russell 93-yd fumble recovery return (Gerela PAT)

TEAM	FD	YDS	RUSH	PASS	RTN	A-C-I	SACKED	PUNT	FUMB	PEN
Bal	10	154	41-82	72	97	22-8-2	5-28	9-40	2-1	6-53
Pit	16	287	43-211	76	72	13-8-2	3-27	4-40	3-3	5-45

Pit-Franco Harris 153R

Pittsburgh's Steel Curtain defense limited Baltimore to 152 total yards. Each team completed only 8 passes, but the Steelers didn't need to throw. They ran for 211 yards, with Franco Harris rushing for 153 and the game's first touchdown. The Colts were deep in Pittsburgh territory in the fourth quarter when Andy Russell's 93-yard fumble return sealed the win.

1975 NFC DIVISIONAL PLAYOFF

Saturday, December 27, 1975 at Los Angeles, Memorial Coliseum, attendance 73,459

ST. LOUIS	0	9	7	7	—	23
LOS ANGELES	14	14	0	7	—	**35**

SCORING LA—Jaworski 5-yd run (Dempsey PAT), LA—Jack Youngblood 47-yd interception return (Dempsey PAT), LA—Simpson 65-yd interception return (Dempsey PAT), StL—Otis 2-yd run (PAT failed), LA—H. Jackson 66-yd pass from Jaworski (Dempsey PAT), StL—FG Bakken 29 yds, StL—M. Gray 11-yd pass from Hart (Bakken PAT), LA—Jessie 2-yd fumble recovery (Dempsey PAT), StL—Jones 3-yd run (Bakken PAT)

TEAM	FD	YDS	RUSH	PASS	RTN	A-C-I	SACKED	PUNT	FUMB	PEN
SL	22	363	27-95	268	6	41-22-3	2-23	6-43	3-2	6-70
LA	26	440	50-237	203	137	23-12-0	0-0	5-32	5-3	5-38

LA-Lawrence McCutcheon 202R

The Rams ran back 2 Jim Hart passes for touchdowns and later returned a fumble for a score. Even when St. Louis scored in the second quarter, the Rams blocked the extra point and then scored on their first play after the kickoff on a 66-yard pass from Ron Jaworski to Harold Jackson. The ground game was even more deadly as Lawrence McCutcheon rushed for 202 yards on 37 carries.

1975 AFC DIVISIONAL PLAYOFF

Sunday, December 28, 1975 at Oakland, Oakland-Alameda County Coliseum, attendance 53,030

CINCINNATI	0	7	7	14	—	28
OAKLAND	3	14	7	7	—	**31**

SCORING Oak—FG Blanda 27 yds, Oak—Siani 9-yd pass from Stabler (Blanda PAT), Cin—Fritts 1-yd run (Green PAT), Oak—Moore 8-yd pass from Stabler (Blanda PAT), Oak—Banaszak 6-yd run (Blanda PAT), Cin—Elliott 6-yd run (Green PAT), Oak—Casper 2-yd pass from Stabler (Blanda PAT), Cin—Joiner 25-yd pass from Anderson (Green PAT), Cin—Curtis 14-yd pass from Anderson (Green PAT)

TEAM	FD	YDS	RUSH	PASS	RTN	A-C-I	SACKED	PUNT	FUMB	PEN
Cin	17	258	25-97	161	41	27-17-0	5-40	6-36	1-0	5-37
Oak	27	358	51-173	185	64	23-17-1	1-14	1-38	1-1	7-64

The Raiders had 100 more yards of offense than the Bengals and held a 31–14 lead with 10 minutes left. They nearly lost. The Raiders hadn't had a turnover or even punted all afternoon until a fourth-quarter interception fueled a Cincinnati touchdown drive. Ray Guy's first punt was followed by another Ken Anderson touchdown pass. A Pete Banaszak fumble gave the Bengals the ball once more, but Oakland held on.

1975 NFC DIVISIONAL PLAYOFF

Sunday, December 28, 1975 at Bloomington, MN, Metropolitan Stadium, attendance 48,050

DALLAS	0	0	7	10	—	**17**
MINNESOTA	0	7	0	7	—	14

SCORING Min—Foreman 1-yd run (Cox PAT), Dal—Dennison 4-yd run (Fritsch PAT), Dal—FG Fritsch 24 yds, Min—McClanahan 1-yd run (Cox PAT), Dal—D. Pearson 50-yd pass from Staubach (Fritsch PAT)

TEAM	FD	YDS	RUSH	PASS	RTN	A-C-I	SACKED	PUNT	FUMB	PEN
Dal	19	356	42-131	225	18	29-17-0	5-21	6-39	4-1	4-30
Min	12	215	27-115	100	5	26-12-1	4-35	7-40	2-0	7-69

Dallas had outplayed Minnesota for most of the day, but the Cowboys trailed, 14–10, with 1:51 remaining. Roger Staubach converted with Drew Pearson on fourth-and-16, and then found him on a 50-yard heave with 24 seconds left for the winning score. Staubach's bomb, and all late-game desperation attempts to come, would bear the name Hail Mary.

1975 AFC CHAMPIONSHIP

Sunday, January 4, 1976 at Pittsburgh, Three Rivers Stadium, attendance 50,609

OAKLAND	0	0	0	10	—	10
PITTSBURGH	0	3	0	13	—	16

SCORING Pit—FG Gerela 36 yds, Pit—Harris 25-yd run (Gerela PAT), Oak—Siani 14-yd pass from Stabler (Blanda PAT), Pit—Stallworth 20-yd pass from Bradshaw (PAT failed), Oak—FG Blanda 41 yds

TEAM	FD	YDS	RUSH	PASS	RTN	A-C-I	SACKED	PUNT	FUMB	PEN
Oak	18	321	32-93	228	19	42-18-2	2-18	8-38	4-3	4-40
Pit	16	332	39-117	215	62	25-15-3	0-0	4-39	4-4	3-32

OAKLAND				
RUSHING	ATT	YDS	LNG	TD
Pete Banaszak	8	33	10	0
Marv Hubbard	10	30	5	0
RECEIVING	NO	YDS	LNG	TD
Mike Siani	5	80	23	1
Dave Casper	5	67	23	0
Cliff Branch	2	56	37	0
PASSING	PA	PC	YDS	TD	IN
Ken Stabler	42	18	246	1	2

PITTSBURGH				
RUSHING	ATT	YDS	LNG	TD
Franco Harris	27	79	25	1
Terry Bradshaw	2	22	16	0
RECEIVING	NO	YDS	LNG	TD
Franco Harris	5	58	22	0
Randy Grossman	4	36	14	0
PASSING	PA	PC	YDS	TD	IN
Terry Bradshaw	25	15	215	1	3

Neither Pittsburgh nor Oakland could do much offensively for most of the day on the icy field at Three Rivers Stadium. Three quarters had resulted in just a 3–0 Steelers lead. The teams suddenly combined for 21 points in six minutes, but Pittsburgh still held a 16–7 lead. The Raiders decided to kick a field goal—the last of George Blanda's 26-year career—with 17 seconds left. They recovered the onsides kick and then Ken Stabler found Cliff Branch for 37 yards, the longest offensive play of the day, but the receiver couldn't get out of bounds and the game ended with the ball on the 15 and no time left.

1975 NFC CHAMPIONSHIP

Sunday, January 4, 1976 at Los Angeles, Memorial Coliseum, attendance 88,919

DALLAS	7	14	13	3	—	37
LOS ANGELES	0	0	0	7	—	7

SCORING Dal—P. Pearson 18-yd pass from Staubach (Fritsch PAT), Dal—Richards 4-yd pass from Staubach (Fritsch PAT), Dal—P. Pearson 15-yd pass from Staubach (Fritsch PAT), Dal—P. Pearson 19-yd pass from Staubach (Fritsch PAT), Dal—FG Fritsch 40 yds, Dal—FG Fritsch 26 yds, LA—Cappelletti 1-yd run (Dempsey PAT), Dal—FG Fritsch 26 yds

TEAM	FD	YDS	RUSH	PASS	RTN	A-C-I	SACKED	PUNT	FUMB	PEN
Dal	24	441	50-195	246	68	28-18-1	0-0	4-35	1-0	5-59
LA	9	118	16-22	96	40	24-11-3	5-51	7-35	1-0	4-25

DALLAS				
RUSHING	ATT	YDS	LNG	TD
Robert Newhouse	16	64	12	0
Roger Staubach	7	54	15	0
RECEIVING	NO	YDS	LNG	TD
Preston Pearson	7	123	27	3
Drew Pearson	5	46	13	0
PASSING	PA	PC	YDS	TD	IN
Roger Staubach	26	16	220	4	1
Clint Longley	2	2	26	0	0

LOS ANGELES				
RUSHING	ATT	YDS	LNG	TD
Ron Jaworski	2	12	7	0
Lawrence McCutcheon	11	10	6	0
RECEIVING	NO	YDS	LNG	TD
Ron Jessie	4	52	18	0
Lawrence McCutcheon	3	39	14	0
PASSING	PA	PC	YDS	TD	IN
Ron Jaworski	22	11	147	0	0
James Harris	2	0	0	0	1

Dallas dominated the Rams in Los Angeles, taking a 21–0 lead before halftime and scoring 34 points before the Rams broke up the shutout in the fourth quarter. Roger Staubach threw 4 touchdowns and 220 yards. Preston Pearson had 7 catches for 123 yards and 3 touchdowns and Drew Pearson caught 5 for 46 yards. Dallas rolled up 441 total yards to 118 for LA. The Rams were held to just 22 yards rushing a week after piling up 237 against the Cardinals. Lawrence McCutcheon, who'd run for 202 against St. Louis, had 11 carries for 10 yards against the Cowboys.

1976 AFC DIVISIONAL PLAYOFF

Saturday, December 18, 1976 at Oakland, Oakland-Alameda County Coliseum, attendance 53,045

NEW ENGLAND	7	0	14	0	—	21
OAKLAND	3	7	0	14	—	24

SCORING NE—A. Johnson 1-yd run (Smith PAT), Oak—FG Mann 40 yds, Oak—Biletnikoff 31-yd pass from Stabler (Mann PAT), NE—Francis 26-yd pass from Grogan (Smith PAT), NE—Phillips 3-yd run (Smith PAT), Oak—van Eeghen 1-yd run (Mann PAT), Oak—Stabler 1-yd run (Mann PAT)

TEAM	FD	YDS	RUSH	PASS	RTN	A-C-I	SACKED	PUNT	FUMB	PEN
NE	23	331	49-164	167	13	24-12-2	0-0	3-44	1-1	10-83
Oak	20	282	24-81	201	71	32-19-0	4-32	5-38	1-1	11-93

Oak-Fred Biletnikoff 137C

Both teams were penalized plenty—Oakland had 11 for 93 yards and New England 10 for 83—but an illegal motion penalty killed the last Patriots drive and flags for pass interference and roughing the passer kept alive the deciding 68-yard Raiders drive. Ken Stabler's 1-yard run with 10 seconds left completed a comeback from a 21–10 deficit in the third quarter.

1976 NFC DIVISIONAL PLAYOFF

Saturday, December 18, 1976 at Bloomington, MN, Metropolitan Stadium, attendance 47,221

WASHINGTON	3	0	3	14	—	20
MINNESOTA	14	7	14	0	—	35

SCORING Min—Voigt 18-yd pass from Tarkenton (Cox PAT), Was—FG Moseley 47 yds, Min—S. White 27-yd pass from Tarkenton (Cox PAT), Min—Foreman 2-yd run (Cox PAT), Min—Foreman 30-yd run (Cox PAT), Was—FG Moseley 35 yds, Min—S. White 9-yd pass from Tarkenton (Cox PAT), Was—Grant 12-yd pass from Kilmer (Moseley PAT), Was—Jefferson 3-yd pass from Kilmer (Moseley PAT)

TEAM	FD	YDS	RUSH	PASS	RTN	A-C-I	SACKED	PUNT	FUMB	PEN
Was	19	365	18-75	290	80	49-26-2	1-8	6-33	0-0	7-57
Min	21	384	46-221	163	12	22-12-2	1-7	6-46	2-0	5-30

Min-Chuck Foreman 105R, Brent McClanahan 101R

The Vikings did everything right against Washington. On an almost balmy 40-degree December day in Minnesota, the Vikes ran the ball at will, starting with a 41-yard run by Brent McClanahan on the game's opening play. Both Chuck Foreman and McClanahan surpassed 100 yards rushing as Minnesota built a 35–6 lead in the third quarter.

1976 AFC DIVISIONAL PLAYOFF

Sunday, December 19, 1976 at Baltimore, Memorial Stadium, attendance 60,020

PITTSBURGH	9	17	0	14	—	40
BALTIMORE	7	0	0	7	—	14

SCORING Pit—Lewis 76-yd pass from Bradshaw (PAT failed), Pit—FG Gerela 45 yds, Bal—Carr 17-yd pass from Jones (Linhart PAT), Pit—Harrison 1-yd run (Gerela PAT), Pit—Swann 29-yd pass from Bradshaw (Gerela PAT), Pit—FG Gerela 25 yds, Pit—Swann 11-yd pass from Bradshaw (Gerela PAT), Bal—Leaks 1-yd run (Linhart PAT), Pit—Harrison 10-yd run (Mansfield PAT)

TEAM	FD	YDS	RUSH	PASS	RTN	A-C-I	SACKED	PUNT	FUMB	PEN
Pit	29	526	40-225	301	50	24-19-0	1-7	1-33	2-1	12-88
Bal	12	170	23-71	99	11	25-11-2	5-45	4-41	0-0	7-59

Pit-Franco Harris 132R, Frank Lewis 103C

Terry Bradshaw hit Frank Lewis for a 76-yard touchdown pass on the third play of the game. Bradshaw threw 2 touchdowns to Lynn Swann and Reggie Harrison ran for another 2. Franco Harris rushed for 132 of Pittsburgh's 526 total yards. A single-engine plane crashed into Memorial Stadium's upper grandstand right after the game. No one was hurt.

1976 NFC DIVISIONAL PLAYOFF

Sunday, December 19, 1976 at Dallas, Texas Stadium, attendance 62,436

LOS ANGELES	0	7	0	7	—	14
DALLAS	3	7	0	2	—	12

SCORING Dal—FG Herrera 44 yds, LA—Haden 4-yd run (Dempsey PAT), Dal—Laidlaw 1-yd run (Herrera PAT), LA—McCutcheon 1-yd run (Dempsey PAT), Dal—Safety, Jensen tackled R. Jackson in end zone

TEAM	FD	YDS	RUSH	PASS	RTN	A-C-I	SACKED	PUNT	FUMB	PEN
LA	17	250	49-120	130	91	21-10-3	3-22	7-36	0-0	8-94
Dal	14	211	28-85	126	73	37-15-3	4-24	6-39	3-1	6-34

LA-Harold Jackson 116C

Charlie Waters blocked 2 punts, the second giving the Cowboys the ball at the Rams 17 with 1:59 left. Trailing 14–10, Roger Staubach threw an apparent touchdown to Butch Johnson, but the receiver had only one foot in bounds. Dallas turned the ball over on downs and the game ended with beleaguered punter Rusty Jackson purposely stepping out of the end zone for a safety.

1976 AFC CHAMPIONSHIP

Sunday, December 26, 1976 at Oakland, Oakland-Alameda County Coliseum, attendance 53,739

PITTSBURGH	0	7	0	0	—	7
OAKLAND	3	14	7	0	—	24

SCORING Oak—FG Mann 39 yds, Oak—Davis 1-yd run (Mann PAT), Pit—Harrison 3-yd run (Mansfield PAT), Oak—Bankston 4-yd pass from Stabler (Mann PAT), Oak—Banaszak 5-yd pass from Stabler (Mann PAT)

TEAM	FD	YDS	RUSH	PASS	RTN	A-C-I	SACKED	PUNT	FUMB	PEN
Pit	13	237	21-72	165	18	35-14-1	3-11	7-37	1-0	5-29
Oak	15	220	51-157	63	44	16-10-0	2-25	7-44	2-0	7-34

PITTSBURGH				
RUSHING	ATT	YDS	LNG	TD
Reggie Harrison	11	44	14	1
John Fuqua	8	24	8	0
RECEIVING	NO	YDS	LNG	TD
Bennie Cunningham	4	36	29	0
Lynn Swann	3	58	30	0
PASSING	PA	PC	YDS	TD	IN
Terry Bradshaw	35	14	176	0	1

OAKLAND				
RUSHING	ATT	YDS	LNG	TD
Mark van Eeghen	22	66	8	0
Clarence Davis	11	54	16	1
RECEIVING	NO	YDS	LNG	TD
Cliff Branch	3	46	28	0
Warren Bankston	2	11	7	1
PASSING	PA	PC	YDS	TD	IN
Ken Stabler	16	10	88	2	0

The Steelers had reached the past two Super Bowls by beating the Raiders in the AFC Championship Game, but this was Oakland's day. Pittsburgh was without starting running backs Franco Harris and Rocky Bleier, both injured the previous week. Reggie Harrison rushed 11 times for 44 yards for the Steelers, but three Raiders surpassed that total as Oakland churned out 157 yards on 51 carries. Ken Stabler completed just 10 passes for 88 yards, but his touchdown pass off a play fake with 17 seconds left in the first half made it a 17–7 game. He threw another touchdown for the only points of the second half.

1976 NFC CHAMPIONSHIP

Sunday, December 26, 1976 at Bloomington, MN, Metropolitan Stadium, attendance 47,191

LOS ANGELES	0	0	13	0	—	13
MINNESOTA	3	7	7	7	—	24

SCORING Min—Bryant 90-yd blocked field goal recovery (Cox PAT), Min—FG Cox 25 yds, Min—Foreman 1-yd run (Cox PAT), LA—McCutcheon 10-yd run (PAT failed), LA—H. Jackson 5-yd pass from Haden (Dempsey PAT), Min—Johnson 12-yd run (Cox PAT)

TEAM	FD	YDS	RUSH	PASS	RTN	A-C-I	SACKED	PUNT	FUMB	PEN
LA	21	336	46-193	143	50	22-9-2	3-18	7-29	4-2	3-33
Min	13	267	29-158	109	37	27-12-1	4-34	8-35	1-1	4-32

LOS ANGELES				
RUSHING	ATT	YDS	LNG	TD
Lawrence McCutcheon	26	128	15	1
John Cappelletti	16	59	11	0
RECEIVING	NO	YDS	LNG	TD
Harold Jackson	4	70	40	1
Ron Jessie	2	60	41	0
PASSING	PA	PC	YDS	TD	IN
Pat Haden	22	9	161	1	2

MINNESOTA				
RUSHING	ATT	YDS	LNG	TD
Chuck Foreman	15	118	62	1
Robert Miller	10	28	9	0
RECEIVING	NO	YDS	LNG	TD
Chuck Foreman	5	81	57	0
Ahmad Rashad	3	28	14	0
PASSING	PA	PC	YDS	TD	IN
Fran Tarkenton	27	12	143	0	1

The sun was out but the temperature was just 12 degrees with a wind chill below zero at Metropolitan Stadium. The warm-weather Rams moved the ball better than Minnesota, but special teams did in Los Angeles. Tom Dempsey had 2 kicks blocked, the first was returned 90 yards by Bobby Bryant in the first quarter. The Vikings went up 10–0 after Rusty Jackson's third blocked punt in two weeks. Neither kicker ever played again for the Rams. Los Angeles scored 2 touchdowns in the third quarter and was driving in the fourth quarter until Pat Haden was intercepted at the Minnesota 8. The Vikings scored again to clinch their fourth Super Bowl appearance in eight seasons.

1977 AFC DIVISIONAL PLAYOFF

Saturday, December 24, 1977 at Denver, Mile High Stadium, attendance 75,011

PITTSBURGH	0	14	0	7	—	21
DENVER	7	7	7	13	—	34

SCORING Den—Lytle 7-yd run (Turner PAT), Pit—Bradshaw 1-yd run (Gerela PAT), Den—Armstrong 10-yd run (Turner PAT), Pit—Harris 1-yd run (Gerela PAT), Den—Odoms 30-yd pass from Morton (Turner PAT), Pit—Brown 1-yd pass from Bradshaw (Gerela PAT), Den—FG Turner 44 yds, Den—FG Turner 25 yds, Den—Dolbin 34-yd pass from Morton (Turner PAT)

TEAM	FD	YDS	RUSH	PASS	RTN	A-C-I	SACKED	PUNT	FUMB	PEN
Pit	18	304	39-127	177	31	37-19-3	0-0	6-34	2-1	10-67
Den	15	258	37-103	155	76	23-11-0	1-9	5-38	3-1	3-20

The Broncos, playing in their first-ever playoff game, used a fumble recovery and blocked punt in the first half to stay even with the experienced Steelers. The game was tied in the fourth quarter when Jim Turner's field goal gave Denver the lead. Broncos linebacker Tom Jackson intercepted 2 Terry Bradshaw passes in the fourth quarter, leading to 10 points.

1977 AFC DIVISIONAL PLAYOFF

Saturday, December 24, 1977 at Baltimore, Memorial Stadium, attendance 60,763

OAKLAND	7	0	14	10	0	6	—	37
BALTIMORE	0	10	7	14	0	0	—	31

SCORING Oak—Davis 30-yd run (Mann PAT), Bal—Laird 61-yd interception return (Linhart PAT), Bal—FG Linhart 36 yds, Oak—Casper 8-yd pass from Stabler (Mann PAT), Bal—Johnson 87-yd kickoff return (Linhart PAT), Oak—Casper 10-yd pass from Stabler (Mann PAT), Oak—Banaszak 1-yd run (Mann PAT), Bal—R. Lee 1-yd run (Linhart PAT), Bal—R. Lee 13-yd run (Linhart PAT), Oak—FG Mann 22 yds, Oak—Casper 10-yd pass from Stabler (no PAT)

TEAM	FD	YDS	RUSH	PASS	RTN	A-C-I	SACKED	PUNT	FUMB	PEN
Oak	28	491	47-167	324	42	40-21-2	2-21	8-47	4-2	7-65
Bal	22	301	50-187	114	83	26-12-0	6-50	13-37	1-0	8-82

Oak-Cliff Branch 113C, Ken Stabler 345P

This Christmas Eve classic turned into the third-longest game in NFL history. The Raiders rallied to tie the game on a field goal with 26 seconds left, but neither team could score in the first overtime. Ken Stabler, who threw for 345 yards, hit Dave Casper on a post pattern—the Ghost to the Post—for a touchdown in the second quarter of sudden death in Baltimore.

1977 NFC DIVISIONAL PLAYOFF

Monday, December 26, 1977 at Dallas, Texas Stadium, attendance 62,920

CHICAGO	0	0	0	7	—	7
DALLAS	7	10	17	3	—	37

SCORING Dal—Dennison 2-yd run (Herrera PAT), Dal—DuPree 28-yd pass from Staubach (Herrera PAT), Dal—FG Herrera 21 yds, Dal—Dorsett 23-yd run (Herrera PAT), Dal—FG Herrera 31 yds, Dal—Dorsett 7-yd run (Herrera PAT), Dal—FG Herrera 27 yds, Chi—Schubert 34-yd pass from Avellini (Thomas PAT)

TEAM	FD	YDS	RUSH	PASS	RTN	A-C-I	SACKED	PUNT	FUMB	PEN
Chi	15	224	27-81	143	15	25-15-4	3-34	6-43	3-3	4-43
Dal	20	365	48-233	132	114	14-8-1	2-2	3-37	2-2	3-35

The Bears, playing in their first postseason game since 1963, were the sentimental choice, but the Cowboys tore right through Chicago. Dallas had 279 total yards in the first half and a 17–0 lead; the Cowboys scored 17 more points in the third quarter. Charlie Waters set a divisional game mark with 3 interceptions.

1977 NFC DIVISIONAL PLAYOFF

Monday, December 26, 1977 at Los Angeles, Memorial Coliseum, attendance 62,538

MINNESOTA	7	0	0	7	—	14
LOS ANGELES	0	0	0	7	—	7

SCORING Min—Foreman 5-yd run (Cox PAT), Min—S. Johnson 1-yd run (Cox PAT), LA—H. Jackson 1-yd pass from Haden (Septien PAT)

TEAM	FD	YDS	RUSH	PASS	RTN	A-C-I	SACKED	PUNT	FUMB	PEN
Min	14	189	49-144	45	47	10-5-0	1-12	8-41	1-0	7-50
LA	14	267	29-149	118	34	32-14-3	1-12	5-38	1-0	2-15

Min-Chuck Foreman 101R; LA-Lawrence McCutcheon 102R

After meeting—and beating—the Rams three straight times in the playoffs in chilly Minnesota, Los Angeles finally hosted the Vikings. The result? A California mud bath that Minnesota reveled in, intercepting 3 passes and winning despite just 189 yards of offense in the sloppy conditions. The Vikings tried just 10 passes with backup Bob Lee subbing for injured Fran Tarkenton. Chuck Foreman had 101 yards on 31 carries.

1977 AFC CHAMPIONSHIP

Sunday, January 1, 1978 at Denver, Mile High Stadium, attendance 74,982

OAKLAND	3	0	0	14	—	17
DENVER	7	0	7	6	—	20

SCORING Oak—FG Mann 20 yds, Den—Moses 74-yd pass from Morton (Turner PAT), Den—Keyworth 1-yd run (Turner PAT), Oak—Casper 7-yd pass from Stabler (Mann PAT), Den—Moses 12-yd pass from Morton (bad snap, pass failed), Oak—Casper 17-yd pass from Stabler (Mann PAT)

TEAM	FD	YDS	RUSH	PASS	RTN	A-C-I	SACKED	PUNT	FUMB	PEN
Oak	20	298	36-94	204	16	35-17-1	1-11	5-36	2-2	2-6
Den	16	308	37-91	217	26	20-10-1	1-7	4-41	0-0	8-46

OAKLAND

RUSHING	ATT	YDS	LNG	TD
Mark van Eeghen	20	71	13	0
Pete Banaszak	7	22	9	0

RECEIVING	NO	YDS	LNG	TD
Dave Casper	5	71	26	2
Fred Biletnikoff	4	38	15	0
Cliff Branch	3	59	24	0

PASSING	PA	PC	YDS	TD	IN
Ken Stabler	35	17	215	2	1

DENVER

RUSHING	ATT	YDS	LNG	TD
Lonnie Perrin	11	42	10	0
Rob Lytle	7	26	8	0

RECEIVING	NO	YDS	LNG	TD
Haven Moses	5	168	74	2
Lonnie Perrin	2	20	16	0

PASSING	PA	PC	YDS	TD	IN
Craig Morton	20	10	224	2	1

On an 18-degree day, the Raiders began with an 18-play drive that ended with an Errol Mann field goal. Two plays into Denver's possession, Craig Morton connected with Haven Moses for a 74-yard touchdown. The biggest play of the day, though, was a fumble that wasn't. Rob Lytle's fumble at the goal line, initially recovered by Oakland, was ruled dead. Denver scored on the next play. The Raiders scored twice in the fourth quarter, but in between those drives Bob Swenson intercepted Ken Stabler to set up Denver's last touchdown. The Broncos held onto the ball for the final 3:08 to clinch the franchise's first conference title.

1977 NFC CHAMPIONSHIP

Sunday, January 1, 1978 at Dallas, Texas Stadium, attendance 61,968

MINNESOTA	0	6	0	0	—	6
DALLAS	6	10	0	7	—	**23**

SCORING Dal—Richards 32-yd pass from Staubach (PAT failed), Dal—Newhouse 5-yd run (Herrera PAT), Min—FG Cox 32 yds, Min—FG Cox 37 yds, Dal—FG Herrera 21 yds, Dal—Dorsett 11-yd run (Herrera PAT).

TEAM	FD	YDS	RUSH	PASS	RTN	A-C-I	SACKED	PUNT	FUMB	PEN
Min	12	214	30-66	148	2	31-14-1	2-10	8-35	5-3	5-32
Dal	16	328	39-170	158	58	23-12-1	2-7	8-37	1-1	5-84

MINNESOTA

RUSHING	ATT	YDS	LNG	TD
Chuck Foreman	21	59	11	0
Robert Miller	8	5	4	0

RECEIVING	NO	YDS	LNG	TD
Chuck Foreman	5	36	9	0
Sammy White	3	46	28	0

PASSING	PA	PC	YDS	TD	IN
Bob Lee	31	14	158	0	1

DALLAS

RUSHING	ATT	YDS	LNG	TD
Robert Newhouse	15	81	15	1
Tony Dorsett	19	71	13	1

RECEIVING	NO	YDS	LNG	TD
Drew Pearson	4	62	28	0
Preston Pearson	3	48	32	0

PASSING	PA	PC	YDS	TD	IN
Roger Staubach	23	12	165	1	1

The Cowboys defense stifled the Vikings, forcing 5 turnovers. The offense, meanwhile, controlled the ball—even on fourth down. Danny White took off on a fake punt for 14 yards and a first down on Dallas's second touchdown march. Bob Lee, subbing for injured Fran Tarkenton, was forced to throw with Minnesota behind. That didn't help. Nor did 2 fumbles that set up Dallas scoring drives. The Cowboys joined the Vikings with four Super Bowl appearances each. Minnesota had now made five championship game appearances since 1969—and suffered their first loss. It would be Minnesota's last NFC Championship Game until 1987.

1978 AFC WILD CARD GAME

Sunday, December 24, 1978 at Miami, Orange Bowl, attendance 70,036

HOUSTON	7	0	0	10	—	**17**
MIAMI	7	0	0	2	—	9

SCORING Mia—Tillman 13-yd pass from Griese (Yepremian PAT), Hou—T. Wilson 13-yd pass from Pastorini (Fritsch PAT), Hou—FG Fritsch 35 yds, Hou—Campbell 1-yd run (Fritsch PAT), Mia—Safety, Pastorini ran out of end zone

TEAM	FD	YDS	RUSH	PASS	RTN	A-C-I	SACKED	PUNT	FUMB	PEN
Hou	23	455	45-165	290	15	30-20-0	2-16	5-44	3-1	5-37
Mia	14	209	25-91	118	24	30-12-3	2-19	5-49	2-2	1-5

Hou-Ken Burrough 103C, Mike Barber 112C, Dan Pastorini 306P

The first AFC Wild Card Game was tied, 7–7, until midway through the fourth quarter. Toni Fritsch's field goal gave Houston the lead and a Bob Griese interception set up the Oilers on a 50-yard scoring drive. Houston more than doubled host Miami's offensive output, 455–209.

1978 NFC WILD CARD GAME

Sunday, December 24, 1978 at Atlanta, Atlanta-Fulton County Stadium, attendance 49,447

PHILADELPHIA	6	0	7	0	—	13
ATLANTA	0	0	0	14	—	**14**

SCORING Phi—Carmichael 13-yd pass from Jaworski (PAT failed), Phi—Montgomery 1-yd run (Michel PAT), Atl—Mitchell 20-yd pass from Bartkowski (Mazzetti PAT), Atl—Francis 37-yd pass from Bartkowski (Mazzetti PAT)

TEAM	FD	YDS	RUSH	PASS	RTN	A-C-I	SACKED	PUNT	FUMB	PEN
Phi	15	217	32-53	164	75	35-19-0	3-26	9-34	3-2	5-60
Atl	14	298	27-75	223	14	32-18-2	2-20	7-33	3-3	6-63

Phi-Charlie Smith 108C; Atl-Wallace Francis 135C

Steve Bartkowksi threw 2 touchdown in the final five minutes to erase a 13–0 deficit and bring Atlanta its first-ever playoff victory in the inaugural NFC Wild Card Game. Mike Michel, a punter turned emergency kicker for the Eagles, missed an extra point and 2 field goals, including a 34-yarder with 13 seconds left.

1978 AFC DIVISIONAL PLAYOFF

Saturday, December 30, 1978 at Pittsburgh, Three Rivers Stadium, attendance 48,921

DENVER	3	7	0	0	—	10
PITTSBURGH	6	13	0	14	—	**33**

SCORING Den—FG Turner 37 yds, Pit—Harris 1-yd run (PAT failed), Pit—Harris 18-yd run (Gerela PAT), Pit—FG Gerela 24 yds, Den—Preston 3-yd run (Turner PAT), Pit—FG Gerela 27 yds, Pit—Stallworth 45-yd pass from Bradshaw (Gerela PAT), Pit—Swann 38-yd pass from Bradshaw (Gerela PAT)

TEAM	FD	YDS	RUSH	PASS	RTN	A-C-I	SACKED	PUNT	FUMB	PEN
Den	15	218	27-87	131	40	22-12-0	6-37	6-34	2-2	8-104
Pit	24	425	40-153	272	28	29-16-1	0-0	2-36	4-1	11-88

Pit-Franco Harris 105R, John Stallworth 156C

Avenging a playoff loss in Denver a year earlier, the Steelers broke open the game in a 14-second span of the fourth quarter. Terry Bradshaw's touchdown pass to John Stallworth, who caught 10 passes for 156 yards, was followed by Denver's fumble on the kickoff. Bradshaw then teamed with Lynn Swann for the clinching score.

1978 NFC DIVISIONAL PLAYOFF

Saturday, December 30, 1978 at Dallas, Texas Stadium, attendance 60,338

ATLANTA	7	13	0	0	—	20
DALLAS	10	3	7	7	—	**27**

SCORING Dal—FG Septien 34 yds, Atl—Bean 14-yd run (Mazzetti PAT), Dal—Laidlaw 13-yd run (Septien PAT), Atl—FG Mazzetti 42 yds, Dal—FG Septien 48 yds, Atl—Francis 17-yd pass from Bartkowski (Mazzetti PAT), Atl—FG Mazzetti 22 yds, Dal—Smith 2-yd pass from D. White (Septien PAT), Dal—Laidlaw 1-yd run (Septien PAT)

TEAM	FD	YDS	RUSH	PASS	RTN	A-C-I	SACKED	PUNT	FUMB	PEN
Atl	16	216	36-164	52	0	23-8-3	5-43	6-38	0-0	7-69
Dal	26	369	37-148	221	69	37-17-1	1-11	3-36	6-3	7-65

Roger Staubach was knocked out of the game in the first half with a concussion and backup quarterback–punter Danny White led the Cowboys back from a 20–13 deficit. A touchdown pass to Jackie Smith tied it. Following a pressured 10-yard Atlanta punt, the Cowboys took the lead on Scott Laidlaw's touchdown run.

1978 AFC DIVISIONAL PLAYOFF

Sunday, December 31, 1978 at Foxboro, MA, Schaefer Stadium, attendance 60,881

HOUSTON	0	21	3	7	—	**31**
NEW ENGLAND	0	0	7	7	—	14

SCORING Hou—Burrough 71-yd pass from Pastorini (Fritsch PAT), Hou—Barber 19-yd pass from Pastorini (Fritsch PAT), Hou—Barber 13-yd pass from Pastorini (Fritsch PAT), Hou—FG Fritsch 30 yds, NE—Jackson 24-yd pass from Johnson (Posey PAT), NE—Francis 24-yd pass from Owen (Posey PAT), Hou—Campbell 2-yd run (Fritsch PAT)

TEAM	FD	YDS	RUSH	PASS	RTN	A-C-I	SACKED	PUNT	FUMB	PEN
Hou	21	344	54-174	170	52	15-12-1	3-30	5-35	1-0	2-25
NE	15	263	20-83	180	6	35-16-3	4-26	4-43	2-0	8-92

Hou-Earl Campbell 118R; NE-Russ Francis 101C

Confusion reigned in Foxboro, where lame duck coach Chuck Fairbanks's club was victimized by turnovers and big plays. The Oilers went up 21–0 in the second quarter following a 71-yard touchdown pass from Dan Pastorini to Ken Burrough and 2

interceptions by Mike Reinfeldt that led to Mike Barber touchdown catches. Earl Campbell ran over the Patriots in the second half.

1978 NFC DIVISIONAL PLAYOFF
Sunday, December 31, 1978 at Los Angeles, Memorial Coliseum, attendance 69,631

MINNESOTA	3	7	0	0	—	10
LOS ANGELES	0	10	14	10	—	**34**

SCORING Min—FG Danmeier 42 yds, LA—Miller 9-yd pass from Haden (Corral PAT), LA—FG Corral 43 yds, Min—Rashad 1-yd pass from Tarkenton (Danmeier PAT), LA—Bryant 3-yd run (Corral PAT), LA—Jessie 27-yd pass from Haden (Corral PAT), LA—FG Corral 28 yds, LA—Jodat 3-yd run (Corral PAT)

TEAM	FD	YDS	RUSH	PASS	RTN	A-C-I	SACKED	PUNT	FUMB	PEN
Min	12	244	16-36	208	10	38-18-2	1-11	6-41	2-0	2-12
LA	25	409	48-200	209	99	29-15-1	0-0	4-31	1-0	4-35

LA-Cullen Bryant 100R, Ron Jessie 108C

The fifth time finally worked for the Rams. Los Angeles, 0–4 against the Vikings in the postseason, snapped a 10–10 tie in the third quarter on Cullen Bryant's touchdown run. The defense held the Vikings to just 58 yards in the second half and Bill Simpson stopped Minnesota with 2 interceptions.

1978 AFC CHAMPIONSHIP
Sunday, January 7, 1979 at Pittsburgh, Three Rivers Stadium, attendance 49,417

HOUSTON	0	3	2	0	—	5
PITTSBURGH	14	17	3	0	—	**34**

SCORING Pit—Harris 7-yd run (Gerela PAT), Pit—Bleier 15-yd run (Gerela PAT), Hou—FG Fritsch 19 yds, Pit—Swann 29-yd pass from Bradshaw (Gerela PAT), Pit—Stallworth 17-yd pass from Bradshaw (Gerela PAT), Pit—FG Gerela 37 yds, Pit—FG Gerela 22 yds, Hou—Safety, Washington tackled Bleier in end zone

TEAM	FD	YDS	RUSH	PASS	RTN	A-C-I	SACKED	PUNT	FUMB	PEN
Hou	10	142	26-72	70	0	26-12-5	4-26	6-40	6-4	5-48
Pit	21	379	47-179	200	181	19-11-2	0-0	1-53	6-3	4-32

HOUSTON					PITTSBURGH				
RUSHING	ATT	YDS	LNG	TD	**RUSHING**	ATT	YDS	LNG	TD
Earl Campbell	22	62	11	0	Franco Harris	20	51	9	1
					Rocky Bleier	10	45	15	1
RECEIVING	NO	YDS	LNG	TD	**RECEIVING**	NO	YDS	LNG	TD
Rich Caster	5	44	21	0	Lynn Swann	4	98	34	1
Tim Wilson	5	33	8	0	Rocky Bleier	4	42	16	0
PASSING	PA	PC	YDS	TD	IN	**PASSING**	PA	PC	YDS	TD	IN
Dan Pastorini	26	12	96	0	5	Terry Bradshaw	19	11	200	2	2

A steady rain followed a snowstorm the previous day and the Steelers followed a solid first half with 17 points in the final minute before intermission. Already ahead 14–3, Terry Bradshaw found Lynn Swann open for a touchdown with 52 seconds to go. The Oilers fumbled the kickoff and the Steelers immediately scored again, with Bradshaw hitting John Stallworth for 17 yards. Houston fumbled on the first play from scrimmage and Roy Gerela kicked a 37-yard field goal. Another Gerela field goal and a Houston safety accounted for all the scoring in the second half. The slick, soaked turf helped cause a postseason record 12 fumbles (6 per side). Houston lost 4 fumbles and threw 5 interceptions.

1978 NFC CHAMPIONSHIP
Sunday, January 7, 1979 at Los Angeles, Memorial Coliseum, attendance 67,470

DALLAS	0	0	7	21	—	**28**
LOS ANGELES	0	0	0	0	—	0

SCORING Dal—Dorsett 5-yd run (Septien PAT), Dal—Laidlaw 4-yd pass from Staubach (Septien PAT), Dal—DuPree 11-yd pass from Staubach (Septien PAT), Dal—Henderson 68-yd interception return (Septien PAT)

TEAM	FD	YDS	RUSH	PASS	RTN	A-C-I	SACKED	PUNT	FUMB	PEN
Dal	16	235	33-126	109	163	25-13-2	3-17	8-35	2-1	10-85
LA	15	277	31-81	196	22	35-14-5	3-10	5-39	3-2	5-40

DALLAS					LOS ANGELES				
RUSHING	ATT	YDS	LNG	TD	**RUSHING**	ATT	YDS	LNG	TD
Tony Dorsett	17	101	53	1	Cullen Bryant	20	52	11	0
Scott Laidlaw	10	20	4	0	Pat Haden	2	20	18	0
RECEIVING	NO	YDS	LNG	TD	**RECEIVING**	NO	YDS	LNG	TD
Billy Joe DuPree	3	48	23	1	Ron Jessie	4	42	14	0
Butch Johnson	2	19	17	0	Willie Miller	3	96	65	0
PASSING	PA	PC	YDS	TD	IN	**PASSING**	PA	PC	YDS	TD	IN
Roger Staubach	25	13	126	2	2	Vince Ferragamo	16	7	130	0	2
						Pat Haden	19	7	76	0	3

The Rams finally beat the Vikings in the playoffs to reach the championship game, but Los Angeles turned the ball over 5 times

in the second half against Dallas. The game was scoreless until late in the third quarter. Charlie Waters had 2 pickoffs that set up Dallas scores, but Vince Ferragamo, replacing injured Pat Haden, was able to move the Rams into scoring position. A fumble sabotaged that drive and started an 89-yard Cowboys march the other way. A final interception by Thomas Henderson was returned 68 yards for a touchdown to set up the first Super Bowl rematch with Dallas facing Pittsburgh.

1979 AFC WILD CARD GAME
Sunday, December 23, 1979 at Houston, Astrodome, attendance 48,776

DENVER	7	0	0	0	—	7
HOUSTON	3	7	0	3	—	**13**

SCORING Hou—FG Fritsch 31 yds, Den—Preston 7-yd pass from Morton (Turner PAT), Hou—Campbell 3-yd run (Fritsch PAT), Hou—FG Fritsch 20 yds

TEAM	FD	YDS	RUSH	PASS	RTN	A-C-I	SACKED	PUNT	FUMB	PEN
Den	17	216	32-112	104	37	27-14-1	6-40	6-44	1-0	7-70
Hou	15	282	42-135	147	57	22-10-2	1-11	5-43	0-0	2-19

In the first postseason game at the Astrodome, the Oilers lost both Earl Campbell and Dan Pastorini to groin injuries yet won the game. Houston started with a field goal and the Broncos came back with a touchdown. The Oilers scored the only other 10 points of the game. The Houston defense had 6 sacks and held Denver twice in crucial spots at the end of the game.

1979 NFC WILD CARD GAME
Sunday, December 23, 1979 at Philadelphia, Veterans Stadium, attendance 69,397

CHICAGO	7	10	0	0	—	17
PHILADELPHIA	3	7	7	10	—	**27**

SCORING Phi—Carmichael 17-yd pass from Jaworski (Franklin PAT), Chi—Payton 2-yd run (Thomas PAT), Phi—FG Franklin 29 yds, Chi—Payton 1-yd run (Thomas PAT), Chi—FG Thomas 30 yds, Phi—Carmichael 29-yd pass from Jaworski (Franklin PAT), Phi—Campfield 63-yd pass from Jaworski (Franklin PAT), Phi—FG Franklin 34 yds

TEAM	FD	YDS	RUSH	PASS	RTN	A-C-I	SACKED	PUNT	FUMB	PEN
Chi	15	241	29-99	142	25	30-13-2	1-0	6-39	1-1	4-35
Phi	18	315	37-139	176	56	23-12-1	3-28	4-41	4-2	4-46

Phi-Harold Carmichael 111C

Veteran Stadium saw its first football playoff action and the Eagles rallied for 17–10 halftime deficit for their first postseason victory since 1960. With the game tied, Philadelphia's Bobby Howard intercepted Mike Phipps in the end zone. Billy Campfield then took a Ron Jaworski pass 63 yards in the fourth quarter for the go-ahead score.

1979 AFC DIVISIONAL PLAYOFF
Saturday, December 29, 1979 at San Diego, San Diego Stadium, attendance 51,192

HOUSTON	0	10	7	0	—	**17**
SAN DIEGO	7	7	0	0	—	14

SCORING SD—C. Williams 1-yd run (Wood PAT), Hou—FG Fritsch 26 yds, Hou—Clark 1-yd run (Fritsch PAT), SD—Mitchell 8-yd run (Wood PAT), Hou—Renfro 47-yd pass from Nielsen (Fritsch PAT)

TEAM	FD	YDS	RUSH	PASS	RTN	A-C-I	SACKED	PUNT	FUMB	PEN
Hou	15	259	40-148	111	36	19-10-1	0-0	6-41	0-0	5-45
SD	25	380	19-63	317	29	47-25-5	2-16	2-32	0-0	6-30

SD-Dan Fouts 333P

The Oilers played without their starting quarterback (Dan Pastorini) or the NFL's leading rusher (Earl Campbell), but Houston's defense carried the day. Vernon Perry set an NFL postseason record with 4 interceptions, not to mention a 57-yard blocked field goal return. Dan Fouts threw for 333 yards, but Houston sub Gifford Nielsen's 47-yard touchdown pass provided the winning margin.

1979 NFC DIVISIONAL PLAYOFF
Saturday, December 29, 1979 at Tampa, Tampa Stadium, attendance 71,402

PHILADELPHIA	0	7	3	7	—	17
TAMPA BAY	7	10	0	7	—	**24**

SCORING TB—Bell 4-yd run (O'Donoghue PAT), TB—FG O'Donoghue 40 yds, TB—Bell 1-yd run (O'Donoghue PAT), Phi—Smith 11-yd pass from Jaworski (Franklin PAT), Phi—FG

Franklin 42 yds, TB—Giles 9-yd pass from Williams (O'Donoghue PAT), Phi—Carmichael 37-yd pass from Jaworski (Franklin PAT)

TEAM	FD	YDS	RUSH	PASS	RTN	A-C-I	SACKED	PUNT	FUMB	PEN
Phi	15	227	18-48	179	85	38-15-0	2-20	5-44	2-1	8-62
TB	17	318	55-186	132	33	15-7-1	0-0	5-43	0-0	9-105

TB-Ricky Bell 142R

A franchise that took 26 games to get its first victory in 1977 won a playoff game in its first try in 1979. Tampa Bay allowed Philadelphia just 43 yards in the first half as the Buccaneers grabbed a 17–0 lead. Ricky Bell rushed a then-NFL playoff record 38 times for 142 yards for the Bucs.

1979 AFC DIVISIONAL PLAYOFF
Sunday, December 30, 1979 at Pittsburgh, Three Rivers Stadium, attendance 50,214

MIAMI	0	0	7	7	—	14
PITTSBURGH	20	0	7	7	—	34

SCORING Pit—Thornton 1-yd run (Bahr PAT), Pit—Stallworth 17-yd pass from Bradshaw (PAT blocked), Pit—Swann 20-yd pass from Bradshaw (Bahr PAT), Mia—Harris 7-yd pass from Griese (von Schamann PAT), Pit—Bleier 1-yd run (Bahr PAT), Pit—Harris 5-yd run (Bahr PAT), Mia—Csonka 1-yd run (von Schamann PAT)

TEAM	FD	YDS	RUSH	PASS	RTN	A-C-I	SACKED	PUNT	FUMB	PEN
Mia	16	249	22-25	224	0	40-22-2	3-19	4-36	0-0	4-35
Pit	27	379	40-159	220	34	31-21-0	1-10	2-30	3-3	8-41

The Steelers scored the first three times they had the ball to take a 20–0 lead in the first quarter. The Steel Curtain locked down Miami. The Dolphins had just 25 yards rushing. When Miami finally scored in the third quarter, Pittsburgh embarked on a 12-play, 69-yard drive.

1979 NFC DIVISIONAL PLAYOFF
Sunday, December 30, 1979 at Dallas, Texas Stadium, attendance 64,792

LOS ANGELES	0	14	0	7	—	21
DALLAS	2	3	7	7	—	19

SCORING Dal—Safety, R. White tackled Ferragamo in end zone, LA—Tyler 32-yd pass from Ferragamo (Corral PAT), Dal—FG Septien 33 yds, LA—R. Smith 43-yd pass from Ferragamo (Corral PAT), Dal—Springs 1-yd run (Septien PAT), Dal—Saldi 2-yd pass from Staubach (Septien PAT), LA—Waddy 50-yd pass from Ferragamo (Corral PAT)

TEAM	FD	YDS	RUSH	PASS	RTN	A-C-I	SACKED	PUNT	FUMB	PEN
LA	16	361	39-159	202	38	21-9-2	1-8	5-41	0-0	6-44
Dal	17	306	34-156	150	50	29-13-1	1-0	8-37	0-0	7-55

Vince Ferragamo, a replacement for injured Pat Haden, was sacked for a safety in the first quarter, but the Rams quarterback stayed on his feet the rest of the game to lead Los Angeles. His third touchdown pass, a 50-yard heave to Billy Waddy with two minutes left, gave the Rams the lead for good. He'd also led a touchdown drive in the final minute of the first half.

1979 AFC CHAMPIONSHIP
Sunday, January 6, 1980 at Pittsburgh, Three Rivers Stadium, attendance 50,475

HOUSTON	7	3	0	3	—	13
PITTSBURGH	3	14	0	10	—	27

SCORING Hou—Perry 75-yd interception return (Fritsch PAT), Pit—FG Bahr 21 yds, Hou—FG Fritsch 21 yds, Pit—Cunningham 16-yd pass from Bradshaw (Bahr PAT), Pit—Stallworth 20-yd pass from Bradshaw (Bahr PAT), Hou—FG Fritsch 23 yds, Pit—FG Bahr 39 yds, Pit—Bleier 4-yd run (Bahr PAT)

TEAM	FD	YDS	RUSH	PASS	RTN	A-C-I	SACKED	PUNT	FUMB	PEN
Hou	11	227	22-24	203	83	29-20-1	1-9	4-30	4-2	2-10
Pit	22	358	36-161	197	8	30-18-1	3-22	3-51	1-1	5-34

HOUSTON					PITTSBURGH				
RUSHING	ATT	YDS	LNG	TD	**RUSHING**	ATT	YDS	LNG	TD
Earl Campbell	17	15	7	0	Franco Harris	21	85	13	0
Tim Wilson	4	9	5	0	Rocky Bleier	13	52	8	1
RECEIVING	NO	YDS	LNG	TD	**RECEIVING**	NO	YDS	LNG	TD
Tim Wilson	7	60	41	0	Franco Harris	6	50	15	0
Rob Carpenter	5	23	14	0	Lynn Swann	4	64	21	0
Mike Renfro	3	52	19	0	John Stallworth	3	52	20	1
PASSING	PA	PC	YDS	TD	IN	**PASSING**	PA	PC	YDS	TD	IN
Dan Pastorini	28	19	203	0	1	Terry Bradshaw	30	18	219	2	1

The AFC championship again pitted Central Division rivals, but it was not the cakewalk of the previous year. Vernon Perry, coming off a 4-interception game, picked off Terry Bradshaw and returned it 75

yards for the game's first score. Bradshaw threw 2 touchdown passes in the second quarter to give the Steelers a 17–10 lead. That score remained until late in the third quarter when Houston's Mike Renfro caught a pass in the back of the end zone, but officials ruled he did not have possession in bounds. The Oilers settled for a field goal and the Steelers scored 10 more points for their 16th straight win at home and fourth Super Bowl appearance.

1979 NFC CHAMPIONSHIP
Sunday, January 6, 1980 at Tampa, Tampa Stadium, attendance 72,033

LOS ANGELES	0	6	0	3	—	9
TAMPA BAY	0	0	0	0	—	0

SCORING LA—FG Corral 19 yds, LA—FG Corral 21 yds, LA—FG Corral 23 yds

TEAM	FD	YDS	RUSH	PASS	RTN	A-C-I	SACKED	PUNT	FUMB	PEN
LA	23	369	53-216	153	77	23-12-0	1-10	5-37	1-1	3-20
TB	7	177	26-92	85	14	27-5-1	1-11	8-37	1-0	4-45

LOS ANGELES					TAMPA BAY				
RUSHING	ATT	YDS	LNG	TD	**RUSHING**	ATT	YDS	LNG	TD
Cullen Bryant	18	106	12	0	Ricky Bell	20	59	10	0
Wendell Tyler	28	86	15	0					
RECEIVING	NO	YDS	LNG	TD	**RECEIVING**	NO	YDS	LNG	TD
Cullen Bryant	4	39	16	0	Isaac Hagins	2	42	25	0
Preston Dennard	3	56	35	0	Ricky Bell	2	12	11	0
PASSING	PA	PC	YDS	TD	IN	**PASSING**	PA	PC	YDS	TD	IN
Vince Ferragamo	23	12	163	0	0	Jerry Eckwood	1	1	42	0	0
						Mike Rae	13	2	42	0	0

The Rams, losers of four of the past five NFC Championship Games, did not score a touchdown against Tampa Bay, but they did not need to. Their defense held the Buccaneers to just 177 yards and 7 first downs in the first championship game in league history without a touchdown scored. Los Angeles dominated the game, rushing for 216 yards and passing for 153 (including a 10-yard loss on a sack of Vince Ferragamo). Frank Corral's 3 short field goals put the Rams, who had scored just 30 points while going 0–4 in NFC Championship Games, in the Super Bowl.

1980 AFC WILD CARD GAME
Sunday, December 28, 1980 at Oakland, Oakland-Alameda County Coliseum, attendance 52,762

HOUSTON OILERS	7	0	0	0	—	7
OAKLAND RAIDERS	3	7	0	17	—	27

SCORING Oak—FG Bahr 47 yds, Hou—Campbell 10-yd run (Fritsch PAT), Oak—Christensen 1-yd pass from Plunkett (Bahr PAT), Oak—Whittington 44-yd pass from Plunkett (Bahr PAT), Oak—FG Bahr 37 yds, Oak—Hayes 20-yd interception return (Bahr PAT)

TEAM	FD	YDS	RUSH	PASS	RTN	A-C-I	SACKED	PUNT	FUMB	PEN
Hou	18	275	33-97	178	84	27-15-2	7-65	9-44	1-1	8-64
Oak	12	250	35-111	139	55	23-8-1	3-29	9-51	2-0	14-91

Lester Hayes, he of the 13 regular season interceptions and stickum abuse, stole 2 passes thrown by ex-Raider Ken Stabler. The first came in the end zone in the third quarter, protecting a 10–7 lead. The second came with six minutes left, and his 20-yard touchdown return sewed up the win over Houston.

1980 NFC WILD CARD GAME
Sunday, December 28, 1980 at Dallas, Texas Stadium, attendance 64,533

LOS ANGELES RAMS	6	7	0	0	—	13
DALLAS COWBOYS	3	10	14	7	—	34

SCORING Dal—FG Septien 28 yds, LA—Thomas 1-yd run (PAT blocked), Dal—FG Septien 29 yds, LA—Dennard 21-yd pass from Ferragamo (Corral PAT), Dal—Dorsett 12-yd run (Septien PAT), Dal—Dorsett 10-yd pass from White (Septien PAT), Dal—Johnson 35-yd pass from White (Septien PAT), Dal—D. Pearson 11-yd pass from White (Septien PAT)

TEAM	FD	YDS	RUSH	PASS	RTN	A-C-I	SACKED	PUNT	FUMB	PEN
LA	15	260	24-92	168	53	30-14-3	1-8	6-39	1-0	5-50
Dal	29	528	46-338	190	103	25-12-3	0-0	2-45	2-0	11-79

LA-Preston Dennard 117C; Dal-Tony Dorsett 160R

The Cowboys and Rams had their accustomed postseason date—albeit in the unfamiliar setting of the wild-card game—and the clubs were locked in a 13–13 tie at halftime. Danny White threw 2 touchdown passes in the second half as Dallas racked up 528 total yards. Of that, 338 came via the run. Tony Dorsett rushed for 160 yards.

1980 AFC DIVISIONAL PLAYOFF
Saturday, January 3, 1981 at San Diego, San Diego Stadium, attendance 52,028

BUFFALO BILLS	0	14	0	0	—	14
SAN DIEGO CHARGERS	3	0	7	10	—	20

SCORING SD—FG Benirschke 22 yds, Buf—Leaks 1-yd run (Mike-Mayer PAT), Buf—Lewis 9-yd pass from Ferguson (Mike-Mayer PAT), SD—Joiner 9-yd pass from Fouts (Benirschke PAT), SD—FG Benirschke 22 yds, SD—Smith 50-yd pass from Fouts (Benirschke PAT)

TEAM	FD	YDS	RUSH	PASS	RTN	A-C-I	SACKED	PUNT	FUMB	PEN
Buf	17	244	33-97	147	13	30-15-3	3-33	6-45	0-0	5-40
SD	21	397	25-96	301	76	37-22-1	2-13	4-28	3-2	6-66

SD-John Jefferson 102C, Dan Fouts 314P

The Bills took a 14–3 lead into the half, but Dan Fouts came out of the locker room and moved the Chargers 70 yards in just 4 plays, culminating in a touchdown pass to Charlie Joiner. Buffalo still led, 14–13, when Fouts found Ron Smith for a 50-yard touchdown with 2:08 remaining.

1980 NFC DIVISIONAL PLAYOFF
Saturday, January 3, 1981 at Philadelphia, Veterans Stadium, attendance 68,434

MINNESOTA VIKINGS	7	7	2	0	—	16
PHILADELPHIA EAGLES	0	7	14	10	—	31

SCORING Min—S. White 30-yd pass from Kramer (Danmeier PAT), Min—Brown 1-yd run (Danmeier PAT), Phi—Carmichael 9-yd pass from Jaworski (Franklin PAT), Phi—Montgomery 8-yd run (Franklin PAT), Min—Safety, Martin and Blair tackled Jaworski in end zone, Phi—Montgomery 5-yd run (Franklin PAT), Phi—FG Franklin 33 yds, Phi—Harrington 2-yd run (Franklin PAT)

TEAM	FD	YDS	RUSH	PASS	RTN	A-C-I	SACKED	PUNT	FUMB	PEN
Min	14	215	13-36	179	18	39-19-5	3-30	5-40	3-3	5-27
Phi	24	305	42-126	179	43	38-17-2	2-11	4-34	1-1	4-30

The Vikings took a 14–0 lead but gave the game away with 8 turnovers in the second half. Minnesota's only points after their fast start came on a safety that briefly gave the Vikings the lead again. Wilbert Montgomery scored twice in the third quarter, giving the Eagles the lead for good.

1980 AFC DIVISIONAL PLAYOFF
Sunday, January 4, 1981 at Cleveland, Municipal Stadium, attendance 77,655

OAKLAND RAIDERS	0	7	0	7	—	14
CLEVELAND BROWNS	0	6	6	0	—	12

SCORING Cle—Bolton 42-yd interception return (PAT failed), Oak—van Eeghen 1-yd run (Bahr PAT), Cle—FG Cockroft 30 yds, Cle—FG Cockroft 30 yds, Oak—van Eeghen 1-yd run (Bahr PAT)

TEAM	FD	YDS	RUSH	PASS	RTN	A-C-I	SACKED	PUNT	FUMB	PEN
Oak	12	208	38-76	132	4	30-14-2	2-17	9-38	2-1	5-39
Cle	17	254	27-85	169	123	40-13-3	2-14	6-40	6-1	2-10

With a wind chill of minus 37, it was the coldest game played since 1967's Ice Bowl in Green Bay. Cleveland moved the ball 73 yards to Oakland's 13 in the game's final two minutes. Don Cockroft, in his final game after 13 seasons as a Brown, had missed 3 kicks on the frozen field, so Cleveland called "Red Right 88." Mike Davis intercepted Brian Sipe's pass to send the Raiders to the championship game.

1980 NFC DIVISIONAL PLAYOFF
Sunday, January 4, 1981 at Atlanta, Atlanta-Fulton County Stadium, attendance 60,022

DALLAS COWBOYS	3	7	0	20	—	30
ATLANTA FALCONS	10	7	7	3	—	27

SCORING Atl—FG Mazzetti 38 yds, Atl—Jenkins 60-yd pass from Bartkowski (Mazzetti PAT), Dal—FG Septien 38 yds, Dal—DuPree 5-yd pass from White (Septien PAT), Atl—Cain 1-yd run (Mazzetti PAT), Atl—Andrews 12-yd pass from Bartkowski (Mazzetti PAT), Dal—Newhouse 1-yd run (Septien PAT), Atl—FG Mazzetti 34 yds, Dal—D. Pearson 14-yd pass from White (Septien PAT), Dal—D. Pearson 23-yd pass from White (bad snap, kick failed)

TEAM	FD	YDS	RUSH	PASS	RTN	A-C-I	SACKED	PUNT	FUMB	PEN
Dal	22	422	24-112	310	-4	40-25-1	1-12	4-39	4-1	6-72
Atl	18	371	27-86	285	30	33-18-1	4-35	4-36	1-1	4-48

Dal-Danny White 322P; Atl-Alfred Jenkins 155C, Steve Bartkowski 320P

The Falcons took a 24–10 lead on the Cowboys into the fourth quarter, but Dallas put together an unbelievable finish. The Cowboys drove 85 yards for a touchdown before Atlanta pushed its lead back to 10 points with a field goal. The Cowboys drove 62 yards and then 70, both culminating with Danny White touchdown passes to Drew Pearson, to pull out the win.

1980 AFC CHAMPIONSHIP
Sunday, January 11, 1981 at San Diego, San Diego Stadium, attendance 52,438

OAKLAND RAIDERS	21	7	3	3	—	34
SAN DIEGO CHARGERS	7	7	10	3	—	27

SCORING Oak—Chester 65-yd pass from Plunkett (Bahr PAT), SD—Joiner 48-yd pass from Fouts (Benirschke PAT), Oak—Plunkett 5-yd run (Bahr PAT), Oak—King 21-yd pass from Plunkett (Bahr PAT), Oak—van Eeghen 3-yd run (Bahr PAT), SD—Joiner 8-yd pass from Fouts (Benirschke PAT), SD—FG Benirschke 26 yds, SD—Muncie 6-yd run (Benirschke PAT), Oak—FG Bahr 27 yds, Oak—FG Bahr 33 yds, SD—FG Benirschke 27 yds

TEAM	FD	YDS	RUSH	PASS	RTN	A-C-I	SACKED	PUNT	FUMB	PEN
Oak	21	362	42-138	224	61	18-14-0	6-37	4-56	0-0	7-54
SD	26	434	23-83	351	41	46-23-2	2-13	2-41	5-1	6-45

OAKLAND RAIDERS						SAN DIEGO CHARGERS				
RUSHING	ATT	YDS	LNG	TD		**RUSHING**	ATT	YDS	LNG	TD
Mark van Eeghen	20	85	10	1		Mike Thomas	12	48	9	0
Kenny King	11	35	8	0		Chuck Muncie	9	34	16	1
RECEIVING	NO	YDS	LNG	TD		**RECEIVING**	NO	YDS	LNG	TD
Raymond Chester	5	102	65	1		Charlie Joiner	6	130	48	2
Cliff Branch	3	78	48	0		Mike Thomas	5	40	24	0
						John Jefferson	4	71	28	0
						Ron Smith	3	76	55	0
PASSING	PA	PC	YDS	TD	IN	**PASSING**	PA	PC	YDS	TD	IN
Jim Plunkett	18	14	261	2	0	Dan Fouts	45	22	336	2	2

In a clash between division rivals in the championship game, Oakland got the jump on San Diego. The Raiders scored 3 touchdowns in the first quarter and held a 28–7 second-quarter lead. Dan Fouts, who threw for 336 yards, connected with Charlie Joiner for a touchdown before the half. The Chargers added 10 points on their first two possessions of the second half to make it 28–24. Chris Bahr kicked 2 field goals and Oakland's defense stiffened, holding San Diego to a Rolf Benirschke field goal after a 72-yard drive. The Raiders controlled the ball for the final 6:43 to become the first team to win three playoff games to reach the Super Bowl.

1980 NFC CHAMPIONSHIP
Sunday, January 11, 1981 at Philadelphia, Veterans Stadium, attendance 70,696

DALLAS COWBOYS	0	7	0	0	—	7
PHILADELPHIA EAGLES	7	0	10	3	—	20

SCORING Phi—Montgomery 42-yd run (Franklin PAT), Dal—Dorsett 3-yd run (Septien PAT), Phi—FG Franklin 26 yds, Phi—Harris 9-yd run (Franklin PAT), Phi—FG Franklin 20 yds

TEAM	FD	YDS	RUSH	PASS	RTN	A-C-I	SACKED	PUNT	FUMB	PEN
Dal	11	206	22-90	116	4	32-12-1	1-11	7-34	5-3	5-40
Phi	19	340	40-263	77	74	29-9-2	2-14	4-34	4-0	5-45

DALLAS COWBOYS						PHILADELPHIA EAGLES				
RUSHING	ATT	YDS	LNG	TD		**RUSHING**	ATT	YDS	LNG	TD
Robert Newhouse	7	44	11	0		Wilbert Montgomery	26	194	55	1
Tony Dorsett	13	41	11	1		Leroy Harris	10	60	12	1
RECEIVING	NO	YDS	LNG	TD		**RECEIVING**	NO	YDS	LNG	TD
Tony Dorsett	3	27	18	0		Rodney Parker	4	31	15	0
Preston Pearson	2	32	23	0		Keith Krepfle	2	22	17	0
PASSING	PA	PC	YDS	TD	IN	**PASSING**	PA	PC	YDS	TD	IN
Danny White	31	12	127	0	1	Ron Jaworski	29	9	91	0	2

Running back Wilbert Montgomery ran for 194 yards on 26 carries, including a 42-yard touchdown just 2:11 into the game on a blustery, 16-degree day in Philadelphia. Tony Dorsett, who managed just 41 yards on 13 rushes, scored the lone Dallas touchdown in the second quarter to tie the score. The Cowboys did not get even within field goal range again. Two Dallas fumbles in the second half set up the go-ahead points. The Cowboys, who'd beaten the Eagles in the final week of the season, had no answer for Philadelphia's ground game that rolled up 263 yards rushing; Dallas had just 209 yards of offense all told.

1981 AFC WILD CARD GAME

Sunday, December 27, 1981 at New York, Shea Stadium, attendance 57,050

BUFFALO BILLS	17	7	0	7	—	**31**
NEW YORK JETS	0	10	3	14	—	**27**

SCORING Buf—Romes 26-yd fumble return (Mike-Mayer PAT), Buf—Lewis 50-yd pass from Ferguson (Mike-Mayer PAT), Buf—FG Mike-Mayer 29 yds, Buf—Lewis 26-yd pass from Ferguson (Mike-Mayer PAT), NYJ—Shuler 30-yd pass from Todd (Leahy PAT), NYJ—FG Leahy 26 yds, Buf—Cribbs 45-yd run (Mike-Mayer PAT), NYJ—B. Jones 30-yd pass from Todd (Leahy PAT), NYJ—Long 1-yd run (Leahy PAT).

TEAM	FD	YDS	RUSH	PASS	RTN	A-C-I	SACKED	PUNT	FUMB	PEN
Buf	15	321	22-91	230	90	34-17-4	2-38	4-44	1-0	8-62
NYJ	23	419	22-71	348	93	50-28-4	5-29	4-33	3-1	6-55

Buf-Frank Lewis 158C; NYJ-Mickey Shuler 116C, Richard Todd 377P

The first Jets postseason game since their AFL days started poorly. Bruce Harper fumbled the kickoff and Charles Romes returned it for a touchdown. Buffalo quickly built a 24–0 lead on 2 touchdown passes by Joe Ferguson and a field goal. Richard Todd passed for 377 yards to lead the Jets back. Bill Simpson picked him off near the goal line—Todd's fourth of the day—on the final play.

1981 NFC WILD CARD GAME

Sunday, December 27, 1981 at Philadelphia, Veterans Stadium, attendance 71,611

NEW YORK GIANTS	20	7	0	0	—	**27**
PHILADELPHIA EAGLES	0	7	7	7	—	**21**

SCORING NYG—Bright 9-yd pass from Brunner (PAT failed), NYG—Mistler 10-yd pass from Brunner (Danelo PAT), NYG—Haynes fumble recovery in end zone (Danelo PAT), Phi—Carmichael 15-yd pass from Jaworski (Franklin PAT), NYG—Mullady 22-yd pass from Brunner (Danelo PAT), Phi—Montgomery 6-yd run (Franklin PAT), Phi—Montgomery 1-yd run (Franklin PAT).

TEAM	FD	YDS	RUSH	PASS	RTN	A-C-I	SACKED	PUNT	FUMB	PEN
NYG	16	275	42-183	92	41	14-9-1	1-4	4-45	1-0	5-54
Phi	19	226	29-93	133	17	24-13-0	3-21	7-42	5-2	4-23

NYG-Rob Carpenter 161R

The Giants took a big early lead and then withstood a comeback by the defending conference champs. Wilbert Montgomery scored 2 second-half touchdowns for the Eagles, but New York ran out the clock. Scott Brunner, who threw 3 touchdown passes, became the first Giants quarterback to win a postseason game since Charlie Conerly captured the NFL title at Yankee Stadium in 1956.

1981 AFC DIVISIONAL PLAYOFF

Saturday, January 2, 1982 at Miami (OT), Orange Bowl, attendance 73,735

SAN DIEGO CHARGERS	24	0	7	7	3	—	**41**
MIAMI DOLPHINS	0	17	14	7	0	—	**38**

SCORING SD—FG Benirschke 32 yds, SD—Chandler 56-yd punt return (Benirschke PAT), SD—Muncie 1-yd run (Benirschke PAT), SD—Brooks 8-yd pass from Fouts (Benirschke PAT), Mia—FG von Schamann 34 yds, Mia—Rose 1-yd pass from Strock (von Schamann PAT), Mia—Nathan 25-yd lateral from Harris after 15-yd pass from Strock (von Schamann PAT), Mia—Rose 15-yd pass from Strock (von Schamann PAT), SD—Winslow 25-yd pass from Fouts (Benirschke PAT), Mia—Hardy 50-yd pass from Strock (von Schamann PAT), Mia—Nathan 12-yd run (von Schamann PAT), SD—Brooks 9-yd pass from Fouts (Benirschke PAT), SD—FG Benirschke 29 yds.

TEAM	FD	YDS	RUSH	PASS	RTN	A-C-I	SACKED	PUNT	FUMB	PEN
SD	34	564	29-149	415	99	54-33-1	2-18	4-40	3-3	9-55
Mia	25	472	28-78	394	42	48-31-2	3-29	5-42	2-1	7-50

SD-Chuck Muncie 120R, Kellen Winslow 166C, Charlie Joiner 108C, Wes Chandler 106C, Dan Fouts 433P; Mia-Tony Nathan 114C, Duriel Harris 106C, Don Strock 403P

An early blowout turned into one of the most memorable games in NFL history. Miami's hook-and-ladder play to end the half cut San Diego's huge lead to 24–17. The Dolphins went ahead and the Chargers rallied to tie late in the fourth quarter. Miami seemed poised for the win, but Kellen Winslow blocked a field goal on the last play of regulation. The Chargers won on an overtime field goal. Despite the teams setting postseason marks for combined points and yardage, the superhuman efforts of San Diego's tight end (13 catches for 166 yards) dubbed this the Kellen Winslow Game.

1981 NFC DIVISIONAL PLAYOFF

Saturday, January 2, 1982 at Dallas, Texas Stadium, attendance 64,848

TAMPA BAY BUCCANEERS	0	0	0	0	—	**0**
DALLAS COWBOYS	0	10	21	7	—	**38**

SCORING Dal—Hill 9-yd pass from D. White (Septien PAT), Dal—FG Septien 32 yds, Dal—Springs 1-yd run (Septien PAT), Dal—Dorsett 5-yd run (Septien PAT), Dal—Jones 5-yd run (Septien PAT), Dal—Newsome 1-yd run (Septien PAT).

TEAM	FD	YDS	RUSH	PASS	RTN	A-C-I	SACKED	PUNT	FUMB	PEN
TB	12	222	22-74	148	1	29-10-4	4-39	5-38	2-0 10-105
Dal	26	345	46-212	133	124	26-15-0	1-10	4-30	0-0	8-40

A 10–0 Dallas halftime advantage turned into a rout in the third quarter as 2 Tampa Bay interceptions (there were 4 on the day) were quickly converted into touchdowns. The Cowboys rushed for 212 yards; the Buccaneers ran for 2 yards in the second half.

1981 AFC DIVISIONAL PLAYOFF

Sunday, January 3, 1982 at Cincinnati, Riverfront Stadium, attendance 55,420

BUFFALO BILLS	0	7	7	7	—	**21**
CINCINNATI BENGALS	14	0	7	7	—	**28**

SCORING Cin—Alexander 4-yd run (Breech PAT), Cin—Johnson 1-yd run (Breech PAT), Buf—Cribbs 1-yd run (Mike-Mayer PAT), Buf—Cribbs 44-yd run (Mike-Mayer PAT), Cin—Alexander 20-yd run (Breech PAT), Buf—Butler 21-yd pass from Ferguson (Mike-Mayer PAT), Cin—Collinsworth 16-yd pass from Anderson (Breech PAT).

TEAM	FD	YDS	RUSH	PASS	RTN	A-C-I	SACKED	PUNT	FUMB	PEN
Buf	21	336	28-134	202	8	31-15-2	0-0	3-42	0-0	6-56
Cin	22	305	33-136	169	43	21-14-0	4-23	4-45	0-0	5-44

The Bengals took an early lead , but Buffalo twice rallied for the tie. Ken Anderson's touchdown pass to Chris Collinsworth gave Cincinnati back the lead in the fourth quarter. The Bills drove to the Bengals 21 and converted a fourth-down pass, but it was called back for delay of game. The next pass fell incomplete. Cincinnati won its first playoff game, having lost on the road in 1970, 1973, and 1975.

1981 NFC DIVISIONAL PLAYOFF

Sunday, January 3, 1982 at San Francisco, Candlestick Park, attendance 58,360

NEW YORK GIANTS	7	3	7	7	—	**24**
SAN FRANCISCO 49ERS	7	17	0	14	—	**38**

SCORING SF—Young 8-yd pass from Montana (Wersching PAT), NYG—Gray 72-yd pass from Brunner (Danelo PAT), SF—FG Wersching 22 yds, SF—Solomon 58-yd pass from Montana (Wersching PAT), SF—Patton 25-yd run (Wersching PAT), NYG—FG Danelo 48 yds, SF—Perkins 59-yd pass from Brunner (Danelo PAT), SF—Ring 3-yd run (Wersching PAT), SF—Lott 20-yd interception return (Wersching PAT), NYG—Perkins 17-yd pass from Brunner (Danelo PAT).

TEAM	FD	YDS	RUSH	PASS	RTN	A-C-I	SACKED	PUNT	FUMB	PEN
NYG	13	346	22-65	281	20	37-16-2	2-9	4-44	4-2	9-61
SF	24	423	34-135	288	54	31-20-1	3-16	5-41	2-0	14-145

NYG-Johnny Perkins 121C, Earnest Gray 118C; SF-Freddie Solomon 107C, Dwight Clark 104C, Joe Montana 304P

The Giants were able to move the ball but had trouble holding onto it. Four New York turnovers were too much against a precision 49ers offense. Joe Montana, in his first playoff game, threw for 304 yards and 2 touchdowns. Two receivers on each team surpassed 100 yards receiving.

1981 AFC CHAMPIONSHIP

Sunday, January 10, 1982 at Cincinnati, Riverfront Stadium, attendance 46,302

SAN DIEGO CHARGERS	0	7	0	0	—	**7**
CINCINNATI BENGALS	10	7	3	7	—	**27**

SCORING Cin—FG Breech 31 yds, Cin—M. L. Harris 8-yd pass from Anderson (Breech PAT), Cin—Johnson 1-yd run (Breech PAT), SD—Winslow 33-yd pass from Fouts (Benirschke PAT), Cin—FG Breech 38 yds, Cin—Bass 3-yd pass from Anderson (Breech PAT).

TEAM	FD	YDS	RUSH	PASS	RTN	A-C-I	SACKED	PUNT	FUMB	PEN
SD	18	301	31-128	173	7	28-15-2	2-12	2-30	4-2	2-15
Cin	19	318	36-143	175	24	23-15-0	0-0	3-31	3-1	3-25

SAN DIEGO CHARGERS

RUSHING	ATT	YDS	LNG	TD
Chuck Muncie	23	94	11	0
James Brooks	6	23	9	0

RECEIVING	NO	YDS	LNG	TD
Wes Chandler	6	79	25	0
Kellen Winslow	3	47	33	1

PASSING	PA	PC	YDS	TD	IN
Dan Fouts	28	15	185	1	2

CINCINNATI BENGALS

RUSHING	ATT	YDS	LNG	TD
Pete Johnson	21	80	11	1
Ken Anderson	5	39	13	0

RECEIVING	NO	YDS	LNG	TD
Dan Ross	5	69	19	0
Charles Alexander	3	25	16	0

PASSING	PA	PC	YDS	TD	IN
Ken Anderson	22	14	161	2	0

Rarely has homefield advantage meant so much. The temperature was 9 below zero, but the wind chill reached minus 59. The Chargers wanted to postpone the game; the Bengals said no. Their linemen showed up in short sleeves instead. Ken Anderson was 14 for 22 for 161 yards. Dan Fouts had more yards—and throws—but his 2 interceptions were costly, as was a fumble on a kickoff that helped Cincinnati take a 10–0 first-quarter lead. The Freezer Bowl propelled the Bengals to the Super Bowl for the first time. The talented Chargers, who'd won a classic game in a Miami steam bath the week before, could only shiver and wonder what might have been.

1981 NFC CHAMPIONSHIP

Sunday, January 10, 1982 at San Francisco, Candlestick Park, attendance 60,525

DALLAS COWBOYS	10	7	0	10	—	27
SAN FRANCISCO 49ERS	7	7	7	7	—	28

SCORING SF—Solomon 8-yd pass from Montana (Wersching PAT), Dal—FG Septien 44 yds, Dal—Hill 26-yd pass from D. White (Septien PAT), SF—Clark 20-yd pass from Montana (Wersching PAT), Dal—Dorsett 5-yd run (Septien PAT), SF—Davis 2-yd run (Wersching PAT), Dal—FG Septien 22 yds, Dal—Cosbie 21-yd pass from D. White (Septien PAT), SF—Clark 6-yd pass from Montana (Wersching PAT)

TEAM	FD	YDS	RUSH	PASS	RTN	A-C-I	SACKED	PUNT	FUMB	PEN
Dal	16	250	32-115	135	13	24-16-1	4-38	6-39	4-2	5-39
SF	26	393	31-127	266	29	35-22-3	3-20	3-36	3-3	7-106

DALLAS COWBOYS

RUSHING	ATT	YDS	LNG	TD
Tony Dorsett	22	91	11	1
James Jones	4	14	7	0

RECEIVING	NO	YDS	LNG	TD
James Jones	3	17	10	0
Billy Joe DuPree	3	15	7	0

PASSING	PA	PC	YDS	TD	IN
Danny White	24	16	173	2	1

SAN FRANCISCO 49ERS

RUSHING	ATT	YDS	LNG	TD
Lenvil Elliott	10	48	11	0
Earl Cooper	8	35	11	0

RECEIVING	NO	YDS	LNG	TD
Dwight Clark	8	120	38	2
Freddie Solomon	6	75	21	1
Charle Young	4	45	17	0

PASSING	PA	PC	YDS	TD	IN
Joe Montana	35	22	286	3	3

Despite a phenomenal season, the 49ers were just two years removed from consecutive 2–14 seasons. During their brief glory in the early 1970s, San Francisco had twice lost to Tom Landry's talented Cowboys in the championship game. Dallas caught a break this time when a penalty wiped out an interception and the Cowboys went on to score to take the lead at halftime. A Dallas fumble recovery led to a go-ahead touchdown with five minutes left. San Francisco drove from its 11 to the Dallas 6 when Montana, seemingly throwing the ball away, found a leaping Dwight Clark. The Catch notwithstanding, the 49ers defense stopped the Cowboys in the final minute.

1982 AFC FIRST ROUND PLAYOFF

Saturday, January 8, 1983 at Miami, Orange Bowl, attendance 68,842

NEW ENGLAND PATRIOTS	0	3	3	7	—	13
MIAMI DOLPHINS	0	14	7	7	—	28

SCORING NE—FG J. Smith 23 yds, Mia—Hardy 2-yd pass from Woodley (von Schamann PAT), Mia—Franklin 1-yd run (von Schamann PAT), NE—FG J. Smith 42 yds, Mia—Bennett 2-yd run (von Schamann PAT), Mia—Hardy 2-yd pass from Woodley (von Schamann PAT), NE—Hasselbeck 22-yd pass from Grogan (J. Smith PAT)

TEAM	FD	YDS	RUSH	PASS	RTN	A-C-I	SACKED	PUNT	FUMB	PEN
NE	14	237	18-77	160	0	30-16-2	4-29	5-44	1-1	4-27
Mia	27	448	45-214	234	65	19-16-0	2-12	1-51	3-3	2-15

Mia-Aundra Franklin 112R

A month earlier, a snowplow had cleared a path for Patriot John Smith to kick a game-winning field goal in Foxboro. In warm and sunny Miami, New England got an early field goal from Smith, but Miami scored 4 touchdowns before New England finally found the end zone in the fourth quarter.

1982 AFC FIRST ROUND PLAYOFF

Saturday, January 8, 1983 at Los Angeles, Memorial Coliseum, attendance 56,555

CLEVELAND BROWNS	0	10	0	0	—	10
LOS ANGELES RAIDERS	3	10	7	7	—	27

SCORING LA—FG C. Bahr 27 yds, Cle—FG M. Bahr 52 yds, LA—Allen 2-yd run (C. Bahr PAT), Cle—Feacher 43-yd pass from McDonald (M. Bahr PAT), LA—FG C. Bahr 37 yds, LA—Allen 3-yd run (C. Bahr PAT), LA—Hawkins 1-yd run (C. Bahr PAT)

TEAM	FD	YDS	RUSH	PASS	RTN	A-C-I	SACKED	PUNT	FUMB	PEN
Cle	17	284	18-56	228	13	37-18-0	6-53	6-49	2-1	4-35
LARd	25	510	36-140	370	45	37-24-2	2-16	3-39	2-0	6-65

Cle-Ricky Feacher 124C; LARd-Cliff Branch 121C; Jim Plunkett 386P

Just as they'd done in Oakland, the Los Angeles Raiders lived up to their owner's motto of "just win, baby." Brothers Matt and Chris Bahr traded field goals early and the Raiders took a 13–10 halftime lead. The Raiders rolled up 510 yards, with Jim Plunkett throwing for 386, as they slowly pulled away from the Browns.

1982 NFC FIRST ROUND PLAYOFF

Saturday, January 8, 1983 at Washington, RFK Stadium, attendance 55,045

DETROIT LIONS	0	0	7	0	—	7
WASHINGTON REDSKINS	10	14	7	0	—	31

SCORING Was—White 77-yd interception return (Moseley PAT), Was—FG Moseley 26 yds, Was—Garrett 21-yd pass from Theismann (Moseley PAT), Was—Garrett 21-yd pass from Theismann (Moseley PAT), Was—Garrett 27-yd pass from Theismann (Moseley PAT), Det—Hill 15-yd pass from Hipple (Murray PAT)

TEAM	FD	YDS	RUSH	PASS	RTN	A-C-I	SACKED	PUNT	FUMB	PEN
Det	20	364	21-95	269	13	38-22-2	4-29	3-38	3-3	5-29
Was	18	366	38-175	191	137	19-14-0	2-19	4-31	0-0	4-20

Det-Leonard Thompson 150C; Was-John Riggins 119R, Alvin Garrett 110C

Washington's Jeris White intercepted an Eric Hipple pass and ran 77 yards for a touchdown. Hipple fumbled on the next possession. Washington's lead was 31–0 before Hipple connected on a touchdown. Joe Theismann threw for 210 yards, plus 3 touchdowns to Alvin Garrett. John Riggins bulled for 119 yards.

1982 NFC FIRST ROUND PLAYOFF

Saturday, January 8, 1983 at Green Bay, Lambeau Field, attendance 54,282

ST. LOUIS CARDINALS	3	6	0	7	—	16
GREEN BAY PACKERS	7	21	10	3	—	41

SCORING StL—FG O'Donoghue 18 yds, GB—Jefferson 60-yd pass from Dickey (Stenerud PAT), GB—Lofton 20-yd pass from Dickey (Stenerud PAT), GB—Ivery 2-yd run (Stenerud PAT), GB—Ivery 4-yd pass from Dickey (Stenerud PAT), StL—Tilley 5-yd pass from Lomax (PAT blocked), GB—FG Stenerud 46 yds, GB—Jefferson 7-yd pass from Dickey (Stenerud PAT), GB—FG Stenerud 34 yds, StL—Shumann 18-yd pass from Lomax (O'Donoghue PAT)

TEAM	FD	YDS	RUSH	PASS	RTN	A-C-I	SACKED	PUNT	FUMB	PEN
SL	27	453	23-106	347	0	51-32-2	5-38	0-0	3-2	6-78
GB	22	394	31-108	286	22	26-19-0	0-0	1-28	1-1	5-35

SL-Roy Green 113C; Neil Lomax 385P; GB-John Jefferson 148C

Neil Lomax passed for 385 yards for the Cardinals, but Lynn Dickey threw 4 touchdown passes as Green Bay was in control the whole way. The Packers won their first postseason game since Super Bowl II and their first in Green Bay since the Ice Bowl in 1967.

1982 AFC FIRST ROUND PLAYOFF

Sunday, January 9, 1983 at Cincinnati, Riverfront Stadium, attendance 57,560

NEW YORK JETS	3	17	3	21	—	44
CINCINNATI BENGALS	14	0	3	0	—	17

SCORING Cin—Curtis 32-yd pass from Anderson (Breech PAT), NYJ—FG Leahy 33 yds, Cin—Ross 2-yd pass from Anderson (Breech PAT), NYJ—Gaffney 14-yd pass from McNeil (Leahy PAT), NYJ—Walker 4-yd pass from Todd (Leahy PAT), NYJ—FG Leahy 24 yds, NYJ—FG Leahy 47 yds, Cin—FG Breech 20 yds, NYJ—McNeil 20-yd run (Leahy PAT), NYJ—Ray 98-yd interception return (Leahy PAT), NYJ—Crutchfield 1-yd run (Leahy PAT)

TEAM	FD	YDS	RUSH	PASS	RTN	A-C-I	SACKED	PUNT	FUMB	PEN
NYJ	27	517	34-234	283	140	29-21-1	0-0	0-0	2-1	12-95
Cin	23	395	21-62	333	0	36-26-3	4-21	2-43	2-1	7-60

NYJ-Freeman McNeil 202R, Wesley Walker 145C; Cin-Cris Collinsworth 120C, Ken Anderson 354P

The defending AFC champs took a 14–3 lead in the first quarter, but the Jets were in control from there, outscoring Cincinnati, 41–3. New York racked up 517 total yards, including 202 yards rushing on 21

carries by Freeman McNeil. The Jets did not punt. Cincinnati's Ken Anderson had 354 passing yards.

1982 AFC FIRST ROUND PLAYOFF

Sunday, January 9, 1983 at Pittsburgh, Three Rivers Stadium, attendance 53,546

SAN DIEGO CHARGERS	3	14	0	14	—	**31**
PITTSBURGH STEELERS	14	0	7	7	—	**28**

SCORING Pit—Ruff fumble recovery in end zone (Anderson PAT), SD—FG Benirschke 25 yds, Pit—Bradshaw 1-yd run (Anderson PAT), SD—Brooks 18-yd run (Benirschke PAT), SD—Sievers 10-yd pass from Fouts (Benirschke PAT), Pit—Cunningham 2-yd pass from Bradshaw (Anderson PAT), Pit—Stallworth 14-yd pass from Bradshaw (Anderson PAT), SD—Winslow 8-yd pass from Fouts (Benirschke PAT), SD—Winslow 12-yd pass from Fouts (Benirschke PAT)

TEAM	FD	YDS	RUSH	PASS	RTN	A-C-I	SACKED	PUNT	FUMB	PEN
SD	29	479	29-146	333	43	42-27-0	0-0	1-48	3-2	6-51
Pit	26	422	23-97	325	12	39-28-2	0-0	2-33	1-0	6-54

SD-Chuck Muncie 126R, Wes Chandler 124C, Kellen Winslow 102C, Dan Fouts 333P; Pit-John Stallworth 116C, Terry Bradshaw 325P

Pittsburgh scored on the opening kickoff when James Brooks fumbled in his end zone and Guy Hoff recovered for a touchdown. The Steelers led in the fourth quarter, 28–17, but Dan Fouts twice found Kellen Winslow for touchdown passes, the second coming in the final minute. Terry Bradshaw threw for 325 yards in his 19th and final playoff game.

1982 NFC FIRST ROUND PLAYOFF

Sunday, January 9, 1983 at Dallas, Texas Stadium, attendance 65,042

TAMPA BAY BUCCANEERS	0	10	7	0	—	**17**
DALLAS COWBOYS	6	7	3	14	—	**30**

SCORING Dal—FG Septien 33 yds, Dal—FG Septien 33 yds, TB—Green 60-yd fumble return (Capece PAT), TB—FG Capece 32 yds, Dal—Springs 6-yd pass from D. White (Septien PAT), Dal—FG Septien 19 yds, TB—Jones 49-yd pass from Williams (Capece PAT), Dal—Hunter 19-yd interception return (Septien PAT), Dal—Newsome 10-yd pass from D. White (Septien PAT)

TEAM	FD	YDS	RUSH	PASS	RTN	A-C-I	SACKED	PUNT	FUMB	PEN
TB	8	218	21-105	113	58	28-8-3	0-0	6-44	0-0	4-41
Dal	29	456	42-179	277	87	45-27-2	5-35	3-37	1-1	6-45

Dal-Tony Dorsett 110R, Danny White 312P

Dallas thoroughly outplayed Tampa Bay, but the Buccaneers held the lead in the fourth quarter. After an interception of Danny White, Doug Williams threw 49 yards to Gordon Jones for a Buccaneers touchdown. Cowboys rookie Monty Hunter intercepted Williams and returned it for the go-ahead score. White later added an insurance touchdown.

1982 NFC FIRST ROUND PLAYOFF

Sunday, January 9, 1983 at Minneapolis, MN, Metrodome, attendance 60,560

ATLANTA FALCONS	7	0	14	3	—	**24**
MINNESOTA VIKINGS	3	10	3	14	—	**30**

SCORING Atl—Rogers recovered blocked punt in end zone (Luckhurst PAT), Min—FG Danmeier 33 yds, Min—White 36-yd pass from Kramer (Danmeier PAT), Min—FG Danmeier 30 yds, Atl—Luckhurst 17-yd run (Luckhurst PAT), Atl—Glazebrook 35-yd interception return (Luckhurst PAT), Min—FG Danmeier 39 yds, Min—McCullum 11-yd pass from Kramer (Danmeier PAT), Atl—FG Luckhurst 41 yds, Min—Brown 5-yd run (Danmeier PAT)

TEAM	FD	YDS	RUSH	PASS	RTN	A-C-I	SACKED	PUNT	FUMB	PEN
Atl	24	235	24-120	115	35	23-9-2	3-19	5-43	1-0	7-98
Min	30	378	42-125	253	90	34-20-1	0-0	5-32	4-0	10-84

The Vikings, playing an indoor playoff game for the first time, marched down the field and scored the winning touchdown on Ted Brown's 5-yard run with 1:44 left. Atlanta had no offensive touchdowns, scoring on a blocked punt, an interception return, and a 17-yard run for a touchdown by kicker Mick Luckhurst on a fake field goal.

1982 AFC DIVISIONAL PLAYOFF

Saturday, January 15, 1983 at Los Angeles, Memorial Coliseum, attendance 90,037

NEW YORK JETS	7	3	0	7	—	**17**
LOS ANGELES RAIDERS	0	0	14	0	—	**14**

SCORING NYJ—Walker 20-yd pass from Todd (Leahy PAT), NYJ—FG Leahy 30 yds, LA—Allen 3-yd run (Bahr PAT), LA—Barnwell 57-yd pass from Plunkett (Bahr PAT), NYJ—Dierking 1-yd run (Leahy PAT)

TEAM	FD	YDS	RUSH	PASS	RTN	A-C-I	SACKED	PUNT	FUMB	PEN
NYJ	21	391	34-139	252	34	24-15-2	4-25	2-32	4-3	7-64
LARd	19	339	30-93	246	0	33-21-3	2-20	4-41	2-2	5-55

NYJ-Freeman McNeil 105R, Wesley Walker 169C

The Jets dominated three quarters of the game, but the Raiders commanded the third quarter, scoring twice and wiping out New York's 10–0 lead. The Raiders had another chance following a Lester Hayes interception, but Marcus Allen subsequently fumbled. Wesley Walker, with 7 catches for 169 yards, went 45 yards to the Raiders 1. Scott Dierking scored with 3:45 remaining, and Lance Mehl twice picked off Jim Plunkett in the closing minutes.

1982 NFC DIVISIONAL PLAYOFF

Saturday, January 15, 1983 at Washington, RFK Stadium, attendance 54,593

MINNESOTA VIKINGS	0	7	0	0	—	**7**
WASHINGTON REDSKINS	14	7	0	0	—	**21**

SCORING Was—Warren 3-yd pass from Theismann (Moseley PAT), Was—Riggins 2-yd run (Moseley PAT), Min—Brown 18-yd run (Danmeier PAT), Was—Garrett 18-yd pass from Theismann (Moseley PAT)

TEAM	FD	YDS	RUSH	PASS	RTN	A-C-I	SACKED	PUNT	FUMB	PEN
Min	15	317	18-79	238	0	39-18-0	2-14	4-39	1-0	5-39
Was	23	415	42-204	211	9	23-17-1	2-2	2-30	0-0	3-25

Was-John Riggins 185R

Washington controlled the ball for 12 minutes in the opening quarter, scoring twice. Minnesota cut the lead to 14–7, but Joe Theismann found Alvin Garrett for the day's final points. From there, it was the Riggo Show, with John Riggins rolling up 185 yards on 37 carries.

1982 AFC DIVISIONAL PLAYOFF

Sunday, January 16, 1983 at Miami, Orange Bowl, attendance 71,383

SAN DIEGO CHARGERS	0	13	0	0	—	**13**
MIAMI DOLPHINS	7	20	0	7	—	**34**

SCORING Mia—Moore 3-yd pass from Woodley (von Schamann PAT), Mia—Franklin 3-yd run (von Schamann PAT), Mia—Lee 6-yd pass from Woodley (von Schamann PAT), Mia—FG von Schamann 24 yds, SD—Joiner 28-yd pass from Fouts (PAT failed), Mia—FG von Schamann 23 yds, SD—Muncie 1-yd run (Benirschke PAT), Mia—Woodley 7-yd run (von Schamann PAT)

TEAM	FD	YDS	RUSH	PASS	RTN	A-C-I	SACKED	PUNT	FUMB	PEN
SD	17	247	17-79	168	34	34-15-5	3-23	4-41	3-2	7-62
Mia	29	413	56-214	199	58	23-18-1	1-16	3-40	2-1	6-70

The rematch of the previous year's epic Kellen Winslow Game in Miami was pretty one-sided. Winslow caught just 1 pass while Dan Fouts threw 5 interceptions. Turnovers gave Dolphin David Woodley the ball in scoring position and he responded with 2 touchdown passes and a 24–0 second-quarter lead. Woodley ran for the only score of the second half.

1982 NFC DIVISIONAL PLAYOFF

Sunday, January 16, 1983 at Dallas, Texas Stadium, attendance 63,972

GREEN BAY PACKERS	0	7	6	13	—	**26**
DALLAS COWBOYS	6	14	3	14	—	**37**

SCORING Dal—FG Septien 50 yds, Dal—FG Septien 34 yds, GB—Lofton 6-yd pass from Dickey (Stenerud PAT), Dal—Newsome 2-yd run (Septien PAT), Dal—Thurman 39-yd interception return (Septien PAT), GB—FG Stenerud 30 yds, GB—FG Stenerud 33 yds, Dal—FG Septien 24 yds, GB—Lofton 71-yd run (PAT failed), Dal—Cosbie 7-yd pass from D. White (Septien PAT), GB—Lee 22-yd interception return (Stenerud PAT), Dal—Newhouse 1-yd run (Septien PAT)

TEAM	FD	YDS	RUSH	PASS	RTN	A-C-I	SACKED	PUNT	FUMB	PEN
GB	21	466	17-158	308	30	36-19-3	4-24	4-42	4-2	3-35
Dal	24	375	39-109	266	81	37-24-1	1-8	4-35	1-1	5-30

GB-James Lofton 109C, Lynn Dickey 332P; Dal-Tony Hill 142C

The Packers and Cowboys met in the postseason for the first time since the Ice Bowl 15 years earlier. There were plenty of points to go around. Green Bay's Lynn Dickey threw for 332 yards, but his 3 interceptions—all by Dennis Thurman—came at crucial times. The Packers scored in the final quarter on James Lofton's 71-yard reverse and Mark Lee's interception return, but the Cowboys countered each with scores of their own.

1982 NFC CHAMPIONSHIP

Saturday, January 22, 1983 at Washington, RFK Stadium, attendance 55,045

DALLAS COWBOYS	3	0	14	0	—	17
WASHINGTON REDSKINS	7	7	7	10	—	**31**

SCORING Dal—FG Septien 27 yds, Was—Brown 19-yd pass from Theismann (Moseley PAT), Was—Riggins 1-yd run (Moseley PAT), Dal—Pearson 6-yd pass from Hogeboom (Septien PAT), Was—Riggins 4-yd run (Moseley PAT), Dal—Johnson 23-yd pass from Hogeboom (Septien PAT), Was—FG Moseley 29 yds, Was—Grant 10-yd interception return (Moseley PAT)

TEAM	FD	YDS	RUSH	PASS	RTN	A-C-I	SACKED	PUNT	FUMB	PEN
Dal	21	340	21-65	275	10	44-23-2	0-0	3-31	2-1	3-15
Was	18	260	40-137	123	26	20-12-0	3-27	5-40	1-0	3-25

DALLAS COWBOYS				
RUSHING	ATT	YDS	LNG	TD
Tony Dorsett	15	57	17	0
Ron Springs	4	15	12	0
RECEIVING	NO	YDS	LNG	TD
Butch Johnson	5	73	23	1
Tony Hill	5	59	15	0
Drew Pearson	5	55	16	1
PASSING	PA	PC	YDS	TD	IN
Gary Hogeboom	29	14	162	2	2
Danny White	15	9	113	0	0

WASHINGTON REDSKINS				
RUSHING	ATT	YDS	LNG	TD
John Riggins	36	140	17	2
Joe Washington	2	2	2	0
RECEIVING	NO	YDS	LNG	TD
Alvin Garrett	4	46	22	0
Charlie Brown	3	54	22	1
PASSING	PA	PC	YDS	TD	IN
Joe Theismann	20	12	150	1	0

The intense Dallas–Washington rivalry reached a fever pitch in this game. The Redskins had a 7–3 second-quarter lead when a muffed punt gave the Redskins the ball at the Dallas 11. They went up 14–3 on a 1-yard plunge by John Riggins, who ran 36 times for 140 yards and 2 touchdowns. Dallas lost its quarterback shortly thereafter as Danny White suffered a concussion. Gary Hogeboom came off the bench and threw for 162 yards and 2 touchdowns. His fourth-quarter interception, deflected by Dexter Manley to Darryl Grant, resulted in a clinching touchdown that sent the Redskins to their first Super Bowl in a decade.

1982 AFC CHAMPIONSHIP

Sunday, January 23, 1983 at Miami, Orange Bowl, attendance 67,396

NEW YORK JETS	0	0	0	0	—	0
MIAMI DOLPHINS	0	0	7	7	—	**14**

SCORING Mia—Bennett 7-yd run (von Schamann PAT), Mia—Duhe 35-yd interception return (von Schamann PAT)

TEAM	FD	YDS	RUSH	PASS	RTN	A-C-I	SACKED	PUNT	FUMB	PEN
NYJ	10	139	24-62	77	66	37-15-5	4-26	10-36	1-0	6-42
Mia	13	198	41-138	60	68	21-9-3	4-27	10-33	3-1	3-15

NEW YORK JETS				
RUSHING	ATT	YDS	LNG	TD
Freeman McNeil	17	46	9	0
Richard Todd	4	10	10	0
RECEIVING	NO	YDS	LNG	TD
Bruce Harper	4	14	14	0
Lam Jones	3	35	18	0
PASSING	PA	PC	YDS	TD	IN
Richard Todd	37	15	103	0	5

MIAMI DOLPHINS.				
RUSHING	ATT	YDS	LNG	TD
David Woodley	8	46	17	0
Aundra Franklin	13	44	8	0
RECEIVING	NO	YDS	LNG	TD
Tommy Vigorito	3	29	20	0
Duriel Harris	2	28	14	0
PASSING	PA	PC	YDS	TD	IN
David Woodley	21	9	87	0	3

For year afterward, Jets fans would lament that the tarp was left off the field prior to the game and heavy rain turned Miami's field into a mess, slowing down New York's potent offense. NFL rushing leader Freeman McNeil had just 46 yards rushing. The Dolphins, controlling the clock, ran 41 times for 138 yards. The clubs combined for 8 sacks and 8 interceptions. A.J. Duhe picked off 3 Richard Todd passes. His third-quarter interception set up the game's first points and he took his fourth-quarter pick 35 yards for the score that dashed New York's dreams of a Super Bowl. Miami was off to its fourth Super Bowl.

1983 AFC WILD CARD GAME

Saturday, December 24, 1983 at Seattle, Kingdome, attendance 64,275

DENVER BRONCOS	7	0	0	0	—	7
SEATTLE SEAHAWKS	3	7	7	14	—	**31**

SCORING Sea—Largent 17-yd pass from Krieg (N. Johnson PAT), Den—Myles 13-yd pass from DeBerg (Karlis PAT), Sea—FG N. Johnson 37 yds, Sea—Metzelaars 5-yd pass from Krieg (N. Johnson PAT), Sea—Johns 18-yd pass from Krieg (N. Johnson PAT), Sea—Hughes 2-yd run (N. Johnson PAT)

TEAM	FD	YDS	RUSH	PASS	RTN	A-C-I	SACKED	PUNT	FUMB	PEN
Den	21	360	33-125	235	10	34-24-2	2-19	4-48	1-1	5-35
Sea	17	324	38-145	179	103	13-12-0	2-21	3-42	1-0	3-34

The Seahawks, playing in their first playoff game at the deafening Kingdome, forced 3 Denver turnovers deep in Seattle territory.

Dave Krieg, who started just half Seattle's games during the season, completed 12 of 13 passes for 200 yards and 3 touchdowns. Rookie Curt Warner, who led the AFC in rushing, ran for 99 yards.

1983 NFC WILD CARD GAME

Monday, December 26, 1983 at Dallas, Texas Stadium, attendance 62,118

LOS ANGELES RAMS	7	0	7	10	—	24
DALLAS COWBOYS	0	7	3	7	—	17

SCORING LA—D. Hill 18-yd pass from Ferragamo (Lansford PAT), Dal—T. Hill 14-yd pass from D. White (Septien PAT), Dal—FG Septien 41 yds, LA—Dennard 16-yd pass from Ferragamo (Lansford PAT), LA—Farmer 8-yd pass from Ferragamo (Lansford PAT), LA—FG Lansford 20 yds, Dal—Cosbie 2-yd pass from D. White (Septien PAT)

TEAM	FD	YDS	RUSH	PASS	RTN	A-C-I	SACKED	PUNT	FUMB	PEN
LARm	19	243	30-94	149	121	31-16-0	2-14	6-37	0-0	4-18
Dal	24	363	20-63	300	16	53-32-3	3-30	5-31	2-1	6-40

Dal—Tony Hill 115C, Danny White 330P

The Cowboys took a 10–7 lead early in the third quarter before disintegrating. Dallas fumbled away a punt, and the Rams scored on the next play. Three consecutive Dallas drives ended with interceptions thrown by Danny White, who put the ball up 52 times for 330 yards. Vince Ferragamo didn't have half that yardage, but he had 3 touchdown passes.

1983 AFC DIVISIONAL PLAYOFF

Saturday, December 31, 1983 at Miami, Orange Bowl, attendance 74,136

SEATTLE SEAHAWKS	0	7	7	13	—	**27**
MIAMI DOLPHINS	0	13	0	7	—	20

SCORING Mia—Johnson 19-yd pass from Marino (PAT failed), Sea—C. Bryant 6-yd pass from Krieg (N. Johnson PAT), Mia—Duper 32-yd pass from Marino (von Schamann PAT), Sea—Warner 1-yd run (N. Johnson PAT), Sea—FG N. Johnson 27 yds, Mia—Bennett 3-yd run (von Schamann PAT), Sea—Warner 2-yd run (N. Johnson PAT), Sea—FG N. Johnson 37 yds

TEAM	FD	YDS	RUSH	PASS	RTN	A-C-I	SACKED	PUNT	FUMB	PEN
Sea	21	334	42-151	183	0	29-15-1	1-9	4-38	0-0	2-15
Mia	21	321	30-128	193	50	26-15-2	0-0	4-36	3-3	5-30

Sea-Curt Warner 113R; Mia-Mark Duper 117C

Rookie Dan Marino helped the Dolphins take a fourth-quarter lead, but Seattle rookie Curt Warner scored his second touchdown to put the Seahawks ahead. Miami had plenty of time to regain the lead, but Fulton Walker fumbled the kickoff. After a Seattle field goal, Walker fumbled again and the Seahawks had the upset.

1983 NFC DIVISIONAL PLAYOFF

Saturday, December 31, 1983 at San Francisco, Candlestick Park, attendance 59,979

DETROIT LIONS	3	6	0	14	—	23
SAN FRANCISCO 49ERS	7	7	3	7	—	**24**

SCORING Det—FG Murray 37 yds, SF—Craig 1-yd run (Wersching PAT), SF—Tyler 1-yd run (Wersching PAT), Det—FG Murray 21 yds, Det—FG Murray 54 yds, SF—FG Wersching 19 yds, Det—Sims 11-yd run (Murray PAT), Det—Sims 3-yd run (Murray PAT), SF—Solomon 14-yd pass from Montana (Wersching PAT)

TEAM	FD	YDS	RUSH	PASS	RTN	A-C-I	SACKED	PUNT	FUMB	PEN
Det	22	412	35-188	224	54	38-24-5	2-12	2-37	2-0	7-63
SF	20	291	27-103	188	41	31-18-1	2-13	5-35	2-1	5-25

Det-Billy Sims 114R

Eddie Murray kicked 3 field goals, including a playoff-record 54-yarder, but with five seconds remaining he missed a 43-yard kick that would have given the Lions their first postseason win since 1957. Although Gary Danielson threw 5 interceptions, the Lions had a lead with five minutes left on a Billy Sims touchdown run. Joe Montana was perfect in the ensuing drive for the 49ers.

1983 AFC DIVISIONAL PLAYOFF

Sunday, January 1, 1984 at Los Angeles, Memorial Coliseum, attendance 90,380

PITTSBURGH STEELERS	3	0	7	0	—	10
LOS ANGELES RAIDERS	7	10	21	0	—	**38**

SCORING Pit—FG Anderson 17 yds, LA—Hayes 18-yd interception return (Bahr PAT), LA—Allen 4-yd run (Bahr PAT), LA—FG Bahr 45 yds, LA—King 9-yd run (Bahr PAT), LA—Allen 49-yd run (Bahr PAT), Pit—Stallworth 58-yd pass from Stoudt (Anderson PAT), LA—Hawkins 2-yd run (Bahr PAT)

TEAM	FD	YDS	RUSH	PASS	RTN	A-C-I	SACKED	PUNT	FUMB	PEN
Pit	17	331	32-162	169	21	27-13-1	5-40	9-36	2-1	4-30
LARd	24	413	33-188	225	70	34-21-0	1-7	6-41	2-0	2-15

LARd–Marcus Allen 121R

The Raiders–Steelers playoff rivalry moved south to Los Angeles, but it quickly turned into a rout in front of a playoff-record crowd of 90,380. Marcus Allen had a lot to do with that. He gained 121 yards on 13 carries, an average of 9.3 yards, and scored twice. He also caught 5 passes for 38 yards.

1983 NFC DIVISIONAL PLAYOFF

Sunday, January 1, 1984 at Washington, RFK Stadium, attendance 54,440

LOS ANGELES RAMS	0	7	0	—	7
WASHINGTON REDSKINS	17	21	6	7	— 51

SCORING Was—Riggins 3-yd run (Moseley PAT), Was—Monk 40-yd pass from Theismann (Moseley PAT), Was—FG Moseley 42 yds, Was—Riggins 1-yd run (Moseley PAT), LA—Dennard 32-yd pass from Ferragamo (Lansford PAT), Was—Monk 21-yd pass from Theismann (Moseley PAT), Was—Riggins 1-yd run (Moseley PAT), Was—FG Moseley 36 yds, Was—FG Moseley 41 yds, Was—Green 72-yd interception return

TEAM	FD	YDS	RUSH	PASS	RTN	A-C-I	SACKED	PUNT	FUMB	PEN
LARm	12	204	16-51	153	4	43-20-3	3-22	7-34	2-1	7-41
Was	23	445	40-130	315	128	25-20-0	0-0	3-28	2-1	6-55

Was–John Riggins 119R, Charlie Brown 171C, Joe Theismann 302P

The Redskins, who averaged a remarkable 33 points per game during the season, reached that number in the second quarter as they shellacked the Rams. Washington held Eric Dickerson, with 1,808 yards rushing during the season, to 16 yards on 10 carries. John Riggins did the heavy lifting, running for 119 yards and 3 touchdowns. Joe Theismann threw for 302 yards.

1983 AFC CHAMPIONSHIP

Sunday, January 8, 1984 at Los Angeles, Memorial Coliseum, attendance 88,734

SEATTLE SEAHAWKS	0	0	7	7	— 14
LOS ANGELES RAIDERS	3	17	7	3	— 30

SCORING LA—FG Bahr 20 yds, LA—Hawkins 1-yd run (Bahr PAT), LA—Hawkins 5-yd run (Bahr PAT), LA—FG Bahr 45 yds, LA—Allen 3-yd pass from Plunkett (Bahr PAT), Sea—Doornink 11-yd pass from Zorn (N. Johnson PAT), LA—FG Bahr 35 yds, Sea—Young 9-yd pass from Zorn (N. Johnson PAT)

TEAM	FD	YDS	RUSH	PASS	RTN	A-C-I	SACKED	PUNT	FUMB	PEN
Sea	16	167	18-65	102	8	36-17-5	4-44	5-32	1-0	2-20
LARd	21	401	46-205	196	54	24-17-2	2-18	2-34	3-2	7-53

SEATTLE SEAHAWKS

RUSHING	ATT	YDS	LNG	TD
Curt Warner	11	26	7	0
Zachary Dixon	3	24	10	0

RECEIVING	NO	YDS	LNG	TD
Don Doornink	6	48	12	1
Paul Johns	5	49	14	0

PASSING	PA	PC	YDS	TD	IN
Jim Zorn	27	14	134	2	2
Dave Krieg	9	3	12	0	3

LOS ANGELES RAIDERS

RUSHING	ATT	YDS	LNG	TD
Marcus Allen	25	154	43	0
Jim Plunkett	7	26	10	0
Frank Hawkins	10	24	8	2

RECEIVING	NO	YDS	LNG	TD
Marcus Allen	7	62	16	1
Malcolm Barnwell	5	116	49	0

PASSING	PA	PC	YDS	TD	IN
Jim Plunkett	24	17	214	1	2

The Raiders defense stifled the Seahawks, allowing just 167 yards. The Raiders, meanwhile, cranked up 401, including 216 by Marcus Allen (154 rushing, 62 receiving). The Seahawks had beaten the Raiders twice during the season, but Seattle's magical run was over by halftime. Dave Krieg was yanked and the score was 27–0 before Seahawks finally scored on a Jim Zorn pass. Some said the Seahawks, making the playoffs for the first time ever, were just happy to be there. They better have been. It would be 22 years before they went to another championship game. For the Raiders, it was there fourth trip to the Super Bowl.

1983 NFC CHAMPIONSHIP

Sunday, January 8, 1984 at Washington, RFK Stadium, attendance 55,363

SAN FRANCISCO 49ERS	0	0	0	21	— 21
WASHINGTON REDSKINS	0	7	14	3	— 24

SCORING Was—Riggins 4-yd run (Moseley PAT), Was—Riggins 1-yd run (Moseley PAT), Was—Brown 70-yd pass from Theismann (Moseley PAT), SF—Wilson 5-yd pass from Montana (Wersching PAT), SF—Solomon 76-yd pass from Montana (Wersching PAT), SF—Wilson 12-yd pass from Montana (Wersching PAT), Was—FG Moseley 25 yds

TEAM	FD	YDS	RUSH	PASS	RTN	A-C-I	SACKED	PUNT	FUMB	PEN
SF	19	434	16-87	347	7	48-27-1	0-0	7-34	4-2	6-72
Was	24	410	45-172	238	36	27-15-1	3-27	5-40	2-1	4-35

SAN FRANCISCO 49ERS

RUSHING	ATT	YDS	LNG	TD
Wendell Tyler	8	44	10	0
Joe Montana	5	40	18	0

RECEIVING	NO	YDS	LNG	TD
Mike Wilson	8	57	22	2
Freddie Solomon	4	106	76	1
Russ Francis	4	48	13	0

PASSING	PA	PC	YDS	TD	IN
Joe Montana	48	27	347	3	1

WASHINGTON REDSKINS

RUSHING	ATT	YDS	LNG	TD
John Riggins	36	123	23	2
Joe Washington	6	23	8	0

RECEIVING	NO	YDS	LNG	TD
Charlie Brown	5	137	70	1
Clint Didier	3	61	46	0

PASSING	PA	PC	YDS	TD	IN
Joe Theismann	26	14	229	1	1

A pass interference call on a ball that, according to 49ers coach Bill Walsh, "couldn't have been caught by a 10-foot tall Boston Celtic," gave the Redskins a first down at the San Francisco 18 in the closing minutes of a tie game. Another questionable call brought the Redskins even closer. Mark Mosely, with 3 misses on the day, drilled a 25-yarder to win the game and nullify a 21-point San Francisco rally in the fourth quarter. Joe Montana completed 27 passes for 347 yards, but there wasn't enough time left for any more miracles. The Redskins were NFC champions for the second straight year.

1984 AFC WILD CARD GAME

Saturday, December 22, 1984 at Seattle, Kingdome, attendance 62,049

LOS ANGELES RAIDERS	0	0	0	7	— 7
SEATTLE SEAHAWKS	0	7	3	3	— 13

SCORING Sea—Turner 26-yd pass from Krieg (Johnson PAT), Sea—FG Johnson 35 yds, Sea—FG Johnson 44 yds, LA—Allen 46-yd pass from Plunkett (Bahr PAT)

TEAM	FD	YDS	RUSH	PASS	RTN	A-C-I	SACKED	PUNT	FUMB	PEN
LARd	14	240	25-105	135	5	27-14-2	6-49	8-42	2-1	8-68
Sea	17	251	51-205	46	73	10-4-0	2-24	8-38	0-0	7-55

Sea–Don Doornink 126R

The Seahawks brought the Raiders inside the Kingdome and smothered them. Dan Doornink bulled for 126 yards on 29 carries. In all, 205 of Seattle's 251 total yards came on the ground. Dave Krieg, a 3,671-yard passer, threw sparingly, going just 4 for 10 with a touchdown. The Seahawks would not win another playoff game until 2005.

1984 NFC WILD CARD GAME

Sunday, December 23, 1984 at Anaheim, CA, Anaheim Stadium, attendance 67,037

NEW YORK GIANTS	10	0	6	0	— 16
LOS ANGELES RAMS	0	3	7	3	— 13

SCORING NYG—FG Haji-Sheikh 37 yds, NYG—Carpenter 1-yd run (Haji-Sheikh PAT), LA—FG Lansford 38 yds, NYG—FG Haji-Sheikh 39 yds, LA—Dickerson 14-yd run (Lansford PAT), NYG—FG Haji-Sheikh 36 yds, LA—FG Lansford 22 yds

TEAM	FD	YDS	RUSH	PASS	RTN	A-C-I	SACKED	PUNT	FUMB	PEN
NYG	16	192	27-40	152	25	31-22-0	4-27	4-39	3-0	5-81
LARm	12	214	26-107	107	17	15-11-0	2-2	4-38	2-2	10-65

LARm–Eric Dickerson 107R

Eric Dickerson, who set the single-season rushing mark, ran for 107 yards and a touchdown, but he fumbled twice, as did Rams quarterback Jeff Kemp in the closing minutes, to seal the game for the Giants. New York rushed for just 40 yards, but Phil Simms moved them to the next round with an effective short-passing game.

1984 AFC DIVISIONAL PLAYOFF

Saturday, December 29, 1984 at Miami, Orange Bowl, attendance 73,469

SEATTLE SEAHAWKS	0	10	0	0	— 10
MIAMI DOLPHINS	7	7	14	3	— 31

SCORING Mia—Nathan 14-yd run (von Schamann PAT), Sea—FG Johnson 27 yds, Mia—Cefalo 34-yd pass from Marino (von Schamann PAT), Sea—Largent 56-yd pass from Krieg (Johnson PAT), Mia—Hardy 3-yd pass from Marino (von Schamann PAT), Mia—Clayton 33-yd pass from Marino (von Schamann PAT), Mia—FG von Schamann 37 yds

TEAM	FD	YDS	RUSH	PASS	RTN	A-C-I	SACKED	PUNT	FUMB	PEN
Sea	18	267	18-51	216	50	35-20-0	2-18	7-37	1-1	4-20
Mia	22	405	36-143	262	36	34-21-2	0-0	3-37	0-0	1-5

Sea–Steve Largent 128C

Dan Marino, the first 5,000-yard passer in history, threw for 262 yards—below his season average of 318—but the Dolphins still won

handily. Miami led the whole way and relied on the ground game in the second half to chew up the clock and spit out Seattle at the Orange Bowl.

1984 NFC DIVISIONAL PLAYOFF
Saturday, December 29, 1984 at San Francisco, Candlestick Park, attendance 60,303

NEW YORK GIANTS	0	10	0	0	—	10
SAN FRANCISCO 49ERS	14	7	0	0	—	21

SCORING SF—Clark 21-yd pass from Montana (Wersching PAT), SF—Francis 9-yd pass from Montana (Wersching PAT), NYG—FG Haji-Sheikh 46 yds, NYG—Carson 14-yd interception return (Haji-Sheikh PAT), SF—Solomon 29-yd pass from Montana (Wersching PAT)

TEAM	FD	YDS	RUSH	PASS	RTN	A-C-I	SACKED	PUNT	FUMB	PEN
NYG	18	260	25-87	173	69	44-25-2	6-45	6-38	2-1	2-25
SF	22	412	28-131	281	52	39-25-3	4-28	5-42	0-0	5-29

SF-Dwight Clark 112C, Joe Montana 309P

The 49ers took a 14–0 lead in the first 6:38 of the first quarter. After the Giants put up 10 points, Joe Montana threw his third touchdown pass to his third different receiver with 4:38 remaining in the first half. Neither team scored again. San Francisco's defense had 6 sacks of Phil Simms and forced 2 interceptions.

1984 AFC DIVISIONAL PLAYOFF
Sunday, December 30, 1984 at Denver, Mile High Stadium, attendance 74,981

PITTSBURGH STEELERS	0	10	7	7	—	24
DENVER BRONCOS	7	0	10	0	—	17

SCORING Den—Wright 9-yd pass from Elway (Karlis PAT), Pit—FG Anderson 28 yds, Pit—Pollard 1-yd run (Anderson PAT), Den—FG Karlis 21 yds, Den—Watson 20-yd pass from Elway (Karlis PAT), Pit—Lipps 10-yd pass from Malone (Anderson PAT), Pit—Pollard 2-yd run (Anderson PAT)

TEAM	FD	YDS	RUSH	PASS	RTN	A-C-I	SACKED	PUNT	FUMB	PEN
Pit	25	381	40-169	212	43	28-17-0	2-12	3-28	3-2	4-30
Den	15	250	22-51	199	17	38-20-2	4-37	4-42	2-0	1-5

Den-Steve Watson 177C

Pittsburgh, which had rudely welcomed John Elway to the NFL in his 1983 pro debut, wasn't any kinder in his first home playoff game. With the game tied and three minutes to play, Elway was intercepted by Eric Williams, who returned the ball to the Denver 2. Frank Pollard scored his second touchdown of the day to claim the victory.

1984 NFC DIVISIONAL PLAYOFF
Sunday, December 30, 1984 at Washington, RFK Stadium, attendance 55,431

CHICAGO BEARS	0	10	13	0	—	23
WASHINGTON REDSKINS	3	0	14	2	—	19

SCORING Was—FG Moseley 25 yds, Chi—FG B. Thomas 34 yds, Chi—Dunsmore 19-yd pass from Payton (B. Thomas PAT), Chi—Gault 75-yd pass from Fuller (PAT failed), Was—Riggins 1-yd run (Moseley PAT), Chi—McKinnon 16-yd pass from Fuller (B. Thomas PAT), Was—Riggins 1-yd run (Moseley PAT), Was—Safety, Finzer stepped out of end zone

TEAM	FD	YDS	RUSH	PASS	RTN	A-C-I	SACKED	PUNT	FUMB	PEN
Chi	13	310	35-114	196	17	17-10-0	5-34	5-39	2-1	6-34
Was	22	336	27-93	243	29	42-22-1	7-49	5-37	0-0	7-55

Chi-Walter Payton 104R; Was-Art Monk 122C

Steve Fuller, one of four quarterbacks the Bears used to win the NFC Central, led Chicago to its first playoff victory since 1963. Fuller did what everyone expected—he handed off to Walter Payton (24 rushes for 102 yards)—but his 9 completions covered 211 yards, including a 75-yard touchdown to Willie Gault. Payton even added a 19-yard touchdown pass in Washington.

1984 AFC CHAMPIONSHIP
Sunday, January 6, 1985 at Miami, Orange Bowl, attendance 76,029

PITTSBURGH STEELERS	7	7	7	7	—	28
MIAMI DOLPHINS	7	17	14	7	—	45

SCORING Mia—Clayton 40-yd pass from Marino (von Schamann PAT), Pit—Erenberg 7-yd run (Anderson PAT), Mia—FG von Schamann 26 yds, Pit—Stallworth 65-yd pass from Malone (Anderson PAT), Mia—Duper 41-yd pass from Marino (von Schamann PAT), Mia—Nathan 2-yd run (von Schamann PAT), Mia—Duper 36-yd pass from Marino (von Schamann PAT), Pit—Stallworth 19-yd pass from Malone (Anderson PAT), Mia—Bennett 1-yd run (von Schamann PAT), Mia—Moore 6-yd pass from Marino (von Schamann PAT), Pit—Capers 29-yd pass from Malone (Anderson PAT)

TEAM	FD	YDS	RUSH	PASS	RTN	A-C-I	SACKED	PUNT	FUMB	PEN
Pit	22	455	32-143	312	25	36-20-3	0-0	3-44	2-1	3-30
Mia	28	569	38-134	435	54	33-22-1	0-0	2-43	1-1	3-25

PITTSBURGH STEELERS

RUSHING
	ATT	YDS	LNG	TD
Walter Abercrombie	15	68	20	0
Frank Pollard	11	48	9	0

RECEIVING
	NO	YDS	LNG	TD
Rich Erenberg	5	59	24	0
John Stallworth	4	111	65	2

PASSING
	PA	PC	YDS	TD	IN
Mark Malone	36	20	312	3	3

MIAMI DOLPHINS

RUSHING
	ATT	YDS	LNG	TD
Tony Nathan	19	64	16	1
Pete Johnson	10	39	12	0

RECEIVING
	NO	YDS	LNG	TD
Tony Nathan	8	114	30	0
Mark Duper	5	148	41	2
Mark Clayton	4	95	40	1

PASSING
	PA	PC	YDS	TD	IN
Dan Marino	32	21	421	4	1

The Steelers were one step from their fifth Super Bowl date, but Pittsburgh native Dan Marino threw for 421 yards and 4 touchdowns. Marino moved the Dolphins with lightning efficiency, following a 4-play, 65-yard touchdown drive with a 5-play drive for 77 yards. Pittsburgh retook the lead in the second quarter, but the Dolphins scored the next 3 touchdowns and were never headed. No Steel Curtain or No-Name Defense need apply. The offenses combined for 1,024 yards, Miami accounting for 569. Mark Malone passed for 312 yards and 3 touchdowns for a distant second to Marino.

1984 NFC CHAMPIONSHIP
Sunday, January 6, 1985 at San Francisco, Candlestick Park, attendance 61,040

CHICAGO BEARS	0	0	0	0	—	0
SAN FRANCISCO 49ERS	3	3	7	10	—	23

SCORING SF—FG Wersching 21 yds, SF—FG Wersching 22 yds, SF—Tyler 9-yd run (Wersching PAT), SF—Solomon 10-yd pass from Montana (Wersching PAT), SF—FG Wersching 34 yds

TEAM	FD	YDS	RUSH	PASS	RTN	A-C-I	SACKED	PUNT	FUMB	PEN
Chi	13	186	32-149	37	17	22-13-1	9-50	7-43	1-0	7-50
SF	25	387	29-159	228	69	35-19-2	3-8	3-39	1-0	3-20

CHICAGO BEARS

RUSHING
	ATT	YDS	LNG	TD
Walter Payton	22	92	20	0
Steve Fuller	6	39	23	0

RECEIVING
	NO	YDS	LNG	TD
Matt Suhey	4	11	7	0
Dennis McKinnon	3	48	21	0

PASSING
	PA	PC	YDS	TD	IN
Steve Fuller	22	13	87	0	1

SAN FRANCISCO 49ERS

RUSHING
	ATT	YDS	LNG	TD
Wendell Tyler	10	68	25	1
Roger Craig	8	44	39	0

RECEIVING
	NO	YDS	LNG	TD
Freddie Solomon	7	73	15	1
Dwight Clark	4	83	38	0

PASSING
	PA	PC	YDS	TD	IN
Joe Montana	34	18	233	1	2

Three times in the first half the 49ers penetrated inside the Chicago 5, and only came away with 2 Ray Wersching field goals. The Bears offense had trouble staying upright, much less kicking a ball through them. After Bob Thomas missed a 41-yard field goal on the opening drive, the Bears never got that close again until the final play of the game. Walter Payton ran to the San Francisco 23, but 49ers fans ran on the field and the referees called the game with two seconds remaining. After watching Joe Montana throw for 228 yards and the defense gather up 9 sacks for San Francisco's 17th win in 18 games, the fans knew when it was over.

1985 AFC WILD CARD GAME
Saturday, December 28, 1985 at East Rutherford, NJ ., Giants Stadium, attendance 75,945

NEW ENGLAND PATRIOTS	3	10	10	3	—	26
NEW YORK JETS	0	7	7	0	—	14

SCORING NE—FG Franklin 33 yds, NYJ—Hector 11-yd pass from O'Brien (Leahy PAT), NE—FG Franklin 41 yds, NE—Morgan 36-yd pass from Eason (Franklin PAT), NE—FG Franklin 20 yds, NE—Rembert 15-yd fumble return (Franklin PAT), NYJ—Shuler 12-yd pass from Ryan (Leahy PAT), NE—FG Franklin 26 yds

TEAM	FD	YDS	RUSH	PASS	RTN	A-C-I	SACKED	PUNT	FUMB	PEN
NE	12	258	39-99	159	58	16-12-0	3-20	5-40	2-0	1-10
NYJ	15	240	21-58	182	49	34-23-2	5-51	5-38	3-2	6-48

New York's first playoff game in New Jersey belonged to New England. The Jets held a 7–6 lead when Ken O'Brien was intercepted to squash a promising drive; the quarterback was injured near the end of the half and things unraveled for New York. Tony Franklin's kickoff—the barefoot kicker had 4 field goals—was stripped by Johnny Rembert and returned for a touchdown as the Patriots earned their first playoff win since 1963.

1985 NFC WILD CARD GAME

Sunday, December 29, 1985 at East Rutherford, NJ, Giants Stadium, attendance 75,131

SAN FRANCISCO 49ERS	0	3	0	0	—	3
NEW YORK GIANTS	3	7	7	0	—	**17**

SCORING NYG—FG Schubert 47 yds, NYG—Bavaro 18-yd pass from Simms (Schubert PAT), SF—FG Wersching 21 yds, NYG—Hasselbeck 3-yd pass from Simms (Schubert PAT)

TEAM	FD	YDS	RUSH	PASS	RTN	A-C-I	SACKED	PUNT	FUMB	PEN
SF	19	362	22-94	268	7	48-26-1	4-28	6-38	2-1	6-41
NYG	21	355	41-174	181	44	31-15-1	0-0	5-37	0-0	5-45

SF-Dwight Clark 120C; NYG-Joe Morris 141R

In the second game at the stadium in as many days—and the first Giants home playoff game since 1962—Joe Morris rushed for 141 yards as New York kept the ball out of Joe Montana's hands. Even when Montana had the ball, it wasn't for long. Four sacks, 9 dropped passes, and an interception made for a tough day for the 49ers at Giants Stadium.

1985 AFC DIVISIONAL PLAYOFF

Saturday, January 4, 1986 at Miami, Orange Bowl, attendance 74,667

CLEVELAND BROWNS	7	7	7	0	—	21
MIAMI DOLPHINS	3	0	14	7	—	**24**

SCORING Mia—FG Reveiz 51 yds, Cle—Newsome 16-yd pass from Kosar (Bahr PAT), Cle—Byner 21-yd run (Bahr PAT), Cle—Byner 66-yd run (Bahr PAT), Mia—Moore 6-yd pass from Marino (Reveiz PAT), Mia—Davenport 31-yd run (Reveiz PAT), Mia—Davenport 1-yd run (Reveiz PAT)

TEAM	FD	YDS	RUSH	PASS	RTN	A-C-I	SACKED	PUNT	FUMB	PEN
Cle	17	313	37-251	62	46	19-10-1	1-4	6-37	1-0	6-49
Mia	20	330	19-92	238	25	45-25-1	0-0	5-42	1-0	2-20

Cle-Earnest Byner 161R; Mia-Tony Nathan 101C

The Browns took a 21–3 lead in the third quarter on 2 touchdown runs by Earnest Byner, but they could not hold back Dan Marino. Three straight drives resulted in touchdowns, with Ron Davenport scoring twice. Browns quarterback Bernie Kosar, who played his college games at the Orange Bowl, felt comfortable yet stifled there against the Dolphins. He complained that Cleveland got too conservative after taking the lead.

1985 NFC DIVISIONAL PLAYOFF

Saturday, January 4, 1986 at Anaheim, CA, Anaheim Stadium, attendance 66,581

DALLAS COWBOYS	0	0	0	0	—	0
LOS ANGELES RAMS	3	0	10	7	—	**20**

SCORING LA—FG Lansford 33 yds, LA—Dickerson 55-yd run (Lansford PAT), LA—FG Lansford 34 yds, LA—Dickerson 40-yd run (Lansford PAT)

TEAM	FD	YDS	RUSH	PASS	RTN	A-C-I	SACKED	PUNT	FUMB	PEN
Dal	15	243	18-61	182	50	43-24-3	5-35	7-47	3-3	5-30
LARm	15	316	41-269	47	103	22-6-1	1-3	7-41	3-1	4-29

LARm-Eric Dickerson 248R

Eric Dickerson piled up 248 yards rushing—more than the entire Dallas offense—and the Rams played close to perfect defense. Dieter Brock, 34, in his only NFL season, completed just 6 passes for 50 yards, but what did he need to throw for? Dickerson had 173 yards in the second half alone, plus touchdown runs of 55 and 44 yards.

1985 AFC DIVISIONAL PLAYOFF

Sunday, January 5, 1986 at Los Angeles, Memorial Coliseum, attendance 87,163

NEW ENGLAND PATRIOTS	7	10	10	0	—	**27**
LOS ANGELES RAIDERS	3	17	0	0	—	20

SCORING NE—Dawson 13-yd pass from Eason (Franklin PAT), LA—FG Bahr 29 yds, LA—Hester 16-yd pass from Wilson (Bahr PAT), LA—Allen 11-yd run (Bahr PAT), NE—C. James 2-yd run (Franklin PAT), NE—FG Franklin 45 yds, LA—FG Bahr 32 yds, NE—FG Franklin 32 yds, NE—Bowman fumble recovery in end zone (Franklin PAT)

TEAM	FD	YDS	RUSH	PASS	RTN	A-C-I	SACKED	PUNT	FUMB	PEN
NE	15	254	49-156	98	23	15-8-0	3-27	6-38	3-2	6-45
LARd	17	287	27-163	124	36	27-11-3	2-11	2-34	5-3	6-53

NE-Craig James 104R; LARd-Marcus Allen 121R

New England trailed, 17–7, in the first half even though Raiders quarterback Marc Wilson didn't complete a pass for the first 17

minutes. Turnovers set up the next 20 points for the Patriots, with Jim Bowman's second fumble recovery giving the Patriots the go-ahead score. Craig James was the first 100-yard rusher against the Raiders all season. Patriots general manager Pat Sullivan was hit in the head by Matt Millen's helmet because of a running dialogue throughout the game.

1985 NFC DIVISIONAL PLAYOFF

Sunday, January 5, 1986 at Chicago, Soldier Field, attendance 65,670

NEW YORK GIANTS	0	0	0	0	—	0
CHICAGO BEARS	7	0	14	0	—	**21**

SCORING Chi—Gayle 5-yd punt return (Butler PAT), Chi—McKinnon 23-yd pass from McMahon (Butler PAT), Chi—McKinnon 20-yd pass from McMahon (Butler PAT)

TEAM	FD	YDS	RUSH	PASS	RTN	A-C-I	SACKED	PUNT	FUMB	PEN
NYG	10	181	14-32	149	9	35-14-0	6-60	9-38	3-1	4-25
Chi	17	363	44-147	216	27	21-11-0	0-0	6-37	0-0	2-20

The game-time temperature was 14 degrees, but it felt like 13 degrees below zero. From the end zone, Sean Landetta's wind-mangled punt grazed his foot and only reached the 5. The punt went for minus 7 yards and a 7–0 Chicago lead. The wind contributed to 4 missed field goals. The Bears' only other scores came on Jim McMahon passes to Doug McKinnon in the second half.

1985 AFC CHAMPIONSHIP

Sunday, January 12, 1986 at Miami, Orange Bowl, attendance 75,662

NEW ENGLAND PATRIOTS	3	14	7	7	—	**31**
MIAMI DOLPHINS	0	7	0	7	—	14

SCORING NE—FG Franklin 23 yds, Mia—Johnson 10-yd pass from Marino (Reveiz PAT), NE—Collins 4-yd pass from Eason (Franklin PAT), NE—D. Ramsey 1-yd pass from Eason (Franklin PAT), NE—Weathers 2-yd pass from Eason (Franklin PAT), Mia—Nathan 10-yd pass from Marino (Reveiz PAT), NE—Tatupu 1-yd run (Franklin PAT)

TEAM	FD	YDS	RUSH	PASS	RTN	A-C-I	SACKED	PUNT	FUMB	PEN
NE	21	326	59-255	71	23	12-10-0	0-0	5-40	2-2	2-15
Mia	18	302	13-68	234	8	48-20-2	1-14	4-41	5-4	4-35

NEW ENGLAND PATRIOTS					MIAMI DOLPHINS				
RUSHING	ATT	YDS	LNG	TD	RUSHING	ATT	YDS	LNG	TD
Craig James	22	105	13	0	Joe Carter	6	56	19	0
Robert Weathers	16	87	45	0	Ron Davenport	3	6	3	0
Tony Collins	12	61	14	0					
RECEIVING	NO	YDS	LNG	TD	RECEIVING	NO	YDS	LNG	TD
Derrick Ramsey	3	18	15	1	Tony Nathan	5	57	20	1
Tony Collins	3	15	9	1	Bruce Hardy	3	52	29	0
PASSING	PA	PC	YDS	TD	IN	PASSING	PA	PC	YDS	TD	IN
Tony Eason	12	10	71	3	0	Dan Marino	48	20	248	2	2

The Patriots had lost 18 consecutive games at the Orange Bowl dating back to 1966. They faced a franchise—a division rival, no less—with a 5–0 mark in the AFC Championship Game. Writers were already preparing columns dissecting how the Dolphins had been the only team to beat NFC champion Chicago during the season. That all went out the window with the first play when the Dolphins fumbled. Five more turnovers were cashed in for 24 points. Patriots quarterback Tony Eason threw just 12 times, but 3 were touchdowns. New England bulled ahead for 255 yards on 59 carries, with Craig James gaining 105 to lead the way to the franchise's first Super Bowl.

1985 NFC CHAMPIONSHIP

Sunday, January 12, 1986 at Chicago, Soldier Field, attendance 66,030

LOS ANGELES RAMS	0	0	0	0	—	0
CHICAGO BEARS	10	0	7	7	—	**24**

SCORING Chi—McMahon 16-yd run (Butler PAT), Chi—FG Butler 34 yds, Chi—Gault 22-yd pass from McMahon (Butler PAT), Chi—Marshall 52-yd fumble return (Butler PAT)

TEAM	FD	YDS	RUSH	PASS	RTN	A-C-I	SACKED	PUNT	FUMB	PEN
LARm	9	130	26-86	44	16	31-10-1	3-22	11-39	4-2	4-25
Chi	13	232	33-91	141	18	25-16-0	3-23	10-36	3-1	6-48

LOS ANGELES RAMS

RUSHING	ATT	YDS	LNG	TD
Eric Dickerson	17	46	9	0
Barry Redden	9	40	12	0

RECEIVING	NO	YDS	LNG	TD
Tony Hunter	3	29	15	0
Eric Dickerson	3	10	7	0

PASSING	PA	PC	YDS	TD	IN
Dieter Brock	31	10	66	0	1

CHICAGO BEARS

RUSHING	ATT	YDS	LNG	TD
Walter Payton	18	32	8	0
Jim McMahon	4	28	16	1

RECEIVING	NO	YDS	LNG	TD
Walter Payton	7	48	19	0
Willie Gault	4	56	22	1

PASSING	PA	PC	YDS	TD	IN
Jim McMahon	25	16	164	1	0

The goalposts were greased to keep fans from tearing them down. That's confidence from a team that cut a rap song about going to the Super Bowl before qualifying for it. Chicago's complete domination made pregame jinx talk ridiculous. The Bears became the first team to record back-to-back shutouts in the same postseason. They held Eric Dickerson to 46 yards a week after he gained 248 in his team's shutout in Los Angeles. Jim McMahon, humorous headband and all, accounted for 2 touchdowns for a 17–0 lead. Even as a comeback seemed remote, Wilbur Marshall returned a fumble 52 yards for a touchdown. Fans left the goalposts alone and did "The Super Bowl Shuffle" in their seats.

1986 AFC WILD CARD GAME
Sunday, December 28, 1986 at East Rutherford, NJ, Giants Stadium, attendance 75,210

KANSAS CITY CHIEFS	6	0	0	9	—	15
NEW YORK JETS	7	14	7	7	—	**35**

SCORING KC—Smith 1-yd run (PAT failed), NYJ—McNeil 1-yd run (Leahy PAT), NYJ—McNeil 1-yd pass from Ryan (Leahy PAT), NYJ—Toon 11-yd pass from Ryan (Leahy PAT), NYJ—McArthur 21-yd interception return (Leahy PAT), KC—Lewis recovered blocked punt in end zone (Lowery PAT), NYJ—Griggs 6-yd pass from Ryan (Leahy PAT), KC—Safety, Jennings ran out of end zone

TEAM	FD	YDS	RUSH	PASS	RTN	A-C-I	SACKED	PUNT	FUMB	PEN
KC	15	241	20-67	174	5	37-20-2	2-3	3-41	2-1	1-5
NYJ	19	306	36-165	141	37	23-16-0	2-12	4-29	1-0	8-54

NYJ-Freeman McNeil 135R

Minds in New York were set on "explode" as the 10–1 Jets lost their last five games but still made the playoffs. The Chiefs hadn't been to the playoffs since 1971 and would fire their coach days after the game. Backup quarterback Pat Ryan had the big play for the Jets, a 24-yard run on fourth-and-6 that set up New York's first touchdown. Freeman McNeil ran for 135 yards.

1986 NFC WILD CARD GAME
Sunday, December 28, 1986 at Washington, RFK Stadium, attendance 54,567

LOS ANGELES RAMS	0	0	0	7	—	7
WASHINGTON REDSKINS	10	3	3	3	—	**19**

SCORING Was—FG Atkinson 25 yds, Was—Bryant 14-yd pass from Schroeder (Atkinson PAT), Was—FG Atkinson 20 yds, Was—FG Atkinson 38 yds, LA—House 12-yd pass from Everett (Lansford PAT), Was—FG Atkinson 19 yds

TEAM	FD	YDS	RUSH	PASS	RTN	A-C-I	SACKED	PUNT	FUMB	PEN
LARm	16	324	34-198	126	23	18-9-2	1-10	3-38	4-4	8-78
Was	15	228	41-138	90	26	23-13-0	0-0	5-42	1-0	6-45

LARm-Eric Dickerson 158R; Was-George Rogers 115R

Jess Atkinson hadn't kicked a field goal in a year, but Washington's late-season replacement booted 4 field goals against Los Angeles. Eric Dickerson ran for 158 yards as the Rams outgained the Redskins, 324–228. Six turnovers—including 3 fumbles by Dickerson—kept LA from scoring until late in the fourth quarter.

1986 AFC DIVISIONAL PLAYOFF
Saturday, January 3, 1987 at Cleveland (OT), Municipal Stadium, attendance 79,720

NEW YORK JETS	7	3	3	7	0	0	—	20
CLEVELAND BROWNS	7	3	0	10	0	3	—	**23**

SCORING NYJ—Walker 42-yd pass from Ryan (Leahy PAT), Cle—Fontenot 37-yd pass from Kosar (Moseley PAT), Cle—FG Moseley 38 yds, NYJ—FG Leahy 46 yds, NYJ—FG Leahy 37 yds, NYJ—McNeil 25-yd run (Leahy PAT), Cle—Mack 1-yd run (Moseley PAT), Cle—FG Moseley 22 yds, Cle—FG Moseley 27 yds

TEAM	FD	YDS	RUSH	PASS	RTN	A-C-I	SACKED	PUNT	FUMB	PEN
NYJ	14	287	31-104	183	23	30-17-0	9-54	14-38	0-0	10-94
Cle	33	558	27-75	483	65	65-34-2	4-11	8-39	2-0	4-40

Cle-Ozzie Newsome 114C, Bernie Kosar 489P

Bernie Kosar threw for 489 yards as the Browns had 19 more first downs and double the yardage of the Jets, yet Cleveland scrambled to come up with 10 points in the last 4:14 to force overtime. Mark Moseley, who tied the game with seven seconds left, kicked the winner in the second overtime period to end the third-longest game in NFL history. For the Jets, who lost five straight heading into the playoffs, it was a devastating finish.

1986 NFC DIVISIONAL PLAYOFF
Saturday, January 3, 1987 at Chicago, Soldier Field, attendance 65,524

WASHINGTON REDSKINS	7	0	7	13	—	27
CHICAGO BEARS	0	13	0	0	—	13

SCORING Was—Monk 28-yd pass from Schroeder (Atkinson PAT), Chi—Gault 50-yd pass from Flutie (Butler PAT), Chi—FG Butler 23 yds, Chi—FG Butler 41 yds, Was—Monk 23-yd pass from Schroeder (Atkinson PAT), Was—Rogers 1-yd run (Atkinson PAT), Was—FG Atkinson 35 yds, Was—FG Atkinson 25 yds

TEAM	FD	YDS	RUSH	PASS	RTN	A-C-I	SACKED	PUNT	FUMB	PEN
Was	19	302	39-134	168	55	32-15-1	2-16	7-39	2-0	8-65
Chi	14	220	24-93	127	70	31-11-2	1-7	5-41	3-2	4-42

The 14-2 Bears hadn't played a winning team in seven weeks and only faced five all season; they had a rude wakeup call against the Redskins. A Doug Flutie interception and a Walter Payton fumble on successive drives in the third quarter turned a 13–7 Chicago lead into a 21–13 deficit.

1986 AFC DIVISIONAL PLAYOFF
Sunday, January 4, 1987 at Denver, Mile High Stadium, attendance 75,262

NEW ENGLAND PATRIOTS	0	10	7	0	—	17
DENVER BRONCOS	3	7	10	2	—	**22**

SCORING Den—FG Karlis 27 yds, NE—Morgan 19-yd pass from Eason (Franklin PAT), Den—Elway 22-yd run (Karlis PAT), NE—FG Franklin 38 yds, Den—FG Karlis 22 yds, NE—Morgan 45-yd pass from Eason (Franklin PAT), Den—Johnson 48-yd pass from Elway (Karlis PAT), Den—Safety, Jones tackled Eason in end zone

TEAM	FD	YDS	RUSH	PASS	RTN	A-C-I	SACKED	PUNT	FUMB	PEN
NE	12	271	24-121	150	15	24-13-0	6-44	9-50	1-0	5-45
Den	23	441	42-188	253	35	32-13-2	1-4	6-46	0-0	3-20

NE-Stanley Morgan 100C; Den-Sammy Winder 102R

John Elway played with a sprained ankle, but he still managed to run for a 22-yard touchdown and throw for 257 yards, including a 47-yard scoring bomb to Vance Johnson to end the third quarter. The free play—New England was offside—produced the fifth, and last, lead change of the game as Denver won its first playoff game in nine seasons.

1986 NFC DIVISIONAL PLAYOFF
Sunday, January 4, 1987 at East Rutherford, NJ, Giants Stadium, attendance 75,691

SAN FRANCISCO 49ERS	3	0	0	0	—	3
NEW YORK GIANTS	7	21	21	0	—	**49**

SCORING NYG—Bavaro 24-yd pass from Simms (Allegre PAT), SF—FG Wersching 26 yds, NYG—Morris 45-yd run (Allegre PAT), NYG—Johnson 15-yd pass from Simms (Allegre PAT), NYG—Taylor 34-yd interception return (Allegre PAT), NYG—McConkey 28-yd pass from Simms (Allegre PAT), NYG—Mowatt 29-yd pass from Simms (Allegre PAT), NYG—Morris 2-yd run (Allegre PAT)

TEAM	FD	YDS	RUSH	PASS	RTN	A-C-I	SACKED	PUNT	FUMB	PEN
SF	9	184	20-29	155	11	37-15-3	1-7	10-40	2-1	11-62
NYG	21	366	44-216	150	134	20-10-0	1-9	7-44	0-0	3-23

NYG-Joe Morris 159R

For the first time in Bill Walsh's tenure, an opponent made the 49ers look bad in the playoffs. Jerry Rice fumbled a sure touchdown in a scoreless game, Joe Montana left with a concussion, and San Francisco allowed twice as many yards as it produced. The Giants could do nothing wrong: Phil Simms threw 4 touchdown passes and Joe Morris had 159 yards rushing and 2 scores as New York put up 42 points in the second and third quarters.

1986 AFC CHAMPIONSHIP

Sunday, January 11, 1987 at Cleveland (OT), Municipal Stadium, attendance 79,973

DENVER BRONCOS	0	10	3	7	3	—	**23**
CLEVELAND BROWNS	7	3	0	10	0	—	20

SCORING Cle—Fontenot 6-yd pass from Kosar (Moseley PAT), Den—FG Karlis 19 yds, Den—Willhite 1-yd run (Karlis PAT), Cle—FG Moseley 29 yds, Den—FG Karlis 26 yds, Cle—FG Moseley 24 yds, Cle—Brennan 48-yd pass from Kosar (Moseley PAT), Den—Jackson 5-yd pass from Elway (Karlis PAT), Den—FG Karlis 33 yds

TEAM	FD	YDS	RUSH	PASS	RTN	A-C-I	SACKED	PUNT	FUMB	PEN
Den	22	374	37-149	225	50	38-22-1	2-19	7-38	2-0	6-39
Cle	17	356	33-100	256	37	32-18-2	1-3	6-43	3-1	9-76

DENVER BRONCOS RUSHING	ATT	YDS	LNG	TD
Sammy Winder	26	83	9	0
John Elway	4	56	34	0
RECEIVING	**NO**	**YDS**	**LNG**	**TD**
Steve Watson	3	55	28	0
Steve Sewell	3	47	22	0
PASSING	**PA**	**PC**	**YDS**	**TD**	**IN**
John Elway	38	22	244	1	1

CLEVELAND BROWNS RUSHING	ATT	YDS	LNG	TD
Kevin Mack	26	94	15	0
Herman Fontenot	3	3	4	0
RECEIVING	**NO**	**YDS**	**LNG**	**TD**
Herman Fontenot	7	66	24	1
Brian Brennan	4	72	48	1
PASSING	**PA**	**PC**	**YDS**	**TD**	**IN**
Bernie Kosar	32	18	259	2	2

A cold, tension-filled AFC Championship Game was tied in the fourth quarter. Cleveland's Bernie Kosar found Brian Brennan for a 48-yard touchdown as Municipal Stadium erupted. The Broncos started at their own 2 with 5:43 to go. The Drive marched the length of the field, with John Elway converting 3 third downs and finding Mark Jackson for the tying score. Although the Browns had played and won three overtime games, including one against the Jets to reach the championship game, this time it was different. The Broncos won the coin flip and Rich Karlis kicked Denver into the Super Bowl and Cleveland in the pants.

1986 NFC CHAMPIONSHIP

Sunday, January 11, 1987 at East Rutherford, NJ, Giants Stadium, attendance 76,891

WASHINGTON REDSKINS	0	0	0	0	—	0
NEW YORK GIANTS	10	7	0	0	—	**17**

SCORING NYG—FG Allegre 47 yds, NYG—Manuel 11-yd pass from Simms (Allegre PAT), NYG—Morris 1-yd run (Allegre PAT)

TEAM	FD	YDS	RUSH	PASS	RTN	A-C-I	SACKED	PUNT	FUMB	PEN
Was	12	190	16-40	150	19	50-20-1	4-45	9-36	3-1	3-15
NYG	12	199	46-117	82	42	14-7-0	1-8	6-42	4-3	6-48

WASHINGTON REDSKINS RUSHING	ATT	YDS	LNG	TD
Kelvin Bryant	6	25	9	0
George Rogers	9	15	4	0
RECEIVING	**NO**	**YDS**	**LNG**	**TD**
Art Monk	8	126	48	0
Kelvin Bryant	7	45	24	0
PASSING	**PA**	**PC**	**YDS**	**TD**	**IN**
Jay Schroeder	50	20	195	0	1

NEW YORK GIANTS RUSHING	ATT	YDS	LNG	TD
Joe Morris	29	87	22	1
Maurice Carthon	7	28	10	0
RECEIVING	**NO**	**YDS**	**LNG**	**TD**
Maurice Carthon	3	18	8	0
Mark Bavaro	2	36	30	0
PASSING	**PA**	**PC**	**YDS**	**TD**	**IN**
Phil Simms	14	7	90	1	0

The biggest crowd in the 10-year history of Giants Stadium saw the most important game the Giants had played since the club's last great run in the early 1960s at Yankee Stadium. The Giants won the opening coin toss and chose to have the stiff wind at their backs. The wind aided Raul Allegre's 47-field goal, and helped Phil Simms zip a touchdown to Lionel Manuel. Washington tried a long field goal with the wind in the second quarter, but the Giants recovered the botched snap. New York drove against the wind and scored again. From there, the Giants knew what to do. They beat the Redskins for the third time since the season began for their first NFC title.

1987 NFC WILD CARD GAME

Sunday, January 3, 1988 at New Orleans, Louisiana Superdome, attendance 68,546

MINNESOTA VIKINGS	10	21	3	10	—	**44**
NEW ORLEANS SAINTS	7	3	0	0	—	10

SCORING NO—Martin 10-yd pass from Hebert (Andersen PAT), Min—FG C. Nelson 42 yds, Min—Carter 84-yd punt return (C. Nelson PAT), Min—Jordan 5-yd pass from Wilson (C. Nelson PAT), Min—Carter 10-yd pass from Rice (C. Nelson PAT), NO—FG Andersen 40 yds, Min—Jones 44-yd pass from Wilson (C. Nelson PAT), Min—FG C. Nelson 32 yds, Min—FG C. Nelson 19 yds, Min—Dozier 8-yd run (C. Nelson PAT)

TEAM	FD	YDS	RUSH	PASS	RTN	A-C-I	SACKED	PUNT	FUMB	PEN
Min	28	417	50-210	207	188	30-17-0	6-42	3-32	4-2	5-42
NO	9	149	14-53	96	0	31-11-4	2-8	6-44	3-2	4-26

New Orleans had waited 20 years for a playoff game and it was over by halftime. Anthony Carter, feeling he wasn't playing enough, volunteered to return punts; his 84-yard runback started the avalanche. Carter scored again in the second quarter—as a receiver—and Wade Wilson heaved a 44-yard touchdown pass to Hassan Jones as the first half expired.

1987 AFC WILD CARD GAME

Sunday, January 3, 1988 at Houston (OT), Astrodome, attendance 50,519

SEATTLE SEAHAWKS	7	3	7	0	—	20
HOUSTON OILERS	3	10	7	0	3	—	**23**

SCORING Sea—Largent 20-yd pass from Krieg (Johnson PAT), Hou—FG Zendejas 47 yds, Hou—Rozier 1-yd run (Zendejas PAT), Hou—FG Zendejas 49 yds, Sea—FG Johnson 33 yds, Sea—FG Johnson 41 yds, Hou—Drewery 29-yd pass from Moon (Zendejas PAT), Sea—Largent 12-yd pass from Krieg (Johnson PAT), Hou—FG Zendejas 42 yds

TEAM	FD	YDS	RUSH	PASS	RTN	A-C-I	SACKED	PUNT	FUMB	PEN
Sea	11	250	11-29	221	94	39-16-0	2-16	7-44	1-1	3-20
Hou	27	437	50-178	259	27	32-21-1	2-14	3-35	2-1	4-25

Sea-Steve Largent 132C

Houston had trouble both selling tickets for the game and finishing off their opponent. Tony Zendejas missed a 29-yard field goal with 1:29 left that enabled the Seahawks to tie the game in the closing minutes on a Dave Krieg touchdown pass to Steve Largent. After a Seahawks punt, Warren Moon led the Oilers down the field and Zendejas was good this time.

1987 NFC DIVISIONAL PLAYOFF

Saturday, January 9, 1988 at San Francisco, Candlestick Park, attendance 63,008

MINNESOTA VIKINGS	3	3	10	6	—	**36**
SAN FRANCISCO 49ERS	3	0	14	7	—	24

SCORING Min—FG C. Nelson 21 yds, SF—FG Wersching 43 yds, Min—Hilton 7-yd pass from Wilson (C. Nelson PAT), Min—FG C. Nelson 23 yds, Min—Mustafaa 45-yd interception return (C. Nelson PAT), SF—Fuller 48-yd interception return (Wersching PAT), Min—Jones 5-yd pass from Wilson (C. Nelson PAT), SF—Young 5-yd run (Wersching PAT), Min—FG C. Nelson 40 yds, Min—FG C. Nelson 46 yds, SF—Frank 16-yd pass from Young (Wersching PAT), Min—FG C. Nelson 23 yds

TEAM	FD	YDS	RUSH	PASS	RTN	A-C-I	SACKED	PUNT	FUMB	PEN
Min	22	397	34-117	280	69	34-20-1	2-18	5-36	0-0	2-20
SF	17	358	18-115	243	65	43-24-2	4-24	6-41	1-0	8-75

Min-Anthony Carter 227C

Vikings quarterback Wade Wilson connected with Anthony Carter 10 times for a playoff-record 227 yards as San Francisco dropped its opening playoff game for the third straight year. The only thing Carter, with 500 all-purpose yards in two playoff games, didn't do was score against the 49ers. Than was Chuck Nelson's job. He was perfect on 5 field goals and 3 extra-point attempts.

1987 AFC DIVISIONAL PLAYOFF

Saturday, January 9, 1988 at Cleveland, Municipal Stadium, attendance 79,372

INDIANAPOLIS COLTS	7	7	0	7	—	21
CLEVELAND BROWNS	7	7	17	7	—	**38**

SCORING Cle—Byner 10-yd pass from Kosar (Bahr PAT), Ind—Beach 2-yd pass from Trudeau (Biasucci PAT), Cle—Langhorne 39-yd pass from Kosar (Bahr PAT), Ind—Dickerson 19-yd pass from Trudeau (Biasucci PAT), Cle—Byner 2-yd run (Bahr PAT), Cle—FG Bahr 22 yds, Cle—Brennan 2-yd pass from Kosar (Bahr PAT), Ind—Bentley 1-yd run (Biasucci PAT), Cle—Minnifield 48-yd interception return (Bahr PAT)

TEAM	FD	YDS	RUSH	PASS	RTN	A-C-I	SACKED	PUNT	FUMB	PEN
Ind	23	315	21-63	252	0	39-22-2	2-14	4-44	1-0	7-75
Cle	25	404	34-175	229	80	31-20-1	0-0	1-37	2-0	4-20

Cle-Earnest Byner 122R

Cleveland's running back tandem was a man down after Kevin Mack became sick early in the game, but Earnest Byner took both roles and rushed for 122 yards and scored twice. The Colts were in their first playoff game since 1977, and their first since moving to Indianapolis four years earlier. It was tied at the half, but Cleveland dominated the latter stages.

1987 NFC DIVISIONAL PLAYOFF

Sunday, January 10, 1988 at Chicago, Soldier Field, attendance 65,268

WASHINGTON REDSKINS	0	14	7	0	—	21
CHICAGO BEARS	7	7	3	0	—	17

SCORING Chi—Thomas 2-yd run (Butler PAT), Chi—Morris 14-yd pass from McMahon (Butler PAT), Was—Rogers 3-yd run (Haji-Sheikh PAT), Was—Didier 18-yd pass from Williams (Haji-Sheikh PAT), Was—Green 52-yd punt return (Haji-Sheikh PAT), Chi—FG Butler 25 yds

TEAM	FD	YDS	RUSH	PASS	RTN	A-C-I	SACKED	PUNT	FUMB	PEN
Was	17	272	29-72	200	88	29-14-1	1-7	4-42	1-1	3-20
Chi	15	280	30-110	170	12	29-15-3	5-27	4-36	1-0	5-50

For the second straight year, the Redskins went to Soldier Field and beat the Bears. Jim McMahon returned from a leg injury and helped Chicago go up, 14–0, but Washington's pursuit paid off with 3 interceptions (all in the second half) and 5 sacks. Walter Payton, playing the final game of his fantastic career, rushed for 85 yards but only 11 of those came in the second half. He was stopped short on fourth down with 31 seconds remaining.

1987 AFC DIVISIONAL PLAYOFF

Sunday, January 10, 1988 at Denver, Mile High Stadium, attendance 75,440

HOUSTON OILERS	0	3	0	7	—	10
DENVER BRONCOS	14	10	3	7	—	34

SCORING Den—Lang 1-yd run (Karlis PAT), Den—Kay 27-yd pass from Elway (Karlis PAT), Den—FG Karlis 43 yds, Hou—FG Zendejas 46 yds, Den—Kay 1-yd pass from Elway (Karlis PAT), Den—FG Karlis 23 yds, Hou—Givins 19-yd pass from Moon (Zendejas PAT), Den—Elway 3-yd run (Karlis PAT)

TEAM	FD	YDS	RUSH	PASS	RTN	A-C-I	SACKED	PUNT	FUMB	PEN
Hou	20	337	26-73	264	2	43-24-2	0-0	3-45	2-1	10-73
Den	19	316	29-61	255	90	25-14-1	1-4	2-46	0-0	4-35

Den-Vance Johnson 105C

The Broncos were in control from the start, but much of it was Houston's doing. The Oilers made mistakes in bad places, fumbling once at their own 5 and being intercepted twice inside the Denver 10. The Broncos led 24–3 at the half as John Elway threw 2 touchdown passes to Clarence Kay. Elway ran for a score in the fourth quarter.

1987 NFC CHAMPIONSHIP

Sunday, January 17, 1988 at Washington, RFK Stadium, attendance 55,212

MINNESOTA VIKINGS	0	7	0	3	—	10
WASHINGTON REDSKINS	7	0	3	7	—	17

SCORING Was—Bryant 42-yd pass from Williams (Haji-Sheikh PAT), Min—Lewis 23-yd pass from W. Wilson (C. Nelson PAT), Was—FG Haji-Sheikh 28 yds, Min—FG C. Nelson 18 yds, Was—Clark 7-yd pass from Williams (Haji-Sheikh PAT)

TEAM	FD	YDS	RUSH	PASS	RTN	A-C-I	SACKED	PUNT	FUMB	PEN
Min	16	259	21-76	183	57	39-19-1	8-60	10-33	0-0	2-10
Was	11	280	34-161	119	20	26-9-0	0-0	8-39	0-0	3-18

MINNESOTA VIKINGS				
RUSHING	ATT	YDS	LNG	TD
Wade Wilson	4	28	11	0
Alfred Anderson	4	25	9	0
RECEIVING	NO	YDS	LNG	TD
Anthony Carter	7	85	23	0
Leo Lewis	4	54	23	1
Steve Jordan	3	56	36	0
PASSING	PA	PC	YDS	TD	IN
Wade Wilson	39	19	243	1	1

WASHINGTON REDSKINS				
RUSHING	ATT	YDS	LNG	TD
Timmy Smith	13	72	34	0
George Rogers	12	46	9	0
RECEIVING	NO	YDS	LNG	TD
Kelvin Bryant	4	47	42	1
Gary Clark	3	57	43	1
PASSING	PA	PC	YDS	TD	IN
Doug Williams	26	9	119	2	0

The Vikings snuck into the playoffs at 8–7, won the first two postseason games in franchise history not coached by Bud Grant, and Jerry Burns's team nearly made the Redskins victim number three. The crowd noise helped produce 8 sacks and Minnesota had 4 drops in the third quarter alone. An interception by Washington in that quarter set up a field goal that snapped a 7–7 tie. The Vikings drove inside the Redskins 1 before settling for a tying field goal. Washington's ensuing 18-play, 70-yard drive ended with Doug Williams passing to Gary Clark. Minnesota moved deep into Washington territory. The ball, Darrin Nelson, and Darrell Green all met at the same spot at the goal line on fourth down. The ball landed on the grass and the Redskins headed to the Super Bowl.

1987 AFC CHAMPIONSHIP

Sunday, January 17, 1988 at Denver, Mile High Stadium, attendance 76,197

CLEVELAND BROWNS	0	3	21	9	—	33
DENVER BRONCOS	14	7	10	7	—	38

SCORING Den—Nattiel 8-yd pass from Elway (Karlis PAT), Den—Sewell 1-yd run (Karlis PAT), Cle—FG Bahr 24 yds, Den—Lang 1-yd run (Karlis PAT), Cle—Langhorne 18-yd pass from Kosar (Bahr PAT), Den—Jackson 80-yd pass from Elway (Karlis PAT), Cle—Byner 32-yd pass from Kosar (Bahr PAT), Cle—Byner 4-yd run (Bahr PAT), Den—FG Karlis 38 yds, Cle—Slaughter 4-yd pass from Kosar (Bahr PAT), Den—Winder 20-yd pass from Elway (Karlis PAT), Cle—Safety, Horan ran out of end zone

TEAM	FD	YDS	RUSH	PASS	RTN	A-C-I	SACKED	PUNT	FUMB	PEN
Cle	25	464	27-128	336	37	41-26-1	2-20	2-48	3-3	7-59
Den	24	412	39-156	256	13	26-14-1	2-25	3-34	2-0	7-44

CLEVELAND BROWNS				
RUSHING	ATT	YDS	LNG	TD
Earnest Byner	15	67	16	1
Kevin Mack	12	61	14	0
RECEIVING	NO	YDS	LNG	TD
Earnest Byner	7	120	53	1
Webster Slaughter	4	53	24	1
Brian Brennan	4	48	19	0
Kevin Mack	4	28	9	0
PASSING	PA	PC	YDS	TD	IN
Bernie Kosar	41	26	356	3	1

DENVER BRONCOS				
RUSHING	ATT	YDS	LNG	TD
Sammy Winder	20	72	10	0
Gene Lang	5	51	42	1
RECEIVING	NO	YDS	LNG	TD
Ricky Nattiel	5	95	26	1
Mark Jackson	4	134	80	1
PASSING	PA	PC	YDS	TD	IN
John Elway	26	14	281	3	1

A year after Cleveland's toughest championship game loss since Paul Brown roamed the sidelines, Denver took a big early lead in the rematch. Denver grabbed a 21–3 halftime lead, but the teams traded blows in the third quarter. Bernie Kosar found Reggie Langhorne and Earnest Byner scored twice; all that was wrapped around a John Elway 80-yard touchdown pass and field goal. Denver grabbed the lead with 3:53 remaining. The same situation of a year before—teams reversed—with the visitors driving, home team on the ropes, and then it changed completely . . . except for Cleveland fans. Byner, with 187 all-purpose yards, was stripped of the ball at the 3 by Jeremiah Castille with 1:05 left. Denver took a safety and celebrated.

1988 AFC WILD CARD GAME

Saturday, December 24, 1988 at Cleveland, Municipal Stadium, attendance 74,977

HOUSTON OILERS	0	14	0	10	—	24
CLEVELAND BROWNS	3	6	7	7	—	23

SCORING Cle—FG Bahr 33 yds, Hou—Pinkett 14-yd pass from Moon (Zendejas PAT), Hou—Pinkett 16-yd run (Zendejas PAT), Cle—FG Bahr 26 yds, Cle—FG Bahr 28 yds, Cle—Slaughter 14-yd pass from Pagel (Bahr PAT), Hou—White 1-yd run (Zendejas PAT), Hou—FG Zendejas 49 yds, Cle—Slaughter 2-yd pass from Pagel (Bahr PAT)

TEAM	FD	YDS	RUSH	PASS	RTN	A-C-I	SACKED	PUNT	FUMB	PEN
Hou	19	334	35-129	205	-	26-16-3	1-8	3-38	2-0	13-118
Cle	19	260	26-68	192	76	28-19-1	0-0	3-35	1-1	9-75

A tight game in Cleveland the week before had resulted in the Browns beating the Oilers to earn both a wild-card spot and home field advantage. The Browns took an early lead in the rematch, but Allen Pinkett scored twice in a seven-second span in the second quarter. Pinkett later dropped what appeared to be a lateral that the Browns recovered for a touchdown; the replay booth upheld the call but the play had been whistled dead.

1988 NFC WILD CARD GAME

Monday, December 26, 1988 at Minneapolis, MN, Metrodome, attendance 57,666

LOS ANGELES RAMS	0	7	3	7	—	17
MINNESOTA VIKINGS	14	0	7	7	—	28

SCORING Min—Anderson 7-yd run (C. Nelson PAT), Min—Rice 17-yd run (C. Nelson PAT), LA—D. Johnson 3-yd pass from Everett (Lansford PAT), Min—Anderson 1-yd run (C. Nelson PAT), LA—FG Lansford 43 yds, Min—Hilton 5-yd pass from Wilson (C. Nelson PAT), LA—Holohan 11-yd pass from Everett (Lansford PAT)

TEAM	FD	YDS	RUSH	PASS	RTN	A-C-I	SACKED	PUNT	FUMB	PEN
LARm	19	342	24-107	235	60	45-19-3	1-12	5-48	0-0	10-54
Min	11	310	33-103	207	55	28-17-0	5-46	7-42	1-0	6-40

Min-Anthony Carter 102C

The great Vikings–Rams clashes of the 1970s at chilly Metropolitan Stadium were long gone. This indoor rematch was warm and dry, with the familiar result. Two interceptions snagged by Minnesota safety Joey Brower in the first quarter resulted in a 14–0 lead. The Vikings went on to their fourth straight playoff win over the Rams in Minnesota.

1988 NFC DIVISIONAL PLAYOFF

Saturday, December 31, 1988 at Chicago, Soldier Field, attendance 65,534

PHILADELPHIA EAGLES	3	6	3	0	—	12
CHICAGO BEARS	7	10	0	3	—	20

SCORING Chi—McKinnon 64-yd pass from Tomczak (Butler PAT), Phi—FG Zendejas 42 yds, Phi—FG Zendejas 29 yds, Chi—Anderson 4-yd run (Butler PAT), Chi—FG Butler 46 yds, Phi—FG Zendejas 30 yds, Phi—FG Zendejas 35 yds, Chi—FG Butler 27 yds

TEAM	FD	YDS	RUSH	PASS	RTN	A-C-I	SACKED	PUNT	FUMB	PEN
Phi	22	430	16-52	378	27	55-27-3	4-29	4-33	0-0	7-60
Chi	14	341	33-164	177	98	23-12-3	1-8	2-43	1-1	1-5

Phi-Keith Byars 103C, Keith Jackson 142C, Randall Cunningham 407P; Chi-Dennis McKinnon 108C

No one could see a darned thing; not the coaches on the sidelines, the fans in the stands, the viewers at home, or the players themselves. The Bears held a 17–6 first-half lead when a thick fog shrouded Soldier Field. The Bears kept it on the ground, but Philadelphia's Randall Cunning managed to throw the ball 54 times—completing half—for 407 yards in the Fog Bowl.

1988 AFC DIVISIONAL PLAYOFF

Saturday, December 31, 1988 at Cincinnati, Riverfront Stadium, attendance 58,560

SEATTLE SEAHAWKS	0	0	0	13	—	13
CINCINNATI BENGALS	7	14	0	0	—	21

SCORING Cin—Wilson 3-yd run (Breech PAT), Cin—Wilson 3-yd run (Breech PAT), Cin—Woods 1-yd run (Breech PAT), Sea—J. Williams 7-yd pass from Krieg (N. Johnson PAT), Sea—Krieg 1-yd run (PAT failed)

TEAM	FD	YDS	RUSH	PASS	RTN	A-C-I	SACKED	PUNT	FUMB	PEN
Sea	19	294	17-18	276	30	50-24-2	2-21	6-44	1-1	5-45
Cin	22	345	47-254	91	19	19-7-0	2-17	6-46	3-2	2-29

Sea-John L. Williams 137C; Cin-Ickey Woods 126R

Ickey Woods ran for 126 yards and gave the crowd his Ickey Shuffle when his touchdown made it 21–0 in the second quarter. Seattle nose guard Joe Nash stayed on the turf four times as trainers came out; fans booed, believing he was trying to stall Cincinnati's No-Huddle offense. The Seahawks scored late in the game, but a missed extra point eliminated any chance for overtime.

1988 NFC DIVISIONAL PLAYOFF

Sunday, January 1, 1989 at San Francisco, Candlestick Park, attendance 61,848

MINNESOTA VIKINGS	3	0	6	0	—	9
SAN FRANCISCO 49ERS	7	14	0	13	—	34

SCORING Min—FG C. Nelson 47 yds, SF—Rice 2-yd pass from Montana (Cofer PAT), SF—Rice 4-yd pass from Montana (Cofer PAT), SF—Rice 11-yd pass from Montana (Cofer PAT), Min—Jones 5-yd pass from Wilson (PAT failed), SF—Craig 4-yd run (Cofer PAT), SF—Craig 80-yd run (PAT failed)

TEAM	FD	YDS	RUSH	PASS	RTN	A-C-I	SACKED	PUNT	FUMB	PEN
Min	20	262	19-54	208	27	47-23-2	6-47	7-39	1-1	9-90
SF	20	372	34-201	171	37	28-17-1	1-6	5-36	2-1	6-60

SF-Roger Craig 135R

Three consecutive playoff losses, including one a year earlier to underdog Minnesota, had the 49ers out to prove something. They did. Jerry Rice caught scoring passes of 2, 4, and 11 yards for a 21–3 second-quarter lead. At the same time, San Francisco's defense had 5 sacks of Wade Wilson before halftime. Roger Craig scored twice in the fourth quarter, capped by an 80-yard run.

1988 AFC DIVISIONAL PLAYOFF

Sunday, January 1, 1989 at Orchard Park, NY, Rich Stadium, attendance 79,532

HOUSTON OILERS	0	3	0	7	—	10
BUFFALO BILLS	0	7	7	3	—	17

SCORING Buf—Riddick 1-yd run (Norwood PAT), Hou—FG Zendejas 35 yds, Buf—Thomas 11-yd run (Norwood PAT), Buf—FG Norwood 27 yds, Hou—Rozier 1-yd run (Zendejas PAT)

TEAM	FD	YDS	RUSH	PASS	RTN	A-C-I	SACKED	PUNT	FUMB	PEN
Hou	20	351	26-125	226	6	33-17-1	2-14	6-37	5-2	8-60
Buf	18	372	29-135	237	84	33-19-1	1-7	4-39	1-0	8-57

The Bills came out throwing in the first playoff game in Buffalo in 22 years. Jim Kelly threw for 244 yards and helped make the Buffalo running game even more effective. Rookie Thurman Thomas ran

for 75 yards on just 7 carries. Special teams also proved vital as a Houston fumble on a punt enabled the Bills to run out the clock.

1988 NFC CHAMPIONSHIP

Sunday, January 8, 1989 at Chicago, Soldier Field, attendance 66,946

SAN FRANCISCO 49ERS	7	7	7	7	—	28
CHICAGO BEARS	0	3	0	0	—	3

SCORING SF—Rice 61-yd pass from Montana (Cofer PAT), SF—Rice 27-yd pass from Montana (Cofer PAT), Chi—FG Butler 25 yds, SF—Frank 5-yd pass from Montana (Cofer PAT), SF—Rathman 4-yd run (Cofer PAT)

TEAM	FD	YDS	RUSH	PASS	RTN	A-C-I	SACKED	PUNT	FUMB	PEN
SF	21	406	37-138	268	24	27-17-0	2-20	6-35	1-1	0-0
Chi	15	267	25-91	176	1	41-20-1	0-0	7-31	2-1	3-35

SAN FRANCISCO 49ERS					CHICAGO BEARS				
RUSHING	ATT	YDS	LNG	TD	**RUSHING**	ATT	YDS	LNG	TD
Roger Craig	18	68	11	0	Neal Anderson	14	59	16	0
Tom Rathman	10	36	12	1	Thomas Sanders	7	22	14	0
RECEIVING	NO	YDS	LNG	TD	**RECEIVING**	NO	YDS	LNG	TD
Jerry Rice	5	133	61	2	Neal Anderson	5	31	13	0
Tom Rathman	5	51	22	0	James Thornton	4	52	18	0
John Taylor	3	51	32	0	Dennis McKinnon	4	32	13	0
PASSING	PA	PC	YDS	TD	IN	**PASSING**	PA	PC	YDS	TD	IN
Joe Montana	27	17	288	3	0	Jim McMahon	29	14	121	0	1
						Mike Tomczak	12	6	55	0	0

Playing in bone-numbing Soldier Field, the 49ers controlled the ball, if not the temperature. On a 17-degree day that felt like minus 26 with the wind, the 49ers scored a touchdown in each quarter. The first pair came on long scores from Joe Montana to Jerry rice. The Bears, who bragged about thriving in the cold, managed just a field goal. In the second half the 49ers put together scoring drives of 13 and 12 plays. No road team had won the NFC Championship Game in the 1980s and San Francisco hadn't won a road playoff game in 18 years. Both streaks came to an end as the 49ers qualified for their third Super Bowl in eight seasons.

1988 AFC CHAMPIONSHIP

Sunday, January 8, 1989 at Cincinnati, Riverfront Stadium, attendance 59,747

BUFFALO BILLS	0	10	0	0	—	10
CINCINNATI BENGALS	7	7	0	7	—	21

SCORING Cin—Woods 1-yd run (Breech PAT), Buf—Reed 9-yd pass from Kelly (Norwood PAT), Cin—Brooks 10-yd pass from Esiason (Breech PAT), Buf—FG Norwood 39 yds, Cin—Woods 1-yd run (Breech PAT)

TEAM	FD	YDS	RUSH	PASS	RTN	A-C-I	SACKED	PUNT	FUMB	PEN
Buf	10	181	17-45	136	27	30-14-3	3-27	6-45	0-0	5-50
Cin	23	249	50-175	74	47	20-11-2	3-20	6-37	2-0	4-45

BUFFALO BILLS					CINCINNATI BENGALS				
RUSHING	ATT	YDS	LNG	TD	**RUSHING**	ATT	YDS	LNG	TD
Jamie Mueller	8	21	13	0	Ickey Woods	29	102	16	2
Jim Kelly	2	10	5	0	Stanley Wilson	5	29	9	0
RECEIVING	NO	YDS	LNG	TD	**RECEIVING**	NO	YDS	LNG	TD
Andre Reed	5	55	18	1	Rodney Holman	4	38	21	0
Robb Riddick	3	28	14	0	James Brooks	2	21	11	1
PASSING	PA	PC	YDS	TD	IN	**PASSING**	PA	PC	YDS	TD	IN
Jim Kelly	30	14	163	1	3	Boomer Esiason	20	11	94	1	2

The pregame activity was better than the game. Commissioner Pete Rozelle decreed two hours before kickoff that officials could wave off too many men on the field penalties caused by Cincinnati's No-Huddle offense. The Bills, in turn, agreed not to fake injuries to buy time on defense, as Seattle had been accused of doing a week earlier. The Bengals chose not to hurry and gobbled up 40 minutes. Cincinnati's defense harassed Jim Kelly, intercepting 2 of his first 3 passes. With the Bengals leading in the third quarter, 14–10, Cincinnati pulled off a fake punt. It led to the second touchdown of the day for Ickey Woods, who rushed for 102 yards on 29 carries to send Cincy to the Super Bowl.

1989 NFC WILD CARD GAME

Sunday, December 31, 1989 at Philadelphia, Veterans Stadium, attendance 65,479

LOS ANGELES RAMS	14	0	0	7	—	21
PHILADELPHIA EAGLES	0	0	0	7	—	7

SCORING LA—Ellard 39-yd pass from Everett (Lansford PAT), LA—Johnson 4-yd pass from Everett (Lansford PAT), Phi—Toney 1-yd run (Ruzek PAT), LA—Bell 7-yd run (Lansford PAT)

TEAM	FD	YDS	RUSH	PASS	RTN	A-C-I	SACKED	PUNT	FUMB	PEN
LARm	19	409	36-144	265	15	33-18-2	2-16	7-37	1-1	1-5
Phi	14	306	20-95	211	39	40-24-1	2-27	9-36	6-2	4-35

LARm-Greg Bell 124R

The Rams were 0–9 in cold-weather playoff games since the franchise moved to Los Angeles from Cleveland in 1946, but Jim Everett went right to work on that. He threw for 173 yards in the first quarter—and 281 in the game—as the Rams took a quick 14–0 lead in cold, rainy Philadelphia. Greg Bell's 52-yard run set up his clinching touchdown.

1989 AFC WILD CARD GAME

Sunday, December 31, 1989 at Houston (OT), Astrodome, attendance 59,406

PITTSBURGH STEELERS	7	3	3	10	3	— 26
HOUSTON OILERS	0	6	3	14	0	— 23

SCORING Pit—Worley 9-yd run (Anderson PAT), Hou—FG Zendejas 26 yds, Hou—FG Zendejas 35 yds, Pit—FG Anderson 25 yds, Hou—FG Anderson 30 yds, Pit—FG Anderson 48 yds, Hou—Givins 18-yd pass from Moon (Zendejas PAT), Hou—Givins 9-yd pass from Moon (Zendejas PAT), Pit—Hoge 2-yd run (Anderson PAT), Pit—FG Anderson 50 yds

TEAM	FD	YDS	RUSH	PASS	RTN	A-C-I	SACKED	PUNT	FUMB	PEN
Pit	17	289	30-177	112	20	33-15-0	1-15	6-25	1-1	5-40
Hou	22	380	25-65	315	0	48-29-0	0-0	4-33	3-2	8-45

Pit-Merril Hoge 100R; Hou-Ernest Givins 136C, Warren Moon 315P

Gary Anderson booted a 50-yard field goal in overtime to give Chuck Noll's Steelers their first playoff win in five years, an eternity in Pittsburgh. The Oilers had beaten the Steelers twice during the season, but Houston dropped to 0–3 in the playoffs against their rival. The winning kick was set up by a Houston fumble. Merrill Hoge's 2-yard scoring run sent the game into overtime.

1989 NFC DIVISIONAL PLAYOFF

Saturday, January 6, 1990 at San Francisco, Candlestick Park, attendance 64,918

MINNESOTA VIKINGS	3	0	3	7	—	13
SAN FRANCISCO 49ERS	7	20	0	14	—	41

SCORING Min—FG Karlis 38 yds, SF—Rice 72-yd pass from Montana (Cofer PAT), SF—Jones 8-yd pass from Montana (Cofer PAT), SF—Taylor 8-yd pass from Montana (PAT failed), SF—Rice 13-yd pass from Montana (Cofer PAT), Min—FG Karlis 44 yds, SF—Lott 58-yd interception return (Cofer PAT), SF—Craig 4-yd run (Cofer PAT), Min—Fenney 3-yd run (Karlis PAT)

TEAM	FD	YDS	RUSH	PASS	RTN	A-C-I	SACKED	PUNT	FUMB	PEN
Min	25	385	21-86	299	18	54-31-4	4-39	4-32	1-1	4-31
SF	22	403	32-162	241	133	25-17-0	0-0	4-31	1-1	9-65

Min-Steve Jordan 149C; SF-Roger Craig 125R, Jerry Rice 114C

The Vikings and 49ers hooked up in the divisional round for the third straight year and San Francisco took the rubber match handily. Minnesota, with the league's most dominant pass rush, allowed 4 Joe Montana scoring passes in the first half. Three Vikings quarterbacks threw 4 interceptions, including a 58-yard touchdown return by Ronnie Lott.

1989 AFC DIVISIONAL PLAYOFF

Saturday, January 6, 1990 at Cleveland, Municipal Stadium, attendance 78,921

BUFFALO BILLS	7	7	7	9	—	30
CLEVELAND BROWNS	3	14	14	3	—	34

SCORING Buf—Reed 72-yd pass from Kelly (Norwood PAT), Cle—FG Bahr 45 yds, Cle—Slaughter 52-yd pass from Kosar (Bahr PAT), Buf—Lofton 33-yd pass from Kelly (Norwood PAT), Cle—Middleton 3-yd run (Bahr PAT), Cle—Slaughter 44-yd pass from Kosar (Bahr PAT), Buf—Thomas 6-yd pass from Kelly (Norwood PAT), Cle—Metcalf 90-yd kickoff return (Bahr PAT), Buf—FG Norwood 30 yds, Cle—FG Bahr 47 yds, Buf—Thomas 3-yd pass from Kelly (PAT failed)

TEAM	FD	YDS	RUSH	PASS	RTN	A-C-I	SACKED	PUNT	FUMB	PEN
Buf	24	453	18-49	404	4	54-28-2	1-1	3-41	2-1	6-35
Cle	18	325	30-90	235	0	29-20-0	2-16	3-38	1-1	5-30

Buf-Thurman Thomas 150C, Andre Reed 115C, Jim Kelly 405P; Cle-Webster Slaughter 114C

The Bills and Browns battled it out through the air, with Jim Kelly throwing for 405 yards and 4 touchdown and Bernie Kosar collecting 251 yards and 3 scores. A missed extra point after Buffalo's last touchdown meant the Bills couldn't settle for a tying field goal.

With three second left, Kelly's pass was picked off at the 2 by Clay Matthews.

1989 NFC DIVISIONAL PLAYOFF

Sunday, January 7, 1990 at East Rutherford, NJ, Giants Stadium, attendance 76,526

LOS ANGELES RAMS	0	7	0	6	6	— 19
NEW YORK GIANTS	6	0	7	0	—	13

SCORING NYG—FG Allegre 35 yds, NYG—FG Allegre 41 yds, LA—Anderson 20-yd pass from Everett (Lansford PAT), NYG—Anderson 2-yd run (Allegre PAT), LA—FG Lansford 31 yds, LA—FG Lansford 22 yds, LA—Anderson 30-yd pass from Everett (no PAT)

TEAM	FD	YDS	RUSH	PASS	RTN	A-C-I	SACKED	PUNT	FUMB	PEN
LARm	26	448	24-146	302	28	44-25-1	2-13	4-30	1-1	5-35
NYG	20	344	36-171	173	0	30-14-1	1-7	5-37	3-0	4-59

LARm=Henry Ellard 125C, Jim Everett 315P; NYG-Ottis Anderson 120R

The Giants dominated the first half, but looked at their 6–0 lead and opted for more in the closing minute. Giants quarterback Phil Simms was intercepted by Michael Stewart, who returned it 29 yards. On the next play Jim Everett hit Flipper Anderson for a 20-yard touchdown. Everett hooked up with Anderson on almost the same play just 1:06 into overtime.

1989 AFC DIVISIONAL PLAYOFF

Sunday, January 7, 1990 at Denver, Mile High Stadium, attendance 75,477

PITTSBURGH STEELERS	3	14	3	3	—	23
DENVER BRONCOS	0	10	7	7	—	24

SCORING Pit—FG Anderson 32 yds, Pit—Hoge 7-yd run (Anderson PAT), Den—Bratton 1-yd run (Treadwell PAT), Pit—Lipps 9-yd pass from Brister (Anderson PAT), Den—FG Treadwell 43 yds, Den—Johnson 37-yd pass from Elway (Treadwell PAT), Pit—FG Anderson 35 yds, Pit—FG Anderson 32 yds, Den—Bratton 1-yd run (Treadwell PAT)

TEAM	FD	YDS	RUSH	PASS	RTN	A-C-I	SACKED	PUNT	FUMB	PEN
Pit	19	404	32-175	229	26	29-19-0	0-0	2-43	2-2	8-50
Den	19	364	31-138	226	6	20-12-1	1-13	4-38	1-0	2-19

Pit-Merril Hoge 120R; Den-Mark Jackson 111C

John Elway did it again. With Denver trailing Pittsburgh late in the fourth quarter, 23–17, Elway led the Broncos on a 71-yard drive. A flea-flicker to Vance Johnson gained 36 yards to the 26. Five plays later Melvin Bratton scored. The loss dropped Steelers coach Chuck Noll's remarkable playoff record to 16–8. It would be his final postseason game.

1989 NFC CHAMPIONSHIP

Sunday, January 14, 1990 at San Francisco, Candlestick Park, attendance 65,634

LOS ANGELES RAMS	3	0	0	0	—	3
SAN FRANCISCO 49ERS	0	21	3	6	—	30

SCORING LA—FG Lansford 23 yds, SF—Jones 20-yd pass from Montana (Cofer PAT), SF—Craig 1-yd run (Cofer PAT), SF—Taylor 18-yd pass from Montana (Cofer PAT), SF—FG Cofer 28 yds, SF—FG Cofer 36 yds, SF—FG Cofer 25 yds

TEAM	FD	YDS	RUSH	PASS	RTN	A-C-I	SACKED	PUNT	FUMB	PEN
LARm	9	156	10-26	130	10	36-16-3	1-11	7-31	1-0	1-10
SF	29	442	44-179	263	58	31-27-0	1-5	2-31	3-2	4-40

LOS ANGELES RAMS				
RUSHING	ATT	YDS	LNG	TD
Greg Bell	8	20	5	0
RECEIVING	NO	YDS	LNG	TD
Buford McGee	7	53	17	0
Pete Holohan	3	26	18	0
PASSING	PA	PC	YDS	TD	IN
Jim Everett	36	16	141	0	3

SAN FRANCISCO 49ERS				
RUSHING	ATT	YDS	LNG	TD
Roger Craig	23	93	13	1
Tom Rathman	10	63	17	0
RECEIVING	NO	YDS	LNG	TD
Jerry Rice	6	55	19	0
Tom Rathman	6	48	13	0
Brent Jones	4	46	20	1
John Taylor	4	45	18	1
PASSING	PA	PC	YDS	TD	IN
Joe Montana	30	26	262	2	0

In almost 40 years together in the NFL, the Rams and 49ers had never met in the playoffs. Los Angeles got off to a good start on Mike Lansford's field goal. Jim Everett seemingly had Flipper Anderson all alone for a touchdown, but Ronnie Lott raced across the field and swatted the ball away at the last second. The Rams did not score on that drive or the rest of the game. Montana set a championship game record by completing 86.7 percent of his passes (26 of 30), but his longest was only 20 yards, a touchdown to Brent Jones for the lead in the second quarter. Nine seconds before the half he hit John Taylor from 18 yards up to make it 21–3 and get the Rams thinking about home.

1989 AFC CHAMPIONSHIP

Sunday, January 14, 1990 at Denver, Mile High Stadium, attendance 76,046

CLEVELAND BROWNS	0	0	21	0	—	21
DENVER BRONCOS	3	7	14	13	—	**37**

SCORING Den—FG Treadwell 29 yds, Den—Young 70-yd pass from Elway (Treadwell PAT), Cle—Brennan 27-yd pass from Kosar (Bahr PAT), Den—Mobley 5-yd pass from Elway (Treadwell PAT), Den—Winder 7-yd run (Treadwell PAT), Cle—Brennan 10-yd pass from Kosar (Bahr PAT), Cle—Manoa 2-yd run (Bahr PAT), Den—Winder 39-yd pass from Elway (Treadwell PAT), Den—FG Treadwell 34 yds, Den—FG Treadwell 31 yds

TEAM	FD	YDS	RUSH	PASS	RTN	A-C-I	SACKED	PUNT	FUMB	PEN
Cle	14	256	14-66	190	7	44-19-3	4-20	8-42	3-0	8-55
Den	22	497	39-120	377	50	36-20-0	1-8	5-46	2-2	1-5

CLEVELAND BROWNS

RUSHING	ATT	YDS	LNG	TD
Kevin Mack	6	36	19	0
Bernie Kosar	2	22	16	0

RECEIVING	NO	YDS	LNG	TD
Reggie Langhorne	5	78	27	0
Brian Brennan	5	58	27	2

PASSING	PA	PC	YDS	TD	IN
Bernie Kosar	44	19	210	2	3

DENVER BRONCOS

RUSHING	ATT	YDS	LNG	TD
John Elway	5	39	25	0
Sammy Winder	21	37	9	1

RECEIVING	NO	YDS	LNG	TD
Vance Johnson	7	91	23	0
Steve Sewell	3	55	43	0
Michael Young	2	123	70	1

PASSING	PA	PC	YDS	TD	IN
John Elway	36	20	385	3	0

For the third time in four years, the Broncos and Browns met in the AFC Championship Game. And Denver headed to the Super Bowl for the third time. This was not the angst-filled afternoon that the first two were for Cleveland, but the Browns had their chances. With the score 10–7 in the third quarter, Denver put up 2 quick touchdowns, but the Browns fought back. Bernie Kosar, battling elbow and finger injuries, hit a diving Brian Brennan for a touchdown. After a Denver fumble, the Browns scored immediately to make it 24–21 at the end of the third quarter. Two interceptions quickly changed into Denver touchdowns to derail any thoughts of another fourth-quarter classic.

1990 NFC WILD CARD GAME

Saturday, January 5, 1991 at Philadelphia, Veterans Stadium, attendance 65,287

WASHINGTON REDSKINS	0	10	10	0	—	**20**
PHILADELPHIA EAGLES	3	3	0	0	—	6

SCORING Phi—FG Ruzek 37 yds, Phi—FG Ruzek 28 yds, Was—Monk 16-yd pass from Rypien (Lohmiller PAT), Was—FG Lohmiller 20 yds, Was—FG Lohmiller 19 yds, Was—Clark 2-yd pass from Rypien (Lohmiller PAT)

TEAM	FD	YDS	RUSH	PASS	RTN	A-C-I	SACKED	PUNT	FUMB	PEN
Was	15	299	35-93	206	41	31-15-1	0-0	9-38	2-1	3-23
Phi	16	318	28-148	170	36	32-15-1	5-35	7-39	2-2	4-40

Phi-Keith Jackson 116C

A key Washington fumble was overturned by instant replay, and 2 Mark Rypien touchdown passes were the difference. Randall Cunningham was Philadelphia's leading rusher with 80 yards and passed for 205 yards, yet a frustrated Buddy Ryan yanked him for a series in the third quarter. He came back, but the Eagles did not.

1990 AFC WILD CARD GAME

Saturday, January 5, 1991 at Miami, Joe Robbie Stadium, attendance 67,276

KANSAS CITY CHIEFS	3	7	6	0	—	16
MIAMI DOLPHINS	0	3	0	14	—	**17**

SCORING KC—FG Lowery 27 yds, Mia—FG Stoyanovich 58 yds, KC—S. Paige 26-yd pass from DeBerg (Lowery PAT), KC—FG Lowery 25 yds, KC—FG Lowery 38 yds, Mia—T. Paige 1-yd pass from Marino (Stoyanovich PAT), Mia—Clayton 12-yd pass from Marino (Stoyanovich PAT)

TEAM	FD	YDS	RUSH	PASS	RTN	A-C-I	SACKED	PUNT	FUMB	PEN
KC	16	367	24-103	264	16	30-17-1	1-5	4-35	0-0	4-35
Mia	23	311	32-98	213	4	39-19-0	2-8	3-40	2-2	2-22

KC-Stephone Paige 142C

The Dolphins rallied from a 13-point, fourth-quarter deficit with touchdown drives of 66 and 85 yards. Before that, Miami's only points of the game came on Pete Stoyanovich's playoff-record 58-yard field goal in the second quarter. Kansas City Pro Bowl kicker Nick Lowery's 52-yard try fell just a yard short with 49 seconds left; it was his first miss in 24 tries.

1990 NFC WILD CARD GAME

Sunday, January 6, 1991 at Chicago, Soldier Field, attendance 60,767

NEW ORLEANS SAINTS	0	3	0	3	—	6
CHICAGO BEARS	3	7	3	3	—	**16**

SCORING Chi—FG Butler 19 yds, Chi—Thornton 18-yd pass from Tomczak (Butler PAT), NO—FG Andersen 47 yds, Chi—FG Butler 22 yds, NO—FG Andersen 38 yds, Chi—FG Butler 21 yds

TEAM	FD	YDS	RUSH	PASS	RTN	A-C-I	SACKED	PUNT	FUMB	PEN
NO	11	193	18-65	128	2	34-11-3	2-25	3-30	1-0	2-10
Chi	18	365	43-189	176	49	26-13-0	2-12	2-28	2-1	7-57

Chi-Neal Anderson 102R

The Saints thought they had blocked a field goal and returned it for a game-tying touchdown, but the play was called back by an offside call. Awarded a first down, the Bears soon kicked a successful field goal for a 13–3 lead. Mike Tomczak, who threw for the game's only touchdown in the second quarter, hit Dennis Gentry for 38 yards in the last five minutes. Kevin Butler's third field goal iced the game.

1990 AFC WILD CARD GAME

Sunday, January 6, 1991 at Cincinnati, Riverfront Stadium, attendance 60,012

HOUSTON OILERS	0	0	7	7	—	14
CINCINNATI BENGALS	10	10	14	7	—	**41**

SCORING Cin—Woods 1-yd run (Breech PAT), Cin—FG Breech 27 yds, Cin—Green 2-yd pass from Esiason (Breech PAT), Cin—FG Breech 30 yds, Cin—Ball 3-yd run (Breech PAT), Cin—Esiason 10-yd run (Breech PAT), Hou—Givins 16-yd pass from Carlson (Garcia PAT), Cin—Kattus 9-yd pass from Esiason (Breech PAT), Hou—Givins 5-yd pass from Carlson (Garcia PAT)

TEAM	FD	YDS	RUSH	PASS	RTN	A-C-I	SACKED	PUNT	FUMB	PEN
Hou	13	226	13-67	159	19	33-16-1	1-6	6-43	2-1	5-33
Cin	24	349	44-187	162	85	25-15-0	0-0	3-45	1-0	4-40

Boomer Esiason passed for 150 yards and was the game's leading rusher with 57 yards, accounting for 3 touchdowns with his arm and his feet for the Bengals. With Cody Carlson subbing for injured Warren Moon, Houston's offense didn't score until it was already 30–0. In their last four games in Cincinnati, the Oilers were outscored, 186–62.

1990 NFC DIVISIONAL PLAYOFF

Saturday, January 12, 1991 at San Francisco, Candlestick Park, attendance 65,292

WASHINGTON REDSKINS	10	0	0	0	—	10
SAN FRANCISCO 49ERS	7	14	0	7	—	**28**

SCORING Was—Monk 31-yd pass from Rypien (Lohmiller PAT), SF—Rathman 1-yd run (Cofer PAT), Was—FG Lohmiller 44 yds, SF—Rice 10-yd pass from Montana (Cofer PAT), SF—Sherrard 8-yd pass from Montana (Cofer PAT), SF—Carter 61-yd interception return (Cofer PAT)

TEAM	FD	YDS	RUSH	PASS	RTN	A-C-I	SACKED	PUNT	FUMB	PEN
Was	25	441	24-80	361	35	48-27-3	0-0	4-33	0-0	1-15
SF	20	338	24-46	292	57	32-23-1	2-10	5-42	0-0	4-25

Was-Art Monk 163C, Mark Rypien 361P; SF-Brent Jones 103C

Joe Montana's dissection of the Redskins was artistic at times, finding intriguing ways to place the ball in the hands of seven different receivers for 274 yards. Washington's Mark Rypien threw for 361 yards, but he had 3 interceptions. Michael Carter's 61-yard interception return for a touchdown capped San Francisco's day.

1990 AFC DIVISIONAL PLAYOFF

Saturday, January 12, 1991 at Orchard Park, NY, Rich Stadium, attendance 77,087

MIAMI DOLPHINS	3	14	3	14	—	34
BUFFALO BILLS	13	14	3	14	—	**44**

SCORING Buf—Reed 40-yd pass from Kelly (Norwood PAT), Mia—FG Stoyanovich 49 yds, Buf—FG Norwood 24 yds, Buf—FG Norwood 22 yds, Buf—Thomas 5-yd run (Norwood PAT), Mia—Duper 64-yd pass from Marino (Stoyanovich PAT), Buf—Lofton 13-yd pass from Kelly (Norwood PAT), Mia—Marino 2-yd run (Stoyanovich PAT), Mia—FG Stoyanovich 22 yds, Buf—FG Norwood 28 yds, Mia—Foster 2-yd pass from Marino (Stoyanovich PAT), Buf—Thomas 5-yd run (Norwood PAT), Buf—Reed 26-yd pass from Kelly (Norwood PAT), Mia—Martin 8-yd pass from Marino (Stoyanovich PAT)

TEAM	FD	YDS	RUSH	PASS	RTN	A-C-I	SACKED	PUNT	FUMB	PEN
Mia	24	430	27-107	323	3	49-23-2	0-0	2-40	1-1	4-32
Buf	24	493	37-154	339	26	29-19-1	0-0	1-47	3-1	4-30

Mia-Mark Duper 113C, Dan Marino 323P; Buf-Thurman Thomas 117R, James Lofton 149C, Andre Reed 122C, Jim Kelly 339P

Jim Kelly completed 19 passes for 339 yards against a Miami defense that looked cold and tired from the No-Huddle offense in snowy Buffalo. Kelly and Dan Marino each threw 3 touchdown passes, but the Bills worked up a big early lead and answered every time Marino tried to bring the Dolphins closer. Neither defense managed a sack in the slippery conditions.

1990 NFC DIVISIONAL PLAYOFF

Sunday, January 13, 1991 at East Rutherford, NJ, Giants Stadium, attendance 77,025

CHICAGO BEARS	0	3	0	0	—	3
NEW YORK GIANTS	10	7	7	7	—	**31**

SCORING NYG—FG Bahr 46 yds, NYG—Baker 21-yd pass from Hostetler (Bahr PAT), Chi—FG Butler 33 yds, NYG—Cross 5-yd pass from Hostetler (Bahr PAT), NYG—Hostetler 3-yd run (Bahr PAT), NYG—Carthon 1-yd run (Bahr PAT)

TEAM	FD	YDS	RUSH	PASS	RTN	A-C-I	SACKED	PUNT	FUMB	PEN
Chi	11	232	16-27	205	3	36-17-2	0-0	2-42	0-0	4-30
NYG	23	288	48-194	94	61	17-10-0	3-18	3-41	1-1	2-15

The Giants dominated the Bears, but New York thrived when pushed. Twice the Bears turned the ball over on downs inside the Giants 5. Chicago's only points came on a second-quarter field goal set up by a fumble that resulted in a broken leg for running back Rodney Hampton. Five other made up for the rookie's loss with 191 yards rushing. Jeff Hostetler, who ran for 43 yards and a touchdown, also threw for 2 scores and 112 yards.

1990 AFC DIVISIONAL PLAYOFF

Sunday, January 13, 1991 at Los Angeles, Memorial Coliseum, attendance 92,045

CINCINNATI BENGALS	0	3	0	7	—	10
LOS ANGELES RAIDERS	0	7	3	10	—	**20**

SCORING Cin—FG Breech 27 yds, LA—Fernandez 13-yd pass from Schroeder (Jaeger PAT), LA—FG Jaeger 49 yds, Cin—Jennings 8-yd pass from Esiason (Breech PAT), LA—Horton 41-yd pass from Schroeder (Jaeger PAT), LA—FG Jaeger 25 yds

TEAM	FD	YDS	RUSH	PASS	RTN	A-C-I	SACKED	PUNT	FUMB	PEN
Cin	12	182	29-124	58	11	15-8-0	4-46	5-52	1-0	1-5
LARd	20	389	32-235	154	40	21-11-1	3-18	2-40	0-0	0-0

LARd-Marcus Allen 140R

Bo Jackson, along with the Nike company, purchased 18,000 tickets so the game could be televised locally. Everyone at the Los Angeles Coliseum, and many more at home, watched in silence as Jackson was taken off the field after a 34-yard run. One of the most electrifying men in two sports, Jackson never played football again and played baseball sparingly with an artificial hip. The Raiders won the game behind a superb effort by Marcus Allen and a running attack that produced 235 yards.

1990 NFC CHAMPIONSHIP

Sunday, January 20, 1991 at San Francisco, Candlestick Park, attendance 65,750

NEW YORK GIANTS	3	3	3	6	—	**15**
SAN FRANCISCO 49ERS	3	3	7	0	—	13

SCORING SF—FG Cofer 47 yds, NYG—FG Bahr 28 yds, NYG—FG Bahr 42 yds, SF—FG Cofer 35 yds, SF—Taylor 61-yd pass from Montana (Cofer PAT), NYG—FG Bahr 46 yds, NYG—FG Bahr 38 yds, NYG—FG Bahr 42 yds

TEAM	FD	YDS	RUSH	PASS	RTN	A-C-I	SACKED	PUNT	FUMB	PEN
NYG	20	311	36-152	159	42	29-15-0	3-17	3-41	0-0	5-45
SF	13	240	11-39	201	40	27-19-0	3-14	5-40	3-1	9-63

NEW YORK GIANTS						SAN FRANCISCO 49ERS				
RUSHING	ATT	YDS	LNG	TD		RUSHING	ATT	YDS	LNG	TD
Ottis Anderson	20	67	27	0		Roger Craig	8	26	7	0
Dave Meggett	10	36	8	0		Joe Montana	2	9	6	0
RECEIVING	NO	YDS	LNG	TD		RECEIVING	NO	YDS	LNG	TD
Mark Ingram	5	82	21	0		Jerry Rice	5	54	19	0
Mark Bavaro	5	54	13	0		Tom Rathman	4	16	12	0
						John Taylor	2	75	61	1
PASSING	PA	PC	YDS	TD	IN	PASSING	PA	PC	YDS	TD	IN
Jeff Hostetler	27	15	176	0	0	Joe Montana	26	18	190	1	0

The Giants and 49ers had met during the regular season, with San Francisco winning, 7–3. The NFC Championship Game rematch was again dominated by defense . . . not to mention kicking. Matt Bahr accounted for all New York's offense, but the Giants still trailed because of a 61-yard touchdown pass from Joe Montana to John Taylor in the third quarter. With the 49ers trying to run out the clock and reach their third straight Super Bowl, Erik Howard eluded a double team and forced a fumble by Roger Craig. New York quarterback Jeff Hostetler, playing for injured Phil Simms, had briefly been knocked out of the game earlier, but his 2 completions under pressure put the Giants in position for Matt Bahr's fifth field goal.

1990 AFC CHAMPIONSHIP

Sunday, January 20, 1991 at Orchard Park, NY, Rich Stadium, attendance 80,325

LOS ANGELES RAIDERS	3	0	0	0	—	3
BUFFALO BILLS	21	20	0	10	—	**51**

SCORING Buf—Lofton 13-yd pass from Kelly (Norwood PAT), LA—FG Jaeger 41 yds, Buf—Thomas 12-yd run (Norwood PAT), Buf—Talley 27-yd interception return (Norwood PAT), Buf—Davis 1-yd run (PAT blocked), Buf—Davis 3-yd run (Norwood PAT), Buf—Lofton 8-yd pass from Kelly (Norwood PAT), Buf—Davis 1-yd run (Norwood PAT), Buf—FG Norwood 39 yds

TEAM	FD	YDS	RUSH	PASS	RTN	A-C-I	SACKED	PUNT	FUMB	PEN
LARd	21	320	28-151	169	22	39-15-6	1-7	3-40	1-1	2-28
Buf	30	502	46-202	300	143	23-17-1	0-0	2-38	3-0	6-32

LOS ANGELES RAIDERS						BUFFALO BILLS				
RUSHING	ATT	YDS	LNG	TD		RUSHING	ATT	YDS	LNG	TD
Greg Bell	5	36	11	0		Thurman Thomas	25	138	15	1
Vince Evans	4	33	15	0						
						Kenneth Davis	10	21	6	3
RECEIVING	NO	YDS	LNG	TD		RECEIVING	NO	YDS	LNG	TD
Mervyn Fernandez	4	57	26	0		James Lofton	5	113	41	2
Ethan Horton	3	25	11	0		Thurman Thomas	5	61	17	0
						Steve Tasker	2	53	44	0
PASSING	PA	PC	YDS	TD	IN	PASSING	PA	PC	YDS	TD	IN
Jay Schroeder	31	13	150	0	5	Jim Kelly	23	17	300	2	1
Vince Evans	8	2	26	0	1						

The Bills fumbled twice on their first possession. The second pulled Howie Long out of position as Bills quarterback Jim Kelly picked up the loose ball and calmly threw 13 yards to James Lofton for the score. The Raiders came back with a field goal, but Thurman Thomas ran for a touchdown and Darryl Talley, who had 2 interceptions, returned Jay Schroeder's pass 27 yards for a score. The Raiders changed defensive fronts and called timeouts to slow the No-Huddle offense, but it did no good. Buffalo's 41 points became the highest-scoring first half in NFL playoff history. Despite January in Buffalo and war in the Persian Gulf, there were just 38 no-shows in a crowd of 80,324 to see the Bills clinch their first Super Bowl berth.

1991 AFC WILD CARD GAME

Saturday, December 28, 1991 at Kansas City, Arrowhead Stadium, attendance 75,827

LOS ANGELES RAIDERS	0	3	3	0	—	6
KANSAS CITY CHIEFS	0	7	0	3	—	**10**

SCORING KC—F. Jones 11-yd pass from DeBerg (Lowery PAT), LA—FG Jaeger 32 yds, LA—FG Jaeger 26 yds, KC—FG Lowery 18 yds

TEAM	FD	YDS	RUSH	PASS	RTN	A-C-I	SACKED	PUNT	FUMB	PEN
LARd	16	276	30-152	124	58	23-12-4	2-16	1-20	2-2	9-75
KC	16	204	39-131	73	76	14-9-1	2-16	2-46	2-1	3-29

LARd-Nick Bell 107R; KC-Barry Word 130R

The word according to Chiefs coach Marty Schottenheimer always involved a conservative brand of football, but this Saturday, the Word was Barry. Word's 130 yards helped the Chiefs grind up the clock, while the Raiders self-destructed, drawing 9 penalties while Art Shell's surprise choice at quarterback, rookie Todd Marinovich, threw 4 drive-killing interceptions.

1991 NFC WILD CARD GAME

Saturday, December 28, 1991 at New Orleans, Louisiana Superdome, attendance 68,794

ATLANTA FALCONS	0	10	7	10	—	**27**
NEW ORLEANS SAINTS	7	6	0	7	—	20

SCORING NO—Turner 26-yd pass from Hebert (Andersen PAT), NO—FG Andersen 45 yds, Atl—Rison 24-yd pass from Miller (Johnson PAT), Atl—FG Johnson 44 yds, NO—FG Andersen 35 yds, Atl—Haynes 20-yd pass from Miller (Johnson PAT), NO—Hilliard 1-yd run (Andersen PAT), Atl—FG Johnson 36 yds, Atl—Haynes 61-yd pass from Miller (Johnson PAT)

TEAM	FD	YDS	RUSH	PASS	RTN	A-C-I	SACKED	PUNT	FUMB	PEN
Atl	20	334	22-79	255	53	30-18-1	5-36	1-42	3-1	6-48
NO	23	330	22-65	265	0	44-26-2	1-8	3-54	2-1	5-49

Atl-Michael Haynes 144C

Two negatives did not make a positive: Atlanta might not have been able to stop the run, but the Saints lacked a running game, making this an aerial duel. Showing his mastery of the Run-and-Shoot, Falcon Chris Miller burned the league's best defense by tossing 3 touchdown passes, including a game-winning 61-yard strike to Michael Haynes.

1991 AFC WILD CARD GAME
Sunday, December 29, 1991 at Houston, Astrodome, attendance 61,485

NEW YORK JETS	0	10	0	0	—	10
HOUSTON OILERS	7	7	0	3	—	17

SCORING Hou—Givins 5-yd pass from Moon (Del Greco PAT), NYJ—Toon 10-yd pass from O'Brien (Allegre PAT), Hou—Givins 20-yd pass from Moon (Del Greco PAT), NYJ—FG Allegre 33 yds, Hou—FG Del Greco 53 yds

TEAM	FD	YDS	RUSH	PASS	RTN	A-C-I	SACKED	PUNT	FUMB	PEN
NYJ	18	285	23-71	214	0	31-21-3	1-7	2-36	0-0	5-45
Hou	21	303	20-71	232	32	40-28-1	4-39	2-45	3-1	8-55

The Jets' first playoff appearance in five years reflected the same weaknesses that made them a .500 team: an inconsistent running game further undermined by Ken O'Brien's uncanny ability to kill his own drives with a pick. Warren Moon's 2 first-half touchdown throws would be enough for the win as Houston's defense shut out the Jets in the second half.

1991 NFC WILD CARD GAME
Sunday, December 29, 1991 at Chicago, Soldier Field, attendance 62,594

DALLAS COWBOYS	10	0	7	0	—	17
CHICAGO BEARS	0	3	3	7	—	13

SCORING Dal—FG Willis 27 yds, Dal—E. Smith 1-yd run (Willis PAT), Chi—FG Butler 19 yds, Chi—FG Butler 43 yds, Dal—Novacek 3-yd pass from Beuerlein (Willis PAT), Chi—Waddle 6-yd pass from Harbaugh (Butler PAT)

TEAM	FD	YDS	RUSH	PASS	RTN	A-C-I	SACKED	PUNT	FUMB	PEN
Dal	15	288	30-108	180	7	18-9-0	0-0	3-45	2-0	2-16
Chi	26	372	34-150	222	5	45-23-2	3-11	1-0	1-1	4-16

Dal-Emmitt Smith 105R; Chi-Tom Waddle 104C

With Troy Aikman out, Dallas coach Jimmy Johnson simplified the game plan by placing everything on Emmitt Smith's shoulders. Dallas reaped the benefit by controlling the clock after a quick 10 points in the first quarter. That kept the Bears playing catch-up. Chicago's new-look, pass-happy offense couldn't build sustained drives, and Jim Harbaugh couldn't work a late miracle.

1991 AFC DIVISIONAL PLAYOFF
Saturday, January 4, 1992 at Denver, Mile High Stadium, attendance 75,301

HOUSTON OILERS	14	7	0	3	—	24
DENVER BRONCOS	6	7	3	10	—	26

SCORING Hou—Jeffires 15-yd pass from Moon (Del Greco PAT), Hou—Hill 9-yd pass from Moon (Del Greco PAT), Den—V. Johnson 10-yd pass from Elway (PAT failed), Hou—Duncan 6-yd pass from Moon (Del Greco PAT), Den—Lewis 1-yd run (Treadwell PAT), Den—FG Treadwell 49 yds, Hou—FG Del Greco 25 yds, Den—Lewis 1-yd run (Treadwell PAT), Den—FG Treadwell 28 yds

TEAM	FD	YDS	RUSH	PASS	RTN	A-C-I	SACKED	PUNT	FUMB	PEN
Hou	23	422	19-97	325	25	36-27-1	0-0	1-44	0-0	13-85
Den	26	418	31-151	267	0	34-20-1	0-0	2-41	3-0	6-70

Hou-Ernest Givins 111C, Warren Moon 325P

Three first-half touchdown passes by Warren Moon would seem to have greased the wheels for an Oilers win, but the Broncos defense rallied to shut out the Oilers in the third quarter. That set up another clutch performance from John Elway, who led the Broncos on an 80-yard drive late in the fourth quarter. Elway converted twice on fourth down to set up the winning kick.

1991 NFC DIVISIONAL PLAYOFF
Saturday, January 4, 1992 at Washington, RFK Stadium, attendance 55,181

ATLANTA FALCONS	0	7	0	0	—	7
WASHINGTON REDSKINS	0	14	3	7	—	24

SCORING Was—Ervins 17-yd run (Lohmiller PAT), Was—Riggs 2-yd run (Lohmiller PAT), Atl—T. Johnson 1-yd run (Johnson PAT), Was—FG Lohmiller 24 yds, Was—Riggs 1-yd run (Lohmiller PAT)

TEAM	FD	YDS	RUSH	PASS	RTN	A-C-I	SACKED	PUNT	FUMB	PEN
Atl	12	193	14-43	150	15	32-17-4	4-28	4-42	3-2	3-19
Was	22	332	45-162	170	55	29-14-1	0-0	4-39	0-0	4-23

Was-Ricky Ervins 104R

Washington's pass defense didn't generate sacks like the Eagles or interceptions like the Saints, but a unit keyed around all-world corner Darrell Green could take away Michael Haynes, the NFL's leading deep threat in 1991. That left Falcons quarterback Chris Miller struggling to hit secondary targets, forcing 4 interceptions while the no-nonsense Redskins offense pounded out 162 yards and 3 touchdowns on the ground.

1991 AFC DIVISIONAL PLAYOFF
Sunday, January 5, 1992 at Buffalo, Rich Stadium, attendance 80,182

KANSAS CITY CHIEFS	0	0	7	7	—	14
BUFFALO BILLS	7	10	7	13	—	37

SCORING Buf—Reed 25-yd pass from Kelly (Norwood PAT), Buf—Reed 53-yd pass from Kelly (Norwood PAT), Buf—FG Norwood 33 yds, Buf—Lofton 10-yd pass from Kelly (Norwood PAT), KC—Word 3-yd run (Lowery PAT), Buf—FG Norwood 20 yds, Buf—FG Norwood 47 yds, Buf—Davis 5-yd run (Norwood PAT), KC—F. Jones 20-yd pass from Vlasic (Lowery PAT)

TEAM	FD	YDS	RUSH	PASS	RTN	A-C-I	SACKED	PUNT	FUMB	PEN
KC	14	213	24-77	136	39	29-14-4	1-10	7-40	3-0	10-59
Buf	29	448	46-180	268	38	35-23-3	1-5	3-33	0-0	6-40

Buf-Thurman Thomas 100R, Andre Reed 100C

Deep down, Bills coach Marv Levy had to be especially happy to beat his previous team. While the defense forced Chiefs quarterback Steve DeBerg from the game and derailed Kansas City's offense, the Bills ran amok in every sense, scoring on the ground, in the air, and with reserves, despite a trio of Jim Kelly interceptions. Levy's five seasons as head coach in Kansas City had to seem almost as distant as the 33–6 Chiefs win over the Bills at Arrowhead Stadium in October.

1991 NFC DIVISIONAL PLAYOFF
Sunday, January 5, 1992 at Detroit, Pontiac Silverdome, attendance 79,835

DALLAS COWBOYS	3	3	0	0	—	6
DETROIT LIONS	7	10	14	7	—	38

SCORING Det—Green 31-yd pass from Kramer (Murray PAT), Dal—FG Willis 28 yds, Det—Jenkins 41-yd interception return (Murray PAT), Dal—FG Willis 28 yds, Det—FG Murray 36 yds, Det—Green 9-yd pass from Kramer (Murray PAT), Det—Moore 7-yd pass from Kramer (Murray PAT), Det—Sanders 47-yd run (Murray PAT)

TEAM	FD	YDS	RUSH	PASS	RTN	A-C-I	SACKED	PUNT	FUMB	PEN
Dal	16	276	22-97	179	18	29-18-2	3-26	5-45	3-2	3-19
Det	23	421	16-84	337	67	38-29-0	1-4	5-46	0-0	4-39

Det-Willie Green 115C, Erik Kramer 341P

The Lions simply were not to be denied. Their defense beat on Cowboys quarterbacks and forced 4 turnovers, included a second-quarter interception run into the end zone by Melvin Jenkins. Veteran quarterback Erik Kramer threw for 341 yards, dissecting the young Dallas defense with a clinical precision in the Run-and-Shoot and hitting his wideouts an overwhelming 24 times. More remarkable still was that this represented Detroit's first postseason win since 1957, three years before Dallas entered the league.

1991 AFC CHAMPIONSHIP
Sunday, January 12, 1992 at Buffalo, Rich Stadium, attendance 80,272

DENVER BRONCOS	0	0	0	7	—	7
BUFFALO BILLS	0	0	7	3	—	10

SCORING Buf—Bailey 11-yd interception return (Norwood PAT), Buf—FG Norwood kick 44 yds, Den—Kubiak 3-yd run (Treadwell PAT)

TEAM	FD	YDS	RUSH	PASS	RTN	A-C-I	SACKED	PUNT	FUMB	PEN
Den	20	304	32-81	223	41	33-22-1	4-34	6-44	4-1	4-20
Buf	12	213	35-104	109	11	25-13-2	1-8	8-38	0-0	6-35

DENVER BRONCOS				
RUSHING	ATT	YDS	LNG	TD
Gaston Green	19	53	18	0
Gary Kubiak	3	22	11	0
RECEIVING	NO	YDS	LNG	TD
Vance Johnson	8	104	24	0
Steve Sewell	7	78	26	0
PASSING	PA	PC	YDS	TD	IN
Gary Kubiak	12	11	136	0	0
John Elway	21	11	121	0	1

BUFFALO BILLS				
RUSHING	ATT	YDS	LNG	TD
Thurman Thomas	26	72	9	0
RECEIVING	NO	YDS	LNG	TD
Keith McKeller	3	39	25	0
Thurman Thomas	3	15	8	0
PASSING	PA	PC	YDS	TD	IN
Jim Kelly	25	13	117	0	2

If fans expected a showdown between Jim Kelly and John Elway, two of the three great quarterbacks of the Class of 1983, they were in for a surprise. The game's first touchdown came with Denver pinned back against its own end zone in the third quarter. Nose tackle Jeff Wright tipped Elway's pass and it fell into the arms of linebacker Carlton Bailey, who scampered in for his club's lone touchdown. The Bills defense forced Elway from the game with a bruised thigh in the fourth quarter. Backup Gary Kubiak, who had announced this would be his last game, ran for Denver's lone score with 1:43 remaining. Not even a successful onside kick could save the Broncos, as Steve Sewell's fumble clinched the win for Buffalo.

1991 NFC CHAMPIONSHIP
Sunday, January 12, 1992 at Washington, RFK Stadium, attendance 55,585

DETROIT LIONS	0	10	0	0	—	10
WASHINGTON REDSKINS	10	7	10	14	—	**41**

SCORING Was—Riggs 2-yd run (Lohmiller PAT), Was—FG Lohmiller 20 yds, Det—W. Green 18-yd pass from Kramer (Murray PAT), Was—Riggs 3-yd run (Lohmiller PAT), Det—FG Murray 30 yds, Was—FG Lohmiller 28 yds, Was—Clark 45-yd pass from Rypien (Lohmiller PAT), Was—Monk 21-yd pass from Rypien (Lohmiller PAT), Was—D. Green 32-yd interception return (Lohmiller PAT)

TEAM	FD	YDS	RUSH	PASS	RTN	A-C-I	SACKED	PUNT	FUMB	PEN
Det	20	304	18-72	232	13	42-25-2	5-32	3-47	3-1	7-46
Was	17	345	35-117	228	83	17-12-0	0-0	3-36	0-0	4-46

DETROIT LIONS				
RUSHING	ATT	YDS	LNG	TD
Barry Sanders	11	44	23	0
Andre Ware	2	25	14	0
RECEIVING	NO	YDS	LNG	TD
Mike Farr	6	73	26	0
Brett Perriman	5	43	14	0
Herman Moore	4	69	21	0
Willie Green	4	54	18	1
Barry Sanders	4	15	10	0
PASSING	PA	PC	YDS	TD	IN
Erik Kramer	33	21	249	1	1
Andre Ware	9	4	15	0	1

WASHINGTON REDSKINS				
RUSHING	ATT	YDS	LNG	TD
Earnest Byner	17	62	9	0
Ricky Ervins	13	53	11	0
Gerald Riggs	2	5	3	2
RECEIVING	NO	YDS	LNG	TD
Art Monk	5	94	45	1
Gary Clark	4	77	45	1
PASSING	PA	PC	YDS	TD	IN
Mark Rypien	17	12	228	2	0

If Detroit's season had been defined by what they drew from Mike Utley's tragic injury, they had taken that inspiration as far as it could go against the juggernaut Redskins. The Lions couldn't afford spotting Washington a quick 10 points at RFK on 2 first quarter turnovers. Still, they kept it close, trailing only 17–10 at the half. The floodgates opened in the second half, as the combination of power running and Mark Rypien's downfield strikes to wideouts Gary Clark and Art Monk turned the game into a rout, culminated by Darrell Green's interception of Andre Ware for a touchdown.

1992 NFC WILD CARD GAME
Saturday, January 2, 1993 at Minneapolis, MN, Metrodome, attendance 57,353

WASHINGTON REDSKINS	3	14	7	0	—	**24**
MINNESOTA VIKINGS	7	0	0	0	—	7

SCORING Min—Allen 1-yd run (Reveiz PAT), Was—FG Lohmiller 44 yds, Was—Byner 3-yd run (Lohmiller PAT), Was—Mitchell 8-yd run (Lohmiller PAT), Was—Clark 24-yd pass from Rypien (Lohmiller PAT)

TEAM	FD	YDS	RUSH	PASS	RTN	A-C-I	SACKED	PUNT	FUMB	PEN
Was	24	358	47-196	162	120	25-16-1	1-10	3-37	0-0	2-15
Min	9	148	17-73	75	34	20-6-2	4-38	7-43	1-0	7-53

Was-Brian Mitchell 109R

Washington's defense dominated. After scoring on their first drive, the Vikings managed just 69 total yards, 7 punts, and 2 interceptions as their offensive achievements from there. Return specialist Brian Mitchell was Washington's surprise weapon, producing 209 total

yards, and breaking the game open on a 36-yard run on a second quarter punt fake from Minnesota's 44.

1992 AFC WILD CARD GAME
Saturday, January 2, 1993 at San Diego, Jack Murphy Stadium, attendance 58,278

KANSAS CITY CHIEFS	0	0	0	0	—	0
SAN DIEGO CHARGERS	0	0	10	7	—	**17**

SCORING SD—Butts 54-yd run (Carney PAT), SD—FG Carney 34 yds, SD—Hendrickson 5-yd run (Carney PAT)

TEAM	FD	YDS	RUSH	PASS	RTN	A-C-I	SACKED	PUNT	FUMB	PEN
KC	17	251	19-61	190	5	34-16-2	7-43	8-45	2-1	7-62
SD	18	342	35-192	150	78	23-14-0	5-49	6-44	2-1	5-44

SD-Marion Butts 119R

Two good defensive teams combined for a mutual shutout in the first half, but the Chiefs cracked first when San Diego's Marion Butts was sprung for a 54-yard TD run in the third period. The coup de grace came in the fourth, as the Chargers made a 10-play, 90-yard drive culminating in taking a page from the Fridge's playbook and having linebacker Steve Hendrickson plunge in for the last score.

1992 NFC WILD CARD GAME
Sunday, January 3, 1993 at New Orleans, Louisiana Superdome, attendance 68,591

PHILADELPHIA EAGLES	7	0	3	26	—	**36**
NEW ORLEANS SAINTS	7	10	3	0	—	20

SCORING NO—Heyward 1-yd run (Andersen PAT), Phi—Barnett 57-yd pass from Cunningham (Ruzek PAT), NO—FG Andersen 35 yds, NO—Early 7-yd pass from Hebert (Andersen PAT), NO—FG Andersen 42 yds, Phi—FG Ruzek 40 yds, Phi—Barnett 35-yd pass from Cunningham (Ruzek PAT), Phi—Sherman 6-yd run (Ruzek PAT), Phi—Safety, White sacked Hebert in end zone, Phi—FG Ruzek 39 yds, Phi—Allen 18-yd interception return (Ruzek PAT)

TEAM	FD	YDS	RUSH	PASS	RTN	A-C-I	SACKED	PUNT	FUMB	PEN
Phi	19	349	28-136	213	44	35-19-0	1-6	5-51	1-1	4-37
NO	20	360	20-76	284	31	39-23-3	1-7	3-45	1-1	4-35

Phi-Heath Sherman 105R, Fred Barnett 102C

New Orleans appeared on the verge of its first playoff win with a 20–10 lead with 11 minutes to go. Then Randall Cunningham threw a touchdown pass, Bobby Hebert tossed an interception, Heath Sherman scored to give the Eagles the lead, Reggie White sacked Hebert for a safety, followed by an Eagles field goal, and finally Eric Allen's TD return of another Hebert interception produced a stunning reversal of fortune against the NFL's top defense.

1992 AFC WILD CARD GAME
Sunday, January 3, 1993 at Buffalo (OT), Rich Stadium, attendance 75,141

HOUSTON OILERS	7	21	7	3	0	—	38
BUFFALO BILLS	3	0	28	7	3	—	**41**

SCORING Hou—Jeffires 3-yd pass from Moon (Del Greco PAT), Buf—FG Christie 36 yds, Hou—Slaughter 7-yd pass from Moon (Del Greco PAT), Hou—Duncan 26-yd pass from Moon (Del Greco PAT), Hou—Jeffires 27-yd pass from Moon (Del Greco PAT), Hou—McDowell 58-yd interception return (Del Greco PAT), Buf—K. Davis 1-yd run (Christie PAT), Buf—Beebe 38-yd pass from Reich (Christie PAT), Buf—Reed 26-yd pass from Reich (Christie PAT), Buf—Reed 18-yd pass from Reich (Christie PAT), Buf—Reed 17-yd pass from Reich (Christie PAT), Hou—FG Del Greco 26 yds, Buf—FG Christie 32 yds

TEAM	FD	YDS	RUSH	PASS	RTN	A-C-I	SACKED	PUNT	FUMB	PEN
Hou	27	429	22-82	347	65	50-36-2	4-24	2-25	2-0	4-30
Buf	19	366	26-98	268	17	34-21-1	3-21	2-35	0-0	4-30

Hou-Ernest Givins 117C, Warren Moon 371P; Buf-Andre Reed 136C

Warren Moon's 4 first-half TD strikes and a 35–3 lead sure seemed like enough early in the third quarter, but Bills quarterback Frank Reich, playing in place of injured Jim Kelly, orchestrated a comeback for the ages with 4 second-half touchdown passes of his own. Moon had to lead the Oilers to a last-second field goal just to force overtime, but he threw an interception on the extra period's first possession. Steve Christie booted the game-winning field goal for the Bills.

1992 NFC DIVISIONAL PLAYOFF

Saturday, January 9, 1993 at San Francisco, Candlestick Park, attendance 64,991

WASHINGTON REDSKINS	3	0	3	7	— 13
SAN FRANCISCO 49ERS	7	10	0	3	— **20**

SCORING SF—Taylor 5-yd pass from Young (Cofer PAT), Was—FG Lohmiller 19 yds, SF—FG Cofer 23 yds, SF—Jones 16-yd pass from Young (Cofer PAT), Was—FG Lohmiller 32 yds, Was—Rypien 1-yd run (Lohmiller PAT), SF—FG Cofer 33 yds

TEAM	FD	YDS	RUSH	PASS	RTN	A-C-I	SACKED	PUNT	FUMB	PEN
Was	20	323	21-73	250	0	41-20-2	5-30	2-36	3-2	4-23
SF	22	401	31-187	214	4	30-20-1	2-13	2-40	4-3	4-35

Was-Gary Clark 100C

Steve Young was responsible for much that went right for both teams. Four turnovers from Redskins quarterback Mark Rypien certainly helped, too. Washington's lone touchdown—set up by a Young fumble—closed the margin to 17–13, but Rypien would later fumble just shy of the San Francisco 20. Young cashed in the payback with a clock-killing drive that culminated in a final field goal.

1992 AFC DIVISIONAL PLAYOFF

Saturday, January 9, 1993 at Pittsburgh, Three Rivers Stadium, attendance 60,407

BUFFALO BILLS	0	7	7	10	— **24**
PITTSBURGH STEELERS	3	0	0	0	— 3

SCORING Pit—FG Anderson 38 yds, Buf—Frerotte 1-yd pass from Reich (Christie PAT), Buf—Lofton 17-yd pass from Reich (Christie PAT), Buf—FG Christie 43 yds, Buf—Gardner 1-yd run (Christie PAT)

TEAM	FD	YDS	RUSH	PASS	RTN	A-C-I	SACKED	PUNT	FUMB	PEN
Buf	19	325	39-169	156	1	23-16-0	1-4	4-42	0-0	4-33
Pit	18	240	27-129	111	14	29-15-2	7-52	3-37	4-1	2-23

Buf-Kenneth Davis 104R; Pit-Barry Foster 104R

Rookie Steelers coach Bill Cowher had a rude introduction to postseason play as the Bills slowly ground up Pittsburgh. On offense, Buffalo's stars were from the team's second rank: Frank Reich, fullback Kenneth Davis, and wideout Don Beebe took over for injured All-Pros. The more experienced Bills tacked on 10 late points to widen the margin in this otherwise tight contest.

1992 NFC DIVISIONAL PLAYOFF

Sunday, January 10, 1993 at Dallas, Texas Stadium, attendance 63,721

PHILADELPHIA EAGLES	3	0	0	7	— 10
DALLAS COWBOYS	7	10	10	7	— **34**

SCORING Phi—FG Ruzek 32 yds, Dal—Tennell 1-yd pass from Aikman (Elliott PAT), Dal—Novacek 6-yd pass from Aikman (Elliott PAT), Dal—FG Elliott 20 yds, Dal—E. Smith 23-yd run (Elliott PAT), Dal—FG Elliott 43 yds, Dal—Gainer 1-yd run (Elliott PAT), Phi—C. Williams 18-yd pass from Cunningham (Ruzek PAT)

TEAM	FD	YDS	RUSH	PASS	RTN	A-C-I	SACKED	PUNT	FUMB	PEN
Phi	12	178	17-63	115	24	30-17-0	5-45	7-41	4-2	6-76
Dal	22	346	38-160	186	5	25-15-0	2-14	4-43	2-1	5-30

Dal-Emmitt Smith 114R

There would be no late comeback for the Eagles this time around, as a multi-faceted Cowboys defense pummeled Randall Cunningham all afternoon. Dallas took an early lead on Troy Aikman's pair of first-half touchdown passes, and then slowly built up a rout by relying on Emmitt Smith and their enormous offensive line.

1992 AFC DIVISIONAL PLAYOFF

Sunday, January 10, 1993 at Miami, Joe Robbie Stadium, attendance 71,224

SAN DIEGO CHARGERS	0	0	0	0	— 0
MIAMI DOLPHINS	0	21	0	10	— **31**

SCORING Mia—Paige 1-yd pass from Marino (Stoyanovich PAT), Mia—K. Jackson 9-yd pass from Marino (Stoyanovich PAT), Mia—K. Jackson 30-yd pass from Marino (Stoyanovich PAT), Mia—FG Stoyanovich 22 yds, Mia—Craver 25-yd run (Stoyanovich PAT)

TEAM	FD	YDS	RUSH	PASS	RTN	A-C-I	SACKED	PUNT	FUMB	PEN
SD	10	202	16-70	132	7	45-18-4	1-8	7-46	3-1	4-39
Mia	18	324	40-157	167	75	29-17-0	0-0	8-41	3-1	0-0

The game was effectively decided within six minutes late in the second quarter. Thee times Chargers quarterback Stan Humphries was intercepted: twice by cornerback Troy Vincent, and the third time by

linebacker Brian Cox. Each pick set up a quick touchdown strike by Dan Marino. Staked to that lead, the Dolphins settled for controlling the clock and blanking a team coming off a playoff shutout.

1992 NFC CHAMPIONSHIP

Sunday, January 17, 1993 at San Francisco, Candlestick Park, attendance 64,920

DALLAS COWBOYS	3	7	7	13	— **30**
SAN FRANCISCO 49ERS	7	3	3	7	— 20

SCORING Dal—FG Elliott 20 yds, SF—Young 1-yd run (Cofer PAT), Dal—E. Smith 5-yd run (Elliott PAT), SF—FG Cofer 28 yds, Dal—Johnston 4-yd run (Elliott PAT), SF—FG Cofer 42 yds, Dal—E. Smith 16-yd pass from Aikman (Elliott PAT), SF—Rice 5-yd pass from Young (Cofer PAT), Dal—K. Martin 6-yd pass from Aikman (PAT failed)

TEAM	FD	YDS	RUSH	PASS	RTN	A-C-I	SACKED	PUNT	FUMB	PEN
Dal	24	416	30-121	295	43	34-24-0	4-27	4-36	1-0	4-25
SF	24	415	21-114	301	30	35-25-2	3-12	1-57	2-2	4-38

DALLAS COWBOYS				
RUSHING	ATT	YDS	LNG	TD
Emmitt Smith	24	114	28	1
Daryl Johnston	2	7	4	1
RECEIVING	NO	YDS	LNG	TD
Emmitt Smith	7	59	16	1
Michael Irvin	6	86	21	0
Daryl Johnston	4	26	10	0
Alvin Harper	3	117	70	0
PASSING	PA	PC	YDS	TD	IN
Troy Aikman	34	24	322	2	0

SAN FRANCISCO 49ERS				
RUSHING	ATT	YDS	LNG	TD
Ricky Watters	11	69		0
Steve Young	8	33		1
RECEIVING	NO	YDS	LNG	TD
Jerry Rice	8	123	36	1
Ricky Watters	6	69	17	0
Tom Rathman	4	33	12	0
PASSING	PA	PC	YDS	TD	IN
Steve Young	35	25	313	1	2

The matchup between the NFC's two top teams was pretty even, but the difference on this afternoon was the quarterbacks. Troy Aikman enjoyed his best postseason game yet, clinching the win with 2 late scores while San Francisco's Steve Young threw a pair of picks. Young's late strike to Jerry Rice narrowed the margin to 24–20, but on the next play from scrimmage, wide receiver Alvin Harper juked a short Aikman completion into a 70-yard gain that set up the clinching Aikman touchdown pass. Dallas was headed to its sixth Super Bowl, and its first without Tom Landry stoically pacing the sidelines.

1992 AFC CHAMPIONSHIP

Sunday, January 17, 1993 at Miami, Joe Robbie Stadium, attendance 72,703

BUFFALO BILLS	3	10	10	6	— **29**
MIAMI DOLPHINS	3	0	7	0	— 10

SCORING Buf—FG Christie 21 yds, Mia—FG Stoyanovich 51 yds, Buf—Thomas 17-yd pass from Kelly (Christie PAT), Buf—FG Christie 33 yds, Buf—K. Davis 2-yd run (Christie PAT), Buf—FG Christie 21 yds, Buf—FG Christie 31 yds, Mia—Duper 15-yd pass from Marino (Stoyanovich), Buff—FG Christie 38 yds

TEAM	FD	YDS	RUSH	PASS	RTN	A-C-I	SACKED	PUNT	FUMB	PEN
Buf	20	358	48-182	176	47	24-17-2	1-1	2-35	1-0	3-20
Mia	15	276	11-33	243	46	45-22-2	4-25	4-37	4-3	5-40

BUFFALO BILLS				
RUSHING	ATT	YDS	LNG	TD
Thurman Thomas	20	96	24	0
Kenneth Davis	19	61	12	1
RECEIVING	NO	YDS	LNG	TD
Thurman Thomas	5	70	19	1
Kenneth Davis	4	52	30	0
PASSING	PA	PC	YDS	TD	IN
Jim Kelly	24	17	177	1	2

MIAMI DOLPHINS				
RUSHING	ATT	YDS	LNG	TD
Bobby Humphrey	8	22	6	0
Aaron Craver	2	13	11	0
RECEIVING	NO	YDS	LNG	TD
Keith Jackson	5	71	24	0
Bobby Humphrey	5	41	16	0
Tony Martin	3	55	22	0
PASSING	PA	PC	YDS	TD	IN
Dan Marino	45	22	268	1	2

The absence of an effective Miami running game meant that if you stopped Dan Marino, you stopped Miami. The Bills defense answered the challenge with 4 sacks of Marino and by picking him off twice. Bills coach Marv Levy nipped a quarterback controversy in the bud by benching playoff hero Frank Reich for a now-healthy Jim Kelly. Kelly responded with a solid game while directing a running attack that buried the Dolphins. The game was broken open on the opening kick of the second half, when a fumbled return set up Buffalo's second touchdown, opening their lead to 20–3.

1993 AFC WILD CARD GAME

Saturday, January 8, 1994 at Kansas City (OT), Arrowhead Stadium, attendance 74,515

PITTSBURGH STEELERS	7	10	0	7	0	— 24
KANSAS CITY CHIEFS	7	0	3	14	3	— **27**

SCORING Pit—Cooper 10-yd pass from O'Donnell (Anderson PAT), KC—Birden 23-yd pass from Krieg (Lowery PAT), Pit—FG Anderson 30 yds, Pit—Mills 26-yd pass from O'Donnell

(Anderson PAT), KC—FG Lowery 23 yds, KC—Allen 2-yd run (Lowery PAT), Pit—Green 22-yd pass from O'Donnell (Anderson PAT), KC—Barnett 7-yd pass from Montana (Lowery PAT), KC—FG Lowery 32 yds

TEAM	FD	YDS	RUSH	PASS	RTN	A-C-I	SACKED	PUNT	FUMB	PEN
Pit	21	369	35-97	272	18	42-23-0	3-14	7-38	1-0	5-40
KC	28	401	33-125	276	36	44-29-0	4-23	6-45	0-0	5-25

Joe Montana added a Kansas City chapter to his reputation for clutch playoff performances. He returned from an in-game injury to throw a fourth-down touchdown pass to wideout Tim Barnett in the fourth quarter. Kicker Nick Lowery went from goat to hero: an earlier missed field goal would have won it in regulation as time expired, but Lowery later hit the game-winner in overtime.

1993 NFC WILD CARD GAME
Saturday, January 8, 1994 at Pontiac, MI, Pontiac Silverdome, attendance 68,479

GREEN BAY PACKERS	0	7	14	7	—	**28**
DETROIT LIONS	3	7	7	7	—	24

SCORING Det—FG Hanson 47 yds, GB—Sharpe 12-yd pass from Favre (Jacke PAT), Det—Perriman 1-yd pass from Kramer (Hanson PAT), Det—Jenkins 15-yd interception return (Hanson PAT), GB—Sharpe 28-yd pass from Favre (Jacke PAT), GB—Teague 101-yd interception return (Jacke PAT), Det—D. Moore 5-yd run (Hanson PAT), GB—Sharpe 40-yd pass from Favre (Jacke PAT)

TEAM	FD	YDS	RUSH	PASS	RTN	A-C-I	SACKED	PUNT	FUMB	PEN
GB	16	293	25-89	204	144	26-15-1	0-0	4-40	2-0	6-49
Det	25	410	29-175	235	37	31-22-2	4-13	3-48	2-0	5-35

GB-Sterling Sharpe 101C; Det-Barry Sanders 169R, Brett Perriman 150C

The see-saw matchup saw both teams score on interception returns, but Packers rookie George Teague's runback from his own end zone was the game's largest reversal of fortune. Brett Favre made a trio of touchdown hookups with wide receiver Sterling Sharpe. The third connection came with less than a minute left, the sixth—and final—lead change of the game.

1993 AFC WILD CARD GAME
Sunday, January 9, 1994 at Los Angeles, Memorial Coliseum, attendance 65,314

DENVER BRONCOS	7	14	0	3	—	24
LOS ANGELES RAIDERS	14	7	14	7	—	**42**

SCORING LA—Horton 9-yd pass from Hostetler (Jaeger PAT), Den—Sharpe 23-yd pass from Elway (Elam PAT), LA—Brown 65-yd pass from Hostetler (Jaeger PAT), Den—R. Johnson 16-yd pass from Elway (Elam PAT), LA—Jett 54-yd pass from Hostetler (Jaeger PAT), Den—Russell 6-yd pass from Elway (Elam PAT), LA—McCallum 26-yd run (Jaeger PAT), LA—McCallum 2-yd run (Jaeger PAT), Den—FG Elam 33 yds, LA—McCallum 1-yd run (Jaeger PAT)

TEAM	FD	YDS	RUSH	PASS	RTN	A-C-I	SACKED	PUNT	FUMB	PEN
Den	26	387	18-56	331	38	54-32-1	1-5	4-34	2-0	10-97
LARd	19	427	32-136	291	1	19-13-0	2-3	4-43	0-0	4-55

Den-Shannon Sharpe 156C, John Elway 302P; LARd-James Jett 111C

There was little that Denver's defense could stop, not Jeff Hostetler, not the wideouts, not the tight end, and not Napoleon McCallum anywhere close to the end zone. A pair of short Bronco punts in the second half ended up being the difference after the teams threw a combined 6 touchdown scores in the first 30 minutes. The Raiders capitalized on field position to turn the game into a rout.

1993 NFC WILD CARD GAME
Sunday, January 9, 1994 at East Rutherford, NJ, Giants Stadium, attendance 75,089

MINNESOTA VIKINGS	0	10	0	0	—	10
NEW YORK GIANTS	3	0	14	0	—	**17**

SCORING NYG—FG Treadwell 26 yds, Min—C. Carter 40-yd pass from McMahon (Reveiz PAT), Min—FG Reveiz 52 yds, NYG—Hampton 51-yd run (Treadwell PAT), NYG—Hampton 2-yd run (Treadwell PAT)

TEAM	FD	YDS	RUSH	PASS	RTN	A-C-I	SACKED	PUNT	FUMB	PEN
Min	11	260	22-79	181	22	34-15-0	3-11	8-38	2-1	6-28
NYG	17	270	41-176	94	5	26-17-0	0-0	7-32	0-0	2-20

NYG-Rodney Hampton 161R

Snow piled on the sidelines, flurries, and a bitter wind might have a playoff picture postcard for the Vikings of old, but the latter-day indoor Vikes weren't ready for brutal New Jersey weather. Minnesota took a first-half lead, but the Giants persevered. They played

mistake-free football on offense and special teams, and let running back Rodney Hampton control the clock as well as dominate the scoreboard.

1993 AFC DIVISIONAL PLAYOFF
Saturday, January 15, 1994 at Orchard Park, NY, Rich Stadium, attendance 61,923

LOS ANGELES RAIDERS	0	17	6	0	—	23
BUFFALO BILLS	0	13	9	7	—	**29**

SCORING LA—FG Jaeger 30 yds, Buf—Davis 1-yd run (PAT failed), LA—McCallum 1-yd run (Jaeger PAT), LA—McCallum 1-yd run (Jaeger PAT), Buf—Thomas 8-yd run (Christie PAT), Buf—Brooks 25-yd pass from Kelly (PAT failed), Buf—FG Christie 29 yds, LA—Brown 86-yd pass from Hostetler (PAT failed), Buf—Brooks 22-yd pass from Kelly (Christie PAT)

TEAM	FD	YDS	RUSH	PASS	RTN	A-C-I	SACKED	PUNT	FUMB	PEN
LARd	15	325	35-110	215	7	20-14-0	2-15	6-37	2-1	9-77
Buf	25	355	30-75	280	7	37-27-0	3-7	3-36	3-1	2-15

LARd-Tim Brown 127C

When it comes to cold, Buffalo trumps them all. Despite a minus-32 wind chill, Bills quarterback Jim Kelly showed his mettle with 2 second-half touchdown strikes, the last a game-winner that answered Tim Brown's busting loose for a long score on a short catch. Penalties hurt the Raiders, particularly a pass interference call that set up a Thurman Thomas touchdown run to make the game 17–13 at the end of the first half.

1993 NFC DIVISIONAL PLAYOFF
Saturday, January 15, 1994 at San Francisco, Candlestick Park, attendance 67,143

NEW YORK GIANTS	0	3	0	0	—	3
SAN FRANCISCO 49ERS	9	14	14	7	—	**44**

SCORING SF—Watters 1-yd run (PAT failed), SF—FG Cofer 29 yds, SF—Watters 1-yd run (Cofer PAT), SF—Watters 2-yd run (Cofer PAT), NYG—FG Treadwell 25 yds, SF—Watters 6-yd run (Cofer PAT), SF—Watters 2-yd run (Cofer PAT), SF—Logan 2-yd run (Cofer PAT)

TEAM	FD	YDS	RUSH	PASS	RTN	A-C-I	SACKED	PUNT	FUMB	PEN
NYG	12	194	19-41	153	3	35-18-3	4-27	5-40	0-0	4-24
SF	25	413	40-178	235	60	24-19-0	1-6	3-45	2-1	6-50

SF-Ricky Watters 118R

Ricky Watters set an NFL playoff record with 5 touchdowns, as the 49ers rolled out to an early lead and simply added to it all afternoon. San Francisco's defense held up its end of the bargain by picking off 3 passes, generating 4 sacks, and allowing the Giants barely 2 yards per carry.

1993 AFC DIVISIONAL PLAYOFF
Sunday, January 16, 1994 at Houston, Astrodome, attendance 64,011

KANSAS CITY CHIEFS	0	0	7	21	—	**28**
HOUSTON OILERS	10	0	0	10	—	20

SCORING Hou—FG Del Greco 49 yds, Hou—Brown 2-yd run (Del Greco PAT), KC—Cash 7-yd pass from Montana (Lowery PAT), Hou—FG Del Greco 43 yds, KC—Birden 11-yd pass from Montana (Lowery PAT), KC—Davis 18-yd pass from Montana (Lowery PAT), Hou—Givins 7-yd pass from Moon (Del Greco PAT), KC—Allen 21-yd run (Lowery PAT)

TEAM	FD	YDS	RUSH	PASS	RTN	A-C-I	SACKED	PUNT	FUMB	PEN
KC	18	354	18-71	283	56	38-22-2	2-16	5-45	0-0	7-51
Hou	19	277	14-39	238	26	43-32-1	9-68	5-49	7-2	3-63

Hou-Warren Moon 306P

Houston's snakebit ways in postseason way continued, as a first-half 10 0 lead was frittered away by a defense that allowed 3 second-half touchdown passes by Joe Montana. Battered by 9 sacks, Warren Moon nevertheless got his team back to within a point with 3:45 remaining, only to watch Montana engineer a clinching drive capped by Marcus Allen's touchdown run.

1993 NFC DIVISIONAL PLAYOFF
Sunday, January 16, 1994 at Dallas, Texas Stadium, attendance 64,790

GREEN BAY PACKERS	3	0	7	7	—	17
DALLAS COWBOYS	0	17	7	3	—	**27**

SCORING GB—FG Jacke 30 yds, Dal—Harper 25-yd pass from Aikman (Murray PAT), Dal—FG Murray 41 yds, Dal—Novacek 6-yd pass from Aikman (Murray PAT), Dal—Irvin 19-yd pass from Aikman (Murray PAT), GB—Brooks 13-yd pass from Favre (Jacke PAT), Dal—FG Murray 38 yds, GB—Sharpe 29-yd pass from Favre (Jacke PAT)

TEAM	FD	YDS	RUSH	PASS	RTN	A-C-I	SACKED	PUNT	FUMB	PEN
GB	19	358	13-31	327	73	45-28-2	2-4	3-39	3-2	4-30
Dal	23	381	27-97	284	19	37-28-2	4-18	3-44	2-1	5-39

GB-Sterling Sharpe 128C, Brett Favre 331P; Dal-Michael Irvin 126C, Troy Aikman 302P

Dallas coach Jimmy Johnson, the reigning on-field architect of playoff victory, provided a seminar to Green Bay's Mike Holmgren, who would eventually garner similar acclaim. Troy Aikman exploited a late turnover to throw his second touchdown pass of the second quarter to build a 24–3 lead. It proved to be a margin that a furious Packers rally led by Brett Favre couldn't surmount.

1993 AFC CHAMPIONSHIP

Sunday, January 23, 1994 at Orchard Park, NY, Rich Stadium, attendance 76,642

KANSAS CITY CHIEFS	6	0	7	0	— 13
BUFFALO BILLS	7	13	0	10	— **30**

SCORING Buf—Thomas 12-yd run (Christie PAT), KC—FG Lowery 31 yds, KC—FG Lowery 31 yds, Buf—Thomas 3-yd run (Christie PAT), Buf—FG Christie 23 yds, Buf—FG Christie 25 yds, KC—Allen 1-yd run (Lowery PAT), Buf—FG Christie 18 yds, Buf—Thomas 3-yd run (Christie PAT)

TEAM	FD	YDS	RUSH	PASS	RTN	A-C-I	SACKED	PUNT	FUMB	PEN
KC	22	338	21-52	286	11	52-25-2	4-37	6-41	1-0	6-29
Buf	30	389	46-229	160	85	27-17-0	0-0	4-33	1-1	2-10

KANSAS CITY CHIEFS						BUFFALO BILLS				
RUSHING	ATT	YDS	LNG	TD		**RUSHING**	ATT	YDS	LNG	TD
Marcus Allen	18	50	24	1		Thurman Thomas	33	186	33	3
Kimble Anders	2	1	3	0		Kenneth Davis	10	32	15	0
RECEIVING	NO	YDS	LNG	TD		**RECEIVING**	NO	YDS	LNG	TD
Keith Cash	6	87	19	0		Andre Reed	4	49	28	0
Willie Davis	5	57	17	0		Bill Brooks	4	34	11	0
J.J. Birden	4	60	26	0		Pete Metzelaars	4	29	12	0
PASSING	PA	PC	YDS	TD	IN	**PASSING**	PA	PC	YDS	TD	IN
Dave Krieg	29	16	198	0	1	Jim Kelly	27	17	160	0	0
Joe Montana	23	9	125	0	1						

The Bills had made a habit of winning playoff games at home, winning the first seven postseason games played in Orchard Park heading in to the championship game. Even with late-game magician Joe Montana in the house for Kansas City, the breaks went the Bills way. Montana's seeming end-zone strike to an open Kimble Anders popped out of the running back's hands and into those of Bills safety Henry Jones, preserving a 20–6 first-half Buffalo lead. The Bills drove Montana from the game, and then went to work on his replacement, veteran Dave Krieg. Buffalo ground up Kansas City's defense with Thurman Thomas's 186 yards and 3 touchdowns. The win made the Bills the first team to qualify for four consecutive Super Bowls.

1993 NFC CHAMPIONSHIP

Sunday, January 23, 1994 at Dallas, Texas Stadium, attendance 64,902

SAN FRANCISCO 49ERS	0	7	7	7	— 21
DALLAS COWBOYS	7	21	7	3	— **38**

SCORING Dal—E. Smith 5-yd run (Murray PAT), SF—Rathman 7-yd pass from Young (Cofer PAT), Dal—Johnston 4-yd run (Murray PAT), Dal—E. Smith 11-yd pass from Aikman (Murray PAT), SF—Watters 4-yd run (Cofer PAT), Dal—Novacek 19-yd pass from Aikman (Murray PAT), SF—Watters 4-yd run (Cofer PAT), Dal—Harper 42-yd pass from Kosar (Murray PAT), Dal—FG Murray 50 yds, SF—Young 1-yd run (Cofer PAT)

TEAM	FD	YDS	RUSH	PASS	RTN	A-C-I	SACKED	PUNT	FUMB	PEN
SF	24	359	21-84	275	9	45-27-1	4-12	4-46	2-0	6-46
Dal	24	377	33-124	253	20	27-19-0	2-7	4-41	0-0	4-29

SAN FRANCISCO 49ERS						DALLAS COWBOYS				
RUSHING	ATT	YDS	LNG	TD		**RUSHING**	ATT	YDS	LNG	TD
Steve Young	7	38	18	1		Emmitt Smith	23	88	9	1
Ricky Watters	12	37	6	1		Troy Aikman	3	25	12	0
RECEIVING	NO	YDS	LNG	TD		**RECEIVING**	NO	YDS	LNG	TD
Ricky Watters	7	33	9	0		Emmitt Smith	7	85	28	1
Jerry Rice	6	83	23	0		Alvin Harper	4	78	42	1
John Taylor	3	61	22	0		Jay Novacek	4	57	20	1
PASSING	PA	PC	YDS	TD	IN	**PASSING**	PA	PC	YDS	TD	IN
Steve Young	45	27	287	1	1	Troy Aikman	18	14	177	2	0
						Bernie Kosar	9	5	83	1	0

A rematch of the previous year's conference championship game prefigured a repeat of the last Super Bowl matchup, as the Cowboys kept the end result from ever being in doubt. The Cowboys scored touchdowns in four of their first five possessions. Not even a concussion dealt to Troy Aikman could keep Dallas off the board, as reserve Bernie Kosar delivered a touchdown strike to Alvin Harper

to keep the game well out of reach. Emmitt Smith had a touchdown running and receiving as the Cowboys won their seventh NFC championship.

1994 NFC WILD CARD GAME

Saturday, December 31, 1994 at Green Bay, Lambeau Field, attendance 58,125

DETROIT LIONS	0	0	3	9	— 12
GREEN BAY PACKERS	7	3	3	3	— **16**

SCORING GB—Levens 3-yd run (Jacke PAT), GB—FG Jacke 51 yds, Det—FG Hanson 38 yds, GB—FG Jacke 32 yds, Det—Perriman 3-yd pass from Krieg (Hanson PAT), GB—FG Jacke 28 yds, Det—Safety, Hentrich ran out of end zone

TEAM	FD	YDS	RUSH	PASS	RTN	A-C-I	SACKED	PUNT	FUMB	PEN
Det	9	171	15-4	175	17	35-17-0	4-24	8-37	1-0	4-30
GB	18	336	35-81	255	15	38-23-0	1-7	5-39	0-0	3-35

The Lions made it a game despite a defense keyed up to obliterate league rushing leader Barry Sanders. Sanders only got 3 yards on 16 touches, including minus-1 yard rushing, but the game was decided when Detroit's Dave Krieg hit Herman Moore in the end zone on fourth down, only to see the officials rule Moore out of bounds. Green Bay ran out of the end zone for a safety and escaped with the win.

1994 AFC WILD CARD GAME

Saturday, December 31, 1994 at Miami, Joe Robbie Stadium, attendance 67,487

KANSAS CITY CHIEFS	14	3	0	0	— 17
MIAMI DOLPHINS	7	10	10	0	— **27**

SCORING KC—Walker 1-yd pass from Montana (Elliot PAT), Mia—Parmalee 1-yd run (Stoyanovich PAT), KC—Anders 57-yd pass from Montana (Elliot PAT), Mia—FG Stoyanovich 40 yds, KC—FG Elliot 21 yds, Mia—R. Williams 1-yd pass from Marino (Stoyanovich PAT), Mia—Fryar 7-yd pass from Marino (Stoyanovich PAT), Mia—FG Stoyanovich 40 yds

TEAM	FD	YDS	RUSH	PASS	RTN	A-C-I	SACKED	PUNT	FUMB	PEN
KC	24	414	23-100	314	7	37-26-1	0-0	2-40	3-1	4-15
Mia	22	381	31-132	249	24	29-22-0	1-8	3-43	0-0	6-50

KC-Kimble Anders 103C, Joe Montana 314P

The Montana vs. Marino clash of titans lived up to its initial billing, as each quarterback led his team to points each time they had the ball in the first half. Dan Marino broke the tie in the third quarter, adding a second touchdown pass while Kansas City's best pair of opportunities ended with turnovers. Joe Montana's career ended with this last defeat.

1994 AFC WILD CARD GAME

Sunday, January 1, 1995 at Cleveland, Cleveland Stadium, attendance 77,452

NEW ENGLAND PATRIOTS	0	10	0	3	— 13
CLEVELAND BROWNS	3	7	7	3	— **20**

SCORING Cle—FG Stover 30 yds, NE—Thompson 13-yd pass from Bledsoe (Bahr PAT), Cle—Carrier 5-yd pass from Testaverde (Stover PAT), NE—FG Bahr 23 yds, Cle—Hoard 10-yd run (Stover PAT), Cle—FG Stover 21 yds, NE—FG Bahr 33 yds

TEAM	FD	YDS	RUSH	PASS	RTN	A-C-I	SACKED	PUNT	FUMB	PEN
NE	20	303	16-57	246	5	51-22-3	1-10	4-42	0-0	3-21
Cle	22	379	34-125	254	48	30-20-0	2-14	3-38	2-1	4-25

Cle-Michael Jackson 122C

The headline was about Browns coach Bill Belichick going up against his former mentor, Patriots coach Bill Parcells, but the pupil's veteran club played a better second half. Vinny Testaverde played error-free football, and forged a 20–10 lead after the teams had been tied at the half. After getting a field goal on the board with 1:30 left, the Patriots recovered the onside kick. Drew Bledsoe moved the chains once before 4 incompletions turned the ball over on downs.

1994 NFC WILD CARD GAME

Sunday, January 1, 1995 at Minneapolis, MN, Metrodome, attendance 60,347

CHICAGO BEARS	0	14	7	14	— **35**
MINNESOTA VIKINGS	3	6	3	6	— 18

SCORING Min—FG Reveiz 29 yds, Chi—Tillman 1-yd run (Butler PAT), Chi—Jennings 9-yd pass from Walsh (Butler PAT), Min—Carter 4-yd pass from Moon (pass failed), Chi—Harris 29-yd run (Butler PAT), Min—FG Reveiz 48 yds, Min—Graham 21-yd pass from Walsh (Butler PAT), Min—Lee 11-yd pass from Moon (pass failed), Chi—Miniefield 48-yd fumble return (Butler PAT)

TEAM	FD	YDS	RUSH	PASS	RTN	A-C-I	SACKED	PUNT	FUMB	PEN
Chi	18	308	30-94	214	20	23-15-1	1-7	3-39	1-1	6-30
Min	22	389	19-49	340	10	61-33-2	2-11	4-33	3-2	11-85

Chi-Jeff Graham 108C; Min-Amp Lee 159C

Warren Moon's association with upset losses in the postseason followed him to his new team. Chicago quarterback Steve Walsh exploited a Minnesota defense incapable of stopping a controlled passing game, while the Bears defense set things up nicely by stuffing the run, nabbing 4 turnovers, and scoring the last touchdown on Kevin Miniefield's fumble return.

1994 AFC DIVISIONAL PLAYOFF
Saturday, January 7, 1995 at Pittsburgh, Three Rivers Stadium, attendance 58,185

CLEVELAND BROWNS	0	3	0	6	— 9
PITTSBURGH STEELERS	3	21	3	2	— **29**

SCORING Pit—FG Anderson 39 yds, Pit—Green 2-yd pass from O'Donnell (Anderson PAT), Pit—J. Williams 26-yd run (Anderson PAT), Cle—FG Stover 22 yds, Pit—Thigpen 9-yd pass from O'Donnell (Anderson PAT), Pit—FG Anderson 40 yds, Cle—McCardell 20-yd pass from Testaverde (pass failed), Pit—Safety, Lake sacked Testaverde in end zone

TEAM	FD	YDS	RUSH	PASS	RTN	A-C-I	SACKED	PUNT	FUMB	PEN
Cle	10	186	17-55	131	40	31-13-2	2-13	5-38	0-0	2-17
Pit	23	424	51-238	186	21	23-16-0	0-0	5-38	2-1	4-50

Pit-Barry Foster 133R, Ernie Mills 117C

Bill Cowher's team played its brand of fundamentally sound football, as the best run defense shut down Cleveland's backfield. Meanwhile, the Steelers simply overpowered the aging Browns defense, as Pittsburgh alternated handoffs to Barry Foster and Bam Morris. Steelers quarterback Neil O'Donnell delivered 2 second-quarter TD passes, the second set up by cornerback Tim McKyer's pick. It was the first playoff game ever between these longtime rivals.

1994 AFC DIVISIONAL PLAYOFF
Sunday, January 8, 1995 at San Diego, Jack Murphy Stadium, attendance 63,381

MIAMI DOLPHINS	7	14	0	0	— 21
SAN DIEGO CHARGERS	0	6	9	7	— **22**

SCORING Mia—K. Jackson 8-yd pass from Marino (Stoyanovich PAT), SD—FG Carney 20 yds, Mia—K. Jackson 9-yd pass from Marino (Stoyanovich PAT), SD—FG Carney 21 yds, Mia—M. Williams 16-yd pass from Marino (Stoyanovich PAT), SD—Safety, R. Davis tackled Parmalee in end zone, SD—Means 24-yd run (Carney PAT), SD—Seay 8-yd pass from Humphries (Carney PAT)

TEAM	FD	YDS	RUSH	PASS	RTN	A-C-I	SACKED	PUNT	FUMB	PEN
Mia	17	282	8-26	256	28	38-24-0	1-6	5-45	1-0	7-47
SD	28	466	40-202	264	14	43-28-2	2-12	2-44	2-1	5-67

Mia-Keith Jackson 109C; SD-Natrone Means 139R

The Dolphins rolled to an early 21–6 lead on Dan Marino's 3 first-half touchdown strikes, but the Chargers won the day by shutting down Miami in the second half. San Diego's run-stuffing added a crucial safety that then set up a touchdown by Natrone Means, who had 139 of his club's 202 yards on the ground. San Diego took the lead with 35 seconds left, but Marino almost brought Miami back. The game ended on a missed field goal attempt.

1994 NFC DIVISIONAL PLAYOFF
Saturday, January 7, 1995 at San Francisco, Candlestick Park, attendance 64,644

CHICAGO BEARS	3	0	0	12	— 15
SAN FRANCISCO 49ERS	7	23	7	7	— **44**

SCORING Chi—FG Butler 39 yds, SF—Floyd 2-yd run (Brien PAT), SF—Jones 8-yd pass from Young (PAT failed), SF—Floyd 4-yd run (Brien PAT), SF—FG Brien 36 yds, SF—Young 6-yd run (Brien PAT), SF—Floyd 1-yd run (Brien PAT), Chi—Flanigan 2-yd pass from Kramer (pass failed), SF—Walker 1-yd run (Brien PAT), Chi—Tillman 1-yd run (pass failed)

TEAM	FD	YDS	RUSH	PASS	RTN	A-C-I	SACKED	PUNT	FUMB	PEN
Chi	20	247	18-39	208	0	47-29-2	4-31	4-37	2-0	4-32
SF	27	330	37-145	185	37	26-18-0	1-5	2-39	3-1	3-16

The overmatched Bears weren't going to upset the masters of the West Coast offense with their dink-and-duck offense, not on San Francisco's home turf. The 49ers instead wore out the Chicago's defense by scoring on 6 straight possessions. George Seifert emptied his bench early in the third quarter as the 49ers coasted to an easy win.

1994 NFC DIVISIONAL PLAYOFF
Sunday, January 8, 1995 at Dallas, Texas Stadium, attendance 64,745

GREEN BAY PACKERS	3	6	0	0	— 9
DALLAS COWBOYS	14	14	0	7	— **35**

SCORING Dal—E. Smith 5-yd run (Boniol PAT), GB—FG Jacke 50 yds, Dal—Harper 94-yd pass from Aikman (Boniol PAT), Dal—B. Thomas 1-yd run (Boniol PAT), GB—Bennett 1-yd run (pass failed), Dal—Galbraith 1-yd pass from Aikman (Boniol PAT), Dal—B. Thomas 2-yd run (Boniol PAT)

TEAM	FD	YDS	RUSH	PASS	RTN	A-C-I	SACKED	PUNT	FUMB	PEN
GB	18	327	23-99	228	57	46-21-1	1-8	4-44	0-0	8-43
Dal	27	450	32-120	330	2	32-23-1	1-7	4-46	1-1	7-46

GB-Robert Brooks 138C; Dal-Jay Novacek 104C, Michael Irvin 111C, Alvin Harper 108C, Troy Aikman 337P

Losing Emmitt Smith to an early hamstring injury only got Dallas angry. Troy Aikman shredded the Green Bay pass defense by spreading the ball around—three different receivers topped 100 yards, and Alvin Harper's 94-yard touchdown reception set a postseason record for longest play from scrimmage. Smith's replacement, Blair Thomas, even matched his season touchdown total with 2 scores.

1994 AFC CHAMPIONSHIP
Sunday, January 15, 1995 at Pittsburgh, Three Rivers Stadium, attendance 61,545

SAN DIEGO CHARGERS	0	3	7	7	— **17**
PITTSBURGH STEELERS	7	3	3	0	— 13

SCORING Pit—Williams 16-yd pass from O'Donnell (Anderson PAT), SD—FG Carney 20 yds, Pit—FG Anderson 39 yds, Pit—FG Anderson 23 yds, SD—Pupunu 43-yd pass from Humphries (Carney PAT), SD—Martin 43-yd pass from Humphries (Carney PAT)

TEAM	FD	YDS	RUSH	PASS	RTN	A-C-I	SACKED	PUNT	FUMB	PEN
SD	13	226	24-66	160	2	22-11-1	1-5	5-38	0-0	3-15
Pit	22	415	26-66	349	16	54-32-0	0-0	5-44	3-1	8-111

SAN DIEGO CHARGERS					PITTSBURGH STEELERS				
RUSHING	ATT	YDS	LNG	TD	**RUSHING**	ATT	YDS	LNG	TD
Natrone Means	20	69	17	0	Barry Foster	20	47	11	0
Stan Humphries	4	-3			John L. Williams	3	16	11	0
RECEIVING	NO	YDS	LNG	TD	**RECEIVING**	NO	YDS	LNG	TD
Alfred Pupunu	4	76	43	1	Ernie Mills	8	106	19	0
Natrone Means	2	19	15	0	John L. Williams	7	45	16	1
					Andre Hastings	5	55	18	0
					Eric Green	4	80	33	0
PASSING	PA	PC	YDS	TD	IN	**PASSING**	PA	PC	YDS	TD	IN
Stan Humphries	22	11	165	2	1	Neil O'Donnell	54	32	349	1	0

The Chargers defense again set the tempo by taking out Pittsburgh's running game. While Steelers quarterback Neil O'Donnell adapted well enough while setting conference title-game records for completions and attempts (32 of 54), the Steelers were not so adept at punching the ball into the end zone. That kept the Chargers still hanging on in the third quarter when Stan Humphries connected for a pair of long touchdown strikes. O'Donnell directed a desperate drive to reach first-and-goal at the San Diego 9, but the Chargers rallied, clinching the win when linebacker Dennis Gibson blocked O'Donnell's fourth down pass. In their third AFC Championship Game, the Chargers were finally heading to the Super Bowl; going all the way back to their early AFL glory, the club had just one title in five title championship games in that league.

1994 NFC CHAMPIONSHIP
Sunday, January 15, 1995 at San Francisco, Candlestick Park, attendance 69,125

DALLAS COWBOYS	7	7	7	7	— 28
SAN FRANCISCO 49ERS	21	10	7	0	— **38**

SCORING SF—Davis 44-yd interception return (Brien PAT), SF—Watters 29-yd pass from Young (Brien PAT), SF—Floyd 1-yd run (Brien PAT), Dal—Irvin 44-yd pass from Aikman (Boniol PAT), SF—FG Brien 34 yds, Dal—E. Smith 1-yd run (Boniol PAT), SF—Rice 28-yd pass from Young (Brien PAT), Dal—E. Smith 4-yd run (Boniol PAT), SF—Young 3-yd run (Brien PAT), Dal—Irvin 10-yd pass from Aikman (Boniol PAT)

TEAM	FD	YDS	RUSH	PASS	RTN	A-C-I	SACKED	PUNT	FUMB	PEN
Dal	29	451	24-99	352	10	53-30-3	4-28	1-23	2-2	9-98
SF	19	294	31-139	155	44	29-13-0	0-0	5-36	1-1	4-30

DALLAS COWBOYS					SAN FRANCISCO 49ERS				
RUSHING	ATT	YDS	LNG	TD	**RUSHING**	ATT	YDS	LNG	TD
Emmitt Smith	20	74	14	2	Ricky Watters	14	72	15	0
Kevin Williams	2	12	8	0	Steve Young	10	47	24	1

RECEIVING	NO	YDS	LNG	TD
Michael Irvin	12	192	44	2
Kevin Williams	6	78	22	0
Jay Novacek	5	72	20	0

PASSING	PA	PC	YDS	TD	IN
Troy Aikman	53	30	380	2	3

RECEIVING	NO	YDS	LNG	TD
Brent Jones	3	37	15	0
William Floyd	3	16	7	0

PASSING	PA	PC	YDS	TD	IN
Steve Young	29	13	155	2	0

TEAM	FD	YDS	RUSH	PASS	RTN	A-C-I	SACKED	PUNT	FUMB	PEN
Det	26	422	16-72	350	0	52-27-6	2-11	5-37	2-1	7-65
Phi	22	452	43-189	263	132	25-17-0	1-7	4-43	1-1	8-80

Det-Herman Moore 133C; Phi-Fred Barnett 109C

A combination of repeated interceptions and quick conversions by Eagles quarterback Rodney Peete generated a ridiculous 51–7 lead for Philly in the third quarter. Don Majkowski's "Magic Man" rep got a late reprise with his trio of touchdown passes coming off of the bench for Detroit. Philadelphia's second touchdown return of an interception—one of 6 picks thrown by the Lions—highlighted the pointlessness of the exercise.

The third time was the charm for San Francisco. After losing consecutive NFC Championship Games to Dallas, the 49ers got out to an early lead thanks to the play of cornerback Eric Davis. First, Davis returned a Troy Aikman interception for a quick score a minute into the game. Three plays later he forced a fumble that set up a Steve Young scoring strike. Niners kicker Doug Brien recovered a fumble of the subsequent kickoff, and San Francisco capitalized with a third touchdown. Spotted 21 points, the 49ers outlasted repeated comeback attempts by Dallas. Aikman threw 53 passes for 380 yards, including 2 touchdowns to Michael Irvin (with 12 catches for 192 yards), but it was finally San Francisco's—and Young's—year.

1995 AFC WILD CARD GAME
Saturday, December 30, 1995 at Buffalo, Rich Stadium, attendance 73,103

MIAMI DOLPHINS	0	0	3	22	— 22
BUFFALO BILLS	10	14	3	10	— 37

SCORING Buf—Thomas 1-yd run (Christie PAT), Buf—FG Christie 48 yds, Buf—Holmes 21-yd run (Christie PAT), Buf—Tasker 37-yd pass from Kelly (Christie PAT), Buf—FG Christie 23 yds, Mia—McDuffie 5-yd pass from Marino (Stoyanovich PAT), Buf—Tindale 44-yd run (Christie PAT), Mia—Hill 45-yd pass from Marino (Stoyanovich PAT), Buf—FG Christie 42 yds, Mia—Kirby 1-yd run (McDuffie pass from Marino)

TEAM	FD	YDS	RUSH	PASS	RTN	A-C-I	SACKED	PUNT	FUMB	PEN
Mia	26	502	14-70	432	38	66-34-3	0-0	3-38	2-1	4-15
Buf	27	536	52-341	195	5	22-12-2	0-0	4-35	1-0	5-29

Mia-O.J. McDuffie 154C, Dan Marino 422P; Buf-Thurman Thomas 158R, Steve Tasker 108C

Although Dan Marino would pass for an impressive 422 yards in an even more incredible 64 attempts, much of these feats were the products of desperate necessity well after the outcome was decided. The Bills humiliated the Dolphins defense with a playoff-record 341 yards on the ground while opening up a 27–0 lead through the third quarter. Each team surpassed 500 yards of offense.

1995 AFC WILD CARD GAME
Sunday, December 31, 1995 at San Diego, Jack Murphy Stadium, attendance 61,182

INDIANAPOLIS COLTS	0	14	7	14	— 35
SAN DIEGO CHARGERS	3	7	7	3	— 20

SCORING SD—FG Carney 54 yds, Ind—Dilger 2-yd pass from Harbaugh (Blanchard PAT), SD—Pupunu 6-yd pass from Humphries (Carney PAT), Ind—Crockett 33-yd run (Blanchard PAT), SD—Jefferson 11-yd pass from Humphries (Carney PAT), Ind—Dawkins 42-yd pass from Harbaugh (Blanchard PAT), SD—FG Carney 30 yds, Ind—Crockett 66-yd run (Blanchard PAT), Ind—Harbaugh 3-yd run (Blanchard PAT)

TEAM	FD	YDS	RUSH	PASS	RTN	A-C-I	SACKED	PUNT	FUMB	PEN
Ind	19	333	29-178	155	133	27-16-1	2-20	5-37	2-0	4-30
SD	27	429	32-145	284	0	47-23-4	1-8	2-55	0-0	4-24

Ind-Zack Crockett 147R; SD-Ronnie Harmon 133C

It looked bad for the Colts when Marshall Faulk went down on the first play from scrimmage. Fullback Zack Crockett dialed in for his 15 minutes of fame with 2 touchdowns on runs totaling 99 yards (the rest of the day he carried 11 times for 48 yards). Four Stan Humphries interceptions doomed the defending conference champs. Jason Belser's second pick set up the clinching score for Indianapolis.

1995 NFC WILD CARD GAME
Saturday, December 30, 1995 at Philadelphia, Veterans Stadium, attendance 66,099

DETROIT LIONS	7	0	14	16	— 37
PHILADELPHIA EAGLES	7	31	13	7	— 58

SCORING Phi—Garner 15-yd run (Anderson PAT), Det—Sloan 32-yd pass from Mitchell (Hanson PAT), Phi—FG Anderson 21 yds, Phi—Barnett 22-yd pass from Peete (Anderson PAT), Phi—Wilburn 24-yd interception return (Anderson PAT), Phi—Watters 1-yd run (Anderson PAT), Phi—Carpenter 43-yd pass from Peete (Anderson PAT), Phi—Watters 45-yd pass from Peete (Anderson PAT), Phi—FG Anderson 31 yds, Phi—FG Anderson 39 yds, Det—Moore 68-yd pass from Majkowski (Hanson PAT), Det—Morton 7-yd pass from Majkowski (Hanson PAT), Phi—Thomas 30-yd interception return (Anderson PAT), Det—Sloan 2-yd pass from Majkowski (Rivers run), Det—Rivers 1-yd run (Moore pass from Majkowski)

1995 NFC WILD CARD GAME
Sunday, December 31, 1995 at Green Bay, Lambeau Field, attendance 60,453

ATLANTA FALCONS	7	3	0	10	— 20
GREEN BAY PACKERS	14	13	0	10	— 37

SCORING Atl—Metcalf 65-yd pass from George (Andersen PAT), GB—Bennett 8-yd run (Jacke PAT), GB—Brooks 14-yd pass from Favre (Jacke PAT), Atl—FG Andersen 31 yds, GB—Freeman 76-yd punt return (bad snap, kick failed), GB—Chmura 2-yd pass from Favre (Jacke PAT), Atl—Birden 27-yd pass from George (Andersen PAT), GB—Levens 18-yd pass from Favre (Jacke PAT), Atl—FG Andersen 22 yds, GB—FG Jacke 25 yds

TEAM	FD	YDS	RUSH	PASS	RTN	A-C-I	SACKED	PUNT	FUMB	PEN
Atl	18	360	10-21	339	6	54-30-2	3-27	5-37	1-0	5-67
GB	23	307	29-117	190	102	35-24-0	1-9	4-43	0-0	5-36

Atl-Eric Metcalf 114C, Jeff George 366P; GB-Edgar Bennett 108R

What started off a see-saw affair turned into a Packers rout in the second quarter. Antonio Freeman's 76-yard punt return for a touchdown was followed by a long drive capped by Brett Favre's second touchdown pass in the half. Up 27–10, the Pack cruised behind Edgar Bennett's 108 yards rushing.

1995 AFC DIVISIONAL PLAYOFF
Saturday, January 6, 1996 at Pittsburgh, Three Rivers Stadium, attendance 59,072

BUFFALO BILLS	0	7	7	7	— 21
PITTSBURGH STEELERS	7	16	3	14	— 40

SCORING Pit—J. L. Williams 1-yd run (N. Johnson PAT), Pit—Mills 10-yd pass from O'Donnell (N. Johnson PAT), Pit—FG N. Johnson 45 yds, Pit—FG N. Johnson 38 yds, Buf—Thomas 1-yd run (Christie PAT), Pit—FG N. Johnson 34 yds, Pit—FG N. Johnson 39 yds, Buf—Cline 2-yd pass from Van Pelt (Christie PAT), Buf—Thomas 9-yd pass from Kelly (Christie PAT), Pit—Morris 13-yd run (N. Johnson PAT), Pit—Morris 2-yd run (N. Johnson PAT)

TEAM	FD	YDS	RUSH	PASS	RTN	A-C-I	SACKED	PUNT	FUMB	PEN
Buf	18	250	21-94	156	26	39-18-3	2-6	5-40	3-1	5-25
Pit	23	409	43-147	262	25	35-19-2	0-0	5-33	1-0	5-41

Pit-Bam Morris 106R

Pittsburgh's punishing defense and Norm Johnson's accurate leg helped the Steelers build up a 26–7 lead, but the Bills snapped back on a pair of touchdown passes by reserve Alex Van Pelt and a banged-up Jim Kelly to close within a touchdown. A long drive capped by a Bam Morris touchdown was followed by a Kelly interception. Morris's subsequent touchdown handed the Bills their first loss in 10 AFC playoff games dating back to 1990.

1995 AFC DIVISIONAL PLAYOFF
Sunday, January 7, 1996 at Kansas City, Arrowhead Stadium, attendance 77,594

INDIANAPOLIS COLTS	0	7	3	0	— 10
KANSAS CITY CHIEFS	0	7	0	0	— 7

SCORING KC—Dawson 20-yd pass from Bono (Elliot PAT), Ind—Turner 5-yd pass from Harbaugh (Blanchard PAT), Ind—FG Blanchard 30 yds

TEAM	FD	YDS	RUSH	PASS	RTN	A-C-I	SACKED	PUNT	FUMB	PEN
Ind	16	249	39-147	102	35	27-12-1	2-10	6-37	4-0	6-38
KC	15	281	28-129	152	34	33-16-3	0-0	4-37	1-1	3-29

The Colts continued to blaze their upset trail despite Marshall Faulk's absence, as they took advantage of 3 missed field goals and 4 Chiefs turnovers to shock the AFC's best team at Arrowhead Stadium. Jim Harbaugh was frequently heroic in doing just enough to twice keep drives alive. Kansas City kicker Lin Elliott missed 3 field-goal tries, the second with 37 seconds left.

1995 NFC DIVISIONAL PLAYOFF

Saturday, January 6, 1996 at San Francisco, 3Com Park, attendance 69,311

GREEN BAY PACKERS	14	7	3	3	— **27**
SAN FRANCISCO 49ERS	0	3	7	7	— 17

SCORING GB—Newsome 31-yd fumble return (Jacke PAT), GB—Jackson 3-yd pass from Favre (Jacke PAT), GB—Chmura 13-yd pass from Favre (Jacke PAT), SF—FG Wilkins 21 yds, SF—Young 1-yd run (Wilkins PAT), GB—FG Jacke 27 yds, GB—FG Jacke 26 yds, SF—Loville 2-yd run (Wilkins PAT)

TEAM	FD	YDS	RUSH	PASS	RTN	A-C-I	SACKED	PUNT	FUMB	PEN
GB	18	368	28-74	294	21	28-21-0	1-5	5-39	0-0	5-35
SF	26	395	18-87	308	14	65-32-2	3-20	5-44	2-2	8-72

GB-Robert Brooks 103C, Keith Jackson 101C; SF-Jerry Rice 117C, Brent Jones 112C, Steve Young 328P

The game started ugly, with the 49ers blocking Green Bay's first field-goal attempt. The Packers scored on a fumble recovery before Brett Favre got on track with a pair of touchdown passes to his tight ends for a 21–0 lead. Steve Young's attempt to mount a comeback generated a playoff-record 65 pass attempts, but the Niners couldn't make up the difference.

1995 NFC DIVISIONAL PLAYOFF

Sunday, January 7, 1996 at Dallas, Texas Stadium, attendance 64,371

PHILADELPHIA EAGLES	0	3	0	8	— 11
DALLAS COWBOYS	3	14	6	7	— **30**

SCORING Dal—FG Boniol 24 yds, Phi—FG Anderson 26 yds, Dal—Sanders 21-yd run (Boniol PAT), Dal—E. Smith 1-yd run (Boniol PAT), Dal—FG Boniol 18 yds, Dal—FG Boniol 51 yds, Dal—Irvin 9-yd pass from Aikman (Boniol PAT), Phi—Cunningham 4-yd run (R. Johnson pass from Cunningham)

TEAM	FD	YDS	RUSH	PASS	RTN	A-C-I	SACKED	PUNT	FUMB	PEN
Phi	13	227	22-74	153	42	31-14-1	5-36	8-41	1-0	3-21
Dal	21	397	38-153	244	33	24-17-1	1-9	4-42	0-0	7-89

Dal-Kevin Williams 124C

With Rodney Peete hurt early on, the Eagles would be hard-pressed to keep up with the league's best offense. The alternating razzle-dazzle of a Deion Sanders end-around for a touchdown was followed by a more traditional Emmitt Smith scoring plunge and a fourth-quarter pass from Troy Aikman to Michael Irvin. The Cowboys had 5 sacks of Eagles quarterbacks in the mismatch.

1995 AFC CHAMPIONSHIP

Sunday, January 14, 1996 at Pittsburgh, Three Rivers Stadium, attendance 61,062

INDIANAPOLIS COLTS	3	3	3	7	— 16
PITTSBURGH STEELERS	3	7	3	7	— **20**

SCORING Ind—FG Blanchard 34 yds, Pit—FG N. Johnson 31 yds, Ind—FG Blanchard 36 yds, Pit—Stewart 5-yd pass from O'Donnell (N. Johnson PAT), Ind—FG Blanchard 37 yds, Pit—FG N. Johnson 36 yds, Ind—Turner 47-yd pass from Harbaugh (Blanchard PAT), Pit—Morris 1-yd run (N. Johnson PAT)

TEAM	FD	YDS	RUSH	PASS	RTN	A-C-I	SACKED	PUNT	FUMB	PEN
Ind	16	328	23-83	245	22	34-21-0	3-22	4-50	1-0	5-57
Pit	21	285	24-80	205	53	41-25-1	1-0	4-39	0-0	4-25

INDIANAPOLIS COLTS

RUSHING	ATT	YDS	LNG	TD
Lamont Warren	15	53	10	0
Jim Harbaugh	6	29	9	0

RECEIVING	NO	YDS	LNG	TD
Sean Dawkins	7	96	30	0
Lamont Warren	7	37	7	0
Floyd Turner	2	55	47	0

PASSING	PA	PC	YDS	TD	IN
Jim Harbaugh	33	21	267	1	0

PITTSBURGH STEELERS

RUSHING	ATT	YDS	LNG	TD
Erric Pegram	10	46	9	0
Kordell Stewart	4	12	5	0

RECEIVING	NO	YDS	LNG	TD
Yancey Thigpen	6	65	14	0
John L. Williams	4	21	7	0
Bam Morris	4	11	6	0
Ernie Mills	3	52	37	0

PASSING	PA	PC	YDS	TD	IN
Neil O'Donnell	41	25	205	1	1

The Colts played perhaps their most inspired game yet, taking the Steelers to the wire. Pittsburgh's defense kept Colts quarterback Jim Harbaugh under control, but the Steelers couldn't put up many points against Indianapolis. The Colts slipped ahead with Harbaugh's strike to Floyd Turner, but with little more than three minutes left, Pittsburgh's Neil O'Donnell produced a crucial drive of his own. He converted on fourth-and-3, followed by a 37-yard completion that set up an end zone dive by Bam Morris. A final Colts rally came up short when Harbaugh's Hail Mary was bobbled and dropped in the end zone as time expired. After disappointment in Pittsburgh in the

last championship game, this time there was relief, jubilation, and the franchise's fifth Super Bowl appearance.

1995 NFC CHAMPIONSHIP

Sunday, January 14, 1996 at Dallas, Texas Stadium, attendance 65,135

GREEN BAY PACKERS	10	7	10	0	— 27
DALLAS COWBOYS	14	10	0	14	— **38**

SCORING GB—FG Jacke 46 yds, Dal—Irvin 6-yd pass from Aikman (Boniol PAT), Dal—Irvin 4-yd pass from Aikman (Boniol PAT), GB—Brooks 73-yd pass from Favre (Jacke PAT), GB—Jackson 24-yd pass from Favre (Jacke PAT), Dal—FG Boniol 34 yds, Dal—E. Smith 1-yd run (Boniol PAT), GB—FG Jacke 37 yds, GB—Brooks 1-yd pass from Favre (Jacke PAT), Dal—E. Smith 5-yd run (Boniol PAT), Dal—E. Smith 16-yd run (Boniol PAT)

TEAM	FD	YDS	RUSH	PASS	RTN	A-C-I	SACKED	PUNT	FUMB	PEN
GB	17	328	12-48	280	54	39-21-2	4-27	3-48	0-0	11-84
Dal	27	419	43-169	250	33	33-21-0	1-5	5-37	0-0	6-65

GREEN BAY PACKERS

RUSHING	ATT	YDS	LNG	TD
Edgar Bennett	9	46		0

RECEIVING	NO	YDS	LNG	TD
Robert Brooks	6	105	73	2
Keith Jackson	5	99		1

PASSING	PA	PC	YDS	TD	IN
Brett Favre	39	21	307	3	2

DALLAS COWBOYS

RUSHING	ATT	YDS	LNG	TD
Emmitt Smith	35	150	23	3
Daryl Johnston	2	8	6	0

RECEIVING	NO	YDS	LNG	TD
Michael Irvin	7	100	36	2
Jay Novacek	5	56	25	0

PASSING	PA	PC	YDS	TD	IN
Troy Aikman	33	21	255	2	0

The contest started off with both quarterbacks throwing with aplomb, as both Troy Aikman and Brett Favre threw a quick pair of scoring strikes. But in the half as in the game, Emmitt Smith was the difference. Smith produced a score late in the second quarter to put Dallas ahead at the half, 24–17. Favre helped put another 10 points on the board in the third quarter to push the Packers ahead, but a classic long drive saw Smith score his second touchdown to retake the lead. Larry Brown's snare of a Favre interception set up a third Smith touchdown, climaxing his 150-yard rushing day. The Cowboys were ready for eighth trip to the Super Bowl and their third date in the big game with Pittsburgh.

1996 AFC WILD CARD GAME

Saturday, December 28, 1996 at Buffalo, Rich Stadium, attendance 70,213

JACKSONVILLE JAGUARS	10	7	3	10	— **30**
BUFFALO BILLS	14	3	3	7	— 27

SCORING Buf—Thomas 7-yd pass from Kelly (Christie PAT), Jax—Simmons 20-yd interception return (Hollis PAT), Buf—Thomas 2-yd run (Christie PAT), Jax—FG Hollis 27 yds, Jax—Means 30-yd run (Hollis PAT), Buf—FG Christie 33 yds, Buf—FG Christie 47 yds, Jax—FG Hollis 24 yds, Buf—Burris 38-yd interception return (Christie PAT), Jax—Smith 2-yd pass from Brunell (Hollis PAT), Jax—FG Hollis 45 yds

TEAM	FD	YDS	RUSH	PASS	RTN	A-C-I	SACKED	PUNT	FUMB	PEN
Jax	18	409	35-184	225	31	33-18-2	2-14	5-51	0-0	6-42
Buf	19	308	29-92	216	70	36-22-1	3-30	5-43	4-2	6-39

Jax-Natrone Means 175R; Buf-Quinn Early 122C

The Bills seemed easy favorites with a 9–0 playoff record in Rich Stadium while going up against the second-year Jaguars. But when a shuffle pass by Jim Kelly, playing in his final game, was picked off by Jags lineman Clyde Simmons and returned for a score, the game degenerated into a slugging match. It was decided on a Mike Hollis field goal that hit the upright and bounced through.

1996 NFC WILD CARD GAME

Saturday, December 28, 1996 at Dallas, Texas Stadium, attendance 64,682

MINNESOTA VIKINGS	0	0	7	8	— 15
DALLAS COWBOYS	7	23	3	7	— **40**

SCORING Dal—Aikman 2-yd run (Boniol PAT), Dal—FG Boniol 28 yds, Dal—E. Smith 37-yd run (Boniol PAT), Dal—Teague 29-yd interception return (Boniol PAT), Dal—FG Boniol 31 yds, Dal—FG Boniol 22 yds, Min—Carter 30-yd pass from B. Johnson (Sisson PAT), Dal—E. Smith 1-yd run (Boniol PAT), Dal—FG Boniol 25 yds, Min—B. Johnson 5-yd run (Carter pass from B. Johnson)

TEAM	FD	YDS	RUSH	PASS	RTN	A-C-I	SACKED	PUNT	FUMB	PEN
Min	12	268	15-63	205	12	27-15-2	2-3	2-40	4-4	3-15
Dal	27	438	46-255	183	57	31-21-1	1-9	1-43	2-1	5-54

Dal-Emmitt Smith 116R, Michael Irvin 103C

The Cowboys bullied the Vikings, with safety George Teague starring. In the first half, he prevented a touchdown by poking the ball out of

Amp Lee's hands on the 1-yard line for a touchback, forced a fumble that set up Emmitt Smith's first TD run, and then intercepted a Brad Johnson pass and returned it for a score. Five Minnesota turnovers produced 23 Dallas points in the rout.

1996 AFC WILD CARD GAME
Sunday, December 29, 1996 at Pittsburgh, Three Rivers Stadium, attendance 58,078

INDIANAPOLIS COLTS	0	14	0	0	— 14
PITTSBURGH STEELERS	10	3	8	21	— **42**

SCORING Pit—FG N. Johnson 29 yds, Pit—Stewart 1-yd run (N. Johnson PAT), Pit—FG N. Johnson 50 yds, Ind—Daniel 59-yd interception return (Blanchard PAT), Ind—Bailey 9-yd pass from Harbaugh (Blanchard PAT), Pit—Bettis 1-yd run (Farquhar pass from Stewart), Pit—Bettis 1-yd run (N. Johnson PAT), Pit—Witman 31-yd run (N. Johnson PAT), Pit—Stewart 3-yd run (N. Johnson PAT)

TEAM	FD	YDS	RUSH	PASS	RTN	A-C-I	SACKED	PUNT	FUMB	PEN
Ind	8	146	15-41	105	63	33-13-1	4-35	8-42	1-1	6-30
Pit	24	407	51-231	176	77	22-14-2	0-0	2-42	2-1	3-19

Pit-Jerome Bettis 102R, Charles Johnson 109C

This rematch of the previous year's conference championship featured two former Bears quarterbacks and some early suspense. Jim Harbaugh and the Colts overtook the Steelers in the first half to lead 14–13, but that only got Pittsburgh angry. Mike Tomczak led a second-half slaughter spiced up with a 100-yard day by Jerome Bettis and some Kordell Stewart showboating.

1996 NFC WILD CARD GAME
Sunday, December 29, 1996 at San Francisco, 3Com Park, attendance 56,460

PHILADELPHIA EAGLES	0	0	0	0	— 0
SAN FRANCISCO 49ERS	0	7	7	0	— **14**

SCORING SF—S. Young 9-yd run (Wilkins PAT), SF—Rice 3-yd pass from S. Young (Wilkins PAT)

TEAM	FD	YDS	RUSH	PASS	RTN	A-C-I	SACKED	PUNT	FUMB	PEN
Phi	16	283	26-71	212	17	33-19-3	3-13	5-36	1-0	3-20
SF	17	279	34-118	161	15	21-14-0	1-0	6-37	0-0	4-38

The weather was the third team on the field in Candlestick, as winds of 50 miles per hour and steady rain discouraged anything fancy on the field. The Niners settled for wrestling matches in the trenches to push their way down for a pair of scores, while the Eagles tried to pass and paid with 3 interceptions and a quick playoff exit.

1996 AFC DIVISIONAL PLAYOFF
Saturday, January 4, 1997 at Denver, Mile High Stadium, attendance 75,678

JACKSONVILLE JAGUARS	0	13	7	10	— **30**
DENVER BRONCOS	12	0	0	15	— 27

SCORING Den—Hebron 1-yd run (PAT blocked), Den—Sharpe 18-yd pass from Elway (pass failed), Jax—FG Hollis 46 yds, Jax—Means 8-yd run (Hollis PAT), Jax—FG Hollis 42 yds, Jax—McCardell 31-yd pass from Brunell (Hollis PAT), Jax—FG Hollis 22 yds, Den—Davis 2-yd run (Davis run), Jax—Smith 16-yd pass from Brunell (Hollis PAT), Den—McCaffrey 15-yd pass from Elway (Elam PAT)

TEAM	FD	YDS	RUSH	PASS	RTN	A-C-I	SACKED	PUNT	FUMB	PEN
Jax	22	443	36-203	240	3	29-18-0	2-5	3-40	0-0	3-18
Den	21	351	21-126	225	12	38-25-0	1-1	5-43	1-0	8-64

Jax-Natrone Means 140R

The Jaguars were 14-point underdogs and the Broncos boasted the best defense in the AFC, but Jacksonville's offense failed to get the memo, scoring on 6 straight possessions. The Broncos might have had more options late in the game if they hadn't blown both their conversion tries in the first quarter. Denver did not score again until the fourth quarter, and a patented late rally from John Elway came up short.

1996 NFC DIVISIONAL PLAYOFF
Saturday, January 4, 1997 at Green Bay, Lambeau Field, attendance 60,787

SAN FRANCISCO 49ERS	0	7	7	0	— 14
GREEN BAY PACKERS	14	7	7	7	— **35**

SCORING GB—Howard 71-yd punt return (Jacke PAT), GB—Rison 4-yd pass from Favre (Jacke PAT), GB—Bennett 2-yd run (Jacke PAT), SF—Kirby 8-yd pass from Grbac (Wilkins PAT), SF—Grbac 2-yd run (Wilkins PAT), GB—Freeman recovered fumble in end zone (Jacke PAT), GB—Bennett 11-yd run (Jacke PAT)

TEAM	FD	YDS	RUSH	PASS	RTN	A-C-I	SACKED	PUNT	FUMB	PEN
SF	12	196	18-68	128	23	41-21-3	1-5	6-36	3-2	6-42
GB	15	210	39-139	71	122	15-11-0	1-8	6-43	5-1	1-5

Playing in the mud the previous week didn't prepare San Francisco's special teams, as Packers return man Desmond Howard scored Green Bay's first touchdown and set up the second. In the mire, misplays set up the Packers' third score and both of San Francisco's, but the Packers settled down to add 2 more touchdowns. The Niners, bereft of Steve Young after an early injury, could not rally.

1996 AFC DIVISIONAL PLAYOFF
Sunday, January 5, 1997 at New England, Foxboro Stadium, attendance 60,188

PITTSBURGH STEELERS	0	0	3	0	— 3
NEW ENGLAND PATRIOTS	14	7	0	7	— **28**

SCORING NE—Martin 2-yd run (Vinatieri PAT), NE—Byars 34-yd pass from Bledsoe (Vinatieri PAT), NE—Martin 78-yd run (Vinatieri PAT), Pit—FG N. Johnson 29 yds, NE—Martin 23-yd run (Vinatieri PAT)

TEAM	FD	YDS	RUSH	PASS	RTN	A-C-I	SACKED	PUNT	FUMB	PEN
Pit	12	213	27-123	90	34	39-16-2	3-20	9-42	0-0	3-15
NE	17	346	32-194	152	86	26-15-2	2-15	7-44	0-0	2-21

NE-Curtis Martin 166R

The Steelers are always supposed to be able to stop the run, but Bill Parcells decided to overpower them anyway. New England relied on Curtis Martin to run over and through crossed-up Pittsburgh after first showcasing the long passing game. The Pats picked up an early big-gainer to Terry Glenn and a rumbling score on a screen to Keith Byars. Martin, who rushed for 166 yards, scored twice in the second half on runs of 78 and 33 yards.

1996 NFC DIVISIONAL PLAYOFF
Sunday, January 5, 1997 at Charlotte, NC, Ericsson Stadium, attendance 72,808

DALLAS COWBOYS	3	8	3	3	— 17
CAROLINA PANTHERS	7	10	3	6	— **26**

SCORING Dal—FG Boniol 22 yds, Car—Walls 1-yd pass from Collins (Kasay PAT), Car—W. Green 10-yd pass from Collins (Kasay PAT), Dal—Johnston 2-yd pass from Aikman (pass failed), Dal—Safety, Carolina bad snap on punt went out of end zone, Car—FG Kasay 24 yds, Dal—FG Boniol 21 yds, Car—FG Kasay 40 yds, Car—FG Kasay 40 yds, Dal—FG Boniol 21 yds, Car—FG Kasay 32 yds

TEAM	FD	YDS	RUSH	PASS	RTN	A-C-I	SACKED	PUNT	FUMB	PEN
Dal	21	244	24-96	148	0	36-18-3	2-17	3-51	1-0	6-61
Car	18	227	37-127	100	139	22-12-1	0-0	1-39	2-1	5-38

Car-Anthony Johnson 104R

The second-year Panthers weren't upset-dependent: they played sound defense and balanced offense, utilized their home-field advantage, and relied on the kicking of John Kasay. Losing Michael Irvin to a shoulder injury took the spark out of the Cowboys offense, and the game degenerated into solid possession football and field goal exchanges, exactly the sort of game Carolina could win. And they did.

1996 AFC CHAMPIONSHIP
Sunday, January 12, 1997 at Foxboro, MA, Foxboro Stadium, attendance 60,190

JACKSONVILLE JAGUARS	0	3	3	0	— 6
NEW ENGLAND PATRIOTS	7	6	0	7	— **20**

SCORING NE—Martin 1-yd run (Vinatieri PAT), Jax—FG Hollis 32 yds, NE—FG Vinatieri 29 yds, NE—FG Vinatieri 20 yds, Jax—FG Hollis 28 yds, NE—Smith 47-yd fumble return (Vinatieri PAT)

TEAM	FD	YDS	RUSH	PASS	RTN	A-C-I	SACKED	PUNT	FUMB	PEN
Jax	18	289	33-101	188	30	38-20-2	1-2	5-36	3-2	4-23
NE	13	234	24-73	161	41	33-20-1	2-17	6-40	2-1	2-5

JACKSONVILLE JAGUARS					NEW ENGLAND PATRIOTS				
RUSHING	ATT	YDS	LNG	TD	RUSHING	ATT	YDS	LNG	TD
Natrone Means	19	43	9	0	Curtis Martin	19	59	15	1
James Stewart	7	40	16	0	Dave Meggett	3	9	8	0
RECEIVING	NO	YDS	LNG	TD	RECEIVING	NO	YDS	LNG	TD
Pete Mitchell	7	63	13	0	Terry Glenn	5	33	11	0
Keenan McCardell	6	62	15	0	Shawn Jefferson	4	91	38	0
					Keith Byars	4	16	6	0
PASSING	PA	PC	YDS	TD	IN	PASSING	PA	PC	YDS	TD	IN
Mark Brunell	38	20	190	0	2	Drew Bledsoe	33	20	178	0	1

The Patriots got their first 10 points off special teams play mistakes by Jacksonville. But the second-year Jaguars hadn't gotten this far

without being resilient. Even after waiting around in the cold during a power failure, the Jags kept New England's defense shackled, restricting the score to 13–6 into the fourth quarter. Jacksonville seemed ready to capitalize until Mark Brunell threw an interception in the end zone on what looked like the tying drive, followed by a fumble on their next possession that was recovered and taken in for the clinching score by the Pats cornerback Otis Smith. Bill Parcells joined Don Shula in having coached two different franchises to the Super Bowl.

1996 NFC CHAMPIONSHIP

Sunday, January 12, 1997 at Green Bay, Lambeau Field, attendance 60,216

CAROLINA PANTHERS	7	3	3	0	— 13
GREEN BAY PACKERS	0	17	10	3	— 30

SCORING Car—Griffith 3-yd pass from Collins (Kasay PAT), GB—Levens 29-yd pass from Favre (Jacke PAT), Car—FG Kasay 22 yds, GB—Freeman 6-yd pass from Favre (Jacke PAT), GB—FG Jacke 31 yds, GB—FG Jacke 32 yds, Car—FG Kasay 23 yds, GB—Bennett 4-yd run (Jacke PAT), GB—FG Jacke 28 yds

TEAM	FD	YDS	RUSH	PASS	RTN	A-C-I	SACKED	PUNT	FUMB	PEN
Car	12	251	14-45	206	14	37-19-2	2-9	5-36	2-1	4-25
GB	22	479	45-201	278	38	29-19-1	1-14	2-36	2-1	5-45

CAROLINA PANTHERS

RUSHING	ATT	YDS	LNG	TD
Anthony Johnson	11	31	7	0
Winslow Oliver	2	15	11	0

RECEIVING	NO	YDS	LNG	TD
Willie Green	5	51	19	0
Mark Carrier	4	65	27	0
Howard Griffith	4	23	9	1

PASSING	PA	PC	YDS	TD	IN
Kerry Collins	37	19	215	1	2

GREEN BAY PACKERS

RUSHING	ATT	YDS	LNG	TD
Edgar Bennett	25	99	13	1
Dorsey Levens	10	88	35	0

RECEIVING	NO	YDS	LNG	TD
Dorsey Levens	5	117	66	1
Antonio Freeman	4	43	25	1
Andre Rison	3	53	23	0

PASSING	PA	PC	YDS	TD	IN
Brett Favre	29	19	292	2	1

Packers fans had been waiting 29 years for a Super Bowl game, the Panthers less than two, but rather than count on karma, the Packers did their homework. Green Bay defanged Carolina's highly-touted blitzing schemes with tremendous pass protection early on, followed by pounding the ball with the ground game in the second half to pummel Carolina into submission. The slowly-amassed Packers lead took the running game off Carolina's tactical menu, forcing a reliance on quarterback Kerry Collins that didn't pay off. Frigid yet raucous Lambeau Field was almost like séance trying to conjure up the spirit of Vince Lombardi in the final quarter, but the 201 yards rushing couldn't have made the old coach smile more than Mike Holmgren.

1997 NFC WILD CARD GAME

Saturday, December 27, 1997 at East Rutherford, NJ, Giants Stadium, attendance 77,710

MINNESOTA VIKINGS	0	3	7	13	— 23
NEW YORK GIANTS	6	13	0	3	— 22

SCORING NYG—FG Daluiso 43 yds, NYG—FG Daluiso 22 yds, NYG—Pierce 2-yd pass from Kanell (Daluiso PAT), NYG—FG Daluiso 41 yds, Min—FG Murray 26 yds, NYG—FG Daluiso 51 yds, Min—Hoard 4-yd run (Murray PAT), Min—FG Murray 26 yds, NYG—FG Daluiso 22 yds, Min—Reed 30-yd pass from Cunningham (Murray PAT), Min—FG Murray 24 yds

TEAM	FD	YDS	RUSH	PASS	RTN	A-C-I	SACKED	PUNT	FUMB	PEN
Min	16	293	28-106	187	23	36-15-1	2-16	6-39	4-2	3-21
NYG	13	266	36-76	190	47	32-16-0	1-9	6-38	2-2	4-28

The Giants got out to an early 19–3 lead on field position generated by Vikings quarterback Randall Cunningham's 3 interceptions. Cunningham straightened out in the second half, hitting Jake Reed with 90 seconds left. After recovering an onside kick, Cunningham maneuvered his team into position for the winning field by Eddie Murray before a stunned crowd at Giants Stadium.

1997 NFC WILD CARD GAME

Sunday, December 28, 1997 at Tampa, Houlihan's Stadium, attendance 73,361

DETROIT LIONS	0	0	3	7	— 10
TAMPA BAY BUCCANEERS	3	10	7	0	— 20

SCORING TB—FG Husted 22 yds, TB—Copeland 9-yd pass from Dilfer (Husted PAT), TB—FG Husted 42 yds, TB—Alstott 31-yd run (Husted PAT), Det—FG Hanson 33 yds, Det—Vardell 1-yd run (Hanson PAT)

TEAM	FD	YDS	RUSH	PASS	RTN	A-C-I	SACKED	PUNT	FUMB	PEN
Det	18	307	27-109	198	7	40-21-1	2-9	4-38	1-0	4-20
TB	15	316	32-141	175	27	26-13-1	2-6	5-40	2-1	4-25

Coach Tony Dungy's new-look Buccaneers played football the way the Steelers did when he was a defensive coordinator: crushing defense and a strong running game. The Lions got heavy doses of both as Tampa built up a 20–0 lead and then coasted in the face of a too-late rally led by Frank Reich. Barry Sanders, a 2,000-yard rusher, was held to 65 yards as Tampa Bay won for the first time in the playoffs since 1979.

1997 AFC WILD CARD GAME

Saturday, December 27, 1997 at Denver, Mile High Stadium, attendance 74,481

JACKSONVILLE JAGUARS	0	7	10	0	— 17
DENVER BRONCOS	14	7	0	21	— 42

SCORING Den—Te. Davis 2-yd run (Elam PAT), Den—R. Smith 43-yd pass from Elway (Elam PAT), Den—Te. Davis 5-yd run (Elam PAT), Jax—Means 2-yd run (Hollis PAT), Jax—FG Hollis 38 yds, Jax—T. Davis 29-yd return of blocked punt (Hollis PAT), Den—Loville 25-yd run (Elam PAT), Den—Loville 8-yd run (Elam PAT), Den—Hebron 6-yd run (Elam PAT)

TEAM	FD	YDS	RUSH	PASS	RTN	A-C-I	SACKED	PUNT	FUMB	PEN
Jax	14	237	14-50	187	5	32-18-1	3-16	4-30	1-1	9-54
Den	28	511	49-310	201	14	24-16-0	3-22	3-50	3-2	9-94

Den-Terrell Davis 184R, Derek Loville 103R

Broncos fans might have worried about repeating the previous year's blown playoff lead against the Jaguars, but the defense never let Jacksonville get anything established. Denver's reliance on bruising running—despite forcing Terrell Davis from the game with bruised ribs—left the Jaguars defense in even worse shape. Davis still amassed 184 yards on the ground and Derek Loville had 103 in a colossal 301-yard rushing day.

1997 AFC WILD CARD GAME

Sunday, December 28, 1997 at Foxboro, MA, Foxboro Stadium, attendance 60,041

MIAMI DOLPHINS	0	0	0	3	— 3
NEW ENGLAND PATRIOTS	0	7	10	0	— 17

SCORING NE—Brown 24-yd pass from Bledsoe (Vinatieri PAT), NE—Collins 40-yd interception return (Vinatieri PAT), NE—FG Vinatieri 22 yds, Mia—FG Mare 38 yds

TEAM	FD	YDS	RUSH	PASS	RTN	A-C-I	SACKED	PUNT	FUMB	PEN
Mia	10	162	17-42	120	45	43-17-2	4-21	7-37	1-1	5-21
NE	15	228	31-108	120	72	32-16-0	3-19	7-37	2-0	5-31

The penalty of falling into habits on offense was perfectly illustrated by Patriots linebacker Todd Collins's recognition of a Dan Marino audible from the team's two previous matchups. Collins put himself in the right place, picked off Marino's pass, and rumbled for a touchdown. Miami could do nothing against the Pats, putting together just 162 yards and only avoiding a shutout because of a fourth-quarter field goal.

1997 NFC DIVISIONAL PLAYOFF

Saturday, January 3, 1998 at San Francisco, 3Com Park, attendance 65,018

MINNESOTA VIKINGS	7	0	7	8	— 22
SAN FRANCISCO 49ERS	7	14	10	7	— 38

SCORING SF—Floyd 1-yd run (Anderson PAT), Min—Carter 66-yd pass from Cunningham (Murray PAT), SF—Kirby 1-yd run (Anderson PAT), SF—Norton 23-yd interception return (Anderson PAT), SF—FG Anderson 34 yds, Min—Carter 3-yd pass from Cunningham (Murray PAT), SF—Owens 15-yd pass from Young (Anderson PAT), SF—Kirby 1-yd run (Anderson PAT), Min—Hatchette 13-yd pass from Cunningham (Walsh pass from Cunningham)

TEAM	FD	YDS	RUSH	PASS	RTN	A-C-I	SACKED	PUNT	FUMB	PEN
Min	16	378	16-57	321	22	40-18-1	1-10	7-30	1-0	12-91
SF	31	394	41-175	219	23	30-21-0	1-5	6-39	0-0	7-69

Min-Jake Reed 114C, Randall Cunningham 331P; SF-Terry Kirby 120R, J.J. Stokes 101C

Injuries robbed the 49ers of both Jerry Rice and Garrison Hearst, but Steve Young directed an offense that instead relied on second-rank heroes Terry Kirby and J.J. Stokes to step up. The Vikings lived and died on Randall Cunningham's inconsistency, effectively dying when an interception was taken for a score near the end of the first half by

49er linebacker Ken Norton, Jr. San Francisco scored enough in the second half to stay comfortable.

1997 NFC DIVISIONAL PLAYOFF

Sunday, January 4, 1998 at Green Bay, Lambeau Field, attendance 60,327

TAMPA BAY BUCCANEERS	0	0	7	0	—	7
GREEN BAY PACKERS	7	6	0	8	—	21

SCORING GB—Chmura 3-yd pass from Favre (Longwell PAT), GB—FG Longwell 21 yds, GB—FG Longwell 32 yds, TB—Alstott 6-yd run (Husted PAT), GB—Levens 2-yd run (Favre run)

TEAM	FD	YDS	RUSH	PASS	RTN	A-C-I	SACKED	PUNT	FUMB	PEN
TB	15	263	27-90	173	21	37-12-2	2-27	4-42	2-0	3-38
GB	16	289	32-118	171	74	28-15-2	4-19	5-43	3-1	7-90

GB-Dorsey Levens 112R

The Packers won sloppily, in part because the Buccaneers were even more sloppy, missing 3 field goals and failing to get their passing game working. Despite a rough afternoon at the hands of Warren Sapp, who sacked Brett Favre twice and forced a pair of fumbles, the Packers offense managed just enough yardage and points to keep the game from being in doubt.

1997 AFC DIVISIONAL PLAYOFF

Saturday, January 3, 1998 at Pittsburgh, Three Rivers Stadium, attendance 61,228

NEW ENGLAND PATRIOTS	0	3	0	3	—	6
PITTSBURGH STEELERS	7	0	0	0	—	7

SCORING Pit—Stewart 40-yd run (Johnson PAT), NE—FG Vinatieri 31 yds, NE—FG Vinatieri 46 yds

TEAM	FD	YDS	RUSH	PASS	RTN	A-C-I	SACKED	PUNT	FUMB	PEN
NE	15	280	19-36	244	24	44-23-2	2-20	7-42	2-2	7-68
Pit	16	279	37-145	134	126	31-14-1	2-0	9-33	0-0	5-41

NE-Shawn Jefferson 104C

The Steelers avenged the previous season's playoff loss to the Patriots, not through any offensive exploits—although Kordell Stewart's long touchdown run gave them the margin they needed—but by the defense's settling the previous season's debt by crushing New England's rushing game. Four Drew Bledsoe turnovers could not be overcome in a tight game.

1997 AFC DIVISIONAL PLAYOFF

Sunday, January 4, 1998 at Kansas City, Arrowhead Stadium, attendance 76,965

DENVER BRONCOS	0	7	0	7	—	14
KANSAS CITY CHIEFS	0	0	10	0	—	10

SCORING Den—Davis 1-yd run (Elam PAT), KC—FG Stoyanovich 20 yds, KC—Gonzalez 12-yd pass from Grbac (Stoyanovich PAT), Den—Davis 1-yd run (Elam PAT)

TEAM	FD	YDS	RUSH	PASS	RTN	A-C-I	SACKED	PUNT	FUMB	PEN
Den	16	272	32-109	163	36	19-10-0	1-7	6-36	4-2	8-64
KC	18	303	24-77	226	10	37-24-0	4-34	5-46	2-0	7-65

Den-Terrell Davis 101R; KC-Andre Rison 110C

The Broncos had the right tool for this sort of tight, defensive-minded game: Terrell Davis. Back from the previous week's rib injury, Davis took the ball 25 times for a pair of scores. The game was decided when Broncos cornerback Darrien Gordon batted away Elvis Grbac's fourth-and-2 pass in the end zone with 19 seconds left.

1997 AFC CHAMPIONSHIP

Sunday, January 11, 1998 at Pittsburgh, Three Rivers Stadium, attendance 61,382

DENVER BRONCOS	7	17	0	0	—	24
PITTSBURGH STEELERS	7	7	0	7	—	21

SCORING Den—Davis 8-yd run (Elam PAT), Pit—Stewart 33-yd run (N. Johnson PAT), Pit—Bettis 1-yd run (N. Johnson PAT), Den—FG Elam 43 yds, Den—Griffith 16-yd pass from Elway (Elam PAT), Den—McCaffrey 1-yd pass from Elway (Elam PAT), Pit—C. Johnson 15-yd pass from Stewart (N. Johnson PAT)

TEAM	FD	YDS	RUSH	PASS	RTN	A-C-I	SACKED	PUNT	FUMB	PEN
Den	23	345	30-150	195	25	31-18-1	2-15	5-31	2-1	4-21
Pit	23	354	27-161	193	19	36-18-3	3-8	4-42	1-1	4-71

DENVER BRONCOS

RUSHING	ATT	YDS	LNG	TD
Terrell Davis	26	139	43	1
John Elway	2	9	10	0

RECEIVING	NO	YDS	LNG	TD
Rod Smith	6	87	20	0
Ed McCaffrey	5	37	11	1

PASSING	PA	PC	YDS	TD	IN
John Elway	31	18	210	2	1

PITTSBURGH STEELERS

RUSHING	ATT	YDS	LNG	TD
Jerome Bettis	23	105	16	1
Kordell Stewart	3	44	33	1

RECEIVING	NO	YDS	LNG	TD
Yancey Thigpen	6	92	27	0
Courtney Hawkins	4	30	9	0

PASSING	PA	PC	YDS	TD	IN
Kordell Stewart	36	18	201	1	3

Against the vaunted Steelers defense, it was an open question whether or not the Broncos would be able to move the ball better than they had against Kansas City. The combination of Terrell Davis's running prowess and John Elway's savvy and passing touch helped put 24 first-half points on the board. From there, the Steelers simply couldn't close the distance. In a game where the statistics were almost dead even—the Steelers had a 9-yard edge in total offense and the clubs had the same number of first downs and completions—Kordell Stewart's 4 turnovers, including 2 interceptions in the end zone, made all the difference. The Broncos headed to their fifth Super Bowl looking for their first win.

1997 NFC CHAMPIONSHIP

Sunday, January 11, 1998 at San Francisco, 3Com Park, attendance 68,987

GREEN BAY PACKERS	3	10	0	10	—	23
SAN FRANCISCO 49ERS	0	3	7	0	—	10

SCORING GB—FG Longwell 19 yds, GB—Freeman 27-yd pass from Favre (Longwell PAT), SF—FG Anderson 28 yds, GB—FG Longwell 43 yds, GB—FG Longwell 25 yds, GB—Levens 5-yd run (Longwell PAT), SF—Levy 95-yd kickoff return (Anderson PAT)

TEAM	FD	YDS	RUSH	PASS	RTN	A-C-I	SACKED	PUNT	FUMB	PEN
GB	19	325	32-106	219	85	27-16-0	1-3	5-37	1-0	9-62
SF	15	257	18-33	224	2	38-23-1	4-26	6-34	4-1	6-64

GREEN BAY PACKERS

RUSHING	ATT	YDS	LNG	TD
Dorsey Levens	27	114	12	1
William Henderson	3	2	3	0

RECEIVING	NO	YDS	LNG	TD
Antonio Freeman	4	107	40	1
Dorsey Levens	4	27	11	0

PASSING	PA	PC	YDS	TD	IN
Brett Favre	27	16	222	1	0

SAN FRANCISCO 49ERS

RUSHING	ATT	YDS	LNG	TD
Terry Kirby	6	21	6	0
Garrison Hearst	8	12	9	0

RECEIVING	NO	YDS	LNG	TD
Terrell Owens	6	100	48	0
J.J. Stokes	6	87	43	0
Terry Kirby	4	7	5	0

PASSING	PA	PC	YDS	TD	IN
Steve Young	38	23	250	0	1

Not having Garrison Hearst at full speed proved deadly. Without a running game, San Francisco couldn't effectively set up long pass plays, restricting Steve Young to hitting receivers underneath coverage and not stretching the field. Playing on the road, the Packers kept Young under pressure all day, getting 4 sacks and Eugene Robinson's 58-yard interception return to set up Green Bay's first touchdown. By contrast, Brett Favre and Dorsey Levens had the benefits of one another's strong play and controlled the clock. That set up the immediate question: Would the Pack repeat as champs?

1998 AFC WILD CARD GAME

Saturday, January 2, 1999 at Miami, Pro Player Stadium, attendance 72,698

BUFFALO BILLS	0	7	3	7	—	17
MIAMI DOLPHINS	3	3	8	10	—	24

SCORING Mia—FG Mare 31 yds, Mia—FG Mare 40 yds, Buf—Thomas 1-yd run (Christie PAT), Mia—Abdul-Jabbar 3-yd run (Pritchett run), Buf—Moulds 32-yd pass from Flutie (Christie PAT), Mia—FG Mare 23 yds, Mia—Thomas 12-yd pass from Marino (Mare PAT), Buf—FG Christie 33 yds

TEAM	FD	YDS	RUSH	PASS	RTN	A-C-I	SACKED	PUNT	FUMB	PEN
Buf	23	416	18-77	339	0	36-21-1	3-21	2-37	4-4	9-93
Mia	25	345	34-117	228	39	34-23-1	1-7	1-34	0-0	6-75

Buf-Eric Moulds 240C, Doug Flutie 360P

In Jimmy Johnson's return to the postseason, the game looked seemed secure a 24–14 lead with 3:42 left, but Miami would have to sweat this one out. Doug Flutie took the Bills to the Miami 1, but Andre Reed, incensed about the spot, bumped an official and was penalized and ejected. Buffalo kicked a field goal, got the ball back, and closed in on a game-tying touchdown when Flutie was sacked and fumbled with seven second left. Bills wide receiver Eric Moulds set a playoff record with 240 receiving yards.

1998 NFC WILD CARD GAME
Saturday, January 2, 1999 at Dallas, Texas Stadium, attendance 62,969

ARIZONA CARDINALS	7	3	7	3	—	**20**	
DALLAS COWBOYS	0	0	0	7	—	7	

SCORING Ariz—Murrell 12-yd pass from Plummer (Jacke PAT), Ariz—FG Jacke 37 yds, Ariz—Centers 3-yd pass from Plummer (Jacke PAT), Ariz—FG Jacke 46 yds, Dal—Davis 6-yd pass from Aikman (Cunningham PAT)

TEAM	FD	YDS	RUSH	PASS	RTN	A-C-I	SACKED	PUNT	FUMB	PEN
Arz	14	346	29-133	213	53	36-19-2	0-0	8-38	0-0	7-55
Dal	20	260	20-96	164	71	49-22-3	4-27	6-41	2-0	5-35

The Cardinals got their first postseason win since 1947. Although quarterback Jake Plummer connected for a pair of touchdown passes and running back Adrian Murrell broke a 74-yard run, the star of the game was Vince Tobin's defense. Arizona corralled Emmitt Smith, erased Michael Irvin, and picked off Troy Aikman 3 times and sacked him 4 times to secure the upset against a team that had beaten Arizona in 16 of the past 17 meetings.

1998 AFC WILD CARD GAME
Sunday, January 3, 1999 at Jacksonville, Alltel Stadium, attendance 71,139

NEW ENGLAND PATRIOTS	0	0	7	3	—	10	
JACKSONVILLE JAGUARS	6	6	0	13	—	**25**	

SCORING Jax—FG Hollis 35 yds, Jax—FG Hollis 24 yds, Jax—Taylor 13-yd run (run failed), NE—Edwards 1-yd run (Vinatieri PAT), NE—FG Vinatieri 27 yds, NE—Smith 37-yd pass from Brunell (Hollis PAT), Jax—FG Hollis 34 yds, Jax—FG Hollis 21 yds

TEAM	FD	YDS	RUSH	PASS	RTN	A-C-I	SACKED	PUNT	FUMB	PEN
NE	14	206	19-35	171	27	44-21-1	2-19	8-47	4-2	6-50
Jax	17	308	37-160	148	89	34-14-0	2-13	6-45	1-0	4-35

Jax-Fred Taylor 162R

Patriots reserve quarterback Scott Zolak's best effort helped get the Patriots close to 12–10 early in the fourth quarter, but an inspired day's work from New England's defensive backs would go for naught. The Pats' inability to mount extended drives left the defense worn out and unable to prevent the Jaguars from padding their lead late in the game. Jacksonville rookie running back Fred Taylor piled up 162 yards.

1998 NFC WILD CARD GAME
Sunday, January 3, 1999 at San Francisco, 3Com Park, attendance 66,506

GREEN BAY PACKERS	3	14	0	10	—	27	
SAN FRANCISCO 49ERS	7	3	10	10	—	**30**	

SCORING GB—FG Longwell 23 yds, SF—Clark 1-yd pass from Young (Richey PAT), GB—Freeman 2-yd pass from Favre (Longwell PAT), SF—FG Richey 34 yds, GB—Levens 2-yd run (Longwell PAT), SF—Clark 8-yd pass from Young (Richey PAT), SF—FG Richey 48 yds, GB—FG Longwell 37 yds, SF—FG Richey 40 yds, GB—Freeman 15-yd pass from Favre (Longwell PAT), SF—Owens 25-yd pass from Young (Richey PAT)

TEAM	FD	YDS	RUSH	PASS	RTN	A-C-I	SACKED	PUNT	FUMB	PEN
GB	24	403	28-121	282	0	35-20-2	1-10	2-51	3-2	4-42
SF	20	347	31-178	169	46	32-18-2	2-13	3-40	1-1	6-50

GB-Dorsey Levens 116R; SF-Garrison Hearst 128R

After five straight losses to the Pack, the 49ers were due, but it took Steve Young's masterful clock management and 7-for-9 passing on the decisive drive to pull off the come-from-behind win. Terrell Owens went from goat to hero by catching the game-winning touchdown with three seconds on the clock; he had dropped 4 passes beforehand, and lost a fumble.

1998 NFC DIVISIONAL PLAYOFF
Saturday, January 9, 1999 at Atlanta, Georgia Dome, attendance 70,262

SAN FRANCISCO 49ERS	0	10	0	8	—	18	
ATLANTA FALCONS	7	7	3	3	—	**20**	

SCORING Atl—Anderson 2-yd run (Andersen PAT), Atl—Anderson 34-yd run (Andersen PAT), SF—Rice 17-yd pass from Young (Richey PAT), SF—FG Richey 36 yds, Atl—FG Andersen 29 yds, Atl—FG Andersen 32 yds, SF—Young 8-yd run (Clark pass from Detmer)

TEAM	FD	YDS	RUSH	PASS	RTN	A-C-I	SACKED	PUNT	FUMB	PEN
SF	15	334	20-46	288	-3	37-23-3	1-1	4-47	2-0	8-47
Atl	16	289	33-136	153	131	19-13-1	2-16	3-41	0-0	6-51

Atl-Jamal Anderson 113R

Though still recovering from a heart attack, Dan Reeves nonetheless was on the sidelines for Atlanta. A tough defensive backfield helped

keep Steve Young from bringing San Francisco back, while the broken leg suffered by Garrison Hearst kept San Francisco's ground game from getting on track. Jamal Anderson, who ran for 113 yards, scored 2 touchdowns early on, and the Falcons held on to beat their division rival.

1998 AFC DIVISIONAL PLAYOFF
Saturday, January 9, 1999 at Denver, Mile High Stadium, attendance 75,729

MIAMI DOLPHINS	0	3	0	0	—	3	
DENVER BRONCOS	14	7	3	14	—	**38**	

SCORING Den—Davis 1-yd run (Elam PAT), Den—Davis 20-yd run (Elam PAT), Mia—FG Mare 22 yds, Den—Loville 11-yd run (Elam PAT), Den—FG Elam 32 yds, Den—R. Smith 28-yd pass from Elway (Elam PAT), Den—N. Smith 79-yd fumble return (Elam PAT)

TEAM	FD	YDS	RUSH	PASS	RTN	A-C-I	SACKED	PUNT	FUMB	PEN
Mia	14	252	13-14	238	11	37-26-2	1-5	5-46	1-1	10-57
Den	24	424	38-250	174	62	23-14-0	1-8	2-49	0-0	5-41

Mia-O.J. McDuffie 118C; Den-Terrell Davis 199R

Miami had won the matchup between the clubs to end the regular season, but the Broncos, who'd long before locked up home-field advantage, made it plain that the stakes were different now. Terrell Davis rolled for 199 yards and 2 touchdowns, and insult was added to injury when the Broncos defense was rewarded with defensive end Neil Smith's slow-motion rumble for a final Denver score on a fumble recovery.

1998 AFC DIVISIONAL PLAYOFF
Sunday, January 10, 1999 at East Rutherford, NJ, Giants Stadium, attendance 78,817

JACKSONVILLE JAGUARS	0	7	7	10	—	24	
NEW YORK JETS	7	10	14	3	—	**34**	

SCORING NYJ—K. Johnson 21-yd pass from Testaverde (Hall PAT), NYJ—FG Hall 52 yds, NYJ—K. Johnson 10-yd run (Hall PAT), Jax—Smith 52-yd pass from Brunell (Hollis PAT), NYJ—Martin 1-yd run (Hall PAT), Jax—McCardell 3-yd pass from Brunell (Hollis PAT), NYJ—Martin 1-yd run (Hall PAT), Jax—Smith 19-yd pass from Brunell (Hollis PAT), Jax—FG Hollis 37 yds, NYJ—FG Hall 30 yds

TEAM	FD	YDS	RUSH	PASS	RTN	A-C-I	SACKED	PUNT	FUMB	PEN
Jax	14	251	22-95	156	-2	31-12-3	0-0	3-37	1-1	3-25
NYJ	29	429	39-151	278	44	36-24-1	2-6	2-35	2-2	5-38

Jax-Jimmy Smith 104C; NYJ-Curtis Martin 124R, Keyshawn Johnson 121C

The Jets rolled behind a great day for Curtis Martin and a surprisingly multi-faceted effort from Keyshawn Johnson. A hobbled Mark Brunell managed to sling the Jaguars back into the game, but the Jets' late prevent defense ended the game with Johnson, who scored touchdowns rushing and receiving, adding an interception to his already impressive totals.

1998 NFC DIVISIONAL PLAYOFF
Sunday, January 10, 1999 at Minneapolis, MN, Metrodome, attendance 63,760

ARIZONA CARDINALS	0	7	7	7	—	21	
MINNESOTA VIKINGS	7	17	10	7	—	**41**	

SCORING Min—Hoard 1-yd run (Anderson PAT), Min—Glover 15-yd pass from Cunningham (Anderson PAT), Min—FG Anderson 34 yds, Ariz—Bates 1-yd run (Jacke PAT), Min—Hoard 16-yd run (Anderson PAT), Ariz—Bates 1-yd run (Jacke PAT), Min—FG Anderson 20 yds, Min—Moss 2-yd pass from Cunningham (Anderson PAT), Ariz—Bates 1-yd run (Jacke PAT), Min—Hoard 6-yd run (Anderson PAT)

TEAM	FD	YDS	RUSH	PASS	RTN	A-C-I	SACKED	PUNT	FUMB	PEN
Arz	23	316	23-74	242	83	41-23-2	0-0	2-36	2-1	13-68
Min	26	416	36-188	228	48	28-17-1	1-8	1-44	0-0	9-38

Min-Robert Smith 124R

Beating the Cowboys expended whatever Cardinals mojo there was, as Minnesota's high-powered offense overwhelmed the Arizona defense. Randall Cunningham, Randy Moss, Cris Carter, and Robert Smith all had great days at the office, while the Cards undermined themselves with 3 turnovers and 13 penalties, scotching any idea of their keeping up. Arizona running back Mario Bates carried 4 times for 3 yards but 3 touchdowns; Minnesota was much more efficient with 188 yards on the ground.

1998 NFC CHAMPIONSHIP

Sunday, January 17, 1999 at Minnesota (OT), Metrodome, attendance 64,060

ATLANTA FALCONS	7	7	3	10	3	—	**30**
MINNESOTA VIKINGS	7	13	0	7	0	—	27

SCORING Atl—J. Anderson 5-yd pass from Chandler (Andersen PAT), Min—Moss 31-yd pass from Cunningham (Anderson PAT), Min—FG Anderson 29 yds, Min—Cunningham 1-yd run (Anderson PAT), Min—FG Anderson 35 yds, Atl—Mathis 14-yd pass from Chandler (Andersen PAT), Atl—FG Andersen 27 yds, Min—Hatchette 5-yd pass from Cunningham (Anderson PAT), Atl—FG Andersen 24 yds, Atl—Mathis 16-yd pass from Chandler (Andersen PAT), Atl—FG Andersen 38 yds

TEAM	FD	YDS	RUSH	PASS	RTN	A-C-I	SACKED	PUNT	FUMB	PEN
Atl	25	427	29-110	317	35	43-27-0	3-23	4-45	2-2	4-65
Min	26	356	34-102	254	0	48-29-0	3-12	4-51	3-2	6-30

ATLANTA FALCONS

RUSHING	ATT	YDS	LNG	TD
Jamal Anderson	23	67	11	0
Tim Dwight	3	28	21	0

RECEIVING	NO	YDS	LNG	TD
Terance Mathis	6	73	19	2
Jamal Anderson	6	33	11	1
Tony Martin	5	129	70	0
O.J. Santiago	3	54	26	0

PASSING	PA	PC	YDS	TD	IN
Chris Chandler	43	27	340	3	0

MINNESOTA VIKINGS

RUSHING	ATT	YDS	LNG	TD
Robert Smith	21	71	16	0
Randall Cunningham	6	13	7	1

RECEIVING	NO	YDS	LNG	TD
Randy Moss	6	75	31	1
Cris Carter	6	67	17	0
Andrew Glover	4	34	11	0
Matthew Hatchette	4	34	14	1

PASSING	PA	PC	YDS	TD	IN
Randall Cunningham	48	29	266	2	0

Minnesota managed to add to its history for postseason disappointment, as the Falcons overcame a 10-point deficit in the fourth quarter with a superb performance by a limping Chris Chandler. The Vikings could have put the game out of reach with 2:07 remaining in regulation, but kicker Gary Anderson missed his first kick of the entire season—regular and postseason games combined—on a 38-yard attempt. That left Chandler enough time to tie the game with a touchdown pass to Terance Mathis. Nearly 12 minutes into overtime, Morten Andersen made his 38-yarder to send Atlanta to the Super Bowl for the first time in 32 seasons of existence.

1998 AFC CHAMPIONSHIP

Sunday, January 17, 1999 at Denver, Mile High Stadium, attendance 75,482

NEW YORK JETS	0	3	7	0	—	10
DENVER BRONCOS	0	0	20	3	—	**23**

SCORING NYJ—FG Hall 32 yds, NYJ—Martin 1-yd run (Hall PAT), Den—Griffith 11-yd pass from Elway (Elam PAT), Den—FG Elam 44 yds, Den—FG Elam 48 yds, Den—Davis 31-yd run (Elam PAT), Den—FG Elam 35 yds

TEAM	FD	YDS	RUSH	PASS	RTN	A-C-I	SACKED	PUNT	FUMB	PEN
NYJ	18	370	13-14	356	43	52-31-2	0-0	7-48	4-4	6-49
Den	14	331	38-178	153	127	34-13-0	3-20	8-45	2-0	6-47

NEW YORK JETS

RUSHING	ATT	YDS	LNG	TD
Curtis Martin	13	14	4	1

RECEIVING	NO	YDS	LNG	TD
Wayne Chrebet	8	121	28	0
Keyshawn Johnson	7	73	25	0
Dedric Ward	5	61	26	0
Curtis Martin	4	39	27	0

PASSING	PA	PC	YDS	TD	IN
Vinny Testaverde	52	31	356	0	2

DENVER BRONCOS

RUSHING	ATT	YDS	LNG	TD
Terrell Davis	32	167	31	1
John Elway	3	13	9	0

RECEIVING	NO	YDS	LNG	TD
Ed McCaffrey	3	66	47	0
Rod Smith	3	37	15	0

PASSING	PA	PC	YDS	TD	IN
John Elway	34	13	173	1	0

The game was filled with odd streaks and crippling failures. New York's Vinny Testaverde completed his first 13 passes, but Curtis Martin couldn't get free running the ball. Despite that—not to mention more than 100 first-half rushing yards from Denver's Terrell Davis—the Jets held a 10–0 lead into the third quarter. That changed when John Elway finally slipped into gear, firing long strikes to set up 4 scoring drives in the third quarter. Davis kept rolling, running for a 31-yard touchdown while amassing 167 yards on the ground, while the Jets self-destructed with 3 fourth-quarter turnovers. Denver became the first team with six AFC championships, surpassing both Pittsburgh and Miami.

1999 AFC WILD CARD GAME

Saturday, January 8, 2000 at Nashville, Adelphia Coliseum, attendance 66,672

BUFFALO BILLS	0	0	7	9	—	16
TENNESSEE TITANS	0	12	0	10	—	**22**

SCORING Ten—Safety, Kearse sacked Johnson in end zone, Ten—McNair 1-yd run (Del Greco PAT), Ten—FG Del Greco 40 yds, Buf—Smith 4-yd run (Christie PAT), Buf—Smith 1-yd run (pass failed), Ten—FG Del Greco 36 yds, Buf—FG Christie 41 yds, Ten—Dyson 75-yd kickoff return lateral from Wycheck (Del Greco PAT)

TEAM	FD	YDS	RUSH	PASS	RTN	A-C-I	SACKED	PUNT	FUMB	PEN
Buf	13	219	27-123	96	10	22-10-0	6-35	8-39	2-2	10-59
Ten	16	194	39-139	55	32	24-13-1	3-21	7-41	2-1	2-12

Ten-Eddie George 106R

A 12–0 Tennessee halftime lead disappeared as Buffalo's Antowain Smith had 2 touchdown runs. Bills kicker Steve Christie's field goal put Tennessee in a corner with 16 seconds left. Lorenzo Neal fielded the kickoff, handed off to H-back Frank Wycheck, who then made a cross-field lateral to a streaking Kevin Dyson to produce the Music City Miracle. Skeptics shook their heads over whether Wycheck made an illegal forward pass, but subsequent instant replay upheld the ruling and the miracle was complete.

1999 NFC WILD CARD GAME

Saturday, January 8, 2000 at Washington, FedEx Field, attendance 79,411

DETROIT LIONS	0	0	13	0	—	13
WASHINGTON REDSKINS	14	13	0	0	—	**27**

SCORING Was—Davis 1-yd run (Conway PAT), Was—Davis 4-yd run (Conway PAT), Was—FG Conway 33 yds, Was—FG Conway 23 yds, Was—Connell 30-yd pass from Johnson (Conway PAT), Det—Rice 94-yd blocked field goal return (pass failed), Det—Rivers 5-yd pass from Frerotte (Hanson PAT)

TEAM	FD	YDS	RUSH	PASS	RTN	A-C-I	SACKED	PUNT	FUMB	PEN
Det	14	258	10-45	213	18	46-21-2	5-38	7-42	3-0	12-126
Was	23	389	46-223	166	23	31-15-2	1-8	4-41	1-0	6-75

Was-Stephen Davis 119R

Stephen Davis ran rampant in the first half, scoring a pair of touchdowns and gaining 119 yards before eventually making way for Skip Hicks in the blowout. Washington relentlessly pounded the ball on the ground for 223 yards. Detroit, trailing 27–0 at the half, had to throw and quarterback Gus Frerotte hit the turf on 5 sacks when not chucking and ducking.

1999 NFC WILD CARD GAME

Sunday, January 9, 2000 at Minneapolis, MN, Metrodome, attendance 64,056

DALLAS COWBOYS	10	0	0	0	—	10
MINNESOTA VIKINGS	3	14	3	7	—	**27**

SCORING Dal—FG Murray 18 yds, Min—FG Anderson 47 yds, Dal—E. Smith 5-yd run (Murray PAT), Min—R. Smith 26-yd pass from George (Anderson PAT), Min—Moss 58-yd pass from George (Anderson PAT), Min—FG Anderson 38 yds, Min—Carter 5-yd pass from George (Anderson PAT)

TEAM	FD	YDS	RUSH	PASS	RTN	A-C-I	SACKED	PUNT	FUMB	PEN
Dal	18	389	16-111	278	6	38-22-1	1-8	4-46	3-2	7-60
Min	20	374	38-175	199	9	25-12-0	3-13	5-41	0-0	7-50

Dal-Rocket Ismail 163C; Min-Robert Smith 140R, Randy Moss 127C

Dennis Green's in-season decision to turn over the Vikings offense over to quarterback Jeff George paid off. Randy Moss, Cris Carter, and Robert Smith each scored and George threw for 212 yards. Smith rushed for a team playoff record 140 yards. The defense kept Dallas off the scoreboard after the first quarter and the veteran Cowboys committed 3 turnovers.

1999 AFC WILD CARD GAME

Sunday, January 9, 2000 at Seattle, Kingdome, attendance 66,170

MIAMI DOLPHINS	3	0	10	7	—	**20**
SEATTLE SEAHAWKS	7	3	7	0	—	17

SCORING Sea—Dawkins 9-yd pass from Kitna (Peterson PAT), Mia—FG Mare 32 yds, Sea—FG Peterson 50 yds, Mia—Gadsden 1-yd pass from Marino (Mare PAT), Sea—Rogers 85-yd kickoff return (Peterson PAT), Mia—FG Mare 50 yds, Mia—Johnson 2-yd run (Mare PAT)

TEAM	FD	YDS	RUSH	PASS	RTN	A-C-I	SACKED	PUNT	FUMB	PEN
Mia	18	299	37-108	191	100	30-17-0	1-5	8-41	0-0	6-67
Sea	12	171	20-41	130	24	30-14-2	6-32	7-48	0-0	2-10

The last game in the Kingdome was the scene of Dan Marino's last late-game rally, as Miami came back from blowing an early lead to win the game with an 11-play, 85-yard drive to score with less than five minutes left. Dolphin Trace Armstrong logged 3 of the 6 sacks of

Jon Kitna, but the game remained close to thanks to Charles Rogers's 85-yard kickoff return for a touchdown.

1999 AFC DIVISIONAL PLAYOFF

Saturday, January 15, 2000 at Jacksonville, Alltel Stadium, attendance 75,173

MIAMI DOLPHINS	0	7	0	0	— 7
JACKSONVILLE JAGUARS	24	17	14	7	— 62

SCORING Jax—Smith 8-yd pass from Brunell (Hollis PAT), Jax—FG Hollis 45 yds, Jax—Taylor 90-yd run (Hollis PAT), Jax—Brackens 16-yd fumble return (Hollis PAT), Jax—Taylor 39-yd pass from Brunell (Hollis PAT), Jax—Stewart 25-yd run (Hollis PAT), Jax—FG Hollis 28 yds, Mia—Gadsden 20-yd pass from Marino (Mare PAT), Jax—Smith 70-yd pass from Fiedler (Hollis PAT), Jax—Whitted 38-yd pass from Fiedler (Hollis PAT), Jax—Howard 5-yd run (Hollis PAT)

TEAM	FD	YDS	RUSH	PASS	RTN	A-C-I	SACKED	PUNT	FUMB	PEN
Mia	10	131	18-21	110	70	41-16-2	5-31	9-45	6-5	9-88
Jax	21	520	46-257	263	49	20-12-1	2-14	5-39	1-1	7-51

Jax-Fred Taylor 135R, Jimmy Smith 136C

The AFC's best team strutted its stuff and made a place for itself in the record book. Fred Taylor's 90-yard run became the longest rushing play in playoff history, the 62 points Jacksonville scored were the most in an AFC playoff game, and were the most points scored by Jacksonville or allowed by Miami. The Dolphins were brutal in the final game of Dan Marino's career, with 5 fumbles and 2 interceptions.

1999 NFC DIVISIONAL PLAYOFF

Saturday, January 15, 2000 at Tampa, Raymond James Stadium, attendance 65,835

WASHINGTON REDSKINS	0	3	10	0	— 13
TAMPA BAY BUCCANEERS	0	0	7	7	— 14

SCORING Was—FG Conway 28 yds, Was—Mitchell 100-yd kickoff return (Conway PAT), Was—FG Conway 48 yds, TB—Alstott 2-yd run (Gramatica PAT), TB—Davis 1-yd pass from King (Gramatica PAT)

TEAM	FD	YDS	RUSH	PASS	RTN	A-C-I	SACKED	PUNT	FUMB	PEN
Was	10	157	22-46	111	56	32-20-1	4-38	8-42	2-1	4-61
TB	12	186	27-44	142	7	32-15-1	2-15	10-42	1-0	2-25

Neither team could move the ball. The only break in the pattern for Washington was Brian Mitchell's 100-yard kickoff return to open the second half. The Redskins were up, 13–0, when safety John Lynch intercepted Brad Johnson. Tampa Bay scored and Warren Sapp recovered a fumble on the next series. Shaun King found John Davis, with just 2 catches all year, for the go-ahead score.

1999 NFC DIVISIONAL PLAYOFF

Sunday, January 16, 2000 at St. Louis, Trans World Dome, attendance 66,194

MINNESOTA VIKINGS	3	14	0	20	— 37
ST. LOUIS RAMS	14	0	21	14	— 49

SCORING Min—FG Anderson 31 yds, StL—Bruce 77-yd pass from Warner (Wilkins PAT), StL—Faulk 41-yd pass from Warner (Wilkins PAT), Min—Carter 22-yd pass from George (Anderson PAT), Min—Hoard 4-yd run (Anderson PAT), StL—Horne 95-yd kickoff return (Wilkins PAT), StL—Faulk 1-yd run (Wilkins PAT), StL—Robinson 13-yd pass from Warner (Wilkins PAT), StL—Tucker 1-yd run from Warner (Wilkins PAT), StL—Williams 2-yd pass from Warner (Wilkins PAT), Min—Reed 4-yd pass from George (Hoard run), Min—Moss 44-yd pass from George (pass failed), Min—Moss 2-yd pass from George (pass failed)

TEAM	FD	YDS	RUSH	PASS	RTN	A-C-I	SACKED	PUNT	FUMB	PEN
Min	27	475	29-87	388	23	50-29-1	4-35	5-48	2-2	10-57
SL	23	405	17-31	374	68	33-27-1	2-17	3-44	2-2	10-70

Min-Randy Moss 188C, Cris Carter 106C, Jeff George 423P; SL-Isaac Bruce 133C, Kurt Warner 391P

Although the game ranks as the second-highest playoff game for combined points and yardage gained, it seemed pretty pointless. The Rams opened up a 32-point lead in the fourth quarter, adding an element of desperation to a game that was already resembling a track meet. Neither team got its ground game working all that well, but Kurt Warner hit five different receivers for touchdown strikes.

1999 AFC DIVISIONAL PLAYOFF

Sunday, January 16, 2000 at Indianapolis, RCA Dome, attendance 57,097

TENNESSEE TITANS	0	6	7	6	— 19
INDIANAPOLIS COLTS	3	6	0	7	— 16

SCORING Ind—FG Vanderjagt 40 yds, Ten—FG Del Greco 49 yds, Ind—FG Vanderjagt 40 yds, Ten—FG Del Greco 37 yds, Ind—FG Vanderjagt 34 yds, Ten—George 68-yd run (Del Greco PAT), Ten—FG Del Greco 25 yds, Ten—FG Del Greco 43 yds, Ind—Manning 15-yd run (Vanderjagt PAT)

TEAM	FD	YDS	RUSH	PASS	RTN	A-C-I	SACKED	PUNT	FUMB	PEN
Ten	13	309	33-197	112	49	24-13-0	0-0	5-52	1-1	9-78
Ind	19	305	22-78	227	24	42-19-0	0-0	7-49	1-0	7-60

Ten-Eddie George 162R

The tension only mounted as each team exchanged field goals in the first half. Tennessee contained the Indianapolis running game and put pressure on quarterback Peyton Manning to beat a talented defensive backfield. The conservative Titans offense finally cracked daylight to spring Eddie George for a 68-yard touchdown run in the third quarter. Both teams would get special attention all day, combining for 16 penalties.

1999 AFC CHAMPIONSHIP

Sunday, January 23, 2000 at Jacksonville, Alltel Stadium, attendance 75,206

TENNESSEE TITANS	7	3	16	7	— 33
JACKSONVILLE JAGUARS	7	7	0	0	— 14

SCORING Jax—Brady 7-yd pass from Brunell (Hollis PAT), Ten—Thigpen 9-yd pass from McNair (Del Greco PAT), Jax—Stewart 33-yd run (Hollis PAT), Ten—FG Del Greco 34 yds, Ten—McNair 1-yd run (Del Greco PAT), Ten—Safety, Evans sacked Brunell in end zone, Ten—Mason 80-yd kickoff return (Del Greco PAT), Ten—McNair 1-yd run (Del Greco PAT)

TEAM	FD	YDS	RUSH	PASS	RTN	A-C-I	SACKED	PUNT	FUMB	PEN
Ten	18	289	34-177	112	14	23-14-1	1-0	5-40	5-3	5-39
Jax	20	355	23-144	211	3	38-19-2	3-15	3-45	5-4	9-100

TENNESSEE TITANS				
RUSHING	**ATT**	**YDS**	**LNG**	**TD**
Steve McNair	9	91	51	2
Eddie George	25	86	20	0
RECEIVING	**NO**	**YDS**	**LNG**	**TD**
Jackie Harris	3	33	15	0
Eddie George	3	19	15	0
PASSING	**PA**	**PC**	**YDS**	**TD**	**IN**
Steve McNair	23	14	112	1	1

JACKSONVILLE JAGUARS				
RUSHING	**ATT**	**YDS**	**LNG**	**TD**
Fred Taylor	19	110	31	0
James Stewart	3	35	33	1
RECEIVING	**NO**	**YDS**	**LNG**	**TD**
Keenan McCardell	6	67	18	0
Jimmy Smith	5	92	37	0
Kyle Brady	5	44		1
PASSING	**PA**	**PC**	**YDS**	**TD**	**IN**
Mark Brunell	38	19	226	1	2

While Jacksonville had the best defense in football, that was mostly against conventional offenses. It was much different with Tennessee quarterback Steve McNair working as a second powerful ball carrier in an otherwise straightforward one-back setup. McNair created yardage on several broken plays to keep the chains moving, breaking out for a 51-yard gain as well as a pair of scores. Otherwise, the game was characterized by sloppy play. Jacksonville was doomed by 6 turnovers and a special teams breakdown that allowed Derrick Mason's 80-yard kickoff return. The Jaguars scored 48 fewer points than the previous week and had no points after the second quarter. For Tennessee, with roots in Houston and known as the Oilers until this season, it was the franchise's first Super Bowl.

1999 NFC CHAMPIONSHIP

Sunday, January 23, 2000 at St. Louis, Trans World Dome, attendance 66,396

TAMPA BAY BUCCANEERS	0	3	0	3	— 6
ST. LOUIS RAMS	3	2	0	6	— 11

SCORING TB—FG Gramatica 25 yds, StL—FG Wilkins 24 yds, StL—Safety, Mayberry's Shotgun snap went out of end zone, TB—FG Gramatica 23 yds, StL—Proehl 30-yd pass from Warner (pass failed)

TEAM	FD	YDS	RUSH	PASS	RTN	A-C-I	SACKED	PUNT	FUMB	PEN
TB	12	203	23-77	126	66	29-13-2	5-37	5-40	3-0	3-15
SL	17	309	21-51	258	53	43-26-3	0-0	4-44	2-0	7-48

TAMPA BAY BUCCANEERS				
RUSHING	**ATT**	**YDS**	**LNG**	**TD**
Mike Alstott	12	39	9	0
Warrick Dunn	9	35	13	0
RECEIVING	**NO**	**YDS**	**LNG**	**TD**
Jacquez Green	4	59	32	0
Warrick Dunn	4	37	12	0
PASSING	**PA**	**PC**	**YDS**	**TD**	**IN**
Shaun King	29	13	163	0	2

ST. LOUIS RAMS				
RUSHING	**ATT**	**YDS**	**LNG**	**TD**
Marshall Faulk	17	44	9	0
RECEIVING	**NO**	**YDS**	**LNG**	**TD**
Torry Holt	7	68	30	0
Ricky Proehl	6	100	30	1
PASSING	**PA**	**PC**	**YDS**	**TD**	**IN**
Kurt Warner	43	26	258	1	3

A matchup between the Greatest Show on Turf and the Buccaneers' daunting defense was a clash of power against power for the ages. Tampa Bay's defense shut down the St. Louis air show for most of the day. The surprise result was that it would be the Rams defense that

did an even better job of rising to the occasion, sacking Shaun King 5 times plus 2 interceptions. A fourth-quarter field goal gave the Bucs a 6–5 lead, but Kurt Warner hit fourth wideout Ricky Proehl for a 30-yard score with less than five minutes left. The Rams would go to the Super Bowl against the Titans, another recently relocated franchise.

2000 AFC WILD CARD GAME
Saturday, December 30, 2000 at Miami (OT), Pro Player Stadium, attendance 73,193

INDIANAPOLIS COLTS	3	11	0	3	0	— 17
MIAMI DOLPHINS	0	0	7	10	6	— **23**

SCORING Ind—FG Vanderjagt 32 yds, Ind—FG Vanderjagt 26 yds, Ind—Pathon 17-yd pass from Manning (Dilger pass from Manning), Mia—Smith 4-yd run (Mare PAT), Mia—FG Mare 38 yds, Ind—FG Vanderjagt 50 yds, Mia—Weaver 9-yd pass from Fiedler (Mare PAT), Mia—Smith 17-yd run (no PAT)

TEAM	FD	YDS	RUSH	PASS	RTN	A-C-I	SACKED	PUNT	FUMB	PEN
Ind	14	293	23-99	194	27	32-17-0	0-0	4-43	0-0	1-10
Mia	26	434	48-258	176	30	34-19-3	2-9	3-46	0-0	7-55

Ind-Edgerrin James 107R; Mia-Lamar Smith 209R

The Colts opened up a 14-point lead, set up largely by Dolphins quarterback Jay Fielder's 3 first-half interceptions, but the story changed in the second half. The Fish tied it with a rally capped by Fiedler's touchdown pass to Jed Weaver with 34 seconds on the clock. The Colts missed a field goal in overtime, which the Dolphins followed up driving downfield to score on the last 17 yards of Lamar Smith's 209-yard day. The only Miamians who could see the game were at the stadium; it was the first playoff game blacked out in seven years.

2000 NFC WILD CARD GAME
Saturday, December 30, 2000 at New Orleans, Louisiana Superdome, attendance 64,900

ST. LOUIS RAMS	7	0	0	21	— 28
NEW ORLEANS SAINTS	0	10	7	14	— **31**

SCORING StL—Bruce 17-yd pass from Warner (Wilkins PAT), NO—Wilson 12-yd pass from Brooks (Brien PAT), NO—FG Brien 33 yds, NO—Jackson 10-yd pass from Brooks (Brien PAT), NO—Jackson 49-yd pass from Brooks (Brien PAT), NO—Jackson 16-yd pass from Brooks (Brien PAT), StL—Proehl 17-yd pass from Warner (run failed), StL—Faulk 25-yd pass from Warner (Wilkins PAT), StL—Warner 5-yd run (Faulk pass from Warner)

TEAM	FD	YDS	RUSH	PASS	RTN	A-C-I	SACKED	PUNT	FUMB	PEN
SL	17	384	16-34	350	65	40-24-3	2-15	5-43	3-2	9-60
NO	17	301	32-50	251	96	29-16-1	2-15	6-41	4-1	5-40

SL-Isaac Bruce 127C, Kurt Warner 365P; NO-Willie Jackson 142C

The first playoff win in Saints history was not without fear. Quarterback Aaron Brooks threw 4 touchdown passes to spot New Orleans a 31–7 lead. Kurt Warner led a frantic rally, scoring 3 touchdowns on 4 possessions in the last 12 minutes, coming up short only when a fumbled punt return—the fifth St. Louis turnover—kept the Rams and Warner from a final shot.

2000 AFC WILD CARD GAME
Sunday, December 31, 2000 at Baltimore, PSINet Stadium, attendance 69,638

DENVER BRONCOS	0	3	0	0	— 3
BALTIMORE RAVENS	0	14	7	0	— **21**

SCORING Bal—Ja. Lewis 1-yd run (Stover PAT), Den—FG Elam 31 yds, Bal—Sharpe 58-yd pass from Dilfer (Stover PAT), Bal—Ja. Lewis 27-yd run (Stover PAT)

TEAM	FD	YDS	RUSH	PASS	RTN	A-C-I	SACKED	PUNT	FUMB	PEN
Den	9	177	18-42	135	13	38-18-1	5-43	9-38	0-0	6-33
Bal	13	240	38-122	118	30	15-9-0	2-12	10-38	1-0	4-30

Bal-Jamal Lewis 110R

The Ravens' defense was one of the most dominating in history, and they underscored the point by limiting the Broncos to 3 points, 9 first downs, and 177 total yards, while sacking Denver quarterbacks 5 times. Ravens running back Jamal Lewis provided Baltimore's usual dose of offense with 110 yards and 2 touchdowns.

2000 NFC WILD CARD GAME
Sunday, December 31, 2000 at Philadelphia, Veterans Stadium, attendance 65,813

TAMPA BAY BUCCANEERS	0	3	0	0	— 3
PHILADELPHIA EAGLES	0	14	0	7	— **21**

SCORING TB—FG Gramatica 29 yds, Phi—McNabb 5-yd run (Akers PAT), Phi—Brown 5-yd pass from McNabb (Akers PAT), Phi—Thomason 2-yd pass from McNabb (Akers PAT)

TEAM	FD	YDS	RUSH	PASS	RTN	A-C-I	SACKED	PUNT	FUMB	PEN
TB	11	199	19-50	149	12	31-17-0	4-22	6-41	2-1	7-62
Phi	20	277	33-126	151	38	33-24-1	2-10	5-37	1-0	2-20

TB-Keyshawn Johnson 106C

The Eagles completely swamped Tampa Bay's offense, crushing the running game, sacking Shaun King 6 times, and forcing a fumble that set up Philly's first touchdown, a 5-yard run by quarterback Donovan McNabb. McNabb would add a pair of touchdown tosses, the last with less than a minute left to kill off the Bucs by the same score that the Ravens beat the Broncos earlier in the day.

2000 NFC DIVISIONAL PLAYOFF
Saturday, January 6, 2001 at Minneapolis, MN, Metrodome, attendance 63,881

NEW ORLEANS SAINTS	3	0	7	6	— 16
MINNESOTA VIKINGS	10	7	10	7	— **34**

SCORING Min—Moss 53-yd pass from Culpepper (Anderson PAT), NO—FG Brien 33 yds, Min—FG Anderson 24 yds, Min—Carter 17-yd pass from Culpepper (Anderson PAT), Min—Moss 68-yd pass from Culpepper (Anderson PAT), NO—Stachelski 2-yd pass from Brooks (Brien PAT), Min—FG Anderson 44 yds, Min—Smith 2-yd run (Anderson PAT), NO—Jackson 48-yd pass from Brooks (pass failed)

TEAM	FD	YDS	RUSH	PASS	RTN	A-C-I	SACKED	PUNT	FUMB	PEN
NO	19	355	17-69	286	33	48-30-2	2-9	5-39	0-0	7-40
Min	18	429	32-127	302	27	31-17-0	0-0	5-45	1-0	5-60

NO-Chad Morton 106C, Willie Jackson 125C; Min-Cris Carter 120C, Randy Moss 121C, Daunte Culpepper 302P

Daunte Culpepper teamed up with wideout Randy Moss for long touchdowns on the third play of each half. Saints defensive backs were toasted for 302 yards, including a shorter touchdown strike to Cris Carter. Robert Tate's interception in the third quarter set up Robert Smith's rushing touchdown to build an insurmountable lead.

2000 AFC DIVISIONAL PLAYOFF
Saturday, January 6, 2001 at Oakland, Network Associates Coliseum, attendance 61,998

MIAMI DOLPHINS	0	0	0	0	— 0
OAKLAND RAIDERS	10	10	7	0	— **27**

SCORING Oak—James 90-yd interception return (Janikowski PAT), Oak—FG Janikowski 36 yds, Oak—FG Janikowski 33 yds, Oak—Jett 6-yd pass from Gannon (Janikowski PAT), Oak—Wheatley 2-yd run (Janikowski PAT)

TEAM	FD	YDS	RUSH	PASS	RTN	A-C-I	SACKED	PUNT	FUMB	PEN
Mia	10	204	17-40	164	76	37-18-3	2-12	6-34	1-1	8-55
Oak	20	269	43-142	127	124	18-12-0	3-16	5-47	1-1	6-40

Jay Fiedler learned the hard way that throwing 3 interceptions per playoff game is no way to keep winning. His first pick was returned 90 yards for a score to squelch a Miami scoring opportunity. The Raiders dominated with a conservative game plan, cranking out 142 yards on the ground in what became a flag-happy bore. But earning the franchise's first trip to a championship game in a decade—and its first in Oakland in 20 years—caused few complaints.

2000 AFC DIVISIONAL PLAYOFF
Sunday, January 7, 2001 at Nashville, Adelphia Coliseum, attendance 68,527

BALTIMORE RAVENS	0	7	3	14	— **24**
TENNESSEE TITANS	7	0	3	0	— 10

SCORING Ten—George 2-yd run (Del Greco PAT), Bal—Ja. Lewis 1-yd run (Stover PAT), Ten—FG Del Greco 21 yds, Bal—FG Stover 38 yds, Bal—Mitchell 90-yd blocked field goal return (Stover PAT), Bal—R. Lewis 50-yd interception return (Stover PAT)

TEAM	FD	YDS	RUSH	PASS	RTN	A-C-I	SACKED	PUNT	FUMB	PEN
Bal	6	134	23-49	85	54	17-5-0	3-32	6-37	0-0	7-50
Ten	23	317	33-126	191	5	47-25-1	1-4	5-38	0-0	6-55

The defensive slugfest limited each team's offense to a single first-half touchdown, plus a field goal apiece in the third quarter. Baltimore's special teams won the game, twice blocking Titans kicker Al Del Greco field goal tries, the second block going for a touchdown in the fourth quarter to take the lead. Ray Lewis's interception return for a touchdown with 6:55 left sealed it. Del Greco was 1 of 4 kicking and the Ravens won despite being outgained, 317–134.

2000 NFC DIVISIONAL PLAYOFF
Sunday, January 7, 2001 at East Rutherford, NJ, Giants Stadium, attendance 78,765

PHILADELPHIA EAGLES	0	3	0	7	— 10
NEW YORK GIANTS	7	10	0	3	— 20

SCORING NYG—Dixon 97-yd kickoff return (Daluiso PAT), NYG—FG Daluiso 37 yds, NYG—Sehorn 32-yd interception return (Daluiso PAT), Phi—FG Akers 28 yds, NYG—FG Daluiso 25 yds, Phi—Small 10-yd pass from McNabb (Akers PAT)

TEAM	FD	YDS	RUSH	PASS	RTN	A-C-I	SACKED	PUNT	FUMB	PEN
Phi	11	186	14-46	140	2	41-20-1	6-41	8-42	3-2	6-50
NYG	15	237	43-112	125	68	19-12-0	1-0	7-32	3-3	4-18

The Giants took a quick lead when Ron Dixon returned the opening kickoff for a score. Both defenses had great games, as New York's offense only generates a pair of field goals while Philly's generated a field goal and an irrelevant late touchdown. Both units collected 3 turnovers apiece, but it was Jason Sehorn's interception return that gave the Giants a second touchdown and the win.

2000 NFC CHAMPIONSHIP
Sunday, January 14, 2001 at East Rutherford, NJ, Giants Stadium, attendance 79,310

MINNESOTA VIKINGS	0	0	0	0	— 0
NEW YORK GIANTS	14	20	7	0	— 41

SCORING NYG—Hilliard 46-yd pass from Collins (Daluiso PAT), NYG—Comella 18-yd pass from Collins (Daluiso PAT), NYG—FG Daluiso 21 yds, NYG—Jurevicius 8-yd pass from Collins (Daluiso PAT), NYG—FG Daluiso 22 yds, NYG—Hilliard 7-yd pass from Collins (Daluiso PAT), NYG—Toomer 7-yd pass from Collins (Daluiso PAT)

TEAM	FD	YDS	RUSH	PASS	RTN	A-C-I	SACKED	PUNT	FUMB	PEN
Min	9	114	9-54	60	5	28-13-3	4-18	6-35	2-2	5-61
NYG	31	518	41-138	380	15	40-29-2	1-5	1-30	1-0	4-36

MINNESOTA VIKINGS				
RUSHING	**ATT**	**YDS**	**LNG**	**TD**
Robert Smith	7	44	25	0
Daunte Culpepper	2	10	6	0
RECEIVING	**NO**	**YDS**	**LNG**	**TD**
Cris Carter	3	24	13	0
Chris Walsh	3	23	11	0

NEW YORK GIANTS				
RUSHING	**ATT**	**YDS**	**LNG**	**TD**
Tiki Barber	12	69	21	0
Joe Montgomery	16	43	8	0
RECEIVING	**NO**	**YDS**	**LNG**	**TD**
Ike Hilliard	10	155	46	2
Amani Toomer	6	88	24	1
Greg Comella	4	36	18	1
Tiki Barber	4	21	11	0
Ron Dixon	2	62	43	0

PASSING	PA	PC	YDS	TD	IN
Daunte Culpepper	28	13	78	0	3

PASSING	PA	PC	YDS	TD	IN
Kerry Collins	39	28	381	5	2

The air show people anticipated did make its appearance, but it didn't involve Daunte Culpepper's arm or Randy Moss's speed. Instead, it was Giants Kerry Collins and Ike Hilliard who had the big games. Collins threw 5 touchdown passes, 4 in the first half, and 2 to Hilliard, who had 10 catches for 155 yards. Contributing greatly to Collins's 381-yard day—and New York's 518 yards in total offense—was a defense that produced outstanding field position by forcing 5 turnovers and sacking a harried Culpepper 4 times. The Giants qualified for the third Super Bowl.

2000 AFC CHAMPIONSHIP
Sunday, January 14, 2001 at Oakland, Network Associates Coliseum, attendance 62,784

BALTIMORE RAVENS	0	10	3	3	— 16
OAKLAND RAIDERS	0	0	3	0	— 3

SCORING Bal—Sharpe 96-yd pass from Dilfer (Stover PAT), Bal—FG Stover 31 yds, Oak—FG Janikowski 24 yds, Bal—FG Stover 28 yds, Bal—FG Stover 21 yds

TEAM	FD	YDS	RUSH	PASS	RTN	A-C-I	SACKED	PUNT	FUMB	PEN
Bal	12	282	46-110	172	117	18-9-1	2-18	7-41	2-1	10-95
Oak	12	191	17-24	167	11	37-19-4	4-20	7-45	2-1	5-36

BALTIMORE RAVENS				
RUSHING	**ATT**	**YDS**	**LNG**	**TD**
Jamal Lewis	29	79	13	0
Priest Holmes	9	31	11	0
RECEIVING	**NO**	**YDS**	**LNG**	**TD**
Brandon Stokley	3	34	14	0
Jermaine Lewis	3	21	15	0
Shannon Sharpe	1	96	96	1

OAKLAND RAIDERS				
RUSHING	**ATT**	**YDS**	**LNG**	**TD**
Bobby Hoying	3	13	5	0
Tyrone Wheatley	12	7	4	0
RECEIVING	**NO**	**YDS**	**LNG**	**TD**
Tim Brown	5	48	17	0
James Jett	3	16	12	0

PASSING	PA	PC	YDS	TD	IN
Trent Dilfer	18	9	190	1	1

PASSING	PA	PC	YDS	TD	IN
Bobby Hoying	16	8	107	0	2
Rich Gannon	21	11	80	0	2

The game was scoreless into the second quarter when Trent Dilfer hit tight end Shannon Sharpe with a short pass on third-and-18, only to see Sharpe spring loose and rumble for a 96-yard score. That was

enough offense in another game won by Baltimore's defense, which stuffed Tyrone Wheatley repeatedly while logging 4 interceptions and 4 sacks. Baltimore defensive tackle Tony Siragusa injured Oakland quarterback Rich Gannon on a particularly hard hit in the first half. His replacement, Bobby Hoying, wasn't treated much better. It was the first Super Bowl trip for the Ravens, whose official history dated back only to 1996.

2001 AFC WILD CARD GAME
Saturday, January 12, 2002 at Oakland, Network Associates Coliseum, attendance 61,503

NEW YORK JETS	0	3	7	14	— 24
OAKLAND RAIDERS	6	10	0	22	— 38

SCORING Oak—FG Janikowski 21 yds, Oak—FG Janikowski 41 yds, NYJ—FG Hall 45 yds, Oak—FG Janikowski 45 yds, Oak—Brown 2-yd pass from Gannon (Janikowski PAT), NYJ—Chrebet 17-yd pass from Testaverde (Hall PAT), Oak—Crockett 2-yd run (Garner run), NYJ—Anderson 3-yd pass from Testaverde (Hall PAT), Oak—Rice 21-yd pass from Gannon (Janikowski PAT), NYJ—Chrebet 4-yd pass from Testaverde (Hall PAT), Oak—Garner 80-yd run (Janikowski PAT)

TEAM	FD	YDS	RUSH	PASS	RTN	A-C-I	SACKED	PUNT	FUMB	PEN
NYJ	23	410	22-136	274	0	41-27-0	1-3	1-24	2-2	0-0
Oak	23	502	31-215	287	0	29-23-0	1-7	2-45	0-0	5-76

NYJ-Curtis Martin 106R, Laveranues Coles 123C; Oak-Charlie Garner 158R, Jerry Rice 183C

After the Jets won in Oakland the previous week to reach the playoffs, a back-and-forth final quarter made the rematch another entertaining game. The Raiders opened up an early lead on Rich Gannon's efficient 23-for-29 passing, but Vinny Testaverde had 3 second-half touchdowns passes. Gannon would hit Jerry Rice for a score—and 183 yards—while Charlie Garner's 80-yard touchdown run with 1:27 remaining sealed the win.

2001 AFC WILD CARD GAME
Sunday, January 13, 2002 at Miami, Pro Player Stadium, attendance 72,251

BALTIMORE RAVENS	0	7	7	6	— 20
MIAMI DOLPHINS	3	0	0	0	— 3

SCORING Mia—FG Mare 33 yds, Bal—Allen 4-yd run (Stover PAT), Bal—Taylor 4-yd pass from Grbac (Stover PAT), Bal—FG Stover 35 yds, Bal—FG Stover 40 yds

TEAM	FD	YDS	RUSH	PASS	RTN	A-C-I	SACKED	PUNT	FUMB	PEN
Bal	20	347	50-226	121	29	18-12-0	1-12	4-46	1-1	5-35
Mia	9	151	15-46	105	9	28-15-1	3-17	5-47	3-2	6-36

Bal-Terry Allen 109R

Although Miami drew first blood with an early field goal, that was all Baltimore allowed. The outcome was slowly ground out beyond doubt as the Ravens rolled for 226 rushing yards. Baltimore's defense was typically ferocious, snagging a trio of turnovers and 3 sacks, and limiting the Dolphins to 151 total yards.

2001 NFC WILD CARD GAME
Saturday, January 12, 2002 at Philadelphia, Veterans Stadium, attendance 65,847

TAMPA BAY BUCCANEERS	6	3	0	0	— 9
PHILADELPHIA EAGLES	3	14	7	7	— 31

SCORING TB—FG Gramatica 36 yds, Phi—FG Akers 26 yds, Phi—Lewis 16-yd pass from McNabb (Akers PAT), TB—FG Gramatica 32 yds, Phi—Staley 23-yd pass from McNabb (Akers PAT), TB—FG Gramatica 27 yds, Phi—Buckhalter 25-yd run (Akers PAT), Phi—Moore 59-yd interception return (Akers PAT)

TEAM	FD	YDS	RUSH	PASS	RTN	A-C-I	SACKED	PUNT	FUMB	PEN
TB	16	258	24-63	195	19	36-22-4	1-7	5-42	1-0	4-28
Phi	17	334	29-148	186	69	25-16-1	3-8	6-38	1-0	7-59

Donovan McNabb scalded Tampa Bay's vaunted defense with a pair of first-half touchdowns, but Philly only got real breathing space in the second half on Correll Buckhalter's 25-yard scoring run. Although sacked only once, Bucs quarterback Brad Johnson was in trouble all day, throwing 4 interceptions, 2 by Damon Moore, including a 59-yard return for a touchdown to finish off the scoring.

2001 NFC WILD CARD GAME
Sunday, January 13, 2002 at Green Bay, Lambeau Field, attendance 59,825

SAN FRANCISCO 49ERS	0	7	0	8	— 15
GREEN BAY PACKERS	6	0	9	10	— 25

SCORING GB—Freeman 5-yd pass from Favre (PAT blocked), SF—Hearst 2-yd run (Cortez PAT), GB—FG Longwell 26 yds, GB—Franks 19-yd pass from Favre (pass failed),

SF—Streets 14-yd pass from Garcia (Streets pass from Garcia), GB—FG Longwell 45 yds, GB—Green 9-yd run (Longwell PAT)

TEAM	FD	YDS	RUSH	PASS	RTN	A-C-I	SACKED	PUNT	FUMB	PEN
SF	19	290	21-71	219	4	32-22-1	2-14	5-37	2-1	3-30
GB	21	368	28-106	262	35	29-22-1	1-7	3-48	1-0	3-25

The game was tight early, as neither team got its offense on track in the first half. Brett Favre put the Pack up, 15–7, with a touchdown pass, but Jeff Garcia responded by hitting Tai Streets for a touchdown and then a two-point conversion. The Packers took the lead on a field goal, but San Francisco's chance was squelched when Tyrone Williams intercepted Garcia. Ahman Green scored the clinching touchdown in the closing minutes.

2001 AFC DIVISIONAL PLAYOFF
Saturday, January 19, 2002 at Foxboro, MA (OT), Foxboro Stadium, attendance 60,292

OAKLAND RAIDERS	0	7	6	0	—	13
NEW ENGLAND PATRIOTS	0	0	3	10	3	—	16

SCORING Oak—Jett 13-yd pass from Gannon (Janikowski PAT), NE—FG Vinatieri 23 yds, Oak—FG Janikowski 38 yds, Oak—FG Janikowski 45 yds, NE—Brady 6-yd run (Vinatieri PAT), NE—FG Vinatieri 45 yds, NE—FG Vinatieri 23 yds

TEAM	FD	YDS	RUSH	PASS	RTN	A-C-I	SACKED	PUNT	FUMB	PEN
Oak	14	230	30-77	153	2	31-17-0	1-6	9-39	0-0	4-20
NE	22	365	30-68	297	49	52-32-1	2-15	8-35	3-0	1-15

NE–David Patten 107C, Tom Brady 312P

The outcome of the infamous Tuck Rule game was decided when the officials overturned a Tom Brady lost fumble, electing to judge it as an incomplete pass. With the ball back in the Patriots' possession, Adam Vinatieri hit the tying 45-yard field goal in a driving snowstorm. New England won the game in overtime with another clutch Vinatieri kick.

2001 AFC DIVISIONAL PLAYOFF
Sunday, January 20, 2002 at Pittsburgh, Heinz Field, attendance 63,976

BALTIMORE RAVENS	0	3	7	0	—	10
PITTSBURGH STEELERS	10	10	0	7	—	27

SCORING Pit—FG Brown 21 yds, Pit—Zereoue 1-yd run (Brown PAT), Pit—Zereoue 1-yd run (Brown PAT), Pit—FG Brown 46 yds, Bal—FG Stover 26 yds, Bal—Je. Lewis 88-yd punt return (Stover PAT), Pit—Burress 32-yd pass from Stewart (Brown PAT)

TEAM	FD	YDS	RUSH	PASS	RTN	A-C-I	SACKED	PUNT	FUMB	PEN
Bal	7	150	11-22	128	117	37-18-3	3-25	8-37	1-1	9-65
Pit	21	297	49-154	143	118	22-12-1	2-11	6-40	3-0	5-50

The hoped-for return of "the Bus," Jerome Bettis, from injury to christen Heinz Field's first playoff game would have to wait another week, but in his place, Amos Zereoue scored a pair of first-half touchdowns. The Steelers had 3 sacks and 3 interceptions of Elvis Grbac, blotting out all attempts by Baltimore offense to find the end zone. The team's only score came on an 88-yard punt return by Jermaine Lewis.

2001 NFC DIVISIONAL PLAYOFF
Saturday, January 19, 2002 at Chicago, Soldier Field, attendance 66,944

PHILADELPHIA EAGLES	6	7	7	13	—	33
CHICAGO BEARS	0	7	7	5	—	19

SCORING Phi—FG Akers 34 yds, Phi—FG Akers 23 yds, Chi—Merritt 47-yd run (Edinger PAT), Phi—Martin 13-yd pass from McNabb (Akers PAT), Chi—Azumah 39-yd interception return (Edinger PAT), Phi—Staley 6-yd pass from McNabb (Akers PAT), Chi—FG Edinger 38 yds, Phi—FG Akers 40 yds, Phi—FG Akers 46 yds, Phi—McNabb 5-yd run (Akers PAT), Chi—Safety, Landeta ran out of end zone

TEAM	FD	YDS	RUSH	PASS	RTN	A-C-I	SACKED	PUNT	FUMB	PEN
Phi	19	336	31-87	249	60	40-26-1	2-13	4-42	0-0	6-60
Chi	10	184	23-111	73	52	22-11-3	2-16	5-38	1-1	1-5

The Bears greatly depended on quarterback Jim Miller to manage an offense laden with trick plays, but when Miller went down with a separated shoulder early in the second quarter, Chicago's ability to keep up with Donovan McNabb and the Eagles took a mortal hit. McNabb would pass for a pair of scores and rush for a third as the Eagles ended what had been a remarkable season for the Bears.

2001 NFC DIVISIONAL PLAYOFF
Sunday, January 20, 2002 at St. Louis, Dome at America's Center, attendance 66,338

GREEN BAY PACKERS	7	3	0	7	—	17
ST. LOUIS RAMS	7	17	14	7	—	45

SCORING StL—Williams 29-yd interception return (Wilkins PAT), GB—Freeman 22-yd pass from Favre (Longwell PAT), StL—Holt 4-yd pass from Warner (Wilkins PAT), StL—Hodgins 4-yd pass from Warner (Wilkins PAT), GB—FG Longwell 28 yds, StL—FG Wilkins 27 yds, StL—Faulk 7-yd run (Wilkins PAT), StL—Polley 34-yd interception return (Wilkins PAT), StL—Williams 32-yd interception return (Wilkins PAT), GB—Freeman 8-yd pass from Favre (Longwell PAT)

TEAM	FD	YDS	RUSH	PASS	RTN	A-C-I	SACKED	PUNT	FUMB	PEN
GB	19	383	22-118	265	6	44-26-6	2-16	3-44	3-2	3-20
SL	13	292	22-91	201	167	30-18-1	2-15	5-42	0-0	4-30

If the matchup between Brett Favre and Kurt Warner promised a high-scoring party, it was crashed by an uninvited guest, the massively improved Rams defense. Although both QBs tossed a pair of touchdowns, Favre had 6 interceptions, 3 of which were returned for touchdowns, including twice by Aeneas Williams.

2001 AFC CHAMPIONSHIP
Sunday, January 27, 2002 at Pittsburgh, Heinz Field, attendance 64,704

NEW ENGLAND PATRIOTS	7	7	7	3	—	24
PITTSBURGH STEELERS	0	3	14	0	—	17

SCORING NE—T. Brown 55-yd punt return (Vinatieri PAT), Pit—FG K. Brown 30 yds, NE—Patten 11-yd pass from Bledsoe (Vinatieri PAT), NE—Harris 49-yd blocked field goal return (Vinatieri PAT), Pit—Bettis 1-yd run (K. Brown PAT), Pit—Zereoue 11-yd run (K. Brown PAT), NE—FG Vinatieri 44 yds

TEAM	FD	YDS	RUSH	PASS	RTN	A-C-I	SACKED	PUNT	FUMB	PEN
NE	15	259	25-67	192	110	39-22-0	4-25	7-39	0-0	12-87
Pit	23	306	22-58	248	29	42-24-3	3-7	6-43	2-1	3-25

NEW ENGLAND PATRIOTS				
RUSHING	ATT	YDS	LNG	TD
Antowain Smith	15	47	19	0
J.R. Redmond	3	13	7	0
RECEIVING	NO	YDS	LNG	TD
Troy Brown	8	121	28	0
David Patten	4	39	15	1
Marc Edwards	4	26	7	0
PASSING	PA	PC	YDS	TD	IN
Tom Brady	18	12	115	0	0
Drew Bledsoe	21	10	102	1	0

PITTSBURGH STEELERS				
RUSHING	ATT	YDS	LNG	TD
Kordell Stewart	8	41	34	0
Amos Zereoue	4	11	11	1
RECEIVING	NO	YDS	LNG	TD
Hines Ward	6	64	24	0
Plaxico Burress	5	67	16	0
Amos Zereoue	4	50	19	0
PASSING	PA	PC	YDS	TD	IN
Kordell Stewart	42	24	255	0	3

The Steelers might have been the better defensive club, but New England's ability to anticipate Pittsburgh's running game forced an unhealthy reliance on Kordell Stewart. Patriots quarterback Tom Brady injured his ankle and Drew Bledsoe entered to throw for the lone score by New England's offense. Patriots special teams decided the game, scoring on a punt return and a blocked field goal. Troy Brown had a hand in both, running back the punt, and later picking up the loose ball after the blocked kick, running 11 yards, and lateraling to Antwan Harris, who went the last 49 yards for the score. The defense picked off Stewart twice in the final three minutes to send the Patriots to their third Super Bowl under their third different coach.

2001 NFC CHAMPIONSHIP
Sunday, January 27, 2002 at St. Louis, Dome at America's Center, attendance 66,502

PHILADELPHIA EAGLES	3	14	0	7	—	24
ST. LOUIS RAMS	10	3	7	9	—	29

SCORING StL—Bruce 5-yd pass from Warner (Wilkins PAT), Phi—FG Akers 46 yds, StL—FG Wilkins 27 yds, Phi—Staley 1-yd run (Akers PAT), StL—FG Wilkins 39 yds, Phi—Pinkston 12-yd pass from McNabb (Akers PAT), StL—FG Wilkins 41 yds, StL—Faulk 1-yd run (pass failed), StL—Faulk 1-yd run (Wilkins PAT), Phi—McNabb 3-yd run (Akers PAT)

TEAM	FD	YDS	RUSH	PASS	RTN	A-C-I	SACKED	PUNT	FUMB	PEN
Phi	16	256	22-110	146	20	30-18-1	3-25	4-39	1-1	2-15
SL	22	371	33-161	210	0	33-22-0	1-2	3-45	2-0	6-38

PHILADELPHIA EAGLES				
RUSHING	**ATT**	**YDS**	**LNG**	**TD**
Correll Buckhalter	6	50	31	0
Duce Staley	11	39	20	1
RECEIVING	**NO**	**YDS**	**LNG**	**TD**
Duce Staley	8	58	10	0
Chad Lewis	5	53	14	0
PASSING	**PA**	**PC**	**YDS**	**TD**	**IN**
Donovan McNabb	30	18	171	1	1

ST. LOUIS RAMS				
RUSHING	**ATT**	**YDS**	**LNG**	**TD**
Marshall Faulk	31	159	31	2
Kurt Warner	2	2	3	0
RECEIVING	**NO**	**YDS**	**LNG**	**TD**
Isaac Bruce	8	84	17	1
Torry Holt	5	58	21	0
Marshall Faulk	4	13	10	0
PASSING	**PA**	**PC**	**YDS**	**TD**	**IN**
Kurt Warner	33	22	212	1	0

The Eagles got out to an early 17–13 lead as the offense seemed to be clicking as usual under Donovan McNabb's direction. Philly's defense hadn't allowed more than 21 points during the season, but Kurt Warner stepped up yet again, bringing the Rams in close while running back Marshall Faulk punched in a pair of second-half scores while rushing for 159 yards on the day. (Warner had the only other 2 rushing yards by the team.) The St. Louis defense rose to the occasion, shutting out the Eagles in the second half until a late score by McNabb. The Rams did not turn the ball over all day in assuring their second Super Bowl appearance in three seasons.

2002 AFC WILD CARD GAME

Saturday, January 4, 2003 at East Rutherford, NJ, Giants Stadium, attendance 78,524

INDIANAPOLIS COLTS	0	0	0	0	—	0
NEW YORK JETS	7	17	10	7	—	**41**

SCORING NYJ—Anderson 56-yd pass from Pennington (Hall PAT), NYJ—FG Hall 41 yds, NYJ—Jordan 1-yd run (Hall PAT), NYJ—Moss 4-yd pass from Pennington (Hall PAT), NYJ—FG Hall 39 yds, NYJ—Baker 3-yd pass from Pennington (Hall PAT), NYJ—Jordan 1-yd run (Hall PAT)

TEAM	FD	YDS	RUSH	PASS	RTN	A-C-I	SACKED	PUNT	FUMB	PEN
Ind	10	176	14-52	124	0	31-14-2	1-13	5-34	2-1	2-10
NYJ	26	396	42-180	216	39	25-19-0	2-6	2-30	0-0	3-30

NYJ-LaMont Jordan 102R

New York dominated every segment of the game. First-year Jets starter Chad Pennington threw 3 touchdowns, while LaMont Jordan, rushing in relief for Curtis Martin in the blowout, ran for 2 scores and 102 yards. Veteran Colts quarterback Peyton Manning did little to add to his postseason reputation, completing 14 of 31 passes and guiding an offense that produced only 176 yards and zero points.

2002 NFC WILD CARD GAME

Saturday, January 4, 2003 at Green Bay, Lambeau Field, attendance 65,358

ATLANTA FALCONS	14	10	3	0	—	**27**
GREEN BAY PACKERS	0	0	7	0	—	7

SCORING Atl—Jefferson 10-yd pass from Vick (Feely PAT), Atl—Ulmer 1-yd blocked punt return (Feely PAT), Atl—Duckett 6-yd run (Feely PAT), Atl—FG Feely 22 yds, GB—Driver 14-yd pass from Favre (Longwell PAT), Atl—FG Feely 23 yds

TEAM	FD	YDS	RUSH	PASS	RTN	A-C-I	SACKED	PUNT	FUMB	PEN
Atl	21	309	44-192	117	5	25-13-0	0-0	15-34	1-0	3-20
GB	17	289	19-56	233	0	42-20-2	2-14	1-0	3-3	3-15

GB-Javon Walker 104C

A night game at Lambeau Field in January didn't faze the Falcons at all. Atlanta opened up an early lead with a second quarter touchdown scored on a blocked punt. The three-headed backfield of Warrick Dunn, T.J. Duckett, and Michael Vick shredded the Pack with 192 rushing yards. Five Green Bay turnovers assured the Packers of their first ever playoff loss at home.

2002 AFC WILD CARD GAME

Sunday, January 5, 2003 at Pittsburgh, Heinz Field, attendance 62,595

CLEVELAND BROWNS	7	10	7	9	—	33
PITTSBURGH STEELERS	0	7	7	22	—	**36**

SCORING Cle—Green 1-yd run (Dawson PAT), Cle—Northcutt 32-yd pass from Holcomb (Dawson PAT), Pit—Randle El 66-yd punt return (Reed PAT), Cle—FG Dawson 31 yds, Cle—Northcutt 15-yd pass from Holcomb (Dawson PAT), Pit—Burress 6-yd pass from Maddox (Reed PAT), Cle—FG Dawson 24 yds, Pit—Tuman 3-yd pass from Maddox (Reed PAT), Cle—Andre' Davis 22-yd pass from Holcomb (pass failed), Pit—Ward 5-yd pass from Maddox (Reed PAT), Pit—Fuamatu-Ma'afala 3-yd run (Tuman pass from Randle El)

TEAM	FD	YDS	RUSH	PASS	RTN	A-C-I	SACKED	PUNT	FUMB	PEN
Cle	21	447	28-38	409	111	43-26-1	2-20	7-39	0-0	9-75
Pit	30	432	20-89	343	91	48-30-2	3-24	6-35	1-1	4-35

Cle-Kevin Johnson 140C, Kelly Holcomb 429P; Pit-Hines Ward 104C, Plaxico Burress 100C, Tommy Maddox 367P

Two unknown quarterbacks—XFL vet Tommy Maddox of the Steelers and Cleveland's Kelly Holcomb—put on an air show. Both tossed 3 touchdowns, but Maddox led the Steelers back from a 24–7 third-quarter deficit to score 22 fourth-quarter points. That proved just enough to withstand Cleveland's comeback. Browns wideout Andre King was tackled in bounds within field goal range as the clock ran out in the first postseason game for the expansion Browns.

2002 NFC WILD CARD GAME

Sunday, January 5, 2003 at San Francisco, 3Com Park, attendance 66,318

NEW YORK GIANTS	7	21	10	0	—	38
SAN FRANCISCO 49ERS	7	7	8	17	—	**39**

SCORING SF—Owens 76-yd pass from Garcia (Chandler PAT), NYG—Toomer 12-yd pass from Collins (Bryant PAT), NYG—Shockey 2-yd pass from Collins (Bryant PAT), SF—Barlow 1-yd run (Chandler PAT), NYG—Toomer 8-yd pass from Collins (Bryant PAT), NYG—Toomer 24-yd pass from Collins (Bryant PAT), NYG—Barber 6-yd run (Bryant PAT), NYG—FG Bryant 21 yds, SF—Owens 26-yd pass from Garcia (Owens pass from Garcia), SF—Garcia 14-yd run (Owens pass from Garcia), SF—FG Chandler 25 yds, SF—Streets 13-yd pass from Garcia (pass failed)

TEAM	FD	YDS	RUSH	PASS	RTN	A-C-I	SACKED	PUNT	FUMB	PEN
NYG	26	446	29-119	327	33	44-29-1	2-15	4-39	1-0	5-50
SF	23	446	20-90	356	0	45-28-1	0-0	3-47	1-1	2-20

NYG-Tiki Barber 115R, Amani Toomer 136C, Kerry Collins 342P; SF-Terrell Owens 177C, Jeff Garcia 331P

Jeff Garcia rallied the 49ers back from a 38–14 deficit to score 25 unanswered points, reducing Kerry Collins's 4 touchdown passes and Amani Toomer's 8-catch, 3-touchdown, 136-yard effort to historical footnotes. The Giants had a chance to win on the last play, but a botched snap resulted in an incomplete pass, with a mistaken ruling that New York had an illegal man downfield to end the game.

2002 AFC DIVISIONAL PLAYOFF

Saturday, January 11, 2003 at Nashville (OT), The Coliseum, attendance 68,809

PITTSBURGH STEELERS	0	13	7	11	0	—	31
TENNESSEE TITANS	14	0	14	3	3	—	**34**

SCORING Ten—McNair 8-yd run (Nedney PAT), Ten—George 1-yd run (Nedney PAT), Pit—Ward 8-yd pass from Maddox (Reed PAT), Pit—FG Reed 30 yds, Pit—FG Reed 39 yds, Ten—Zereoue 31-yd run (Reed PAT), Ten—Wycheck 7-yd pass from McNair (Nedney PAT), Ten—Kinney 2-yd pass from McNair (Nedney PAT), Pit—Ward 21-yd pass from Maddox (Burress pass from Ward), Pit—FG Reed 40 yds, Ten—FG Nedney 42 yds, Ten—FG Nedney 26 yds

TEAM	FD	YDS	RUSH	PASS	RTN	A-C-I	SACKED	PUNT	FUMB	PEN
Pit	21	324	20-67	257	14	42-21-1	1-9	6-32	0-0	6-41
Ten	29	430	36-99	331	25	45-27-2	1-7	4-29	2-2	8-92

Ten-Frank Wycheck 123C, Steve McNair 338P

This see-saw matchup saw the Steelers score 20 points off 3 Tennessee turnovers. Titans kicker Joe Nedney went from goat to hero. He missed a game-winner at the end of the fourth quarter, and then another kick in overtime, only to get a third bite of the apple because of a controversial roughing call, which he finally made for the win.

2002 NFC DIVISIONAL PLAYOFF

Saturday, January 11, 2003 at Philadelphia, Veterans Stadium, attendance 66,452

ATLANTA FALCONS	0	6	0	0	—	6
PHILADELPHIA EAGLES	10	3	0	7	—	**20**

SCORING Phi—Taylor 39-yd interception return (Akers PAT), Phi—FG Akers 34 yds, Phi—FG Akers 39 yds, Atl—FG Feely 34 yds, Atl—FG Feely 52 yds, Phi—Thrash 35-yd pass from McNabb (Akers PAT)

TEAM	FD	YDS	RUSH	PASS	RTN	A-C-I	SACKED	PUNT	FUMB	PEN
Atl	19	354	24-93	261	26	39-23-2	3-27	5-38	2-0	9-95
Phi	15	318	26-91	227	64	30-20-0	2-20	5-41	2-0	3-30

A rough day for Michael Vick—including 2 interceptions and 3 sacks—was almost redeemed by a third-quarter game-tying touchdown run … only to see it called back on a holding penalty. The

drive ended with a missed field goal; Vick's 274 passing yards were no consolation. Donovan McNabb clinched the victory with a late TD pass.

2002 NFC DIVISIONAL PLAYOFF

Sunday, January 12, 2003 at Tampa, Raymond James Stadium, attendance 65,599

SAN FRANCISCO 49ERS	3	3	0	0	—	6
TAMPA BAY BUCCANEERS	7	21	3	0	—	31

SCORING TB—Alstott 2-yd run (Gramatica PAT), SF—FG Chandler 24 yds, TB—Jurevicius 20-yd pass from B. Johnson (Gramatica PAT), SF—FG Chandler 40 yds, TB—Dudley 12-yd pass from B. Johnson (Gramatica PAT), TB—Alstott 2-yd run (Gramatica PAT), TB—FG Gramatica 19 yds

TEAM	FD	YDS	RUSH	PASS	RTN	A-C-I	SACKED	PUNT	FUMB	PEN
SF	14	228	13-62	166	38	41-22-3	4-27	3-34	4-2	6-71
TB	21	329	38-121	208	43	32-16-1	1-9	4-47	2-1	10-100

Buccaneers quarterback Brad Johnson returned from a month lost to injury to toss a pair of touchdowns. Tampa Bay's crushing defense ground the 49ers to powder, sacking Jeff Garcia 4 times, forcing 5 turnovers, and holding San Francisco to a pair of first-half field goals while taking a 28–6 halftime lead. The Buccaneers controlled the ball and the tempo in the second half.

2002 AFC DIVISIONAL PLAYOFF

Sunday, January 12, 2003 at Oakland, Network Associates Coliseum, attendance 62,207

NEW YORK JETS	3	7	0	0	—	10
OAKLAND RAIDERS	3	7	7	13	—	30

SCORING NYJ—FG Hall 38 yds, Oak—FG Janikowski 29 yds, Oak—Crockett 1-yd run (Janikowski PAT), NYJ—Sowell 1-yd pass from Pennington (Hall PAT), Oak—Porter 29-yd pass from Gannon (Janikowski PAT), Oak—Rice 9-yd pass from Gannon (Janikowski PAT), Oak—FG Janikowski 34 yds, Oak—FG Janikowski 31 yds

TEAM	FD	YDS	RUSH	PASS	RTN	A-C-I	SACKED	PUNT	FUMB	PEN
NYJ	20	287	24-120	167	0	47-21-2	4-16	2-39	3-2	5-30
Oak	20	399	30-127	272	1	30-20-1	2-11	3-36	2-0	8-70

Oak-Jerry Porter 123C

A tight first half put both teams on the spot in the second, with Oakland's Rich Gannon rising to the occasion with a pair of touchdown strikes, including Jerry Rice's 22nd and last career postseason touchdown. The Jets and Chad Pennington self-destructed, committing 4 turnovers and allowing 4 sacks as the Raiders pulled away. Nine different Jets caught passes, but only 1 touchdown.

2002 NFC CHAMPIONSHIP

Sunday, January 19, 2003 at Philadelphia, Veterans Stadium, attendance 66,713

TAMPA BAY BUCCANEERS	10	7	3	7	—	27
PHILADELPHIA EAGLES	7	3	0	0	—	10

SCORING Phi—Staley 20-yd run (Akers PAT), TB—FG Gramatica 48 yds, TB—Alstott 1-yd run (Gramatica PAT), Phi—FG Akers 30 yds, TB—K. Johnson 9-yd pass from B. Johnson (Gramatica PAT), TB—FG Gramatica 27 yds, TB—Barber 92-yd interception return (Gramatica PAT)

TEAM	FD	YDS	RUSH	PASS	RTN	A-C-I	SACKED	PUNT	FUMB	PEN
TB	15	308	32-49	259	104	33-20-1	0-0	7-36	0-0	3-16
Phi	20	312	21-80	232	35	49-26-1	2-11	7-40	2-2	5-45

TAMPA BAY BUCCANEERS

RUSHING	ATT	YDS	LNG	TD
Mike Alstott	17	25	6	1
Michael Pittman	8	17	9	0

RECEIVING	NO	YDS	LNG	TD
Michael Pittman	5	53	14	0
Keenan McCardell	5	37	11	0
Joe Jurevicius	1	71	71	0

PASSING	PA	PC	YDS	TD	IN
Brad Johnson	33	20	259	1	1

PHILADELPHIA EAGLES

RUSHING	ATT	YDS	LNG	TD
Duce Staley	13	58	20	1
Donovan McNabb	3	17	11	0

RECEIVING	NO	YDS	LNG	TD
Chad Lewis	6	65	16	0
Duce Staley	6	26	12	0
Antonio Freeman	5	66	23	0
James Thrash	4	23	11	0
Todd Pinkston	3	51	24	0

PASSING	PA	PC	YDS	TD	IN
Donovan McNabb	49	26	243	0	1

The Buccaneers were 1–21 in games played below 40 degrees and were due an especially rude reception for what would be the final NFL game played at Veteran's Stadium, where the past two Bucs seasons had ended in the playoffs. Despite Philly's touchdown in the opening minute, Tampa Bay pulled off the big play on offense when Brad Johnson hit Joe Jurevicius for a 71-yard gain. That set up a 1-yard touchdown plunge by Mike Alstott. The Eagles fumbled twice, and the Bucs defense sealed the win when cornerback Ronde

Barber intercepted Donovan McNabb and ran it back for a 92-yard touchdown, closing down the Vet and sending the Bucs to their first Super Bowl.

2002 AFC CHAMPIONSHIP

Sunday, January 19, 2003 at Oakland, Network Associates Coliseum, attendance 62,544

TENNESSEE TITANS	7	10	7	0	—	24
OAKLAND RAIDERS	14	10	3	14	—	41

SCORING Oak—Porter 3-yd pass from Gannon (Janikowski PAT), Ten—Bennett 33-yd pass from McNair (Nedney PAT), Oak—Garner 12-yd pass from Gannon (Janikowski PAT), Ten—FG Nedney 29 yds, Ten—McNair 9-yd run (Nedney PAT), Oak—Jolley 1-yd pass from Gannon (Janikowski PAT), Oak—FG Janikowski 43 yds, Oak—FG Janikowski 32 yds, Ten—McNair 13-yd run (Hentrich PAT), Oak—Gannon 2-yd run (Janikowski PAT), Oak—Crockett 7-yd run (Janikowski PAT)

TEAM	FD	YDS	RUSH	PASS	RTN	A-C-I	SACKED	PUNT	FUMB	PEN
Ten	28	312	30-138	174	11	36-21-0	2-20	3-32	2-2	7-60
Oak	25	375	17-89	286	0	41-29-0	0-0	3-40	3-1	14-127

TENNESSEE TITANS

RUSHING	ATT	YDS	LNG	TD
Eddie George	15	67	17	0
Steve McNair	5	53	16	2

RECEIVING	NO	YDS	LNG	TD
Derrick Mason	5	41	14	0
Robert Holcombe	5	25	9	0
Frank Wycheck	4	41	18	0
Drew Bennett	3	58	33	1

PASSING	PA	PC	YDS	TD	IN
Steve McNair	36	21	194	1	0

OAKLAND RAIDERS

RUSHING	ATT	YDS	LNG	TD
Rich Gannon	8	41	14	1
Charlie Garner	7	36	18	0

RECEIVING	NO	YDS	LNG	TD
Tim Brown	9	73	14	0
Charlie Garner	7	55	17	1
Jerry Rice	5	79	29	0
Jerry Porter	4	52	31	1

PASSING	PA	PC	YDS	TD	IN
Rich Gannon	41	29	286	3	0

The offensive fireworks centered on the rival quarterbacks, as Steve McNair and Rich Gannon traded scores in the early going. Gannon had the benefit of particularly outstanding protection, placing incredible pressure on Titans defensive backs charged with guarding Raiders wideouts Jerry Rice, Tim Brown, and Jerry Porter. Gannon piled up 286 yards and 3 touchdowns. After abstaining from running the ball for three quarters, Raiders coach Bill Callahan protected the lead in the fourth quarter with a late but effective introduction of the running game against an exhausted Tennessee defense. It was the franchise's first conference championship clinched on the field in Oakland since John Madden's Raiders did it in 1976.

2003 AFC WILD CARD GAME

Saturday, January 3, 2004 at Baltimore, M & T Bank Stadium, attendance 69,452

TENNESSEE TITANS	7	0	7	6	—	20
BALTIMORE RAVENS	3	7	0	7	—	17

SCORING Ten—Brown 6-yd run (Anderson PAT), Bal—Demps 56-yd interception return (Stover PAT), Bal—FG Stover 43 yds, Ten—McCareins 49-yd pass from McNair (Anderson PAT), Ten—FG Anderson 45 yds, Bal—Heap 35-yd pass from Wright (Stover PAT), Ten—FG Anderson 46 yds

TEAM	FD	YDS	RUSH	PASS	RTN	A-C-I	SACKED	PUNT	FUMB	PEN
Ten	16	324	40-165	159	71	23-14-3	0-0	6-45	0-0	6-55
Bal	12	255	16-54	201	81	37-20-2	2-13	8-49	1-0	8-70

Someone had to win. Titans quarterback Steve McNair's 3 interceptions short-circuited the offense and helped keep the Ravens in the game, thanks to a Will Demps 56-yard runback for a score. An unnecessary roughness penalty on the Ravens forced them to punt and Tennessee got great field position to set up Gary Anderson's winning field-goal drive.

2003 NFC WILD CARD GAME

Saturday, January 3, 2004 at Charlotte, NC, Ericsson Stadium, attendance 73,014

DALLAS COWBOYS	0	3	0	7	—	10
CAROLINA PANTHERS	6	10	7	6	—	29

SCORING Car—FG Kasey 18 yds, Car—FG Kasey 38 yds, Car—Davis 23-yd run (Kasey PAT), Dal—FG Cundiff 37 yds, Car—FG Kasey 19 yds, Car—Smith 32-yd pass from Delhomme (Kasey PAT), Car—FG Kasey 32 yds, Dal—Carter 9-yd run (Cundiff PAT), Car—FG Kasey 34 yds

TEAM	FD	YDS	RUSH	PASS	RTN	A-C-I	SACKED	PUNT	FUMB	PEN
Dal	10	204	18-72	132	22	36-21-1	3-22	6-42	1-1	2-11
Car	16	380	34-107	273	47	29-18-0	1-5	5-48	1-0	0-0

Car-Stephen Davis 104R, Steve Smith 135C, Muhsin Muhammad 103C

A resurrected Cowboys team couldn't win with the virtues of its faults. While the defense was able to force the Panthers to settle

for field goal after field goal, outscoring Carolina's mistake-free offense—fueled by Stephen Davis's 104 rushing yards—was more than Dallas could get from quarterback Quincy Carter. Kicker John Kasey's 5 field goals were more than enough against the Cowboys.

2003 NFC WILD CARD GAME

Sunday, January 4, 2004 at Green Bay (OT), Lambeau Field, attendance 71,457

SEATTLE SEAHAWKS	3	3	14	7	0	— 27
GREEN BAY PACKERS	0	13	0	14	6	— 33

SCORING Sea—FG Brown 30 yds, GB—FG Longwell 31 yds, Sea—FG Brown 35 yds, GB—Franks 23-yd pass from Favre (Longwell PAT), GB—FG Longwell 27 yds, Sea—Alexander 1-yd run (Brown PAT), Sea—Alexander 1-yd run (Brown PAT), GB—Green 1-yd run (Longwell PAT), GB—Green 1-yd run (Longwell PAT), Sea—Alexander 1-yd run (Brown PAT), GB—Harris 52-yd interception return (no PAT)

TEAM	FD	YDS	RUSH	PASS	RTN	A-C-I	SACKED	PUNT	FUMB	PEN
Sea	22	340	21-49	291	16	45-25-1	2-14	6-38	1-0	2-15
GB	22	397	32-78	319	91	38-26-0	0-0	5-38	0-0	5-30

Sea-Matt Hasselbeck 305P; GB-Javon Walker 111C, Brett Favre 319P

There were a lot of firsts: the first NFC playoff appearance for Seattle, the first time coach Mike Holmgren faced his former team in the playoffs, and the first known recorded trash-talking coin flip. Shaun Alexander scored 3 touchdown for Seattle and Ahman Green 2 for the Packers, but it was the matchup between Brett Favre and his former backup, Matt Hasselbeck, that kept the ball moving. After winning the coin toss in overtime, Hasselbeck confidently said, "We'll take the ball and we're going to score." He threw an interception that Al Harris returned for the winning touchdown.

2003 AFC WILD CARD GAME

Sunday, January 4, 2004 at Indianapolis, RCA Dome, attendance 56,586

DENVER BRONCOS	3	0	0	7	— 10
INDIANAPOLIS COLTS	14	17	10	0	— 41

SCORING Ind—Stokley 31-yd pass from Manning (Vanderjagt PAT), Den—FG Elam 49 yds, Ind—Harrison 46-yd pass from Manning (Vanderjagt PAT), Ind—Harrison 23-yd pass from Manning (Vanderjagt PAT), Ind—Stokley 87-yd pass from Manning (Vanderjagt PAT), Ind—FG Vanderjagt 27 yds, Ind—Wayne 7-yd pass from Manning (Vanderjagt PAT), Ind—FG Vanderjagt 20 yds, Den—Smith 7-yd pass from Plummer (Elam PAT)

TEAM	FD	YDS	RUSH	PASS	RTN	A-C-I	SACKED	PUNT	FUMB	PEN
Den	20	322	26-146	176	0	30-23-2	2-5	2-42	2-1	5-55
Ind	23	479	23-85	394	52	31-26-0	0-0	0-0	3-1	5-40

Ind-Marvin Harrison 133C, Brandon Stokley 144C, Peyton Manning 377P

The Colts, Tony Dungy, and Peyton Manning all shed their reputations as playoff losers with a blowout win over Denver. Manning lit up the Broncos by throwing 5 touchdowns on 22-for-26 passing for 377 yards and achieving an almost unattainable 158.3 quarterback rating, before taking most of the second half off.

2003 NFC DIVISIONAL PLAYOFF

Saturday, January 10, 2004 at St. Louis, Edwards Jones Dome, attendance 66,165

CAROLINA PANTHERS	0	10	6	7	0	6	— 29
ST. LOUIS RAMS	3	6	3	11	0	0	— 23

SCORING StL—FG Wilkins 20 yds, StL—FG Wilkins 26 yds, Car—Muhammad fumble recovery in end zone (Kasey PAT), StL—FG Wilkins 24 yds, Car—FG Kasey 45 yds, StL—FG Wilkins 51 yds, Car—FG Kasey 52 yds, Car—FG Kasey 34 yds, Car—Hoover 7-yd run (Kasey PAT), StL—Faulk 1-yd run (Looker pass from Bulger), StL—FG Wilkins 33 yds, Car—Smith 69-yd pass from Delhomme (no PAT)

TEAM	FD	YDS	RUSH	PASS	RTN	A-C-I	SACKED	PUNT	FUMB	PEN
Car	24	485	41-216	269	15	27-16-1	3-21	2-37	1-0	13-92
SL	23	380	23-64	316	37	46-27-3	2-16	1-46	0-0	5-33

Car-Steve Smith 163C; SL-Isaac Bruce 116C, Marc Bulger 332P

Despite losing Stephen Davis early on, the Panthers won a stunning victory in the second overtime when Jake Delhomme hit Steve Smith for a 69-yard score on the first play of the sixth quarter, this after both team missed potential game-winning field goals in the first overtime. Although he threw a trio of interceptions on the day, Marc Bulger helped rally the Rams for 11 fourth-quarter points. Coach Mike Martz was criticized for settling for the tie at the end of regulation instead of trying for the win.

2003 AFC DIVISIONAL PLAYOFF

Saturday, January 10, 2004 at Foxboro, MA, Gillette Stadium, attendance 68,436

TENNESSEE TITANS	7	0	7	0	— 14
NEW ENGLAND PATRIOTS	7	7	0	3	— 17

SCORING NE—Be. Johnson 41-yd pass from Brady (Vinatieri PAT), Ten—Brown 5-yd run (Anderson PAT), NE—Smith 1-yd run (Vinatieri PAT), Ten—Mason 11-yd pass from McNair (Anderson PAT), NE—FG Vinatieri 46 yds

TEAM	FD	YDS	RUSH	PASS	RTN	A-C-I	SACKED	PUNT	FUMB	PEN
Ten	16	284	26-84	200	0	26-18-1	3-10	4-34	0-0	9-55
NE	18	297	27-96	201	16	41-21-0	0-0	4-27	1-1	2-14

Winter cold was a major factor, as the teams endured a night game played at 4 degrees. After exchanging a pair of touchdowns in the second half, Adam Vinatieri's field goal with 4:06 remaining broke the tie. It held up when the Titans lost the ball on downs trying to reach field goal range.

2003 AFC DIVISIONAL PLAYOFF

Sunday, January 11, 2004 at Kansas City, Arrowhead Stadium, attendance 79,159

INDIANAPOLIS COLTS	14	7	10	7	— 38
KANSAS CITY CHIEFS	3	7	14	7	— 31

SCORING Ind—Stokley 29-yd pass from Manning (Vanderjagt PAT), KC—FG Andersen 22 yds, Ind—James 11-yd run (Vanderjagt PAT), KC—Hall 9-yd pass from Green (Andersen PAT), Ind—Lopienski 2-yd pass from Manning (Vanderjagt PAT), Ind—FG Vanderjagt 45 yds, KC—Holmes 1-yd run (Andersen PAT), Ind—Wayne 19-yd pass from Manning (Vanderjagt PAT), KC—Hall 92-yd kickoff return (Andersen PAT), Ind—James 1-yd run (Vanderjagt PAT), KC—Holmes 1-yd run (Andersen PAT)

TEAM	FD	YDS	RUSH	PASS	RTN	A-C-I	SACKED	PUNT	FUMB	PEN
Ind	27	434	32-142	292	0	30-22-0	1-12	0-0	0-0	1-5
KC	24	408	30-196	212	0	30-18-0	0-0	0-0	1-1	4-30

Ind-Edgerrin James 125R, Peyton Manning 304P; KC-Priest Holmes 176R

The first punt-free playoff game in NFL history featured 2 scores and 176 yards for Priest Holmes of the Chiefs, 125 yards and 2 scores by Edgerrin James of the Colts, and Dante Hall's reaching the end zone both as a receiver and a return man for Kansas City. Despite all that scoring, the key moments were Holmes's third-quarter fumble, the game's only turnover, and coach Dick Vermeil's decision not to try an onside kick with four minutes left after closing to within a touchdown. The Chiefs never saw the ball again.

2003 NFC DIVISIONAL PLAYOFF

Sunday, January 11, 2004 at Philadelphia (OT), Lincoln Financial Field, attendance 67,707

GREEN BAY PACKERS	14	0	0	3	0	— 17
PHILADELPHIA EAGLES	0	7	0	10	3	— 20

SCORING GB—Ferguson 40-yd pass from Favre (Longwell PAT), GB—Ferguson 17-yd pass from Favre (Longwell PAT), Phi—Staley 7-yd pass from McNabb (Akers PAT), Phi—Pinkston 12-yd pass from McNabb (Akers PAT), GB—FG Longwell 21 yds, Phi—FG Akers 37 yds, Phi—FG Akers 31 yds

TEAM	FD	YDS	RUSH	PASS	RTN	A-C-I	SACKED	PUNT	FUMB	PEN
GB	16	381	37-210	171	27	28-15-1	1-9	7-42	0-0	6-45
Phi	19	363	25-164	199	69	39-21-0	8-49	7-43	3-1	3-25

GB-Ahman Green 156R; Phi-Donovan McNabb 107R

A pair of first-quarter touchdown passes from Bret Favre might have augured a big day for the Packers, but such was not the case. With their running game absent, the Eagles put it all on Donovan McNabb. The quarterback took 8 sacks yet scrambled for 107 yards. Facing fourth-and-26 late in the fourth quarter and trailing by a field goal, McNabb kept the tying drive alive by hitting Freddie Mitchell for a 28-yard completion. David Akers tied the game and then booted the game-winner in overtime.

2003 AFC CHAMPIONSHIP

Sunday, January 18, 2004 at Foxboro, MA, Gillette Stadium, attendance 68,436

INDIANAPOLIS COLTS	0	0	7	7	— 14
NEW ENGLAND PATRIOTS	7	8	6	3	— 24

SCORING NE—Givens 7-yd pass from Brady (Vinatieri PAT), NE—FG Vinatieri 31 yds, NE—FG Vinatieri 25 yds, NE—Safety, Snow's snap sailed over punter's head and was kicked through end zone, Ind—James 2-yd run (Vanderjagt PAT), NE—FG Vinatieri 27 yds, NE—FG Vinatieri 21 yds, Ind—Pollard 7-yd pass from Manning (Vanderjagt PAT), NE—FG Vinatieri 34 yds

TEAM	FD	YDS	RUSH	PASS	RTN	A-C-I	SACKED	PUNT	FUMB	PEN
Ind	21	306	25-98	208	0	47-23-4	4-29	1-55	2-1	4-20
NE	20	349	32-112	237	42	37-22-1	0-0	2-37	1-1	3-15

INDIANAPOLIS COLTS

RUSHING	ATT	YDS	LNG	TD
Edgerrin James	19	78	12	1
Dominic Rhodes	3	16	11	0

RECEIVING	NO	YDS	LNG	TD
Marcus Pollard	6	90	32	1
Reggie Wayne	4	46	20	0

PASSING	PA	PC	YDS	TD	IN
Peyton Manning	47	23	237	1	4

NEW ENGLAND PATRIOTS

RUSHING	ATT	YDS	LNG	TD
Antowain Smith	22	100	35	0
Kevin Faulk	3	8	6	0

RECEIVING	NO	YDS	LNG	TD
David Givens	8	68	18	1
Troy Brown	7	88	18	0

PASSING	PA	PC	YDS	TD	IN
Tom Brady	37	22	237	1	1

After the previous week's bitter cold in New England, this game featured snow. The weather—and the relentless New England coverage—hampered the high-flying Colts air attack. Cornerback Ty Law had Peyton Manning's number, grabbing 3 interceptions, while the Patriots defense outscored Indianapolis in the first half, 2–0. New England's offense moved the ball enough to make it a 15–0 advantage over all. After a first-quarter touchdown, though, the Colts prevented the Patriots from finding the end zone again. Adam Vinatieri continued to be easy money in the playoffs, hitting 5 field goals, and Antowain Smith ran for 100 yards to put the Pats in the Super Bowl for the fourth time.

2003 NFC CHAMPIONSHIP

Sunday, January 18, 2004 at Philadelphia, Lincoln Financial Field, attendance 67,862

CAROLINA PANTHERS	0	7	7	0	— **14**
PHILADELPHIA EAGLES	0	3	0	0	— 3

SCORING Car—Muhammad 24-yd pass from Delhomme (Kasey PAT), Phi—FG Akers 41 yds, Car—Foster 1-yd run (Kasey PAT)

TEAM	FD	YDS	RUSH	PASS	RTN	A-C-I	SACKED	PUNT	FUMB	PEN
Car	14	256	40-155	101	13	14-9-0	0-0	8-38	1-0	5-35
Phi	18	289	26-137	152	14	36-17-4	5-36	4-37	1-0	4-34

CAROLINA PANTHERS

RUSHING	ATT	YDS	LNG	TD
Stephen Davis	19	76	15	0
DeShaun Foster	14	60	13	1

RECEIVING	NO	YDS	LNG	TD
Steve Smith	3	26	15	0
Muhsin Muhammad	2	39	24	1

PASSING	PA	PC	YDS	TD	IN
Jake Delhomme	14	9	101	1	0

PHILADELPHIA EAGLES

RUSHING	ATT	YDS	LNG	TD
Duce Staley	13	79	18	0
Correll Buckhalter	11	48	9	0

RECEIVING	NO	YDS	LNG	TD
Chad Lewis	4	69	27	0
Freddie Mitchell	4	38	12	0
Duce Staley	4	33	19	0

PASSING	PA	PC	YDS	TD	IN
Donovan McNabb	22	10	100	0	3
Koy Detmer	14	7	88	0	1

The Panthers throttled the Eagles with much the same game plan they'd used to beat Dallas two weeks earlier. The difference was that this time Carolina did it against Donovan McNabb, forcing him into a trio of picks before forcing him from the game with an injured ribcage. Rookie cornerback Ricky Manning had 3 of Carolina's 4 interceptions on the day, while the offense ground down the clock with conservative play-calling. Jake Delhomme threw just 14 times, notching 101 yards, while the Panthers ran the ball 40 times for 155 yards to reach the franchise's first Super Bowl. The Eagles, meanwhile, lost in the championship game for the third straight year.

2004 NFC WILD CARD GAME

Saturday, January 8, 2005 at Seattle, Qwest Field, attendance 65,397

ST. LOUIS RAMS	7	7	3	10	— **27**
SEATTLE SEAHAWKS	3	7	3	7	— 20

SCORING StL—Holt 15-yd pass from Bulger (Wilkins PAT), Sea—FG Brown 47 yds, StL—Faulk 1-yd run (Wilkins PAT), Sea—Engram 19-yd pass from Hasselbeck (Brown PAT), Sea—FG Brown 30 yds, StL—FG Wilkins 38 yds, Sea—Jackson 23-yd pass from Hasselbeck (Brown PAT), StL—FG Wilkins 27 yds, StL—Cleeland 17-yd pass from Bulger (Wilkins PAT)

TEAM	FD	YDS	RUSH	PASS	RTN	A-C-I	SACKED	PUNT	FUMB	PEN
SL	22	396	27-102	294	14	32-18-1	5-19	3-29	0-0	4-30
Sea	24	413	20-81	332	9	43-27-1	3-9	3-44	2-0	9-61

SL-Torry Holt 108C, Kevin Curtis 107C, Marc Bulger 313P; Sea-Darrell Jackson 128C, Matt Hasselbeck 341P

After losing both regular-season games against the Rams, the Seahawks had another shot in the playoffs, only to suffer the same result. Both teams made inspired rallies, the Rams to better effect when Marc Bulger passed for a touchdown with 2:11 left. Seattle

answered with a drive to the St. Louis 5, but Bobby Engram's dropped a fourth-down pass. St. Louis became the first .500 team to win a playoff game; Minnesota would make it two the next day.

2004 AFC WILD CARD GAME

Saturday, January 8, 2005 at San Diego (OT), Qualcomm Stadium, attendance 67,536

NEW YORK JETS	0	7	10	0	3	— **20**
SAN DIEGO CHARGERS	0	7	0	10	0	— 17

SCORING SD—McCardell 26-yd pass from Brees (Kaeding PAT), NYJ—Becht 13-yd pass from Pennington (Brien PAT), NYJ—Moss 47-yd pass from Pennington (Brien PAT), NYJ—FG Brien 42 yds, SD—FG Kaeding 35 yds, SD—Gates 1-yd pass from Brees (Kaeding PAT), NYJ—FG Brien 28 yds

TEAM	FD	YDS	RUSH	PASS	RTN	A-C-I	SACKED	PUNT	FUMB	PEN
NYJ	20	396	28-126	270	22	33-23-0	2-9	5-40	0-0	8-49
SD	24	408	33-100	308	11	42-31-1	2-11	5-36	1-0	9-75

NYJ-Santana Moss 100C; SD-Drew Brees 319P

The heavily-favored Chargers came up just short, but not before a late rally. A roughing the passer call negated Drew Brees's fourth-down incompletion with 20 seconds left. Given another chance, Brees hit Antonio Gates for the tie. The Jets caught a break when the Chargers missed a field goal, and Doug Brien made the winning field goal for the Jets.

2004 AFC WILD CARD GAME

Sunday, January 9, 2005 at Indianapolis, RCA Dome, attendance 56,609

DENVER BRONCOS	0	3	14	7	— 24
INDIANAPOLIS COLTS	14	21	0	14	— **49**

SCORING Ind—Mungro 2-yd run from Manning (Vanderjagt PAT), Ind—James 1-yd run (Vanderjagt PAT), Ind—Clark 19-yd pass from Manning (Vanderjagt PAT), Den—FG Elam 33 yds, Ind—Wayne 35-yd pass from Manning (Vanderjagt PAT), Ind—Manning 1-yd run (Vanderjagt PAT), Den—Smith 9-yd pass from Plummer (Elam PAT), Den—Putzier 35-yd pass from Plummer (Elam PAT), Ind—Wayne 43-yd pass from Manning (Vanderjagt PAT), Den—Bell 1-yd run (Elam PAT), Ind—Rhodes 2-yd run (Vanderjagt PAT)

TEAM	FD	YDS	RUSH	PASS	RTN	A-C-I	SACKED	PUNT	FUMB	PEN
Den	18	338	21-78	260	-1	34-24-1	3-24	4-38	1-0	5-24
Ind	27	529	24-76	453	9	33-27-1	1-4	2-38	0-0	4-25

Ind-Reggie Wayne 221C, Dallas Clark 112C, Peyton Manning 457P

The Colts rolled with their second postseason blowout victory over the Broncos in as many years. Peyton Manning was peerless on 27-for-33 passing for 457 yards and 4 touchdown passes, while rushing for a fifth. Reggie Wayne was Manning's weapon of choice, logging 221 yards and a pair of scores.

2004 NFC WILD CARD GAME

Sunday, January 9, 2005 at Green Bay, Lambeau Field, attendance 71,075

MINNESOTA VIKINGS	17	7	0	7	— **31**
GREEN BAY PACKERS	3	7	0	7	— 17

SCORING Min—Williams 68-yd pass from Culpepper (Andersen PAT), Min—Moss 20-yd pass from Culpepper (Andersen PAT), Min—FG Andersen 35 yds, GB—FG Longwell 43 yds, GB—Franks 4-yd pass from Favre (Longwell PAT), Min—Burleson 19-yd pass from Culpepper (Andersen PAT), GB—Davenport 1-yd run (Longwell PAT), Min—Moss 34-yd pass from Culpepper (Andersen PAT)

TEAM	FD	YDS	RUSH	PASS	RTN	A-C-I	SACKED	PUNT	FUMB	PEN
Min	18	384	26-123	261	51	29-19-0	4-23	4-32	2-0	7-56
GB	24	306	29-105	201	-4	33-22-4	2-15	3-41	3-0	8-55

Daunte Culpepper led the Vikings to an early lead with a pair of first-quarter touchdown strikes. Brett Favre struggled, throwing 4 interceptions. On his second score, wideout Randy Moss let Packers fans know how he felt, pantomiming a mooning of the crowd—something Green Bay fans did to defeated teams on the bus out of town. The league felt a professional should know better, fining Moss ,000.

2004 AFC DIVISIONAL PLAYOFF

Saturday, January 15, 2005 at Pittsburgh (OT), Heinz Field, attendance 64,915

NEW YORK JETS	0	10	7	0	0	— 17
PITTSBURGH STEELERS	10	0	0	7	3	— **20**

SCORING Pit—FG Reed 45 yds, Pit—Bettis 3-yd run (Reed PAT), NYJ—FG Brien 42 yds, NYJ—Moss 75-yd punt return (Brien PAT), NYJ—Tongue 86-yd interception return (Brien PAT), Pit—Ward 4-yd pass from Roethlisberger (Reed PAT), Pit—FG Reed 33 yds

TEAM	FD	YDS	RUSH	PASS	RTN	A-C-I	SACKED	PUNT	FUMB	PEN
NYJ	17	275	27-110	165	193	33-21-1	3-17	6-39	0-0	4-35
Pit	23	364	43-193	171	39	30-17-2	1-10	5-40	1-1	6-45

Pit-Jerome Bettis 101R, Hines Ward 105C

New York's first touchdown came on an interception returned for touchdowns, but the same crew blew a fourth-quarter lead for the second time in two weeks when Steelers rookie Ben Roethlisberger hit Hines Ward for a tying score. Last week's hero was this week's goat. Jets kicker Doug Brien twice missed potential game-winning kicks; something Jeff Reed didn't do when the opportunity came his way in overtime.

2004 NFC DIVISIONAL PLAYOFF

Saturday, January 15, 2005 at Atlanta, Georgia Dome, attendance 70,709

ST. LOUIS RAMS	7	10	0	0	— 17
ATLANTA FALCONS	14	14	10	9	— 47

SCORING Atl—Crumpler 18-yd pass from Vick (Feely PAT), StL—Curtis 57-yd pass from Bulger (Wilkins PAT), Atl—Dunn 62-yd run (Feely PAT), StL—Holt 28-yd pass from Bulger (Wilkins PAT), Atl—Dunn 19-yd run (Feely PAT), StL—FG Wilkins 55 yds, Atl—Price 6-yd pass from Vick (Feely PAT), Atl—Rossum 68-yd punt return (Feely PAT), StL—FG Wilkins 55 yds, Atl—Price 6-yd pass from Vick (Feely PAT), Atl—FG Feely 38 yds, Atl—Safety, Smith sacked Bulger in end zone, Atl—Duckett 4-yd run (Feely PAT)

TEAM	FD	YDS	RUSH	PASS	RTN	A-C-I	SACKED	PUNT	FUMB	PEN
SL	19	339	18-77	262	0	35-23-1	4-37	4-46	1-1	4-26
Atl	18	397	40-327	70	152	17-13-0	1-14	2-42	1-1	4-32

SL-Kevin Curtis 128C; Atl-Warrick Dunn 142R, Michael Vick 119R

The Falcons dominated from the start. Warrick Dunn rushed for 142 yards and a pair of scores, and Michael Vick added 119 yards more on 8 attempts. Return man Allen Rossum returned punts for a record 152 yards, including his 68-yard touchdown in the second quarter. The passing game took the night off, with just 90 yards in the 30-point win.

2004 NFC DIVISIONAL PLAYOFF

Sunday, January 16, 2005 at Philadelphia, Lincoln Financial Field, attendance 67,722

MINNESOTA VIKINGS	0	7	0	7	— 14
PHILADELPHIA EAGLES	7	14	0	6	— 27

SCORING Phi—Mitchell 2-yd pass from McNabb (Akers PAT), Phi—Westbrook 7-yd pass from McNabb (Akers PAT), Min—Culpepper 7-yd run (Andersen PAT), Phi—Mitchell fumble recovery in end zone (Akers PAT), Phi—FG Akers 21 yds, Phi—FG Akers 23 yds, Min—Robinson 32-yd pass from Culpepper (Andersen PAT)

TEAM	FD	YDS	RUSH	PASS	RTN	A-C-I	SACKED	PUNT	FUMB	PEN
Min	21	385	21-97	288	7	47-24-2	3-28	4-35	1-0	
7-108										
Phi	23	395	25-109	286	45	33-21-0	1-0	3-37	3-1	4-20

Min-Marcus Robinson 119C, Daunte Culpepper 316P

The Eagles caught a break when L.J. Smith's fumble into the end zone was recovered by teammate Freddie Mitchell. Mitchell also scored on a more convention play when quarterback Donovan McNabb hit him from 2 yards out. The Vikings may have lost momentum when a field-goal attempt was botched into an unsuccessful fake through a miscommunication. Seven penalties for 108 yards didn't help Minnesota, either.

2004 AFC DIVISIONAL PLAYOFF

Sunday, January 16, 2005 at Foxboro, MA, Gillette Stadium, attendance 68,756

INDIANAPOLIS COLTS	0	3	0	0	— 3
NEW ENGLAND PATRIOTS	0	6	7	7	— 20

SCORING NE—FG Vinatieri 24 yds, NE—FG Vinatieri 31 yds, Ind—FG Vanderjagt 23 yds, NE—Givens 5-yd pass from Brady (Vinatieri PAT), NE—Brady 1-yd run (Vinatieri PAT)

TEAM	FD	YDS	RUSH	PASS	RTN	A-C-I	SACKED	PUNT	FUMB	PEN
Ind	18	276	15-46	230	0	42-27-1	1-8	6-41	3-2	4-44
NE	21	325	39-210	115	37	27-18-0	3-29	5-39	0-0	5-35

NE-Corey Dillon 144R

The Patriots once again took advantage of foul weather at home to help Bill Belichick's always-intricate defense shut down a great offense. The Colts running attack disappeared while Corey Dillon rambled for 144 yards and the Patriots amassed 210 yards on the ground. Indy couldn't even play catch-up, not while the Patriots held onto the ball for 21:26 in the second half.

2004 NFC CHAMPIONSHIP

Sunday, January 23, 2005 at Philadelphia, Lincoln Financial Field, attendance 67,717

ATLANTA FALCONS	0	10	0	0	— 10
PHILADELPHIA EAGLES	7	7	6	7	— 27

SCORING Phi—Levens 4-yd run (Akers PAT), Atl—FG Feely 23 yds, Phi—C. Lewis 3-yd pass from McNabb (Akers PAT), Atl—Dunn 10-yd run (Feely PAT), Phi—FG Akers 31 yds, Phi—C. Lewis 34-yd pass from McNabb (Akers PAT), Phi—C. Lewis 2-yd pass from McNabb (Akers PAT)

TEAM	FD	YDS	RUSH	PASS	RTN	A-C-I	SACKED	PUNT	FUMB	PEN
Atl	14	202	26-99	103	20	24-11-1	4-33	5-26	1-0	5-24
Phi	22	326	33-156	170	15	27-18-0	2-13	3-38	2-0	6-59

ATLANTA FALCONS				
RUSHING	ATT	YDS	LNG	TD
Warrick Dunn	15	59	10	1
Michael Vick	4	26	13	0
RECEIVING	NO	YDS	LNG	TD
Alge Crumpler	4	49	31	0
Peerless Price	2	37	23	0
PASSING	PA	PC	YDS	TD	IN
Michael Vick	24	11	136	0	1

PHILADELPHIA EAGLES				
RUSHING	ATT	YDS	LNG	TD
Brian Westbrook	16	96	36	0
Donovan McNabb	10	32	8	0
RECEIVING	NO	YDS	LNG	TD
Brian Westbrook	5	39	14	0
Chad Lewis	4	20	12	2
Greg Lewis	2	65	45	0
PASSING	PA	PC	YDS	TD	IN
Donovan McNabb	26	17	180	2	0

Philadelphia's defense stopped up Atlanta's running game on a bitterly cold day. That forcing the Falcons to try to win on Michael Vick's passing. The dangerous Vick was a non-factor, throwing for just 136 yards and being sacked 4 times. Atlanta couldn't stop Donovan McNabb and Brian Westbrook, who combined for 128 yards on the ground. McNabb also hit tight end Chad Lewis for 2 touchdowns. Lewis, however, sustained a foot injury and would miss the Super Bowl, so even with wide receiver Terrell Owens expected back, the Eagles wouldn't be at full strength in Jacksonville. But winning the NFC title after three straight losses in the championship game was enough for now.

2004 AFC CHAMPIONSHIP

Sunday, January 23, 2005 at Pittsburgh, Heinz Field, attendance 65,242

NEW ENGLAND PATRIOTS	10	14	7	10	— 41
PITTSBURGH STEELERS	3	0	14	10	— 27

SCORING NE—FG Vinatieri 48 yds, NE—Branch 60-yd pass from Brady (Vinatieri PAT), Pit—FG Reed 43 yds, NE—Givens 9-yd pass from Brady (Vinatieri PAT), NE—Harrison 87-yd interception return (Vinatieri PAT), Pit—Bettis 5-yd run (Reed PAT), NE—Dillon 25-yd run (Vinatieri PAT), Pit—Ward 30-yd pass from Roethlisberger (Reed PAT), Pit—FG Reed 20 yds, NE—FG Vinatieri 31 yds, NE—Branch 23-yd run (Vinatieri PAT), Pit—Burress 7-yd pass from Roethlisberger (Reed PAT)

TEAM	FD	YDS	RUSH	PASS	RTN	A-C-I	SACKED	PUNT	FUMB	PEN
NE	18	322	32-126	196	93	21-14-0	2-11	4-40	1-0	1-5
Pit	19	388	37-163	225	40	24-14-3	1-1	3-43	2-1	2-20

NEW ENGLAND PATRIOTS				
RUSHING	ATT	YDS	LNG	TD
Corey Dillon	24	73	25	1
Deion Branch	2	37	23	1
RECEIVING	NO	YDS	LNG	TD
David Givens	5	59	18	1
Deion Branch	4	116	60	1
PASSING	PA	PC	YDS	TD	IN
Tom Brady	21	14	207	2	0

PITTSBURGH STEELERS				
RUSHING	ATT	YDS	LNG	TD
Jerome Bettis	17	64	25	1
Ben Roethlisberger	5	45	13	0
RECEIVING	NO	YDS	LNG	TD
Hines Ward	5	109	30	1
Antwaan Randle El	3	52	34	0
PASSING	PA	PC	YDS	TD	IN
Ben Roethlisberger	24	14	226	2	3

A bitterly cold day on the East Coast didn't seem to promise the fireworks that followed, although the final score sounds closer than it was. The Pats got out to an early lead with Tom Brady's efficient passing, notably his long strike to Deion Branch to burn both the Steelers and critics who felt the New England quarterback couldn't hit deep routes. New England's defense stuffed Pittsburgh's feature backs, and intercepted Ben Roethlisberger 3 times, including a return of 87 yards for a touchdown by Rodney Harrison to open up a 24–3 lead. Roethlisberger's record 14-game win streak as a rookie came to an end and the Patriots claimed their third conference title in four years.

2005 NFC WILD CARD GAME

Saturday, January 7, 2006 at Tampa, Raymond James Stadium, attendance 65,514

WASHINGTON REDSKINS	14	3	0	0	— 17
TAMPA BAY BUCCANEERS	0	3	7	0	— 10

SCORING Was—Portis 6-yd run (Hall PAT), Was—Taylor 51-yd fumble recovery (Hall PAT), TB—FG Bryant 43 yds, Was—FG Hall 47 yds, TB—Simms 2-yd run (Bryant PAT)

TEAM	FD	YDS	RUSH	PASS	RTN	A-C-I	SACKED	PUNT	FUMB	PEN
Was	9	120	31-95	25	53	16-7-1	2-16	7-38	3-0	4-30
TB	17	243	25-75	168	40	38-25-2	3-30	5-39	3-1	3-30

Washington's 120 total offensive yards was half that of Tampa Bay's and it was the fewest in playoff history for a winning playoff team, but the defense made sure points got on the board. The Redskins' first touchdown was set up by an interception, and the second came on a twice-fumbled fumble return. A game-tying touchdown pass by Chris Simms was nullified when receiver Edell Shepherd was ruled not in control of the ball.

2005 AFC WILD CARD GAME

Saturday, January 7, 2006 at Foxboro, MA, Gillette Stadium, attendance 68,756

JACKSONVILLE JAGUARS	0	3	0	0	— 3
NEW ENGLAND PATRIOTS	0	7	14	7	— 28

SCORING NE—Brown 11-yd pass from Brady (Vinatieri PAT), Jax—FG Scobee 36 yds, NE—Givens 3-yd pass from Brady (Vinatieri PAT), NE—Watson 63-yd pass from Brady (Vinatieri PAT), NE—Samuel 73-yd interception return (Vinatieri PAT)

TEAM	FD	YDS	RUSH	PASS	RTN	A-C-I	SACKED	PUNT	FUMB	PEN
Jax	15	292	17-87	205	12	39-21-1	6-42	5-42	2-1	8-40
NE	17	307	28-118	189	104	27-15-0	4-12	5-39	4-0	4-32

Bill Belichick's Patriots won their 10th straight playoff game, eclipsing Vince Lombardi's record. The defense was in especially fine form, scoring the final touchdown on cornerback Asante Samuel's 73-yard interception return, and recording 6 sacks—including a playoff-record 4 ½ by linebacker Willie McGinest—and holding the Jaguars to a field goal. Tom Brady's tossed 3 touchdowns for the Pats.

2005 NFC WILD CARD GAME

Sunday, January 8, 2006 at East Rutherford, NJ, Giants Stadium, attendance 79,378

CAROLINA PANTHERS	0	10	7	6	— 23
NEW YORK GIANTS	0	0	0	0	— 0

SCORING Car—Smith 22-yd pass from Delhomme (Kasay PAT), Car—FG Kasay 31 yds, Car—Smith 12-yd run (Kasay PAT), Car—FG Kasay 45 yds, Car—FG Kasay 18 yds

TEAM	FD	YDS	RUSH	PASS	RTN	A-C-I	SACKED	PUNT	FUMB	PEN
Car	23	335	45-223	112	5	22-15-0	4-28	4-38	1-0	7-52
NYG	9	132	13-41	91	5	18-10-3	4-22	4-39	2-2	2-15

Car-DeShaun Foster 151R

The Panthers' ball-control offense fulfilled its duties with DeShaun Foster's 151 yards and 64 by Nick Goings, but the defense made sure that Eli Manning's first playoff appearance was one to forget. Carolina sacked him 4 times and had 3 interceptions among a total of 5 turnovers in the first road-team shutout in the playoffs since 1980.

2005 AFC WILD CARD GAME

Sunday, January 8, 2006 at Cincinnati, Paul Brown Stadium, attendance 65,870

PITTSBURGH STEELERS	0	14	14	3	— 31
CINCINNATI BENGALS	10	7	0	0	— 17

SCORING Cin—FG Graham 23 yds, Cin—Johnson 20-yd run (Graham PAT), Pit—Parker 19-yd pass from Roethlisberger (Reed PAT), Cin—Houshmandzadeh 7-yd pass from Kitna (Graham PAT), Pit—Ward 5-yd pass from Roethlisberger (Reed PAT), Pit—Bettis 5-yd run (Reed PAT), Pit—Wilson 43-yd pass from Roethlisberger (Reed PAT), Pit—FG Reed 21 yds

TEAM	FD	YDS	RUSH	PASS	RTN	A-C-I	SACKED	PUNT	FUMB	PEN
Pit	19	346	34-144	202	52	21-14-0	1-6	3-47	0-0	6-39
Cin	19	327	20-84	243	15	41-25-2	4-20	3-44	2-0	7-90

Pit-Cedrick Wilson 104C

Scripts went out the window when Bengals quarterback Carson Palmer suffered a season-ending knee injury on the second play from scrimmage. The play still went for 66 yards and Cincinnati—playing its first playoff game in 15 years—opened up a 10-point lead, but a botched field-goal attempt was Cincy's lone second-half scoring opportunity. Ben Roethlisberger rallied the Steelers with a trick play: Antwaan Randle El took a direct snap, lateraled to Roethlisberger, who then hit Cedrick Wilson for a touchdown and a decisive lead.

2005 NFC DIVISIONAL PLAYOFF

Saturday, January 14, 2006 at Seattle, Qwest Field, attendance 67,551

WASHINGTON REDSKINS	0	3	0	7	— 10
SEATTLE SEAHAWKS	0	7	7	6	— 20

SCORING Was—FG Hall 26 yds, Sea—Jackson 29-yd pass from Hasselbeck (Brown PAT), Sea—Hasselbeck 6-yd run (Brown PAT), Sea—FG Brown 33 yds, Was—Moss 20-yd pass from Brunell (Hall PAT), Sea—FG Brown 31 yds

TEAM	FD	YDS	RUSH	PASS	RTN	A-C-I	SACKED	PUNT	FUMB	PEN
Was	11	289	25-59	230	3	38-22-0	2-12	7-43	1-1	7-50
Sea	15	334	33-119	215	-1	26-16-0	0-0	5-42	5-3	2-10

Was-Santana Moss 103C; Sea-Darrell Jackson 143C

Shaun Alexander's concussion created early worry for the Seahawks, but the defense kept Washington in check all game—the Redskins lucked into a touchdown on Santana Moss's reception of a deflected pass. The Seahawks methodically put together 4 scoring drives in their star's absence to win the team's first playoff game since 1984.

2005 AFC DIVISIONAL PLAYOFF

Saturday, January 14, 2006 at Denver, Invesco Field at Mile High, attendance 76,238

NEW ENGLAND PATRIOTS	0	3	3	7	— 13
DENVER BRONCOS	0	10	7	10	— 27

SCORING NE—FG Vinatieri 40 yds, Den—Anderson 1-yd run (Elam PAT), Den—FG Elam 50 yds, NE—FG Vinatieri 32 yds, Den—Anderson 1-yd run (Elam PAT), Den—Smith 4-yd pass from Plummer (Elam PAT), NE—Givens 4-yd pass from Brady (Vinatieri PAT), Den—FG Elam 34 yds

TEAM	FD	YDS	RUSH	PASS	RTN	A-C-I	SACKED	PUNT	FUMB	PEN
NE	15	420	21-79	341	37	36-20-2	0-0	3-49	3-3	8-82
Den	16	286	32-96	190	115	26-15-1	2-7	6-46	1-0	4-24

NE-Deion Branch 153C, Tom Brady 341P

A tight defensive matchup degenerated into an upset as the Patriots committed 5 turnovers, which the Broncos opportunistically converted into 24 points. The turning point was Tom Brady's interception in the end zone; Champ Bailey returned it 100 yards to the New England 1-yard line. A chance for the lead quickly turned into a 17–6 hole. From there, the two-time champs muffed a punt and even a rare Adam Vinatieri miss, bringing their postseason streak to an end at 10.

2005 AFC DIVISIONAL PLAYOFF

Sunday, January 15, 2006 at Indianapolis, RCA Dome, attendance 57,449

PITTSBURGH STEELERS	14	0	7	0	— 21
INDIANAPOLIS COLTS	0	3	0	15	— 18

SCORING Pit—Randle El 6-yd pass from Roethlisberger (Reed PAT), Pit—Miller 7-yd pass from Roethlisberger (Reed PAT), Ind—FG Vanderjagt 20 yds, Pit—Bettis 1-yd run (Reed PAT), Ind—Clark 50-yd pass from Manning (Vanderjagt PAT), Ind—James 3-yd run (Wayne pass from Manning)

TEAM	FD	YDS	RUSH	PASS	RTN	A-C-I	SACKED	PUNT	FUMB	PEN
Pit	21	295	42-112	183	50	24-14-1	2-14	5-42	1-1	2-8
Ind	15	305	14-58	247	3	38-22-0	5-43	6-45	1-0	9-67

The Steelers managed the upset by rolling to an early lead, scoring 3 touchdowns on solid drives, and then fending off a furious late Colts rally. The second Indianapolis score shouldn't have happened, as a Peyton Manning interception was incorrectly ruled incomplete. Steelers quarterback Ben Roethlisberger made a game-saving tackle on Nick Harper after recovering a Jerome Bettis fumble. Colts kicker Mike Vanderjagt subsequently missed a tying field goal.

2005 NFC DIVISIONAL PLAYOFF

Sunday, January 15, 2006 at Chicago, Soldier Field, attendance 62,209

CAROLINA PANTHERS	7	9	7	6	— 29
CHICAGO BEARS	0	7	7	7	— 21

SCORING Car—Smith 58-yd pass from Delhomme (Kasay PAT), Car—FG Kasay 20 yds, Car—FG Kasay 38 yds, Chi—Peterson 1-yd run (Gould PAT), Car—FG Kasay 37 yds, Chi—Clark 1-yd pass from Grossman (Gould PAT), Car—Smith 39-yd pass from Delhomme (Kasay PAT), Chi—McKie 3-yd run (Gould PAT), Car—Mangum 1-yd pass from Delhomme (PAT failed)

TEAM	FD	YDS	RUSH	PASS	RTN	A-C-I	SACKED	PUNT	FUMB	PEN
Car	21	434	31-123	311	0	33-24-1	1-8	5-41	3-0	9-50
Chi	23	282	27-97	185	21	41-17-1	1-7	7-35	0-0	4-19

Car-Steve Smith 218C, Jake Delhomme 319P

Despite losing DeShaun Foster for the rest of the playoffs with a broken ankle, Carolina generated 434 total yards on offense. Jake Delhomme and Steve Smith opened things up, combining for 2 long scoring strikes, 12 receptions, and 218 yards. The Bears struggled back to within a field goal on their first possession in the third quarter, and made it 23–21 in the fourth quarter, but Carolina never lost the lead.

2005 AFC CHAMPIONSHIP

Sunday, January 22, 2006 at Denver, Invesco Field at Mile High, attendance 76,775

PITTSBURGH STEELERS	3	21	0	10	—	**34**
DENVER BRONCOS	0	3	7	7	—	17

SCORING Pit—FG Reed 47 yds, Pit—Wilson 12-yd pass from Roethlisberger (Reed PAT), Den—FG Elam 23 yds, Pit—Bettis 3-yd run (Reed PAT), Pit—Ward 17-yd pass from Roethlisberger (Reed PAT), Den—Lelie 30-yd pass from Plummer (Elam PAT), Pit—FG Reed 42 yds, Den—Anderson 3-yd run (Elam PAT), Pit—Roethlisberger 4-yd run (Reed PAT)

TEAM	FD	YDS	RUSH	PASS	RTN	A-C-I	SACKED	PUNT	FUMB	PEN
Pit	20	358	33-90	268	28	29-21-0	2-7	4-37	1-0	8-61
Den	16	308	21-97	211	0	30-18-2	3-12	2-44	2-2	4-20

PITTSBURGH STEELERS					DENVER BRONCOS				
RUSHING	ATT	YDS	LNG	TD	RUSHING	ATT	YDS	LNG	TD
Jerome Bettis	15	39	7	1	Mike Anderson	9	36	7	1
Willie Parker	14	35	14	0	Tatum Bell	5	31	11	0
RECEIVING	NO	YDS	LNG	TD	RECEIVING	NO	YDS	LNG	TD
Cedrick Wilson	5	92	30	1	Tatum Bell	5	28	9	0
Hines Ward	5	59	21	1	Rod Smith	4	61	32	0
Antwaan Randle El	4	52	20	0	Jeb Putzier	4	55	19	0
					Ashley Lelie	2	68	38	1
PASSING	PA	PC	YDS	TD	IN	PASSING	PA	PC	YDS	TD	IN
Ben Roethlisberger	29	21	275	2	0	Jake Plummer	30	18	223	1	2

The Steelers managed to jump out to an early 24–3 lead despite having their running game clogged up by Denver's defense, but Ben Roethlisberger was exceptionally accurate. The Broncos rallied to score on a couple of long second-half scoring drives, but in a game in which Pittsburgh's defense grabbed 4 turnovers, the last—a fumble by Jake Plummer—clinched matters. The Steelers converted the miscue into Roethlisberger's late touchdown run. Pittsburgh had been 1–4 in AFC Championship Games since 1994, all at home. The Steelers looked great on the road for the third straight Sunday, qualifying for their sixth Super Bowl, the same number Denver reached seven years earlier.

2005 NFC CHAMPIONSHIP

Sunday, January 22, 2006 at Seattle, Qwest Field, attendance 67,837

CAROLINA PANTHERS	0	7	0	7	—	14
SEATTLE SEAHAWKS	10	10	7	7	—	**34**

SCORING Sea—Stevens 17-yd pass from Hasselbeck (Brown PAT), Sea—FG Brown 24 yds, Sea—Alexander 1-yd run (Brown PAT), Car—Smith 59-yd punt return (Kasay PAT), Sea—FG Brown 39 yds, Sea—Jackson 20-yd pass from Hasselbeck (Brown PAT), Sea—Alexander 1-yd run (Brown PAT), Car—Carter 47-yd pass from Delhomme (Kasay PAT)

TEAM	FD	YDS	RUSH	PASS	RTN	A-C-I	SACKED	PUNT	FUMB	PEN
Car	11	212	12-36	176	59	35-15-3	2-20	7-35	1-1	5-57
Sea	27	393	51-190	203	74	28-20-0	2-16	5-39	0-0	7-63

CAROLINA PANTHERS					SEATTLE SEAHAWKS				
RUSHING	ATT	YDS	LNG	TD	RUSHING	ATT	YDS	LNG	TD
Jamal Robertson	4	19	15	0	Shaun Alexander	34	132	18	2
Jake Delhomme	3	15	6	0	Matt Hasselbeck	6	27	15	0
RECEIVING	NO	YDS	LNG	TD	RECEIVING	NO	YDS	LNG	TD
Jamal Robertson	5	37	18	0	Darrell Jackson	6	75	20	1
Steve Smith	5	33	12	0	Jeremy Stevens	6	66	17	1
Drew Carter	2	88	47	1					
PASSING	PA	PC	YDS	TD	IN	PASSING	PA	PC	YDS	TD	IN
Jake Delhomme	35	15	196	1	3	Matt Hasselbeck	28	20	219	2	0

Without DeShaun Foster, the Panthers would have to put on another air show, but the Seahawks weren't in the mood, squelching Jake Delhomme with 3 interceptions and a pair of sacks. Seattle also kept Steve Smith from getting out from underneath coverage to do any serious damage, save on his 59-yard punt return for a score. Seahawks quarterback Matt Hasselback threw for 219 yards and 2 touchdowns. Shaun Alexander seemed none the worse for the previous week's concussion, running 34 times for 132 yards and 2 scores as Seattle pounded its way to its first Super Bowl appearance.

THE SUPER BOWL

Today's NFL moves so effortlessly from week to week and is so clearly a successful money-making entity, it is hard to imagine a time in the last half century when there might have been any question about its prolonged health. Given the way the NFL has shrugged off every recent football competitor with the ease of Walter Payton shedding a tackler, it's hard to imagine any league that could threaten the NFL's stability. Yet the threat from the American Football League was very real. As much as commissioner Pete Rozelle and the other owners resisted, merger was a choice they had to make.

Every January—make that February, now—comes the lasting legacy of that peace between leagues. An event so big that it swallows the media for several days and takes over cities for two weeks at a time. An event that affects company budgets in dozens of different fields, is a major coup for one TV network, is broadcast to 234 countries (most recent figure), and is the most important day on the advertising calendar. Is that enough hype yet? Well, it is also a day of such special significance to pro football, that old rock superstars are dusted off and put on the field moments after players have rushed off it for halftime, that wardrobe malfunctions cause national outrage, and that, lost amid the countless pieces of choreographed confetti falling from above onto the field, there is a winner and a loser. And then there is a postgame show presented by yet another sponsor. And finally, this day of sports excess rivaled nowhere else in the world, is over. Super Bowl Sunday has come and gone.

It was not always this way. Before 1933 the NFL did not even have a championship game on the schedule. One was needed to decide a clear NFL champion in the cluttered 1932 standings between the Portsmouth Spartans, now the Detroit Lions, and the Chicago Bears. Even though a blizzard forced it to be played indoors on a jury-rigged field, and the game's lone touchdown was a controversial play, the NFL founding fathers found it appealing enough to actually schedule a championship. The first 25 scheduled championship produced some great moments—the Sneakers Game, the Bears' record 73–0 rout of the Redskins, and Sammy Baugh's pass hitting the crossbar to cause a safety that was the difference in the 1945 game—but the country mostly yawned. The NFL Championship Game was chump change compared to the World Series and it paled by comparison to college football's annual spectacles like the Rose Bowl or the Cotton Bowl. That changed when the New York Giants played the Baltimore Colts for the 1958 title.

A tight game turned epic when Johnny Unitas moved the Colts down the field to tie the game with a last-second field goal. His hand guided Baltimore to its first title in the first sudden death game ever played. Television glued fans to the game the Sunday after Christmas. Football was never viewed the same again. The NFL, in its fourth decade, had reached the big leagues.

The National Football League tried to push off the American Football League as an inferior circuit right from the start. The truth was, there were plenty of geographical areas ignored or underserved by the NFL—as there had been when the All-America Football Conference was founded after World War II—and the AFL was a high-flying league that drew a lot of interest. The longer it stayed around, the more trouble it made for the NFL. When the league got a large television contract and then threw the money from it at some of the game's biggest stars, most notably Joe Namath, the NFL realized that, like National League baseball came to understand six-plus decades earlier, that it was time to change the model. Either take the competition in as a partner or watch both leagues slowly strangle each other. A merger was first discussed in a parking lot in Dallas and by June 8, 1966, it was announced.

The "new NFL" would have 26 teams in 25 cities—New York was the only city with two clubs—with Pete Rozelle at its head. The merged league would feature expansion, a common draft, interleague games starting in 1970, and, starting after the 1966 season, an AFL–NFL Championship Game, the ultimate sign that the two leagues were equal. Only when it came game time they weren't considered equal at all.

Kansas City Chiefs owner Lamar Hunt came up with the term Super Bowl, basing it on the popular children's toy of the time his daughter enjoyed that bounced very high when thrown against something. The other owners thought it funny when he brought it up at a meeting. Many others tried to come up with a better name, but none did. And Super Bowl sure sounded better than AFL–NFL Championship Game. Like a super ball, the name kept bouncing and bouncing until it finally stuck.

The first game was shown on both CBS and NBC. Half a minute of commercial time went for $85,000 on CBS; about $75,000 on NBC. The cost for the same spot on Super Bowl XL—on just one network, ABC—was $2.5 million. The team's did use separate balls for that first game. Green Bay used the NFL ball when it was on offense and Kansas City used the AFL ball when it called the signals. The site of the first game was cavernous Memorial Coliseum in Los Angeles, a favorite site for the NFL's Pro Bowl, but a place almost impossible to fill. The first game was 32,000 short of a sellout, but the 65 million people watching at home created the largest crowd in the NFL's 46-year history. Six years later Rozelle, a Los Angeles native who came to the commissioner's office from the Rams and had a soft spot for the old building, let the Coliseum host another Super Bowl; it had 90,182—the largest crowd for any of the first 10 Super Bowls—although it was still blacked out in the Los Angeles area because tickets hadn't been purchased within the 72-hour window. There were no more Super Bowl blackouts … and no more Super Bowls at the Coliseum.

Finding hosts for the Super Bowl haven't been hard since then. Warm weather cities have spent hundreds of millions on new stadiums, or renovations to existing facilities, with the promise of a Super Bowl. Some cold weather cities have spent lavishly on domes that have limited use after the football season ends with the promise that the Super Bowl will come to their town. Municipalities that figured they could never afford—or be awarded—an Olympics bid, could manage to host a Super Bowl and bring an estimated $300 million into the host city, the NFL estimates. What is does do is make a city—maybe one that is rarely talked about, like Jacksonville, or receives mostly negative press, like Detroit—get two weeks of publicity that the municipality could never otherwise buy and it might put their venue in line for other big-time events like a Republican or Democratic national convention, an NCAA Final Four, or the next YourProductHere.com Bowl. Whether it's perception or reality, the Super Bowl is about going for the brass ring, even for people who've never played football—or in the case of the Super Bowl, never watched football—in their lives.

The Super Bowl is also about the pre-game hype, the players, some laboring in obscurity for most of their careers, only to be placed under the media microscope that can only happen when media outlets demand countless stories in exchange for putting up reporters in environments far removed from the strained light of the sports desk. One thing the week before the Super Bowl has taught people is that it doesn't matter what the story is, just keep hitting on it and the game will get here soon enough. Many times, especially in the first 24 affairs, the game didn't come close to living up to the hype. For whatever reason, the games have generally gotten better, but fans know—and even those who simply watch this one game of the year—that the game can turn into a stinker at any time. That's just the way the Super Bowl is; but the world certainly seems to like it just the way it is.

SUPER BOWLS PAST

This section is designed to provide details and statistics of every game, but a list of vital information for every game is provided below for easy reference. the list below includes game, city, stadium, score, and Most Valuable Player. (See Player Register for a list of position abbreviations.) In 39 of 40 instances, counting the year the award was shared as one, the MVP has been awarded to a player from the winning team. In Super Bowl V, however, the MVP came from the losing side. That winner, Chuck Howley, has his team (Cowboys) listed in parentheses.

GAME	CITY	STADIUM	DATE	SCORE	MVP
Super Bowl I	Los Angeles	LA Coliseum	January 15, 1967	Packers 35, Chiefs 10	Bart Starr, QB
Super Bowl II	Miami	Orange Bowl	January 14, 1968	Packers 33, Raiders 14	Bart Starr, QB
Super Bowl III	Miami	Orange Bowl	January 12, 1969	Jets 16, Colts 7	Joe Namath, QB
Super Bowl IV	New Orleans	Tulane Stadium	January 11, 1970	Chiefs 23, Vikings 7	Len Dawson, QB
Super Bowl V	Miami	Orange Bowl	January 17, 1971	Colts 16, Cowboys 13	Chuck Howley, LB (Cowboys)
Super Bowl VI	New Orleans	Tulane Stadium	January 16, 1972	Cowboys 24, Dolphins 3	Roger Staubach, QB
Super Bowl VII	Los Angeles	LA Coliseum	January 14, 1973	Dolphins 14, Redskins 7	Jake Scott, S
Super Bowl VIII	Houston	Rice Stadium	January 13, 1974	Dolphins 24, Vikings 7	Larry Csonka, RB
Super Bowl IX	New Orleans	Tulane Stadium	January 12, 1975	Steelers 16, Vikings 6	Franco Harris, RB
Super Bowl X	Miami	Orange Bowl	January 18, 1976	Steelers 21, Cowboys 17	Lynn Swann, WR
Super Bowl XI	Pasadena, CA	Rose Bowl	January 9, 1977	Raiders 32, Vikings 14	Fred Biletnikoff, WR
Super Bowl XII	New Orleans	Superdome	January 15, 1978	Cowboys 27, Broncos 10	Harvey Martin, DE; Randy White, DT
Super Bowl XIII	Miami	Orange Bowl	January 21, 1979	Steelers 35, Cowboys 31	Terry Bradshaw, QB
Super Bowl XIV	Pasadena, CA	Rose Bowl	January 20, 1980	Steelers 31, Rams 19	Terry Bradshaw, QB
Super Bowl XV	New Orleans	Superdome	January 25, 1981	Raiders 27, Eagles 10	Jim Plunkett, QB
Super Bowl XVI	Pontiac, MI	Silverdome	January 24, 1982	49ers 26, Bengals 21	Joe Montana, QB
Super Bowl XVII	Pasadena, CA	Rose Bowl	January 30, 1983	Redskins 27, Dolphins 17	John Riggins, RB
Super Bowl XVIII	Tampa	Tampa Stadium	January 22, 1984	Raiders 38, Redskins 9	Marcus Allen, RB
Super Bowl XIX	Stanford, CA	Stanford Stadium	January 20, 1985	49ers 38, Dolphins 16	Joe Montana, QB
Super Bowl XX	New Orleans	Superdome	January 26, 1986	Bears 46, Patriots 10	Richard Dent, DE
Super Bowl XXI	Pasadena, CA	Rose Bowl	January 25, 1987	Giants 39, Broncos 20	Phil Simms, QB
Super Bowl XXII	San Diego	Jack Murphy Stadium	January 31, 1988	Redskins 42, Broncos 10	Doug Williams, QB
Super Bowl XXIII	Miami	Joe Robbie Stadium	January 22, 1989	49ers 20, Bengals 16	Jerry Rice, WR
Super Bowl XXIV	New Orleans	Superdome	January 28, 1990	49ers 55, Broncos 10	Joe Montana, QB
Super Bowl XXV	Tampa	Tampa Stadium	January 27, 1991	Giants 20, Bills 19	Ottis Anderson, MVP
Super Bowl XXVI	Minneapolis	Metrodome	January 26, 1992	Redskins 37, Bills 24	Mark Rypien, QB
Super Bowl XXVII	Pasadena, CA	Rose Bowl	January 31, 1993	Cowboys 52, Bills 17	Troy Aikman, QB
Super Bowl XXVIII	Atlanta	Georgia Dome	January 30, 1994	Cowboys 30, Bills 13	Emmitt Smith, RB
Super Bowl XXIX	Miami	Joe Robbie Stadium	January 29, 1995	49ers 49, Chargers 26	Steve Young, QB
Super Bowl XXX	Tempe, AZ	Sun Devil Stadium	January 28, 1996	Cowboys 27, Steelers 17	Larry Brown, CB
Super Bowl XXXI	New Orleans	Superdome	January 26, 1997	Packers 35, Patriots 21	Desmond Howard, KR
Super Bowl XXXII	San Diego	Qualcomm Stadium	January 25, 1998	Broncos 34, Falcons 19	John Elway, QB
Super Bowl XXXIII	Miami	Pro Player Stadium	January 31, 1999	Broncos 34, Falcons 19	John Elway, QB
Super Bowl XXXIV	Atlanta	Georgia Dome	January 30, 2000	Rams 23, Titans 16	Kurt Warner, QB
Super Bowl XXXV	Tampa	Raymond James Stadium	January 28, 2001	Ravens 34, Giants 7	Ray Lewis, LB
Super Bowl XXXVI	New Orleans	Superdome	February 3, 2002	Patriots 20, Rams 17	Tom Brady, QB
Super Bowl XXXVII	San Diego	Qualcomm Stadium	January 26, 2003	Buccaneers 48, Raiders 21	Dexter Jackson, FS
Super Bowl XXXVIII	Houston	Reliant Stadium	February 1, 2004	Patriots 32, Panthers 29	Tom Brady, QB
Super Bowl XXXIX	Jacksonville	Alltell Stadium	February 6, 2005	Patriots 24, Eagles 21	Deion Branch, WR
Super Bowl XL	Detroit	Ford Field	February 5, 2006	Steelers 21, Seahawks 10	Hines Ward, WR

SUPER BOWLS FUTURE

Although the Super Bowl has probably single-handedly taught two generations of people how to count by Roman numerals, the information below goes beyond the dead language numbers. The chart includes Super Bowl, host city, stadium, date, the network broadcasting the game, and how many times the game has been played in that city or region. Some locales, just like some teams, see a lot more Super Bowls than others.

GAME	CITY	STADIUM	DATE	NETWORK	PREV.
Super Bowl XLI	Miami	Dolphin Stadium	February 4, 2007	CBS	9
Super Bowl XLII	Glendale, AZ	Cardinals Stadium	February 3, 2008	Fox	2
Super Bowl XLIII	Tampa	Raymond James Stadium	February 1, 2009	NBC	4
Super Bowl XLIV	Miami	Dolphin Stadium	TBA	CBS	10

KEY TO THE SUPER BOWL SECTION

This chapter includes a writeup of every Super Bowl, plus all the vital statistics about the most-anticipated and most-watched sporting event each year. It includes the date, location, attendance, and the scoring of the game by quarter. Common abbreviation to keep in mind in the statistical section are **Att-Comp-Int**, referring to Attempts-Completions-Interceptions by all the players throwing passes for that team in that game, and **PAT** meaning point after touchdown (two-point conversions are described as passes or runs and if they failed or succeeded). In the sacks section, **NO** stands for the number of quarterback sacks by a defensive player. Other abbreviations are listed below.

Rushing

ATT Rushing Attempts
YDS Yards Gained
LNG Longest Run
TD Rushing Touchdowns

Receiving and Returns

NO Number of Catches
YDS Yards Gained
LNG Longest Play
TD Touchdowns

Passing

PA Pass Attempts
PC Pass Completions
YDS Yards Passing
TD Touchdowns
IN Interceptions

Punting

NO Number of Punts
YDS Yards Per Punt
LNG Longest Punt
BLK Blocked Punts

As for the stadiums, keep in mind that a few of the names have changed over the years, but the sites are still the same. Miami's Joe Robbie Stadium became Pro Player Stadium and has seen been renamed Dolphin Stadium, amid other things. Likewise, Jack Murphy Stadium was later dubbed mellifluous Qualcomm Stadium.

SUPER BOWL I

Sunday, January 15, 1967 at Los Angeles, Memorial Coliseum, attendance 61,946   MVP: Bart Starr

KANSAS CITY CHIEFS (AFL)	0	10	0	0	—	10
GREEN BAY PACKERS (NFL)	7	7	14	7	—	35

SCORING GB—McGee 37-yd pass from Starr (Chandler PAT), KC—McClinton 7-yd pass from Dawson (Mercer PAT), GB—Taylor 14-yd run (Chandler PAT), KC—FG Mercer 31 yds, GB—Pitts 5-yd run (Chandler PAT), GB—McGee 13-yd pass from Starr (Chandler PAT), GB—Pitts 1-yd run (Chandler PAT)

TEAM	FIRST DOWNS	TOTAL YARDAGE	RUSHING	PASSING	RETURNS	ATT-COMP-INT	SACKED	PUNTING	FUMBLES	PENALTIES
KC	17	239	19-72	167	19	32-17-1	6-61	7-45	1-0	4-26
GB	21	358	33-130	228	73	24-16-1	3-22	4-43	1-0	4-40

KANSAS CITY CHIEFS (AFL)

RUSHING	ATT	YDS	LNG	TD
Len Dawson	3	24	15	0
Mike Garrett	6	17	9	0
Curtis McClinton	6	16	6	0
Pete Beathard	1	14	14	0
Bert Coan	3	1	3	0

RECEIVING	NO	YDS	LNG	TD
Chris Burford	4	67	27	0
Otis Taylor	4	57	31	0
Mike Garrett	3	28	17	0
Curtis McClinton	2	34	27	1
Fred Arbanas	2	30	18	0
Reggie Carolan	1	7	7	0
Bert Coan	1	5	5	0

PASSING	PA	PC	YDS	TD	IN
Len Dawson	27	16	211	1	1
Pete Beathard	5	1	17	0	0

GREEN BAY PACKERS (NFL)

RUSHING	ATT	YDS	LNG	TD
Jim Taylor	16	53	14	1
Elijah Pitts	11	45	12	2
Donny Anderson	4	30	13	0
Jim Grabowski	2	2	2	0

RECEIVING	NO	YDS	LNG	TD
Max McGee	7	138	37	2
Carroll Dale	4	59	25	0
Elijah Pitts	2	32	22	0
Marv Fleming	2	22	11	0
Jim Taylor	1	-1	-1	0

PASSING	PA	PC	YDS	TD	IN
Bart Starr	23	16	250	2	1
Zeke Bratkowski	1	0	0	0	0

KANSAS CITY CHIEFS (AFL)

KICKOFF RETURNS	NO	YDS	LNG	TD
Bert Coan	4	87	31	0
Mike Garrett	2	43	23	0

PUNT RETURNS	NO	YDS	LNG	TD
Mike Garrett	2	17	9	0
Emmitt Thomas	1	2	2	0

INTERCEPTION RETURNS	NO	YDS	LNG	TD
Willie Mitchell	1	0	0	0

PUNTING	NO	YDS	LNG	BLK
Jerrel Wilson	7	45	61	0

GREEN BAY PACKERS (NFL)

KICKOFF RETURNS	NO	YDS	LNG	TD
Herb Adderley	2	40	20	0
Donny Anderson	1	25	25	0

PUNT RETURNS	NO	YDS	LNG	TD
Donny Anderson	3	25	15	0
Willie Wood	1	-2	-2	0

INTERCEPTION RETURNS	NO	YDS	LNG	TD
Willie Wood	1	50	50	0

PUNTING	NO	YDS	LNG	BLK
Don Chandler	3	43	50	0
Donny Anderson	1	43	43	0

FOR STARTERS, IT'S GREEN BAY

The Kansas City Chiefs were the best team in the AFL. They probably could have beaten any number of NFL teams—contrary to Vince Lombardi's postgame comments—but they could only stay with the Green Bay Packers for a half.

Little-used veteran Max McGee, who'd stayed out all night, was the surprise star of the game. Pressed into duty when Boyd Dowler was injured in the first quarter, McGee caught 7 passes for 138 and 2 touchdowns from MVP Bart Starr. The biggest play, though, came in the third quarter with the Packers clinging to a 13–10 lead. Lombardi reluctantly blitzed on third down and Chiefs quarterback Len Dawson was intercepted by Willie Wood, who took the ball to the Kansas City 5. Elijah Pitts scored on the next play and the Packers breathed much easier.

Amid the array of firsts for the Super Bowl, Fred "The Hammer" Williamson was the first player to shoot off his mouth for the amassed press. By the fourth quarter the Hammer was carried off the field and the Packers carried the day.

SUPER BOWL II

Sunday, January 14, 1968 at Miami, Orange Bowl, attendance 75,546   MVP: Bart Starr

GREEN BAY PACKERS (NFL)	3	13	10	7	—	33
OAKLAND RAIDERS (AFL)	0	7	0	7	—	14

SCORING GB —FG Chandler 39 yds, GB —FG Chandler 20 yds, GB —Dowler 62-yd pass from Starr (Chandler PAT), Oak—Miller 23-yd pass from Lamonica (Blanda PAT), GB —FG Chandler 43 yds, GB —Anderson 2-yd run (Chandler PAT), GB —FG Chandler 31 yds, GB —Adderley 60-yd interception return (Chandler PAT), Oak—Miller 23-yd pass from Lamonica (Blanda PAT)

TEAM	FIRST DOWNS	TOTAL YARDAGE	RUSHING	PASSING	RETURNS	ATT-COMP-INT	SACKED	PUNTING	FUMBLES	PENALTIES
GB	19	322	41-160	162	95	24-13-0	4-40	6-39	0-0	1-12
Oak	16	293	20-107	186	12	34-15-1	3-22	6-44	3-2	4-31

GREEN BAY PACKERS (NFL)

RUSHING	ATT	YDS	LNG	TD
Ben Wilson	17	62	13	0
Donny Anderson	14	48	8	1
Travis Williams	8	36	18	0
Bart Starr	1	14	14	0
Chuck Mercein	1	0	0	0

RECEIVING	NO	YDS	LNG	TD
Carroll Dale	4	43	17	0
Marv Fleming	4	35	11	0
Boyd Dowler	2	71	62	1
Donny Anderson	2	18	12	0
Max McGee	1	35	35	0

PASSING	PA	PC	YDS	TD	IN
Bart Starr	24	13	202	1	0

OAKLAND RAIDERS (AFL)

RUSHING	ATT	YDS	LNG	TD
Hewritt Dixon	12	54	14	0
Larry Todd	2	37	32	0
Pete Banaszak	6	16	5	0

RECEIVING	NO	YDS	LNG	TD
Bill Miller	5	84	23	2
Pete Banaszak	4	69	41	0
Billy Cannon	2	25	15	0
Fred Biletnikoff	2	10	6	0
Warren Wells	1	17	17	0
Hewritt Dixon	1	3	3	0

PASSING	PA	PC	YDS	TD	IN
Daryle Lamonica	34	15	208	2	1

GREEN BAY PACKERS (NFL)

KICKOFF RETURNS	NO	YDS	LNG	TD
Herb Adderley	1	24	24	0
Travis Williams	1	18	18	0
Tommy Crutcher	1	7	7	0

PUNT RETURNS	NO	YDS	LNG	TD
Willie Wood	5	35	31	0

INTERCEPTION RETURNS	NO	YDS	LNG	TD
Herb Adderley	1	60	60	1

PUNTING	NO	YDS	LNG	BLK
Donny Anderson	6	39	48	0

OAKLAND RAIDERS (AFL)

KICKOFF RETURNS	NO	YDS	LNG	TD
Larry Todd	3	63	23	0
Dave Grayson	2	61	25	0
Wayne Hawkins	1	3	3	0
Dave Kocourek	1	0	0	0

PUNT RETURNS	NO	YDS	LNG	TD
Rodger Bird	2	12	12	0
Warren Wells	1	0	0	0

INTERCEPTION RETURNS	NO	YDS	LNG	TD

PUNTING	NO	YDS	LNG	BLK
Mike Eischeid	6	44	55	0

LOMBARDI PACKS IT IN

The last thing the AFL wanted was a repeat of the previous year's game. Vince Lombardi's blunt assessment of the league's caliber of play had hurt. The Oakland Raiders hoped to provide the proper response, but this time it was never close.

The Packers went up 13–0 in the second quarter when MVP Bart Starr hit Boyd Dowler for a 62-yard touchdown. An 8-play, 78-yard drive put Oakland on the scoreboard, but a fumble on a fair catch gave the Packers another chance. Don Chandler kicked his third field goal just before the half. Amid speculation that Lombardi would quit (something that proved true), veteran Jerry Kramer told the Packers at halftime to "win one for the old man." Green Bay thoroughly dominated the second half. Herb Adderley returned a Daryle Lamonica pass 60 yards for a score.

After the game, Lombardi let slip that Green Bay's effort "wasn't our best." The Raiders had gone 13–1 and won the AFL Championship Game by 33 points. Now an NFL team not even playing at top form had whipped them.

SUPER BOWL III

Sunday, January 12, 1969 at Miami, Orange Bowl, attendance 75,377   MVP: Joe Namath

NEW YORK JETS (AFL)	0	7	6	3	—	16
BALTIMORE COLTS (NFL)	0	0	0	7	—	7

SCORING NYJ—Snell 4-yd run (Turner PAT), NYJ—FG Turner 32 yds, NYJ—FG Turner 30 yds, NYJ—FG Turner 9 yds, Bal—Hill 1-yd run (Michaels PAT)

TEAM	FIRST DOWNS	TOTAL YARDAGE	RUSHING	PASSING	RETURNS	ATT-COMP-INT	SACKED	PUNTING	FUMBLES	PENALTIES
NYJ	21	337	43-142	195	9	29-17-0	2-11	4-39	1-1	5-28
Bal	18	324	23-143	181	34	41-17-4	0-0	3-44	1-1	3-23

NEW YORK JETS (AFL)

RUSHING	ATT	YDS	LNG	TD
Matt Snell	30	121	12	1
Emerson Boozer	10	19	8	0
Bill Mathis	3	2	1	0

RECEIVING	NO	YDS	LNG	TD
George Sauer	8	133	39	0
Matt Snell	4	40	14	0
Bill Mathis	3	20	13	0
Pete Lammons	2	13	11	0

PASSING	PA	PC	YDS	TD	IN
Joe Namath	28	17	206	0	0
Babe Parilli	1	0	0	0	0

BALTIMORE COLTS (NFL)

RUSHING	ATT	YDS	LNG	TD
Tom Matte	11	116	58	0
Jerry Hill	9	29	12	1
John Unitas	1	0	0	0
Earl Morrall	2	-2		0

RECEIVING	NO	YDS	LNG	TD
Willie Richardson	6	58	21	0
Jimmy Orr	3	42	17	0
John Mackey	3	35	19	0
Tom Matte	2	30	30	0
Jerry Hill	2	1	1	0
Tom Mitchell	1	15	15	0

PASSING	PA	PC	YDS	TD	IN
John Unitas	24	11	110	0	1
Earl Morrall	17	6	71	0	3

NEW YORK JETS (AFL)

KICKOFF RETURNS	NO	YDS	LNG	TD
Earl Christy	1	25	25	0

PUNT RETURNS	NO	YDS	LNG	TD
Bill Baird	1	0	0	0

INTERCEPTION RETURNS	NO	YDS	LNG	TD
Randy Beverly	2	0	0	0
Jim Hudson	1	9	9	0
Johnny Sample	1	0	0	0

PUNTING	NO	YDS	LNG	BLK
Curley Johnson	4	38	39	0

BALTIMORE COLTS (NFL)

KICKOFF RETURNS	NO	YDS	LNG	TD
Preston Pearson	2	59	33	0
Timmy Brown	2	46	25	0

PUNT RETURNS	NO	YDS	LNG	TD
Timmy Brown	4	34	21	0

INTERCEPTION RETURNS	NO	YDS	LNG	TD

PUNTING	NO	YDS	LNG	BLK
David Lee	3	44	51	0

GUARANTEED PANDEMONIUM

The first two games of this interleague championship, now officially called the Super Bowl, seemed decidedly one-sided. The Baltimore Colts were without doubt the best team in pro football, evidenced by the 19-point spread. Joe Namath thought otherwise, and said so. He even guaranteed it.

The Jets quarterback was loose yet sharp, audibling repeatedly and leading New York to a 7–0 halftime lead. When the lead grew to 13–0, NFL MVP Earl Morrall was removed for Johnny Unitas, who threw just 32 passes all year because of an elbow injury. The Jets defense wasn't any kinder to him, stopping his first drive and picking him off in the end zone on his second. Unitas finally led Baltimore to a touchdown with 3:19 left, but the onside kick—like Baltimore's 5 turnovers—bounced New York's way.

On the same field a year before, it seemed like the AFL–NFL championship was doomed. Commissioner Pete Rozelle even mentioned he was considering changing the format to allow NFL teams to play each other. That wouldn't be necessary now.

SUPER BOWL IV

Sunday, January 11, 1970 at New Orleans, Tulane Stadium, attendance 80,562   MVP: Len Dawson

MINNESOTA VIKINGS (NFL)	0	0	7	0	—	7
KANSAS CITY CHIEFS (AFL)	3	13	7	0	—	23

SCORING KC —FG Stenerud 48 yds, KC —FG Stenerud 32 yds, KC —FG Stenerud 25 yds, KC —Garrett 5-yd run (Stenerud PAT), Min—Osborn 4-yd run (Cox PAT), KC —Taylor 46-yd pass from Dawson (Stenerud PAT)

TEAM	FIRST DOWNS	TOTAL YARDAGE	RUSHING	PASSING	RETURNS	ATT-COMP-INT	SACKED	PUNTING	FUMBLES	PENALTIES
Min	13	239	19-67	172	18	28-17-3	3-27	3-37	3-2	6-67
KC	18	273	42-151	122	24	17-12-1	3-20	4-49	0-0	4-47

MINNESOTA VIKINGS (NFL)

RUSHING	ATT	YDS	LNG	TD
Bill Brown	6	26	10	0
Oscar Reed	4	17	15	0
Dave Osborn	7	15	4	1
Joe Kapp	2	9	7	0

RECEIVING	NO	YDS	LNG	TD
John Henderson	7	111	28	0
Bill Brown	3	11	11	0
John Beasley	2	41	26	0
Oscar Reed	2	16	12	0
Dave Osborn	2	11	10	0
Gene Washington	1	9	9	0

PASSING	PA	PC	YDS	TD	IN
Joe Kapp	25	16	183	0	2
Gary Cuozzo	3	1	16	0	1

KANSAS CITY CHIEFS (AFL)

RUSHING	ATT	YDS	LNG	TD
Mike Garrett	11	39	6	1
Frank Pitts	3	37	19	0
Wendell Hayes	8	31	13	0
Warren McVea	12	26	9	0
Len Dawson	3	11	11	0
Robert Holmes	5	7	7	0

RECEIVING	NO	YDS	LNG	TD
Otis Taylor	6	81	46	1
Frank Pitts	3	33	20	0
Mike Garrett	2	25	17	0
Wendell Hayes	1	3	3	0

PASSING	PA	PC	YDS	TD	IN
Len Dawson	17	12	142	1	1

MINNESOTA VIKINGS (NFL)

KICKOFF RETURNS	NO	YDS	LNG	TD
Charlie West	3	46	27	0
Clint Jones	1	33	33	0

PUNT RETURNS	NO	YDS	LNG	TD
Charlie West	2	18	11	0

INTERCEPTION RETURNS	NO	YDS	LNG	TD
Paul Krause	1	0	0	0

PUNTING	NO	YDS	LNG	BLK
Bob Lee	3	37	50	0

KANSAS CITY CHIEFS (AFL)

KICKOFF RETURNS	NO	YDS	LNG	TD
Mike Garrett	1	18	18	0
Wendell Hayes	1	18	18	0

PUNT RETURNS	NO	YDS	LNG	TD
Mike Garrett	1	0	0	0

INTERCEPTION RETURNS	NO	YDS	LNG	TD
Willie Lanier	1	9	9	0
Johnny Robinson	1	9	9	0
Emmitt Thomas	1	6	6	0

PUNTING	NO	YDS	LNG	BLK
Jerrel Wilson	4	48	59	0

CHIEFS AND AFL HAVE ONE FOR THE ROAD

A few days before what would be the last game ever played by an AFL team, Kansas City coach Hank Stram was asked by NFL Films to wear a microphone. The dapper, ebullient football strategist reluctantly agreed. His entertaining sideline chatter outlived the AFL, spreading the word of a league that stuck around longer than anyone ever thought. And won in the end.

Super Bowl IV wasn't a drama, though. Stram's club thoroughly dominated Minnesota, a 14-point favorite going in. When the Vikings defense stiffened, Jan Stenerud came out and kicked field goals. It was 9–0 in the second quarter when the Vikings fumbled a kickoff and the Chiefs recovered. Mike Garrett ran it in for a touchdown.

Len Dawson completed just 12 passes for 142 yards, but he had survived the test. A federal gambling probe had brought up his name and the assembled media in New Orleans descended upon him. He was exhausted, stressed, and completely innocent. His 46-yard touchdown pass to Lionel Taylor assured him of MVP.

SUPER BOWL V

Sunday, January 17, 1971 at Miami, Orange Bowl, attendance 79,204   MVP: Chuck Howley

BALTIMORE COLTS	0	6	0	10	—	**16**
DALLAS COWBOYS	3	10	0	0	—	13

SCORING Dal—FG Clark 14 yds, Dal—FG Clark 30 yds, Bal—Mackey 75-yd pass from Unitas (O'Brien kick blocked), Dal—Thomas 7-yd pass from Morton (Clark PAT), Bal—Nowatzke 2-yd run (O'Brien PAT), Bal—FG O'Brien 32 yds

TEAM	FIRST DOWNS	TOTAL YARDAGE	RUSHING	PASSING	RETURNS	ATT-COMP-INT	SACKED	PUNTING	FUMBLES	PENALTIES
Bal	14	329	31-69	260	69	25-11-3	0-0	4-42	5-4	4-31
Dal	9	215	31-102	113	31	26-12-3	2-14	9-42	1-1	10-133

BALTIMORE COLTS					DALLAS COWBOYS				
RUSHING	ATT	YDS	LNG	TD	RUSHING	ATT	YDS	LNG	TD
Tom Nowatzke	10	33	9	1	Walt Garrison	12	65	19	0
Norm Bulaich	18	28	8	0	Duane Thomas	18	35	7	0
John Unitas	1	4	4	0	Craig Morton	1	2	2	0
Sam Havrilak	1	3	3	0					
Earl Morrall	1	1	1	0					
RECEIVING	NO	YDS	LNG	TD	RECEIVING	NO	YDS	LNG	TD
Roy Jefferson	3	52	23	0	Dan Reeves	5	46	17	0
John Mackey	2	80	75	1	Duane Thomas	4	21	7	1
Eddie Hinton	2	51	26	0	Walt Garrison	2	19	14	0
Sam Havrilak	2	27	25	0	Bob Hayes	1	41	41	0
Tom Nowatzke	1	45	45	0					
Norm Bulaich	1	5	5	0					
PASSING	PA	PC	YDS	TD	IN	PASSING	PA	PC	YDS	TD	IN
Earl Morrall	15	7	147	0	1	Craig Morton	26	12	127	1	3
John Unitas	9	3	88	1	2						
Sam Havrilak	1	1	25	0	0						

BALTIMORE COLTS					DALLAS COWBOYS				
KICKOFF RETURNS	NO	YDS	LNG	TD	KICKOFF RETURNS	NO	YDS	LNG	TD
Jim Duncan	4	90	30	0	Cliff Harris	1	18	18	0
					Calvin Hill	1	14	14	0
					D.D. Lewis	1	2	2	0
PUNT RETURNS	NO	YDS	LNG	TD	PUNT RETURNS	NO	YDS	LNG	TD
Ron Gardin	4	4	2	0	Bob Hayes	3	9	7	0
Jerry Logan	1	8	8	0					
INTERCEPTION RETURNS	NO	YDS	LNG	TD	INTERCEPTION RETURNS	NO	YDS	LNG	TD
Rick Volk	1	30	30	0	Chuck Howley	2	22	22	0
Jerry Logan	1	14	14	0	Mel Renfro	1	0	0	0
Mike Curtis	1	13	13	0					
PUNTING	NO	YDS	LNG	BLK	PUNTING	NO	YDS	LNG	BLK
David Lee	4	41	56	0	Ron Widby	9	41	49	0

COLTS TRY FROM THE OTHER SIDE

The Baltimore Colts returned to the scene of the greatest disaster in franchise history. Two years earlier they had lost here to the New York Jets in Super Bowl III, an unthinkable feat. Now the teams were in the same division as part of the AFC. The Colts didn't care how it looked; they just wanted to win.

It was good that style points weren't given. The Colts had 7 turnovers, the Cowboys 4, and even balls that weren't turned over turned a few stomachs. A second-quarter Johnny Unitas pass intended for Eddie Hinton bounced off the receiver's hands, then out of Cowboy Mel Renfro's clutches, and finally to Baltimore's John Mackey, who ran 75 yards for a touchdown. The extra point was blocked.

The game was tied in the final minute when Colt Mike Curtis intercepted Craig Morton in Dallas territory. First-year coach Don McCafferty sent in his rookie kicker to win it. Jim O'Brien's kick sailed through with five seconds left, giving Baltimore a dramatic victory in what was by all accounts the sloppiest Super Bowl on record.

SUPER BOWL VI

Sunday, January 16, 1972 at New Orleans, Tulane Stadium, attendance 81,023   MVP: Roger Staubach

DALLAS COWBOYS	3	7	7	7	—	**24**
MIAMI DOLPHINS	0	3	0	0	—	3

SCORING Dal—FG Clark 9 yds, Dal—Alworth 7-yd pass from Staubach (Clark PAT), Mia—FG Yepremian 31 yds, Dal—D. Thomas 3-yd run (Clark PAT), Dal—Ditka 7-yd pass from Staubach (Clark PAT)

TEAM	FIRST DOWNS	TOTAL YARDAGE	RUSHING	PASSING	RETURNS	ATT-COMP-INT	SACKED	PUNTING	FUMBLES	PENALTIES
Dal	23	352	48-252	100	40	19-12-0	2-19	5-37	1-1	3-15
Mia	10	185	20-80	105	21	23-12-1	1-29	5-40	2-2	0-0

DALLAS COWBOYS					MIAMI DOLPHINS				
RUSHING	ATT	YDS	LNG	TD	RUSHING	ATT	YDS	LNG	TD
Duane Thomas	19	95	23	1	Larry Csonka	9	40	12	0
Walt Garrison	14	74	17	0	Jim Kiick	10	40	9	0
Calvin Hill	7	25	13	0	Bob Griese	1	0	0	0
Roger Staubach	5	18	5	0					
Mike Ditka	1	17	17	0					
Bob Hayes	1	16	16	0					
Dan Reeves	1	7	7	0					
RECEIVING	NO	YDS	LNG	TD	RECEIVING	NO	YDS	LNG	TD
Duane Thomas	3	17	11	0	Paul Warfield	4	39	23	0
Lance Alworth	2	28	21	1	Jim Kiick	3	21	11	0
Mike Ditka	2	28	21	1	Larry Csonka	2	18	16	0
Bob Hayes	2	23	18	0	Marv Fleming	1	27	27	0
Walt Garrison	2	11	7	0	Howard Twilley	1	20	20	0
Calvin Hill	1	12	12	0	Jim Mandich	1	9	9	0
PASSING	PA	PC	YDS	TD	IN	PASSING	PA	PC	YDS	TD	IN
Roger Staubach	19	12	119	2	0	Bob Griese	23	12	134	0	1

DALLAS COWBOYS					MIAMI DOLPHINS				
KICKOFF RETURNS	NO	YDS	LNG	TD	KICKOFF RETURNS	NO	YDS	LNG	TD
Ike Thomas	1	23	23	0	Mercury Morris	4	90	37	0
Charlie Waters	1	11	11	0	Hubert Ginn	1	32	32	0
PUNT RETURNS	NO	YDS	LNG	TD	PUNT RETURNS	NO	YDS	LNG	TD
Bob Hayes	1	-1	-1	0	Jake Scott	1	21	21	0
INTERCEPTION RETURNS	NO	YDS	LNG	TD	INTERCEPTION RETURNS	NO	YDS	LNG	TD
Chuck Howley	1	41	41	0					
PUNTING	NO	YDS	LNG	BLK	PUNTING	NO	YDS	LNG	BLK
Ron Widby	5	37	47	0	Larry Seiple	5	40	45	0

THE COWBOYS FINALLY FIND A WAY

Teams from the AFL, and now the AFC, had won three straight Super Bowls. The Cowboys had lost two epic battles with Green Bay for NFL titles in the 1960s, and in Super Bowl V had thrown away a chance for the championship trophy, renamed for late Packers coach Vince Lombardi.

Tom Landry, who'd coached with Lombardi for the Giants in the 1950s, had the Cowboys ready. Chuck Howley, who recovered 3 turnovers as MVP in a losing cause in the previous Super Bowl, picked up a rare Larry Csonka fumble in the first quarter. Dallas turned it into a field goal. Roger Staubach, finally inserted as the regular starter in 1971, capped a 76-yard drive in the second quarter with a 7-yard pass to Lance Alworth. Garo Yepremian's field goal before the half made it 10–3.

The Cowboys embarked on long scoring drives in both the third and fourth quarters. Duane Thomas, who'd been as mute throughout the week as Miami's offense was in the game, ran for 95 yards. Patient and pinpoint Staubach was named MVP.

SUPER BOWL VII

Sunday, January 14, 1973 at Los Angeles, Memorial Coliseum, attendance 90,182   MVP: Jake Scott

MIAMI DOPHINS	7	7	0	0	—	**14**
WASHINGTON REDSKINS	0	0	0	7	—	7

SCORING Mia—Twilley 28-yd pass from Griese (Yepremian PAT), Mia—Kiick 1-yd run (Yepremian PAT), Was—Bass 49-yd fumble return (Knight PAT)

TEAM	FIRST DOWNS	TOTAL YARDAGE	RUSHING	PASSING	RETURNS	ATT-COMP-INT	SACKED	PUNTING	FUMBLES	PENALTIES
Mia	12	253	37-184	69	99	11-8-1	2-19	7-43	2-1	3-35
Was	16	228	36-141	87	9	28-14-3	2-17	5-31	1-0	3-25

MIAMI DOLPHINS

RUSHING	ATT	YDS	LNG	TD
Larry Csonka	15	112	49	0
Jim Kiick	12	38	8	1
Mercury Morris	10	34	6	0

RECEIVING	NO	YDS	LNG	TD
Paul Warfield	3	36	18	0
Jim Kiick	2	6	4	0
Howard Twilley	1	28	28	1
Jim Mandich	1	19	19	0
Larry Csonka	1	-1	-1	0

PASSING	PA	PC	YDS	TD	IN
Bob Griese	11	8	88	1	1

WASHINGTON REDSKINS

RUSHING	ATT	YDS	LNG	TD
Larry Brown	22	72	11	0
Charlie Harraway	10	37	8	0
Billy Kilmer	2	18	9	0
Charley Taylor	1	8	8	0
Jerry Smith	1	6	6	0

RECEIVING	NO	YDS	LNG	TD
Roy Jefferson	5	50	15	0
Larry Brown	5	26	12	0
Charley Taylor	2	20	15	0
Jerry Smith	1	11	11	0
Charlie Harraway	1	-3	-3	0

PASSING	PA	PC	YDS	TD	IN
Billy Kilmer	28	14	104	0	3

MIAMI DOLPHINS

KICKOFF RETURNS	NO	YDS	LNG	TD
Mercury Morris	2	33	17	0

PUNT RETURNS	NO	YDS	LNG	TD
Jake Scott	2	4	4	0

INTERCEPTION RETURNS	NO	YDS	LNG	TD
Jake Scott	2	63	55	0
Nick Buoniconti	1	32	32	0

PUNTING	NO	YDS	LNG	BLK
Larry Seiple	7	43	50	0

WASHINGTON REDSKINS

KICKOFF RETURNS	NO	YDS	LNG	TD
Alvin Haymond	2	30	18	0
Herb Mul-Key	1	15	15	0

PUNT RETURNS	NO	YDS	LNG	TD
Alvin Haymond	4	9	7	0

INTERCEPTION RETURNS	NO	YDS	LNG	TD
Brig Owens	1	0	0	0

PUNTING	NO	YDS	LNG	BLK
Mike Bragg	5	31	38	0

ALL TOO PERFECT

The Miami Dolphins were perfect, but people loved George Allen's Over the Hill Gang. Washington had held playoff opponents Green Bay and Dallas to just a field goal apiece. President Richard Nixon, who once even recommended a play that Allen tried, befriended the Redskins; so did Las Vegas, which installed Washington as the favorite.

Miami was nearly flawless in the first half. The Redskins moved the ball in the second half but missed a field goal by Curt Knight.

It was a field-goal try by Miami, though, that forever stamped this game. With two minutes left, the Dolphins lined up for a 42-yard attempt that would have been all too perfect: 17–0 on the scoreboard and in the record books.

Garo Yepremian's kick was blocked. He picked up the ball and tried to throw it. The ball slipped and then he batted it in the air . . . right to Mike Bass, who took it 49 yards for a touchdown. Washington got the ball back with 1:14 to go, but Miami's defense suffocated the Redskins one last time.

SUPER BOWL VIII

Sunday, January 13, 1974 at Houston, Rice Stadium, attendance 71,882   MVP: Larry Csonka

MINNESOTA VIKINGS	0	0	0	7	—	7
MIAMI DOLPHINS	14	3	7	0	—	24

SCORING Mia—Csonka 5-yd run (Yepremian PAT), Mia—Kiick 1-yd run (Yepremian PAT), Mia—FG Yepremian 28 yds, Mia—Csonka 2-yd run (Yepremian PAT), Min—Tarkenton 4-yd run (Cox PAT)

TEAM	FIRST DOWNS	TOTAL YARDAGE	RUSHING	PASSING	RETURNS	ATT-COMP-INT	SACKED	PUNTING	FUMBLES	PENALTIES
Min	14	238	24-72	166	0	28-18-1	2-16	5-42	2-1	7-65
Mia	21	259	53-196	63	30	7-6-0	1-10	3-40	1-0	1-4

MINNESOTA VIKINGS

RUSHING	ATT	YDS	LNG	TD
Oscar Reed	11	32	9	0
Chuck Foreman	7	18	5	0
Fran Tarkenton	4	17	8	1
Ed Marinaro	1	3	3	0
Bill Brown	1	2	2	0

RECEIVING	NO	YDS	LNG	TD
Chuck Foreman	5	27	10	0
John Gilliam	4	44	30	0
Stu Voigt	3	46	17	0
Ed Marinaro	2	39	27	0
Bill Brown	1	9	9	0
Doug Kingsriter	1	9	9	0
Jim Lash	1	9	9	0
Oscar Reed	1	-1	-1	0

PASSING	PA	PC	YDS	TD	IN
Fran Tarkenton	28	18	182	0	1

MIAMI DOLPHINS

RUSHING	ATT	YDS	LNG	TD
Larry Csonka	33	145	16	2
Mercury Morris	11	34	14	0
Jim Kiick	7	10	5	1
Bob Griese	2	7	5	0

RECEIVING	NO	YDS	LNG	TD
Paul Warfield	2	33	27	0
Jim Mandich	2	21	13	0
Marlin Briscoe	2	19	13	0

PASSING	PA	PC	YDS	TD	IN
Bob Griese	7	6	73	0	0

MINNESOTA VIKINGS

KICKOFF RETURNS	NO	YDS	LNG	TD
John Gilliam	2	41	21	0
Charlie West	2	28	15	0

PUNT RETURNS	NO	YDS	LNG	TD

INTERCEPTION RETURNS	NO	YDS	LNG	TD

PUNTING	NO	YDS	LNG	BLK
Mike Eischeid	5	42	48	0

MIAMI DOLPHINS

KICKOFF RETURNS	NO	YDS	LNG	TD
Jake Scott	2	47	31	0

PUNT RETURNS	NO	YDS	LNG	TD
Jake Scott	3	20	12	0

INTERCEPTION RETURNS	NO	YDS	LNG	TD
Curtis Johnson	1	10	10	0

PUNTING	NO	YDS	LNG	BLK
Larry Seiple	3	39	57	0

ANOTHER DAY OF THE DOLPHIN

For once, no one gave the NFC team extra credence because they came from the conference of elders. The Dolphins were clearly better than the Vikings and proved it. Like Washington the year before, Minnesota was fortunate not to get shut out by the No-Name Defense.

The Dolphins marched down the field twice in the first quarter and came away with touchdowns. Larry Csonka, who gained 112 yards on just 15 carries the previous year, got the ball a lot more in Super Bowl VIII. He bulled ahead for 145 yards on 33 carries. Bob

Griese threw just 7 passes (6 completions), while Fran Tarkenton threw 28 times (completing 18). A holding call on Minnesota nullified John Gilliam's 65-yard, second-half kickoff return. The Vikings punted back to Miami and Csonka did what Super Bowl MVPs do: Make Vikings Pay.

The Dolphins were the first team to go to three straight Super Bowls. Don Shula, with the Colts in Super Bowl III, was head coach in four of the first eight Super Bowls.

SUPER BOWL IX

Sunday, January 12, 1975 at New Orleans, Tulane Stadium, attendance 80,997

MVP: Franco Harris

PITTSBURGH STEELERS	0	2	7	7	—	16
MINNESOTA VIKINGS	0	0	0	6	—	6

SCORING Pit—Safety, White downed Tarkenton in end zone, Pit—Harris 9-yd run (Gerela PAT), Min—T. Brown recovered blocked punt in end zone (PAT failed), Pit—L. Brown 4-yd pass from Bradshaw (Gerela PAT)

TEAM	FIRST DOWNS	TOTAL YARDAGE	RUSHING	PASSING	RETURNS	ATT-COMP-INT	SACKED	PUNTING	FUMBLES	PENALTIES
Pit	17	333	57-249	84	82	14-9-0	2-12	7-35	4-2	8-122
Min	9	119	21-17	102	12	26-11-3	0-0	6-37	3-2	4-18

PITTSBURGH STEELERS

RUSHING	ATT	YDS	LNG	TD
Franco Harris	34	158	25	1
Rocky Bleier	17	65	18	0
Terry Bradshaw	5	33	17	0
Lynn Swann	1	-7	-7	0

RECEIVING	NO	YDS	LNG	TD
Larry Brown	3	49	20	1
John Stallworth	3	24	22	0
Rocky Bleier	2	11	6	0
Frank Lewis	1	12	12	0

PASSING	PA	PC	YDS	TD	IN
Terry Bradshaw	14	9	96	1	0

MINNESOTA VIKINGS

RUSHING	ATT	YDS	LNG	TD
Chuck Foreman	12	18	12	0
Fran Tarkenton	1	0	0	0
Dave Osborn	8	-1	2	0

RECEIVING	NO	YDS	LNG	TD
Chuck Foreman	5	50	17	0
Stu Voigt	2	31	28	0
Dave Osborn	2	7	4	0
John Gilliam	1	16	16	0
Oscar Reed	1	-2	-2	0

PASSING	PA	PC	YDS	TD	IN
Fran Tarkenton	26	11	102	0	3

PITTSBURGH STEELERS

KICKOFF RETURNS	NO	YDS	LNG	TD
Reggie Harrison	2	17	17	0
Preston Pearson	1	15	15	0

PUNT RETURNS	NO	YDS	LNG	TD
Lynn Swann	3	34	17	0
Glen Edwards	2	2	2	0

INTERCEPTION RETURNS	NO	YDS	LNG	TD
Mike Wagner	1	26	26	0
Mel Blount	1	10	10	0
Joe Greene	1	10	10	0

PUNTING	NO	YDS	LNG	BLK
Bobby Walden	6	40	52	1

MINNESOTA VIKINGS

KICKOFF RETURNS	NO	YDS	LNG	TD
Sam McCullum	1	26	26	0
Brent McClanahan	1	22	22	0
Bill Brown	1	2	2	0

PUNT RETURNS	NO	YDS	LNG	TD
Sam McCullum	3	11	6	0
Nate Wright	1	1	1	0

INTERCEPTION RETURNS	NO	YDS	LNG	TD

PUNTING	NO	YDS	LNG	BLK
Mike Eischeid	6	37	42	0

JUST GETTING STARTED

Pittsburgh had gone without an NFL championship since 1933, when Art Rooney founded the franchise, then called the Pirates, with $2,500 he won at the track. Pennsylvania added two teams that year because the state legalized professional sports on Sunday. Now, 42 seasons later, Super Bowl Sunday was practically a national holiday.

It was one of nastiest days ever for a Super Bowl, cold and drizzly, and the defenses kept the game tight. This Super Bowl lacked action in the traditional sense, but it did have the first Super Bowl safety, by Dwight White. Those were the only points of the first half.

The Vikings screwed up the second-half kickoff for the second straight year. Following Bill Brown's fumble, Franco Harris, who ran for a then-record 158 yards, scored from the 9 for a 9-0 lead. The Vikings made it close when Matt Blair blocked a punt and Terry Brown recovered it for a touchdown, but the Steelers were in command. The Steel Curtain limited Minnesota to just 119 total yards. And Mr. Rooney finally had his trophy.

SUPER BOWL X

Sunday, January 18, 1976 at Miami, Orange Bowl, attendance 80,187

MVP: Lynn Swann

DALLAS COWBOYS	7	3	0	7	—	17
PITTSBURGH STEELERS	7	0	0	14	—	21

SCORING Dal—D. Pearson 29-yd pass from Staubach (Fritsch PAT), Pit—Grossman 7-yd pass from Bradshaw (Gerela PAT), Dal—FG Fritsch 36 yds, Pit—Safety, Harrison blocked Hoopes' kick through end zone, Pit—FG Gerela 36 yds, Pit—FG Gerela 18 yds, Pit—Swann 64-yd pass from Bradshaw (Gerela kick failed), Dal—P. Howard 34-yd pass from Staubach (Fritsch PAT)

TEAM	FIRST DOWNS	TOTAL YARDAGE	RUSHING	PASSING	RETURNS	ATT-COMP-INT	SACKED	PUNTING	FUMBLES	PENALTIES
Dal	14	270	31-108	162	5	24-15-3	7-42	7-35	4-0	2-20
Pit	13	339	46-149	190	120	19-9-0	2-19	4-40	4-0	0-0

DALLAS COWBOYS

RUSHING	ATT	YDS	LNG	TD
Robert Newhouse	16	56	16	0
Roger Staubach	5	22	11	0
Doug Dennison	5	16	5	0
Preston Pearson	5	14	9	0

RECEIVING	NO	YDS	LNG	TD
Preston Pearson	5	53	14	0
Charley Young	3	31	14	0
Drew Pearson	2	59	30	1
Robert Newhouse	2	12	8	0
Percy Howard	1	34	34	1
Jean Fugett	1	9	9	0
Doug Dennison	1	6	6	0

PASSING	PA	PC	YDS	TD	IN
Roger Staubach	24	15	204	2	3

PITTSBURGH STEELERS

RUSHING	ATT	YDS	LNG	TD
Franco Harris	27	82	11	0
Rocky Bleier	15	51	8	0
Terry Bradshaw	4	16	8	0

RECEIVING	NO	YDS	LNG	TD
Lynn Swann	4	161	74	1
John Stallworth	2	8	13	0
Franco Harris	1	26	26	0
Larry Brown	1	7	7	0
Randy Grossman	1	7	7	1

PASSING	PA	PC	YDS	TD	IN
Terry Bradshaw	19	9	209	2	0

DALLAS COWBOYS

KICKOFF RETURNS	NO	YDS	LNG	TD
Preston Pearson	4	48	24	0
Thomas Henderson	0	48	48	0

PUNT RETURNS	NO	YDS	LNG	TD
Golden Richards	1	5	5	0

INTERCEPTION RETURNS	NO	YDS	LNG	TD

PUNTING	NO	YDS	LNG	BLK
Mitch Hoopes	6	40	48	1

PITTSBURGH STEELERS

KICKOFF RETURNS	NO	YDS	LNG	TD
Mel Blount	3	64	27	0
Mike Collier	1	25	25	0

PUNT RETURNS	NO	YDS	LNG	TD
Dave Brown	3	14	9	0
Glen Edwards	2	17	10	0

INTERCEPTION RETURNS	NO	YDS	LNG	TD
Glen Edwards	1	35	35	0
J.T. Thomas	1	35	35	0
Mike Wagner	1	19	19	0

PUNTING	NO	YDS	LNG	BLK
Bobby Walden	4	39	59	0

BACK AGAIN SO SOON?

After waiting more than four decades for their first NFL title, the Steelers went for seconds right away. It was a thrilling matchup: America's Team against the Steel Curtain. Pittsburgh resented Dallas's moniker and the Cowboys wanted their second Super Bowl title as badly as the Steelers did.

With 11 minutes left in the game, Dallas led, 10-7. Pittsburgh's Reggie Harrison blocked a punt. The ball struck him in the face, split his tongue, and bounced through the end zone for a safety. The Steelers took the lead on 2 field goals by Roy Gerela, playing with a cracked rib, and a 64-yard bomb from Terry Bradshaw to Lynn Swann, the game's MVP with 4 catches for 161 yards.

Dallas quickly moved 80 yards and scored on Percy Howard's touchdown grab. (It was his only career catch.) Roger Staubach, just three weeks removed from his Hail Mary pass that beat the Vikings, drove the Cowboys to the Pittsburgh 38 with five seconds left. Steelers safety Mike Wagner deflected Staubach's last-gasp pass to teammate Glen Edwards. Pittsburgh's prayers were answered.

SUPER BOWL XI

Sunday, January 9, 1977 at Pasadena, CA, Rose Bowl, attendance 103,438

MVP: Fred Biletnikoff

OAKLAND RAIDERS	0	16	3	13	—	32
MINNESOTA VIKINGS	0	0	7	7	—	14

SCORING Oak—FG Mann 24 yds, Oak—Casper 1-yd pass from Stabler (Mann PAT), Oak—Banaszak 1-yd run (PAT failed), Oak—FG Mann 40 yds, Min—S. White 8-yd pass from Tarkenton (Cox PAT), Oak—Banaszak 2-yd run (Mann PAT), Oak—Brown 75-yd interception return (PAT failed), Min—Voigt 13-yd pass from Lee (Cox PAT)

TEAM	FIRST DOWNS	TOTAL YARDAGE	RUSHING	PASSING	RETURNS	ATT-COMP-INT	SACKED	PUNTING	FUMBLES	PENALTIES
Oak	21	429	52-266	163	134	19-12-0	2-17	5-32	0-0	4-30
Min	20	353	26-71	282	14	44-24-2	1-4	7-38	1-1	2-25

OAKLAND RAIDERS

RUSHING	ATT	YDS	LNG	TD
Clarence Davis	16	137	35	0
Mark van Eeghen	18	73	11	0
Pete Banaszak	10	19	6	2
Carl Garrett	4	19	13	0
Hubert Ginn	2	9	9	0
Mike Rae	2	9	11	0

RECEIVING	NO	YDS	LNG	TD
Fred Biletnikoff	4	79	48	0
Dave Casper	4	70	26	1
Cliff Branch	3	20	10	0
Carl Garrett	1	11	11	0

PASSING	PA	PC	YDS	TD	IN
Ken Stabler	19	12	180	1	0

MINNESOTA VIKINGS

RUSHING	ATT	YDS	LNG	TD
Chuck Foreman	17	44	7	0
Sammy Johnson	2	9	8	0
Sammy White	1	7	7	0
Bob Lee	1	4	4	0
Robert Miller	2	4	3	0
Brent McClanahan	3	3	2	0

RECEIVING	NO	YDS	LNG	TD
Sammy White	5	77	20	1
Chuck Foreman	5	62	26	0
Stu Voigt	4	49	15	1
Robert Miller	4	19	13	0
Ahmad Rashad	3	53	25	0
Sammy Johnson	3	26	17	0

PASSING	PA	PC	YDS	TD	IN
Fran Tarkenton	35	17	205	1	2
Bob Lee	9	7	81	1	0

OAKLAND RAIDERS

KICKOFF RETURNS	NO	YDS	LNG	TD
Carl Garrett	2	47	24	0

PUNT RETURNS	NO	YDS	LNG	TD
Neal Colzie	4	43	25	0

INTERCEPTION RETURNS	NO	YDS	LNG	TD
Willie Brown	1	75	75	1
Willie Hall	1	16	16	0

PUNTING	NO	YDS	LNG	BLK
Ray Guy	4	40	51	1

MINNESOTA VIKINGS

KICKOFF RETURNS	NO	YDS	LNG	TD
Sammy White	4	79	26	0
Leonard Willis	3	57	20	0

PUNT RETURNS	NO	YDS	LNG	TD
Leonard Willis	3	14	8	0

INTERCEPTION RETURNS	NO	YDS	LNG	TD

PUNTING	NO	YDS	LNG	BLK
Neil Clabo	7	37	46	0

RAIDERS COME UP ROSES

The only thing new about this game was the Rose Bowl: the first Super Bowl venue to have never hosted pro football. Few people who weren't Vikings fans had the vibe Minnesota would end its 0-for-3 Super drought against the dominant Raiders.

The Vikings had a brief chance. Minnesota blocked a Ray Guy punt but quickly fumbled right back. The Raiders drove 90 yards for Erroll Mann's field goal. Oakland added 2 touchdowns before the half arrived. Pete Banaszak followed Minnesota's first score with his second touchdown of the day. The Vikings did change one thing: After scoring a single touchdown in each of their Super Bowl losses, this time they added a second. It came after Fran Tarkenton had been removed; his last pass wound up in Willie Brown's hands for a 75-yard interception return.

The toughest part was picking an MVP: Fred Biletnikoff (4 catches, 79 yards), Dave Casper (4 catches, 70 yards), Ken Stabler (180 yards passing) Clarence Davis (16 carries, 137 yards) or Willie Brown? In the end, it was Biletnikoff. And all Raiders.

SUPER BOWL XII

Sunday, January 15, 1978 at New Orleans, Louisiana Superdome, attendance 75,583

MVP: Harvey Martin, Randy White

DALLAS COWBOYS (NFC)	10	3	7	7	—	27
DENVER BRONCOS (AFC)	0	0	10	0	—	10

SCORING Dal—Dorsett 3-yd run (Herrera PAT), Dal—FG Herrera 35 yds, Dal—FG Herrera 43 yds, Den—FG Turner 47 yds, Dal—Johnson 45-yd pass from Staubach (Herrera PAT), Den—Lytle 1-yd run (Turner PAT), Dal—Richards 29-yd pass from Newhouse (Herrera PAT)

TEAM	FIRST DOWNS	TOTAL YARDAGE	RUSHING	PASSING	RETURNS	ATT-COMP-INT	SACKED	PUNTING	FUMBLES	PENALTIES
Dal	17	325	38-143	182	46	28-19-0	5-35	5-42	6-2	12-94
Den	11	156	29-121	35	22	25-8-4	4-26	4-38	4-4	8-60

DALLAS COWBOYS (NFC)

RUSHING	ATT	YDS	LNG	TD
Tony Dorsett	15	66	19	1
Robert Newhouse	14	55	10	0
Danny White	1	13	13	0
Preston Pearson	3	11	5	0
Roger Staubach	3	6	5	0
Scott Laidlaw	1	1	1	0
Butch Johnson	1	-9	-9	0

RECEIVING	NO	YDS	LNG	TD
Preston Pearson	5	37	11	0
Billy Joe DuPree	4	66	19	0
Robert Newhouse	3	-1	5	0
Butch Johnson	2	53	45	1
Golden Richards	2	38	29	1
Tony Dorsett	2	11	15	0
Drew Pearson	1	13	13	0

PASSING	PA	PC	YDS	TD	IN
Roger Staubach	25	17	183	1	0
Robert Newhouse	1	1	29	1	0
Danny White	2	1	5	0	0

DENVER BRONCOS (AFC)

RUSHING	ATT	YDS	LNG	TD
Rob Lytle	10	35	16	1
Otis Armstrong	7	27	18	0
Norris Weese	3	26	10	0
Jim Jensen	1	16	16	0
Jon Keyworth	5	9	6	0
Lonnie Perrin	3	8	4	0

RECEIVING	NO	YDS	LNG	TD
Jack Dolbin	2	24	15	0
Riley Odoms	2	9	10	0
Haven Moses	1	21	21	0
Rick Upchurch	1	9	9	0
Jim Jensen	1	5	5	0
Lonnie Perrin	1	-7	-7	0

PASSING	PA	PC	YDS	TD	IN
Craig Morton	15	4	39	0	4
Norris Weese	10	4	22	0	0

DALLAS COWBOYS (NFC)

KICKOFF RETURNS	NO	YDS	LNG	TD
Butch Johnson	2	29	15	0
Larry Brinson	1	22	22	0

PUNT RETURNS	NO	YDS	LNG	TD
Tony Hill	1	0	0	0

INTERCEPTION RETURNS	NO	YDS	LNG	TD
Mark Washington	1	27	27	0
Aaron Kyle	1	19	19	0
Benny Barnes	1	0	0	0
Randy Hughes	1	0	0	0

PUNTING	NO	YDS	LNG	BLK
Danny White	5	41	53	0

DENVER BRONCOS (AFC)

KICKOFF RETURNS	NO	YDS	LNG	TD
Rick Upchurch	3	94	67	0
John Schultz	2	62	37	0
Jim Jensen	1	17	17	0

PUNT RETURNS	NO	YDS	LNG	TD
Rick Upchurch	3	22	8	0
John Schultz	1	0	0	0

INTERCEPTION RETURNS	NO	YDS	LNG	TD

PUNTING	NO	YDS	LNG	BLK
Bucky Dilts	4	38	46	0

AN INDOOR DOOMSDAY BLAST

The Super Bowl hype machine was set to maximum for New Orleans. The first indoor Super Bowl would be, according to the papers, a battle of great defenses (Doomsday vs. Orange Crush); revenge for a spurned former Cowboys quarterback (Craig Morton); a comeuppance for brash Dallas rookie Tony Dorsett; and an epic clash of two 12–2 teams. In reality, it turned out to be just another one-sided game.

Two Morton interceptions became a quick 10–0 lead, with Dorsett scoring the first points. By halftime it was 13–0; Denver had 7 turnovers and 2 first downs. The Broncos managed 10 points in the third quarter, but Roger Staubach tossed a 45-yard touchdown pass hauled in by a diving Butch Johnson. A halfback option pass from Robert Newhouse to Golden Richards made the rout official.

Two teammates shared MVP for the first time—Harvey Martin and Randy White—but it could have gone to whole Dallas defense. Or the whole Cowboys team, for that matter.

SUPER BOWL XIII

Sunday, January 21, 1979 at Miami, Orange Bowl, attendance 79,484   MVP: Terry Bradshaw

PITTSBURGH STEELERS (AFC)	7	14	0	14	—	35
DALLAS COWBOYS (NFC)	7	7	3	14	—	31

SCORING Pit—Stallworth 28-yd pass from Bradshaw (Gerela PAT), Dal—Hill 39-yd pass from Staubach (Septien PAT), Dal—Hegman 37-yd fumble recovery return (Septien PAT), Pit—Stallworth 75-yd pass from Bradshaw (Gerela PAT), Pit—Bleier 7-yd pass from Bradshaw (Gerela PAT), Dal—FG Septien 27 yds, Pit—Harris 22-yd run (Gerela PAT), Pit—Swann 18-yd pass from Bradshaw (Gerela PAT), Dal—DuPree 7-yd pass from Staubach (Septien PAT), Dal—B. Johnson 4-yd pass from Staubach (Septien PAT)

TEAM	FIRST DOWNS	TOTAL YARDAGE	RUSHING	PASSING	RETURNS	ATT-COMP-INT	SACKED	PUNTING	FUMBLES	PENALTIES
Pit	19	357	24-66	291	40	30-17-1	4-27	3-43	2-2	5-35
Dal	20	330	32-154	176	54	30-17-1	5-52	5-40	3-2	9-89

PITTSBURGH STEELERS (AFC)

RUSHING	ATT	YDS	LNG	TD
Franco Harris	20	68	22	1
Rocky Bleier	2	3	2	0
Terry Bradshaw	2	-5	2	0

RECEIVING	NO	YDS	LNG	TD
Lynn Swann	7	124	29	1
John Stallworth	3	115	75	2
Randy Grossman	3	29	10	0
Theo Bell	2	21	12	0
Franco Harris	1	22	22	0
Rocky Bleier	1	7	7	1

PASSING	PA	PC	YDS	TD	IN
Terry Bradshaw	30	17	318	4	1

DALLAS COWBOYS (NFC)

RUSHING	ATT	YDS	LNG	TD
Tony Dorsett	16	96	29	0
Roger Staubach	4	37	18	0
Scott Laidlaw	3	12	7	0
Preston Pearson	1	6	6	0
Robert Newhouse	8	3	5	0

RECEIVING	NO	YDS	LNG	TD
Tony Dorsett	5	44	13	0
Drew Pearson	4	73	25	0
Tony Hill	2	49	39	1
Butch Johnson	2	30	26	1
Billy Joe DuPree	2	17	10	1
Preston Pearson	2	15	8	0

PASSING	PA	PC	YDS	TD	IN
Roger Staubach	30	17	228	3	1

PITTSBURGH STEELERS (AFC)

KICKOFF RETURNS	NO	YDS	LNG	TD
Larry Anderson	3	45	24	0

PUNT RETURNS	NO	YDS	LNG	TD
Theo Bell	4	27	12	0

INTERCEPTION RETURNS	NO	YDS	LNG	TD
Mel Blount	1	13	13	0

PUNTING	NO	YDS	LNG	BLK
Craig Colquitt	3	43	52	0

DALLAS COWBOYS (NFC)

KICKOFF RETURNS	NO	YDS	LNG	TD
Butch Johnson	3	63	23	0
Larry Brinson	2	41	25	0
Randy White	1	0	0	0

PUNT RETURNS	NO	YDS	LNG	TD
Butch Johnson	2	33	21	0

INTERCEPTION RETURNS	NO	YDS	LNG	TD
D.D. Lewis	1	21	21	0

PUNTING	NO	YDS	LNG	BLK
Danny White	5	39	50	0

A COPY BETTER THAN THE ORIGINAL

Thirteen Super Bowls wasn't unlucky—well, maybe for a future Hall of Fame tight end—but this was probably the most entertaining game to date. It certainly lived up to the standards of the first Dallas–Pittsburgh encounter at the Orange Bowl.

These two great defensive teams put up plenty of offense. Terry Bradshaw hit John Stallworth twice for touchdowns and tossed another to Rocky Bleier. Roger Staubach wasn't quite as successful, but his touchdown pass and Mike Hegman's 37-yard fumble recovery kept the score at 21–14, the highest-scoring first half yet in the Super Bowl.

The third quarter had a heartbreaking end zone drop by Jackie Smith in the last game of a brilliant career. Four lost points would come to mind during the frenzied final period. Bradshaw threw his fourth touchdown of the day and racked up 318 passing yards, the most to that point, but his MVP wasn't secure. Staubach fired a touchdown with 2:27 left and another with 22 seconds remaining. The onside kick didn't work, ending a fine game with a familiar result.

SUPER BOWL XIV

Sunday, January 20, 1980 at Pasadena, CA, Rose Bowl, attendance 103,985   MVP: Terry Bradshaw

LOS ANGELES RAMS (NFC)	7	6	6	0	—	19
PITTSBURGH STEELERS (AFC)	3	7	7	14	—	31

SCORING Pit—FG Bahr 41 yds, LA—Bryant 1-yd run (Corral PAT), Pit—Harris 1-yd run (Bahr PAT), LA—FG Corral 31 yds, LA—FG Corral 45 yds, Pit—Swann 47-yd pass from Bradshaw (Bahr PAT), LA—Smith 24-yd pass from McCutcheon (PAT failed), Pit—Stallworth 73-yd pass from Bradshaw (Bahr PAT), Pit—Harris 1-yd run (Bahr PAT)

TEAM	FIRST DOWNS	TOTAL YARDAGE	RUSHING	PASSING	RETURNS	ATT-COMP-INT	SACKED	PUNTING	FUMBLES	PENALTIES
LA	16	301	29-107	194	25	26-16-1	4-42	5-44	0-0	2-26
Pit	19	393	37-84	309	47	21-14-3	0-0	2-43	0-0	6-65

LOS ANGELES RAMS (NFC)

RUSHING	ATT	YDS	LNG	TD
Wendell Tyler	17	60	39	0
Cullen Bryant	6	30	14	1
Lawrence McCutcheon	5	10	6	0
Vince Ferragamo	1	7	7	0

RECEIVING	NO	YDS	LNG	TD
Billy Waddy	3	75	50	0
Cullen Bryant	3	21	12	0
Wendell Tyler	3	20	11	0
Preston Dennard	2	32	24	0
Terry Nelson	2	20	14	0
Drew Hill	1	28	28	0
Ron Smith	1	24	24	1
Lawrence McCutcheon	1	16	16	0

PASSING	PA	PC	YDS	TD	IN
Vince Ferragamo	25	15	212	0	1
Lawrence McCutcheon	1	1	24	1	0

PITTSBURGH STEELERS (AFC)

RUSHING	ATT	YDS	LNG	TD
Franco Harris	20	46	12	2
Rocky Bleier	10	25	9	0
Terry Bradshaw	3	9	6	0
Sidney Thornton	4	4	5	0

RECEIVING	NO	YDS	LNG	TD
Lynn Swann	5	79	47	1
John Stallworth	3	121	73	1
Franco Harris	3	66	32	0
Bennie Cunningham	2	21	13	0
Sidney Thornton	1	22	22	0

PASSING	PA	PC	YDS	TD	IN
Terry Bradshaw	21	14	309	2	3

LOS ANGELES RAMS (NFC)

KICKOFF RETURNS	NO	YDS	LNG	TD
Eddie Hill	3	47	27	0
Jim Jodat	2	32	16	0
George Andrews	1	0	0	0

PUNT RETURNS	NO	YDS	LNG	TD
Eddie Brown	1	4	4	0

INTERCEPTION RETURNS	NO	YDS	LNG	TD
Dave Elmendorf	1	10	10	0
Eddie Brown	1	6	6	0
Rod Perry	1	-1	-1	0
Pat Thomas	0	6	6	0

PUNTING	NO	YDS	LNG	BLK
Ken Clark	5	44	59	0

PITTSBURGH STEELERS (AFC)

KICKOFF RETURNS	NO	YDS	LNG	TD
Larry Anderson	5	162	45	0

PUNT RETURNS	NO	YDS	LNG	TD
Theo Bell	2	17	11	0
Jim Smith	2	14	7	0

INTERCEPTION RETURNS	NO	YDS	LNG	TD
Jack Lambert	1	16	16	0

PUNTING	NO	YDS	LNG	BLK
Craig Colquitt	2	42	50	0

STEELERS GO FOR A NIGHTCAP

Of course, the Steelers were the favorite. They had won three of the last five Super Bowls and were a full-on dynasty. As if more mojo was necessary, the team they'd originally been named after, the Pittsburgh Pirates, had won the World Series in the fall. Yet this one was hard.

The Rams, the first team to play a Super Bowl in their back yard, led in every quarter and had many in the record crowd of 103,985 thinking upset. Quarterback Vince Ferragamo was efficient, as were the Los Angeles runners. Lawrence McCutcheon brought the crowd to its feet when his halfback option pass found Ron Smith for the lead.

Bradshaw had seen this before. John Stallworth, who'd hauled in a 75-yard pass in the previous year's Super Bowl, caught a pass in stride for 73 yards and a 24–19 lead. Bradshaw and Stallworth worked their deep magic again—this time for 45 yards—to set up a Franco Harris touchdown run. No team had won four Super Bowls before and Bradshaw joined Bart Starr as a back-to-back MVP.

SUPER BOWL XV

Sunday, January 25, 1981 at New Orleans, Louisiana Superdome, attendance 75,500   MVP: Jim Plunkett

	1	2	3	4	—	Final
OAKLAND RAIDERS	14	0	10	3	—	27
PHILADELPHIA EAGLES	0	3	0	7	—	10

SCORING Oak—Branch 2-yd pass from Plunkett (Bahr PAT), Oak—King 80-yd pass from Plunkett (Bahr PAT), Phi—FG Franklin 30 yds, Oak—Branch 29-yd pass from Plunkett (Bahr PAT), Oak—FG Bahr 46 yds, Phi—Krepfle 8-yd pass from Jaworski (Franklin PAT), Oak—FG Bahr 35 yds

TEAM	FIRST DOWNS	TOTAL YARDAGE	RUSHING	PASSING	RETURNS	ATT-COMP-INT	SACKED	PUNTING	FUMBLES	PENALTIES
Oak	17	377	34-117	260	45	21-13-0	1-1	3-42	0-0	5-37
Phi	19	360	26-69	291	20	38-18-3	0-0	3-37	1-1	6-57

OAKLAND RAIDERS

RUSHING	ATT	YDS	LNG	TD
Mark van Eeghen	19	80	8	0
Kenny King	6	18	6	0
Derrick Jensen	3	12	6	0
Jim Plunkett	3	9	5	0
Arthur Whittington	3	-2	2	0

RECEIVING	NO	YDS	LNG	TD
Cliff Branch	5	67	29	2
Bob Chandler	4	77	32	0
Kenny King	2	93	80	1
Raymond Chester	2	24	16	0

PASSING	PA	PC	YDS	TD	IN
Jim Plunkett	21	13	261	3	0

PHILADELPHIA EAGLES

RUSHING	ATT	YDS	LNG	TD
Wilbert Montgomery	16	44	8	0
Leroy Harris	7	14	5	0
Louie Giammona	1	7	7	0
Perry Harrington	1	4	4	0
Ron Jaworski	1	0	0	0

RECEIVING	NO	YDS	LNG	TD
Wilbert Montgomery	6	91	25	0
Harold Carmichael	5	83	29	0
Charlie Smith	2	59	43	0
Keith Krepfle	2	16	8	1
John Spagnola	1	22	22	0
Rodney Parker	1	19	19	0
Leroy Harris	1	1	1	0

PASSING	PA	PC	YDS	TD	IN
Ron Jaworski	38	18	291	1	3

OAKLAND RAIDERS

KICKOFF RETURNS	NO	YDS	LNG	TD
Ira Matthews	2	29	21	0
Keith Moody	1	19	19	0

PUNT RETURNS	NO	YDS	LNG	TD
Ira Matthews	2	1	2	0

INTERCEPTION RETURNS	NO	YDS	LNG	TD
Rod Martin	3	44	25	0

PUNTING	NO	YDS	LNG	BLK
Ray Guy	3	42	44	0

PHILADELPHIA EAGLES

KICKOFF RETURNS	NO	YDS	LNG	TD
Billy Campfield	5	87	21	0
Perry Harrington	1	0	0	0

PUNT RETURNS	NO	YDS	LNG	TD
John Sciarra	2	18	12	0
Wally Henry	1	2	2	0

INTERCEPTION RETURNS	NO	YDS	LNG	TD

PUNTING	NO	YDS	LNG	BLK
Max Runager	3	36	46	0

WILD CARDS TAKE OVER NEW ORLEANS

This was the fifth Super Bowl played in New Orleans, but the Oakland Raiders were the first team to discover that people there liked to have fun. At least that's what the reports coming out of the city indicated. The pleasures of the Big Easy were off limits to the Philadelphia Eagles; that apparently included any celebration the night of the game.

Jim Plunkett had filled in for injured Dan Pastorini, and led the Raiders to the wild card and the Super Bowl. He also led Oakland to a touchdown on its first possession. The Raiders faced third-and-4 when Plunkett threw to Kenny King, who raced 80 yards for a 14–0 lead on the final play of the first quarter. Cue the jazz music.

The game wasn't over, but it sure seemed that way. Rod Martin still had to collect the last of his 3 interceptions from Ron Jaworski, Plunkett had to amass the last of his 261 passing yards to be MVP, and the Raiders had to decide how to celebrate the NFL's first wild card Super Bowl championship.

SUPER BOWL XVI

Sunday, January 24, 1982 at Pontiac, MI, Pontiac Silverdome, attendance 81,270   MVP: Joe Montana

	1	2	3	4	—	Final
SAN FRANCISCO 49ERS	7	13	0	6	—	26
CINCINNATI BENGALS	0	0	7	14	—	21

SCORING SF —Montana 1-yd run (Wersching PAT), SF —Cooper 11-yd pass from Montana (Wersching PAT), SF —FG Wersching 22 yds, SF —FG Wersching 26 yds, Cin—Anderson 5-yd run (Breech PAT), Cin—Ross 4-yd pass from Anderson (Breech PAT), SF —FG Wersching 40 yds, SF —FG Wersching 23 yds, Cin—Ross 3-yd pass from Anderson (Breech PAT)

TEAM	FIRST DOWNS	TOTAL YARDAGE	RUSHING	PASSING	RETURNS	ATT-COMP-INT	SACKED	PUNTING	FUMBLES	PENALTIES
SF	20	275	40-127	148	58	22-14-0	1-9	4-46	2-1	8-65
Cin	24	356	24-72	284	35	34-25-2	5-16	3-44	2-2	8-57

SAN FRANCISCO 49ERS

RUSHING	ATT	YDS	LNG	TD
Ricky Patton	17	55	10	0
Earl Cooper	9	34	14	0
Joe Montana	6	18	7	1
Bill Ring	5	17	7	0
Johnny Davis	2	5	4	0
Dwight Clark	1	-2	-2	0

RECEIVING	NO	YDS	LNG	TD
Freddie Solomon	4	52	20	0
Dwight Clark	4	45	17	0
Earl Cooper	2	15	11	0
Mike Wilson	1	22	22	0
Charle Young	1	14	14	0
Ricky Patton	1	6	6	0
Bill Ring	1	3	3	0

PASSING	PA	PC	YDS	TD	IN
Joe Montana	22	14	157	1	0

CINCINNATI BENGALS

RUSHING	ATT	YDS	LNG	TD
Pete Johnson	14	36	5	0
Charles Alexander	5	17	13	0
Ken Anderson	4	15	6	1
Archie Griffin	1	4	4	0

RECEIVING	NO	YDS	LNG	TD
Dan Ross	11	104	16	2
Cris Collinsworth	5	107	49	0
Isaac Curtis	3	42	21	0
Steve Kreider	2	36	19	0
Pete Johnson	2	8	5	0
Charles Alexander	2	3	3	0

PASSING	PA	PC	YDS	TD	IN
Ken Anderson	34	25	300	2	2

SAN FRANCISCO 49ERS

KICKOFF RETURNS	NO	YDS	LNG	TD
Dwight Hicks	1	23	23	0
Amos Lawrence	1	17	17	0

PUNT RETURNS	NO	YDS	LNG	TD
Dwight Hicks	1	6	6	0

INTERCEPTION RETURNS	NO	YDS	LNG	TD
Dwight Hicks	1	27	27	0
Eric Wright	1	25	25	0

PUNTING	NO	YDS	LNG	BLK
Jim Miller	4	46	50	0

CINCINNATI BENGALS

KICKOFF RETURNS	NO	YDS	LNG	TD
David Verser	5	52	16	0
Guy Frazier	1	0	0	0
Archie Griffin	1	0	0	0

PUNT RETURNS	NO	YDS	LNG	TD
Mike Fuller	4	35	17	0

INTERCEPTION RETURNS	NO	YDS	LNG	TD

PUNTING	NO	YDS	LNG	BLK
Pat McInally	3	43	53	0

THE BIG GAME COMES TO MONTANA

Another year, another dome. But for the first time the Super Bowl was played in a place that needed it for warmth. The streets of Detroit seemed almost as cold as Riverfront Stadium, where the Bengals had survived the elements and the frozen San Diego Chargers to reach their first Super Bowl. San Francisco, a 2–14 team just two years earlier, was in town for its first big game, too.

MVP Joe Montana led the 49ers to a 20–0 lead, with 2 field goals coming in the last 18 seconds of the half. Ken Anderson, who had trained under 49ers coach Bill Walsh in Cincinnati, brought the Bengals back. After his touchdown run, Anderson moved Cincinnati to the San Francisco 3. Massive fullback Pete Johnson reached the 1 on first down, but the Bengals got no closer.

Cincinnati scored on its next possession, but the lost opportunity haunted them as Ray Wersching kicked another 2 field goals. Although Anderson's second touchdown to Dan Ross with 16 seconds left made it close, Cincinnati was out in the cold.

SUPER BOWL XVII

Sunday, January 30, 1983 at Pasadena, CA, Rose Bowl, attendance 103,667

MVP: John Riggins

MIAMI DOLPHINS	7	10	0	0	—	17
WASHINGTON REDSKINS	0	10	3	14	—	27

SCORING Mia—Cefalo 76-yd pass from Woodley (von Schamann PAT), Was—FG Moseley 31 yds, Mia—FG von Schamann 20 yds, Was—Garrett 4-yd pass from Theismann (Moseley PAT), Mia—Walker 98-yd kickoff return (von Schamann PAT), Was—FG Moseley 20 yds, Was—Riggins 43-yd run (Moseley PAT), Was—Brown 6-yd pass from Theismann (Moseley PAT)

TEAM	FIRST DOWNS	TOTAL YARDAGE	RUSHING	PASSING	RETURNS	ATT-COMP-INT	SACKED	PUNTING	FUMBLES	PENALTIES
Mia	9	176	29-96	80	22	17-4-1	1-17	6-38	2-1	4-55
Was	24	400	52-276	124	52	23-15-2	3-19	4-42	0-0	5-36

MIAMI DOLPHINS

RUSHING	ATT	YDS	LNG	TD
Aundra Franklin	16	49	9	0
Tony Nathan	7	26	12	0
David Woodley	4	16	7	0
Tommy Vigorito	1	4	4	0
Duriel Harris	1	1	1	0

RECEIVING	NO	YDS	LNG	TD
Jimmy Cefalo	2	82	76	1
Duriel Harris	2	15	8	0

PASSING	PA	PC	YDS	TD	IN
David Woodley	14	4	97	1	1
Don Strock	3	0	0	0	0

WASHINGTON REDSKINS

RUSHING	ATT	YDS	LNG	TD
John Riggins	38	166	43	1
Alvin Garrett	1	44	44	0
Clarence Harmon	9	40	12	0
Joe Theismann	3	20	23	0
Rick Walker	1	6	6	0

RECEIVING	NO	YDS	LNG	TD
Charlie Brown	6	60	26	1
Don Warren	5	28	10	0
Alvin Garrett	2	13	9	1
Rick Walker	1	27	27	0
John Riggins	1	15	15	0

PASSING	PA	PC	YDS	TD	IN
Joe Theismann	23	15	143	2	2

MIAMI DOLPHINS

KICKOFF RETURNS	NO	YDS	LNG	TD
Fulton Walker	4	190	98	1
Lyle Blackwood	2	32	17	0

PUNT RETURNS	NO	YDS	LNG	TD
Tommy Vigorito	2	22	12	0

INTERCEPTION RETURNS	NO	YDS	LNG	TD
Lyle Blackwood	1	0	0	0
A.J. Duhe	1	0	0	0

PUNTING	NO	YDS	LNG	BLK
Tom Orosz	6	37	46	0

SACKS				NO
Bob Baumhower				1
Larry Gordon				1
Earnest Rhone				1

WASHINGTON REDSKINS

KICKOFF RETURNS	NO	YDS	LNG	TD
Mike Nelms	2	44	24	0
Otis Wonsley	1	13	13	0

PUNT RETURNS	NO	YDS	LNG	TD
Mike Nelms	6	52	12	0

INTERCEPTION RETURNS	NO	YDS	LNG	TD
Mark Murphy	1	0	0	0

PUNTING	NO	YDS	LNG	BLK
Jeff Hayes	4	42	54	0

SACKS				NO
Dexter Manley				1

SKINS STRIKE GOLD

The NFL carried a lot of baggage to Pasadena: A strike had wiped seven weeks off the regular season, the "come on down" 16-team playoff system was like those mocked in basketball and hockey, and a new pro football league was finalizing plans for the spring. Miami and Washington had met in Super Bowl VII, Don Shula's "perfect" season. This season was anything but.

David Woodley wasn't much of a passer and the Dolphins didn't put together much offense, only 177 yards in the game, but they managed big plays. Woodley found Jimmy Cefalo in a seam for 76 yards and Fulton Walker returned the first kickoff for a touchdown in Super Bowl history. Miami led at the half, 17–10.

The Dolphins still led in the fourth quarter when John Riggins ran left on fourth down. He shook off a defender and rumbled 43 yards for the deciding touchdown. Riggins, the game's outspoken MVP, ran for 166 yards, his teammates rushed for 110 more, and coach Joe Gibbs and the Redskins had their first Super Bowl title.

SUPER BOWL XVIII

Sunday, January 22, 1984 at Tampa, Tampa Stadium, attendance 72,920

MVP: Marcus Allen

WASHINGTON REDSKINS	0	3	6	0	—	9
LOS ANGELES RAIDERS	7	14	14	3	—	38

SCORING LA—Jensen recovered blocked punt in end zone (Bahr PAT), LA—Branch 12-yd pass from Plunkett (Bahr PAT), Was—FG Moseley 24 yds, LA—Squirek 5-yd interception return (Bahr PAT), Was—Riggins 1-yd run (PAT blocked), LA—Allen 5-yd run (Bahr PAT), LA—Allen 74-yd run (Bahr PAT), LA—FG Bahr 21 yds

TEAM	FIRST DOWNS	TOTAL YARDAGE	RUSHING	PASSING	RETURNS	ATT-COMP-INT	SACKED	PUNTING	FUMBLES	PENALTIES
Was	19	283	32-90	193	35	35-16-2	6-50	8-32	1-1	4-62
LARd	18	385	33-231	154	13	25-16-0	2-18	7-43	3-2	7-56

WASHINGTON REDSKINS

RUSHING	ATT	YDS	LNG	TD
John Riggins	26	64	8	1
Joe Theismann	3	18	8	0
Joe Washington	3	8	5	0

RECEIVING	NO	YDS	LNG	TD
Clint Didier	5	65	20	0
Charlie Brown	3	93	60	0
Joe Washington	3	20	10	0
Nick Giaquinto	2	21	14	0
Art Monk	1	26	26	0
Alvin Garrett	1	17	17	0
John Riggins	1	1	1	0

PASSING	PA	PC	YDS	TD	IN
Joe Theismann	35	16	243	0	2

LOS ANGELES RAIDERS

RUSHING	ATT	YDS	LNG	TD
Marcus Allen	20	191	74	2
Greg Pruitt	5	17	11	0
Kenny King	3	12	10	0
Chester Willis	1	7	7	0
Frank Hawkins	3	6	3	0
Jim Plunkett	1	-2	-2	0

RECEIVING	NO	YDS	LNG	TD
Cliff Branch	6	94	50	1
Todd Christensen	4	32	14	0
Frank Hawkins	2	20	14	0
Marcus Allen	2	18	12	0
Kenny King	2	8	7	0

PASSING	PA	PC	YDS	TD	IN
Jim Plunkett	25	16	172	1	0

WASHINGTON REDSKINS

KICKOFF RETURNS	NO	YDS	LNG	TD
Alvin Garrett	5	100	35	0
Darryl Grant	1	32	32	0
Bruce Kimball	1	0	0	0

PUNT RETURNS	NO	YDS	LNG	TD
Darrell Green	1	34	34	0
Nick Giaquinto	1	1	1	0

INTERCEPTION RETURNS	NO	YDS	LNG	TD

PUNTING	NO	YDS	LNG	BLK
Jeff Hayes	7	37	48	1

SACKS				NO
Monte Coleman				1
Darryl Grant				1

LOS ANGELES RAIDERS

KICKOFF RETURNS	NO	YDS	LNG	TD
Greg Pruitt	1	17	17	0

PUNT RETURNS	NO	YDS	LNG	TD
Greg Pruitt	1	8	8	0
Ted Watts	1	0	0	0

INTERCEPTION RETURNS	NO	YDS	LNG	TD
Jack Squirek	1	5	5	1
Mike Haynes	1	0	0	0

PUNTING	NO	YDS	LNG	BLK
Ray Guy	7	42	47	0

SACKS				NO
Jeff Barnes				1
Mike Davis				1
Rod Martin				1
Hugh Millen				1
Bill Pickel				1
Greg Townsend				1

ALLEN WRENCHES REDSKINS REPEAT

The Raiders, following a contentious move to Los Angeles, were the best team in the AFC. The Redskins were still rolling from the previous season. They lost just twice, both times by a single point.

The Raiders pounded Washington's vaunted offensive line—the Hogs—scrubbing the best running game this side of Walter Payton. This harassment extended to special teams. Derrick Jensen blocked a punt and scored the first points of the game. Forced to put the ball up, Joe Theismann completed 16 passes, the same number as Raider Jim Plunkett, but it required 10 more attempts. The one Theismann regretted most came on first down on his own 12 with 12 seconds left in the half. His swing pass landed in the arms of Jack Squirek, who waltzed 5 yards for the score.

Marcus Allen took over. His 191-yard performance—breaking the mark set a year earlier by Redskin John Riggins—was punctuated by a 74-yard weave across the field in the third quarter that locked up the MVP as surely as it cemented the game.

SUPER BOWL XIX

Sunday, January 20, 1985 at Palo Alto, CA, Stanford Stadium, attendance 84,059 — MVP: Joe Montana

MIAMI DOLPHINS	10	6	0	0 —	16
SAN FRANCISCO 49ERS	7	21	10	0 —	38

SCORING Mia—FG von Schamann 37 yds, SF —Monroe 33-yd pass from Montana (Wersching PAT), Mia—D. Johnson 2-yd pass from Marino (von Schamann PAT), SF —Craig 8-yd pass from Montana (Wersching PAT), SF —Montana 6-yd run (Wersching PAT), SF —Craig 2-yd run (Wersching PAT), Mia—FG von Schamann 31 yds, Mia—FG von Schamann 30 yds, SF —FG Wersching 27 yds, SF —Craig 16-yd pass from Montana (Wersching PAT)

TEAM	FIRST DOWNS	TOTAL YARDAGE	RUSHING	PASSING	RETURNS	ATT-COMP-INT	SACKED	PUNTING	FUMBLES	PENALTIES
Mia	19	314	9-25	289	15	50-29-2	4-29	6-39	1-0	1-10
SF	31	537	40-211	326	51	35-24-0	1-5	3-33	2-2	2-10

MIAMI DOLPHINS

RUSHING	ATT	YDS	LNG	TD
Tony Nathan	5	18	16	0
Woody Bennett	3	7	7	0
Dan Marino	1	0	0	0

RECEIVING	NO	YDS	LNG	TD
Tony Nathan	10	83	25	0
Mark Clayton	6	92	27	0
Joe Rose	6	73	30	0
Dan Johnson	3	28	21	1
Nat Moore	2	17	9	0
Jimmy Cefalo	1	14	14	0
Mark Duper	1	11	11	0

PASSING	PA	PC	YDS	TD	IN
Dan Marino	50	29	318	1	2

SAN FRANCISCO 49ERS

RUSHING	ATT	YDS	LNG	TD
Wendell Tyler	13	65	9	0
Joe Montana	5	59	19	1
Roger Craig	15	58	10	1
Derrick Harmon	5	20	7	0
Freddie Solomon	1	5	5	0
Earl Cooper	1	4	4	0

RECEIVING	NO	YDS	LNG	TD
Roger Craig	7	77	20	2
Dwight Clark	6	77	33	0
Russ Francis	5	60	19	0
Wendell Tyler	4	70	40	0
Carl Monroe	1	33	33	1
Freddie Solomon	1	14	14	0

PASSING	PA	PC	YDS	TD	IN
Joe Montana	35	24	331	3	0

MIAMI DOLPHINS

KICKOFF RETURNS	NO	YDS	LNG	TD
Fulton Walker	4	93	28	0
Bruce Hardy	2	31	16	0
Eddie Hill	1	16	16	0

PUNT RETURNS	NO	YDS	LNG	TD
Fulton Walker	2	15	9	0

INTERCEPTION RETURNS	NO	YDS	LNG	TD

PUNTING	NO	YDS	LNG	BLK
Reggie Roby	6	39	51	0

SACKS				NO
Doug Betters				1

SAN FRANCISCO 49ERS

KICKOFF RETURNS	NO	YDS	LNG	TD
Derrick Harmon	2	24	23	0
Carl Monroe	1	16	16	0
Guy McIntyre	1	0	0	0

PUNT RETURNS	NO	YDS	LNG	TD
Dana McLemore	5	51	28	0

INTERCEPTION RETURNS	NO	YDS	LNG	TD
Carlton Williamson	1	0	0	0
Eric Wright	1	0	0	0

PUNTING	NO	YDS	LNG	BLK
Max Runager	3	32	35	0

SACKS				NO
Dwaine Board				2
Gary Johnson				1
Manu Tuiasosopo				1

A San Francisco Treat

There was enough hype about quarterbacks coming into this game to fill Stanford Stadium, the first Northern California location to host a Super Bowl and the place where Bill Walsh had worked before he got the call to coach in San Francisco. It was home in many ways, and it showed.

Joe Montana felt plenty comfortable, throwing for a then-record 331 yards. Dan Marino had 318 yards, but the San Francisco defense limited an already sketchy Miami running game to just 25 yards. The 49ers knew what was coming, and between MVP Montana and Roger Craig—the first player to score 3 touchdowns in a Super Bowl—San Francisco was able to keep a comfortable lead throughout the game. Miami held two leads; both came in the first quarter.

It seemed that Marino, 23, would get more chances in future Super Bowls, but he never did. Miami coach Don Shula's sixth Super Bowl was also his last. For the 49ers there was more yet to come.

SUPER BOWL XX

Sunday, January 26, 1986 at New Orleans, Louisiana Superdome, attendance 73,818 — MVP: Richard Dent

CHICAGO BEARS	13	10	21	2 —	46
NEW ENGLAND PATRIOTS	3	0	0	7 —	10

SCORING NE —FG Franklin 36 yds, Chi—FG Butler 28 yds, Chi—FG Butler 24 yds, Chi—Suhey 11-yd run (Butler PAT), Chi—McMahon 2-yd run (Butler PAT), Chi—FG Butler 24 yds, Chi—McMahon 1-yd run (Butler PAT), Chi—Phillips 28-yd interception return (Butler PAT), Chi—Perry 1-yd run (Butler PAT), NE —Fryar 8-yd pass from Grogan (Franklin PAT), Chi—Safety, Waechter tackled Grogan in end zone

TEAM	FIRST DOWNS	TOTAL YARDAGE	RUSHING	PASSING	RETURNS	ATT-COMP-INT	SACKED	PUNTING	FUMBLES	PENALTIES
Chi	23	408	49-167	241	95	24-12-0	3-15	4-43	3-2	6-35
NE	12	123	11-7	116	22	36-17-2	7-61	6-44	4-4	5-35

CHICAGO BEARS

RUSHING	ATT	YDS	LNG	TD
Walter Payton	22	61	7	0
Matt Suhey	11	52	11	1
Dennis Gentry	3	15	8	0
Thomas Sanders	4	15	7	0
Jim McMahon	5	14	7	2
Calvin Thomas	2	8	7	0
Steve Fuller	1	1	1	0
William Perry	1	1	1	1

RECEIVING	NO	YDS	LNG	TD
Willie Gault	4	129	60	0
Dennis Gentry	2	41	27	0
Ken Margerum	2	36	29	0
Emery Moorehead	2	22	14	0
Matt Suhey	1	24	24	0
Calvin Thomas	1	4	4	0

PASSING	PA	PC	YDS	TD	IN
Jim McMahon	20	12	256	0	0
Steve Fuller	4	0	0	0	0

NEW ENGLAND PATRIOTS

RUSHING	ATT	YDS	LNG	TD
Tony Collins	3	4	3	0
Steve Grogan	1	3	3	0
Robert Weathers	1	3	3	0
Craig James	5	1	3	0
Greg Hawthorne	1	-4	-4	0

RECEIVING	NO	YDS	LNG	TD
Stanley Morgan	7	70	19	0
Stephen Starring	2	39	24	0
Irving Fryar	2	24	16	1
Tony Collins	2	19	11	0
Derrick Ramsey	2	16	11	0
Craig James	1	6	6	0
Robert Weathers	1	3	3	0

PASSING	PA	PC	YDS	TD	IN
Steve Grogan	30	17	177	1	2
Tony Eason	6	0	0	0	0

CHICAGO BEARS

KICKOFF RETURNS	NO	YDS	LNG	TD
Keith Ortego	2	20	12	0

PUNT RETURNS	NO	YDS	LNG	TD
Keith Ortego	2	20	12	0

INTERCEPTION RETURNS	NO	YDS	LNG	TD
Jim Morrisey	1	47	47	0
Reggie Phillips	1	28	47	1

PUNTING	NO	YDS	LNG	BLK
Maury Buford	4	43	52	0

SACKS				NO
Otis Wilson				2
Richard Dent				1
Dan Hampton				1
Steve McMichael				1
Henry Waechter				1
Wilber Marshall				0

NEW ENGLAND PATRIOTS

KICKOFF RETURNS	NO	YDS	LNG	TD
Irving Fryar	2	22	12	0

PUNT RETURNS	NO	YDS	LNG	TD
Irving Fryar	2	22	12	0

INTERCEPTION RETURNS	NO	YDS	LNG	TD

PUNTING	NO	YDS	LNG	BLK
Rich Camarillo	6	43	62	0

SACKS				NO
Dennis Owens				2
Ben Thomas				1

Bears on a Rampage

The Bears recorded their out-of-tune rap single, "The Super Bowl Shuffle," a few weeks before the game, so they needed a win in New Orleans to increase its air play. They took care of business quickly.

New England had reached its first Super Bowl because of the run; Chicago didn't let anyone run. The leading Patriots rusher, Tony Collins, had 4 yards. Quarterback Tony Eason was removed before he could complete a pass. Replacement Steve Grogan finally found the end zone in the fourth quarter—making it 44–10—but he was soon on his back in his own end zone on a Henry Waechter safety. Bears quarterback Jim McMahon was effective, whether it was throwing for 256 yards or wearing the right headband in his feud with the commissioner.

The defense was very busy … scoring. Reggie Phillips returned an interception 28 yards for a touchdown and defensive tackle William "Refrigerator" Perry ran for a touchdown while Walter Payton watched. MVP Richard Dent wasn't involved in the scoring, but he made sure that the Patriots did precious little.

SUPER BOWL XXI

Sunday, January 25, 1987 at Pasadena, CA, Rose Bowl, attendance 101,063

MVP: Phil Simms

DENVER BRONCOS	10	0	0	10	—	20
NEW YORK GIANTS	7	2	17	13	—	39

SCORING Den—FG Karlis 48 yds, NYG—Mowatt 6-yd pass from Simms (Allegre PAT), Den—Elway 4-yd run (Karlis PAT), NYG—Safety, Martin tackled Elway in end zone, NYG—Bavaro 13-yd pass from Simms (Allegre PAT), NYG—FG Allegre 21 yds, NYG—Morris 1-yd run (Allegre PAT), NYG—McConkey 6-yd pass from Simms (Allegre PAT), Den—FG Karlis 28 yds, NYG—Anderson 2-yd run (PAT failed), Den—V. Johnson 47-yd pass from Elway (Karlis PAT)

TEAM	FIRST DOWNS	TOTAL YARDAGE	RUSHING	PASSING	RETURNS	ATT-COMP-INT	SACKED	PUNTING	FUMBLES	PENALTIES
Den	24	372	19-52	320	9	41-26-1	4-32	2-41	2-0	4-28
NYG	24	399	38-136	263	18	25-22-0	1-5	3-46	0-0	6-48

DENVER BRONCOS

RUSHING	ATT	YDS	LNG	TD
John Elway	6	27	10	1
Gerald Willhite	4	19	11	0
Steve Sewell	3	4	12	0
Gene Lang	2	2	4	0
Sammy Winder	4	0		0

RECEIVING	NO	YDS	LNG	TD
Vance Johnson	5	121	54	1
Gerald Willhite	5	39	11	0
Sammy Winder	4	34	14	0
Mark Jackson	3	51	24	0
Steve Watson	2	54	31	0
Clint Sampson	2	20	11	0
Orson Mobley	2	17	11	0
Steve Sewell	2	12	7	0
Gene Lang	1	4	4	0

PASSING	PA	PC	YDS	TD	IN
John Elway	37	22	304	1	1
Gary Kubiak	4	4	48	0	0

NEW YORK GIANTS

RUSHING	ATT	YDS	LNG	TD
Joe Morris	20	67	11	1
Phil Simms	3	25	22	0
Lee Rouson	3	22	18	0
Tony Galbreath	4	17	7	0
Maurice Carthon	3	4	2	0
Ottis Anderson	2	1	2	1
Jeff Rutledge	3	0		0

RECEIVING	NO	YDS	LNG	TD
Mark Bavaro	4	51	17	1
Joe Morris	4	20	12	0
Maurice Carthon	4	13	7	0
Stacy Robinson	3	62	36	0
Lionel Manuel	3	43	17	0
Phil McConkey	2	50	44	1
Lee Rouson	1	23	23	0
Zeke Mowatt	1	6	6	1

PASSING	PA	PC	YDS	TD	IN
Phil Simms	25	22	268	3	0

DENVER BRONCOS

KICKOFF RETURNS	NO	YDS	LNG	TD
Ken Bell	3	48	28	0
Gene Lang	2	36	23	0

PUNT RETURNS	NO	YDS	LNG	TD
Gerald Willhite	1	9	9	0

INTERCEPTION RETURNS	NO	YDS	LNG	TD

PUNTING	NO	YDS	LNG	BLK
Mike Horan	2	41	42	0

SACKS				NO
Freddie Gilbert				0
Ken Woodard				0

NEW YORK GIANTS

KICKOFF RETURNS	NO	YDS	LNG	TD
Lee Rouson	3	56	33	0
Tom Flynn	1	-3	-3	0

PUNT RETURNS	NO	YDS	LNG	TD
Phil McConkey	1	25	25	0

INTERCEPTION RETURNS	NO	YDS	LNG	TD
Elvis Patterson	1	-7	-7	0

PUNTING	NO	YDS	LNG	BLK
Sean Landeta	3	46	59	0

SACKS				NO
Leonard Marshall				2
Eric Dorsey				1
George Martin				1

A GIANT IN THE SADDLE

The New York Giants hadn't won a championship in 30 years; the Denver Broncos had never won one, not even in the AFL. Something had to give.

The Giants were heavy favorites, but Denver looked good early. John Elway ran for a touchdown, but Rich Karlis was just 1-for-3 in field goals. Denver took a slim 10–9 lead into the half. Then Phil Simms went from having a good game to an all-time great one. He completed a Super Bowl-record 10 straight passes, finishing the day with 22 completions in 25 tries for 268 yards and 3 touchdowns to claim MVP. His 13-yard pass to Mark Bavarro in the third quarter gave the Giants the lead for good. New York put up 17 more points before Denver scored again.

Bill Parcells's first championship ended a long period of darkness for owner Wellington Mara that started to brighten with the drafting of Simms in 1979. For Denver coach Dan Reeves, whose team put together an epic drive in Cleveland to get to Pasadena, his club had been picked apart.

SUPER BOWL XXII

Sunday, January 31, 1988 at San Diego, Jack Murphy Stadium, attendance 73,302

MVP: Doug Williams

WASHINGTON REDSKINS	0	35	0	7	—	42
DENVER BRONCOS	10	0	0	0	—	10

SCORING Den—Nattiel 56-yd pass from Elway (Karlis PAT), Den—FG Karlis 24 yds, Was—Sanders 80-yd pass from Williams (Haji-Sheikh PAT), Was—Clark 27-yd pass from Williams (Haji-Sheikh PAT), Was—Smith 58-yd run (Haji-Sheikh PAT), Was—Sanders 50-yd pass from Williams (Haji-Sheikh PAT), Was—Didier 8-yd pass from Williams (Haji-Sheikh PAT), Was—Smith 4-yd run (Haji-Sheikh PAT)

TEAM	FIRST DOWNS	TOTAL YARDAGE	RUSHING	PASSING	RETURNS	ATT-COMP-INT	SACKED	PUNTING	FUMBLES	PENALTIES
Was	25	602	40-280	322	11	30-18-1	2-18	4-38	1-0	6-65
Den	18	327	17-97	230	18	39-15-3	5-50	7-36	0-0	5-26

WASHINGTON REDSKINS

RUSHING	ATT	YDS	LNG	TD
Timmy Smith	22	204	58	2
Kelvin Bryant	8	38	15	0
Gary Clark	1	25	25	0
George Rogers	5	17	5	0
Keith Griffin	1	2	2	0
Doug Williams	2	-2	-1	0
Ricky Sanders	1	-4	-4	0

RECEIVING	NO	YDS	LNG	TD
Ricky Sanders	9	193	80	2
Gary Clark	3	55	27	1
Don Warren	2	15	9	0
Art Monk	1	40	40	0
Kelvin Bryant	1	20	20	0
Timmy Smith	1	9	9	0
Clint Didier	1	8	8	1

PASSING	PA	PC	YDS	TD	IN
Doug Williams	29	18	340	4	1
Jay Schroeder	1	0	0	0	0

DENVER BRONCOS

RUSHING	ATT	YDS	LNG	TD
Gene Lang	5	38	13	0
John Elway	3	32	21	0
Sammy Winder	8	30	13	0
Steve Sewell	1	-3	-3	0

RECEIVING	NO	YDS	LNG	TD
Mark Jackson	4	76	32	0
Steve Sewell	4	41	18	0
Ricky Nattiel	2	69	56	1
Clarence Kay	2	38	27	0
Sammy Winder	1	26	26	0
John Elway	1	23	23	0
Gene Lang	1	7	7	0

PASSING	PA	PC	YDS	TD	IN
John Elway	38	14	257	1	3
Steve Sewell	1	1	23	0	0

WASHINGTON REDSKINS

KICKOFF RETURNS	NO	YDS	LNG	TD
Ricky Sanders	3	46	16	0

PUNT RETURNS	NO	YDS	LNG	TD
Darrell Green	1	0	0	0

INTERCEPTION RETURNS	NO	YDS	LNG	TD
Barry Wilburn	2	11	11	0
Brian Davis	1	0	0	0

PUNTING	NO	YDS	LNG	BLK
Steve Cox	4	37	42	0

SACKS				NO
Alvin Walton				2
Dexter Manley				1
Charles Mann				1
Monte Coleman				0

DENVER BRONCOS

KICKOFF RETURNS	NO	YDS	LNG	TD
Ken Bell	5	88	21	0

PUNT RETURNS	NO	YDS	LNG	TD
Kevin Clark	2	18	9	0

INTERCEPTION RETURNS	NO	YDS	LNG	TD
Jeremiah Castille	1	0	0	0

PUNTING	NO	YDS	LNG	BLK
Mike Horan	7	36	43	0

SACKS				NO
Rulon Jones				1
Karl Mecklenburg				1

IT ONLY LASTS A SECOND (QUARTER)

Although the replacements from the NFL strike were long gone, Doug Williams still replaced Jay Schroeder, who had been injured late in the season. Williams endured two weeks of nonsense about being the first African American starting quarterback in the Super Bowl. He was actually asked, "How long have you been a black quarterback?" Williams shut up everybody with an incredible performance.

The Broncos led in the first quarter, 10–0, and it looked like maybe this was Denver's year. Then the second quarter started.

Washington scored 5 touchdowns: Williams threw 4 and another came on a 58-yard run by rookie Timmy Smith. Smith had his own remarkable day with a record 204 yards rushing, but Williams was the MVP. He threw for 228 yards in the second quarter alone and finished with a then-record 340 passing yards. Washington amassed 602 yards of total offense.

Only in four Super Bowls—the last four, it so happened—had a team even scored 35 points in a game, much less a quarter. *Sports Illustrated* summed it up best on its cover: "Wow!"

SUPER BOWL XXIII

Sunday, January 22, 1989 at Miami, Joe Robbie Stadium, attendance 75,129

MVP: Jerry Rice

CINCINNATI BENGALS	0	3	10	3	—	16
SAN FRANCISCO 49ERS	3	0	3	14	—	20

SCORING SF —FG Cofer 41 yds, Cin—FG Breech 34 yds, Cin—FG Breech 43 yds, SF —FG Cofer 32 yds, Cin—Jennings 93-yd kickoff return (Breech PAT), SF —Rice 14-yd pass from Montana (Cofer PAT), Cin—FG Breech 40 yds, SF —Taylor 10-yd pass from Montana (Cofer PAT)

TEAM	FIRST DOWNS	TOTAL YARDAGE	RUSHING	PASSING	RETURNS	ATT-COMP-INT	SACKED	PUNTING	FUMBLES	PENALTIES
Cin	13	229	28-106	123	5	25-11-1	5-21	5-45	1-0	7-65
SF	23	453	27-112	341	56	36-23-0	3-16	4-37	4-2	4-32

CINCINNATI BENGALS

RUSHING	ATT	YDS	LNG	TD
Ickey Woods	20	79	10	0
James Brooks	6	24	11	0
Stanford Jennings	1	3	3	0
Boomer Esiason	1	0	0	0

RECEIVING	NO	YDS	LNG	TD
Eddie Brown	4	44	17	0
Cris Collinsworth	3	40	23	0
Tim McGee	2	23	18	0
James Brooks	1	20	20	0
Ira Hillary	1	17	17	0

PASSING	PA	PC	YDS	TD	IN
Boomer Esiason	25	11	144	0	1

SAN FRANCISCO 49ERS

RUSHING	ATT	YDS	LNG	TD
Roger Craig	17	71	13	0
Tom Rathman	5	23	11	0
Joe Montana	4	13	11	0
Jerry Rice	1	5	5	0

RECEIVING	NO	YDS	LNG	TD
Jerry Rice	11	215	44	1
Roger Craig	8	101	40	0
John Frank	2	15	8	0
Tom Rathman	1	16	16	0
John Taylor	1	10	10	1

PASSING	PA	PC	YDS	TD	IN
Joe Montana	36	23	357	2	0

CINCINNATI BENGALS

KICKOFF RETURNS	NO	YDS	LNG	TD
Stanford Jennings	2	117	93	1
James Brooks	1	15	15	0

PUNT RETURNS	NO	YDS	LNG	TD
Ray Horton	1	5	5	0
Ira Hillary	1	0	0	0

INTERCEPTION RETURNS	NO	YDS	LNG	TD

PUNTING	NO	YDS	LNG	BLK
Lee Johnson	5	44	63	0

SACKS	NO
Jason Buck	1
David Fulcher	1
Reggie Williams	1

SAN FRANCISCO 49ERS

KICKOFF RETURNS	NO	YDS	LNG	TD
Del Rodgers	3	53	22	0
John Taylor	1	13	13	0
Harry Sydney	1	11	11	0

PUNT RETURNS	NO	YDS	LNG	TD
John Taylor	3	56	45	0

INTERCEPTION RETURNS	NO	YDS	LNG	TD
Bill Romanowski	1	0	0	0

PUNTING	NO	YDS	LNG	BLK
Barry Helton	4	37	55	0

SACKS	NO
Charles Haley	2
Michael Carter	1
Kevin Fagan	1
Danny Stubbs	1

FOR ONCE, A SUPER ENDING

This rematch of Super Bowl XVI arrived with tragedy in the air. There were riots that week in a nearby section of Miami, and Bengals fullback Stanley Wilson missed the game because of a cocaine relapse.

The game was tied in the third quarter, 6–6, when Cincinnati's Stanford Jennings returned the kickoff 93 yards for a touchdown. Joe Montana, in the midst of another brilliant Super Bowl, teamed with Jerry Rice on an acrobatic 14-yard touchdown to tie the game in the fourth quarter. Jim Breech's field goal put the Bengals up with 3:10 remaining.

Taking over at his own 8, Montana got into field goal range with 1:15 left on a 27-yard pass to Rice, the game's MVP with 215 receiving yards. The 49ers wanted more. Montana found John Taylor in the end zone with 34 seconds remaining.

Cincinnati coach Sam Wyche had begun as a quarterback under Bill Walsh, a first-year assistant for the expansion Bengals, in 1968; Wyche knew he'd been beaten by the best. San Francisco's third championship was Walsh's last game in the NFL.

SUPER BOWL XXIV

Sunday, January 28, 1990 at New Orleans, Louisiana Superdome, attendance 72,919

MVP: Joe Montana

SAN FRANCISCO 49ERS	13	14	14	14	—	55
DENVER BRONCOS	3	0	7	0	—	10

SCORING SF —Rice 20-yd pass from Montana (Cofer PAT), Den—FG Treadwell 42 yds, SF —Jones 7-yd pass from Montana (PAT failed), SF —Rathman 1-yd run (Cofer PAT), SF —Rice 38-yd pass from Montana (Cofer PAT), SF —Rice 28-yd pass from Montana (Cofer PAT), SF —Taylor 35-yd pass from Montana (Cofer PAT), Den—Elway 3-yd run (Treadwell PAT), SF —Rathman 3-yd run (Cofer PAT), SF —Craig 1-yd run (Cofer PAT)

TEAM	FIRST DOWNS	TOTAL YARDAGE	RUSHING	PASSING	RETURNS	ATT-COMP-INT	SACKED	PUNTING	FUMBLES	PENALTIES
SF	28	461	44-144	317	80	32-24-0	1-0	4-40	0-0	4-38
Den	12	167	17-64	103	11	29-11-2	6-33	6-39	3-2	0-0

SAN FRANCISCO 49ERS

RUSHING	ATT	YDS	LNG	TD
Roger Craig	20	69	18	1
Tom Rathman	11	38	18	2
Joe Montana	2	15	10	0
Terrence Flagler	6	14	10	0
Steve Young	4	6	11	0
Harry Sydney	1	2	2	0

RECEIVING	NO	YDS	LNG	TD
Jerry Rice	7	148	38	3
Roger Craig	5	34	12	0
Tom Rathman	4	43	18	0
John Taylor	3	49	35	1
Mike Sherrard	1	13	13	0
Wesley Walls	1	9	9	0
Brent Jones	1	7	7	1
Harry Sydney	1	7	7	0
Jamie Williams	1	7	7	0

PASSING	PA	PC	YDS	TD	IN
Joe Montana	29	22	297	5	0
Steve Young	3	2	20	0	0

DENVER BRONCOS

RUSHING	ATT	YDS	LNG	TD
Bobby Humphrey	12	61	34	0
John Elway	4	8	3	1
Sammy Winder	1	-5	-5	0

RECEIVING	NO	YDS	LNG	TD
Bobby Humphrey	3	38	27	0
Steve Sewell	2	22	12	0
Vance Johnson	2	21	13	0
Ricky Nattiel	1	28	28	0
Mel Bratton	1	14	14	0
Sammy Winder	1	7	7	0
Clarence Kay	1	6	6	0

PASSING	PA	PC	YDS	TD	IN
John Elway	26	10	108	0	2
Gary Kubiak	3	1	28	0	0

SAN FRANCISCO 49ERS

KICKOFF RETURNS	NO	YDS	LNG	TD
Terrence Flagler	3	49	22	0

PUNT RETURNS	NO	YDS	LNG	TD
John Taylor	3	38	17	0

INTERCEPTION RETURNS	NO	YDS	LNG	TD
Chet Brooks	1	38	38	0
Mike Walter	1	4	4	0

PUNTING	NO	YDS	LNG	BLK
Barry Helton	4	39	47	0

SACKS	NO
Danny Stubbs	2
Kevin Fagan	1
Don Griffin	1
Pete Kugler	1
Larry Roberts	1

DENVER BRONCOS

KICKOFF RETURNS	NO	YDS	LNG	TD
Darren Carrington	6	146	39	0
Ken Bell	2	41	24	0
Tyrone Braxton	1	9	9	0

PUNT RETURNS	NO	YDS	LNG	TD
Vance Johnson	2	11	7	0

INTERCEPTION RETURNS	NO	YDS	LNG	TD

PUNTING	NO	YDS	LNG	BLK
Mike Horan	6	38	43	0

SACKS	NO
Tyrone Braxton	1

SUPERDOME SUPER ROUT

The 49ers were 11½-point favorites going in; that spread was covered before halftime. San Francisco scored 2 touchdowns each quarter, abetted by 4 Denver turnovers.

San Francisco led, 7–3, when the Broncos fumbled at midfield in the first quarter. Joe Montana quickly moved the 49ers down the field, culminating with a 7-yard touchdown pass to Brent Jones. If Mike Cofer's missed PAT was seen by anyone as some sort of sign, the sign most certainly wasn't "yield." Three plays later, Denver punted; 13 plays after that, aided by a Tom Rathman fourth-down conversion, it was 20–3. The blowout was at hand.

Joe Montana won his third Super Bowl MVP, throwing for 297 yards and a then-record 5 touchdowns. Jerry Rice caught 3 touchdown passes; Rathman scored twice. Nine different 49ers caught passes on the day.

For San Francisco's George Seifert, it was the end of a sensational first season as a head coach. For Denver coach Dan Reeves and quarterback John Elway, it was their third Super Bowl humiliation in four years.

SUPER BOWL XXV

Sunday, January 27, 1991 at Tampa, Tampa Stadium, attendance 73,813

MVP: Ottis Anderson

BUFFALO BILLS	3	9	0	7	—	19
NEW YORK GIANTS	3	7	7	3	—	20

SCORING NYG—FG Bahr 28 yds, Buf—FG Norwood 23 yds, Buf—D. Smith 1-yd run (Norwood PAT), Buf—Safety, Smith tackled Hostetler in end zone, NYG—Baker 14-yd pass from Hostetler (Bahr PAT), NYG—Anderson 1-yd run (Bahr PAT), Buf—Thomas 31-yd run (Norwood PAT), NYG—FG Bahr 21 yds

TEAM	FIRST DOWNS	TOTAL YARDAGE	RUSHING	PASSING	RETURNS	ATT-COMP-INT	SACKED	PUNTING	FUMBLES	PENALTIES
Buf	18	371	25-166	205	0	30-18-0	1-7	6-39	1-0	6-35
NYG	24	386	39-172	214	37	32-20-0	2-8	4-44	0-0	5-31

BUFFALO BILLS

RUSHING	ATT	YDS	LNG	TD
Thurman Thomas	15	135	31	1
Jim Kelly	6	23	9	0
Kenneth Davis	2	4	3	0
Jamie Mueller	1	3	3	0
Don Smith	1	1	1	1

RECEIVING	NO	YDS	LNG	TD
Andre Reed	8	62	20	0
Thurman Thomas	5	55	15	0
Kenneth Davis	2	23	19	0
Keith McKeller	2	11	6	0
James Lofton	1	61	61	0

PASSING	PA	PC	YDS	TD	IN
Jim Kelly	30	18	212	0	0

NEW YORK GIANTS

RUSHING	ATT	YDS	LNG	TD
Ottis Anderson	21	102	24	1
Dave Meggett	9	48	17	0
Maurice Carthon	3	12	5	0
Jeff Hostetler	6	10	5	0

RECEIVING	NO	YDS	LNG	TD
Mark Ingram	5	74	22	0
Mark Bavaro	5	50	19	0
Howard Cross	4	39	13	0
Stephen Baker	2	31	17	1
Dave Meggett	2	18	11	0
Ottis Anderson	1	7	7	0
Maurice Carthon	1	3	3	0

PASSING	PA	PC	YDS	TD	IN
Jeff Hostetler	32	20	222	1	0

BUFFALO BILLS

KICKOFF RETURNS	NO	YDS	LNG	TD
Don Smith	4	66	24	0
Al Edwards	2	48	33	0

PUNT RETURNS	NO	YDS	LNG	TD

PUNTING	NO	YDS	LNG	BLK
Rick Tuten	6	38	47	0

SACKS	NO
Bruce Smith	1
Jeff Wright	1

NEW YORK GIANTS

KICKOFF RETURNS	NO	YDS	LNG	TD
Dave Meggett	2	26	16	0
Dave Duerson	1	22	22	0

PUNT RETURNS	NO	YDS	LNG	TD
Dave Meggett	2	37	20	0

PUNTING	NO	YDS	LNG	BLK
Sean Landeta	4	43	54	0

SACKS	NO
Leonard Marshall	1

SAILING RIGHT FOR GIANTS

There was a lot on people's minds heading into the Super Bowl. The Gulf War was in its second week and Tampa Stadium exuded both patriotism and uneasiness. ABC showed a live news broadcast at halftime and the Disney-themed halftime show was on tape delay.

The game itself was a classic. Giants coach Bill Parcells figured the best way to handle the quick-strike, no-huddle Bills was to keep them off the field. New York controlled the ball for more than 40 minutes. And they did it with a backup quarterback. Jeff Hostetler had started just twice in seven seasons until Phil Simms got hurt late in the year. Hostetler completed 20 passes for 222 yards, but New York relied heavily on Ottis Anderson, who rushed for 102 yards to earn MVP.

The lead fluctuated until Matt Bahr's field goal put the Giants ahead in the fourth quarter. Buffalo's Scott Norwood had a long-range shot at winning the game, but his 47-yard kick sailed wide right with four seconds left. It was the narrowest margin ever in a Super Bowl.

SUPER BOWL XXVI

Sunday, January 26, 1992 at Bloomington, MN, Metrodome, attendance 63,130

MVP: Mark Rypien

WASHINGTON REDSKINS	0	17	14	6	—	37
BUFFALO BILLS	0	0	10	14	—	24

SCORING Was—FG Lohmiller 34 yds, Was—Byner 10-yd pass from Rypien (Lohmiller PAT), Was—Riggs 1-yd run (Lohmiller PAT), Was—Riggs 2-yd run (Lohmiller PAT), Buf—FG Norwood 21 yds, Buf—Thomas 1-yd run (Norwood PAT), Was—Clark 30-yd pass from Rypien (Lohmiller PAT), Was—FG Lohmiller 25 yds, Was—FG Lohmiller 39 yds, Buf—Metzelaars 2-yd pass from Kelly (Norwood PAT), Buf—Beebe 4-yd pass from Kelly (Norwood PAT)

TEAM	FIRST DOWNS	TOTAL YARDAGE	RUSHING	PASSING	RETURNS	ATT-COMP-INT	SACKED	PUNTING	FUMBLES	PENALTIES
Was	24	417	40-125	292	79	33-18-1	0-0	4-38	1-0	5-82
Buf	25	283	18-43	240	13	59-29-4	5-46	6-35	6-1	6-50

WASHINGTON REDSKINS

RUSHING	ATT	YDS	LNG	TD
Ricky Ervins	13	72	21	0
Earnest Byner	14	49	19	0
Gerald Riggs	5	7	4	2
Ricky Sanders	1	1	1	0
Jeff Rutledge	1	0	0	0
Mark Rypien	6	-4	2	0

RECEIVING	NO	YDS	LNG	TD
Gary Clark	7	114	34	1
Art Monk	7	113	31	0
Earnest Byner	3	24	10	1
Ricky Sanders	1	41	41	0

PASSING	PA	PC	YDS	TD	IN
Mark Rypien	33	18	292	2	1

BUFFALO BILLS

RUSHING	ATT	YDS	LNG	TD
Kenneth Davis	4	17	13	0
Jim Kelly	3	16	9	0
Thurman Thomas	10	13	6	1
James Lofton	1	-3	-3	0

RECEIVING	NO	YDS	LNG	TD
James Lofton	7	92	18	0
Andre Reed	5	34	12	0
Don Beebe	4	61	43	1
Kenneth Davis	4	38	12	0
Thurman Thomas	4	27	8	0
Keith McKeller	2	29	21	0
Al Edwards	1	11	11	0
Pete Metzelaars	1	2	2	1
Jim Kelly	1	-8	-8	0

PASSING	PA	PC	YDS	TD	IN
Jim Kelly	58	28	275	2	4
Frank Reich	1	1	11	0	0

WASHINGTON REDSKINS

KICKOFF RETURNS	NO	YDS	LNG	TD
Brian Mitchell	1	16	16	0

PUNT RETURNS	NO	YDS	LNG	TD

INTERCEPTION RETURNS	NO	YDS	LNG	TD
Brad Edwards	2	56	35	0
Kurt Gouveia	1	23	23	0
Darrell Green	1	0	0	0

PUNTING	NO	YDS	LNG	BLK
Kelly Goodburn	4	37	45	0

SACKS	NO
Jason Buck	1
Jumpy Geathers	1
Wilber Marshall	1
Alvoid Mays	1
Fred Stokes	1

BUFFALO BILLS

KICKOFF RETURNS	NO	YDS	LNG	TD
Al Edwards	4	77	24	0

PUNT RETURNS	NO	YDS	LNG	TD
Cliff Hicks	3	9	7	0

INTERCEPTION RETURNS	NO	YDS	LNG	TD
Kirby Jackson	1	4	4	0

PUNTING	NO	YDS	LNG	BLK
Chris Mohr	6	35	53	0

SACKS	NO

RYPIEN ROARING FOR REDSKINS

It was so cold in Minneapolis they skated on the field. Actually, the field was quite warm indoors and former Olympic gold medallists Brian Boitano and Dorothy Hamill did the skating on ice embedded on large platforms on the field. Not coincidentally, the game was shown by CBS, which was to broadcast the upcoming Winter Olympics.

The Redskins slipped up on their first 2 possessions, but they rallied for 17 second-quarter points. The second touchdown run by Gerald Riggs made it 24–0 before Buffalo scored on successive possessions. The Redskins ran off the next 13 points. Two Jim Kelly touchdown passes in the fourth quarter—he threw 58 times on the day—made the game sound remotely close. It wasn't.

Mark Rypien passed for 292 yards and 3 touchdown to earn MVP. Rypien was the third different quarterback Washington coach Joe Gibbs had used to win a championship. Thurman Thomas, who'd rushed for 135 in the previous year's Super Bowl, ran for 13 yards against Washington. He missed part of the opening series because he couldn't find his helmet.

SUPER BOWL XXVII

Sunday, January 31, 1993 at Los Angeles, Rose Bowl, attendance 98,374   MVP: Troy Aikman

BUFFALO BILLS	7	3	7	0	—	17
DALLAS COWBOYS	**14**	**14**	**3**	**21**	**—**	**52**

SCORING Buf—Thomas 2-yd run (Christie PAT), Dal—Novacek 23-yd pass from Aikman (Elliott PAT), Dal—J. Jones 2-yd fumble return (Elliott PAT), Buf—FG Christie 21 yds, Dal—Irvin 19-yd pass from Aikman (Elliott PAT), Dal—Irvin 18-yd pass from Aikman (Elliott PAT), Dal—FG Elliott 20 yds, Buf—Beebe 40-yd pass from Reich (Christie PAT), Dal—Harper 45-yd pass from Aikman (Elliott PAT), Dal—E. Smith 10-yd run (Elliott PAT), Dal—Norton 9-yd fumble return (Elliott PAT)

TEAM	FIRST DOWNS	TOTAL YARDAGE	RUSHING	PASSING	RETURNS	ATT-COMP-INT	SACKED	PUNTING	FUMBLES	PENALTIES
Buf	22	362	29-108	254	0	38-22-4	4-22	3-45	8-5	4-30
Dal	20	408	29-137	271	70	30-22-0	1-2	4-33	3-1	8-53

BUFFALO BILLS

RUSHING	ATT	YDS	LNG	TD
Kenneth Davis	15	86	14	0
Thurman Thomas	11	19	9	1
Carwell Gardner	1	3	3	0
Frank Reich	2	0	0	0

RECEIVING	NO	YDS	LNG	TD
Andre Reed	8	152	40	0
Thurman Thomas	4	10	7	0
Kenneth Davis	3	16	13	0
Don Beebe	2	50	40	1
Steve Tasker	2	30	16	0
Pete Metzelaars	2	12	7	0
Keith McKeller	1	6	6	0

PASSING	PA	PC	YDS	TD	IN
Frank Reich	31	18	194	1	2
Jim Kelly	7	4	82	0	2

DALLAS COWBOYS

RUSHING	ATT	YDS	LNG	TD
Emmitt Smith	22	108	38	1
Troy Aikman	3	28	19	0
Derrick Gainer	2	1	1	0
Steve Beuerlein	1	0	0	0
Daryl Johnston	1	0	0	0

RECEIVING	NO	YDS	LNG	TD
Jay Novacek	7	72	23	1
Michael Irvin	6	114	25	2
Emmitt Smith	6	27	18	0
Daryl Johnston	2	15	8	0
Alvin Harper	1	45	45	1

PASSING	PA	PC	YDS	TD	IN
Troy Aikman	30	22	273	4	0

BUFFALO BILLS

KICKOFF RETURNS	NO	YDS	LNG	TD
Brad Lamb	2	49	33	0
Kenneth Davis	1	21	21	0
Cliff Hicks	1	20	20	0

PUNT RETURNS	NO	YDS	LNG	TD
Cliff Hicks	1	0	0	0

INTERCEPTION RETURNS	NO	YDS	LNG	TD

PUNTING	NO	YDS	LNG	BLK
Chris Mohr	3	45	48	0

SACKS				NO
Bruce Smith				1

DALLAS COWBOYS

KICKOFF RETURNS	NO	YDS	LNG	TD
Kelvin Martin	4	79	22	0

PUNT RETURNS	NO	YDS	LNG	TD
Kelvin Martin	3	35	30	0

INTERCEPTION RETURNS	NO	YDS	LNG	TD
Thomas Everett	2	22	22	0
James Washington	1	13	13	0
Larry Brown	1	0	0	0

PUNTING	NO	YDS	LNG	BLK
Mike Saxon	3	43	57	1

SACKS				NO
Thomas Everett				1
Charles Haley				1
Jim Jeffcoat				1
Leon Lett				1

Cowboys Overrun Buffalo

Dallas hadn't been to a Super Bowl since 1979. Buffalo hadn't been to a Super Bowl since, well, last year . . . and the year before that. Still, the Cowboys were favored by a touchdown.

Steve Tasker blocked a punt after the first Cowboys possession. The Bills scored a touchdown. Dallas punted again and the Bills moved to midfield. Then Buffalo's nightmare began. Jim Kelly was intercepted and Dallas marched to a tying touchdown. Charles Haley sacked Kelly and Jimmie Jones snagged the ball for a touchdown.

Two scores 15 seconds apart was a new Super Bowl record. A Buffalo field goal was offset by a pair of touchdowns from MVP Troy Aikman to Michael Irvin. Buffalo had 9 turnovers; the points piled up like snow in Buffalo.

The Bills had one moment. Leon Lett took off with a fourth-quarter fumble, slowing down to showboat as he neared the goal line. Hustling Bills wide receiver Don Beebe knocked the ball away for a touchback. It was a small victory, but Buffalo was still 0–3 in the big game.

SUPER BOWL XXVIII

Sunday, January 30, 1994 at Atlanta, Georgia Dome, attendance 72,817   MVP: Emmitt Smith

DALLAS COWBOYS	**6**	**0**	**14**	**10**	**—**	**30**
BUFFALO BILLS	3	10	0	0	—	13

SCORING Dal—FG Murray 41 yds, Buf—FG Christie 54 yds, Dal—FG Murray 24 yds, Buf—Thomas 4-yd run (Christie PAT), Buf—FG Christie 28 yds, Dal—Washington 48-yd fumble return (Murray PAT), Dal—E. Smith 15-yd run (Murray PAT), Dal—E. Smith 1-yd run (Murray PAT), Dal—FG Murray 20 yds

TEAM	FIRST DOWNS	TOTAL YARDAGE	RUSHING	PASSING	RETURNS	ATT-COMP-INT	SACKED	PUNTING	FUMBLES	PENALTIES
Dal	20	341	35-137	204	17	27-19-1	2-3	4-44	0-0	6-50
Buf	22	314	27-87	227	46	50-31-1	3-33	5-38	3-2	1-10

DALLAS COWBOYS

RUSHING	ATT	YDS	LNG	TD
Emmitt Smith	30	132	15	2
Kevin Williams	1	6	6	0
Troy Aikman	1	3	3	0
Daryl Johnston	1	0	0	0
Bernie Kosar	1	-1	-1	0
Lincoln Coleman	1	-3	-3	0

RECEIVING	NO	YDS	LNG	TD
Michael Irvin	5	66	20	0
Jay Novacek	5	26	9	0
Emmitt Smith	4	26	10	0
Alvin Harper	3	75	35	0
Daryl Johnston	2	14	11	0

PASSING	PA	PC	YDS	TD	IN
Troy Aikman	27	19	207	0	1

BUFFALO BILLS

RUSHING	ATT	YDS	LNG	TD
Kenneth Davis	9	38	11	0
Thurman Thomas	16	37	6	1
Jim Kelly	2	12	8	0

RECEIVING	NO	YDS	LNG	TD
Bill Brooks	7	63	15	0
Thurman Thomas	7	52	24	0
Andre Reed	6	75	22	0
Don Beebe	6	60	18	0
Kenneth Davis	3	-5	7	0
Pete Metzelaars	1	8	8	0
Keith McKeller	1	7	7	0

PASSING	PA	PC	YDS	TD	IN
Jim Kelly	50	31	260	0	1

DALLAS COWBOYS

KICKOFF RETURNS	NO	YDS	LNG	TD
Kevin Williams	1	50	50	0
Kenneth Gant	1	22	22	0

PUNT RETURNS	NO	YDS	LNG	TD
Kevin Williams	1	5	5	0

INTERCEPTION RETURNS	NO	YDS	LNG	TD
James Washington	1	12	12	0

PUNTING	NO	YDS	LNG	BLK
John Jett	4	43	47	0

SACKS				NO
Jim Jeffcoat				1
Tony Casillas				0
Charles Haley				0
Tony Tolbert				0

BUFFALO BILLS

KICKOFF RETURNS	NO	YDS	LNG	TD
Russell Copeland	4	82	22	0
Don Beebe	2	62	34	0

PUNT RETURNS	NO	YDS	LNG	TD
Russell Copeland	1	5	5	0

INTERCEPTION RETURNS	NO	YDS	LNG	TD
Nate Odomes	1	41	41	0

PUNTING	NO	YDS	LNG	BLK
Chris Mohr	5	37	52	0

SACKS				NO
Jeff Wright				3

A Super Bowl Rerun

This Super Bowl rematch at the Georgia Dome would need more than a country music salute to make people forget the shellacking Dallas had inflicted on Buffalo in Pasadena. The Bills were the first team to reach four straight Super Bowls, and they desperately wanted to avoid losing them all.

Buffalo's Steve Christie kicked the longest field goal in Super Bowl history, a 54-yarder in the first quarter. Trailing, 6–3, the Bills caught a rare break when a running into the kicker penalty awarded them a first down. Thurman Thomas converted it into a touchdown and Christie added another field goal. Buffalo had its first halftime lead in the Super Bowl in three years.

In the first minute of the second half, Thomas fumbled and James Washington zigged his way for a game-tying score. Then Emmitt Smith took over the game. He scored twice, racking up 132 rushing yards on 30 carries to earn MVP. The Bills, on the other hand, had become pro football's Rodney Dangerfield, earning no respect despite being the second-best team each year.

SUPER BOWL XXIX

Sunday, January 29, 1995 at Miami, Joe Robbie Stadium, attendance 74,107

MVP: Steve Young

SAN DIEGO CHARGERS	7	3	8	8	—	26
SAN FRANCISCO 49ERS	14	14	14	7	—	49

SCORING SF—Rice 44-yd pass from Young (Brien PAT), SF—Watters 51-yd pass from Young (Brien PAT), SD—Means 1-yd run (Carney PAT), SF—Floyd 5-yd pass from Young (Brien PAT), SF—Watters 8-yd pass from Young (Brien PAT), SD—FG Carney 31 yds, SF—Watters 9-yd run (Brien PAT), SF—Coleman 98-yd kickoff return (Seay pass from Humphries), SF—Rice 15-yd pass from Young (Brien PAT), SF—Rice 7-yd pass from Young (Brien PAT), SD—Martin 30-yd pass from Humphries (Pupunu pass from Humphries)

TEAM	FIRST DOWNS	TOTAL YARDAGE	RUSHING	PASSING	RETURNS	ATT-COMP-INT	SACKED	PUNTING	FUMBLES	PENALTIES
SD	20	354	19-67	287	1	55-27-3	2-18	4-49	1-0	6-63
SF	28	455	32-139	316	28	38-25-0	3-15	5-40	2-0	3-18

SAN DIEGO CHARGERS

RUSHING	ATT	YDS	LNG	TD
Natrone Means	13	33	11	1
Ronnie Harmon	2	10	10	0
Shawn Jefferson	1	10	10	0
Gale Gilbert	1	8	8	0
Eric Bieniemy	1	3	3	0
Stan Humphries	1	3	3	0

RECEIVING	NO	YDS	LNG	TD
Ronnie Harmon	8	68	20	0
Mark Seay	7	75	22	0
Alfred Pupunu	4	48	23	0
Tony Martin	3	59	30	1
Shawn Jefferson	2	15	9	0
Eric Bieniemy	1	33	33	0
Natrone Means	1	4	4	0
Duane Young	1	3	3	0

PASSING	PA	PC	YDS	TD	IN
Stan Humphries	49	24	275	1	2
Gale Gilbert	6	3	30	0	1

SAN FRANCISCO 49ERS

RUSHING	ATT	YDS	LNG	TD
Steve Young	5	49	21	0
Ricky Watters	15	47	13	1
William Floyd	9	32	6	0
Jerry Rice	1	10	10	0
Dexter Carter	1	1	1	0
Elvis Grbac	1	0	0	0

RECEIVING	NO	YDS	LNG	TD
Jerry Rice	10	149	44	3
John Taylor	4	43	16	0
William Floyd	4	26	9	0
Ricky Watters	3	61	51	2
Brent Jones	2	41	33	0
Ted Popson	1	6	6	0
Ed McCaffrey	1	5	5	0

PASSING	PA	PC	YDS	TD	IN
Steve Young	36	24	325	6	0
Bill Musgrave	1	1	6	0	0
Elvis Grbac	1	0	0	0	0

SAN DIEGO CHARGERS

KICKOFF RETURNS	NO	YDS	LNG	TD
Andre Coleman	8	242	98	1

PUNT RETURNS	NO	YDS	LNG	TD
Darrien Gordon	3	1	1	0

INTERCEPTION RETURNS	NO	YDS	LNG	TD

PUNTING	NO	YDS	LNG	BLK
Bryan Wagner	4	48	55	0

SACKS				NO
Raylee Johnson				2
Junior Seau				1

SAN FRANCISCO 49ERS

KICKOFF RETURNS	NO	YDS	LNG	TD
Dexter Carter	4	48	18	0

PUNT RETURNS	NO	YDS	LNG	TD
Dexter Carter	2	12	11	0

INTERCEPTION RETURNS	NO	YDS	LNG	TD
Deion Sanders	1	15	15	0
Toi Cook	1	1	1	0
Eric Davis	1	0	0	0

PUNTING	NO	YDS	LNG	BLK
Klaus Wilmsmeyer	5	39	46	0

SACKS				NO
Dana Stubblefield				1
Dennis Brown				0
Tim Harris				0

GAME IS FOR YOUNG

Of San Francisco's first four Super Bowl wins, one was decided in the last minute, two weren't that close, and one was an absolute blowout. Super Bowl XXXIX went in that third category. Steve Young, living in the shadow of Joe Montana despite overtaking the former 49ers quarterback as the most efficient passer in history, didn't mind the lopsided score.

Young threw a 44-yard touchdown pass to Jerry Rice, Montana's old favorite, on the third play of the game. He connected with Ricky Watters for a 51-yard touchdown just 4:55 into the game. It was 28–10 at the half and Young wasn't close to done. He broke Montana's Super Bowl record with 6 touchdown passes—3 to Rice—and was also the game's leading rusher with 49 yards. Young was the clear MVP.

San Francisco became the first five-time Super Bowl champion. George Seifert, living under the smaller but omnipresent shadow of Bill Walsh, had his second title. The Chargers, under no one's shadow despite coming from sunny San Diego, had to remain content with their first AFC crown.

SUPER BOWL XXX

Sunday, January 28, 1996 at Phoenix, Sun Devil Stadium, attendance 76,347

MVP: Larry Brown

DALLAS COWBOYS	10	3	7	7	—	27
PITTSBURGH STEELERS	0	7	0	10	—	17

SCORING Dal—FG Boniol 42 yds, Dal—Novacek 3-yd pass from Aikman (Boniol PAT), Dal—FG Boniol 35 yds, Pit—Thigpen 6-yd pass from O'Donnell (N. Johnson PAT), Dal—E. Smith 1-yd run (Boniol PAT), Pit—FG N. Johnson 46 yds, Pit—Morris 1-yd run (N. Johnson PAT), Dal—E. Smith 4-yd run (Boniol PAT)

TEAM	FIRST DOWNS	TOTAL YARDAGE	RUSHING	PASSING	RETURNS	ATT-COMP-INT	SACKED	PUNTING	FUMBLES	PENALTIES
Dal	15	254	25-56	198	88	23-15-0	2-11	5-38	0-0	5-25
Pit	25	310	31-103	207	18	49-28-3	4-32	4-45	2-0	2-15

DALLAS COWBOYS

RUSHING	ATT	YDS	LNG	TD
Emmitt Smith	18	49	23	2
Daryl Johnston	2	8	4	0
Kevin Williams	1	2	2	0
Troy Aikman	4	-3		0

RECEIVING	NO	YDS	LNG	TD
Michael Irvin	5	76	20	0
Jay Novacek	5	50	19	1
Kevin Williams	2	29	22	0
Deion Sanders	1	47	47	0
Daryl Johnston	1	4	4	0
Emmitt Smith	1	3	3	0

PASSING	PA	PC	YDS	TD	IN
Troy Aikman	23	15	209	1	0

PITTSBURGH STEELERS

RUSHING	ATT	YDS	LNG	TD
Bam Morris	19	73	15	1
Erric Pegram	6	15	4	0
Kordell Stewart	4	15	7	0
Neil O'Donnell	1	0	0	0
John L. Williams	1	0	0	0

RECEIVING	NO	YDS	LNG	TD
Andre Hastings	10	98	19	0
Ernie Mills	8	78	17	0
Yancey Thigpen	3	19	10	1
Bam Morris	3	18	10	0
Corey Holliday	2	19	10	0
John L. Williams	2	7	5	0

PASSING	PA	PC	YDS	TD	IN
Neil O'Donnell	49	28	239	1	3

DALLAS COWBOYS

KICKOFF RETURNS	NO	YDS	LNG	TD
Kevin Williams	2	24	18	0
Brock Marion	1	13	13	0

PUNT RETURNS	NO	YDS	LNG	TD
Deion Sanders	1	11	11	0

INTERCEPTION RETURNS	NO	YDS	LNG	TD
Larry Brown	2	77	44	0
Brock Marion	1	0	0	0

PUNTING	NO	YDS	LNG	BLK
John Jett	5	38	51	0

SACKS				NO
Chad Hennings				2
Charles Haley				1
Tony Tolbert				1

PITTSBURGH STEELERS

KICKOFF RETURNS	NO	YDS	LNG	TD
Ernie Mills	4	79	22	0
Fred McAfee	1	17	17	0

PUNT RETURNS	NO	YDS	LNG	TD
Andre Hastings	2	18	11	0

INTERCEPTION RETURNS	NO	YDS	LNG	TD

PUNTING	NO	YDS	LNG	BLK
Rohn Stark	4	44	55	0

SACKS				NO
Levon Kirkland				1
Ray Seals				1

THIRD TIME'S THE CHARM

For the first time two teams met in the Super Bowl for the third time. The Cowboys were two years removed from consecutive Super Bowl titles, although that happened under Jimmy Johnson, not second-year coach Barry Switzer. The Steelers reached the playoffs each of the four seasons since Pittsburgh native Bill Cowher had replaced legend Chuck Noll, who'd twice beaten Dallas for titles in the 1970s.

The heavily-favored Cowboys took a 13–0 lead, but Pittsburgh managed a fourth-down conversion by Kordell Stewart and a Neil O'Donnell touchdown pass with 13 seconds to go in the first half. After Norm Johnson's field goal in the fourth quarter, the Steelers tried an unexpected onside kick with 11:25 left in the game. Pittsburgh recovered, scored a touchdown, held Dallas, and got the ball back down by only 20–17.

O'Donnell, at the time the NFL's all-time leader in fewest interceptions per pass attempt, was picked off for the second time by MVP Larry Brown. Emmitt Smith scored his second touchdown and the Cowboys had finally taken a Super Bowl from the Steelers.

SUPER BOWL XXXI

Sunday, January 26, 1997 at New Orleans, Louisiana Superdome, attendance 72,301

MVP: Desmond Howard

NEW ENGLAND PATRIOTS	14	0	7	0	—	21
GREEN BAY PACKERS	**10**	**17**	**8**	**0**	—	**35**

SCORING GB—Rison 54-yd pass from Favre (Jacke PAT), GB—FG Jacke 37 yds, NE—Byars 1-yd pass from Bledsoe (Vinatieri PAT), NE—Coates 4-yd pass from Bledsoe (Vinatieri PAT), GB—Freeman 81-yd pass from Favre (Jacke PAT), GB—FG Jacke 31 yds, GB—Favre 2-yd run (Jacke PAT), NE—Martin 18-yd run (Vinatieri PAT), GB—Howard 99-yd kickoff return (Chmura pass from Favre)

TEAM	FIRST DOWNS	TOTAL YARDAGE	RUSHING	PASSING	RETURNS	ATT-COMP-INT	SACKED	PUNTING	FUMBLES	PENALTIES
NE	16	257	13-43	214	30	48-25-4	5-39	8-45	0-0	2-22
GB	16	323	36-115	208	114	27-14-0	5-38	7-43	0-0	3-41

NEW ENGLAND PATRIOTS

RUSHING	ATT	YDS	LNG	TD
Curtis Martin	11	42	18	1
Drew Bledsoe	1	1	1	0
Dave Meggett	1	0	0	0

RECEIVING	NO	YDS	LNG	TD
Ben Coates	6	67	19	1
Terry Glenn	4	62	44	0
Keith Byars	4	42	32	1
Shawn Jefferson	3	34	14	0
Curtis Martin	3	28	20	0
Dave Meggett	3	8	5	0
Vincent Brisby	2	12	7	0

PASSING	PA	PC	YDS	TD	IN
Drew Bledsoe	48	25	253	2	4

GREEN BAY PACKERS

RUSHING	ATT	YDS	LNG	TD
Dorsey Levens	14	61	12	0
Edgar Bennett	17	40	10	0
Brett Favre	4	12	12	1
William Henderson	1	2	2	0

RECEIVING	NO	YDS	LNG	TD
Antonio Freeman	3	105	81	1
Dorsey Levens	3	23	14	0
Andre Rison	2	77	54	1
William Henderson	2	14	8	0
Mark Chmura	2	13	8	0
Keith Jackson	1	10	10	0
Edgar Bennett	1	4	4	0

PASSING	PA	PC	YDS	TD	IN
Brett Favre	27	14	246	2	0

NEW ENGLAND PATRIOTS

KICKOFF RETURNS	NO	YDS	LNG	TD
Dave Meggett	5	117	26	0
Hason Graham	1	18	18	0

PUNT RETURNS	NO	YDS	LNG	TD
Dave Meggett	4	30	20	0

INTERCEPTION RETURNS	NO	YDS	LNG	TD

PUNTING	NO	YDS	LNG	BLK
Tom Tupa	8	45	53	0

SACKS				NO
Tedy Bruschi				2
Ferric Collons				1
Willie McGinest				1
Otis Smith				1

GREEN BAY PACKERS

KICKOFF RETURNS	NO	YDS	LNG	TD
Desmond Howard	4	154	99	1

PUNT RETURNS	NO	YDS	LNG	TD
Desmond Howard	6	90	34	0

INTERCEPTION RETURNS	NO	YDS	LNG	TD
Brian Williams	1	16	16	0
Mike Prior	1	8	8	0
Doug Evans	1	0	0	0
Craig Newsome	1	0	0	0

PUNTING	NO	YDS	LNG	BLK
Craig Hentrich	7	42	58	0

SACKS				NO
Reggie White				3
LeRoy Butler				1
Santana Dotson				1

PACKERS LOOK GOOD IN RETURN

Green Bay thrived at Lambeau Field, winning 18 straight home games there (including playoffs). Super Bowl XXXI at the Louisiana Superdome was not far from the Mississippi home of Packers hero Brett Favre. The Patriots had been to just one Super Bowl—11 years earlier in New Orleans—and it had gone very badly against the Bears.

The Packers took a 10–0 lead and still trailed after the first quarter on 2 touchdown passes by Drew Bledsoe. Favre found Antonio Freeman for an 81-yard touchdown pass, the longest in a Super Bowl. Green Bay took a 27–14 halftime lead.

The Patriots drew within a touchdown, but Desmond Howard returned the ensuing kickoff 99 yards. Howard had 244 return yards, including a 34-yard punt return, becoming the first special teams player to be named MVP. The defensive rush produced 5 sacks, 3 by Reggie White, and 4 interceptions. The Packers had their first championship since Super Bowl II. Coach Bill Parcells left New England a few weeks after the game and joined the division rival Jets.

SUPER BOWL XXXII

Sunday, January 25, 1998 at San Diego, Qualcomm Stadium, attendance 68,912

MVP: Terrell Davis

GREEN BAY PACKERS	7	7	3	7	—	24
DENVER BRONCOS	**7**	**10**	**7**	**7**	—	**31**

SCORING GB —Freeman 22-yd pass from Favre (Longwell PAT), Den—Davis 1-yd run (Elam PAT), Den—Elway 1-yd run (Elam PAT), Den—FG Elam 51 yds, GB —Chmura 6-yd pass from Favre (Longwell PAT), GB —FG Longwell 27 yds, Den—Davis 1-yd run (Elam PAT), GB —Freeman 13-yd pass from Favre (Longwell PAT), Den—Davis 1-yd run (Elam PAT)

TEAM	FIRST DOWNS	TOTAL YARDAGE	RUSHING	PASSING	RETURNS	ATT-COMP-INT	SACKED	PUNTING	FUMBLES	PENALTIES
GB	21	350	20-95	255	17	42-25-1	1-1	4-18	2-2	9-59
Den	21	302	39-179	123	0	22-12-1	0-0	4-37	1-1	7-65

GREEN BAY PACKERS

RUSHING	ATT	YDS	LNG	TD
Dorsey Levens	19	90	16	0
Robert Brooks	1	5	5	0

RECEIVING	NO	YDS	LNG	TD
Antonio Freeman	9	126	27	2
Dorsey Levens	6	56	22	0
Mark Chmura	4	43	21	1
Robert Brooks	3	16	10	0
William Henderson	2	9	7	0
Terry Mickens	1	6	6	0

PASSING	PA	PC	YDS	TD	IN
Brett Favre	42	25	256	3	1

DENVER BRONCOS

RUSHING	ATT	YDS	LNG	TD
Terrell Davis	30	157	27	3
John Elway	5	17	10	1
Vaughn Hebron	3	3	2	0
Howard Griffith	1	2	2	0

RECEIVING	NO	YDS	LNG	TD
Shannon Sharpe	5	38	12	0
Ed McCaffrey	2	45	36	0
Terrell Davis	2	8	4	0
Howard Griffith	1	23	23	0
Vaughn Hebron	1	5	5	0
Dwayne Carswell	1	4	4	0

PASSING	PA	PC	YDS	TD	IN
John Elway	22	12	123	0	1

GREEN BAY PACKERS

KICKOFF RETURNS	NO	YDS	LNG	TD
Antonio Freeman	6	104	22	0

INTERCEPTION RETURNS	NO	YDS	LNG	TD
Eugene Robinson	1	17	17	0

PUNTING	NO	YDS	LNG	BLK
Craig Hentrich	4	18	51	0

SACKS				NO
Atwater				1

DENVER BRONCOS

KICKOFF RETURNS	NO	YDS	LNG	TD
Vaughn Hebron	4	79	2	0
Keith Burns	1	16	16	0

INTERCEPTION RETURNS	NO	YDS	LNG	TD
Tyrone Braxton	1	0	0	0

PUNTING	NO	YDS	LNG	BLK
Tom Rouen	4	37	47	0

SACKS				NO
				Steve

LONG WAIT ENDS FOR DENVER

The Packers were hungry to link their storied past to their thriving present. Green Bay had won the first two Super Bowls ever played and was also the defending champion. Denver, on the other hand, was 0–4 in Super Bowls, and represented a conference that had lost 13 straight Super Bowls. Green Bay was an 11 ½-point favorite.

The Packers looked impressive out of the gate, marching 76 yards and scoring on a 22-yard pass from Brett Favre to Antonio Freeman. The Broncos responded by scoring the next 17 points, even with

running back Terrell Davis missing almost all of the second quarter with a severe migraine headache.

Although Green Bay tied the game in the third quarter and again in the fourth, Denver pulled ahead with 1:24 left on the third touchdown of the day by Davis, who earned MVP with 157 rushing yards despite the headache. Green Bay had a final chance, but linebacker John Mobley broke up a fourth-down pass to give Denver, John Elway, and the AFC a long-sought victory.

SUPER BOWL XXXIII

Sunday, January 31, 1999 at Miami, Pro Player Stadium, attendance 74,803

MVP: John Elway

	1	2	3	4		Final
DENVER BRONCOS	7	10	0	17	—	34
ATLANTA FALCONS	3	3	0	13	—	19

SCORING Atl—FG Andersen 32 yds, Den—Griffith 1-yd run (Elam PAT), Den—FG Elam 26 yds, Den—R. Smith 80-yd pass from Elway (Elam PAT), Atl—FG Andersen 28 yds, Den—Griffith 1-yd run (Elam PAT), Den—Elway 3-yd run (Elam PAT), Atl—Dwight 94-yd kickoff return (Andersen PAT), Den—FG Elam 37 yds, Atl—Mathis 3-yd pass from Chandler (pass failed)

TEAM	FIRST DOWNS	TOTAL YARDAGE	RUSHING	PASSING	RETURNS	ATT-COMP-INT	SACKED	PUNTING	FUMBLES	PENALTIES
Den	22	457	36-121	336	136	29-18-1	0-0	1-35	0-0	4-61
Atl	21	337	23-131	206	1	35-19-3	2-13	1-39	1-1	0-0

DENVER BRONCOS

RUSHING	ATT	YDS	LNG	TD
Terrell Davis	25	102	15	0
Howard Griffith	4	9	4	2
Derek Loville	2	8	6	0
John Elway	3	2	3	1
Rod Smith	1	1	1	0
Bubby Brister	1	-1	-1	0

RECEIVING	NO	YDS	LNG	TD
Rod Smith	5	152	80	1
Ed McCaffrey	5	72	25	0
Byron Chamberlain	3	29	13	0
Terrell Davis	2	50	39	0
Shannon Sharpe	2	26	14	0
Howard Griffith	1	7	7	0

PASSING	PA	PC	YDS	TD	IN
John Elway	29	18	336	1	1

ATLANTA FALCONS

RUSHING	ATT	YDS	LNG	TD
Jamal Anderson	18	96	15	0
Chris Chandler	4	30	12	0
Tim Dwight	1	5	5	0

RECEIVING	NO	YDS	LNG	TD
Terance Mathis	7	85	30	1
Tony Martin	5	79	23	0
Jamal Anderson	3	16	9	0
Ronnie Harris	2	21	13	0
O.J. Santiago	1	13	13	0
Brian Kozlowski	1	5	5	0

PASSING	PA	PC	YDS	TD	IN
Chris Chandler	35	19	219	1	3

DENVER BRONCOS

KICKOFF RETURNS	NO	YDS	LNG	TD
Vaughn Hebron	2	42	26	0
Byron Chamberlain	1	2	2	0

INTERCEPTION RETURNS	NO	YDS	LNG	TD
Darrien Gordon	2	108	58	0
Darrius Johnson	1	28	28	0

PUNTING	NO	YDS	LNG	BLK
Tom Rouen	1	35	35	0

SACKS		NO
Orson Mobley		1
Bill Romanowski		1

ATLANTA FALCONS

KICKOFF RETURNS	NO	YDS	LNG	TD
Tim Dwight	5	210	94	1
Brian Kozlowski	2	17	16	0

INTERCEPTION RETURNS	NO	YDS	LNG	TD
Ronnie Bradford	1	1	1	0

PUNTING	NO	YDS	LNG	BLK
Dan Stryzinski	1	39	39	0

SACKS		NO
		NO

ELWAY RIDES INTO SUNSET

John Elway faced Dan Reeves, who had coached Denver to three Super Bowl appearances (and losses) in the 1980s. Falcons safety Eugene Robinson faced a mug shot camera the same day he received the Bart Starr Award winner as "the NFL player who best exemplifies outstanding character and leadership in the home, on the field, and in the community." He was arrested the night before the game for soliciting a prostitute.

Elway found Rod Smith for a 41-yard play to set up Denver's first score; the pair teamed up for an 80-yard completion to give the Broncos a 17–3 lead. After a scoreless third quarter, Elway made it 24–6 with a 3-yard run. Tim Dwight returned the kickoff 94 yards for Atlanta's first touchdown. Elway, who finished with 336 yards passing, led Denver right back; Jason Elam kicked his second field goal.

The 38-year-old Elway, the first quarterback to appear in five Super Bowls, became the oldest player ever to be named the game's MVP. He retired not long after the game.

SUPER BOWL XXXIV

Sunday, January 30, 2000 at Atlanta, Georgia Dome, attendance 72,625

MVP: Kurt Warner

	1	2	3	4		Final
ST. LOUIS RAMS	3	6	7	7	—	23
TENNESSEE TITANS	0	0	6	10	—	16

SCORING StL—FG Wilkins 27 yds, StL—FG Wilkins 29 yds, StL—FG Wilkins 28 yds, StL—Holt 9-yd pass from Warner (Wilkins PAT), Ten—George 1-yd run (pass failed), Ten—George 2-yd run (Del Greco PAT), Ten—FG Del Greco 43 yds, StL—Bruce 73-yd pass from Warner (Wilkins PAT)

TEAM	FIRST DOWNS	TOTAL YARDAGE	RUSHING	PASSING	RETURNS	ATT-COMP-INT	SACKED	PUNTING	FUMBLES	PENALTIES
SL	23	436	13-29	407	8	45-24-0	1-7	2-39	2-0	8-60
Ten	27	367	36-159	208	-1	36-22-0	1-6	3-43	1-0	7-45

ST. LOUIS RAMS

RUSHING	ATT	YDS	LNG	TD
Marshall Faulk	10	17	4	0
Robert Holcombe	1	11	11	0
Kurt Warner	1	1	1	0
Mike Horan	1	0	0	0

RECEIVING	NO	YDS	LNG	TD
Torry Holt	7	109	32	1
Isaac Bruce	6	162	73	1
Marshall Faulk	5	90	52	0
Az-Zahir Hakim	1	17	17	0
Ernie Conwell	1	16	16	0
Ricky Proehl	1	11	11	0
Roland Williams	1	9	11	0
Robert Holcombe	1	1	1	0
Fred Miller	1	-1	-1	0

PASSING	PA	PC	YDS	TD	IN
Kurt Warner	45	24	414	2	0

TENNESSEE TITANS

RUSHING	ATT	YDS	LNG	TD
Eddie George	28	95	13	2
Steve McNair	8	64	23	0

RECEIVING	NO	YDS	LNG	TD
Jackie Harris	7	64	21	0
Frank Wycheck	5	35	13	0
Kevin Dyson	4	41	16	0
Eddie George	2	35	32	0
Isaac Byrd	2	21	21	0
Derrick Mason	2	18	9	0

PASSING	PA	PC	YDS	TD	IN
Steve McNair	36	22	214	0	0

ST. LOUIS RAMS

KICKOFF RETURNS	NO	YDS	LNG	TD
Tony Horne	4	55	25	0

PUNT RETURNS	NO	YDS	LNG	TD
Az-Zahir Hakim	2	8	10	0

PUNTING	NO	YDS	LNG	BLK
Mike Horan	2	38	49	0

SACKS		NO
Kevin Carter		1

TENNESSEE TITANS

KICKOFF RETURNS	NO	YDS	LNG	TD
Derrick Mason	5	122	35	0

PUNT RETURNS	NO	YDS	LNG	TD
Derrick Mason	1	-1	-1	0

PUNTING	NO	YDS	LNG	BLK
Craig Hentrich	3	43	49	0

SACKS		NO
Jason Fisk		1

NOW IN NEW LOCATION: SUPER BOWL

Two recently relocated franchises faced off in Super Bowl XXXIV. The Rams had lost a Super Bowl while in Los Angeles; their AFC counterpart had not owned a title since winning the first two AFL championships as the Houston Oilers.

Tennessee's defense did just enough to keep the Titans alive in the first half. The Rams were in position for 5 field goal tries: Jeff Wilkins made 3, missed 1, and another snap was mishandled.

Kurt Warner's touchdown pass in the third quarter gave St. Louis a 16–0 lead, but Eddie George scored twice and Al Del Greco kicked a tying field goal. On the next play Warner hit Isaac Bruce for a 73-yard touchdown with two minutes remaining. The play broke the tie and made MVP Warner the first quarterback to throw for 400 yards in a Super Bowl. Steve McNair brought the Titans to the Rams 10 with five seconds remaining. McNair hit Kevin Dyson, but Mike Jones pulled him down just short of the goal line to end the game.

SUPER BOWL XXXV

Sunday, January 28, 2001 at Tampa, Raymond James Stadium, attendance 71,921

MVP: Ray Lewis

BALTIMORE RAVENS	7	3	14	10	—	**34**
NEW YORK GIANTS	0	0	7	0	—	7

SCORING Bal—Stokley 38-yd pass from Dilfer (Stover PAT), Bal—FG Stover 47 yds, Bal—Starks 49-yd interception return (Stover PAT), NYG—Dixon 97-yd kickoff return (Daluiso PAT), Bal—Je. Lewis 84-yd kickoff return (Stover PAT), Bal—Ja. Lewis 3-yd run (Stover PAT), Bal—FG Stover 34 yds

TEAM	FIRST DOWNS	TOTAL YARDAGE	RUSHING	PASSING	RETURNS	ATT-COMP-INT	SACKED	PUNTING	FUMBLES	PENALTIES
Bal	13	244	33-111	133	93	26-12-0	3-20	10-43	2-0	9-70
NYG	11	152	16-66	86	46	39-15-4	4-26	11-38	2-1	6-27

BALTIMORE RAVENS

RUSHING	ATT	YDS	LNG	TD
Jamal Lewis	27	102	19	1
Priest Holmes	4	8	6	0
Jermaine Lewis	1	1	1	0
Trent Dilfer	1	0	0	0

RECEIVING	NO	YDS	LNG	TD
Brandon Stokley	3	52	38	1
Ben Coates	3	30	17	0
Qadry Ismail	1	44	44	0
Patrick Johnson	1	8	8	0
Jermaine Lewis	1	6	6	0
Shannon Sharpe	1	5	5	0
Priest Holmes	1	4	4	0
Jamal Lewis	1	4	4	0

PASSING	PA	PC	YDS	TD	IN
Trent Dilfer	25	12	153	1	0
Tony Banks	1	0	0	0	0

NEW YORK GIANTS

RUSHING	ATT	YDS	LNG	TD
Tiki Barber	11	49	27	0
Kerry Collins	3	12	5	0
Joe Montgomery	2	5	4	0

RECEIVING	NO	YDS	LNG	TD
Tiki Barber	6	26	7	0
Ike Hilliard	3	30	13	0
Amani Toomer	2	24	19	0
Ron Dixon	1	16	16	0
Howard Cross	1	7	7	0
Pete Mitchell	1	7	7	0
Greg Comella	1	2	2	0

PASSING	PA	PC	YDS	TD	IN
Kerry Collins	39	15	112	0	4

BALTIMORE RAVENS

KICKOFF RETURNS	NO	YDS	LNG	TD
Jermaine Lewis	2	111	84	1

PUNT RETURNS	NO	YDS	LNG	TD
Jermaine Lewis	3	34	34	0

INTERCEPTION RETURNS	NO	YDS	LNG	TD
Duane Starks	1	49	49	1
Chris McAlister	1	4	4	0
Jamie Sharper	1	4	4	0
Kim Herring	1	2	2	0

PUNTING	NO	YDS	LNG	BLK
Kyle Richardson	10	43	53	0

SACKS				NO
Michael McCrary				2
Rob Burnett				1
Keith Washington				1

NEW YORK GIANTS

KICKOFF RETURNS	NO	YDS	LNG	TD
Ron Dixon	6	154	97	1
Damon Washington	1	17	17	0

PUNT RETURNS	NO	YDS	LNG	TD
Ike Hilliard	3	33	19	0
Tiki Barber	2	13	9	0

INTERCEPTION RETURNS	NO	YDS	LNG	TD

PUNTING	NO	YDS	LNG	BLK
Brad Maynard	11	38	46	0

SACKS				NO
Cornelius Griffin				1
Michael Strahan				1

LORD BALTIMORE

The Baltimore Ravens and New York Giants each rallied to get to the Super Bowl. While the superstitious Ravens refused to even utter the word "playoffs" while winning seven straight games, Giants coach Jim Fassel boldly guaranteed on November 22 that his slumping club would make the playoffs. Silent or loud, both teams proved right.

The Super Bowl turned on big plays, even one that wasn't. Jesse Armstead's interception return for a touchdown was nullified by defensive holding. The Giants, on the other hand, constantly sent the ball back Baltimore's way on 5 turnovers and 11 punts.

An unprecedented Super Bowl feat occurred on three successive plays in the third quarter. Duane Starks ran an interception back for a Ravens touchdown. Then Ron Dixon returned the kick 97 yards for a score. Jermaine Lewis took the ensuing kickoff 84 yards for a touchdown. Although not possessing a nickname like the No-Name Defense (Super Bowl VII) or Steel Curtain (Super Bowl IX), Baltimore's defense—led by MVP Ray Lewis—joined those clubs in allowing only a special teams touchdown.

SUPER BOWL XXXVI

Sunday, February 3, 2002 at New Orleans, Louisiana Superdome, attendance 72,922

MVP: Tom Brady

ST. LOUIS RAMS	3	0	0	14	—	17
NEW ENGLAND PATRIOTS	0	14	3	3	—	**20**

SCORING StL—FG Wilkins 50 yds, NE—Law 47-yd interception return (Vinatieri PAT), NE—Patten 8-yd pass from Brady (Vinatieri PAT), NE —FG Vinatieri 37 yds, StL—Warner 2-yd run (Wilkins PAT), StL—Proehl 26-yd pass from Warner (Wilkins PAT), NE —FG Vinatieri 48 yds

TEAM	FIRST DOWNS	TOTAL YARDAGE	RUSHING	PASSING	RETURNS	ATT-COMP-INT	SACKED	PUNTING	FUMBLES	PENALTIES
SL	26	427	22-90	337	6	44-28-2	3-28	4-40	2-1	6-39
NE	15	267	25-133	134	81	27-16-0	2-11	8-43	0-0	5-31

ST. LOUIS RAMS

RUSHING	ATT	YDS	LNG	TD
Marshall Faulk	17	76	15	0
Kurt Warner	3	6	5	1
Az-Zahir Hakim	1	5	5	0
James Hodgins	1	3	3	0

RECEIVING	NO	YDS	LNG	TD
Az-Zahir Hakim	5	90	29	0
Isaac Bruce	5	56	22	0
Torry Holt	5	49	18	0
Marshall Faulk	4	54	18	0
Ricky Proehl	3	71	30	1
Jeff Robinson	2	18	12	0
Ernie Conwell	2	8	9	0
Yo Murphy	1	11	11	0
James Hodgins	1	8	8	0

PASSING	PA	PC	YDS	TD	IN
Kurt Warner	44	28	365	1	2

NEW ENGLAND PATRIOTS

RUSHING	ATT	YDS	LNG	TD
Antowain Smith	18	92	17	0
David Patten	1	22	22	0
Kevin Faulk	2	15	8	0
Marc Edwards	2	5	3	0
Tom Brady	1	3	3	0
J.R. Redmond	1	-4	-4	0

RECEIVING	NO	YDS	LNG	TD
Troy Brown	6	89	23	0
J.R. Redmond	3	24	11	0
Jermaine Wiggins	2	14	8	0
Marc Edwards	2	7	5	0
David Patten	1	8	8	1
Antowain Smith	1	4	4	0
Kevin Faulk	1	-1	-1	0

PASSING	PA	PC	YDS	TD	IN
Tom Brady	27	16	145	1	0

ST. LOUIS RAMS

KICKOFF RETURNS	NO	YDS	LNG	TD
Yo Murphy	3	81	30	0
Marshall Faulk	1	1	1	0

PUNT RETURNS	NO	YDS	LNG	TD
Dre' Bly	3	6	7	0

INTERCEPTION RETURNS	NO	YDS	LNG	TD

PUNTING	NO	YDS	LNG	BLK
John Baker	4	39	49	0

SACKS				NO
Leonard Little				1
Grant Wistrom				1

NEW ENGLAND PATRIOTS

KICKOFF RETURNS	NO	YDS	LNG	TD
Patrick Pass	3	85	35	0
Troy Brown	1	15	15	0

PUNT RETURNS	NO	YDS	LNG	TD
Troy Brown	1	4	4	0

INTERCEPTION RETURNS	NO	YDS	LNG	TD
Ty Law	1	47	47	0
Otis Smith	1	30	30	0

PUNTING	NO	YDS	LNG	BLK
Ken Walter	8	43	53	0

SACKS				NO
Bobby Hamilton				1
Willie McGinest				1
Richard Seymour				1

PATRIOT UPRISING

The St. Louis Rams, two years removed from a Super Bowl victory, were 14-point favorites in Super Bowl XXXVI. The New England Patriots, who'd already lost two Super Bowls at the Superdome, surged under inexperienced Tom Brady after veteran Drew Bledsoe was injured early in the season.

Three turnovers gave the Patriots a shocking 17–3 lead. Ty Law intercepted a Kurt Warner pass and rumbled 47 yards for a touchdown. A fumble set up Brady's touchdown pass eight seconds before halftime. An Otis Smith 30-yard interception return positioned the Pats for Adam Vinatieri's 37-yard field goal.

The only points the Patriots didn't score off turnovers came after St. Louis tied the score late in the fourth quarter. New England started at its own 17 with 1:21 left. J.R. Redmond moved the chains and stopped the clock after a key catch and Troy Brown's 23-yard reception from MVP Brady pushed the Pats past midfield. Vinatieri's 48-yard kick—the first game-ending field goal in 31 Super Bowls—gave the Patriots their first championship ever.

SUPER BOWL XXXVII

Sunday, January 26, 2003 at San Diego, Qualcomm Stadium, attendance 67,603

MVP: Dexter Jackson

OAKLAND RAIDERS	3	0	6	12	—	21
TAMPA BAY BUCCANEERS	**3**	**17**	**14**	**14**	—	**48**

SCORING Oak—FG Janikowski 40 yds, TB —FG Gramatica 31 yds, TB —FG Gramatica 43 yds, TB —Alstott 2-yd run (Gramatica PAT), TB —McCardell 5-yd pass from B. Johnson (Gramatica PAT), TB —McCardell 8-yd pass from B. Johnson (Gramatica PAT), TB —D. Smith 44-yd interception return (Gramatica PAT), Oak—Porter 39-yd pass from Gannon (pass failed), Oak—E. Johnson 13-yd blocked punt return (pass failed), Oak—Rice 48-yd pass from Gannon (pass failed), TB —Brooks 44-yd interception return (Gramatica PAT), TB —D. Smith 50-yd interception return (Gramatica PAT)

TEAM	FIRST DOWNS	TOTAL YARDAGE	RUSHING	PASSING	RETURNS	ATT-COMP-INT	SACKED	PUNTING	FUMBLES	PENALTIES
Oak	11	269	11-19	250	41	44-24-5	5-22	5-39	1-0	7-51
TB	24	365	42-150	215	197	34-18-1	0-0	5-31	1-0	5-41

OAKLAND RAIDERS

RUSHING	ATT	YDS	LNG	TD
Charlie Garner	7	10	4	0
Zack Crockett	2	6	4	0
Rich Gannon	2	3	2	0

RECEIVING	NO	YDS	LNG	TD
Charlie Garner	7	51	9	0
Jerry Rice	5	77	48	1
Doug Jolley	5	59	25	0
Jerry Porter	4	62	39	1
Tim Brown	1	9	9	0
Jon Ritchie	1	7	7	0
Tyrone Wheatley	1	7	7	0

PASSING	PA	PC	YDS	TD	IN
Rich Gannon	44	24	272	2	5

TAMPA BAY BUCCANEERS

RUSHING	ATT	YDS	LNG	TD
Michael Pittman	29	124	24	0
Mike Alstott	10	15	5	1
Brad Johnson	1	10	10	0
Aaron Stecker	1	1	1	0
Tom Tupa	1	0	0	0

RECEIVING	NO	YDS	LNG	TD
Keyshawn Johnson	6	69	18	0
Mike Alstott	5	43	16	0
Joe Jurevicius	4	78	33	0
Keenan McCardell	2	13	8	2
Ken Dilger	1	12	12	0

PASSING	PA	PC	YDS	TD	IN
Brad Johnson	34	18	215	2	1

OAKLAND RAIDERS

KICKOFF RETURNS	NO	YDS	LNG	TD
Marcus Knight	8	143	29	0
Chris Cooper	1	6	6	0

PUNT RETURNS	NO	YDS	LNG	TD
Darrien Gordon	3	29	17	0

INTERCEPTION RETURNS	NO	YDS	LNG	TD
Charles Woodson	1	12	12	0

PUNTING	NO	YDS	LNG	BLK
Shane Lechler	5	39	53	0

SACKS	NO

TAMPA BAY BUCCANEERS

KICKOFF RETURNS	NO	YDS	LNG	TD
Aaron Stecker	3	67	27	0
Dwight Smith	1	23	23	0

PUNT RETURNS	NO	YDS	LNG	TD
Karl Williams	1	25	25	0

INTERCEPTION RETURNS	NO	YDS	LNG	TD
Dwight Smith	2	94	50	2
Dexter Jackson	2	34	24	0
Derrick Brooks	1	44	44	1

PUNTING	NO	YDS	LNG	BLK
Tom Tupa	4	38	43	1

SACKS	NO
Simeon Rice	2
Warren Sapp	1
Greg Spires	1
Ellis Wyms	1

RAIDERS TAKE CASH, GRUDEN TAKES TITLE

John Gruden had built the Raiders into one of the game's top teams. Then he left—for four high draft picks and $8 million. Gruden took over a Buccaneers franchise that had never been to the Super Bowl and took them to the big game his first year. The Raiders still had a high-powered offense led by quarterback Rich Gannon, but Gruden had driven it before. The club also used a backup center after Barrett Robbins went missing and was later hospitalized.

Tampa Bay's lone turnover led to an early Oakland field goal, but the Buccaneers dominated the rest of the game. Brad Johnson's second-touchdown pass to Keenan McCardell made it 27–3 in the third quarter.

The Bucs became the first team with 3 defensive touchdowns in a Super Bowl. Dwight Smith scored twice and Derrick Brooks once on interception returns, yet Dexter Jackson, with 2 picks in the first half, was named MVP. The Raiders had to go for two points after each late touchdown, leaving them with 21 points despite 3 touchdowns and 1 field goal.

SUPER BOWL XXXVIII

Sunday, February 1, 2004 at Houston, Reliant Stadium, attendance 71,525

MVP: Tom Brady

CAROLINA PANTHERS	0	10	0	19	—	29
NEW ENGLAND PATRIOTS	**0**	**14**	**0**	**18**	—	**32**

SCORING NE —Branch 5-yd pass from Brady (Vinatieri PAT), Car—Smith 39-yd pass from Delhomme (Kasey PAT), NE —Givens 5-yd pass from Brady (Vinatieri PAT), Car—FG Kasey 50 yds, NE —Smith 2-yd run (Vinatieri PAT), Car—Foster 33-yd run (pass failed), Car—Muhammad 85-yd pass from Delhomme (pass failed), NE —Vrabel 1-yd pass from Brady (Faulk run), Car—Proehl 12-yd pass from Delhomme (Kasey PAT), NE —FG Vinatieri 41 yds

TEAM	FIRST DOWNS	TOTAL YARDAGE	RUSHING	PASSING	RETURNS	ATT-COMP-INT	SACKED	PUNTING	FUMBLES	PENALTIES
Car	17	387	16-92	295	14	33-16-0	4-28	7-44	1-1	12-73
NE	29	481	35-127	354	42	48-32-1	0-0	5-35	1-0	8-60

CAROLINA PANTHERS

RUSHING	ATT	YDS	LNG	TD
Stephen Davis	13	49	21	0
DeShaun Foster	3	43	33	1

RECEIVING	NO	YDS	LNG	TD
Muhsin Muhammad	4	140	85	1
Steve Smith	4	80	39	1
Ricky Proehl	4	71	31	1
Jermaine Wiggins	2	21	15	0
DeShaun Foster	1	9	9	0
Kris Mangum	1	2	2	0

PASSING	PA	PC	YDS	TD	IN
Jake Delhomme	33	16	323	3	0

NEW ENGLAND PATRIOTS

RUSHING	ATT	YDS	LNG	TD
Antowain Smith	26	83	9	1
Kevin Faulk	6	42	23	0
Tom Brady	2	12	12	0
Troy Brown	1	-10	-10	0

RECEIVING	NO	YDS	LNG	TD
Deion Branch	10	143	52	1
Troy Brown	8	76	13	0
David Givens	5	69	25	1
Daniel Graham	4	46	33	0
Kevin Faulk	4	19	7	0
Mike Vrabel	1	1	1	1

PASSING	PA	PC	YDS	TD	IN
Tom Brady	48	32	354	3	1

CAROLINA PANTHERS

KICKOFF RETURNS	NO	YDS	LNG	TD
Rod Smart	4	74	22	0
Steve Smith	1	30	30	0
Kris Mangum	1	12	12	0

PUNT RETURNS	NO	YDS	LNG	TD
Steve Smith	1	2	2	0

INTERCEPTION RETURNS	NO	YDS	LNG	TD
Reggie Howard	1	12	12	0

PUNTING	NO	YDS	LNG	BLK
Todd Sauerbrun	7	44	51	0

SACKS	NO

NEW ENGLAND PATRIOTS

KICKOFF RETURNS	NO	YDS	LNG	TD
Bethel Johnson	4	78	29	0

PUNT RETURNS	NO	YDS	LNG	TD
Troy Brown	4	40	28	0
Deion Branch	1	2	2	0

INTERCEPTION RETURNS	NO	YDS	LNG	TD

PUNTING	NO	YDS	LNG	BLK
Ken Walter	5	34	51	0

SACKS	NO
Mike Vrabel	2
Rodney Harrison	1
Willie McGinest	1

VINATIERI PROVIDES ANOTHER IN THE HEAD

Super Bowl XXXVIII followed a familiar script, only this time Bill Belichick's Patriots were the favorites. Like Super Bowl XXXVI, it featured MVP Tom Brady's aerial show, an undrafted quarterback's comeback (this time Carolina's Jake Delhomme), and Adam Vinatieri's heroic finish.

Neither team scored in the first quarter (or the third quarter), and the game was tight throughout. Antowain Smith's touchdown for New England began an unprecedented fourth-quarter scoring frenzy. The Panthers responded with DeShaun Foster's 33-yard touchdown run. After an interception of Brady in the end zone, Delhomme found Muhsin Muhammad for 85 yards, the longest play in Super Bowl history. Carolina missed two-point conversions each time, but the Panthers emerged with a 22–21 lead.

Brady and Delhomme exchanged touchdown passes—plus New England's two-point conversion—and the game was tied at 29–29. John Kasay's kickoff went out of bounds and the Patriots took over at their own 40 with 1:08 to go and three timeouts. Deion Branch's 10th catch of the game set up Vinatieri's second championship-deciding kick in three years.

SUPER BOWL XXXIX

Sunday, February 6, 2005 at Jacksonville, Alltel Stadium, attendance 78,125

MVP: Deion Branch

NEW ENGLAND PATRIOTS	0	7	7	10	—	24
PHILADELPHIA EAGLES	0	7	7	7	—	21

SCORING Phi—Smith 6-yd pass from McNabb (Akers PAT), NE—Givens 4-yd pass from Brady (Vinatieri PAT), NE—Vrabel 2-yd pass from Brady (Vinatieri PAT), Phi—Westbrook 10-yd pass from McNabb (Akers PAT), NE—Dillon 2-yd run (Vinatieri PAT), NE—FG Vinatieri 22 yds, Phi—Lewis 30-yd pass from McNabb (Akers PAT)

TEAM	FIRST DOWNS	TOTAL YARDAGE	RUSHING	PASSING	RETURNS	ATT-COMP-INT	SACKED	PUNTING	FUMBLES	PENALTIES
NE	21	331	28-112	219	31	33-23-0	2-17	7-45	1-1	7-47
Phi	24	369	17-45	324	19	51-30-3	4-33	5-43	2-1	3-35

NEW ENGLAND PATRIOTS

RUSHING	ATT	YDS	LNG	TD
Corey Dillon	18	75	25	1
Kevin Faulk	8	38	12	0
Patrick Pass	1	0	0	0
Tom Brady	1	-1	-1	0

RECEIVING	NO	YDS	LNG	TD
Deion Branch	11	133	27	0
Corey Dillon	3	31	16	0
David Givens	3	19	13	1
Kevin Faulk	2	27	14	0
Troy Brown	2	17	12	0
Daniel Graham	1	7	7	0
Mike Vrabel	1	2	2	1

PASSING	PA	PC	YDS	TD	IN
Tom Brady	33	23	236	2	0

PHILADELPHIA EAGLES

RUSHING	ATT	YDS	LNG	TD
Brian Westbrook	15	44	22	0
Dorsey Levens	1	1	1	0
Donovan McNabb	1	0	0	0

RECEIVING	NO	YDS	LNG	TD
Terrell Owens	9	122	36	0
Brian Westbrook	7	60	15	1
Todd Pinkston	4	82	40	0
Greg Lewis	4	53	30	1
L.J. Smith	4	27	9	1
Freddie Mitchell	1	11	11	0
Josh Parry	1	2	2	0

PASSING	PA	PC	YDS	TD	IN
Donovan McNabb	51	30	357	3	3

NEW ENGLAND PATRIOTS

KICKOFF RETURNS	NO	YDS	LNG	TD
Bethel Johnson	2	44	26	0
Patrick Pass	1	17	17	0
Christian Fauria	1	2	2	0

PUNT RETURNS	NO	YDS	LNG	TD
Troy Brown	3	12	8	0
Bethel Johnson	1	14	14	0

INTERCEPTION RETURNS	NO	YDS	LNG	TD
Rodney Harrison	2	5	6	0
Tedy Bruschi	1	0	0	0

PUNTING	NO	YDS	LNG	BLK
Josh Miller	7	45	50	0

SACKS				NO
Tedy Bruschi				1
Rodney Harrison				1
Richard Seymour				1
Mike Vrabel				1

PHILADELPHIA EAGLES

KICKOFF RETURNS	NO	YDS	LNG	TD
J.R. Reed	4	82	26	0
Roderick Hood	1	32	32	0

PUNT RETURNS	NO	YDS	LNG	TD
Brian Westbrook	3	19	10	0

INTERCEPTION RETURNS	NO	YDS	LNG	TD

PUNTING	NO	YDS	LNG	BLK
Dirk Johnson	5	42	52	0

SACKS				NO
Derrick Burgess				1
team sack				1

EAGLES FIND PATRIOTS AT NEXT STEP

After three years of frustration, Philadelphia survived the NFC Championship Game only to run into the powerful Patriots. Philadelphia would have back Terrell Owens, a receiver as talented as he was exasperating, who'd sprained his ankle and missed the playoffs.

Eagles quarterback Donovan McNabb twice turned the ball over in the first quarter, only to have it overturned by replay and nullified by penalty. Two more turnovers stuck, yet the Eagles still scored the first points of the game on a touchdown pass to L.J. Smith. New England tied it with 1:10 left in the half. Linebacker Mike Vrabel, lined up as a tight end, caught a touchdown from Tom Brady to give the Patriots the lead. McNabb's touchdown to Brian Westbrook made it the first Super Bowl ever tied going into the fourth quarter. It wasn't tied long.

The Patriots scored 10 points in the fourth quarter, as MVP Deion Branch finished with 11 catches. Philadelphia put together a late rally and got the ball a final time, but McNabb's third interception made the Patriots three-time champions.

SUPER BOWL XL

Sunday, February 5, 2006 at Detroit, Ford Field, attendance 68,206

MVP: Hines Ward

SEATTLE SEAHAWKS	3	0	7	0	—	10
PITTSBURGH STEELERS	0	7	7	7	—	21

SCORING Sea—FG Brown 47 yds, Pit—Roethlisberger 1-yd run (Reed PAT), Pit—Parker 75-yd run (Reed PAT), Sea—Stevens 16-yd pass from Hasselbeck (Brown PAT), Pit—Ward 43-yd pass from Randle El (Reed PAT)

TEAM	FIRST DOWNS	TOTAL YARDAGE	RUSHING	PASSING	RETURNS	ATT-COMP-INT	SACKED	PUNTING	FUMBLES	PENALTIES
Sea	20	396	25-137	259	103	49-26-1	3-14	6-50	0-0	7-70
Pit	14	339	33-181	158	56	22-10-2	1-8	6-49	0-0	3-20

SEATTLE SEAHAWKS

RUSHING	ATT	YDS	LNG	TD
Shaun Alexander	20	95	21	0
Matt Hasselbeck	3	35	18	0
Mack Strong	2	7	7	0

RECEIVING	NO	YDS	LNG	TD
Bobby Engram	6	70	21	0
Joe Jurevicius	5	93	35	0
Darrell Jackson	5	50	20	0
Jerramy Stevens	3	25	16	1
Mack Strong	2	15	13	0
Ryan Hannam	2	12	9	0
Shaun Alexander	2	2	4	0
Maurice Morris	1	6	6	0

PASSING	PA	PC	YDS	TD	IN
Matt Hasselbeck	49	26	273	1	1

PITTSBURGH STEELERS

RUSHING	ATT	YDS	LNG	TD
Willie Parker	10	93	75	1
Jerome Bettis	14	43	12	0
Ben Roethlisberger	7	25	10	1
Hines Ward	1	18	18	0
Verron Haynes	1	2	2	0

RECEIVING	NO	YDS	LNG	TD
Hines Ward	5	123	43	1
Antwaan Randle El	3	22	8	0
Cedrick Wilson	1	20	20	0
Willie Parker	1	1	1	0

PASSING	PA	PC	YDS	TD	IN
Ben Roethlisberger	21	9	123	0	2
Antwaan Randle El	1	1	43	1	0

SEATTLE SEAHAWKS

KICKOFF RETURNS	NO	YDS	LNG	TD
Josh Scobey	3	55	25	0
Maurice Morris	1	16	16	0

PUNT RETURNS	NO	YDS	LNG	TD
Peter Warrick	4	27	15	0

INTERCEPTION RETURNS	NO	YDS	LNG	TD
Kelly Herndon	1	76	76	0
Michael Boulware	1	0	0	0

PUNTING	NO	YDS	LNG	BLK
Tom Rouen	6	50	57	0

SACKS				NO
Grant Wistrom				1

PITTSBURGH STEELERS

KICKOFF RETURNS	NO	YDS	LNG	TD
Ricardo Colclough	2	43	22	0

PUNT RETURNS	NO	YDS	LNG	TD
Antwaan Randle El	2	32	20	0

INTERCEPTION RETURNS	NO	YDS	LNG	TD
Ike Taylor	1	24	24	0

PUNTING	NO	YDS	LNG	BLK
Chris Gardocki	6	48	60	0

SACKS				NO
Clark Haggans				1
Casey Hampton				1
Deshea Townsend				1

POLISHING OFF A FIFTH IN PITTSBURGH

Low-key Seattle played in its first Super Bowl. Pittsburgh, one of the NFL's most popular teams—and a franchise with a Super Bowl winning percentage of .800 heading in—was ready to crown beloved coach Bill Cowher with his first title. There was just the matter of the game.

Several crucial calls went Pittsburgh's way, but the Seahawks made three huge mistakes on defense. They let Pittsburgh quarterback Ben Roethlisberger complete a third-and-28 to MVP Hines Ward that led to the first score, surrendered the longest running play in Super Bowl history (75 yards by Willie Parker early in the second half), and bit on a trick play with wide receiver Antwaan Randle El, a quarterback at Indiana, throwing to Ward for a touchdown. The biggest play by Seattle's Matt Hasselback (273 passing yards) was called back by a penalty.

Although he played poorly, the 23-year-old Roethlisberger became the youngest starting quarterback to win a Super Bowl. Jerome Bettis went out happy in his final career game in his native Detroit, carrying Pittsburgh's fifth Lombardi Trophy.

THE ALL-TIME LEADERS

The first recorded scoring leader in pro football history was Elmer Oliphant of the Buffalo All-Americans. Since scoring records weren't kept during the league's first season in 1920, Oliphant's mark of 47 points in year two lasted about as long as the league's name. In 1922 the American Professional Football Association became the National Football League, and Hank Gillo of the Racine Legion became the NFL's new single-season scoring leader with 52 points. Oliphant's other records set or shared for that season—touchdown passes (7), extra points (26), and field goals (5)—also soon passed into history. The mark for rushing and total touchdowns, set by or shared by Akron Pros player–coach Fritz Pollard in 1921, was soon erased; as was that year's mark for receiving touchdowns set by another player–coach, George Halas of the Chicago Staleys (forerunner of the Bears), who tied for the league lead with Heinie Miller. As scoring increased and teams played more games, single-season records fell, career totals started to pile up, and all-time leaders were formed. So it goes.

Each generation passes the one before it as changes to the game and schedule create new all-time leaders. None of Oliphant's contemporaries appear on the lists here, and even a revolutionary player like Don Hutson, whose receiving totals once looked like they would never be passed, is now far down on the list. Even forward-looking Halas would be surprised. Three touchdown catches that once tied for the league lead might be good for a share of the league lead for a week.

But the records don't take into account the different circumstances men in different eras played under. This section does two things: It counts the stats as they were recorded, in the context of the total number of games and it also pro-rates these numbers—or normalizes them—so that players from different eras with shorter schedules can be compared. Otherwise, most players from 12-game schedules, when a 1,000-yard rushing season was a major achievement, don't measure up against players who competed in 16-game seasons where 1,000 yards came to 62.5 yards per game.

All season leaders are normalized to the 16-game schedule and the number of games is shown except for average categories. All career leaders are normalized to the 16-game schedule each year, a multiplier is shown which is used to multiply the raw number to get the normalized number. In both cases, the normalized number is italicized and the rank using the raw number is shown in parentheses. Active players through the 2005 season are bold-faced.

The upshot of the process is that a player like Walter Payton, whose 339 rushing attempts in 1977—the last season before the schedule increased from 14 to 16 games—ranked 67th when counted against players whose achievements have occurred since 1978 with the longer schedule. When normalized for a 16-game schedule, Payton's carries come to 387, tied for 11th with several players, including Jim Brown. Brown's 290 carries in a 12-game schedule in 1959 ranked 207th when compared against players in later eras. Their raw numbers would appear in the far right column under rushing attempt leaders as 290(207) for Brown and 339(67) for Payton. Tied with them for 11th place on this list are active running backs Edgerrin James and Jamal Lewis, who each carried the ball 387 times in 16-game seasons since 2000.

AAFC NOT INCLUDED

The All-America Football Conference stats were not considered for all-time leaders. There are several players who would have ranked or ranked higher if the AAFC was included, like Joe Perry, Y.A. Tittle, Otto Graham, Lou Groza, Glenn Dobbs, and Frankie Albert, among others. Based on the records of the Cleveland Browns and San Francisco 49ers, who joined the NFL in 1950, each AAFC team was probably about 2 or 3 wins a year lower in quality than the NFL. This would amount to about 100 points or maybe 7 points per game. A 7-point favorite would win the game about two-thirds of the time. The early American Football League was probably as weak or weaker, but the NFL has officially recognized all AFL stats; so do the editors of this book.

Those who would rank in the top 25, if the AAFC was included would be the following.

Rushing

Joe Perry Attempts number 18, yards No.12, average No. 9, touchdowns No. 11, rank No. 12, combined net yards No. 19, total touchdowns No. 14, overall rank No. 21
Marion Motley Average No. 2
Johnny Strzykalski Average No. 8

Passing

Y.A. Tittle Yards No. 11, average gain No. 20, touchdowns No. 5, touchdown percentage No. 24, attempts No. 12, completions No. 12, interceptions No. 2
Otto Graham Average gain No. 1, touchdown percentage No. 5, rating No. 11
George Ratterman Average gain No. 22, TD percentage 6
Frankie Albert Touchdown percentage No. 2

Kicking

Lou Groza Total points No. 4, field goals No. 15, field goals attempted No. 5
Glenn Dobbs Punt average No. 1
Horace Gillom Punt average No. 23

Returns

Buddy Young Kickoff return average No. 4, kickoff return touchdowns No. 9, punt/kick return touchdowns No 12
Harry Clarke Kickoff return average No. 5
Jim Cason Punt return average No. 2
Chuck Fenenbock Punt return average No. 7
Bob Smith Interception return yards No 17
Ned Mathews Kickoff return touchdowns No. 21

KEY TO THE LEADERS SECTION

The comparison between eras is the result of taking the numbers actually gained by a player in past eras with shorter seasons and creating a new number for comparison with players competing in 16-game schedules. (This does not take into account games missed by an individual because of injury, benching, or other reasons.) Statistics that are untouched—that is, raw and without being normalized—are listed as unadjusted or **UNADJ**. The aforementioned multiplier is under the heading **RATIO**. Multiplying the unadjusted number by the ratio produces the adjusted numbers or **ADJ**. Keep in mind, however, that the actual ratio is usually several decimal places longer than the one listed and the actual results are within 0.5–1 percent. Players from 16-game schedules are simply listed with a ratio of 1.00. In the section for single season, the number of games scheduled in a season is listed under **G**.

Not only is the ability to compare players from different eras important, but so is making sure that a star performer isn't overtaken in the record book by a flash in the pan. While this can't happen in the counting statistical categories—a player with the highest number in almost any category is worthy of inclusion in this section no matter how long he played—but minimums must be set in the average and percentage categories to make sure that a durable player with many years in the league isn't passed by a player with a short career and a relatively small sample size. This way, someone who returned 10 kicks for 320 yards in his career can't supplant Gale Sayers and his 30.56 average set over five seasons with at least 14 returns per year. Likewise, Travis Williams's 1967 season average of 41.06 can't be overtaken by some with 2 returns of 100 yards.

Minimum requirements	Season	Lifetime
Passing pct, average gain, rating	10 attempts/game	1,500 attempts
Rushing average gain	5 attempts/game	50 attempts
Receiving average gain	2 attempts/game	200 receptions
Punt average	2 punts/game	250 punts
Field goal percentage	1 field goal/game	100 field goals
Punt Return Average	1 return/game	75 returns
Kickoff return average	1 return/game	75 returns

YEARS

	NAME	UNADJ
1	George Blanda	26
2	Morten Andersen	23
	Gary Anderson	23
4	Sean Landeta	21
	Earl Morrall	21
6	Darrell Green	20
	Trey Junkin	20
	Jim Marshall	20
	Jerry Rice	20
	Jackie Slater	20
11	Ray Brown	19
	Len Dawson	19
	Jim Hart	19
	Dave Krieg	19
	Bruce Matthews	19
	Clay Matthews	19
	Eddie Murray	19
	Bruce Smith	19
	Jan Stenerud	19
	Vinny Testaverde	19
21	Lomas Brown	18
	John Carney	18
	Jeff Feagles	18
	Lee Johnson	18
	Norm Johnson	18
	Charlie Joiner	18
	Sonny Jurgensen	18
	Pat Leahy	18
	Nick Lowery	18
	Ron McDole	18
	Craig Morton	18
	Fran Tarkenton	18
	Johnny Unitas	18
	Jeff Van Note	18
35	Doug Atkins	17
	Matt Bahr	17
	Jim Bakken	17
	John Brodie	17
	Tim Brown	17
	Blair Bush	17
	Chris Chandler	17
	Steve DeBerg	17
	Al Del Greco	17
	Ray Donaldson	17
	Joe Ferguson	17
	Pat Fischer	17
	Irving Fryar	17
	Rich Gannon	17
	Lou Groza	17
	Mike Kenn	17
	Dan Marino	17
	Warren Moon	17
	Mick Tingelhoff	17
	Mike Webster	17
	Ed White	17
	Wade Wilson	17
	Rod Woodson	17
58	53 players tied	16

GAMES PLAYED

	NAME	ADJ	RATIO	UNADJ
1	George Blanda	411	1.21	340(3)
2	Morten Andersen	361	1.02	354(1)
	Gary Anderson	361	1.02	353(2)
4	Jim Marshall	318	1.13	282(9)
5	Jerry Rice	304	1.00	303(4)
6	Earl Morrall	301	1.18	255(20)
7	Bruce Matthews	297	1.00	296(5)
8	Darrell Green	296	1.00	295(6)
9	Jan Stenerud	292	1.11	263(14)
10	Jeff Feagles	288	1.00	288(7)
11	Sean Landeta	285	1.00	284(8)
12	Trey Junkin	282	1.00	281(10)
13	Norm Johnson	281	1.03	273(13)
	Clay Matthews	281	1.01	278(12)
15	Bruce Smith	280	1.00	279(11)
16	Fran Tarkenton	279	1.13	246(28)
17	Ron McDole	273	1.14	240(38)
18	Mick Tingelhoff	272	1.13	240(38)
19	Jackie Slater	271	1.05	259(18)
20	Lou Groza	269	1.25	216(101)
21	Nick Lowery	268	1.03	260(17)
	Jeff Van Note	268	1.09	246(28)
23	Ed White	266	1.10	241(37)
24	Jim Bakken	265	1.13	234(51)
	Pat Leahy	265	1.06	250(24)
26	Lomas Brown	264	1.00	263(14)
27	Ray Brown	262	1.00	262(16)
28	Charlie Joiner	261	1.09	239(40)
	Mike Webster	261	1.07	245(31)
30	Lee Johnson	260	1.00	259(18)
31	Mike Kenn	259	1.03	251(23)
32	Irving Fryar	256	1.00	255(20)
	John Hadl	256	1.14	224(76)
	Sonny Jurgensen	256	1.17	218(90)
	Eddie Murray	256	1.02	250(24)
	Jim Turner	256	1.12	228(62)
37	Tim Brown	255	1.00	255(20)
38	Paul Krause	254	1.12	226(69)
39	Blair Bush	253	1.03	246(28)
	Carl Eller	253	1.12	225(72)
41	Ray Donaldson	252	1.03	244(33)
42	Eugene Robinson	251	1.00	250(24)
	Johnny Unitas	251	1.19	211(123)
44	Doug Atkins	250	1.22	205(165)
45	Al Del Greco	248	1.00	248(27)
46	Jerrel Wilson	246	1.13	217(96)
47	John Carney	245	1.00	245(31)
	Jimmy Johnson	245	1.15	213(111)
49	Len Dawson	244	1.16	211(123)
	Pat Fischer	244	1.15	213(111)
51	Dan Marino	243	1.00	242(35)
	Pete Metzelaars	243	1.03	235(49)
	Bill Romanowski	243	1.00	243(34)
54	Matt Bahr	242	1.03	235(49)
	Stan Brock	242	1.03	234(51)
	Ricky Proehl	242	1.00	242(35)
57	James Lofton	241	1.03	233(56)
	Rohn Stark	241	1.03	233(56)
59	Fred Cox	240	1.14	210(131)
	Ted Hendricks	240	1.12	215(106)
	Too Tall Jones	240	1.07	224(76)
	Jim Otto	240	1.14	210(131)
	Alan Page	240	1.10	218(90)
64	Jerry Fontenot	239	1.00	239(40)
	Chris Mohr	239	1.00	239(40)
	Reggie Roby	239	1.00	238(44)
	Matt Stover	239	1.00	239(40)
	Gene Upshaw	239	1.10	217(96)
	Rod Woodson	239	1.00	238(44)
70	Bryan Barker	238	1.00	238(44)
	Merlin Olsen	238	1.14	208(139)
	Len Rohde	238	1.14	208(139)
	Jackie Smith	238	1.13	210(131)
74	Mel Hein	237	1.39	170
	Clyde Simmons	237	1.00	236(47)
76	Sammy Baugh	236	1.43	165
	Elvin Bethea	236	1.12	210(131)
	John Brodie	236	1.17	201(194)
	Charley Cowan	236	1.15	206(156)
	Carl Hairston	236	1.05	224(76)
	Gene Hickerson	236	1.17	202(188)
82	Sam Baker	235	1.21	195(239)
	Cris Carter	235	1.00	234(50)
	John Elway	235	1.00	234(50)
	Rickey Jackson	235	1.04	227(67)
	Guy Morriss	235	1.08	217(96)
	Andre Reed	235	1.00	234(50)
89	Grady Alderman	234	1.15	204(172)
	Bart Starr	234	1.19	196(227)
90	Chris Doleman	233	1.00	232(57)
	Art Shell	233	1.13	207(147)
	Wayne Walker	233	1.16	200(202)
	Reggie White	233	1.00	232(57)
	Ron Yary	233	1.13	207(147)
95	Dave Butz	232	1.07	216(101)
	Art Monk	232	1.04	224(76)
	Mark Moseley	232	1.09	213(111)
	Ken Riley	232	1.12	207(147)
	Frank Winters	232	1.00	231(59)

RUSHING ATTEMPTS

	NAME	ADJ	RATIO	UNADJ
1	Emmitt Smith	4409	1.00	4409(1)
2	Walter Payton	4084	1.06	3838(2)
3	Curtis Martin	3518	1.00	3518(3)
4	Jerome Bettis	3479	1.00	3479(4)
5	Franco Harris	3263	1.11	2949(8)
6	John Riggins	3219	1.10	2916(10)
7	Marcus Allen	3160	1.05	3022(6)
8	Tony Dorsett	3112	1.06	2936(9)
9	Barry Sanders	3062	1.00	3062(5)
10	Eric Dickerson	3015	1.01	2996(7)
11	Thurman Thomas	2877	1.00	2877(11)
12	Eddie George	2865	1.00	2865(12)
13	Jim Brown	2839	1.20	2359(18)
14	Marshall Faulk	2836	1.00	2836(13)
15	O.J. Simpson	2707	1.13	2404(17)
16	Ottis Anderson	2675	1.04	2562(15)
17	Ricky Watters	2622	1.00	2622(14)
18	Corey Dillon	2419	1.00	2419(16)
19	Earl Campbell	2309	1.06	2187(20)
20	Joe Perry	2255	1.30	1737(39)
21	Jim Taylor	2251	1.16	1941(27)
22	Edgerrin James	2188	1.00	2188(19)
23	Terry Allen	2152	1.00	2152(21)
24	Larry Csonka	2117	1.12	1891(29)
25	Earnest Byner	2102	1.00	2095(22)
26	Gerald Riggs	2063	1.04	1989(24)
27	Roger Craig	2005	1.01	1991(23)
28	Leroy Kelly	1974	1.14	1727(41)
29	Warrick Dunn	1970	1.00	1970(25)
30	Mike Pruitt	1969	1.07	1844(31)
31	Herschel Walker	1968	1.01	1954(26)
32	Freeman McNeil	1924	1.07	1798(35)
33	Stephen Davis	1905	1.00	1905(28)
34	Tiki Barber	1890	1.00	1890(30)
	John Henry Johnson	1890	1.20	1571(55)
36	Bill Brown	1885	1.14	1649(50)
37	Floyd Little	1875	1.14	1641(51)
38	Lydell Mitchell	1874	1.12	1675(47)
39	Ken Willard	1854	1.14	1622(52)
40	Steve Van Buren	1834	1.39	1320(82)
41	Garrison Hearst	1831	1.00	1831(32)
	Fred Taylor	1831	1.00	1831(32)
43	Rodney Hampton	1824	1.00	1824(34)
44	Mark van Eeghen	1819	1.10	1652(49)
45	Rick Casares	1810	1.26	1431(69)
46	George Rogers	1798	1.06	1692(45)
47	Chris Warren	1791	1.00	1791(36)
48	Antowain Smith	1784	1.00	1784(37)
49	James Brooks	1759	1.04	1685(46)
50	Ricky Williams	1757	1.00	1757(38)
51	Larry Brown	1749	1.14	1530(60)
52	Priest Holmes	1734	1.00	1734(40)
53	Chuck Foreman	1729	1.11	1556(57)
54	Chuck Muncie	1718	1.10	1561(56)
55	Shaun Alexander	1717	1.00	1717(42)
56	Don Perkins	1714	1.14	1500(64)
	Curt Warner	1714	1.01	1698(44)
58	LaDainian Tomlinson	1702	1.00	1702(43)
59	Lawrence McCutcheon	1699	1.12	1521(61)
60	James Wilder	1658	1.05	1586(54)
61	Terrell Davis	1655	1.00	1655(48)
62	Calvin Hill	1640	1.13	1452(68)
63	Wilbert Montgomery	1635	1.06	1540(58)
64	Pete Johnson	1632	1.10	1489(66)
65	Ahman Green	1605	1.00	1605(53)
66	Clarke Hinkle	1589	1.36	1171(110)
67	Sammy Winder	1560	1.04	1495(65)
68	John Brockington	1539	1.14	1347(76)
69	Charlie Garner	1537	1.00	1537(59)
70	Jim Nance	1533	1.14	1341(79)
71	Sam Cunningham	1525	1.10	1385(74)
72	Neal Anderson	1524	1.01	1515(62)
73	Ollie Matson	1513	1.29	1170(111)
74	Jamal Lewis	1508	1.00	1508(63)
75	Mike Garrett	1495	1.14	1308(86)
76	Alex Webster	1485	1.24	1196(103)
77	James Stewart	1478	1.00	1478(67)
78	Emerson Boozer	1475	1.14	1291(88)
79	Wendell Tyler	1459	1.09	1344(78)
80	Joe Morris	1436	1.02	1411(71)
81	Hugh McElhenny	1434	1.28	1124(125)
82	Tony Canadeo	1431	1.40	1025(149)
83	Duce Staley	1430	1.00	1430(70)
84	William Andrews	1423	1.08	1315(83)
85	Joe Cribbs	1418	1.08	1309(85)
86	Robert Smith	1411	1.00	1411(71)
87	Natrone Means	1409	1.00	1409(73)
88	Delvin Williams	1408	1.07	1312(84)
89	Dick Bass	1392	1.14	1218(95)
90	Ron Johnson	1376	1.14	1204(97)
91	Adrian Murrell	1375	1.00	1375(75)
92	MacArthur Lane	1371	1.14	1206(96)
	Tom Matte	1371	1.14	1200(100)
94	Donny Anderson	1368	1.14	1197(102)
95	John David Crow	1359	1.17	1157(117)
96	Dave Osborn	1347	1.14	1179(107)
97	Marion Butts	1345	1.00	1345(77)
98	Altie Taylor	1337	1.14	1170(111)
99	Jamal Anderson	1329	1.00	1329(80)

RUSHING YARDS

	NAME	ADJ	RATIO	UNADJ
1	Emmitt Smith	18355	1.00	18355(1)
2	Walter Payton	17785	1.06	16726(2)
3	Barry Sanders	15269	1.00	15269(3)
4	Jim Brown	14794	1.20	12312(8)
5	**Curtis Martin**	**14101**	**1.00**	**14101(4)**
6	**Jerome Bettis**	**13662**	**1.00**	**13662(5)**
7	Tony Dorsett	13493	1.06	12739(7)
8	Franco Harris	13489	1.11	12120(11)
9	Eric Dickerson	13345	1.01	13259(6)
10	Marcus Allen	12835	1.05	12243(10)
11	O.J. Simpson	12691	1.13	11236(14)
12	John Riggins	12447	1.10	11352(13)
13	**Marshall Faulk**	**12279**	**1.00**	**12279(9)**
14	Thurman Thomas	12074	1.00	12074(12)
15	Joe Perry	10937	1.31	8378(24)
16	Ottis Anderson	10730	1.04	10273(18)
17	Ricky Watters	10643	1.00	10643(15)
18	Eddie George	10441	1.00	10441(16)
19	**Corey Dillon**	**10429**	**1.00**	**10429(17)**
20	Jim Taylor	9958	1.16	8597(23)
21	Earl Campbell	9825	1.04	9407(19)
22	**Edgerrin James**	**9226**	**1.00**	**9226(20)**
23	Larry Csonka	9071	1.12	8081(31)
24	**Tiki Barber**	**8787**	**1.00**	**8787(21)**
25	Freeman McNeil	8721	1.08	8074(32)
26	Terry Allen	8614	1.00	8614(22)
27	Gerald Riggs	8479	1.04	8188(30)
28	**Fred Taylor**	**8367**	**1.00**	**8367(25)**
29	**Warrick Dunn**	**8321**	**1.00**	**8321(26)**
30	James Brooks	8316	1.04	7962(35)
31	Leroy Kelly	8313	1.14	7274(43)
32	Earnest Byner	8290	1.00	8261(27)
33	Herschel Walker	8284	1.01	8225(28)
34	Roger Craig	8243	1.01	8189(29)
35	Steve Van Buren	8218	1.40	5860(69)
36	John Henry Johnson	8193	1.20	6803(51)
37	**Priest Holmes**	**8035**	**1.00**	**8035(33)**
38	Garrison Hearst	7966	1.00	7966(34)
39	**Stephen Davis**	**7875**	**1.00**	**7875(36)**
40	Mike Pruitt	7828	1.06	7378(41)
41	**Shaun Alexander**	**7817**	**1.00**	**7817(37)**
42	Chris Warren	7696	1.00	7696(38)
43	George Rogers	7633	1.06	7176(44)
44	Terrell Davis	7607	1.00	7607(39)
45	**Ahman Green**	**7432**	**1.00**	**7432(40)**
46	Mark van Eeghen	7383	1.11	6651(55)
47	Lawrence McCutcheon	7367	1.12	6578(56)
48	**LaDainian Tomlinson**	**7361**	**1.00**	**7361(42)**
49	Rick Casares	7358	1.27	5797(72)
50	Chuck Muncie	7355	1.10	6702(53)
51	Lydell Mitchell	7318	1.12	6534(57)
52	Floyd Little	7226	1.14	6323(59)
53	Wilbert Montgomery	7216	1.06	6789(52)
54	Don Perkins	7105	1.14	6217(60)
55	Charlie Garner	7097	1.00	7097(45)
	Ricky Williams	**7097**	**1.00**	**7097(45)**
57	Ken Willard	6977	1.14	6105(62)
58	Curt Warner	6910	1.01	6844(49)
59	Rodney Hampton	6897	1.00	6897(47)
60	**Antowain Smith**	**6881**	**1.00**	**6881(48)**
61	Calvin Hill	6878	1.13	6083(63)
62	Wendell Tyler	6862	1.08	6378(58)
63	Robert Smith	6818	1.00	6818(50)
64	Hugh McElhenny	6786	1.29	5281(85)
65	Larry Brown	6714	1.14	5875(68)
66	Ollie Matson	6711	1.30	5173(91)
67	Bill Brown	6672	1.14	5838(71)
68	**Jamal Lewis**	**6669**	**1.00**	**6669(54)**
69	Chuck Foreman	6652	1.12	5950(66)
70	William Andrews	6432	1.07	5986(65)
71	Lenny Moore	6324	1.22	5174(90)
72	James Wilder	6293	1.05	6008(64)
73	Greg Pruitt	6269	1.11	5672(74)
74	Mike Garrett	6264	1.14	5481(78)
75	Neal Anderson	6205	1.01	6166(61)
76	Pete Johnson	6193	1.10	5626(75)
77	Dick Bass	6191	1.14	5417(81)
78	Jim Nance	6173	1.14	5401(82)
79	Delvin Williams	6022	1.08	5598(76)
80	Sam Cunningham	6017	1.10	5453(79)
81	**Clinton Portis**	**5930**	**1.00**	**5930(67)**
82	John Brockington	5926	1.14	5185(88)
83	Tony Canadeo	5873	1.40	4197(142)
84	Clem Daniels	5872	1.14	5138(92)
85	Emerson Boozer	5869	1.14	5135(93)
86	Joe Cribbs	5868	1.10	5356(83)
87	John David Crow	5841	1.18	4963(99)
	James Stewart	5841	1.00	5841(70)
89	**Duce Staley**	**5785**	**1.00**	**5785(73)**
90	Alex Webster	5768	1.24	4638(118)
91	Paul Lowe	5709	1.14	4995(98)
92	Sammy Winder	5678	1.05	5427(80)
93	Joe Morris	5666	1.01	5585(77)
94	Gale Sayers	5664	1.14	4956(102)
95	Billy Sims	5603	1.10	5106(95)
96	J.D. Smith	5577	1.19	4672(113)
97	Dexter Bussey	5484	1.07	5105(96)
98	Donny Anderson	5367	1.14	4696(112)
99	Alan Ameche	5343	1.32	4045(153)

RUSHING AVERAGE GAIN

	NAME	ADJ	UNADJ
1	Randall Cunningham	6.36	6.36(1)
2	Fran Tarkenton	5.47	5.44(2)
3	Jim Brown	5.21	5.22(3)
4	Dan Towler	5.20	5.20(4)
5	Mercury Morris	5.14	5.14(5)
6	Charlie Trippi	5.10	5.10(6)
7	Gale Sayers	5.00	5.00(7)
8	Barry Sanders	4.99	4.99(8)
9	Tobin Rote	4.95	4.93(9)
10	Napoleon Kaufman	4.90	4.90(10)
	Lenny Moore	4.90	4.84(12)
12	Paul Lowe	4.87	4.87(11)
13	Joe Perry	4.85	4.82(15)
14	Robert Smith	4.83	4.83(14)
15	Ernie Green	4.80	4.80(16)
16	Marv Hubbard	4.78	4.78(17)
17	Tony Nathan	4.75	4.84(12)
	Greg Pruitt	4.75	4.74(19)
19	James Brooks	4.73	4.73(20)
	Hugh McElhenny	4.73	4.70(24)
	Tank Younger	4.73	4.73(20)
22	Stump Mitchell	4.71	4.72(22)
	Clinton Portis	**4.71**	**4.71(23)**
24	Wendell Tyler	4.70	4.75(18)
25	O.J. Simpson	4.69	4.67(25)
26	**Tiki Barber**	**4.65**	**4.65(26)**
27	**Ahman Green**	**4.63**	**4.63(27)**
	Priest Holmes	**4.63**	**4.63(27)**
29	Charlie Garner	4.62	4.62(29)
30	Terrell Davis	4.60	4.60(30)
31	Terry Metcalf	4.57	4.57(32)
	Fred Taylor	**4.57**	**4.57(32)**
33	**Shaun Alexander**	**4.55**	**4.55(35)**
	Dutch Clark	4.55	4.57(32)
35	Clarence Davis	4.54	4.53(38)
	Hoyle Granger	4.54	4.54(37)
37	Gerry Ellis	4.53	4.58(31)
	Freeman McNeil	4.53	4.49(40)
39	William Andrews	4.52	4.55(35)
40	Clem Daniels	4.48	4.48(41)
	Essex Johnson	4.48	4.48(41)
	Steve Van Buren	4.48	4.44(47)
43	Abner Haynes	4.47	4.47(43)
44	Keith Lincoln	4.46	4.46(44)
45	Dick Bass	4.45	4.45(46)
46	Willie Galimore	4.44	4.46(44)
	Ollie Matson	4.44	4.42(50)
48	Eric Dickerson	4.43	4.43(48)
	Billy Sims	4.43	4.51(39)
50	**Mike Anderson**	**4.42**	**4.42(50)**
	Jamal Lewis	**4.42**	**4.42(50)**
	Jim Taylor	4.42	4.43(48)
53	Wilbert Montgomery	4.41	4.41(53)
54	John Elway	4.40	4.40(54)
55	Bronko Nagurski	4.39	4.39(56)
56	Otis Armstrong	4.37	4.35(58)
57	Walter Payton	4.36	4.36(57)
58	Garrison Hearst	4.35	4.35(58)
59	Timmy Brown	4.34	4.34(61)
	Tony Dorsett	4.34	4.34(61)
	John Henry Johnson	4.34	4.33(63)
	Lawrence McCutcheon	4.34	4.32(65)
63	**Marshall Faulk**	**4.33**	**4.33(63)**
64	Walt Garrison	4.32	4.32(65)
	Darrin Nelson	4.32	4.35(58)
	LaDainian Tomlinson	**4.32**	**4.32(65)**
67	**Corey Dillon**	**4.31**	**4.31(68)**
	Cid Edwards	4.31	4.31(68)
	Barry Foster	4.31	4.31(68)
	Frank Gifford	4.31	4.30(71)
71	John David Crow	4.30	4.29(76)
	Amos Marsh	4.30	4.30(71)
	Deuce McAllister	**4.30**	**4.30(71)**
	Chris Warren	4.30	4.30(71)
75	Larry Csonka	4.29	4.27(81)
	Eddie Lee Ivery	4.29	4.40(54)
77	Willie Ellison	4.28	4.28(79)
	Chuck Muncie	4.28	4.29(76)
	J.D. Smith	4.28	4.25(86)
	Delvin Williams	4.28	4.27(81)
	Tom Woodeshick	4.28	4.28(79)
82	Elmer Angsman	4.27	4.26(85)
	Les Josephson	4.27	4.27(81)
84	Earl Campbell	4.26	4.30(71)
	Kenneth Davis	4.26	4.27(81)
86	Curtis Dickey	4.25	4.29(76)
	Cookie Gilchrist	4.25	4.25(86)
	Rob Goode	4.25	4.25(86)
	George Rogers	4.25	4.24(89)
90	Nick Pietrosante	4.24	4.22(92)
91	**Rudi Johnson**	**4.23**	**4.23(91)**
92	**Warrick Dunn**	**4.22**	**4.22(92)**
	John Fuqua	4.22	4.22(92)
	Edgerrin James	**4.22**	**4.22(92)**
95	Alan Ameche	4.21	4.20(99)
	Dexter Bussey	4.21	4.24(89)
	Leroy Kelly	4.21	4.21(97)
	Herschel Walker	4.21	4.21(97)
99	Thurman Thomas	4.20	4.20(99)

RUSHING TDS

	NAME	ADJ	RATIO	UNADJ
1	Emmitt Smith	164	1.00	164(1)
2	Marcus Allen	132	1.07	123(2)
3	Jim Brown	129	1.21	106(4)
4	Walter Payton	116	1.05	110(3)
5	John Riggins	110	1.06	104(5)
6	**Marshall Faulk**	**100**	**1.00**	**100(6)**
	Franco Harris	100	1.10	91(8)
8	Barry Sanders	99	1.00	99(7)
9	Steve Van Buren	98	1.42	69(24)
10	Jim Taylor	96	1.16	83(14)
11	**Jerome Bettis**	**91**	**1.00**	**91(8)**
12	Eric Dickerson	90	1.00	90(10)
	Curtis Martin	**90**	**1.00**	**90(10)**
14	**Shaun Alexander**	**89**	**1.00**	**89(12)**
15	**Priest Holmes**	**86**	**1.00**	**86(13)**
16	Leroy Kelly	85	1.14	74(19)
17	Ottis Anderson	83	1.03	81(15)
	Tony Dorsett	83	1.07	77(17)
19	Pete Johnson	82	1.08	76(18)
20	Chuck Muncie	78	1.10	71(23)
	Ricky Watters	78	1.00	78(16)
22	Earl Campbell	76	1.02	74(19)
	Lenny Moore	76	1.20	63(32)
24	Terry Allen	73	1.00	73(21)
	Gerald Riggs	73	1.06	69(24)
26	**LaDainian Tomlinson**	**72**	**1.00**	**72(22)**
27	Larry Csonka	71	1.10	64(30)
28	Joe Perry	70	1.32	53(42)
29	**Corey Dillon**	**69**	**1.00**	**69(24)**
	O.J. Simpson	69	1.13	61(33)
31	Eddie George	68	1.00	68(27)
32	**Stephen Davis**	**65**	**1.00**	**65(28)**
	Thurman Thomas	65	1.00	65(28)
34	**Edgerrin James**	**64**	**1.00**	**64(30)**
35	Rick Casares	62	1.28	49(55)
36	Herschel Walker	61	1.01	61(33)
37	Terrell Davis	60	1.00	60(35)
38	Emerson Boozer	59	1.14	52(44)
	Bill Brown	59	1.14	52(44)
	Chuck Foreman	59	1.12	53(42)
	Paul Hornung	59	1.19	50(51)
42	John Henry Johnson	58	1.22	48(59)
43	Earnest Byner	57	1.01	56(36)
	George Rogers	57	1.05	54(40)
	Dan Towler	57	1.33	43(72)
	Wendell Tyler	57	1.15	50(51)
	Curt Warner	57	1.01	56(36)
48	Roger Craig	56	1.00	56(36)
49	**Mike Alstott**	**55**	**1.00**	**55(39)**
50	Pete Banaszak	54	1.14	47(61)
	James Brooks	54	1.10	49(55)
	Antowain Smith	**54**	**1.00**	**54(40)**
53	Alan Ameche	53	1.32	40(82)
	Abner Haynes	53	1.14	46(63)
	Ernie Nevers	53	1.39	38(97)
	Mike Pruitt	53	1.05	51(47)
57	Chris Warren	52	1.00	52(44)
58	Neal Anderson	51	1.00	51(47)
	Greg Bell	51	1.00	51(47)
	Ollie Matson	51	1.29	40(82)
	Tom Matte	51	1.14	45(65)
	Wilbert Montgomery	51	1.13	45(65)
	Joe Morris	51	1.02	50(51)
	Jim Nance	51	1.14	45(65)
	Fred Taylor	**51**	**1.00**	**51(47)**
	Ken Willard	51	1.14	45(65)
67	**Tiki Barber**	**50**	**1.00**	**50(51)**
	Hugh McElhenny	50	1.32	38(97)
69	**Ahman Green**	**49**	**1.00**	**49(55)**
	Rodney Hampton	49	1.00	49(55)
	Floyd Little	49	1.14	43(72)
	Pug Manders	49	1.52	32(141)
	Tobin Rote	49	1.32	37(106)
	Alex Webster	49	1.26	39(91)
75	Calvin Hill	48	1.14	42(77)
	Clarke Hinkle	48	1.37	35(119)
	Don Perkins	48	1.14	42(77)
	J.D. Smith	48	1.20	40(82)
	James Stewart	48	1.00	48(59)
80	Donny Anderson	47	1.14	41(80)
	Sam Cunningham	47	1.09	43(72)
	Verne Lewellen	47	1.26	37(106)
	Ricky Williams	**47**	**1.00**	**47(61)**
84	Dutch Clark	46	1.28	36(112)
	Ted Fritsch	46	1.50	31(150)
	Ron Johnson	46	1.14	40(82)
	Jack Kemp	46	1.14	40(82)
	Kevin Mack	46	1.01	46(63)
89	Larry Kinnebrew	45	1.01	44(71)
	Natrone Means	45	1.00	45(65)
	Clinton Portis	**45**	**1.00**	**45(65)**
	Gale Sayers	45	1.14	39(91)
	Billy Sims	45	1.07	42(77)
	Tank Younger	45	1.33	34(126)
95	John David Crow	44	1.17	38(97)
	Frank Gifford	44	1.30	34(126)
	Otto Graham	44	1.33	33(134)
	Pat Harder	44	1.35	33(134)
	Don McCauley	44	1.11	40(82)

PASS ATTEMPTS

	NAME	ADJ	RATIO	UNADJ
1	Dan Marino	*8388*	1.00	8358(1)
2	**Brett Favre**	***7611***	**1.00**	**7611(2)**
3	Fran Tarkenton	*7309*	1.13	6467(7)
4	John Elway	*7277*	1.00	7250(3)
5	Warren Moon	*6848*	1.00	6823(4)
6	**Drew Bledsoe**	***6548***	**1.00**	**6548(5)**
7	**Vinny Testaverde**	***6537***	**1.00**	**6526(6)**
8	Johnny Unitas	*6142*	1.18	5186(12)
9	Dan Fouts	*6041*	1.08	5604(8)
10	Joe Montana	*5687*	1.05	5391(9)
11	Jim Hart	*5591*	1.10	5076(14)
12	Dave Krieg	*5391*	1.02	5311(10)
13	John Hadl	*5357*	1.14	4687(19)
14	Boomer Esiason	*5234*	1.01	5205(11)
15	Steve DeBerg	*5216*	1.04	5024(15)
16	John Brodie	*5182*	1.15	4491(23)
17	Roman Gabriel	*5141*	1.14	4498(22)
18	**Kerry Collins**	***5082***	**1.00**	**5082(13)**
19	Ken Anderson	*5019*	1.12	4475(24)
20	Norm Snead	*4975*	1.14	4353(25)
21	Jim Everett	*4943*	1.00	4923(16)
22	Joe Ferguson	*4914*	1.09	4519(21)
23	Sonny Jurgensen	*4889*	1.15	4262(29)
24	Bobby Layne	*4821*	1.30	3700(47)
25	Y.A. Tittle	*4816*	1.26	3817(40)
26	Jim Kelly	*4807*	1.01	4779(17)
27	George Blanda	*4768*	1.19	4007(34)
28	Troy Aikman	*4715*	1.00	4715(18)
29	Phil Simms	*4666*	1.00	4647(20)
30	Ron Jaworski	*4407*	1.07	4117(32)
31	Terry Bradshaw	*4376*	1.12	3901(38)
32	**Mark Brunell**	***4334***	**1.00**	**4334(26)**
33	**Peyton Manning**	***4333***	**1.00**	**4333(27)**
34	Randall Cunningham	*4316*	1.01	4289(28)
35	Joe Namath	*4299*	1.14	3762(44)
36	Sammy Baugh	*4284*	1.43	2995(70)
37	Len Dawson	*4279*	1.14	3741(45)
38	Rich Gannon	*4206*	1.00	4206(30)
39	Jim Plunkett	*4189*	1.13	3701(46)
40	Ken Stabler	*4165*	1.10	3793(42)
41	Craig Morton	*4156*	1.10	3786(43)
42	Steve Young	*4154*	1.00	4149(31)
43	**Jake Plummer**	***4033***	**1.00**	**4033(33)**
44	Chris Chandler	*4005*	1.00	4005(35)
45	Archie Manning	*3987*	1.09	3642(49)
46	Jeff George	*3967*	1.00	3967(36)
47	Babe Parilli	*3930*	1.18	3330(58)
48	Jim Harbaugh	*3919*	1.00	3918(37)
49	Tommy Kramer	*3904*	1.07	3651(48)
50	Charley Johnson	*3877*	1.14	3392(56)
51	**Steve McNair**	***3871***	**1.00**	**3871(39)**
52	Joe Theismann	*3852*	1.07	3602(50)
53	Bob Griese	*3827*	1.12	3429(55)
54	Steve Grogan	*3824*	1.06	3593(52)
55	Norm Van Brocklin	*3806*	1.31	2895(78)
56	**Brad Johnson**	***3798***	**1.00**	**3798(41)**
57	Tobin Rote	*3789*	1.30	2907(77)
58	Steve Bartkowski	*3733*	1.08	3456(53)
59	Charlie Conerly	*3732*	1.32	2833(81)
60	Bart Starr	*3704*	1.18	3149(64)
61	Brian Sipe	*3683*	1.07	3439(54)
62	Ken O'Brien	*3628*	1.01	3602(50)
63	Jack Kemp	*3515*	1.14	3073(68)
64	Jim Zorn	*3441*	1.09	3149(64)
65	Billy Kilmer	*3404*	1.14	2984(71)
66	Lynn Dickey	*3403*	1.09	3125(66)
67	Bernie Kosar	*3391*	1.01	3365(57)
68	Dan Pastorini	*3352*	1.10	3055(69)
69	Neil Lomax	*3343*	1.06	3153(63)
70	**Trent Green**	***3329***	**1.00**	**3329(59)**
71	Steve Beuerlein	*3328*	1.00	3328(60)
72	Roger Staubach	*3256*	1.10	2958(73)
73	**Jeff Blake**	***3241***	**1.00**	**3241(61)**
74	Richard Todd	*3231*	1.09	2967(72)
75	Neil O'Donnell	*3229*	1.00	3229(62)
76	Earl Morrall	*3184*	1.18	2689(85)
77	Danny White	*3171*	1.07	2950(75)
78	Bobby Hebert	*3141*	1.01	3121(67)
79	Billy Wade	*3061*	1.21	2523(93)
80	Daryle Lamonica	*2973*	1.14	2601(89)
81	**Trent Dilfer**	***2953***	**1.00**	**2953(74)**
82	**Donovan McNabb**	***2943***	**1.00**	**2943(76)**
83	Chris Miller	*2898*	1.00	2892(79)
84	Milt Plum	*2866*	1.18	2419(99)
85	**Jon Kitna**	***2837***	**1.00**	**2837(80)**
86	Bert Jones	*2827*	1.11	2551(91)
87	Jay Schroeder	*2826*	1.01	2808(82)
88	**Jeff Garcia**	***2785***	**1.00**	**2785(83)**
89	**Aaron Brooks**	***2771***	**1.00**	**2771(84)**
90	Doug Williams	*2755*	1.10	2507(95)
91	Jim McMahon	*2750*	1.07	2573(90)
92	Don Meredith	*2638*	1.14	2308(108)
93	**Gus Frerotte**	***2635***	**1.00**	**2635(86)**
94	Julie Rykovich	*2613*	1.00	2613(87)
95	**Daunte Culpepper**	***2607***	**1.00**	**2607(88)**
96	Bill Kenney	*2580*	1.06	2430(97)
97	Sid Luckman	*2549*	1.46	1744(129)
98	**Tom Brady**	***2548***	**1.00**	**2548(92)**
99	Greg Landry	*2539*	1.10	2300(109)

PASS COMPLETIONS

	NAME	ADJ	RATIO	UNADJ
1	Dan Marino	*4985*	1.00	4967(1)
2	**Brett Favre**	***4678***	**1.00**	**4678(2)**
3	Fran Tarkenton	*4163*	1.13	3686(7)
4	John Elway	*4138*	1.00	4123(3)
5	Warren Moon	*4000*	1.00	3988(4)
6	**Drew Bledsoe**	***3749***	**1.00**	**3749(5)**
7	**Vinny Testaverde**	***3696***	**1.00**	**3691(6)**
8	Joe Montana	*3592*	1.05	3409(8)
9	Dan Fouts	*3553*	1.08	3297(9)
10	Johnny Unitas	*3351*	1.18	2830(16)
11	Dave Krieg	*3155*	1.02	3105(10)
12	Ken Anderson	*2996*	1.13	2654(20)
13	Steve DeBerg	*2986*	1.04	2874(13)
14	Boomer Esiason	*2985*	1.01	2969(11)
15	Troy Aikman	*2898*	1.00	2898(12)
16	Jim Kelly	*2891*	1.01	2874(13)
17	Jim Hart	*2854*	1.10	2593(21)
18	Jim Everett	*2852*	1.00	2841(15)
19	John Brodie	*2849*	1.15	2469(25)
20	**Kerry Collins**	***2826***	**1.00**	**2826(17)**
21	Sonny Jurgensen	*2790*	1.15	2433(26)
22	**Peyton Manning**	***2769***	**1.00**	**2769(18)**
23	Roman Gabriel	*2704*	1.14	2366(29)
24	John Hadl	*2701*	1.14	2363(30)
25	Y.A. Tittle	*2672*	1.26	2118(41)
26	Steve Young	*2669*	1.00	2667(19)
27	Norm Snead	*2601*	1.14	2276(37)
28	Phil Simms	*2587*	1.00	2576(22)
29	**Mark Brunell**	***2576***	**1.00**	**2576(22)**
30	Joe Ferguson	*2575*	1.09	2369(28)
31	Rich Gannon	*2533*	1.00	2533(24)
32	Ken Stabler	*2496*	1.10	2270(38)
33	Randall Cunningham	*2444*	1.01	2429(27)
34	Len Dawson	*2442*	1.14	2136(40)
35	Sammy Baugh	*2426*	1.43	1693(69)
36	Bobby Layne	*2363*	1.30	1814(62)
37	**Brad Johnson**	***2350***	**1.00**	**2350(31)**
38	Ron Jaworski	*2348*	1.07	2187(39)
39	Chris Chandler	*2328*	1.00	2328(32)
40	**Jake Plummer**	***2309***	**1.00**	**2309(33)**
41	Jim Harbaugh	*2306*	1.00	2305(34)
42	**Steve McNair**	***2305***	**1.00**	**2305(34)**
43	Jeff George	*2298*	1.00	2298(36)
44	George Blanda	*2269*	1.19	1911(54)
45	Terry Bradshaw	*2268*	1.12	2025(45)
46	Craig Morton	*2249*	1.10	2053(43)
47	Jim Plunkett	*2202*	1.13	1943(51)
48	Joe Theismann	*2195*	1.07	2044(44)
49	Archie Manning	*2186*	1.09	2011(48)
50	Tommy Kramer	*2156*	1.07	2012(47)
51	Joe Namath	*2155*	1.14	1886(56)
52	Bob Griese	*2146*	1.11	1926(53)
53	Ken O'Brien	*2126*	1.01	2110(42)
54	Bart Starr	*2121*	1.17	1808(63)
55	Steve Bartkowski	*2095*	1.08	1932(52)
56	Brian Sipe	*2079*	1.07	1944(50)
57	Norm Van Brocklin	*2042*	1.31	1553(81)
58	**Trent Green**	***2022***	**1.00**	**2022(46)**
59	Bernie Kosar	*2010*	1.01	1994(49)
60	Steve Grogan	*2000*	1.06	1879(57)
61	Charley Johnson	*1985*	1.14	1737(66)
62	Neil Lomax	*1920*	1.06	1817(61)
63	Danny White	*1899*	1.08	1761(64)
64	Lynn Dickey	*1898*	1.09	1747(65)
65	Steve Beuerlein	*1894*	1.00	1894(55)
66	Charlie Conerly	*1870*	1.32	1418(93)
67	Neil O'Donnell	*1865*	1.00	1865(58)
68	Roger Staubach	*1855*	1.10	1685(70)
69	Bobby Hebert	*1850*	1.01	1839(59)
70	**Jeff Blake**	***1827***	**1.00**	**1827(60)**
	Babe Parilli	*1827*	1.18	1552(82)
72	Jim Zorn	*1813*	1.09	1669(72)
73	Billy Kilmer	*1808*	1.14	1585(76)
74	Richard Todd	*1757*	1.09	1610(75)
75	Tobin Rote	*1725*	1.30	1329(101)
76	**Donovan McNabb**	***1718***	**1.00**	**1718(67)**
77	Dan Pastorini	*1708*	1.10	1556(80)
78	**Jeff Garcia**	***1695***	**1.00**	**1695(68)**
79	**Daunte Culpepper**	***1678***	**1.00**	**1678(71)**
80	**Jon Kitna**	***1667***	**1.00**	**1667(73)**
81	Billy Wade	*1660*	1.21	1370(96)
82	**Trent Dilfer**	***1646***	**1.00**	**1646(74)**
83	Jack Kemp	*1643*	1.14	1436(88)
84	Earl Morrall	*1627*	1.18	1379(95)
85	Jim McMahon	*1594*	1.07	1492(84)
86	Bert Jones	*1584*	1.11	1430(90)
87	Chris Miller	*1583*	1.00	1580(77)
88	**Tom Brady**	***1577***	**1.00**	**1577(78)**
89	**Aaron Brooks**	***1563***	**1.00**	**1563(79)**
90	Milt Plum	*1550*	1.19	1306(104)
91	**Kurt Warner**	***1537***	**1.00**	**1537(83)**
92	Daryle Lamonica	*1472*	1.14	1288(106)
93	Julie Rykovich	*1466*	1.00	1466(85)
94	**Brian Griese**	***1463***	**1.00**	**1463(86)**
95	Elvis Grbac	*1446*	1.00	1446(87)
96	Jay Schroeder	*1435*	1.01	1426(91)
97	Stan Humphries	*1431*	1.00	1431(89)
98	**Gus Frerotte**	***1426***	**1.00**	**1426(91)**
99	Bill Kenney	*1414*	1.06	1330(100)

PASSING YARDS

	NAME	ADJ	RATIO	UNADJ
1	Dan Marino	*61577*	1.00	61361(1)
2	**Brett Favre**	***53615***	**1.00**	**53615(2)**
3	Fran Tarkenton	*53222*	1.13	47003(5)
4	John Elway	*51688*	1.00	51475(3)
5	Warren Moon	*49512*	1.00	49325(4)
6	Johnny Unitas	*47693*	1.19	40239(10)
7	Dan Fouts	*46544*	1.08	43040(8)
8	**Vinny Testaverde**	***45324***	**1.00**	**45252(6)**
9	**Drew Bledsoe**	***43447***	**1.00**	**43447(7)**
10	Joe Montana	*42787*	1.06	40551(9)
11	Dave Krieg	*38679*	1.01	38147(11)
12	John Hadl	*38289*	1.14	33503(18)
13	Jim Hart	*38230*	1.10	34665(15)
14	Boomer Esiason	*38141*	1.01	37920(12)
15	Ken Anderson	*36989*	1.13	32838(23)
16	Sonny Jurgensen	*36971*	1.15	32224(24)
17	John Brodie	*36386*	1.15	31548(25)
18	Y.A. Tittle	*35665*	1.26	28339(34)
19	Jim Kelly	*35654*	1.01	35467(13)
20	Steve DeBerg	*35460*	1.04	34241(16)
21	Norm Snead	*35197*	1.14	30797(26)
22	Jim Everett	*34975*	1.00	34837(14)
23	Bobby Layne	*34794*	1.30	26768(45)
24	Roman Gabriel	*33650*	1.14	29444(30)
25	**Kerry Collins**	***33637***	**1.00**	**33637(17)**
26	Phil Simms	*33611*	1.00	33462(19)
27	**Peyton Manning**	***33189***	**1.00**	**33189(20)**
28	Steve Young	*33162*	1.00	33124(21)
29	Troy Aikman	*32942*	1.00	32942(22)
30	Len Dawson	*32831*	1.14	28711(32)
31	Joe Ferguson	*32322*	1.08	29817(29)
32	George Blanda	*31896*	1.18	26920(43)
33	Joe Namath	*31615*	1.14	27663(39)
34	Sammy Baugh	*31265*	1.43	21886(67)
35	Terry Bradshaw	*31261*	1.12	27989(36)
36	Norm Van Brocklin	*31011*	1.31	23611(60)
37	Ken Stabler	*30771*	1.10	27938(37)
38	Craig Morton	*30621*	1.10	27908(38)
39	Ron Jaworski	*30219*	1.07	28190(35)
40	Randall Cunningham	*30165*	1.01	29979(28)
41	**Mark Brunell**	***30037***	**1.00**	**30037(27)**
42	Jim Plunkett	*29353*	1.13	25882(47)
43	Bart Starr	*28946*	1.17	24718(54)
44	Rich Gannon	*28744*	1.00	28743(31)
45	Steve Grogan	*28551*	1.06	26886(44)
46	Chris Chandler	*28484*	1.00	28484(33)
47	Bob Griese	*27999*	1.12	25092(52)
48	Charley Johnson	*27897*	1.14	24410(55)
49	Jeff George	*27602*	1.00	27602(40)
50	**Jake Plummer**	***27259***	**1.00**	**27259(41)**
51	**Steve McNair**	***27141***	**1.00**	**27141(42)**
52	Joe Theismann	*27126*	1.08	25206(50)
53	Babe Parilli	*26758*	1.18	22681(65)
54	Tommy Kramer	*26452*	1.07	24777(53)
55	Jim Harbaugh	*26292*	1.00	26288(46)
56	Steve Bartkowski	*26054*	1.08	24124(56)
57	Archie Manning	*26022*	1.09	23911(58)
58	**Brad Johnson**	***25798***	**1.00**	**25798(48)**
59	Charlie Conerly	*25682*	1.32	19488(78)
60	**Trent Green**	***25621***	**1.00**	**25621(49)**
61	Lynn Dickey	*25395*	1.09	23322(61)
62	Ken O'Brien	*25274*	1.01	25094(51)
63	Brian Sipe	*25166*	1.06	23713(59)
64	Roger Staubach	*24975*	1.10	22700(64)
65	Earl Morrall	*24560*	1.18	20809(73)
66	Tobin Rote	*24427*	1.30	18850(86)
67	Jack Kemp	*24266*	1.14	21218(71)
68	Neil Lomax	*24060*	1.06	22771(63)
69	Steve Beuerlein	*24046*	1.00	24046(57)
70	Danny White	*23786*	1.08	21959(66)
71	Bernie Kosar	*23503*	1.01	23301(62)
72	Billy Kilmer	*23378*	1.14	20495(75)
73	Jim Zorn	*22934*	1.09	21115(72)
74	Billy Wade	*22563*	1.22	18530(87)
75	Richard Todd	*22526*	1.09	20610(74)
76	Daryle Lamonica	*21890*	1.14	19154(84)
77	Bobby Hebert	*21824*	1.01	21683(70)
78	**Jeff Blake**	***21711***	**1.00**	**21711(68)**
79	Neil O'Donnell	*21690*	1.00	21690(69)
80	Sid Luckman	*21578*	1.47	14686(115)
81	Milt Plum	*20841*	1.19	17536(95)
82	Dan Pastorini	*20272*	1.09	18515(88)
83	Jay Schroeder	*20188*	1.01	20063(77)
84	**Daunte Culpepper**	***20162***	**1.00**	**20162(76)**
85	Bert Jones	*20089*	1.10	18190(91)
86	Don Meredith	*19656*	1.14	17199(98)
87	**Donovan McNabb**	***19433***	**1.00**	**19433(79)**
88	Jim McMahon	*19425*	1.07	18148(92)
89	Chris Miller	*19357*	1.00	19320(81)
90	**Trent Dilfer**	***19352***	**1.00**	**19352(80)**
91	Ed Brown	*19329*	1.24	15600(110)
92	**Kurt Warner**	***19214***	**1.00**	**19214(82)**
93	**Aaron Brooks**	***19156***	**1.00**	**19156(83)**
94	**Jeff Garcia**	***19076***	**1.00**	**19076(85)**
95	Doug Williams	*18686*	1.10	16998(100)
96	Frank Ryan	*18475*	1.15	16042(107)
97	Julie Rykovich	*18473*	1.00	18473(89)
98	Bill Kenney	*18345*	1.06	17277(97)
99	**Jon Kitna**	***18259***	**1.00**	**18259(90)**

PASSING AVERAGE GAIN

NAME	ADJ	UNADJ
1 Otto Graham	8.63	8.63(1)
2 Sid Luckman	8.47	8.42(2)
3 Kurt Warner	8.21	8.21(3)
4 Norm Van Brocklin	8.15	8.16(4)
5 Steve Young	7.98	7.98(5)
6 Marc Bulger	7.86	7.86(6)
7 Ed Brown	7.85	7.85(7)
8 Bart Starr	7.82	7.85(7)
9 Johnny Unitas	7.77	7.76(9)
10 Daunte Culpepper	7.73	7.73(11)
11 Earl Morrall	7.71	7.74(10)
12 Dan Fouts	7.70	7.68(13)
Trent Green	7.70	7.70(12)
14 Len Dawson	7.67	7.67(14)
Roger Staubach	7.67	7.67(14)
16 Peyton Manning	7.66	7.66(16)
17 Sonny Jurgensen	7.56	7.56(17)
18 Joe Montana	7.52	7.52(18)
Frank Ryan	7.52	7.52(18)
20 Danny White	7.50	7.44(24)
21 Steve Grogan	7.47	7.48(20)
22 Lynn Dickey	7.46	7.46(21)
23 Eddie LeBaron	7.45	7.46(21)
Don Meredith	7.45	7.45(23)
25 Bill Nelsen	7.44	7.44(24)
26 Jake Delhomme	7.43	7.43(26)
27 Jim Kelly	7.42	7.42(27)
28 Y.A. Tittle	7.41	7.42(27)
29 Ken Stabler	7.39	7.37(29)
30 Ken Anderson	7.37	7.34(33)
Craig Morton	7.37	7.37(29)
Billy Wade	7.37	7.34(33)
Bob Waterfield	7.37	7.33(36)
34 Daryle Lamonica	7.36	7.36(31)
Joe Namath	7.35	7.35(32)
36 Dan Marino	7.34	7.34(33)
37 Bob Griese	7.32	7.32(37)
38 Sammy Baugh	7.30	7.31(38)
39 Boomer Esiason	7.29	7.29(39)
40 Fran Tarkenton	7.28	7.27(41)
41 Milt Plum	7.27	7.25(42)
42 Tommy Thompson	7.26	7.29(39)
43 Steve Beuerlein	7.23	7.23(43)
Warren Moon	7.23	7.23(43)
45 Matt Hasselbeck	7.22	7.22(46)
Bobby Layne	7.22	7.23(43)
47 Charley Johnson	7.20	7.20(48)
Neil Lomax	7.20	7.22(46)
Phil Simms	7.20	7.20(48)
50 Dave Krieg	7.17	7.18(50)
51 John Hadl	7.15	7.15(52)
52 Terry Bradshaw	7.14	7.17(51)
Jay Schroeder	7.14	7.14(53)
54 Tony Eason	7.12	7.12(55)
Wade Wilson	7.12	7.12(55)
56 Chris Chandler	7.11	7.11(58)
Bert Jones	7.11	7.13(54)
Bill Kenney	7.11	7.11(58)
59 John Elway	7.10	7.10(60)
60 Gary Danielson	7.09	7.12(55)
61 Tom Brady	7.08	7.08(61)
Jim Everett	7.08	7.08(61)
Vince Ferragamo	7.08	7.02(70)
64 Julie Rykovich	7.07	7.07(63)
Norm Snead	7.07	7.07(63)
66 Jim McMahon	7.06	7.05(65)
67 Brian Griese	7.05	7.05(65)
68 Brett Favre	7.04	7.04(67)
Joe Theismann	7.04	7.00(73)
Bobby Thomason	7.04	7.04(67)
71 Jeff Hostetler	7.03	7.03(69)
72 John Brodie	7.02	7.02(70)
73 Steve McNair	7.01	7.01(72)
Jim Plunkett	7.01	6.99(74)
75 Greg Landry	7.00	6.98(77)
76 Troy Aikman	6.99	6.99(74)
Randall Cunningham	6.99	6.99(74)
78 Steve Bartkowski	6.98	6.98(77)
Zeke Bratkowski	6.98	6.97(79)
80 Tom Flores	6.97	6.97(79)
Ken O'Brien	6.97	6.97(79)
Richard Todd	6.97	6.95(84)
83 Jeff George	6.96	6.96(82)
Rodney Peete	6.96	6.96(82)
85 Bobby Hebert	6.95	6.95(84)
86 Mark Brunell	6.93	6.93(86)
Bernie Kosar	6.93	6.92(89)
Vinny Testaverde	6.93	6.93(86)
89 Marc Wilson	6.92	6.92(89)
90 Aaron Brooks	6.91	6.91(91)
91 Jay Fiedler	6.90	6.90(92)
Jack Kemp	6.90	6.90(92)
93 Arnie Herber	6.89	6.84(102)
94 Charlie Conerly	6.88	6.88(95)
Mike Tomczak	6.88	6.88(95)
96 Gus Frerotte	6.87	6.87(97)
Billy Kilmer	6.87	6.87(97)
98 Elvis Grbac	6.86	6.86(99)
Ron Jaworski	6.86	6.85(100)

COMPLETION PERCENT

NAME	ADJ	UNADJ
1 Kurt Warner	65.68	65.68(1)
2 Marc Bulger	65.02	65.02(2)
3 Daunte Culpepper	64.37	64.37(3)
4 Steve Young	64.27	64.28(4)
5 Peyton Manning	63.90	63.90(5)
6 Joe Montana	63.17	63.24(6)
7 Brian Griese	63.11	63.11(7)
8 Drew Brees	62.19	62.19(8)
9 Tom Brady	61.89	61.89(9)
10 Brad Johnson	61.87	61.87(10)
11 Troy Aikman	61.46	61.46(11)
Brett Favre	61.46	61.46(11)
13 Jeff Garcia	60.86	60.86(13)
Matt Hasselbeck	60.86	60.86(13)
15 Trent Green	60.74	60.74(15)
16 Rich Gannon	60.22	60.22(16)
17 Jim Kelly	60.14	60.14(17)
18 Ken Stabler	59.92	59.85(18)
19 Danny White	59.90	59.69(20)
20 Tim Couch	59.80	59.80(19)
21 Ken Anderson	59.69	59.31(24)
22 Steve McNair	59.55	59.55(21)
23 Mark Brunell	59.44	59.44(22)
24 Dan Marino	59.43	59.43(23)
25 Bernie Kosar	59.28	59.26(25)
26 Elvis Grbac	59.14	59.14(26)
27 Jake Delhomme	59.08	59.08(27)
28 Bobby Hebert	58.90	58.92(28)
29 Jim Harbaugh	58.83	58.83(29)
30 Dan Fouts	58.81	58.83(29)
31 Jon Kitna	58.76	58.76(31)
32 Jay Fiedler	58.71	58.71(32)
33 Ken O'Brien	58.59	58.58(33)
34 Dave Krieg	58.52	58.46(34)
35 Warren Moon	58.42	58.45(35)
36 Donovan McNabb	58.38	58.38(36)
37 Tony Eason	58.23	58.25(37)
38 Chris Chandler	58.13	58.13(38)
39 Jeff Hostetler	58.04	58.04(39)
40 Jim McMahon	57.94	57.99(40)
41 Jeff George	57.93	57.93(41)
42 David Carr	57.80	57.80(42)
43 Neil O'Donnell	57.76	57.76(43)
44 Jim Everett	57.69	57.71(44)
45 Neil Lomax	57.43	57.63(45)
46 Rodney Peete	57.29	57.29(47)
47 Bart Starr	57.28	57.42(46)
48 Steve DeBerg	57.26	57.21(52)
Erik Kramer	57.26	57.29(47)
Wade Wilson	57.26	57.29(47)
51 Drew Bledsoe	57.25	57.25(50)
Jake Plummer	57.25	57.25(50)
53 Len Dawson	57.08	57.10(54)
54 Sonny Jurgensen	57.06	57.09(55)
55 Boomer Esiason	57.03	57.04(56)
56 Joe Theismann	56.99	56.75(62)
57 Roger Staubach	56.96	56.96(58)
Fran Tarkenton	56.96	57.00(57)
59 Steve Beuerlein	56.91	56.91(59)
60 Stan Humphries	56.88	56.88(60)
61 John Elway	56.86	56.87(61)
62 Gary Danielson	56.64	57.19(53)
63 Sammy Baugh	56.62	56.53(65)
Randall Cunningham	56.62	56.63(63)
65 Vinny Testaverde	56.54	56.56(64)
66 Brian Sipe	56.44	56.53(65)
67 Aaron Brooks	56.41	56.41(67)
68 Jeff Blake	56.37	56.37(68)
69 Steve Bartkowski	56.12	55.90(72)
70 Julie Rykovich	56.10	56.10(70)
71 Bob Griese	56.08	56.17(69)
72 Bert Jones	56.05	56.06(71)
73 Vince Ferragamo	55.91	55.85(74)
74 Kordell Stewart	55.81	55.81(75)
75 Lynn Dickey	55.78	55.90(72)
76 Trent Dilfer	55.74	55.74(76)
77 Otto Graham	55.72	55.72(77)
78 Kerry Collins	55.61	55.61(78)
79 Y.A. Tittle	55.47	55.49(79)
80 Scott Mitchell	55.46	55.46(81)
81 Phil Simms	55.44	55.43(82)
82 Greg Landry	55.38	55.48(80)
Don Majkowski	55.38	55.43(82)
84 Tommy Kramer	55.22	55.11(85)
85 John Brodie	54.99	54.98(86)
86 Steve Bono	54.88	54.91(87)
87 Archie Manning	54.84	55.22(84)
88 Bill Kenney	54.82	54.73(88)
89 Doug Flutie	54.72	54.72(89)
Joey Harrington	54.72	54.72(89)
91 Chris Miller	54.61	54.63(91)
92 Dave Brown	54.59	54.59(92)
93 Bubby Brister	54.56	54.57(93)
94 Johnny Unitas	54.55	54.57(93)
95 Richard Todd	54.39	54.26(96)
96 Tony Banks	54.24	54.24(97)
Billy Wade	54.24	54.30(95)
98 Craig Morton	54.13	54.23(98)
99 Gus Frerotte	54.12	54.12(99)

TD PASSES

NAME	ADJ	RATIO	UNADJ
1 Dan Marino	422	1.00	420(1)
2 Brett Favre	396	1.00	396(2)
3 Fran Tarkenton	387	1.13	342(3)
4 Johnny Unitas	347	1.20	290(6)
5 John Elway	301	1.00	300(4)
6 Sonny Jurgensen	293	1.15	255(10)
7 Warren Moon	292	1.00	291(5)
8 Joe Montana	288	1.06	273(7)
9 George Blanda	279	1.18	236(18)
John Hadl	279	1.14	244(13)
11 Len Dawson	273	1.14	239(16)
Dan Fouts	273	1.07	254(11)
13 Vinny Testaverde	269	1.00	269(8)
14 Sammy Baugh	267	1.43	187(35)
15 Dave Krieg	264	1.01	261(9)
Y.A. Tittle	264	1.24	212(21)
17 Bobby Layne	255	1.30	196(29)
18 Boomer Esiason	248	1.00	247(12)
19 John Brodie	246	1.15	214(20)
20 Drew Bledsoe	244	1.00	244(13)
Peyton Manning	244	1.00	244(13)
22 Terry Bradshaw	239	1.13	212(21)
23 Jim Kelly	238	1.01	237(17)
24 Steve Young	233	1.00	232(19)
25 Jim Hart	231	1.11	209(23)
26 Roman Gabriel	230	1.14	201(26)
27 Charlie Conerly	228	1.32	173(42)
28 Norm Van Brocklin	226	1.31	173(42)
29 Norm Snead	224	1.14	196(29)
30 Ken Anderson	220	1.12	197(28)
31 Bob Griese	215	1.12	192(34)
32 Ken Stabler	214	1.10	194(33)
33 Joe Ferguson	210	1.07	196(29)
Babe Parilli	210	1.18	178(40)
35 Randall Cunningham	209	1.01	207(24)
36 Jim Everett	204	1.00	203(25)
37 Steve DeBerg	202	1.03	196(29)
Sid Luckman	202	1.48	137(69)
39 Craig Morton	201	1.10	183(36)
40 Phil Simms	200	1.01	199(27)
41 Joe Namath	198	1.14	173(42)
42 Steve Grogan	195	1.07	182(37)
43 Charley Johnson	194	1.14	170(46)
44 Tobin Rote	192	1.30	148(66)
45 Ron Jaworski	191	1.07	179(39)
46 Earl Morrall	188	1.17	161(51)
47 Daryle Lamonica	187	1.14	164(49)
Jim Plunkett	187	1.14	164(49)
49 Rich Gannon	180	1.00	180(38)
50 Bart Starr	177	1.17	152(61)
51 Mark Brunell	174	1.00	174(41)
52 Kerry Collins	173	1.00	173(42)
Billy Kilmer	173	1.14	152(61)
Joe Theismann	173	1.08	160(52)
55 Tommy Kramer	172	1.08	159(53)
56 Frank Ryan	171	1.15	149(65)
57 Chris Chandler	170	1.00	170(46)
58 Danny White	169	1.09	155(56)
59 Roger Staubach	167	1.09	153(60)
60 Troy Aikman	165	1.00	165(48)
Steve Bartkowski	165	1.06	156(54)
62 Brian Sipe	161	1.05	154(58)
63 Steve McNair	156	1.00	156(54)
64 Brad Johnson	155	1.00	155(56)
65 Jeff George	154	1.00	154(58)
Don Meredith	154	1.14	135(71)
67 Lynn Dickey	153	1.09	141(68)
68 Trent Green	150	1.00	150(63)
Jake Plummer	150	1.00	150(63)
Billy Wade	150	1.21	124(80)
71 Steve Beuerlein	147	1.00	147(67)
72 Milt Plum	145	1.19	122(86)
73 Neil Lomax	141	1.04	136(70)
74 Archie Manning	138	1.10	125(79)
75 Richard Todd	137	1.10	124(80)
76 Bobby Hebert	136	1.01	135(71)
Bert Jones	136	1.09	124(80)
78 Daunte Culpepper	135	1.00	135(71)
Bob Waterfield	135	1.39	97(107)
80 Jeff Blake	134	1.00	134(74)
Donovan McNabb	134	1.00	134(74)
82 Jack Kemp	130	1.14	114(91)
Eddie LeBaron	130	1.25	104(97)
84 Jim Harbaugh	129	1.00	129(76)
Ken O'Brien	129	1.01	128(77)
86 Ed Brown	126	1.24	102(100)
Jeff Garcia	126	1.00	126(78)
88 Bernie Kosar	125	1.01	124(80)
89 Tommy Thompson	124	1.36	91(114)
90 Tom Brady	123	1.00	123(84)
Chris Miller	123	1.00	123(84)
92 Aaron Brooks	120	1.00	120(87)
Neil O'Donnell	120	1.00	120(87)
Jim Zorn	120	1.09	111(93)
95 Kurt Warner	119	1.00	119(89)
96 Otto Graham	117	1.33	88(116)
97 Julie Rykovich	115	1.00	115(90)
Jay Schroeder	115	1.01	114(91)
99 2 players tied			98

INT PERCENT

	NAME	ADJ	UNADJ
1	Neil O'Donnell	2.11	2.11(1)
2	**Donovan McNabb**	2.24	2.24(2)
3	**Mark Brunell**	2.35	2.35(3)
4	Steve Bono	2.47	2.47(4)
	Rich Gannon	2.47	2.47(4)
6	**Jeff Garcia**	2.55	2.55(6)
7	Bernie Kosar	2.58	2.59(9)
	Steve Young	2.58	2.58(7)
9	**Tom Brady**	2.59	2.59(9)
	Matt Hasselbeck	2.59	2.59(9)
11	Joe Montana	2.61	2.58(7)
12	**Steve McNair**	2.66	2.66(12)
13	**Brad Johnson**	2.69	2.69(13)
14	Ken O'Brien	2.72	2.72(14)
15	**Trent Green**	2.76	2.76(15)
16	Jeff George	2.85	2.85(16)
17	Neil Lomax	2.86	2.85(16)
18	**Drew Brees**	2.93	2.93(18)
19	Troy Aikman	2.99	2.99(19)
	Jim Harbaugh	2.99	2.99(19)
21	**Gus Frerotte**	3.00	3.00(21)
	Peyton Manning	3.00	3.00(21)
23	Dan Marino	3.01	3.02(23)
24	**Drew Bledsoe**	3.02	3.02(23)
25	**Aaron Brooks**	3.03	3.03(25)
26	Jeff Hostetler	3.04	3.04(26)
27	**Jeff Blake**	3.05	3.05(27)
28	**Tony Banks**	3.10	3.10(28)
29	Randall Cunningham	3.12	3.12(29)
	John Elway	3.12	3.12(29)
31	**Doug Flutie**	3.16	3.16(31)
32	**David Carr**	3.26	3.26(32)
	Tony Eason	3.26	3.26(32)
34	**Kerry Collins**	3.27	3.27(34)
35	**Daunte Culpepper**	3.30	3.30(35)
36	Roman Gabriel	3.31	3.31(36)
	Elvis Grbac	3.31	3.31(36)
38	**Kurt Warner**	3.33	3.33(38)
39	Stan Humphries	3.34	3.34(39)
40	**Brett Favre**	3.35	3.35(40)
41	**Marc Bulger**	3.36	3.36(41)
	Brian Griese	3.36	3.36(41)
43	Steve Beuerlein	3.37	3.37(43)
	Julie Rykovich	3.37	3.37(43)
45	Phil Simms	3.38	3.38(45)
46	Warren Moon	3.42	3.41(46)
47	**Joey Harrington**	3.44	3.44(47)
	Erik Kramer	3.44	3.44(47)
49	Scott Mitchell	3.45	3.45(49)
50	**Jake Delhomme**	3.46	3.46(50)
51	Jim McMahon	3.49	3.50(51)
52	Don Majkowski	3.51	3.52(52)
53	Ken Anderson	3.52	3.58(60)
54	Bubby Brister	3.53	3.53(53)
55	Boomer Esiason	3.54	3.54(55)
	Bill Kenney	3.54	3.54(55)
	Chris Miller	3.54	3.53(53)
58	Dave Brown	3.55	3.55(57)
59	Jim Everett	3.56	3.55(57)
	Kordell Stewart	3.56	3.56(59)
61	Chris Chandler	3.65	3.65(61)
62	Jim Kelly	3.66	3.66(62)
63	**Jon Kitna**	3.67	3.67(63)
	Jake Plummer	3.67	3.67(63)
65	Doug Williams	3.70	3.71(66)
66	Roger Staubach	3.71	3.68(65)
67	Rick Mirer	3.72	3.72(67)
68	Dave Krieg	3.74	3.75(68)
69	Billy Joe Tolliver	3.75	3.75(68)
70	**Jay Fiedler**	3.84	3.84(71)
71	Jay Schroeder	3.85	3.85(72)
	Joe Theismann	3.85	3.83(70)
73	Tim Couch	3.91	3.91(73)
74	Rodney Peete	3.92	3.92(74)
75	Bert Jones	3.95	3.96(75)
76	**Trent Dilfer**	3.96	3.96(75)
77	Bobby Hebert	3.97	3.97(77)
78	**Vinny Testaverde**	4.00	4.00(79)
79	Ron Jaworski	4.03	3.98(78)
80	Bill Munson	4.04	4.04(80)
81	Mike Pagel	4.07	4.17(84)
82	Steve DeBerg	4.08	4.06(82)
83	Fran Tarkenton	4.10	4.11(83)
84	Jack Trudeau	4.18	4.20(86)
85	Wade Wilson	4.21	4.20(86)
86	Steve Bartkowski	4.23	4.17(84)
87	Gary Danielson	4.26	4.04(80)
88	Dan Fouts	4.30	4.32(88)
89	Tommy Kramer	4.31	4.33(89)
90	Brian Sipe	4.36	4.33(89)
91	Bart Starr	4.42	4.38(91)
92	Sonny Jurgensen	4.45	4.43(92)
93	Greg Landry	4.51	4.48(94)
	Danny White	4.51	4.47(93)
95	Eric Hipple	4.53	4.53(96)
96	Mike Tomczak	4.54	4.54(97)
	Jim Zorn	4.54	4.48(94)
98	Joe Ferguson	4.69	4.62(98)
99	Mike Livingston	4.75	4.74(99)

PASSER RATING

	NAME	ADJ	UNADJ
1	Steve Young	96.8	96.8(1)
2	**Kurt Warner**	94.1	94.1(2)
3	**Peyton Manning**	93.5	93.5(3)
4	Joe Montana	92.1	92.2(4)
5	**Daunte Culpepper**	91.4	91.4(5)
6	**Marc Bulger**	90.6	90.6(6)
7	**Tom Brady**	88.4	88.4(7)
8	**Trent Green**	88.2	88.2(8)
9	**Matt Hasselbeck**	86.6	86.6(9)
10	Dan Marino	86.3	86.3(10)
11	**Brett Favre**	86.0	86.0(11)
12	**Jeff Garcia**	85.8	85.8(12)
13	**Drew Brees**	84.8	84.8(13)
14	**Brian Griese**	84.8	84.8(14)
15	Rich Gannon	84.7	84.7(15)
16	**Jake Delhomme**	84.4	84.4(16)
17	Jim Kelly	84.3	84.3(17)
18	**Brad Johnson**	84.3	84.3(18)
19	**Donovan McNabb**	84.0	84.0(19)
20	**Mark Brunell**	84.0	84.0(20)
21	**Steve McNair**	83.2	83.2(22)
22	Roger Staubach	83.2	83.4(21)
23	Sonny Jurgensen	82.5	82.6(24)
24	Len Dawson	82.5	82.5(25)
25	Ken Anderson	82.4	81.8(26)
26	Danny White	82.2	81.7(29)
27	Neil Lomax	82.1	82.6(23)
28	Bernie Kosar	81.9	81.8(27)
29	Neil O'Donnell	81.8	81.8(28)
30	Troy Aikman	81.6	81.6(30)
31	Dave Krieg	81.4	81.5(31)
32	Randall Cunningham	81.4	81.4(32)
33	Boomer Esiason	81.0	81.0(33)
34	Warren Moon	80.8	80.9(34)
35	Jeff Hostetler	80.4	80.4(35)
	Fran Tarkenton	80.4	80.3(39)
37	Ken O'Brien	80.4	80.4(37)
38	Jeff George	80.4	80.4(38)
39	Dan Fouts	80.3	80.2(41)
40	Steve Beuerlein	80.3	80.3(40)
41	Bart Starr	79.9	80.4(36)
42	John Elway	79.8	79.8(42)
43	**Aaron Brooks**	79.7	79.7(44)
	Tony Eason	79.7	79.7(43)
45	Elvis Grbac	79.6	79.6(45)
46	Chris Chandler	79.1	79.1(46)
47	Julie Rykovich	78.9	78.9(47)
48	Jim Everett	78.5	78.5(48)
49	Phil Simms	78.5	78.4(49)
	Johnny Unitas	78.5	78.2(51)
51	Jim McMahon	78.3	78.1(52)
52	Otto Graham	78.1	78.1(52)
53	**Jeff Blake**	78.0	78.0(54)
	Bobby Hebert	78.0	78.0(55)
55	Bert Jones	77.9	78.2(50)
56	Joe Theismann	77.8	77.3(58)
57	Jim Harbaugh	77.6	77.6(57)
58	Frank Ryan	77.4	77.6(56)
59	**Drew Bledsoe**	77.2	77.2(59)
60	**Jay Fiedler**	77.1	77.1(61)
61	Bob Griese	77.1	77.1(60)
62	Bill Kenney	77.0	76.9(62)
63	Erik Kramer	76.6	76.6(63)
64	**Doug Flutie**	76.3	76.3(65)
65	Stan Humphries	75.8	75.8(66)
66	Sid Luckman	75.8	75.0(78)
67	Ken Stabler	75.6	75.3(70)
68	Wade Wilson	75.5	75.5(67)
69	**Gus Frerotte**	75.3	75.3(69)
70	Steve Bono	75.2	75.2(73)
	Jon Kitna	75.2	75.2(71)
	Scott Mitchell	75.2	75.2(71)
73	Gary Danielson	75.1	76.5(64)
74	**Vinny Testaverde**	75.1	75.1(74)
75	Tim Couch	75.1	75.1(75)
76	**Jake Plummer**	75.0	75.0(77)
77	Steve Bartkowski	75.0	75.4(68)
78	Norm Van Brocklin	74.9	75.0(76)
79	Don Meredith	74.8	74.8(80)
80	Chris Miller	74.8	74.9(79)
81	Roman Gabriel	74.2	74.2(82)
82	Steve DeBerg	74.0	74.2(83)
83	Brian Sipe	73.9	74.7(81)
84	**Kerry Collins**	73.7	73.7(85)
85	**David Carr**	73.7	73.7(86)
86	Earl Morrall	73.5	74.0(84)
87	Rodney Peete	73.3	73.3(89)
88	Craig Morton	73.1	73.5(88)
89	Y.A. Tittle	73.0	73.6(87)
90	Tommy Kramer	73.0	72.7(94)
91	Greg Landry	72.9	72.9(91)
92	Daryle Lamonica	72.9	72.9(91)
	Don Majkowski	72.9	72.9(90)
94	Ron Jaworski	72.7	72.7(93)
95	Milt Plum	72.4	72.2(98)
96	**Tony Banks**	72.3	72.3(95)
97	Sammy Baugh	72.2	72.2(99)
98	Bubby Brister	72.2	72.2(96)
99	John Brodie	72.0	72.2(97)

RECEPTIONS

	NAME	ADJ	RATIO	UNADJ
1	Jerry Rice	1553	1.00	1549(1)
2	Cris Carter	1101	1.00	1101(2)
3	Tim Brown	1094	1.00	1094(3)
4	Art Monk	970	1.03	940(5)
5	Andre Reed	955	1.00	951(4)
6	**Marvin Harrison**	927	1.00	927(6)
7	Steve Largent	862	1.05	819(11)
	Jimmy Smith	862	1.00	862(7)
9	Irving Fryar	853	1.00	851(8)
10	Larry Centers	827	1.00	827(9)
11	**Keenan McCardell**	825	1.00	825(10)
12	Henry Ellard	817	1.00	814(13)
13	Shannon Sharpe	815	1.00	815(12)
14	Charlie Joiner	814	1.08	750(18)
15	**Isaac Bruce**	813	1.00	813(14)
16	**Rod Smith**	797	1.00	797(15)
17	James Lofton	794	1.04	764(17)
18	**Marshall Faulk**	767	1.00	767(16)
19	Raymond Berry	763	1.21	631(35)
20	Michael Irvin	750	1.00	750(18)
21	**Keyshawn Johnson**	744	1.00	744(20)
22	Andre Rison	743	1.00	743(21)
23	Charley Taylor	742	1.14	649(29)
24	Don Hutson	726	1.49	488(100)
25	Don Maynard	724	1.14	633(34)
26	**Terrell Owens**	716	1.00	716(22)
27	Gary Clark	703	1.01	699(23)
28	Ozzie Newsome	702	1.06	662(28)
29	Terance Mathis	689	1.00	689(24)
30	**Eric Moulds**	675	1.00	675(25)
31	Fred Biletnikoff	670	1.14	589(45)
	Herman Moore	670	1.00	670(26)
33	**Ricky Proehl**	666	1.00	666(27)
34	Harold Carmichael	660	1.12	590(44)
35	**Tony Gonzalez**	648	1.00	648(30)
	Lionel Taylor	648	1.14	567(56)
37	Drew Hill	643	1.01	634(32)
38	**Muhsin Muhammad**	642	1.00	642(31)
39	Billy Howton	640	1.27	503(91)
40	Harold Jackson	638	1.10	579(52)
41	**Randy Moss**	634	1.00	634(32)
42	Rob Moore	628	1.00	628(36)
43	**Johnnie Morton**	624	1.00	624(37)
44	Marcus Allen	620	1.06	587(46)
45	Lance Alworth	619	1.14	542(67)
	Torry Holt	619	1.00	619(38)
47	Keith Byars	611	1.00	610(39)
48	Bobby Mitchell	605	1.16	521(80)
49	Wes Chandler	600	1.07	559(60)
50	Anthony Miller	595	1.00	595(40)
	Sterling Sharpe	595	1.00	595(40)
52	Curtis Conway	594	1.00	594(42)
53	Tony Martin	593	1.00	593(43)
54	Roy Green	587	1.05	559(60)
	Kellen Winslow	587	1.08	541(69)
56	Bill Brooks	586	1.01	583(47)
	Ronnie Harmon	586	1.01	582(48)
58	Mark Clayton	585	1.01	582(48)
59	Stanley Morgan	584	1.05	557(62)
60	Tommy McDonald	582	1.18	495(95)
61	Brian Blades	581	1.00	581(50)
62	**Wayne Chrebet**	580	1.00	580(51)
63	Ernest Givins	575	1.01	571(54)
64	**Hines Ward**	574	1.00	574(53)
65	John Stallworth	573	1.07	537(74)
66	Mark Carrier	571	1.00	569(55)
67	Roger Craig	570	1.01	566(57)
68	Webster Slaughter	566	1.01	563(59)
69	Ed McCaffrey	565	1.00	565(58)
70	J.T. Smith	558	1.03	544(66)
71	Eric Martin	556	1.01	553(63)
72	Cliff Branch	555	1.11	501(92)
73	Dwight Clark	554	1.10	506(89)
74	**Joey Galloway**	550	1.00	550(64)
75	Jackie Smith	549	1.14	480(105)
	John L. Williams	549	1.00	546(65)
77	Boyd Dowler	548	1.16	474(110)
78	Art Powell	547	1.14	479(107)
79	Drew Pearson	543	1.11	489(99)
80	Jeff Graham	542	1.00	542(67)
	Billy Wilson	542	1.33	407(153)
82	Eric Metcalf	541	1.00	541(69)
	Ahmad Rashad	541	1.09	495(95)
84	Carl Pickens	540	1.00	540(71)
85	**Joe Horn**	539	1.00	539(72)
	Derrick Mason	539	1.00	539(72)
	Nat Moore	539	1.06	510(87)
88	Pete Retzlaff	538	1.19	452(118)
89	Haywood Jeffires	535	1.00	535(75)
90	Tom Fears	533	1.33	400(160)
91	Walter Payton	530	1.08	492(97)
92	**Amani Toomer**	529	1.00	529(76)
93	**Tiki Barber**	528	1.00	528(77)
94	Brett Perriman	525	1.00	525(78)
95	**Terry Glenn**	523	1.00	523(79)
96	Al Toon	522	1.01	517(81)
97	Tony Galbreath	519	1.06	490(98)
98	Herschel Walker	516	1.01	512(84)
99	3 players tied			515

RECEIVING YARDS

	NAME	ADJ	RATIO	UNADJ
1	Jerry Rice	*22967*	1.00	22895(1)
2	Tim Brown	*14934*	1.00	14934(2)
3	James Lofton	*14604*	1.04	14004(3)
4	Cris Carter	*13905*	1.00	13899(4)
5	Henry Ellard	*13830*	1.00	13777(5)
6	Steve Largent	*13726*	1.05	13089(7)
7	Don Maynard	*13541*	1.14	11834(15)
8	Andre Reed	*13248*	1.00	13198(6)
9	Charlie Joiner	*13219*	1.09	12146(13)
10	Art Monk	*13101*	1.03	12721(9)
11	Irving Fryar	*12816*	1.00	12785(8)
12	**Marvin Harrison**	***12331***	**1.00**	**12331(10)**
13	**Jimmy Smith**	***12287***	**1.00**	**12287(11)**
14	**Isaac Bruce**	***12278***	**1.00**	**12278(12)**
15	Michael Irvin	*11904*	1.00	11904(14)
16	Don Hutson	*11868*	1.49	7991(64)
17	Lance Alworth	*11733*	1.14	10266(22)
18	Harold Jackson	*11384*	1.10	10372(21)
19	Stanley Morgan	*11278*	1.05	10716(18)
20	Raymond Berry	*11240*	1.21	9275(30)
21	Gary Clark	*10927*	1.01	10856(17)
22	**Rod Smith**	***10877***	**1.00**	**10877(16)**
23	Billy Howton	*10828*	1.28	8459(51)
24	**Keenan McCardell**	***10680***	**1.00**	**10680(19)**
25	**Terrell Owens**	***10535***	**1.00**	**10535(20)**
26	Charley Taylor	*10411*	1.14	9110(33)
27	Fred Biletnikoff	*10215*	1.14	8974(37)
28	Andre Rison	*10205*	1.00	10205(23)
29	**Randy Moss**	***10147***	**1.00**	**10147(24)**
30	Shannon Sharpe	*10060*	1.00	10060(25)
31	Harold Carmichael	*9996*	1.11	8985(36)
32	Drew Hill	*9968*	1.01	9831(26)
33	Tommy McDonald	*9931*	1.18	8410(52)
34	Wes Chandler	*9810*	1.09	8966(39)
35	Paul Warfield	*9789*	1.14	8565(48)
36	**Keyshawn Johnson**	***9756***	**1.00**	**9756(27)**
37	Cliff Branch	*9699*	1.12	8685(47)
38	**Torry Holt**	***9487***	**1.00**	**9487(28)**
39	Carroll Dale	*9459*	1.14	8277(54)
40	Rob Moore	*9368*	1.00	9368(29)
41	Roy Green	*9366*	1.04	8965(40)
42	Jimmy Orr	*9333*	1.18	7914(69)
43	John Stallworth	*9327*	1.07	8723(45)
44	Art Powell	*9195*	1.14	8046(62)
45	Bobby Mitchell	*9182*	1.15	7954(67)
46	Herman Moore	*9174*	1.00	9174(31)
47	Anthony Miller	*9148*	1.00	9148(32)
48	**Eric Moulds**	***9096***	**1.00**	**9096(34)**
49	Tony Martin	*9065*	1.00	9065(35)
50	Jackie Smith	*9049*	1.14	7918(68)
51	Mark Clayton	*9026*	1.01	8974(37)
52	Mark Duper	*8909*	1.00	8869(41)
53	Wesley Walker	*8907*	1.07	8306(53)
54	Haven Moses	*8874*	1.10	8091(61)
55	**Ricky Proehl**	***8848***	**1.00**	**8848(42)**
56	Terance Mathis	*8809*	1.00	8809(43)
57	Mark Carrier	*8791*	1.00	8763(44)
58	Pete Retzlaff	*8783*	1.19	7412(82)
59	**Johnnie Morton**	***8719***	**1.00**	**8719(46)**
60	Drew Pearson	*8687*	1.11	7822(70)
61	Roy Jefferson	*8616*	1.14	7539(78)
62	Gary Garrison	*8615*	1.14	7538(79)
63	**Joey Galloway**	***8501***	**1.00**	**8501(49)**
	Muhsin Muhammad	***8501***	**1.00**	**8501(49)**
65	Ozzie Newsome	*8497*	1.06	7980(66)
66	Bob Hayes	*8473*	1.14	7414(81)
67	Boyd Dowler	*8413*	1.16	7270(86)
68	Tony Hill	*8400*	1.05	7988(65)
69	Elroy Hirsch	*8399*	1.33	6299(127)
70	Otis Taylor	*8350*	1.14	7306(85)
71	Ernest Givins	*8277*	1.01	8215(56)
72	Curtis Conway	*8230*	1.00	8230(55)
73	Lionel Taylor	*8223*	1.14	7195(88)
74	Eric Martin	*8213*	1.01	8161(58)
75	Jeff Graham	*8172*	1.00	8172(57)
76	Webster Slaughter	*8165*	1.01	8111(60)
77	Sterling Sharpe	*8134*	1.00	8134(59)
78	John Gilliam	*8064*	1.14	7056(94)
79	Bill Brooks	*8049*	1.01	8001(63)
80	Nat Moore	*7995*	1.06	7546(77)
81	Billy Wilson	*7860*	1.33	5902(140)
82	Isaac Curtis	*7852*	1.11	7101(92)
83	**Joe Horn**	***7822***	**1.00**	**7822(70)**
84	Ken Burrough	*7812*	1.10	7102(91)
85	**Tony Gonzalez**	***7810***	**1.00**	**7810(72)**
86	Gene Washington	*7808*	1.14	6856(102)
87	Charley Hennigan	*7798*	1.14	6823(104)
88	**Amani Toomer**	***7797***	**1.00**	**7797(73)**
89	Anthony Carter	*7794*	1.01	7733(75)
90	Del Shofner	*7782*	1.20	6470(118)
91	**Terry Glenn**	***7776***	**1.00**	**7776(74)**
92	Max McGee	*7679*	1.21	6346(123)
93	Reggie Rucker	*7654*	1.08	7065(93)
94	Brian Blades	*7620*	1.00	7620(76)
95	Pete Pihos	*7492*	1.33	5619(153)
96	Dwight Clark	*7479*	1.11	6750(106)
97	Pat Tilley	*7434*	1.06	7005(97)
98	Ed McCaffrey	*7422*	1.00	7422(80)
99	Ahmad Rashad	*7397*	1.08	6831(103)

RECEIVING AVERAGE GAIN

	NAME	ADJ	UNADJ
1	Ken Kavanaugh	*22.37*	22.38(1)
2	Homer Jones	*22.26*	22.26(2)
3	Buddy Dial	*20.89*	20.83(3)
4	Bob Boyd	*20.52*	20.52(4)
5	Harlon Hill	*20.28*	20.24(5)
6	Flipper Anderson	*20.06*	20.06(6)
	Paul Warfield	*20.06*	20.06(6)
8	Bob Hayes	*19.98*	19.98(8)
9	Willie Gault	*19.93*	19.92(9)
10	Jimmy Orr	*19.85*	19.78(10)
11	Ray Renfro	*19.69*	19.60(11)
12	Stanley Morgan	*19.30*	19.24(12)
13	Hugh Taylor	*19.24*	19.24(12)
14	Mel Gray	*18.95*	18.93(16)
15	Lance Alworth	*18.94*	18.94(15)
16	Carroll Dale	*18.90*	18.90(17)
17	Roger Carr	*18.86*	18.71(18)
18	Wesley Walker	*18.79*	18.96(14)
19	Don Maynard	*18.69*	18.70(19)
20	Frank Clarke	*18.66*	18.65(20)
21	Del Shofner	*18.64*	18.54(22)
22	Gary Garrison	*18.61*	18.61(21)
23	John Gilliam	*18.47*	18.47(23)
24	Max McGee	*18.41*	18.39(24)
25	James Lofton	*18.39*	18.33(26)
26	Elroy Hirsch	*18.36*	18.36(25)
27	Ben Hawkins	*18.25*	18.25(27)
28	Carlos Carson	*18.07*	18.05(29)
29	Haven Moses	*18.06*	18.06(28)
30	Elbert Dubenion	*18.01*	18.01(30)
	Lance Rentzel	*18.01*	18.01(30)
32	Mervyn Fernandez	*18.00*	18.01(30)
33	Pete Brewster	*17.90*	17.90(34)
34	Harold Jackson	*17.84*	17.91(33)
35	Gene Washington	*17.83*	17.81(36)
36	Otis Taylor	*17.82*	17.82(35)
37	Gene Washington	*17.79*	17.79(38)
38	Mike Quick	*17.76*	17.81(36)
39	Jack Snow	*17.68*	17.68(39)
40	Jim Colclough	*17.67*	17.67(40)
41	Cliff Branch	*17.49*	17.34(45)
42	Bob Schnelker	*17.43*	17.38(42)
43	Aaron Thomas	*17.38*	17.38(42)
44	Mark Duper	*17.36*	17.36(44)
45	Jim Doran	*17.33*	17.30(47)
46	Bill Anderson	*17.32*	17.12(52)
47	Alfred Jenkins	*17.31*	17.41(41)
48	James Jett	*17.25*	17.25(49)
49	Bobby Walston	*17.24*	17.24(50)
50	Rich Caster	*17.22*	17.13(51)
51	Jack Ferrante	*17.18*	17.07(53)
52	Kevin House	*17.17*	17.29(48)
	Steve Watson	*17.17*	17.31(46)
54	Isaac Curtis	*17.08*	17.07(53)
55	Tommy McDonald	*17.07*	16.99(56)
56	John Greene	*17.02*	16.94(58)
57	Ray Mathews	*17.01*	17.01(55)
58	Lionel Manuel	*17.00*	16.99(56)
59	Leonard Thompson	*16.97*	16.90(61)
60	Henry Ellard	*16.92*	16.93(60)
	Billy Howton	*16.92*	16.82(66)
62	Ken Burrough	*16.89*	16.87(64)
63	Ernie Jones	*16.88*	16.88(63)
64	Eddie Brown	*16.87*	16.90(61)
65	Frank Lewis	*16.85*	16.94(58)
66	Randy Vataha	*16.83*	16.83(65)
67	Stephone Paige	*16.82*	16.82(66)
68	Art Powell	*16.80*	16.80(68)
69	Terry Barr	*16.79*	16.78(69)
70	Jim Benton	*16.76*	16.67(80)
	Dub Jones	*16.76*	16.76(71)
	Louis Lipps	*16.76*	16.77(70)
73	Jim Mutscheller	*16.74*	16.75(72)
74	Derrick Alexander	*16.72*	16.72(74)
	Roy Jefferson	*16.72*	16.72(74)
	Hassan Jones	*16.72*	16.70(76)
77	Doak Walker	*16.70*	16.70(76)
78	Charlie Brown	*16.69*	16.13(112)
79	Charley Frazier	*16.68*	16.68(78)
	Lenny Moore	*16.68*	16.64(81)
81	Duriel Harris	*16.67*	16.74(73)
82	Charley Hennigan	*16.64*	16.64(81)
83	Gary Ballman	*16.61*	16.61(83)
84	**Santana Moss**	***16.59***	**16.59(85)**
85	Stacey Bailey	*16.58*	16.61(83)
	Tony Hill	*16.58*	16.68(78)
87	Bo Roberson	*16.57*	16.57(86)
88	Frank Pitts	*16.55*	16.55(87)
89	Jackie Smith	*16.50*	16.50(89)
90	Rick Upchurch	*16.48*	16.36(95)
91	Ray Butler	*16.46*	16.52(88)
92	Al Denson	*16.44*	16.44(90)
93	Dave Kocourek	*16.43*	16.43(91)
94	Sonny Randle	*16.41*	16.43(91)
95	Sammy White	*16.40*	16.28(98)
96	Wes Chandler	*16.36*	16.04(118)
97	Don Hutson	*16.35*	16.38(94)
98	Freddie Scott	*16.34*	16.30(97)
99	2 players tied		16.33

RECEIVING TDS

	NAME	ADJ	RATIO	UNADJ
1	Jerry Rice	*198*	1.01	197(1)
2	Don Hutson	*147*	1.48	99(7)
3	Cris Carter	*130*	1.00	130(2)
4	**Marvin Harrison**	***110***	**1.00**	**110(3)**
5	Steve Largent	*105*	1.05	100(5)
6	Don Maynard	*101*	1.14	88(9)
	Terrell Owens	***101***	**1.00**	**101(4)**
8	Tim Brown	*100*	1.00	100(5)
	Tommy McDonald	*100*	1.19	84(13)
10	**Randy Moss**	***98***	**1.00**	**98(8)**
11	Lance Alworth	*97*	1.14	85(11)
	Paul Warfield	*97*	1.14	85(11)
13	Art Powell	*93*	1.14	81(17)
14	Charley Taylor	*90*	1.14	79(18)
15	Harold Carmichael	*88*	1.11	79(18)
16	Fred Biletnikoff	*87*	1.14	76(21)
	Andre Reed	*87*	1.00	87(10)
18	Raymond Berry	*84*	1.23	68(29)
	Mark Clayton	*84*	1.01	84(13)
	Irving Fryar	*84*	1.00	84(13)
	Harold Jackson	*84*	1.11	76(21)
	Andre Rison	*84*	1.00	84(13)
23	Bob Hayes	*81*	1.14	71(26)
	Pete Pihos	*81*	1.33	61(51)
25	Gary Collins	*80*	1.14	70(28)
26	Billy Howton	*78*	1.28	61(51)
	James Lofton	*78*	1.05	75(23)
	Nat Moore	*78*	1.05	74(24)
	Jimmy Orr	*78*	1.18	66(33)
30	**Isaac Bruce**	***77***	**1.00**	**77(20)**
	Hugh Taylor	*77*	1.33	58(60)
32	Cliff Branch	*76*	1.14	67(31)
	Bobby Mitchell	*76*	1.16	65(35)
	Wesley Walker	*76*	1.07	71(26)
35	Stanley Morgan	*75*	1.04	72(25)
36	Sonny Randle	*74*	1.15	65(35)
37	Elroy Hirsch	*71*	1.33	53(73)
	John Stallworth	*71*	1.12	63(44)
39	Ken Kavanaugh	*70*	1.40	50(85)
40	Roy Green	*69*	1.04	66(33)
	Charlie Joiner	*69*	1.07	65(35)
	Art Monk	*69*	1.02	68(29)
	Jerry Smith	*69*	1.14	60(55)
44	Gene Washington	*68*	1.14	60(55)
45	Jim Benton	*67*	1.49	45(119)
	Jimmy Smith	***67***	**1.00**	**67(31)**
47	Gary Garrison	*66*	1.14	58(60)
48	Gary Clark	*65*	1.01	65(35)
	Henry Ellard	*65*	1.00	65(35)
	Michael Irvin	*65*	1.00	65(35)
	Sterling Sharpe	*65*	1.00	65(35)
	Rod Smith	***65***	**1.00**	**65(35)**
	Otis Taylor	*65*	1.14	57(62)
	Billy Wilson	*65*	1.33	49(92)
55	**Joey Galloway**	***64***	**1.00**	**64(43)**
	Ray Renfro	*64*	1.28	50(85)
57	Chris Burford	*63*	1.14	55(67)
	Wes Chandler	*63*	1.13	56(63)
	Terance Mathis	*63*	1.00	63(44)
	Anthony Miller	*63*	1.00	63(44)
	Carl Pickens	*63*	1.00	63(44)
	Mike Quick	*63*	1.02	61(51)
63	**Keenan McCardell**	***62***	**1.00**	**62(48)**
	Herman Moore	*62*	1.00	62(48)
	Haven Moses	*62*	1.10	56(63)
	Shannon Sharpe	*62*	1.00	62(48)
67	Antonio Freeman	*61*	1.00	61(51)
	Max McGee	*61*	1.23	50(85)
	Kyle Rote	*61*	1.27	48(99)
	Del Shofner	*61*	1.20	51(81)
71	Dave Casper	*60*	1.14	52(76)
	Mark Duper	*60*	1.01	59(59)
	Drew Hill	*60*	1.01	60(55)
	Keyshawn Johnson	***60***	**1.00**	**60(55)**
	Bobby Walston	*60*	1.31	46(116)
76	Isaac Curtis	*59*	1.11	53(73)
	Carroll Dale	*59*	1.14	52(76)
	Roy Jefferson	*59*	1.14	52(76)
	Lenny Moore	*59*	1.23	48(99)
80	Charley Hennigan	*58*	1.14	51(81)
81	Frank Clarke	*57*	1.14	50(85)
	Sammy White	*57*	1.13	50(85)
83	**Tony Gonzalez**	***56***	**1.00**	**56(63)**
	Tony Martin	*56*	1.00	56(63)
85	Anthony Carter	*55*	1.01	55(67)
	John Gilliam	*55*	1.14	48(99)
	Ed McCaffrey	*55*	1.00	55(67)
88	Ken Burrough	*54*	1.10	49(92)
	Billy Cannon	*54*	1.14	47(110)
	Frank Gifford	*54*	1.24	43(132)
	Torry Holt	***54***	**1.00**	**54(70)**
	Joe Morrison	*54*	1.15	47(110)
	Ricky Proehl	***54***	**1.00**	**54(70)**
	Pete Retzlaff	*54*	1.16	47(110)
	Lynn Swann	*54*	1.06	51(81)
	Wesley Walls	*54*	1.00	54(70)
97	5 players tied			53

COMBINED NET YARDS

#	NAME	ADJ	RATIO	UNADJ
1	Jerry Rice	23621	1.00	23546(1)
2	Brian Mitchell	23330	1.00	23330(2)
3	Walter Payton	23286	1.07	21803(3)
4	Emmitt Smith	21564	1.00	21564(4)
5	Tim Brown	19682	1.00	19682(5)
6	Marshall Faulk	19190	1.00	19190(6)
7	Marcus Allen	18580	1.05	17648(9)
8	Jim Brown	18521	1.20	15459(16)
9	Barry Sanders	18308	1.00	18308(7)
10	Herschel Walker	18275	1.01	18168(8)
11	Curtis Martin	17421	1.00	17421(10)
12	Tony Dorsett	17270	1.06	16326(13)
13	Eric Metcalf	17230	1.00	17230(11)
14	Ollie Matson	16623	1.29	12884(39)
15	Bobby Mitchell	16614	1.18	14078(27)
16	Thurman Thomas	16532	1.00	16532(12)
17	Franco Harris	16332	1.12	14622(23)
18	O.J. Simpson	16239	1.13	14368(24)
19	James Brooks	16026	1.07	14910(21)
20	Henry Ellard	15779	1.00	15718(14)
21	Irving Fryar	15648	1.00	15594(15)
22	Eric Dickerson	15508	1.01	15411(17)
23	Tiki Barber	15232	1.00	15232(18)
24	Lenny Moore	15199	1.22	12451(46)
25	Jerome Bettis	15113	1.00	15113(19)
26	James Lofton	14956	1.05	14277(25)
27	Glyn Milburn	14911	1.00	14911(20)
28	Ricky Watters	14891	1.00	14891(22)
29	Greg Pruitt	14839	1.12	13262(36)
30	John Riggins	14772	1.10	13435(31)
31	Hugh McElhenny	14646	1.29	11375(66)
32	Timmy Brown	14496	1.14	12684(41)
33	Don Maynard	14248	1.15	12379(47)
34	Cris Carter	14206	1.00	14184(26)
35	Leroy Kelly	14091	1.14	12330(51)
36	Steve Largent	14071	1.05	13396(32)
37	Dave Meggett	13996	1.00	13996(28)
38	Floyd Little	13912	1.14	12173(54)
39	Ottis Anderson	13902	1.04	13362(33)
40	Abner Haynes	13789	1.14	12065(56)
41	Andre Reed	13762	1.00	13712(29)
42	Joe Perry	13608	1.30	10456(86)
43	Earnest Byner	13563	1.00	13497(30)
44	Drew Hill	13507	1.01	13337(34)
45	Charlie Joiner	13473	1.09	12367(49)
46	Art Monk	13463	1.03	13063(38)
47	Mel Gray	13349	1.01	13279(35)
48	Roger Craig	13230	1.01	13143(37)
49	Don Hutson	12980	1.49	8709(169)
50	Jimmy Smith	12875	1.00	12875(40)
51	Stump Mitchell	12738	1.06	11985(58)
52	Steve Van Buren	12724	1.42	8958(149)
53	Frank Gifford	12686	1.29	9870(104)
54	Eddie George	12669	1.00	12669(42)
55	Marvin Harrison	12551	1.00	12551(43)
56	Desmond Howard	12519	1.00	12519(44)
57	Jon Arnett	12489	1.22	10214(94)
58	Isaac Bruce	12484	1.00	12484(45)
59	Lance Alworth	12480	1.14	10920(74)
60	Stanley Morgan	12432	1.05	11835(61)
61	Corey Dillon	12376	1.00	12376(48)
62	Bruce Harper	12360	1.08	11429(63)
63	Chris Warren	12349	1.00	12349(50)
64	Charley Taylor	12346	1.14	10803(76)
65	Warrick Dunn	12281	1.00	12281(52)
66	Derrick Mason	12275	1.00	12275(53)
67	Jim Taylor	12240	1.16	10539(84)
68	Kevin Williams	12085	1.00	12085(55)
69	Edgerrin James	12065	1.00	12065(56)
70	Rod Smith	11979	1.00	11979(59)
71	Billy Johnson	11973	1.11	10785(77)
72	Michael Irvin	11910	1.00	11910(60)
73	Tommy McDonald	11898	1.20	9896(103)
74	Freeman McNeil	11828	1.07	11018(72)
75	Roy Green	11820	1.04	11393(65)
76	Carl Garrett	11793	1.14	10319(90)
77	Harold Jackson	11640	1.10	10601(81)
78	Charlie Garner	11516	1.00	11516(62)
79	Wes Chandler	11430	1.08	10561(82)
80	Bill Dudley	11409	1.39	8217(205)
81	Eric Moulds	11405	1.00	11405(64)
82	Darrin Nelson	11367	1.03	11025(71)
83	Terance Mathis	11350	1.00	11350(67)
84	Terry Metcalf	11294	1.13	10001(102)
85	Raymond Berry	11276	1.21	9302(131)
86	Rick Upchurch	11258	1.12	10081(98)
87	Dick James	11216	1.20	9369(126)
88	Ahman Green	11207	1.00	11207(68)
89	Clem Daniels	11167	1.14	9771(106)
90	Keenan McCardell	11140	1.00	11140(69)
91	Gary Clark	11043	1.01	10972(73)
92	Priest Holmes	11032	1.00	11032(70)
93	Lydell Mitchell	10896	1.12	9752(108)
94	Billy Howton	10869	1.28	8492(179)
95	Wilbert Montgomery	10833	1.07	10105(97)
96	Allen Rossum	10820	1.00	10820(75)
97	Terrell Owens	10785	1.00	10785(77)
98	Gale Sayers	10783	1.14	9435(122)
99	Preston Pearson	10738	1.12	9545(117)

TOTAL TDS

#	NAME	ADJ	RATIO	UNADJ
1	Jerry Rice	210	1.01	208(1)
2	Emmitt Smith	175	1.00	175(2)
3	Marcus Allen	156	1.08	145(3)
4	Don Hutson	155	1.48	105(12)
5	Jim Brown	152	1.21	126(6)
6	Lenny Moore	137	1.21	113(9)
7	Marshall Faulk	136	1.00	136(4)
8	Cris Carter	131	1.00	131(5)
	Walter Payton	131	1.05	125(7)
10	John Riggins	124	1.07	116(8)
11	Franco Harris	110	1.10	100(16)
	Marvin Harrison	110	1.00	110(10)
	Steve Van Buren	110	1.43	77(48)
14	Barry Sanders	109	1.00	109(11)
15	Jim Taylor	108	1.16	93(23)
16	Bobby Mitchell	107	1.18	91(24)
17	Steve Largent	106	1.05	101(15)
18	Tim Brown	105	1.00	105(12)
19	Leroy Kelly	103	1.14	90(27)
	Terrell Owens	103	1.00	103(14)
	Charley Taylor	103	1.14	90(27)
22	Tommy McDonald	102	1.19	85(36)
23	Don Maynard	101	1.14	88(29)
24	Shaun Alexander	100	1.00	100(16)
	Curtis Martin	100	1.00	100(16)
26	Lance Alworth	99	1.14	87(33)
	Frank Gifford	99	1.27	78(46)
	Randy Moss	99	1.00	99(19)
29	Paul Warfield	98	1.14	86(34)
30	Tony Dorsett	97	1.06	91(24)
31	Eric Dickerson	96	1.00	96(20)
32	Jerome Bettis	94	1.00	94(21)
	Priest Holmes	94	1.00	94(21)
	Ollie Matson	94	1.29	73(63)
	Art Powell	94	1.15	82(40)
36	Ricky Watters	91	1.00	91(24)
37	Ottis Anderson	88	1.03	86(34)
	Fred Biletnikoff	88	1.14	77(48)
	Harold Carmichael	88	1.11	79(43)
	Irving Fryar	88	1.00	88(29)
	Pete Johnson	88	1.07	82(40)
	Andre Reed	88	1.00	88(29)
	Thurman Thomas	88	1.00	88(29)
44	Bill Brown	87	1.14	76(51)
	John David Crow	87	1.18	74(60)
	Bob Hayes	87	1.14	76(51)
47	O.J. Simpson	86	1.13	76(51)
48	Mark Clayton	85	1.01	85(36)
	Chuck Foreman	85	1.12	76(51)
	Herschel Walker	85	1.01	84(38)
51	Raymond Berry	84	1.23	68(76)
	James Brooks	84	1.06	79(43)
	Harold Jackson	84	1.11	76(51)
	Pete Pihos	84	1.33	63(100)
	Andre Rison	84	1.00	84(38)
56	Chuck Muncie	82	1.11	74(60)
57	Gary Collins	80	1.14	70(69)
	James Lofton	80	1.06	76(51)
	Joe Perry	80	1.32	61(109)
	LaDainian Tomlinson	80	1.00	80(42)
61	Terry Allen	79	1.00	79(43)
	Abner Haynes	79	1.14	69(71)
	Nat Moore	79	1.05	75(58)
64	Eddie George	78	1.00	78(46)
	Billy Howton	78	1.28	61(109)
	Hugh McElhenny	78	1.30	60(115)
	Jimmy Orr	78	1.18	66(84)
68	Isaac Bruce	77	1.00	77(48)
	Hugh Taylor	77	1.33	58(121)
	Wendell Tyler	77	1.16	66(84)
71	Cliff Branch	76	1.14	67(82)
	Earl Campbell	76	1.02	74(60)
	Rick Casares	76	1.27	60(115)
	Corey Dillon	76	1.00	76(51)
	Stanley Morgan	76	1.04	73(63)
	Wesley Walker	76	1.07	71(67)
77	Larry Csonka	75	1.10	68(76)
	Edgerrin James	75	1.00	75(58)
	Joe Morrison	75	1.15	65(88)
80	Emerson Boozer	74	1.14	65(88)
	Billy Cannon	74	1.14	65(88)
	Sonny Randle	74	1.15	65(88)
83	Timmy Brown	73	1.14	64(97)
	Earnest Byner	73	1.01	72(66)
	Roger Craig	73	1.00	73(63)
	Elroy Hirsch	73	1.33	55(141)
	Paul Hornung	73	1.18	62(104)
	Ken Kavanaugh	73	1.40	52(168)
	Gerald Riggs	73	1.06	69(71)
90	Jim Benton	72	1.49	48(203)
	Roy Green	72	1.04	69(71)
	Calvin Hill	72	1.10	65(88)
	John Stallworth	72	1.12	64(97)
94	Neal Anderson	71	1.01	71(67)
	Alex Webster	71	1.26	56(134)
	Ken Willard	71	1.14	62(104)
97	Joey Galloway	70	1.00	70(69)
	Ray Renfro	70	1.28	55(141)
99	6 players tied.................69			

TOTAL POINTS

#	NAME	ADJ	RATIO	UNADJ
1	Gary Anderson	2480	1.02	2434(1)
2	George Blanda	2391	1.19	2002(3)
3	Morten Andersen	2375	1.01	2358(2)
4	Jan Stenerud	1903	1.12	1699(6)
5	Norm Johnson	1775	1.02	1736(4)
6	Nick Lowery	1774	1.04	1711(5)
7	Lou Groza	1683	1.25	1349(20)
8	Eddie Murray	1638	1.03	1594(8)
9	John Carney	1634	1.00	1634(7)
10	Jim Turner	1625	1.13	1439(14)
11	Matt Stover	1594	1.00	1594(8)
12	Al Del Greco	1587	1.00	1584(10)
13	Jim Bakken	1569	1.14	1380(18)
14	Fred Cox	1560	1.14	1365(19)
15	Jason Elam	1557	1.00	1557(11)
16	Pat Leahy	1552	1.06	1470(13)
17	Mark Moseley	1511	1.09	1382(17)
18	Steve Christie	1476	1.00	1476(12)
19	Matt Bahr	1453	1.02	1422(15)
20	Jason Hanson	1420	1.00	1420(16)
21	Jim Breech	1305	1.05	1246(23)
	John Kasay	1305	1.00	1305(21)
23	Gino Cappelletti	1291	1.14	1130(29)
24	Chris Bahr	1290	1.06	1213(25)
25	Jerry Rice	1265	1.01	1256(22)
26	Pete Stoyanovich	1236	1.00	1236(24)
27	Don Hutson	1229	1.49	823(58)
28	Kevin Butler	1214	1.00	1208(26)
29	Ray Wersching	1201	1.07	1122(30)
30	Don Cockroft	1196	1.11	1080(31)
31	Garo Yepremian	1190	1.11	1074(32)
32	Jeff Wilkins	1188	1.00	1188(27)
33	Bruce Gossett	1178	1.14	1031(36)
34	Sam Baker	1167	1.19	977(39)
35	Adam Vinatieri	1158	1.00	1158(28)
36	Bobby Walston	1127	1.28	881(49)
37	Lou Michaels	1099	1.15	955(42)
38	Ryan Longwell	1054	1.00	1054(33)
39	Emmitt Smith	1052	1.00	1052(34)
40	Todd Peterson	1043	1.00	1043(35)
41	Roy Gerela	1019	1.13	903(48)
42	Rafael Septien	1017	1.06	960(41)
43	Jeff Jaeger	1013	1.00	1008(37)
44	Mike Vanderjagt	995	1.00	995(38)
45	Pete Gogolak	986	1.14	863(54)
46	Greg Davis	963	1.00	962(40)
47	Errol Mann	957	1.13	846(56)
48	Olindo Mare	948	1.00	948(43)
49	Chris Jacke	944	1.00	944(44)
50	Marcus Allen	939	1.08	872(52)
51	Fuad Reveiz	935	1.00	931(45)
52	Doug Brien	915	1.00	915(46)
53	Chip Lohmiller	913	1.00	913(47)
54	Jim Brown	912	1.21	756(66)
55	Tony Franklin	909	1.04	872(52)
56	Paul Hornung	903	1.19	760(64)
57	Tony Zendejas	880	1.01	874(51)
58	Mike Hollis	879	1.00	879(50)
59	Gordie Soltau	859	1.33	644(85)
60	Tommy Davis	856	1.16	738(69)
61	John Hall	853	1.00	853(55)
62	Rich Karlis	842	1.05	799(60)
63	Rolf Benirschke	839	1.09	766(63)
64	Mike Lansford	834	1.06	789(62)
65	Toni Fritsch	831	1.10	758(65)
66	Marshall Faulk	830	1.00	830(57)
67	Dean Biasucci	829	1.01	823(58)
68	Mike Clark	827	1.14	724(71)
69	Lenny Moore	823	1.21	678(78)
70	Tom Dempsey	822	1.13	729(70)
71	Bob Thomas	813	1.08	756(66)
72	Horst Muhlmann	808	1.14	707(72)
73	Cris Carter	797	1.00	796(61)
74	Walter Payton	788	1.05	750(68)
	Bob Waterfield	788	1.38	573(107)
76	John Smith	753	1.09	692(75)
77	John Riggins	742	1.07	696(74)
78	Pat Summerall	720	1.28	563(114)
79	Gene Mingo	719	1.14	629(89)
80	Pat Harder	712	1.34	531(127)
	Doak Walker	712	1.33	534(124)
82	Joe Danelo	704	1.10	639(87)
83	Mike Cofer	703	1.00	702(73)
84	David Akers	689	1.00	689(76)
85	Cary Blanchard	683	1.00	683(77)
86	Mike Mercer	679	1.14	594(98)
87	Ben Agajanian	675	1.29	525(131)
	Kris Brown	675	1.00	675(79)
89	Scott Norwood	674	1.01	670(80)
	Ken Strong	674	1.39	484(147)
91	Marvin Harrison	670	1.00	670(80)
92	Joe Nedney	669	1.00	669(82)
93	Efren Herrera	665	1.10	604(94)
94	Steve Van Buren	664	1.43	464(161)
95	Bill Dudley	661	1.37	484(147)
96	Doug Pelfrey	660	1.00	660(83)
97	Franco Harris	657	1.10	600(95)
98	Barry Sanders	654	1.00	654(84)
99	Fred Cone	651	1.32	494(142)

KICKOFF RETURNS

	NAME	ADJ	RATIO	UNADJ
1	Brian Mitchell	607	1.00	607(1)
2	Mel Gray	423	1.00	421(2)
3	Glyn Milburn	407	1.00	407(3)
4	**Allen Rossum**	**375**	**1.00**	**375(4)**
5	Michael Bates	373	1.00	373(5)
6	Desmond Howard	359	1.00	359(6)
7	Kevin Williams	322	1.00	322(7)
8	Ron Smith	314	1.14	275(11)
9	**Dante Hall**	**307**	**1.00**	**307(8)**
10	Tyrone Hughes	283	1.00	283(9)
11	Eric Metcalf	280	1.00	280(10)
12	Bruce Harper	263	1.08	243(14)
13	Dave Meggett	252	1.00	252(12)
14	Dexter Carter	250	1.00	250(13)
15	Al Carmichael	247	1.30	191(33)
16	Corey Harris	238	1.00	238(15)
	Clarence Verdin	238	1.00	237(16)
18	Vai Sikahema	237	1.01	235(17)
19	Dick James	226	1.20	189(35)
	Tamarick Vanover	226	1.00	226(18)
21	Abe Woodson	225	1.17	193(30)
22	Rod Woodson	221	1.00	220(19)
23	Charlie Rogers	217	1.00	217(20)
24	Herschel Walker	215	1.00	215(21)
25	Jermaine Lewis	212	1.00	212(22)
	Steve Odom	212	1.09	194(29)
27	Larry Anderson	210	1.11	189(35)
	Timmy Brown	210	1.14	184(39)
29	**Reggie Swinton**	**208**	**1.00**	**208(23)**
30	Speedy Duncan	206	1.14	180(40)
	Michael Lewis	**206**	**1.00**	**206(24)**
32	**Tim Dwight**	**202**	**1.00**	**202(25)**
33	Ron Brown	201	1.01	199(26)
	Dennis Gentry	201	1.05	192(32)
35	David Dunn	198	1.00	198(27)
	Chad Morton	**198**	**1.00**	**198(27)**
37	Alvin Haymond	194	1.14	170(47)
38	Andre Coleman	193	1.00	193(30)
	Mike Nelms	193	1.10	175(42)
40	Ronney Jenkins	190	1.00	190(34)
41	Qadry Ismail	189	1.00	189(35)
	Stump Mitchell	189	1.07	177(41)
43	Dwight Stone	188	1.01	186(38)
44	Joe Arenas	185	1.33	139(73)
45	Woodley Lewis	183	1.33	137(75)
	Ollie Matson	183	1.28	143(71)
	Fulton Walker	183	1.09	167(49)
48	Bobby Jancik	181	1.14	158(51)

KICKOFF RETURN AVERAGE

	NAME	ADJ	UNADJ
1	Gale Sayers	30.56	30.56(1)
2	Lynn Chandnois	29.57	29.57(2)
3	Abe Woodson	28.64	28.69(3)
4	Buddy Young	27.93	27.93(4)
5	Travis Williams	27.46	27.46(5)
6	Joe Arenas	27.32	27.32(6)
7	Tommy Wilson	27.24	27.24(7)
8	Clarence Davis	27.09	27.09(8)
9	Steve Van Buren	26.93	26.71(9)
10	Lenny Lyles	26.68	26.68(10)
11	Gary Ballman	26.58	26.58(11)
12	Mercury Morris	26.55	26.55(12)
13	Tom Moore	26.51	26.51(13)
14	Bobby Jancik	26.49	26.49(14)
15	Mel Renfro	26.42	26.42(15)
16	Ollie Matson	26.35	26.20(18)
17	Cullen Bryant	26.32	26.28(17)
18	Bobby Mitchell	26.26	26.37(16)
19	Alvin Haymond	26.11	26.11(19)
20	Noland Smith	26.06	26.06(20)
21	Al Nelson	25.99	25.99(21)
22	Timmy Brown	25.98	25.98(22)
23	Vic Washington	25.90	25.90(23)
24	Dave Hampton	25.87	25.87(24)
25	Larry Garron	25.83	25.83(25)
26	Clarence Childs	25.78	25.78(26)
27	Herb Adderley	25.67	25.67(27)
28	Pat Studstill	25.65	25.65(28)
29	Terry Metcalf	25.59	25.51(29)
30	Walter Roberts	25.50	25.50(30)
31	Vitamin Smith	25.49	25.49(31)
32	John Gilliam	25.46	25.46(32)
33	Dave Grayson	25.44	25.44(33)
34	Billy Cannon	25.43	25.43(34)
	Charley Warner	25.43	25.43(34)
36	Don Shy	25.27	25.27(36)
37	Speedy Duncan	25.22	25.22(37)
38	Al Carmichael	25.17	25.12(39)
	Ron Smith	25.17	25.17(38)
40	Bobby Williams	25.12	25.12(39)
41	Charlie West	25.03	25.02(41)
42	Abner Haynes	25.00	25.00(42)
43	George Atkinson	24.91	24.91(43)
44	Larry Jones	24.88	24.88(44)
45	Don Paul	24.86	24.86(45)
46	Tom Watkins	24.85	24.85(46)
47	Rick Upchurch	24.82	24.79(47)
48	2 players tied		24.73

KICKOFF RETURN YARDS

	NAME	ADJ	RATIO	UNADJ
1	Brian Mitchell	14014	1.00	14014(1)
2	Mel Gray	10292	1.00	10250(2)
3	Glyn Milburn	9788	1.00	9788(3)
4	Michael Bates	9110	1.00	9110(4)
5	**Allen Rossum**	**8553**	**1.00**	**8553(5)**
6	Desmond Howard	7959	1.00	7959(6)
7	Ron Smith	7911	1.14	6922(10)
8	**Dante Hall**	**7437**	**1.00**	**7437(7)**
9	Kevin Williams	7309	1.00	7309(8)
10	Tyrone Hughes	6999	1.00	6999(9)
11	Abe Woodson	6447	1.16	5538(13)
12	Al Carmichael	6228	1.30	4798(25)
13	Bruce Harper	5841	1.08	5407(17)
14	Eric Metcalf	5813	1.00	5813(11)
15	Dave Meggett	5566	1.00	5566(12)
16	Dick James	5564	1.19	4676(29)
17	Corey Harris	5528	1.00	5528(14)
18	Timmy Brown	5464	1.14	4781(26)
19	Tamarick Vanover	5422	1.00	5422(15)
20	Dexter Carter	5412	1.00	5412(16)
21	Speedy Duncan	5187	1.14	4539(33)
22	Herschel Walker	5084	1.00	5084(18)
23	Alvin Haymond	5072	1.14	4438(37)
24	Joe Arenas	5064	1.33	3798(49)
25	**Michael Lewis**	**4989**	**1.00**	**4989(19)**
26	Vai Sikahema	4984	1.01	4933(20)
27	Clarence Verdin	4946	1.00	4930(21)
28	**Reggie Swinton**	**4919**	**1.00**	**4919(22)**
29	Rod Woodson	4913	1.00	4894(23)
30	Charlie Rogers	4877	1.00	4877(24)
31	Steve Odom	4855	1.09	4451(36)
32	Ollie Matson	4818	1.29	3746(52)
33	Bobby Jancik	4783	1.14	4185(40)
34	**Chad Morton**	**4731**	**1.00**	**4731(27)**
35	**Tim Dwight**	**4723**	**1.00**	**4723(28)**
36	Larry Anderson	4619	1.10	4217(39)
37	Jermaine Lewis	4611	1.00	4611(30)
38	David Dunn	4597	1.00	4597(31)
39	Mike Nelms	4561	1.10	4128(42)
40	Ronney Jenkins	4550	1.00	4550(32)
41	Ron Brown	4532	1.01	4493(34)
42	Dennis Gentry	4520	1.04	4353(38)
43	Andre Coleman	4466	1.00	4466(35)
44	Woodley Lewis	4433	1.33	3325(71)
45	Stump Mitchell	4290	1.07	4007(44)
46	Carl Garrett	4233	1.14	3704(53)
47	Bruce Laird	4230	1.13	3748(51)
48	Qadry Ismail	4135	1.00	4135(41)
49	Fulton Walker	4116	1.09	3779(50)
50	Kermit Alexander	4098	1.14	3586(58)

KICKOFF RETURN TDS

	NAME	ADJ	RATIO	UNADJ
1	Ollie Matson	8	1.33	6(1)
2	Gale Sayers	7	1.14	6(1)
	Travis Williams	7	1.14	6(1)
4	Timmy Brown	6	1.14	5(6)
	Mel Gray	6	1.00	6(1)
	Dante Hall	**6**	**1.00**	**6(1)**
	Bobby Mitchell	6	1.18	5(6)
	Abe Woodson	6	1.18	5(6)
9	Michael Bates	5	1.00	5(6)
	Cecil Turner	5	1.14	4(10)
	Steve Van Buren	5	1.51	3(16)
12	Ron Brown	4	1.02	4(10)
	Lynn Chandnois	4	1.33	3(16)
	Andre Coleman	4	1.00	4(10)
	Lenny Lyles	4	1.27	3(16)
	Brian Mitchell	4	1.00	4(10)
	Vitamin Smith	4	1.33	3(16)
	Tamarick Vanover	4	1.00	4(10)
	Jon Vaughn	4	1.00	4(10)
20	Cullen Bryant	3	1.14	3(16)
	Al Carmichael	3	1.33	2(35)
	Raymond Clayborn	3	1.14	3(16)
	Andy Farkas	3	1.45	2(35)
	Dennis Gentry	3	1.02	3(16)
	Dave Hampton	3	1.14	3(16)
	Tyrone Hughes	3	1.00	3(16)
	Ronney Jenkins	3	1.00	3(16)
	Terry Kirby	3	1.00	3(16)
	Michael Lewis	**3**	**1.00**	**3(16)**
	Dante Magnani	3	1.53	2(35)
	George McAfee	3	1.45	2(35)
	Mercury Morris	3	1.14	3(16)
	Chad Morton	**3**	**1.00**	**3(16)**
	Allen Rossum	**3**	**1.00**	**3(16)**
	Eddie Saenz	3	1.33	2(35)
	Deion Sanders	**3**	**1.00**	**3(16)**
	Ron Smith	3	1.14	3(16)
	Charley Warner	3	1.14	3(16)
	Dave Williams	3	1.05	3(16)
	Buddy Young	3	1.33	2(35)
41	43 players tied			2

PUNT RETURNS

	NAME	ADJ	RATIO	UNADJ
1	Brian Mitchell	463	1.00	463(1)
2	Eric Metcalf	351	1.00	351(2)
3	Dave Meggett	349	1.00	349(3)
4	Emlen Tunnell	344	1.33	258(13)
5	Tim Brown	326	1.00	326(4)
6	Billy Johnson	322	1.14	282(9)
7	Darrien Gordon	314	1.00	314(5)
8	Glyn Milburn	304	1.00	304(6)
9	Jermaine Lewis	295	1.00	295(7)
	Vai Sikahema	295	1.01	292(8)
11	Alvin Haymond	289	1.14	253(15)
12	Mike Fuller	279	1.11	252(16)
13	Rick Upchurch	276	1.11	248(18)
14	J.T. Smith	269	1.01	267(10)
	Ron Smith	269	1.14	235(21)
16	Kelvin Martin	262	1.01	261(11)
17	Rod Woodson	261	1.00	260(12)
18	Karl Williams	255	1.00	255(14)
19	Mel Gray	254	1.01	252(16)
20	**Troy Brown**	**244**	**1.00**	**244(19)**
	Desmond Howard	244	1.00	244(19)
22	Mike Nelms	237	1.12	212(25)
23	Speedy Duncan	231	1.14	202(29)
	Phil McConkey	231	1.01	228(23)
	Kevin Williams	231	1.00	231(22)
26	Danny Reece	229	1.03	222(24)
27	Greg Pruitt	223	1.15	194(32)
28	Willie Wood	214	1.14	187(36)
29	**Deion Sanders**	**212**	**1.00**	**212(25)**
30	Irving Fryar	207	1.01	206(28)
	Allen Rossum	**207**	**1.00**	**207(27)**
32	Bruce Harper	206	1.12	183(37)
33	Theo Bell	202	1.07	189(35)
	Leo Lewis	202	1.01	201(30)
35	Freddie Solomon	197	1.11	177(40)
	Tamarick Vanover	197	1.00	197(31)
37	Robbie Martin	195	1.12	175(41)
38	Gerald McNeil	193	1.01	191(34)
39	Willie Drewrey	192	1.00	192(33)
40	Eddie Brown	188	1.10	172(44)
41	Neal Colzie	187	1.10	170(46)
42	Howard Stevens	186	1.14	163(51)
43	Woodley Lewis	184	1.33	138(78)
	Larry Marshall	184	1.14	162(52)
45	**Derrick Mason**	**182**	**1.00**	**182(38)**
46	Charlie West	180	1.14	158(59)
47	Bill Thompson	179	1.14	157(61)

PUNT RETURN AVERAGE

	NAME	ADJ	UNADJ
1	Ernie Steele	14.67	14.71(1)
2	Charlie Trippi	13.71	13.71(2)
3	Dick Christy	13.32	13.51(3)
4	George McAfee	12.85	12.78(4)
5	Ray Mathews	12.77	12.77(5)
6	Jack Christiansen	12.75	12.75(6)
7	Claude Gibson	12.55	12.55(7)
8	Andy Farkas	12.39	12.39(8)
9	Rick Upchurch	12.34	12.13(10)
10	Bill Dudley	12.21	12.22(9)
11	Desmond Howard	11.86	11.86(11)
12	Billy Johnson	11.85	11.76(12)
13	Mack Herron	11.69	11.69(13)
14	Frank Seno	11.65	11.67(14)
15	Bill Thompson	11.56	11.55(15)
16	**Santana Moss**	**11.49**	**11.49(16)**
17	Darrien Gordon	11.47	11.47(17)
18	Paul Johns	11.34	11.39(18)
19	Bosh Pritchard	11.30	11.28(20)
20	Henry Ellard	11.28	11.31(19)
21	Terry Metcalf	11.19	11.14(21)
22	Bob Hayes	11.13	11.13(22)
	Jermaine Lewis	11.13	11.13(22)
24	Jim Bertelsen	11.09	11.09(24)
25	Floyd Little	11.02	11.02(25)
26	Louis Lipps	11.00	11.02(25)
27	Bobby Joe Edmonds	10.99	10.98(27)
28	Mel Gray	10.95	10.92(28)
29	Dana McLemore	10.94	10.51(45)
30	Speedy Duncan	10.90	10.90(29)
	Eddie Saenz	10.90	10.90(29)
32	**Michael Lewis**	**10.88**	**10.88(31)**
33	Vai Sikahema	10.87	10.85(32)
34	Vitamin Smith	10.85	10.85(32)
35	Winslow Oliver	10.83	10.83(34)
36	Brian Mitchell	10.80	10.80(35)
37	**Allen Rossum**	**10.77**	**10.77(36)**
38	**Az-Zahir Hakim**	**10.75**	**10.75(37)**
39	Jo-Jo Townsell	10.73	10.71(38)
40	Dan Sandifer	10.65	10.65(39)
41	Dave Meggett	10.62	10.62(40)
42	**Phillip Buchanon**	**10.61**	**10.61(41)**
43	**Dennis Northcutt**	**10.56**	**10.56(42)**
44	Mike Haynes	10.53	10.43(51)
	Leroy Kelly	10.53	10.53(44)
46	Stanley Morgan	10.52	10.43(51)
47	Keith Moody	10.51	10.45(49)
48	Jeff Burris	10.50	10.50(47)
49	Neal Colzie	10.49	10.35(58)

PUNT RETURN YARDS

	NAME	ADJ	RATIO	UNADJ
1	Brian Mitchell	4999	1.00	4999(1)
2	Billy Johnson	3821	1.15	3317(6)
3	Dave Meggett	3708	1.00	3708(2)
4	Darrien Gordon	3601	1.00	3601(3)
5	Eric Metcalf	3453	1.00	3453(4)
6	Rick Upchurch	3411	1.13	3008(9)
7	Tim Brown	3320	1.00	3320(5)
8	Jermaine Lewis	3282	1.00	3282(7)
9	Vai Sikahema	3206	1.01	3169(8)
10	Glyn Milburn	2984	1.00	2984(10)
11	Emlen Tunnell	2945	1.33	2209(21)
12	Mike Fuller	2906	1.09	2660(14)
13	Desmond Howard	2895	1.00	2895(11)
14	J.T. Smith	2784	1.01	2764(12)
15	Mel Gray	2776	1.01	2753(13)
16	Kelvin Martin	2581	1.01	2567(15)
17	Karl Williams	2565	1.00	2565(16)
18	**Troy Brown**	**2554**	**1.00**	**2554(17)**
19	Speedy Duncan	2515	1.14	2201(22)
20	Alvin Haymond	2455	1.14	2148(24)
21	Rod Woodson	2371	1.00	2362(18)
22	Kevin Williams	2295	1.00	2295(19)
23	Greg Pruitt	2264	1.13	2007(27)
24	**Allen Rossum**	**2229**	**1.00**	**2229(20)**
25	**Deion Sanders**	**2199**	**1.00**	**2199(23)**
26	Mike Nelms	2144	1.10	1948(28)
27	Bill Dudley	2105	1.39	1515(57)
28	Bill Thompson	2073	1.14	1814(32)
29	Irving Fryar	2067	1.01	2055(25)
30	Ron Smith	2043	1.14	1788(33)
31	Tamarick Vanover	2016	1.00	2016(26)
32	Bruce Harper	1988	1.11	1784(34)
33	Neal Colzie	1964	1.12	1759(36)
34	George McAfee	1932	1.35	1431(66)
35	Leo Lewis	1886	1.01	1868(29)
36	Robbie Martin	1884	1.13	1670(38)
37	Phil McConkey	1858	1.01	1832(31)
38	**Dennis Northcutt**	**1837**	**1.00**	**1837(30)**
39	Freddie Solomon	1825	1.13	1614(44)
40	Howard Stevens	1782	1.14	1559(52)
41	**Az-Zahir Hakim**	**1773**	**1.00**	**1773(35)**
42	Gerald McNeil	1743	1.01	1717(37)
43	Dana McLemore	1737	1.09	1598(46)
44	Eddie Brown	1678	1.11	1511(58)
45	Larry Marshall	1668	1.14	1466(63)
46	Clarence Verdin	1650	1.00	1650(39)
47	LeRoy Irvin	1645	1.13	1457(64)
48	**Dante Hall**	**1642**	**1.00**	**1642(40)**
49	Reggie Barlow	1639	1.00	1639(41)
50	Walter Stanley	1631	1.01	1619(42)

PUNT RETURN TDS

	NAME	ADJ	RATIO	UNADJ
1	Jack Christiansen	11	1.33	8(3)
2	Eric Metcalf	10	1.00	10(1)
	Rick Upchurch	10	1.28	8(3)
4	Brian Mitchell	9	1.00	9(2)
5	Desmond Howard	8	1.00	8(3)
6	Billy Johnson	7	1.12	6(7)
	Dave Meggett	7	1.00	7(6)
	Emlen Tunnell	7	1.33	5(11)
9	Darrien Gordon	6	1.00	6(7)
	Jermaine Lewis	6	1.00	6(7)
	Curly Oden	6	1.26	5(11)
	Deion Sanders	**6**	**1.00**	**6(7)**
13	Dick Christy	5	1.14	4(15)
	Speedy Duncan	5	1.14	4(15)
	Joey Galloway	**5**	**1.00**	**5(11)**
	LeRoy Irvin	5	1.19	4(15)
	Dana McLemore	5	1.21	4(15)
	Lemar Parrish	5	1.14	4(15)
	Karl Williams	5	1.00	5(11)
20	**Eddie Drummond**	**4**	**1.00**	**4(15)**
	Bill Dudley	4	1.33	3(30)
	Henry Ellard	4	1.00	4(15)
	Dante Hall	**4**	**1.00**	**4(15)**
	Yale Lary	4	1.33	3(30)
	Woodley Lewis	4	1.33	3(30)
	Ray Mathews	4	1.33	3(30)
	Ollie Matson	4	1.33	3(30)
	Ray McLean	4	1.45	3(30)
	Bobby Mitchell	4	1.27	3(30)
	Antwaan Randle El	**4**	**1.00**	**4(15)**
	Vai Sikahema	4	1.02	4(15)
	J.T. Smith	4	1.00	4(15)
	Steve Smith	**4**	**1.00**	**4(15)**
	Freddie Solomon	4	1.07	4(15)
	Dick Todd	4	1.45	3(30)
	Tamarick Vanover	4	1.00	4(15)
	Clarence Verdin	4	1.00	4(15)
38	38 players tied 3			

PUNT/KICK RETURN YARDS

	NAME	ADJ	RATIO	UNADJ
1	Brian Mitchell	19013	1.00	19013(1)
2	Mel Gray	13069	1.01	13003(2)
3	Glyn Milburn	12772	1.00	12772(3)
4	Desmond Howard	10854	1.00	10854(4)
5	**Allen Rossum**	**10782**	**1.00**	**10782(5)**
6	Ron Smith	9954	1.14	8710(11)
7	Kevin Williams	9604	1.00	9604(6)
8	Dave Meggett	9274	1.00	9274(7)
9	Eric Metcalf	9266	1.00	9266(8)
10	Michael Bates	9154	1.00	9154(9)
11	**Dante Hall**	**9079**	**1.00**	**9079(10)**
12	Tyrone Hughes	8410	1.00	8410(12)
13	Vai Sikahema	8189	1.01	8102(13)
14	Jermaine Lewis	7893	1.00	7893(14)
15	Bruce Harper	7829	1.09	7191(17)
16	Speedy Duncan	7703	1.14	6740(19)
17	Abe Woodson	7577	1.17	6494(22)
18	Alvin Haymond	7527	1.14	6586(20)
19	Tamarick Vanover	7438	1.00	7438(15)
20	Al Carmichael	7413	1.30	5710(31)
21	Rod Woodson	7284	1.00	7256(16)
22	Billy Johnson	7161	1.14	6258(25)
23	Dexter Carter	6770	1.00	6770(18)
24	Dick James	6709	1.19	5628(32)
25	Mike Nelms	6705	1.10	6076(28)
26	Clarence Verdin	6596	1.00	6580(21)
27	**Michael Lewis**	**6360**	**1.00**	**6360(23)**
28	**Tim Dwight**	**6296**	**1.00**	**6296(24)**
29	**Reggie Swinton**	**6230**	**1.00**	**6230(26)**
30	Timmy Brown	6194	1.14	5420(34)
31	Charlie Rogers	6125	1.00	6125(27)
32	Joe Arenas	6096	1.33	4572(50)
33	Rick Upchurch	6059	1.13	5363(36)
34	**Chad Morton**	**5894**	**1.00**	**5894(29)**
35	Woodley Lewis	5801	1.33	4351(61)
36	Stump Mitchell	5795	1.08	5384(35)
37	**Deion Sanders**	**5722**	**1.00**	**5722(30)**
38	Ollie Matson	5610	1.29	4341(62)
39	Fulton Walker	5553	1.06	5216(37)
40	Corey Harris	5545	1.00	5545(33)
41	Eddie Payton	5533	1.09	5063(41)
42	Bobby Jancik	5522	1.14	4832(48)
43	Larry Marshall	5517	1.13	4862(46)
44	Steve Odom	5477	1.09	5046(42)
45	Greg Pruitt	5265	1.16	4521(53)
46	Larry Anderson	5243	1.09	4799(49)
47	Bobby Joe Edmonds	5171	1.01	5117(38)
48	**Derrick Mason**	**5086**	**1.00**	**5086(39)**
49	Herschel Walker	5084	1.00	5084(40)
50	Kermit Alexander	5053	1.14	4421(58)

PUNT/KICK RETURN TDS

	NAME	ADJ	RATIO	UNADJ
1	Brian Mitchell	13	1.00	13(1)
2	Ollie Matson	12	1.33	9(4)
	Eric Metcalf	12	1.00	12(2)
4	Jack Christiansen	11	1.33	8(7)
5	**Dante Hall**	**10**	**1.00**	**10(3)**
	Bobby Mitchell	10	1.21	8(7)
	Rick Upchurch	10	1.28	8(7)
8	Mel Gray	9	1.00	9(4)
	Billy Johnson	9	1.13	8(7)
	Deion Sanders	**9**	**1.00**	**9(4)**
	Gale Sayers	9	1.14	8(7)
12	Desmond Howard	8	1.00	8(7)
	Dave Meggett	8	1.00	8(7)
	Emlen Tunnell	8	1.33	6(17)
	Steve Van Buren	8	1.52	5(24)
	Tamarick Vanover	8	1.00	8(7)
	Travis Williams	8	1.14	7(15)
	Abe Woodson	8	1.17	7(15)
19	Timmy Brown	7	1.14	6(17)
20	**Eddie Drummond**	**6**	**1.00**	**6(17)**
	Darrien Gordon	6	1.00	6(17)
	Jermaine Lewis	6	1.00	6(17)
	George McAfee	6	1.42	4(37)
	Curly Oden	6	1.26	5(24)
	Lemar Parrish	6	1.14	5(24)
	Allen Rossum	**6**	**1.00**	**6(17)**
	Ron Smith	6	1.14	5(24)
	Steve Smith	**6**	**1.00**	**6(17)**
29	Michael Bates	5	1.00	5(24)
	Dick Christy	5	1.14	4(37)
	Andre Coleman	5	1.00	5(24)
	Bill Dudley	5	1.36	4(37)
	Speedy Duncan	5	1.14	4(37)
	Tim Dwight	**5**	**1.00**	**5(24)**
	Joey Galloway	**5**	**1.00**	**5(24)**
	Tyrone Hughes	5	1.00	5(24)
	LeRoy Irvin	5	1.19	4(37)
	Woodley Lewis	5	1.33	4(37)
	Dana McLemore	5	1.21	4(37)
	Antwaan Randle El	**5**	**1.00**	**5(24)**
	Vitamin Smith	5	1.33	4(37)
	Freddie Solomon	5	1.09	5(24)
	Cecil Turner	5	1.14	4(37)
	Clarence Verdin	5	1.00	5(24)
	Karl Williams	5	1.00	5(24)
46	24 players tied 4			

PUNTS

	NAME	ADJ	RATIO	UNADJ
1	**Jeff Feagles**	**1437**	**1.00**	**1437(1)**
2	**Sean Landeta**	**1405**	**1.00**	**1401(2)**
3	Dave Jennings	1242	1.08	1154(4)
4	Lee Johnson	1229	1.00	1226(3)
5	Jerrel Wilson	1217	1.14	1072(11)
6	John James	1190	1.10	1083(10)
7	Rohn Stark	1181	1.03	1141(6)
8	Chris Mohr	1152	1.00	1152(5)
9	Ray Guy	1134	1.08	1049(14)
10	**Bryan Barker**	**1132**	**1.00**	**1132(7)**
11	Mark Royals	1117	1.00	1116(8)
12	Bobby Walden	1113	1.14	974(20)
13	**Chris Gardocki**	**1112**	**1.00**	**1112(9)**
14	Bobby Joe Green	1109	1.14	970(21)
15	Mike Bragg	1080	1.10	978(19)
16	Rich Camarillo	1069	1.04	1027(15)
17	Brian Hansen	1060	1.00	1057(12)
18	Dan Stryzinski	1055	1.00	1055(13)
19	Jeff Gossett	1011	1.03	982(18)
20	Mike Horan	1006	1.00	1003(16)
21	Reggie Roby	994	1.00	992(17)
22	Bob Parsons	981	1.11	884(25)
23	John Kidd	961	1.00	957(22)
24	David Lee	945	1.13	838(28)
25	Paul Maguire	909	1.14	795(36)
26	**Craig Hentrich**	**896**	**1.00**	**896(23)**
27	Tom Blanchard	895	1.09	819(33)
28	Tommy Barnhardt	891	1.00	890(24)
29	Greg Coleman	877	1.07	820(32)
30	Tom Tupa	873	1.00	873(26)
31	Jim Arnold	869	1.00	866(27)
32	Sam Baker	846	1.20	703(43)
33	**Brad Maynard**	**837**	**1.00**	**837(29)**
34	**Darren Bennett**	**836**	**1.00**	**836(30)**
35	**Todd Sauerbrun**	**832**	**1.00**	**832(31)**
36	Mike Saxon	818	1.01	813(34)
37	**Tom Rouen**	**810**	**1.00**	**810(35)**
38	Don Chandler	800	1.21	660(48)
39	Matt Turk	790	1.00	790(37)
40	Herman Weaver	764	1.10	693(45)
41	Louie Aguiar	758	1.00	758(38)
42	John Jett	756	1.00	756(39)
43	Pat McInally	745	1.06	700(44)
44	Don Cockroft	744	1.14	651(49)
45	Rick Tuten	741	1.00	741(40)
46	Larry Seiple	723	1.14	633(51)
47	**Mitch Berger**	**710**	**1.00**	**710(41)**
48	**Josh Miller**	**704**	**1.00**	**704(42)**

PUNT AVERAGE

	NAME	ADJ	UNADJ
1	**Shane Lechler**	**45.85**	**45.85(1)**
2	Sammy Baugh	45.05	45.10(2)
3	Tommy Davis	44.70	44.68(3)
4	Yale Lary	44.13	44.29(4)
5	**Todd Sauerbrun**	**43.99**	**43.99(5)**
6	Bob Scarpitto	43.84	43.84(6)
7	Horace Gillom	43.82	43.82(7)
8	Jerry Norton	43.72	43.77(8)
9	Dave Lewis	43.67	43.67(9)
10	Greg Montgomery	43.57	43.57(10)
11	Don Chandler	43.50	43.45(11)
12	**Darren Bennett**	**43.44**	**43.44(12)**
	Tom Rouen	**43.44**	**43.44(12)**
	Rick Tuten	43.44	43.44(12)
15	**Brian Moorman**	**43.43**	**43.43(15)**
16	Rohn Stark	43.38	43.36(17)
17	Tom Tupa	43.37	43.37(16)
18	**Hunter Smith**	**43.36**	**43.36(17)**
19	**Chris Hanson**	**43.33**	**43.33(19)**
	Sean Landeta	**43.33**	**43.33(19)**
21	Reggie Roby	43.30	43.30(21)
22	**Mitch Berger**	**43.21**	**43.21(22)**
23	Jerrel Wilson	43.09	43.04(24)
24	**Josh Miller**	**43.08**	**43.08(23)**
25	**Craig Hentrich**	**42.90**	**42.90(25)**
26	**Scott Player**	**42.88**	**42.88(26)**
27	**Chris Gardocki**	**42.85**	**42.85(27)**
	Norm Van Brocklin	42.85	42.85(27)
29	Rich Camarillo	42.76	42.74(30)
30	Danny Villanueva	42.75	42.75(29)
31	**Leo Araguz**	**42.64**	**42.64(31)**
32	Sam Baker	42.63	42.59(32)
33	Bobby Joe Green	42.59	42.59(32)
34	Harry Newsome	42.50	42.50(34)
35	Ralf Mojsiejenko	42.46	42.45(35)
36	John Jett	42.44	42.44(36)
37	Bob Waterfield	42.42	42.43(37)
38	Lee Johnson	42.39	42.40(39)
39	Matt Turk	42.37	42.37(40)
40	Ray Guy	42.34	42.41(38)
41	Dick Deschaine	42.32	42.32(41)
42	Jim Arnold	42.31	42.31(42)
	Curley Johnson	42.31	42.31(42)
44	Brian Hansen	42.28	42.29(44)
45	Jim Fraser	42.22	42.22(45)
46	Jack Jacobs	42.18	42.17(46)
47	Mike Horan	42.16	42.16(47)
48	**Josh Bidwell**	**42.15**	**42.15(48)**

FIELD GOALS

	NAME	ADJ	RATIO	UNADJ
1	Gary Anderson	547	1.02	538(1)
2	Morten Andersen	523	1.01	520(2)
3	Jan Stenerud	418	1.12	373(6)
4	George Blanda	400	1.19	335(12)
5	Nick Lowery	399	1.04	383(4)
6	John Carney	390	1.00	390(3)
7	Matt Stover	380	1.00	380(5)
8	Norm Johnson	375	1.02	366(7)
9	Eddie Murray	362	1.03	352(8)
10	Al Del Greco	348	1.00	347(9)
11	Jim Turner	344	1.13	304(15)
12	Jason Elam	341	1.00	341(10)
13	Steve Christie	336	1.00	336(11)
14	Mark Moseley	331	1.10	300(17)
15	Jason Hanson	327	1.00	327(13)
16	Fred Cox	322	1.14	282(19)
17	Jim Bakken	321	1.14	282(19)
18	Pat Leahy	320	1.05	304(15)
19	John Kasay	310	1.00	310(14)
20	Matt Bahr	306	1.02	300(17)
21	Lou Groza	292	1.25	234(28)
22	Pete Stoyanovich	272	1.00	272(21)
23	Kevin Butler	266	1.00	265(22)
24	Adam Vinatieri	263	1.00	263(23)
25	Chris Bahr	255	1.06	241(26)
	Jim Breech	255	1.05	243(25)
27	Jeff Wilkins	251	1.00	251(24)
28	Bruce Gossett	250	1.14	219(33)
29	Don Cockroft	239	1.11	216(36)
30	Ray Wersching	238	1.07	222(32)
31	Todd Peterson	235	1.00	235(27)
32	Garo Yepremian	233	1.11	210(37)
33	Jeff Jaeger	230	1.00	229(29)
34	Ryan Longwell	226	1.00	226(30)
35	Greg Davis	224	1.00	224(31)
36	Olindo Mare	219	1.00	219(33)
37	Mike Vanderjagt	217	1.00	217(35)
38	Sam Baker	215	1.20	179(49)
	Lou Michaels	215	1.15	187(44)
40	Roy Gerela	208	1.13	184(47)
41	Doug Brien	207	1.00	207(38)
42	Chip Lohmiller	204	1.00	204(39)
43	Chris Jacke	202	1.00	202(40)
44	Gino Cappelletti	201	1.14	176(52)
	Errol Mann	201	1.13	177(50)
46	Mike Hollis	200	1.00	200(41)
47	Pete Gogolak	198	1.14	173(53)
48	John Hall	194	1.00	194(42)

FIELD GOAL PERCENT

	NAME	ADJ	UNADJ
1	Mike Vanderjagt	87.50	87.50(1)
2	Shayne Graham	84.21	84.21(2)
3	Phil Dawson	83.85	83.85(3)
4	Matt Stover	83.15	83.15(4)
5	Jeff Wilkins	82.03	82.03(5)
6	Olindo Mare	82.02	82.02(6)
7	David Akers	82.01	82.01(7)
8	Adam Vinatieri	81.93	81.93(8)
9	Ryan Longwell	81.59	81.59(9)
10	Jeff Reed	81.42	81.42(10)
11	John Carney	81.25	81.25(11)
12	Jason Hanson	80.94	80.94(12)
13	Doug Brien	80.23	80.23(13)
14	Gary Anderson	80.11	80.06(15)
15	John Kasay	80.10	80.10(14)
16	Richie Cunningham	80.00	80.00(16)
	Mike Hollis	80.00	80.00(16)
18	Nick Lowery	79.94	79.96(18)
19	Pete Stoyanovich	79.53	79.53(19)
20	Todd Peterson	79.39	79.39(20)
21	Jason Elam	79.30	79.30(21)
22	Morten Andersen	78.79	79.03(22)
23	Jay Feely	78.70	78.70(23)
24	Chris Boniol	78.53	78.53(24)
25	Sebastian Janikowski	78.41	78.41(25)
26	Steve Christie	77.96	77.96(26)
27	Rian Lindell	77.58	77.58(27)
28	Joe Nedney	77.27	77.27(29)
	Doug Pelfrey	77.27	77.27(29)
30	Al Del Greco	77.24	77.28(28)
31	David Treadwell	77.14	77.14(31)
32	Cary Blanchard	77.10	77.10(32)
33	Neil Rackers	76.67	76.67(34)
34	Norm Johnson	76.61	76.73(33)
35	Martin Gramatica	76.54	76.54(35)
36	Kris Brown	76.33	76.33(36)
37	Chris Jacke	76.23	76.23(37)
38	Brad Daluiso	76.19	76.19(38)
39	Eddie Murray	75.79	75.54(39)
40	Donald Igwebuike	75.54	75.52(40)
41	Fuad Reveiz	75.22	75.20(41)
42	Paul Edinger	75.00	75.00(42)
43	John Hall	74.33	74.33(43)
44	Jeff Jaeger	74.06	74.11(44)
45	Tony Zendejas	73.83	73.81(45)
46	Raul Allegre	73.55	73.66(46)
47	Paul McFadden	73.49	73.62(47)
48	Kevin Butler	73.38	73.41(48)

INTERCEPTIONS

	NAME	ADJ	RATIO	UNADJ
1	Emlen Tunnell	105	1.33	79(2)
2	Paul Krause	92	1.14	81(1)
3	Night Train Lane	87	1.27	68(4)
4	Ken Riley	75	1.15	65(5)
5	Dick LeBeau	71	1.14	62(7)
	Rod Woodson	71	1.00	71(3)
7	Jack Butler	69	1.33	52(22)
	Bobby Dillon	69	1.33	52(22)
9	Emmitt Thomas	66	1.14	58(9)
10	Bobby Boyd	65	1.14	57(10)
	Ronnie Lott	65	1.03	63(6)
	Johnny Robinson	65	1.14	57(10)
13	Lem Barney	64	1.14	56(15)
	Dave Brown	64	1.03	62(7)
	Pat Fischer	64	1.14	56(15)
16	Mel Blount	63	1.10	57(10)
	Jimmy Patton	63	1.22	52(22)
	Everson Walls	63	1.10	57(10)
19	Willie Brown	62	1.14	54(18)
	Yale Lary	62	1.24	50(29)
21	Don Burroughs	61	1.22	50(29)
	Jack Christiansen	61	1.33	46(45)
23	Mel Renfro	59	1.14	52(22)
	Larry Wilson	59	1.14	52(22)
25	Bobby Bryant	57	1.11	51(27)
	Eugene Robinson	57	1.00	57(10)
27	Ken Houston	56	1.13	49(34)
	Donnie Shell	56	1.09	51(27)
29	Herb Adderley	55	1.14	48(36)
	Don Doll	55	1.33	41(63)
	Dave Grayson	55	1.14	48(36)
	Richie Petitbon	55	1.15	48(36)
	Jake Scott	55	1.12	49(34)
	Aeneas Williams	55	1.00	55(17)
	Willie Wood	55	1.14	48(36)
36	Eric Allen	54	1.00	54(18)
	Darrell Green	54	1.00	54(18)
	Jimmy Johnson	54	1.14	47(41)
39	Erich Barnes	53	1.18	45(51)
	Goose Gonsoulin	53	1.14	46(45)
	John Harris	53	1.07	50(29)
	Tom Keane	53	1.33	40(67)
	Warren Lahr	53	1.33	40(67)
	Eddie Meador	53	1.16	46(45)
	Deion Sanders	53	1.00	53(21)
	Dave Whitsell	53	1.15	46(45)
47	Mike Haynes	51	1.11	46(45)
	Jim Norton	51	1.14	45(51)
	Lemar Parrish	51	1.09	47(41)
50	Terrell Buckley	50	1.00	50(29)
	Deron Cherry	50	1.00	50(29)
	Irv Comp	50	1.48	34(126)
53	Kermit Alexander	49	1.14	43(57)
	Thom Darden	49	1.08	45(51)
55	Sammy Baugh	48	1.54	31(156)
	Lindon Crow	48	1.26	38(81)
	Jim David	48	1.33	36(103)
	Bobby Hunt	48	1.14	42(59)
	Dave Waymer	48	1.01	48(36)
60	Ray Buchanan	47	1.00	47(41)
	Spider Lockhart	47	1.14	41(63)
	Frank Reagan	47	1.34	35(113)
	Johnny Sample	47	1.15	41(63)
	Troy Vincent	47	1.00	47(41)
65	Butch Byrd	46	1.14	40(67)
	W.K. Hicks	46	1.14	40(67)
	Don Hutson	46	1.53	30(172)
	Ty Law	46	1.00	46(45)
	Ed Sharockman	46	1.14	40(67)
70	Steve Foley	45	1.02	44(56)
	James Hasty	45	1.00	45(51)
	Don Paul	45	1.33	34(126)
	Darren Sharper	45	1.00	45(51)
	Don Shinnick	45	1.20	37(91)
	Charlie Waters	45	1.10	41(63)
76	Clarence Scott	44	1.14	39(75)
	Bill Thompson	44	1.09	40(67)
	Roger Wehrli	44	1.10	40(67)
79	Gary Barbaro	43	1.10	39(75)
	Cris Dishman	43	1.00	43(57)
	Glen Edwards	43	1.09	39(75)
	Dick Lynch	43	1.16	37(91)
	Jerry Norton	43	1.23	35(113)
	Rick Volk	43	1.13	38(81)
85	Ashley Ambrose	42	1.00	42(59)
	Ray Brown	42	1.12	38(81)
	Gill Byrd	42	1.00	42(59)
	Tony Greene	42	1.13	37(91)
	Rolland Lawrence	42	1.09	39(75)
	Albert Lewis	42	1.00	42(59)
	Howie Livingston	42	1.46	29(192)
	Ken Reaves	42	1.14	37(91)
93	9 players tied			41

INTERCEPTION RETURN TDS

	NAME	ADJ	RATIO	UNADJ
1	Rod Woodson	12	1.01	12(1)
2	Ken Houston	10	1.14	9(2)
3	Deion Sanders	9	1.00	9(2)
	Aeneas Williams	9	1.00	9(2)
5	Herb Adderley	8	1.14	7(6)
	Eric Allen	8	1.00	8(5)
	Erich Barnes	8	1.17	7(6)
	Lem Barney	8	1.14	7(6)
9	Bobby Bell	7	1.14	6(12)
	Bobby Dillon	7	1.33	5(18)
	Miller Farr	7	1.14	6(12)
	Tom Janik	7	1.14	6(12)
	Warren Lahr	7	1.33	5(18)
	Ty Law	7	1.00	7(6)
	Darren Sharper	7	1.00	7(6)
	Otis Smith	7	1.00	7(6)
17	Johnny Blood	6	1.24	5(18)
	Terrell Buckley	6	1.00	6(12)
	Butch Byrd	6	1.14	5(18)
	Kenny Graham	6	1.14	5(18)
	Dave Grayson	6	1.14	5(18)
	Darrell Green	6	1.00	6(12)
	Dick Harris	6	1.14	5(18)
	Jim Kearney	6	1.14	5(18)
	Night Train Lane	6	1.30	5(18)
	Jerry Logan	6	1.14	5(18)
	Ronnie Lott	6	1.16	5(18)
	Terry McDaniel	6	1.00	6(12)
	Eddie Meador	6	1.14	5(18)
	Jack Pardee	6	1.14	5(18)
	Ken Riley	6	1.21	5(18)
	Emmitt Thomas	6	1.14	5(18)
	Larry Wilson	6	1.14	5(18)
34	Dre' Bly	5	1.00	5(18)
	Bobby Boyd	5	1.14	4(43)
	Charley Brock	5	1.55	3(97)
	Derrick Brooks	5	1.00	5(18)
	Dave Brown	5	1.03	5(18)
	Jack Butler	5	1.33	4(43)
	Pat Fischer	5	1.14	4(43)
	Aaron Glenn	5	1.00	5(18)
	Joe Golding	5	1.33	4(43)
	Dale Hackbart	5	1.14	4(43)
	Jimmy Hitchcock	5	1.00	5(18)
	LeRoy Irvin	5	1.01	5(18)
	Ken Konz	5	1.33	4(43)
	Darryll Lewis	5	1.00	5(18)
	Mike Lucci	5	1.14	4(43)
	Dick Lynch	5	1.14	4(43)
	Rod Martin	5	1.19	4(43)
	Erik McMillan	5	1.00	5(18)
	Bennie McRae	5	1.14	4(43)
	Jerry Norton	5	1.24	4(43)
	Lemar Parrish	5	1.14	4(43)
	John Rowser	5	1.14	4(43)
	Johnny Sample	5	1.14	4(43)
	Dennis Thurman	5	1.19	4(43)
	Emlen Tunnell	5	1.33	4(43)
	Dewayne Washington	5	1.00	5(18)
	Dave Whitsell	5	1.14	4(43)
61	52 players tied			4

	SACKS	ADJ	RATIO	UNADJ
1	Bruce Smith	200.8	1.00	200.0(1)
2	Reggie White	199.4	1.01	198.0(2)
3	Kevin Greene	160.4	1.00	160.0(3)
4	Chris Doleman	151.2	1.00	150.5(4)
5	Lawrence Taylor	139.1	1.05	132.5(7)
6	Richard Dent	138.3	1.01	137.5(5)
7	John Randle	137.5	1.00	137.5(5)
8	Leslie O'Neal	132.5	1.00	132.5(7)
9	Rickey Jackson	132.1	1.03	128.0(10)
10	**Michael Strahan**	**129.5**	**1.00**	**129.5(9)**
11	Derrick Thomas	126.5	1.00	126.5(11)
12	Clyde Simmons	121.9	1.00	121.5(12)
13	**Simeon Rice**	**119.0**	**1.00**	**119.0(13)**
14	Sean Jones	113.4	1.00	113.0(14)
15	Greg Townsend	110.1	1.01	109.5(15)
16	Pat Swilling	108.2	1.01	107.5(16)
17	Trace Armstrong	106.0	1.00	106.0(17)
18	Neil Smith	104.5	1.00	104.5(18)
19	Dexter Manley	103.1	1.06	97.5(23)
20	Jim Jeffcoat	102.8	1.00	102.5(19)
21	Charles Haley	100.9	1.00	100.5(20)
22	Andre Tippett	100.8	1.01	100.0(22)
23	William Fuller	100.6	1.00	100.5(20)
24	Jacob Green	100.5	1.03	97.5(23)
25	Simon Fletcher	97.8	1.00	97.5(23)
26	Steve McMichael	97.4	1.03	95.0(27)
27	Robert Porcher	95.5	1.00	95.5(26)
28	Henry Thomas	93.7	1.00	93.5(28)
29	**Jason Taylor**	**92.5**	**1.00**	**92.5(29)**
30	**Kevin Carter**	**92.0**	**1.00**	**92.0(30)**
31	Ken Harvey	89.0	1.00	89.0(31)
32	Howie Long	88.5	1.05	84.0(33)
33	**Warren Sapp**	**84.5**	**1.00**	**84.5(32)**
34	Leonard Marshall	84.0	1.01	83.5(34)
35	Charles Mann	83.6	1.01	83.0(35)
36	Lee Williams	83.0	1.01	82.5(36)
37	Wayne Martin	82.5	1.00	82.5(36)
38	Tim Harris	81.5	1.01	81.0(38)
39	Hugh Douglas	80.0	1.00	80.0(39)
	Jason Gildon	80.0	1.00	80.0(39)
41	Karl Mecklenburg	79.5	1.01	79.0(41)
42	Mark Gastineau	79.0	1.07	74.0(47)
43	Chad Brown	78.0	1.00	78.0(42)
	Willie McGinest	**78.0**	**1.00**	**78.0(42)**
45	**Bryant Young**	**77.5**	**1.00**	**77.5(44)**
46	Ray Childress	76.9	1.01	76.5(45)
47	Bryce Paup	75.0	1.00	75.0(46)
48	Michael Sinclair	73.5	1.00	73.5(48)
49	Rob Burnett	73.0	1.00	73.0(49)
50	Al Baker	72.3	1.10	65.5(57)
51	Cornelius Bennett	72.1	1.01	71.5(50)
52	**La'Roi Glover**	**71.5**	**1.00**	**71.5(50)**
53	Michael McCrary	71.0	1.00	71.0(52)
54	**Peter Boulware**	**70.0**	**1.00**	**70.0(53)**
	Lance Johnstone	**70.0**	**1.00**	**70.0(53)**
56	Clay Matthews	69.7	1.00	69.5(55)
57	Freddie Joe Nunn	68.2	1.01	67.5(56)
58	Jeff Bryant	65.6	1.04	63.0(61)
59	**Marco Coleman**	**65.5**	**1.00**	**65.5(57)**
60	Tony Bennett	64.5	1.00	64.5(59)
61	Dan Hampton	64.2	1.13	57.0(81)
62	**Trevor Pryce**	**64.0**	**1.00**	**64.0(60)**
63	Mike Cofer	63.1	1.01	62.5(63)
64	Keith Hamilton	63.0	1.00	63.0(61)
65	Too Tall Jones	62.8	1.09	57.5(79)
66	**Jevon Kearse**	**62.5**	**1.00**	**62.5(63)**
67	Jumpy Geathers	62.0	1.00	62.0(65)
68	Phil Hansen	61.5	1.00	61.5(66)
69	**Leonard Little**	**61.0**	**1.00**	**61.0(67)**
	Michael Dean Perry	61.0	1.00	61.0(67)
71	Tracy Scroggins	60.5	1.00	60.5(69)
72	Doug Martin	60.0	1.19	50.5(110)
	Keith Willis	60.0	1.02	59.0(72)
74	Ezra Johnson	59.9	1.08	55.5(84)
75	Jeff Cross	59.5	1.00	59.5(70)
	Alfred Williams	59.5	1.00	59.5(70)
77	Tony Tolbert	59.0	1.00	59.0(72)
78	**Kabeer Gbaja-Biamila**	**58.5**	**1.00**	**58.5(74)**
	Chuck Smith	58.5	1.00	58.5(74)
80	Keith Millard	58.2	1.00	58.0(76)
81	Cortez Kennedy	58.0	1.00	58.0(76)
	Anthony Pleasant	58.0	1.00	58.0(76)
83	Anthony Smith	57.5	1.00	57.5(79)
84	Curtis Greer	56.7	1.12	50.5(110)
85	Chad Bratzke	56.5	1.00	56.5(82)
86	Bill Pickel	56.1	1.00	56.0(83)
87	Greg Brown	55.7	1.06	52.5(95)
88	Tony Brackens	55.0	1.00	55.0(85)
89	Rulon Jones	54.5	1.04	52.5(95)
	Greg Lloyd	54.5	1.00	54.5(86)
	Dan Wilkinson	**54.5**	**1.00**	**54.5(86)**
92	Randy White	54.3	1.05	52.0(100)
93	Frank Warren	53.7	1.02	52.5(95)
94	**John Abraham**	**53.5**	**1.00**	**53.5(88)**
	Duane Bickett	53.5	1.01	53.0(93)
	Phillip Daniels	**53.5**	**1.00**	**53.5(88)**
	Patrick Kerney	**53.5**	**1.00**	**53.5(88)**
	Chris Slade	53.5	1.00	53.5(88)
	Dana Stubblefield	53.5	1.00	53.5(88)

	OVERALL RANK	ADJ	RATIO	UNADJ
1	Dan Marino	22957	1.00	22875(1)
2	John Elway	22074	1.00	21970(2)
3	Walter Payton	21764	1.07	20420(5)
4	Emmitt Smith	21678	1.00	21678(3)
5	Fran Tarkenton	21128	1.14	18560(7)
6	**Brett Favre**	**20449**	**1.00**	**20449(4)**
7	Joe Montana	18884	1.05	17957(9)
8	Warren Moon	18816	1.00	18754(6)
9	Steve Young	18148	1.00	18112(8)
10	Jim Brown	18010	1.20	15008(21)
11	Barry Sanders	17778	1.00	17778(10)
12	Marcus Allen	17296	1.05	16415(13)
13	**Marshall Faulk**	**16885**	**1.00**	**16885(11)**
14	**Curtis Martin**	**16744**	**1.00**	**16744(12)**
15	Tony Dorsett	16245	1.06	15337(16)
16	Randall Cunningham	16044	1.01	15940(14)
17	Johnny Unitas	15962	1.20	13357(34)
18	Franco Harris	15935	1.11	14302(24)
19	**Drew Bledsoe**	**15835**	**1.00**	**15835(15)**
20	**Vinny Testaverde**	**15357**	**1.00**	**15331(17)**
21	Eric Dickerson	15326	1.01	15230(19)
22	**Jerome Bettis**	**15318**	**1.00**	**15318(18)**
23	O.J. Simpson	15315	1.13	13552(30)
24	Ken Anderson	15210	1.13	13424(32)
25	Thurman Thomas	15068	1.00	15068(20)
26	Dan Fouts	14922	1.09	13716(28)
27	John Riggins	14783	1.10	13497(31)
28	Boomer Esiason	14580	1.01	14499(22)
29	**Mark Brunell**	**14358**	**1.00**	**14358(23)**
30	**Steve McNair**	**14032**	**1.00**	**14032(25)**
31	Dave Krieg	14003	1.01	13815(26)
32	Rich Gannon	13767	1.00	13769(27)
33	Ricky Watters	13618	1.00	13618(29)
34	**Peyton Manning**	**13369**	**1.00**	**13369(33)**
35	Herschel Walker	13343	1.01	13255(35)
36	Jerry Rice	13216	1.00	13169(36)
37	Ottis Anderson	13161	1.04	12639(40)
38	Jim Kelly	13138	1.01	13058(37)
39	Roman Gabriel	12993	1.14	11369(48)
40	Joe Perry	12963	1.30	9942(73)
41	Phil Simms	12820	1.00	12762(38)
42	Troy Aikman	12753	1.00	12753(39)
43	**Tiki Barber**	**12426**	**1.00**	**12426(41)**
44	Eddie George	12285	1.00	12285(42)
45	James Brooks	12204	1.06	11509(47)
46	Jim Everett	12113	1.00	12070(45)
47	Jim Taylor	12104	1.16	10435(60)
48	Ollie Matson	12095	1.29	9347(89)
49	**Corey Dillon**	**12078**	**1.00**	**12078(43)**
50	Jim Harbaugh	12075	1.00	12072(44)
51	Sonny Jurgensen	11977	1.14	10469(58)
52	Leroy Kelly	11966	1.14	10470(57)
53	**Kerry Collins**	**11752**	**1.00**	**11752(46)**
54	Lenny Moore	11532	1.22	9451(85)
55	Steve Van Buren	11511	1.42	8123(124)
56	Earnest Byner	11392	1.00	11340(50)
57	Roger Craig	11361	1.01	11288(51)
58	**Edgerrin James**	**11341**	**1.00**	**11341(49)**
59	Roger Staubach	11253	1.10	10213(66)
60	Brian Mitchell	11007	1.00	11007(52)
61	Earl Campbell	10997	1.04	10544(56)
62	Len Dawson	10991	1.14	9614(79)
63	Floyd Little	10862	1.14	9505(83)
64	Freeman McNeil	10781	1.08	10002(71)
65	**Trent Green**	**10756**	**1.00**	**10756(53)**
66	Joe Theismann	10736	1.08	9945(72)
67	Hugh McElhenny	10732	1.29	8342(113)
68	Chris Chandler	10691	1.00	10691(54)
69	**Warrick Dunn**	**10690**	**1.00**	**10690(55)**
70	Greg Pruitt	10683	1.11	9589(80)
71	John Brodie	10596	1.14	9271(91)
72	Bart Starr	10544	1.16	9057(97)
73	Steve DeBerg	10519	1.03	10211(67)
74	Bobby Mitchell	10501	1.19	8847(104)
75	**Donovan McNabb**	**10467**	**1.00**	**10467(59)**
76	Tim Brown	10397	1.00	10397(61)
77	Jeff George	10378	1.00	10378(62)
78	**Jake Plummer**	**10363**	**1.00**	**10363(63)**
79	**Priest Holmes**	**10359**	**1.00**	**10359(64)**
80	Terry Bradshaw	10287	1.11	9232(93)
81	Larry Csonka	10257	1.12	9151(95)
82	**Brad Johnson**	**10251**	**1.00**	**10251(65)**
83	Terry Allen	10180	1.00	10180(68)
84	Gerald Riggs	10121	1.04	9711(76)
85	Neil Lomax	10104	1.06	9540(82)
86	Chris Warren	10088	1.00	10088(69)
87	**Daunte Culpepper**	**10082**	**1.00**	**10082(70)**
88	Ron Jaworski	10035	1.06	9449(86)
89	**Fred Taylor**	**9894**	**1.00**	**9894(74)**
90	Jim Hart	9847	1.11	8863(102)
91	Abner Haynes	9794	1.14	8570(107)
92	Ken O'Brien	9751	1.01	9675(77)
93	John Hadl	9736	1.14	8519(111)
94	**Jeff Blake**	**9733**	**1.00**	**9733(75)**
95	John Henry Johnson	9727	1.21	8064(126)
96	Chuck Muncie	9696	1.10	8804(106)
97	Frank Gifford	9681	1.29	7480(154)
98	Bobby Layne	9680	1.32	7345(160)
99	**Ahman Green**	**9664**	**1.00**	**9664(78)**

RUSHING ATTEMPTS

	NAME	ADJ	G	UNADJ
1	Jamal Anderson, 1998	410	16	410(1)
2	James Wilder, 1984	407	16	407(2)
3	Eric Dickerson, 1986	404	16	404(3)
4	Eddie George, 2000	403	16	403(4)
5	Gerald Riggs, 1985	397	16	397(5)
6	Terrell Davis, 1998	392	16	392(6)
	Ricky Williams, 2003	392	16	392(6)
8	Eric Dickerson, 1983	390	16	390(8)
	Barry Foster, 1992	390	16	390(8)
10	Eric Dickerson, 1988	388	16	388(10)
11	Jim Brown, 1959	387	12	290(207)
	Edgerrin James, 2000	387	16	387(11)
	Jamal Lewis, 2003	387	16	387(11)
	Walter Payton, 1977	387	14	339(67)
15	**Ricky Williams, 2002**	383	16	383(13)
16	Walter Payton, 1984	381	16	381(14)
17	Marcus Allen, 1985	380	16	380(15)
18	Eric Dickerson, 1984	379	16	379(16)
	O.J. Simpson, 1973	379	14	332(85)
20	George Rogers, 1981	378	16	378(17)
21	Emmitt Smith, 1995	377	16	377(18)
22	O.J. Simpson, 1975	376	14	329(92)
23	**Jerome Bettis, 1997**	375	16	375(19)
	John Riggins, 1983	375	16	375(19)
25	Earl Campbell, 1980	373	16	373(21)
	Emmitt Smith, 1992	373	16	373(21)
27	**LaDainian Tomlinson, 2002**	372	16	372(23)
28	**Curtis Martin, 2004**	371	16	371(24)
29	**Shaun Alexander, 2005**	370	16	370(25)
	Christian Okoye, 1989	370	16	370(25)
	Mark van Eeghen, 1977	370	14	324(107)
32	Terrell Davis, 1997	369	16	369(27)
	Edgerrin James, 1999	369	16	369(27)
	Curtis Martin, 1998	369	16	369(27)
	Walter Payton, 1979	369	16	369(27)
36	Earl Campbell, 1979	368	16	368(31)
	Curtis Martin, 1995	368	16	368(31)
	Emmitt Smith, 1994	368	16	368(31)
39	**Curtis Martin, 1999**	367	16	367(34)
40	Emmitt Smith, 1991	365	16	365(35)
	James Wilder, 1985	365	16	365(35)
42	Earl Campbell, 1981	361	16	361(37)
	Rudi Johnson, 2004	361	16	361(37)
	Eddie Price, 1951	361	12	271(283)
	Herschel Walker, 1988	361	16	361(37)
46	**Edgerrin James, 2005**	360	16	360(40)
47	**Tiki Barber, 2005**	357	16	357(41)
	Eddie George, 1997	357	16	357(41)
49	**Stephen Davis, 2001**	356	16	356(43)
50	**Jerome Bettis, 2000**	355	16	355(44)
	Ahman Green, 2003	355	16	355(44)
	Walter Payton, 1976	355	14	311(144)
	Thurman Thomas, 1993	355	16	355(44)
54	**Shaun Alexander, 2004**	353	16	353(47)
	Gerald Riggs, 1984	353	16	353(47)
	Ricky Watters, 1996	353	16	353(47)
57	**Clinton Portis, 2005**	352	16	352(50)
58	**Deuce McAllister, 2003**	351	16	351(51)
	Steve Van Buren, 1949	351	12	263(315)
60	Jim Brown, 1961	349	14	305(161)
61	Eddie George, 1998	348	16	348(52)
62	Terry Allen, 1996	347	16	347(53)
63	Charles White, 1987	346	15	324(107)
64	Terrell Davis, 1996	345	16	345(54)
	Corey Dillon, 2004	345	16	345(54)
	Fred Taylor, 2003	345	16	345(54)
67	Dalton Hilliard, 1989	344	16	344(57)
	Lydell Mitchell, 1977	344	14	301(169)
69	Jim Brown, 1958	343	12	257(343)
	Eddie George, 2002	343	16	343(58)
	Franco Harris, 1977	343	14	300(172)
	Natrone Means, 1994	343	16	343(58)
	Clinton Portis, 2004	343	16	343(58)
	Gerald Riggs, 1986	343	16	343(58)
	Barry Sanders, 1998	343	16	343(58)
76	Tony Dorsett, 1981	342	16	342(63)
	Jim Nance, 1966	342	14	299(177)
	Barry Sanders, 1991	342	16	342(63)
79	Ron Johnson, 1972	341	14	298(179)
	Joe Morris, 1986	341	16	341(65)
81	**Corey Dillon, 2001**	340	16	340(66)
82	Walter Payton, 1981	339	16	339(67)
	James Stewart, 2000	339	16	339(67)
	LaDainian Tomlinson, 2001	339	16	339(67)
	LaDainian Tomlinson, 2004	339	16	339(67)
	LaDainian Tomlinson, 2005	339	16	339(67)
87	Terry Allen, 1995	338	16	338(73)
	Wilbert Montgomery, 1979	338	16	338(73)
89	**Rudi Johnson, 2005**	337	16	337(75)
	Ricky Watters, 1995	337	16	337(75)
91	**Larry Johnson, 2005**	336	16	336(77)
	Lawrence McCutcheon, 1977	336	14	294(191)
93	Eddie George, 1996	335	16	335(78)
	Barry Sanders, 1997	335	16	335(78)
	Curt Warner, 1983	335	16	335(78)
96	**Edgerrin James, 2004**	334	16	334(81)
	O.J. Simpson, 1972	334	14	292(198)
98	5 players tied			333

RUSHING YARDS

	NAME	ADJ	G	UNADJ
1	O.J. Simpson, 1973	2289	14	2003(5)
2	Jim Brown, 1963	2129	14	1863(10)
3	Walter Payton, 1977	2117	14	1852(13)
4	Eric Dickerson, 1984	2105	16	2105(1)
5	O.J. Simpson, 1975	2077	14	1817(16)
6	**Jamal Lewis, 2003**	2066	16	2066(2)
7	Barry Sanders, 1997	2053	16	2053(3)
8	Jim Brown, 1958	2036	12	1527(56)
9	Terrell Davis, 1998	2008	16	2008(4)
10	Earl Campbell, 1980	1934	16	1934(6)
11	**Ahman Green, 2003**	1883	16	1883(7)
	Barry Sanders, 1994	1883	16	1883(7)
13	**Shaun Alexander, 2005**	1880	16	1880(9)
14	**Tiki Barber, 2005**	1860	16	1860(11)
15	**Ricky Williams, 2002**	1853	16	1853(12)
16	Jamal Anderson, 1998	1846	16	1846(14)
17	Eric Dickerson, 1986	1821	16	1821(15)
18	Eric Dickerson, 1983	1808	16	1808(17)
19	Emmitt Smith, 1995	1773	16	1773(18)
20	Jim Brown, 1959	1772	12	1329(140)
21	Jim Brown, 1965	1765	14	1544(53)
22	Marcus Allen, 1985	1759	16	1759(19)
23	Terrell Davis, 1997	1750	16	1750(20)
	Larry Johnson, 2005	1750	16	1750(20)
25	Gerald Riggs, 1985	1719	16	1719(22)
26	O.J. Simpson, 1976	1718	14	1503(67)
27	Emmitt Smith, 1992	1713	16	1713(23)
28	**Edgerrin James, 2000**	1709	16	1709(24)
29	Earl Campbell, 1979	1697	16	1697(25)
	Curtis Martin, 2004	1697	16	1697(25)
31	**Shaun Alexander, 2004**	1696	16	1696(27)
32	Barry Foster, 1992	1690	16	1690(28)
33	Jim Taylor, 1962	1685	14	1474(79)
34	Walter Payton, 1984	1684	16	1684(29)
35	**LaDainian Tomlinson, 2002**	1683	16	1683(30)
36	George Rogers, 1981	1674	16	1674(31)
37	Jim Nance, 1966	1666	14	1458(84)
38	**Jerome Bettis, 1997**	1665	16	1665(32)
39	Eric Dickerson, 1988	1659	16	1659(33)
40	Jim Brown, 1964	1653	14	1446(89)
41	Tony Dorsett, 1981	1646	16	1646(34)
42	**LaDainian Tomlinson, 2003**	1645	16	1645(35)
43	**Deuce McAllister, 2003**	1641	16	1641(36)
44	**Corey Dillon, 2004**	1635	16	1635(37)
45	**Priest Holmes, 2002**	1615	16	1615(38)
46	Walter Payton, 1979	1610	16	1610(39)
47	Jim Brown, 1961	1609	14	1408(103)
48	Otis Armstrong, 1974	1608	14	1407(104)
49	Ottis Anderson, 1979	1605	16	1605(40)
50	**Clinton Portis, 2003**	1591	16	1591(41)
51	Walter Payton, 1976	1589	14	1390(112)
52	**Fred Taylor, 2003**	1572	16	1572(42)
53	Garrison Hearst, 1998	1570	16	1570(43)
54	William Andrews, 1983	1567	16	1567(44)
55	Emmitt Smith, 1991	1563	16	1563(45)
56	**Priest Holmes, 2001**	1555	16	1555(46)
57	**Edgerrin James, 1999**	1553	16	1553(47)
	Barry Sanders, 1996	1553	16	1553(47)
59	Walter Payton, 1985	1551	16	1551(49)
60	**Edgerrin James, 2004**	1548	16	1548(50)
	Barry Sanders, 1991	1548	16	1548(50)
62	Chris Warren, 1994	1545	16	1545(52)
63	James Wilder, 1984	1544	16	1544(53)
64	Terrell Davis, 1996	1538	16	1538(55)
65	Steve Van Buren, 1949	1528	12	1146(269)
66	Robert Smith, 2000	1521	16	1521(57)
67	**Tiki Barber, 2004**	1518	16	1518(58)
68	Joe Morris, 1986	1516	16	1516(59)
	Clinton Portis, 2005	1516	16	1516(59)
70	Herschel Walker, 1988	1514	16	1514(61)
71	**Curtis Martin, 2001**	1513	16	1513(62)
72	Wilbert Montgomery, 1979	1512	16	1512(63)
73	Eddie George, 2000	1509	16	1509(64)
74	**Clinton Portis, 2002**	1508	16	1508(65)
75	**Edgerrin James, 2005**	1506	16	1506(66)
76	Roger Craig, 1988	1502	16	1502(68)
77	Rick Casares, 1956	1501	12	1126(288)
78	Barry Sanders, 1995	1500	16	1500(69)
79	Jim Taylor, 1961	1494	14	1307(157)
80	Barry Sanders, 1998	1491	16	1491(70)
81	**Mike Anderson, 2000**	1487	16	1487(71)
	Curtis Martin, 1995	1487	16	1487(71)
	Thurman Thomas, 1992	1487	16	1487(71)
84	Gerald Riggs, 1984	1486	16	1486(74)
	Emmitt Smith, 1993	1486	16	1486(74)
86	Emmitt Smith, 1994	1484	16	1484(76)
87	Curt Warner, 1986	1481	16	1481(77)
88	Christian Okoye, 1989	1480	16	1480(78)
89	Barry Sanders, 1989	1470	16	1470(80)
90	Charles White, 1987	1466	15	1374(120)
91	**Curtis Martin, 1999**	1464	16	1464(81)
92	**LaDainian Tomlinson, 2005**	1462	16	1462(82)
93	Walter Payton, 1980	1460	16	1460(83)
94	**Rudi Johnson, 2005**	1458	16	1458(84)
95	Mark van Eeghen, 1977	1455	14	1273(173)
96	**Rudi Johnson, 2004**	1454	16	1454(86)
97	Earl Campbell, 1978	1450	16	1450(87)
98	Curt Warner, 1983	1449	16	1449(88)
99	**Stephen Davis, 2003**	1444	16	1444(90)

RUSHING AVERAGE GAIN

	NAME	ADJ	G	UNADJ
1	Beattie Feathers, 1934	8.44	13	8.44(1)
2	Hugh McElhenny, 1954	8.05	12	8.05(2)
3	Randall Cunningham, 1990	7.98	16	7.98(3)
4	Lenny Moore, 1956	7.55	12	7.55(4)
5	**Michael Vick, 2004**	7.52	16	7.52(5)
6	Tommy Wilson, 1956	7.34	12	7.34(6)
7	**Donovan McNabb, 2000**	7.31	16	7.31(7)
8	George McAfee, 1941	7.29	11	7.29(8)
	Lenny Moore, 1958	7.29	12	7.29(8)
10	Skeets Quinlan, 1953	7.27	12	7.27(10)
11	Joe Maniaci, 1939	7.06	11	7.06(11)
12	Lenny Moore, 1961	7.04	14	7.04(12)
13	Hugh McElhenny, 1952	6.98	12	6.98(13)
14	Greg Landry, 1971	6.97	14	6.97(14)
15	Tobin Rote, 1951	6.88	12	6.88(15)
	Michael Vick, 2002	6.88	16	6.88(15)
17	Bobby Douglass, 1972	6.87	14	6.87(17)
18	Bo Jackson, 1987	6.84	15	6.84(18)
19	Dan Towler, 1951	6.78	12	6.78(19)
20	Randall Cunningham, 1988	6.71	16	6.71(20)
21	Tank Younger, 1954	6.70	12	6.70(21)
22	**Steve McNair, 1997**	6.67	16	6.67(22)
23	Steve Grogan, 1978	6.65	16	6.65(23)
	Johnny Olszewski, 1959	6.65	12	6.65(23)
25	Randall Cunningham, 1987	6.64	15	6.64(25)
26	Ward Cuff, 1943	6.54	10	6.54(26)
	Ron Waller, 1956	6.54	12	6.54(26)
28	Tommy Wilson, 1958	6.51	12	6.51(28)
29	Greg Landry, 1972	6.47	14	6.47(29)
30	Keith Lincoln, 1963	6.45	14	6.45(30)
31	Charlie Trippi, 1951	6.42	12	6.42(31)
32	Jim Brown, 1963	6.40	14	6.40(32)
	Mercury Morris, 1973	6.40	14	6.40(32)
34	Ernie Caddel, 1936	6.37	12	6.37(34)
35	Randall Cunningham, 1992	6.31	16	6.31(35)
	Fred Gehrke, 1945	6.31	10	6.31(35)
37	Johnny Lujack, 1950	6.30	12	6.30(37)
38	Paul Lowe, 1960	6.29	14	6.29(38)
39	Bobby Mitchell, 1958	6.25	12	6.25(39)
40	Dick Bass, 1961	6.20	14	6.20(40)
	Dutch Clark, 1934	6.20	13	6.20(40)
	Gale Sayers, 1968	6.20	14	6.20(40)
43	Jim Gillette, 1945	6.19	10	6.19(43)
44	Essex Johnson, 1971	6.14	14	6.14(44)
45	Barry Sanders, 1997	6.13	16	6.13(45)
46	Ronnie Harmon, 1991	6.11	16	6.11(46)
47	Richard Huntley, 1999	6.10	16	6.10(47)
48	Al Grygo, 1944	6.08	10	6.08(48)
	Dante Magnani, 1943	6.08	10	6.08(48)
50	Joe Perry, 1954	6.06	12	6.06(50)
	Joe Perry, 1958	6.06	12	6.06(50)
52	Ernie Green, 1963	6.05	14	6.05(52)
	Dick Hoerner, 1951	6.05	12	6.05(52)
54	Hokie Gajan, 1984	6.03	16	6.03(54)
	Ted McKnight, 1978	6.03	16	6.03(54)
	O.J. Simpson, 1973	6.03	14	6.03(54)
57	Bosh Pritchard, 1949	6.02	12	6.02(57)
58	Skeets Quinlan, 1954	5.98	12	5.98(58)
59	Randall Cunningham, 1989	5.97	16	5.97(59)
60	Jim Brown, 1958	5.94	12	5.94(60)
	Rich Gannon, 2000	5.94	16	5.94(60)
62	Verl Lillywhite, 1951	5.93	12	5.93(62)
63	**Donovan McNabb, 2001**	5.88	16	5.88(63)
	Nick Pietrosante, 1959	5.88	12	5.88(63)
65	Ray Renfro, 1953	5.87	12	5.87(65)
66	Jim Brown, 1960	5.85	14	5.85(66)
	John David Crow, 1960	5.85	14	5.85(66)
	Michael Vick, 2005	5.85	16	5.85(66)
69	Napoleon Kaufman, 1996	5.83	16	5.83(69)
	Dante Magnani, 1942	5.83	11	5.83(69)
71	Steve Van Buren, 1945	5.82	10	5.82(71)
72	Marion Motley, 1950	5.79	12	5.79(72)
73	Bill Osmanski, 1939	5.78	11	5.78(73)
	Dan Towler, 1953	5.78	12	5.78(73)
75	Gene Ronzani, 1934	5.77	13	5.77(75)
76	**Daunte Culpepper, 2002**	5.75	16	5.75(76)
77	Dan Towler, 1952	5.73	12	5.73(77)
78	Billy Grimes, 1950	5.71	12	5.71(78)
	Paul Lowe, 1963	5.71	14	5.71(78)
	Johnny Morris, 1960	5.71	14	5.71(78)
81	**Priest Holmes, 1999**	5.69	16	5.69(81)
	Barry Sanders, 1994	5.69	16	5.69(81)
83	Herman Heard, 1987	5.68	15	5.68(83)
84	Ken Carpenter, 1952	5.67	12	5.67(84)
	Bobby Mitchell, 1959	5.67	12	5.67(84)
86	Jerry Williams, 1953	5.66	12	5.66(86)
87	Ernie Caddel, 1937	5.64	11	5.64(87)
	Wray Carlton, 1962	5.64	14	5.64(87)
89	Bob Thomas, 1972	5.62	14	5.62(89)
90	James Brooks, 1989	5.61	16	5.61(90)
	Franco Harris, 1972	5.61	14	5.61(90)
	Abner Haynes, 1960	5.61	14	5.61(90)
	Bob Hoernschemeyer, 1950	5.61	12	5.61(90)
94	Don Calhoun, 1976	5.59	14	5.59(94)
	Ward Cuff, 1944	5.59	10	5.59(94)
	Bobby Douglass, 1973	5.59	14	5.59(94)
	Kordell Stewart, 2001	5.59	16	5.59(94)
98	4 players tied			5.58

RUSHING TDS

	NAME	ADJ	G	UNADJ
1	Shaun Alexander, 2005	27	16	27(1)
	Priest Holmes, 2003	27	16	27(1)
3	Emmitt Smith, 1995	25	16	25(3)
4	John Riggins, 1983	24	16	24(4)
	Steve Van Buren, 1945	24	10	15(32)
6	Jim Brown, 1958	23	12	17(19)
7	Jim Taylor, 1962	22	14	19(11)
8	Terry Allen, 1996	21	16	21(5)
	Terrell Davis, 1998	21	16	21(5)
	Priest Holmes, 2002	21	16	21(5)
	Joe Morris, 1985	21	16	21(5)
	Emmitt Smith, 1994	21	16	21(5)
13	Marcus Allen, 1982	20	9	11(148)
	Larry Johnson, 2005	20	16	20(10)
15	Jim Brown, 1959	19	12	14(43)
	Jim Brown, 1965	19	14	17(19)
	Earl Campbell, 1979	19	16	19(11)
	Chuck Muncie, 1981	19	16	19(11)
19	Pete Banaszak, 1975	18	14	16(23)
	Eric Dickerson, 1983	18	16	18(14)
	Marshall Faulk, 2000	18	16	18(14)
	Leroy Kelly, 1968	18	14	16(23)
	Tony Latone, 1929	18	8	9
	Lenny Moore, 1964	18	14	16(23)
	George Rogers, 1986	18	16	18(14)
	O.J. Simpson, 1975	18	14	16(23)
	Emmitt Smith, 1992	18	16	18(14)
	LaDainian Tomlinson, 2005	18	16	18(14)
29	Stephen Davis, 1999	17	16	17(19)
	Leroy Kelly, 1966	17	14	15(32)
	Jim Taylor, 1961	17	14	15(32)
	LaDainian Tomlinson, 2004	17	16	17(19)
	Steve Van Buren, 1947	17	12	13(73)
34	Shaun Alexander, 2002	16	16	16(23)
	Shaun Alexander, 2004	16	16	16(23)
	Greg Bell, 1988	16	16	16(23)
	Rick Casares, 1956	16	12	12(109)
	Jimmy Conzelman, 1922	16	7	7
	John David Crow, 1962	16	14	14(43)
	Franco Harris, 1976	16	14	14(43)
	Eddie Lee Ivery, 1982	16	9	9
	Bill Paschal, 1943	16	10	10(204)
	Walter Payton, 1977	16	14	14(43)
	Barry Sanders, 1991	16	16	16(23)
	Gale Sayers, 1965	16	14	14(43)
	Wendell Tyler, 1982	16	9	9
	Ricky Williams, 2002	16	16	16(23)
48	Karim Abdul-Jabbar, 1997	15	16	15(32)
	Mike Anderson, 2000	15	16	15(32)
	Greg Bell, 1989	15	16	15(32)
	Jim Brown, 1962	15	14	13(73)
	Terrell Davis, 1997	15	16	15(32)
	Chuck Foreman, 1975	15	14	13(73)
	Chuck Foreman, 1976	15	14	13(73)
	Cookie Gilchrist, 1962	15	14	13(73)
	Ahman Green, 2003	15	16	15(32)
	Abner Haynes, 1962	15	14	13(73)
	Paul Hornung, 1960	15	14	13(73)
	Johnny Lujack, 1950	15	12	11(148)
	Ernie Nevers, 1929	15	13	12(109)
	Walter Payton, 1976	15	14	13(73)
	Clinton Portis, 2002	15	16	15(32)
	Tobin Rote, 1956	15	12	11(148)
	Dan Towler, 1954	15	12	11(148)
	Steve Van Buren, 1949	15	12	11(148)
	Chris Warren, 1995	15	16	15(32)
	Ickey Woods, 1988	15	16	15(32)
68	38 players tied 14			

PASS ATTEMPTS

	NAME	ADJ	G	UNADJ
1	Drew Bledsoe, 1994	691	16	691(1)
2	Warren Moon, 1991	655	16	655(2)
3	Drew Bledsoe, 1995	636	16	636(3)
4	Drew Bledsoe, 1996	623	16	623(4)
	Dan Marino, 1986	623	16	623(4)
6	Rich Gannon, 2002	618	16	618(6)
7	Dan Marino, 1994	615	16	615(7)
	Joe Montana, 1982	615	9	346
9	Drew Bledsoe, 2002	610	16	610(8)
10	Dan Fouts, 1981	609	16	609(9)
11	Brett Favre, 2005	607	16	607(10)
12	Dan Marino, 1988	606	16	606(11)
	Warren Moon, 1995	606	16	606(11)
14	John Elway, 1985	605	16	605(13)
15	Bill Kenney, 1983	603	16	603(14)
16	Tom Brady, 2002	601	16	601(15)
	Warren Moon, 1994	601	16	601(15)
18	Don Majkowski, 1989	599	16	599(17)
19	Brett Favre, 1999	595	16	595(18)
20	Tommy Kramer, 1981	593	16	593(19)
21	Peyton Manning, 2002	591	16	591(20)
22	Vinny Testaverde, 2000	590	16	590(21)
23	Dan Fouts, 1980	589	16	589(22)
24	Dan Fouts, 1982	587	9	330
25	Warren Moon, 1990	584	16	584(23)
26	Scott Mitchell, 1995	583	16	583(24)
27	Brett Favre, 1994	582	16	582(25)
28	Sonny Jurgensen, 1967	581	14	508(144)
	Jon Kitna, 2001	581	16	581(26)
30	Brett Favre, 2000	580	16	580(27)
31	Steve DeBerg, 1979	578	16	578(28)
32	George Blanda, 1964	577	14	505(149)
33	Peyton Manning, 1998	575	16	575(29)
34	Fran Tarkenton, 1978	572	16	572(30)
35	Steve Beuerlein, 1999	571	16	571(31)
	Peyton Manning, 2000	571	16	571(31)
37	Brett Favre, 1995	570	16	570(33)
	Brad Johnson, 2003	570	16	570(33)
39	Donovan McNabb, 2000	569	16	569(35)
40	Kerry Collins, 2001	568	16	568(36)
41	Jeff Blake, 1995	567	16	567(37)
	Jim Everett, 1995	567	16	567(37)
	Dan Marino, 1985	567	16	567(37)
	Brian Sipe, 1981	567	16	567(37)
45	Tommy Kramer, 1979	566	16	566(41)
	Peyton Manning, 2003	566	16	566(41)
47	Kerry Collins, 2005	565	16	565(43)
48	Dan Marino, 1984	564	16	564(44)
49	Jeff Garcia, 2000	561	16	561(45)
	Joe Namath, 1967	561	14	491(182)
51	Randall Cunningham, 1988	560	16	560(46)
	Neil Lomax, 1984	560	16	560(46)
53	Brad Johnson, 2001	559	16	559(48)
54	Aaron Brooks, 2001	558	16	558(49)
55	Mark Brunell, 1996	557	16	557(50)
	Jeff George, 1995	557	16	557(50)
	Eli Manning, 2005	557	16	557(50)
58	Trent Green, 2004	556	16	556(53)
59	Jim Everett, 1990	554	16	554(54)
	Joey Harrington, 2003	554	16	554(54)
	Dan Marino, 1992	554	16	554(54)
	Brian Sipe, 1980	554	16	554(54)
63	John Elway, 1993	551	16	551(58)
	Brett Favre, 1998	551	16	551(58)
	Brett Favre, 2002	551	16	551(58)
66	Dan Marino, 1989	550	16	550(61)
67	Ken Anderson, 1982	549	9	309
	Jeff Blake, 1996	549	16	549(62)
	Daunte Culpepper, 2002	549	16	549(62)
	Rich Gannon, 2001	549	16	549(62)
	Dan Marino, 1991	549	16	549(62)
	Vinny Testaverde, 1996	549	16	549(62)
73	Daunte Culpepper, 2004	548	16	548(67)
	Tommy Kramer, 1982	548	9	308
	Dan Marino, 1997	548	16	548(67)
76	Elvis Grbac, 2000	547	16	547(69)
	Peyton Manning, 2001	547	16	547(69)
	Jake Plummer, 1998	547	16	547(69)
79	Frank Tripucka, 1960	546	14	478(211)
	Kurt Warner, 2001	546	16	546(72)
	Doug Williams, 1982	546	9	307
82	Kerry Collins, 2002	545	16	545(73)
83	Brett Favre, 1996	543	16	543(74)
84	Aaron Brooks, 2004	542	16	542(75)
	John Elway, 1995	542	16	542(75)
86	Babe Parilli, 1964	541	14	473(230)
	Jay Schroeder, 1986	541	16	541(77)
88	Jim Everett, 1994	540	16	540(78)
	Brett Favre, 2004	540	16	540(78)
	Chris Weinke, 2001	540	16	540(78)
91	Drew Bledsoe, 1999	539	16	539(81)
92	Joe Namath, 1966	538	14	471(237)
93	Dan Marino, 1998	537	16	537(82)
94	Brian Sipe, 1979	535	16	535(83)
95	Steve Bartkowski, 1981	533	16	533(84)
	Steve Beuerlein, 2000	533	16	533(84)
	Jake Delhomme, 2004	533	16	533(84)
	Peyton Manning, 1999	533	16	533(84)
	Phil Simms, 1984	533	16	533(84)
	Danny White, 1983	533	16	533(84)

PASS COMPLETIONS

	NAME	ADJ	G	UNADJ
1	Rich Gannon, 2002	418	16	418(1)
2	Warren Moon, 1991	404	16	404(2)
3	Drew Bledsoe, 1994	400	16	400(3)
4	Peyton Manning, 2002	392	16	392(4)
5	Ken Anderson, 1982	388	9	218
6	Dan Marino, 1994	385	16	385(5)
7	Daunte Culpepper, 2004	379	16	379(6)
	Peyton Manning, 2003	379	16	379(6)
	Joe Montana, 1982	379	9	213
10	Dan Marino, 1986	378	16	378(8)
11	Warren Moon, 1995	377	16	377(9)
12	Drew Bledsoe, 2002	375	16	375(10)
	Kurt Warner, 2001	375	16	375(10)
14	Drew Bledsoe, 1996	373	16	373(12)
	Tom Brady, 2002	373	16	373(12)
16	Brett Favre, 2005	372	16	372(14)
17	Warren Moon, 1994	371	16	371(15)
18	Trent Green, 2004	369	16	369(16)
19	Brett Favre, 1994	363	16	363(17)
	Dan Fouts, 1982	363	9	204
21	Dan Marino, 1984	362	16	362(18)
	Warren Moon, 1990	362	16	362(18)
23	Rich Gannon, 2001	361	16	361(20)
24	Dan Fouts, 1981	360	16	360(21)
25	Brett Favre, 1995	359	16	359(22)
26	Peyton Manning, 2000	357	16	357(23)
27	Jeff Garcia, 2000	355	16	355(24)
28	Brad Johnson, 2003	354	16	354(25)
	Dan Marino, 1988	354	16	354(25)
30	Mark Brunell, 1996	353	16	353(27)
	Don Majkowski, 1989	353	16	353(27)
32	John Elway, 1993	348	16	348(29)
	Dan Fouts, 1980	348	16	348(29)
34	Steve DeBerg, 1979	347	16	347(31)
	Brett Favre, 1998	347	16	347(31)
36	Jim Everett, 1994	346	16	346(33)
	Brett Favre, 2004	346	16	346(33)
	Bill Kenney, 1983	346	16	346(33)
	Scott Mitchell, 1995	346	16	346(33)
40	Jim Everett, 1995	345	16	345(37)
	Neil Lomax, 1984	345	16	345(37)
	Carson Palmer, 2005	345	16	345(37)
	Fran Tarkenton, 1978	345	16	345(37)
44	Steve Beuerlein, 1999	343	16	343(41)
	Peyton Manning, 2001	343	16	343(41)
46	Brett Favre, 1999	341	16	341(43)
	Brett Favre, 2002	341	16	341(43)
48	Brad Johnson, 2001	340	16	340(45)
49	Brett Favre, 2000	338	16	338(46)
50	Brian Sipe, 1980	337	16	337(47)
51	Marc Bulger, 2003	336	16	336(48)
	Jeff George, 1995	336	16	336(48)
	Peyton Manning, 2004	336	16	336(48)
	Dan Marino, 1985	336	16	336(48)
55	Kerry Collins, 2002	335	16	335(52)
56	Tom Brady, 2005	334	16	334(53)
	Danny White, 1983	334	16	334(53)
58	Daunte Culpepper, 2002	333	16	333(55)
59	Dan Fouts, 1979	332	16	332(56)
	Joe Montana, 1983	332	16	332(56)
61	Peyton Manning, 1999	331	16	331(58)
62	Trent Green, 2003	330	16	330(59)
	Dan Marino, 1992	330	16	330(59)
	Donovan McNabb, 2000	330	16	330(59)
65	Sonny Jurgensen, 1967	329	14	288(183)
66	Jeff Garcia, 2002	328	16	328(62)
	Vinny Testaverde, 2000	328	16	328(62)
68	Kerry Collins, 2001	327	16	327(64)
	John Elway, 1985	327	16	327(64)
70	Jeff Blake, 1995	326	16	326(66)
	Elvis Grbac, 2000	326	16	326(66)
	Peyton Manning, 1998	326	16	326(66)
73	Brett Favre, 1996	325	16	325(69)
	Vinny Testaverde, 1996	325	16	325(69)
	Kurt Warner, 1999	325	16	325(69)
76	Steve Beuerlein, 2000	324	16	324(72)
	Jon Kitna, 2003	324	16	324(72)
	Jake Plummer, 1998	324	16	324(72)
	Steve Young, 1994	324	16	324(72)
80	Drew Bledsoe, 1995	323	16	323(76)
	Drew Brees, 2005	323	16	323(76)
82	Jeff George, 1994	322	16	322(78)
	Tommy Kramer, 1981	322	16	322(78)
	Steve Young, 1998	322	16	322(78)
85	Marc Bulger, 2004	321	16	321(81)
	Joe Montana, 1990	321	16	321(81)
87	Drew Brees, 2002	320	16	320(83)
88	Dan Marino, 1997	319	16	319(84)
89	Brett Favre, 1993	318	16	318(85)
	Dan Marino, 1991	318	16	318(85)
91	Tom Brady, 2003	317	16	317(87)
	Dan Fouts, 1984	317	16	317(87)
	Trent Green, 2005	317	16	317(87)
94	John Elway, 1995	316	16	316(90)
	Jeff Garcia, 2001	316	16	316(90)
	Brad Johnson, 1999	316	16	316(90)
97	Erik Kramer, 1995	315	16	315(93)
	Tommy Kramer, 1979	315	16	315(93)
99	3 players tied 314			

PASSING YARDS

	NAME	ADJ	G	UNADJ
1	Dan Fouts, 1982	*5125*	9	2883
2	Dan Marino, 1984	*5084*	16	5084(1)
3	**Kurt Warner, 2001**	***4830***	**16**	**4830(2)**
4	Dan Fouts, 1981	*4802*	16	4802(3)
5	Dan Marino, 1986	*4746*	16	4746(4)
6	**Daunte Culpepper, 2004**	***4717***	**16**	**4717(5)**
7	Dan Fouts, 1980	*4715*	16	4715(6)
8	Warren Moon, 1991	*4690*	16	4690(7)
9	Rich Gannon, 2002	*4689*	16	4689(8)
	Warren Moon, 1990	*4689*	16	4689(8)
11	Joe Montana, 1982	*4645*	9	2613
12	Neil Lomax, 1984	*4614*	16	4614(10)
13	**Trent Green, 2004**	***4591***	**16**	**4591(11)**
14	Joe Namath, 1967	*4579*	14	4007(55)
15	**Peyton Manning, 2004**	***4557***	**16**	**4557(12)**
16	**Drew Bledsoe, 1994**	***4555***	**16**	**4555(13)**
17	Lynn Dickey, 1983	*4458*	16	4458(14)
18	Dan Marino, 1994	*4453*	16	4453(15)
19	Ken Anderson, 1982	*4436*	9	2495
	Steve Beuerlein, 1999	*4436*	16	4436(16)
21	Dan Marino, 1988	*4434*	16	4434(17)
22	**Brett Favre, 1995**	***4413***	**16**	**4413(18)**
	Peyton Manning, 2000	***4413***	**16**	**4413(18)**
24	**Mark Brunell, 1996**	***4367***	**16**	**4367(20)**
25	**Drew Bledsoe, 2002**	***4359***	**16**	**4359(21)**
26	**Kurt Warner, 1999**	***4353***	**16**	**4353(22)**
27	Bill Kenney, 1983	*4348*	16	4348(23)
28	Scott Mitchell, 1995	*4338*	16	4338(24)
29	Don Majkowski, 1989	*4318*	16	4318(25)
30	Jim Everett, 1989	*4310*	16	4310(26)
31	Sonny Jurgensen, 1967	*4282*	14	3747(110)
32	**Jeff Garcia, 2000**	***4278***	**16**	**4278(27)**
33	**Peyton Manning, 2003**	***4267***	**16**	**4267(28)**
34	Warren Moon, 1994	*4264*	16	4264(29)
35	Sonny Jurgensen, 1961	*4255*	14	3723(119)
36	Warren Moon, 1995	*4228*	16	4228(30)
37	**Brett Favre, 1998**	***4212***	**16**	**4212(31)**
38	**Peyton Manning, 2002**	***4200***	**16**	**4200(32)**
39	**Vinny Testaverde, 1996**	***4177***	**16**	**4177(33)**
40	Steve Young, 1998	*4170*	16	4170(34)
41	Elvis Grbac, 2000	*4169*	16	4169(35)
42	Jeff George, 1995	*4143*	16	4143(36)
43	Dan Marino, 1985	*4137*	16	4137(37)
44	**Peyton Manning, 1999**	***4135***	**16**	**4135(38)**
45	Brian Sipe, 1980	*4132*	16	4132(39)
46	**Peyton Manning, 2001**	***4131***	**16**	**4131(40)**
47	Dan Marino, 1992	*4116*	16	4116(41)
48	**Tom Brady, 2005**	***4110***	**16**	**4110(42)**
49	Jay Schroeder, 1986	*4109*	16	4109(43)
50	**Brett Favre, 1999**	***4091***	**16**	**4091(44)**
51	**Jake Plummer, 2004**	***4089***	**16**	**4089(45)**
52	**Brett Favre, 2004**	***4088***	**16**	**4088(46)**
53	**Drew Bledsoe, 1996**	***4086***	**16**	**4086(47)**
54	Dan Fouts, 1979	*4082*	16	4082(48)
55	**Kerry Collins, 2002**	***4073***	**16**	**4073(49)**
56	Phil Simms, 1984	*4044*	16	4044(50)
57	**Trent Green, 2003**	***4039***	**16**	**4039(51)**
58	John Elway, 1993	*4030*	16	4030(52)
59	Steve Young, 1993	*4023*	16	4023(53)
60	**Trent Green, 2005**	***4014***	**16**	**4014(54)**
61	**Brad Johnson, 1999**	***4005***	**16**	**4005(56)**
62	Dan Marino, 1989	*3997*	16	3997(57)
63	Jim Everett, 1990	*3989*	16	3989(58)
64	**Drew Bledsoe, 1999**	***3985***	**16**	**3985(59)**
65	Danny White, 1983	*3980*	16	3980(60)
66	Johnny Unitas, 1963	*3978*	14	3481(186)
67	John Elway, 1995	*3970*	16	3970(61)
	Jim Everett, 1995	*3970*	16	3970(61)
	Dan Marino, 1991	*3970*	16	3970(61)
70	John Hadl, 1968	*3969*	14	3473(189)
	Steve Young, 1994	*3969*	16	3969(64)
72	**Marc Bulger, 2004**	***3964***	**16**	**3964(65)**
	Jim Everett, 1988	*3964*	16	3964(65)
74	Babe Parilli, 1964	*3960*	14	3465(193)
75	Boomer Esiason, 1986	*3959*	16	3959(67)
76	Joe Montana, 1990	*3944*	16	3944(68)
77	**Daunte Culpepper, 2000**	***3937***	**16**	**3937(69)**
78	**Brett Favre, 2001**	***3921***	**16**	**3921(70)**
79	Johnny Unitas, 1967	*3918*	14	3428(208)
80	Sammy Baugh, 1947	*3917*	12	2938
	Jeff George, 1997	*3917*	16	3917(71)
82	Tommy Kramer, 1981	*3912*	16	3912(72)
83	Joe Montana, 1983	*3910*	16	3910(73)
84	**Brett Favre, 1996**	***3899***	**16**	**3899(74)**
85	John Elway, 1985	*3891*	16	3891(75)
86	Ken O'Brien, 1985	*3888*	16	3888(76)
87	**Jake Delhomme, 2004**	***3886***	**16**	**3886(77)**
88	Norm Snead, 1967	*3885*	14	3399(215)
89	**Brett Favre, 1994**	***3882***	**16**	**3882(78)**
90	**Brett Favre, 2005**	***3881***	**16**	**3881(79)**
91	Brian Sipe, 1981	*3876*	16	3876(80)
92	**Donovan McNabb, 2004**	***3875***	**16**	**3875(81)**
93	**Brett Favre, 1997**	***3867***	**16**	**3867(82)**
94	Johnny Unitas, 1959	*3865*	12	2899
95	Joe Namath, 1966	*3862*	14	3379(227)
96	Jim Everett, 1994	*3855*	16	3855(83)
97	Bernie Kosar, 1986	*3854*	16	3854(84)
98	**Daunte Culpepper, 2002**	***3853***	**16**	**3853(85)**
99	John Hadl, 1967	*3846*	14	3365(229)

PASSING AVERAGE GAIN

	NAME	ADJ	G	UNADJ
1	Frank Filchock, 1939	*12.29*	11	12.29(1)
2	Tommy O'Connell, 1957	*11.17*	12	11.17(2)
3	Sid Luckman, 1943	*10.86*	10	10.86(3)
4	Charlie O'Rourke, 1942	*10.81*	11	10.81(4)
5	Otto Graham, 1953	*10.55*	12	10.55(5)
6	Norm Van Brocklin, 1954	*10.14*	12	10.14(6)
7	Ed Brown, 1956	*9.92*	12	9.92(7)
	Sid Luckman, 1941	*9.92*	11	9.92(7)
9	**Kurt Warner, 2000**	***9.88***	**16**	**9.88(9)**
10	Sid Luckman, 1942	*9.75*	11	9.75(10)
11	Chris Chandler, 1998	*9.65*	16	9.65(11)
12	Bart Starr, 1968	*9.46*	14	9.46(12)
13	Len Dawson, 1968	*9.42*	14	9.42(13)
14	Greg Cook, 1969	*9.41*	14	9.41(14)
	Eddie LeBaron, 1958	*9.41*	12	9.41(14)
	Ken Stabler, 1976	*9.41*	14	9.41(14)
	Bob Waterfield, 1945	*9.41*	10	9.41(14)
18	Bob Berry, 1968	*9.37*	14	9.37(18)
19	Otto Graham, 1955	*9.30*	12	9.30(19)
20	Johnny Unitas, 1964	*9.26*	14	9.26(20)
21	James Harris, 1976	*9.24*	14	9.24(21)
22	Lynn Dickey, 1983	*9.21*	16	9.21(22)
	Boomer Esiason, 1988	*9.21*	16	9.21(22)
24	George Blanda, 1961	*9.20*	14	9.20(24)
25	Milt Plum, 1960	*9.19*	14	9.19(25)
26	Earl Morrall, 1968	*9.18*	14	9.18(26)
27	Sammy Baugh, 1945	*9.17*	10	9.17(27)
	Peyton Manning, 2004	***9.17***	**16**	**9.17(27)**
29	John Brodie, 1961	*9.14*	14	9.14(29)
30	Joe Montana, 1989	*9.12*	16	9.12(30)
31	Earl Morrall, 1972	*9.07*	14	9.07(31)
32	Bert Jones, 1976	*9.05*	14	9.05(32)
33	Eddie LeBaron, 1957	*9.03*	12	9.03(33)
	Clyde LeForce, 1948	*9.03*	12	9.03(33)
	Billy Wade, 1961	*9.03*	14	9.03(33)
36	Steve Young, 1991	*9.02*	16	9.02(36)
37	Dan Marino, 1984	*9.01*	16	9.01(37)
38	Bart Starr, 1966	*8.99*	14	8.99(38)
39	Johnny Unitas, 1965	*8.97*	14	8.97(39)
40	Don Horn, 1969	*8.96*	14	8.96(40)
	Sid Luckman, 1940	*8.96*	11	8.96(40)
42	Sonny Jurgensen, 1961	*8.95*	14	8.95(42)
43	Roger Staubach, 1971	*8.92*	14	8.92(43)
44	Sonny Jurgensen, 1962	*8.91*	14	8.91(44)
45	Len Dawson, 1962	*8.90*	14	8.90(45)
	Len Dawson, 1966	*8.90*	14	8.90(45)
	Ben Roethlisberger, 2005	***8.90***	**16**	**8.90(45)**
	Bob Waterfield, 1951	*8.90*	12	8.90(45)
49	Norm Van Brocklin, 1951	*8.89*	12	8.89(49)
50	**Ben Roethlisberger, 2004**	***8.88***	**16**	**8.88(50)**
51	Bob Berry, 1971	*8.87*	14	8.87(51)
52	Bob Griese, 1975	*8.86*	14	8.86(52)
53	Norm Van Brocklin, 1950	*8.85*	12	8.85(53)
	Kurt Warner, 2001	***8.85***	**16**	**8.85(53)**
55	Dave Krieg, 1983	*8.80*	16	8.80(55)
56	Charlie Conerly, 1959	*8.79*	12	8.79(56)
	Craig Morton, 1970	*8.79*	14	8.79(56)
58	Tobin Rote, 1963	*8.78*	14	8.78(58)
59	Dan Fouts, 1983	*8.75*	16	8.75(59)
60	Dan Fouts, 1982	*8.74*	9	8.74(60)
61	Bobby Layne, 1958	*8.73*	12	8.73(61)
62	Randall Cunningham, 1998	*8.72*	16	8.72(62)
	Otto Graham, 1954	*8.72*	12	8.72(62)
	Kurt Warner, 1999	***8.72***	**16**	**8.72(62)**
65	Steve Young, 1993	*8.71*	16	8.71(65)
66	Norm Van Brocklin, 1960	*8.70*	14	8.70(66)
67	Joe Namath, 1972	*8.69*	14	8.69(67)
68	Bobby Layne, 1960	*8.68*	14	8.68(68)
	Bart Starr, 1967	*8.68*	14	8.68(68)
70	Craig Morton, 1969	*8.67*	14	8.67(70)
71	Eddie LeBaron, 1962	*8.65*	14	8.65(71)
72	Roman Gabriel, 1964	*8.64*	14	8.64(72)
73	Tom Flores, 1966	*8.62*	14	8.62(73)
	Steve Young, 1992	*8.62*	16	8.62(73)
75	**Daunte Culpepper, 2004**	***8.61***	**16**	**8.61(75)**
	Steve Grogan, 1981	*8.61*	16	8.61(75)
	Steve Young, 1994	*8.61*	16	8.61(75)
78	**Trent Green, 2000**	***8.60***	**16**	**8.60(78)**
	Y.A. Tittle, 1962	*8.60*	14	8.60(78)
80	Greg Landry, 1971	*8.57*	14	8.57(80)
	Milt Plum, 1958	*8.57*	12	8.57(80)
	Y.A. Tittle, 1963	*8.57*	14	8.57(80)
83	Jeff George, 1999	*8.56*	16	8.56(83)
84	Bart Starr, 1962	*8.55*	14	8.55(84)
85	Bernie Masterson, 1937	*8.54*	11	8.54(85)
86	Jay Schroeder, 1990	*8.53*	16	8.53(86)
87	Johnny Lujack, 1949	*8.52*	12	8.52(87)
88	Tom Flores, 1963	*8.51*	14	8.51(88)
	Steve Young, 1997	*8.51*	16	8.51(88)
90	Craig Morton, 1981	*8.50*	16	8.50(90)
91	Jack Kemp, 1964	*8.49*	14	8.49(91)
	Roger Staubach, 1973	*8.49*	14	8.49(91)
	Johnny Unitas, 1963	*8.49*	14	8.49(91)
94	Mark Rypien, 1991	*8.47*	16	8.47(94)
	Johnny Unitas, 1957	*8.47*	12	8.47(94)
	Norm Van Brocklin, 1952	*8.47*	12	8.47(94)
97	Rudy Bukich, 1965	*8.46*	14	8.46(97)
	Dan Fouts, 1985	*8.46*	16	8.46(97)
99	Eric Hipple, 1981	*8.45*	16	8.45(99)

COMPLETION PERCENT

	NAME	ADJ	G	UNADJ
1	Ken Anderson, 1982	*70.55*	9	70.55(1)
2	Sammy Baugh, 1945	*70.33*	10	70.33(2)
3	Steve Young, 1994	*70.28*	16	70.28(3)
4	Joe Montana, 1989	*70.21*	16	70.21(4)
5	**Brian Griese, 2004**	***69.35***	**16**	**69.35(5)**
6	**Daunte Culpepper, 2004**	***69.16***	**16**	**69.16(6)**
7	Troy Aikman, 1993	*69.13*	16	69.13(7)
8	**Chad Pennington, 2002**	***68.92***	**16**	**68.92(8)**
9	**Kurt Warner, 2001**	***68.68***	**16**	**68.68(9)**
10	Steve Young, 1993	*67.97*	16	67.97(10)
11	**Carson Palmer, 2005**	***67.78***	**16**	**67.78(11)**
12	**Kurt Warner, 2000**	***67.72***	**16**	**67.72(12)**
	Steve Young, 1996	*67.72*	16	67.72(12)
14	Steve Young, 1997	*67.70*	16	67.70(14)
15	Rich Gannon, 2002	*67.64*	16	67.64(15)
16	**Peyton Manning, 2004**	***67.61***	**16**	**67.61(16)**
17	**Kelly Holcomb, 2005**	***67.39***	**16**	**67.39(17)**
18	**Peyton Manning, 2005**	***67.33***	**16**	**67.33(18)**
19	Steve Bartkowski, 1984	*67.29*	16	67.29(19)
20	**Peyton Manning, 2003**	***66.96***	**16**	**66.96(20)**
21	**Marc Bulger, 2005**	***66.90***	**16**	**66.90(21)**
22	Steve Young, 1995	*66.89*	16	66.89(22)
23	Joe Montana, 1987	*66.83*	15	66.83(23)
24	**Brian Griese, 2002**	***66.74***	**16**	**66.74(24)**
25	Ken Anderson, 1983	*66.67*	16	66.67(25)
	Ken Stabler, 1976	*66.67*	14	66.67(25)
	Steve Young, 1992	*66.67*	16	66.67(25)
28	**Ben Roethlisberger, 2004**	***66.44***	**16**	**66.44(28)**
29	Len Dawson, 1975	*66.43*	14	66.43(29)
30	**Trent Green, 2004**	***66.37***	**16**	**66.37(30)**
31	**Peyton Manning, 2002**	***66.33***	**16**	**66.33(31)**
32	**Marc Bulger, 2004**	***66.19***	**16**	**66.19(32)**
33	Rich Gannon, 2001	*65.76*	16	65.76(33)
34	Cody Carlson, 1992	*65.64*	16	65.64(34)
35	Dave Krieg, 1991	*65.61*	16	65.61(35)
36	**Drew Brees, 2004**	***65.50***	**16**	**65.50(36)**
37	**Matt Hasselbeck, 2005**	***65.48***	**16**	**65.48(37)**
38	**Chad Pennington, 2004**	***65.41***	**16**	**65.41(38)**
39	**Brett Favre, 2003**	***65.39***	**16**	**65.39(39)**
40	Troy Aikman, 1991	*65.29*	16	65.29(40)
41	**Kurt Warner, 1999**	***65.13***	**16**	**65.13(41)**
42	**Daunte Culpepper, 2003**	***64.98***	**16**	**64.98(42)**
43	Ken Anderson, 1974	*64.94*	14	64.94(43)
44	Troy Aikman, 1995	*64.81*	16	64.81(44)
45	Warren Moon, 1992	*64.74*	16	64.74(45)
46	Otto Graham, 1953	*64.73*	12	64.73(46)
47	**Drew Brees, 2005**	***64.60***	**16**	**64.60(47)**
48	Joe Montana, 1984	*64.58*	16	64.58(48)
49	Troy Aikman, 1994	*64.54*	16	64.54(49)
50	**Kurt Warner, 2005**	***64.53***	**16**	**64.53(50)**
51	Steve Young, 1991	*64.52*	16	64.52(51)
52	Joe Montana, 1980	*64.47*	16	64.47(52)
	Joe Montana, 1983	*64.47*	16	64.47(52)
54	**Brian Griese, 2000**	***64.29***	**16**	**64.29(54)**
55	Fran Tarkenton, 1975	*64.24*	14	64.24(55)
56	**Daunte Culpepper, 2001**	***64.21***	**16**	**64.21(56)**
57	Dan Marino, 1984	*64.18*	16	64.18(57)
58	Jim Kelly, 1991	*64.14*	16	64.14(58)
59	**Brett Favre, 1992**	***64.12***	**16**	**64.12(59)**
60	Dan Marino, 1995	*64.11*	16	64.11(60)
	Ken Stabler, 1980	*64.11*	16	64.11(60)
62	Jim Everett, 1994	*64.07*	16	64.07(62)
	Brett Favre, 2004	***64.07***	**16**	**64.07(62)**
	Sonny Jurgensen, 1974	*64.07*	14	64.07(62)
65	**Donovan McNabb, 2004**	***63.97***	**16**	**63.97(65)**
66	**Tom Brady, 2001**	***63.92***	**16**	**63.92(66)**
67	**Kelly Holcomb, 2003**	***63.91***	**16**	**63.91(67)**
68	Joe Theismann, 1982	*63.89*	9	63.89(68)
69	Troy Aikman, 1992	*63.85*	16	63.85(69)
70	Bart Starr, 1968	*63.74*	14	63.74(70)
71	Joe Montana, 1981	*63.73*	16	63.73(71)
72	**Matt Hasselbeck, 2002**	***63.72***	**16**	**63.72(72)**
73	Jim Harbaugh, 1995	*63.69*	16	63.69(73)
74	Troy Aikman, 1996	*63.66*	16	63.66(74)
75	Ken Anderson, 1984	*63.64*	16	63.64(75)
	Chad Pennington, 2003	***63.64***	**16**	**63.64(75)**
77	Jim Kelly, 1994	*63.62*	16	63.62(77)
78	Steve Bartkowski, 1983	*63.43*	16	63.43(78)
79	**Mark Brunell, 1996**	***63.38***	**16**	**63.38(79)**
80	Steve Bartkowski, 1982	*63.36*	9	63.36(80)
81	Jim Kelly, 1990	*63.29*	16	63.29(81)
82	**Jeff Garcia, 2000**	***63.28***	**16**	**63.28(82)**
83	Dan Fouts, 1983	*63.24*	16	63.24(83)
84	Chris Chandler, 1995	*63.20*	16	63.20(84)
85	**Marc Bulger, 2003**	***63.16***	**16**	**63.16(85)**
	John Elway, 1993	*63.16*	16	63.16(85)
	Danny White, 1982	*63.16*	9	63.16(85)
88	**Trent Green, 2003**	***63.10***	**16**	**63.10(88)**
89	Y.A. Tittle, 1957	*63.08*	12	63.08(89)
90	**Tom Brady, 2005**	***63.02***	**16**	**63.02(90)**
91	**Brett Favre, 1995**	***62.98***	**16**	**62.98(91)**
	Brett Favre, 1998	***62.98***	**16**	**62.98(91)**
	Bob Griese, 1978	*62.98*	16	62.98(91)
94	Steve Beuerlein, 1998	*62.97*	16	62.97(94)
95	Eric Hipple, 1986	*62.95*	16	62.95(95)
96	Bobby Hebert, 1989	*62.89*	16	62.89(96)
97	**Kurt Warner, 2004**	***62.82***	**16**	**62.82(97)**
98	Jeff Hostetler, 1991	*62.81*	16	62.81(98)
99	Sammy Baugh, 1940	*62.71*	11	62.71(99)
	Peyton Manning, 2001	***62.71***	**16**	**62.71(99)**

TD PASSES

	NAME	ADJ	G	UNADJ
1	**Peyton Manning, 2004**	**49**	**16**	**49(1)**
2	Dan Marino, 1984	48	16	48(2)
3	Sid Luckman, 1943	45	10	28(68)
4	Dan Marino, 1986	44	16	44(3)
5	Johnny Unitas, 1959	43	12	32(26)
6	George Blanda, 1961	41	14	36(8)
	Y.A. Tittle, 1963	41	14	36(8)
	Kurt Warner, 1999	**41**	**16**	**41(4)**
9	**Daunte Culpepper, 2004**	**39**	**16**	**39(5)**
	Brett Favre, 1996	**39**	**16**	**39(5)**
	Daryle Lamonica, 1969	39	14	34(15)
12	**Brett Favre, 1995**	**38**	**16**	**38(7)**
	Y.A. Tittle, 1962	38	14	33(17)
14	Sammy Baugh, 1943	37	10	23(206)
	Sonny Jurgensen, 1961	37	14	32(26)
16	Steve Beuerlein, 1999	36	16	36(8)
	Kurt Warner, 2001	**36**	**16**	**36(8)**
	Steve Young, 1998	36	16	36(8)
19	**Brett Favre, 1997**	**35**	**16**	**35(13)**
	Cecil Isbell, 1942	35	11	24(161)
	Sonny Jurgensen, 1967	35	14	31(35)
	Bobby Layne, 1951	35	12	26(107)
	Babe Parilli, 1964	35	14	31(35)
	Steve Young, 1994	35	16	35(13)
25	John Brodie, 1965	34	14	30(43)
	Randall Cunningham, 1998	34	16	34(15)
	Len Dawson, 1964	34	14	30(43)
	Daryle Lamonica, 1967	34	14	30(43)
29	Sammy Baugh, 1947	33	12	25(137)
	Daunte Culpepper, 2000	**33**	**16**	**33(17)**
	Len Dawson, 1962	33	14	29(54)
	Brett Favre, 1994	**33**	**16**	**33(17)**
	Dan Fouts, 1981	33	16	33(17)
	Jim Kelly, 1991	33	16	33(17)
	Peyton Manning, 2000	**33**	**16**	**33(17)**
	Joe Montana, 1987	33	15	31(35)
	Warren Moon, 1990	33	16	33(17)
	Warren Moon, 1995	33	16	33(17)
	Frank Ryan, 1966	33	14	29(54)
	Norm Snead, 1967	33	14	29(54)
	Fran Tarkenton, 1967	33	14	29(54)
	Vinny Testaverde, 1996	**33**	**16**	**33(17)**
	Tommy Thompson, 1948	33	12	25(137)
44	Lynn Dickey, 1983	32	16	32(26)
	Brett Favre, 2001	**32**	**16**	**32(26)**
	Brett Favre, 2003	**32**	**16**	**32(26)**
	Jeff Garcia, 2001	**32**	**16**	**32(26)**
	Charley Johnson, 1963	32	14	28(68)
	Sonny Jurgensen, 1966	32	14	28(68)
	Dave Krieg, 1984	32	16	32(26)
	Sid Luckman, 1947	32	12	24(161)
	Scott Mitchell, 1995	32	16	32(26)
	Carson Palmer, 2005	**32**	**16**	**32(26)**
	Johnny Unitas, 1957	32	12	24(161)
55	Steve Bartkowski, 1980	31	16	31(35)
	George Blanda, 1962	31	14	27(88)
	Adrian Burk, 1954	31	12	23(206)
	Jim Everett, 1988	31	16	31(35)
	Brett Favre, 1998	**31**	**16**	**31(35)**
	Jeff Garcia, 2000	**31**	**16**	**31(35)**
	John Hadl, 1968	31	14	27(88)
	Johnny Lujack, 1949	31	12	23(206)
	Donovan McNabb, 2004	**31**	**16**	**31(35)**
	Ken Stabler, 1976	31	14	27(88)
65	Steve Bartkowski, 1981	30	16	30(43)
	Terry Bradshaw, 1982	30	9	17
	Randall Cunningham, 1990	30	16	30(43)
	Len Dawson, 1963	30	14	26(107)
	Len Dawson, 1966	30	14	26(107)
	Al Dorow, 1960	30	14	26(107)
	Brett Favre, 2004	**30**	**16**	**30(43)**
	Vince Ferragamo, 1980	30	16	30(43)
	Dan Fouts, 1980	30	16	30(43)
	Dan Fouts, 1982	30	9	17
	Dan Marino, 1985	30	16	30(43)
	Dan Marino, 1994	30	16	30(43)
	Joe Montana, 1982	30	9	17
	Earl Morrall, 1968	30	14	26(107)
	Joe Namath, 1967	30	14	26(107)
	Brian Sipe, 1980	30	16	30(43)
	Ken Stabler, 1974	30	14	26(107)
82	20 players tied 29			

INT PERCENT

	NAME	ADJ	G	UNADJ
1	Joe Ferguson, 1976	.66	14	.66(1)
2	Steve DeBerg, 1990	.90	16	.90(2)
3	Steve Bartkowski, 1983	1.16	16	1.16(3)
4	Neil O'Donnell, 1998	1.17	16	1.17(4)
5	**Brian Griese, 2000**	**1.19**	**16**	**1.19(5)**
6	Bart Starr, 1966	1.20	14	1.20(6)
7	Walt Holmer, 1932	1.28	10	1.28(7)
8	Jim Harbaugh, 1997	1.29	16	1.29(8)
	Phil Simms, 1990	1.29	16	1.29(8)
10	**Doug Flutie, 2000**	**1.30**	**16**	**1.30(10)**
11	**Brad Johnson, 2002**	**1.33**	**16**	**1.33(11)**
12	**Brad Johnson, 2005**	**1.36**	**16**	**1.36(12)**
13	Jeff Hostetler, 1991	1.40	16	1.40(13)
14	Neil O'Donnell, 1993	1.44	16	1.44(14)
	Kurt Warner, 2004	**1.44**	**16**	**1.44(14)**
16	Jeff George, 1993	1.47	16	1.47(16)
	Bart Starr, 1964	1.47	14	1.47(16)
18	**Chad Pennington, 2002**	**1.50**	**16**	**1.50(18)**
19	Neil O'Donnell, 1997	1.52	16	1.52(19)
20	Troy Aikman, 1993	1.53	16	1.53(20)
21	**Aaron Brooks, 2003**	**1.54**	**16**	**1.54(21)**
	Jake Plummer, 2005	**1.54**	**16**	**1.54(21)**
23	Troy Aikman, 1998	1.59	16	1.59(23)
	Jim Harbaugh, 1995	1.59	16	1.59(23)
25	**Mark Brunell, 1997**	**1.61**	**16**	**1.61(25)**
26	Troy Aikman, 1995	1.62	16	1.62(26)
	Bubby Brister, 1993	1.62	16	1.62(26)
	Rich Gannon, 2002	1.62	16	1.62(26)
29	Rich Gannon, 2001	1.64	16	1.64(29)
	Ken O'Brien, 1985	1.64	16	1.64(29)
31	Ken O'Brien, 1988	1.65	16	1.65(31)
32	**Byron Leftwich, 2005**	**1.66**	**16**	**1.66(32)**
	Donovan McNabb, 2002	**1.66**	**16**	**1.66(32)**
	Vinny Testaverde, 1998	**1.66**	**16**	**1.66(32)**
35	**Mark Brunell, 2002**	**1.68**	**16**	**1.68(35)**
	John Friesz, 1993	1.68	16	1.68(35)
	Neil O'Donnell, 1995	1.68	16	1.68(35)
38	Steve Bono, 1991	1.69	16	1.69(38)
	Rich Gannon, 1991	1.69	16	1.69(38)
	Rich Gannon, 1998	1.69	16	1.69(38)
	Steve Young, 1997	1.69	16	1.69(38)
42	Joe Pisarcik, 1984	1.70	16	1.70(42)
43	**Donovan McNabb, 2004**	**1.71**	**16**	**1.71(43)**
44	Jeff George, 1997	1.73	16	1.73(44)
45	Steve Young, 1992	1.74	16	1.74(45)
46	**Drew Brees, 2004**	**1.75**	**16**	**1.75(46)**
	Roman Gabriel, 1969	1.75	14	1.75(46)
	Steve McNair, 2003	**1.75**	**16**	**1.75(46)**
49	**Peyton Manning, 2003**	**1.77**	**16**	**1.77(49)**
50	Rich Gannon, 2003	1.78	16	1.78(50)
	Jeff Garcia, 2000	**1.78**	**16**	**1.78(50)**
52	John Elway, 1993	1.81	16	1.81(52)
53	Bernie Kosar, 1991	1.82	16	1.82(53)
54	Joe Montana, 1994	1.83	16	1.83(54)
55	Rick Mirer, 1994	1.84	16	1.84(55)
56	Tony Eason, 1984	1.86	16	1.86(56)
57	Bernie Kosar, 1986	1.88	16	1.88(57)
58	**Jeff Garcia, 2002**	**1.89**	**16**	**1.89(58)**
59	Chris Miller, 1989	1.90	16	1.90(59)
	Roger Staubach, 1971	1.90	14	1.90(59)
	Michael Vick, 2002	**1.90**	**16**	**1.90(59)**
	Steve Young, 1996	1.90	16	1.90(59)
63	Elvis Grbac, 1997	1.91	16	1.91(63)
64	Steve Bono, 1995	1.92	16	1.92(64)
	Jim Harbaugh, 1990	1.92	16	1.92(64)
	Erik Kramer, 1995	1.92	16	1.92(64)
67	Fran Tarkenton, 1976	1.94	14	1.94(67)
68	Fran Tarkenton, 1969	1.96	14	1.96(68)
69	Jeff George, 1995	1.97	16	1.97(69)
	Trent Green, 2005	**1.97**	**16**	**1.97(69)**
	Brad Johnson, 2001	**1.97**	**16**	**1.97(69)**
	Johnny Unitas, 1964	1.97	14	1.97(69)
73	**Charlie Batch, 1998**	**1.98**	**16**	**1.98(73)**
74	Scott Hunter, 1977	1.99	14	1.99(74)
75	Kent Graham, 1997	2.00	16	2.00(75)
	Matt Hasselbeck, 2005	**2.00**	**16**	**2.00(75)**
	Milt Plum, 1960	2.00	14	2.00(75)
78	**Daunte Culpepper, 2004**	**2.01**	**16**	**2.01(78)**
	Peyton Manning, 2004	**2.01**	**16**	**2.01(78)**
	Dan Marino, 1997	2.01	16	2.01(78)
81	**Mark Brunell, 1995**	**2.02**	**16**	**2.02(81)**
	John Elway, 1994	2.02	16	2.02(81)
83	Dan Marino, 1983	2.03	16	2.03(83)
	Steve McNair, 1998	**2.03**	**16**	**2.03(83)**
85	**Mark Brunell, 1999**	**2.04**	**16**	**2.04(85)**
	Ken O'Brien, 1987	2.04	15	2.04(85)
87	Chris Chandler, 1997	2.05	16	2.05(87)
88	Charlie Conerly, 1959	2.06	12	2.06(88)
	Jim Hart, 1974	2.06	14	2.06(88)
	Scott Mitchell, 1995	2.06	16	2.06(88)
91	Dan Marino, 1990	2.07	16	2.07(91)
	Joe Montana, 1989	2.07	16	2.07(91)
93	**Trent Green, 2000**	**2.08**	**16**	**2.08(93)**
94	Ken Anderson, 1981	2.09	16	2.09(94)
95	Gary Wood, 1964	2.10	14	2.10(95)
96	**Kerry Collins, 2005**	**2.12**	**16**	**2.12(96)**
97	Steve Fuller, 1982	2.15	9	2.15(97)
98	**Trent Green, 1998**	**2.16**	**16**	**2.16(98)**
99	Steve Young, 1994	2.17	16	2.17(99))

PASSER RATING

	NAME	ADJ	G	UNADJ
1	**Peyton Manning, 2004**	**121.1**	**16**	**121.1(1)**
2	Steve Young, 1994	112.7	16	112.7(2)
3	Joe Montana, 1989	112.4	16	112.4(3)
4	Frank Filchock, 1939	111.6	11	111.6(4)
5	**Daunte Culpepper, 2004**	**110.9**	**16**	**110.9(5)**
6	Milt Plum, 1960	110.3	14	110.3(6)
7	Sammy Baugh, 1945	109.8	10	109.8(7)
8	**Kurt Warner, 1999**	**109.2**	**16**	**109.2(8)**
9	Dan Marino, 1984	108.9	16	108.9(9)
10	Sid Luckman, 1943	107.6	10	107.6(10)
11	Steve Young, 1992	107.0	16	107.0(11)
12	Randall Cunningham, 1998	106.0	16	106.0(12)
13	Bart Starr, 1966	104.9	14	104.9(13)
14	Roger Staubach, 1971	104.8	14	104.8(14)
15	**Drew Brees, 2004**	**104.7**	**16**	**104.7(15)**
16	Y.A. Tittle, 1963	104.7	14	104.7(16)
17	**Donovan McNabb, 2004**	**104.7**	**16**	**104.7(17)**
18	Steve Young, 1997	104.7	16	104.7(18)
19	Bart Starr, 1968	104.3	14	104.3(19)
20	**Chad Pennington, 2002**	**104.2**	**16**	**104.2(20)**
21	**Peyton Manning, 2005**	**104.0**	**16**	**104.0(21)**
22	Ken Stabler, 1976	103.4	14	103.4(22)
23	**Brian Griese, 2000**	**102.8**	**16**	**102.8(23)**
24	Joe Montana, 1984	102.8	16	102.8(24)
25	Charlie Conerly, 1959	102.7	12	102.7(25)
26	Bert Jones, 1976	102.4	14	102.4(26)
27	Joe Montana, 1987	102.1	15	102.1(27)
28	Steve Young, 1991	101.8	16	101.8(28)
29	**Trent Green, 2000**	**101.7**	**16**	**101.7(29)**
30	Len Dawson, 1966	101.6	14	101.6(30)
31	**Vinny Testaverde, 1998**	**101.6**	**16**	**101.6(31)**
32	Steve Young, 1993	101.5	16	101.5(32)
33	**Kurt Warner, 2001**	**101.3**	**16**	**101.3(33)**
34	Jim Kelly, 1990	101.1	16	101.1(34)
35	Steve Young, 1998	101.1	16	101.1(35)
36	**Carson Palmer, 2005**	**101.1**	**16**	**101.1(36)**
37	Chris Chandler, 1998	100.8	16	100.8(37)
38	Jim Harbaugh, 1995	100.7	16	100.7(38)
39	**Steve McNair, 2003**	**100.3**	**16**	**100.3(39)**
40	Otto Graham, 1953	99.6	12	99.6(40)
41	**Brett Favre, 1995**	**99.5**	**16**	**99.5(41)**
42	Troy Aikman, 1993	99.0	16	99.0(42)
43	**Peyton Manning, 2003**	**99.0**	**16**	**99.0(43)**
44	Len Dawson, 1968	98.6	14	98.6(44)
45	**Ben Roethlisberger, 2005**	**98.5**	**16**	**98.5(45)**
46	Ken Anderson, 1981	98.4	16	98.4(46)
47	Tommy Thompson, 1948	98.3	12	98.3(47)
48	Len Dawson, 1962	98.3	14	98.3(48)
49	**Kurt Warner, 2000**	**98.2**	**16**	**98.2(49)**
50	**Matt Hasselbeck, 2005**	**98.2**	**16**	**98.2(50)**
51	**Ben Roethlisberger, 2004**	**98.1**	**16**	**98.1(51)**
52	**Daunte Culpepper, 2000**	**98.0**	**16**	**98.0(52)**
53	Mark Rypien, 1991	97.9	16	97.9(53)
54	Steve Bartkowski, 1983	97.6	16	97.6(54)
55	**Jeff Garcia, 2000**	**97.5**	**16**	**97.5(55)**
	Jim Kelly, 1991	97.5	16	97.5(55)
57	**Brian Griese, 2004**	**97.4**	**16**	**97.4(57)**
58	Johnny Unitas, 1965	97.3	14	97.3(58)
59	Boomer Esiason, 1988	97.3	16	97.3(59)
60	Rich Gannon, 2002	97.3	16	97.3(60)
61	Steve Young, 1996	97.1	16	97.1(61)
62	Bart Starr, 1964	97.1	14	97.1(62)
63	Joe Theismann, 1983	96.9	16	96.9(63)
64	Warren Moon, 1990	96.7	16	96.7(64)
65	**Daunte Culpepper, 2003**	**96.4**	**16**	**96.4(65)**
66	Johnny Unitas, 1964	96.4	14	96.4(66)
67	Steve DeBerg, 1990	96.3	16	96.3(67)
68	Ken O'Brien, 1985	96.2	16	96.2(68)
69	Dan Marino, 1983	95.9	16	95.9(69)
70	**Brett Favre, 1996**	**95.8**	**16**	**95.8(70)**
71	Ken Anderson, 1974	95.6	14	95.6(71)
72	Rich Gannon, 2001	95.5	16	95.5(72)
73	Bernie Kosar, 1987	95.4	15	95.4(73)
74	Eddie LeBaron, 1962	95.3	14	95.3(74)
75	John Brodie, 1965	95.3	14	95.3(75)
76	Ken Anderson, 1982	95.3	9	95.3(76)
77	Sid Luckman, 1941	95.2	11	95.2(77)
78	**Trent Green, 2004**	**95.2**	**16**	**95.2(78)**
79	Chris Chandler, 1997	95.0	16	95.0(79)
80	Dave Krieg, 1983	95.0	16	95.0(80)
81	Ken Stabler, 1974	94.9	14	94.9(81)
82	**Jeff Garcia, 2001**	**94.8**	**16**	**94.8(82)**
83	**Peyton Manning, 2000**	**94.7**	**16**	**94.7(83)**
84	Steve Beuerlein, 1999	94.5	16	94.5(84)
85	Dave Krieg, 1988	94.5	16	94.5(85)
	Roger Staubach, 1973	94.5	14	94.5(85)
87	Joe Montana, 1983	94.5	16	94.5(87)
88	Sonny Jurgensen, 1974	94.5	14	94.5(88)
89	**Marc Bulger, 2005**	**94.3**	**16**	**94.3(89)**
90	Jeff George, 1999	94.2	16	94.2(90)
91	**Brett Favre, 2001**	**94.0**	**16**	**94.0(91)**
92	Otto Graham, 1955	94.0	12	94.0(92)
93	Ken Anderson, 1975	93.9	14	93.9(93)
94	John Brodie, 1970	93.8	14	93.8(94)
95	Billy Wade, 1961	93.7	14	93.7(95)
96	Rudy Bukich, 1965	93.7	14	93.7(96)
97	**Marc Bulger, 2004**	**93.7**	**16**	**93.7(97)**
98	Troy Aikman, 1995	93.5	16	93.5(98)
99	Erik Kramer, 1995	93.5	16	93.5(99

RECEPTIONS

	NAME	ADJ	G	UNADJ
1	**Marvin Harrison, 2002**	143	16	143(1)
2	Herman Moore, 1995	123	16	123(2)
3	Cris Carter, 1994	122	16	122(3)
	Cris Carter, 1995	122	16	122(3)
	Jerry Rice, 1995	122	16	122(3)
6	**Isaac Bruce, 1995**	119	16	119(6)
7	**Torry Holt, 2003**	117	16	117(7)
8	**Jimmy Smith, 1999**	116	16	116(8)
9	**Marvin Harrison, 1999**	115	16	115(9)
	Charley Hennigan, 1964	115	14	101(37)
11	Lionel Taylor, 1961	114	14	100(42)
12	**Rod Smith, 2001**	113	16	113(10)
13	Tom Fears, 1950	112	12	84(165)
	Jerry Rice, 1994	112	16	112(11)
	Sterling Sharpe, 1993	112	16	112(11)
	Jimmy Smith, 2001	112	16	112(11)
	Hines Ward, 2002	112	16	112(11)
18	Michael Irvin, 1995	111	16	111(15)
	Terance Mathis, 1994	111	16	111(15)
	Randy Moss, 2003	111	16	111(15)
21	**Marvin Harrison, 2001**	109	16	109(18)
22	Don Hutson, 1942	108	11	74
	Brett Perriman, 1995	108	16	108(19)
	Jerry Rice, 1996	108	16	108(19)
	Sterling Sharpe, 1992	108	16	108(19)
26	Dwight Clark, 1982	107	9	60
27	**Keyshawn Johnson, 2001**	106	16	106(22)
	Art Monk, 1984	106	16	106(22)
	Herman Moore, 1996	106	16	106(22)
	Johnny Morris, 1964	106	14	93(79)
	Randy Moss, 2002	106	16	106(22)
32	Lionel Taylor, 1960	105	14	92(87)
33	Tim Brown, 1997	104	16	104(26)
	Eric Metcalf, 1995	104	16	104(26)
	Herman Moore, 1997	104	16	104(26)
36	**Larry Fitzgerald, 2005**	103	16	103(29)
	Steve Smith, 2005	103	16	103(29)
38	**Anquan Boldin, 2005**	102	16	102(31)
	Robert Brooks, 1995	102	16	102(31)
	Tony Gonzalez, 2004	102	16	102(31)
	Marvin Harrison, 2000	102	16	102(31)
	Torry Holt, 2005	102	16	102(31)
	Muhsin Muhammad, 2000	102	16	102(31)
44	**Anquan Boldin, 2003**	101	16	101(37)
	Troy Brown, 2001	101	16	101(37)
	Larry Centers, 1995	101	16	101(37)
	Ed McCaffrey, 2000	101	16	101(37)
48	**Marty Booker, 2001**	100	16	100(42)
	Haywood Jeffires, 1991	100	16	100(42)
	Eric Moulds, 2002	100	16	100(42)
	Terrell Owens, 2002	100	16	100(42)
	Carl Pickens, 1996	100	16	100(42)
	Jerry Rice, 1990	100	16	100(42)
	Rod Smith, 2000	100	16	100(42)
	LaDainian Tomlinson, 2003	100	16	100(42)
56	Larry Centers, 1996	99	16	99(51)
	Carl Pickens, 1995	99	16	99(51)
58	**David Boston, 2001**	98	16	98(53)
	Jerry Rice, 1993	98	16	98(53)
60	**Marty Booker, 2002**	97	16	97(55)
	Troy Brown, 2002	97	16	97(55)
	Chad Johnson, 2005	97	16	97(55)
	Rob Moore, 1997	97	16	97(55)
	Terrell Owens, 2000	97	16	97(55)
	J.T. Smith, 1987	97	15	91(91)
	Lionel Taylor, 1965	97	14	85(153)
67	Cris Carter, 1996	96	16	96(60)
	Cris Carter, 2000	96	16	96(60)
	Ben Coates, 1994	96	16	96(60)
	Derrick Mason, 2004	96	16	96(60)
	Muhsin Muhammad, 1999	96	16	96(60)
	Kellen Winslow, 1982	96	9	54
73	Todd Christensen, 1986	95	16	95(65)
	Chad Johnson, 2004	95	16	95(65)
	Derrick Mason, 2003	95	16	95(65)
	Hines Ward, 2003	95	16	95(65)
77	**Marvin Harrison, 2003**	94	16	94(69)
	Charley Hennigan, 1961	94	14	82(190)
	Torry Holt, 2004	94	16	94(69)
	Joe Horn, 2000	94	16	94(69)
	Joe Horn, 2004	94	16	94(69)
	Keenan McCardell, 2000	94	16	94(69)
	Eric Moulds, 2000	94	16	94(69)
	Brett Perriman, 1996	94	16	94(69)
	Peerless Price, 2002	94	16	94(69)
	Sterling Sharpe, 1994	94	16	94(69)
	Hines Ward, 2001	94	16	94(69)
	James Wilder, 1982	94	9	53
89	**Tony Gonzalez, 2000**	93	16	93(79)
	Don Hutson, 1944	93	10	58
	Michael Irvin, 1991	93	16	93(79)
	Keenan McCardell, 2001	93	16	93(79)
	Muhsin Muhammad, 2004	93	16	93(79)
	Terrell Owens, 2001	93	16	93(79)
	Andre Rison, 1992	93	16	93(79)
	Al Toon, 1988	93	16	93(79)
97	Todd Christensen, 1983	92	16	92(87)
	Roger Craig, 1985	92	16	92(87)
	Jerry Rice, 2002	92	16	92(87)

RECEIVING YARDS

	NAME	ADJ	G	UNADJ
1	Charley Hennigan, 1961	1995	14	1746(3)
2	Elroy Hirsch, 1951	1993	12	1495(26)
3	Jerry Rice, 1995	1848	16	1848(1)
4	Wes Chandler, 1982	1835	9	1032
5	Lance Alworth, 1965	1831	14	1602(12)
6	**Isaac Bruce, 1995**	1781	16	1781(2)
7	Charley Hennigan, 1964	1767	14	1546(19)
8	Don Hutson, 1942	1761	11	1211(178)
9	**Marvin Harrison, 2002**	1722	16	1722(4)
10	Jim Benton, 1945	1707	10	1067
11	**Torry Holt, 2003**	1696	16	1696(5)
12	Herman Moore, 1995	1686	16	1686(6)
13	Bill Groman, 1960	1683	14	1473(31)
14	**Marvin Harrison, 1999**	1663	16	1663(7)
15	Billy Howton, 1952	1641	12	1231(163)
	Bobby Mitchell, 1963	1641	14	1436(36)
17	Don Maynard, 1967	1639	14	1434(37)
18	**Jimmy Smith, 1999**	1636	16	1636(8)
19	**Torry Holt, 2000**	1635	16	1635(9)
20	**Randy Moss, 2003**	1632	16	1632(10)
21	Dwight Clark, 1982	1623	9	913
22	Bob Boyd, 1954	1616	12	1212(177)
23	Michael Irvin, 1995	1603	16	1603(11)
24	**Rod Smith, 2000**	1602	16	1602(12)
25	**David Boston, 2001**	1598	16	1598(14)
26	Billy Howton, 1956	1584	12	1188(205)
	Rob Moore, 1997	1584	16	1584(15)
28	Bobby Mitchell, 1962	1582	14	1384(59)
29	Lance Alworth, 1966	1581	14	1383(60)
30	Jerry Rice, 1986	1570	16	1570(16)
31	**Steve Smith, 2005**	1563	16	1563(17)
32	Roy Green, 1984	1555	16	1555(18)
	Art Powell, 1964	1555	14	1361(70)
34	Dave Parks, 1965	1536	14	1344(76)
35	**Marvin Harrison, 2001**	1524	16	1524(20)
36	Michael Irvin, 1991	1523	16	1523(21)
37	Harlon Hill, 1956	1504	12	1128(292)
38	Jerry Rice, 1993	1503	16	1503(22)
39	Jerry Rice, 1990	1502	16	1502(23)
40	Lance Alworth, 1968	1499	14	1312(98)
	Harlon Hill, 1954	1499	12	1124(300)
	Jerry Rice, 1994	1499	16	1499(24)
43	Robert Brooks, 1995	1497	16	1497(25)
44	Stanley Morgan, 1986	1491	16	1491(27)
45	Art Powell, 1963	1490	14	1304(105)
46	Tom Fears, 1950	1488	12	1116(307)
	Brett Perriman, 1995	1488	16	1488(28)
48	Raymond Berry, 1960	1483	14	1298(112)
	Santana Moss, 2005	1483	16	1483(29)
	Jerry Rice, 1989	1483	16	1483(29)
51	Don Maynard, 1968	1482	14	1297(113)
	Otis Taylor, 1966	1482	14	1297(113)
53	Buddy Dial, 1963	1480	14	1295(116)
54	**Isaac Bruce, 2000**	1471	16	1471(32)
55	Del Shofner, 1958	1463	12	1097
56	Sterling Sharpe, 1992	1461	16	1461(33)
57	**Terrell Owens, 2000**	1451	16	1451(34)
58	Pat Studstill, 1966	1447	14	1266(131)
59	Ben Hawkins, 1967	1446	14	1265(133)
	Don Maynard, 1960	1446	14	1265(133)
61	Warren Wells, 1969	1440	14	1260(138)
62	**Randy Moss, 2000**	1437	16	1437(35)
63	**Chad Johnson, 2005**	1432	16	1432(38)
64	Antonio Freeman, 1998	1424	16	1424(39)
65	Sterling Sharpe, 1989	1423	16	1423(40)
66	Mark Carrier, 1989	1422	16	1422(41)
67	Henry Ellard, 1988	1414	16	1414(42)
68	**Marvin Harrison, 2000**	1413	16	1413(43)
	Randy Moss, 1999	1413	16	1413(43)
70	**Terrell Owens, 2001**	1412	16	1412(45)
71	Lance Alworth, 1964	1411	14	1235(158)
	Lionel Taylor, 1960	1411	14	1235(158)
73	**Larry Fitzgerald, 2005**	1409	16	1409(46)
	Mike Quick, 1983	1409	16	1409(46)
75	Tim Brown, 1997	1408	16	1408(48)
	Bob Hayes, 1966	1408	14	1232(162)
77	**Muhsin Muhammad, 2004**	1405	16	1405(49)
78	**Anquan Boldin, 2005**	1402	16	1402(50)
79	**Marcus Robinson, 1999**	1400	16	1400(51)
80	**Joe Horn, 2004**	1399	16	1399(52)
	Pete Pihos, 1953	1399	12	1049
82	Yancey Thigpen, 1997	1398	16	1398(53)
83	Henry Ellard, 1994	1397	16	1397(54)
84	Michael Irvin, 1992	1396	16	1396(55)
85	John Stallworth, 1984	1395	16	1395(56)
86	Don Maynard, 1965	1392	14	1218(174)
87	Derrick Alexander, 2000	1391	16	1391(57)
88	Mark Clayton, 1984	1389	16	1389(58)
89	Don Hutson, 1944	1386	10	866
90	Henry Ellard, 1989	1382	16	1382(61)
	Homer Jones, 1967	1382	14	1209(182)
	Javon Walker, 2004	1382	16	1382(61)
93	Lance Alworth, 1963	1377	14	1205(187)
	Anquan Boldin, 2003	1377	16	1377(63)
	Jackie Smith, 1967	1377	14	1205(187)
96	**Jimmy Smith, 2001**	1373	16	1373(64)
97	**Torry Holt, 2004**	1372	16	1372(65)
	Art Monk, 1984	1372	16	1372(65)
99	Cris Carter, 1995	1371	16	1371(67)
	Johnny Morris, 1964	1371	14	1200(193)

RECEIVING AVERAGE GAIN

	NAME	ADJ	G	UNADJ
1	Don Currivan, 1947	32.58	12	32.58(1)
2	Jimmy Orr, 1958	27.58	12	27.58(2)
3	Elbert Dubenion, 1964	27.12	14	27.12(3)
4	Frank Liebel, 1945	26.95	10	26.95(4)
5	Warren Wells, 1969	26.81	14	26.81(5)
6	Jack Snow, 1967	26.25	14	26.25(6)
7	Bob Hayes, 1970	26.15	14	26.15(7)
8	Flipper Anderson, 1989	26.05	16	26.05(8)
9	Roger Carr, 1976	25.86	14	25.86(9)
10	Jimmy Orr, 1968	25.62	14	25.62(10)
11	Ken Kavanaugh, 1947	25.56	12	25.56(11)
12	Paul Warfield, 1970	25.11	14	25.11(12)
13	Harlon Hill, 1954	24.98	12	24.98(13)
14	Alvin Harper, 1994	24.88	16	24.88(14)
	Don Hutson, 1939	24.88	11	24.88(14)
16	Homer Jones, 1967	24.67	14	24.67(16)
17	Elbie Nickel, 1949	24.35	12	24.35(17)
	Wesley Walker, 1978	24.35	16	24.35(17)
19	Buddy Dial, 1960	24.30	14	24.30(19)
20	Anthony Carter, 1987	24.26	15	24.26(20)
21	Cliff Branch, 1976	24.15	14	24.15(21)
22	Roy Jefferson, 1966	24.13	14	24.13(22)
23	Stanley Morgan, 1978	24.12	16	24.12(23)
24	Eddie Brown, 1988	24.02	16	24.02(24)
25	Bob Hayes, 1971	24.00	14	24.00(25)
	Harlon Hill, 1956	24.00	12	24.00(25)
27	Ray Renfro, 1958	23.88	12	23.88(27)
28	Billy Dewell, 1946	23.81	11	23.81(28)
29	John Greene, 1948	23.80	12	23.80(29)
30	Jim Benton, 1945	23.71	10	23.71(30)
31	Ron Shanklin, 1973	23.70	14	23.70(31)
32	Carroll Dale, 1966	23.68	14	23.68(32)
33	Elroy Hirsch, 1952	23.60	12	23.60(33)
34	Chris Sanders, 1995	23.51	16	23.51(34)
35	Bill Groman, 1961	23.50	14	23.50(35)
36	Homer Jones, 1968	23.49	14	23.49(36)
37	Mal Kutner, 1946	23.48	11	23.48(37)
38	Hugh Taylor, 1952	23.44	12	23.44(38)
39	Stanley Morgan, 1981	23.39	16	23.39(39)
40	James Jett, 1993	23.36	16	23.36(40)
41	Harry Clarke, 1943	23.26	10	23.26(41)
42	Billy Howton, 1952	23.23	12	23.23(42)
43	Lance Alworth, 1965	23.22	14	23.22(43)
44	Max McGee, 1959	23.17	12	23.17(44)
45	Paul Warfield, 1971	23.16	14	23.16(45)
46	Ron Shanklin, 1970	23.03	14	23.03(46)
47	Mal Kutner, 1948	23.00	12	23.00(47)
48	Ron Jessie, 1976	22.91	14	22.91(48)
49	Chris Burkett, 1986	22.88	16	22.88(49)
50	Bob Boyd, 1954	22.87	12	22.87(50)
51	Gary Garrison, 1970	22.86	14	22.86(51)
52	Bob Boyd, 1953	22.83	12	22.83(52)
	Clem Daniels, 1963	22.83	14	22.83(52)
54	Stanley Morgan, 1979	22.77	16	22.77(54)
55	Don Maynard, 1968	22.75	14	22.75(55)
56	Shawn Jefferson, 1998	22.68	16	22.68(56)
57	Elroy Hirsch, 1951	22.65	12	22.65(57)
58	Ken Kavanaugh, 1949	22.59	12	22.59(58)
59	Bob Trumpy, 1969	22.57	14	22.57(59)
60	Harold Jackson, 1979	22.51	16	22.51(60)
61	Ken Burrow, 1971	22.45	14	22.45(61)
62	Michael Haynes, 1991	22.44	16	22.44(62)
63	Frank Clarke, 1961	22.41	14	22.41(63)
	James Lofton, 1983	22.41	16	22.41(63)
65	Otis Taylor, 1966	22.36	14	22.36(65)
66	Lance Rentzel, 1969	22.33	14	22.33(66)
67	Frank Clarke, 1962	22.19	14	22.19(67)
68	Jack Ferrante, 1945	22.10	10	22.10(68)
69	John Gilliam, 1972	22.02	14	22.02(69)
	Stanley Morgan, 1980	22.02	16	22.02(69)
71	Cloyce Box, 1952	22.00	12	22.00(71)
	Harry Jacunski, 1943	22.00	10	22.00(71)
73	Charlie Joiner, 1971	21.97	14	21.97(73)
74	Mal Kutner, 1947	21.95	12	21.95(74)
	James Lofton, 1984	21.95	16	21.95(74)
76	Paul Warfield, 1967	21.94	14	21.94(76)
77	Stephone Paige, 1985	21.93	16	21.93(77)
78	Fred Biletnikoff, 1967	21.90	14	21.90(78)
79	Mark Nichols, 1984	21.88	16	21.88(79)
80	Harold Jackson, 1973	21.85	14	21.85(80)
81	Frank Pitts, 1968	21.83	14	21.83(81)
82	Bob Hayes, 1965	21.80	14	21.80(82)
83	Homer Jones, 1966	21.75	14	21.75(83)
84	Warren Wells, 1970	21.74	14	21.74(84)
85	Ken Kavanaugh, 1945	21.72	10	21.72(85)
86	Jim Colclough, 1962	21.70	14	21.70(86)
87	Jimmy Orr, 1964	21.67	14	21.67(87)
88	John Gilliam, 1973	21.60	14	21.60(88)
	Billy Howton, 1956	21.60	12	21.60(88)
90	Buddy Dial, 1963	21.58	14	21.58(90)
	Alvin Harper, 1993	21.58	16	21.58(90)
92	Charlie Brown, 1982	21.56	9	21.56(92)
93	Jackie Smith, 1967	21.52	14	21.52(93)
94	Flipper Anderson, 1990	21.51	16	21.51(94)
	Del Shofner, 1958	21.51	12	21.51(94)
96	Gary Ballman, 1965	21.48	14	21.48(96)
97	James Lofton, 1987	21.46	15	21.46(97)
98	Roy Green, 1981	21.45	16	21.45(98)
	Warren Wells, 1968	21.45	14	21.45(98)

RECEIVING TDS

	NAME	ADJ	G	UNADJ
1	Don Hutson, 1942	25	11	17(4)
2	Elroy Hirsch, 1951	23	12	17(4)
	Jerry Rice, 1987	23	15	22(1)
4	Cloyce Box, 1952	20	12	15(15)
5	Raymond Berry, 1959	19	12	14(24)
	Bill Groman, 1961	19	14	17(4)
	Mal Kutner, 1948	19	12	14(24)
8	Mark Clayton, 1984	18	16	18(2)
	Don Hutson, 1943	18	10	11(127)
	Art Powell, 1963	18	14	16(12)
	Sterling Sharpe, 1994	18	16	18(2)
12	Cris Carter, 1995	17	16	17(4)
	Billy Howton, 1952	17	12	13(42)
	Ken Kavanaugh, 1947	17	12	13(42)
	Randy Moss, 1998	**17**	**16**	**17(4)**
	Randy Moss, 2003	**17**	**16**	**17(4)**
	Carl Pickens, 1995	17	16	17(4)
	Sonny Randle, 1960	17	14	15(15)
	Jerry Rice, 1989	17	16	17(4)
20	Lance Alworth, 1965	16	14	14(24)
	Wes Chandler, 1982	16	9	9
	Frank Clarke, 1962	16	14	14(24)
	Leon Hart, 1951	16	12	12(72)
	Harlon Hill, 1954	16	12	12(72)
	Billy Howton, 1956	16	12	12(72)
	Frank Liebel, 1945	16	10	10(181)
	Don Maynard, 1965	16	14	14(24)
	Muhsin Muhammad, 2004	**16**	**16**	**16(12)**
	Terrell Owens, 2001	**16**	**16**	**16(12)**
	Art Powell, 1960	16	14	14(24)
	Bob Shaw, 1950	16	12	12(72)
	Hugh Taylor, 1952	16	12	12(72)
	Warren Wells, 1969	16	14	14(24)
34	Lance Alworth, 1964	15	14	13(42)
	Lance Alworth, 1966	15	14	13(42)
	Terry Barr, 1963	15	14	13(42)
	Cloyce Box, 1950	15	12	11(127)
	Cliff Branch, 1974	15	14	13(42)
	Gary Collins, 1963	15	14	13(42)
	Dick Gordon, 1970	15	14	13(42)
	Marvin Harrison, 2001	**15**	**16**	**15(15)**
	Marvin Harrison, 2004	**15**	**16**	**15(15)**
	Bob Hayes, 1966	15	14	13(42)
	Harlon Hill, 1956	15	12	11(127)
	Don Hutson, 1941	15	11	10(181)
	Harold Jackson, 1973	15	14	13(42)
	Homer Jones, 1967	15	14	13(42)
	Tommy McDonald, 1960	15	14	13(42)
	Tommy McDonald, 1961	15	14	13(42)
	Randy Moss, 2000	**15**	**16**	**15(15)**
	Pete Pihos, 1948	15	12	11(127)
	Jerry Rice, 1986	15	16	15(15)
	Jerry Rice, 1993	15	16	15(15)
	Jerry Rice, 1995	15	16	15(15)
	Andre Rison, 1993	15	16	15(15)
	Bobby Walston, 1954	15	12	11(127)
57	Fred Biletnikoff, 1969	14	14	12(72)
	Cliff Branch, 1976	14	14	12(72)
	Charlie Brown, 1982	14	9	8
	Chris Burford, 1962	14	14	12(72)
	Mark Clayton, 1988	14	16	14(24)
	Gary Collins, 1966	14	14	12(72)
	Buddy Dial, 1961	14	14	12(72)
	Mike Ditka, 1961	14	14	12(72)
	Charley Frazier, 1966	14	14	12(72)
	Antonio Freeman, 1998	14	16	14(24)
	Gary Garrison, 1970	14	14	12(72)
	Roy Green, 1983	14	16	14(24)
	Bill Groman, 1960	14	14	12(72)
	Marvin Harrison, 2000	**14**	**16**	**14(24)**
	Bob Hayes, 1965	14	14	12(72)
	Charley Hennigan, 1961	14	14	12(72)
	Don Hutson, 1944	14	10	9
	Don Hutson, 1945	14	10	9
	Michael Jackson, 1996	14	16	14(24)
	Tony Martin, 1996	14	16	14(24)
	Anthony Miller, 1995	14	16	14(24)
	Herman Moore, 1995	14	16	14(24)
	Nat Moore, 1977	14	14	12(72)
	Terrell Owens, 1998	**14**	**16**	**14(24)**
	Terrell Owens, 2004	**14**	**16**	**14(24)**
	Dave Parks, 1965	14	14	12(72)
	Art Powell, 1965	14	14	12(72)
	Sonny Randle, 1963	14	14	12(72)
	Lance Rentzel, 1969	14	14	12(72)
	Jerry Rice, 1991	14	16	14(24)
	Del Shofner, 1962	14	14	12(72)
	Jerry Smith, 1967	14	14	12(72)
	Charley Taylor, 1966	14	14	12(72)
	Lionel Taylor, 1960	14	14	12(72)
	Paul Warfield, 1968	14	14	12(72)
	Gene Washington, 1970	14	14	12(72)
	Gene Washington, 1972	14	14	12(72)
94	45 players tied			13

COMBINED NET YARDS

	NAME	ADJ	G	UNADJ
1	Terry Metcalf, 1975	2814	14	2462(5)
2	Mack Herron, 1974	2793	14	2444(7)
3	Gale Sayers, 1966	2789	14	2440(8)
4	Timmy Brown, 1963	2775	14	2428(10)
5	**Derrick Mason, 2000**	**2690**	**16**	**2690(1)**
6	**Michael Lewis, 2002**	**2647**	**16**	**2647(2)**
7	Timmy Brown, 1962	2635	14	2306(19)
8	Gale Sayers, 1965	2597	14	2272(23)
9	Harry Clarke, 1943	2571	10	1607
10	O.J. Simpson, 1975	2563	14	2243(27)
11	Lionel James, 1985	2535	16	2535(3)
12	Walter Payton, 1977	2533	14	2216(32)
13	Billy Grimes, 1950	2528	12	1896(139)
14	Otis Armstrong, 1974	2512	14	2198(37)
15	Brian Mitchell, 1994	2477	16	2477(4)
16	Eddie Saenz, 1947	2461	12	1846(170)
17	James Brooks, 1982	2459	9	1383
18	Dick Christy, 1962	2454	14	2147(47)
19	**Dante Hall, 2003**	**2446**	**16**	**2446(6)**
20	Jim Brown, 1963	2435	14	2131(50)
21	**Marshall Faulk, 1999**	**2429**	**16**	**2429(9)**
22	MarTay Jenkins, 2000	2402	16	2402(11)
23	Bill Dudley, 1946	2400	11	1650
	Abner Haynes, 1960	2400	14	2100(55)
25	**Tiki Barber, 2005**	**2390**	**16**	**2390(12)**
26	**LaDainian Tomlinson, 2003**	**2370**	**16**	**2370(13)**
27	O.J. Simpson, 1973	2369	14	2073(63)
28	Steve Van Buren, 1945	2365	10	1478
29	Barry Sanders, 1997	2358	16	2358(14)
30	Brian Mitchell, 1998	2357	16	2357(15)
31	Terry Metcalf, 1974	2352	14	2058(67)
32	Brian Mitchell, 1995	2348	16	2348(16)
33	Billy Cannon, 1961	2335	14	2043(71)
34	Jim Brown, 1958	2319	12	1739(250)
35	Tim Brown, 1988	2317	16	2317(17)
36	Terry Metcalf, 1977	2311	14	2022(83)
37	Marcus Allen, 1985	2308	16	2308(18)
	Jon Arnett, 1958	2308	12	1731(260)
	Hugh McElhenny, 1952	2308	12	1731(260)
40	**Edgerrin James, 2000**	**2303**	**16**	**2303(20)**
41	Leroy Kelly, 1966	2302	14	2014(86)
42	**Priest Holmes, 2002**	**2287**	**16**	**2287(21)**
43	**Dante Hall, 2005**	**2283**	**16**	**2283(22)**
	Amos Marsh, 1962	2283	14	1998(90)
45	**Jamal Lewis, 2003**	**2271**	**16**	**2271(24)**
46	Vic Washington, 1971	2270	14	1986(95)
47	Eric Dickerson, 1984	2259	16	2259(25)
48	**Ahman Green, 2003**	**2250**	**16**	**2250(26)**
49	**Marshall Faulk, 1998**	**2240**	**16**	**2240(28)**
50	**Dante Hall, 2004**	**2236**	**16**	**2236(29)**
51	James Wilder, 1984	2229	16	2229(30)
52	Terrell Davis, 1998	2225	16	2225(31)
53	Jerry LeVias, 1969	2224	14	1946(107)
54	Ollie Matson, 1954	2221	12	1666
55	**Ricky Williams, 2002**	**2216**	**16**	**2216(32)**
56	Eric Dickerson, 1983	2212	16	2212(34)
57	**Wes Welker, 2005**	**2208**	**16**	**2208(35)**
58	**Marshall Faulk, 2000**	**2207**	**16**	**2207(36)**
59	Rick Upchurch, 1975	2205	14	1929(117)
60	Jim Brown, 1961	2191	14	1917(124)
	Kevin Williams, 1997	2191	16	2191(38)
62	Lenny Moore, 1958	2184	12	1638
63	Carl Garrett, 1969	2182	14	1909(128)
64	William Andrews, 1983	2176	16	2176(39)
	Steve Bagarus, 1945	2176	10	1360
66	**LaDainian Tomlinson, 2002**	**2172**	**16**	**2172(40)**
67	**Priest Holmes, 2001**	**2169**	**16**	**2169(41)**
68	Barry Sanders, 1994	2166	16	2166(42)
69	Jamal Anderson, 1998	2165	16	2165(43)
70	Ray Mathews, 1952	2163	12	1622
71	Bruce Harper, 1978	2157	16	2157(44)
72	**Deuce McAllister, 2003**	**2154**	**16**	**2154(45)**
73	Larry Garron, 1963	2153	14	1884(144)
74	Emmitt Smith, 1995	2148	16	2148(46)
75	**Marshall Faulk, 2001**	**2147**	**16**	**2147(47)**
76	Jim Brown, 1959	2143	12	1607
77	Jim Brown, 1965	2139	14	1872(147)
	Edgerrin James, 1999	**2139**	**16**	**2139(49)**
79	Bruce Harper, 1977	2134	14	1867(155)
80	Abner Haynes, 1961	2131	14	1865(159)
81	Lynn Chandnois, 1953	2124	12	1593
82	**Dante Hall, 2002**	**2120**	**16**	**2120(51)**
83	Bobby Mitchell, 1963	2117	14	1852(166)
84	Thurman Thomas, 1992	2113	16	2113(52)
85	**Priest Holmes, 2003**	**2110**	**16**	**2110(53)**
86	Paul Lowe, 1960	2106	14	1843(171)
87	Garrison Hearst, 1998	2105	16	2105(54)
88	Mack Herron, 1973	2102	14	1839(174)
89	**Tiki Barber, 2004**	**2096**	**16**	**2096(56)**
90	James Brooks, 1981	2093	16	2093(57)
	Larry Johnson, 2005	**2093**	**16**	**2093(57)**
92	Terrence Wilkins, 1999	2089	16	2089(59)
93	Floyd Little, 1968	2086	14	1825(183)
94	**Tiki Barber, 2000**	**2085**	**16**	**2085(60)**
95	Dick Bass, 1962	2082	14	1822(188)
96	Brian Mitchell, 1997	2081	16	2081(61)
97	Billy Johnson, 1975	2080	14	1820(190)
	Glyn Milburn, 1995	2080	16	2080(62)
99	Bruce Harper, 1980	2072	16	2072(64)

TOTAL TDS

	NAME	ADJ	G	UNADJ
1	Steve Van Buren, 1945	29	10	18(29)
2	**Shaun Alexander, 2005**	**28**	**16**	**28(1)**
3	**Priest Holmes, 2003**	**27**	**16**	**27(2)**
4	**Marshall Faulk, 2000**	**26**	**16**	**26(3)**
	O.J. Simpson, 1975	26	14	23(7)
6	Marcus Allen, 1982	25	9	14(127)
	Chuck Foreman, 1975	25	14	22(10)
	Don Hutson, 1942	25	11	17(42)
	Jerry Rice, 1987	25	15	23(7)
	Gale Sayers, 1965	25	14	22(10)
	Emmitt Smith, 1995	25	16	25(4)
12	Jim Brown, 1958	24	12	18(29)
	Jim Brown, 1965	24	14	21(13)
	Priest Holmes, 2002	**24**	**16**	**24(5)**
	John Riggins, 1983	24	16	24(5)
16	Terrell Davis, 1998	23	16	23(7)
	Elroy Hirsch, 1951	23	12	17(42)
	Leroy Kelly, 1968	23	14	20(18)
	Lenny Moore, 1964	23	14	20(18)
	Gene Roberts, 1949	23	12	17(42)
	Wendell Tyler, 1982	23	9	13(181)
22	Abner Haynes, 1962	22	14	19(24)
	Emmitt Smith, 1994	22	16	22(10)
	Jim Taylor, 1962	22	14	19(24)
25	Terry Allen, 1996	21	16	21(13)
	Jim Brown, 1962	21	14	18(29)
	Marshall Faulk, 2001	**21**	**16**	**21(13)**
	Bill Groman, 1961	21	14	18(29)
	Larry Johnson, 2005	**21**	**16**	**21(13)**
	Joe Morris, 1985	21	16	21(13)
31	**Shaun Alexander, 2004**	**20**	**16**	**20(18)**
	Cloyce Box, 1952	20	12	15(84)
	Eric Dickerson, 1983	20	16	20(18)
	Ahman Green, 2003	**20**	**16**	**20(18)**
	Mal Kutner, 1948	20	12	15(84)
	LaDainian Tomlinson, 2005	**20**	**16**	**20(18)**
37	Raymond Berry, 1959	19	12	14(127)
	Jim Brown, 1959	19	12	14(127)
	Earl Campbell, 1979	19	16	19(24)
	Rick Casares, 1956	19	12	14(127)
	John David Crow, 1962	19	14	17(42)
	Don Hutson, 1943	19	10	12
	Lenny Moore, 1958	19	12	14(127)
	Chuck Muncie, 1981	19	16	19(24)
	Bill Paschal, 1943	19	10	12
	Emmitt Smith, 1992	19	16	19(24)
	Steve Van Buren, 1947	19	12	14(127)
48	**Shaun Alexander, 2002**	**18**	**16**	**18(29)**
	Marcus Allen, 1984	18	16	18(29)
	Pete Banaszak, 1975	18	14	16(61)
	Greg Bell, 1988	18	16	18(29)
	Bill Brown, 1964	18	14	16(61)
	Mark Clayton, 1984	18	16	18(29)
	Dalton Hilliard, 1989	18	16	18(29)
	Eddie Lee Ivery, 1982	18	9	10
	Edgerrin James, 2000	**18**	**16**	**18(29)**
	Leroy Kelly, 1966	18	14	16(61)
	Tony Latone, 1929	18	8	9
	Walter Payton, 1977	18	14	16(61)
	Art Powell, 1963	18	14	16(61)
	Dan Reeves, 1966	18	14	16(61)
	George Rogers, 1986	18	16	18(29)
	Sterling Sharpe, 1994	18	16	18(29)
	Jim Taylor, 1961	18	14	16(61)
	LaDainian Tomlinson, 2004	**18**	**16**	**18(29)**
66	Lance Alworth, 1964	17	14	15(84)
	Jim Brown, 1963	17	14	15(84)
	Billy Cannon, 1961	17	14	15(84)
	Cris Carter, 1995	17	16	17(42)
	Stephen Davis, 1999	**17**	**16**	**17(42)**
	Chuck Foreman, 1974	17	14	15(84)
	Cookie Gilchrist, 1962	17	14	15(84)
	Paul Hornung, 1960	17	14	15(84)
	Billy Howton, 1952	17	12	13(181)
	Don Hutson, 1941	17	11	12
	Edgerrin James, 1999	**17**	**16**	**17(42)**
	Ken Kavanaugh, 1947	17	12	13(181)
	Curtis Martin, 1996	**17**	**16**	**17(42)**
	George McAfee, 1941	17	11	12
	Lydell Mitchell, 1975	17	14	15(84)
	Lenny Moore, 1961	17	14	15(84)
	Randy Moss, 1998	**17**	**16**	**17(42)**
	Randy Moss, 2003	**17**	**16**	**17(42)**
	Joe Perry, 1953	17	12	13(181)
	Carl Pickens, 1995	17	16	17(42)
	Clinton Portis, 2002	**17**	**16**	**17(42)**
	Sonny Randle, 1960	17	14	15(84)
	Jerry Rice, 1989	17	16	17(42)
	Jerry Rice, 1995	17	16	17(42)
	Barry Sanders, 1991	17	16	17(42)
	Charley Taylor, 1966	17	14	15(84)
	Fred Taylor, 1998	**17**	**16**	**17(42)**
	Jim Taylor, 1964	17	14	15(84)
	LaDainian Tomlinson, 2003	**17**	**16**	**17(42)**
	Wendell Tyler, 1981	17	16	17(42)
	Ricky Williams, 2002	**17**	**16**	**17(42)**
97	48 players tied			16

TOTAL POINTS

	NAME	ADJ	G	UNADJ
1	Paul Hornung, 1960	201	14	176(1)
	Don Hutson, 1942	201	11	138(29)
3	Don Hutson, 1943	187	10	117(169)
4	Gino Cappelletti, 1964	177	14	155(9)
5	Steve Van Buren, 1945	176	10	110(284)
6	Doak Walker, 1950	171	12	128(67)
7	**Shaun Alexander, 2005**	168	16	168(2)
	Gino Cappelletti, 1961	168	14	147(13)
9	Paul Hornung, 1961	167	14	146(14)
10	Jim Turner, 1968	166	14	145(15)
11	Gary Anderson, 1998	164	16	164(3)
12	**Jeff Wilkins, 2003**	163	16	163(4)
13	**Priest Holmes, 2003**	162	16	162(5)
14	Mark Moseley, 1983	161	16	161(6)
15	**Marshall Faulk, 2000**	160	16	160(7)
16	O.J. Simpson, 1975	158	14	138(29)
17	Gene Mingo, 1962	157	14	137(34)
	Mike Vanderjagt, 2003	157	16	157(8)
19	Don Hutson, 1945	155	10	97
20	Gordie Soltau, 1953	152	12	114(223)
	Bobby Walston, 1954	152	12	114(223)
22	Gino Cappelletti, 1965	151	14	132(44)
	Chuck Foreman, 1975	151	14	132(44)
	Gale Sayers, 1965	151	14	132(44)
25	Emmitt Smith, 1995	150	16	150(10)
26	Marcus Allen, 1982	149	9	84
	Chip Lohmiller, 1991	149	16	149(11)
	David Ray, 1973	149	14	130(57)
29	**Jay Feely, 2005**	148	16	148(12)
30	Pat Harder, 1948	147	12	110(284)
	Jerry Rice, 1987	147	15	138(29)
	Jan Stenerud, 1968	147	14	129(62)
	Jim Turner, 1969	147	14	129(62)
34	Gino Cappelletti, 1962	146	14	128(67)
	Cookie Gilchrist, 1962	146	14	128(67)
	Chester Marcol, 1972	146	14	128(67)
37	Ted Fritsch, 1946	145	11	100
	John Kasay, 1996	145	16	145(15)
	Johnny Lujack, 1950	145	12	109
	Mike Vanderjagt, 1999	145	16	145(15)
41	Jim Brown, 1958	144	12	108
	Jim Brown, 1965	144	14	126(84)
	Kevin Butler, 1985	144	16	144(18)
	Lou Groza, 1953	144	12	108
	Priest Holmes, 2002	144	16	144(18)
	Olindo Mare, 1999	144	16	144(18)
	John Riggins, 1983	144	16	144(18)
48	Fred Cox, 1970	143	14	125(93)
49	Rolf Benirschke, 1982	142	9	80
50	Roy Gerela, 1973	141	14	123(105)
	Norm Johnson, 1995	141	16	141(22)
	Gene Mingo, 1960	141	14	123(105)
	Adam Vinatieri, 2004	141	16	141(22)
	Doak Walker, 1954	141	12	106
55	Steve Christie, 1998	140	16	140(24)
	Tony Franklin, 1986	140	16	140(24)
	Neil Rackers, 2005	140	16	140(24)
58	Gary Anderson, 1985	139	16	139(27)
	Nick Lowery, 1990	139	16	139(27)
	Wendell Tyler, 1982	139	9	78
61	Fred Cox, 1969	138	14	121(114)
	Terrell Davis, 1998	138	16	138(29)
	Jay Feely, 2002	138	16	138(29)
	Bobby Howfield, 1972	138	14	121(114)
	Don Hutson, 1941	138	11	95
	David Ray, 1970	138	14	121(114)
67	Leroy Kelly, 1968	137	14	120(128)
	Lenny Moore, 1964	137	14	120(128)
69	Gino Cappelletti, 1966	136	14	119(153)
	Mike Cofer, 1989	136	16	136(35)
	Al Del Greco, 1998	136	16	136(35)
	Roy Gerela, 1972	136	14	119(153)
	Pat Harder, 1947	136	12	102
	Pat Harder, 1949	136	12	102
	Elroy Hirsch, 1951	136	12	102
	Don Hutson, 1944	136	10	85
	Gene Roberts, 1949	136	12	102
	Jan Stenerud, 1969	136	14	119(153)
79	Cary Blanchard, 1996	135	16	135(37)
	John Carney, 1994	135	16	135(37)
	Mark Moseley, 1982	135	9	76
	Matt Stover, 2000	135	16	135(37)
83	Jim Bakken, 1967	134	14	117(169)
	George Blanda, 1968	134	14	117(169)
	Mike Hollis, 1997	134	16	134(40)
	Todd Peterson, 1999	134	16	134(40)
	Matt Stover, 2003	134	16	134(40)
	Garo Yepremian, 1971	134	14	117(169)
89	**David Akers, 2002**	133	16	133(43)
	George Blanda, 1967	133	14	116(189)
	Jan Stenerud, 1970	133	14	116(189)
92	**Jason Elam, 1995**	132	16	132(44)
	Jason Hanson, 1995	132	16	132(44)
	Jeff Jaeger, 1993	132	16	132(44)
	Bobby Layne, 1956	132	12	99
	Nick Lowery, 1982	132	9	74
	Fuad Reveiz, 1994	132	16	132(44)
	Emmitt Smith, 1994	132	16	132(44)
99	11 players tied			131

KICKOFF RETURNS

	NAME	ADJ	G	UNADJ
1	MarTay Jenkins, 2000	82	16	82(1)
2	**Chris Carr, 2005**	73	16	73(2)
	Josh Scobey, 2003	73	16	73(2)
4	Tyrone Hughes, 1996	70	16	70(4)
	Michael Lewis, 2002	70	16	70(4)
6	**Dante Hall, 2004**	68	16	68(6)
7	Ronney Jenkins, 2000	67	16	67(7)
8	Tyrone Hughes, 1995	66	16	66(8)
	Charlie Rogers, 2000	66	16	66(8)
10	**Dante Hall, 2005**	65	16	65(10)
11	Glyn Milburn, 1996	64	16	64(11)
	Tab Perry, 2005	64	16	64(11)
	Charlie Rogers, 2002	64	16	64(11)
14	Tyrone Hughes, 1994	63	16	63(14)
	Glyn Milburn, 2000	63	16	63(14)
	Darren Sproles, 2005	63	16	63(14)
	Reggie Swinton, 2005	63	16	63(14)
18	Andre Coleman, 1995	62	16	62(18)
	Brock Marion, 1999	62	16	62(18)
	Glyn Milburn, 1998	62	16	62(18)
	Allen Rossum, 2003	62	16	62(18)
22	Desmond Howard, 1997	61	16	61(22)
	Glyn Milburn, 1999	61	16	61(22)
	Darrick Vaughn, 2001	61	16	61(22)
	Wes Welker, 2005	61	16	61(22)
26	Drew Hill, 1981	60	16	60(26)
	Justin Miller, 2005	60	16	60(26)
28	Michael Bates, 1998	59	16	59(28)
	James Brooks, 1982	59	9	33
	Brian Mitchell, 1998	59	16	59(28)
	J.J. Moses, 2004	59	16	59(28)
	B.J. Sams, 2004	59	16	59(28)
	Josh Scobey, 2005	59	16	59(28)
	Kevin Williams, 1997	59	16	59(28)
35	Bobby Joe Edmonds, 1995	58	16	58(34)
	Ronney Jenkins, 2001	58	16	58(34)
	Brian Mitchell, 1994	58	16	58(34)
	Chad Morton, 2002	58	16	58(34)
	J.J. Moses, 2003	58	16	58(34)
	Allen Rossum, 2004	58	16	58(34)
41	**Dante Hall, 2002**	57	16	57(40)
	Dante Hall, 2003	57	16	57(40)
	Tony Horne, 2000	57	16	57(40)
	Desmond Howard, 2000	57	16	57(40)
	Desmond Howard, 2001	57	16	57(40)
	Eric Metcalf, 1998	57	16	57(40)
	Roell Preston, 1998	57	16	57(40)
	Tyson Thompson, 2005	57	16	57(40)
	Wes Welker, 2004	57	16	57(40)

KICKOFF RETURN AVERAGE

	NAME	ADJ	G	UNADJ
1	Travis Williams, 1967	41.06	14	41.06(1)
2	Gale Sayers, 1967	37.69	14	37.69(2)
3	Ollie Matson, 1958	35.50	12	35.50(3)
4	Jim Duncan, 1970	35.35	14	35.35(4)
5	Lynn Chandnois, 1952	35.24	12	35.24(5)
6	Preston Pearson, 1968	35.13	14	35.13(6)
7	Joe Arenas, 1953	34.44	12	34.44(7)
8	Tom Watkins, 1965	34.35	14	34.35(8)
9	Vitamin Smith, 1950	33.73	12	33.73(9)
10	Bobby Williams, 1969	33.12	14	33.12(10)
11	Duriel Harris, 1976	32.88	14	32.88(11)
12	Ron Brown, 1985	32.79	16	32.79(12)
13	Cecil Turner, 1970	32.70	14	32.70(13)
14	Lynn Chandnois, 1951	32.50	12	32.50(14)
15	Abe Woodson, 1963	32.24	14	32.24(15)
16	Tommy Wilson, 1956	31.80	12	31.80(16)
17	Gary Ballman, 1963	31.73	14	31.73(17)
18	Walter Payton, 1975	31.71	14	31.71(18)
19	Jack Salscheider, 1949	31.60	12	31.60(19)
20	**Najeh Davenport, 2003**	31.56	16	31.56(20)
21	Gale Sayers, 1965	31.43	14	31.43(21)
22	Frank Seno, 1946	31.38	11	31.38(22)
23	Abe Woodson, 1962	31.27	14	31.27(23)
24	Ken Hall, 1960	31.26	14	31.26(24)
25	Gale Sayers, 1966	31.22	14	31.22(25)
26	Ollie Matson, 1952	31.20	12	31.20(26)
27	Terry Metcalf, 1974	31.15	14	31.15(27)
28	Raymond Clayborn, 1977	31.04	14	31.04(28)
29	Lenny Lyles, 1960	30.94	14	30.94(29)
30	Frank Minini, 1948	30.83	12	30.83(30)
31	Ron Smith, 1972	30.80	14	30.80(31)
32	Alvin Haymond, 1965	30.70	14	30.70(32)
33	Bobby Humphery, 1984	30.68	16	30.68(33)
34	Buddy Young, 1951	30.50	12	30.50(34)
35	Harold Hart, 1975	30.47	14	30.47(35)
36	Carl Garrett, 1973	30.38	14	30.38(36)
37	Dick Bass, 1961	30.35	14	30.35(37)
38	Bobby Jancik, 1962	30.25	14	30.25(38)
39	Michael Bates, 1996	30.24	16	30.24(39)
	Terrence McGee, 2005	30.24	16	30.24(39)
41	Johnny Counts, 1962	30.15	14	30.15(41)
42	Corey Harris, 1993	30.13	16	30.13(42)
	Lemar Parrish, 1970	30.13	14	30.13(42)
44	John Gilliam, 1967	30.06	14	30.06(44)
45	Mel Renfro, 1965	30.00	14	30.00(45)
46	Wallace Francis, 1973	29.87	14	29.87(46)
47	Al Carmichael, 1955	29.86	12	29.86(47)

KICKOFF RETURN YARDS

	NAME	ADJ	G	UNADJ
1	MarTay Jenkins, 2000	2186	16	2186(1)
2	**Michael Lewis, 2002**	1807	16	1807(2)
3	Tyrone Hughes, 1996	1791	16	1791(3)
4	**Chris Carr, 2005**	1752	16	1752(4)
5	**Dante Hall, 2004**	1718	16	1718(5)
6	**Josh Scobey, 2003**	1684	16	1684(6)
7	Charlie Rogers, 2000	1629	16	1629(7)
8	Glyn Milburn, 1996	1627	16	1627(8)
9	Tyrone Hughes, 1995	1617	16	1617(9)
10	**Justin Miller, 2005**	1577	16	1577(10)
11	**Tab Perry, 2005**	1562	16	1562(11)
12	**Dante Hall, 2005**	1560	16	1560(12)
13	Tyrone Hughes, 1994	1556	16	1556(13)
14	Glyn Milburn, 1998	1550	16	1550(14)
15	**Jerome Mathis, 2005**	1542	16	1542(15)
16	Ronney Jenkins, 2001	1541	16	1541(16)
17	Ronney Jenkins, 2000	1531	16	1531(17)
18	**Darren Sproles, 2005**	1528	16	1528(18)
19	Brock Marion, 1999	1524	16	1524(19)
20	**Chad Morton, 2002**	1509	16	1509(20)
21	Bobby Jancik, 1963	1505	14	1317(50)
22	Dave Hampton, 1971	1502	14	1314(52)
23	Roell Preston, 1998	1497	16	1497(21)
24	Darrick Vaughn, 2001	1491	16	1491(22)
25	Michael Bates, 1998	1480	16	1480(23)
26	**Dante Hall, 2003**	1478	16	1478(24)
	Brian Mitchell, 1994	1478	16	1478(24)
28	Glyn Milburn, 2000	1468	16	1468(26)
29	Kevin Williams, 1997	1458	16	1458(27)
30	**Reggie Swinton, 2005**	1456	16	1456(28)
31	Desmond Howard, 2001	1446	16	1446(29)
32	**Steve Smith, 2001**	1431	16	1431(30)
33	**Terry Fair, 1998**	1428	16	1428(31)
34	Glyn Milburn, 1999	1426	16	1426(32)
35	Odell Barry, 1964	1423	14	1245(72)
36	Chuck Latourette, 1968	1414	14	1237(73)
37	Andre Coleman, 1995	1411	16	1411(33)
38	Brian Mitchell, 1995	1408	16	1408(34)
39	Desmond Howard, 2000	1401	16	1401(35)
40	**Tyson Thompson, 2005**	1399	16	1399(36)
41	**Terrence McGee, 2005**	1391	16	1391(37)
42	Tremain Mack, 1999	1382	16	1382(38)
43	Tony Horne, 2000	1379	16	1379(39)
	Wes Welker, 2005	1379	16	1379(39)
45	**Terrence McGee, 2004**	1370	16	1370(41)
46	**J.J. Moses, 2003**	1355	16	1355(42)
47	**Dante Hall, 2002**	1354	16	1354(43)

KICKOFF RETURN TDS

	NAME	ADJ	G	UNADJ
1	Cecil Turner, 1970	5	14	4(1)
	Travis Williams, 1967	5	14	4(1)
3	Vitamin Smith, 1950	4	12	3(3)
4	Ron Brown, 1985	3	16	3(3)
	Lynn Chandnois, 1952	3	12	2(11)
	Raymond Clayborn, 1977	3	14	3(3)
	Les Goble, 1954	3	12	2(11)
	Mel Gray, 1994	3	16	3(3)
	Lenny Lyles, 1958	3	12	2(11)
	Ollie Matson, 1952	3	12	2(11)
	Ollie Matson, 1958	3	12	2(11)
	Terrence McGee, 2004	3	16	3(3)
	Eddie Saenz, 1947	3	12	2(11)
	Gale Sayers, 1967	3	14	3(3)
	Darrick Vaughn, 2000	3	16	3(3)
	Abe Woodson, 1963	3	14	3(3)
17	**Jerry Azumah, 2003**	2	16	2(11)
	Michael Bates, 1999	2	16	2(11)
	Timmy Brown, 1966	2	14	2(11)
	Leon Burton, 1960	2	14	2(11)
	Andre Coleman, 1994	2	16	2(11)
	Andre Coleman, 1995	2	16	2(11)
	Eddie Drummond, 2004	2	16	2(11)
	Terry Fair, 1998	2	16	2(11)
	Kevin Faulk, 2002	2	16	2(11)
	Wallace Francis, 1973	2	14	2(11)
	Dante Hall, 2003	2	16	2(11)
	Dante Hall, 2004	2	16	2(11)
	Byron Hanspard, 1997	2	16	2(11)
	Tony Horne, 1999	2	16	2(11)
	Tyrone Hughes, 1994	2	16	2(11)
	Ronney Jenkins, 2001	2	16	2(11)
	Ron Jessie, 1971	2	14	2(11)
	Michael Lewis, 2002	2	16	2(11)
	Jerome Mathis, 2005	2	16	2(11)
	Eric Metcalf, 1990	2	16	2(11)
	Glyn Milburn, 1998	2	16	2(11)
	Chad Morton, 2002	2	16	2(11)
	Paul Palmer, 1987	2	15	2(11)
	Preston Pearson, 1968	2	14	2(11)
	Roell Preston, 1998	2	16	2(11)
	Deion Sanders, 1992	2	16	2(11)
	Gale Sayers, 1966	2	14	2(11)
	Goldie Sellers, 1966	2	14	2(11)
	Steve Smith, 2001	2	16	2(11)
	Ike Thomas, 1971	2	14	2(11)
	Tamarick Vanover, 1995	2	16	2(11)
	Charley Warner, 1965	2	14	2(11)
	Derrick Witherspoon, 1996	2	16	2(11)

PUNT RETURNS

	NAME	ADJ	G	UNADJ
1	Danny Reece, 1979	70	16	70(1)
2	Leon Bright, 1982	66	9	37(206)
3	Eddie Brown, 1977	65	14	57(7)
4	Rolland Lawrence, 1976	62	14	54(15)
	Fulton Walker, 1985	62	16	62(2)
6	Alvin Haymond, 1970	61	14	53(19)
	Larry Jones, 1975	61	14	53(19)
8	Desmond Howard, 1996	58	16	58(3)
	Rolland Lawrence, 1977	58	14	51(32)
	Leo Lewis, 1988	58	16	58(3)
	Greg Pruitt, 1983	58	16	58(3)
	J.T. Smith, 1979	58	16	58(3)
	Rick Upchurch, 1977	58	14	51(32)
14	Lew Barnes, 1986	57	16	57(7)
	Jeff Fisher, 1984	57	16	57(7)
	Butch Johnson, 1977	57	14	50(40)
	Jermaine Lewis, 1999	57	16	57(7)
	Mike Nelms, 1982	57	9	32
	Danny Reece, 1980	57	16	57(7)
20	Eddie Brown, 1979	56	16	56(12)
21	Eddie Brown, 1976	55	14	48(47)
	Neal Colzie, 1975	55	14	48(47)
	B.J. Sams, 2004	**55**	**16**	**55(13)**
	Steve Smith, 2002	**55**	**16**	**55(13)**
25	Gary Allen, 1984	54	16	54(15)
	Wally Henry, 1981	54	16	54(15)
	James Jones, 1980	54	16	54(15)
	Manfred Moore, 1977	54	14	47(53)
29	Rodger Bird, 1967	53	14	46(61)
	Rod Harris, 1991	53	16	53(19)
	Todd Kinchen, 1995	53	16	53(19)
	Louis Lipps, 1984	53	16	53(19)
	Larry Marshall, 1977	53	14	46(61)
	Phil McConkey, 1985	53	16	53(19)
	Greg Pruitt, 1984	53	16	53(19)
36	Leon Bright, 1981	52	16	52(26)
	Todd Kinchen, 1997	52	16	52(26)
	Robbie Martin, 1981	52	16	52(26)
	Dave Meggett, 1996	52	16	52(26)
	Winslow Oliver, 1996	52	16	52(26)
	Jackie Wallace, 1978	52	16	52(26)
42	Mike Haynes, 1976	51	14	45(70)
	Butch Johnson, 1976	51	14	45(70)
	Butch Johnson, 1978	51	16	51(32)
	Leon Johnson, 1997	51	16	51(32)
	Mark Jones, 2005	**51**	**16**	**51(32)**
	Derrick Mason, 2000	**51**	**16**	**51(32)**
	Emlen Tunnell, 1953	51	12	38(181)
	Tamarick Vanover, 1995	51	16	51(32)
	Tamarick Vanover, 1999	51	16	51(32)

PUNT RETURN AVERAGE

	NAME	ADJ	G	UNADJ
1	Herb Rich, 1950	23.00	12	23.00(1)
2	Jack Christiansen, 1952	21.47	12	21.47(2)
3	Dick Christy, 1961	21.28	14	21.28(3)
4	Red Cochran, 1949	20.93	12	20.93(4)
5	Jerry Davis, 1948	20.88	12	20.88(5)
6	Bob Hayes, 1968	20.80	14	20.80(6)
7	Frankie Sinkwich, 1943	20.73	10	20.73(7)
8	Buddy Young, 1951	19.25	12	19.25(8)
9	Billy Grimes, 1950	19.14	12	19.14(9)
10	Jack Christiansen, 1951	19.06	12	19.06(10)
11	Ollie Matson, 1955	18.85	12	18.85(11)
12	Lemar Parrish, 1974	18.78	14	18.78(12)
13	Woodley Lewis, 1952	18.47	12	18.47(13)
14	Frank Seno, 1947	17.75	12	17.75(14)
15	Jeff Ogden, 2000	17.00	16	17.00(15)
	Dick Todd, 1941	17.00	11	17.00(15)
17	Floyd Little, 1967	16.88	14	16.88(17)
18	Dick Jauron, 1974	16.82	14	16.82(18)
19	**Jimmy Williams, 2002**	**16.80**	**16**	**16.80(19)**
20	Dick Christy, 1962	16.67	14	16.67(20)
21	Andy Tomasic, 1942	16.58	11	16.58(21)
22	Art Jones, 1941	16.57	11	16.57(22)
23	**Amani Toomer, 1996**	**16.56**	**16**	**16.56(23)**
24	**Santana Moss, 2002**	**16.52**	**16**	**16.52(24)**
25	Ernie Steele, 1944	16.45	10	16.45(25)
26	**Dante Hall, 2003**	**16.28**	**16**	**16.28(26)**
27	Rick Upchurch, 1982	16.13	9	16.13(27)
28	Willie Wood, 1961	16.07	14	16.07(28)
29	Jermaine Lewis, 2000	16.06	16	16.06(29)
30	Bob Gage, 1949	15.88	12	15.88(30)
31	Harry Clarke, 1943	15.80	10	15.80(31)
32	Pat Studstill, 1962	15.76	14	15.76(32)
33	Mike Martin, 1984	15.67	16	15.67(33)
34	**Deion Sanders, 1998**	**15.63**	**16**	**15.63(34)**
35	Jermaine Lewis, 1997	15.61	16	15.61(35)
36	Leroy Kelly, 1965	15.59	14	15.59(36)
37	Walt Slater, 1947	15.54	12	15.54(37)
38	Bert Zagers, 1957	15.50	12	15.50(38)
39	Speedy Duncan, 1965	15.47	14	15.47(39)
40	Merle Hapes, 1942	15.45	11	15.45(40)
41	Bill Dudley, 1950	15.42	12	15.42(41)
42	Mel Gray, 1991	15.40	16	15.40(42)
	Billy Johnson, 1977	15.40	14	15.40(42)
	Ray Mathews, 1951	15.40	12	15.40(42)
45	Ken Ellis, 1972	15.36	14	15.36(45)
	Abner Haynes, 1960	15.36	14	15.36(45)

PUNT RETURN YARDS

	NAME	ADJ	G	UNADJ
1	Desmond Howard, 1996	875	16	875(1)
2	Neal Colzie, 1975	749	14	655(6)
3	Rick Upchurch, 1977	746	14	653(7)
4	Billy Grimes, 1950	740	12	555(29)
5	Eddie Brown, 1976	738	14	646(8)
6	Rodger Bird, 1967	699	14	612(14)
	Billy Johnson, 1975	699	14	612(14)
8	Mike Haynes, 1976	695	14	608(17)
9	Fulton Walker, 1985	692	16	692(2)
10	Greg Pruitt, 1983	666	16	666(3)
11	**Derrick Mason, 2000**	**662**	**16**	**662(4)**
12	Lynn Swann, 1974	659	14	577(25)
13	Louis Lipps, 1984	656	16	656(5)
14	Emlen Tunnell, 1951	652	12	489(66)
15	Tamarick Vanover, 1999	627	16	627(9)
16	**Michael Lewis, 2002**	**625**	**16**	**625(10)**
17	Leon Johnson, 1997	619	16	619(11)
18	Jackie Wallace, 1978	618	16	618(12)
19	Billy Johnson, 1977	616	14	539(39)
20	LeRoy Irvin, 1981	615	16	615(13)
21	Rick Upchurch, 1976	613	14	536(41)
22	J.T. Smith, 1979	612	16	612(14)
23	Brian Mitchell, 1991	600	16	600(18)
24	Winslow Oliver, 1996	598	16	598(19)
25	Karl Williams, 1997	597	16	597(20)
26	Mack Herron, 1974	591	14	517(48)
27	Bruce Taylor, 1970	590	14	516(49)
28	Dave Meggett, 1996	588	16	588(21)
29	Vai Sikahema, 1987	587	15	550(31)
30	Dave Meggett, 1989	582	16	582(22)
31	J.T. Smith, 1980	581	16	581(23)
32	Walt Slater, 1947	580	12	435(128)
33	Leon Bright, 1982	578	9	325(331)
	Jermaine Lewis, 2000	578	16	578(24)
35	**B.J. Sams, 2004**	**575**	**16**	**575(26)**
36	Brian Mitchell, 2002	567	16	567(27)
37	George Atkinson, 1968	560	14	490(65)
	Bill Dudley, 1946	560	11	385(203)
39	Butch Johnson, 1976	559	14	489(66)
	Larry Marshall, 1977	559	14	489(66)
41	George McAfee, 1948	556	12	417(147)
	John Taylor, 1988	556	16	556(28)
43	Reggie Barlow, 1998	555	16	555(29)
	Ron Smith, 1974	555	14	486(74)
45	Leo Lewis, 1988	550	16	550(31)
46	James Jones, 1980	548	16	548(33)
	Emlen Tunnell, 1952	548	12	411(158)
48	**Allen Rossum, 2003**	**545**	**16**	**545(34)**
49	Darrien Gordon, 1997	543	16	543(35)
50	**Antwaan Randle El, 2003**	**542**	**16**	**542(36)**

PUNT RETURN TDS

	NAME	ADJ	G	UNADJ
1	Jack Christiansen, 1951	5	12	4(1)
	Rick Upchurch, 1976	5	14	4(1)
3	Curly Oden, 1926	4	13	3(3)
	Emlen Tunnell, 1951	4	12	3(3)
	Rick Upchurch, 1982	4	9	2(10)
6	Jack Christiansen, 1952	3	12	2(10)
	Red Cochran, 1949	3	12	2(10)
	Jerry Davis, 1948	3	12	2(10)
	Darrien Gordon, 1997	3	16	3(3)
	Billy Grimes, 1950	3	12	2(10)
	Desmond Howard, 1996	3	16	3(3)
	LeRoy Irvin, 1981	3	16	3(3)
	Billy Johnson, 1975	3	14	3(3)
	Woodley Lewis, 1952	3	12	2(10)
	Ray Mathews, 1952	3	12	2(10)
	Ollie Matson, 1955	3	12	2(10)
	Eric Metcalf, 1997	3	16	3(3)
	Billy Stacy, 1959	3	12	2(10)
	Charlie Trippi, 1948	3	12	2(10)
	Johnny Williams, 1952	3	12	2(10)
	Bert Zagers, 1957	3	12	2(10)
22	60 players tied 2			

PUNT/KICK RETURN YARDS

	NAME	ADJ	G	UNADJ
1	**Michael Lewis, 2002**	**2432**	**16**	**2432(1)**
2	MarTay Jenkins, 2000	2187	16	2187(2)
3	Charlie Rogers, 2000	1992	16	1992(3)
4	**Dante Hall, 2003**	**1950**	**16**	**1950(4)**
	Dante Hall, 2004	**1950**	**16**	**1950(4)**
6	Tyrone Hughes, 1996	1943	16	1943(6)
7	**Chris Carr, 2005**	**1938**	**16**	**1938(7)**
8	Brian Mitchell, 1994	1930	16	1930(8)
9	Kevin Williams, 1997	1920	16	1920(9)
10	Glyn Milburn, 1996	1911	16	1911(10)
11	Roell Preston, 1998	1895	16	1895(11)
12	Tyrone Hughes, 1995	1879	16	1879(12)
13	Desmond Howard, 2000	1858	16	1858(13)
14	Brian Mitchell, 1998	1843	16	1843(14)
15	Glyn Milburn, 1998	1841	16	1841(15)
16	**Dante Hall, 2005**	**1836**	**16**	**1836(16)**
	Allen Rossum, 2003	**1836**	**16**	**1836(16)**
18	**B.J. Sams, 2004**	**1826**	**16**	**1826(18)**
19	Chuck Latourette, 1968	1808	14	1582(51)
20	**Steve Smith, 2001**	**1795**	**16**	**1795(19)**
21	**Derrick Mason, 2000**	**1794**	**16**	**1794(20)**
22	**Reggie Swinton, 2005**	**1790**	**16**	**1790(21)**
23	**Wes Welker, 2004**	**1777**	**16**	**1777(22)**
24	Glyn Milburn, 1999	1772	16	1772(23)
25	**Wes Welker, 2005**	**1769**	**16**	**1769(24)**
26	Glyn Milburn, 2000	1768	16	1768(25)
27	Glyn Milburn, 1997	1748	16	1748(26)
28	**Dante Hall, 2002**	**1744**	**16**	**1744(27)**
29	**Reggie Swinton, 2001**	**1741**	**16**	**1741(28)**
30	Andre Coleman, 1995	1737	16	1737(29)
	Stump Mitchell, 1981	1737	16	1737(29)
32	Brian Mitchell, 2002	1729	16	1729(31)
33	Brian Mitchell, 1995	1723	16	1723(32)
34	**Allen Rossum, 2004**	**1707**	**16**	**1707(33)**
35	Larry Jones, 1975	1706	14	1493(69)
36	Tyrone Hughes, 1994	1699	16	1699(34)
37	Tamarick Vanover, 1997	1691	16	1691(35)
38	**Josh Scobey, 2003**	**1684**	**16**	**1684(36)**
39	Bobby Jancik, 1963	1671	14	1462(77)
40	Bruce Harper, 1977	1669	14	1460(78)
41	Bruce Harper, 1978	1658	16	1658(37)
42	Desmond Howard, 2001	1647	16	1647(38)
43	Mel Renfro, 1964	1640	14	1435(84)
44	**Darren Sproles, 2005**	**1636**	**16**	**1636(39)**
45	Tamarick Vanover, 1995	1635	16	1635(40)
46	Eric Guliford, 1997	1626	16	1626(41)
47	Glyn Milburn, 1995	1623	16	1623(42)
48	**Terry Fair, 1998**	**1617**	**16**	**1617(43)**

PUNT AVERAGE

	NAME	ADJ	G	UNADJ
1	Sammy Baugh, 1940	51.40	11	51.40(1)
2	Yale Lary, 1963	48.94	14	48.94(2)
3	Sammy Baugh, 1941	48.73	11	48.73(3)
4	Yale Lary, 1961	48.44	14	48.44(4)
5	Sammy Baugh, 1942	48.24	11	48.24(5)
6	**Todd Sauerbrun, 2001**	**47.52**	**16**	**47.52(6)**
7	Joe Muha, 1948	47.26	12	47.26(7)
8	**Craig Hentrich, 1998**	**47.22**	**16**	**47.22(8)**
9	George Gulyanics, 1949	47.17	12	47.17(9)
10	Yale Lary, 1959	47.13	12	47.13(10)
11	Bobby Joe Green, 1961	47.00	14	47.00(11)
12	Greg Montgomery, 1992	46.92	16	46.92(12)
	Tom Rouen, 1998	**46.92**	**16**	**46.92(12)**
14	**Shane Lechler, 2003**	**46.91**	**16**	**46.91(14)**
15	Pat Brady, 1953	46.90	12	46.90(15)
16	**Shane Lechler, 2004**	**46.70**	**16**	**46.70(16)**
17	Gary Collins, 1965	46.69	14	46.69(17)
18	Don Chandler, 1959	46.64	12	46.64(18)
19	**Tom Rouen, 1999**	**46.52**	**16**	**46.52(19)**
20	Bobby Joe Green, 1963	46.47	14	46.47(20)
21	Bobby Walden, 1964	46.40	14	46.40(21)
22	John Kidd, 1996	46.29	16	46.29(22)
23	Yale Lary, 1964	46.25	14	46.25(23)
24	**Shane Lechler, 2001**	**46.23**	**16**	**46.23(24)**
25	Dave Lewis, 1970	46.22	14	46.22(25)
26	**Darren Bennett, 2000**	**46.17**	**16**	**46.17(26)**
27	Rohn Stark, 1985	45.95	16	45.95(27)
28	**Shane Lechler, 2000**	**45.91**	**16**	**45.91(28)**
29	Sammy Baugh, 1943	45.90	10	45.90(29)
30	Mark Royals, 1997	45.89	16	45.89(30)
31	Tommy Davis, 1965	45.76	14	45.76(31)
	Tom Tupa, 1997	45.76	16	45.76(31)
33	Horace Gillom, 1952	45.69	12	45.69(33)
34	Reggie Roby, 1991	45.67	16	45.67(34)
35	Tommy Davis, 1959	45.66	12	45.66(35)
	Chris Gardocki, 1996	**45.66**	**16**	**45.66(35)**
	Shane Lechler, 2005	**45.66**	**16**	**45.66(35)**
	Brian Moorman, 2005	**45.66**	**16**	**45.66(35)**
39	Mark Royals, 1998	45.65	16	45.65(39)
40	Bob Cifers, 1946	45.63	11	45.63(40)
41	**Darren Bennett, 1996**	**45.60**	**16**	**45.60(41)**
42	Don Chandler, 1964	45.59	14	45.59(42)
	Greg Montgomery, 1993	45.59	16	45.59(42)
44	Tommy Davis, 1962	45.58	14	45.58(44)
45	**Josh Bidwell, 2005**	**45.57**	**16**	**45.57(45)**
	David Lee, 1966	45.57	14	45.57(45)
47	Tommy Davis, 1964	45.56	14	45.56(47)
	Jerry Norton, 1960	45.56	14	45.56(47)

FIELD GOALS

	NAME	ADJ	G	UNADJ
1	Neil Rackers, 2005	40	16	40(1)
2	Olindo Mare, 1999	39	16	39(2)
	Jim Turner, 1968	39	14	34(13)
	Jeff Wilkins, 2003	39	16	39(2)
5	Chester Marcol, 1972	38	14	33(22)
6	John Kasay, 1996	37	16	37(4)
	Jim Turner, 1969	37	14	32(28)
	Mike Vanderjagt, 2003	37	16	37(4)
9	Cary Blanchard, 1996	36	16	36(6)
	Al Del Greco, 1998	36	16	36(6)
	Mark Moseley, 1982	36	9	20
12	Gary Anderson, 1998	35	16	35(8)
	Jay Feely, 2005	35	16	35(8)
	Ali Haji-Sheikh, 1983	35	16	35(8)
	Jeff Jaeger, 1993	35	16	35(8)
	Matt Stover, 2000	35	16	35(8)
17	John Carney, 1994	34	16	34(13)
	Fred Cox, 1970	34	14	30(54)
	Richie Cunningham, 1997	34	16	34(13)
	Jason Hanson, 1993	34	16	34(13)
	Norm Johnson, 1995	34	16	34(13)
	Nick Lowery, 1982	34	9	19
	Nick Lowery, 1990	34	16	34(13)
	Todd Peterson, 1999	34	16	34(13)
	David Ray, 1973	34	14	30(54)
	Fuad Reveiz, 1994	34	16	34(13)
	Jan Stenerud, 1968	34	14	30(54)
	Jan Stenerud, 1970	34	14	30(54)
	Mike Vanderjagt, 1999	34	16	34(13)
30	Gary Anderson, 1985	33	16	33(22)
	Steve Christie, 1998	33	16	33(22)
	Roy Gerela, 1973	33	14	29(71)
	Curt Knight, 1971	33	14	29(71)
	Ryan Longwell, 2000	33	16	33(22)
	Mark Moseley, 1983	33	16	33(22)
	David Ray, 1970	33	14	29(71)
	Matt Stover, 2003	33	16	33(22)
38	Cary Blanchard, 1997	32	16	32(28)
	Chris Boniol, 1996	32	16	32(28)
	Bill Capece, 1982	32	9	18
	Al Del Greco, 1996	32	16	32(28)
	Jay Feely, 2002	32	16	32(28)
	Tony Franklin, 1986	32	16	32(28)
	Roy Gerela, 1972	32	14	28(93)
	Pete Gogolak, 1965	32	14	28(93)
	Bruce Gossett, 1966	32	14	28(93)
	Martin Gramatica, 2002	32	16	32(28)
	John Kasay, 2003	32	16	32(28)
	Scott Norwood, 1988	32	16	32(28)
	Garo Yepremian, 1971	32	14	28(93)

FIELD GOAL PERCENT

	NAME	ADJ	G	UNADJ
1	Gary Anderson, 1998	100.00	16	100.00(1)
	Mike Vanderjagt, 2003	100.00	16	100.00(1)
	Jeff Wilkins, 2000	100.00	16	100.00(1)
	Tony Zendejas, 1991	100.00	16	100.00(1)
5	Chris Boniol, 1995	96.43	16	96.43(5)
6	Norm Johnson, 1993	96.30	16	96.30(6)
	Pete Stoyanovich, 1997	96.30	16	96.30(6)
8	Gary Anderson, 2000	95.65	16	95.65(8)
	Jason Hanson, 2003	95.65	16	95.65(8)
10	Mark Moseley, 1982	95.24	9	95.24(10)
	Eddie Murray, 1988	95.24	16	95.24(10)
	Eddie Murray, 1989	95.24	16	95.24(10)
	Neil Rackers, 2005	95.24	16	95.24(10)
14	Adam Vinatieri, 2004	93.94	16	93.94(14)
15	Gary Anderson, 1993	93.33	16	93.33(15)
16	Phil Dawson, 2005	93.10	16	93.10(16)
17	Joe Nedney, 2000	92.86	16	92.86(17)
	Joe Nedney, 2005	92.86	16	92.86(17)
	Matt Stover, 1994	92.86	16	92.86(17)
	Jeff Wilkins, 2003	92.86	16	92.86(17)
21	Mike Vanderjagt, 2000	92.59	16	92.59(21)
22	Al Del Greco, 1998	92.31	16	92.31(22)
	Mike Hollis, 2000	92.31	16	92.31(22)
24	Josh Brown, 2004	92.00	16	92.00(24)
	Todd Peterson, 2005	92.00	16	92.00(24)
	Mike Vanderjagt, 2005	92.00	16	92.00(24)
27	Richie Cunningham, 1997	91.89	16	91.89(27)
	Nick Lowery, 1990	91.89	16	91.89(27)
29	Nick Lowery, 1992	91.67	16	91.67(29)
	Eddie Murray, 1982	91.67	9	91.67(29)
	Jan Stenerud, 1981	91.67	16	91.67(29)
32	Wade Richey, 1999	91.30	16	91.30(32)
33	Doug Brien, 1998	90.91	16	90.91(33)
34	Matt Stover, 2004	90.63	16	90.63(34)
35	John Carney, 1990	90.48	16	90.48(35)
	Olindo Mare, 2001	90.48	16	90.48(35)
37	Olindo Mare, 2000	90.32	16	90.32(37)
38	Cary Blanchard, 1996	90.00	16	90.00(38)
	Adam Vinatieri, 2002	90.00	16	90.00(38)
40	Matt Stover, 2000	89.74	16	89.74(40)
41	Jason Hanson, 1997	89.66	16	89.66(41)
42	John Carney, 1994	89.47	16	89.47(42)
	Jeff Reed, 2002	89.47	16	89.47(42)
	Mike Vanderjagt, 1999	89.47	16	89.47(42)
45	Sebastian Janikowski, 2004	89.29	16	89.29(45)
46	4 players tied			88.89

INTERCEPTIONS

	NAME	ADJ	G	UNADJ
1	Night Train Lane, 1952	19	12	14(1)
2	Sammy Baugh, 1943	18	10	11(14)
3	Spec Sanders, 1950	17	12	13(2)
	Dan Sandifer, 1948	17	12	13(2)
5	Jack Christiansen, 1953	16	12	12(5)
	Irv Comp, 1943	16	10	10(27)
	Don Doll, 1950	16	12	12(5)
	Woodley Lewis, 1950	16	12	12(5)
	Bob Nussbaumer, 1949	16	12	12(5)
10	Lindon Crow, 1956	15	12	11(14)
	Don Doll, 1949	15	12	11(14)
	Bill Dudley, 1946	15	11	10(27)
	Tom Keane, 1953	15	12	11(14)
	Jimmy Patton, 1958	15	12	11(14)
	Otto Schnellbacher, 1951	15	12	11(14)
	Will Sherman, 1955	15	12	11(14)
17	Fred Glick, 1963	14	14	12(5)
	Paul Krause, 1964	14	14	12(5)
	Howie Livingston, 1944	14	10	9(71)
	Dainard Paulson, 1964	14	14	12(5)
	Emmitt Thomas, 1974	14	14	12(5)
22	Mel Blount, 1975	13	14	11(14)
	Bill Bradley, 1971	13	14	11(14)
	Jack Butler, 1957	13	12	10(27)
	Jack Christiansen, 1957	13	12	10(27)
	Milt Davis, 1957	13	12	10(27)
	Don Doll, 1953	13	12	10(27)
	Goose Gonsoulin, 1960	13	14	11(14)
	Ron Hall, 1964	13	14	11(14)
	Howard Hartley, 1951	13	12	10(27)
	Lester Hayes, 1980	13	16	13(2)
	Don Hutson, 1943	13	10	8(142)
	Tom Keane, 1952	13	12	10(27)
	Night Train Lane, 1954	13	12	10(27)
	Ray Ramsey, 1953	13	12	10(27)
	Frank Reagan, 1947	13	12	10(27)
	Lee Riley, 1962	13	14	11(14)
	Frank Seno, 1947	13	12	10(27)
	Emlen Tunnell, 1949	13	12	10(27)
40	Dick Alban, 1954	12	12	9(71)
	Bibbles Bawel, 1955	12	12	9(71)
	Don Burroughs, 1955	12	12	9(71)
	Jack Butler, 1953	12	12	9(71)
	Jack Butler, 1958	12	12	9(71)
	Jerry Davis, 1950	12	12	9(71)
	Bobby Dillon, 1953	12	12	9(71)
	Bobby Dillon, 1955	12	12	9(71)
	Bobby Dillon, 1957	12	12	9(71)
	Bob Forte, 1947	12	12	9(71)
	Tommy James, 1950	12	12	9(71)
	Frank Reagan, 1948	12	12	9(71)
	Mike Reinfeldt, 1979	12	16	12(5)
	Bob Smith, 1949	12	12	9(71)
	Bob Smith, 1952	12	12	9(71)
	John Symank, 1957	12	12	9(71)
	Emlen Tunnell, 1951	12	12	9(71)
	Bulldog Turner, 1942	12	11	8(142)
	Lowell Wagner, 1951	12	12	9(71)
	Everson Walls, 1982	12	9	7
60	46 players tied			11

SACKS

	NAME	ADJ	G	UNADJ
1	Michael Strahan, 2001	22.5	16	22.5(1)
2	Mark Gastineau, 1984	22.0	16	22.0(2)
3	Chris Doleman, 1989	21.0	16	21.0(3)
	Reggie White, 1987	21.0	15	21.0(3)
5	Lawrence Taylor, 1986	20.5	16	20.5(5)
6	Derrick Thomas, 1990	20.0	16	20.0(6)
7	Tim Harris, 1989	19.5	16	19.5(7)
8	Mark Gastineau, 1983	19.0	16	19.0(8)
	Clyde Simmons, 1992	19.0	16	19.0(8)
	Bruce Smith, 1990	19.0	16	19.0(8)
11	Dexter Manley, 1986	18.5	16	18.5(11)
	Michael Strahan, 2003	18.5	16	18.5(11)
	Jason Taylor, 2002	18.5	16	18.5(11)
	Andre Tippett, 1984	18.5	16	18.5(11)
15	Keith Millard, 1989	18.0	16	18.0(15)
	Reggie White, 1986	18.0	16	18.0(15)
	Reggie White, 1988	18.0	16	18.0(15)
18	Fred Dean, 1983	17.5	16	17.5(18)
	Richard Dent, 1984	17.5	16	17.5(18)
	Bryce Paup, 1995	17.5	16	17.5(18)
21	Kevin Carter, 1999	17.0	16	17.0(21)
	Richard Dent, 1985	17.0	16	17.0(21)
	La'Roi Glover, 2000	17.0	16	17.0(21)
	Tim Harris, 1992	17.0	16	17.0(21)
	Leslie O'Neal, 1992	17.0	16	17.0(21)
	Pat Swilling, 1991	17.0	16	17.0(21)
27	Trace Armstrong, 2000	16.5	16	16.5(27)
	Kevin Greene, 1988	16.5	16	16.5(27)
	Kevin Greene, 1989	16.5	16	16.5(27)
	Simeon Rice, 1999	16.5	16	16.5(27)
	Warren Sapp, 2000	16.5	16	16.5(27)
	Michael Sinclair, 1998	16.5	16	16.5(27)
	Pat Swilling, 1989	16.5	16	16.5(27)
	Andre Tippett, 1985	16.5	16	16.5(27)
35	Doug Betters, 1983	16.0	16	16.0(35)
	Greg Brown, 1984	16.0	16	16.0(35)
	Derrick Burgess, 2005	16.0	16	16.0(35)
	Simon Fletcher, 1992	16.0	16	16.0(35)
	Dwight Freeney, 2004	16.0	16	16.0(35)
	Jacob Green, 1983	16.0	16	16.0(35)
	Curtis Greer, 1983	16.0	16	16.0(35)
	Charles Haley, 1990	16.0	16	16.0(35)
	Reggie White, 1998	16.0	16	16.0(35)
44	Sean Jones, 1986	15.5	16	15.5(44)
	Leonard Marshall, 1985	15.5	16	15.5(44)
	Wayne Martin, 1992	15.5	16	15.5(44)
	John Randle, 1997	15.5	16	15.5(44)
	Simeon Rice, 2002	15.5	16	15.5(44)
	Clyde Simmons, 1989	15.5	16	15.5(44)
	Lawrence Taylor, 1988	15.5	16	15.5(44)
51	Peter Boulware, 2001	15.0	16	15.0(51)
	Chris Doleman, 1998	15.0	16	15.0(51)
	Hugh Douglas, 2000	15.0	16	15.0(51)
	William Fuller, 1991	15.0	16	15.0(51)
	Kevin Greene, 1998	15.0	16	15.0(51)
	Dexter Manley, 1985	15.0	16	15.0(51)
	Mike Merriweather, 1984	15.0	16	15.0(51)
	Adewale Ogunleye, 2003	15.0	16	15.0(51)
	Robert Porcher, 1999	15.0	16	15.0(51)
	Simeon Rice, 2003	15.0	16	15.0(51)
	Bruce Smith, 1986	15.0	16	15.0(51)
	Neil Smith, 1993	15.0	16	15.0(51)
	Michael Strahan, 1998	15.0	16	15.0(51)
	Dana Stubblefield, 1997	15.0	16	15.0(51)
	Lawrence Taylor, 1989	15.0	16	15.0(51)
	Reggie White, 1991	15.0	16	15.0(51)
	Lee Williams, 1986	15.0	16	15.0(51)
68	Bertrand Berry, 2004	14.5	16	14.5(68)
	Jeff Bryant, 1984	14.5	16	14.5(68)
	Chris Doleman, 1992	14.5	16	14.5(68)
	Kevin Greene, 1996	14.5	16	14.5(68)
	Ezra Johnson, 1983	14.5	16	14.5(68)
	Jevon Kearse, 1999	14.5	16	14.5(68)
	Leonard Little, 2001	14.5	16	14.5(68)
	Charles Mann, 1985	14.5	16	14.5(68)
	Michael McCrary, 1998	14.5	16	14.5(68)
	Neil Smith, 1992	14.5	16	14.5(68)
	Art Still, 1984	14.5	16	14.5(68)
	Jason Taylor, 2000	14.5	16	14.5(68)
	Derrick Thomas, 1992	14.5	16	14.5(68)
	Osi Umenyiora, 2005	14.5	16	14.5(68)
82	Doug Betters, 1984	14.0	16	14.0(82)
	Reggie Camp, 1984	14.0	16	14.0(82)
	Bryan Cox, 1992	14.0	16	14.0(82)
	Kevin Greene, 1994	14.0	16	14.0(82)
	Curtis Greer, 1984	14.0	16	14.0(82)
	Eric Hicks, 2000	14.0	16	14.0(82)
	Jim Jeffcoat, 1986	14.0	16	14.0(82)
	Cortez Kennedy, 1992	14.0	16	14.0(82)
	Freddie Joe Nunn, 1988	14.0	16	14.0(82)
	Simeon Rice, 2005	14.0	16	14.0(82)
	Bruce Smith, 1992	14.0	16	14.0(82)
	Bruce Smith, 1993	14.0	16	14.0(82)
	Bruce Smith, 1997	14.0	16	14.0(82)
	Michael Strahan, 1997	14.0	16	14.0(82)
	Reggie White, 1990	14.0	16	14.0(82)
	Reggie White, 1992	14.0	16	14.0(82)
	Lee Williams, 1989	14.0	16	14.0(82)
	Keith Willis, 1983	14.0	16	14.0(82)

OVERALL RANK			
NAME	ADJ	G	UNADJ
1 O.J. Simpson, 1975	2543	14	2225(11)
2 Daunte Culpepper, 2004	**2540**	**16**	**2540(1)**
3 Walter Payton, 1977	2516	14	2202(15)
4 O.J. Simpson, 1973	2465	14	2157(24)
5 Jim Brown, 1963	2437	14	2132(27)
6 Jim Brown, 1958	2400	12	1800(115)
7 Randall Cunningham, 1990	2355	16	2355(2)
8 Jeff Garcia, 2000	**2348**	**16**	**2348(3)**
9 Terrell Davis, 1998	2337	16	2337(4)
10 Barry Sanders, 1997	2331	16	2331(5)
11 Jamal Lewis, 2003	**2309**	**16**	**2309(6)**
12 Steve Young, 1998	2299	16	2299(7)
13 Eric Dickerson, 1984	2275	16	2275(8)
14 Rich Gannon, 2002	2261	16	2261(9)
15 Ahman Green, 2003	**2242**	**16**	**2242(10)**
16 Tiki Barber, 2005	**2225**	**16**	**2225(11)**
Warren Moon, 1990	2225	16	2225(11)
18 Gale Sayers, 1966	2218	14	1941(68)
19 Emmitt Smith, 1995	2211	16	2211(14)
20 Eric Dickerson, 1983	2200	16	2200(16)
Ricky Williams, 2002	**2200**	**16**	**2200(16)**
22 Jim Brown, 1965	2197	14	1923(72)
23 Shaun Alexander, 2005	**2194**	**16**	**2194(18)**
24 Priest Holmes, 2002	**2176**	**16**	**2176(19)**
25 LaDainian Tomlinson, 2003	**2173**	**16**	**2173(20)**
26 Marcus Allen, 1985	2170	16	2170(21)
27 Peyton Manning, 2004	**2162**	**16**	**2162(22)**
28 Edgerrin James, 2000	**2161**	**16**	**2161(23)**
29 Jamal Anderson, 1998	2156	16	2156(25)
30 Steve Young, 1992	2155	16	2155(26)
31 Larry Johnson, 2005	**2127**	**16**	**2127(28)**
32 Otis Armstrong, 1974	2126	14	1861(93)
33 Jim Brown, 1959	2123	12	1592(259)
Steve Young, 1994	2123	16	2123(29)
35 Earl Campbell, 1980	2121	16	2121(30)
36 Steve Van Buren, 1945	2116	10	1323
37 Barry Sanders, 1994	2100	16	2100(31)
38 Dan Marino, 1984	2095	16	2095(32)
39 Michael Vick, 2002	**2093**	**16**	**2093(33)**
40 Brett Favre, 1995	**2088**	**16**	**2088(34)**
41 LaDainian Tomlinson, 2002	**2073**	**16**	**2073(35)**
42 Randall Cunningham, 1988	2068	16	2068(36)
43 Emmitt Smith, 1992	2066	16	2066(37)
44 Gale Sayers, 1965	2063	14	1805(112)
45 Eric Dickerson, 1986	2046	16	2046(38)
46 Terrell Davis, 1997	2044	16	2044(39)
47 Priest Holmes, 2003	**2035**	**16**	**2035(40)**
48 Daunte Culpepper, 2000	**2034**	**16**	**2034(41)**
49 James Wilder, 1984	2030	16	2030(42)
50 Jim Brown, 1961	2024	14	1771(135)
51 Donovan McNabb, 2004	**2023**	**16**	**2023(43)**
52 Neil Lomax, 1984	2021	16	2021(44)
53 Terry Metcalf, 1975	2012	14	1761(145)
54 Marshall Faulk, 1999	**2000**	**16**	**2000(45)**
55 Marshall Faulk, 2000	**1997**	**16**	**1997(46)**
56 Edgerrin James, 1999	**1996**	**16**	**1996(47)**
57 Eric Dickerson, 1988	1993	16	1993(48)
Scott Mitchell, 1995	1993	16	1993(48)
59 Rich Gannon, 2000	1984	16	1984(50)
60 Deuce McAllister, 2003	**1979**	**16**	**1979(51)**
61 Barry Foster, 1992	1972	16	1972(52)
Walter Payton, 1984	1972	16	1972(52)
63 Dan Fouts, 1982	1964	9	1105
Kurt Warner, 1999	**1964**	**16**	**1964(54)**
65 O.J. Simpson, 1976	1963	14	1718(165)
66 William Andrews, 1983	1962	16	1962(55)
Jim Taylor, 1962	1962	14	1717(166)
68 Shaun Alexander, 2004	**1961**	**16**	**1961(56)**
69 Donovan McNabb, 2000	**1959**	**16**	**1959(57)**
70 Gerald Riggs, 1985	1953	16	1953(58)
71 Ken Anderson, 1981	1952	16	1952(59)
Priest Holmes, 2001	**1952**	**16**	**1952(59)**
73 Jim Brown, 1964	1951	14	1708(172)
Mack Herron, 1974	1951	14	1707(174)
75 Curtis Martin, 2004	**1950**	**16**	**1950(61)**
76 Walter Payton, 1979	1949	16	1949(62)
77 Tiki Barber, 2004	**1947**	**16**	**1947(63)**
78 Walter Payton, 1985	1946	16	1946(64)
79 Steve Young, 1993	1945	16	1945(65)
80 Steve Beuerlein, 1999	1942	16	1942(66)
Dan Fouts, 1981	1942	16	1942(66)
82 Rich Gannon, 2001	1940	16	1940(69)
83 Earl Campbell, 1979	1934	16	1934(70)
84 Marshall Faulk, 2001	**1930**	**16**	**1930(71)**
85 Joe Montana, 1982	1919	9	1080
86 Garrison Hearst, 1998	1918	16	1918(73)
87 Joe Montana, 1983	1909	16	1909(74)
88 Ken Anderson, 1982	1907	9	1073
89 Timmy Brown, 1963	1905	14	1667(194)
Mark Brunell, 1996	**1905**	**16**	**1905(75)**
Thurman Thomas, 1992	1905	16	1905(75)
92 Peyton Manning, 2003	**1904**	**16**	**1904(77)**
93 Don Majkowski, 1989	1902	16	1902(78)
94 Peyton Manning, 2000	**1898**	**16**	**1898(79)**
95 John Elway, 1993	1893	16	1893(80)
96 Steve McNair, 1998	**1888**	**16**	**1888(81)**
Clinton Portis, 2003	**1888**	**16**	**1888(81)**
98 Daunte Culpepper, 2003	**1887**	**16**	**1887(83)**
99 Eddie George, 2000	1886	16	1886(84)

CHRONOLOGY OF NFL RECORDS

Most fans know that Emmitt Smith holds the NFL career rushing record and that Walter Payton and Jim Brown held it before him. But whose record did Jim Brown break? (Joe Perry's.) And who held it before that? (Steve Van Buren.) The chronology of National Football League records is a layering of history. The league did not begin 85 years ago with an array of icons holding every major record. Men whose names mean little to most modern readers slugged it out in front of only hundreds of fans—on dusty fields in obscure locations, never dreaming of the fame, riches, and success that would await those to come.

Official records were not kept during the league's first dozen seasons, but marks are known for categories such as years of service. George Halas began an association with a team, the Decatur Staleys, and a league, the American Professional Football Association, which would last for six decades. His team would transform itself into a powerhouse known as the Chicago Bears and his league would become the National Football League, the most potent assemblage of sports franchises in the country. While his longevity mark as a player was surpassed in 1929, Halas outlasted everyone as a head coach.

Papa Bear passed longtime rival Curly Lambeau of the Green Bay Packers for most years as a head coach, and then passed him for most career wins—and losses—during his 40-year tenure calling the plays for the Bears. (His record for longevity as a head coach seems pretty safe, given that Halas also owned the team.) Don Shula eventually broke his record for most wins, and so too did Tom Landry surpass Halas for most losses. Dan Reeves later exceeded Landry for the top spot in that category. Not all records are necessarily bad for the person who was superseded.

Not all record-setters are well known. Todd Heap, for example, set the NFL record in 2003 by scoring four two-point conversions as a member of the Baltimore Ravens—he actually had more two-point conversions than touchdowns that year. Heap's example also shows how records can go from one league to another. Heap broke a mark originally set by Gino Cappelletti of the Boston Patriots in the first year of the American Football League in 1960. The mark was tied the next year by Richie Lucas of the Buffalo Bills and lay dormant for 33 more years with the AFL joining the NFL and the two-point conversion fading into the deepest recesses of memory in the pro game. The rule was added much later to spice up the NFL in 1994, and all AFL stats were folded into those of the NFL after the merger. Tom Tupa, a punter for the Cleveland Browns, scored the first two-point conversion since the merger in the 1994 season opener against Cincinnati. Tupa, the holder on extra points as well as a former quarterback, managed to tie the single-season record with two more two-pointers that year. Ronnie Harmon of the San Diego Chargers and Haywood Jeffires of the Houston Oilers—playing for a pair of old AFL franchises, no less—also scored three two-point conversions. Six more players would match the mark until Heap climbed on top in 2003.

Granted, that's not the kind of important mark for career rushing yardage or most wins and losses by a head coach, but it illustrates the ups and downs that a record can have. That's what this section is all about. And what's best about this section is that the players who came before aren't expunged from the books. Even in the All-Time Leaders section, with normalized numbers that allow for comparisons between eras, the early record holders generally fade away as their achievements are quickly surpassed by later generations of players who play more games under different rules.

This section honors those who set the standard in their day, knowing that the old cliché would eventually rear its head: that records really were meant to be broken. Here is the chronicle of just how that came to pass and who was passed in the process.

Since official statistics weren't kept until 1932, most of the records date back to that year. Scoring plays and records are available for earlier games and those have been used where possible. References for this section include several editions of *The NFL Record Manual* and *The NFL Record and Fact Book*. The second edition of *Total Football*, published in 1999, was used as a source for single-season and career data since it contained the latest official stats.

One exception is sacks, which became an official statistic only in 1982 and are difficult to track before that. For scoring records, the source was the scoring summaries compiled by Pro Football Researchers Association members along with some data compiled from other sources.

AFL and NFL stats are considered one and the same in this section, following the ruling made after the merger of the two leagues in 1970. (Records originally set in the AFL are indicated with an asterisk, however.) Thus George Blanda set the NFL record for TD passes in a year (1961) while he was playing for the Oilers in the AFL. At that time, Sonny Jurgensen was credited with tying Johnny Unitas's mark of 32 touchdown passes in 1961; Y.A. Tittle was credited with breaking it with 33 in 1962 and 36 in 1963, retiring as the single-season leader in the category. For the purpose of record-keeping throughout this book, the NFL and AFL are considered equals, but the reader should be aware that this was not the case when some of these records were set.

Although a few players fall through the cracks, this section revives many names long forgotten as all-time leaders in pro football history. Once a player sets a record and maintains it through the end of a given season, he's in this section forever. It's easy to see from the records they set how players such as Cliff Battles, Steve Van Buren, Sammy Baugh, and Don Hutson truly dominated their eras.

SERVICE

MOST SEASONS AS PLAYER

9   George Halas, 1920–28
    Paddy Driscoll, 1920–28
    Jimmy Conzelman, 1920–20–28
    Al Nesser, 1920–28
10 Paddy Driscoll, 1920–29
    Jimmy Conzelman, 1920–29
    George Trafton, 1920–21, 23–30
    Jug Earp, 1921–30
11 George Trafton, 1920–21, 1923–31
    Jug Earp, 1921–31
12 George Trafton, 1920–21, 1923–32
    Jug Earp, 1921–32
    Johnny Blood, 1925–36
13 Johnny Blood, 1925–37
14 Johnny Blood, 1925–38
    Mel Hein, 1931–44
15 Mel Hein, 1931–45
    Sammy Baugh, 1937–51
16 Sammy Baugh, 1937–52
    George Blanda, 1949–58, 1960–65
17 George Blanda, 1949–58, 1960–66
18 George Blanda, 1949–58, 1960–67
19 George Blanda, 1949–58, 1960–68
20 George Blanda, 1949–58, 1960–69
21 George Blanda, 1949–58, 1960–70
22 George Blanda, 1949–58, 1960–71
23 George Blanda, 1949–58, 1960–72
24 George Blanda, 1949–58, 1960–73
25 George Blanda, 1949–58, 1960–74
26 George Blanda, 1949–58, 1960–75

MOST GAMES AS PLAYER

59   George Halas, 1920–24
76   George Halas, 1920–25
91   George Halas, 1920–26
101 George Halas, 1920–27
105 George Halas, 1920–28
118 Paddy Driscoll, 1920–29
127 George Trafton, 1920–21, 1923–30
138 George Trafton, 1920–21, 1923–31
149 George Trafton, 1920–21, 1923–32
150 Mel Hein, 1931–43
160 Mel Hein, 1931–44
170 Mel Hein, 1931–45
175 Bobby Layne, 1948–62
176 Y.A. Tittle, 1950–64
186 George Blanda, 1949–58, 1960–64
200 George Blanda, 1949–58, 1961–65
214 George Blanda, 1949–58, 1960–66
228 George Blanda, 1949–58, 1960–67
242 George Blanda, 1949–58, 1960–68
256 George Blanda, 1949–58, 1960–69
270 George Blanda, 1949–58, 1960–70
284 George Blanda, 1949–58, 1960–71
298 George Blanda, 1949–58, 1960–72
312 George Blanda, 1949–58, 1960–73
326 George Blanda, 1949–58, 1960–74
340 George Blanda, 1949–58, 1960–75
354 Morten Andersen, 1982–2004

MOST SEASONS ONE CLUB

9   George Halas, 1920–28
    George Trafton, 1920–21, 1923–29
10 George Trafton, 1920–21, 1923–30
11 George Trafton, 1920–21, 1923–31
12 George Trafton, 1920–21, 1923–32
    Mel Hein, 1931–42
13 Mel Hein, 1931–43
14 Mel Hein, 1931–44

MOST SEASONS ONE CLUB

15 Mel Hein, 1931–45
    Sammy Baugh, 1937–51
16 Sammy Baugh, 1937–52
    Lou Groza, 1950–59, 1961–66
17 Lou Groza, 1950–59, 1961–67
    John Unitas, 1956–72
    Jim Marshall, 1961–77
18 Jim Marshall, 1961–78
19 Jim Marshall, 1971–79
    Jackie Slater, 1976–94
20 Jackie Slater, 1977–95
    Darrell Green, 1983–2002

MOST CONSECUTIVE GAMES PLAYED

114 Sid Luckman, 1939–49
     Emlen Tunnell, 1948–57
126 Emlen Tunnell, 1948–58
138 Emlen Tunnell, 1948–59
150 Emlen Tunnell, 1948–60
158 Emlen Tunnell, 1948–61
160 Leo Nomellini, 1950–62
174 Leo Nomellini, 1950–63
180 Dick Modzelewski, 1953–66
182 Jim Ringo, 1953–67
187 Forrest Gregg, 1956, 1958–70
188 Forrest Gregg, 1956, 1958–71
196 George Blanda, 1960–73
     Jim Otto, 1960–73
210 Jim Otto, 1960–74
     George Blanda, 1960–74
224 George Blanda, 1960–75
236 Jim Marshall, 1960–76
250 Jim Marshall, 1960–77
266 Jim Marshall, 1960–78
282 Jim Marshall, 1960–79
288 Jeff Feagles, 1988–2005

HEAD COACH

MOST SEASONS AS HEAD COACH

10 George Halas, 1920–29
    Curly Lambeau, 1921–30
11 Curly Lambeau, 1921–31
12 Curly Lambeau, 1921–32
13 Curly Lambeau, 1921–33
14 Curly Lambeau, 1921–34
15 Curly Lambeau, 1921–35
16 Curly Lambeau, 1921–36
17 Curly Lambeau, 1921–37
18 Curly Lambeau, 1921–38
19 Curly Lambeau, 1921–39
20 Curly Lambeau, 1921–40
21 Curly Lambeau, 1921–41
22 Curly Lambeau, 1921–42
23 Curly Lambeau, 1921–43
24 Curly Lambeau, 1921–44
25 Curly Lambeau, 1921–45
26 Curly Lambeau, 1921–46
27 Curly Lambeau, 1921–47
28 Curly Lambeau, 1921–48
29 Curly Lambeau, 1921–49
30 Curly Lambeau, 1921–50
31 Curly Lambeau, 1921–51
32 Curly Lambeau, 1921–52
33 Curly Lambeau, 1921–53
    George Halas, 1920–29, 1933–42, 1946–55,
    1958–60
34 George Halas, 1920–29, 1933–42, 1946–55,
    1958–61
35 George Halas, 1920–29, 1933–42, 1946–55,
    1958–62
36 George Halas, 1920–29, 1933–42, 1946–55,
    1958–63
37 George Halas, 1920–29, 1933–42, 1946–55,
    1958–64
38 George Halas, 1920–28, 1933–42, 1946–55,
    1958–65
39 George Halas, 1920–29, 1933–42, 1946–55,
    1958–66
40 George Halas, 1920–29, 1933–42, 1946–55,
    1958–67

MOST GAMES WON AS HEAD COACH

19   George Halas, 1920–21
28   George Halas, 1920–22
37   George Halas, 1920–23
43   George Halas, 1920–24
52   George Halas, 1920–25
64   George Halas, 1920–26
73   George Halas, 1920–27
80   George Halas, 1920–28
84   George Halas, 1920–29
93   Curly Lambeau, 1921–32
98   Curly Lambeau, 1921–33
107 George Halas, 1920–29, 1933–34
113 George Halas, 1920–29, 1933–35
     Curly Lambeau, 1921–35
123 Curly Lambeau, 1921–36
131 George Halas, 1920–29, 1933–37
138 Curly Lambeau, 1921–38
147 Curly Lambeau, 1921–39
153 Curly Lambeau, 1921–40
     George Halas, 1920–29, 1933–40
163 George Halas, 1920–29, 1933–41
     Curly Lambeau, 1921–41
171 Curly Lambeau, 1921–42
178 Curly Lambeau, 1921–43
186 Curly Lambeau, 1921–44
192 Curly Lambeau, 1921–45
198 Curly Lambeau, 1921–46

MOST GAMES WON AS HEAD COACH (CONT.)

204 Curly Lambeau, 1921–47
207 Curly Lambeau, 1921–48
209 Curly Lambeau, 1921–49
214 Curly Lambeau, 1921–50
219 George Halas, 1920–29, 1933–42, 1946–51
224 George Halas, 1920–29, 1933–42, 1946–52
227 George Halas, 1920–29, 1933–42, 1946–53
235 George Halas, 1920–29, 1933–42, 1946–54
243 George Halas, 1920–29, 1933–42, 1946–55
251 George Halas, 1920–29, 1933–42, 1946–55,
     1958
259 George Halas, 1920–29, 1933–42, 1946–55,
     1958–59
264 George Halas, 1920–29, 1933–42, 1946–55,
     1958–60
272 George Halas, 1920–29, 1933–42, 1946–55,
     1958–61
281 George Halas, 1920–29, 1933–42, 1946–55,
     1958–62
292 George Halas, 1920–29, 1933–42, 1946–55,
     1958–63
297 George Halas, 1920–29, 1933–42, 1946–55,
     1958–64
306 George Halas, 1920–29, 1933–42, 1946–55,
     1958–65
311 George Halas, 1920–29, 1933–42, 1946–55,
     1958–66
318 George Halas, 1920–29, 1933–42, 1946–55,
     1958–67
319 Don Shula, 1963–94
328 Don Shula, 1963–95

MOST GAMES LOST AS HEAD COACH

14   Ted Nesser, 1920–21
15   Jim Thorpe, 1920–22
25   Jim Thorpe, 1920–23
26   Carl Storck, 1922–26
31   George Halas, 1920–29
32   Jimmy Conzelman, 1921–23, 1925–30
33   Curly Lambeau, 1921–32
40   Curly Lambeau, 1921–33
46   Curly Lambeau, 1921–34
50   Curly Lambeau, 1921–35
51   Curly Lambeau, 1921–36
55   Curly Lambeau, 1921–37
58   Curly Lambeau, 1921–38
60   Curly Lambeau, 1921–39
64   Curly Lambeau, 1921–40
65   Curly Lambeau, 1921–41
67   Curly Lambeau, 1921–42
69   Curly Lambeau, 1921–43
71   Curly Lambeau, 1921–44
75   Curly Lambeau, 1921–45
80   Curly Lambeau, 1921–46
85   Curly Lambeau, 1921–47
94   Curly Lambeau, 1921–48
104 Curly Lambeau, 1921–49
111 Curly Lambeau, 1921–50

MOST GAMES LOST AS HEAD COACH

119 Curly Lambeau, 1921–51
127 Curly Lambeau, 1922–52
132 Curly Lambeau, 1922–53
135 Halas, 1920–29, 1933–42, 1946–55, 1958–65
142 Halas, 1920–29, 1933–42, 1946–55, 1958–66
148 Halas, 1920–29, 1933–42, 1946–55, 1958–67
149 Tom Landry, 1960–87
162 Tom Landry, 1960–88
166 Dan Reeves, 1981–2003

SCORING

MOST SEASONS SCORING LEADER

2   Paddy Driscoll, 1923, 1926
    Jack McBride, 1927, 1930
    Dutch Clark, 1932, 1935
3   Dutch Clark, 1932, 1935, 1936
    Don Hutson, 1940–42
4   Don Hutson, 1940–43
5   Don Hutson, 1940–44
    Gino Cappelletti, 1961, 1963–66*

MOST CONS SEASONS SCORING LEADER

2   Dutch Clark, 1935–36
    Don Hutson, 1940–41
3   Don Hutson, 1940–42
4   Don Hutson, 1940–43
5   Don Hutson, 1940–44

POINTS

MOST POINTS SCORED, CAREER
77	Dutch Sternaman, 1920–22
143	Paddy Driscoll, 1920–23
177	Paddy Driscoll, 1920–24
244	Paddy Driscoll, 1920–25
330	Paddy Driscoll, 1920–26
373	Paddy Driscoll, 1920–27
393	Paddy Driscoll, 1920–28
402	Paddy Driscoll, 1920–29
524	Don Hutson, 1935–42
641	Don Hutson, 1935–43
726	Don Hutson, 1935–44
823	Don Hutson, 1935–45
833	Bobby Walston, 1951–61
902	Lou Groza, 1950–59, 1961–62
987	Lou Groza, 1950–59, 1961–63
1102	Lou Groza, 1950–59, 1961–64
1195	Lou Groza, 1950–59, 1961–65
1273	Lou Groza, 1950–59, 1961–66
1349	Lou Groza, 1950–60, 1961–67
1477	George Blanda, 1949–58, 1960–69
1561	George Blanda, 1949–58, 1960–70
1647	George Blanda, 1949–58, 1960–71
1742	George Blanda, 1949–58, 1960–72
1842	George Blanda, 1949–58, 1960–73
1919	George Blanda, 1949–58, 1960–74
2002	George Blanda, 1949–58, 1960–75
2059	Gary Anderson, 1982–2000
2133	Gary Anderson, 1982–2001
2223	Gary Anderson, 1982–2002
2346	Gary Anderson, 1982–2003
2434	Gary Anderson, 1982–2004

MOST POINTS SCORED, SEASON
47	Elmer Oliphant, 1921
52	Hank Gillo, 1922
78	Paddy Driscoll, 1923
86	Paddy Driscoll, 1926
95	Don Hutson, 1941
138	Don Hutson, 1942
176	Paul Hornung, 1960

MOST POINTS SCORED, ROOKIE SEASON
32	Benny Boynton, 1921
	Joey Sternaman, 1922
37	Gus Tebell, 1923
72	Tex Hamer, 1924
	Bill Paschal, 1943
128	Doak Walker, 1950
132	Gale Sayers, 1965
144	Kevin Butler, 1985

MOST POINTS SCORED, NO TDS, SEASON
24	Russ Hathaway, 1921
31	Frank Morrissey, 1923
38	Jim Welsh, 1924
45	Bob Snyder, 1943
51	Ward Cuff, 1947
74	Cliff Patton, 1948
89	Lou Groza, 1952
108	Lou Groza, 1953
112	George Blanda, 1962*
115	Lou Groza, 1964
	Jim Bakken, 1964
	Pete Gogolak, 1965*
117	Jim Bakken, 1967
145	Jim Turner, 1968*
161	Mark Moseley, 1983
164	Gary Anderson, 1998

MOST SEASONS SCORING 100 POINTS
2	Don Hutson, 1942, 43
	Pat Harder, 1947–48
3	Pat Harder, 1947–49
	Gino Cappelletti, 1961–63*
4	Gino Cappelletti, 1961–64*
5	Gino Cappelletti, 1961–65*
6	Gino Cappelletti, 1961–66*
	George Blanda, 1960–61, 1967–69, 1973
	Bruce Gossett, 1966–67, 1969–71, 1973
	Jan Stenerud, 1967–71, 1981
7	Jan Stenerud, 1967–71, 1981, 1983
	Nick Lowery, 1981, 1983–86, 1988–89
8	Nick Lowery, 1981, 1983–86, 1988–90
9	Nick Lowery, 1981, 1983–86, 1988–91
10	Nick Lowery, 1981, 1983–86, 1988–92
11	Nick Lowery, 1981, 1983–86, 1988–93
	Morten Andersen, 1985–89, 1991–95, 1997
12	Morten Andersen, 85–89, 1991–95, 1997–98
	Gary Anderson, 1983–85, 1988, 1991–94, 1996–99

MOST SEASONS SCORING 100 POINTS (CONT.)
13	Gary Anderson, 1983–85, 1988, 1991–94, 1996–2000
	Morten Andersen, 1985–89, 1991–95, 1997–98, 2002
14	Morten Andersen, 1985–89, 1991–95, 1997–98, 2002–03
	Gary Anderson, 1983–85, 1988, 1991–94, 1996–2000, 2003

MOST POINTS SCORED, GAME
24	Frank Bacon, Day-Col, 10-2-21
	Herb Henderson, Evv-Ham, 10–16–21
	Doc Elliott, Cle-Mil, 11–27–24
30	Jimmy Conzelman, RI-Evv, 10–15–22
40	Ernie Nevers, ChiC-ChiB, 11–28–29

MOST CONSECUTIVE GAMES SCORING
10	Dutch Sternaman, 1921
16	Pete Henry, 1922–23
19	Pete Henry, 1922–23, 1925
24	Don Hutson, 1940–42
34	Don Hutson, 1940–43
40	Don Hutson, 1940–44
45	Lou Groza, 1950–53
57	Lou Groza, 1950–54
69	Lou Groza, 1950–55
81	Lou Groza, 1950–56
93	Lou Groza, 1950–57
105	Lou Groza, 1950–58
107	Lou Groza, 1950–59

MOST CONSECUTIVE GAMES SCORING
110	Sam Baker, 1962–69
112	Fred Cox, 1963–70
126	Fred Cox, 1963–71
140	Fred Cox, 1963–72
151	Fred Cox, 1963–73
165	Jim Breech, 1979–90
181	Jim Breech, 1979–91
186	Jim Breech, 1979–92
190	Morten Andersen, 1983–95
206	Morten Andersen, 1983–96
222	Morten Andersen, 1983–97
238	Morten Andersen, 1983–98
254	Morten Andersen, 1983–99
270	Morten Andersen, 1983–2000
286	Morten Andersen, 1983–2001
300	Morten Andersen, 1983–2002
316	Morten Andersen, 1983–2003
332	Morten Andersen, 1983–2004

POINTS: TOUCHDOWNS

MOST SEASONS TOUCHDOWN LEADER
2	Tex Hamer, 1924, 1925
	Paddy Driscoll, 1923, 1927
	Vern Lewellen, 1928, 1930
	Don Hutson, 1935–36
3	Don Hutson, 1935–37
4	Don Hutson, 1935–38
5	Don Hutson, 1935–38, 1941
6	Don Hutson, 1935–38, 1941–42
7	Don Hutson, 1935–38, 1941–43
8	Don Hutson, 1935–38, 1941–44

MOST CONSECUTIVE SEASONS TD LEADER
2	Tex Hamer, 1924–25
	Don Hutson, 1935–36
3	Don Hutson, 1935–37
4	Don Hutson, 1935–38
	Don Hutson, 1941–44

MOST TOUCHDOWNS SCORED, CAREER
11	Carl Cramer, 1920–22
13	Jimmy Conzelman, 1920–23
14	Jimmy Conzelman, 1920–24
	Guy Chamberlin, 1920–24
19	Joey Sternaman, 1922–25
23	Ben Jones, 1923–26
	Paddy Driscoll, 1920–26
28	Paddy Driscoll, 1920–27
30	Paddy Driscoll, 1920–28
35	Vern Lewellen, 1924–29
44	Vern Lewellen, 1924–30
50	Vern Lewellen, 1924–31
51	Vern Lewellen, 1924–32
57	Don Hutson, 1935–41
74	Don Hutson, 1935–42
86	Don Hutson, 1935–43
95	Don Hutson, 1935–44
105	Don Hutson, 1935–45
	Don Hutson, Jim Brown, 1957–64

MOST TOUCHDOWNS SCORED, CAREER (CONT.)
126	Jim Brown, 1957–65
139	Jerry Rice, 1985–94
156	Jerry Rice, 1985–95
165	Jerry Rice, 1985–96
166	Jerry Rice, 1985–97
175	Jerry Rice, 1985–98
180	Jerry Rice, 1985–99
187	Jerry Rice, 1985–2000
196	Jerry Rice, 1985–2001
203	Jerry Rice, 1985–2002
205	Jerry Rice, 1985–2003
208	Jerry Rice, 1985–2004

MOST TOUCHDOWNS SCORED, SEASON
7	Ookie Anderson, 1921
	Fritz Pollard, 1921
	Jimmy Conzelman, 1922
	Guy Chamberlin, 1922
	Paddy Driscoll, 1923
	Lou Smyth, 1923
12	Tex Hamer, 1924
	Ernie Nevers, 1929
14	Johnny Blood, 1931
17	Don Hutson, 1942
18	Steve Van Buren, 1945
	Jim Brown, 1958
	Bill Groman, 1961*
19	Jim Taylor, 1962
	Abner Haynes, 1962*
20	Lenny Moore, 1964
22	Gale Sayers, 1965
23	O.J. Simpson, 1975
24	John Riggins, 1983
25	Emmitt Smith, 1995
26	Marshall Faulk, 2000
27	Priest Holmes, 2003
28	Shaun Alexander, 2005

MOST TDS SCORED, ROOKIE SEASON
4	Herb Henderson, 1921
	Pete Stinchcomb, 1921
5	Joey Sternaman, 1922
	Dutch Lauer, 1922
6	Ben Jones, 1923
12	Tex Hamer, 1924
	Bill Paschal, 1943
13	Bill Howton, 1952
22	Gale Sayers, 1965

MOST TOUCHDOWNS SCORED, GAME
4	Frank Bacon, Day-Col, 10-2-21
	Herb Henderson, Evv-Ham, 10–16–21
	Doc Elliott, Cle-Mil, 11–27–24
5	Jimmy Conzelman, RI-EVV, 10–15–22
6	Ernie Nevers, ChiC-ChiB, 11–28–29
	Dub Jones, Cle-Chi, 11–25–51
	Gale Sayers, Chi-SF, 12–12–65

MOST CONSECUTIVE GAMES SCORING TDS
3	Fritz Pollard, 1921
	Ookie Anderson, 1921
	Johnny Scott, 1921
	Heinie Miller, 1921
	Duncan Annan, 1922
	Buck Gavin, 1922
	Dutch Sternaman, 1922
4	Guy Chamberlin, 1922
	Dutch Sternaman, 1923
	Tex Hamer, 1924
5	Tex Hamer, 1924–25
	Eddie Tryon, 1927
	Tony Latone, 1929
6	Beattie Feathers, 1934
7	John Drake, 1939
	Don Hutson, 1941–42
	Bill Paschal, 1943
	Don Hutson, 1943–44
8	Steve Van Buren, 1947
11	Elroy Hirsch, 1950–51
	Buddy Dial, 1959–60
17	Lenny Moore, 1963–64
18	Lenny Moore, 1963–65
	LaDainian Tomlinson, 2004–05

POINTS: EXTRA POINTS

MOST SEASONS EXTRA POINT LEADER
2	Jim Welch, 1924, 1926
	Jack McBride, 1926–27
	Benny Friedman, 1928–29
	Red Dunn, 1930–31

MOST SEASONS EXTRA POINT LEADER
- 2 Jack Manders, 1933–34
- 3 Jack Manders, 1933–35
-    Dutch Clark, 1932, 1935–36
-    Don Hutson, 1941–42, 1945
-    Bob Waterfield, 1945–46, 1950
- 4 Bob Waterfield, 1945–46, 1950, 1952
-    George Blanda, 1956, 1961–62, 1967
- 5 George Blanda, 1956, 1961–62, 1967–68
- 6 George Blanda, 1956, 1961–62, 1967–69
- 7 George Blanda, 1956, 1961–62, 1967–69, 1972
- 8 Blanda, 1956, 1961–62, 1967–69, 1972, 1974

MOST EXTRA POINT ATTEMPTS, CAREER
- 26 Elmer Oliphant, 1920–21
- 39 Pete Henry, 1920–23
- 44 Pete Henry, 1920–25
- 57 Paddy Driscoll, 1920–26
- 71 Paddy Driscoll, 1920–27
- 82 Paddy Driscoll, 1920–28
- 86 Paddy Driscoll, 1920–29
- 95 Red Dunn, 1924–30
- 115 Red Dunn, 1924–31
- 116 Jack Manders, 1933–38
- 136 Jack Manders, 1933–39
- 154 Jack Manders, 1933–40
- 184 Don Hutson, 1935–45
- 190 Bob Waterfield, 1945–49
- 248 Bob Waterfield, 1945–50
- 291 Bob Waterfield, 1945–51
- 336 Bob Waterfield, 1945–52
- 352 Lou Groza, 1950–59
- 390 Lou Groza, 1950–59, 1961
- 425 Lou Groza, 1950–59, 1961–62
- 468 Lou Groza, 1950–59, 1961–63
- 517 Lou Groza, 1950–59, 1961–64
- 562 Lou Groza, 1950–59, 1961–65
- 614 Lou Groza, 1950–59, 1961–66
- 657 Lou Groza, 1950–59, 1961–67
- 667 George Blanda, 1949–58, 1960–68
- 712 George Blanda, 1949–58, 1960–69
- 748 George Blanda, 1949–58, 1960–70
- 790 George Blanda, 1949–58, 1960–71
- 834 George Blanda, 1949–58, 1960–72
- 865 George Blanda, 1949–58, 1960–73
- 911 George Blanda, 1949–58, 1960–74
- 959 George Blanda, 1949–58, 1960–75

MOST EXTRA POINT ATTEMPTS, SEASON
- 26 Elmer Oliphant, 1921
- 30 Pete Henry, 1923
- 34 Charlie Berry, 1925
-    Don Hutson, 1942
- 42 Bob Snyder, 1943
- 52 Ray McLean, 1947
- 53 Pat Harder, 1948
- 58 Bob Waterfield, 1950
- 65 George Blanda, 1961*
- 70 Uwe Von Schamann, 1984

MOST EXTRA POINT ATTEMPTS, GAME
- 6 Russ Hathaway, Day-Col, 10-2-21
- 7 Elmer Oliphant, Buf-NYBG, 10-16-21
-    Frank Morrisey, Buf-OOr, 10-21-23
-    Riley Smith, Was-NYG, 12-5-37
-    Bob Snyder, Chi-PP, 10-17-43
- 8 Bob Snyder, Chi-NYG, 11-14-43
-    Don Hutson, GB-Det, 10-7-45
- 9 Pat Harder, ChiC-NYG, 10-17-48
-    Pat Harder, ChiC-NYB, 11-13-49
-    Bob Waterfield, LA-Bal, 10-22-50
- 10 Charley Gogolak, Was-NYG, 11-27-66

MOST EXTRA POINTS, CAREER
- 26 Elmer Oliphant, 1920–22
- 29 Pete Henry, 1920–23
- 35 Pete Henry, 1920–25
- 45 Paddy Driscoll, 1920–26
- 52 Paddy Driscoll, 1920–27
- 60 Paddy Driscoll, 1920–28
- 63 Paddy Driscoll, 1920–29
- 75 Red Dunn, 1924–31
-    Jack Manders, 1933–36
- 89 Jack Manders, 1933–37
- 99 Jack Manders, 1933–38
- 117 Jack Manders, 1933–39
- 133 Jack Manders, 1933–40
- 141 Don Hutson, 1935–44
- 172 Don Hutson, 1935–45
- 176 Bob Waterfield, 1945–49
- 230 Bob Waterfield, 1945–50
- 271 Bob Waterfield, 1945–51
- 315 Bob Waterfield, 1945–52
- 343 Lou Groza, 1950–59
- 380 Lou Groza, 1950–59, 1961

MOST EXTRA POINTS, CAREER (CONT.)
- 413 Lou Groza, 1950–59, 1961–62
- 453 Lou Groza, 1950–59, 1961–63
- 502 Lou Groza, 1950–59, 1961–64
- 547 Lou Groza, 1950–59, 1961–65
- 598 Lou Groza, 1950–59, 1961–66
- 641 Lou Groza, 1950–59, 1961–67
- 703 George Blanda, 1949–58, 1960–69
- 739 George Blanda, 1949–58, 1960–70
- 780 George Blanda, 1949–58, 1960–71
- 824 George Blanda, 1949–58, 1960–72
- 855 George Blanda, 1949–58, 1960–73
- 899 George Blanda, 1949–58, 1960–74
- 943 George Blanda, 1949–58, 1960–75

MOST EXTRA POINTS, SEASON
- 26 Elmer Oliphant, 1921
- 29 Charlie Berry, 1925
- 31 Jack Manders, 1934
- 33 Don Hutson, 1942
- 39 Bob Snyder, 1943
- 44 Ray McLean, 1947
- 53 Pat Harder, 1948
- 54 Bob Waterfield, 1950
- 64 George Blanda, 1961*
- 66 Uwe Von Schhamann, 1984

MOST EXTRA POINTS, GAME
- 6 Russ Hathaway, Day-Col, 10-2-21
- 7 Elmer Oliphant, Buf-NYBG, 10-16-21
-    Riley Smith, Was-NYG, 12-5-37
- 8 Bob Snyder, Chi-NYG, 11-14-43
- 9 Pat Harder, ChiC-NYG, 10-17-48
-    Bob Waterfield, LA-Bal, 10-22-50
-    Charley Gogolak, Was-NYG, 11-27-66

MOST CONSECUTIVE EXTRA POINTS
- 72 Jack Manders, 1933–37
- 84 Cliff Patton, 1947–49
- 104 Lou Groza, 1950–52
- 109 Lou Groza, 1950–53
- 143 George Blanda, 1951–55
- 156 George Blanda, 1951–56
- 156 Tommy Davis, 1959–63
- 186 Tommy Davis, 1959–64
- 234 Tommy Davis, 1959–65
- 250 Eddie Murray, 1988–95, 97
- 255 Norm Johnson, 1991–97
- 276 Norm Johnson, 1991–98
- 301 Norm Johnson, 1991–99
- 313 Jason Elam, 1993–2000
- 344 Jason Elam, 1993–2001
- 371 Jason Elam, 1993–2002

HIGHEST XP PCT., CAREER (200 XPA)
- 92.7 Bob Waterfield, 1945–50
- 93.1 Bob Waterfield, 1945–51
- 93.8 Bob Waterfield, 1945–52
- 98.7 Lou Groza, 1950–55
- 98.8 Lou Groza, 1950–56
- 99.1 George Blanda, 1949–57
- 98.8 George Blanda, 1949–58
- 98.7 George Blanda, 1949–58, 1960
- 98.6 George Blanda, 1949–58, 1960–61
- 98.5 George Blanda, 1949–58, 1960–62
- 98.7 George Blanda, 1949–58, 1960–63
- 98.6 George Blanda, 1949–58, 1960–64
- 99.6 Tommy Davis, 1959–65
- 99.3 Tommy Davis, 1959–66
- 99.4 Tommy Davis, 1959–67
- 99.5 Jim Bakken, 1962–68
- 99.4 Tommy Davis, 1959–68
- 99.5 Jan Stenerud, 1967–72
- 99.4 Tommy Davis, 1959–68
- 99.5 Chip Lohmiller, 1988–92
- 99.4 Tommy Davis, 1959–68
- 99.5 Jason Elam, 1993–97
- 99.6 Jason Elam, 1993–98
- 99.7 Jason Elam, 1993–99
- 100.0 Todd Peterson, 1994–2000
- 99.7 Jason Elam, 1993–2001
- 99.5 Jason Elam, 1993–2002
- 99.6 Mike Vanderjagt, 1998–2003
- 99.6 Jason Elam, 1993–2004
- 99.4 Jason Elam, 1993–2005

MOST EXTRA POINTS, NO MISSES, SEASON
- 26 Elmer Oliphant, 1921
- 36 Don Hutson, 1943
- 37 Bob Waterfield, 1946
- 53 Pat Harder, 1948
- 56 Danny Villanueva, 1966
-    Ray Wersching, 1984
-    Chip Lohmiller, 1991
- 59 Gary Anderson, 1998
- 64 Jeff Wilkins, 1999

MOST EXTRA POINTS, NO MISSES, GAME
- 6 Russ Hathaway, Day-Col, 10-2-21
- 7 Elmer Oliphant, Buf-NYBG, 10-16-21
-    Riley Smith, Was-NYG, 12-5-37
- 8 Bob Snyder, Chi-NYG, 11-14-43
- 9 Pat Harder, ChiC-NYG, 10-17-48
-    Bob Waterfield, LA-Bal, 10-22-50

MOST 2-PT. CONVERSIONS, CAREER
- 4 Gino Cappelletti, 1960–69
- 5 Terance Mathis, 1994–95
- 6 Terance Mathis, 1994–96
-    Marshall Faulk, 1994–2004
- 7 Marshall Faulk, 1994–2005

MOST 2-PT. CONVERSIONS, SEASON
- 3 Gino Cappelletti, 1960
-    Richie Lucas, 1961
-    Ronnie Harmon, 1994
-    Heywood Jeffires, 1994
-    Tom Tupa, 1994
-    Terance Mathis, 1995
-    Lamar Smith, 1996
-    Cris Carter, 1997
-    Terrell Davis, 1997
-    James Stewart, 2000
-    Hines Ward, 2002
- 4 Todd Heap, 2003

MOST 2-PT. COVERSIONS, GAME
- 1 by many, 1960–69
- 2 Brett Perriman, Det-GB, 11–6-94
-    Michael Jackson, Bal-NE, 10-6-96
-    Terrell Davis, Den-Atl, 9–28-97

MOST 2-PT. COVERSIONS, GAME
- 2 Charles Johnson, Pit-Ten, 11-1-98
-    Marshall Faulk, SL-Atl, 10-15-2000
-    Todd Heap, Bal-Cin, 10-19-03

POINTS: FIELD GOALS

MOST SEASONS FIELD GOAL LEADER
- 2 Paddy Driscoll, 1922–23
- 3 Paddy Driscoll, 1922–23, 1925
- 4 Paddy Driscoll, 1922–23, 1925–26
-    Jack Manders, 1933–34, 1936–37
-    Ward Cuff, 1938–39, 1943, 1947
-    Lou Groza, 1950, 1952–54
- 5 Lou Groza, 1950, 1952–54, 1957

MOST CONSECUTIVE SEASONS FG LEADER
- 2 Paddy Driscoll, 1922–23
-    Paddy Driscoll, 1925–26
-    Jack Manders, 1933–34
-    Armand Niccolai, 1935–36
-    Jack Manders, 1936–37
-    Ward Cuff, 1938–39
-    Cliff Patton, 1948–49
-    Lou Groza, 1952–53
- 3 Lou Groza, 1952–54

MOST FIELD GOAL ATTEMPTS, CAREER
- 15 Elmer Oliphant, 1920–21
- 23 Dutch Sternamam, 1920–22
- 37 Pete Henry, 1920–23
- 54 Paddy Driscoll, 1920–24
- 73 Paddy Driscoll, 1920–25
- 103 Paddy Driscoll, 1920–26
- 113 Paddy Driscoll, 1920–27
- 117 Paddy Driscoll, 1920–28
- 118 Paddy Driscoll, 1920–29
- 125 Lou Groza, 1950–54
- 147 Lou Groza, 1950–55
- 167 Lou Groza, 1950–56
- 189 Lou Groza, 1950–57
- 208 Lou Groza, 1950–58
- 224 Lou Groza, 1950–59
- 234 George Blanda, 1949–58, 1960
- 260 George Blanda, 1949–58, 1960–61
- 286 George Blanda, 1949–58, 1960–62
- 308 George Blanda, 1949–58, 1960–63
- 337 George Blanda, 1949–58, 1960–64
- 359 George Blanda, 1949–58, 1960–65
- 388 George Blanda, 1949–58, 1960–66
- 418 George Blanda, 1949–58, 1960–67
- 452 George Blanda, 1949–58, 1960–68
- 489 George Blanda, 1949–58, 1960–69
- 518 George Blanda, 1949–58, 1960–70
- 540 George Blanda, 1949–58, 1960–71
- 566 George Blanda, 1949–58, 1960–72
- 599 George Blanda, 1949–58, 1960–73
- 616 George Blanda, 1949–58, 1960–74
- 637 George Blanda, 1949–58, 1960–75

MOST FIELD GOAL ATTEMPTS, CAREER (CONT.)
650	Gary Anderson, 1982–2003
672	Gary Anderson, 1982–2004

MOST FIELD GOAL ATTEMPTS, SEASON
15	Elmer Oliphant, 1921
25	Pete Henry, 1923
30	Paddy Driscoll, 1926
33	Lou Groza, 1952
39	Steve Myrah, 1961
42	Lou Michaels, 1962
46	Pete Gogolak, 1965*
49	Bruce Gossett, 1966
	Curt Knight, 1971

MOST FIELD GOAL ATTEMPTS, GAME
6	Ted Fritsch, GB-NYB, 10-7-49
7	Bob Waterfield, LA-Det, 12-9-51
8	Lou Michaels, Pit-SL, 12-2-62
	Garo Yepremian, Det-Min, 11-13-66
9	Jim Bakken, SL-Pit, 9-24-67

MOST FIELD GOALS, CAREER
9	Paddy Driscoll, 1920–22
19	Paddy Driscoll, 1920–23
26	Paddy Driscoll, 1920–24
37	Paddy Driscoll, 1920–25
49	Paddy Driscoll, 1920–26
51	Paddy Driscoll, 1920–27
60	Bob Waterfield, 1945–52
65	Lou Groza, 1950–53
81	Lou Groza, 1950–54
92	Lou Groza, 1950–55
103	Lou Groza, 1950–56
118	Lou Groza, 1950–57
126	Lou Groza, 1950–58
131	Lou Groza, 1950–59
147	Lou Groza, 1950–59, 1961
161	Lou Groza, 1950–59, 1961–62
176	Lou Groza, 1950–59, 1961–63
198	Lou Groza, 1950–59, 1961–64
214	Lou Groza, 1950–59, 1961–65
223	Lou Groza, 1950–59, 1961–66
234	Lou Groza, 1950–59, 1961–67
240	George Blanda, 1949–58, 1960–69
256	George Blanda, 1949–58, 1960–70
271	George Blanda, 1949–58, 1960–71
288	George Blanda, 1949–58, 1960–72
311	George Blanda, 1949–58, 1960–73
322	George Blanda, 1949–58, 1960–74
335	George Blanda, 1949–58, 1960–75
338	Jan Stenerud, 1967–81
358	Jan Stenerud, 1967–82
373	Jan Stenerud, 1967–83
383	Nick Lowery, 1978, 1980–96
385	Gary Anderson, 1982–97
420	Gary Anderson, 1982–98
439	Gary Anderson, 1982–99
461	Gary Anderson, 1982–2000
476	Gary Anderson, 1982–2001
494	Gary Anderson, 1982–2002
521	Gary Anderson, 1982–2003
538	Gary Anderson, 1982–2004

MOST FIELD GOALS, SEASON
5	Dutch Sternaman, 1921
	Elmer Oliphant, 1921
8	Paddy Driscoll, 1922
10	Paddy Driscoll, 1923
11	Paddy Driscoll, 1925
12	Paddy Driscoll, 1926
13	Lou Groza, 1950
	Bob Waterfield, 1951
19	Lou Groza, 1952
23	Lou Groza, 1953
27	Gene Mingo, 1962*
28	Bruce Gossett, 1966
	Pete Gogolak, 1966*
34	Jim Turner, 1968*
35	Ali Haji-Sheikh, 1983
	Jeff Jaeger, 1993
37	John Kasay, 1996
39	Olindo Mare, 1999
	Jeff Wilkins	2003
40	Neil Rackers	2005

MOST FIELD GOALS, ROOKIE
3	Benny Boynton, 1921
	Curly Lambeau, 1922
4	Gus Tebell, 1923
7	Red Dunn, 1924
	George Blanda, 1949
8	Doak Walker, 1950
	Les Richter, 1954
9	Dick Bielski, 1955

MOST FIELD GOALS, ROOKIE (CONT.)
11	Paige Cothren, 1957
14	Tom Miner, 1958
18	Gene Mingo, 1960*
19	Pete Gogolak, 1964*
	Booth Lusteg, 1966*
22	Tom Dempsey, 1969
	Dennis Partee, 1968*
33	Chester Marcol, 1972
35	Ali Haji-Sheikh, 1983

MOST FIELD GOALS, GAME
3	Hank Gillo, Rac-Roc, 10–29–22
	Paddy Driscoll, ChiC-ChiB, 12–10–22
	Pete Henry, Can-Day, 10–14–23
	Paddy Driscoll, ChiC-Min, 10–21–23
	Hank Gillo, Rac-Akr, 10–21–23
	Ben Winkelman, Mil-Rac, 11–29–23
4	Paddy Driscoll, ChiC-Col, 10–11–25
	Al Bloodgood, KC-Dul, 12–12–26
5	Bob Waterfield, LA-Det, 12–9–51
	Roger LeClerc, Chi-Det, 12–3–61
	Jim Bakken, SL-Phi, 12–13–64
	Lou Michaels, Bal-SF, 9–25–66
6	Garo Yepremian, Det-Min, 11–13–66
7	Jim Bakken, SL-Pit, 9–24–67
	Rich Karlis, Min-Rams, 11–5–89
	Chris Boniol, Dal-GB, 11–18–96
	Billy Cundiff, Dal-NYG, 9–15–03

MOST FIELD GOALS, ONE QUARTER
4	Garo Yepremian, Det-Min, 11–13–66
	Curt Knight, Was-NYG, 11–15–70
	Roger Ruzek, Dal-NYG, 11–2–87
	Cary Blanchard, Ind-Buf, 9–21–97
	Sebastian Janikowski, Oka-Chi, 10–5–03
	Jeff Wilkins, SL-Bal, 11–9–03
	Lawrence Tynes, KC-NE, 11–27–05

MOST CONSECUTIVE GAMES, FIELD GOALS
3	Elmer Oliphant, 1921
4	Paddy Driscoll, 1922
5	Pete Henry, 1922–23
6	Howard Buck, 1923
7	Hank Gillo, 1924
8	Lou Groza, 1950
12	Lou Groza, 1950–51
19	Jim Bakken, 1966–67
	Bruce Gossett, 1967–68
	Fred Cox, 1968–69
31	Fred Cox, 1968–70
38	Matt Stover, 1999–2001

MOST CONSECUTIVE FIELD GOALS MADE
12	Lou Groza, 1953
	Bobby Layne, 1956–57
16	Jan Stenerud, 1969*
	Don Cockroft, 1974–75
	Garo Yepremian, 1978
20	Garo Yepremian, 1978–79
23	Mark Moseley, 1981–82
24	Kevin Butler, 1988–89
25	Morten Andersen, 1992–93
29	John Carney, 1992–93
31	Fuad Reveiz, 1994–95
40	Gary Anderson, 1997–98
41	Mike Vanderjagt, 2002–03
42	Mike Vanderjagt, 2002–04

LONGEST FIELD GOAL
50	Hank Gillo, Rac-Akr, 10–21–23
	Ave Kaplan, Min-RI, 11–11–23
52	Paddy Driscoll, ChiC-Mil, 9–28–24
	Gus Sonnenberg, Det-Fra, 11–27–26
54	Glen Presnell, Det-GB, 10–3–34
56	Bert Rechichar, Bal-Chi, 9–27–53
63	Tom Dempsey, NO-Det, 11–8–70
	Jason Elam, Den-Jax, 10–25–98

HIGHEST FG PCT., CAREER (100 FGS)
61.7	Lou Groza, 1950–56
62.4	Lou Groza, 1950–57
60.6	Lou Groza, 1950–58
58.5	Lou Groza, 1950–59
59.5	Lou Groza, 1950–59, 1961
57.9	Lou Groza, 1950–59, 1961–62
58.5	Lou Groza, 1950–59, 1961–63
59.3	Lou Groza, 1950–59, 1961–64
59.6	Lou Groza, 1950–59, 1961–65
58.4	Lou Groza, 1950–59, 1961–66
62.9	Jim Bakken, 1962–67
62.9	Jim Bakken, 1962–68
61.5	Jim Bakken, 1962–69
70.6	Jan Stenerud, 1967–70

HIGHEST FG PCT., CAREER (100 FGS) (CONT.)
68.0	Jan Stenerud, 1967–71
66.5	Jan Stenerud, 1967–72
66.7	Garo Yepremian, 1966–67, 1970–73
67.3	Don Cockroft, 1968–74
68.0	Don Cockroft, 1968–75
67.1	Garo Yepremian, 1966–67, 1970–76
66.9	Don Cockroft, 1968–77
67.0	Don Cockroft, 1968–78
67.1	Garo Yepremian, 1966–67, 1970–79
68.6	John Smith, 1974–80
68.8	Efren Herrera, 1974, 1976–81
68.0	Toni Fritsch, 1971–82
72.0	Ralf Benirschke, 1977–83
74.7	Nick Lowery, 1978, 1980–84
76.8	Nick Lowery, 1978, 1980–85
77.2	Gary Anderson, 1982–86
79.6	Morten Andersen, 1982–87
78.2	Morten Andersen, 1982–88
77.3	Nick Lowery, 1978, 1980–89
79.0	Nick Lowery, 1978, 1980–90
79.3	Nick Lowery, 1978, 1980–91
80.8	Pete Stoyanovich, 1989–92
80.0	Nick Lowery, 1978, 1980–93
80.4	Nick Lowery, 1978, 1980–94
80.6	Matt Stover, 1991–95
81.3	Doug Pelfrey, 1993–96
83.1	Chris Boniol 1994–97
81.6	Mike Hollis, 1995–98
81.7	John Carney, 1988–99
84.7	Ryan Longwell, 1997–2000
87.7	Mike Vanderjagt, 1998–2001
85.1	Mike Vanderjagt, 1998–2002
87.9	Mike Vanderjagt, 1998–2003
87.0	Mike Vanderjagt, 1998–2004
87.5	Mike Vanderjagt, 1998–2005

HIGHEST FG PCT., SEASON
41.7	Dutch Sternaman, 1921
61.5	Paddy Driscoll, 1922
71.4	Paddy Driscoll, 1923
76.9	Bill Dudley, 1951
88.5	Lou Groza, 1953
91.7	Jan Stenerud, 1981
95.2	Mark Moseley, 1982
	Eddie Murray, 1988, 1989
100.0	Tony Zendejas, 1991
	Gary Anderson, 1998
	Jeff Wilkins, 2000
	Mike Vanderjagt, 2003

MOST FIELD GOALS, NO MISSES, GAME
5	Roger LeClerc, Chi-Det, 12–3–61
6	Gino Cappelletti, Bos-SD, 9–20–64*
	Joe Danelo, NYG-Sea, 10–18–81
	Ray Wersching, SF-NO, 10–16–83
	Gary Anderson, Pit-Den, 10–23–88
7	Rich Karlis, Min-Rams, 11–5–89
	Chris Boniol, Dal-GB, 11–18–96

MOST 50-YARD FIELD GOALS, CAREER
2	Paddy Driscoll, 1920–25
	Bert Rechichar, 1952–53
4	Bert Rechichar, 1952–55
5	George Blanda, 1949–58, 60–61
6	George Blanda, 1949–58, 60–62
7	George Blanda, 1949–58, 60–66
8	George Blanda, 1949–68, 60–70
	Jan Stenerud, 1967–71
9	Jan Stenerud, 1967–72
10	Tom Dempsey, 1969–73
	Jan Stenerud, 1967–74
12	Tom Dempsey, 1969–75
	Jan Stenerud, 1967–76
14	Jan Stenerud, 1967–81
17	Jan Stenerud, 1967–84
	Nick Lowery, 1978, 1980–88
18	Nick Lowery, 1978, 1980–89
	Morten Andersen, 1982–91
21	Morten Andersen, 1982–92
22	Morten Andersen, 1982–93
30	Morten Andersen, 1982–95
31	Morten Andersen, 1982–96
33	Morten Andersen, 1982–97
35	Morten Andersen, 1982–98
37	Morten Andersen, 1982–2000
39	Morten Andersen, 1982–2001
40	Morten Andersen, 1982–2002

MOST 50-YARD FIELD GOALS, SEASON
2	Bert Rechichar, 1953, 1955
	Lou Michaels, 1960
	Jim Martin, 1960
	George Blanda, 1960, 1961
	Gene Mingo, 1963

MOST 50-YARD FIELD GOALS, SEASON (CONT.)

  Jan Stenerud, 1967, 1968, 1969
4 Horst Muhlmann, 1970
  Mark Moseley, 1977
  Fred Steinfort, 1980
  Norm Johnson, 1986
6 Dean Biasucci, 1988
  Tony Zendejas, 1993
  Chris Jacke, 1993
8 Morten Andersen, 1995

MOST 50-YARD FIELD GOALS, GAME

2 Jim Martin, Det-Bal, 10–23–60
  Tom Dempsey, NO-LA, 12–6–70
  Chris Bahr, Cin-Hou, 9–23–79
  Nick Lowery, KC-Sea, 9–14–80
  Mark Moseley, Was-NO, 10–26–80
  Fred Steinfort, Den-Sea, 12–21–80
  Mick Luckhurst, Atl-Den, 12–5–82
  Morten Andersen, NO-Phi, 12–11–83
  Mick Luckhurst, Atl-Rams, 10–7–84
  Paul McFadden, Phi-Det, 11–4–84
  Nick Lowery, KC-NO, 9–8–85
  Pat Leahy, NYJ-NE, 10–20–85
  Tony Zendejas, Hou-SD, 11–24–85
  Norm Johnson, Sea-Rdrs, 12–8–86
  Raul Allegre, NYG-Phi, 11–15–87
  Dean Biasucci, Ind-Mia, 9–25–88
  Paul McFadden, Atl-Buf, 11–5–89
  Kevin Butler, Chi-Min, 9–23–90
  Chip Lohmiller, Was-Ind, 12–22–90
  Chip Lohmiller, Was-Dal, 9–9–91
  John Kasay, Sea-SD, 10–27–91

MOST 50-YARD FIELD GOALS, GAME

  Fuad Reveiz, Min-TB, 12–8–91
  John Carney, SD-Sea, 9–5–93
  Tony Zendejas, LA-Pit, 9–12–93
  Doug Pelfrey, Cin-Hou, 10–24–93
  Eddie Murray, Dal-Min, 12–12–93
  Greg Davis, Phx-Sea, 12–19–93
3 Morten Andersen, Atl-NO, 12–10–95
  Neil Rackers, Arz-Sea, 10–24–04

POINTS: SAFETIES

MOST SAFETIES, CAREER

2 Tom Nash, 1932
  Bill McPeak, 1954, 1956
3 Bill McPeak, 1954, 1956, 1957
  Charlie Krueger, 1959–61
  Ernie Stautner, 1950, 1958, 1962
  Jim Katkavage, 1958, 1961, 1965
  Roger Brown, 1962, 1965
  Bruce Maher, 1960, 1963, 1967
  Ron McDole, 1964, 1968*
  Ted Hendricks, 1974, 1975, 1976
4 Ted Hendricks, 1974, 1975, 1976, 1977
  Doug English, 1977, 1979, 1983
  Derrick Thomas, 1994, 1996–98

MOST SAFETIES, SEASON

2 Tom Nash, 1932
  Roger Brown, 1962
  Ron McDole, 1964*
  Alan Page, 1971
  Fred Dryer, 1973
  Benny Barnes, 1973
  James Young, 1977
  Tom Hannon, 1981
  Doug English, 1983
  Don Blackmon, 1985
  Tim Harris, 1988
  Brian Jordan, 1991
  Burt Grossman, 1992
  Rod Stephens, 1993
  Bryant Young, 1996

MOST SAFETIES, GAME

2 Fred Dryer, LA-GB, 10–21–73

RUSHING

MOST SEASONS RUSHING LEADER

2 Cliff Battles, 1932, 1937
  Whizzer White, 1938, 1940
  Bill Paschal, 1943–44
  Bill Dudley, 1942, 1946
  Steve Van Buren, 1945, 1947
3 Steve Van Buren, 1945, 1947–48
4 Steve Van Buren, 1945, 1947–49
  Jim Brown, 1957–60
5 Jim Brown, 1957–61
6 Jim Brown, 1957–61, 1963
7 Jim Brown, 1957–61, 1963–64
8 Jim Brown, 1957–61, 1963–65

MOST CONS SEASONS RUSHING LEADER

2 Bill Paschal, 1943–44
  Steve Van Buren, 1947–48
3 Steve Van Buren, 1947–49
  Jim Brown, 1957–59
4 Jim Brown, 1957–60
5 Jim Brown, 1957–61

RUSHING: ATTEMPTS

MOST SEASONS RUSHING ATTEMPTS LEADER

2 Cliff Battles, 1932, 1937
  Whizzer White, 1938, 1940
  Bill Paschal, 1943–44
  Bill Dudley, 1942, 1946

MOST SEASONS RUSHING ATTEMPTS LEADER

2 Steve Van Buren, 1947–48
3 Steve Van Buren, 1947–49
4 Steve Van Buren, 1947–50
  Jim Brown, 1958–59, 1961, 1963
5 Jim Brown, 1958–59, 1961, 1963–64
6 Jim Brown, 1958–59, 1961, 1963–65

MOST CONS SEASONS RUSH ATTS LEADER

2 Bill Paschal, 1943–44
  Steve Van Buren, 1947–48
3 Steve Van Buren, 1947–49
4 Steve Van Buren, 1947–50
  Walter Payton, 1976–79

MOST RUSHING ATTEMPTS, CAREER

 284 Cliff Battles, 1932–33
 380 Cliff Battles, 1932–34
 455 Clarke Hinkle, 1932–35
 623 Cliff Battles, 1932–36
 839 Cliff Battles, 1932–37
 864 Ace Gutowsky, 1932–38
 933 Clarke Hinkle, 1932–39
1042 Clarke Hinkle, 1932–40
1171 Clarke Hinkle, 1932–41
1208 Steve Van Buren, 1944–50
1320 Steve Van Buren, 1944–51
1415 Joe Perry, 1950–59
1451 Joe Perry, 1950–60
1619 Joe Perry, 1950–61
1713 Joe Perry, 1950–62
1790 Jim Brown, 1957–63
2070 Jim Brown, 1957–64
2359 Jim Brown, 1957–65
2404 O.J. Simpson, 1969–79
2462 Franco Harris, 1972–81
2602 Franco Harris, 1972–82
2881 Franco Harris, 1972–83
3047 Walter Payton, 1975–84
3371 Walter Payton, 1975–85
3692 Walter Payton, 1975–86
3828 Walter Payton, 1975–87
4052 Emmitt Smith, 1990–2002
4142 Emmitt Smith, 1990–2003
4409 Emmitt Smith, 1990–2004

MOST RUSHING ATTEMPTS, SEASON

148 Cliff Battles, 1932
173 Jim Musick, 1933
206 Tuffy Leemans, 1936
216 Cliff Battles, 1937
217 Steve Van Buren, 1947
263 Steve Van Buren, 1949
271 Eddie Price, 1951
290 Jim Brown, 1959
305 Jim Brown, 1961
332 O.J. Simpson, 1973
339 Walter Payton, 1977
369 Walter Payton, 1979
373 Earl Campbell, 1980
378 George Rogers, 1981
390 Eric Dickerson, 1983
407 James Wilder, 1984
410 Jamal Anderson, 1998

MOST RUSHING ATTEMPTS, ROOKIE

148 Cliff Battles, 1932
206 Tuffy Leemans, 1936
213 Alan Ameche, 1955
215 Matt Snell, 1964*
238 Paul Robinson, 1968*
254 Booby Clark, 1973
302 Earl Campbell, 1978
331 Ottis Anderson, 1979
378 George Rogers, 1981
390 Eric Dickerson, 1983

MOST RUSHING ATTEMPTS, GAME

38 Harry Newman, NYG-GB, 11–11–34
   Jim Nance, Bos-Oak 10–30–66*
39 O.J. Simpson, Buf-KC, 10–29–73
40 Lydell Mitchell, Bal-NYJ, 10–20–74
41 Franco Harris, Pit-Cin, 10–17–76
42 James Wilder, TB-Pit, 10–30–83
43 Butch Woolfolk, NYG-Phi, 11–20–83
   James Wilder, TB-GB, 9–30–84
45 Jamie Morris, Was-Cin, 12–17–84

RUSHING: YARDS

MOST RUSHING YARDS, CAREER

 1313 Cliff Battles, 1932–33
 1793 Cliff Battles, 1932–34
 2023 Cliff Battles, 1932–35
 2637 Cliff Battles, 1932–36
 3511 Cliff Battles, 1932–37
 3860 Clarke Hinkle, 1932–41
 4904 Steve Van Buren, 1944–49
 5533 Steve Van Buren, 1944–50
 5860 Steve Van Buren, 1944–51
 6549 Joe Perry, 1950–58
 7151 Joe Perry, 1950–59
 7246 Joe Perry, 1950–60
 7921 Joe Perry, 1950–61
 8280 Joe Perry, 1950–62
 9322 Jim Brown, 1957–63
10768 Jim Brown, 1957–64
12312 Jim Brown, 1957–65
13309 Walter Payton, 1975–84
14860 Walter Payton, 1975–85
16193 Walter Payton, 1975–86
16726 Walter Payton, 1975–87
17162 Emmitt Smith, 1990–2002
17418 Emmitt Smith, 1990–2003
18355 Emmitt Smith, 1990–2004

MOST 1000-YARD RUSHING SEASONS

 2 Steve van Buren, 1947, 1949
   Joe Perry, 1953–54
   Jim Brown, 1958–59
 3 Jim Brown, 1958–60
 4 Jim Brown, 1958–61
 5 Jim Brown, 1958–61, 1963
 6 Jim Brown, 1958–61, 1963–64
 7 Jim Brown, 1958–61, 1963–65
   Franco Harris, 1972, 1974–79
 8 Franco Harris, 1972, 1974–79, 1983
   Walter Payton, 1976–81, 1983–84
 9 Walter Payton, 1976–81, 1983–85
10 Walter Payton, 1976–81, 1983–86
   Barry Sanders, 1989–98
   Emmitt Smith, 1991–2000
11 Emmitt Smith, 1991–2001

MOST CONS 1000-YARD RUSHING SEASONS

 2 Joe Perry, 1953–54
   Jim Brown, 1958–59
 3 Jim Brown, 1958–60
 4 Jim Brown, 1958–61
   Jim Taylor, 1960–63
 5 Jim Taylor, 1960–64
   O.J. Simpson, 1972–76
   Franco Harris, 1974–78
 6 Franco Harris, 1974–79
   Walter Payton, 1976–81
   Eric Dickerson, 1983–88
 7 Eric Dickerson, 1983–89
   Barry Sanders, 1989–95
   Thurman Thomas, 1989–95
 8 Barry Sanders, 1989–96
   Thurman Thomas, 1989–96

MOST CONS 1000-YARD RUSHING SEASONS

 9 Barry Sanders, 1989–97
10 Barry Sanders, 1989–98
   Emmitt Smith, 1991–2000
11 Emmitt Smith, 1991–2001

MOST YARDS RUSHING, SEASON

 576 Cliff Battles, 1932
 809 Jim Musick, 1933
1004 Beattie Feathers, 1934
1008 Steve Van Buren, 1947
1146 Steve Van Buren, 1949
1527 Jim Brown, 1958
1863 Jim Brown, 1963
2003 O.J. Simpson, 1973
2105 Eric Dickerson, 1983

MOST YARDS RUSHING, ROOKIE

576	Cliff Battles	1932
1004	Beattie Feathers, 1934	
1023	Paul Robinson, 1968*	
1105	John Brockington, 1971	
1162	Don Woods, 1974	
1450	Earl Campbell, 1978	
1605	Ottis Anderson, 1979	
1674	George Rogers, 1981	
1808	Eric Dickerson, 1983	

MOST YARDS RUSHING, GAME

215	Cliff Battles, Bos-NYG, 10–8–33
218	Gene Roberts, NYG-ChiC, 11–12–50
223	Tom Wilson, LA-GB, 12–16–56
237	Jim Brown, Cle-LA, 11–24–57
	Jim Brown, Cle-Phi, 11–19–61
243	Cookie Gilchrist, Buf-NYJ, 12–8–63*
247	Willie Ellison, LA-NO, 12–5–71
250	O.J. Simpson, Buf-NE, 9–16–73
273	O.J. Simpson, Buf-Det, 11–25–76
275	Walter Payton, Chi-Min, 11–20–77
278	Corey Dillon, Cin-Den, 10–22–2000
295	Jamal Lewis, Bal-Cle, 9–14–03

MOST 200-YARD RUSHING GAMES, CAREER

2	Jim Brown, 1957, 1961
4	Jim Brown, 1957, 1961, 1963
	O.J. Simpson, 1973, 1975
6	O.J. Simpson, 1973, 1975–76

MOST 200-YARD RUSHING GAMES, SEASON

2	Jim Brown, 1963
3	O.J. Simpson, 1973
4	Earl Campbell, 1980

MOST CONSECUTIVE 200-YARD RUSHING GAMES

2	O.J. Simpson, 1973
	Earl Campbell, 1980
	Ricky Williams 2002

MOST 100-YARD RUSHING GAMES, CAREER

5	Beattie Feathers, 1934
6	Steve Van Buren, 1944–45
9	Steve Van Buren, 1944–47
13	Steve Van Buren, 1944–48
17	Steve Van Buren, 1944–49
18	Steve Van Buren, 1944–50
19	Joe Perry, 1950–58
20	Joe Perry, 1950–59
26	Jim Brown, 1957–60
32	Jim Brown, 1957–61
35	Jim Brown, 1957–62
44	Jim Brown, 1957–63
50	Jim Brown, 1957–64
58	Jim Brown, 1957–65
63	Walter Payton, 1975–84

MOST 100-YARD RUSHING GAMES, CAREER

73	Walter Payton, 1975–85
77	Walter Payton, 1975–86
78	Emmitt Smith, 1990–2004

MOST 100-YARD RUSHING GAMES, SEASON

5	Beattie Fethers, 1934
	Tony Canadeo, 1949
7	Rob Goode, 1951
	Rick Casares, 1956
9	Jim Brown, 1958
	Jim Brown, 1963
11	O.J. Simpson, 1973
	Earl Campbell, 1979
12	Eric Dickerson, 1984
	Barry Foster, 1992
14	Barry Sanders, 1997

MOST CONSECUTIVE 100-YARD RUSHING GAMES

3	Beattie Feathers, 1934
4	Steve Van Buren, 1951
5	Rob Goode, 1951
6	Jim Brown, 1958
	Franco Harris, 1972
7	O.J. Simpson, 1972–73
	Earl Campbell, 1979
9	Walter Payton, 1985
10	Marcus Allen, 1985
11	Marcus Allen, 1985–86
14	Barry Sanders, 1997

LONGEST RUN FROM SCRIMMAGE

85	Pete Stinchcomb, ChiS-Cle, 11–20–21
91	Hap Moran, NYG-GB, 11–23–30
97	Andy Uram, GB-ChiC, 10–8–39
	Bob Gage, Pit-Chi, 12–4–49
99	Tony Dorsett, Dal-Min, 1–8–83

RUSHING: AVERAGE GAIN

HIGH AVG. GAIN RUSHING, CAREER

4.2	Cliff Battles, 1932–37
5.0	Steve Van Buren, 1944–48
4.8	Steve Van Buren, 1944–49
4.6	Steve Van Buren, 1944–50
4.4	Steve Van Buren, 1944–51
5.3	Joe Perry, 1950–54
5.1	Joe Perry, 1950–55
5.1	Joe Perry, 1950–56
5.0	Joe Perry, 1950–57
5.1	Joe Perry, 1950–58
5.1	Jim Brown, 1957–59
5.2	Jim Brown, 1957–60
5.1	Jim Brown, 1957–61
5.0	Jim Brown, 1957–62
5.2	Jim Brown, 1957–63
5.3	Lenny Moore, 1956–64
5.2	Jim Brown, 1957–65
5.3	Gale Sayers, 1965–68
5.2	Jim Brown, 1957–65
6.4	Randall Cunningham, 1985–95, 1997–2000
6.4	Randall Cunningham, 1985–95, 1997–2001

HIGH AVG. GAIN RUSHING, SEASON (100 ATT)

4.8	Bob Campiglio, 1932
5.0	Cliff Battles, 1933
8.4	Beattie Feathers, 1934

HIGH AVG. GAIN RUSHING, GAME (10 ATTS)

13.4	Cliff Battles, Bos-NYG, 10–8–33
16.7	Bill Grimes, GB-NYY, 10–8–50
17.1	Marion Motley, Cle-Pit, 10–29–50
17.3	Michael Vick, Atl-Min, 12–1–02

RUSHING: TOUCHDOWNS

MOST SEASONS TD RUN LEADER

2	Jack McBride, 1927, 1930
	Vern Lewellen, 1928, 1930
	Dutch Clark, 1931, 1934
3	Dutch Clark, 1931, 1934, 1936
4	Dutch Clark, 1931, 1934, 1936–37
	Steve Van Buren, 1945, 1947–49
	Jim Brown, 1957–59, 1963
5	Jim Brown, 1957–59, 1963, 1965

MOST CONS SEASONS AS TD RUN LEADER

2	Dutch Clark, 1936–37
	Johnny Drake, 1939–40
	Bill Paschal, 1943–44
	Steve Van Buren, 1947–48
3	Steve Van Buren, 1947–49
	Jim Brown, 1957–59
	Abner Haynes, 1960–62*
	Cookie Gilchrist, 1962–64*
	Leroy Kelly, 1966–68

MOST TOUCHDOWN RUNS, CAREER

6	Fritz Pollard, 1920–21
10	Carl Cramer, 1920–22
11	Jimmy Conzelman, 1920–23
12	Dutch Sternaman, 1920–24
	Tex Hamer, 1924
17	Tex Hamer, 1924–25
19	Tex Hamer, 1924–26
	Ben Jones, 1923–26
22	Paddy Driscoll, 1920–27
24	Paddy Driscoll, 1920–28
25	Paddy Driscoll, 1920–29
31	Vern Lewellen, 1924–30
38	Ernie Nevers, 1926–31
	Steve Van Buren, 1944–47
48	Steve Van Buren, 1944–48
59	Steve Van Buren, 1944–49
63	Steve Van Buren, 1944–50
69	Steve Van Buren, 1944–51
70	Jim Brown, 1957–62
82	Jim Brown, 1957–63
89	Jim Brown, 1957–64
106	Jim Brown, 1957–65
	Walter Payton, 1975–86
110	Walter Payton, 1975–87
112	Marcus Allen, 1982–96

MOST TOUCHDOWN RUNS, CAREER (CONT.)

123	Marcus Allen, 1982–97
125	Emmitt Smith, 1990–98
136	Emmitt Smith, 1990–99
145	Emmitt Smith, 1990–2000
148	Emmitt Smith, 1990–2001
153	Emmitt Smith, 1990–2002
155	Emmitt Smith, 1990–2003
164	Emmitt Smith, 1990–2004

MOST TOUCHDOWN RUNS, SEASON

6	Fritz Pollard, 1921
7	Jimmy Conzelman, 1922
	Lou Smyth, 1923
12	Tex Hamer, 1924
	Ernie Nevers, 1929
15	Steve Van Buren, 1945
17	Jim Brown, 1958
19	Jim Taylor, 1962
	Earl Campbell, 1979
	Chuck Muncie, 1981
24	John Riggins, 1983
25	Emmitt Smith, 1995
27	Priest Holmes 2003
	Shaun Alexander 2005

MOST TOUCHDOWN RUNS, ROOKIE

4	Herb Henderson, 1921
	Pete Stinchcomb, 1921
5	Joey Sternaman, 1922

MOST TOUCHDOWN RUNS, ROOKIE

5	Dutch Lauer, 1922
6	Ben Jones, 1923
12	Tex Hamer, 1924
14	Gale Sayers, 1965
18	Eric Dickerson, 1983

MOST TOUCHDOWN RUNS, GAME

3	Frank Pollard, Akr-Cin, 10–21–21
	Frank Bacon, Day-Col, 10–2–21
4	Herb Henderson, Evv-Ham, 10–16–21
	Doc Elliott, Cle-Mil, 11–27–24
5	Jimmy Conzelman, RI-EVV, 10–15–22
6	Ernie Nevers, ChiC-ChiB, 11–28–29

MOST CONSECUTIVE GAMES TD RUNS

3	Fritz Pollard, 1921
	Lou Smyth, 1923
	Doc Elliott, 1923
	Ben Jones, 1923–24
4	Tex Hamer, 1924
5	Tex Hamer, 1924–25
	Tony Latone, 1929
6	Beattie Feathers, 1934
7	Johnny Drake, 1939
	Bill Paschal, 1943
8	Steve Van Buren, 1947
11	Lenny Moore, 1963–64
13	John Riggins, 1983–84
	George Rogers, 1985–86
18	LaDainian Tomlinson, 2004–05

PASSING

MOST SEASONS LEADING PASSER

2	Arnold Herber, 1932, 1934
3	Arnold Herber, 1932, 1934, 1936
	Sammy Baugh, 1937, 1940, 1943
4	Sammy Baugh, 1937, 1940, 1943, 1945
5	Sammy Baugh, 1937, 1940, 1943, 1945, 1947
6	Sammy Baugh, 1937, 1940, 1943, 1945, 1947, 1949
	Steve Young, 1991–94, 1996–97

MOST CONSECUTIVE SEASONS LEADING PASSER

2	Cecil Isbell, 1941–42
	Milt Plum, 1960–61
	Ken Anderson, 1974–75
	Roger Staubach, 1978–79
	Ken Anderson, 1981–82
	Steve Young, 1991–92
3	Steve Young, 1991–93
4	Steve Young, 1991–94

PASSING: RATING

HIGHEST RATING, CAREER (1500 ATTS)

71.1	Sammy Baugh, 1937–45
69.1	Sammy Baugh, 1937–46
73.0	Sammy Baugh, 1937–47
77.0	Sid Luckman, 1939–48
75.8	Sid Luckman, 1939–49
75.0	Sid Luckman, 1939–50

HIGHEST RATING, CAREER (1500 ATTS) (CONT.)

78.2	Otto Graham, 1950–55
83.9	John Unitas, 1956–60
80.0	John Unitas, 1956–61
79.4	John Unitas, 1956–62
81.0	John Unitas, 1956–63
82.5	John Unitas, 1956–64
83.8	John Unitas, 1956–65
87.6	Len Dawson, 1957–66
86.9	Len Dawson, 1957–67
88.1	Len Dawson, 1957–68
86.8	Len Dawson, 1957–69
85.3	Len Dawson, 1957–70
84.9	Len Dawson, 1957–71
83.8	Len Dawson, 1957–72

HIGHEST RATING, CAREER (1500 ATTS)

83.4	Len Dawson 1957–73
82.6	Sonny Jurgensen, 1957–74
82.6	Sonny Jurgensen, 1957–75
83.9	Ken Anderson, 1971–76
83.9	Ken Stabler, 1970–77
82.6	Sonny Jurgensen, 1957–74
83.4	Roger Staubach, 1969–79
90.0	Joe Montana, 1979–83
92.7	Joe Montana, 1979–84
92.4	Joe Montana, 1979–85
95.2	Dan Marino, 1983–86
94.1	Dan Marino, 1983–87
92.0	Joe Montana, 1979–88
94.0	Joe Montana, 1979–89
93.4	Joe Montana, 1979–90
93.5	Joe Montana, 1979–90, 92
93.1	Joe Montana, 1979–90, 1992–93
96.8	Steve Young, 1985–94
96.1	Steve Young, 1985–95
96.2	Steve Young, 1985–96
97.0	Steve Young, 1985–97
97.6	Steve Young, 1985–98
96.8	Steve Young, 1985–99
98.2	Kurt Warner, 1998–2002
97.2	Kurt Warner, 1998–2003
96.8	Steve Young, 1985–99

HIGHEST PASSER RATING, SEASON

51.5	Arnie Herber, 1932
51.7	Harry Newman, 1933
69.8	Ed Danowski, 1935
85.4	Sammy Baugh, 1940
87.0	Cecil Isbell, 1942
107.6	Sid Luckman, 1943
109.9	Sammy Baugh, 1945
110.4	Milt Plum, 1960
112.4	Joe Montana, 1989
112.8	Steve Young, 1994
121.1	Peyton Manning, 2004

HIGHEST PASSER RATING, ROOKIE

51.7	Harry Newman, 1933
58.4	Parker Hall, 1939
72.5	Bob Waterfield, 1945
84.0	Charlie Conerly, 1948
88.2	Greg Cook, 1969*
96.0	Dan Marino, 1983
98.1	Ben Roethlisberger, 2004

PASSING: ATTEMPTS

MOST SEASONS PASS ATTEMPTS LEADER

2	Arnie Herber, 1932, 1934
3	Arnie Herber, 1932, 1934, 1936
	Arnie Herber, 1937, 1943, 1945
4	Sammy Baugh, 1937, 1943, 1945, 1947
	John Unitas, 1957, 1959–61
	George Blanda, 1956, 1963–65
	Dan Marino, 1984, 1986, 1988, 1992
5	Dan Marino, 1984, 1986, 1988, 1992, 1997

MOST CONS SEASONS PASS ATTS LEADER

2	Sammy Baugh, 1947–48
	Bobby Layne, 1950–51
	John Unitas, 1959–60
3	John Unitas, 1959–61
	George Blanda, 1963–65*
	Drew Bledsoe, 1995–97

MOST PASS ATTEMPTS, CAREER

225	Arnie Herber, 1930–33
340	Arnie Herber, 1930–34
449	Arnie Herber, 1930–35
622	Arnie Herber, 1930–36
726	Arnie Herber, 1930–37

MOST PASS ATTEMPTS, CAREER

781	Arnie Herber, 1930–38
920	Arnie Herber, 1930–39
1009	Arnie Herber, 1930–40
1229	Sammy Baugh, 1937–43
1375	Sammy Baugh, 1937–44
1557	Sammy Baugh, 1937–45
1718	Sammy Baugh, 1937–46
2072	Sammy Baugh, 1937–47
2387	Sammy Baugh, 1937–48
2642	Sammy Baugh, 1937–49
2808	Sammy Baugh, 1937–50
2962	Sammy Baugh, 1937–51
2995	Sammy Baugh, 1937–52
3109	Bobby Layne, 1948–59
3318	Bobby Layne, 1948–60
3467	Bobby Layne, 1948–61
3700	Bobby Layne, 1948–62
3817	Y.A. Tittle, 1950–64
4097	John Unitas, 1956–67
4129	John Unitas, 1956–68
4456	John Unitas, 1956–69
4777	John Unitas, 1956–70
4953	John Unitas, 1956–71
5110	John Unitas, 1956–72
5186	John Unitas, 1956–73
5225	Fran Tarkenton, 1961–75
5637	Fran Tarkenton, 1961–76
5895	Fran Tarkenton, 1961–77
6467	Fran Tarkenton, 1961–78
6531	Dan Marino, 1983–95
6904	Dan Marino, 1983–96
7452	Dan Marino, 1983–97
7989	Dan Marino, 1983–98
8358	Dan Marino, 1983–99

MOST PASS ATTEMPTS, SEASON

101	Arnie Herber, 1932
136	Harry Newman, 1933
173	Arnie Herber, 1936
208	Parker Hall, 1939
277	Davey O'Brien, 1940
295	Bud Schwenk, 1942
354	Sammy Baugh, 1947
364	Otto Graham, 1952
382	Tobin Rote, 1954
478	Frank Tripucka, 1960*
505	George Blanda, 1964*
508	Sonny Jurgensen, 1967
572	Fran Tarkenton, 1978
578	Steve DeBerg, 1979
589	Dan Fouts, 1980
609	Dan Fouts, 1981
623	Dan Marino, 1986
655	Warren Moon, 1991
691	Drew Bledsoe, 1994

MOST PASS ATTEMPTS, ROOKIE

136	Harry Newman, 1933
171	Sammy Baugh, 1937
208	Parker Hall, 1939
295	Bud Schwenk, 1942
298	Charlie Conerly, 1948
375	Norm Snead, 1961
439	Jim Zorn, 1976
486	Rick Mirer, 1993
575	Peyton Manning, 1998

MOST PASS ATTEMPTS, GAME

60	Davey O'Brien, Phi-Was, 12–1–40
68	George Blanda, Hou-Buf, 11–1–64*
70	Drew Bledsoe, NE-Min, 11–13–94

PASSING: COMPLETIONS

MOST SEASONS PASS COMPLETION LEADER

2	Arnie Herber, 1932, 1934
3	Arnie Herber, 1932, 1934, 1936
	Sammy Baugh, 1937, 1943, 1945
4	Sammy Baugh, 1937, 1943, 1945, 1947
5	Sammy Baugh, 1937, 1943, 1945, 1947, 1948
	Dan Marino, 1984–86, 1988, 1992
6	Dan Marino, 1984–86, 1988, 1992, 1997

MOST CONS SEASONS AS COMP LEADER

2	Cecil Isbell, 1941–42
	Sammy Baugh, 1947–48
	John Unitas, 1959–60
	George Blanda, 1963–64*
3	George Blanda, 1963–65*
	Dan Marino, 1984–86

MOST PASS COMPLETIONS, CAREER

87	Arnie Herber, 1930–33
129	Arnie Herber, 1930–34
169	Arnie Herber, 1930–35
246	Arnie Herber, 1930–36
293	Arnie Herber, 1930–37
315	Arnie Herber, 1930–38
372	Arnie Herber, 1930–39
410	Arnie Herber, 1930–40
414	Sammy Baugh, 1937–41
546	Sammy Baugh, 1937–42
679	Sammy Baugh, 1937–43
761	Sammy Baugh, 1937–44
889	Sammy Baugh, 1937–45
976	Sammy Baugh, 1937–46
1186	Sammy Baugh, 1937–47
1371	Sammy Baugh, 1937–48
1516	Sammy Baugh, 1937–49
1606	Sammy Baugh, 1937–50
1673	Sammy Baugh, 1937–51
1693	Sammy Baugh, 1937–52
1698	Bobby Layne, 1948–61
1814	Bobby Layne, 1948–62
1971	Y.A. Tittle, 1950–63
2118	Y.A. Tittle, 1950–64
2261	John Unitas, 1956–67
2272	John Unitas, 1956–68
2450	John Unitas, 1956–69
2616	John Unitas, 1956–70
2708	John Unitas, 1956–71
2796	John Unitas, 1956–72
2830	John Unitas, 1956–73
2931	Fran Tarkenton, 1961–75
3186	Fran Tarkenton, 1961–77
3341	Fran Tarkenton, 1961–76
3686	Fran Tarkenton, 1961–78
3913	Dan Marino, 1983–95
4134	Dan. Marino, 1983–96
4453	Dan Marino, 1983–97
4763	Dan Marino, 1983–98
4967	Dan Marino, 1983–99

MOST PASS COMPLETIONS, SEASON

37	Arnie Herber, 1932
53	Harry Newman, 1933
57	Ed Danowski, 1934
77	Arnie Herber, 1936
81	Sammy Baugh, 1937
106	Parker Hall, 1939
124	Davey O'Brien, 1940
146	Cecil Isbell, 1942
210	Sammy Baugh, 1947
248	Frank Tripucka, 1960*
262	George Blanda, 1964*
288	Sonny Jurgensen, 1967
345	Fran Tarkenton, 1978
347	Steve DeBerg, 1979
348	Dan Fouts, 1980

MOST PASS COMPLETIONS, SEASON

360	Dan Fouts, 1981
362	Dan Marino, 1984
378	Dan Marino, 1986
404	Warren Moon, 1991
418	Rich Gannon, 2002

MOST PASS COMPLETIONS, ROOKIE

53	Harry Newman, 1933
81	Sammy Baugh, 1937
106	Parker Hall, 1939
126	Bud Schwenk, 1942
162	Charlie Conerly, 1948
172	Norm Snead, 1961
208	Jim Zorn, 1976
274	Rick Mirer, 1993
326	Peyton Manning, 1998

MOST PASS COMPLETIONS, GAME

14	Arnie Herber, GB-Phi, 12–3–33
15	Pat Coffee, ChiC-ChiB, 12–5–37
	Ace Parker, Bkn-Was, 10–8–39
	Dwight Sloan, Det-NYG, 11–5–39
19	Davey O'Brien, Phi-GB, 11–12–39
21	Davey O'Brien, Phi-Chi, 11–19–39
23	Sammy Baugh, Was-Bkn, 11–10–40
33	Davey O'Brien, Phi-Was, 12–1–40
36	Charlie Conerly, NYG-Pit, 12–5–48
37	George Blanda, Hou-Buf, 11–1–64*
42	Richard Todd, NYJ-SF, 9–21–80
45	Drew Bledsoe, NE-Min, 11–13–94

MOST CONSECUTIVE COMPLETIONS

10	Norm Van Brocklin, LA-Det, 10–15–50	
11	Norm Van Brocklin, LA-Bal, 10–22–50	
	George Ratterman, Cle-Pit, 10–6–56	
	Milt Plum, Cle-Was, 10–30–60	
13	Fran Tarkenton, Min-LA, 12–3–61	
	Rudy Bukich, Chi-Det, 11–26–64	
15	Len Dawson, KC-Hou, 9–9–67*	
	Joe Namath, NYJ-Bos, 10–29–67*	
16	Ken Anderson, Cin-Pit, 12–10–74	
17	Bert Jones, Bal-NYJ, 12–15–74	
	Steve DeBerg, Den-Rams, 12–12–82	
18	Steve DeBerg, Den-KC, 12–19–82	
20	Ken Anderson, Cin-Hou, 1–2–83	
22	Joe Montana, SF-GB, 12–6–87	
24	Donovan McNabb, Phi-GB, 12–5–04 (2 games)	

PASSING: COMPLETION PERCENTAGE

MOST SEASONS COMPLETION PCT. LEADER

2	Dutch Clark, 1934, 1936
	Bob Monnett, 1937, 1938
	Sammy Baugh, 1940, 1942
3	Sammy Baugh, 1940, 1942–43
4	Sammy Baugh, 1940, 1942–43, 1945
5	Sammy Baugh, 1940, 1942–43, 1945, 1947

MOST SEASONS COMPLETION PCT. LEADER

6	Sammy Baugh, 1940, 1942–43, 1945, 1947–48
7	Sammy Baugh, 1940, 1942–43, 1945, 1947–49
	Len Dawson, 1962, 1964–69*
8	Len Dawson, 1962, 1964–69, 1975

MOST CONS SEASONS AS COMP PCT. LEADER

2	Bob Monnett, 1937–38
	Sammy Baugh, 1942–43
	Sammy Baugh, 1947–48
3	Sammy Baugh, 1947–49
	Otto Graham, 1953–55
	Milt Plum, 1959–61
	Len Dawson, 1964–66*
4	Len Dawson, 1964–67*
5	Len Dawson, 1964–68*
6	Len Dawson, 1964–69*

HIGH COMP PERCENTAGE, CAREER

57.1	Sammy Baugh, 1937–45
56.8	Sammy Baugh, 1937–46
57.2	Sammy Baugh, 1937–47
57.4	Sammy Baugh, 1937–48
57.4	Sammy Baugh, 1937–49
57.2	Sammy Baugh, 1937–50
56.5	Sammy Baugh, 1937–51
56.5	Sammy Baugh, 1937–52
56.8	Bart Starr, 1956–64
56.6	Bart Starr, 1956–65
57.2	Bart Starr, 1956–66
57.0	Bart Starr, 1956–67
57.5	Bart Starr, 1956–68
57.7	Bart Starr, 1956–69
57.5	Bart Starr, 1956–70
57.4	Bart Starr, 1956–71
57.8	Ken Anderson, 1971–76
59.9	Ken Stabler, 1970–77
59.6	Ken Stabler, 1970–78
59.9	Ken Stabler, 1970–79
60.6	Ken Stabler, 1970–80
60.3	Ken Stabler, 1970–81
60.4	Ken Stabler, 1970–82
63.5	Joe Montana, 1979–83
63.7	Joe Montana, 1979–84
63.3	Joe Montana, 1979–85
63.2	Joe Montana, 1979–86
63.6	Joe Montana, 1979–87
63.2	Joe Montana, 1979–88
63.9	Joe Montana, 1979–89
63.6	Joe Montana, 1979–90
63.7	Joe Montana, 1979–90, 1992
63.5	Joe Montana, 1979–90, 1992–93
63.6	Steve Young, 1985–94
64.2	Steve Young, 1985–95
64.5	Steve Young, 1985–96
64.8	Steve Young, 1985–97
64.5	Steve Young, 1985–98
64.3	Steve Young, 1985–99
66.7	Kurt Warner, 1998–2002
66.4	Kurt Warner, 1998–2003
65.9	Kurt Warner, 1998–2004
65.7	Kurt Warner, 1998–2005

HIGHEST PASS COMP PERCENTAGE, SEASON

40.7	Keith Molesworth, 1932
52.5	Benny Friedman, 1933
53.5	Dutch Clark, 1936
54.4	Bob Monnett, 1938
61.8	Frank Filchock, 1939
62.7	Sammy Baugh, 1940
70.3	Sammy Baugh, 1945
70.6	Ken Anderson, 1982

HIGHEST PASS COMP PERCENTAGE, ROOKIE

39.0	Harry Newman, 1933
47.4	Sammy Baugh, 1937
51.0	Parker Hall, 1939
51.5	Bob Waterfield, 1945
53.7	Clyde LaForce, 1947
54.2	Charlie Conerly, 1948
55.6	John Unitas, 1956
56.1	Fran Tarkenton, 1961
57.5	Jim McMahon, 1982
58.5	Dan Marino, 1983
66.4	Ben Roethlisberger, 2004

HIGHEST PASS COMP PCT., GAME (20 ATTS)

75.0	Sammy Baugh, Was-Phi, 10–20–40
75.7	Frank Filchock, Was-Phi, 10–8–44
85.7	Sammy Baugh, Was-Phi, 10–14–45
86.2	Ken Stabler, Oak-Bal, 10–28–73
90.9	Ken Anderson, Cin-Pit, 11–10–74
91.3	Vinny Testaverde, Cle-Rams, 12–26–93

PASSING: YARDS

MOST SEASONS PASSING YARDS LEADER

2	Arnie Herber, 1932, 1934
3	Arnie Herber, 1932, 1934, 1936
	Sid Luckman, 1943, 1945–46
	Sammy Baugh, 1937, 1940, 1947
4	Sammy Baugh, 1937, 1940, 1947–48
	John Unitas, 1957, 1959–60, 1963
	Sonny Jurgensen, 1961–62, 1966–67
5	Sonny Jurgensen, 1961–62, 1966–67, 1969
	Dan Marino, 1984–86, 1988, 1992

MOST CONSE SEASONS PASSING YDS LEADER

2	Cecil Isbell, 1941–42
	Sid Luckman, 1945–46
	Sammy Baugh, 1947–48
	Bobby Layne, 1950–51
	Otto Graham, 1952–53
	John Unitas, 1959–60
	Sonny Jurgensen, 1961–62
	Sonny Jurgensen, 1966–67
	Joe Namath, 1966–67*
	Ken Anderson 1974–75
	Dan Fouts, 1979–80
3	Dan Fouts, 1979–81
4	Dan Fouts, 1979–82

MOST YARDS PASSING LIFE

1295	Arnie Herber, 1930–33
2094	Arnie Herber, 1930–34
2823	Arnie Herber, 1930–35
4062	Arnie Herber, 1930–36
4746	Arnie Herber, 1930–37
5082	Arnie Herber, 1930–38
6189	Arnie Herber, 1930–39
6749	Arnie Herber, 1930–40
8379	Sammy Baugh, 1937–43
9228	Sammy Baugh, 1937–44
10897	Sammy Baugh, 1937–45
12060	Sammy Baugh, 1937–46
14998	Sammy Baugh, 1937–47
17597	Sammy Baugh, 1937–48
19500	Sammy Baugh, 1937–49
20630	Sammy Baugh, 1937–50
21734	Sammy Baugh, 1937–51
21886	Sammy Baugh, 1937–52
22063	Bobby Layne, 1948–59
23877	Bobby Layne, 1948–60
25082	Bobby Layne, 1948–61
26768	Bobby Layne, 1948–62
28339	Y.A. Tittle, 1950–64
29593	John Unitas, 1956–66
33021	John Unitas, 1956–67
33160	John Unitas, 1956–68
35502	John Unitas, 1956–69
37715	John Unitas, 1956–70
38657	John Unitas, 1956–71
39768	John Unitas, 1956–72
40239	John Unitas, 1956–73
41801	Fran Tarkenton, 1961–76
43535	Fran Tarkenton, 1961–77
47003	Fran Tarkenton, 1961–78
48841	Dan Marino, 1983–95

MOST YARDS PASSING LIFE (CONT.)

51636	Dan Marino, 1983–96
55416	Dan Marino, 1983–97
58913	Dan Marino, 1983–98
61361	Dan Marino, 1983–99

MOST SEASONS 3000 YARDS PASSING

2	Sonny Jurgensen, 1961–62
	John Unitas, 1960, 1963
	Y.A. Tittle, 1962–63
3	Sonny Jurgensen, 1961–62, 1966
4	Sonny Jurgensen, 1961–62, 1966–67
5	Sonny Jurgensen, 1961–62, 1966–67, 1969
	Dan Fouts, 1979, 1980–81, 1984–85

MOST SEASONS 3000 YARDS PASSING

6	Dan Fouts, 1979, 1980–8l, 1984–86
	Joe Montana, 1981, 1983–85, 1987, 1989
	Dan Marino, 1984–89
7	Joe Montana, 1981, 1983–85, 1987, 1989–90
	Dan Marino, 1984–90
8	Dan Marino, 1984–91
9	Dan Marino, 1984–92
10	Dan Marino, 1984–92, 1994
11	Dan Marino, 1984–92, 1994–95
	John Elway, 1985–91, 1993–96
12	Dan Marino, 1984–92, 1994–95, 1997
	John Elway, 1985–91, 1993–97
13	Dan Marino, 1984–92, 1994–95, 1997–98
	Brett Favre, 1992–2004
14	Brett Favre, 1992–2005

MOST PASSING YARDS, SEASON

639	Arnie Herber, 1932
973	Harry Newman, 1933
1239	Arnie Herber, 1936
1324	Davey O'Brien, 1939
1367	Sammy Baugh, 1940
1479	Cecil Isbell, 1941
2021	Cecil Isbell, 1942
2194	Sid Luckman, 1943
2938	Sammy Baugh, 1947
3099	John Unitas, 1960
3723	Sonny Jurgensen, 1961
4007	Joe Namath, 1967*
4082	Dan Fouts, 1979
4715	Dan Fouts, 1980
4802	Dan Fouts, 1981
5084	Dan Marino, 1984

MOST PASSING YARDS, ROOKIE

973	Harry Newman, 1933
1127	Sammy Baugh, 1937
1324	Davey O'Brien, 1939
1360	Bud Schwenk, 1942
1609	Bob Waterfield, 1945
2175	Charlie Conerly, 1948
2337	Norm Snead, 1961
2507	Dennis Shaw, 1970
2571	Jim Zorn, 1976
2833	Rick Mirer, 1993
3739	Peyton Manning, 1998

MOST PASSING YARDS, GAME

306	Pat Coffee, ChiC-ChiB, 12–5–37
316	Davey O'Brien, Phi-Was, 12–1–40
333	Cecil Isbell, GB-ChiC, 11–1–42
376	Sammy Baugh, Was-Bkn, 10–31–43
433	Sid Luckman, Chi-NYG, 11–14–43
446	Sammy Baugh, Was-Bos, 10–31–48
468	John Lujack, ChiB-ChiC, 12–11–49
554	Norm Van Brocklin, LA-NYY, 9–28–51

MOST GAMES 400 YARDS PASSING, CAREER

2	George Blanda, 1949–58, 1960–61
	Sonny Jurgensen, 1957–61
3	Sonny Jurgensen, 1957–62
4	Sonny Jurgensen, 1957–65
5	Sonny Jurgensen, 1957–67
6	Dan Fouts, 1973–85
7	Dan Marino, 1983–86
9	Dan Marino, 1983–88
10	Dan Marino, 1983–89
12	Dan Marino, 1983–94
13	Dan Marino, 1983–95

MOST GAMES 400 YARDS PASSING, SEASON

2	Sonny Jurgensen, 1961
	George Blanda, 1961*
	Joe Namath, 1972
	Dan Fouts, 1982
4	Dan Marino, 1984

MOST CONS GAMES 400 YARDS PASSING

2	Dan Fouts, 1982	
	Dan Marino, 1984	
	Phil Simms, 1985	
	Billy Volek	2004

MOST GAMES 300 YARDS PASSING, CAREER

2	Bob Waterfield, 1945–46
4	Sammy Baugh, 1937–47
6	Sammy Baugh, 1937–48
7	Sammy Baugh, 1937–49
	Bobby Layne, 1948–55
10	Bobby Layne, 1948–58
11	John Unitas, 1956–62
15	John Unitas, 1956–63
18	John Unitas, 1956–65
20	John Unitas, 1956–66
23	John Unitas, 1956–67
25	John Unitas, 1956–69
26	John Unitas, 1956–72
30	Dan Fouts, 1973–82
35	Dan Fouts, 1973–83
40	Dan Fouts, 1973–84
47	Dan Fouts, 1973–85
48	Dan Fouts, 1973–86
51	Dan Fouts, 1973–87
52	Dan Marino, 1983–95
56	Dan Marino, 1983–97
60	Dan Marino, 1983–98
63	Dan Marino, 1983–99

MOST GAMES 300 YARDS PASSING, SEASON

3	Sammy Baugh, 1947
	Otto Graham, 1950
	Bob Thomason, 1953
	Y.A. Tittle, 1953
	Bobby Layne, 1958
4	John Unitas, 1960
5	Sonny Jurgensen, 1961
6	Joe Namath, 1967*
	Dan Fouts, 1979
8	Dan Fouts, 1980
9	Dan Marino, 1984
	Warren Moon, 1991
	Kurt Warner, 1999, 2001
10	Rich Gannon, 2002

MOST CONS GAMES 300 YARDS PASSING

2	Sid Luckman, 1947
	Otto Graham, 1953
	Bob Thomason, 1953
	Y.A. Tittle, 1953
	George Blanda, 1954
	Bobby Layne, 1958
	Frank Tripucka, 1960*
	John Unitas, 1960
	Sonny Jurgensen, 1961
	Charley Johnson, 1962
	John Unitas, 1962
	Billy Wade, 1962
	Charley Johnson, 1963
	Don Meredith, 1963
3	John Unitas, 1963
	Cotton Davidson, 1964*
	George Blanda, 1964*
	Sonny Jurgensen, 1967
	John Hadl, 1967*
	Joe Namath, 1967–68*
	Darryl Lamonica, 1968*
4	Dan Fouts, 1979
5	Joe Montana, 1982
6	Steve Young, 1998
	Kurt Warner, 2000
	Rich Gannon, 2002

LONGEST PASS PLAY

70	Benny Boynton, Was-Cle, 12–11–21
	Sonny Winters, Col-Oor, 11–25–23
	Sonny Winters, Col-Day, 12–3–23
78	Phil White, KC-RI, 11–15–25
83	Arnie Herber, GB-Chi, 9–22–35
86	Rabbit Keen, Phi-GB, 11–14–37
97	Pat Coffee, ChiC-ChiB, 12–5–37
98	Doug Russell, ChiC-Cle, 11–27–38
99	Frank Filchock, Was-Pit, 10–15–39
	George Izo, Was-Cle, 9–15–63
	Karl Sweetan, Det-Bal, 10–16–66
	Sonny Jurgensen, Was-Chi, 9–15–68
	Jim Plunkett, Rdrs-Was, 10–2–83
	Ron Jaworski, Phi-Atl, 11–10–85
	Stan Humphries, SD-Sea, 9–18–94
	Brett Favre, GB-Chi, 9–11–95
	Trent Green, KC-SD, 12–22–02
	Jeff Garcia, Cle-Cin, 10–17–04

PASSING: AVERAGE GAIN

MOST SEASONS AVG. GAIN LEADER

2	Arnie Herber, 1932, 1934
3	Arnie Herber, 1932, 1934, 1936
	Sid Luckman, 1939–41
4	Sid Luckman, 1939–42
5	Sid Luckman, 1939–43
6	Sid Luckman, 1939–43, 1946
7	Sid Luckman, 1939–43, 1946–47

MOST CONS SEASONS AVG. GAIN LEADER

2	Sid Luckman, 1939–40
3	Sid Luckman, 1939–41
4	Sid Luckman, 1939–42
5	Sid Luckman, 1939–43

HIGHEST AVG. GAIN, CAREER (1500 ATTS)

7.00	Sammy Baugh, 1937–45
7.02	Sammy Baugh, 1937–46
7.24	Sammy Baugh, 1937–47
8.63	Sid Luckman, 1939–48
8.50	Sid Luckman, 1939–49
8.42	Sid Luckman, 1939–50
8.65	Norm Van Brocklin, 1949–55
8.63	Otto Graham, 1950–55
8.68	Kurt Warner, 1998–2002
8.63	Otto Graham, 1950–55

HIGHEST AVERAGE PASSING GAIN, SEASON

6.33	Arnie Herber, 1932
7.15	Harry Newman, 1933
7.16	Arnie Herber, 1936
8.09	Bob Masterson, 1939
9.92	Sid Luckman, 1941
10.86	Sid Luckman, 1943
11.17	Tommy O'Connell, 1957

HIGHEST AVERAGE PASSING GAIN, ROOKIE

7.15	Harry Newman, 1933
9.409	Bob Waterfield, 1945
9.411	Greg Cook, 1969*

HIGHEST AVG. GAIN, GAME (20 ATTS)

9.27	Pat Coffee, ChiC-ChiB, 12–5–37
15.86	Cecil Isbell, GB-ChiC, 11–1–42
18.58	Sammy Baugh, Was-Bos, 10–31–48

PASSING: TOUCHDOWN PASSES

MOST SEASONS TOUCHDOWN PASS LEADER

2	Benny Friedman, 1927–28
3	Benny Friedman, 1927–29
4	Benny Friedman, 1927–30
	John Unitas, 1957–60
	Len Dawson, 1962–63, 1965–66*
	Steve Young, 1992–94, 1998
	Brett Favre, 1995, 1996, 1997, 2003

MOST CONS SEASONS TD PASS LEADER

2	Benny Friedman, 1927–28
3	Benny Friedman, 1927–29
4	Benny Friedman, 1927–30
	John Unitas, 1957–60

MOST TOUCHDOWN PASSES, CAREER

7	Elmer Oliphant, 1920–21
8	Lou Smyth, 1920–23
14	Curly Lambeau, 1921–24
19	Curly Lambeau, 1921–25
22	Curly Lambeau, 1921–26
23	Curly Lambeau, 1921–27
24	Curly Lambeau, 1921–28
	Red Dunn, 1924–28
40	Benny Friedman, 1927–29
53	Benny Friedman, 1927–30
56	Benny Friedman, 1927–31
61	Benny Friedman, 1927–32
66	Benny Friedman, 1927–33
	Arnie Herber, 1930–40
80	Sammy Baugh, 1937–43
84	Sammy Baugh, 1937–44
95	Sammy Baugh, 1937–45
103	Sammy Baugh, 1937–46
128	Sammy Baugh, 1937–47
150	Sammy Baugh, 1937–48
168	Sammy Baugh, 1937–49
178	Sammy Baugh, 1937–50
185	Sammy Baugh, 1937–51
187	Sammy Baugh, 1937–52
	Bobby Layne, 1948–61
196	Bobby Layne, 1948–62
202	Y.A. Tittle, 1950–63
212	Y.A. Tittle, 1950–64

MOST TOUCHDOWN PASSES, CAREER (CONT.)

232	John Unitas, 1956–66
252	John Unitas, 1956–67
254	John Unitas, 1956–68
266	John Unitas, 1956–69
280	John Unitas, 1956–70
283	John Unitas, 1956–71
287	John Unitas, 1956–72
290	John Unitas, 1956–73
291	Fran Tarkenton, 1961–75
308	Fran Tarkenton, 1961–76
317	Fran Tarkenton, 1961–77
342	Fran Tarkenton, 1961–78
352	Dan Marino, 1983–95
369	Dan Marino, 1983–96
385	Dan Marino, 1983–97
408	Dan Marino, 1983–98
420	Dan Marino, 1983–99

MOST TOUCHDOWN PASSES, SEASON

7	Elmer Oliphant, 1921
9	Hoge Workman, 1924
	Red Dunn, 1925
11	Benny Friedman, 1927
20	Benny Friedman, 1929
24	Cecil Isbell, 1942
28	Sid Luckman, 1943
32	John Unitas, 1959
36	George Blanda, 1961*
	Y.A. Tittle, 1963
48	Dan Marino, 1984
49	Peyton Manning 2004

MOST TOUCHDOWN PASSES, ROOKIE

5	Benny Boynton, 1921
9	Hoge Workman, 1924
11	Benny Friedman, 1927
	Harry Newman, 1933
	Charlie O'Rourke, 1942
14	Bob Waterfield, 1945
22	Charlie Conerly, 1948
26	Peyton Manning, 1998

MOST TOUCHDOWN PASSES, GAME

4	Elmer Oliphant, Buf-NY, 10–16–21
	Red Dunn, ChiC-Mil, 12–10–25
	Ernie Nevers, Dul-Pot, 10–23–27
	Benny Friedman, NY-ChiB, 11–17–29
5	Benny Friedman, NY-Fra, 10–19–30
	Ray Buivid, ChiB-ChiC, 12–5–37
	Cecil Isbell, GB-ChiC, 11–1–42
6	Sammy Baugh, Was-Bkn, 10–31–43
7	Sid Luckman, Chi-NYG, 11–14–43
	Adrian Burk, Phi-Was, 11–28–54
	George Blanda, Hou-NYT, 11–19–61*
	Y.A. Tittle, NYG-Was, 10–28–62
	Joe Kapp, Min-Dal, 9–28–69

MOST CONS GAMES THROWING TD PASSES

4	Benny Boynton, 1921
	Hoge Workman, 1924
	Bill Kelly, 1928–29
7	Benny Friedman, 1929
9	Arnie Herber, 1936
11	Cecil Isbell, 1941
22	Cecil Isbell, 1941–42
25	John Unitas, 1956–58
37	John Unitas, 1956–59
47	John Unitas, 1956–60

MOST GAMES FOUR TD PASSES, CAREER

3	Sammy Baugh, 1937–43
	Sid Luckman, 1939–45
5	Sammy Baugh, 1937–47
7	Sammy Baugh, 1937–48
8	Sammy Baugh, 1937–49
	John Unitas, 1956–61
11	John Unitas, 1956–62
12	John Unitas, 1956–63
13	John Unitas, 1956–65
16	John Unitas, 1956–66
17	John Unitas, 1956–67
	Dan Marino, 1983–92
19	Dan Marino, 1983–94
20	Dan Marino, 1983–95
21	Dan Marino, 1983–98

MOST GAMES FOUR TD PASSES, SEASON

3	Sammy Baugh, 1943
	John Unitas, 1960
4	George Blanda, 1961*
	Vince Ferragamo, 1980
6	Dan Marino, 1984
	Peyton Manning, 2004

MOST CONSECUTIVE GAMES FOUR TD PASSES

2	Norm Van Brocklin, 1957
	Bobby Layne, 1959–60
	John Unitas, 1960
	John Unitas, 1962
	Tom Flores, 1963*
	Cotton Davidson, 1964*
	Len Dawson, 1964*
	Tommy Kramer, 1981
4	Dan Marino, 1984
5	Peyton Manning 2004

PASSING: INTERCEPTIONS

MOST PASSES THROWN WITHOUT INT

114	Jim Hardy, 1948
208	Milt Plum, 1959–60
	Milt Plum, 1960–61
225	Bart Starr, 1964
294	Bart Starr, 1964–65
308	Bernie Kosar, 1991

MOST PASSES HAD INTERCEPTED, CAREER

21	Arnie Herber, 1930–33
33	Arnie Herber, 1930–34
47	Arnie Herber, 1930–35
60	Arnie Herber, 1930–36
70	Arnie Herber, 1930–37
74	Arnie Herber, 1930–38
83	Arnie Herber, 1930–39
90	Arnie Herber, 1930–40
93	Sammy Baugh, 1937–43
101	Sammy Baugh, 1937–44
106	Arnie Herber, 1930–40, 1944–45
122	Sammy Baugh, 1937–46
137	Sammy Baugh, 1937–47
160	Sammy Baugh, 1937–48
174	Sammy Baugh, 1937–49
185	Sammy Baugh, 1937–50
202	Sammy Baugh, 1937–51
203	Sammy Baugh, 1937–52
210	Bobby Layne, 1948–60
226	Bobby Layne, 1948–61
243	Bobby Layne, 1948–62
259	George Blanda, 1949–58, 1960–66
262	George Blanda, 1949–58, 1960–67
264	George Blanda, 1949–58, 1960–68
265	George Blanda, 1949–58, 1960–69
270	George Blanda, 1949–58, 1960–70
276	George Blanda, 1949–58, 1960–71
277	George Blanda, 1949–58, 1960–75

MOST PASSES HAD INTERCEPTED, SEASON

9	Arnie Herber, 1932
17	Harry Newman, 1933
18	Whizzer White, 1938
21	Hugh McCullough, 1940
27	Bud Schwenk, 1942
31	Sid Luckman, 1947
34	Frank Tripucka, 1960*
42	George Blanda, 1962*

MOST PASSES HAD INTERCEPTED, GAME

5	Harry Newman, NYG-Por, 9–24–33
	Ernest Rentner, Bos-Pit, 12–1–35
	Jack Gildea, Pit-Bos, 12–1–35
	Cecil Isbell, GB-NYG, 11–20–38
	Sammy Baugh, Was-GB, 10–29–39
	Hugh McCullough, Pit-NYG, 11–19–39
	Tommy Thompson, Phi-Was, 10–23–41
7	Parker Hall, Cle-GB, 11–8–42
	Frank Sinkwich, Det-GB, 10–24–43
	Bob Waterfield, LA-GB, 10–17–48
8	Jim Hardy, ChiC-Phi, 9–24–50

PASSING: INTERCEPTION PERCENTAGE

MOST SEASONS PASS INT PCT. LEADER

2	Bob Monnett, 1933, 1936
	Sammy Baugh, 1940, 1942
3	Sammy Baugh, 1940, 1942, 1944
4	Sammy Baugh, 1940, 1942, 1944–45
5	Sammy Baugh, 1940, 1942, 1944–45, 1947

LOWEST PASS INT PCT., CAREER–(1500 ATTS)

6.7	Sammy Baugh, 1937–45
7.1	Sammy Baugh, 1937–46
6.6	Sammy Baugh, 1937–47
6.7	Sammy Baugh, 1937–48
6.6	Sammy Baugh, 1937–49
6.6	Sammy Baugh, 1937–50
6.8	Sammy Baugh, 1937–51
6.8	Sammy Baugh, 1937–52

LOWEST PASS INT PCT., CAREER (1500 ATTS)

6.5	Bobby Layne, 1948–53
6.2	Bobby Layne, 1948–54
6.0	Otto Graham, 1950–55
5.9	Charlie Conerly, 1948–59
4.8	John Unitas, 1956–60
5.0	John Unitas, 1956–61
5.1	John Unitas, 1956–62
4.8	John Unitas, 1956–63
4.3	Bart Starr, 1956–64
4.3	Bart Starr, 1956–65
3.9	Bart Starr, 1956–66
4.3	Bart Starr, 1956–67
3.7	Roman Gabriel, 1962–68
3.4	Roman Gabriel, 1962–69
3.3	Roman Gabriel, 1962–70
3.2	Roman Gabriel, 1962–71
3.4	Roman Gabriel, 1962–72
3.3	Roman Gabriel, 1962–73
3.3	Roman Gabriel, 1962–74
3.3	Roman Gabriel, 1962–75
3.2	Ken Anderson, 1971–76
3.2	Ken Anderson, 1971–77
3.3	Roman Gabriel, 1971–77
2.7	Joe Montana, 1979–83
2.6	Joe Montana, 1979–84
2.6	Joe Montana, 1979–85
2.6	Joe Montana, 1979–86
2.7	Joe Montana, 1979–87
2.5	Ken O'Brien, 1983–88
2.4	Bernie Kosar, 1985–89
2.6	Bernie Kosar, 1985–90
2.5	Bernie Kosar, 1985–91
2.6	Bernie Kosar, 1985–92
2.5	Bernie Kosar, 1985–93
2.5	Jeff Hostetler, 1985–94
2.1	Neil O'Donnell, 1991–95
2.2	Neil O'Donnell, 1991–96
2.1	Neil O'Donnell, 1991–97
2.0	Neil O'Donnell, 1991–98
2.0	Neil O'Donnell, 1991–99
2.1	Neil O'Donnell, 1991–2000
2.1	Neil O'Donnell, 1991–2001
2.1	Neil O'Donnell, 1991–2002
2.1	Neil O'Donnell, 1991–2003

LOWEST PASS INT PERCENTAGE, SEASON

8.9	Arnie Herber, 1932
6.5	Bob Monnett, 1933
5.5	Harry Newman, 1934
3.8	Bob Monnett, 1936
3.7	Ed Danowski, 1937
2.8	Dwight Sloan, 1939
2.2	Sammy Baugh, 1945
2.1	Charlie Conerly, 1959
2.0	Milt Plum, 1960
1.98	Roman Gabriel, 1962
1.5	Bart Starr, 1964
1.2	Bart Starr, 1966
0.7	Joe Ferguson, 1976

LOWEST PASS INT PERCENTAGE, ROOKIE

12.5	Harry Newman, 1933
8.2	Sammy Baugh, 1937
6.3	Parker Hall, 1939
5.5	Paul Christman, 1945
5.2	Paul Governali, 1946
4.4	Charlie Conerly, 1948
2.1	Gary Wood, 1964
2.03	Dan Marino, 1983
1.98	Charlie Batch, 1998

MOST PASSES THROWN WITHOUT INT, GAME

60	Davey O'Brien, Phi-Was, 12–1–40
63	Rich Gannon, Min-NE, 10–20–91
70	Drew Bledsoe, NE-Min, 11–13–94

PASSING: SACKS

MOST TIMES SACKED, CAREER (SINCE 1963)

92	Don Meredith, 1960–64
131	Don Meredith, 1960–65
168	Don Meredith, 1960–66
189	Don Meredith, 1960–67
219	Don Meredith, 1960–68
245	Fran Tarkenton, 1961–69
281	Fran Tarkenton, 1961–70
308	Fran Tarkenton, 1961–71
334	Fran Tarkenton, 1961–72
365	Fran Tarkenton, 1961–73
382	Fran Tarkenton, 1961–74
409	Fran Tarkenton, 1961–75
434	Fran Tarkenton, 1961–76
456	Fran Tarkenton, 1961–77
483	Fran Tarkenton, 1961–78

MOST TIMES SACKED, CAREER (SINCE 1963) (CONT.)

492	Dave Krieg, 1980–96
498	John Elway, 1983–97
516	John Elway, 1983–98

MOST TIMES SACKED, SEASON

59	Tony Eason, 1984
62	Ken O'Brien, 1985
72	Randall Cunningham, 1986
76	David Carr, 2002

MOST TIMES SACKED, GAME

11	Charley Johnson, SL-NYG, 11–1–64
	Bart Starr, GB-Det, 11–7–65
	Jack Kemp, Buf-Oak, 10–15–67*
	Bob Berry, Atl-SL, 11–24–68
12	Bert Jones, Bal-SL, 10–26–80
	Warren Moon, Hou-Dal, 9–29–85

RECEIVING

MOST SEASONS LEADING RECEIVER

2	Don Hutson, 1936–37
3	Don Hutson, 1936–37, 1939
4	Don Hutson, 1936–37, 1939, 1941
5	Don Hutson, 1936–37, 1939, 1941–42
6	Don Hutson, 1936–37, 1939, 1941–43
7	Don Hutson, 1936–37, 1939, 1941–44
8	Don Hutson, 1936–37, 1939, 1941–45

MOST CONS SEASONS LEADING RECEIVER

2	Don Hutson, 1936–37
	Don Hutson, 1941–42
3	Don Hutson, 1941–43
4	Don Hutson, 1941–44
5	Don Hutson, 1941–45

MOST PASS RECEPTIONS, CAREER

32	Ray Flaherty, 1927–33
40	Ray Flaherty, 1927–34
53	Luke Johnsos, 1929–35
61	Dale Burnett, 1930–36
93	Don Hutson, 1935–37
125	Don Hutson, 1935–38
159	Don Hutson, 1935–39
204	Don Hutson, 1935–40
262	Don Hutson, 1935–41
336	Don Hutson, 1935–42
383	Don Hutson, 1935–43
441	Don Hutson, 1935–44
488	Don Hutson, 1935–45
503	Bill Howton, 1952–63
506	Raymond Berry, 1955–64
564	Raymond Berry, 1955–65
620	Raymond Berry, 1955–66
631	Raymond Berry, 1955–67
632	Don Maynard, 1958, 1960–72
633	Don Maynard, 1958, 1960–73
635	Charley Taylor, 1964–75
649	Charley Taylor, 1964–75, 1977

MOST PASS RECEPTIONS, CAREER

657	Charlie Joiner, 1969–84
716	Charlie Joiner, 1969–85
750	Charlie Joiner, 1969–86
752	Steve Largent, 1976–87
791	Steve Largent, 1976–88
819	Steve Largent, 1976–89
847	Art Monk, 1980–92
888	Art Monk, 1980–93
934	Art Monk, 1980–94
942	Jerry Rice, 1985–95
1050	Jerry Rice, 1985–96
1057	Jerry Rice, 1985–97
1139	Jerry Rice, 1985–98
1206	Jerry Rice, 1985–99
1281	Jerry Rice, 1985–2000
1364	Jerry Rice, 1985–2001
1456	Jerry Rice, 1985–2002
1519	Jerry Rice, 1985–2003
1549	Jerry Rice, 1985–2004

MOST SEASONS FIFTY RECEPTIONS

2	Don Hutson, 1935–42
3	Don Hutson, 1935–43
	Tom Fears, 1948–50
	Pete Pihos, 1947–55
	Billy Wilson, 1951–55
4	Billy Wilson, 1951–56
5	Billy Wilson, 1951–57
	Raymond Berry, 1955–62
6	Raymond Berry, 1955–65
	Lionel Taylor, 1960–65*
	Art Powell, 1960–65*

MOST SEASONS FIFTY RECEPTIONS (CONT.)

7	Raymond Berry, 1955–66
	Art Powell, 1960–66*
	Lance Alworth, 1962–69*
	Charley Taylor, 1964–75
	Steve Largent, 1976–84
8	Steve Largent, 1976–85
9	Steve Largent, 1976–86
10	Steve Largent, 1976–87
	Gary Clark, 1985–94
	Jerry Rice, 1986–95
11	Jerry Rice, 1986–96
	Andre Reed, 1986–94, 1996–97
12	Jerry Rice, 1986–96, 1998
	Andre Reed, 1986–94, 1996–98
13	Jerry Rice, 1986–96, 1998–99
	Andre Reed, 1986–94, 1996–99
14	Jerry Rice, 1986–96, 1998–2000
15	Jerry Rice, 1986–96, 1998–2001
16	Jerry Rice, 1986–96, 1998–2002
17	Jerry Rice, 1986–96, 1998–2003

MOST PASS RECEPTIONS, SEASON

21	Ray Flaherty, 1932
22	John Kelly, 1933
26	Tod Goodwin, 1935
34	Don Hutson, 1936
41	Don Hutson, 1937
	Gaynell Tinsley, 1938
58	Don Looney, 1940
	Don Hutson, 1941
74	Don Hutson, 1942
77	Tom Fears, 1949
84	Tom Fears, 1950
92	Lionel Taylor, 1960*
100	Lionel Taylor, 1961*
101	Charlie Hennigan, 1964*
106	Art Monk, 1984
108	Sterling Sharpe, 1992
112	Sterling Sharpe, 1993
122	Cris Carter, 1994
123	Herman Moore, 1995
143	Marvin Harrison, 2002

MOST PASS RECEPTIONS, ROOKIE

13	Paul Moss, 1933
26	Tod Goodwin, 1935
36	Gaynell Tinsley, 1937
58	Don Looney, 1940
72	Bill Groman, 1960*
83	Earl Cooper, 1983
90	Terry Glenn, 1996
101	Anquan Boldin 2003

MOST PASS RECEPTIONS, GAME

8	Johnny Blood, GB-ChiC, 11–28–35
	Gaynell Tinsley, ChiC-GB, 9–25–38
	Gaynell Tinsley, ChiC-Phi, 10–26–38
	Red Ramsey, Phi-Chi, 11–19–39
	Don Looney, Phi-GB, 9–15–40
	Don Looney, Phi-Cle, 9–22–40
	Don Hutson, GB-Chi, 11–3–40
14	Don Looney, Phi-Was, 12–1–40
	Don Hutson, GB-NYG, 11–22–42
	Jim Keane, Chi-NYG, 10–23–49
	Ralph Heywood, NYB-Det, 12–4–49
18	Tom Fears, LA-Bal, 12–3–50
20	Terrell Owens, SF-Chi, 12–17–2000

MOST CONSECUTIVE GAMES RECEIVING

32	Don Hutson, 1937–39
43	Don Hutson, 1937–40
44	Don Hutson, 1937–41
50	Don Hutson, 1941–45
51	Tom Fears, 1947–51
52	Tommy McDonald, 1957–61
66	Tommy McDonald, 1957–62
80	Tommy McDonald, 1957–63
93	Tommy McDonald, 1957–64
94	Bobby Joe Conrad, 1961–68
96	Lance Alworth, 1962–69*
104	Dan Abramowicz, 1967–74
112	Harold Carmichael, 1972–79
127	Harold Carmichael, 1972–80
139	Steve Largent, 1976–86
152	Steve Largent, 1976–87
167	Steve Largent, 1976–88
177	Steve Largent, 1976–89
180	Art Monk, 1983–94
183	Art Monk, 1983–95
193	Jerry Rice, 1985–98
209	Jerry Rice, 1985–99
225	Jerry Rice, 1985–2000
241	Jerry Rice, 1985–2001

MOST CONSECUTIVE GAMES RECEIVING (CONT.)

257	Jerry Rice, 1985–2002
273	Jerry Rice, 1985–2003
274	Jerry Rice, 1985–2004

RECEIVING: YARDS

MOST SEASONS RECEIVING YARDS LEADER

2	Don Hutson, 1936, 1938
3	Don Hutson, 1936, 1938–39
4	Don Hutson, 1936, 1938–39, 1941
5	Don Hutson, 1936, 1938–39, 1941–42
6	Don Hutson, 1936, 1938–39, 1941–43
7	Don Hutson, 1936, 1938–39, 1941–44

MOST CONS SEASONS REC YARDS LEADER

2	Don Hutson, 1938–39
	Don Hutson, 1941–42
3	Don Hutson, 1941–43
4	Don Hutson, 1941–44

MOST YARDS RECEIVING, CAREER

527	Ray Flaherty, 1927–33
603	Ray Flaherty, 1927–34
864	Luke Johnsos, 1929–35
985	Luke Johnsos, 1929–36
1508	Don Hutson, 1935–37
2056	Don Hutson, 1935–38

MOST YARDS RECEIVING, CAREER

2902	Don Huston, 1935–39
3566	Don Huston, 1935–40
4304	Don Huston, 1935–41
5515	Don Huston, 1935–42
6291	Don Huston, 1935–43
7157	Don Huston, 1935–44
7991	Don Huston, 1935–45
8459	Bill Howton, 1952–63
9108	Raymond Berry, 1955–66
9275	Raymond Berry, 1955–67
9435	Don Maynard, 1958, 1960–68
10373	Don Maynard, 1958, 1960–69
10898	Don Maynard, 1958, 1960–70
11306	Don Maynard, 1958, 1960–71
11816	Don Maynard, 1958, 1960–72
11834	Don Maynard, 1958, 1960–73
12146	Charlie Joiner, 1969–86
12686	Steve Largent, 1976–88
13089	Steve Largent, 1976–89
13821	James Lofton, 1978–92
14004	James Lofton, 1978–93
15123	Jerry Rice, 1985–95
16377	Jerry Rice, 1985–96
16455	Jerry Rice, 1985–97
17612	Jerry Rice, 1985–98
18442	Jerry Rice, 1985–99
19247	Jerry Rice, 1985–2000
20386	Jerry Rice, 1985–2001
21597	Jerry Rice, 1985–2002
22466	Jerry Rice, 1985–2003
22895	Jerry Rice, 1985–2004

MOST SEASONS 1000 YARDS RECEIVING

2	Tom Fears, 1949–50
	Billy Howton, 1952, 1956
	Harlon Hill, 1954, 1956
	Del Shofner, 1958, 1961
3	Del Shofner, 1958, 1961–62
4	Del Shofner, 1958, 1961–63
	Art Powell, 1960, 1962–64*
	Lionel Taylor, 1960–61, 1963, 1965*
5	Art Powell, 1960, 1962–64, 1966*
	Lance Alworth, 1963–67*
6	Lance Alworth, 1963–68*
7	Lance Alworth, 1963–68*
	Steve Largent, 1978–81, 1983–85
8	Steve Largent, 1978–81, 1983–86
	Jerry Rice, 1986–93
9	Jerry Rice, 1986–94
10	Jerry Rice, 1986–95
11	Jerry Rice, 1986–96
12	Jerry Rice, 1986–96, 1998
13	Jerry Rice, 1986–96, 1998, 2001
14	Jerry Rice, 1986–96, 1998, 2002

MOST RECEIVING YARDS, SEASON

350	Ray Flaherty, 1932
433	Charley Malone, 1935
536	Don Hutson, 1936
675	Gaynell Tinsley, 1937
846	Don Hutson, 1939
1211	Don Hutson, 1942
1495	Elroy Hirsch, 1951
1746	Charlie Hennigan, 1961*
1848	Jerry Rice, 1995

MOST RECEIVING YARDS, ROOKIE

283	Paul Moss, 1933
432	Tod Goodwin, 1935
675	Gaynell Tinsley, 1937
707	Don Looney, 1940
1231	Billy Howton, 1952
1473	Bill Groman, 1960*

MOST GAMES 200 YARDS RECEIVING, CAREER

2	Don Hutson, 1935–42
3	Don Hutson, 1935–43
4	Don Hutson, 1935–44
	Charlie Hennigan, 1960–62*
	Lance Alworth, 1962–65*
5	Lance Alworth, 1962–67*

MOST GAMES 200 YARDS RECEIVING, SEASON

2	Don Hutson, 1942
	Gene Roberts, 1949
3	Charlie Hennigan, 1961*

MOST GAMES 100 YARDS RECEIVING, CAREER

3	Don Hutson, 1935–37
	Gaynell Tinsley, 1937
4	Gaynell Tinsley, 1937–38
8	Don Hutson, 1935–39
10	Don Hutson, 1935–41
16	Don Hutson, 1935–42
18	Don Hutson, 1935–43
20	Don Hutson, 1935–44
24	Don Hutson, 1935–45
28	Charlie Hennigan, 1960–64*
29	Charlie Hennigan, 1960–65*
31	Art Powell, 1959–66
34	Don Maynard, 1958, 1960–67
41	Don Maynard, 1958, 1960–68
46	Don Maynard, 1958, 1960–69
48	Don Maynard, 1958, 1960–70
49	Don Maynard, 1958, 1960–71
50	Don Maynard, 1958, 1960–72
58	Jerry Rice, 1985–95
61	Jerry Rice, 1985–96
64	Jerry Rice, 1985–98
66	Jerry Rice, 1985–99
68	Jerry Rice, 1985–2001
68	Jerry Rice, 1985–2001
73	Jerry Rice, 1985–2002
75	Jerry Rice, 1985–2003
76	Jerry Rice, 1985–2004

MOST GAMES 100 YARDS RECEIVING, SEASON

2	Don Hutson, 1935
3	Gaynell Tinsley, 1937
4	Don Hutson, 1939
6	Don Hutson, 1942
9	Elroy Hirsch, 1951
	Bill Groman, 1960*
10	Charlie Hennigan, 1961*
11	Michael Irvin, 1995

MOST CONS GAMES 100 YARDS RECEIVING

2	Don Hutson, 1939
	Don Hutson, 1941–42
	Don Hutson, 1942
4	Don Hutson, 1945
5	Elroy Hirsch, 1951
	Bob Boyd, 1954
6	Raymond Berry, 1960
7	Bill Groman, 1961*
	Charlie Hennigan, 1961*
	Michael Irvin, 1995

MOST YARDS RECEIVING, GAME

167	Gaynell Tinsley, ChiC-Was, 9–24–37
	Gaynell Tinsley, ChiC-Cle, 11–27–38
180	Don Looney, Phi-Was, 12–1–40
209	Don Hutson, GB-Cle, 10–18–42
213	Wilbur Moore, Was-Bkn, 10–31–43
237	Don Hutson, GB-Bkn, 11–21–43
303	Jim Benton, Cle-Det, 11–27–45
309	Stephone Paige, KC-SD, 12–22–85
336	Willie Anderson, Rams-NO, 11–26–89

LONGEST PASS RECEPTION

70	Bullets Walson, Was-Cle, 12–11–21
	Bob Rapp, Col-Oor, 11–25–23
	Bob Rapp, Col-Day, 12–3–23
78	Chuck Corgan, KC-RI, 11–15–25
83	Don Hutson, GB-Chi, 9–22–35
86	Joe Carter, Phi-GB, 11–14–37
97	Gaynell Tinsley, ChiC-ChiB, 12–5–37
98	Gaynell Tinsley, ChiC-Cle, 11–27–38
99	Andy Farkas, Was-Pit, 10–15–39
	Bobby Mitchell, Was-Cle, 9–15–63

LONGEST PASS RECEPTION (CONT.)
Pat Studstill, Det-Bal, 10–16–66
Gerry Allen, Was-Chi, 9–15–68
Cliff Branch, Rdrs-Was, 10–2–83
Mike Quick, Phi-Atl, 11–10–85
Tony Martin, SD-Sea, 9–18–94
Robert Brooks, GB-Chi, 9–11–95
Mark Boerigter, KC-SD, 12–22–02
Andre' Davis, Cle-Cin, 10–17–04

RECEIVING: TOUCHDOWNS
MOST SEASONS TD RECEPTION LEADER
2	Ray Flaherty, 1927, 1929
	Johnny Blood, 1930–31
3	Ray Flaherty, 1927, 1929, 1932
	Don Hutson, 1935–37
4	Don Hutson, 1935–38
5	Don Hutson, 1935–38, 1940
6	Don Hutson, 1935–38, 1940–41
7	Don Hutson, 1935–38, 1940–42
8	Don Hutson, 1935–38, 1940–43
9	Don Hutson, 1935–38, 1940–44

MOST CONSECUTIVE SEASONS TD REC LEADER
2	Johnny Blood, 1930–31
	Don Hutson, 1935–36
3	Don Hutson, 1935–37
4	Don Hutson, 1935–38
	Don Hutson, 1940–43
5	Don Hutson, 1940–44

MOST TOUCHDOWN RECEPTIONS, CAREER
3	Heine Miller, 1920–21
	George Halas, 1920–21
4	George Halas, 1920–22
5	Guy Chamberlin, 1920–23
	Scotty Bierce, 1921–23
8	Bob Rapp, 1920–24
9	Bob Rapp, 1920–25
10	Jimmy Conzelman, 1921–28
13	Ray Flaherty, 1927–29
22	Johnny Blood, 1925–31
25	Johnny Blood, 1925–32
28	Johnny Blood, 1925–33
31	Johnny Blood, 1925–35
33	Johnny Blood, 1925–36
37	Johnny Blood, 1925–37
43	Don Hutson, 1935–40
53	Don Hutson, 1935–41
70	Don Hutson, 1935–42
81	Don Hutson, 1935–43
90	Don Hutson, 1935–44
99	Don Hutson, 1935–45
100	Steve Largent, 1976–89
103	Jerry Rice, 1985–92
118	Jerry Rice, 1985–93
131	Jerry Rice, 1985–94
146	Jerry Rice, 1985–95
154	Jerry Rice, 1985–96
155	Jerry Rice, 1985–97
164	Jerry Rice, 1985–98
169	Jerry Rice, 1985–99
176	Jerry Rice, 1985–2000

MOST TOUCHDOWN RECEPTIONS, CAREER
185	Jerry Rice, 1985–2001
192	Jerry Rice, 1985–2002
194	Jerry Rice, 1985–2003
197	Jerry Rice, 1985–2004

MOST TOUCHDOWN RECEPTIONS, SEASON
3	Heine Miller, 1921
	George Halas, 1921
	Bob Rapp, 1923
5	Bob Rapp, 1924
	Tillie Voss, 1924
6	Gibby Welch, 1928
8	Ray Flaherty, 1929
11	Johnny Blood, 1931
17	Don Hutson, 1942
	Elroy Hirsch, 1951
	Bill Groman, 1961*
18	Mark Clayton, 1984
22	Jerry Rice, 1987

MOST TOUCHDOWN RECEPTIONS, ROOKIE
2	Jerry Noonan, 1921
	Gus Tebell, 1923
3	Evar Swanson, 1924
4	Charlie Berry, 1925
	Ray Flaherty, 1927
6	Gibby Welch, 1928
	Don Hutson, 1935
10	Bill Swiacki, 1948

MOST TOUCHDOWN RECEPTIONS, ROOKIE (CONT.)
13	Billy Howton, 1952
	John Jefferson, 1979
17	Randy Moss, 1998

MOST TOUCHDOWN RECEPTIONS, GAME
2	Gus Tebell, Col-OOr, 11–25–23
	Bob Rapp, Col-Roc, 10–12–24
	Hal Erickson, Mil-Ken, 10–12–24
	Bob Rapp, Col-Akr, 11–2–24
	Tillie Voss, GB-KC, 11–27–24
	John Armstrong, RI-Dul, 10–11–25
	Marty Norton, GB-Mil, 10–11–25
	Hal Erickson, ChiC-KC, 10–18–25
	Myrt Basing, GB-Roc, 10–25–25
	Ray Crowther, Fra-Akr, 11–7–25
	Jimmy Conzelman, Det-Cle, 11–11–25
	Charlie Berry, Pot-GB, 11–26–25
	Walt French, Pot-Fra, 11–29–25
	Herb Blumer, ChiC-Mil, 12–10–25
	Dick O'Donnell, GB-Det, 9–19–26
3	Joe Rooney, Dul-Pot, 10–23–27
	Ray Flaherty, NYY-ChiB, 11–8–27
	Gibby Welch, Pro-Day, 9–29–29
	Johnny Blood, GB-Pro, 11–26–31
	Joe Carter, Phi-Cin, 11–6–34
	Bill Karr, ChiB-Det, 11–24–35
	Gaynell Tinsley, ChiC-Was, 9–24–37
	Don Hutson, GB-Cle, 10–17–37
	Les McDonald ChiB-ChiC, 12–5–37
	Don Hutson, GB-Cle, 9–11–38
	Don Hutson, GB-Cle, 10–30–38
	Don Hutson, GB-Was, 11–30–41
	Don Hutson, GB-ChiC, 11–1–42
	Andy Uram, GB-ChiC, 11–1–42
	Don Hutson, GB-Cle, 11–8–42
	Jim Benton, Cle-CP, 9–24–44
	Dave Diehl, Det-Cle, 11–26–44
4	Don Hutson, GB-Det, 10–7–45
	Bob Shaw, LA-Was, 12–11–49
5	Bob Shaw, ChiC-Bal, 10–1–50
	Kellen Winslow, SD-Oak, 11–22–81
	Jerry Rice, SF-Atl, 10–14–90

MOST CONSECUTIVE GAMES TD RECEPTIONS
3	Heine Miller, 1921
	Hinkey Haines, 1927
	Gibby Welch, 1928
4	Gibby Welch, 1928–29
	Rex Thomas, 1930
	Johnny Blood, 1931
	Bill McKalip, 1931
	Don Hutson, 1936
	Bill Hewitt, 1938
5	Jim Benton, 1939–40
7	Don Hutson, 1941–42
	Don Hutson, 1943–44
	Ken Kavanaugh, 1947
	Mal Kutner, 1947–48
11	Elroy Hirsch, 1950–51
	Buddy Dial, 1959–60
13	Jerry Rice, 1986–87

RECEIVING: AVERAGE GAIN
HIGHEST AVERAGE GAIN, CAREER (200 REC)
17.4	Don Hutson, 1935–40
16.4	Don Hutson, 1935–41
16.4	Don Hutson, 1935–42
16.4	Don Hutson, 1935–43
16.2	Don Hutson, 1935–44
16.4	Don Hutson, 1935–45
17.0	Jim Benton, 1938–46
16.7	Jim Benton, 1938–47
19.4	Hugh Taylor, 1947–52
19.5	Hugh Taylor, 1947–53
19.2	Hugh Taylor, 1947–54
20.5	Harlon Hill, 1954–58
20.5	Harlon Hill, 1954–59
20.5	Harlon Hill, 1954–60
20.4	Harlon Hill, 1954–61
20.2	Harlon Hill, 1954–62
21.6	Buddy Dial, 1959–63
21.3	Buddy Dial, 1959–64
21.2	Lance Alworth, 1962–65*
20.8	Buddy Dial, 1959–66
22.6	Homer Jones, 1964–69
22.3	Homer Jones, 1964–70
22.5	Stanley Morgan, 1977–82
22.3	Homer Jones, 1964–70

HIGHEST AVG. GAIN, SEASON (24 REC)
16.4	Tod Goodwin, 1935
18.8	Gaynell Tinsley, 1937
24.9	Don Hutson, 1939
32.4	Dan Currivan, 1947

HIGHEST AVG. GAIN, GAME (3 REC)
55.7	Gaynell Tinsley, ChiC-Was, 9–24–37
60.3	Dan Currivan, Bos-Was, 11–30–47
60.7	Bill Groman, Hou-Den, 11–20–60*
	Homer Jones, NYG-Was, 12–12–65
63.0	Torry Holt, SL-Atl, 9–24–2000

YARDS FROM SCRIMMAGE
MOST SCRIMMAGE YARDS, CAREER
1,558	Cliff Battles, 1932–33
2,133	Cliff Battles, 1932–34
2,385	Cliff Battles, 1932–35
3,102	Cliff Battles, 1932–36
4,057	Cliff Battles, 1932–37
4,397	Clarke Hinkle, 1932–41
5,611	Don Hutson, 1935–42
6,428	Don Hutson, 1935–43
7,381	Don Hutson, 1935–44
8,275	Don Hutson, 1935–45
8,422	Joe Perry, 1950–59
8,514	Joe Perry, 1950–60
9,511	Joe Perry, 1950–61

MOST SCRIMMAGE YARDS, CAREER
10,064	Joe Perry, 1950–62
11,153	Jim Brown, 1957–63
12,939	Jim Brown, 1957–64
14,811	Jim Brown, 1957–65
16,765	Walter Payton, 1975–84
18,799	Walter Payton, 1975–85
20,514	Walter Payton, 1975–86
21,264	Walter Payton, 1975–87
22,242	Jerry Rice, 1985–2002
23,111	Jerry Rice, 1985–2003
23,540	Jerry Rice, 1985–2004

MOST SCRIMMAGE YARDS, SEASON
636	Cliff Battles, 1932
922	Cliff Battles, 1933
1,178	Beattie Feathers, 1934
1,215	Don Hutson, 1942
1,345	Gene Roberts, 1949
1,498	Elroy Hirsch, 1951
1,665	Jim Brown, 1958
1,867	Jim Brown, 1961
2,131	Jim Brown, 1963
2,243	O.J. Simpson, 1975
2,244	Eric Dickerson, 1984
2,314	Marcus Allen, 1985
2,358	Barry Sanders, 1997
2,429	Marshall Faulk, 1999

MOST SCRIMMAGE YARDS, ROOKIE
636	Cliff Battles, 1932
1,178	Beattie Feathers, 1934
1,231	Billy Howton, 1952
1,473	Bill Groman, 1960
1,569	Charley Taylor, 1964
1,908	Ottis Anderson, 1979
1,924	Billy Sims, 1980
2,212	Eric Dickerson, 1983

MOST SCRIMMAGE YARDS, GAME
215	Cliff Battles, Bos-NYG, 10–8–33
248	Andy Farkas, Was-Phi, 11–1–42
303	Jim Benton, Cle-Det, 11–27–45
330	Billy Cannon, Hou-NYY, 12–10–61*
336	Flipper Anderson, LARm-NO, 11–26–89

INTERCEPTIONS
MOST SEASONS INTERCEPTION LEADER
2	Dick Lane, 1952, 1954
	Jack Christiansen, 1953, 1957
	Milt Davis, 1957, 1959
	Dick Lynch, 1961, 1963
	Johnny Robinson, 1966, 1970
	Bill Bradley, 1971–72
	Emmitt Thomas, 1969, 1974
	Everson Walls, 1981–82
3	Everson Walls, 1981–82, 1985

MOST PASS INTERCEPTIONS, CAREER
10	George McAfee, 1940–41
14	Don Hutson, 1935–42
23	Sammy Baugh, 1937–43
27	Sammy Baugh, 1937–44
31	Sammy Baugh, 1937–45
	Irv Comp, 1943–48
34	Irv Comp, 1953–49
35	Frank Reagan, 1941, 1946–51
40	Emlen Tunnell, 1948–52
46	Emlen Tunnell, 1948–53

MOST PASS INTERCEPTIONS, CAREER (CONT.)

54	Emlen Tunnell, 1948–54
61	Emlen Tunnell, 1948–55
67	Emlen Tunnell, 1948–56
73	Emlen Tunnell, 1948–57
74	Emlen Tunnell, 1948–58

MOST PASS INTERCEPTIONS, CAREER

76	Emlen Tunnell, 1948–59
79	Emlen Tunnell, 1948–60
81	Paul Krause, 1964–79

MOST PASS INTERCEPTIONS, SEASON

6	Ace Parker, 1940
	Kent Ryan, 1940
	Don Hutson, 1940
7	Marshall Goldberg, 1941
	Art Jones, 1941
8	Clyde Turner, 1942
11	Sammy Baugh, 1943
13	Dan Sandifer, 1948
	Spec Sanders, 1950
14	Dick Lane, 1952

MOST PASS INTERCEPTIONS, ROOKIE

7	Art Jones, 1941
10	Irv Comp, 1943
13	Dan Sandifer, 1948
14	Dick Lane, 1952

MOST PASS INTERCEPTIONS, GAME

4	Sammy Baugh, Was-Det, 11–14–43
	Dan Sandifer, Was-Bos, 10–31–48
	Don Doll, Det-ChiC, 10–23–49
	Bob Nussbaumer, ChiC-NYB, 11–13–49
	Russ Craft, Phi-ChiC, 9–24–50
	Bobby Dillon, GB-Det, 11–26–53
	Jack Butler, Pit-Was, 12–13–53
	Goose Gonsoulin, Den-Buf, 9–18–60*
	Jerry Norton, SL-Was, 11–20–60
	Dave Baker, SF-LA, 12–4–60
	Jerry Norton, SL-Pit, 11–26–61
	Bobby Ply, Tex-SD, 12–16–62*
	Bobby Hunt, KC-Hou, 10–4–64*
	Willie Brown, Den-NYJ, 11–15–64*
	Dick Anderson, Mia-Pit, 12–3–73
	Willie Buchanon, GB-SD, 9–24–78
	Deron Cherry, KC-Sea, 9–29–85
	Kwamie Lassiter, Arz-SD, 12–27–98
	Deltha O'Neal, Den-KC, 10–7–2001

MOST CONSECUTIVE GAMES PASS INTS

4	Bulldog Turner, 1942
	Don Hutson, 1942
5	Irv Comp, 1943
6	Frank Seno, 1947
	Dan Sandifer, 1948
	Spec Sanders, 1950
7	Tom Landry, 1950–51
8	Tommy Morrow, 1962–63*

INTERCEPTIONS: YARDS

MOST SEASON PASS INT YARDS LEADER

2	Dick Lane, 1952, 1954
	Herb Adderly, 1966, 1969
	Dick Anderson, 1968, 1970

MOST PASS INTERCEPTION YARDS, CAREER

168	Ward Cuff, 1937–41
244	Sammy Baugh, 1937–42
356	Sammy Baugh, 1937–43
377	Sammy Baugh, 1937–44
491	Sammy Baugh, 1937–45
522	Frank Reagan, 1941, 1946–49
654	Frank Reagan, 1941, 1946–50
714	Frank Reagan, 1941, 1946–51
757	Emlen Tunnell, 1948–52
874	Emlen Tunnell, 1948–53
982	Emlen Tunnell, 1948–54
1058	Emlen Tunnell, 1948–55
1145	Emlen Tunnell, 1948–56
1232	Emlen Tunnell, 1948–57
1240	Emlen Tunnell, 1948–58
1260	Emlen Tunnell, 1948–59

MOST PASS INTERCEPTION YARDS, CAREER

1282	Emlen Tunnell 1948–60
1465	Rod Woodson, 1987–2002
1483	Rod Woodson, 1987–2003

MOST PASS INTERCEPTION YARDS, SEASON

146	Ace Parker, 1940
152	Ward Cuff, 1941
197	Don Hutson, 1943
242	Bill Dudley, 1946
258	Dan Sandifer, 1948
301	Don Doll, 1949
339	Charley McNeil, 1961*
358	Ed Reed, 2004

MOST PASS INTERCEPTION YARDS, ROOKIE

128	Ned Mathews, 1941
149	Irv Comp, 1943
172	Howard Livingston, 1944
258	Dan Sandifer, 1948
301	Don Doll, 1949

MOST PASS INTERCEPTION YARDS, GAME

111	Ace Parker, Bkn-Cle, 11–17–40
121	Milt Davis, Bal-Chi, 11–17–57
177	Charlie McNeil, SD-Hou, 9–24–61*

LONGEST PASS INTERCEPTION RETURN

85	Howard Berry, Roc-ChiS, 10–16–21
96	Joe Guyon, Oor-ChiC, 12–2–23
99	Martin Kottler, Pit-ChiC, 9–27–33
100	Vern Huffman, Det-Bkn, I0-I7–37
102	Bob Smith, Det-Chi, 11–24–49
	Erich Barnes, NYG-Dal, 10–15–61
	Gary Barbaro, KC-Sea, 12–11–77
	Louis Breeden, Cin-SD, 11–8–81
103	Vencie Glenn, SD-Den, 11–29–87
	Louis Oliver, Mia-Buf, 10–4–92
106	Ed Reed, Bal-Cle, 11–7–04

INTERCEPTIONS: TOUCHDOWNS

MOST PASS INTERCEPTION TDS, CAREER

3	Guy Chamberlin, 1921–22
	Duke Hanny, 1923–28
	Len Sedbrook, 1928–30
	Johnny Blood, 1925–32
4	Johnny Blood, 1925–35
5	Johnny Blood, 1925–36
	Warren Lahr, 1950–54
	Bobby Dillon, 1952–58
	Dick Lane, 1952–60
	Dick Harris, 1960–63
	Larry Wilson, 1960–66
	Herb Adderley, 1961–66
6	Herb Adderley, 1961–67
7	Herb Adderley, 1961–69
	Erich Barnes, 1958–70
9	Ken Houston, 1967–71
	Rod Woodson, 1987–99
10	Rod Woodson, 1987–2001
12	Rod Woodson, 1987–2002

MOST PASS INTERCEPTION TDS, SEASON

2	by many, 1922–60
3	Dick Harris, 1961*
	Dick Lynch, 1963
	Herb Adderley, 1965
	Lem Barney, 1967
	Miller Farr, 1967*
4	Ken Houston, 1971
	Jim Kearney, 1972
	Eric Allen, 1993

MOST PASS INTERCEPTION TDS, ROOKIE

2	Tom Leary, 1930
	Bill Petrilas, 1944
	Dan Sandifer, 1948
	Jerry Weatherly, 1950
	Dick Lane, 1952
	J.C. Caroline, 1956
	Milt Davis, 1957
	Bobby Franklin, 1960
	Dave Webster, 1960*
	Don Webb, 1961*
	Gus Otto, 1965*
3	Lem Barney, 1967
	Ronnie Lott, 1981

MOST PASS INTERCEPTION TDS, GAME

2	Guy Chamberlin, Can-ChiC, 11–26–22
	Hoot Flanagan, Pot-Fra, 11–29–25
	Tom Leary, Nwk-Fra, 10–4–30
	Bi11 Blackburn, ChiC-Bos, 10–24–48
	Dan Sandifer, Was-Bos, 10–31–48
	Bob Franklin, Cle-Chi, 12–11–60
	Bill Stacy, SL-Dal, 11–5-61
	Jerry Norton, SL-Pit, 11–26–61
	Miller Farr, Hou-Buf, 12–7-68*

MOST PASS INTERCEPTION TDS, GAME (CONT.)

	Ken Houston, Hou-SD, 12–19–71
	Jim Kearney, KC-Den, 10–1–72
	Lemar Parrish, Cin-Hou, 12–17–72
	Dick Anderson, Mia-Pit, 12–3–73
	Prentice McCray, NE-NYJ, 11–21–76
	Kenny Johnson, Atl-GB, 11–27–83
	Mike Kozlowski, Mia-NYJ, 12–16–83
	Dave Brown, Sea-KC, 11–4–84
	Lloyd Burruss, KC-SD, 10–19–86
	Henry Jones, Buf-Ind, 9–20–92
	Robert Massey, Phx-Was, 10–4–92
	Eric Allen, Phi-NO, 12–26–93
	Ken Norton, SF-SL, 10–22–95
	Otis Smith, NYJ-TB, 12–14–97
	Dewayne Washington, Pit-Jax, 11–22–98
	Aaron Glenn, Hou-Pit, 12–8–02

PUNTING

MOST SEASONS PUNT LEADER

2	Sammy Baugh, 1940–41
3	Sammy Baugh, 1940–42
4	Sammy Baugh, 1940–43
	Jerrel Wilson, 1965, 1968, 1972–73

MOST CONSECUTIVE SEASONS PUNT LEADER

2	Sammy Baugh, 1940–41
3	Sammy Baugh, 1940–42
4	Sammy Baugh, 1940–43

MOST PUNTS, CAREER

115	Parker Hall, 1939–40
164	Parker Hall, 1939–41
200	Parker Hall, 1939–42
222	Sammy Baugh, 1937–44
255	Sammy Baugh, 1937–45
288	Sammy Baugh, 1937–46
323	Sammy Baugh, 1937–47
324	Sammy Baugh, 1937–49
333	Sammy Baugh, 1937–50
337	Sammy Baugh, 1937–51
338	Sammy Baugh, 1937–52
345	Adrian Burk, 1950–54
406	Adrian Burk, 1950–55
474	Adrian Burk, 1950–56
523	Norm Van Brocklin, 1949–60
525	Don Chandler, 1956–64
598	Don Chandler, 1956–65
659	Don Chandler, 1956–66
660	Don Chandler, 1956–67

MOST PUNTS, CAREER

703	Sam Baker, 1953, 1956–68
712	Paul Maguire, 1960–69*
795	Paul Maguire, 1960–70
821	Bobby Joe Green, 1960–71
888	Bobby Joe Green, 1960–72
970	Bobby Joe Green, 1960–73
1018	Jerrel Wilson, 1963–77
1072	Jerrel Wilson, 1963–78
1083	John James, 1972–84
1090	Dave Jennings, 1974–86
1154	Dave Jennings, 1974–87
1163	Lee Johnson, 1985–2000
1216	Sean Landeta, 1987–2001
1268	Sean Landeta, 1987–2002
1327	Sean Landeta, 1987–2003
1367	Sean Landeta, 1987–2004
1437	Jeff Feagles, 1988–2005

MOST PUNTS, SEASON

58	Parker Hall, 1939
64	Roy McKay, 1946
92	Howard Maley, 1947
101	Bob Scarpitto, 1967*
	John James, 1977
109	John James, 1978
114	Bob Parson, 1981
	Chad Stanley, 2002

MOST PUNTS, ROOKIE

60	Howard Maley, 1946
81	Adrian Burk, 1950
88	Bill Van Heusen, 1968*
93	Wilbur Summers, 1977
96	Mike Connell, 1978
	Chris Norman, 1986
108	John Teltchik, 1986
111	Brad Maynard, 1997

MOST PUNTS, GAME

14	Dick Nesbitt, ChiC-ChiB, 11–30–33
	Keith Molesworth, Chi-GB, 12–10–33
	Sammy Baugh, Was-Phi, 11–5–39
	Carl Kinscherf, NYG-Det, 11–7–43
	George Taliaferro, NYY-LA, 9–28–51
15	John Teltchik, Phi-NYG, 12–6–87
16	Leo Araguz, Oak-SD, 10–11–98

LONGEST PUNT

94	Joe Lintzenich, Chi-NYG, 11–16–31
98	Steve O'Neal, NYJ-Den, 9–21–69

PUNTING: AVERAGE

HIGHEST PUNTING AVE, CAREER (250 PUNTS)

45.3	Sammy Baugh, 1937–45
45.3	Sammy Baugh, 1937–46
45.1	Sammy Baugh, 1937–47
45.1	Sammy Baugh, 1937–49
45.0	Sammy Baugh, 1937–50
45.1	Sammy Baugh, 1937–51
45.1	Sammy Baugh, 1937–52
45.3	Bobby Joe Green, 1960–63
45.3	Tommy Davis, 1959–64
45.3	Tommy Davis, 1959–65
45.1	Sammy Baugh, 1937–52
45.2	Rohn Stark, 1982–85
45.2	Rohn Stark, 1982–86
45.1	Sammy Baugh, 1937–52
45.7	Shane Lechler, 2000–03
45.9	Shane Lechler, 2000–04
45.9	Shane Lechler, 2000–05

HIGHEST PUNTING AVERAGE, SEASON

40.8	Parker Hall, 1939
51.4	Sammy Baugh, 1940

HIGHEST PUNTING AVERAGE, ROOKIE

40.8	Parker Hall, 1939
41.0	Ray Mallouf, 1941
41.3	Bob Trocolor, 1942
45.9	Frank Sinkwich, 1943

HIGHEST PUNTING AVERAGE, GAME

59.4	Sammy Baugh, Was-Det, 10–27–40
61.6	Roy McKay, GB-ChiC, 10–28–45
61.8	Bob Cifers, Det-Chi, 11–24–46

PUNTING: BLOCKED

MOST CONSECUTIVE PUNTS, NONE BLOCKED

533	Bobby Joe Green, 1960–68
578	Bobby Walden, 1964–72
623	Dave Jennings, 1976–83
726	Chris Gardocki, 1991–2000
825	Chris Gardocki, 1991–2001
906	Chris Gardocki, 1991–2002
978	Chris Gardocki, 1991–2003
1045	Chris Gardocki, 1991–2004
1112	Chris Gardocki, 1991–2005

MOST PUNTS HAD BLOCKED, CAREER

3	Sammy Baugh, 1937–43
	Roy Zimmerman, 1940–43
4	Sammy Baugh, 1937–44
	Roy Zimmerman, 1940–44
6	Sammy Baugh, 1937–47
7	Sammy Baugh, 1937–50
	Tom Yewcic, 1961–65*
8	Tom Yewcic, 1961–66*
9	Jerrel Wilson, 1963–74
10	Jerrel Wilson, 1963–75
11	Jerrel Wilson, 1963–76
12	Jerrel Wilson, 1963–77
	Herman Weaver, 1970–79
14	Herman Weaver, 1970–80
	Harry Newsome, 1985–92

MOST PUNTS HAD BLOCKED, SEASON

3	Sammy Baugh, 1943
	Howard Maley, 1947
	Jug Girard, 1949
	Bob Luna, 1955
	Horace Gillom, 1955
	Dennis Partee, 1973
	Jim McCann, 1973
	Greg Gantt, 1973
	Tom Blanchard, 1975
	Steve Broussard, 1975
	Tom Wittum, 1975
	Dave Jennings, 1976
	Don Cockroft, 1976
	Spike Jones, 1976

MOST PUNTS HAD BLOCKED, SEASON (CONT.)

	Mike Patrick, 1977
	Tom Wittum, 1977
	Herman Weaver, 1979
	Dave Jennings, 1979
	Rich Camarillo, 1986
	Harry Newsome, 1986
	Bill Renner, 1986
6	Harry Newsome, 1988

PUNTING: INSIDE THE 20

MOST PUNTS INSIDE THE 20, CAREER (SINCE 1976)

47	John James, 1972–77
71	John James, 1972–78
83	John James, 1972–79
108	John James, 1972–80
128	Bob Parsons, 1973–81
138	Bob Parsons, 1973–82
159	Bob Parsons, 1973–83
170	Dave Jennings, 1974–84
193	Dave Jennings, 1974–85
220	Dave Jennings, 1974–86
232	Dave Jennings, 1974–87
253	Rich Camarillo, 1981–94
279	Rich Camarillo, 1981–95
284	Reggie Roby, 1983–97
298	Reggie Roby, 1983–98
304	Jeff Feagles, 1988–99
328	Jeff Feagles, 1988–2000
354	Jeff Feagles, 1988–2001
376	Jeff Feagles, 1988–2002
407	Jeff Feagles, 1988–2003
430	Jeff Feagles, 1988–2004
456	Jeff Feagles, 1988–2005

MOST PUNTS INSIDE THE 20, SEASON

28	John James, 1976
29	Mike Bragg, 1977
31	Bob Parsons, 1981
33	John Kidd, 1985
35	Rich Camarillo, 1994
	Mark Royals, 1994
39	Kyle Richardson, 1994

MOST PUNTS INSIDE THE 20, GAME

8	Mark Royals, Pit-Hou, 11–6–94
	Bryan Barker, Jax-Bal, 11–14–99

PUNT RETURNS

MOST SEASONS PUNT RETURN LEADER

1	by many (1941–61)
2	Dick Christy, 1961–62*
	Speedy Duncan, 1965–66*
3	Speedy Duncan, 1965–66, 1971
	Rick Upchurch, 1976, 1978, 1982

MOST PUNT RETURNS, CAREER

30	Andy Farkas, 1938–42
45	Andy Farkas, 1938–43
52	Andy Farkas, 1938–44
59	Andy Farkas, 1938–45
63	Bill Dudley, 1942 45–47
71	Bosh Pritchard, 1942, 1946–48
84	Bosh Pritchard, 1942, 1946–49
112	George McAfee, 1940–41, 1945–50
116	Bill Dudley, 1942, 1945–51
133	Emlen Tunnell, 1948–52
171	Emlen Tunnell, 1948–53
192	Emlen Tunnell, 1948–54
217	Emlen Tunnell, 1948–55
239	Emlen Tunnell, 1948–56
251	Emlen Tunnell, 1948–57
257	Emlen Tunnell, 1948–58
258	Emlen Tunnell, 1948–59
	Billy Johnson, 1974–80, 1982–86
279	Billy Johnson, 1974–80, 1982–87
282	Billy Johnson, 1974–80, 1982–88
292	Vai Sikahema, 1986–93
301	Tim Brown, 1988–96
344	Dave Meggett, 1989–97
349	Dave Meggett, 1989–98
	Brian Mitchell, 1990–2000
388	Brian Mitchell, 1990–2001
434	Brian Mitchell, 1990–2002
463	Brian Mitchell, 1990–2003

MOST PUNT RETURNS, SEASON

19	Whizzer White, 1941
21	Meryl Condit, 1942
22	Bob Davis, 1944
27	Bill Dudley, 1946
28	Duke Slater, 1947
30	George McAfee, 1948

MOST PUNT RETURNS, SEASON (CONT.)

33	George McAfee, 1950
34	Emlen Tunnell, 1951
	Bibbles Bawel, 1952

MOST PUNT RETURNS, SEASON

38	Emlen Tunnell, 1953
41	Alvin Haymond, 1965
53	Alvin Haymond, 1970
	Larry Jones, 1975
54	Rolland Lawrence, 1976
70	Danny Reece, 1979

MOST PUNT RETURNS, ROOKIE

14	Art Jones, 1941
20	Bill Dudley, 1942
21	Steve Bagarus, 1945
28	Walt Slater, 1947
34	Bibbles Bawel, 1952
37	Rodger Bird, 1966*
43	Bruce Taylor, 1970
48	Neal Colzie, 1975
	Kevin Miller, 1978
54	James Jones, 1980
57	Lew Barnes, 1986

MOST PUNT RETURNS, GAME

7	Bosh Pritchard, Phi-GB, 11–29–42
	George McAfee, Chi-GB, 10–15–50
8	Emlen Tunnell, NYG-NYY, 12–3–50
	Joe Arenas, SF-Det, 10–16–55
	Hugh McElhenny, SF-Det, 11–2–58
9	Rodger Bird, Oak-Den, 9–10–67*
	Ralph McGill, SF-Atl, 10–29–72
	Ed Podolak, KC-SD, 11–10–74
	Tony Leonard, SF-NO, 10–17–76
	Butch Johnson, Dal-Buf, 11–15–76
	Larry Marshall, Phi-TB, 9–18–77
11	Eddie Brown, Was-TB, 10–9–77

PUNT RETURNS: FAIR CATCHES

MOST FAIR CATCHES, CAREER

29	Willie Wood, 1960–63
40	Willie Wood, 1960–64
50	Willie Wood, 1960–65
59	Willie Wood, 1960–66
65	Willie Wood, 1960–67
76	Willie Wood, 1960–68
82	Willie Wood, 1960–69
100	Willie Wood, 1960–70
102	Willie Wood, 1960–71
111	Tim Brown, 1988–96
121	Mel Gray, 1986–97
137	Brian Mitchell, 1990–98
151	Brian Mitchell, 1990–99
184	Brian Mitchell, 1990–2000
206	Brian Mitchell, 1990–2001
217	Brian Mitchell, 1990–2002
231	Brian Mitchell, 1990–2003

MOST FAIR CATCHES, SEASON

15	Billy Gambrell, 1963
17	Billy Gambrell, 1964
18	Abe Woodson 1965
	Johnny Roland, 1966
24	Kenny Graham, 1969*
25	Mark Konecny, 1988
	Phil McConkey, 1988
27	Leo Lewis, 1989
33	Brian Mitchell, 2000

MOST FAIR CATCHES, GAME

4	Eddie Dove, NYG-Cle, 10–27–63
5	Bill Butler, Min-Bal, 11–17–63
	Tommy Watkins, Det-LA, 9–19–65
	Johnny Roland, SL-GB, 10–30–67
	Kenny Graham, SD-Cin, 10–4–69*
	Walt Sumner, Cle-Mia, 10–25–70
	Willie Wood, GB-Chi, 11–15–70
6	Jake Scott, Mia-Buf, 12–20–70
7	Lem Barney, Det-Chi, 11–21–76
	Bobby Morse, Phi-Buf, 12–27–87

PUNT RETURNS: YARDS

MOST SEASONS PUNT RET YARDAGE LEADER

2	Bill Dudley, 1942, 1946
	Emlen Tunnell, 1951–52
	Dick Christy, 1961–62*
	Claude Gibson, 1963–64*
	Alvin Haymond, 1965–66
3	Alvin Haymond, 1965–66, 1969

MOST PUNT RETURN YARDS, CAREER

371	Andy Farkas, 1938–42
539	Andy Farkas, 1938–43
630	Andy Farkas, 1938–44
731	Andy Farkas, 1938–45
884	Ernie Steele, 1942, 1944–47
925	Bill Dudley, 1942, 1945–49
1147	George McAfee, 1940–41, 1945–49
1431	George McAfee, 1940–41, 1945–50
1481	Bill Dudley, 1942, 1945–51
1635	Emlen Tunnell, 1948–52
1858	Emlen Tunnell, 1948–53
1928	Emlen Tunnell, 1948–54
2026	Emlen Tunnell, 1948–55
2146	Emlen Tunnell, 1948–56
2206	Emlen Tunnell, 1948–57
2209	Emlen Tunnell, 1948–59
2298	Rick Upchurch, 1975–79
2651	Rick Upchurch, 1975–80
2714	Rick Upchurch, 1975–81
2956	Rick Upchurch, 1975–82
3008	Rick Upchurch, 1975–83
3036	Billy Johnson, 1974–80, 1982–85
3123	Billy Johnson, 1974–80, 1982–86
3291	Billy Johnson, 1974–80, 1982–87
3317	Billy Johnson, 1974–80, 1982–88
3668	Dave Meggett, 1989–97
3708	Dave Meggett, 1989–98
3811	Brian Mitchell, 1990–2000
4278	Brian Mitchell, 1990–2001
4845	Brian Mitchell, 1990–2002
4999	Brian Mitchell, 1990–2003

MOST PUNT RETURN YARDS, SEASON

262	Whizzer White, 1941
271	Bill Dudley, 1942
	Bob Davis, 1944
385	Bill Dudley, 1946
435	Walt Slater, 1947
555	Bill Grimes, 1950
612	Rodger Bird, 1967*
655	Neal Colzie, 1975
666	Greg Pruitt, 1983
692	Fulton Walker, 1985
875	Desmond Howard, 1996

MOST PUNT RETURN YARDS, ROOKIE

271	Bill Dudley, 1942
435	Duke Slater, 1947
490	George Atkinson, 1968*
516	Bruce Taylor, 1970
577	Lynn Swann, 1974
655	Neal Colzie, 1975
656	Louis Lipps, 1984

MOST PUNT RETURN YARDS, GAME

147	Emlen Tunnell, NYG-ChiC, 10–14–51
175	Jack Christiansen, Det-GB, 11–22–51
184	Tommy Watkins, Det-SF, 10–6–63
205	George Atkinson, Oak-Buf, 9–15–68*
207	Leroy Irvin, Rams-Atl, 10–11–81

LONGEST PUNT RETURN

75	Paddy Driscoll, ChiC-RI, 10–16–21
78	Benny Boynton, Buf-Roc, 10–19–24
90	Roddy Lamb, RI-Mil, 11–22–25
95	Al Bloodgood, NYG-Pot, 9–30–28

LONGEST PUNT RETURN

98	Gil LeFebvre, Cin-Bkn, 12–3–33
	Charlie West, Min-Was, 11–3–68
	Dennis Morgan, Dal-SL, 10–13–74
	Terance Mathis, NYJ-Dal, 11–4–90
103	Robert Bailey, Rams-NO, 10–23–94

PUNT RETURNS: AVERAGE

HIGHEST AVG. PUNT RET, CAREER (75 RET)

14.5	George McAfee, 1940–41, 1945–49
13.9	Bill Dudley, 1945–46–50
12.8	George McAfee, 1940–41, 1945–50
13.1	Jack Christiansen, 1951–55
13.1	Jack Christiansen, 1951–56
12.8	George McAfee, 1940–41, 1945–50
13.0	Claude Gibson, 1961–64
12.8	George McAfee, 1940–41, 1945–50
13.1	Speedy Duncan, 1964–67
12.8	Speedy Duncan, 1964–68
12.8	George McAfee, 1940–41, 1945–50
13.2	Billy Johnson, 1974–76
13.7	Billy Johnson, 1974–77
13.4	Billy Johnson, 1974–78
13.2	Billy Johnson, 1974–79
12.8	George McAfee, 1940–41, 1945–50
12.9	Billy Johnson, 1974–80, 1982

HIGHEST AVG. PUNT RET, CAREER (75 RET) (CONT.)

12.8	George McAfee, 1940–41, 1945–50
13.5	Henry Ellard, 1983–85
12.9	Henry Ellard, 1983–86
12.8	George McAfee, 1940–41, 1945–50
13.7	Darrien Gordon, 1994, 1996
13.6	Darrien Gordon, 1994, 1996–97
13.2	Darrien Gordon, 1994, 1986–98
12.8	George McAfee, 1940–41, 1945–50

HIGHEST AVERAGE PUNT RETURN, SEASON

17.0	Dick Todd, 1941
20.7	Frank Sinkwich, 1943
20.88	Jerry Davis, 1948
20.93	Red Cochran, 1949
23.0	Herb Rich, 1950

HIGHEST AVERAGE PUNT RETURN, ROOKIE

20.7	Frank Sinkwich, 1943
20.9	Jerry Davis, 1948
23.0	Herb Rich, 1950

HIGHEST AVERAGE PUNT RETURN, GAME

37.7	Frank Seno, Bos-Chi, 11–2–47
43.8	Jack Christiansen, Det-GB, 11–22–51
47.7	Chuck Latourette, SL-NO, 9–29–68
51.0	Steve Smith, Car-Cin, 12–8–2002

PUNT RETURNS: TOUCHDOWNS

MOST PUNT RETURN TOUCHDOWNS, CAREER

1	by several, 1921–25
3	Curly Oden, 1925–26
4	Curly Oden, 1925–27
5	Curly Oden, 1925–31
6	Jack Christiansen, 1951–52
7	Jack Christiansen, 1951–54
8	Jack Christiansen, 1951–56
	Rick Upchurch, 1975–82
9	Eric Metcalf, 1989–97
10	Eric Metcalf, 1989–99, 2001

MOST PUNT RETURN TOUCHDOWNS, SEASON

1	by several, 1921–25
3	Curly Oden, 1926
4	Jack Christiansen, 1951

MOST PUNT RETURN TOUCHDOWNS, ROOKIE

2	Jerry Davis, 1948
4	Jack Christiansen, 1951

MOST PUNT RETURN TOUCHDOWNS, GAME

2	Jack Christiansen, Det-LA, 10–14–51
	Jack Christiansen, Det-GB, 10–22–51
	Dick Christy, NYT-Den, 9–24–61*
	Rick Upchurch, Den-Cle, 9–26–76
	Leroy Irvin, LA-Atl, 10–11–81
	Vai Sikahema, SL-TB, 12–21–86
	Todd Kinchen, Rams-Atl, 12–27–92
	Eric Metcalf, Cle-Pit, 10–24–93
	Eric Metcalf, SD-Cin, 11–2–97
	Darrien Gordon, Den-Car, 11–9–97
	Jermaine Lewis, Bal-Sea, 12–7–97
	Steve Smith, Car-Cin, 12–8–2002
	Eddie Drummond, Det-Jax, 11–14–04

KICK RETURNS

MOST SEASONS KICK RETURN LEADER

2	Marshall Goldberg, 1941–42
	Lynn Chandnois, 1951–52
	Abe Woodson, 1959, 1962
3	Abe Woodson, 1959, 1962–63

MOST KICK RETURNS, CAREER

27	Marshall Goldberg, 1939–42
29	Marshall Goldberg, 1939–43
30	Andy Farkas, 1938–44
38	Andy Farkas, 1938–45
43	Frank Seno, 1943–46
70	Frank Seno, 1943–47
78	Frank Seno, 1943–48
80	Frank Seno, 1943–49
84	Eddie Saenz, 1946–50
93	Eddie Saenz, 1946–51
108	Woodley Lewis, 1950–55
115	Joe Arenas, 1951–56
139	Joe Arenas, 1951–57
153	Al Carmichael, 1953–58
175	Al Carmichael, 1953–58, 1960
191	Al Carmichael, 1953–58, 1960–61
193	Abe Woodson, 1958–65
220	Ron Smith, 1965–72

MOST KICK RETURNS, CAREER (CONT.)

256	Ron Smith, 1965–73
275	Ron Smith, 1965–74
309	Mel Gray, 1986–94
362	Mel Gray, 1986–95
412	Mel Gray, 1986–96
421	Mel Gray, 1986–97
	Brian Mitchell, 1990–99
468	Brian Mitchell, 1990–2000
509	Brian Mitchell, 1990–2001
552	Brian Mitchell, 1990–2002
607	Brian Mitchell, 1990–2003

MOST KICK RETURNS, SEASON

15	Marshall Goldberg, 1941
16	Ken Heineman, 1942
23	Johnny Grigas, 1943
29	Eddie Saenz, 1947
32	Woodley Lewis, 1953
34	Woodley Lewis, 1954
37	Abe Woodson, 1962
47	Odell Barry, 1964*
	Larry Jones, 1975

MOST KICK RETURNS, SEASON

55	Bruce Harper, 1978
	Bruce Harper, 1979
	David Turner, 1979
60	Drew Hill, 1981
63	Tyrone Hughes, 1994
66	Tyrone Hughes, 1995
70	Tyrone Hughes, 1996
82	MarTay Jenkins 2000

MOST KICK RETURNS, ROOKIE

11	Bill Dudley, 1942
	Chuck Fenenbock, 1943
	Johnny Butler, 1943
12	Albie Reisz, 1944
	Hank Margarita, 1944
	Steve Bagarus, 1945
22	Walt Slater, 1947
26	Dan Sandifer, 1948
28	Don Paul, 1950
31	Leon Burton, 1960*
47	Odell Barry, 1964*
50	Nesby Glasgow, 1979
	Dino Hall, 1979
55	Stump Mitchell, 1981
56	Tony Horne, 1998
67	Ronnie Jenkins, 2000
73	Josh Scobey, 2003
	Chris Carr, 2005

MOST KICK RETURNS, GAME

7	Joe Watt, Det-ChiC, 11–7–48
8	George Taliaferro, NYY-NYG, 12–3–50
	Mel Renfro, Dal-GB, 11–29–64
9	Noland Smith, KC-Oak, 11–23–67*
	Dino Hall, Cle-Pit, 10–7–79
	Paul Palmer, KC-Sea, 9–20–87
	Eric Metcalf, Atl-SF, 9–29–96
	Eric Metcalf, Atl-SL, 11–10–96
10	Desmond Howard, Oak-Sea, 10–26–97
	Richard Alston, Cle-Cin, 11–28–2004

KICK RETURNS: YARDS

MOST SEASONS KICK RETURN YARDAGE LEADER

2	Marshall Goldberg, 1941–42
	Woodley Lewis, 1953–54
	Al Carmichael, 1956–57
	Timmy Brown, 1961, 1963
	Bobby Jancik, 1962–63*
	Ron Smith, 1966–67

MOST SEASONS KICK RETURN YARDAGE LEADER

2	Bruce Harper, 1977–78
3	Bruce Harper, 1977–79
	Tyrone Hughes, 1994–96

MOST KICK RETURN YARDS, CAREER

683	Marshall Goldberg, 1941–42
736	Marshall Goldberg, 1941–43
819	Andy Farkas, 1938–44
984	Andy Farkas, 1938–45
1070	Frank Seno, 1943–46
1706	Frank Seno, 1943–47
1877	Frank Seno, 1943–48
1920	Steve Van Buren, 1944–49
2046	Eddie Saenz, 1946–50
2191	Eddie Saenz, 1946–51
2292	Buddy Young, 1950–54
2575	Woodley Lewis, 1950–55

MOST KICK RETURN YARDS, CAREER (CONT.)
3141 Joe Arenas, 1951–56
3798 Joe Arenas, 1951–57
3907 Al Carmichael, 1953–58
4488 Al Carmichael, 1953–58, 1960
4798 Al Carmichael, 1953–58, 1960–61
4873 Abe Woodson, 1958–64
5538 Abe Woodson, 1958–65

MOST KICK RETURN YARDS, CAREER
5555 Ron Smith, 1965–72
6502 Ron Smith, 1965–73
6922 Ron Smith, 1965–74
7650 Mel Gray, 1986–94
8833 Mel Gray, 1986–95
10057 Mel Gray, 1986–96
10250 Mel Gray, 1986–97
10710 Brian Mitchell, 1990–2000
11735 Brian Mitchell, 1990–2001
12897 Brian Mitchell, 1990–2002
14014 Brian Mitchell, 1990–2003

MOST KICK RETURN YARDS, SEASON
290 Marshall Goldberg, 1941
393 Marshall Goldberg, 1942
442 Ken Heineman, 1943
471 Johnny Grigas, 1944
599 Abe Karnofsky, 1946
797 Eddie Saenz, 1947
830 Woodley Lewis, 1953
836 Woodley Lewis, 1954
927 Al Carmichael, 1956
1157 Abe Woodson, 1962
1317 Bobby Jancik, 1963*
1345 Buster Rhymes, 1985
1556 Tyrone Hughes, 1994
1617 Tyrone Hughes, 1995
1791 Tyrone Hughes, 1996
2186 MarTay Jenkins 2000

MOST KICK RETURN YARDS, ROOKIE
298 Bill Dudley, 1942
325 Steve Bagarus, 1945
480 Walt Slater, 1947
594 Dan Sandifer, 1948
693 Don Paul, 1950
749 Les Goble, 1954
897 Leon Burton, 1960*
1245 Odell Barry, 1964*
1293 Andre Coleman, 1994
1428 Terry Fair, 1998
1531 Ronnie Jenkins, 2000
1684 Josh Scobey, 2003
1752 Chris Carr, 2005

MOST KICK RETURN YARDS, GAME
164 Marshall Goldberg, ChiC-GB, 11-1-42
207 Joe Scott, NYG-LA, 11-14-48
294 Wally Triplett, Det-LA, 10-29-50
304 Tyrone Hughes, NO-Rams, 10-23-94

LONGEST KICK RETURN
92 Cy Wentworth, Pro-NYG, 10-11-25
98 Chief Elkins, Fra-ChiC, 11-24-28
102 Doug Russell, ChiC-Cin, 9-24-34
105 Frank Seno, ChiC-NYG, 10-20-46
106 Al Carmichael, GB-Chi, 10-7-56
    Noland Smith, KC-Den, 12-17-67
    Roy Green, SL-Dal, 10-21-79

KICK RETURNS: AVERAGE
HIGHEST AVG. KICK RET., CAREER (75 RET)
24.1 Frank Seno, 1943–48
24.0 Frank Seno, 1943–49
26.7 Steve Van Buren, 1944–50
29.4 Lynn Chandnois, 1950–54
28.9 Lynn Chandnois, 1950–55
29.6 Lynn Chandnois, 1950–56
29.8 Abe Woodson, 1958–63
29.6 Lynn Chandnois, 1950–56
31.7 Gale Sayers, 1965–68
30.6 Gale Sayers, 1965–69

HIGHEST AVERAGE KICK RETURN, SEASON
24.2 Marshall Goldberg, 1941
27.1 Bill Dudley, 1942
27.6 Ken Heineman, 1943
28.7 Steve Van Buren, 1945
31.4 Frank Seno, 1946
31.6 Jack Salscheider, 1949
33.7 Vitamin Smith, 1950
35.2 Lynn Chandnois, 1952
35.5 Ollie Matson, 1958
41.1 Travis Williams, 1967

HIGHEST AVERAGE KICK RETURN, ROOKIE
27.1 Bill Dudley, 1942
27.1 Steve Bagarus, 1945
31.8 Tom Wilson, 1956
33.1 Tom Moore, 1960
41.1 Travis Williams, 1967

HIGHEST AVG. KICK RETURN, GAME (3 RET)
41.0 Marshall Goldberg, ChiC-GB, 11-1-42
51.8 Joe Scott, NYG-LA, 11-14-48
73.6 Wally Triplett   Det-LA, 10-29-50

KICK RETURNS: TOUCHDOWNS
MOST KICK RETURN TOUCHDOWNS, CAREER
1 by many, 1921–39
2 George McAfee, 1940–41
  Andy Farkas, 1938–41
  Dante Magnani, 1940–43
  Steve Van Buren, 1944–45
3 Steve Van Buren, 1944–47
  Vitamin Smith, 1949–50
  Lynn Chandnois, 1950–53
  Ollie Matson, 1952, 1954
4 Ollie Matson, 1952, 1954–56
6 Ollie Matson, 1952, 1954–58
  Gale Sayers, 1965–67
  Travis Williams, 1967–71
  Mel Gray, 1986–94
  Dante Hall, 2000–05

MOST KICK RETURN TOUCHDOWNS, SEASON
1 by many, 1921–46
2 Eddie Saenz, 1947
3 Vitamin Smith, 1950
  Abe Woodson, 1963
4 Travis Williams, 1967
  Cecil Turner, 1970

MOST KICK RETURN TOUCHDOWNS, ROOKIE
1 by many, 1921–51
2 Ollie Matson, 1952
  Les Goble, 1954
  Lenny Lyles, 1958
  Leon Burton, 1960*
  Goldie Sellers, 1966*
4 Travis Williams, 1967

MOST KICK RETURN TOUCHDOWNS, GAME
1 by many, 1941–65
2 Timmy Brown, Phi-Dal, 11-6-66
  Travis Williams, GB-Cle, 11-12-67
  Ron Brown, Rams-GB, 11-24-86
  Tyrone Hughes, NO-Rams, 10-23-94
  Chad Morton, NYJ-Buf, 9-8-2002

COMBINED RETURNS
MOST COMBINED RETURNS, CAREER
45 Marshall Goldberg, 1939–42
64 Andy Farkas, 1938–43
82 Andy Farkas, 1938–44
97 Andy Farkas, 1938–45
121 Frank Seno, 1943–47
142 Frank Seno, 1943–48

MOST COMBINED RETURNS, CAREER
148 Bill Dudley, 1942, 1945–49
161 Bill Dudley, 1942, 1945–50
194 Bill Dudley, 1942, 1945–51
212 Emlen Tunnell, 1948–53
238 Emlen Tunnell, 1948–54
263 Emlen Tunnell, 1948–55
285 Emlen Tunnell, 1948–56
297 Emlen Tunnell, 1948–57
303 Emlen Tunnell, 1948–58
304 Emlen Tunnell, 1948–59
313 Al Carmichael, 1953–58, 1960–61
316 Alvin Haymond, 1964–70
332 Alvin Haymond, 1964–70
365 Alvin Haymond, 1964–71
387 Ron Smith, 1965–72
450 Ron Smith, 1965–73
510 Ron Smith, 1965–74
527 Vai Sikahema, 1986–93
573 Mel Gray, 1986–95
645 Mel Gray, 1986–96
673 Mel Gray, 1986–97
738 Brian Mitchell, 1990–99
817 Brian Mitchell, 1990–2000
897 Brian Mitchell, 1990–2001
986 Brian Mitchell, 1990–2002
1070 Brian Mitchell, 1990–2003

MOST COMBINED RETURNS, SEASON
24 Marshall Goldberg, 1941
31 Bill Dudley, 1942
33 Steve Bagarus, 1945
41 Bill Dudley, 1946
53 Eddie Saenz, 1947
55 Billy Grimes, 1950
67 Woodley Lewis, 1953
72 Mel Renfro, 1964
74 Chuck Latourette, 1968
88 Alvin Haymond, 1970
100 Larry Jones, 1975
    Tyrone Hughes, 1996
102 Glyn Milburn, 1997
103 Brian Mitchell, 1998
114 Michael Lewis, 2002
    B.J. Sams, 2004

MOST COMBINED RETURNS, GAME
12 Mel Renfro, Dal-GB, 11-29-64
   Larry Jones, Was-Dal, 12-13-75
   Eddie Brown, Was-TB, 10-9-77
   Nesby Glasgow, Bal-Den, 9-2-79
13 Stump Mitchell, SL-Atl, 10-18-81
   Ronnie Harris, NE-Pit, 12-5-93

COMBINED RETURNS: YARDS
MOST COMBINED RETURN YARDS, CAREER
895 Marshall Goldberg, 1939–42
1129 Andy Farkas, 1938–43
1449 Andy Farkas, 1938–44
1715 Andy Farkas, 1938–45
2354 Frank Seno, 1943–47
2624 Frank Seno, 1943–48
2663 Frank Seno, 1943–49
2804 Bill Dudley, 1942, 1945–50
3224 Bill Dudley, 1942, 1945–51
3258 Bill Dudley, 1942, 1945–51, 1953
3392 Woodley Lewis   1050–55
3835 Joe Arenas, 1951–56
4572 Joe Arenas, 1951–57
4660 Al Carmichael, 1953–58
5342 Al Carmichael, 1953–58, 1960
5720 Al Carmichael, 1953–58, 1960–61
5822 Abe Woodson, 1958–64
6494 Abe Woodson, 1958–65

MOST COMBINED RETURN YARDS, CAREER
6505 Ron Smith, 1965–72
7804 Ron Smith, 1965–73
8710 Ron Smith, 1965–74
9734 Mel Gray, 1986–94
11220 Mel Gray, 1986–95
12649 Mel Gray, 1986–96
13003 Mel Gray, 1986–97
13062 Brian Mitchell, 1990–99
14521 Brian Mitchell, 1990–2000
16013 Brian Mitchell, 1990–2001
17742 Brian Mitchell, 1990–2002
19103 Brian Mitchell, 1990–2003

MOST COMBINED RETURN YARDS, SEASON
442 Marshall Goldberg, 1941
569 Bill Dudley, 1942
576 Steve Bagarus, 1945
665 Bill Dudley, 1946
1105 Eddie Saenz, 1947
1155 Bill Grimes, 1950
1336 Abe Woodson, 1962
1462 Bobby Jancik, 1963*
1582 Chuck Latourette, 1968
1658 Bruce Harper, 1978
1737 Stump Mitchell, 1981
1930 Brian Mitchell, 1994
1943 Tyrone Hughes, 1996
2187 MarTay Jenkins   2000
2432 Michael Lewis   2002

MOST COMBINED RETURN YARDS, GAME
294 Wally Triplett, Det-LA, 10-29-50
    Woodley Lewis, LA-Det, 10-18-53
347 Tyrone Hughes, NO-Rams, 10-23-94

COMBINED RETURNS: TOUCHDOWNS
MOST COMBINED RETURN TDS, CAREER
1 by several, 1921–25
3 Curly Oden, 1925–26
4 Curly Oden, 1925–27
5 Curly Oden, 1925–31
  Steve Van Buren, 1944–45
  Emlen Tunnell, 1948–51
6 Jack Christiansen, 1951–52
7 Jack Christiansen, 1951–54

MOST COMBINED RETURN TDS, CAREER (CONT.)

8	Jack Christiansen, 1951–56
9	Ollie Matson, 1952, 1954–58
	Mel Gray, 1986–95
11	Eric Metcalf, 1989–97
	Brian Mitchell, 1990–2000
12	Brian Mitchell, 1990–2001
	Eric Metcalf, 1989–99, 2001
13	Brian Mitchell, 1990–2002

MOST COMBINED RETURN TDS, SEASON

1	by several, 1921–25
3	Curly Oden, 1926
	Vitamin Smith, 1950
4	Emlen Tunnell, 1951
	Jack Christiansen, 1951
	Gale Sayers, 1967
	Travis Williams, 1967
	Cecil Turner, 1970
	Billy Johnson, 1975
	Rick Upchurch, 1976
	Dante Hall, 2003
	Eddie Drummond 2004

MOST COMBINED RETURN TDS, GAME

2	Jack Christiansen, Det-LA, 10–14–51
	Jack Christiansen, Det-GB, 11–22–51
	Jimmy Patton, NYG-Was, 10–30–55
	Bobby Mitchell, Cle-Phi, 11–23–58
	Dick Christy, NYT-Den, 9–24–61*
	Al Frazier, Den-Bos, 12–3–61*

MOST COMBINED RETURN TDS, GAME

2	Timmy Brown, Phi-Dal , 11–6–66
	Travis Williams, GB-Cle, 11–12–67
	Gale Sayers, Chi-SF, 12–3–67
	Travis Williams, GB-Pit, 11–2–69
	Rick Upchurch, Den-Cle, 9–26–76
	Eddie Payton, Det-Min, 12–17–77
	Leroy Irvin, LA-Atl, 10–11–81
	Ron Brown, Rams-GB, 11–24–85
	Vai Sikahema, SL-TB, 12–21–86
	Todd Kinchen, Rams-Atl, 12–27–92
	Eric Metcalf, Cle-Pit, 10–24–93
	Tyrone Hughes, NO-Rams, 10–23–94
	Eric Metcalf, SD-Cin, 11–2–97
	Darrien Gordon, Den-Car, 11–9–97
	Jermaine Lewis, Bal-Sea, 12–7–97
	Jermaine Lewis, Bal-NYJ, 12–24–00
	Chad Morton, NYJ-Buf, 9–8–02
	Michael Lewis, NO-Was, 10–13–02
	Steve Smith, Car-Cin, 12–8–02
	Dante Hall, KC-SL, 12–8–02
	Eddie Drummond, Det-Jax, 11–14–04

FUMBLES

MOST FUMBLES, CAREER

27	Paul Christman, 1945–46
30	Paul Christman, 1945–47
34	Sammy Baugh, 1937–48
40	Sammy Baugh, 1937–50
46	Sammy Baugh, 1937–51
47	Sammy Baugh, 1937–52
	Bobby Layne, 1948–53
49	Bobby Layne, 1948–54
53	Bobby Layne, 1948–55
56	Bobby Layne, 1948–56
59	Bobby Layne, 1948–57
66	Bobby Layne, 1948–58
68	Bobby Layne, 1948–59
69	Bobby Layne, 1948–60
73	Bobby Layne, 1948–61
80	Bobby Layne, 1948–62
82	John Unitas, 1956–68
84	John Unitas, 1956–69
86	John Unitas, 1956–70
89	John Unitas, 1956–71
92	John Unitas, 1956–72
95	John Unitas, 1956–73
96	Roman Gabriel, 1962–76
105	Roman Gabriel, 1962–77
106	Dan Fouts, 1973–87
108	Dave Krieg, 1980–91
118	Dave Krieg, 1980–92
124	Dave Krieg, 1980–93
128	Dave Krieg, 1980–94
144	Dave Krieg, 1980–95
150	Dave Krieg, 1980–96
152	Warren Moon, 1984–97
160	Warren Moon, 1984–98
161	Warren Moon, 1984–2000

MOST FUMBLES, SEASON

12	Paul Christman, 1945
15	Paul Christman, 1945

MOST FUMBLES, SEASON (CONT.)

	Sammy Baugh, 1947
	Sam Etcheverry, 1961
16	Don Meredith, 1964
17	Dan Pastorini, 1973
	Warren Moon, 1984
18	Dave Krieg, 1989
	Warren Moon, 1990
21	Tony Banks, 1996
23	Kerry Collins, 2001
	Daunte Culpepper, 2002

MOST FUMBLES, GAME

5	Paul Christman, ChiC-GB, 11–10–46
	Charlie Conerly, NYG-SF, 12–1–57
6	Sam Etcheverry, SL-NYG, 9–17–61
7	Len Dawson, KC-SD, 11–15–64*

FUMBLES: RECOVERIES (OWN & OPP)

MOST RECOVERIES (OWN & OPP) CAREER

12	Steve Van Buren 1944–46
15	Tommy Thompson, 1940–47
17	Steve Van Buren, 1944–48
18	Bob Waterfield, 1945–49
19	Bob Waterfield, 1945–50
	Steve Van Buren, 1944–50
	Sammy Baugh, 1937–50
21	Sammy Baugh, 1937–51
23	Bob Waterfield, 1945–52
24	Bobby Layne, 1948–60
	Charlie Conerly, 1948–60
26	Charlie Conerly, 1948–61
27	Bobby Layne, 1948–62
	Jack Kemp, 1958, 1960–66
33	Jack Kemp, 1958, 1960–67
38	Jack Kemp, 1958, 1960–67, 1969
43	Fran Tarkenton, 1961–78
44	Warren Moon, 1984–93
46	Warren Moon, 1984–94
51	Warren Moon, 1984–95
53	Warren Moon, 1984–96
54	Warren Moon, 1984–97
55	Warren Moon, 1984–98
56	Warren Moon, 1984–2000

MOST RECOVERIES (OWN & OPP), SEASON

8	Paul Christman, 1945
	Joe Schmidt, 1955
9	Don Hultz, 1963
	Dave Krieg, 1989
	Brian Griese, 1999
	Jon Kitna, 2000
12	David Carr, 2002

MOST RECOVERIES (OWN & OPP), GAME

4	Otto Graham, Cle-NYG, 10–25–53
	Sam Etcheverry, SL-NYG, 9–17–61
	Roman Gabriel, LA-SF, 10–12–69
	Joe Ferguson, Buf-Mia, 9–18–77
	Randall Cunningham, Phi-Rdrs, 11–30–88

FUMBLES: OWN RECOVERIES

MOST OWN FUMBLE RECOVERIES, CAREER

11	Paul Christman, 1945–46
16	Sammy Baugh, 1937–48
17	Sammy Baugh, 1937–49
19	Sammy Baugh, l937–50
21	Sammy Baugh, 1937–51
22	Charlie Conerly, 1948–58
	Bobby Layne, 1948–59
24	Bobby Layne, 1948–60
	Charlie Conerly, 1948–60
26	Charlie Conerly, 1948–61
27	Bobby Layne, 1948–62
	Jack Kemp, 1958, 1960–66
33	Jack Kemp, 1958, 1960–67
38	Jack Kemp, 1958, 1960–67, 1969
43	Fran Tarkenton, 1961–78
44	Warren Moon, 1984–93
46	Warren Moon, 1984–94
51	Warren Moon, 1984–95
53	Warren Moon, 1984–96
54	Warren Moon, 1984–97
55	Warren Moon, 1984–98
56	Warren Moon, 1984–2000

MOST OWN FUMBLE RECOVERIES, SEASON

8	Paul Christman, 1945
	Bill Butler, 1963
	Danny White, 1981
9	Dave Krieg, 1989
	Brian Griese, 1999
	Jon Kitna, 2000
12	David Carr, 2002

MOST OWN FUMBLE RECOVERIES, GAME

4	Otto Graham, Cle-NYG, 10–25–53
	Sam Etcheverry, SL-NYG, 9–17–61
	Roman Gabriel, LA-SF, 10–12–69
	Joe Ferguson, Buf-Mia, 9–18–77
	Randall Cunningham, Phi-Rdrs, 11–30–88

FUMBLES: OPPONENT RECOVERIES

MOST OPPONENTS RECOVERIES, CAREER

10	Charley Brock, 1939–46
11	Charley Brock, 1939–47
	Gil Bouley, 1945–49
13	Gil Bouley, 1945–50
	Paul Lipscomb, 1945–53
15	Len Ford, 1950–54
16	Len Ford, 1950–55
	Mike Jarmoluk, 1946–55
18	Len Ford, 1950–56
19	Len Ford, 1950–57
20	Len Ford, 1950–58
21	Andy Robustelli, 1951–62
	Ernie Stautner, 1950–63
22	Andy Robustelli 1951–64
	Joe Fortunato, 1955–66
	Jim Marshall, 1960–71
24	Dick Butkus, 1965–72
25	Dick Butkus, 1965–73
26	Jim Marshall, 1960–75
28	Jim Marshall, 1960–78
29	Jim Marshall, 1960–79

MOST OPPONENTS RECOVERIES, SEASON

5	Charley Brock, 1945
	Charley Brock, 1946
	Paul Lipscomb, 1946
	Frank Maznicki, 1947
	Tom Wham, 1950
	Ray Poole, 1950
	Thurman McGraw, 1950
	Blaine Earon, 1952
6	Barney Poole, 1953
8	Joe Schmidt, 1955
9	Don Hultz, 1963

MOST OPPONENTS RECOVERIES, GAME

3	Corwin Clatt, ChiC-Det, 11–6–49
	Vic Sears, Phi-GB, 11–2–52
	Ed Beatty, SF-LA, 10–7–56
	Ron Carroll, Hou-Cin, 10–27–74
	Maurice Spencer, NO-Atl, 10–10–76
	Steve Nelson, NE-Phi, 10–8–78
	Charles Jackson, KC-Pit, 9–6–81
	Willie Buchanon, SD-Den, 9–27–81
	Ray Childress, Hou-Was, 10–30–88
	John Thiery, Chi-Hou, 10–22–95
	Stephen Boyd, Det-Chi, 10–4–98
	Darryl Williams, Sea-KC, 10–4–98
	Rod Woodson, Oak-Pit, 9–15–2002
	Brian Young, SL-Bal, 11–9–2003

FUMBLES: LONGEST RETURN

LONGEST FUMBLE RETURN

98	George Halas, Chi-Oor, 11–4–23
104	Jack Tatum, Oak-GB, 9–24–72
	Aeneas Williams, Arz-Was, 11–5–00

FUMBLES: RECOVERY TOUCHDOWNS

MOST FUMBLE REC TDS (OWN & OPP), CAREER

2	Tille Voss, 1921–22
3	Link Lyman, 1922–24
4	Link Lyman, 1922–31
	Bill Thompson, 1969–80
	Jessie Tuggle, 1987–92
5	Jessie Tuggle, 1987–98
	Jason Taylor, 1997–2005

MOST FUMBLE REC TDS (OWN & OPP), SEASON

3	Link Lyman, 1924

MOST FUMBLE RECOVERY TDS (OWN), CAREER

2	Ken Kavanaugh, 1940–41, 1945–50
	Mike Ditka, 1961–72
	Gail Cogdill, 1960–70
	Ahmad Rashad, 1974
	Jim Mitchell, 1969–79
	Drew Pearson, 1973–83
	Del Rodgers, 1982, 1984, 1987–88
	Ahmad Rashad, 1974
	Del Rodgers, 1982

MOST FUMBLE RECOVERY TDS (OPP), CAREER

3	Link Lyman, 1922–24	
	Leo Sugar, 1954–57	
	Bud McFadin, 1960–63*	
	Tony Cline, 1960–66*	
	Bob Lilly, 1961–71	
	Chris Hanburger, 1965–74	
	Lemar Parrish, 1970–74	
	Paul Krause, 1964–75	
	Brad Dusek, 1974–78	
	Bill Thompson, 1969–79	
	David Logan, 1979–83	
	Thomas Howard, 1977–84	
	Greg Townsend, 1983–91	
	Chris Martin, 1983–91	
	Jessie Tuggle, 1987–91	
4	Jessie Tuggle, 1987–92	
5	Jessie Tuggle, 1987–98	
	Jason Taylor, 1997–2005	

MOST FUMBLE RECOVERY TDS (OPP), SEASON

3   Link Lyman, 1924

MOST FUMBLE RECOVERY TDS (OPP), GAME

2   Fred Evans, Chi-Was, 11–28–48

COMBINED NET YARDS

MOST SEASONS NET YARDAGE LEADER

2	Cliff Battles, 1932–33
3	Cliff Battles, 1932–33, 1937
	Jim Brown, 1958–60
4	Jim Brown, 1958–61
5	Jim Brown, 1958–61, 1964

MOST CONS SEASONS NET YARDAGE LEADER

2	Cliff Battles, 1932–33
	Charley Trippi, 1948–49
	Jim Brown, 1958–59
3	Jim Brown, 1958–60
4	Jim Brown, 1958–61

MOST NET YARDS ATTEMPTS, CAREER

299	Cliff Battles, 1932–33
400	Cliff Battles, 1932–34
470	Cliff Battles, 1932–35
652	Cliff Battles, 1932–36
877	Cliff Battles, 1932–37
970	Clarke Hinkle, 1932–39
1085	Clarke Hinkle, 1932–40
1228	Clarke Hinkle, 1932–41
1382	Steve Van Buren, 1944–50
1498	Steve Van Buren, 1944–51

MOST NET YARDS ATTEMPTS, CAREER

1622	Joe Perry, 1950–59
1662	Joe Perry, 1950–60
1864	Joe Perry, 1950–61
1980	Joe Perry, 1950–62
2017	Jim Brown, 1957–63
2335	Jim Brown, 1957–64
2658	Jim Brown, 1957–65
2728	Franco Harris, 1972–81
2899	Franco Harris, 1972–82
3212	Franco Harris, 1972–83
3457	Walter Payton, 1975–84
3831	Walter Payton, 1975–85
4189	Walter Payton, 1975–86
4368	Walter Payton, 1975–87
4551	Emmitt Smith, 1990–2002
4655	Emmitt Smith, 1990–2003
4939	Emmitt Smith, 1990–2004

MOST NET YARDS ATTEMPTS, SEASON

159	Cliff Battles, 1932
173	Jim Musick, 1933
210	Tuffy Leemans, 1936
215	Cliff Battles, 1937
240	Steve Van Buren, 1947
279	Steve Van Buren, 1949
319	Jim Brown, 1959
354	Jim Brown, 1961
358	O.J. Simpson, 1975
373	Walter Payton, 1977
	Lydell Mitchell, 1977
385	Walter Payton, 1978
402	Walter Payton, 1979
442	Eric Dickerson, 1983
496	James Wilder, 1984

MOST NET YARDS ATTEMPTS, ROOKIE

159	Cliff Battles, 1932
210	Tuffy Leemans, 1936
244	Alan Ameche, 1955
248	Abner Haynes, 1960*
259	Don Perkins, 1961
278	Matt Snell, 1964*
299	Booby Clark, 1973
314	Earl Campbell, 1978
373	Ottis Anderson, 1979
390	Joe Cribbs, 1980

MOST NET YARDS ATTEMPTS, ROOKIE (CONT.)

395	George Rogers, 1981
442	Eric Dickerson, 1983

MOST NET YARDS ATTEMPTS, GAME

38	Harry Newman, NYG-GB, 11–11–34
39	Jim Brown, Cle-ChiC, 10–4–59
41	Ron Johnson, NYG-Phi, 10–2–72
43	Lydell Mitchell, Bal-NYJ, 10–20–74
48	James Wilder, TB-Pit, 10–30–83
	LaDainian Tomlinson, SD-Den, 12–1–02

MOST NET YARDS, CAREER

1558	Cliff Battles, 1932–33
2133	Cliff Battles, 1932–34
2385	Cliff Battles, 1932–35
3102	Cliff Battles, 1932–36
4057	Cliff Battles, 1932–37
4509	Clarke Hinkle, 1932–41
5746	Don Hutson, 1935–42
6760	Don Hutson, 1935–43
7763	Don Hutson, 1935–44
8709	Don Hutson, 1935–45
8958	Steve Van Buren, 1944–51
9965	Ollie Matson, 1952–59
10449	Ollie Matson, 1952–60
11167	Ollie Matson, 1952–61
11216	Ollie Matson, 1952–62

MOST NET YARDS, CAREER

11801	Jim Brown, 1957–63
13587	Jim Brown, 1957–64
15459	Jim Brown, 1957–65
17304	Walter Payton, 1975–84
19338	Walter Payton, 1975–85
21053	Walter Payton, 1975–86
21803	Walter Payton, 1975–87
22248	Jerry Rice, 1985–2002
23330	Brian Mitchell, 1990–2003
23546	Jerry Rice, 1985–2004

MOST NET YARDS, SEASON

709	Cliff Battles, 1932
922	Cliff Battles, 1933
1181	Beattie Feathers, 1934
1236	Marshall Goldberg, 1941
1349	Bill Dudley, 1942
1607	Harry Clark, 1943
1620	Bill Dudley, 1946
1846	Eddie Saenz, 1947
1896	Billy Grimes, 1950
2100	Abner Haynes, 1960*
2147	Dick Christy, 1961*
2306	Timmy Brown, 1962
2428	Timmy Brown, 1963
2440	Gale Sayers, 1966
2444	Mac Herron, 1974
2462	Terry Metcalf, 1975
2535	Lionel James, 1985
2690	Derrick Mason, 2000

MOST NET YARDS, ROOKIE

709	Cliff Battles, 1932
1181	Beattie Feathers, 1934
1349	Bill Dudley, 1942
1731	Hugh McElhenny, 1952
2100	Abner Haynes, 1960*
2272	Gale Sayers, 1965
2317	Tim Brown, 1988

MOST NET YARDS, GAME

331	Wally Triplett, Det-LA, 10–29–50
373	Billy Cannon, Hou-NYT, 12–10–61*
404	Glyn Milburn, Den-Sea, 12–10–95

SACKS

MOST SEASONS LEADING LEAGUE

2	Mark Gastineau, 1983–84
	Reggie White, 1987–88
	Kevin Greene, 1994, 1996
	Michael Strahan 2001, 2003

MOST SACKS, CAREER (SINCE 1982)

25.0	Mark Gastineau, 1982–83
47.0	Mark Gastineau, 1982–84
60.5	Mark Gastineau, 1982–85
64.5	Dexter Manley, 1982–86
73.5	Lawrence Taylor, 1981–87
89.0	Lawrence Taylor, 1981–88
104.0	Lawrence Taylor, 1981–89
114.5	Lawrence Taylor, 1981–90
121.5	Lawrence Taylor, 1981–91
126.5	Lawrence Taylor, 1981–92
137.0	Reggie White, 1985–93
145.0	Reggie White, 1985–94
157.0	Reggie White, 1985–95
165.5	Reggie White, 1985–96

MOST SACKS, CAREER (SINCE 1982) (CONT.)

176.5	Reggie White, 1985–97
192.5	Reggie White, 1985–98
198.0	Reggie White, 1985–98, 2000
200.0	Bruce Smith, 1986–2003

MOST SACKS, SEASON

11.5	Doug Martin, 1982
19.0	Mark Gastineau, 1983
22.0	Mark Gastineau, 1984
22.5	Michael Strahan, 2001

MOST SACKS, ROOKIE

5.5	Chip Banks, 1982
	Bruce Clark, 1982
11.0	Vernon Maxwell, 1983
12.5	Leslie O'Neal, 1986
	Simeon Rice, 1996
14.5	Jevon Kearse, 1999

MOST SACKS GAME

4.0	Doug English, Det-GB, 12–12–82
5.5	William Gay, Det-TB, 9–4–83
6.0	Fred Dean, SF-NO, 11–13–83
7.0	Derrick Thomas, KC-Sea, 11–11–90

MOST SEASONS 10 SACKS

2	Doug Martin, 1982–83
	Dennis Harrison, 1982–83
3	Dennis Harrison, 1982–84
	Dwaine Board, 1983–85
	Mark Gastineau, 1983–85
	Jacob Green, 1983–85
	Rickey Jackson, 1983–85
	Howie Long, 1983–85
	Randy White, 1983–85
	Dexter Manley, 1983–85
4	Jacob Green, 1983–86
	Dexter Manley, 1983–86
	Richard Dent, 1984–87
	Lawrence Taylor, 1984–87
5	Richard Dent, 1984–88
	Lawrence Taylor, 1984–88
6	Lawrence Taylor, 1984–89
7	Lawrence Taylor, 1984–90
	Greg Townsend, 1983, 1985–86, 1988–91
	Reggie White, 1985–91
8	Reggie White, 1985–92
9	Reggie White, 1985–93
10	Reggie White, 1985–93, 1995
	Bruce Smith, 1986–90, 1992–96
11	Bruce Smith, 1986–90, 1992–97
	Reggie White, 1985–93, 1995, 1997
12	Reggie White, 1985–93, 1995, 1997–98
	Bruce Smith, 1986–90, 1992–98
13	Bruce Smith, 1986–90, 1992–98, 2000

MOST CONSECUTIVE SEASONS 10 SACKS

2	Doug Martin, 1982–83
	Dennis Harrison, 1982–83
3	Dennis Harrison, 1982–84
	Dwaine Board, 1983–85
	Mark Gastineau, 1983–85
	Jacob Green, 1983–85
	Rickey Jackson, 1983–85
	Howie Long, 1983–85
	Randy White, 1983–85
	Dexter Manley, 1983–85
4	Jacob Green, 1983–86
	Dexter Manley, 1983–86
	Richard Dent, 1984–87
	Lawrence Taylor, 1984–87
5	Richard Dent, 1984–88
	Lawrence Taylor, 1984–88
6	Lawrence Taylor, 1984–89
7	Lawrence Taylor, 1984–90
	Reggie White, 1985–91
8	Reggie White, 1985–92
9	Reggie White, 1985–93

MOST CONSECUTIVE GAMES, SACK

8	Dennis Harrison, 1982
	Dwaine Board, 1983
	Andre Tippett, 1984–85
	Greg Brown, 1985
9	Bruce Smith, 1986–87
10	Simon Fletcher, 1992–93

MISCELLANEOUS

LONGEST RETURN OF A MISSED FIELD GOAL

99	Jerry Williams, LA-GB, 12–16–51
	Carl Taseff, Bal-LA, 12–12–59
	Timmy Brown, Phi-SL, 9–16–62
100	Al Nelson, Phi-Cle, 12–11–66
	Ken Ellis, GB-NYG, 9–19–71
101	Al Nelson, Phi-Dal, 9–26–71
104	Aaron Glenn, NYJ-Ind, 11–15–98
107	Chris McAlister, Bal-Den, 9–30–02
108	Nathan Vasher, Chi-SF, 11–13–05

THE PRO FOOTBALL HALL OF FAME

"The milestone men of pro football … their deeds and dogged faith wrote the history of this great game."
—The official announcement of the first selections for the Pro Football Hall of Fame

The idea of a hall of fame or a museum to honor the great figures in pro football history had been bouncing around for years. In 1947 a group from Latrobe, Pennsylvania, sought permission to serve as the host for such an undertaking. National Football League commissioner Bert Bell agreed, recognizing that the small western Pennsylvania mining town had been the home of both the first professional football player and the first professional game. Everybody agreed that the concept was a good one, but nobody actually did anything to turn the idea into a reality.

Two developments during the 1950s prompted action. First, the rising popularity of the league was spurring interest in the history of the game. Pro football was now viewed as one of the major sports, and building a hall of fame would signify that it truly did belong on the same level as the others. Secondly, and perhaps more importantly, those other sports were opening their own halls. The National Baseball Hall of Fame opened in 1939. Hockey inducted its first class in 1945, and basketball did the same thing in 1959. Even tennis had a Hall of Fame, which opened its doors in 1954 in Newport, Rhode Island.

Football was lagging behind, and on December 6, 1959, Canton, Ohio, sportswriter Chuck Such issued a call to action. The headline on his article read, "Pro Football Needs a Hall of Fame and Logical Site Is Here." He laid out a compelling case. Canton was the home of the Bulldogs, the most dominant pro team of pro football's early years. Jim Thorpe started his pro football career in Canton, and he helped put the pro game on the map while playing for the Bulldogs. Perhaps most importantly, the National Football League was born in Canton, at a meeting of independent team owners in 1920, at a crowded gathering at the offices of Ralph Hay's Hupmobile car dealership to forge an alliance.

Such's article caught the attention of the community and energized local business leaders. Among them was Henry Timken, president of Canton's largest employer, the Timken Ball Bearing Company. He pledged his support to the project, offering $100,000 toward construction of a building and launching a committee to help make it happen.

Timken's committee made a presentation to the NFL owners in January 1961, showing a model of the proposed building and pledging that the community would raise the money necessary to build it. The owners gave their approval, and the people of Canton reached their fundraising goals less than three months later.

Dick McCann, longtime general manager of the Washington Redskins, was hired as the Hall of Fame's director in April of that year. He set about the task of collecting memorabilia to illustrate the game's history. On August 11, 1962, a groundbreaking ceremony was held for a 19,000 square foot building. Commissioner Pete Rozelle was among the dignitaries in attendance. The ceremony was followed by an exhibition game between the Giants and Cardinals at the adjacent Fawcett Stadium, beginning an annual tradition that continues to this day.

The duty of selecting the players to be enshrined in Canton was given to a Board of Selectors, comprised of representatives of each of the 14 cities that hosted an NFL team. (American Football League teams were not represented until after the 1970 merger.) Although this board was not given specific instructions about how to make their selections, they agreed that for the first class, a unanimous vote would be required for any nominee to be inducted. There was no shortage of worthy nominees.

Their first class included some obvious selections, giants of football's early decades such as Jim Thorpe, Red Grange, Don Hutson, and Sammy Baugh. It also included two coaches, two team owners, two former commissioners, and three linemen. In all, 17 men were chosen for the Hall's inaugural class, which was inducted on September 7, 1963.

By 1970 a more formal selection process was unveiled. Selectors first whittled down the list of eligible candidates to 15 finalists. Then they voted on that list of finalists to determine which players would be inducted. In 1972 an Old Timers Committee was formed to nominate one finalist each year that had been previously overlooked. (The name was later changed to the Seniors Committee after some players objected to being referred to as "old timers.")

Changes to the selection process have been implemented over the years. There are currently 39 men on the Board of Selectors—one representing the hometown of each NFL team and seven at-large Selectors. Nine of those Selectors comprise the Seniors Committee. The names of the 15 finalist are announced during the month of November, and the Board meets each year during Super Bowl week to discuss and vote on each candidate. Current rules stipulate that between three and six new members will be selected each year.

KEY TO THE HALL OF FAME INDUCTEES

The section that follows lists the 235 individuals who have been inducted into the Pro Football Hall of Fame, including the six men in the class of 2006. The list gives the name, the year they were inducted, the number of years they were selected as a finalist, the number of years they were eligible for selection, their primary position, and the years during which they played.

Players who were named as finalists but not inducted appear in a separate list. That is followed by a year-by-year list of the finalists. Players who were nominated by the Old Timers/Seniors Committee are noted with a dagger (†). The names of inductees appear in bold.

INDUCTEES TO THE PRO FOOTBALL HALL OF FAME

FULL NAME	INDUCTED	FINAL	ELIG	POS	SERVICE
Herb Adderley	1980	3	3	CB	1961–72
Troy Aikman	2006	1	1	QB	1989–2000
†George Allen	2002	4	24	Coach	1966–77
Marcus Allen	2003	1	1	RB	1982–97
Lance Alworth	1978	1	1	WR	1962–72
Doug Atkins	1982	6	8	DE	1953–69
†Red Badgro	1981	1	19	E	1927; 1930–36
Lem Barney	1992	2	10	CB	1967–77
Cliff Battles	1968	—	6	HB	1932–37
Sammy Baugh	1963	—	1	QB	1937–52
Chuck Bednarik	1967	—	1	C-LB	1949–62
Bert Bell	1963	—	1	Exec	1933–59
Bobby Bell	1983	1	3	LB	1963–74
Raymond Berry	1973	1	1	WR	1955–67
Elvin Bethea	2003	1	15	DE	1968–83
Charles Bidwill, Sr.	1967	—	5	Exec	1933–47
Fred Biletnikoff	1988	5	5	WR	1965–78
George Blanda	1981	1	1	QB	1949–58; 1960–75
Mel Blount	1989	1	1	CB	1970–83
Terry Bradshaw	1989	1	1	QB	1970–83
Bob Brown	2004	5	26	T	1964–73
Jim Brown	1971	1	1	FB	1957–65
Paul Brown	1967	—	3	Coach	1946–62; 1968–75
Roosevelt Brown	1975	5	9	T	1953–65
Willie Brown	1984	1	1	CB	1963–78
Buck Buchanan	1990	5	10	DT	1963–75
†Nick Buoniconti	2001	1	20	LB	1962–74; 1976
Dick Butkus	1979	1	1	LB	1965–73
Earl Campbell	1991	1	1	RB	1978–85
†Tony Canadeo	1974	4	12	HB	1941–44; 1946–52
Joe Carr	1963	—	1	Exec	1921–39
Harry Carson	2006	7	13	LB	1976–88
Dave Casper	2002	3	13	TE	1974–84
Guy Chamberlin	1965	—	3	Coach	1922–27
Jack Christiansen	1970	1	7	S	1951–58
Dutch Clark	1963	—	1	QB	1931–32; 1934–38
George Connor	1975	2	13	LB	1948–55
Jimmy Conzelman	1964	—	2	Coach	1921–30; 1940–42; 1946–48
†Lou Creekmur	1996	2	32	T-G	1950–59
Larry Csonka	1987	2	3	FB	1968–79
Al Davis	1992	7	—	Exec	1963–present
Willie Davis	1981	6	7	DE	1958–69
Len Dawson	1987	3	7	QB	1957–75
Joe DeLamielleure	2003	1	13	G	1973–85
Eric Dickerson	1999	1	1	RB	1983–93
Dan Dierdorf	1996	5	8	T	1971–83
Mike Ditka	1988	2	12	TE	1961–72
Art Donovan	1968	—	2	DT	1950–61
Tony Dorsett	1994	1	1	RB	1977–88
Paddy Driscoll	1965	—	3	QB	1920–29
Bill Dudley	1966	—	4	HB	1942; 1945–51; 1953
Turk Edwards	1969	—	7	T	1932–40
Carl Eller	2004	13	20	DE	1964–79
John Elway	2004	1	1	QB	1983–98
Weeb Ewbank	1978	3	5	Coach	1954–73
Tom Fears	1970	1	8	WR	1948–56
Jim Finks	1995	1	—	Exec	1964–82; 1986–92
†Ray Flaherty	1976	1	14	Coach	1936–49
Len Ford	1976	5	13	DE	1948–58
Dan Fortmann	1965	—	3	G	1936–43
Dan Fouts	1993	1	1	QB	1973–87
†Benny Friedman	2005	1	43	B	1927–34
†Frank Gatski	1985	2	23	C	1946–57
Bill George	1974	2	3	LB	1952–66
Joe Gibbs	1996	1	4	Coach	1981–92
Frank Gifford	1977	6	8	HB-FL	1952–60; 1962–64
Sid Gillman	1983	2	2	Coach	1955–69; 1971–74
Otto Graham	1965	—	3	QB	1946–55
Red Grange	1963	—	1	HB	1925–34
Bud Grant	1994	4	7	Coach	1967–83; 1985
Joe Greene	1987	1	1	DT	1969–81
Forrest Gregg	1977	1	1	T-G	1956; 1958–71
Bob Griese	1990	5	5	QB	1967–80
Lou Groza	1974	2	2	T	1946–59; 1961–67
Joe Guyon	1966	—	4	HB	1919–25; 1927
George Halas	1963	—	1	Coach	1920–29; 1933–42; 1946–67
Jack Ham	1988	1	1	LB	1971–82
Dan Hampton	2002	2	7	DT-DE	1979–90
John Hannah	1991	1	1	G	1973–85
Franco Harris	1990	1	1	RB	1972–84
Mike Haynes	1997	3	3	CB	1976–89
Ed Healey	1964	—	2	T	1920–27
Mel Hein	1963	—	1	C	1931–45
Ted Hendricks	1990	2	2	LB	1969–83
Pete Henry	1963	—	1	T	1920–28
Arnie Herber	1966	—	4	QB	1930–40; 1944–45
Bill Hewitt	1971	2	9	E	1932–39; 1943
Clarke Hinkle	1964	—	2	FB	1932–41
Crazylegs Hirsch	1968	—	6	WR	1946–56
Paul Hornung	1986	12	15	HB	1957–62; 1964–66
Ken Houston	1986	1	1	S	1967–80
Cal Hubbard	1963	—	1	T	1927–33; 1935–36
Sam Huff	1982	3	8	LB	1956–67; 1969
Lamar Hunt	1972	1	—	Exec	1959–present
Don Hutson	1963	—	1	E	1935–45
Jimmy Johnson	1994	1	13	CB	1961–76
†John Henry Johnson	1987	9	16	FB	1954–66
Charlie Joiner	1996	5	5	WR	1969–86
Deacon Jones	1980	1	1	DE	1961–74
†Stan Jones	1991	1	19	T-G	1954–66
†Henry Jordan	1995	4	21	DT	1957–69
Sonny Jurgensen	1983	3	4	QB	1957–74
Jim Kelly	2002	1	1	QB	1986–96
†Leroy Kelly	1994	4	16	RB	1964–73
Walt Kiesling	1966	—	4	G	1926–38
Bruiser Kinard	1971	2	2	T	1938–47
Paul Krause	1998	3	14	S	1964–79
Curly Lambeau	1963	—	1	Coach	1919–53
Jack Lambert	1990	1	1	LB	1974–84
Tom Landry	1990	1	1	Coach	1960–88
Dick Lane	1974	4	4	CB	1952–65
Jim Langer	1987	1	1	C	1970–81
Willie Lanier	1986	3	4	LB	1967–77
Steve Largent	1995	1	1	WR	1976–89
Yale Lary	1979	6	10	S	1952–53; 1956–64
Dante Lavelli	1975	6	13	WR	1946–56
Bobby Layne	1967	—	1	QB	1948–62
†Tuffy Leemans	1978	1	16	HB-FB	1936–43
Marv Levy	2001	3	3	Coach	1978–82; 1986–97
Bob Lilly	1980	1	1	DT	1961–74
Larry Little	1993	4	8	G	1967–80
James Lofton	2003	3	5	WR	1978–93
Vince Lombardi	1971	1	3	Coach	1959–67; 1969
Howie Long	2000	2	2	DE	1981–93
Ronnie Lott	2000	1	1	CB-S	1981–94
Sid Luckman	1965	—	3	QB	1939–50
Link Lyman	1964	—	1	T	1922–28; 1930–31; 1933–34
Tom Mack	1999	11	16	G	1966–78
John Mackey	1992	5	15	TE	1963–72
John Madden	2006	2	23	Coach	1969–78
Tim Mara	1963	—	1	Exec	1925–59
Wellington Mara	1997	2	—	Exec	1937–2005
Gino Marchetti	1972	1	1	DE	1952–64; 1966
Dan Marino	2005	1	1	QB	1983–99
George Marshall	1963	—	1	Exec	1932–69
Ollie Matson	1972	1	1	HB	1952; 1954–66
Don Maynard	1987	8	9	WR	1958; 1960–73
George McAfee	1966	—	4	HB	1940–41; 1945–50
Mike McCormack	1984	4	17	T	1951; 1954–62
†Tommy McDonald	1998	2	25	WR	1957–68
Hugh McElhenny	1970	1	1	HB	1952–64
Blood McNally	1963	—	1	HB	1925–38
Mike Michalske	1964	—	2	G	1926–35; 1937
Wayne Millner	1968	—	6	E	1936–41; 1945
Bobby Mitchell	1983	1	10	WR	1958–68
Ron Mix	1979	1	3	T	1960–69; 1971
Joe Montana	2000	1	1	QB	1979–94
Warren Moon	2006	1	1	QB	1984–2000
Lenny Moore	1975	2	3	HB	1956–67
Marion Motley	1968	—	6	FB	1946–53; 1955
Mike Munchak	2001	2	3	G	1982–93
Anthony Muñoz	1998	1	1	T	1980–92
†George Musso	1982	1	20	T-G	1933–44
Bronko Nagurski	1963	—	1	FB	1930–37; 1943
Joe Namath	1985	3	3	QB	1965–77
Greasy Neale	1969	—	7	Coach	1941–50
Ernie Nevers	1963	—	1	FB	1926–27; 1929–31
Ozzie Newsome	1999	3	4	TE	1978–90
Ray Nitschke	1978	1	1	LB	1958–72
Chuck Noll	1993	1	1	Coach	1969–91
Leo Nomellini	1969	—	2	DT	1950–63
Merlin Olsen	1982	1	1	DT	1962–76
Jim Otto	1980	1	1	C	1960–74
Steve Owen	1966	—	4	Coach	1930–53
Alan Page	1988	2	2	DT	1967–81
†Ace Parker	1972	1	10	QB	1937–41; 1945–46
Jim Parker	1973	1	1	G-T	1957–67
Walter Payton	1993	1	1	RB	1975–87
Joe Perry	1969	—	2	FB	1948–63
Pete Pihos	1970	1	8	WR	1947–55
†Fritz Pollard	2005	1	43	B	1919–26
Shorty Ray	1966	—	4	Exec	1938–52
Dan Reeves	1967	—	4	Exec	1941–71
Mel Renfro	1996	4	14	S-CB	1964–77
John Riggins	1992	2	2	RB	1971–79; 1981–85
Jim Ringo	1981	7	9	C	1953–67
Andy Robustelli	1971	2	2	DE	1951–64
Art Rooney	1964	—	1	Exec	1933–88
Dan Rooney	2000	3	—	Exec	1955–present
Pete Rozelle	1985	8	1	Exec	1960–89
Barry Sanders	2004	1	1	RB	1989–98
Gale Sayers	1977	1	1	HB	1965–71
Joe Schmidt	1973	3	3	LB	1953–65
Tex Schramm	1991	1	—	Exec	1947–56; 1960–90
Lee Roy Selmon	1995	1	6	DE	1976–84
†Billy Shaw	1999	1	25	G	1961–69
Art Shell	1989	1	1	T	1968–82
Don Shula	1997	1	1	Coach	1963–95

FULL NAME	INDUCTED	FINAL	ELIG	POS	SERVICE
O.J. Simpson	1985	1	1	RB	1969–79
Mike Singletary	1998	1	1	LB	1981–92
Jackie Slater	2001	1	1	T	1976–95
Jackie Smith	1994	2	12	TE	1963–78
†Bob St. Clair	1990	1	24	T	1953–63
John Stallworth	2002	8	10	WR	1974–87
Bart Starr	1977	1	1	QB	1956–71
Roger Staubach	1985	1	1	QB	1969–79
Ernie Stautner	1969	—	2	DT	1950–63
Jan Stenerud	1991	1	1	K	1967–85
Dwight Stephenson	1998	5	6	C	1980–87
Hank Stram	2003	1	20	Coach	1960–74; 1976–77
Ken Strong	1967	—	5	HB	1929–37; 1939; 1944–47
Joe Stydahar	1967	—	5	T	1936–42; 1945–46
Lynn Swann	2001	14	14	WR	1974–82
Fran Tarkenton	1986	3	3	QB	1961–78
Charley Taylor	1984	2	2	WR	1964–75; 1977
Jim Taylor	1976	4	4	FB	1958–67
Lawrence Taylor	1999	1	1	LB	1981–93
Jim Thorpe	1963	—	1	HB	1915–17; 1919–26; 1928
Y.A. Tittle	1971	2	2	QB	1948–64
George Trafton	1964	—	2	C	1920–21; 1923–32
Charley Trippi	1968	—	6	HB	1947–55
Emlen Tunnell	1967	—	2	S	1948–61
Bulldog Turner	1966	—	4	C	1940–52
Johnny Unitas	1979	1	1	QB	1956–73
Gene Upshaw	1987	1	1	G	1967–81
Norm Van Brocklin	1971	2	6	QB	1949–60
Steve Van Buren	1965	—	3	HB	1944–51
†Doak Walker	1986	5	24	HB	1950–55
Bill Walsh	1993	2	4	Coach	1979–88
Paul Warfield	1983	1	1	WR	1964–77
Bob Waterfield	1965	—	3	QB	1945–52
Mike Webster	1997	2	2	C	1974–90
†Arnie Weinmeister	1984	1	22	DT	1948–53
Randy White	1994	1	1	DT	1975–88
Reggie White	2006	1	1	DT–DE	1985–88; 2000
†Dave Wilcox	2000	1	21	LB	1964–74
†Bill Willis	1977	1	15	MG	1946–53
Larry Wilson	1978	1	1	S	1960–72
Kellen Winslow	1995	3	3	TE	1979–87
Alex Wojciechowicz	1968	—	6	C	1938–50
Willie Wood	1989	10	13	S	1960–71
Rayfield Wright	2006	2	22	T	1967–79
Ron Yary	2001	6	14	T	1968–82
Steve Young	2005	1	1	QB	1985–99
Jack Youngblood	2001	8	12	DE	1971–84

FINALISTS WHO WERE NOT INDUCTED

FULL NAME	FINAL	ELIG	POS	SERVICE
Ken Anderson	2	15	QB	1971–86
Blanton Collier	1	36	Coach	1963–70
Charley Conerly	7	40	QB	1948–61
Richard Dent	2	4	DE	1983–97
Beattie Feathers	1	44	B	1934–40
†Willie Galimore	1	38	HB	1957–63
†Marshall Goldberg	1	44	B	1939–43; 1946–48
Randy Gradishar	1	18	LB	1974–83
L.C. Greenwood	6	20	DE	1969–81
Rosey Grier	1	35	DT–DE	1955–66
Russ Grimm	2	10	G–C	1981–91
Ray Guy	5	15	P	1973–86
Cliff Harris	1	22	DB	1970–79
†Ole Haugsrud	1	—	Exec	1961–76
Bob Hayes	1	26	WR	1965–75
Lester Hayes	3	15	DB	1977–86
Gene Hickerson	3	28	G	1958–73
Claude Humphrey	3	20	DE	1968–81
Michael Irvin	2	2	WR	1988–99
Lee Roy Jordan	1	25	LB	1963–76
†Jerry Kramer	10	33	G	1958–68
Bob Kuechenberg	5	18	G–T–C	1970–83
Gene Lipscomb	2	39	DT–DE	1953–62
Jim Marshall	1	22	DE	1960–79
Art Modell	1	—	Exec	1961–2004
Art Monk	6	6	WR	1980–95
Tony Morabito	1	—	Exec	1946–57
Bill Parcells	2	5	Coach	1983–90; 1993–99; 2003–present
Johnny Robinson	6	30	DB	1960–71
†Lou Rymkus	1	44	Coach	1960–61
Clark Shaughnessy	3	44	Coach	1948–49
Donnie Shell	1	14	DB	1974–87
Duke Slater	2	44	T	1922–31
†Mac Speedie	3	44	WR	1946–52
Ken Stabler	3	17	QB	1970–84
†Dick Stanfel	1	43	G	1952–58
Derrick Thomas	2	2	LB	1989–99
Thurman Thomas	1	1	RB	1988–2000
Jim Tyrer	1	27	T	1961–74
Roger Wehrli	1	19	DB	1969–82
Ralph Wilson. Jr.	2	—	Exec	1960–present
George Young	3	—	Exec	1968–2001
Gary Zimmerman	3	4	T	1986–97

YEARLY FINALISTS

1963
Sammy Baugh, Bert Bell, Joe Carr, Dutch Clark, Red Grange, George Halas, Mel Hein, Pete Henry, Cal Hubbard, Don Hutson, Curly Lambeau, Tim Mara, George Marshall, Blood McNally, Bronko Nagurski, Ernie Nevers, Jim Thorpe, Arnie Herber, Walt Kiesling, George McAfee, Steve Owen, Shorty Ray, Bulldog Turner, Gene "Big Daddy" Lipscomb, **Hugh McElhenny**, **Pete Pihos**, Andy Robustelli, Clark Shaugnessy, Duke Slater, Mac Speedie, Y.A. Tittle

1964
Jimmy Conzelman, Ed Healey, Clarke Hinkle, Link Lyman, Mike Michalske, Art Rooney, George Trafton

1965
Guy Chamberlin, Paddy Driscoll, Dan Fortmann, Otto Graham, Sid Luckman, Steve Van Buren, Bob Waterfield

1966
Bill Dudley, Joe Guyon

1967
Chuck Bednarik, Charles Bidwill, Sr., Paul Brown, Bobby Layne, Dan Reeves, Ken Strong, Joe Stydahar, Emlen Tunnell

1968
Cliff Battles, Art Donovan, Crazylegs Hirsch, Wayne Millner, Marion Motley, Charley Trippi, Alex Wojciechowicz

1969
Turk Edwards, Greasy Neale, Leo Nomellini, Joe Perry, Ernie Stautner

1970
Jack Christiansen, Tom Fears, Beattie Feathers, Bill Hewitt, Bruiser Kinard, Dante Lavelli, Tuffy Leemans

1971
Norm Van Brocklin, **Jim Brown**, Roosevelt Brown, Tony Canadeo, Charley Conerly, Len Ford, Frank Gifford, **Bill Hewitt**, **Bruiser Kinard**, †Dick "Night Train" Lane, Dante Lavelli, **Vince Lombardi**, **Andy Robustelli**, Joe Schmidt, Duke Slater, **Y.A. Tittle**, **Norm Van Brocklin**

1972
Roosevelt Brown, Tony Canadeo, Charley Conerly, Bill George, Frank Gifford, Paul Hornung, **Lamar Hunt**, Dick "Night Train" Lane, Dante Lavelli, **Gino Marchetti**, **Ollie Matson**, **Ace Parker**, Joe Schmidt, Mac Speedie, Doak Walker

1973
Raymond Berry, Roosevelt Brown, Tony Canadeo, Len Ford, Rosey Grier, Lou Groza, †Ole Haugsrud, Paul Hornung, Dick "Night Train" Lane, Dante Lavelli, Tony Morabito, **Jim Parker**, **Joe Schmidt**, Jim Taylor, Doak Walker

1974
Roosevelt Brown, **Tony Canadeo**, Charley Conerly, George Connor, Len Ford, **Bill George**, Frank Gifford, **Lou Groza**, Jerry Kramer, Yale Lary, Dante Lavelli, Lenny Moore, †**Dick "Night Train" Lane**, Jim Taylor, Doak Walker

1975
Doug Atkins, **Roosevelt Brown**, Charley Conerly, George Connor, Len Ford, Frank Gifford, John Henry Johnson, Jerry Kramer, Yale Lary, Dante Lavelli, Lenny Moore, Jim Ringo, Clark Shaughnessy, Jim Taylor

1976
Charley Conerly, Willie Davis, Weeb Ewbank, **Ray Flaherty**, **Len Ford**, Frank Gatski, Frank Gifford, Paul Hornung, John Henry Johnson, Henry Jordan, Jerry Kramer, Jim Ringo, Clark Shaughnessy, **Jim Taylor**, Doak Walker

1977
Doug Atkins, Willie Davis, Weeb Ewbank, **Frank Gifford**, **Forrest Gregg**, Sam Huff, John Henry Johnson, Yale Lary, Gene "Big Daddy" Lipscomb, Jim Ringo, Pete Rozelle, **Gale Sayers**, **Bart Starr**, **Bill Willis**, Willie Wood

1978
Herb Adderley, **Lance Alworth**, Doug Atkins, Charley Conerly, Willie Davis, **Weeb Ewbank**, Paul Hornung, Sam Huff, John Henry Johnson, Jerry Kramer, Yale Lary, **Tuffy Leemans**, **Ray Nitschke**, Jim Ringo, **Larry Wilson**, Willie Wood

1979
Herb Adderley, Doug Atkins, **Dick Butkus**, Willie Davis, †Marshall Goldberg, Paul Hornung, John Henry Johnson, Jerry Kramer, **Yale Lary**, John Mackey, **Ron Mix**, Jim Ringo, Pete Rozelle, **Johnny Unitas**, Willie Wood

1980

Herb Adderley
Charley Conerly
†Lou Creekmur
Willie Davis
Paul Hornung
John Henry Johnson
Deacon Jones
Sonny Jurgensen
Jerry Kramer
Bob Lilly
Don Maynard
Jim Otto
Jim Ringo
Johnny Robinson
Pete Rozelle
Willie Wood
Willie Lanier
Don Maynard
Mike McCormack
Joe Namath
Pete Rozelle
Fran Tarkenton
Charley Taylor
Arnie Weinmeister
Willie Wood

1981

Doug Atkins
Red Badgro
George Blanda
Willie Davis
Mike Ditka
Gene Hickerson
Paul Hornung
Jerry Kramer
Don Maynard
Mike McCormack
Jim Ringo
Johnny Robinson
Pete Rozelle
Jim Tyrer
Willie Wood

1982

Doug Atkins
Len Dawson
Sid Gillman
Gene Hickerson
Paul Hornung
Sam Huff
Sonny Jurgensen
Leroy Kelly
Don Maynard
Mike McCormack
George Musso
Merlin Olsen
Johnny Robinson
Pete Rozelle
Willie Wood

1983

Bobby Bell
Sid Gillman
Gene Hickerson
Paul Hornung
John Henry Johnson
Sonny Jurgensen
Don Maynard
Mike McCormack
Bobby Mitchell
Joe Namath
Johnny Robinson
Pete Rozelle
†Mac Speedie
Charley Taylor
Paul Warfield
Willie Wood

1984

Fred Biletnikoff
Willie Brown
Buck Buchanan
Paul Hornung
Henry Jordan
Jerry Kramer

1985

Fred Biletnikoff
Buck Buchanan
Carl Eller
Frank Gatski
Paul Hornung
Willie Lanier
John Madden
Don Maynard
Joe Namath
Johnny Robinson
Pete Rozelle
O.J. Simpson
Roger Staubach
Fran Tarkenton
Willie Wood

1986

Fred Biletnikoff
Larry Csonka
Al Davis
Len Dawson
Bob Griese
Paul Hornung
Ken Houston
John Henry Johnson
Willie Lanier
Larry Little
Tom Mack
Don Maynard
Johnny Robinson
Fran Tarkenton
Doak Walker

1987

Fred Biletnikoff
Bob Brown
Blanton Collier
Larry Csonka
Al Davis
Len Dawson
Joe Greene
Bob Griese
John Henry Johnson
Jerry Kramer
Jim Langer
Larry Little
Don Maynard
Tommy Mcdonald
Alan Page
Gene Upshaw

1988

George Allen
Fred Biletnikoff
Buck Buchanan
Al Davis
Mike Ditka
Bud Grant
Bob Griese
Jack Ham
Lee Roy Jordan
Leroy Kelly
Tom Mack
Alan Page
†Lou Rymkus
Art Shell
Lynn Swann

1989

Mel Blount
Terry Bradshaw
Buck Buchanan
Al Davis
Carl Eller
Bud Grant
Bob Griese
Ted Hendricks
†Henry Jordan
Leroy Kelly
Tom Mack
John Mackey
Art Shell
Lynn Swann
Willie Wood

1990

Buck Buchanan
Al Davis
Dan Dierdorf
Bob Griese
Franco Harris
Ted Hendricks
Jack Lambert
Tom Landry
Larry Little
John Mackey
Bob St. Clair
Ken Stabler
Lynn Swann
Ron Yary
Jack Youngblood

1991

Lem Barney
Bob Brown
Earl Campbell
Al Davis
Carl Eller
L.C. Greenwood
John Hannah
Stan Jones
John Mackey
John Riggins
Tex Schramm
Ken Stabler
Jan Stenerud
Lynn Swann
Jack Youngblood

1992

Lem Barney
Bob Brown
Al Davis
Dan Dierdorf
Carl Eller
†Willie Galimore
Bud Grant
Ray Guy
Charlie Joiner
Tom Mack
John Mackey
Wellington Mara
John Riggins
Lynn Swann
Bill Walsh

1993

Bob Brown
Carl Eller
Dan Fouts
Charlie Joiner
Larry Little
Tom Mack
Chuck Noll
Walter Payton

Mel Renfro
Jackie Smith
†Dick Stanfel
Dwight Stephenson
Lynn Swann
Bill Walsh
Kellen Winslow

1994

Dan Dierdorf
Tony Dorsett
Carl Eller
Bud Grant
Jimmy Johnson
Charlie Joiner
Leroy Kelly
Paul Krause
Tom Mack
Mel Renfro
Jackie Smith
John Stallworth
Lynn Swann
Randy White
Kellen Winslow

1995

Dan Dierdorf
Carl Eller
Jim Finks
L.C. Greenwood
Ray Guy
Mike Haynes
Charlie Joiner
Henry Jordan
Steve Largent
Tom Mack
Mel Renfro
Lee Roy Selmon
Dwight Stephenson
Lynn Swann
Kellen Winslow

1996

Ken Anderson
Lou Creekmur
Dan Dierdorf
Carl Eller
Joe Gibbs
L.C. Greenwood
Mike Haynes
Charlie Joiner
Tom Mack
Mel Renfro
John Stallworth
Dwight Stephenson
Lynn Swann
Mike Webster
Jack Youngblood

1997

Carl Eller
Ray Guy
Mike Haynes
†Jerry Kramer
Paul Krause
Tom Mack
Wellington Mara
Ozzie Newsome
Don Shula
John Stallworth
Dwight Stephenson
Lynn Swann
Mike Webster
Ron Yary
Jack Youngblood

1998

George Allen
Ken Anderson
Carl Eller
Paul Krause
Tom Mack
Tommy McDonald
Anthony Munoz
Ozzie Newsome
Dan Rooney
Mike Singletary
John Stallworth
Dwight Stephenson
Lynn Swann
Ron Yary
Jack Youngblood

1999

George Allen
Eric Dickerson
Carl Eller
Ray Guy
Marv Levy
Howie Long
Tom Mack
Ozzie Newsome
Dan Rooney
Billy Shaw
John Stallworth
Lynn Swann
Lawrence Taylor
Ron Yary
Jack Youngblood

2000

Harry Carson
Dave Casper
Carl Eller
Marv Levy
James Lofton
Howie Long
Ronnie Lott
Joe Montana
Mike Munchak
Dan Rooney
John Stallworth
Lynn Swann
Dave Wilcox
Ron Yary
Jack Youngblood

2001

Nick Buoniconti
Harry Carson
Dave Casper
Dan Hampton
Lester Hayes
Marv Levy
Art Monk
Mike Munchak
Bill Parcells
Jackie Slater
John Stallworth
Lynn Swann
Ralph Wilson, Jr.
Ron Yary
Jack Youngblood

2002

George Allen
Harry Carson
Dave Casper
L.C. Greenwood
Ray Guy
Dan Hampton
Lester Hayes
Jim Kelly

Bob Kuechenberg
James Lofton
Art Modell
Art Monk
Bill Parcells
Donnie Shell
John Stallworth

2003

Marcus Allen
Elvin Bethea
Harry Carson
Joe Delamielleure
Randy Gradishar
Lester Hayes
Claude Humphrey
Bob Kuechenberg
James Lofton
Art Monk
Ken Stabler
Hank Stram
Ralph Wilson
George Young
Gary Zimmerman

2004

Bob Brown
Harry Carson
Richard Dent
Carl Eller
John Elway
Cliff Harris
†Bob Hayes
Lester Hayes
Bob Kuechenberg
Jim Marshall
Art Monk
Barry Sanders
Rayfield Wright
George Young
Gary Zimmerman

2005

Harry Carson
Richard Dent
Benny Friedman
L.C. Greenwood
Russ Grimm
Claude Humphrey
Michael Irvin
Bob Kuechenberg
Dan Marino
Art Monk
Fritz Pollard
Derrick Thomas
Roger Wehrli
George Young
Steve Young

2006

Troy Aikman
Harry Carson
L.C. Greenwood
Russ Grimm
Claude Humphrey
Michael Irvin
Bob Kuechenberg
John Madden
Art Monk
Warren Moon
Derrick Thomas
Thurman Thomas
Reggie White
Rayfield Wright
Gary Zimmerman

ALL-PRO TEAMS

Walter Camp is rightly regarded as the father of American football, and among his many contributions was a public relations gimmick in 1889 that endures to this day. To help bring some attention to the burgeoning sport of college football, he published a list of the best players in the country, dubbed "The All America Team." He continued the practice each season until his death 36 years later. The Walter Camp Foundation has continued that practice in the 80 years that have followed, and a plethora of other organizations have seen fit to name their own All-American teams, too.

The idea of naming an all-star team after each season for the professional ranks seemed natural. Over the years many different organizations have named their own All-Pro team at the end of a season. We've included selections from 21 of them here, those deemed by the research community to be the most important and respected.

Some might wonder why All-Pro selections are interesting or relevant. After all, they represent someone's opinion, whether individually or collectively, and opinion is subject to bias, ignorance, or whimsy. But they provide a valuable glimpse of how players were rated by their contemporaries. Since there is little objective data with which to rank players from pro football's early years—particularly linemen—the All-Pro rosters sometimes offer us an otherwise unavailable insight into a player's performance.

All-Pro selections come in three varieties. Some list the best players in one league. Others pick one roster of players across multiple leagues. A third option is to pick teams from each conference, essentially two separate All-Pro rosters from one league. Some organizations produced more than one of these varieties for the same season. For example, *Pro Football Weekly* named both an All-Pro team and All-Conference teams throughout the 1970s and 1980s. In 1968 and 1969 they selected one All-Pro team that included players from both the AFL and NFL.

The *Chicago Herald American* started the practice of naming separate All-Pro teams for offense and defense in 1947. The *New York Daily News* followed the practice in 1950, and everyone else followed suit by 1951. Special teams players were ignored until 1964, when *The Sporting News* included kickers and punters on their All-Pro roster. Kick returners were first honored by the Pro Football Writers Association in 1975. Separate selections were added for special teamers in 1984 and punt returners in 1996.

CONSENSUS PICKS

In some years there have been as many as 10 different All-Pro teams named by various organizations. In 1969, 13 different offensive tackles were named All-Pro. How do we sort through those 13 players to determine which players were consensus selections and which were anomalies? The answer goes a little beyond the traditional All-Pro approach. By assigning a weighted value to each selection, we can calculate a total for each player, and rank them to determine the top players at each position. This helps easily identify the difference between a player like Bob Brown, named first team on all 10 All-Pro rosters in 1969, and his teammate Charley Cowgan, who was named second team by one organization and not mentioned by the other nine.

Six players were named to All-Pro teams at two different positions in the same season. This generally occurred when a player started at one position and also played on special teams. Deion Sanders and Rod Woodson are the only players to accomplish the feat more than once.

KEY TO YEARLY ALL-PRO ROSTERS

The first section that follows lists the players that were named to an All-Pro team each season and the organization that honored them. The number in each column indicates whether a player was first, second, or third team selection (i.e., 1, 2, 3 on the list). If there was a tie, then the number is preceded by †. If a player was selected at a different position, the position will appear before the number.

The first column, **TT**, stands for Total Score, a weighted value of the player's selections. This allows us to determine consensus picks from the years when several different organizations named All-Pro teams. Players whose names are bolded were the consensus picks for that season.

SELECTING ORGANIZATIONS

All League Teams

AAFC	Official AAFC , 1946–49
AFL	Official AFL, 1960–66
AP	Associated Press, 1940–2005
BU	*Buffalo Evening News*, 1921
CN	*Canton Daily News*, 1922–23
CDN	*Chicago Daily News*, 1933–36
CHA	*Chicago Herald American*, 1939–48
CHT	*Chicago Tribune*, 1926–29
CL	*Collyer's Eye magazine*, 1923–41
GB	*Green Bay Press-Gazette*, 1923–35
HG	George Halas (syndicated), 1922
FW	Professional Football Writers of America, 1938–39; 1968; 1970–2005
INS	International News Service, 1937–451937–45
NE	Newspaper Enterprise Association, 1955–92
NFL	Official NFL, 1931–42
NY	*New York Daily News*, 1937–61; 1963–69
UP	United Press International, 1931–41; 1943–69
PFI	*Pro Football Illustrated*, 1943–48
PW	*Pro Football Weekly*, 1968–84; 1986–91
RI	*Rock Island Argus*, 1920
SN	*The Sporting News*, 1954–61; 1969; 1980–81, 1983–2005

All-Pro Teams (one team for multiple leagues)

*AP	Associated Press, 1946–49
*CHA	*Chicago Herald American*, 1946–46
*FW	Professional Football Writers of America, 1969
*HF	Pro Football Hall of Fame, 1969
*INS	International News Service, 1949
*NE	Newspaper Enterprise Association, 1969
*PW	*Pro Football Weekly*, 1968–69
*SN	*The Sporting News*, 1948

All-Conference Teams (multiple teams for one league)

+AP	Associated Press, 1970–76
+PW	Pro Football Weekly, 1970–84; 1986–2005
+SN	The Sporting News, 1962–79
+UP	United Press International, 1970–96

KEY TO ALPHABETICAL LIST

Pos Positions at which a player was selected.

Tot The total number of seasons in which a player was named to an All-Pro team. (If a player was named to an All-Pro team at different positions during the same season, that is considered two selections.)

Cons The number of times that a player was a consensus All-Pro.

Years The years in which the player was selected.

Additionally, † before the player's name indicates that he was selected to an All-Pro team at more than one position in the same season.

1920 APFA

NAME	POS	TT	RI
Oak Smith, RI	E	3	1
Guy Chamberlin, Dec	E	3	1
Obe Wenig, RI	E	2	2
George Halas, Dec	E	2	2
Bob Nash, Akr	E	1	3
Bobby Marshall, RI	E	1	3
Pete Henry, Can	T	3	1
Hugh Blacklock, Dec	T	3	1
Ed Shaw, RI	T	2	2
Cub Buck, Can	T	2	2
Burt Ingwersen, Dec	T	1	3
Walt Buland, RI	T	1	3
Dewey Lyle, RI	G	3	1
Fred Denfeld, RI	G	3	1
Harrie Dadmun, Can	G	2	2
Alf Cobb, Akr	G	2	2
Tommy Tomlin, Akr	G	1	3
Ross Petty, Dec	G	1	3
George Trafton, Dec	C	3	1
Paul Des Jardien, ChiT	C	2	2
Freeman Fitzgerald, RI	C	1	3
Fritz Pollard, Akr	B	3	1
Eddie Novak, RI	B	3	1
Rip King, Akr	B	3	1
Paddy Driscoll, ChiC	B	3	1
Norb Sacksteder, Day	B	2	2
Al Mahrt, Day	B	2	2
Joe Guyon, Can	B	2	2
Guil Falcon, ChiT	B	2	2
Dutch Sternaman, Dec	B	1	3
Milt Ghee, ChiT	B	1	3
Pete Calac, Can	B	1	3
Frank Bacon, Day	B	1	3

1921 APFA

NAME	POS	TT	BU
Luke Urban, Buf	E	3	1
Bob Nash, Buf	E	3	1
Belf West, Can	T	3	1
Pete Henry, Can	T	3	1
Al Nesser, Akr	G	3	1
Bull Lowe, Cle	G	3	1
Doc Alexander, Roc	C	3	1
Pete Stinchcomb, ChiS	B	3	1
Elmer Oliphant, Buf	B	3	1
Rip King, Akr	B	3	1
Benny Boynton, Was	B	3	1

1922 NFL

NAME	POS	TT	CN	HG
Eddie Anderson, ChiC	E	5	1	2
Luke Urban, Buf	E	3	—	1
Guy Chamberlin, Can	E	3	—	1
Bird Carroll, Can	E	3	1	—
Tillie Voss, RI	E	2	—	2
Pete Henry, Can	T	6	1	1
Steamer Horning, Tol	T	3	1	—
Hugh Blacklock, ChiB	T	3	—	1
Russ Hathaway, Day	T	2	—	2
Fred Gillies, ChiC	T	2	—	2
Herb Stein, Tol	G	6	1	1
Duke Osborn, Can	G	3	1	—
Ed Healey, ChiB	G	3	—	1
Al Nesser, Akr	G	2	—	2
Hunk Anderson, ChiB	G	2	—	2
Doc Alexander, Roc	C	6	1	1
Jim Flower, Akr	C	2	—	2
Pete Stinchcomb, ChiB	B	6	1	1
Paddy Driscoll, ChiC	B	6	1	1
Harry Robb, Can	B	3	1	—
Rip King, Akr	B	3	—	1
Tommy Hughitt, Buf	B	3	—	1
Doc Elliott, Can	B	3	1	—
Dutch Sternaman, ChiB	B	2	—	2
Curly Lambeau, GB	B	2	—	2
Jim Laird, Buf	B	2	—	2
Benny Boynton, Roc	B	2	—	2

1923 NFL

NAME	POS	TT	CL	GB	CN
Luke Urban, Buf	E	6	1	—	1
Gus Tebell, Col	E	6	—	1	1
Guy Chamberlin, Can	E	5	1	2	—
Tillie Voss, Tol	E	4	—	T3	1
Duke Hanny, ChiB	E	4	2	2	—
Inky Williams, Ham	E	3	—	1	—
Paul Goebel, Col	E	3	—	—	1
Bird Carroll, Can	E	3	—	—	1
Glenn Carberry, Buf	E	3	—	—	1
Dick Reichle, Mil	E	2	2	—	—
Ben Winkelman, Mil	E	1	—	3	—
Dick O'Donnell, Dul	E	1	—	3	—
Pete Henry, Can	T	9	1	1	G1
Ed Healey, ChiB	T	6	—	1	G1

1923 NFL (CONT.)

NAME	POS	TT	CL	GB	CN
Duke Slater, RI	T	5	1	2	—
Link Lyman, Can	T	5	2	—	1
Russ Hathaway, Day	T	5	—	2	1
Gus Sonnenberg, Col	T	3	—	—	1
Ralph Scott, ChiB	T	3	—	—	1
Ed Sauer, Day	T	3	—	—	1
Steamer Horning, Tol	T	3	—	—	1
Elmer McCormick, Buf	T	2	2	—	—
Cub Buck, GB	T	1	—	3	—
Hec Garvey, ChiB	G	8	1	2	1
Swede Youngstrom, Buf	G	6	1	1	—
Clyde Zoia, ChiC	G	3	—	—	1
Bub Weller, SL	G	3	—	1	—
John Sack, Col	G	3	—	—	1
Duke Osborn, Can	G	3	—	—	1
Rudy Comstock, Can	G	3	—	—	1
Herb Sies, RI	G	2	2	—	—
Frank Morrissey, Buf	G	2	—	2	—
Stan Keck, Cle	G	2	2	—	—
Al Nesser, Akr	G	1	—	3	—
Tom McNamara, Tol	G	1	—	3	—
George Trafton, ChiB	C	5	2	—	1
Larry Conover, Can	C	5	—	2	1
Charlie Guy, Cle	C	4	—	3	1
Harry Mehre, Min	C	3	—	1	—
Walt Kreinheder, SL	C	3	1	—	—
Paddy Driscoll, ChiC	B	9	1	1	1
Harry Robb, Can	B	7	2	2	1
Tex Grigg, Can	B	6	1	—	1
Doc Elliott, Can	B	6	—	1	1
Joey Sternaman, Dul	B	5	2	—	1
Jimmy Conzelman, Mil	B	5	—	2	1
Hal Erickson, Mil	B	4	1	3	—
Jim Thorpe, Oor	B	3	—	1	—
Dutch Sternaman, ChiB	B	3	—	—	1
Lou Smyth, Can	B	3	—	—	1
Bob Rapp, Col	B	3	—	—	1
Al Michaels, Akr	B	3	—	1	—
Ben Jones, Can	B	3	—	—	1
Hank Gillo, Rac	B	3	1	—	—
Pete Stinchcomb, Cle	B	2	2	—	—
Curly Lambeau, GB	B	2	—	2	—
Dinger Doane, Mil	B	2	—	2	—
Jack Crangle, ChiC	B	2	2	—	—
Milt Romney, Rac	B	1	—	3	—
Johnny Kyle, Cle	B	1	—	3	—
John Armstrong, RI	B	1	—	3	—

1924 NFL

NAME	POS	TT	CL	GB
Paul Goebel, Col	E	4	2	2
Guy Chamberlin, Cle	E	4	1	3
Mike Wilson, RI	E	3	1	—
Tillie Voss, GB	E	3	—	1
Joe Little Twig, RI	E	3	—	1
Duke Hanny, ChiB	E	2	2	—
Eddie Anderson, ChiC	E	2	—	2
Oscar Christianson, Min	E	1	—	3
Link Lyman, Cle	T	5	1	2
Ed Healey, ChiB	T	5	2	1
Bub Weller, Mil	T	3	1	—
Boni Petcoff, Col	T	3	—	1
Olin Smith, Cle	T	2	2	—
Duke Slater, RI	T	2	—	2
Mike Gulian, Fra	T	1	—	3
Cub Buck, GB	T	1	—	3
Jim McMillen, ChiB	G	5	1	2
Swede Youngstrom, Buf	G	3	—	1
Stan Muirhead, Day	G	3	—	1
George Berry, Akr	G	3	1	—
Doc Williams, Dul	G	2	—	2
Jim Welsh, Fra	G	2	2	—
Walt LeJeune, Mil	G	2	—	2
Al Nesser, Akr	G	1	—	3
Ralph King, Rac	G	1	—	3
George Trafton, ChiB	C	3	—	1
Elmer McCormick, Buf	C	3	1	—
Herb Stein, Fra	C	2	2	—
Andy Nemecek, Col	C	2	—	2
Carl Peterson, KC	C	1	—	3
Charlie Way, Fra	B	6	1	1
Joey Sternaman, ChiB	B	6	1	1
Benny Boynton, Buf	B	6	1	1
Tex Hamer, Fra	B	5	1	2
Doc Elliott, Cle	B	3	—	1
Hoge Workman, Cle	B	2	2	—
Dave Noble, Cle	B	2	—	2
Curly Lambeau, GB	B	2	—	2
John Hurlburt, ChiC	B	2	2	—
Ken Huffine, Day	B	2	2	—
Red Dunn, Mil	B	2	—	2
Paddy Driscoll, ChiC	B	2	—	2
Sonny Winters, Col	B	1	—	3
Joe Guyon, RI	B	1	—	3
Hank Gillo, Rac	B	1	—	3
Wayne Brenkert, Akr	B	1	—	3

1925 NFL

NAME	POS	TT	CL	GB
Charlie Berry, Pot	**E**	6	1	1
Ed Lynch, Roc	**E**	3	—	1
Rae Crowther, Fra	**E**	3	1	—
Red Maloney, Pro	E	2	—	2
Duke Hanny, ChiB	E	2	2	—
Lynn Bomar, NYG	E	2	—	2
Eddie Anderson, ChiC	E	2	2	—
Tillie Voss, Det	E	1	3	—
Paul Goebel, Col	E	1	3	—
Ed Healey, ChiB	**T**	6	1	1
Duke Slater, RI	**T**	5	1	2
Gus Sonnenberg, Det	T	3	—	1
Russ Stein, Pot	T	2	2	—
Dick Stahlman, Akr	T	2	—	2
Link Lyman, Can	T	2	2	—
Norm Harvey, Buf	T	1	3	—
Cub Buck, GB	T	1	3	—
Jim McMillen, ChiB	**G**	5	2	1
Swede Youngstrom, Buf	**G**	3	1	—
Century Milstead, NYG	**G**	3	1	—
Art Carney, NYG	**G**	3	—	1
Chet Widerquist, RI	G	2	2	—
Duke Osborn, Pot	G	2	—	2
George Abramson, GB	G	2	—	2
Al Nesser, Akr	G	1	3	—
Willis Brennan, ChiC	G	1	3	—
George Trafton, ChiB	**C**	3	1	—
Ralph Claypool, ChiC	**C**	3	—	1
Dolph Eckstein, Pro	C	2	—	2
Frank Culver, Can	C	2	2	—
Ernie Vick, Det	C	1	3	—
Paddy Driscoll, ChiC	**B**	6	1	1
Joey Sternaman, ChiB	**B**	5	2	1
Jack McBride, NYG	**B**	4	3	1
Tex Hamer, Fra	**B**	4	2	2
Barney Wentz, Pot	B	3	1	—
Dave Noble, Cle	B	3	—	1
Walter French, Pot	B	3	1	—
Heinie Benkert, NYG	B	3	1	—
Cy Wentworth, Pro	B	2	—	2
James Robertson, Akr	B	2	—	2
Verne Lewellen, GB	B	2	—	2
Bob Koehler, ChiC	B	2	2	—
Jimmy Conzelman, Det	B	2	2	—
Hinkey Haines, NYG	B	1	3	—
Hal Erickson, ChiC	B	1	3	—
Al Bloodgood, KC	B	1	3	—

1926 NFL

NAME	POS	TT	CL	GB	CT
Brick Muller, LA	**E**	8	1	1	2
Lavvie Dilweg, Mil	**E**	8	1	2	1
Charlie Berry, Pot	E	4	3	1	—
Frank Bissell, Akr	E	3	3	2	—
Duke Hanny, ChiB	E	2	2	—	—
Ed Healey, ChiB	**T**	9	1	1	1
Frank Racis, Pot	**T**	3	1	—	—
Walt Ellis, ChiC	**T**	3	—	1	—
Bub Weller, ChiC	T	2	—	—	2
John Thurman, LA	T	2	—	2	—
Steve Owen, NYG	T	2	—	2	—
Paul Jappe, Bkn	T	1	3	—	—
Jim McMillen, ChiB	**G**	6	1	—	1
Johnny Budd, Fra	**G**	6	—	1	1
Gus Sonnenberg, Det	**G**	5	T2	1	—
Bill Buckler, ChiB	G	4	—	2	2
Jim Welsh, Pot	G	3	1	—	—
Joe Williams, NYG	G	2	2	—	—
Rudy Comstock, Fra	G	2	2	—	—
Willis Brennan, ChiC	G	2	—	—	2
Jay Berquist, KC	G	2	—	—	—
Chet Widerquist, ChiC	G	1	3	—	—
George Trafton, ChiB	**C**	5	2	—	1
Clyde Smith, KC	C	3	1	—	—
Ralph Claypool, ChiC	C	3	—	1	—
John Alexander, NYG	C	3	G3	—	2
Herb Stein, Pot	C	2	—	2	—
Ernie Nevers, Dul	**B**	9	1	1	1
Paddy Driscoll, ChiB	**B**	9	1	1	1
Al Bloodgood, KC	**B**	5	1	2	—
Verne Lewellen, GB	**B**	3	—	1	—
Tony Latone, Pot	**B**	3	—	—	1
Tut Imlay, LA	**B**	3	—	1	—
Hust Stockton, Fra	B	2	—	2	—
Curly Oden, Pro	B	2	—	2	—
Cully Lidberg, GB	B	2	2	—	—
Tex Hamer, Fra	B	2	—	2	2
Hinkey Haines, NYG	B	2	—	2	—
Jack McBride, NYG	B	1	3	—	—
Two-Bits Homan, Fra	B	1	3	—	—
Herb DeWitz, KC	B	1	3	—	—
Heinie Benkert, Pot	B	1	3	—	—

1927 NFL

NAME	POS	TT	GB	CT
Lavvie Dilweg, GB	**E**	6	1	1
Cal Hubbard, NYG	**E**	3	1	1
Carl Bacchus, Cle	**E**	3	—	1
Ed Lynch, Pro	E	2	2	—
George Kenneally, Pot	E	2	2	—
Century Milstead, NYG	**T**	5	2	1
Ed Weir, Fra	**T**	3	1	1
Gus Sonnenberg, Pro	**T**	3	1	—
Joe Kozlowsky, Pro	**T**	3	—	1
Duke Slater, ChiC	T	2	2	—
Mike Michalske, NYY	**G**	6	1	1
Steve Owen, NYG	**G**	3	1	—
Jim McMillen, ChiB	**G**	3	—	1
Milt Rehnquist, Cle	G	2	2	—
Al Graham, Day	G	2	2	—
George Trafton, ChiB	**C**	5	2	1
Clyde Smith, Cle	C	3	1	—
Verne Lewellen, NYY	**B**	6	1	1
Benny Friedman, Cle	**B**	6	1	1
Paddy Driscoll, ChiB	**B**	6	1	1
Jack McBride, NYG	**B**	5	2	1
Ernie Nevers, Dul	B	3	1	—
Eddie Tryon, NYY	B	2	2	—
Bill Senn, ChiB	B	2	2	—
Hinkey Haines, NYG	B	2	2	—

1928 NFL

NAME	POS	TT	GB	CT
Lavvie Dilweg, GB	**E**	6	1	1
Cal Hubbard, NYG	**E**	5	2	1
Ray Flaherty, NYG	**E**	5	1	2
George Kenneally, Pot	E	2	—	2
Carl Bacchus, Det	E	2	2	—
Bill Owen, Det	**T**	6	1	1
Gus Sonnenberg, Pro	**T**	5	2	1
Bull Behman, Fra	**T**	5	1	G2
Don Murry, ChiB	T	2	—	2
Link Lyman, ChiB	T	2	2	—
Roger Ashmore, GB	T	2	—	2
Mike Michalske, NYY	**G**	6	1	1
Jim McMillen, ChiB	**G**	6	1	1
Al Graham, Day	G	4	2	2
Milt Rehnquist, Pro	G	2	2	—
Joe Wostoupal, Det	**C**	5	2	1
Clyde Smith, Pro	**C**	5	1	2
Wildcat Wilson, Pro	**B**	6	1	1
Verne Lewellen, GB	**B**	6	1	1
Benny Friedman, Det	**B**	6	1	1
Paddy Driscoll, ChiB	**B**	5	2	1
Wally Diehl, Fra	**B**	5	1	2
Curly Oden, Pro	B	4	2	2
Eddie Kotal, GB	B	4	2	2
Ken Mercer, Fra	B	2	—	2
Tony Latone, Pot	B	2	2	—

1929 NFL

NAME	POS	TT	CL	GB	CT
Ray Flaherty, NYG	**E**	9	1	1	1
Lavvie Dilweg, GB	**E**	9	1	1	1
Luke Johnsos, ChiB	E	4	2	2	—
Jack Spellman, Pro	E	2	2	—	—
Bob Lundell, Min	E	2	—	2	—
Bull Behman, Fra	**T**	9	1	1	1
Duke Slater, ChiC	**T**	5	—	2	1
Cal Hubbard, GB	**T**	5	2	—	G1
Bob Beattie, Ora	**T**	5	2	1	—
Steve Owen, NYG	T	3	1	—	—
Bill Kern, GB	T	2	—	2	—
Mike Michalske, GB	**G**	9	1	1	1
Milt Rehnquist, Pro	**G**	5	2	1	—
Walt Kiesling, ChiC	G	3	1	—	—
Frank Racis, Bos	G	2	—	2	—
Hal Hanson, Fra	G	2	—	2	—
Herb Blumer, ChiC	G	2	2	—	—
Joe Wostoupal, NYG	**C**	9	1	1	1
Joey Maxwell, Fra	C	2	2	—	—
Jug Earp, GB	C	2	—	2	—
Tony Plansky, NYG	**B**	9	1	1	1
Ernie Nevers, ChiC	**B**	9	1	1	1
Verne Lewellen, GB	**B**	9	1	1	1
Benny Friedman, NYG	**B**	9	1	1	1
Ken Strong, SI	B	4	2	2	—
George Pease, Ora	B	4	2	2	—
Doug Wycoff, SI	B	2	2	—	—
Walt Holmer, ChiB	B	2	—	—	—
Wally Diehl, Fra	B	2	—	2	—
Johnny Blood, GB	B	2	—	2	—

1930 NFL

NAME	POS	TT	CL	GB
Luke Johnsos, ChiB	**E**	6	1	1
Lavvie Dilweg, GB	**E**	6	1	1
Tom Nash, GB	E	4	2	2
Chuck Kassel, ChiC	E	3	2	3

1930 NFL (CONT.)

NAME	POS	TT	CL	GB
Red Badgro, NYG	E	2	—	2
Tony Kostos, Min	E	1	—	3
Link Lyman, ChiB	**T**	**6**	**1**	**1**
Jap Douds, Por	**T**	**5**	**2**	**1**
Duke Slater, ChiC	T	3	2	3
Bill Owen, NYG	T	3	1	—
Jim Mooney, Bkn	T	2	—	2
Bill Kern, GB	T	2	—	2
Cal Hubbard, GB	T	1	—	3
Mike Michalske, GB	**G**	**6**	**1**	**1**
Walt Kiesling, ChiC	**G**	**6**	**1**	**1**
Hal Hanson, Min	G	2	—	2
George Gibson, Min	G	2	2	—
Rudy Comstock, NYG	G	2	—	2
Zuck Carlson, ChiB	G	2	2	—
Al Graham, Por	G	1	—	3
Les Caywood, NYG	G	1	—	3
Joe Wostoupal, NYG	**C**	**4**	**2**	**2**
Nate Barragar, Min	**C**	**4**	**1**	**3**
Swede Hagberg, Bkn	C	3	—	1
Ken Strong, SI	**B**	**6**	**1**	**1**
Ernie Nevers, ChiC	**B**	**6**	**1**	**1**
Red Grange, ChiB	**B**	**6**	**1**	**1**
Benny Friedman, NYG	**B**	**6**	**1**	**1**
Bronko Nagurski, ChiB	B	4	2	2
Red Dunn, GB	B	4	2	2
Johnny Blood, GB	B	3	2	3
Stumpy Thomason, Bkn	B	2	—	2
Father Lumpkin, Por	B	2	—	2
Bill Glassgow, Por	B	2	2	—
Jack McBride, Bkn	B	1	—	3
Carl Brumbaugh, ChiB	B	1	—	3
Chuck Bennett, Por	B	1	—	3

1931 NFL

NAME	POS	TT	UP	CL	NL
Lavvie Dilweg, GB	**E**	**8**	**1**	**2**	**1**
Bill McKalip, Por	**E**	**7**	**2**	**1**	**2**
Luke Johnsos, ChiB	**E**	**7**	**1**	**2**	**2**
Tom Nash, GB	E	3	—	1	—
Red Badgro, NYG	E	3	—	—	1
Chuck Braidwood, Cle	E	2	2	—	—
Al Rose, Pro	E	1	—	—	3
Ray Flaherty, NYG	E	1	—	—	3
Bill Owen, NYG	**T**	**6**	**2**	**1**	**3**
Cal Hubbard, GB	**T**	**6**	**1**	**—**	**1**
Dick Stahlman, GB	T	5	—	1	2
Len Grant, NYG	T	5	1	2	2
Jap Douds, Por	T	4	—	2	2
George Christensen, Por	T	3	—	—	1
Link Lyman, ChiB	T	2	2	—	—
Lou Gordon, Bkn	T	1	—	—	3
Butch Gibson, NYG	**G**	**9**	**1**	**1**	**1**
Mike Michalske, GB	**G**	**8**	**1**	**2**	**1**
Walt Kiesling, ChiC	G	6	2	2	2
Zuck Carlson, ChiB	G	4	—	1	3
Dave Myers, Bkn	G	2	—	—	2
Al Graham, Pro	G	2	—	—	2
Maury Bodenger, Por	G	1	—	—	3
Frank McNally, ChiC	**C**	**6**	**1**	**—**	**1**
Nate Barragar, GB	**C**	**6**	**2**	**1**	**3**
Bert Pearson, ChiB	C	2	—	2	—
Mel Hein, NYG	C	2	—	—	2
Ernie Nevers, ChiC	**B**	**9**	**1**	**1**	**1**
Red Grange, ChiB	**B**	**9**	**1**	**1**	**1**
Dutch Clark, Por	**B**	**9**	**1**	**1**	**1**
Ken Strong, SI	**B**	**8**	**1**	**1**	**2**
Johnny Blood, GB	B	7	2	2	1
Red Dunn, GB	B	4	2	2	2
Dick Nesbitt, ChiB	B	3	—	2	3
Glenn Presnell, Por	B	2	—	2	—
Bronko Nagurski, ChiB	B	2	—	2	—
Hap Moran, NYG	B	2	—	2	—
Bo Molenda, GB	B	2	—	—	2
Dutch Kitzmiller, NYG	B	2	2	—	—
Carl Brumbaugh, ChiB	B	2	—	2	—
Father Lumpkin, Por	B	1	—	—	3
Herb Joesting, ChiB	B	1	—	—	3
Benny Friedman, NYG	B	1	—	—	3

1932 NFL

NAME	POS	TT	UP	CL	NL
Ray Flaherty, NYG	**E**	**9**	**1**	**1**	**1**
Bill Hewitt, ChiB	**E**	**7**	**2**	**1**	**2**
Tom Nash, GB	E	5	1	2	—
Luke Johnsos, ChiB	E	5	—	2	1
Lavvie Dilweg, GB	E	4	2	—	2
Cal Hubbard, GB	**T**	**9**	**1**	**1**	**1**
Len Grant, NYG	**T**	**6**	**1**	**1**	**—**
George Christensen, Por	**T**	**6**	**2**	**2**	**2**
Turk Edwards, Bos	T	5	—	2	1
Jake Williams, ChiC	T	2	—	—	2
Lou Gordon, ChiC	T	2	—	—	2
Zuck Carlson, ChiB	**G**	**9**	**1**	**1**	**1**
Ox Emerson, Por	**G**	**6**	**1**	**1**	**—**

1932 NFL (CONT.)

NAME	POS	TT	UP	CL	NL
Joe Kopcha, ChiB	G	4	2	2	—
Walt Kiesling, ChiC	G	3	—	—	1
Joe Zeller, GB	G	2	2	—	—
George Hurley, Bos	G	2	—	—	2
Butch Gibson, NYG	G	2	—	—	2
Maury Bodenger, Por	G	2	—	—	2
Tim Moynihan, ChiC	**C**	**7**	**1**	**1**	**3**
Nate Barragar, GB	**C**	**7**	**2**	**2**	**1**
Mel Hein, NYG	C	2	—	—	2
Bronko Nagurski, ChiB	**B**	**9**	**1**	**1**	**1**
Dutch Clark, Por	**B**	**9**	**1**	**1**	**1**
Arnie Herber, GB	**B**	**8**	**1**	**2**	**1**
Clarke Hinkle, GB	**B**	**7**	**2**	**1**	**2**
Keith Molesworth, ChiB	B	6	2	2	2
Father Lumpkin, Por	B	6	1	—	—
Jack Grossman, Bkn	B	4	—	2	2
Cliff Battles, Bos	B	3	—	1	—
Glenn Presnell, Por	B	2	2	—	—
Ace Gutowsky, Por	B	2	—	2	—
Red Grange, ChiB	B	2	—	2	—
Bob Campiglio, SI	B	2	2	—	—

1933 NFL

NAME	POS	TT	UP	CL	GB	NL	CD
Bill Hewitt, ChiB	**E**	**15**	**1**	**1**	**1**	**1**	**1**
Ray Flaherty, NYG	**E**	**12**	**1**	**2**	**2**	**2**	**1**
Harry Ebding, Por	E	9	1	—	2	2	2
Red Badgro, NYG	E	8	—	1	1	1	2
Lavvie Dilweg, GB	E	2	2	—	—	—	—
Cal Hubbard, GB	**T**	**15**	**1**	**1**	**G1**	**1**	**1**
Turk Edwards, Bos	**T**	**11**	**2**	**—**	**1**	**1**	**1**
George Christensen, Por	**T**	**11**	**1**	**1**	**1**	**1**	**2**
Len Grant, NYG	T	4	—	—	2	2	—
Lou Gordon, ChiC	T	4	2	—	2	—	—
George Musso, ChiB	T	2	—	—	2	—	—
Link Lyman, ChiB	T	2	—	—	—	—	2
Joe Kopcha, ChiB	**G**	**14**	**1**	**1**	**2**	**1**	**1**
Ox Emerson, Por	**G**	**9**	**1**	**1**	**—**	**1**	**1**
Herman Hickman, Bkn	G	8	2	—	1	1	—
Zuck Carlson, ChiB	G	8	2	—	2	2	2
George Hurley, Bos	G	2	—	—	—	—	2
Butch Gibson, NYG	G	2	—	—	—	2	—
Ookie Miller, ChiB	**C**	**14**	**1**	**1**	**2**	**1**	**1**
Mel Hein, NYG	C	9	2	—	2	1	2
Glenn Presnell, Por	**B**	**15**	**1**	**1**	**1**	**1**	**1**
Bronko Nagurski, ChiB	**B**	**15**	**1**	**1**	**1**	**1**	**1**
Cliff Battles, Bos	**B**	**15**	**1**	**1**	**1**	**1**	**1**
Ken Strong, NYG	**B**	**14**	**1**	**1**	**1**	**2**	**1**
Harry Newman, NYG	B	9	2	—	2	1	2
Jim Musick, Bos	B	6	2	—	2	2	—
Clarke Hinkle, GB	B	6	—	2	—	2	2
Swede Hanson, Phi	B	6	—	1	—	2	2
Shipwreck Kelly, Bkn	B	4	2	—	2	—	—
Benny Friedman, Bkn	B	2	—	—	—	2	—

1934 NFL

NAME	POS	TT	UP	CL	GB	NL	CD
Bill Hewitt, ChiB	**E**	**15**	**1**	**1**	**1**	**1**	**1**
Bill McKalip, Det	**E**	**9**	**2**	**—**	**1**	**2**	**2**
Red Badgro, NYG	E	6	—	—	—	1	1
Ray Flaherty, NYG	E	5	2	1	—	—	—
Bill Karr, ChiB	E	4	—	—	2	—	2
Buster Mitchell, Det	E	3	1	—	—	—	—
Bill Smith, ChiC	E	2	—	—	2	—	—
Harry Ebding, Det	E	2	—	—	—	—	2
Link Lyman, ChiB	**T**	**13**	**1**	**1**	**1**	**2**	**2**
Turk Edwards, Bos	**T**	**10**	**1**	**—**	**2**	**2**	**1**
George Christensen, Det	**T**	**10**	**2**	**1**	**2**	**1**	**1**
Bill Morgan, NYG	T	9	—	—	1	1	1
Harry Field, ChiC	T	4	2	—	—	2	—
Joe Kopcha, ChiB	**G**	**12**	**1**	**1**	**1**	**1**	**1**
Ox Emerson, Det	**G**	**11**	**1**	**1**	**—**	**1**	**1**
Potsy Jones, NYG	G	9	2	1	2	—	2
Mike Michalske, GB	G	7	—	1	2	2	—
Butch Gibson, NYG	G	3	—	—	2	1	—
Herman Hickman, Bkn	G	2	—	—	2	—	—
Zuck Carlson, ChiB	G	2	2	—	—	—	—
Mel Hein, NYG	**C**	**15**	**1**	**1**	**1**	**1**	**1**
Eddie Kawal, ChiB	C	4	—	—	2	†2	—
Cap Oehler, Pit	C	2	—	—	—	—	2
Bernie Hughes, ChiC	C	2	—	—	2	—	—
Nate Barragar, GB	C	2	—	—	—	†2	—
Bronko Nagurski, ChiB	**B**	**15**	**1**	**1**	**1**	**1**	**1**
Beattie Feathers, ChiB	**B**	**15**	**1**	**1**	**1**	**1**	**1**
Dutch Clark, Det	**B**	**15**	**1**	**1**	**1**	**1**	**1**
Ken Strong, NYG	**B**	**14**	**2**	**1**	**1**	**1**	**1**
Cliff Battles, Bos	B	9	1	—	2	2	2
Harry Newman, NYG	B	8	2	—	2	2	2
Jack Manders, ChiB	B	5	U1	—	—	2	2
Glenn Presnell, Det	B	4	2	—	—	1	1
Clarke Hinkle, GB	B	4	—	2	—	2	—
Swede Hanson, Phi	B	4	—	2	—	2	2
Ace Gutowsky, Det	B	2	—	—	2	—	2

ALL-PRO TEAMS

1935 NFL

NAME	POS	TT	UP	CL	GB	NL	CD
Bill Smith, ChiC	E	15	1	1	1	1	1
Bill Karr, ChiB	E	15	1	1	1	1	1
Tod Goodwin, NYG	E	6	2	—	2	2	—
Don Hutson, GB	E	5	2	—	3	2	—
Eggs Manske, Phi	E	2	—	—	2	—	—
Joe Carter, Phi	E	1	—	—	3	—	—
Bill Morgan, NYG	T	15	1	1	1	1	1
George Musso, ChiB	T	13	2	1	2	1	1
Ade Schwammel, GB	T	4	1	—	3	—	—
Armand Niccolai, Pit	T	3	2	—	3	—	—
Turk Edwards, Bos	T	3	—	—	1	—	—
Bill Lee, Bkn	T	2	—	—	2	—	—
George Christensen, Det	T	2	—	—	—	2	—
Tony Blazine, ChiC	T	2	—	—	—	2	—
Ox Emerson, Det	G	14	1	1	1	2	1
Mike Michalske, GB	G	11	2	—	1	1	1
Joe Kopcha, ChiB	G	8	1	—	2	1	—
Potsy Jones, NYG	G	4	—	1	3	—	—
Phil Handler, ChiC	G	2	2	—	—	—	—
Lon Evans, GB	G	2	—	—	2	—	—
Bree Cuppoletti, ChiC	G	2	—	—	2	—	—
Rick Concannon, Bos	G	1	—	—	3	—	—
Mel Hein, NYG	C	15	1	1	1	1	1
Clare Randolph, Det	C	4	2	—	—	2	—
Nate Barragar, GB	C	2	—	—	—	2	—
Frank Bausch, Bos	C	1	—	—	3	—	—
Ed Danowski, NYG	B	15	1	1	1	1	1
Dutch Clark, Det	B	15	1	1	1	1	1
Ernie Caddel, Det	B	8	2	—	—	1	1
Arnie Herber, GB	B	7	—	1	2	2	—
Phil Sarboe, ChiC	B	6	2	—	2	2	—
Gene Ronzani, ChiB	B	6	1	—	3	2	—
Mike Mikulak, ChiC	B	6	—	—	1	1	—
Jack Manders, ChiB	B	6	—	—	1	1	—
Bill Shepherd, Det	B	4	2	—	—	—	—
George Sauer, GB	B	3	—	—	1	—	—
Clarke Hinkle, GB	B	3	1	—	—	—	—
Cliff Battles, Bos	B	3	—	—	3	2	—
Kink Richards, NYG	B	2	2	—	—	—	—
Ralph Kercheval, Bkn	B	2	—	—	2	—	—
Ken Strong, NYG	B	1	—	—	3	—	—
Glenn Presnell, Det	B	1	—	—	3	—	—

1936 NFL

NAME	POS	TT	UP	CL	NL	CD
Bill Hewitt, ChiB	E	12	1	1	1	1
Don Hutson, GB	E	10	2	1	1	2
Milt Gantenbein, GB	E	10	1	2	2	1
Bill Smith, ChiC	E	4	2	—	2	—
Joe Carter, Phi	E	4	—	2	—	2
Joe Stydahar, ChiB	T	9	2	1	2	2
Turk Edwards, Bos	T	9	1	—	1	1
Ernie Smith, GB	T	6	1	—	1	—
George Christensen, Det	T	5	—	2	2	1
Jack Johnson, Det	T	3	—	1	—	—
Ade Schwammel, GB	T	2	—	2	—	—
Armand Niccolai, Pit	T	2	2	—	—	—
Jim MacMurdo, Phi	T	2	—	2	—	—
Bill Lee, Bkn	T	2	—	—	2	—
Lon Evans, GB	G	12	1	1	1	1
Ox Emerson, Det	G	8	1	2	1	—
Bree Cuppoletti, ChiC	G	7	2	—	2	1
George Rado, Pit	G	5	—	1	—	2
Danny Fortmann, ChiB	G	4	2	—	2	1
Les Olsson, Bos	G	2	—	—	—	2
Eddie Kahn, Bos	G	2	—	2	—	—
Mel Hein, NYG	C	11	2	1	1	1
Frank Bausch, Bos	C	7	1	2	2	—
Eddie Kawal, ChiB	C	2	—	—	—	2
Dutch Clark, Det	B	12	1	1	1	1
Cliff Battles, Bos	B	12	1	1	1	1
Bronko Nagurski, ChiB	B	11	1	1	1	1
Tuffy Leemans, NYG	B	10	2	1	1	2
Arnie Herber, GB	B	7	—	2	2	1
Clarke Hinkle, GB	B	6	1	—	1	—
Ace Gutowsky, Det	B	6	2	2	—	—
Beattie Feathers, ChiB	B	4	2	2	—	—
Ernie Caddel, Det	B	4	—	—	2	2
Riley Smith, Bos	B	2	—	—	2	2
Bernie Masterson, ChiB	B	2	—	—	2	—
Ralph Kercheval, Bkn	B	2	—	2	—	—
George Grosvenor, ChiC	B	2	2	—	—	—

1937 NFL

NAME	POS	TT	UP	NY	CL	NL	IN
Gaynell Tinsley, ChiC	E	14	1	1	1	1	2
Don Hutson, GB	E	13	2	1	1	2	1
Bill Hewitt, Phi	E	10	2	2	—	1	1
Ed Klewicki, Det	E	5	1	—	2	—	—
Bill Karr, ChiB	E	4	—	2	2	—	—
Wayne Millner, Was	E	2	—	—	2	—	—
Milt Gantenbein, GB	E	2	—	—	—	2	—
Turk Edwards, Was	T	15	1	1	1	1	1
Joe Stydahar, ChiB	T	14	1	1	1	1	2
Ed Widseth, NYG	T	11	2	2	2	2	1

1937 NFL (CONT.)

NAME	POS	TT	UP	NY	CL	NL	IN
Ernie Smith, GB	T	6	—	2	—	2	2
Lou Gordon, GB	T	4	2	—	2	—	2
George Musso, ChiB	G	15	1	1	1	1	1
Danny Fortmann, ChiB	G	11	2	1	2	2	2
Lon Evans, GB	G	8	1	2	—	1	—
Johnny Dell Isola, NYG	G	7	—	2	1	2	—
Ox Emerson, Det	G	3	—	—	—	—	1
Orville Tuttle, NYG	G	2	—	—	—	—	—
Les Olsson, Was	G	2	2	—	—	—	—
Russ Letlow, GB	G	2	—	—	2	—	—
Mel Hein, NYG	C	13	2	1	2	1	1
Frank Bausch, ChiB	C	7	—	2	1	2	—
Mike Basrak, Pit	C	5	1	—	—	—	2
Clarke Hinkle, GB	B	15	1	1	1	1	1
Dutch Clark, Det	B	15	1	1	1	1	1
Cliff Battles, Was	B	13	2	1	2	1	1
Sammy Baugh, Was	B	12	1	1	—	1	1
Jack Manders, ChiB	B	8	1	2	1	—	—
Bronko Nagurski, ChiB	B	5	—	1	2	—	—
Tuffy Leemans, NYG	B	4	—	2	—	2	—
Ace Gutowsky, Det	B	4	2	—	—	—	—
Johnny Drake, Cle	B	4	2	2	—	—	—
Ed Danowski, NYG	B	4	—	—	2	2	—
Ernie Caddel, Det	B	4	—	2	—	2	—
Riley Smith, Was	B	2	2	—	—	—	—
Bill Shepherd, Det	B	2	—	—	—	—	2
Ace Parker, Bkn	B	2	—	—	—	—	2
Ray Nolting, ChiB	B	2	—	—	—	—	2
Bull Karcis, Pit	B	2	—	—	2	—	—
Johnny Gildea, Pit	B	2	—	—	—	—	2

1938 NFL

NAME	POS	TT	UP	NY	FW	CL	NL	IN
Gaynell Tinsley, ChiC	E	16	2	2	1	1	1	1
Don Hutson, GB	E	15	1	1	1	—	1	1
Bill Hewitt, Phi	E	15	1	1	2	2	2	2
Milt Gantenbein, GB	E	4	2	—	—	2	—	—
Joe Carter, Phi	E	4	—	2	2	—	—	—
Bill Smith, ChiC	E	2	—	—	—	2	—	—
Jim Poole, NYG	E	2	—	—	—	—	—	2
Ed Klewicki, Det	E	2	—	—	2	—	—	—
Ed Widseth, NYG	T	18	1	1	1	1	1	1
Joe Stydahar, ChiB	T	16	1	1	2	2	1	1
Bruiser Kinard, Bkn	T	11	2	2	1	—	2	2
Turk Edwards, Was	T	9	—	2	2	1	2	—
Jack Johnson, Det	T	2	—	—	—	—	—	2
John Golemgeske, Bkn	T	2	—	—	—	—	—	—
Conway Baker, ChiC	T	2	2	—	—	—	—	—
Danny Fortmann, ChiB	G	18	1	1	1	1	1	1
Russ Letlow, GB	G	16	2	2	1	1	1	1
Johnny Dell Isola, NYG	G	8	—	2	2	2	—	2
Orville Tuttle, NYG	G	6	2	—	2	—	—	2
Les Olsson, Was	G	3	—	1	—	—	—	—
Byron Gentry, Pit	G	3	1	—	—	—	—	—
George Musso, ChiB	G	2	—	—	—	—	2	—
Jim Karcher, Was	G	2	—	—	—	—	2	—
Ross Carter, ChiC	G	2	—	—	—	—	2	—
Mel Hein, NYG	C	14	1	1	2	—	1	1
Frank Bausch, ChiB	C	12	2	2	1	2	—	—
Chuck Cherundolo, Cle	C	2	—	—	—	—	—	—
Mike Basrak, Pit	C	2	—	—	—	—	—	2
Clarke Hinkle, GB	B	18	1	1	1	1	1	1
Ed Danowski, NYG	B	18	1	1	1	1	1	1
Ace Parker, Bkn	B	17	1	1	1	1	1	1
Whizzer White, Pit	B	16	1	2	1	1	2	1
Bill Shepherd, Det	B	10	—	1	2	1	—	2
Cecil Isbell, GB	B	10	2	2	—	2	2	—
Tuffy Leemans, NYG	B	8	2	2	2	2	—	—
Sammy Baugh, Was	B	6	2	—	2	2	—	—
Lloyd Cardwell, Det	B	5	—	2	—	—	1	—
Riley Smith, Was	B	4	—	—	—	2	2	—
Johnny Drake, Cle	B	4	—	—	—	—	2	2
Ace Gutowsky, Det	B	2	—	—	—	—	—	—
Ward Cuff, NYG	B	2	—	—	—	—	—	2

1939 NFL

NAME	POS	TT	UP	NY	FW	CL	NL	IN	CH
Don Hutson, GB	E	21	1	1	1	1	1	1	1
Jim Poole, NYG	E	17	1	2	—	1	1	1	1
Perry Schwartz, Bkn	E	15	2	1	2	2	2	2	2
Dick Plasman, ChiB	E	11	2	2	2	1	—	—	2
Bill Smith, ChiC	E	3	—	—	—	1	—	—	—
Jim Lee Howell, NYG	E	2	—	—	—	—	—	2	—
Jim Benton, Cle	E	2	—	—	—	—	—	—	—
Joe Stydahar, ChiB	T	21	1	1	1	1	1	1	1
Jim Barber, Was	T	11	1	—	1	—	1	—	2
John Mellus, NYG	T	9	—	2	2	2	—	2	1
Baby Ray, GB	T	7	2	—	—	1	—	—	—
Bruiser Kinard, Bkn	T	6	2	2	—	2	—	—	—
Turk Edwards, Was	T	6	—	—	2	—	2	2	—
Ed Widseth, NYG	T	4	—	2	—	2	—	—	—
Jack Johnson, Det	T	4	—	—	2	—	2	—	—
Bo Russell, Was	T	2	—	—	—	—	—	—	2
Danny Fortmann, ChiB	G	21	1	1	1	1	1	1	1
Johnny Dell Isola, NYG	G	14	2	1	1	1	1	—	—

1939 NFL (CONT.)

NAME	POS	TT	UP	NY	FW	CL	NL	IN	CH
Socko Wiethe, Det	G	11	1	2	2	2	—	—	2
George Musso, ChiB	G	6	—	—	2	—	2	—	2
Orville Tuttle, NYG	G	4	2	—	—	2	—	—	—
Russ Letlow, GB	G	4	—	2	—	2	—	—	—
Buckets Goldenberg, GB	G	3	—	—	—	—	—	—	1
Byron Gentry, Pit	G	3	—	—	—	—	—	1	—
Kayo Lunday, NYG	G	2	—	—	—	—	—	2	—
Jim Karcher, Was	G	2	—	—	—	—	—	2	—
Mel Hein, NYG	C	17	1	1	1	2	1	1	—
Ki Aldrich, ChiC	C	10	2	—	2	—	2	2	2
Alex Wojciechowicz, Det	C	8	—	2	—	1	—	1	1
Bill Osmanski, ChiB	B	21	1	1	1	1	1	1	1
Parker Hall, Cle	B	19	1	1	1	2	2	1	1
Andy Farkas, Was	B	18	1	1	1	1	1	—	1
Tuffy Leemans, NYG	B	16	1	1	2	2	1	1	1
Ace Parker, Bkn	B	14	—	2	1	1	2	2	1
Johnny Drake, Cle	B	12	2	2	2	2	2	—	2
Davey O'Brien, Phi	B	11	2	2	2	2	—	1	—
Frank Filchock, Was	B	7	2	2	—	—	—	1	—
Ward Cuff, NYG	B	6	—	—	2	—	—	2	2
Lloyd Cardwell, Det	B	5	—	—	—	1	2	—	—
Larry Craig, GB	B	3	—	—	—	—	—	—	1
Fred Vanzo, Det	B	2	—	—	—	—	—	—	2
Bill Shepherd, Det	B	2	—	—	—	—	—	2	—
Cecil Isbell, GB	B	2	—	—	—	—	—	2	—
Clarke Hinkle, GB	B	2	—	—	—	—	—	—	2

1940 NFL

NAME	POS	TT	AP	UP	NY	CL	NL	IN	CH
Perry Schwartz, Bkn	E	20	1	2	1	1	1	1	1
Don Hutson, GB	E	20	1	1	1	1	1	2	1
Jim Poole, NYG	E	14	—	1	2	2	2	1	2
Don Looney, Phi	E	8	—	2	2	2	2	—	—
Carl Mulleneaux, GB	E	2	—	2	—	—	—	—	—
Chuck Hanneman, Det	E	2	—	—	—	—	—	2	—
Bruiser Kinard, Bkn	T	21	1	1	1	1	1	1	1
Joe Stydahar, ChiB	T	17	1	—	1	1	1	1	2
Jim Barber, Was	T	9	—	1	2	2	2	—	—
John Mellus, NYG	T	6	—	2	—	2	2	—	—
Frank Cope, NYG	T	4	—	—	—	—	2	2	—
Chet Adams, Cle	T	4	—	2	—	2	—	2	—
Lee Artoe, ChiB	T	2	—	—	—	—	—	—	1
Ed Kolman, ChiB	T	2	—	2	—	—	—	—	—
Danny Fortmann, ChiB	G	21	1	1	1	1	1	1	1
Socko Wiethe, Det	G	16	1	2	1	1	1	—	2
Steve Slivinski, Was	G	10	—	1	2	—	2	1	—
Russ Letlow, GB	G	6	—	—	2	2	—	—	2
Dick Bassi, Phi	G	5	—	—	2	—	2	—	1
Doug Oldershaw, NYG	G	4	2	—	—	2	—	—	—
Orville Tuttle, NYG	G	2	—	—	—	—	—	2	—
Dick Farman, Was	G	2	—	2	—	—	—	—	—
Mel Hein, NYG	C	17	1	1	1	—	1	1	2
Bulldog Turner, ChiB	C	13	—	2	2	2	2	2	1
Charley Brock, GB	C	3	—	—	—	1	—	—	—
Ace Parker, Bkn	B	21	1	1	1	1	1	1	1
Johnny Drake, Cle	B	20	1	1	1	1	1	2	1
Whizzer White, Det	B	19	1	1	1	1	1	1	2
Sammy Baugh, Was	B	19	1	1	1	1	1	1	2
Dick Todd, Was	B	11	—	2	2	2	2	1	—
Sid Luckman, ChiB	B	7	—	—	—	2	—	2	1
Clarke Hinkle, GB	B	7	—	—	—	2	2	1	2
Cecil Isbell, GB	B	6	—	2	2	—	2	—	—
Parker Hall, Cle	B	4	—	2	—	2	—	—	—
Gary Famiglietti, ChiB	B	4	—	2	2	—	—	—	—
Fred Vanzo, Det	B	3	—	—	—	2	—	—	1
Lloyd Cardwell, Det	B	3	—	—	—	1	—	—	—
Davey O'Brien, Phi	B	2	—	—	2	—	—	2	—
George McAfee, ChiB	B	2	—	—	2	—	2	—	—
Pug Manders, Bkn	B	2	—	—	—	—	—	2	—
Tuffy Leemans, NYG	B	2	—	—	—	—	—	2	—

1941 NFL

NAME	POS	TT	AP	UP	NY	CL	NL	CH
Don Hutson, GB	E	18	1	1	1	1	1	1
Perry Schwartz, Bkn	E	16	1	2	1	1	1	2
Dick Plasman, ChiB	E	7	—	1	—	2	2	—
Jim Lee Howell, NYG	E	5	2	—	—	—	—	1
Billy Dewell, ChiC	E	4	—	2	—	2	—	—
George Wilson, ChiB	E	2	—	—	—	—	—	2
Ray Riddick, GB	E	2	—	—	—	—	2	—
Bob Nowaskey, ChiB	E	2	—	—	2	—	—	—
Wayne Millner, Was	E	2	—	—	2	—	—	—
Dick Humbert, Phi	E	2	—	—	2	—	—	—
Willie Wilkin, Was	T	14	1	2	1	—	1	1
Bruiser Kinard, Bkn	T	14	2	1	1	—	1	1
John Mellus, NYG	T	10	1	—	—	1	2	2
Baby Ray, GB	T	8	—	—	2	1	—	2
Lee Artoe, ChiB	T	6	2	—	—	2	—	—
Ed Kolman, ChiB	T	4	—	—	2	—	2	—
Phil Ragazzo, Phi	T	2	—	—	—	2	—	—
Chet Adams, Cle	T	2	—	—	2	—	—	—
Danny Fortmann, ChiB	G	18	1	1	1	1	1	1
Joe Kuharich, ChiC	G	14	1	2	—	1	1	2
Pete Tinsley, GB	G	6	2	—	2	—	—	2
Augie Lio, Det	G	6	2	—	2	—	—	2

1941 NFL (CONT.)

NAME	POS	TT	AP	UP	NY	CL	NL	CH
Riley Matheson, Cle	G	5	—	1	—	—	2	—
Bob Suffridge, Phi	G	3	—	—	1	—	—	—
Len Younce, NYG	G	2	—	2	—	—	—	—
Doug Oldershaw, NYG	G	2	—	—	—	—	—	2
Aldo Forte, ChiB	G	2	—	—	—	2	—	—
Monk Edwards, NYG	G	2	—	—	—	—	2	—
Bulldog Turner, ChiB	C	18	1	1	1	1	1	1
George Svendsen, GB	C	6	—	2	—	2	2	2
Mel Hein, NYG	C	6	2	—	2	—	—	2
George McAfee, ChiB	B	18	1	1	1	1	1	1
Cecil Isbell, GB	B	18	1	1	1	1	1	1
Pug Manders, Bkn	B	16	1	1	1	1	1	1
Sid Luckman, ChiB	B	14	1	2	1	1	1	1
Whizzer White, Det	B	8	2	—	—	2	2	2
Tuffy Leemans, NYG	B	8	2	—	2	—	—	2
Marshall Goldberg, ChiC	B	8	—	2	2	—	2	—
Clarke Hinkle, GB	B	7	2	—	2	—	—	2
Sammy Baugh, Was	B	6	—	2	2	—	2	—
Norm Standlee, ChiB	B	5	—	2	1	—	—	—
Ward Cuff, NYG	B	5	1	—	—	2	—	—
Bill Osmanski, ChiB	B	3	—	—	—	1	—	—
Art Jones, Pit	B	2	—	—	—	2	—	—
Johnny Drake, Cle	B	2	—	—	—	2	—	—

1942 NFL

NAME	POS	TT	AP	NY	NL	IN
Don Hutson, GB	E	12	1	1	1	1
George Wilson, ChiB	E	10	1	1	2	2
Perry Schwartz, Bkn	E	8	2	2	2	2
Bob Masterson, Was	E	7	2	2	1	—
Ed Cifers, Was	E	3	—	—	—	1
Lee Artoe, ChiB	T	11	1	1	1	2
Willie Wilkin, Was	T	9	1	1	1	—
Bruiser Kinard, Bkn	T	9	2	2	2	1
Ed Kolman, ChiB	T	5	—	2	—	1
Chet Adams, Cle	T	4	2	—	2	—
Joe Stydahar, ChiB	T	2	—	—	—	2
Danny Fortmann, ChiB	G	12	1	1	1	1
Monk Edwards, NYG	G	10	2	2	1	2
Milt Simington, Pit	G	5	—	1	—	2
Riley Matheson, Cle	G	5	1	—	2	—
Buckets Goldenberg, GB	G	4	2	—	2	—
Steve Slivinski, Was	G	2	—	—	—	2
Dick Farman, Was	G	2	2	—	2	—
Bulldog Turner, ChiB	C	12	1	1	1	1
Chuck Cherundolo, Pit	C	8	2	2	2	2
Sid Luckman, ChiB	B	12	1	1	1	1
Bill Dudley, Pit	B	12	1	1	1	1
Sammy Baugh, Was	B	11	1	1	2	1
Cecil Isbell, GB	B	10	2	1	1	2
Gary Famiglietti, ChiB	B	10	2	2	1	1
Andy Farkas, Was	B	7	1	2	2	—
Merl Condit, Bkn	B	6	2	2	—	—
Tommy Thompson, Phi	B	4	—	2	—	2
Tuffy Leemans, NYG	B	4	2	—	—	2
Ray McLean, ChiB	B	2	—	—	—	2
Dante Magnani, Cle	B	2	—	—	—	2

1943 NFL

NAME	POS	TT	AP	UP	NY	IN	CH	FI
Don Hutson, GB	E	18	1	1	1	1	1	1
Ed Rucinski, ChiC	E	13	1	1	2	—	1	2
George Wilson, ChiB	E	11	2	2	2	—	2	1
Bob Masterson, Was	E	9	2	2	1	—	—	—
Joe Aguirre, Was	E	3	—	—	1	—	—	—
Bill Fisk, Det	E	2	—	—	—	—	—	2
Al Blozis, NYG	T	15	1	1	1	1	—	1
Vic Sears, P-P	T	10	2	1	2	1	—	1
Baby Ray, GB	T	10	—	2	1	—	G2	1
Bruiser Kinard, Bkn	T	7	—	1	—	—	2	2
Chet Adams, GB	T	7	2	—	2	—	1	—
Chet Bulger, ChiC	T	4	2	—	2	—	—	—
Lou Rymkus, Was	T	3	—	—	1	—	—	—
Danny Fortmann, ChiB	G	15	1	1	1	1	—	1
Dick Farman, Was	G	12	1	1	1	1	—	—
Augie Lio, Det	G	11	2	2	2	—	1	T2
Steve Slivinski, Was	G	4	—	—	2	—	—	—
Riley Matheson, Det	G	4	2	—	2	—	—	—
Len Younce, NYG	G	3	—	—	—	—	—	1
Elbie Schultz, P-P	G	2	—	—	—	—	—	1
Clyde Shugart, Was	G	2	—	—	2	—	—	—
Frank Cope, NYG	G	2	—	—	—	—	—	1
Bulldog Turner, ChiB	C	18	1	1	1	1	1	1
Charley Brock, GB	C	6	2	—	—	—	—	2
George Smith, Was	C	4	—	2	2	—	—	—
Sid Luckman, ChiB	B	18	1	1	1	1	1	1
Sammy Baugh, Was	B	18	1	1	1	1	1	1
Tony Canadeo, GB	B	15	1	2	1	1	—	2
Ward Cuff, NYG	B	13	2	1	2	1	—	2
Harry Clarke, ChiB	B	13	1	1	2	1	—	2
Bill Paschal, NYG	B	8	1	—	—	2	—	—
Jack Hinkle, P-P	B	8	2	—	1	2	—	—
Andy Farkas, Was	B	8	1	—	2	—	—	—
Frankie Sinkwich, Det	B	5	—	—	—	—	—	2
Roy Zimmerman, P-P	B	2	—	—	—	—	—	2
Ernie Steele, P-P	B	2	2	—	—	—	—	—
Wilbur Moore, Was	B	2	—	—	—	—	—	2

1944 NFL

NAME	POS	TT	AP	UP	NY	IN	FI
Don Hutson, GB	E	15	1	1	1	1	1
Joe Aguirre, Was	E	15	1	1	1	1	1
George Wilson, ChiB	E	6	—	2	2	2	—
Jim Benton, Cle	E	6	—	2	2	2	—
Al Wistert, Phi	T	12	1	1	1	1	—
Frank Cope, NYG	T	11	—	1	2	1	1
Bruiser Kinard, Bkn	T	10	1	2	1	2	—
Baby Ray, GB	T	9	—	2	2	2	1
Len Younce, NYG	G	15	1	1	1	1	1
Riley Matheson, Cle	G	14	1	1	1	2	1
Augie Lio, Bos	G	7	—	2	2	1	—
George Zorich, ChiB	G	4	—	2	—	2	—
Pete Gudauskas, ChiB	G	2	—	—	2	—	—
Bulldog Turner, ChiB	C	12	1	1	1	1	—
Mel Hein, NYG	C	4	—	—	2	2	—
Alex Wojciechowicz, Det	C	3	—	—	—	—	1
Charley Brock, GB	C	2	—	2	—	—	—
Frankie Sinkwich, Det	B	15	1	1	1	1	1
Bill Paschal, NYG	B	15	1	1	1	1	1
Sid Luckman, ChiB	B	14	1	2	1	1	1
John Grigas, C-P	B	8	—	2	1	1	—
Ward Cuff, NYG	B	8	—	1	—	2	1
Roy Zimmerman, Phi	B	7	—	1	2	2	—
Steve Van Buren, Phi	B	7	1	2	2	—	—
Frank Filchock, Was	B	6	—	2	2	2	—
Pug Manders, Bkn	B	4	—	—	2	2	—

1945 NFL

NAME	POS	TT	AP	UP	NY	IN	CH	FI
Don Hutson, GB	E	16	1	1	1	2	2	1
Jim Benton, Cle	E	16	1	2	1	1	2	1
Steve Pritko, Cle	E	8	—	1	—	1	—	2
Joe Aguirre, Was	E	8	—	—	2	1	1	—
Jack Ferrante, Phi	E	4	—	2	2	—	—	—
Ed Rucinski, ChiC	E	2	—	2	—	—	—	—
Frank Liebel, NYG	E	2	—	—	—	—	—	2
Al Wistert, Phi	T	18	1	1	1	1	1	1
Frank Cope, NYG	T	9	1	2	2	—	—	G2
Emil Uremovich, Det	T	8	—	1	1	—	2	2
John Adams, Was	T	7	—	—	—	G2	2	1
Elbie Schultz, Cle	T	6	—	—	—	1	1	—
Vic Sears, Phi	T	4	—	2	—	2	—	—
Lee Artoe, ChiB	T	4	—	2	2	—	—	—
George Sergienko, Bos	T	2	—	—	—	2	—	—
Chet Bulger, ChiC	T	2	—	—	—	—	2	—
Riley Matheson, Cle	G	17	1	1	1	2	1	1
Bill Radovich, Det	G	14	1	1	2	1	1	—
Augie Lio, Bos	G	12	—	2	1	1	2	2
Stan Batinski, Det	G	5	—	2	—	—	—	1
Bob Zimny, ChiC	G	2	—	—	—	—	2	—
Bruno Banducci, Phi	G	2	—	2	—	—	—	—
Charley Brock, GB	C	17	1	1	1	1	2	1
Mike Scarry, Cle	C	7	—	2	—	1	—	2
Mel Hein, NYG	C	2	—	—	—	2	—	—
Ki Aldrich, Was	C	2	—	—	2	—	—	—
Steve Van Buren, Phi	B	18	1	1	1	1	1	1
Bob Waterfield, Cle	B	17	1	1	1	2	1	1
Bob Margarita, ChiB	B	12	—	2	1	2	1	2
Sammy Baugh, Was	B	11	—	1	1	1	—	2
Ted Fritsch, GB	B	10	—	1	2	2	1	—
Frank Akins, Was	B	10	—	2	2	1	—	1
Sid Luckman, ChiB	B	8	—	2	2	—	2	2
Fred Gehrke, Cle	B	7	—	2	—	2	1	1
Steve Bagarus, Was	B	7	1	—	2	—	2	2
Bob Westfall, Det	B	5	1	—	—	—	—	—
Jim Gillette, Cle	B	3	—	—	1	—	—	—
Bill Paschal, NYG	B	2	—	—	—	2	—	—
Don Greenwood, Cle	B	2	—	—	—	2	—	—

1946 NFL

NAME	POS	TT	UP	NY	FI	*AP	*CH
Jim Benton, LARm	E	16	1	1	1	1	1
Jim Poole, NYG	E	8	—	2	1	1	—
Ken Kavanaugh, ChiB	E	7	1	2	2	—	—
Billy Dewell, ChiC	E	5	2	1	—	—	—
Nolan Luhn, GB	E	2	—	—	2	—	—
Frank Liebel, NYG	E	2	2	—	—	—	—
Jim White, NYG	T	14	1	1	2	2	1
Al Wistert, Phi	T	12	1	1	1	1	—
John Adams, Was	T	7	2	2	1	—	—
Fred Davis, ChiB	T	4	2	—	2	—	—
Frank Cope, NYG	T	2	—	2	—	—	—
Riley Matheson, LARm	G	16	1	1	1	1	1
Len Younce, NYG	G	7	2	1	—	—	—
Buster Ramsey, ChiC	G	6	2	—	2	—	—
Augie Lio, Phi	G	5	—	2	—	—	1
Ray Bray, ChiB	G	3	—	1	—	—	—
Monk Edwards, NYG	G	2	2	—	—	—	—
Bulldog Turner, ChiB	C	15	1	1	2	1	1
Charley Brock, GB	C	5	2	—	—	—	—
Vince Banonis, ChiC	C	2	—	1	—	—	—
Sid Luckman, ChiB	QB	14	2	1	1	2	1
Bob Waterfield, LARm	QB	10	1	2	2	1	—
Paul Christman, ChiC	QB	2	2	—	—	—	—
Bill Dudley, Pit	HB	15	1	1	1	2	1
Steve Van Buren, Phi	HB	7	2	1	2	—	—
Hugh Gallarneau, ChiB	HB	5	—	2	1	—	—
Frank Filchock, NYG	HB	5	1	2	—	—	—
Fred Gehrke, LARm	HB	2	—	2	—	1	—
Steve Bagarus, Was	HB	2	—	2	—	1	—
Ted Fritsch, GB	FB	16	1	1	1	1	1
Bill Osmanski, ChiB	FB	2	2	—	—	—	—
Pat Harder, ChiC	FB	2	—	—	2	—	—

1946 AAFC

NAME	POS	TT	UP	NY	AA	*AP	*CH
Dante Lavelli, Cle	E	9	2	2	1	2	—
Mac Speedie, Cle	E	8	1	1	2	—	—
Jack Russell, NYY	E	8	—	2	2	2	1
Alyn Beals, SF	E	8	1	2	1	—	—
Joe Aguirre, LAD	E	5	2	1	—	—	—
Bruiser Kinard, NYY	T	12	1	1	1	1	—
Martin Ruby, Bkn	T	11	1	1	1	2	—
Lee Artoe, LAD	T	6	2	2	2	—	—
Lou Rymkus, Cle	T	4	—	—	—	—	1
Bob Reinhard, LAD	T	4	—	2	2	—	—
Lou Groza, Cle	T	2	2	—	—	—	—
Bill Radovich, LAD	G	11	1	1	2	1	—
Bruno Banducci, SF	G	11	1	1	1	2	—
Bill Willis, Cle	G	7	—	—	1	—	1
Ed Ulinski, Cle	G	4	2	2	—	—	—
Buddy Jungmichel, Mia	G	4	2	—	2	—	—
Garland Gregory, SF	G	2	2	—	—	—	—
Robert Nelson, LAD	C	10	1	2	1	2	—
Mike Scarry, Cle	C	7	1	1	2	—	—
Frankie Albert, SF	QB	9	2	1	2	2	—
Otto Graham, Cle	QB	8	1	2	1	—	—
Ace Parker, NYY	QB	2	2	—	—	—	—
Glenn Dobbs, Bkn	HB	16	1	1	1	1	1
Spec Sanders, NYY	HB	12	1	1	1	1	—
Bob Hoernschemeyer, ChiR	HB	6	2	2	2	—	—
Steve Juzwik, Buf	HB	4	—	2	2	—	—
Marion Motley, Cle	FB	11	1	1	2	—	—
Norm Standlee, SF	FB	6	2	2	2	—	—

1947 NFL

NAME	POS	TT	UP	NY	CH	FI	*AP
Ken Kavanaugh, ChiB	E	13	1	—	o1	2	2
Mal Kutner, ChiC	E	11	1	—	od1	1	2
Larry Craig, GB	E	7	3	—	d1	1	—
Val Jansante, Pit	E	5	2	1	—	—	—
Charley Mehelich, Pit	E	3	—	—	d1	—	—
Pete Pihos, Phi	E	2	—	—	—	2	—
Jim Keane, ChiB	E	2	2	—	—	—	—
Jim Benton, LARm	E	1	3	—	—	—	—
Al Wistert, Phi	T	14	1	1	o1	2	1
Fred Davis, ChiB	T	12	1	1	od1	1	—
Dick Huffman, LARm	T	5	2	—	—	—	—
Stan Mauldin, ChiC	T	4	3	—	—	1	—
Gil Bouley, LARm	T	3	—	—	d1	—	—
Jim White, NYG	T	2	2	—	—	—	—
Russ Thomas, Det	T	2	—	—	—	2	—
Walt Stickel, ChiB	T	1	3	—	—	—	—
Riley Matheson, LARm	G	13	2	1	d1	2	1
Buster Ramsey, ChiC	G	11	—	1	o1	1	2
Dick Wildung, GB	G	8	2	—	o1	1	—
John Badaczewski, Bos	G	6	3	—	d1	2	—
Len Younce, NYG	G	3	1	—	—	—	—
Red Moore, Pit	G	3	1	—	—	—	—
Roger Eason, LARm	G	1	3	—	—	—	—
Bulldog Turner, ChiB	C	13	3	1	od1	1	1
Vince Banonis, ChiC	C	3	1	—	—	—	—
Fred Naumetz, LARm	C	2	—	—	—	2	—
Chuck Cherundolo, Pit	C	2	2	—	—	—	—
Sid Luckman, ChiB	QB	12	1	1	—	1	1
Sammy Baugh, Was	QB	10	1	—	o1	2	2
Paul Christman, ChiC	QB	2	2	—	—	—	—
Boley Dancewicz, Bos	QB	2	2	—	—	—	—
Steve Van Buren, Phi	HB	12	1	1	—	1	1
Bill Dudley, Det	HB	10	3	1	od1	1	—
Johnny Clement, Pit	HB	6	2	—	—	2	2
Elmer Angsman, ChiC	HB	5	—	—	o1	2	—
Marshall Goldberg, ChiC	HB	3	—	—	d1	—	—
Charlie Trippi, ChiC	HB	2	2	—	—	—	—
Tony Canadeo, GB	HB	1	3	—	—	—	—
Pat Harder, ChiC	FB	9	1	1	—	2	2
Walt Schlinkman, GB	FB	7	2	—	—	1	—
John Cannady, NYG	FB	3	—	—	d1	—	—
Camp Wilson, Det	FB	1	3	—	—	—	—

1947 AAFC

NAME	POS	TT	NY	AA	*AP
Mac Speedie, Cle	E	9	1	1	1
Jack Russell, NYY	E	5	1	2	2
Dante Lavelli, Cle	E	3	—	1	—
Bruce Alford, NYY	E	3	—	—	1
Alyn Beals, SF	E	2	—	2	—
Lou Rymkus, Cle	T	6	1	1	—
Nate Johnson, NYY	T	6	1	1	—

1947 AAFC (CONT.)

NAME	POS	TT	NY	AA	*AP
John Woudenberg, SF	T	4	—	2	2
Martin Ruby, Bkn	T	4	—	2	2
Bruno Banducci, SF	**G**	9	1	1	1
Dick Barwegan, NYY	**G**	7	1	2	2
Bill Willis, Cle	G	3	—	1	—
Len Levy, LAD	G	2	—	2	—
Robert Nelson, LAD	**C**	8	1	1	2
Lou Sossamon, NYY	C	2	—	2	—
Otto Graham, Cle	**QB**	9	1	1	1
George Ratterman, Buf	QB	2	—	2	—
Frankie Albert, SF	QB	2	—	2	2
Spec Sanders, NYY	**HB**	9	1	1	1
Chet Mutryn, Buf	**HB**	6	1	1	—
Buddy Young, NYY	HB	2	—	2	—
Johnny Strzykalski, SF	HB	2	—	2	—
Marion Motley, Cle	**FB**	8	1	1	2
Norm Standlee, SF	FB	2	—	2	—

1948 NFL

NAME	POS	TT	UP	NY	CH	FI	*AP	*SN
Mal Kutner, ChiC	**E**	19	1	1	o1	1	1	1
Pete Pihos, Phi	**E**	17	1	1	d1	1	2	2
Ken Kavanaugh, ChiB	E	9	2	2	o1	2	—	—
Tom Fears, LARm	E	4	2	2	—	—	—	—
Ed Cifers, ChiB	E	3	—	—	d1	—	—	—
Bill Swiacki, NYG	E	2	—	—	—	2	—	—
Al Wistert, Phi	**T**	16	1	1	o1	1	—	1
Dick Huffman, LARm	**T**	16	1	1	—	1	1	1
Fred Davis, ChiB	T	14	2	2	o1	2	2	2
Tex Coulter, NYG	T	4	2	—	2	—	—	—
Chet Bulger, ChiC	T	3	—	—	d1	—	—	—
Gil Bouley, LARm	T	3	—	—	d1	—	—	—
Dick Wildung, GB	T	2	—	2	—	—	—	—
Buster Ramsey, ChiC	**G**	19	1	1	o1	1	1	1
Ray Bray, ChiB	**G**	15	1	1	o1	1	—	2
Chuck Drulis, ChiB	G	6	2	2	—	—	2	—
Mike Lazetich, LARm	G	5	—	—	d1	2	—	—
Len Younce, NYG	G	3	—	—	d1	—	—	—
Wash Serini, ChiB	G	3	—	—	d1	—	—	—
Bucko Kilroy, Phi	G	2	2	—	—	—	—	—
Don Ettinger, NYG	G	2	—	2	—	—	—	—
Bulldog Turner, ChiB	**C**	18	1	2	o1	1	1	1
Vince Banonis, ChiC	C	11	2	1	d1	—	—	2
Fred Naumetz, LARm	C	2	—	—	—	2	—	—
Sammy Baugh, Was	**QB**	17	1	1	o1	1	2	2
Tommy Thompson, Phi	QB	8	2	2	—	2	2	—
Johnny Lujack, ChiB	QB	3	—	—	d1	—	—	—
Sid Luckman, ChiB	QB	2	—	2	—	—	—	—
Charlie Trippi, ChiC	**HB**	19	1	1	o1	1	1	1
Steve Van Buren, Phi	**HB**	16	1	1	—	1	1	1
George McAfee, ChiB	HB	7	2	2	d1	—	—	—
Elmer Angsman, ChiC	HB	7	—	2	o1	2	—	—
Tony Canadeo, GB	HB	4	2	—	—	—	—	—
Bill Dudley, Det	HB	3	—	—	d1	—	—	—
Pat Harder, ChiC	**FB**	15	1	1	o1	1	—	2
Joe Muha, Phi	FB	7	2	—	d1	2	—	—

1948 AAFC

NAME	POS	TT	UP	NY	AA	*AP	*SN
Mac Speedie, Cle	**E**	16	1	1	1	1	1
Alyn Beals, SF	**E**	14	1	1	1	2	2
Dante Lavelli, Cle	E	6	2	2	2	—	—
Al Baldwin, Buf	E	6	2	2	2	—	—
Bob Reinhard, LAD	**T**	15	1	1	1	1	2
Lou Rymkus, Cle	**T**	10	1	2	1	2	—
John Woudenberg, SF	T	7	2	1	2	—	—
Martin Ruby, Bkn	T	4	—	2	—	—	—
Arnie Weinmeister, NYY	T	2	—	2	—	—	—
Dick Barwegan, Bal	**G**	16	1	1	1	1	1
Bill Willis, Cle	**G**	14	1	1	1	2	2
Ed Ulinski, Cle	G	4	2	—	2	—	—
Riley Matheson, SF	G	4	—	2	2	—	—
Weldon Humble, Cle	G	4	2	2	—	—	—
Lou Saban, Cle	**C**	8	1	1	2	—	—
Robert Nelson, LAD	C	7	2	2	1	—	—
George Strohmeyer, Bkn	C	2	—	—	2	—	—
Otto Graham, Cle	**QB**	14	1	2	1	1	2
Frankie Albert, SF	QB	11	2	1	2	—	1
Johnny Strzykalski, SF	**HB**	11	1	1	2	—	—
Chet Mutryn, Buf	**HB**	11	1	1	1	—	—
Glenn Dobbs, LAD	HB	9	2	2	2	—	2
Billy Hillenbrand, Bal	HB	6	2	2	2	—	—
Spec Sanders, NYY	HB	2	—	—	—	—	—
Marion Motley, Cle	**FB**	16	1	1	1	1	1
Mickey Colmer, Bkn	FB	4	2	—	2	—	—

1949 NFL

NAME	POS	TT	UP	NY	*AP	*IN
Pete Pihos, Phi	**E**	13	1	1	1	d1
Ed Sprinkle, ChiB	**E**	8	2	2	—	d1
Tom Fears, LARm	**E**	8	1	1	2	—
Jim Keane, ChiB	E	2	2	—	—	—
Jack Ferrante, Phi	E	2	—	2	—	—
Dick Huffman, LARm	**T**	13	1	1	1	d1

1949 NFL (CONT.)

NAME	POS	TT	UP	NY	*AP	*IN
George Connor, ChiB	**T**	6	2	2	2	—
Dick Wildung, GB	T	5	1	2	1	—
Vic Sears, Phi	T	5	1	2	—	—
Al Wistert, Phi	T	4	—	—	—	o1
Buster Ramsey, ChiC	**G**	8	1	2	1	—
Ray Bray, ChiB	**G**	8	1	1	2	—
Bucko Kilroy, Phi	G	5	2	1	—	—
Wash Serini, ChiB	G	4	—	—	—	o1
Mike Lazetich, LARm	G	4	—	—	—	d1
Darrell Hogan, Pit	G	4	—	—	—	o1
Cliff Patton, Phi	G	2	2	—	—	—
Chuck DeShane, Det	G	2	2	2	—	—
Fred Naumetz, LARm	**C**	9	1	1	1	—
Vince Banonis, ChiC	C	6	2	2	—	o1
Bill Walsh, Pit	C	2	—	2	—	—
Bob Waterfield, LARm	**QB**	6	1	—	1	—
Tommy Thompson, Phi	QB	4	2	2	—	—
Johnny Lujack, ChiB	QB	3	—	1	—	—
Steve Van Buren, Phi	**HB**	13	1	1	1	o1
Tony Canadeo, GB	**HB**	11	1	2	2	o1
Elmer Angsman, ChiC	**HB**	6	2	2	2	—
Gene Roberts, NYG	HB	5	2	1	—	—
Emlen Tunnell, NYG	HB	4	—	—	—	d1
Don Doll, Det	HB	4	—	—	—	d1
Pat Harder, ChiC	**FB**	6	1	1	1	—
Dick Hoerner, LARm	FB	4	2	2	—	—

1949 AAFC

NAME	POS	TT	UP	NY	AA	*AP	*IN
Mac Speedie, Cle	**E**	16	1	1	1	1	o1
Alyn Beals, SF	**E**	15	1	1	1	2	o1
Dante Lavelli, Cle	E	6	2	2	2	—	—
Al Baldwin, Buf	E	4	2	—	2	—	—
Jack Russell, NYY	E	2	—	2	—	—	—
Arnie Weinmeister, NYY	**T**	12	1	1	1	1	—
Lou Rymkus, Cle	**T**	9	1	—	2	—	o1
John Kissell, Buf	**T**	9	2	1	—	—	d1
Bob Reinhard, LAD	T	7	—	2	1	2	—
Martin Ruby, NYY	T	6	2	2	2	—	—
Dick Barwegan, Bal	**G**	12	1	1	1	1	—
Visco Grgich, SF	**G**	11	1	1	1	2	—
Joe Signaigo, NYY	G	10	2	2	2	—	o1
Bill Willis, Cle	G	6	2	2	2	—	—
Lou Saban, Cle	**C**	15	1	1	1	2	d1
Robert Nelson, LAD	C	4	2	2	—	—	—
John Rapacz, ChiH	C	2	—	—	2	—	—
Otto Graham, Cle	**QB**	16	1	1	1	1	o1
Frankie Albert, SF	QB	9	2	2	1	2	—
Chet Mutryn, Buf	**HB**	15	1	2	1	1	o1
Buddy Young, NYY	**HB**	8	1	1	2	—	—
George Taliaferro, LAD	HB	6	2	2	—	—	—
Herm Wedemeyer, Bal	HB	4	—	—	—	—	d1
Bob Hoernschemeyer, ChiH	HB	4	2	—	2	—	—
Jim Cason, SF	HB	4	—	—	—	—	d1
Johnny Clement, ChiH	HB	2	—	2	—	—	—
Joe Perry, SF	**FB**	11	1	1	1	2	—
Marion Motley, Cle	FB	7	2	1	2	—	—

1950 NFL

NAME	POS	TT	AP	UP	NY
Tom Fears, LARm	**E**	9	1	1	o1
Mac Speedie, Cle	**E**	8	2	1	o1
Bob Shaw, ChiC	E	4	—	2	o2
Pete Pihos, Phi	E	4	—	2	o2
Ed Sprinkle, ChiB	E	3	—	—	d1
Ray Poole, NYG	E	3	—	—	d1
Dan Edwards, NYY	E	3	1	—	—
Tom Wham, ChiC	E	2	—	—	d2
Jack Russell, NYY	E	2	—	—	d2
Cloyce Box, Det	E	2	2	—	—
Arnie Weinmeister, NYG	**T**	9	1	1	d1
George Connor, ChiB	**T**	9	1	1	o1
Bob Reinhard, LARm	T	7	2	2	d1
Dick Huffman, LARm	T	7	2	2	o1
Al Wistert, Phi	T	2	—	—	o2
Vic Sears, Phi	T	2	—	—	d2
Carl Samuelson, Pit	T	2	—	—	d2
Lou Rymkus, Cle	T	2	—	—	o2
Dick Barwegan, ChiB	**G**	9	1	1	o1
Bill Willis, Cle	**G**	6	—	1	d1
Bucko Kilroy, Phi	G	5	—	—	o1
Ray Bray, ChiB	G	5	2	—	d1
Les Bingaman, Det	G	4	—	2	d2
Joe Signaigo, NYY	G	3	1	—	—
Buster Ramsey, ChiC	G	2	2	—	—
Ed Neal, GB	G	2	—	—	d2
John Mastrangelo, NYG	G	2	—	—	o2
Lin Houston, Cle	G	2	—	—	o2
Clayton Tonnemaker, GB	**C**	8	2	1	d1
John Rapacz, NYG	C	5	—	—	o1
Chuck Bednarik, Phi	C	5	1	—	d2
Joe Muha, Phi	C	3	—	—	d1
Fred Naumetz, LARm	C	2	—	—	o2
Tony Adamle, Cle	C	2	—	—	d2
Johnny Lujack, ChiB	**QB**	9	1	1	o1

ALL-PRO TEAMS

1950 NFL (CONT.)

NAME	POS	TT	AP	UP	NY
Bob Waterfield, LARm	QB	2	2	—	—
George Ratterman, NYY	QB	2	—	—	o2
Otto Graham, Cle	QB	2	—	2	—
Joe Geri, Pit	**HB**	9	1	1	o1
Doak Walker, Det	**HB**	8	1	1	o2
Billy Joe Grimes, GB	HB	5	2	—	o1
Steve Van Buren, Phi	HB	4	—	2	o2
Otto Schnellbacher, NYG	HB	3	—	—	d1
Spec Sanders, NYY	HB	3	—	—	d1
Don Doll, Det	HB	3	—	—	d1
Buddy Young, NYY	HB	2	—	2	—
Emlen Tunnell, NYG	HB	2	—	—	d2
Johnny Strzykalski, SF	HB	2	—	—	d2
Tommy James, Cle	HB	2	—	—	d2
Bill Dudley, Was	HB	2	—	—	d2
Marion Motley, Cle	**FB**	9	1	1	o1
Dick Hoerner, LARm	FB	4	2	—	o2
Pat Harder, ChiC	FB	2	—	2	—

1951 NFL

OFFENSE	POS	TT	AP	UP	NY
Elroy Hirsch, LARm	**E**	9	1	1	1
Dante Lavelli, Cle	**E**	6	—	1	1
Bobby Walston, Phi	E	2	—	2	—
Gordie Soltau, SF	E	2	—	2	—
Fran Polsfoot, ChiC	E	2	—	—	2
Tom Fears, LARm	E	2	—	—	2
Leo Nomellini, SF	**T**	7	1	2	2
Lou Groza, Cle	**T**	6	—	1	1
Tex Coulter, NYG	**T**	6	—	1	1
Lou Rymkus, Cle	T	2	—	2	—
Paul Lipscomb, Was	T	2	—	—	2
Bill Fischer, ChiC	T	2	—	—	2
Lou Creekmur, Det	**G**	9	1	1	1
Dick Barwegan, ChiB	**G**	9	1	1	1
Al Wistert, Phi	G	2	—	—	2
Lin Houston, Cle	G	2	—	2	—
Abe Gibron, Cle	G	2	—	2	—
Bruno Banducci, SF	G	2	—	2	—
Frank Gatski, Cle	**C**	6	—	1	1
Vic Lindskog, Phi	C	3	1	—	—
Jay Rhodemyre, GB	C	2	—	—	2
John Rapacz, NYG	C	2	—	2	—
Otto Graham, Cle	**QB**	9	1	1	1
Bob Waterfield, LARm	QB	4	—	2	2
Doak Walker, Det	**RB**	9	1	1	1
Dub Jones, Cle	**RB**	9	1	1	1
Dan Towler, LARm	**RB**	6	—	1	1
Eddie Price, NYG	RB	5	1	2	—
Joe Geri, Pit	RB	4	—	2	2
Bob Hoernschemeyer, Det	RB	2	—	—	—
John Dottley, ChiB	RB	2	—	—	—

DEFENSE	POS	TT	AP	UP	NY
Len Ford, Cle	**DE**	9	1	1	1
Leon Hart, Det	**DE**	8	0T1	1	2
Larry Brink, LARm	**DE**	8	1	2	1
Ed Sprinkle, ChiB	DE	4	—	2	2
Arnie Weinmeister, NYG	**DT**	9	1	1	1
George Connor, ChiB	**DT**	9	0T1	1	1
Al DeRogatis, NYG	DT	7	1	2	2
John Kissell, Cle	DT	2	—	—	2
Bill Willis, Cle	**MG**	9	1	1	1
Stan West, LARm	**MG**	5	—	2	1
Les Bingaman, Det	**MG**	5	1	—	2
Jon Baker, NYG	MG	3	—	1	—
Bob Momsen, Det	MG	2	—	2	—
Bucko Kilroy, Phi	MG	2	—	—	2
Chuck Bednarik, Phi	**LB**	9	1	1	1
Tony Adamle, Cle	**LB**	6	—	1	1
Tank Younger, LARm	LB	3	1	—	—
Tommy Thompson, Cle	LB	2	—	2	—
John Cannady, NYG	LB	2	—	2	—
Hardy Brown, SF	LB	2	—	—	2
Emlen Tunnell, NYG	**DB**	9	1	1	1
Otto Schnellbacher, NYG	**DB**	9	1	1	1
Warren Lahr, Cle	**DB**	6	—	1	1
Jerry Shipkey, Pit	DB	5	1	—	LB2
Johnny Lujack, ChiB	DB	4	—	2	2
Don Doll, Det	DB	4	—	2	2
Woodley Lewis, LARm	DB	2	—	2	—
Bill Dudley, Was	DB	2	—	—	2

1952 NFL

OFFENSE	POS	TT	AP	UP	NY
Gordie Soltau, SF	**E**	9	1	1	1
Mac Speedie, Cle	**E**	7	2	2	1
Billy Howton, GB	**E**	7	2	2	1
Elroy Hirsch, LARm	E	4	—	2	2
Cloyce Box, Det	E	3	1	—	—
Leo Nomellini, SF	**T**	9	1	1	1
Lou Groza, Cle	**T**	9	G1	1	1
Bob Toneff, SF	T	6	2	2	2
Tex Coulter, NYG	T	4	2	2	—
Lum Snyder, Phi	T	2	—	—	2

1952 NFL (CONT.)

	POS	TT	AP	UP	NY
Lou Creekmur, Det	**G**	9	1	1	1
Bruno Banducci, SF	**G**	7	2	2	1
Bill Fischer, ChiC	G	5	—	1	2
Dick Barwegan, ChiB	G	4	—	2	2
John Wozniak, DalT	G	2	2	—	—
Frank Gatski, Cle	**C**	8	1	2	1
Bill Johnson, SF	C	4	2	—	2
Bill Walsh, Pit	C	3	—	1	—
Otto Graham, Cle	**QB**	8	2	1	1
Bobby Layne, Det	QB	5	1	—	2
Norm Van Brocklin, LARm	QB	2	—	2	—
Eddie Price, NYG	**RB**	9	1	1	1
Hugh McElhenny, SF	**RB**	9	1	1	1
Dan Towler, LARm	**RB**	8	1	1	2
Bob Hoernschemeyer, Det	RB	7	2	2	1
Ray Mathews, Pit	RB	4	—	—	2
Charlie Trippi, ChiC	RB	2	—	—	2
George Taliaferro, DalT	RB	2	2	—	—
Pat Harder, Det	RB	2	2	—	—

DEFENSE	POS	TT	AP	UP	NY
Len Ford, Cle	**DE**	9	1	1	1
Pete Pihos, Phi	**DE**	8	1	2	1
Andy Robustelli, LARm	DE	4	2	—	2
Ed Henke, SF	DE	4	—	2	2
Larry Brink, LARm	DE	3	—	1	—
Ed Sprinkle, ChiB	DE	2	2	—	—
Arnie Weinmeister, NYG	**DT**	9	1	1	1
Thurman McGraw, Det	**DT**	9	1	1	1
Ernie Stautner, Pit	DT	4	2	2	—
Vic Sears, Phi	DT	4	2	—	2
Al DeRogatis, NYG	DT	2	—	—	2
Stan West, LARm	**MG**	9	1	1	1
Bill Willis, Cle	**MG**	8	1	2	1
Les Bingaman, Det	MG	5	—	1	2
Bucko Kilroy, Phi	MG	4	2	2	—
Dale Dodrill, Pit	MG	2	—	—	2
Jon Baker, NYG	MG	2	—	—	2
George Connor, ChiB	**LB**	9	0T1	1	1
Jerry Shipkey, Pit	**LB**	8	1	2	1
Chuck Bednarik, Phi	LB	6	1	1	—
Tommy Thompson, Cle	LB	4	2	—	2
Tank Younger, LARm	LB	2	—	2	—
Don Paul, LARm	LB	2	2	—	—
Hardy Brown, SF	LB	2	—	—	2
Emlen Tunnell, NYG	**DB**	8	1	1	2
Bob Smith, Det	**DB**	8	2	1	1
Herb Rich, LARm	**DB**	8	2	1	1
Johnny Williams, Was	DB	7	2	2	1
Ollie Matson, ChiC	DB	5	1	o2	—
Jack Christiansen, Det	DB	5	1	2	—
Warren Lahr, Cle	DB	4	—	2	2
Lowell Wagner, SF	DB	2	—	—	2

1953 NFL

OFFENSE	POS	TT	AP	UP	NY
Pete Pihos, Phi	**E**	9	1	1	1
Elroy Hirsch, LARm	**E**	7	1	2	2
Dante Lavelli, Cle	E	6	—	1	1
Hugh Taylor, Was	E	2	—	—	2
Gordie Soltau, SF	E	2	—	2	—
Lou Groza, Cle	**T**	9	1	1	1
Lou Creekmur, Det	**T**	9	G1	1	1
Frank Wydo, Phi	T	2	—	—	2
Clayton Tonnemaker, GB	T	2	—	—	2
Bob St. Clair, SF	T	2	—	2	—
Lum Snyder, Phi	T	2	—	2	—
Dick Stanfel, Det	**G**	9	1	1	1
Abe Gibron, Cle	**G**	5	—	2	1
Bruno Banducci, SF	**G**	5	—	1	2
Bud McFadin, LARm	G	2	—	—	2
Bill Lange, Bal	G	2	—	2	—
Frank Gatski, Cle	**C**	9	1	1	1
Bill Johnson, SF	C	2	—	2	—
Brad Ecklund, Bal	C	2	—	2	—
Otto Graham, Cle	**QB**	9	1	1	1
Bobby Thomason, Phi	QB	2	—	—	2
Bobby Layne, Det	QB	2	—	2	—
Joe Perry, SF	**RB**	9	1	1	1
Hugh McElhenny, SF	**RB**	9	1	1	1
Doak Walker, Det	**RB**	7	1	2	2
Dan Towler, LARm	RB	5	—	1	2
Bob Hoernschemeyer, Det	RB	5	—	2	1
Johnny Olszewski, ChiC	RB	2	—	—	2
Chick Jagade, Cle	RB	2	—	2	—

DEFENSE	POS	TT	AP	UP	NY
Len Ford, Cle	**DE**	9	1	1	1
Andy Robustelli, LARm	**DE**	7	1	2	2
Norm Willey, Phi	DE	6	—	1	2
Bill McPeak, Pit	DE	2	—	2	—
Larry Brink, LARm	DE	2	—	—	2
Arnie Weinmeister, NYG	**DT**	9	1	1	1
Leo Nomellini, SF	**DT**	9	1	1	MG1
Thurman McGraw, Det	DT	5	—	2	1

1953 NFL (CONT.)

DEFENSE

DEFENSE	POS	TT	AP	UP	NY
Ernie Stautner, Pit	DT	4	—	2	2
Don Colo, Cle	DT	2	—	—	2
Les Bingaman, Det	**MG**	9	1	1	1
Bill Willis, Cle	**MG**	5	1	2	—
Bucko Kilroy, Phi	MG	4	—	2	2
Dale Dodrill, Pit	MG	3	—	1	—
Art Michalik, SF	MG	2	—	—	2
George Connor, ChiB	**LB**	9	OT1	1	1
Tommy Thompson, Cle	**LB**	8	DB1	1	2
Chuck Bednarik, Phi	**LB**	8	1	2	1
Don Paul, LARm	LB	7	1	2	2
Tom Keane, Bal	**DB**	9	1	1	1
Jack Christiansen, Det	**DB**	9	1	1	1
Ken Gorgal, Cle	**DB**	6	—	1	1
Bert Rechichar, Bal	DB	4	—	2	2
Woodley Lewis, LARm	DB	2	—	2	—
Warren Lahr, Cle	DB	2	—	2	—
Frank Gifford, NYG	DB	2	—	—	2
Bobby Dillon, GB	DB	2	—	—	2

1954 NFL

OFFENSE

OFFENSE	POS	TT	AP	UP	NY	SN
Pete Pihos, Phi	**E**	11	1	1	2	1
Harlon Hill, ChiB	**E**	11	2	1	1	1
Bob Boyd, LARm	E	8	1	2	1	—
Billy Wilson, SF	E	6	2	2	2	—
Dorne Dibble, Det	E	2	—	—	—	2
Lou Groza, Cle	**T**	12	1	1	1	1
Lou Creekmur, Det	**T**	12	1	1	1	1
Bob St. Clair, SF	T	6	2	2	2	—
Lum Snyder, Phi	T	6	2	2	2	—
Bruno Banducci, SF	**G**	12	1	1	1	1
Dick Stanfel, Det	**G**	11	1	1	1	2
Abe Gibron, Cle	G	4	2	2	—	—
Duane Putnam, LARm	G	2	2	—	—	—
George Connor, ChiB	G	2	—	2	—	—
Bill Walsh, Pit	**C**	8	1	1	2	—
Frank Gatski, Cle	C	6	2	2	2	—
Bill Johnson, SF	C	3	—	—	1	—
Otto Graham, Cle	**QB**	12	1	1	1	1
Bobby Layne, Det	QB	6	2	2	—	2
Norm Van Brocklin, LARm	QB	4	—	—	2	2
Doak Walker, Det	**RB**	12	1	1	1	1
Joe Perry, SF	**RB**	12	1	1	1	1
Ollie Matson, ChiC	**RB**	12	1	1	d1	1
Hugh McElhenny, SF	RB	9	2	2	1	2
Tank Younger, LARm	RB	4	2	2	—	—
John Henry Johnson, SF	RB	4	—	2	—	—
Billy Wells, Was	RB	2	—	—	2	—
Dan Towler, LARm	RB	2	2	—	—	—
Bill Bowman, Det	RB	2	—	—	2	—

DEFENSE

DEFENSE	POS	TT	AP	UP	NY	SN
Len Ford, Cle	**DE**	11	1	1	1	2
Norm Willey, Phi	**DE**	9	1	1	1	—
Andy Robustelli, LARm	DE	6	2	2	2	—
Ed Sprinkle, ChiB	DE	2	—	—	2	—
John Martinkovic, GB	DE	2	—	—	2	—
Leon Hart, Det	DE	2	—	2	—	—
Leo Nomellini, SF	**DT**	11	1	1	1	2
Art Donovan, Bal	**DT**	10	1	1	2	2
Ernie Stautner, Pit	DT	6	2	2	2	—
Ray Krouse, NYG	DT	5	—	1	—	—
Don Colo, Cle	DT	2	—	2	—	—
Les Bingaman, Det	**MG**	12	1	1	1	1
Bucko Kilroy, Phi	**MG**	7	2	1	—	2
Dale Dodrill, Pit	**MG**	7	1	2	2	—
Mike McCormack, Cle	MG	2	—	2	—	—
Chuck Bednarik, Phi	**LB**	12	1	1	1	1
Clayton Tonnemaker, GB	**LB**	7	2	2	1	—
Joe Schmidt, Det	**LB**	7	1	2	2	—
Roger Zatkoff, GB	LB	5	MG2	1	—	—
LaVern Torgeson, Det	LB	2	—	—	2	—
Don Paul, LARm	LB	2	2	—	—	—
Tom Catlin, Cle	LB	2	—	2	—	—
Jack Christiansen, Det	**DB**	11	1	1	1	2
Tom Landry, NYG	**DB**	8	1	1	2	—
Jim David, Det	**DB**	8	2	1	1	—
Night Train Lane, ChiC	DB	6	2	2	2	—
Emlen Tunnell, NYG	DB	5	2	—	1	—
Bobby Dillon, GB	DB	5	1	1	2	—
Warren Lahr, Cle	DB	2	—	2	—	—
Tommy James, Cle	DB	2	—	—	2	—

1955 NFL

OFFENSE

OFFENSE	POS	TT	AP	NE	UP	NY	SN
Harlon Hill, ChiB	**E**	15	1	1	1	1	1
Billy Wilson, SF	**E**	14	2	1	1	1	1
Pete Pihos, Phi	E	12	1	2	2	2	1
Kyle Rote, NYG	E	5	—	2	—	2	—
Billy Howton, GB	E	4	—	2	—	2	—
Tom Fears, LARm	E	2	2	—	—	—	—
Lou Groza, Cle	**T**	15	1	1	1	1	1
Bob St. Clair, SF	**T**	10	2	1	1	2	—
Mike McCormack, Cle	**T**	10	—	2	2	1	1

1955 NFL (CONT.)

OFFENSE

OFFENSE	POS	TT	AP	NE	UP	NY	SN
Lou Creekmur, Det	T	6	2	—	2	2	—
Bill Wightkin, ChiB	T	3	1	—	—	—	—
Jack Jennings, ChiC	T	3	—	—	—	—	1
Lum Snyder, Phi	T	2	—	2	—	—	—
Duane Putnam, LARm	**G**	14	1	1	2	1	1
Stan Jones, ChiB	**G**	12	1	2	2	2	1
Abe Gibron, Cle	G	11	2	1	1	1	—
Bill Austin, NYG	G	5	—	—	1	2	—
Herman Clark, ChiB	G	3	—	—	—	—	1
Red Stephens, Was	G	2	2	—	—	—	—
Harley Sewell, Det	G	2	—	2	—	—	—
Frank Gatski, Cle	**C**	15	1	1	1	1	1
Dick Szymanski, Bal	C	6	2	—	2	2	—
Bill Johnson, SF	C	2	—	2	—	—	—
Otto Graham, Cle	**QB**	14	1	2	1	1	1
Tobin Rote, GB	QB	7	2	1	—	2	—
Norm Van Brocklin, LARm	QB	5	—	—	2	—	1
Ollie Matson, ChiC	**RB**	15	1	1	1	1	1
Alan Ameche, Bal	**RB**	14	1	2	1	1	1
Howie Ferguson, GB	**RB**	12	2	1	2	2	1
Frank Gifford, NYG	RB	9	1	1	—	—	1
Doak Walker, Det	RB	7	—	2	—	2	1
Alex Webster, NYG	RB	6	2	—	2	2	—
Ron Waller, LARm	RB	5	2	—	—	—	1
Fred Morrison, Cle	RB	5	—	2	2	—	—
Rick Casares, ChiB	RB	3	—	—	—	1	—
Ray Renfro, Cle	RB	2	—	2	—	—	—

DEFENSE

DEFENSE	POS	TT	AP	NE	UP	NY	SN
Andy Robustelli, LARm	**DE**	13	1	2	2	1	1
Len Ford, Cle	**DE**	11	2	1	1	1	—
Gene Brito, Was	**DE**	11	1	1	1	2	—
Gino Marchetti, Bal	DE	6	2	2	—	2	—
Tom Scott, Phi	DE	3	—	—	—	—	1
Norm Willey, Phi	DE	2	—	—	2	—	—
Art Donovan, Bal	**DT**	15	1	1	1	1	1
Bob Toneff, SF	**DT**	13	1	2	2	1	1
Don Colo, Cle	DT	10	2	1	1	2	—
Ernie Stautner, Pit	DT	5	—	—	2	—	1
Bud McFadin, LARm	DT	4	2	—	2	—	—
Ray Krouse, NYG	DT	4	—	—	2	DG2	—
Dale Dodrill, Pit	**LB**	14	DG2	1	1	1	1
George Connor, ChiB	**LB**	11	2	1	1	1	—
Roger Zatkoff, GB	**LB**	10	1	2	—	2	1
Chuck Bednarik, Phi	**LB**	10	2	1	1	2	—
Joe Schmidt, Det	LB	8	1	1	2	—	—
LaVern Torgeson, Was	LB	5	—	2	2	—	—
Les Richter, LARm	LB	5	—	—	2	1	—
Bill George, ChiB	LB	5	DG1	2	—	—	1
Wayne Robinson, Phi	LB	3	—	—	—	—	1
Bob Gain, Cle	LB	2	—	—	2	—	—
Will Sherman, LARm	**DB**	15	1	1	1	1	1
Bobby Dillon, GB	**DB**	15	1	1	1	1	1
Jack Christiansen, Det	**DB**	15	1	1	1	1	1
Emlen Tunnell, NYG	**DB**	12	1	2	2	2	1
Bert Rechichar, Bal	DB	10	2	1	2	1	—
Warren Lahr, Cle	DB	6	—	2	2	2	—
Don Paul, LARm	DB	5	2	—	1	—	—
Night Train Lane, ChiC	DB	4	—	2	2	—	—
Dick Alban, Was	DB	3	—	—	—	—	1
Joe Scudero, Was	DB	2	2	—	—	—	—
Tom Landry, NYG	DB	2	—	—	2	—	—
Ken Konz, Cle	DB	2	—	—	2	—	—
Jim David, Det	DB	2	—	2	—	—	—
Rex Berry, SF	DB	2	—	2	—	—	—

1956 NFL

OFFENSE

OFFENSE	POS	TT	AP	NE	UP	NY	SN
Billy Howton, GB	**E**	15	1	1	1	1	1
Harlon Hill, ChiB	**E**	15	1	1	1	1	1
Kyle Rote, NYG	E	9	2	—	2	2	1
Billy Wilson, SF	E	6	2	2	2	—	—
John Carson, Was	E	3	—	—	—	—	1
Elroy Hirsch, LARm	E	2	—	—	—	2	—
Pete Brewster, Cle	E	2	—	2	—	—	—
Rosey Brown, NYG	**T**	15	1	1	1	1	1
Lou Creekmur, Det	**T**	11	1	1	1	1	1
Bill Wightkin, ChiB	T	10	—	2	2	1	1
Lou Groza, Cle	T	6	2	—	2	2	—
Mike McCormack, Cle	T	5	—	2	—	1	—
Bob St. Clair, SF	T	3	—	2	—	—	1
Don Boll, Was	T	2	—	—	—	—	—
Dick Stanfel, Was	**G**	14	1	1	1	1	1
Stan Jones, ChiB	**G**	14	1	2	1	1	1
Duane Putnam, LARm	G	13	2	1	2	1	1
Herman Clark, ChiB	G	4	—	2	—	—	—
Red Stephens, Was	G	3	—	—	—	—	1
Jack Stroud, NYG	G	2	—	—	—	—	—
Harley Sewell, Det	G	2	—	2	—	—	—
Larry Strickland, ChiB	**C**	13	1	2	2	1	1
Charlie Ane, Det	C	8	2	1	1	—	—
Ray Wietecha, NYG	C	5	—	—	—	2	—
Bobby Layne, Det	**QB**	15	1	1	1	1	1
Tobin Rote, GB	QB	8	2	2	2	2	—
Charlie Conerly, NYG	QB	3	—	—	1	—	—

1956 NFL (CONT.)

OFFENSE	POS	TT	AP	NE	UP	NY	SN
Ollie Matson, ChiC	RB	15	1	1	1	1	1
Frank Gifford, NYG	RB	15	1	1	1	1	1
Rick Casares, ChiB	RB	15	1	1	1	1	1
Hugh McElhenny, SF	RB	11	2	2	2	2	1
Alan Ameche, Bal	RB	9	2	2	—	2	1
Johnny Olszewski, ChiC	RB	3	—	—	—	—	1
Alex Webster, NYG	RB	2	2	—	—	—	—
Ron Waller, LARm	RB	2	—	2	—	—	—
Lenny Moore, Bal	RB	2	—	—	—	2	—
Leon Hart, Det	RB	2	—	—	2	—	—
Preston Carpenter, Cle	RB	2	—	—	2	—	—

DEFENSE	POS	TT	AP	NE	UP	NY	SN
Andy Robustelli, NYG	DE	14	1	2	1	1	1
Gene Brito, Was	DE	14	1	1	1	2	1
Gino Marchetti, Bal	DE	13	2	1	2	1	1
John Martinkovic, GB	DE	3	—	—	—	—	1
Tom Scott, Phi	DE	2	—	2	—	—	—
Ed Meadows, ChiB	DE	2	2	—	—	—	—
Bob Gain, Cle	DE	2	—	—	2	—	—
Len Ford, Cle	DE	2	—	—	—	2	—
Rosey Grier, NYG	DT	14	1	2	1	1	1
Art Donovan, Bal	DT	13	1	1	2	2	1
Ernie Stautner, Pit	DT	11	2	1	1	1	—
Bud McFadin, LARm	DT	4	—	2	—	2	—
Don Colo, Cle	DT	4	—	2	—	—	—
Bob Miller, Det	DT	3	—	—	—	—	1
Ray Krouse, Det	DT	3	—	—	—	—	1
Joe Schmidt, Det	LB	15	1	1	1	1	1
Bill George, ChiB	LB	12	1	1	1	—	1
Chuck Bednarik, Phi	LB	11	2	1	1	1	1
Bill Svoboda, NYG	LB	9	—	2	2	2	1
Les Richter, LARm	LB	9	1	—	—	1	1
Chuck Drazenovich, Was	LB	9	2	2	2	—	1
Dale Dodrill, Pit	LB	6	—	2	2	2	—
Roger Zatkoff, GB	LB	4	—	2	—	2	—
Wayne Robinson, Phi	LB	3	—	—	—	—	1
Night Train Lane, ChiC	DB	15	1	1	1	1	1
Jack Christiansen, Det	DB	15	1	1	1	1	1
Bobby Dillon, GB	DB	14	2	1	1	1	1
Yale Lary, Det	DB	12	1	2	2	2	1
Emlen Tunnell, NYG	DB	11	1	1	1	2	—
Jim David, Det	DB	8	2	2	2	2	—
Jack Butler, Pit	DB	7	2	2	—	—	—
Ken Konz, Cle	DB	5	—	—	2	—	1
Dicky Moegle, SF	DB	3	—	—	—	—	1
Warren Lahr, Cle	DB	3	—	—	—	—	1
J.C. Caroline, ChiB	DB	3	—	—	—	1	—
Ray Gene Smith, ChiB	DB	2	—	—	—	2	—
Will Sherman, LARm	DB	2	—	2	—	—	—
Lindon Crow, ChiC	DB	2	2	—	—	—	—

1957 NFL

OFFENSE	POS	TT	AP	NE	UP	NY	SN
Billy Wilson, SF	E	15	1	1	1	1	1
Billy Howton, GB	E	12	1	1	1	1	—
Pete Brewster, Cle	E	9	2	2	2	—	1
Jim Mutscheller, Bal	E	6	—	2	2	2	—
Raymond Berry, Bal	E	5	2	—	—	—	1
John Carson, Was	E	3	—	—	—	—	1
Clyde Conner, SF	E	2	—	—	—	2	—
Rosey Brown, NYG	T	15	1	1	1	1	1
Mike McCormack, Cle	T	10	2	1	2	—	1
Lou Groza, Cle	T	10	2	2	1	1	—
Lou Creekmur, Det	T	10	1	—	2	2	1
Jim Parker, Bal	T	3	—	—	—	—	1
Art Spinney, Bal	T	2	—	—	—	2	—
Charlie Ane, Det	T	2	—	2	—	—	—
Dick Stanfel, Was	G	15	1	1	1	1	1
Duane Putnam, LARm	G	15	1	1	1	1	1
Jack Stroud, NYG	G	8	2	2	2	2	—
Harley Sewell, Det	G	7	2	—	2	—	1
Stan Jones, ChiB	G	4	—	2	—	2	—
Jim Ray Smith, Cle	G	3	—	—	—	—	1
Larry Strickland, ChiB	C	8	2	—	1	1	—
Jim Ringo, GB	C	8	1	1	2	—	—
Ray Wietecha, NYG	C	7	—	2	—	2	1
Frank Morze, SF	C	3	—	—	—	—	1
Y.A. Tittle, SF	QB	14	1	2	1	1	1
Johnny Unitas, Bal	QB	9	2	1	2	2	—
Charlie Conerly, NYG	QB	3	—	—	—	—	1
Ollie Matson, ChiC	RB	15	1	1	1	1	1
Frank Gifford, NYG	RB	15	1	1	1	1	1
Jim Brown, Cle	RB	15	1	1	1	1	1
Tommy Wilson, LARm	RB	9	2	—	2	2	1
Rick Casares, ChiB	RB	9	2	2	—	2	1
Lenny Moore, Bal	RB	7	—	2	—	2	—
Hugh McElhenny, SF	RB	4	2	—	2	—	—
Willie Galimore, ChiB	RB	2	2	—	—	—	—
Don Bosseler, Was	RB	2	2	—	—	—	—

DEFENSE	POS	TT	AP	NE	UP	NY	SN
Gino Marchetti, Bal	DE	15	1	1	1	1	1
Gene Brito, Was	DE	13	1	1	2	2	1
Andy Robustelli, NYG	DE	10	2	2	1	—	1

1957 NFL (CONT.)

DEFENSE	POS	TT	AP	NE	UP	NY	SN
Doug Atkins, ChiB	DE	6	2	2	—	2	—
Bill Quinlan, Cle	DE	3	—	—	—	—	1
Ed Henke, SF	DE	3	—	—	—	—	1
Len Ford, Cle	DE	2	—	—	2	—	—
Art Donovan, Bal	DT	15	1	1	1	1	1
Leo Nomellini, SF	DT	10	1	2	1	2	—
Don Colo, Cle	DT	10	2	1	2	1	—
Bob Gain, Cle	DT	8	—	—	2	1	1
Ernie Stautner, Pit	DT	7	2	—	—	2	1
Dave Hanner, GB	DT	3	—	—	—	—	1
Dick Modzelewski, NYG	DT	2	—	2	—	—	—
Joe Schmidt, Det	LB	15	1	1	1	1	1
Marv Matuszak, SF	LB	14	1	1	1	2	1
Bill George, ChiB	LB	12	1	1	1	1	1
Chuck Bednarik, Phi	LB	12	2	2	2	1	1
Les Richter, LARm	LB	7	2	—	2	—	1
Sam Huff, NYG	LB	5	2	—	—	—	1
Chuck Drazenovich, Was	LB	5	—	2	—	—	1
Walt Michaels, Cle	LB	4	—	2	—	—	1
LaVern Torgeson, Was	LB	2	—	—	—	2	—
Dick Daugherty, LARm	LB	2	—	—	—	2	—
Bobby Dillon, GB	DB	15	1	1	1	1	1
Jack Butler, Pit	DB	15	1	1	1	1	1
Jack Christiansen, Det	DB	12	1	1	1	1	—
Emlen Tunnell, NYG	DB	11	2	2	2	2	1
Yale Lary, Det	DB	11	2	1	1	—	1
Milt Davis, Bal	DB	10	1	—	2	2	1
Dicky Moegle, SF	DB	9	2	2	—	2	1
Night Train Lane, ChiC	DB	7	—	2	—	2	1
Jim David, Det	DB	6	—	2	2	—	—
Will Sherman, LARm	DB	3	—	—	—	—	1
Ken Konz, Cle	DB	3	—	—	—	—	1
Don Paul, Cle	DB	2	2	—	—	—	—

1958 NFL

OFFENSE	POS	TT	AP	NE	UP	NY	SN
Del Shofner, LARm	E	15	1	1	1	1	1
Raymond Berry, Bal	E	15	1	1	1	1	1
Pete Retzlaff, Phi	E	11	2	2	2	2	1
Billy Wilson, SF	E	4	—	2	—	2	—
Jimmy Orr, Pit	E	4	2	—	2	—	—
Woodley Lewis, ChiC	E	3	—	—	—	—	1
Rosey Brown, NYG	T	15	1	1	1	1	1
Jim Parker, Bal	T	12	1	1	1	1	—
Mike McCormack, Cle	T	11	2	2	2	2	1
Bob St. Clair, SF	T	10	2	2	—	1	1
Lou Creekmur, Det	T	5	—	2	—	2	—
Frank Varrichione, Pit	T	2	—	—	—	—	1
Dick Stanfel, Was	G	15	1	1	1	1	1
Duane Putnam, LARm	G	15	1	1	1	1	1
Jim Ray Smith, Cle	G	11	2	2	2	2	1
Art Spinney, Bal	G	9	2	2	2	—	1
Harley Sewell, Det	G	2	—	—	—	2	—
Ray Wietecha, NYG	C	14	1	1	1	2	1
Jim Ringo, GB	C	12	2	2	2	1	1
Johnny Unitas, Bal	QB	15	1	1	1	1	1
Bobby Layne, Pit	QB	11	2	1	1	1	1
Lenny Moore, Bal	RB	15	1	1	1	1	1
Jim Brown, Cle	RB	15	1	1	1	1	1
Jon Arnett, LARm	RB	15	1	1	1	1	1
Ollie Matson, ChiC	RB	9	—	2	2	2	1
Frank Gifford, NYG	RB	9	2	2	2	—	1
Alan Ameche, Bal	RB	8	2	2	†2	—	1
Willie Galimore, ChiB	RB	4	2	—	—	2	—
Joe Perry, SF	RB	3	—	—	—	—	1
Rick Casares, ChiB	RB	2	—	—	†2	—	—

DEFENSE	POS	TT	AP	NE	UP	NY	SN
Gino Marchetti, Bal	DE	15	1	1	1	1	1
Gene Brito, Was	DE	13	2	1	1	2	1
Doug Atkins, ChiB	DE	12	2	2	2	1	1
Andy Robustelli, NYG	DE	10	1	2	2	—	1
Lou Michaels, LARm	DE	2	—	—	—	2	—
Gene Lipscomb, Bal	DT	15	1	1	1	1	1
Ernie Stautner, Pit	DT	10	1	2	1	2	—
Art Donovan, Bal	DT	9	2	2	2	1	—
Bob Gain, Cle	DT	8	—	1	2	—	1
Rosey Grier, NYG	DT	5	2	—	—	—	1
Fred Williams, ChiB	DT	3	—	—	—	—	1
Don Colo, Cle	DT	2	—	—	—	2	—
Joe Schmidt, Det	LB	15	1	1	1	1	1
Sam Huff, NYG	LB	12	1	1	1	1	—
Bill George, ChiB	LB	12	1	1	1	1	—
Les Richter, LARm	LB	11	2	2	2	2	1
Walt Michaels, Cle	LB	9	2	2	2	—	1
Bill Pellington, Bal	LB	5	—	—	—	—	1
Chuck Drazenovich, Was	LB	5	—	—	—	—	1
Dale Dodrill, Pit	LB	3	—	—	—	—	1
Harland Svare, NYG	LB	2	—	—	—	2	—
Joe Fortunato, ChiB	LB	2	—	—	—	2	—
Bobby Dillon, GB	DB	15	1	1	1	1	1
Jack Butler, Pit	DB	15	1	1	1	1	1
Jimmy Patton, NYG	DB	14	1	1	1	2	1
Andy Nelson, Bal	DB	12	2	2	2	1	1
Yale Lary, Det	DB	12	1	1	1	1	—

1958 NFL (CONT.)

DEFENSE	POS	TT	AP	NE	UP	NY	SN
Will Sherman, LARm	DB	11	2	2	2	2	1
Night Train Lane, ChiC	DB	6	2	2	—	2	—
Don Paul, Cle	DB	5	—	—	2	—	1
Carl Taseff, Bal	DB	4	2	—	2	—	—
Stan Wallace, ChiB	DB	3	—	—	—	—	1
Jerry Norton, Phi	DB	3	—	—	—	—	1
Jim David, Det	DB	2	—	2	—	—	—
Terry Barr, Det	DB	2	—	—	—	2	—

1959 NFL

OFFENSE	POS	TT	AP	NE	UP	NY	SN
Del Shofner, LARm	**E**	15	1	1	1	1	1
Raymond Berry, Bal	**E**	15	1	1	1	1	1
Tommy McDonald, Phi	E	7	2	—	2	—	1
Jimmy Orr, Pit	E	5	2	—	—	—	1
Bob Schnelker, NYG	E	2	—	—	2	—	—
Ray Renfro, Cle	E	2	—	—	—	2	—
Billy Howton, Cle	E	2	—	—	—	2	—
Jim Parker, Bal	**T**	15	1	1	1	1	1
Rosey Brown, NYG	**T**	15	1	1	1	1	1
Mike McCormack, Cle	T	9	2	—	2	2	—
Forrest Gregg, GB	T	7	2	—	2	—	1
Frank Varrichione, Pit	T	2	—	—	—	2	—
Jim Ray Smith, Cle	**G**	15	1	1	1	1	1
Art Spinney, Bal	**G**	8	2	—	1	1	—
Stan Jones, ChiB	**G**	8	1	—	2	—	1
Duane Putnam, LARm	G	5	—	1	—	2	—
Bruce Bosley, SF	G	5	2	—	—	—	1
Jack Stroud, NYG	G	4	—	—	2	2	—
John Nisby, Pit	G	3	—	—	—	—	1
Jim Ringo, GB	**C**	15	1	1	1	1	1
Ray Wietecha, NYG	C	9	2	—	2	2	1
Johnny Unitas, Bal	**QB**	15	1	1	1	1	1
Charlie Conerly, NYG	QB	9	†2	2	—	2	1
Bobby Layne, Pit	QB	2	†2	—	—	—	—
Frank Gifford, NYG	**RB**	15	1	1	1	1	1
Jim Brown, Cle	**RB**	15	1	1	1	1	1
Lenny Moore, Bal	**RB**	14	1	1	2	1	1
J.D. Smith, SF	RB	8	2	—	—	2	—
Ollie Matson, LARm	RB	5	—	—	2	—	1
John David Crow, ChiC	RB	5	—	—	—	2	1
Paul Hornung, GB	RB	4	2	—	2	—	—
Alan Ameche, Bal	RB	4	2	—	—	2	—
Bobby Mitchell, Cle	RB	2	—	—	—	2	—

DEFENSE	POS	TT	AP	NE	UP	NY	SN
Andy Robustelli, NYG	**DE**	15	1	1	1	1	1
Gino Marchetti, Bal	**DE**	15	1	1	1	1	1
Doug Atkins, ChiB	DE	9	2	—	2	2	1
Bob Gain, Cle	DE	3	—	—	—	—	1
George Tarasovic, Pit	DE	2	—	—	2	—	—
Lou Michaels, LARm	DE	2	2	—	—	—	—
Jim Katcavage, NYG	DE	2	—	—	—	2	—
Leo Nomellini, SF	**DT**	15	1	1	1	1	1
Gene Lipscomb, Bal	**DT**	9	1	—	1	1	—
Ernie Stautner, Pit	DT	7	—	1	2	2	—
Rosey Grier, NYG	DT	4	2	—	2	—	—
Frank Fuller, ChiC	DT	4	2	—	—	—	1
Bob Toneff, Was	DT	3	—	—	—	—	1
Jess Richardson, Phi	DT	3	—	—	—	—	1
Dave Hanner, GB	DT	3	—	—	—	—	1
Joe Schmidt, Det	**LB**	15	1	1	1	1	1
Sam Huff, NYG	**LB**	15	1	1	1	1	1
Bill George, ChiB	**LB**	14	1	1	1	2	1
Walt Michaels, Cle	LB	10	2	—	2	1	1
John Reger, Pit	LB	7	2	—	—	1	—
Matt Hazeltine, SF	LB	3	—	—	—	—	1
Don Shinnick, Bal	LB	2	—	—	2	—	—
Les Richter, LARm	LB	2	2	—	—	—	—
Bill Forester, GB	LB	2	—	—	—	2	—
Jimmy Patton, NYG	**DB**	12	1	—	1	1	1
Jack Butler, Pit	**DB**	12	1	—	1	1	1
Andy Nelson, Bal	**DB**	11	1	—	2	1	1
Yale Lary, Det	**DB**	10	2	1	2	1	—
Tom Brookshier, Phi	**DB**	10	2	1	2	1	—
Abe Woodson, SF	DB	8	1	—	1	2	—
Dean Derby, Pit	DB	8	2	—	1	1	—
Milt Davis, Bal	DB	7	—	1	2	2	—
Erich Barnes, ChiB	DB	5	2	—	—	2	—
Jesse Whittenton, GB	DB	3	—	—	—	—	1
Jerry Norton, ChiC	DB	3	—	—	—	—	1
Night Train Lane, ChiC	DB	3	—	1	—	—	—
Bobby Dillon, GB	DB	2	—	—	—	2	—
Lindon Crow, NYG	DB	2	—	—	—	2	—

1960 NFL

OFFENSE	POS	TT	AP	NE	UP	NY	SN
Raymond Berry, Bal	**E**	15	1	1	1	1	1
Sonny Randle, SL	**E**	13	1	2	1	2	1
Tommy McDonald, Phi	E	11	—	1	2	1	1
Red Phillips, LARm	E	7	2	—	2	—	—
Kyle Rote, NYG	E	2	2	—	—	—	—
R.C. Owens, SF	E	2	2	—	—	—	—
Willard Dewveall, ChiB	E	2	—	—	—	2	—
Jim Parker, Bal	**T**	15	1	1	1	1	1

1960 NFL (CONT.)

OFFENSE	POS	TT	AP	NE	UP	NY	SN
Rosey Brown, NYG	**T**	13	2	2	1	1	1
Forrest Gregg, GB	T	9	1	2	2	2	—
Bob St. Clair, SF	T	8	2	1	—	—	1
Mike McCormack, Cle	T	7	—	—	2	2	1
Jim Ray Smith, Cle	**G**	15	1	1	1	1	1
Stan Jones, ChiB	**G**	14	2	1	1	1	1
Jerry Kramer, GB	G	7	1	—	2	2	—
Bruce Bosley, SF	G	6	—	2	2	2	—
Harley Sewell, Det	G	3	—	—	—	—	1
John Nisby, Pit	G	3	—	—	—	—	1
Jack Stroud, NYG	G	2	2	—	—	—	—
Art Spinney, Bal	G	2	—	2	—	—	—
Jim Ringo, GB	**C**	15	1	1	1	1	1
Art Hunter, LARm	C	6	2	2	2	—	—
Jim Schrader, Was	C	3	—	—	—	—	1
Chuck Bednarik, Phi	C	2	—	—	2	—	—
Norm Van Brocklin, Phi	**QB**	15	1	1	1	1	1
Johnny Unitas, Bal	QB	9	—	2	2	2	1
Milt Plum, Cle	QB	2	2	—	—	—	—
Lenny Moore, Bal	**RB**	15	1	1	1	1	1
Paul Hornung, GB	**RB**	15	1	1	1	1	1
Jim Brown, Cle	**RB**	15	1	1	1	1	1
Jim Taylor, GB	RB	11	2	2	2	2	1
Tom Tracy, Pit	RB	9	2	2	—	2	1
John David Crow, SL	RB	9	2	—	2	2	1
Bobby Mitchell, Cle	RB	4	—	2	2	—	—

DEFENSE	POS	TT	AP	NE	UP	NY	SN
Doug Atkins, ChiB	**DE**	14	2	1	1	1	—
Gino Marchetti, Bal	**DE**	12	1	1	1	1	—
Andy Robustelli, NYG	DE	9	1	2	2	2	—
Bob Gain, Cle	DE	5	—	DT2	—	—	1
Bill Quinlan, GB	DE	3	—	—	—	—	1
Marion Campbell, Phi	DE	3	—	—	—	—	1
John Paluck, Was	DE	2	—	2	—	—	—
Charlie Krueger, SF	DE	2	2	—	—	—	—
Gene Brito, LARm	DE	2	—	—	—	2	—
Ordell Braase, Bal	DE	2	—	—	—	2	—
Henry Jordan, GB	**DT**	11	1	2	1	1	—
Gene Lipscomb, Bal	**DT**	9	—	1	—	1	1
Alex Karras, Det	DT	8	1	—	1	2	—
Leo Nomellini, SF	DT	7	2	—	—	2	1
Bob Toneff, Was	DT	3	—	1	—	—	—
Rosey Grier, NYG	DT	3	—	—	—	—	1
Frank Fuller, SL	DT	3	—	—	—	—	1
Ernie Stautner, Pit	DT	2	—	—	—	—	1
Jess Richardson, Phi	DT	2	—	—	2	—	—
Art Donovan, Bal	DT	2	2	—	—	—	—
Bill George, ChiB	**LB**	15	1	1	1	1	1
Sam Huff, NYG	**LB**	13	2	1	2	1	1
Bill Forester, GB	**LB**	13	1	2	1	2	1
Chuck Bednarik, Phi	LB	12	1	—	1	1	1
Joe Schmidt, Det	LB	10	2	1	2	—	1
John Reger, Pit	LB	7	—	2	2	—	1
Wayne Walker, Det	LB	2	—	—	—	—	1
Les Richter, LARm	LB	2	2	—	—	—	—
Bill Pellington, Bal	LB	2	—	2	—	—	—
Walt Michaels, Cle	LB	2	—	—	2	—	—
Tom Brookshier, Phi	**CB**	15	1	1	1	1	1
Abe Woodson, SF	**CB**	13	1	2	2	1	1
Night Train Lane, Det	CB	11	—	1	1	2	1
Jesse Whittenton, GB	CB	4	2	—	—	2	—
Johnny Sample, Bal	CB	4	—	S2	2	—	—
Dean Derby, Pit	CB	3	—	—	—	—	1
Erich Barnes, ChiB	CB	3	—	—	—	—	1
Eddie Meador, LARm	CB	2	2	—	—	—	—
Yale Lary, Det	CB	2	—	2	—	—	—
Jimmy Patton, NYG	**S**	15	1	1	1	1	1
Jerry Norton, SL	**S**	15	1	1	1	1	1
Dave Baker, SF	S	8	2	2	2	2	—
Don Burroughs, Phi	S	6	2	2	—	2	—
Andy Nelson, Bal	S	3	—	—	—	—	1

1960 AFL

OFFENSE	POS	TT	AP	UP	AL
Lionel Taylor, Den	**E**	9	1	1	1
Art Powell, NYT	**E**	7	1	2	2
Bill Groman, Hou	E	6	—	1	1
Don Maynard, NYT	E	4	—	2	B2
Howard Clark, LAC	E	2	—	—	2
Ron Mix, LAC	**T**	9	1	1	1
Rich Michael, Hou	**T**	6	—	1	1
Al Jamison, Hou	T	5	1	—	2
Ernie Wright, LAC	T	4	—	2	2
Jerry Cornelison, DalT	T	2	—	2	—
Bob Mischak, NYT	**G**	9	1	1	1
Billy Krisher, DalT	**G**	8	1	2	1
Jack Davis, Bos	G	3	—	1	—
Don Manoukian, Oak	G	2	—	—	2
Charley Leo, Bos	G	2	—	2	—
Ken Adamson, Den	G	2	—	2	—
Jim Otto, Oak	**C**	8	1	2	1
Walt Cudzik, Bos	C	3	—	1	—
Dan McGrew, Buf	C	2	—	—	2
Jack Kemp, LAC	**QB**	9	1	1	1

1960 AFL (CONT.)

OFFENSE	POS	TT	AP	UP	AL
Frank Tripucka, Den	QB	2	—	2	—
Al Dorow, NYT	QB	2	—	—	2
Dave Smith, Hou	**RB**	9	1	1	1
Paul Lowe, LAC	**RB**	9	1	1	1
Abner Haynes, DalT	**RB**	9	1	1	1
Billy Cannon, Hou	RB	4	—	2	2
Elbert Dubenion, Buf	RB	2	—	2	—
Wray Carlton, Buf	RB	2	—	—	2

DEFENSE	POS	TT	AP	UP	AL
LaVerne Torczon, Buf	**DE**	9	1	1	1
Mel Branch, DalT	**DE**	9	1	1	1
Paul Miller, DalT	DE	4	—	2	2
Ron Nery, LAC	DE	2	—	2	—
Bob Dee, Bos	DE	2	—	—	2
Bud McFadin, Den	**DT**	9	1	1	1
Chuck McMurtry, Buf	**DT**	6	1	1	—
Orville Trask, Hou	DT	4	—	2	2
Volney Peters, LAC	DT	3	—	—	1
Sid Youngelman, NYT	DT	2	—	—	2
Dick Chorovich, LAC	DT	2	—	2	—
Archie Matsos, Buf	**LB**	9	1	1	1
Sherrill Headrick, DalT	**LB**	8	1	2	1
Larry Grantham, NYT	**LB**	7	1	2	2
Paul Maguire, LAC	LB	5	—	1	2
Mike Dukes, Hou	LB	3	—	1	—
Tom Addison, Bos	LB	3	—	—	1
Dennit Morris, Hou	LB	2	—	—	2
Bob Dougherty, Oak	LB	2	—	2	—
Goose Gonsoulin, Den	**CB**	8	1	2	1
Dick Harris, LAC	**CB**	6	1	—	1
Eddie Macon, Oak	CB	5	—	1	2
Julian Spence, Hou	CB	3	—	1	—
Dave Webster, DalT	CB	2	—	—	2
Joe Cannavino, Oak	CB	2	—	—	2
Richie McCabe, Buf	**S**	8	1	2	1
Mark Johnston, Hou	**S**	7	1	2	2
Ross O'Hanley, Bos	S	3	—	—	1
Fred Bruney, Bos	S	3	—	1	—
Johnny Bookman, DalT	S	3	—	1	—
Jim Wagstaff, Buf	S	2	—	—	2

1961 NFL

OFFENSE	POS	TT	AP	NE	UP	NY	SN
Del Shofner, NYG	**E**	15	1	1	1	1	1
Red Phillips, LARm	**E**	14	1	2	1	1	1
Mike Ditka, ChiB	E	10	—	1	2	2	1
Buddy Dial, Pit	E	5	—	—	—	2	1
Raymond Berry, Bal	E	4	—	2	2	—	—
Rosey Brown, NYG	**T**	15	1	1	1	1	1
Jim Parker, Bal	**T**	14	1	1	2	1	1
Mike McCormack, Cle	T	9	—	2	2	2	1
Bob St. Clair, SF	T	5	—	2	—	—	1
Forrest Gregg, GB	T	5	—	—	1	2	—
Fuzzy Thurston, GB	**G**	15	1	1	1	1	1
Jim Ray Smith, Cle	**G**	15	1	1	1	1	1
John Nisby, Pit	G	5	—	—	—	—	1
Bruce Bosley, SF	G	5	—	2	—	—	1
Jack Stroud, NYG	G	4	—	—	2	2	—
Jerry Kramer, GB	G	2	—	—	—	2	—
Stan Jones, ChiB	G	2	—	—	2	—	—
Jim Ringo, GB	**C**	15	1	1	1	1	1
Ray Wietecha, NYG	C	7	—	2	—	2	1
Chuck Bednarik, Phi	C	2	—	—	2	—	—
Sonny Jurgensen, Phi	**QB**	9	1	—	1	—	1
Y.A. Tittle, NYG	QB	8	—	1	2	1	—
Bart Starr, GB	QB	7	—	2	—	2	1
Lenny Moore, Bal	**RB**	15	1	1	1	1	1
Jim Brown, Cle	**RB**	15	1	1	1	1	1
Paul Hornung, GB	**RB**	14	1	2	1	1	1
Jim Taylor, GB	RB	10	—	1	2	2	1
Tommy McDonald, Phi	RB	9	—	2	2	2	1
Jon Arnett, LARm	RB	6	—	2	2	2	—
Don Perkins, Dal	RB	3	—	—	—	—	1

DEFENSE	POS	TT	AP	NE	UP	NY	SN
Gino Marchetti, Bal	**DE**	15	1	1	1	1	1
Jim Katcavage, NYG	**DE**	11	1	1	1	1	1
Andy Robustelli, NYG	DE	9	—	2	2	2	1
Doug Atkins, ChiB	DE	8	—	1	—	2	1
Ernie Stautner, Pit	DE	3	—	—	—	—	1
Leo Sugar, Phi	DE	2	—	—	2	—	—
Henry Jordan, GB	**DT**	15	1	1	1	1	1
Alex Karras, Det	**DT**	11	1	—	1	2	1
Roger Brown, Det	DT	4	—	2	2	—	—
Bob Toneff, Was	DT	3	—	—	—	—	1
Jess Richardson, Phi	DT	3	—	—	—	—	1
Dick Modzelewski, NYG	DT	3	—	—	—	1	—
Gene Lipscomb, Pit	DT	3	—	1	—	—	—
Leo Nomellini, SF	DT	2	—	—	—	—	1
Rosey Grier, NYG	DT	2	—	—	—	2	—
Bob Gain, Cle	DT	2	—	—	2	—	—
Joe Schmidt, Det	**LB**	15	1	1	1	1	1
Bill Forester, GB	**LB**	14	1	2	1	1	1
Bill George, ChiB	**LB**	8	1	1	2	—	—

1961 NFL (CONT.)

DEFENSE	POS	TT	AP	NE	UP	NY	SN
John Reger, Pit	LB	7	—	2	—	2	1
Dan Currie, GB	LB	6	—	1	1	—	—
Maxie Baughan, Phi	LB	5	—	—	2	1	—
Cliff Livingston, NYG	LB	4	—	—	2	2	—
Sam Huff, NYG	LB	4	—	2	—	2	—
Walt Michaels, Cle	LB	3	—	—	—	—	1
Matt Hazeltine, SF	LB	3	—	—	—	—	1
Chuck Bednarik, Phi	LB	3	—	—	—	—	1
Night Train Lane, Det	**CB**	13	S1	1	2	2	1
Erich Barnes, NYG	**CB**	12	1	—	1	1	1
Jesse Whittenton, GB	CB	10	1	2	1	2	—
Abe Woodson, SF	CB	3	—	—	—	1	—
Eddie Meador, LARm	CB	3	—	—	—	—	1
Jimmy Hill, SL	CB	3	—	1	—	—	—
Don Bishop, Dal	CB	3	—	—	—	—	1
Dick Lynch, NYG	CB	2	—	—	2	—	—
Jimmy Patton, NYG	**S**	15	1	1	1	1	1
Johnny Sample, Pit	**S**	8	—	2	1	1	—
Jerry Norton, SL	**S**	8	—	1	—	2	1
Don Burroughs, Phi	S	6	—	2	2	—	2
Andy Nelson, Bal	S	3	—	—	—	—	1
Dave Baker, SF	S	3	—	—	—	—	1
Yale Lary, Det	S	2	—	2	—	2	—
Eddie Dove, SF	S	2	—	—	2	—	—

1961 AFL

OFFENSE	POS	TT	AP	UP	NY	SN	AL
Charley Hennigan, Hou	**E**	15	B1	1	1	1	1
Lionel Taylor, Den	**E**	12	1	1	1	—	1
Bill Groman, Hou	E	10	1	2	2	1	—
Gino Cappelletti, Bos	E	6	—	B2	2	—	2
Dave Kocourek, SD	E	4	—	2	—	—	2
Al Jamison, Hou	**T**	15	1	1	1	1	1
Ron Mix, SD	**T**	12	1	1	1	—	1
Ken Rice, Buf	T	6	—	2	2	—	2
Jerry Cornelison, DalT	T	5	—	2	—	1	—
Ernie Wright, SD	T	2	—	—	2	—	—
Jerry DeLucca, Bos	T	2	—	—	—	—	2
Bob Mischak, NYT	**G**	15	1	1	1	1	1
Ken Adamson, Den	**G**	9	1	2	2	—	2
Tony Sardisco, Bos	G	6	—	1	1	—	—
Bob Talamini, Hou	G	4	—	2	—	—	2
Billy Krisher, DalT	G	4	—	2	2	—	—
Charley Leo, Bos	G	3	—	—	—	—	1
Wayne Hawkins, Oak	G	3	—	—	1	—	—
Jim Otto, Oak	**C**	15	1	1	1	1	1
Don Rogers, SD	C	4	—	2	2	—	—
Bob Schmidt, Hou	C	2	—	—	—	—	2
George Blanda, Hou	**QB**	15	1	1	1	1	1
Jack Kemp, SD	QB	6	—	2	2	—	2
Bill Mathis, NYT	**RB**	15	1	1	1	1	1
Billy Cannon, Hou	**RB**	15	1	1	1	1	1
Abner Haynes, DalT	**RB**	12	—	1	1	1	1
Paul Lowe, SD	RB	6	—	2	2	—	2
Charley Tolar, Hou	RB	4	—	2	—	—	2
Donnie Stone, Den	RB	2	—	—	2	—	—
Alan Miller, Oak	RB	2	—	—	—	—	2
Larry Garron, Bos	RB	2	—	—	—	—	2

DEFENSE	POS	TT	AP	UP	NY	SN	AL
Earl Faison, SD	**DE**	15	1	1	1	1	1
Ron Nery, SD	**DE**	10	1	2	2	1	—
LaVerne Torczon, Buf	DE	8	—	1	1	—	2
Don Floyd, Hou	DE	3	—	—	—	—	1
Sid Youngelman, NYT	DE	2	—	—	2	—	—
Larry Eisenhauer, Bos	DE	2	—	—	2	—	—
Bob Dee, Bos	DE	2	—	—	—	—	2
Bud McFadin, Den	**DT**	15	1	1	1	1	1
Ernie Ladd, SD	**DT**	14	1	1	1	1	2
Ed Husmann, Hou	DT	4	—	2	2	—	—
Bill Hudson, SD	DT	4	—	2	2	—	—
Chuck McMurtry, Buf	DT	3	—	—	—	1	—
Jim Hunt, Bos	DT	2	—	—	—	—	2
Sherrill Headrick, DalT	**LB**	15	1	1	1	1	1
Larry Grantham, NYT	**LB**	14	1	1	1	1	2
Tom Addison, Bos	**LB**	13	1	1	2	1	2
Archie Matsos, Buf	LB	8	—	2	1	1	—
E.J. Holub, DalT	LB	6	—	2	2	—	1
Chuck Allen, SD	LB	5	—	—	2	—	1
Ralph Felton, Buf	LB	2	—	—	—	—	2
Dick Harris, SD	**CB**	15	1	1	1	1	1
Tony Banfield, Hou	**CB**	14	1	1	2	1	1
Fred Williamson, Oak	CB	4	—	2	—	—	2
Claude Gibson, SD	CB	4	—	2	2	—	—
Dick Felt, NYT	CB	2	—	—	—	—	2
Charlie McNeil, SD	**S**	15	1	1	1	1	1
Billy Atkins, Buf	**S**	11	—	1	B1	1	2
Dave Webster, DalT	S	6	1	—	—	—	1
Jim Norton, Hou	S	4	—	2	2	—	—
Goose Gonsoulin, Den	S	4	—	2	—	—	2
Mark Johnston, Hou	S	3	—	—	1	—	—
Ross O'Hanley, Bos	S	2	—	—	2	—	—

1962 NFL

Offense

OFFENSE	POS	TT	+SN	AP	NE	UP
Del Shofner, NYG	E	11	1	1	1	1
Bobby Mitchell, Was	E	11	1	1	1	1
Gail Cogdill, Det	E	8	1	2	2	2
Tommy McDonald, Phi	E	4	—	2	2	—
Sonny Randle, SL	E	2	1	—	—	2
Boyd Dowler, GB	E	2	1	—	—	—
Mike Ditka, ChiB	TE	10	1	2	1	1
Ron Kramer, GB	TE	7	—	1	2	2
Preston Carpenter, Pit	TE	2	1	—	—	—
Forrest Gregg, GB	T	11	1	1	1	1
Jim Parker, Bal	T	10	1	G1	1	2
Rosey Brown, NYG	T	8	—	1	2	1
Jack Stroud, NYG	T	6	1	2	1	2
Mike McCormack, Cle	T	4	1	—	2	—
Bob St. Clair, SF	T	2	—	—	—	2
Fuzzy Thurston, GB	G	9	1	2	2	1
Jim Ray Smith, Cle	G	9	1	2	1	2
Jerry Kramer, GB	G	9	—	1	1	1
Harley Sewell, Det	G	2	—	—	2	—
Mike Sandusky, Pit	G	2	1	—	—	2
Ray Lemek, Pit	G	2	1	—	—	—
Ted Connolly, SF	G	2	1	—	—	—
Jim Ringo, GB	C	11	1	1	1	1
Ray Wietecha, NYG	C	4	—	2	—	2
Jim Schrader, Phi	C	2	1	—	—	—
Buzz Nutter, Pit	C	2	—	—	2	—
Y.A. Tittle, NYG	QB	11	1	1	1	1
Bart Starr, GB	QB	6	—	2	2	2
Billy Wade, ChiB	QB	2	1	—	—	—
Jim Taylor, GB	RB	11	1	1	1	1
Dick Bass, LARm	RB	9	1	2	†2	1
Don Perkins, Dal	RB	8	—	1	1	2
John Henry Johnson, Pit	RB	6	—	2	2	2
John David Crow, SL	RB	4	1	—	†2	—
Jim Brown, Cle	RB	4	1	—	—	—

Defense

DEFENSE	POS	TT	+SN	AP	NE	UP
Gino Marchetti, Bal	DE	11	1	1	1	1
Jim Katcavage, NYG	DE	10	1	2	1	1
Willie Davis, GB	DE	5	—	1	—	2
Andy Robustelli, NYG	DE	4	—	2	—	†2
Bill Glass, Cle	DE	4	1	—	2	—
Doug Atkins, ChiB	DE	4	1	—	2	—
Lou Michaels, Pit	DE	2	—	—	—	†2
Alex Karras, Det	DT	10	1	2	1	1
Henry Jordan, GB	DT	9	1	1	2	2
Roger Brown, Det	DT	9	—	1	1	1
Bob Toneff, Was	DT	4	—	1	2	—
Leo Nomellini, SF	DT	2	—	—	—	2
Rosey Grier, NYG	DT	2	1	—	—	—
Bob Gain, Cle	DT	2	—	2	—	—
Bill Forester, GB	OLB	11	1	1	1	1
Dan Currie, GB	OLB	9	—	1	1	1
Matt Hazeltine, SF	OLB	6	—	2	2	2
Galen Fiss, Cle	OLB	6	1	—	2	2
Joe Fortunato, ChiB	OLB	2	—	2	—	—
Carl Brettschneider, Det	OLB	2	1	—	—	—
Rod Breedlove, Was	OLB	2	1	—	—	—
Joe Schmidt, Det	MLB	11	1	1	1	1
Ray Nitschke, GB	MLB	4	—	2	2	—
Jerry Tubbs, Dal	MLB	2	1	—	—	—
Bill Pellington, Bal	MLB	2	—	—	—	2
Night Train Lane, Det	CB	11	1	1	1	1
Herb Adderley, GB	CB	8	—	1	2	1
Abe Woodson, SF	CB	7	1	—	1	2
Jimmy Hill, SL	CB	6	1	2	2	—
Erich Barnes, NYG	CB	6	1	2	—	2
Jimmy Patton, NYG	S	11	1	1	1	1
Yale Lary, Det	S	11	1	1	1	1
Willie Wood, GB	S	8	1	2	2	2
Clendon Thomas, Pit	S	2	1	—	—	—
Richie Petitbon, ChiB	S	2	—	2	—	—
Don Fleming, Cle	S	2	1	—	—	—
Don Burroughs, Phi	S	2	—	—	—	2

1962 AFL

Offense

OFFENSE	POS	TT	AP	UP	AL
Charley Hennigan, Hou	E	9	1	1	1
Chris Burford, DalT	E	9	1	1	1
Lionel Taylor, Den	E	5	1	2	—
Art Powell, NYT	E	2	—	2	—
Dave Kocourek, SD	TE	8	2	1	1
Fred Arbanas, DalT	TE	4	2	2	—
Eldon Danenhauer, Den	T	7	2	2	1
Al Jamison, Hou	T	6	1	1	—
Harold Olson, Buf	T	5	1	2	—
Charley Long, Bos	T	5	2	1	—
Jim Tyrer, DalT	T	3	—	—	1
Ron Mix, SD	G	9	1	1	1
Bob Talamini, Hou	G	6	1	1	—
Billy Shaw, Buf	G	5	1	2	—
Billy Neighbors, Bos	G	4	2	2	—
Bob Mischak, NYT	G	2	2	—	—
Jim Otto, Oak	C	9	1	1	1
Bob Schmidt, Hou	C	4	2	2	—

1962 AFL (CONT.)

Offense

OFFENSE	POS	TT	AP	UP	AL
Len Dawson, DalT	QB	9	1	1	1
George Blanda, Hou	QB	4	2	2	—
Abner Haynes, DalT	RB	9	1	1	1
Cookie Gilchrist, Buf	RB	9	1	1	1
Charley Tolar, Hou	RB	4	2	2	—
Gene Mingo, Den	RB	2	—	2	—
Curtis McClinton, DalT	RB	2	—	2	—

Defense

DEFENSE	POS	TT	AP	UP	AL
Don Floyd, Hou	DE	9	1	1	1
Mel Branch, DalT	DE	7	2	2	1
Larry Eisenhauer, Bos	DE	6	1	1	—
Earl Faison, SD	DE	2	—	2	—
Bob Dee, Bos	DE	2	2	—	—
Bud McFadin, Den	DT	9	1	1	1
Jerry Mays, DalT	DT	7	2	2	1
Ed Husmann, Hou	DT	6	1	1	—
Tom Sestak, Buf	DT	4	2	2	—
E.J. Holub, DalT	OLB	9	1	1	1
Larry Grantham, NYT	OLB	9	1	1	1
Doug Cline, Hou	OLB	4	2	2	—
Tom Addison, Bos	OLB	4	2	2	—
Sherrill Headrick, DalT	MLB	9	1	1	1
Nick Buoniconti, Bos	MLB	2	—	2	—
Chuck Allen, SD	MLB	2	2	—	—
Fred Williamson, Oak	CB	9	1	1	1
Tony Banfield, Hou	CB	9	1	1	1
Dick Harris, SD	CB	4	2	2	—
Dick Felt, Bos	CB	4	2	2	—
Goose Gonsoulin, Den	S	8	1	2	1
Bob Zeman, Den	S	7	2	2	1
Bobby Hunt, DalT	S	6	1	1	—
Jim Norton, Hou	S	5	2	1	—

1963 NFL

Offense

OFFENSE	POS	TT	+SN	AP	NE	UP	NY
Del Shofner, NYG	E	14	1	1	1	1	1
Bobby Joe Conrad, SL	E	11	—	1	2	1	1
Bobby Mitchell, Was	E	9	1	—	1	2	2
Terry Barr, Det	E	6	1	2	2	—	—
Gail Cogdill, Det	E	4	1	2	—	—	—
Sonny Randle, SL	E	2	—	—	—	—	2
Buddy Dial, Pit	E	2	—	—	—	2	—
Mike Ditka, ChiB	TE	14	1	1	1	1	1
Ron Kramer, GB	TE	8	—	2	2	2	2
Pete Retzlaff, Phi	TE	2	1	—	—	—	—
Forrest Gregg, GB	T	14	1	1	1	1	1
Rosey Brown, NYG	T	13	1	2	1	1	1
Dick Schafrath, Cle	T	11	1	1	2	2	2
Charlie Bradshaw, Pit	T	6	—	2	—	2	2
Bob Wetoska, ChiB	T	2	1	—	—	—	—
Bob St. Clair, SF	T	2	1	—	—	—	—
Jerry Kramer, GB	G	14	1	1	1	1	1
Ken Gray, SL	G	12	1	2	2	1	1
Jim Parker, Bal	G	10	—	1	1	2	2
Darrell Dess, NYG	G	8	1	2	2	—	2
Fuzzy Thurston, GB	G	2	—	—	—	—	—
John Gordy, Det	G	2	1	—	—	—	—
Jim Ringo, GB	C	12	—	1	1	1	1
Bob DeMarco, SL	C	6	1	2	2	2	2
Mike Pyle, ChiB	C	4	1	—	—	—	—
Buzz Nutter, Pit	C	2	1	—	—	—	—
Y.A. Tittle, NYG	QB	14	1	1	1	1	1
Johnny Unitas, Bal	QB	8	—	2	2	2	2
Billy Wade, ChiB	QB	2	1	—	—	—	—
Tommy Mason, Min	RB	14	1	1	1	1	1
Jim Brown, Cle	RB	14	1	1	1	1	1
Jim Taylor, GB	RB	10	1	2	2	2	2
Timmy Brown, Phi	RB	8	1	2	2	2	2
Tom Moore, GB	RB	2	—	2	—	—	—

Defense

DEFENSE	POS	TT	+SN	AP	NE	UP	NY
Doug Atkins, ChiB	DE	14	1	1	1	1	1
Jim Katcavage, NYG	DE	13	1	1	1	1	1
Gino Marchetti, Bal	DE	11	1	2	2	2	2
Willie Davis, GB	DE	6	—	2	2	2	—
Bill Glass, Cle	DE	4	1	2	—	—	—
Henry Jordan, GB	DT	14	1	1	1	1	1
Roger Brown, Det	DT	12	—	1	1	1	1
Merlin Olsen, LARm	DT	8	—	2	2	2	2
Bob Gain, Cle	DT	6	1	2	2	2	2
Rosey Grier, LARm	DT	4	1	2	—	—	—
Luke Owens, SL	DT	2	1	—	—	—	—
Dick Modzelewski, NYG	DT	2	1	—	—	—	2
Joe Fortunato, ChiB	OLB	12	—	1	1	1	1
Larry Morris, ChiB	OLB	8	—	2	2	2	1
Dan Currie, GB	OLB	8	—	2	1	1	1
Jack Pardee, LARm	OLB	7	1	1	2	—	1
Bill Forester, GB	OLB	7	1	2	—	1	—
Wayne Walker, Det	OLB	7	1	2	—	—	—
Bill Koman, SL	OLB	2	—	2	—	—	—
Chuck Howley, Dal	OLB	2	1	—	—	—	—
Rip Hawkins, Min	OLB	2	1	—	—	—	—
Bill George, ChiB	MLB	13	1	2	1	1	1
Myron Pottios, Pit	MLB	7	1	2	1	—	—

1963 NFL (CONT.)

DEFENSE	POS	TT	+SN	AP	NE	UP	NY
Joe Schmidt, Det	MLB	3	—	—	1	—	—
Ray Nitschke, GB	MLB	2	—	—	—	—	2
Sam Huff, NYG	MLB	2	—	—	—	2	—
Dick Lynch, NYG	CB	14	1	1	1	1	1
Night Train Lane, Det	CB	12	1	2	2	1	1
Herb Adderley, GB	CB	9	1	1	—	2	2
Abe Woodson, SF	CB	5	—	2	1	—	—
Eddie Meador, LARm	CB	4	—	—	2	—	2
Jimmy Hill, SL	CB	4	1	—	—	2	—
Rosey Taylor, ChiB	S	13	1	1	1	2	1
Larry Wilson, SL	S	9	1	—	2	1	2
Richie Petitbon, ChiB	S	9	—	1	—	1	1
Clendon Thomas, Pit	S	6	1	2	—	—	2
Willie Wood, GB	S	5	—	—	1	2	—
Yale Lary, Det	S	4	1	2	—	—	—
Jimmy Patton, NYG	S	2	—	—	2	—	—

1963 AFL

OFFENSE	POS	TT	AP	NE	UP	NY	AL
Art Powell, Oak	E	15	1	1	1	1	1
Lance Alworth, SD	E	15	1	1	1	1	1
Elbert Dubenion, Buf	E	4	2	—	—	2	—
Lionel Taylor, Den	E	2	—	—	2	—	—
Bill Miller, Buf	E	2	2	—	—	—	—
Charley Hennigan, Hou	E	2	—	—	2	—	—
Gino Cappelletti, Bos	E	2	—	2	—	—	—
Fred Arbanas, KC	TE	11	1	—	1	2	1
Dave Kocourek, SD	TE	10	2	1	2	1	—
Ron Mix, SD	T	15	1	1	1	1	1
Jim Tyrer, KC	T	12	2	1	2	2	1
Stew Barber, Buf	T	9	1	—	1	1	—
Dick Guesman, NYJ	T	2	—	—	2	—	—
Eldon Danenhauer, Den	T	2	—	—	2	—	—
Billy Shaw, Buf	G	15	1	1	1	1	1
Bob Talamini, Hou	G	14	1	1	2	1	1
Billy Neighbors, Bos	G	7	2	—	1	2	—
Charley Long, Bos	G	4	T2	—	2	—	—
Wayne Hawkins, Oak	G	2	2	—	—	—	—
Jim Otto, Oak	C	15	1	1	1	1	1
Don Rogers, SD	C	4	2	—	—	2	—
Bob Schmidt, Hou	C	2	—	—	2	—	—
Tobin Rote, SD	QB	15	1	1	1	1	1
George Blanda, Hou	QB	4	2	—	—	2	—
Jack Kemp, Buf	QB	2	—	—	2	—	—
Clem Daniels, Oak	RB	15	1	1	1	1	1
Keith Lincoln, SD	RB	14	1	1	1	2	1
Cookie Gilchrist, Buf	RB	7	2	—	2	1	—
Paul Lowe, SD	RB	4	2	—	2	—	—
Billy Joe, Den	RB	2	—	—	2	—	—

DEFENSE	POS	TT	AP	NE	UP	NY	AL
Larry Eisenhauer, Bos	DE	15	1	1	1	1	1
Earl Faison, SD	DE	12	1	—	1	1	1
Dalva Allen, Oak	DE	7	2	1	2	2	—
Mel Branch, KC	DE	6	2	—	2	2	—
Don Floyd, Hou	DE	2	—	—	2	—	—
Tom Sestak, Buf	DT	15	1	1	1	1	1
Houston Antwine, Bos	DT	15	1	1	1	1	1
Jerry Mays, KC	DT	6	2	—	2	2	—
Bud McFadin, Den	DT	4	2	—	2	—	—
Ed Husmann, Hou	DT	2	—	—	2	—	—
E.J. Holub, KC	OLB	15	1	1	1	1	1
Larry Grantham, NYJ	OLB	12	1	1	1	1	1
Tom Addison, Bos	OLB	9	2	—	2	2	1
Doug Cline, Hou	OLB	6	2	—	2	2	—
Archie Matsos, Oak	MLB	12	1	—	1	1	1
Nick Buoniconti, Bos	MLB	9	2	1	2	2	—
Fred Williamson, Oak	CB	15	1	1	1	1	1
Dick Westmoreland, SD	CB	9	2	1	2	2	—
Tony Banfield, Hou	CB	9	1	—	1	1	—
Dave Grayson, KC	CB	5	—	—	—	—	—
Dick Harris, SD	CB	2	2	—	—	—	—
Ron Hall, Bos	CB	2	—	—	2	—	—
Fred Glick, Hou	S	15	1	1	1	1	1
Tommy Morrow, Oak	S	12	1	1	1	1	—
Joe Krakoski, Oak	S	4	2	—	—	—	—
George Blair, SD	S	4	2	—	2	—	—
Goose Gonsoulin, Den	S	3	—	—	—	—	1
Johnny Robinson, KC	S	2	—	—	2	—	—
Bobby Jancik, Hou	S	2	—	—	2	—	—

1964 NFL

OFFENSE	POS	TT	+SN	AP	NE	UP	NY
Johnny Morris, ChiB	E	14	1	1	1	1	1
Frank Clarke, Dal	E	10	—	1	2	2	1
Bobby Mitchell, Was	E	9	—	2	2	1	2
Paul Warfield, Cle	E	4	—	1	—	—	2
Gail Cogdill, Det	E	4	2	—	—	—	—
Max McGee, GB	E	2	—	1	—	—	—
Bobby Joe Conrad, SL	E	2	—	—	—	2	—
Gary Ballman, Pit	E	2	1	—	—	—	—
Mike Ditka, ChiB	TE	14	1	1	1	1	1
Pete Retzlaff, Phi	TE	10	1	2	2	2	2
Dick Schafrath, Cle	T	13	1	1	2	1	1
Forrest Gregg, GB	T	12	—	1	1	1	1

1964 NFL (CONT.)

OFFENSE	POS	TT	+SN	AP	NE	UP	NY
Charlie Bradshaw, Pit	T	8	1	—	2	2	2
George Preas, Bal	T	4	—	2	—	2	2
Bob Vogel, Bal	T	3	—	—	1	—	2
Bob Wetoska, ChiB	T	2	1	—	—	—	—
Frank Varrichione, LARm	T	2	1	—	—	—	—
Ernie McMillan, SL	T	2	—	—	—	—	2
Bob Brown, Phi	T	2	—	2	—	—	—
Jim Parker, Bal	G	14	1	1	1	1	1
Ken Gray, SL	G	13	1	1	2	1	1
John Gordy, Det	G	9	1	2	1	2	—
Alex Sandusky, Bal	G	6	—	2	2	—	2
Fuzzy Thurston, GB	G	2	—	—	—	—	2
Gene Hickerson, Cle	G	2	—	—	2	—	—
Ed Blaine, Phi	G	2	1	—	—	—	—
Mick Tingelhoff, Min	C	10	1	1	2	1	—
Jim Ringo, Phi	C	8	—	2	2	2	2
Bob DeMarco, SL	C	8	1	—	1	—	1
Johnny Unitas, Bal	QB	14	1	1	1	1	1
Sonny Jurgensen, Was	QB	8	1	—	2	2	2
Bart Starr, GB	QB	2	—	2	—	—	—
Lenny Moore, Bal	RB	14	1	1	1	1	1
Jim Brown, Cle	RB	14	1	1	1	1	1
Jim Taylor, GB	RB	8	1	—	2	2	2
Charley Taylor, Was	RB	6	1	2	—	2	—
Tommy Mason, Min	RB	4	—	—	2	2	—
Bill Brown, Min	RB	2	—	—	2	—	—

DEFENSE	POS	TT	+SN	AP	NE	UP	NY
Gino Marchetti, Bal	DE	14	1	1	1	1	1
Willie Davis, GB	DE	12	—	1	1	1	1
Deacon Jones, LARm	DE	8	—	2	2	2	2
John Paluck, Was	DE	2	—	2	—	—	—
Jim Marshall, Min	DE	2	—	—	2	—	—
Jim Katcavage, NYG	DE	2	1	—	—	—	—
Bill Glass, Cle	DE	2	1	—	—	—	—
John Baker, Pit	DE	2	—	—	—	—	2
Doug Atkins, ChiB	DE	2	—	—	2	—	—
Lionel Aldridge, GB	DE	2	1	—	—	—	—
Bob Lilly, Dal	DT	14	1	1	1	1	1
Merlin Olsen, LARm	DT	11	1	2	1	2	2
Henry Jordan, GB	DT	9	—	1	—	1	1
Alex Karras, Det	DT	8	—	2	1	—	—
Roger Brown, Det	DT	4	1	—	2	—	—
Floyd Peters, Phi	DT	2	1	—	—	—	—
Joe Fortunato, ChiB	OLB	14	1	1	1	1	1
Wayne Walker, Det	OLB	11	1	2	2	1	2
Maxie Baughan, Phi	OLB	8	1	1	—	—	1
Matt Hazeltine, SF	OLB	6	—	2	2	2	—
Steve Stonebreaker, Bal	OLB	4	—	—	—	2	2
Jim Houston, Cle	OLB	3	—	1	—	—	—
Bill Koman, SL	OLB	2	1	—	—	—	—
Ray Nitschke, GB	MLB	9	—	1	—	1	1
Dale Meinert, SL	MLB	7	—	1	1	2	2
Bill Pellington, Bal	MLB	6	1	2	2	—	—
Sam Huff, Was	MLB	2	1	—	—	—	—
Pat Fischer, SL	CB	14	1	1	1	1	1
Herb Adderley, GB	CB	10	1	2	2	2	2
Bobby Boyd, Bal	CB	9	—	1	—	1	2
Erich Barnes, NYG	CB	5	—	1	—	1	—
Bernie Parrish, Cle	CB	4	1	2	—	—	—
Dick LeBeau, Det	CB	4	—	—	2	—	—
Ed Sharockman, Min	CB	2	1	—	—	—	—
Jimmy Johnson, SF	CB	2	—	—	2	—	—
Paul Krause, Was	S	14	1	1	1	1	1
Willie Wood, GB	S	11	—	1	1	1	2
Mel Renfro, Dal	S	9	—	2	2	2	1
Rosey Taylor, ChiB	S	6	1	—	2	—	2
Jimmy Ridlon, Dal	S	2	1	—	—	—	—
Eddie Meador, LARm	S	2	1	—	—	—	—
Jerry Logan, Bal	S	2	—	—	2	—	—

SPECIALISTS	POS	TT	+SN	AP	NE	UP	NY
Lou Groza, Cle	K	2	1	—	—	—	—
Bruce Gossett, LARm	K	2	1	—	—	—	—
Yale Lary, Det	P	2	1	—	—	—	—
Don Chandler, NYG	P	2	1	—	—	—	—

1964 AFL

OFFENSE	POS	TT	AP	NE	UP	NY	AL
Charley Hennigan, Hou	E	15	1	1	1	1	†1
Lance Alworth, SD	E	15	1	1	1	1	1
Art Powell, Oak	E	11	2	2	2	2	†1
Elbert Dubenion, Buf	E	4	2	—	—	2	—
Gino Cappelletti, Bos	E	2	—	2	2	—	—
Fred Arbanas, KC	TE	15	1	1	1	1	1
Dave Kocourek, SD	TE	8	2	2	2	2	—
Ron Mix, SD	T	15	1	1	1	1	1
Stew Barber, Buf	T	12	1	1	1	1	—
Jim Tyrer, KC	T	11	2	2	2	2	1
Eldon Danenhauer, Den	T	4	2	—	2	—	—
Winston Hill, NYJ	T	2	—	—	—	—	2
Sonny Bishop, Hou	T	2	—	2	—	—	—
Billy Shaw, Buf	G	15	1	1	1	1	1
Bob Talamini, Hou	G	12	2	2	2	2	1
Billy Neighbors, Bos	G	9	1	—	2	1	—

1964 AFL (CONT.)

OFFENSE	POS	TT	AP	NE	UP	NY	AL
Charley Long, Bos	G	6	—	2	2	2	—
Bob Mischak, Oak	G	2	—	2	—	—	—
Wayne Hawkins, Oak	G	2	2	—	—	—	—
Jim Otto, Oak	**C**	15	1	1	1	1	1
Jon Morris, Bos	C	6	2	2	—	2	—
Mike Hudock, NYJ	C	2	—	—	2	—	—
Babe Parilli, Bos	**QB**	15	1	1	1	1	1
Len Dawson, KC	QB	8	2	2	2	2	—
Keith Lincoln, SD	**RB**	15	1	1	1	1	1
Cookie Gilchrist, Buf	**RB**	15	1	1	1	1	1
Matt Snell, NYJ	RB	8	2	2	2	2	—
Abner Haynes, KC	RB	4	2	—	—	—	1
Clem Daniels, Oak	RB	2	—	2	—	—	—
Sid Blanks, Hou	RB	2	—	—	2	—	—

DEFENSE	POS	TT	AP	NE	UP	NY	AL
Earl Faison, SD	**DE**	15	1	1	1	1	1
Larry Eisenhauer, Bos	**DE**	14	1	1	2	1	1
Bobby Bell, KC	DE	9	2	2	1	2	—
Bob Dee, Bos	DE	4	2	—	—	2	—
Don Floyd, Hou	DE	2	—	—	2	—	—
Tom Day, Buf	DE	2	—	2	—	—	—
Tom Sestak, Buf	**DT**	15	1	1	1	1	1
Ernie Ladd, SD	**DT**	12	1	1	1	1	—
Buck Buchanan, KC	DT	8	2	2	2	2	—
Jerry Mays, KC	DT	7	2	2	—	—	1
Houston Antwine, Bos	DT	4	—	—	2	2	—
Larry Grantham, NYJ	**OLB**	15	1	1	1	1	1
Tom Addison, Bos	**OLB**	12	2	1	2	2	1
Mike Stratton, Buf	OLB	11	1	2	1	1	—
Frank Buncom, SD	OLB	6	2	—	2	2	—
E.J. Holub, KC	OLB	2	—	2	—	—	—
Nick Buoniconti, Bos	**MLB**	15	1	1	1	1	1
Chuck Allen, SD	MLB	4	—	2	2	—	—
Archie Matsos, Oak	MLB	2	—	—	—	2	—
Sherrill Headrick, KC	MLB	2	2	—	—	—	—
Willie Brown, Den	**CB**	15	1	1	1	1	1
Dave Grayson, KC	**CB**	13	1	2	1	1	1
Dick Westmoreland, SD	CB	9	2	1	2	2	—
Fred Williamson, Oak	CB	5	—	1	1	2	—
Pete Jaquess, Hou	CB	2	—	—	—	2	—
Butch Byrd, Buf	CB	2	—	2	—	—	—
Dainard Paulson, NYJ	**S**	13	2	1	1	2	1
Ron Hall, Bos	**S**	12	1	1	1	1	—
George Saimes, Buf	S	10	1	2	2	1	—
Fred Glick, Hou	S	5	—	2	—	—	1
Bobby Hunt, KC	S	4	2	—	—	2	—
Goose Gonsoulin, Den	S	2	—	—	2	—	—

1965 NFL

OFFENSE	POS	TT	+SN	AP	NE	UP	NY
Dave Parks, SF	**E**	14	1	1	1	1	1
Jimmy Orr, Bal	**E**	12	1	1	1	2	2
Gary Collins, Cle	E	10	1	2	—	1	1
Bob Hayes, Dal	E	4	1	—	—	2	—
Raymond Berry, Bal	E	4	—	2	—	—	2
Pete Retzlaff, Phi	**TE**	14	1	1	1	1	1
Mike Ditka, ChiB	TE	8	1	2	2	—	2
Bob Vogel, Bal	**T**	12	1	2	1	2	1
Dick Schafrath, Cle	**T**	11	1	1	—	1	1
Forrest Gregg, GB	T	10	1	G1	—	1	2
Bob Brown, Phi	T	8	—	1	1	—	2
Bob Wetoska, ChiB	T	4	1	—	—	2	—
Rosey Brown, NYG	T	4	1	—	—	—	2
Grady Alderman, Min	T	2	—	2	—	—	—
Jim Parker, Bal	**G**	14	1	1	1	1	1
Ken Gray, SL	**G**	10	1	2	—	1	1
John Gordy, Det	G	7	—	—	1	2	2
Gene Hickerson, Cle	G	4	—	2	—	2	—
John Wooten, Cle	G	2	1	—	—	—	1
Mick Tingelhoff, Min	**C**	14	1	1	1	1	1
Bob DeMarco, SL	C	4	1	—	—	2	—
Mike Pyle, ChiB	C	2	—	—	—	—	2
John Morrow, Cle	C	2	—	2	—	—	—
Johnny Unitas, Bal	**QB**	12	—	1	1	1	1
Rudy Bukich, ChiB	QB	4	—	—	—	2	2
John Brodie, SF	QB	4	1	2	—	—	—
Frank Ryan, Cle	QB	2	1	—	—	—	—
Gale Sayers, ChiB	**RB**	14	1	1	1	1	1
Jim Brown, Cle	**RB**	14	1	1	1	1	1
Timmy Brown, Phi	RB	8	1	2	—	2	2
Ken Willard, SF	RB	6	1	2	—	2	—
Bill Brown, Min	RB	2	—	—	—	—	2

DEFENSE	POS	TT	+SN	AP	NE	UP	NY
Willie Davis, GB	**DE**	14	1	1	1	1	1
Deacon Jones, LARm	**DE**	12	—	1	1	1	1
Bill Glass, Cle	DE	8	1	2	—	2	2
Doug Atkins, ChiB	DE	6	1	2	—	2	—
Ordell Braase, Bal	DE	2	—	—	—	—	2
John Baker, Pit	DE	2	1	—	—	—	—
Bob Lilly, Dal	**DT**	14	1	1	1	1	1
Alex Karras, Det	**DT**	12	1	1	1	1	1
Merlin Olsen, LARm	DT	8	1	2	—	2	2
Roger Brown, Det	DT	6	1	—	—	2	—

1965 NFL (CONT.)

DEFENSE	POS	TT	+SN	AP	NE	UP	NY
Sam Silas, SL	DT	2	1	—	—	—	—
Charlie Krueger, SF	DT	2	—	2	—	—	—
Wayne Walker, Det	**OLB**	14	1	1	1	1	1
Joe Fortunato, ChiB	**OLB**	10	—	1	1	2	2
Jim Houston, Cle	OLB	9	1	2	—	1	1
Steve Stonebreaker, Bal	OLB	7	1	—	—	2	1
Maxie Baughan, Phi	OLB	4	1	2	—	—	—
Dick Butkus, ChiB	**MLB**	11	—	1	1	2	1
Ray Nitschke, GB	MLB	9	1	2	—	1	2
Sam Huff, Was	MLB	2	1	—	—	—	—
Bobby Boyd, Bal	**CB**	12	—	1	1	1	1
Herb Adderley, GB	**CB**	12	—	1	1	1	1
Pat Fischer, SL	CB	6	1	—	—	2	2
Bennie McRae, ChiB	CB	4	1	—	2	—	—
Dick LeBeau, Det	CB	4	1	2	—	—	—
Johnny Sample, Was	CB	2	—	—	—	2	—
Dick Lynch, NYG	CB	2	1	—	—	—	2
Jimmy Johnson, SF	CB	2	—	2	—	—	—
Willie Wood, GB	**S**	14	1	1	1	1	1
Mel Renfro, Dal	**S**	11	1	2	1	2	2
Paul Krause, Was	**S**	11	1	1	—	1	1
Larry Wilson, SL	S	4	—	—	2	—	2
Rosey Taylor, ChiB	S	2	—	2	—	—	—
Eddie Meador, LARm	S	2	1	—	—	—	—

SPECIALISTS	POS	TT	+SN	AP	NE	UP	NY
Lou Groza, Cle	K	2	1	—	—	—	—
Don Chandler, GB	K	2	1	—	—	—	—
Tommy Davis, SF	P	2	1	—	—	—	—
Gary Collins, Cle	P	2	1	—	—	—	—

1965 AFL

OFFENSE	POS	TT	AP	NE	UP	NY	AL
Lionel Taylor, Den	**E**	15	1	1	1	1	†1
Lance Alworth, SD	**E**	15	1	1	1	1	1
Art Powell, Oak	E	9	2	—	2	2	†1
Don Maynard, NYJ	E	4	2	—	—	2	—
Willie Frazier, Hou	**TE**	15	1	1	1	1	1
Dave Kocourek, SD	TE	4	2	—	—	2	—
Fred Arbanas, KC	TE	2	—	2	—	—	—
Jim Tyrer, KC	**T**	15	1	1	1	1	1
Ron Mix, SD	**T**	12	1	1	1	1	1
Eldon Danenhauer, Den	T	9	2	—	2	2	1
Stew Barber, Buf	T	4	—	2	2	—	—
Sherman Plunkett, NYJ	T	2	2	—	—	—	—
Billy Shaw, Buf	**G**	15	1	1	1	1	1
Bob Talamini, Hou	**G**	12	1	—	1	1	1
Wayne Hawkins, Oak	G	7	2	1	2	—	—
Walt Sweeney, SD	G	4	2	—	—	2	—
Dan Ficca, NYJ	G	2	—	2	—	—	—
Sonny Bishop, Hou	G	2	—	—	—	2	—
Jim Otto, Oak	**C**	15	1	1	1	1	1
Jon Morris, Bos	C	4	2	—	2	2	—
Mike Hudock, NYJ	C	2	—	—	—	—	2
Jack Kemp, Buf	**QB**	15	1	1	1	1	1
John Hadl, SD	QB	6	2	2	—	2	2
Paul Lowe, SD	**RB**	15	1	1	1	1	1
Cookie Gilchrist, Den	**RB**	15	1	1	1	1	1
Matt Snell, NYJ	RB	4	2	2	—	—	—
Curtis McClinton, KC	RB	2	2	—	—	—	—
Mack Lee Hill, KC	RB	2	—	—	2	—	—
Clem Daniels, Oak	RB	2	—	2	—	—	—
Ode Burrell, Hou	RB	2	—	—	—	2	—

DEFENSE	POS	TT	AP	NE	UP	NY	AL
Earl Faison, SD	**DE**	15	1	1	1	1	1
Jerry Mays, KC	**DE**	14	1	2	1	1	1
Tom Day, Buf	DE	4	2	—	—	2	—
Ben Davidson, Oak	DE	4	2	—	2	—	—
Ron McDole, Buf	DE	3	—	1	—	—	1
Verlon Biggs, NYJ	DE	2	—	—	2	—	—
Tom Sestak, Buf	**DT**	15	1	1	1	1	1
Ernie Ladd, SD	**DT**	15	1	1	1	1	1
Buck Buchanan, KC	DT	6	2	—	2	2	—
Jim Dunaway, Buf	DT	4	—	2	—	2	—
Ray Jacobs, Den	DT	2	2	—	—	—	—
Mike Stratton, Buf	**OLB**	15	1	1	1	1	1
Bobby Bell, KC	**OLB**	15	1	1	1	1	1
Larry Grantham, NYJ	OLB	6	2	—	2	2	—
John Bramlett, Den	OLB	4	—	2	—	2	—
E.J. Holub, KC	OLB	2	—	2	—	—	—
Frank Buncom, SD	OLB	2	2	—	—	—	—
Nick Buoniconti, Bos	**MLB**	15	1	1	1	1	1
John Tracey, Buf	MLB	4	2	—	—	2	—
Dave Grayson, Oak	**CB**	15	1	1	1	1	1
Butch Byrd, Buf	**CB**	11	1	—	2	1	1
W.K. Hicks, Hou	CB	6	2	—	2	2	—
Speedy Duncan, SD	CB	5	2	1	—	—	—
Fred Williamson, KC	CB	3	—	—	1	—	—
Willie Mitchell, KC	CB	2	—	2	—	—	—
Willie Brown, Den	CB	2	2	—	—	—	—
George Saimes, Buf	**S**	15	1	1	1	1	1
Dainard Paulson, NYJ	**S**	11	2	1	1	1	1
Johnny Robinson, KC	S	10	1	—	2	2	1
Kenny Graham, SD	S	2	2	—	—	—	—

1965 AFL (CONT.)

SPECIALISTS	POS	TT	AP	NE	UP	NY	AL
Pete Gogolak, Buf	K	3	—	—	—	—	1
Curley Johnson, NYJ	P	3	—	—	—	—	1

1966 NFL

OFFENSE	POS	TT	+SN	AP	NE	UP	NY	FW
Bob Hayes, Dal	E	17	1	1	1	1	1	1
Pat Studstill, Det	E	14	1	1	—	1	1	1
Dave Parks, SF	E	9	1	2	1	—	2	—
Gary Collins, Cle	E	6	—	2	—	2	2	—
Charley Taylor, Was	E	4	1	—	—	2	—	—
John Mackey, Bal	TE	17	1	1	1	1	1	1
Mike Ditka, ChiB	TE	4	—	2	—	2	—	—
Jackie Smith, SL	TE	2	1	—	—	—	—	—
Pete Retzlaff, Phi	TE	2	—	—	—	—	2	—
Bob Brown, Phi	T	17	1	1	1	1	1	1
Forrest Gregg, GB	T	15	—	1	1	1	1	1
Ralph Neely, Dal	T	8	1	2	—	2	2	—
Ernie McMillan, SL	T	4	—	2	—	2	2	—
Bob Vogel, Bal	T	2	1	—	—	—	—	—
Walt Rock, SF	T	2	1	—	—	—	—	—
Jim Parker, Bal	T	2	—	—	—	—	2	—
Jerry Kramer, GB	G	14	1	1	—	1	1	1
John Thomas, SF	G	10	—	1	1	2	2	—
John Gordy, Det	G	7	1	2	—	—	—	—
John Wooten, Cle	G	6	—	—	—	—	1	1
Gene Hickerson, Cle	G	5	1	—	1	—	—	—
Ken Gray, SL	G	4	1	—	—	—	—	—
Fuzzy Thurston, GB	G	2	—	—	—	—	2	—
Tony Liscio, Dal	G	2	—	2	—	—	—	—
Mick Tingelhoff, Min	C	17	1	1	1	1	1	1
Jim Ringo, Phi	C	2	—	2	—	—	—	—
Greg Larson, NYG	C	2	1	—	—	—	—	—
Bob DeMarco, SL	C	2	—	—	2	—	—	—
Bruce Bosley, SF	C	2	—	—	—	—	2	—
Bart Starr, GB	QB	17	1	1	1	1	1	1
Don Meredith, Dal	QB	6	—	2	—	2	2	—
Sonny Jurgensen, Was	QB	2	1	—	—	—	—	—
Gale Sayers, ChiB	RB	17	1	1	1	1	1	1
Leroy Kelly, Cle	RB	17	1	1	1	1	1	1
Dick Bass, LARm	RB	6	—	2	—	2	2	—
Jim Taylor, GB	RB	4	1	—	—	2	—	—
Dan Reeves, Dal	RB	4	1	2	—	—	—	—
Timmy Brown, Phi	RB	2	—	—	—	—	2	—

DEFENSE	POS	TT	+SN	AP	NE	UP	NY	FW
Deacon Jones, LARm	DE	17	1	1	1	1	1	1
Willie Davis, GB	DE	17	1	1	1	1	1	1
Joe Robb, SL	DE	4	—	—	—	—	—	—
Ordell Braase, Bal	DE	4	—	2	—	—	—	—
George Andrie, Dal	DE	4	—	—	—	2	2	—
Ben McGee, Pit	DE	2	1	—	—	—	—	—
Jim Katcavage, NYG	DE	2	1	—	—	—	—	—
Merlin Olsen, LARm	DT	17	1	1	1	1	1	1
Bob Lilly, Dal	DT	17	1	1	1	1	1	1
Alex Karras, Det	DT	6	—	2	—	2	2	—
Henry Jordan, GB	DT	6	—	2	—	2	2	—
Floyd Peters, Phi	DT	2	1	—	—	—	—	—
Roger Brown, Det	DT	2	1	—	—	—	—	—
Chuck Howley, Dal	OLB	14	—	1	1	1	2	1
Wayne Walker, Det	OLB	10	—	2	—	2	1	—
Lee Roy Caffey, GB	OLB	9	—	1	—	1	1	—
Maxie Baughan, LARm	OLB	7	1	2	1	—	—	—
Dave Wilcox, SF	OLB	2	—	—	—	2	—	—
Dave Robinson, GB	OLB	2	1	—	—	—	—	—
Jim Houston, Cle	OLB	2	1	—	—	—	—	—
Joe Fortunato, ChiB	OLB	2	—	—	—	—	2	—
John Campbell, Pit	OLB	2	—	—	—	—	2	—
Ray Nitschke, GB	MLB	15	—	1	1	1	1	1
Dick Butkus, ChiB	MLB	8	1	2	—	2	2	—
Lee Roy Jordan, Dal	MLB	2	—	—	—	—	—	—
Herb Adderley, GB	CB	17	1	1	1	1	1	1
Cornell Green, Dal	CB	13	1	1	1	2	1	—
Bobby Boyd, Bal	CB	10	—	2	—	1	2	1
Jimmy Johnson, SF	CB	6	1	2	—	—	2	—
Erich Barnes, Cle	CB	2	—	—	—	—	—	—
Larry Wilson, SL	S	17	1	1	1	1	1	1
Willie Wood, GB	S	15	—	1	1	1	1	1
Jerry Stovall, SL	S	8	1	2	—	2	2	—
Ross Fichtner, Cle	S	4	—	2	—	—	CB2	—
Clendon Thomas, Pit	S	2	—	—	—	2	—	—
Mel Renfro, Dal	S	2	—	—	—	2	—	—
Richie Petitbon, ChiB	S	2	1	—	—	—	—	—
Eddie Meador, LARm	S	2	1	—	—	—	—	—

SPECIALISTS	POS	TT	+SN	AP	NE	UP	NY	FW
Bruce Gossett, LARm	K	2	1	—	—	—	—	—
Charlie Gogolak, Was	K	2	1	—	—	—	—	—
David Lee, Bal	P	2	1	—	—	—	—	—
Sam Baker, Phi	P	2	1	—	—	—	—	—

1966 AFL

OFFENSE	POS	TT	AP	NE	UP	NY	AL
Lance Alworth, SD	E	15	1	1	1	1	1
Otis Taylor, KC	E	13	1	1	1	2	2
Art Powell, Oak	E	12	2	2	2	1	1

1966 AFL (CONT.)

OFFENSE	POS	TT	AP	NE	UP	NY	AL
George Sauer, NYJ	E	8	2	2	—	2	2
Gino Cappelletti, Bos	E	2	—	—	2	—	—
Fred Arbanas, KC	TE	15	1	1	1	1	1
Al Denson, Den	TE	8	2	—	2	2	2
Dave Costa, Buf	TE	2	—	2	—	—	—
Jim Tyrer, KC	T	15	1	1	1	1	1
Ron Mix, SD	T	14	1	1	1	1	2
Dick Hudson, Buf	T	6	2	1	2	—	—
Stew Barber, Buf	T	6	2	—	—	2	2
Sherman Plunkett, NYJ	T	5	—	—	—	2	1
Walt Suggs, Hou	T	4	—	2	2	—	—
Billy Shaw, Buf	G	15	1	1	1	1	1
Wayne Hawkins, Oak	G	13	2	1	1	1	2
Bob Talamini, Hou	G	9	—	2	2	2	1
Ed Budde, KC	G	9	1	2	—	2	2
Sam DeLuca, NYJ	G	4	2	—	2	—	—
Jim Otto, Oak	C	14	2	1	1	1	1
Jon Morris, Bos	C	11	1	2	2	2	2
Len Dawson, KC	QB	15	1	1	1	1	1
Jack Kemp, Buf	QB	6	2	—	2	2	2
Joe Namath, NYJ	QB	2	—	2	—	—	—
John Hadl, SD	QB	2	—	—	2	—	—
Jim Nance, Bos	RB	15	1	1	1	1	1
Clem Daniels, Oak	RB	12	1	1	1	—	1
Bobby Burnett, Buf	RB	11	2	2	2	1	2
Wray Carlton, Buf	RB	10	2	2	2	2	2
Mike Garrett, KC	RB	2	—	—	—	—	—

DEFENSE	POS	TT	AP	NE	UP	NY	AL
Jerry Mays, KC	DE	15	1	1	1	1	1
Verlon Biggs, NYJ	DE	12	2	1	1	2	2
Ron McDole, Buf	DE	10	1	2	2	1	—
Larry Eisenhauer, Bos	DE	7	—	2	2	2	1
Ike Lassiter, Oak	DE	2	2	—	—	—	—
Tom Day, Buf	DE	2	—	—	—	—	—
Ben Davidson, Oak	DE	2	—	—	2	—	—
Houston Antwine, Bos	DT	14	2	†1	1	1	1
Buck Buchanan, KC	DT	13	1	2	2	2	1
Tom Keating, Oak	DT	9	2	1	2	—	2
Tom Sestak, Buf	DT	8	—	†1	—	1	2
Jim Dunaway, Buf	DT	7	1	—	2	—	—
Jim Hunt, Bos	DT	2	—	2	—	—	—
Mike Stratton, Buf	OLB	15	1	1	1	1	1
Bobby Bell, KC	OLB	15	1	1	1	1	1
E.J. Holub, KC	OLB	8	—	2	2	2	2
John Bramlett, Den	OLB	6	2	2	2	—	—
Larry Grantham, NYJ	OLB	2	—	—	—	—	—
Frank Buncom, SD	OLB	2	—	—	—	—	—
Johnny Baker, Hou	OLB	2	—	—	—	—	—
Nick Buoniconti, Bos	MLB	15	1	1	1	1	1
Sherrill Headrick, KC	MLB	6	2	2	—	2	—
Harry Jacobs, Buf	MLB	4	—	—	2	—	2
Butch Byrd, Buf	CB	15	1	1	1	1	1
Dave Grayson, Oak	CB	13	1	2	1	2	1
Kent McCloughan, Oak	CB	10	1	2	1	—	2
Speedy Duncan, SD	CB	8	2	—	2	2	2
Johnny Sample, NYJ	CB	2	—	—	—	—	—
Willie Brown, Den	CB	2	—	—	—	—	—
Johnny Robinson, KC	S	15	1	1	1	1	1
Kenny Graham, SD	S	13	1	1	1	2	2
George Saimes, Buf	S	10	—	2	2	1	2
Bobby Hunt, KC	S	6	2	—	—	—	2
Hagood Clarke, Buf	S	4	2	—	2	—	—
Willie West, Mia	S	2	—	—	2	—	—

SPECIALISTS	POS	TT	AP	NE	UP	NY	AL
Gino Cappelletti, Bos	K	3	—	—	—	—	1
George Blanda, Hou	K	2	—	—	—	—	2
Bob Scarpitto, Den	P	3	—	—	—	—	1
Jerrel Wilson, KC	P	2	—	—	—	—	2

1967 NFL

OFFENSE	POS	TT	+SN	AP	NE	UP	NY
Homer Jones, NYG	E	13	1	2	1	1	1
Charley Taylor, Was	E	11	—	1	1	1	2
Willie Richardson, Bal	E	11	1	1	2	2	1
Bob Hayes, Dal	E	11	1	2	2	2	1
Boyd Dowler, GB	E	2	1	—	—	—	—
John Mackey, Bal	TE	13	1	1	1	2	1
Jerry Smith, Was	TE	9	1	2	—	1	2
Jackie Smith, SL	TE	2	—	—	—	—	—
Ralph Neely, Dal	T	13	1	1	2	1	1
Forrest Gregg, GB	T	13	1	1	2	1	1
Ernie McMillan, SL	T	7	—	2	1	—	2
Bob Brown, Phi	T	6	1	2	—	—	—
Bob Vogel, Bal	T	5	1	—	1	—	—
Charley Cowan, LARm	T	4	—	—	—	2	—
Gene Hickerson, Cle	G	14	1	1	1	1	1
Jerry Kramer, GB	G	13	1	1	2	1	1
Ken Gray, SL	G	8	1	2	—	2	2
John Gordy, Det	G	8	—	2	2	—	2
Howard Mudd, SF	G	5	1	—	—	1	—
Mick Tingelhoff, Min	C	13	1	1	1	1	1
Bob DeMarco, SL	C	9	1	2	—	2	2
Johnny Unitas, Bal	QB	14	1	1	1	1	1

1967 NFL (CONT.)

OFFENSE	POS	TT	+SN	AP	NE	UP	NY
Sonny Jurgensen, Was	QB	10	1	2	2	2	2
Gale Sayers, ChiB	**RB**	14	1	1	1	1	1
Leroy Kelly, Cle	**RB**	14	1	1	1	1	1
Johnny Roland, SL	RB	10	1	2	2	2	2
Dave Osborn, Min	RB	6	1	—	2	2	—
Don Perkins, Dal	RB	4	—	2	—	—	2

DEFENSE	POS	TT	+SN	AP	NE	UP	NY
Deacon Jones, LARm	**DE**	14	1	1	1	1	1
Willie Davis, GB	**DE**	14	1	1	1	1	1
Ordell Braase, Bal	DE	8	—	2	2	2	2
Carl Eller, Min	DE	4	—	—	2	2	—
George Andrie, Dal	DE	4	1	2	—	—	—
Lamar Lundy, LARm	DE	2	—	—	—	—	2
Bill Glass, Cle	DE	2	1	—	—	—	—
Merlin Olsen, LARm	**DT**	14	1	1	1	1	1
Bob Lilly, Dal	**DT**	14	1	1	1	1	1
Alex Karras, Det	DT	10	1	2	2	2	2
Chuck Walker, SL	DT	4	—	2	—	2	—
Floyd Peters, Phi	DT	2	1	—	—	—	—
Fred Miller, Bal	DT	2	—	—	2	—	—
Henry Jordan, GB	DT	2	—	—	—	—	2
Dave Robinson, GB	**OLB**	14	1	1	1	1	1
Maxie Baughan, LARm	**OLB**	12	1	2	2	1	1
Chuck Howley, Dal	OLB	11	1	1	2	2	2
Dave Wilcox, SF	OLB	9	—	2	—	2	2
Andy Russell, Pit	OLB	2	—	—	—	—	2
Tommy Nobis, Atl	**MLB**	12	1	1	2	2	1
Dick Butkus, ChiB	MLB	6	—	—	1	1	—
Ray Nitschke, GB	MLB	4	—	2	—	—	2
Dale Meinert, SL	MLB	2	1	—	—	—	—
Cornell Green, Dal	**CB**	14	1	1	1	1	1
Bob Jeter, GB	**CB**	12	—	1	1	1	1
Herb Adderley, GB	CB	8	1	2	2	—	2
Dave Whitsell, NO	CB	6	1	2	—	2	—
Bobby Boyd, Bal	CB	4	1	—	—	—	—
Lem Barney, Det	CB	4	—	2	—	2	2
Willie Wood, GB	**S**	13	1	1	2	1	1
Larry Wilson, SL	**S**	13	1	1	1	2	1
Eddie Meador, LARm	S	12	1	2	1	1	2
Richie Petitbon, ChiB	S	8	—	2	2	2	2
Mel Renfro, Dal	S	2	1	—	—	—	—

SPECIALISTS	POS	TT	+SN	AP	NE	UP	NY
Don Chandler, GB	K	2	1	—	—	—	—
Jim Bakken, SL	K	2	1	—	—	—	—
Pat Studstill, Det	P	2	1	—	—	—	—
Gary Collins, Cle	P	2	1	—	—	—	—

1967 AFL

OFFENSE	POS	TT	+SN	AP	NE	UP	NY
Lance Alworth, SD	**E**	14	1	1	1	1	1
George Sauer, NYJ	**E**	13	1	1	2	1	1
Al Denson, Den	E	10	2	—	1	2	2
Don Maynard, NYJ	E	8	—	2	2	2	2
Otis Taylor, KC	E	1	2	—	—	—	—
Fred Arbanas, KC	**TE**	10	—	2	1	2	1
Billy Cannon, Oak	TE	9	2	1	—	1	2
Willie Frazier, SD	TE	4	1	—	2	—	—
Ron Mix, SD	**T**	13	2	1	1	1	1
Jim Tyrer, KC	**T**	12	1	1	2	2	1
Harry Schuh, Oak	T	11	2	2	1	1	2
Walt Suggs, Hou	T	8	1	2	2	2	—
Sherman Plunkett, NYJ	T	2	—	—	—	—	2
Walt Sweeney, SD	**G**	13	2	1	1	1	1
Bob Talamini, Hou	**G**	11	1	1	1	-1	—
Wayne Hawkins, Oak	G	7	2	—	—	2	2
Gene Upshaw, Oak	G	6	1	—	2	2	—
Ed Budde, KC	G	6	—	2	2	—	2
Dave Herman, NYJ	G	3	—	—	—	—	1
Jim Otto, Oak	**C**	14	1	1	1	1	1
Bobby Maples, Hou	C	6	—	2	—	2	2
Jon Morris, Bos	C	3	2	—	2	—	—
Daryle Lamonica, Oak	**QB**	12	1	1	2	1	2
Joe Namath, NYJ	QB	11	2	2	1	2	1
Mike Garrett, KC	**RB**	14	1	1	1	1	1
Jim Nance, Bos	**RB**	13	2	1	1	1	1
Hewritt Dixon, Oak	RB	8	1	—	—	2	2
Hoyle Granger, Hou	RB	6	—	2	2	2	—
Dickie Post, SD	RB	4	—	2	—	—	2
Emerson Boozer, NYJ	RB	1	2	—	—	—	—

DEFENSE	POS	TT	+SN	AP	NE	UP	NY
Ben Davidson, Oak	**DE**	13	1	1	2	1	1
Pat Holmes, Hou	**DE**	12	2	1	1	1	2
Ron McDole, Buf	DE	7	—	2	1	2	—
Jerry Mays, KC	DE	6	1	2	—	2	—
Gerry Philbin, NYJ	DE	5	—	—	2	—	1
Verlon Biggs, NYJ	DE	3	2	—	2	—	—
Buck Buchanan, KC	**DT**	14	1	1	1	1	1
Tom Keating, Oak	**DT**	13	1	1	1	1	2
Dave Costa, Den	DT	8	—	2	2	2	—
Houston Antwine, Bos	DT	8	2	2	—	2	1
Jim Hunt, Bos	DT	3	2	—	—	—	—
George Webster, Hou	**OLB**	14	1	1	1	1	1

1967 AFL (CONT.)

DEFENSE	POS	TT	+SN	AP	NE	UP	NY
Bobby Bell, KC	**OLB**	13	1	1	2	1	1
Mike Stratton, Buf	OLB	8	2	2	1	—	2
Larry Grantham, NYJ	OLB	4	—	2	—	—	2
Gus Otto, Oak	OLB	3	2	—	—	2	—
Bill Laskey, Oak	OLB	2	—	—	—	—	—
Frank Buncom, SD	OLB	2	—	—	—	—	—
Nick Buoniconti, Bos	**MLB**	13	1	1	2	1	1
Dan Conners, Oak	MLB	10	2	2	1	2	2
Kent McCloughan, Oak	**CB**	14	1	1	1	1	1
Miller Farr, Hou	**CB**	14	1	1	1	1	1
Speedy Duncan, SD	CB	7	2	2	2	—	2
Willie Brown, Oak	CB	7	2	2	—	2	2
Dick Westmoreland, Mia	CB	4	—	2	2	2	—
George Saimes, Buf	**S**	14	1	1	1	1	1
Johnny Robinson, KC	**S**	13	2	1	1	1	2
Jim Norton, Hou	S	6	—	2	—	2	—
Kenny Graham, SD	S	6	1	—	2	—	2
Rodger Bird, Oak	S	4	—	2	2	—	2
Don Webb, Bos	S	2	—	—	—	—	—
Jimmy Warren, Mia	S	1	2	—	—	—	—

SPECIALISTS	POS	TT	+SN	AP	NE	UP	NY
George Blanda, Oak	K	2	1	—	—	—	—
Jan Stenerud, KC	K	1	2	—	—	—	—
Bob Scarpitto, Den	P	2	1	—	—	—	—
Paul Maguire, Buf	P	1	2	—	—	—	—

1968 NFL

OFFENSE	POS	TT	+SN	AP	NE	UP	NY	FW	PW	*PW
Clifton McNeil, SF	**E**	20	1	1	1	1	1	1	1	—
Paul Warfield, Cle	**E**	11	—	2	1	1	—	1	1	1
Bob Hayes, Dal	E	10	1	1	—	2	1	—	—	—
Roy Jefferson, Pit	E	8	†1	2	2	2	—	—	—	—
Homer Jones, NYG	E	4	†1	—	—	—	2	—	—	—
Carroll Dale, GB	E	4	1	—	2	—	—	—	—	—
Charley Taylor, Was	E	2	—	—	—	2	—	—	—	—
Willie Richardson, Bal	E	2	—	—	—	—	2	—	—	—
Lance Rentzel, Dal	E	2	†1	—	—	—	—	—	—	—
John Mackey, Bal	**TE**	24	1	1	1	1	1	1	1	1
Jackie Smith, SL	TE	10	†1	2	2	2	2	—	—	—
Milt Morin, Cle	TE	2	†1	—	—	—	—	—	—	—
Ralph Neely, Dal	**T**	24	1	1	1	1	1	1	1	1
Bob Brown, Phi	**T**	17	1	1	1	2	2	1	—	—
Bob Vogel, Bal	T	15	1	2	2	1	1	—	—	1
Charley Cowan, LARm	T	6	1	2	—	—	2	—	—	—
Ernie McMillan, SL	T	4	—	—	2	—	2	—	—	—
Gene Hickerson, Cle	**G**	24	1	1	1	1	1	1	1	1
Howard Mudd, SF	**G**	17	1	1	1	1	1	1	1	—
Tom Mack, LARm	G	4	—	—	2	—	2	—	—	—
Ken Gray, SL	G	4	1	—	—	2	—	—	—	—
Gale Gillingham, GB	G	4	—	2	—	—	2	—	—	—
Dan Sullivan, Bal	G	2	1	—	—	—	—	—	—	—
George Seals, ChiB	G	2	—	2	—	—	—	—	—	—
Glenn Ressler, Bal	G	2	—	—	—	2	—	—	—	—
Jerry Kramer, GB	G	2	—	—	—	—	2	—	—	—
Pete Case, NYG	G	2	—	—	—	—	—	2	—	—
Mick Tingelhoff, Min	**C**	20	1	1	1	1	1	1	1	—
Bob DeMarco, SL	C	10	1	2	2	2	2	—	—	—
Earl Morrall, Bal	**QB**	19	1	1	1	1	2	1	1	—
Bill Nelsen, Cle	QB	6	1	2	2	—	1	—	—	—
Don Meredith, Dal	QB	2	—	2	—	—	—	—	—	—
Roman Gabriel, LARm	QB	2	—	—	—	2	—	—	—	—
Gale Sayers, ChiB	**RB**	24	1	1	1	1	1	1	1	1
Leroy Kelly, Cle	**RB**	24	1	1	1	1	1	1	1	1
Bill Brown, Min	RB	12	1	2	2	2	2	—	—	—
Ken Willard, SF	RB	4	—	—	—	—	2	—	—	—
Tom Woodeshick, Phi	RB	2	—	—	—	—	—	—	2	—
Don Perkins, Dal	RB	2	—	2	—	—	—	—	—	—
Dick Hoak, Pit	RB	2	1	—	—	—	—	—	—	—

DEFENSE	POS	TT	+SN	AP	NE	UP	NY	FW	PW	*PW
Deacon Jones, LARm	**DE**	24	1	1	1	1	1	1	1	1
Carl Eller, Min	**DE**	20	1	1	1	1	1	1	1	—
Bubba Smith, Bal	DE	8	—	2	—	2	2	2	—	—
Doug Atkins, NO	DE	6	1	2	2	—	—	—	—	—
George Andrie, Dal	DE	6	1	—	2	2	—	—	—	—
Jim Marshall, Min	DE	2	—	—	—	—	2	—	—	—
Merlin Olsen, LARm	**DT**	24	1	1	1	1	1	1	1	1
Bob Lilly, Dal	**DT**	24	1	1	1	1	1	1	1	1
Fred Miller, Bal	DT	6	—	2	—	2	2	—	—	—
Alex Karras, Det	DT	6	1	2	2	—	—	—	—	—
Billy Ray Smith, Bal	DT	2	2	—	—	—	—	—	—	—
Jethro Pugh, Dal	DT	2	—	—	2	—	—	—	—	—
Alan Page, Min	DT	2	—	—	—	2	—	—	—	—
Bob Lurtsema, NYG	DT	2	—	—	—	—	2	—	—	—
Walter Johnson, Cle	DT	2	—	—	—	—	—	2	—	—
Mike Curtis, Bal	**OLB**	21	—	1	2	1	1	1	1	1
Chuck Howley, Dal	**OLB**	17	1	1	1	2	2	1	—	—
Dave Robinson, GB	OLB	15	1	2	1	2	2	—	1	—
Maxie Baughan, LARm	OLB	6	1	2	—	—	2	—	—	—
Dave Wilcox, SF	OLB	4	—	—	2	—	2	—	—	—
Andy Russell, Pit	OLB	2	—	—	—	—	—	—	—	—
Chris Hanburger, Was	OLB	2	—	1	—	2	1	1	—	1
Dick Butkus, ChiB	**MLB**	21	1	1	2	1	1	1	1	1
Tommy Nobis, Atl	MLB	13	2	2	1	2	2	1	2	—

1968 NFL (CONT.)

DEFENSE	POS	TT	+SN	AP	NE	UP	NY	FW	PW	*PW
Lee Roy Jordan, Dal	MLB	2	1	—	—	—	—	—	—	—
Lem Barney, Det	**CB**	**24**	**1**	**1**	**1**	**1**	**1**	**1**	**1**	**1**
Bobby Boyd, Bal	**CB**	**17**	**†1**	**1**	—	**1**	**1**	**1**	**1**	—
Cornell Green, Dal	CB	13	1	2	1	2	2	2	—	—
Ben Davis, Cle	CB	4	†1	2	—	—	—	—	—	—
Kermit Alexander, SF	CB	4	—	—	—	2	2	—	—	—
Jimmy Johnson, SF	CB	2	—	—	2	—	—	—	—	—
Bob Jeter, GB	CB	2	—	—	2	—	—	—	—	—
Pat Fischer, Was	CB	2	†1	—	—	—	—	—	—	—
Erich Barnes, Cle	CB	2	†1	—	—	—	—	—	—	—
Herb Adderley, GB	CB	2	†1	—	—	—	—	—	—	—
Larry Wilson, SL	**S**	**24**	**1**	**1**	**1**	**1**	**1**	**1**	**1**	**1**
Willie Wood, GB	**S**	**15**	**1**	**2**	**2**	**1**	**1**	—	**1**	—
Eddie Meador, LARm	S	13	1	1	2	2	2	2	—	—
Rick Volk, Bal	S	8	—	—	1	2	—	1	—	—
Mel Renfro, Dal	S	2	†1	—	—	—	—	—	—	—
Jerry Logan, Bal	S	2	—	—	—	—	—	2	—	—
Spider Lockhart, NYG	S	2	†1	—	—	—	—	—	—	—
Paul Krause, Min	S	2	—	2	—	—	—	—	—	—

SPECIALISTS	POS	TT	+SN	AP	NE	UP	NY	FW	PW	*PW
Mac Percival, ChiB	K	2	1	—	—	—	—	—	—	—
Jim Bakken, SL	K	2	1	—	—	—	—	—	—	—
Billy Lothridge, Atl	P	5	1	—	—	—	—	1	—	—
Ron Widby, Dal	P	2	1	—	—	—	—	—	—	—

1968 AFL

OFFENSE	POS	TT	+SN	AP	NE	UP	NY	FW	PW	*PW
Lance Alworth, SD	**E**	**24**	**1**	**1**	**1**	**1**	**1**	**1**	**1**	**1**
George Sauer, NYJ	**E**	**23**	**1**	**1**	**1**	**1**	**2**	**1**	**1**	**1**
Don Maynard, NYJ	E	8	2	2	—	2	1	—	—	—
Karl Noonan, Mia	E	6	—	2	—	2	2	—	—	—
Gary Garrison, SD	E	1	2	—	—	—	—	—	—	—
Jim Whalen, Bos	**TE**	**14**	—	**1**	**1**	**1**	**2**	—	**1**	—
Alvin Reed, Hou	TE	9	1	2	—	2	1	—	—	—
Jacque MacKinnon, SD	TE	3	2	—	2	—	—	—	—	—
Billy Cannon, Oak	TE	2	—	—	—	—	—	2	—	—
Ron Mix, SD	**T**	**23**	**1**	**1**	**1**	**1**	**1**	**2**	**1**	**1**
Jim Tyrer, KC	**T**	**13**	**2**	**1**	**1**	**1**	—	—	**1**	—
Harry Schuh, Oak	T	9	—	2	2	2	1	—	—	—
Walt Suggs, Hou	T	8	1	2	2	2	—	—	—	—
Winston Hill, NYJ	T	3	2	—	—	—	2	—	—	—
Stew Barber, Buf	T	2	—	—	—	—	2	—	—	—
Walt Sweeney, SD	**G**	**21**	**1**	**1**	**1**	**1**	**1**	—	**1**	**1**
Gene Upshaw, Oak	**G**	**17**	**1**	**1**	**2**	**1**	**2**	**2**	**1**	—
Ed Budde, KC	G	10	2	2	2	2	1	—	—	—
Dave Herman, NYJ	G	5	—	—	1	—	2	—	—	—
Billy Shaw, Buf	G	3	2	2	—	—	—	—	—	—
Jim Otto, Oak	**C**	**20**	**1**	**1**	**1**	**1**	**2**	—	**1**	**1**
John Schmitt, NYJ	C	7	—	2	—	2	1	—	—	—
Bob Johnson, Cin	C	2	—	—	2	—	—	—	—	—
Jon Morris, Bos	C	1	2	—	—	—	—	—	—	—
Joe Namath, NYJ	**QB**	**24**	**1**	**1**	**1**	**1**	**1**	**1**	**1**	**1**
Len Dawson, KC	QB	4	—	2	—	2	—	—	—	—
Daryle Lamonica, Oak	QB	2	—	—	—	—	2	—	—	—
Bob Griese, Mia	QB	2	—	—	2	—	—	—	—	—
John Hadl, SD	QB	1	2	—	—	—	—	—	—	—
Paul Robinson, Cin	**RB**	**19**	**1**	**1**	**1**	**1**	**1**	**2**	**1**	—
Hewritt Dixon, Oak	**RB**	**17**	**1**	**1**	**1**	**1**	**1**	—	**1**	—
Dickie Post, SD	RB	9	2	2	2	2	2	—	—	—
Robert Holmes, KC	RB	7	2	2	2	2	—	—	—	—
Matt Snell, NYJ	RB	2	—	—	—	—	2	—	—	—

DEFENSE	POS	TT	+SN	AP	NE	UP	NY	FW	PW	*PW
Gerry Philbin, NYJ	**DE**	**23**	**1**	**1**	**1**	**1**	**1**	**2**	**1**	**1**
Rich Jackson, Den	**DE**	**12**	**2**	**1**	—	**1**	**2**	—	**1**	—
Ron McDole, Buf	DE	8	2	2	1	—	2	—	—	—
Jerry Mays, KC	DE	8	1	2	2	2	—	—	—	—
Ike Lassiter, Oak	DE	7	—	—	2	2	1	—	—	—
Buck Buchanan, KC	**DT**	**18**	**2**	**1**	**1**	**1**	**1**	**2**	**1**	—
Dan Birdwell, Oak	**DT**	**13**	**1**	**1**	**2**	**1**	—	—	**1**	—
Houston Antwine, Bos	DT	9	1	2	1	2	—	—	—	—
John Elliott, NYJ	DT	7	—	2	—	2	1	—	—	—
Dave Costa, Den	DT	3	2	—	2	—	—	—	—	—
Tom Sestak, Buf	DT	2	—	—	—	—	2	—	—	—
Jim Hunt, Bos	DT	2	—	—	—	—	2	—	—	—
George Webster, Hou	**OLB**	**24**	**1**	**1**	**1**	**1**	**1**	**1**	**1**	**1**
Bobby Bell, KC	**OLB**	**17**	**1**	**1**	**1**	**1**	**1**	—	**1**	—
Jim Lynch, KC	OLB	6	—	2	2	2	—	—	—	—
Mike Stratton, Buf	OLB	5	2	—	2	—	2	—	—	—
Larry Grantham, NYJ	OLB	4	—	2	—	—	2	—	—	—
Frank Buncom, Cin	OLB	2	—	—	—	2	—	—	—	—
Gus Otto, Oak	OLB	1	2	—	—	—	—	—	—	—
Dan Conners, Oak	**MLB**	**13**	—	**2**	**†2**	**1**	**1**	—	**1**	—
Willie Lanier, KC	MLB	9	2	1	1	—	2	—	—	—
Nick Buoniconti, Bos	MLB	4	1	—	—	2	—	—	—	—
Al Atkinson, NYJ	MLB	2	—	—	†2	—	—	—	—	—
Miller Farr, Hou	**CB**	**21**	**1**	**1**	**1**	**1**	**1**	—	**1**	**1**
Willie Brown, Oak	**CB**	**16**	**1**	**1**	**1**	**1**	—	**2**	**1**	—
Butch Byrd, Buf	CB	7	—	2	2	—	1	—	—	—
Johnny Sample, NYJ	CB	4	—	—	—	2	2	—	—	—
Leroy Mitchell, Bos	CB	4	—	2	—	2	—	—	—	—
Jimmy Warren, Mia	CB	3	2	—	2	—	—	—	—	—
Kent McCloughan, Oak	CB	3	2	—	—	—	2	—	—	—
Johnny Robinson, KC	**S**	**21**	**1**	**1**	**1**	**1**	**1**	—	**1**	**1**

1968 AFL (CONT.)

DEFENSE	POS	TT	+SN	AP	NE	UP	NY	FW	PW	*PW
Dave Grayson, Oak	**S**	**15**	**2**	**1**	**1**	**1**	**2**	—	**1**	—
Kenny Graham, SD	S	10	1	2	2	2	2	—	—	—
George Saimes, Buf	S	6	2	—	—	2	1	—	—	—
Jim Hudson, NYJ	S	5	—	2	—	—	1	—	—	—
Ken Houston, Hou	S	2	—	—	2	—	—	—	—	—

SPECIALISTS	POS	TT	+SN	AP	NE	UP	NY	FW	PW	*PW
Jim Turner, NYJ	K	7	2	—	—	—	—	1	1	—
Jan Stenerud, KC	K	4	1	—	—	—	—	2	—	—
Jerrel Wilson, KC	P	7	1	—	—	—	—	2	1	—
Curley Johnson, NYJ	P	1	2	—	—	—	—	—	—	—

1969 NFL

OFFENSE	POS	TT	+SN	AP	NE	UP	NY	PW	*HF	*FW	*NE	*PW
Paul Warfield, Cle	**E**	**19**	—	—	**1**	—	**2**	**1**	**1**	**2**	**1**	—
Roy Jefferson, Pit	**E**	**14**	**1**	**†1**	**1**	**1**	**1**	—	—	—	—	—
Gene Washington, Min	E	12	1	2	—	2	1	1	—	—	—	—
Gary Collins, Cle	E	9	—	1	—	1	—	—	—	2	—	—
Danny Abramowicz, NO	E	9	1	†1	—	2	2	—	—	—	—	—
Charley Taylor, Was	E	5	—	—	2	—	—	—	—	—	2	—
Lance Rentzel, Dal	E	4	—	2	2	—	—	—	—	—	—	—
Gene Washington, SF	E	2	1	—	—	—	—	—	—	—	—	—
Jerry Smith, Was	**TE**	**25**	**1**	**1**	**1**	**1**	**1**	**1**	—	**1**	**1**	—
Charlie Sanders, Det	TE	9	1	2	—	2	—	—	2	—	—	—
Jackie Smith, SL	TE	7	—	—	2	—	2	—	—	—	2	—
Bob Brown, LARm	**T**	**33**	**1**	**1**	**1**	**1**	**1**	**1**	**1**	**1**	**1**	**1**
Ralph Neely, Dal	**T**	**26**	**1**	**1**	**1**	**1**	**1**	**1**	**2**	**2**	**2**	—
Grady Alderman, Min	T	11	†1	2	2	2	—	—	—	2	—	—
Bob Vogel, Bal	T	6	†1	—	—	2	2	—	—	—	—	—
Dick Schafrath, Cle	T	2	1	—	—	—	—	—	—	—	—	—
Len Rohde, SF	T	2	—	—	2	—	—	—	—	—	—	—
Ernie McMillan, SL	T	2	—	—	—	—	2	—	—	—	—	—
Charley Cowan, LARm	T	2	—	2	—	—	—	—	—	—	—	—
Gene Hickerson, Cle	**G**	**24**	**1**	**1**	**2**	**1**	**1**	**1**	**1**	—	—	**1**
Tom Mack, LARm	**G**	**21**	**1**	**2**	**1**	**1**	**2**	—	**2**	**2**	**2**	—
John Niland, Dal	G	17	—	1	2	2	1	1	1	—	—	—
Gale Gillingham, GB	G	16	1	1	1	2	—	—	2	—	2	—
George Seals, ChiB	G	2	—	—	—	—	2	—	—	—	—	—
Ken Gray, SL	G	2	1	—	—	—	—	—	—	—	—	—
Mick Tingelhoff, Min	**C**	**33**	**1**	**1**	**1**	**1**	**1**	**1**	**1**	**1**	**1**	**1**
Bill Curry, Bal	C	4	—	2	—	2	—	—	—	—	—	—
Ken Iman, LARm	C	2	—	—	—	—	2	—	—	—	—	—
Ed Flanagan, Det	C	2	—	—	2	—	—	—	—	—	—	—
Bob DeMarco, SL	C	2	1	—	—	—	—	—	—	—	—	—
Gale Sayers, ChiB	**B**	**33**	**1**	**1**	**1**	**1**	**1**	**1**	**1**	**1**	**1**	**1**
Roman Gabriel, LARm	**QB**	**23**	**1**	**1**	**2**	**1**	**1**	**1**	**1**	**2**	—	—
Sonny Jurgensen, Was	QB	14	1	2	1	2	2	—	—	—	2	—
Calvin Hill, Dal	**RB**	**27**	**1**	**1**	**2**	**1**	**1**	**1**	**1**	**1**	**2**	—
Leroy Kelly, Cle	RB	19	—	2	1	2	2	—	2	2	1	—
Tom Woodeshick, Phi	RB	7	—	2	—	2	1	—	—	—	—	—
Tom Matte, Bal	RB	4	1	—	2	—	—	—	—	—	—	—

DEFENSE	POS	TT	+SN	AP	NE	UP	NY	PW	*HF	*FW	*NE	*PW
Deacon Jones, LARm	**DE**	**33**	**1**	**1**	**1**	**1**	**1**	**1**	**1**	**1**	**1**	**1**
Carl Eller, Min	**DE**	**33**	**1**	**1**	**1**	**1**	**1**	**1**	**1**	**1**	**1**	**1**
Jim Marshall, Min	DE	11	—	2	2	2	2	—	—	—	2	—
Claude Humphrey, Atl	DE	4	—	2	2	—	—	—	—	—	—	—
George Andrie, Dal	DE	4	1	—	—	2	—	—	—	—	—	—
Chuck Walker, SL	DE	2	†1	—	—	—	—	—	—	—	—	—
Ron Snidow, Cle	DE	2	†1	—	—	—	—	—	—	—	—	—
Jack Gregory, Cle	DE	2	—	—	—	—	2	—	—	—	—	—
Merlin Olsen, LARm	**DT**	**33**	**1**	**1**	**1**	**1**	**1**	**1**	**1**	**1**	**1**	**1**
Bob Lilly, Dal	**DT**	**28**	**1**	**1**	**1**	**2**	**1**	**1**	**1**	**1**	**1**	—
Alan Page, Min	DT	20	1	2	2	1	2	—	2	2	2	—
Alex Karras, Det	DT	6	—	2	2	2	—	—	—	—	—	—
Joe Greene, Pit	DT	4	1	—	—	—	2	—	—	—	—	—
Chuck Howley, Dal	**OLB**	**32**	**1**	**1**	**1**	**1**	**1**	**1**	**1**	**2**	**1**	**1**
Dave Robinson, GB	**OLB**	**24**	—	**1**	**1**	**1**	**1**	**1**	**2**	**2**	**2**	—
Chris Hanburger, Was	OLB	8	1	2	2	2	—	—	—	—	—	—
Mike Curtis, Bal	OLB	6	1	—	*2	—	2	—	—	—	—	—
Maxie Baughan, LARm	OLB	6	1	2	—	—	2	—	—	—	—	—
Dave Wilcox, SF	OLB	4	—	—	2	2	—	—	—	—	—	—
Dick Butkus, ChiB	**MLB**	**33**	**1**	**1**	**1**	**1**	**1**	**1**	**1**	**1**	**1**	**1**
Ray Nitschke, GB	MLB	6	—	—	—	—	—	—	—	2	2	—
Mike Lucci, Det	MLB	4	—	2	—	2	—	—	—	—	—	—
Lee Roy Jordan, Dal	MLB	4	1	—	—	—	2	—	—	—	—	—
Lem Barney, Det	**CB**	**33**	**1**	**1**	**1**	**1**	**1**	**1**	**1**	**1**	**1**	**1**
Jimmy Johnson, SF	**CB**	**18**	**1**	—	**1**	**2**	**2**	—	**2**	**2**	**2**	—
Herb Adderley, GB	CB	14	—	1	—	—	2	1	2	2	—	—
Bobby Bryant, Min	CB	12	—	2	2	2	1	—	—	—	2	—
Cornell Green, Dal	CB	9	1	2	2	1	—	—	—	—	—	—
Pat Fischer, Was	CB	2	1	—	—	—	—	—	—	—	—	—
Mel Renfro, Dal	**S**	**26**	**1**	**2**	**1**	—	**2**	**1**	**2**	**2**	**1**	**1**
Larry Wilson, SL	**S**	**25**	**1**	**1**	**1**	**1**	**1**	—	**1**	**1**	**2**	—
Eddie Meador, LARm	S	17	1	1	—	1	1	1	—	2	—	—
Willie Wood, GB	S	4	1	—	2	—	—	—	—	—	—	—
Rick Volk, Bal	S	2	—	—	2	—	—	—	—	—	—	—
Paul Krause, Min	S	2	—	2	—	—	—	—	—	—	—	—
Ernie Kellermann, Cle	S	2	—	—	—	—	2	—	—	—	—	—
Karl Kassulke, Min	S	2	—	—	—	2	—	—	—	—	—	—
Mike Howell, Cle	S	2	—	—	—	2	—	—	—	—	—	—

* Received for MLB

SPECIALISTS	POS	TT	+SN	AP	NE	UP	NY	PW	*HF	*FW	*NE	*PW
Fred Cox, Min	K	5	1	—	—	—	—	1	—	—	—	—
Tom Dempsey, NO	K	2	1	—	—	—	—	—	—	—	—	—
David Lee, Bal	**P**	**17**	**1**	—	—	—	—	**1**	**1**	**1**	**1**	—
Ron Widby, Dal	P	5	1	—	—	—	—	—	—	2	—	—

1969 AFL

OFFENSE	POS	TT	AP	NE	UP	NY	SN	PW	*HF	*FW	*NE	*PW
Fred Biletnikoff, Oak	**E**	**32**	**1**	**1**	**2**	**1**	**1**	**1**	**2**	**1**	**1**	**1**
Lance Alworth, SD	**E**	**30**	**2**	**1**	**1**	**2**	**1**	**1**	**2**	**1**	**2**	**1**
Don Maynard, NYJ	E	20	1	2	2	1	2	—	1	1	—	—
Warren Wells, Oak	E	7	2	2	1	—	—	—	—	—	—	—
Al Denson, Den	E	4	—	—	—	2	2	—	—	—	—	—
Bob Trumpy, Cin	**TE**	**28**	**1**	**1**	**1**	**1**	**2**	**1**	**1**	**2**	**—**	**1**
Alvin Reed, Hou	TE	11	2	2	2	2	1	—	—	—	—	—
Jim Tyrer, KC	**T**	**33**	**1**	**1**	**1**	**1**	**1**	**1**	**1**	**1**	**2**	**1**
Harry Schuh, Oak	**T**	**18**	**1**	**2**	**1**	**2**	**2**	**1**	**2**	**—**	**—**	**—**
Winston Hill, NYJ	T	17	2	1	2	1	1	—	—	—	1	—
Walt Suggs, Hou	T	8	2	2	2	2	—	—	—	—	—	—
Dave Hill, KC	T	2	—	—	—	—	2	—	—	—	—	—
Ed Budde, KC	**G**	**24**	**1**	**1**	**2**	**1**	**1**	**1**	**—**	**2**	**1**	**—**
Gene Upshaw, Oak	**G**	**21**	**1**	**2**	**1**	**1**	**1**	**—**	**2**	**1**	**—**	**—**
Walt Sweeney, SD	**G**	**21**	**2**	**1**	**1**	**2**	**—**	**1**	**—**	**—**	**1**	**1**
Mo Moorman, KC	G	4	2	—	—	—	2	—	—	—	—	—
Dave Herman, NYJ	G	4	—	—	2	2	—	—	—	—	—	—
Billy Shaw, Buf	G	2	—	2	—	—	—	—	—	—	—	—
Sonny Bishop, Hou	G	2	—	—	—	—	2	—	—	—	—	—
Jim Otto, Oak	**C**	**27**	**1**	**1**	**1**	**1**	**1**	**1**	**2**	**2**	**2**	**—**
John Schmitt, NYJ	C	8	†2	—	2	2	2	—	—	—	—	—
Jon Morris, Bos	C	4	†2	2	—	—	—	—	—	—	—	—
E.J. Holub, KC	C	2	†2	—	—	—	—	—	—	—	—	—
Daryle Lamonica, Oak	**QB**	**27**	**1**	**2**	**1**	**2**	**1**	**1**	**2**	**1**	**—**	**1**
Joe Namath, NYJ	QB	16	2	1	2	1	2	—	—	—	1	—
Matt Snell, NYJ	**RB**	**25**	**1**	**1**	**1**	**1**	**1**	**1**	**—**	**—**	**2**	**1**
Floyd Little, Den	**RB**	**24**	**1**	**1**	**1**	**1**	**1**	**1**	**2**	**2**	**—**	**—**
Dickie Post, SD	RB	8	2	—	2	2	2	—	—	—	—	—
Jim Nance, Bos	RB	8	2	—	2	2	2	—	—	—	—	—
Mike Garrett, KC	RB	2	—	2	—	—	—	—	—	—	—	—
Carl Garrett, Bos	RB	2	—	2	—	—	—	—	—	—	—	—

DEFENSE	POS	TT	AP	NE	UP	NY	SN	PW	*HF	*FW	*NE	*PW
Rich Jackson, Den	**DE**	**27**	**1**	**1**	**1**	**1**	**1**	**1**	**2**	**2**	**2**	**—**
Gerry Philbin, NYJ	**DE**	**23**	**1**	**2**	**1**	**1**	**1**	**1**	**2**	**2**	**—**	**—**
Ike Lassiter, Oak	DE	6	2	—	2	2	—	—	—	—	—	—
Jerry Mays, KC	DE	4	2	—	—	—	2	—	—	—	—	—
Aaron Brown, KC	DE	4	—	—	—	2	2	—	—	—	—	—
Ron McDole, Buf	DE	3	—	1	—	—	—	—	—	—	—	—
Steve DeLong, SD	DE	2	—	2	—	—	—	—	—	—	—	—
Elvin Bethea, Hou	DE	2	—	—	2	—	—	—	—	—	—	—
Buck Buchanan, KC	**DT**	**24**	**1**	**2**	**1**	**1**	**1**	**1**	**2**	**—**	**—**	**1**
John Elliott, NYJ	**DT**	**20**	**1**	**1**	**1**	**1**	**2**	**1**	**—**	**2**	**—**	**—**
Tom Keating, Oak	DT	12	2	1	2	2	—	—	—	—	2	—
Houston Antwine, Bos	DT	5	2	—	—	—	1	—	—	—	—	—
Jim Dunaway, Buf	DT	4	—	2	—	2	—	—	—	—	—	—
Dave Costa, Den	DT	4	—	—	2	—	2	—	—	—	—	—
Bobby Bell, KC	**OLB**	**34**	**1**	**1**	**1**	**1**	**1**	**1**	**1**	**1**	**1**	**1**
George Webster, Hou	**OLB**	**28**	**1**	**1**	**1**	**1**	**1**	**1**	**2**	**1**	**2**	**—**
Jim Lynch, KC	OLB	6	2	2	2	—	—	—	—	—	—	—
Larry Grantham, NYJ	OLB	6	—	—	2	2	2	—	—	—	—	—
Mike Stratton, Buf	OLB	4	—	2	—	2	—	—	—	—	—	—
Gus Otto, Oak	OLB	4	†2	—	—	—	2	—	—	—	—	—
Pete Barnes, SD	OLB	2	†2	—	—	—	—	—	—	—	—	—
Willie Lanier, KC	**MLB**	**15**	**—**	**2**	**2**	**1**	**†2**	**1**	**2**	**—**	**—**	**—**
Nick Buoniconti, Mia	MLB	11	1	1	1	—	†2	—	—	—	—	—
Dan Conners, Oak	MLB	7	2	—	—	2	1	—	—	—	—	—
Willie Brown, Oak	**CB**	**34**	**1**	**1**	**1**	**1**	**1**	**1**	**1**	**1**	**1**	**1**
Butch Byrd, Buf	**CB**	**17**	**1**	**1**	**1**	**1**	**2**	**1**	**—**	**—**	**—**	**—**
Miller Farr, Hou	CB	11	2	2	2	2	1	—	—	—	—	—
Bill Thompson, Den	CB	4	2	2	—	—	—	—	—	—	—	—
Booker Edgerson, Buf	CB	4	—	—	2	2	—	—	—	—	—	—
Emmitt Thomas, KC	CB	2	—	—	—	—	2	—	—	—	—	—
Dave Grayson, Oak	**S**	**32**	**1**	**1**	**1**	**2**	**1**	**1**	**2**	**1**	**1**	**1**
Johnny Robinson, KC	**S**	**25**	**1**	**1**	**1**	**1**	**1**	**1**	**1**	**—**	**2**	**—**
Ken Houston, Hou	S	11	2	2	2	1	2	—	—	—	—	—
Kenny Graham, SD	S	8	2	—	2	2	2	—	—	—	—	—
George Atkinson, Oak	S	2	—	2	—	—	—	—	—	—	—	—

SPECIALISTS	POS	TT	AP	NE	UP	NY	SN	PW	*HF	*FW	*NE	*PW
Jan Stenerud, KC	**K**	**17**	**—**	**—**	**—**	**—**	**1**	**1**	**1**	**2**	**1**	**—**
Jim Turner, NYJ	K	9	—	—	—	—	2	—	2	1	—	—
Paul Maguire, Buf	P	6	—	—	—	—	—	1	2	—	—	—
Dennis Partee, SD	P	3	—	—	—	—	1	—	—	—	—	—
Larry Seiple, Mia	P	2	—	—	—	—	2	—	—	—	—	—

1970 NFL

OFFENSE	POS	TT	+AP	+SN	+PW	+UP	AP	NE	FW	PW
Gene Washington, SF	**WR**	**20**	**1**	**1**	**1**	**1**	**1**	**1**	**1**	**1**
Dick Gordon, ChiB	**WR**	**20**	**1**	**1**	**1**	**1**	**1**	**1**	**1**	**1**
Marlin Briscoe, Buf	WR	10	1	†1	1	1	—	—	2	—
Warren Wells, Oak	WR	8	—	†1	1	1	—	2	—	—
Fred Biletnikoff, Oak	WR	5	1	—	—	2	—	—	2	—
Paul Warfield, Mia	WR	4	—	1	—	—	—	2	—	—
Charley Taylor, Was	WR	1	—	—	—	2	—	—	—	—
Clifton McNeil, NYG	WR	1	—	—	—	2	—	—	—	—
Gary Garrison, SD	WR	1	—	—	—	2	—	—	—	—
Charlie Sanders, Det	**TE**	**20**	**1**	**1**	**1**	**1**	**1**	**1**	**1**	**1**
Bob Trumpy, Cin	TE	8	1	1	—	—	—	2	2	—
Alvin Reed, Hou	TE	4	—	—	1	1	—	—	—	—
Jackie Smith, SL	TE	1	—	—	—	2	—	—	—	—
Raymond Chester, Oak	TE	1	—	—	—	2	—	—	—	—
Jim Tyrer, KC	**T**	**20**	**1**	**1**	**1**	**1**	**1**	**1**	**1**	**1**
Bob Brown, LARm	**T**	**18**	**1**	**—**	**1**	**1**	**1**	**1**	**1**	**1**
Winston Hill, NYJ	T	10	1	1	—	1	—	2	2	—

1970 NFL (CONT.)

OFFENSE	POS	TT	+AP	+SN	+PW	+UP	AP	NE	FW	PW
Ernie McMillan, SL	T	6	—	1	—	1	—	2	—	—
Ron Yary, Min	T	4	—	1	—	—	—	—	2	—
Harry Schuh, Oak	T	3	—	—	1	2	—	—	—	—
Rocky Freitas, Det	T	3	—	—	1	2	—	—	—	—
Cas Banaszek, SF	T	3	1	—	—	2	—	—	—	—
Bob Vogel, Bal	T	1	—	—	—	2	—	—	—	—
Gene Upshaw, Oak	**G**	**16**	**1**	**1**	**1**	**2**	**1**	**—**	**1**	**1**
Gale Gillingham, GB	**G**	**16**	**1**	**1**	**1**	**1**	**1**	**1**	**2**	**—**
Tom Mack, LARm	G	13	—	1	1	1	—	2	2	1
Walt Sweeney, SD	G	8	1	—	1	2	—	1	—	—
Gene Hickerson, Cle	G	5	—	—	—	1	—	—	1	—
Ed Budde, KC	G	4	—	1	—	1	—	—	—	—
John Niland, Dal	G	3	1	—	—	2	—	—	—	—
Irv Goode, SL	G	3	—	—	—	2	—	2	—	—
Jim Otto, Oak	**C**	**14**	**1**	**1**	**1**	**1**	**1**	**1**	**—**	**—**
Mick Tingelhoff, Min	C	13	1	—	1	2	—	2	1	1
Ed Flanagan, Det	C	6	—	1	—	1	—	—	2	—
Bob Johnson, Cin	C	1	—	—	—	2	—	—	—	—
John Brodie, SF	**QB**	**20**	**1**	**1**	**1**	**1**	**1**	**1**	**1**	**1**
Daryle Lamonica, Oak	QB	6	1	—	1	1	—	—	—	—
Bob Griese, Mia	QB	4	—	1	—	—	—	2	—	—
Fran Tarkenton, NYG	QB	2	—	—	—	—	—	—	2	—
Johnny Unitas, Bal	QB	1	—	—	—	2	—	—	—	—
Larry Brown, Was	**RB**	**20**	**1**	**1**	**1**	**1**	**1**	**1**	**1**	**1**
Ron Johnson, NYG	**RB**	**16**	**1**	**—**	**1**	**2**	**1**	**2**	**1**	**1**
Floyd Little, Den	RB	8	1	1	1	—	—	—	2	—
MacArthur Lane, SL	RB	7	—	1	—	—	—	1	2	—
Mel Farr, Det	RB	3	—	—	—	2	—	2	—	—
Larry Csonka, Mia	RB	3	—	—	1	2	—	—	—	—
Jess Phillips, Cin	RB	2	—	1	—	—	—	—	—	—
Hewritt Dixon, Oak	RB	2	1	—	—	—	—	—	—	—
Ed Podolak, KC	RB	1	—	—	—	2	—	—	—	—

DEFENSE	POS	TT	+AP	+SN	+PW	+UP	AP	NE	FW	PW
Carl Eller, Min	**DE**	**20**	**1**	**1**	**1**	**1**	**1**	**1**	**1**	**1**
Rich Jackson, Den	**DE**	**17**	**1**	**1**	**1**	**1**	**1**	**1**	**1**	**—**
Deacon Jones, LARm	DE	13	—	1	1	1	—	2	2	1
Claude Humphrey, Atl	DE	7	1	—	1	2	—	2	—	—
Bubba Smith, Bal	DE	6	—	1	—	1	—	—	2	—
Aaron Brown, KC	DE	2	1	—	—	—	—	—	—	—
Jerry Mays, KC	DE	1	—	—	—	2	—	—	—	—
Larry Hand, Det	DE	1	—	—	—	2	—	—	—	—
Jack Gregory, Cle	DE	1	—	—	—	2	—	—	—	—
Alan Page, Min	**DT**	**20**	**1**	**1**	**1**	**1**	**1**	**1**	**1**	**1**
Merlin Olsen, LARm	**DT**	**20**	**1**	**1**	**1**	**1**	**1**	**1**	**1**	**1**
John Elliott, NYJ	DT	8	1	—	1	1	—	—	2	—
Bob Lilly, Dal	DT	5	—	—	—	2	—	2	2	—
Tom Keating, Oak	DT	5	—	1	1	2	—	—	—	—
Joe Greene, Pit	DT	4	—	1	—	1	—	—	—	—
Buck Buchanan, KC	DT	3	1	—	—	2	—	—	—	—
Manny Fernandez, Mia	DT	2	—	—	—	—	—	2	—	—
Charlie Krueger, SF	DT	1	—	—	—	2	—	—	—	—
Bobby Bell, KC	**OLB**	**20**	**1**	**1**	**1**	**1**	**1**	**1**	**1**	**1**
Chuck Howley, Dal	**OLB**	**19**	**1**	**1**	**1**	**1**	**1**	**2**	**1**	**1**
Andy Russell, Pit	OLB	10	1	1	1	1	—	2	—	—
Paul Naumoff, Det	OLB	6	1	—	1	—	—	—	2	—
Dave Wilcox, SF	OLB	4	—	—	—	2	—	1	—	—
Larry Stallings, SL	OLB	2	—	—	—	1	—	—	—	—
Gus Otto, Oak	OLB	2	—	—	—	—	—	—	2	—
Chris Hanburger, Was	OLB	2	—	1	—	—	—	—	—	—
Ron Pritchard, Hou	OLB	1	—	—	—	2	—	—	—	—
Paul Guidry, Buf	OLB	1	—	—	—	2	—	—	—	—
Fred Carr, GB	OLB	1	—	—	—	2	—	—	—	—
Dick Butkus, ChiB	**MLB**	**20**	**1**	**1**	**1**	**1**	**1**	**1**	**1**	**1**
Willie Lanier, KC	MLB	12	1	1	1	1	—	2	2	—
Mike Lucci, Det	MLB	1	—	—	—	2	—	—	—	—
Mike Curtis, Bal	MLB	1	—	—	—	2	—	—	—	—
Jimmy Johnson, SF	**CB**	**20**	**1**	**1**	**1**	**1**	**1**	**1**	**1**	**1**
Jim Marsalis, KC	**CB**	**16**	**1**	**1**	**1**	**1**	**1**	**—**	**2**	**1**
Willie Brown, Oak	CB	13	1	1	1	1	—	2	1	—
Roger Wehrli, SL	CB	9	—	1	1	1	—	1	—	—
Lem Barney, Det	CB	3	—	—	—	2	—	2	—	—
Mel Renfro, Dal	CB	2	1	—	—	—	—	—	—	—
Dick LeBeau, Det	CB	2	—	—	—	—	—	—	2	—
Emmitt Thomas, KC	CB	1	—	—	—	2	—	—	—	—
Bruce Taylor, SF	CB	1	—	—	—	2	—	—	—	—
Kent McCloughan, Oak	CB	1	—	—	—	2	—	—	—	—
Larry Wilson, SL	**S**	**20**	**1**	**1**	**1**	**1**	**1**	**1**	**1**	**1**
Johnny Robinson, KC	**S**	**20**	**1**	**1**	**1**	**1**	**1**	**1**	**1**	**1**
Spider Lockhart, NYG	S	7	1	—	1	2	—	—	2	—
Willie Wood, GB	S	5	—	1	—	2	—	2	—	—
Ken Houston, Hou	S	5	—	—	1	2	—	2	—	—
Jerry Logan, Bal	S	4	1	—	—	1	—	—	—	—
Dave Grayson, Oak	S	3	—	—	—	2	—	—	2	—
Rick Volk, Bal	S	2	—	1	—	—	—	—	—	—
Paul Krause, Min	S	2	—	—	—	1	—	—	—	—

SPECIALISTS	POS	TT	+AP	+SN	+PW	+UP	AP	NE	FW	PW
Jan Stenerud, KC	K	10	1	1	—	—	1	—	1	—
Fred Cox, Min	K	4	1	1	—	—	—	—	—	—
George Blanda, Oak	K	2	—	—	—	—	—	—	2	—
Dave Lewis, Cin	P	8	1	—	—	—	1	—	1	—
David Lee, Bal	P	4	—	1	—	—	—	—	2	—
Julian Fagan, NO	P	4	1	1	—	—	—	—	—	—

1971 NFL

OFFENSE	POS	TT	+AP	+SN	+PW	+UP	AP	NE	FW	PW
Paul Warfield, Mia	**WR**	**20**	**1**	**1**	**1**	**1**	**1**	**1**	**1**	**1**
Otis Taylor, KC	**WR**	**20**	**1**	**1**	**1**	**1**	**1**	**1**	**1**	**1**
Gene Washington, SF	WR	12	1	1	1	1	—	2	2	—
Roy Jefferson, Was	WR	5	1	—	1	2	—	—	—	—
Fred Biletnikoff, Oak	WR	5	—	—	—	2	—	2	2	—
Bob Grim, Min	WR	4	—	1	—	1	—	—	—	—
Dick Gordon, ChiB	WR	1	—	—	—	2	—	—	—	—
Gary Garrison, SD	WR	1	—	—	—	2	—	—	—	—
Charlie Sanders, Det	**TE**	**20**	**1**	**1**	**1**	**1**	**1**	**1**	**1**	**1**
Ted Kwalick, SF	TE	5	—	—	—	2	—	2	2	—
Raymond Chester, Oak	TE	5	—	1	1	2	—	—	—	—
Milt Morin, Cle	TE	4	1	—	—	1	—	—	—	—
Ron Yary, Min	**T**	**20**	**1**	**1**	**1**	**1**	**1**	**1**	**1**	**1**
Jim Tyrer, KC	**T**	**15**	**1**	**1**	**1**	**1**	—	**2**	**2**	**1**
Bob Brown, Oak	T	10	1	1	—	2	—	1	2	—
Rayfield Wright, Dal	T	9	1	—	—	2	1	—	1	—
Winston Hill, NYJ	T	4	—	—	—	1	—	2	—	—
Bob Vogel, Bal	T	3	—	—	1	2	—	—	—	—
Cas Banaszek, SF	T	3	—	—	1	2	—	—	—	—
Ernie McMillan, SL	T	2	—	—	—	1	—	—	—	—
Charley Cowan, LARm	T	2	—	1	—	—	—	—	—	—
Larry Little, Mia	**G**	**17**	**1**	**1**	**1**	**1**	**1**	—	**1**	**1**
John Niland, Dal	**G**	**16**	**1**	**1**	**1**	**2**	**1**	—	**1**	**1**
Gale Gillingham, GB	G	11	—	1	1	1	—	1	2	—
Tom Mack, LARm	G	9	1	—	—	1	—	1	2	—
Gene Upshaw, Oak	G	7	—	1	1	2	—	2	—	—
Walt Sweeney, SD	G	6	1	—	—	1	—	2	—	—
Woody Peoples, SF	G	1	—	—	—	2	—	—	—	—
Ed Budde, KC	G	1	—	—	—	2	—	—	—	—
Forrest Blue, SF	**C**	**15**	**1**	—	**1**	**1**	**1**	—	**1**	**1**
Bill Curry, Bal	C	10	1	—	1	1	—	2	2	—
Jim Otto, Oak	C	5	—	1	—	—	—	1	—	—
Len Hauss, Was	C	3	—	†1	—	2	—	—	—	—
Ed Flanagan, Det	C	2	—	†1	—	—	—	—	—	—
Bob DeMarco, Mia	C	1	—	—	—	2	—	—	—	—
Bob Griese, Mia	**QB**	**20**	**1**	**1**	**1**	**1**	**1**	**1**	**1**	**1**
Roger Staubach, Dal	QB	11	1	1	1	2	—	2	2	—
Greg Landry, Det	QB	2	—	—	—	1	—	—	—	—
Len Dawson, KC	QB	1	—	—	—	2	—	—	—	—
John Brockington, GB	**RB**	**20**	**1**	**1**	**1**	**1**	**1**	**1**	**1**	**1**
Larry Csonka, Mia	**RB**	**16**	**1**	**1**	**1**	**1**	**1**	**2**	**1**	—
Floyd Little, Den	RB	13	1	1	1	1	—	—	2	1
Larry Brown, Was	RB	8	—	1	1	1	—	2	—	—
Leroy Kelly, Cle	RB	6	—	—	—	2	—	1	2	—
Steve Owens, Det	RB	3	1	—	—	2	—	—	—	—
Willie Ellison, LARm	RB	1	—	—	—	2	—	—	—	—
Norm Bulaich, Bal	RB	1	—	—	—	2	—	—	—	—

DEFENSE	POS	TT	+AP	+SN	+PW	+UP	AP	NE	FW	PW
Carl Eller, Min	**DE**	**20**	**1**	**1**	**1**	**1**	**1**	**1**	**1**	**1**
Bubba Smith, Bal	**DE**	**19**	**1**	**1**	**1**	**1**	**1**	**2**	**1**	**1**
Claude Humphrey, Atl	DE	13	1	1	1	1	—	1	2	—
Cedrick Hardman, SF	DE	3	—	—	—	2	—	—	2	—
Aaron Brown, KC	DE	3	1	—	—	2	—	—	—	—
Elvin Bethea, Hou	DE	3	—	—	1	2	—	—	—	—
Bill Stanfill, Mia	DE	2	—	—	—	1	—	—	—	—
Rich Jackson, Den	DE	2	—	1	—	—	—	—	—	—
Coy Bacon, LARm	DE	2	—	—	—	—	—	2	—	—
Jim Marshall, Min	DE	1	—	—	—	2	—	—	—	—
Alan Page, Min	**DT**	**20**	**1**	**1**	**1**	**1**	**1**	**1**	**1**	**1**
Bob Lilly, Dal	**DT**	**20**	**1**	**1**	**1**	**1**	**1**	**1**	**1**	**1**
Joe Greene, Pit	DT	12	1	1	1	1	—	2	2	—
Mike Reid, Cin	DT	6	1	†1	—	1	—	—	—	—
Buck Buchanan, KC	DT	5	—	—	1	2	—	2	—	—
Manny Fernandez, Mia	DT	3	—	†1	—	2	—	—	—	—
Curley Culp, KC	DT	2	—	—	—	—	—	—	2	—
Merlin Olsen, LARm	DT	1	—	—	—	2	—	—	—	—
Robert Brown, GB	DT	1	—	—	—	2	—	—	—	—
Ted Hendricks, Bal	**OLB**	**20**	**1**	**1**	**1**	**1**	**1**	**1**	**1**	**1**
Dave Wilcox, SF	**OLB**	**17**	**1**	**1**	**1**	**1**	**1**	**1**	**1**	—
Bobby Bell, KC	OLB	15	1	1	1	1	—	2	2	1
Jack Pardee, Was	OLB	6	1	—	1	1	—	—	—	—
Isiah Robertson, LARm	OLB	5	—	1	—	2	—	2	—	—
Chuck Howley, Dal	OLB	3	—	—	—	2	—	—	2	—
Ron Pritchard, Hou	OLB	1	—	—	—	2	—	—	—	—
Larry Grantham, NYJ	OLB	1	—	—	—	2	—	—	—	—
Willie Lanier, KC	**MLB**	**20**	**1**	**1**	**1**	**1**	**1**	**1**	**1**	**1**
Dick Butkus, ChiB	MLB	10	1	—	1	1	—	2	2	—
Mike Lucci, Det	MLB	3	—	1	—	2	—	—	—	—
Mike Curtis, Bal	MLB	1	—	—	—	2	—	—	—	—
Jimmy Johnson, SF	**CB**	**20**	**1**	**1**	**1**	**1**	**1**	**1**	**1**	**1**
Willie Brown, Oak	**CB**	**19**	**1**	**1**	**1**	**1**	**1**	**2**	**1**	**1**
Roger Wehrli, SL	CB	8	—	1	1	1	—	2	—	—
Mel Renfro, Dal	CB	8	1	—	—	2	—	1	2	—
Emmitt Thomas, KC	CB	7	1	—	1	2	—	—	2	—
Jim Marsalis, KC	CB	4	—	1	—	1	—	—	—	—
Earlie Thomas, NYJ	CB	1	—	—	—	2	—	—	—	—
Dick LeBeau, Det	CB	1	—	—	—	2	—	—	—	—
Bill Bradley, Phi	**S**	**17**	**1**	**†1**	**1**	**1**	**1**	—	**1**	**1**
Rick Volk, Bal	**S**	**14**	**1**	—	**1**	**2**	**1**	**1**	**1**	—
Ken Houston, Hou	S	13	—	†1	1	1	—	2	2	1
Paul Krause, Min	S	9	—	1	1	1	—	1	—	—
Jake Scott, Mia	S	8	1	—	—	1	—	2	2	—
Jerry Logan, Bal	S	3	—	†1	—	2	—	—	—	—
Willie Wood, GB	S	2	—	†1	—	—	—	—	—	—

1971 NFL (CONT.)

DEFENSE	POS	TT	+AP	+SN	+PW	+UP	AP	NE	FW	PW
Johnny Robinson, KC	S	2	—	1	—	—	—	—	—	—
Cornell Green, Dal	S	2	1	—	—	—	—	—	—	—
Larry Wilson, SL	S	1	—	—	—	2	—	—	—	—
Richie Petitbon, Was	S	1	—	—	—	2	—	—	—	—

SPECIALISTS	POS	TT	+AP	+SN	+PW	+UP	AP	NE	FW	PW
Garo Yepremian, Mia	**K**	**14**	**1**	**1**	**1**	—	**1**	**2**	**†1**	—
Curt Knight, Was	K	7	1	1	—	—	—	1	—	—
Jan Stenerud, KC	K	3	—	—	—	—	—	—	†1	—
Fred Cox, Min	K	2	—	—	1	—	—	—	—	—
Jerrel Wilson, KC	P	7	—	1	1	—	—	—	1	—
Ron Widby, Dal	P	2	—	1	—	—	—	—	—	—
Tom McNeill, Phi	P	2	—	—	1	—	—	—	—	—
Dave Lewis, Cin	P	2	—	—	—	—	—	—	2	—

1972 NFL

OFFENSE	POS	TT	+AP	+SN	+PW	+UP	AP	NE	FW	PW
Gene Washington, SF	**WR**	**19**	**1**	**1**	**1**	**1**	**1**	**2**	**1**	**1**
Fred Biletnikoff, Oak	**WR**	**19**	**1**	**1**	**1**	**1**	**1**	**1**	**2**	**1**
Harold Jackson, Phi	WR	12	1	1	—	1	2	2	2	—
Paul Warfield, Mia	WR	10	1	1	—	2	2	1	—	—
Otis Taylor, KC	WR	5	—	—	—	1	—	—	1	—
Charley Taylor, Was	WR	1	—	—	—	2	—	—	—	—
John Gilliam, Min	WR	1	—	—	—	2	—	—	—	—
Gary Garrison, SD	WR	1	—	—	—	2	—	—	—	—
Ted Kwalick, SF	**TE**	**17**	**1**	—	**1**	**1**	**1**	**1**	**2**	**1**
Bob Tucker, NYG	TE	8	—	1	—	2	2	—	1	—
Raymond Chester, Oak	TE	6	1	1	—	1	—	—	—	—
Jim Mitchell, Atl	TE	2	—	—	—	—	—	2	—	—
Rich Caster, NYJ	TE	1	—	—	—	2	—	—	—	—
Rayfield Wright, Dal	**T**	**20**	**1**	**1**	**1**	**1**	**1**	**1**	**1**	**1**
Bob Brown, Oak	**T**	**16**	**1**	**1**	**1**	**1**	**2**	—	**1**	**1**
Ron Yary, Min	T	13	1	1	—	1	1	2	2	—
Winston Hill, NYJ	T	10	1	1	—	1	—	2	2	—
George Kunz, Atl	T	4	—	—	—	2	—	1	—	—
Rocky Freitas, Det	T	3	—	—	—	2	2	—	—	—
Art Shell, Oak	T	1	—	—	—	2	—	—	—	—
Terry Owens, SD	T	1	—	—	—	2	—	—	—	—
Larry Little, Mia	**G**	**20**	**1**	**1**	**1**	**1**	**1**	**1**	**1**	**1**
John Niland, Dal	**G**	**18**	**1**	**1**	**1**	**1**	**1**	**2**	**2**	**1**
Tom Mack, LARm	G	10	1	1	—	1	2	2	—	—
Gene Upshaw, Oak	G	9	1	—	—	1	2	—	1	—
Bruce Van Dyke, Pit	G	5	—	1	—	2	—	—	2	—
Blaine Nye, Dal	G	3	—	—	—	—	—	1	—	—
John Wilbur, Was	G	1	—	—	—	2	—	—	—	—
Randy Rasmussen, NYJ	G	1	—	—	—	2	—	—	—	—
Woody Peoples, SF	G	1	—	—	—	2	—	—	—	—
Forrest Blue, SF	**C**	**19**	**1**	**1**	**1**	**1**	**1**	**2**	**1**	**1**
Jim Otto, Oak	C	6	1	1	—	—	2	—	—	—
Len Hauss, Was	C	6	—	—	—	2	—	1	2	—
Bob Johnson, Cin	C	2	—	—	—	1	—	—	—	—
Ray Mansfield, Pit	C	1	—	—	—	2	—	—	—	—
Joe Namath, NYJ	**QB**	**17**	—	**1**	**1**	**1**	**2**	**1**	**1**	**1**
Earl Morrall, Mia	QB	7	1	—	—	—	1	2	—	—
Fran Tarkenton, Min	QB	4	—	1	—	1	—	—	—	—
Daryle Lamonica, Oak	QB	3	—	—	—	2	—	—	2	—
Billy Kilmer, Was	QB	3	1	—	—	2	—	—	—	—
Larry Brown, Was	**RB**	**20**	**1**	**1**	**1**	**1**	**1**	**1**	**1**	**1**
O.J. Simpson, Buf	**RB**	**15**	**1**	**†1**	—	**1**	**1**	**1**	**1**	—
Larry Csonka, Mia	**RB**	**15**	**1**	**†1**	**1**	**1**	**2**	—	**2**	**1**
John Brockington, GB	RB	8	1	1	—	1	—	2	—	—
Franco Harris, Pit	RB	7	—	1	—	2	2	2	—	—
Ron Johnson, NYG	RB	3	—	—	—	2	—	—	2	—
Floyd Little, Den	RB	1	—	—	—	2	—	—	—	—
Dave Hampton, Atl	RB	1	—	—	—	2	—	—	—	—

DEFENSE	POS	TT	+AP	+SN	+PW	+UP	AP	NE	FW	PW
Claude Humphrey, Atl	**DE**	**20**	**1**	**1**	**1**	**1**	**1**	**1**	**1**	**1**
Jack Gregory, NYG	**DE**	**17**	**1**	—	**1**	**1**	**2**	**1**	**1**	**1**
Bill Stanfill, Mia	DE	9	1	1	—	1	1	—	—	—
Carl Eller, Min	DE	5	—	1	—	2	2	—	—	—
Deacon Jones, SD	DE	3	—	—	—	2	—	2	—	—
Elvin Bethea, Hou	DE	3	—	1	—	2	—	—	—	—
Dwight White, Pit	DE	2	—	—	—	1	—	—	—	—
Larry Hand, Det	DE	2	—	—	—	—	—	2	—	—
Vern Den Herder, Mia	DE	2	1	—	—	—	—	—	—	—
Verlon Biggs, Was	DE	2	—	—	—	—	—	—	2	—
Coy Bacon, LARm	DE	2	—	—	—	—	—	—	2	—
John Zook, Atl	DE	1	—	—	—	2	—	—	—	—
Joe Greene, Pit	**DT**	**20**	**1**	**1**	**1**	**1**	**1**	**1**	**1**	**1**
Bob Lilly, Dal	**DT**	**17**	**1**	**1**	**1**	**1**	**2**	**2**	**2**	**1**
Mike Reid, Cin	DT	15	1	1	—	1	1	1	1	—
Alan Page, Min	DT	12	1	1	—	1	2	2	2	—
Paul Smith, Den	DT	1	—	—	—	2	—	—	—	—
Merlin Olsen, LARm	DT	1	—	—	—	2	—	—	—	—
Manny Fernandez, Mia	DT	1	—	—	—	2	—	—	—	—
Robert Brown, GB	DT	1	—	—	—	2	—	—	—	—
Dave Wilcox, SF	**OLB**	**20**	**1**	**1**	**1**	**1**	**1**	**1**	**1**	**1**
Chris Hanburger, Was	**OLB**	**20**	**1**	**1**	**1**	**1**	**1**	**1**	**1**	**1**
Andy Russell, Pit	OLB	12	1	1	—	1	2	2	2	—
Ted Hendricks, Bal	OLB	8	1	—	—	1	2	2	—	—
Jack Ham, Pit	OLB	3	—	—	—	2	—	—	2	—
Bobby Bell, KC	OLB	2	—	1	—	—	—	—	—	—
Phil Villapiano, Oak	OLB	1	—	—	—	2	—	—	—	—
Isiah Robertson, LARm	OLB	1	—	—	—	2	—	—	—	—

1972 NFL (CONT.)

DEFENSE	POS	TT	+AP	+SN	+PW	+UP	AP	NE	FW	PW
Fred Carr, GB	OLB	1	—	—	—	2	—	—	—	—
Dick Butkus, ChiB	**MLB**	**15**	**1**	**1**	**—**	**1**	**1**	**1**	**1**	**—**
Willie Lanier, KC	MLB	11	—	1	1	1	—	2	—	1
Nick Buoniconti, Mia	MLB	7	1	—	—	2	2	—	2	—
Jim Carter, GB	MLB	1	—	—	—	2	—	—	—	—
Jimmy Johnson, SF	**CB**	**19**	**1**	**1**	**1**	**2**	**1**	**1**	**1**	**1**
Willie Brown, Oak	**CB**	**19**	**1**	**1**	**1**	**1**	**2**	**1**	**1**	**1**
Ken Ellis, GB	CB	9	1	—	—	1	1	—	2	—
Mel Renfro, Dal	CB	7	—	—	—	2	2	2	2	—
Robert James, Buf	CB	4	1	—	—	1	—	—	—	—
Lem Barney, Det	CB	4	—	1	—	1	—	—	—	—
Lemar Parrish, Cin	CB	2	—	1	—	—	—	—	—	—
Pat Fischer, Was	CB	2	—	—	—	—	—	2	—	—
Emmitt Thomas, KC	CB	1	—	—	—	2	—	—	—	—
Clarence Scott, Cle	CB	1	—	—	—	2	—	—	—	—
Bill Bradley, Phi	**S**	**20**	**1**	**1**	**1**	**1**	**1**	**1**	**1**	**1**
Jake Scott, Mia	**S**	**17**	**1**	**1**	**1**	**1**	**2**	**2**	**2**	**1**
Dick Anderson, Mia	S	15	1	1	—	1	1	1	1	—
Paul Krause, Min	S	8	1	1	—	1	2	—	—	—
Ken Houston, Hou	S	5	—	—	—	2	—	2	2	—
Cornell Green, Dal	S	1	—	—	—	2	—	—	—	—
Dave Elmendorf, LARm	S	1	—	—	—	2	—	—	—	—
Tommy Casanova, Cin	S	1	—	—	—	2	—	—	—	—

SPECIALISTS	POS	TT	+AP	+SN	+PW	+UP	AP	NE	FW	PW
Chester Marcol, GB	**K**	**18**	**1**	**1**	**1**	**—**	**1**	**1**	**1**	**1**
Roy Gerela, Pit	K	10	1	1	—	—	2	2	2	—
Jerrel Wilson, KC	**P**	**12**	**—**	**1**	**1**	**—**	**—**	**2**	**1**	**1**
Dave Chapple, LARm	P	4	—	1	—	—	—	—	2	—
Don Cockroft, Cle	P	3	—	—	—	—	—	1	—	—

1973 NFL

OFFENSE	POS	TT	+AP	+SN	+PW	+UP	AP	NE	FW	PW
Harold Jackson, LARm	**WR**	**20**	**1**	**1**	**1**	**1**	**1**	**1**	**1**	**1**
Paul Warfield, Mia	**WR**	**15**	**1**	**1**	**1**	**1**	**1**	**2**	**2**	**—**
Harold Carmichael, Phi	**WR**	**15**	**1**	**—**	**1**	**2**	**2**	**2**	**1**	**1**
John Gilliam, Min	WR	11	—	1	—	1	2	1	2	—
Fred Biletnikoff, Oak	WR	7	1	1	1	2	—	—	—	—
Ron Shanklin, Pit	WR	2	—	—	—	1	—	—	—	—
Charley Taylor, Was	WR	1	—	—	—	2	—	—	—	—
Isaac Curtis, Cin	WR	1	—	—	—	2	—	—	—	—
Charle Young, Phi	**TE**	**16**	**1**	**—**	**1**	**2**	**1**	**2**	**1**	**1**
Riley Odoms, Den	TE	15	1	1	1	1	2	1	2	—
Ted Kwalick, SF	TE	4	—	1	—	1	—	—	—	—
Milt Morin, Cle	TE	1	—	—	—	2	—	—	—	—
Ron Yary, Min	**T**	**19**	**1**	**1**	**1**	**1**	**1**	**2**	**1**	**1**
Rayfield Wright, Dal	**T**	**14**	**1**	**1**	**—**	**1**	**1**	**2**	**1**	**—**
George Kunz, Atl	T	13	—	—	1	2	2	1	2	1
Art Shell, Oak	T	9	1	—	1	1	—	1	—	—
Winston Hill, NYJ	T	6	—	1	1	1	—	—	—	—
Charley Cowan, LARm	T	5	—	—	—	2	2	—	2	—
Russ Washington, SD	T	3	—	1	—	2	—	—	—	—
Norm Evans, Mia	T	3	1	—	—	2	—	—	—	—
Larry Little, Mia	**G**	**20**	**1**	**1**	**1**	**1**	**1**	**1**	**1**	**1**
Tom Mack, LARm	**G**	**15**	**1**	**1**	**1**	**1**	**2**	**—**	**2**	**1**
Reggie McKenzie, Buf	G	14	1	1	—	1	1	2	1	—
Gene Upshaw, Oak	G	7	—	—	1	2	2	2	—	—
John Niland, Dal	G	6	1	1	—	1	—	—	—	—
Gale Gillingham, GB	G	5	—	—	1	2	—	—	2	—
Joe Scibelli, LARm	G	4	—	—	—	2	—	1	—	—
Bruce Van Dyke, Pit	G	1	—	—	—	2	—	—	—	—
Forrest Blue, SF	**C**	**16**	**1**	**1**	**1**	**1**	**2**	**—**	**1**	**1**
Jim Langer, Mia	C	9	—	1	1	1	1	—	—	—
Jack Rudnay, KC	C	5	1	—	—	2	—	2	—	—
Bob Johnson, Cin	C	3	—	—	—	—	—	1	—	—
Len Hauss, Was	C	3	—	—	—	2	—	—	2	—
John Hadl, LARm	**QB**	**19**	**1**	**1**	**1**	**1**	**1**	**2**	**1**	**1**
Fran Tarkenton, Min	QB	8	—	—	—	2	2	1	2	—
Charley Johnson, Den	QB	4	—	—	1	1	—	—	—	—
Bob Griese, Mia	QB	3	—	1	—	2	—	—	—	—
Ken Stabler, Oak	QB	2	1	—	—	3	—	—	—	—
O.J. Simpson, Buf	**RB**	**20**	**1**	**1**	**1**	**1**	**1**	**1**	**1**	**1**
Larry Csonka, Mia	**RB**	**18**	**1**	**1**	**1**	**1**	**1**	**2**	**2**	**1**
John Brockington, GB	RB	15	1	1	1	1	2	1	2	—
Calvin Hill, Dal	RB	13	1	1	1	1	2	—	1	—
Lawrence McCutcheon, LARm	RB	3	—	—	—	2	—	2	—	—
Mercury Morris, Mia	RB	1	—	—	—	2	—	—	—	—
Floyd Little, Den	RB	1	—	—	—	2	—	—	—	—
Dave Hampton, Atl	RB	1	—	—	—	2	—	—	—	—

DEFENSE	POS	TT	+AP	+SN	+PW	+UP	AP	NE	FW	PW
Claude Humphrey, Atl	**DE**	**17**	**1**	**1**	**1**	**1**	**1**	**—**	**1**	**1**
Bill Stanfill, Mia	**DE**	**16**	**1**	**1**	**1**	**1**	**2**	**1**	**1**	**—**
Carl Eller, Min	**DE**	**16**	**1**	**1**	**1**	**1**	**1**	**—**	**2**	**1**
Dwight White, Pit	DE	6	1	1	—	1	—	—	—	—
Jack Youngblood, LARm	DE	5	—	—	—	2	2	—	2	—
John Zook, Atl	DE	3	—	—	—	2	—	2	—	—
L.C. Greenwood, Pit	DE	3	—	—	1	2	—	—	—	—
Elvin Bethea, Hou	DE	3	—	—	—	2	—	2	—	—
Alan Page, Min	**DT**	**20**	**1**	**1**	**1**	**1**	**1**	**DE1**	**1**	**1**
Joe Greene, Pit	**DT**	**20**	**1**	**1**	**1**	**1**	**1**	**1**	**1**	**1**
Mike Reid, Cin	DT	13	1	1	—	1	2	1	2	—
Merlin Olsen, LARm	DT	10	1	1	1	1	2	—	—	—
Paul Smith, Den	DT	7	—	—	1	2	—	2	2	—
Manny Fernandez, Mia	DT	3	—	—	—	2	—	2	—	—

1973 NFL (CONT.)

DEFENSE	POS	TT	+AP	+SN	+PW	+UP	AP	NE	FW	PW
Diron Talbert, Was	DT	1	—	—	—	2	—	—	—	—
Bob Lilly, Dal	DT	1	—	—	—	2	—	—	—	—
Chris Hanburger, Was	**OLB**	**19**	**1**	**1**	**1**	**1**	**1**	**1**	**2**	**1**
Dave Wilcox, SF	**OLB**	**17**	**—**	**1**	**1**	**1**	**2**	**1**	**1**	**1**
Jack Ham, Pit	OLB	14	1	1	1	1	2	2	2	—
Isiah Robertson, LARm	OLB	9	1	—	—	2	1	—	1	—
Andy Russell, Pit	OLB	6	—	1	1	1	—	—	—	—
Ted Hendricks, Bal	OLB	5	1	—	—	2	—	2	—	—
Phil Villapiano, Oak	OLB	1	—	—	—	2	—	—	—	—
Wally Hilgenberg, Min	OLB	1	—	—	—	2	—	—	—	—
Lee Roy Jordan, Dal	**MLB**	**19**	**1**	**1**	**1**	**1**	**2**	**1**	**1**	**1**
Willie Lanier, KC	MLB	16	1	1	1	1	1	1	2	—
Jeff Siemon, Min	MLB	1	—	—	—	2	—	—	—	—
Nick Buoniconti, Mia	MLB	1	—	—	—	2	—	—	—	—
Mel Renfro, Dal	**CB**	**19**	**1**	**1**	**1**	**1**	**2**	**1**	**1**	**1**
Willie Brown, Oak	**CB**	**19**	**1**	**1**	**1**	**2**	**1**	**1**	**1**	**1**
Ken Ellis, GB	CB	10	1	1	1	1	—	—	2	—
Robert James, Buf	CB	9	1	1	—	1	1	—	—	—
Lem Barney, Det	CB	7	—	—	—	2	2	2	2	—
Clarence Scott, Cle	CB	4	—	—	—	1	—	2	—	—
Bobby Bryant, Min	CB	3	—	—	1	2	—	—	—	—
Lemar Parrish, Cin	CB	1	—	—	—	2	—	—	—	—
Dick Anderson, Mia	**S**	**20**	**1**	**1**	**1**	**1**	**1**	**1**	**1**	**1**
Jake Scott, Mia	**S**	**14**	**1**	**1**	**—**	**1**	**1**	**2**	**1**	**—**
Ken Houston, Was	**S**	**14**	**1**	**1**	**1**	**1**	**2**	**2**	**2**	**—**
Paul Krause, Min	S	8	1	1	1	1	—	—	—	—
Bill Bradley, Phi	S	8	—	—	—	2	2	1	2	—
Mike Wagner, Pit	S	6	—	—	1	2	—	—	—	1
Jack Tatum, Oak	S	2	—	—	1	—	—	—	—	—
Brig Owens, Was	S	1	—	—	—	2	—	—	—	—
Glen Edwards, Pit	S	1	—	—	—	2	—	—	—	—

SPECIALISTS	POS	TT	+AP	+SN	+PW	+UP	AP	NE	FW	PW
Garo Yepremian, Mia	**K**	**18**	**1**	**†1**	**1**	**—**	**1**	**1**	**1**	**1**
Roy Gerela, Pit	K	6	—	—	—	—	2	2	2	—
Nick Mike-Mayer, Atl	K	4	1	†1	—	—	—	—	—	—
Bruce Gossett, SF	K	4	—	†1	1	—	—	—	—	—
George Blanda, Oak	K	2	—	†1	—	—	—	—	—	—
Ray Guy, Oak	**P**	**13**	**—**	**1**	**1**	**—**	**—**	**1**	**1**	**1**
Tom Wittum, SF	P	4	—	1	1	—	—	—	—	—
Jerrel Wilson, KC	P	4	—	—	—	—	—	2	2	—

1974 NFL

OFFENSE	POS	TT	+AP	+SN	+PW	+UP	AP	NE	FW	PW
Cliff Branch, Oak	**WR**	**20**	**1**	**1**	**1**	**1**	**1**	**1**	**1**	**1**
Drew Pearson, Dal	**WR**	**19**	**1**	**1**	**1**	**1**	**1**	**2**	**1**	**1**
Isaac Curtis, Cin	WR	12	1	1	—	1	2	2	2	—
Charley Taylor, Was	WR	8	1	1	—	1	2	—	—	—
Mel Gray, SL	WR	6	—	—	1	2	—	1	—	—
Paul Warfield, Mia	WR	3	—	—	1	2	—	—	—	—
Fred Biletnikoff, Oak	WR	2	—	—	—	—	—	—	2	—
Ahmad Rashad, Buf	WR	1	—	—	—	2	—	—	—	—
Harold Carmichael, Phi	WR	1	—	—	—	2	—	—	—	—
Riley Odoms, Den	**TE**	**20**	**1**	**1**	**1**	**1**	**1**	**1**	**1**	**1**
Charle Young, Phi	TE	14	1	1	1	1	2	2	2	—
Charlie Sanders, Det	TE	1	—	—	—	2	—	—	—	—
Rich Caster, NYJ	TE	1	—	—	—	2	—	—	—	—
Ron Yary, Min	**T**	**20**	**1**	**1**	**1**	**1**	**1**	**1**	**1**	**1**
Art Shell, Oak	**T**	**20**	**1**	**1**	**1**	**1**	**1**	**1**	**1**	**1**
Rayfield Wright, Dal	T	12	1	1	1	1	2	—	2	—
Russ Washington, SD	T	7	1	†1	—	2	—	2	—	—
Dan Dierdorf, SL	T	7	—	—	—	2	2	2	2	—
Winston Hill, NYJ	T	4	—	—	1	1	—	—	—	—
Norm Evans, Mia	T	2	—	†1	—	—	—	—	—	—
George Kunz, Atl	T	1	—	—	—	2	—	—	—	—
Jon Kolb, Pit	T	1	—	—	—	2	—	—	—	—
Tom Mack, LARm	**G**	**16**	**1**	**1**	**1**	**1**	**2**	**—**	**1**	**1**
Gene Upshaw, Oak	**G**	**15**	**1**	**—**	**1**	**2**	**1**	**2**	**2**	**1**
Larry Little, Mia	G	12	1	†1	—	1	1	—	1	—
Gale Gillingham, GB	G	9	1	1	—	1	—	1	—	—
Reggie McKenzie, Buf	G	8	—	1	—	1	2	—	2	—
Ed White, Min	G	4	—	—	—	2	—	1	—	—
John Niland, Dal	G	3	—	—	1	2	—	—	—	—
Bob Kuechenberg, Mia	G	3	—	—	1	2	—	—	—	—
John Hannah, NE	G	2	—	†1	—	—	—	—	—	—
Joe DeLamielleure, Buf	G	2	—	—	—	—	—	2	—	—
Jim Langer, Mia	**C**	**20**	**1**	**1**	**1**	**1**	**1**	**1**	**1**	**1**
Len Hauss, Was	C	7	1	†1	—	2	2	—	—	—
Forrest Blue, SF	C	6	—	†1	1	1	—	—	—	—
Jack Rudnay, KC	C	2	—	—	—	—	—	2	—	—
Bobby Maples, Den	C	2	—	—	—	—	—	—	2	—
Bob Johnson, Cin	C	1	—	—	—	2	—	—	—	—
Ken Stabler, Oak	**QB**	**20**	**1**	**1**	**1**	**1**	**1**	**1**	**1**	**1**
Jim Hart, SL	QB	12	1	1	1	1	2	—	2	—
Ken Anderson, Cin	QB	3	—	—	—	2	—	2	—	—
Fran Tarkenton, Min	QB	1	—	—	—	2	—	—	—	—
O.J. Simpson, Buf	**RB**	**20**	**1**	**1**	**1**	**1**	**1**	**1**	**1**	**1**
Otis Armstrong, Den	**RB**	**19**	**1**	**1**	**1**	**1**	**1**	**2**	**1**	**1**
Lawrence McCutcheon, LARm	RB	15	1	1	1	1	2	1	2	—
Chuck Foreman, Min	RB	14	1	1	1	1	2	2	2	—
Terry Metcalf, SL	RB	1	—	—	—	2	—	—	—	—
Calvin Hill, Dal	RB	1	—	—	—	2	—	—	—	—
Franco Harris, Pit	RB	1	—	—	—	2	—	—	—	—
Sam Cunningham, NE	RB	1	—	—	—	2	—	—	—	—

1974 NFL (CONT.)

DEFENSE	POS	TT	+AP	+SN	+PW	+UP	AP	NE	FW	PW
L.C. Greenwood, Pit	**DE**	**19**	**1**	**1**	**1**	**1**	**1**	**2**	**1**	**1**
Claude Humphrey, Atl	**DE**	**18**	**1**	**1**	**1**	**1**	**2**	**1**	**2**	**1**
Jack Youngblood, LARm	DE	14	1	1	1	1	1	—	1	—
Bill Stanfill, Mia	DE	10	1	1	—	1	—	2	2	—
Fred Dryer, LARm	DE	6	—	—	—	2	2	1	—	—
Elvin Bethea, Hou	DE	3	—	—	1	2	—	—	—	—
Dwight White, Pit	DE	1	—	—	—	2	—	—	—	—
Carl Eller, Min	DE	1	—	—	—	2	—	—	—	—
Alan Page, Min	**DT**	**20**	**1**	**1**	**1**	**1**	**1**	**1**	**1**	**1**
Joe Greene, Pit	**DT**	**20**	**1**	**1**	**1**	**1**	**1**	**1**	**1**	**1**
Wally Chambers, ChiB	DT	7	1	1	—	2	2	—	—	—
Otis Sistrunk, Oak	DT	6	1	—	—	1	2	—	—	—
John Mendenhall, NYG	DT	4	—	—	—	1	—	—	2	—
Larry Brooks, LARm	DT	4	—	—	1	—	—	2	—	—
Art Thoms, Oak	DT	3	—	1	—	2	—	—	—	—
Mike Reid, Cin	DT	3	—	—	1	2	—	—	—	—
Merlin Olsen, LARm	DT	3	—	—	—	2	—	—	2	—
Ernie Holmes, Pit	DT	2	—	—	—	—	—	2	—	—
Ted Hendricks, GB	**OLB**	**20**	**1**	**1**	**1**	**1**	**1**	**1**	**1**	**1**
Jack Ham, Pit	**OLB**	**20**	**1**	**1**	**1**	**1**	**1**	**1**	**1**	**1**
Chris Hanburger, Was	OLB	14	1	1	1	1	2	2	2	—
Isiah Robertson, LARm	OLB	7	—	—	—	2	2	2	2	—
Phil Villapiano, Oak	OLB	6	1	1	—	1	—	—	—	—
Andy Russell, Pit	OLB	3	—	—	1	2	—	—	—	—
Dave Washington, Buf	OLB	1	—	—	—	2	—	—	—	—
Fred Carr, GB	OLB	1	—	—	—	2	—	—	—	—
Bill Bergey, Phi	**MLB**	**19**	**1**	**1**	**1**	**1**	**1**	**2**	**1**	**1**
Willie Lanier, KC	MLB	15	1	1	1	1	2	1	2	—
Jeff Siemon, Min	MLB	1	—	—	—	2	—	—	—	—
Mike Curtis, Bal	MLB	1	—	—	—	2	—	—	—	—
Robert James, Buf	**CB**	**17**	**1**	**1**	**1**	**1**	**1**	**1**	**1**	**—**
Emmitt Thomas, KC	**CB**	**16**	**1**	**1**	**1**	**1**	**1**	**2**	**1**	**—**
Roger Wehrli, SL	CB	15	1	1	1	1	2	1	2	—
Mike Bass, Was	CB	8	1	1	—	1	2	—	—	—
Lemar Parrish, Cin	CB	5	—	—	—	2	—	2	2	—
Nate Wright, Min	CB	2	—	—	1	—	—	—	—	—
Jimmy Johnson, SF	CB	1	—	—	—	2	—	—	—	—
Ken Ellis, GB	CB	1	—	—	—	2	—	—	—	—
Willie Brown, Oak	CB	1	—	—	—	2	—	—	—	—
Tony Greene, Buf	**S**	**20**	**1**	**1**	**1**	**1**	**1**	**1**	**1**	**1**
Jake Scott, Mia	**S**	**13**	**1**	**—**	**1**	**2**	**1**	**—**	**2**	**1**
Ken Houston, Was	**S**	**13**	**1**	**1**	**1**	**1**	**—**	**2**	**1**	**—**
Dick Anderson, Mia	S	10	—	1	—	2	2	1	2	—
Cliff Harris, Dal	S	8	—	1	1	1	—	2	—	—
Jack Tatum, Oak	S	4	—	—	—	1	2	—	—	—
Dave Elmendorf, LARm	S	2	1	—	—	—	—	—	—	—
Ray Brown, Atl	S	1	—	—	—	2	—	—	—	—
Bill Bradley, Phi	S	1	—	—	—	2	—	—	—	—

SPECIALISTS	POS	TT	+AP	+SN	+PW	+UP	AP	NE	FW	PW
Chester Marcol, GB	**K**	**15**	**—**	**1**	**1**	**1**	**1**	**—**	**1**	**1**
Roy Gerela, Pit	K	10	—	1	—	1	2	2	2	—
Jan Stenerud, KC	K	3	—	—	—	—	—	1	—	—
John Leypoldt, Buf	K	3	—	—	1	2	—	—	—	—
Jim Bakken, SL	K	1	—	—	—	2	—	—	—	—
Ray Guy, Oak	**P**	**15**	**—**	**1**	**1**	**1**	**—**	**1**	**1**	**1**
Tom Wittum, SF	P	6	—	1	1	1	—	—	—	—
Jerrel Wilson, KC	P	3	—	—	—	2	—	2	—	—
Billy Van Heusen, Den	P	2	—	—	—	—	—	—	2	—

1975 NFL

OFFENSE	POS	TT	+AP	+SN	+PW	+UP	AP	NE	FW	PW
Mel Gray, SL	**WR**	**19**	**1**	**1**	**1**	**1**	**1**	**2**	**1**	**1**
Lynn Swann, Pit	**WR**	**15**	**1**	**1**	**1**	**1**	**2**	**2**	**1**	**—**
Isaac Curtis, Cin	**WR**	**15**	**—**	**1**	**1**	**2**	**2**	**1**	**2**	**1**
Cliff Branch, Oak	WR	12	1	—	—	1	1	1	2	—
John Gilliam, Min	WR	5	—	1	1	2	—	—	—	—
Charley Taylor, Was	WR	4	1	—	—	1	—	—	—	—
Drew Pearson, Dal	WR	2	—	—	1	—	—	—	—	—
Ken Payne, GB	WR	1	—	—	—	2	—	—	—	—
Bob Chandler, Buf	WR	1	—	—	—	2	—	—	—	—
Charle Young, Phi	**TE**	**19**	**1**	**1**	**1**	**1**	**2**	**1**	**1**	**1**
Riley Odoms, Den	TE	10	1	1	—	2	1	2	—	—
Rich Caster, NYJ	TE	6	—	—	1	1	—	—	2	—
Charlie Sanders, Det	TE	1	—	—	—	2	—	—	—	—
Ron Yary, Min	**T**	**20**	**1**	**1**	**1**	**1**	**1**	**1**	**1**	**1**
George Kunz, Bal	**T**	**16**	**1**	**1**	**1**	**1**	**1**	**—**	**2**	**1**
Dan Dierdorf, SL	T	13	1	—	1	1	2	2	1	—
Art Shell, Oak	T	12	1	1	—	1	2	2	2	—
Rayfield Wright, Dal	T	6	—	1	—	2	—	1	—	—
Jon Kolb, Pit	T	3	—	—	1	2	—	—	—	—
Ralph Neely, Dal	T	1	—	—	—	2	—	—	—	—
Vern Holland, Cin	T	1	—	—	—	2	—	—	—	—
Larry Little, Mia	**G**	**17**	**1**	**—**	**1**	**1**	**1**	**2**	**1**	**1**
Joe DeLamielleure, Buf	**G**	**17**	**1**	**1**	**1**	**1**	**1**	**—**	**1**	**1**
Tom Mack, LARm	G	12	1	1	1	1	—	2	2	—
Ed White, Min	G	11	1	1	1	1	—	1	—	—
Bob Kuechenberg, Mia	G	8	—	1	—	2	—	1	2	—
Reggie McKenzie, Buf	G	3	—	—	—	2	2	—	—	—
Conrad Dobler, SL	G	3	—	—	1	2	—	—	—	—
Gene Upshaw, Oak	G	2	—	—	—	—	2	—	—	—
Blaine Nye, Dal	G	1	—	—	—	2	—	—	—	—
Jim Langer, Mia	**C**	**20**	**1**	**1**	**1**	**1**	**1**	**1**	**1**	**1**
Len Hauss, Was	C	8	1	1	—	1	2	—	—	—
Jack Rudnay, KC	C	2	—	—	—	—	—	2	—	—

1975 NFL (CONT.)

OFFENSE	POS	TT	+AP	+SN	+PW	+UP	AP	NE	FW	PW
Bob Johnson, Cin	C	2	—	—	—	—	—	—	2	—
Tom Banks, SL	C	2	—	—	1	—	—	—	—	—
Jeff Van Note, Atl	C	1	—	—	—	2	—	—	—	—
Ray Mansfield, Pit	C	1	—	—	—	2	—	—	—	—
Fran Tarkenton, Min	**QB**	**20**	**1**	**1**	**1**	**1**	**1**	**1**	**1**	**1**
Ken Anderson, Cin	QB	14	1	1	1	1	2	2	2	—
Billy Kilmer, Was	QB	1	—	—	—	2	—	—	—	—
Terry Bradshaw, Pit	QB	1	—	—	—	2	—	—	—	—
O.J. Simpson, Buf	**RB**	**20**	**1**	**1**	**1**	**1**	**1**	**1**	**1**	**1**
Chuck Foreman, Min	**RB**	**20**	**1**	**1**	**1**	**1**	**1**	**1**	**1**	**1**
Terry Metcalf, SL	RB	16	1	1	1	1	2	2	2	2
Franco Harris, Pit	RB	16	1	1	1	1	2	2	2	2
John Riggins, NYJ	RB	1	—	—	—	2	—	—	—	—
Lydell Mitchell, Bal	RB	1	—	—	—	2	—	—	—	—
Lawrence McCutcheon, LARm	RB	1	—	—	—	2	—	—	—	—
Dave Hampton, Atl	RB	1	—	—	—	2	—	—	—	—

DEFENSE	POS	TT	+AP	+SN	+PW	+UP	AP	NE	FW	PW
Jack Youngblood, LARm	**DE**	**20**	**1**	**1**	**1**	**1**	**1**	**1**	**1**	**1**
L.C. Greenwood, Pit	**DE**	**20**	**1**	**1**	**1**	**1**	**1**	**1**	**1**	**1**
John Dutton, Bal	DE	10	1	1	—	1	2	—	2	—
Cedrick Hardman, SF	DE	5	—	1	—	2	—	2	—	—
Dwight White, Pit	DE	4	—	—	1	—	—	—	2	—
Carl Eller, Min	DE	4	1	—	—	1	—	—	—	—
Elvin Bethea, Hou	DE	4	—	—	—	—	2	2	—	—
Fred Dryer, LARm	DE	3	—	—	1	2	—	—	—	—
Curley Culp, Hou	**DT**	**20**	**1**	**1**	**1**	**1**	**1**	**1**	**1**	**1**
Alan Page, Min	**DT**	**19**	**1**	**1**	**1**	**1**	**1**	**2**	**1**	**1**
Wally Chambers, ChiB	DT	15	1	1	1	1	2	1	2	—
Joe Greene, Pit	DT	12	1	—	1	1	2	2	2	—
Jerry Sherk, Cle	DT	3	—	1	—	2	—	—	—	—
Otis Sistrunk, Oak	DT	2	—	—	1	—	—	—	—	—
Herb Orvis, Det	DT	1	—	—	—	2	—	—	—	—
Merlin Olsen, LARm	DT	1	—	—	—	2	—	—	—	—
Ernie Holmes, Pit	DT	1	—	—	—	2	—	—	—	—
Jack Ham, Pit	**OLB**	**20**	**1**	**1**	**1**	**1**	**1**	**1**	**1**	**1**
Isiah Robertson, LARm	**OLB**	**16**	**1**	**—**	**1**	**1**	**2**	**1**	**2**	**†1**
Chris Hanburger, Was	OLB	15	1	1	1	1	1	2	2	—
Phil Villapiano, Oak	OLB	10	1	—	1	2	2	—	—	†1
Andy Russell, Pit	OLB	5	—	—	—	1	—	—	1	—
Fred Carr, GB	OLB	5	—	1	—	2	—	2	—	—
Tom MacLeod, Bal	OLB	2	—	1	—	—	—	—	—	—
Paul Naumoff, Det	OLB	1	—	—	—	2	—	—	—	—
Robert Brazile, Hou	OLB	1	—	—	—	2	—	—	—	—
Jack Lambert, Pit	**MLB**	**16**	**1**	**1**	**1**	**1**	**2**	**—**	**1**	**1**
Bill Bergey, Phi	MLB	9	1	—	—	1	1	2	—	—
Willie Lanier, KC	MLB	6	—	—	—	2	—	1	2	—
Lee Roy Jordan, Dal	MLB	4	—	1	1	—	—	—	—	—
Jeff Siemon, Min	MLB	1	—	—	—	2	—	—	—	—
Mel Blount, Pit	**CB**	**20**	**1**	**1**	**1**	**1**	**1**	**1**	**1**	**1**
Roger Wehrli, SL	**CB**	**19**	**1**	**1**	**1**	**1**	**1**	**2**	**1**	**1**
Emmitt Thomas, KC	CB	9	—	—	1	1	2	1	—	—
Ken Riley, Cin	CB	9	1	1	—	2	2	—	2	—
Rolland Lawrence, Atl	CB	4	—	1	—	1	—	—	—	—
Lemar Parrish, Cin	CB	3	—	—	—	2	—	2	—	—
Bobby Bryant, Min	CB	3	—	—	—	2	—	—	2	—
Lem Barney, Det	CB	3	—	—	1	2	—	—	—	—
Pat Fischer, Was	CB	2	1	—	—	—	—	—	—	—
Ken Houston, Was	**S**	**20**	**1**	**1**	**1**	**1**	**1**	**1**	**1**	**1**
Paul Krause, Min	**S**	**19**	**1**	**1**	**1**	**1**	**1**	**2**	**1**	**1**
Jake Scott, Mia	S	8	—	1	—	1	2	—	2	—
Dave Elmendorf, LARm	S	7	1	—	—	2	2	2	—	—
Jack Tatum, Oak	S	6	—	1	1	1	—	—	—	—
Cliff Harris, Dal	S	6	—	—	—	2	—	1	2	—
Tommy Casanova, Cin	S	3	1	—	—	2	—	—	—	—
Mike Wagner, Pit	S	2	—	—	1	—	—	—	—	—
Glen Edwards, Pit	S	1	—	—	—	2	—	—	—	—

SPECIALISTS	POS	TT	+AP	+SN	+PW	+UP	AP	NE	FW	PW
Jim Bakken, SL	**K**	**20**	**1**	**1**	**1**	**1**	**1**	**1**	**1**	**1**
Jan Stenerud, KC	K	14	1	1	1	1	2	2	2	—
Roy Gerela, Pit	K	1	—	—	—	2	—	—	—	—
Toni Fritsch, Dal	K	1	—	—	—	2	—	—	—	—
Ray Guy, Oak	**P**	**15**	**—**	**1**	**1**	**1**	**—**	**1**	**1**	**1**
John James, Atl	P	6	—	1	1	1	—	—	—	—
Jerrel Wilson, KC	P	2	—	—	—	—	—	2	—	—
Neil Clabo, Min	P	2	—	—	—	—	—	—	2	—
Herman Weaver, Det	P	1	—	—	—	2	—	—	—	—
Bobby Walden, Pit	P	1	—	—	—	2	—	—	—	—
Billy Johnson, Hou	KR	5	—	—	1	—	—	—	—	1
Terry Metcalf, SL	KR	2	—	—	1	—	—	—	—	—

1976 NFL

OFFENSE	POS	TT	+AP	+SN	+PW	+UP	AP	NE	FW	PW
Cliff Branch, Oak	**WR**	**20**	**1**	**1**	**1**	**1**	**1**	**1**	**1**	**1**
Drew Pearson, Dal	**WR**	**17**	**1**	**1**	**1**	**1**	**1**	**—**	**1**	**1**
Roger Carr, Bal	WR	13	1	1	1	2	2	2	2	—
Isaac Curtis, Cin	WR	11	—	1	—	1	2	1	2	—
Sammy White, Min	WR	4	—	—	1	1	—	—	—	—
Charlie Joiner, SD	WR	3	—	—	—	2	—	2	—	—
Mel Gray, SL	WR	2	1	—	—	—	—	—	—	—
Harold Jackson, LARm	WR	1	—	—	—	2	—	—	—	—
Frank Grant, Was	WR	1	—	—	—	2	—	—	—	—
Dave Casper, Oak	**TE**	**20**	**1**	**1**	**1**	**1**	**1**	**1**	**1**	**1**
Russ Francis, NE	TE	9	—	1	—	2	2	2	2	—

1976 NFL (CONT.)

OFFENSE	POS	TT	+AP	+SN	+PW	+UP	AP	NE	FW	PW
Billy Joe DuPree, Dal	TE	6	1	—	1	1	—	—	—	—
Charlie Sanders, Det	TE	1	—	—	—	2	—	—	—	—
Riley Odoms, Den	TE	1	—	—	—	2	—	—	—	—
Dan Dierdorf, SL	**T**	**20**	**1**	**1**	**1**	**1**	**1**	**1**	**1**	**1**
Ron Yary, Min	**T**	**17**	**1**	**1**	**1**	**1**	**1**	**1**	**1**	**—**
George Kunz, Bal	T	14	1	1	1	1	2	2	2	—
Art Shell, Oak	T	11	1	1	1	1	—	—	—	1
Rayfield Wright, Dal	T	7	—	—	—	2	2	2	2	—
Jon Kolb, Pit	T	1	—	—	—	2	—	—	—	—
Leon Gray, NE	T	1	—	—	—	2	—	—	—	—
Lionel Antoine, ChiB	T	1	—	—	—	2	—	—	—	—
Joe DeLamielleure, Buf	**G**	**20**	**1**	**1**	**1**	**1**	**1**	**1**	**1**	**1**
John Hannah, NE	**G**	**19**	**1**	**1**	**1**	**1**	**1**	**2**	**1**	**1**
Conrad Dobler, SL	G	13	1	1	1	1	2	1	—	—
Gene Upshaw, Oak	G	7	—	—	—	2	2	2	2	—
Ed White, Min	G	6	—	1	—	1	—	—	2	—
Blaine Nye, Dal	G	5	1	—	1	2	—	—	—	—
Reggie McKenzie, Buf	G	1	—	—	—	2	—	—	—	—
Tom Mack, LARm	G	1	—	—	—	2	—	—	—	—
Jim Langer, Mia	**C**	**19**	**1**	**1**	**1**	**1**	**2**	**1**	**1**	**1**
Tom Banks, SL	C	15	1	1	1	1	1	2	2	—
Bob Johnson, Cin	C	1	—	—	—	2	—	—	—	—
Len Hauss, Was	C	1	—	—	—	2	—	—	—	—
Ken Stabler, Oak	**QB**	**14**	**—**	**1**	**1**	**2**	**2**	**2**	**2**	**1**
Bert Jones, Bal	QB	13	1	—	—	1	1	1	1	—
Roger Staubach, Dal	QB	5	1	1	—	2	—	—	—	—
Fran Tarkenton, Min	QB	4	—	—	1	1	—	—	—	—
O.J. Simpson, Buf	**RB**	**20**	**1**	**1**	**1**	**1**	**1**	**1**	**1**	**1**
Walter Payton, ChiB	**RB**	**19**	**1**	**1**	**1**	**1**	**1**	**2**	**1**	**1**
Chuck Foreman, Min	RB	15	1	1	1	1	2	1	2	—
Lydell Mitchell, Bal	RB	8	1	1	—	1	2	—	—	—
Franco Harris, Pit	RB	7	—	—	1	2	—	2	2	—
Mike Thomas, Was	RB	1	—	—	—	2	—	—	—	—
Greg Pruitt, Cle	RB	1	—	—	—	2	—	—	—	—
Lawrence McCutcheon, LARm	RB	1	—	—	—	2	—	—	—	—

DEFENSE	POS	TT	+AP	+SN	+PW	+UP	AP	NE	FW	PW
Jack Youngblood, LARm	**DE**	**20**	**1**	**1**	**1**	**1**	**1**	**1**	**1**	**1**
Tommy Hart, SF	**DE**	**19**	**1**	**1**	**1**	**1**	**2**	**1**	**1**	**1**
John Dutton, Bal	DE	13	1	1	1	1	1	—	2	—
Coy Bacon, Cin	DE	12	1	1	1	1	—	2	2	—
Harvey Martin, Dal	DE	3	—	—	—	2	2	—	—	—
Claude Humphrey, Atl	DE	3	—	—	—	2	—	2	—	—
L.C. Greenwood, Pit	DE	1	—	—	—	2	—	—	—	—
Fred Cook, Bal	DE	1	—	—	—	2	—	—	—	—
Jerry Sherk, Cle	**DT**	**20**	**1**	**1**	**1**	**1**	**1**	**1**	**1**	**1**
Wally Chambers, ChiB	**DT**	**20**	**1**	**1**	**1**	**1**	**1**	**1**	**1**	**1**
Alan Page, Min	DT	14	1	1	1	1	2	2	2	—
Joe Greene, Pit	DT	7	1	—	†1	2	2	—	—	—
Curley Culp, Hou	DT	5	—	1	†1	2	—	—	—	—
Joe Ehrmann, Bal	DT	4	—	—	—	1	—	—	2	—
Cleveland Elam, SF	DT	3	—	—	—	2	—	2	—	—
Larry Brooks, LARm	DT	1	—	—	—	2	—	—	—	—
Jack Ham, Pit	**OLB**	**20**	**1**	**1**	**1**	**1**	**1**	**1**	**1**	**1**
Isiah Robertson, LARm	**OLB**	**13**	**1**	**1**	**1**	**1**	**1**	**—**	**2**	**—**
Chris Hanburger, Was	OLB	12	—	1	1	1	—	1	—	1
Robert Brazile, Hou	OLB	11	—	1	1	1	2	—	1	—
Ted Hendricks, Oak	OLB	9	1	—	—	2	2	2	2	—
Phil Villapiano, Oak	OLB	3	—	—	—	2	—	2	—	—
Brad Van Pelt, NYG	OLB	2	1	—	—	—	—	—	—	—
Charlie Weaver, Det	OLB	1	—	—	—	2	—	—	—	—
Fred Carr, GB	OLB	1	—	—	—	2	—	—	—	—
Jack Lambert, Pit	**MLB**	**20**	**1**	**1**	**1**	**1**	**1**	**1**	**1**	**1**
Bill Bergey, Phi	MLB	14	1	1	1	1	2	2	2	—
Jeff Siemon, Min	MLB	1	—	—	—	2	—	—	—	—
Randy Gradishar, Den	MLB	1	—	—	—	2	—	—	—	—
Monte Jackson, LARm	**CB**	**20**	**1**	**1**	**1**	**1**	**1**	**1**	**1**	**1**
Roger Wehrli, SL	**CB**	**14**	**1**	**1**	**1**	**1**	**1**	**—**	**1**	**—**
Mike Haynes, NE	**CB**	**14**	**1**	**1**	**1**	**1**	**2**	**2**	**2**	**—**
Mel Blount, Pit	CB	11	—	1	1	1	—	2	—	1
Ken Riley, Cin	CB	7	1	—	—	2	2	—	2	—
Lemar Parrish, Cin	CB	4	—	—	—	2	—	1	—	—
Nate Wright, Min	CB	1	—	—	—	2	—	—	—	—
Joe Lavender, Was	CB	1	—	—	—	2	—	—	—	—
Cliff Harris, Dal	**S**	**20**	**1**	**1**	**1**	**1**	**1**	**1**	**1**	**1**
Ken Houston, Was	**S**	**17**	**1**	**1**	**1**	**1**	**—**	**1**	**1**	**1**
Tommy Casanova, Cin	S	13	1	—	1	1	1	2	2	—
Mike Wagner, Pit	S	8	—	1	1	1	2	—	—	—
Glen Edwards, Pit	S	7	1	—	—	2	2	2	—	—
Jack Tatum, Oak	S	2	—	1	—	—	—	—	—	—
Thom Darden, Cle	S	2	—	—	—	—	—	—	2	—
Charlie West, Det	S	1	—	—	—	2	—	—	—	—
James Hunter, Det	S	1	—	—	—	2	—	—	—	—
George Atkinson, Oak	S	1	—	—	—	2	—	—	—	—

SPECIALISTS	POS	TT	+AP	+SN	+PW	+UP	AP	NE	FW	PW
Jim Bakken, SL	**K**	**20**	**1**	**1**	**1**	**1**	**1**	**1**	**1**	**1**
Toni Linhart, Bal	K	6	—	1	1	1	—	—	—	—
Efren Herrera, Dal	K	5	—	—	—	2	2	—	2	—
Jan Stenerud, KC	K	4	1	—	—	—	—	2	—	—
Jim Turner, Den	K	1	—	—	—	2	—	—	—	—
Ray Guy, Oak	**P**	**20**	**1**	**1**	**1**	**1**	**1**	**1**	**1**	**1**
John James, Atl	P	14	1	1	1	1	2	2	2	—
Dave Jennings, NYG	P	1	—	—	—	2	—	—	—	—
Marv Bateman, Buf	P	1	—	—	—	2	—	—	—	—

1976 NFL (CONT.)

SPECIALISTS	POS	TT	+AP	+SN	+PW	+UP	AP	NE	FW	PW
Rick Upchurch, Den	**KR**	**8**	**—**	**—**	**pr1**	**—**	**1**	**—**	**—**	**pr1**
Duriel Harris, Mia	KR	5	—	—	kr1	—	—	—	—	kr1
Eddie Brown, Was	KR	4	—	—	pr1	—	2	—	—	—
Cullen Bryant, LARm	KR	2	—	—	kr1	—	—	—	—	—

1977 NFL

OFFENSE	POS	TT	+SN	+PW	+UP	AP	NE	FW	PW
Drew Pearson, Dal	**WR**	**18**	**1**	**1**	**1**	**1**	**1**	**1**	**1**
Nat Moore, Mia	**WR**	**12**	**1**	**1**	**1**	**1**	**—**	**1**	**—**
Lynn Swann, Pit	WR	11	1	1	1	2	—	—	1
Harold Jackson, LARm	WR	6	1	—	1	—	2	—	—
Ken Burrough, Hou	WR	5	—	—	2	2	2	—	—
Sammy White, Min	WR	3	—	1	2	—	—	—	—
Cliff Branch, Oak	WR	3	—	—	—	—	1	—	—
Bob Chandler, Buf	WR	1	—	—	2	—	—	—	—
Harold Carmichael, Phi	WR	1	—	—	2	—	—	—	—
Dave Casper, Oak	**TE**	**18**	**1**	**1**	**1**	**1**	**1**	**1**	**1**
Jean Fugett, Was	TE	6	1	1	1	—	—	—	—
Riley Odoms, Den	TE	3	—	—	2	2	—	—	—
Russ Francis, NE	TE	2	—	—	—	—	2	—	—
Billy Joe DuPree, Dal	TE	1	—	—	2	—	—	—	—
Art Shell, Oak	**T**	**18**	**1**	**1**	**1**	**1**	**1**	**1**	**1**
Dan Dierdorf, SL	**T**	**18**	**1**	**1**	**1**	**1**	**1**	**1**	**1**
Ron Yary, Min	T	10	1	1	1	2	2	—	—
George Kunz, Bal	T	10	1	1	1	2	2	—	—
Russ Washington, SD	T	1	—	—	2	—	—	—	—
Stan Walters, Phi	T	1	—	—	2	—	—	—	—
Dennis Lick, ChiB	T	1	—	—	2	—	—	—	—
Leon Gray, NE	T	1	—	—	2	—	—	—	—
Gene Upshaw, Oak	**G**	**17**	**1**	**1**	**1**	**1**	**2**	**1**	**1**
Joe DeLamielleure, Buf	**G**	**17**	**1**	**1**	**2**	**1**	**1**	**†1**	**1**
John Hannah, NE	G	7	—	—	1	2	1	—	—
Tom Mack, LARm	G	6	1	1	1	—	—	—	—
Larry Little, Mia	G	6	—	—	2	2	—	†1	—
Revie Sorey, ChiB	G	4	—	1	1	—	—	—	—
Bob Young, SL	G	2	1	—	—	—	—	—	—
Bob Kuechenberg, Mia	G	2	—	—	—	—	2	—	—
Ed White, Min	G	1	—	—	2	—	—	—	—
Conrad Dobler, SL	G	1	—	—	2	—	—	—	—
Jim Langer, Mia	**C**	**18**	**1**	**1**	**1**	**1**	**1**	**1**	**1**
Tom Banks, SL	C	10	1	1	1	2	2	—	—
Mike Webster, Pit	C	1	—	—	2	—	—	—	—
Len Hauss, Was	C	1	—	—	2	—	—	—	—
Bob Griese, Mia	**QB**	**16**	**—**	**1**	**1**	**1**	**1**	**1**	**1**
Roger Staubach, Dal	QB	6	1	1	1	—	—	—	—
Bert Jones, Bal	QB	5	—	—	2	2	2	—	—
Craig Morton, Den	QB	2	1	—	—	—	—	—	—
Pat Haden, LARm	QB	1	—	—	2	—	—	—	—
Walter Payton, ChiB	**RB**	**18**	**1**	**1**	**1**	**1**	**1**	**1**	**1**
Franco Harris, Pit	**RB**	**18**	**1**	**1**	**1**	**1**	**1**	**1**	**1**
Lydell Mitchell, Bal	RB	8	1	1	1	2	—	—	—
Chuck Foreman, Min	RB	7	1	1	2	—	2	—	—
Mark van Eeghen, Oak	RB	3	—	—	2	2	—	—	—
Greg Pruitt, Cle	RB	3	—	—	2	—	2	—	—
Lawrence McCutcheon, LARm	RB	2	—	—	1	—	—	—	—
Tony Dorsett, Dal	RB	1	—	—	2	—	—	—	—

DEFENSE	POS	TT	+SN	+PW	+UP	AP	NE	FW	PW
Harvey Martin, Dal	**DE**	**18**	**1**	**1**	**1**	**1**	**1**	**1**	**1**
Lyle Alzado, Den	**DE**	**17**	**1**	**1**	**1**	**1**	**2**	**1**	**1**
Jack Youngblood, LARm	DE	8	1	—	1	2	2	—	—
Claude Humphrey, Atl	DE	8	—	1	2	2	1	—	—
Coy Bacon, Cin	DE	4	1	—	1	—	—	—	—
Fred Cook, Bal	DE	3	—	1	2	—	—	—	—
Lee Roy Selmon, TB	DE	1	—	—	2	—	—	—	—
Cleveland Elam, SF	**DT**	**18**	**1**	**1**	**1**	**1**	**1**	**1**	**1**
Louie Kelcher, SD	**DT**	**11**	**1**	**1**	**1**	**2**	**1**	**—**	**—**
Larry Brooks, LARm	DT	7	1	—	—	—	2	1	—
Randy White, Dal	DT	6	—	1	2	—	—	—	1
Joe Greene, Pit	DT	5	—	—	1	1	—	—	—
Curley Culp, Hou	DT	4	—	1	—	—	2	—	—
Rubin Carter, Den	DT	3	—	—	2	2	—	—	—
Mike Barnes, Bal	DT	3	1	—	2	—	—	—	—
Alan Page, Min	DT	2	—	—	1	—	—	—	—
Dave Pear, TB	DT	1	—	—	2	—	—	—	—
Jack Ham, Pit	**OLB**	**18**	**1**	**1**	**1**	**1**	**1**	**1**	**1**
Tom Jackson, Den	**OLB**	**15**	**1**	**1**	**1**	**1**	**—**	**1**	**1**
Isiah Robertson, LARm	OLB	10	1	1	1	2	2	—	—
Robert Brazile, Hou	OLB	6	—	—	2	2	1	—	—
Brad Van Pelt, NYG	OLB	4	—	1	1	—	—	—	—
Matt Blair, Min	OLB	3	1	—	2	—	—	—	—
Ted Hendricks, Oak	OLB	2	—	—	—	—	2	—	—
Stan White, Bal	OLB	1	—	—	2	—	—	—	—
Thomas Henderson, Dal	OLB	1	—	—	2	—	—	—	—
Randy Gradishar, Den	**MLB**	**14**	**1**	**1**	**1**	**1**	**2**	**—**	**1**
Bill Bergey, Phi	**MLB**	**14**	**1**	**1**	**1**	**2**	**1**	**1**	**—**
Jeff Siemon, Min	MLB	1	—	—	2	—	—	—	—
Jack Lambert, Pit	MLB	1	—	—	2	—	—	—	—
Rolland Lawrence, Atl	**CB**	**17**	**1**	**1**	**1**	**1**	**2**	**1**	**1**
Monte Jackson, LARm	**CB**	**11**	**1**	**1**	**1**	**2**	**—**	**1**	**—**
Mike Haynes, NE	CB	9	—	1	1	2	—	—	1
Louis Wright, Den	CB	8	1	1	1	—	2	—	—
Roger Wehrli, SL	CB	7	—	—	2	1	1	—	—
Mel Blount, Pit	CB	6	1	—	2	—	1	—	—
Lemar Parrish, Cin	CB	1	—	—	2	—	—	—	—

1977 NFL (CONT.)

DEFENSE	POS	TT	+SN	+PW	+UP	AP	NE	FW	PW
Allan Ellis, ChiB	CB	1	—	—	2	—	—	—	—
Cliff Harris, Dal	**S**	18	1	1	1	1	1	1	1
Ken Houston, Was	**S**	10	—	1	1	—	1	—	1
Bill Thompson, Den	S	9	1	1	1	1	—	—	—
Charlie Waters, Dal	S	8	—	—	2	2	2	1	—
Jack Tatum, Oak	S	6	—	1	1	—	2	—	—
Bill Simpson, LARm	S	3	1	—	2	—	—	—	—
Tommy Casanova, Cin	S	2	—	1	—	—	—	—	—
Lyle Blackwood, Bal	S	2	—	—	—	2	—	—	—
Tony Greene, Buf	S	2	—	—	2	—	—	—	—
Tim Foley, Mia	S	1	—	—	2	—	—	—	—

SPECIALISTS	POS	TT	+SN	+PW	+UP	AP	NE	FW	PW
Efren Herrera, Dal	**K**	18	1	1	1	1	1	1	1
Errol Mann, Oak	K	6	—	—	1	2	2	—	—
Chris Bahr, Cin	K	2	1	—	—	—	—	—	—
Mark Moseley, Was	K	1	—	—	2	—	—	—	—
Toni Linhart, Bal	K	1	—	—	2	—	—	—	—
Ray Guy, Oak	**P**	18	1	1	1	1	1	1	1
John James, Atl	P	10	1	1	1	2	2	—	—
Bob Parsons, ChiB	P	1	—	—	2	—	—	—	—
Pat McInally, Cin	P	1	—	—	2	—	—	—	—
Billy Johnson, Hou	**KR**	11	—	pr1	—	1	—	1	pr1
Raymond Clayborn, NE	KR	5	—	kr1	—	—	—	—	kr1
Rick Upchurch, Den	KR	2	—	—	—	2	—	—	—
Bobby Hammond, NYG	KR	2	—	pr1	—	—	—	—	—
Eddie Brown, Was	KR	2	—	kr1	—	—	—	—	—

1978 NFL

OFFENSE	POS	TT	+SN	+PW	+UP	AP	NE	FW	PW
Lynn Swann, Pit	**WR**	18	1	1	1	1	1	1	1
Wesley Walker, NYJ	**WR**	16	—	1	1	1	1	1	1
Steve Largent, Sea	WR	7	1	—	2	2	2	—	—
Harold Carmichael, Phi	WR	6	1	1	1	—	—	—	—
John Jefferson, SD	WR	5	—	—	2	2	2	—	—
Ahmad Rashad, Min	WR	3	1	—	2	—	—	—	—
Sammy White, Min	WR	2	—	—	1	—	—	—	—
Tony Hill, Dal	WR	2	—	1	—	—	—	—	—
Drew Pearson, Dal	WR	1	—	—	2	—	—	—	—
Dave Casper, Oak	**TE**	18	1	1	1	1	1	1	1
Billy Joe DuPree, Dal	TE	6	1	1	1	—	—	—	—
Russ Francis, NE	TE	5	—	—	2	2	2	—	—
Henry Childs, NO	TE	1	—	—	2	—	—	—	—
Dan Dierdorf, SL	**T**	18	1	1	1	1	1	1	1
Leon Gray, NE	**T**	17	1	1	1	1	2	1	1
Doug France, LARm	T	9	1	1	2	2	2	—	—
Art Shell, Oak	T	4	—	—	1	2	—	—	—
Russ Washington, SD	T	3	—	—	2	—	—	—	—
Jon Kolb, Pit	T	3	—	1	2	—	—	—	—
Stan Walters, Phi	T	3	—	—	1	—	—	—	—
Greg Sampson, Hou	T	1	—	—	2	—	—	—	—
Pat Donovan, Dal	T	1	—	—	2	—	—	—	—
John Hannah, NE	**G**	18	1	1	1	1	1	1	1
Joe DeLamielleure, Buf	**G**	17	1	†1	1	2	1	1	†1
Bob Kuechenberg, Mia	G	12	T1	†1	—	1	2	—	†1
Larry Little, Mia	G	5	—	—	2	2	2	—	—
Bob Young, SL	G	4	1	1	—	—	—	—	—
Dennis Harrah, LARm	G	4	—	1	1	—	—	—	—
Tom Mack, LARm	G	3	1	—	2	—	—	—	—
Herb Scott, Dal	G	2	—	—	1	—	—	—	—
Revie Sorey, ChiB	G	1	—	—	2	—	—	—	—
Tom Lynch, Sea	G	1	—	—	2	—	—	—	—
Mike Webster, Pit	**C**	18	1	1	1	1	1	1	1
Tom Banks, SL	C	6	1	1	1	—	—	—	—
Jim Langer, Mia	C	5	—	—	2	2	2	—	—
Jim Clack, NYG	C	1	—	—	2	—	—	—	—
Terry Bradshaw, Pit	**QB**	17	1	1	1	1	2	1	1
Jim Zorn, Sea	QB	6	—	—	2	1	2	—	—
Archie Manning, NO	QB	4	1	—	1	—	—	—	—
Roger Staubach, Dal	QB	3	—	1	2	—	—	—	—
Earl Campbell, Hou	**RB**	18	1	1	1	1	1	1	1
Walter Payton, ChiB	**RB**	17	1	1	1	2	1	1	1
Delvin Williams, Mia	RB	11	1	1	1	1	2	—	—
Wilbert Montgomery, Phi	RB	5	—	1	2	2	—	—	—
Terdell Middleton, GB	RB	3	1	—	1	—	—	—	—
Franco Harris, Pit	RB	3	—	—	2	2	—	—	—
Tony Dorsett, Dal	RB	2	—	—	2	—	—	—	—
Sam Cunningham, NE	RB	1	—	—	2	—	—	—	—

DEFENSE	POS	TT	+SN	+PW	+UP	AP	NE	FW	PW
Jack Youngblood, LARm	**DE**	18	1	1	1	1	1	1	1
Al Baker, Det	**DE**	15	—	1	2	1	1	1	1
Lee Roy Selmon, TB	DE	8	1	1	2	2	—	—	—
Lyle Alzado, Den	DE	8	1	1	1	2	—	—	—
Elvin Bethea, Hou	DE	6	—	1	1	—	2	—	—
L.C. Greenwood, Pit	DE	1	—	—	2	—	—	—	—
Joe Klecko, NYJ	DE	1	—	—	2	—	—	—	—
Too Tall Jones, Dal	DE	1	—	—	2	—	—	—	—
Randy White, Dal	**DT**	18	1	1	1	1	1	1	1
Louie Kelcher, SD	**DT**	18	1	1	1	1	1	1	1
Larry Brooks, LARm	DT	10	1	1	1	2	—	—	—
Curley Culp, Hou	DT	5	—	—	2	2	—	—	—
Joe Greene, Pit	DT	3	—	1	2	—	—	—	—
Dave Pear, TB	DT	1	—	—	2	—	—	—	—
Doug English, Det	DT	1	—	—	2	—	—	—	—

1978 NFL (CONT.)

DEFENSE	POS	TT	+SN	+PW	+UP	AP	NE	FW	PW
Jack Ham, Pit	**OLB**	18	1	1	1	1	1	1	1
Robert Brazile, Hou	**OLB**	18	1	1	1	1	1	1	1
Matt Blair, Min	OLB	6	1	1	1	—	—	—	—
Brad Van Pelt, NYG	OLB	5	1	—	2	—	2	—	—
Harry Carson, NYG	OLB	5	—	1	mlb2	2	—	—	—
Fulton Kuykendall, Atl	OLB	3	—	1	2	—	—	—	—
Tom Jackson, Den	OLB	3	—	—	2	2	—	—	—
Ted Hendricks, Oak	OLB	3	—	—	2	2	—	—	—
Jim Youngblood, LARm	OLB	2	—	1	—	—	—	—	—
Randy Gradishar, Den	**MLB**	18	1	1	1	1	1	1	1
Jack Lambert, Pit	MLB	11	1	1	1	2	—	—	1
Bill Bergey, Phi	MLB	11	1	1	1	2	—	—	1
Steve Nelson, NE	MLB	1	—	—	2	—	—	—	—
Louis Wright, Den	**CB**	18	1	1	1	1	1	1	1
Willie Buchanon, GB	**CB**	17	1	1	1	1	2	†1	1
Mike Haynes, NE	CB	14	1	1	1	2	1	†1	—
Pat Thomas, LARm	CB	6	—	1	1	—	2	—	—
Rod Perry, LARm	CB	3	1	—	2	—	—	—	—
Mel Blount, Pit	CB	3	—	—	2	2	—	—	—
Rolland Lawrence, Atl	CB	1	—	—	2	—	—	—	—
Steve Foley, Den	CB	1	—	—	2	—	—	—	—
Cliff Harris, Dal	**S**	17	1	1	1	1	2	†1	1
Thom Darden, Cle	**S**	17	1	1	1	2	1	†1	1
Charlie Waters, Dal	S	12	1	—	1	2	—	—	—
Bill Thompson, Den	S	6	1	1	1	—	—	—	—
Ken Houston, Was	S	4	—	2	1	—	—	—	—
Bill Simpson, LARm	S	3	—	1	2	—	—	—	—
Donnie Shell, Pit	S	3	—	—	2	2	—	—	—
Mike Wagner, Pit	S	1	—	—	2	—	—	—	—

SPECIALISTS	POS	TT	+SN	+PW	+UP	AP	NE	FW	PW
Frank Corral, LARm	**K**	17	1	1	1	2	1	1	1
Pat Leahy, NYJ	K	9	1	1	1	1	—	—	—
Mark Moseley, Was	K	3	—	—	2	2	—	—	—
Don Cockroft, Cle	K	1	—	—	2	—	—	—	—
Ray Guy, Oak	**P**	18	1	1	1	1	1	1	1
Tom Skladany, Det	P	6	1	1	1	—	—	—	—
Dave Jennings, NYG	P	5	—	—	2	2	2	—	—
Pat McInally, Cin	P	1	—	—	2	—	—	—	—
Rick Upchurch, Den	**KR**	8	—	pr1	—	1	—	—	pr1
Tony Green, Was	KR	7	—	kr1	—	2	—	—	kr1
Keith Wright, Cle	KR	2	—	kr1	—	—	—	—	—
Jackie Wallace, LARm	KR	2	—	pr1	—	—	—	—	—

1979 NFL

OFFENSE	POS	TT	+SN	+PW	+UP	AP	NE	FW	PW
John Stallworth, Pit	**WR**	18	1	1	1	1	1	1	1
John Jefferson, SD	**WR**	18	1	1	1	1	1	1	1
Ahmad Rashad, Min	WR	8	1	1	1	—	2	—	—
Harold Carmichael, Phi	WR	8	1	1	1	2	—	—	—
Steve Largent, Sea	WR	3	—	—	2	2	—	—	—
Wes Chandler, NO	WR	3	—	—	2	2	—	—	—
Nat Moore, Mia	WR	1	—	—	2	—	—	—	—
Tony Hill, Dal	WR	1	—	—	2	—	—	—	—
Dave Casper, Oak	**TE**	10	—	1	—	1	2	—	1
Ozzie Newsome, Cle	TE	9	1	—	1	2	—	—	—
Keith Krepfle, Phi	TE	4	1	1	1	—	—	—	—
Raymond Chester, Oak	TE	4	—	—	2	2	1	—	—
Henry Childs, NO	TE	3	—	1	2	—	—	—	—
Leon Gray, Hou	**T**	18	1	1	1	1	1	1	1
Marvin Powell, NYJ	**T**	17	1	1	1	1	2	1	1
Stan Walters, Phi	T	8	1	1	1	2	—	—	—
Pat Donovan, Dal	T	6	1	1	1	—	—	—	—
Russ Washington, SD	T	5	—	—	2	2	2	—	—
Jon Kolb, Pit	T	4	—	—	2	2	1	—	—
Jerry Sisemore, Phi	T	1	—	—	2	—	—	—	—
Doug France, LARm	T	1	—	—	2	—	—	—	—
John Hannah, NE	**G**	18	1	1	1	1	1	1	1
Joe DeLamielleure, Buf	**G**	14	1	1	1	2	1	1	1
Bob Young, SL	G	12	1	1	1	1	—	—	1
Herb Scott, Dal	G	4	1	1	1	—	—	—	—
Ed White, SD	G	3	—	2	2	—	—	—	—
Doug Wilkerson, SD	G	2	—	—	2	—	2	—	—
Gerry Mullins, Pit	G	2	—	—	2	—	—	—	—
Dennis Harrah, LARm	G	2	1	—	1	—	—	—	—
Revie Sorey, ChiB	G	1	—	—	2	—	—	—	—
Randy Rasmussen, NYJ	G	1	—	—	2	—	—	—	—
Conrad Dobler, NO	G	1	—	—	2	—	—	—	—
Mike Webster, Pit	**C**	18	1	1	1	1	1	1	1
Tom Banks, SL	C	4	1	—	1	—	—	—	—
Jeff Van Note, Atl	C	2	—	—	2	—	—	—	—
Rich Saul, LARm	C	2	—	—	1	—	2	—	—
Jack Rudnay, KC	C	2	—	—	2	—	—	—	—
Carl Mauck, Hou	C	1	—	—	2	—	—	—	—
Jim Clack, NYG	C	1	—	—	2	—	—	—	—
Dan Fouts, SD	**QB**	18	1	1	1	1	1	1	1
Roger Staubach, Dal	QB	6	1	1	1	—	—	—	—
Terry Bradshaw, Pit	QB	3	—	—	2	2	2	—	—
Brian Sipe, Cle	QB	2	—	—	2	—	2	—	—
Joe Theismann, Was	QB	1	—	—	2	—	—	—	—
Earl Campbell, Hou	**RB**	18	1	1	1	1	1	1	1
Walter Payton, ChiB	**RB**	14	1	1	1	2	1	—	1
Ottis Anderson, SL	**RB**	14	1	1	1	2	1	—	1
Mike Pruitt, Cle	RB	6	1	1	1	—	—	—	—
Wilbert Montgomery, Phi	RB	3	—	—	2	2	—	—	—

1979 NFL (CONT.)

OFFENSE	POS	TT	+SN	+PW	+UP	AP	NE	FW	PW
Franco Harris, Pit	RB	3	—	—	2	—	2	—	—
Sherman Smith, Sea	RB	1	—	—	2	—	—	—	—
Chuck Muncie, NO	RB	1	—	—	2	—	—	—	—

DEFENSE	POS	TT	+SN	+PW	+UP	AP	NE	FW	PW
Jack Youngblood, LARm	**DE**	**18**	**1**	**1**	**1**	**1**	**1**	**1**	**1**
Lee Roy Selmon, TB	**DE**	**18**	**1**	**1**	**1**	**1**	**1**	**1**	**1**
Fred Dean, SD	DE	6	1	1	1	—	—	—	—
Harvey Martin, Dal	DE	5	—	—	2	2	2	—	—
L.C. Greenwood, Pit	DE	4	1	—	1	—	—	—	—
Lyle Alzado, Cle	DE	3	—	1	2	—	—	—	—
Elvin Bethea, Hou	DE	2	—	—	—	2	—	—	—
Al Baker, Det	DE	2	—	—	—	—	2	—	—
Art Still, KC	DE	1	—	—	2	—	—	—	—
Carl Hairston, Phi	DE	1	—	—	2	—	—	—	—
Randy White, Dal	**DT**	**18**	**1**	**1**	**1**	**1**	**1**	**1**	**1**
Joe Greene, Pit	**DT**	**14**	**1**	**1**	**1**	**—**	**2**	**1**	**1**
Charlie Johnson, Phi	DT	9	1	1	1	—	1	—	—
Bob Baumhower, Mia	DT	6	1	1	—	2	—	—	—
Larry Brooks, LARm	DT	4	—	—	2	1	—	—	—
Curley Culp, Hou	DT	3	—	—	2	2	—	—	—
Wilbur Young, SD	DT	2	—	—	1	—	—	—	—
Gary Johnson, SD	DT	2	—	—	—	—	2	—	—
Joe Klecko, NYJ	DT	1	—	—	2	—	—	—	—
Dave Butz, Was	DT	1	—	—	2	—	—	—	—
Jack Ham, Pit	**OLB**	**18**	**1**	**1**	**1**	**1**	**1**	**1**	**1**
Robert Brazile, Hou	**OLB**	**18**	**1**	**1**	**1**	**1**	**1**	**1**	**1**
Brad Van Pelt, NYG	OLB	6	1	1	1	—	—	—	—
Jim Youngblood, LARm	OLB	4	1	—	—	2	—	—	—
Dave Lewis, TB	OLB	4	—	—	1	—	2	—	—
Matt Blair, Min	OLB	3	—	1	2	—	—	—	—
Dewey Selmon, TB	OLB	2	—	—	—	2	—	—	—
Tom Jackson, Den	OLB	2	—	—	—	—	2	—	—
Bob Swenson, Den	OLB	1	—	—	2	—	—	—	—
Steve Nelson, NE	OLB	1	—	—	2	—	—	—	—
Brad Dusek, Was	OLB	1	—	—	2	—	—	—	—
Jack Lambert, Pit	**MLB**	**15**	**1**	**1**	**1**	**1**	**1**	**—**	**1**
Randy Gradishar, Den	**MLB**	**15**	**1**	**1**	**2**	**2**	**2**	**1**	**1**
Harry Carson, NYG	MLB	6	1	1	1	—	—	—	—
Jack Reynolds, LARm	MLB	3	1	—	2	—	—	—	—
Bob Breunig, Dal	MLB	2	—	1	—	—	—	—	—
Louis Wright, Den	**CB**	**18**	**1**	**1**	**1**	**1**	**1**	**1**	**1**
Lemar Parrish, Was	**CB**	**18**	**1**	**1**	**1**	**1**	**1**	**1**	**1**
Mike Haynes, NE	CB	10	1	1	1	2	2	—	—
Roger Wehrli, SL	CB	6	1	1	1	—	—	—	—
Mel Blount, Pit	CB	5	—	—	2	2	2	—	—
Rolland Lawrence, Atl	CB	1	—	—	2	—	—	—	—
Joe Lavender, Was	CB	1	—	—	2	—	—	—	—
Lester Hayes, Oak	CB	1	—	—	2	—	—	—	—
Mike Reinfeldt, Hou	**S**	**18**	**1**	**1**	**1**	**1**	**1**	**1**	**1**
Donnie Shell, Pit	**S**	**8**	**1**	**—**	**—**	**1**	**1**	**—**	**—**
Gary Fencik, ChiB	**S**	**8**	**1**	**1**	**2**	**—**	**—**	**1**	**—**
Tom Myers, NO	S	7	—	1	1	—	—	—	1
Thom Darden, Cle	S	5	—	1	2	2	—	—	—
Bill Thompson, Den	S	4	—	—	1	—	2	—	—
Ken Houston, Was	S	4	—	—	1	2	—	—	—
Cliff Harris, Dal	S	3	1	—	2	—	—	—	—
Tim Foley, Mia	S	3	—	—	2	—	2	—	—

SPECIALISTS	POS	TT	+SN	+PW	+UP	AP	NE	FW	PW
Toni Fritsch, Hou	**K**	**15**	**1**	**1**	**1**	**1**	**1**	**1**	**—**
Mark Moseley, Was	K	13	1	1	1	2	2	—	1
Efren Herrera, Sea	K	1	—	—	2	—	—	—	—
Tony Franklin, Phi	K	1	—	—	2	—	—	—	—
Bob Grupp, KC	**P**	**15**	**1**	**1**	**1**	**—**	**1**	**1**	**1**
Dave Jennings, NYG	P	9	1	1	1	1	—	—	—
Ray Guy, Oak	P	3	—	—	2	—	2	—	—
Danny White, Dal	P	1	—	—	2	—	—	—	—
Rick Upchurch, Den	**KR**	**7**	**—**	**pr1**	**—**	**2**	**—**	**—**	**pr1**
Ira Matthews, Oak	**KR**	**7**	**kr1**	**kr1**	**—**	**—**	**—**	**—**	**kr1**
Tony Nathan, Mia	KR	5	pr1	—	—	1	—	—	—
Wally Henry, Phi	KR	4	pr1	pr1	—	—	—	—	—
Roy Green, SL	KR	4	kr1	kr1	—	—	—	—	—

1980 NFL

OFFENSE	POS	TT	+PW	+UP	AP	NE	FW	SN	PW
John Jefferson, SD	**WR**	**19**	**1**	**1**	**1**	**1**	**1**	**1**	**1**
James Lofton, GB	**WR**	**18**	**1**	**1**	**2**	**1**	**1**	**1**	**1**
Stanley Morgan, NE	WR	8	1	1	2	2	—	—	—
Ahmad Rashad, Min	WR	4	1	1	—	—	—	—	—
Charlie Joiner, SD	WR	4	—	2	1	—	—	—	—
Harold Carmichael, Phi	WR	3	—	2	—	2	—	—	—
Pat Tilley, SL	WR	1	—	2	—	—	—	—	—
Jerry Butler, Buf	WR	1	—	2	—	—	—	—	—
Kellen Winslow, SD	**TE**	**19**	**1**	**1**	**1**	**1**	**1**	**1**	**1**
Junior Miller, Atl	TE	6	1	1	2	—	—	—	—
Ozzie Newsome, Cle	TE	2	—	—	—	2	—	—	—
Jimmie Giles, TB	TE	1	—	2	—	—	—	—	—
Russ Francis, NE	TE	1	—	2	—	—	—	—	—
Mike Kenn, Atl	**T**	**19**	**1**	**1**	**1**	**1**	**1**	**1**	**1**
Leon Gray, Hou	**T**	**18**	**1**	**1**	**1**	**2**	**1**	**1**	**1**
Marvin Powell, NYJ	T	8	1	1	2	2	—	—	—
Dan Dierdorf, SL	T	6	—	2	2	1	—	—	—
Doug France, LARm	T	3	1	2	—	—	—	—	—
Pat Donovan, Dal	T	2	—	1	—	—	—	—	—

1980 NFL (CONT.)

OFFENSE	POS	TT	+PW	+UP	AP	NE	FW	SN	PW
Ken Jones, Buf	T	1	—	2	—	—	—	—	—
Doug Dieken, Cle	T	1	—	2	—	—	—	—	—
John Hannah, NE	**G**	**19**	**1**	**1**	**1**	**1**	**1**	**1**	**1**
Joe DeLamielleure, Cle	**G**	**12**	**1**	**1**	**2**	**—**	**1**	**1**	**—**
Kent Hill, LARm	G	9	1	1	2	—	—	—	1
Herbert Scott, Dal	G	8	—	1	1	1	—	—	—
Randy Cross, SF	G	4	1	—	—	2	—	—	—
Doug Wilkerson, SD	G	3	—	2	—	2	—	—	—
Reggie McKenzie, Buf	G	1	—	2	—	—	—	—	—
Noah Jackson, ChiB	G	1	—	2	—	—	—	—	—
Dennis Harrah, LARm	G	1	—	2	—	—	—	—	—
Mike Webster, Pit	**C**	**19**	**1**	**1**	**1**	**1**	**1**	**1**	**1**
Rich Saul, LARm	C	5	—	2	2	2	—	—	—
Jeff Van Note, Atl	C	4	1	1	—	—	—	—	—
Tom DeLeone, Cle	C	1	—	2	—	—	—	—	—
Brian Sipe, Cle	**QB**	**19**	**1**	**1**	**1**	**1**	**1**	**1**	**1**
Ron Jaworski, Phi	QB	4	1	1	—	—	—	—	—
Dan Fouts, SD	QB	3	—	2	2	—	—	—	—
Steve Bartkowski, Atl	QB	1	—	2	—	—	—	—	—
Walter Payton, ChiB	**RB**	**19**	**1**	**1**	**1**	**1**	**1**	**1**	**1**
Earl Campbell, Hou	**RB**	**19**	**1**	**1**	**1**	**1**	**1**	**1**	**1**
Billy Sims, Det	RB	8	1	1	2	2	—	—	—
Ottis Anderson, SL	RB	5	—	2	2	2	—	—	—
Joe Cribbs, Buf	RB	4	1	1	—	—	—	—	—
Mike Pruitt, Cle	RB	1	—	2	—	—	—	—	—
Kenny King, Oak	RB	1	—	2	—	—	—	—	—
William Andrews, Atl	RB	1	—	2	—	—	—	—	—

DEFENSE	POS	TT	+PW	+UP	AP	NE	FW	SN	PW
Art Still, KC	**DE**	**18**	**1**	**1**	**2**	**1**	**1**	**1**	**1**
Lee Roy Selmon, TB	**DE**	**13**	**—**	**1**	**2**	**1**	**1**	**1**	**—**
Fred Dean, SD	DE	9	1	2	1	—	—	—	1
Dan Hampton, ChiB	DE	5	1	2	—	2	—	—	—
Lyle Alzado, Cle	DE	5	—	1	1	—	—	—	—
Jack Youngblood, LARm	DE	4	—	1	—	2	—	—	—
Carl Hairston, Phi	DE	3	1	2	—	—	—	—	—
Ben Williams, Buf	DE	1	—	2	—	—	—	—	—
Gary Johnson, SD	**DT**	**19**	**1**	**1**	**1**	**1**	**1**	**1**	**1**
Randy White, Dal	**DT**	**18**	**1**	**1**	**2**	**1**	**1**	**1**	**1**
Fred Smerlas, Buf	DT	9	1	1	—	2	—	—	1
Charlie Johnson, Phi	DT	9	1	1	1	2	—	—	—
Louie Kelcher, SD	DT	5	1	2	2	—	—	—	—
Alan Page, ChiB	DT	3	1	2	—	—	—	—	—
Reggie Kinlaw, Oak	DT	1	—	2	—	—	—	—	—
Larry Brooks, LARm	DT	1	—	2	—	—	—	—	—
Ted Hendricks, Oak	**OLB**	**19**	**1**	**1**	**1**	**1**	**1**	**1**	**1**
Robert Brazile, Hou	**OLB**	**18**	**1**	**1**	**2**	**1**	**1**	**1**	**1**
Matt Blair, Min	OLB	9	1	1	1	2	—	—	—
Jerry Robinson, Phi	OLB	6	1	1	2	—	—	—	—
Jack Ham, Pit	OLB	3	—	2	—	2	—	—	—
Brad Van Pelt, NYG	OLB	1	—	2	—	—	—	—	—
Al Richardson, Atl	OLB	1	—	2	—	—	—	—	—
Woodrow Lowe, SD	OLB	1	—	2	—	—	—	—	—
Jack Lambert, Pit	**ILB**	**14**	**1**	**—**	**1**	**1**	**1**	**—**	**1**
Steve Nelson, NE	ILB	9	1	2	—	—	—	1	1
Randy Gradishar, Den	ILB	5	—	—	—	2	—	1	—
Bob Breunig, Dal	ILB	4	—	1	2	—	—	—	—
Bill Bergey, Phi	ILB	3	1	2	—	—	—	—	—
Jim Haslett, Buf	ILB	2	—	1	—	—	—	—	—
Buddy Curry, Atl	ILB	2	1	—	—	—	—	—	—
Lester Hayes, Oak	**CB**	**19**	**1**	**1**	**1**	**1**	**1**	**1**	**1**
Lemar Parrish, Was	**CB**	**18**	**1**	**1**	**2**	**1**	**1**	**1**	**1**
Pat Thomas, LARm	CB	9	1	1	1	2	—	—	—
Mike Haynes, NE	CB	8	1	1	2	2	—	—	—
Louis Wright, Den	CB	1	—	2	—	—	—	—	—
Greg Stemrick, Hou	CB	1	—	2	—	—	—	—	—
Rod Perry, LARm	CB	1	—	2	—	—	—	—	—
Herman Edwards, Phi	CB	1	—	2	—	—	—	—	—
Nolan Cromwell, LARm	**S**	**19**	**1**	**1**	**1**	**1**	**1**	**1**	**1**
Donnie Shell, Pit	**S**	**16**	**†1**	**1**	**1**	**1**	**1**	**1**	**—**
Gary Barbaro, KC	S	8	1	1	2	2	—	—	—
Gary Fencik, ChiB	S	7	1	1	—	—	—	—	1
Randy Logan, Phi	S	5	—	2	2	2	—	—	—
Bruce Laird, Bal	S	2	†1	—	—	—	—	—	—
Mike Reinfeldt, Hou	S	1	—	2	—	—	—	—	—
Vernon Perry, Hou	S	1	—	2	—	—	—	—	—

SPECIALISTS	POS	TT	+PW	+UP	AP	NE	FW	SN	PW
Eddie Murray, Det	**K**	**13**	**1**	**1**	**1**	**1**	**1**	**—**	**—**
Fred Steinfort, Den	K	12	†1	1	—	2	—	1	†1
John Smith, NE	K	6	†1	2	—	—	—	—	†1
Tim Mazzetti, Atl	K	1	—	2	—	—	—	—	—
Dave Jennings, NYG	**P**	**19**	**1**	**1**	**1**	**1**	**1**	**1**	**1**
Ray Guy, Oak	P	6	1	1	—	2	—	—	—
Luke Prestridge, Den	P	1	—	2	—	—	—	—	—
John James, Atl	P	1	—	2	—	—	—	—	—
J.T. Smith, KC	**KR**	**11**	**pr1**	**—**	**1**	**—**	**—**	**pr1**	**pr1**
Horace Ivory, NE	**KR**	**11**	**kr1**	**—**	**—**	**—**	**1**	**kr1**	**kr1**
Freddie Solomon, SF	KR	2	pr1	—	—	—	—	—	—
Rich Mauti, NO	KR	2	kr1	—	—	—	—	—	—

1981 NFL

OFFENSE	POS	TT	+PW	+UP	AP	NE	FW	SN	PW
James Lofton, GB	**WR**	**19**	**1**	**1**	**1**	**1**	**1**	**1**	**1**
Alfred Jenkins, Atl	**WR**	**19**	**1**	**1**	**1**	**1**	**1**	**1**	**†1**

1981 NFL (CONT.)

OFFENSE	POS	TT	+PW	+UP	AP	NE	FW	SN	PW
Steve Watson, Den	WR	11	1	1	2	2	—	—	†1
Frank Lewis, Buf	WR	6	1	1	—	2	—	—	—
Cris Collinsworth, Cin	WR	3	—	2	2	—	—	—	—
Ahmad Rashad, Min	WR	1	—	2	—	—	—	—	—
Steve Largent, Sea	WR	1	—	2	—	—	—	—	—
Dwight Clark, SF	WR	1	—	2	—	—	—	—	—
Kellen Winslow, SD	**TE**	19	1	1	1	1	1	1	1
Joe Senser, Min	TE	6	1	1	—	2	—	—	—
Ozzie Newsome, Cle	TE	2	—	—	2	—	—	—	—
Dan Ross, Cin	TE	1	—	2	—	—	—	—	—
Jimmie Giles, TB	TE	1	—	2	—	—	—	—	—
Marvin Powell, NYJ	**T**	19	1	1	1	1	1	1	1
Anthony Munoz, Cin	**T**	19	1	1	1	1	1	1	1
Mike Kenn, Atl	T	8	1	1	2	2	—	—	—
Pat Donovan, Dal	T	7	1	2	2	2	—	—	—
Keith Dorney, Det	T	2	—	1	—	—	—	—	—
Chris Ward, NYJ	T	1	—	2	—	—	—	—	—
Jerry Sisemore, Phi	T	1	—	2	—	—	—	—	—
Leon Gray, Hou	T	1	—	2	—	—	—	—	—
John Hannah, NE	**G**	19	1	1	1	1	1	1	1
Randy Cross, SF	**G**	15	1	1	2	1	1	—	1
Herbert Scott, Dal	G	12	1	1	1	2	—	1	—
Ed Newman, Mia	G	5	—	2	2	2	—	—	—
Doug Wilkerson, SD	G	4	1	1	—	—	—	—	—
Greg Roberts, TB	G	1	—	2	—	—	—	—	—
Wes Hamilton, Min	G	1	—	2	—	—	—	—	—
Joe DeLamielleure, Cle	G	1	—	2	—	—	—	—	—
Mike Webster, Pit	**C**	19	1	1	1	1	1	1	1
Joe Fields, NYJ	C	3	—	2	2	—	—	—	—
Rich Saul, LARm	C	2	—	—	2	—	—	—	—
Guy Morriss, Phi	C	2	—	1	—	—	—	—	—
Larry McCarren, GB	C	2	1	—	—	—	—	—	—
Jeff Van Note, Atl	C	1	—	2	—	—	—	—	—
Ken Anderson, Cin	**QB**	19	1	1	1	1	1	1	1
Joe Montana, SF	QB	8	1	1	2	2	—	—	—
Danny White, Dal	QB	1	—	2	—	—	—	—	—
Dan Fouts, SD	QB	1	—	2	—	—	—	—	—
Tony Dorsett, Dal	**RB**	19	1	1	1	1	1	1	1
Billy Sims, Det	**RB**	14	1	2	2	1	1	—	—
George Rogers, NO	RB	10	—	1	1	2	—	1	—
Chuck Muncie, SD	RB	4	1	1	—	—	—	—	—
Joe Delaney, KC	RB	4	1	1	—	—	—	—	—
William Andrews, Atl	RB	3	—	2	2	—	—	—	—
Joe Cribbs, Buf	RB	2	—	—	2	—	—	—	—
Pete Johnson, Cin	RB	1	—	2	—	—	—	—	—
Earl Campbell, Hou	RB	1	—	2	—	—	—	—	—

DEFENSE	POS	TT	+PW	+UP	AP	NE	FW	SN	PW
Joe Klecko, NYJ	**DE**	19	1	1	1	1	1	1	1
Fred Dean, SF	**DE**	18	1	1	1	2	1	1	1
Too Tall Jones, Dal	DE	9	1	1	2	1	—	—	—
Mark Gastineau, NYJ	DE	8	1	1	2	2	—	—	—
Ben Williams, Buf	DE	1	—	2	—	—	—	—	—
Carl Hairston, Phi	DE	1	—	2	—	—	—	—	—
Eddie Edwards, Cin	DE	1	—	2	—	—	—	—	—
Mike Butler, GB	DE	1	—	2	—	—	—	—	—
Randy White, Dal	**DT**	19	1	1	1	1	1	1	1
Doug English, Det	**DT**	11	1	2	1	—	—	—	1
Bob Baumhower, Mia	**DT**	11	1	1	2	2	—	1	—
Gary Johnson, SD	DT	9	1	2	1	—	1	—	—
Charlie Johnson, Phi	DT	7	1	1	1	—	—	—	—
Fred Smerlas, Buf	DT	6	1	1	—	2	—	—	—
Louie Kelcher, SD	DT	3	—	2	2	—	—	—	—
Don Smith, Atl	DT	1	—	2	—	—	—	—	—
Lawrence Taylor, NYG	**OLB**	19	1	1	1	1	1	1	1
Bob Swenson, Den	**OLB**	12	1	2	1	1	1	—	1
Jerry Robinson, Phi	OLB	9	1	1	2	—	1	—	—
Matt Blair, Min	OLB	5	1	2	—	2	—	—	—
Ted Hendricks, Oak	OLB	4	1	1	—	—	—	—	—
Robert Brazile, Hou	OLB	3	—	2	2	—	—	—	—
Rod Martin, Oak	OLB	2	—	—	2	—	—	—	—
A.J. Duhe, Mia	OLB	2	—	1	—	—	—	—	—
Mike Douglass, GB	OLB	1	—	2	—	—	—	—	—
Jack Lambert, Pit	**ILB**	18	1	2	1	1	1	1	1
Randy Gradishar, Den	ILB	14	1	2	2	—	—	1	1
Harry Carson, NYG	ILB	7	1	1	—	—	—	—	1
Jack Reynolds, SF	ILB	1	—	2	—	—	—	—	—
Ronnie Lott, SF	**CB**	19	1	1	1	1	1	1	1
Mark Haynes, NYG	**CB**	11	1	2	2	1	—	—	1
Mel Blount, Pit	CB	10	1	1	1	—	1	—	—
Roynell Young, Phi	CB	6	—	1	2	2	—	—	—
Gary Green, KC	CB	6	1	1	—	2	—	—	—
Lester Hayes, Oak	CB	4	—	2	—	—	—	1	—
Louis Wright, Den	CB	1	—	†2	—	—	—	—	—
Dennis Thurman, Dal	CB	1	—	2	—	—	—	—	—
Ken Riley, Cin	CB	1	—	†2	—	—	—	—	—
Eric Harris, KC	CB	1	—	†2	—	—	—	—	—
Mario Clark, Buf	CB	1	—	†2	—	—	—	—	—
Nolan Cromwell, LARm	**S**	18	1	2	1	1	1	1	1
Dwight Hicks, SF	**S**	11	1	1	2	2	—	—	1
Gary Fencik, ChiB	S	10	—	1	1	2	—	1	—
Gary Barbaro, KC	S	9	1	2	1	1	—	—	—
Darrol Ray, NYJ	S	4	1	1	—	—	—	—	—
Donnie Shell, Pit	S	3	—	2	2	—	—	—	—
Bill Thompson, Den	S	2	—	1	—	—	—	—	—
Randy Logan, Phi	S	1	—	2	—	—	—	—	—

1981 NFL (CONT.)

SPECIALISTS	POS	TT	+PW	+UP	AP	NE	FW	SN	PW
Rafael Septien, Dal	**K**	16	1	1	1	—	1	1	1
Nick Lowery, KC	K	9	1	1	2	1	—	—	—
Eddie Murray, Det	K	2	—	—	—	2	—	—	—
Jan Stenerud, GB	K	1	—	2	—	—	—	—	—
Pat Leahy, NYJ	K	1	—	2	—	—	—	—	—
Pat McInally, Cin	**P**	15	1	1	1	2	1	1	—
Tom Skladany, Det	P	10	1	1	—	2	—	—	—
Dave Jennings, NYG	P	3	—	2	2	—	—	—	—
Ray Guy, Oak	P	1	—	2	—	—	—	—	—
LeRoy Irvin, LARm	**KR**	14	pr1	—	1	—	pr1	pr1	pr1
Mike Nelms, Was	KR	13	kr1	—	2	—	kr1	kr1	kr1
J.T. Smith, KC	KR	2	pr1	—	—	—	—	—	—
Carl Roaches, Hou	KR	2	kr1	—	—	—	—	—	—

1982 NFL

OFFENSE	POS	TT	+PW	AP	NE	FW	PW
Dwight Clark, SF	**WR**	14	1	1	1	1	1
Wes Chandler, SD	**WR**	14	1	1	1	1	1
James Lofton, GB	WR	6	1	2	2	—	—
Charlie Brown, Was	WR	3	2	—	2	—	—
Wesley Walker, NYJ	WR	2	1	—	—	—	—
Cris Collinsworth, Cin	WR	2	—	2	—	—	—
Kellen Winslow, SD	**TE**	14	1	1	1	1	1
Dan Ross, Cin	TE	3	2	2	—	—	—
Ozzie Newsome, Cle	TE	2	—	—	2	—	—
Jimmie Giles, TB	TE	2	1	—	—	—	—
Marvin Powell, NYJ	**T**	14	1	1	1	1	1
Anthony Munoz, Cin	**T**	14	1	1	1	1	1
Mike Kenn, Atl	T	6	1	2	2	—	—
Russ Washington, SD	T	2	—	2	—	—	—
Greg Koch, GB	T	2	—	—	2	—	—
Pat Donovan, Dal	T	2	1	—	—	—	—
Doug Wilkerson, SD	**G**	14	1	1	1	1	1
John Hannah, NE	**G**	11	2	2	2	1	1
Ed Newman, Mia	G	7	1	2	1	—	—
R.C. Thielemann, Atl	G	5	1	1	—	—	—
Kurt Petersen, Dal	G	2	—	2	—	—	—
Kent Hill, LARm	G	2	1	—	—	—	—
Russ Grimm, Was	G	1	2	—	—	—	—
Mike Webster, Pit	**C**	10	1	—	2	1	1
Joe Fields, NYJ	C	7	2	1	2	—	—
Jeff Van Note, Atl	C	2	—	2	—	—	—
Larry McCarren, GB	C	2	1	—	—	—	—
Dan Fouts, SD	**QB**	14	1	1	1	1	1
Joe Theismann, Was	QB	4	1	2	—	—	—
Danny White, Dal	QB	3	2	2	—	—	—
Ken Anderson, Cin	QB	1	2	—	—	—	—
Freeman McNeil, NYJ	**RB**	14	1	1	1	1	1
Marcus Allen, LARd	**RB**	14	1	1	1	1	1
Tony Dorsett, Dal	RB	6	1	2	2	—	—
William Andrews, Atl	RB	6	1	2	2	—	—
Billy Sims, Det	RB	1	2	—	—	—	—
George Rogers, NO	RB	1	2	—	—	—	—
Chuck Muncie, SD	RB	1	2	—	—	—	—
Andra Franklin, Mia	RB	1	2	—	—	—	—

DEFENSE	POS	TT	+PW	AP	NE	FW	PW
Mark Gastineau, NYJ	**DE**	14	1	1	1	1	1
Lee Roy Selmon, TB	**DE**	10	1	2	1	1	—
Too Tall Jones, Dal	DE	6	2	1	2	—	—
Doug Martin, Min	DE	5	1	—	2	—	1
Ben Williams, Buf	DE	3	2	—	2	—	—
Harvey Martin, Dal	DE	2	—	2	—	—	—
Lyle Alzado, LARd	DE	2	1	—	—	—	—
Art Still, KC	DE	1	2	—	—	—	—
Dennis Harrison, Phi	DE	1	2	—	—	—	—
Randy White, Dal	**DT**	14	1	1	1	1	1
Dan Hampton, ChiB	**DT**	12	2	2	1	1	1
Bob Baumhower, Mia	DT	6	1	2	2	—	—
Doug English, Det	DT	5	—	1	2	—	—
Fred Smerlas, Buf	DT	3	—	1	2	—	—
Gary Johnson, SD	DT	2	1	—	—	—	—
Lawrence Taylor, NYG	**OLB**	14	1	1	1	1	1
Hugh Green, TB	**OLB**	12	1	2	2	1	1
Ted Hendricks, LARd	OLB	5	1	1	—	—	—
Rod Martin, LARd	OLB	3	—	—	1	—	—
Joel Williams, Atl	OLB	2	—	2	—	—	—
Keena Turner, SF	OLB	2	—	—	2	—	—
Robert Brazile, Hou	OLB	2	1	—	—	—	—
Lance Mehl, NYJ	OLB	2	1	—	—	—	—
Chip Banks, Cle	OLB	1	2	—	—	—	—
Jack Lambert, Pit	**ILB**	14	1	1	1	1	1
Harry Carson, NYG	ILB	4	1	2	—	—	—
Mike Douglass, GB	ILB	3	—	—	2	—	—
Randy Gradishar, Den	ILB	2	1	2	—	—	—
George Cumby, GB	ILB	2	—	2	—	—	—
Bob Breunig, Dal	ILB	2	1	—	—	—	—
Jim LeClair, Cin	ILB	1	2	—	—	—	—
Buddy Curry, Atl	ILB	1	2	—	—	—	—
Everson Walls, Dal	**CB**	12	1	2	2	1	1
Mark Haynes, NYG	**CB**	11	1	1	—	1	1
Mike Haynes, NE	CB	7	1	2	1	—	—
Louis Breeden, Cin	CB	4	1	2	—	—	—
Lester Hayes, LARd	CB	4	1	2	—	—	—
Gary Green, KC	CB	1	2	—	—	—	—

1982 NFL (CONT.)

DEFENSE	POS	TT	+UP	AP	NE	FW	PW
Herman Edwards, Phi	CB	1	2	—	—	—	—
Vernon Dean, Was	CB	1	2	—	—	—	—
Donnie Shell, Pit	**S**	8	—	1	2	1	—
Kenny Easley, Sea	**S**	8	1	—	1	—	1
Nolan Cromwell, LARm	**S**	8	1	1	—	1	—
Gary Barbaro, KC	S	5	1	—	1	—	—
Gary Fencik, ChiB	S	4	2	—	—	—	1
Darrol Ray, NYJ	S	3	2	—	2	—	—
Tony Peters, Was	S	2	1	—	—	—	—
Tim Fox, SD	S	2	—	2	—	—	—
Neal Colzie, TB	S	2	—	2	—	—	—

SPECIALISTS	POS	TT	+UP	AP	NE	FW	PW
Mark Moseley, Was	**K**	14	1	1	1	1	1
Uwe von Schamann, Mia	K	2	—	2	—	—	—
Eddie Murray, Det	K	2	—	—	2	—	—
Rolf Benirschke, SD	K	2	1	—	—	—	—
Nick Lowery, KC	K	1	2	—	—	—	—
Dave Jennings, NYG	**P**	13	1	2	1	1	1
Luke Prestridge, Den	P	5	1	1	—	—	—
Rich Camarillo, NE	P	2	—	—	2	—	—
Rohn Stark, Bal	P	1	2	—	—	—	—
Carl Birdsong, SL	P	1	2	—	—	—	—
Mike Nelms, Was	**KR**	8	—	2	—	kr1	kr1
Rick Upchurch, Den	KR	6	—	1	—	—	pr1
LeRoy Irvin, LARm	KR	3	—	—	—	pr1	—

1983 NFL

OFFENSE	POS	TT	+PW	+UP	AP	NE	FW	SN	PW
Roy Green, SL	**WR**	19	1	1	1	1	1	1	1
Mike Quick, Phi	**WR**	13	1	1	1	1	—	—	1
James Lofton, GB	WR	8	—	2	2	2	1	—	—
Cris Collinsworth, Cin	WR	8	1	1	2	2	—	—	—
Steve Largent, Sea	WR	4	—	2	—	—	—	1	—
Tim Smith, Hou	WR	2	1	—	—	—	—	—	—
Carlos Carson, KC	WR	2	—	1	—	—	—	—	—
Mark Duper, Mia	WR	1	—	2	—	—	—	—	—
Charlie Brown, Was	WR	1	—	2	—	—	—	—	—
Todd Christensen, LARd	**TE**	19	1	1	1	1	1	1	1
Ozzie Newsome, Cle	TE	5	—	2	2	2	—	—	—
Paul Coffman, GB	TE	4	1	1	—	—	—	—	—
Mike Barber, LARm	TE	1	—	2	—	—	—	—	—
Joe Jacoby, Was	**T**	19	1	1	1	1	1	1	1
Anthony Munoz, Cin	**T**	8	1	2	—	1	—	—	1
Mike Kenn, Atl	**T**	8	1	2	2	—	—	—	1
Jackie Slater, LARm	T	6	—	1	2	2	—	—	—
Cody Risien, Cle	T	4	—	1	—	2	—	—	—
Marvin Powell, NYJ	T	3	1	2	—	—	—	—	—
Eric Laakso, Mia	T	3	—	—	—	—	—	—	—
Keith Fahnhorst, SF	T	3	—	—	1	—	—	—	—
Brian Holloway, NE	T	2	1	—	—	—	—	—	—
Henry Lawrence, LARd	T	1	—	2	—	—	—	—	—
Pat Donovan, Dal	T	1	—	2	—	—	—	—	—
John Hannah, NE	**G**	19	1	1	1	1	1	1	1
Russ Grimm, Was	**G**	16	1	1	1	1	1	—	1
Kent Hill, LARm	G	7	1	1	—	—	—	1	—
Ed Newman, Mia	G	6	—	1	2	2	—	—	—
Chris Hinton, Bal	G	3	1	2	—	—	—	—	—
Mike Munchak, Hou	G	2	—	—	2	—	—	—	—
Joe DeLamielleure, Cle	G	2	—	1	—	—	—	—	—
R.C. Thielemann, Atl	G	1	—	2	—	—	—	—	—
Herbert Scott, Dal	G	1	—	2	—	—	—	—	—
Bob Kuechenberg, Mia	G	1	—	2	—	—	—	—	—
Dwight Stephenson, Mia	**C**	15	1	1	2	1	1	—	1
Mike Webster, Pit	C	7	—	2	1	—	—	1	—
Jeff Bostic, Was	C	4	1	1	—	—	—	—	—
Larry McCarren, GB	C	3	—	2	—	2	—	—	—
Joe Theismann, Was	**QB**	19	1	1	1	1	1	1	1
Dan Marino, Mia	QB	6	1	1	2	—	—	—	—
Joe Montana, SF	QB	2	—	—	2	—	—	—	—
Dan Fouts, SD	QB	1	—	2	—	—	—	—	—
Lynn Dickey, GB	QB	1	—	2	—	—	—	—	—
Eric Dickerson, LARm	**RB**	19	1	1	1	1	1	1	1
John Riggins, Was	**RB**	15	1	1	2	1	—	—	1
Curt Warner, Sea	RB	6	1	1	2	—	—	—	—
William Andrews, Atl	RB	6	—	—	1	—	1	—	—
Joe Cribbs, Buf	RB	4	1	1	—	—	—	—	—
Walter Payton, ChiB	RB	3	—	2	—	1	—	—	—
Tony Dorsett, Dal	RB	3	—	2	2	—	—	—	—
Mike Pruitt, Cle	RB	1	—	2	—	—	—	—	—
Tony Collins, NE	RB	1	—	2	—	—	—	—	—

DEFENSE	POS	TT	+PW	+UP	AP	NE	FW	SN	PW
Doug Betters, Mia	**DE**	19	1	1	1	1	1	1	1
Howie Long, LARd	**DE**	17	1	2	2	1	1	1	1
Too Tall Jones, Dal	DE	8	1	1	2	2	—	—	—
Mark Gastineau, NYJ	DE	5	—	1	1	—	—	—	—
Jacob Green, Sea	DE	3	—	2	—	2	—	—	—
Fred Dean, SF	DE	3	1	2	—	—	—	—	—
William Gay, Det	DE	2	—	1	—	—	—	—	—
Lee Roy Selmon, TB	DE	1	—	2	—	—	—	—	—
Randy White, Dal	**DT**	19	1	1	1	1	1	1	1
Dave Butz, Was	**DT**	15	1	2	1	1	—	1	1
Bob Baumhower, Mia	DT	10	1	1	1	—	—	—	—
Fred Smerlas, Buf	DT	8	1	2	1	1	—	—	—

1983 NFL (CONT.)

DEFENSE	POS	TT	+PW	+UP	AP	NE	FW	SN	PW
Doug English, Det	DT	7	—	—	2	2	1	—	—
Joe Klecko, NYJ	DT	4	—	1	2	—	—	—	—
David Logan, TB	DT	2	1	—	—	—	—	—	—
Lawrence Taylor, NYG	**OLB**	19	1	1	1	1	1	1	1
Chip Banks, Cle	**OLB**	15	1	1	2	1	—	—	1
Rod Martin, LARd	OLB	12	1	1	2	1	—	1	—
Hugh Green, TB	OLB	11	1	1	2	2	—	1	—
Lance Mehl, NYJ	OLB	3	1	2	—	—	—	—	—
Rickey Jackson, NO	OLB	2	1	—	—	—	—	—	—
Ted Hendricks, LARd	OLB	1	—	2	—	—	—	—	—
Jack Lambert, Pit	**ILB**	19	1	1	1	1	1	1	1
Mike Singletary, ChiB	ILB	10	1	1	—	1	—	—	1
Tom Cousineau, Cle	ILB	4	—	1	2	—	—	—	—
Randy Gradishar, Den	ILB	3	—	2	2	—	—	—	—
Jerry Robinson, Phi	ILB	2	—	2	—	—	—	—	—
Bob Breunig, Dal	ILB	2	—	2	—	—	—	—	—
Jim Kovach, NO	ILB	1	—	2	—	—	—	—	—
A.J. Duhe, Mia	ILB	1	—	2	—	—	—	—	—
Jim Collins, LARm	ILB	1	—	2	—	—	—	—	—
Ken Riley, Cin	**CB**	12	1	2	1	—	—	1	1
Lester Hayes, LARd	**CB**	11	1	1	2	2	—	—	1
Gary Green, KC	CB	8	—	1	—	1	1	—	—
Everson Walls, Dal	CB	6	1	2	1	—	—	—	—
Ronnie Lott, SF	CB	6	1	2	—	1	—	—	—
Johnnie Poe, NO	CB	4	—	1	2	—	—	—	—
Raymond Clayborn, NE	CB	4	—	2	—	—	—	—	—
Louis Wright, Den	CB	3	—	1	—	—	—	—	—
Eric Wright, SF	CB	2	—	1	—	—	—	—	—
Mark Haynes, NYG	CB	2	—	2	—	—	—	—	—
Mark Murphy, Was	**S**	18	1	1	1	2	1	1	1
Kenny Easley, Sea	**S**	16	1	1	1	1	—	1	1
Deron Cherry, KC	S	6	1	1	2	—	—	—	—
Nolan Cromwell, LARm	S	5	1	2	—	1	—	—	—
Johnnie Johnson, LARm	S	4	—	2	—	1	—	—	—
Vann McElroy, LARd	S	3	2	2	—	—	—	—	—
Steve Freeman, Buf	S	3	—	1	—	—	—	—	—
Russell Gary, NO	S	2	—	1	—	—	—	—	—
Roland James, NE	S	1	—	2	—	—	—	—	—

SPECIALISTS	POS	TT	+PW	+UP	AP	NE	FW	SN	PW
Ali Haji-Sheikh, NYG	**K**	19	1	1	1	1	1	1	1
Gary Anderson, Pit	K	6	1	1	2	—	—	—	—
Raul Allegre, Bal	K	3	—	2	2	—	—	—	—
Mark Moseley, Was	K	1	—	2	—	—	—	—	—
Rich Camarillo, NE	**P**	18	1	1	2	1	1	1	1
Rohn Stark, Bal	P	6	—	2	1	2	—	—	—
Carl Birdsong, SL	P	4	1	1	—	—	—	—	—
Frank Garcia, TB	P	1	—	2	—	—	—	—	—
Billy Johnson, Atl	**KR**	13	pr1	—	2	—	pr1	pr1	pr1
Fulton Walker, Mia	KR	11	kr1	—	—	kr1	kr1	kr1	—
Mike Nelms, Was	KR	5	kr1	—	1	—	—	—	—
Greg Pruitt, LARd	KR	2	pr1	—	—	—	—	—	—

1984 NFL

OFFENSE	POS	TT	+PW	+UP	AP	NE	FW	SN	PW
Roy Green, SL	**WR**	19	1	1	1	1	1	1	1
Art Monk, Was	**WR**	18	1	1	1	2	1	1	1
John Stallworth, Pit	WR	6	1	1	—	2	—	—	—
Mark Clayton, Mia	WR	5	1	2	2	—	—	—	—
James Lofton, GB	WR	4	—	2	—	1	—	—	—
Steve Largent, Sea	WR	3	—	2	2	—	—	—	—
Mark Duper, Mia	WR	2	—	1	—	—	—	—	—
Kevin House, TB	WR	1	—	2	—	—	—	—	—
Ozzie Newsome, Cle	**TE**	19	1	1	1	1	1	1	1
Paul Coffman, GB	TE	6	1	1	—	—	—	—	—
Todd Christensen, LARd	TE	3	—	2	2	—	—	—	—
Doug Cosbie, Dal	TE	1	—	2	—	—	—	—	—
Keith Fahnhorst, SF	**T**	16	1	1	1	1	—	1	—
Joe Jacoby, Was	**T**	13	1	1	1	2	1	—	—
Anthony Munoz, Cin	T	12	1	1	2	1	—	1	—
Bill Bain, LARm	T	7	1	2	—	—	—	—	1
Brian Holloway, NE	T	5	1	2	2	—	—	—	—
Henry Lawrence, LARd	T	2	—	1	—	—	—	—	—
Luis Sharpe, SL	T	1	—	1	—	—	—	—	—
Mike Kenn, Atl	T	1	—	2	—	—	—	—	—
Jon Giesler, Mia	T	1	—	2	—	—	—	—	—
John Hannah, NE	**G**	13	—	1	2	1	1	1	—
Russ Grimm, Was	**G**	11	1	1	1	1	—	—	—
Randy Cross, SF	**G**	11	1	1	2	2	—	—	1
Ed Newman, Mia	G	10	1	1	1	—	—	—	—
Mike Munchak, Hou	G	5	1	2	—	—	—	—	—
Sean Farrell, TB	G	3	—	2	—	—	—	—	—
John Ayers, SF	G	2	1	—	—	—	—	—	—
Kent Hill, LARm	G	2	—	2	—	—	—	—	—
Dennis Harrah, LARm	G	2	—	2	—	—	—	—	—
Roy Foster, Mia	G	1	—	2	—	—	—	—	—
Dwight Stephenson, Mia	**C**	19	1	1	1	1	1	1	1
Fred Quillan, SF	C	4	1	1	—	—	—	—	—
Mike Webster, Pit	C	2	—	2	—	—	—	—	—
Randy Clark, SL	C	2	—	2	—	—	—	—	—
Larry McCarren, GB	C	1	—	2	—	—	—	—	—
Dan Marino, Mia	**QB**	19	1	1	1	1	1	1	1
Joe Montana, SF	QB	8	1	1	2	2	—	—	—
Neil Lomax, SL	QB	1	—	2	—	—	—	—	—
Dave Krieg, Sea	QB	1	—	2	—	—	—	—	—

ALL-PRO TEAMS

1984 NFL (CONT.)

OFFENSE	POS	TT	+PW	+UP	AP	NE	FW	SN	PW
Walter Payton, ChiB	**RB**	19	1	1	1	1	1	1	1
Eric Dickerson, LARm	**RB**	19	1	1	1	1	1	1	1
Marcus Allen, LARd	RB	8	1	1	2	2	—	—	—
James Wilder, TB	RB	5	—	2	2	2	—	—	—
Earnest Jackson, SD	RB	3	1	2	—	—	—	—	—
Freeman McNeil, NYJ	RB	2	—	1	—	—	—	—	—
Sammy Winder, Den	RB	1	—	2	—	—	—	—	—
Gerald Riggs, Atl	RB	1	—	2	—	—	—	—	—

DEFENSE	POS	TT	+PW	+UP	AP	NE	FW	SN	PW
Mark Gastineau, NYJ	**DE**	19	1	1	1	1	1	1	1
Howie Long, LARd	**DE**	13	1	1	1	1	1	1	—
Richard Dent, ChiB	DE	9	1	1	2	—	—	—	1
Lee Roy Selmon, TB	DE	6	1	1	—	2	—	—	—
Jacob Green, Sea	DE	5	—	—	2	—	1	—	—
Art Still, KC	DE	3	—	2	2	—	—	—	—
Jack Youngblood, LARm	DE	1	—	2	—	—	—	—	—
Curtis Greer, SL	DE	1	—	2	—	—	—	—	—
Jeff Bryant, Sea	DE	1	—	2	—	—	—	—	—
Randy White, Dal	**DT**	16	1	1	1	1	1	—	1
Dan Hampton, ChiB	**DT**	15	1	2	1	1	—	1	1
Joe Nash, Sea	DT	12	1	1	1	2	—	—	1
David Logan, TB	DT	5	1	—	—	—	—	1	—
Bob Baumhower, Mia	DT	3	—	2	2	—	—	—	—
Doug English, Det	DT	2	—	—	2	—	—	—	—
Gary Dunn, Pit	DT	2	—	—	2	—	—	—	—
Dave Butz, Was	DT	2	—	2	—	—	—	—	—
Lawrence Taylor, NYG	**OLB**	19	1	1	1	1	1	1	1
Clay Matthews, Cle	**OLB**	10	1	—	2	1	—	—	1
Mike Merriweather, Pit	OLB	9	1	1	—	2	—	—	1
Rod Martin, LARd	OLB	8	—	1	1	—	1	—	—
Rickey Jackson, NO	OLB	8	1	1	2	2	—	—	—
Andre Tippett, NE	OLB	3	1	2	—	—	—	—	—
Tom Jackson, Den	OLB	3	1	2	—	—	—	—	—
Otis Wilson, ChiB	OLB	1	—	2	—	—	—	—	—
Keena Turner, SF	OLB	1	—	2	—	—	—	—	—
Mike Singletary, ChiB	**ILB**	19	1	1	1	1	1	1	1
E.J. Junior, SL	**ILB**	11	—	1	1	1	1	—	—
Jim Collins, LARm	ILB	8	1	2	2	—	—	—	1
Harry Carson, NYG	ILB	5	—	—	—	2	—	1	—
Steve Nelson, NE	ILB	4	—	1	—	—	—	—	—
Tom Cousineau, Cle	ILB	4	—	1	2	—	—	—	—
Scott Studwell, Min	ILB	1	—	2	—	—	—	—	—
Matt Millen, LARd	ILB	1	—	2	—	—	—	—	—
Robin Cole, Pit	ILB	1	—	2	—	—	—	—	—
Mike Haynes, LARd	**CB**	19	1	1	1	1	1	1	1
Louis Wright, Den	**CB**	11	1	2	—	2	—	1	1
Mark Haynes, NYG	CB	10	1	1	1	1	—	—	—
Lester Hayes, LARd	CB	5	—	1	—	1	—	—	—
Eric Wright, SF	CB	4	1	—	2	—	—	—	—
Dave Brown, Sea	CB	3	—	2	2	—	—	—	—
Everson Walls, Dal	CB	2	—	2	—	—	—	—	—
Gary Green, LARm	CB	2	—	—	2	—	—	—	—
Ronnie Lott, SF	CB	1	—	2	—	—	—	—	—
Tim Lewis, GB	CB	1	—	2	—	—	—	—	—
Kenny Easley, Sea	**S**	19	1	1	1	1	1	1	1
Todd Bell, ChiB	**S**	8	1	2	2	—	—	1	—
Michael Downs, Dal	S	7	—	1	2	—	1	—	—
Deron Cherry, KC	S	7	—	1	1	2	—	—	—
Dennis Smith, Den	S	6	1	—	—	—	—	—	1
Wes Hopkins, Phi	S	5	1	—	—	1	—	—	—
Vann McElroy, LARd	S	3	—	1	2	—	—	—	—
Dwight Hicks, SF	S	2	—	1	—	—	—	—	—
Gary Fencik, ChiB	S	1	—	2	—	—	—	—	—

SPECIALISTS	POS	TT	+PW	+UP	AP	NE	FW	SN	PW
Norm Johnson, Sea	**K**	18	1	1	1	2	1	1	1
Jan Stenerud, Min	K	9	1	1	2	1	—	—	—
Paul McFadden, Phi	K	1	—	2	—	—	—	—	—
Gary Anderson, Pit	K	1	—	2	—	—	—	—	—
Reggie Roby, Mia	**P**	19	1	1	1	1	1	1	1
Rohn Stark, Ind	P	3	—	2	2	—	—	—	—
Bucky Scribner, GB	P	2	—	1	—	—	—	—	—
Mike Horan, Phi	P	2	1	—	—	—	—	—	—
Jim Arnold, KC	P	2	1	—	—	—	—	—	—
Brian Hansen, NO	P	1	—	2	—	—	—	—	—
Fredd Young, Sea	ST	5	1	—	—	—	—	—	1
Bill Bates, Dal	ST	2	1	—	—	—	—	—	—
Bobby Humphery, NYJ	**KR**	11	kr1	—	—	kr1	kr1	kr1	
Louis Lipps, Pit	KR	10	pr1	—	2	pr1	—	pr1	
Henry Ellard, LARm	KR	8	pr1	—	1	—	pr1	—	
Stump Mitchell, SL	KR	2	kr1	—	—	—	—	—	

1985 NFL

OFFENSE	POS	TT	+UP	AP	NE	FW	SN
Mike Quick, Phi	**WR**	11	1	1	1	—	1
Louis Lipps, Pit	**WR**	10	1	2	1	1	—
Steve Largent, Sea	**WR**	10	1	1	2	1	—
Art Monk, Was	WR	7	1	2	—	—	1
James Lofton, GB	WR	3	2	—	—	—	—
Tony Hill, Dal	WR	1	2	—	—	—	—
Cris Collinsworth, Cin	WR	1	2	—	—	—	—
Mark Clayton, Mia	WR	1	2	—	—	—	—
Todd Christensen, LARd	**TE**	14	1	1	1	1	1
Ozzie Newsome, Cle	TE	3	2	2	—	—	—

1985 NFL (CONT.)

OFFENSE	POS	TT	+UP	AP	NE	FW	SN
Mickey Shuler, NYJ	TE	2	—	—	2	—	—
Doug Cosbie, Dal	TE	2	1	—	—	—	—
Jimmie Giles, TB	TE	1	2	—	—	—	—
Anthony Munoz, Cin	**T**	14	1	1	1	1	1
Jimbo Covert, ChiB	**T**	14	1	1	1	1	1
Chris Hinton, Ind	T	6	1	2	2	—	—
Brian Holloway, NE	T	3	2	2	—	—	—
Keith Fahnhorst, SF	T	2	—	—	2	—	—
Keith Dorney, Det	T	2	1	—	—	—	—
Jackie Slater, LARm	T	1	2	—	—	—	—
Jim Lachey, SD	T	1	2	—	—	—	—
Joe Jacoby, Was	T	1	2	—	—	—	—
Russ Grimm, Was	**G**	14	1	1	1	1	1
John Hannah, NE	**G**	13	1	1	2	1	1
Mike Munchak, Hou	G	5	2	2	2	—	—
Kent Hill, LARm	G	3	2	2	—	—	—
Randy Cross, SF	G	3	—	—	1	—	—
Dennis Harrah, LARm	G	2	1	—	—	—	—
Roy Foster, Mia	G	2	1	—	—	—	—
John Ayers, SF	G	1	2	—	—	—	—
Dan Alexander, NYJ	G	1	2	—	—	—	—
Dwight Stephenson, Mia	**C**	14	1	1	1	1	1
Jay Hilgenberg, ChiB	C	2	1	—	—	—	—
Joe Fields, NYJ	C	2	—	—	2	—	—
Bill Bryan, Den	C	2	—	—	2	—	—
Mike Webster, Pit	C	1	2	—	—	—	—
Fred Quillan, SF	C	1	2	—	—	—	—
Dan Marino, Mia	**QB**	13	1	1	2	1	1
Dan Fouts, SD	QB	6	2	2	—	—	—
Joe Montana, SF	QB	2	1	—	—	—	—
Jim McMahon, ChiB	QB	1	2	—	—	—	—
Walter Payton, ChiB	**RB**	14	1	1	1	1	1
Marcus Allen, LARd	**RB**	14	1	1	1	1	1
Roger Craig, SF	RB	5	2	2	2	—	—
Gerald Riggs, Atl	RB	4	1	2	—	—	—
Freeman McNeil, NYJ	RB	4	1	—	2	—	—
Curt Warner, Sea	RB	2	1	—	—	—	—
Joe Morris, NYG	RB	1	2	—	—	—	—
Lionel James, SD	RB	1	2	—	—	—	—

DEFENSE	POS	TT	+UP	AP	NE	FW	SN
Howie Long, LARd	**DE**	11	1	1	1	1	—
Rulon Jones, Den	**DE**	9	1	2	2	—	1
Richard Dent, ChiB	DE	8	1	1	—	1	—
Mark Gastineau, NYJ	DE	7	2	—	1	—	1
Leonard Marshall, NYG	DE	6	1	2	2	—	—
Too Tall Jones, Dal	DE	1	2	—	—	—	—
Jacob Green, Sea	DE	1	2	—	—	—	—
Randy White, Dal	**DT**	11	1	1	1	1	—
Joe Klecko, NYJ	**DT**	11	1	1	1	1	—
Bob Golic, Cle	DT	6	2	2	—	—	1
Dan Hampton, ChiB	DT	5	de2	2	2	—	—
Steve McMichael, ChiB	DT	4	2	1	—	—	—
Joe Nash, Sea	DT	2	—	—	2	—	—
Michael Carter, SF	DT	2	—	2	—	—	—
Andre Tippett, NE	**OLB**	14	1	1	1	1	1
Lawrence Taylor, NYG	**OLB**	14	1	1	1	1	1
Otis Wilson, ChiB	OLB	4	1	2	—	—	—
Keena Turner, SF	OLB	3	2	—	2	—	—
Mike Merriweather, Pit	OLB	3	2	—	2	—	—
Rickey Jackson, NO	OLB	3	2	2	—	—	—
Chip Banks, Cle	OLB	2	1	—	—	—	—
Rod Martin, LARd	OLB	1	2	—	—	—	—
Mike Singletary, ChiB	**ILB**	14	1	1	1	1	1
Karl Mecklenburg, Den	**ILB**	11	1	1	1	1	—
Lance Mehl, NYJ	ILB	6	1	2	2	—	—
Harry Carson, NYG	ILB	5	2	2	2	—	1
Jim Collins, LARm	ILB	4	2	—	—	—	1
E.J. Junior, SL	ILB	2	1	—	—	—	—
Steve Nelson, NE	ILB	1	2	—	—	—	—
Matt Millen, LARd	ILB	1	2	—	—	—	—
Mike Haynes, LARd	**CB**	14	1	1	1	1	1
Eric Wright, SF	**CB**	11	1	1	—	1	1
Everson Walls, Dal	CB	9	1	2	2	1	—
LeRoy Irvin, LARm	CB	3	2	2	—	—	—
Raymond Clayborn, NE	CB	3	2	2	—	—	—
Louis Wright, Den	CB	2	1	—	—	—	—
Gary Green, LARm	CB	1	2	—	—	—	—
Dave Brown, Sea	CB	1	2	—	—	—	—
Wes Hopkins, Phi	**S**	14	1	1	1	1	1
Kenny Easley, Sea	**S**	14	1	1	1	1	1
Deron Cherry, KC	S	6	1	2	2	—	—
Gary Fencik, ChiB	S	3	2	2	—	—	—
Bo Eason, Hou	S	2	—	—	2	—	—
Michael Downs, Dal	S	2	1	—	—	—	—
Dennis Smith, Den	S	1	2	—	—	—	—
Fred Marion, NE	S	1	2	—	—	—	—
Joey Browner, Min	S	1	2	—	—	—	—

SPECIALISTS	POS	TT	+UP	AP	NE	FW	SN
Nick Lowery, KC	**K**	7	2	1	1	—	—
Morten Andersen, NO	**K**	7	1	2	—	—	1
Gary Anderson, Pit	K	5	1	—	—	1	—
Kevin Butler, ChiB	K	3	2	—	2	—	—
Dale Hatcher, LARm	**P**	11	1	1	—	1	1

1985 NFL (CONT.)

SPECIALISTS	POS	TT	+UP	AP	NE	FW	SN
Rohn Stark, Ind	P	7	1	2	1	—	—
Reggie Roby, Mia	P	3	2	—	2	—	—
Sean Landeta, NYG	P	1	2	—	—	—	—
Ron Brown, LARm	**KR**	9	—	1	—	1	kr1
Henry Ellard, LARm	KR	3	—	—	—	—	pr1
Irving Fryar, NE	KR	2	—	2	—	—	—

1986 NFL

OFFENSE	POS	TT	+PW	+UP	AP	NE	FW	SN	PW
Jerry Rice, SF	**WR**	19	1	1	1	1	1	1	1
Al Toon, NYJ	**WR**	16	1	1	1	1	1	—	1
Stanley Morgan, NE	WR	11	1	1	2	2	—	1	—
Gary Clark, Was	WR	6	1	1	2	—	—	—	—
Steve Largent, Sea	WR	3	—	2	—	—	—	—	—
Wesley Walker, NYJ	WR	1	—	2	—	—	—	—	—
Mike Quick, Phi	WR	1	—	2	—	—	—	—	—
Art Monk, Was	WR	1	—	2	—	—	—	—	—
Mark Bavaro, NYG	**TE**	18	1	1	1	2	1	1	1
Todd Christensen, LARd	TE	9	1	1	2	1	—	—	—
Mickey Shuler, NYJ	TE	1	—	2	—	—	—	—	—
Steve Jordan, Min	TE	1	—	2	—	—	—	—	—
Anthony Munoz, Cin	**T**	19	1	1	1	1	1	1	1
Jimbo Covert, ChiB	**T**	16	1	1	1	—	1	1	1
Jackie Slater, LARm	T	8	1	1	2	2	—	—	—
Gary Zimmerman, Min	T	3	—	2	—	—	—	—	—
Cody Risien, Cle	T	3	1	2	—	—	—	—	—
Brian Holloway, NE	T	3	—	—	—	1	—	—	—
Chris Hinton, Ind	T	2	—	1	—	—	—	—	—
Brad Benson, NYG	T	2	—	—	2	—	—	—	—
Joe Jacoby, Was	T	1	—	2	—	—	—	—	—
Jon Giesler, Mia	T	1	—	2	—	—	—	—	—
Dennis Harrah, LARm	**G**	16	1	1	1	—	1	1	1
Bill Fralic, Atl	**G**	15	1	2	1	1	—	1	1
Russ Grimm, Was	G	10	—	1	2	1	1	—	—
Max Montoya, Cin	G	4	1	1	—	—	—	—	—
Roy Foster, Mia	G	4	1	1	—	—	—	—	—
Randy Cross, SF	G	4	—	—	2	2	—	—	—
Dan Fike, Cle	G	2	—	—	—	2	—	—	—
Chris Godfrey, NYG	G	1	—	2	—	—	—	—	—
Keith Bishop, Den	G	1	—	2	—	—	—	—	—
Dan Alexander, NYJ	G	1	—	2	—	—	—	—	—
Dwight Stephenson, Mia	**C**	19	1	1	1	1	1	1	1
Jay Hilgenberg, ChiB	C	8	1	1	2	2	—	—	—
Doug Smith, LARm	C	1	—	2	—	—	—	—	—
Ray Donaldson, Ind	C	1	—	2	—	—	—	—	—
Dan Marino, Mia	**QB**	18	1	1	1	2	1	1	1
Tommy Kramer, Min	QB	6	1	1	2	—	—	—	—
Phil Simms, NYG	QB	3	—	—	—	1	—	—	—
Jay Schroeder, Was	QB	1	—	2	—	—	—	—	—
John Elway, Den	QB	1	—	2	—	—	—	—	—
Joe Morris, NYG	**RB**	19	1	1	1	1	1	1	1
Eric Dickerson, LARm	**RB**	19	1	1	1	1	1	1	1
Curt Warner, Sea	RB	8	1	1	2	2	—	—	—
Walter Payton, ChiB	RB	5	—	2	2	2	—	—	—
James Brooks, Cin	RB	4	1	1	—	—	—	—	—
Gerald Willhite, Den	RB	1	—	2	—	—	—	—	—
Rueben Mayes, NO	RB	1	—	2	—	—	—	—	—
Marcus Allen, LARd	RB	1	—	2	—	—	—	—	—

DEFENSE	POS	TT	+PW	+UP	AP	NE	FW	SN	PW
Dexter Manley, Was	**DE**	19	1	1	1	1	1	1	1
Rulon Jones, Den	**DE**	18	1	1	1	2	1	1	1
Dan Hampton, ChiB	DE	7	—	1	2	1	—	—	—
Howie Long, LARd	DE	4	1	—	—	2	—	—	—
Leonard Marshall, NYG	DE	3	—	2	2	—	—	—	—
Art Still, KC	DE	2	—	1	—	—	—	—	—
Lee Williams, SD	DE	1	—	2	—	—	—	—	—
Bruce Smith, Buf	DE	1	—	2	—	—	—	—	—
Rick Bryan, Atl	DE	1	—	2	—	—	—	—	—
Steve McMichael, ChiB	**DT**	14	1	2	2	—	1	1	1
Reggie White, Phi	**DT**	13	de1	1	1	1	1	—	—
Bill Pickel, LARd	DT	8	—	1	1	—	—	1	—
Bill Maas, KC	DT	7	1	—	2	—	—	—	1
Michael Carter, SF	DT	3	—	—	1	—	—	—	—
Keith Millard, Min	DT	2	—	—	2	—	—	—	—
Bob Golic, Cle	DT	2	—	—	2	—	—	—	—
Jim Burt, NYG	DT	2	1	—	—	—	—	—	—
Joe Klecko, NYJ	DT	1	—	2	—	—	—	—	—
Lawrence Taylor, NYG	**OLB**	19	1	1	1	1	1	1	1
Wilber Marshall, ChiB	**OLB**	18	1	1	1	2	1	1	1
Andre Tippett, NE	OLB	8	1	1	2	2	—	—	—
Rickey Jackson, NO	OLB	6	—	2	2	1	—	—	—
Chip Banks, Cle	OLB	4	1	1	—	—	—	—	—
Keena Turner, SF	OLB	1	—	2	—	—	—	—	—
Bryan Hinkle, Pit	OLB	1	—	2	—	—	—	—	—
Don Blackmon, NE	OLB	1	—	2	—	—	—	—	—
Mike Singletary, ChiB	**ILB**	19	1	1	1	1	1	1	1
Karl Mecklenburg, Den	**ILB**	19	1	1	1	1	1	1	1
Harry Carson, NYG	ILB	8	1	1	2	2	—	—	—
John Offerdahl, Mia	ILB	6	1	1	2	—	—	—	—
Kyle Clifton, NYJ	ILB	2	—	2	—	—	—	—	—
Fredd Young, Sea	ILB	1	—	2	—	—	—	—	—
Billy Ray Smith, SD	ILB	1	—	2	—	—	—	—	—
Mark Jerue, LARm	ILB	1	—	2	—	—	—	—	—
Carl Ekern, LARm	ILB	1	—	2	—	—	—	—	—

1986 NFL (CONT.)

DEFENSE	POS	TT	+PW	+UP	AP	NE	FW	SN	PW
Hanford Dixon, Cle	**CB**	19	1	1	1	1	1	1	1
LeRoy Irvin, LARm	**CB**	13	—	1	1	2	1	1	—
Darrell Green, Was	CB	8	1	2	2	1	—	—	—
Jerry Gray, LARm	CB	6	1	1	2	—	—	—	—
Raymond Clayborn, NE	CB	5	1	—	—	—	—	—	1
Albert Lewis, KC	CB	3	—	2	—	2	—	—	—
Ronnie Lippett, NE	CB	2	—	1	—	—	—	—	—
Mike Richardson, ChiB	CB	1	—	2	—	—	—	—	—
Frank Minnifield, Cle	CB	1	—	2	—	—	—	—	—
Ronnie Lott, SF	**S**	16	1	1	1	1	1	—	1
Dave Duerson, ChiB	**S**	15	1	1	2	—	1	1	1
Deron Cherry, KC	S	12	1	1	1	2	—	—	—
Leonard Smith, SL	S	5	—	2	2	2	—	—	—
Dennis Smith, Den	S	5	1	—	—	1	—	—	—
Lloyd Burruss, KC	S	2	—	1	—	—	—	—	—
Vince Newsome, LARm	S	1	—	2	—	—	—	—	—
Vann McElroy, LARd	S	1	—	2	—	—	—	—	—
Kenny Easley, Sea	S	1	—	2	—	—	—	—	—

SPECIALISTS	POS	TT	+PW	+UP	AP	NE	FW	SN	PW
Morten Andersen, NO	**K**	19	1	1	1	1	1	1	1
Tony Franklin, NE	K	6	1	1	2	—	—	—	—
Pat Leahy, NYJ	K	2	—	—	—	2	—	—	—
Ray Wersching, SF	K	1	—	2	—	—	—	—	—
Nick Lowery, KC	K	1	—	2	—	—	—	—	—
Sean Landeta, NYG	**P**	18	1	1	1	2	1	1	1
Rohn Stark, Ind	P	9	1	1	2	1	—	—	—
Reggie Roby, Mia	P	1	—	2	—	—	—	—	—
Steve Cox, Was	P	1	—	2	—	—	—	—	—
Mosi Tatupu, NE	ST	5	1	—	—	—	—	—	1
Neal Anderson, ChiB	ST	2	1	—	—	—	—	—	—
Bobby Joe Edmonds, Sea	**KR**	14	pr1	—	1	—	1	pr1	pr1
Dennis Gentry, ChiB	KR	5	kr1	—	—	—	—	—	kr1
Vai Sikahema, SL	KR	4	pr1	2	—	—	—	—	—
Mel Gray, NO	KR	3	—	—	—	—	—	kr1	—
Tim McGee, Cin	KR	2	kr1	—	—	—	—	—	—

1987 NFL

OFFENSE	POS	TT	+PW	+UP	AP	NE	FW	SN	PW
Jerry Rice, SF	**WR**	19	1	1	1	1	1	1	1
J.T. Smith, SL	**WR**	12	1	1	2	—	—	1	1
Steve Largent, Sea	WR	11	1	1	2	2	1	—	—
Gary Clark, Was	WR	5	—	—	1	2	—	—	—
Al Toon, NYJ	WR	4	1	1	—	—	—	—	—
Mike Quick, Phi	WR	4	—	2	2	—	—	—	—
Anthony Carter, Min	WR	1	—	2	—	—	—	—	—
Carlos Carson, KC	WR	1	—	2	—	—	—	—	—
Chris Burkett, Buf	WR	1	—	2	—	—	—	—	—
Mark Bavaro, NYG	**TE**	19	1	1	1	1	1	1	1
Kellen Winslow, SD	TE	4	—	1	2	—	—	—	—
Todd Christensen, LARd	TE	3	1	2	—	—	—	—	—
Robert Awalt, SL	TE	2	—	—	2	—	—	—	—
Steve Jordan, Min	TE	1	—	2	—	—	—	—	—
Gary Zimmerman, Min	**T**	17	1	2	1	2	1	1	1
Anthony Munoz, Cin	**T**	13	1	1	1	—	1	1	1
Jackie Slater, LARm	T	9	1	1	2	1	—	—	—
Chris Hinton, Ind	T	6	1	2	—	1	—	—	—
Jim Lachey, SD	T	4	—	1	2	—	—	—	—
Jimbo Covert, ChiB	T	4	—	1	—	2	—	—	—
Joe Jacoby, Was	T	3	—	—	1	—	—	—	—
Luis Sharpe, SL	T	1	—	2	—	—	—	—	—
Cody Risien, Cle	T	1	—	2	—	—	—	—	—
Mike Munchak, Hou	**G**	19	1	1	1	1	1	1	1
Bill Fralic, Atl	**G**	18	1	1	1	2	1	1	1
Ron Solt, Ind	G	9	1	1	2	1	—	—	—
Tom Newberry, LARm	G	6	1	1	2	—	—	—	—
Keith Bishop, Den	G	3	—	2	2	—	—	—	—
Dennis Harrah, LARm	G	1	—	2	—	—	—	—	—
Dan Fike, Cle	G	1	—	2	—	—	—	—	—
Brad Edelman, NO	G	1	—	2	—	—	—	—	—
Dwight Stephenson, Mia	**C**	13	1	1	1	—	1	1	1
Jay Hilgenberg, ChiB	C	7	1	1	2	—	—	—	—
Ray Donaldson, Ind	C	5	1	2	2	2	—	—	—
Mike Webster, Pit	C	3	—	—	1	—	—	—	—
Bart Oates, NYG	C	1	—	2	—	—	—	—	—
Randy Cross, SF	C	1	—	2	—	—	—	—	—
Joe Montana, SF	**QB**	15	1	1	1	2	1	—	1
John Elway, Den	QB	12	1	1	2	1	—	1	—
Neil Lomax, SL	QB	1	—	2	—	—	—	—	—
Bernie Kosar, Cle	QB	1	—	2	—	—	—	—	—
Eric Dickerson, Ind	**RB**	19	1	1	1	1	1	1	1
Charles White, LARm	**RB**	18	1	1	1	2	1	1	1
Curt Warner, Sea	RB	9	1	1	2	1	—	—	—
Herschel Walker, Dal	RB	7	1	2	2	2	—	—	—
Rueben Mayes, NO	RB	2	—	1	—	—	—	—	—
Mike Rozier, Hou	RB	2	—	1	—	—	—	—	—
Roger Craig, SF	RB	1	—	2	—	—	—	—	—
Earnest Byner, Cle	RB	1	—	2	—	—	—	—	—

DEFENSE	POS	TT	+PW	+UP	AP	NE	FW	SN	PW
Reggie White, Phi	**DE**	19	1	1	1	1	1	1	1
Bruce Smith, Buf	**DE**	18	1	1	1	2	1	1	1
Chris Doleman, Min	DE	9	1	1	2	1	—	—	—
Jacob Green, Sea	DE	4	1	1	—	—	—	—	—
Charles Mann, Was	DE	3	—	2	2	—	—	—	—

1987 NFL (CONT.)

OFFENSE	POS	TT	+PW	+UP	AP	NE	FW	SN	PW
Bruce Clark, NO	DE	2	—	—	—	2	—	—	—
Dexter Manley, Was	DE	1	—	2	—	—	—	—	—
Rulon Jones, Den	DE	1	—	2	—	—	—	—	—
Carl Hairston, Cle	DE	1	—	2	—	—	—	—	—
Michael Carter, SF	**DT**	16	1	1	1	1	1	1	—
Steve McMichael, ChiB	DT	12	1	2	1	—	—	1	1
Bill Maas, KC	DT	9	1	1	—	2	—	—	1
Tim Krumrie, Cin	DT	3	—	2	2	—	—	—	—
Keith Millard, Min	DT	2	—	2	—	—	—	—	—
Andre Tippett, NE	**OLB**	15	1	1	1	2	1	—	1
Carl Banks, NYG	**OLB**	14	—	1	1	1	1	1	—
Lawrence Taylor, NYG	OLB	8	1	2	2	—	—	—	1
Duane Bickett, Ind	OLB	8	1	1	2	2	—	—	—
Rickey Jackson, NO	OLB	6	—	—	1	—	1	—	—
Wilber Marshall, ChiB	OLB	3	1	2	—	—	—	—	—
Pat Swilling, NO	OLB	2	—	1	—	—	—	—	—
Mike Merriweather, Pit	OLB	1	—	2	—	—	—	—	—
Chip Banks, SD	OLB	1	—	2	—	—	—	—	—
Fredd Young, Sea	**ILB**	19	1	1	1	1	1	1	1
Mike Singletary, ChiB	**ILB**	18	1	1	1	2	1	1	1
Karl Mecklenburg, Den	ILB	9	1	1	2	1	—	—	—
Vaughan Johnson, NO	ILB	4	1	1	—	—	—	—	—
Shane Conlan, Buf	ILB	4	—	2	2	—	—	—	—
Billy Ray Smith, SD	ILB	1	—	2	—	—	—	—	—
Ervin Randle, TB	ILB	1	—	2	—	—	—	—	—
John Offerdahl, Mia	ILB	1	—	2	—	—	—	—	—
Brian Noble, GB	ILB	1	—	2	—	—	—	—	—
Hanford Dixon, Cle	**CB**	19	1	1	1	1	1	1	1
Frank Minnifield, Cle	**CB**	17	1	1	2	2	1	1	1
Barry Wilburn, Was	CB	7	1	1	1	—	—	—	—
Jerry Gray, LARm	CB	5	1	2	—	2	—	—	—
Dave Waymer, NO	CB	4	—	1	2	—	—	—	—
Darrell Green, Was	CB	3	—	—	—	1	—	—	—
Ronnie Lippett, NE	CB	1	—	2	—	—	—	—	—
Albert Lewis, KC	CB	1	—	2	—	—	—	—	—
Don Griffin, SF	CB	1	—	2	—	—	—	—	—
Joey Browner, Min	**S**	19	1	1	1	1	1	1	1
Ronnie Lott, SF	**S**	18	1	1	1	2	1	1	1
Keith Bostic, Hou	S	9	1	1	2	1	—	—	—
Kenny Easley, Sea	S	5	1	2	—	2	—	—	—
Dave Duerson, ChiB	S	3	—	2	2	—	—	—	—
Vann McElroy, LARd	S	2	—	1	—	—	—	—	—
Alvin Walton, Was	S	1	—	2	—	—	—	—	—
Deron Cherry, KC	S	1	—	2	—	—	—	—	—

SPECIALISTS	POS	TT	+PW	+UP	AP	NE	FW	SN	PW
Morten Andersen, NO	**K**	19	1	1	1	1	1	1	1
Dean Biasucci, Ind	K	8	1	1	2	2	—	—	—
Roger Ruzek, Dal	K	1	—	2	—	—	—	—	—
Pat Leahy, NYJ	K	1	—	2	—	—	—	—	—
Jim Arnold, Det	**P**	19	1	1	1	1	1	1	1
Ralf Mojsiejenko, SD	P	6	—	1	2	2	—	—	—
Reggie Roby, Mia	P	3	1	2	—	—	—	—	—
Rick Donnelly, Atl	P	1	—	2	—	—	—	—	—
Ron Wolfley, SL	ST	5	1	—	—	—	—	—	1
Steve Tasker, Buf	ST	2	1	—	—	—	—	—	—
Mel Gray, NO	**KR**	11	pr1	—	—	—	pr1	pr1	pr1
Sylvester Stamps, Atl	KR	8	kr1	—	—	—	—	kr1	kr1
Dennis Gentry, ChiB	KR	5	—	—	2	—	kr1	—	—
Vai Sikahema, SL	KR	3	—	1	—	—	—	—	—
Paul Palmer, KC	KR	2	kr1	—	—	—	—	—	—
Lionel James, SD	KR	2	pr1	—	—	—	—	—	—

1988 NFL

OFFENSE	POS	TT	+PW	+UP	AP	NE	FW	SN	PW
Jerry Rice, SF	**WR**	18	1	1	1	2	1	1	1
Henry Ellard, LARm	**WR**	16	1	1	1	1	1	1	—
Al Toon, NYJ	WR	11	1	1	2	2	—	—	1
Eddie Brown, Cin	WR	9	1	1	2	1	—	—	—
Drew Hill, Hou	WR	1	—	2	—	—	—	—	—
Mark Clayton, Mia	WR	1	—	2	—	—	—	—	—
Anthony Carter, Min	WR	1	—	2	—	—	—	—	—
Keith Jackson, Phi	**TE**	18	1	1	1	1	1	1	1
Mickey Shuler, NYJ	TE	9	1	1	2	1	—	—	—
Rodney Holman, Cin	TE	1	—	2	—	—	—	—	—
Anthony Munoz, Cin	**T**	19	1	1	1	1	1	1	1
Gary Zimmerman, Min	**T**	10	—	1	1	2	1	—	—
Bruce Armstrong, NE	T	7	—	1	2	—	—	—	—
Jackie Slater, LARm	T	6	1	1	2	—	—	—	1
Luis Sharpe, Phx	T	6	1	1	2	—	—	—	—
Irv Pankey, LARm	T	3	—	—	1	—	—	—	—
Tunch Ilkin, Pit	T	3	1	2	—	—	—	—	—
Chris Hinton, Ind	T	3	—	2	—	2	—	—	—
Bruce Matthews, Hou	**G**	18	1	1	1	2	1	1	1
Tom Newberry, LARm	**G**	16	1	1	1	1	1	1	1
Mike Munchak, Hou	G	8	1	2	2	1	—	—	—
Bill Fralic, Atl	G	7	1	2	1	—	—	—	—
Max Montoya, Cin	G	4	—	1	2	—	—	—	—
Mark May, Was	G	2	1	—	2	—	—	—	—
Bryan Millard, Sea	G	1	—	2	—	—	—	—	—
Randall McDaniel, Min	G	1	—	2	—	—	—	—	—
Jay Hilgenberg, ChiB	**C**	19	1	1	1	1	1	1	1
Ray Donaldson, Ind	C	5	1	2	—	2	—	—	—
Kent Hull, Buf	C	4	—	1	2	—	—	—	—
Boomer Esiason, Cin	**QB**	19	1	1	1	1	1	1	1

1988 NFL (CONT.)

OFFENSE	POS	TT	+PW	+UP	AP	NE	FW	SN	PW
Randall Cunningham, Phi	QB	6	1	1	2	—	—	—	—
Dan Marino, Mia	QB	2	—	—	—	2	—	—	—
Warren Moon, Hou	QB	1	—	2	—	—	—	—	—
Jim Everett, LARm	QB	1	—	2	—	—	—	—	—
Eric Dickerson, Ind	**RB**	19	1	1	1	1	1	1	1
Roger Craig, SF	**RB**	19	1	1	1	1	1	1	1
Herschel Walker, Dal	RB	8	1	1	2	2	—	—	—
Ickey Woods, Cin	RB	5	—	2	2	2	—	—	—
John Stephens, NE	RB	4	1	1	—	—	—	—	—
James Brooks, Cin	RB	1	—	2	—	—	—	—	—
Neal Anderson, ChiB	RB	1	—	2	—	—	—	—	—

DEFENSE	POS	TT	+PW	+UP	AP	NE	FW	SN	PW
Reggie White, Phi	**DE**	19	1	1	1	1	1	1	1
Bruce Smith, Buf	**DE**	19	1	1	1	1	1	1	1
Richard Dent, ChiB	DE	8	1	1	2	2	—	—	—
Ray Childress, Hou	DE	8	1	1	2	2	—	—	—
Lee Williams, SD	DE	1	—	2	—	—	—	—	—
Greg Townsend, LARd	DE	1	—	2	—	—	—	—	—
Freddie Joe Nunn, Phx	DE	1	—	2	—	—	—	—	—
Chris Doleman, Min	DE	1	—	2	—	—	—	—	—
Tim Krumrie, Cin	**DT**	15	1	2	1	—	1	1	1
Dan Hampton, ChiB	**DT**	12	1	1	2	1	—	—	1
Keith Millard, Min	DT	11	—	1	2	1	1	—	—
Michael Carter, SF	DT	7	1	—	2	1	—	—	—
Fred Smerlas, Buf	DT	2	—	1	—	—	—	—	—
Steve McMichael, ChiB	DT	1	—	2	—	—	—	—	—
Cornelius Bennett, Buf	**OLB**	19	1	1	1	1	1	1	1
Lawrence Taylor, NYG	**OLB**	18	1	1	1	2	1	1	1
Andre Tippett, NE	OLB	8	1	1	2	2	—	—	—
Tim Harris, GB	OLB	7	1	—	†2	1	—	—	—
Mike Cofer, Det	OLB	3	—	2	†2	—	—	—	—
Charles Haley, SF	OLB	2	—	1	—	—	—	—	—
Clay Matthews, Cle	OLB	1	—	2	—	—	—	—	—
Duane Bickett, Ind	OLB	1	—	2	—	—	—	—	—
Mike Singletary, ChiB	**ILB**	19	1	1	1	1	1	1	1
Shane Conlan, Buf	**ILB**	15	1	1	2	—	1	1	1
Vaughan Johnson, NO	ILB	7	1	1	—	1	—	—	—
John Offerdahl, Mia	ILB	6	1	1	2	—	—	—	—
Scott Studwell, Min	ILB	2	—	—	2	—	—	—	—
Johnny Rembert, NE	ILB	1	—	2	—	—	—	—	—
Dino Hackett, KC	ILB	1	—	2	—	—	—	—	—
Frank Minnifield, Cle	**CB**	19	1	1	1	1	1	1	1
Carl Lee, Min	**CB**	18	1	1	1	2	1	1	1
Albert Lewis, KC	CB	4	1	1	—	—	—	—	—
Jerry Gray, LARm	CB	4	1	—	—	2	—	—	—
Scott Case, Atl	CB	4	—	1	2	—	—	—	—
Ronnie Lippett, NE	CB	3	—	—	1	—	—	—	—
Hanford Dixon, Cle	CB	2	—	—	2	—	—	—	—
Eric Thomas, Cin	CB	1	—	2	—	—	—	—	—
Tim McKyer, SF	CB	1	—	2	—	—	—	—	—
Raymond Clayborn, NE	CB	1	—	2	—	—	—	—	—
Joey Browner, Min	**S**	19	1	1	1	1	1	1	1
Deron Cherry, KC	**S**	18	1	1	1	2	1	1	1
Ronnie Lott, SF	S	7	—	1	2	1	—	—	—
David Fulcher, Cin	S	6	1	1	2	—	—	—	—
Dave Duerson, ChiB	S	2	1	—	—	—	—	—	—
Bennie Blades, Det	S	2	—	—	2	—	—	—	—
Erik McMillan, NYJ	S	1	—	2	—	—	—	—	—
Terry Hoage, Phi	S	1	—	2	—	—	—	—	—
Lloyd Burruss, KC	S	1	—	2	—	—	—	—	—

SPECIALISTS	POS	TT	+PW	+UP	AP	NE	FW	SN	PW
Scott Norwood, Buf	**K**	13	1	1	1	—	1	—	1
Dean Biasucci, Ind	K	5	—	—	2	—	—	1	—
Nick Lowery, KC	K	4	—	2	—	1	—	—	—
Morten Andersen, NO	K	4	—	1	—	2	—	—	—
Eddie Murray, Det	K	2	1	—	—	—	—	—	—
Chuck Nelson, Min	K	1	—	2	—	—	—	—	—
Mike Horan, Den	**P**	15	1	1	1	2	1	1	—
Jim Arnold, Det	P	12	1	1	2	1	—	—	1
Ralf Mojsiejenko, SD	P	1	—	2	—	—	—	—	—
Rick Donnelly, Atl	P	1	—	2	—	—	—	—	—
Eugene Seale, Hou	ST	5	1	—	—	—	—	—	1
Robert Delpino, LARm	ST	2	1	—	—	—	—	—	—
John Taylor, SF	**KR**	11	pr1	—	—	—	pr1	pr1	pr1
Tim Brown, LARd	**KR**	11	kr1	—	—	—	kr1	kr1	kr1
Jo-Jo Townsell, NYJ	KR	2	pr1	—	—	—	—	—	—
Dennis Gentry, ChiB	KR	2	kr1	—	—	—	—	—	—

1989 NFL

OFFENSE	POS	TT	+PW	+UP	AP	NE	FW	SN	PW
Sterling Sharpe, GB	**WR**	19	1	1	1	1	1	1	1
Jerry Rice, SF	**WR**	19	1	1	1	1	1	1	1
Andre Reed, Buf	WR	8	1	1	2	2	—	—	—
Webster Slaughter, Cle	WR	4	—	1	2	—	—	—	—
Anthony Miller, SD	WR	3	1	2	—	—	—	—	—
Mark Carrier, TB	WR	3	—	2	2	—	—	—	—
Henry Ellard, LARm	WR	2	1	2	—	—	—	—	—
Brian Blades, Sea	WR	1	—	2	—	—	—	—	—
Keith Jackson, Phi	**TE**	13	1	1	1	1	1	1	1
Rodney Holman, Cin	TE	12	1	1	2	1	—	—	1
Steve Jordan, Min	TE	3	—	2	2	—	—	—	—
Ferrell Edmunds, Mia	TE	1	—	2	—	—	—	—	—
Anthony Munoz, Cin	**T**	19	1	1	1	1	1	1	1

1989 NFL (CONT.)

OFFENSE	POS	TT	+PW	+UP	AP	NE	FW	SN	PW
Jim Lachey, Was	T	13	1	1	1	—	—	1	1
Jackie Slater, LARm	T	8	1	2	2	1	—	—	—
Chris Hinton, Ind	T	8	1	1	2	2	—	—	—
Gary Zimmerman, Min	T	4	—	2	—	—	1	—	—
Paul Gruber, TB	T	2	—	1	—	—	—	—	—
Lomas Brown, Det	T	2	—	—	2	—	—	—	—
Bruce Armstrong, NE	T	1	—	2	—	—	—	—	—
John Alt, KC	T	1	—	2	—	—	—	—	—
Tom Newberry, LARm	G	18	1	1	1	2	1	1	1
Mike Munchak, Hou	G	15	1	1	2	1	1	—	†1
Bruce Matthews, Hou	G	15	1	1	1	2	—	1	†1
Rich Moran, GB	G	3	—	—	—	1	—	—	—
Max Montoya, Cin	G	3	—	2	2	—	—	—	—
Randall McDaniel, Min	G	3	1	2	—	—	—	—	—
Bill Fralic, Atl	G	2	—	1	—	—	—	—	—
Ron Hallstrom, GB	G	1	—	2	—	—	—	—	—
Roy Foster, Mia	G	1	—	2	—	—	—	—	—
Jay Hilgenberg, ChiB	C	16	1	1	1	1	1	—	1
Kent Hull, Buf	C	9	1	1	2	—	—	1	—
Kirk Lowdermilk, Min	C	3	—	2	2	—	—	—	—
Ray Donaldson, Ind	C	1	—	2	—	—	—	—	—
Joe Montana, SF	QB	19	1	1	1	1	1	1	1
Don Majkowski, GB	QB	3	—	2	2	—	—	—	—
Boomer Esiason, Cin	QB	3	1	2	—	—	—	—	—
Warren Moon, Hou	QB	2	—	1	—	—	—	—	—
Jim Everett, LARm	QB	2	—	—	—	2	—	—	—
Christian Okoye, KC	RB	19	1	1	1	1	1	1	1
Barry Sanders, Det	RB	18	1	1	1	2	1	1	1
Thurman Thomas, Buf	RB	9	1	1	2	1	—	—	—
Dalton Hilliard, NO	RB	5	—	2	2	—	—	—	—
Neal Anderson, ChiB	RB	4	1	1	—	—	—	—	—
Bo Jackson, LARd	RB	1	—	2	—	—	—	—	—
Roger Craig, SF	RB	1	—	2	—	—	—	—	—
James Brooks, Cin	RB	1	—	2	—	—	—	—	—

DEFENSE	POS	TT	+PW	+UP	AP	NE	FW	SN	PW
Chris Doleman, Min	DE	19	1	1	1	1	1	1	1
Reggie White, Phi	DE	16	1	1	1	1	1	—	1
Lee Williams, SD	DE	9	1	1	2	—	—	1	—
Bruce Smith, Buf	DE	8	1	1	2	2	—	—	—
Howie Long, LARd	DE	2	—	2	—	—	—	—	—
Greg Townsend, LARd	DE	1	—	2	—	—	—	—	—
Clyde Simmons, Phi	DE	1	—	2	—	—	—	—	—
Charles Mann, Was	DE	1	—	2	—	—	—	—	—
Keith Millard, Min	DT	19	1	1	1	1	1	1	1
Michael Dean Perry, Cle	DT	16	1	1	1	1	1	—	—
Jerry Ball, Det	DT	7	1	—	—	2	—	—	1
Ray Childress, Hou	DT	3	—	de2	2	—	—	—	—
Tony Casillas, Atl	DT	3	—	1	2	—	—	—	—
Greg Kragen, Den	DT	2	1	—	—	—	—	—	—
Jerome Brown, Phi	DT	2	—	—	2	—	—	—	—
Fred Smerlas, Buf	DT	1	—	2	—	—	—	—	—
Tim Harris, GB	OLB	19	1	1	1	1	1	1	1
Lawrence Taylor, NYG	OLB	15	1	1	1	2	1	—	1
Kevin Greene, LARm	OLB	9	—	2	2	1	—	1	—
Pat Swilling, NO	OLB	5	—	2	2	2	—	—	—
Derrick Thomas, KC	OLB	4	1	1	—	—	—	—	—
Leslie O'Neal, SD	OLB	4	1	1	—	—	—	—	—
Clay Matthews, Cle	OLB	1	—	2	—	—	—	—	—
Cornelius Bennett, Buf	OLB	1	—	2	—	—	—	—	—
Mike Singletary, ChiB	ILB	16	1	1	1	—	—	1	1
Karl Mecklenburg, Den	ILB	16	1	1	1	1	—	—	1
Vaughan Johnson, NO	ILB	9	1	1	2	1	—	—	—
Eugene Lockhart, Dal	ILB	5	—	—	2	—	—	1	—
Mike Johnson, Cle	ILB	4	1	1	—	—	—	—	—
Mike Walter, SF	ILB	2	—	—	2	—	—	—	—
Billy Ray Smith, SD	ILB	2	—	—	2	—	—	—	—
Scott Studwell, Min	ILB	1	—	2	—	—	—	—	—
Chris Spielman, Det	ILB	1	—	2	—	—	—	—	—
John Offerdahl, Mia	ILB	1	—	2	—	—	—	—	—
John Grimsley, Hou	ILB	1	—	2	—	—	—	—	—
Albert Lewis, KC	CB	19	1	1	1	1	1	1	1
Eric Allen, Phi	CB	12	1	1	1	2	—	—	1
Jerry Gray, LARm	CB	8	1	2	2	—	—	—	—
Frank Minnifield, Cle	CB	6	—	1	2	2	—	—	—
Mark Collins, NYG	CB	3	—	—	2	—	—	—	—
Gill Byrd, SD	CB	3	—	—	—	—	—	1	—
Rod Woodson, Pit	CB	2	—	1	—	—	—	—	—
Don Griffin, SF	CB	2	—	1	—	—	—	—	—
Kevin Ross, KC	CB	1	—	2	—	—	—	—	—
Nate Odomes, Buf	CB	1	—	2	—	—	—	—	—
Carl Lee, Min	CB	1	—	2	—	—	—	—	—
David Fulcher, Cin	S	18	1	1	1	2	1	1	1
Ronnie Lott, SF	S	13	1	1	1	—	1	—	1
Joey Browner, Min	S	8	†1	2	2	—	—	—	—
Tim McDonald, Phx	S	7	†1	1	—	—	—	—	—
Dennis Smith, Den	S	5	1	2	—	—	—	—	—
Erik McMillan, NYJ	S	4	—	1	—	—	—	—	—
Harry Hamilton, TB	S	4	—	2	—	—	—	1	—
Deron Cherry, KC	S	1	—	2	—	—	—	—	—

SPECIALISTS	POS	TT	+PW	+UP	AP	NE	FW	SN	PW
Eddie Murray, Det	K	10	1	—	2	—	—	1	1
Mike Cofer, SF	K	8	—	1	1	1	—	—	—
Mike Lansford, LARm	K	5	—	—	—	2	—	1	—

1989 NFL (CONT.)

SPECIALISTS	POS	TT	+PW	+UP	AP	NE	FW	SN	PW
David Treadwell, Den	K	4	1	1	—	—	—	—	—
Tony Zendejas, Hou	K	1	—	2	—	—	—	—	—
Kevin Butler, ChiB	K	1	—	2	—	—	—	—	—
Sean Landeta, NYG	P	16	1	1	1	—	1	1	1
Greg Montgomery, Hou	P	7	1	1	—	1	—	—	—
Reggie Roby, Mia	P	3	—	2	—	2	—	—	—
Rich Camarillo, Phx	P	3	—	2	2	—	—	—	—
Rufus Porter, Sea	ST	5	1	—	—	—	—	—	1
Ron Wolfley, Phx	ST	2	1	—	—	—	—	—	—
Rod Woodson, Pit	KR	14	kr1	—	1	—	kr1	kr1	kr1
Walter Stanley, Det	KR	8	pr1	—	—	—	—	pr1	pr1
Dave Meggett, NYG	KR	3	—	—	—	pr1	—	—	—
Clarence Verdin, Ind	KR	2	pr1	—	—	—	—	—	—
John Taylor, SF	KR	2	—	1	—	—	—	—	—
Mel Gray, Det	KR	2	kr1	—	—	—	—	—	—

1990 NFL

OFFENSE	POS	TT	+PW	+UP	AP	NE	FW	SN	PW
Andre Rison, Atl	WR	19	1	1	1	1	1	1	1
Jerry Rice, SF	WR	19	1	1	1	1	1	1	1
Andre Reed, Buf	WR	8	1	1	2	2	—	—	—
Ernest Givins, Hou	WR	4	—	1	2	—	—	—	—
Sterling Sharpe, GB	WR	3	—	2	2	—	—	—	—
Anthony Miller, SD	WR	3	1	2	—	—	—	—	—
Drew Hill, Hou	WR	1	—	2	—	—	—	—	—
Gary Clark, Was	WR	1	—	2	—	—	—	—	—
Keith Jackson, Phi	TE	19	1	1	1	1	1	1	1
Rodney Holman, Cin	TE	8	1	1	2	2	—	—	—
Jay Novacek, Dal	TE	1	—	2	—	—	—	—	—
Eric Green, Pit	TE	1	—	2	—	—	—	—	—
Jim Lachey, Was	T	19	1	1	1	1	1	1	1
Anthony Munoz, Cin	T	16	1	1	1	1	1	—	1
John Alt, KC	T	7	—	1	2	—	—	1	—
Lomas Brown, Det	T	4	—	2	—	—	—	—	—
Bruce Armstrong, NE	T	4	1	—	—	—	—	—	—
Jackie Slater, LARm	T	3	1	2	—	—	—	—	—
Luis Sharpe, Phx	T	2	—	—	2	—	—	—	—
Richmond Webb, Mia	T	1	—	2	—	—	—	—	—
Jimbo Covert, ChiB	T	1	—	2	—	—	—	—	—
Howard Ballard, Buf	T	1	—	2	—	—	—	—	—
Bruce Matthews, Hou	G	19	1	1	1	1	1	1	1
Steve Wisniewski, LARd	G	17	1	1	2	2	1	—	1
Randall McDaniel, Min	G	9	1	1	1	2	—	—	—
Mark Bortz, ChiB	G	6	1	2	—	1	—	—	—
Mike Munchak, Hou	G	3	—	2	2	—	—	—	—
Guy McIntyre, SF	G	2	—	1	—	—	—	—	—
Jim Ritcher, Buf	G	1	—	2	—	—	—	—	—
Tom Newberry, LARm	G	1	—	2	—	—	—	—	—
Kent Hull, Buf	C	19	1	1	1	1	1	1	1
Jay Hilgenberg, ChiB	C	6	1	1	2	—	—	—	—
Don Mosebar, LARd	C	3	—	2	2	—	—	—	—
Randall Cunningham, Phi	QB	10	1	1	—	—	—	1	1
Warren Moon, Hou	QB	9	1	1	2	—	—	—	—
Joe Montana, SF	QB	7	—	2	1	1	—	—	—
Jim Kelly, Buf	QB	3	—	2	2	—	—	—	—
Thurman Thomas, Buf	RB	19	1	1	1	1	1	1	1
Barry Sanders, Det	RB	19	1	1	1	1	1	1	1
Marion Butts, SD	RB	8	1	1	2	—	—	—	—
Neal Anderson, ChiB	RB	8	1	2	—	—	—	—	—
Bo Jackson, LARd	RB	1	—	2	—	—	—	—	—
Earnest Byner, Was	RB	1	—	2	—	—	—	—	—
Keith Byars, Phi	RB	1	1	—	—	—	—	—	—
James Brooks, Cin	RB	1	—	2	—	—	—	—	—

DEFENSE	POS	TT	+PW	+UP	AP	NE	FW	SN	PW
Bruce Smith, Buf	DE	19	1	1	1	1	1	—	1
Reggie White, Phi	DE	16	1	1	1	DT1	1	—	1
Greg Townsend, LARd	DE	12	1	1	2	1	—	1	—
Richard Dent, ChiB	DE	6	1	1	2	—	—	—	—
Chris Doleman, Min	DE	3	—	2	2	—	—	—	—
Jeff Cross, Mia	DE	3	—	2	2	—	—	—	—
Howie Long, LARd	DE	1	—	2	—	—	—	—	—
Kevin Fagan, SF	DE	1	—	2	—	—	—	—	—
Michael Dean Perry, Cle	DT	19	1	1	1	1	1	1	1
Ray Childress, Hou	DT	11	—	2	2	2	1	1	1
Dan Saleaumua, KC	DT	7	1	—	—	2	—	—	1
Jerome Brown, Phi	DT	7	1	1	—	—	—	—	—
Jerry Ball, Det	DT	5	1	2	2	—	—	—	—
Alvin Wright, LARd	DT	1	—	2	—	—	—	—	—
Derrick Thomas, KC	OLB	19	1	1	1	1	1	1	1
Charles Haley, SF	OLB	16	1	1	1	1	1	—	1
Lawrence Taylor, NYG	OLB	6	1	1	2	—	—	—	—
Darryl Talley, Buf	OLB	6	1	1	2	—	—	—	—
Pat Swilling, NO	OLB	3	—	2	2	—	—	—	—
Leslie O'Neal, SD	OLB	3	—	2	2	—	—	—	—
Mike Cofer, Det	OLB	3	—	2	2	—	—	—	—
Cornelius Bennett, Buf	OLB	2	—	1	—	—	—	—	—
John Offerdahl, Mia	ILB	19	1	1	1	1	1	1	1
Pepper Johnson, NYG	ILB	19	1	1	1	1	1	1	1
Mike Singletary, ChiB	ILB	6	1	1	2	—	—	—	—
David Little, Pit	ILB	4	1	1	—	—	—	—	—
Vaughan Johnson, NO	ILB	3	—	2	2	—	—	—	—
Shane Conlan, Buf	ILB	3	—	2	2	—	—	—	—
Byron Evans, Phi	ILB	2	—	1	—	—	—	—	—
Eugene Lockhart, Dal	ILB	1	—	2	—	—	—	—	—

1990 NFL (CONT.)

DEFENSE	POS	TT	+PW	+UP	AP	NE	FW	SN	PW
Rod Woodson, Pit	**CB**	19	1	1	1	1	1	1	1
Albert Lewis, KC	**CB**	16	1	1	1	1	1	1	—
Darrell Green, Was	CB	9	1	1	2	—	—	—	1
Kevin Ross, KC	CB	3	—	2	2	—	—	—	—
Tim McKyer, Mia	CB	3	—	2	—	2	—	—	—
Wayne Haddix, TB	CB	2	1	—	—	—	—	—	—
Mark Collins, NYG	CB	2	—	1	—	—	—	—	—
Gill Byrd, SD	CB	2	—	—	—	2	—	—	—
Issiac Holt, Dal	CB	1	—	2	—	—	—	—	—
Don Griffin, SF	CB	1	—	2	—	—	—	—	—
Joey Browner, Min	**S**	19	1	1	1	1	1	1	1
Ronnie Lott, SF	**S**	13	—	2	1	1	1	1	—
Mark Carrier, ChiB	S	9	1	1	2	—	—	—	1
David Fulcher, Cin	S	6	1	1	2	—	—	—	—
Steve Atwater, Den	S	6	1	1	—	2	—	—	—
Tim McDonald, Phx	S	3	—	2	—	2	—	—	—
Louis Oliver, Mia	S	1	—	2	—	—	—	—	—
Carnell Lake, Pit	S	1	—	2	—	—	—	—	—

SPECIALISTS	POS	TT	+PW	+UP	AP	NE	FW	SN	PW
Nick Lowery, KC	**K**	19	1	1	1	1	1	1	1
Steve Christie, TB	K	4	1	1	—	—	—	—	—
Pete Stoyanovich, Mia	K	3	—	2	2	—	—	—	—
John Carney, SD	K	2	—	—	—	2	—	—	—
Chris Jacke, GB	K	1	—	2	—	—	—	—	—
Sean Landeta, NYG	**P**	19	1	1	1	1	1	1	1
Rohn Stark, Ind	P	8	1	1	2	2	—	—	—
Mike Horan, Den	P	1	—	2	—	—	—	—	—
Rich Camarillo, Phx	P	1	—	2	—	—	—	—	—
Reyna Thompson, NYG	ST	5	1	—	—	—	—	—	1
Steve Tasker, Buf	ST	2	1	—	—	—	—	—	—
Mel Gray, Det	**KR**	16	kr1	kr1	1	—	kr1	kr1	kr1
Dave Meggett, NYG	KR	12	pr1	pr1	2	—	pr1	pr1	—
Clarence Verdin, Ind	KR	7	pr1	pr1	—	—	—	—	pr1
Rod Woodson, Pit	KR	4	kr1	kr1	—	—	—	—	—

1991 NFL

OFFENSE	POS	TT	+PW	+UP	AP	NE	FW	SN	PW
Michael Irvin, Dal	**WR**	19	1	1	1	1	1	1	1
Haywood Jeffires, Hou	**WR**	12	1	1	1	2	1	—	1
Jerry Rice, SF	WR	10	1	—	—	2	—	1	1
Gary Clark, Was	WR	7	—	1	2	1	—	—	—
Andre Reed, Buf	WR	6	1	1	—	2	—	—	—
Andre Rison, Atl	WR	5	—	—	2	1	—	—	—
Marv Cook, NE	**TE**	19	1	1	1	1	1	1	1
Jay Novacek, Dal	TE	8	1	1	2	2	—	—	—
Jim Lachey, Was	**T**	19	1	1	1	1	1	1	1
Mike Kenn, Atl	**T**	15	1	1	1	2	1	—	1
Anthony Munoz, Cin	T	5	—	—	2	—	—	1	—
Lomas Brown, Det	T	5	—	2	2	1	—	—	—
Bruce Armstrong, NE	T	4	1	1	—	1	—	—	—
Paul Gruber, TB	T	2	—	—	2	—	—	—	—
Howard Ballard, Buf	T	2	1	—	—	—	—	—	—
John Alt, KC	T	2	—	1	—	—	—	—	—
Steve Wisniewski, LARd	**G**	19	1	1	1	1	1	1	1
Mike Munchak, Hou	**G**	15	1	1	1	2	1	—	1
Randall McDaniel, Min	G	10	1	—	2	1	—	1	—
Jim Ritcher, Buf	G	4	—	—	2	2	—	—	—
Guy McIntyre, SF	G	4	1	1	—	—	—	—	—
Raleigh McKenzie, Was	G	2	—	1	—	—	—	—	—
Bruce Matthews, Hou	**C**	10	1	—	2	1	—	—	1
Kent Hull, Buf	C	8	—	1	1	—	1	—	—
Don Mosebar, LARd	C	5	—	—	2	—	1	—	—
Jay Hilgenberg, ChiB	C	4	1	1	—	—	—	—	—
Jim Kelly, Buf	**QB**	19	1	1	1	1	1	1	1
Mark Rypien, Was	QB	8	1	1	2	2	—	—	—
Thurman Thomas, Buf	**RB**	19	1	1	1	1	1	1	1
Barry Sanders, Det	**RB**	19	1	1	1	1	1	1	1
Emmitt Smith, Dal	RB	8	1	1	—	2	—	—	—
Christian Okoye, KC	RB	4	1	—	2	—	—	—	—
Gaston Green, Den	RB	2	—	1	—	—	—	—	—
Earnest Byner, Was	RB	2	—	2	—	—	—	—	—

DEFENSE	POS	TT	+PW	+UP	AP	NE	FW	SN	PW
Reggie White, Phi	**DE**	19	1	1	1	1	1	1	1
Clyde Simmons, Phi	**DE**	19	1	1	1	1	1	1	1
Greg Townsend, LARd	DE	8	1	1	2	2	—	—	—
William Fuller, Hou	DE	4	1	1	—	—	—	—	—
Charles Mann, Was	DE	2	—	—	2	—	—	—	—
Jeff Lageman, NYJ	DE	2	—	—	2	—	—	—	—
Jerome Brown, Phi	**DT**	16	1	1	1	—	1	1	1
Jerry Ball, Det	**DT**	16	1	1	1	1	1	1	—
Michael Dean Perry, Cle	DT	9	1	—	2	2	—	1	—
Ray Childress, Hou	DT	7	1	1	—	1	—	—	—
Steve McMichael, ChiB	DT	2	—	—	2	—	—	—	—
Greg Kragen, Den	DT	2	—	1	—	—	—	—	—
Cortez Kennedy, Sea	DT	2	—	2	—	—	—	—	—
Pat Swilling, NO	**OLB**	19	1	1	1	1	1	1	1
Derrick Thomas, KC	**OLB**	15	1	1	1	2	—	1	1
Seth Joyner, Phi	OLB	10	1	—	2	1	1	—	—
Cornelius Bennett, Buf	OLB	7	1	1	—	2	—	—	—
Wilber Marshall, Was	OLB	6	—	1	2	2	—	—	—
Sam Mills, NO	**ILB**	15	1	1	—	2	2	1	1
Al Smith, Hou	**ILB**	10	1	1	1	—	1	—	1
Mike Singletary, ChiB	ILB	8	—	1	1	—	—	1	—

1991 NFL (CONT.)

DEFENSE	POS	TT	+PW	+UP	AP	NE	FW	SN	PW
Vincent Brown, NE	ILB	6	1	—	2	2	—	—	—
Chris Spielman, Det	ILB	3	—	1	—	1	—	—	—
Junior Seau, SD	ILB	3	—	—	1	—	1	—	—
Jessie Tuggle, Atl	ILB	2	1	—	—	1	—	—	—
Karl Mecklenburg, Den	ILB	2	—	—	2	—	—	—	—
Vaughan Johnson, NO	ILB	2	1	—	—	—	—	—	—
Darrell Green, Was	**CB**	19	1	1	1	1	1	1	1
Deion Sanders, Atl	**CB**	15	1	1	2	1	1	1	—
Cris Dishman, Hou	CB	10	1	1	1	—	—	—	1
Eric Allen, Phi	CB	4	—	—	2	2	—	—	—
Rod Woodson, Pit	CB	2	—	—	2	—	—	—	—
Nate Odomes, Buf	CB	2	—	1	—	—	—	—	—
Gill Byrd, SD	CB	2	1	—	—	—	—	—	—
Ronnie Lott, LARd	**S**	16	1	1	1	—	1	1	1
Steve Atwater, Den	**S**	16	1	1	1	1	1	1	—
Tim McDonald, Phx	S	6	1	—	2	2	—	—	—
Mark Carrier, ChiB	S	6	—	—	1	—	1	—	1
Bennie Blades, Det	S	6	1	1	—	1	—	—	—
Andre Waters, Phi	S	2	—	1	—	—	—	—	—
Bubba McDowell, Hou	S	2	—	2	—	—	—	—	—

SPECIALISTS	POS	TT	+PW	+UP	AP	NE	FW	SN	PW
Jeff Jaeger, LARd	**K**	15	1	1	1	2	1	—	1
Chip Lohmiller, Was	K	9	1	1	2	—	1	—	—
Pete Stoyanovich, Mia	K	3	—	—	1	—	—	1	—
Jeff Gossett, LARd	**P**	19	1	1	1	1	1	1	1
Reggie Roby, Mia	P	4	—	—	2	2	—	—	—
Rich Camarillo, Phx	P	4	1	1	—	1	—	—	—
Steve Tasker, Buf	ST	5	1	—	—	—	—	—	1
Bennie Thompson, NO	ST	2	1	—	—	—	—	—	—
Mel Gray, Det	**KR**	11	1	—	1	—	1	1	1
Brian Mitchell, Was	KR	2	—	—	2	—	—	—	—
Nate Lewis, SD	KR	2	kr1	—	—	—	—	—	—
Tim Brown, LARd	KR	2	pr1	—	—	—	—	—	—

1992 NFL

OFFENSE	POS	TT	+PW	+UP	AP	NE	FW	SN
Sterling Sharpe, GB	**WR**	16	1	1	1	1	1	1
Jerry Rice, SF	**WR**	16	1	1	1	1	1	1
Andre Rison, Atl	WR	4	—	—	2	2	—	—
Anthony Miller, SD	WR	4	1	1	—	—	—	—
Haywood Jeffires, Hou	WR	4	1	1	—	—	—	—
Michael Irvin, Dal	WR	4	—	—	2	2	—	—
Jay Novacek, Dal	**TE**	13	1	1	1	—	1	1
Keith Jackson, Mia	TE	6	1	1	2	—	—	—
Brent Jones, SF	TE	3	—	—	1	—	1	—
Jackie Harris, GB	TE	2	—	—	2	—	—	—
Harris Barton, SF	**T**	13	1	1	1	2	1	1
Richmond Webb, Mia	**T**	10	1	1	1	—	—	—
Steve Wallace, SF	T	9	1	1	2	—	1	—
Gary Zimmerman, Min	T	5	—	1	1	—	—	—
Paul Gruber, TB	T	5	—	2	1	—	—	—
Howard Ballard, Buf	T	4	1	1	—	—	—	—
Lomas Brown, Det	T	3	—	—	2	1	—	—
Will Wolford, Buf	T	2	—	—	1	—	—	—
Randall McDaniel, Min	**G**	14	1	—	1	1	1	1
Steve Wisniewski, LARd	**G**	11	1	—	1	—	1	1
Mike Munchak, Hou	G	6	1	1	2	—	—	—
Guy McIntyre, SF	G	6	1	1	2	—	—	—
David Richards, SD	G	2	—	—	2	—	—	—
Nate Newton, Dal	G	2	—	1	—	—	—	—
Derek Kennard, NO	G	2	—	1	—	—	—	—
Carlton Haselrig, Pit	G	2	—	2	—	—	—	—
Bruce Matthews, Hou	**C**	16	1	1	1	G1	1	1
Mark Stepnoski, Dal	C	9	1	1	2	1	—	—
Kirk Lowdermilk, Min	C	2	—	1	—	—	—	—
Steve Young, SF	**QB**	16	1	1	1	1	1	1
Dan Marino, Mia	QB	6	1	1	2	2	—	—
Jim Kelly, Buf	QB	2	—	—	†2	—	—	—
Randall Cunningham, Phi	QB	2	—	—	†2	—	—	—
Emmitt Smith, Dal	**RB**	16	1	1	1	1	1	1
Barry Foster, Pit	**RB**	16	1	1	1	1	1	1
Thurman Thomas, Buf	RB	8	1	1	2	2	—	—
Barry Sanders, Det	RB	8	1	1	2	2	—	—

DEFENSE	POS	TT	+PW	+UP	AP	NE	FW	SN
Chris Doleman, Min	**DE**	16	1	1	1	1	1	1
Reggie White, Phi	**DE**	12	1	1	2	1	1	—
Bruce Smith, Buf	DE	11	1	1	2	†2	—	1
Leslie O'Neal, SD	DE	6	1	1	2	1	—	—
Clyde Simmons, Phi	DE	3	—	—	1	—	1	—
Neil Smith, KC	DE	2	—	—	—	†2	—	—
Cortez Kennedy, Sea	**DT**	16	1	1	1	1	1	1
Ray Childress, Hou	**DT**	11	1	1	1	1	1	1
Pierce Holt, SF	DT	8	1	1	2	2	—	—
Michael Dean Perry, Cle	DT	3	—	—	1	—	—	1
Henry Thomas, Min	DT	2	1	—	—	—	—	—
Wayne Martin, NO	DT	2	1	—	—	—	—	—
Greg Kragen, Den	DT	2	—	—	2	—	—	—
Wilber Marshall, Was	**OLB**	13	1	1	1	1	1	1
Rickey Jackson, NO	**OLB**	11	1	1	2	2	1	—
Derrick Thomas, KC	OLB	10	1	1	1	1	—	1
Pat Swilling, NO	OLB	6	—	—	1	—	1	—
Seth Joyner, Phi	OLB	4	1	—	2	2	—	—
Bryan Cox, Mia	OLB	4	1	1	2	—	—	—

1992 NFL (CONT.)

DEFENSE	POS	TT	+PW	+UP	AP	NE	FW	SN
Junior Seau, SD	**ILB**	16	1	1	1	1	1	1
Sam Mills, NO	**ILB**	12	1	1	2	—	1	1
Al Smith, Hou	ILB	7	1	—	1	2	—	—
Byron Evans, Phi	ILB	4	1	—	—	2	—	—
Cornelius Bennett, Buf	ILB	3	—	—	—	1	—	—
Chris Spielman, Det	ILB	2	—	—	2	—	—	—
Vaughan Johnson, NO	ILB	2	—	1	—	—	—	—
Vincent Brown, NE	ILB	2	1	—	—	—	—	—
Rod Woodson, Pit	**CB**	16	1	1	1	1	1	1
Audray McMillian, Min	**CB**	10	1	1	—	1	—	1
Deion Sanders, Atl	CB	8	—	—	2	1	—	1
Gill Byrd, SD	CB	6	1	1	2	—	—	—
Ricky Reynolds, TB	CB	2	1	—	—	—	—	—
Terry McDaniel, LARd	CB	2	—	—	2	—	—	—
Carl Lee, Min	CB	2	—	—	2	—	—	—
Eric Allen, Phi	CB	2	—	1	—	—	—	—
Steve Atwater, Den	**S**	14	1	—	1	1	1	1
Henry Jones, Buf	**S**	13	1	1	1	—	1	1
Tim McDonald, Phx	S	7	1	—	2	1	—	—
Louis Oliver, Mia	S	4	1	—	1	—	—	—
Todd Scott, Min	S	2	—	1	—	—	—	—
Carnell Lake, Pit	S	2	—	—	2	—	—	—
Brad Edwards, Was	S	2	1	—	—	—	—	—
Chuck Cecil, GB	S	2	1	—	—	—	—	—
Bennie Blades, Det	S	2	—	—	2	—	—	—

SPECIALISTS	POS	TT	+PW	+UP	AP	NE	FW	SN
Pete Stoyanovich, Mia	**K**	12	1	1	1	2	—	1
Morten Andersen, NO	**K**	12	1	1	2	1	1	—
Rich Camarillo, Phx	**P**	12	1	1	2	1	—	—
Rohn Stark, Ind	P	10	1	—	2	1	—	1
Greg Montgomery, Hou	P	2	—	1	—	—	—	—
Steve Tasker, Buf	ST	5	1	—	—	—	1	—
Elbert Shelley, Atl	ST	2	1	—	—	—	—	—
Deion Sanders, Atl	**KR**	11	kr1	—	1	—	kr1	kr1
Mel Gray, Det	KR	8	—	—	2	1	—	pr1
Kelvin Martin, Dal	KR	5	pr1	—	—	—	pr1	—
Clarence Verdin, Ind	KR	4	pr1	1	—	—	—	—
Jon Vaughn, NE	KR	2	kr1	—	—	—	—	—
Vai Sikahema, Phi	KR	2	—	—	2	—	—	—
Johnny Bailey, Phx	KR	2	—	1	—	—	—	—

1993 NFL

OFFENSE	POS	TT	+PW	+UP	AP	FW	SN
Sterling Sharpe, GB	**WR**	13	1	1	1	1	1
Jerry Rice, SF	**WR**	13	1	1	1	1	1
Anthony Miller, SD	WR	4	1	1	—	—	—
Tim Brown, LARd	WR	4	1	1	—	—	—
Andre Rison, Atl	WR	2	—	—	2	—	—
Michael Irvin, Dal	WR	2	—	—	2	—	—
Shannon Sharpe, Den	**TE**	13	1	1	1	1	1
Brent Jones, SF	TE	6	1	1	2	—	—
Erik Williams, Dal	**T**	13	1	1	1	1	1
Harris Barton, SF	**T**	13	1	1	1	1	1
Gary Zimmerman, Den	T	4	1	—	2	—	—
Richmond Webb, Mia	T	4	—	1	2	—	—
John Jackson, Pit	T	2	1	—	—	—	—
Howard Ballard, Buf	T	2	—	1	2	—	—
Randall McDaniel, Min	**G**	13	1	1	1	1	1
Steve Wisniewski, LARd	**G**	12	1	1	2	1	1
Mike Munchak, Hou	G	6	1	1	2	—	—
Chris Hinton, Atl	G	5	—	1	1	—	—
Nate Newton, Dal	G	2	1	—	—	—	—
Bruce Matthews, Hou	**C**	12	1	1	2	1	1
Mark Stepnoski, Dal	C	4	1	1	—	—	—
Dermontti Dawson, Pit	C	3	—	1	1	—	—
Steve Young, SF	**QB**	10	1	1	1	1	—
John Elway, Den	QB	6	1	1	2	—	—
Troy Aikman, Dal	QB	3	—	—	—	—	1
Emmitt Smith, Dal	**RB**	13	1	1	1	1	1
Jerome Bettis, LARm	**RB**	10	1	1	1	1	—
Thurman Thomas, Buf	RB	6	1	1	2	—	—
Barry Sanders, Det	RB	5	—	—	2	—	1
Marcus Allen, KC	RB	4	1	1	—	—	—

DEFENSE	POS	TT	+PW	+UP	AP	FW	SN
Bruce Smith, Buf	**DE**	13	1	1	1	1	1
Neil Smith, KC	**DE**	10	1	1	1	1	—
Reggie White, GB	DE	9	1	1	2	—	—
Chris Doleman, Min	DE	4	—	1	2	—	—
Richard Dent, ChiB	DE	2	1	—	—	—	—
Cortez Kennedy, Sea	**DT**	13	1	1	1	1	1
John Randle, Min	**DT**	10	1	1	1	1	—
Ray Childress, Hou	DT	6	1	1	2	—	—
Sean Gilbert, LARm	DT	4	1	—	—	—	—
Michael Dean Perry, Cle	DT	3	—	—	—	—	—
Henry Thomas, Min	DT	2	—	—	2	—	—
Greg Lloyd, Pit	**OLB**	10	1	1	1	1	—
Rickey Jackson, NO	**OLB**	9	1	1	2	—	1
Renaldo Turnbull, NO	OLB	5	—	1	—	—	—
Darryl Talley, Buf	OLB	5	1	—	—	—	—
Seth Joyner, Phi	OLB	5	—	—	1	—	—
Derrick Thomas, KC	OLB	4	1	1	—	—	—
Junior Seau, SD	**ILB**	13	1	1	1	1	1
Hardy Nickerson, TB	**ILB**	11	1	—	1	1	1

1993 NFL (CONT.)

DEFENSE	POS	TT	+PW	+UP	AP	FW	SN
Michael Brooks, NYG	ILB	6	1	1	2	—	—
Ken Norton, Dal	ILB	2	—	—	2	—	—
Vincent Brown, NE	ILB	2	1	—	—	—	—
Rod Woodson, Pit	**CB**	13	1	1	1	1	1
Deion Sanders, Atl	**CB**	13	1	1	1	1	1
Eric Allen, Phi	CB	6	1	1	2	—	—
Nate Odomes, Buf	CB	4	—	1	2	—	—
Terry McDaniel, LARd	CB	2	1	—	—	—	—
LeRoy Butler, GB	**S**	13	1	1	1	1	1
Marcus Robertson, Hou	**S**	10	1	1	1	—	1
Eugene Robinson, Sea	S	7	1	—	2	1	—
Tim McDonald, SF	S	6	1	1	2	—	—
Steve Atwater, Den	S	2	1	—	—	—	—

SPECIALISTS	POS	TT	+PW	+UP	AP	FW	SN
Norm Johnson, Atl	**K**	9	1	1	2	1	—
Gary Anderson, Pit	K	4	1	1	—	—	—
Chris Jacke, GB	K	3	—	—	1	—	—
Jason Hanson, Det	K	3	—	—	—	—	1
Greg Montgomery, Hou	**P**	13	1	1	1	1	1
Rich Camarillo, Phx	P	6	1	1	2	—	—
Steve Tasker, Buf	ST	5	1	—	—	1	—
Elbert Shelley, Atl	ST	2	1	—	—	—	—
Eric Metcalf, Cle	**KR**	13	pr1	1	1	pr1	pr1
Tyrone Hughes, NO	KR	9	pr1	1	2	kr1	—
Mel Gray, Det	KR	3	—	—	—	—	kr1
O.J. McDuffie, Mia	KR	2	kr1	—	—	—	—

1994 NFL

OFFENSE	POS	TT	+PW	+UP	AP	FW	SN
Jerry Rice, SF	**WR**	13	1	1	1	1	1
Cris Carter, Min	**WR**	13	1	1	1	1	1
Andre Reed, Buf	WR	4	1	1	—	—	—
Irving Fryar, Mia	WR	4	—	1	2	—	—
Terance Mathis, Atl	WR	3	—	1	2	—	—
Tim Brown, LARd	WR	3	1	—	2	—	—
Sterling Sharpe, GB	WR	1	—	2	—	—	—
Carl Pickens, Cin	WR	1	—	2	—	—	—
Ben Coates, NE	**TE**	13	1	1	1	1	1
Brent Jones, SF	TE	6	1	1	2	—	—
Shannon Sharpe, Den	TE	1	—	2	—	—	—
Jay Novacek, Dal	TE	1	—	2	—	—	—
Richmond Webb, Mia	**T**	13	1	1	1	1	1
Willie Roaf, NO	**T**	13	1	1	1	1	1
Lomas Brown, Det	T	6	1	1	2	—	—
Tony Jones, Cle	T	5	1	—	2	—	—
Bruce Armstrong, NE	T	2	—	1	—	—	—
Gary Zimmerman, Den	T	1	—	2	—	—	—
Steve Wallace, SF	T	1	—	2	—	—	—
Mark Tuinei, Dal	T	1	—	2	—	—	—
Randall McDaniel, Min	**G**	13	1	1	1	1	1
Nate Newton, Dal	**G**	10	1	1	1	1	—
Steve Wisniewski, LARd	G	9	1	1	2	—	1
Keith Sims, Mia	G	6	1	1	2	—	—
Lance Smith, NYG	G	1	—	2	—	—	—
Jesse Sapolu, SF	G	1	—	2	—	—	—
Duval Love, Pit	G	1	—	2	—	—	—
Bob Kratch, NE	G	1	—	2	—	—	—
Dermontti Dawson, Pit	**C**	13	1	1	1	1	1
Mark Stepnoski, Dal	C	4	—	1	2	—	—
Kevin Glover, Det	C	2	1	—	—	—	—
Bart Oates, SF	C	1	—	2	—	—	—
Courtney Hall, SD	C	1	—	2	—	—	—
Steve Young, SF	**QB**	13	1	1	1	1	1
Dan Marino, Mia	QB	6	1	1	2	—	—
Drew Bledsoe, NE	QB	1	—	2	—	—	—
Troy Aikman, Dal	QB	1	—	2	—	—	—
Emmitt Smith, Dal	**RB**	13	1	1	1	1	1
Barry Sanders, Det	**RB**	13	1	1	1	1	1
Chris Warren, Sea	RB	6	1	1	2	—	—
Marshall Faulk, Ind	RB	6	1	1	2	—	—
Ricky Watters, SF	RB	1	—	2	—	—	—
Thurman Thomas, Buf	RB	1	—	2	—	—	—
Natrone Means, SD	RB	1	—	2	—	—	—
Terry Allen, Min	RB	1	—	2	—	—	—

DEFENSE	POS	TT	+PW	+UP	AP	FW	SN
Bruce Smith, Buf	**DE**	13	1	1	1	1	1
Charles Haley, Dal	**DE**	13	1	1	1	1	1
Reggie White, GB	DE	6	1	1	2	—	—
Leslie O'Neal, SD	DE	6	1	1	2	—	—
Neil Smith, KC	DE	1	—	2	—	—	—
Sean Jones, GB	DE	1	—	2	—	—	—
William Fuller, Phi	DE	1	—	2	—	—	—
Rob Burnett, Cle	DE	1	—	2	—	—	—
John Randle, Min	**DT**	13	1	1	1	1	1
Chester McGlockton, LARd	**DT**	11	1	2	2	1	1
Cortez Kennedy, Sea	DT	7	1	1	2	—	—
Michael Dean Perry, Cle	DT	4	—	1	2	—	—
Dana Stubblefield, SF	DT	3	—	1	2	—	—
Leon Lett, Dal	DT	2	—	1	—	—	—
Henry Thomas, Min	DT	1	—	2	—	—	—
Tim Bowens, Mia	DT	1	—	2	—	—	—
Greg Lloyd, Pit	**OLB**	13	1	1	1	1	1
Kevin Greene, Pit	**OLB**	9	1	2	1	1	—

1994 NFL (CONT.)

DEFENSE	POS	TT	+PW	+UP	AP	FW	SN
Ken Harvey, Was	OLB	6	1	1	2	—	—
Derrick Thomas, KC	OLB	4	—	1	2	—	—
Bryce Paup, GB	OLB	4	1	1	—	—	—
Seth Joyner, Arz	OLB	1	—	2	—	—	—
Cornelius Bennett, Buf	OLB	1	—	2	—	—	—
Junior Seau, SD	**ILB**	13	1	1	1	1	1
Chris Spielman, Det	**ILB**	12	1	1	2	1	1
Jack Del Rio, Min	ILB	3	1	2	—	—	—
Bryan Cox, Mia	ILB	2	1	—	—	—	—
Jessie Tuggle, Atl	ILB	1	—	2	—	—	—
Pepper Johnson, Cle	ILB	1	—	2	—	—	—
Rod Woodson, Pit	**CB**	13	1	1	1	1	1
Deion Sanders, SF	**CB**	13	1	1	1	1	1
Terry McDaniel, LARd	CB	6	1	1	2	—	—
Aeneas Williams, Arz	CB	4	—	1	2	—	—
Donnell Woolford, ChiB	CB	3	1	2	—	—	—
Dale Carter, KC	CB	1	—	2	—	—	—
Ray Buchanan, Ind	CB	1	—	2	—	—	—
Eric Allen, Phi	CB	1	—	2	—	—	—
Darren Woodson, Dal	**S**	13	1	1	1	1	1
Eric Turner, Cle	**S**	10	1	1	1	1	—
Merton Hanks, SF	S	9	1	1	2	—	1
Carnell Lake, Pit	S	6	1	1	2	—	—
Stanley Richard, SD	S	1	—	2	—	—	—
Darren Perry, Pit	S	1	—	2	—	—	—
Tim McDonald, SF	S	1	—	2	—	—	—
Mark Carrier, ChiB	S	1	—	2	—	—	—

SPECIALISTS	POS	TT	+PW	+UP	AP	FW	SN
John Carney, SD	**K**	10	1	1	1	—	1
Fuad Reveiz, Min	K	9	1	1	2	1	—
Matt Stover, Cle	K	1	—	2	—	—	—
Eddie Murray, Phi	K	1	—	2	—	—	—
Reggie Roby, Was	**P**	13	1	1	1	1	1
Rick Tuten, Sea	P	6	1	1	2	—	—
Tom Rouen, Den	P	1	—	2	—	—	—
Sean Landeta, LARm	P	1	—	2	—	—	—
Steve Tasker, Buf	ST	5	1	—	—	1	—
Maurice Douglass, ChiB	ST	2	1	—	—	—	—
Mel Gray, Det	**KR**	11	kr1	—	1	kr1	kr1
Brian Mitchell, Was	KR	7	pr1	—	2	pr1	—
Eric Metcalf, Cle	KR	3	—	—	—	—	pr1
Darrien Gordon, SD	KR	2	pr1	—	—	—	—
Andre Coleman, SD	KR	2	kr1	—	—	—	—

1995 NFL

OFFENSE	POS	TT	+PW	+UP	AP	FW	SN
Jerry Rice, SF	**WR**	13	1	1	1	1	1
Herman Moore, Det	**WR**	13	1	1	1	1	1
Carl Pickens, Cin	WR	6	1	1	2	—	—
Tim Brown, Oak	WR	4	1	1	—	—	—
Cris Carter, Min	WR	3	—	2	2	—	—
Yancey Thigpen, Pit	WR	1	—	2	—	—	—
Tony Martin, SD	WR	1	—	2	—	—	—
Isaac Bruce, SL	WR	1	—	2	—	—	—
Ben Coates, NE	**TE**	13	1	1	1	1	1
Shannon Sharpe, Den	TE	3	—	2	2	—	—
Mark Chmura, GB	TE	3	1	2	—	—	—
Jay Novacek, Dal	TE	2	—	1	—	—	—
Willie Roaf, NO	**T**	13	1	1	1	1	1
Lomas Brown, Det	**T**	10	1	1	1	1	—
Richmond Webb, Mia	T	6	1	1	2	—	—
Gary Zimmerman, Den	T	4	—	1	2	—	—
Erik Williams, Dal	T	3	—	—	—	—	1
Bruce Armstrong, NE	T	3	1	2	—	—	—
Mark Tuinei, Dal	T	1	—	2	—	—	—
Leon Searcy, Pit	T	1	—	2	—	—	—
Andy Heck, ChiB	T	1	—	2	—	—	—
Nate Newton, Dal	**G**	13	1	1	1	1	1
Randall McDaniel, Min	**G**	10	1	1	1	1	—
Steve Wisniewski, Oak	G	6	1	1	2	—	—
Larry Allen, Dal	G	6	—	2	2	—	1
Bruce Matthews, Hou	G	4	1	1	—	—	—
Dave Szott, KC	G	1	—	2	—	—	—
Keith Sims, Mia	G	1	—	2	—	—	—
Jesse Sapolu, SF	G	1	—	2	—	—	—
Dermontti Dawson, Pit	**C**	13	1	1	1	1	1
Kevin Glover, Det	C	6	1	1	2	—	—
Bart Oates, SF	C	1	—	2	—	—	—
Kent Hull, Buf	C	1	—	2	—	—	—
Brett Favre, GB	**QB**	13	1	1	1	1	1
Jim Harbaugh, Ind	QB	4	1	1	—	—	—
Dan Marino, Mia	QB	3	—	2	†2	—	—
Steve Young, SF	QB	2	—	—	†2	—	—
Troy Aikman, Dal	QB	1	—	2	—	—	—
Emmitt Smith, Dal	**RB**	13	1	1	1	1	1
Barry Sanders, Det	**RB**	13	1	1	1	1	1
Chris Warren, Sea	RB	6	1	1	2	—	—
Curtis Martin, NE	RB	4	1	1	—	—	—
Marshall Faulk, Ind	RB	3	—	2	2	—	—
Ricky Watters, Phi	RB	1	—	2	—	—	—
Terrell Davis, Den	RB	1	—	2	—	—	—
Terry Allen, Was	RB	1	—	2	—	—	—

1995 NFL (CONT.)

DEFENSE	POS	TT	+PW	+UP	AP	FW	SN
Reggie White, GB	**DE**	13	1	1	1	1	1
Bruce Smith, Buf	**DE**	13	1	1	1	1	1
Neil Smith, KC	DE	6	1	1	2	—	—
William Fuller, Phi	DE	6	1	1	2	—	—
Ray Seals, Pit	DE	1	—	2	—	—	—
Leslie O'Neal, SD	DE	1	—	2	—	—	—
Sean Jones, GB	DE	1	—	2	—	—	—
Charles Haley, Dal	DE	1	—	2	—	—	—
John Randle, Min	**DT**	13	1	1	1	1	1
Chester McGlockton, Oak	**DT**	10	1	1	1	1	—
Dana Stubblefield, SF	DT	6	1	1	2	—	—
Eric Swann, Arz	DT	4	—	2	—	—	1
Dan Saleaumua, KC	DT	4	1	1	—	—	—
Andy Harmon, Phi	DT	3	—	2	2	—	—
Michael Dean Perry, Den	DT	1	—	2	—	—	—
Cortez Kennedy, Sea	DT	1	—	2	—	—	—
Bryce Paup, Buf	**OLB**	13	1	1	1	1	1
Greg Lloyd, Pit	**OLB**	13	1	1	1	1	1
Ken Harvey, Was	OLB	6	1	1	2	—	—
William Thomas, Phi	OLB	5	1	2	—	—	—
Lee Woodall, SF	OLB	2	—	1	—	—	—
Derrick Thomas, KC	OLB	1	—	2	—	—	—
Pat Swilling, Oak	OLB	1	—	2	—	—	—
Chris Spielman, Det	OLB	1	—	2	—	—	—
Junior Seau, SD	**ILB**	12	1	1	2	1	1
Ken Norton, SF	ILB	7	1	1	1	—	—
Sam Mills, Car	ILB	1	—	2	—	—	—
Bryan Cox, Mia	ILB	1	—	2	—	—	—
Aeneas Williams, Arz	**CB**	13	1	1	1	1	1
Eric Davis, SF	**CB**	10	1	1	1	1	—
Dale Carter, KC	CB	6	1	1	2	—	—
Terry McDaniel, Oak	CB	5	1	2	2	—	—
Deion Sanders, Dal	CB	4	—	2	—	—	1
Darryll Lewis, Hou	CB	1	—	2	—	—	—
Eric Allen, NO	CB	1	—	2	—	—	—
Darren Woodson, Dal	**S**	13	1	1	1	1	1
Merton Hanks, SF	**S**	13	1	1	1	1	1
Carnell Lake, Pit	S	6	1	cb1	2	—	—
Blaine Bishop, Hou	S	4	1	1	—	—	—
Tim McDonald, SF	S	3	—	2	2	—	—
Steve Atwater, Den	S	2	—	1	—	—	—
Orlando Thomas, Min	S	1	—	2	—	—	—
Kurt Schulz, Buf	S	1	—	2	—	—	—
Robert Blackmon, Sea	S	1	—	2	—	—	—

SPECIALISTS	POS	TT	+PW	+UP	AP	FW	SN
Morten Andersen, Atl	**K**	13	1	1	1	1	1
Jason Elam, Den	K	6	1	1	2	—	—
Darren Bennett, SD	**P**	13	1	1	1	1	1
Jeff Feagles, Arz	P	4	1	1	—	—	—
Louie Aguiar, KC	P	2	—	2	—	—	—
Steve Tasker, Buf	ST	5	1	—	—	1	—
Elbert Shelley, Atl	ST	2	1	—	—	—	—
Brian Mitchell, Was	**KR**	11	pr1	—	1	1	pr1
Glyn Milburn, Den	KR	7	kr1	—	2	—	kr1
Andre Coleman, SD	KR	2	pr1	—	—	—	—

1996 NFL

OFFENSE	POS	TT	+PW	+UP	AP	FW	SN
Jerry Rice, SF	**WR**	13	1	1	1	1	1
Herman Moore, Det	**WR**	10	1	1	1	—	1
Carl Pickens, Cin	WR	9	1	1	2	1	—
Tony Martin, SD	WR	5	1	2	2	—	—
Terry Glenn, NE	WR	2	—	1	—	—	—
Cris Carter, Min	WR	1	—	2	—	—	—
Isaac Bruce, SL	WR	1	—	2	—	—	—
Tim Brown, Oak	WR	1	—	2	—	—	—
Shannon Sharpe, Den	**TE**	13	1	1	1	1	1
Wesley Walls, Car	TE	6	1	1	2	—	—
Keith Jackson, GB	TE	1	—	2	—	—	—
Ben Coates, NE	TE	1	—	2	—	—	—
Gary Zimmerman, Den	**T**	13	1	1	1	1	1
Willie Roaf, NO	**T**	12	1	1	2	1	1
Bruce Armstrong, NE	T	6	1	1	2	—	—
Erik Williams, Dal	T	4	—	2	2	—	—
Lomas Brown, Arz	T	4	1	1	—	—	—
Bob Whitfield, Atl	T	1	—	2	—	—	—
John Jackson, Pit	T	1	—	2	—	—	—
Tony Boselli, Jax	T	1	—	2	—	—	—
Randall McDaniel, Min	**G**	13	1	1	1	1	1
Larry Allen, Dal	**G**	13	1	1	1	1	1
Bruce Matthews, Hou	G	6	1	1	2	—	—
Steve Wisniewski, Oak	G	4	1	2	—	—	—
Will Shields, KC	G	3	1	2	—	—	—
Will Wolford, Pit	G	1	—	2	—	—	—
Nate Newton, Dal	G	1	—	2	—	—	—
Bob Dahl, Was	G	1	—	2	—	—	—
Dermontti Dawson, Pit	**C**	13	1	1	1	1	1
Kevin Glover, Det	C	4	1	1	—	—	—
Mark Stepnoski, Hou	C	3	—	2	2	—	—
Ray Donaldson, Dal	C	1	—	2	—	—	—
Brett Favre, GB	**QB**	13	1	1	1	1	1
John Elway, Den	QB	6	1	1	2	—	—
Steve Young, SF	QB	2	—	1	—	—	—
Drew Bledsoe, NE	QB	1	—	2	—	—	—

1996 NFL (CONT.)

OFFENSE	POS	TT	+PW	+UP	AP	FW	SN
Terrell Davis, Den	RB	13	1	1	1	1	1
Barry Sanders, Det	RB	12	1	1	2	1	1
Jerome Bettis, Pit	RB	7	1	1	1	—	—
Terry Allen, Was	RB	6	1	1	2	—	—
Ricky Watters, Phi	RB	1	—	2	—	—	—
Emmitt Smith, Dal	RB	1	—	2	—	—	—
Curtis Martin, NE	RB	1	—	2	—	—	—
Eddie George, Hou	RB	1	—	2	—	—	—
Larry Centers, Arz	FB	3	—	—	1	—	—
Mike Alstott, TB	FB	2	—	—	2	—	—

DEFENSE	POS	TT	+PW	+UP	AP	FW	SN
Alfred Williams, Den	DE	13	1	1	1	1	1
Bruce Smith, Buf	DE	13	1	1	1	1	1
Reggie White, GB	DE	6	1	1	2	—	—
Tony Tolbert, Dal	DE	6	1	1	2	—	—
Neil Smith, KC	DE	1	—	2	—	—	—
Michael Sinclair, Sea	DE	1	—	2	—	—	—
Simeon Rice, Arz	DE	1	—	2	—	—	—
William Fuller, Phi	DE	1	—	2	—	—	—
Bryant Young, SF	DT	13	1	1	1	1	1
John Randle, Min	DT	13	1	1	1	1	1
Chester McGlockton, Oak	DT	6	1	1	2	—	—
Cortez Kennedy, Sea	DT	6	1	1	2	—	—
Eric Swann, Arz	DT	1	—	2	—	—	—
Dana Stubblefield, SF	DT	1	—	2	—	—	—
Michael Dean Perry, Den	DT	1	—	2	—	—	—
John Jurkovic, Jax	DT	1	—	2	—	—	—
Chad Brown, Pit	OLB	13	1	1	1	1	1
Kevin Greene, Car	OLB	10	1	1	1	—	1
Lamar Lathon, Car	OLB	9	1	1	2	—	1
Derrick Thomas, KC	OLB	6	1	1	2	—	—
Bill Romanowski, Den	OLB	1	—	2	—	—	—
Bryce Paup, Buf	OLB	1	—	2	—	—	—
Seth Joyner, Arz	OLB	1	—	2	—	—	—
Ken Harvey, Was	OLB	1	—	2	—	—	—
Sam Mills, Car	ILB	10	1	1	1	1	—
Junior Seau, SD	ILB	8	—	1	1	—	1
Levon Kirkland, Pit	ILB	5	1	1	2	2	—
Hardy Nickerson, TB	ILB	3	—	2	2	—	—
Deion Sanders, Dal	CB	13	1	1	1	1	1
Aeneas Williams, Arz	CB	9	1	1	2	1	—
Dale Carter, KC	CB	9	1	1	2	—	1
Ashley Ambrose, Cin	CB	7	1	1	1	—	—
Rod Woodson, Pit	CB	1	—	2	—	—	—
Kevin Smith, Dal	CB	1	—	2	—	—	—
Eric Davis, Car	CB	1	—	2	—	—	—
Mark Collins, KC	CB	1	—	2	—	—	—
Darren Woodson, Dal	S	13	1	1	1	1	1
LeRoy Butler, GB	S	13	1	1	1	1	1
Steve Atwater, Den	S	6	1	1	2	—	—
Carnell Lake, Pit	S	4	1	1	—	—	—
Merton Hanks, SF	S	3	—	2	2	—	—
Tim McDonald, SF	S	1	—	2	—	—	—
Tyrone Braxton, Den	S	1	—	2	—	—	—
Blaine Bishop, Hou	S	1	—	2	—	—	—

SPECIALISTS	POS	TT	+PW	+UP	AP	FW	SN
Cary Blanchard, Ind	K	13	1	1	1	1	1
John Kasay, Car	K	6	1	1	2	—	—
Al Del Greco, Hou	K	1	—	2	—	—	—
Chris Boniol, Dal	K	1	—	2	—	—	—
Chris Gardocki, Ind	P	13	1	1	†1	1	1
Matt Turk, Was	P	7	1	1	†1	—	—
Todd Sauerbrun, ChiB	P	1	—	2	—	—	—
John Kidd, Mia	P	1	—	2	—	—	—
Jim Schwantz, Dal	ST	5	1	—	—	1	—
John Henry Mills, Hou	ST	2	1	—	—	—	—
Desmond Howard, GB	PR	10	1	1	—	1	1
Darrien Gordon, SD	PR	3	1	2	—	—	—
Michael Bates, Car	KR	12	1	2	1	1	—
Dave Meggett, NE	KR	4	—	1	2	—	—
Tamarick Vanover, KC	KR	2	1	—	—	—	—

1997 NFL

OFFENSE	POS	TT	+PW	AP	FW	SN
Herman Moore, Det	WR	11	1	1	1	1
Rob Moore, Arz	WR	8	1	1	1	—
Tim Brown, Oak	WR	7	1	2	—	—
Yancey Thigpen, Pit	WR	4	1	2	—	—
Shannon Sharpe, Den	TE	11	1	1	1	1
Wesley Walls, Car	TE	4	1	2	—	—
Jonathan Ogden, Bal	T	11	1	1	1	1
Tony Boselli, Jax	T	11	1	1	1	1
Todd Steussie, Min	T	4	1	2	—	—
Willie Roaf, NO	T	4	1	2	—	—
Larry Allen, Dal	G	11	1	1	1	1
Dave Szott, KC	G	8	1	1	1	—
Randall McDaniel, Min	G	7	1	2	—	—
Will Shields, KC	G	2	—	2	—	—
Bruce Matthews, Ten	G	2	1	—	—	—
Dermontti Dawson, Pit	C	11	1	1	1	1
Kevin Glover, Det	C	2	1	—	—	—
Brett Favre, GB	QB	11	1	1	1	1
Steve Young, SF	QB	2	—	2	—	—

1997 NFL (CONT.)

OFFENSE	POS	TT	+PW	AP	FW	SN
John Elway, Den	QB	2	1	—	—	—
Barry Sanders, Det	RB	11	1	1	1	1
Terrell Davis, Den	RB	11	1	1	1	1
Jerome Bettis, Pit	RB	4	1	2	—	—
Dorsey Levens, GB	RB	2	1	—	—	—
Mike Alstott, TB	FB	3	—	1	—	—
Charles Way, NYG	FB	2	—	2	—	—

DEFENSE	POS	TT	+PW	AP	FW	SN
Michael Strahan, NYG	DE	11	1	1	1	1
Bruce Smith, Buf	DE	11	1	1	1	1
Chuck Smith, Atl	DE	4	†1	2	—	—
Reggie White, GB	DE	2	—	†2	—	—
Neil Smith, Den	DE	2	—	†2	—	—
Michael Sinclair, Sea	DE	2	1	—	—	—
Robert Porcher, Det	DE	2	†1	—	—	—
Dana Stubblefield, SF	DT	11	1	1	1	1
John Randle, Min	DT	11	1	1	1	1
Ted Washington, Buf	DT	4	1	2	—	—
Joel Steed, Pit	DT	2	1	—	—	—
Warren Sapp, TB	DT	2	—	2	—	—
John Mobley, Den	OLB	11	1	1	1	1
Jessie Armstead, NYG	OLB	11	1	1	1	1
Chris Slade, NE	OLB	4	1	2	—	—
Derrick Brooks, TB	OLB	4	1	2	—	—
Levon Kirkland, Pit	ILB	11	1	1	1	1
Hardy Nickerson, TB	ILB	5	1	1	—	—
Winfred Tubbs, NO	ILB	4	1	†2	—	—
Junior Seau, SD	ILB	4	1	†2	—	—
Ray Lewis, Bal	ILB	2	—	†2	—	—
Aeneas Williams, Arz	CB	11	1	1	1	1
Deion Sanders, Dal	CB	11	1	1	1	1
James Hasty, KC	CB	4	†1	2	—	—
Aaron Glenn, NYJ	CB	2	1	—	—	—
Doug Evans, GB	CB	2	—	†2	—	—
Cris Dishman, Was	CB	2	—	†2	—	—
Dale Carter, KC	CB	2	†1	—	—	—
Carnell Lake, Pit	S	11	1	1	1	1
LeRoy Butler, GB	S	11	1	1	1	1
Darryl Williams, Sea	S	4	1	2	—	—
Merton Hanks, SF	S	4	1	2	—	—

SPECIALISTS	POS	TT	+PW	AP	FW	SN
Richie Cunningham, Dal	K	6	—	1	—	1
Pete Stoyanovich, KC	K	5	1	—	1	—
Jason Hanson, Det	K	4	1	2	—	—
Bryan Barker, Jax	P	8	1	1	1	—
Matt Turk, Was	P	7	1	2	—	1
Travis Jervey, GB	ST	5	1	—	1	—
Larry Whigham, NE	ST	2	1	—	—	—
Darrien Gordon, Den	PR	10	1	†2	1	1
David Palmer, Min	PR	2	1	—	—	—
Michael Bates, Car	KR	10	1	†2	1	1
Eric Metcalf, SD	KR	3	—	1	—	—
Tamarick Vanover, KC	KR	2	1	—	—	—

1998 NFL

OFFENSE	POS	TT	+PW	AP	FW	SN
Randy Moss, Min	WR	11	1	1	1	1
Antonio Freeman, GB	WR	11	1	1	1	1
Eric Moulds, Buf	WR	4	1	†2	—	—
Jimmy Smith, Jax	WR	2	—	†2	—	—
Ed McCaffrey, Den	WR	2	—	2	—	—
Keyshawn Johnson, NYJ	WR	2	1	—	—	—
Shannon Sharpe, Den	TE	11	1	1	1	1
Ben Coates, NE	TE	2	—	2	—	—
Mark Chmura, GB	TE	2	1	—	—	—
Tony Boselli, Jax	T	11	1	1	1	1
Larry Allen, Dal	T	11	1	1	1	1
Todd Steussie, Min	T	4	1	2	—	—
Jonathan Ogden, Bal	T	4	1	2	—	—
Randall McDaniel, Min	G	11	1	1	1	1
Bruce Matthews, Ten	G	11	1	1	1	1
Kevin Gogan, SF	G	4	1	2	—	—
Ruben Brown, Buf	G	4	1	2	—	—
Dermontti Dawson, Pit	C	11	1	1	1	1
Jeff Christy, Min	C	4	1	†2	—	—
Kevin Mawae, NYJ	C	2	—	†2	—	—
Randall Cunningham, Min	QB	8	1	1	1	—
Steve Young, SF	QB	5	—	2	—	1
Vinny Testaverde, NYJ	QB	2	1	—	—	—
Terrell Davis, Den	RB	11	1	1	1	1
Jamal Anderson, Atl	RB	11	1	1	1	1
Marshall Faulk, Ind	RB	4	1	2	—	—
Barry Sanders, Det	RB	2	2	—	—	—
Garrison Hearst, SF	RB	2	1	—	—	—
Mike Alstott, TB	FB	3	—	1	—	—
Sam Gash, Buf	FB	2	1	—	—	—

DEFENSE	POS	TT	+PW	AP	FW	SN
Reggie White, GB	DE	11	1	1	1	1
Michael Strahan, NYG	DE	8	1	1	1	—
Michael McCrary, Bal	DE	5	1	—	—	1
Michael Sinclair, Sea	DE	4	1	2	—	—
Bruce Smith, Buf	DE	2	—	2	—	—

1998 NFL (CONT.)

DEFENSE	POS	TT	+PW	AP	FW	SN
John Randle, Min	**DT**	**11**	**1**	**1**	**1**	**1**
Darrell Russell, Oak	**DT**	**8**	**1**	**1**	**1**	—
Bryant Young, SF	DT	5	—	†2	—	1
Warren Sapp, TB	DT	4	1	†2	—	—
Ted Washington, Buf	DT	2	1	—	—	—
La'Roi Glover, NO	DT	2	—	2	—	—
Chad Brown, Sea	**OLB**	**11**	**1**	**1**	**1**	**1**
Mo Lewis, NYJ	**OLB**	**8**	**1**	**1**	**1**	—
Derrick Brooks, TB	OLB	4	1	2	—	—
Dwayne Rudd, Min	OLB	2	—	2	—	—
Jessie Armstead, NYG	OLB	2	1	—	—	—
Junior Seau, SD	**ILB**	**9**	—	**1**	**1**	**1**
Ray Lewis, Bal	ILB	5	—	2	—	1
Jessie Tuggle, Atl	ILB	4	1	2	—	—
Zach Thomas, Mia	ILB	3	—	1	—	—
Deion Sanders, Dal	**CB**	**11**	**1**	**1**	**1**	**1**
Ty Law, NE	**CB**	**11**	**1**	**1**	**1**	**1**
Ray Buchanan, Atl	CB	4	1	2	—	—
Sam Madison, Mia	CB	2	—	2	—	—
Aaron Glenn, NYJ	CB	2	1	—	—	—
Rodney Harrison, SD	**S**	**11**	**1**	**1**	**1**	**†1**
LeRoy Butler, GB	**S**	**11**	**1**	**1**	**1**	**1**
Robert Griffith, Min	S	5	—	2	—	†1
Lawyer Milloy, NE	S	4	1	2	—	—
Darren Woodson, Dal	S	3	—	1	—	†1
Eugene Robinson, Atl	S	2	1	—	—	—

SPECIALISTS	POS	TT	+PW	AP	FW	SN
Gary Anderson, Min	**K**	**11**	**1**	**1**	**1**	**1**
Jason Elam, Den	K	4	1	2	—	—
Craig Hentrich, Ten	**P**	**11**	**1**	**1**	**1**	**1**
Matt Turk, Was	P	4	1	2	—	—
Bennie Thompson, Bal	ST	5	1	—	1	—
Michael Bates, Car	ST	2	1	—	—	—
Jermaine Lewis, Bal	**PR**	**8**	**1**	**1**	—	**1**
Deion Sanders, Dal	PR	5	1	—	1	—
Roell Preston, GB	**KR**	**7**	**1**	**2**	**†1**	—
Terry Fair, Det	KR	6	—	—	†1	1
Vaughn Hebron, Den	KR	2	1	—	—	—

1999 NFL

OFFENSE	POS	TT	+PW	AP	FW	SN
Marvin Harrison, Ind	**WR**	**11**	**1**	**1**	**1**	**1**
Cris Carter, Min	**WR**	**8**	**1**	**1**	**1**	—
Isaac Bruce, SL	WR	7	1	2	—	1
Jimmy Smith, Jax	WR	4	1	2	—	—
Tony Gonzalez, KC	**TE**	**11**	**1**	**1**	**1**	**1**
Wesley Walls, Car	TE	4	1	2	—	—
Orlando Pace, SL	**T**	**11**	**1**	**1**	**1**	**1**
Tony Boselli, Jax	**T**	**11**	**1**	**1**	**1**	**1**
Jonathan Ogden, Bal	T	4	1	†2	—	—
Willie Roaf, NO	T	2	1	—	—	—
Leon Searcy, Jax	T	2	—	†2	—	—
Jon Runyan, Ten	T	2	—	2	—	—
Larry Allen, Dal	**G**	**11**	**1**	**1**	**1**	**1**
Bruce Matthews, Ten	**G**	**8**	**1**	**1**	**1**	—
Tre' Johnson, Was	G	4	1	2	—	—
Ruben Brown, Buf	G	4	1	2	—	—
Will Shields, KC	G	3	—	—	—	1
Kevin Mawae, NYJ	**C**	**8**	**1**	**1**	—	**†1**
Tom Nalen, Den	C	5	—	2	—	†1
Jeff Christy, Min	C	5	1	—	1	—
Kurt Warner, SL	**QB**	**11**	**1**	**1**	**1**	**1**
Peyton Manning, Ind	QB	4	1	2	—	—
Edgerrin James, Ind	**RB**	**11**	**1**	**1**	**1**	**1**
Marshall Faulk, SL	**RB**	**11**	**1**	**1**	**1**	**1**
Eddie George, Ten	RB	4	1	†2	—	—
Stephen Davis, Was	RB	4	1	2	—	—
Curtis Martin, NYJ	RB	2	—	†2	—	—
Mike Alstott, TB	FB	3	—	1	—	—
Sam Gash, Buf	FB	2	—	2	—	—

DEFENSE	POS	TT	+PW	AP	FW	SN
Jevon Kearse, Ten	**DE**	**11**	**1**	**1**	**1**	**1**
Kevin Carter, SL	**DE**	**11**	**1**	**1**	**1**	**1**
Tony Brackens, Jax	DE	4	1	2	—	—
Robert Porcher, Det	DE	2	1	—	—	—
Simeon Rice, Arz	DE	2	—	2	—	—
Warren Sapp, TB	**DT**	**11**	**1**	**1**	**1**	**1**
Darrell Russell, Oak	**DT**	**10**	**1**	**2**	**1**	**1**
Trevor Pryce, Den	DT	5	1	1	—	—
Luther Elliss, Det	DT	2	1	—	—	—
Bryant Young, SF	DT	2	—	2	—	—
Ray Lewis, Bal	**LB**	**11**	**1**	**1**	**1**	**1**
Kevin Hardy, Jax	**LB**	**11**	**1**	**1**	**1**	**1**
Derrick Brooks, TB	**LB**	**11**	**1**	**1**	**1**	**1**
Hardy Nickerson, TB	LB	4	1	2	—	—
Peter Boulware, Bal	LB	4	1	2	—	—
Jessie Armstead, NYG	LB	4	1	2	—	—
Zach Thomas, Mia	LB	3	—	1	—	—
Junior Seau, SD	LB	2	—	2	—	—
Sam Madison, Mia	**CB**	**11**	**1**	**1**	**1**	**1**
Charles Woodson, Oak	**CB**	**8**	**1**	**1**	**1**	—
Deion Sanders, Dal	CB	7	1	2	—	1
Todd Lyght, SL	CB	4	1	2	—	—

1999 NFL (CONT.)

DEFENSE	POS	TT	+PW	AP	FW	SN
John Lynch, TB	**S**	**11**	**1**	**1**	**1**	**1**
Lawyer Milloy, NE	**S**	**8**	**1**	**1**	—	**1**
Carnell Lake, Jax	S	7	1	2	1	—
Brian Dawkins, Phi	S	2	1	—	—	—
Robert Griffith, Min	S	2	—	2	—	—

SPECIALISTS	POS	TT	+PW	AP	FW	SN
Olindo Mare, Mia	**K**	**11**	**1**	**1**	**1**	**1**
Jason Hanson, Det	K	2	1	—	—	—
Mike Vanderjagt, Ind	K	2	—	2	—	—
Mitch Berger, Min	**P**	**10**	**1**	**2**	**1**	**1**
Tom Tupa, NYJ	P	5	1	1	—	—
Michael Bates, Car	ST	5	1	—	—	—
Detron Smith, Den	ST	2	1	—	—	—
Charlie Rogers, Sea	**PR**	**8**	**1**	**1**	—	**1**
Glyn Milburn, ChiB	**KR**	**8**	**pr1**	**1**	—	**1**
Tony Horne, SL	KR	7	1	2	1	—
Tremain Mack, Cin	KR	2	1	—	—	—

2000 NFL

OFFENSE	POS	TT	+PW	AP	FW	SN
Randy Moss, Min	**WR**	**11**	**1**	**1**	**1**	**1**
Marvin Harrison, Ind	**WR**	**10**	**1**	**2**	**1**	**1**
Terrell Owens, SF	WR	5	1	1	—	—
Rod Smith, Den	WR	2	1	—	—	—
Tony Gonzalez, KC	**TE**	**11**	**1**	**1**	**1**	**1**
Chad Lewis, Phi	TE	4	1	†2	—	—
Frank Wycheck, Ten	TE	2	—	†2	—	—
Jonathan Ogden, Bal	**T**	**11**	**1**	**1**	**1**	**1**
Willie Roaf, NO	**T**	**7**	**1**	**2**	**1**	—
Orlando Pace, SL	**T**	**7**	**1**	**2**	—	**1**
Kyle Turley, NO	T	3	—	1	—	—
Brad Hopkins, Ten	T	2	1	—	—	—
Bruce Matthews, Ten	**G**	**11**	**1**	**1**	**1**	**1**
Larry Allen, Dal	**G**	**11**	**1**	**1**	**1**	**1**
Steve Wisniewski, Oak	G	4	1	2	—	—
Ron Stone, NYG	G	2	1	—	—	—
Ruben Brown, Buf	G	2	—	2	—	—
Tom Nalen, Den	**C**	**8**	**1**	**1**	**1**	**1**
Kevin Mawae, NYJ	C	5	—	2	1	—
Matt Birk, Min	C	2	1	—	—	—
Rich Gannon, Oak	**QB**	**11**	**1**	**1**	**1**	**1**
Daunte Culpepper, Min	QB	2	1	—	—	—
Peyton Manning, Ind	QB	2	—	2	—	—
Marshall Faulk, SL	**RB**	**11**	**1**	**1**	**1**	**1**
Eddie George, Ten	**RB**	**8**	**1**	**1**	**1**	—
Edgerrin James, Ind	RB	7	1	1	—	1
Robert Smith, Min	RB	2	1	—	—	—

DEFENSE	POS	TT	+PW	AP	FW	SN
Jason Taylor, Mia	**DE**	**11**	**1**	**1**	**1**	**1**
Hugh Douglas, Phi	**DE**	**11**	**1**	**1**	**1**	**1**
Trace Armstrong, Mia	DE	4	1	2	—	—
Joe Johnson, NO	DE	2	1	—	—	—
Rob Burnett, Bal	DE	2	—	2	—	—
Warren Sapp, TB	**DT**	**11**	**1**	**1**	**1**	**1**
La'Roi Glover, NO	**DT**	**11**	**1**	**1**	**1**	**1**
Sam Adams, Bal	DT	4	1	2	—	—
Trevor Pryce, Den	DT	2	1	—	—	—
Keith Hamilton, NYG	DT	2	—	2	—	—
Junior Seau, SD	**LB**	**11**	**1**	**1**	**1**	**1**
Ray Lewis, Bal	**LB**	**11**	**1**	**1**	**1**	**1**
Derrick Brooks, TB	**LB**	**11**	**1**	**1**	**1**	**1**
Jeremiah Trotter, Phi	LB	5	1	1	—	—
Mo Lewis, NYJ	LB	4	1	2	—	—
Keith Mitchell, NO	LB	2	1	—	—	—
Randall Godfrey, Ten	LB	2	—	†2	—	—
Sam Cowart, Buf	LB	2	—	2	—	—
Stephen Boyd, Det	LB	2	—	†2	—	—
Jessie Armstead, NYG	LB	2	—	2	—	—
Samari Rolle, Ten	**CB**	**11**	**1**	**1**	**1**	**1**
Sam Madison, Mia	**CB**	**11**	**1**	**1**	**1**	**1**
Champ Bailey, Was	CB	4	1	2	—	—
Troy Vincent, Phi	CB	2	1	—	—	—
Charles Woodson, Oak	CB	2	—	2	—	—
Darren Sharper, GB	**S**	**11**	**1**	**1**	**1**	**1**
John Lynch, TB	**S**	**11**	**1**	**1**	**1**	**1**
Rod Woodson, Bal	S	4	1	2	—	—
Brock Marion, Mia	S	2	1	—	—	—
Blaine Bishop, Ten	S	2	—	2	—	—

SPECIALISTS	POS	TT	+PW	AP	FW	SN
Matt Stover, Bal	**K**	**11**	**1**	**1**	**1**	**1**
Martin Gramatica, TB	K	4	1	2	—	—
Shane Lechler, Oak	**P**	**6**	—	**1**	—	**1**
Darren Bennett, SD	P	5	1	1	—	—
Scott Player, Arz	P	2	1	—	—	—
Chris Gardocki, Cle	P	2	—	2	—	—
Michael Bates, Car	ST	5	1	—	—	1
Larry Izzo, Mia	ST	2	1	—	—	—
Az-Zahir Hakim, SL	**PR**	**6**	—	**1**	**1**	**1**
Desmond Howard, Det	PR	2	1	—	—	—
Derrick Mason, Ten	**KR**	**11**	***2**	**1**	**1**	**1**
Darrick Vaughn, Atl	KR	4	1	2	—	—

* received 1 for **kr** and 1 for **pr**

2001 NFL

OFFENSE	POS	TT	+PW	AP	FW	SN
Terrell Owens, SF	**WR**	11	1	1	1	1
David Boston, Arz	**WR**	11	1	1	1	—
Rod Smith, Den	WR	4	1	2	—	—
Marvin Harrison, Ind	WR	4	1	2	—	—
Tony Gonzalez, KC	**TE**	11	1	1	1	1
Wesley Walls, Car	TE	2	1	—	—	—
Ernie Conwell, SL	TE	2	—	2	—	—
Orlando Pace, SL	**T**	11	1	1	1	1
Jonathan Ogden, Bal	**T**	10	1	2	1	1
Walter Jones, Sea	T	5	1	1	—	—
Chris Samuels, Was	T	2	1	—	—	—
James Williams, ChiB	T	2	—	†2	—	—
Lincoln Kennedy, Oak	T	2	—	†2	—	—
Alan Faneca, Pit	**G**	11	1	1	1	1
Larry Allen, Dal	**G**	11	1	1	1	1
Ray Brown, SF	G	4	1	2	—	—
Will Shields, KC	G	2	1	—	—	—
Adam Timmerman, SL	G	2	—	2	—	—
Kevin Mawae, NYJ	**C**	11	1	1	1	1
Olin Kreutz, ChiB	C	2	1	—	—	—
Jeff Hartings, Pit	C	2	—	2	—	—
Kurt Warner, SL	**QB**	11	1	1	1	1
Rich Gannon, Oak	QB	2	1	—	—	—
Brett Favre, GB	QB	2	—	2	—	—
Marshall Faulk, SL	**RB**	11	1	1	1	1
Curtis Martin, NYJ	**RB**	10	1	2	1	1
Priest Holmes, KC	RB	5	1	1	—	—
Ahman Green, GB	RB	4	1	2	—	—

DEFENSE	POS	TT	+PW	AP	FW	SN
Michael Strahan, NYG	**DE**	11	1	1	1	1
John Abraham, NYJ	**DE**	11	1	1	1	1
Marcellus Wiley, SD	DE	4	1	2	—	—
Robert Porcher, Det	DE	2	1	—	—	—
Jason Taylor, Mia	DE	2	—	2	—	—
Warren Sapp, TB	**DT**	11	1	1	1	1
Ted Washington, ChiB	**DT**	6	—	1	1	—
Sam Adams, Bal	DT	5	1	—	1	—
Bryant Young, SF	DT	4	1	2	—	—
John Randle, Sea	DT	2	1	—	—	—
Trevor Pryce, Den	DT	2	—	2	—	—
Brian Urlacher, ChiB	**LB**	11	1	1	1	1
Jamir Miller, Cle	**LB**	8	1	1	1	—
Ray Lewis, Bal	**LB**	8	1	1	—	1
Jason Gildon, Pit	**LB**	8	1	1	1	—
Derrick Brooks, TB	LB	4	1	2	—	—
LaVar Arrington, Was	LB	4	1	2	—	—
Jeremiah Trotter, Phi	LB	2	—	†2	—	—
Zach Thomas, Mia	LB	2	—	2	—	—
Kendrell Bell, Pit	LB	2	—	†2	—	—
Aeneas Williams, SL	**CB**	11	1	1	1	1
Ronde Barber, TB	**CB**	6	—	1	1	1
Charles Woodson, Oak	CB	5	†1	—	—	1
Troy Vincent, Phi	CB	4	1	2	—	—
Sam Madison, Mia	CB	4	†1	2	—	—
Deltha O'Neal, Den	CB	2	1	—	—	—
Brian Dawkins, Phi	**S**	11	1	1	1	1
John Lynch, TB	**S**	7	1	2	1	—
Rodney Harrison, SD	S	5	1	—	—	1
Mike Brown, ChiB	S	3	—	1	—	—
Lawyer Milloy, NE	S	2	1	—	—	—
Sammy Knight, NO	S	2	—	2	—	—

SPECIALISTS	POS	TT	+PW	AP	FW	SN
David Akers, Phi	**K**	11	1	1	1	1
Jason Elam, Den	K	4	1	2	—	—
Todd Sauerbrun, Car	**P**	11	1	1	1	1
Shane Lechler, Oak	P	4	1	2	—	—
Larry Whigham, ChiB	ST	5	1	—	1	—
Ian Gold, Den	ST	2	1	—	—	—
Troy Brown, NE	PR	5	1	—	1	—
Darrien Gordon, Atl	PR	2	1	—	—	—
Steve Smith, Car	**KR**	11	1	1	1	1
Jermaine Lewis, Bal	KR	7	1	2	—	pr1

2002 NFL

OFFENSE	POS	TT	+PW	AP	FW	SN
Terrell Owens, SF	**WR**	11	1	1	1	1
Marvin Harrison, Ind	**WR**	11	1	1	1	1
Hines Ward, Pit	WR	4	1	2	—	—
Randy Moss, Min	WR	2	1	—	—	—
Jerry Rice, Oak	WR	2	—	2	—	—
Eric Moulds, Buf	WR	2	—	2	—	—
Tony Gonzalez, KC	**TE**	10	1	2	1	1
Jeremy Shockey, NYG	TE	5	1	1	—	—
Jonathan Ogden, Bal	**T**	11	1	1	1	1
Tra Thomas, Phi	**T**	7	1	2	—	1
Lincoln Kennedy, Oak	T	5	1	1	—	—
Walter Jones, Sea	T	5	1	1	—	—
Willie Roaf, KC	T	2	—	2	—	—
Will Shields, KC	**G**	11	1	1	1	1
Alan Faneca, Pit	**G**	11	1	1	1	1
Jermane Mayberry, Phi	G	4	1	2	—	—
Ron Stone, SF	G	2	1	—	—	—
Ruben Brown, Buf	G	2	—	2	—	—

2002 NFL (CONT.)

OFFENSE	POS	TT	+PW	AP	FW	SN
Kevin Mawae, NYJ	**C**	10	1	2	1	1
Barret Robbins, Oak	C	3	—	1	—	—
Jeremy Newberry, SF	C	2	1	—	—	—
Rich Gannon, Oak	**QB**	11	1	1	1	1
Brett Favre, GB	QB	4	1	2	—	—
Ricky Williams, Mia	**RB**	11	1	1	1	1
Priest Holmes, KC	**RB**	11	1	1	1	1
Deuce McAllister, NO	RB	2	1	—	—	—
Tiki Barber, NYG	RB	2	1	—	—	—
LaDainian Tomlinson, SD	RB	2	—	2	—	—
Fred Beasley, SF	RB	2	—	2	—	—

DEFENSE	POS	TT	+PW	AP	FW	SN
Jason Taylor, Mia	**DE**	11	1	1	1	1
Simeon Rice, TB	**DE**	11	1	1	1	1
Hugh Douglas, Phi	DE	4	1	2	—	—
John Abraham, NYJ	DE	2	1	—	—	—
Michael Strahan, NYG	DE	2	—	2	—	—
Warren Sapp, TB	**DT**	11	1	1	1	1
La'Roi Glover, Dal	**DT**	10	1	2	1	1
Kris Jenkins, Car	DT	3	—	1	—	—
Gary Walker, Hou	DT	2	1	—	—	—
Richard Seymour, NE	DT	2	1	—	—	—
Chris Hovan, Min	DT	2	—	2	—	—
Brian Urlacher, ChiB	**LB**	11	1	1	1	1
Joey Porter, Pit	**LB**	11	1	1	1	1
Derrick Brooks, TB	**LB**	11	1	1	1	1
Zach Thomas, Mia	LB	5	1	1	—	—
Keith Bulluck, Ten	LB	4	1	2	—	—
LaVar Arrington, Was	LB	2	1	—	—	—
Julian Peterson, SF	LB	2	—	2	—	—
Donnie Edwards, SD	LB	2	—	2	—	—
Keith Brooking, Atl	LB	2	—	2	—	—
Patrick Surtain, Mia	**CB**	11	1	1	1	1
Bobby Taylor, Phi	**CB**	7	1	2	1	1
Troy Vincent, Phi	CB	5	1	1	—	—
Aaron Glenn, Hou	CB	5	1	—	—	1
Ronde Barber, TB	CB	2	—	2	—	—
Brian Dawkins, Phi	**S**	9	—	1	1	1
Rod Woodson, Oak	**S**	8	1	1	1	—
Darren Sharper, GB	S	5	—	—	—	1
Lance Schulters, Ten	S	2	1	—	—	—
John Lynch, TB	S	2	—	2	—	—

SPECIALISTS	POS	TT	+PW	AP	FW	SN
Adam Vinatieri, NE	**K**	8	1	1	1	—
David Akers, Phi	K	7	1	2	—	1
Todd Sauerbrun, Car	**P**	11	1	1	1	1
Chris Hanson, Jax	P	4	1	2	—	—
Fred McAfee, NO	ST	5	1	—	—	1
Larry Izzo, NE	ST	2	1	—	—	—
Santana Moss, NYJ	**PR**	8	1	—	1	1
Michael Lewis, NO	**KR**	11	*2	1	1	1
Chad Morton, NYJ	KR	2	1	—	—	—
Dante Hall, KC	KR	2	—	2	—	—

* received 1 for **kr** and 1 for **pr**

2003 NFL

OFFENSE	POS	TT	+PW	AP	FW	SN
Torry Holt, SL	**WR**	11	1	1	1	1
Randy Moss, Min	**WR**	8	1	1	1	—
Marvin Harrison, Ind	WR	7	1	2	—	1
Chad Johnson, Cin	WR	4	1	†2	—	—
Hines Ward, Pit	WR	2	—	†2	—	—
Tony Gonzalez, KC	**TE**	11	1	1	1	1
Alge Crumpler, Atl	TE	2	1	—	—	—
Todd Heap, Bal	TE	2	—	2	—	—
Jonathan Ogden, Bal	**T**	11	1	1	1	1
Orlando Pace, SL	**T**	8	1	1	1	—
Willie Roaf, KC	T	7	1	2	—	1
Walter Jones, Sea	T	2	1	—	—	—
Willie Anderson, Cin	T	2	—	2	—	—
Will Shields, KC	**G**	11	1	1	1	1
Steve Hutchinson, Sea	**G**	11	1	1	1	1
Marco Rivera, GB	G	4	1	2	—	—
Alan Faneca, Pit	G	2	1	—	—	—
Tom Nalen, Den	**C**	8	1	1	1	—
Matt Birk, Min	C	7	1	2	—	1
Peyton Manning, Ind	**QB**	11	1	1	1	1
Brett Favre, GB	QB	2	1	—	—	—
Steve McNair, Ten	QB	2	—	2	—	—
Jamal Lewis, Bal	**RB**	11	1	1	1	1
Priest Holmes, KC	**RB**	11	1	1	1	1
Deuce McAllister, NO	RB	2	1	—	—	—
Ahman Green, GB	RB	2	1	—	—	—
LaDainian Tomlinson, SD	RB	2	—	2	—	—
Fred Beasley, SF	RB	2	—	2	—	—

DEFENSE	POS	TT	+PW	AP	FW	SN
Michael Strahan, NYG	**DE**	11	1	1	1	1
Leonard Little, SL	**DE**	8	1	1	1	—
Simeon Rice, TB	DE	5	—	2	—	1
Dwight Freeney, Ind	DE	4	1	2	—	—
Adewale Ogunleye, Mia	DE	2	1	—	—	—
Richard Seymour, NE	**DT**	11	1	1	1	1

2003 NFL (CONT.)

DEFENSE	POS	TT	+PW	AP	FW	SN
Kris Jenkins, Car	DT	11	1	1	1	1
Marcus Stroud, Jax	DT	4	1	2	—	—
La'Roi Glover, Dal	DT	4	1	2	—	—
Julian Peterson, SF	LB	11	1	1	1	1
Ray Lewis, Bal	LB	11	1	1	1	1
Keith Bulluck, Ten	LB	8	1	1	1	—
Derrick Brooks, TB	LB	5	—	2	—	1
Dat Nguyen, Dal	LB	4	1	2	—	—
LaVar Arrington, Was	LB	4	1	2	—	—
Zach Thomas, Mia	LB	3	—	1	—	—
Takeo Spikes, Buf	LB	2	1	—	—	—
Tedy Bruschi, NE	LB	2	—	2	—	—
Ty Law, NE	CB	8	1	1	1	—
Patrick Surtain, Mia	CB	7	1	2	—	1
Champ Bailey, Was	CB	7	1	2	—	1
Chris McAlister, Bal	CB	6	—	1	1	—
Dre' Bly, Det	CB	2	1	—	—	—
Roy Williams, Dal	S	11	1	1	1	1
Ed Reed, Bal	S	10	1	2	1	1
Rodney Harrison, NE	S	5	1	1	—	—
Tony Parrish, SF	S	4	1	2	—	—

SPECIALISTS	POS	TT	+PW	AP	FW	SN
Mike Vanderjagt, Ind	K	11	1	1	1	1
Jeff Wilkins, SL	K	4	1	2	—	—
Todd Sauerbrun, Car	P	7	1	2	—	1
Shane Lechler, Oak	P	6	—	1	1	—
Craig Hentrich, Ten	P	2	1	—	—	—
Alex Bannister, Sea	ST	5	1	—	1	—
Adalius Thomas, Bal	ST	2	1	—	—	—
Brian Westbrook, Phi	PR	2	1	—	—	—
Dante Hall, KC	KR	11	*2	1	*2	pr1
Jerry Azumah, ChiB	KR	7	1	2	—	1

* in both cases received 1 for **kr** and 1 for **pr**

2004 NFL

OFFENSE	POS	TT	+PW	AP	FW	SN
Terrell Owens, Phi	WR	11	1	1	1	1
Muhsin Muhammad, Car	WR	8	1	1	1	—
Marvin Harrison, Ind	WR	7	1	2	—	1
Chad Johnson, Cin	WR	2	1	—	—	—
Hines Ward, Pit	WR	2	—	2	—	—
Antonio Gates, SD	TE	11	1	1	1	1
Jason Witten, Dal	TE	2	1	—	—	—
Tony Gonzalez, KC	TE	2	—	2	—	—
Walter Jones, Sea	T	11	1	1	1	1
Willie Roaf, KC	T	8	1	†1	1	—
Jonathan Ogden, Bal	T	4	1	2	—	—
Orlando Pace, SL	T	3	—	—	—	1
Willie Anderson, Cin	T	3	—	†1	—	—
Tra Thomas, Phi	T	2	1	—	—	—
Alan Faneca, Pit	G	11	1	1	1	1
Brian Waters, KC	G	9	1	1	1	1
Will Shields, KC	G	4	1	2	—	—
Steve Hutchinson, Sea	G	4	1	2	—	—
Marco Rivera, GB	G	2	1	—	—	—
Kevin Mawae, NYJ	C	7	1	2	1	—
Jeff Hartings, Pit	C	6	—	1	—	1
Olin Kreutz, ChiB	C	2	1	—	—	—
Peyton Manning, Ind	QB	11	1	1	1	1
Daunte Culpepper, Min	QB	2	1	—	—	—
Curtis Martin, NYJ	RB	11	1	1	1	1
Edgerrin James, Ind	RB	7	1	2	—	1
Shaun Alexander, Sea	RB	7	1	2	1	—
LaDainian Tomlinson, SD	RB	3	—	1	—	—
Tiki Barber, NYG	RB	2	1	—	—	—
William Henderson, GB	FB	3	—	1	—	—
Tony Richardson, KC	FB	2	—	2	—	—

DEFENSE	POS	TT	+PW	AP	FW	SN
Julius Peppers, Car	DE	11	1	1	1	1
Dwight Freeney, Ind	DE	11	1	1	1	1
Bertrand Berry, Arz	DE	4	1	2	—	—
Jason Taylor, Mia	DE	2	1	—	—	—
Patrick Kerney, Atl	DE	2	—	2	—	—
Richard Seymour, NE	DT	11	1	1	1	1
Kevin Williams, Min	DT	9	—	1	1	1
Kevin Williams, Min	DT	2	1	—	—	—
Marcus Stroud, Jax	DT	2	1	—	—	—
Roderick Coleman, Atl	DT	2	1	—	—	—
Jamal Williams, SD	DT	2	—	2	—	—
Shaun Rogers, Det	DT	2	—	2	—	—
Takeo Spikes, Buf	LB	11	1	1	1	1
James Farrior, Pit	LB	11	1	1	1	1
Derrick Brooks, TB	LB	8	1	1	1	—
Ray Lewis, Bal	LB	6	—	1	—	1
Joey Porter, Pit	LB	4	1	2	—	—
Keith Brooking, Atl	LB	4	1	2	—	—
Dan Morgan, Car	LB	2	1	—	—	—
Donnie Edwards, SD	LB	2	—	2	—	—
Tedy Bruschi, NE	LB	2	—	2	—	—
Champ Bailey, Den	CB	11	1	†1	1	1
Lito Sheppard, Phi	CB	8	1	†1	1	—
Chris McAlister, Bal	CB	7	1	2	—	1

2004 NFL (CONT.)

DEFENSE	POS	TT	+PW	AP	FW	SN
Ronde Barber, TB	CB	3	—	1	—	—
Shawn Springs, Was	CB	2	1	—	—	—
Ed Reed, Bal	S	11	1	1	1	1
Brian Dawkins, Phi	S	11	1	1	1	1
Troy Polamalu, Pit	S	4	1	2	—	—
Michael Lewis, Phi	S	2	1	—	—	—
Rodney Harrison, NE	S	2	—	2	—	—

SPECIALISTS	POS	TT	+PW	AP	FW	SN
Adam Vinatieri, NE	K	11	1	1	1	1
David Akers, Phi	K	4	1	2	—	—
Shane Lechler, Oak	P	11	1	1	1	1
Mitch Berger, NO	P	2	1	—	—	—
Brad Maynard, ChiB	P	2	—	2	—	—
Larry Izzo, NE	ST	5	1	—	1	—
Ike Reese, Phi	ST	2	1	—	—	—
B.J. Sams, Bal	PR	2	1	—	—	—
Eddie Drummond, Det	KR	11	*2	1	pr1	pr1
Terrence McGee, Buf	KR	10	1	2	1	1

* received 1 for **kr** and 1 for **pr**

2005 NFL

OFFENSE	POS	TT	+PW	AP	FW	SN
Steve Smith, Car	WR	11	1	1	1	1
Chad Johnson, Cin	WR	11	1	1	1	1
Santana Moss, Was	WR	4	1	2	—	—
Marvin Harrison, Ind	WR	4	1	2	—	—
Antonio Gates, SD	TE	11	1	1	1	1
Chris Cooley, Was	TE	2	1	—	—	—
Walter Jones, Sea	T	11	1	1	1	1
Willie Anderson, Cin	T	8	1	1	1	—
Willie Roaf, KC	T	7	1	2	—	—
Orlando Pace, SL	T	2	1	—	—	—
Jon Jansen, Was	T	2	—	2	—	—
Steve Hutchinson, Sea	G	11	1	1	1	1
Alan Faneca, Pit	G	11	1	†1	1	1
Will Shields, KC	G	4	1	2	—	—
Brian Waters, KC	G	3	—	†1	—	—
Olin Kreutz, ChiB	C	10	1	2	1	1
Jeff Saturday, Ind	C	5	1	1	—	—
Mike Wahle, Car	C	2	1	—	—	—
Peyton Manning, Ind	QB	11	1	1	1	1
Matt Hasselbeck, Sea	QB	2	1	—	—	—
Tom Brady, NE	QB	2	—	2	—	—
Shaun Alexander, Sea	RB	11	1	1	1	1
Tiki Barber, NYG	RB	8	1	1	1	—
LaDainian Tomlinson, SD	RB	5	—	2	—	1
Larry Johnson, KC	RB	4	1	2	—	—
Edgerrin James, Ind	RB	2	1	—	—	—
Mack Strong, Sea	FB	3	—	1	—	—
Lorenzo Neal, SD	FB	2	—	2	—	—

DEFENSE	POS	TT	+PW	AP	FW	SN
Dwight Freeney, Ind	DE	11	1	1	1	—
Osi Umenyiora, NYG	DE	8	1	1	1	—
Michael Strahan, NYG	DE	7	1	2	—	1
Derrick Burgess, Oak	DE	4	1	2	—	—
Jamal Williams, SD	DT	8	1	1	—	1
Richard Seymour, NE	DT	8	1	1	—	1
Roderick Coleman, Atl	DT	7	1	2	1	—
Tommie Harris, ChiB	DT	4	1	2	—	—
Marcus Stroud, Jax	DT	3	—	—	—	1
Brian Urlacher, ChiB	LB	11	1	1	1	1
Al Wilson, Den	LB	8	1	1	—	1
Lance Briggs, ChiB	LB	8	1	1	1	—
Cato June, Ind	LB	7	1	2	1	—
Derrick Brooks, TB	LB	5	1	1	—	—
Joey Porter, Pit	LB	4	1	2	—	—
Shawne Merriman, SD	LB	3	—	—	—	1
Zach Thomas, Mia	LB	2	1	1	—	—
Mike Peterson, Jax	LB	2	1	2	—	—
Champ Bailey, Den	CB	11	1	1	1	1
Nathan Vasher, ChiB	CB	7	1	2	1	—
Deltha O'Neal, Cin	CB	7	1	2	—	1
Ronde Barber, TB	CB	5	1	1	—	—
Troy Polamalu, Pit	S	11	1	1	1	1
Darren Sharper, Min	S	10	1	2	1	1
Bob Sanders, Ind	S	5	1	1	—	—
Mike Brown, ChiB	S	4	1	2	—	—

SPECIALISTS	POS	TT	+PW	AP	FW	SN
Neil Rackers, Arz	K	11	1	1	1	1
Shayne Graham, Cin	K	4	1	2	—	—
Brian Moorman, Buf	P	11	1	1	1	1
Josh Bidwell, TB	P	4	1	2	—	—
David Tyree, NYG	ST	5	1	—	1	—
Hanik Milligan, SD	ST	2	1	—	—	—
Antwaan Randle El, Pit	PR	5	1	—	—	—
B.J. Sams, Bal	PR	3	—	—	—	1
Reno Mahe, Phi	PR	2	1	—	—	—
Jerome Mathis, Hou	KR	11	1	1	1	1
Koren Robinson, Min	KR	2	1	—	—	—
Terrence McGee, Buf	KR	2	—	2	—	—

NAME	POS	TOT	CONS	YEARS
Abraham, John	DE	2	2	2001–02
Abramowicz, Danny	E	1	0	1969
Abramson, George	G	1	0	1925
Adamle, Tony	C–LB	2	1	1950–51
Adams, Chet	T	4	0	1940–43
Adams, John	T	2	0	1945–46
Adams, Sam	DT	2	2	2000–01
Adamson, Ken	G	2	1	1960–61
Adderley, Herb	CB	8	4	1962–69
Addison, Tom	LB–OLB	5	2	1960–64
Aguiar, Louie	P	1	0	1995
Aguirre, Joe	E	4	1	1943–46
Aikman, Troy	QB	3	0	1993–95
Akers, David	K	3	3	2001–02; 2004
Akins, Frank	B	1	0	1945
Alban, Dick	DB	1	0	1955
Albert, Frankie	QB	4	1	1946–49
Alderman, Grady	T	2	0	1965; 1969
Aldrich, Ki	C	2	0	1939; 1945
Aldridge, Lionel	DE	1	0	1964
Alexander, Dan	G	2	0	1985–86
Alexander, Doc	C	2	2	1921–22
Alexander, John	C	1	0	1926
Alexander, Kermit	CB	1	0	1968
Alexander, Shaun	RB	2	2	2004–05
Alford, Bruce	E	1	0	1947
Allegre, Raul	K	1	0	1983
Allen, Chuck	LB–MLB	3	0	1961–62; 1964
Allen, Dalva	DE	1	0	1963
Allen, Eric	CB	6	3	1989; 1991–95
Allen, Larry	G–T	7	7	1995–2001
Allen, Marcus	RB	4	4	1982; 1984–86; 1993
Allen, Terry	RB	3	1	1994–96
Alstott, Mike	FB	4	3	1996–99
Alt, John	T	3	1	1989–91
Alworth, Lance	E	7	7	1963–69
Alzado, Lyle	DE	5	2	1977–80; 1982
Ambrose, Ashley	CB	1	1	1996
Ameche, Alan	RB	4	1	1955–56; 1958–59
Andersen, Morten	K	6	6	1985–88; 1992; 1995
Anderson, Dick	S	3	3	1972–74
Anderson, Eddie	E	3	1	1922; 1924–25
Anderson, Gary	K	5	3	1983–85; 1993; 1998
Anderson, Hunk	G	1	0	1922
Anderson, Jamal	RB	1	1	1998
Anderson, Ken	QB	4	2	1974–75; 1981–82
Anderson, Neal	ST–RB	4	2	1986; 1988–90
Anderson, Ottis	RB	2	2	1979–80
Anderson, Willie	T	3	2	2003–05
Andrews, William	RB	4	2	1980–83
Andrie, George	DE	4	0	1966–69
Ane, Charlie	C–T	2	0	1956–57
Angsman, Elmer	HB	3	0	1947–49
Antoine, Lionel	T	1	0	1976
Antwine, Houston	DT	6	2	1963–64; 1966–69
Arbanas, Fred	TE	6	4	1962–67
Armstead, Jessie	OLB–LB	4	1	1997–2000
Armstrong, Bruce	T	7	5	1988–91; 1994–96
Armstrong, John	B	1	0	1923
Armstrong, Otis	RB	1	0	1974
Armstrong, Trace	DE	1	1	2000
Arnett, Jon	RB	2	1	1958; 1961
Arnold, Jim	P	3	2	1984; 1987–88
Arrington, LaVar	LB	3	3	2001–03
Artoe, Lee	T	5	1	1940–42; 1945–46
Ashmore, Roger	T	1	0	1928
Atkins, Billy	S	1	1	1961
Atkins, Doug	DE	10	2	1957–65; 1968
Atkinson, Al	MLB	1	0	1968
Atkinson, George	S	2	0	1969; 1976
Atwater, Steve	S	6	4	1990–93; 1995–96
Austin, Bill	G	1	0	1955
Awalt, Robert	TE	1	0	1987
Ayers, John	G	2	0	1984–85
Azumah, Jerry	KR	1	1	2003
Bacchus, Carl	E	2	1	1927–28
Bacon, Coy	DE	4	1	1971–72; 1976–77
Bacon, Frank	B	1	0	1920
Badaczewski, John	G	1	0	1947
Badgro, Red	E	4	0	1930–31; 1933–34
Bagarus, Steve	B–HB	2	0	1945–46
Bahr, Chris	K	1	0	1977
Bailey, Champ	CB	4	4	2000; 2003–05
Bailey, Johnny	KR	1	0	1992
Bain, Bill	T	1	1	1984
Baker, Al	DE	2	1	1978–79
Baker, Conway	T	1	0	1938
Baker, Dave	S	2	0	1960–61
Baker, John	DE	2	0	1964–65
Baker, Johnny	OLB	1	0	1966
Baker, Jon	MG	2	0	1951–52
Baker, Sam	P	1	0	1966
Bakken, Jim	K	5	2	1967–68; 1974–76
Baldwin, Al	E	2	0	1948–49
Ball, Jerry	DT	3	2	1989–91
Ballard, Howard	T	4	1	1990–93

NAME	POS	TOT	CONS	YEARS
Ballman, Gary	E	1	0	1964
Banaszek, Cas	T	2	0	1970–71
Banducci, Bruno	G	7	5	1945–47; 1951–54
Banfield, Tony	CB	3	3	1961–63
Banks, Carl	OLB	1	1	1987
Banks, Chip	OLB	5	1	1982–83; 1985–87
Banks, Tom	C	5	4	1975–79
Bannister, Alex	ST	1	1	2003
Banonis, Vince	C	4	0	1946–49
Barbaro, Gary	S	3	3	1980–82
Barber, Jim	T	2	1	1939–40
Barber, Mike	TE	1	0	1983
Barber, Ronde	CB	4	2	2001–02; 2004–05
Barber, Stew	T	5	1	1963–66; 1968
Barber, Tiki	RB	3	2	2002; 2004–05
Barker, Bryan	P	1	1	1997
Barnes, Erich	DB–CB	7	1	1959–62; 1964; 1966; 1968
Barnes, Mike	DT	1	0	1977
Barnes, Pete	OLB	1	0	1969
Barney, Lem	CB	7	2	1967–70; 1972–73; 1975
Barr, Terry	DB–E	2	0	1958; 1963
Barragar, Nate	C	5	3	1930–32; 1934–35
Bartkowski, Steve	QB	1	0	1980
Barton, Harris	T	2	2	1992–93
Barwegan, Dick	G	6	5	1947–52
Basrak, Mike	C	2	0	1937–38
Bass, Dick	RB	2	1	1962; 1966
Bass, Mike	CB	1	0	1974
Bassi, Dick	G	1	0	1940
Bateman, Marv	P	1	0	1976
Bates, Bill	ST	1	0	1984
Bates, Michael	KR–ST	5	4	1996–2000
Batinski, Stan	G	1	0	1945
Battles, Cliff	B	6	3	1932–37
Baugh, Sammy	B–QB	9	6	1937–38; 1940–43; 1945; 1947–48
Baughan, Maxie	LB–OLB	7	1	1961; 1964–69
Baumhower, Bob	DT	5	4	1979; 1981–84
Bausch, Frank	C	4	0	1935–38
Bavaro, Mark	TE	2	2	1986–87
Beals, Alyn	E	4	3	1946–49
Beasley, Fred	RB	2	0	2002–03
Beattie, Bob	T	1	1	1929
Bednarik, Chuck†	C–LB	12	7	1950–57; 1960–61
Behman, Bull	T	3	2	1926; 1928–29
Bell, Bobby	DE–OLB	9	7	1964–72
Bell, Kendrell	LB	1	0	2001
Bell, Todd	S	1	1	1984
Benirschke, Rolf	K	1	0	1982
Benkert, Heinie	B	2	0	1925–26
Bennett, Chuck	B	1	0	1930
Bennett, Cornelius	OLB–ILB	6	2	1988–92; 1994
Bennett, Darren	P	2	2	1995; 2000
Benson, Brad	T	1	0	1986
Benton, Jim	E	5	2	1939; 1944–47
Berger, Mitch	P	2	2	1999; 2004
Bergey, Bill	MLB–ILB	6	6	1974–78; 1980
Berquist, Jay	G	1	0	1926
Berry, Bert	DE	1	1	2004
Berry, Charlie	E	2	1	1925–26
Berry, George	G	1	0	1924
Berry, Raymond	E	6	3	1957–61; 1965
Berry, Rex	DB	1	0	1955
Bethea, Elvin	DE	8	1	1969; 1971–75; 1978–79
Betters, Doug	DE	1	1	1983
Bettis, Jerome	RB	3	3	1993; 1996–97
Biasucci, Dean	K	2	2	1987–88
Bickett, Duane	OLB	2	1	1987–88
Bidwell, Josh	P	1	0	2005
Biggs, Verlon	DE	4	1	1965–67; 1972
Biletnikoff, Fred	E–WR	6	2	1969–74
Bingaman, Les	G–MG	5	3	1950–54
Bird, Rodger	S	1	0	1967
Birdsong, Carl	P	2	0	1982–83
Birdwell, Dan	DT	1	1	1968
Birk, Matt	C	2	1	2000; 2003
Bishop, Blaine	S	3	1	1995–96; 2000
Bishop, Don	CB	1	0	1961
Bishop, Keith	G	2	1	1986–87
Bishop, Sonny	T–G	3	0	1964–65; 1969
Bissell, Frank	E	1	0	1926
Blacklock, Hugh	T	2	2	1920; 1922
Blackmon, Don	OLB	1	0	1986
Blackmon, Robert	S	1	0	1995
Blackwood, Lyle	S	1	0	1977
Blades, Bennie	S	3	1	1988; 1991–92
Blades, Brian	WR	1	0	1989
Blaine, Ed	G	1	0	1964
Blair, George	S	1	0	1963
Blair, Matt	OLB	5	4	1977–81
Blanchard, Cary	K	1	1	1996
Blanda, George	QB–K	7	1	1961–63; 1966–67; 1970; 1973

NAME	POS	TOT	CONS	YEARS
Blanks, Sid	RB	1	0	1964
Blazine, Tony	T	1	0	1935
Bledsoe, Drew	QB	2	0	1994; 1996
Blood, Johnny	B	3	0	1929–31
Bloodgood, Al	B	2	1	1925–26
Blount, Mel	CB	6	3	1975–79; 1981
Blozis, Al	T	1	1	1943
Blue, Forrest	C	4	3	1971–74
Blumer, Herb	G	1	0	1929
Bly, Dre'	CB	1	0	2003
Bodenger, Maury	G	2	0	1931–32
Boll, Don	T	1	0	1956
Bomar, Lynn	E	1	0	1925
Boniol, Chris	K	1	0	1996
Bookman, Johnny	S	1	0	1960
Boozer, Emerson	RB	1	0	1967
Bortz, Mark	G	1	1	1990
Boselli, Tony	T	4	3	1996–99
Bosley, Bruce	G–C	4	0	1959–61; 1966
Bosseler, Don	RB	1	0	1957
Bostic, Jeff	C	1	0	1983
Bostic, Keith	S	1	0	1987
Boston, David	WR	1	0	2001
Bouley, Gil	T	2	0	1947–48
Boulware, Peter	LB	1	1	1999
Bowens, Tim	DT	1	0	1994
Bowman, Bill	RB	1	0	1954
Box, Cloyce	E	2	0	1950; 1952
Boyd, Bob	E	1	0	1954
Boyd, Bob	CB	5	2	1964–68
Boyd, Stephen	LB	1	0	2000
Boynton, Benny	B	3	2	1921–22; 1924
Braase, Ordell	DE	4	0	1960; 1965–67
Brackens, Tony	DE	1	1	1999
Bradley, Bill	S	4	2	1971–74
Bradshaw, Charlie	T	2	0	1963–64
Bradshaw, Jim	B	1	0	1926
Bradshaw, Terry	QB	3	1	1975; 1978–79
Brady, Tom	QB	1	0	2005
Braidwood, Chuck	E	1	0	1931
Bramlett, John	OLB	2	0	1965–66
Branch, Cliff	WR	4	3	1974–77
Branch, Mel	DE	3	2	1960; 1962–63
Braxton, Tyrone	S	1	0	1996
Bray, Ray	G	4	3	1946; 1948–50
Brazile, Robert	OLB	8	6	1975–82
Breeden, Louis	CB	1	1	1982
Breedlove, Rod	OLB	1	0	1962
Brenkert, Wayne	B	1	0	1924
Brennan, Willis	G	2	0	1925–26
Brettschneider, Carl	OLB	1	0	1962
Breunig, Bob	MLB–ILB	4	2	1979–80; 1982–83
Brewster, Pete	E	2	0	1956–57
Briggs, Lance	LB	1	1	2005
Brink, Larry	DE	3	1	1951–53
Briscoe, Marlin	WR	1	1	1970
Brito, Gene	DE	5	4	1955–58; 1960
Brock, Charley	C	5	1	1940; 1943–46
Brockington, John	RB	3	3	1971–73
Brodie, John	QB	2	1	1965; 1970
Brooking, Keith	LB	2	1	2002; 2004
Brooks, Derrick	OLB–LB	9	9	1997–2005
Brooks, James	RB	4	1	1986; 1988–90
Brooks, Larry	DT	6	2	1974; 1976–80
Brooks, Michael	ILB	1	1	1993
Brookshier, Tom	DB–CB	2	1	1959–60
Brown, Aaron	DE	3	1	1969–71
Brown, Bill	RB	3	0	1964–65; 1968
Brown, Bob	T	9	6	1964–72
Brown, Chad	OLB	2	1	1996; 1998
Brown, Charlie	WR	1	1	1982–83
Brown, Dave	CB	2	0	1984–85
Brown, Eddie	KR	2	0	1976–77
Brown, Eddie	WR	1	1	1988
Brown, Hardy	LB	2	0	1951–52
Brown, Jerome	DT	2	1	1989–91
Brown, Jim	RB	9	8	1957–65
Brown, Larry	RB	3	3	1970–72
Brown, Lomas	T	7	5	1989–92; 1994–96
Brown, Mike	S	2	2	2001; 2005
Brown, Ray	S	1	0	1974
Brown, Ray	G	1	0	2001
Brown, Robert	DT	2	0	1971–72
Brown, Roger	DT	6	1	1961–66
Brown, Ron	KR	1	0	1985
Brown, Rosey	T	9	7	1956–63; 1965
Brown, Ruben	G	4	2	1998–2000; 2002
Brown, Tim	KR–WR	7	5	1988; 1991; 1993–97
Brown, Timmy	RB	3	0	1963; 1965–66
Brown, Troy	PR	1	1	2001
Brown, Vincent	ILB	3	1	1991–93
Brown, Willie	CB	11	1	1964–74
Browner, Joey	S	5	4	1985; 1987–90
Bruce, Isaac	WR	3	1	1995–96; 1999
Brumbaugh, Carl	B	2	0	1930–31
Bruney, Fred	S	1	0	1960

ALL-PRO TEAMS: ALPHABETICAL LIST

NAME	POS	TOT	CONS	YEARS
Bruschi, Tedy	LB	2	0	2003–04
Bryan, Bill	C	1	0	1985
Bryan, Rick	DE	1	0	1986
Bryant, Bobby	CB	3	0	1969; 1973; 1975
Bryant, Cullen	KR	1	0	1976
Bryant, Jeff	DE	1	0	1984
Buchanan, Buck	DT	8	4	1964–71
Buchanan, Ray	CB	2	1	1994; 1998
Buchanon, Willie	CB	1	0	1978
Buck, Cub	T	4	0	1920; 1923–25
Buckler, Bill	G	1	0	1926
Budd, Johnny	G	1	0	1926
Budde, Ed	G	6	1	1966–71
Bukich, Rudy	QB	1	0	1965
Bulaich, Norm	RB	1	0	1971
Buland, Walt	T	1	0	1920
Bulger, Chet	T	3	0	1943; 1945; 1948
Bulluck, Keith	LB	2	2	2002–03
Buncom, Frank	OLB	5	0	1964–68
Buoniconti, Nick	MLB	10	4	1962–69; 1972–73
Burford, Chris	E	1	1	1962
Burgess, Derrick	DE	1	1	2005
Burkett, Chris	WR	1	0	1987
Burnett, Bobby	RB	1	0	1966
Burnett, Rob	DE	2	0	1994; 2000
Burrell, Ode	RB	1	0	1965
Burrough, Ken	WR	1	0	1977
Burroughs, Don	S	3	0	1960–62
Burruss, Lloyd	S	2	0	1986; 1988
Burt, Jim	DT	1	0	1986
Butkus, Dick	MLB	8	6	1965–72
Butler, Jack	DB	4	3	1956–59
Butler, Jerry	WR	1	0	1980
Butler, Kevin	K	2	0	1985; 1989
Butler, LeRoy	S	4	4	1993; 1996–98
Butler, Mike	DE	1	0	1981
Butts, Marion	RB	1	0	1990
Butz, Dave	DT	3	1	1979; 1983–84
Byars, Keith	RB	1	0	1990
Byner, Earnest	RB	3	0	1987; 1990–91
Byrd, Butch	CB	5	3	1964–66; 1968–69
Byrd, Gill	CB	4	1	1989–92
Caddel, Ernie	B	3	1	1935–37
Caffey, Lee Roy	OLB	1	0	1966
Calac, Pete	B	1	0	1920
Camarillo, Rich	P	7	4	1982–83; 1989–93
Campbell, Earl	RB	4	3	1978–81
Campbell, John	OLB	1	0	1966
Campbell, Marion	DE	1	0	1960
Campiglio, Bob	B	1	0	1932
Canadeo, Tony	B–HB	4	2	1943; 1947–49
Cannady, John	FB–LB	2	0	1947; 1951
Cannavino, Joe	CB	1	0	1960
Cannon, Billy	RB–TE	4	2	1960–61; 1967–68
†Cappelletti, Gino	E–K	5	0	1961; 1963–64; 1966
Carberry, Glenn	E	1	0	1923
Cardwell, Lloyd	B	3	0	1938–40
Carlson, Zuck	G	5	1	1930–34
Carlton, Wray	RB	2	0	1960; 1966
Carmichael, Harold	WR	6	3	1973–74; 1977–80
Carney, Art	G	1	1	1925
Carney, John	K	2	1	1990; 1994
Caroline, J.C.	DB	1	0	1956
Carpenter, Preston	RB–TE	2	0	1956; 1962
Carr, Fred	OLB	5	0	1970; 1972; 1974–76
Carr, Roger	WR	1	0	1976
Carrier, Mark	S	2	0	1991; 1994
Carrier, Mark	WR	1	0	1989
Carrier, Mark	S	1	0	1990
Carroll, Bird	E	2	1	1922–23
Carson, Carlos	WR	2	0	1983; 1987
Carson, Harry	OLB–MLB –ILB	7	7	1978–79; 1981–82; 1984–86
Carson, John	E	2	0	1956–57
Carter, Anthony	WR	2	0	1987–88
Carter, Cris	WR	4	2	1994–96; 1999
Carter, Dale	CB	4	3	1994–97
Carter, Jim	MLB	1	0	1972
Carter, Joe	E	3	0	1935–36; 1938
Carter, Kevin	DE	1	1	1999
Carter, Michael	DT	4	1	1985–88
Carter, Ross	G	1	0	1938
Carter, Rubin	DT	1	0	1977
Casanova, Tommy	S	4	1	1972; 1975–77
Casares, Rick	RB	4	1	1955–58
Case, Pete	G	1	0	1968
Case, Scott	CB	1	1	1988
Casillas, Tony	DT	1	0	1989
Cason, Jim	HB	1	0	1949
Casper, Dave	TE	4	4	1976–79
Caster, Rich	TE	3	0	1972; 1974–75
Catlin, Tom	LB	1	0	1954
Caywood, Les	G	1	0	1930
Cecil, Chuck	S	1	0	1992
Centers, Larry	FB	1	0	1996
Chamberlin, Guy	E	4	3	1920; 1922–24

NAME	POS	TOT	CONS	YEARS
Chambers, Wally	DT	3	3	1974–76
Chandler, Bob	WR	2	0	1975; 1977
Chandler, Don	P–K	3	0	1964–65; 1967
Chandler, Wes	WR	2	1	1979; 1982
Chapple, Dave	P	1	0	1972
Cherry, Deron	S	7	5	1983–89
Cherundolo, Chuck	C	3	0	1938; 1942; 1947
Chester, Raymond	TE	4	1	1970–72; 1979
Childress, Ray	DE–DT	6	5	1988–93
Childs, Henry	TE	2	0	1978–79
Chmura, Mark	TE	2	2	1995; 1998
Chorovich, Dick	DT	1	0	1960
Christensen, George	T	6	3	1931–36
Christensen, Todd	TE	5	4	1983–87
Christiansen, Jack	DB	6	5	1952–57
Christianson, Oscar	E	1	0	1924
Christie, Steve	K	1	1	1990
Christman, Paul	QB	2	0	1946–47
Christy, Jeff	C	2	2	1998–99
Cifers, Ed	E	2	0	1942; 1948
Clabo, Neil	P	1	0	1975
Clack, Jim	C	2	0	1978–79
Clark, Bruce	DE	1	0	1987
Clark, Dutch	B	6	6	1931–32; 1934–37
Clark, Dwight	WR	2	1	1981–82
Clark, Gary	WR	4	2	1986–87; 1990–91
Clark, Herman	G	2	0	1955–56
Clark, Howard	E	1	0	1960
Clark, Mario	CB	1	0	1981
Clark, Randy	C	1	0	1984
Clarke, Frank	E	1	1	1964
Clarke, Hagood	S	1	0	1966
Clarke, Harry	B	1	1	1943
Clayborn, Raymond	KR–CB	5	1	1977; 1983; 1985–86; 1988
Claypool, Ralph	C	2	1	1925–26
Clayton, Mark	WR	3	1	1984–85; 1988
Clement, Johnny	HB	2	0	1947; 1949
Clifton, Kyle	ILB	1	0	1986
Cline, Doug	OLB	2	0	1962–63
Coates, Ben	TE	4	2	1994–96; 1998
Cobb, Alf	G	1	0	1920
Cockroft, Don	P–K	2	0	1972; 1978
Cofer, Mike	OLB–K	3	1	1988–90
Coffman, Paul	TE	3	2	1983–84
Cogdill, Gail	E	3	0	1962–64
Cole, Robin	ILB	1	0	1984
Coleman, Andre	KR	2	0	1994–95
Coleman, Rod	DT	1	1	2004
Coleman, Roderick	DT	1	0	2005
†Collins, Gary	E–P	5	0	1965–67; 1969
Collins, Jim	ILB	3	1	1983–85
Collins, Mark	CB	3	0	1989–90; 1996
Collins, Tony	RB	1	0	1983
Collinsworth, Cris	WR	4	1	1981–83; 1985
Colmer, Mickey	FB	1	0	1948
Colo, Don	DT	6	0	1953–58
Colzie, Neal	S	1	0	1982
Comstock, Rudy	G	3	0	1923; 1926; 1930
Concannon, Rick	G	1	0	1935
Condit, Merl	B	1	0	1942
Conerly, Charlie	QB	3	0	1956–57; 1959
Conlan, Shane	ILB	3	1	1987–88; 1990
Conner, Clyde	E	1	0	1957
Conners, Dan	MLB	3	1	1967–69
Connolly, Ted	G	1	0	1962
Connor, George	T–DT –LB–G	7	6	1949–55
Conover, Larry	C	1	1	1923
Conrad, Bobby Joe	E	2	1	1963–64
Conwell, Ernie	TE	1	0	2001
Conzelman, Jimmy	B	2	0	1923; 1925
Cook, Fred	DE	2	0	1976–77
Cook, Marv	TE	1	1	1991
Cooley, Chris	TE	1	0	2005
Cope, Frank	T–G	5	2	1940; 1943–46
Cornelison, Jerry	T	2	0	1960–61
Corral, Frank	K	1	1	1978
Cosbie, Doug	TE	2	0	1984–85
Costa, Dave	TE–DT	4	3	1966–69
Coulter, Tex	T	3	1	1948; 1951–52
Cousineau, Tom	ILB	2	2	1983–84
Covert, Jimbo	T	4	2	1985–87; 1990
Cowan, Charley	T	5	0	1967–69; 1971; 1973
Cowart, Sam	LB	1	0	2000
Cox, Bryan	OLB–ILB	3	1	1992; 1994–95
Cox, Fred	K	3	0	1969–71
Cox, Steve	P	1	0	1986
Craig, Larry	B–E	2	0	1939; 1947
Craig, Roger	RB	4	2	1985; 1987–89
Crangle, Jack	B	1	0	1923
Creekmur, Lou	G–T	8	6	1951–58
Cribbs, Joe	RB	3	2	1980–81; 1983
Cromwell, Nolan	S	4	4	1980–83
Cross, Jeff	DE	1	0	1990
Cross, Randy	G–C	6	2	1980–81; 1984–87

NAME	POS	TOT	CONS	YEARS
Crow, John David	RB	3	0	1959–60; 1962
Crow, Lindon	DB	2	0	1956; 1959
Crowther, Rae	E	1	1	1925
Crumpler, Alge	TE	1	1	2003
Csonka, Larry	RB	4	3	1970–73
Cudzik, Walt	C	1	0	1960
Cuff, Ward	B	5	2	1938–39; 1941; 1943–44
Culp, Curley	DT	6	2	1971; 1975–79
Culpepper, Daunte	QB	2	2	2000; 2004
Culver, Frank	C	1	0	1925
Cumby, George	ILB	1	0	1982
Cunningham, Randall	QB	4	3	1988; 1990; 1992; 1998
Cunningham, Richie	K	1	1	1997
Cunningham, Sam	RB	2	0	1974; 1978
Cuppoletti, Bree	G	2	0	1935–36
Currie, Dan	LB–OLB	3	2	1961–63
Curry, Bill	C	2	1	1969; 1971
Curry, Buddy	ILB	2	0	1980; 1982
Curtis, Isaac	WR	4	3	1973–76
Curtis, Mike	OLB–MLB	5	1	1968–71; 1974
Dadmun, Harrie	G	1	0	1920
Dahl, Bob	G	1	0	1996
Dale, Carroll	E	1	0	1968
Dancewicz, Boley	QB	1	0	1947
Danenhauer, Eldon	T	4	0	1962–65
Daniels, Clem	RB	4	2	1963–66
Danowski, Ed	B	3	2	1935; 1937–38
Darden, Thom	S	3	1	1976; 1978–79
Daugherty, Dick	LB	1	0	1957
David, Jim	DB	5	1	1954–58
Davidson, Ben	DE	3	1	1965–67
Davis, Ben	CB	1	0	1968
Davis, Eric	CB	2	1	1995–96
Davis, Fred	T	3	1	1946–48
Davis, Jack	G	1	0	1960
Davis, Milt	DB	2	0	1957; 1959
Davis, Stephen	RB	1	1	1999
Davis, Terrell	RB	4	3	1995–98
Davis, Tommy	P	1	0	1965
Davis, Willie	DE	6	4	1962–67
Dawkins, Brian	S	4	4	1999; 2001–02; 2004
Dawson, Dermontti	C	6	5	1993–98
Dawson, Len	QB	5	2	1962; 1964; 1966; 1968; 1971
Day, Tom	DE	3	0	1964–66
Dean, Fred	DE	4	3	1979–81; 1983
Dean, Vernon	CB	1	0	1982
Dee, Bob	DE	4	0	1960–62; 1964
Del Greco, Al	K	1	0*	1996
Del Rio, Jack	ILB	1	1	1994
DeLamielleure, Joe	G	9	6	1974–81; 1983
Delaney, Joe	RB	1	1	1981
DeLeone, Tom	C	1	0	1980
Dell Isola, Johnny	G	3	1	1937–39
DeLong, Steve	DE	1	0	1969
Delpino, Robert	ST	1	0	1988
DeLuca, Sam	G	1	0	1966
DeLucca, Jerry	T	1	0	1961
DeMarco, Bob	C	8	0	1963–69; 1971
Dempsey, Tom	K	1	0	1969
Den Herder, Vern	DE	1	0	1972
Denfeld, Fred	G	1	0	1920
Denson, Al	TE–E	3	0	1966–67; 1969
Dent, Richard	DE	5	4	1984–85; 1988; 1990; 1993
Derby, Dean	DB–CB	2	0	1959–60
DeRogatis, Al	DT	2	0	1951–52
DeShane, Chuck	G	1	0	1949
DesJardien, Shorty	C	1	0	1920
Dess, Darrell	G	1	0	1963
Dewell, Billy	E	2	0	1941; 1946
DeWitz, Herb	B	1	0	1926
Dewveall, Willard	E	1	0	1960
Dial, Buddy	E	2	0	1961; 1963
Dibble, Dorne	E	1	0	1954
Dickerson, Eric	RB	5	5	1983–84; 1986–88
Dickey, Lynn	QB	1	0	1983
Diehl, Wally	B	2	1	1928–29
Dieken, Doug	T	1	0	1980
Dierdorf, Dan	T	6	5	1974–78; 1980
Dillon, Bobby	DB	7	4	1953–59
Dilweg, Lavvie	E	8	6	1926–33
Dishman, Cris	CB	2	1	1991; 1997
Ditka, Mike	E–TE	6	3	1961–66
Dixon, Hanford	CB	3	2	1986–88
Dixon, Hewritt	RB	3	1	1967–68; 1970
Doane, Dinger	B	1	0	1923
Dobbs, Glenn	HB	2	1	1946; 1948
Dobler, Conrad	G	4	0	1975–77; 1979
Dodrill, Dale	MG–LB	6	2	1952–56; 1958
Doleman, Chris	DE	6	4	1987–90; 1992–93
Doll, Don	HB–DB	3	1	1949–51
Donaldson, Ray	C	5	1	1986–89; 1996
Donnelly, Rick	P	2	0	1987–88

NAME	POS	TOT	CONS	YEARS
Donovan, Art	DT	6	4	1954–58; 1960
Donovan, Pat	T	6	3	1978–83
Dorney, Keith	T	2	0	1981; 1985
Dorow, Al	QB	1	0	1960
Dorsett, Tony	RB	5	2	1977–78; 1981–83
Dottley, John	RB	1	0	1951
Douds, Jap	T	2	1	1930–31
Dougherty, Bob	LB	1	0	1960
Douglas, Hugh	DE	2	2	2000; 2002
Douglass, Maurice	ST	1	0	1994
Douglass, Mike	OLB–ILB	2	1	1981–82
Dove, Eddie	S	1	0	1961
Dowler, Boyd	E	2	0	1962; 1967
Downs, Michael	S	2	1	1984–85
Drake, Johnny	B	5	1	1937–41
Drazenovich, Chuck	LB	3	0	1956–58
Driscoll, Paddy	B	8	7	1920; 1922–28
Drulis, Chuck	G	1	0	1948
Drummond, Eddie	KR	1	1	2004
Dryer, Fred	DE	2	0	1974–75
Dubenion, Elbert	RB–E	3	0	1960; 1963–64
Dudley, Bill	B–HB–DB	6	3	1942; 1946–48; 1950–51
Duerson, Dave	S	3	1	1986–88
Duhe, A.J.	OLB–ILB	2	0	1981; 1983
Dukes, Mike	LB	1	0	1960
Dunaway, Jim	DT	3	0	1965–66; 1969
Duncan, Speedy	CB	3	0	1965–67
Dunn, Gary	DT	1	0	1984
Dunn, Red	B	3	0	1924; 1930–31
Duper, Mark	WR	2	0	1983–84
DuPree, Billy Joe	TE	3	1	1976–78
Dusek, Brad	OLB	1	0	1979
Dutton, John	DE	2	2	1975–76
Earp, Jugger	C	1	0	1929
Easley, Kenny	S	6	5	1982–87
Eason, Bo	S	1	0	1985
Eason, Roger	G	1	0	1947
Ebding, Harry	E	2	0	1933–34
Ecklund, Brad	C	1	0	1953
Eckstein, Dolph	C	1	0	1925
Edelman, Brad	G	1	0	1987
Edgerson, Booker	CB	1	0	1969
Edmonds, Bobby Joe	KR	1	1	1986
Edmunds, Ferrell	TE	1	0	1989
Edwards, Brad	S	1	0	1992
Edwards, Dan	E	1	0	1950
Edwards, Donnie	LB	2	0	2002; 2004
Edwards, Eddie	DE	1	0	1981
Edwards, Glen	S	3	0	1973; 1975–76
Edwards, Herman	CB	2	0	1980; 1982
Edwards, Monk	G	3	1	1941–42; 1946
Edwards, Turk	T	8	4	1932–39
Ehrmann, Joe	DT	1	0	1976
Eisenhauer, Larry	DE	5	2	1961–64; 1966
Ekern, Carl	ILB	1	0	1986
Elam, Cleveland	DT	2	1	1976–77
Elam, Jason	K	3	3	1995; 1998; 2001
Ellard, Henry	KR–WR	4	1	1984–85; 1988–89
Eller, Carl	DE	9	6	1967–75
Elliott, Doc	B	3	2	1922–24
Elliott, John	DT	3	2	1968–70
Ellis, Allan	CB	1	0	1977
Ellis, Ken	CB	3	2	1972–74
Ellis, Walt	T	1	1	1926
Ellison, Willie	RB	1	0	1971
Elliss, Luther	DT	1	0	1999
Elmendorf, Dave	S	3	1	1972; 1974–75
Elway, John	QB	5	4	1986–87; 1993; 1996–97
Emerson, Ox	G	6	5	1932–37
English, Doug	DT	5	2	1978; 1981–84
Erickson, Hal	B	2	0	1923; 1925
Esiason, Boomer	QB	2	2	1988–89
Ettinger, Don	G	1	0	1948
Evans, Byron	ILB	2	1	1990; 1992
Evans, Doug	CB	1	0	1997
Evans, Lon	G	3	1	1935–37
Evans, Norm	T	2	0	1973–74
Everett, Jim	QB	2	0	1988–89
Fagan, Julian	P	1	0	1970
Fagan, Kevin	DE	1	0	1990
Fahnhorst, Keith	T	3	1	1983–85
Fair, Terry	KR	1	1	1998
Faison, Earl	DE	5	4	1961–65
Falcon, Guil	B	1	0	1920
Famiglietti, Gary	B	2	1	1940; 1942
Faneca, Alan	G	5	5	2001–05
Farkas, Andy	B	3	1	1939; 1942–43
Farman, Dick	G	3	1	1940; 1942–43
Farr, Mel	RB	1	0	1970
Farr, Miller	CB	3	2	1967–69
Farrell, Sean	G	1	0	1984
Farrior, James	LB	1	1	2004
Faulk, Marshall	RB	6	5	1994–95; 1998–2001
Favre, Brett	QB	6	5	1995–97; 2001–03
Feagles, Jeff	P	1	1	1995
Fears, Tom	E	5	2	1948–51; 1955
Feathers, Beattie	B	1	1	1934; 1936
Felt, Dick	CB	2	0	1961–62
Felton, Ralph	LB	1	0	1961
Fencik, Gary	S	6	4	1979–82; 1984–85
Ferguson, Howie	RB	1	0	1955
Fernandez, Manny	DT	4	0	1970–73
Ferrante, Jack	E	2	0	1945; 1949
Ficca, Dan	G	1	0	1965
Fichtner, Ross	S	1	0	1966
Field, Harry	T	1	0	1934
Fields, Joe	C	3	2	1981–82; 1985
Fike, Dan	G	2	0	1986–87
Filchock, Frank	B–HB	3	0	1939; 1944; 1946
Fischer, Bill	T–G	2	1	1951–52
Fischer, Pat	CB	6	1	1964–65; 1968–69; 1972; 1975
Fisk, Bill	E	1	0	1943
Fiss, Galen	OLB	1	0	1962
Fitzgerald, Freeman	C	1	0	1920
Flaherty, Ray	E	7	4	1926; 1928–29; 1931–34
Flanagan, Ed	C	3	0	1969–71
Fleming, Don	S	1	0	1962
Flower, Jim	C	1	0	1922
Floyd, Don	DE	4	1	1961–64
Foley, Steve	CB	1	0	1978
Foley, Tim	S	2	0	1977; 1979
Ford, Len	DE	7	5	1951–57
Foreman, Chuck	RB	4	4	1974–77
Forester, Bill	LB–OLB	5	4	1959–63
Forte, Aldo	G	1	0	1941
Fortmann, Danny	G	8	7	1936–43
Fortunato, Joe	LB–OLB	6	3	1958; 1962–66
Foster, Barry	RB	1	1	1992
Foster, Roy	G	4	1	1984–86; 1989
Fouts, Dan	QB	6	3	1979–83; 1985
Fox, Tim	S	1	0	1982
Fralic, Bill	G	4	3	1986–89
France, Doug	T	3	1	1978–80
Francis, Russ	TE	4	1	1976–78; 1980
Franklin, Andra	RB	1	0	1982
Franklin, Tony	K	2	1	1979; 1986
Frazier, Willie	TE	2	1	1965; 1967
Freeman, Antonio	WR	1	1	1998
Freeman, Steve	S	1	0	1983
Freeney, Dwight	DE	3	3	2003–05
Freitas, Rocky	T	2	0	1970; 1972
French, Walter	B	1	0	1925
Friedman, Benny	B	6	4	1927–31; 1933
Fritsch, Ted	B–FB	2	1	1945–46
Fritsch, Toni	K	2	1	1975; 1979
Fryar, Irving	KR–WR	2	1	1985; 1994
Fugett, Jean	TE	1	1	1977
Fulcher, David	S	3	3	1988–90
Fuller, Frank	DT	2	0	1959–60
Fuller, William	DE	4	1	1991; 1994–96
Gabriel, Roman	QB	2	1	1968–69
Gain, Bob	LB–DE–DT	9	0	1955–63
Galimore, Willie	RB	2	0	1957–58
Gallarneau, Hugh	HB	1	0	1946
Gannon, Rich	QB	3	3	2000–02
Gantenbein, Milt	E	3	1	1936–38
Garcia, Frank	P	1	0	1983
Gardocki, Chris	P	2	1	1996; 2000
Garrett, Carl	RB	1	0	1969
Garrett, Mike	RB	3	1	1966–67; 1969
Garrison, Gary	E–WR	4	0	1968; 1970–72
Garron, Larry	RB	1	0	1961
Garvey, Hec	G	1	1	1923
Gary, Russell	S	1	0	1983
Gash, Sam	FB	2	0	1998–99
Gastineau, Mark	DE	5	5	1981–85
Gates, Antonio	TE	2	2	2004–05
Gatski, Frank	C	5	4	1951–55
Gay, William	DE	1	0	1983
Gehrke, Fred	B–HB	2	0	1945–46
Gentry, Byron	G	2	0	1938–39
Gentry, Dennis	KR	3	1	1986–88
George, Bill	LB–MLB	8	7	1955–61; 1963
George, Eddie	RB	3	2	1996; 1999–2000
Gerela, Roy	K	3	1	1972–75
Geri, Joe	HB–RB	2	1	1950–51
Ghee, Milt	B	1	0	1920
Gibron, Abe	G	4	1	1951; 1953–55
Gibson, Butch	G	4	0	1931–34
Gibson, Claude	CB	1	0	1961
Gibson, George	G	1	0	1930
Giesler, Jon	T	2	0	1984; 1986
Gifford, Frank	DB–RB	6	3	1953; 1955–59
Gilbert, Sean	DT	1	0	1993
Gilchrist, Cookie	RB	4	3	1962–65
Gildea, Johnny	B	1	0	1937
Gildon, Jason	LB	1	0	2001
Giles, Jimmie	TE	4	0	1980–82; 1985
Gillette, Jim	B	1	0	1945
Gilliam, John	WR	3	1	1972–73; 1975
Gillies, Fred	T	1	0	1922
Gillingham, Gale	G	6	3	1968–71; 1973–74
Gillo, Hank	B	2	0	1923–24
Givins, Ernest	WR	1	1	1990
Glass, Bill	DE	5	0	1962–65; 1967
Glassgow, Bill	B	1	0	1930
Glenn, Aaron	CB	3	3	1997–98; 2002
Glenn, Terry	WR	1	0	1996
Glick, Fred	S	2	1	1963–64
Glover, Kevin	C	4	3	1994–97
Glover, La'Roi	DT	4	3	1998; 2000; 2002–03
Godfrey, Chris	G	1	0	1986
Godfrey, Randall	LB	1	0	2000
Goebel, Paul	E	4	1	1923–26
Gogan, Kevin	G	1	1	1998
Gogolak, Charlie	K	1	0	1966
Gogolak, Pete	K	1	0	1965
Gold, Ian	ST	1	0	2001
Goldberg, Marshall	B–HB	2	0	1941; 1947
Goldenberg, Buckets	G	2	0	1939; 1942
Golembeske, John	T	1	0	1938
Golic, Bob	DT	2	1	1985–86
Gonsoulin, Goose	CB–S	5	2	1960–64
Gonzalez, Tony	TE	6	5	1999–2004
Goode, Irv	G	1	0	1970
Goodwin, Tod	E	1	0	1935
Gordon, Darrien	KR–PR	4	1	1994; 1996–97; 2001
Gordon, Dick	WR	2	0	1970–71
Gordon, Lou	T	4	0	1931–33; 1937
Gordy, John	G	5	0	1963–67
Gorgal, Ken	DB	1	0	1953
Gossett, Bruce	K	3	1	1964; 1966; 1973
Gossett, Jeff	P	1	1	1991
Gradishar, Randy	MLB–ILB	8	6	1976–83
Graham, Al	G	4	0	1927–28; 1930–31
Graham, Kenny	S	5	1	1965–69
Graham, Otto	QB	10	9	1946–55
Graham, Shayne	K	1	1	2005
Gramatica, Martin	K	1	0	2000
Grange, Red	B	4	2	1926; 1930–32
Granger, Hoyle	RB	1	0	1967
Grant, Frank	WR	1	0	1976
Grant, Len	T	3	1	1931–33
Grantham, Larry	LB–OLB	11	5	1960–69; 1971
Gray, Jerry	CB	4	4	1986–89
Gray, Ken	G	7	3	1963–69
Gray, Leon	T	6	3	1976–81
Gray, Mel	WR	3	1	1974–76
Gray, Mel	KR	8	6	1986–87; 1989–94
Grayson, Dave	CB–S	7	5	1963–66; 1968–70
Green, Ahman	RB	2	2	2001; 2003
Green, Cornell	CB–S	6	2	1966–69; 1971–72
Green, Darrell	CB	4	3	1986–87; 1990–91
Green, Eric	TE	1	0	1990
Green, Gary	CB	5	2	1981–85
Green, Gaston	RB	1	0	1991
Green, Hugh	OLB	2	2	1982–83
Green, Jacob	DE	4	1	1983–85; 1987
Green, Roy	KR–WR	3	2	1979; 1983–84
Green, Tony	KR	1	0	1978
Greene, Joe	DT	11	7	1969–79
Greene, Kevin	OLB	3	3	1989; 1994; 1996
Greene, Tony	S	2	1	1974; 1977
Greenwood, Don	B	1	0	1945
Greenwood, L.C.	DE	6	3	1973–76; 1978–79
Greer, Curtis	DE	1	0	1984
Gregg, Forrest	T	9	5	1959–67
Gregory, Garland	G	1	0	1946
Gregory, Jack	DE	3	1	1969–70; 1972
Grgich, Visco	G	1	0	1949
Grier, Rosey	DT	7	1	1956; 1958–63
Griese, Bob	QB	5	2	1968; 1970–71; 1973; 1977
Griffin, Don	CB	3	0	1987; 1989–90
Griffith, Robert	S	2	1	1998–99
Grigas, John	B	1	1	1944
Grigg, Tex	B	1	1	1923
Grim, Bob	WR	1	0	1971
Grimes, Billy Joe	HB	1	1	1950
Grimm, Russ	G	5	4	1982–86
Grimsley, John	ILB	1	0	1989
Groman, Bill	E	2	0	1960–61
Grossman, Jack	B	1	0	1932
Grosvenor, George	B	1	0	1936
Groza, Lou	T–K	10	6	1946; 1951–57; 1964–65
Gruber, Paul	T	3	0	1989; 1991–92
Grupp, Bob	P	1	1	1979
Gudauskas, Pete	G	1	0	1944
Guesman, Dick	T	1	0	1963
Guidry, Paul	OLB	1	0	1970
Gulian, Mike	B	1	0	1924
Gutowsky, Ace	B	5	0	1932; 1934; 1936–38
Guy, Charlie	C	1	0	1923

ALL-PRO TEAMS: ALPHABETICAL LIST

NAME	POS	TOT	CONS	YEARS
Guy, Ray	P	9	7	1973–81
Guyon, Joe	B	2	0	1920; 1924
Hackett, Dino	ILB	1	0	1988
Haddix, Wayne	CB	1	0	1990
Haden, Pat	QB	1	0	1977
Hadl, John	QB	4	1	1965–66; 1968; 1973
Hagberg, Swede	C	1	0	1930
Haines, Hinkey	B	3	0	1925–27
Hairston, Carl	DE	4	0	1979–81; 1987
Haji–Sheikh, Ali	K	1	1	1983
Hakim, Az–Zahir	PR	1	1	2000
Halas, George	E	1	0	1920
Haley, Charles	OLB–DE	4	2	1988; 1990; 1994–95
Hall, Courtney	C	1	0	1994
Hall, Dante	KR	2	1	2002–03
Hall, Parker	B	2	1	1939–40
Hall, Ron	CB–S	2	1	1963–64
Hallstrom, Ron	G	1	0	1989
Ham, Jack	OLB	9	7	1972–80
Hamer, Tex	B	3	2	1924–26
Hamilton, Harry	S	1	0	1989
Hamilton, Keith	DT	1	0	2000
Hamilton, Wes	G	1	0	1981
Hammond, Bobby	KR	1	0	1977
Hampton, Dan	DE–DT	6	6	1980; 1982; 1984–86; 1988
Hampton, Dave	RB	3	0	1972–73; 1975
Hanburger, Chris	OLB	8	5	1968–70; 1972–76
Hand, Larry	DE	2	0	1970; 1972
Handler, Phil	G	1	0	1935
Hanks, Merton	S	4	3	1994–97
Hannah, John	G	11	10	1974; 1976–85
Hanneman, Chuck	E	1	0	1940
Hanner, Dave	DT	2	0	1957; 1959
Hanny, Duke	E	4	0	1923–26
Hansen, Brian	P	1	0	1984
Hanson, Chris	P	1	1	2002
Hanson, Hal	G	2	0	1929–30
Hanson, Jason	K	3	1	1993; 1997; 1999
Hanson, Swede	B	2	0	1933–34
Harbaugh, Jim	QB	1	1	1995
Harder, Pat	FB–RB	6	3	1946–50; 1952
Hardman, Cedrick	DE	2	1	1971; 1975
Hardy, Kevin	LB	1	1	1999
Harmon, Andy	DT	1	0	1995
Harrah, Dennis	G	7	2	1978–80; 1984–87
Harris, Cliff	S	6	3	1974–79
Harris, Dick	CB	4	1	1960–63
Harris, Duriel	KR	1	0	1976
Harris, Eric	CB	1	0	1981
Harris, Franco	RB	7	2	1972; 1974–79
Harris, Jackie	TE	1	0	1992
Harris, Tim	OLB	2	2	1988–89
Harris, Tommie	DT	1	1	2005
Harrison, Dennis	DE	1	0	1982
Harrison, Marvin	WR	7	7	1999–2005
Harrison, Rodney	S	4	3	1998; 2001; 2003–04
Hart, Jim	QB	1	1	1974
Hart, Leon	DE–RB	3	1	1951; 1954; 1956
Hart, Tommy	DE	1	1	1976
Hartings, Jeff	C	2	1	2001; 2004
Harvey, Ken	OLB	3	2	1994–96
Harvey, Norm	T	1	0	1925
Haselrig, Carlton	G	1	0	1992
Haslett, Jim	ILB	1	0	1980
Hasselbeck, Matt	QB	1	0	2005
Hasty, James	CB	1	1	1997
Hatcher, Dale	P	1	1	1985
Hathaway, Russ	T	2	0	1922–23
Hauss, Len	C	7	2	1971–77
Hawkins, Rip	OLB	1	0	1963
Hawkins, Wayne	G	6	1	1961; 1963–67
Hayes, Bob	E	4	3	1965–68
Hayes, Lester	CB	6	3	1979–84
Haynes, Abner	RB	4	1	1960–62; 1964
Haynes, Mark	CB	4	3	1981–84
Haynes, Mike	CB	8	8	1976–80; 1982; 1984–85
Hazeltine, Matt	LB–OLB	4	0	1959; 1961–62; 1964
Headrick, Sherrill	LB–MLB	5	3	1960–62; 1964; 1966
Healey, Ed	G–T	5	5	1922–26
Heap, Todd	TE	1	0	2003
Hearst, Garrison	RB	1	1	1998
Hebron, Vaughn	KR	1	0	1998
Heck, Andy	T	1	0	1995
Hein, Mel	C	13	7	1931–41; 1944–45
Henderson, Thomas	OLB	1	0	1977
Henderson, William	FB	1	1	2004
Hendricks, Ted	OLB	11	5	1971–74; 1976–78; 1980–83
Henke, Ed	DE	2	0	1952; 1957
Hennigan, Charley	E	4	3	1961–64
Henry, Pete	T	4	4	1920–23
Henry, Wally	KR	1	0	1979
Hentrich, Craig	P	2	1	1998; 2003
Herber, Arnie	B	4	2	1932; 1935–36

NAME	POS	TOT	CONS	YEARS
Herman, Dave	G	3	0	1967–69
Herrera, Efren	K	3	1	1976–77; 1979
Hewitt, Bill	E	6	5	1932–34; 1936–38
Hickerson, Gene	G	7	3	1964–70
Hickman, Herman	G	2	0	1933–34
Hicks, Dwight	S	2	1	1981; 1984
Hicks, W.K.	CB	1	0	1965
Hilgenberg, Jay	C	7	6	1985–91
Hilgenberg, Wally	OLB	1	0	1973
Hill, Calvin	RB	3	2	1969; 1973–74
Hill, Dave	T	1	0	1969
Hill, Drew	WR	2	0	1988; 1990
Hill, Harlon	E	3	3	1954–56
Hill, Jimmy	CB	3	0	1961–63
Hill, Kent	G	5	3	1980; 1982–85
Hill, Mack Lee	RB	1	0	1965
Hill, Tony	WR	3	0	1978–79; 1985
Hill, Winston	T	8	2	1964; 1968–74
Hillenbrand, Billy	HB	1	0	1948
Hilliard, Dalton	RB	1	1	1989
Hinkle, Bryan	OLB	1	0	1986
Hinkle, Clarke	B	10	3	1932–41
Hinkle, Jack	B	1	0	1943
Hinton, Chris	G–T	7	4	1983; 1985–89; 1993
Hirsch, Elroy	E	4	2	1951–53; 1956
Hoage, Terry	S	1	0	1988
Hoak, Dick	RB	1	0	1968
Hoerner, Dick	FB	2	1	1949–50
Hoernschemeyer, Bob	HB–RB	5	0	1946; 1949; 1951–53
Hogan, Darrell	G	1	0	1949
Holland, Vern	T	1	0	1975
Holloway, Brian	T	4	1	1983–86
Holman, Rodney	TE	3	2	1988–90
Holmer, Walt	B	1	0	1929
Holmes, Ernie	DT	2	0	1974–75
Holmes, Pat	DE	1	0	1967
Holmes, Priest	RB	3	3	2001–03
Holmes, Robert	RB	1	0	1968
Holt, Issiac	CB	1	0	1990
Holt, Pierce	DT	1	1	1992
Holt, Torry	WR	1	0	2003
Holub, E.J.	LB–OLB–C	7	2	1961–66; 1969
Homan, Two–Bits	B	1	0	1926
Hopkins, Brad	T	1	1	2000
Hopkins, Wes	S	2	1	1984–85
Horan, Mike	P	3	1	1984; 1988; 1990
Horne, Tony	KR	1	1	1999
Horning, Steamer	T	2	1	1922–23
Hornung, Paul	RB	3	2	1959–61
House, Kevin	WR	1	0	1984
Houston, Jim	OLB	3	1	1964–66
Houston, Ken	S	12	7	1968–79
Houston, Lin	G	2	0	1950–51
Hovan, Chris	DT	1	0	2002
Howard, Desmond	PR	2	1	1996; 2000
Howell, Jim Lee	E	2	0	1939; 1941
Howell, Mike	S	1	0	1966
Howley, Chuck	OLB	7	4	1963; 1966–71
Howton, Billy	E	5	3	1952; 1955–57; 1959
Hubbard, Cal	E–T	7	6	1927–33
Hudock, Mike	C	2	0	1964–65
Hudson, Bill	DT	1	0	1961
Hudson, Dick	T	1	0	1966
Hudson, Jim	S	1	0	1968
Huff, Sam	LB–MLB	8	3	1957–61; 1963–65
Huffine, Ken	B	1	0	1924
Huffman, Dick	T	4	3	1947–50
Hughes, Bernie	C	1	0	1934
Hughes, Tyrone	KR	1	1	1993
Hughitt, Tommy	B	1	1	1922
Hull, Kent	C	5	3	1988–91; 1995
Humbert, Dick	E	1	0	1941
Humble, Weldon	G	1	0	1948
Humphery, Bobby	KR	1	1	1984
Humphrey, Claude	DE	8	6	1969–74; 1976–77
Hunt, Bobby	S	3	0	1962; 1964; 1966
Hunt, Jim	DT	4	0	1961; 1966–68
Hunter, Art	C	1	0	1960
Hunter, James	S	1	0	1976
Hurlburt, John	B	1	0	1924
Hurley, George	G	2	0	1932–33
Husmann, Ed	DT	3	0	1961–63
Hutchinson, Steve	G	3	3	2003–05
Hutson, Don	E	11	10	1935–45
Ilkin, Tunch	T	1	0	1988
Iman, Ken	C	1	0	1969
Imlay, Tut	B	1	0	1926
Ingwersen, Burt	T	1	0	1920
Irvin, LeRoy	KR–CB	4	3	1981–82; 1985–86
Irvin, Michael	WR	3	1	1991–93
Isbell, Cecil	B	2	1	1938–42
Ivory, Horace	KR	1	0	1980
Izzo, Larry	ST	3	1	2000; 2002; 2004
Jacke, Chris	K	2	0	1990; 1993
Jackson, Bo	RB	2	0	1989–90
Jackson, Earnest	RB	1	0	1984

NAME	POS	TOT	CONS	YEARS
Jackson, Harold	WR	4	3	1972–73; 1976–77
Jackson, John	T	2	0	1993; 1996
Jackson, Keith	TE	5	4	1988–90; 1992; 1996
Jackson, Monte	CB	2	2	1976–77
Jackson, Noah	G	1	0	1980
Jackson, Rich	DE	4	3	1968–71
Jackson, Rickey	OLB	7	5	1983–87; 1992–93
Jackson, Tom	OLB	4	1	1977–79; 1984
Jacobs, Harry	MLB	1	0	1966
Jacobs, Ray	DT	1	0	1965
Jacoby, Joe	T	5	2	1983–87
Jaeger, Jeff	K	1	1	1991
Jagade, Chick	RB	1	0	1953
James, Edgerrin	RB	4	3	1999–2000; 2004–05
James, John	P	4	3	1975–77; 1980
James, Lionel	RB–KR	2	0	1985; 1987
James, Robert	CB	3	2	1972–74
James, Roland	S	1	0	1983
James, Tommy	HB–DB	2	0	1950; 1954
Jamison, Al	T	3	2	1960–62
Jancik, Bobby	S	1	0	1963
Jansante, Val	E	1	0	1947
Jansen, Jon	T	1	0	2005
Jappe, Paul	E	1	0	1926
Jaquess, Pete	CB	1	0	1964
Jaworski, Ron	QB	1	1	1980
Jefferson, John	WR	3	2	1978–80
Jefferson, Roy	E–WR	3	2	1968–69; 1971
Jeffires, Haywood	WR	2	1	1991–92
Jenkins, Alfred	WR	1	1	1981
Jenkins, Kris	DT	2	2	2002–03
Jennings, Dave	P	6	3	1976; 1978–82
Jennings, Jack	T	1	0	1955
Jerue, Mark	ILB	1	0	1986
Jervey, Travis	ST	1	1	1997
Jeter, Bob	CB	2	1	1967–68
Joe, Billy	RB	1	0	1963
Joesting, Herb	B	1	0	1931
Johnson, Bill	C	4	0	1952–55
Johnson, Billy	KR	3	2	1975; 1977; 1983
Johnson, Bob	C	7	0	1968; 1970; 1972–76
Johnson, Chad	WR	3	0	2003–05
Johnson, Charley	QB	1	0	1973
Johnson, Charlie	DT	3	3	1979–81
Johnson, Curley	P	2	0	1965; 1968
Johnson, Gary	DT	4	2	1979–82
Johnson, Jack	T	3	0	1936; 1938–39
Johnson, Jimmy	CB	9	4	1964–66; 1968–72; 1974
Johnson, Joe	DE	1	1	2000
Johnson, John Henry	RB	2	0	1954; 1962
Johnson, Johnnie	S	2	1	1983
Johnson, Keyshawn	WR	1	1	1998
Johnson, Larry	RB	1	1	2005
Johnson, Mike	ILB	1	1	1989
Johnson, Nate	T	1	1	1947
Johnson, Norm	K	2	1	1984; 1993
Johnson, Pepper	ILB	2	1	1990; 1994
Johnson, Pete	RB	1	0	1981
Johnson, Ron	RB	2	0	1970; 1972
Johnson, Tre	G	1	1	1999
Johnson, Vaughan	ILB	6	3	1987–92
Johnson, Walter	DT	1	0	1968
Johnsos, Luke	E	4	2	1929–32
Johnston, Mark	S	2	1	1960–61
Joiner, Charlie	WR	2	0	1976; 1980
Jones, Art	B	1	0	1941
Jones, Ben	B	1	0	1923
Jones, Bert	QB	2	1	1976–77
Jones, Brent	TE	3	2	1992–94
Jones, Deacon	DE	8	6	1964–70; 1972
Jones, Dub	RB	1	1	1951
Jones, Henry	S	1	1	1992
Jones, Homer	E	2	1	1967–68
Jones, Ken	T	1	0	1980
Jones, Potsy	G	2	0	1934–35
Jones, Rulon	DE	3	2	1985–87
Jones, Sean	DE	2	0	1994–95
Jones, Stan	G	6	4	1955–57; 1959–61
Jones, Tony	T	1	1	1994
Jones, Too Tall	DE	3	0	1978; 1981–83; 1985
Jones, Walter	T	5	5	2001–05
Jordan, Henry	DT	7	4	1960–64; 1966–67
Jordan, Lee Roy	MLB	5	1	1966; 1968–69; 1973; 1975
Jordan, Steve	TE	3	0	1986–87; 1989
Joyner, Seth	OLB	5	2	1991–94; 1996
June, Cato	LB	1	1	2005
Jungmichel, Buddy	G	1	0	1946
Junior, E.J.	ILB	2	1	1984–85
Jurgensen, Sonny	QB	5	1	1961; 1964; 1966–67; 1969
Jurkovic, John	DT	1	0	1996
Juzwik, Steve	HB	1	0	1946
Kahn, Eddie	G	1	0	1936
Karcher, Jim	G	2	0	1938–39

NAME	POS	TOT	CONS	YEARS
Maynard, Don	E	5	0	1960; 1965; 1967–69
Mays, Jerry	DT–DE	9	3	1962–70
Mazzetti, Tim	K	1	0	1980
McAfee, Fred	ST	1	1	2002
McAfee, George	B–HB	3	1	1940–41; 1948
McAlister, Chris	CB	2	1	2003–04
McAllister, Deuce	RB	2	2	2002–03
McBride, Jack	B	4	2	1925–27; 1930
McCabe, Richie	S	1	1	1960
McCaffrey, Ed	WR	1	0	1998
McCarren, Larry	C	4	0	1981–84
McClinton, Curtis	RB	2	0	1962; 1965
McCloughan, Kent	CB	4	1	1966–68; 1970
McCormack, Mike	MG–T	9	2	1954–62
McCormick, Elmer	T–C	2	1	1923–24
McCrary, Michael	DE	1	1	1998
McCutcheon, Lawrence	RB	5	1	1973–77
McDaniel, Randall	G	11	10	1988–98
McDaniel, Terry	CB	4	2	1992–95
McDole, Ron	DE	5	0	1965–69
McDonald, Tim	S	8	4	1989–96
McDonald, Tommy	E–RB	4	0	1959–62
McDowell, Bubba	S	1	0	1991
McDuffie, O.J.	KR	1	1	1993
McElhenny, Hugh	RB	5	2	1952–54; 1956–57
McElroy, Vann	S	4	0	1983–84; 1986–87
McFadden, Paul	K	1	1	1984
McFadin, Bud	G–DT	7	3	1953; 1955–56; 1960–63
McGee, Ben	DE	1	0	1966
McGee, Max	E	1	0	1964
McGee, Terrence	KR	2	1	2004–05
McGee, Tim	KR	1	0	1986
McGlockton, Charles	DT	1	1	1996
McGlockton, Chester	DT	2	2	1994–95
McGraw, Thurman	DT	2	1	1952–53
McGrew, Dan	C	1	0	1960
McInally, Pat	P	3	1	1977–78; 1981
McIntyre, Guy	G	3	1	1990–92
McKalip, Bill	E	2	2	1931; 1934
McKenzie, Raleigh	G	1	0	1991
McKenzie, Reggie	G	5	0	1973–76; 1980
McKyer, Tim	CB	2	1	1988; 1990
McLean, Ray	B	1	0	1942
McMahon, Jim	QB	1	0	1985
McMichael, Steve	DT	5	2	1985–88; 1991
McMillan, Erik	S	2	0	1988–89
McMillan, Ernie	T	7	1	1964; 1966–71
McMillen, Jim	G	5	5	1924–28
McMillian, Audry	CB	1	1	1992
McMurtry, Chuck	DT	2	1	1960–61
McNair, Steve	QB	1	0	2003
McNally, Frank	C	1	1	1931
McNamara, Tom	G	1	0	1923
McNeil, Charlie	S	1	1	1961
McNeil, Clifton	E–WR	2	1	1968; 1970
McNeil, Freeman	RB	3	2	1982; 1984–85
McNeill, Tom	P	1	0	1971
McPeak, Bill	DE	1	0	1953
McRae, Bennie	CB	1	0	1965
Meador, Eddie	CB–S	9	0	1960–61; 1963–69
Meadows, Ed	DE	1	0	1956
Means, Natrone	RB	1	0	1994
Mecklenburg, Karl	ILB	5	4	1985–87; 1989; 1991
Meggett, Dave	KR	3	2	1989–90; 1996
Mehelich, Charley	E	1	0	1947
Mehl, Lance	OLB–ILB	3	1	1982–83; 1985
Mehre, Harry	C	1	0	1923
Meinert, Dale	MLB	2	0	1964; 1967
Mellus, John	T	3	0	1939–41
Mendenhall, John	DT	1	0	1974
Mercer, Ken	B	1	0	1928
Meredith, Don	QB	2	0	1966; 1968
Merriman, Shawne	LB	1	0	2005
Merriweather, Mike	OLB	3	2	1984–85; 1987
Metcalf, Eric	KR	3	2	1993–94; 1997
†Metcalf, Terry	RB–KR	3	1	1974–75
Michael, Rich	T	1	1	1960
Michaels, Al	B	1	0	1923
Michaels, Lou	DE	3	1	1958–59; 1962
Michaels, Walt	LB	5	1	1957–61
Michalik, Art	MG	1	0	1953
Michalske, Mike	G	7	6	1927–31; 1934–35
Middleton, Terdell	RB	1	0	1978
Mike–Mayer, Nick	K	1	1	1973
Mikulak, Mike	B	1	0	1935
Milburn, Glyn	KR	2	2	1995; 1999
Millard, Bryan	G	1	0	1988
Millard, Keith	DT	4	2	1986–89
Millen, Matt	ILB	2	0	1984–85
Miller, Alan	RB	1	0	1961
Miller, Anthony	WR	4	4	1989–90; 1992–93
Miller, Bill	E	1	0	1963
Miller, Bob	DT	1	0	1956
Miller, Fred	DT	2	0	1967–68
Miller, Jamir	LB	1	1	2001

NAME	POS	TOT	CONS	YEARS
Miller, Junior	TE	1	1	1980
Miller, Ookie	C	1	1	1933
Miller, Paul	DE	1	0	1960
Milligan, Hanik	ST	1	0	2005
Millner, Wayne	E	2	0	1937; 1941
Milloy, Lawyer	S	3	3	1998–99; 2001
Mills, John Henry	ST	1	0	1996
Mills, Sam	ILB	4	3	1991–92; 1995–96
Milstead, Century	G–T	3	2	1925–27
Mingo, Gene	RB	1	0	1962
Minnifield, Frank	CB	4	3	1986–89
Mischak, Bob	G	4	2	1960–62; 1964
Mitchell, Bobby	RB–E	5	1	1959–60; 1962–64
Mitchell, Brian	KR	3	2	1991; 1994–95
Mitchell, Buster	E	1	0	1934
Mitchell, Jim	TE	1	0	1972
Mitchell, Keith	LB	1	1	2000
Mitchell, Leroy	CB	1	0	1968
Mitchell, Lydell	RB	3	2	1975–77
Mitchell, Stump	KR	1	0	1984
Mitchell, Willie	CB	1	0	1965
Mix, Ron	T–G	9	9	1960–68
Mobley, John	OLB	1	1	1997
Modzelewski, Dick	DT	3	0	1957; 1961; 1963
Moegle, Dicky	DB	2	0	1956–57
Mojsiejenko, Ralf	P	2	1	1987–88
Molenda, Bo	B	1	0	1931
Molesworth, Keith	B	1	0	1932
Momsen, Bob	MG	1	0	1951
Monk, Art	WR	3	2	1984–86
Montana, Joe	QB	7	4	1981; 1983–85; 1987; 1989–90
Montgomery, Greg	P	3	2	1989; 1992–93
Montgomery, Wilbert	RB	2	1	1978–79
Montoya, Max	G	3	1	1986; 1988–89
Moon, Warren	QB	3	1	1988–90
Mooney, Jim	T	1	0	1930
Moore, Herman	WR	3	3	1995–97
Moore, Lenny	RB	7	5	1956–61; 1964
Moore, Nat	WR	2	1	1977; 1979
Moore, Red	G	1	0	1947
Moore, Rob	WR	1	1	1997
Moore, Tom	RB	1	0	1963
Moore, Wilbur	B	1	0	1943
Moorman, Brian	P	1	1	2005
Moorman, Mo	G	1	0	1969
Moran, Hap	B	1	0	1931
Moran, Rich	G	1	0	1989
Morgan, Bill	T	2	1	1934–35
Morgan, Dan	LB	1	0	2004
Morgan, Stanley	WR	2	0	1980; 1986
Morin, Milt	TE	3	0	1968; 1971; 1973
Morrall, Earl	QB	2	0	1968; 1972
Morris, Dennit	LB	1	0	1960
Morris, Joe	RB	2	1	1985–86
Morris, Johnny	E	1	1	1964
Morris, Jon	C	6	0	1964–69
Morris, Larry	OLB	1	1	1963
Morris, Mercury	RB	1	0	1973
Morrison, Fred	RB	1	0	1955
Morriss, Guy	C	1	0	1981
Morrissey, Frank	C	1	0	1923
Morrow, John	C	1	0	1965
Morrow, Tommy	S	1	0	1963
Morton, Chad	KR	1	0	2002
Morton, Craig	QB	1	0	1977
Morze, Frank	C	1	0	1957
Mosebar, Don	C	2	0	1990–91
Moseley, Mark	K	5	2	1977–79; 1982–83
Moss, Randy	WR	4	4	1998; 2000; 2002–03
Moss, Santana	PR–WR	2	2	2002; 2005
Motley, Marion	FB	5	4	1946–50
Moulds, Eric	WR	2	1	1998; 2002
Moynihan, Tim	C	1	1	1932
Mudd, Howard	G	2	1	1967–68
Muha, Joe	FB–C	2	0	1948; 1950
Muhammad, Muhsin	WR	1	0	2004
Muirhead, Stan	G	1	1	1924
Mulleneaux, Carl	E	1	0	1940
Muller, Brick	E	1	0	1926
Mullins, Gerry	G	1	0	1979
Munchak, Mike	G	10	7	1983–85; 1987–93
Muncie, Chuck	RB	3	1	1979; 1981–82
Munoz, Anthony	T	11	11	1981–91
Murphy, Mark	S	1	1	1983
Murray, Eddie	K	6	2	1980–82; 1988–89; 1994
Murry, Don	T	1	0	1928
Musick, Jim	B	1	0	1933
Musso, George	T–G	5	2	1933; 1935; 1937–39
Mutryn, Chet	HB	3	3	1947–49
Mutscheller, Jim	E	1	0	1957
Myers, Dave	G	1	0	1931
Myers, Tom	S	1	1	1979
Nagurski, Bronko	B	7	4	1930–34; 1936–37
Nalen, Tom	C	3	2	1999–2000; 2003

NAME	POS	TOT	CONS	YEARS
Namath, Joe	QB	5	2	1966–69; 1972
Nance, Jim	RB	3	2	1966–67; 1969
Nash, Bob	E	2	1	1920–21
Nash, Joe	DT	2	1	1984–85
Nash, Tom	E	3	0	1930–32
Nathan, Tony	KR	1	0	1979
Naumetz, Fred	C	4	1	1947–50
Naumoff, Paul	OLB	2	1	1970; 1975
Neal, Ed	G	1	0	1950
Neal, Lorenzo	FB	1	0	2005
Neely, Ralph	T	5	3	1966–69; 1975
Neighbors, Billy	G	3	0	1962–64
Nelms, Mike	KR	3	2	1981–83
Nelsen, Bill	QB	1	0	1968
Nelson, Andy	DB–S	4	2	1958–61
Nelson, Chuck	K	1	0	1988
Nelson, Robert	C	4	2	1946–49
Nelson, Steve	MLB–OLB–ILB	5	2	1978–80; 1984–85
Nemecek, Andy	C	1	0	1924
Nery, Ron	DE	2	1	1960–61
Nesbitt, Dick	B	1	0	1931
Nesser, Al	G	5	1	1921–25
Nevers, Ernie	B	4	3	1926–27; 1929–31
Newberry, Jeremy	C	1	1	2002
Newberry, Tom	G	4	3	1987–90
Newman, Ed	G	4	4	1981–84
Newman, Harry	B	2	2	1933–34
Newsome, Ozzie	TE	7	4	1979–85
Newsome, Vince	S	1	0	1986
Newton, Nate	G	5	2	1992–96
Nguyen, Dat	LB	1	1	2003
Niccolai, Armand	T	2	0	1935–36
Nickerson, Hardy	ILB–LB	4	3	1993; 1996–97; 1999
Niland, John	G	6	3	1969–74
Nisby, John	G	3	0	1959–61
Nitschke, Ray	MLB	7	1	1962–67; 1969
Nobis, Tommy	MLB	2	1	1967–68
Noble, Brian	ILB	1	0	1987
Noble, Dave	B	2	0	1924–25
Nolting, Ray	B	1	0	1937
Nomellini, Leo	T–DT	9	6	1951–54; 1957; 1959–62
Noonan, Karl	E	1	0	1968
Norton, Jerry	DB–S	4	2	1958–61
Norton, Jim	S	3	0	1961–62; 1967
Norton, Ken	ILB	2	1	1993; 1995
Norwood, Scott	K	1	1	1988
Novacek, Jay	TE	5	2	1990–92; 1994–95
Novak, Eddie	B	1	1	1920
Nowaskey, Bob	E	1	0	1941
Nunn, Freddie Joe	DE	1	0	1988
Nutter, Buzz	C	2	0	1962–63
Nye, Blaine	G	3	1	1972; 1975–76
Oates, Bart	C	3	0	1987; 1994–95
O'Brien, Davey	B	2	0	1939–40
Oden, Curly	B	2	0	1926; 1928
Odomes, Nate	CB	3	1	1989; 1991; 1993
Odoms, Riley	TE	5	3	1973–77
O'Donnell, Dick	E	1	0	1923
Oehler, Cap	C	1	0	1934
Offerdahl, John	ILB	5	3	1986–90
Ogden, Jonathan	T	8	8	1997–2004
Ogunleye, Adewale	DE	1	0	2003
O'Hanley, Ross	S	2	0	1960–61
Okoye, Christian	RB	2	1	1989; 1991
Oldershaw, Doug	G	2	0	1940–41
Oliphant, Elmer	B	1	1	1921
Oliver, Louis	S	2	1	1990; 1992
Olsen, Merlin	DT	13	7	1963–75
Olson, Harold	T	1	0	1962
Olsson, Les	G	3	0	1936–38
Olszewski, Johnny	RB	2	0	1953; 1956
O'Neal, Deltha	CB	2	1	2001; 2005
O'Neal, Leslie	OLB–DE	5	3	1989–90; 1992; 1994–95
Orr, Jimmy	E	3	1	1958–59; 1965
Orvis, Herb	DT	1	0	1975
Osborn, Dave	RB	1	0	1967
Osborn, Duke	G	3	1	1922–23; 1925
Osmanski, Bill	B–FB	3	1	1939; 1941; 1946
Otto, Gus	OLB	4	0	1967–70
Otto, Jim	C	13	12	1960–72
Owen, Bill	T	3	2	1928; 1930–31
Owen, Steve	T–G	3	1	1926–27; 1929
Owens, Brig	S	1	0	1973
Owens, Luke	DT	1	0	1963
Owens, R.C.	E	1	0	1960
Owens, Steve	RB	1	0	1971
Owens, Terrell	WR	4	4	2000–02; 2004
Owens, Terry	T	1	0	1972
Pace, Orlando	T	6	6	1999–2001; 2003–05
Page, Alan	DT	11	7	1968–77; 1980
Palmer, David	PR	1	1	1997
Palmer, Paul	KR	1	0	1987
Paluck, John	DE	2	0	1960; 1964

NAME	POS	TOT	CONS	YEARS
Pankey, Irv	T	1	0	1988
Pardee, Jack	OLB	2	2	1963; 1971
Parilli, Babe	QB	1	1	1964
Parker, Ace	B–QB	5	2	1937–40; 1946
Parker, Jim	T–G	10	7	1957–66
Parks, Dave	E	2	1	1965–66
Parrish, Bernie	CB	1	0	1964
Parrish, Lemar	CB	8	2	1972–77; 1979–80
Parrish, Tony	S	1	1	2003
Parsons, Bob	P	1	0	1977
Partee, Dennis	P	1	0	1969
Paschal, Bill	B	3	1	1943–45
Patton, Cliff	G	1	0	1949
Patton, Jimmy	DB–S	6	5	1958–63
Paul, Don	LB–DB	6	0	1952–55; 1957–58
Paulson, Dainard	S	2	2	1964–65
Paup, Bryce	OLB	3	2	1994–96
Payne, Ken	WR	1	0	1975
Payton, Walter	RB	9	8	1976–80; 1983–86
Pear, Dave	DT	2	0	1977–78
Pearson, Bert	C	1	0	1931
Pearson, Drew	WR	5	3	1974–78
Pease, George	B	1	0	1929
Pellington, Bill	LB–MLB	4	0	1958; 1960; 1962; 1964
Peoples, Woody	G	2	0	1971–72
Peppers, Julius	DE	1	1	2004
Percival, Mac	K	1	0	1968
Perkins, Don	RB	4	0	1961–62; 1967–68
Perry, Darren	S	1	0	1994
Perry, Joe	FB–RB	4	3	1949; 1953–54; 1958
Perry, Michael Dean	DT	8	4	1989–96
Perry, Rod	CB	2	0	1978; 1980
Perry, Vernon	S	1	0	1980
Petcoff, Boni	T	1	0	1924
Peters, Floyd	DT	3	0	1964; 1966–67
Peters, Tony	S	1	0	1982
Peters, Volney	DT	1	0	1960
Petersen, Kurt	G	1	0	1982
Peterson, Carl	C	1	0	1924
Peterson, Julian	LB	2	1	2002–03
Peterson, Mike	LB	1	0	2005
Petitbon, Richie	S	5	0	1962–63; 1966–67; 1971
Petty, Ross	G	1	0	1920
Philbin, Gerry	DE	3	2	1967–69
Phillips, Jess	RB	1	0	1970
Phillips, Red	E	2	1	1960–61
Pickel, Bill	DT	1	1	1986
Pickens, Carl	WR	3	2	1994–96
Pihos, Pete	E–DE	8	6	1947–50; 1952–55
Plansky, Tony	B	1	1	1929
Plasman, Dick	E	2	0	1939; 1941
Player, Scott	P	1	0	2000
Plum, Milt	QB	1	0	1960
Plunkett, Sherman	T	3	0	1965–67
Podolak, Ed	RB	1	0	1970
Poe, Johnnie	CB	1	0	1983
Polamalu, Troy	S	2	2	2004–05
Pollard, Fritz	B	1	1	1920
Polsfoot, Fran	E	1	0	1951
Poole, Jim	E	4	2	1938–40; 1946
Poole, Ray	E	1	0	1950
Porcher, Robert	DE	3	3	1997; 1999; 2001
Porter, Joey	LB	3	3	2002; 2004–05
Porter, Rufus	ST	1	1	1989
Post, Dickie	RB	3	0	1967–69
Pottios, Myron	MLB	1	0	1963
Powell, Art	E	6	2	1960; 1962–66
Powell, Marvin	T	5	4	1979–83
Preas, George	T	1	0	1964
Presnell, Glenn	B	5	1	1931–35
Preston, Roell	KR	1	1	1998
Prestridge, Luke	P	2	1	1980; 1982
Price, Eddie	RB	2	1	1951–52
Pritchard, Ron	OLB	2	0	1970–71
Pritko, Steve	E	1	0	1945
Pruitt, Greg	RB–KR	3	0	1976–77; 1983
Pruitt, Mike	RB	3	1	1979–80; 1983
Pryce, Trevor	DT	3	2	1999–2001
Pugh, Jethro	DT	1	0	1968
Putnam, Duane	G	6	3	1954–59
Pyle, Mike	C	2	0	1963; 1965
Quick, Mike	WR	4	3	1983; 1985–87
Quillan, Fred	C	2	1	1984–85
Quinlan, Bill	DE	2	0	1957; 1960
Racis, Frank	T–G	2	1	1926; 1929
Rackers, Neil	K	1	1	2005
Rado, George	G	1	0	1936
Radovich, Bill	G	2	0	1945–46
Ragazzo, Phil	T	1	0	1941
Ramsey, Buster	B	5	3	1946–50
Randle, Ervin	ILB	1	0	1987
Randle, John	DT	7	6	1993–98; 2001
Randle, Sonny	E	3	1	1960; 1962–63
Randle El, Antwaan	PR	1	1	2005

NAME	POS	TOT	CONS	YEARS
Randolph, Clare	C	1	0	1935
Rapacz, John	C	3	1	1949–51
Rapp, Bob	B	1	0	1923
Rashad, Ahmad	WR	5	2	1974; 1978–81
Rasmussen, Randy	G	2	0	1972; 1979
Ratterman, George	QB	1	1	1947; 1950
Ray, Baby	T	4	1	1939; 1941; 1943–44
Ray, Darrol	S	2	0	1981–82
Rechichar, Bert	DB	2	0	1953; 1955
Reed, Alvin	TE	3	0	1968–70
Reed, Andre	WR	5	1	1989–91; 1994
Reed, Ed	S	2	2	2003–04
Reese, Ike	ST	1	0	2004
Reeves, Dan	RB	1	0	1966
Reger, John	LB	3	1	1959–61
Rehnquist, Milt	G	3	1	1927–29
Reichle, Dick	E	1	0	1923
Reid, Mike	DT	4	3	1971–74
Reinfeldt, Mike	S	2	1	1979–80
Reinhard, Bob	T	4	1	1946; 1948–50
Rembert, Johnny	ILB	1	0	1988
Renfro, Mel	S–CB	10	5	1964–73
Renfro, Ray	RB–E	2	0	1955; 1959
Rentzel, Lance	E	2	0	1968–69
Ressler, Glenn	G	1	0	1968
Retzlaff, Pete	E–TE	5	1	1958; 1963–66
Reveiz, Fuad	K	1	1	1994
Reynolds, Jack	MLB–ILB	2	0	1979; 1981
Reynolds, Ricky	CB	1	0	1992
Rhodemyre, Jay	C	1	0	1951
Rice, Jerry	WR	12	11	1986–96; 2002
Rice, Ken	T	1	0	1961
Rice, Simeon	DE	4	2	1996; 1999; 2002–03
Rich, Herb	DB	1	0	1952
Richard, Stanley	S	1	0	1994
Richards, David	G	1	0	1992
Richards, Kink	B	1	0	1935
Richardson, Al	OLB	1	0	1980
Richardson, Jess	DT	3	0	1959–61
Richardson, Mike	CB	1	0	1986
Richardson, Tony	FB	1	0	2004
Richardson, Willie	E	2	1	1967–68
Richter, Les	LB	6	0	1955–60
Riddick, Ray	E	1	0	1941
Ridlon, Jimmy	S	1	0	1964
Riggins, John	RB	2	1	1975; 1983
Riggs, Gerald	RB	2	1	1984–85
Riley, Ken	CB	4	2	1975–76; 1981; 1983
Ringo, Jim	C	9	6	1957–64; 1966
Rison, Andre	WR	4	1	1990–93
Ritcher, Jim	G	2	0	1990–91
Rivera, Marco	G	2	1	2003–04
Roaches, Carl	KR	1	0	1981
Roaf, Willie	T	10	9	1994–97; 1999–2000; 2002–05
Robb, Harry	B	2	2	1922–23
Robb, Joe	DE	1	0	1966
Robbins, Barret	C	1	1	2002
Roberts, Gene	HB	1	0	1949
Roberts, Greg	G	1	0	1981
Robertson, Isiah	OLB	7	4	1971–77
Robertson, James	B	1	0	1925
Robertson, Marcus	S	1	1	1993
Robinson, Dave	OLB	4	2	1966–69
Robinson, Eugene	S	2	1	1993; 1998
Robinson, Jerry	OLB–ILB	3	2	1980–81; 1983
Robinson, Johnny	S	8	3	1963; 1965–71
Robinson, Koren	KR	1	1	2005
Robinson, Paul	RB	1	0	1968
Robinson, Wayne	LB	2	0	1955–56
Robustelli, Andy	DE	11	4	1952–62
Roby, Reggie	P	7	2	1984–87; 1989; 1991; 1994
Rock, Walt	T	1	0	1966
Rogers, Charlie	PR	1	1	1999
Rogers, Don	C	2	0	1961; 1963
Rogers, George	RB	2	1	1981–82
Rogers, Shaun	DT	1	0	2004
Rohde, Len	T	1	0	1969
Roland, Johnny	RB	1	0	1967
Rolle, Samari	CB	1	1	2000
Romanowski, Bill	OLB	1	0	1996
Romney, Milt	B	1	0	1923
Ronzani, Gene	B	1	0	1935
Rose, Al	E	1	0	1931
Ross, Dan	TE	2	1	1981–82
Ross, Kevin	CB	2	0	1989–90
Rote, Kyle	E	3	0	1955–56; 1960
Rote, Tobin	QB	3	1	1955–56; 1963
Rouen, Tom	P	1	0	1994
Rozier, Mike	RB	1	0	1987
Ruby, Martin	T	4	1	1946–49
Rucinski, Ed	E	2	1	1943; 1945
Rudd, Dwayne	OLB	1	0	1998
Rudnay, Jack	C	4	0	1973–75; 1979

NAME	POS	TOT	CONS	YEARS
Runyan, Jon	T	1	0	1999
Russell, Andy	OLB	7	2	1967–68; 1970; 1972–75
Russell, Bo	T	1	0	1939
Russell, Darrell	DT	2	2	1998–99
Russell, Jack	E	4	1	1946–47; 1949–50
Ruzek, Roger	K	1	0	1987
Ryan, Frank	QB	1	0	1965
Rymkus, Lou	T	3	1	1943; 1946–51
Rypien, Mark	QB	1	1	1991
Saban, Lou	C	2	2	1948–49
Sack, John	G	1	0	1923
Sacksteder, Norb	B	1	0	1920
Saimes, George	S	5	2	1964–68
Saleaumua, Dan	DT	2	1	1990; 1995
Sample, Johnny	CB–S	5	1	1960–61; 1965–66; 1968
Sampson, Greg	T	1	0	1978
Sams, B.J.	PR	2	0	2004–05
Samuels, Chris	T	1	1	2001
Samuelson, Carl	T	1	0	1950
Sanders, Barry	RB	10	8	1989–98
Sanders, Bob	S	1	1	2005
Sanders, Charlie	TE	6	2	1969–71; 1974–76
†Sanders, Deion	CB–KR–PR	11	10	1991–99
Sanders, Spec	HB	4	3	1946–48; 1950
Sandusky, Alex	G	1	0	1964
Sandusky, Mike	G	1	0	1962
Sapolu, Jesse	G	2	0	1994–95
Sapp, Warren	DT	6	5	1997–2002
Sarboe, Phil	B	1	0	1935
Sardisco, Tony	G	1	0	1961
Saturday, Jeff	C	1	1	2005
Sauer, Ed	T	1	0	1923
Sauer, George	B	1	0	1935
Sauer, George	E	2	0	1966–68
Sauerbrun, Todd	P	4	3	1996; 2001–03
Saul, Rich	C	3	1	1979–81
Sayers, Gale	RB–B	5	5	1965–69
Scarpitto, Bob	P	2	0	1966–67
Scarry, Mike	C	2	0	1945–46
Schafrath, Dick	T	4	2	1963–65; 1969
Schlinkman, Walt	FB	1	0	1947
Schmidt, Bob	C	3	0	1961–63
Schmidt, Joe	LB–MLB	10	7	1954–63
Schmitt, John	C	2	0	1968–69
Schnelker, Bob	E	1	0	1959
Schnellbacher, Otto	HB–DB	2	1	1950–51
Schrader, Jim	C	2	0	1960; 1962
Schroeder, Jay	QB	1	0	1986
Schuh, Harry	T	4	1	1967–70
Schulters, Lance	S	1	0	2002
Schultz, Elbie	G–T	2	0	1943; 1945
Schulz, Kurt	S	1	0	1995
Schwammel, Ade	T	2	0	1935–36
Schwantz, Jim	ST	1	1	1996
Schwartz, Perry	E	2	0	1939–42
Scibelli, Joe	G	1	0	1973
Scott, Clarence	CB	2	0	1972–73
Scott, Herb	G	2	1	1978–79
Scott, Herbert	G	3	2	1980–81; 1983
Scott, Jake	S	5	4	1971–75
Scott, Ralph	T	1	0	1923
Scott, Todd	S	1	0	1992
Scott, Tom	DE	2	0	1955–56
Scribner, Bucky	P	1	0	1984
Scudero, Joe	DB	1	0	1955
Seale, Eugene	ST	1	1	1988
Seals, George	G	2	0	1968–69
Seals, Ray	DE	1	0	1995
Searcy, Leon	T	2	0	1995; 1999
Sears, Vic	T–DT	5	1	1943; 1945; 1949–50; 1952
Seau, Junior	ILB–LB	10	8	1991–2000
Seiple, Larry	P	1	0	1969
Selmon, Dewey	OLB	1	0	1979
Selmon, Lee Roy	DE	7	5	1977–80; 1982–84
Senn, Bill	B	1	0	1927
Senser, Joe	TE	1	1	1981
Septien, Rafael	K	1	1	1981
Sergienko, George	T	1	0	1945
Serini, Wash	G	2	0	1948–49
Sestak, Tom	DT	6	3	1962–66; 1968
Sewell, Harley	G	6	3	1955–58; 1960; 1962
Seymour, Richard	DT	4	4	2002–05
Shanklin, Ron	WR	1	0	1973
Sharockman, Ed	CB	1	0	1964
Sharpe, Luis	T	4	1	1984; 1987–88; 1990
Sharpe, Shannon	TE	6	4	1993–98
Sharpe, Sterling	WR	5	3	1989–90; 1992–94
Sharper, Darren	S	3	3	2000; 2002; 2005
Shaw, Billy	G	7	4	1962–66; 1968–69
Shaw, Bob	E	1	0	1950
Shaw, Ed	T	1	0	1920
Shell, Art	T	7	6	1972–78
Shell, Donnie	S	5	3	1978–82

NAME	POS	TOT	CONS	YEARS
Shelley, Elbert	ST	3	0	1992–93; 1995
Shepherd, Bill	B	4	0	1935; 1937–39
Sheppard, Lito	CB	1	1	2004
Sherk, Jerry	DT	2	1	1975–76
Sherman, Will	DB	4	1	1955–58
Shields, Will	G	8	6	1996–97; 1999; 2001–05
Shinnick, Don	LB	1	0	1959
Shipkey, Jerry	DB–LB	2	1	1951–52
Shockey, Jeremy	TE	1	1	2002
Shofner, Del	E	5	5	1958–59; 1961–63
Shugart, Clyde	G	1	0	1943
Shuler, Mickey	TE	2	1	1985–86; 1988
Siemon, Jeff	MLB	5	0	1973–77
Sies, Herb	G	1	0	1923
Signaigo, Joe	G	2	0	1949–50
Sikahema, Vai	KR	3	0	1986–87; 1992
Silas, Sam	DT	1	0	1965
Simington, Milt	G	1	0	1942
Simmons, Clyde	DE	3	1	1989; 1991–92
Simms, Phil	QB	1	0	1986
Simpson, Bill	S	2	0	1977–78
Simpson, O.J.	RB	5	5	1972–76
Sims, Billy	RB	3	2	1980–82
Sims, Keith	G	2	1	1994–95
Sinclair, Michael	DE	3	2	1996–98
Singletary, Mike	ILB	9	9	1983–91
Sinkwich, Frankie	B	2	1	1943–44
Sipe, Brian	QB	2	1	1979–80
Sisemore, Jerry	T	2	0	1979; 1981
Sistrunk, Otis	DT	2	1	1974–75
Skladany, Tom	P	2	1	1978; 1981
Slade, Chris	OLB	1	1	1997
Slater, Duke	T	7	2	1923–27; 1929–30
Slater, Jackie	T	7	6	1983; 1985–90
Slaughter, Webster	WR	1	1	1989
Slivinski, Steve	G	3	0	1940; 1942–43
Smerlas, Fred	DT	6	2	1980–83; 1988–89
Smith, Al	ILB	2	2	1991–92
Smith, Bill	E	5	1	1934–36; 1938–39
Smith, Billy Ray	DT	1	0	1968
Smith, Billy Ray	ILB	3	0	1986–87; 1989
Smith, Bob	DB	1	1	1952
Smith, Bruce	DE	12	10	1986–90; 1992–98
Smith, Bubba	DE	3	1	1968; 1970–71
Smith, Chuck	DE	1	1	1997
Smith, Clyde	C	3	1	1926–28
Smith, Dave	RB	1	1	1960
Smith, Dennis	S	4	2	1984–86; 1989
Smith, Detron	ST	1	0	1999
Smith, Don	DT	1	0	1981
Smith, Doug	C	1	0	1986
Smith, Emmitt	RB	6	5	1991–96
Smith, Ernie	T	2	0	1936–37
Smith, George	C	1	0	1943
Smith, J.D.	RB	1	0	1959
Smith, J.T.	KR–WR	3	2	1980–81; 1987
Smith, Jackie	TE	5	0	1966–70
Smith, Jerry	TE	2	1	1967; 1969
Smith, Jim Ray	G	6	4	1957–62
Smith, Jimmy	WR	2	1	1998–99
Smith, John	K	1	0	1980
Smith, Kevin	CB	1	1	1996
Smith, Lance	G	1	0	1994
Smith, Leonard	S	1	1	1986
Smith, Neil	DE	6	2	1992–97
Smith, Oak	E	1	1	1920
Smith, Olin	T	1	0	1924
Smith, Paul	DT	2	0	1972–73
Smith, Ray Gene	DB	1	0	1956
Smith, Riley	B	3	0	1936–38
Smith, Robert	RB	1	1	2000
Smith, Rod	WR	2	0	2000–01
Smith, Sherman	RB	1	0	1979
Smith, Steve	KR–WR	2	2	2001; 2005
Smith, Tim	WR	1	0	1983
Smyth, Lou	B	1	0	1923
Snell, Matt	RB	4	1	1964–65; 1968–69
Snidow, Ron	DE	1	0	1969
Snyder, Lum	T	4	0	1952–55
Solomon, Freddie	KR	1	0	1980
Solt, Ron	G	1	1	1987
Soltau, Gordie	E	3	1	1951–53
Sonnenberg, Gus	T–G	5	3	1923; 1925–28
Sorey, Revie	G	3	0	1977–79
Sossamon, Lou	C	1	0	1947
Speedie, Mac	E	6	6	1946–50; 1952
Spellman, Jack	E	1	0	1929
Spence, Julian	CB	1	0	1960
Spielman, Chris	ILB–OLB	5	1	1989; 1991–92; 1994–95
Spikes, Takeo	LB	2	1	2003–04
Spinney, Art	T–G	4	1	1957–60
Springs, Shawn	CB	1	1	2004
Sprinkle, Ed	E–DE	5	0	1949–52; 1954

NAME	POS	TOT	CONS	YEARS
St. Clair, Bob	T	9	1	1953–56; 1958; 1960–63
Stabler, Ken	QB	3	2	1973–74; 1976
Stahlman, Dick	T	2	0	1925; 1931
Stallings, Larry	OLB	1	0	1970
Stallworth, John	WR	2	0	1979; 1984
Stamps, Sylvester	KR	1	1	1987
Standlee, Norm	B–FB	3	0	1941; 1946–47
Stanfel, Dick	G	5	3	1953–54; 1956–58
Stanfill, Bill	DE	4	3	1971–74
Stanley, Walter	KR	1	1	1989
Stark, Rohn	P	7	6	1982–86; 1990; 1992
Starr, Bart	QB	4	1	1961–62; 1964; 1966
Staubach, Roger	QB	5	3	1971; 1976–79
Stautner, Ernie	DT–DE	10	4	1952–61
Steed, Joel	DT	1	1	1997
Steele, Ernie	B	1	0	1943
Stein, Herb	G–C	3	1	1922; 1924; 1926
Stein, Russ	T	1	0	1925
Steinfort, Fred	K	1	1	1980
Stemrick, Greg	CB	1	0	1980
Stenerud, Jan	K	10	4	1967–71; 1974–76; 1981; 1984
Stephens, John	RB	1	1	1988
Stephens, Red	G	2	0	1955–56
Stephenson, Dwight	C	5	5	1983–87
Stepnoski, Mark	C	4	2	1992–94; 1996
Sternaman, Dutch	B	3	0	1920; 1922–23
Sternaman, Joey	B	4	2	1923–26
Steussie, Todd	T	2	2	1997–98
Stickel, Walt	T	1	0	1947
Still, Art	DE	5	1	1979–80; 1982; 1984; 1986
Stinchcomb, Pete	B	3	2	1921–23
Stockton, Hust	B	1	0	1926
Stone, Donnie	RB	1	0	1961
Stone, Ron	G	2	2	2000; 2002
Stonebreaker, Steve	OLB	2	0	1964–65
Stovall, Jerry	S	1	0	1966
Stover, Matt	K	2	1	1994; 2000
Stoyanovich, Pete	K	4	2	1990–92; 1997
Strahan, Michael	DE	6	5	1997–98; 2001–03; 2005
Stratton, Mike	OLB	6	2	1964–69
Strickland, Larry	C	2	2	1956–57
Strohmeyer, George	C	1	0	1948
Strong, Ken	B	6	4	1929–31; 1933–35
Strong, Mack	FB	1	1	2005
Stroud, Jack	G–T	6	0	1956–57; 1959–62
Stroud, Marcus	DT	3	2	2003–05
Strzykalski, Johnny	HB	3	1	1947–48; 1950
Stubblefield, Dana	DT	4	3	1994–97
Studstill, Pat	E–P	2	1	1966–67
Studwell, Scott	ILB	3	1	1984; 1988–89
Stydahar, Joe	T	6	5	1936–40; 1942
Suffridge, Bob	G	1	0	1941
Sugar, Leo	DE	1	0	1961
Suggs, Walt	T	4	0	1966–69
Sullivan, Dan	G	1	0	1968
Surtain, Patrick	CB	2	0	2002–03
Svare, Harland	LB	1	0	1958
Svendsen, George	C	1	0	1941
Svoboda, Bill	LB	1	0	1956
Swann, Eric	DT	2	0	1995–96
Swann, Lynn	WR	3	3	1975; 1977–78
Sweeney, Walt	G	6	6	1965; 1967–71
Swenson, Bob	OLB	2	1	1979; 1981
Swiacki, Bill	E	1	0	1948
Swilling, Pat	OLB	6	3	1987; 1989–92; 1995
Szott, Dave	G	2	1	1995; 1997
Szymanski, Dick	C	1	0	1955
Talamini, Bob	G	7	5	1961–67
Talbert, Diron	DT	1	0	1973
Taliaferro, George	HB–RB	2	1	1949; 1952
Talley, Darryl	OLB	2	0	1990; 1993
Tarasovic, George	DE	1	0	1959
Tarkenton, Fran	QB	6	2	1970; 1972–76
Taseff, Carl	DB	1	0	1958
Tasker, Steve	ST	7	5	1987; 1990–95
Tatum, Jack	S	3	1	1973–77
Tatupu, Mosi	ST	1	1	1986
Taylor, Bobby	CB	1	1	2002
Taylor, Bruce	CB	1	0	1970
Taylor, Charley	RB–E–WR	10	1	1964; 1966–70; 1972–75
Taylor, Hugh	E	1	0	1953
Taylor, Jason	DE	4	2	2000–02; 2004
Taylor, Jim	RB	6	1	1960–64; 1966
Taylor, John	KR	2	1	1988–89
Taylor, Lawrence	OLB	10	10	1981–90
Taylor, Lionel	E	5	3	1960–63; 1965
Taylor, Otis	E–WR	4	2	1966–67; 1971–72
Taylor, Rosey	S	3	1	1963–65
Tebell, Gus	E	1	1	1923
Testaverde, Vinny	QB	1	0	1998
Theismann, Joe	QB	3	2	1979; 1982–83

NAME	POS	TOT	CONS	YEARS
Thielemann, R.C.	G	2	1	1982–83
Thigpen, Yancey	WR	2	1	1995; 1997
Thomas, Adalius	ST	1	0	2003
Thomas, Clendon	S	3	0	1962–63; 1966
Thomas, Derrick	OLB	8	5	1989–96
Thomas, Earlie	CB	1	0	1971
Thomas, Emmitt	CB	6	3	1969–72; 1974–75
Thomas, Eric	CB	1	0	1988
Thomas, Henry	DT	3	0	1992–94
Thomas, John	G	1	1	1966
Thomas, Mike	RB	1	0	1976
Thomas, Orlando	S	1	0	1995
Thomas, Pat	CB	2	2	1978; 1980
Thomas, Russ	T	1	0	1947
Thomas, Thurman	RB	6	5	1989–94
Thomas, Tra	T	2	2	2002; 2004
Thomas, William	OLB	1	1	1995
Thomas, Zach	ILB–LB	6	1	1998–99; 2001–03; 2005
Thomason, Bobby	QB	1	0	1953
Thomason, Stumpy	B	1	0	1930
Thompson, Bennie	ST	2	1	1991; 1998
Thompson, Bill	CB–S	5	2	1969; 1977–79; 1981
Thompson, Reyna	ST	1	1	1990
Thompson, Tommy	B–QB	3	0	1942; 1948–49
Thompson, Tommy	LB	3	1	1951–53
Thoms, Art	DT	1	0	1974
Thorpe, Jim	B	1	0	1923
Thurman, Dennis	CB	1	0	1981
Thurman, John	T	1	0	1926
Thurston, Fuzzy	G	5	2	1961–64; 1966
Tilley, Pat	WR	1	0	1980
Timmerman, Adam	G	2	0	2001
Tingelhoff, Mick	C	7	7	1964–70
Tinsley, Gaynell	E	2	2	1937–38
Tinsley, Pete	G	1	0	1941
Tippett, Andre	OLB	5	4	1984–88
Tittle, Y.A.	QB	4	3	1957; 1961–63
Todd, Dick	B	1	0	1940
Tolar, Charley	RB	2	0	1961–62
Tolbert, Tony	DE	1	1	1996
Tomlin, Tommy	G	1	0	1920
Tomlinson, LaDainian	RB	4	2	2002–05
Toneff, Bob	T–DT	6	1	1952; 1955; 1959–62
Tonnemaker, Clayton	C–T–LB	3	2	1950; 1953–54
Toon, Al	WR	3	3	1986–88
Torczon, Lavern	DE	2	1	1960–61
Torgeson, LaVern	LB	3	0	1954–55; 1957
Towler, Dan	RB	4	2	1951–54
Townsell, Jo Jo	KR	1	0	1988
Townsend, Greg	DE	4	2	1988–91
Tracey, John	MLB	1	0	1965
Tracy, Tom	RB	1	0	1960
Trafton, George	C	6	6	1920; 1923–27
Trask, Orville	DT	1	0	1960
Treadwell, David	K	1	0	1989
Trippi, Charlie	HB–RB	3	1	1947–48; 1952
Tripucka, Frank	QB	1	0	1960
Trotter, Jeremiah	LB	2	1	2000–01
Trumpy, Bob	TE	2	2	1969–70
Tryon, Eddie	B	2	1	1926–27
Tubbs, Jerry	MLB	1	0	1962
Tubbs, Winfred	ILB	1	1	1997
Tucker, Bob	TE	1	1	1972
Tuggle, Jessie	ILB	3	1	1991; 1994; 1998
Tuinei, Mark	T	2	0	1994–95
Tully, George	E	1	0	1926
Tunnell, Emlen	HB–DB	8	4	1949–52; 1954–57
Tupa, Tom	P	1	1	1999
Turk, Matt	P	3	3	1996–98
Turley, Kyle	T	1	1	2000
Turnbull, Renaldo	OLB	1	1	1993
Turner, Bulldog	C	8	7	1940–44; 1946–48
Turner, Eric	S	1	1	1994
Turner, Jim	K	3	0	1968–69; 1976
Turner, Keena	OLB	4	1	1982; 1984–86
Tuten, Rick	P	1	1	1994
Tuttle, Orville	G	4	0	1937–40
Tyree, David	ST	1	1	2005
Tyrer, Jim	T	10	8	1962–71
Ulinski, Ed	G	2	0	1946; 1948
Umenyiora, Osi	DE	1	0	2005
Unitas, Johnny	QB	9	5	1957–60; 1963–65; 1967; 1970
Upchurch, Rick	KR	5	3	1976–79; 1982
Upshaw, Gene	G	11	8	1967–77
Urban, Luke	E	3	3	1921–23
Uremovich, Emil	T	1	0	1945
Urlacher, Brian	LB	3	3	2001–02; 2005
Van Brocklin, Norm	QB	4	1	1952; 1954–55; 1960
Van Buren, Steve	B–HB	7	6	1944–50
Van Dyke, Bruce	G	2	0	1972–73
van Eeghen, Mark	RB	1	0	1977
Van Heusen, Billy	P	1	0	1974
Van Note, Jeff	C	5	1	1975; 1979–82

NAME	POS	TOT	CONS	YEARS
Van Pelt, Brad	OLB	5	2	1976–80
Vanderjagt, Mike	K	2	1	1999; 2003
Vanover, Tamarick	KR	2	1	1996–97
Vanzo, Fred	B	2	0	1939–40
Varrichione, Frank	T	3	0	1958–59; 1964
Vasher, Nathan	CB	1	1	2005
Vaughn, Darrick	KR	1	1	2000
Vaughn, Jon	KR	1	0	1992
Verdin, Clarence	KR	3	2	1989–90; 1992
Vick, Ernie	C	1	0	1925
Villapiano, Phil	OLB	5	2	1972–76
Vinatieri, Adam	K	2	2	2002; 2004
Vincent, Troy	CB	3	3	2000–02
Vogel, Bob	T	8	1	1964–71
Volk, Rick	S	4	4	1968–71
von Schamann, Uwe	K	1	0	1982
Voss, Tillie	E	4	0	1922–25
Wade, Billy	QB	2	0	1962–63
Wagner, Lowell	DB	1	0	1952
Wagner, Mike	S	4	1	1973; 1975–76; 1978
Wagstaff, Jim	S	1	0	1960
Wahle, Mike	C	1	0	2005
Walden, Bobby	P	1	0	1975
Walker, Chuck	DT–DE	2	0	1967; 1969
Walker, Doak	HB–RB	5	4	1950–51; 1953–55
Walker, Fulton	KR	1	1	1983
Walker, Gary	DT	1	0	2002
Walker, Herschel	RB	2	2	1987–88
Walker, Wayne	LB–OLB	5	3	1960; 1963–66
Walker, Wesley	WR	3	1	1978; 1982; 1986
Wallace, Jackie	KR	1	0	1978
Wallace, Stan	DB	1	0	1958
Wallace, Steve	T	2	1	1992; 1994
Waller, Ron	RB	2	0	1955–56
Walls, Everson	CB	4	3	1982–85
Walls, Wesley	TE	4	1	1996–97; 1999; 2001
Walsh, Bill	C	3	1	1949; 1952; 1954
Walston, Bobby	E	1	0	1951
Walter, Mike	ILB	1	0	1989
Walters, Stan	T	3	1	1977–79
Walton, Alvin	S	1	0	1987
Ward, Chris	T	1	0	1981
Ward, Hines	WR	3	1	2002–04
Warfield, Paul	E–WR	8	5	1964; 1968–74
Warner, Curt	RB	4	1	1983; 1985–87
Warner, Kurt	QB	2	2	1999; 2001
Warren, Chris	RB	2	2	1994–95
Warren, Jimmy	S–CB	2	0	1967–68
Washington, Dave	OLB	1	0	1974
Washington, Gene	E	1	0	1969
Washington, Gene	E–WR	3	1	1969–72
Washington, Russ	T	6	1	1973–74; 1977–79; 1982
Washington, Ted	DT	3	2	1997–98; 2001
Waterfield, Bob	B–QB	5	3	1945–46; 1949–51
Waters, Andre	S	1	0	1991
Waters, Brian	G	2	2	2004–05
Waters, Charlie	S	2	2	1977–78
Watson, Steve	WR	1	1	1981
Watters, Ricky	RB	3	0	1994–96
Way, Charles	FB	1	0	1997
Way, Charlie	B	1	0	1924
Waymer, Dave	CB	1	0	1987
Weaver, Charlie	OLB	1	0	1976
Weaver, Herman	P	1	0	1975
Webb, Don	S	1	0	1967
Webb, Richmond	T	5	4	1990; 1992–95
Webster, Alex	RB	2	0	1955–56
Webster, Dave	CB–S	2	0	1960–61
Webster, George	OLB	3	3	1967–69
Webster, Mike	C	10	6	1977–85; 1987
Wedemeyer, Herm	HB	1	0	1949
Wehrli, Roger	CB	7	6	1970–71; 1974–77; 1979

NAME	POS	TOT	CONS	YEARS
Weinmeister, Arnie	T–DT	6	5	1948–53
Weir, Ed	T	1	1	1927
Weller, Bub	G–T	3	0	1923–24; 1926
Wells, Billy	RB	1	0	1954
Wells, Warren	E–WR	2	1	1969–70
Welsh, Jim	G	2	0	1924; 1926
Wenig, Obe	E	1	0	1920
Wentworth, Cy	B	1	0	1925
Wentz, Barney	B	1	0	1925
Wersching, Ray	K	1	0	1986
West, Belf	T	1	1	1921
West, Charlie	S	1	0	1976
West, Stan	MG	2	2	1951–52
West, Willie	S	1	0	1966
Westbrook, Brian	PR	1	0	2003
Westfall, Bob	B	1	0	1945
Westmoreland, Dick	CB	3	1	1963–64; 1967
Wetoska, Bob	T	3	0	1963–65
Whalen, Jim	TE	1	1	1968
Wham, Tom	E	1	0	1950
Whigham, Larry	ST	2	1	1997; 2001
White, Charles	RB	1	1	1987
White, Danny	P–QB	3	0	1979; 1981–82
White, Dwight	DE	4	1	1972–75
White, Ed	G	5	2	1974–77; 1979
White, Jim	T	1	1	1946–47
White, Randy	DT	9	9	1977–85
White, Reggie	DT–DE	13	12	1986–98
White, Sammy	WR	3	0	1976–78
White, Stan	OLB	1	0	1977
White, Whizzer	B	3	2	1938; 1940–41
Whitfield, Bob	T	1	0	1996
Whitsell, Dave	CB	1	0	1967
Whittenton, Jesse	DB–CB	3	0	1959–61
Widby, Ron	P	3	0	1968–69; 1971
Widerquist, Chet	G	2	0	1925–26
Widseth, Ed	T	3	1	1937–39
Wietecha, Ray	C	6	1	1956–59; 1961–62
Wiethe, Socko	G	2	1	1939–40
Wightkin, Bill	T	2	0	1955–56
Wilbur, John	G	1	0	1972
Wilburn, Barry	CB	1	1	1987
Wilcox, Dave	OLB	8	3	1966–73
Wilder, James	RB	1	1	1984
Wildung, Dick	G–T	3	0	1947–49
Wiley, Marcellus	DE	1	1	2001
Wilkerson, Doug	G	4	2	1979–82
Wilkin, Willie	T	2	0	1941–42
Wilkins, Jeff	K	1	1	2003
Willard, Ken	RB	2	0	1965; 1968
Willey, Norm	DE	3	1	1953–55
Willhite, Gerald	RB	1	0	1986
Williams, Aeneas	CB	5	5	1994–97; 2001
Williams, Alfred	DE	1	1	1996
Williams, Ben	DE	3	0	1980–82
Williams, Darryl	S	1	1	1997
Williams, Delvin	RB	1	1	1978
Williams, Doc	G	1	0	1924
Williams, Erik	T	3	1	1993; 1995–96
Williams, Fred	DT	1	0	1958
Williams, Inky	E	1	0	1923
Williams, Jake	T	1	0	1932
Williams, Jamal	DT	2	1	2004–05
Williams, James	T	1	0	2001
Williams, Joe	G	1	0	1926
Williams, Joel	OLB	1	0	1982
Williams, Johnny	DB	1	0	1952
Williams, Kevin	DT	1	1	2004
Williams, Lee	DE	3	1	1986; 1988–89
Williams, Ricky	RB	1	1	2002
Williams, Roy	S	1	1	2003
Williamson, Fred	CB	5	2	1961–65
Willis, Bill	G–MG	8	5	1946–53
Wilson, Al	LB	1	1	2005

NAME	POS	TOT	CONS	YEARS
Wilson, Billy	E	5	2	1954–58
Wilson, Camp	FB	1	0	1947
Wilson, George	E	4	1	1941–44
Wilson, Jerrel	P	7	2	1966; 1968; 1971–75
Wilson, Larry	S	8	6	1963; 1965–71
Wilson, Mike	E	1	0	1924
Wilson, Otis	OLB	2	1	1984–85
Wilson, Tommy	RB	1	0	1957
Wilson, Wildcat	B	2	1	1926; 1928
Winder, Sammy	RB	1	0	1984
Winkelman, Ben	E	1	0	1923
Winslow, Kellen	TE	4	4	1980–82; 1987
Winters, Sonny	B	1	0	1924
Wisniewski, Steve	G	8	8	1990–96; 2000
Wistert, Al	T–G	8	5	1944–51
Witten, Jason	TE	1	1	2004
Wittum, Tom	P	2	0	1973–74
Wojciechowicz, Alex	C	2	0	1939; 1944
Wolfley, Ron	ST	2	1	1987; 1989
Wolford, Will	T–G	2	0	1992; 1996
Wood, Willie	S	10	6	1962–71
Woodall, Lee	OLB	1	0	1995
Woodeshick, Tom	RB	2	0	1968–69
Woods, Ickey	RB	1	1	1988
Woodson, Abe	DB–CB	5	2	1959–63
Woodson, Charles	CB	3	2	1999–2001
Woodson, Darren	S	4	3	1994–96; 1998
†Woodson, Rod	CB–KR–S	11	7	1989–94; 1996; 2000; 2002
Woolford, Donnell	CB	1	1	1994
Wooten, John	G	2	0	1965–66
Workman, Hoge	B	1	0	1924
Wostoupal, Joe	C	3	3	1928–30
Woudenberg, John	T	2	0	1947–48
Wozniak, John	G	1	0	1952
Wright, Alvin	DT	1	0	1990
Wright, Eric	CB	3	1	1983–85
Wright, Ernie	T	2	0	1960–61
Wright, Keith	KR	1	0	1978
Wright, Louis	CB	8	4	1977–81; 1983–85
Wright, Nate	CB	2	0	1974; 1976
Wright, Rayfield	T	6	4	1971–76
Wycheck, Frank	TE	1	0	2000
Wycoff, Doug	B	1	0	1929
Wydo, Frank	T	1	0	1953
Yary, Ron	T	8	7	1970–77
Yepremian, Garo	K	2	1	1971; 1973
Younce, Len	G	6	2	1941; 1943–44; 1946–48
Young, Bob	G	3	2	1977–79
Young, Bryant	DT	4	3	1996; 1998–99; 2001
Young, Buddy	HB	3	1	1947; 1949–50
Young, Charle	TE	3	3	1973–75
Young, Fredd	ST–ILB	3	2	1984; 1986–87
Young, Roynell	CB	1	0	1981
Young, Steve	QB	7	4	1992–98
Young, Wilbur	DT	1	0	1979
Youngblood, Jack	DE	9	6	1973–80; 1984
Youngblood, Jim	OLB	2	1	1978–79
Youngelman, Sid	DT–DE	2	0	1960–61
Younger, Tank	LB–RB	3	1	1951–52; 1954
Youngstrom, Swede	G	3	3	1923–25
Zatkoff, Roger	LB	3	1	1954–56
Zeller, Joe	G	1	0	1932
Zeman, Bob	S	1	1	1962
Zendejas, Tony	K	1	0	1989
Zimmerman, Gary	T	9	6	1986–89; 1992–96
Zimmerman, Roy	B	2	0	1943–44
Zimny, Bob	G	1	0	1945
Zoia, Clyde	G	1	0	1923
Zook, John	DE	2	0	1972–73
Zorich, George	G	1	0	1944

THE PRO-BOWL

The idea of an all-star football game with a team of the very best professionals is older than the National Football League. The first such game took place on December 3, 1898 at Exposition Park in Pittsburgh. On one side was the Duquesne Country & Athletic Club, which had dominated the Pittsburgh football season that year. Opposing the DC & AC was a team consisting of the best players from all the teams in the Pittsburgh area. The *Pittsburgh Press* reported that the All-Stars were probably as talented as the Duquesne team, but they were unable to work as a team and were beaten easily that day, 16–0. The game only attracted about 1,500 fans and was not considered a success. It would be more than three decades before the idea of all-star games would be widely adopted by various sports.

The first all-star game the NFL regularly participated in was not an NFL game. In August 1934 the Chicago Bears faced a team of college football all-stars in a game that ended in a scoreless tie. Arch Ward of the *Chicago Tribune*, who started the major league baseball All-Star Game a year earlier, organized that first College All-Star Game, as he would organize the All-America Football Conference a dozen years later. Attended by almost 80,000 fans at Soldier Field, the game quickly became an annual tradition that would last for over 40 years. Each year the best team in the NFL would come to Chicago before the start of training camp to face the best talent college football had to offer. At first, the All-Stars were competitive with the pros, winning or tying half of the first 14 games, but as the NFL became more and more competitive, victories for the College All-Stars occurred less and less frequently. The 20–17 victory over the Green Bay Packers in 1963 would be the last for the collegians. As the game grew less and less competitive, fan interest and attendance sharply declined. The 1976 game, which would be called after the fans stormed the field during a rain delay late in the third quarter, was the last of the series.

The first NFL sponsored All-Star Game took place after the 1938 season. On January 15, 1939, the New York Giants edged an assortment of talent from other NFL teams and two independent teams 13–10 at Wrigley Field in Los Angeles. The NFL would continue to schedule a postseason game between its best team and a group of All-Stars from the rest of the league for four additional seasons. The All-Stars would lose all five games. As a result of the United States' entrance into World War II, this All-Star Game series was cancelled after 1942.

The next pro football All-Star Game would be held not by the NFL but by the upstart All-American Football Conference. Houston oil tycoon Glenn McCarthy, who hoped to use the game to attract a professional football franchise to Houston, sponsored the first and only AAFC All-Star Game. The Shamrock Charity Bowl All-Star Game was held on December 17, 1949 at Rice Stadium in Houston. The game pit the undefeated AAFC champion Cleveland Browns against the best of the AAFC. The Browns were upset by the All-Stars, 13–7. By the time the game was held, a merger between the NFL and the AAFC had already been announced, so the game served as a celebration of and farewell to the league. That 12,000 fans attended the game and star-studded entertainment event despite terrible rains made it a success

At the end of the following season, 1950, the NFL hosted its first Pro Bowl in a format similar to that of the game still held annually. The first three Pro Bowls pitted the all-stars of the American Conference versus the all-stars of the National Conference. After the NFL was slightly realigned into East and West divisions in 1953, the Pro Bowl pitted the best of the East against the best of the West. That arrangement would continue until the merger with the AFL in 1970, even after the NFL split into four divisions in 1967. All of the Pro Bowls between 1951 and 1970 were held at the Los Angeles Memorial Coliseum.

The next league to compete with the NFL, the American Football League, began its own All-Star Game after the 1961 season. All but one of the AFL All-Star Games pitted the East's All-Stars versus the West's All-Stars. (The other game, held following the 1965 season, pitted the AFL champion Bills against the rest of the league's All-Stars). The AFL All-Star Games were only mildly successful; attendance was usually only amounted to about half of the year's

NFL Pro Bowl attendance. The most memorable AFL All-Star Game, which took place in 1965, was memorable because of what happened off the field. The game was originally scheduled to take place in New Orleans. But many of the African American players selected to play were angered by the racism and hostility that greeted them after they arrived in the city. As a result they voted to leave the city and refused to play there. The league initially resisted moving the game but eventually agreed to transfer it to Houston.

The merger of the AFL and the NFL in 1970 led to the Pro Bowl becoming a contest between the AFC and the NFC. The Pro Bowl has had a permanent home in Honolulu since 1980. Pro Bowl week has grown to include numerous parties, a celebrity golf tournament, an alumni touch football game, and a skills contest. Players are selected by a vote conducted among fans, players, and coaches, with each of those three groups given one-third of the voting power. Despite the NFL's attempts to make the Pro Bowl more attractive, the game has lost much of its luster. Many players develop minor injuries just in time to keep them from making the trip to Hawaii. Television ratings have fallen sharply. As the amount of attention paid to the Super Bowl continues to expand, perhaps it's inevitable that an all-star exhibition the week after the big game will strike many fans as anti-climactic.

KEY TO THE PRO BOWL

The Pro Bowl may be the least intense game on the NFL calendar, but it does take that calendar seriously. While the NFL playoffs and Super Bowl always go under the heading of the year in which the season began—the 2005 NFC Championship Game, for example, was played on January 22, 2006—the Pro Bowl is listed by the year in which the game was actually played. This dates back to the Pro Bowl's birth in 1951 as a January contest after the NFL postseason and college bowl season had concluded. The NFL postseason, on the other hand, ended in December every year until 1965. The NFL postseason calendar has snuck into the next calendar year every season since.

Most of the Pro Bowl leaders in this section are based on the results of the Pro Bowls that were held after the 1970 merger, when the Pro Bowl became a contest between the AFC and NFC. But also included is a list of the men who were most frequently selected to the Pro Bowl from 1951 to the present.

For the Pro Bowl statistical leaders, which take into account the games played from 1971 forward, most categories include those who have the highest totals for both a single-season and career. Abbreviations for those categories include:

Passing
- **PA** Passes Attempted
- **PC** Passes Completed
- **PY** Passing Yards
- **TD** Touchdowns
- **INT** Interceptions

Rushing
- **ATT** Attempts
- **YDS** Yards

Receiving
- **REC** Receiving
- **YDS** Yards

Scoring
- **XP** Extra Points
- **FG** Field Goals
- **PTS** Points

After the leaders is an alphabetical list of every Pro Bowl player. This list takes into account appearances in the contest since it was introduced in 1951. This list includes the **TOTAL** number of Pro Bowls appeared in, followed by the player's **NAME**, **POSITION**, and the **YEARS** he played in the Pro Bowl.

CHICAGO ALL–STARS GAME

DATE	NFL TEAM	SCORE	ATTENDANCE	ALL–STARS MVP	ALL–STARS COACH
Aug 31, 1934	Chicago Bears	0–0	79,432		Noble Kizer, Purdue
Aug 29, 1935	**Chicago Bears**	5–0	77,450		Frank Thomas, Alabama
Sep 2, 1936	Detroit Lions	7–7	76,000		Bernie Bierman, Minnesota
Sep 1, 1937	Green Bay Packers	0–6	84,560		Charles E. Dorais, Detroit
Aug 31, 1938	Washington Redskins	16–28	74,250	Cecil Isbell, B, Purdue (Packers)	Bo McMillan, Indiana
Aug 30, 1939	**New York Giants**	9–0	81,456	Bill Osmanski, FB, Holy Cross (Bears)	Elmer Layden, Notre Dame
Aug 29, 1940	**Green Bay Packers**	45–28	84,567	Ambrose Schindler, B, USC (Packers)	Eddie Anderson, Holy Cross
Aug 28, 1941	**Chicago Bears**	37–13	98,203	George Franck, B, Minnesota (Bears)	Carl Snavely, Cornell University
Aug 28, 1942	**Chicago Bears**	21–0	101,103	Bruce Smith, B, Minnesota (Packers)	Robert Zuppke, Illinois
Aug 25, 1943*	Washington Redskins	7–27	48,437	Pat Harder, B, Wisconsin (Cardinals)	Harry Stuhldreher, Wisconsin
Aug 30, 1944*	**Chicago Bears**	24–21	49,246*	Glenn Dobbs, B, Tulsa (Cardinals)	Lynn Waldorf, Northwestern
Aug 30, 1945	**Green Bay Packers**	19–7	92,753	Charlie Trippi, B, Georgia (Cardinals)	Bernie Bierman, Minnesota
Aug 23, 1946	Los Angeles Rams	0–16	97,380	Elroy Hirsch, B, Wisconsin (Rams‡)	Bo McMillan, Indiana
Aug 22, 1947	Chicago Bears	0–16	105,840	Buddy Young, B, Illinois (AAFC Yankees)	Frank Leahy, Notre Dame
Aug 20, 1948	**Chicago Cardinals**	28–0	101,220	Jay Rhodemyre, C, Kentucky (Packers)	Frank Leahy, Notre Dame
Aug 12, 1949	**Philadelphia Eagles**	38–0	93,780	Bill Fischer, G, Notre Dame (Cardinals)	Bud Wilkinson, Oklahoma
Aug 11, 1950	Philadelphia Eagles	7–17	88,885	Charlie Justice, B, North Carolina (Redskins)	Eddie Anderson, Holy Cross
Aug 17, 1951	**Cleveland Browns**	33–0	92,180	Bud McFadin, G, Texas (Rams)	Herman Hickman, Yale
Aug 15, 1952	**Los Angeles Rams**	10–7	88,316	Vito Parilli, LB, Kentucky (49ers)	Bobby Dodd, Georgia Tech
Aug 14, 1953	**Detroit Lions**	24–10	93,818	Gib Dawson, HB, Texas (Packers)	Bobby Dodd, Georgia Tech
Aug 13, 1954	**Detroit Lions**	31–6	93,470	Carlton Massey, E, Texas (Browns)	Jim Tatum, Maryland
Aug 12, 1955	Cleveland Browns	27–30	75,000	Ralph Guglielmi, QB, Notre Dame (Redskins)	Curly Lambeau
Aug 10, 1956	**Cleveland Browns**	26–0	75,000	Bob Pellegrini, LB/C, Maryland (Eagles)	Curly Lambeau
Aug 9, 1957	**New York Giants**	22–12	75,000	John Brodie, QB, Stanford (49ers)	Curly Lambeau
Aug 15, 1958	Detroit Lions	19–35	70,000	Bob Mitchell, HB, Illinois (Browns); Jim Ninowski, QB, Michigan St. (Browns)	Otto Graham
Aug 14, 1959	**Baltimore Colts**	29–0	70,000	Bob Ptacek, QB, Michigan (Browns)	Otto Graham
Aug 12, 1960	**Baltimore Colts**	32–7	70,000	Jim Leo, DE, Cincinnati (Giants)	Otto Graham
Aug 4, 1961	**Philadelphia Eagles**	28–14	66,000	Billy Kilmer, QB, UCLA (49ers)	Otto Graham
Aug 3, 1962	**Green Bay Packers**	42–20	65,000	John Hadl, QB, Kansas (Lions‡)	Otto Graham
Aug 2, 1963	Green Bay Packers	17–20	65,000	Ron Vander Kelen, QB, Wisconsin (Vikings†)	Otto Graham
Aug 7, 1964	**Chicago Bears**	28–17	65,000	Charley Taylor, HB, Arizona State (Redskins)	Otto Graham
Aug 6, 1965	**Cleveland Browns**	24–16	68,000	John Huarte, QB, Notre Dame (Eagles‡)	Otto Graham
Aug 5, 1966	**Green Bay Packers**	38–0	72,000	Gary Lane, QB, Missouri (Browns)	John Sauer
Aug 4, 1967	**Green Bay Packers**	27–0	70,934	Bubba Smith, DT, Michigan State (Colts)	John Sauer
Aug 2, 1968	**Green Bay Packers**	34–17	69,917	Larry Csonka, RB, Syracuse (Dolphins)	Norm Van Brocklin
Aug 1, 1969	**New York Jets**	26–24	74,208	Greg Cook, QB, Cincinnati (Bengals)	Otto Graham
Jul 31, 1970	**Kansas City Chiefs**	24–3	69,940	Bruce Taylor, DB, Boston University (49ers)	Otto Graham
Jul 30, 1971	**Baltimore Colts**	24–17	52,289	Richard Harris, DE, Grambling State (Eagles)	Blanton Collier
Jul 28, 1972	**Dallas Cowboys**	20–7	54,162	Pat Sullivan, QB, Auburn (Falcons)	Bob Devaney, Nebraska
Jul 27, 1973	**Miami Dolphins**	14–3	54,103	Ray Guy, P, Southern Mississippi (Raiders)	John McKay, USC
Jul 26, 1974**	Miami Dolphins	—	—	—	John McKay, USC
Aug 1, 1975	**Pittsburgh Steelers**	21–17	54,562	Steve Bartkowski, QB, California (Falcons)	John McKay, USC
Aug 23, 1976***	**Pittsburgh Steelers**	24–0	52,895		Ara Parseghian

* The game was played in Northwestern University's Dyche Stadium in Evanston, IL these years

** The game was canceled after the College All–Stars voted not to play as a result of the then ongoing strike by the NFL players

***The game was stopped with 1:22 left in the 3rd quarter as a result of torrential rain and then a decision was made not to resume the game after several thousand fans then stormed the field and tore down the goal posts.

†Was drafted by AFL Titans but not by Vikings, who signed him as a free agent

‡Was drafted by this NFL team but first played with AAFC Rockets (Hirsch), AFL Chargers (Hadl), and AFL Patriots (Huarte)

PRO ALL–STAR GAME

DATE	WINNER	LOSER	SCORE	CITY	STADIUMS	ATTENDANCE
Jan 15, 1939	New York Giants	NFL All–Stars	13–10	Los Angeles, CA	Wrigley Field	20,000
Jan 14, 1940	Green Bay Packers	NFL All–Stars	16–7	Los Angeles, CA	Gilmore Stadium	18,000
Dec 29, 1940	Chicago Bears	NFL All–Stars	28–14	Los Angeles, CA	Gilmore Stadium	21,624
Jan 4, 1942	Chicago Bears	NFL All–Stars	35–24	New York, NY	Polo Grounds	17,725
Dec 27, 1942	NFL All–Stars	Washington Redskins	17–14	Philadelphia, PA	Shibe Park	18,671

THE SHAMROCK BOWL (AAFC ALL–STAR GAME)

DATE	WINNER	LOSER	SCORE	CITY	STADIUMS	ATTENDANCE
Dec 17, 1949	AAFC All–Stars	Cleveland Browns	12–7	Houston, TX	Rice Stadium	12,000

NFL PRO BOWL

DATE	WINNER	SCORE	CITY	STADIUMS	ATTENDANCE	MVP
Jan 14, 1951	American Conference	28–27	Los Angeles, CA	Los Angeles Memorial Coliseum	53,676	Otto Graham, QB, Browns
Jan 12, 1952	National Conference	30–13	Los Angeles, CA	Los Angeles Memorial Coliseum	19,400	Dan Towler, FB, Rams
Jan 10, 1953	National Conference	27–7	Los Angeles, CA	Los Angeles Memorial Coliseum	34,208	Don Doll, DB, Lions
Jan 17, 1954	East	20–9	Los Angeles, CA	Los Angeles Memorial Coliseum	44,214	Chuck Bednarik, LB, Eagles
Jan 16, 1955	West	26–19	Los Angeles, CA	Los Angeles Memorial Coliseum	43,972	Billy Wilson, RE, 49ers
Jan 15, 1956	East	31–30	Los Angeles, CA	Los Angeles Memorial Coliseum	37,867	Ollie Matson, HB, Cardinals
Jan 13, 1957	West	19–10	Los Angeles, CA	Los Angeles Memorial Coliseum	44,177	Bert Rechichar, DB, Colts; Ernie Stautner, DT, Steelers
Jan 12, 1958	West	26–7	Los Angeles, CA	Los Angeles Memorial Coliseum	66,634	Hugh McElhenny, HB, 49ers; Gene Brito, DE, Redskins
Jan 11, 1959	East	28–21	Los Angeles, CA	Los Angeles Memorial Coliseum	72,250	Frank Gifford, HB, Giants: Doug Atkins, DE, Bears
Jan 17, 1960	West	38–21	Los Angeles, CA	Los Angeles Memorial Coliseum	56,876	Johnny Unitas, QB, Colts; Gene Lipscomb, DT, Steelers
Jan 15, 1961	West	35–31	Los Angeles, CA	Los Angeles Memorial Coliseum	62,971	Johnny Unitas, QB, Colts; Sam Huff, LB, Giants
Jan 14, 1962	West	31–30	Los Angeles, CA	Los Angeles Memorial Coliseum	57,409	Jim Brown, FB, Browns; Henry Jordan, DT, Packers
Jan 13, 1963	East	30–20	Los Angeles, CA	Los Angeles Memorial Coliseum	61,374	Jim Brown, FB, Browns; Gene Lipscomb, DT, Steelers
Jan 12, 1964	West	31–17	Los Angeles, CA	Los Angeles Memorial Coliseum	67,242	Johnny Unitas, QB, Colts; Gino Marchetti, DE, Colts
Jan 10, 1965	West	34–14	Los Angeles, CA	Los Angeles Memorial Coliseum	60,598	Fran Tarkenton, QB, Vikings; Terry Barr, WR, Lions
Jan 15, 1966	East	36–7	Los Angeles, CA	Los Angeles Memorial Coliseum	60,124	Jim Brown, FB, Browns; Dale Meinhart, LB, Cardinals
Jan 22, 1967	East	20–10	Los Angeles, CA	Los Angeles Memorial Coliseum	15,062	Gale Sayers, HB, Bears; Floyd Peters, DT, Eagles
Jan 21, 1968	West	38–20	Los Angeles, CA	Los Angeles Memorial Coliseum	53,289	Gale Sayers, HB, Bears; Dave Robinson, LB, Packers
Jan 19, 1969	West	10–7	Los Angeles, CA	Los Angeles Memorial Coliseum	32,050	Roman Gabriel, QB, Rams; Merlin Olsen, DT, Rams
Jan 18, 1970	West	16–13	Los Angeles, CA	Los Angeles Memorial Coliseum	57,786	Gale Sayers, HB, Bears; George Andrie, DE, Cowboys

AFL All–Star Game

DATE	WINNER	SCORE	CITY	STADIUMS	ATTENDANCE	MVP
Jan 7, 1962	West	47–27	San Diego, CA	Balboa Stadium	20,973	Cotton Davidson, QB, Texans
Jan 13, 1963	West	21–14	San Diego, CA	Balboa Stadium	27,641	Curtis McClinton, FB, Texans; Earl Faison, DE, Chargers
Jan 19, 1964	West	27–24	San Diego, CA	Balboa Stadium	20,016	Keith Lincoln, FB, Chargers; Archie Matsos, LB, Raiders
Jan 16, 1965*	West	38–14	Houston, TX	Jeppesen Stadium	15,446	Keith Lincoln, FB, Chargers; Willie Brown, CB, Broncos
Jan 15, 1966**	AFL All–Stars	30–19	Houston, TX	Rice Stadium	35,572	Joe Namath, QB, Jets; Frank Buncum, LB, Chargers
Jan 21, 1967	East	30–23	Oakland, CA	Oakland–Alameda County Coliseum	18,876	Babe Parilli, QB, Boston Patriots; Verlon Biggs, DE, New York Jets
Jan 21, 1968	East	25–24	Jacksonville, FL	Gator Bowl	40,103	Joe Namath, QB, Jets; Don Maynard, FL, Jets; Speedy Duncan, CB, Chargers
Jan 19, 1969	West	38–25	Jacksonville, FL	Gator Bowl	41,058	Len Dawson, QB, Chiefs; George Webster, LB, Oilers
Jan 17, 1970	West	26–3	Houston, TX	Astrodome	30,170	John Hadl, QB, Chargers

* The game was originally scheduled to take place at Tulane Stadium in New Orleans, but a players boycott against the racist conditions of New Orleans triggered a move of the game to Houston
** The Buffalo Bills were the losing team in the only AFL All–Star Game not to pit East All–Stars vs. West All–Stars

NFL Pro Bowl

DATE	WINNER	SCORE	CITY	STADIUMS	ATTENDANCE	MVP
Jan 24, 1971	NFC	27–6	Los Angeles, CA	Los Angeles Memorial Coliseum	48,222	Mel Renfro, CB, Cowboys; Fred Carr, LB, Packers
Jan 23, 1972	AFC	26–13	Los Angeles, CA	Los Angeles Memorial Coliseum	53,647	Jan Stenerud, K, Chiefs; Willie Lanier, LB, Chiefs
Jan 21, 1973	AFC	33–28	Dallas, TX	Texas Stadium	37,091	O. J. Simpson, RB, Bills
Jan 20, 1974	AFC	15–13	Kansas City, MO	Arrowhead Stadium	68,918	Garo Yepremian, K, Dolphins
Jan 20, 1975	NFC	17–10	Miami, FL	Orange Bowl,	26,484	James Harris, QB, Rams
Jan 26, 1976	NFC	23–20	New Orleans, LA	Louisiana Superdome	30,546	Billy Johnson, KR, Oilers
Jan 17, 1977	AFC	24–14	Seattle, WA	Kingdome	64,752	Mel Blount, CB, Steelers
Jan 23, 1978	NFC	14–13	Tampa, FL	Tampa Stadium	51,337	Walter Payton, RB, Bears
Jan 29, 1979	NFC	13–7	Los Angeles, CA	Los Angeles Memorial Coliseum	46,281	Ahmad Rashad, WR, Vikings
Jan 27, 1980	NFC	37–27	Honolulu, HI	Aloha Stadium	49,800	Chuck Muncie, RB, Saints
Feb 1, 1981	NFC	21–7	Honolulu, HI	Aloha Stadium	50,360	Eddie Murray, K, Lions
Jan 31, 1982	AFC	16–13	Honolulu, HI	Aloha Stadium	50,402	Kellen Winslow, TE, Chargers; Lee Roy Selmon, DE, Buccaneers
Feb 6, 1983	NFC	20–19	Honolulu, HI	Aloha Stadium	49,883	Dan Fouts, QB, Chargers; John Jefferson, WR, Packers
Jan 29, 1984	NFC	45–3	Honolulu, HI	Aloha Stadium	50,445	Joe Theismann, QB, Redskins
Jan 27, 1985	AFC	22–14	Honolulu, HI	Aloha Stadium	50,385	Mark Gastineau, DE, Jets
Feb 2, 1986	NFC	28–24	Honolulu, HI	Aloha Stadium	50,101	Phil Simms, QB, Giants
Feb 1, 1987	AFC	10–6	Honolulu, HI	Aloha Stadium	50,101	Reggie White, DE, Eagles
Feb 7, 1988	AFC	15–6	Honolulu, HI	Aloha Stadium	50,113	Bruce Smith, DE, Bills
Jan 29, 1989	NFC	34–3	Honolulu, HI	Aloha Stadium	50,113	Randall Cunningham, QB, Eagles
Feb 4, 1990	NFC	27–21	Honolulu, HI	Aloha Stadium	50,445	Jerry Gray, CB, Rams
Feb 3, 1991	AFC	23–21	Honolulu, HI	Aloha Stadium	50,345	Jim Kelly, QB, Bills
Feb 2, 1992	NFC	21–15	Honolulu, HI	Aloha Stadium	50,209	Michael Irvin, WR, Cowboys
Feb 7, 1993	AFC	23–20 (OT)	Honolulu, HI	Aloha Stadium	50,007	Steve Tasker, Special Teams, Bills
Feb 6, 1994	NFC	17–3	Honolulu, HI	Aloha Stadium	50,026	Andre Rison, WR, Falcons
Feb 5, 1995	AFC	41–13	Honolulu, HI	Aloha Stadium	49,121	Marshall Faulk, RB, Colts
Feb 4, 1996	NFC	20–13	Honolulu, HI	Aloha Stadium	50,034	Jerry Rice, WR, 49ers
Feb 2, 1997	AFC	26–23	Honolulu, HI	Aloha Stadium	50,031	Mark Brunell, QB, Jaguars
Feb 1, 1998	AFC	39–24	Honolulu, HI	Aloha Stadium	49,995	Warren Moon, QB, Seahawks
Feb 7, 1999	AFC	23–10	Honolulu, HI	Aloha Stadium	50,075	Ty Law, CB, Patriots; Keyshawn Johnson, WR, Jets
Feb 6, 2000	NFC	51–31	Honolulu, HI	Aloha Stadium	50,112	Randy Moss, WR, Vikings
Feb 4, 2001	AFC	38–17	Honolulu, HI	Aloha Stadium	50,128	Rich Gannon, QB, Raiders
Feb 10, 2002	AFC	38–30	Honolulu, HI	Aloha Stadium	50,310	Rich Gannon, QB, Raiders
Feb 2, 2003	AFC	45–20	Honolulu, HI	Aloha Stadium	50,125	Ricky Williams, RB, Dolphins
Feb 8, 2004	NFC	55–52	Honolulu, HI	Aloha Stadium	50,127	Marc Bulger, QB, Ram
Feb 13, 2005	AFC	38–27	Honolulu, HI	Aloha Stadium	50,125	Peyton Manning, QB,Colts
Feb 12, 2006	NFL	23–17	Honolulu, HI	Aloha Stadium	51,190	Derrick Brooks, LB, Bucaneers

PRO BOWL LEADERS

MOST GAMES PLAYED (1971–PRESENT)

- 12 Randall McDaniel (Minnesota 1990 – 2000; Tampa Bay 2001)
- **11 Reggie White (Philadelphia, 1987–93 and Green Bay, 1994, 1996–97, 1999)
- 11 Junior Seau (San Diego, 1992–2002)
- 11 Rod Woodson (Pittsburgh, 1990–95, 1997; Baltimore 2000–02; Oakland 2003)
- 10 Lawrence Taylor (N.Y. Giants, 1982–91)
- 10 Ronnie Lott (San Francisco, 1982–85, 1987–91 and L.A. Raiders, 1992)
- 10 Mike Singletary (Chicago, 1984–93)
- ****10 Bruce Matthews (Houston, 1989–95, 1997; Tennessee, 2000, 2002)
- ***10 Jerry Rice (San Francisco, 1987–88, 1990–94, 1996, 1999; Oakland, 2003)

* Each star represents a an additional Pro Bowl the player was selected for but did not play

MOST GAMES SELECTED (INCLUDING 1951–70)

- 14 Merlin Olsen (Rams 1963–76)
- 12 Ken Houston (Oilers 1969–73; Redskins 1974–80)
- 12 Randall McDaniel (Vikings 1990–2000; Buccaneers 2001)
- 12 Jim Otto (Raiders 1962–73)
- 12 Jerry Rice (49ers 1987–94, 1996–97, 1999; Raiders 2003)
- 12 Junior Seau (Chargers 1992–2003)
- 11 Bob Lilly (Cowboys 1963, 1965–74)
- 11 Tom Mack (Rams 1968–76, 1978–79)
- 11 Anthony Munoz (Bengals 1982–92)
- 11 Wilie Roaf (Saints 1995–2001; Chiefs 2003–06)
- 11 Will Shields (Chiefs 1996–2006)
- 11 Bruce Smith (Bills 1988–91, 1993–99)
- 11 Rod Woodson (Steelers 1990–96; Ravens 2000–2002; Raiders 2003)
- 10 Larry Allen (Cowboys 1996–2002, 2004–06)
- 10 Joe Greene (Steelers 1970–77, 1979–80)
- 10 Ronnie Lott (49ers 1982–1985, 1987–91; Raiders 1992)
- 10 Gino Marchetti (Colts 1955–58, 1960–65)
- 10 Leo Nomenilli (49ers 1951–54, 1957–62)
- 10 Mel Renfro (Cowboys 1965–74)
- 10 Jim Ringo (Packers 1958–64;1965–66, 1968)
- 10 Barry Sanders (Lions 1989–99)
- 10 Mike Singletary (Bears 1984–93)
- 10 Lawrence Taylor (Giants 1982–91)
- 10 Johnny Unitas (Colts 1958–65, 1967–68)

PASSING, CAREER	PA	PC	PY	TD	INT
Manning, Peyton	134	79	1131	12	8
Fouts, Dan	120	63	890	1	8
Young, Steve	101	48	614	4	3
Griese, Bob	88	44	554	2	3
Moon, Warren	90	45	465	1	3
Favre, Brett	57	31	463	2	2
Gannon, Rich	53	36	434	7	1
Cunningham, Randall	52	29	419	1	3
Anderson, Ken	56	33	398	2	3
Brunell, Mark	47	24	378	3	2

PASSING, SINGLE GAME	YEAR	CONF	PA	PC	PY	TD	INT
Manning, Peyton	2004	AFC	41	22	342	3	2
Fouts, Dan	1983	AFC	30	17	274	1	1
Manning, Peyton	2000	AFC	23	17	270	2	2
Theismann, Joe	1984	NFC	27	21	242	3	0
Brunell, Mark	1997	AFC	22	12	236	1	0
Simms, Phil	1986	NFC	27	15	212	3	0
Kelly, Jim	1991	AFC	19	13	210	2	0
Vick, Michael	2005	NFC	24	14	205	1	1
Young, Steve	1993	NFC	32	18	196	1	3
Frerotte, Gus	1997	NFC	25	13	193	1	1

RUSHING, CAREER	ATT	YDS	TD
Payton, Walter	81	368	2
Simpson, O.J.	68	356	2
Faulk, Marshall	42	271	1
Warren, Chris	25	234	1
Campbell, Earl	46	220	1
McCutcheon, Lawrence	44	215	1
Sanders, Barry	66	215	2
Hubbard, Marv	36	209	1
Dickerson, Eric	63	195	1
Harris, Franco	46	161	0

RUSHING, SINGLE GAME	YEAR	CONF	ATT	YDS	TD
Faulk, Marshall	1995	AFC	13	180	1
Warren, Chris	1995	AFC	14	127	1
Simpson, O.J.	1973	AFC	16	112	1
Hubbard, Marv	1974	AFC	17	104	0
Anderson, Neal	1989	NFC	13	85	0
Holmes, Priest	2002	AFC	7	77	1
Payton, Walter	1978	NFC	13	77	1
Payton, Walter	1985	NFC	11	76	1
Simpson, O.J.	1974	AFC	19	76	0
McCutcheon, Lawrence	1976	NFC	7	75	0

RECEIVING, CAREER	REC	YDS	TD
Rice, Jerry	37	495	2
Harrison, Marvin	30	462	5
Carter, Cris	27	335	3
Gonzalez, Tony	26	378	4
Brown, Tim	23	408	1
Holt, Torry	21	348	3
Irvin, Michael	18	274	2
Owens, Terrell	18	242	2
Johnson, Keyshawn	18	172	0
Payton, Walter	18	146	0

RECEIVING, GAME	YEAR	CONF	REC	YDS	TD
Moss, Randy	2000	NFC	9	212	1
Johnson, Chad	2004	AFC	5	156	1
Brown, Troy	1997	AFC	5	137	1
Brown, Tim	1998	AFC	5	129	0
Holt, Torry	2004	NFC	7	128	1
Irvin, Michael	1992	NFC	8	125	1
Owens, Terrell	2002	NFC	8	122	1
Smith, Jimmy	2000	AFC	8	119	3
Chandler, Wes	1986	AFC	4	114	1
Mason, Derrick	2004	AFC	6	113	0

SCORING, CAREER	TD	XP	FG	PTS
Andersen, Morten	0	15	10	45
Stenerud, Jan	0	6	8	30
Smith, Jimmy	5	0	0	30
Harrison, Marvin	5	0	0	30
Akers, David	0	8	7	29
Lowery, Nick	0	6	7	26
Ward, Hines	4	0	0	24
Gonzalez, Tony	4	0	0	24
Alstott, Mike	4	0	0	24
Murray, Eddie	0	4	6	22

SCORING, GAME	YEAR	CONF	TD	XP	FG	PTS
Alexander, Shaun	2004	NFC	3	0	0	18
Brockington, John	1973	NFC	3	0	0	18
Smith, Jimmy	2000	AFC	3	0	0	18
Alstott, Mike	2000	NFC	3	0	0	18
Yepremian, Garo	1974	AFC	0	0	5	15
Hanson, Jason	2000	NFC	0	6	3	15
Stenerud, Jan	1972	AFC	0	2	4	14
Wilkins, Jeff	2004	NFC	0	7	2	13
Murray, Eddie	1981	NFC	0	1	4	13
Johnson, Johnny	1991	NFC	2	0	0	12
Muncie, Chuck	1980	NFC	2	0	0	12
Ward, Hines	2005	AFC	2	0	0	12
Williams, Ricky	2003	AFC	2	0	0	12
Green, Eric	1995	AFC	2	0	0	12
Andrews, William	1984	NFC	2	0	0	12
Harrison, Marvin	2001	AFC	2	0	0	12
Campbell, Earl	1980	AFC	2	0	0	12
Walker, Herschel	1989	NFC	2	0	0	12
Renfro, Mel	1971	NFC	2	0	0	12
Akers, David	2002	NFC	0	3	3	12

TOTAL	NAME, POSITION, YEARS
1	Abraham, Donnie, DB, 2000
3	Abraham, John, DE, 2001, 2002, 2004
2	Adamle, Tony, LB-FB, 1950, 1951
2	Adams, Chet, T-E-DT, 1941, 1942
2	Adams, Flozell, T-G-TE, 2003, 2004
1	Adams, Julius, DE-DT, 1980
3	Adams, Sam, DT-DE, 2000, 2001, 2004
1	Adamson, Ken, G, 1961
5	Adderley, Herb, DB, 1963, 1964, 1965, 1966, 1967
4	Addison, Tom, LB, 1961, 1962, 1963, 1964
6	Aikman, Troy, QB, 1991, 1992, 1993, 1994, 1995, 1996
3	Akers, David, K, 2001, 2002, 2004
1	Alban, Dick, DB, 1954
1	Albert, Frankie, QB-DB, 1950
6	Alderman, Grady, T-G, 1963, 1964, 1965, 1966, 1967, 1969
2	Aldrich, Ki, C-LB-G, 1939, 1942
1	Alexander, Kermit, DB, 1968
3	Alexander, Shaun, RB, 2003, 2004, 2005
1	Alexander, Stephen, TE, 2000
2	Allen, Chuck, LB, 1963, 1964
6	Allen, Eric, DB, 1989, 1991, 1992, 1993, 1994, 1995
10	Allen, Larry, G-T, 1995, 1996, 1997, 1998, 1999, 2000, 2001, 2003, 2004, 2005
6	Allen, Marcus, RB, 1982, 1984, 1985, 1986, 1987, 1993
1	Allen, Terry, RB, 1996
6	Alstott, Mike, RB, 1997, 1998, 1999, 2000, 2001, 2002
2	Alt, John, T, 1992, 1993
7	Alworth, Lance, FL-WR, 1963, 1964, 1965, 1966, 1967, 1968, 1969
2	Alzado, Lyle, DE-DT, 1977, 1978
1	Ambrose, Ashley, DB, 1996
4	Ameche, Alan, FB, 1955, 1956, 1957, 1958
3	Anders, Kimble, RB, 1995, 1996, 1997
7	Andersen, Morten, K, 1985, 1986, 1987, 1988, 1990, 1992, 1995
2	Anderson, Bill, E-TE, 1959, 1960
3	Anderson, Dick, DB, 1972, 1973, 1974
1	Anderson, Donny, RB, 1968
4	Anderson, Gary, K, 1984, 1985, 1993, 1998
1	Anderson, Gary, W, 1986
1	Anderson, Jamal, RB, 1998
4	Anderson, Ken, QB, 1975, 1976, 1981, 1982
4	Anderson, Neal, RB, 1988, 1989, 1990, 1991
2	Anderson, Ottis, RB, 1979, 1980
1	Anderson, Richie, FB, 2000
3	Anderson, Willie, T, 2003, 2004, 2005
4	Andrews, William, RB, 1980, 1981, 1982, 1983
5	Andrie, George, DE, 1965, 1966, 1967, 1968, 1969
2	Ane, Charlie, T-C, 1956, 1958
1	Angsman, Elmer, HB, 1950
6	Antwine, Houston, DT-DE, 1963, 1964, 1965, 1966, 1967, 1968
1	Apolskis, Ray, C-G-LB, 1941
5	Arbanas, Fred, TE, 1962, 1963, 1964, 1965, 1967
5	Armstead, Jessie, LB, 1997, 1998, 1999, 2000, 2001
6	Armstrong, Bruce, T-G, 1990, 1991, 1994, 1995, 1996, 1997
2	Armstrong, Otis, RB, 1974, 1976
1	Armstrong, Trace, DE, 2000
5	Arnett, Jon, HB-E, 1957, 1958, 1959, 1960, 1961
2	Arnold, Jim, P, 1987, 1988
4	Arrington, LaVar, LB, 2001, 2002, 2003
3	Artoe, Lee, T, 1940, 1941, 1942
1	Atkins, Billy, DB-HB, 1961
8	Atkins, Doug, DE, 1957, 1958, 1959, 1960, 1961, 1962, 1963, 1965
1	Atkinson, Al, LB, 1968
2	Atkinson, George, DB, 1968, 1969
8	Atwater, Steve, DB, 1990, 1991, 1992, 1993, 1994, 1995, 1996, 1998
1	Austin, Bill, G-T, 1954
1	Azumah, Jerry, DB, 2003
3	Bacon, Coy, DE-DT, 1972, 1976, 1977
6	Bailey, Champ, DB, 2000, 2001, 2002, 2003, 2004, 2005
1	Bailey, Johnny, RB, 1992
2	Baisi, Al, G, 1940, 1941
3	Baker, Al, DE, 1978, 1979, 1980
1	Baker, Dave, DB, 1959
2	Baker, Jon, DG-LB-G, 1951, 1952
4	Baker, Sam, K-FB, 1956, 1963, 1964, 1968
1	Baker, Tony, RB, 1969
4	Bakken, Jim, K, 1965, 1967, 1975, 1976
1	Balasz, Frank, FB-LB-DB, 1939
3	Ball, Jerry, NT-DT, 1989, 1990, 1991
1	Ballard, Howard, T, 1992, 1993
2	Ballman, Gary, FL-TE-SE-WR, 1964, 1965
1	Banducci, Bruno, G, 1954

TOTAL	NAME, POSITION, YEARS
3	Banfield, Tony, DB, 1961, 1962, 1963
1	Banks, Carl, LB, 1987
4	Banks, Chip, LB, 1982, 1983, 1985, 1986
4	Banks, Tom, C-G, 1975, 1976, 1977, 1978
1	Bannister, Alex, WR, 2003
3	Barbaro, Gary, DB, 1980, 1981, 1982
1	Barber, Jim, T, 1940
3	Barber, Ronde, DB, 2001, 2004, 2005
5	Barber, Stew, T-LB-G, 1963, 1964, 1965, 1966, 1967
2	Barber, Tiki, RB, 2004, 2005
1	Barker, Bryan, P, 1997
1	Barkum, Jerome, TE-WR, 1973
1	Barnard, Charles, E, 1938
3	Barnes, Billy Ray, HB, 1957, 1958, 1959
6	Barnes, Erich, DB, 1959, 1961, 1962, 1963, 1964, 1968
1	Barnes, Mike, DT-DE, 1977
1	Barnes, Walt, G, 1950
1	Barnett, Fred, WR, 1992
7	Barney, Lem, DB, 1967, 1968, 1969, 1972, 1973, 1975, 1976
2	Barr, Terry, HB-DB-FL, 1963, 1964
2	Bartkowski, Steve, QB, 1980, 1981
1	Barton, Harris, T-G, 1993
1	Bartrum, Mike, TE-C, 2005
4	Barwegan, Dick, G, 1950, 1951, 1952, 1953
3	Bass, Dick, FB-HB, 1962, 1963, 1966
1	Bassi, Dick, G, 1940
1	Bates, Bill, DB, 1984
5	Bates, Michael, RB, 1996, 1997, 1998, 1999, 2000
6	Baugh, Sammy, QB-TB, 1938, 1939, 1940, 1941, 1942, 1951
9	Baughan, Maxie, LB, 1960, 1961, 1963, 1964, 1965, 1966, 1967, 1968, 1969
5	Baumhower, Bob, NT, 1979, 1981, 1982, 1983, 1984
1	Bausch, Frank, C, 1940
2	Bavaro, Mark, TE, 1986, 1987
1	Beasley, Fred, FB, 2003
8	Bednarik, Chuck, LB-C, 1950, 1951, 1952, 1953, 1954, 1956, 1957, 1960
1	Behrman, Dave, C-T, 1965
1	Beinor, Ed, T-DE, 1942
1	Beirne, Jim, WR-TE, 1969
9	Bell, Bobby, LB-DE, 1964, 1965, 1966, 1967, 1968, 1969, 1970, 1971, 1972
1	Bell, Greg, RB, 1984
1	Bell, Kendrell, LB, 2001
1	Bell, Todd, DB-LB, 1984
1	Bemiller, Al, C-G-T, 1965
1	Benirschke, Rolf, K, 1982
5	Bennett, Cornelius, LB, 1988, 1990, 1991, 1992, 1993
2	Bennett, Darren, P, 1995, 2000
1	Bennett, Michael, RB, 2002
1	Benson, Brad, T-G-C, 1986
2	Bentley, LeCharles, G-C, 2003, 2005
1	Benton, Jim, E, 1939
2	Berger, Mitch, P, 1999, 2004
5	Bergey, Bill, LB, 1969, 1974, 1976, 1977, 1978
1	Berry, Bertrand, DE, 2004
1	Berry, Bob, QB, 1969
5	Berry, Raymond, E, 1958, 1959, 1961, 1963, 1964
1	Bertelsen, Jim, RB, 1973
8	Bethea, Elvin, DE, 1969, 1971, 1972, 1973, 1974, 1975, 1978, 1979
6	Bettis, Jerome, RB, 1993, 1994, 1996, 1997, 2001, 2004
1	Beuerlein, Steve, QB, 1999
1	Biasucci, Dean, K, 1987
1	Bickett, Duane, LB, 1987
1	Bidwell, Josh, P, 2005
1	Bielski, Dick, E-FB, 1961
3	Biggs, Verlon, DE, 1966, 1967, 1968
6	Biletnikoff, Fred, WR-FL, 1967, 1969, 1970, 1971, 1973, 1974
2	Bingaman, Les, DG-G, 1951, 1953
1	Birdsong, Carl, P, 1983
1	Birdwell, Dan, DT-DE, 1968
4	Birk, Matt, C, 2000, 2001, 2003, 2004
1	Bishop, Bill, DT-T, 1954
4	Bishop, Blaine, DB, 1995, 1996, 1997, 2000
1	Bishop, Don, B, 1962
2	Bishop, Keith, G-C, 1986, 1987
1	Bishop, Sonny, G-T, 1968
1	Bjork, Del, T, 1938
1	Blades, Bennie, DB, 1991
1	Blades, Brian, WR, 1989
1	Blair, George, DB-K, 1961
6	Blair, Matt, LB, 1977, 1978, 1979, 1980, 1981, 1982
1	Blake, Jeff, QB, 1995

TOTAL	NAME, POSITION, YEARS
1	Blanchard, Cary, K, 1996
4	Blanda, George, QB, 1961, 1962, 1963, 1967
1	Blanks, Sid, RB, 1964
1	Blazine, Tony, T, 1939
4	Bledsoe, Drew, QB, 1994, 1996, 1997, 2002
5	Blount, Mel, DB, 1975, 1976, 1978, 1979, 1981
1	Blozis, Al, T, 1942
4	Blue, Forrest, C, 1971, 1972, 1973, 1974
2	Bly, Dre', DB, 2003, 2004
1	Bokamper, Kim, DE-LB, 1979
1	Boldin, Anquan, WR, 2003
1	Bono, Steve, QB, 1995
1	Booker, Marty, WR, 2002
2	Boozer, Emerson, RB, 1966, 1968
2	Bortz, Mark, G, 1988, 1990
1	Boryla, Mike, QB, 1975
5	Boselli, Tony, T, 1996, 1997, 1998, 1999, 2000
4	Bosley, Bruce, C-G-DE, 1960, 1965, 1966, 1967
1	Bosseler, Don, FB, 1959
1	Bostic, Jeff, C, 1983
1	Bostic, Keith, DB, 1987
1	Boston, David, WR, 2001
4	Boulware, Peter, LB-DE, 1998, 1999, 2002, 2003
2	Bowens, Tim, DT, 1998, 2002
2	Box, Cloyce, E-HB, 1950, 1952
2	Boyd, Bob, E-DB, 1954
2	Boyd, Bobby, DB, 1964, 1968
2	Boyd, Stephen, LB, 1999, 2000
2	Boyette, Garland, LB-DE, 1968, 1969
2	Braase, Ordell, DE, 1966, 1967
1	Brackens, Tony, DE, 1999
3	Bradley, Bill, DB, 1971, 1972, 1973
2	Bradshaw, Charlie, T, 1963, 1964
3	Bradshaw, Terry, QB, 1975, 1978, 1979
3	Brady, Tom, QB, 2001, 2004, 2005
2	Bramlett, John, LB, 1966, 1967
4	Branch, Cliff, WR, 1974, 1975, 1977
3	Branch, Mel, DE, 1961, 1962, 1963
1	Braxton, Tyrone, DB, 1996
4	Bray, Ray, G-DG, 1940, 1941, 1950, 1951
7	Brazile, Robert, LB, 1976, 1977, 1978, 1979, 1980, 1981, 1982
1	Breedlove, Rod, LB, 1962
1	Brees, Drew, QB, 2004
1	Brenner, Hoby, TE, 1987
3	Breunig, Bob, LB, 1979, 1980, 1982
1	Brewer, Johnny, TE-LB-DE, 1966
2	Brewster, Pete, E, 1955, 1956
1	Brezina, Greg, LB, 1969
1	Briggs, Lance, LB, 2005
2	Brink, Larry, DE-E, 1950, 1951
1	Briscoe, Marlin, WR-QB-FL, 1970
5	Brito, Gene, DE-E, 1953, 1955, 1956, 1957, 1958
3	Brock, Charley, C-HB-FB, 1939, 1940, 1942
3	Brockington, John, RB, 1971, 1972, 1973
2	Brodie, John, QB, 1965, 1970
1	Brooker, Tommy, E-K, 1964
5	Brooking, Keith, LB, 2001, 2002, 2003, 2004, 2005
9	Brooks, Derrick, LB, 1997, 1998, 1999, 2000, 2001, 2002, 2003, 2004, 2005
4	Brooks, James, RB, 1986, 1988, 1989, 1990
5	Brooks, Larry, DT, 1976, 1977, 1978, 1979, 1980
1	Brooks, Lee, DT, 1976
1	Brooks, Michael, LB, 1992
2	Brookshier, Tom, DB, 1959, 1960
4	Brown, Bill, RB, 1964, 1965, 1967, 1968
6	Brown, Bob, T, 1965, 1966, 1968, 1969, 1970, 1971
3	Brown, Chad, LB, 1996, 1998, 1999
2	Brown, Charlie, WR, 1982, 1983
1	Brown, Dave, DB, 1984
2	Brown, Ed, QB, 1955, 1956
2	Brown, Eddie, DB, 1976, 1977
1	Brown, Eddie, WR, 1988
1	Brown, Hardy, LB-DB-FB, 1952
2	Brown, Jerome, DT, 1990, 1991
9	Brown, Jim, FB, 1957, 1958, 1959, 1960, 1961, 1962, 1963, 1964, 1965
1	Brown, Larry, T-TE, 1982
4	Brown, Larry, RB, 1969, 1970, 1971, 1972
7	Brown, Lomas, T, 1990, 1991, 1992, 1993, 1994, 1995, 1996
1	Brown, Mike, DB, 2005
1	Brown, Ray, G-T, 2001
1	Brown, Robert, DT-DE, 1972
6	Brown, Roger, DT, 1962, 1963, 1964, 1965, 1966, 1967
1	Brown, Ron, WR, 1985
9	Brown, Rosey, T, 1955, 1956, 1957, 1958, 1959, 1960, 1962, 1964, 1965
8	Brown, Ruben, G, 1996, 1997, 1998, 1999, 2000, 2001, 2002, 2003
9	Brown, Tim, WR, 1988, 1991, 1993, 1994, 1995, 1997, 1999, 2001
3	Brown, Timmy, RB, 1962, 1963, 1965

TOTAL	NAME, POSITION, YEARS
1	Brown, Troy, WR, 2001
9	Brown, Willie, DB, 1964, 1965, 1967, 1968, 1969, 1970, 1971, 1972, 1973
6	Browner, Joey, DB, 1985, 1986, 1987, 1988, 1989, 1990
4	Bruce, Isaac, WR, 1996, 1999, 2000, 2001
1	Bruder, Hank, B, 1939
1	Brumm, Don, DE, 1968
3	Brunell, Mark, QB, 1996, 1997, 1999
2	Bruney, Fred, DB, 1961, 1962
1	Bruschi, Tedy, LB, 2004
2	Bryant, Bobby, DB, 1975, 1976
8	Buchanan, Buck, DT, 1964, 1965, 1966, 1967, 1968, 1969, 1970, 1971
1	Buchanan, Ray, DB, 1998
3	Buchanon, Willie, DB, 1973, 1974, 1978
7	Budde, Ed, G, 1963, 1966, 1967, 1968, 1969, 1970, 1971
1	Buhler, Larry, B, 1939
1	Bulaich, Norm, RB, 1971
1	Bulger, Marc, QB, 2003
1	Bulluck, Keith, LB, 2003
3	Buncom, Frank, LB, 1964, 1965, 1967
8	Buoniconti, Nick, LB, 1963, 1964, 1965, 1966, 1967, 1969, 1972, 1973
1	Burford, Chris, SE-WR, 1961
1	Burgess, Derrick, DE-LB, 2005
2	Burk, Adrian, QB, 1954, 1955
1	Burnett, Bobby, RB, 1966
1	Burnett, Dale, B, 1938
1	Burnett, Rob, DE, 1994
1	Burrell, Ode, RB-WR-P, 1965
2	Burrough, Ken, WR, 1975, 1977
1	Burruss, Lloyd, DB, 1986
1	Burt, Jim, NT-DT, 1986
1	Bussey, Young, QB, 1941
8	Butkus, Dick, LB, 1965, 1966, 1967, 1968, 1969, 1970, 1971, 1972
1	Butler, Cannonball, RB, 1969
4	Butler, Jack, DB, 1955, 1956, 1957, 1958
1	Butler, Jerry, WR, 1980
4	Butler, LeRoy, DB, 1993, 1996, 1997, 1998
2	Butts, Marion, RB, 1990, 1991
1	Butz, Dave, DT-DE, 1983
1	Byars, Keith, RB-TE, 1993
2	Byner, Earnest, RB, 1990, 1991
5	Byrd, Butch, DB, 1964, 1965, 1966, 1968, 1969
1	Byrd, Gill, DB, 1991
1	Caffey, Lee Roy, LB, 1965
5	Camarillo, Rich, P, 1983, 1989, 1991, 1992, 1993
5	Campbell, Earl, RB, 1978, 1979, 1980, 1981, 1983
2	Campbell, Marion, DE-DT-MG-G-T, 1959, 1960
1	Campbell, Woody, RB, 1967
1	Cannady, John, LB-C, 1950, 1952
2	Cannon, Billy, TE-HB-FB, 1961, 1969
5	Cappelletti, Gino, FL-SE-DB-WR-K, 1961, 1963, 1964, 1965, 1966
1	Carapella, Al, DT-MG-T-LB, 1954
1	Cardwell, Lloyd, WB-DB-FB, 1938
1	Carlton, Wray, HB-FB, 1966
4	Carmichael, Harold, WR-TE, 1973, 1978, 1979, 1980
1	Carney, John, K, 1994
1	Carolan, Reggie, TE, 1962
1	Caroline, J.C., DB-HB, 1956
1	Carollo, Joe, T, 1968
1	Carpenter, Ken, HB-FL, 1951
1	Carpenter, Preston, E-HB, 1962
3	Carr, Fred, LB, 1970, 1972, 1975
1	Carr, Roger, WR, 1976
1	Carrier, Mark, WR, 1989
3	Carrier, Mark, DB, 1990, 1991, 1993
1	Carroll, Victor, T-C-G, 1942
1	Carson, Carlos, WR, 1987
6	Carson, Harry, LB, 1978, 1979, 1981, 1985, 1986, 1987
1	Carson, John, E, 1957
1	Carswell, Dwayne, TE, 2001
2	Carter, Anthony, WR, 1987, 1988
8	Carter, Cris, WR, 1993, 1994, 1995, 1996, 1997, 1998, 1999, 2000
4	Carter, Dale, DB, 1994, 1995, 1996, 1997
1	Carter, Jim, LB-G, 1973
1	Carter, Joe, E, 1938, 1939
2	Carter, Kevin, DE-DT, 1999, 2002
3	Carter, Michael, NT, 1985, 1987, 1988
3	Casanova, Tommy, DB, 1974, 1976, 1977
5	Casares, Rick, FB, 1955, 1956, 1957, 1958, 1959
1	Case, Scott, DB, 1988
1	Casey, Bernie, HB-FL-TE-WR, 1967
2	Cason, Jim, DB-HB, 1951, 1954
5	Casper, Dave, TE, 1976, 1977, 1978, 1979, 1980
3	Caster, Rich, TE-WR, 1972, 1974, 1975
1	Cecil, Chuck, DB, 1992
3	Centers, Larry, FB, 1995, 1996, 2001

TOTAL	NAME, POSITION, YEARS
1	Chamberlain, Byron, TE, 2001
1	Chambers, Chris, WR, 2005
3	Chambers, Wally, DT-DE, 1973, 1975, 1976
2	Chandler, Chris, QB, 1997, 1998
1	Chandler, Don, FB-P-K, 1967
4	Chandler, Wes, WR, 1979, 1982, 1983, 1985
2	Chandnois, Lynn, HB-WB-TB, 1952, 1953
1	Chapple, Dave, P, 1972
1	Chavous, Corey, DB, 2003
6	Cherry, Deron, DB, 1983, 1984, 1985, 1986, 1987, 1988
2	Cherundolo, Chuck, C-LB, 1941, 1942
1	Chesney, Chet, C-LB, 1940
4	Chester, Raymond, TE, 1970, 1971, 1972, 1979
5	Childress, Ray, DT-DE, 1988, 1990, 1991, 1992, 1993
1	Childs, Henry, TE, 1979
3	Chmura, Mark, TE, 1995, 1997, 1998
5	Christensen, Todd, TE-FB, 1983, 1984, 1985, 1986, 1987
5	Christiansen, Jack, DB, 1953, 1954, 1955, 1956, 1957
1	Christy, Dick, HB, 1962
3	Christy, Jeff, C, 1998, 1999, 2000
1	Cifers, Ed, E, 1942
1	Clancy, Jack, SE-WR, 1967
1	Clark, Bruce, DE-DT, 1984
2	Clark, Dwight, WR, 1981, 1982
4	Clark, Gary, WR, 1986, 1987, 1990, 1991
1	Clark, Mike, K, 1966
1	Clarke, Hagood, DB, 1965
2	Clarke, Harry, HB-DB, 1940, 1941
1	Clarke, Leon, E-FL, 1956
3	Clayborn, Raymond, DB, 1983, 1985, 1986
5	Clayton, Mark, WR, 1984, 1985, 1986, 1988, 1991
1	Clements, Nate, DB, 2004
3	Coakley, Dexter, LB, 1999, 2001, 2003
5	Coates, Ben, TE, 1994, 1995, 1996, 1997, 1998
1	Cofer, Mike, LB-DE, 1988
3	Coffman, Paul, TE, 1982, 1983, 1984
3	Cogdill, Gail, WR, 1960, 1962, 1963
1	Colclough, Jim, E, 1962
1	Cole, Pete, G-T, 1938
1	Cole, Robin, LB-DE, 1984
1	Coleman, Marco, DE-LB, 2000
1	Coleman, Roderick, DT, 2005
1	Coles, Laveranues, WR, 2003
2	Collins, Gary, FL-WR-P, 1965, 1966
1	Collins, Jim, LB, 1985
1	Collins, Kerry, QB, 1996
1	Collins, Ray, DT-T, 1951
1	Collins, Tony, RB, 1983
3	Collinsworth, Cris, WR, 1981, 1982, 1983
3	Colo, Don, DT, 1954, 1955, 1958
1	Condit, Merl, HB, 1940, 1942
2	Conerly, Charlie, QB, 1950, 1956
3	Conlan, Shane, LB, 1988, 1989, 1990
3	Conners, Dan, LB, 1966, 1967, 1968
1	Connolly, Ted, G, 1961
4	Connor, George, T-LB-DT-G, 1950, 1951, 1952, 1953
1	Conrad, Bobby Joe, FL-DB-HB-WR-K, 1964
1	Conti, Enio, G, 1942
2	Cook, Marv, TE, 1991, 1992
1	Cooke, Ed, DE-LB, 1966
1	Coomer, Joe, T-G, 1941
2	Cope, Frank, T, 1938, 1940
1	Cordill, Ollie, WB-HB-P, 1940
1	Corey, Walt, LB, 1963
1	Cornelison, Jerry, T, 1962
1	Corral, Frank, K, 1978
3	Cosbie, Doug, TE, 1983, 1984, 1985
4	Costa, Dave, DT-DE, 1963, 1967, 1968, 1969
2	Costa, Paul, TE-T, 1965, 1966
2	Coulter, Tex, T-C-E, 1951, 1952
2	Covert, Jimbo, T, 1985, 1986
3	Cowan, Charley, T-G, 1968, 1969, 1970
1	Cowart, Sam, LB, 2000
3	Cox, Bryan, LB, 1994, 1994, 1995
1	Cox, Fred, K, 1970
2	Craft, Russ, DB-HB, 1951, 1952
3	Craig, Larry, B-E, 1939, 1941, 1942
4	Craig, Roger, RB, 1985, 1987, 1988, 1989
8	Creekmur, Lou, T-G-DG-DT, 1950, 1951, 1952, 1953, 1954, 1955, 1956, 1957
3	Cribbs, Joe, RB, 1980, 1981, 1983
4	Cromwell, Nolan, DB, 1980, 1981, 1982, 1983
2	Cross, Irv, DB, 1964, 1965
1	Cross, Jeff, DE, 1990
3	Cross, Randy, G-C, 1981, 1982, 1984
4	Crow, John David, HB-TE-FB, 1959, 1960, 1962, 1965
3	Crow, Lindon, DB, 1956, 1957, 1959
3	Crumpler, Alge, TE, 2003, 2004, 2005

TOTAL	NAME, POSITION, YEARS
5	Csonka, Larry, RB, 1970, 1971, 1972, 1973, 1974
3	Cuff, Ward, WB-QB-HB, 1938, 1939, 1941
6	Culp, Curley, DT-NT-G, 1969, 1971, 1975, 1976, 1977, 1978
3	Culpepper, Daunte, QB, 2000, 2003, 2004
4	Cunningham, Randall, QB, 1988, 1989, 1990, 1998
1	Cunningham, Sam, RB, 1978
1	Current, Mike, T, 1969
1	Currie, Dan, LB, 1960
2	Curry, Bill, C-LB, 1971, 1972
4	Curtis, Isaac, WR, 1973, 1974, 1975, 1976
4	Curtis, Mike, LB-FB, 1968, 1970, 1971, 1974
1	Dalby, Dave, C, 1977
3	Dale, Carroll, WR-TE-FL, 1968, 1969, 1970
2	Danenhauer, Eldon, T, 1962, 1965
4	Daniels, Clem, HB-DB, 1963, 1964, 1965, 1966
1	Danowski, Ed, B, 1938
1	Darden, Thom, DB, 1978
1	Daugherty, Dick, G-LB-C, 1957
6	David, Jim, DB, 1954, 1955, 1956, 1957, 1958, 1959
3	Davidson, Ben, DE-DT, 1966, 1967, 1968
2	Davidson, Cotton, QB, 1961, 1963
1	Davis, Ben, DB, 1972
1	Davis, Eric, DB, 1995
2	Davis, Fred, T-DT, 1942, 1950
1	Davis, Glenn, HB, 1950
3	Davis, Stephen, RB, 1999, 2000, 2003
3	Davis, Terrell, RB, 1996, 1997, 1998
2	Davis, Tommy, K-P, 1962, 1963
5	Davis, Willie, DE-DT, 1963, 1964, 1965, 1966, 1967
5	Dawkins, Brian, DB, 1999, 2001, 2002, 2004, 2005
7	Dawson, Dermontti, C-G, 1992, 1993, 1994, 1995, 1996, 1997, 1998
7	Dawson, Len, QB, 1962, 1964, 1966, 1967, 1968, 1969, 1971
1	Day, Tom, DE-G-DT-T, 1965
1	Deal, Rufus, B, 1942
4	Dean, Fred, DE, 1979, 1980, 1981, 1983
1	Dean, Ted, FB-HB, 1961
4	Dee, Bob, DE-DT, 1961, 1963, 1964, 1965
1	Del Rio, Jack, LB, 1994
6	DeLamielleure, Joe, G, 1975, 1976, 1977, 1978, 1979, 1980
1	Delaney, Joe, RB, 1981
2	DeLeone, Tom, C, 1979, 1980
1	Delhomme, Jake, QB, 2005
1	DeLong, Steve, DE-DT, 1969
3	DeMarco, Bob, C-G, 1963, 1965, 1967
1	Dempsey, Tom, K, 1969
2	Denson, Al, FL-TE-SE-WR, 1967, 1969
4	Dent, Richard, DE, 1984, 1985, 1990, 1993
1	Derby, Dean, DB, 1959
2	DeRogatis, Al, DT-T, 1950, 1951
2	Dess, Darrell, G-T, 1962, 1963
1	Dewell, Billy, E, 1941
1	Dewveall, Willard, E, 1962
2	Dial, Buddy, SE-FL, 1961, 1963
6	Dickerson, Eric, RB, 1983, 1984, 1986, 1987, 1988, 1989
1	Dieken, Doug, T, 1980
6	Dierdorf, Dan, T-G-C, 1974, 1975, 1976, 1977, 1978, 1980
1	Dilfer, Trent, QB, 1997
1	Dilger, Ken, TE, 2001
4	Dillon, Bobby, DB, 1955, 1956, 1957, 1958
4	Dillon, Corey, RB, 1999, 2000, 2001, 2004
2	Dishman, Cris, DB, 1991, 1997
5	Ditka, Mike, TE, 1961, 1962, 1963, 1964, 1965
3	Dixon, Hanford, DB, 1986, 1987, 1988
4	Dixon, Hewritt, RB-TE, 1966, 1967, 1968, 1970
3	Dobler, Conrad, G, 1975, 1976, 1977
4	Dodrill, Dale, MG-LB, 1953, 1954, 1955, 1957
8	Doleman, Chris, DE-LB, 1987, 1988, 1989, 1990, 1992, 1993, 1995, 1997
4	Doll, Don, DB, 1950, 1951, 1952, 1953
6	Donaldson, Ray, C, 1986, 1987, 1988, 1989, 1995, 1996
5	Donovan, Art, DT-T, 1953, 1954, 1955, 1956, 1957
4	Donovan, Pat, T, 1979, 1980, 1981, 1982
1	Doran, Jim, E-DE, 1960
1	Dorney, Keith, T-G, 1982
1	Dorow, Al, QB, 1956, 1961
4	Dorsett, Tony, RB, 1978, 1981, 1982, 1983
1	Dottley, John, FB, 1951
1	Dougherty, Phil, C, 1938
3	Douglas, Hugh, DE, 2000, 2001, 2002
1	Dove, Bob, DE-E, 1950
1	Dove, Eddie, DB, 1961
2	Dowler, Boyd, FL-SE-WR, 1965, 1967
3	Drake, Johnny, B, 1938, 1939, 1940

TOTAL	NAME, POSITION, YEARS
4	Drazenovich, Chuck, LB-FB, 1955, 1956, 1957, 1958
1	Driver, Donald, WR, 2002
1	Drulis, Chuck, G-LB, 1942
1	Drummond, Eddie, WR, 2004
1	Dryer, Fred, DE, 1975
1	Dubenion, Elbert, FL-WR-HB, 1964
3	Dudley, Bill, HB-TB-QB, 1942, 1950, 1951
4	Duerson, Dave, DB, 1985, 1986, 1987, 1988
1	Duhe, A.J., LB-DE, 1984
4	Dunaway, Jim, DT, 1965, 1966, 1967, 1968
1	Duncan, Curtis, WR, 1992
4	Duncan, Speedy, DB, 1965, 1966, 1967, 1971
3	Dunn, Warrick, RB, 1997, 2000, 2005
3	Duper, Mark, WR, 1983, 1984, 1986
3	DuPree, Billy Joe, TE, 1976, 1977, 1978
3	Dutton, John, DT-DE, 1975, 1976, 1977
5	Easley, Kenny, DB, 1982, 1983, 1984, 1985, 1987
2	Ecklund, Brad, C-LB, 1950, 1951
1	Edelman, Brad, G, 1987
1	Edgerson, Booker, DB, 1965
1	Edmonds, Bobby Joe, RB, 1986
2	Edmunds, Ferrell, TE, 1989, 1990
1	Edwards, Dan, E, 1950
1	Edwards, Donnie, LB, 2002
2	Edwards, Glen, DB, 1975, 1976
1	Edwards, Turk, T, 1939
4	Eisenhauer, Larry, DE, 1962, 1963, 1964, 1966
1	Ekern, Carl, LB, 1986
2	Elam, Cleveland, DT-DE, 1976, 1977
3	Elam, Jason, K, 1995, 1998, 2001
3	Ellard, Henry, WR, 1984, 1988, 1989
6	Eller, Carl, DE, 1968, 1969, 1970, 1971, 1973, 1974
3	Elliott, John, DT-DE, 1968, 1969, 1970
1	Elliott, Jumbo, T, 1993
1	Ellis, Allan, DB, 1977
2	Ellis, Ken, DB, 1973, 1974
1	Ellis, Shaun, DE, 2003
1	Ellison, Willie, RB, 1971
2	Elliss, Luther, DT-DE, 1999, 2000
1	Elter, Leo, FB-HB, 1956
9	Elway, John, QB, 1986, 1987, 1989, 1991, 1993, 1994, 1996, 1997, 1998
4	English, Doug, DT-NT, 1978, 1981, 1982, 1983
1	Erlandson, Tom, LB, 1966
4	Esiason, Boomer, QB, 1986, 1988, 1989, 1993
1	Etter, Bob, K, 1969
2	Evans, Norm, T, 1972, 1974
1	Everett, Jim, QB, 1990
1	Everett, Thomas, DB, 1993
1	Fahnhorst, Keith, T, 1984
5	Faison, Earl, DE, 1961, 1962, 1963, 1964, 1965
3	Falaschi, Nello, BB, 1938, 1939, 1941
3	Famiglietti, Gary, FB-HB, 1940, 1941, 1942
5	Faneca, Alan, G-T, 2001, 2002, 2003, 2004, 2005
2	Farkas, Andy, FB-HB-WB, 1939, 1942
1	Farman, Dick, G, 1942
2	Farr, Mel, RB, 1967, 1970
3	Farr, Miller, DB, 1967, 1968, 1969
1	Farragut, Ken, C-LB, 1953
1	Farrior, James, LB, 2004
7	Faulk, Marshall, RB, 1994, 1995, 1998, 1999, 2000, 2001, 2002
8	Favre, Brett, QB, 1992, 1993, 1995, 1996, 1997, 2001, 2002, 2003
1	Feagles, Jeff, P, 1995
1	Fears, Tom, E, 1950
1	Federovitch, John, T, 1941
2	Felt, Dick, DB, 1961, 1962
2	Fencik, Gary, DB, 1980, 1981
1	Ferguson, Charley, WR-TE, 1965
1	Ferguson, Howie, FB-HB, 1955
2	Fields, Joe, C-G, 1981, 1982
2	Fields, Mark, LB, 2000, 2004
2	Filchock, Frank, TB-QB-HB, 1939, 1941
1	Finks, Jim, QB-DB-TB, 1952
3	Fischer, Bill, T-G-DT, 1950, 1951, 1952
3	Fischer, Pat, DB, 1964, 1965, 1969
2	Fiss, Galen, LB, 1962, 1963
1	Fitzgerald, Larry, WR, 2005
4	Flanagan, Ed, C, 1969, 1970, 1971, 1973
1	Flanagan, Mike, C-T, 2003
1	Flatley, Paul, WR-FL, 1966
1	Flint, George, G, 1965
1	Flores, Tom, QB, 1966
2	Floyd, Don, DE, 1961, 1962
1	Flutie, Doug, QB, 1998
1	Foley, Dave, T-C, 1973
1	Foley, Tim, DB, 1979
1	Folkins, Lee, TE-DE, 1963
4	Ford, Len, DE-E, 1951, 1952, 1953, 1954
5	Foreman, Chuck, RB, 1973, 1974, 1975, 1976, 1977
4	Forester, Bill, LB-MG-DT, 1959, 1960, 1961, 1962

TOTAL	NAME, POSITION, YEARS
2	Forte, Aldo, G-T, 1940, 1941
3	Fortmann, Danny, G-LB, 1940, 1941, 1942
5	Fortunato, Joe, LB, 1958, 1962, 1963, 1964, 1965
1	Foster, Barry, RB, 1992
2	Foster, Roy, G-T, 1985, 1986
6	Fouts, Dan, QB, 1979, 1980, 1981, 1982, 1983, 1985
1	Fox, Tim, DB, 1980
4	Fralic, Bill, G-T, 1986, 1987, 1988, 1989
2	France, Doug, T, 1977, 1978
1	Francis, Russ, TE, 1980
1	Franklin, Andra, RB, 1982
1	Franklin, Tony, K, 1986
3	Franks, Bubba, TE, 2001, 2002, 2003
3	Fraser, Jim, LB-P, 1962, 1963, 1964
1	Frazier, Charley, WR, 1966
3	Frazier, Willie, TE, 1965, 1967, 1969
1	Frederickson, Tucker, RB, 1965
1	Freeman, Antonio, WR, 1998
3	Freeney, Dwight, DE, 2003, 2004, 2005
1	Freitas, Rocky, T, 1972
1	Frerotte, Gus, QB, 1996
1	Fritsch, Toni, K, 1979
5	Fryar, Irving, WR, 1985, 1993, 1994, 1996, 1997
1	Fugett, Jean, TE, 1977
3	Fulcher, David, DB, 1988, 1989, 1990
1	Fuller, Frank, DT-T-G-C-DE, 1959
4	Fuller, William, DE, 1991, 1994, 1995, 1996
1	Fullwood, Brent, RB, 1989
4	Gabriel, Roman, QB, 1967, 1968, 1969, 1973
5	Gain, Bob, DT-DE-MG-T, 1957, 1958, 1959, 1961, 1962
1	Galazin, Stan, C, 1938
1	Galimore, Willie, HB, 1958
1	Gallarneau, Hugh, HB, 1941
1	Gammon, Kendall, C-TE, 2004
4	Gannon, Rich, QB, 1999, 2000, 2001, 2002
1	Gantenbein, Milt, E-DE, 1939
4	Garcia, Jeff, QB, 2000, 2001, 2002
1	Gardocki, Chris, P, 1996
1	Garner, Charlie, RB, 2000
1	Garrett, Carl, RB, 1969
2	Garrett, Mike, RB, 1966, 1967
4	Garrison, Gary, WR-SE, 1968, 1970, 1971, 1972
1	Garrison, Walt, RB, 1972
4	Garron, Larry, HB-FB, 1961, 1963, 1964, 1967
2	Gash, Sam, FB, 1998, 1999
5	Gastineau, Mark, DE, 1981, 1982, 1983, 1984, 1985
2	Gates, Antonio, TE, 2004, 2005
1	Gatski, Frank, C-LB, 1955
1	Gayle, Shaun, DB, 1991
1	Gbaja-Biamila, Kabeer, DE, 2003
1	Gelatka, Chuck, E, 1938
2	Gentry, Byron, G, 1938, 1939
8	George, Bill, LB-G-MG-DT, 1954, 1955, 1956, 1957, 1958, 1959, 1960, 1961
4	George, Eddie, RB, 1997, 1998, 1999, 2000
1	George, Ray, T, 1939
2	Gerela, Roy, K, 1972, 1974
2	Geri, Joe, TB-HB, 1950, 1951
3	Gibbons, Jim, E-TE, 1960, 1961, 1964
2	Gibron, Abe, G, 1952, 1953, 1955
7	Gifford, Frank, HB-FL-DB-WR, 1953, 1954, 1955, 1956, 1958, 1959, 1963
1	Gilbert, Kline, T-G, 1957
1	Gilbert, Sean, DT-DE, 1993
4	Gilchrist, Cookie, FB, 1962, 1963, 1964, 1965
1	Gildea, Johnny, B, 1938
3	Gildon, Jason, LB, 2000, 2001, 2002
4	Giles, Jimmie, TE, 1980, 1981, 1982, 1985
3	Gilliam, John, WR-FL, 1972, 1973, 1974, 1975
1	Gilliam, Jon, C, 1961
5	Gillingham, Gale, G-DT, 1969, 1970, 1971, 1973, 1974
1	Gillom, Horace, E-DE, 1952
2	Gilmer, Harry, QB-HB, 1950, 1952
2	Givins, Ernest, WR-TE, 1990, 1992
4	Glass, Bill, DE-C-T, 1962, 1963, 1964, 1967
3	Glenn, Aaron, DB, 1997, 1998, 2002
2	Glenn, Tarik, T-G, 2004, 2005
3	Glick, Fred, DB, 1962, 1963, 1964
3	Glover, Kevin, C-G, 1995, 1996, 1997
5	Glover, La'Roi, DT-NT, 2000, 2001, 2002, 2003, 2004
1	Goddard, Ed, B, 1938
1	Goeddeke, George, G-C-T, 1969
2	Gogan, Kevin, G-T, 1994, 1997, 1998
1	Gogolak, Pete, K, 1965
1	Gold, Ian, LB, 2001
1	Goldberg, Marshall, B, 1941
1	Goldenberg, Buckets, G-BB, 1939
2	Golic, Bob, NT-DT-LB-DE, 1985, 1986
5	Gonsoulin, George, DB, 1961, 1962, 1963, 1964, 1966

TOTAL	NAME, POSITION, YEARS
7	Gonzalez, Tony, TE, 1999, 2000, 2001, 2002, 2003, 2004, 2005
2	Goode, Irv, G-T-C, 1964, 1967
2	Goode, Rob, B, 1951, 1954
1	Goode, Tom, C-LB, 1969
2	Gordon, Dick, WR-SE-FL, 1970, 1971
3	Gordy, John, G-T, 1963, 1964, 1965
2	Gossett, Bruce, K, 1966, 1968
1	Gossett, Jeff, P, 1991
7	Gradishar, Randy, LB, 1975, 1977, 1978, 1979, 1981, 1982, 1983
4	Graham, Kenny, DB, 1965, 1967, 1968, 1969
5	Graham, Otto, QB-DB, 1950, 1951, 1952, 1953, 1954
1	Graham, Shayne, K, 2005
1	Gramatica, Martin, K, 2000
2	Granger, Hoyle, RB, 1967, 1968
5	Grantham, Larry, LB, 1962, 1963, 1964, 1966, 1969
4	Gray, Jerry, DB, 1986, 1987, 1988, 1989
6	Gray, Ken, G-LB, 1961, 1963, 1964, 1966, 1967, 1968
4	Gray, Leon, T-G, 1976, 1978, 1979, 1981
4	Gray, Mel, WR, 1974, 1975, 1976, 1977
4	Gray, Mel, RB-WR, 1990, 1991, 1992, 1994
6	Grayson, Dave, DB, 1962, 1963, 1964, 1965, 1966, 1969
1	Grbac, Elvis, QB, 2000
5	Green, Ahman, RB, 2001, 2002, 2003, 2004
1	Green, Bobby Joe, P, 1970
5	Green, Cornell, DB, 1965, 1966, 1967, 1971, 1972
7	Green, Darrell, DB, 1984, 1986, 1987, 1990, 1991, 1996, 1997
2	Green, Eric, TE, 1993, 1994
2	Green, Ernie, HB-FB, 1966, 1967
4	Green, Gary, DB, 1981, 1982, 1983, 1985
1	Green, Gaston, RB, 1991
1	Green, Harold, RB, 1992
2	Green, Hugh, LB, 1982, 1983
2	Green, Jacob, DE, 1986, 1987
1	Green, John, DE-E, 1950
2	Green, Roy, WR-DB, 1983, 1984
1	Green, Tony, RB, 1978
2	Green, Trent, QB, 2003, 2005
10	Greene, Joe, DT, 1969, 1970, 1971, 1972, 1973, 1974, 1975, 1976, 1978, 1979
5	Greene, Kevin, LB-DE, 1989, 1994, 1995, 1996, 1998
1	Greene, Tony, DB, 1977
1	Greenfield, Tom, C-LB, 1939
6	Greenwood, L.C., DE, 1973, 1974, 1975, 1976, 1978, 1979
9	Gregg, Forrest, T-G-DT, 1959, 1960, 1961, 1962, 1963, 1964, 1966, 1967, 1968
2	Gregory, Jack, DE, 1969, 1972
1	Grgich, Visco, G-MG-T-LB, 1950
2	Grier, Rosey, DT-DE, 1956, 1960
8	Griese, Bob, QB, 1967, 1968, 1970, 1971, 1973, 1974, 1977, 1978
1	Griese, Brian, QB, 2000
1	Griffith, Robert, DB, 2000
1	Grim, Bob, WR, 1971
2	Grimes, Billy, HB, 1950, 1951
4	Grimm, Russ, G-C, 1983, 1984, 1985, 1986
1	Grimsley, John, LB, 1988
1	Groom, Jerry, MG-DT-C-LB, 1954
9	Groza, Lou, T-C-DT-K, 1950, 1951, 1952, 1953, 1954, 1955, 1957, 1958, 1959
1	Grupp, Bob, P, 1979
7	Guy, Ray, P, 1973, 1974, 1975, 1976, 1977, 1978, 1980
1	Hackett, Dino, LB, 1988
1	Haddix, Wayne, DB, 1990
1	Haden, Jack, T, 1938
1	Haden, Pat, QB, 1977
6	Hadl, John, QB, 1964, 1965, 1968, 1969, 1972, 1973
1	Haji-Sheikh, Ali, K, 1983
5	Haley, Charles, DE-LB, 1988, 1990, 1991, 1994, 1995
2	Hall, Dante, WR, 2002, 2003
1	Hall, DeAngelo, DB, 2005
1	Hall, Parker, TB-HB, 1939
1	Hall, Ron, DB, 1963
8	Ham, Jack, LB, 1973, 1974, 1975, 1976, 1977, 1978, 1979, 1980
2	Hampton, Casey, NT-DT, 2003, 2005
4	Hampton, Dan, DE-DT, 1980, 1982, 1984, 1985
2	Hampton, Rodney, RB, 1992, 1993
9	Hanburger, Chris, LB, 1966, 1966, 1967, 1969, 1973, 1974, 1975, 1976
1	Hanken, Ray, E, 1938
4	Hanks, Merton, DB, 1994, 1995, 1996, 1997
9	Hannah, John, G, 1976, 1978, 1979, 1980, 1981, 1982, 1983, 1984, 1985

TOTAL	NAME, POSITION, YEARS
2	Hanner, Dave, DT, 1953, 1954
1	Hansen, Brian, P, 1984
1	Hanson, Chris, P, 2002
2	Hanson, Jason, K, 1997, 1999
1	Harbaugh, Jim, QB, 1995
2	Harder, Pat, FB-LB, 1950, 1952
2	Hardman, Cedrick, DE, 1971, 1975
1	Hardy, Jim, QB-DB, 1950
1	Hardy, Kevin, LB, 1999
2	Hare, Cece, B, 1941, 1942
1	Hare, Ray, B, 1942
1	Harmon, Ronnie, RB-WR, 1992
6	Harrah, Dennis, G-C, 1978, 1979, 1980, 1985, 1986, 1987
5	Harris, Cliff, DB, 1974, 1975, 1977, 1978, 1979
1	Harris, Dick, DB, 1961
9	Harris, Franco, RB, 1972, 1973, 1974, 1975, 1976, 1977, 1978, 1979, 1980
1	Harris, James, QB, 1974
1	Harris, Tim, LB-DE, 1989
1	Harris, Tommie, DT, 2005
1	Harrison, Dennis, DE, 1982
7	Harrison, Marvin, WR, 1999, 2000, 2001, 2002, 2003, 2004, 2005
2	Harrison, Rodney, DB, 1998, 2001
4	Hart, Jim, QB, 1974, 1975, 1976, 1977
1	Hart, Leon, E-FB-DE, 1951
1	Hart, Tommy, DE-LB, 1976
2	Hartings, Jeff, C-G, 2004, 2005
4	Harvey, Ken, LB, 1994, 1995, 1996, 1997
1	Haselrig, Carlton, G, 1992
2	Hasselbeck, Matt, QB, 2003, 2005
2	Hasty, James, DB, 1997, 1999
1	Hatcher, Dale, P, 1985
5	Hauss, Len, C, 1966, 1968, 1969, 1970, 1972
1	Hawkins, Rip, LB, 1963
5	Hawkins, Wayne, G, 1963, 1964, 1965, 1966, 1967
3	Hayes, Bob, SE-WR, 1965, 1966, 1967
5	Hayes, Lester, DB, 1980, 1981, 1982, 1983, 1984
3	Haynes, Abner, HB, 1961, 1962, 1964
3	Haynes, Mark, DB, 1982, 1983, 1984
9	Haynes, Mike, DB, 1976, 1977, 1978, 1979, 1980, 1982, 1984, 1985, 1986
2	Hazeltine, Matt, LB, 1962, 1964
4	Headrick, Sherrill, LB, 1961, 1962, 1965, 1966
2	Heap, Todd, TE, 2002, 2003
2	Hearst, Garrison, RB, 1998, 2001
1	Hebert, Bobby, QB, 1993
4	Hein, Mel, C-LB, 1938, 1939, 1940, 1941
1	Henderson, John, DT, 2004
1	Henderson, Thomas, LB, 1978
1	Henderson, William, FB, 2004
8	Hendricks, Ted, LB, 1971, 1972, 1973, 1974, 1980, 1981, 1982, 1983
1	Henke, Ed, DE-LB-G, 1952
5	Hennigan, Charley, WR, 1961, 1962, 1963, 1964, 1965
1	Henry, Travis, RB, 2002
1	Henry, Wally, WR, 1979
2	Hentrich, Craig, P, 1998, 2003
1	Herber, Arnie, TB-HB-DB-QB-BB, 1939
2	Herman, Dave, G-T, 1968, 1969
1	Herrera, Efren, K, 1977
1	Heyward, Craig, RB, 1995
6	Hickerson, Gene, G, 1965, 1966, 1967, 1968, 1969, 1970
4	Hicks, Dwight, DB, 1981, 1982, 1983, 1984
1	Hicks, W.K., DB, 1966
7	Hilgenberg, Jay, C-G, 1985, 1986, 1987, 1988, 1989, 1990, 1991
1	Hilgenberg, Joel, C-G, 1992
4	Hill, Calvin, RB, 1969, 1972, 1973, 1974
2	Hill, David, TE, 1978, 1979
2	Hill, Drew, WR, 1988, 1990
3	Hill, Harlon, E-DB, 1954, 1955, 1956
1	Hill, J.D., WR, 1972
3	Hill, Jimmy, DB, 1960, 1961, 1962
5	Hill, Kent, G-T, 1980, 1982, 1983, 1984, 1985
1	Hill, Mack Lee, FB-HB, 1964
3	Hill, Tony, WR, 1978, 1979, 1985
8	Hill, Winston, T, 1964, 1967, 1968, 1969, 1970, 1971, 1972, 1973
1	Hilliard, Dalton, RB, 1989
1	Hines, Glen Ray, T, 1968, 1969
3	Hinkle, Clarke, FB-LB-HB-DB, 1938, 1939, 1940
7	Hinton, Chris, T-G, 1983, 1985, 1986, 1987, 1988, 1989, 1991
3	Hirsch, Elroy, E-HB-DE, 1951, 1952, 1953
1	Hoaglin, Fred, C, 1969
1	Hoak, Dick, RB-FL, 1968
1	Hoard, Leroy, RB, 1994
1	Hock, John, G, 1956
1	Hoerner, Dick, FB, 1950
2	Hoernschemeyer, Bob, B, 1951, 1952
2	Hoffman, John, HB-FB-E-LB, 1953, 1955

TOTAL	NAME, POSITION, YEARS
1	Hollis, Mike, K, 1997
3	Holloway, Brian, T-G, 1983, 1984, 1985
3	Holman, Rodney, TE, 1988, 1989, 1990
2	Holmes, Pat, DE-DT, 1967, 1968
3	Holmes, Priest, RB, 2001, 2002, 2003
1	Holmes, Robert, RB, 1969
1	Holt, Pierce, DE-DT, 1992
5	Holt, Torry, WR, 2000, 2001, 2003, 2004, 2005
5	Holub, E.J., LB-C, 1962, 1962, 1964, 1965, 1966
1	Hopkins, Brad, T, 2000
1	Hopkins, Wes, DB, 1985
1	Hopp, Harry, B, 1942
1	Horan, Mike, P, 1988
4	Horn, Joe, WR, 2000, 2001, 2002, 2004
2	Hornung, Paul, HB-FB-QB, 1959, 1960
1	Horton, Ethan, TE-RB, 1991
1	Hostetler, Jeff, QB, 1994
4	Houston, Jim, LB-DE, 1964, 1965, 1969, 1970
12	Houston, Ken, DB, 1968, 1969, 1970, 1971, 1972, 1973, 1974, 1975, 1976, 1977, 1978, 1979
1	Howard, Desmond, WR, 2000
1	Howard, Erik, NT-DT-DE, 1990
1	Howell, Jim Lee, E, 1938
6	Howley, Chuck, LB, 1965, 1966, 1967, 1968, 1969, 1971
4	Howton, Billy, E, 1952, 1955, 1956, 1957
3	Hubbard, Marv, RB, 1971, 1972, 1973
1	Hubbert, Brad, RB, 1967
1	Hudson, Bill, DT, 1961
1	Hudson, Dick, T-G, 1965
5	Huff, Sam, LB, 1958, 1959, 1960, 1961, 1964
1	Huffman, Dick, T, 1950
1	Hughes, Bill, G-C, 1941
2	Hughes, George, T-G, 1951, 1953
1	Hughes, Tyrone, DB, 1993
3	Hull, Kent, C, 1988, 1989, 1990
1	Humbert, Dick, E-DE, 1941
1	Humble, Weldon, G, 1950
1	Humphrey, Bobby, RB, 1990
6	Humphrey, Claude, DE, 1970, 1971, 1972, 1973, 1974, 1977
1	Hunt, Bobby, DB, 1964
4	Hunt, Jim, DT-DE, 1961, 1966, 1967, 1969
1	Hunter, Art, C-T, 1959
3	Husmann, Ed, DT-G-DE-LB, 1961, 1962, 1963
3	Hutchinson, Steve, G, 2003, 2004, 2005
4	Hutson, Don, E-DB-DE, 1939, 1940, 1941, 1942
2	Ilkin, Tunch, T-G-C, 1988, 1989
2	Irvin, LeRoy, DB, 1985, 1986
5	Irvin, Michael, WR, 1991, 1992, 1993, 1994, 1995
4	Isbell, Cecil, TB-HB, 1938, 1939, 1941, 1942
1	Ivy, Pop, E, 1942
3	Izzo, Larry, LB, 2000, 2002, 2004
1	Jackson, Bo, RB, 1990
2	Jackson, Earnest, RB, 1984, 1986
1	Jackson, Frank, FL-FB-SE-WR-HB, 1965
5	Jackson, Harold, WR-FL, 1969, 1972, 1973, 1975, 1977
5	Jackson, Keith, TE, 1988, 1989, 1990, 1992, 1996
2	Jackson, Monte, DB, 1976, 1977
3	Jackson, Rich, DE-LB, 1968, 1969, 1970
6	Jackson, Rickey, LB-DE, 1983, 1984, 1985, 1986, 1992, 1993
3	Jackson, Tom, LB, 1977, 1978, 1979
2	Jacobs, Harry, LB-DE, 1965, 1969
4	Jacoby, Joe, T-G, 1983, 1984, 1985, 1986
1	Jacunski, Harry, E, 1939
1	Jaeger, Jeff, K, 1991
1	Jagade, Chick, FB, 1953
1	James, Craig, RB, 1985
1	James, Dick, HB-DB, 1961
4	James, Edgerrin, RB, 1999, 2000, 2004, 2005
3	James, John, P, 1975, 1976, 1977
3	James, Robert, DB, 1972, 1973, 1974
1	James, Tommy, DB-HB, 1953
1	James, Tory, DB, 2004
2	Jamison, Al, T, 1961, 1962
2	Janik, Tom, DB, 1965, 1967
1	Jankowski, Ed, FB, 1939
1	Jaquess, Pete, DB, 1964
1	Jarmoluk, Mike, DT-T-MG, 1951
1	Jauron, Dick, DB, 1974
1	Jaworski, Ron, QB, 1980
4	Jefferson, John, WR, 1978, 1979, 1980, 1982
3	Jefferson, Roy, WR-SE, 1968, 1969, 1971
3	Jeffires, Haywood, WR, 1991, 1992, 1993
2	Jenkins, Alfred, WR, 1980, 1981
2	Jenkins, Kris, DT, 2002, 2003
1	Jennings, Brian, TE, 2004
4	Jennings, Dave, P, 1978, 1979, 1980, 1982
1	Jervey, Travis, RB, 1997
1	Jessie, Ron, WR, 1976
2	Jeter, Bob, DB-WR, 1967, 1969

TOTAL	NAME, POSITION, YEARS
1	Joe, Billy, RB, 1965
1	Johnson, Andre, WR, 2004
2	Johnson, Bill, C-LB, 1952, 1953
3	Johnson, Billy, WR, 1975, 1977, 1983
1	Johnson, Bob, C, 1968
2	Johnson, Brad, QB, 1999, 2002
3	Johnson, Chad, WR, 2003, 2004, 2005
1	Johnson, Charley, QB, 1963
3	Johnson, Charlie, NT, 1979, 1980, 1981
1	Johnson, Curley, RB-P-TE, 1965
1	Johnson, Ezra, DE, 1978
4	Johnson, Gary, DT-DE-NT, 1979, 1980, 1981, 1982
1	Johnson, Jack, T, 1939
5	Johnson, Jimmy, DB-HB, 1969, 1970, 1971, 1972, 1974
2	Johnson, Joe, DE, 1998, 2000
4	Johnson, John Henry, FB-HB, 1954, 1962, 1963, 1964
1	Johnson, Johnny, RB, 1990
3	Johnson, Keyshawn, WR, 1998, 1999, 2001
1	Johnson, Larry, LB-C-E, 1938
1	Johnson, Larry, RB, 2005
2	Johnson, Mike, LB, 1989, 1990
2	Johnson, Norm, K, 1984, 1993
2	Johnson, Pepper, LB, 1990, 1994
1	Johnson, Pete, RB, 1981
2	Johnson, Ron, RB, 1970, 1972
1	Johnson, Rudi, RB, 2004
1	Johnson, Tre', G-T, 1999
4	Johnson, Vaughan, LB, 1989, 1990, 1991, 1992
3	Johnson, Walter, DT, 1967, 1968, 1969
2	Johnston, Daryl, RB, 1993, 1994
1	Johnston, Mark, DB, 1961
1	Joiner, Charlie, WR, 1976, 1979, 1980
1	Jones, Art, WB-DB-HB-TB, 1941
1	Jones, Bert, QB, 1976
4	Jones, Brent, TE, 1992, 1993, 1994, 1995
1	Jones, Cody, DT-DE, 1978
8	Jones, Deacon, DE, 1964, 1965, 1966, 1967, 1968, 1969, 1970, 1972
1	Jones, Dub, HB-DB-WB-TB, 1951
1	Jones, Henry, DB, 1992
2	Jones, Homer, SE-WR, 1967, 1968
2	Jones, Rulon, DE, 1985, 1986
1	Jones, Sean, DE, 1993
7	Jones, Stan, G-DT-T, 1955, 1956, 1957, 1958, 1959, 1960, 1961
1	Jones, Tony, T-G, 1998
3	Jones, Too Tall, DE, 1981, 1982, 1983
6	Jones, Walter, T, 1999, 2001, 2002, 2003, 2004, 2005
4	Jordan, Henry, DT-DE, 1960, 1961, 1963, 1966
5	Jordan, Lee Roy, LB, 1967, 1968, 1969, 1973, 1974
6	Jordan, Steve, TE, 1986, 1987, 1988, 1989, 1990, 1991
1	Josephson, Les, RB, 1967
1	Joyce, Don, DE-DT, 1958
3	Joyner, Seth, LB-DB, 1991, 1993, 1994
1	June, Cato, LB, 2005
5	Junior, E.J., LB, 1984, 1985
5	Jurgensen, Sonny, QB, 1961, 1964, 1966, 1967, 1969
1	Justice, Ed, WB-HB, 1942
1	Kaminski, Larry, C, 1967
1	Kapp, Joe, QB, 1969
3	Karas, Emil, LB, 1961, 1962, 1963
1	Karcis, Bull, FB-BB-HB, 1938
4	Karras, Alex, DT, 1960, 1961, 1962, 1965
1	Kasay, John, K, 1996
1	Kassulke, Karl, DB, 1970
3	Katcavage, Jim, DE-DT, 1961, 1962, 1963
2	Kavanaugh, Ken, E, 1940, 1941
1	Keane, Tom, DB-E, 1953
3	Kearse, Jevon, DE, 1999, 2000, 2001
2	Keating, Tom, DT, 1966, 1967
3	Kelcher, Louie, DT-NT, 1977, 1978, 1980
1	Kell, Paul, T, 1939
1	Kellermann, Ernie, DB, 1968
4	Kelly, Jim, QB, 1987, 1990, 1991, 1992
6	Kelly, Leroy, RB, 1966, 1967, 1968, 1969, 1970, 1971
7	Kemp, Jack, QB, 1961, 1962, 1963, 1964, 1965, 1966, 1969
5	Kenn, Mike, T, 1980, 1981, 1982, 1983, 1984
8	Kennedy, Cortez, DT, 1991, 1992, 1993, 1994, 1995, 1996, 1998, 1999
3	Kennedy, Lincoln, T-G, 2000, 2001, 2002
1	Kenney, Bill, QB, 1983
1	Kerney, Patrick, DE, 2004
1	Keys, Brady, DB-HB, 1966
1	Khayat, Bob, G-K-C, 1960
2	Kiick, Jim, RB, 1968, 1969
1	Kilmer, Billy, QB-HB, 1972
3	Kilroy, Bucko, G-MG-T-DT, 1952, 1953, 1954

THE PRO BOWL: ALPHABETICAL LIST

TOTAL	NAME, POSITION, YEARS
1	Mehl, Lance, LB, 1985
3	Meinert, Dale, LB-G, 1963, 1965, 1967
2	Mellus, John, T, 1938, 1941
1	Mercer, Mike, K, 1967
3	Meredith, Don, QB, 1966, 1967, 1968
1	Meredith, Dudley, DT, 1965
1	Merriman, Shawne, LB, 2005
3	Merriweather, Mike, LB, 1984, 1985, 1986
1	Mertens, Jerry, DB, 1958
3	Metcalf, Eric, RB-WR, 1993, 1994, 1997
3	Metcalf, Terry, RB-WR, 1974, 1975, 1977
2	Michael, Rich, T, 1962, 1963
2	Michaels, Lou, DE-K, 1962, 1963
5	Michaels, Walt, LB, 1955, 1956, 1957, 1958, 1959
1	Michalik, Art, MG-LB-G, 1953
1	Middleton, Terdell, RB, 1978
2	Mihal, Joe, T, 1940, 1941
1	Mike-Mayer, Nick, K, 1973
2	Milburn, Glyn, RB-WR, 1995, 1999
2	Millard, Keith, DT-NT-DE, 1988, 1989
1	Millen, Matt, LB, 1988
1	Miller, Alan, FB, 1961
5	Miller, Anthony, WR, 1989, 1990, 1992, 1993, 1995
1	Miller, Chris, QB, 1991
3	Miller, Fred, DT, 1967, 1968, 1969
1	Miller, Jamir, LB, 2001
2	Miller, Junior, TE, 1980, 1981
2	Miller, Paul, DE, 1955, 1956
1	Milligan, Hanik, DB, 2005
4	Milloy, Lawyer, DB, 1998, 1999, 2001, 2002
1	Mills, John Henry, LB, 1996
1	Mills, Pete, WR, 1965
5	Mills, Sam, LB, 1987, 1988, 1991, 1992, 1996
1	Mingo, Gene, HB-K, 1962
4	Minnifield, Frank, DB, 1986, 1987, 1988, 1989
2	Mischak, Bob, G-TE, 1961, 1962
4	Mitchell, Bobby, FL-HB-WR, 1960, 1962, 1963, 1964
1	Mitchell, Brian, RB, 1995
2	Mitchell, Jim, TE, 1969, 1972
1	Mitchell, Keith, LB, 2000
1	Mitchell, Leroy, DB, 1968
3	Mitchell, Lydell, RB, 1975, 1976, 1977
8	Mix, Ron, T-G, 1961, 1962, 1963, 1964, 1965, 1966, 1967, 1968
1	Modzelewski, Dick, DT, 1964
1	Moegle, Dicky, DB-HB-FB, 1955
1	Mojsiejenko, Ralf, P, 1987
3	Monk, Art, WR, 1984, 1985, 1986
8	Montana, Joe, QB, 1981, 1983, 1984, 1985, 1987, 1989, 1990, 1993
1	Montgomery, Greg, P, 1993
2	Montgomery, Wilbert, RB, 1978, 1979
4	Montoya, Max, G, 1986, 1988, 1989, 1993
9	Moon, Warren, QB, 1988, 1989, 1990, 1991, 1992, 1993, 1994, 1995, 1997
1	Moore, Allen, DE, 1939
4	Moore, Herman, WR, 1994, 1995, 1996, 1997
7	Moore, Lenny, HB-FL, 1956, 1958, 1959, 1960, 1961, 1962, 1964
1	Moore, Nat, WR-RB, 1977
2	Moore, Rob, WR, 1994, 1997
1	Moore, Tom, HB-FB, 1962
1	Moore, Wayne, T, 1973
1	Moore, Wilbur, WB-HB-DB-FB, 1942
2	Moore, Zeke, DB, 1969, 1970
1	Moorman, Brian, P, 2005
1	Morgan, Dan, LB, 2004
4	Morgan, Stanley, WR, 1979, 1980, 1986, 1987
2	Morin, Milt, TE, 1968, 1971
2	Morrall, Earl, QB, 1957, 1968
1	Morris, Dennit, LB, 1961
2	Morris, Joe, RB, 1985, 1986
1	Morris, Johnny, FL-HB, 1960
7	Morris, Jon, C, 1964, 1965, 1966, 1967, 1968, 1969, 1970
3	Morris, Mercury, RB, 1971, 1972, 1973
1	Morrison, Fred, FB-HB, 1955
3	Morrow, John, C-G, 1961, 1963
3	Mosebar, Don, C-T-G, 1986, 1990, 1991
2	Moseley, Mark, K, 1979, 1982
2	Moses, Haven, WR-SE, 1969, 1973
5	Moss, Randy, WR, 1998, 1999, 2000, 2002, 2003
1	Moss, Santana, WR, 2005
1	Motley, Marion, FB-LB, 1950
3	Moulds, Eric, WR, 1998, 2000, 2002
3	Mudd, Howard, G, 1966, 1967, 1968
2	Muhammad, Muhsin, WR, 1999, 2004
1	Mul-Key, Herb, RB, 1973
2	Mulleneaux, Carl, E, 1939, 1940
9	Munchak, Mike, G, 1984, 1985, 1987, 1988, 1989, 1990, 1991, 1992, 1993
3	Muncie, Chuck, RB, 1979, 1981, 1982

TOTAL	NAME, POSITION, YEARS
11	Munoz, Anthony, T, 1981, 1982, 1983, 1984, 1985, 1986, 1987, 1988, 1989, 1990, 1991
1	Murphy, Mark, DB, 1983
2	Murray, Eddie, K, 1980, 1989
3	Musso, George, G-T, 1939, 1940, 1941
1	Mutscheller, Jim, E-DE, 1957
1	Myers, Chip, WR, 1972
1	Myers, Tom, DB, 1979
1	Nagler, Gern, E, 1958
5	Nalen, Tom, C, 1997, 1998, 1999, 2000, 2003
5	Namath, Joe, QB, 1965, 1967, 1968, 1969, 1972
1	Nance, Jim, RB, 1966, 1967
1	Nash, Joe, NT-DT, 1984
1	Naumoff, Paul, LB, 1970
1	Neal, Ed, MG-C-G-T, 1950
2	Neal, Lorenzo, FB, 2002, 2005
2	Neely, Ralph, T-G, 1967, 1969
1	Neighbors, Billy, G, 1963
3	Nelms, Mike, DB, 1980, 1981, 1982
1	Nelsen, Bill, QB, 1969
1	Nelson, Andy, DB, 1960
3	Nelson, Steve, LB, 1980, 1984, 1985
1	Neville, Tom, T, 1966
2	Newberry, Jeremy, C-G, 2001, 2002
2	Newberry, Tom, G-C, 1988, 1989
4	Newman, Ed, G, 1981, 1982, 1983, 1984
5	Newsome, Ozzie, TE, 1981, 1984, 1985
6	Newton, Nate, G-T, 1992, 1993, 1994, 1995, 1996, 1998
3	Nickel, Elbie, E-DE, 1952, 1953, 1956
5	Nickerson, Hardy, LB, 1993, 1996, 1997, 1998, 1999
2	Niemi, Laurie, T-DT, 1951, 1952
6	Niland, John, G, 1968, 1969, 1970, 1971, 1972, 1973
3	Nisby, John, G, 1959, 1961, 1962
1	Nitschke, Ray, LB, 1964
5	Nobis, Tommy, LB, 1966, 1967, 1968, 1970, 1972
2	Nolting, Ray, HB, 1940, 1941
10	Nomellini, Leo, DT-T, 1950, 1951, 1952, 1953, 1956, 1957, 1958, 1959, 1960, 1961
1	Noonan, Karl, SE-FL-WR, 1968
2	Norton, Don, E, 1961, 1962
5	Norton, Jerry, DB-HB, 1957, 1958, 1959, 1961, 1962
3	Norton, Jim, DB-P, 1962, 1963, 1967
3	Norton, Ken, LB, 1993, 1995, 1997
1	Norwood, Scott, K, 1988
5	Novacek, Jay, TE, 1991, 1992, 1993, 1994, 1995
2	Nowaskey, Bob, E-DE, 1940, 1941
1	Nutter, Buzz, C-LB, 1962
2	Nye, Blaine, G, 1974, 1976
1	Oakes, Don, T-DT, 1967
5	Oates, Bart, C, 1990, 1991, 1993, 1994, 1995
1	O'Brien, Davey, QB-TB, 1939
2	O'Brien, Ken, QB, 1985, 1991
1	Odom, Steve, WR, 1975
2	Odomes, Nate, DB, 1992, 1993
4	Odoms, Riley, TE, 1973, 1974, 1975, 1978
1	O'Donnell, Joe, G-T, 1965
1	O'Donnell, Neil, QB, 1992
5	Offerdahl, John, LB, 1986, 1987, 1988, 1989, 1990
9	Ogden, Jonathan, T-G, 1997, 1998, 1999, 2000, 2001, 2002, 2003, 2004, 2005
1	Ogunleye, Adewale, DE, 2003
2	Okoye, Christian, RB, 1989, 1991
1	Oldershaw, Doug, G-E, 1940
14	Olsen, Merlin, DT, 1962, 1963, 1964, 1965, 1966, 1967, 1968, 1969, 1970, 1971, 1972, 1973, 1974, 1975
1	Olson, Harold, T, 1961
2	Olszewski, Johnny, FB-HB, 1953, 1955
2	O'Neal, Deltha, DB, 2001, 2005
6	O'Neal, Leslie, DE-LB, 1989, 1990, 1992, 1993, 1994, 1995
2	Orr, Jimmy, FL-E-SE-WR, 1959, 1965
1	Osborn, Dave, RB, 1970
3	Osmanski, Bill, FB, 1939, 1940, 1941
1	Otis, Jim, RB, 1975
1	Otto, Gus, LB, 1969
12	Otto, Jim, C, 1961, 1962, 1963, 1964, 1965, 1966, 1967, 1968, 1969, 1970, 1971, 1972
1	Owens, Steve, RB, 1971
5	Owens, Terrell, WR, 2000, 2001, 2002, 2003, 2004
7	Pace, Orlando, T, 1999, 2000, 2001, 2002, 2003, 2004, 2005
9	Page, Alan, DT, 1968, 1969, 1970, 1971, 1972, 1973, 1974, 1975, 1976
1	Palmer, Carson, QB, 2005
1	Paluck, John, DE, 1964
1	Panfil, Ken, T, 1959
1	Pardee, Jack, LB, 1963
3	Parilli, Babe, QB, 1963, 1964, 1966

TOTAL	NAME, POSITION, YEARS
8	Parker, Jim, T-G, 1958, 1959, 1960, 1961, 1962, 1963, 1964, 1965
3	Parks, Dave, SE-TE-WR, 1964, 1965, 1966
2	Parrish, Bernie, DB, 1960, 1963
8	Parrish, Lemar, DB, 1970, 1971, 1974, 1975, 1976, 1977, 1979, 1980
1	Parry, Ox, T, 1938
1	Pastorini, Dan, QB, 1975
5	Patton, Jimmy, DB, 1958, 1959, 1960, 1961, 1962
3	Paul, Don, LB-MG-C, 1951, 1952, 1953
4	Paul, Don, DB-HB, 1953, 1956, 1957, 1958
2	Paulson, Dainard, DB, 1964, 1965
4	Paup, Bryce, LB, 1994, 1995, 1996, 1997
9	Payton, Walter, RB, 1976, 1977, 1978, 1979, 1980, 1983, 1984, 1985, 1986
1	Pear, Dave, NT-DT, 1978
3	Pearson, Drew, WR, 1974, 1976, 1977
2	Peoples, Woody, G, 1972, 1973
2	Peppers, Julius, DE, 2004, 2005
6	Perkins, Don, FB-HB, 1961, 1962, 1963, 1966, 1967, 1968
3	Perry, Joe, FB, 1952, 1953, 1954
6	Perry, Michael Dean, DT-DE, 1989, 1990, 1991, 1993, 1994, 1996
2	Perry, Rod, DB, 1978, 1980
3	Peters, Floyd, DT, 1964, 1966, 1967
1	Peters, Tony, DB, 1982
1	Peters, Volney, DT-T-DE, 1955
2	Peterson, Julian, LB, 2002, 2003
4	Petitbon, Richie, DB, 1962, 1963, 1966, 1967
1	Petty, John, FB, 1942
2	Philbin, Gerry, DE, 1968, 1969
3	Phillips, Red, E, 1960, 1961, 1962
2	Pickens, Carl, WR, 1995, 1996
2	Pietrosante, Nick, FB, 1960, 1961
6	Pihos, Pete, E-DE, 1950, 1951, 1952, 1953, 1954, 1955
2	Pinckert, Ernie, B, 1938, 1939
2	Plasman, Dick, E-T, 1940, 1941
1	Player, Scott, P, 2000
2	Plum, Milt, QB, 1960, 1961
1	Plummer, Jake, QB, 2005
2	Plunkett, Sherman, T, 1964, 1966
1	Podoley, Jim, HB-E, 1957
1	Poillon, Dick, B, 1942
2	Polamalu, Troy, DB, 2004, 2005
1	Polsfoot, Fran, E, 1951
2	Pool, Hampton, E, 1940, 1941
2	Poole, Jim, E, 1938, 1939, 1940
3	Porcher, Robert, DE-DT, 1997, 1999, 2001
3	Porter, Joey, LB, 2002, 2004, 2005
2	Porter, Rufus, LB-DE, 1988, 1989
1	Portis, Clinton, RB, 2003
2	Post, Dickie, RB, 1967, 1969
3	Pottios, Myron, LB, 1961, 1963, 1964
4	Powell, Art, SE-DB-WR, 1963, 1964, 1965, 1966
5	Powell, Marvin, T, 1979, 1980, 1981, 1982, 1983
1	Preston, Roell, WR, 1998
1	Prestridge, Luke, P, 1982
1	Price, Cotton, TB-DB-QB, 1940
3	Price, Eddie, FB, 1951, 1952, 1954
1	Pritchard, Bosh, HB, 1942
2	Promuto, Vince, G, 1963, 1964
5	Pruitt, Greg, RB, 1973, 1974, 1976, 1977, 1983
2	Pruitt, Mike, RB, 1979, 1980
4	Pryce, Trevor, DT-DE, 1999, 2000, 2001, 2002
4	Putnam, Duane, G, 1954, 1955, 1957, 1958
1	Pyle, Mike, C, 1963
1	Quarles, Shelton, LB, 2002
2	Quick, Mike, WR, 1983, 1984, 1985, 1986, 1987
2	Quillan, Fred, C, 1984, 1985
1	Quinlan, Skeets, HB, 1954
1	Rackers, Neil, K, 2005
1	Radovich, Bill, G, 1938
7	Randle, John, DT-DE, 1993, 1994, 1995, 1996, 1997, 1998, 2001
4	Randle, Sonny, E-WR, 1960, 1961, 1962, 1965
4	Rashad, Ahmad, WR, 1978, 1979, 1980, 1981
1	Ray, Baby, T, 1939
1	Reaves, Ken, DB, 1969
3	Rechichar, Bert, DB-LB-HB-E, 1955, 1956, 1957
1	Redman, Rick, LB-P, 1967
2	Reed, Alvin, TE, 1968, 1969
7	Reed, Andre, WR, 1988, 1989, 1990, 1991, 1992, 1993, 1994
1	Reed, Ed, DB, 2003, 2004
1	Reese, Ike, LB, 2004
3	Reger, John, LB-G, 1959, 1960, 1961
1	Reichow, Jerry, E-QB, 1961
2	Reid, Mike, DT, 1972, 1973
1	Reinfeldt, Mike, DB, 1979
2	Rembert, Johnny, LB, 1988, 1989
10	Renfro, Mel, DB-RB, 1964, 1965, 1966, 1967, 1968, 1969, 1970, 1971, 1972, 1973
3	Renfro, Ray, HB-FL, 1953, 1957, 1960

THE PRO BOWL: ALPHABETICAL LIST

TOTAL	NAME, POSITION, YEARS
5	Retzlaff, Pete, E-HB-TE, 1958, 1960, 1963, 1964, 1965
1	Reveiz, Fuad, K, 1994
3	Reynolds, Bob, T, 1966, 1968, 1969
2	Reynolds, Jack, LB, 1975, 1980
12	Rice, Jerry, WR, 1986, 1987, 1988, 1989, 1990, 1991, 1992, 1993, 1995, 1996, 1998, 2002
1	Rice, Ken, T-G, 1961
3	Rice, Simeon, DE, 1999, 2002, 2003
1	Richards, Kink, B, 1938
1	Richardson, Jess, DT, 1959
2	Richardson, Tony, FB, 2003, 2004
2	Richardson, Willie, FL-WR, 1967, 1968
8	Richter, Les, LB-MG, 1954, 1955, 1956, 1957, 1958, 1959, 1960, 1961
1	Riffle, Dick, B, 1941
1	Riggins, John, RB, 1975
3	Riggs, Gerald, RB, 1985, 1986, 1987
10	Ringo, Jim, C, 1957, 1958, 1959, 1960, 1961, 1962, 1963, 1964, 1965, 1967
1	Risien, Cody, T-G, 1986, 1987
5	Rison, Andre, WR, 1990, 1991, 1992, 1993, 1997
2	Ritcher, Jim, G, 1991, 1992
3	Rivera, Marco, G, 2002, 2003, 2004
1	Roaches, Carl, WR, 1981
11	Roaf, Willie, T, 1994, 1995, 1996, 1997, 1998, 1999, 2000, 2002, 2003, 2004, 2005
1	Robb, Joe, DE-LB, 1966
1	Robbins, Barret, C, 2002
1	Roberson, Bo, FL-HB-WR, 1965
1	Roberts, Gene, HB-FB, 1950
1	Roberts, William, G-T, 1990
6	Robertson, Isiah, LB, 1971, 1973, 1974, 1975, 1976, 1977
3	Robinson, Dave, LB, 1966, 1967, 1969
3	Robinson, Eugene, DB, 1992, 1993, 1998
1	Robinson, Jerry, LB, 1981
7	Robinson, Johnny, DB-FL-HB, 1963, 1964, 1965, 1966, 1967, 1968, 1970
1	Robinson, Koren, WR, 2005
2	Robinson, Paul, RB, 1968, 1969
2	Robinson, Wayne, LB-C, 1954, 1955
7	Robustelli, Andy, DE, 1953, 1955, 1956, 1957, 1959, 1960, 1961
3	Roby, Reggie, P, 1984, 1989, 1994
1	Rochester, Paul, DT, 1961
1	Rock, Walt, T-DT, 1965
1	Rogel, Fran, FB, 1956
2	Rogers, George, RB, 1981, 1982
2	Rogers, Shaun, DT, 2004, 2005
1	Rohde, Len, T, 1970
2	Roland, Johnny, RB, 1966, 1967
1	Rolle, Samari, DB, 2000
2	Romanowski, Bill, LB, 1996, 1998
1	Ross, Dan, TE, 1982
2	Ross, Kevin, DB, 1989, 1990
1	Rossovich, Tim, LB-DE, 1969
1	Rossum, Allen, DB, 2004
4	Rote, Kyle, E-HB, 1953, 1954, 1955, 1956
2	Rote, Tobin, QB, 1956, 1963
1	Rowe, Bob, DT-DE, 1968
2	Rozier, Mike, RB, 1987, 1988
1	Rucinski, Ed, E, 1942
1	Ruddy, Tim, C, 2000
4	Rudnay, Jack, C, 1973, 1974, 1975, 1976
1	Runyan, Jon, T, 2002
7	Russell, Andy, LB, 1968, 1970, 1971, 1972, 1973, 1974, 1975
2	Russell, Darrell, DT-DE, 1998, 1999
2	Rutgens, Joe, DT, 1963, 1965
1	Rutkowski, Ed, QB-HB-SE-WR, 1965
3	Ryan, Frank, QB, 1964, 1965, 1966
2	Rypien, Mark, QB, 1989, 1991
5	Saimes, George, DB, 1964, 1965, 1966, 1967, 1968
1	Saleaumua, Dan, DT-NT-DE, 1995
3	Samuels, Chris, T, 2001, 2002, 2005
10	Sanders, Barry, RB, 1989, 1990, 1991, 1992, 1993, 1994, 1995, 1996, 1997, 1998
1	Sanders, Bob, DB, 2005
7	Sanders, Charlie, TE, 1968, 1969, 1970, 1971, 1974, 1975, 1976
8	Sanders, Deion, DB-WR, 1991, 1992, 1993, 1994, 1996, 1997, 1998, 1999
1	Sanders, Spec, TB-DB-HB, 1950
1	Sandusky, Mike, G, 1960
2	Sanford, Leo, LB, 1956, 1957
2	Sapolu, Jesse, C-G, 1993, 1994
7	Sapp, Warren, DT, 1997, 1998, 1999, 2000, 2001, 2002, 2003
1	Saturday, Jeff, C, 2005
4	Sauer, George, SE-WR, 1966, 1967, 1968, 1969
3	Sauerbrun, Todd, P, 2001, 2002, 2003
6	Saul, Rich, C-G-T, 1976, 1977, 1978, 1979, 1980, 1981
4	Sayers, Gale, RB, 1965, 1966, 1967, 1969

TOTAL	NAME, POSITION, YEARS
1	Scarpitto, Bob, FL-WR-P, 1966
6	Schafrath, Dick, T-G-DE, 1963, 1964, 1965, 1966, 1967, 1968
2	Schlereth, Mark, G-C, 1991, 1998
3	Schmidt, Bob, C-T-G, 1961, 1962, 1963
1	Schmidt, Henry, DT-E, 1965
9	Schmidt, Joe, LB, 1954, 1955, 1956, 1957, 1958, 1959, 1960, 1961, 1962
1	Schneck, Mike, C, 2005
2	Schnelker, Bob, E, 1958, 1959
2	Schnellbacher, Otto, DB-E, 1950, 1951
1	Schottenheimer, Marty, LB, 1965
3	Schrader, Jim, C-T, 1958, 1959, 1961
1	Schroeder, Gene, E-DB, 1952
1	Schroeder, Jay, QB, 1986
3	Schuh, Harry, T, 1967, 1969, 1970
1	Schulters, Lance, DB, 1999
1	Schultz, Charlie, T, 1939
1	Schwantz, Jim, LB, 1996
4	Schwartz, Perry, E, 1938, 1939, 1941, 1942
1	Scibelli, Joe, G-T, 1968
1	Scott, Clarence, DB, 1973
3	Scott, Herbert, G-T, 1979, 1980, 1981
5	Scott, Jake, DB, 1971, 1972, 1973, 1974, 1975
1	Scott, Todd, DB, 1992
2	Scott, Tom, DE-LB, 1957, 1958
1	Scudero, Joe, DB-HB, 1955
1	Searcy, Leon, T, 1999
12	Seau, Junior, LB, 1991, 1992, 1993, 1994, 1995, 1996, 1997, 1998, 1999, 2000, 2001, 2002
1	Sellers, Ron, WR, 1969
6	Selmon, Lee Roy, DE-DT, 1979, 1980, 1981, 1982, 1983, 1984
1	Senser, Joe, TE, 1981
1	Septien, Rafael, K, 1981
4	Sestak, Tom, DT, 1962, 1963, 1964, 1965
1	Settle, John, RB, 1988
4	Sewell, Harley, G-LB, 1957, 1958, 1959, 1962
1	Seymour, Bob, HB-FB, 1942
4	Seymour, Richard, DE-DT, 2002, 2003, 2004, 2005
1	Shaffer, Lee, B, 1938
1	Shanklin, Ron, WR, 1973
3	Sharpe, Luis, T, 1987, 1988, 1989
8	Sharpe, Shannon, TE, 1992, 1993, 1994, 1995, 1996, 1997, 1998, 2001
5	Sharpe, Sterling, WR, 1989, 1990, 1992, 1993, 1994
3	Sharper, Darren, DB, 2000, 2002, 2005
8	Shaw, Billy, G, 1962, 1963, 1964, 1965, 1966, 1967, 1968, 1969
1	Shaw, Bob, E, 1950
8	Shell, Art, T, 1972, 1973, 1974, 1975, 1976, 1977, 1978, 1980
5	Shell, Donnie, DB, 1978, 1979, 1980, 1981, 1982
4	Shelley, Elbert, DB, 1992, 1993, 1994, 1995
1	Sheppard, Lito, DB, 2004
4	Sherk, Jerry, DT-DE-NT, 1973, 1974, 1975, 1976
1	Sherman, Solly, QB, 1940
2	Sherman, Will, DB, 1955, 1958
11	Shields, Will, G, 1995, 1996, 1997, 1998, 1999, 2000, 2001, 2002, 2003, 2004, 2005
3	Shipkey, Jerry, LB-FB-DB, 1950, 1951, 1952
1	Shirk, John, E-DE, 1940
3	Shockey, Jeremy, TE, 2002, 2003, 2005
5	Shofner, Del, E-DB, 1958, 1959, 1961, 1962, 1963
1	Shonta, Chuck, DB, 1966
2	Shugart, Clyde, G-T, 1941, 1942
2	Shuler, Mickey, TE, 1986, 1988
3	Siegal, John, E-DE, 1940, 1941, 1942
4	Siemon, Jeff, LB, 1973, 1975, 1976, 1977
2	Sikahema, Vai, RB, 1986, 1987
1	Silas, Sam, DT, 1965
1	Simington, Milt, G, 1942
2	Simmons, Clyde, DE-DT, 1991, 1992
1	Simmons, Jack, C-G-T, 1956
2	Simms, Phil, QB, 1985, 1993
1	Simon, Corey, DT, 2003
6	Simpson, O.J., RB, 1969, 1972, 1973, 1974, 1975, 1976
3	Sims, Billy, RB, 1980, 1981, 1982
3	Sims, Keith, G, 1993, 1994, 1995
3	Sinclair, Michael, DE, 1996, 1997, 1998
10	Singletary, Mike, LB, 1983, 1984, 1985, 1986, 1987, 1988, 1989, 1990, 1991, 1992
1	Sipe, Brian, QB, 1980
2	Sisemore, Jerry, T-G, 1979, 1981
1	Sistrunk, Otis, DT-DE-NT, 1974
1	Sivell, Jim, G, 1941
1	Skladany, Tom, P, 1981
1	Skoronski, Bob, T-C, 1966
1	Slade, Chris, LB, 1997
7	Slater, Jackie, T-G, 1983, 1985, 1986, 1987, 1988, 1989, 1990
2	Slaughter, Webster, WR, 1989, 1993

TOTAL	NAME, POSITION, YEARS
1	Slivinski, Steve, G-LB, 1942
1	Sloan, David, TE, 1999
5	Smerlas, Fred, NT-DT, 1980, 1981, 1982, 1983, 1988
1	Smith, Aaron, DE, 2004
2	Smith, Al, LB, 1991, 1992
1	Smith, Bill, E-DE, 1939
1	Smith, Bob, DB-HB-WB, 1952
1	Smith, Bobby, HB, 1965
11	Smith, Bruce, DE, 1987, 1988, 1989, 1990, 1992, 1993, 1994, 1995, 1996, 1997, 1998
2	Smith, Bubba, DE-DT, 1970, 1971
6	Smith, Dennis, DB, 1985, 1986, 1989, 1990, 1991, 1993
1	Smith, Detron, RB, 1999
6	Smith, Doug, C-G-T, 1984, 1985, 1986, 1987, 1988, 1989
8	Smith, Emmitt, RB, 1990, 1991, 1992, 1993, 1994, 1995, 1998, 1999
1	Smith, Ernie, T, 1939
1	Smith, George, C, 1942
1	Smith, Harry, T, 1940
2	Smith, J.D., FB-HB-DB, 1959, 1962
1	Smith, J.D., T, 1961
2	Smith, J.T., WR, 1980, 1988
5	Smith, Jackie, TE, 1966, 1967, 1968, 1969, 1970
2	Smith, Jerry, TE-SE-FL, 1967, 1969
5	Smith, Jim Ray, G-T-DE, 1958, 1959, 1960, 1961, 1962
5	Smith, Jimmy, WR, 1997, 1998, 1999, 2000, 2001
1	Smith, John, K, 1980
1	Smith, Marvel, T, 2004
6	Smith, Neil, DE, 1991, 1992, 1993, 1994, 1995, 1997
2	Smith, Paul, DT-DE, 1972, 1973
2	Smith, Robert, RB, 1998, 2000
3	Smith, Rod, WR, 2000, 2001, 2005
1	Smith, Ron, DB-WR, 1972
2	Smith, Steve, WR, 2001, 2005
1	Smith, Stu, FB-LB-TB-DB, 1938
3	Snead, Norm, QB, 1963, 1965, 1972
3	Snell, Matt, RB, 1964, 1966, 1969
1	Snow, Jack, WR-SE, 1967
2	Snyder, Bob, TB-QB, 1940, 1941
2	Snyder, Lum, T, 1953, 1954
1	Soar, Hank, B, 1938
1	Sochia, Brian, NT-DE, 1988
1	Solt, Ron, G, 1987
3	Soltau, Gordie, E, 1951, 1952, 1953
1	Spadaccini, Vic, B, 1940
1	Speedie, Mac, E, 1950
4	Spielman, Chris, LB, 1989, 1990, 1991, 1994
2	Spikes, Takeo, LB, 2003, 2004
2	Spinney, Art, G-DE, 1959, 1960
1	Springs, Shawn, DB, 1998
4	Sprinkle, Ed, DE-E-G-LB, 1950, 1951, 1952, 1954
5	St. Clair, Bob, T, 1956, 1958, 1959, 1960, 1961
1	St. Jean, Len, G, 1966
4	Stabler, Ken, QB, 1973, 1974, 1976, 1977
1	Stacy, Billy, DB-FL, 1961
1	Stallings, Larry, LB, 1970
4	Stallworth, John, WR, 1979, 1982, 1983, 1984
2	Standlee, Norm, FB-LB, 1941, 1950
5	Stanfel, Dick, G, 1953, 1955, 1956, 1957, 1958
5	Stanfill, Bill, DE, 1969, 1971, 1972, 1973, 1974
4	Stark, Rohn, P, 1985, 1986, 1990, 1992
4	Starr, Bart, QB, 1960, 1961, 1962, 1966
6	Staubach, Roger, QB, 1971, 1975, 1976, 1977, 1978, 1979
9	Stautner, Ernie, DT-DE-G, 1952, 1953, 1955, 1956, 1957, 1958, 1959, 1960, 1961
1	Steed, Joel, NT, 1997
1	Stemrick, Greg, DB, 1980
6	Stenerud, Jan, K, 1968, 1969, 1970, 1971, 1975, 1984
1	Stephens, John, RB, 1988
5	Stephenson, Dwight, C-T, 1983, 1984, 1985, 1986, 1987
5	Stepnoski, Mark, C-G, 1992, 1993, 1994, 1995, 1996
2	Steussie, Todd, T, 1997, 1998
1	Stewart, Kordell, QB, 2001
4	Still, Art, DE, 1980, 1981, 1982, 1984
1	Stits, Bill, DB-HB, 1954
1	Stone, Donnie, HB-FB, 1961
3	Stone, Ron, G, 2000, 2001, 2002
3	Stovall, Jerry, DB-P, 1966, 1967, 1969
1	Stover, Matt, K, 2000
7	Strahan, Michael, DE, 1997, 1998, 1999, 2001, 2002, 2003, 2005
1	Stralka, Clem, G-T, 1942
6	Stratton, Mike, LB, 1963, 1964, 1965, 1966, 1967, 1968
1	Strickland, Larry, C, 1956
1	Stringer, Korey, T, 2000

TOTAL	NAME, POSITION, YEARS
1	Strong, Mack, FB, 2005
3	Stroud, Jack, G-T, 1955, 1957, 1960
3	Stroud, Marcus, DT, 2003, 2004, 2005
1	Strzykalski, Johnny, HB, 1950
3	Stubblefield, Dana, DT, 1994, 1995, 1997
2	Studstill, Pat, FL-HB-WR-P, 1965, 1966
2	Studwell, Scott, LB, 1987, 1988
2	Sturm, Jerry, C-T-G, 1964, 1966
4	Stydahar, Joe, T, 1938, 1939, 1940, 1941
2	Sugar, Leo, DE, 1958, 1960
1	Suggs, Terrell, LB-DE, 2004
2	Suggs, Walt, T-C, 1967, 1968
1	Sunde, Milt, G, 1966
2	Surtain, Patrick, DB, 2002, 2003
2	Svendsen, Bud, C-LB-G, 1939
1	Svoboda, Bill, LB-FB, 1953
2	Swann, Eric, DT-DE, 1995, 1996
3	Swann, Lynn, WR, 1975, 1978, 1978
9	Sweeney, Walt, G, 1964, 1965, 1966, 1967, 1968, 1969, 1970, 1971, 1972
1	Swenson, Bob, LB, 1981
5	Swilling, Pat, LB-DE, 1989, 1990, 1991, 1991, 1993
2	Swisher, Bob, HB, 1940, 1941
3	Szymanski, Dick, C-LB, 1955, 1962, 1964
6	Talamini, Bob, G, 1962, 1963, 1964, 1965, 1966, 1967
1	Talbert, Diron, DT-DE, 1974
3	Taliaferro, George, HB-TB-QB-DB, 1951, 1952, 1953
1	Taliaferro, Mike, QB, 1969
2	Talley, Darryl, LB, 1990, 1991
9	Tarkenton, Fran, QB, 1964, 1965, 1967, 1968, 1969, 1970, 1974, 1975, 1976
7	Tasker, Steve, WR, 1987, 1990, 1991, 1992, 1993, 1994, 1995
3	Tatum, Jack, DB, 1973, 1974, 1975
1	Tatupu, Lofa, LB, 2005
1	Tatupu, Mosi, RB, 1986
1	Taylor, Bobby, DB, 2002
1	Taylor, Bruce, DB, 1971
8	Taylor, Charley, WR-SE-RB, 1964, 1965, 1966, 1967, 1972, 1973, 1974, 1975
2	Taylor, Hugh, E, 1952, 1954
4	Taylor, Jason, DE, 2000, 2002, 2004, 2005
5	Taylor, Jim, FB, 1960, 1961, 1962, 1963, 1964
2	Taylor, John, WR, 1988, 1989
10	Taylor, Lawrence, LB, 1981, 1982, 1983, 1984, 1985, 1986, 1987, 1988, 1989, 1990
3	Taylor, Lionel, E-WR-FL, 1961, 1962, 1965
3	Taylor, Otis, WR-FL, 1966, 1971, 1972
2	Taylor, Rosey, DB, 1963, 1968
1	Terrell, Marvin, G, 1962
2	Testaverde, Vinny, QB, 1996, 1998
1	Teteak, Deral, LB-G, 1952
2	Theismann, Joe, QB, 1982, 1983
3	Thielemann, R.C., G-C, 1981, 1982, 1983
2	Thigpen, Yancey, WR, 1995, 1997
1	Thomas, Aaron, TE-SE, 1964
1	Thomas, Adalius, LB-DE, 2003
1	Thomas, Clendon, DB-E-FL-HB, 1963
9	Thomas, Derrick, LB, 1989, 1990, 1991, 1992, 1993, 1994, 1995, 1996, 1997
5	Thomas, Emmitt, DB, 1968, 1971, 1972, 1974, 1975
1	Thomas, Eric, DB, 1988
2	Thomas, Henry, DT-NT, 1991, 1992
1	Thomas, J.T., DB, 1976
1	Thomas, John, G-T-LB, 1966
1	Thomas, Mike, RB, 1976
2	Thomas, Pat, DB, 1978, 1980
5	Thomas, Thurman, RB, 1989, 1990, 1991, 1992, 1993
3	Thomas, Tra, T, 2001, 2002, 2004
2	Thomas, William, LB, 1995, 1996
6	Thomas, Zach, LB, 1999, 2000, 2001, 2002, 2003, 2005
3	Thomason, Bobby, QB, 1953, 1955, 1956
2	Thompson, Bennie, DB, 1991, 1998
3	Thompson, Bill, DB, 1977, 1978, 1981
1	Thompson, Reyna, DB, 1990
1	Thompson, Tommy, QB, 1942
1	Tilley, Pat, WR, 1980
1	Timmerman, Adam, G, 2001
6	Tingelhoff, Mick, C, 1964, 1965, 1966, 1967, 1968, 1969
1	Tinsley, Gaynell, E, 1938
1	Tinsley, Pete, G, 1939
5	Tippett, Andre, LB, 1984, 1985, 1986, 1987, 1988
1	Titchenal, Bob, E-C-LB-DE, 1942
6	Tittle, Y.A., QB, 1953, 1954, 1957, 1959, 1961, 1962
1	Tobeck, Robbie, C-G, 2005
2	Todd, Dick, B, 1940, 1942
2	Tolar, Charley, FB, 1961, 1962
1	Tolbert, Tony, DE, 1996

TOTAL	NAME, POSITION, YEARS
3	Tomlinson, LaDainian, RB, 2002, 2004, 2005
4	Toneff, Bob, DT-DE-T-LB-G, 1955, 1959, 1960, 1961
1	Tonnemaker, Clayton, LB-C, 1953
3	Toon, Al, WR, 1986, 1987, 1988
1	Torczon, LaVerne, DE, 1961
3	Torgeson, LaVern, LB-C, 1954, 1955, 1956
1	Torrance, Jack, T, 1940
1	Toth, Zollie, FB, 1950
4	Towler, Dan, FB, 1951, 1952, 1953, 1954
2	Townsend, Greg, DE-LB-DT-NT, 1990, 1991
2	Tracey, John, LB-E-DE, 1965, 1966
2	Tracy, Tom, HB-FB, 1958, 1960
1	Treadwell, David, K, 1989
2	Trippi, Charlie, HB-QB-DB, 1952, 1953
1	Tripson, John, T, 1941
1	Tripucka, Frank, QB, 1962
4	Trotter, Jeremiah, LB, 2000, 2001, 2004, 2005
4	Trumpy, Bob, TE-WR, 1968, 1969, 1970, 1973
1	Tubbs, Jerry, LB-C, 1962
1	Tubbs, Winfred, LB, 1998
5	Tuggle, Jessie, LB, 1992, 1994, 1995, 1997, 1998
2	Tuinei, Mark, T-C-DT, 1994, 1995
9	Tunnell, Emlen, DB, 1950, 1951, 1952, 1953, 1954, 1955, 1956, 1957, 1959
1	Tupa, Tom, QB-P, 1999
1	Turk, Matt, P, 1996, 1997, 1998
1	Turnbull, Renaldo, DE-LB, 1993
1	Turner, Bake, WR-SE, 1963
4	Turner, Bulldog, C-T-LB-G, 1940, 1941, 1950, 1951
1	Turner, Cecil, FL-WR, 1970
2	Turner, Eric, DB, 1994, 1996
2	Turner, Jim, K, 1968, 1969
1	Turner, Keena, LB, 1984
1	Tuten, Rick, P, 1994
2	Tuttle, Orville, G, 1938, 1939
1	Tyler, Wendell, RB, 1984
1	Tyree, David, WR, 2005
9	Tyrer, Jim, T, 1962, 1963, 1964, 1965, 1966, 1968, 1969, 1970, 1971
1	Ulinski, Harry, C, 1955
1	Umenyiora, Osi, DE, 2005
10	Unitas, Johnny, QB, 1957, 1958, 1959, 1960, 1961, 1962, 1963, 1964, 1966, 1967
4	Upchurch, Rick, WR, 1978, 1979, 1980, 1982
7	Upshaw, Gene, G, 1968, 1972, 1973, 1974, 1975, 1976, 1977
1	Uram, Andy, RB, 1939
5	Urlacher, Brian, LB, 2000, 2001, 2002, 2003, 2005
9	Van Brocklin, Norm, QB, 1950, 1951, 1952, 1953, 1954, 1955, 1958, 1959, 1960
1	Van Dyke, Bruce, G, 1973
5	Van Note, Jeff, C-G-LB, 1974, 1975, 1980, 1981, 1982
5	Van Pelt, Brad, LB, 1976, 1977, 1978, 1979, 1980
1	Van Raaphorst, Dick, K, 1966
1	Vanden Bosch, Kyle, DE, 2005
1	Vanderjagt, Mike, K, 2003
1	Vanzo, Fred, BB-LB, 1939
5	Varrichione, Frank, T, 1955, 1957, 1958, 1960, 1962
1	Vasher, Nathan, DB, 2005
2	Verdin, Clarence, WR, 1990, 1992
3	Vick, Michael, QB, 2002, 2004, 2005
4	Villapiano, Phil, LB, 1973, 1974, 1975, 1976
1	Vilma, Jonathan, LB, 2005
2	Vinatieri, Adam, K, 2002, 2004
5	Vincent, Troy, DB, 1999, 2000, 2001, 2002, 2003
5	Vogel, Bob, T, 1964, 1965, 1967, 1968, 1971
3	Volk, Rick, DB, 1967, 1969, 1971
2	Wade, Billy, QB, 1958, 1963
2	Wagner, Mike, DB, 1975, 1976
1	Wahle, Mike, G-T, 2005
1	Walden, Bobby, P, 1969
1	Walker, Chuck, DT-DE, 1966
5	Walker, Doak, HB-DB, 1950, 1951, 1953, 1954, 1955
2	Walker, Gary, DT-DE, 2001, 2002
2	Walker, Herschel, RB, 1987, 1988
1	Walker, Javon, WR, 2004
3	Walker, Wayne, LB, 1963, 1964, 1965
2	Walker, Wesley, WR, 1978, 1982
1	Wallace, Steve, T-G, 1992
1	Waller, Ron, HB, 1955
1	Wallner, Fred, LB-G, 1955
4	Walls, Everson, DB, 1981, 1982, 1983, 1985
5	Walls, Wesley, TE, 1996, 1997, 1998, 1999, 2001
2	Walsh, Bill, C, 1950, 1951
2	Walston, Bobby, E-HB-K, 1960, 1961
2	Walters, Stan, T, 1978, 1979
4	Ward, Hines, WR, 2001, 2002, 2003, 2004
8	Warfield, Paul, WR-SE, 1964, 1968, 1969, 1970, 1971, 1972, 1973, 1974

TOTAL	NAME, POSITION, YEARS
4	Warlick, Ernie, TE, 1962, 1963, 1964, 1965
1	Warner, Charley, DB-HB, 1965
3	Warner, Curt, RB, 1983, 1986, 1987
3	Warner, Kurt, QB, 1999, 2000, 2001
3	Warren, Chris, RB, 1993, 1994, 1995
1	Warren, Jimmy, DB, 1966
1	Washington, Dave, LB-TE, 1976
2	Washington, Gene, WR, 1969, 1970
4	Washington, Gene, WR-SE, 1969, 1970, 1971, 1972
1	Washington, Joe, RB, 1979
1	Washington, Marcus, LB, 2004
5	Washington, Russ, T-DT, 1974, 1975, 1977, 1978, 1979
4	Washington, Ted, NT-DT, 1997, 1998, 2000, 2001
1	Washington, Vic, RB-DB-WR, 1971
2	Waterfield, Bob, QB, 1950, 1951
2	Waters, Brian, G, 2004, 2005
3	Waters, Charlie, DB, 1976, 1977, 1978
1	Watson, Steve, WR, 1981
5	Watters, Ricky, RB, 1992, 1993, 1994, 1995, 1996
1	Watts, George, T, 1942
1	Waymer, Dave, DB, 1987
2	Weatherall, Jim, DT-T, 1955, 1956
1	Webb, Don, DB, 1969
7	Webb, Richmond, T, 1990, 1991, 1992, 1993, 1994, 1995, 1996
2	Webster, Alex, HB-FB, 1958, 1961
1	Webster, Dave, DB, 1961
3	Webster, George, LB, 1967, 1968, 1969
9	Webster, Mike, C-G, 1978, 1979, 1980, 1981, 1982, 1983, 1984, 1985, 1987
7	Wehrli, Roger, DB, 1970, 1971, 1974, 1975, 1976, 1977, 1979
4	Weinmeister, Arnie, DT-T, 1950, 1951, 1952, 1953
1	Weisgerber, Dick, B, 1939
1	Wells, Billy, HB, 1954
2	Wells, Warren, SE-WR, 1968, 1970
2	West, Stan, DG-G-C, 1951, 1952
2	West, Willie, DB, 1963, 1966
1	Westbrook, Brian, RB, 2004
1	Westmoreland, Dick, DB, 1967
1	Wham, Tom, DE-E, 1951
2	Whigham, Larry, DB, 1997, 2001
1	White, Charles, RB, 1987
1	White, Danny, QB-P, 1982
2	White, Dwight, DE, 1972, 1973
3	White, Ed, G-T, 1975, 1976, 1977, 1979
1	White, Lorenzo, RB, 1992
9	White, Randy, DT-LB-DE, 1977, 1978, 1979, 1980, 1981, 1982, 1983, 1984, 1985
13	White, Reggie, DE-DT, 1986, 1987, 1988, 1989, 1990, 1991, 1992, 1993, 1994, 1995, 1996, 1997, 1998
2	White, Sammy, WR, 1976, 1977
1	White, Tarzan, G, 1938
1	Whited, Marv, G-BB, 1942
1	Whitfield, Bob, T, 1998
1	Whitsell, Dave, DB, 1967
2	Whittenton, Jesse, DB, 1961, 1963
1	Widby, Ron, P, 1971
1	Widseth, Ed, T, 1938
2	Wietecha, Ray, C, 1957, 1958, 1960, 1962
2	Wiggin, Paul, DE, 1965, 1967
1	Wightkin, Bill, T-DE-E, 1955
7	Wilcox, Dave, LB, 1966, 1968, 1969, 1970, 1971, 1972, 1973
1	Wilder, James, RB, 1984
1	Wildung, Dick, T-DT-G, 1951
1	Wiley, Marcellus, DE, 2001
3	Wilkerson, Doug, G, 1980, 1981, 1982
3	Wilkin, Willie, T, 1940, 1941, 1942
1	Wilkins, Jeff, K, 2003
4	Willard, Ken, RB, 1965, 1966, 1968, 1969
2	Wiley, Norm, DE-G-E, 1954, 1955
8	Williams, Aeneas, DB, 1994, 1995, 1996, 1997, 1998, 1999, 2001, 2003
1	Williams, Ben, DE-NT, 1982
1	Williams, Darryl, DB, 1997
2	Williams, Delvin, RB, 1976, 1978
4	Williams, Erik, T, 1993, 1996, 1997, 1999
4	Williams, Fred, DT-G, 1952, 1953, 1958, 1959
1	Williams, Jamal, DT-NT, 2005
1	Williams, James, T-DE-DT, 2001
2	Williams, John L., FB, 1990, 1991
1	Williams, Johnny, DB-HB, 1952
1	Williams, Kevin, DT-DE, 2004
2	Williams, Lee, DE-DT, 1988, 1989
1	Williams, Ricky, RB, 2002
3	Williams, Roy, DB, 2003, 2004, 2005
1	Williams, Willie, DB, 1969
2	Williamson, Carlton, DB, 1984, 1985
3	Williamson, Fred, DB, 1961, 1962, 1963
3	Willis, Bill, DG-G, 1950, 1951, 1952

THE PRO BOWL: ALPHABETICAL LIST

TOTAL	NAME, POSITION, YEARS
3	Wilson, Al, LB, 2001, 2002, 2005
6	Wilson, Billy, E-FL, 1954, 1955, 1956, 1957, 1958, 1959
3	Wilson, George, E-DE, 1940, 1941, 1942
3	Wilson, Jerrel, RB-P, 1970, 1971, 1972
8	Wilson, Larry, DB, 1962, 1963, 1965, 1966, 1967, 1968, 1969, 1970
1	Wilson, Nemiah, DB, 1967
1	Wilson, Otis, LB, 1985
1	Wilson, Tommy, HB-FB, 1957
1	Wilson, Wade, QB, 1988
1	Wimberly, Ab, DE-E, 1952
2	Winder, Sammy, RB, 1984, 1986
1	Winkler, Jim, DT-G, 1952
5	Winslow, Kellen, TE, 1980, 1981, 1982, 1983, 1987
1	Winters, Frank, C-G, 1996
8	Wisniewski, Steve, G, 1990, 1991, 1992, 1993, 1994, 1995, 1997, 2000
1	Wistert, Al, T-G-DT, 1950
2	Witten, Jason, TE, 2004, 2005
2	Wittum, Tom, P, 1973, 1974
1	Wolfe, Red, FB, 1938
4	Wolfley, Ron, RB, 1986, 1987, 1988, 1989
3	Wolford, Will, T-G, 1990, 1992, 1995
1	Wood, Duane, DB, 1963

TOTAL	NAME, POSITION, YEARS
8	Wood, Willie, DB, 1962, 1964, 1965, 1966, 1967, 1968, 1969, 1970
2	Woodall, Lee, LB, 1995, 1997
1	Woodeshick, Tom, RB, 1968
1	Woods, Jerome, DB, 2003
5	Woodson, Abe, DB-HB, 1959, 1960, 1961, 1962, 1963
4	Woodson, Charles, DB, 1998, 1999, 2000, 2001
5	Woodson, Darren, DB, 1994, 1995, 1996, 1997, 1998
1	Woodson, Marv, DB-HB, 1967
11	Woodson, Rod, DB, 1989, 1990, 1991, 1992, 1993, 1994, 1995, 1999, 2000, 2001, 2002
1	Woody, Damien, C-G, 2002
1	Woolford, Donnell, DB, 1993
2	Wooten, John, G, 1965, 1966
1	Woudenberg, John, T, 1942
1	Wozniak, John, G-LB, 1952
2	Wright, Eric, DB, 1984, 1985
3	Wright, Ernie, T, 1961, 1963, 1965
5	Wright, Louis, DB, 1977, 1978, 1979, 1983, 1985
6	Wright, Rayfield, T-TE, 1971, 1972, 1973, 1974, 1975, 1976
3	Wycheck, Frank, TE, 1998, 1999, 2000
7	Yary, Ron, T, 1971, 1972, 1973, 1974, 1975, 1976, 1977

TOTAL	NAME, POSITION, YEARS
2	Yepremian, Garo, K, 1973, 1978
1	Young, Bill, T, 1942
2	Young, Bob, G-DE-DT, 1978, 1979
4	Young, Bryant, DT-DE, 1996, 1999, 2001, 2002
1	Young, Buddy, HB-FB-DB, 1954
3	Young, Charle, TE, 1973, 1974, 1975
4	Young, Fredd, LB, 1984, 1985, 1986, 1987
1	Young, Roynell, DB, 1981
7	Young, Steve, QB, 1992, 1993, 1994, 1995, 1996, 1997, 1998
7	Youngblood, Jack, DE, 1973, 1974, 1975, 1976, 1977, 1978, 1979
1	Youngblood, Jim, LB, 1979
4	Younger, Tank, FB-LB-HB, 1951, 1952, 1953, 1955
1	Zarnas, Gust, G, 1939
3	Zatkoff, Roger, LB-DE, 1954, 1955, 1956
1	Zeman, Bob, DB, 1962
1	Zeno, Joe, G-T, 1942
7	Zimmerman, Gary, T, 1987, 1988, 1989, 1992, 1994, 1995, 1996
1	Zimmerman, Roy, QB-WB-K, 1942
1	Zook, John, DE, 1973

In most American sports, it's clear who wins the most valuable player and rookie of the year. Everyone recognizes the same awards given by the same groups as authoritative. In major league baseball, for example, the honors awarded annually by the Baseball Writers Association of America are accepted as the gold standard. Other organizations, including major league baseball itself, give out similar awards, but virtually no one pays attention to them. When it comes to the NFL, however, asking who the MVP was in any given year can seem like a trick question.

It is far from clear which organization gives out the most prestigious awards. The organizations whose awards carry the most weight today are not the same organizations whose awards had a similar stature 40 years ago. In fact, some of the awards that used to garner the greatest amount of media attention, such as the United Press International awards, no longer exist. And some of today's more widely publicized awards, such as the extensive set of awards given out by *Pro Football Weekly* and the Pro Football Writers of America, didn't exist as late as 1967.

Even when it's clear who is giving what type of awards, the historical record of pro football awards is still very complicated. Sometimes a Player of the Year or Rookie of the Year award is given out to only one professional football player in the country. Other times, however, a version of an award is given to a player in each league or conference. In still other years, parallel versions of the same awards are given to both an offensive player and a defensive player. And then there are the years where both a back and a lineman each get versions of the same awards. Many awards are split not just two but four ways. From 1983–96 UPI gave out separate annual awards for the AFC Offensive Player of the Year, AFC Defensive Player of the Year, NFC Offensive Player of the Year, and an NFC Defensive Player of the Year. Before 1983, however, UPI had only split its Player of the Year award by league or conference. And after 1996 they left the football awards business altogether. Other award presenters, including *The Sporting News*, have been equally inconsistent at times, switching from two Rookie of the Year selections to four Rookie of the Year selections in 1970 before switching back to two a decade later.

The award with the most different varieties over the years is the MVP/Player of the Year awards (some of the presenters use both terms interchangeably to describe their award, so we won't even try to distinguish between Most Valuable Player and Player of the Year honors). No less than 10 organizations have handed out awards for either in a given year. Among them, the Associated Press has given out an award since 1972, the Newspaper Enterprise Association gave out a player of the year trophy from 1955–88, while Philadelphia's Maxwell Club has honored former commissioner Bert Bell with an award in his name since the year he died in 1959.

Two other popular awards are the Coach of the Year and Rookie of the Year awards. There are also two competing Executive of the Year awards. It actually isn't all that hard for a mediocre pro football coach that happens to be in charge of the right team in the right year to dominate the Coach of the Year awards in an individual year. Since 1963, 18 coaches in 23 years have swept all the Coach of the Year awards available in a given year. It is actually a more significant historical achievement for a coach to earn at least one Coach of the Year award in at least two different years. Of the 16 coaches who have done that, 11 of the 12 of those coaches who have retired (one of whom, Joe Gibbs, has since un-retired) have been inducted into the Hall of Fame. Of those 12, only Chuck Knox, who won 11 Coach of the Year awards, is clearly retired and has not been elected to the Hall. The four coaches who have earned coach of the year honors in multiple years and are still active (or could still possibly coach again) are Bill Parcells, Andy Reid, Dom Capers, and Dan Reeves.

THE BIG PICTURE

In this section each set of parallel awards is presented side-by-side in one large table in an effort to bring as much clarity to this data as possible. This presentation should make it relatively easy to see the many variations of all the awards with the least amount of confusion. This will reveal where there was unanimity and where there were significant differences of opinion on the identity of the most worthy candidates for the annual awards

Also in this section are the results of various more unique awards, most of which, though not all, are awarded by *Pro Football Weekly*

and the PFWA. Some, including the Comeback Player of the Year award, are classics of the sports awards genre. Others, though, such as the Assistant Coach of the Year and the Most Improved Player of the Year awards, acknowledge the achievements of individuals who don't normally get recognized. The Golden Toe award has been given to the NFL's best kicker *Pro Football Weekly* every year since 1971. Both placekickers and punters are eligible, but placekickers have won 27 of the 34 Golden Toes. The Pete Rozelle Radio–Television Award, has been presented annually by the Pro Football Hall of Fame since 1989, and it is given to individuals who have made "longtime exceptional contributions to radio and television in professional football." In addition to over-the-air broadcasters, media executives and production personnel are also eligible for this honor.

The Walter Payton NFL Man of the Year award, which was renamed after the Hall of Fame running back in 1999, is an official NFL award that is given to a player who performs well both on the field and in their community. Each team nominates a player and a special panel that includes the NFL commissioner, Walter Payton's widow, the previous year's winner, and various retired players and members of the media, decides the winner. While other sports leagues present similar awards to players who strive to contribute to society, this NFL award is unusual in that it explicitly takes into account the nominees' on-field performance as well. The Byron "Whizzer" White award, named after the former NFL running back and U.S. Supreme Court judge, is a similar award that the NFL Players Association presents annually to a player who best serves "his team, community and country." Unlike the NFL award, the NFLPA award is often given to lesser players who perform many charitable works in their community.

The Joe E. Carr Trophy, which was handed out annually by the NFL to the league's most valuable player from 1938 through 1946. This award, named after the league's first president a year before he left his position, was the only significant honor available to NFL players in those years other than being named an All-Pro. After the NFL ceased giving out the Carr Trophy, there would be no award for the best player or players in the NFL until seven years later, when in 1953 UPI recognized Otto Graham as its first NFL Player of the Year. The All-America Football Conference, however, did recognize a most valuable player in 1946 (halfback Glenn Dobbs of the Brooklyn Dodgers), as well as 1947 and 1948 (Cleveland Browns quarterback Otto Graham both years).

Counting the AAFC awards, Hall of Famer Graham won a player of the year award after four different years. A feat matched by Cleveland's Jim Brown, Lawrence Taylor of the New York Giants, Jerry Rice of the San Francisco 49ers, and Mike Singletary of the Chicago Bears. Reggie White and Y.A. Tittle won the award after four different seasons for more than one team. The all-time record holder, however, is Buffalo Bill defensive end Bruce Smith, who received at least one player of the year award after five different seasons: 1987, 1988, 1990, 1993, and 1996. Three players received player of the year awards in three consecutive years: Brett Favre of the Green Bay Packers, Earl Campbell of the Houston Oilers, and Marshall Faulk of the St. Louis Rams. The only other three players to receive such an award in three different years are Johnny Unitas of the Baltimore Colts, O.J. Simpson of the Buffalo Bills, Walter Payton of the Chicago Bears, and Eric Dickerson of the Los Angeles Rams.

With such a large variety of organizations presenting their own Player of the Year awards, it is difficult for a player to win every award they are eligible for in a single year. No player has achieved this type of unanimous acclaim more than once. There have been several unanimous Players of the Year: Norm Van Brocklin for the Philadelphia Eagles in 1960, Unitas in 1967, Roman Gabriel of the Rams in 1969, Larry Brown for the Washington Redskins in 1972, Simpson in 1973, Fran Tarkenton of the Minnesota Vikings in 1974, Ken Anderson of the Cincinnati Bengals in 1981, Dan Marino of the Miami Dolphins in 1984, Joe Montana of the 49ers in 1989, Favre in 1995, Barry Sanders of the Detroit Lions in 1997.

It is virtually impossible for a defensive player to win every possible award due to the obvious bias toward offense by most voters. The only two defensive players who have come close by winning four player of the year awards in one year are Alan Page, the Vikings defensive tackle in 1971, and Lawrence Taylor, a linebacker. But it's not about the consensus, it's about recognition. As they like to say—while smiling factitiously—at Hollywood's annual awards haul, the Oscars, "It's an honor just to be nominated."

AWARDS

MVPs/PLAYERS OF THE YEAR

YEAR	JOE E. CARR TROPHY
1938	Mel Hein, C, Giants
1939	Parker Hall, HB, Rams
1940	Ace Parker, HB, Dodgers
1941	Don Hutson, E, Packers
1942	Don Hutson, E, Packers
1943	Sid Luckman, QB, Bears
1944	Frank Sinkwich, HB - Lions
1945	Bob Waterfield, QB, Rams
1946	Bill Dudley, HB, Steelers

YEAR	AP NFL MVP	AP NFL OFF PLAYER OF THE YEAR	AP NFL DEF PLAYER OF THE YEAR	NEA NFL PLAYER OF THE YEAR	PFW/PFWA OFF PLAYER OF THE YEAR
1953					
1954					
1955				Harlon Hill, OE, Bears	
1956				Frank Gifford, HB, Giants	
1957	Jim Brown, FB, Browns			Johnny Unitas, QB, Colts	
1958	Gino Marchetti, DE, Colts			Jim Brown, FB, Browns	
1959	Charley Conerly, QB, Giants			Charley Conerly, QB, Giants	
1960	Norm Van Brocklin, QB, Eagles; Joe Schmidt, LB, Lions			Norm Van Brocklin, QB, Eagles	
1961	Paul Hornung, HB, Packers			Y.A. Tittle, QB, Giants	
1962	Jim Taylor, FB, Packers			Jim Taylor, FB, Packers	
1963	Y.A. Tittle, QB, Giants			Jim Brown, FB Browns; Y.A. Tittle, QB, Giants	
1964	Johnny Unitas, QB, Colts			Lenny Moore, HB, Colts	
1965	Jim Brown, FB, Browns			Jim Brown, FB, Browns	
1966	Bart Starr, QB, Packers			Bart Starr, QB, Packers	
1967	Johnny Unitas, QB, Colts			Johnny Unitas, QB, Colts	
1968	Earl Morrall, QB, Colts			Earl Morrall, QB, Colts	Joe Namath, QB, Jets (AFL) Earl Morrall, QB, Colts (NFL)
1969	Roman Gabriel, QB, Rams			Roman Gabriel, QB, Rams	Daryle Lamonica, QB, Raiders (AFL) Roman Gabriel, QB, Rams (NFL)
1970	John Brodie, QB, 49ers			John Brodie, QB, 49ers	John Brodie, QB, 49ers
1971	Alan Page, DT, Vikings		Alan Page, DT, Vikings	Bob Griese, QB, Dolphins	Otis Taylor, WR, Chiefs
1972	Larry Brown, RB, Redskins	Larry Brown, RB, Redskins	Joe Greene, DT, Steelers	Larry Brown, RB, Redskins	Larry Brown, RB, Redskins
1973	O.J. Simpson, RB, Bills	O.J. Simpson, RB, Bills	Dick Anderson, S, Dolphins	O.J. Simpson, RB, Bills	O.J. Simpson, RB, Bills
1974	Ken Stabler, QB, Raiders	Ken Stabler, QB, Raiders	Joe Greene, DT, Steelers	Ken Stabler, QB, Raiders	Jim Hart, QB, Cardinals
1975	Fran Tarkenton, QB, Vikings	Fran Tarkenton, QB, Vikings	Mel Blount, CB, Steelers	Fran Tarkenton, QB, Min	Fran Tarkenton, QB, Vikings
1976	Bert Jones, QB, Colts	Bert Jones, QB, Colts	Jack Lambert, LB, Steelers	Bert Jones, QB, Colts	Ken Stabler, QB, Raiders
1977	Walter Payton, RB, Bears	Walter Payton, RB, Bears	Harvey Martin, DE, Cowboys	Walter Payton, RB, Bears	Walter Payton, RB, Bears
1978	Terry Bradshaw, QB, Steelers	Earl Campbell, RB, Oilers	Randy Gradishar, LB, Broncos	Earl Campbell, RB, Oilers	Earl Campbell, RB, Oilers
1979	Earl Campbell, RB, Oilers	Earl Campbell, RB, Oilers	Lee Roy Selmon, DE, Buccaneers	Earl Campbell, RB, Oilers	Earl Campbell, RB, Oilers
1980	Brian Sipe, QB, Browns	Earl Campbell, RB, Oilers	Lester Hayes, CB, Raiders	Earl Campbell, RB, Oilers	Brian Sipe, QB, Browns
1981	Ken Anderson, QB, Bengals	Ken Anderson, QB, Bengals	Lawrence Taylor, LB, Giants	Ken Anderson, QB, Bengals	Ken Anderson, QB, Bengals
1982	Mark Moseley, PK, Redskins	Dan Fouts, QB, Chargers	Lawrence Taylor, LB, Giants	Dan Fouts, QB, Chargers	Dan Fouts, QB, Chargers
1983	Joe Theismann, QB, Redskins	Joe Theismann, QB, Redskins	Doug Betters, DE, Dolphins	Joe Theismann, QB, Redskins	Joe Theismann, QB, Redskins
1984	Dan Marino, QB, Dolphins	Dan Marino, QB, Dolphins	Kenny Easley, S, Seahawks	Dan Marino, QB, Dolphins	Dan Marino, QB, Dolphins
1985	Marcus Allen, RB, Raiders	Marcus Allen, RB, Raiders	Mike Singletary, LB, Bears	Walter Payton, RB, Bears	No Award
1986	Lawrence Taylor, LB, Giants	Eric Dickerson, RB, Rams	Lawrence Taylor, LB, Giants	Phil Simms, QB, Giants	Jerry Rice, WR, 49ers
1987	John Elway, QB, Denver	Jerry Rice, WR, 49ers	Reggie White, DE, Packers	Jerry Rice, WR, 49ers	Jerry Rice, WR, 49ers
1988	Boomer Esiason, QB, Bengals	Roger Craig, RB 49ers	Mike Singletary, LB, Bears	Roger Craig, RB, 49ers	Boomer Esiason, QB, Bengals
1989	Joe Montana, QB, 49ers	Joe Montana, QB, 49ers	Keith Millard, DT, Vikings		Joe Montana, QB, 49ers
1990	Joe Montana, QB, 49ers	Warren Moon, QB, Oilers	Bruce Smith, DE, Bills		Randall Cunningham, QB, Eagles
1991	Thurman Thomas, RB, Bills	Thurman Thomas, RB Bills	Pat Swilling, LB, Saints		Thurman Thomas, RB, Bills
1992	Steve Young, QB, 49ers	Steve Young, QB, 49ers	Cortez Kennedy, DT, Seahawks		Steve Young, QB, 49ers
1993	Emmitt Smith, RB, Cowboys	Jerry Rice, WR, 49ers	Rod Woodson, CB, Steelers		Emmitt Smith, RB, Cowboys
1994	Steve Young, QB 49ers	Baeet Sanders, RB, Lions	Deion Sanders, CB, 49ers		Steve Young, QB, 49ers
1995	Brett Favre, QB, Packers	Brett Favre, QB, Packers	Bryce Paup, LB, Bills		Brett Favre, QB, Packers
1996	Brett Favre, QB, Packers	Terrell Davis, RB Broncos	Bruce Smith, DE, Bills		Brett Favre, QB, Packers
1997	Brett Favre, QB, Packers; Barry Sanders, RB, Lions	Barry Sanders, RB, Lions	Dana Stubblefield, DT, 49ers		Barry Sanders, RB, Lions
1998	Terrell Davis, RB, Broncos	Terrell Davis, RB, Broncos	Reggie White, DE, Packers		Terrell Davis, RB, Broncos
1999	Kurt Warner, QB, Rams	Marshall Faulk, RB, Rams	Warren Sapp, DT, Buccaneers		Kurt Warner, QB, Rams
2000	Marshall Faulk, RB, Rams	Marshall Faulk, RB, Rams	Ray Lewis, LB, Ravens		Marshall Faulk, RB, Rams
2001	Kurt Warner, QB, Rams	Marshall Faulk, RB, Rams	Michael Strahan, DE, Giants		Marshall Faulk, RB, Rams
2002	Rich Gannon, QB, Raiders	Priest Holmes, RB Chiefs	Derrick Brooks, LB, Buccaneers		Rich Gannon, QB, Raiders
2003	Steve Mcnair; QB, Titans; Peyton Manning, QB, Colts	Jamal Lewis, RB, Ravens	Ray Lewis, LB, Ravens		Jamal Lewis, RB, Ravens
2004	Peyton Manning, QB, Colts	Peyton Manning, QB, Colts	Ed Reed, S, Ravens		Peyton Manning, QB, Colts
2005	Shaun Alexander, RB, Seahawks	Shaun Alexander, RB, Seahawks	Brian Urlacher, LB, Bears		Shaun Alexander, RB, Seahawks

YEAR	PFW/PFWA DEF PLAYER OF THE YEAR	UPI AFL/AFC PLAYER OF THE YEAR	UPI NFL/NFC PLAYER OF THE YEAR	BERT BELL TROPHY (MAXWELL CLUB)	SPORTING NEWS NFL PLAYER OF THE YEAR
1953			Otto Graham, QB, Browns		Lou Groza, T–K, Browns
1954			Joe Perry, FB, 49ers		Otto Graham, QB, Browns
1955			Otto Graham, QB, Browns		Frank Gifford, HB, Giants
1956			Frank Gifford, HB, Giants		Jim Brown, RB, Browns
1957			Y.A. Tittle, QB, Giants		Jim Brown, RB, Browns
1958			Jim Brown, RB, Browns	Johnny Unitas, QB, Colts	Johnny Unitas, QB, Colts
1959			Johnny Unitas, QB, Colts	Norm Van Brocklin, QB, Eagles	Norm Van Brocklin, QB, Eagles
1960		Abner Haynes, HB, Texans	Norm Van Brocklin, QB, Eagles	Paul Hornung, HB, Packers	Paul Hornung, HB, Packers
1961		George Blanda, QB–K, Oilers	Paul Hornung, HB, Packers	Andy Robustelli, DE, Giants	Y.A. Tittle, QB, Giants
1962		Cookie Gilchrist, FB, Bills	Y.A. Tittle, QB, Giants	Jim Brown, RB, Browns	Y.A. Tittle, QB, Giants
1963		Lance Alworth, FL, Chargers	Jim Brown, RB, Browns		
1964		Gino Cappelletti, SE, Patriots	Johnny Unitas, QB, Colts	Johnny Unitas, QB, Colts	Johnny Unitas, QB, Colts
1965		Paul Lowe, HB, Chargers	Jim Brown, RB, Browns	Pete Retzlaff, TE, Eagles	Jim Brown, RB, Browns
1966		Jim Nance, RB, Patriots	Bart Starr, QB, Packers	Don Meredith, QB, Cowboys	Bart Starr, QB, Packers
1967		Daryle Lamonica, QB, Raiders	Johnny Unitas, QB, Colts	Johnny Unitas, QB, Colts	Johnny Unitas, QB, Colts
1968		Joe Namath, QB, Jets	Earl Morrall, QB, Colts	Leroy Kelly, RB, Browns	Earl Morrall, QB, Colts
1969		Daryle Lamonica, QB, Raiders	Roman Gabriel, QB, Rams	Roman Gabriel, QB, Rams	Roman Gabriel, QB, Rams
1970	Dick Butkus, LB, Bears	George Blanda, QB–PK, Raiders	John Brodie, QB, 49ers	George Blanda, QB–/K, Raiders	John Brodie, QB, 49ers (NFC) George Blanda, QB–K, Raiders (AFC)
1971	Alan Page, DT, Vikings	Otis Taylor, WR, Chiefs	Alan Page, DT, Vikings	Roger Staubach, QB, Cowboys	Roger Staubach, QB, Cowboys (NFC) Bob Griese, QB, Dolphins (AFC)
1972	Joe Greene, DT, Steelers	O.J. Simpson, RB, Bills	Larry Brown, RB, Redskins	Larry Brown, RB, Redskins	Larry Brown, RB, Redskins (NFC) Earl Morrall, QB, Dolphins (AFC)
1973	Alan Page, DT, Vikings; Paul Smith, DT, Broncos	O.J. Simpson, RB, Bills	John Hadl, QB, Rams	O.J. Simpson, RB, Bills	John Hadl, QB, Rams (NFC) O.J. Simpson, RB, Bills (AFC)
1974	Joe Greene, DT, Steelers	Ken Stabler, QB, Raiders	Jim Hart, QB, Cardinals	Merlin Olsen, DT, Rams	Chuck Foreman, RB, Vikings (NFC) Ken Stabler, QB, Raiders (AFC)
1975	Jack Ham, LB, Steelers	O.J. Simpson, RB, Bills	Fran Tarkenton, QB, Vikings	Fran Tarkenton, QB, Vikings	Fran Tarkenton, QB, Vikings (NFC) O.J. Simpson, RB, Bills (AFC)
1976	Jack Lambert, LB, Steelers	Bert Jones, QB, Colts	Chuck Foreman, RB, Vikings	Ken Stabler, QB, Raiders	Walter Payton, RB, Bears (NFC) Ken Stabler, QB, Raiders (AFC)
1977	Harvey Martin, DE, Cowboys.	Craig Morton, QB, Broncos	Walter Payton, RB, Bears	Bob Griese, QB, Dolphins	Walter Payton, RB, Bears (NFC) Craig Morton, QB, Broncos (AFC)
1978	Randy Gradishar, LB, Broncos	Earl Campbell, RB, Oilers	Archie Manning, QB, Saints	Terry Bradshaw, QB, Steelers	Archie Manning, QB, Saints (NFC) Earl Campbell, RB, Oilers (AFC)
1979	Lee Roy Selmon, DE, Buccaneers	Dan Fouts, QB, Chargers	Ottis Anderson, RB, Cardinals	Earl Campbell, RB, Oilers	Ottis Anderson, RB, Cardinals (NFC) Dan Fouts, QB, San Chargers (AFC)
1980	Lester Hayes, CB, Raiders	Brian Sipe, QB, Browns	Ron Jaworski, QB, Eagles	Ron Jaworski, QB, Eagles	Brian Sipe, QB, Browns
1981	Joe Klecko, DE, Jets	Ken Anderson, QB, Bengals	Tony Dorsett, RB, Cowboys	Ken Anderson, QB, Bengals	Ken Anderson, QB, Bengals
1982	Dan Hampton, DT, Bears	Dan Fouts, QB, Chargers	Mark Moseley, K, Redskins	Joe Theismann, QB, Redskins	Mark Moseley, PK, Redskins
1983	Bob Baumhower, NT, Dolphins	Curt Warner, RB, Seahawks (OFF) Rod Martin, LB, Raiders (DEF)	Eric Dickerson, RB, Rams (OFF) Mike Singletary, LB, Bears (DEF)	John Riggins, RB, Redskins	Eric Dickerson, RB, Rams
1984	Kenny Easley, S, Seahawks	Dan Marino, QB, Dolphins (OFF) Mark Gastineau, DE, Jets (DEF)	Eric Dickerson, RB, Rams (OFF) Lawrence Taylor, LB, Giants (DEF)	Dan Marino, QB, Dolphins	Dan Marino, QB, Dolphins
1985	No Award	Marcus Allen, RB, Raiders (OFF) Andre Tippett, LB, Patriots (DEF)	Walter Payton, RB, Bears (OFF) Mike Singletary, LB, Bears (DEF)	Walter Payton, RB, Bears	Marcus Allen, RB, Raiders
1986	Lawrence Taylor, LB, Giants	Curt Warner, RB, Seahawks (OFF) Rulon Jones, DE, Broncos (DEF)	Eric Dickerson, RB, Rams (OFF) Lawrence Taylor, LB, Giants (DEF)	Lawrence Taylor, LB, Giants	Lawrence Taylor, LB, Giants
1987	Reggie White, DE, Packers	John Elway, QB, Denver (OFF) Bruce Smith, DE, Bills (DEF)	Jerry Rice, WR, 49ers (OFF) Reggie White, DE, Packers (DEF)	Jerry Rice, WR, 49ers	Jerry Rice, WR, 49ers
1988	Mike Singletary, LB, Bears	Boomer Esiason, QB, Bengals (OFF) Bruce Smith, DE, Bills (DEF); Cornelius Bennett, LB, Bills (DEF)	Roger Craig, RB, 49ers (OFF) Mike Singletary, LB, Bears (DEF)	Randall Cunningham, QB, Eagles	Boomer Esiason, QB, Bengals
1989	Keith Millard, DT, Vikings	Christian Okoye, RB, Chiefs (OFF) Michael Dean Perry, DT, Browns (DEF)	Joe Montana, QB, 49ers (OFF) Keith Millard, DT, Vikings (DEF)	Joe Montana, QB, 49ers	Joe Montana, QB, 49ers
1990	Bruce Smith, DE, Bills	Warren Moon, QB, Oilers (OFF) Bruce Smith, DE, Bills (DEF)	Randall Cunningham, QB, Eagles (OFF) Charles Haley, LB, 49ers (DEF)	Randall Cunningham, QB, Eagles	Jerry Rice, WR, 49ers
1991	Reggie White, DE, Eagles.	Thurman Thomas, RB, Bills (OFF) Cornelius Bennett, LB, Bills (DEF)	Mark Rypien, QB, Redskins (OFF) Reggie White, DE, Packers (DEF)	Barry Sanders, RB, Lions	Thurman Thomas, RB, Bills
1992	Cortez Kennedy, DT, Seahawks	Barry Foster, RB, Steelers (OFF) Junior Seau, LB, Chargers (DEF)	Steve Young, QB, 49ers (OFF) Chris Doleman, LB, Vikings (DEF)	Steve Young, QB, 49ers	Steve Young, QB, 49ers
1993	Bruce Smith, DE, Bills	John Elway, QB, Denver (OFF) Rod Woodson, CB, Steelers (DEF)	Emmitt Smith, RB, Cowboys (OFF) Eric Allen, CB, Eagles (DEF)	Emmitt Smith, RB, Cowboys	Emmitt Smith, RB, Cowboys
1994	Deion Sanders, CB, 49ers	Dan Marino, QB, Dolphins (OFF) Greg Lloyd, LB, Steelers (DEF)	Steve Young, QB, 49ers (OFF) Charles Haley, DE, Cowboys (DEF)	Steve Young, QB, 49ers	Steve Young, QB, 49ers
1995	Bryce Paup, LB, Bills	Jim Harbaugh, QB, Colts (OFF) Bryce Paup, LB, Bills (DEF)	Brett Favre, QB, Packers (OFF) Reggie White, DE, Packers (DEF)	Brett Favre, QB, Packers	Brett Favre, QB, Packers
1996	Bruce Smith, DE, Bills	Terrell Davis, RB, Broncos (OFF) Bruce Smith, DE, Bills (DEF)	Brett Favre, QB, Packers (OFF) Kevin Greene, LB, Panthers (DEF)	Brett Favre, QB, Packers	Brett Favre, QB, Packers
1997	Dana Stubblefield, DT, 49ers			Barry Sanders, RB, Lions	Barry Sanders, RB, Lions
1998	Reggie White, DE, Packers			Randall Cunningham, QB, Eagles	Terrell Davis, RB, Broncos
1999	Warren Sapp, DT, Buccaneers			Kurt Warner, QB, Rams	Kurt Warner, QB, Rams
2000	Ray Lewis, LB, Ravens			Rich Gannon, QB, Raiders	Marshall Faulk, RB, Rams
2001	Michael Strahan Giants			Marshall Faulk, RB, Rams	Marshall Faulk, RB, Rams
2002	Derrick Brooks, LB, Buccaneers			Rich Gannon, QB, Raiders	Rich Gannon, QB, Raiders
2003	Ray Lewis, LB, Ravens			Peyton Manning, QB, Colts	Peyton Manning, QB, Colts
2004	Ed Reed, S, Ravens.			Peyton Manning, QB, Colts	Peyton Manning, QB, Colts
2005	Brian Urlacher, LB, Bears			Shaun Alexander, RB, Seahawks	Shaun Alexander, RB, Seahawks

ROOKIES OF THE YEAR

YEAR	UPI NFL/NFC ROOKIE OF THE YEAR	UPI AFL/AFC ROOKIE OF THE YEAR	AP NFL OFF ROOKIE OF THE YEAR	AP NFL DEF ROOKIE OF THE YEAR	SPORTING NEWS NFL ROOKIE OF THE YEAR
1955	Alan Ameche, FB, Colts				Alan Ameche, FB, Colts
1956	Lenny Moore, HB, Colts				J.C. Caroline, HB, Bears
1957	Jim Brown, FB, Browns				Jim Brown, FB, Browns
1958	Jimmy Orr, FL, Steelers				Bobby Mitchell, HB, Browns
1959	Boyd Dowler, FL, Packers				Nick Pietrosante, FB, Lions
1960	Gail Cogdill, FL, Lions	Abner Haynes, HB, Texans			Gail Codgill, E, Lions
1961	Mike Ditka, TE, Bears	Earl Faison, DE, Chargers			Mike Ditka, E, Bears
1962	Ronnie Bull, FB, Bears	Curtis McClinton, FB, Texans			Ronnie Bull, HB, Bears
1963	Paul Flatley, FL, Vikings	Billy Joe, FB, Broncos			Paul Flatley, WR, Vikings
1964	Charley Taylor, HB, Redskins	Matt Snell, FB, Jets			Charley Taylor, HB, Redskins
1965	Gale Sayers, HB, Bears	Joe Namath, QB, Jets			Gale Sayers, RB, Bears
1966	Johnny Roland, HB, Cardinals	Bobby Burnett, HB, Bills			Tommy Nobis, LB, Falcons
1967	Mel Farr, RB, Lions	George Webster, LB, Oilers		Lem Barney, CB, Lions	Mel Farr, RB, Lions
1968	Earl McCullough, FL, Lions	Paul Robinson, RB, Bengals		Claude Humphrey, DE, Falcons	Earl McCullouch, WR, Lions
1969	Calvin Hill, RB, Cowboys	Greg Cook, QB, Bengals		Joe Greene, DT, Steelers	Calvin Hill, RB, Cowboys
1970	Bruce Taylor, DB, 49ers	Dennis Shaw, QB, Bills	Dennis Shaw, QB, Bills	Bruce Taylor, CB, 49ers	Bruce Taylor, CB, 49ers (NFC) Dennis Shaw, QB, Bills (AFC)
1971	John Brockington, RB, Packers	Jim Plunkett, QB, Patriots	John Brockington, RB, Packers	Isiah Robertson, LB, Rams	John Brockington, RB, Packers (NFC) Jim Plunkett, QB, Patriots (AFC)
1972	Chester Marcol, K, Packers	Franco Harris, RB, Steelers	Franco Harris, RB, Steelers	Willie Buchanon, CB, Packers	Chester Marcol, PK, Packers (NFC) Franco Harris, RB, Steelers (AFC)
1973	Charlie Young, TE, Eagles	Bobbie Clark, RB, Bengals	Chuck Foreman, RB, Vikings	Wally Chambers, DT, Bears	Chuck Foreman, RB, Vikings (NFC) Boobie Clark, RB, Bengals (AFC)
1974	John Hicks, G, Giants	Don Woods, RB, Chargers	Don Woods, RB, Chargers	Jack Lambert, LB, Steelers	Wilbur Jackson, RB, 49ers (NFC) Don Woods, RB, Chargers (AFC)
1975	Mike Thomas, RB, Redskins	Robert Brazile, LB, Oilers	Mike Thomas, RB, Redskins	Robert Brazile, LB, Oilers	Steve Bartkowski, QB, Falcons (NFC) Robert Brazile, LB, Oilers (AFC)
1976	Sammy White, WR, Vikings	Mike Haynes, DB, Patriots	Sammy White, WR, Vikings	Mike Haynes, CB, Patriots	Sammy White, WR, Vikings (NFC) Mike Haynes, CB, Patriots (AFC)
1977	Tony Dorsett, RB, Cowboys	A.J. Duhe, DE, Dolphins	Tony Dorsett, RB, Cowboys	A.J. Duhe, DE, Dolphins	Tony Dorsett, RB, Cowboys (NFC) A.J. Duhe, DT, Dolphins (AFC)
1978	Bubba Baker, DE, Lions	Earl Campbell, RB, Oilers	Earl Campbell, RB, Oilers	Al Baker, DE, Lions	Al Baker, DE, Lions (NFC) Earl Campbell, RB, Oilers (AFC)
1979	Ottis Anderson, RB, Cardinals	Jerry Butler, WR, Bills	Ottis Anderson, RB, Cardinals	Jim Haslett, LB, Bills	Otis Anderson, RB, Cardinals (NFC) Jerry Butler, WR, Bills (AFC)
1980	Billy Sims, RB, Lions	Joe Cribbs, RB, Bills	Billy Sims, RB, Lions	Al Richardson, LB, Falcons; Buddy Curry, LB, Falcons	Billy Sims, RB, Lions
1981	George Rogers, RB, Saints	Joe Delaney, RB, Chiefs	George Rogers, RB, Saints	Lawrence Taylor, LB, Giants	George Rogers, RB, Saints
1982	Jim McMahon, QB, Bears	Marcus Allen, RB, Raiders	Marcus Allen, RB, Raiders	Chip Banks, LB, Browns	Marcus Allen, RB, Raiders
1983	Eric Dickerson, RB, Rams	Curt Warner, RB, Seahawks	Eric Dickerson, RB, Rams	Vernon Maxwell, LB, Colts	Dan Marino, QB, Dolphins
1984	Paul McFadden, K, Eagles	Louis Lipps, WR, Steelers	Louis Lipps, WR, Steelers	Bill Maas, DT, Chiefs	Louis Lipps, WR, Steelers
1985	Jerry Rice, WR, 49ers	Kevin Mack, RB, Browns	Eddie Brown, WR, Bengals	Duane Bickett, LB, Colts	Eddie Brown, WR, Bengals
1986	Reuben Mayes, RB, Saints	Leslie O'Neal, DE, Chargers	Reuben Mayes, RB, Saints	Leslie O'Neal, DE, Chargers	Rueben Mayes, RB, Saints
1987	Robert Awalt, TE, Cardinals	Shane Conlan, LB, Bills	Troy Stradford, RB, Dolphins	Shane Conlan, LB, Bills	Robert Awalt, TE, Cardinals
1988	Keith Jackson, TE, Eagles	John Stephens, RB, Patriots	John Stephens, RB, Patriots	Eric McMillan, S, Jets	Keith Jackson, TE, Eagles
1989	Barry Sanders, RB, Lions	Derrick Thomas, LB, Chiefs	Barry Sanders, RB, Lions	Derrick Thomas, LB, Chiefs	Barry Sanders, RB, Lions
1990	Mark Carrier, S, Bears	Richmond Webb, T, Dolphins	Emmitt Smith, RB, Cowboys	Mark Carrier, S, Bears	Richmond Webb, T, Dolphins
1991	Lawrence Dawsey, WR, Buccaneers	Mike Croel, LB, Broncos	Leonard Russell, RB, Patriots	Mike Croel, LB, Broncos	Mike Croel, LB, Broncos
1992	Robert Jones, LB, Cowboys	Dale Carter, CB, Chiefs	Carl Pickens, WR, Bengals	Dale Carter, CB, Chiefs	Santana Dotson, DL, Buccaneers
1993	Jerome Bettis, RB, Rams	Rick Mirer, QB, Seahawks	Jerome Bettis, RB, Rams	Dana Stubblefield, DT, 49ers	Jerome Bettis, RB, Rams
1994	Bryant Young, DT, 49ers	Marshall Faulk, RB, Colts	Marshall Faulk, RB, Colts	Tim Bowens, DT, Dolphins	Marshall Faulk, RB, Colts
1995	Rashaan Salaam, RB, Bears	Curtis Martin, RB, Patriots	Curtis Martin, RB, Patriots	Hugh Douglas, DE, Jets	Curtis Martin, RB, Patriots
1996	Simeon Rice, DE, Cardinals	Terry Glenn, WR, Patriots	Eddie George, RB, Oilers	Simeon Rice, DE, Cardinals	Eddie George, RB, Oilers
1997			Warrick Dunn, RB, Buccaneers	Peter Boulware, LB, Ravens	Warrick Dunn, RB, Buccaneers
1998			Randy Moss, WR, Vikings	Charles Woodson, CB, Raiders	Randy Moss, WR, Vikings
1999			Edgerrin James, RB, Colts	Jevon Kearse, DE, Titans	Edgerrin James, RB, Colts
2000			Mike Anderson, RB, Broncos	Brian Urlacher, LB, Bears	Brian Urlacher, LB, Bears
2001			Anthony Thomas, RB, Bears	Kendrell Bell, LB, Steelers	Kendrell Bell, LB, Steelers
2002			Clinton Portis, RB, Broncos	Julius Peppers, DE, Panthers	Clinton Portis, RB, Broncos
2003			Anquan Boldin, WR, Cardinals	Terrell Suggs, LB, Ravens	Anquan Boldin, WR, Cardinals
2004			Ben Roethlisberger, QB, Steelers	Jonathan Vilma, LB, Jets	Ben Roethlisberger, QB, Steelers
2005			Cadillac Williams, RB, Buccaneers	Shawne Merriman, LB, Chargers	Shawne Merriman, LB, Chargers

COACH OF THE YEAR

YEAR	AP NFL COACH OF THE YEAR	PFW/PFWA COACH OF THE YEAR	SPORTING NEWS NFL COACH OF THE YEAR	UPI NFL/NFC COACH OF THE YEAR	UPI AFL/AFC COACH OF THE YEAR	EARLE NEALE AWARD
1947			Jimmy Conzelman, Cardinals			
1948			Earle (Greasy) Neale, Eagles			
1949			Paul Brown, Browns (AAFC)			
1950			Steve Owen, Giants			
1951			Paul Brown, Browns			
1952			J. Hampton Pool, Rams			
1953			Paul Brown, Browns			
1954			None			
1955			Joe Kuharich, Redskins	Joe Kuharich, Redskins		
1956			Jim Lee Howell, Giants	Buddy Parker, Lions		
1957	George Wilson, Lions		None	Paul Brown, Browns		
1958	Weeb Ewbank, Colts		None	Weeb Ewbank, Colts		
1959	Vince Lombardi, Packers		None	Vince Lombardi, Packers		
1960	Buck Shaw, Eagles		None	Buck Shaw, Eagles		
1961	Allie Sherman, Giants		Vince Lombardi, Packers	Allie Sherman, Giants	Lou Rymkus, Oilers	
1962	Allie Sherman, Giants		None	Allie Sherman, Giants	Wally Lemm, Oilers	
1963	George Halas, Bears		George Halas, Bears	George Halas, Bears	Jack Faulkner, Broncos	
1964	Don Shula, Colts		Don Shula, Colts	Don Shula, Colts	Al Davis, Raiders	
1965	George Halas, Bears		George Halas, Bears	George Halas, Bears	Lou Saban, Bills	
1966	Tom Landry, Cowboys		Tom Landry, Cowboys	Tom Landry, Cowboys	Lou Saban, Bills	
1967	George Allen, Rams; Don Shula, Colts		George Allen, Rams	George Allen, Rams	Mike Holovak, Boston John Rauch, Raiders	
1968	Don Shula, Colts	Hank Stram, Chiefs; Don Shula, Colts	Don Shula, Colts	Don Shula, Colts	Hank Stram, Chiefs	
1969	Bud Grant, Vikings	John Madden, Raiders; Bud Grant, Vikings	Bud Grant, Vikings	Bud Grant, Vikings	Paul Brown, Bengals	
1970	Dick Nolan, 49ers	Don Shula, Dolphins	Don Shula, Dolphins	Alex Webster, Giants	Paul Brown, Bengals	
1971	George Allen, Redskins	George Allen, Redskins	George Allen, Redskins	George Allen, Redskins	Paul Brown, Bengals	
1972	Dan Devine, Packers	Don Shula, Dolphins	Don Shula, Dolphins	Dan Devine, Packers	Don Shula, Dolphins	
1973	Chuck Knox, Rams	Chuck Knox, Rams	Chuck Knox, Rams	Chuck Knox, Rams	Chuck Noll, Steelers	
1974	Don Coryell, Cardinals	Don Coryell, Cardinals	Don Coryell, Cardinals	Don Coryell, Cardinals	John Ralston, Broncos	
1975	Ted Marchibroda, Colts	Ted Marchibroda, Colts	Ted Marchibroda, Colts	Tom Landry, Cowboys	Sid Gillman, Oilers; Ted Marchibroda, Colts	

	NEA NFL ROOKIE OF THE YEAR	PFW/PFWA OFF ROOKIE OF THE YEAR	PFW/PFWA DEF ROOKIE OF THE YEAR	PEPSI NFL ROOKIE OF THE YEAR
1955				
1956				
1957				
1958				
1959				
1960				
1961				
1962				
1963				
1964	Charley Taylor, HB, Redskins			
1965	Gale Sayers, HB, Bears			
1966	Tommy Nobis, LB, Falcons			
1967	Mel Farr, HB, Lions			
1968	Earl McCullouch, OE, Lions			
1969	Calvin Hill, HB, Cowboys	Greg Cook, QB, Bengals (AFL); Calvin Hill, RB, Cowboys (NFL)	Joe Greene, DT, Steelers (NFL); James Marsalis, CB Chiefs (AFL)	
1970	Raymond Chester, TE, Raiders	Dennis Shaw, QB, Bills	Bruce Taylor, CB, 49ers	
1971	John Brockington, RB, Packers (NFC); Jim Plunkett, QB, Patriots (AFC)	Jim Plunkett, QB, Patriots	Isiah Robertson, LB, Rams	
1972	Willie Buchanon, CB, Packers (NFC); Franco Harris, RB, Steelers (AFC)	Franco Harris, RB, Steelers	Sherman White, DE, Bengals	
1973	Chuck Foreman, RB, Vikings (NFC); Boobie Clark, RB, Bengals (AFC)	Chuck Foreman, RB, Vikings	Wally Chambers, DT, Bears	
1974	Wilbur Jackson, RB, 49ers (NFC); Don Woods, RB, Chargers (AFC)	Don Woods, RB, Chargers	Jack Lambert, LB, Steelers	
1975	Steve Bartkowski, QB, Falcons (NFC); Robert Brazile, LB, Oilers (AFC)	Mike Thomas, RB, Redskins; Steve Bartkowski, QB, Falcons	Robert Brazile, LB, Oilers	
1976	Sammy White, WR, Vikings (NFC); Mike Haynes, CB, Patriots (AFC)	Sammy White, WR, Vikings	Mike Haynes, CB, Patriots	
1977	Tony Dorsett, RB, Cowboys	Tony Dorsett, RB, Cowboys	A.J. Duhe, DT, Dolphins	
1978	Earl Campbell, RB, Oilers	Earl Campbell, RB, Oilers	Al Baker, DE, Lions	
1979	Ottis Anderson, RB, Cardinals	Ottis Anderson, RB, Cardinals	Jesse Baker, DE, Oilers	
1980	Billy Sims, RB, Lions	Billy Sims, RB, Lions	Buddy Curry, LB, Falcons	
1981	Lawrence Taylor, LB, Giants	George Rogers, RB, Saints	Lawrence Taylor, LB, Giants	
1982	Marcus Allen, RB, Raiders	Marcus Allen, RB, Raiders	Chip Banks, LB, Browns	
1983	Eric Dickerson, RB, Rams	Eric Dickerson, RB, Rams	Vernon Maxwell, LB, Colts	
1984	Louis Lipps, WR, Steelers	Louis Lipps, WR, Steelers	Tom Flynn, S, Packers	
1985	Eddie Brown, WR, Bengals	No Award	No Award	
1986	Reuben Mayes, RB, Saints	Reuben Mayes, RB, Saints	Leslie O'Neal, DE, Chargers; John Offerdahl, LB, Dolphins	
1987	Bo Jackson, RB, Raiders	Troy Stradford, RB, Dolphins	Shane Conlan, LB, Bills	
1988	John Stephens, RB, Patriots	Ickey Woods, RB, Bengals; John Stephens, RB, Patriots	Eric McMillan, S, Jets	
1989	Barry Sanders, RB, Lions	Barry Sanders, RB, Lions	Derrick Thomas, LB, Chiefs	
1990		Emmitt Smith, RB, Cowboys	Mark Carrier, S, Bears	
1991		Leonard Russell, RB, Patriots	Mike Croel, LB, Broncos	
1992		Jason Hanson, PK, Lions.	Dale Carter, CB, Chiefs	
1993		Jerome Bettis, RB, Rams	Dana Stubblefield, DT, 49ers	
1994		Curtis Martin, RB, Patriots	Tim Bowens, DT, Dolphins	
1995		Curtis Martin, RB, Patriots	Hugh Douglas, DE, Jets	
1996		Eddie George, RB, Oilers	Simeon Rice, DE, Cardinals	
1997		Warrick Dunn, RB, Buccaneers	Peter Boulware, LB, Ravens	
1998		Randy Moss, WR, Vikings	Charles Woodson, CB, Raiders	
1999		Edgerrin James, RB, Colts	Jevon Kearse, DE, Titans	
2000		Mike Anderson, RB, Broncos	Brian Urlacher, LB, Bears	
2001		Anthony Thomas, RB, Bears	Kendrell Bell, LB, Steelers	
2002		Clinton Portis, RB, Broncos	Julius Peppers, DE, Panthers	Jeremy Shockey, TE, Giants
2003		Anquan Boldin, WR, Cardinals	Terrell Suggs, LB, Ravens	Domanick Davis, RB, Texans
2004		Ben Roethlisberger, QB, Steelers	Dunta Robinson, CB, Texans	Ben Roethlisberger, QB, Steelers
2005		Cadillac Williams, RB, Buccaneers	Shawne Merriman, LB, Chargers	Cadillac Williams, RB, Buccaneers

COACH OF THE YEAR (CONT.)

YEAR	AP NFL COACH OF THE YEAR	PFW/PFWA COACH OF THE YEAR	SPORTING NEWS NFL COACH OF THE YEAR	UPI NFL/NFC COACH OF THE YEAR	UPI AFL/AFC COACH OF THE YEAR	EARLE NEALE AWARD
1976	Forrest Gregg, Browns	Chuck Fairbanks, Patriots	Chuck Fairbanks, Patriots	Jack Pardee, Bears	Chuck Fairbanks, Patriots	
1977	Red Miller, Broncos	Red Miller, Broncos	Red Miller, Broncos	Leeman Bennett, Falcons	Red Miller, Broncos	
1978	Jack Patera, Seahawks	Walt Michaels, Jets	Jack Patera, Seattle	Dick Vermeil, Eagles	Walt Michaels, Jets	
1979	Jack Pardee, Redskins	Dick Vermeil, Eagles	Dick Vermeil, Eagles	Jack Pardee, Redskins	Sam Rutigliano, Browns	
1980	Chuck Knox, Bills	Chuck Knox, Bills	Chuck Knox, Bills	Leeman Bennett, Falcons	Sam Rutigliano, Browns	
1981	Bill Walsh, 49ers	Bill Walsh, 49ers	Bill Walsh, 49ers	Bill Walsh, 49ers	Forrest Gregg, Bengals	
1982	Joe Gibbs, Redskins	Joe Gibbs, Redskins	Joe Gibbs, Redskins	Joe Gibbs, Redskins	Tom Flores, Raiders	
1983	Joe Gibbs, Redskins	Joe Gibbs, Redskins	Joe Gibbs, Redskins	John Robinson, Rams	Chuck Knox, Seattle	
1984	Chuck Knox, Seahawks	No Award	Chuck Knox, Seattle	Bill Walsh, 49ers	Chuck Knox, Seattle	
1985	Mike Ditka, Bears	Dan Reeves, Broncos	Mike Ditka, Bears	Mike Ditka, Bears	Raymond Berry, Patriots	
1986	Bill Parcells, Giants	Bill Parcells, Giants	Bill Parcells, Giants	Bill Parcells, New York	Marty Schottenheimer, Browns	
1987	Jim Mora, Saints	Jim Mora, Saints	Jim Mora, Saints	Jim Mora, Saints	Ron Meyer, Colts	
1988	Mike Ditka, Bears	Mike Ditka, Bears	Marv Levy, Bills	Mike Ditka, Bears	Marv Levy, Bills	
1989	Lindy Infante, Packers	George Seifert, 49ers	Lindy Infante, Packers	Lindy Infante, Packers	Dan Reeves, Broncos	Chuck Noll, Steelers
1990	Jimmy Johnson, Cowboys	Art Shell, Raiders	George Seifert, 49ers	Jimmy Johnson, Cowboys	Art Shell, Los Angeles	Art Shell, Raiders
1991	Wayne Fontes, Lions	Wayne Fontes, Lions	Joe Gibbs, Redskins	Wayne Fontes, Lions	Dan Reeves, Broncos	Wayne Fontes, Lions
1992	Bill Cowher, Steelers	Bobby Ross, Chargers	Bill Cowher, Steelers	Dennis Green, Vikings	Bobby Ross, San Diego	Bobby Ross, Chargers
1993	Dan Reeves, Giants	Dan Reeves, Giants	Dan Reeves, Giants	Dan Reeves, Giants	Marv Levy, Bills	Dan Reeves, Giants
1994	Bill Parcells, Patriots	Bill Parcells, Patriots	George Seifert, 49ers	Dave Wannstedt, Bears	Bill Parcells, Patriots	Bill Parcells, Patriots
1995	Ray Rhodes, Eagles	Dom Capers, Panthers	Ray Rhodes, Eagles	Ray Rhodes, Eagles	Marty Schottenheimer, Chiefs	Ray Rhodes, Eagles
1996	Dom Capers, Panthers	Dom Capers, Panthers	Dom Capers, Panthers	Dom Capers, Panthers	Tom Coughlin, Jaguars	Dom Capers, Panthers
1997	Jim Fassel, Giants	Jim Fassel, Giants	Jim Fassel, Giants			Tony Dungy, Buccaneers
1998	Dan Reeves, Falcons	Dan Reeves, Falcons	Dan Reeves, Falcons			Dennis Green, Vikings
1999	Dick Vermeil, Rams	Dick Vermeil, Rams	Dick Vermeil, Cardinals			Dick Vermeil, Rams
2000	Jim Haslett, Saints	Jim Haslett, Saints	Andy Reid, Eagles			Andy Reid, Eagles
2001	Dick Jauron, Bears	Dick Jauron, Bears	Dick Jauron, Bears			Dick Jauron, Bears
2002	Andy Reid, Eagles	Andy Reid, Eagles	Andy Reid, Eagles			Andy Reid, Eagles
2003	Bill Belichick, Patriots	Bill Belichick, Patriots	Bill Belichick, Patriots			Dick Vermeil, Chiefs
2004	Marty Schottenheimer, Chargers	Marty Schottenheimer, Chargers	Bill Cowher, Steelers			Marty Schottenheimer, Chargers
2005	Lovie Smith, Bears	Lovie Smith, Bears	Tony Dungy, Colts			Tony Dungy, Colts

PFW/PFWA Comeback Player of The Year

1972 Earl Morrall, QB, Dolphins
1973 Roman Gabriel, QB, Eagles
1974 Joe Namath, QB, Jets
1975 Dave Hampton, RB, Falcons
1976 Greg Landry, QB, Lions
1977 Craig Morton, QB, Broncos
1978 John Riggens, RB, Redskins
1979 Larry Csonka, RB, Dolphins
1980 Jim Plunkett, QB, Raiders
1981 Ken Anderson, QB, Bengals
1982 Lyle Alzado, DE, Raiders
1983 Billy Johnson, WR, Falcons
1984 John Stallworth, WR, Steelers
1985 No award given
1986 Joe Montana, QB, 49ers;Tommy Kramer, QB, Vikings
1987 Charles White, RB, Rams
1988 Greg Bell, RB, Rams
1989 Ottis Anderson, RB, Giants
1990 Barry Word, RB, Chiefs
1991 Jim McMahon, QB, Eagles
1992 Randall Cunningham, QB, Eagles
1993 Marcus Allen, RB, Chiefs
1994 Dan Marino, QB, Dolphins
1995 Jim Harbaugh, QB, Colts
1996 Jerome Bettis, RB, Steelers
1997 Robert Brooks, WR, ackers
1998 Doug Flutie, QB, Bills
1999 Bryant Young, DT, 49ers
2000 Joe Johnson, DE, Saints
2001 Garrison Hearst, RB, 49ers
2002 Tommy Maddox, QB, Steelers
2003 Jon Kitna, QB, Bengals
2004 William McGahee, RB, Bills
2005 Steve Smith, WR, Panthers

PFW/PFWA Most Improved Player Of the Year

2000 Jeff Garcia, QB, 49ers
2001 Kordell Stewart, QB, Steelers
2002 Chad Pennington, QB, Jets
2003 Jon Kitna, QB, Bengals
2004 Drew Brees, QB, Chargers
2005 Osi Umenyiora; DE, Giants

Executive of the Year

YEAR	SPORTING NEWS GEORGE YOUNG NFL EXEC OF THE YEAR AWARD	PFW/PFWA EXEC OF THE YEAR
1955	Dan Reeves, Rams	
1956	George Halas, Bears	
1972	Dan Rooney, Steelers	
1973	Jim Finks, Vikings	
1974	Art Rooney, Steelers	
1975	Joe Thomas, Colts	
1976	Al Davis, Raiders	
1977	Tex Schramm, Cowboys	
1978	John Thompson, Seahawks	
1979	John Sanders, Chargers	
1980	Eddie LeBaron, Falcons	
1981	Paul Brown, Bengals	
1982	Bobby Beathard, Redskins	
1983	Bobby Beathard, Redskins	
1984	George Young, Giants	
1985	Mike McCaskey, Bears	
1986	George Young, Giants	
1987	Jim Finks, Saints	
1988	Bill Polian, Bills	
1989	John McVay, 49ers	
1990	George Young, Giants	
1991	Bill Polian, Bills	
1992	Ron Wolf, Packers	
1993	George Young, Giants	George Young, Giants
1994	Carmen Policy, 49ers	Carmen Policy, 49ers
1995	Bill Polian, Panthers	Bill Polian, Panthers
1996	Bill Polian, Panthers	Bill Polian, Panthers
1997	George Young, Giants	George Young, Giants
1998	Jeff Diamond, Vikings	Vikings Front Office
1999	Bill Polian, Colts	Bill Polian, Colts
2000	Randy Mueller, Saints	Randy Mueller, Saints
2001	Dan Rooney, Steelers	Charley Armey, Rams
2002	Bruce Allen, Raiders	Al Davis, Raiders
2003	Scott Pioli, Patriots	Scott Pioli, Patriots
2004	Scott Pioli, Patriots	A.J. Smith, Chargers
2005	Art Rooney II, Steelers	Bill Polian, Colts

PFW/PFWA Golden Toe Award

1971 Garo Yepremian, K, Dolphins
1972 Don Cockroft, PK, Browns
1973 David Ray, K, Rams
1974 Roy Gerela, K, Steelers
1975 Ray Guy, P, Raiders
1976 Toni Linhart, K, Colts
1977 Mark Moseley, K, Redskins
1978 Frank Corral, K, Rams
1979 Bob Grupp, P, Chiefs
1980 Fred Steinfort, K, Broncos
1981 Rafael Septien, K, Cowboys
1982 Mark Moseley, K, Redskins
1983 Ali Haji-Sheikh, K, Giants
1984 Norm Johnson, K, Seahawks
1985 No Selection
1986 Morten Andersen, K, Saints
1987 Jim Arnold, P, Lions
1988 Scott Norwood, K, Bills
1989 Eddie Murray, K, Lions
1990 Nick Lowery, K, Chiefs
1991 Jeff Gossett, P, Raiders
1992 Rich Camarillo, P, Cardinals
1993 Norm Johnson, K, Falcons
1994 Fuad Reveiz, K, Vikings
1995 Morten Andersen, K, Falcons
1996 Cary Blanchard, K, Colts
1997 Pete Stoyanovich, K, Chiefs
1998 Gary Anderson, K, Vikings
1999 Craig Hentrich, P, Titans
2000 Matt Stover, K, Ravens
2001 Todd Sauerbrun, P, Panthers
2002 Adam Vinatieri, K, Patriots
2003 Mike Vanderjagt, K, Colts
2004 Adam Vinatieri, K, Patriots
2005 Neil Rackers, K, Cardinals

PFW/PFWA Assistant Coach of the Year

1993 Ray Rhodes, Packers
1994 Dom Capers, Steelers
1995 Pete Carroll, 49ers
1996 Dave Campo, Cowboys
1997 John Fox, Giants
1998 Brian Billick, Vikings
1999 Dom Capers, Jaguars
2000 Marvin Lewis, Ravens
2001 Mike Mularkey, Steelers
2002 Monte Kiffin, Buccaneers
2003 Romeo Crennel, Patriots
2004 Dick LeBeau, Steelers
2005 Ron Rivera, Bears

Byron "Whizzer" White Award

1967 Bart Starr, QB, Packers
1968 Willie Davis, DE, Packers
1969 Eddie Meador, DB, Rams
1970 Gale Sayers, HB, Bears
1971 Kermit Alexander, LB, Rams
1972 Ray May, LB, Colts
1973 Andy Russell, LB, Steelers
1974 Floyd Little, RB, Broncos
1975 Rocky Bleier, RB, Steelers
1976 Jim Hart, QB, Cardinals
1977 Lyle Alzado, DE, Broncos
1978 Archie Manning, QB, Saints
1979 Roger Staubach, QB, Cowboys
1980 Gene Upshaw, G, Raiders
1981 Ken Houston, LB, Redskins
1982 Franco Harris, RB, Steelers
1983 Doug Dieken, T, Browns
1984 Stump Mitchell, RB, Cardinals
1985 Reggie Williams, LB, Bengals
1986 Nat Moore, WR, Dolphins
1987 George Martin, DE, Giants
1988 Deron Cherry, DB, Chiefs
1989 Mike Singletary, LB, Bears
1990 Ozzie Newsome, TE, Browns
1991 Mike Kenn, T, Falcons
1992 Reggie White, DE, Eagles
1993 Nick Lowery, K, Chiefs
1994 Mark Kelso, DB, Bills
1995 Derrick Thomas, LB, Chiefs
1996 Bill Brooks, WR, Bills
1997 Chris Zorich, DT, Bears
1998 Hardy Nickerson, LB, Buccaneers
1999 Cris Carter, WR, Vikings
2000 Doug Pelfrey, K, Bengals
2001 Michael McCrary, DE, Ravens
2002 Mark Brunell, QB, Jaguars
2003 Troy Vincent, CB, Eagles
2004 Derrick Brooks, Buccaneers
2005 Payton Manning, QB, Colts
2006 Steve McNair, QB, Titans

PETE ROZELLE RADIO-TELEVISION AWARD

1989 Bill McPhail
1990 Lindsey Nelson
1991 Ed Sabol
1992 Chris Schenkel
1993 Curt Gowdy
1994 Pat Summerall
1995 Frank Gifford
1996 Jack Buck
1997 Charlie Jones
1998 Val Pinchbeck
1999 Dick Enberg
2000 Ray Scott
2001 Roone Arledge
2002 John Madden
2003 Don Criqui
2004 Van Miller
2005 Myron Cope

WALTER PAYTON NFL MAN OF THE YEAR

1970 Johnny Unitas, QB, Colts
1971 John Hadl, QB, Chargers
1972 Willie Lanier, LB, Chiefs
1973 Len Dawson, QB, Chiefs
1974 George Blanda, QB, Raiders
1975 Ken Anderson, QB, Bengals
1976 Franco Harris, RB, Steelers
1977 Walter Payton, RB , Bears

WALTER PAYTON NFL MAN OF THE YEAR (CONT.)

1978 Roger Staubach, QB, Cowboys
1979 Joe Greene, DT, Steelers
1980 Harold Carmichael, WR, Eagles
1981 Lynn Swann, WR, Steelers
1982 Joe Theismann, QB, Redskins
1983 Rolf Benirschke, K, Chargers
1984 Marty Lyons, Tackle, Jets
1985 Dwight Stephenson, C, Dolphins
1986 Reggie Williams, LB, Bengals
1987 Dave Duerson, S, Bears
1988 Steve Largent, WR, Seahawks
1989 Warren Moon, QB, Oilers
1990 Mike Singletary, LB, Bears
1991 Anthony Munoz, Tackle, Bengals
1992 John Elway, QB, Broncos
1993 Derrick Thomas, LB, Chiefs
1994 Junior Seau, LB, Chargers
1995 Boomer Esiason, QB , Jets
1996 Darrell Green, CB, Redskins
1997 Troy Aikman, QB, Cowboys
1998 Dan Marino, QB, Dolphins
1999 Cris Carter, WR, Vikings
2000 Derrick Brooks, Buccaneers; Jim Flanigan, Bears
2001 Jerome Bettis, RB, Steelers
2002 Troy Vincent, DE, Eagles
2003 Will Shields, G, Chiefs
2004 Warrick Dunn, RB, Falcons
2005 Peyton Manning, QB, Colts

RETIRED UNIFORM NUMBERS

In 1973 the National Football League codified a system of assigning uniform numbers, setting up ranges of numbers to be assigned to players depending on their positions. The league actually initiated many of the uniform number standards back in 1952, but those rules were not strictly enforced and what enforcement there was focused on only players at certain positions. The 1973 rules limited every player to a relatively small range of possible numbers and strict enforcement began immediately. Quarterbacks and all types of kickers were eligible for numbers from 1 to 19. For running backs and various defensive backs, the possibilities were 20 through 49. The 80s were set aside for wide receivers and tight ends. Offensive and defensive linemen were assigned numbers in the 60s and 70s. Numbers in the 50s were given to centers and linebackers.

As a result of larger rosters and retired numbers, these policies have had to be relaxed somewhat to ensure there is a number for every player. Linebackers and defensive linemen, for example, now wear numbers in the 90s as well as the lower ranges assigned to them. The most recent change occurred in 2004, when the NFL authorized teams to allow the use of 10 to 19 by wide receivers and linebackers

While the NFL has shown flexibility about the uniform number policy when absolutely necessary, it has been unwilling to make any exception to its rules for specific players interested in specific numbers. In the mid-1980s rookie Seattle Seahawks linebacker Brian Bosworth campaigned to use his college number 44. The Seahawks tried to get around the rules and awarded him that number, but the NFL intervened and forced Bosworth to switch to 55. In 2006 Reggie Bush campaigned to use his college number (5) with the New Orleans Saints, but even his offer of donating revenues from his uniform sales to victims of Hurricane Katrina failed to persuade the league to allow an exception.

The retired uniform numbers listed in this section show that each player once had a much larger palette of uniform numbers to choose from. The NFL, however, believes that fans are better able to follow the game when they can identify players playing specific positions by their uniform number. Officials clearly benefit from the system; it is much easier, for example, to spot an ineligible receiver downfield on a pass play when any offensive player downfield not wearing a number in a certain range is clearly violating the rules.

Beyond the range of numbers comes the decision of when to retire numbers. Entering 2006, 27 NFL teams have retired uniform numbers. The storied Dallas Cowboys and Oakland Raiders have chosen not to retire any uniform numbers, although Dallas does honor former greats in the Ring of Honor at Texas Stadium and Jim Otto's number (00) is in essence retired because the league no longer issues double zero. The Jacksonville Jaguars, Baltimore Ravens, and Houston Texans, meanwhile, are new franchises and have not yet had a player worthy of having his number retired.

Even within the teams of the NFL that do retire numbers, it's clear that approaches vary. The Chicago Bears have retired 13 numbers, while the Pittsburgh Steelers have retired only one, for Ernie Stautner. Just because a team hasn't retired a number, however, doesn't mean that current players can wear them. The Steelers, for example, may not have retired the numbers of 1970s greats like Terry Bradshaw and Franco Harris, but the club hasn't used their uniform numbers since those players retired. Most retired numbers are retired in honor of the career achievements of the player who wore that number, but there are exceptions. Several uniform numbers have been retired in tribute to players who died in the middle of their careers. Other teams have honored former players who died prematurely. Pat Tillman, who was killed while fighting for the U.S. military in Afghanistan in 2004, had his number 40 retired by the Arizona Cardinals. Sam Mills, one of the first stars for the Carolina Panthers who later served as the team's linebackers coach after he finished playing, had his number 51 retired in 2005 shortly after his death from intestinal cancer at age 45.

BEARS
Bronko Nagurski	3
George McAfee	5
George Halas	7
Willie Galimore	28
Walter Payton	34
Gale Sayers	40
Brian Piccolo	41
Sid Luckman	42
Dick Butkus	51
Bill Hewitt	56
Bill George	61
Bulldog Turner	66
Red Grange	77

BENGALS
Bob Johnson	54

BILLS
Jim Kelly	12

BRONCOS
John Elway	7
Frank Tripucka	18
Floyd Little	44

BROWNS
Otto Graham	14
Jim Brown	32
Ernie Davis	45
Don Fleming	46
Lou Groza	76

BUCCANEERS
Lee Roy Selmon	63

CARDINALS
Larry Wilson	8
Pat Tillman	40
Stan Mauldin	77
J.V. Cain	88
Marshall Goldberg	99

CHARGERS
Dan Fouts	14

CHIEFS
Jan Stenerud	3
Len Dawson	16
Abner Haynes	28
Stone Johnson	33
Mack Lee Hill	36
Willie Lanier	63
Bobby Bell	78
Buck Buchanan	86

COLTS
Johnny Unitas	19
Buddy Young	22
Lenny Moore	24
Art Donovan	70
Jim Parker	77
Raymond Berry	82
Gino Marchetti	89

DOLPHINS
Bob Griese	12
Dan Marino	13
Larry Csonka	39

EAGLES
Steve Van Buren	15
Tom Brookshier	40
Pete Retzlaff	44
Chuck Bednarik	60
Al Wistert	70
Reggie White	92
Jerome Brown	99

FALCONS
Steve Bartkowski	10
William Andrews	31
Jeff Van Note	57
Tommy Nobis	60

49ERS
John Brodie	12
Joe Montana	16
Joe Perry	34
Jimmy Johnson	37
Hugh McElhenny	39
Charlie Krueger	70
Leo Nomellini	73
Bob St. Clair	79
Dwight Clark	87

GIANTS
Ray Flaherty	1
Tuffy Leemans	4
Mel Hein	7
Phil Simms	11
Y.A. Tittle	14
Frank Gifford	16
Al Blozis	32
Joe Morrison	40
Charlie Conerly	42
Ken Strong	50
Lawrence Taylor	56

JETS
Joe Namath	12
Don Maynard	13
Joe Klecko	73

LIONS
Dutch Clark	7
Bobby Layne	22
Doak Walker	37
Joe Schmidt	56
Chuck Hughes	85

PACKERS
Tony Canadeo	3
Don Hutson	14
Bart Starr	15
Ray Nitschke	66
Reggie White	92

PANTHERS
Sam Mills	51

PATRIOTS
Bruce Armstrong	78
Gino Cappelletti	20
Mike Haynes	40
Steve Nelson	57
John Hannah	73
Jim Lee Hunt	79
Bob Dee	89

RAMS
Bob Waterfield	7
Eric Dickerson	29
Merlin Olsen	74
Jackie Slater	78
Jack Youngblood	85

REDSKINS
Sammy Baugh	33

SAINTS
Jim Taylor	31
Doug Atkins	81

SEAHAWKS
Fans/The 12th Man	12
Steve Largent	80

STEELERS
Ernie Stautner	70

TITANS (OILERS)
Earl Campbell	34
Jim Norton	43
Mike Munchak	63
Elvin Bethea	65
Bruce Matthews	74

VIKINGS
Fran Tarkenton	10
Mick Tingelhoff	53
Jim Marshall	70
Korey Stringer	77
Cris Carter	80
Alan Page	88

GREAT PERFORMANCES

Robert Bailey of the Rams returned only 1 punt in his career, but it was quite an effort. Against the Saints on October 23, 1994, Bailey returned a punt a league-record 103 yards. He went on to play seven more years until 2001, when his career was cut short by a neck injury, but he never returned another punt. His record return occurred while the punt lay on the ground in the end zone and some of the Saints left the field, thinking it had been ruled dead. Bailey picked it up and ran for the touchdown. The Saints still won the game, largely due to 347 return yards by Tyrone Hughes, who set records with 7 kickoff returns for 304 yards and 2 touchdowns and 43 more yards on 3 punt returns.

Bailey's return is an example of the kind of long play that takes a team from one end of the field to the other and can dramatically alter the course of any football game in only a few moments. It can happen any number of different ways. A running back breaks a few tackles on a play early in the game and then is able to sail down the field. The quarterback throws a long Hail Mary in the final moments of the game and it is caught by a receiver in the end zone. A tipped pass falls into the hands of a defensive end on his own 2-yard line and he just runs as fast as he can till he scores. This section features the longest plays in NFL history in several different categories.

Top 100 Rushing Plays

99 Tony Dorsett, Cowboys, Jan. 3, 1983
98 Ahman Green, Packers, Dec. 28, 2003
97 Andy Uram, Packers, Oct. 8, 1939
97 Bob Gage, Steelers, Dec. 4, 1949
96 Jim Spavital, Colts, Nov. 5, 1950
96 Bob Hoernschemeyer, Lions, Nov. 23, 1950
96 Garrison Hearst, 49ers, Sept. 6, 1998
96 Corey Dillon, Bengals, Oct. 28, 2001
95 Tiki Barber, Giants, Dec. 31, 2005
94 O.J. Simpson, Bills, Oct. 29, 1972
92 Kenny Washington, Rams, Nov. 2, 1947
92 Bo Jackson, Raiders, Nov. 5, 1989
91 Sid Blanks, Oilers, Dec. 13, 1964
91 Bo Jackson, Raiders, Nov. 30, 1987
91 Herschel Walker, Eagles, Nov. 27, 1994
90 Bobby Mitchell, Browns, Nov. 15, 1959
90 Wilbert Montgomery, Eagles, Dec. 19, 1982
90 Fred Taylor, Jaguars, Jan. 15, 2000 (playoff)
90 Ahman Green, Packers, Oct. 24, 2004
90 Johnny Johnson, Jets, Sept. 25, 1994 (no td)
89 Hugh McElhenny, 49ers, Oct. 5, 1952
89 Kenny King, Raiders, Oct. 12, 1980
88 Parker Hall, Rams, Oct. 29, 1939
88 Billy Wells, Redskins, Nov. 21, 1954
88 O.J. Simpson, Bills, Sept. 28, 1975
88 Shaun Alexander, Seahawks, Nov. 11, 2001
88 Shaun Alexander, Seahawks, Nov. 6, 2005
88 Bo Jackson, Raiders, Dec. 16, 1990 (no td)
87 John Henry Johnson, Steelers, Dec. 11, 1960
87 Jack Larscheid, Raiders, Oct. 16, 1960
87 Paul Lowe, Chargers, Sept. 10, 1961
87 Paul Robinson, Bengals, Oct. 27, 1968
86 Bill Osmanski, Bears, Oct. 15, 1939
86 Hugh McElhenny, 49ers, Nov. 18, 1956
86 Keith Lincoln, Chargers, Sept. 30, 1962
86 Essex Johnson, Bengals, Dec. 5, 1971
86 Joey Galloway, Seahawks, Nov. 12, 1995
85 Pete Stinchcomb, Chicago Staleys, Nov. 20, 1921
85 Len Sedbrook, Giants, Oct. 16, 1930
85 Bob Hoernschemeyer, Lions, Nov. 22, 1951
85 Larry Garron, Patriots, Oct. 22, 1961
85 John Fuqua, Steelers, Dec. 20, 1970
85 Eric Dickerson, Rams, Sept. 25, 1983
85 Greg Bell, Bills, Nov. 18, 1984
85 Reggie Brooks, Redskins, Sept. 19, 1993
85 Brian Mitchell, Eagles, Oct. 1, 2000
85 Michael Bennett, Vikings, Nov. 3, 2002
85 Barry Sanders, Lions, Oct. 2, 1994 (no td)
84 Ike Peterson, Lions, Nov. 8, 1936
84 Tom Harmon, Rams, Oct. 13, 1946
84 Bob Hoernschemeyer, Brooklyn Dodgers (AAFC), Oct. 17, 1947
84 Jim Taylor, Packers, Nov. 8, 1964
84 Tony Dorsett, Cowboys, Dec. 4, 1977
84 Ted McKnight, Chiefs, Sept. 30, 1979
84 Herschel Walker, Cowboys, Dec. 14, 1986
83 Hugh McElhenny, 49ers, Oct. 26, 1952
83 John David Crow, Cardinals, Oct. 4, 1958
83 Tony Teresa, Raiders, Nov. 13, 1960
83 James Lofton, Packers, Sept. 20, 1982
83 Napoleon Kaufman, Raiders, Oct. 19, 1997
83 Ahman Green, Packers, Sept. 9, 2001
83 Jess Phillips, Bengals, Nov. 2, 1969 (no td)
83 Michael Turner, Chargers, Dec. 18, 2005

82 Beattie Feathers, Bears, Oct. 10, 1934
82 Dutch Clark, Lions, Oct. 28, 1934
82 Elmer Angsman, Cardinals, Oct. 23, 1949
82 Tommy Wilson, Rams, Oct. 12, 1958
82 Gene Mingo, Broncos, Oct. 5, 1962
82 Joe Delaney, Chiefs, Oct. 18, 1981
82 Barry Sanders, Lions, Oct. 12, 1997
82 Derrick Alexander, Chiefs, Dec. 18, 1999
82 Jamal Lewis, Ravens, Sept. 14, 2003
81 Glenn Presnell, Portland Spartans, Nov. 5, 1933
81 Swede Hanson, Eagles, Sept. 16, 1934
81 Rick Casares, Bears, Oct. 16, 1955
81 Earl Campbell, Oilers, Nov. 20, 1978
81 Billy Sims, Lions, Sept. 30, 1984 (no td)
80 Paddy Driscoll, Cardinals, Oct. 18, 1925
80 Hinkey Haines, Giants, Nov. 7, 1926
80 Harry Newman, Giants, Oct. 8, 1933
80 Lloyd Cardwell, Lions, Nov. 15, 1942
80 Wally Triplett, Lions, Oct. 30, 1949
80 Rob Goode, Redskins, Sept. 24, 1950
80 Eddie Price, Giants, Dec. 9, 1951
80 J.D. Smith, 49ers, Dec. 7, 1958
80 Jon Arnett, Rams, Nov. 22, 1959
80 Jim Brown, Browns, Sept. 15, 1963
80 Tom Matte, Colts, Oct. 12, 1964
80 Abner Haynes, Chiefs, Nov. 29, 1964
80 Wray Carlton, Bills, Dec. 5, 1965
80 Brad Hubbert, Chargers, Dec. 24, 1967
80 Warren McVea, Bengals, Sept. 22, 1968
80 Clint Jones, Vikings, Nov. 2, 1969
80 Warren McVea, Chiefs, Oct. 26, 1969
80 Carl Garrett, Patriots, Nov. 9, 1969
80 Floyd Little, Broncos, Oct. 25, 1970
80 Willie Ellison, Rams, Dec. 5, 1971
80 O.J. Simpson, Bills, Sept. 16, 1973
80 Delvin Williams, 49ers, Nov. 7, 1976
80 Neal Anderson, Bears, Nov. 27, 1988
80 Roger Craig, 49ers, Jan. 1, 1989 (playoff)
80 Thurman Thomas, Bills, Nov. 18, 1990
80 Kordell Stewart, Steelers, Dec. 22, 1996
80 Barry Sanders, Lions, Oct. 12, 1997
80 Barry Sanders, Lions, Nov. 23, 1997
80 Napoleon Kaufman, Raiders, Sept. 13, 1998
80 Corey Dillon, Bengals, Oct. 8, 2000
80 Tyrone Wheatley, Raiders, Oct. 22, 2000
80 Mike Anderson, Broncos, Nov. 26, 2000
80 Charlie Garner, Raiders, Jan. 12, 2002 (playoff)
80 Jessie Clark, Packers, Sept. 29, 1985 (not TD)
80 Bob Davis, Yanks, Nov. 19, 1944 (not TD)
80 Troy Hambrick, Cowboys, Sept. 30, 2001 (not TD)
80 Leroy Harris, Eagles, Nov. 25, 1979 (not TD)
80 Wilbur Jackson, 49ers, Nov. 27, 1977 (not TD)
80 Larry Moriarty, Oilers, Sept. 11, 1983 (not TD)
80 Willie Parker, Steelers, Dec. 24, 2005

Top 100 Passing Plays

99 Andy Farkas from Frank Filchock, Redskins, Oct. 15, 1939
99 Mac Speedie from Otto Graham, Browns (AAFC), Nov. 2, 1947
99 Bobby Mitchell from George Izo, Redskins, Sept. 15, 1963
99 Pat Studstill from Karl Sweetan, Lions, Oct. 16, 1966
99 Gerry Allen from Sonny Jurgensen, Redskins, Sept. 15, 1968
99 Cliff Branch from Jim Plunkett, Raiders, Oct. 2, 1983
99 Mike Quick from Ron Jaworski, Eagles, Nov. 10, 1985
99 Tony Martin from Stan Humphries, Chargers, Sept. 18, 1994
99 Robert Brooks from Brett Favre, Packers, Sept. 11, 1995
99 Marc Boerigter from Trent Green, Chiefs, Dec. 22, 2002
99 Andre' Davis from Jeff Garcia, Browns, Oct. 17, 2004
98 Gaynell Tinsley from Doug Russell, Cardinals, Nov. 27, 1938
98 Night Train Lane from Ogden Compton, Cardinals, Nov. 13, 1955
98 Bo Farrington from Billy Wade, Bears, Oct. 8, 1961
98 Willard Dewveall from Jacky Lee, Oilers, Nov. 25, 1962
98 Homer Jones from Earl Morrall, Giants, Sept. 11, 1966
98 Michael Haynes from Bobby Hebert, Falcons, Sept. 12, 1993
98 Johnnie Morton from Charlie Batch, Lions, Oct. 4, 1998
98 Bobby Moore (Ahman Rashad) from Jim Hart, Cardinals, Dec. 10, 1972 (not TD)
97 Gaynell Tinsley from Doug Russell, Cardinals, Dec. 5, 1937
97 Cloyce Box from Bobby Layne, Lions, Dec. 5, 1953
97 Jerry Tarr from George Shaw, Broncos, Sept. 21, 1962
97 Webster Slaughter from Bernie Kosar, Browns, Oct. 23, 1989
97 John Taylor from Steve Young, 49ers, Nov. 3, 1991
96 Billy Grimes from Tobin Rote, Packers, Dec. 10, 1950
96 Ollie Matson from Frank Ryan, Rams, Oct. 1, 1961
96 Al Frazier from Frank Tripucka, Broncos, Sept. 15, 1962
96 Frank Grant from Billy Kilmer, Redskins, Nov. 9, 1975
96 Wesley Walker from Ken O'Brien, Jets, Dec. 8, 1985
96 Jerry Rice from Joe Montana, 49ers, Oct. 27, 1988
96 Shannon Sharpe from Trent Dilfer, Ravens, Jan. 14, 2001 (playoff)
96 Walter Roberts from Billy Kilmer, Saints, Nov. 19, 1967 (not TD)
95 Bucky Pope from Bill Munson, Rams, Dec. 13, 1964
95 Dick Compton from George Blanda, Oilers, Dec. 5, 1965
95 Bob Hayes from Don Meredith, Cowboys, Nov. 13, 1966
95 Steve Odom from Lynn Dickey, Packers, Oct. 2, 1977

TOP 100 PASSING PLAYS (CONT.)

95 Steve Watson from Craig Morton, Broncos, Oct. 11, 1981
95 John Taylor from Joe Montana, 49ers, Dec. 11, 1989
95 Fred Barnett from Randall Cunningham, Eagles, Dec. 2, 1990
95 Quinn Early from Todd Collins, Bills, Dec. 1, 1996
94 Glenn Bass from Jack Kemp, Bills, Oct. 11, 1964
94 Warren Wells from George Blanda, Raiders, Nov. 10, 1968
94 Rich Houston from Norm Snead, Giants, Sept. 24, 1972
94 Billy Brooks from Ken Anderson, Bengals, Nov. 13, 1977
94 Leonard Thompson from Eric Hipple, Lions, Oct. 19, 1981
94 Alvin Harper from Troy Aikman, Cowboys, Jan. 8, 1995 (playoff)
94 Jamal Anderson from Chris Chandler, Falcons, Sept. 23, 2001
93 Red Phillips from Billy Wade, Rams, Nov. 16, 1958
93 Dobie Craig from Tom Flores, Raiders, Oct. 20, 1963
93 Elbert Dubenion from Tom Flores, Bills, Dec. 28, 1963 (playoff)
93 Dick Gordon from Jack Concannon, Bears, Nov. 19, 1967
93 Wendell Tucker from Roman Gabriel, Rams, Nov. 9, 1969
93 Robert Holmes 14, lateral from Otis Taylor 79 from Mike Livingston, Chiefs, Nov. 20, 1969
93 Freddie Solomon from Steve DeBerg, 49ers, Sept. 28, 1980
93 Steve Watson from Craig Morton, Broncos, Sept. 27, 1981
93 Ernie Jones from Neil Lomax, Cardinals, Dec. 10, 1988
93 Herman Moore from Rodney Peete, Lions, Oct. 31, 1993
93 Herschel Walker from Randall Cunningham, Eagles, Sept. 4, 1994 (not TD)
92 Don Hutson from Arnie Herber, Packers, Oct. 8, 1939
92 Del Shofner from Billy Wade, Rams, Oct. 19, 1958
92 Bill Groman from Jacky Lee, Oilers, Nov. 20, 1960
92 Tommy Brooker from Len Dawson, Cowboys, Nov. 18, 1962
92 Dan Lewis from Milt Plum, Lions, Nov. 15, 1964
92 Ben Hawkins from Len Dawson, Eagles, Sept. 22, 1968
92 Gloster Richardson from Len Dawson, Chiefs, Nov. 3, 1968
92 Frank Lewis from Joe Ferguson, Bills, Sept. 17, 1978
92 John Taylor from Joe Montana, 49ers, Dec. 11, 1989
92 Derrick Alexander from Eric Zeier, Ravens, Dec. 7, 1997 (not TD)
92 Marcus Allen from Marc Wilson, Raiders, Oct. 7, 1984 (not TD)
91 Elroy Hirsch from Bob Waterfield, Rams, Dec. 2, 1951
91 Tommy McDonald from M.C. Reynolds, Eagles, Oct. 5, 1958
91 John David Crow from M.C. Reynolds, Cardinals, Oct. 12, 1958
91 Willard Dewveall from Ed Brown, Bears, Oct. 16, 1960
91 Boyd Dowler from Ed Brown, Packers, Dec. 17, 1960
91 Keith Lincoln from Jack Kemp, Chargers, Nov. 12, 1961
91 Tony Dorsett from Roger Staubach, Cowboys, Sept. 4, 1978
91 Brett Perriman from Scott Mitchell, Lions, Dec. 23, 1995
91 David Patten from Tom Brady, Patriots, Oct. 21, 2001
91 Rich Caster from Joe Namath, Jets, Oct. 26, 1975 (not TD)
91 Terrell Owens from Donovan McNabb, Eagles, Oct. 30, 2005
90 Billy Howton from Babe Parilli, Packers, Dec. 14, 1952
90 Dick Dorsey from Cotton Davidson, Raiders, Dec. 2, 1962
90 Bob Scarpitto from John McCormick, Broncos, Oct. 17, 1965
90 Frank Pitts from Len Dawson, Chiefs, Nov. 17, 1968
90 Speedy Thomas from Virgil Carter, Bengals, Sept. 19, 1971
90 Rick Upchurch from Charley Johnson, Broncos, Sept. 21, 1975
90 Roger Carr from Charley Johnson, Colts, Nov. 16, 1975
90 Mark Malone from Terry Bradshaw, Steelers, Nov. 8, 1981
90 Mike Quick from Ron Jaworski, Eagles, Oct. 28, 1984
90 Craig James from Tony Eason, Patriots, Sept. 15, 1985
90 J.J. Birden from Bubby Brister, Chiefs, Nov. 18, 1990
90 Eddie Kennison from Troy Aikman, Saints, Oct. 10, 1999
90 Jason Tucker from Troy Aikman, Cowboys, Jan. 2, 2000
90 Bobby Shaw from Kordell Stewart, Steelers, Dec. 16, 2001
90 Alvin Harper from Troy Aikman, Cowboys, Nov. 13, 1994 (not TD)
90 Dwight Stone from Bubby Brister, Steelers, Oct. 14, 1990 (not TD)
89 Billy Howton from Babe Parilli, Packers, Oct. 5, 1952
89 Bobby Mitchell from Milt Plum, Browns, Jan. 7, 1961 (playoff)
89 Charley Ferguson from Fran Tarkenton, Vikings, Nov. 11, 1962
89 Elbert Dubenion from Jack Kemp, Bills, Oct. 13, 1963
89 Homer Jones from Earl Morrall, Giants, Oct. 17, 1965
89 John Mackey from Len Dawson, Colts, Oct. 30, 1966
89 Otis Taylor from Len Dawson, Chiefs, Nov. 13, 1966 (not TD)
89 Carroll Dale from Don Horn, Packers, Sept. 27, 1970
89 Bob Hayes from Don Horn, Cowboys, Oct. 25, 1970
89 Larry Brown from Billy Kilmer, Redskins, Nov. 5, 1972
89 Rich Caster from Joe Namath, Jets, Oct. 7, 1974
89 Roger Carr from Bert Jones, Colts, Nov. 9, 1975
89 Rickey Watts from Vince Evans, Bears, Sept. 21, 1980
89 Louis Lipps from Bubby Brister, Steelers, Nov. 13, 1988
89 Willie Drewrey from Vinny Testaverde, Buccaneers, Dec. 2, 1990
89 Dwight Stone from Neil O'Donnell, Steelers, Sept. 1, 1991
89 Michael Haynes from Chris Miller, Falcons, Sept. 13, 1992
89 Willie Green from Kerry Collins, Car, Dec. 17, 1995
89 Randal Hill from Heath Shuler, Saints, Oct. 5, 1997
89 Andre Hastings from Kerry Collins, Saints, Dec. 6, 1998
89 Brandon Lloyd from Tim Rattay, 49ers, Sept. 25, 2005

TOP 50 KICKOFF RETURNS

106 Al Carmichael, Packers, Oct. 7, 1956
106 Noland Smith, Chiefs, Dec. 17, 1967
106 Roy Green, Cardinals, Oct. 21, 1979
105 Frank Seno, Cardinals, Oct. 20, 1946
105 Ollie Matson, Cardinals, Oct. 14, 1956
105 Abe Woodson, 49ers, Nov. 8, 1959
105 Timmy Brown, Eagles, Sept. 17, 1961
105 Jon Arnett, Rams, Oct. 29, 1961
105 Mercury Morris, Mia, Sept. 14, 1969

TOP 50 KICKOFF RETURNS (CONT.)

105 Travis Williams, Rams, Dec. 5, 1971
105 Terry Fair, Lions, Sept. 28, 1998
104 Buddy Young, Colts, Nov. 15, 1953
104 Terry Barr 86, lateral from Gene Gedman 18, Lions, Oct. 26, 1958
104 Ken Hall, Oilers, Oct. 23, 1960
104 Carl Ward, Browns, Nov. 26, 1967
104 Travis Williams, Packers, Dec. 9, 1967
104 Ira Matthews, Raiders, Oct. 25, 1979
104 Terrence McGee, Bills, Dec. 5, 2004
103 Spec Sanders, New York Yankees (AAFC), Oct. 27, 1946
103 Russ Craft, Eagles, Oct. 7, 1950
103 Tommy Wilson, Rams, Nov. 25, 1956
103 Lenny Lyles, Colts, Oct. 4, 1958
103 Herb Adderley, Packers, Nov. 18, 1962
103 Keith Lincoln, Chargers, Sept. 16, 1962
103 Abe Woodson, 49ers, Sept. 14, 1963
103 Gale Sayers, Bears, Sept. 17, 1967
103 George Hoey, Cardinals, Nov. 21, 1971
103 Bob Gresham, Oilers, Sept. 23, 1973
103 Tony Horne, Rams, Oct. 15, 2000
102 Doug Russell, Cardinals, Sept. 23, 1934
102 Leroy Bolden, Browns, Oct. 26, 1958
102 Charley Warner, Bills, Nov. 7, 1965
102 Preston Pearson, Colts, Nov. 10, 1968
102 Ron Jessie, Lions, Oct. 24, 1971
102 Larry Jones, Redskins, Nov. 24, 1974
102 Harold Hart, Raiders, Sept. 22, 1975
102 Curtis Brown, Bills, Sept. 24, 1978
102 Alexander Wright, Cowboys, Dec. 22, 1991
102 Mel Gray, Lions, Oct. 23, 1994
102 Eric Guliford, Saints, Aug. 31, 1997
102 Eric Bieniemy, Bengals, Oct. 26, 1997
102 Tony Horne, Rams, Nov. 29, 1998
101 Dave Smukler, Eagles, Nov. 13, 1938
101 Billy Jefferson, Lions, Nov. 23, 1941
101 Lenny Lyles, Colts, Oct. 26, 1958
101 Ollie Matson, Cardinals, Nov. 23, 1958
101 Amos Marsh, Cowboys, Oct. 14, 1962
101 Leon Burton, Titans, Oct. 28, 1960
101 Lance Rentzel, Vikings, Nov. 14, 1965
101 Don McCall, Steelers, Nov. 23, 1969
101 Dave Hampton, Packers, Oct. 4, 1970
101 Ike Thomas, Cowboys, Dec. 4, 1971
101 Wallace Francis, Bills, Oct. 7, 1973
101 Cotton Speyrer, Colts, Nov. 25, 1973
101 Raymond Clayborn, Patriots, Dec. 18, 1977
101 James Owens, 49ers, Nov. 2, 1980
101 Mel Gray, Saints, Sept. 21, 1986
101 Eric Metcalf, Browns, Dec. 9, 1990
101 Terry Kirby, 49ers, Nov. 16, 1997
101 Leon Johnson, Jets, Dec. 14, 1997
101 Terry Fair, Lions, Sept. 6, 1998
101 Roell Preston, Packers, Oct. 5, 1998
101 Brian Mitchell, Redskins, Dec. 6, 1998
101 Tony Horne, Rams, Oct. 17, 1999
101 Derrick Mason, Titans, Nov. 18, 2001

TOP 50 PUNT RETURNS

103 Robert Bailey, Rams, Oct. 23, 1994
98 Gil LeFebvre, Bengals, Dec. 3, 1933
98 Charlie West, Vikings, Nov. 3, 1968
98 Dennis Morgan, Cowboys, Oct. 13, 1974
98 Terance Mathis, Jets, Nov. 4, 1990
97 Greg Pruitt, Raiders, Oct. 2, 1983
96 Bill Dudley, Redskins, Dec. 3, 1950
95 Al Bloodgood, Giants, Sept. 30, 1928
95 Frank Bernardi, Cardinals, Oct. 14, 1956
95 Speedy Duncan, Chargers, Nov. 24, 1968
95 Steve Odom, Packers, Nov. 10, 1974
95 John Taylor, 49ers, Nov. 21, 1988
95 Johnny Bailey, Bears, Dec. 29, 1990
95 Carl Pickens, Bengals, Sept. 20, 1992
95 Desmond Howard, Lions, Sept. 3, 2000
95 Lamont Brightful, Ravens, Nov. 10, 2002
95 Jacquez Green, Buccaneers, Sept. 13, 1998
94 Tom Casey, New York Yankees (AAFC), Aug. 27, 1948
94 Mark Lee, Packers, Nov. 8, 1981
94 Dennis McKinnon, Bears, Sept. 14, 1987
94 Darrien Gordon, Broncos, Sept. 14, 1997
94 Charlie Rogers, Seahawks, Sept. 26, 1999
94 Hugh McElhenny, 49ers, Oct. 19, 1952
93 Veryl Switzer, Packers, Nov. 7, 1954
93 Dana McLemore, 49ers, Jan. 2, 1983
93 Glyn Milburn, Bears, Sept. 20, 1998
93 Dante Hall, Chiefs, Oct. 5, 2003
93 Bill Baird, Jets, Nov. 10, 1963
92 Bob Pfohl, Colts (AAFC), Sept. 26, 1948
92 Rick Upchurch, Broncos, Oct. 3, 1976
92 Eric Metcalf, Browns, Sept. 4, 1994
92 Desmond Howard, Packers, Dec. 15, 1996
91 Rex Bumgardner, Buffalo Bills (AAFC), Oct. 24, 1948
91 Keith Moody, Bills, Oct. 23, 1977
91 Jo-Jo Townsell, Jets, Nov. 9, 1987

TOP 50 PUNT RETURNS (CONT.)

91 Eric Metcalf, Browns, Oct. 24, 1993
91 Nate Burleson, Vikings, Nov. 8, 2004
90 Roddy Lamb, Rock Island Independents, Nov. 22, 1925
90 Andy Uram, Packers, Oct. 12, 1941
90 Rex Bumgardner, Buffalo Bills (AAFC), Nov. 25, 1948
90 Carl Taseff, Colts, Oct. 14, 1956
90 Tom Watkins, Lions, Oct. 6, 1963
90 Brady Keys, Steelers, Sept. 20, 1964 (not TD)
90 Bob Hayes, Cowboys, Dec. 8, 1968
90 Lemar Parrish, Bengals, Oct. 6, 1974
90 Phil Epps, Packers, Oct. 2, 1983
90 Darrien Gordon, Chargers, Sept. 25, 1994
90 Jacquez Green, Redskins, Sept. 16, 2002
90 Dante Hall, Chiefs, Dec. 1, 2002
90 Dick Bass, Rams, Dec. 17, 1961

TOP 50 INTERCEPTIONS

106 Ed Reed, Ravens, Nov. 7, 2004
104 Troy Vincent 90, lateral from James Willis 14, Eagles, Nov. 3, 1996
103 Pete Barnum, Col, Sept. 26, 1926
103 Vencie Glenn, Chargers, Nov. 29, 1987
103 Louis Oliver, Dolphins, Oct. 4, 1992
102 Bob Smith, Lions, Nov. 24, 1949
102 Erich Barnes, Giants, Oct. 15, 1961
102 Gary Barbaro, Chiefs, Dec. 11, 1977
102 Louis Breeden, Bengals, Nov. 8, 1981
102 Eddie Anderson, Raiders, Dec. 14, 1992
102 Donald Frank, Chargers, Oct. 31, 1993
102 Artrell Hawkins, Bengals, Nov. 3, 2002
102 Marcus Coleman, Texans, Sept. 26, 2004
101 Richie Petitbon, Bears, Dec. 9, 1962
101 Henry Carr, Giants, Nov. 13, 1966
101 Tony Greene, Bills, Oct. 3, 1976
101 Tom Pridemore, Falcons, Sept. 20, 1981
101 George Teague, Packers, Jan. 8, 1994 (playoff)
101 Bryant Westbrook, Lions, Nov. 23, 2000
101 Lito Sheppard, Eagles, Nov. 15, 2004
100 Vern Huffman, Lions, Oct. 17, 1937
100 Mike Gaechter, Cowboys, Oct. 14, 1962
100 Speedy Duncan, Chargers, Oct. 15, 1967
100 Tom Janik, Bills, Sept. 29, 1968
100 Tim Collier, Chiefs, Dec. 18, 1977
100 Barry Wilburn, Redskins, Dec. 26, 1987
100 Aaron Glenn, Jets, Sept. 15, 1996
100 Jimmy Hitchcock, Patriots, Nov. 23, 1997
100 Brock Marion, Dolphins, Jan. 6, 2002
100 Champ Bailey, Broncos, Jan. 14, 2006 (playoff, not TD)
99 Marty Kottler, Steelers, Sept. 27, 1933
99 Ernie Zalejski 81, lateral from George Buksar 18, Colts, Nov. 26, 1950
99 Jerry Norton, Eagles, Oct. 5, 1957
99 Dave Grayson, Cowboys, Dec. 17, 1961
99 Johnnie Johnson, Rams, Sept. 21, 1980
99 Rick Sanford, Patriots, Dec. 5, 1982
99 Gill Byrd, Chargers, Oct. 14, 1984
99 Tim Lewis, Packers, Nov. 18, 1984
99 Kevin Ross, Chiefs, Sept. 6, 1992
99 Stanley Richard, Chargers, Sept. 4, 1994
99 Shaun Gayle, Chargers, Dec. 23, 1995
98 Bob Suci, Patriots, Nov. 1, 1963
98 Pete Jaquess, Oilers, Sept. 19, 1964
98 Darrol Ray, Jets, Jan. 9, 1983 (playoff)
98 Darryll Lewis, Oilers, Oct. 22, 1995
98 Bennie Blades, Lions, Sept. 29, 1996
98 Marcus Coleman, Jets, Dec. 27, 1999
98 Chris McAlister, Ravens, Dec. 24, 2000
98 Shelton Quarles, Buccaneers, Oct. 7, 2001
98 Rod Woodson, Raiders, Nov. 11, 2002
98 Chad Williams, Ravens, Dec. 1, 2002

THE KICKING GAME

There is an obscure rule in football stating that a team may elect to attempt a field goal from the spot of a fair catch after a punt. This is usually only tried as the last play of a half, since otherwise the team would probably be able to get closer by electing to run plays after the punt. The coaches know the rule and you would think it would come up from time to time, but it hasn't. Looking at the results of normal field goals, which often sail well above the crossbar and even above the ends of the goal posts themselves, it would appear that there would be a good chance of making a field goal from 70 yards or more under these conditions, where there would be no rush and no worry about kicking too low. We may yet see it happen. On October 9, 2005 at Houston, Tennessee tried a 58-yarder as the final play of the first half, but it fell short. There have been a number of cases in the past 10 years where a 60-to 70-yard attempt could have been made, but the coach chose to run a play instead. Here is a list of the longest field goals that were attempted ... and good.

LONGEST FIELD GOALS

63 Tom Dempsey, Saints, Nov. 8, 1970
63 Jason Elam, Broncos, Oct. 25, 1998
60 Steve Cox, Browns, Oct. 21, 1984
60 Morten Andersen, Saints , Oct. 27, 1991
59 Tony Franklin, Eagles, Nov. 12, 1979
59 Pete Stoyanovich, Dolphins, Nov. 12, 1989
59 Steve Christie, Bills, Sept. 26, 1993
59 Morten Andersen, Falcons, Dec. 24, 1995
58 Josh Brown, Seahawks, Oct. 5, 2003
58 Pete Stoyanovich, Dolphins, Jan 5, 1991
58 Nick Lowery, Chiefs, Sept. 12, 1985
58 Steve Cox, Browns, Dec. 4, 1983
58 Nick Lowery, Chiefs, Sept. 18, 1983
58 Dan Miller, Colts, Dec. 26, 1982
58 Michael Koenen, Falcons, Oct. 9, 2005
57 David Akers, Eagles, Sept. 14, 2003
57 Adam Vinateri, Patriots, Nov. 10, 2002
57 Jeff Wilkins, Rams, Sept. 27, 1998
57 Michael Husted, Buccaneers, Dec. 19, 1993
57 Mark Moseley, Redskins, Sept. 28, 1986
57 Fred Steinfort, Broncos, Oct. 13, 1980
57 Nick Lowery, Chiefs, Sept. 14, 1980
57 Don Cockroft, Browns, Oct. 29, 1972

LONGEST PUNTS

98 Steve O'Neal, Jets, Sept. 21, 1969
94 Joe Lintzenich, Bears, Nov. 16, 1931
93 Shawn McCarthy, Patriots, Nov. 3, 1991
91 Randall Cunningham, Eagles, Dec. 3, 1989
90 Don Chandler, Packers, Oct. 10, 1965
90 Rodney Williams, Giants, Sept. 10, 2001
89 Luke Prestridge, Patriots, Oct. 21, 1984
88 Bob Waterfield, Rams, Oct. 17, 1948
87 Bob Scarpitto, Patriots, Sept. 29, 1968
87 Dave Finzer, Bears, Oct. 7, 1984
86 Bob Waterfield, Rams, Oct. 5, 1947
86 Larry Barnes, 49ers, Sept. 29, 1957
85 Bill Shepherd, Lions, Nov. 15, 1936
85 Sammy Baugh, Redskins, Dec. 1, 1940
84 Doug Russell, Cardinals, Sept. 11, 1938
84 Spec Sanders, New York Yankees (AAFC), Oct. 5, 1947
84 Ron Widby, Cowboys, Nov. 3, 1968
84 Harry Newsome, Vikings, Dec. 20, 1992
84 Brian Moorman, Bills, Dec. 22, 2002
83 Chris Norman, Broncos, Sept. 23, 1984
83 Bryan Barker, Jaguars, Oct. 11, 1999
82 Frankie Albert, 49ers (AAFC), Aug. 29, 1948
82 Joe Muha, Eagles, Oct. 10, 1948
82 Joe Geri, Steelers, Nov. 20, 1949
82 Paul Maguire, Chargers, Nov. 19, 1961
82 Tommy Davis, 49ers, Sept. 30, 1962
81 Sammy Baugh, Raiders, Nov. 14, 1943
81 Billy deCorrevont, Lions, Oct. 6, 1946
81 Bob Reinhard, Los Angeles Dons (AAFC), Sept. 7, 1947
81 Spec Sanders, New York Yankees (AAFC), Sept. 21, 1947
81 Tom McNeill, Saints, Sept. 28, 1969
81 Mike Wood, Cardinals, Dec. 10, 1978
81 Bob Parsons, Bears, Dec. 5, 1982
81 Andy Lee, 49ers, Nov. 21, 2004
80 Parker Hall, Rams, 1940
80 Glenn Dobbs, Los Angeles Dons (AAFC), 1949
80 Horace Gillom, Browns, Nov. 28, 1954
80 King Hill, Eagles, Nov. 11, 1962
80 Jim Miller, 49ers, Sept. 19, 1982
80 Randall Cunningham, Eagles, Oct. 16, 1994
80 Chris Mohr, Bills, Oct. 13, 1996
80 Brian Moorman, Bills, Sept. 12, 2004
79 George McAfee, Bears, Nov. 17, 1940
79 Tommy Davis, 49ers, Oct. 14, 1962
79 Jim Norton, Oilers, Nov. 22, 1964
79 Chuck Ramsey, Jets, Oct. 15, 1978
78 Ernie Nevers, Cardinals, Nov. 13, 1930
78 Parker Hall, Rams, 1940
78 Sid Luckman, Bears, Oct. 31, 1943
78 Glenn Dobbs, Brooklyn Dodgers (AAFC), Nov. 24, 1946
78 Jack Jacobs, Packers, Oct. 10, 1948
78 Jerry Norton, Cardinals, Nov. 5, 1961
78 Ed Brown, Steelers, Oct. 28, 1962
78 Pat Studstill, Lions, Oct. 8, 1967
78 Paul Maguire, Bills, Sept. 21, 1969
78 Billy Van Heusen, Broncos, Dec. 2, 1973
78 Marv Bateman, Bills, Sept. 19, 1976
78 Craig Hentrich, Titans, Jan. 2, 2000

THE 2,000-YARDS RUSHING CLUB

Only five men in NFL history have rushed for more than 2,000 yards in one season. O.J. Simpson did it first in 1973, and he needed only 14 games, the length of a season at that time. Eric Dickerson was the second to achieve the mark. He broke the 2,000-yard barrier in his 15th game (of a 16-game schedule) and is the only player to rush more than

2,100 yards in a season. In the last decade, three more running backs have made it 2,000 yards in a season: Barry Sanders, Terrell Davis, and Jamal Lewis. All needed the full 16-game schedule (and had a bye week). Note that Sanders did achieve 2,000 yards in 14 games with the Lions in 1997, but they were his last 14 games of the season; he gained a total of just 53 yards in his first two games. The week-by-week progress of each 2,000-yard seasons is presented below, with the rushing attempts, rushing yards, and opposition for each game.

O.J. Simpson, Bills 1973

WEEK	ATTEMPTS	YARDS	OPPONENT
1	29	250	Patriots
2	22	103	Chargers
3	24	123	Jets
4	27	171	Eagles
5	22	166	Colts
6	14	55	Dolphins
7	39	157	Chiefs
8	20	79	Saints
9	20	99	Bengals
10	20	120	Dolphins
11	15	124	Colts
12	24	137	Falcons
13	22	219	Patriots
14	34	200	Jets
Total	332	2003	

Eric Dickerson, Rams 1984

WEEK	ATTEMPTS	YARDS	OPPONENT
1	21	138	Cowboys
2	27	102	Browns
3	23	49	Steelers
4	22	89	Bengals
5	22	120	Giants
6	19	107	Falcons
7	20	175	Saints
8	24	145	Falcons
9	13	38	Rams
10	21	208	Cardinals
11	28	149	Bears
12	25	132	Packers
13	28	191	Buccaneers
14	33	149	Saints
15	27	215	Oilers
16	26	98	49ers
Total	379	2105	

Barry Sanders, Lions 1997

WEEK	ATTEMPTS	YARDS	OPPONENT
1	15	33	Falcons
2	10	20	Buccaneers
3	19	161	Bears
4	18	113	Saints
5	28	139	Packers
6	25	107	Bills
7	24	215	Buccaneers
8	24	105	Giants
10	23	105	Packers
11	15	105	Redskins
12	19	108	Vikings
13	24	216	Colts
14	19	167	Bears
15	30	137	Dolphins
16	19	138	Vikings
17	23	184	Jets
Total	335	2053	

Terrell Davis, Broncos 1998

WEEK	ATTEMPTS	YARDS	OPPONENT
1	22	75	Patriots
2	23	191	Cowboys
3	28	104	Raiders
4	21	119	Redskins
5	20	168	Eagles
6	30	208	Seahawks
8	31	136	Jaguars
9	27	149	Bengals
10	20	69	Chargers
11	18	111	Chiefs
12	31	162	Raiders
13	24	74	Chargers
14	24	88	Chiefs
15	28	147	Giants
16	16	29	Dolphins
17	29	178	Seahawks
Total	392	2008	

Jamal Lewis, Ravens 2003

GAME	ATTEMPTS	YARDS	OPPONENT
1	5	69	Steelers
2	30	295	Browns
3	23	132	Chargers
4	26	115	Chiefs
6	21	131	Cardinals
7	19	101	Bengals
8	32	134	Broncos
9	21	68	Jaguars
10	27	111	Rams
11	25	91	Dolphins
12	26	117	Seahawks
13	19	78	49ers
14	30	180	Bengals
15	24	125	Raiders
16	22	205	Browns
17	27	114	Steelers
Total	387	2066	

CONSECUTIVE WINS

The New England Patriots set an all-time record by winning 21 consecutive games, including playoff games, in 2003 and 2004. Several teams have had 18 consecutive wins, including the Chicago Bears of 1933–34 and also 1941–42, the Cleveland Browns (AAFC) of 1947–48, the Miami Dolphins of 1972–73, the San Francisco 49ers of 1989–90, and the Denver Broncos of 1997–98. The Patriots won 18 straight regular-season games during their streak. Miami won the most consecutive games in one season, including 14 during the regular season and 3 in the playoffs, thus posting a perfect 17–0 record in 1972. As a result of the extension of the schedule to 16 games in 1978, the 49ers were able to top Miami's regular-season mark for most overall wins in a season with 15 in 1984. The 1985 Bears and 1998 Minnesota Vikings duplicated this feat.

Below are the game-by-game details of the Patriots' historic winning streak. The opposition is in bold for away games. Playoff games are italicized.

GAME	DATE	OPPONENT	SCORE
1	October 5, 2003	Titans	38–30
2	October 12, 2003	Giants	17–6
3	October 19, 2003	**Dolphins**	19–13 (OT)
4	October 26, 2003	Browns	9–3
5	November 3, 2003	**Broncos**	30–26
6	November 16, 2003	Cowboys	12–0
7	November 23, 2003	**Texans**	23–20 (OT)
8	November 30, 2003	**Colts**	38–34
9	December 7, 2003	Dolphins	12–0
10	December 14, 2003	Jaguars	27–13
11	December 20, 2003	**Jets**	21–16
12	December 27, 2003	Bills	31–0
13	*January 10, 2004*	*Titans*	*17–14*
14	*January 18, 2004*	*Colts*	*24–14*
15	*February 1, 2004*	*Panthers*	*32–29*
16	September 9, 2004	Colts	27–24
17	September 19, 2004	**Cardinals**	23–12
18	October 3, 2004	**Bills**	31–17
19	October 10, 2004	Dolphins	24–10
20	October 17, 2004	Seahawks	30–20
21	October 24, 2004	Jets	13–7

The streak ended on October 31, 2004, with a 34–20 loss to the Steelers in Pittsburgh.

CONSECUTIVE GAMES AND STREAKS

Through the end of the 2005 season, Brett Favre had started 221 consecutive games at quarterback for the Green Bay Packers, more than any other quarterback in NFL history. After much vacillating, he decided to return for another season in 2006. Favre was originally drafted in the second round by Atlanta in 1991, but did not get along with coach Jerry Glanville and played poorly, so the Falcons were happy to get rid of him for a first-round draft choice from Green Bay. This choice had been obtained from Philadelphia and was later traded by Atlanta to Dallas who used it to draft defensive back Kevin Smith. Green Bay general manager Ron Wolf had recognized Favre's ability earlier and had been looking for an opportunity to obtain him.

Peyton Manning has not missed a game in his career and his streak is currently at 128. Ron Jaworski of the Eagles started 116 consecutive games after being obtained in a trade from the Rams until he was injured in 1982. Joe Ferguson had a 107-game streak and Roman Gabriel made 89. Dan Marino caught a break in this regard during the 1987 strike. He stands second among quarterbacks with 145 because of an NFL policy that says that consecutive game streaks continued even when players missed games as a result of the 1987 strike.

The all-time record for any position was held more than two decades by Jim Marshall, who started 282 games in a row at defensive end, all but the first 12 for the Minnesota Vikings. On November 27, 2005, however, veteran punter Jeff Feagles played for the New York Giants and became the new record holder. Marshall's streak, it should be noted, was as a starter and was achieved while playing a far more physically demanding position. Below we present top football streaks of all kinds.

Consecutive Games Played

288	Jeff Feagles, Patriots, 1988–89; Eagles, 1990–93, Cardinals, 1994–97; Seahawks, 1998–2002; Giants, 2003–05
282	Jim Marshall, Browns, 1960; Vikings, 1961–1979
248	Morten Andersen, Saints, 1987–1994; Falcons, 1995–2000; Giants, 2001; Chiefs, 2002
240	Mick Tingelhoff, Vikings, 1962–1978 Bill Romanowski, 49ers, 1989–1993; Eagles, 1994–95; Broncos, 1996–2001; Raiders, 2002

Consecutive Games Scored In

332	Morten Andersen, Saints, 1982–1994; Falcons, 1995–2000; Giants, 2001; Chiefs, 2002–03 Vikings, 2004
204	Jason Elam, Broncos, 1993–2005
186	Jim Breech, Raiders, 1979; Bengals, 1980–1992

Consecutive Games with a Touchdown

18	Lenny Moore, Colts, 1963–65
18	LaDainian Tomlinson Chargers 2004–5
14	O. J. Simpson, Bills, 1975
13	John Riggins, Redskins, 1982–83
13	George Rogers, Redskins, 1985–86
13	Jerry Rice, 49ers, 1986–87

Consecutive Games with a Field Goal

38	Matt Stover, Ravens, 1999–2001
31	Fred Cox, Vikings, 1968–1970
28	Jim Turner, Jets, 1970; Broncos, 1971–72
28	Chip Lohmiller, Redskins, 1988–1990

Consecutive Field Goals

42	Mike Vanderjagt, Colts, 2002–03
40	Gary Anderson, 49ers, 1997; Vikings, 1998
31	Fuad Reveiz, Vikings, 1994–95
31	Neil Rackers, Cardinals, 2005

Consecutive Points after Touchdown

371	Jason Elam, Broncos, 1993–2002
311	Jeff Wilkins Rams 1999–2005
301	Norm Johnson, Falcons, 1991–94; Steelers, 1995–98; Eagles, 1999
250	Eddie Murray, Lions, 1988–1991; Chiefs, 1992; Buccaneers, 1992; Cowboys, 1993; Eagles, 1994; Redskins, 1995; Vikings, 1997

Consecutive Seasons, 1,000-Plus Yards Rushing

11	Emmitt Smith, Cowboys, 1991–2001
10	Barry Sanders, Lions, 1989–1998
10	Curtis Martin, Patriots, 1995–97; Jets, 1998–2004

Consecutive Games, 200-Plus Yards Rushing

2	O. J. Simpson, Bills, 1973, 1976
2	Earl Campbell, Oilers, 1980
2	Ricky Williams, Dolphins, 2002

Consecutive Games, 100-Plus Yards Rushing

14	Barry Sanders, Lions, 1997
11	Marcus Allen, Raiders, 1985–86
9	Walter Payton, Bears, 1985
9	Fred Taylor, Jaguars, 2000
9	Deuce McAllister, Saints, 2003

Consecutive Games With a Rushing TD

18	LaDainian Tomlinson Chargers 2004–5
13	John Riggins, Redskins, 1982–83
13	George Rogers, Redskins, 1985–86
11	Lenny Moore, Colts, 1963–64
11	Emmitt Smith, Cowboys, 1994–95
11	Emmitt Smith, Cowboys, 1995
11	Priest Holmes, Chiefs, 2002
10	Greg Bell, Rams, 1988–89
10	Terry Allen, Redskins, 1995–96

Consecutive Passes Completed

24	Donavan McNabb Eagles (10 vs Giants 11–28 2004 14 vs. Packers 12–5–2004)
22	Joe Montana, 49ers vs. Browns (5), Nov. 29, 1987; vs. Packers (17), Dec. 6, 1987
21	Rich Gannon, Raiders vs. Broncos, Nov. 11, 2002
20	Ken Anderson, Bengals vs. Oilers, Jan. 2, 1983
20	Hugh Millen, Broncos vs. Raiders (7), Dec. 11, 1994; vs. 49ers (13), Dec. 17, 1994
20	Steve Young, 49ers vs. Redskins, Nov. 24, 1996

Consecutive Games, 400-Plus Yards Passing
2 Dan Fouts, Chargers, 1982
2 Dan Marino, Dolphins, 1984
2 Phil Simms, Giants, 1985
2 Billy Volek, Titans 2004

Consecutive Games, 300-Plus Yards Passing
6 Steve Young, 49ers, 1998
6 Kurt Warner, Rams, 2000
6 Rich Gannon, Raiders, 2002
5 Joe Montana, 49ers, 1982
5 Kerry Collins, Giants, 2001–02
4 Dan Fouts, Chargers, 1979
4 Dan Fouts, Chargers, 1980–81
4 Bill Kenney, Chiefs, 1983
4 Joe Montana, 49ers, 1985–86
4 Joe Montana, 49ers, 1990
4 Warren Moon, Oilers, 1990
4 Drew Bledsoe, Patriots, 1993–94
4 Kurt Warner, Rams, 1999
4 Brian Griese, Broncos, 2002
4 Daunte Culpepper, Vikings 2004
4 Trent Chiefs 2004.

Consecutive Games, 4 or More Touchdown Passes
5 Peyton Manning Colts 2004
4 Dan Marino, Dolphins, 1984

Consecutive Games with a TD Pass
47 Johnny Unitas, Colts, 1956–1960
36 Brett Favre, Packers, 2002–4
30 Dan Marino, Dolphins, 1985–87
28 Dave Krieg, Seahawks, 1983–85

Consecutive Passes Without an Interception
308 Bernie Kosar, Browns, 1990–91
294 Bart Starr, Packers, 1964–65
279 Jeff George, Colts, 1993; Falcons, 1994

Consecutive Games with a Reception
274 Jerry Rice, 49ers, 1985–2000; Raiders, 2001–04
183 Art Monk, Redskins, 1983–1993; Jets, 1994; Eagles, 1995
179 Tim Brown (1993–94 Raiders, 1995–2003 Oak, 2004 Buccaneers)
177 Steve Largent, Seahawks, 1977–1989

Consecutive Games, 100-Plus Yards Receiving
7 Charley Hennigan, Oilers, 1961
7 Michael Irvin, Cowboys, 1995
6 Raymond Berry, Colts, 1960
6 Bill Groman, Oilers, 1961
6 Pat Studstill, Lions, 1966
6 Isaac Bruce, Rams, 1995
5 Elroy "Crazy Legs" Hirsch, Rams, 1951
5 Bob Boyd, Rams, 1954
5 Terry Barr, Lions, 1963
5 Lance Alworth, Chargers, 1966
5 Don Maynard, Jets, 1968–69
5 Harold Jackson, Eagles, 1971–72
5 Patrick Jeffers, Panthers, 1999
5 Terrell Owens, Eagles, 2004
5 Anquan Boldin, Cardinals, 2005.

Consecutive Games with a Touchdown Reception
13 Jerry Rice, 49ers, 1986–87
11 Elroy "Crazy Legs" Hirsch, Rams, 1950–51
11 Buddy Dial, Steelers, 1959–1960
10 Carl Pickens, Bengals, 1994–95
10 Randy Moss Vikings 2003–04

Consecutive Games with an Interception
8 Tom Morrow, Raiders, 1962–63
7 Tom Landry, Giants, 1950–51
7 Paul Krause, Redskins, 1964
7 Larry Wilson, Cardinals, 1966
7 Ben Davis, Browns, 1968

Consecutive Seasons with 10 or More Sacks
9 Reggie White, Eagles, 1985–1992; Packers, 1993
8 John Randle, Vikings, 1992–99
7 Lawrence Taylor, Giants, 1984–1990
7 Bruce Smith, Bills, 1992–98

Consecutive Games with a Sack
10 Simon Fletcher, Broncos, Nov. 15, 1992–Sept. 20, 1993
9 Bruce Smith, Bills, Nov. 16, 1986–Oct. 25, 1987
9 Kevin Greene, 49ers–Panthers, Dec. 7, 1997–Oct. 18, 1998

Consecutive Punts without a Block
1,112 Chris Gardocki, Bears, 1992–94; Colts, 1995–98; Browns, 1999–2003; Steelers, 2004–05
878 Bryan Barker, Chiefs, 1993; Eagles, 1994; Jaguars, 1995–2000; Redskins, 2001–03; Packers, 2004; Rams, 2005
638 Tom Tupa Patriots 97–98, Jets 99–01, Buccaneers 02–03; Redskins 2004
623 Dave Jennings, Giants, 1976–1983

THE PRO FOOTBALL DRAFT

Philadelphia Eagles owner Bert Bell came up with the idea for a draft of amateur players. He was tired of being outbid for the services of college stars by big-spending owners in New York and Chicago. The inability to land talented players was keeping his team in the cellar, but Bell's motives weren't entirely selfish. He argued that the league would be stronger if all of the teams were competitive, and he proposed the draft as a way for the teams that were struggling to be replenished and revitalized with the best college players of the day.

The other owners agreed, and on February 8, 1936, representatives of each team gathered at the Ritz-Carlton hotel in Philadelphia for the first NFL draft. The order of selection was based on the previous season's standings, with the worst record receiving the first pick. The dubious honor went to Bell's Eagles, who selected University of Chicago running back Jay Berwanger. Unfortunately for Bell, Berwanger didn't have much interest in playing pro football. He felt he could make more money as a businessman, (and he would eventually make a fortune with his foam rubber and plastics company). Thus, the league was rejected by its first ever draft pick. More would follow.

Only 24 of the 81 players selected in that first draft signed NFL contracts. All nine Eagles drafted that day refused to sign with Philadelphia and never played a game in the NFL. Times quickly changed, though. Over the next decade, the draft would help dramatically increase the flow of collegiate players into the pro ranks. Owners expanded the draft from nine to ten rounds in 1937. By 1939 there were 20 rounds. During World War II teams filled their depleted ranks with a 32-round draft, renamed "the preferred negotiations list" so as not to confuse two drafts with far different ramifications.

By the 1950s teams were dedicating significant resources to scouting, realizing that one good draft could launch a dynasty. The great Green Bay Packers teams of the 1960s were born from the team's remarkable success in the drafts of the late 1950s. Over three seasons, the Packers drafted five Hall of Famers. Tackle Forrest Gregg and quarterback Bart Starr were selected in the 1956 draft, Paul Hornung their first pick in 1957, and Jim Taylor and Ray Nitschke were picked in 1958. Green Bay was 1–10–1 in 1958, but by 1960 they had advanced to the NFL title game and would go on to win five titles over the next seven seasons.

The Pittsburgh Steelers can also point to their scouting department as a major contributor to their dominating run during the 1970s. They drafted at least one future Hall of Famer each year from 1969 to 1972, and added four more in a remarkable 1974 draft class. Those players formed the core of a Steelers team that won four Super Bowls in six seasons.

Of course, the NFL draft provides just as many heartbreaks. Ernie Davis, the first overall pick in 1962, was diagnosed with leukemia and died without playing a single NFL game. Thirty-three of the men who were first-round draft picks never played pro football.

There are many more examples of players who did play, but they never lived up to the great expectations that accompanied their selection. Archie Griffin, the only two-time Heisman Trophy winner in history, ran for 2,808 yards in seven NFL seasons after amassing almost twice that in 50 fewer games at Ohio State. Some, like running backs Ki-Jana Carter and Steve Emtman had their pro careers derailed by injury. Others, like Ryan Leaf, Art Schlichter, and Lawrence Phillips self-destructed under the weight of their own personal problems.

The worst heartbreak of all might be the failure to recognize the talent that was available when a team made its selection. Notre Dame quarterback Joe Montana was a third-round pick, meaning that every team passed on him at least twice. Johnny Unitas wasn't selected until the ninth round. Deacon Jones was a 14th-round pick. New York Jets fans have as much right to lament as anyone. They watched their team select quarterback Ken O'Brien four picks ahead of Dan Marino in 1983, take receiver Al Toon six picks ahead of Jerry Rice in 1985, and pick running back Blair Thomas 15 spots ahead of Emmitt Smith in 1990.

STRUCTURAL CHANGES

The first major change brought about by the NFL–AFL merger was the implementation of a common draft, held for the first time in 1967. The number of rounds dropped from 20 to 17, and 10 years later it dropped to 12. As teams invested more resources into scouting, their ability to identify the best pro prospects increased, and there simply wasn't as much need for teams to bring so many rookies to camp each year. The draft was shortened to eight rounds in 1993 and seven a year later.

In 1993 the NFL began the practice of awarding extra draft picks to teams who lost significant players through free agency. These compensatory picks came at the end of rounds three through seven, depending on how good the free agent player was determined to be. The practice of trading draft picks was used strategically in the draft's early days, and that practice has grown dramatically. About 3 percent of picks were traded in 1950, 11 percent in 1970, and 21 percent in 1990. Picks are sometimes traded for veteran players, but most often, teams jostle for position, moving up in one round to get a player they covet, or trading down when their draft board doesn't show any attractive names.

Some coaches, like George Allen, felt draftees were a bad risk and often traded his choices for veterans. From 1971–79 the Washington Redskins typically had one or two choices in the first 10 rounds, usually nothing better than fifth. Since they made the playoffs almost every year, even after Allen moved on, it seemed to like a good strategy.

On February 11, 1992, Green Bay sent Atlanta a first-round draft choice for a young backup quarterback, Brett Favre. Some scoffed at what seemed like giving away a high-draft pick for a questionable talent. The talent proved to be beyond question, but what did the Falcons get in return for Favre? Following the bouncing pick.

On April 26, 1992, Atlanta sent the first-round choice as well as a fifth-rounder to Dallas for their first- and fourth-round picks. Atlanta picked running back Tony Smith (Southern Mississippi) in the first and Frankie Smith (defensive back, Baylor) in the fourth round. The Cowboys got defensive backs Kevin Smith (Texas A&M) in the first round and Greg Briggs (Texas Southern) in the fifth. Green Bay used its own first-round draft choice—and fifth overall selection—to pick Terrell Buckley. In 1991 Green Bay and Philadelphia had swapped first-round picks (Green Bay was number eight and Philadelphia had been number 19). For this trade the Packers also got Philly's first pick in 1992, which was traded to Atlanta for Favre and Atlanta later traded it to Dallas. The 1991 picks were Antone Davis for Philadelphia and Vinnie Clark for Green Bay. Buckley played three years for Green Bay and Clark two and then they were traded for more picks. Eventually Green Bay ended up with tight end Keith Jackson, who played only two years for Green Bay but helped the team—along with this guy Favre—reach the Super Bowl XXXI. Antone Davis started 74 of 78 games for the Eagles over five years but was released in 1996 and signed with Atlanta.

After all that, the only thing that seems sure is that Atlanta would like to do that trade all over again. It's hard to know what you've got, no matter how excited everyone seems to be. The draft has grown in popularity, sprouting experts to cater to the draftniks who follow the two-day, televised ritual with an almost religious-like obsession. Despite all the information and hype, the draft is still like a game of poker where the winning hand sometimes takes years to be revealed.

DRAFTED MORE THAN ONCE

Some players have been selected in more than one draft, and some by more than one league. The players in the list below were drafted one year and re-entered the draft another season. The year listed before each name represents the draft the player was selected in, the abbreviation means the team that chose him the first time, and the number indicates the round he was originally drafted in. When (D) appears on the line, it means that the player was disqualified and wasn't eligible for that year's draft despite being picked by the

team. DNS means the player did not sign and was later drafted again. Sometimes both things happened to the same player. Jim Beaver was drafted by both the NFL and AFL in 1960 and signed with neither. (He has a zero listed next to the Dallas Texans because the AFL teams did not use a real order for rounds in its first draft.) Beaver was later drafted again in 1961, by the Philadelphia Eagles. Despite being drafted three times, he played just 1 NFL game.

Bo Jackson is probably the most famous redrafted player, choosing to play major league baseball as a Kansas City Royal rather than go to the Tampa Bay Buccaneers, who used the first pick in the 1986 draft on him. When the Los Angeles Raiders drafted him in the seventh round the next year—after 182 other players had been picked—Jackson indeed signed and went on to become a two-sport icon.

1940	Al Matuza, GB 19 DNS, redraft 1941
1940	Bob Hoffman, Was 14 DNS, redraft 1940
1941	Lloyd Cheatham, Bkn 14 DNS, redraft 1942
1943	Solon Barnett, GB 10 DNS, redraft 1945
1943	Don Nolander, Was 21 DNS, redraft 1945
1944	Joe Golding, Bkn, 27 DNS, redraft 1946
1945	Johnny Strzykalski, Bos 5 DNS (D), redraft 1946
1945	George Connor, Pit 15 DNS (D), redraft 1946
1945	Bob McClure, GB 15 DNS (D), redraft 1946
1945	John Cannady, ChiC 16 DNS (D), redraft 1947
1945	Ed Stacco, Was 18 DNS (D), redraft 1946
1945	Ham Nichols, GB 30 DNS, redraft 1946
1946	Don Paul, LARm 5 DNS (D), redraft 1947
1946	Ben Raimondi, Phi 26 DNS (D), redraft 1947
1946	Bob Skoglund, Was 9 DNS, redraft 1947
1946	Bob Hazelhurst, NYG 14 DNS, redraft 1947
1946	Alton Baldwin, ChiC 29 DNS, redraft 1947
1947	Herb St. John, GB 24 DNS, redraft 1948
1948	Rob Goode, ChiB 15 DNS (D), redraft 1949
1948	Jim Duncan, ChiB 23 DNS, redraft 1949, DNS, redraft 1950
1948	Stan Heath, GB 25 DNS, redraft 1949
1948	John Panelli, GB 29 DNS (D), redraft 1949
1948	Truett Smith, ChiB 32 DNS (D), redraft 1950
1948	Bill Fischer, ChiC 32 DNS (D), redraft 1949
1949	Dick McKissack, ChiC 2 DNS (D), redraft 1950
1949	Jim Duncan, ChiB 21 DNS, redraft 1950
1949	Jim Cullom, Was 24 DNS (D), redraft 1950
1950	Ebert Van Buren, NYG 8 DNS (D), redraft 1951
1950	Charley Toogood, Cle 26 DNS (D), redraft 1951
1950	Tom Bienemann, ChiC 27 DNS, redraft 1951
1950	Johnny Karras, Det 28 DNS (D), redraft 1952
1951	Jack Bighead, Phi 23 DNS (D), redraft 1952
1951	Fred Williams, Cle 26 DNS, redraft 1952
1953	Bill Lucky, GB 19 DNS, redraft 1954
1954	Sam Palumbo, SF 15 DNS, redraft 1955
1954	Tom Feamster, ChiB 25 DNS, redraft 1955
1956	George Herring, SF 16 DNS, redraft 1960 AFL

1958	Dave Lloyd, Bal 18 DNS (D), redraft 1959
1958	Gene Gossage, Phi 28 DNS, redraft 1960 AFL
1959	Blanche Martin, LARm 4 DNS, redraft 1960 AFL
1959	Zeke Smith, Bal 4 DNS, redraft 1960 AFL
1959	Bobby Joe Green, SF 9 DNS, redraft 1960 AFL
1959	Alan Goldstein, LA 10 DNS, redraft 1960 AFL
1959	Ron Stehouwer, Det 12 DNS, redraft 1960 AFL
1959	Mike Connelly, LARm 12 DNS, redraft 1960 AFL
1959	Charlie Flowers, NYG 12 DNS, redraft 1960 AFL
1959	Bill Lopasky, SF 13 DNS, redraft 1960 AFL
1959	Pete Davidson, LARm, 14 DNS, redraft 1960 AFL
1959	Bob Bercich, NYG 15 DNS, redraft 1960 AFL
1959	Jack Rudolph, Det 17 DNS, redraft 1960 AFL
1959	Goose Gonsoulin, NYG 17 DNS (D), redraft 1960 AFL
1959	Billy Brewer, Was 20 DNS, redraft 1960 AFL
1959	Lebron Shields, Det 22 DNS, redraft 1960 AFL
1959	Alex Kroll, LARm 27 DNS, redraft 1962 AFL
1960	Jim Beaver, Bal 17 DNS, redraft 1961
1960	Jim Beaver, DalT 0 DNS, redraft 1961
1971	Moses Denson, Hou 16 DNS (D), redraft 1972
1972	Bob Maddox, SF 15 DNS, redraft 1973
1973	Monroe Eley, KC 11 DNS (D), redraft 1974
1974	John Tate, NYJ 13 DNS (D), redraft 1975
1980	Matthew Teague, Dal 10 DNS, redraft 1980 Supp
1985	Matt Darwin, Dal 5 DNS, redraft 1986
1986	Bo Jackson, TB 1 DNS, redraft 1987
1988	Melvin Bratton, Mia 6 DNS, redraft 1989
1991	Craig Erickson, Phi 5 DNS, redraft 1992

KEY TO DRAFT DATA

In the section that follows, every player selected in the draft who played in the NFL is listed. The first column contains the round the players were drafted in, followed by their name, the college they attended, and the position they played. That's followed by the number of games they played for the team that selected them, and the number of total games they played in the NFL. For example, "6. Joe Maniaci, Fordham, B, 24/60" listed under the Brooklyn Dodgers entry for 1936 means that Maniaci, a back, was selected in the sixth round of the first draft by the football Dodgers. He played 24 games for Brooklyn, and a total of 60 NFL games (the rest were with the Chicago Bears). All players selected in the first 15 rounds of each draft are listed, which is why many selections, especially those in the early days of the draft are listed as 0/0. Draftees who later played at least 50 games with the team that drafted them are shown in bold to make them more visible.

The list of drafted players who played in the NFL gets longer as time wears on as more and more players decided there was good money, not to mention fame, awaiting them in professional football. The draft was the perfect melding of college and pro football and a business-school study in how the NFL latched onto, and eventually surpassed, the college game in terms of national interest and influence.

1936 NFL

BROOKLYN DODGERS
1. Dick Crayne, Iowa, FB, 22/22
2. Vernal (Babe) LeVoir, Minnesota, B, 0/0
3. Wagner Jorgensen, St. Mary's (CA), C, 18/18
4. Paul (Bear) Bryant, Alabama, E, 0/0
5. Bobby Wilson, SMU, TB, 12/12
6. Joe Maniaci, Fordham, B, 24/60
7. Herb Schreiber, St. Mary's (CA), B, 0/0
8. Bob (Bones) Hamilton, Stanford, B, 0/0
9. Monk Moscrip, Stanford, E, 0/22

BOSTON REDSKINS
1. Riley Smith, Alabama, BB, 30/30
2. Keith Topping, Stanford, E, 0/0
3. Ed Smith, NYU, BB, 8/10
4. Paul Tangora, Northwestern, G, 0/0
5. Wilson Groseclose, Texas Christian, T, 0/0
6. Larry Lutz, California, T, 0/0
7. Don Irwin, Colgate, FB, 29/29
8. **Wayne Millner, Notre Dame, E, 76/76**
9. Marcel Saunders, Loyola (CA), G, 0/0

CHICAGO BEARS
1. **Joe Stydahar, West Virginia, T, 84/84**
2. Eddie Michaels, Villanova, G, 12/62
3. George Roscoe, Minnesota, B, 0/0
4. Bob Allman, Michigan State, E, 1/1
5. Verne Oech, Minnesota, G, 8/8
6. Ted Christofferson, Washington State, B, 0/0
7. Dick Smith, Minnesota, T, 0/0
8. John Sylvester, Rice, E, 0/0
9. **Danny Fortmann, Colgate, G, 86/86**

CHICAGO CARDINALS
1. Jimmy Lawrence, TCU, WB, 30/33
2. Gomer Jones, Ohio State, C, 0/0
3. Eddie Erdelalz, St. Mary's (CA), E, 0/0
4. Jeep Brett, Washington State, E, 1/19
5. Stan Riordan, Oregon, E, 0/0
6. Ettore Antonini, Indiana, E, 0/0
7. Tack Dennis, Tulsa, B, 0/0
8. Ross Carter, Oregon, G, 42/42
9. Niels Larsen, Stanford, T, 0/0

DETROIT LIONS
1. Sid Wagner, Michigan State, G, 27/27
2. Chuck Cheshire, UCLA, B, 0/0
3. Andy Pilney, Notre Dame, B, 0/0
4. Sheldon Biese, Minnesota, B, 0/0
5. Kavanaugh Francis, Alabama, C, 0/0
6. Abe Mickal, Louisiana State, B, 0/0
7. Charlie Wasicek, Colgate, T, 0/0
8. Dale Rennebohm, Minnesota, C, 0/0
9. Bob (Choo-Choo) Train, Yale, E, 0/0

GREEN BAY PACKERS
1. **Russ Letlow, San Francisco, G, 71/71**
2. J.W. Wheeler, Oklahoma, T, 0/0
3. Bernie Scherer, Nebraska, E, 26/35
4. Theron Ward, Idaho, B, 0/0
5. Darrell Lester, TCU, C, 16/16
6. Bob Reynolds, Stanford, T, 0/20
7. Wally Fromhart, Notre Dame, B, 0/0
8. Wally Cruice, Northwestern, B, 0/0
9. J.C. Wetsel, Southern Methodist, G, 0/0

NEW YORK GIANTS
1. Art Lewis, Ohio University, T, 12/28
2. **Tuffy Leemans, George Washington, FB, 80/80**
3. Frank (Butch) Loebs, Purdue, E, 0/0
4. Gene Rose, Tennessee, E, 7/7
5. Ed Jontos, Syracuse, G, 0/0
6. Gus Durner, Duke, T, 0/0
7. Bob Peeples, Marquette, T, 0/0
8. Dick Heekin, Ohio State, B, 0/0
9. Phil Flanagan, Holy Cross, G, 0/0

PHILADELPHIA EAGLES
1. Jay Berwanger, Chicago, B, 0/0
2. John McCauley, Rice, B, 0/0
3. Wes Muller, Stanford, C, 0/0
4. Bill Wallace, Rice, B, 0/0
5. Harry Shuford, Southern Methodist, B, 0/0
6. Al Barabas, Columbia, B, 0/0
7. Jack Weller, Princeton, G, 0/0
8. Pepper Constable, Princeton, B, 0/0
9. Paul Pauk, Princeton, B, 0/0

PITTSBURGH PIRATES
1. Bill Shakespeare, Notre Dame, B, 0/0
2. Len Barnum, West Virginia Wesleyan, B, 0/52
3. Bobby Grayson, Stanford, B, 0/0
4. Truman Spain, Southern Methodist, T, 0/0
5. Dick Sandefur, Purdue, FB, 9/9
6. Maurice Orr, Southern Methodist, T, 0/0
7. Marty Peters, Notre Dame, E, 0/0
8. Ed Karpowich, Catholic, T, 36/36
9. Joe Meglen, Georgetown (DC), B, 0/0

1937 NFL

BROOKLYN DODGERS
1. Ed Goddard, Washington State, B, 4/18
2. Ace Parker, Duke, TB, 48/68
3. Max Starcevich, Washington, G, 0/0
4. Bill Kurlish, Pennsylvania, B, 0/0
5. Bert Johnson, Kentucky, FB, 10/56
6. John Golemgeske, Wisconsin, T, 42/42
7. Fred Funk, UCLA, B, 0/0
8. Steve Reid, Northwestern, G, 0/0
9. Ed Nowogrowski, Washington, B, 0/0
10. Gil Kuhn, Southern California, T, 0/0

CHICAGO BEARS
1. Les McDonald, Nebraska, E, 29/39
2. Marv Stewart, Louisiana State, C, 0/0
3. **Dick Plasman, Vanderbilt, E, 52/59**
4. Henry Hammond, Rhodes, E, 6/6
5. Bill Conkright, Oklahoma, C, 17/62
6. Del Bjork, Oregon, T, 20/20
7. J.W. (Buck) Friedman, Rice, B, 0/0
8. Steve Toth, Northwestern, B, 0/0
9. Al Guepe, Marquette, B, 0/0
10. Ed (Red) Wade, Utah State, T, 0/0

CHICAGO CARDINALS
1. Ray Buivid, Marquette, B, 0/17
2. Gaynell Tinsley, LSU, E, 29/29
3. Art Guepe, Marquette, B, 0/0
4. H.K. (Bucky) Bryan, Tulane, B, 0/0
5. Ham Harmon, Tulsa, C, 6/6
6. Phil Dickens, Tennessee, B, 0/0
7. Herm Dickerson, Virginia Tech, B, 0/0
8. John Reynolds, Baylor, C, 5/5
9. Dwight Hafeli, Washington (St. Louis), E, 0/0
10. Middleton Fitzsimmons, Georgia Tech, G, 0/0

CLEVELAND RAMS
1. **Johnny Drake, Purdue, B, 55/55**
2. Julie Alfonse, Minnesota, WB, 20/20
3. Bobby LaRue, Pittsburgh, B, 0/0
4. John Wiatrak, Washington, C, 0/1
5. Inwood Smith, Ohio State, G, 0/0
6. Chris Del Sasso, Indiana, T, 0/0
7. Norm Schoen, Baldwin-Wallace, B, 0/0
8. Herm Schmarr, Catholic, DE, 0/5
9. Ray Johnson, Denver, DB, 3/4
10. Solon Holt, Texas Christian, G, 0/0

DETROIT LIONS
1. **Lloyd Cardwell, Nebraska, WB, 57/57**
2. Charley Hamrick, Ohio State, T, 0/0
3. Vern Huffman, Indiana, BB, 22/22
4. Bill Glassford, Pittsburgh, G, 0/0
5. Maury Patt, Carnegie Mellon, E, 10/48
6. George Bell, Purdue, G, 0/0
7. John Sprague, Southern Methodist, E, 0/0
8. Elvin Sayre, Illinois, C, 0/0
9. Larry Kelley, Yale, E, 0/0
10. Kay Bell, Washington State, T, 0/21

GREEN BAY PACKERS
1. **Ed Jankowski, Wisconsin, FB, 50/50**
2. Averell Daniell, Pittsburgh, T, 5/9
3. Charles (Bud) Wilkinson, Minnesota, T, 0/0
4. Bud Svendsen, Minnesota, C, 21/57
5. Dewitt Gibson, Northwestern, T, 0/0
6. Merle Wendt, Ohio State, E, 0/0
7. Marv Baldwin, Texas Christian, T, 0/0
8. Les Chapman, Tulsa, T, 0/0
9. Gordon Dahlgren, Michigan State, G, 0/0
10. Dave Gavin, Holy Cross, T, 0/0

NEW YORK GIANTS
1. Ed Widseth, Minnesota, T, 44/44
2. Tarzan White, Alabama, G, 32/50
3. Jerry Dennerlein, St. Mary's (CA), T, 22/22
4. **Ward Cuff, Marquette, WB, 90/110**
5. Mickey Kobrosky, Trinity (CT), QB, 7/7
6. Jim Farley, Virginia Military, G, 0/0
7. **Jim Poole, Mississippi, E, 69/78**
8. Gene Meyers, Kentucky, G, 0/0
9. Dwight Scheyer, Washington State, T, 0/0
10. Chuck Gelatka, Mississippi State, E, 34/34

PHILADELPHIA EAGLES
1. Sam Francis, Nebraska, FB, 0/40
2. Fran Murray, Pennsylvania, B, 22/22
3. Drew Ellis, TCU, T, 22/22
4. Walt Gilbert, Auburn, B, 0/0
5. Alex Drobnitch, Denver, G, 0/0
6. Bill Guckeyson, Maryland, B, 0/0
7. Herb Barna, West Virginia, E, 0/0
8. Nestor Hennon, Carnegie-Mellon, E, 0/0
9. Paul Fanning, Kansas State, T, 0/0
10. Ray Antil, Minnesota, E, 0/0

PITTSBURGH PIRATES
1. Mike Basrak, Duquesne, C, 15/15
2. Bob Finley, Southern Methodist, B, 0/0
3. Bill Breeden, Oklahoma, B, 9/9
4. Elmo (Bo) Hewes, Oklahoma, B, 0/0
5. Jack Frye, Missouri, B, 0/0
6. Walt Roach, Texas Christian, E, 0/0
7. By Haines, Washington, HB, 5/5
8. Marty Kordick, St. Mary's (CA), G, 0/0
9. Matt Patanelli, Michigan, E, 0/0
10. Stan Nevers, Kentucky, T, 0/0

WASHINGTON REDSKINS
1. **Sammy Baugh, TCU, QB, 165/165**
2. Nello Falaschi, Santa Clara, BB, 0/42
3. Maurice Eldar, Kansas State, B, 0/0
4. Dick Bassi, Santa Clara, G, 0/57
5. Chuck Bond, Washington, T, 22/22
6. Jimmie Cain, Washington, B, 0/0
7. Rotta Holland, Kansas State, G, 0/0
8. Joel Eaves, Auburn, E, 0/0
9. Bill Docherty, Temple, T, 0/0
10. Mac Cara, North Carolina State, E, 0/19

1938 NFL

BROOKLYN DODGERS
1. Boyd Brumbaugh, Duquesne, B, 12/36
2. Joe Kilgrow, Alabama, B, 0/0
3. **Bruiser Kinard, Mississippi, T, 73/101**
4. Gene Moore, Colorado, C, 7/7
5. Ed Merlin, Vanderbilt, G, 16/16
6. **Perry Schwartz, California, E, 54/68**
7. Leroy Monsky, Alabama, G, 0/0
8. Len Noyes, Montana, G, 5/5
9. John Stringham, BYU, B, 0/0
10. **Jim Sivell, Auburn, G, 56/80**
11. Johnny Druze, Fordham, E, 10/10
12. Lou Mark, North Carolina State, C, 33/39

CHICAGO BEARS
1. Joe Gray, Oregon State, B, 0/0
3. **Gary Famiglietti, Boston University, FB, 77/88**
5. Gust Zarnas, Ohio State, G, 10/28
6. Bob Masterson, Miami (FL), E, 0/98
7. Frank Ramsey, Oregon State, T, 9/9
8. Fletcher Sims, Georgia Tech, B, 0/0
9. Alex Schwarz, San Francisco, T, 0/0
10. John Wager, Butler, T, 0/0
11. Ray Mickovsky, Case Western Reserve, B, 0/0
12. Fred Dreher, Denver, E, 3/3

CHICAGO CARDINALS
1. Jack Robbins, Arkansas, TB, 17/17
2. Milt Popovich, Montana, B, 43/43
3. Frank Patrick, Pittsburgh, B, 15/15
4. Bob Herwig, California, C, 0/0
5. Al Babartsky, Fordham, T, 27/54
6. Joe Brunansky, Duke, T, 0/0
7. Ed Cherry, Hardin-Simmons, FB, 6/8
8. Leon Lavington, Colorado, E, 0/0
9. Phil Dougherty, Santa Clara, C, 8/8
10. Dwight Sloan, Arkansas, B, 10/31
11. Bob Kenderdine, Indiana, E, 0/0
12. Bob Mautner, Holy Cross, C, 0/0

CLEVELAND RAMS
1. Corby Davis, Indiana, BB, 39/39
2. **Jim Benton, Arkansas, E, 82/91**
3. Joe Routt, Texas A&M, G, 0/0
4. Vic Markov, Washington, T, 10/10
5. Ed Franco, Fordham, T, 0/10
6. **Ray Hamilton, Arkansas, E, 50/58**
7. Red Chesbro, Colgate, G, 8/8
8. Walt (Tiger) Mayberry, Florida, B, 0/0
9. Charles Ream, Ohio State, T, 10/10
10. Joe Maras, Duquesne, C, 0/17
11. Al Hoptowit, Washington State, T, 0/41
12. Vic Spadaccini, Minnesota, B, 30/30

DETROIT LIONS
1. **Alex Wojciechowicz, Fordham, C, 86/134**
3. Pete Smith, Oklahoma, E, 0/0
5. Andy Bershak, North Carolina, E, 0/0
6. Karl Schleckman, Utah, T, 0/0
7. Paul Szakash, Montana, E, 38/38
8. Dick Nardi, Ohio State, B, 8/14
9. Jim Sirtosky, Indiana, G, 0/0
10. Ralph Wolf, Ohio State, C, 0/0
11. Clarence Douglass, Kansas, B, 0/0
12. Clint Frank, Yale, B, 0/0

GREEN BAY PACKERS
1. **Cecil Isbell, Purdue, TB, 54/54**
3. Marty Schreyer, Purdue, T, 0/0
5. Chuck Sweeney, Notre Dame, E, 0/0
6. **Andy Uram, Minnesota, RB, 62/62**
7. Johnny Kovatch, Northwestern, E, 0/6
8. Phil Ragazzo, Case Western Reserve, T, 0/63
9. John Howell, Nebraska, HB, 6/6
10. Frank Barnhart, Northern Colorado, G, 0/0
11. **Pete Tinsley, Georgia, G, 76/76**
12. Tony Falkenstein, St. Mary's (CA), FB, 10/18

NEW YORK GIANTS
1. George Karamatic, Gonzaga, FB, 0/10
3. Fred Vanzo, Northwestern, BB, 0/39
5. Marion (Dutch) Konemann, Georgia Tech, B, 0/0
6. Frank Souchak, Pittsburgh, E, 0/4
7. Kelly Moan, West Virginia, TB, 0/2
8. Ted Doyle, Nebraska, T, 0/74
9. John Mellus, Villanova, T, 41/95
10. Bob Grimstead, Washington State, T, 0/0
11. Doug Oldershaw, California-Santa Barbara, G, 31/31
12. Elmore Hackney, Duke, B, 0/0

PHILADELPHIA EAGLES
1. Jim McDonald, Ohio State, B, 0/20
2. Dick Riffle, Albright, B, 32/53
3. Joe Bukant, Washington-St. Louis, B, 33/51
4. John Meek, California, B, 0/0
5. Fred Shirey, Nebraska, T, 0/12
6. Red Ramsey, Texas Tech, E, 35/35
7. Bob Lannon, Iowa, E, 0/0
8. Clem Woltman, Purdue, T, 31/31
9. Elmer Kolberg, Oregon State, HB, 18/22
10. Emmett Kriel, Baylor, G, 1/1
11. Carl Hinkle, Vanderbilt, C, 0/0
12. Johnny Michelosen, Pittsburgh, B, 0/0

PITTSBURGH PIRATES
1. Whizzer White, Colorado, TB, 11/33
2. Frank Filchock, Indiana, TB, 6/76
3. Red Wolfe, Texas, FB, 0/8
4. Tony Matisi, Pittsburgh, T, 0/5
5. Lou Midler, Minnesota, G, 11/18
6. George Platukis, Duquesne, E, 38/47
7. Ray King, Minnesota, E, 0/0
8. Tom Burnette, North Carolina, BB, 6/14
9. Paul McDonough, Utah, E, 6/38
10. Pat McCarty, Notre Dame, C, 0/0
11. Bill Krause, Baldwin-Wallace, G, 0/2
12. Joe Kuharich, Notre Dame, G, 0/27

WASHINGTON REDSKINS
1. **Andy Farkas, Detroit Mercy, FB, 62/70**
3. Sam Chapman, California, B, 0/0
5. Dave Price, Mississippi State, C, 0/0
6. Elmer Dohrmann, Nebraska, E, 0/0
7. Roy Young, Texas A&M, T, 9/9
8. Bill Hartman, Georgia, B, 10/10
9. Mickey Parks, Oklahoma, C, 24/37
10. Jack Abbitt, Elon, B, 0/0
11. Dick Johnston, Washington, E, 0/0
12. Hank Bartos, North Carolina, G, 7/7

1939 NFL

BROOKLYN DODGERS
1. Bob MacLeod, Dartmouth, HB, 0/9
1. Bob Haak, Indiana, G, 10/10
2. **Pug Manders, Drake, FB, 64/90**
3. Waddy Young, Oklahoma, E, 22/22
4. Vic Bottari, California, B, 0/0
5. Jack Kinnison, Missouri, C, 0/0
6. Ed Beinor, Notre Dame, T, 0/33
6. Len Janiak, Ohio University, B, 10/40
7. Alex Schoenbaum, Ohio State, T, 0/0
8. Dan (Tiger) Hill, Duke, C, 0/0
9. Forrest Kline, Texas Christian, G, 0/0
10. Kimble Bradley, Mississippi, B, 0/0
11. George Lenc, Augustana (IL), E, 2/2
12. Ralph Heikkinen, Michigan, G, 3/3
12. Carl Kaplanoff, Ohio State, G, 11/11
13. George Gembis, Wayne State, B, 0/0
14. Ray Carnelly, Carnegie Mellon, HB, 9/9
15. Lou Trunzo, Wake Forest, G, 0/0
17. John Siegal, Columbia, E, 0/43

CHICAGO BEARS
1. **Sid Luckman, Columbia, QB, 128/128**
1. Bill Osmanski, Holy Cross, FB, 46/46
3. John Wysocki, Villanova, E, 0/0
5. Joe Delaney, Holy Cross, T, 0/0
7. Charles Heileman, Iowa State, E, 2/2
8. Bob Dannies, Pittsburgh, C, 0/0
9. **Ray Bray, North Carolina, G, 109/121**
10. Walt Wood, Tennessee, B, 0/0
11. Al Braga, San Francisco, B, 0/0
12. Hal Roise, Idaho, B, 0/0
13. Ed Bock, Iowa State, G, 0/0
14. Anton Stolfa, Luther, QB, 1/1
15. Bob Voigts, Northwestern, T, 0/0

18. Solly Sherman, Chicago, QB, 14/14
21. Aldo Forte, Montana, G, 36/49

CHICAGO CARDINALS

1. Ki Aldrich, TCU, C, 22/73
2. **Marshall Goldberg, Pittsburgh, B, 77/77**
3. Alvord Wolff, Santa Clara, T, 0/0
4. Hal (Curly) Stebbins, Pittsburgh, B, 0/0
5. Bill Daddio, Pittsburgh, E, 22/25
6. George Faust, Minnesota, BB, 9/9
7. Bill Dwyer, New Mexico, B, 0/0
8. Sherm Hinkebein, Kentucky, C, 0/0
9. Earl Brown, Notre Dame, E, 0/0
10. Earl Crowder, Oklahoma, BB, 6/9
11. Bowden Wyatt, Tennessee, E, 0/0
12. Jim Thomas, Oklahoma, G, 13/13
13. Andy Sabados, The Citadel, G, 18/18
14. Blase Miatovich, San Francisco, T, 0/0
15. Russ Clarke, Santa Clara, G, 0/0
17. Ev Elkins, Marshall, B, 1/1
18. Frank Huffman, Marshall, T, 28/28
19. Mike Kochel, Fordham, G, 8/8

CLEVELAND RAMS

1. Parker Hall, Mississippi, TB, 42/53
2. Gaylon Smith, Rhodes, FB, 37/51
3. Elmer Tarbox, Texas Tech, B, 0/0
4. Wally Garard, St. Mary's (CA), T, 0/0
5. Eddie Gallo, Louisiana State, T, 0/0
6. Barney McGarry, Utah, G, 37/37
7. Jerry Dowd, St. Mary's (CA), C, 9/9
8. Warren (Bronco) Brunner, Tulane, B, 0/0
9. Lew Bostick, Alabama, G, 8/8
10. Frank Petrick, Indiana, E, 0/0
11. Sid Roth, Cornell, G, 0/0
12. Chet Adams, Ohio University, T, 42/117
13. Joel Hitt, Mississippi College, E, 3/3
14. John Ryland, UCLA, C, 0/0
15. Ben Friend, LSU, T, 10/10
17. Mike Perrie, St. Mary's (CA), QB, 2/2
18. Alex Atty, West Virginia, G, 3/3

DETROIT LIONS

1. Johnny Pingel, Michigan State, TB, 9/9
3. Howie Weiss, Wisconsin, FB, 20/20
5. Steve Maronic, North Carolina, T, 15/15
6. Joe Wendlick, Oregon State, E, 0/19
7. Darrell Tully, Texas A&M-Commerce, TB, 9/9
8. Dick Trzuskowski, Idaho, T, 0/0
9. **Bill Callihan, Nebraska, B, 62/62**
10. Ray George, USC, T, 11/13
11. Tony Calvelli, Stanford, C, 18/31
12. Jim Coughlan, Santa Clara, E, 0/0
13. Prescott Hutchins, Oregon State, G, 0/0
14. Art Means, Washington., G, 0/0
15. Gene Hodge, East Texas State, E, 0/0
16. Bill Lazetich, Montana, WB, 0/15
17. Ralph Niehaus, Dayton, T, 0/6
19. Tony Tonelli, USC, C, 9/9

GREEN BAY PACKERS

1. Larry Buhler, Minnesota, B, 21/21
3. **Charley Brock, Nebraska, C, 92/92**
5. Lynn Hovland, Wisconsin, G, 0/0
6. **Larry Craig, South Carolina, B, 121/121**
7. Frank Twedell, Minnesota, G, 4/4
8. Paul Kell, Notre Dame, T, 20/20
9. Johnny Hall, TCU, WB, 0/37
10. Vince Gavre, Wisconsin, B, 0/0
11. Charley Sprague, Southern Methodist, E, 0/0
13. Dan Elmer, Minnesota, C, 0/0
14. Bill Badgett, Georgia, T, 0/0
15. Tom Greenfield, Arizona, C, 22/22
18. Frank Balasz, Iowa, FB, 13/24
19. John Brennan, Michigan, G, 2/2
20. Charlie Schultz, Minnesota, T, 21/21

NEW YORK GIANTS

1. Walt Nielsen, Arizona, FB, 9/9
2. John Chickerneo, Pittsburgh, B, 4/4
5. Don Willis, Clemson, B, 0/0
6. Jerry Ginney, Santa Clara, G, 0/1
7. Lloyd Woodell, Arkansas, C, 0/0
8. Pete Zagar, Stanford, T, 0/0
9. Bob Mills, Nebraska, T, 0/0
10. Tom Roberts, DePaul, T, 9/25
11. Merl Miller, Washington, B, 0/0
12. Bruno Schroeder, Texas A&M, E, 0/0
13. Sam Allis, Centenary, B, 0/0
14. George Watson, North Carolina, B, 0/0
15. Gil Duggan, Oklahoma, T, 10/72
17. Jack Sanders, SMU, G, 0/33
21. Mario Tonelli, Notre Dame, FB, 0/9

PHILADELPHIA EAGLES

1. Davey O'Brien, TCU, QB, 22/22
2. Chuck Newton, Washington, FB, 12/12
3. Joe Mihal, Purdue, T, 0/33
4. Billy Dewell, SMU, E, 0/69
5. Zed Coston, Texas A&M, C, 1/1
6. Jake Schuehle, Rice, HB, 2/2
7. Tony Ippolito, Purdue, G, 0/9
8. George Somers, La Salle, T, 19/40
9. Rankin Britt, Texas A&M, E, 1/1
10. Bill McKeever, Cornell, T, 0/0
11. Paul Humphrey, Purdue, C, 0/11
12. Jack Kraynick, North Carolina, B, 0/0
13. Allie White, TCU, G, 7/7
14. Joe Aleskus, Ohio State, T, 0/0
15. Foster Watkins, West Texas A&M, QB, 20/20
16. Irv Hall, Brown, FB, 8/8
18. Charlie Gainor, North Dakota, DE, 0/1

PITTSBURGH PIRATES

3. Billy Patterson, Baylor, B, 11/19
4. Hugh McCullough, Oklahoma, TB, 10/36
5. Ernie Wheeler, North Dakota State, DB, 5/10
6. Sam Boyd, Baylor, E, 14/14
7. Eddie Palumbo, Detroit, B, 0/0
8. Ole Nelson, Michigan State, E, 0/0
9. Steve Petro, Pittsburgh, G, 0/17
10. Jack Lee, Carnegie Mellon, BB, 5/5
11. Lou Tomasetti, Bucknell, FB, 21/94
12. Denny Cochran, St. Louis, B, 0/0
13. Fabian Hoffman, Pittsburgh, E, 0/0
14. Ed Clary, South Carolina, B, 0/0
15. John Tosi, Niagara, C, 3/4

WASHINGTON REDSKINS

1. I.B. Hale, Texas Christian, T, 0/0
3. Charley Holm, Alabama, B, 0/0
5. **Dick Todd, Texas A&M, B, 79/79**
6. Dave Anderson, California, B, 0/0
7. Quinton Lumpkin, Georgia, C, 0/0
8. Bo Russell, Auburn, T, 22/22
9. **Wilbur Moore, Minnesota, WB, 72/72**
10. Jimmy Johnston, Washington, B, 22/28
11. Jimmy German, Centre, TB, 8/9
12. Bob O'Mara, Duke, B, 0/0
13. **Steve Slivinski, Washington, G, 53/53**
15. Eric Tipton, Duke, B, 0/0
16. Dick Farman, Washington State, G, 49/49
17. **Clyde Shugart, Iowa State, G, 56/56**
18. Boyd Morgan, USC, B, 11/11

1940 NFL

BROOKLYN DODGERS

1. Banks McFadden, Clemson, HB, 11/11
2. Nile Kinnick, Iowa, B, 0/0
3. Rhoten Shetley, Furman, B, 25/38
4. Bill Bailey, Duke, E, 15/15
5. Walt Merrill, Alabama, T, 28/28
6. Jack Murray, Wisconsin, C, 0/0
7. Ty Coon, North Carolina State, G, 9/9
8. Frank Zadworney, Ohio State, HB, 3/3
9. Art Jocher, Manhattan, G, 21/21
10. Jim Turner, Holy Cross, G, 0/0
11. Nick Cutlich, Northwestern, T, 0/0
12. George Dougherty, Howard, B, 0/0
13. Mike Gussie, West Virginia, G, 8/8
14. Len Coffman, Tennessee, B, 0/0
15. Jim Conlin, NYU, C, 0/0

CHICAGO BEARS

1. **Bulldog Turner, Hardin-Simmons, C, 138/138**
3. **Ken Kavanaugh, LSU, E, 90/90**
5. **Ed Kolman, Temple, T, 55/66**
6. John Woudenberg, St. Mary's (CA), T, 0/83
7. Len Akin, Baylor, G, 11/11
8. Jim Fordham, Georgia, FB, 19/19
9. Hampton Pool, Stanford, E, 33/37
10. Tom Pace, Utah, B, 0/0
11. Lee Artoe, California, T, 42/84
12. Bill McCubbin, Kentucky, E, 0/0
13. Harry Clarke, West Virginia, HB, 41/74
14. Frank Crisci, Case Western Reserve, T, 0/0
15. Sherm Barnes, Baylor, E, 0/0
20. Young Bussey, LSU, QB, 10/10
21. **Ray McLean, St. Anselm, HB, 76/76**
22. Walt Kichefski, Miami (FL), E, 0/43

CHICAGO CARDINALS

1. George Cafego, Tennessee, FB, 0/35
2. George (Snuffy) Stirnweiss, North Carolina, B, 0/0
3. Lloyd Madden, Colorado Mines, WB, 9/9
4. John Shirk, Oklahoma, E, 11/11
5. Marty Christiansen, Minnesota, FB, 6/6
6. Vic Reginato, Oregon, E, 0/0
7. Andy Chisick, Villanova, C, 22/22
8. Ben Kish, Pittsburgh, B, 0/83
9. Luke Pappas, Utah, T, 0/0
10. Jack Roche, Santa Clara, B, 0/0
11. Bill Davis, Texas Tech, T, 20/40
12. Stan Andersen, Stanford, T, 0/22
13. Al Coppage, Oklahoma, E, 31/58
14. Judson Hudson, Davis & Elkins, B, 0/0
15. Joe Ziembra, St. Benedict's, E, 0/0
16. Beryl Clark, Oklahoma, B, 9/9
17. Ralph Foster, Oklahoma State, T, 19/19
20. Rupert Pate, Wake Forest, G, 1/9

CLEVELAND RAMS

1. Olie Cordill, Rice, WB, 10/10
2. Merl Condit, Carnegie Mellon, HB, 0/54
3. Jack Haman, Northwestern, C, 21/21
4. Bobby Wood, Alabama, T, 0/3
5. Park Myers, Texas, T, 0/0
6. Ken Heineman, Texas-El Paso, TB, 3/11
7. Bob Nowaskey, George Washington, E, 0/95
8. Bob Anahu, Santa Clara, E, 0/0
9. Wilfred Thorpe, Arkansas, G, 16/16
10. Herb Smith, St. Mary's (CA), B, 0/0
11. Boyd Clay, Tennessee, T, 34/34
12. Shag Goolsby, Mississippi State, C, 8/8
13. Jack Gregory, Tennessee-Chattanooga, G, 7/7
14. Pete Bogden, Utah, E, 0/0
15. Owen Goodnight, Hardin-Simmons, HB, 9/9
17. Jack Nix, Mississippi State, WB, 1/1
18. Ralph Stevenson, Oklahoma, G, 3/3
19. **Dante Magnani, St. Mary's (CA), HB, 51/84**
20. Luke Lindon, Kentucky, T, 0/14

DETROIT LIONS

1. Doyle Nave, Southern California, B, 0/0
3. Bill Fisk, USC, E, 42/83
5. Harry Smith, USC, T, 10/10
6. Jim Rike, Tennessee, C, 0/0
7. Bob Winslow, USC, DE, 8/10
8. Bill Tranavitch, Rutgers, B, 0/0
9. Bob Haas, Missouri, T, 0/0
10. Leon DeWitte, Purdue, B, 0/0
11. Erwin Prasse, Iowa, E, 0/0
12. Ken Binder, Carroll, B, 0/0
13. Justin Bowers, Oklahoma, T, 0/0
14. Jack Morlock, Marshall, WB, 4/4
15. Stillman Rouse, Missouri, E, 10/10
17. Johnny Hackenbruck, Oregon State, T, 7/7
18. Frank Ribar, Duke, G, 0/2

GREEN BAY PACKERS

1. Hal Van Every, Minnesota, TB, 20/20
3. **Lou Brock, Purdue, B, 58/58**
5. Esco Sarkkinen, Ohio State, E, 0/0
6. Dick Cassiano, Pittsburgh, B, 0/10
7. Millard White, Tulane, T, 0/0
8. George Seeman, Nebraska, E, 1/1
9. J.R. Manley, Oklahoma, G, 0/0
10. Jack Brown, Purdue, B, 0/0
11. Don Guritz, Northwestern, G, 0/0
12. Phil Gaspar, Southern California, T, 0/0
13. Ambrose Schindler, Southern California, B, 0/0
14. Bill Kerr, Notre Dame, E, 0/11
15. Mel Brewer, Illinois, G, 0/0
18. Jim Gillette, Virginia, HB, 10/52

NEW YORK GIANTS

1. Grenny Lansdell, USC, HB, 2/2
3. John McLaughry, Brown, BB, 9/9
5. Carl Tomasello, Scranton, E, 1/1
6. Lou Smith, California, B, 0/0
7. Rex Williams, Texas Tech, C, 0/3
8. Win Pedersen, Minnesota, T, 13/23
9. Dom Principe, Fordham, B, 25/35
10. Earl Clark, Texas Christian, B, 0/0
11. John McKibben, Tulsa, E, 0/0
12. Ed McGee, Temple, T, 3/32
13. Joe Payne, Clemson, G, 0/0
14. Bob Smith, Oregon, B, 0/0
15. Othel Turner, Tulsa, T, 0/0
17. John Rogalla, Scranton, FB, 0/8
18. Monk Edwards, Baylor, G, 41/41

PHILADELPHIA EAGLES

1. George McAfee, Duke, HB, 0/75
2. John Schiechl, Santa Clara, C, 0/49
3. Dick Favor, Oklahoma, B, 0/0
4. Elbie Schultz, Oregon State, T, 11/86
5. Frank Emmons, Oregon, B, 11/11
6. Saul Singer, Arkansas, T, 0/0
7. Hal (Mike) Pegg, Bucknell, C, 0/0
8. Don Looney, TCU, E, 11/23
9. Don Jones, Washington, B, 0/0
10. Frank Maher, Toledo, B, 0/4
11. Elmer Hackney, Kansas State, FB, 8/61
12. Durward Hoerner, Texas Christian, E, 0/0
13. Ted Hennis, Purdue, B, 0/0
14. Bill Bunsen, Kansas, B, 0/0
15. Don Crumbaker, Kansas State, E, 0/0

PITTSBURGH STEELERS

1. Kay Eakin, Arkansas, HB, 0/31
2. Ralph Wenzel, Tulane, E, 6/6
3. George Kiick, Bucknell, FB, 17/17
4. Pop Ivy, Oklahoma, E, 4/57
5. Clark Goff, Florida, T, 11/11
6. Frank Bykowski, Purdue, G, 1/1
7. Pete Cignetti, Boston College, B, 0/0
8. Carl Nery, Duquesne, G, 22/22
9. Dick Boisseau, Washington & Lee, T, 0/0
10. Paul Shu, Virginia Military, B, 0/0
11. Cary Cox, Alabama, C, 0/0
12. Rocco Pirro, Catholic, G, 20/71
13. John Noppenberg, Miami (FL), B, 13/15
14. Nick Stublar, Santa Clara, T, 0/0
15. Ray McCarthy, Santa Clara, B, 0/0

WASHINGTON REDSKINS

1. Ed Boell, NYU, B, 0/0
3. Burt (Buddy) Banker, Tulane, B, 0/0
5. Bill Kirchem, Tulane, T, 0/0
6. Joe Boyd, Texas A&M, T, 0/0
7. Roy Zimmerman, San Jose State, QB, 22/84
8. Roland (Bud) Orf, Missouri, E, 0/0
9. Bob Hoffman, USC, B, 11/54
10. **Bob Seymour, Oklahoma, HB, 60/73**
11. Howard Stoecker, Southern California, T, 0/0
12. Allen Johnson, Duke, G, 0/0
13. Sam Bartholomew, Tennessee, FB, 0/9
14. Ernie Lain, Rice, B, 0/0
15. Sandy Sanford, Alabama, E, 7/7
16. Bolo Perdue, Arkansas, DE, 0/20
17. Steve Andrako, Ohio State, C, 5/5

1941 NFL

BROOKLYN DODGERS

1. Dean McAdams, Washington, TB, 30/30
3. Leo Stasica, Colorado, B, 5/18
5. Ray Frick, Pennsylvania, C, 3/3
6. Ed Rucinski, Indiana, E, 22/60
7. Hal Newman, Alabama, E, 0/0
8. Glenn Jackson, Texas, C, 0/0
9. Henry Toczylowski, Boston College, B, 0/0
10. Jim Langhurst, Ohio State, B, 0/0
11. Bernie Weiner, Kansas State, G, 10/10
12. Harvey Johnson, Mississippi State, B, 0/0
13. George Kinard, Mississippi, G, 18/29
15. Mike Jurich, Denver, T, 15/15
16. Warren Alfson, Nebraska, G, 11/11
19. Dave Parker, Hardin-Simmons, E, 7/7
20. Joe Ungerer, Fordham, T, 0/15
21. Julie Koshlap, Georgetown (DC), B, 0/1
22. Ken Whitlow, Rice, C, 0/13

CHICAGO BEARS

1. Tom Harmon, Michigan, HB, 0/22
1. Norm Standlee, Stanford, FB, 10/86
1. Don Scott, Ohio State, B, 0/0
3. **Hugh Gallarneau, Stanford, HB, 52/52**
5. Charlie O'Rourke, Boston College, QB, 11/58
6. Tom O'Boyle, Tulane, G, 0/0
7. John Federovitch, Davis & Elkins, T, 14/14
8. Fred Hartman, Rice, T, 11/23
8. Al Matuza, Georgetown (DC), C, 31/31
8. Dave Rankin, Purdue, E, 0/0
9. Hal Lahar, Oklahoma, G, 8/47
10. Jim (Sweet) Lalanne, North Carolina, B, 0/0
11. Jim Hardin, Kentucky, E, 0/0
12. Bob Morrow, Illinois Wesleyan, B, 0/43
13. Jim Johnson, Santa Clara, B, 0/0
14. Johnny Martin, Oklahoma, WB, 0/45
15. Jack Mulkey, Fresno State, E, 0/0
17. Bill Glenn, Eastern Illinois, QB, 2/2

CHICAGO CARDINALS

1. John Kimbrough, Texas A&M, FB, 0/38
2. **Paul Christman, Missouri, QB, 50/61**
3. Bob Foxx, Tennessee, B, 0/0
4. Johnny Clement, SMU, TB, 9/47
5. **Ray Apolskis, Marquette, C, 74/74**
6. Marshall Robnett, Texas A&M, C, 14/22
7. John Kuzman, Fordham, T, 5/29
8. George Kracum, Pittsburgh, FB, 0/11
9. Tom Vargo, Penn State, E, 0/0
10. Ray Mallouf, SMU, QB, 37/48
11. Jack Sommers, UCLA, C, 0/8
12. Charlie Armstrong, Mississippi College, DB, 0/10
13. Wayne Pitts, Arizona State, B, 0/0
14. Joe Lokanc, Northwestern, G, 9/9
15. Claude White, Ohio State, C, 0/0

CLEVELAND RAMS

1. Rudy Mucha, Washington, G, 13/22
2. Abe Shires, Tennessee, T, 0/7
3. Jay MacDowell, Washington, T, 0/62
4. Walt (Butch) Luther, Nebraska, B, 0/0

5. Chet Haliska, Oregon, B, 0/0
6. Jim Kisselburgh, Oregon State, B, 0/0
7. Ray Prochaska, Nebraska, E, 8/8
8. Tony Gallovich, Wake Forest, WB, 3/3
9. Milt Simington, Arkansas, G, 7/18
10. John Pendergast, Wake Forest, C, 0/0
11. Nick Drahos, Cornell, T, 0/0
12. Harold Punches, Colorado, G, 0/0
13. Bill McMurray, Murray State, E, 0/0
14. Bill Elmore, California, B, 0/0
15. Warren Desmore, Toledo, C, 0/0
16. Gordon Wilson, Texas-El Paso, G, 1/39
17. Kirk Hershey, Cornell, E, 2/8

DETROIT LIONS

1. Jim Thomason, Texas A&M, WB, 5/5
2. Gene Goodreault, Boston College, E, 0/0
3. Harry Hopp, Nebraska, B, 30/51
4. Augie Lio, Georgetown (DC), G, 31/72
5. Robert Nelson, Baylor, C, 18/71
6. John Tripson, Mississippi State, T, 11/11
7. John Jett, Wake Forest, E, 5/5
8. Joseph Manzo, Boston College, T, 3/3
9. Jasper Davis, Duke, B, 0/0
10. Ted Pavelec, Detroit Mercy, G, 25/25
11. Milt Piepul, Notre Dame, FB, 11/11
12. Billy Jefferson, Mississippi State, HB, 11/19
13. Maurice Britt, Arkansas, E, 9/9
14. Alex Schibanoff, Franklin & Marshall, T, 8/8
15. Perry Scott, Muhlenberg, E, 7/7

GREEN BAY PACKERS

1. George Paskvan, Wisconsin, FB, 7/7
3. Bob Paffrath, Minnesota, B, 0/12
5. Ed Frutig, Michigan, E, 9/24
6. Herm Rohrig, Nebraska, WB, 25/25
7. Bill Telesmanic, San Francisco, E, 0/0
8. **Bill Kuusisto, Minnesota, G, 54/54**
9. **Tony Canadeo, Gonzaga, HB, 116/116**
10. Mike Byelene, Purdue, B, 0/0
11. Paul Heimenz, Northwestern, C, 0/0
12. Mike Enich, Iowa, T, 0/0
13. Ed Heffernan, St. Mary's (CA), B, 0/0
14. Del Lyman, UCLA, T, 5/11
15. Johnny Frieberger, Arkansas, E, 0/0
16. Ernie Pannell, Texas A&M, T, 22/22
20. Jimmy Strausbaugh, Ohio State, HB, 0/11

NEW YORK GIANTS

1. George Franck, Minnesota, HB, 33/33
3. Frank Reagan, Pennsylvania, B, 32/68
5. Len Eshmont, Fordham, HB, 9/57
6. Lou DeFilippo, Fordham, T, 36/36
7. Don Vosberg, Marquette, E, 7/7
8. **Len Younce, Oregon State, G, 65/65**
9. Ben Sohn, USC, G, 11/11
10. Walt Matuszczak, Cornell, B, 0/0
11. Bobby Peoples, Southern California, B, 0/0
12. Andy Marefos, St. Mary's (CA), FB, 21/34
13. Cass Brovarney, Detroit, G, 0/0
14. Arnie Moore, Mississippi State, E, 0/0
15. Johnny Black, Arizona, B, 0/0

PHILADELPHIA EAGLES

2. Art Jones, Richmond, WB, 0/18
3. Marion Pugh, Texas A&M, B, 0/24
4. Al Ghesquiere, Detroit, B, 0/0
5. Royal Kahler, Nebraska, T, 0/16
6. Red Hickey, Arkansas, E, 0/49
7. Julius (Mush) Battista, Florida, G, 0/0
9. P.K. Rogers, East Texas State, B, 0/0
10. Don Williams, Texas, G, 0/6
11. Marshall Stenstrom, Oregon, B, 0/0
12. John Patrick, Penn State, BB, 0/18
13. Joe Hoague, Colgate, FB, 0/28
14. Les Dodson, Mississippi, B, 0/2
15. Alex Lukachick, Boston College, E, 0/0
19. John Shonk, West Virginia, E, 10/10

PITTSBURGH STEELERS

2. Chet Gladchuk, Boston College, C, 0/28
3. Johnny Knolla, Creighton, HB, 0/18
4. Jim Ringgold, Wake Forest, B, 0/0
5. Vic Sears, Oregon State, T, 0/131
6. Bob Suffridge, Tennessee, G, 0/20
7. Jim Roberts, Marshall, C, 0/0
9. Ervin (Buddy) Elrod, Mississippi State, E, 0/0
10. Ralph Fritz, Michigan, G, 0/10
11. Emil Uremovich, Indiana, T, 0/48
12. Paul Severin, North Carolina, E, 0/0
13. Russ Cotton, Texas-El Paso, QB, 11/11
14. J.W. Goree, Louisiana State, G, 0/0
15. John Eibner, Kentucky, T, 0/30
16. Wes McAfee, Duke, HB, 0/8
17. Terry Fox, Miami (FL), FB, 0/21
20. Bob Bjorklund, Minnesota, C, 0/7
22. Jim Castiglia, Georgetown (DC), FB, 0/42
22. Mort Landsberg, Cornell, HB, 0/17

WASHINGTON REDSKINS

1. Forest Evashevski, Michigan, B, 0/0
3. Fred Davis, Alabama, T, 26/97
5. Jim Stuart, Oregon, T, 5/5
6. Ed Cifers, Tennessee, E, 33/56
7. Al Krueger, USC, HB, 18/28
8. Henry Wilder, Iowa State, B, 0/0
9. Bill Grimmett, Tulsa, E, 0/0
10. Ed Hickerson, Alabama, G, 0/0
11. Joe Aguirre, St. Mary's (CA), E, 40/83
12. Jack Banta, USC, HB, 1/53
13. Roy Conn, Arizona, T, 0/0
14. Deward Tornell, San Jose State, B, 0/0
15. Morris Buckingham, San Jose State, C, 0/0
16. Ken Dow, Oregon State, FB, 2/2
18. Joe Osmanski, Holy Cross, FB, 0/42
22. Lee Gentry, Tulsa, HB, 5/5

1942 NFL

BROOKLYN DODGERS

1. Bobby Robertson, St. Mary's (CA), C, 11/11
3. Curt Mecham, Oregon, TB, 8/8
5. Vike Francis, Nebraska, B, 0/0
6. Henry Stanton, Arizona, E, 0/15
7. Wayne Goldsmith, Emporia State, B, 0/0
8. Preston Flanagan, Texas, E, 0/0
9. Bob Gifford, Denver, BB, 5/5
10. Joe Petro, Muhlenberg, G, 0/0
11. Fraser (Pat) Donlan, Manhattan, T, 0/0
12. Jim Thibaut, Tulane, FB, 0/3
13. Art Deremer, Niagara, C, 5/5
14. Stan Gervelis, Pittsburgh, E, 0/0
15. Gene Davis, Pennsylvania, B, 0/0
22. Walt Fedora, George Washington, FB, 8/8

CHICAGO BEARS

1. Frankie Albert, Stanford, QB, 0/90
3. Joe Boratyn, Holy Cross, B, 0/0
5. Martin Ruby, Texas A&M, T, 0/65
6. Harry Burrus, Hardin-Simmons, B, 0/38
7. Bob Jeffries, Missouri, G, 0/4
8. Frank Maznicki, Boston College, HB, 15/27
9. John Petty, Purdue, FB, 10/10
10. Noah Mullins, Kentucky, HB, 34/45
11. Bill Geyer, Colgate, HB, 9/9
12. Jim Daniell, Ohio State, T, 7/21
13. Jackie Hunt, Marshall, FB, 4/4
14. Henry Gude, Vanderbilt, C, 0/2
15. Joe Krutulis, Miami (FL), E, 0/0
19. Edgar Jones, Pittsburgh, HB, 1/44
21. Adolph Kissell, Boston College, HB, 4/4
22. **Stu Clarkson, Texas A&M-Kingsville, LB, 74/74**

CHICAGO CARDINALS

1. Steve Lach, Duke, WB, 9/32
2. Lloyd Cheatham, Auburn, B, 11/50
3. Bud Schwenk, Washington-St. Louis, QB, 11/37
4. **Vince Banonis, Detroit Mercy, C, 70/108**
5. Bob Reinhard, California, T, 0/66
6. Chal Daniel, Texas, G, 0/0
7. Rupe Thornton, Santa Clara, G, 0/25
8. Doug Renzel, Marquette, B, 0/0
9. Chet Wetterlund, Illinois Wesleyan, TB, 0/6
10. Jud Ringer, Minnesota, E, 0/0
11. Jim Fitzharris, St. Thomas (MN), E, 0/0
12. Dick Brye, Marquette, T, 0/0
13. Charley Givler, Wake Forest, G, 0/0
14. Hugh Swink, Oklahoma State, T, 0/0
15. Marv Harshman, Pacific Lutheran, B, 0/0
19. Jimmy Nelson, Alabama, B, 0/14

CLEVELAND RAMS

1. Jack Wilson, Baylor, HB, 10/10
2. Jack Jacobs, Oklahoma, QB, 10/55
3. Roger Eason, Oklahoma, G, 32/44
4. Len Levy, Minnesota, G, 17/42
5. Orville Matthews, Oklahoma, B, 0/0
6. Mike Sweeney, Texas, E, 0/0
7. Italo Rossi, Purdue, T, 0/0
8. Bob Brumley, Rice, WB, 0/1
9. Hub Ulrich, Kansas, E, 0/14
10. Bob deLauer, USC, C, 13/13
11. Ben Hightower, Sam Houston State, E, 10/18
12. Walt Zirinsky, Lafayette, HB, 5/5
13. Ray Bradfield, Santa Clara, E, 0/0
14. Tom Greene, Georgia, T, 0/0
15. Ike Peel, Tennessee, B, 0/0

DETROIT LIONS

1. Bob Westfall, Michigan, FB, 41/41
2. Alf Bauman, Northwestern, DT, 0/34
3. Bob Dethman, Oregon State, B, 0/0
4. Mickey Sanzotta, Case Western Reserve, B, 20/20
5. Joe Blalock, Clemson, E, 0/0
6. Murray Evans, Hardin-Simmons, BB, 19/19
7. Tom Colella, Canisius, HB, 17/89
8. Joe Franceski, Scranton, T, 0/0
9. Emil Banjavic, Arizona, WB, 10/10
10. Bill Diehl, Iowa, C, 0/0
11. John Polanski, Wake Forest, FB, 3/16
12. Joe Stringfellow, Southern Mississippi, TB, 9/9
13. Tony Arena, Michigan State, C, 1/1
14. Wolf Heinberg, Cal-Santa Barbara, T, 0/0
15. Mac Speedie, Utah, E, 0/86
18. George Speth, Murray State, T, 10/10

GREEN BAY PACKERS

1. Urban Odson, Minnesota, T, 39/39
3. Ray Frankowski, Washington, G, 2/42
5. Bill Green, Iowa, B, 0/0
6. Joe Krivonak, South Carolina, G, 0/4
7. Pres Johnston, SMU, HB, 0/11
8. Joe Rogers, Michigan, E, 0/0
9. Noah Langdale, Alabama, T, 0/0
10. Gene Flick, Minnesota, C, 0/0
11. Tom Farris, Wisconsin, QB, 0/33
12. Jimmy Richardson, Marquette, B, 0/0
13. Bruce Smith, Minnesota, HB, 23/31
14. Bill Applegate, South Carolina, G, 0/0
15. Jim Trimble, Indiana, T, 0/0
18. Bob Ingalls, Michigan, C, 10/10
19. George Benson, Northwestern, B, 0/1

NEW YORK GIANTS

1. Merle Hapes, Mississippi, FB, 21/21
3. Bob Sweiger, Minnesota, WB, 0/53
5. Al Blozis, Georgetown (DC), T, 23/23
6. Bob Glass, Tulane, B, 0/0
7. Tommy Prothro, Duke, B, 0/0
8. Tom Kearns, Miami (FL), T, 3/12
9. Bob Merker, Millikin, E, 0/0
10. Mike Kopcik, Georgetown (DC), E, 0/0
11. John Solic, St. Francis (NY), C, 0/0
12. Len Krouse, Penn State, B, 0/0
13. Bob Barnett, Duke, C, 0/0
14. Pete Layden, Texas, B, 0/31
15. Buddy Jungmichel, Texas, G, 0/14
18. Junie Hovious, Mississippi, HB, 6/6
21. Jim Blumenstock, Fordham, FB, 10/10

PHILADELPHIA EAGLES

1. Pete Kmetovic, Stanford, HB, 5/16
2. **Vic Lindskog, Stanford, C, 78/78**
3. Ted Williams, Boston College, B, 11/21
4. Gordon Paschka, Minnesota, FB, 0/16
5. Ernie Blandin, Tulane, T, 0/71
6. Earl Younglove, Washington, E, 0/0
7. Billy Sewell, Washington State, B, 0/0
8. Bill Halverson, Oregon State, T, 8/8
9. Ray Graves, Tennessee, C, 18/28
10. Jack Stackpool, Washington, FB, 8/8
11. Noble Doss, Texas, HB, 20/24
12. Fred Meyer, Stanford, E, 18/18
13. Bob Brenton, Missouri, T, 0/0
14. John Wyhonic, Alabama, G, 23/39
15. O'Dell Griffin, Baylor, G, 0/0

PITTSBURGH STEELERS

1. Bill Dudley, Virginia, HB, 26/90
2. Vern Martin, Texas, BB, 11/11
3. Ken Casanega, Santa Clara, QB, 0/15
4. Mal Kutner, Texas, E, 0/56
5. Curt Sandig, St. Mary's (TX), HB, 11/20
6. Charley Greene, Tulsa, T, 0/0
7. Johnny Butler, Tennessee, HB, 0/26
8. Floyd Spendlove, Utah, T, 0/0
9. Rayburn Chase, Missouri, B, 0/0
10. Ernie Steele, Washington, HB, 0/69
11. Thornley Wood, Columbia, B, 0/0
12. Bill Roach, Texas Christian, E, 0/0
13. Wayne Holt, Tulsa, G, 0/0
14. Clure Mosher, Louisville, C, 2/2
15. Hubbard Law, Sam Houston State, G, 17/17
16. Andy Tomasic, Temple, TB, 15/15
17. Garth Chamberlain, Brigham Young, G, 3/3
18. John Rokisky, Duquesne, DE, 0/25

WASHINGTON REDSKINS

1. Spec Sanders, Texas, TB, 0/52
3. Rufus Deal, Auburn, B, 6/6
5. Joe Zeno, Holy Cross, G, 29/42
6. Harley McCollum, Tulane, T, 0/23
7. Bob Fitch, Minnesota, E, 0/0
8. George Peters, Oregon State, B, 0/0
9. Frank Swiger, Duke, B, 0/0
10. John Goodyear, Marquette, B, 3/3
11. **Al DeMao, Duquesne, C, 97/97**
12. Phil Ahwesh, Duquesne, B, 0/0
13. John Kovatch, Notre Dame, E, 18/21
14. Billy deCorrevont, Northwestern, B, 10/49
15. Marv Whited, Oklahoma, G, 15/15
17. George Watts, Appalachian State, T, 8/8
19. Charlie Timmons, Georgia, FB, 0/13
20. Tiny Croft, Ripon, T, 0/51
21. Steve Juzwik, Notre Dame, HB, 2/29
22. Al Couppee, Iowa, G, 7/7

1943 NFL

BROOKLYN DODGERS

1. Paul Governali, Columbia, QB, 0/32
2. Blondy Black, Mississippi State, B, 0/9
3. George Ceithaml, Michigan, B, 0/0
4. Joe Domnanovich, Alabama, C, 0/67
5. Marty Comer, Tulane, DE, 0/27
6. Harvey Johnson, William & Mary, T, 0/65
7. John Matisi, Duquesne, T, 4/16
8. John Ferguson, California, E, 0/0
9. Ray Rason, Southern Methodist, G, 0/0
10. Vic Schleich, Nebraska, T, 0/11
11. Joe Sabasteanski, Fordham, G, 0/34
12. Lou Thomas, Tulane, B, 0/0
13. Bert Stiff, Pennsylvania, B, 0/0
14. John Fekete, Ohio University, HB, 0/3
15. Floyd Rhea, Oregon, G, 8/19
22. Don Reece, Missouri, FB, 0/13
25. Gene Lee, Florida, C, 0/11

CHICAGO BEARS

1. Bob Steuber, Depauw, HB, 1/19
3. Fred Evans, Notre Dame, HB, 3/22
5. Ed Stamm, Stanford, T, 0/0
6. Derrell Palmer, TCU, DT, 0/96
7. Milt Vucinich, Stanford, C, 3/3
8. Alyn Beals, Santa Clara, E, 0/77
9. Jim Jurkovich, California, B, 0/0
10. Walt Lamb, Oklahoma, E, 11/11
11. Ray (Duke) Hammett, Stanford, B, 0/0
12. Al Zikmund, Nebraska, B, 0/0
13. Clark Wood, Kentucky, T, 0/0
14. Loyd Arms, Oklahoma State, G, 0/27
15. Lyle Sturdy, Wichita State, B, 0/0
17. Pat Preston, Duke, G, 38/38
18. Hank Norberg, Stanford, E, 10/35
22. Bill Johnson, SMU, G, 6/6

CHICAGO CARDINALS

1. Glenn Dobbs, Tulsa, TB, 0/49
2. John Grigas, Holy Cross, FB, 10/49
3. Don Currivan, Boston College, E, 7/75
4. Al Hust, Tennessee, E, 10/10
5. George Hecht, Alabama, G, 0/10
6. Al Klug, Marquette, T, 0/36
7. Stan Mauldin, Texas, T, 19/19
8. Bill Godwin, Georgia, C, 0/24
9. Moffatt Storer, Duke, B, 0/0
10. Fondren Mitchell, Florida, HB, 0/7
11. Emil Lussow, Dubuque, E, 0/0
12. Paul Hirsbrunner, Wisconsin, T, 0/0
13. Bill Baumgartner, Minnesota, E, 0/2
14. **Buster Ramsey, William & Mary, G, 57/57**
15. Earl Doloway, Indiana, B, 0/0
17. Bill Campbell, Oklahoma, T, 34/38
18. Clarence Booth, SMU, T, 6/11
21. George Smith, Villanova, FB, 3/3
22. George Sutch, Temple, B, 3/3
24. Weldon Humble, Louisiana-Lafayette, G, 0/58
25. Cal Purdin, Tulsa, B, 4/13
27. Al Drulis, Temple, B, 14/24

CLEVELAND RAMS

1. Mike Holovak, Boston College, FB, 11/34
2. Tom Farmer, Iowa, HB, 8/27
3. **Fred Naumetz, Boston College, C, 58/58**
4. Chuck Taylor, Stanford, G, 0/14
5. Clyde Johnson, Kentucky, T, 23/32
6. Les Horvath, Ohio State, HB, 22/34
7. Bill Henderson, Texas A&M, E, 0/0
8. Bill Parker, Iowa, E, 0/0
9. Al Solari, UCLA, B, 0/0
10. Homer Simmons, Oklahoma, T, 0/0
11. Tom Roblin, Oregon, B, 0/0
12. Bill Vickroy, Ohio State, C, 0/0
13. Tom Alberghini, Holy Cross, G, 0/1
14. Sam Sharp, Alabama, E, 0/0
15. Dick Kieppe, Michigan State, B, 0/0
16. Cullen Rogers, Texas A&M, HB, 0/5
28. Steve Pritko, Villanova, E, 42/86
29. Floyd Konetsky, Florida, E, 18/24

DETROIT LIONS

1. Frankie Sinkwich, Georgia, B, 20/35
2. Dave Schreiner, Wisconsin, E, 0/0
3. Dick Ashcom, Oregon, T, 0/0

4. Ralph Hamer, Furman, B, 0/0
5. Lloyd Wickett, Oregon State, T, 14/14
6. Jim Jones, Union (TN), T, 2/2
7. Paul Sizemore, Furman, E, 0/0
8. George Poschner, Georgia, E, 0/0
9. Jack Irish, Arizona, T, 0/0
10. Jack Fenton, Michigan State, B, 0/0
11. Dick Renfro, Washington State, FB, 0/3
12. Bob Kolesar, Michigan, G, 0/2
13. Del Huntsinger, Portland, B, 0/0
14. Ellard Dernoncourt, St. Louis, E, 0/0
15. Dick Woodward, Colorado, E, 0/0
18. Chet Maeda, Colorado State, HB, 0/1
19. Bert Kuczynski, Pennsylvania, E, 2/5
24. Bill Remington, Washington State, C, 0/9

GREEN BAY PACKERS

1. **Dick Wildung, Minnesota, T, 83/83**
3. **Irv Comp, Benedictine, B, 69/69**
5. Roy McKay, Texas, TB, 35/35
6. Nick Susoeff, Washington State, E, 0/44
7. Ken Snelling, UCLA, FB, 2/2
8. Les Gatewood, Tulane, C, 23/23
9. Norm Verry, USC, T, 0/11
11. **Bob Forte, Arkansas, HB, 80/80**
12. Van Davis, Georgia, DE, 0/37
13. Tom Brock, Notre Dame, C, 0/0
14. Ralph Tate, Oklahoma State, B, 0/0
15. Don Carlson, Denver, T, 0/0
19. Hal Prescott, Hardin-Simmons, E, 2/33
20. Eddie Forrest, Santa Clara, G, 0/25
21. Lloyd Wasserbach, Wisconsin, T, 0/17
23. Jug Bennett, Hardin-Simmons, G, 3/3
32. Ken Roskie, South Carolina, FB, 6/21

NEW YORK GIANTS

1. Steve Filipowicz, Fordham, FB, 21/21
3. Dewey Proctor, Furman, FB, 0/25
5. Val Culwell, Oregon, G, 0/0
6. Jim Reynolds, Auburn, FB, 0/7
7. Lou Palazzi, Penn State, C, 16/16
8. Larry Visnic, Benedictine, G, 22/22
9. Doyle Caraway, Texas Tech, G, 0/0
10. Bill Piccolo, Canisius, C, 18/18
11. Glenn Knox, William & Mary, E, 0/0
12. Walt Domina, Norwich, B, 0/0
13. Don McCafferty, Ohio State, E, 9/9
14. Jay Stoves, Washington State, B, 0/0
15. Howard Currie, Geneva, T, 0/0
24. Keith Beebe, Occidental, B, 5/5
25. Dave Brown, Alabama, WB, 24/24
27. Ed McNamara, Holy Cross, T, 0/1
31. Verlin Adams, Charleston (WV), DE, 12/12

PHILADELPHIA EAGLES

1. **Joe Muha, VMI, FB, 56/56**
2. Lamar Davis, Georgia, E, 0/53
3. Monk Gafford, Auburn, B, 0/39
4. Bob Kennedy, Washington State, B, 0/58
5. **Al Wistert, Michigan, T, 86/95**
6. Bruno Banducci, Stanford, G, 19/122
7. Walt Harrison, Washington, C, 0/0
8. Bruce Alford, TCU, E, 0/75
9. Rocco Canale, Boston College, T, 12/38
10. Zuehl Conoly, Texas, G, 0/9
11. John Billman, Minnesota, G, 0/5
12. Jack Donaldson, Pennsylvania, T, 0/0
13. Bill Erickson, Georgetown (DC), C, 0/0
14. George Weeks, Alabama, DE, 0/3
15. **Russ Craft, Alabama, DB, 89/100**
17. Walt Gorinski, LSU, FB, 0/6
18. Bob Friedman, Washington, T, 10/10
20. Chet Mutryn, Xavier (OH), HB, 0/65
21. Bap Manzini, St. Vincent, C, 22/23
27. Art Macioszczyk, Western Michigan, FB, 21/22

PITTSBURGH STEELERS

1. Bill Daley, Columbia, FB, 0/24
3. Jack Russell, Baylor, E, 0/65
5. Harry Connolly, Boston College, TB, 0/3
6. Lou Sossamon, South Carolina, C, 0/42
7. Al Ratto, St. Mary's (CA), C, 0/0
8. Ray Curry, St. Mary's (CA), E, 0/0
9. Ed Murphy, Holy Cross, E, 0/0
10. Dick Dwelle, Rice, B, 0/0
11. Al Wukits, Duquesne, C, 3/38
12. Joe Repko, Boston College, T, 17/37
13. Pete Boltrek, North Carolina State, T, 0/0
14. Mort Shiekman, Pennsylvania, G, 0/0
15. Milt Crain, Baylor, FB, 0/10
16. Max Kielbasa, Duquesne, HB, 2/2
17. Nick Skorich, Cincinnati, G, 32/32
19. Ray Bucek, Texas A&M, G, 11/11
21. Tony Compagno, St. Mary's (CA), FB, 34/34
24. Harry Wynne, Arkansas, E, 0/15
25. Joe Cibulas, Duquesne, T, 5/5
27. Jack Freeman, Texas, G, 0/12
29. Jack Durishan, Pittsburgh, T, 0/6

WASHINGTON REDSKINS

1. Jack Jenkins, Vanderbilt, FB, 22/22
3. Bill Dutton, Pittsburgh, HB, 0/11
5. Bob Dove, Notre Dame, DE, 0/106
6. Wally Ziemba, Notre Dame, C, 0/0
7. Lou Rymkus, Notre Dame, T, 10/86
8. Tony Leon, Alabama, G, 6/36
9. Bob Motl, Northwestern, E, 0/14
10. Walt McDonald, Tulane, B, 0/46
11. George Perpich, Georgetown (DC), T, 0/27
12. Dan Wood, Mississippi, C, 0/0
13. Harry Wright, Notre Dame, G, 0/0
14. Oscar Britt, Mississippi, G, 1/1
15. Dick Weber, Syracuse, G, 0/0
25. Roman Bentz, Tulane, G, 0/34
27. Vince Pacewic, San Francisco, HB, 2/2
29. Johnny Jaffurs, Penn State, G, 8/8
30. Frank Akins, Washington State, FB, 28/28

1944 NFL

BROOKLYN TIGERS

1. Creighton Miller, Notre Dame, B, 0/0
2. Jim Callahan, Texas, TB, 0/9
3. Ralph Park, Texas, B, 0/0
4. Rudy Sikich, Minnesota, T, 0/6
5. Verne Ullom, Cincinnati, E, 0/0
6. Bruce McDonald, Illinois State, E, 0/0
7. Bob Graiziger, Minnesota, G, 0/0
8. Jack Sachse, Texas, C, 0/4
9. Mitch Olenski, Alabama, T, 0/26
10. Aldo Cenci, Penn State, B, 0/0
11. John Bicaninch, Minnesota, G, 0/0
12. Jim Tyree, Oklahoma, E, 0/12
13. Jim Wright, SMU, G, 0/12
14. John Genis, Illinois, T, 0/0
15. Billie (Spook) Murphy, Mississippi State, B, 0/0
17. Howard Maley, SMU, HB, 0/23
20. George Doherty, Louisiana Tech, T, 10/43
22. Ted Cook, Alabama, E, 0/46
24. Jack Baldwin, Centenary, C, 0/15
28. Bob Zimny, Indiana, T, 0/52

BOSTON YANKS

1. Angelo Bertelli, Notre Dame, QB, 0/16
2. Babe Dimancheff, Purdue, HB, 13/63
5. Larry Rice, Tulane, C, 0/0
6. John (Butch) Parker, Loyola (LA), T, 0/0
7. Mike Andrews, North Carolina State, E, 0/0
8. Bob Musick, Southern California, B, 0/0
9. Tex Warrington, Auburn, G, 0/39
10. Angelo Sisti, Boston College, T, 0/0
11. Gene Long, Kansas, G, 0/0
12. Ed Fiorentino, Brown, DE, 4/4
13. Mike Zeleznak, Kansas State, B, 0/0
14. John Maskas, Virginia Tech, G, 0/18
15. John Bond, Texas Christian, B, 0/0
17. Marshall Shurnas, Missouri, E, 0/11
19. Art Faircloth, Guilford, B, 0/5
31. Ralph Calcagni, Pennsylvania, T, 11/20

CHICAGO BEARS

1. Ray Evans, Kansas, TB, 0/9
3. Rudy Smeja, Michigan, E, 18/29
5. Abe Croft, SMU, E, 11/11
6. C.B. Stanley, Tulsa, T, 0/13
7. Darwin Seeley, Stanford, C, 0/0
8. Randall (Buck) Fawcett, Stanford, B, 0/0
9. Jack Morton, Purdue, E, 8/22
10. Bill Stanford, Wake Forest, C, 0/0
11. Lin Houston, Ohio State, G, 0/98
12. J.P. Moore, Vanderbilt, B, 0/0
13. Bill Duffey, Georgetown (DC), E, 0/0
14. Joe Hartley, Louisiana State, T, 0/0
15. Bill Milner, Duke, LB, 36/48
16. Buckets Hirsch, Northwestern, QB, 0/34
19. Barry French, Purdue, G, 0/49
21. Bob Margarita, Brown, HB, 21/21
25. Roy Ruskusky, St. Mary's (CA), E, 0/11
28. Charlie Mitchell, Tulsa, HB, 8/10

CHICAGO CARDINALS

1. **Pat Harder, Wisconsin, FB, 58/86**
2. Paul Mitchell, Minnesota, DT, 0/69
3. Saxon Judd, Tulsa, E, 0/41
4. John Tavener, Indiana, C, 0/3
5. **Bill Blackburn, Rice, C, 59/59**
6. Bill Garnaas, Minnesota, QB, 0/26
7. Rodger Smith, Texas Tech, B, 0/0
8. Red Cochran, Wake Forest, QB, 36/36
9. Frank Scanlan, Loyola (LA), B, 0/0
10. Lou Saban, Indiana, C, 0/54
11. Fran Griffin, Holy Cross, T, 0/0
12. Leo Daniels, Texas A&M, B, 0/0
13. Bobby Dobbs, Tulsa, B, 0/0
14. Van Hall, Texas Christian, B, 0/0
15. Jack Carpenter, Michigan, T, 0/36
17. Joe Magliolo, Texas, LB, 0/13
18. Walt Szot, Bucknell, DT, 33/56
20. Ray Kuffel, Notre Dame, E, 0/23

CLEVELAND RAMS

1. Tony Butkovich, Illinois, B, 0/0
3. **Gil Bouley, Boston College, T, 64/64**
5. **Bob Waterfield, UCLA, QB, 91/91**
6. Al Akins, Washington State, HB, 0/25
7. George Cheverko, Fordham, B, 0/19
8. Stan Stasica, Illinois, HB, 0/1
9. Fred Boensch, Stanford, G, 0/24
10. Bob Shaw, Ohio State, E, 26/38
11. Joe Andrejco, Fordham, B, 0/0
12. Pat Filley, Notre Dame, G, 0/0
13. Bob Erickson, Washington, B, 0/0
14. Mel Maceau, Marquette, C, 0/37
15. Frank Hubbell, Tennessee, E, 36/36
20. Joe Yackanich, Fordham, G, 0/26
27. Jim Smith, Colorado, T, 0/7

DETROIT LIONS

1. Otto Graham, Northwestern, QB, 0/126
2. Bob Cifers, Tennessee, HB, 11/42
3. Ralph Heywood, USC, E, 14/48
4. George Betteridge, Utah, B, 0/0
5. **John Greene, Michigan, E, 78/78**
6. Ed Alliquie, Santa Clara, T, 0/0
7. Paul Briggs, Colorado, T, 12/12
8. Red Giske, Washington State, G, 0/0
9. Matthew Bolger, Notre Dame, E, 0/0
10. Herb Hein, Minnesota, E, 0/0
11. Paul White, Michigan, HB, 0/11
12. Jack Lescoulie, UCLA, G, 0/0
13. Doug Rehor, Dickinson, B, 0/0
14. Bill Pritula, Michigan, C, 0/0
15. Jim Molich, Fresno State, E, 0/0
17. Jack Helms, Georgia Tech, DE, 7/7
18. Elmer Madarik, Detroit Mercy, HB, 22/23
21. Alex Kapter, Northwestern, G, 0/6
29. Robert Derleth, Michigan, T, 1/1

GREEN BAY PACKERS

1. Merv Pregulman, Michigan, C, 11/47
3. Tom Kuzma, Michigan, B, 0/0
5. Bill McPartland, St. Mary's (CA), T, 0/0
6. Mickey McCardle, Southern California, B, 0/0
7. Jack Tracy, Washington, E, 0/0
8. Alex Agase, Illinois, LB, 0/70
9. Don Whitmire, Alabama/Navy, T, 0/0
10. Bob Koch, Oregon, B, 0/0
11. Virgil Johnson, Arkansas, E, 0/0
12. Roy Giusti, St. Mary's (CA), B, 0/0
13. Bill Baughman, Alabama, C, 0/0
14. Don Griffin, Illinois, HB, 0/13
15. Bert Gissler, Nebraska, E, 0/0
21. Jim Cox, Stanford, G, 0/14

NEW YORK GIANTS

1. Billy Hillenbrand, Indiana, HB, 0/41
2. Lamar Blount, Mississippi State, E, 0/22
3. Clyde Flowers, Texas Christian, T, 0/0
4. Herb Kane, East Central (OK), T, 8/8
5. Vic Maitland, Hobart, T, 0/0
6. Jack Okland, Utah State, T, 0/0
7. Herm Frickey, Minnesota, B, 0/0
8. Roy Clay, Colorado State, WB, 1/1
9. John Sanchez, San Francisco, T, 20/41
10. Ernie Beamer, Duke, E, 0/0
11. Carl Grate, Georgia, G, 6/6
12. Tommy Mont, Maryland, QB, 0/27
13. **Ray Poole, Mississippi, DE, 71/71**
14. Bert Corley, Mississippi State, C, 0/22
15. Ollie Poole, Mississippi, DE, 0/22

PHILADELPHIA EAGLES

1. **Steve Van Buren, LSU, HB, 83/83**
3. Loren LaPrade, Stanford, G, 0/0
5. Joe Parker, Texas, E, 0/20
6. Hillary Horne, Mississippi State, T, 0/0
7. Vic Kulbitski, Notre Dame, FB, 0/40
8. George Phillips, UCLA, LB, 0/1
9. Paul Sarringhaus, Ohio State, HB, 0/7
10. John Perko, Notre Dame, G, 0/14
11. Elliott Ormsbee, Bradley, HB, 4/4
12. Earle Parsons, USC, HB, 0/21
13. Bob Hanzlik, Wisconsin, E, 0/0
14. Jim Talley, Louisiana State, C, 0/0
15. Dom Fusci, South Carolina, T, 0/0
16. John Green, Tulsa, DE, 44/44
22. Al Postus, Villanova, TB, 0/2
23. Milt Smith, UCLA, DB, 5/5
24. Earl Klapstein, Pacific, T, 0/9
26. Ed Eiden, Scranton, C, 0/1
28. Nick Daukas, Dartmouth, T, 0/15

PITTSBURGH STEELERS

1. Johnny Podesto, St. Mary's (CA), B, 0/0
2. Bob Odell, Pennsylvania, E, 0/0
3. Bob Gantt, Duke, E, 0/0
4. Art McCaffray, Pacific, T, 11/11
5. George Owen, Wake Forest, G, 0/0
6. Dan Savage, Brown, B, 0/0
7. Jesse Freitas, Santa Clara, QB, 0/31
8. George Titus, Holy Cross, C, 11/11
9. Ed Stofko, St. Francis (PA), TB, 2/2
10. **Val Jansante, Villanova, E, 65/68**
11. Carl Buda, Tulsa, G, 3/3
12. Sam Gray, Tulsa, E, 16/16
13. Bob Longacre, William & Mary, B, 0/0
14. Les Zetty, Muhlenberg, E, 0/0
15. Jim Myers, Tennessee, G, 0/0

WASHINGTON REDSKINS

1. Mike Micka, Colgate, FB, 16/54
3. Earl Audet, USC, T, 10/51
5. Ed Doherty, Boston College, B, 0/0
6. Jackie Fellows, Fresno State, B, 0/0
7. Hal Fischer, Texas, G, 0/0
8. Cliff White, Murray State, T, 0/0
9. Ted Ogdahl, Willamette, B, 0/0
10. Bob Sneddon, St. Mary's (CA), DB, 10/22
11. Bill Aldworth, Minnesota, T, 0/0
12. Bill Joslyn, Stanford, B, 0/0
13. Charley Walker, Kentucky, C, 0/0
14. Boyd Clement, Oregon State, C, 0/0
15. Jim Gaffney, Tennessee, QB, 12/12
16. Ted Ossowski, Oregon State, T, 0/3
18. John Batorski, Colgate, E, 0/8
19. Clyde Ehrhardt, Georgia, C, 34/34
23. Bill Reinhard, California, B, 0/22

1945 NFL

BROOKLYN TIGERS

1. Joe Renfroe, Tulane, B, 0/0
2. Wayne Williams, Minnesota, B, 0/0
3. Cecil Gray, Oregon, C, 0/0
4. Steve Enich, Marquette, G, 0/5
5. Adolph Kowalski, Tulsa, BB, 0/10
6. Dick Barwegan, Purdue, G, 0/92
7. Louie Futrell, Fresno State, B, 0/0
8. John Dodds, California, G, 0/0
9. Elting Johnson, Bucknell, B, 0/0
10. Roy Cross, Tennessee, E, 0/0
11. Earl Haury, Kansas State, T, 0/0
12. John Martin, East Tennessee State, B, 0/0
13. George McDonald, South Carolina, T, 0/0
14. Hal Self, Alabama, B, 0/0
15. Tom Reilly, Fordham, G, 0/0
17. Arnie Weinmeister, Washington, DT, 0/71
18. Charley Eikenberg, Rice, QB, 0/9

BOSTON YANKS

1. Eddie Prokop, Georgia Tech, B, 0/40
2. Tom Dean, SMU, T, 21/21
3. Damon Tassos, Texas A&M, G, 0/55
4. Don Deeks, Washington, T, 18/29
6. Jim Mello, Notre Dame, DB, 9/28
7. Marty Silovich, Marquette, C, 0/0
8. Ellis Jones, Tulsa, G, 8/8
9. Earl Lambert, Manhattan, B, 0/0
10. Don Kasprzak, Dartmouth, B, 0/0
11. Ben Jones, Arkansas, E, 0/0
12. Herb Coleman, Notre Dame, C, 0/37
13. Joe Pezelski, Villanova, B, 0/0
14. John DiGangi, Holy Cross, T, 0/0
15. Chan Highsmith, North Carolina, C, 0/0
20. Mario Gianelli, Boston College, MG, 0/44
28. John Morelli, Georgetown (DC), G, 19/19

CHICAGO BEARS

1. Don Lund, Michigan, B, 0/0
3. Charley Allen, Southern Methodist, B, 0/0
5. Forrest Masterson, Iowa, C, 7/7
6. Wayne Shaw, Southern Methodist, B, 0/0
7. Glen Burgeis, Tulsa, T, 3/3
8. Pat O'Brien, Purdue, T, 0/0
9. Bill Mayther, Oregon, C, 0/0
10. Bill Poe, Clemson, B, 0/0
11. Chuck Avery, Minnesota, B, 0/0
12. Jack Boyd, UCLA, B, 0/0
13. Ralph Ellsworth, Texas, B, 0/0
14. Frank Mattioli, Pittsburgh, G, 0/11
15. Merle Gibson, Texas Christian, E, 0/0
17. Nick Sacrinty, Wake Forest, QB, 11/11
18. **Jim Keane, Northwestern, E, 70/81**
19. Bruno Niedziela, Iowa, T, 0/12
21. Walt Stickel, Pennsylvania, T, 45/68
22. Bob Livingstone, Notre Dame, HB, 0/35
26. Lu Gambino, Maryland, FB, 0/19
29. Nick Forkovitch, William & Mary, FB, 0/9
32. George Groves, Marquette, G, 0/9

CHICAGO CARDINALS

1. **Charlie Trippi, Georgia, HB, 99/99**
2. Paul Collins, Missouri, QB, 3/3
3. Walt Watt, Miami (FL), HB, 4/4
4. Bob Dobelstein, Tennessee, G, 0/41
5. Zeke Chronister, Texas Christian, E, 0/0
6. Corwin Clatt, Notre Dame, FB, 24/24
7. Ziggy Czarobski, Notre Dame, T, 0/26
8. John Harrington, Marquette, E, 0/25
9. Gene Meeks, Kentucky, B, 0/0
10. Bill Huber, Notre Dame, E, 0/0
11. Halley Heard, Louisiana State, T, 0/0
12. Bob Cowan, Indiana, B, 0/33
13. Elmore (Buddy) Luper, Duke, B, 0/0
14. Solon Barnett, Baylor, T, 0/5
15. Gordon Carver, Duke, B, 0/0
20. Jack Kramer, Marquette, T, 0/13
28. Garland Williams, Georgia, T, 0/26

CLEVELAND RAMS

1. **Elroy Hirsch, Michigan, E, 103/127**
2. **Mike Lazetich, Michigan, G, 59/59**
3. W.G. (Dub) Wooten, Oklahoma, E, 0/0
4. **Jack Zilly, Notre Dame, DE, 52/64**
5. Roger Harding, California, C, 16/42
6. Gerry Cowhig, Notre Dame, LB, 31/54
7. Fred Negus, Wisconsin, C, 0/49
8. Johnny August, Alabama, B, 0/0
9. Dick Huffman, Tennessee, T, 47/47
10. Vern Walters, Alma, B, 0/0
11. **Tom Fears, UCLA, E, 87/87**
12. Joe Winkler, Purdue, C, 8/8
13. Jack Aland, Alabama, T, 0/0
14. Chuck Uknes, Iowa, B, 0/0
15. Bill Lund, Case Western Reserve, HB, 0/18
17. **Dick Hoerner, Iowa, FB, 52/63**
23. Luke Higgins, Notre Dame, G, 0/11
28. Pat West, USC, FB, 36/39

DETROIT LIONS

1. Frank Szymanski, Notre Dame, C, 27/47
3. Stan Mohrbacher, Iowa, G, 0/0
5. Bob Wiese, Michigan, B, 16/16
6. Gene Fekete, Ohio State, FB, 0/6
7. Mike Jarmoluk, Temple, DT, 0/118
8. Jackie Lowther, Detroit Mercy, B, 8/10
9. Les Joop, Illinois, T, 0/0
10. Paul Walker, Yale, E, 0/12
11. Howie Hansen, Utah State, T, 0/0
12. Mike Kasap, Purdue, T, 0/12
13. Wally Hopp, Nebraska, B, 0/0
14. Ben Trickey, Iowa, B, 0/0
15. Windell Williams, Louisiana-Lafayette, E, 0/26
19. Clyde LeForce, Tulsa, QB, 32/32
24. Russ Morrow, Tennessee, C, 0/10
26. Bob Ivory, Detroit Mercy, G, 3/3

GREEN BAY PACKERS

1. Walt Schlinkman, Texas Tech, FB, 46/46
3. Clyde Goodnight, Tulsa, E, 38/58
5. Joe Graham, Florida, E, 0/0
6. Don Wells, Georgia, DE, 38/38
7. Casey Stephenson, Tennessee, B, 0/0
8. Toby Collins, Tulsa, T, 0/0
9. Lamar Dingler, Arkansas, E, 0/0
10. Hal Helscher, Louisiana State, B, 0/0
11. Ralph Hammond, Pittsburgh, C, 0/0
12. Ed Podgorski, Lafayette, T, 0/0
13. Bill Hackett, Ohio State, G, 0/0
14. Marv Lindsey, Arkansas, B, 0/0
19. Ed Jeffers, Oklahoma State, G, 0/14
24. Lloyd Baxter, SMU, C, 11/11
25. **Nolan Luhn, Tulsa, E, 56/56**

NEW YORK GIANTS

1. Elmer Barbour, Wake Forest, BB, 3/3
3. Gordon Appleby, Ohio State, C, 0/0
5. Ed Castleberry, West Texas State, B, 0/0
6. Barney Poole, Army, DE, 11/69
7. Jack Mead, Wisconsin, E, 20/20
8. Nick Vodick, Northwestern, B, 0/0
9. John Rudan, Marquette, B, 0/0
10. Vic Smith, UCLA, B, 0/0
11. Jim Young, Arkansas, T, 0/0
12. Billy Bevis, Tennessee, B, 0/0
13. Bob Boozer, Arkansas, T, 0/0
14. Stan Rhoades, Mississippi State, B, 0/0
15. Jack Wink, Wisconsin, B, 0/0
16. Jim Little, Kentucky, T, 3/3
21. Sam Vacanti, Nebraska, QB, 0/39

PHILADELPHIA EAGLES

1. John Yonakor, Notre Dame, E, 0/74
3. Alvin Dark, Louisiana State, B, 0/0
5. **Pete Pihos, Indiana, E, 107/107**
6. Chuck Dellago, Minnesota, G, 0/0
7. Gonzalo Morales, St. Mary's (CA), HB, 0/18
8. Sam Robinson, Washington, B, 0/0
9. Forrest Hall, San Francisco, B, 0/14
10. Joe Sadonis, Fordham, T, 0/0
11. Rudy Mobley, Hardin-Simmons, HB, 0/14
12. Jim Newmeyer, St. Vincent, T, 0/0
13. Bill Chambers, UCLA, G, 0/25
14. John Duda, Virginia, B, 0/0
15. Bill Montgomery, LSU, HB, 0/3
18. Quentin Klenk, USC, T, 0/10
19. Joe Spencer, Oklahoma State, T, 0/48
22. **John Magee, Louisiana-Lafayette, G, 91/91**
23. Norm Mosley, Alabama, TB, 0/5
26. Dan Talcott, UNLV, T, 8/8
31. Ken Reese, Alabama, HB, 0/4

PITTSBURGH STEELERS

1. Paul Duhart, Florida, B, 2/13
2. Jack Dugger, Ohio State, T, 0/37
3. Bill Dellastatious, Missouri, B, 0/0
4. Roger Adams, Florida, C, 0/0
5. **Charley Mehelich, Duquesne, DE, 59/59**
6. Gregg Browning, Denver, E, 0/3
7. Mike Wolak, Duquesne, B, 0/0
8. Tom Hughes, Missouri, T, 0/0
9. Leon Pense, Arkansas, BB, 10/10
10. Art Brandau, Tennessee, C, 6/6
11. Ray Ball, Holy Cross, B, 0/0
12. Frank Basilone, Duquesne, B, 0/0
13. John Monahan, Dartmouth, E, 0/0
14. Mel O'Delli, Duquesne, HB, 2/2
17. Jack Itzel, Pittsburgh, FB, 10/10
18. Alex Wizbicki, Holy Cross, DB, 0/45
19. Jim Landrigan, Dartmouth, T, 0/5
27. Glen Stough, Duke, T, 10/10
30. John Kondrla, St. Vincent, T, 1/1

WASHINGTON REDSKINS

1. Jim Hardy, USC, QB, 0/69
3. **John Adams, Notre Dame, T, 55/55**
5. George Bujan, Oregon, C, 0/0
6. John North, Vanderbilt, E, 0/29
7. **John Steber, Vanderbilt, G, 55/55**
8. Art Porter, Tulane, E, 0/0
9. Curt Kuykendall, Auburn, B, 0/0
10. Frank Brogger, Michigan State, E, 0/0
11. Mack Creger, Northwestern, B, 0/0
12. Paul McKee, Syracuse, E, 23/23
13. Charlie Conerly, Mississippi, QB, 0/161
14. John Putnik, Utah State, E, 0/0
15. **Eddie Saenz, USC, HB, 50/50**
25. Cecil Souders, Ohio State, E, 0/35
32. Don Nolander, Minnesota, C, 0/11

1946 NFL

BOSTON YANKS

1. Boley Dancewicz, Notre Dame, QB, 23/23
2. Nick Scollard, St. Joseph's (IN), E, 47/47
3. Bob McClure, Nevada-Reno, G, 22/22
4. Jack Breslin, Michigan State, B, 0/0
5. Gaston Bourgeois, Tulane, B, 0/0
6. Thurman Tigart, Oklahoma, G, 0/0
7. Ed Mieszkowski, Notre Dame, T, 0/23
8. Chet Lipka, Boston College, E, 0/0
9. Al Dekdebrun, Cornell, B, 2/32
10. Rex John, Wisconsin, T, 0/0
11. Bob West, Colorado, B, 0/0
12. Max Dodge, Nevada-Reno, E, 0/0
13. Joe Kirkland, Virginia, T, 0/0
14. Ralph Ventresco, Penn State, B, 0/0
15. John Furey, Boston College, T, 0/0
16. Bill Swiacki, Columbia, E, 0/59
24. Mike Karmazin, Duke, G, 0/10
30. Nick Klutka, Florida, E, 0/11

CHICAGO BEARS

1. Johnny Lujack, Notre Dame, QB, 45/45
2. Julie Rykovich, Illinois, HB, 35/82
3. Frank Broyles, Georgia Tech, QB, 0/0
4. Ernie Knotts, Duke, G, 0/0
5. Don Schneider, Pennsylvania, HB, 0/9
6. Ted Scruggs, Rice, E, 0/26
7. Wendell Beard, California, T, 0/0
8. John Ziegler, Colorado, B, 0/0
9. Walt Dropo, Connecticut, E, 0/0
10. Bill Harris, Auburn, C, 0/0
11. Eddie Allen, Pennsylvania, FB, 9/9
12. Frank Bauman, Illinois, E, 0/0
13. Reed Nostrum, Utah, T, 0/0
14. Dick Chatterton, BYU, B, 0/0
15. Johnny Timko, Temple, C, 0/0
16. Ted Hazelwood, North Carolina, T, 0/15
24. Visco Grgich, Santa Clara, G, 0/78

CHICAGO CARDINALS

1. Dub Jones, LSU, HB, 0/114
2. Mac Wenskunas, Illinois, C, 0/0
3. **Elmer Angsman, Notre Dame, HB, 83/83**
4. Hamilton Nichols, Rice, G, 34/43
5. Joe Golding, Oklahoma, HB, 0/58
6. Len Dickey, Texas A&M, T, 0/0
7. Pat Lenshan, Tennessee, E, 0/0
8. Phil Tinsley, Alabama, E, 0/0
9. Jake Colhouer, Oklahoma State, G, 32/40
10. Tom Barber, Tennessee-Chattanooga, T, 0/0
11. Dick Loepfe, Wisconsin, T, 13/13
12. Vinnie Yablonski, Columbia, FB, 40/40
13. Lee Lewis, Washington, B, 0/0
14. Bob Russell, Miami (OH), B, 0/0
15. Fred Rovai, Notre Dame, G, 0/0
16. Ray Evans, Texas-El Paso, G, 0/22

DETROIT LIONS

1. Bill Dellastatious, Missouri, B, 0/0
3. Russ Thomas, Ohio State, T, 44/44
5. Dave Harris, Wake Forest, E, 0/0
6. Joe Eddins, Auburn, G, 0/0
7. Pete Berezney, Notre Dame, T, 0/25
8. Keith DeCourcey, Washington, B, 0/0
9. Bill Hedges, West Texas State, T, 0/0
10. Thornton Dixon, Ohio State, T, 0/0
11. Bob Stevens, Oregon State, B, 0/0
12. Pat Farris, Texas Tech, T, 0/0
13. Paul Copoulos, Marquette, B, 0/0
14. Ty Irby, Auburn, B, 0/0
15. Pat Thrash, South Carolina, E, 0/0
16. Kelley Mote, Duke, E, 36/69
21. Ned Maloney, Purdue, E, 0/26
22. Jack Simmons, Detroit Mercy, C, 24/106
25. Ed Stacco, Colgate, T, 10/14

GREEN BAY PACKERS

1. Johnny Strzykalski, Marquette, HB, 0/81
3. Bob Nussbaumer, Michigan, HB, 14/49
5. Ed Cody, Purdue, FB, 20/38
6. John Ferraro, Southern California, T, 0/0
7. Art Renner, Michigan, E, 0/0
8. Bert Cole, Oklahoma State, T, 0/0
9. Grant Darnell, Texas A&M, G, 0/0
10. Joe McAfee, Holy Cross, B, 0/0
11. Steve Conroy, Holy Cross, B, 0/0
12. Billy Hildebrand, Mississippi State, E, 0/0
13. Tom Hand, Iowa, C, 0/0
14. George Hills, Georgia Tech, G, 0/0
15. Jim Hough, Clemson, B, 0/0
22. Howie Brown, Indiana, G, 0/36
30. Al Sparlis, UCLA, G, 3/3

LOS ANGELES RAMS

1. Emil Sitko, Notre Dame, HB, 0/30
3. Don Samuel, Oregon State, DB, 0/6
6. Newell (Ace) Oestreich, California, B, 0/0
7. Fay King, Georgia, E, 0/50
8. Joe Whisler, Ohio State, B, 0/0
9. Mike Schumchyk, Arkansas, E, 0/0
10. Joe Signaigo, Notre Dame, G, 0/38
11. Tom Phillips, Ohio State, B, 0/0
12. Ted Strojny, Holy Cross, T, 0/0
13. George Strohmeyer, Notre Dame, C, 0/26
14. Bob Palladino, Notre Dame, B, 0/0
15. Dick Lorenz, Oregon State, E, 0/0
17. Gasper Urban, Notre Dame, G, 0/14
21. Cliff Lewis, Duke, DB, 0/71

NEW YORK GIANTS

1. George Connor, Notre Dame, T, 0/90
2. Elmer Jones, Wake Forest, G, 0/31
3. Hosea Rodgers, North Carolina, FB, 0/12
4. Paul Duke, Georgia Tech, C, 0/10
5. Pete Stout, TCU, FB, 0/14
6. Jim Lalikos, Brown, T, 0/0
7. Jim Plyler, Texas, T, 0/0
8. Gene Roberts, Tennessee-Chattanooga, HB, 44/44
9. Mike Harris, Mississippi State, G, 0/0
10. Walt Clay, Colorado, B, 0/47
11. Warren Amling, Ohio State, G, 0/0
12. Al Bush, Duke, T, 0/0
13. Bob Reiman, Oregon State, B, 0/0
15. Stan Stapley, Utah, T, 0/0
18. Bob Morris, USC, HB, 1/1

PHILADELPHIA EAGLES

1. Leo Riggs, Southern California, B, 0/0
3. Gordon Gray, Southern California, E, 0/0
5. Walt Slater, Tennessee, TB, 0/11
6. Felto Prewitt, Tulsa, C, 0/46
7. George Robotham, UCLA, E, 0/0
8. Jim Lecture, Northwestern, G, 0/1
9. Ernie Lewis, Colorado, FB, 0/46
10. Al Vandeweghe, William & Mary, E, 0/5
11. Bill Iancelli, Franklin & Marshall, E, 0/0
12. **Pat McHugh, Georgia Tech, DB, 51/51**
13. John Wingender, Washington, B, 0/0
14. Homer Paine, Oklahoma, T, 0/12
15. John Kerns, North Carolina, T, 0/40
28. Bob Long, Tennessee, HB, 0/2

PITTSBURGH STEELERS

1. Felix (Doc) Blanchard, Army, B, 0/0
2. George Clark, Duke, B, 0/0
3. Harmon Rowe, San Francisco, DB, 0/57
4. Joe Tepsic, Penn State, B, 0/0
5. Jack Seiferling, Utah State, B, 0/0
6. Marion Woods, Clemson, G, 0/0
7. Tom Reinhardt, Minnesota, T, 0/0
8. Joe Ponsetto, Michigan, B, 0/0
9. Bob Evans, Pennsylvania, B, 0/0
10. Mel Bonwell, Central (IA), B, 0/0
11. Doc Holloway, William & Mary, G, 0/0
12. Carroll Owen, Catawba, B, 0/0
13. George Poppin, New Mexico, T, 0/0
14. Bob McCain, Mississippi, E, 0/11
15. Tom Tallchief, Oklahoma, T, 0/0
30. Gail Bruce, Washington, DE, 0/50

WASHINGTON REDSKINS

1. Cal Rossi, UCLA, B, 0/0
3. Stan Kozlowski, Holy Cross, FB, 0/5
5. Gay Adelt, Utah, B, 0/0
6. Walt Trojanowski, Connecticut, B, 0/0
7. Bob Hendren, USC, T, 36/36
8. George Callanan, Southern California, B, 0/0
10. Jake Leicht, Oregon, HB, 0/26
11. Chick Maggioli, Illinois, DB, 0/27
12. Monte Moncrief, Texas A&M, T, 0/0
13. **Joe Tereshinski, Georgia, DE, 86/86**
14. Stan Sprague, Illinois, E, 0/0
15. Harry Adelman, Southern California, E, 0/0
18. Ed Robnett, Texas Tech, FB, 0/4

1947 NFL

BOSTON YANKS

1. Fritz Barzilauskas, Yale, G, 29/36
2. Walt Heap, Texas, B, 0/27
3. John Rapacz, Oklahoma, C, 0/76
4. Al Baldwin, Arkansas, E, 0/51
5. Carroll Vogelaar, San Francisco, T, 46/46
6. George Sullivan, Notre Dame, E, 1/1
7. Joe Watt, Syracuse, HB, 6/26
8. Bill Chipley, Washington & Lee, E, 30/30
9. Gene Malinowski, Detroit Mercy, B, 12/12
10. Robert Hazelhurst, Denver, HB, 12/12
11. Alex Sidorik, Mississippi State, T, 12/33
12. Wally Roberts, Holy Cross, E, 0/0
13. Bob Sullivan, Iowa, HB, 0/5
14. Leo Long, Duke, B, 0/0
15. Frank Parker, Holy Cross, T, 0/0
16. Hugo Marcolini, St. Bonaventure, B, 0/10
17. Marion Shirley, Oklahoma City, T, 0/20
18. Roland Nabors, Texas Tech, LB, 0/10
27. Odell Stautzenberger, Texas A&M, G, 0/9
29. Tom Rodgers, Bucknell, T, 9/9
30. John Prchlik, Yale, DT, 0/59

CHICAGO BEARS

B1. Bob Fenimore, Oklahoma State, HB, 10/10
1. **Don Kindt, Wisconsin, DB, 108/108**
3. Frank Minini, San Jose State, HB, 24/36
5. Jim Canady, Texas, B, 8/15
5. Lloyd Merriman, Stanford, B, 0/0
6. Harlan Wetz, Texas, T, 0/11
6. Roger Stephens, Cincinnati, B, 0/0
7. Reid Moseley, Georgia, E, 0/0
8. Allen Smith, Mississippi, E, 22/22
9. Dwight (Dike) Eddleman, Illinois, B, 0/0
10. Arnold Tucker, Army, B, 0/0
11. Larry Hatch, Washington, B, 0/0
12. Tony Adamle, Ohio State, LB, 0/75
13. Emil Fritz, Maryland, G, 0/0
14. Jim Turner, California, T, 0/0
15. Wayne Goodall, Oklahoma City, E, 0/0
17. Wally Dreyer, Michigan, DB, 12/24
21. Russ Reader, Michigan State, DB, 2/2
23. Al Lawler, Texas, HB, 7/7
26. Max Morris, Northwestern, E, 0/38
28. Joe Billy Baumgardner, Texas, HB, 0/2

CHICAGO CARDINALS

1. Tex Coulter, Army, T, 0/69
3. Ermal Allen, Kentucky, QB, 0/12
6. Ben Raimondi, Indiana, TB, 0/7
7. Howard Turner, North Carolina State, B, 0/0
8. George Maddock, Northwestern, T, 0/0
9. Art Dufelmeier, Illinois, B, 0/0
10. Ray Ramsey, Bradley, B, 37/74
11. Dave Wallace, Oklahoma, B, 0/0
12. Charley Sarratt, Oklahoma, QB, 0/8
13. Hardin Cooper, Tulsa, T, 0/0
14. Carl Russ, Rice, B, 0/0
15. Buddy Mulligan, Duke, B, 0/0
16. Charles Smith, Georgia, HB, 7/7

17. Bob Ravensberg, Indiana, E, 23/23
20. Clarence Esser, Wisconsin, E, 7/7
25. Otto Schnellbacher, Kansas, DB, 0/50
26. Larry Joe, Penn State, B, 0/1
28. Joe Smith, Texas Tech, E, 0/12
31. Bob Callahan, Michigan, C, 0/7

DETROIT LIONS

1. Glenn Davis, Army, HB, 0/23
3. Jim Kekeris, Missouri, T, 0/15
4. Charley Hoover, Vanderbilt, C, 0/0
5. Bob Chappuis, Michigan, TB, 0/19
6. Bernie Gallagher, Pennsylvania, G, 0/8
7. Ed Grain, Pennsylvania, G, 0/23
8. Harvey James, Miami (FL), C, 0/0
9. Kale Alexander, South Carolina, T, 0/0
10. Chalmers (Bump) Elliott, Michigan, B, 0/0
11. Pete Sullivan, Detroit, T, 0/0
12. LaVerne Camaratta, Iowa State, B, 0/0
13. Walt Vezmar, Michigan State, G, 13/13
14. Dick Hagen, Washington, E, 0/0
15. J.W. Meeks, East Texas State, B, 0/0
16. Reed Nilsen, Brigham Young, C, 2/2
17. Tommy James, Ohio State, DB, 2/98
20. Elmer Madar, Michigan, E, 0/9
22. Carl Schuette, Marquette, LB, 0/48
26. Earl Maves, Wisconsin, WB, 1/1
27. Bill Hillman, Tennessee, B, 2/2

GREEN BAY PACKERS

1. Ernie Case, UCLA, QB, 0/14
3. Burr Baldwin, UCLA, E, 0/34
5. Buddy Burris, Oklahoma, G, 29/29
6. Gene Wilson, SMU, E, 21/21
7. Dick Connors, Northwestern, B, 0/0
8. Monte Moncrief, Texas A&M, T, 0/0
9. Bob McDougal, Miami (FL), FB, 1/1
10. Bob Kelly, Navy, HB, 0/26
11. Tom Moulton, Oklahoma State, C, 0/0
12. George Hills, Georgia Tech, G, 0/0
13. Bob Skoglund, Notre Dame, DE, 9/9
14. Jack Mitchell, Oklahoma, B, 0/0
15. Denny Crawford, Tennessee, G, 0/8
17. Ted Scalissi, Ripon, HB, 0/10
20. Brad Ecklund, Oregon, C, 0/60
32. Ralph Olsen, Utah, DE, 4/4

LOS ANGELES RAMS

1. Herm Wedemeyer, St. Mary's (CA), B, 0/25
3. **Don Paul, UCLA, LB, 87/87**
5. Gordon Gray, Southern California, B, 0/0
6. Paul Evenson, Oregon State, T, 0/0
7. Bill Smyth, Penn State, DE, 46/46
8. Bill McGovern, Washington, C, 0/0
9. Max Partin, Tennessee, B, 0/0
10. Carl Samuelson, Nebraska, DT, 0/43
11. Russ Steger, Illinois, B, 0/0
12. Dante Lavelli, Ohio State, E, 0/123
13. Mike Dimitro, UCLA, G, 0/0
14. John Kissell, Boston College, DT, 0/98
15. George Fuchs, Wisconsin, B, 0/0
18. Ed Champagne, LSU, T, 39/39
19. Jim Dewar, Indiana, B, 0/11
21. **Leon McLaughlin, UCLA, C, 60/60**
22. Charlie Elliott, Oregon, T, 0/14
23. Lou Levanti, Illinois, C, 0/6
27. Bob David, Villanova, G, 11/15
28. Jim Hunnicutt, South Carolina, G, 0/1
30. Hal Dean, Ohio State, G, 35/35

NEW YORK GIANTS

1. Vic Schwall, Northwestern, HB, 0/41
3. **John Cannady, Indiana, LB, 92/92**
5. Nelson Greene, Tulsa, T, 0/14
6. Bob Davis, Georgia Tech, T, 0/12
7. Duke Iverson, Oregon, B, 8/46
8. Frank Muehlheuser, Colgate, FB, 0/20
9. John Novitsky, Oklahoma City, T, 0/0
10. Fred Mullis, Tennessee-Chattanooga, B, 0/0
11. Bob Hoernschemeyer, Navy, B, 0/113
12. Hardy Brown, Tulsa, LB, 0/115
13. Bill Hachten, Stanford, G, 8/8
14. Herschel (Ug) Fuson, Army, B, 0/0
15. John Fallon, Notre Dame, T, 0/0
20. **Tom Landry, Texas, DB, 70/82**
22. Art Donovan, Boston College, DT, 0/138
23. Hal Shoener, Iowa, E, 0/38
26. Ralph Stewart, Missouri, C, 0/24
30. John Wright, Georgia, B, 0/13
31. Bill Schuler, Yale, T, 23/23

PHILADELPHIA EAGLES

1. **Neill Armstrong, Oklahoma State, E, 54/54**
3. Bill Mackrides, Nevada-Reno, QB, 39/46
5. George Savitsky, Pennsylvania, T, 24/24
7. Tony Yovicsin, Miami (FL), E, 0/0
8. Al Satterfield, Vanderbilt, T, 0/12
9. Bob Leonetti, Wake Forest, G, 0/11
10. Ulysses Cornogg, Wake Forest, T, 0/0
11. Alex Sarkisian, Northwestern, C, 0/0
12. Jerry D'Arcy, Tulsa, C, 0/0
13. John Hamberger, Southern Methodist, T, 0/0
14. Al Johnson, Hardin-Simmons, QB, 5/5
15. Joe Cook, Hardin-Simmons, B, 0/0
16. Jeff Durkota, Penn State, FB, 0/12
17. Hubert Shurtz, LSU, T, 0/12
19. T.J. Campion, Southeastern Louisiana, T, 5/5
23. Joe Haynes, Tulsa, C, 0/9
30. Bernie Winkler, Texas Tech, T, 0/4

PITTSBURGH STEELERS

1. Hub Bechtol, Texas Tech, E, 0/38
3. John Mastrangelo, Notre Dame, T, 23/44
5. **Frank Wydo, Cornell, T, 60/132**
6. Frank Aschenbrenner, Northwestern, RB, 0/6
7. Bryant Meeks, South Carolina, C, 18/18
8. **Jerry Shipkey, UCLA, LB, 58/66**
9. Bert Vander Clute, Wesleyan, G, 0/0
10. Paul Gibson, North Carolina State, E, 0/30
11. Jack Medd, Wesleyan, C, 0/0
12. Jack Fitch, North Carolina, B, 0/0
13. Ara Parseghian, Miami (OH), HB, 0/14
14. Red Moore, Penn State, G, 36/36
15. Larry Bruno, Geneva, B, 0/0
17. **Elbie Nickel, Cincinnati, E, 131/131**
18. Bill Cregar, Holy Cross, G, 23/23
19. Jerry Mulready, North Dakota State, E, 0/9
24. Paul Davis, Otterbein, FB, 11/11
25. Tommy Kalmanir, Nevada-Reno, HB, 0/43
28. Ralph Sazio, William & Mary, T, 0/13
32. Warren Lahr, Case Western Reserve, DB, 0/125

WASHINGTON REDSKINS

1. Cal Rossi, UCLA, B, 0/0
3. Gene (Red) Knight, Louisiana State, B, 0/0
5. Hank Foldberg, Army, E, 0/25
6. Mike Garzoni, USC, G, 10/17
7. Bill Gray, Oregon State, G, 24/24
8. Hank Harris, Texas, G, 12/12
9. Roy Karrasch, UCLA, E, 0/0
10. Ernie Williamson, North Carolina, T, 9/23
11. L.G. Carmody, Central Washington, B, 0/0
12. U.S. Savage, Richmond, E, 0/0
13. Bob Steckroth, William & Mary, E, 0/0
14. Weldon Edwards, TCU, T, 5/5
15. Earl Wheeler, Arkansas, C, 0/0
19. **Harry Dowda, Wake Forest, DB, 60/84**
24. Bob Smith, Iowa, DB, 0/78
31. Herb Shoener, Iowa, E, 18/18

1947 AAFC

BROOKLYN DODGERS

S. Gene Roberts, Tennessee-Chattanooga, HB, 0/44
1. Neill Armstrong, Oklahoma State, E, 0/54
2. Charlie Conerly, Mississippi, QB, 0/161
3. Fritz Barzilauskas, Yale, G, 0/36
4. Jim Wright, SMU, G, 0/12
5. Harlan Wetz, Texas, T, 11/11
6. Binks Bushmaier, Vanderbilt, B, 0/0
7. Garland Williams, Georgia, T, 26/26
8. Jim Hefti, St. Lawrence, B, 0/0
9. Buddy Burris, Oklahoma, G, 0/29
10. Bill Milner, Duke, LB, 0/48
11. Bob Smith, Iowa, DB, 10/78
12. Marv Goodman, Willamette, E, 0/0
13. Ted Scruggs, Rice, E, 26/26
14. Reed Nilsen, Brigham Young, C, 0/2
15. Gus Shannon, Colorado, G, 0/0
20. Hank Foldberg, Army, E, 13/25
25. Ray Evans, Texas-El Paso, G, 0/22

BUFFALO BISONS

S. Frank Aschenbrenner, Northwestern, RB, 0/6
S. Red Cochran, Wake Forest, QB, 0/36
S. Bob Fenimore, Oklahoma State, HB, 0/10
1. Al Baldwin, Arkansas, E, 39/51
2. Bob Davis, Georgia Tech, T, 0/12
3. Ray Kuffel, Notre Dame, E, 7/23
4. Joe Andrejko, Fordham, B, 0/0
5. John Mastrangelo, Notre Dame, T, 0/44
6. Bert Corley, Mississippi State, C, 13/22
7. Ernie Knotts, Duke, G, 0/0
8. Joe Watt, Syracuse, HB, 0/26
9. Paul Gibson, North Carolina State, E, 30/30
10. John Maskas, Virginia Tech, G, 18/18
11. Baxter Jarrell, North Carolina, T, 0/0
12. Chet Liptka, Boston College, T, 0/0
13. Joe Sowinski, Indiana, G, 0/0
14. Bill Chipley, Washington & Lee, E, 0/30
15. Bronco Kosanovich, Penn State, C, 0/0
18. Vinnie Yablonski, Columbia, FB, 0/40
20. Bill Swiacki, Columbia, E, 0/59
21. Hamilton Nichols, Rice, G, 0/43
23. Don Schneider, Pennsylvania, HB, 9/9
25. Frank Wydo, Cornell, T, 0/132

CHICAGO ROCKETS

S. Bernie Gallagher, Pennsylvania, G, 0/8
S. Johnny Lujack, Notre Dame, QB, 0/45
1. George Sullivan, Notre Dame, E, 0/1
2. Ray Manieri, Wake Forest, B, 0/0
3. Robert Derleth, Michigan, T, 0/1
4. Johnny Reagan, Montana State, B, 0/0
5. Jim Pharr, Auburn, C, 0/0
6. Bob Sandberg, Minnesota, B, 0/0
7. Eddie Allen, Pennsylvania, FB, 0/9
8. Matt Bolger, Notre Dame, E, 0/0
9. Charley Eikenberg, Rice, QB, 0/9
10. Ermal Allen, Kentucky, QB, 0/12
11. Marty Chaves, Oregon State, G, 0/0
12. George Jernigan, Georgia, G, 0/0
13. R.J. Jordan, Georgia Tech, E, 0/0
14. Bob Livingstone, Notre Dame, HB, 19/35
15. Bill Ivy, Northwestern, T, 0/0
16. Bruno Niedziela, Iowa, T, 12/12
17. Bill Mackrides, Nevada-Reno, QB, 0/46
22. Sam Vacanti, Nebraska, QB, 22/39

CLEVELAND BROWNS

S. Dick Hoerner, Iowa, FB, 0/63
1. Bob Chappuis, Michigan, TB, 0/19
2. Gerry Cowhig, Notre Dame, LB, 0/54
3. Jack Carpenter, Michigan, T, 0/36
4. Bob Cowan, Indiana, B, 24/33
5. Bill Griffen, Kentucky, T, 0/0
6. Jack Bush, Georgia, T, 0/0
7. John Rapacz, Oklahoma, C, 0/76
8. Robert Hazelhurst, Denver, HB, 0/12
9. Ralph Ellsworth, Texas, B, 0/0
10. Jim Dewar, Indiana, B, 10/11
11. Bill Huber, Illinois, E, 0/0
12. Mario Gianelli, Boston College, MG, 0/44
13. Marshall Shurnas, Missouri, E, 11/11
14. Joe Signaigo, Notre Dame, G, 0/38
15. Dean Widseth, Minnesota, T, 0/0

LOS ANGELES DONS

S. Herm Wedemeyer, St. Mary's (CA), B, 14/25
1. Burr Baldwin, UCLA, E, 34/34
2. Jerry Shipkey, UCLA, LB, 0/66
3. Lloyd Merriman, Stanford, B, 0/0
4. Cal Rossi, UCLA, B, 0/0
5. Boyd Clement, Oregon State, T, 0/0
6. Willie Zapalac, Texas A&M, B, 0/0
7. George Savitsky, Pennsylvania, T, 0/24
8. Don Paul, UCLA, LB, 0/87
9. Paul Hart, Delaware, B, 0/0
10. Walt Heap, Texas, B, 27/27
11. Mike Dimitro, UCLA, G, 0/0
12. Red Moore, Penn State, G, 0/36
13. Joe Martin, Cornell, B, 0/0
14. Gene Wilson, SMU, E, 0/21
15. Frank Muehlheuser, Colgate, FB, 0/20
16. Ed Cody, Purdue, FB, 0/38
17. Bob Sullivan, Iowa, HB, 0/5

MIAMI SEAHAWKS

S. Ernie Case, UCLA, QB, 14/14
1. Elmer Madar, Michigan, E, 9/9
2. Hub Bechtol, Texas Tech, E, 38/38
3. Tommy Mont, Maryland, QB, 0/27
4. Weldon Humble, Louisiana-Lafayette, G, 0/58
5. Russ Deal, Indiana, T, 0/0
6. Don Malmberg, UCLA, T, 0/0
7. Vic Schwall, Northwestern, HB, 0/41
8. Howard Turner, North Carolina State, B, 0/0
9. Frank Hubbell, Tennessee, E, 0/36
10. Gaston Burgeois, Tulane, G, 0/0
11. Jim Brieske, Michigan, C, 0/0
12. Rudy Mobley, Hardin-Simmons, HB, 14/14
13. Gerry Doherty, Delaware, B, 0/0
14. Bill Baumgartner, Minnesota, E, 2/2
15. Jim Kekeris, Missouri, T, 0/15
16. John North, Vanderbilt, E, 29/29
17. Jim Canady, Texas, B, 0/15
18. Howie Brown, Indiana, G, 0/36
25. Jim Landrigan, Dartmouth, T, 5/5

NEW YORK YANKEES

S. Charlie Trippi, Georgia, HB, 0/99
1. Ben Raimondi, Indiana, TB, 7/7
2. Monte Moncreif, Texas A&M, T, 0/0
4. Joe Tereshinski, Georgia, DE, 0/86
5. Jack Durishan, Pittsburgh, T, 6/6
6. Walt Dropo, Connecticut, E, 0/0
7. Roland Nabors, Texas Tech, LB, 10/10
8. George Strohmeyer, Notre Dame, C, 0/26
9. Ted Ossowski, Oregon State, T, 3/3
11. Bill Healey, Georgia Tech, G, 0/0
12. Ed Sikorski, Muhlenberg, B, 0/0
14. Charlie Elliott, Oregon, T, 10/14
15. Ed Grain, Pennsylvania, G, 2/23

SAN FRANCISCO 49ERS

S. Glenn Davis, Army, HB, 0/23
1. Clyde LeForce, Tulsa, QB, 0/32
2. Bob Wiese, Michigan, B, 0/16
3. Paul Duke, Georgia Tech, C, 0/10
4. Don Samuel, Oregon State, DB, 0/6
5. Al Satterfield, Vanderbilt, T, 12/12
6. Jack Zilly, Notre Dame, DE, 0/64
7. Gene (Red) Knight, Louisiana State, B, 0/0
8. Charlie Malmberg, Rice, T, 0/0
9. Bob Leonetti, Wake Forest, G, 0/11
10. Frank Broyles, Georgia Tech, QB, 0/0
11. Jim Tyree, Oklahoma, E, 0/12
12. Ed Robnett, Texas Tech, FB, 4/4
13. Walt Slater, Tennessee, TB, 0/11
14. Earl Wheeler, Arkansas, C, 0/0
15. Les Proctor, Texas, G, 0/0
16. Al DeRogatis, Duke, DT, 0/46
18. Bryant Meeks, South Carolina, C, 0/18
19. Ed Royston, Wake Forest, G, 0/21
20. Max Bumgardner, Texas, DE, 0/11

1948 NFL

BOSTON YANKS

1. Vaughn Mancha, Alabama, C, 12/12
3. John Nolan, Penn State, T, 36/36
5. Bill Healey, Georgia Tech, G, 0/0
6. Phil Slosburg, Temple, B, 15/15
8. Robert (Tex) Furse, Yale, B, 0/0
9. Jim Burton, Wesleyan, E, 0/0
10. Bob Forbes, Florida, B, 0/0
11. George Roman, Case Western Reserve, T, 20/26
12. Ab Wimberly, LSU, DE, 0/47
13. Bob Jensen, Iowa State, DE, 0/34
14. Hal (Bus) Entsminger, Missouri, B, 0/0
15. Carmen Ragonese, New Hampshire, B, 0/0
16. George Ratterman, Notre Dame, QB, 18/92
20. Frank Nelson, Utah, B, 16/16
21. Jim Lukens, Washington & Lee, E, 0/11

CHICAGO BEARS

1. Max Bumgardner, Texas, DE, 0/11
1. Bobby Layne, Texas, QB, 11/175
3. Dub Garrett, Mississippi State, G, 3/28
5. Knox Ramsey, William & Mary, G, 0/69
6. Bob Brugge, Ohio State, B, 0/0
8. Shorty McWilliams, Army, DB, 0/22
9. Malachi Mills, Virginia Military, T, 0/0
10. Dick Flanagan, Ohio State, LB, 24/84
11. Jim McDowell, William & Mary, G, 0/0
12. Mel Sheehan, Missouri, E, 0/0
13. Dick Scott, Navy, C, 0/0
14. Ollie Cline, Ohio State, FB, 0/64
22. J.R. Boone, Tulsa, E, 43/63

CHICAGO CARDINALS

1. Jim Spavital, Oklahoma State, FB, 0/23
3. Bill Smith, North Carolina, T, 0/12
5. Jay Smith, Southern Mississippi, E, 0/0
7. Jim Cason, LSU, DB, 0/89
8. Jim Camp, North Carolina, QB, 0/12
10. Carl Weisner, St. Louis, E, 0/0
11. Gene Corum, West Virginia, G, 0/0
12. Clarence Self, Wisconsin, DB, 12/62
13. John Hollar, Appalachian State, FB, 0/17
14. Bob Hanlon, Loras, HB, 10/22
15. George Petrovich, Texas, G, 22/22
16. Jim Still, Georgia Tech, B, 0/21
19. Jerry Davis, Southeastern Louisiana, DB, 39/46
24. Dick Wedel, Wake Forest, G, 1/1
25. Paul Shoults, Miami (OH), HB, 0/12

DETROIT LIONS

1. Y.A. Tittle, LSU, QB, 0/203
2. George Quist, Stanford, B, 0/0
3. **Les Bingaman, Illinois, DG, 78/78**
4. Jim Minor, Arkansas, T, 0/0
6. Bob Williamson, Hobart, T, 0/0
7. Fred Enke, Arizona, QB, 48/68
7. Moroni Schwab, Utah State, T, 0/0
9. Don Doll, USC, DB, 47/71
10. Paul Cleary, USC, E, 0/23
11. Fred Land, LSU, T, 0/2
13. Russ Steger, Illinois, B, 0/0

14. Hal Enstice, Union (NY), B, 0/0
15. Pete Elliott, Michigan, B, 0/0
18. Jim Spruill, Rice, T, 0/28
19. Barney Hafen, Utah, DE, 24/24

GREEN BAY PACKERS

1. Jug Girard, Wisconsin, E, 46/114
3. Ed Smith, Texas-El Paso, HB, 15/23
5. Don Richards, Arkansas, T, 0/0
5. Weyman Sellers, Georgia, E, 0/0
6. Larry Olsonoski, Minnesota, G, 16/24
7. Jay Rhodemyre, Kentucky, C, 45/45
8. Bob Cunz, Illinois, T, 0/0
10. George Walmsley, Rice, B, 0/0
11. Bob Hodges, Bradley, T, 0/0
12. Bob Rennebohm, Wisconsin, E, 0/0
13. Perry Moss, Illinois, QB, 6/6
14. Fred Provo, Washington, HB, 9/9
15. Lou Agase, Illinois, T, 0/0
21. Herb St. John, Georgia, G, 0/21
30. Clarence McGeary, North Dakota State, DT, 12/12
32. Ralph Earhart, Texas Tech, HB, 24/24

LOS ANGELES RAMS

3. Tom Keane, West Virginia, DB, 40/87
5. Bruce Bailey, Virginia, B, 0/0
6. George Grimes, Virginia, DB, 0/9
7. Gene Ruszkowski, Ohio U., T, 0/0
7. Noel Cudd, West Texas State, T, 0/0
8. Bob Walker, Colorado Mines, B, 0/0
9. Mike Graham, Cincinnati, B, 0/14
10. Glenn Johnson, Arizona State, T, 0/17
11. Johnny Zisch, Colorado, E, 0/0
12. Atherton (Pinky) Phleger, Stanford, T, 0/0
13. Bob Heck, Purdue, DE, 0/4
14. Bill Schroll, LSU, LB, 0/36
15. Bob Dement, Southern Mississippi, T, 0/0
17. **Larry Brink, Northern Illinois, DE, 70/82**
18. Bill O'Connor, Notre Dame, E, 0/35
22. Ray Yagiello, Catawba, G, 24/24
27. Jim Wade, Oklahoma City, HB, 0/10

NEW YORK GIANTS

1. Skippy Minisi, Pennsylvania, HB, 12/12
2. **Joe Scott, San Francisco, HB, 51/51**
4. Bruce Gehrke, Columbia, E, 8/8
5. Johnny Wolosky, Penn State, C, 0/0
6. Bill Erickson, Mississippi, G, 9/15
7. Bob Pfohl, Purdue, B, 0/26
8. Ray Coates, LSU, HB, 21/21
8. Ralph Hutchinson, Tennessee-Chattanooga, T, 10/10
9. Dick Ottele, Washington, BB, 0/8
9. Ed Royston, Wake Forest, G, 21/21
9. Ken Wiltgen, Northwestern, E, 0/0
10. Stan Magdziak, William & Mary, B, 0/0
11. Pete Lanzl, Youngstown State, E, 0/0
12. Len Modzeleski, Scranton, T, 0/0
12. Jim Brieske, Michigan, C, 0/0
13. Bob Hatch, Boston, B, 0/0
14. John Hansel, Guilford, G, 0/0
15. Dan Garza, Oregon, E, 0/23
19. Don Ettinger, Kansas, LB, 33/33
20. Frank Williams, Utah State, FB, 9/9
21. Dick Woodard, Iowa, LB, 35/59
22. George Kisiday, Columbia, E, 0/14
24. Walter McCormick, USC, C, 0/9
25. Dick Wilkins, Oregon, E, 6/29
29. Bob Greenhalgh, San Francisco, FB, 10/10
30. Ed Kelley, Texas, T, 0/12

PHILADELPHIA EAGLES

1. Clyde Scott, Arkansas, HB, 23/28
3. Paul Campbell, Texas, QB, 0/0
5. Jack Myers, UCLA, FB, 36/48
6. Howard Duncan, Ohio State, C, 0/1
7. Buddy Tinsley, Baylor, T, 0/10
8. Martin Wendell, Notre Dame, G, 0/10
9. Scott Beasley, Nevada-Reno, E, 0/0
10. Ray Richeson, Alabama, G, 0/12
11. Gil Johnson, SMU, QB, 0/9
12. Bill Wyman, Rice, T, 0/0
13. Jim Waithall, West Virginia, B, 0/0
14. Dick Kempthorn, Michigan, B, 0/0
15. Dick Rifenburg, Michigan, E, 0/12
18. Aubrey Fowler, Arkansas, HB, 0/13
25. **Jim Parmer, Oklahoma State, FB, 88/88**
26. Lou Creekmur, William & Mary, T, 0/116
27. Bill Stanton, North Carolina State, DE, 0/10
29. Rex Grossman, Indiana, LB, 0/37
31. Art Statuto, Notre Dame, C, 0/38

PITTSBURGH STEELERS

1. Dan Edwards, Georgia, E, 0/70
3. Jerry Nuzum, New Mexico State, HB, 45/45
5. John Wozniak, Alabama, G, 0/62
6. Joe Gasparella, Notre Dame, BB, 24/26
7. Bill Luongo, Pennsylvania, B, 0/0
8. Jim Cooper, North Texas, C, 0/1
9. Ed Ryan, St. Mary's (CA), E, 9/9
10. Dick Deranek, Indiana, B, 0/0
11. Paul Redfield, Colgate, T, 0/0
12. George Papach, Purdue, FB, 22/22
13. Tom Finical, Princeton, E, 0/0
14. Clayton Lane, New Hampshire, T, 0/1
15. Dick Mazuca, Canisius, G, 0/0
16. **Bill McPeak, Pittsburgh, DE, 105/105**
19. Pete Barbolak, Purdue, T, 10/10
24. Floyd Simmons, Notre Dame, B, 0/11

WASHINGTON REDSKINS

B1. **Harry Gilmer, Alabama, QB, 57/76**
1. Lowell Tew, Alabama, FB, 0/15
3. Tommy Thompson, William & Mary, LB, 0/54
5. Dan Sandifer, LSU, DB, 24/64
6. Jack Weisenburger, Michigan, B, 0/0
7. Jack Kurkowski, Detroit, B, 0/0
8. Jerry Cady, Gustavus Adolphus, T, 0/0
9. Bob Anderson, Stanford, B, 0/0
10. Mike Katrishen, Southern Mississippi, G, 23/23
11. Ed Marshall, Pennsylvania, T, 0/0
12. Ted Andrus, Southwestern Louisiana, G, 0/0
13. Carl Russ, Rice, B, 0/0
14. Chick Jagade, Indiana, FB, 0/68
15. Ed Quirk, Missouri, FB, 38/38
20. Cloyce Box, West Texas A&M, E, 0/57
22. Joel Williams, Texas, C, 0/26
28. Don Corbitt, Arizona, C, 3/3

1948 AAFC

BALTIMORE COLTS

1. Bobby Layne, Texas, QB, 0/175
2. Dub Garrett, Mississippi State, G, 25/28
3. Earl Cooke, Southern Methodist, G, 0/0
4. Dan Sandifer, LSU, DB, 0/64
5. Joe Smith, Texas Tech, E, 12/12
6. Gene Raczkowski, Ohio U, T, 0/0
7. Jim Batchelor, East Texas State, B, 0/0
8. Rex Olson, BYU, B, 0/0
9. Aubrey Fowler, Arkansas, HB, 13/13
10. Jack Fitch, North Carolina, B, 0/0
11. Don Ettinger, Kansas, LB, 0/33
12. Paul Redfield, Colgate, T, 0/0
13. Stan Madgziak, William & Mary, B, 0/0
14. Dick Deranek, Indiana, B, 0/0
15. Dike Norman, Washington & Lee, B, 0/0
19. Norm Mosley, Alabama, TB, 0/5
24. Bob Pfohl, Purdue, B, 26/26
25. Lou Levanti, Illinois, C, 0/6
27. Chick Jagade, Indiana, FB, 10/68
29. Rex Grossman, Indiana, LB, 33/37

BROOKLYN DODGERS

1. Harry Gilmer, Alabama, QB, 0/76
3. Dan Edwards, Georgia, E, 11/70
4. Joe Spencer, Oklahoma State, T, 13/48
5. Les Bingaman, Illinois, DG, 0/78
6. Jim Smith, Southern Mississippi, E, 0/0
7. Homer Paine, Oklahoma, T, 0/12
8. Bruce Gehrke, Columbia, E, 0/8
9. Jim Minor, Arkansas, T, 0/0
10. Herb St. John, Georgia, G, 10/21
11. Chuck Newman, Louisiana Tech, E, 0/0
12. Jim Camp, North Carolina, QB, 12/12
13. Bob Koch, Oregon, B, 0/0
14. John White, Michigan, C, 0/0
15. Bob Terry, Texas A&M, T, 0/0
16. John Wozniak, Alabama, G, 14/62
17. Bob Jensen, Iowa State, DE, 0/34
26. Ray Richeson, Alabama, G, 0/12
30. Clarence McGeary, North Dakota State, DT, 0/12

BUFFALO BISONS

1. Clyde Scott, Arkansas, HB, 0/28
4. Bill O'Connor, Notre Dame, E, 14/35
6. Martin Wendell, Notre Dame, G, 0/10
7. Bob Brugge, Ohio State, B, 0/0
9. Lou King, Iowa, B, 0/0
11. John Finney, Compton J.C., B, 0/0
12. Dick Johnson, Baylor, G, 0/0
13. George Grimes, Virginia, DB, 0/9
14. Larry Joe, Penn State, B, 1/1
15. Frank Ballard, Virginia Tech, G, 0/0
17. Ray Coates, LSU, HB, 0/21
22. Ralph Sazio, William & Mary, T, 0/13

CHICAGO ROCKETS

1. Skippy Minisi, Pennsylvania, HB, 0/12
2. Carl Samuelson, Nebraska, DT, 0/43
3. John Nolan, Penn State, T, 0/36
4. Paul Cleary, USC, E, 10/23
6. Vince DiFrancisca, Northwestern, G, 0/0
7. Jay Rhodemyre, Kentucky, C, 0/45
8. Jim Turner, California, T, 0/0
9. Myron Miller, Oklahoma State, C, 0/0
10. Phil Slosburg, Temple, B, 0/15
11. Jack Swaner, California, B, 0/0
12. Thurman Gay, Oklahoma State, T, 0/0
13. Frank Parker, Holy Cross, T, 0/0
14. Lou Agase, Illinois, T, 0/0
15. J.F. McCarthy, Pennsylvania, E, 0/0
17. Dick Flanagan, Ohio State, LB, 0/84
18. Ed Ryan, St. Mary's (CA), E, 0/9
20. Don Doll, USC, DB, 0/71
21. Fred Provo, Washington, HB, 0/9
29. Dick Wedel, Wake Forest, G, 0/1

CLEVELAND BROWNS

1. Jeff Durkota, Penn State, FB, 0/12
3. Ollie Cline, Ohio State, FB, 11/64
7. **Tommy Thompson, William & Mary, LB, 54/54**
9. Bill Smith, North Carolina, T, 0/12
11. Ralph Maughan, Utah State, C, 0/0
13. Mike Rubish, North Carolina, E, 0/0
14. Alex Sarkesian, Northwestern, C, 0/0
15. Dan Dworsky, Michigan, LB, 0/11
22. Lu Gambino, Maryland, FB, 0/19
25. Ara Parseghian, Miami (OH), HB, 14/14
29. George Roman, Case Western Reserve, T, 0/26

LOS ANGELES DONS

1. Vaughn Mancha, Alabama, C, 0/12
4. John Novitsky, Oklahoma City, T, 0/0
7. Weldon Edwards, TCU, T, 0/5
8. Jim Spavital, Oklahoma State, FB, 12/23
9. Knox Ramsey, William & Mary, G, 25/69
10. Malachi Mills, Virginia Military, G, 0/0
12. Harper Davis, Mississippi State, DB, 11/35
13. Mike Graham, Cincinnati, B, 14/14
14. Bernie Winkler, Texas Tech, T, 4/4
15. Bill Erickson, Mississippi, G, 0/15
16. Shorty McWilliams, Army, DB, 12/22
19. Ab Wimberly, LSU, DE, 12/47
20. Frank Ziegler, Georgia Tech, HB, 0/57
21. Ed Smith, Texas-El Paso, HB, 0/23
26. Jim Still, Georgia Tech, B, 0/21
28. Lou Creekmur, William & Mary, T, 0/116
29. Leon McLaughlin, UCLA, C, 0/60

NEW YORK YANKEES

1. Lowell Tew, Alabama, FB, 15/15
3. Otto Schnellbacher, Kansas, DB, 26/50
7. Pete Stout, TCU, FB, 0/14
9. Barney Poole, Army, DE, 11/69
11. Jack Weisenberger, Michigan, B, 0/0
12. Bob Hendren, USC, T, 0/36
13. Dick Ottele, Washington, BB, 0/8
15. Joe Magliolo, Texas, LB, 13/13
18. Marion Shirley, Oklahoma City, T, 20/20
19. Tom Landry, Texas, DB, 12/82
22. Fred Enke, Arizona, QB, 0/68
27. Jug Girard, Wisconsin, E, 0/114
29. Frank Nelson, Utah, B, 0/16

SAN FRANCISCO 49ERS

1. Joe Scott, San Francisco, HB, 0/51
3. **Jim Cason, LSU, DB, 65/89**
4. Walter McCormick, USC, C, 9/9
6. Fred Land, LSU, T, 2/2
7. Phil O'Reilly, Purdue, T, 0/0
9. Bill Luongo, Pennsylvania, B, 0/0
11. Bob Steckroth, William & Mary, E, 0/0
12. Gene Malinowski, Detroit Mercy, B, 0/12
13. Len Modzelski, Scranton, T, 0/0
14. Les Rideout, Bowling Green, T, 0/0
15. Larry Olsonoski, Minnesota, G, 0/24
17. Bob Ravensberg, Indiana, E, 0/23
20. Pete Barbolak, Purdue, T, 0/10
21. Dick Loepfe, Wisconsin, T, 0/13
22. Bob Heck, Purdue, DE, 0/4
27. Perry Moss, Illinois, QB, 0/6
29. Herb Siegert, Illinois, G, 0/36
30. Frank Williams, Utah State, FB, 0/9

1949 NFL

CHICAGO BEARS

1. Dick Harris, Texas, C, 0/0
2. Billy Grimes, Oklahoma State, HB, 0/48
3. Red O'Quinn, Wake Forest, DB, 14/19
4. Ben Bendrick, Wisconsin, B, 0/0
5. **John Hoffman, Arkansas, HB, 88/88**
6. Gerry Krall, Ohio State, DB, 0/7
7. Wally (Wah-Wah) Jones, Kentucky, E, 0/0
8. Bones Weatherly, Rice, LB, 35/35
8. **Bill Wightkin, Notre Dame, T, 92/92**
9. Dolph Tokarczyk, Pennsylvania, G, 0/0
10. Lee Malley, Vanderbilt, B, 0/0
11. Jerry Tiblier, Mississippi, B, 0/0
12. **George Blanda, Kentucky, QB, 115/340**
13. George Taliaferro, Indiana, HB, 0/72
14. Ernie Keily, Texas-El Paso, G, 0/0
15. Hal Faverty, Wisconsin, LB, 0/11

CHICAGO CARDINALS

1. **Bill Fischer, Notre Dame, T, 59/59**
4. John Goldsberry, Indiana, DT, 20/20
5. Tom Wham, Furman, DE, 35/35
6. Bernie Hanula, Wake Forest, T, 0/0
7. Jim Cain, Alabama, DE, 12/60
7. Myrl Greathouse, Oklahoma, B, 0/0
8. Joe E Brown, Georgia Tech, B, 0/0
9. Hal Herring, Auburn, LB, 0/46
10. Bob Hecker, Baldwin-Wallace, B, 0/0
11. Stan Flowers, Redlands, E, 0/0
12. Billy Stone, Bradley, HB, 0/66
13. Bob Todd, Louisville, T, 0/0
14. Tony Klimek, Illinois, DE, 24/24
15. Bob McQuade, Xavier, B, 0/0

DETROIT LIONS

1. John Rauch, Georgia, QB, 0/27
2. John Panelli, Notre Dame, LB, 19/51
3. Lou Kusserow, Columbia, LB, 0/22
4. Joe Sullivan, Dartmouth, B, 0/0
6. Bob Meinert, Oklahoma State, B, 0/0
9. Chuck Drazenovich, Penn State, LB, 0/113
10. Bill Davis, Duke, G, 0/0
11. Ernie Settembre, Miami (FL), T, 0/0
12. Virgil Boteler, New Mexico, C, 0/0
13. Al Russas, Tennessee, T, 9/9
14. Dale Panter, Utah State, T, 0/0
15. Bob Pifferini, San Jose State, C, 12/12
19. Wally Triplett, Penn State, HB, 18/24
21. Jack Lininger, Ohio State, LB, 24/24

GREEN BAY PACKERS

1. Stan Heath, Nevada-Reno, QB, 12/12
2. Dan Dworsky, Michigan, LB, 0/11
3. Lou Ferry, Villanova, DT, 12/71
4. Bob Summerhays, Utah, LB, 35/35
5. Glenn Lewis, Texas Tech, B, 0/0
6. Joe Ethridge, SMU, TE, 12/12
8. Dan Orlich, UNLV, DE, 36/36
9. Everett Faunce, Minnesota, B, 0/0
11. Harry Larche, Arkansas State, T, 0/0
12. Rebel Steiner, Alabama, DB, 24/24
13. Al Mastrangeli, Illinois, C, 0/0
14. Bobby Williams, Texas Tech, C, 0/0
15. Ken Cooper, Vanderbilt, G, 0/24
21. Ken Kranz, Wisconsin-Milwaukee, DB, 7/7
23. Bill Kelley, Texas Tech, E, 12/12

LOS ANGELES RAMS

1. Bobby Thomason, VMI, QB, 6/85
2. George Sims, Baylor, DB, 21/21
3. Jim Winkler, Texas A&M, DT, 23/32
4. **Norm Van Brocklin, Oregon, QB, 104/140**
5. Earl Howell, Mississippi, HB, 0/12
6. Charles Reynolds, Texas Tech, B, 0/0
7. Jon Baker, California, DG, 0/46
7. Jerry Williams, Washington State, DB, 46/69
8. John Waldrum, Sul Ross, G, 0/0
9. Johnny Smith, Arizona, E, 0/0
10. George Buksar, San Francisco, LB, 0/36
10. Max Minnich, Bowling Green, B, 0/0
11. Jim Cozad, Iowa, T, 0/0
12. Bill Renna, Santa Clara, C, 0/0
13. Paul Barry, Tulsa, FB, 18/42
14. Ed Carmichael, Oregon State, T, 0/0
15. J.C. Dodd, Sul Ross, B, 0/0
16. Joe Morgan, Southern Mississippi, T, 0/8
25. Clay Matthews, Georgia Tech, DE, 0/45

NEW YORK BULLDOGS

1. Doak Walker, SMU, HB, 0/67
2. Bob DeMoss, Purdue, QB, 3/3
3. Phil Colella, St. Bonaventure, B, 0/0
3. Lynn Chewning, Hampden-Sydney, B, 0/0
4. Huey Keeney, Rice, B, 0/0
5. Mike Boyda, Washington & Lee, LB, 9/9
6. Rip Collins, LSU, HB, 0/31
6. Sam Tamburo, Penn State, DE, 12/12
7. Pete Wissman, St. Louis, LB, 0/48
8. Mike Rubish, North Carolina, E, 0/0
9. Bernie Craig, Denver, T, 0/0
10. John Geary, Wesleyan, T, 0/0
11. Edo Mencotti, Detroit, B, 0/0
12. Mornane Maenhout, St. John's (MN), E, 0/0
13. Jim Dieckelman, Holy Cross, E, 0/0
14. Ed Toscani, Dayton, B, 0/0
15. George Ramacorti, Boston, G, 0/0
17. Warren Beson, Minnesota, C, 0/3
20. Frank Gaul, Notre Dame, T, 12/12

NEW YORK GIANTS

1. Paul Page, SMU, HB, 0/8
2. Al DeRogatis, Duke, DT, 46/46
3. Bill Olson, Columbia, B, 0/0

4. Bill Kay, Iowa, T, 0/0
5. J.D. Cheek, Oklahoma State, G, 0/0
6. Abe Gibron, Purdue, G, 0/125
7. Frank LoVuolo, St. Bonaventure, E, 11/11
8. Jack Salscheider, St. Thomas, HB, 11/11
9. Joe Soboleski, Michigan, G, 0/27
10. Gene Rossides, Columbia, B, 0/0
11. Dick Hensley, Kentucky, E, 11/33
12. George Sundheim, Northwestern, B, 0/0
13. **Bill Austin, Oregon State, G, 75/75**
14. Norb Adams, Purdue, B, 0/0
15. Ralph Pickelsimer, Otterbein, C, 0/0
23. Clete Fischer, Nebraska, HB, 11/11

PHILADELPHIA EAGLES

B1. **Chuck Bednarik, Pennsylvania, LB, 169/169**
1. Frank Tripucka, Notre Dame, QB, 0/75
2. Frank Burns, Rutgers, B, 0/0
3. **Frank Ziegler, Georgia Tech, HB, 57/57**
4. Don Panciera, San Francisco, QB, 0/26
5. Terry Brennan, Notre Dame, B, 0/0
6. Warren Huey, Michigan State, E, 0/0
7. Frank Gillespie, Clemson, G, 0/0
8. Bob Dean, Cornell, B, 0/0
9. Jon Jenkins, Dartmouth, T, 0/15
10. Roy Lester, West Virginia, E, 0/0
11. Bobby Wilson, Mississippi, B, 0/0
12. Dale Armstrong, Dartmouth, E, 0/0
13. Lyle Button, Illinois, T, 0/0
14. Bobby Lund, Tennessee, B, 0/0
15. Carl Copp, Vanderbilt, T, 0/0
17. Leo Skladany, Pittsburgh, E, 3/7
25. John Schweder, Pennsylvania, G, 0/71

PITTSBURGH STEELERS

1. Bob Gage, Clemson, DB, 22/22
2. Harper Davis, Mississippi State, DB, 0/35
3. **Bill Walsh, Notre Dame, C, 72/72**
4. Joe Geri, Georgia, TB, 36/48
5. Bill Long, Oklahoma State, E, 10/10
6. Doug Brightwell, Texas Christian, C, 0/0
7. Bill Talarico, Pennsylvania, B, 0/0
8. George Brown, TCU, G, 0/20
9. Tom Brennan, Boston College, T, 0/0
10. Bob Hood, Alabama, E, 0/0
11. Al Sanders, Southern Mississippi, C, 0/0
12. **Jim Finks, Tulsa, QB, 79/79**
13. R.R. Walston, North Texas State, G, 0/0
14. Dave Moon, Southern Methodist, B, 0/0
15. Ed Sobczak, Michigan, E, 0/0
17. Vito Kissell, Holy Cross, LB, 0/20
23. Jim Owens, Oklahoma, E, 0/9

WASHINGTON REDSKINS

1. **Rob Goode, Texas A&M, B, 51/59**
2. **Laurie Niemi, Washington State, T, 56/56**
3. Len Szafaryn, North Carolina, T, 12/75
4. Mike DeNoia, Scranton, B, 0/0
5. Ed Berrang, Villanova, DE, 31/42
7. Chet Fritz, Missouri, G, 0/0
8. Bob Kennedy, North Carolina, DB, 0/10
9. Ed McNeil, Michigan, E, 0/0
10. Vic Vasicek, Texas, LB, 0/24
11. Homer Hobbs, Georgia, G, 0/22
12. Harry Varner, Arizona, T, 0/0
13. Ed Henke, USC, DE, 0/123
14. Pat Haggerty, William & Mary, E, 0/0
15. Gene Frassetto, California, T, 0/0
18. Herb Siegert, Illinois, G, 36/36
20. Oliver Fletcher, USC, G, 0/3
25. Nick Sebek, Indiana, QB, 2/2

1949 AAFC

BALTIMORE COLTS

1. George Sims, Baylor, DB, 0/21
2. Bob Gage, Clemson, DB, 0/22
4. Ralph Kohl, Michigan, T, 0/0
5. Wally (Wah-Wah) Jones, Kentucky, E, 0/0
6. Frank Pattee, Kansas, B, 0/0
7. Frank Folger, Duke, B, 0/0
8. Bob Prymuski, Illinois, T, 0/0
9. Everett Faunce, Minnesota, B, 0/0
10. Kale Alexander, South Carolina, T, 0/0
11. Paul Page, SMU, HB, 8/8
12. Jim Owens, Oklahoma, E, 9/9
13. Warren Beson, Minnesota, C, 3/3
14. David Moon, Southern Methodist, B, 0/0
15. Jon Jenkins, Dartmouth, T, 14/15
16. Red O'Quinn, Wake Forest, DB, 0/19
28. Bob DeMoss, Purdue, QB, 0/3

BROOKLYN DODGERS

S1. Chuck Bednarik, Pennsylvania, LB, 0/169
1. Joe Sullivan, Dartmouth, B, 0/0
2. Lou Ferry, Villanova, DT, 0/71
2. Len Szafaryn, North Carolina, T, 0/75
2. Bill Walsh, Notre Dame, C, 0/72
3. Wally Triplett, Penn State, HB, 0/24
4. Dolph Tokarczyk, Penn, G, 0/0
5. Joe Quinn, Cornell, G, 0/0
6. Leo Skladany, Pittsburgh, E, 0/7
7. Lynn Chewning, Hampden-Sydney, B, 0/0
8. Bob McCurry, Michigan State, C, 0/0
9. Chuck Klemovitch, Columbia, G, 0/0
10. Bob Duncan, Duke, E, 0/0
11. Hilary Chollet, Cornell, B, 0/0
12. Bill Davis, Duke, G, 0/0
14. Murry Alexander, Mississippi State, E, 0/0
15. Howard Derrick, Tennessee-Chattanooga, B, 0/0
20. Eddie Price, Tulane, FB, 0/63
25. Bill Long, Oklahoma State, E, 0/10

BUFFALO BISONS

S1. Abe Gibron, Purdue, G, 10/125
1. Bill Kay, Iowa, T, 0/0
S2. Frank Tripucka, Notre Dame, QB, 0/75
3. Vito Kissell, Holy Cross, LB, 9/20
3. Hugh Keeney, Rice, B, 0/0
5. Frank Gaul, Notre Dame, T, 0/12
6. Frank Guess, Texas, B, 0/0
7. Harold Ensminger, Missouri, QB, 0/0
8. Vic Vasicek, Texas, LB, 12/24
9. Alex Verdova, Ohio State, B, 0/0
10. Al Russas, Tennessee, T, 0/9
11. Ernie Settembre, Miami, T, 0/0
12. Milt Kormarnicki, Villanova, C, 0/0
13. Butch Songin, Boston College, QB, 0/35
14. Leon Cooper, Hardin-Simmons, T, 0/0
15. Clayton Tonnemaker, Minnesota, LB, 0/36
16. Rob Goode, Texas A&M, B, 0/59
17. Art Donovan, Boston College, DT, 0/138

CHICAGO HORNETS

1. Stan Heath, Nevada-Reno, QB, 0/12
2. George Blanda, Kentucky, QB, 0/340
4. Jim Finks, Tulsa, QB, 0/79
5. Carmen Falcone, Penn, B, 0/0
6. Sam Tamburo, Penn State, DE, 0/12
7. Ralph Hutchinson, Tennessee-Chattanooga, T, 0/10
8. Jim Cain, Alabama, DE, 0/60
10. Warren Huey, Michigan State, E, 0/0
11. Norm Van Brocklin, Oregon, QB, 0/140
12. Jay Van Noy, Utah State, B, 0/0
13. Tom Wham, Furman, DE, 0/35
14. Ivan Snowden, Texas A&I, T, 0/0
15. Abbie Reynolds, Texas Tech, B, 0/0

CHICAGO ROCKETS

S2. Bill Fischer, Notre Dame, T, 0/59

CLEVELAND BROWNS

1. Jack Mitchell, Oklahoma, QB, 0/0
3. Rip Collins, LSU, HB, 0/31
4. Bill McLellan, Brown, T, 0/0
5. Ed McNeill, Michigan, E, 0/0
7. Phil Alexander, South Carolina, T, 0/0
8. Mike Cannevino, Ohio State, B, 0/0
9. Doak Walker, SMU, HB, 0/67
10. Norb Adams, Purdue, B, 0/0
11. Negley Norton, Penn State, T, 0/0
12. Frank Burns, Rutgers, B, 0/0
13. Clarence Self, Wisconsin, DB, 0/62
14. Walt Kersulis, Illinois, E, 0/0
15. Bobby Jack Stuart, Army, B, 0/0
26. Jack Lininger, Ohio State, LB, 0/24
29. Joe Soboleski, Michigan, G, 0/27

LOS ANGELES DONS

1. George Taliaferro, Indiana, HB, 11/72
3. Hosea Rodgers, North Carolina, FB, 12/12
4. Bob Meinert, Oklahoma State, B, 0/0
5. Billy Grimes, Oklahoma State, HB, 12/48
6. Joe Geri, Georgia, TB, 0/48
7. Bill Renna, Santa Clara, C, 0/0
8. Bill Austin, Oregon State, G, 0/75
9. Mike Rubish, North Carolina, E, 0/0
10. Gerry Krall, Ohio State, DB, 0/7
11. Chuck Drazenovich, Penn State, LB, 0/113
12. Larry Klosterman, North Carolina, G, 0/0
14. Dick Lorenz, Oregon St., E, 0/0
15. Bob Bastian, Southern California, G, 0/0
29. Joe Ethridge, SMU, TE, 0/12

NEW YORK YANKEES

1. Bobby Thomason, VMI, QB, 0/85
S2. Lou Kusserow, Columbia, LB, 11/22
2. John Panelli, Notre Dame, LB, 0/51
S2. John Rauch, Georgia, QB, 0/27
6. Don Panciera, San Francisco, QB, 12/26
7. Dan Garza, Oregon, E, 12/23
8. Brian Bell, Washington & Lee, B, 0/0
9. Al Mastrangeli, Illinois, C, 0/0
10. John Goldsberry, Indiana, DT, 0/20
11. Ben Bendrick, Wisconsin, B, 0/0
12. Frank Van Deren, California, E, 0/0
13. Ed Berrang, Villanova, DE, 0/42
14. Bob Doormink, Washington State, T, 0/0
15. Jack Glenn, Georgia Tech, T, 0/0
17. Gil Johnson, SMU, QB, 9/9
18. Barney Hafen, Utah, DE, 0/24
20. Tommy Kalmanir, Nevada-Reno, HB, 0/43

SAN FRANCISCO 49ERS

S1. Ernie Stautner, Boston College, DT, 0/173
1. Chester Fritz, Missouri, T, 0/0
S2. Jim Winkler, Texas A&M, DT, 0/32
3. Frank LoVuolo, St. Bonaventure, E, 0/11
4. Mike De Noia, Scranton, B, 0/0
5. George Brodnax, Georgia Tech, E, 0/0
6. John Hamberger, Southern Methodist, T, 0/0
7. Dan Steigman, North Carolina, C, 0/0
8. Bernie Reid, Georgia, G, 0/0
9. Fred Wendt, Texas-El Paso, B, 0/0
10. Dick Flowers, Alabama, T, 0/0
11. Bob Lund, Tennessee, B, 0/0
12. Jon Baker, California, DG, 0/46
13. Jim Reichert, Arkansas, G, 0/0
15. Pete Wissman, St. Louis, LB, 48/48
16. Homer Hobbs, Georgia, G, 22/22
25. Paul Shoults, Miami (OH), HB, 0/12

1950 NFL

BALTIMORE COLTS

1. Adrian Burk, Baylor, QB, 12/82
2. Leon Campbell, Arkansas, FB, 3/41
3. Don Colo, Brown, DT, 12/100
4. Bill Murray, Purdue, G, 12/35
5. Jack Halliday, SMU, T, 0/11
6. Herb Rich, Vanderbilt, DB, 12/64
7. Art Bok, Dayton, B, 0/0
8. Dick Harris, Texas, C, 0/0
9. Bill Bass, Arkansas, B, 0/0
10. Errol Fry, Texas, G, 0/0
11. Joe Romanosky, St. Bonaventure, T, 0/0
12. Bill Dey, Dartmouth, B, 0/0
13. Ray Stone, Texas, E, 0/0
14. Mitch Smiarowski, St. Bonaventure, C, 0/0
15. Art Spinney, Boston College, G, 2/94
26. Geno Mazzanti, Arkansas, HB, 4/4

CHICAGO BEARS

1. Chuck Hunsinger, Florida, HB, 34/34
1. Fred Morrison, Ohio State, FB, 48/84
2. John Dottley, Mississippi, FB, 27/27
3. Steve Romanik, Villanova, QB, 24/38
4. Tom Novak, Nebraska, C, 0/0
4. Dom Papaleo, Boston College, G, 0/0
5. Ernie Zalejski, Notre Dame, DB, 0/11
6. **Wayne Hansen, Texas-El Paso, LB, 99/111**
6. Gaspar Perricone, Northwestern, B, 0/0
7. Rollin Prather, Kansas State, E, 0/0
8. Sam Nevills, Oregon, T, 0/0
9. Breezy Reid, Georgia, HB, 0/78
9. Dick Braznell, Missouri, B, 0/0
10. Al Wahl, Michigan, T, 0/0
11. John Helwig, Notre Dame, LB, 42/42
12. Kenny Roof, Oklahoma State, B, 0/0
13. Frank Dempsey, Florida, LB, 39/39
14. Al Hover, Louisiana State, G, 0/0
15. Jimmy Glisson, Tulane, B, 0/0
16. Ed Bradley, Wake Forest, G, 12/12

CHICAGO CARDINALS

2. **Jack Jennings, Ohio State, T, 90/90**
3. Fran Polsfoot, Washington State, E, 27/37
3. Bill Svoboda, Tulane, LB, 45/100
4. Don Paul, Washington State, DB, 41/100
5. Carl Kiilsgaard, Idaho, T, 0/0
6. Warren Wood, Puget Sound, G, 0/0
7. Ed Bagdon, Michigan State, G, 23/26
7. Billy Gay, Notre Dame, DB, 3/3
8. John Hock, Santa Clara, G, 12/57
9. Vito Ragazzo, William & Mary, E, 0/0
10. Walt Grothaus, Notre Dame, C, 0/0
10. Milt Lavigne, Southeastern Louisiana, B, 0/0
11. J.D. Ison, Baylor, E, 0/0
12. Frank Wallheiser, Western Kentucky, E, 0/0
12. Bob Sharpe, Davidson, G, 0/0
13. Jerry Hennessy, Santa Clara, DE, 19/39
14. Dee Andros, Oklahoma, G, 0/0
15. Al Langford, Howard Payne, B, 0/0
17. Tom Palmer, Wake Forest, DT, 0/18
22. Jim Lipinski, Fairmont State, T, 1/1
24. Bob Gambold, Washington State, QB, 0/3

CLEVELAND BROWNS

1. Ken Carpenter, Oregon State, HB, 43/49
2. Jim Martin, Notre Dame, G, 12/166
2. **John Sandusky, Villanova, T, 70/82**
3. Jimmy Joe Robinson, Pittsburgh, B, 0/0
4. Bob (Red) Wilson, Wisconsin, C, 0/0
5. Don Phelps, Kentucky, HB, 17/17
6. Ken Gorgal, Purdue, DB, 35/58
7. Win Carter, Missouri, B, 0/0
8. Russ Frizzell, Tulsa, T, 0/0
9. Jim Duncan, Wake Forest, DE, 0/43
10. Frank O'Pella, William & Mary, B, 0/0
11. Bob Plotz, Pittsburgh, G, 0/0
12. Emerson Cole, Toledo, FB, 30/31
13. Rupe Wright, Baylor, G, 0/0
14. Packard Harrington, St. Mary's (CA), C, 0/0
15. Ted Meland, Oregon, G, 0/0
19. Butch Songin, Boston College, QB, 0/35
23. Dom Moselle, Wisconsin-Superior, DB, 11/43
29. Bob Schnelker, Bowling Green State, E, 0/105

DETROIT LIONS

B1. **Leon Hart, Notre Dame, E, 92/92**
1. Joe Watson, Rice, C, 8/8
2. Thurman McGraw, Colorado State, DT, 49/49
3. Art Murakowski, Northwestern, FB, 12/12
4. Ernie Kiely, Texas-El Paso, G, 0/0
5. Hal Fitkin, Dartmouth, B, 0/0
6. Floyd Jaszewski, Minnesota, T, 24/24
7. Bill Leverman, St. Edward's, B, 0/0
8. Ralph McAllister, Minnesota, B, 0/0
9. Ed Wood, Detroit, G, 0/0
10. Roland Malcolm, Gustavus Adolphus, B, 0/0
11. Jack Wilson, Ohio State, T, 0/0
12. Bucky Walters, Brown, T, 0/0
13. Jim Ryan, San Francisco, B, 0/0
14. Cliff Squires, Nebraska Wesleyan, C, 0/0
15. Tom Worthington, Northwestern, B, 0/0
18. Don Stansauk, Denver, DT, 0/15
19. Gus Cifelli, Notre Dame, T, 36/60

GREEN BAY PACKERS

1. Clayton Tonnemaker, Minnesota, LB, 36/36
2. **Tobin Rote, Rice, QB, 84/149**
3. Gordie Soltau, Minnesota, E, 0/107
4. Larry Coutre, Notre Dame, HB, 19/22
6. Jack Cloud, William & Mary, LB, 13/33
7. Willie Manley, Oklahoma, T, 24/24
8. Harry Szulborski, Purdue, B, 0/0
9. Roger Wilson, South Carolina, E, 0/0
10. Bob Mealey, Minnesota, T, 0/0
11. Gene Lorendo, Georgia, E, 0/0
12. Andy Pavich, Denver, E, 0/0
13. Carl Elliott, Virginia, DE, 48/48
14. Fred Leon, Nevada-Reno, T, 0/0
15. Gene Huebner, Baylor, C, 0/0
18. Arnie Galiffa, Army, QB, 0/7

LOS ANGELES RAMS

1. Ralph Pasquariello, Villanova, FB, 9/29
1. **Stan West, Oklahoma, DG, 57/84**
2. Bob Fuchs, Missouri, C, 0/0
3. Don Murray, Penn State, T, 0/0
4. Ben Proctor, Texas, E, 0/0
5. Dick McKissack, SMU, DB, 0/1
6. Orville Langrell, Oklahoma City, T, 0/0
7. Cliff Coggin, Southern Mississippi, E, 0/0
8. **Woodley Lewis, Oregon, DB, 72/126**
9. Les Cowan, McMurry, DT, 0/9
10. Jay Van Noy, Utah State, B, 0/0
11. Jay Roundy, Southern California, B, 0/0
11. Fred Stuvek, West Virginia, G, 0/0
12. John Lunney, Arkansas, G, 0/0
13. Tom Winbigler, College of Idaho, B, 0/0
14. Bill Trautwein, Ohio State, T, 0/0
15. Dave Stephenson, West Virginia, G, 12/61
18. Bobby Collier, SMU, T, 11/11
25. **Dan Towler, Washington & Jefferson, FB, 67/67**
30. Bill Lange, Dayton, G, 22/56

LOS ANGELES RAMS

7. Don Narrell, Texas Christian, T, 0/0
8. Jack Archer, Texas Christian, B, 0/0
10. Melvin Lyle, Louisiana State, E, 0/0
11. Roger McAuley, Texas Christian, G, 0/0
12. Andy Hillhouse, Texas A&M, E, 0/0
13. Jack Morton, West Virginia, B, 0/0
14. Ed Carmichael, Oregon State, G, 0/0
15. Norm Messeroll, Tennessee, T, 0/0

NEW YORK GIANTS

1. Travis Tidwell, Auburn, QB, 14/14
2. **Eddie Price, Tulane, FB, 63/63**

3. Randy Clay, Texas, HB, 24/24
4. Porter Payne, Georgia, G, 0/0
5. Forrest Griffith, Kansas, HB, 16/16
9. Vince Cisterna, Northern Arizona, E, 0/0
10. Bob Wilkinson, UCLA, E, 19/19
12. **Ray Wietecha, Northwestern, C, 124/124**
13. Joe Kelly, Wisconsin, C, 0/0
14. Gene Fritz, Minnesota, T, 0/0
15. Bill Roberson, Stephen F. Austin, T, 0/0
16. Bob Jackson, North Carolina A&T, FB, 24/24
21. Bill Stribling, Mississippi, E, 30/56
24. Tom Finnin, Detroit Mercy, DT, 0/55
30. Hamp Tanner, Georgia, T, 0/22

NEW YORK YANKS
2. Art Weiner, North Carolina, E, 12/12
4. Zollie Toth, LSU, FB, 33/45
5. Mike Swistowicz, Notre Dame, HB, 1/9
6. Bennie Aldridge, Oklahoma State, DB, 24/43
18. Jim Champion, Mississippi State, LB, 19/19
19. Bobbie Griffin, Baylor, DB, 12/12

PHILADELPHIA EAGLES
1. Bud Grant, Minnesota, E, 24/24
3. Bob Sanders, Oregon, B, 0/0
4. Bob McChesney, Hardin-Simmons, E, 0/36
5. Mike Kaysserian, Detroit, B, 0/0
6. Lloyd McDermott, Kentucky, DT, 0/24
7. Mel Olix, Miami (OH), B, 0/0
8. Dick O'Hanlon, Ohio State, T, 0/0
9. Bobby Wilson, Mississippi, B, 0/0
10. Ernie Johnson, UCLA, B, 0/0
11. Bobby Lantrip, Rice, B, 0/0
12. Frank Mahoney, Brown, E, 0/0
13. **Norm Willey, Marshall, DE, 92/92**
14. Billy Hix, Arkansas, E, 11/11
15. Herb Carey, Dartmouth, B, 0/0

PITTSBURGH STEELERS
1. **Lynn Chandnois, Michigan State, HB, 72/72**
2. **Ernie Stautner, Boston College, DT, 173/173**
3. **George Hughes, William & Mary, T, 60/60**
5. Lou Allen, Duke, T, 24/24
5. Tom Rowe, Dartmouth, E, 0/0
6. Ed Mattson, Trinity (TX), B, 0/0
7. Truett Smith, Mississippi State, BB, 20/20
8. **Fran Rogel, Penn State, FB, 96/96**
9. Max Druen, Tulane, T, 0/0
11. Charley Williams, Sam Houston State, E, 0/0
13. Negley Norton, Penn State, T, 0/0
14. Jim Kynes, Florida, C, 0/0
15. Harry Russell, San Jose State, B, 0/0
21. Dick Tomlinson, Kansas, G, 23/23

SAN FRANCISCO 49ERS
1. **Leo Nomellini, Minnesota, DT, 174/174**
2. Don Campora, Pacific, T, 20/25
3. Ray Collins, LSU, DT, 32/71
4. Morris Bailey, Texas Christian, E, 0/0
5. Harry Kane, Pacific, C, 0/0
6. Don Van Pool, Oklahoma State, E, 0/0
7. Lindy Berry, Texas Christian, B, 0/0
8. Ellery Williams, Santa Clara, E, 0/12
9. Pete Zinach, West Virginia, B, 0/0
10. Bob Celeri, California, QB, 0/19
11. Harley Dow, San Jose State, G, 12/12
12. Don Burke, USC, LB, 39/39
13. Lou (Bimbo) Cecconi, Pittsburgh, B, 0/0
14. Tom Payne, Santa Clara, E, 0/0
15. Leo Crampsey, St. Bonaventure, E, 0/0
16. Charlie Shaw, Oklahoma State, G, 6/6
20. Jack Nix, USC, E, 9/9
22. **Billy Wilson, San Jose State, E, 100/100**
26. Jim Powers, USC, DB, 46/46

WASHINGTON REDSKINS
1. George Thomas, Oklahoma, HB, 24/31
2. Hall Haynes, Santa Clara, DB, 20/40
3. Lou Karras, Purdue, DT, 26/26
4. **Harry Ulinski, Kentucky, C, 72/72**
5. Frank Spaniel, Notre Dame, HB, 6/12
6. Gene Pepper, Missouri, G, 41/44
7. Jerry Houghton, Washington State, T, 12/14
8. John Rohde, Pacific, E, 0/0
9. Don Winslow, Iowa, T, 0/0
10. **Eddie LeBaron, Pacific, QB, 82/134**
11. Dan Brown, Villanova, DE, 11/11
12. Bill Chauncey, Iowa State, B, 0/0
13. Clay Davis, Oklahoma State, C, 0/0
14. Lyle Button, Illinois, T, 0/0
15. Alex Loyd, Oklahoma State, E, 0/12
16. Charlie Justice, North Carolina, HB, 43/43
17. Jim Cullom, California, G, 0/2
21. **Cas Witucki, Indiana, G, 54/54**

1951 NFL

CHICAGO BEARS
1. **Gene Schroeder, Virginia, E, 64/64**
1. Bob Williams, Notre Dame, QB, 29/29
2. **Bill George, Wake Forest, LB, 159/173**
3. Wilford White, Arizona State, HB, 17/17
4. Tom Jelley, Miami (FL), DE, 0/5
4. Bob Moser, Pacific, C, 30/30
5. Brad Rowland, McMurry, HB, 12/12
6. Herb Falkenberg, Trinity (TX), B, 0/0
7. Paul Lea, Tulane, DT, 0/9
8. Clair Mayes, Oklahoma, G, 0/0
9. Bill Gregus, Wake Forest, B, 0/0
10. J.W. Sherrill, Tennessee, B, 0/0
11. Tom Hardiman, Georgetown (DC), B, 0/0
12. Lawrence (Punjab) Hairston, Nevada-Reno, T, 0/0
13. Charley Wright, West Texas State, B, 0/0
14. Bailey Woods, Abilene Christian, B, 0/0
15. Sid Hall, Pacific, C, 0/0

CHICAGO CARDINALS
1. **Jerry Groom, Notre Dame, MG, 58/58**
2. Don Joyce, Tulane, DE, 34/135
3. **Don Stonesifer, Northwestern, E, 72/72**
4. Dick Doyne, Lehigh, B, 0/0
5. Lynn Lynch, Illinois, G, 3/3
6. Ed Jasonek, Furman, B, 0/0
7. Dick Punches, Colorado, T, 0/0
8. **Leo Sanford, Louisiana Tech, LB, 84/93**
9. Neil Schmidt, Purdue, B, 0/0
11. **Tom Bienemann, Drake, DE, 65/65**
12. Jack Landry, Notre Dame, B, 0/0
13. Volney Peters, USC, DT, 24/104
14. Bill Leskovar, Kentucky, B, 0/0
15. John Simcic, Wisconsin, G, 0/0
20. Fred Wallner, Notre Dame, LB, 45/52
22. S.J. Whitman, Tulsa, DB, 22/39
24. Billy Cross, West Texas A&M, HB, 36/36
27. Ken Huxhold, Wisconsin, G, 0/59

CLEVELAND BROWNS
1. **Ken Konz, LSU, DB, 84/84**
2. Bucky Curtis, Vanderbilt, E, 0/0
3. Jerry Helluin, Tulane, DT, 18/80
4. Bob Smith, Texas A&M, FB, 0/15
5. Ace Loomis, Wisconsin-LaCrosse, DB, 0/33
6. Dan Rogas, Tulane, G, 0/22
7. **Walt Michaels, Washington & Lee, LB, 120/133**
7. Irv Holdash, North Carolina, C, 0/0
8. Max Clark, Houston, B, 0/0
9. Don Shula, John Carroll, DB, 17/73
9. Burl Toler, San Francisco, G, 0/0
10. Chet Gierula, Maryland, G, 0/0
11. Bernie Custis, Syracuse, B, 0/0
12. Milan Seillers, Florida State, B, 0/0
12. Stew Kirtley, Morehead State, E, 0/0
13. Bob Voskuhl, Georgetown (KY), C, 0/0
14. Rudy Cernoch, Northwestern, T, 0/0
15. Joe Skibinski, Purdue, G, 12/36
22. Carl Taseff, John Carroll, DB, 9/116
30. Sisto Averno, Muhlenberg, LB, 0/51

DETROIT LIONS
2. Dick Stanfel, San Francisco, G, 39/73
3. **Dorne Dibble, Michigan State, E, 68/68**
4. Pete D'Alonzo, Villanova, FB, 16/16
5. **Jim Doran, Iowa State, E, 89/115**
5. LaVern Torgeson, Washington State, LB, 47/82
6. **Jack Christiansen, Colorado State, DB, 89/89**
7. Bob Momsen, Ohio State, MG, 12/22
8. Dick Raklovits, Illinois, B, 0/0
10. Jim Shoaf, Louisiana State, G, 0/0
11. Frankie Anderson, Oklahoma, E, 0/0
13. Wayne Siegert, Illinois, T, 0/4
14. Lee Wittmer, Detroit, T, 0/0
15. Jim Hill, Tennessee, DB, 21/31
17. Darrel Meisenheimer, Oklahoma State, DB, 0/9
29. Bruce Womack, West Texas A&M, G, 3/3

GREEN BAY PACKERS
1. Bob Gain, Kentucky, DT, 0/125
3. **Fred Cone, Clemson, FB, 82/94**
5. Wade Stinson, Kansas, B, 0/0
6. Sig Holowenko, John Carroll, T, 0/0
7. Bill Sutherland, St. Vincent, E, 0/0
9. Dick McWilliams, Michigan, T, 0/0
10. Bob Noppinger, Georgetown (DC), T, 0/0
11. George Rooks, Morgan State, B, 0/0
12. Carl Kreager, Michigan, C, 0/0
13. Ed Stephens, Missouri, B, 0/0
14. Ray Bauer, Montana, E, 0/0
15. Joe Ernst, Tulane, B, 0/0
16. Dick Afflis, Nevada-Reno, T, 48/48
17. Ray Pelfrey, Eastern Kentucky, E, 13/32

LOS ANGELES RAMS
1. Bud McFadin, Texas, DT, 43/125
3. **Charlie Toogood, Nebraska, DT, 61/67**
4. George Kinek, Tulane, E, 0/12
5. Tony Momsen, Michigan, C, 0/13
6. Norb Hecker, Baldwin-Wallace, DB, 32/64
7. Alan Egler, Colgate, B, 0/0
8. Hugo Primiani, Boston, T, 0/0
9. Nolan Lang, Oklahoma, B, 0/0
10. Roland Kirkby, Washington, B, 0/0
11. John Natyshak, Tampa, B, 0/0
12. Don Hardey, Pacific, B, 0/0
13. Joe Reid, LSU, LB, 11/22
14. Rob McCoy, Georgia Tech, B, 0/0
15. Obie Posey, Southern, B, 0/0
18. **Dick Daugherty, Oregon, G, 69/69**
19. **Andy Robustelli, Arnold, DE, 59/175**
22. Billy Baggett, LSU, HB, 0/11
26. Howie Ruetz, Loras, DT, 0/20
27. Al Brosky, Illinois, DB, 0/9

NEW YORK GIANTS
B1. **Kyle Rote, SMU, E, 121/121**
2. **Ray Krouse, Maryland, DT, 58/118**
3. Sonny Grandelius, Michigan State, HB, 12/12
5. **Jack Stroud, Tennessee, G, 132/132**
6. Herb Hannah, Alabama, T, 12/12
8. Fred Benners, SMU, QB, 6/6
9. Holland Donan, Princeton, T, 0/0
11. Reds Bagnell, Pennsylvania, B, 0/0
12. Bob Hudson, Clemson, DB, 23/106
13. Paul Douglass, Illinois, B, 0/0
14. Pat Flanagan, Marquette, T, 0/0
15. Gene Vykukal, Texas, T, 0/0
17. Bud Sherrod, Tennessee, E, 11/11
20. Bill Albright, Wisconsin, G, 47/47
23. **Dick Yelvington, Georgia, T, 62/62**
25. Chet Lagod, Tennessee-Chattanooga, G, 11/11
26. Quincy Armstrong, North Texas, C, 0/2

NEW YORK YANKS
2. Ken Jackson, Texas, T, 12/68
3. Mike McCormack, Kansas, T, 12/119
4. Elmer Wingate, Maryland, DE, 0/12
6. George Musacco, Loyola (CA), B, 0/0
8. Larry Lauer, Alabama, C, 0/18
10. Jesse Thomas, Michigan State, DB, 0/36
11. Steve Wyndham, Clemson, B, 0/0
12. Al Lary, Alabama, E, 0/0
13. John Thomas, Oregon State, E, 0/0
14. Charley Rapp, Duquesne, B, 0/0
15. Bill Wanamaker, Kentucky, G, 0/0
21. Al Pollard, Army, HB, 6/36
24. James Stroschein, UCLA, DE, 11/11
26. Will Sherman, St. Mary's (CA), DB, 2/87

PHILADELPHIA EAGLES
1. Ebert Van Buren, LSU, DB, 36/36
3. Al Bruno, Kentucky, E, 0/0
4. Fran Nagle, Nebraska, B, 0/0
5. Jack Dwyer, Loyola Marymount, DB, 0/46
6. Ken Farragut, Mississippi, C, 43/43
7. Frank Boydston, Baylor, B, 0/0
8. Jack Richards, Arkansas, E, 0/0
9. Denny Doyle, Tulane, G, 0/0
10. Louis Schaufele, Arkansas, B, 0/0
11. Bob Pope, Kentucky, T, 0/0
12. Henry Rich, Arizona State, B, 0/0
13. Pete Mastellone, Miami (FL), C, 0/0
14. **Bobby Walston, Georgia, E, 148/148**
15. Bobby North, Georgia Tech, B, 0/0
29. Roscoe Hansen, North Carolina, T, 9/9

PITTSBURGH STEELERS
1. Butch Avinger, Alabama, FB, 0/12
2. Chuck Ortmann, Michigan, B, 12/15
3. George Sulima, Boston University, E, 31/31
5. Floyd Sampson, McMurry, B, 0/0
6. **Dale Dodrill, Colorado State, MG, 103/103**
7. **Ray Mathews, Clemson, HB, 108/114**
8. Henry Minarik, Michigan State, E, 11/11
11. Joe McCutcheon, Washington & Lee, C, 0/0
12. Jim Brandt, St. Thomas, DB, 33/33
13. Bill Szabo, Bucknell, T, 0/0
14. Mike Mizerany, Alabama, G, 0/0
15. Clay Webb, Kentucky, B, 0/0
21. Ernie Cheatham, Loyola Marymount, DT, 4/6
22. Dick Hendley, Clemson, BB, 7/7
25. Tom Calvin, Alabama, HB, 30/30

SAN FRANCISCO 49ERS
2. Pete Schabarum, California, HB, 34/34
3. Billy Mixon, Georgia, HB, 22/22
5. **Al Carapella, Miami (FL), DT, 60/60**
5. Dick Steere, Drake, G, 0/5
6. Bishop Strickland, South Carolina, FB, 9/9
7. Dick Forbes, St. Ambrose, E, 0/0
8. **Joe Arenas, Nebraska-Omaha, HB, 84/84**
9. Bruce Van Alstyne, Stanford, E, 0/0
10. Nick Feher, Georgia, G, 40/42
11. **Bill Jessup, USC, E, 53/62**
12. Jim Monachino, California, HB, 13/20
13. Dick Harvin, Georgia Tech, E, 0/0
14. **Rex Berry, Brigham Young, DB, 66/66**
15. Dave Sparks, South Carolina, G, 8/18
16. Bob White, Stanford, HB, 24/35
17. Art Michalik, St. Ambrose, MG, 14/38

WASHINGTON REDSKINS
1. Leon Heath, Oklahoma, FB, 31/31
2. Ed Salem, Alabama, DB, 12/12
2. Jim Staton, Wake Forest, DT, 8/8
3. Walt Yowarsky, Kentucky, DE, 22/64
4. Paul Giroski, Rice, T, 0/0
6. John Martinkovic, Xavier (OH), DE, 0/84
7. Johnny Papit, Virginia, HB, 25/29
8. Billy Cox, Duke, DE, 26/26
9. Jake Rowden, Maryland, C, 0/0
10. James Janosek, Purdue, T, 0/0
11. Bill DeChard, Holy Cross, B, 0/0
12. Al Applegate, Scranton, G, 0/0
13. Dick Campbell, Wyoming, B, 0/0
15. Vic Thomas, Colorado, T, 0/0
17. **Gene Brito, Loyola Marymount, DE, 84/97**
18. Dom Fucci, Kentucky, DB, 0/12
19. Buddy Brown, Arkansas, G, 24/71
26. Johnny Williams, USC, DB, 24/35
30. Nick Bolkovac, Pittsburgh, DT, 0/17

1952 NFL

CHICAGO BEARS
1. **Jim Dooley, Miami (FL), B, 81/81**
2. Eddie Macon, Pacific, DB, 23/37
3. **Bill McColl, Stanford, E, 96/96**
4. **Herman Clark, Oregon State, G, 52/52**
5. **Jack Hoffman, Xavier (OH), DE, 55/55**
5. **Fred Williams, Arkansas, DT, 140/168**
6. **Ed Brown, San Francisco, QB, 98/154**
7. **Joe Fortunato, Mississippi State, LB, 155/155**
8. **Bill Bishop, North Texas, DT, 107/117**
8. Billy Jurney, Arkansas, E, 0/0
9. Bobby Cross, Stephen F. Austin State, T, 12/87
11. Bill Miller, Wake Forest, B, 0/0
12. Andy Kozar, Tennessee, B, 0/0
13. Rich Athan, Northwestern, B, 0/0
14. Gale Galloway, Baylor, C, 0/0
15. Dick Kazmaier, Princeton, B, 0/0
18. Tommy O'Connell, Illinois, QB, 12/45
20. Jimmy Lesane, Virginia, DB, 13/17
21. Ted Daffer, Tennessee, DE, 12/12

CHICAGO CARDINALS
1. **Ollie Matson, San Francisco, RB, 72/171**
2. Pete Brewster, Purdue, E, 0/104
2. Johnny Karras, Illinois, HB, 10/10
5. Dick Fugler, Tulane, T, 12/24
6. John Hancock, Baylor, G, 0/0
7. Harry Jabbusch, South Carolina, C, 0/0
8. Don Coleman, Michigan State, G, 0/0
9. Malcolm Cook, Georgia, B, 0/0
10. John Feltch, Holy Cross, T, 0/0
11. **Leo Sugar, Purdue, DE, 84/104**
12. Joe Masnaghetti, Marquette, T, 0/0
13. Mel Massucco, Holy Cross, B, 0/0
14. Tom Tofaute, North Carolina State, C, 0/0
15. John Davis, Indiana, B, 0/0
16. Mike Mergen, San Francisco, T, 12/12
19. Ed Listopad, Wake Forest, G, 4/4
23. Red Stephens, San Francisco, G, 0/70
25. Cliff Anderson, Indiana, E, 13/21

CLEVELAND BROWNS
1. Bert Rechichar, Tennessee, DB, 12/99
1. Harry Agganis, Boston, QB, 0/0
2. Bill Hughes, Michigan State, C, 0/0
3. Joe Campanella, Ohio State, LB, 0/68
3. Don Klosterman, Loyola Marymount, QB, 0/2
4. **Ray Renfro, North Texas, HB, 142/142**
4. Elmer Costa, North Carolina State, G, 0/0
5. Keever Jankovich, Pacific, LB, 0/12
6. Burrell Shields, John Carroll, HB, 0/14
7. John Pace, Mississippi State, T, 0/0
8. Herschel Forester, SMU, G, 48/48
8. Stan Williams, Baylor, DB, 0/12
9. Bob Finnell, Xavier, B, 0/0
10. Pat Ribiero, Pacific, T, 0/0
11. Dick Logan, Ohio State, G, 0/19

12. Roy Thompson, Florida State, B, 0/0
13. Tom Cosgrove, Maryland, C, 0/0
14. Steve Ruzich, Ohio State, G, 0/36
15. Holly Alpin, Tampa, E, 0/0
24. Junior Wren, Missouri, DB, 48/62

DALLAS TEXANS

1. Les Richter, California, LB, 0/112
2. Gino Marchetti, San Francisco, DE, 12/161
7. Johnny Petitbon, Notre Dame, DB, 11/47
9. Jim Lansford, Texas, T, 12/12
11. Pat Cannamela, USC, LB, 12/12
12. Jim Mutscheller, Notre Dame, E, 0/95
15. Jack Bighead, Pepperdine, DE, 0/13
17. Dick Horn, Stanford, QB, 0/5
19. Gene Felker, Wisconsin, E, 6/6
21. Harry Hugasian, Stanford, HB, 0/6

DETROIT LIONS

3. **Yale Lary, Texas A&M, DB, 133/133**
4. Pat Summerall, Arkansas, DE, 2/109
5. **Bob Miller, Virginia, DT, 81/81**
6. Gordon Cooper, Denver, E, 0/0
7. Wes Gardner, Utah, C, 0/0
8. Tom Dublinski, Utah, QB, 25/29
9. **Sonny Gandee, Ohio State, LB, 51/53**
10. Steve Dowden, Baylor, T, 0/12
11. Keith Flowers, TCU, C, 3/9
12. Jim Roshto, Louisiana State, B, 0/0
13. Carroll McDonald, Florida, C, 0/0
14. Ray Oliverson, BYU, B, 0/0
15. John Burgamy, Georgia, G, 0/0
17. Hank Lauricella, Tennessee, HB, 0/11
18. Stan Campbell, Iowa State, G, 41/92
19. Blaine Earon, Duke, DE, 18/18
20. **Gil Mains, Murray State, DT, 85/85**
22. **Jim David, Colorado State, DB, 96/96**
25. Byron Bailey, Washington State, HB, 8/18
28. Hal Turner, Tennessee State, DE, 3/3

GREEN BAY PACKERS

1. Babe Parilli, Kentucky, QB, 48/189
2. **Billy Howton, Rice, E, 80/142**
3. **Bobby Dillon, Texas, DB, 94/94**
5. **Dave Hanner, Arkansas, DT, 160/160**
6. Tom Johnson, Michigan, DT, 8/8
7. Bill Reichardt, Iowa, FB, 12/12
8. Mel Becket, Indiana, C, 0/0
9. Deral Teteak, Wisconsin, LB, 49/49
10. Bill Roffler, Washington State, DB, 0/3
10. Art Kleinschmidt, Tulane, G, 0/0
11. Billy Burkhalter, Rice, B, 0/0
12. Bill Wilson, Texas, T, 0/0
13. Billy Hair, Clemson, B, 0/0
14. Jack Morgan, Michigan State, T, 0/0
15. Bobby Jack Floyd, TCU, FB, 12/20
20. Chuck Boerio, Illinois, LB, 1/1

LOS ANGELES RAMS

1. Bob Carey, Michigan State, E, 21/32
B1. **Billy Wade, Vanderbilt, QB, 69/128**
2. Bob Griffin, Arkansas, LB, 44/49
3. Dewey McConnell, Wyoming, DB, 0/9
4. Ken Casner, Baylor, DT, 11/11
4. Skeets Quinlan, San Diego State, HB, 43/49
5. Gordon Polofsky, Tennessee, LB, 0/26
6. Jerrell Price, Texas Tech, T, 0/0
7. Burt Delevan, Pacific, T, 0/14
8. Tom McCormick, Pacific, HB, 26/32
9. Byron Townsend, Texas, B, 0/0
10. Luke Welch, Baylor, T, 0/0
11. Sam Baker, Oregon State, K, 0/195
12. Jake Roberts, Tulsa, B, 0/0
13. Aubrey (Red) Phillips, Texas Tech, C, 0/0
14. Joe Moss, Maryland, T, 0/12
15. Bill Hegarty, Villanova, DE, 0/3
18. Bob Dees, Southwest Missouri State, DT, 0/9
25. Len Teeuws, Tulane, DT, 24/72
26. Frank Fuller, Kentucky, DT, 43/95
29. Gerry Perry, California, T, 0/96

NEW YORK GIANTS

1. **Frank Gifford, USC, HB, 136/136**
2. Ray Beck, Georgia Tech, G, 46/46
3. Don Heinrich, Washington, QB, 43/56
4. Merwin Hodel, Colorado, FB, 2/2
4. Don Menasco, Texas, DB, 20/26
5. Robert Patton, Clemson, G, 12/12
6. Jim MacKenzie, Kentucky, T, 0/0
7. Val Joe Walker, SMU, DB, 0/58
9. John Kastan, Boston, B, 0/0
10. Pat Knight, SMU, LB, 20/20
11. Charlie Harris, California, C, 0/0
12. Dick Ochoa, Texas, B, 0/0
13. Pat Brady, Nevada-Reno, QB, 0/36
14. Hal Mitchell, UCLA, T, 11/11
15. Paul Bischoff, West Virginia, E, 0/0
20. Rex Boggan, Mississippi, DT, 11/11

NEW YORK GIANTS

5. Jack Jorgenson, Colorado, T, 0/0
5. Mel Sinquefield, Mississippi, C, 0/0
6. Dave Cianelli, Maryland, C, 0/0
10. Jim Hammond, Wisconsin, B, 0/0
13. Bill Ward, Arkansas, G, 0/0
14. Paul Williams, Texas, E, 0/0

PHILADELPHIA EAGLES

1. Johnny Bright, Drake, B, 0/0
2. Jim Weatherall, Oklahoma, DT, 36/65
3. **Lum Snyder, Georgia Tech, T, 59/59**
4. Chuck Ulrich, Illinois, DT, 0/51
6. Dick Lemmon, California, B, 0/0
7. John Thomas, Oregon State, E, 0/0
8. **Wayne Robinson, Minnesota, LB, 58/58**
9. Maury Nipp, Loyola Marymount, G, 25/25
10. Gerry McGinley, Pennsylvania, G, 0/0
11. Ralph Goldston, Youngstown State, HB, 27/27
12. Jack Blount, Mississippi State, T, 0/0
13. Ed Hamilton, Kentucky, B, 0/0
14. Bob Stringer, Tulsa, LB, 24/24
15. Malcolm Schmidt, Iowa State, E, 0/0
24. Joe Tyrrell, Temple, G, 2/2
25. Bob Kelley, West Texas A&M, C, 24/24
28. John Brewer, Louisville, FB, 18/18
30. Don Stevens, Illinois, HB, 15/15

PITTSBURGH STEELERS

1. Ed Modzelewski, Maryland, FB, 10/66
2. **George Tarasovic, LSU, DE, 118/155**
3. Steve Wadiak, South Carolina, B, 0/0
4. Jack Gearding, Xavier, T, 0/0
7. Claude Hipps, Georgia, DB, 17/17
9. Hal (Herky) Payne, Tennessee, B, 0/0
10. George Gilmartin, Xavier, B, 0/0
11. Jack Spinks, Alcorn State, T, 10/30
12. Marv McFadden, Michigan State, G, 24/24
13. Dave Flood, Notre Dame, B, 0/0
14. June Davis, Texas, G, 0/0
15. Dick Pivirotto, Princeton, B, 0/0
16. Pete Ladygo, Maryland, G, 24/24
19. Gary Kerkorian, Stanford, QB, 12/32
25. Bill Robinson, Lincoln (MO), HB, 0/3
27. Dick Doyle, Ohio State, DB, 12/18
30. Ed Kissell, Wake Forest, DB, 13/13

SAN FRANCISCO 49ERS

1. **Hugh McElhenny, Washington, HB, 97/143**
2. **Bob Toneff, Notre Dame, DT, 69/149**
3. Billy Tidwell, Texas A&M, HB, 10/10
3. Gene Shannon, Houston, B, 0/0
4. Marion Campbell, Georgia, DE, 23/94
5. Pat O'Donahue, Wisconsin, DE, 8/20
6. Jim Beasley, Tulsa, C, 0/0
7. Don Robison, California, B, 0/0
8. Jerry Smith, Wisconsin, G, 26/29
9. Glen Christian, Idaho, B, 0/0
10. Carl West, Mississippi, B, 0/0
11. J.D. Kimmel, Houston, DT, 0/36
12. Fred Snyder, Loyola (CA), E, 0/0
13. Rudy Yeager, Louisiana State, T, 0/0
14. Frank Simons, Nebraska, E, 0/0
15. Haldo Norman, Gustavus Adolphus, E, 0/0
16. Bob Meyers, Stanford, HB, 1/1
25. Bud Laughlin, Kansas, FB, 10/10

WASHINGTON REDSKINS

1. Larry Isbell, Baylor, B, 0/0
2. Andy Davis, George Washington, DB, 6/6
3. Al Dorow, Michigan State, QB, 31/69
4. Dick Hightower, Southern Methodist, C, 0/0
5. Jim Clark, Oregon State, T, 24/24
6. Ed Kensler, Maryland, G, 0/0
7. Vic Janowicz, Ohio State, HB, 22/22
8. Hubert Johnston, Iowa, T, 0/0
9. Dick Alban, Northwestern, DB, 48/96
10. **Chet Ostrowski, Notre Dame, DE, 68/68**
11. Orlando Mazza, Michigan State, E, 0/0
12. Frank Middendorf, Cincinnati, C, 0/0
13. Ray Potter, Louisiana State, T, 0/0
14. Doug Conway, Texas Christian, T, 0/0
15. Julius Wittman, Ohio State, T, 0/0
16. Marv Berschet, Illinois, G, 16/16
23. Ken Barfield, Mississippi, T, 8/8

1953 NFL

BALTIMORE COLTS

1. Billy Vessels, Oklahoma, HB, 12/12
2. Bernie Flowers, Purdue, E, 1/1
3. Buck McPhail, Oklahoma, FB, 12/12
4. Tom Catlin, Oklahoma, LB, 0/51
5. Jack Little, Texas A&M, T, 20/20
6. Jimmy Sears, USC, DB, 0/37
7. Bill Athey, Baylor, G, 0/0
8. Jim Prewett, Tulsa, T, 0/0
9. Bob Blair, Texas Christian, E, 0/0
10. John Cole, Arkansas, B, 0/0
11. Gene Rossi, Cincinnati, B, 0/0
12. Kaye Vaughn, Tulsa, G, 0/0
13. Bobby Morehead, Georgia Tech, B, 0/0
14. Frank Continetti, George Washington, G, 0/0
15. Buddy Sutton, Arkansas, B, 0/0
24. Monte Brethauer, Oregon, DB, 24/24

CHICAGO BEARS

1. Billy Anderson, Compton CC (CA), DB, 19/19
2. **Zeke Bratkowski, Georgia, QB, 59/132**
3. Bill Rowekamp, Army/Missouri, B, 0/0
4. Joe Koch, Wake Forest, B, 0/0
5. **Stan Jones, Maryland, G, 144/157**
6. Art DeCarlo, Georgia, DB, 0/61
6. **Kline Gilbert, Mississippi, T, 60/60**
7. Don Bingham, Sul Ross State, HB, 12/12
7. Bucky McElroy, Southern Mississippi, HB, 1/1
8. John Kreamcheck, William & Mary, DT, 36/36
9. Bruno Ashley, East Texas State, T, 0/0
10. Jimmy Moore, Florida A&M, B, 0/0
11. Ralph Charney, Kentucky, B, 0/0
11. Jim Slowey, Georgetown (DC), C, 0/0
12. Jim Lawrence, Duke, T, 0/0
13. **Larry Strickland, North Texas, C, 62/62**
14. Harland Carl, Wisconsin, HB, 9/9
15. Ralph Jecha, Northwestern, G, 12/19
16. Johnny Hatley, Sul Ross State, G, 10/48

CHICAGO CARDINALS

1. **Johnny Olszewski, California, FB, 56/113**
2. Jim Psaltis, USC, DB, 24/35
3. Dale Samuels, Purdue, QB, 0/0
4. Gerdes (Buck) Martin, Georgia Tech, E, 0/0
5. Bill Shalosky, Cincinnati, G, 0/0
6. Tony Curcillo, Ohio State, DB, 12/12
7. Tom Higgins, North Carolina, T, 12/29
8. Jerry Watford, Alabama, G, 24/24
9. **Ed Husmann, Nebraska, DT, 52/134**
9. Avatus Stone, Syracuse, HB, 0/1
10. Charley Berndt, Wisconsin, T, 0/0
11. Ed Woodsum, Yale, E, 0/0
12. Chuck Spaulding, Wyoming, B, 0/0
13. Frank McPhee, Princeton, DB, 7/7
13. Ronnie Morris, Tulsa, B, 0/0
14. Dick Sprague, Washington, B, 0/0
15. Nick Chickillo, Miami (FL), LB, 12/12
23. Jim Root, Miami (OH), QB, 20/20

CLEVELAND BROWNS

1. Doug Atkins, Tennessee, DE, 20/205
2. Billy Reynolds, Pittsburgh, HB, 36/54
3. Fred Bruney, Ohio State, DB, 0/77
3. Gene Donaldson, Kentucky, G, 11/11
4. Dick Tamburo, Michigan State, C, 0/0
5. Bob Van Doren, USC, DE, 0/10
6. Don Steinbrunner, Washington State, T, 8/8
7. Gene Filipski, Villanova, HB, 0/24
8. Carlton Massey, Texas, DE, 35/49
9. Bob McNamara, Minnesota, DB, 0/28
10. Elmo Natali, California (PA), B, 0/0
11. Dick Hilinski, Ohio State, T, 0/0
12. Elmer Willhoite, Southern California, G, 0/0
13. **Galen Fiss, Kansas, LB, 139/139**
14. Gern Nagler, Santa Clara, E, 25/91
15. John Carson, Georgia, E, 0/71
20. **Chuck Noll, Dayton, LB, 77/77**

DETROIT LIONS

1. **Harley Sewell, Texas, G, 120/122**
2. Gene Gedman, Indiana, HB, 45/45
4. **Charlie Ane, USC, T, 83/83**
6. **Ollie Spencer, Kansas, T, 61/99**
7. **Joe Schmidt, Pittsburgh, LB, 155/155**
8. Lew Carpenter, Arkansas, HB, 35/123
9. Carlton McCormick, Texas Christian, C, 0/0
10. Dreher Gaskin, Clemson, E, 0/0
11. Elmer Messenger, Washington State, G, 0/0
12. Larry Spencer, Wake Forest, B, 0/0
13. Bob Thomas, Washington & Lee, E, 0/0
14. Jack Barger, New Mexico, T, 0/0
15. Ted Topor, Michigan, LB, 6/6
18. Ed Mioduszewski, William & Mary, QB, 0/12
19. Paul Held, San Jose State, QB, 0/10
22. Pete Retzlaff, South Dakota State, E, 0/132
23. **Carl Karilivacz, Syracuse, DB, 58/85**
25. Marv Brown, Texas A&M-Commerce, HB, 4/4

GREEN BAY PACKERS

1. **Al Carmichael, USC, HB, 68/84**
2. Gil Reich, Army/Kansas, B, 0/0
3. **Bill Forester, SMU, LB, 138/138**
4. Gib Dawson, Texas, HB, 7/7
5. Roger Zatkoff, Michigan, LB, 48/72
6. Bob Kennedy, Wisconsin, G, 0/0
7. **Jim Ringo, Syracuse, C, 131/187**
8. Lauren Hargrove, Georgia, B, 0/0
9. Floyd Harrawood, Tulsa, T, 0/0
10. Vic Rimkus, Holy Cross, G, 0/0
11. **Joe Johnson, Boston College, HB, 53/66**
12. Dick Curran, Arizona State, B, 0/0
13. Bob Orders, Army/West Virginia, C, 0/0
14. Charley Wrenn, Texas Christian, T, 0/0
15. Gene Helwig, Tulsa, B, 0/0
30. Al Barry, USC, G, 24/53

LOS ANGELES RAMS

1. Ed Barker, Washington State, E, 0/18
1. Donn Moomaw, UCLA, C, 0/0
2. Rudy Bukich, USC, QB, 11/103
3. **Bob Fry, Kentucky, T, 60/126**
4. Willie Roberts, Tulsa, E, 0/0
5. Tom Scott, Virginia, DE, 0/150
6. Paul Miller, LSU, DE, 48/78
6. Howie Waugh, Tulsa, B, 0/0
7. Bobby Reynolds, Nebraska, B, 0/0
8. Bob Morgan, Maryland, DT, 0/10
9. Brad Myers, Bucknell, B, 17/26
10. Mick Lakos, Vanderbilt, B, 0/0
11. Jim Bailey, Miami (OH), B, 0/0
12. Chuck Doud, UCLA, G, 0/0
13. Andy Matto, Cincinnati, T, 0/0
14. Frank James, Houston, G, 0/0
15. Tom Carroll, Oklahoma, B, 0/0
17. Harland Svare, Washington State, LB, 20/89
19. Jack Ellena, UCLA, G, 21/21

NEW YORK GIANTS

1. Bobby Marlow, Alabama, B, 0/0
2. Eddie Crowder, Oklahoma, QB, 0/0
3. Cal Roberts, Gustavus Adolphus, T, 0/0
4. Everett Douglas, Florida, T, 10/10
5. Buford Long, Florida, DB, 26/26
6. Bob Peviani, USC, LB, 12/12
7. Don Branby, Colorado, E, 0/0
8. Don Beck, Army/Notre Dame, B, 0/0
9. Jim Gray, Panola J.C., B, 0/0
10. Darrow Cooper, Texas A&M, E, 0/0
10. Charlie Maloy, Holy Cross, QB, 0/0
11. Jim Ruehl, Ohio State, C, 0/0
12. Joe Matesic, Arizona State, T, 0/1
13. Jack McShulski, Army/Kansas State, E, 0/0
14. J.L. Hall, Florida, B, 0/0
15. Dick Bowman, Oklahoma, G, 0/0
27. **Rosey Brown, Morgan State, T, 162/162**
28. Joe Ramona, Santa Clara, G, 8/8

PHILADELPHIA EAGLES

2. Al Conway, Army/William Jewell, B, 0/0
3. Don Johnson, California, HB, 20/20
4. George Mrkonic, Kansas, T, 10/10
5. Eddie Bell, Pennsylvania, DB, 48/62
5. Rex Smith, Illinois, E, 0/0
7. Jack Erickson, Army/Beloit, T, 0/0
7. Ray Malavasi, Army/Mississippi, G, 0/0
8. **Jess Richardson, Alabama, DT, 97/139**
9. Roger French, Minnesota, E, 0/0
10. **Tom Brookshier, Colorado, DB, 76/76**
11. Bob Pollard, Penn State, B, 0/0
12. George Porter, San Jose State, T, 0/0
13. Ray Westort, Utah, G, 0/0
14. Roy Bailey, Tulane, B, 0/0
15. Willie Irvin, Florida A&M, DE, 3/3
25. John Michels, Tennessee, G, 11/11

PITTSBURGH STEELERS

1. Ted Marchibroda, Detroit Mercy, QB, 23/30
2. **John Henry Johnson, Arizona State, FB, 67/143**
3. Marv Matuszak, Tulsa, LB, 25/123
4. Lloyd Colteryahn, Maryland, E, 0/27
5. Bob Gaona, Wake Forest, T, 48/60
6. Tom Barton, Clemson, G, 0/0
7. John Alderton, Maryland, DE, 10/10
8. Lowell Perry, Michigan, E, 6/6
9. Pat Sarnese, Temple, T, 0/0
10. Frank Holohan, Tennessee, T, 0/0
12. Jerry Robertson, Kansas, B, 0/0
13. Leo Davis, Bradley, E, 0/0
14. Charley Montgomery, Mississippi, T, 0/0
15. Bob O'Neil, Notre Dame, G, 24/38

26. Jack McClairen, Bethune-Cookman, E, 45/45
30. Lou Tepe, Duke, C, 34/34

SAN FRANCISCO 49ERS

B1. Harry Babcock, Georgia, E, 30/30
1. Tom Stolhandske, Texas, LB, 12/12
2. George Morris, Georgia Tech, C, 12/12
3. **Bob St. Clair, Tulsa, T, 119/119**
4. Ed Fullerton, Maryland, DB, 0/1
5. Hal Miller, Georgia Tech, T, 12/12
7. Paul Carr, Houston, DB, 30/30
8. Doug Hogland, Oregon State, G, 36/72
9. Hal Ledyard, Tennessee-Chattanooga, QB, 10/10
10. Pete Brown, Georgia Tech, C, 24/24
11. Al Charlton, Washington State, B, 0/0
12. Carson (Red) Leach, Duke, G, 0/0
13. Bill Earley, Washington, B, 0/0
14. Tom Fletcher, Arizona State, B, 0/0
15. Charley Genthner, Texas, T, 0/0
21. Ken Bahnsen, North Texas, FB, 7/7

WASHINGTON REDSKINS

1. Jack Scarbath, Maryland, QB, 22/29
2. Dick Modzelewski, Maryland, DT, 24/180
3. Paul Dekker, Michigan State, E, 11/11
4. **Don Boll, Nebraska, T, 81/92**
5. Nick Carras, Missouri, B, 0/0
8. Lew Weidensaul, Maryland, E, 0/0
11. Alex Webster, North Carolina State, HB, 0/109
12. Buzz Nutter, Virginia Tech, C, 0/153
14. Ed Timmerman, Michigan State, B, 0/0
15. Dave Suminski, Wisconsin, G, 2/8

1954 NFL

BALTIMORE COLTS

1. Cotton Davidson, Baylor, QB, 24/111
2. Larry Grigg, Oklahoma, B, 0/0
5. Don Ellis, Texas A&M, B, 0/0
7. Glenn Turner, Georgia Tech, B, 0/0
8. Dennis McCotter, Detroit, G, 0/0
9. Bob Adams, Shippensburg, G, 0/0
10. Bob Schoonmaker, Missouri, B, 0/0
11. Bob Leberman, Syracuse, DB, 12/12
12. Donald Chelf, Iowa, T, 0/28
13. Chuck McMillan, John Carroll, DB, 6/6
14. **Ordell Braase, South Dakota, DE, 157/157**
15. Joe D'Agostino, Florida, G, 0/0
16. **Alex Sandusky, Clarion, G, 166/166**
20. **Raymond Berry, SMU, E, 154/154**

CHICAGO BEARS

1. Stan Wallace, Illinois, DB, 37/37
2. **Rick Casares, Florida, FB, 121/130**
3. Ed Meadows, Duke, DE, 36/65
4. Fran Paterra, Notre Dame, B, 0/0
5. Bob Griffis, Furman, G, 0/0
6. John Hudson, Rice, G, 0/0
7. Ralph Cecere, Villanova, B, 0/0
8. Tom Garlington, Arkansas, T, 0/0
9. Paul Giel, Minnesota, B, 0/0
10. D.C. Andrews, Hardin-Simmons, E, 0/0
11. Ron Wallin, Minnesota, B, 0/0
12. Joe Faragalli, Villanova, G, 0/0
13. Julius Seaholm, Texas, G, 0/0
14. Ken Miller, Illinois, B, 0/0
15. **Harlon Hill, North Alabama, E, 89/103**
18. McNeil Moore, Sam Houston State, DB, 35/35
20. Jim Ladd, Bowling Green State, E, 0/11
22. Charlie Sumner, William & Mary, DB, 46/73
23. **Herman Lee, Florida A&M, T, 119/127**
30. Jim Haluska, Wisconsin, QB, 5/5

CHICAGO CARDINALS

1. **Lamar McHan, Arkansas, QB, 60/113**
2. Gary Knafelc, Colorado, E, 1/101
3. Bobby Cavazos, Texas Tech, B, 0/0
4. Bill Bredde, Oklahoma State, DB, 12/12
5. Don Dohoney, Michigan State, E, 0/0
6. Tom McHugh, Notre Dame, B, 0/0
7. Dave Mann, Oregon State, HB, 36/36
8. Paul Larson, California, QB, 5/6
9. Dean Chambers, Washington, T, 0/0
10. Tommy Lewis, Alabama, B, 0/0
11. Homer Smith, Princeton, B, 0/0
12. Howard Pitt, Duke, E, 0/0
13. Les Goble, Alfred, HB, 21/21
14. Sammy Dumas, Arkansas, G, 0/0
15. Cecil Harp, Pacific, E, 0/0
18. Dick Young, Tennessee-Chattanooga, FB, 0/34
22. Ledio Fanucchi, Fresno State, T, 12/12
23. Charley Oakley, LSU, DB, 1/1
30. Alex Burl, Colorado State, HB, 8/8

CLEVELAND BROWNS

1. John Bauer, Illinois, T, 0/2
B1. Bobby Garrett, Stanford, QB, 0/9
2. Chet Hanulak, Maryland, HB, 24/24
3. Maurice Bassett, Langston, FB, 36/36
4. Jerry Hilgenberg, Iowa, C, 0/0
5. Bill Lucky, Baylor, DT, 0/12
6. **Jim Ray Smith, Baylor, G, 81/93**
6. Asa Jenkins, Toledo, B, 0/0
7. Don Miller, SMU, HB, 0/3
8. Bill Barbish, Tennessee, B, 0/0
8. Charlie Harris, Georgia, B, 0/0
9. Tom Jones, Miami (OH), RB, 2/2
10. Donald Goss, SMU, T, 6/6
10. Tom Pagna, Miami (OH), B, 0/0
11. Max Schuebel, Rice, T, 0/0
12. Tom Bruenich, Maryland, T, 0/0
13. George Cummins, Tulane, T, 0/0
14. Jim Head, Iowa, B, 0/0
15. Chet Lyssy, Hardin-Simmons, B, 0/0
23. Bob Mischak, Army, G, 0/79

DETROIT LIONS

1. Dick Chapman, Rice, T, 0/0
2. Jim Neal, Michigan State, C, 0/0
3. Bill Bowman, William & Mary, FB, 18/23
4. Bill Stits, UCLA, DB, 36/92
4. Howard McCants, Washington State, E, 0/0
5. George Parozzo, William & Mary, T, 0/0
6. Dick Kercher, Tulsa, HB, 7/7
6. Pence Dacus, Southwest Texas State, B, 0/0
7. Jack Cross, Utah, B, 0/0
8. Milt Davis, UCLA, DB, 0/45
9. Bob Lawson, Cal Poly-SLO, B, 0/0
10. Jack Carroll, Holy Cross, E, 0/0
11. Milt Schwenk, Washington State, T, 0/0
12. Bob Hartman, Oregon State, T, 0/0
13. Jim Swierczek, Marshall, B, 0/0
14. Ray Novak, Nebraska, B, 0/0
15. Kirk Hinderlider, Colorado State, E, 0/0
22. Dewey Brundage, Brigham Young, DE, 0/11
25. Richie Woit, Arkansas State, DB, 1/1

GREEN BAY PACKERS

1. Art Hunter, Notre Dame, C, 12/119
1. Veryl Switzer, Kansas State, HB, 24/24
2. Bob Fleck, Syracuse, T, 0/0
3. George Timberlake, USC, LB, 6/6
4. Tommy Allman, West Virginia, B, 0/0
5. **Max McGee, Tulane, E, 148/148**
7. Sam Marshall, Florida A&M, T, 0/0
8. Jimmie Williams, Texas Tech, T, 0/0
9. Dave Davis, Georgia Tech, E, 0/0
10. Gene Knutson, Michigan, DE, 18/18
11. Ken Hall, North Texas State, E, 0/0
12. Bill Oliver, Alabama, B, 0/0
13. Mike Takacs, Ohio State, G, 0/0
14. Dave (Kosse) Johnson, Rice, B, 0/0
18. Emery Barnes, Oregon, DE, 2/2

LOS ANGELES RAMS

1. Ed Beatty, Mississippi, C, 0/80
2. Buddy Gillioz, Houston, T, 0/0
3. Jim Kincaid, South Carolina, DB, 0/2
3. Tom Nickoloff, Southern California, E, 0/0
3. Henry Hair, Georgia Tech, E, 0/0
4. Lester McClelland, Syracuse, T, 0/0
4. Norm Nygaard, San Diego State, B, 0/0
5. Art Hauser, Xavier (OH), DT, 48/76
5. Charlie Allen, San Jose State, T, 0/0
6. Ken Panfil, Purdue, T, 30/58
7. Charley Weeks, Southern California, T, 0/0
8. George Black, Washington, E, 0/0
9. Alex Bravo, Cal Poly-San Luis Obispo, DB, 15/43
10. Ed Hughes, Tulsa, DB, 23/53
10. Joe Katchik, Notre Dame, DT, 0/2
11. Duane Wardlow, Washington, DE, 21/21
12. Jack Maultsby, North Carolina, T, 0/0
13. Sam Hensley, Georgia Tech, E, 0/0
14. Mitchell Johnson, Bishop, B, 0/0
15. Ed Elliot, Richmond, B, 0/0
18. Stan Sheriff, Cal Poly-San Luis Obispo, LB, 0/24
20. Bob Dougherty, Kentucky, LB, 10/69
26. Glenn Holtzman, North Texas, T, 48/48

NEW YORK GIANTS

2. Ken Buck, Pacific, E, 0/0
3. Clyde Bennett, South Carolina, E, 0/0
4. **Dick Nolan, Maryland, DB, 76/99**
5. Earl Putman, Arizona State, C, 0/11
6. George Jacoby, Ohio State, T, 0/0
7. Wayne Berry, Washington State, HB, 10/10
8. Ralph Starkey, West Virginia, T, 0/0
9. Pete O'Garra, UCLA, E, 0/0
10. John Steinberg, Stanford, E, 0/0
11. Tom Fitzpatrick, Villanova, G, 0/0
12. Wendell Gulseth, Wisconsin, T, 0/0
13. Bob Topp, Michigan, E, 6/6
14. Bobby Epps, Pittsburgh, FB, 31/31
15. Jim Swan, Denver, G, 0/0
23. Pete Mangum, Mississippi, LB, 2/16
27. Bob Clatterbuck, Houston, QB, 16/18

PHILADELPHIA EAGLES

1. Neil Worden, Notre Dame, FB, 24/24
2. Rocky Ryan, Illinois, DB, 24/28
3. Ted Connor, Nebraska, T, 0/0
4. Menil Mavraides, Notre Dame, G, 24/24
6. Hal Lambert, Texas Christian, T, 0/0
7. **Jerry Norton, SMU, DB, 51/131**
8. Dan Hunter, Florida, T, 0/0
9. Phil Branch, Texas, G, 0/0
11. Dave McLaughlin, Dartmouth, E, 0/0
12. Dick Clasby, Harvard, B, 0/0
13. Joe Mehalick, Virginia, T, 0/0
14. Hal Patterson, Kansas, B, 0/0
15. Ray McKown, Texas Christian, B, 0/0

PITTSBURGH STEELERS

1. Johnny Lattner, Notre Dame, HB, 12/12
2. Pat Stark, Syracuse, B, 0/0
3. Tom Miner, Tulsa, K, 12/12
6. Laurin Pepper, Southern Mississippi, B, 0/0
7. Jack O'Brien, Florida, E, 31/31
8. Paul Cameron, UCLA, DB, 12/12
9. Joe Zombek, Pittsburgh, DE, 9/9
10. Bob Fisher, Tennessee, T, 0/0
11. Lou Cimarolli, Pittsburgh, B, 0/0
12. Don Fritz, Cincinnati, E, 0/0
13. Charley Lattimer, Maryland, C, 0/0
14. Roger Bradford, Waynesburg, E, 0/0
15. Tom Drake, Tennessee-Chattanooga, G, 0/0
27. Tom Yewcic, Michigan State, QB, 0/77

SAN FRANCISCO 49ERS

1. Bernie Faloney, Maryland, B, 0/0
2. Leo Rucka, Rice, LB, 5/5
3. Steve Korcheck, George Washington, C, 0/0
4. Charlie Boxold, Maryland, B, 0/0
5. Bob Hantla, Kansas, G, 24/24
5. Frank Mincevich, South Carolina, G, 0/0
6. Floyd Sagely, Arkansas, DB, 15/25
7. Sid Youngelman, Alabama, DT, 10/107
9. **Ted Connolly, Tulsa, G, 82/92**
11. John Skocko, Southern California, E, 0/0
12. Hal Easterwood, Mississippi State, C, 0/0
13. Morgan Williams, Texas Christian, G, 0/0
14. Sammy Williams, California, B, 0/0
15. Ed Gossage, Georgia Tech, T, 0/0

WASHINGTON REDSKINS

1. Steve Meilinger, Kentucky, E, 24/52
2. **Jim Schrader, Notre Dame, C, 76/116**
4. **Ralph Felton, Maryland, LB, 75/93**
5. Billy Wells, Michigan State, HB, 20/54
6. Bill McHenry, Washington & Lee, C, 0/0
7. Harry Jagielski, Indiana, DT, 5/36
8. Bill Marker, West Virginia, E, 0/0
9. Jerry Minnick, Nebraska, T, 0/0
10. Merrill Green, Oklahoma, B, 0/0
11. Gene Wilson, South Carolina, B, 0/0
12. Ben Dunkerly, West Virginia, T, 0/0
13. Roger Dornburg, Wisconsin, B, 0/0
14. Roger Nelson, Oklahoma, T, 0/0
15. Hugh Merck, South Carolina, T, 0/0
18. Walt Cudzik, Purdue, C, 1/71
20. Sam Morley, Stanford, E, 1/1
24. Will Renfro, Memphis, DT, 34/60
25. George Rosso, Ohio State, DB, 12/12
28. Ron Hansen, Minnesota, G, 12/12

1955 NFL

BALTIMORE COLTS

1. **Alan Ameche, Wisconsin, FB, 70/70**
B1. George Shaw, Oregon, QB, 36/71
2. **Dick Szymanski, Notre Dame, C, 157/157**
3. L.G. Dupre, Baylor, HB, 48/69
4. Jack Patera, Oregon, LB, 36/61
5. **George Preas, Virginia Tech, T, 140/140**
6. Leo Lewis, Lincoln (MO), B, 0/0
7. Frank McDonald, Miami (FL), E, 0/0
8. Dale Meinert, Oklahoma State, LB, 0/125
9. Walter Bryan, Texas Tech, DB, 10/10
9. Bill Evans, Miami (OH), G, 0/0
11. Emil Radik, Nebraska-Omaha, B, 0/0
12. Dick Chorovich, Miami (OH), DT, 14/28
13. Pat Abbruzzi, Rhode Island, B, 0/0
14. John Lee, Georgia Tech, B, 0/0
15. Jerry Peterson, Texas, DT, 1/1
18. Charlie Shepard, North Texas, HB, 0/12
28. Bob Myers, Ohio State, DT, 1/1

CHICAGO BEARS

1. Ron Drzewiecki, Marquette, HB, 20/20
2. Bobby Watkins, Ohio State, HB, 33/38
4. Joe O'Malley, Georgia, DE, 0/22
5. Leland Kendall, Oklahoma State, T, 0/0
6. Henry Mosley, Morris Brown, HB, 1/1
6. Dan Shannon, Notre Dame, E, 0/0
7. Bruce Sturgess, William & Mary, B, 0/0
8. Gene Verkerk, North Texas State, T, 0/0
9. Jim Lavery, Scranton, B, 0/0
10. John Allen, Arizona State, E, 0/0
11. Tom Redfield, Delaware, E, 0/0
12. Clarence Bratt, Wisconsin, B, 0/0
13. Norm Cash, Sul Ross, B, 0/0
14. Ed Nickla, Maryland, T, 12/12
15. J.D. Smith, North Carolina A&T, FB, 6/131
24. Joe Young, Arizona, DE, 0/20
26. Perry Jeter, Cal Poly-San Luis Obispo, HB, 16/16
29. Dick Klein, Iowa, T, 24/85

CHICAGO CARDINALS

1. Max Boydston, Oklahoma, E, 43/82
2. Lindon Crow, USC, DB, 36/123
3. **Mal Hammack, Florida, FB, 128/128**
3. Tony Pasquesi, Notre Dame, DT, 29/29
4. Frank Bernardi, Colorado, DB, 35/41
5. Mario De Ra, Southern California, T, 0/0
6. Jack Bowersox, Maryland, G, 0/0
7. Dave Leggett, Ohio State, QB, 4/4
8. Sam Irvine, Maryland, C, 0/0
9. Charlie McGinty, North Texas State, E, 0/0
10. Frank Scaffidi, Marquette, T, 0/0
11. Tom Pepsin, Miami (FL), E, 0/0
12. Dale Sandstrom, Concordia (MN), B, 0/0
13. Tom McLuckie, Maryland, G, 0/0
14. Gordy Brown, Louisiana Tech, E, 0/0
15. Dick Brubaker, Ohio State, E, 13/22

CLEVELAND BROWNS

1. Kurt Burris, Oklahoma, C, 0/0
2. Dean Renfro, North Texas, HB, 0/7
3. Bobby Freeman, Auburn, DB, 21/73
3. John Hall, Iowa, DE, 0/2
4. Sam Palumbo, Notre Dame, LB, 21/31
4. Paul Reynolds, Notre Dame, B, 0/0
5. Aramis Dandoy, Southern California, B, 0/0
6. Leroy Bolden, Michigan State, HB, 23/23
7. Jack Locklear, Auburn, C, 0/0
9. Henry Ford, Pittsburgh, HB, 2/14
10. Glen Dillon, Pittsburgh, E, 0/0
11. Eric Knebel, Southern Methodist, T, 0/0
12. Jack Eaton, New Mexico, T, 0/0
13. John Borton, Ohio State, QB, 5/5
14. Fred Robinson, Washington, G, 12/12
15. Bob Smith, Nebraska, HB, 12/16
23. Jim Greer, Elizabeth City State, E, 0/14

DETROIT LIONS

1. **Dave Middleton, Auburn, E, 63/75**
2. Jim Salsbury, UCLA, G, 23/47
3. **Darris McCord, Tennessee, DE, 168/168**
4. Lee Riley, Detroit Mercy, DB, 12/83
4. Gordon Malloy, Miami (FL), B, 0/0
5. Bud Brooks, Arkansas, G, 1/1
6. Elijah Childers, Prairie View A&M, T, 0/0
7. Bert Zagers, Michigan State, DB, 0/32
8. Leon Cunningham, South Carolina, LB, 8/8
8. Bill Walker, Maryland, E, 0/0
8. Lamoine Holland, Rice, E, 0/0
9. Walt Jenkins, Wayne State (MI), DE, 2/2
10. Tom Gastall, Boston, B, 0/0
11. Herb McDermott, Iowa State, T, 0/0
12. Dick Goist, Cincinnati, B, 0/0
13. Don Henderson, Utah, T, 0/0
14. Jerry Gajda, St. Benedict's (KS), B, 0/0
15. George Atkins, Auburn, G, 12/12

GREEN BAY PACKERS

1. **Tom Bettis, Purdue, LB, 84/109**
2. Jim Temp, Wisconsin, DE, 43/43
3. Buddy Leake, Oklahoma, B, 0/0
5. Hank Bullough, Michigan State, G, 20/20
6. Norm Amundsen, Wisconsin, G, 12/12
7. Bob Clemens, Georgia, FB, 2/2
8. Johnny Crouch, Texas Christian, E, 0/0
9. Ed Culpepper, Alabama, DT, 0/74
10. George Rogers, Auburn, T, 0/0
11. Ron Clark, Nebraska, B, 0/0
12. Art Walker, Michigan, T, 0/0
13. Ed Adams, South Carolina, B, 0/0
14. Fred Baer, Michigan, B, 0/0
15. George Machoukas, Toledo, C, 0/0
16. Charlie Brackins, Prairie View A&M, QB, 7/7
18. Doyle Nix, SMU, DB, 12/54

25. **Nate Borden, Indiana, DE, 57/92**
26. Jim Jennings, Missouri, DE, 4/4

LOS ANGELES RAMS

1. Larry Morris, Georgia Tech, LB, 25/124
2. Sid Fournet, LSU, G, 24/82
2. Bob Long, UCLA, LB, 23/89
2. Corky Taylor, Kansas State, DB, 12/12
2. Ron Waller, Maryland, HB, 42/44
4. Tom Feamster, Florida State, T, 0/12
4. Ed Fouch, Southern California, T, 0/0
5. Edward Kelley, Texas, DB, 0/14
6. Corky Tharp, Alabama, DB, 0/9
7. Frank Clayton, Southern California, B, 0/0
8. Billy Teas, Georgia Tech, B, 0/0
9. John Witte, Oregon State, T, 0/0
10. Jesse Arnelle, Penn State, E, 0/0
10. Claude Harland, Texas Tech, E, 0/0
11. Joe Ray, UCLA, T, 0/0
12. Jim Hanifan, California, E, 0/0
13. Dave Parkinson, Texas, B, 0/0
14. George Elliot, Northeastern Oklahoma, B, 0/0
15. Bob Hoerning, St. Norbert, B, 0/0
17. Gene Mitcham, Arizona State, E, 0/2

NEW YORK GIANTS

1. Joe Heap, Notre Dame, HB, 12/12
3. **Rosey Grier, Penn State, DT, 85/141**
5. **Mel Triplett, Toledo, FB, 69/97**
6. Ron Locklin, Wisconsin, E, 0/0
8. **Jimmy Patton, Mississippi, DB, 153/153**
10. Lea Paslay, Mississippi, B, 0/0
11. Bill Hillen, West Virginia, E, 0/0
12. Hank Burnine, Missouri, E, 3/17
13. John Damore, Northwestern, C, 0/12
14. Elwood Kettler, Texas A&M, B, 0/0
15. Ed Stowers, Wake Forest, E, 0/0
26. Abe Cohen, Tennessee-Chattanooga, G, 0/14
28. Al Crow, William & Mary, DT, 0/3

PHILADELPHIA EAGLES

1. **Dick Bielski, Maryland, E, 60/114**
2. Buck Lansford, Texas, G, 34/61
3. Frank Eidom, Southern Methodist, B, 0/0
4. Dean Dugger, Ohio State, E, 0/0
5. Gene Lamone, West Virginia, G, 0/0
6. Billy Quinn, Texas, B, 0/0
7. Bill McKenna, Brandeis, E, 0/0
8. Herman Watson, Vanderbilt, T, 0/0
9. Von Morgan, Abilene Christian, E, 0/0
10. Talmadge (Duke) Washington, Washington State, B, 0/0
11. Bob Hardy, Kentucky, B, 0/0
12. Andy Nacrelli, Fordham, E, 2/2
13. Jerry Krisher, Ohio State, C, 0/0
14. Tommy Bell, Army, B, 0/0
15. Don Brougher, Maryland, C, 0/0

PITTSBURGH STEELERS

1. **Frank Varrichione, Notre Dame, T, 72/133**
3. Ed Bernet, SMU, E, 12/21
4. Fred Broussard, Northwestern State (LA), C, 6/8
5. George Mason, Alabama, T, 0/0
6. Lem Harkey, College of Emporia, FB, 0/4
7. Hal Reeve, Oregon, T, 0/0
9. Johnny Unitas, Louisville, QB, 0/211
10. Terry Boyle, Cincinnati, T, 0/0
11. Vic Eaton, Missouri, QB, 12/12
12. Jim Cooke, Lincoln (PA), E, 0/0
13. Jim Whitmer, Purdue, B, 0/0
14. John (Buck) Byrne, John Carroll, G, 0/0
15. Ellis Duckett, Michigan State, B, 0/0
22. Richie McCabe, Pittsburgh, DB, 19/52
23. Gordy Holz, Minnesota, DT, 0/70

SAN FRANCISCO 49ERS

1. Dicky Moegle, Rice, DB, 47/73
2. **Frank Morze, Boston College, C, 68/84**
3. Carroll Hardy, Colorado, HB, 10/10
4. **Matt Hazeltine, California, LB, 176/190**
5. Eldred Kraemer, Pittsburgh, G, 12/12
6. Bobby Luna, Alabama, DB, 12/24
7. Johnny Dean, Virginia Tech, B, 0/0
8. Freddie Meyers, Oklahoma State, B, 0/0
9. Fred Preziosio, Purdue, T, 0/0
10. Ron Ashbacker, Oregon State, E, 0/0
11. Rudy Rotella, Nebraska-Omaha, E, 0/0
12. Lou Palatella, Pittsburgh, G, 43/43
13. Richie Gaskell, George Washington, E, 0/0
14. Nick McKeithan, Duke, B, 0/0
15. Burdette Hess, Idaho, G, 0/0
21. George Maderos, Cal State-Chico, DB, 20/20

WASHINGTON REDSKINS

1. Ralph Guglielmi, Notre Dame, QB, 37/66
3. Ray Perkins, Syracuse, B, 0/0
5. Don Glantz, Nebraska, T, 0/0
7. Erik Christensen, Richmond, DE, 2/2
7. Ron Marciniak, Kansas State, G, 12/12
8. Johnny Allen, Purdue, C, 48/48
9. Johnny Miller, Boston College, T, 36/41
10. Tom Louderback, San Jose State, LB, 0/54
11. Larry Parker, North Carolina, B, 0/0
12. John Barish, Waynesburg, T, 0/0
13. Len Oniskey, Cornell, T, 0/0
14. Tom Braatz, Marquette, LB, 25/38
15. Charley Horton, Vanderbilt, B, 0/0
16. Hal Norris, California, LB, 13/13
19. Bob Dee, Holy Cross, DE, 22/134
26. Walt Houston, Purdue, G, 10/10

1956 NFL

BALTIMORE COLTS

1. **Lenny Moore, Penn State, HB, 143/143**
2. Dick Donlin, Hamline, E, 0/0
3. Bob Pascal, Duke, B, 0/0
4. Ben Inabinet, Clemson, T, 0/0
5. Herb Gray, Texas, E, 0/0
6. Don Schmidt, Texas Tech, B, 0/0
7. Bill Waters, Austin, T, 0/0
8. Bill Koman, North Carolina, LB, 12/156
9. John Lewis, Michigan State, E, 0/0
10. Gene Scott, Centre, B, 0/0
11. Dennis Shaw, North Texas State, E, 0/0
12. **Steve Myhra, North Dakota, G, 62/62**
13. Jack Hill, Utah State, WR, 0/14
14. Ted Schwanger, Tennessee Tech, B, 0/0
15. John Polzer, Virginia, QB, 0/0
17. Bill Danenhauer, Emporia State, DE, 0/7
21. Jim Harness, Mississippi State, DB, 1/1

CHICAGO BEARS

1. Menan (Tex) Schriewer, Texas, E, 0/0
2. M.L. Brackett, Auburn, DE, 20/32
4. **John Mellekas, Arizona, C, 62/84**
5. **Willie Galimore, Florida A&M, HB, 82/82**
7. **J.C. Caroline, Illinois, DB, 118/118**
8. Dick Klawitter, South Dakota State, C, 5/5
9. Ken Vargo, Ohio State, C, 0/0
10. Dick Lucas, Boston College, E, 0/42
11. John Jankans, Arizona State, E, 0/0
12. Buddy Cruze, Tennessee, E, 0/0
13. Dick Grogg, Minnesota, G, 0/0
14. Milt Graham, Colgate, T, 0/28
15. Dick Fitzgerald, Notre Dame, B, 0/0
24. Jesse Castete, McNeese State, DB, 8/22

CHICAGO CARDINALS

1. **Joe Childress, Auburn, HB, 96/96**
2. Norm Masters, Michigan State, T, 0/104
3. John Roach, SMU, QB, 32/64
4. Sam Salerno, Coloraoo, T, 0/0
6. John Dittrich, Wisconsin, G, 12/47
6. Charlie Dupre, Baylor, DB, 0/14
7. Bob Konovsky, Wisconsin, G, 36/49
8. Dave Lunceford, Baylor, T, 12/12
9. Bob Lovely, Tampa, T, 0/0
10. Willis Towne, Wichita State, E, 0/0
11. Fob James, Auburn, B, 0/0
12. Jerry Walker, Texas Tech, T, 0/0
13. Bo Bolinger, Oklahoma, G, 0/0
14. Carnell Neuman, Illinois, B, 0/0
15. Charlie Anderson, Louisiana Tech, E, 2/2
15. Tom Spiers, Arkansas State, QB, 0/0
24. Orville Trask, Rice, DT, 0/35

CLEVELAND BROWNS

1. Preston Carpenter, Arkansas, E, 48/149
2. Billy Kinard, Mississippi, DB, 7/45
3. Bill Quinlan, Michigan State, DE, 22/111
3. Larry Ross, Denver, E, 0/0
4. Bobby Moss, West Virginia, B, 0/0
5. Frank Clarke, Colorado, E, 36/140
6. Sherman Plunkett, Maryland-Eastern Shore, T, 0/132
6. **Paul Wiggin, Stanford, DE, 146/146**
7. Chuck Griffith, Southern California, E, 0/0
8. Len Hellyer, Marshall, B, 0/0
9. Jack Hecker, Bowling Green, E, 0/0
10. Eddie Rayburn, Rice, T, 0/0
11. Bill Underdonk, West Virginia, T, 0/0
12. Harry Javernick, Colorado, T, 0/0
13. Jim Furey, Kansas State, LB, 0/9
14. Charlie Sidwell, William & Mary, B, 0/0
15. Willie Davis, Grambling State, DE, 24/162
16. Thurlow Cooper, Maine, TE, 0/41

DETROIT LIONS

1. **Howard Cassady, Ohio State, HB, 74/84**
3. Don McIlhenny, SMU, HB, 9/64
4. Jerry Reichow, Iowa, E, 29/95
5. Tom Tracy, Tennessee, HB, 13/89
6. Bob Lusk, William & Mary, C, 5/5
7. Gene Cronin, Pacific, DE, 48/87
8. Jack Powell, Texas A&M, T, 0/0
9. Calvin Jones, Iowa, G, 0/0
10. Joe Silas, South Carolina, DE, 0/0
11. Lew Wacker, Richmond, B, 0/0
11. Tom Selep, Maryland, B, 0/0
12. R.B. Nunnery, LSU, T, 0/6
13. O.K. Ferguson, Louisiana State, B, 0/0
14. Ronnie Falls, Duke, LB, 0/0
15. Horace (Buzzy) Allert, Southwest Texas State, DE, 0/0

GREEN BAY PACKERS

1. Jack Losch, Miami (FL), HB, 12/12
2. **Forrest Gregg, SMU, T, 187/193**
4. Cecil Morris, Oklahoma, G, 0/0
5. **Bob Skoronski, Indiana, T, 146/146**
6. Bob Burris, Oklahoma, B, 0/0
7. **Hank Gremminger, Baylor, DB, 123/131**
8. Russ Dennis, Maryland, E, 0/0
9. Gordy Duvall, Southern California, B, 0/0
10. Bob Laugherty, Maryland, B, 0/0
11. Mike Hudock, Miami (FL), C, 0/96
12. Max Burnett, Arizona, B, 0/0
13. Jim Mense, Notre Dame, C, 0/0
14. Charlie Thomas, Wisconsin, B, 0/0
15. Buddy Alliston, Mississippi, LB, 0/11
17. **Bart Starr, Alabama, QB, 196/196**

LOS ANGELES RAMS

1. **Joe Marconi, West Virginia, FB, 71/135**
1. Charlie Horton, Vanderbilt, B, 0/0
2. Leon Clarke, USC, E, 43/79
2. Hugh Pitts, TCU, LB, 9/21
3. A.D. Williams, Pacific, E, 0/37
3. John Marshall, Southern Methodist, B, 0/0
4. Will Berzinski, Wisconsin-LaCrosse, HB, 0/4
4. Jim Carmichael, California, E, 0/0
5. Jesse Whittenton, Texas-El Paso, DB, 24/112
5. Jim Freeman, Iowa, E, 0/0
5. Herb Nakken, Utah, B, 0/0
6. Eddie Vincent, Iowa, B, 0/0
7. Jack Morris, Oregon, DB, 27/45
8. George Boyer, Florida State, LB, 0/0
9. Maury Woolford, Louisville, T, 0/0
10. Charlie Sticka, Trinity (CT), B, 0/0
11. Jim Decker, UCLA, B, 0/0
12. Em Lindbeck, Illinois, QB, 0/0
13. Mike Norcia, Kent State, B, 0/0
14. Tommy Runnels, North Texas, HB, 0/21
15. Dick Shatto, Kentucky, B, 0/0
18. Jack Klotz, Widener, T, 0/55
24. Sam Williams, Michigan State, DE, 12/119
28. John Morrow, Michigan, C, 35/125

NEW YORK GIANTS

2. Henry Moore, Arkansas, DB, 5/16
3. **Sam Huff, West Virginia, LB, 102/168**
4. **Jim Katcavage, Dayton, DE, 165/165**
5. **Don Chandler, Florida, FB, 112/154**
6. Fred Cason, Florida, B, 0/0
7. Ron Nery, Kansas State, DE, 0/50
8. Don Holleder, Army, E, 0/0
9. Ken Braden, East Texas State, C, 0/0
10. Johnny Hermann, UCLA, DB, 2/10
11. Dick Moloney, Kentucky, B, 0/0
13. Ed Crawford, Mississippi, DB, 12/12
14. John McMullan, Notre Dame, G, 0/28
15. Ron Melnik, Army, T, 0/0
20. Mike Falls, Minnesota, G, 0/25
21. Don McComb, Villanova, DE, 0/1
24. Jerry Huth, Wake Forest, G, 11/74

PHILADELPHIA EAGLES

1. **Bob Pellegrini, Maryland, LB, 59/107**
2. Frank D'Agostino, Auburn, G, 12/14
3. Don Schaefer, Notre Dame, FB, 12/12
5. Fuzzy Thurston, Valparaiso, G, 0/116
6. Tirrel Burton, Miami (OH), B, 0/0
7. John Waedekin, Hardin-Simmons, T, 0/0
8. Elroy Payne, McMurry, B, 0/0
9. John Bredice, Boston University, E, 12/12
10. Tom Dimmick, Houston, C, 12/25
11. Ken Keller, North Carolina, HB, 23/23
12. Tommy Harkins, Vanderbilt, E, 0/0
13. James Sides, Texas Tech, B, 0/0
14. Frank Reich, Penn State, C, 0/0
15. Don Brant, Montana, B, 0/0

PITTSBURGH STEELERS

1. Art Davis, Mississippi State, DB, 9/9
B1. Gary Glick, Colorado State, DB, 34/71
2. **Joe Krupa, Purdue, DT, 110/110**
3. Jim Taylor, Baylor, C, 12/29
4. Dick Murley, Purdue, T, 2/7
5. Bill Murakowski, Purdue, B, 0/0
6. Ray Taylor, Texas Christian, B, 0/0
7. Dick Gaspari, George Washington, C, 0/0
8. Vere Wellman, Wichita State, G, 0/0
9. Wayne Edmonds, Notre Dame, G, 0/0
10. Lou Baldacci, Michigan, HB, 10/10
10. Bob Nolan, Miami (FL), E, 0/0
12. Phil Tarasovic, Yale, E, 0/0
13. Weldon Holley, Baylor, B, 0/0
14. Jim Emmons, Alabama, T, 0/0
20. Fred Glatz, Pittsburgh, E, 4/4

SAN FRANCISCO 49ERS

1. Earl Morrall, Michigan State, QB, 12/255
2. **Bruce Bosley, West Virginia, C, 163/175**
3. Bill Herchman, Texas Tech, DT, 48/85
4. Frank Pajaczkowski, Richmond, B, 0/0
6. Tony Sardisco, Tulane, G, 3/50
7. Larry Barnes, Colorado State, FB, 10/24
8. Charlie Smith, Abilene Christian, DE, 12/12
9. Jim Cox, Cal Poly-SLO, E, 0/0
10. Jerry Zaleski, Colorado State, B, 0/0
11. Stew Pell, North Carolina, T, 0/0
12. Roger Swedberg, Iowa, T, 0/0
13. Ralph Moody, Kansas, B, 0/0
14. **R.C. Owens, College of Idaho, HB, 62/90**
15. Reed Henderson, Utah State, T, 0/0
15. Gene Boyd, Abilene Christian, B, 0/0
18. Bill Yelverton, Mississippi, DE, 0/10
21. L.C. Joyner, Contra Costa JC, HB, 0/2
25. Paul Goad, Abilene Christian, FB, 4/4
26. Rommie Loudd, UCLA, LB, 0/41

WASHINGTON REDSKINS

1. Ed Vereb, Maryland, HB, 9/9
2. **John Paluck, Pittsburgh, DE, 105/105**
3. Fred Wyant, West Virginia, QB, 10/10
4. Fran Machinsky, Ohio State, T, 0/0
5. Gary Lowe, Michigan State, DB, 12/97
7. Donnie Caraway, Houston, B, 0/0
8. **Dick James, Oregon, HB, 99/117**
9. Francis (Whitey) Rouviere, Miami (FL), B, 0/0
11. Tom Powell, Colgate, G, 0/0
12. Jerry Planutis, Michigan State, HB, 3/3
12. Gil Moreno, UCLA, T, 0/0
13. Jerry Ward, Dayton, G, 0/0
14. Pat Uebel, Army, B, 0/0
17. Eagle Day, Mississippi, QB, 16/16
19. **Ray Lemek, Notre Dame, T, 61/117**

1957 NFL

BALTIMORE COLTS

1. **Jim Parker, Ohio State, T, 135/135**
2. **Don Shinnick, UCLA, LB, 159/159**
3. Luke Owens, Kent State, DE, 11/115
4. Jackie Simpson, Florida, B, 0/0
5. Ronnie Underwood, Arkansas, B, 0/0
6. Billy Pricer, Oklahoma, FB, 48/54
7. Reuben Saage, Baylor, B, 0/0
8. Jack Harmon, Eastern Oregon, E, 0/0
9. Bob White, Otterbein, T, 0/0
10. Joe Grisham, Austin Peay, E, 0/0
11. **Andy Nelson, Memphis, DB, 89/103**
12. Don Simonic, Tennessee Tech, T, 0/0
13. Jack Call, Colgate, HB, 24/28
14. Joe Guido, Youngstown State, B, 0/0
15. Hall Whitley, Texas A&M-Kingsville, LB, 0/4
16. Joe Cannavino, Ohio State, DB, 0/32
20. Walt Livingston, Heidelberg, HB, 0/3

CHICAGO BEARS

1. **Earl Leggett, LSU, DT, 102/132**
2. Jim Swink, TCU, HB, 0/5
3. Ronnie Knox, UCLA, QB, 1/1
4. Jack Johnson, Miami (FL), DB, 29/45
5. Vic Zucco, Michigan State, DB, 38/38
6. Bo Dickinson, Southern Mississippi, FB, 0/60
7. Jerry DeLucca, Middle Tennessee State, T, 0/59
8. **Bob Kilcullen, Texas Tech, DT, 104/104**
8. Al Ward, Yale, B, 0/0
9. Bill Brown, Syracuse, LB, 0/14
10. Bill Murphy, Fresno State, E, 0/0
11. Roger Hampton, McNeese State, B, 0/0
12. Larry Sorenson, Utah State, T, 0/0
13. Don Williams, Texas Tech, B, 0/0
14. Bob Schmidt, Memphis State, B, 0/0
15. Tony Hosek, West Virginia, E, 0/0
20. Al Frazier, Florida A&M, FL, 0/31
25. Joe Ryan, Villanova, DE, 0/4

CHICAGO CARDINALS

1. Jerry Tubbs, Oklahoma, LB, 18/119
2. Tom Maentz, Michigan, E, 0/0
3. Bill Hudson, Clemson, DT, 0/32
5. Wayne Bock, Illinois, DT, 4/4
9. Don McCumby, Washington, T, 0/0

10. Don Carothers, Bradley, E, 0/3
11. Bob Kraus, Kansas, G, 0/0
12. Bob Derrick, Oklahoma, B, 0/0
13. Ed Ritt, Montana State, T, 0/0
14. Bob Fee, Indiana, B, 0/0
15. Bill Livingston, Southern Methodist, C, 0/0
18. Hal Smith, UCLA, DT, 0/21

CLEVELAND BROWNS

1. **Jim Brown, Syracuse, FB, 118/118**
2. **Milt Plum, Penn State, QB, 59/129**
3. George Walker, Arkansas, B, 0/0
4. Paul Camera, Stanford, E, 0/0
5. Milt Campbell, Indiana, HB, 9/9
5. Henry Jordan, Virginia, DT, 24/163
6. Joe Amstutz, Indiana, C, 11/11
6. Harley Martin, California, T, 0/0
7. **Gene Hickerson, Mississippi, G, 202/202**
7. Mike Rotunno, Michigan, C, 0/0
8. Don Gillis, Rice, C, 0/45
9. Don Comstock, Alabama, B, 0/0
10. Bob Reinhart, San Jose State, B, 0/0
11. Bill Cummings, Ohio State, T, 0/0
12. Rudy Spitzenberger, Houston, G, 0/0
13. Jerry Sansom, Auburn, E, 0/0
14. Don Feller, Kansas, B, 0/0
15. Dave Kaiser, Michigan State, E, 0/0
18. LaVerne Torczon, Nebraska, DE, 0/98
25. Tom Dimitroff, Miami (OH), QB, 0/3
28. Gene Cockrell, Hardin-Simmons, T, 0/42

DETROIT LIONS

1. **Bill Glass, Baylor, DE, 50/144**
2. **John Gordy, Tennessee, G, 134/134**
3. **Terry Barr, Michigan, HB, 102/102**
4. Steve Junker, Xavier (OH), E, 30/55
5. John Barrow, Florida, G, 0/0
6. Ken Russell, Bowling Green State, T, 26/26
7. Jerry Leahy, Colorado, T, 0/1
8. Dave Liddick, George Washington, DT, 0/4
9. John Nikkel, Texas Christian, E, 0/0
10. Tom Rychlec, American International, E, 12/49
11. Carl Osterich, Missouri, C, 0/0
12. Charlie O'Brien, Valparaiso, E, 0/0
13. Bill West, Eastern Oregon, B, 0/0
14. Phil Smith, Jacksonville State, B, 0/0
15. Gene Alderton, Maryland, C, 0/0
17. Jack Kemp, Occidental, QB, 0/122
19. Bob Gunderman, Virginia, E, 0/1
21. Dudley Meredith, Lamar, DT, 0/77
26. Chuck Muelhaupt, Iowa State, G, 0/28

GREEN BAY PACKERS

B1. **Paul Hornung, Notre Dame, HB, 104/104**
1. **Ron Kramer, Michigan, E, 89/128**
2. Joel Wells, Clemson, HB, 0/14
3. Dalton Truax, Tulane, T, 0/14
4. Carl Vereen, Georgia Tech, T, 12/12
6. John Nisby, Pacific, G, 0/102
7. Frank Gilliam, Iowa, E, 0/0
8. George Belotti, USC, C, 0/20
9. Ken Wineberg, Texas Christian, B, 0/0
10. Gary Gustafson, Gustavus Adolphus, G, 0/0
11. Jim Roseboro, Ohio State, B, 0/0
12. Ed Sullivan, Notre Dame, C, 0/0
12. Glenn Bestor, Wisconsin, B, 0/0
13. Jim Morse, Notre Dame, B, 0/0
14. Rudy Schoendorf, Miami (OH), T, 0/0
15. Pat Hinton, Louisiana Tech, G, 0/0
19. Ernie Danjean, Auburn, LB, 12/12
23. **John Symank, Florida, DB, 76/89**

LOS ANGELES RAMS

1. **Jon Arnett, USC, HB, 81/123**
1. Del Shofner, Baylor, E, 47/125
2. **Jack Pardee, Texas A&M, LB, 169/196**
3. Billy Ray Sr. Smith, Arkansas, DT, 12/166
3. **George Strugar, Washington, DT, 57/78**
4. **Lamar Lundy, Purdue, DE, 152/152**
4. Bobby Cox, Minnesota, QB, 0/0
5. Dean Derby, Washington, DB, 0/68
5. Dick Enright, Southern California, G, 0/0
6. Roy Wilkins, Georgia, LB, 24/50
7. Ed Gray, Oklahoma, T, 0/0
8. Charlie Bradshaw, Baylor, T, 36/145
8. Roy Hord, Duke, G, 29/53
9. John Mitchell, Texas Christian, C, 0/0
10. Warren Spragg, Hillsdale, T, 0/0
11. Don Smith, Miami (OH), T, 0/0
12. Don Klochak, North Carolina, B, 0/0
13. Bob Wolfenden, Virginia Tech, B, 0/0
14. Joe Lazzarino, Maryland, T, 0/0
15. Ed Hinman, Wichita State, B, 0/0
20. Byron Beams, Notre Dame, T, 0/16
22. Paige Cothren, Mississippi, K, 24/31
23. Dalva Allen, Houston, DE, 0/70
25. Jimmy Orr, Georgia, FL, 0/149
27. Clancy Osborne, Arizona State, LB, 0/72

NEW YORK GIANTS

2. Sam DeLuca, South Carolina, G, 0/81
3. Dennis Mendyk, Michigan State, B, 0/0
5. Larry Wesley, Florida, T, 0/0
6. Bob Hobert, Minnesota, T, 0/0
7. Chuck Curtis, Texas Christian, QB, 0/0
8. Johnny Bookman, Miami (FL), DB, 11/33
9. Don Maynard, Texas-El Paso, E, 12/186
10. Gordon Massa, Holy Cross, C, 0/0
11. Pat Burke, Michigan State, G, 0/0
13. Ron Bennett, Mississippi State, E, 0/0
14. Dean Hesse, East Texas State, T, 0/0
15. Julius Derrick, South Carolina, E, 0/0

PHILADELPHIA EAGLES

1. **Clarence Peaks, Michigan State, FB, 83/105**
2. **Billy Ray Barnes, Wake Forest, HB, 60/98**
3. **Tommy McDonald, Oklahoma, FL, 88/152**
4. **Sonny Jurgensen, Duke, QB, 83/218**
5. Jimmy Harris, Oklahoma, DB, 12/49
7. Tom Saidock, Michigan State, DT, 11/41
8. Hal McElhaney, Duke, B, 0/0
9. Hal Davis, Westminster (PA), B, 0/0
10. Don Bruhns, Drake, C, 0/0
11. Gil Shoaf, Wabash, T, 0/0
12. Buddy Dike, Texas Christian, B, 0/0
13. Hubert Bobo, Ohio State, LB, 0/31
14. Jerry Cashman, Syracuse, T, 0/0
15. Mort Moriarity, Texas, E, 0/0
16. John Nocera, Iowa, LB, 48/57
22. John Simerson, Purdue, C, 16/43
26. Al Richardson, Grambling State, DE, 0/3

PITTSBURGH STEELERS

1. Len Dawson, Purdue, QB, 19/211
2. Bill Michael, Ohio State, G, 3/3
3. Don Owens, Southern Mississippi, DT, 0/87
5. Perry Richards, Detroit Mercy, E, 7/47
6. George Volkert, Georgia Tech, B, 0/0
7. Curley Johnson, Houston, RB, 0/129
9. Charley Hutchings, Miami (FL), T, 0/0
10. Ralph Jelic, Pittsburgh, B, 0/0
11. Dick Hughes, Tulsa, HB, 1/1
12. Vern Ellison, Oregon State, G, 0/0
13. Dwaine Underwood, Oklahoma State, T, 0/0
14. Jim Crawford, Wyoming, HB, 0/54
15. Herman Canil, Pittsburgh, T, 0/0
19. Phil Bennett, Miami (FL), LB, 0/2
21. Chick Cichowski, Indiana, DB, 12/14

SAN FRANCISCO 49ERS

1. **John Brodie, Stanford, QB, 201/201**
2. **Abe Woodson, Illinois, DB, 89/116**
4. **Jimmy Ridlon, Syracuse, DB, 68/89**
4. Mike Sandusky, Maryland, G, 0/104
5. **Karl Rubke, USC, LB, 104/143**
6. Bill Rhodes, Western State (CO), B, 0/0
6. Jim Hunter, Missouri, B, 0/0
7. Fred Dugan, Dayton, E, 24/75
8. Ernie Pitts, Denver, E, 0/0
9. Charlie Brueckman, Pittsburgh, LB, 0/23
10. Jerry Hurst, Middle Tennessee State, E, 0/0
11. **Tommy Davis, LSU, K, 138/138**
12. Fred Sington, Alabama, T, 0/0
13. Charley Mackey, Arizona State, E, 0/0
14. Ron Warzeka, Montana State, DT, 0/14
15. Earl Kaiser, Houston, B, 0/0
19. Gene Babb, Austin, LB, 24/76
23. **John Thomas, Pacific, G, 122/122**

WASHINGTON REDSKINS

1. **Don Bosseler, Miami (FL), FB, 96/96**
2. Joe Walton, Pittsburgh, E, 45/82
3. Ed Sutton, North Carolina, HB, 33/45
4. Jim Podoley, Central Michigan, HB, 43/43
4. Vince Scorsone, Pittsburgh, G, 0/0
6. J.T. Frankenberger, Kentucky, T, 0/0
7. Wally Merz, Colorado, T, 0/0
8. Paul Lopata, Yale, E, 0/0
9. Galen Laack, Pacific, G, 0/8
10. Don Dobrino, Iowa, B, 0/0
11. Dick Foster, Idaho, T, 0/0
12. Wade Mitchell, Georgia Tech, QB, 0/0
13. Claude Austin, George Washington, B, 0/0
14. George Rice, Wofford, T, 0/0
15. Brad Bomba, Indiana, E, 0/0
22. Ed Voytek, Purdue, G, 24/24

1958 NFL

BALTIMORE COLTS

1. **Lenny Lyles, Louisville, DB, 125/149**
2. Bob Stransky, Colorado, HB, 0/14
3. Joe Nicely, West Virginia, G, 0/0
4. Les Walters, Penn State, DB, 0/8
5. Ray Brown, Mississippi, DB, 36/36
6. Bob Taylor, Vanderbilt, E, 0/0
7. John Diehl, Virginia, DT, 45/53
7. Johnny Sample, Maryland-Eastern Shore, DB, 35/125
8. Floyd Peters, San Francisco State, DT, 0/145
9. Hal Bullard, Lenoir-Rhyne, B, 0/0
10. Ray Schamber, South Dakota, E, 0/0
11. Bobby Jordan, Virginia Military, B, 0/0
12. Tom Addison, South Carolina, LB, 0/106
13. Jerry Richardson, Wofford, FL, 22/22
14. Ken Hall, Texas A&M, HB, 0/34
15. Les Carney, Ohio U., B, 0/0
16. Archie Matsos, Michigan State, LB, 0/95

CHICAGO BEARS

1. Chuck Howley, West Virginia, LB, 15/180
2. Willard Dewveall, SMU, E, 23/72
3. Ed Cooke, Maryland, DE, 3/117
3. Don Healy, Maryland, DT, 24/51
4. Erich Barnes, Purdue, DB, 36/177
5. Bob Jewett, Michigan State, E, 12/12
6. Merrill Douglas, Utah, FB, 36/55
7. Gene Bentley, Texas Tech, B, 0/0
8. Ed Rutsch, George Washington, T, 0/0
9. Ralph Anderson, Los Angeles State, E, 12/22
10. Aubrey Lewis, Notre Dame, B, 0/0
11. Rocco Cinelli, Wisconsin, T, 0/0
12. **Johnny Morris, California-Santa Barbara, FL, 121/121**
14. Bill Melnik, Army, T, 0/0
15. Jim Harryman, Compton J.C., B, 0/0
19. Bill Roehnelt, Bradley, LB, 24/54
21. Bill Miller, New Mexico Highlands, DT, 0/4

CHICAGO CARDINALS

1. **John David Crow, Texas A&M, HB, 69/125**
B1. King Hill, Rice, QB, 44/123
2. Jim McCusker, Pittsburgh, T, 11/83
2. Bobby Jack Oliver, Rice, T, 0/0
3. Larry Cowart, Baylor, C, 0/0
6. Bobby Gordon, Tennessee, DB, 12/25
7. Jon Jelacic, Minnesota, DE, 0/44
9. John Keelan, Kansas State, T, 0/0
10. Gil Robertshaw, Brown, T, 0/0
11. Dean Philpott, Fresno State, FB, 9/9
11. Bill Hinton, Louisiana Tech, G, 0/0
13. Charlie Jackson, SMU, DB, 10/13
14. Bob Schmidt, Minnesota, C, 0/98
15. Ray Dunlap, Marshall, B, 0/0
19. **Sonny Randle, Virginia, E, 97/120**

CLEVELAND BROWNS

1. **Jim Shofner, TCU, DB, 76/76**
2. Charley Mitchell, Florida, G, 0/0
3. Buzz Guy, Duke, G, 0/44
4. Jim Ninowski, Michigan State, QB, 40/89
5. Jim Gibbons, Iowa, E, 0/140
5. Farrell Funston, Pacific, E, 0/0
6. Jim Wulff, Michigan State, DB, 0/17
7. **Bobby Mitchell, Illinois, FL, 50/148**
8. Bert Lattimore, Duke, E, 0/0
9. **Bernie Parrish, Florida, DB, 94/105**
10. Leo Russavage, North Carolina, T, 0/0
11. Russ Bowermaster, Ohio State, E, 0/0
12. Bob Brodhead, Duke, QB, 0/4
13. Hal Williams, Miami (OH), B, 0/0
14. Ken Miller, Texas Christian, T, 0/0
15. Howard Hoelscher, Rice, B, 0/0
16. Jerry Cornelison, SMU, T, 0/70
22. Bob Renn, Florida State, HB, 0/12

DETROIT LIONS

1. **Alex Karras, Iowa, DT, 161/161**
4. **Wayne Walker, Idaho, LB, 200/200**
6. **Dan Lewis, Wisconsin, HB, 84/110**
7. Ralph Pfeifer, Kansas State, B, 0/0
7. Hal Outten, Virginia, T, 0/0
8. Phil Blazer, North Carolina, G, 0/14
8. Karl Koepfer, Bowling Green State, G, 1/1
9. Ben Paolucci, Wayne State (MI), DT, 4/4
9. Jim Loftin, Alabama, B, 0/0
10. Elliot Schaubach, William & Mary, T, 0/0
11. Claude Chaney, Dayton, B, 0/0
12. Hal Boutte, San Jose State, E, 0/0
13. Barry Maroney, Cincinnati, B, 0/0
14. **Ken Webb, Presbyterian, HB, 61/73**
15. John Scheldrup, Iowa State, E, 0/0
15. Jerry Mohlman, Benedictine, B, 0/0
21. Jim Wagstaff, Idaho State, DB, 0/31
24. Dave Whitsell, Indiana, DB, 35/161

GREEN BAY PACKERS

1. **Dan Currie, Michigan State, LB, 90/118**
2. **Jim Taylor, LSU, FB, 118/132**
3. Dick Christy, North Carolina State, HB, 0/64
3. **Ray Nitschke, Illinois, LB, 190/190**
4. **Jerry Kramer, Idaho, G, 130/130**
5. Joe Francis, Oregon State, QB, 24/24
6. Ken Gray, Howard Payne, G, 0/162
7. Doug Mainson, Hillsdale, B, 0/0
8. Mike Bill, Syracuse, C, 0/0
9. Norm Jarock, St. Norbert, B, 0/0
10. Carl Johnson, Illinois, T, 0/0
11. Harry Horton, Wichita State, E, 0/0
12. Wayne Miller, Baylor, E, 0/0
13. Gene Cook, Toledo, E, 0/1
14. Harry Hauffe, South Dakota, T, 0/0
15. Tom Newell, Drake, B, 0/0

LOS ANGELES RAMS

1. Lou Michaels, Kentucky, DE, 35/171
1. **Red Phillips, Auburn, E, 82/119**
2. Clendon Thomas, Oklahoma, DB, 41/137
3. Jim Jones, Washington, DB, 12/13
4. John Guzik, Pittsburgh, LB, 24/27
4. Urban Henry, Georgia Tech, DT, 14/38
4. Frank Woidzik, Buffalo, T, 0/0
5. John Baker, North Carolina Central, DE, 49/131
5. Frank Ryan, Rice, QB, 40/126
6. Floyd Iglehart, Wiley, HB, 1/1
7. **Bill Jobko, Ohio State, LB, 57/107**
8. Bobby Marks, Texas A&M, B, 0/0
9. Gene Selawski, Purdue, T, 12/32
10. Al Jacks, Penn State, QB, 0/0
11. Gerry Schweitzer, Pacific, E, 0/0
12. Ron Clairborne, Kansas, T, 0/0
13. Tony Kolodziej, Michigan State, E, 0/0
14. Bill Mason, UCLA, B, 0/0
15. Dick Johnston, Southern Mississippi, C, 0/0
19. Dick Dorsey, Oklahoma, SE, 0/11

NEW YORK GIANTS

1. **Phil King, Vanderbilt, HB, 67/103**
2. Frank Youso, Minnesota, T, 36/92
4. Donnie Caraway, Houston, B, 0/0
5. Bobby Joe Conrad, Texas A&M, FL, 0/156
5. Dick Day, Washington, T, 0/0
6. Billy Lott, Mississippi, FB, 12/61
7. Vernon Vaughn, Maryland-Eastern Shore, E, 0/0
8. Don Sutherin, Ohio State, DB, 2/12
9. Ron Kissell, Pittsburgh, T, 0/0
10. Herb Drummond, Central State (OH), B, 0/0
11. Sid Williams, Wisconsin, B, 0/0
12. Gerry Hershey, Syracuse, T, 0/0
13. Don Herndon, Tampa, HB, 0/8
13. George Kurker, Tufts, T, 0/0
14. C.R. Roberts, USC, FB, 0/27
15. Norm Sixta, Minnesota, T, 0/0
28. Bob Watters, Lincoln (MO), DE, 0/29

PHILADELPHIA EAGLES

1. Walt Kowalczyk, Michigan State, FB, 24/40
2. Proverb Jacobs, California, T, 12/54
4. Frank Rigney, Iowa, T, 0/0
5. Bobby Mulgado, Arizona State, B, 0/0
6. John Kersey, Duke, T, 0/0
7. Len Mansfield, Pittsburg State, T, 0/0
8. Bill Striegel, Pacific, G, 12/18
10. Theron Sapp, Georgia, FB, 47/82
11. Mel Dillard, Purdue, B, 0/0
12. Jack Crabtree, Oregon, B, 0/0
13. Mickey Trimarki, West Virginia, QB, 0/0
14. Bill Lapham, Iowa, C, 12/26
15. Stan Hinos, Mississippi Valley State, T, 0/0
19. Ron Sabal, Purdue, T, 0/28
29. Don McDonald, Houston, DB, 0/11

PITTSBURGH STEELERS

2. Larry Krutko, West Virginia, FB, 25/25
3. Billy Krisher, Oklahoma, G, 8/35
6. Dick Lasse, Syracuse, LB, 24/54
9. Mike Henry, USC, LB, 34/76
10. Dick Campbell, Marquette, LB, 36/36
11. Larry Aldrich, Idaho, E, 0/0
12. Leroy Reed, Mississippi, B, 0/0
14. Doyle Jennings, Oklahoma, T, 0/0
15. Ed Sears, Florida, B, 0/0
17. Joe Lewis, Compton CC (CA), DT, 29/53
26. Jon Evans, Oklahoma State, E, 1/1

SAN FRANCISCO 49ERS

1. **Charlie Krueger, Texas A&M, DT, 198/198**
1. James Pace, Michigan, HB, 12/12
2. Bob Newman, Washington State, B, 0/0
3. Bob Hoppe, Auburn, B, 0/0
4. John Varone, Miami (FL), B, 0/0
5. Billy Atkins, Auburn, DB, 23/64

6. Henry Schmidt, Trinity (TX), DT, 24/99
8. Leon Burton, Arizona State, HB, 0/14
8. Ron Mills, West Texas State, B, 0/0
9. George Troutman, Capital, T, 0/0
10. Vel Heckman, Florida, T, 0/0
11. Hogan Wharton, Houston, G, 0/56
12. Pete Williams, Lehigh, T, 0/0
13. Jim Yore, Indiana, B, 0/0
13. Hal Dukes, Michigan State, E, 0/0
14. Max Fields, Whittier, B, 0/0
16. George Shirkey, Stephen F. Austin State, DT, 0/35
17. John Wittenborn, Southeast Missouri State, G, 28/116
18. Dennit Morris, Oklahoma, LB, 12/40
20. **Jerry Mertens, Drake, DB, 91/91**
24. Dee Mackey, Texas A&M-Commerce, E, 12/78

WASHINGTON REDSKINS

2. Mike Sommer, George Washington, HB, 5/22
3. **Bill Anderson, Tennessee, E, 74/98**
3. Stan Flowers, Georgia Tech, B, 0/0
4. Dan Nolan, Lehigh, QB, 0/0
5. Jim Van Pelt, Michigan, QB, 0/0
6. Dick Lynch, Notre Dame, DB, 12/109
7. Leon Bennett, Boston College, T, 0/0
8. Buddy Payne, North Carolina, E, 0/0
9. Frank Kuchta, Notre Dame, LB, 14/26
10. Ben Preston, Auburn, T, 0/0
11. Darrell Dess, North Carolina State, G, 14/146
12. Eddie Michaels, Villanova, G, 0/0
13. Ken (Model-T) Ford, Hardin-Simmons, QB, 0/0
14. Jack Farls, Penn State, E, 0/0
15. Jack Davis, Maryland, G, 0/2
21. Jackie Simpson, Mississippi, LB, 0/36

1959 NFL

BALTIMORE COLTS

1. **Jackie Burkett, Auburn, LB, 79/121**
2. Dave Sherer, SMU, E, 12/23
5. Don Churchwell, Mississippi, DT, 0/11
6. Palmer Pyle, Michigan State, G, 38/61
7. Hal Lewis, Houston, FB, 12/26
8. Tommy Joe Coffey, West Texas State, B, 0/0
9. Tom Brown, Minnesota, G, 0/0
10. Don Stewart, Southern Methodist, E, 0/0
11. Thomas Stephens, Syracuse, TE, 0/49
12. Dick Wood, Auburn, QB, 0/60
13. Rudi Smith, Mississippi, T, 0/0
14. Ferdie Burket, Southeastern Oklahoma, B, 0/0
15. Ted Foret, Auburn, T, 0/0

CHICAGO BEARS

1. Don Clark, Ohio State, B, 0/0
2. **Richie Petitbon, Tulane, DB, 136/179**
3. Pete Johnson, VMI, DB, 7/7
5. **John Adams, Los Angeles State, E, 51/64**
6. Fred Cole, Maryland, G, 0/14
7. Jim Tucker, Tennessee-Chattanooga, E, 0/0
8. Willie Smith, Michigan, G, 0/28
8. Dick Clark, Baylor, B, 0/0
9. Maury Youmans, Syracuse, DE, 28/56
10. Bob Coronado, Pacific, WR, 0/5
11. Ed Gray, North Texas State, T, 0/0
12. Justin Rowland, TCU, DB, 6/21
13. Gene Jones, Rice, LB, 0/1
14. Joe Robb, TCU, DE, 0/159
15. **Roger LeClerc, Trinity (CT), LB, 96/104**
21. Donnie Stone, Arkansas, HB, 0/67
27. John Aveni, Indiana, K, 24/38

CHICAGO CARDINALS

1. **Billy Stacy, Mississippi State, DB, 58/58**
2. Jerry Wilson, Auburn, DE, 0/22
3. Jimmy Butler, Vanderbilt, B, 0/0
4. Ken Beck, Texas A&M, DT, 0/24
5. Ted Bates, Oregon State, LB, 46/54
5. Maury Schleicher, Penn State, DE, 10/40
6. Mac Lewis, Iowa, T, 8/8
6. **Tom Redmond, Vanderbilt, DE, 60/60**
9. Gary Ferguson, Southern Methodist, T, 0/0
10. Emil DeCantis, North Carolina, B, 0/0
11. Floyd Faucette, Georgia Tech, B, 0/0
12. Ted Edmondson, Hardin-Simmons, E, 0/0
13. Pat Lamberti, Richmond, LB, 0/12
14. Bob Bobo, Texas-El Paso, T, 0/0
15. John Schroeder, North Carolina, E, 0/0
17. Pete Hart, Hardin-Simmons, FB, 0/14
21. Dale Memmelaar, Wyoming, G, 32/107
23. Fred Glick, Colorado State, DB, 5/83
28. Don Fleming, Florida, DB, 0/38

CLEVELAND BROWNS

1. **Rich Kreitling, Illinois, E, 65/79**
2. **Dick Schafrath, Ohio State, T, 176/176**
3. Fran O'Brien, Michigan State, T, 12/124
4. Dave Lloyd, Georgia, LB, 38/157
4. Gary Prahst, Michigan, E, 0/0
5. Dick LeBeau, Ohio State, DB, 0/185
5. **John Wooten, Colorado, G, 122/136**
6. Bob Denton, Pacific, DE, 12/68
6. Jim Prestel, Idaho, DT, 6/96
7. Gene Miller, Rice, T, 0/0
8. Bob Ptacek, Michigan, QB, 12/12
9. Kirk Wilson, UCLA, B, 0/0
10. Bob Zeman, Wisconsin, DB, 0/82
11. Jerry King, Kent State, G, 0/0
12. Frank Palandrani, North Carolina State, T, 0/0
13. Ray Reese, Bowling Green, B, 0/0
14. Elbert Dubenion, Bluffton, FL, 0/103
15. Tom Salwocki, Pittsburgh, C, 0/0
16. Jamie Caleb, Grambling State, HB, 17/27
21. Jim Fraser, Wisconsin, LB, 0/72
27. Larry Baker, Bowling Green State, T, 0/2

DETROIT LIONS

1. **Nick Pietrosante, Notre Dame, FB, 89/116**
2. Mike Rabold, Indiana, G, 12/105
2. Charley Horton, Baylor, G, 0/0
3. Ron Koes, North Carolina, C, 0/0
3. Ron Luciano, Syracuse, T, 0/0
4. Bob Grottkau, Oregon, G, 17/30
4. Art Brandriff, Virginia Military, B, 0/0
6. Dick Guesman, West Virginia, DT, 0/59
7. Ben Donnell, Vanderbilt, DE, 0/3
8. Jim Lenden, Oregon, T, 0/0
9. Carl Smith, Tennessee, FB, 0/14
10. Jack Laraway, Purdue, LB, 0/22
11. Harry Jacobs, Bradley, LB, 0/134
13. Jim Steffen, UCLA, DB, 28/88
14. Jim Baldwin, McMurry, C, 0/0
15. **Bruce Maher, Detroit Mercy, DB, 108/136**
16. George McGee, Southern (LA), T, 0/14
19. Rufus Granderson, Prairie View A&M, DT, 0/6
20. Dan McGrew, Purdue, C, 0/14
25. Dan Chamberlain, Sacramento State, E, 0/15

GREEN BAY PACKERS

1. Randy Duncan, Iowa, QB, 0/14
2. Alex Hawkins, South Carolina, HB, 0/125
3. **Boyd Dowler, Colorado, FL, 150/162**
5. Andy Cvercko, Northwestern, G, 12/47
6. Willie Taylor, Florida A&M, C, 0/0
7. Bobby Jackson, Alabama, DB, 0/21
7. Gary Raid, Willamette, T, 0/0
8. Bob Laraba, Texas-El Paso, LB, 0/28
8. Buddy Mayfield, South Carolina, E, 0/0
9. George Dixon, Bridgeport, B, 0/0
10. Sam Tuccio, Southern Mississippi, T, 0/0
11. Bob Webb, St. Ambrose, B, 0/0
12. Larry Hall, Missouri Valley, G, 0/0
13. Jim Hurd, Albion, B, 0/0
14. Ken Kerr, Arizona State, G, 0/0
15. Dick Teteak, Wisconsin, G, 0/0
19. Bill Butler, Tennessee-Chattanooga, DB, 11/75
21. Dave Smith, Ripon, FB, 0/65
24. Joe Hergert, Florida, LB, 0/19
27. Timmy Brown, Ball State, RB, 1/108

LOS ANGELES RAMS

1. **Dick Bass, Pacific, FB, 112/112**
1. Paul Dickson, Baylor, DT, 10/152
2. Don Brown, Houston, HB, 0/3
2. Buddy Humphrey, Baylor, QB, 6/26
3. Tom Franckhauser, Purdue, DB, 12/58
3. Larry Hickman, Baylor, FB, 0/24
4. Bob Reifsnyder, Navy, DE, 0/16
4. John Tracey, Texas A&M, LB, 0/110
5. John Lands, Montana State, E, 0/0
6. Dave Painter, Tulane, C, 0/0
7. **Eddie Meador, Arkansas Tech, DB, 163/163**
8. Bill Conner, Jackson State, E, 0/0
9. Larry Cundiff, Michigan State, T, 0/0
11. Joe Kelly, New Mexico State, B, 0/0
13. Al Witcher, Baylor, E, 0/14
15. Walt Kelly, Houston, B, 0/0
19. Carver Shannon, Southern Illinois, DB, 38/38
20. Ross Coyle, Oklahoma, DB, 13/13

NEW YORK GIANTS

1. Lee Grosscup, Utah, QB, 8/16
2. Buddy Dial, Rice, SE, 0/98
3. **Joe Morrison, Cincinnati, HB, 184/184**
5. Ellison Kelly, Michigan State, G, 12/12
9. Jack Delveaux, Illinois, B, 0/0
10. Bob Pepe, North Carolina State, E, 0/0
11. Bob Sawyer, Wyoming, B, 0/0
13. John Kompara, South Carolina, DT, 0/7
14. Roger Ellis, Maine, LB, 0/43
16. Bob Soltis, Minnesota, DB, 0/17
19. George Scott, Miami (OH), HB, 7/7
27. Joe Biscaha, Richmond, E, 8/9

PHILADELPHIA EAGLES

2. **J.D. 3 Smith, Rice, T, 65/86**
3. Wray Carlton, Duke, HB, 0/87
4. Jim Grazione, Villanova, QB, 0/0
5. Nick Mumley, Purdue, DE, 0/42
6. Al Benecick, Syracuse, G, 0/0
8. Willmer Fowler, Northwestern, HB, 0/13
9. Gene Johnson, Cincinnati, DB, 23/30
10. Rollie West, Villanova, B, 0/0
11. Art Powell, San Jose State, SE, 12/117
12. Howard Keys, Oklahoma State, C, 41/41
13. Dick Stillwagon, Purdue, B, 0/0
14. Jack Smith, Clemson, T, 0/0
15. Jim Poteete, Mississippi State, C, 0/0
19. Alan Miller, Boston College, FB, 0/70
25. Dick Jamieson, Bradley, QB, 0/14

PITTSBURGH STEELERS

8. Tom Barnett, Purdue, HB, 24/24
9. Hal Davis, Houston, G, 0/0
10. Riley Gunnels, Georgia, DT, 28/91
11. Overton Curtis, Utah State, B, 0/0
12. Bill Pavliska, Baylor, B, 0/0
13. Dewey Bohling, Hardin-Simmons, HB, 0/26
14. John Peppercorn, Kansas, E, 0/0
15. J.W. Brodnax, LSU, FB, 0/14
19. Dave Kocourek, Wisconsin, TE, 0/115
20. Rudy Hayes, Clemson, LB, 28/28
21. Johnny Green, Tennessee-Chattanooga, QB, 0/30
26. Jack Scott, Ohio State, DT, 0/21
27. Charley Tolar, Northwestern State (LA), FB, 0/95
28. Ron Hall, Missouri Valley, DB, 2/90

SAN FRANCISCO 49ERS

1. Dave Baker, Oklahoma, DB, 38/38
1. Dan James, Ohio State, T, 0/93
2. **Bob Harrison, Oklahoma, LB, 73/106**
3. **Eddie Dove, Colorado, DB, 54/66**
4. Monte Clark, USC, T, 36/139
5. Frank Geremia, Notre Dame, T, 0/0
6. Tony Bavaro, Holy Cross, T, 0/0
7. **Daniel Colchico, San Jose State, DE, 67/76**
7. Don Rogers, South Carolina, C, 0/68
8. Lew Aiken, Vanderbilt, E, 0/0
10. Bronko Nagurski, Notre Dame, T, 0/0
11. Jack Hayes, Trinity (TX), B, 0/0
12. Bill Korutz, Dayton, C, 0/0
14. Mike Dukes, Clemson, LB, 0/81
15. Joe Belland, Arizona State, B, 0/0
19. Tom Osborne, Hastings, WR, 0/24

WASHINGTON REDSKINS

1. Don Allard, Boston College, QB, 0/5
3. Emil Karas, Dayton, LB, 11/71
4. Jim Wood, Oklahoma State, E, 0/0
5. Bob Wetoska, Notre Dame, T, 0/128
6. Jim McFalls, Virginia Military, T, 0/0
7. Don Lawrence, Notre Dame, DT, 35/35
7. Mitch Ogiego, Iowa, QB, 0/0
7. Jim Kenney, Boston, E, 0/0
8. Gene O'Pella, Villanova, E, 0/0
9. Dick Haley, Pittsburgh, DB, 22/75
10. Ron Toth, Notre Dame, B, 0/0
11. Gerry Marciniak, Michigan, G, 0/0
12. Roger Wypyszynski, St. Norbert, T, 0/0
13. Billy Shoemake, Louisiana State, E, 0/0
14. Kurt Schwarz, Maryland, G, 0/0
15. Fred Hood, Northeastern Oklahoma, E, 0/0
18. Joe Kapp, California, QB, 0/51
22. Art Gob, Pittsburgh, DE, 12/15
26. Gene Grabosky, Syracuse, DT, 0/3
30. Jim Colclough, Boston College, E, 0/126

1960 NFL

BALTIMORE COLTS

1. Ron Mix, USC, T, 0/142
2. Don Floyd, TCU, DE, 0/97
2. Marvin Terrell, Mississippi, G, 0/38
3. **Jim Welch, SMU, DB, 100/114**
4. Gerhard Schwedes, Syracuse, HB, 0/10
5. Marv Lasater, Texas Christian, B, 0/0
6. Al Bansavage, USC, LB, 0/17
7. Jerry Beabout, Purdue, T, 0/0
8. **Jim Colvin, Houston, DT, 53/103**
9. Don Perkins, New Mexico, FB, 0/107
9. Bob Hall, Army, T, 0/0
10. Ernie Barnes, North Carolina Central, G, 0/43
10. **Bobby Boyd, Oklahoma, DB, 121/121**
11. Bob Wehking, Florida, C, 0/0
12. Bill Bucek, Rice, HB, 0/0
13. Jim Nemeth, South Carolina, C, 0/0
14. Dale Johannsen, Augustana (SD), T, 0/0
15. Larry Grantham, Mississippi, LB, 0/175
16. George Boynton, Texas A&M-Commerce, DB, 0/3

CHICAGO BEARS

1. Roger Davis, Syracuse, G, 48/72
3. Don Meredith, SMU, QB, 0/104
4. Billy Martin, Minnesota, HB, 32/32
5. Dick Norman, Stanford, QB, 3/3
6. Ed Kovac, Cincinnati, HB, 0/15
7. **Charlie Bivins, Morris Brown, HB, 91/102**
8. Pete Manning, Wake Forest, DB, 9/9
9. Ken Kirk, Mississippi, LB, 22/44
11. Stan Fanning, Idaho, T, 30/52
11. Glenn Shaw, Kentucky, FB, 12/29
12. Tom Budrewicz, Brown, G, 0/2
13. Bob Spada, Duke, E, 0/0
14. Jim Sorey, Texas Southern, DT, 0/42
15. Warren Lashua, Whitworth, B, 0/0
16. Bo Farrington, Prairie View A&M, SE, 45/45
18. Claude King, Houston, HB, 0/25
20. Angelo Coia, USC, SE, 44/77

CHICAGO BEARS

4. Silas Woods, Marquette, E, 0/0
5. Bill Burrell, Illinois, LB, 0/0
5. George Phelps, Cornell College (IA), B, 0/0
5. Ed Mazurek, Xavier, T, 0/0
9. Dewitt Hoopes, Northwestern, T, 0/0
12. Tom Chapman, Detroit, E, 0/0
13. Vic Jones, Indiana, HB, 0/0

CLEVELAND BROWNS

1. **Jim Houston, Ohio State, LB, 177/177**
2. Prentice Gautt, Oklahoma, HB, 12/88
2. Larry Stephens, Texas, DE, 26/103
3. **Ross Fichtner, Purdue, DB, 102/106**
4. **Johnny Brewer, Mississippi, TE, 98/135**
4. Jim Marshall, Ohio State, DE, 12/282
5. Bob Jarus, Purdue, FB, 0/0
6. Bob Khayat, Mississippi, G, 0/40
7. Taz Anderson, Georgia Tech, TE, 0/62
8. Bob White, Ohio State, FB, 0/6
9. Chris Burford, Stanford, SE, 0/103
10. Clyde Washington, Purdue, DB, 0/63
11. **Bobby Franklin, Mississippi, DB, 86/86**
12. Rich Mostardo, Kent State, DB, 10/26
13. Dick Grecni, Ohio University, LB, 0/12
14. Bill Dumbauld, West Virginia, T, 0/0
15. Tom Watkins, Iowa State, HB, 10/75

DETROIT LIONS

1. Johnny Robinson, LSU, DB, 0/164
2. Warren Rabb, LSU, QB, 7/30
3. **Bob Scholtz, Notre Dame, C, 60/81**
4. **Roger Brown, Maryland-Eastern Shore, DT, 96/138**
4. Jim Andreotti, Northwestern, C, 0/0
6. **Gail Cogdill, Washington State, SE, 103/127**
7. Jim Norton, Idaho, DB, 0/125
9. Max Messner, Cincinnati, LB, 43/70
10. Grady Alderman, Detroit Mercy, T, 11/204
10. Jim O'Brien, Boston College, T, 0/0
11. Ted Aucerman, Indiana, E, 0/0
12. Dave Ross, Los Angeles State, E, 0/12
13. Pete Tunney, Occidental, HB, 0/0
14. Jim Glasgow, Jacksonville State, T, 0/0
15. Darrell Harper, Michigan, HB, 0/4
19. Gene Prebola, Boston University, TE, 0/56
20. Dean Look, Michigan State, QB, 0/1

GREEN BAY PACKERS

1. **Tom Moore, Vanderbilt, HB, 78/102**
2. **Bob Jeter, Iowa, DB, 107/139**
5. Dale Hackbart, Wisconsin, DB, 14/152
6. Mike Wright, Minnesota, T, 0/0
7. Kirk Phares, South Carolina, G, 0/0
8. Don Hitt, Oklahoma State, C, 0/0
9. Frank Brixius, Minnesota, T, 0/0
11. Ron Ray, Howard Payne, T, 0/0
12. Harry Ball, Boston College, T, 0/0
13. Paul Winslow, North Carolina Central, DB, 12/12
14. Jon Gilliam, Texas A&M-Commerce, C, 0/76
15. Garney Henley, Huron, B, 0/0

LOS ANGELES RAMS

1. Billy Cannon, LSU, TE, 0/133
3. Pervis Atkins, New Mexico State, FL, 42/78

3. Charley Britt, Georgia, DB, 44/49
5. Chuck Janerette, Penn State, DT, 12/80
6. Don Ellersick, Washington State, DB, 12/12
6. Jerry Stalcup, Wisconsin, LB, 12/34
7. Ron Morrison, New Mexico, T, 0/0
8. **Carroll Dale, Virginia Tech, WR, 65/189**
9. Marv Luster, UCLA, E, 0/0
10. Curtis McClinton, Kansas, FB, 0/107
11. Ken Young, Valparaiso, HB, 0/0
12. Doug Brown, Fresno State, DT, 1/13
13. James Jones, Southern Methodist, E, 0/0
14. Harold Stanger, North Texas State, C, 0/0
15. Harry Rakowski, Citadel, C, 0/0
19. **Jim Boeke, Heidelberg, T, 54/119**

NEW YORK GIANTS

1. Lou Cordileone, Clemson, DT, 11/75
3. Jim Leo, Cincinnati, DE, 12/40
6. George Blair, Mississippi, DB, 0/46
7. Bob Yates, Syracuse, T, 0/68
8. Fred Hageman, Kansas, C, 0/55
9. Bob Anderson, Army, HB, 1/1
10. Bob Simms, Rutgers, LB, 28/31
11. Dale Rems, Purdue, T, 0/0
12. Pete Hall, Marquette, E, 12/12
13. Jim Varnado, Southern, FB, 0/0
14. Doug Cline, Clemson, LB, 0/95
15. Walter Beach, Central Michigan, DB, 0/48

PHILADELPHIA EAGLES

1. Ron Burton, Northwestern, HB, 0/69
2. **Maxie Baughan, Georgia Tech, LB, 80/147**
3. Curt Merz, Iowa, G, 0/92
4. Ted Dean, Wichita State, FB, 42/44
4. Jack Cummings, North Carolina, QB, 0/0
5. Don Norton, Iowa, E, 0/91
6. Emmett Wilson, Georgia Tech, T, 0/0
7. John Wilkins, Southern California, T, 0/0
8. Monte Lee, Texas, LB, 0/39
12. Dave Grosz, Oregon, QB, 0/0
13. **Dave Graham, Virginia, T, 83/83**
14. Ray Petersen, West Virginia, B, 0/0
15. John Wilcox, Oregon, DT, 12/12
20. Ray Armstrong, TCU, DT, 0/14

PITTSBURGH STEELERS

1. Jack Spikes, TCU, FB, 0/86
5. Abner Haynes, North Texas, HB, 0/112
7. Leonard Wilson, Purdue, B, 0/0
7. Lonnie Dennis, BYU, G, 0/0
8. Dan Lanphear, Wisconsin, DE, 0/16
9. Marshall Harris, Texas Christian, G, 0/0
10. John Kapele, Brigham Young, DE, 32/38
10. Arvie Martin, Texas Christian, C, 0/0
12. Earl Butler, North Carolina, T, 0/0
13. Joe Womack, Los Angeles State, HB, 11/11
14. **Brady Keys, Colorado State, DB, 85/100**
15. Larry Essenmacker, Alma, T, 0/0
16. Dave Ames, Richmond, HB, 0/12

SAN FRANCISCO 49ERS

1. **Monty Stickles, Notre Dame, TE, 102/115**
2. Carl Kammerer, Pacific, DE, 28/123
2. **Mike Magac, Missouri, G, 56/78**
3. Rod Breedlove, Maryland, LB, 0/101
4. Ray Norton, San Jose State, HB, 9/9
5. **Len Rohde, Utah State, T, 208/208**
6. Lee Murchison, Pacific, WR, 0/14
7. Bob Waters, Presbyterian, QB, 30/30
8. Bill Mathis, Clemson, FB, 0/137
8. Max Fugler, Louisiana State, C, 0/0
9. Bobby Wasden, Auburn, E, 0/0
10. Mel Branch, LSU, DE, 0/126
11. Ed Pitts, South Carolina, T, 0/0
11. Ernie Hansen, Northern Arizona, C, 0/0
12. Jim Williams, North Carolina, G, 0/0
13. Dean Hinshaw, Stanford, T, 0/0
14. Gary Campbell, Whittier, B, 0/0
15. **Mike Dowdle, Texas, LB, 51/81**
17. Goose Gonsoulin, Baylor, DB, 14/108

ST. LOUIS CARDINALS

1. George Izo, Notre Dame, QB, 2/26
2. Mike McGee, Duke, G, 37/37
2. Harold Olson, Clemson, T, 0/70
3. Charley Ellzey, Southern Mississippi, C, 14/14
3. Hugh McInnis, Southern Mississippi, TE, 24/38
4. Willie West, Oregon, DB, 21/105
6. Jacky Lee, Cincinnati, QB, 0/100
7. **Larry Wilson, Utah, DB, 169/169**
8. Wayne Crow, California, HB, 0/47
10. **Charley Johnson, New Mexico State, QB, 87/165**
10. Paul Oglesby, UCLA, T, 0/14
11. Bobby Towns, Georgia, DB, 4/6
14. **Bob DeMarco, Dayton, C, 107/185**
15. Frank Mestnik, Marquette, FB, 22/33
16. Jim Hunt, Prairie View A&M, DT, 0/146
20. Tom Day, North Carolina A&T, DE, 10/117

WASHINGTON REDSKINS

1. Richie Lucas, Penn State, QB, 0/22
2. Sam Horner, VMI, HB, 24/33
3. **Andy Stynchula, Penn State, DE, 53/104**
4. **Vince Promuto, Holy Cross, G, 130/130**
5. Don Stallings, North Carolina, DT, 9/9
6. Dave Hudson, Florida, E, 0/0
8. Earl Kohlhaas, Penn State, G, 0/0
9. Dwight Bumgarner, Duke, E, 0/0
11. Jim Eifrid, Colorado State, LB, 0/1
12. Jim Crotty, Notre Dame, DB, 14/22
13. Bill Herron, Georgia, E, 0/0
14. Charlie Milstead, Texas A&M, QB, 0/22
15. Bernie Darre, Tulane, G, 12/12
16. Joe Kulbacki, Purdue, HB, 0/14

1960 AFL

BOSTON PATRIOTS

1. Buddy Allen, Utah State, HB, 0/1
1. **Ron Burton, Northwestern, HB, 69/69**
1. Daniel Colchico, San Jose State, DE, 0/76
1. Joe Kulbacki, Purdue, HB, 0/14
1. Dee Mackey, Texas A&M-Commerce, E, 0/78
1. Pete Manning, Wake Forest, DB, 0/9
1. Frank Mestnik, Marquette, FB, 0/33
1. Ron Mix, USC, T, 0/142
1. Jim Prestel, Idaho, DT, 0/96
1. Gerhard Schwedes, Syracuse, HB, 7/10
1. Harvey White, Clemson, QB, 9/9
1. Gary Wisener, Baylor, DB, 0/15
2. Dave Ames, Richmond, HB, 0/12
2. Jim Boeke, Heidelberg, T, 0/119
2. Billy Brewer, Mississippi, DB, 0/11
2. Bo Farrington, Prairie View A&M, SE, 0/45
2. Dick Grecni, Ohio University, LB, 0/12
2. **Jack Rudolph, Georgia Tech, LB, 64/75**
2. John Wilcox, Oregon, DT, 0/12

BUFFALO BILLS

1. Charlie Bivins, Morris Brown, HB, 9/102
1. Mike Connelly, Utah State, C, 0/120
1. Lou Cordileone, Clemson, DT, 0/75
1. Ted Dean, Wichita State, FB, 0/44
1. Ross Fichtner, Purdue, DB, 0/106
1. Jon Gilliam, Texas A&M-Commerce, C, 0/76
1. Alan Goldstein, North Carolina, E, 0/14
1. Jim Houston, Ohio State, LB, 0/177
1. Bob Khayat, Mississippi, G, 0/40
1. Ken Kirk, Mississippi, LB, 0/44
1. Jim Leo, Cincinnati, DE, 0/40
1. Richie Lucas, Penn State, QB, 22/22
1. Chuck McMurtry, Whittier, DT, 28/53
1. Harold Olson, Clemson, T, 42/70
1. Vince Promuto, Holy Cross, G, 0/130
1. Len Rohde, Utah State, T, 0/208
1. Joe Schaffer, Tennessee, LB, 14/14
1. Larry Wilson, Utah, DB, 0/169
2. **Tom Day, North Carolina A&T, DE, 96/117**
2. Pete Hall, Marquette, E, 0/12
2. Darrell Harper, Michigan, HB, 4/4
2. Jim Sorey, Texas Southern, DT, 42/42

DALLAS TEXANS

1. Jack Atchason, Western Illinois, E, 0/3
1. **Chris Burford, Stanford, SE, 103/103**
1. Gail Cogdill, Washington State, SE, 0/127
1. Jim Crotty, Notre Dame, DB, 0/22
1. Gene Gossage, Northwestern, DE, 0/40
1. John Kapele, Brigham Young, DE, 0/38
1. Don Meredith, SMU, QB, 0/104
1. Tom Moore, Vanderbilt, HB, 0/102
1. Lee Murchison, Pacific, WR, 0/14
1. Jim Norton, Idaho, DB, 0/125
1. Warren Rabb, LSU, QB, 0/30
1. **Johnny Robinson, LSU, DB, 164/164**
1. Glenn Shaw, Kentucky, FB, 0/29
1. Jack Stone, Oregon, T, 14/42
1. Marvin Terrell, Mississippi, G, 38/38
1. Carroll Zaruba, Nebraska, DB, 7/7
2. Grady Alderman, Detroit Mercy, T, 0/204
2. Taz Anderson, Georgia Tech, TE, 0/62
2. Doug Brown, Fresno State, DT, 0/13
2. Charley Ellzey, Southern Mississippi, C, 0/14
2. Goose Gonsoulin, Baylor, DB, 0/108
2. Paul Winslow, North Carolina Central, DB, 0/12

DENVER BRONCOS

1. Charley Britt, Georgia, DB, 0/49
1. Bernie Darre, Tulane, G, 0/12
1. Roger Davis, Syracuse, G, 0/72
1. Mike Dowdle, Texas, LB, 0/81
1. Wayne Hawkins, Pacific, G, 0/136
1. Claude King, Houston, HB, 0/25
1. Roger LeClerc, Trinity (CT), LB, 8/104
1. Dean Look, Michigan State, QB, 0/1
1. Bill Mathis, Clemson, FB, 0/137
1. Ray Norton, San Jose State, HB, 0/9
1. Lebron Shields, Tennessee, DE, 0/18
1. Jack Spikes, TCU, FB, 0/86
1. Willie West, Oregon, DB, 7/105
1. Bob Yates, Syracuse, T, 0/68
2. Mel Branch, LSU, DE, 0/126
2. Jim Colvin, Houston, DT, 0/103
2. Bobby Joe Green, Florida, P, 0/187
2. Sam Horner, VMI, HB, 0/33

HOUSTON OILERS

1. Dick Bass, Pacific, FB, 0/112
1. Billy Cannon, LSU, TE, 48/133
1. **Doug Cline, Clemson, LB, 93/95**
1. George Herring, Southern Mississippi, QB, 0/28
1. **Jacky Lee, Cincinnati, QB, 68/100**
1. Bruce Maher, Detroit Mercy, DB, 0/136
1. Mike McGee, Duke, G, 0/37
1. Hugh McInnis, Southern Mississippi, TE, 0/38
1. Max Messner, Cincinnati, LB, 0/70
1. Gene Prebola, Boston University, TE, 0/56
1. Palmer Pyle, Michigan State, G, 0/61
1. Bob Simms, Rutgers, LB, 0/31
1. Bob White, Ohio State, FB, 6/6
1. Maury Youmans, Syracuse, DE, 0/56
2. Stan Fanning, Idaho, T, 5/52
2. Dave Graham, Virginia, T, 0/83
2. Jim Marshall, Ohio State, DE, 0/282
2. Ron Morrison, New Mexico, DT, 1/1
2. Paul Oglesby, UCLA, T, 0/14
2. **Bob Talamini, Kentucky, G, 112/126**
2. Bobby Towns, Georgia, DB, 0/6
2. Jim Welch, SMU, DB, 0/114

LOS ANGELES CHARGERS

1. Bob Bercich, Michigan State, DB, 0/18
1. Bobby Boyd, Oklahoma, DB, 0/121
1. Byron Bradfute, Southern Mississippi, T, 0/17
1. Rod Breedlove, Maryland, LB, 0/101
1. Jake Crouthamel, Dartmouth, HB, 0/2
1. Pete Davidson, The Citadel, DT, 0/1
1. Charlie Flowers, Mississippi, FB, 24/28
1. Bobby Franklin, Mississippi, DB, 0/86
1. Bob Jeter, Iowa, DB, 0/139
1. Billy Locklin, New Mexico State, LB, 0/2
1. Bill Lopasky, West Virginia, G, 0/10
1. **Paul Maguire, The Citadel, LB, 53/151**
1. Wahoo McDaniel, Oklahoma, LB, 0/105
1. Charlie Milstead, Texas A&M, QB, 0/22
1. Bob Scholtz, Notre Dame, C, 0/81
1. Ron Stehouwer, Colorado State, G, 0/68
1. Monty Stickles, Notre Dame, TE, 0/115
1. **Bob Zeman, Wisconsin, DB, 54/82**
2. George Blair, Mississippi, DB, 46/46
2. Bob DeMarco, Dayton, C, 0/185
2. Gorden Kelley, Georgia, LB, 0/51
2. Bob Waters, Presbyterian, QB, 0/30

NEW YORK TITANS

1. Jackie Burkett, Auburn, LB, 0/121
1. Angelo Coia, USC, SE, 0/77
1. Jim Eifrid, Colorado State, LB, 0/1
1. Don Ellersick, Washington State, DB, 0/12
1. Don Floyd, TCU, DE, 0/97
1. Prentice Gautt, Oklahoma, HB, 0/88
1. **Larry Grantham, Mississippi, LB, 175/175**
1. George Izo, Notre Dame, QB, 0/26
1. Ed Kovac, Cincinnati, HB, 3/15
1. Mike Magac, Missouri, G, 0/78
1. Blanche Martin, Michigan State, FB, 4/13
1. Curt Merz, Iowa, G, 0/92
1. Eddie Meyer, West Texas A&M, T, 0/9
1. Jim Mooty, Arkansas, DB, 0/7
1. Don Perkins, New Mexico, FB, 0/107
1. Dave Ross, Los Angeles State, E, 12/12
1. Zeke Smith, Auburn, LB, 0/24
1. Don Stallings, North Carolina, DT, 0/9
1. Larry Stephens, Texas, DE, 0/103
1. James Stinnette, Oregon State, FB, 0/24
2. Ray Armstrong, TCU, DT, 0/14
2. Roger Brown, Maryland-Eastern Shore, DT, 0/138
2. Tom Budrewicz, Brown, G, 2/2
2. Andy Stynchula, Penn State, DE, 0/104

OAKLAND RAIDERS

1. Maxie Baughan, Georgia Tech, LB, 0/147
1. Carmen Cavalli, Richmond, DE, 14/14
1. Don Deskins, Michigan, DT, 14/14
1. Leon Dombrowski, Delaware, LB, 0/1
1. Dale Hackbart, Wisconsin, DB, 0/152
1. Abner Haynes, North Texas, HB, 0/112
1. Don Norton, Iowa, E, 0/91
1. **Jim Otto, Miami (FL), C, 210/210**
1. Jerry Stalcup, Wisconsin, LB, 0/34
1. Al Witcher, Baylor, E, 0/14
2. Pervis Atkins, New Mexico State, FL, 19/78
2. Al Bansavage, USC, LB, 14/17
2. Walter Beach, Central Michigan, DB, 0/48
2. Johnny Brewer, Mississippi, TE, 0/135
2. Joe Cannavino, Ohio State, DB, 28/32
2. Don Churchwell, Mississippi, DT, 1/11
2. Fred Hageman, Kansas, C, 0/55
2. Billy Lott, Mississippi, FB, 14/61
2. Rich Mostardo, Kent State, DB, 5/26

1961 NFL

BALTIMORE COLTS

1. **Tom Matte, Ohio State, RB, 142/142**
2. **Tom Gilburg, Syracuse, T, 69/69**
3. **Jerry Hill, Wyoming, RB, 102/102**
4. Ken Gregory, Whittier, E, 14/30
5. Ed Dyas, Auburn, B, 0/0
5. Ron Osborne, Clemson, T, 0/0
6. Don Kern, Virginia Military, HB, 0/0
7. Ike Grimsley, Michigan State, HB, 0/0
8. Paul Terhes, Bucknell, B, 0/0
9. Pete Nicklas, Baylor, T, 0/14
10. Bob Clemens, Pittsburgh, FB, 9/9
11. Ralph White, Bowling Green, T, 0/0
12. Dick Reynolds, North Carolina State, T, 0/0
13. Dallas Garber, Marietta, B, 0/0
14. Bob Hunt, Southern Methodist, T, 0/0
15. E.A. Sims, New Mexico State, E, 0/0
19. Joe Novsek, Tulsa, DE, 0/14

CHICAGO BEARS

1. **Mike Ditka, Pittsburgh, TE, 84/158**
2. Bill Brown, Illinois, RB, 14/194
3. Claude Gibson, North Carolina State, DB, 0/70
4. Ernie Ladd, Grambling State, DT, 0/112
5. Keith Lincoln, Washington State, FB, 0/99
6. George Fleming, Washington, HB, 0/14
7. **Mike Pyle, Yale, C, 121/121**
8. Ed Ryan, Michigan State, B, 0/0
9. Bobby Bethune, Mississippi State, DB, 0/10
10. Jason Harness, Michigan State, E, 0/0
11. Sam Fewell, South Carolina, T, 0/0
12. Howard Dyer, Virginia Military, QB, 0/0
13. Bob McLeod, Abilene Christian, TE, 0/84
14. Jim Tyrer, Ohio State, T, 0/194
15. Chuck Linning, Miami (FL), T, 0/0
16. Wayne Frazier, Auburn, C, 0/48

CLEVELAND BROWNS

1. Bobby Crespino, Mississippi, SE, 41/107
2. Ed Nutting, Georgia Tech, T, 4/18
4. **John Brown, Syracuse, T, 67/136**
5. Mike Lucci, Tennessee, LB, 37/154
6. **Frank Parker, Oklahoma State, DT, 60/78**
7. Preston Powell, Grambling State, FB, 12/12
8. Fred Cox, Pittsburgh, K, 0/210
8. John Frongillo, Baylor, C, 0/54
9. Jake Gibbs, Mississippi, QB, 0/0
10. Wayne Wolff, Wake Forest, G, 0/2
10. Ken Ericson, Syracuse, E, 0/0
11. Billy Gault, TCU, HB, 0/4
12. Dick Lage, Lenoir-Rhyne, E, 0/1
13. Jack Wilson, Duke, B, 0/0
14. Phil Lohman, Oklahoma, C, 0/0
15. Charley Taylor, Mississippi, B, 0/0
16. Roger Shoals, Maryland, T, 16/104

DALLAS COWBOYS

1. **Bob Lilly, TCU, DT, 196/196**
2. E.J. Holub, Texas Tech, LB, 0/127
3. Stew Barber, Penn State, T, 0/125
4. Sonny Davis, Baylor, LB, 2/2
7. Art Gilmore, Oregon State, B, 0/0
8. Don Talbert, Texas, T, 37/103
9. Glynn Gregory, SMU, E, 20/20
11. Norris Stevenson, Missouri, B, 0/0
12. Lowndes Shingler, Clemson, QB, 0/0
13. Don Goodman, Florida, B, 0/0
14. Billy Shaw, Georgia Tech, G, 0/119

15. Julius Varnado, Cal State-San Francisco, T, 0/0
19. Lynn Hoyem, Long Beach State, G, 28/84

DETROIT LIONS

2. Dan LaRose, Missouri, T, 37/65
3. Houston Antwine, Southern Illinois, DT, 0/156
3. Dick Mills, Pittsburgh, G, 22/22
4. Ron Hartline, Oklahoma, FB, 0/0
5. Earl Faison, Indiana, DE, 0/73
5. Ron Puckett, Cal State-Los Angeles, T, 0/0
8. Larry Muff, Benedictine, E, 0/0
9. Bob Brooks, Ohio University, FB, 0/14
10. Errol Linden, Houston, T, 0/134
11. Larry Vargo, Detroit Mercy, DB, 23/57
12. Tom Rodgers, Kentucky, B, 0/0
13. Paul Hodge, Pittsburgh, LB, 0/0
14. Charley Bowers, Arizona State, HB, 0/0
15. Mike Lauber, Wisconsin-River Falls, E, 0/0
17. Tom Goode, Mississippi State, C, 0/113

GREEN BAY PACKERS

1. **Herb Adderley, Michigan State, DB, 125/164**
2. **Ron Kostelnik, Cincinnati, DT, 110/120**
3. Phil Nugent, Tulane, DB, 0/12
4. Paul Dudley, Arkansas, HB, 0/21
4. Joe LeSage, Tulane, G, 0/0
5. Jack Novak, Miami (FL), G, 0/0
6. Lee Folkins, Washington, TE, 14/63
7. Lewis Johnson, Florida A&M, B, 0/0
9. Vester Flanagan, Cal State-Humboldt, T, 0/0
10. Roger Hagberg, Minnesota, FB, 0/68
10. Buck McLeod, Baylor, T, 0/0
11. Val Keckin, Southern Mississippi, QB, 0/6
12. John Denvir, Colorado, G, 0/11
13. **Elijah Pitts, Philander Smith, HB, 126/134**
14. Nelson Toburen, Wichita State, LB, 24/24
15. Ray Lardani, Miami (FL), T, 0/0
17. Jim Brewington, North Carolina Central, T, 0/14
20. Ray Ratkowski, Notre Dame, HB, 0/1

LOS ANGELES RAMS

1. **Marlin McKeever, USC, LB, 95/162**
2. Elbert Kimbrough, Northwestern, DB, 5/85
3. Ron Miller, Wisconsin, QB, 6/6
3. Harold Beaty, Oklahoma State, G, 0/0
4. **Charley Cowan, New Mexico Highlands, T, 206/206**
5. Willie Hector, Pacific, T, 12/12
6. Bruce Olderman, Allegheny, T, 0/0
6. Larry Wood, Northwestern, B, 0/0
7. Bobby Smith, UCLA, DB, 49/69
8. Reggie Carolan, Idaho, TE, 0/80
9. Duane Allen, Mt.San Antonio J.C., TE, 31/49
10. **Joe Scibelli, American International, G, 202/202**
11. Bobby Lane, Baylor, LB, 0/8
12. Walt Mince, Arizona, B, 0/0
13. Mike McKeever, Southern California, G, 0/0
14. **Deacon Jones, Mississippi Valley State, DE, 151/191**
15. Ernie Wright, Ohio State, T, 0/174
17. Chuck Allen, Washington, LB, 0/144

MINNESOTA VIKINGS

1. **Tommy Mason, Tulane, RB, 70/124**
2. **Rip Hawkins, North Carolina, LB, 70/70**
3. **Fran Tarkenton, Georgia, QB, 177/246**
4. Chuck Lamson, Wyoming, DB, 26/67
5. **Ed Sharockman, Pittsburgh, DB, 142/142**
6. Jerry Burch, Georgia Tech, WR, 0/14
7. Allan Ferrie, Wagner, E, 0/0
8. Paul Lindquist, New Hampshire, DT, 0/2
9. Dan Sheehan, Tennessee-Chattanooga, T, 0/0
10. Doug Mayberry, Utah State, FB, 17/19
11. Jerry Mays, SMU, DE, 0/140
12. Steve Stonebreaker, Detroit Mercy, LB, 28/84
13. Ray Hayes, Central Oklahoma, FB, 13/13
14. Ken Petersen, Utah, G, 12/12
15. Mike Mercer, Arizona State, K, 18/119
17. Willie Jones, Purdue, FB, 0/10
18. Bob Voight, Los Angeles State, DT, 0/14

NEW YORK GIANTS

2. Bob Gaiters, New Mexico State, HB, 16/31
2. Bruce Tarbox, Syracuse, G, 0/7
4. Ben Davidson, Washington, DE, 0/152
5. Jerry Daniels, Mississippi, E, 0/0
6. **Greg Larson, Minnesota, C, 179/179**
7. Jim Collier, Arkansas, TE, 13/27
8. Allen Green, Mississippi, K, 0/14
9. Moses Gray, Indiana, T, 0/5
10. Glen Knight, Shaw, E, 0/0
11. Bob Benton, Mississippi, T, 0/0
12. Jack Moynihan, Holy Cross, QB, 0/0
13. Jerry Fields, Ohio State, LB, 0/19
14. Gene White, Florida A&M, HB, 0/7
15. Cody Binkley, Vanderbilt, C, 0/0

PHILADELPHIA EAGLES

1. Art Baker, Syracuse, FB, 0/17
2. Bo Strange, Louisiana State, C, 0/0
3. Don Oakes, Virginia Tech, T, 22/104
3. Jim Wright, Memphis, DB, 0/10
4. Dan Ficca, USC, G, 0/70
6. Ben Balme, Yale, G, 0/0
7. **Irv Cross, Northwestern, DB, 83/125**
8. Jim Beaver, Florida, DT, 1/1
9. Wayne Fontes, Michigan State, DB, 0/9
10. Luther Hayes, USC, E, 0/14
11. L.E. Hicks, Florida, T, 0/0
12. Billy Majors, Tennessee, DB, 0/1
13. Don Jonas, Penn State, HB, 1/1
14. Willie Fleming, Iowa, HB, 0/0
15. **Bobby Richards, LSU, DE, 56/84**
20. Jacque MacKinnon, Colgate, TE, 0/118

PITTSBURGH STEELERS

2. Myron Pottios, Notre Dame, LB, 41/129
5. Fred Mautino, Syracuse, E, 0/0
7. **Dick Hoak, Penn State, RB, 135/135**
8. George Balthazar, Tennessee State, T, 0/0
10. Red Mack, Notre Dame, TE, 41/58
11. Henry Clement, North Carolina, TE, 14/14
12. Frank Jackunas, Detroit Mercy, C, 0/3
14. Bob Schmitz, Montana State, LB, 49/51
15. Ray McCown, West Texas State, B, 0/0
16. Wilbert Scott, Indiana, LB, 4/4
17. Terry Nofsinger, Utah, QB, 9/24

SAN FRANCISCO 49ERS

1. **Bernie Casey, Bowling Green State, HB, 79/105**
1. **Jimmy Johnson, UCLA, DB, 213/213**
1. Billy Kilmer, UCLA, QB, 39/170
2. **Roland Lakes, Wichita State, DT, 140/154**
3. Bill Cooper, Muskingum, FB, 38/38
4. Dale Messer, Fresno State, HB, 46/46
4. Aaron Thomas, Oregon State, TE, 16/133
5. Bob McCreary, Wake Forest, T, 0/9
5. **Clark Miller, Utah State, DE, 89/97**
6. Mike McClellan, Oklahoma, DB, 0/24
7. Ray Purdin, Northwestern, B, 0/0
8. Neill Plumley, Oregon, T, 0/0
9. Leon Donohue, San Jose State, G, 42/84
9. Everisto Nino, East Texas State, T, 0/0
10. Paul Hynes, Louisiana Tech, DB, 0/23
11. Tony Parrilli, Illinois, G, 0/0
12. Donald Coffey, Memphis, WR, 0/3
13. Tommy Hackler, Tennessee Tech, E, 0/0
13. Julius Fincke, McNeese State, T, 0/0
14. Bill Worrell, Georgia, T, 0/0
15. Bob Sams, Central State (OK), T, 0/0
16. Charley Fuller, San Francisco State, HB, 0/17
18. **Kay McFarland, Colorado State, WR, 63/63**

ST. LOUIS CARDINALS

1. Ken Rice, Auburn, T, 0/79
2. Fred Arbanas, Michigan State, TE, 0/118
3. Billy Wilson, Auburn, T, 0/0
4. Ron McDole, Nebraska, DE, 13/240
5. Glenn Bass, East Carolina, SE, 0/79
6. Dale Evans, Kansas State, HB, 0/5
6. Dick Thornton, Northwestern, QB, 0/0
7. Al Bemiller, Syracuse, C, 0/126
7. George Hultz, Southern Mississippi, DT, 13/13
8. Marshall Starks, Illinois, DB, 0/18
9. Chick Graning, Georgia Tech, HB, 0/0
10. Jimmy King, Clemson, T, 0/0
11. Bill Kinnune, Washington, G, 0/0
12. Mike Stock, Northwestern, B, 0/0
13. **Ernie McMillan, Illinois, T, 178/190**
14. Bob Elliot, North Carolina, FB, 0/0
15. Mel West, Missouri, HB, 0/16
17. **Pat Fischer, Nebraska, DB, 87/213**
20. Leo Reed, Colorado State, T, 0/9

WASHINGTON REDSKINS

1. **Joe Rutgens, Illinois, DT, 110/110**
1. Norm Snead, Wake Forest, QB, 42/178
3. Jim Cunningham, Pittsburgh, FB, 42/42
6. Joe Krakoski, Illinois, DB, 11/62
6. John O'Day, Miami (FL), T, 0/0
7. Jim Kerr, Penn State, DB, 24/24
8. Charlie Barnes, Louisiana-Monroe, E, 0/4
9. Joel Arrington, Duke, B, 0/0
11. **Riley Mattson, Oregon, T, 56/68**
12. Bob Coolbaugh, Richmond, FL, 0/14
13. Doug Elmore, Mississippi, P, 14/14
14. Doyle Schick, Kansas, DB, 5/5
15. Bob Johnson, Michigan, E, 0/0
17. Joe Bellino, Navy, HB, 0/35
19. Tony Romeo, Florida State, TE, 0/89

1961 AFL

BOSTON PATRIOTS

1. Tommy Mason, Tulane, RB, 0/124
2. Rip Hawkins, North Carolina, LB, 0/70
3. Dan LaRose, Missouri, T, 0/65
5. Fran Tarkenton, Georgia, QB, 0/246
6. **Larry Eisenhauer, Boston College, DE, 115/115**
7. Paul Terhes, Bucknell, QB, 0/0
8. **Charley Long, Tennessee-Chattanooga, G, 124/124**
9. Roland Lakes, Wichita State, DT, 0/154
11. Mel West, Missouri, HB, 4/16
13. Dan Underwood, McNeese State, T, 0/0
14. Jim Wright, Memphis, DB, 0/10
17. Ray Ratkowski, Notre Dame, HB, 1/1
19. Joe Bellino, Navy, HB, 35/35
20. Clarence Childs, Florida A&M, DB, 0/59
21. **Don Oakes, Virginia Tech, T, 82/104**
24. **Don Webb, Iowa State, DB, 134/134**
26. Charley Granger, Southern (LA), T, 0/14
29. Ernie McMillan, Illinois, T, 0/190
30. George Hultz, Southern Mississippi, DT, 0/13

BUFFALO BILLS

1. Ken Rice, Auburn, T, 28/79
2. **Billy Shaw, Georgia Tech, G, 119/119**
3. Art Baker, Syracuse, FB, 17/17
3. Tom Gilburg, Syracuse, T, 0/69
4. **Stew Barber, Penn State, T, 125/125**
5. Norm Snead, Wake Forest, QB, 0/178
6. Fred Brown, Georgia, HB, 9/9
7. **Al Bemiller, Syracuse, C, 126/126**
9. Billy Majors, Tennessee, DB, 1/1
10. Don Kern, Virginia Military, HB, 0/0
12. Floyd Powers, Mississippi State, G, 0/0
14. Ron Kostelnik, Cincinnati, DT, 0/120
17. Wayne Wolff, Wake Forest, G, 2/2
19. Charlie Barnes, Louisiana-Monroe, E, 0/4
21. Larry Vargo, Detroit Mercy, DB, 0/57
23. Red Mack, Notre Dame, TE, 0/58
24. Frank Jackunas, Detroit Mercy, C, 3/3
30. Billy Martin, Minnesota, HB, 0/32

DALLAS TEXANS

1. **E.J. Holub, Texas Tech, LB, 127/127**
2. Bob Lilly, TCU, DT, 0/196
3. **Jim Tyrer, Ohio State, T, 180/194**
4. Claude Moorman, Duke, E, 0/0
5. **Jerry Mays, SMU, DE, 140/140**
7. **Fred Arbanas, Michigan State, TE, 118/118**
8. John O'Day, Miami (FL), T, 0/0
9. Dick Mills, Pittsburgh, G, 0/22
10. Jerry Daniels, Mississippi, E, 0/0
11. Marvin Tibbets, Georgia Tech, HB, 0/0
12. Paul Hynes, Louisiana Tech, DB, 1/23
13. Glynn Gregory, SMU, E, 0/20
14. **Curtis McClinton, Kansas, FB, 107/107**
15. Ed Nutting, Georgia Tech, T, 0/18
16. Aaron Thomas, Oregon State, TE, 0/133
19. **Frank Jackson, SMU, FL, 70/90**
20. Bobby Lane, Baylor, LB, 0/8
22. Ed Sharockman, Pittsburgh, DB, 0/142

DENVER BRONCOS

1. Bob Gaiters, New Mexico State, HB, 6/31
2. Jerry Hill, Wyoming, RB, 0/102
4. Ron McDole, Nebraska, DE, 0/240
5. Charley Cowan, New Mexico Highlands, T, 0/206
6. Dale Evans, Kansas State, HB, 5/5
7. Pat Patchen, Florida, E, 0/0
9. Phil Nugent, Tulane, DB, 12/12
10. Charley Sturgeon, Kentucky, HB, 0/0
11. John Simko, Augustana (SD), E, 0/0
12. Jerry Miller, Howard Payne, E, 0/0
13. Ron Greene, Washington State, G, 0/0
14. Bill Cooper, Muskingum, FB, 0/38
15. Willie Crafts, Texas A&I, G, 0/0

HOUSTON OILERS

1. Mike Ditka, Pittsburgh, TE, 0/158
2. **Tom Goode, Mississippi State, C, 56/113**
3. **Walt Suggs, Mississippi State, T, 137/137**
4. Bobby Walden, Georgia, P, 0/194
5. Monte Lee, Texas, LB, 0/39
6. Jake Gibbs, Mississippi, QB, 0/0
7. Dick Reynolds, North Carolina State, T, 0/0
8. Houston Antwine, Southern Illinois, DT, 0/156
9. Ralph White, Bowling Green, T, 0/0
11. Bob Bird, Bowling Green, G, 0/0
12. **Bob McLeod, Abilene Christian, TE, 84/84**
13. Gerald Hinton, Louisiana Tech, G, 0/0
14. Jimmy King, Clemson, T, 0/0
15. Dennis Ferriter, Marquette, C, 0/0
21. Ron Miller, Wisconsin, QB, 0/6
22. Bob Kelly, New Mexico State, T, 32/39
24. Ken Gregory, Whittier, E, 0/30
28. **John Frongillo, Baylor, C, 54/54**
29. Errol Linden, Houston, T, 0/134

HOUSTON OILERS

6. Calvin Bird, Kentucky, HB, 0/0
6. Cliff Roberts, Illinois, T, 0/0
10. Willie Hector, Pacific, G, 0/0
14. Billy Wilson, Auburn, T, 0/0

NEW YORK TITANS

2. Herb Adderley, Michigan State, DB, 0/164
5. Tom Matte, Ohio State, RB, 0/142
6. Bill Brown, Illinois, RB, 0/194
8. Harold Beaty, Oklahoma State, T, 0/0
9. Bernie Casey, Bowling Green State, HB, 0/105
10. Joe Scibelli, American International, G, 0/202
11. Art Gilmore, Oregon State, HB, 0/0
12. Norris Stevenson, Missouri, HB, 0/0
13. Joe Wendryhoski, Illinois, C, 0/59
14. Jim Cunningham, Pittsburgh, FB, 0/42
15. Irv Cross, Northwestern, E, 0/0
19. Jim Kerr, Penn State, DB, 0/24
21. Bob Brooks, Ohio University, FB, 14/14
22. Wayne Fontes, Michigan State, DB, 9/9
23. Mickey Walker, Michigan State, G, 0/52
26. Bobby Smith, UCLA, DB, 0/69
27. Moses Gray, Indiana, T, 5/5
28. Fred Cox, Pittsburgh, K, 0/210

OAKLAND RAIDERS

1. Joe Rutgens, Illinois, DT, 0/110
2. George Fleming, Washington, HB, 14/14
4. Elbert Kimbrough, Northwestern, DB, 0/85
5. Dick Norman, Stanford, QB, 0/3
6. Bobby Crespino, Mississippi, SE, 0/107
7. Tom Watkins, Iowa State, HB, 0/75
8. Dick Price, Mississippi, G, 0/0
10. Ken Peterson, Utah, T, 0/0
11. Doug Mayberry, Utah State, FB, 0/0
12. Bob Schmitz, Montana State, G, 0/0
13. Jerry Burch, Georgia Tech, WR, 14/14
13. Gerald Burch, Georgia Tech, E, 0/0
14. Clark Miller, Utah State, DE, 0/97
15. Bob Coolbaugh, Richmond, FL, 14/14
17. Joe Novsek, Tulsa, DE, 14/14
18. **Joe Krakoski, Illinois, DB, 51/62**
19. Charley Fuller, San Francisco State, HB, 17/17
20. Preston Powell, Grambling State, FB, 0/12

SAN DIEGO CHARGERS

1. **Earl Faison, Indiana, DE, 67/73**
2. **Keith Lincoln, Washington State, FB, 81/99**
3. Marlin McKeever, USC, LB, 0/162
4. Jimmy Johnson, UCLA, DB, 0/213
5. Billy Kilmer, UCLA, QB, 0/170
6. Cliff Roberts, Illinois, T, 0/10
7. Claude Gibson, North Carolina State, DB, 28/70
8. Charley Johnson, New Mexico State, QB, 0/165
9. Bob Scarpitto, Notre Dame, FL, 7/102
11. Greg Larson, Minnesota, C, 0/179
12. Hezekiah Braxton, Virginia Union, FB, 8/9
13. Dale Messer, Fresno State, HB, 0/46
15. **Ernie Ladd, Grambling State, DT, 70/112**
16. **Bud Whitehead, Florida State, DB, 94/94**
17. Reggie Carolan, Idaho, TE, 18/80
23. Glenn Bass, East Carolina, SE, 0/79
25. Donald Coffey, Memphis, WR, 0/3
27. Luther Hayes, USC, E, 14/14
28. **Chuck Allen, Washington, LB, 108/144**
29. Dan Ficca, USC, G, 0/70

1962 NFL

BALTIMORE COLTS

1. **Wendell Harris, LSU, DB, 56/83**
2. Bill Saul, Penn State, LB, 28/88
3. **Dan Sullivan, Boston College, G, 140/140**

4. Jim Dillard, Oklahoma State, B, 0/0
5. Jerry Croft, Bowling Green, G, 0/0
7. **Fred Miller, LSU, DT, 133/133**
8. Pete Brokaw, Syracuse, B, 0/0
9. Roy Walker, Purdue, FB, 0/0
9. Walt Rappold, Duke, QB, 0/0
10. Fred Moore, Memphis, DT, 0/29
11. Scott Tyler, Miami (OH), B, 0/0
12. Bake Turner, Texas Tech, WR, 14/118
13. Charles Holmes, Maryland-Eastern Shore, FB, 0/0
14. Stinson Jones, Virginia Military, B, 0/0
15. Joe Monte, Furman, G, 0/0
16. Ray Abruzzese, Alabama, B, 0/61
19. Fred Gillett, Los Angeles State, C, 0/9

CHICAGO BEARS

1. **Ronnie Bull, Baylor, RB, 110/123**
2. Clyde Brock, Utah State, T, 0/24
2. **Bennie McRae, Michigan, DB, 125/133**
3. Bill Hull, Wake Forest, DE, 0/14
3. Jim Bates, Southern California, E, 0/0
4. **Jim Cadile, San Jose State, G, 128/128**
5. Mac Burton, San Jose State, E, 0/0
5. Bill Tunnicliff, Michigan, FB, 0/0
7. **Ed O'Bradovich, Illinois, DE, 124/124**
8. Larry Onesti, Northwestern, LB, 0/38
8. Ed Reynolds, Tulane, T, 0/0
9. Kelton Winston, Wiley, DB, 0/20
10. LeRoy Weaver, Adams State, B, 0/0
11. Jerry Robinson, Grambling State, FL, 0/46
12. Bill Watts, Miami (FL), T, 0/0
13. Joe Perkowski, Notre Dame, B, 0/0
14. Andy Von Sonn, UCLA, LB, 0/14
15. Kent Martin, Wake Forest, T, 0/0
17. Glenn Glass, Tennessee, DB, 0/55
18. Tommy Neck, LSU, DB, 1/1

CLEVELAND BROWNS

1. **Gary Collins, Maryland, FL, 127/127**
1. Leroy Jackson, Western Illinois, HB, 0/15
2. Chuck Hinton, North Carolina Central, DT, 0/123
2. Sandy Stephens, Minnesota, B, 0/0
3. John Furman, Texas-El Paso, QB, 0/0
4. Stan Sczurek, Purdue, LB, 34/45
5. Hank Rivera, Oregon State, DB, 0/12
6. Sam Tidmore, Ohio State, LB, 18/18
7. John Havlicek, Ohio State, E, 0/0
9. Charles Dickerson, Illinois, T, 0/0
10. Jerry Goerlitz, Northern Michigan, C, 0/0
10. Albert White, Capital, B, 0/0
11. Clifton McNeil, Grambling State, WR, 43/105
11. Ronnie Meyers, Villanova, E, 0/0
12. Ted Stute, Ohio U., E, 0/0
13. Frank Gardner, North Carolina Central, T, 0/0
14. Jim Shorter, Detroit Mercy, DB, 20/87
15. Tom Goosby, Baldwin-Wallace, G, 1/15
18. Sonny Bishop, Fresno State, G, 0/110

DALLAS COWBOYS

2. Sonny Gibbs, TCU, QB, 0/2
3. Bobby Plummer, Texas Christian, T, 0/0
6. **George Andrie, Marquette, DE, 141/141**
6. Donnie Davis, Southern (LA), WR, 11/25
8. Ken Tureaud, Michigan, B, 0/0
10. John Longmeyer, Southern Illinois, G, 0/0
11. Larry Hudas, Michigan State, E, 0/0
13. Bob Moses, Texas, E, 0/0
14. **Harold Hays, Southern Mississippi, LB, 70/96**
15. Guy Reese, SMU, DT, 28/57
17. Ray Jacobs, Howard Payne, DT, 0/79
18. Dave Cloutier, Maine, DB, 0/12
20. Amos Bullocks, Southern Illinois, HB, 26/34

DETROIT LIONS

1. John Hadl, Kansas, QB, 0/224
2. Eddie Wilson, Arizona, QB, 0/56
3. **Bobby Thompson, Arizona, DB, 65/72**
4. Larry Ferguson, Iowa, HB, 7/7
4. John Lomakoski, Western Michigan, T, 3/3
5. Dan Birdwell, Houston, DT, 0/96
6. Mike Bundra, USC, DT, 26/48
7. Tom Hall, Minnesota, WR, 27/96
8. Murdock Hooper, Houston, T, 0/0
8. Frank Imperiale, Southern Illinois, G, 0/0
9. Todd Grant, Michigan, C, 0/0
10. Jerry Archer, Pittsburg State, C, 0/0
11. Karl Anderson, Bowling Green, T, 0/0
12. Gale Sprute, Winona State, C, 0/0
13. Sherlock Knight, Central State (OH), T, 0/0
14. Jim Davidson, Maryland, B, 0/0
15. Dick Broadbent, Delaware, E, 0/0
16. Tom Sestak, McNeese State, DT, 0/96

GREEN BAY PACKERS

1. Earl Gros, LSU, FB, 28/108
2. Ed Blaine, Missouri, G, 14/70
3. Gary Barnes, Clemson, WR, 13/60
4. Ron Gassert, Virginia, DT, 10/10
5. Chuck Morris, Mississippi, B, 0/0
5. Jon Schopf, Michigan, G, 0/0
6. Oscar Donahue, San Jose State, WR, 0/13
6. John Sutro, San Jose State, T, 0/5
7. Gary Cutsinger, Oklahoma State, DE, 0/84
8. Jim Tullis, Florida A&M, B, 0/0
9. Peter Schenck, Washington State, B, 0/0
10. Gale Weidner, Colorado, QB, 0/0
11. Jim Thrush, Xavier, T, 0/0
12. Tom Pennington, Georgia, K, 0/3
12. Joe Thorne, South Dakota State, B, 0/0
13. Tom Kepner, Villanova, T, 0/0
14. Ernie Green, Louisville, HB, 0/89
15. Roger Holdinsky, West Virginia, B, 0/0

LOS ANGELES RAMS

1. **Roman Gabriel, North Carolina State, QB, 130/183**
1. **Merlin Olsen, Utah State, DT, 208/208**
2. **Joe Carollo, Notre Dame, T, 108/150**
3. John Meyers, Washington, DT, 0/84
3. John Cornett, Rice, T, 0/0
4. Art Perkins, North Texas, FB, 26/26
5. Ben Wilson, USC, FB, 41/55
5. Jim Smith, Penn State, T, 0/0
7. Jim Bakken, Wisconsin, K, 0/234
7. Sherwyn Thorson, Iowa, G, 0/0
8. Dick Farris, North Texas State, G, 0/0
9. Ike Lassiter, St. Augustine's, DE, 0/112
10. Jim Norris, Houston, DT, 0/22
11. Bert Wilder, North Carolina State, DE, 0/55
12. Marv Marinovich, USC, G, 0/1
13. Bob Fearnside, Bowling Green, HB, 0/0
14. Gary Henson, Colorado, E, 0/12
15. Walter Nikirk, Houston, T, 0/0

MINNESOTA VIKINGS

3. Bill Miller, Miami (FL), SE, 0/66
4. **Roy Winston, LSU, LB, 191/191**
6. **Larry Bowie, Purdue, G, 92/92**
8. Paul White, Florida, HB, 0/0
9. Marshall Shirk, UCLA, T, 0/0
12. Gary Fallon, Syracuse, HB, 0/0
13. Roger Van Cleef, Southwestern Oklahoma, T, 0/0
14. Pat Russ, Purdue, DT, 14/14
15. Larry Guilford, Pacific, E, 0/0
16. John Contoulis, Connecticut, DT, 0/12
19. Tom Minter, Baylor, DB, 0/12

NEW YORK GIANTS

1. Jerry Hillebrand, Colorado, LB, 49/99
2. Bob Bill, Notre Dame, T, 0/0
4. Glynn Griffing, Mississippi, QB, 13/13
5. **Bookie Bolin, Mississippi, G, 77/89**
5. Curtis Miranda, Florida A&M, C, 0/0
6. Bill Triplett, Miami (OH), RB, 11/128
7. Ken Byers, Cincinnati, G, 36/56
9. Reed Bohovich, Lehigh, G, 10/10
10. J.R. Williams, Fresno State, C, 0/0
11. Dave Bishop, Connecticut, B, 0/0
12. Albert Gursky, Penn State, LB, 2/2
13. Billy Joe Booth, Louisiana State, T, 0/0
14. Greg Mather, Navy, E, 0/0
18. Bill Winter, St. Olaf, LB, 33/33

PHILADELPHIA EAGLES

2. Pete Case, Georgia, G, 40/117
3. Pat Holmes, Texas Tech, DE, 0/108
4. Bill Byrne, Boston College, G, 12/12
6. John McGeever, Auburn, DB, 0/67
6. Gus Gonzales, Tulane, G, 0/0
7. Frank Budd, Villanova, WR, 13/27
7. Jim Perkins, Colorado, T, 0/42
8. Ralph Smith, Mississippi, TE, 38/108
9. Bob Butler, Kentucky, G, 3/4
10. **Jim Skaggs, Washington, G, 100/100**
11. George Horne, BYU, T, 0/0
12. Larry Thompson, Tulane, C, 0/0
13. George McKinney, Arkansas, B, 0/0
14. Jim Schwab, Penn State, E, 0/0
15. Mike Woulfe, Colorado, LB, 13/13
16. Jerry Mazzanti, Arkansas, DE, 5/30

PITTSBURGH STEELERS

1. Bob Ferguson, Ohio State, FB, 18/20
7. Jack Collins, Texas, HB, 0/0
8. **Gary Ballman, Michigan State, FL, 57/131**
9. John Powers, Notre Dame, TE, 44/49
10. Larry Vignali, Pittsburgh, G, 0/0
11. Bob Wills, California, E, 0/0
12. Sam Mudie, Rutgers, B, 0/0
13. Dave Woodward, Auburn, T, 0/0
14. Jim Whitaker, Nevada-Reno, E, 0/0
15. Vern Hatch, North Carolina Central, E, 0/0
16. Bobby Ply, Baylor, DB, 0/77

SAN FRANCISCO 49ERS

1. Lance Alworth, Arkansas, FL, 0/136
2. Ed Pine, Utah, LB, 42/50
3. Billy Ray Adams, Mississippi, FB, 0/0
4. Floyd Dean, Florida, LB, 15/15
4. Chuck Sieminski, Penn State, DT, 42/78
5. Mike Lind, Notre Dame, FB, 24/44
5. Ted Woods, Colorado, HB, 0/0
6. Keith Luhnow, Santa Ana, B, 0/0
6. Jerry Brown, Mississippi, G, 0/0
6. Bill Winter, West Virginia, T, 0/0
7. John Burrell, Rice, WR, 0/56
8. Jim Vollenweider, Miami (FL), HB, 27/27
9. Jim Roberts, Mississippi, T, 0/0
10. Regis Coustillac, Pittsburgh, G, 0/0
11. Larry Jepson, Furman, C, 0/0
12. Milt McPike, Kirksville, E, 0/0
13. George Pierovich, California, B, 0/0
14. Dick Easterly, Syracuse, B, 0/0
15. Ray Osborne, Mississippi State, T, 0/0

ST. LOUIS CARDINALS

1. Fate Echols, Northwestern, T, 8/8
1. **Irv Goode, Kentucky, G, 134/162**
2. Bobby Jackson, New Mexico State, FB, 0/50
3. Chuck Bryant, Ohio State, E, 13/13
4. Roger Kochman, Penn State, HB, 0/5
5. Bill Rice, Alabama, E, 0/0
6. Jack Elwell, Purdue, WR, 13/13
7. Bill Kirchiro, Maryland, G, 0/8
8. George Gross, Auburn, DT, 0/70
9. Wilburn Hollis, Iowa, QB, 0/0
10. George Francovitch, Syracuse, G, 0/0
11. Jimmy Saxton, Texas, HB, 0/13
12. Bob O'Billovich, Montana State, B, 0/0
13. Bill Diamond, Miami (FL), G, 0/5
14. George Mans, Michigan, E, 0/0
15. Dick Barlund, Maryland, E, 0/0
16. Bucky Wegener, Missouri, G, 0/18

WASHINGTON REDSKINS

1. Ernie Davis, Syracuse, B, 0/0
2. Joe Hernandez, Arizona, WR, 14/14
3. Bob Mitinger, Penn State, LB, 0/42
4. Billy Neighbors, Alabama, G, 0/112
7. Bert Coan, Kansas, HB, 0/72
8. Ron Hatcher, Michigan State, FB, 3/3
9. Dave Viti, Boston, E, 0/0
10. John Childress, Arkansas, G, 0/0
11. Carl Palazzo, Adams State, T, 0/0
12. Terry Terrebonne, Tulane, HB, 0/0
13. Bill Whisler, Iowa, E, 0/0
14. Jim Costen, South Carolina, HB, 0/0
15. Len Velia, Georgia, T, 0/0
16. Tommy Brooker, Alabama, E, 0/55
17. Al Miller, Ohio University, LB, 25/25
18. Carl Charon, Michigan State, DB, 0/26
19. Claude Crabb, Colorado, DB, 26/80

1962 AFL

BOSTON PATRIOTS

1. Gary Collins, Maryland, FL, 0/127
2. Leroy Jackson, Western Illinois, HB, 0/15
3. Sherwyn Thorson, Iowa, G, 0/0
5. Bill Hull, Wake Forest, DE, 0/14
6. **Billy Neighbors, Alabama, G, 56/112**
7. John Schopf, Michigan, T, 0/0
8. Bennie McRae, Michigan, DB, 0/133
9. Bill Triplett, Miami (OH), RB, 0/128
10. John Knight, Valparaiso, HB, 0/0
13. **Nick Buoniconti, Notre Dame, LB, 91/183**
14. Chuck Sieminski, Penn State, DT, 0/78
15. Gerry Goerlitz, Northern Michigan, C, 0/0
16. Ken Byers, Cincinnati, G, 0/56
20. Tommy Neck, LSU, DB, 0/1
27. Albert Gursky, Penn State, LB, 0/2

BUFFALO BILLS

1. Ernie Davis, Syracuse, HB, 0/0
2. Glenn Glass, Tennessee, DB, 0/55
3. Jack Elwell, Purdue, WR, 0/13
5. Tom Dellinger, North Carolina State, HB, 0/0
6. Dave Viti, Boston, E, 0/0
7. Jim LeCompte, North Carolina, G, 0/0
8. Paul White, Florida, HB, 0/0
9. Bill Saul, Penn State, LB, 0/88
10. Amos Bullocks, Southern Illinois, HB, 0/34
11. Tom Pennington, Georgia, K, 0/3
11. Jerry Croft, Bowling Green, G, 0/0
13. Ron Gassert, Virginia, DT, 0/10
13. **Mike Stratton, Tennessee, LB, 142/156**
14. Ron Scufca, Purdue, T, 0/0
15. Roger Kochman, Penn State, HB, 5/5
17. **Tom Sestak, McNeese State, DT, 96/96**
20. Sam Tidmore, Ohio State, LB, 0/18
21. Carey Henley, Tennessee-Chattanooga, HB, 1/1
22. Tom Hall, Minnesota, WR, 0/96
23. Ray Abruzzese, Alabama, B, 35/61
24. Stan Sczurek, Purdue, LB, 0/45
27. Claude Crabb, Colorado, DB, 0/80
29. Jim Beaver, Florida, DT, 0/1
31. Jim Collier, Arkansas, TE, 0/27

DALLAS TEXANS

1. Ronnie Bull, Baylor, RB, 0/123
2. Bill Miller, Miami (FL), SE, 14/66
3. Eddie Wilson, Arizona, QB, 42/56
4. Irv Goode, Kentucky, G, 0/162
4. Chuck Hinton, North Carolina Central, DT, 0/123
5. Bobby Plummer, Texas Christian, T, 0/0
6. Al Hinton, Iowa, E, 0/0
8. Larry Bowie, Purdue, G, 0/92
9. Marshall Shirk, UCLA, T, 0/0
10. Jimmy Saxton, Texas, HB, 13/13
11. **Bobby Hunt, Auburn, DB, 84/112**
11. Guy Reese, SMU, DT, 0/57
12. Bobby Thompson, Arizona, DB, 0/72
14. Bookie Bolin, Mississippi, G, 0/89
16. Pettis Norman, Johnson C. Smith, TE, 0/162
17. **Tommy Brooker, Alabama, E, 55/55**
18. Joe Carollo, Notre Dame, T, 0/150
25. John Burrell, Rice, WR, 0/56
34. Roger Shoals, Maryland, T, 0/104

DENVER BRONCOS

1. Merlin Olsen, Utah State, DT, 0/208
2. Jerry Hillebrand, Colorado, LB, 0/99
3. Charles Holmes, Maryland-Eastern Shore, FB, 0/0
4. John Furman, Texas-El Paso, QB, 0/0
7. **John McGeever, Auburn, DB, 55/67**
8. Elbert Harris, Southeastern Louisiana, HB, 0/0
9. Larry Jepson, Furman, C, 0/0
10. Gale Weidner, Colorado, QB, 0/0
11. Mike Kline, Oregon State, G, 0/0
13. Bob Cegelski, Montana State, C, 0/0
14. Sonny Gibbs, TCU, QB, 0/2
15. Bill Louden, Benedictine, G, 0/0
16. Gary Ballman, Michigan State, FL, 0/131
17. Jerry Tarr, Oregon, WR, 14/14
21. Jim Perkins, Colorado, T, 42/42
25. Dave Edwards, Auburn, LB, 0/181
27. Andy Von Sonn, UCLA, LB, 0/14
29. Lynn Hoyem, Long Beach State, G, 0/84
33. Duane Allen, Mt.San Antonio J.C., TE, 0/49
34. Steve Stonebreaker, Detroit Mercy, LB, 0/84

HOUSTON OILERS

1. Ray Jacobs, Howard Payne, DT, 0/79
2. Earl Gros, LSU, FB, 0/108
3. Pete Case, Georgia, G, 0/117
4. **Gary Cutsinger, Oklahoma State, DE, 84/84**
5. Bill Rice, Alabama, E, 0/0
6. Ray Pinion, Texas Christian, G, 0/0
7. Gus Gonzales, Tulane, G, 0/0
8. Clyde Brock, Utah State, T, 0/24
9. Larry Onesti, Northwestern, LB, 38/38
10. Bob Moses, Texas, E, 0/0
11. John Thomas, McMurry, G, 0/0
12. Jack Collins, Texas, HB, 0/0
13. Royce Cassell, New Mexico State, E, 0/0
14. Glynn Griffing, Mississippi, QB, 0/13
15. Ken Shaffer, Marquette, T, 0/0
17. Bill Miller, New Mexico Highlands, DT, 4/4
18. Art Perkins, North Texas, FB, 0/26
19. **Bobby Jancik, Lamar, DB, 81/81**
20. Joe Bob Isbell, Houston, G, 0/45
21. Roland Jackson, Rice, FB, 0/5
26. Harold Hays, Southern Mississippi, LB, 0/96
28. Gary Henson, Colorado, E, 0/12
30. Bob Clemens, Pittsburgh, FB, 0/9
34. Don Talbert, Texas, T, 0/103

NEW YORK TITANS

1. Sandy Stephens, Minnesota, QB, 0/0
2. Alex Kroll, Rutgers, T, 14/14
3. Fate Echols, Northwestern, T, 0/8
4. Ed Blaine, Missouri, G, 0/70
5. Bobby Ply, Baylor, DB, 0/77
6. Mel Melin, Washington State, QB, 0/0
7. George Mans, Michigan, E, 0/0
8. John Lomakoski, Western Michigan, T, 0/3

9. Gary Barnes, Clemson, WR, 0/60
10. Ted Stute, Ohio U., T, 0/0
11. Curtis Miranda, Florida A&M, C, 0/0
12. Bill Winter, West Virginia, T, 0/0
13. Wilburn Hollis, Iowa, QB, 0/0
14. **Bert Wilder, North Carolina State, DE, 55/55**
15. Sam Mudie, Rutgers, HB, 0/0
17. Al Miller, Ohio University, LB, 0/25
19. Reed Bohovich, Lehigh, G, 0/10
21. Ron Hatcher, Michigan State, FB, 0/3
24. Johnny Counts, Illinois, HB, 0/17
29. Frank Parker, Oklahoma State, DT, 0/78
30. Mike McClellan, Oklahoma, DB, 0/24
32. Don Jonas, Penn State, HB, 0/1

OAKLAND RAIDERS

1. Roman Gabriel, North Carolina State, QB, 0/183
2. Lance Alworth, Arkansas, FL, 0/136
3. Ed Pine, Utah, LB, 0/50
4. John Meyers, Washington, DT, 0/84
5. Joe Hernandez, Arizona, WR, 0/14
6. **Dan Birdwell, Houston, DT, 96/96**
7. Jim Norris, Houston, DT, 22/22
8. Ferrell Yarborough, Northwestern State (LA), E, 0/0
9. Jim Dillard, Oklahoma State, HB, 0/0
10. Hank Rivera, Oregon State, DB, 9/12
12. Oscar Donahue, San Jose State, WR, 0/13
12. Jim Skaggs, Washington, G, 0/100
12. Gary Schwertfeger, Montana, LB, 0/0
13. George Pierovich, California, FB, 0/0
14. Bert Coan, Kansas, HB, 0/72
15. Floyd Dean, Florida, LB, 0/15
16. Pat Russ, Purdue, DT, 0/14
17. Larry Ferguson, Iowa, HB, 0/7
18. Jim Vollenweider, Miami (FL), HB, 0/27
20. John Sutro, San Jose State, T, 0/5
22. Jim Cadile, San Jose State, G, 0/128
26. Fred Miller, LSU, DT, 0/133
28. Marv Marinovich, USC, G, 1/1
29. Leon Donohue, San Jose State, G, 0/84
30. Pete Nicklas, Baylor, T, 14/14
32. Bobby Richards, LSU, DE, 0/84
33. Gene White, Florida A&M, HB, 7/7

SAN DIEGO CHARGERS

1. Bob Ferguson, Ohio State, FB, 0/20
2. Dick Hudson, Memphis, T, 14/66
3. **John Hadl, Kansas, QB, 154/224**
4. Bob Bill, Notre Dame, T, 0/0
4. Mack Burton, San Jose State, HB, 0/0
5. Bob Mitinger, Penn State, LB, 42/42
5. John Cornett, Rice, T, 0/0
6. **Frank Buncom, USC, LB, 84/96**
6. Roy Winston, LSU, LB, 0/191
7. Wendell Harris, LSU, DB, 0/83
7. Bobby Jackson, New Mexico State, FB, 26/50
8. Jerry Robinson, Grambling State, FL, 42/46
9. Tom Minter, Baylor, DB, 0/12
10. Dan Sullivan, Boston College, G, 0/140
11. Sonny Bishop, Fresno State, G, 0/110
12. George Andrie, Marquette, DE, 0/141
12. Ralph Smith, Mississippi, TE, 0/108
13. Chuck Bryant, Ohio State, E, 0/13
14. Jim Bates, Southern California, HB, 0/0
15. Fred Moore, Memphis, DT, 29/29
16. **George Gross, Auburn, DT, 70/70**
18. Dennis Biodrowski, Memphis, G, 0/30
19. Mike Lind, Notre Dame, FB, 0/44
22. Jim Thibert, Toledo, LB, 0/13
25. **Sam Gruneisen, Villanova, C, 120/130**
26. Mike Woulfe, Colorado, LB, 0/13
28. Ben Wilson, USC, FB, 0/55
29. Paul Dudley, Arkansas, HB, 0/21
30. John Denvir, Colorado, G, 0/11
31. Doug Elmore, Mississippi, P, 0/14
32. Wayne Frazier, Auburn, C, 7/48
33. **Jacque MacKinnon, Colgate, TE, 114/118**

1963 NFL

BALTIMORE COLTS

1. **Bob Vogel, Ohio State, T, 139/139**
2. **John Mackey, Syracuse, TE, 126/139**
2. **Butch Wilson, Alabama, TE, 54/82**
4. **Jerry Logan, West Texas A&M, DB, 140/140**
4. Harlow Fullwood, Virginia, G, 0/0
5. Bill Ventura, Richmond, T, 0/0
6. Jerry Cook, Texas, B, 0/0
7. **Willie Richardson, Jackson State, FL, 99/109**
8. Dave Hayes, Penn State, B, 0/0
9. Don Trull, Baylor, QB, 0/77
10. Bill Sierkerski, Missouri, G, 0/0
11. Winston Hill, Texas Southern, T, 0/198
12. Butch Maples, Baylor, LB, 5/5
13. Paul Watters, Miami (OH), T, 0/0
14. Neal Petties, San Diego State, E, 33/33
15. Leon Mavity, Colorado, DB, 0/0
17. Kern Carson, San Diego State, HB, 0/13

CHICAGO BEARS

1. Dave Behrman, Michigan State, C, 0/39
2. Steve Barnett, Oregon, T, 13/27
2. Bob Jencks, Miami (OH), TE, 28/42
3. Larry Glueck, Villanova, DB, 37/37
4. Charley Mitchell, Washington, HB, 0/59
4. Stan Sanders, Whittier, E, 0/0
6. **John Johnson, Indiana, DT, 81/85**
6. Dave Mathieson, Washington State, QB, 0/0
7. Paul Underhill, Missouri, B, 0/0
8. Dennis Harmon, Southern Illinois, DB, 0/0
9. Dave Watson, Georgia Tech, G, 0/28
9. Monte Day, Fresno State, T, 0/0
10. Ed Hoerster, Notre Dame, LB, 0/0
11. James Tullis, Florida A&M, DB, 0/0
12. Dick Drummond, George Washington, B, 0/0
13. John Szumczyk, Trinity (CT), B, 0/0
14. Gordon Banks, Fisk, B, 0/0
15. Bob Dentel, Miami (FL), C, 0/0
16. Lowell Caylor, Miami (OH), DB, 0/13
17. John Jr. Sisk, Miami (FL), DB, 3/3

CLEVELAND BROWNS

1. Tom Hutchinson, Kentucky, TE, 42/47
2. **Jim Kanicki, Michigan State, DT, 88/116**
4. Bill Munsey, Minnesota, B, 0/0
5. Frank Baker, Toledo, B, 0/0
6. Ernie Borghetti, Pittsburgh, T, 0/0
6. Tom Bloom, Purdue, B, 0/0
8. Walt Sweeney, Syracuse, G, 0/181
9. Dave Raimey, Michigan, DB, 5/5
10. Jim Bobbitt, Michigan State, G, 0/0
11. Art Graham, Boston College, SE, 0/75
12. Lindy Infante, Florida, B, 0/0
13. Dave Katterhenrich, Ohio State, B, 0/0
14. Staley Faulkner, Texas, T, 0/1
15. Lynn Reade, Southern California, T, 0/0

DALLAS COWBOYS

1. **Lee Roy Jordan, Alabama, LB, 186/186**
3. Jim Price, Auburn, LB, 0/20
4. Whaley Hall, Mississippi, T, 0/0
7. Marv Clothier, Kansas, G, 0/0
10. Rod Scheyer, Washington, T, 0/0
11. Ray Schoenke, SMU, G, 23/145
12. Bill Perkins, Iowa, HB, 0/4
13. Paul Wicker, Fresno State, T, 0/0
14. Lou Cioci, Boston College, LB, 0/0
15. Jerry Overton, Utah, DB, 10/10
18. Bill Frank, Colorado, T, 4/4
19. Jim Stiger, Washington, HB, 33/58

DETROIT LIONS

1. **Daryl Sanders, Ohio State, T, 56/56**
2. Roy Williams, Pacific, DT, 0/7
4. **Chuck Walton, Iowa State, G, 98/98**
6. Don King, Syracuse, HB, 0/0
7. John Gamble, Pacific, G, 0/0
8. Dennis Gaubatz, LSU, LB, 28/95
9. Ken Dill, Mississippi, LB, 0/0
10. Nick Ryder, Miami (FL), FB, 24/24
11. Karl Kassulke, Drake, DB, 0/131
12. Tom Janik, Texas A&M-Kingsville, DB, 0/114
13. **Ernie Clark, Michigan State, LB, 68/82**
14. Bill O'Brien, Xavier, T, 0/0
15. Jim Simon, Miami (FL), G, 41/82
18. Al Greer, Jackson State, E, 1/1
19. Lucien Reeberg, Hampton, T, 14/14

GREEN BAY PACKERS

1. **Dave Robinson, Penn State, LB, 127/155**
2. **Tom Brown, Maryland, DB, 70/71**
3. Dennis Claridge, Nebraska, QB, 1/8
3. Tony Liscio, Tulsa, T, 0/89
4. **Lionel Aldridge, Utah State, DE, 123/147**
4. Carlton Simons, Stanford, C, 0/0
5. Dan Grimm, Colorado, G, 42/80
5. Jack Cverko, Northwestern, G, 0/0
6. Jan Barrett, Fresno State, E, 3/20
6. John Simmons, Tulsa, E, 0/0
7. Gary Kroner, Wisconsin, DB, 0/31
7. Olin Hill, Furman, T, 0/0
7. Turnley Todd, Virginia, LB, 0/0
8. Keith Kinderman, Florida State, FB, 0/15
8. Louis Rettino, Villanova, B, 0/0
9. Bill Freeman, Southern Mississippi, T, 0/0
10. Earl McQuiston, Iowa, G, 0/0
11. **Marv Fleming, Utah, TE, 95/162**
12. Daryle Lamonica, Notre Dame, QB, 0/151
13. Bill Kellum, Tulane, T, 0/0
14. Ed Holler, South Carolina, LB, 2/15
15. Gene Breen, Virginia Tech, LB, 6/32
20. Bobby Brezina, Houston, HB, 0/1

LOS ANGELES RAMS

1. Terry Baker, Oregon State, QB, 18/18
1. Rufus Guthrie, Georgia Tech, G, 0/0
2. Tom Nomina, Miami (OH), DT, 0/67
3. Johnny Baker, Mississippi State, LB, 0/51
3. Dave Costa, Utah, DT, 0/168
4. John Griffin, Memphis, DB, 10/36
5. Joe Auer, Georgia Tech, RB, 0/51
5. **Don Chuy, Clemson, G, 74/82**
5. Roland Benson, Miami (FL), T, 0/0
6. George Saimes, Michigan State, DB, 0/121
6. Terry Monaghan, Penn State, T, 0/0
7. Bill Zorn, Michigan State, T, 0/0
8. Anton Peters, Florida, DT, 0/10
9. Mel Profit, UCLA, E, 0/0
10. Curt Farrier, Montana State, DT, 0/27
11. Dave Theisen, Nebraska, B, 0/0
12. Billy Moody, Arkansas, B, 0/0
13. Al Hildebrand, Stanford, T, 0/0
14. Alan Arbuse, Rhode Island, T, 0/0
15. Larry Campbell, Toledo, E, 0/0
17. Jerrel Wilson, Southern Mississippi, RB, 0/217

MINNESOTA VIKINGS

1. Jim Dunaway, Mississippi, DT, 0/132
2. Bobby Bell, Minnesota, LB, 0/168
3. Ray Poage, Texas, TE, 7/86
4. **Paul Flatley, Northwestern, WR, 64/106**
5. Gary Kaltenbach, Pittsburgh, T, 0/0
8. Jim O'Mahoney, Miami (FL), LB, 0/26
9. Bob Hoover, Florida, B, 0/0
10. Terry Kosens, Hofstra, DB, 8/8
11. John Campbell, Minnesota, LB, 28/88
12. John Sklopan, Southern Mississippi, DB, 0/3
13. Dave O'Brien, Boston College, T, 28/60
14. Ralph Ferrisi, Southern Connecticut State, B, 0/0
15. John Murio, Whitworth, E, 0/0
16. Rex Mirich, Arizona State, DT, 0/83

NEW YORK GIANTS

2. Frank Lasky, Florida, T, 18/18
3. Dick Skelly, Florida, B, 0/0
5. Dave Hill, Auburn, T, 0/150
5. Lou Slaby, Pittsburgh, LB, 26/39
6. Bob Petrich, West Texas A&M, DE, 0/62
7. Dave Hoppmann, Iowa State, B, 0/0
7. Burt Petkus, Northwestern, G, 0/0
8. Dave Herman, Michigan State, G, 0/128
9. Bob Taylor, Maryland-Eastern Shore, DE, 28/28
10. Mike Taliaferro, Illinois, QB, 0/82
11. Don McKinnon, Dartmouth, LB, 0/17
12. Ed Adamchik, Pittsburgh, C, 2/4
13. Jim Moss, West Virginia, B, 0/0
14. Joe Williams, Iowa, B, 0/0
15. Lane Howell, Grambling State, T, 28/91
16. Charlie Killett, Memphis, HB, 13/13
17. Bob McAdams, North Carolina Central, DT, 0/26
18. Bill Pashe, George Washington, DB, 0/4
19. Buck Buchanan, Grambling State, DT, 0/182
20. **Homer Jones, Texas Southern, SE, 73/87**

PHILADELPHIA EAGLES

1. Ed Budde, Michigan State, G, 0/177
2. Ray Mansfield, Washington, C, 14/196
3. Dave Crossan, Maryland, C, 0/59
3. Louis Guy, Mississippi, DB, 0/11
7. Lee Roy Caffey, Texas A&M, LB, 14/129
8. Eugene Sykes, LSU, DB, 0/27
8. **Tom Woodeshick, West Virginia, RB, 111/115**
9. Dennis Ward, Oklahoma, T, 0/0
10. Pete Liske, Penn State, QB, 28/48
11. Ralph Heck, Colorado, LB, 40/120
12. Roger Gill, Texas Tech, WR, 25/25
13. Joe Iacone, West Chester, B, 0/0
14. **Nate Ramsey, Indiana State, DB, 134/138**
15. George Heard, New Mexico, E, 0/0
16. **Ron Goodwin, Baylor, FL, 56/56**

PITTSBURGH STEELERS

8. Frank Atkinson, Stanford, DT, 14/17
9. Gene Carrington, Boston College, T, 0/0
10. Bill Nelsen, USC, QB, 32/90
11. Hewritt Dixon, Florida A&M, RB, 0/99
12. Roy Curry, Jackson State, WR, 6/6
13. Harold Gray, Cal State-Los Angeles, LB, 0/0
14. Robert Dickerson, Bethune-Cookman, E, 0/0
15. Matt Szykowny, Iowa, B, 0/0
16. **Andy Russell, Missouri, LB, 168/168**
18. **Jim Bradshaw, Tennessee-Chattanooga, DB, 62/62**

SAN FRANCISCO 49ERS

1. **Kermit Alexander, UCLA, DB, 94/143**
2. **Walt Rock, Maryland, T, 63/137**
3. Don Lisbon, Bowling Green State, HB, 20/20
4. Hatch Rosdahl, Penn State, DE, 0/32
4. Hugh Campbell, Washington State, E, 0/0
5. Vern Burke, Oregon State, SE, 3/24
5. Jim (Preacher) Pilot, New Mexico State, B, 0/0
5. Gary Moeller, Ohio State, G, 0/0
6. Pat Emerick, Western Michigan, G, 0/0
7. Ernest DeCourley, Moorhead State, T, 0/0
8. Roger Locke, Arizona State, E, 0/0
9. John Maczuzak, Pittsburgh, DT, 0/1
10. Dick Lopour, Huron, B, 0/0
11. Steve Shafer, Utah State, B, 0/0
12. Bob Benton, Mississippi State, T, 0/0
13. Dick Schultz, Ohio, T, 0/0
14. Bill Tobin, Missouri, HB, 0/10
15. Oliver Ross, West Texas State, B, 0/0

ST. LOUIS CARDINALS

1. **Don Brumm, Purdue, DE, 95/111**
1. **Jerry Stovall, LSU, DB, 97/97**
2. **Bob Reynolds, Bowling Green State, T, 122/138**
3. Danny Brabham, Arkansas, LB, 0/65
3. Mike Fracchia, Alabama, B, 0/0
4. Don Estes, LSU, G, 0/5
5. Bill Thornton, Nebraska, FB, 47/47
6. Bob Paremore, Florida A&M, HB, 18/18
7. Jim Moss, South Carolina, T, 0/0
8. Jim Cook, Oklahoma, G, 0/0
9. **Willis Crenshaw, Kansas State, RB, 84/96**
10. **Jackie Smith, Northwestern State (LA), TE, 198/210**
11. **Jimmy Burson, Auburn, DB, 51/65**
12. **Chuck Walker, Duke, DT, 96/143**
13. Alex Zyskowski, Wichita State, B, 0/0
14. Paul Lea, Oklahoma, B, 0/0
15. Ed Scrutchins, Toledo, DE, 0/4
17. **Dave Meggyesy, Syracuse, LB, 82/82**
18. **Larry Stallings, Georgia Tech, LB, 181/181**

WASHINGTON REDSKINS

1. **Pat Richter, Wisconsin, TE, 103/103**
2. **Lonnie Sanders, Michigan State, DB, 57/71**
3. **Ron Snidow, Oregon, DE, 69/126**
6. Charley Nickoson, Ohio U., T, 0/0
7. Dave Francis, Ohio State, FB, 8/8
9. Billy Joe, Villanova, RB, 0/78
10. Rod Foster, Ohio State, G, 0/0
11. Allen Schau, Western Michigan, E, 0/0
12. Bob Caldwell, Georgia Tech, C, 0/0
13. John Greiner, Purdue, E, 0/0
14. Tom Winingder, Georgia Tech, B, 0/0
15. Harry Butsko, Maryland, LB, 4/4
19. Jim Turner, Utah State, K, 0/228

1963 AFL

BOSTON PATRIOTS

1. **Art Graham, Boston College, SE, 75/75**
2. Lee Roy Jordan, Alabama, LB, 0/186
3. Bob Vogel, Ohio State, T, 0/139
4. Bob Reynolds, Bowling Green State, T, 16/138
5. Lou Cioci, Boston College, G, 0/0
6. Sam Silas, Southern Illinois, DT, 0/100
7. Dick Williamson, Alabama, E, 0/0
8. Rod Foster, Ohio State, G, 0/0
9. Jim Simon, Miami (FL), G, 0/82
10. Don McKinnon, Dartmouth, LB, 17/17
11. Dave Watson, Georgia Tech, G, 28/28
11. Dave Hayes, Penn State, FB, 0/0
12. Billy Gambrell, South Carolina, SE, 0/78
12. Tim Gauntner, John Carroll, HB, 0/0
13. Dave Adams, Arkansas, T, 0/0
13. Ralph Ferrissi, Southern Connecticut State, FB, 0/0
14. Whaley Hall, Mississippi, T, 0/0
15. Bob Dentel, Miami (FL), C, 0/0
17. Tom Neumann, Northen Michigan, HB, 10/10
18. Dave O'Brien, Boston College, T, 0/60
20. Jim Bradshaw, Tennessee-Chattanooga, DB, 0/62
22. Nate Craddock, Parsons, FB, 0/3
23. Al Snyder, Holy Cross, WR, 2/7
25. Dennis Gaubatz, LSU, LB, 0/95

BUFFALO BILLS

1. Dave Behrman, Michigan State, C, 28/39
2. **Jim Dunaway, Mississippi, DT, 126/132**
2. Tom Hutchinson, Kentucky, TE, 0/47
3. Tom Brown, Maryland, DB, 0/71
4. Tom Woodeshick, West Virginia, RB, 0/115
5. Bob Jencks, Miami (OH), TE, 0/42
6. Jim Moss, South Carolina, LB, 0/0
7. Jim Kanicki, Michigan State, DT, 0/116
9. Larry Stallings, Georgia Tech, LB, 0/181
10. Ron Snidow, Oregon, DE, 0/126
11. Ron Goodwin, Baylor, FL, 0/56
14. J.B. Simmons, Tulsa, E, 0/0
15. Paul Underhill, Missouri, FB, 0/0
18. Herb Paterra, Michigan State, LB, 10/10
19. Eugene Sykes, LSU, DB, 23/27
21. Ed Adamchik, Pittsburgh, C, 0/4
22. Chuck Walker, Duke, DT, 0/143
24. **Daryle Lamonica, Notre Dame, QB, 56/151**
26. Willis Crenshaw, Kansas State, RB, 0/96
29. Charlie Killett, Memphis, HB, 0/13

BUFFALO BILLS

11. Lindy Infante, Florida, HB, 0/0
13. Dennis Ward, Oklahoma, G, 0/0
14. Stone Johnson, Grambling, HB, 0/0
14. Jim (Preacher) Pilot, New Mexico State, HB, 0/0

DENVER BRONCOS

1. Kermit Alexander, UCLA, DB, 0/143
2. Tom Nomina, Miami (OH), DT, 37/67
2. Ray Poage, Texas, TE, 0/86
3. Tom Janik, Texas A&M-Kingsville, DB, 23/114
4. Lou Slaby, Pittsburgh, LB, 0/39
5. Ray Mansfield, Washington, C, 0/196
6. Anton Peters, Florida, DT, 10/10
7. Paul Flatley, Northwestern, WR, 0/106
7. Mickey Slaughter, Louisiana Tech, QB, 40/40
8. Hewritt Dixon, Florida A&M, RB, 33/99
8. John Griffin, Memphis, DB, 26/36
9. Marv Fleming, Utah, TE, 0/162
10. Pat Richter, Wisconsin, TE, 0/103
10. Lonnie Sanders, Michigan State, DB, 0/71
11. Billy Joe, Villanova, RB, 28/78
12. John Gamble, Pacific, E, 0/0
13. Butch Maples, Baylor, LB, 0/5
15. Winston Freeman, North Texas State, E, 0/0
16. Dave Crossan, Maryland, C, 0/59
17. Bob Paremore, Florida A&M, HB, 0/18
18. **Charley Mitchell, Washington, HB, 56/59**
20. Dan Grimm, Colorado, G, 0/80
29. Kern Carson, San Diego State, HB, 0/13

HOUSTON OILERS

1. **Danny Brabham, Arkansas, LB, 56/65**
2. Don Estes, LSU, G, 0/5
3. Jerry Cook, Texas, HB, 0/0
4. Lee Roy Caffey, Texas A&M, LB, 0/129
4. Jerry Hopkins, Texas A&M, LB, 0/67
5. Don Chuy, Clemson, G, 0/82
5. Homer Jones, Texas Southern, SE, 0/87
6. Lionel Aldridge, Utah State, DE, 0/147
7. Johnny Baker, Mississippi State, LB, 41/51
8. Jimmy Burson, Auburn, DB, 0/65
9. Ed Burke, Notre Dame, T, 0/0
11. Tom Brown, Pittsburgh, G, 0/0
14. **Don Trull, Baylor, QB, 70/77**
21. Staley Faulkner, Texas, T, 1/1

KANSAS CITY CHIEFS

1. **Buck Buchanan, Grambling State, DT, 182/182**
1. **Ed Budde, Michigan State, G, 177/177**
2. Walt Rock, Maryland, T, 0/137
3. Don Brumm, Purdue, DE, 0/111
4. Daryl Sanders, Ohio State, T, 0/56
5. John Campbell, Minnesota, LB, 0/88
6. George Saimes, Michigan State, DB, 0/121
7. **Bobby Bell, Minnesota, LB, 168/168**
8. John Sklopan, Southern Mississippi, DB, 0/3
9. Jan Barrett, Fresno State, E, 0/20
10. Curt Farrier, Montana State, DT, 27/27
11. **Jerrel Wilson, Southern Mississippi, RB, 203/217**
15. Joe Auer, Georgia Tech, RB, 0/51
22. John Maczuzak, Pittsburgh, DT, 1/1
24. **Dave Hill, Auburn, T, 150/150**
29. John Jr. Sisk, Miami (FL), DB, 0/3

NEW YORK JETS

1. Jerry Stovall, LSU, DB, 0/97
3. Willie Richardson, Jackson State, FL, 0/109
4. John Contoulis, Connecticut, DT, 0/12
5. John Mackey, Syracuse, TE, 0/139
6. Jim Price, Auburn, LB, 14/20
7. Louis Guy, Mississippi, DB, 0/11
10. Tony Liscio, Tulsa, T, 0/89
15. Pete Liske, Penn State, QB, 2/48
16. Nick Ryder, Miami (FL), FB, 0/24
19. Gary Kroner, Wisconsin, DB, 0/31
20. John Johnson, Indiana, DT, 0/85
21. Ron Vander Kelen, Wisconsin, QB, 0/29
22. Bill Thornton, Nebraska, FB, 0/47
24. Lowell Caylor, Miami (OH), DB, 0/13
27. **Dave Herman, Michigan State, G, 128/128**
28. Mike Taliaferro, Illinois, QB, 45/82

NEW YORK JETS

8. Bill King, Dartmouth, QB, 0/0
9. Stan Sanders, Whittier, E, 0/0
12. Joe Craver, North Carolina, LB, 0/0
12. Tommy Lucas, Texas, E, 0/0
13. Olin Hill, Furman, T, 0/0

OAKLAND RAIDERS

6. Butch Wilson, Alabama, TE, 0/82
7. Dave Costa, Utah, DT, 42/168
8. Roger Locke, Arizona State, E, 0/0
9. Jerry Logan, West Texas A&M, DB, 0/140
10. Ray Schoenke, SMU, G, 0/145
12. Walt Burdin, McNeese State, LB, 0/0
12. Doyle Branson, Southern Oregon, HB, 0/0
13. Darnel Haney, Utah State, E, 0/0
13. Drew Roberts, Cal State-Humboldt, E, 0/0
15. Vern Burke, Oregon State, SE, 0/24
18. Terry Dillon, Montana, DB, 0/7
20. Rex Mirich, Arizona State, DT, 42/83
21. Neal Petties, San Diego State, E, 0/33
26. Dennis Claridge, Nebraska, QB, 0/8

SAN DIEGO CHARGERS

1. **Walt Sweeney, Syracuse, G, 154/181**
2. Rufus Guthrie, Georgia Tech, G, 0/0
3. Keith Kinderman, Florida State, FB, 11/15
3. Dave Robinson, Penn State, LB, 0/155
4. Roy Williams, Pacific, DT, 0/7
5. Larry Glueck, Villanova, DB, 0/37
6. Pat Emerick, Western Michigan, LB, 0/0
8. Gene Heeter, West Virginia, TE, 0/25
9. Steve Barnett, Oregon, T, 0/27
10. Don Scott, Tampa, T, 0/0
11. **Bob Petrich, West Texas A&M, DE, 56/62**
12. Terry Baker, Oregon State, QB, 0/18
13. Chuck Walton, Iowa State, G, 0/98
14. Frank Lasky, Florida, T, 0/18
14. Hatch Rosdahl, Penn State, DE, 0/32
14. Jack Cvercko, Northwestern, G, 0/0
15. Mike Fracchia, Alabama, HB, 0/0
16. Gene Breen, Virginia Tech, LB, 0/32
19. Ernie Park, McMurry, G, 35/74
22. Roger Gill, Texas Tech, WR, 0/25
24. Bill Frank, Colorado, T, 0/4
25. Jerry Mazzanti, Arkansas, DE, 0/30
27. Harry Butsko, Maryland, LB, 0/4

1964 NFL

BALTIMORE COLTS

1. Marv Woodson, Indiana, DB, 0/72
2. **Tony Lorick, Arizona State, RB, 56/83**
4. Ted Davis, Georgia Tech, LB, 38/90
5. Ed Lothamer, Michigan State, DT, 0/88
6. Jim Mazurek, Syracuse, T, 0/0
7. Ken Sugarman, Whitworth, T, 0/0
8. J.R. Williamson, Louisiana Tech, LB, 0/93
9. Vince Turner, Missouri, DB, 0/6
11. John Paglio, Syracuse, T, 0/0
12. Kenny Graham, Washington State, DB, 0/90
13. Charlie Parker, Southern Mississippi, G, 0/14
14. John Case, Clemson, E, 0/0
15. Larry Kramer, Nebraska, T, 0/0
18. Alvin Haymond, Southern (LA), DB, 45/104

CHICAGO BEARS

1. **Dick Evey, Tennessee, DT, 82/102**
2. Bill Martin, Georgia Tech, TE, 28/70
2. Pat Crain, Clemson, HB, 0/0
3. Sid Blanks, Texas A&M-Kingsville, RB, 0/83
4. Frank Budka, Notre Dame, DB, 0/14
4. **Mike Reilly, Iowa, LB, 64/74**
5. Dan Conners, Miami (FL), LB, 0/141
6. Jim Jones, Wisconsin, SE, 41/54
7. Chuck Logan, Northwestern, TE, 0/46
8. Larry Rakestraw, Georgia, QB, 13/13
9. Jay Wilkinson, Duke, HB, 0/0
10. Mike Brown, Delaware, B, 0/0
11. Dick Leeuwenburg, Stanford, T, 9/9
12. Bob Horton, Boston University, LB, 0/22
13. Cloyd Webb, Iowa, E, 0/0
14. Kent Francisco, UCLA, T, 0/0
15. George Burman, Northwestern, C, 14/85

CLEVELAND BROWNS

1. **Paul Warfield, Ohio State, WR, 97/157**
2. Billy Truax, LSU, TE, 0/114
4. Don Shackelford, Pacific, G, 0/8
5. Dick Klein, Wichita State, T, 0/0
7. Sammy Odom, Northwestern State (LA), DT, 0/14
8. **Leroy Kelly, Morgan State, RB, 136/136**
9. John Briscoe, Arizona, LB, 0/0
10. Dick Van Raaphorst, Ohio State, K, 0/42
10. Bobby Robinson, Mississippi, G, 0/0
11. Eddie Versprille, Alabama, FB, 0/0
12. Ed Mitchell, Southern (LA), G, 0/21
13. Bob Meehan, Syracuse, G, 0/0
14. Terry Sieg, Virginia, HB, 0/0
15. John Houtman, Michigan, T, 0/0
16. Sid Williams, Southern (LA), LB, 41/70
18. Sherman Lewis, Michigan State, DB, 0/10
19. Jim Higgins, Xavier (OH), T, 0/7

DALLAS COWBOYS

1. Scott Appleton, Texas, DT, 0/70
2. **Mel Renfro, Oregon, DB, 174/174**
4. Perry Lee Dunn, Mississippi, RB, 27/74
6. Jim Evans, Texas-El Paso, WR, 0/21
6. Billy Lothridge, Georgia Tech, DB, 14/104
6. Jim Curry, Cincinnati, E, 0/0
7. **Bob Hayes, Florida A&M, SE, 128/132**
8. Al Geverink, UCLA, HB, 0/0
9. Jake Kupp, Washington, G, 28/154
10. **Roger Staubach, Navy, QB, 131/131**
11. Bob Crenshaw, Baylor, G, 0/0
12. Johnny Norman, Northwestern State (LA), E, 0/0
13. Jerry Rhome, Tulsa, QB, 33/71
14. Jim Worden, Wittenberg, LB, 0/0
15. Bill Van Burkleo, Tulsa, B, 0/0
17. Bud Abell, Missouri, LB, 0/40
18. Theophile Viltz, USC, DB, 0/14

DETROIT LIONS

1. Pete Beathard, USC, QB, 0/110
2. Matt Snorton, Michigan State, TE, 0/5
3. Pat Batten, Hardin-Simmons, FB, 3/3
3. Gerry Philbin, Buffalo, DE, 0/123
4. Wally Hilgenberg, Iowa, LB, 41/199
5. Benny Nelson, Alabama, DB, 0/14
6. John Hilton, Richmond, TE, 19/106
7. Bill Parcells, Wichita State, T, 0/0
9. **Wayne Rasmussen, South Dakota State, DB, 112/112**
10. **Larry Hand, Appalachian State, DE, 164/164**
10. Glenn Holton, West Virginia, HB, 0/0
11. Don Hyne, Baldwin-Wallace, T, 0/0
12. Warren Wells, Texas Southern, SE, 9/65
13. John Miller, Idaho State, T, 0/0
14. Doug Bickle, Hillsdale, E, 0/0
15. Roger LaLonde, Muskingum, DT, 14/25

GREEN BAY PACKERS

1. Lloyd Voss, Nebraska, DE, 28/123
2. Jon Morris, Holy Cross, C, 0/182
3. Ode Burrell, Mississippi State, RB, 0/59
3. **Tommy Crutcher, TCU, LB, 80/108**
3. Joe O'Donnell, Michigan, G, 0/91
4. Paul Costa, Notre Dame, TE, 0/100
4. Bob Long, Wichita State, FL, 35/61
5. **Steve Wright, Alabama, T, 56/101**
5. Duke Carlisle, Texas, B, 0/0
7. Dick Herzing, Drake, T, 0/0
8. **Ken Bowman, Wisconsin, C, 123/123**
9. John McDowell, St. John's (MN), T, 12/27
10. Allen Jacobs, Utah, FB, 14/34
11. Jack Petersen, Nebraska-Omaha, T, 0/0
12. Dwain Bean, North Texas State, B, 0/0
13. Jack Mauro, Northern Michigan, T, 0/0
14. Tom O'Grady, Northwestern, E, 0/0
15. Alex Zenko, Kent State, T, 0/0
17. Len St. Jean, Northern Michigan, G, 0/140
19. John Baker, Norfolk State, DE, 0/14
20. Bill Curry, Georgia Tech, C, 28/123

LOS ANGELES RAMS

1. Bill Munson, Utah State, QB, 31/107
3. Willie Brown, USC, WR, 23/30
3. Roger Pillath, Wisconsin, T, 14/20
3. Jerry Richardson, West Texas A&M, DB, 28/55
3. John Mims, Rice, T, 0/0
5. Ken Henson, TCU, C, 0/4
6. Herman Johnson, Michigan State, HB, 0/0
7. John Varnell, West Texas State, T, 0/0
8. Bucky Pope, Catawba, FL, 30/33
9. Jerry Burton, Northwestern State (LA), B, 0/0
10. Gary Larsen, Concordia (IL), DT, 14/149
10. Ron Smith, Richmond, QB, 1/10
11. John Farris, San Diego State, G, 0/28
12. Bill Dawson, Florida State, TE, 0/9
13. Marv Harris, Stanford, LB, 14/14
14. John Garrett, Oklahoma, LB, 0/0
15. Mike Mayne, Idaho, E, 0/0
20. Bob Hohn, Nebraska, DB, 0/46

MINNESOTA VIKINGS

1. **Carl Eller, Minnesota, DE, 209/225**
2. Hal Bedsole, USC, TE, 24/24
3. George Rose, Auburn, DB, 34/47
4. Tom Keating, Michigan, DT, 0/114
5. **John Kirby, Nebraska, LB, 68/94**
6. Bob Lacey, North Carolina, WR, 1/1
7. Wes Bryant, Arkansas, T, 0/0
8. Bill McWatters, North Texas, FB, 11/11
9. Darrell Lester, McNeese State, FB, 6/29
11. H.O. Estes, East Central (OK), G, 0/0
12. Sandy Sands, Texas, E, 0/0
13. Russ Vollmer, Memphis State, HB, 0/0
14. Tom Michel, East Carolina, HB, 11/11
15. Monte Kiffin, Nebraska, T, 0/0
16. Carleton Oats, Florida A&M, DT, 0/111
20. **Milt Sunde, Minnesota, G, 147/147**

NEW YORK GIANTS

1. Joe Don Looney, Oklahoma, HB, 0/42
2. Steve Thurlow, Stanford, RB, 26/50
4. George Seals, Missouri, G, 0/134
4. Matt Snell, Ohio State, RB, 0/87
5. Tony DiMidio, West Chester, T, 0/26
6. Henry Schichtle, Wichita State, QB, 1/1
7. Roger Anderson, Virginia Union, DT, 37/37
8. **Gary Wood, Cornell, QB, 61/63**
8. Ray Popp, Pittsburgh, G, 0/0
9. Mickey Bitsko, Dayton, LB, 0/0
10. Jim Moran, Idaho, DT, 28/28
11. Glen Condren, Oklahoma, DT, 34/79
12. Jim McNaughton, Utah State, E, 0/0
13. John Deibert, Penn State, T, 0/0
14. Bill Harris, Colorado, HB, 0/0
15. Chuck Hinton, Mississippi, C, 32/32
18. J.D. Garrett, Grambling State, HB, 0/50

PHILADELPHIA EAGLES

1. **Bob Brown, Nebraska, T, 64/126**
2. Jack Concannon, Boston College, QB, 18/90
4. Ray Kubala, Texas A&M, C, 0/41
5. Mickey Babb, Georgia, E, 0/0
6. Al Denson, Florida A&M, FL, 0/98
7. Pete Goimarac, West Virginia, C, 0/0
9. Larry Smith, Mississippi, B, 0/0
10. Tom Boris, Purdue, B, 0/0
11. Bob Berry, Oregon, QB, 0/78
12. John Sapinsky, William & Mary, T, 0/0
13. Howard Kindig, Los Angeles State, DE, 0/112
14. Ernie Arizzi, Maryland, B, 0/0
15. Bob Burrows, East Texas State, T, 0/0
17. **Mike Morgan, LSU, LB, 50/87**
18. **Izzy Lang, Tennessee State, RB, 65/77**

PITTSBURGH STEELERS

1. **Paul Martha, Pittsburgh, DB, 75/88**
2. Jim Kelly, Notre Dame, TE, 6/19
3. Ralph Baker, Penn State, LB, 0/142
4. **Ben McGee, Jackson State, DE, 120/120**
5. T.W. Alley, William & Mary, T, 0/0
6. Tom Gibson, South Carolina, G, 0/0
7. Bobby Smith, North Texas, HB, 8/36
8. Bobby Currington, North Carolina Central, HB, 0/0
9. Bob Nichols, Stanford, T, 14/41
11. Robert Soleau, William & Mary, LB, 14/14
12. Bob Sherman, Iowa, DB, 25/25
13. Glenn Baker, Washington State, T, 0/0
14. Tom Jenkins, Ohio State, G, 0/0
18. Oliver Dobbins, Morgan State, DB, 0/14

SAN FRANCISCO 49ERS

1. **Dave Parks, Texas Tech, SE, 50/118**
2. George Mira, Miami (FL), QB, 47/60
3. **Dave Wilcox, Oregon, LB, 153/153**
4. Jim Wilson, Georgia, G, 25/46
5. Rudy Johnson, Nebraska, HB, 19/20
6. **Gary Lewis, Arizona State, RB, 72/73**
7. Hagood Clarke, Florida, DB, 0/67

8. Bob Daugherty, Tulsa, HB, 4/4
8. Bob Poole, Clemson, TE, 22/50
9. **Howard Mudd, Hillsdale, G, 75/93**
10. Fred Polser, East Texas State, T, 0/0
11. Dennis Almquist, Idaho, G, 0/0
12. Jim Long, Fresno State, B, 0/0
13. Robert Brown, Arkansas-Pine Bluff, DT, 0/146
14. **Ed Beard, Tennessee, LB, 97/97**
15. Jim Griffin, Grambling State, DE, 0/42
16. Cornell Gordon, North Carolina A&T, DB, 0/83

ST. LOUIS CARDINALS

1. Ken Kortas, Louisville, DT, 14/73
2. Herschel Turner, Kentucky, T, 27/27
3. Remi Prudhomme, LSU, C, 0/79
5. Charley Brooks, Memphis State, E, 0/0
6. Dick Bowman, Syracuse, E, 0/0
7. Jerry Lamb, Arkansas, E, 0/0
8. George Bednar, Notre Dame, G, 0/0
8. Bob Johnson, Wisconsin, E, 0/0
9. Willie Ross, Nebraska, FB, 0/12
10. Tony Lawrence, Bowling Green, T, 0/0
11. Richard Hard, Wenatchee Valley J.C., T, 0/0
12. **Rick Sortun, Washington, G, 82/82**
13. Jake Adams, Virginia Tech, E, 0/0
14. Len Slaby, Syracuse, C, 0/0
15. Cliff Stallings, New Mexico, B, 0/0
19. **Bob Young, Howard Payne, G, 105/194**

WASHINGTON REDSKINS

1. **Charley Taylor, Arizona State, WR, 165/165**
2. **Paul Krause, Iowa, DB, 54/226**
5. **Jim Snowden, Notre Dame, T, 98/98**
6. Russ Brown, Florida, E, 0/0
7. Dick Shiner, Maryland, QB, 29/99
9. **Len Hauss, Georgia, C, 196/196**
10. Rick Leeson, Pittsburgh, B, 0/0
11. Gene Donaldson, Purdue, RB, 0/2
12. Bob Zvolerin, Tennessee, T, 0/0
13. Tom MacDonald, Notre Dame, B, 0/0
14. Tom Urbanik, Penn State, B, 0/0
15. Dick Evers, Colorado State, T, 0/0
16. Tom Walters, Southern Mississippi, DB, 49/49
17. Ozzie Clay, Iowa State, WR, 14/14
19. John Seedborg, Arizona State, P, 1/1

1964 AFL

BOSTON PATRIOTS

1. Jack Concannon, Boston College, QB, 0/90
2. Jim Kelly, Notre Dame, TE, 0/19
4. **Jon Morris, Holy Cross, C, 130/182**
6. Jim Mazurek, Syracuse, G, 0/0
7. T.W. Alley, William & Mary, T, 0/0
8. **J.D. Garrett, Grambling State, HB, 50/50**
8. Roger LaLonde, Muskingum, DT, 0/25
9. **Len St. Jean, Northern Michigan, G, 140/140**
11. John Barrett, Boston College, HB, 0/0
13. Joe Scarpati, North Carolina State, DB, 0/96
14. Jim Wilson, Georgia, G, 0/46
15. Tony Gibbons, John Carroll, T, 0/0
17. Gary Wood, Cornell, QB, 0/63
19. Bill Dawson, Florida State, TE, 9/9
20. Lonnie Farmer, Tennessee-Chattanooga, LB, 31/31

BUFFALO BILLS

1. Carl Eller, Minnesota, DE, 0/225
2. Dick Evey, Tennessee, DT, 0/102
3. George Rose, Auburn, DB, 0/47
4. **Butch Byrd, Boston University, DB, 98/112**
4. Paul Warfield, Ohio State, WR, 0/157
5. Mike Reilly, Iowa, LB, 0/74
7. Roger Pillath, Wisconsin, T, 0/20
9. Paul Martha, Pittsburgh, DB, 0/88
10. Howard Simpson, Auburn, DE, 0/3
10. Earl Lattimer, Michigan State, FB, 0/0
11. Bobby Smith, North Texas, HB, 28/36
11. Cloyd Webb, Iowa, E, 0/0
12. Pete Gogolak, Cornell, K, 28/149
12. Willie Ross, Nebraska, FB, 12/12
13. **Joe O'Donnell, Michigan, G, 91/91**
14. Remi Prudhomme, LSU, C, 32/79
15. Bill Simpson, Baylor, T, 0/0
16. John Hilton, Richmond, TE, 0/106
18. **Hagood Clarke, Florida, DB, 67/67**
26. Allen Jacobs, Utah, FB, 0/34

DENVER BRONCOS

1. Robert Brown, Arkansas-Pine Bluff, DT, 0/146
3. Matt Snorton, Michigan State, TE, 5/5
3. Marv Woodson, Indiana, DB, 0/72
6. **Al Denson, Florida A&M, FL, 91/98**
6. Don Shackelford, Pacific, G, 8/8
7. Ray Kubala, Texas A&M, C, 41/41
7. Jerry Richardson, West Texas A&M, DB, 0/55
8. Wally Hilgenberg, Iowa, LB, 0/199
9. John Mims, Rice, T, 0/0
12. Paul Krause, Iowa, DB, 0/226
13. Charlie Parker, Southern Mississippi, G, 14/14
14. Bob Hayes, Florida A&M, SE, 0/132
15. Chuck Logan, Northwestern, TE, 0/46
18. George Mira, Miami (FL), QB, 0/60
19. Odell Barry, Findlay, WR, 26/26
22. Gary Lewis, Arizona State, RB, 0/73
25. Jim Jones, Wisconsin, SE, 13/54
26. Bob Berry, Oregon, QB, 0/78

HOUSTON OILERS

1. Scott Appleton, Texas, DT, 42/70
2. Charley Taylor, Arizona State, WR, 0/165
2. Billy Truax, LSU, TE, 0/114
3. Bobby Crenshaw, Baylor, T, 0/0
4. **Ode Burrell, Mississippi State, RB, 59/59**
5. **Sid Blanks, Texas A&M-Kingsville, RB, 55/83**
5. John Varnell, West Texas State, T, 0/0
6. Dave Wilcox, Oregon, LB, 0/153
8. Ezell Seals, Prairie View A&M, HB, 0/0
9. Jerry Burton, Northwestern State (LA), HB, 0/0
10. Sammy Odom, Northwestern State (LA), DT, 14/14
11. Owen Dejanovich, Northern Arizona, G, 0/0
12. Benny Nelson, Alabama, DB, 14/14
14. Ken Henson, TCU, C, 0/4
15. Pat Crain, Clemson, FB, 0/0
16. Bill Munson, Utah State, QB, 0/107
17. Dick Leeuwenburg, Stanford, T, 0/9
18. Bob Nichols, Stanford, T, 0/41
20. Pete Jaquess, Eastern New Mexico, DB, 28/85

KANSAS CITY CHIEFS

1. **Pete Beathard, USC, QB, 52/110**
2. Bill Martin, Georgia Tech, TE, 0/70
3. Ken Kortas, Louisville, DT, 0/73
4. **Ed Lothamer, Michigan State, DT, 88/88**
5. Tom Keating, Michigan, DT, 23/114
6. Joe Don Looney, Oklahoma, HB, 0/42
6. Duke Carlisle, Texas, DB, 0/0
7. John Simon, Notre Dame, E, 0/0
8. Hal Bedsole, USC, TE, 0/24
9. Tony DiMidio, West Chester, T, 26/26
10. Clay Stephens, Notre Dame, E, 0/0
11. Tommy Crutcher, TCU, LB, 0/108
12. Jack Adams, Virginia Tech, E, 0/0
13. Orville Hudson, East Texas State, E, 0/0
13. Jay Wilkinson, Duke, HB, 0/0
14. Paul Costa, Notre Dame, TE, 0/100
15. Jim Snowden, Notre Dame, T, 0/98
16. Roger Staubach, Navy, QB, 0/131
20. Bob Hohn, Nebraska, DB, 0/46
23. Bud Abell, Missouri, LB, 40/40

NEW YORK JETS

1. **Matt Snell, Ohio State, RB, 87/87**
2. Lloyd Voss, Nebraska, DE, 0/123
3. **Gerry Philbin, Buffalo, DE, 110/123**
4. Jim Evans, Texas-El Paso, WR, 21/21
5. Ben McGee, Jackson State, DE, 0/120
6. **Ralph Baker, Penn State, LB, 142/142**
8. Steve Wright, Alabama, T, 0/101
9. Sherman Lewis, Michigan State, DB, 10/10
10. Ken Bowman, Wisconsin, C, 0/123
11. Bob Lacey, North Carolina, WR, 0/1
12. Rudy Johnson, Nebraska, HB, 0/20
13. Jeff Ware, Pittsburgh, LB, 0/0
14. Charley Brooks, Memphis State, E, 0/0
15. Herman Johnson, Michigan State, DB, 0/0
19. Glen Condren, Oklahoma, DT, 0/79
20. Dick Shiner, Maryland, QB, 0/99
21. Larry Hand, Appalachian State, DE, 0/164
23. **Cornell Gordon, North Carolina A&T, DB, 54/83**
25. Jerry Rhome, Tulsa, QB, 0/71

OAKLAND RAIDERS

1. Tony Lorick, Arizona State, RB, 0/83
2. **Dan Conners, Miami (FL), LB, 141/141**
3. George Bednar, Notre Dame, T, 0/0
4. **Bill Budness, Boston University, LB, 92/92**
5. Don Green, Susquehanna, DB, 0/0
7. John Sapinsky, William & Mary, T, 0/0
8. Vince Petno, Citadel, DB, 0/0
9. Herschel Turner, Kentucky, T, 0/27
9. **J.R. Williamson, Louisiana Tech, LB, 54/93**
10. Mel Renfro, Oregon, DB, 0/174
11. Larry Rakestraw, Georgia, QB, 0/13
12. Billy Lothridge, Georgia Tech, DB, 0/104
13. Mickey Babb, Georgia, E, 0/0
14. Fred Polser, East Texas State, G, 0/0
15. Mike Geirs, Southern California, T, 0/0
19. Tom Michel, East Carolina, HB, 0/11
20. Ed Beard, Tennessee, LB, 0/97
21. **Carleton Oats, Florida A&M, DT, 103/111**
23. Bill Curry, Georgia Tech, C, 0/123

SAN DIEGO CHARGERS

1. Ted Davis, Georgia Tech, LB, 0/90
2. John Kirby, Nebraska, LB, 0/94
3. Perry Lee Dunn, Mississippi, RB, 0/74
4. Dave Parks, Texas Tech, SE, 0/118
5. **Gary Kirner, USC, G, 77/77**
5. Pete Goimarac, West Virginia, C, 0/0
6. Willie Brown, USC, WR, 0/30
7. Roger Anderson, Virginia Union, DT, 0/37
7. Pat Batten, Hardin-Simmons, FB, 0/3
8. George Seals, Missouri, G, 0/134
10. Bob Long, Wichita State, FL, 0/61
10. Dick Bowman, Syracuse, E, 0/0
11. Bob Horton, Boston University, LB, 22/22
12. Ron Carpenter, Texas A&M, LB, 18/18
13. **Kenny Graham, Washington State, DB, 82/90**
14. Howard Kindig, Los Angeles State, DE, 35/112
15. Ed Mitchell, Southern (LA), G, 21/21
16. Bob Daugherty, Tulsa, HB, 0/4
17. John Farris, San Diego State, G, 28/28
22. Chuck Hinton, Mississippi, C, 0/32
23. Ron Smith, Richmond, QB, 0/10

1965 NFL

BALTIMORE COLTS

1. **Mike Curtis, Duke, LB, 125/166**
2. Ralph Neely, Oklahoma, T, 0/172
3. **Glenn Ressler, Penn State, G, 125/125**
4. Marty Schottenheimer, Pittsburgh, LB, 0/79
4. Dave Johnson, San Jose State, E, 0/0
5. John McGuire, Syracuse, E, 0/0
6. Al Atkinson, Villanova, LB, 0/120
6. Bobby Felts, Florida A&M, HB, 7/38
7. John Kolocek, Corpus Christi State, T, 0/0
8. Rosey Davis, Tennessee State, DE, 0/22
9. Tom Bleick, Georgia Tech, DB, 7/9
10. George Harold, Allen, DB, 14/22
11. Lamar Richardson, Fisk, E, 0/0
12. Ted Rodosovich, Cincinnati, G, 0/0
13. Bruce Airheart, North Dakota State, HB, 0/0
14. Jerry Fishman, Maryland, LB, 0/0
15. **Roy Hilton, Jackson State, DE, 125/151**
16. Steve Tensi, Florida State, QB, 0/56
18. Charlie King, Purdue, DB, 0/51
19. Barry Brown, Florida, TE, 24/57

CHICAGO BEARS

1. **Dick Butkus, Illinois, LB, 119/119**
1. Steve DeLong, Tennessee, DE, 14/103
1. **Gale Sayers, Kansas, RB, 68/68**
4. Jim Nance, Syracuse, RB, 0/101
6. Tony Carey, Notre Dame, HB, 0/0
7. **Dick Gordon, Michigan State, WR, 97/115**
7. Mickey Sutton, Auburn, DB, 0/5
8. Brian Schweda, Kansas, DE, 14/38
9. Ken Ambrusko, Maryland, B, 0/0
10. Dennis Murphy, Florida, DT, 2/2
11. **Frank Cornish, Grambling State, DT, 55/83**
12. Steve Cox, South Carolina, T, 0/0
13. Dave Daniels, Florida A&M, DT, 0/14
14. Dave Pivec, Notre Dame, TE, 0/45
15. Art Robinson, Cal State-Los Angeles, B, 0/0
16. Frank Pitts, Southern (LA), WR, 0/127
20. **Ralph Kurek, Wisconsin, RB, 81/81**

CLEVELAND BROWNS

2. Gerry Bussell, Georgia Tech, DB, 0/6
2. Jim Garcia, Purdue, DE, 12/35
2. **Walter Johnson, Los Angeles State, DT, 168/182**
3. Bobby Maples, Baylor, C, 0/184
3. **Bo Scott, Ohio State, RB, 73/73**
5. Bill Irwin, Mississippi, T, 0/0
6. Arnie Simkus, Michigan, DE, 0/12
6. Corwyn Aldredge, Northwestern State (LA), E, 0/0
7. **Dale Lindsey, Western Kentucky, LB, 106/111**
8. **Mike Howell, Grambling State, DB, 102/103**
9. Gary Lane, Missouri, QB, 11/18
10. Pat Screen, Louisiana State, QB, 0/0
11. Ollie Cordill, Memphis, DB, 0/16
12. Justin Canale, Mississippi State, G, 0/64
13. Henry Pickett, Baylor, HB, 0/0
14. Dan Simrell, Toledo, QB, 0/0

DALLAS COWBOYS

1. **Craig Morton, California, QB, 97/203**
2. Malcolm Walker, Rice, C, 47/58
4. Jimmy Sidle, Auburn, RB, 0/6
4. Bob Svihus, USC, T, 0/122
5. Roger Pettee, Florida, LB, 0/0
6. Sonny Utz, Virginia Tech, FB, 0/0
7. Brig Owens, Cincinnati, DB, 0/158
8. Russell Wayt, Rice, LB, 9/9
9. Jim Zanios, Texas Tech, FB, 0/0
10. Gaylon McCullough, Alabama, C, 0/0
11. **Jethro Pugh, Elizabeth City State, DT, 183/183**
12. Ernie Kellermann, Miami (OH), DB, 0/105
13. Jack Schraub, California, E, 0/0
14. Garry Porterfield, Tulsa, DE, 2/2
15. Gene Foster, Arizona State, RB, 0/68
17. Mitch Johnson, UCLA, T, 12/79
18. Marty Amsler, Evansville, DE, 0/37

DETROIT LIONS

1. **Tom Nowatzke, Indiana, FB, 65/96**
2. **Jerry Rush, Michigan State, DT, 89/89**
3. Fred Biletnikoff, Florida State, WR, 0/190
4. Tom Myers, Northwestern, QB, 2/2
5. **Ed Flanagan, Purdue, C, 139/165**
5. **Tom Vaughn, Iowa State, DB, 88/88**
5. John Flynn, Oklahoma, E, 0/0
6. Earl Hawkins, Emory & Henry, B, 0/0
7. Greg Kent, Utah, T, 5/12
7. **Bob Kowalkowski, Virginia, G, 138/142**
8. Larry Harbin, Appalachian State, B, 0/0
9. Bruce McLenna, Hillsdale, HB, 9/9
10. Frank Pennie, Florida, T, 0/0
11. Jim Kearney, Prairie View A&M, DB, 13/142
12. Jim Moore, North Texas State, LB, 0/0
13. Jack Jacobson, Oklahoma State, DB, 0/3
14. Larry Brown, Oklahoma, B, 0/0
15. Wallace Dickey, Southwest Texas State, T, 0/22
18. Karl Sweetan, Wake Forest, QB, 20/36
20. George Wilson, Xavier (OH), QB, 0/14

GREEN BAY PACKERS

1. **Donny Anderson, Texas Tech, RB, 84/126**
1. Larry Elkins, Baylor, WR, 0/18
2. Al Dotson, Grambling State, DT, 0/47
3. Allen Brown, Mississippi, TE, 19/19
4. Wally Mahle, Syracuse, B, 0/0
5. Doug Goodwin, Maryland-Eastern Shore, RB, 0/5
5. Jim Harvey, Mississippi, G, 0/78
6. Dick Koeper, Oregon State, T, 0/3
6. Bill Symons, Colorado, HB, 0/0
7. Junior Coffey, Washington, RB, 13/59
7. Jerry Roberts, Baldwin Wallace, B, 0/0
7. Roger Jacobazzi, Wisconsin, T, 0/0
8. Mike Shinn, Kansas, E, 0/0
9. Larry Bulaich, Texas Christian, B, 0/0
10. Bud Marshall, Stephen F. Austin State, DT, 14/48
11. Jim Weatherwax, Los Angeles State, DT, 34/34
12. Gene Jeter, Texas Southern, LB, 0/30
13. Roy Schmidt, Long Beach State, G, 0/43
14. John Putnam, Drake, FB, 0/0
15. Chuck Hurston, Auburn, DE, 0/93
16. Phil Vandersea, Massachusetts, LB, 38/46

LOS ANGELES RAMS

1. **Clancy Williams, Washington State, DB, 97/97**
3. Fred Brown, Miami (FL), LB, 14/40
4. Mike Strofolino, Villanova, LB, 9/35
5. Frank Marchlewski, Minnesota, C, 32/74
5. **Doug Woodlief, Memphis, LB, 69/69**
6. Bill Harrison, Elon, E, 0/0
7. Tony Guillory, Lamar, LB, 41/53
8. Stan Dzura, California, T, 0/0
9. Ronnie Caveness, Arkansas, LB, 0/46
10. Jim Burt, Western Kentucky, HB, 0/0
11. Merlin Walet, McNeese State, FB, 0/0
12. Bob Werl, Miami (FL), DE, 0/8
13. Brent Berry, San Jose State, T, 0/0
14. Bill Robertson, Austin, E, 0/0
15. Marvin Davis, Wichita State, DE, 0/1
19. Billy Guy Anderson, Tulsa, QB, 0/8

MINNESOTA VIKINGS

1. Jack Snow, Notre Dame, WR, 0/150
2. Lance Rentzel, Oklahoma, WR, 20/115
2. Archie Sutton, Illinois, T, 19/19
4. Jim Jr. Harris, Utah State, DT, 0/42

4. Jim Whalen, Boston College, TE, 0/89
6. Jim Grisham, Oklahoma, B, 0/0
8. Jeff Jordan, Tulsa, DB, 37/37
8. John Hankinson, Minnesota, QB, 0/0
9. Frank McClendon, Alabama, T, 0/0
10. Jerald Schweiger, Wisconsin-Superior, T, 0/0
11. John Thomas, Southern California, E, 0/0
12. Mike Tilleman, Montana, DT, 12/149
13. **Dave Osborn, North Dakota, RB, 137/143**
14. Max Leetzow, Idaho, DE, 0/28
15. Phillip Morgan, East Tennessee State, B, 0/0
18. Rich Kotite, Wagner, TE, 0/35
19. Ellis Johnson, Southeastern Louisiana, HB, 0/28
20. Cosmo Iacavazzi, Princeton, HB, 0/2

NEW YORK GIANTS

1. **Tucker Frederickson, Auburn, RB, 66/66**
3. Chuck Mercein, Yale, RB, 27/58
3. Bob Timberlake, Michigan, K, 12/12
4. Henry Carr, Arizona State, DB, 37/37
5. Frank Lambert, Mississippi, P, 0/28
8. **Willie Williams, Grambling State, DB, 100/106**
9. John Frick, Ohio U., E, 0/0
10. Ben Crenshaw, Jackson State, B, 0/0
11. **Ernie Koy, Texas, RB, 79/79**
12. Jim Carroll, Notre Dame, LB, 15/61
13. **Spider Lockhart, North Texas, DB, 145/145**
14. Olen Underwood, Texas, LB, 10/89
15. Mike Giers, Southern California, G, 0/0
16. Tom Good, Marshall, LB, 0/2
18. Mike Ciccolella, Dayton, LB, 35/35
19. Smith Reed, Alcorn State, HB, 11/11

PHILADELPHIA EAGLES

2. Ray Rissmiller, Georgia, T, 1/16
3. **Al Nelson, Cincinnati, DB, 105/105**
4. **Fred Hill, USC, TE, 83/83**
5. John Henderson, Michigan, WR, 0/93
6. Gary Garrison, San Diego State, WR, 0/134
6. John Huarte, Notre Dame, QB, 2/24
7. Erwin Will, Dayton, DT, 5/5
8. Al Piraino, Wisconsin, T, 0/0
9. Floyd Hudlow, Arizona, DB, 0/24
10. Rick Redman, Washington, LB, 0/100
11. Louis James, Texas-El Paso, HB, 0/0
12. John Kuznieski, Purdue, HB, 0/0
13. John Fouse, Arizona, E, 0/0
14. Tom Longo, Notre Dame, DB, 0/29
15. Otis Taylor, Prairie View A&M, WR, 0/130
16. Jim Gray, Toledo, DB, 3/9
20. Bob Shann, Boston College, DB, 10/10

PITTSBURGH STEELERS

2. **Roy Jefferson, Utah, WR, 65/162**
7. Charlie Browning, Washington, HB, 0/1
8. Bill Howley, Pittsburgh, E, 0/0
9. Tom Neville, Mississippi State, T, 0/190
10. Dave Tobey, Oregon, LB, 0/23
11. Frank Molden, Jackson State, DT, 0/31
12. Craig Lofquist, Minnesota, B, 0/0
13. **J.R. Wilburn, South Carolina, FL, 58/58**
14. Cannonball Butler, Edward Waters, RB, 39/97
15. John Carrell, Texas Tech, LB, 0/6
17. Whit Canale, Tennessee, DE, 0/16

SAN FRANCISCO 49ERS

1. George Donnelly, Illinois, DB, 33/33
1. **Ken Willard, North Carolina, RB, 125/132**
2. Joe Cerne, Northwestern, C, 39/45
3. Jack Chapple, Stanford, LB, 14/14
3. Jim Norton, Washington, DE, 28/64
3. Bob Schweickert, Virginia Tech, QB, 0/6
4. Larry Todd, Arizona State, RB, 0/57
5. Dave McCormick, LSU, T, 14/16
9. Wayne Swinford, Georgia, DB, 26/26
10. Bob Cappadona, Northeastern, RB, 0/41
11. Steve Mass, Detroit, T, 0/0
12. Dave Plump, Fresno State, DB, 0/14
13. Gregg Schumacher, Illinois, DE, 0/25
14. Frank Andruski, Utah, HB, 0/0
15. Joe Pabian, West Virginia, T, 0/0
16. Dave Hettema, New Mexico, T, 7/13

ST. LOUIS CARDINALS

1. Joe Namath, Alabama, QB, 0/140
2. Dave Simmons, Georgia Tech, LB, 20/44
3. Ray Ogden, Alabama, TE, 17/70
4. **Johnny Roland, Missouri, RB, 96/103**
5. Bob Bonds, San Jose State, HB, 0/0
6. Glen Ray Hines, Arkansas, T, 0/112
7. Frank Roy, Utah, G, 11/11
8. John Meyer, Notre Dame, LB, 0/14
9. Jimmy Heidel, Mississippi, DB, 14/28
10. Chuck Drulis, Duke, E, 0/0
11. Bud French, Alabama, B, 0/0
12. Glen Sasser, North Carolina State, E, 0/0
13. Steve Murphy, Northwestern, HB, 0/0
14. Mike Alford, Auburn, C, 13/25
15. Harlan Lane, Baylor, B, 0/0
16. Carl Silvestri, Wisconsin, DB, 14/17
17. Mike Melinkovich, Washington, DE, 24/31
18. Ed McQuarters, Oklahoma, DT, 1/1
19. **Roy Shivers, Utah State, RB, 73/73**

WASHINGTON REDSKINS

2. Bob Breitenstein, Tulsa, T, 0/58
3. Kent McCloughan, Nebraska, DB, 0/67
8. Don Croftcheck, Indiana, G, 26/35
9. **Jerry Smith, Arizona State, TE, 168/168**
10. Bob Briggs, Central Oklahoma, FB, 7/7
11. Willie Adams, New Mexico State, DE, 28/28
12. John Strohmeyer, Nebraska, T, 0/0
13. Biff Bracy, Duke, HB, 0/0
14. Dave Estrada, Arizona State, HB, 0/0
15. Ben Baldwin, Vanderbilt, B, 0/0
16. Robert Reed, Tennessee State, G, 8/8
18. **Chris Hanburger, North Carolina, LB, 187/187**

1965 AFL

BOSTON PATRIOTS

1. Jerry Rush, Michigan State, DT, 0/89
3. **Jim Whalen, Boston College, TE, 70/89**
4. Ellis Johnson, Southeastern Louisiana, HB, 28/28
5. Corwyn Aldredge, Northwestern State (LA), E, 0/0
6. **Justin Canale, Mississippi State, G, 56/64**
7. **Tom Neville, Mississippi State, T, 160/190**
8. Fred Brown, Miami (FL), LB, 0/40
9. Bob Malone, Louisiana Tech, T, 0/0
11. John Frechette, Boston College, T, 0/0
12. Jim Weatherly, Mississippi, DB, 0/0
13. Charlie Green, Wittenberg, QB, 0/14
14. Jay Cunningham, Bowling Green State, DB, 40/40
15. Ted Rodosevitch, Cincinnati, G, 0/0
16. George Pyne, Olivet, DT, 14/14
17. White Graves, LSU, DB, 40/42
18. Ed Meixler, Boston University, LB, 4/4
19. **Jim Nance, Syracuse, RB, 94/101**

R1. Dave McCormick, LSU, T, 0/16
R2. Bob Kowalkowski, Virginia, G, 0/142
R3. Bob Cappadona, Northeastern, RB, 27/41
R10. Dave Hettema, New Mexico, T, 0/13
R11. Roy Schmidt, Long Beach State, G, 0/43

BUFFALO BILLS

1. Jim Davidson, Ohio State, T, 0/0
3. Al Atkinson, Villanova, LB, 0/120
5. Dave Simmons, Georgia Tech, LB, 0/44
6. Lance Rentzel, Oklahoma, WR, 0/115
7. **Marty Schottenheimer, Pittsburgh, LB, 56/79**
8. Ray Rissmiller, Georgia, T, 4/16
9. Al Nelson, Cincinnati, DB, 0/105
10. Floyd Hudlow, Arizona, DB, 7/24
10. Chuck Mercein, Yale, RB, 0/58
11. Doug Goodwin, Maryland-Eastern Shore, RB, 3/5
12. Chuck Hurston, Auburn, DE, 9/93
12. Pete Mills, Wichita State, WR, 3/3
13. Bob Timberlake, Michigan, K, 0/12
14. Lyn Hart, Virginia State, DB, 0/0
15. John Meyer, Notre Dame, LB, 0/14
17. John Henderson, Michigan, WR, 0/93
19. Frank Marchlewski, Minnesota, C, 13/74

R2. Gary Lane, Missouri, QB, 0/18
R7. J.R. Wilburn, South Carolina, FL, 0/58
R8. Charlie King, Purdue, DB, 28/51
R12. George Wilson, Xavier (OH), QB, 0/14

DENVER BRONCOS

2. Dick Butkus, Illinois, LB, 0/119
3. Glenn Ressler, Penn State, G, 0/125
4. George Donnelly, Illinois, DB, 0/33
5. Bob Breitenstein, Tulsa, T, 30/58
5. Max Leetzow, Idaho, DE, 28/28
6. Tom Wilhelm, Syracuse, T, 0/0
7. Jim Garcia, Purdue, DE, 0/35
8. Jon Hohman, Wisconsin, G, 24/24
9. Gerry Bussell, Georgia Tech, DB, 6/6
10. Gene Jeter, Texas Southern, LB, 30/30
11. Tom Vaughn, Iowa State, DB, 0/88
12. Tom Myers, Northwestern, QB, 0/2
13. Mike Strofolino, Villanova, LB, 0/35
14. John Frick, Ohio U., G, 0/0
15. Jeff Jordan, Tulsa, DB, 0/37
16. Brian Schweda, Kansas, DE, 0/38

R1. Miller Farr, Wichita State, DB, 7/113
R2. Walter Johnson, Los Angeles State, DT, 0/182
R3. Marvin Davis, Wichita State, DE, 1/1
R4. Barry Brown, Florida, TE, 0/57
R6. **Jerry Inman, Oregon, DT, 82/82**
R9. Phil Vandersea, Massachusetts, LB, 0/46

HOUSTON OILERS

1. Larry Elkins, Baylor, WR, 18/18
2. Ralph Neely, Oklahoma, T, 0/172
2. Malcolm Walker, Rice, C, 0/58
3. Ernie Koy, Texas, RB, 0/79
4. **Bobby Maples, Baylor, C, 83/184**
5. Frank Molden, Jackson State, DT, 0/31
6. Dennis Murphy, Florida, DT, 0/2
6. Russell Wayt, Rice, LB, 0/9
8. Roy Hilton, Jackson State, DE, 0/151
8. Ray Ogden, Alabama, TE, 0/70
9. George Kinney, Wiley, DE, 1/1
10. Maxie Williams, Southeastern Louisiana, G, 14/83
11. Kent McCloughan, Nebraska, DB, 0/67
12. Robert Reed, Tennessee State, G, 0/8
13. Bobby Felts, Florida A&M, HB, 0/38
14. Norm Evans, TCU, T, 14/188
15. Tony Guillory, Lamar, LB, 0/53
16. Junior Coffey, Washington, RB, 0/59
19. Braden Beck, Stanford, K, 2/2

R1. Donny Anderson, Texas Tech, RB, 0/126
R2. **Glen Ray Hines, Arkansas, T, 70/112**
R4. Ollie Cordill, Memphis, DB, 0/16
R6. Dave Daniels, Florida A&M, DT, 0/14
R9. Tom Bleick, Georgia Tech, DB, 0/9
R11. Billy Guy Anderson, Tulsa, QB, 8/8

KANSAS CITY CHIEFS

1. Gale Sayers, Kansas, RB, 0/68
2. Ronnie Caveness, Arkansas, LB, 7/46
2. Jack Chapple, Stanford, LB, 0/14
3. Mike Curtis, Duke, LB, 0/166
4. **Frank Pitts, Southern (LA), WR, 74/127**
4. **Otis Taylor, Prairie View A&M, WR, 130/130**
5. Smith Reed, Alcorn State, HB, 0/11
6. Mickey Sutton, Auburn, DB, 0/5
7. **Gloster Richardson, Jackson State, WR, 51/92**
7. Lou Bobich, Michigan State, DB, 0/0
8. Danny Thomas, Southern Methodist, QB, 0/0
9. Joe Cerne, Northwestern, C, 0/45
10. Bob Howard, Stanford, DB, 0/0
11. Al Piraino, Wisconsin, T, 0/0
12. Mike Cox, Iowa State, LB, 0/0
13. Bob Bonds, San Jose State, DB, 0/0
14. Fred Dolson, Wiley, DB, 0/0
15. Dave Powless, Illinois, G, 0/0
17. Don Croftcheck, Indiana, G, 0/35
18. Jerry Smith, Arizona State, TE, 0/168
19. Mike Alford, Auburn, C, 0/25

R1. Al Dotson, Grambling State, DT, 1/47
R2. Frank Cornish, Grambling State, DT, 0/83
R3. Henry Carr, Arizona State, DB, 0/37
R9. Bruce McLenna, Hillsdale, HB, 0/9

NEW YORK JETS

1. **Joe Namath, Alabama, QB, 136/140**
1. Tom Nowatzke, Indiana, FB, 0/96
2. John Huarte, Notre Dame, QB, 0/24
3. **Verlon Biggs, Jackson State, DE, 80/135**
4. Bob Schweickert, Virginia Tech, QB, 6/6
5. Glenn Sasser, North Carolina State, DE, 0/0
6. Don Hoovler, Ohio U., LB, 0/0
7. Jim Jr. Harris, Utah State, DT, 42/42
7. Archie Roberts, Columbia, QB, 0/1
8. Rick McCurdy, Oklahoma, DE, 0/0
9. Jimmy Sidle, Auburn, RB, 0/6
10. Frank Lambert, Mississippi, P, 0/28
11. Jim Gray, Toledo, DB, 6/9
12. John Berrington, Iowa State, LB, 0/0
13. Sonny Utz, Virginia Tech, FB, 0/0
14. Gary Plumlee, New Mexico, DT, 0/0
15. Jim Burt, Western Kentucky, DB, 0/0
17. Charlie Browning, Washington, HB, 1/1
19. Mitch Dudek, Xavier (OH), T, 14/14

R1. Johnny Roland, Missouri, RB, 0/103
R3. Jimmy Heidel, Mississippi, DB, 0/28
R4. Bob Werl, Miami (FL), DE, 8/8
R5. **George Sauer, Texas, SE, 84/84**
R6. Dale Lindsey, Western Kentucky, LB, 0/111
R9. Rich Kotite, Wagner, TE, 0/35
R11. Bud Marshall, Stephen F. Austin State, DT, 0/48

OAKLAND RAIDERS

1. **Harry Schuh, Memphis, T, 84/140**
2. **Fred Biletnikoff, Florida State, WR, 190/190**
3. **Bob Svihus, USC, T, 82/122**
4. **Gus Otto, Missouri, LB, 102/102**
9. Rich Zecher, Utah State, DT, 14/40
10. Craig Morton, California, QB, 0/203
11. Bill Minor, Illinois, LB, 0/0
13. Wally Mahle, Syracuse, DB, 0/0
14. Loren Hawley, California, DB, 0/0
15. Bill Cronin, Boston College, TE, 0/16
16. Fred Hill, USC, TE, 0/83
17. Garry Porterfield, Tulsa, DE, 0/2
20. Bo Scott, Ohio State, RB, 0/73

R1. **Larry Todd, Arizona State, RB, 57/57**
R2. **Jim Harvey, Mississippi, G, 78/78**
R6. Greg Kent, Utah, T, 7/12
R7. John Carrell, Texas Tech, LB, 0/6
R11. Tom Longo, Notre Dame, DB, 0/29

SAN DIEGO CHARGERS

1. **Steve DeLong, Tennessee, DE, 89/103**
2. Roy Jefferson, Utah, WR, 0/162
3. Allen Brown, Mississippi, TE, 0/19
4. Steve Tensi, Florida State, QB, 15/56
5. **Rick Redman, Washington, LB, 100/100**
6. Will Beasley, North Carolina A&T, FB, 0/0
7. Jack Snow, Notre Dame, WR, 0/150
8. Clancy Williams, Washington State, DB, 0/97
9. Jerry Whelchel, Massachusetts, QB, 0/0
10. **Gene Foster, Arizona State, RB, 68/68**
11. Veran Smith, Utah State, G, 0/0
12. Jim Allison, San Diego State, RB, 43/43
13. Bill Quigley, Villanova, LB, 0/0
14. Don Floyd, Florida State, E, 0/0
15. Mike Howell, Grambling State, DB, 0/103
18. Bob Evans, Texas A&M, DE, 0/4

R1. **Gary Garrison, San Diego State, WR, 131/134**
R2. Larry Martin, San Diego State, DT, 1/1
R4. Doug Woodlief, Memphis, LB, 0/69
R5. Jim Weatherwax, Los Angeles State, DT, 0/34
R6. Tom Good, Marshall, LB, 2/2
R8. Roy Shivers, Utah State, RB, 0/73
R10. Dave Plump, Fresno State, DB, 14/14
R12. Mike Ciccolella, Dayton, LB, 0/35

1966 NFL

ATLANTA FALCONS

1. Randy Johnson, Texas A&M-Kingsville, QB, 46/75
1. **Tommy Nobis, Texas, LB, 133/133**
2. Jerry Jones, Bowling Green State, T, 7/44
2. Nick Rassas, Notre Dame, DB, 27/27
3. Mike Dennis, Mississippi, RB, 0/15
3. Phil Sheridan, Notre Dame, E, 0/0
4. Willie Asbury, Kent State, RB, 0/33
4. **Ken Reaves, Norfolk State, DB, 112/164**
5. Bill Wolski, Notre Dame, FB, 2/2
5. Martin Kahn, North Texas State, T, 0/0
6. Charley Casey, Florida, FL, 0/0
7. William Johnson, University of the South, FB, 0/0
8. Bill Goss, Tulane, LB, 0/0
9. Bob Sanders, North Texas, LB, 9/9
10. Mike Bender, Arkansas, G, 0/0
11. Steve Sloan, Alabama, QB, 8/8
12. Ken Hollister, Indiana, T, 0/0
13. Bob Collins, South Carolina, T, 0/0
14. Steve Ecker, Shippensburg, K, 0/0
15. Tommy Tolleson, Alabama, WR, 8/8
20. Bob Riggle, Penn State, DB, 25/25

BALTIMORE COLTS

1. **Sam Ball, Kentucky, T, 61/61**
2. Butch Allison, Missouri, T, 0/0
3. Rick Kestner, Kentucky, FL, 0/0
4. Hoyle Granger, Mississippi State, RB, 0/83
4. Rod Sherman, USC, WR, 0/83
6. Stas Maliszewski, Princeton, LB, 0/0
7. **Ray Perkins, Alabama, WR, 58/58**
7. Dave Ellis, North Carolina State, DE, 0/0
8. Gerry Allen, Nebraska-Omaha, RB, 4/28
8. Jack White, Penn State, QB, 0/0
9. Jerry Gross, Auburn, HB, 0/0
10. Claude Brownlee, Benedictine, DT, 0/3
11. Eric Crabtree, Pittsburgh, WR, 0/83
12. Jim Carter, Tennessee State, G, 0/0
13. Bob Hadrick, Purdue, E, 0/0
14. Jim Ward, Gettysburg, QB, 11/13
15. Lee Garner, Mississippi, LB, 0/0
18. Ed Toner, Massachusetts, DT, 0/26
20. Tom Carr, Morgan State, DT, 0/4

1404 THE PRO FOOTBALL DRAFT

CHICAGO BEARS
1. George Rice, LSU, DT, 0/37
2. Charlie Brown, Syracuse, DB, 22/30
3. Bob Pickens, Nebraska, T, 20/20
4. **Doug Buffone, Louisville, LB, 186/186**
4. **Randy Jackson, Florida, T, 105/105**
6. Frank McRae, Tennessee State, DT, 6/6
6. Dennis Brewster, BYU, T, 0/0
7. Ron Meyer, South Dakota State, QB, 0/4
8. Doug McFalls, Georgia, DB, 0/0
9. Fritz Greenlee, Northern Arizona, LB, 0/4
10. Bobby Burnett, Arkansas, RB, 0/25
11. Terry Owens, Jacksonville State, T, 0/132
12. Wayne Page, Clemson, DE, 0/0
13. Wayne Becker, Montana, T, 0/0
14. Mike Buckner, Northwestern, DB, 0/0
15. Jim Kollman, Oregon, G, 0/0
17. Curt Gentry, Maryland-Eastern Shore, DB, 38/38
20. Goldie Sellers, Grambling State, DB, 0/55

CLEVELAND BROWNS
1. **Milt Morin, Massachusetts, TE, 129/129**
2. Rick Norton, Kentucky, QB, 0/32
4. Pete Duranko, Notre Dame, DE, 0/98
5. Randy Schultz, Northern Iowa, RB, 14/31
5. Dan Fulford, Auburn, E, 0/0
6. Jim Battle, Southern (LA), T, 6/6
6. **Fred Hoaglin, Pittsburgh, C, 87/142**
7. Leroy Carter, Grambling, FL, 0/0
8. Tom Talaga, Notre Dame, E, 0/0
9. **Jack Gregory, Delta State, DE, 86/182**
10. Monte Ledbetter, Northwestern State (LA), WR, 0/21
11. Tony Fire, Bowling Green, T, 0/0
12. Rich Czap, Nebraska, T, 0/0
13. Jim Boudreaux, Louisiana Tech, T, 0/12
14. Pete Lammons, Texas, TE, 0/95
15. Bob Ellis, Massachusetts, DE, 0/0
16. David Ray, Alabama, K, 0/70
18. Charlie Harraway, San Jose State, RB, 41/110
19. Karl Singer, Purdue, T, 0/39

DALLAS COWBOYS
1. **John Niland, Iowa, G, 124/138**
2. Willie Townes, Tulsa, DE, 32/38
5. **Walt Garrison, Oklahoma State, RB, 119/119**
6. Bob Dunlevy, West Virginia, E, 0/0
7. Arthur Robinson, Florida A&M, E, 0/0
8. Don Kunit, Penn State, HB, 0/0
9. Darrell Elam, West Virginia Tech, E, 0/0
10. Mason Mitchell, Washington, HB, 0/0
11. Austin Denney, Tennessee, TE, 0/50
12. Craig Baynham, Georgia Tech, HB, 38/50
12. **Les Shy, Long Beach State, RB, 52/65**
13. Ron Lamb, South Carolina, RB, 0/56
14. Lewis Turner, Norfolk State, HB, 0/0
15. Mark Gartung, Oregon State, T, 0/0
17. George Allen, West Texas A&M, T, 0/9

DETROIT LIONS
2. Nick Eddy, Notre Dame, RB, 29/29
3. Bill Malinchak, Indiana, SE, 48/106
4. Doug Van Horn, Ohio State, G, 14/172
4. Willie Walker, Tennessee State, WR, 9/9
5. Bill Cody, Auburn, LB, 1/52
6. Wayne DeSutter, Western Illinois, T, 0/14
7. Johnnie Robinson, Tennessee State, DB, 14/14
8. John Pincavage, Virginia, HB, 0/0
9. Dick Cunningham, Arkansas, T, 0/66
10. Bruce Yates, Auburn, T, 0/0
10. Tom Brigham, Wisconsin, DE, 0/0
11. Jack O'Billovich, Oregon State, LB, 0/0
12. Randy Winkler, Tarleton State, T, 8/27
13. Bill Maselter, Wisconsin, T, 0/0
14. Denis Moore, USC, DT, 31/33
15. Bill Sullivan, West Virginia, DE, 0/0
20. Allen Smith, Findlay, HB, 0/1

GREEN BAY PACKERS
1. **Gale Gillingham, Minnesota, G, 128/128**
1. **Jim Grabowski, Illinois, RB, 63/75**
2. Tom Cichowski, Maryland, T, 0/13
3. Fred Heron, San Jose State, DT, 0/79
3. Tony Jeter, Nebraska, TE, 0/11
4. John Roderick, SMU, WR, 0/18
7. Ray Miller, Idaho, DE, 0/0
8. Ken McLean, Texas A&M, FL, 0/0
9. Ron Rector, Northwestern, RB, 0/20
10. Sam Montgomery, Southern, DE, 0/0
11. Ralph Wenzel, San Diego State, G, 0/71
12. Jim Mankins, Florida State, RB, 0/11
13. Ed King, Southern California, LB, 0/0
14. Ron Hanson, North Dakota State, FL, 0/0
15. Grady Bolton, Mississippi State, T, 0/0
17. Dave Hathcock, Memphis, DB, 14/20

LOS ANGELES RAMS
1. **Tom Mack, Michigan, G, 184/184**
2. Mike Garrett, USC, RB, 0/104
3. Dick Tyson, Tulsa, G, 0/10
4. Henry Dyer, Grambling State, RB, 16/41
5. Dick Arndt, Idaho, DT, 0/34
5. Diron Talbert, Texas, DT, 44/186
6. Bruce Anderson, Willamette, DE, 7/59
7. George Youngblood, Los Angeles State, DB, 14/44
8. Vilnis Ezerins, Wisconsin-Whitewater, RB, 14/14
9. Burton Matthies, Wayne State, HB, 0/0
10. Mike Capshaw, Abilene Christian, T, 0/0
11. Darrell Hoover, Arizona, HB, 0/0
12. George Clayton, Fairmont State, DB, 0/0
13. Jake David, Lamar, HB, 0/0
14. Terry Parks, Cal State-Los Angeles, T, 0/0
15. Mike Sullivan, Oregon State, E, 0/0

MINNESOTA VIKINGS
1. Jerry Shay, Purdue, DT, 15/63
2. **Jim Lindsey, Arkansas, RB, 84/84**
3. Don Hansen, Illinois, LB, 25/142
4. Ron Acks, Illinois, LB, 0/105
5. **Doug Davis, Kentucky, T, 79/79**
5. Bob Hall, Brown, DB, 0/0
6. Wilbur Aylor, Southwest Texas State, T, 0/0
7. Bob Meers, Massachusetts, E, 0/0
9. Ron Green, North Dakota, WR, 0/5
11. Stan Quintana, New Mexico, DB, 0/0
12. Bob Petrella, Tennessee, DB, 0/61
13. Larry Martin, San Diego State, DT, 0/1
14. Howard Twilley, Tulsa, WR, 0/120
15. Hugh Wright, Adams State, HB, 0/0
19. Jesse Stokes, Corpus Christi, DB, 0/2

NEW YORK GIANTS
1. Francis Peay, Missouri, T, 22/103
2. Don Davis, Los Angeles State, DT, 14/14
3. Tom Fisher, Tennessee, LB, 0/0
5. Bill Briggs, Iowa, DE, 0/23
7. Phil Harris, Texas, DB, 14/14
8. **Charlie Harper, Oklahoma State, T, 85/85**
8. Bill Matan, Kansas State, DE, 3/3
9. **Freeman White, Nebraska, TE, 55/55**
10. Jeff Smith, USC, LB, 14/14
11. Cliff Wilder, Iowa, E, 0/0
12. Ken Avery, Southern Mississippi, LB, 27/123
13. Jim Fulgham, Minnesota, T, 0/0
14. Howard McCard, Syracuse, G, 0/0
15. Steve Bowman, Alabama, HB, 4/4
16. Sammy Price, Illinois, RB, 0/36
19. Bobby Crockett, Arkansas, SE, 0/28
20. Randy Minniear, Purdue, RB, 19/27

PHILADELPHIA EAGLES
1. Randy Beisler, Indiana, G, 36/118
2. **Gary Pettigrew, Stanford, DT, 106/111**
3. **Ben Hawkins, Arizona State, WR, 102/104**
4. Frank Emanuel, Tennessee, LB, 0/59
5. Dan Berry, California, HB, 0/0
6. Bob Sherlag, Memphis, WR, 0/9
6. **Mel Tom, San Jose State, DE, 88/117**
7. Dave Lince, North Dakota, TE, 18/18
8. John Mason, Stanford, E, 0/0
9. Jim Todd, Ball State, HB, 0/10
10. John Osmond, Tulsa, C, 0/0
11. Welford Walton, Nevada-Reno, DE, 0/0
12. Bruce Van Dyke, Missouri, G, 4/128
13. Jim Bohl, New Mexico State, HB, 0/0
14. **Ron Medved, Washington, DB, 51/51**
15. Harry Day, Memphis State, T, 0/0
16. Arunas Vasys, Notre Dame, LB, 22/22
17. **Ike Kelley, Ohio State, LB, 67/67**
19. Taft Reed, Jackson State, DB, 6/6

PITTSBURGH STEELERS
1. Dick Leftridge, West Virginia, FB, 4/4
2. **Larry Gagner, Florida, G, 52/59**
3. Pat Killorin, Syracuse, C, 5/5
7. Emerson Boozer, Maryland-Eastern Shore, RB, 0/118
9. Dale Stewart, Pittsburgh, DE, 0/0
10. Jerry Marion, Wyoming, WR, 7/7
11. Charley Washington, Grambling, HB, 0/0
13. Benjy Dial, Eastern New Mexico, QB, 0/1
14. Joe Novogratz, Pittsburgh, LB, 0/0
15. Joe Dobson, Idaho, T, 0/0

SAN FRANCISCO 49ERS
1. **Stan Hindman, Mississippi, DE, 76/76**
2. **Bob Windsor, Kentucky, TE, 69/117**
3. **Al Randolph, Iowa, DB, 75/111**
3. Dan Bland, Mississippi State, DB, 0/0
4. Don Parker, Virginia, G, 12/12
5. **Mel Phillips, North Carolina A&T, DB, 147/147**
5. Steve Smith, Michigan, T, 0/100
6. Charlie Johnson, Louisville, DT, 29/29
8. **Dick Witcher, UCLA, WR, 109/109**
9. Kent Kramer, Minnesota, TE, 14/97
10. Ronald Sbranti, Utah State, LB, 0/14
11. Preston Ridlehuber, Georgia, RB, 0/22
12. Lyle Loebach, Simpson, T, 0/0
13. Jim Jackson, Western Illinois, DB, 13/13
14. **Elmer Collett, San Francisco State, G, 84/145**
15. Saint Saffold, San Jose State, SE, 0/14
16. Jim LeClair, C.W. Post, QB, 0/8

ST. LOUIS CARDINALS
1. Carl McAdams, Oklahoma, DT, 0/26
2. Harold Lucas, Michigan State, T, 0/0
3. Dave Long, Iowa, DE, 42/96
4. Gary Snook, Iowa, QB, 0/0
5. Jack Clancy, Michigan, SE, 0/36
6. Tim Van Galder, Iowa State, QB, 5/5
7. Charley Arkwright, Georgia, T, 0/0
8. Dan Goich, California, DT, 0/56
9. Charlie Bryant, Allen, RB, 18/34
10. Mike Ringer, Oklahoma, HB, 0/0
11. Bobby Williams, Central Oklahoma, DB, 28/69
12. Rickey Johnson, Clemson, T, 0/0
13. Jim Brown, Nebraska, G, 0/0
14. LaVerle Pratt, Idaho, LB, 0/0
15. Darryl Alleman, Wyoming, E, 0/0
16. Dick Kasperek, Iowa State, C, 20/20
17. Benny Russell, Louisville, QB, 0/1
18. Willie Jones, Kansas State, DT, 0/22

WASHINGTON REDSKINS
1. Charlie Gogolak, Princeton, K, 29/55
2. Walt Barnes, Nebraska, DT, 42/61
3. Tom Barrington, Ohio State, RB, 6/57
4. Billy Clay, Mississippi, DB, 6/6
5. Dick Lemay, Vanderbilt, T, 0/0
6. Earl Yates, Duke, T, 0/0
7. George Patton, Georgia, T, 0/0
8. Stan Mitchell, Tennessee, RB, 0/42
9. Jack Shinholser, Florida State, LB, 0/0
10. Ceasar Belser, Arkansas-Pine Bluff, DB, 0/60
11. Dick Reding, Northwestern State (LA), FL, 0/0
12. John Stipech, Utah, LB, 0/0
13. Heath Wingate, Bowling Green State, C, 3/3
14. Jerry Lovelace, Texas Tech, HB, 0/0
15. Hal Seymour, Florida, HB, 0/0
16. Hal Wantland, Tennessee, DB, 0/2
19. Andre White, Florida A&M, TE, 0/22
20. John Kelly, Florida A&M, T, 16/16

1966 AFL

BOSTON PATRIOTS
1. Karl Singer, Purdue, T, 39/39
2. Jim Boudreaux, Louisiana Tech, T, 12/12
3. Harold Lucas, Michigan State, T, 0/0
5. John Mangum, Southern Mississippi, DT, 28/28
6. Dan Irby, Louisiana Tech, T, 0/0
7. Jim Battle, Southern (LA), T, 0/6
8. Sam Montgomery, Southern, DB, 0/0
9. Doug Satcher, Southern Mississippi, LB, 42/42
10. Dennis Brewster, BYU, T, 0/0
12. Dick Fugere, Cincinnati, LB, 0/0
13. Tom Carr, Bates, FB, 0/0
14. Bob Hall, Brown, DB, 0/0
15. Billy Laird, Louisiana Tech, QB, 0/0
17. Dick Capp, Boston College, TE, 0/16
R1. Willie Townes, Tulsa, DE, 0/38
R2. Ken Avery, Southern Mississippi, LB, 0/123
R3. Ed Toner, Massachusetts, DT, 26/26
R4. Heath Wingate, Bowling Green State, C, 0/3
R5. Ray Perkins, Alabama, WR, 0/58
R6. Joe Avezzano, Florida State, C, 3/3
R11. Jerry Marion, Wyoming, WR, 0/7

BUFFALO BILLS
1. Mike Dennis, Mississippi, RB, 0/15
2. Jim Lindsey, Arkansas, RB, 0/84
3. Randy Jackson, Florida, T, 0/105
4. Bobby Burnett, Arkansas, RB, 22/25
5. Bob Sherlag, Memphis, WR, 0/9
6. Bill Johnson, University of the South, HB, 0/0
8. **Paul Guidry, McNeese State, LB, 92/106**
9. Jim Carter, Tennessee State, DE, 0/0
10. Bobby Crockett, Arkansas, SE, 28/28
11. Dale Stewart, Pittsburgh, HB, 0/0
12. Wayne DeSutter, Western Illinois, T, 14/14
13. Al McFarlane, Louisville, HB, 0/0
14. Tony Golmont, North Carolina State, DB, 0/0
15. Allen Smith, Fort Valley State, RB, 19/19
19. Mel Phillips, North Carolina A&T, DB, 0/147
R1. Jack Gregory, Delta State, DE, 0/182
R2. Johnnie Robinson, Tennessee State, DB, 0/14
R3. Tony King, Findlay, DB, 7/7
R4. **Dick Cunningham, Arkansas, T, 56/66**
R11. Benny Russell, Louisville, QB, 1/1

DENVER BRONCOS
1. Jerry Shay, Purdue, DT, 0/63
2. Freeman White, Nebraska, TE, 0/55
3. Bob Hadrick, Purdue, E, 0/0
4. Randy Johnson, Texas A&M-Kingsville, QB, 0/75
5. Billy Clay, Mississippi, DB, 0/6
6. James Fulgham, Minnesota, T, 0/0
7. Scotty Glacken, Duke, QB, 10/10
7. Jerry Jones, Bowling Green State, T, 0/44
8. Goldie Sellers, Grambling State, DB, 27/55
9. Ronald Sbranti, Utah State, LB, 14/14
10. Larry Cox, Abilene Christian, DT, 33/33
11. James Burns, Northwestern, G, 0/0
13. Eric Crabtree, Pittsburgh, WR, 42/83
14. **Fred Forsberg, Washington, LB, 53/69**
15. Mike Ringer, Oklahoma, DB, 0/0
R1. Nick Eddy, Notre Dame, RB, 0/29
R2. **Pete Duranko, Notre Dame, DE, 98/98**
R3. Dick Arndt, Idaho, DT, 0/34
R8. Henry Sorrell, Tennessee-Chattanooga, LB, 10/10
R10. Andre White, Florida A&M, TE, 14/22

HOUSTON OILERS
1. Tommy Nobis, Texas, LB, 0/133
2. Stan Hindman, Mississippi, DE, 0/76
3. George Rice, LSU, DT, 37/37
4. George Allen, West Texas A&M, T, 9/9
5. **Hoyle Granger, Mississippi State, RB, 69/83**
6. Dave Long, Iowa, DE, 0/96
7. Pep Menefee, New Mexico State, WR, 0/7
8. Dan Bland, Mississippi State, HB, 0/0
9. Dick Suffel, Southwest Texas State, DB, 0/0
10. Wilbur Aylor, Southwest Texas State, DT, 0/0
11. Monte Ledbetter, Northwestern State (LA), WR, 5/21
12. Harry Day, Memphis State, DE, 0/0
13. Fred Zimmerman, Toledo, LB, 0/0
14. Dave Lince, North Dakota, TE, 0/18
15. Tom Dillard, Austin Peay, T, 0/0
16. Steve Smith, Michigan, T, 0/100
R2. Tim Van Galder, Iowa State, QB, 0/5
R10. Dan Goich, California, DT, 0/56

KANSAS CITY CHIEFS
1. **Aaron Brown, Minnesota, DE, 78/88**
2. Francis Peay, Missouri, T, 19/103
3. Walt Barnes, Nebraska, DT, 0/61
4. Elijah Gibson, Bethune-Cookman, HB, 0/0
5. Doug Van Horn, Ohio State, G, 0/172
6. John Osmond, Tulsa, C, 0/0
7. Charlie Gogolak, Princeton, K, 0/55
8. Fletcher Smith, Tennessee State, DB, 24/80
9. Dick Smith, Northwestern, DB, 0/20
10. Fred Dawston, South Carolina State, DB, 0/0
11. Willie Ray Smith, Kansas, DB, 0/0
12. Bill Bonds, McMurry, DB, 0/0
13. Wayne Walker, Northwestern State (LA), P, 4/12
14. Charlie Harraway, San Jose State, RB, 0/110
15. Bruce Van Dyke, Missouri, G, 0/128
16. Tom Barrington, Ohio State, RB, 0/57
17. Walt Garrison, Oklahoma State, RB, 0/119
20. **Mike Garrett, USC, RB, 58/104**
R1. George Youngblood, Los Angeles State, DB, 0/44
R2. Bob Pickens, Nebraska, T, 0/20
R3. **Jan Stenerud, Montana State, K, 186/263**
R10. Elmer Collett, San Francisco State, G, 0/145
R11. Denis Moore, USC, DT, 0/33

MIAMI DOLPHINS

1. Jim Grabowski, Illinois, RB, 0/75
1. Rick Norton, Kentucky, QB, 31/32
2. **Frank Emanuel, Tennessee, LB, 56/59**
3. Larry Gagner, Florida, G, 0/59
4. Dick Leftridge, West Virginia, FB, 0/4
5. Grady Bolton, Mississippi State, T, 0/0
6. Ed Weisacosky, Miami (FL), LB, 25/67
7. Don Hansen, Illinois, LB, 0/142
8. **Bob Petrella, Tennessee, DB, 61/61**
9. Bill Matan, Kansas State, DE, 0/3
10. Pat Killorin, Syracuse, C, 0/5
11. Sammy Price, Illinois, RB, 36/36
12. **Howard Twilley, Tulsa, WR, 120/120**
13. Kent Kramer, Minnesota, TE, 0/97
14. Phil Scoggin, Texas A&M, K, 0/0
15. Jerry Oliver, Southwest Texas State, T, 0/0
19. Doug Moreau, LSU, TE, 33/33

R1. John Roderick, SMU, WR, 7/18
R3. Jack Clancy, Michigan, SE, 22/36
R4. Jim Mankins, Florida State, RB, 0/11
R5. Fritz Greenlee, Northern Arizona, LB, 0/4
R6. Bill Darnall, North Carolina, WR, 13/13
R8. Jon Brittenum, Arkansas, QB, 0/14
R9. Craig Baynham, Georgia Tech, HB, 0/50
R10. Randy Winkler, Tarleton State, T, 0/27

NEW YORK JETS

1. William Yearby, Michigan, DE, 9/9
2. Sam Ball, Kentucky, T, 0/61
3. Carl McAdams, Oklahoma, DT, 26/26
4. Jim Waskiewicz, Wichita State, C, 27/39
4. Phil Sheridan, Notre Dame, E, 0/0
5. Ben Hawkins, Arizona State, WR, 0/104
6. **Emerson Boozer, Maryland-Eastern Shore, RB, 118/118**
6. Dick Lemay, Vanderbilt, G, 0/0
7. Joe Dobson, Idaho, T, 0/0
8. **Pete Lammons, Texas, TE, 83/95**
9. James Jones, Nebraska-Omaha, E, 0/0
10. Bill Wolski, Notre Dame, FB, 0/2
11. Gerry Allen, Nebraska-Omaha, RB, 0/28
11. Bob Walton, Auburn, T, 0/0
12. Steve Chomyszak, Syracuse, DT, 2/79
12. Ken Hollister, Indiana, DE, 0/0
13. Stas Maliszewski, Princeton, LB, 0/0
14. Stan Quintana, New Mexico, DB, 0/0
15. Bill Cody, Auburn, LB, 0/52
16. Ron Acks, Illinois, LB, 0/105
17. Tommy Tolleson, Alabama, WR, 0/8
19. Preston Ridlehuber, Georgia, RB, 0/22
20. Randy Schultz, Northern Iowa, RB, 0/31

R1. Don Parker, Virginia, G, 0/12
R2. Austin Denney, Tennessee, TE, 0/50
R6. Allen Smith, Findlay, HB, 1/1

OAKLAND RAIDERS

1. Rodger Bird, Kentucky, DB, 38/38
2. Butch Allison, Missouri, T, 0/0
3. Tom Mitchell, Bucknell, TE, 14/145
4. Dick Tyson, Tulsa, G, 3/10
5. **Pete Banaszak, Miami (FL), RB, 173/173**
7. Frank McRae, Tennessee State, DT, 0/6
9. Clifton Kinney, San Diego State, LB, 0/0
10. Tony Jeter, Nebraska, TE, 0/11
11. Joe Labruzzo, Louisiana State, HB, 0/0
12. Wayne Foster, Washington State, T, 0/0
13. John Niland, Iowa, G, 0/138
14. Mike Johnson, Kansas, DB, 0/54
15. Steve Renko, Kansas, FB, 0/0
20. Steve Bowman, Alabama, HB, 0/4

R1. **Rod Sherman, USC, WR, 53/83**
R2. Tom Cichowski, Maryland, T, 0/13
R6. Dan Archer, Oregon, G, 14/22
R8. Ray Schmautz, San Diego, LB, 10/10
R9. Mel Tom, San Jose State, DE, 0/117

SAN DIEGO CHARGERS

1. Don Davis, Los Angeles State, DT, 0/14
2. Nick Rassas, Notre Dame, DB, 0/27
3. Milt Morin, Massachusetts, TE, 0/129
4. Charlie Brown, Syracuse, DB, 0/30
5. **Russ Smith, Miami (FL), RB, 52/52**
6. Gary Pettigrew, Stanford, DT, 0/111
7. **Jim Tolbert, Lincoln (MO), DB, 61/105**
8. Doug Buffone, Louisville, LB, 0/186
9. Taft Reed, Jackson State, DB, 0/6
10. Dan Pride, Jackson State, LB, 0/6
11. **Terry Owens, Jacksonville State, T, 132/132**
12. Ray Jones, Cal State-Los Angeles, HB, 0/0
13. Houston Ridge, San Diego State, DE, 44/44
14. Mike London, Wisconsin, LB, 3/3
15. Shelly Novack, Long Beach State, E, 0/0
16. Bill Scott, Idaho, DB, 0/14
18. John Travis, San Jose State, FB, 6/6

R1. Bob Windsor, Kentucky, TE, 0/117
R2. Diron Talbert, Texas, DT, 0/186
R3. **Jeff Staggs, San Diego State, LB, 61/82**
R6. **Joe Beauchamp, Iowa State, DB, 117/117**
R7. Saint Saffold, San Jose State, SE, 0/14
R8. Brad Hubbert, Arizona, RB, 38/38

1967 NFL

ATLANTA FALCONS

2. Leo Carroll, San Diego State, DE, 0/27
3. Jimmy Jordan, Florida, RB, 0/1
5. Bill Delaney, American International, TE, 0/0
5. Randy Matson, Texas A&M, DT, 0/0
6. Eugene Snipes, Elizabeth City, HB, 0/0
6. Martine Bircher, Arkansas, DB, 0/0
7. Corey Colehour, North Dakota, QB, 0/0
9. Bobby Moten, Bishop, WR, 0/3
10. Dick Schafroth, Iowa State, T, 0/0
11. John Walker, Jackson State, LB, 0/0
12. Bill Gentry, North Carolina State, LB, 0/0
13. Sandor Szabo, Ithaca, K, 0/0
14. Tom Bryan, Auburn, FB, 0/0
15. Al Nicholas, Cal State-Sacramento, FB, 0/0

BALTIMORE COLTS

1. **Bubba Smith, Michigan State, DE, 69/111**
1. Jim Detwiler, Michigan, HB, 0/0
2. **Rick Volk, Michigan, DB, 123/150**
3. Norman Davis, Grambling State, G, 14/40
3. Leon Ward, Oklahoma State, LB, 0/0
4. **Charlie Stukes, Maryland-Eastern Shore, DB, 79/107**
5. Ron Porter, Idaho, LB, 30/93
6. Terry Southall, Baylor, QB, 0/0
7. Bo Rein, Ohio State, FL, 0/0
8. **Cornelius Johnson, Virginia Union, G, 74/74**
8. Lee Anderson, Bishop, T, 0/0
9. Ron Kirkland, Nebraska, HB, 0/0
10. Leigh Gilbert, Northern Illinois, TE, 0/0
12. Preston Pearson, Illinois, RB, 35/176
12. Herman Reed, St. Augustine, T, 0/0
12. J.B. Christian, Oklahoma State, G, 0/0
13. Marc Allen, West Texas State, DE, 0/0
14. Pat Conley, Purdue, LB, 0/0
15. Bob Wade, Morgan State, DB, 0/30
16. Don Alley, Adams State, WR, 10/18

BOSTON PATRIOTS

1. John Charles, Purdue, DB, 39/79
4. **Ed Philpott, Miami (OH), LB, 68/68**
5. Mel Witt, Texas-Arlington, DE, 35/35
6. Ron Medlen, Southern Methodist, DE, 0/0
7. Bobby Leo, Harvard, RB, 3/3
8. Thomas Fussell, LSU, DE, 12/12
9. Charlie Thornhill, Michigan State, DB, 0/0
10. John Runnels, Penn State, LB, 0/0
11. Leroy Mitchell, Texas Southern, DB, 28/82
12. Dave Davis, Harvard, T, 0/0
13. Ray Ilg, Colgate, LB, 28/28
14. Bobby Beaird, Auburn, DB, 0/0
15. Tom Folliard, Mississippi State, LB, 0/0
17. Bobby Nichols, Boston University, TE, 15/15

BUFFALO BILLS

1. **John Pitts, Arizona State, DB, 87/115**
2. Jim LeMoine, Utah State, TE, 8/35
3. Tom Rhoads, Notre Dame, DE, 0/0
4. Gary Bugenhagen, Syracuse, G, 14/24
6. Bill Wilkerson, Texas-El Paso, DE, 0/0
7. George Gaiser, SMU, T, 0/10
8. Tommy Luke, Mississippi, DB, 0/7
9. Gerald Seither, Kent State, E, 0/0
10. Tom Croft, Louisiana Tech, DB, 0/0
11. Paul Tomich, Drake, T, 0/0
12. Ernie Ames, Kent State, DT, 0/0
12. Bob Bonner, Southern, DT, 0/0
13. Howard Finley, Tennessee State, DB, 0/0
13. George Carter, St. Bonaventure, HB, 0/0
13. Randy Wheeler, Georgia, HB, 0/0
14. Vern Moore, Central State (OK), HB, 0/0
15. Grant Martinsen, Utah State, DB, 0/0

CHICAGO BEARS

1. Loyd Phillips, Arkansas, DE, 32/32
2. Bob Jones, San Diego State, WR, 15/15
3. **Garry Lyle, George Washington, DB, 84/84**
4. Al Dodd, Northwestern State (LA), WR, 6/71
4. Tom Greenlee, Washington, DB, 0/0
5. Bruce Alford, TCU, K, 0/27
6. Virgil Carter, Brigham Young, QB, 18/52
6. Doug Kriewald, West Texas A&M, G, 15/15
7. John Truitt, Indiana State, E, 0/0
8. Roger Murphy, Northwestern, E, 0/0
8. Jerry Griffin, Southern Methodist, LB, 0/0
9. Greg Cass, Washington, C, 0/0
11. Earl Mayo, Morgan State, HB, 0/0
12. Bruce Green, Midland Lutheran, E, 0/0
13. Kaye Carstens, Nebraska, DB, 0/0
14. Lynn Nesbitt, Wake Forest, G, 0/0
15. Terry Oakes, Cal State-San Francisco, DE, 0/0

CLEVELAND BROWNS

1. **Bob Matheson, Duke, LB, 55/180**
2. Larry Conjar, Notre Dame, RB, 12/35
3. Eppie Barney, Iowa State, FL, 26/26
3. **Don Cockroft, Adams State, K, 188/188**
4. **Joe Taffoni, Tennessee-Martin, T, 55/78**
4. Carl Ward, Michigan, DB, 28/30
6. **John Demarie, LSU, G, 123/132**
7. Bill House, Youngstown State, T, 0/0
8. Bill Devrow, Southern Mississippi, DB, 0/0
9. Cecil Dowdy, Alabama, LB, 0/0
10. **Jim Copeland, Virginia, C, 81/81**
11. Bill Sabatino, Colorado, DT, 7/13
12. Charlie Fowler, Houston, G, 0/20
13. **Billy Andrews, Southeastern Louisiana, LB, 100/142**
14. Floyd Rogers, Clemson, T, 0/0
15. Dennis Williamson, Wisconsin-Whitewater, DB, 0/0
17. **Ben Davis, Defiance, DB, 75/109**

DALLAS COWBOYS

3. Phil Clark, Northwestern, DB, 37/52
4. Curtis Marker, Northern Michigan, G, 0/0
6. Sims Stokes, Northern Arizona, WR, 3/3
7. **Rayfield Wright, Fort Valley State, T, 166/166**
8. Steve Laub, Illinois Wesleyan, QB, 0/0
9. Byron Morgan, Findlay, DB, 0/0
10. Eugene Bowens, Tennessee State, HB, 0/0
11. Pat Riley, Kentucky, FL, 0/0
12. Harold Deters, North Carolina State, K, 3/3
13. Al Kerkian, Akron, DE, 0/0
14. Tommy Boyd, Tarleton State, G, 0/0
15. Leavie David, Edward Waters, DB, 0/0

DENVER BRONCOS

1. **Floyd Little, Syracuse, RB, 117/117**
2. Tom Beer, Houston, TE, 37/79
3. **Mike Current, Ohio State, T, 108/169**
3. **George Goeddeke, Notre Dame, G, 66/66**
4. **Carl Cunningham, Houston, LB, 55/68**
5. John Huard, Maine, LB, 42/43
5. **Fran Lynch, Hofstra, RB, 99/99**
6. Neal Sweeney, Tulsa, WR, 10/10
7. Frank Richter, Georgia, LB, 34/34
8. Tom Cassese, C.W. Post, DB, 14/14
9. Jim Summers, Michigan State, DB, 11/11
10. Paul Krause, Dubuque, QB, 0/0
11. Lou Andrus, Brigham Young, LB, 8/8
13. Dennis Furjanic, Houston, DE, 0/0
14. Tom Francisco, Virginia Tech, HB, 0/0
15. Don Smith, Florida A&M, G, 2/2
16. Jack Lentz, Holy Cross, DB, 26/26

DETROIT LIONS

1. **Mel Farr, UCLA, RB, 69/69**
2. **Lem Barney, Jackson State, DB, 140/140**
3. **Paul Naumoff, Tennessee, LB, 168/168**
4. Lew Kamanu, Weber State, DE, 12/12
6. John McCambridge, Northwestern, DE, 6/6
6. Tim Jones, Weber State, QB, 0/0
7. Ted Tuinstra, Iowa State, T, 0/0
9. **Mike Weger, Bowling Green State, DB, 108/123**
10. Jerry Hayhoe, Southern California, G, 0/0
11. Ray Shirley, Arizona State, T, 0/0
12. Eric Watts, San Jose State, DB, 0/0
13. Lamar Wright, Georgia Tech, G, 0/0
14. Cleveland Robinson, South Carolina State, DE, 0/0
15. Sam Burke, Georgia Tech, DB, 0/0
16. Jerry Zawadzkas, Columbia, TE, 2/2

GREEN BAY PACKERS

1. Don Horn, San Diego State, QB, 20/57
1. **Bob Hyland, Boston College, C, 56/136**
2. Dave Dunaway, Duke, WR, 2/13
2. Jim Flanigan, Pittsburgh, LB, 40/54
3. John Rowser, Michigan, DB, 42/127
4. Travis Williams, Arizona State, RB, 48/62
5. Jay Bachman, Cincinnati, C, 0/45
5. Dwight Hood, Baylor, DT, 0/0
5. Richard Tate, Utah, DB, 0/0
6. Stew Williams, Bowling Green, FB, 0/0
7. Bob Ziolkowski, Iowa, T, 0/0
7. Bill Powell, Missouri, LB, 0/0
8. Clarence Miles, Trinity (TX), DT, 0/0
9. Harlan Reed, Mississippi State, TE, 0/0
10. Bill Shear, Cortland State, K, 0/0
11. Dave Bennett, Springfield, QB, 0/0
12. Mike Bass, Michigan, DB, 0/100
13. Keith Brown, Central Missouri State, FL, 0/0
14. Claudis James, Jackson State, WR, 15/15
15. Jim Schneider, Colgate, DT, 0/0

HOUSTON OILERS

1. **Tom Regner, Notre Dame, G, 67/67**
1. **George Webster, Michigan State, LB, 64/119**
2. Bob Davis, Virginia, QB, 10/40
2. **Roy Hopkins, Texas Southern, RB, 53/53**
3. Larry Carwell, Iowa State, DB, 23/74
4. Carel Stith, Nebraska, DT, 31/31
5. Pete Johns, Tulane, DB, 22/22
5. **Zeke Moore, Lincoln (MO), DB, 145/145**
5. **Willie Parker, Arkansas-Pine Bluff, DT, 54/54**
6. Pete Barnes, Southern (LA), LB, 21/142
7. Ed Carrington, Virginia, TE, 15/15
8. John Brunson, Benedictine, HB, 0/0
8. Sharon Washington, Northeast Missouri State, FL, 0/0
9. **Ken Houston, Prairie View A&M, DB, 84/196**
10. **Woody Campbell, Northwestern, RB, 50/50**
10. Tim Sheehan, Stanford, C, 0/0
11. Harold Decker, Kalamazoo, DE, 0/0
14. Henry Hailstock, Lincoln (MO), G, 0/0
15. Marvin McQueen, Mississippi, LB, 0/0
16. Rex Keeling, Samford, P, 0/1

KANSAS CITY CHIEFS

1. Gene Trosch, Miami (FL), DE, 27/27
2. **Willie Lanier, Morgan State, LB, 149/149**
2. **Jim Lynch, Notre Dame, LB, 151/151**
3. Billy Masters, LSU, TE, 24/132
4. Ron Zwernemann, East Texas State, G, 0/0
6. Noland Smith, Tennessee State, WR, 32/39
7. Dick Erickson, Wisconsin-Stout, C, 0/0
8. Tom Altemeier, Luther, T, 0/0
9. Ed Pope, Jackson State, DT, 0/0
11. Bill Braswell, Auburn, G, 0/0
12. Dick Kolonski, Lake Forest, C, 0/0
12. Kent Lashley, Northeastern Oklahoma, FL, 0/0
13. Linwood Simmons, Edward Waters, FB, 0/0
14. John Bishop, Delta State, DT, 0/0
15. Dennis Caponi, Xavier, FB, 0/0

LOS ANGELES RAMS

2. **Willie Ellison, Texas Southern, RB, 83/98**
5. Nate Shaw, USC, DB, 15/15
9. Tommie Smith, San Jose State, WR, 0/2
10. Leon Moore, Tennessee State, DB, 0/0
11. Frank Horak, Texas Christian, DB, 0/0
12. Pat Badjek, Franklin, LB, 0/0
13. John Erisman, Miami (OH), E, 0/0
14. Walt Richardson, Fresno State, DT, 0/0
15. Steve Bunker, Oregon, TE, 0/0

MIAMI DOLPHINS

1. **Bob Griese, Purdue, QB, 161/161**
2. **Jim Riley, Oklahoma, DE, 68/68**
4. Bob Greenlee, Yale, T, 0/0
5. Gary Tucker, Tennessee Chattanooga, RB, 14/14
6. Bud Norris, Washington State, TE, 0/0
7. **Larry Seiple, Kentucky, TE, 150/150**
9. **John Richardson, UCLA, DT, 63/88**
10. Tom Beier, Miami (FL), DB, 28/28
11. Jack Pyburn, Texas A&M, T, 23/23
12. Stan Juk, South Carolina, LB, 0/0
12. Jim Whitaker, Missouri, DB, 0/0
14. Charles Stikes, Kent State, DB, 0/0
15. Jake Ferro, Youngstown State, LB, 0/0

MINNESOTA VIKINGS

1. **Clint Jones, Michigan State, RB, 75/87**
1. **Alan Page, Notre Dame, DT, 160/218**
1. **Gene Washington, Michigan State, WR, 81/95**
2. **Bob Grim, Oregon State, WR, 79/134**
3. Earl Denny, Missouri, RB, 27/27
4. Al Coleman, Tennessee State, DB, 2/57
5. Ken Last, Minnesota, E, 0/0
7. **Bobby Bryant, South Carolina, DB, 161/161**
8. **John Beasley, California, TE, 75/97**
9. Bill Morris, Holy Cross, G, 0/0
10. Pete Tatman, Nebraska, RB, 5/5
11. Bob Trygstad, Washington State, DT, 0/0

12. Fred Cremer, St. John's (MN), G, 0/0
13. Charley Hardt, Tulsa, DB, 0/0
14. Jim Hargrove, Howard Payne, LB, 32/56
15. Jimmy Shea, Eastern New Mexico, DB, 0/0

NEW ORLEANS SAINTS

1. Les Kelley, Alabama, LB, 30/30
2. Bo Burris, Houston, DB, 40/40
2. John Gilliam, South Carolina State, WR, 37/151
2. **Dave Rowe, Penn State, DT, 56/165**
3. Ben Hart, Oklahoma, E, 1/1
3. **Del Williams, Florida State, G, 92/92**
4. Ron Widby, Tennessee, P, 0/81
4. Bill Carr, Florida, C, 0/0
4. Tom Stangle, Dayton, T, 0/0
5. John Douglas, Texas Southern, DB, 28/36
5. Don McCall, USC, RB, 29/42
6. George Harvey, Kansas, T, 6/6
6. Bo Wood, North Carolina, DE, 0/14
7. Gary Hertzog, Willamette, G, 0/0
7. Bob McKelvey, Northwestern, HB, 0/0
8. Sam Harris, Colorado, TE, 0/0
8. Barry Siler, Albion, LB, 0/0
9. Tim Lavens, Idaho, TE, 0/0
9. Eugene Ross, Oklahoma, DB, 0/0
10. Charlie Brown, Missouri, RB, 6/6
10. Roosevelt Robertson, North Carolina Central, FL, 0/0
11. Jim Benson, Florida, C, 0/0
11. Bernard Corbin, Alabama A&M, DB, 0/0
12. Ronnie Pack, Texas Tech, G, 0/0
12. John Robinson, Tennessee State, FL, 0/0
13. Bill Stetz, Boston College, G, 0/2
13. Gary Grossnickle, Missouri, DB, 0/0
14. Jimmy Hester, North Dakota, TE, 29/34
14. George Stetter, Virginia, DB, 0/0
15. John Snow, Wake Forest, T, 0/0
15. Darrell Johnson, Lamar, HB, 0/0
16. Bruce Cortez, Parsons, DB, 1/1
17. **Danny Abramowicz, Xavier (OH), E, 85/111**

NEW YORK GIANTS

4. Louis Thompson, Alabama, DT, 0/0
5. Dave Lewis, Stanford, QB, 0/56
8. **Scott Eaton, Oregon State, DB, 60/60**
9. Fred Freeman, Mississippi Valley State, T, 0/0
10. Dick Stebbins, Grambling, E, 0/0
11. Pete Pifer, Oregon State, FB, 0/0
12. Bob Shortal, Dayton, LB, 0/0
13. Tom Stidham, Oklahoma, K, 0/0
14. Bill Bates, Missouri, K, 0/0
15. Tom Reale, Southern Connecticut State, T, 0/0

NEW YORK JETS

1. Paul Seiler, Notre Dame, C, 13/39
2. Rich Sheron, Washington State, TE, 0/0
3. Henry King, Utah State, DB, 13/13
3. Dennis Randall, Oklahoma State, DE, 7/20
4. Julian Gray, Grambling, DB, 0/0
5. Louis Jackson, Grambling, DB, 0/0
6. Jeff Richardson, Michigan State, T, 25/28
7. **John Elliott, Texas, DT, 85/85**
8. Gene Bledsoe, Texas, G, 0/0
9. Ray Scott, Prairie View A&M, DE, 0/0
10. Raymond Brown, Alcorn State, DB, 0/0
11. Herb Slattery, Delaware, G, 0/0
12. **Randy Rasmussen, Nebraska-Kearney, G, 207/207**
13. Jack Emmer, Rutgers, FL, 0/0
14. Michael Stromberg, Temple, LB, 2/2
15. Jack Schweberger, Vermont, FL, 0/0

OAKLAND RAIDERS

1. **Gene Upshaw, Texas A&M-Kingsville, G, 217/217**
3. Bill Fairband, Colorado, LB, 9/9
4. James Roy Jackson, Oklahoma, E, 0/0
5. Mike Hibler, Stanford, LB, 0/11
5. Gerald Warfield, Mississippi, HB, 0/0
6. Rick Egloff, Wyoming, QB, 0/0
7. Ron Lewellen, Tennessee-Martin, DT, 0/0
8. Estes Banks, Colorado, RB, 9/23
9. Mark Devilling, Muskingum, LB, 0/0
10. Richard Sligh, North Carolina Central, DT, 8/8
11. **Duane Benson, Hamline, LB, 62/121**
12. Bob Kruse, Wayne State (NE), G, 25/28
13. Len Kleinpeter, Southwestern Louisiana, E, 0/0
14. Casey Boyett, BYU, E, 0/0
15. Ben Woodson, Utah, HB, 0/0

PHILADELPHIA EAGLES

1. Harry Jones, Arkansas, RB, 29/29
2. John Brooks, Kent State, G, 0/0
3. Harry Wilson, Nebraska, RB, 6/6
4. Chuck Hughes, Texas-El Paso, WR, 22/38
5. Dick Absher, Maryland, LB, 8/58
5. Bob Van Pelt, Indiana, C, 0/0
6. Bob Hughes, Jackson State, DE, 0/16
7. John Williams, San Diego State, DB, 0/0
7. Bob Crenshaw, New Mexico State, G, 0/0
8. Don Klacking, Wyoming, FB, 0/0
9. Harold Stancell, Tennessee, DB, 0/0
10. Maurice Bates, Northern State (SD), DE, 0/0
11. Omar Parker, Washington, G, 0/0
12. Ben Monroe, New Mexico, QB, 0/0
13. Bill Downs, Louisville, DT, 0/0
14. Dick Kenney, Michigan State, K, 0/0
15. David Poche, McNeese State, T, 0/0

PITTSBURGH STEELERS

2. Don Shy, San Diego State, RB, 27/84
3. Rocky Freitas, Oregon State, T, 0/134
4. Ray May, USC, LB, 40/118
6. Mike Haggerty, Miami (FL), T, 43/60
8. John Foruria, Idaho, DB, 9/9
8. Mike Barnes, Purdue, T, 0/0
9. Paul Otis, Houston, DT, 0/0
10. Bill Wilsey, Fresno State, LB, 0/0
11. Jim Whitcomb, Emporia State, FL, 0/0
13. Jim Homan, Southern California, G, 0/0
14. Chet Anderson, Minnesota, TE, 14/14
15. Mike Love, Abilene Christian, FB, 0/0

SAN DIEGO CHARGERS

1. Ron Billingsley, Wyoming, DT, 44/61
2. **Bob Howard, San Diego State, DB, 102/169**
2. Ron McCall, Weber State, LB, 5/5
3. Harold Akin, Oklahoma State, T, 13/13
4. Dickie Post, Houston, RB, 49/62
5. Bernie Erickson, Abilene Christian, LB, 21/26
6. Nate Johns, San Diego State, FL, 0/0
7. Dave Conway, Texas, K, 0/1
8. John Mills, Tennessee, E, 0/0
9. Steve Newell, Long Beach State, WR, 7/7
10. Torre Ossmo, Western Michigan, T, 0/0
11. Carroll Jarvis, Virginia, HB, 0/0
13. Leon Carr, Prairie View A&M, DB, 0/0
14. Marty Baccaglio, San Jose State, DE, 9/40
15. Craig Scoggins, San Diego State, E, 0/0

SAN FRANCISCO 49ERS

1. **Cas Banaszek, Northwestern, T, 120/120**
1. **Steve Spurrier, Florida, QB, 92/106**
2. Tom Holzer, Louisville, DE, 14/14
3. **Frank Nunley, Michigan, LB, 137/137**
3. **Bill Tucker, Tennessee State, RB, 55/69**
4. Wayne Trimble, Alabama, DB, 1/1
6. **Doug Cunningham, Mississippi, RB, 82/84**
7. Milt Jackson, Tulsa, DB, 0/0
8. Walter Johnson, Tuskegee, DE, 1/1
9. Bob Briggs, Heidelberg, DE, 0/84
10. Chip Myers, Northwestern Oklahoma State, WR, 12/108
11. Ken Carmann, Kearney State, DT, 0/0
12. James Hall, Tuskegee, LB, 0/0
13. Rich Gibbs, Iowa, DB, 0/0
14. Dalton Leblanc, Northeast Louisiana, FL, 0/0
15. Clarence Spencer, Louisville, FL, 0/0

ST. LOUIS CARDINALS

1. **Dave Williams, Washington, WR, 67/86**
2. **Bob Rowe, Western Michigan, DT, 122/122**
3. Vidal Carlin, North Texas State, QB, 0/0
4. Mike Barnes, Texas-Arlington, DB, 17/17
4. Andy Bowling, Virginia Tech, LB, 0/6
5. **Jamie Rivers, Bowling Green State, LB, 57/76**
6. Mike Campbell, Lenoir-Rhyne, RB, 0/3
7. Joe Randall, Brown, K, 0/0
8. Mike Gold, Utah State, T, 0/0
9. Ted Wheeler, West Texas A&M, G, 9/15
10. Lavern Barrs, Furman, DB, 0/0
11. Ed Marcontell, Lamar, G, 2/4
12. Steve Dundas, Pomona, FL, 0/0
13. Bob Duncum, West Texas A&M, T, 4/4
14. Bo Hickey, Maryland, RB, 0/12
15. Bill Wosilius, Syracuse, LB, 0/0
16. Philip Spiller, Los Angeles State, DB, 14/25

WASHINGTON REDSKINS

1. Ray McDonald, Idaho, RB, 13/13
2. Spain Musgrove, Utah State, DE, 30/37
3. Curg Belcher, BYU, DB, 0/0
6. Don Bandy, Tulsa, G, 26/26
7. John Love, North Texas, WR, 13/18
7. Bruce Matte, Miami (OH), QB, 0/0
8. Larry Hendershot, Arizona State, LB, 4/4
9. Pete Larson, Cornell, RB, 22/22
10. Tim Houlton, St. Norbert, DT, 0/0
10. Bruce Sullivan, Illinois, DB, 0/0
11. Bill Brown, Texas-El Paso, C, 0/0
12. Ron Sepic, Ohio State, E, 0/0
13. Bob Rodwell, Eastern Michigan, LB, 0/0
14. Andy Socha, Marshall, HB, 0/0
15. Ed Breding, Texas A&M, LB, 28/28

1968 NFL

ATLANTA FALCONS

1. **Claude Humphrey, Tennessee State, DE, 127/171**
2. Carlton Dabney, Morgan State, DT, 14/14
2. John Wright, Illinois, WR, 5/19
6. Rick Eber, Tulsa, WR, 1/12
6. Jim Hagle, Southern Methodist, RB, 0/0
6. Joe Wynns, South Carolina State, DB, 0/0
8. Ray Jeffords, Georgia, TE, 0/0
9. Henry Holland, North Texas State, C, 0/0
10. Mike Tomasini, Colorado State, DT, 0/0
11. **Greg Brezina, Houston, LB, 151/151**
12. A.J. Vaughn, Wayne State, RB, 0/0
13. Billy Harris, Colorado, RB, 6/20
14. Joe Polk, Livingstone, RB, 0/0
15. Don Bean, Houston, FL, 0/0

BALTIMORE COLTS

1. **John Williams, Minnesota, T, 55/166**
2. Bob Grant, Wake Forest, LB, 35/41
3. Rich O'Hara, Northern Arizona, FL, 0/0
4. Jim Duncan, Maryland-Eastern Shore, DB, 38/38
5. Paul Elzey, Toledo, LB, 0/5
7. Anthony Andrews, Hampton, RB, 0/0
8. Tommy Davis, Tennessee State, G, 0/0
9. Terry Cole, Indiana, RB, 23/37
10. Ocie Austin, Utah State, DB, 28/49
10. Ed Tomlin, Hampton, RB, 0/0
11. Bill Pickens, Houston, G, 0/0
12. James Jackson, Jackson State, T, 0/0
13. Howard Tennebar, Kent State, T, 0/0
14. Charles Mitchell, Alabama State, TE, 0/0
15. Jeff Beaver, North Carolina, QB, 0/0

BOSTON PATRIOTS

1. Dennis Byrd, North Carolina State, DE, 14/14
2. Tom Funchess, Jackson State, T, 39/87
3. Aaron Marsh, Eastern Kentucky, WR, 28/28
4. R.C. Gamble, South Carolina State, RB, 27/27
5. Jim Smithberger, Notre Dame, DB, 0/0
7. John Schneider, Toledo, QB, 0/0
8. Daryl Johnson, Morgan State, DB, 42/42
10. John Outlaw, Jackson State, DB, 34/110
11. Paul Feldhausen, Northland (WI), T, 2/2
12. **Jim Cheyunski, Syracuse, LB, 66/121**
13. Max Huber, BYU, T, 0/0
14. Henry McKay, Guilford, E, 0/0
15. Art McMahon, North Carolina State, DB, 43/43
17. Ed Koontz, Catawba, LB, 6/6

BUFFALO BILLS

1. **Haven Moses, San Diego State, WR, 59/199**
2. Bob Tatarek, Miami (FL), DT, 47/49
3. Richard Trapp, Florida, FL, 14/22
4. **Edgar Chandler, Georgia, LB, 56/68**
5. Max Anderson, Arizona State, RB, 25/25
5. Ben Gregory, Nebraska, RB, 6/6
5. **Mike McBath, Penn State, DE, 50/50**
7. Pete Richardson, Dayton, DB, 39/39
8. Bob Kalsu, Oklahoma, G, 14/14
9. Gary McDermott, Tulsa, RB, 14/18
10. Jerry Lawson, Utah, DB, 1/1
11. Dick Plagge, Auburn, RB, 0/0
12. Greg Pipes, Baylor, LB, 0/0
13. Dan Darragh, William & Mary, QB, 17/17
14. Chuck DeVleigher, Memphis, DT, 4/4
15. John Gilmore, Peru State, DT, 0/0
16. John Frantz, California, C, 2/2

CHICAGO BEARS

1. Mike Hull, USC, RB, 37/89
2. **Bob Wallace, Texas-El Paso, WR, 59/59**
3. Major Hazelton, Florida A&M, DB, 23/26
4. Wayne Mass, Clemson, T, 39/59
4. Alan Bush, Mississippi, G, 0/0
5. **Cecil Turner, Cal Poly-San Luis Obispo, FL, 76/76**
6. Jim Schmedding, Weber State, G, 0/24
7. **Willie Holman, South Carolina State, DE, 66/71**
8. Wayne Bell, Lenoir-Rhyne, RB, 0/0
9. Sam Moore, Mississippi Valley State, T, 0/0
10. Fred Davis, Doane, G, 0/0
11. **Rich Coady, Memphis, C, 67/67**
12. Emilio Vallez, New Mexico, TE, 9/9
13. Willie Dearion, Prairie View A&M, FL, 0/0
14. Harold Gargus, New Mexico State, DT, 0/0
15. Rich Jaeger, Gustavus Adolphus, C, 0/0

CINCINNATI BENGALS

1. **Bob Johnson, Tennessee, C, 154/154**
2. Tommie Smiley, Lamar, RB, 8/29
2. Bill Staley, Utah State, DT, 23/49
3. Dale Livingston, Western Michigan, K, 24/38
3. **Paul Robinson, Arizona, RB, 60/79**
3. Gary Davis, Vanderbilt, QB, 0/0
4. Warren McVea, Houston, RB, 12/56
4. **Jess Phillips, Michigan State, RB, 69/138**
5. **Al Beauchamp, Southern (LA), LB, 111/125**
5. Dave Middendorf, Washington State, G, 26/34
6. **Howard Fest, Texas, G, 112/127**
6. **Essex Johnson, Grambling State, RB, 98/112**
6. Jim Johnson, South Carolina State, DB, 11/11
6. Bill Kindricks, Alabama A&M, DT, 9/9
6. John Neidert, Louisville, LB, 8/30
6. Dewey Warren, Tennessee, QB, 7/7
6. Monk Williams, Arkansas-Pine Bluff, FL, 2/2
6. Elmo Maple, Southern, FL, 0/0
6. Sidney Ellis, Jackson State, DB, 0/0
7. Steve Smith, Miami (FL), TE, 0/0
7. Wes Bean, Grambling, LB, 0/0
8. Harry Gunner, Oregon State, DE, 28/42
8. Ed Brantley, North Texas State, T, 0/0
9. Phil Johnson, Long Beach State, DB, 0/0
9. Steve Hanrahan, Weber State, DT, 0/0
10. Wayne Patrick, Louisville, RB, 0/53
10. James Russell, North Texas State, E, 0/0
11. Wally Scott, Arizona, DB, 0/0
11. Jeff Banks, Pacific, LB, 0/0
12. **Bob Trumpy, Utah, TE, 128/128**
12. Harold Jones, Grambling, T, 0/0
13. Teddy Washington, San Diego State, RB, 1/1
13. James Bivins, Texas Southern, LB, 0/0
14. Les Webster, Iowa State, RB, 0/0
14. Steve Lewicke, Texas-El Paso, E, 0/0
15. Harvey Palmore, Morgan State, G, 0/0
15. Joe Mira, Miami (FL), FL, 0/0

CLEVELAND BROWNS

1. Marvin Upshaw, Trinity (TX), DE, 28/99
2. **John Garlington, LSU, LB, 128/128**
3. **Reece Morrison, Southwest Texas State, RB, 54/63**
3. Harry Olszewski, Clemson, G, 0/0
4. Wayne Meylan, Nebraska, LB, 27/29
5. Mike Wempe, Missouri, T, 0/0
5. Jackie Jackson, Clemson, RB, 0/0
6. Nate James, Florida A&M, DB, 12/12
7. Dale Brady, Memphis State, RB, 0/0
8. Tom Schoen, Notre Dame, DB, 4/4
9. David Porter, Michigan, DT, 0/0
10. Alvin Mitchell, Morgan State, DB, 26/28
10. James Greer, Stephen F. Austin, DE, 0/0
11. Jim Alcorn, Clarion, QB, 0/0
12. Tom Beutler, Toledo, LB, 4/8
13. Terry Sellers, Georgia, DB, 0/0
14. Edgar Whipps, Jackson State, RB, 0/0
15. Bob Baxter, Memphis State, FL, 0/0

DALLAS COWBOYS

1. Dennis Homan, Alabama, WR, 31/46
2. Dave McDaniels, Mississippi Valley State, WR, 4/4
3. Ed Harmon, Louisville, LB, 0/11
4. John Douglas, Missouri, LB, 0/56
5. **Blaine Nye, Stanford, G, 125/125**
6. **D.D. Lewis, Mississippi State, LB, 186/186**
7. Bob Taucher, Nebraska, T, 0/0
8. Frank Brown, Albany State, DT, 0/0
9. Ken Kmiec, Illinois, DB, 0/0
10. Ben Olison, Kansas, FL, 0/0
11. Ron Shotts, Oklahoma, RB, 0/0
12. Wilson Whitty, Boston, LB, 0/0
13. Carter Lord, Harvard, FL, 0/0
14. Ron Williams, West Virginia, DB, 0/0
15. Tony Lunceford, Auburn, K, 0/0
16. **Larry Cole, Hawaii, DE, 176/176**

DENVER BRONCOS

2. Curley Culp, Arizona State, DT, 0/179
3. Garrett Ford, West Virginia, RB, 14/14
3. Bob Vaughn, Mississippi, G, 1/1
4. Drake Garrett, Michigan State, DB, 15/15
4. Gus Hollomon, Houston, DB, 27/66
4. Gordon Lambert, Tennessee-Martin, LB, 14/14
8. Steve Holloway, Weber State, DB, 0/0
9. **Paul Smith, New Mexico, DT, 133/164**
10. Bob Langford, Middle Tennessee State, T, 0/0
12. Bobby Hendrix, Mississippi, T, 0/0
13. **Charlie Greer, Colorado, DB, 88/88**
14. Marlin Briscoe, Nebraska-Omaha, WR, 11/105
15. Jeff Kuhman, Vermont, LB, 0/0

DETROIT LIONS

1. **Greg Landry, Massachusetts, QB, 102/146**
1. **Earl McCullouch, USC, WR, 72/75**
2. Jerry DePoyster, Wyoming, K, 14/40
3. **Charlie Sanders, Minnesota, TE, 128/128**
4. **Ed Mooney, Texas Tech, LB, 56/69**
5. Phil Odle, Brigham Young, WR, 31/31
6. Mike Spitzer, San Jose State, DE, 0/0
8. Terry Miller, Illinois, LB, 1/41
9. Greg Barton, Tulsa, QB, 1/1
10. Granville Liggins, Oklahoma, LB, 0/0
11. Dwight Little, Kentucky, G, 0/0
12. Ed Caruthers, Arizona, DB, 0/0
13. Chuck Bailey, Cal State-Humboldt, T, 0/0
14. Richie Davis, Upsala, E, 0/0
15. Jim Oliver, Colorado State, RB, 0/0

GREEN BAY PACKERS

1. **Fred Carr, Texas-El Paso, LB, 140/140**
1. **Bill Lueck, Arizona, G, 90/101**
3. **Dick Himes, Ohio State, T, 135/135**
3. Billy Stevens, Texas-El Paso, QB, 3/3
4. Brendan McCarthy, Boston College, RB, 0/15
4. John Robinson, Tennessee State, FL, 0/0
5. Steve Duich, San Diego State, G, 0/23
5. Francis Winkler, Memphis, DE, 21/21
6. Walter Chadwick, Tennessee, RB, 0/0
7. Andy Beath, Duke, DB, 0/0
8. Tom Owens, Missouri-Rolla, G, 0/0
9. Bob Apisa, Michigan State, RB, 0/0
10. Rick Cash, Truman State, DE, 0/64
10. Ron Worthen, Arkansas State, C, 0/0
11. Gordon Rule, Dartmouth, DB, 15/15
12. Dennis Porter, Northern Michigan, T, 0/0
13. Frank Geiselman, Rhode Island, FL, 0/0
14. John Farler, Colorado, E, 0/0
15. Ridley Gibson, Baylor, DB, 0/0

HOUSTON OILERS

2. Mac Haik, Mississippi, WR, 44/44
3. **Elvin Bethea, North Carolina A&T, DE, 210/210**
4. **Jim Beirne, Purdue, WR, 80/94**
5. Bob Longo, Pittsburgh, E, 0/0
7. Paul Toscano, Wyoming, DB, 0/0
9. Bob Robertson, Illinois, T, 14/14
10. Tom Domres, Wisconsin, DT, 47/63
10. Joe Peace, Louisiana Tech, LB, 0/0
11. Bill Halley, La Verne, E, 0/0
12. Barry Lischner, Missouri, RB, 0/0
13. Jimmy Dousay, Louisiana State, RB, 0/0
14. Richard Stotter, Houston, LB, 3/3
16. Bob Smith, Miami (OH), DB, 6/6

KANSAS CITY CHIEFS

1. **George Daney, Texas-El Paso, G, 97/97**
1. **Mo Moorman, Texas A&M, G, 72/72**
2. **Mike Livingston, SMU, QB, 91/91**
4. Mickey McCarty, TCU, TE, 3/3
7. Sammy Grezaffi, Louisiana State, DB, 0/0
8. Lindon Endsley, North Texas State, C, 0/0
9. Wayne McClure, Mississippi, LB, 0/27
10. Jack Gehrke, Utah, WR, 2/26
11. Tom Nosewicz, Tulane, DE, 0/0
12. Bobby Johns, Alabama, DB, 0/0
13. Jim Kavanagh, Boston College, FL, 0/0
14. Robert Holmes, Southern (LA), RB, 48/89
15. Bill Chambless, Miami (FL), G, 0/0

LOS ANGELES RAMS

2. Gary Beban, UCLA, QB, 0/5
2. Mike LaHood, Wyoming, G, 37/51
5. Don Martin, Washington, K, 0/0
6. Bobby Webb, Southern Mississippi, C, 0/0
8. Joe Williams, Florida A&M, FL, 0/0
9. Bob Richardson, Washington, T, 0/0
10. Allen Marcelin, Parsons, FL, 0/0
11. **John Pergine, Notre Dame, LB, 50/90**
12. **Harold Jackson, Jackson State, WR, 72/208**
13. Dean Halverson, Washington, LB, 27/66
14. Cephus Jackson, Jackson State, DB, 0/0
15. Dennis Yell, Moorhead State, T, 0/0
16. Jimmy Raye, Michigan State, DB, 0/2

MIAMI DOLPHINS

1. **Doug Crusan, Indiana, T, 82/82**
1. **Larry Csonka, Syracuse, RB, 106/146**
2. Jim Cox, Miami (FL), TE, 13/13
2. Jimmy Keyes, Mississippi, LB, 17/17
3. **Dick Anderson, Colorado, DB, 121/121**
3. Jim Urbanek, Mississippi, DT, 8/8
5. **Jim Kiick, Wyoming, RB, 97/115**
6. Kim Hammond, Florida State, QB, 3/6
6. Jimmy Hines, Texas Southern, WR, 9/10
7. John Boynton, Tennessee, T, 14/14
8. Randy Edmunds, Georgia Tech, LB, 28/45
9. Sam McDowell, Southwest Missouri State, T, 0/0
9. Tom Paciorek, Houston, DB, 0/0
10. Joe Mirto, Miami (FL), T, 0/0
11. Cornelius Cooper, Prairie View A&M, T, 0/0
12. Paul Paxton, Akron, T, 0/0
13. Bob Joswick, Tulsa, DE, 6/6
14. Ray Blunk, Xavier, TE, 0/0
15. Ken Corbin, Miami (FL), LB, 0/0

MINNESOTA VIKINGS

1. **Ron Yary, USC, T, 199/207**
2. **Charlie West, Texas-El Paso, DB, 75/161**
3. Mike McGill, Notre Dame, LB, 38/53
4. Mike Freeman, Fresno State, DB, 0/37
6. Bob Goodridge, Vanderbilt, WR, 11/11
7. **Oscar Reed, Colorado State, RB, 79/86**
7. Lenny Snow, Georgia Tech, RB, 0/0
8. Hank Urbanowicz, Miami (FL), DT, 0/0
9. Mike Donohoe, San Francisco, TE, 0/64
10. Tom Sakal, Minnesota, DB, 0/0
11. Bill Haas, Nebraska-Omaha, E, 0/0
12. Howie Small, Rhode Island, C, 0/0
13. Rich Wherry, Northern State (SD), E, 0/0
14. Don Evans, Arkansas-Pine Bluff, T, 0/0
15. Jim Haynie, West Chester, QB, 0/0
17. **Bob Lee, Pacific, QB, 52/77**

NEW ORLEANS SAINTS

1. Kevin Hardy, Notre Dame, DT, 0/45
3. Dave Szymakowski, West Texas A&M, WR, 3/3
4. Dan Sartin, Mississippi, DT, 0/13
4. Willie Crittendon, Tulsa, DT, 0/0
5. Ronnie Lee South, Arkansas, QB, 4/4
7. Gene Howard, Langston, DB, 36/63
7. Ray Phillips, Michigan, G, 0/0
8. Richard Swatland, Notre Dame, G, 0/4
9. Joe Blake, Tulsa, T, 0/0
10. Doug Robinson, Iowa State, DB, 0/0
11. Bennie Blocker, South Carolina State, RB, 0/0
12. John Beck, San Diego State, DB, 0/0
13. K.O. Trepanier, Montana State, DE, 0/0
14. Herb Covington, Memphis State, RB, 0/0
15. Wilmer Cooks, Colorado, RB, 0/0
17. James Ferguson, USC, C, 4/10

NEW YORK GIANTS

2. Rich Buzin, Penn State, T, 42/49
3. Bobby Duhon, Tulane, RB, 44/44
7. Doug Chatman, Jackson State, DE, 0/0
9. Joe Koontz, San Francisco State, WR, 14/14
11. Henry Davis, Grambling State, LB, 27/83
12. Jim Holifield, Jackson State, DB, 28/28
13. John Gallagher, Boston, DE, 0/0
14. Bill Moreman, Florida State, RB, 0/0
15. McKinley Boston, Minnesota, DE, 27/27
16. Kenny Parker, Fordham, DB, 14/14

NEW YORK JETS

1. Lee White, Weber State, RB, 29/44
2. Steve Thompson, Washington, DT, 43/43
3. Sam Walton, Texas A&M-Commerce, T, 20/34
4. Gary Magner, Southern California, DT, 0/0
5. Lee Jacobsen, Kearney State, LB, 0/0
7. Oscar Lubke, Ball State, T, 0/0
8. Karl Henke, Tulsa, DE, 6/16
8. Jim Richards, Virginia Tech, DB, 26/26
8. Bob Taylor, Maryland-Eastern Shore, RB, 0/0
9. Gary Houser, Oregon State, TE, 0/0
10. Mike D'Amato, Hofstra, DB, 13/13
11. Henry Owens, Weber State, FL, 0/0
12. Raymond Hayes, Toledo, DT, 6/6
13. Tom Myslinski, Maryland, G, 0/0
14. Harvey Nairn, Southern, RB, 0/0
15. Ronnie Ehrig, Texas, DB, 0/0

OAKLAND RAIDERS

1. Eldrige Dickey, Tennessee State, WR, 18/18
2. **Ken Stabler, Alabama, QB, 130/184**
3. **Art Shell, Maryland-Eastern Shore, T, 207/207**
4. **Charlie Smith, Utah, RB, 91/95**
5. John Naponick, Virginia, T, 0/0
7. **George Atkinson, Morris Brown, DB, 138/144**
7. John Harper, Adams State, C, 0/0
9. John Eason, Florida A&M, WR, 3/3
10. Rick Owens, Pennsylvania, DB, 0/0
11. **Marv Hubbard, Colgate, RB, 90/103**
11. Chip Oliver, USC, LB, 28/28
12. Larry Plantz, Colorado, FL, 0/0
13. Larry Blackstone, Fairmont State, RB, 0/0
14. Ray Carlson, Hamline, LB, 0/0
15. Mike Leinert, Texas Tech, RB, 0/0

PHILADELPHIA EAGLES

1. **Tim Rossovich, USC, LB, 55/88**
2. Cyril Pinder, Illinois, RB, 42/72
3. Adrian Young, USC, LB, 40/52
4. Len McNeil, Fresno State, G, 0/0
5. Mike Dirks, Wyoming, DT, 43/43
5. **Mark Nordquist, Pacific, G, 96/111**
6. Dave Martin, Notre Dame, LB, 0/10
6. Thurman Randle, Texas-El Paso, T, 0/0
7. Joe Przybycki, Michigan State, G, 0/0
8. Al Lavan, Colorado State, DB, 0/24
9. **Mike Evans, Boston College, C, 73/73**
10. John Mallory, West Virginia, DB, 14/55
11. Len Persin, Boston College, DE, 0/0
12. Thurston Taylor, Florida State, TE, 0/0
13. George Barron, Mississippi State, T, 0/0
14. Dan Williamson, West Virginia, LB, 0/0
15. Joe Graham, Tennessee, G, 0/0

PITTSBURGH STEELERS

1. Mike Taylor, USC, T, 23/46
2. Ernie Ruple, Arkansas, DE, 14/14
3. Ken Hebert, Houston, WR, 3/3
3. Jon Henderson, Colorado State, WR, 23/37
7. Doug Dalton, New Mexico State, RB, 0/0
7. Bill Glennon, Washington, DT, 0/0
8. Danny Holman, San Jose State, QB, 0/0
9. John Knight, Weber State, DE, 0/0
11. Kim King, Georgia Tech, QB, 0/0
12. Sam Wheeler, Wisconsin, LB, 0/0
13. Joe Roundy, Puget Sound, G, 0/0
14. Lou Harris, Kent State, DB, 14/14
15. Bob Lanning, Northern Montana, DE, 0/0
16. **Rocky Bleier, Notre Dame, RB, 140/140**

SAN DIEGO CHARGERS

1. Jim Hill, Texas A&M-Kingsville, DB, 42/94
1. **Russ Washington, Missouri, T, 200/200**
2. Bill Lenkaitis, Penn State, C, 29/180
4. Ken Dyer, Arizona State, DB, 14/27
5. Bill Perry, Kent State, TE, 0/0
7. Lane Fenner, Florida State, WR, 11/11
8. Elliot Gammage, Tennessee, TE, 0/0
9. Grundy Harris, Southern, RB, 0/0
11. **Dennis Partee, SMU, K, 111/111**
12. Jeff Queen, Morgan State, RB, 42/76
13. Fred Combs, North Carolina State, DB, 0/0
14. Jim Campbell, West Texas A&M, LB, 1/1
15. Bob Wells, Johnson C. Smith, T, 20/20
15. Dan Kramarczyk, Dayton, T, 0/0
16. Dick Farley, Boston University, DB, 24/24

SAN FRANCISCO 49ERS

1. **Forrest Blue, Auburn, C, 96/148**
3. Lance Olssen, Purdue, T, 9/9
3. **Skip Vanderbundt, Oregon State, LB, 119/134**
4. **Johnny Fuller, Lamar, DB, 63/99**
5. Dwight Lee, Michigan State, RB, 2/13
6. **Bill Belk, Maryland-Eastern Shore, DE, 87/87**
6. Lee Johnson, Tennessee State, WR, 21/21
7. Jerry Richardson, Mississippi, LB, 0/0
8. Charley Brown, Augustana (SD), T, 0/0
8. Tom Gray, Morehead State, FL, 0/0
9. Casey Boyett, BYU, E, 0/0
10. **Tommy Hart, Morris Brown, DE, 131/177**
11. Dennis Fitzgibbons, Syracuse, G, 0/0
12. Henry Johnson, Fisk, QB, 0/0
13. Tom Mitrakos, Pittsburgh, C, 0/0
14. Alex Moore, Norfolk State, RB, 0/3
15. Clarence Spencer, Louisville, FL, 0/0
17. Dennis Patera, Brigham Young, K, 5/5

ST. LOUIS CARDINALS

1. **MacArthur Lane, Utah State, RB, 50/133**
2. Bob Atkins, Grambling State, DB, 27/114
2. Fred Hyatt, Auburn, WR, 43/45
4. Don Fitzgerald, Kent State, RB, 0/0
4. Joe Schniesing, New Mexico State, LB, 0/0
5. Rocky Rosema, Michigan, LB, 32/32
6. Frank Lane, Stephen F. Austin, LB, 0/0
7. Ken Henry, Wake Forest, FL, 0/0
8. Jerry Daanen, Miami (FL), WR, 37/37
9. Billy Sinkule, Central Michigan, DE, 0/0
10. Tom Busch, Iowa State, FL, 0/0
11. Larry Slagle, UCLA, G, 0/0
12. Vern Emerson, Minnesota-Duluth, T, 23/23
13. Mack Sauls, Southwest Texas State, DB, 10/10
14. Vic Bender, Northeast Louisiana, C, 0/0
15. Dave Lovich, Northwestern State (LA), DE, 0/0
17. Bobby Lee, Minnesota, WR, 4/6

WASHINGTON REDSKINS

1. Jim Smith, Oregon, DB, 14/14
2. Tom Roussel, Southern Mississippi, LB, 42/66
4. Dennis Crane, USC, DT, 24/33
5. Ken Barefoot, Virginia Tech, TE, 8/8
5. **Mike Bragg, Richmond, P, 172/188**
6. Willie Banks, Alcorn State, G, 19/37
7. **Bob Brunet, Louisiana Tech, RB, 81/81**
8. Brian Magnuson, Montana, RB, 0/0
9. Frank Liberatore, Clemson, DB, 0/0
11. Tom Garretson, Northwestern, DB, 0/0
12. Dave Weedman, Western Washington, DT, 0/0
13. Mike St. Louis, Central Missouri State, T, 0/0
14. Dave Zivich, Cal-Santa Barbara, T, 0/0
15. Coger Coverson, Texas Southern, G, 0/0
17. Frank Bosch, Colorado, DT, 39/39

1969 NFL

ATLANTA FALCONS

1. **George Kunz, Notre Dame, T, 79/129**
2. Paul Gipson, Houston, RB, 23/33
3. Mal Snider, Stanford, G, 41/83
3. Jon Sandstrom, Oregon State, G, 0/0
4. Dicky Lyons, Kentucky, DB, 0/4
4. **Jim Mitchell, Prairie View A&M, TE, 155/155**
5. Tony Pleviak, Illinois, DE, 0/0
6. Wally Oyler, Louisville, DB, 0/0
7. Ted Cottrell, Delaware Valley, LB, 24/24
7. Dick Enderle, Minnesota, G, 40/96
8. Jim Callahan, Temple, FL, 0/0
10. Jeff Stanciel, Mississippi Valley State, RB, 2/2
11. **Jeff Van Note, Kentucky, C, 246/246**
12. Denver Samples, Texas-El Paso, DT, 0/0
13. Harry Carpenter, Tennessee State, T, 0/0
14. Billy Hunt, Kansas, DB, 0/0
15. Jim Weatherford, Tennessee, DB, 14/14

BALTIMORE COLTS

1. Eddie Hinton, Oklahoma, WR, 47/67
2. **Ted Hendricks, Miami (FL), LB, 70/215**
2. Tommy Maxwell, Texas A&M, DB, 27/68
3. **Dennis Nelson, Illinois State, T, 61/77**
4. Jacky Stewart, Texas Tech, RB, 0/0
5. King Dunlap, Tennessee State, DT, 0/0
6. Bill Fortier, Louisiana State, T, 0/0
7. Roland Moss, Toledo, TE, 6/26
7. Gary Fleming, Samford, DE, 0/0
8. **Sam Havrilak, Bucknell, WR, 69/75**
9. George Wright, Sam Houston State, DT, 12/16
9. Larry Good, Georgia Tech, QB, 0/0
10. Marion Griffin, Purdue, TE, 0/0
11. Ken Delaney, Akron, T, 0/0
12. Butch Riley, Texas A&M-Kingsville, LB, 11/11
13. Carl Mauck, Southern Illinois, C, 4/166
14. Dave Bartelt, Colorado, LB, 0/0
15. George Thompson, Marquette, DB, 0/0

BOSTON PATRIOTS

1. Ron Sellers, Florida State, WR, 35/52
2. **Mike Montler, Colorado, C, 53/123**
3. **Carl Garrett, New Mexico Highlands, RB, 51/110**
5. Onree Jackson, Alabama A&M, QB, 0/0
7. Rick Hackley, New Mexico State, T, 0/0
8. Bob Gladieux, Notre Dame, RB, 43/45
9. Steve Alexakos, San Jose State, G, 0/18
9. Joe Walker, Albany State, DE, 0/0
10. Dennis Devlin, Wyoming, DB, 0/0
11. Barry Gallup, Boston College, WR, 0/0
12. Richard Lee, Grambling, DT, 0/0

13. Joe Leasy, Alcorn State, LB, 0/0
14. John Cagle, Clemson, DE, 6/6
15. Brant Conley, Tulsa, RB, 0/0

BUFFALO BILLS

1. **O.J. Simpson, USC, RB, 112/135**
2. Bill Enyart, Oregon State, RB, 28/29
3. Julian Nunamaker, Tennessee-Martin, DE, 18/18
4. Mike Richey, North Carolina, T, 14/19
5. Ben Mayes, Drake, DE, 0/5
7. John Helton, Arizona State, DE, 0/0
8. James Harris, Grambling State, QB, 18/83
8. Waddey Harvey, Virginia Tech, DT, 28/28
10. Ron Baines, Montana, FL, 0/0
11. Bobby Hall, North Carolina State, RB, 0/0
12. Lloyd Pate, Cincinnati, RB, 9/9
13. Leon Lovelace, Texas Tech, T, 0/0
14. Bubba Thornton, TCU, WR, 14/14
15. Karl Wilson, Olivet, RB, 0/0

CHICAGO BEARS

1. Rufus Mayes, Ohio State, T, 13/139
2. **Bobby Douglass, Kansas, QB, 61/91**
3. Ross Montgomery, TCU, RB, 26/26
4. Rudy Redmond, Pacific, DB, 0/50
5. Jim Winegardner, Notre Dame, TE, 0/0
6. Bill Nicholson, Stanford, DE, 0/0
7. Ron Copeland, UCLA, WR, 6/6
8. Webb Hubbell, Arkansas, G, 0/0
9. Joe Aluise, Arizona, RB, 0/0
10. Ron Pearson, Maryland, TE, 0/0
11. Sam Campbell, Iowa State, DT, 0/0
12. Dave Hale, Ottawa (KS), DT, 30/30
13. Tom Quinn, Notre Dame, DB, 0/0
14. Ronnie Ehrig, Texas, DB, 0/0
15. Bob Coble, Kansas State, P, 0/0

CINCINNATI BENGALS

1. Greg Cook, Cincinnati, QB, 12/12
2. **Bill Bergey, Arkansas State, LB, 68/159**
3. **Speedy Thomas, Utah, WR, 51/58**
4. Clem Turner, Cincinnati, RB, 14/51
5. **Guy Dennis, Florida, G, 55/89**
6. **Ken Riley, Florida A&M, DB, 207/207**
7. **Royce Berry, Houston, DE, 82/94**
8. Tim Buchanan, Hawaii, LB, 14/14
9. Mike Stripling, Tulsa, RB, 0/0
10. Steve Howell, Ohio State, TE, 0/0
11. Mark Stewart, Georgia, DB, 0/0
12. Lonnie Paige, North Carolina Central, DT, 0/0
13. Chuck Benson, Southern Illinois, WR, 0/0
14. Mike Wilson, Dayton, T, 17/26
15. Bill Shoemaker, Stanford, K, 0/0

CLEVELAND BROWNS

1. Ron Johnson, Michigan, RB, 14/81
3. **Chip Glass, Florida State, TE, 68/81**
3. Al Jenkins, Tulsa, G, 13/40
4. Freddie Summers, Washington (MD), DB, 23/23
5. **Fair Hooker, Arizona State, WR, 74/74**
6. Joe Righetti, Waynesburg, DT, 23/23
6. Larry Adams, Texas Christian, DT, 0/0
7. **Walt Sumner, Florida State, DB, 76/76**
8. Chuck Reynolds, Tulsa, C, 25/25
9. Ron Kamzelski, Minnesota, DT, 0/0
10. Greg Shelly, Virginia, G, 0/0
11. Dave Jones, Kansas State, WR, 41/41
12. Dick Davis, Nebraska, RB, 0/6
13. Tommy Boutwell, Southern Mississippi, WR, 0/5
14. Jiggy Smaha, Georgia, DT, 0/0
15. Joe Stevenson, Georgia Tech, TE, 0/0
17. Bob Oliver, Abilene Christian, DE, 8/8

DALLAS COWBOYS

1. **Calvin Hill, Yale, RB, 73/156**
2. Richmond Flowers, Tennessee, DB, 25/55
3. Halvor Hagen, Weber State, G, 18/70
3. Thomas Stincic, Michigan, LB, 35/42
5. Chuck Kyle, Purdue, LB, 0/0
6. Rick Shaw, Arizona State, FL, 0/0
7. Larry Bales, Emory & Henry, FL, 0/0
8. Elmer Benhardt, Missouri, LB, 0/0
9. Claxton Welch, Oregon, RB, 28/31
10. Stuart Gottlieb, Weber State, T, 0/0
11. Sweeny Williams, Prairie View A&M, DE, 0/111
12. Bob Belden, Notre Dame, QB, 0/0
13. Rene Matison, New Mexico, FL, 0/0
14. Gerald Lutri, Northern Michigan, T, 0/0
15. Bill Justus, Tennessee, DB, 0/0

DENVER BRONCOS

2. Grady Cavness, Texas-El Paso, DB, 14/18
3. **Bill Thompson, Maryland-Eastern Shore, DB, 179/179**
4. Ed Hayes, Morgan State, DB, 0/4
4. **Mike Schnitker, Colorado, G, 74/74**
5. Frank Quayle, Virginia, RB, 11/11
6. Wandy Williams, Hofstra, RB, 12/12
6. Mike Coleman, Tampa, RB, 0/0
7. Al Giffin, Auburn, TE, 0/0
9. Henry Jones, Grambling State, RB, 2/2
10. Jimmy Smith, Utah State, DB, 2/2
11. Chuck Pastrana, Maryland, QB, 7/7
12. Wes Plummer, Arizona State, DB, 0/0
13. Johnny Sias, Georgia Tech, WR, 0/0
14. Gary Crane, Arkansas State, LB, 6/6
15. Errol Kahoun, Miami (OH), G, 0/0

DETROIT LIONS

2. **Altie Taylor, Utah State, RB, 91/102**
2. **Jim Yarbrough, Florida, T, 112/112**
3. **Larry Walton, Arizona State, WR, 95/107**
8. Jim Carr, Jackson State, T, 0/0
9. Rocky Rasley, Oregon State, G, 48/74
10. Bob Bergum, Wisconsin-Platteville, DE, 0/0
11. Ron Walker, Morris Brown, DE, 0/0
12. Bob Hadlock, George Fox, DT, 0/0
13. Wilson Bowie, Southern California, RB, 0/0
14. George Hoey, Michigan, DB, 0/50
15. Fred Gough, Texas-Arlington, LB, 0/0

GREEN BAY PACKERS

1. Rich Moore, Villanova, DT, 20/20
2. Dave Bradley, Penn State, G, 15/16
3. John Spilis, Northern Illinois, WR, 40/40
4. **Perry Williams, Purdue, RB, 69/83**
5. **Bill Hayhoe, USC, T, 61/61**
6. Ron Jones, Texas-El Paso, TE, 6/6
6. Ken Vinyard, Texas Tech, K, 0/14
7. Larry Agajanian, UCLA, DT, 0/0
8. Doug Gosnell, Utah State, C, 0/0
9. Dave Hampton, Wyoming, RB, 33/93
10. Bruce Nelson, North Dakota State, T, 0/0
11. Lee Harden, Texas-El Paso, DB, 8/8
12. Tom Buckman, Texas A&M, TE, 0/7
13. Craig Koinzan, Doane, LB, 0/0
14. Rich Voltzke, Minnesota, RB, 0/0
15. Dan Eckstein, Presbyterian, DB, 0/0

HOUSTON OILERS

1. Ron Pritchard, Arizona State, LB, 48/105
2. Jerry LeVias, SMU, WR, 28/70
3. **Elbert Drungo, Tennessee State, T, 107/120**
3. Rich Johnson, Illinois, RB, 14/14
4. Roy Gerela, New Mexico State, K, 28/145
4. Charlie Joiner, Grambling State, WR, 36/239
5. Johnny Peacock, Houston, DB, 28/28
6. Willie Grate, South Carolina State, TE, 0/25
7. Mike Richardson, SMU, RB, 35/35
8. Glenn Woods, Prairie View A&M, DE, 7/7
9. Ed Watson, Grambling State, LB, 3/3
10. Bob Naponic, Illinois, QB, 2/2
10. Joe Pryor, Boston College, DE, 0/0
11. Terry May, Southern Methodist, C, 0/0
12. George Resley, Texas A&M, DT, 0/0
13. Richard Pickens, Tennessee, RB, 0/0
14. Roy Reeves, South Carolina, WR, 0/2
15. John Tysziewicz, Tennessee-Chattanooga, G, 0/0
16. Loyd Wainscott, Texas, LB, 25/25
17. Hank Autry, Southern Mississippi, C, 28/28

KANSAS CITY CHIEFS

1. **Jim Marsalis, Tennessee State, DB, 78/90**
2. **Ed Podolak, Iowa, RB, 104/104**
3. **Morris Stroud, Clark Atlanta, TE, 69/69**
4. **Jack Rudnay, Northwestern, C, 178/178**
5. **Bob Stein, Minnesota, LB, 50/89**
6. John Pleasant, Alabama State, RB, 0/0
7. Tom Nettles, San Diego State, FL, 0/0
8. Clanton King, Purdue, T, 0/0
8. Maurice LeBlanc, Louisiana State, DB, 0/0
9. Dan Klepper, Nebraska-Omaha, G, 0/0
10. John Sponheimer, Cornell, DT, 0/0
11. Skip Wupper, C.W. Post, DE, 0/0
12. John Lavin, Notre Dame, LB, 0/0
13. Rick Piland, Virginia Tech, G, 0/0
14. Al Bream, Iowa, DB, 0/0
15. Leland Winston, Rice, T, 0/0

LOS ANGELES RAMS

1. **Bob Klein, USC, TE, 102/145**
1. Jim Seymour, Notre Dame, WR, 0/31
1. **Larry Smith, Florida, RB, 65/72**
4. John Zook, Kansas, DE, 0/144
6. **Pat Curran, Lakeland, TE, 66/122**
6. A.Z. Drones, West Texas State, T, 0/0
7. James Hawkins, Nebraska, DB, 0/0
8. Richard Harvey, Jackson State, DB, 0/7
9. Mike Foote, Oregon State, LB, 0/0
10. Jerry Gordon, Auburn, T, 0/0
11. Dave Svendsen, Eastern Washington, FL, 0/0
12. Tim Carr, C.W. Post, QB, 0/0
13. Roger Williams, Grambling State, DB, 18/18
14. Ray Stephens, Minnesota, RB, 0/0
15. George Jugum, Washington, LB, 0/0

MIAMI DOLPHINS

1. **Bill Stanfill, Georgia, DE, 109/109**
2. **Bob Heinz, Pacific, DT, 109/111**
3. **Mercury Morris, West Texas A&M, RB, 86/99**
4. Norm McBride, Utah, DE, 10/10
5. Karl Kremser, Tennessee, K, 15/15
5. Willie Pearson, North Carolina A&T, DB, 5/5
6. Ed Tuck, Notre Dame, G, 0/0
7. John Eagan, Boston College, C, 0/0
7. John Kulka, Penn State, C, 0/0
8. Bruce Weinstein, Yale, TE, 0/0
9. **Jesse Powell, West Texas A&M, LB, 56/56**
10. Jim Mertens, Fairmont State, TE, 14/14
11. Mike Berdis, North Dakota State, T, 0/0
12. Dale McCullers, Florida State, LB, 14/14
13. Amos Ayres, Arkansas-Pine Bluff, DB, 0/0
14. Glenn Thompson, Troy State, T, 0/0
15. Chick McGeehan, Tennessee, FL, 0/0
16. **Lloyd Mumphord, Texas Southern, DB, 77/122**

MINNESOTA VIKINGS

2. **Ed White, California, G, 122/241**
2. Volly Murphy, Texas-El Paso, FL, 0/0
4. Mike McCaffrey, California, LB, 0/12
5. Jim Barnes, Arkansas, G, 0/0
5. Mike O'Shea, Utah State, WR, 0/0
5. Cornelius Davis, Kansas State, RB, 0/0
6. Marion Bates, Texas Southern, DB, 0/0
8. Harris Wood, Washington, FL, 0/0
9. Tom Fink, Minnesota, G, 0/0
10. Tom McCauley, Wisconsin, DB, 0/32
11. Brian Dowling, Yale, QB, 0/27
12. Noel Jenke, Minnesota, LB, 14/25
13. Jim Moylan, Texas Tech, DT, 0/0
14. Tommy Head, Southwest Texas State, C, 0/0
15. Eugene Mosley, Jackson State, TE, 0/0

NEW ORLEANS SAINTS

1. John Shinners, Xavier (OH), G, 25/97
2. **Richard Neal, Southern (LA), DE, 56/120**
4. Dennis Hale, Minnesota, DB, 0/0
4. Bob Hudspeth, Southern Illinois, T, 0/0
5. Tony Kyasky, Syracuse, DB, 0/0
5. Keith Christensen, Kansas, T, 0/0
6. Bob Miller, Southern California, TE, 0/0
8. Jim Lawrence, Southern California, FL, 0/0
9. **Joe Owens, Alcorn State, DE, 70/87**
10. McKinley Reynolds, Hawaii, RB, 0/0
11. Tommy Morel, Louisiana State, FL, 0/0
12. Tom Broadhead, Cal-Santa Barbara, RB, 0/0
13. Joe Robillard, Linfield, DB, 0/0
14. Gary Loyd, California Lutheran, K, 0/0
15. Bill Waller, Xavier, FL, 0/0
16. Ed Hargett, Texas A&M, QB, 44/49

NEW YORK GIANTS

1. Fred Dryer, San Diego State, DE, 42/176
3. Vern Vanoy, Kansas, DT, 6/20
4. **Rich Houston, Texas A&M-Commerce, WR, 60/60**
7. Al Brenner, Michigan State, DB, 7/7
8. George Irby, Tuskegee, RB, 0/0
9. Ray Hickl, Texas A&M-Kingsville, LB, 10/10
10. Lou Galiardi, Dayton, DT, 0/0
11. John Fuqua, Morgan State, RB, 13/100
12. Harry Blackney, Maryland, RB, 0/0
13. Richard Perrin, Bowling Green, DB, 0/0
14. Steve Smith, Weber State, K, 0/0
15. **Don Herrmann, Waynesburg, WR, 70/100**

NEW YORK JETS

1. Dave Foley, Ohio State, T, 29/110
2. Al Woodall, Duke, QB, 31/31
4. Ezell Jones, Minnesota, T, 0/18
5. Chris Gilbert, Texas, RB, 0/0
6. Jimmie Jones, Wichita State, DE, 17/40
7. Cliff Larson, Houston, DE, 0/0
8. Cecil Leonard, Tuskegee, DB, 13/13
9. Frank Peters, Ohio University, T, 0/3
10. Mike Hall, Alabama, LB, 0/0
11. Gary Roberts, Purdue, G, 0/11
12. Mike Battle, USC, DB, 28/28
13. **Steve O'Neal, Texas A&M, P, 56/70**
14. Roger Finnie, Florida A&M, T, 38/121
15. Wayne Stewart, California, TE, 38/52
16. George Nock, Morgan State, RB, 30/37

OAKLAND RAIDERS

1. **Art Thoms, Syracuse, DT, 86/98**
2. **George Buehler, Stanford, G, 115/137**
3. Lloyd Edwards, San Diego State, TE, 14/14
4. Ruby Jackson, New Mexico State, T, 0/0
6. Jackie Allen, Baylor, DB, 5/34
6. Ken Newfield, Louisiana State, RB, 0/0
7. Finnis Taylor, Prairie View A&M, DB, 0/0
9. Drew Buie, Catawba, WR, 42/46
11. Harold Rice, Tennessee State, DE, 12/12
13. Al Goddard, Johnson C. Smith, DB, 0/0
13. Dave Husted, Wabash, LB, 0/0
14. Harold Busby, UCLA, E, 0/0
15. Alvin Presnell, Alabama A&M, RB, 0/0

PHILADELPHIA EAGLES

1. Leroy Keyes, Purdue, DB, 45/48
2. Ernie Calloway, Texas Southern, DT, 47/47
3. **Bill Bradley, Texas, DB, 110/114**
4. Bob Kuechenberg, Notre Dame, G, 0/196
5. Jim Anderson, Missouri, G, 0/0
6. Dick Barnhorst, Xavier, TE, 0/0
7. Mike Schmeising, St. Olaf, RB, 0/0
8. Bill Hobbs, Texas A&M, LB, 37/43
9. Kent Lawrence, Georgia, WR, 9/10
9. Lynn Buss, Wisconsin, LB, 0/0
10. Sonny Wade, Emory & Henry, QB, 0/0
10. Donnie Shanklin, Kansas, RB, 0/0
11. Jim Marcum, Texas-Arlington, DB, 0/0
12. Gary Adams, Arkansas, DB, 0/0
13. **Wade Key, Southwest Texas State, G, 121/121**
14. Jim Ross, Bishop, T, 0/0
15. Leon Angevine, Penn State, WR, 0/0

PITTSBURGH STEELERS

1. **Joe Greene, North Texas, DT, 181/181**
2. Warren Bankston, Tulane, RB, 39/114
2. Terry Hanratty, Notre Dame, QB, 47/50
3. **Jon Kolb, Oklahoma State, T, 177/177**
4. Bob Campbell, Penn State, WR, 14/14
7. Chuck Beatty, North Texas, DB, 30/34
7. Chadwick Brown, East Texas State, T, 0/0
8. Joe Cooper, Tennessee State, FL, 0/0
9. John Sodaski, Villanova, LB, 3/21
10. **L.C. Greenwood, Arkansas-Pine Bluff, DE, 170/170**
11. Clarence Washington, Arkansas-Pine Bluff, DT, 27/27
12. Doug Fisher, San Diego State, LB, 10/10
13. John Lynch, Drake, LB, 0/0
14. Bob Houmard, Ohio U., RB, 0/0
15. Ken Liberto, Louisiana Tech, WR, 0/0

SAN DIEGO CHARGERS

1. Bob Babich, Miami (OH), LB, 42/125
1. Marty Domres, Columbia, QB, 22/90
2. Ron Sayers, Nebraska-Omaha, RB, 8/8
3. Gene Ferguson, Norfolk State, T, 26/41
5. Harry Orszulak, Pittsburgh, FL, 0/0
6. Terry Swarn, Colorado State, FL, 0/0
8. Craig Cotton, Youngstown State, TE, 9/77
9. Joe Williams, Southern, DB, 0/0
10. David Arnold, Northwestern State (LA), G, 0/0
11. Willie Norwood, Alcorn State, TE, 0/0
12. Jim White, Arkansas-Pine Bluff, RB, 0/0
13. Mike Simpson, Houston, DB, 0/41
14. Bill Ackman, New Mexico State, DT, 0/0
15. Charlie Jarvis, Army, RB, 0/0
17. Larry Rentz, Florida, DB, 2/2

SAN FRANCISCO 49ERS

1. **Ted Kwalick, Penn State, TE, 83/108**
1. **Gene Washington, Stanford, WR, 124/140**
4. Gene Moore, Occidental, RB, 5/5
4. **Jim Sniadecki, Indiana, LB, 58/58**
5. **Earl Edwards, Wichita State, DT, 55/150**
6. **Jimmy Thomas, Texas-Arlington, RB, 63/63**
7. Steve Van Sinderen, Washington State, T, 0/0
8. Mike Loper, BYU, T, 0/0

9. Hilton Crawford, Grambling State, DB, 0/7
10. Dave Chapple, California-Santa Barbara, P, 0/40
11. Willie Peake, Alcorn State, T, 0/0
12. Jack O'Malley, Southern California, T, 0/0
13. Paul Champlin, Eastern Montana, DB, 0/0
14. Tom Black, East Texas State, FL, 0/0
15. Gary Golden, Texas Tech, DB, 0/0
16. **Bob Hoskins, Wichita State, DT, 77/77**

ST. LOUIS CARDINALS

1. **Roger Wehrli, Missouri, DB, 193/193**
2. Rolf Krueger, Texas A&M, DE, 42/69
3. Terry Brown, Oklahoma State, DB, 24/85
3. Chip Healy, Vanderbilt, LB, 28/28
4. Bill Rhodes, Florida State, G, 0/0
5. Gene Huey, Wyoming, DB, 0/4
5. Walt Shockley, San Jose State, RB, 0/0
6. Amos Van Pelt, Ball State, RB, 0/0
8. **Wayne Mulligan, Clemson, C, 60/87**
9. Cal Snowden, Indiana, DE, 21/47
10. Gerald Warren, North Carolina State, K, 0/0
11. Gary Kerl, Utah, LB, 0/0
12. Howard Taylor, New Mexico State, RB, 0/0
13. Dick Heinz, Cal-Santa Barbara, DT, 0/0
14. Ed Roseborough, Arizona State, QB, 0/0
15. Fritz Latham, Tuskegee, T, 0/0

WASHINGTON REDSKINS

2. Eugene Epps, Texas-El Paso, DB, 0/0
3. Ed Cross, Arkansas-Pine Bluff, RB, 0/0
5. Bill Kishman, Colorado State, DB, 0/0
6. **Harold McLinton, Southern (LA), LB, 127/127**
7. John Didion, Oregon State, C, 24/80
7. Jeff Anderson, Virginia, RB, 0/0
8. **Larry Jr. Brown, Kansas State, RB, 102/102**
11. Eric Norri, Notre Dame, DT, 0/0
12. Bob Shannon, Tennessee State, DB, 0/0
13. Mike Shook, North Texas State, DB, 0/0
14. Rick Brand, Virginia, DT, 0/0
15. Paul Rogers, Virginia, T, 0/0

1970 NFL

ATLANTA FALCONS

1. John Small, The Citadel, DT, 33/47
2. **Art Malone, Arizona State, RB, 64/80**
3. **Andy Maurer, Oregon, G, 56/108**
3. Todd Snyder, Ohio University, WR, 30/30
4. Paul Reed, Johnson C. Smith, T, 0/0
5. Ken Mendenhall, Oklahoma, C, 0/143
5. Bruce Van Ness, Rutgers, RB, 0/0
6. Mack Herron, Kansas State, RB, 4/39
6. Randy Marshall, Linfield, DE, 15/15
6. Jade Butcher, Indiana, WR, 0/0
7. Gary Orcutt, Southern California, WR, 0/0
8. Larry Brewer, Louisiana Tech, TE, 0/0
8. Seth Miller, Arizona State, DB, 0/0
9. Roy Robinson, Montana, DB, 0/0
10. Jim Hatcher, Kansas, DB, 0/0
11. Mike Brunson, Arizona State, RB, 8/8
12. Lonnie Holton, Northern Michigan, RB, 0/0
13. Rich Stepanek, Iowa, DT, 0/0
14. Chuck Wald, North Dakota State, WR, 0/0
15. Keith Mauney, Princeton, DB, 0/0
17. Bill Bell, Kansas, K, 28/31

BALTIMORE COLTS

1. Norm Bulaich, TCU, RB, 31/120
2. **Jim Bailey, Kansas, DT, 65/116**
3. Jim O'Brien, Cincinnati, WR, 42/52
3. Ara Person, Morgan State, TE, 0/4
4. Steve Smear, Penn State, LB, 0/0
5. Billy Newsome, Grambling State, DE, 42/99
6. Ron Gardin, Arizona, DB, 14/22
7. Gordon Slade, Davidson, QB, 0/0
8. Bob Bouley, Boston College, T, 0/0
9. Barney Harris, Texas A&M, DB, 0/0
10. Dick Palmer, Kentucky, LB, 0/43
11. George Edwards, Fairmont State, RB, 0/0
12. Don Burrell, Angelo State, WR, 0/0
13. Dave Polak, Bowling Green, LB, 0/0
14. Tom Curtis, Michigan, DB, 24/24
15. Philip Gary, Kentucky State, DE, 0/0
16. Jack Maitland, Williams, RB, 14/41

BOSTON PATRIOTS

1. Phil Olsen, Utah State, DT, 0/79
3. Mike Ballou, UCLA, LB, 14/14
4. Eddie Ray, LSU, RB, 5/48
5. Bob Olson, Notre Dame, LB, 0/0
7. Odell Lawson, Langston, RB, 16/37
9. Dennis Wirgowski, Purdue, DE, 37/50
10. Henry Brown, Missouri, WR, 0/0
11. Dennis Bramlett, Texas-El Paso, T, 0/0
12. Greg Roero, New Mexico Highlands, DT, 0/0
13. Ronnie Shelley, Troy State, DB, 0/0
14. Garvie Craw, Michigan, RB, 0/0
15. Kent Schoolfield, Florida A&M, WR, 0/0

BUFFALO BILLS

1. Al Cowlings, USC, DE, 41/101
2. Dennis Shaw, San Diego State, QB, 45/50
3. Glenn Alexander, Grambling State, WR, 13/13
3. Jim Reilly, Notre Dame, G, 27/27
4. Jerry Gantt, North Carolina Central, T, 6/6
5. Steve Starnes, Tampa, LB, 0/0
6. Grant Guthrie, Florida State, K, 20/20
6. Ken Edwards, Virginia Tech, RB, 0/0
7. Wayne Fowler, Richmond, C, 10/10
8. Richard Cheek, Auburn, G, 14/14
9. Bill Bridges, Houston, G, 0/0
10. Willie Dixon, Albany State, DB, 0/0
11. Terry Williams, Grambling, RB, 0/0
12. Dave Simpson, Drake, T, 0/0
13. Stefan Schroeder, Pacific, K, 0/0
14. Bill Costen, Morris Brown, T, 0/0
15. Dave Farris, Central Michigan, TE, 0/0

CHICAGO BEARS

3. **George Farmer, UCLA, WR, 64/70**
4. **Ross Brupbacher, Texas A&M, LB, 56/56**
4. Lynn Larson, Kansas State, T, 0/1
6. Jeff Curchin, Florida State, T, 26/27
6. Bobby Cutburth, Oklahoma State, QB, 0/0
8. Dana Stephenson, Nebraska, DB, 0/0
9. Linzy Cole, TCU, WR, 7/31
10. **Glen Holloway, North Texas, G, 56/70**
11. Ted Rose, Northern Michigan, TE, 0/0
12. Butch Davis, Missouri, DB, 10/10
13. **Jimmy Gunn, USC, LB, 63/86**
14. Jim Morgan, Henderson State, WR, 0/0
15. Phil Abraira, Florida State, DB, 0/0

CINCINNATI BENGALS

1. **Mike Reid, Penn State, DT, 64/64**
2. **Ron Carpenter, North Carolina State, DT, 97/97**
3. Chip Bennett, Abilene Christian, LB, 0/0
4. Billie Hayes, San Diego State, DB, 0/14
4. Joe Stephen, Jackson State, G, 0/0
6. Sandy Durko, USC, DB, 15/40
7. **Lemar Parrish, Lincoln (MO), DB, 105/166**
8. Bill Trout, Miami (FL), DT, 0/0
9. Bill Bolden, UCLA, RB, 0/0
10. Nick Roman, Ohio State, DE, 16/52
11. Sam Wallace, Grambling, LB, 0/0
12. Tom Truesdell, Ohio Wesleyan, DT, 0/0
13. Paul Dunn, U.S. International, RB, 5/5
14. Joe Johnson, Johnson C. Smith, WR, 0/0
15. Marvin Weeks, Alcorn State, DB, 0/0
16. Larry Ely, Iowa, LB, 17/29

CLEVELAND BROWNS

1. **Bob McKay, Texas, T, 67/105**
1. **Mike Phipps, Purdue, QB, 88/119**
2. **Joe Jones, Tennessee State, DE, 90/134**
2. **Jerry Sherk, Oklahoma State, DT, 147/147**
4. Ricky Stevenson, Arizona, DB, 1/1
5. Steve Engel, Colorado, RB, 3/3
6. Mike Cilek, Iowa, QB, 0/0
7. Craig Wycinski, Michigan State, G, 6/6
8. Honester Davidson, Bowling Green, DB, 0/0
9. Geoff Brown, Pittsburgh, LB, 0/0
10. William Yanchar, Purdue, DT, 5/5
11. Gene Benner, Maine, WR, 0/0
12. Jerry Sanders, Texas Tech, K, 0/0
13. Larry Roberts, Central Missouri State, RB, 0/0
14. Jim Tharpe, Lincoln (MO), LB, 0/0
15. Guy Homoly, Illinois State, DB, 0/0

DALLAS COWBOYS

1. Duane Thomas, West Texas A&M, RB, 25/49
2. Margene Adkins, Henderson J.C., WR, 8/35
2. Bob Asher, Vanderbilt, T, 6/58
3. Steve Kiner, Tennessee, LB, 14/114
3. **Charlie Waters, Clemson, DB, 160/160**
3. Denton Fox, Texas Tech, DB, 0/0
4. **John Fitzgerald, Boston College, C, 137/137**
6. **Pat Toomay, Vanderbilt, DE, 70/142**
7. Don Abbey, Penn State, LB, 0/0
8. Jerry Dossey, Arkansas, G, 0/0
9. Zenon Andrusyshyn, UCLA, P, 0/16
10. Pete Athas, Tennessee, DB, 0/79
11. Ivan Southerland, Clemson, T, 0/0
12. Joe Williams, Wyoming, RB, 12/26
13. **Mark Washington, Morgan State, DB, 106/118**
14. Julian Martin, North Carolina Central, WR, 0/0
15. Ken DeLong, Tennessee, TE, 0/0

DENVER BRONCOS

1. Bobby Anderson, Colorado, RB, 48/54
2. Alden Roche, Southern (LA), DE, 14/120
3. John Kohler, South Dakota, T, 0/0
4. Jerry Hendren, Idaho, WR, 10/10
5. Bill McKoy, Purdue, LB, 30/44
6. John Mosier, Kansas, TE, 11/25
7. Randy Montgomery, Weber State, DB, 26/40
8. Lew Porter, Southern (LA), WR, 0/5
9. Dave Washington, Alcorn State, LB, 27/138
10. Maurice Fullerton, Tuskegee, DT, 0/0
11. Cleve Bryant, Ohio U., DB, 0/0
12. Greg Jones, Wisconsin-Whitewater, RB, 0/0
13. Jim McKoy, Parsons, DB, 0/0
14. Jeff Slipp, BYU, DE, 0/0
15. Maher Barakat, South Dakota Tech, K, 0/0

DETROIT LIONS

1. **Steve Owens, Oklahoma, RB, 53/53**
2. Ray Parson, Minnesota, T, 14/14
3. **Jim Mitchell, Virginia State, DE, 101/101**
5. Bob Parker, Memphis State, G, 0/0
6. Tony Terry, Southern California, DT, 0/0
7. Ken Geddes, Nebraska, LB, 0/95
9. **Herman Weaver, Tennessee, P, 97/158**
10. Bruce Maxwell, Arkansas, RB, 11/11
11. Roger Laird, Kentucky State, DB, 0/0
12. Emanuel Murrell, Cal Poly-SLO, DB, 0/0
13. Dave Haverdick, Morehead State, DT, 8/8
14. Charlie Brown, Northern Arizona, WR, 14/14
15. Bob Haney, Idaho, T, 0/0

GREEN BAY PACKERS

1. **Mike McCoy, Notre Dame, DT, 94/132**
1. **Rich McGeorge, Elon, TE, 116/116**
2. **Al Matthews, Texas A&M-Kingsville, DB, 84/99**
3. **Jim Carter, Minnesota, LB, 106/106**
4. Skip Butler, Texas-Arlington, K, 0/73
4. **Ken Ellis, Southern (LA), DB, 83/115**
5. Cecil Pryor, Michigan, DE, 0/0
6. Ervin Hunt, Fresno State, DB, 6/6
7. Cleo Walker, Louisville, LB, 11/22
8. Tim Mjos, North Dakota State, RB, 0/0
9. Bob Reinhard, Stanford, G, 0/0
10. Frank Patrick, Nebraska, QB, 4/4
10. Russ Melby, Weber State, DT, 0/0
11. Dan Hook, Cal State-Humboldt, LB, 0/0
12. Frank Foreman, Michigan State, WR, 0/0
13. Dave Smith, Utah, RB, 0/7
14. Bob Lints, Eastern Michigan, G, 0/0
15. Mike Carter, Sacramento State, WR, 2/7
17. **Larry Krause, St. Norbert, RB, 51/51**

HOUSTON OILERS

1. Doug Wilkerson, North Carolina Central, G, 9/204
2. Lee Brooks, Texas, DT, 36/79
2. Bill Dusenbery, Johnson C. Smith, RB, 0/8
4. Spike Jones, Georgia, P, 14/103
5. **Ron Saul, Michigan State, G, 61/142**
5. Ed Duley, Northern Arizona, DT, 0/0
6. **Benny Johnson, Johnson C. Smith, DB, 51/60**
7. Charley Olson, Concordia (MN), DB, 0/0
8. Mike McClish, Wisconsin, T, 0/0
9. Charley Blossoms, Texas Southern, DE, 0/0
10. Joe Dawkins, Wisconsin, RB, 34/98
11. Bob Morris, Duke, C, 0/0
12. Richard Dawkins, Johnson C. Smith, TE, 0/0
13. Jess Lewis, Oregon State, LB, 10/10
14. Clair Rasmussen, Wisconsin-Oshkosh, G, 0/0
15. Dave Sharp, Stanford, T, 0/0
17. Julian Fagan, Mississippi, P, 0/56

KANSAS CITY CHIEFS

1. Sid Smith, USC, C, 42/53
2. **Clyde Werner, Washington, LB, 63/63**
3. David Hadley, Alcorn State, DB, 28/28
3. Billy Bob Barnett, Texas A&M, DE, 0/0
5. Mike Oriard, Notre Dame, C, 42/42
6. Bob Hews, Princeton, T, 0/2
7. Clyde Glosson, Texas-El Paso, WR, 0/11
8. Fred Barry, Boston University, DB, 0/9
9. Charley Evans, Texas Tech, T, 0/0
10. Bob Stankovich, Arkansas, G, 0/0
11. Bill O'Neal, Grambling, RB, 0/0
12. Rod Fedorchak, Pittsburgh, G, 0/0
13. Troy Patridge, Texas-Arlington, DE, 0/0
14. Glen Dumont, American International, RB, 0/0
15. Bob Liggett, Nebraska, DT, 7/7

LOS ANGELES RAMS

1. **Jack Reynolds, Tennessee, LB, 145/198**
2. Donnie Williams, Prairie View A&M, WR, 5/5
7. Bill Nelson, Oregon State, DT, 47/47
7. Ted Provost, Ohio State, DB, 0/9
8. **Rich Saul, Michigan State, C, 176/176**
9. Dave Graham, New Mexico Highlands, T, 0/0
10. Vince Opalsky, Miami (FL), RB, 0/0
11. David Bookert, New Mexico, RB, 0/0
12. Larry Arnold, Hawaii, QB, 0/0
13. Melvin Jones, Florida A&M, WR, 0/0
14. Bob Geddes, UCLA, LB, 0/38
15. Dag Azam, West Texas State, G, 0/0

MIAMI DOLPHINS

2. **Jim Mandich, Michigan, TE, 109/119**
3. **Tim Foley, Purdue, DB, 134/134**
4. **Curtis Johnson, Toledo, DB, 125/125**
6. Dave Campbell, Auburn, DE, 0/0
7. **Jake Scott, Georgia, DB, 84/126**
8. Narvel Chavers, Jackson State, RB, 0/0
9. **Hubert Ginn, Florida A&M, RB, 63/90**
10. Dick Nittenger, Tampa, G, 0/0
11. Brownie Wheless, Rice, T, 0/0
12. **Mike Kolen, Auburn, LB, 84/84**
13. Dave Buddington, Springfield, RB, 0/0
14. Gary Brackett, Holy Cross, G, 0/0
15. Pat Hauser, East Tennessee State, WR, 0/0

MINNESOTA VIKINGS

1. **John Ward, Oklahoma State, G, 64/78**
2. Bill Cappleman, Florida State, QB, 1/8
3. Chuck Burgoon, North Park, LB, 0/0
5. Greg Jones, UCLA, RB, 0/24
7. Hap Farber, Mississippi, LB, 3/8
8. Mike Carroll, Missouri, G, 0/0
9. George Morrow, Mississippi, DE, 0/0
10. **Stu Voigt, Wisconsin, TE, 131/131**
11. Godfrey Zaunbrecher, LSU, C, 16/16
12. James Holland, Jackson State, DB, 0/0
13. Bob Pearce, Stephen F. Austin, DB, 0/0
14. Tommy Spinks, Louisiana Tech, WR, 0/0
15. Bennie Francis, Chadron State, DE, 0/0

NEW ORLEANS SAINTS

1. Ken Burrough, Texas Southern, WR, 12/156
3. Clovis Swinney, Arkansas State, DT, 14/18
4. Delles Howell, Grambling State, DB, 37/71
5. Steve Ramsey, North Texas, QB, 1/54
5. Glenn Cannon, Mississippi, DB, 0/0
6. Mel Easley, Oregon State, DB, 0/0
7. Lon Woodard, San Diego State, DE, 0/0
8. Larry Estes, Alcorn State, DE, 22/47
9. Jim Otis, Ohio State, RB, 13/116
10. Jim Brumfield, Indiana State, RB, 0/14
11. Gary Klahr, Arizona, LB, 0/0
12. Willie Davenport, Southern, DB, 0/0
13. Ralph Miller, Alabama State, TE, 0/0
14. Doug Sutherland, Wisconsin-Superior, DT, 10/164
15. Jim Vest, Washington State, DE, 0/0
17. Doug Wyatt, Tulsa, DB, 40/58

NEW YORK GIANTS

1. **Jim Files, Oklahoma, LB, 56/56**
4. Wes Grant, UCLA, DE, 0/11
5. Claude Brumfield, Tennessee State, G, 0/0
6. Duane Miller, Drake, WR, 0/0
9. **Pat Hughes, Boston University, LB, 95/141**
10. Matt Fortier, Fairmont State, DE, 0/0
11. Alan Pitcaithley, Oregon, RB, 0/0
12. Larry Nels, Wyoming, LB, 0/0
13. Gary Inskeep, Wisconsin-Stout, T, 0/0
14. Rodney Brand, Arkansas, C, 0/0
15. Warren Muir, South Carolina, RB, 0/0

NEW YORK JETS

1. **Steve Tannen, Florida, DB, 61/61**
2. **Rich Caster, Jackson State, TE, 107/161**
3. Dennis Onkotz, Penn State, LB, 9/9
4. **John Ebersole, Penn State, LB, 108/108**
5. Gary Arthur, Miami (OH), TE, 21/21
5. Cliff McClain, South Carolina State, RB, 46/46

6. Terry Stewart, Arkansas, DB, 0/0
7. Jim Williams, Virginia State, DB, 0/0
8. **Mark Lomas, Northern Arizona, DE, 67/67**
8. Jack Porter, Oklahoma, C, 0/1
9. **Eddie Bell, Idaho State, WR, 81/86**
10. Cleve Dickerson, Miami (OH), RB, 0/0
11. **Earlie Thomas, Colorado State, DB, 61/71**
12. Bill Pierson, San Diego State, C, 0/0
13. Walter Groth, Baylor, DT, 0/0
14. **John Little, Oklahoma State, DT, 70/110**
15. Tom Bayless, Purdue, DT, 2/2

OAKLAND RAIDERS

1. **Raymond Chester, Morgan State, TE, 103/172**
2. Ted Koy, Texas, TE, 14/67
3. **Gerald Irons, Maryland-Eastern Shore, LB, 77/135**
4. **Tony Cline, Miami (FL), DE, 72/93**
5. Art Laster, Maryland-Eastern Shore, T, 0/14
6. Alvin Wyatt, Bethune-Cookman, DB, 11/43
7. Steve Svitak, Boise State, LB, 0/0
8. Mike Wynn, Nebraska, DE, 0/0
9. Ike Hill, Catawba, WB, 0/49
10. Gordon Bosserman, UCLA, T, 0/0
11. Emery Hicks, Kansas, LB, 0/0
12. Gerry De Loach, Cal-Davis, G, 0/0
13. Don Highsmith, Michigan State, RB, 30/37
14. John Riley, Auburn, K, 0/0

PHILADELPHIA EAGLES

1. **Steve Zabel, Oklahoma, LB, 60/124**
2. Ray Jones, Southern (LA), DB, 12/30
3. Lee Bouggess, Louisville, RB, 32/32
7. Terry Brennan, Notre Dame, T, 0/0
8. Ira Gordon, Kansas State, G, 0/62
9. David King, Stephen F. Austin, LB, 0/0
10. Steve Jaggard, Memphis State, DB, 0/0
11. Billy Walik, Villanova, WR, 32/32
12. Robert Jones, Grambling, DT, 0/0
13. **Dick Stevens, Baylor, T, 60/60**
14. Mark Moseley, Stephen F. Austin State, K, 14/213
15. John Carlos, San Jose State, WR, 0/0
16. Tuufuli Uperesa, Montana, G, 2/2

PITTSBURGH STEELERS

1. **Terry Bradshaw, Louisiana Tech, QB, 168/168**
2. **Ron Shanklin, North Texas, WR, 67/72**
3. **Mel Blount, Southern (LA), DB, 200/200**
4. Ed George, Wake Forest, T, 0/56
4. Jim Evenson, Oregon, RB, 0/0
5. Jon Staggers, Missouri, WR, 26/70
6. Manuel Barrera, Kansas State, LB, 0/0
6. Clarence Kegler, South Carolina State, T, 0/0
7. Danny Griffin, Texas-Arlington, RB, 0/0
8. Dave Smith, Indiana State, WR, 34/44
9. Carl Crennel, West Virginia, LB, 3/3
10. Isaiah Brown, Stanford, DB, 0/0
11. Calvin Hunt, Baylor, C, 0/21
12. Rick Sharp, Washington, T, 17/29
13. Billy Main, Oregon State, RB, 0/0
14. Bert Askson, Texas Southern, DE, 11/54
15. Glen Keppy, Wisconsin-Platteville, DT, 0/0

SAN DIEGO CHARGERS

1. Walker Gillette, Richmond, WR, 25/91
2. Tom Williams, California-Davis, DT, 27/27
4. Bill Maddox, Syracuse, TE, 0/0
5. Pettus Farrar, Norfolk State, RB, 0/0
6. Billy Parks, Long Beach State, WR, 10/60
7. Jim Fabish, Texas-El Paso, DB, 0/0
8. Wayne Clark, U.S. International, QB, 25/40
9. **Chris Fletcher, Temple, DB, 76/76**
10. Mac Steen, Florida, G, 0/0
11. Jack Protz, Syracuse, LB, 14/14
12. Howard Gravelle, Cal-Davis, TE, 0/0
13. Bernard Bradley, Utah State, DB, 0/0
14. Tyrone Caldwell, South Carolina State, DT, 0/0
15. Eugene Childs, Texas-El Paso, RB, 0/0

SAN FRANCISCO 49ERS

1. **Cedrick Hardman, North Texas, DE, 139/171**
1. **Bruce Taylor, Boston University, DB, 109/109**
2. **John Isenbarger, Indiana, RB, 55/55**
4. Vic Washington, Wyoming, RB, 40/67
5. Gary McArthur, Southern California, T, 0/0
6. Rusty Clark, Houston, QB, 0/0
7. Jim Strong, Houston, RB, 3/31
8. Carter Campbell, Weber State, DE, 1/43
9. Preston Riley, Memphis, WR, 39/40
10. **Larry Schreiber, Tennessee Tech, RB, 60/74**
11. Dan Crockett, Toledo, WR, 0/0
12. Bill Tant, Dayton, T, 0/0
13. Jim Vanderslice, Texas Christian, LB, 0/0
14. Jack King, Clemson, G, 0/0
15. Dave Delsignore, Youngstown State, WR, 0/0

ST. LOUIS CARDINALS

1. Larry Stegent, Texas A&M, RB, 7/7
2. Chuck Hutchison, Ohio State, G, 24/47
2. Jim Corrigall, Kent State, LB, 0/0
3. Charlie Pittman, Penn State, RB, 8/18
3. Eric Harris, Colorado, DB, 0/0
4. Greg Lens, Trinity (TX), DT, 0/21
4. Don Parish, Stanford, LB, 17/19
5. Tom Lloyd, Bowling Green, T, 0/0
5. Barry Pierson, Michigan, DB, 0/0
6. James Manuel, Toledo, T, 0/0
7. **Jim McFarland, Nebraska, TE, 61/68**
8. **Tom Banks, Auburn, C, 116/116**
8. Mike Holmgren, Southern California, QB, 0/0
9. Paul White, Texas-El Paso, RB, 11/11
10. Tony Plummer, Pacific, DB, 1/41
11. Mike Siwek, Western Michigan, DT, 2/2
12. Charles Collins, Kansas State, WR, 0/0
13. Jack Thomas, Mississippi State, G, 0/0
14. Ray Groth, Utah, WR, 0/0
15. Ron Wilson, West Illinois, WR, 0/0

WASHINGTON REDSKINS

2. **Bill Brundige, Colorado, DT, 107/107**
4. **Paul Laaveg, Iowa, G, 72/72**
5. Danny Pierce, Memphis, RB, 2/2
5. **Manny Sistrunk, Arkansas-Pine Bluff, DT, 63/123**
7. Jim Harris, Howard Payne, DB, 3/5
7. Roland Merritt, Maryland, WR, 0/0
8. Paul Johnson, Penn State, DB, 0/0
9. Ralph Sonntag, Maryland, T, 0/0
11. Mack Alston, Maryland-Eastern Shore, TE, 34/145
12. Jim Kates, Penn State, LB, 0/0
13. Joe Patterson, Lawrence, T, 0/0
14. Tony Moro, Dayton, RB, 0/0
15. Vic Lewandowski, Holy Cross, C, 0/0

1971 NFL

ATLANTA FALCONS

1. Joe Profit, Louisiana-Monroe, RB, 15/23
2. **Ken Burrow, San Diego State, WR, 64/64**
3. Leo Hart, Duke, QB, 1/3
4. Mike Potchad, Pittsburg State (KS), T, 0/0
5. Ray Jarvis, Norfolk State, WR, 6/82
6. **Ray Brown, West Texas A&M, DB, 94/137**
6. **Tom Hayes, San Diego State, DB, 69/78**
7. Wes Chesson, Duke, WR, 29/43
8. **Dennis Havig, Colorado, G, 55/76**
9. Alvin Griffin, Tuskegee, WR, 0/0
10. Faddie Tillman, Boise State, DT, 0/1
11. Larry Shears, Lincoln (MO), DB, 10/10
12. Ronnie Lowe, Fort Valley State, WR, 0/0
13. Dan Crooks, Wisconsin, DB, 0/0
14. Deryl Comer, Texas, TE, 0/0
15. Wallace Clark, Auburn, RB, 0/0

BALTIMORE COLTS

1. Lenny Dunlap, North Texas, DB, 4/46
1. **Don McCauley, North Carolina, RB, 156/156**
2. Bill Atessis, Texas, DE, 0/5
3. Karl Douglas, Texas A&I, QB, 0/0
5. John Andrews, Indiana, TE, 22/23
6. Ken Frith, Northeast Louisiana, DT, 0/0
7. Gordon Bowdell, Michigan State, WR, 0/2
8. Willie Bogan, Dartmouth, DB, 0/0
9. Bill Burnett, Arkansas, RB, 0/0
10. Rex Kern, Ohio State, DB, 33/41
11. Dave Jones, Baylor, LB, 0/0
11. Bobby Wuensch, Texas, T, 0/0
12. Bill Triplett, Michigan State, WR, 0/0
13. Tom Neville, Yale, LB, 0/0
14. Mike Mikolayunas, Davidson, RB, 0/0
15. Mike Hogan, Michigan State, LB, 0/0
17. Don Nottingham, Kent State, RB, 31/98

BALTIMORE COLTS

5. Tim Kelly, Notre Dame, LB, 0/0
6. David Hardt, Kentucky, TE, 0/0
10. Layne McDowell, Iowa, T, 0/0
11. Dan Schneiss, Nebraska, TE, 0/0
12. John Rodman, Northwestern, T, 0/0
13. Lewis Swain, Alabama A&M, DB, 0/0
15. Nick McGarry, Massachusetts, TE, 0/0

BUFFALO BILLS

1. **J.D. Hill, Arizona State, WR, 61/73**
2. Jan White, Ohio State, TE, 27/27
3. **Jim Braxton, West Virginia, RB, 80/90**
3. Bruce Jarvis, Washington, C, 24/24
5. Tim Beamer, Illinois, DB, 12/12
5. **Donnie Green, Purdue, T, 75/92**
6. Bill McKinley, Arizona, DE, 7/7
7. **Bob Chandler, USC, WR, 116/145**
8. Louis Ross, South Carolina State, DE, 19/20
8. Tyrone Walls, Missouri, RB, 0/0
9. Bob Strickland, Auburn, LB, 0/0
11. Andy Browder, Texas A&I, T, 0/0
12. Jim Sheffield, Texas A&M, K, 0/0
13. Busty Underwood, Texas Christian, QB, 0/0
14. Jim Hoots, Missouri Southern, DE, 0/0
15. Charley Cole, Toledo, RB, 0/0

CHICAGO BEARS

1. Joe Moore, Missouri, RB, 23/23
2. Charlie Ford, Houston, DB, 41/60
2. Jim Harrison, Missouri, RB, 38/38
3. Tony McGee, Bishop, DE, 42/202
3. **Bob Newton, Nebraska, G, 59/142**
4. Jerry Moore, Arkansas, DB, 24/43
6. Earl Thomas, Houston, WR, 39/71
7. Buddy Lee, Louisiana State, QB, 0/0
7. Dennis Ferris, Pittsburgh, RB, 0/0
8. Karl Weiss, Vanderbilt, T, 0/0
9. Lester McClain, Tennessee, WR, 0/0
10. Larry Rowden, Houston, LB, 16/16
11. Cliff Hardy, Michigan State, DB, 1/1
12. Steve Booras, Mesa J.C., DE, 0/0
13. Ed Nicholas, North Carolina State, T, 0/0
14. Willie Lewis, Arizona, RB, 0/0
15. Ron Maciejowski, Ohio State, QB, 0/0

CINCINNATI BENGALS

1. **Vern Holland, Tennessee State, T, 119/131**
2. Steve Lawson, Kansas, G, 10/64
3. **Ken Anderson, Augustana (IL), QB, 192/192**
4. Fred Willis, Boston College, RB, 19/77
5. Art May, Tuskegee, DE, 0/11
7. Neal Craig, Fisk, DB, 40/79
8. Fred Herring, Tennessee State, DB, 0/0
9. Gary Gustafson, Montana State, LB, 0/0
10. Jack Stambaugh, Oregon, G, 0/0
11. Ed Marshall, Cameron, WR, 13/33
12. James Hayden, Memphis State, DE, 0/0
13. David Knapman, Central Washington, TE, 0/0
14. Irvin Mallory, Virginia Union, DB, 0/2
15. Bob Thomas, Arizona State, RB, 0/48

CLEVELAND BROWNS

1. **Clarence Scott, Kansas State, DB, 186/186**
2. Bo Cornell, Washington, LB, 28/96
3. **Charlie Hall, Houston, LB, 146/146**
3. Paul Staroba, Michigan, WR, 8/10
4. Bubba Pena, Massachusetts, G, 2/2
5. Stan Brown, Purdue, WR, 6/6
6. **Doug Dieken, Illinois, T, 203/203**
6. Jay Dixon, Boston, DE, 0/0
7. Bob Jacobs, Wyoming, K, 0/0
8. Larry Zelina, Ohio State, RB, 0/0
9. Wilmur Levels, North Texas State, DB, 0/0
10. Steve Casteel, Oklahoma, LB, 0/0
11. Mike Sikich, Northwestern, G, 3/3
12. Tony Blanchard, North Carolina, TE, 0/0
13. Thad Jamula, Lehigh, T, 0/0
14. Rick Kingrea, Tulane, LB, 21/91
15. Bill Green, Western Kentucky, DB, 0/0

DALLAS COWBOYS

1. Tody Smith, USC, DE, 17/69
2. Ike Thomas, Bishop, DB, 7/37
3. **Bill Gregory, Wisconsin, DE, 96/142**
3. Sam Scarber, New Mexico, RB, 0/25
4. Joe Carter, Grambling, TE, 0/0
4. Adam Mitchell, Mississippi, T, 0/0
5. Ron Kadziel, Stanford, LB, 0/14
6. Steve Maier, Northern Arizona, WR, 0/0
7. Bill Griffin, Catawba, T, 0/0
8. Ron Jessie, Kansas, WR, 0/138
9. Honor Jackson, Pacific, DB, 0/32
10. Rodney Wallace, New Mexico, T, 37/37
11. Ernest Bonwell, Lane, DT, 0/0
12. Steve Goepel, Colgate, QB, 0/0
13. James Ford, Texas Southern, RB, 0/14
14. Tyrone Covey, Utah State, DB, 0/0
15. Bob Young, Delaware, TE, 0/0

DENVER BRONCOS

1. **Marv Montgomery, USC, T, 57/81**
2. Dwight Harrison, Texas A&M-Kingsville, DB, 12/108
4. **Lyle Alzado, Yankton, DE, 99/196**
4. Cleo Johnson, Alcorn State, DB, 0/0
6. Harold Phillips, Michigan State, DB, 0/0
7. Doug Adams, Ohio State, LB, 0/49
8. Tom Beard, Michigan State, C, 0/12
9. John Handy, Purdue, LB, 0/0
10. Carlis Harris, Idaho State, WR, 0/0
11. Roger Roitsch, Rice, DT, 0/0
12. Floyd Franks, Mississippi, WR, 0/0
13. Craig Blackford, Evansville, QB, 0/0
14. **Tommy Lyons, Georgia, G, 73/73**
15. Larry James, Norfolk State, RB, 0/0

DETROIT LIONS

1. Bob Bell, Cincinnati, DT, 41/100
2. Dave Thompson, Clemson, T, 35/56
2. **Charlie Weaver, USC, LB, 142/147**
3. Al Clark, Eastern Michigan, DB, 9/69
4. Larry Woods, Tennessee State, DT, 13/47
5. Pete Newell, Michigan, G, 0/0
6. Frank Harris, Boston College, QB, 0/0
6. Herman Franklin, Southern California, WR, 0/0
7. Brownie Wheless, Rice, T, 0/0
8. Ken Lee, Washington, LB, 1/13
9. Mickey Zofko, Auburn, RB, 37/44
11. Phil Webb, Colorado State, DB, 0/0
12. Bill Pilconis, Pittsburgh, WR, 0/0
13. David Abercrombie, Tulane, RB, 0/0
14. Tom Lorenz, Iowa State, TE, 0/0
15. Ed Coates, Central Missouri State, WR, 0/0
17. Gordon Jolley, Utah, G, 32/59

GREEN BAY PACKERS

1. **John Brockington, Ohio State, RB, 85/95**
2. Virgil Robinson, Grambling State, RB, 0/14
3. **Charlie Hall, Pittsburgh, DB, 83/83**
5. Donnell Smith, Southern (LA), DE, 4/25
5. Jim Stillwagon, Ohio State, LB, 0/0
6. Scott Hunter, Alabama, QB, 35/64
7. Dave Davis, Tennessee State, WR, 24/33
7. James Johnson, Bishop, WR, 0/0
8. Win Headley, Wake Forest, C, 0/0
9. Barry Mayer, Minnesota, RB, 0/0
10. Kevin Hunt, Doane, T, 3/70
11. John Lanier, Parsons, RB, 0/0
12. Greg Hendren, California, G, 0/0
13. Jack Martin, Angelo State, RB, 0/0
14. LeRoy Spears, Moorhead State, DE, 0/0
15. Len Garrett, New Mexico Highlands, TE, 30/55

HOUSTON OILERS

1. **Dan Pastorini, Santa Clara, QB, 125/140**
3. Lynn Dickey, Kansas State, QB, 47/152
4. Larron Jackson, Missouri, G, 0/83
5. Willie Armstrong, Grambling, RB, 0/0
6. **Willie Alexander, Alcorn State, DB, 122/122**
7. Phil Croyle, California, LB, 27/32
7. Larry Watson, Morgan State, T, 0/0
9. Floyd Rice, Alcorn State, LB, 33/102
10. Russell Price, North Carolina Central, DE, 0/0
11. Macon Hughes, Rice, WR, 0/0
12. John Thompson, Minnesota, G, 0/0
13. Joe Hoing, Arkansas Tech, G, 0/0
14. Dick Adams, Miami (OH), DB, 0/0
15. Andy Hopkins, Stephen F. Austin State, RB, 2/2

KANSAS CITY CHIEFS

1. Elmo Wright, Houston, WR, 45/51
2. **Wilbur Young, William Penn, DE, 94/153**
2. Scott Lewis, Grambling, DE, 0/0
4. David Robinson, Jacksonville State, TE, 0/0
5. Mike Adamle, Northwestern, RB, 22/76
6. **Kerry Reardon, Iowa, DB, 58/58**
8. **Mike Sensibaugh, Ohio State, DB, 63/92**
8. Rick Telander, Northwestern, DB, 0/0
9. Alvin Hawes, Minnesota, T, 0/0
10. Bruce Jankowski, Ohio State, WR, 9/9
11. Nate Allen, Texas Southern, DB, 44/108
12. Tony Esposito, Pittsburgh, RB, 0/0
13. Chuck Hixson, Southern Methodist, QB, 0/0
14. Bruce Bergey, UCLA, DE, 6/7
15. Mike Montgomery, Southwest Texas State, DB, 0/0

LOS ANGELES RAMS

1. **Isiah Robertson, Southern (LA), LB, 111/168**
1. **Jack Youngblood, Florida, DE, 202/202**
3. **Dave Elmendorf, Texas A&M, DB, 130/130**
4. Steve Worster, Texas, RB, 0/0
8. Tony Garay, Hofstra, DE, 0/0
9. Joe Schmidt, Miami (FL), WR, 0/0
10. Don Popplewell, Colorado, C, 0/0
11. Charlie Richards, Richmond, QB, 0/0

12. Kirk Behrendt, Wisconsin-Whitewater, T, 0/0
13. Russell Harrison, Kansas State, RB, 0/0
14. Lionel Coleman, Oregon, DB, 0/0
15. Gary Kos, Notre Dame, G, 0/0
17. Joe Sweet, Tennessee State, WR, 19/34
17. Randy Vataha, Stanford, WR, 0/86

MIAMI DOLPHINS

2. Otto Stowe, Iowa State, WR, 21/36
3. Dale Farley, West Virginia, LB, 4/13
4. Joe Theismann, Notre Dame, QB, 0/167
6. Dennis Coleman, Mississippi, LB, 0/9
7. Ron Dickerson, Kansas State, DB, 0/0
9. **Vern Den Herder, Iowa Central, DE, 166/166**
10. Ron Maree, Purdue, DT, 0/0
11. Vic Surma, Penn State, T, 0/0
12. Leroy Byars, Alcorn State, RB, 0/0
13. Lonnie Hepburn, Texas Southern, DB, 0/31
14. David Vaughn, Memphis State, TE, 0/0
15. Bob Richards, California, G, 0/0

MINNESOTA VIKINGS

1. Leo Hayden, Ohio State, RB, 7/13
3. Eddie Hackett, Alcorn State, WR, 0/0
4. Vince Clements, Connecticut, RB, 0/16
7. Gene Mack, Texas-El Paso, LB, 0/0
8. John Farley, Johnson C. Smith, DE, 0/0
9. Tim Sullivan, Iowa, RB, 0/0
10. Chris Morris, Indiana, T, 0/22
11. Mike Walker, Tulane, DE, 0/5
12. Reggie Holmes, Wisconsin-Stout, DB, 0/0
13. Benny Fry, Houston, C, 0/0
14. Jim Gallagher, Yale, LB, 0/0
15. **Jeff Wright, Minnesota, DB, 83/83**
17. Ken Duncan, Tulsa, P, 0/2

NEW ENGLAND PATRIOTS

1. **Jim Plunkett, Stanford, QB, 61/157**
2. **Julius Adams, Texas Southern, DE, 206/206**
9. Josh Ashton, Tulsa, RB, 38/40
14. Alfred Sykes, Florida A&M, WR, 4/4

NEW ORLEANS SAINTS

1. **Archie Manning, Mississippi, QB, 134/151**
2. Sam Holden, Grambling State, T, 9/9
3. **Bivian Lee, Prairie View A&M, DB, 65/65**
4. Carlos Bell, Houston, TE, 1/1
4. Dee Martin, Kentucky State, DB, 14/14
4. **Don Morrison, Texas-Arlington, T, 94/123**
6. Richard Winther, Mississippi, C, 5/16
6. Don Moorhead, Michigan, RB, 0/0
7. **Bob Newland, Oregon, WR, 56/56**
7. Larry DiNardo, Notre Dame, G, 0/0
8. Bob Gresham, West Virginia, RB, 27/75
8. Jimmy Elder, Southern, DB, 0/0
9. Tom Williams, Willamette, DB, 0/0
10. Rocky Pamplin, Hawaii, RB, 0/0
11. **Bob Pollard, Weber State, DE, 92/154**
12. Ron Gathright, Morehead State, DB, 0/0
13. Don Burchfield, Ball State, TE, 14/14
14. Bobby Scott, Tennessee, QB, 41/41
15. Bart Graves, Tulane, T, 0/0
16. Craig Robinson, Houston, T, 19/19

NEW YORK GIANTS

1. Rocky Thompson, West Texas A&M, RB, 29/29
2. Wayne Walton, Abilene Christian, T, 14/37
3. Ron Hornsby, Southeastern Louisiana, LB, 49/49
4. Dave Tipton, Stanford, DE, 25/62
8. Ted Gregory, Delaware, DE, 0/0
9. Ed Thomas, Lebanon Valley, LB, 0/0
10. **Henry Reed, Weber State, DE, 51/51**
11. Mark Ellison, Dayton, G, 28/28
12. Tom Blanchard, Oregon, P, 42/148
13. Dave Roller, Kentucky, DT, 14/92
14. Charlie Evans, USC, RB, 19/25
15. Jim Wright, Notre Dame, LB, 0/0
17. Coleman Zeno, Grambling State, WR, 2/2

NEW YORK JETS

1. **John Riggins, Kansas, RB, 61/175**
2. John Mooring, Tampa, T, 42/53
3. Chris Farasopoulos, Brigham Young, DB, 36/42
4. Willie Zapalac, Texas, LB, 33/33
6. **Phil Wise, Nebraska-Omaha, DB, 62/92**
7. Scott Palmer, Texas, DT, 2/7
8. Roy Kirksey, Maryland-Eastern Shore, G, 14/34
9. John Curtis, Springfield, TE, 0/0
10. Jim Bettis, Michigan, DB, 0/0
11. Vern Studdard, Mississippi, WR, 8/8
12. **Rich Sowells, Alcorn State, DB, 69/78**
13. John Eggold, Arizona, DE, 0/0
14. John Harpring, Michigan, G, 0/0
15. Dan Dyches, South Carolina, C, 0/0
16. Steve Harkey, Georgia Tech, RB, 25/25

OAKLAND RAIDERS

1. **Jack Tatum, Ohio State, DB, 120/136**
2. **Phil Villapiano, Bowling Green State, LB, 118/163**
3. Warren Koegel, Penn State, C, 16/21
4. **Clarence Davis, USC, RB, 88/88**
5. **Bob Moore, Stanford, TE, 70/93**
6. Greg Slough, USC, LB, 22/22
7. Don Martin, Yale, DB, 0/29
9. Dave Garnett, Pittsburgh, RB, 0/0
10. Bill West, Tennessee State, DB, 0/8
10. Tim Oesterling, UCLA, DT, 0/0
11. Jim Poston, South Carolina, DT, 0/0
12. **Horace Jones, Louisville, DE, 70/71**
13. Mick Natzel, Central Michigan, DB, 0/0
14. Thomas Gipson, North Texas, DT, 4/4
15. Andy Giles, William & Mary, DE, 0/0

PHILADELPHIA EAGLES

1. Richard Harris, Grambling State, DE, 39/93
2. Henry Allison, San Diego State, G, 20/55
4. Happy Feller, Texas, K, 9/21
5. Tom Shellabarger, San Diego State, T, 0/0
6. Jack Smith, Troy State, DB, 5/5
6. Wyck Neely, Mississippi, DB, 0/0
7. **Harold Carmichael, Southern (LA), WR, 180/182**
8. Len Gotshalk, Humboldt State, T, 0/66
9. Len Pettigrew, Ashland, LB, 0/0
10. **Tom Bailey, Florida State, RB, 50/50**
11. Sonny Davis, Tennessee State, RB, 14/14
12. Rich Saathoff, Northern Arizona, DE, 0/0
13. Danny Lester, Texas, DB, 0/0
14. Bob Creech, TCU, LB, 16/18
15. Ed Fisher, Prairie View A&M, G, 0/0

PITTSBURGH STEELERS

1. **Frank Lewis, Grambling State, WR, 75/155**
2. **Jack Ham, Penn State, LB, 162/162**
3. Steve Davis, Delaware State, RB, 39/65
4. **Gerry Mullins, USC, G, 124/124**
4. **Dwight White, Texas A&M-Commerce, DE, 126/126**
5. Ralph Anderson, West Texas A&M, DB, 21/34
5. **Larry Brown, Kansas, T, 167/167**
5. Mel Holmes, North Carolina A&T, G, 29/29
5. Fred Brister, Mississippi, LB, 0/0
6. Craig Hanneman, Oregon State, DE, 27/47
7. Worthy McClure, Mississippi, T, 0/0
8. Larry Crowe, Texas Southern, RB, 0/6
8. **Ernie Holmes, Texas Southern, DT, 81/84**
8. Paul Rogers, Nebraska, K, 0/0
9. Mike Anderson, Louisiana State, LB, 0/0
10. Jim O'Shea, Boston College, TE, 0/0
11. **Mike Wagner, Western Illinois, DB, 119/119**
13. Al Young, South Carolina State, WR, 15/15
14. McKinney Evans, New Mexico Highlands, DB, 0/0
15. Ray Makin, Kentucky, G, 0/0

SAN DIEGO CHARGERS

3. Mike Montgomery, Kansas State, RB, 11/37
5. Bryant Salter, Pittsburgh, DB, 41/71
5. Ray White, Syracuse, LB, 18/38
5. Phil Asack, Duke, DE, 0/0
6. Jacob Mayes, Tennessee State, RB, 0/0
7. Chuck Dicus, Arkansas, WR, 24/24
8. Leon Van Gorkum, San Diego State, DE, 0/0
9. John Tanner, Tennessee Tech, LB, 14/40
10. Gary Nowak, Michigan State, DT, 5/5
11. Leon Burns, Long Beach State, RB, 14/28
11. Don Pinson, Tennessee State, DB, 0/0
12. Wes Garnett, Utah State, WR, 0/0
13. Sammy Milner, Mississippi State, WR, 0/0
14. Edward O'Daniel, Texas Southern, DE, 0/0
15. Eric Humston, Muskingum, LB, 0/0

SAN FRANCISCO 49ERS

1. William Anderson, Ohio State, DB, 12/15
2. Ernie Janet, Washington, G, 0/31
2. Joe Orduna, Nebraska, RB, 0/39
3. Willie Parker, North Texas, C, 0/94
3. Sam Dickerson, Southern California, WR, 0/0
4. Tony Harris, Toledo, DB, 4/4
5. Marty Huff, Michigan, LB, 3/3
5. Dean Shaternick, Kansas State, T, 0/0
5. George Wells, New Mexico State, LB, 0/0
6. Al Bresler, Auburn, WR, 0/0
7. **John Watson, Oklahoma, G, 80/95**
8. Jim McCann, Arizona State, P, 26/31
9. Therman Couch, Iowa State, LB, 0/0
10. Ron Cardo, Wisconsin-Oshkosh, RB, 0/0
10. Ernie Jennings, Air Force, WR, 0/0
11. Joe Reed, Mississippi State, QB, 21/50
12. Jim Bunch, Wisconsin-Platteville, DT, 0/0
13. John Bullock, Purdue, RB, 0/0
14. Bill Dunstan, Utah State, DT, 0/80
15. John Lennon, Colgate, T, 0/0

ST. LOUIS CARDINALS

1. **Norm Thompson, Utah, DB, 76/115**
2. **Dan Dierdorf, Michigan, T, 160/160**
3. Jim Livesay, Richmond, WR, 0/0
4. Larry Willingham, Auburn, DB, 20/20
5. Rocky Wallace, Missouri, LB, 0/0
6. **Mel Gray, Missouri, WR, 145/145**
7. James Cooch, Colorado, DB, 0/0
8. **Ron Yankowski, Kansas State, DE, 128/128**
9. Mike Savoy, Black Hills State, WR, 0/0
10. Ron Miller, McNeese State, T, 0/0
11. Rick Ogle, Colorado, LB, 6/10
12. Tim Von Dulm, Portland State, QB, 0/0
13. Jeff Allen, Iowa State, DB, 1/1
14. Doug Klausen, Arizona, T, 0/0
15. Ted Heiskell, Houston, RB, 0/0

WASHINGTON REDSKINS

2. Cotton Speyrer, Texas, WR, 0/36
6. Conway Hayman, Delaware, G, 0/77
7. Willie Germany, Morgan State, DB, 0/42
9. Mike Fanucci, Arizona State, DE, 14/40
10. Jesse Taylor, Cincinnati, RB, 0/14
11. **George Starke, Columbia, T, 156/156**
12. Jeff Severson, Long Beach State, DB, 12/83
13. Dan Ryczek, Virginia, C, 42/102
14. Bill Bynum, Western New Mexico, QB, 0/0
15. Anthony Christnovich, Wisconsin-LaCrosse, G, 0/0

1972 NFL

ATLANTA FALCONS

1. Clarence Ellis, Notre Dame, DB, 41/41
2. Rosie Manning, Northeastern State (OK), DT, 14/24
2. Steve Okoniewski, Montana, DT, 0/52
2. Pat Sullivan, Auburn, QB, 30/30
3. Les Goodman, Yankton, RB, 0/19
4. Andrew Howard, Grambling, DT, 0/0
5. Ralph Cindrich, Pittsburgh, LB, 0/36
5. Billy Taylor, Michigan, RB, 0/0
6. Mike Perfetti, Minnesota, DB, 0/0
6. Fred Riley, Idaho, WR, 0/0
7. Lance Moon, Wisconsin, RB, 0/0
8. Henry Brandon, Southern, RB, 0/0
9. **Ray Easterling, Richmond, DB, 83/83**
11. Jack Phillips, Grambling, WR, 0/0
12. Larry Mialik, Wisconsin, TE, 42/49
13. Henry Sovio, Hawaii, TE, 0/0
14. Tom Chandler, Minnesota, LB, 0/0
15. Oscar Jenkins, Virginia Union, DB, 0/0

BALTIMORE COLTS

1. Tom Drougas, Oregon, T, 27/65
2. **Glenn Doughty, Michigan, WR, 103/103**
2. Jack Mildren, Oklahoma, DB, 28/42
2. **Lydell Mitchell, Penn State, RB, 81/111**
4. Eric Allen, Michigan State, WR, 0/0
5. Don Croft, Texas-El Paso, DT, 0/34
6. **Bruce Laird, American International, DB, 141/164**
7. John Sykes, Morgan State, WR, 0/2
8. Al Qualls, Oklahoma, LB, 0/0
8. Van Brownson, Nebraska, QB, 0/0
9. Gary Hambell, Dayton, DT, 0/0
10. Dave Schilling, Oregon State, RB, 0/0
11. Fred DeBernardi, Texas-El Paso, DE, 0/7
12. Gary Theiler, Tennessee, TE, 0/0
13. Herb Washington, Michigan, WR, 0/0
14. John Morris, Missouri Valley, C, 0/0
15. Robin Parkhouse, Alabama, LB, 0/0
17. **Stan White, Ohio State, LB, 112/153**

BUFFALO BILLS

1. **Walt Patulski, Notre Dame, DE, 56/70**
2. **Reggie McKenzie, Michigan, G, 147/171**
3. Fred Swendsen, Notre Dame, DE, 0/0
4. Randy Jackson, Wichita State, RB, 5/21
5. Leon Garror, Alcorn State, DB, 16/16
5. Bob Penchion, Alcorn State, G, 17/48
7. Ralph Stepaniak, Notre Dame, DB, 0/0
8. Paul Gibson, Texas-El Paso, WR, 0/1
9. Steve Vogel, Boise State, LB, 0/0
10. Maurice Tyler, Morgan State, DB, 14/86
11. Bill Light, Minnesota, LB, 0/0
12. Jeff Baker, U.S. International, WR, 0/0
13. Eddie Moss, Southeast Missouri State, RB, 0/35
14. Karl Salb, Kansas, DT, 0/0

CHICAGO BEARS

1. **Lionel Antoine, Southern Illinois, T, 68/68**
1. **Craig Clemons, Iowa, DB, 82/82**
3. Johnny Musso, Alabama, RB, 30/30
5. **Bob Parsons, Penn State, TE, 170/170**
6. **Bob Pifferini, UCLA, LB, 52/57**
7. **Jim Osborne, Southern (LA), DT, 186/186**
7. Jim Fassel, Long Beach State, QB, 0/0
8. Ralph Wirtz, North Dakota State, WR, 0/0
9. Larry Horton, Iowa, DE, 10/10
10. Jack Turnbull, Oregon State, C, 0/0
11. Ed Wimberly, Jackson State, DB, 0/0
12. Doug Neill, Texas A&M, RB, 0/0
13. Jay Rood, South Dakota-Springfield, T, 0/0
14. Bob Brown, Rice, WR, 0/0
15. Roger Lawson, Western Michigan, RB, 22/22
16. Bill McKinney, West Texas A&M, LB, 8/8

CINCINNATI BENGALS

1. **Sherman White, California, DE, 52/158**
2. **Tommy Casanova, LSU, DB, 71/71**
3. **Jim LeClair, North Dakota, LB, 158/158**
4. **Bernard Jackson, Washington State, DB, 68/118**
5. Tom DeLeone, Ohio State, C, 27/176
7. Steve Conley, Kansas, LB, 1/8
8. Dan Kratzer, Missouri Valley, WR, 0/1
9. Stan Walters, Syracuse, T, 26/153
10. Brian Foster, Colorado, DB, 0/0
11. Kent Pederson, Cal-Santa Barbara, TE, 0/0
12. Fredrick Wegis, Cal Poly-SLO, DB, 0/0
13. James Hamilton, Arkansas State, QB, 0/0
14. Steve Porter, Indiana, WR, 0/0
15. Hosea Minnieweather, Jackson State, DT, 0/0
17. Dave Green, Ohio University, P, 28/76

CLEVELAND BROWNS

1. **Thom Darden, Michigan, DB, 128/128**
2. Cliff Brooks, Tennessee State, DB, 41/58
2. Lester Sims, Alabama, DE, 0/0
5. George Hunt, Tennessee, K, 0/28
5. Greg Kucera, Northern Colorado, RB, 0/0
6. Leonard Forey, Texas A&M, G, 0/0
7. Don Wesley, Maryland-Eastern Shore, T, 0/0
8. Hugh McKinnis, Arizona State, RB, 41/52
9. Billy Lefear, Henderson State, RB, 43/43
9. Larry McKee, Arizona, G, 0/0
10. Herschell Mosier, Northwestern Oklahoma, DT, 0/0
11. Mel Long, Toledo, LB, 42/42
12. Bernie Chapman, Texas-El Paso, DB, 0/0
13. **Brian Sipe, San Diego State, QB, 125/125**
14. Ed Stewart, East Central (OK), G, 0/0
15. Jewel McCullar, Cal State-Chico, LB, 0/0

DALLAS COWBOYS

1. Bill Thomas, Boston College, RB, 7/27
2. John Babinecz, Villanova, LB, 26/40
2. **Robert Newhouse, Houston, RB, 168/168**
2. Charlie McKee, Arizona, WR, 0/0
3. Marv Bateman, Utah, P, 29/76
3. Mike Keller, Michigan, LB, 5/5
4. Tim Kearney, Northern Michigan, LB, 0/106
4. Robert West, San Diego State, WR, 0/29
4. Charlie Zapiec, Penn State, LB, 0/0
6. Charles Bolden, Iowa, DB, 0/0
8. Ralph Coleman, North Carolina A&T, LB, 1/1
9. Roy Bell, Oklahoma, RB, 0/0
10. Richard Amman, Florida State, DE, 0/28
11. Lonnie Leonard, North Carolina A&T, DE, 0/0
12. Jimmy Harris, Ohio State, WR, 0/0
13. **Jean Fugett, Amherst, TE, 52/103**
14. Alan Thompson, Wisconsin, RB, 0/0
15. Carlos Alvarez, Florida, WR, 0/0

DENVER BRONCOS

1. **Riley Odoms, Houston, TE, 153/153**
3. Bill Phillips, Arkansas State, LB, 0/0
4. Tom Graham, Oregon, LB, 33/88
5. Jim Krieg, Washington, WR, 6/6
8. Ronnie Estay, Louisiana State, DT, 0/0

9. Floyd Priester, Boston, DB, 0/0
10. Richard Wilkins, Maryland-Eastern Shore, DE, 0/0
11. Larry Brunson, Colorado, WR, 13/79
12. Randy McDougall, Weber State, WR, 0/0
13. Bob Warner, Bloomsburg, RB, 0/0
14. Jerome Kundich, Texas-El Paso, G, 0/0
15. Harold Parmenter, Massachusetts, DT, 0/0

DETROIT LIONS
1. **Herb Orvis, Colorado, DT, 72/122**
3. **Ken Sanders, Howard Payne, DE, 85/100**
6. Charlie Potts, Purdue, DB, 10/10
7. Charles Stoudamire, Portland State, WR, 0/0
8. Henry Stuckey, Missouri, DB, 0/27
9. Bill McClintock, Drake, DB, 0/0
10. Jim Teal, Purdue, LB, 14/14
11. Bob Waldron, Tulane, DT, 0/0
12. Paul Bradley, Southern Methodist, WR, 0/0
13. John Kirschner, Memphis State, TE, 0/0
14. Eric Kelly, Whitworth, T, 0/0
15. Steve Roach, Kansas, LB, 0/0
16. Leon Jenkins, West Virginia, DB, 4/4

GREEN BAY PACKERS
1. **Willie Buchanon, San Diego State, DB, 80/137**
1. Jerry Tagge, Nebraska, QB, 18/18
2. **Chester Marcol, Hillsdale, K, 102/103**
4. Eric Patton, Notre Dame, LB, 0/0
6. Bob Hudson, Northeastern State (OK), RB, 12/40
6. **Dave Pureifory, Eastern Michigan, DE, 78/148**
6. Nathaniel Ross, Bethune-Cookman, DB, 0/0
7. Bill Bushong, Kentucky, DT, 0/0
8. Leland Glass, Oregon, WR, 26/26
10. Keith Wortman, Nebraska, T, 46/96
11. David Bailey, Alabama, WR, 0/0
12. Mike Rich, Florida, RB, 0/0
13. Jesse Lakes, Central Michigan, RB, 0/0
14. Larry Hefner, Clemson, LB, 34/34
15. Rich Thone, Arkansas Tech, WR, 0/0

HOUSTON OILERS
1. **Greg Sampson, Stanford, T, 93/93**
3. Solomon Freelon, Grambling State, G, 39/39
3. Lewis Jolley, North Carolina, RB, 17/17
6. Joe Bullard, Tulane, DB, 0/0
6. Elmer Allen, Mississippi, LB, 0/0
7. Eric Hutchinson, Northwestern, DB, 0/0
8. Guy Roberts, Maryland, LB, 49/67
9. Willie Postler. Louiser, Montana, T, 0/0
10. Rhett Dawson, Florida State, WR, 14/16
10. Jim Butler, Tulsa, TE, 0/0
11. Ron Evans, Baylor, T, 0/0
12. Willie Rodgers, Kentucky State, RB, 42/42
13. Willie Roberts, Houston, DB, 0/4
14. Gary Crockett, Lamar, C, 0/0
16. Guy Murdock, Michigan, C, 14/14

KANSAS CITY CHIEFS
1. **Jeff Kinney, Nebraska, RB, 50/62**
4. Andy Hamilton, LSU, WR, 15/24
5. Milt Davis, Texas-Arlington, DE, 0/0
6. John Kahler, Long Beach State, DE, 0/0
7. Dean Carlson, Iowa State, QB, 1/1
8. Scott Mahoney, Colorado, G, 0/0
9. Dave Taylor, Weber State, DT, 0/0
10. Rich Ruppert, Hawaii, T, 0/0
11. Elbert Walker, Wisconsin, T, 0/0
12. Mike Williams, Oregon, DT, 0/0
13. Tyler Hellams, South Carolina, DB, 0/0
14. Dave Chaney, San Jose State, LB, 0/0
15. Larry Marshall, Maryland, DB, 23/75
17. Ted Washington, Mississippi Valley State, LB, 0/128

LOS ANGELES RAMS
2. **Jim Bertelsen, Texas, RB, 68/68**
3. **Lawrence McCutcheon, Colorado State, RB, 89/109**
4. John Saunders, Toledo, DB, 0/9
4. Eddie Phillips, Texas, DB, 0/0
5. Bob Christiansen, UCLA, DT, 0/4
5. Bob Childs, Kansas, G, 0/0
6. Eddie Herbert, Texas Southern, DT, 0/0
8. Tom Graham, Baldwin-Wallace, WR, 0/0
9. Harry Howard, Ohio State, DB, 0/1
10. Jim Massey, Linfield, DB, 0/15
11. Albert Schmidt, Pittsburg State, RB, 0/0
12. Dave Hoot, Texas A&M, DB, 0/0
13. Jaime Nunez, Weber State, K, 0/0
14. **Larry Brooks, Virginia State, DT, 131/131**
15. Kenny Page, Kansas, LB, 0/0

MIAMI DOLPHINS
1. Mike Kadish, Notre Dame, DT, 0/127
3. Gary Kosins, Dayton, RB, 0/40
4. **Larry Ball, Louisville, LB, 52/79**
4. Al Benton, Ohio U., T, 0/0
5. **Charlie Babb, Memphis, DB, 97/97**
6. Ray Nettles, Tennessee, LB, 0/0
7. Bill Adams, Holy Cross, G, 0/46
7. Calvin Harrell, Arkansas State, RB, 0/0
8. Craig Curry, Minnesota, QB, 0/0
9. Greg Johnson, Wisconsin, DB, 0/0
11. Ed Jenkins, Holy Cross, RB, 3/14
12. Ashley Bell, Purdue, TE, 0/0
13. Archie Robinson, Hillsdale, DB, 0/0
14. Willie Jones, Tampa, LB, 0/0
15. Bill Davis, William & Mary, DT, 0/0

MINNESOTA VIKINGS
1. **Jeff Siemon, Stanford, LB, 156/156**
2. **Ed Marinaro, Cornell, RB, 51/58**
3. Bart Buetow, Minnesota, T, 2/9
6. **Amos Martin, Louisville, LB, 52/54**
7. Bill Slater, Western Michigan, DE, 0/0
8. Calvin Demery, Arizona State, WR, 5/5
9. **Charles Goodrum, Florida A&M, G, 95/95**
10. Willie Aldridge, South Carolina State, RB, 0/0
11. Willie McKelton, Southern, DB, 0/0
12. Bob Banaugh, Montana State, DB, 0/0
13. Franklin Roberts, Alcorn State, RB, 0/0
14. Marv Owens, San Diego State, WR, 0/10
15. Mike Sivert, East Tennessee State, G, 0/0
16. Neil Graff, Wisconsin, QB, 0/29

NEW ENGLAND PATRIOTS
2. Tom Reynolds, San Diego State, WR, 12/21
3. Jim White, Colorado State, DE, 13/48
5. **Ron Bolton, Norfolk State, DB, 55/145**
7. Clark Hoss, Oregon State, TE, 0/4
7. John Tarver, Colorado, RB, 31/39
8. Steve Beyrle, Kansas State, G, 0/0
9. Mike Kelson, Arkansas, T, 0/0
10. Mel Caraway, Northwestern Oklahoma, DB, 0/0
11. Rodney Cason, Angelo State, T, 0/0
12. Steve Booras, Mesa J.C., DE, 0/0
13. Sam Elmore, Eastern Michigan, DB, 0/0
14. Eddie Rideout, Boston College, WR, 0/0
15. Joel Klimek, Pittsburgh, TE, 0/0

NEW ORLEANS SAINTS
1. Royce Smith, Georgia, G, 24/62
2. Willie Hall, USC, LB, 21/67
3. Bob Kuziel, Pittsburgh, C, 1/90
3. **Tom Myers, Syracuse, DB, 136/136**
4. Mike Crangle, Tennessee-Martin, DE, 13/13
4. **Joe Federspiel, Kentucky, LB, 130/141**
4. Mike Coleman, Knoxville, DE, 0/0
5. Bill Butler, Kansas State, RB, 41/41
5. Carl Johnson, Nebraska, T, 28/28
5. Bob Davies, South Carolina, DB, 0/0
6. Wayne Dorton, Arkansas State, G, 0/0
6. Curt Watson, Tennessee, RB, 0/0
7. **Ernie Jackson, Duke, DB, 71/89**
8. Ron Vinson, Abilene Christian, WR, 0/0
9. Kent Branstetter, Houston, T, 0/9
10. Andy Kupp, Idaho, G, 0/0
11. Paul Dongieux, Mississippi, LB, 0/0
12. Steve Lockhart, Arkansas State, TE, 0/0
13. Cephus Weatherspoon, Fort Lewis, WR, 1/1
14. Steve Barrios, Tulane, WR, 0/0
15. Rusty Lachaussee, Tulane, QB, 0/0

NEW YORK GIANTS
1. Larry Jacobson, Nebraska, DT, 33/33
1. Eldridge Small, Texas A&M-Kingsville, DB, 34/34
3. **John Mendenhall, Grambling State, DT, 101/116**
3. Tommy Mozisek, Houston, RB, 0/0
5. Tom Gatewood, Notre Dame, TE, 17/17
5. Larry Edwards, Texas A&I, LB, 0/0
6. John Hill, Lehigh, C, 38/177
7. Mike Zikas, Notre Dame, DT, 0/0
8. Tom Mabry, Arkansas, T, 0/0
9. Ed Richardson, Southern, RB, 0/0
10. John Odom, Texas Tech, DB, 0/0
11. John Robertson, Kansas State, DB, 0/0
12. Jay Anderson, Mayville, DT, 0/0
13. Chuck Heard, Georgia, DE, 0/0
14. James Evans, South Carolina State, LB, 0/0
15. Ken Kavanaugh, Louisiana State, TE, 0/0

NEW YORK JETS
1. **Jerome Barkum, Jackson State, TE, 158/158**
1. Michael Taylor, Michigan, LB, 22/22
3. Gary Hammond, SMU, WR, 0/49
4. **Ed Galigher, UCLA, DT, 60/87**
5. Dick Harris, South Carolina, DB, 0/0
6. Joey Jackson, New Mexico State, DE, 17/20
8. Marion Latimore, Kansas State, G, 0/0
9. Jeff Ford, Georgia Tech, DB, 0/0
10. Rocky Turner, Tennessee-Chattanooga, DB, 22/22
11. Robert Stevenson, Tennessee State, LB, 0/0
12. Hank Bjorklund, Princeton, RB, 30/30
13. Steve Sullivan, North Texas State, T, 0/0
14. Louis Age, Southwestern Louisiana, G, 0/0
15. Phil Sullivan, Georgia, DB, 0/0

OAKLAND RAIDERS
1. **Mike Siani, Villanova, WR, 74/101**
2. Kelvin Korver, Northwestern Iowa, DT, 24/24
2. **John Vella, USC, T, 84/92**
3. Mel Lunsford, Central State (OH), DE, 0/92
4. **Cliff Branch, Colorado, WR, 183/183**
4. **Dave Dalby, UCLA, C, 205/205**
6. Dan Medlin, North Carolina State, G, 48/76
7. **Skip Thomas, USC, DB, 82/82**
7. Ray Jamieson, Memphis State, RB, 0/0
7. Dennis Pete, Cal State-San Francisco, DB, 0/0
8. Jackie Brown, Stanford, RB, 0/0
9. Dave Bigler, Morningside, RB, 0/0
10. Phillip Price, Idaho State, DB, 0/0
11. Joe Carroll, Pittsburgh, LB, 22/22
12. Kent Gaydos, Florida State, WR, 0/4
13. Ted Covington, Cal State-Northridge, WR, 0/0
14. Dennis Cambal, William & Mary, TE, 0/8
15. Charles Hester, Central State (OH), RB, 0/0
15. Dave Snesrud, Hamline, LB, 0/0

PHILADELPHIA EAGLES
1. John Reaves, Florida, QB, 16/51
2. Dan Yochum, Syracuse, T, 0/0
3. **Tom Luken, Purdue, G, 64/64**
3. Bobby Majors, Tennessee, DB, 0/9
4. Po James, New Mexico State, RB, 49/49
6. Vernon Winfield, Minnesota, G, 14/14
7. Will Foster, Eastern Michigan, LB, 0/21
8. Larry Ratcliff, Eastern Michigan, RB, 0/0
9. Pat Gibbs, Lamar, DB, 2/2
10. **John Bunting, North Carolina, LB, 132/132**
11. Dennis Sweeney, Western Michigan, DE, 0/0
12. Don Zimmerman, Louisiana-Monroe, WR, 39/41
13. Preston Carpenter, Mississippi, DE, 0/0
14. Bill Overmyer, Ashland University, LB, 6/6
15. **Tom Sullivan, Miami (FL), RB, 80/84**

PITTSBURGH STEELERS
1. **Franco Harris, Penn State, RB, 165/173**
2. **Gordon Gravelle, Brigham Young, T, 54/96**
3. John McMakin, Clemson, TE, 36/60
4. Ed Bradley, Wake Forest, LB, 49/93
4. Lorenzo Brinkley, Missouri, DB, 0/0
5. **Steve Furness, Rhode Island, DT, 97/106**
6. Dennis Meyer, Arkansas State, DB, 11/11
7. Joe Colquitt, Kansas State, DE, 0/0
7. Robert Kelly, Jackson State, DB, 0/0
8. Stahle Vincent, Rice, RB, 0/0
9. Don Kelley, Clemson, DB, 0/0
10. Bob Brown, Tampa, DT, 0/0
11. Joe Gilliam, Tennessee State, QB, 20/20
12. Ron Curl, Michigan State, T, 0/0
13. Ernie Messmer, Villanova, T, 0/0
14. Tommy Durrance, Florida, RB, 0/0
15. John Hulecki, Massachusetts, G, 0/0
15. Charles Harrington, Wichita State, G, 0/0
16. Nate Hawkins, UNLV, WR, 0/11

SAN DIEGO CHARGERS
2. Pete Lazetich, Stanford, DE, 35/62
3. Bill McClard, Arkansas, K, 9/34
5. Jim Bishop, Tennessee Tech, TE, 0/0
5. Harry Gooden, Alcorn State, DE, 0/0
6. Bruce Ward, San Diego State, G, 0/0
9. Fran Schmitz, St. Norbert, DT, 0/0
10. Lon Kolstad, Wisconsin-Whitewater, LB, 0/0
11. John Turner, Long Beach State, TE, 0/0
12. Sam Key, Elon, LB, 0/0
13. Andy Selfridge, Virginia, LB, 0/53
14. John Van Reenen, Washington State, DE, 0/0
15. Charles Neugent, Tuskegee, DB, 0/0
17. Oscar Dragon, Arizona State, RB, 13/13

SAN FRANCISCO 49ERS
1. Terry Beasley, Auburn, WR, 29/29
2. **Jean Barrett, Tulsa, T, 93/93**
2. **Ralph McGill, Tulsa, DB, 70/99**
3. Jubilee Dunbar, Southern (LA), WR, 0/19
4. **Windlan Hall, Arizona State, DB, 54/81**
5. Mike Greene, Georgia, LB, 0/0
6. Jackie Walker, Tennessee, DB, 0/0
7. Ed Hardy, Jackson State, G, 3/3
8. **Tom Wittum, Northern Illinois, P, 70/70**
9. Jerry Brown, Northwestern, DB, 0/0
10. Steve Williams, Western Carolina, DE, 0/12
11. Tom Laputka, Southern Illinois, DE, 0/0
12. Steve Setzler, St. John's (MN), DE, 0/0
13. Leon Pettigrew, Cal State-Northridge, T, 0/0
14. Eric Guthrie, Boise State, QB, 0/0
16. Ron Davis, Virginia State, G, 0/2

ST. LOUIS CARDINALS
1. Ahmad Rashad, Oregon, WR, 27/139
2. **Mark Arneson, Arizona, LB, 127/127**
3. Tom Beckman, Michigan, DE, 2/2
4. Martin Imhof, San Diego State, DE, 13/32
4. Jeff Lyman, Brigham Young, LB, 2/3
5. **Conrad Dobler, Wyoming, G, 80/129**
6. Don Heater, Montana Tech, RB, 2/2
7. Council Rudolph, Kentucky State, DE, 32/72
8. Bob Wicks, Utah State, WR, 9/15
9. Gene Macken, South Dakota, C, 0/0
10. Eric Washington, Texas-El Paso, DB, 15/15
10. Mike Franks, Eastern New Mexico, QB, 0/0
11. Ron Jones, Arkansas, LB, 0/0
12. Tommy Gay, Arkansas-Pine Bluff, DT, 0/0
13. Tom Campana, Ohio State, DB, 0/0
14. Pat McTeer, New Mexico State, K, 0/0
15. Mark Herman, Yankton, TE, 0/0
17. Kent Carter, USC, LB, 0/2

WASHINGTON REDSKINS
8. Moses Denson, Maryland-Eastern Shore, RB, 26/26
9. Steve Boekholder, Drake, DE, 0/0
10. Mike Oldham, Michigan, WR, 0/0
11. Jeff Welch, Arkansas Tech, DB, 0/0
12. Don Bunce, Stanford, QB, 0/0
13. **Frank Grant, Southern Colorado, WR, 75/85**
15. Mike O'Quinn, McNeese State, G, 0/0
15. Carl Taibi, Colorado, DE, 0/0

1973 NFL

ATLANTA FALCONS
2. Greg Marx, Notre Dame, DE, 14/14
4. Tom Geredine, Truman State, WR, 24/34
6. Nick Bebout, Wyoming, T, 40/97
7. Tommy Campbell, Iowa State, DB, 0/14
8. Tom Reed, Arkansas, G, 0/0
9. Russell Ingram, Texas Tech, C, 0/0
10. **Nick Mike-Mayer, Temple, K, 63/125**
11. Byron Buelow, Wisconsin-LaCrosse, DB, 0/0
12. Mike Samples, Drake, LB, 0/0
13. Chris Stecher, Claremont-Mudd-Scripps, T, 0/0
14. John Madeya, Louisville, QB, 0/0
15. Thomas Gage, Lamar, DB, 0/0

BALTIMORE COLTS
1. **Joe Ehrmann, Syracuse, DT, 108/121**
1. **Bert Jones, LSU, QB, 98/102**
2. **Mike Barnes, Miami (FL), DT, 113/113**
3. Bill Olds, Nebraska, RB, 40/52
3. Jamie Rotella, Tennessee, LB, 0/0
4. Gery Palmer, Kansas, T, 0/2
4. Ollie Smith, Tennessee State, WR, 8/33
5. **Dave Taylor, Catawba, T, 72/72**
8. **Ray Oldham, Middle Tennessee State, DB, 69/125**
8. Bill Windauer, Iowa, DT, 11/18
11. Dan Neal, Kentucky, C, 19/134
12. Bernard Thomas, Western Michigan, DE, 0/0
13. Tom Pierantozzi, West Chester, QB, 0/0
14. Ed Williams, West Virginia, RB, 0/0
15. Jackie Brown, South Carolina, DB, 0/0

BUFFALO BILLS

1. **Joe DeLamielleure, Michigan State, G, 112/185**
1. **Paul Seymour, Michigan, TE, 69/69**
2. Jeff Winans, USC, G, 20/35
3. **Joe Ferguson, Arkansas, QB, 164/186**
3. Bob Kampa, California, DT, 9/13
4. Donnie Walker, Central State (OH), DB, 25/27
4. Jeff Yeates, Boston College, DE, 26/138
5. Wallace Francis, Arkansas-Pine Bluff, WR, 26/132
6. **John Skorupan, Penn State, LB, 50/92**
7. Brian McConnell, Michigan State, LB, 1/8
7. John Ford, Henderson State, TE, 0/0
8. Lee Fobbs, Grambling, RB, 0/0
9. Mike Reppond, Arkansas, WR, 0/2
10. Matthew Reed, Grambling, QB, 0/0
10. John LeHeup, South Carolina, LB, 0/0
11. Richard Earl, Tennessee, T, 0/0
12. Ronnie Carroll, Sam Houston State, G, 0/14
14. **Merv Krakau, Iowa State, LB, 71/72**
15. Joe Rizzo, Kings Point, LB, 0/81
15. Vince O'Neil, Kansas, RB, 0/0

CHICAGO BEARS

1. **Wally Chambers, Eastern Kentucky, DT, 60/88**
2. Gary Hrivnak, Purdue, DE, 41/41
2. Gary Huff, Florida State, QB, 43/57
5. **Allan Ellis, UCLA, DB, 94/105**
6. Mike Creaney, Notre Dame, C, 0/0
8. Conrad Graham, Tennessee, DB, 0/0
9. Mike Deutsch, North Dakota, RB, 0/0
10. Bill Barry, Mississippi, WR, 0/0
11. Ed Seigler, Clemson, K, 0/0
12. Mike Griffin, Arkansas, G, 0/0
13. John Cieszkowski, Notre Dame, RB, 0/0
14. Dave Juenger, Ohio University, WR, 1/1
15. **Don Rives, Texas Tech, LB, 74/74**

CINCINNATI BENGALS

1. **Isaac Curtis, San Diego State, WR, 167/167**
2. Al Chandler, Oklahoma, TE, 27/85
3. Tim George, Carson-Newman, WR, 12/20
5. Bob McCall, Arizona, RB, 0/8
6. Bob Jones, Virginia Union, DB, 23/51
7. Bob Maddox, Frostburg State, DT, 14/28
8. Joe Wilson, Holy Cross, RB, 13/25
9. John Dampeer, Notre Dame, G, 0/0
10. **Lenvil Elliott, Truman State, RB, 66/101**
11. William Montgomery, Morehouse, DB, 0/0
12. **Boobie Clark, Bethune-Cookman, RB, 73/94**
13. Brooks West, Texas-El Paso, DT, 0/0
14. Hurles Scales, North Texas, DB, 0/15
15. Ted McNulty, Indiana, QB, 0/0

CLEVELAND BROWNS

1. Pete Adams, USC, G, 25/25
1. Steve Holden, Arizona State, WR, 48/54
2. **Greg Pruitt, Oklahoma, RB, 118/158**
2. Jim Stienke, Southwest Texas State, DB, 7/66
3. Bob Crum, Arizona, DE, 0/14
4. Andy Dorris, New Mexico State, DE, 0/118
4. Randy Mattingly, Evansville, QB, 0/0
6. Van Green, Shaw, DB, 43/48
9. Curtis Wester, East Texas State, G, 0/0
10. Tommy Humphrey, Abilene Christian, C, 0/5
11. Carl Barisich, Princeton, DT, 41/102
12. Stan Simmons, Lewis & Clark, TE, 0/0
13. Jim Romaniszyn, Edinboro, LB, 28/39
14. Robert Popelka, Southern Methodist, DB, 0/0
15. Dave Sullivan, Virginia, WR, 7/7

DALLAS COWBOYS

1. **Billy Joe DuPree, Michigan State, TE, 159/159**
2. **Golden Richards, Brigham Young, WR, 66/86**
3. **Harvey Martin, Texas A&M-Commerce, DE, 158/158**
4. Drane Scrivener, Tulsa, DB, 0/0
5. Bruce Walton, UCLA, T, 33/33
6. Bob Leyen, Yale, G, 0/0
7. Rodrigo Barnes, Rice, LB, 16/32
8. Dan Werner, Michigan State, QB, 0/0
9. Mike White, Minnesota, DB, 0/0
10. Carl Johnson, Tennessee, LB, 0/0
11. Gerald Caswell, Colorado State, G, 0/0
12. Jim Arneson, Arizona, G, 26/33
13. John Smith, UCLA, WR, 0/0
14. Bob Thornton, North Carolina, G, 0/0
15. Walt Baisy, Grambling, LB, 0/0
17. Les Strayhorn, East Carolina, RB, 24/24

DENVER BRONCOS

1. **Otis Armstrong, Purdue, RB, 96/96**
2. **Barney Chavous, South Carolina State, DE, 183/183**
3. **Paul Howard, Brigham Young, G, 187/187**
3. John Wood, LSU, DT, 0/2
4. **Tom Jackson, Louisville, LB, 191/191**
5. Charles McTorry, Tennessee State, DB, 0/0
7. Mike Askea, Stanford, T, 4/4
7. **John Grant, USC, DT, 99/99**
9. Lyle Blackwood, TCU, DB, 0/176
10. Al Marshall, Boise State, WR, 0/4
11. Elton Brown, Utah State, DE, 0/0
12. Jim O'Malley, Notre Dame, LB, 40/40
13. Ed Smith, Colorado College, DE, 16/16
13. Ed White, Tulsa, RB, 0/0
14. John Hufnagel, Penn State, QB, 9/9
15. Calvin Jones, Washington, DB, 46/46
16. Oliver Ross, Alabama A&M, RB, 25/35

DETROIT LIONS

1. **Ernie Price, Texas A&M-Kingsville, DE, 65/81**
2. Leon Crosswhite, Oklahoma, RB, 21/21
3. **Levi Johnson, Texas A&M-Kingsville, DB, 59/59**
3. **Jim Laslavic, Penn State, LB, 68/124**
3. John Brady, Washington, TE, 0/0
4. Mike Hennigan, Tennessee Tech, LB, 26/64
4. Jim Hooks, Central Oklahoma, RB, 32/32
4. **Dick Jauron, Yale, DB, 58/100**
7. John Andrews, Morgan State, DE, 0/28
8. Prentice McCray, Arizona State, DB, 7/88
8. John Bledsoe, Ohio State, RB, 0/0
9. Ira Dean, Baylor, DB, 0/0
10. Ray Bonner, Middle Tennessee State, DB, 0/0
11. Scott Freeman, Wyoming, WR, 0/0
12. Tom Scott, Washington, WR, 0/0
13. John Moss, Pittsburgh, LB, 0/0
14. Jay Corey, Santa Clara, T, 0/0
15. Dan Hansen, BYU, DB, 0/0

GREEN BAY PACKERS

1. Barry Smith, Florida State, WR, 41/54
3. Tom MacLeod, Minnesota, LB, 10/64
6. **Tom Toner, Idaho State, LB, 53/53**
7. John Muller, Iowa, T, 0/0
8. Hise Austin, Prairie View A&M, DB, 9/12
9. Rick Brown, South Carolina, LB, 0/0
10. Larry Allen, Illinois, LB, 0/0
11. Phil Engle, South Dakota State, DT, 0/0
12. **Larry McCarren, Illinois, C, 162/162**
13. Tim Alderson, Minnesota, DB, 0/0
14. James Anderson, Northwestern, DT, 0/0
15. Reggie Echols, UCLA, WR, 0/0

HOUSTON OILERS

1. George Amundson, Iowa State, RB, 23/29
1. John Matuszak, Tampa, DE, 14/123
4. **Gregg Bingham, Purdue, LB, 173/173**
5. Edesel Garrison, Southern California, WR, 0/0
6. Ron Mayo, Morgan State, TE, 13/22
7. Shelby Jordan, Washington-St. Louis, T, 0/151
8. Joe Blahak, Nebraska, DB, 12/44
9. Mark Williams, Rice, K, 0/0
10. Darrell Vaughn, Northern Colorado, DT, 0/0
11. Larry Eaglin, Stephen F. Austin State, DB, 11/11
12. Brad Lyman, UCLA, WR, 0/0
13. Willie Martin, Northeastern Oklahoma, G, 0/0
14. Ron Lou, Arizona State, C, 23/37
15. Roger Goree, Baylor, LB, 0/0

KANSAS CITY CHIEFS

2. Gary Butler, Rice, TE, 14/25
3. Paul Krause, Central Michigan, T, 0/0
4. John Lohmeyer, Emporia State, DT, 41/41
5. Fred Grambau, Michigan, DE, 0/0
6. Doug Jones, Cal State-Northridge, DB, 18/68
7. Donn Smith, Purdue, T, 0/0
8. Al Palewicz, Miami (FL), LB, 36/50
9. Bill Story, Southern Illinois, T, 14/14
10. Willie Osley, Illinois, DB, 3/10
12. Tom Ramsey, Northern Arizona, DT, 0/0
13. Paul Metallo, Massachusetts, DB, 0/0
14. Albert White, Fort Valley State, WR, 0/0

LOS ANGELES RAMS

2. **Cullen Bryant, Colorado, RB, 134/153**
2. Ron Jaworski, Youngstown State, QB, 24/188
2. **Jim Youngblood, Tennessee Tech, LB, 152/156**
3. Tim Stokes, Oregon, T, 6/105
4. Eddie McMillan, Florida State, DB, 42/84
4. **Terry Nelson, Arkansas-Pine Bluff, TE, 87/87**
5. **Cody Jones, San Jose State, DT, 110/110**
5. Steve Jones, Duke, RB, 0/75
6. Jim Peterson, San Diego State, LB, 28/31
6. Jason Caldwell, North Carolina Central, WR, 0/0
7. Bill Dulac, Eastern Michigan, G, 0/26
7. Steve Brown, Oregon State, LB, 0/0
9. Jim Nicholson, Michigan State, T, 0/72
11. Jeff Inmon, North Carolina Central, RB, 0/0
11. Willie Jackson, Florida, WR, 0/0
12. Robert Storck, Wisconsin, DT, 0/0
13. Rod Milburn, Southern, WR, 0/0
13. Clint Spearman, Michigan, LB, 0/0
14. Walter Rhone, Central State (MO), DB, 0/0
15. Jerry Bond, Weber State, DB, 0/0

MIAMI DOLPHINS

2. Chuck Bradley, Oregon, TE, 0/19
3. Leon Gray, Jackson State, T, 0/142
4. Bo Rather, Michigan, WR, 9/64
5. Dave McCurry, Iowa State, DB, 0/2
5. **Don Strock, Virginia Tech, QB, 163/167**
6. **Ed Newman, Duke, G, 167/167**
7. Kevin Reilly, Villanova, LB, 0/25
7. Thomas Smith, Miami (FL), RB, 2/2
7. Benny Shepherd, Arkansas Tech, RB, 0/0
7. Willie Hatter, Northern Illinois, WR, 0/0
8. Archie Pearmon, Northeastern Oklahoma, DE, 0/0
9. Karl Lorch, USC, DE, 0/90
10. Ron Fernandes, Eastern Michigan, DE, 0/40
11. Chris Kete, Boston College, C, 0/0
12. Mike Mullen, Tulane, LB, 0/0
13. Joe Booker, Miami (OH), RB, 0/0
14. Greg Boyd, Arizona, DB, 0/6
15. Bill Palmer, St. Thomas (MN), TE, 0/0
17. Charlie Wade, Tennessee State, WR, 0/22

MINNESOTA VIKINGS

1. **Chuck Foreman, Miami (FL), RB, 93/109**
2. Jackie Wallace, Arizona, DB, 14/70
3. Jim Lash, Northwestern, WR, 42/60
4. Mike Wells, Illinois, QB, 0/7
5. **Brent McClanahan, Arizona State, RB, 95/95**
6. Doug Kingsriter, Minnesota, TE, 28/28
6. Fred Abbott, Florida, LB, 0/0
7. Josh Brown, Southwest Texas State, RB, 0/0
8. Craig Darling, Iowa, T, 0/0
9. Larry Dibbles, New Mexico, DE, 0/0
10. Dave Mason, Nebraska, DB, 0/19
10. Randy Lee, Tulane, DB, 0/0
11. Geary Murdock, Iowa State, G, 0/0
12. Alan Spencer, Pittsburg State (KS), WR, 0/0
13. Ron Just, Minot State, G, 0/0
14. Eddie Bishop, Southern, DB, 0/0
15. Tony Chandler, Missouri Valley, RB, 0/0

NEW ENGLAND PATRIOTS

1. **Sam Cunningham, USC, RB, 107/107**
1. **John Hannah, Alabama, G, 183/183**
1. **Darryl Stingley, Purdue, WR, 60/60**
3. Brad Dusek, Texas A&M, LB, 0/114
3. Charles Davis, Alcorn State, RB, 0/0
4. Allen Gallaher, USC, T, 14/14
5. Doug Dumler, Nebraska, C, 42/70
8. Isaac Brown, Western Kentucky, RB, 0/0
9. David Callaway, Texas A&M, T, 0/0
10. Dan Ruster, Oklahoma, DB, 0/0
11. Homer May, Texas A&M, TE, 0/0
12. Bruce Barnes, UCLA, P, 23/23
13. Alan Lowry, Texas, DB, 0/0
14. **Ray Hamilton, Oklahoma, NT, 132/132**
15. Condie Pugh, Norfolk State, RB, 0/0

NEW ORLEANS SAINTS

2. **Steve Baumgartner, Purdue, DE, 61/95**
2. **Derland Moore, Oklahoma, DT, 170/171**
3. Pete Van Valkenberg, Brigham Young, RB, 0/24
4. **Jim Merlo, Stanford, LB, 88/88**
6. Marty Shuford, Arizona, RB, 0/0
7. Bill Cahill, Washington, DB, 0/19
8. Doug Winslow, Drake, WR, 12/17
8. Bob Peterson, Utah, G, 0/0
9. Mike Fink, Missouri, DB, 13/13
10. Jeff Horsley, North Carolina Central, RB, 0/0
11. James Owens, Auburn, RB, 0/0
12. Paul Orndorff, Tampa, RB, 0/0
13. Richard Watkins, Weber State, DT, 0/0
14. Paul Fersen, Georgia, T, 4/4
15. Mike Evenson, North Dakota State, C, 0/0
16. Howard Stevens, Louisville, RB, 28/66

NEW YORK GIANTS

2. **Brad Van Pelt, Michigan State, LB, 143/184**
3. Rich Glover, Nebraska, DT, 13/27
5. Leon McQuay, Tampa, RB, 13/30
6. Wade Brantley, Troy State, DT, 0/0
7. Rod Freeman, Vanderbilt, TE, 0/0
8. George Hasenohrl, Ohio State, DT, 5/5
9. Ty Paine, Washington State, QB, 0/0
10. Walt Love, Westminster (UT), WR, 12/12
11. William Wideman, North Carolina A&T, DT, 0/0
12. Ron Lumpkin, Arizona State, DB, 1/1
13. Clifton Davis, Alcorn State, RB, 0/0
14. **Brian Kelley, California Lutheran, LB, 143/143**
15. Carl Schaukowitch, Penn State, G, 0/11

NEW YORK JETS

1. **Burgess Owens, Miami (FL), DB, 97/137**
2. **Robert Woods, Tennessee State, T, 54/99**
4. Bill Ferguson, San Diego State, LB, 24/24
5. Bruce Bannon, Penn State, LB, 0/28
6. Rick Harrell, Clemson, C, 4/4
6. Travis Roach, Texas, G, 14/14
7. Mike Haggard, South Carolina, WR, 0/0
8. Rick Seifert, Ohio State, DB, 0/0
9. Rob Spicer, Indiana, LB, 13/13
10. Joe Carbone, Delaware, LB, 0/0
10. James Krempin, Texas A&I, T, 0/0
11. **David Knight, William & Mary, WR, 58/58**
12. **Garry Puetz, Valparaiso, G, 69/119**
13. Robert Parrish, Duke, DT, 0/0
14. Joe Schwartz, Toledo, RB, 0/0
15. Mahlon Williams, North Carolina Central, TE, 0/0

OAKLAND RAIDERS

S1. Blenda Gay, Fayetteville State, DE, 0/30
1. **Ray Guy, Southern Mississippi, P, 207/207**
2. **Monte Johnson, Nebraska, LB, 99/99**
4. Perry Smith, Colorado State, DB, 0/108
4. Joe Wylie, Oklahoma, WR, 0/0
5. Ron Mikolajczyk, Tampa, T, 0/32
5. Louis Neal, Prairie View A&M, WR, 0/15
6. Brent Myers, Purdue, T, 0/0
7. Gary Weaver, Fresno State, LB, 24/87
8. Mike Rae, USC, QB, 17/28
9. Steve Sweeney, California, WR, 14/14
10. Leo Allen, Tuskegee, RB, 0/0
11. Jerry List, Nebraska, RB, 0/0
12. Jim Krapf, Alabama, G, 0/0
14. Bruce Polen, William Penn, DB, 0/0
15. Dave Leffers, Vanderbilt, C, 0/0

PHILADELPHIA EAGLES

1. **Jerry Sisemore, Texas, T, 156/156**
1. **Charle Young, USC, TE, 56/187**
2. **Guy Morriss, TCU, C, 158/217**
3. **Randy Logan, Michigan, DB, 159/159**
6. Bob Picard, Eastern Washington, WR, 46/54
7. **Will Wynn, Tennessee State, DE, 54/55**
8. Dan Lintner, Indiana, DB, 0/0
9. John Nokes, Northern Illinois, LB, 0/0
11. Gary Van Elst, Michigan State, DT, 0/0
12. Joe Lavender, San Diego State, DB, 40/139
13. Stan Davis, Memphis, WR, 8/8
14. Ralph Sacra, Texas A&M, T, 0/0
15. Ken Schlezes, Notre Dame, DB, 0/0
17. Greg Oliver, Trinity (TX), RB, 25/25

PITTSBURGH STEELERS

1. **J.T. Thomas, Florida State, DB, 116/125**
2. Ken Phares, Mississippi State, DB, 0/0
3. Roger Bernhardt, Kansas, G, 0/18
4. Gail Clark, Michigan State, LB, 0/19
5. Dave Reavis, Arkansas, T, 24/121
5. Larry Clark, Northern Illinois, LB, 0/0
6. Glenn Scolnik, Indiana, WR, 1/1
6. Ron Bell, Illinois State, RB, 0/0
7. Nate Dorsey, Mississippi Valley State, WR, 0/2
8. **Loren Toews, California, LB, 149/149**
8. Bill Janssen, Nebraska, T, 0/0
9. Bracey Bonham, North Carolina Central, G, 0/0

10. Don Wunderly, Arkansas, DT, 0/0
11. Bob White, Arizona, DB, 0/0
12. Willie Lee, Indiana State, RB, 0/0
13. Rick Fergerson, Kansas State, WR, 0/0
14. Roger Cowan, Stanford, DE, 0/0
15. Charles Cross, Iowa, DB, 0/0

SAN DIEGO CHARGERS

1. Johnny Rodgers, Nebraska, WR, 17/17
3. **Dan Fouts, Oregon, QB, 181/181**
4. Bill Singletary, Temple, LB, 0/3
4. Jim Thaxton, Tennessee State, TE, 12/54
5. Willie McGee, Alcorn State, WR, 11/56
5. Jon Knoble, Weber State, LB, 0/0
6. Marvin Roberts, Michigan State, C, 0/0
9. Tab Bennett, Illinois, LB, 0/0
10. Cliff Burnett, Montana, DE, 0/0
11. Jay Douglas, Memphis, C, 28/28
12. Lynn Ahrens, Eastern Montana, T, 0/0
13. Alfred Reese, Tennessee State, RB, 0/0
14. Tony Adams, Utah State, QB, 0/53
15. Gary Parris, Florida State, TE, 23/91
17. Barry Darrow, Montana, T, 0/71

SAN FRANCISCO 49ERS

1. Mike Holmes, Texas Southern, DB, 27/31
2. **Willie Harper, Nebraska, LB, 134/134**
5. Ed Beverly, Arizona State, WR, 2/2
5. Mike Fulk, Indiana, LB, 0/0
6. Arthur Moore, Tulsa, NT, 0/29
7. John Mitchell, Alabama, LB, 0/0
8. Dave Atkins, Texas-El Paso, RB, 6/9
9. Roger Praetorius, Syracuse, RB, 0/0
10. Charlie Hunt, Florida State, LB, 8/13
11. Tom Dahlberg, Gustavus Adolphus, RB, 0/0
12. Larry Pettus, Tennessee State, T, 0/0
13. Alan Kelso, Washington, C, 0/0
14. Dennis Morrison, Kansas State, QB, 3/3
15. Mike Bettiga, Humboldt State, WR, 10/10

ST. LOUIS CARDINALS

1. Dave Butz, Purdue, DT, 13/216
2. Gary Keithley, Texas-El Paso, QB, 14/14
3. **Terry Metcalf, Long Beach State, RB, 65/81**
3. Fred Sturt, Bowling Green State, G, 0/95
5. **Tom Brahaney, Oklahoma, C, 134/134**
6. **Dwayne Crump, Fresno State, DB, 55/55**
6. Phil Andre, Washington, DB, 0/0
7. Ken Jones, Oklahoma, T, 0/0
8. Ken Garrett, Wake Forest, RB, 0/0
9. Ken King, Kentucky, LB, 0/0
10. Bonnie Sloan, Austin Peay State, DT, 4/4
11. Dan Sanspree, Auburn, DE, 0/0
12. Dean Unruh, Oklahoma, T, 0/0
13. Ed Robinson, Lamar, DB, 0/0
14. Dan Peiffer, Southeast Missouri State, C, 0/37
15. Mel Parker, Duke, LB, 0/0

WASHINGTON REDSKINS

5. Charley Cantrell, Lamar, G, 0/0
8. Mike Hancock, Idaho State, TE, 21/21
9. Rich Galbos, Ohio State, RB, 0/0
9. Eddie Sheats, Kansas, LB, 0/0
10. Ken Stone, Vanderbilt, DB, 21/101
12. Ernie Webster, Pittsburgh, G, 0/0
13. **Dennis Johnson, Delaware, DE, 51/65**
14. Herb Marshall, Cameron, DB, 0/0

1974 NFL

ATLANTA FALCONS

2. Gerald Tinker, Kent State, WR, 20/26
3. Kim McQuilken, Lehigh, QB, 23/26
3. Mo Spencer, North Carolina Central, DB, 0/56
4. Vince Kendrick, Florida, RB, 14/15
5. Henry Childs, Kansas State, TE, 6/103
5. Monroe Eley, Arizona State, RB, 13/13
6. Doyle Orange, Southern Mississippi, RB, 0/0
7. James Coode, Michigan, T, 0/0
9. Larry Bailey, Pacific, DT, 1/1
10. **Paul Ryczek, Virginia, C, 88/99**
11. Eddie Wilson, Albany State, WR, 0/0
12. Vic Koegel, Ohio State, LB, 0/6
13. Ralph Powell, Nebraska, RB, 0/0
14. John Givens, Villanova, G, 0/0
15. Willie Jones, Iowa State, WR, 0/0
16. Molly McGee, Rhode Island, RB, 10/10

BALTIMORE COLTS

1. **Roger Carr, Louisiana Tech, WR, 102/115**
1. **John Dutton, Nebraska, DT, 68/185**
2. **Fred Cook, Southern Mississippi, DE, 104/104**
2. Ed Shuttlesworth, Michigan, RB, 0/0
3. **Robert Pratt, North Carolina, G, 118/170**
3. Glenn Robinson, Oklahoma State, DE, 11/39
4. Tony Bell, Bowling Green, DB, 0/0
5. **Doug Nettles, Vanderbilt, DB, 71/73**
6. Danny Rhodes, Arkansas, LB, 14/14
7. **Dan Dickel, Iowa, LB, 56/60**
7. Noah Jackson, Tampa, G, 0/131
7. Freddie Scott, Amherst, WR, 46/132
8. Greg Latta, Morgan State, TE, 0/73
8. Paul Miles, Bowling Green, RB, 0/0
10. **Bob Van Duyne, Idaho, G, 88/88**
10. Glenn Ellis, Elon, DT, 0/0
11. Tim Rudnick, Notre Dame, DB, 14/14
12. Dave Simonson, Minnesota, T, 13/29
12. Bo Bobrowski, Purdue, QB, 0/0
13. Randy Hall, Idaho, DB, 27/27
14. Ed Collins, Rice, WR, 0/0
15. Pat Kelly, Richmond, LB, 0/0
17. Tim Berra, Massachusetts, WR, 14/14

BUFFALO BILLS

1. **Reuben Gant, Oklahoma State, TE, 101/101**
2. Doug Allen, Penn State, LB, 28/28
3. Gary Marangi, Boston College, QB, 19/19
4. Carlester Crumpler, East Carolina, RB, 0/0
5. Gary Hayman, Penn State, RB, 15/15
5. Tim Guy, Oregon, T, 0/0
8. Gregg Hare, Ohio State, QB, 0/0
9. Brian Doherty, Notre Dame, P, 0/0
10. Don Calhoun, Kansas State, RB, 20/114
10. Art Cameron, Albany State (GA), TE, 0/0
11. Rod Kirby, Pittsburgh, LB, 0/0
12. Dave Means, Southeast Missouri State, DE, 9/9
13. Ed Gatewood, Tennessee State, LB, 0/0
14. Paul Lamm, North Carolina, DB, 0/0
14. Phil Gurbada, Mayville State, DB, 0/0
15. Ken Williams, Southwestern Louisiana, LB, 0/0

CHICAGO BEARS

1. **Waymond Bryant, Tennessee State, LB, 53/53**
1. Dave Gallagher, Michigan, DE, 14/51
3. Greg Horton, Colorado, G, 0/63
3. Cliff Taylor, Memphis, RB, 14/21
3. Wayne Wheeler, Alabama, WR, 12/12
7. Jack Ettinger, Arkansas, WR, 0/0
8. Ken Grandberry, Washington State, RB, 14/14
8. Alan Chadwick, East Tennessee State, QB, 0/0
11. Norm Hodgins, LSU, DB, 14/14
12. **Jeff Sevy, California, T, 54/73**
13. Joe Barnes, Texas Tech, QB, 3/3
14. Paul Vellano, Maryland, DT, 0/0
15. Oliver Alexander, Grambling, TE, 0/0

CINCINNATI BENGALS

1. Bill Kollar, Montana State, DE, 37/109
S1. Clint Longley, Abilene Christian, QB, 0/9
2. Charlie Davis, Colorado, RB, 14/20
3. Evan Jolitz, Cincinnati, LB, 12/12
3. **Dave Lapham, Syracuse, G, 140/140**
4. Mike Boryla, Stanford, QB, 0/23
4. Daryl White, Nebraska, G, 0/10
4. Richard Williams, Abilene Christian, WR, 0/2
5. Richard Bishop, Louisville, DE, 0/89
5. Haskel Stanback, Tennessee, RB, 0/83
6. Bill Bryant, Grambling State, DB, 0/42
6. Robin Sinclair, Washington State, DB, 0/0
7. Ken Sawyer, Syracuse, DB, 12/12
8. **John McDaniel, Lincoln (MO), WR, 56/96**
9. Ed Johnson, Southern Methodist, DE, 0/0
10. Charles Herd, Penn State, WR, 0/0
11. Ed Kezirian, UCLA, T, 0/0
12. Rudy McClinon, Xavier, DB, 0/0
13. Ted Jornov, Iowa State, LB, 0/0
14. Mike Phillips, Cornell, T, 0/0
15. Isaac Jackson, Kansas State, RB, 0/0

CLEVELAND BROWNS

2. Billy Corbett, Johnson C. Smith, T, 0/0
5. Mark Ilgenfritz, Vanderbilt, DE, 14/14
6. Billy Pritchett, West Texas A&M, RB, 14/29
7. **Gerry Sullivan, Illinois, T, 119/119**
7. Bob Herrick, Purdue, WR, 0/0
8. Eddie Brown, Tennessee, DB, 16/72
9. Dan Scott, Ohio State, G, 0/0
10. Mike Puestow, North Dakota State, WR, 0/0
11. Tom Gooden, Harding, K, 0/0
12. Ron McNeil, North Carolina Central, DE, 0/0
13. Mike Seifert, Wisconsin, DE, 12/12
14. Bob Hunt, Heidelberg, RB, 2/2
15. Ransom Terrell, Arizona, LB, 0/0
16. Preston Anderson, Rice, DB, 14/14

DALLAS COWBOYS

1. **Too Tall Jones, Tennessee State, DE, 224/224**
1. Charley Young, North Carolina State, RB, 37/37
3. Cal Peterson, UCLA, LB, 28/80
3. **Danny White, Arizona State, QB, 166/166**
4. Ken Hutcherson, West Alabama, LB, 14/22
4. Andy Andrade, Northern Michigan, RB, 0/0
5. John Kelsey, Missouri, T, 0/0
6. Jimmy Bright, UCLA, DB, 0/0
7. Raymond Nester, Michigan State, LB, 0/0
8. Mike Holt, Michigan State, DB, 0/0
9. Bill Dulin, Johnson C. Smith, T, 0/0
10. Dennis Morgan, Western Illinois, RB, 13/17
11. Harvey McGee, Southern Mississippi, WR, 0/0
12. Keith Bobo, Southern Methodist, QB, 0/0
13. Fred Lima, Colorado, K, 0/0
14. Doug Richards, BYU, DB, 0/0
15. Bruce Craft, Geneva, T, 0/0
16. Gene Killian, Tennessee, G, 7/7

DENVER BRONCOS

1. **Randy Gradishar, Ohio State, LB, 145/145**
2. Carl Wafer, Tennessee State, DE, 0/3
3. **Claudie Minor, San Diego State, T, 125/125**
4. Ozell Collier, Colorado, DB, 0/0
6. John Winesberry, Stanford, WR, 0/0
10. Charlie Johnson, Southern, DB, 0/0
11. Steve Buchanan, Holy Cross, RB, 0/0
12. Larry Cameron, Alcorn State, LB, 0/0
13. John Clerkley, Fort Valley State, DT, 0/0
14. Rich Marks, Northern Illinois, DB, 0/0
15. Piel Pennington, Massachusetts, QB, 0/0
16. Darrell Austin, South Carolina, G, 0/69
17. Boyd Brown, Alcorn State, TE, 40/46

DETROIT LIONS

1. **Ed O'Neil, Penn State, LB, 88/100**
2. Billy Howard, Alcorn State, DE, 38/38
3. **Dexter Bussey, Texas-Arlington, RB, 150/150**
5. Carl Capria, Purdue, DB, 12/13
6. Willie Burden, North Carolina State, RB, 0/0
6. Jim Davis, Alcorn State, G, 0/0
7. Efren Herrera, UCLA, K, 0/106
8. Mike Denimarck, Emporia State, LB, 0/0
10. David Wooley, Central State (OK), RB, 0/0
11. T.C. Blair, Tulsa, TE, 11/11
12. Mark Wakefield, Tampa, WR, 0/0
13. Fred Rothwell, Kansas State, C, 14/14
14. David Jones, Howard Payne, DB, 0/0
15. John Wells, Kansas State, G, 0/0

GREEN BAY PACKERS

1. **Barty Smith, Richmond, RB, 67/67**
5. **Steve Odom, Utah, WR, 75/81**
6. Ken Payne, Langston, WR, 44/60
6. Don Woods, New Mexico, RB, 0/85
7. Bart Purvis, Maryland, T, 0/0
8. Monte Doris, Southern California, LB, 0/0
8. Ned Guillet, Boston College, DB, 0/0
9. Harold Holton, Texas-El Paso, G, 0/0
10. Doug Troszak, Michigan, DT, 0/0
11. **Eric Torkelson, Connecticut, RB, 93/93**
12. Randy Walker, Northwestern State (LA), P, 14/14
13. Emanuel Armstrong, San Jose State, LB, 0/0
14. Andrew Neloms, Kentucky State, DT, 0/0
15. Dave Wannstedt, Pittsburgh, T, 0/0
16. Mark Cooney, Colorado, LB, 13/13

HOUSTON OILERS

4. Steve Manstedt, Nebraska, LB, 0/0
6. Booker Brown, USC, T, 0/17
7. Leonard Fairley, Alcorn State, DB, 2/2
8. Mike McCoy, Western Kentucky, DB, 0/0
11. Steve Taylor, Auburn, C, 0/0
12. Ricky Browne, Florida, LB, 0/0
13. Dan Dixon, Boise State, G, 0/0
15. **Billy Johnson, Widener, WR, 79/143**

KANSAS CITY CHIEFS

1. Woody Green, Arizona State, RB, 28/28
2. **Charlie Getty, Penn State, T, 119/134**
3. David Jaynes, Kansas, QB, 2/2
4. **Matt Herkenhoff, Minnesota, T, 125/125**
6. Jay Washington, Clemson, RB, 0/0
7. LeRoy Hegge, South Dakota-Springfield, DE, 0/0
9. Jim Jennings, Rutgers, RB, 0/0
10. **Tom Condon, Boston College, G, 147/148**
11. Bob Thornbladh, Michigan, LB, 14/14
12. Carl Brown, West Texas State, WR, 0/0
13. Norm Romagnoli, Kentucky State, LB, 0/0
14. Frank Pomarico, Notre Dame, G, 0/0
15. Lem Burnham, U.S. International, DE, 0/45

LOS ANGELES RAMS

1. **John Cappelletti, Penn State, RB, 69/105**
2. **Bill Simpson, Michigan State, DB, 72/108**
3. Al Oliver, UCLA, T, 0/0
4. Norris Weese, Mississippi, QB, 0/57
4. Frank Johnson, Cal-Riverside, T, 0/0
7. John Harvey, Texas-Arlington, RB, 0/0
9. Don Hutt, Boise State, WR, 0/0
9. Derek Williams, Cal-Riverside, DB, 0/0
11. Rick Hayes, Washington, T, 0/0
12. Roger Freberg, UCLA, G, 0/0
13. Pete Solverson, Drake, T, 0/0
14. Ananias Carson, Langston, WR, 0/0
15. Bob Thomas, Notre Dame, K, 0/144

MIAMI DOLPHINS

1. Don Reese, Jackson State, DT, 41/88
2. **Benny Malone, Arizona State, RB, 57/82**
2. **Andre Tillman, Texas Tech, TE, 58/58**
2. Jeris White, Hawaii, DB, 42/129
3. **Nat Moore, Florida, WR, 183/183**
4. Bill Stevenson, Drake, DB, 0/0
5. Cleveland Vann, Oklahoma State, LB, 0/0
6. Randy Crowder, Penn State, DT, 39/71
6. Bob Wolfe, Nebraska, T, 0/0
7. Carl Swierc, Rice, WR, 0/0
7. Joe Sullivan, Boston College, G, 0/0
8. Melvin Baker, Texas Southern, WR, 9/21
9. Bob Lally, Cornell, LB, 0/2
9. Tom Wickert, Washington State, T, 13/27
10. Gary Valbuena, Tennessee, QB, 0/0
11. Gerry Roberts, UCLA, DE, 0/0
12. Jim Revels, Florida, DB, 0/0
13. Clayton Heath, Wake Forest, RB, 6/8
14. Sam Johnson, Arizona State, LB, 0/0
15. Larry Cates, Western Michigan, DB, 0/0

MINNESOTA VIKINGS

1. **Fred McNeill, UCLA, LB, 167/167**
1. **Steve Riley, USC, T, 138/138**
2. **Matt Blair, Iowa State, LB, 160/160**
2. John Holland, Tennessee State, WR, 10/38
3. Scott Anderson, Missouri, C, 7/7
3. **Steve Craig, Northwestern, TE, 72/72**
4. Mike Townsend, Notre Dame, DB, 0/0
5. Jim Ferguson, Stanford, DB, 0/0
6. Mark Kellar, Northern Illinois, RB, 33/33
7. Fred Tabron, Southwest Missouri State, RB, 0/0
8. Berl Simmons, Texas Christian, K, 0/0
9. Sam McCullum, Montana State, WR, 38/129
10. Barry Reed, Peru State, RB, 0/0
11. Dave Boone, Eastern Michigan, DE, 5/5
12. Randy Poltl, Stanford, DB, 5/44
13. Gary Keller, Utah, DT, 0/0
14. Alan Dixon, Harding, RB, 0/0
15. Kurt Wachtler, St. John's (MN), DT, 0/0

NEW ENGLAND PATRIOTS

2. Steve Corbett, Boston College, G, 14/14
2. **Steve Nelson, North Dakota State, LB, 174/174**
5. **Andy Johnson, Georgia, RB, 94/94**
5. Charlie Battle, Grambling, LB, 0/0
6. Chuck Ramsey, Wake Forest, P, 0/117
7. Maury Damkroger, Nebraska, LB, 13/13
9. Ed McCartney, Northwestern Oklahoma, LB, 0/0
11. Archie Gibson, Utah State, RB, 0/0
12. Eddie Foster, Oklahoma, T, 0/0
13. Phil Bennett, Boston College, RB, 0/0
14. Cecil Bowens, Kentucky, RB, 0/0
15. **Sam Hunt, Stephen F. Austin State, LB, 84/84**

NEW ORLEANS SAINTS

1. Rick Middleton, Ohio State, LB, 28/64
2. Paul Seal, Michigan, TE, 42/85
4. Rod McNeill, USC, RB, 25/36
5. Joel Parker, Florida, WR, 22/22
5. Terry Schmidt, Ball State, DB, 22/143
8. Alvin Maxson, SMU, RB, 41/56
9. Phil LaPorta, Penn State, T, 20/20
10. Frosty Anderson, Nebraska, WR, 0/0
10. Tommy Thibodeaux, Tulane, G, 0/0
11. Kent Merritt, Virginia, WR, 0/0
12. James Buckmon, Pittsburgh, DE, 0/0

13. Mike Truax, Tulane, LB, 0/0
14. Kent Marshall, Texas Christian, DB, 0/0
15. Larry Cipa, Michigan, QB, 8/8
16. Don Coleman, Michigan, LB, 27/27

NEW YORK GIANTS

1. **John Hicks, Ohio State, G, 52/52**
2. Tom Mullen, Southwest Missouri State, G, 43/50
3. Rick Dvorak, Wichita State, DT, 46/47
4. Carl Summerell, East Carolina, QB, 10/10
5. Don Clune, Pennsylvania, WR, 18/28
5. **Clyde Powers, Oklahoma, DB, 56/57**
6. **Jim Pietrzak, Eastern Michigan, C, 61/140**
7. Marty Woolbright, South Carolina, TE, 0/0
8. Ezil Bilbbs, Grambling, DE, 0/0
9. Jim Rathje, Northern Michigan, RB, 0/0
10. **Ray Rhodes, Tulsa, DB, 83/97**
11. Bobby Brooks, Bishop, DB, 32/32
12. Jim Sims, USC, LB, 0/2
13. Dennis Colvin, Southwest Texas State, T, 0/0
14. Mike Hayes, Virginia State, T, 0/0
15. Larry Jones, Truman State, WB, 0/51
17. Steve Crosby, Fort Hays State, RB, 15/15

NEW YORK JETS

1. Carl Barzilauskas, Indiana, DT, 49/70
2. Gordie Browne, Boston College, T, 23/23
3. Godwin Turk, Southern (LA), LB, 14/56
3. Roscoe Word, Jackson State, DB, 30/37
5. Gary Baccus, Oklahoma, LB, 0/0
6. Bill Wyman, Texas, C, 0/0
6. Wayne Jones, Mississippi State, RB, 0/0
7. Burney Veazey, Mississippi, TE, 0/0
8. Greg Gantt, Alabama, P, 28/28
8. Ron Rydalch, Utah, DT, 0/74
8. Larry Lightfoot, Livingston, RB, 0/0
9. Robert Burns, Georgia, RB, 14/14
10. Sam Baker, Georgia, G, 0/0
11. Eugene Bird, Southern Mississippi, DB, 0/0
11. Bill Buckley, Mississippi State, WR, 0/0
12. John Ricca, Duke, DE, 0/0
14. Greg Fountain, Mississippi State, G, 0/0
15. Willie Brister, Southern (LA), TE, 24/24
16. Jazz Jackson, Western Kentucky, RB, 33/33

OAKLAND RAIDERS

1. **Henry Lawrence, Florida A&M, T, 187/187**
2. **Dave Casper, Notre Dame, TE, 99/147**
3. **Mark van Eeghen, Colgate, RB, 112/136**
4. **Morris Bradshaw, Ohio State, WR, 104/112**
5. Pete Wessel, Northwestern, DB, 0/0
6. James McAlister, UCLA, RB, 0/43
7. Rod Garcia, Stanford, K, 0/0
9. Ken Pope, Oklahoma, DB, 0/4
10. Chris Arnold, Virginia State, DB, 0/0
11. Harold Hart, Texas Southern, RB, 29/30
12. Noe Gonzalez, Southwest Texas State, RB, 0/2
13. Mike Dennery, Southern Mississippi, LB, 28/31
14. Don Willingham, Wisconsin-Milwaukee, RB, 0/0
15. Greg Mathis, Idaho State, DB, 0/0

PHILADELPHIA EAGLES

3. Mitch Sutton, Kansas, DE, 18/18
4. **Frank LeMaster, Kentucky, LB, 129/129**
5. Jim Cagle, Georgia, DT, 14/14
5. **Keith Krepfle, Iowa State, TE, 93/97**
7. Willie Cullars, Kansas State, DE, 13/13
8. Robert Woods, Howard Payne, LB, 0/0
9. Mark Sheridan, Holy Cross, WR, 0/0
10. Phil Polak, Bowling Green, RB, 0/0
11. Bill Brittain, Kansas State, C, 0/0
12. Artimus Parker, USC, DB, 42/53
13. Lars Ditley, South Dakota Tech, DE, 0/0
14. Dave Smith, Oklahoma, LB, 0/0
15. Sid Bond, Texas Christian, T, 0/0

PITTSBURGH STEELERS

1. **Lynn Swann, USC, WR, 115/115**
2. **Jack Lambert, Kent State, LB, 146/146**
4. **Jimmy Allen, UCLA, DB, 50/110**
4. **John Stallworth, Alabama A&M, WR, 165/165**
5. **Mike Webster, Wisconsin, C, 220/245**
6. Rich Druschel, North Carolina State, T, 11/11
6. Jim Wolf, Prairie View A&M, DT, 11/25
7. Allen Sitterle, North Carolina State, T, 0/0
7. Scott Garske, Eastern Michigan, TE, 0/0
8. Mark Gefert, Purdue, LB, 0/0
9. Charles Davis, TCU, DT, 14/74
9. Tommy Reamon, Missouri, RB, 0/11
10. Jim Kregel, Ohio State, G, 0/0
10. Dave Atkinson, BYU, DB, 0/0
11. Dickie Morton, Arkansas, RB, 0/0
12. Hugh Lickiss, Simpson, LB, 0/0
13. Frank Kolch, Eastern Michigan, QB, 0/0
14. Bruce Henley, Rice, DB, 0/0
15. Larry Hunt, Iowa State, DT, 0/0

SAN DIEGO CHARGERS

1. **Don Goode, Kansas, LB, 81/112**
1. **Bo Matthews, Colorado, RB, 78/101**
2. Mark Markovich, Penn State, C, 23/41
3. Bill Rudder, Tennessee, RB, 0/0
4. Harrison Davis, Virginia, WR, 12/12
5. John Teerlinck, Western Illinois, DT, 20/20
6. Jesse Freitas, San Diego State, QB, 13/13
8. Bon Boatwright, Oklahoma State, DT, 10/10
8. Tom Forrest, Cincinnati, G, 0/8
9. Danny Colbert, Tulsa, DB, 32/32
10. John Ketchoyian, Santa Clara, LB, 0/0
11. Dave Grannell, Arizona State, TE, 9/9
12. Sam Williams, California, DB, 24/28
13. Brian Vertefeuille, Idaho State, T, 14/14
14. Greg Bailey, Long Beach State, DB, 0/0
15. Charles Anthony, USC, LB, 13/13
15. Greg Meczka, Bowling Green, TE, 0/0
17. **Charles DeJurnett, San Jose State, NT, 66/118**

SAN FRANCISCO 49ERS

1. **Wilbur Jackson, Alabama, RB, 72/94**
1. Bill Sandifer, UCLA, DT, 30/46
2. **Keith Fahnhorst, Minnesota, T, 193/193**
2. **Delvin Williams, Kansas, RB, 54/100**
4. Clint Haslerig, Michigan, WR, 0/26
4. Sammy Johnson, North Carolina, RB, 34/62
6. Mike Raines, Alabama, DT, 2/2
7. Kermit Johnson, UCLA, RB, 22/22
8. Jim Schnietz, Missouri, G, 0/0
9. Manfred Moore, USC, RB, 28/51
10. Glen Gaspard, Texas, LB, 0/0
11. Greg Battle, Colorado State, DB, 0/0
12. Tom Hull, Penn State, LB, 13/25
13. Tom Owen, Wichita State, QB, 14/26
14. Walt Williamson, Michigan, DE, 0/0
15. Leonard Gray, Long Beach State, TE, 0/0

ST. LOUIS CARDINALS

1. **J.V. Cain, Colorado, TE, 55/55**
2. Greg Kindle, Tennessee State, G, 24/35
3. Steve George, Houston, DT, 13/14
4. Ike Harris, Iowa State, WR, 40/88
4. Durwood Keeton, Oklahoma, DB, 0/12
5. **Steve Neils, Minnesota, LB, 88/88**
8. Sergio Albert, U.S. International, K, 12/12
9. Reggie Harrison, Cincinnati, RB, 1/45
10. Reggie Hartle, Newberry, LB, 28/28
12. Roger Wallace, Bowling Green State, WR, 0/3
13. Jimmy Poulos, Georgia, RB, 0/0
14. Charles Smith, Yankton, RB, 0/0
15. Vincent Ancell, Arkansas State, DB, 0/0

WASHINGTON REDSKINS

6. Jon Keyworth, Colorado, RB, 0/95
7. Mike Varty, Northwestern, LB, 2/8
8. Darwin Robinson, Dakota State (San Diego), RB, 0/0
9. Jimmie Kennedy, Colorado State, TE, 0/37
9. Mark Sens, Colorado, DE, 0/0
9. Mike Flater, Colorado Mines, K, 0/0
10. Johnny Vann, South Dakota, DB, 0/0
11. Joe Miller, Villanova, T, 0/0
13. Stu O'Dell, Indiana, LB, 25/39
14. Don Van Galder, Utah, QB, 0/0

1975 NFL

ATLANTA FALCONS

1. **Steve Bartkowski, California, QB, 123/129**
2. **Ralph Ortega, Florida, LB, 57/81**
3. Woody Thompson, Miami (FL), RB, 35/35
4. John Nessel, Penn State, G, 0/0
5. Greg McCrary, Clark Atlanta, TE, 26/74
6. **Fulton Kuykendall, UCLA, LB, 123/124**
6. Doug Payton, Colorado, G, 0/0
7. Mike Esposito, Boston College, RB, 40/40
8. Brent Adams, Tennessee-Chattanooga, T, 41/41
9. Brad Davis, LSU, RB, 4/4
10. Marshall Mills, West Virginia, WR, 0/0
11. **Jeff Merrow, West Virginia, DE, 108/108**
12. Monzo Pickett, Texas Southern, T, 0/0
13. Carl Russ, Michigan, LB, 14/19
14. Steve Robinson, Tuskegee, DT, 0/0
15. Jim Robinson, Georgia Tech, WR, 0/58
16. Steve Knutson, USC, G, 0/40

BALTIMORE COLTS

1. **Ken Huff, North Carolina, G, 102/145**
3. Dave Pear, Washington, NT, 13/79
3. Mike Washington, Alabama, DB, 0/100
4. Marshall Johnson, Houston, WR, 32/32
4. Paul Linford, BYU, DT, 0/0
5. **Roosevelt Leaks, Texas, RB, 54/107**
6. Don Westbrook, Nebraska, WR, 0/71
7. Steve Joachim, Temple, QB, 0/1
7. Kim Jones, Colorado State, RB, 0/43
7. **Derrel Luce, Baylor, LB, 56/85**
8. John Bushong, Western Kentucky, DE, 0/0
8. Greg Denboer, Michigan, TE, 0/0
8. Mario Cage, Northwestern State (LA), RB, 0/0
9. Royce McKinney, Kentucky State, DB, 0/9
10. Phil Wagenheim, Maryland, P, 0/0
11. Dave Hazel, Ohio State, WR, 0/0
12. Brad Storm, Iowa State, LB, 0/0
13. John Roman, Idaho State, T, 0/93
14. Mike Smith, Southern Methodist, C, 0/0
15. John Goodie, Langston, RB, 0/0

BUFFALO BILLS

1. Tom Ruud, Nebraska, LB, 36/59
2. Bob Nelson, Nebraska, LB, 25/72
2. Glenn Lott, Drake, DB, 0/0
4. Tom Donchez, Penn State, RB, 0/14
5. John McCrumbly, Texas A&M, LB, 13/13
7. Gil Chapman, Michigan, WR, 0/9
7. Reggie Cherry, Houston, RB, 0/0
7. Harry Banks, Michigan, DB, 0/0
8. John Hill, Duke, DT, 0/0
10. **Roland Hooks, North Carolina State, RB, 98/98**
11. Tom Drake, Michigan, DB, 0/0
12. Mark Johnson, Missouri, DE, 24/31
13. Mark Dienhart, St. Thomas (MN), T, 0/0
14. Robert Evans, Morris Brown, WR, 0/0
15. Chris Kupec, North Carolina, QB, 0/0

CHICAGO BEARS

1. **Walter Payton, Jackson State, RB, 190/190**
2. **Mike Hartenstine, Penn State, DE, 179/184**
4. **Virgil Livers, Western Kentucky, DB, 68/68**
5. **Revie Sorey, Illinois, G, 109/109**
6. **Bob Avellini, Maryland, QB, 73/73**
6. **Tom Hicks, Illinois, LB, 64/64**
7. Earl Douthitt, Iowa, DB, 9/9
8. Joe Harris, Georgia Tech, LB, 0/83
9. Roger Stillwell, Stanford, DT, 31/31
10. Mike Julius, St. Thomas (MN), G, 0/0
11. Mike Dean, Texas, K, 0/0
12. **Doug Plank, Ohio State, DB, 101/101**
13. Charles McDaniel, Louisiana Tech, RB, 0/0
14. Walter Hartfield, Southwest Texas State, RB, 0/0
15. Steve Marcantonio, Miami (FL), WR, 0/0
17. **Roland Harper, Louisiana Tech, RB, 89/89**

CINCINNATI BENGALS

1. **Glenn Cameron, Florida, LB, 159/159**
2. Al Krevis, Boston College, T, 3/13
3. **Gary Burley, Pittsburgh, DE, 105/117**
3. **Bo Harris, LSU, LB, 103/103**
3. Gary Sheide, BYU, QB, 0/0
4. Stan Fritts, North Carolina State, RB, 26/26
5. **Pat McInally, Harvard, WR, 149/149**
5. Jeff West, Cincinnati, P, 0/123
6. Tom Shuman, Penn State, QB, 0/0
6. Rollen Smith, Arkansas, DB, 0/0
7. Chris Devlin, Penn State, LB, 24/30
8. Ricky Davis, Alabama, DB, 14/38
9. Greg Dubinetz, Yale, G, 0/15
9. Lofell Williams, Virginia Union, WR, 0/0
10. Rocky Felker, Mississippi State, DB, 0/0
11. **Marvin Cobb, USC, DB, 71/79**
12. Jack Novak, Wisconsin, TE, 14/35
13. Ron Rosenberg, Montana, LB, 0/0
14. Frank Haywood, North Carolina State, DT, 0/0
15. Greg Enright, Southern Oregon, K, 0/0

CLEVELAND BROWNS

1. **Mack Mitchell, Houston, DE, 56/69**
3. Oscar Roan, SMU, TE, 49/49
4. **Tony Peters, Oklahoma, DB, 58/133**
5. Jim Cope, Ohio State, LB, 0/6
5. John Zimba, Villanova, DE, 0/0
6. Henry Hynoski, Temple, RB, 14/14
6. Charles Miller, West Virginia, DB, 0/0
7. Merle Wang, Texas Christian, T, 0/0
8. Barry Santini, Purdue, TE, 0/0
9. Larry Poole, Kent State, RB, 29/38
9. Floyd Hogan, Arkansas, DB, 0/0
10. Stan Lewis, Wayne State (NE), DE, 6/6
11. Tom Marinelli, Boston College, G, 0/0
12. **Dick Ambrose, Virginia, LB, 116/116**
13. Willie Armstead, Utah, WR, 0/0
14. Tim Barrett, John Carroll, RB, 0/0
15. Willie Moore, Johnson C. Smith, DT, 0/0
16. John McKay, USC, WR, 0/43
17. **Dave Graf, Penn State, LB, 65/71**

DALLAS COWBOYS

1. **Thomas Henderson, Langston, LB, 67/75**
1. **Randy White, Maryland, DT, 209/209**
2. **Burton Lawless, Florida, G, 73/82**
3. **Bob Breunig, Arizona State, LB, 135/135**
4. **Pat Donovan, Stanford, T, 129/129**
4. **Randy Hughes, Oklahoma, DB, 77/77**
5. Kyle Davis, Oklahoma, C, 14/21
6. Rolly Woolsey, Boise State, DB, 14/44
7. **Mike Hegman, Tennessee State, LB, 170/170**
8. Mitch Hoopes, Arizona, P, 14/25
9. Ed Jones, Rutgers, DB, 0/12
10. Dennis Booker, Millersville, RB, 0/0
11. Greg Krpalek, Oregon State, C, 0/0
12. Chuck Bland, Cincinnati, DB, 0/0
13. **Herbert Scott, Virginia Union, G, 140/140**
14. **Scott Laidlaw, Stanford, RB, 67/74**
15. Willie Hamilton, Arizona, RB, 0/0

DENVER BRONCOS

1. **Louis Wright, San Jose State, DB, 166/166**
2. Charles Smith, North Carolina Central, DE, 0/0
3. Mike Franckowiak, Central Michigan, RB, 28/57
3. Drew Mahalic, Notre Dame, LB, 0/49
4. **Rick Upchurch, Minnesota, WR, 119/119**
4. Steve Taylor, Georgia, DB, 0/0
5. **Rubin Carter, Miami (FL), NT, 166/166**
5. Stan Rogers, Maryland, T, 14/14
8. **Steve Foley, Tulane, DB, 150/150**
9. Roussell Williams, Arizona, DB, 0/0
10. Steve Haggerty, UNLV, WR, 1/1
10. Hank Engelhardt, Pacific, C, 0/0
12. Harry Walters, Maryland, LB, 0/0
13. Eric Penick, Notre Dame, RB, 0/0
14. Jerry Arnold, Oklahoma, G, 0/0
15. Ken Shelton, Virginia, TE, 0/0

DETROIT LIONS

1. **Lynn Boden, South Dakota State, G, 57/67**
2. **Doug English, Texas, DT, 131/131**
4. Craig Hertwig, Georgia, T, 37/37
6. Dennis Franklin, Michigan, WR, 9/9
6. **Horace King, Georgia, RB, 123/123**
6. Fred Cooper, Purdue, DB, 0/0
7. Mike Murphy, Drake, WR, 0/0
8. **Leonard Thompson, Oklahoma State, WR, 175/175**
9. Steve Strinko, Michigan, LB, 0/0
10. Brad Boyd, Louisiana State, TE, 0/0
11. Steve Myers, Ohio State, G, 0/0
12. Andre Roundtree, Iowa State, LB, 0/0
13. Jim Smith, North Carolina Central, RB, 0/0
14. Jim McMillan, Boise State, QB, 0/0
15. Rudy Green, Yale, RB, 0/0

GREEN BAY PACKERS

2. Bill Bain, USC, T, 14/132
3. Willard Harrell, Pacific, RB, 40/136
4. **Steve Luke, Ohio State, DB, 90/90**
7. Tony Giaquinto, Central Connecticut State, WR, 0/0
9. Jay Lynn Hodgin, South Carolina, RB, 0/0
10. Bill Cooke, Massachusetts, DT, 5/75
11. Bob Martin, Washington, DE, 0/0
12. Carlos Brown, Pacific, QB, 26/26
13. Bob Fuhriman, Utah State, DB, 0/0
14. Stan Blackmon, North Texas State, TE, 0/0
15. Randy Allen, Southern, WR, 0/0
16. Bob McCaffrey, USC, C, 11/11

HOUSTON OILERS

1. **Robert Brazile, Jackson State, LB, 147/147**
1. Don Hardeman, Texas A&M-Kingsville, RB, 38/64
2. Emmett Edwards, Kansas, WR, 14/20
6. Jesse O'Neal, Grambling, DE, 0/0
7. Mark Cotney, Cameron, DB, 14/127
7. Mike Biehle, Miami (OH), T, 0/0
8. Jerry Lawrence, South Dakota State, DT, 0/0
9. Bob Bruer, Mankato State, TE, 0/68
10. Alan Pringle, Rice, K, 0/1
11. John Sawyer, Southern Mississippi, TE, 22/110

12. Willie Miller, Colorado State, WR, 0/77
13. Ricky Scales, Virginia Tech, WR, 0/0
14. Jody Medford, Rice, G, 0/0
15. Jack Holmes, Texas Southern, RB, 0/64

KANSAS CITY CHIEFS

2. Elmore Stephens, Kentucky, TE, 0/0
3. Cornelius Walker, Rice, DT, 0/0
6. Morris LaGrand, Tampa, RB, 11/13
6. Dave Wasick, San Jose State, LB, 0/0
8. Wayne Hoffman, Oklahoma, TE, 0/0
11. Dale Hegland, Minnesota, G, 0/0
12. James Rackley, Florida A&M, RB, 0/0
13. John Snider, Stanford, LB, 0/0
14. Gene Moshier, Vanderbilt, G, 0/0

LOS ANGELES RAMS

1. **Mike Fanning, Notre Dame, DT, 107/137**
1. **Doug France, Ohio State, T, 97/110**
1. **Dennis Harrah, Miami (FL), G, 168/168**
2. Monte Jackson, San Diego State, DB, 47/112
2. Leroy Jones, Norfolk State, DE, 0/111
3. Dan Nugent, Auburn, G, 0/58
3. Geoff Reece, Washington State, C, 14/17
4. **Rod Perry, Colorado, DB, 94/118**
5. Wayne Hammond, Montana State, DT, 0/5
5. Rick Nuzum, Kentucky, C, 14/30
6. Darius McCarthy, South Carolina State, WR, 0/0
7. **Pat Haden, USC, QB, 65/65**
8. John Washington, Tulane, DB, 0/0
9. Gordy Riegel, Stanford, LB, 0/0
11. Howard Strickland, California, RB, 0/0
12. Chandler Williams, Lincoln (MO), WR, 0/0
13. A.J. Jacobs, Louisville, DB, 0/0
14. Arthur Allen, Clark, WR, 0/0
15. Alvin White, Oregon State, QB, 0/0

MIAMI DOLPHINS

1. Darryl Carlton, Tampa, T, 28/71
2. Freddie Solomon, Tampa, WR, 37/151
2. Stan Winfrey, Arkansas State, RB, 28/30
3. Gerald Hill, Houston, LB, 0/0
4. Bruce Elia, Ohio State, LB, 14/55
5. Barry Hill, Iowa State, DB, 20/20
5. Morris Owens, Arizona State, WR, 4/62
6. **Steve Towle, Kansas, LB, 78/78**
7. Phillip Kent, Baylor, RB, 0/0
8. Barney Crawford, Harding, DT, 0/0
9. James Wilson, Clark, G, 0/0
10. Joe Danelo, Washington State, K, 0/136
10. Clyde Russell, Oklahoma, RB, 0/0
10. Joe Jackson, Penn State, TE, 0/0
11. John Dilworth, Northwestern State (LA), DB, 0/0
12. Joe Yancey, Henderson State, T, 0/0
13. Leonard Isabell, Tulsa, WR, 0/0
14. James Lewis, Tennessee State, DB, 0/0
14. John Graham, Colorado State, QB, 0/0
15. Skip Johns, Carson-Newman, RB, 0/0

MINNESOTA VIKINGS

1. **Mark Mullaney, Colorado State, DE, 151/151**
2. Art Riley, Southern California, DT, 0/0
4. Champ Henson, Ohio State, RB, 0/6
4. Bruce Adams, Kansas, WR, 0/0
5. **Robert Miller, Kansas, RB, 89/89**
6. Bubba Broussard, Houston, LB, 0/0
7. Henry Greene, Southern, RB, 0/0
8. Joe Hollimon, Arkansas State, DB, 0/0
9. John Passananti, Western Illinois, G, 0/0
10. Neil Clabo, Tennessee, P, 41/41
11. Ike Spencer, Utah, RB, 0/0
12. Autry Beamon, Texas A&M-Commerce, DB, 28/100
13. Mike Hurd, Michigan State, WR, 0/0
14. Mike Strickland, Eastern Michigan, RB, 0/0
15. Ollie Bakken, Minnesota, LB, 0/0

NEW ENGLAND PATRIOTS

1. **Russ Francis, Oregon, TE, 92/167**
2. **Rod Shoate, Oklahoma, LB, 79/79**
3. Peter Cusick, Ohio State, NT, 13/13
4. Steve Burks, Arkansas State, WR, 34/34
4. Allen Carter, USC, RB, 15/15
5. Steve Freeman, Mississippi State, DB, 0/190
5. **Steve Grogan, Kansas State, QB, 149/149**
7. Lawrence Williams, Texas Tech, WR, 0/21
11. Rene Garnett, Idaho State, DB, 0/0
12. Matt Kendon, Idaho State, DT, 0/0
12. Condredge Holloway, Tennessee, QB, 0/0
13. Joe Harvey, Northern Michigan, DE, 0/0
14. Tom Gossom, Auburn, WR, 0/0
15. Don Clayton, Murray State, RB, 0/0

NEW ORLEANS SAINTS

1. Larry Burton, Purdue, WR, 28/43
1. Kurt Schumacher, Ohio State, G, 41/45
2. Lee Gross, Auburn, C, 32/48
3. **Elois Grooms, Tennessee Tech, DE, 99/138**
3. Andrew Jones, Washington State, RB, 15/15
4. John Starkebaum, Nebraska, DB, 0/0
4. Charlie Hall, Tulane, DE, 0/0
6. Mike Lemon, Kansas, LB, 2/22
7. Steve Rogers, LSU, RB, 13/14
9. **Mike Strachan, Iowa State, RB, 62/62**
10. Chuck Heater, Michigan, RB, 0/0
11. Danny Lee, Northeast Louisiana, P, 0/0
12. Ron Gustafson, North Dakota, WR, 0/0
13. Jim Upchurch, Arizona, RB, 0/0
14. Randy Rhino, Georgia Tech, DB, 0/0
15. Grant Burget, Oklahoma, RB, 0/0
16. Mike McDonald, Catawba, LB, 0/4
17. Greg Westbrooks, Colorado, LB, 35/66

NEW YORK GIANTS

2. Al Simpson, Colorado State, G, 23/23
3. Danny Buggs, West Virginia, WR, 19/68
4. Robert Giblin, Houston, DB, 12/23
7. Jim Obradovich, USC, TE, 14/129
8. John Tate, Jackson State, LB, 2/2
9. Mike Mahoney, Richmond, WR, 0/0
10. Terry McClowry, Michigan State, LB, 0/0
11. **George Martin, Oregon, DE, 201/201**
12. Marsh White, Arkansas, RB, 28/28
13. Ricky Townsend, Tennessee, K, 0/0
15. Jim O'Connor, Drake, RB, 0/0
17. Rondy Colbert, Lamar, DB, 28/32

NEW YORK JETS

2. Anthony Davis, USC, RB, 0/15
3. Richard Wood, USC, LB, 14/146
5. Joe Wysocki, Miami (FL), G, 0/0
6. Tom Alward, Nebraska, G, 0/14
8. James Scott, Trinity Valley CC (TX), WR, 0/71
9. Everett Taylor, Memphis State, DB, 0/0
10. Charles James, Jackson State, DB, 0/0
11. Jon Bradford, Central State (OH), RB, 0/0
12. Bert Cooper, Florida State, LB, 0/12
13. Dan Spivey, Georgia, DT, 0/0
14. **Joe Fields, Widener, C, 173/186**
15. Brison Manor, Arkansas, DE, 0/113

OAKLAND RAIDERS

1. **Neal Colzie, Ohio State, DB, 56/118**
2. **Charlie Phillips, USC, DB, 67/67**
3. Louis Carter, Maryland, RB, 8/52
5. **David Humm, Nebraska, QB, 76/95**
7. James Daniels, Texas A&M, DB, 0/0
9. Harry Knight, Richmond, QB, 0/0
10. **Steve Sylvester, Notre Dame, C, 106/106**
12. Jack Magee, Boston College, C, 0/0
14. Tom Doyle, Yale, QB, 0/0
15. Paul Careathers, Tennessee, RB, 0/0

PHILADELPHIA EAGLES

7. Bill Capraun, Miami (FL), T, 0/0
8. Jeff Bleamer, Penn State, T, 24/32
10. Ken Schroy, Maryland, DB, 0/113
11. Keith Rowen, Stanford, G, 0/0
12. Dick Pawlewicz, William & Mary, RB, 0/0
13. Tom Ehlers, Kentucky, LB, 42/50
14. Larry O'Rourke, Ohio State, DT, 0/0
15. Clayton Korver, Northwestern (IA), DE, 0/0

PITTSBURGH STEELERS

1. Dave Brown, Michigan, DB, 13/216
2. Bob Barber, Grambling State, DE, 0/60
3. Walter White, Maryland, TE, 0/63
4. Harold Evans, Houston, LB, 0/0
5. Brent Sexton, Elon, DB, 11/11
6. Marvin Crenshaw, Nebraska, T, 0/0
8. Wayne Mattingly, Colorado, T, 0/0
8. Tom Kropp, Kearney State, LB, 0/0
8. Al Humphrey, Tulsa, DE, 0/0
9. Eugene Clark, UCLA, G, 0/0
9. Bruce Reimer, North Dakota State, RB, 0/0
10. Kirt Heyer, Kearney State, DT, 0/0
10. Archie Gray, Wyoming, WR, 0/0
11. Randy Little, West Liberty, TE, 0/0
12. Greg Murphy, Penn State, DE, 0/0
13. Bob Gaddis, Mississippi Valley State, WR, 0/2
14. Mike Collier, Morgan State, RB, 14/36
15. Marty Smith, Louisville, DT, 0/14
15. James Thatcher, Langston, WR, 0/0

SAN DIEGO CHARGERS

1. **Gary Johnson, Grambling State, DT, 134/157**
1. **Mike Williams, LSU, DB, 107/109**
2. **Fred Dean, Louisiana Tech, DE, 84/141**
2. **Louie Kelcher, SMU, DT, 100/116**
3. **Mike Fuller, Auburn, DB, 90/114**
4. Ken Bernich, Auburn, LB, 0/5
5. Kevin Nosbusch, Notre Dame, DT, 0/0
5. Charles Waddell, North Carolina, TE, 0/0
6. **Billy Shields, Georgia Tech, T, 127/142**
6. John Carroll, Oklahoma, WR, 0/0
7. Rickey Young, Jackson State, RB, 42/131
8. **Ralph Perretta, Purdue, C, 68/73**
8. Barry Collier, Georgia, T, 0/0
9. Larry Keller, Houston, LB, 0/44
10. Otha Bradley, Southern California, DT, 0/0
11. Vince Phason, Arizona, DB, 0/0
11. Ike McBee, San Jose State, WR, 0/0
12. Jerry Dahl, North Dakota State, LB, 0/0
13. Pete Demmerle, Notre Dame, WR, 0/0
13. Glen Printers, South Colorado State, RB, 0/0
14. Reggie Barnett, Notre Dame, DB, 0/0
15. John Roush, Oklahoma, G, 0/0
17. Neal Jeffrey, Baylor, QB, 5/5

SAN FRANCISCO 49ERS

1. **Jimmy Webb, Mississippi State, DT, 90/106**
2. Greg Collins, Notre Dame, LB, 14/38
3. Wayne Baker, Brigham Young, DT, 14/14
3. Jeff Hart, Oregon State, T, 14/99
3. Steve Mike-Mayer, Maryland, K, 28/80
4. **Cleveland Elam, Tennessee State, DT, 54/62**
4. Frank Oliver, Kentucky State, DB, 0/18
5. Wayne Bullock, Notre Dame, RB, 0/0
8. Preston Kendrick, Florida, LB, 0/0
9. James Johnson, Tennessee State, DB, 0/0
9. Dan Natale, Penn State, TE, 0/0
9. Caesar Douglas, Illinois Weslyan, T, 0/0
10. Donnie Layton, South Carolina State, RB, 0/0
11. Gene Hernandez, Texas Christian, DB, 0/0
12. Rick Worley, Howard Payne, QB, 0/0
13. Dale Mitchell, USC, LB, 17/17
14. David Henson, Abilene Christian, WR, 0/0
15. Rich Lavin, Western Illinois, TE, 0/0

ST. LOUIS CARDINALS

1. Tim Gray, Texas A&M, DB, 14/66
2. Jim Germany, New Mexico State, RB, 0/0
5. Harvey Goodman, Colorado, G, 0/14
6. Larry Jameson, Indiana, DT, 0/1
7. Steve Beaird, Baylor, RB, 0/0
8. John Adams, West Virginia, DT, 0/0
8. Louis Lauriano, Long Beach State, DB, 0/0
10. Mike McGraw, Wyoming, LB, 4/5
11. Jerry Latin, Northern Illinois, RB, 37/51
12. Ben Jones, Louisiana State, WR, 0/0
13. Steve Lindgren, Hamline, DE, 0/0
14. Ritch Bahe, Nebraska, WR, 0/0
15. Ron Franklin, Boise State, DT, 0/0

WASHINGTON REDSKINS

5. **Mike Thomas, UNLV, RB, 53/77**
6. Mark Doak, Nebraska, T, 0/0
9. **Dallas Hickman, California, DE, 86/91**
11. Ardell Johnson, Nebraska, DB, 0/0
11. Jerry Hackenbruck, Oregon State, DE, 0/0
14. Morris McKie, North Carolina A&T, DB, 0/0
14. Dave Benson, Weber State, LB, 0/0
15. Art Kuehn, UCLA, C, 0/100

1976 NFL

ATLANTA FALCONS

1. Bubba Bean, Texas A&M, RB, 40/40
2. Sonny Collins, Kentucky, RB, 11/11
3. **Dave Scott, Kansas, G, 98/98**
4. Walt Brett, Montana, G, 0/0
6. Stan Varner, BYU, DT, 0/0
7. Karl Farmer, Pittsburgh, WR, 15/17
8. **Frank Reed, Washington, DB, 71/71**
9. **Phil McKinnely, UCLA, T, 62/77**
11. Chuck Brislin, Mississippi State, T, 0/0
12. Pat Bolton, Montana State, K, 0/0
13. Mike Williams, Florida, T, 0/0
14. Mark Husfloen, Washington State, DE, 0/0
15. Ron Olson, Washington, DB, 0/0

BALTIMORE COLTS

1. Ken Novak, Purdue, DT, 23/23
3. Ron Lee, West Virginia, RB, 42/42
3. **Ed Simonini, Texas A&M, LB, 74/83**
5. Mike Kirkland, Arkansas, QB, 16/16
5. **Sanders Shiver, Carson-Newman, LB, 112/132**
8. Ricky Thompson, Baylor, WR, 14/80
9. Stu Levenick, Illinois, T, 0/0
10. Tim Baylor, Morgan State, DB, 43/59
11. Rick Gibney, Georgia Tech, DT, 0/0
12. Frank Stavroff, Indiana, K, 0/0
14. Jeremiah Cummings, Albany State, DE, 0/0
15. Gary Alexander, Clemson, T, 0/0

BUFFALO BILLS

1. **Mario Clark, Oregon, DB, 115/126**
2. **Joe Devlin, Iowa, T, 191/191**
2. **Ken Jones, Arkansas State, T, 158/163**
3. **Ben Williams, Mississippi, DE, 147/147**
4. **Dan Jilek, Michigan, LB, 58/58**
5. Fred Coleman, Louisiana-Monroe, TE, 7/7
6. Scott Piper, Arizona, WR, 0/13
6. Darnell Powell, Tennessee-Chattanooga, RB, 11/25
6. Leslie Benson, Baylor, DE, 0/0
7. Jackie Williams, Texas A&M, DB, 0/0
8. Scott Gardner, Virginia, QB, 0/0
8. Bobby Joe Easter, Middle Tennessee State, RB, 0/0
8. Art Meadowcroft, Minnesota, G, 0/0
9. Jeff Turner, Kansas, LB, 0/0
9. Bob Kotzur, Southwest Texas State, DT, 0/0
10. **Keith Moody, Syracuse, DB, 58/63**
11. Forry Smith, Iowa State, WR, 0/0
12. Joe Lowery, Jackson State, RB, 0/0
13. Will Wilcox, Texas, G, 0/0
14. Tony Williams, Middle Tennessee State, WR, 0/0
15. Arnold Robinson, Bethune-Cookman, LB, 0/0

CHICAGO BEARS

1. **Dennis Lick, Wisconsin, T, 79/79**
3. **Brian Baschnagel, Ohio State, WR, 129/129**
4. John Sciarra, UCLA, DB, 0/76
4. Wayne Rhodes, Alabama, DB, 0/0
6. **Dan Jiggetts, Harvard, T, 98/98**
7. **Jerry Muckensturm, Arkansas State, LB, 81/81**
11. Norm Andersen, UCLA, WR, 0/0
12. John O'Leary, Nebraska, RB, 0/0
13. Dale Kasowski, North Dakota, RB, 0/0
14. Ron Cuie, Oregon State, RB, 0/0
15. Jerry Meyers, Northern Illinois, DE, 47/49

CINCINNATI BENGALS

1. Billy Brooks, Oklahoma, WR, 45/55
1. **Archie Griffin, Ohio State, RB, 98/98**
2. **Chris Bahr, Penn State, K, 60/210**
2. **Glenn Bujnoch, Texas A&M, G, 89/103**
3. Danny Reece, USC, DB, 0/72
3. **Reggie Williams, Dartmouth, LB, 206/206**
4. Tony Davis, Nebraska, RB, 42/89
4. Greg Fairchild, Tulsa, G, 25/27
5. Scott Perry, Williams, DB, 48/63
5. Willie Shelby, Alabama, RB, 27/30
6. Orlando Nelson, Utah State, TE, 0/0
7. Bob Bateman, Brown, QB, 0/0
7. Pete Rome, Miami (OH), DB, 0/0
7. Ken Kuhn, Ohio State, LB, 0/0
8. Ron Hunt, Oregon, T, 28/28
9. Lonnie Allgood, Syracuse, WR, 0/0
10. Tom Klaban, Ohio State, K, 0/0
11. Melvin Morgan, Mississippi Valley State, DB, 41/55
12. Joe Dale Harris, Alabama, WR, 0/0
13. Randy Walker, Miami (OH), RB, 0/0
14. Greg Coleman, Florida A&M, P, 0/162
15. Lynn Hieber, Indiana (PA), QB, 0/0

CLEVELAND BROWNS

1. **Mike Pruitt, Purdue, RB, 124/152**
3. **Dave Logan, Colorado, WR, 115/119**
4. **Mike St. Clair, Grambling State, DE, 57/91**
4. Gene Swick, Toledo, QB, 0/0
5. **Henry Sheppard, SMU, G, 82/82**
7. Steve Cassidy, Louisiana State, DT, 0/0
9. James Reed, Mississippi, RB, 0/0
9. Craig Nagel, Purdue, QB, 0/0
10. Doug Kleber, Illinois, T, 0/0
11. Doug Celek, Kent State, DE, 0/0
13. Brian Murray, Arizona, T, 0/0
14. Joe Smalzer, Illinois, TE, 0/0
15. Luther Philyaw, Loyola (CA), DB, 0/0

DALLAS COWBOYS

1. **Aaron Kyle, Wyoming, DB, 60/95**
2. Jim Eidson, Mississippi State, G, 9/9
2. Jim Jensen, Iowa, RB, 14/78

3. Duke Fergerson, San Diego State, WR, 0/42
3. **Butch Johnson, California-Riverside, WR, 112/144**
3. John Smith, Boise State, RB, 0/0
4. **Tom Rafferty, Penn State, C, 203/203**
5. Wally Pesuit, Kentucky, G, 0/48
6. Greg McGuire, Indiana, T, 0/0
7. Greg Schaum, Michigan State, DE, 12/26
7. Dave Williams, Colorado, RB, 0/66
8. Henry Laws, South Carolina, DB, 0/0
9. Beasley Reece, North Texas, DB, 10/117
10. Leroy Cook, Alabama, DE, 0/0
11. Cornelius Greene, Ohio State, QB, 0/0
12. Charles McShane, California Lutheran, LB, 0/29
13. Mark Driscoll, Colorado State, QB, 0/0
14. Larry Mushinskie, Nebraska, TE, 0/0
15. Dale Curry, UCLA, LB, 0/0

DENVER BRONCOS

1. **Tom Glassic, Virginia, G, 105/105**
2. Kurt Knoff, Kansas, DB, 0/70
4. Craig Penrose, San Diego State, QB, 18/18
5. Lonnie Perrin, Illinois, RB, 44/58
8. James Betterson, North Carolina, RB, 0/23
9. Jim Czirr, Michigan, C, 0/0
9. Jim Lisko, Arkansas State, LB, 0/0
10. Art Gilliam, Grambling, DE, 0/0
11. Greg Pittman, Iowa State, LB, 0/0
12. Randy Moore, Arizona State, DT, 8/8
13. Donnie McGraw, Houston, RB, 0/0
14. **Larry Evans, Mississippi College, LB, 101/104**
15. Wilbur Summers, Louisville, P, 0/13
16. John Huddleston, Utah, LB, 0/27

DETROIT LIONS

1. Lawrence Gaines, Wyoming, RB, 43/43
1. **James Hunter, Grambling State, DB, 86/86**
2. **David Hill, Texas A&M-Kingsville, TE, 100/176**
2. Ken Long, Purdue, G, 13/13
3. **Russ Bolinger, Long Beach State, G, 83/121**
3. **John Woodcock, Hawaii, DT, 52/70**
5. Steadman Scavella, Miami (FL), LB, 0/0
7. Garth Ten Napel, Texas A&M, LB, 28/29
8. Rich Sorenson, Cal State-Chico, K, 0/0
8. Charles Braswell, West Virginia, DB, 0/0
9. Leanell Jones, Long Beach State, TE, 0/0
10. Bill Bowerman, New Mexico State, QB, 0/0
11. Gary Shugrue, Villanova, DE, 0/0
12. Mike McCabe, South Carolina, C, 0/0
13. Mel Jacobs, San Diego State, WR, 0/0
14. Leonard Elston, Kentucky State, WR, 0/0
15. Trent Smock, Indiana, WR, 0/0

GREEN BAY PACKERS

1. **Mark Koncar, Colorado, T, 53/58**
3. **Mike McCoy, Colorado, DB, 110/110**
4. Tom Perko, Pittsburgh, LB, 14/14
5. **Aundra Thompson, Texas A&M-Commerce, WR, 63/83**
8. Jim Burrow, Nebraska, DB, 3/3
9. **Jim Gueno, Tulane, LB, 75/75**
10. Jessie Green, Tulsa, WR, 1/24
11. Curtis Leak, Johnson C. Smith, WR, 0/0
12. **Melvin Jackson, USC, G, 64/64**
13. Bradley Bowman, Southern Mississippi, DB, 0/0
14. John Henson, Cal Poly-SLO, RB, 0/0
15. Jerry Dandridge, Memphis State, LB, 0/0

HOUSTON OILERS

2. **Mike Barber, Louisiana Tech, TE, 78/129**
4. Steve Largent, Tulsa, WR, 0/200
6. Todd Simonsen, South Dakota State, T, 0/0
7. Larry Harris, Oklahoma State, DT, 0/0
8. Bobby Simon, Grambling, T, 0/0
9. Art Stringer, Ball State, LB, 41/41
10. Steve Kincannon, Cal State-Humboldt, QB, 0/0
11. Skip Walker, Texas A&M, RB, 0/0
12. Larry Bell, East Texas State, DT, 0/0
13. Dan O'Rourke, Colorado, WR, 0/0
14. John Reimer, Wisconsin, T, 0/0
15. Bobby Byars, Cheyney, DB, 0/0

KANSAS CITY CHIEFS

1. **Rod Walters, Iowa, G, 52/55**
2. Cliff Frazier, UCLA, DT, 14/14
3. **Gary Barbaro, Nicholls State, DB, 101/101**
3. **Henry Marshall, Missouri, WR, 165/165**
3. Keith Simons, Minnesota, DT, 20/49
5. Jimbo Elrod, Oklahoma, LB, 36/40
5. Willie Lee, Bethune-Cookman, DT, 28/28
6. Steve Taylor, Kansas, DB, 14/14
6. Bob Gregolunas, Northern Illinois, LB, 0/0
6. Calvin Harper, Illinois State, T, 0/0
7. Rod Wellington, Iowa, RB, 0/0
8. Orrin Olsen, Brigham Young, C, 14/14
9. **Tim Collier, Texas A&M-Commerce, DB, 52/94**
10. **Whitney Paul, Colorado, LB, 100/155**
11. Bob Squires, Hastings, TE, 0/0
12. Harold Porter, Southwestern Louisiana, WR, 0/0
13. Joe Bruner, Northeast Louisiana, QB, 0/0
14. Rick Thurman, Texas, T, 0/0
15. Dave Rozumek, New Hampshire, LB, 45/45
17. Pat McNeil, Baylor, RB, 13/13

LOS ANGELES RAMS

1. Kevin McLain, Colorado State, LB, 48/48
2. Ron McCartney, Tennessee, LB, 0/45
2. **Pat Thomas, Texas A&M, DB, 87/87**
3. **Jackie Slater, Jackson State, T, 259/259**
4. Gerald Taylor, Texas A&I, WR, 0/0
5. Ken Bordelon, LSU, LB, 0/82
5. **Carl Ekern, San Jose State, LB, 166/166**
5. Dwight Scales, Grambling State, WR, 39/90
7. Larry Buie, Mississippi State, DB, 0/0
9. Jeb Church, Stanford, DB, 0/0
10. Freeman Johns, SMU, WR, 7/7
11. Brian Nemeth, South Carolina, TE, 0/0
12. Jim Jodat, Carthage, RB, 37/87
13. Steve Hamilton, Emporia State, QB, 0/0
14. Al Burleson, Washington, DB, 0/0
15. Malcolm Campbell, Cal State-Los Angeles, WR, 0/0

MIAMI DOLPHINS

1. **Kim Bokamper, San Jose State, DE, 127/127**
1. **Larry Gordon, Arizona State, LB, 100/100**
2. Loaird McCreary, Tennessee State, TE, 44/55
3. **Duriel Harris, New Mexico State, WR, 111/127**
4. Melvin Mitchell, Tennessee State, G, 19/34
6. **Gary Davis, Cal Poly-San Luis Obispo, RB, 57/79**
7. Joe Ingersoll, Nevada-Las Vegas, G, 0/0
7. John Owens, Tennessee State, DE, 0/0
8. Bob Simpson, Colorado, DE, 5/5
9. Norris Thomas, Southern Mississippi, DB, 46/112
10. Gary Fencik, Yale, DB, 0/164
10. Don Testerman, Clemson, RB, 5/49
11. Dexter Pride, Minnesota, RB, 0/0
12. Randy Young, Iowa State, T, 0/9
12. Darryl Brandford, Northwestern, DT, 0/0
13. Bernie Head, Tulsa, C, 0/0
14. Bob Gissler, South Dakota State, LB, 0/0
15. Ron Holmes, Utah State, RB, 0/0

MINNESOTA VIKINGS

1. **James White, Oklahoma State, DT, 117/117**
2. **Sammy White, Grambling State, WR, 128/128**
3. **Wes Hamilton, Tulsa, G, 116/116**
4. Leonard Willis, Ohio State, WR, 14/36
5. Steve Wagner, Wisconsin, DB, 0/61
5. Keith Barnette, Boston College, RB, 0/0
6. Terry Egerdahl, Minnesota-Duluth, DB, 0/0
7. Larry Brune, Rice, DB, 16/16
9. Isaac Hagins, Southern (LA), WR, 0/50
10. Bill Salmon, Northern Iowa, QB, 0/0
11. Steve Kracher, Montana State, RB, 0/0
12. Robert Sparks, Cal State-San Francisco, DB, 0/0
13. Gary Pauson, Colorado State, DE, 0/0
14. Jeff Stapleton, Purdue, T, 0/0
15. Ron Groce, Macalester, RB, 4/4

NEW ENGLAND PATRIOTS

1. **Pete Brock, Colorado, C, 154/154**
1. **Tim Fox, Ohio State, DB, 91/141**
1. **Mike Haynes, Arizona State, DB, 90/177**
2. Ike Forte, Arkansas, RB, 23/64
6. Greg Boyd, San Diego State, DE, 23/82
7. Perry Brooks, Southern (LA), DT, 0/92
8. Stu Betts, Northern Michigan, RB, 0/0
9. Doug Beaudoin, Minnesota, DB, 45/59
10. Ricky Feacher, Mississippi Valley State, WR, 3/125
11. Donnie Thomas, Indiana, LB, 3/3
12. Nathaniel Bell, Tulane, DT, 0/0
13. James Jones, Central Michigan, DB, 0/0
14. Dave Quehl, Holy Cross, WR, 0/0
15. Bernard Coleman, Bethune-Cookman, WR, 0/0

NEW ORLEANS SAINTS

1. **Chuck Muncie, California, RB, 59/110**
2. **Tony Galbreath, Missouri, RB, 75/170**
3. Bob Simmons, Texas, G, 0/88
4. Tinker Owens, Oklahoma, WR, 48/48
5. Scott Parrish, Utah State, T, 0/0
6. Terry Stieve, Wisconsin, G, 28/113
7. Ed Bauer, Notre Dame, G, 0/0
8. Craig Cassady, Ohio State, DB, 12/12
9. Warren Peiffer, Iowa, DT, 0/0
10. Junior Hardin, Eastern Kentucky, LB, 0/0
11. Greg Kokal, Kent State, QB, 0/0
12. Milton Butts, North Carolina, T, 0/0
13. Kenny Downing, Missouri, DB, 0/0
14. Rich Hucke, Western Montana, DE, 0/0
15. Steve Seminoff, Wichita State, DT, 0/0

NEW YORK GIANTS

1. Troy Archer, Colorado, DT, 38/38
4. Gordon Bell, Michigan, RB, 24/30
4. **Harry Carson, South Carolina State, LB, 173/173**
5. Melvin Wilson, Cal State-Northridge, DB, 0/0
6. **Dan Lloyd, Washington, LB, 57/57**
8. John Jordan, Indiana, DT, 0/0
10. John Thomas, Valley City, RB, 0/0
11. Craig Brantley, Clemson, WR, 0/0
12. Jerry Golsteyn, Northern Illinois, QB, 13/21
13. Rick Caswell, Western Kentucky, KR, 0/0
14. Jerry Mullane, Lehigh, LB, 0/0
15. Eddie Morgan, Arkansas State, DT, 0/0

NEW YORK JETS

1. **Richard Todd, Alabama, QB, 102/119**
2. **Shafer Suggs, Ball State, DB, 56/60**
3. **Greg Buttle, Penn State, LB, 110/110**
5. Steve King, Michigan, T, 0/0
6. Bob Martin, Nebraska, LB, 36/49
7. **Abdul Salaam, Kent State, DT, 97/97**
7. James Richards, Florida, RB, 0/0
8. Louie Giammona, Utah State, RB, 14/69
8. Joe Davis, Southern California, G, 0/0
9. Ronnie Moore, Virginia Military, WR, 0/0
11. **Lawrence Pillers, Alcorn State, DE, 62/139**
12. Don Buckey, North Carolina State, WR, 4/4
12. Dave Buckey, North Carolina State, QB, 0/0
14. Al Gluchoski, West Virginia, C, 0/0
15. Rick Faulk, Cal State-San Francisco, P, 0/0

OAKLAND RAIDERS

2. Jeb Blount, Tulsa, QB, 0/5
2. Charles Philyaw, Texas Southern, DE, 44/44
3. Rik Bonness, Nebraska, LB, 14/59
4. Herb McMath, Morningside, DT, 14/22
5. Fred Steinfort, Boston College, K, 7/64
7. Clarence Chapman, Eastern Michigan, DB, 0/65
8. Jerome Dove, Colorado State, DB, 0/60
8. Terry Kunz, Colorado, RB, 7/7
10. Dwight Lewis, Purdue, DB, 0/0
11. Rick Jennings, Maryland, RB, 13/16
12. Cedric Brown, Kent State, DB, 0/100
13. Craig Crnick, Idaho, DE, 0/0
13. Mark Young, Washington State, T, 0/0
14. Calvin Young, Fresno State, RB, 0/0
15. Carl Hargrave, Upper Iowa, DB, 0/0

PHILADELPHIA EAGLES

4. Mike Smith, Florida, DE, 0/0
5. Greg Johnson, Florida State, DT, 0/7
6. Kirk Johnson, Howard Payne, T, 0/0
7. **Carl Hairston, Maryland-Eastern Shore, DE, 116/224**
8. Richard La Fargue, Arkansas, C, 0/0
9. Mike Hogan, Tennessee-Chattanooga, RB, 40/49
9. Richard Osborne, Texas A&M, TE, 34/50
10. Herb Lusk, Long Beach State, RB, 28/28
11. Mike Gilbert, San Diego State, DT, 0/0
13. **Terry Tautolo, UCLA, LB, 59/104**
13. Steve Ebbecke, Villanova, DB, 0/0
14. Melvin Shy, Tennessee State, DB, 0/0
15. Brett White, UCLA, P, 0/0

PITTSBURGH STEELERS

1. **Bennie Cunningham, Clemson, TE, 118/118**
2. Mike Kruczek, Boston College, QB, 29/36
2. **Ray Pinney, Washington, T, 125/125**
2. James Files, McNeese State, C, 0/0
3. Ron Coder, Penn State, G, 0/53
3. Ernest Pough, Texas Southern, WR, 28/40
4. **Theo Bell, Arizona, WR, 56/127**
4. Wonder Monds, Nebraska, DB, 0/16
5. Rodney Norton, Rice, LB, 0/0
6. Jack Deloplaine, Salem, RB, 33/40
6. **Gary Dunn, Miami (FL), NT, 146/146**
7. Barry Burton, Vanderbilt, TE, 0/0
8. Ed McAleney, Massachusetts, DE, 0/2
9. Wentford Gaines, Cincinnati, DB, 1/36
10. Gary Campbell, Colorado, LB, 0/93
11. Rolland Fuchs, Arkansas, RB, 0/0
12. Bill Carroll, East Texas State, WR, 0/0
13. Larry Kain, Ohio State, TE, 0/0
14. Wayne Fields, Florida, DB, 0/0
15. Mel Davis, North Texas State, DE, 0/0

SAN DIEGO CHARGERS

1. Joe Washington, Oklahoma, RB, 13/119
2. **Don Macek, Boston College, C, 162/162**
3. Larry Dorsey, Tennessee State, WR, 26/42
4. **Bob Horn, Oregon State, LB, 92/109**
4. **Artie Owens, West Virginia, WR, 57/64**
4. Ron Singleton, Grambling State, T, 13/59
5. **Woodrow Lowe, Alabama, LB, 164/164**
6. Calvin Lane, Fresno State, DB, 0/0
8. Tony DiRienzo, Oklahoma, K, 0/0
9. Glynn Harrison, Georgia, RB, 0/8
10. Jeff Perlinger, Michigan, DE, 0/0
11. **Ray Preston, Syracuse, LB, 122/122**
12. Ron Lee, Oregon, DB, 0/0
12. Herman Harris, Mississippi Valley State, DB, 0/0
13. John Lee, Nebraska, DE, 48/52
14. Ed Jones, Cincinnati, G, 0/0
15. Jack Hoffman, Indiana, DT, 0/0
17. Clarence Sanders, Cincinnati, LB, 0/17

SAN FRANCISCO 49ERS

2. **Randy Cross, UCLA, G, 185/185**
2. **Eddie Lewis, Kansas, DB, 51/73**
4. Steve Rivera, California, WR, 12/15
5. Tony Leonard, Virginia Union, DB, 39/43
6. Scott Bull, Arkansas, QB, 36/36
6. Robert Pennywell, Grambling State, LB, 0/61
7. Jay Chesley, Vanderbilt, DB, 0/0
8. **John Ayers, West Texas A&M, G, 148/157**
9. Kenny Harrison, SMU, WR, 33/42
10. Robin Ross, Washington State, T, 0/0
11. **Paul Hofer, Mississippi, RB, 77/77**
12. Gerald Loper, Florida, G, 0/0
13. Larry Brumfield, Indiana State, DB, 0/0
14. Johnny Miller, Livingstone, G, 6/6
15. Howard Stidham, Tennessee Tech, LB, 4/4
16. Reggie Lewis, San Diego State, DE, 0/34

ST. LOUIS CARDINALS

1. **Mike Dawson, Arizona, DT, 88/113**
3. Brad Oates, Brigham Young, T, 44/67
4. **Pat Tilley, Louisiana Tech, WR, 147/147**
5. **Wayne Morris, SMU, RB, 110/120**
7. Phil Rogers, Virginia Tech, RB, 0/0
8. Randy Burks, Oklahoma State, WR, 0/1
10. Randy Walker, Bethune-Cookman, RB, 0/0
11. Marty Akins, Texas, DB, 0/0
13. Greg Brewton, Michigan State, DT, 0/0
14. Raymond Crosier, Abilene Christian, DE, 0/0
15. **Lee Nelson, Florida State, DB, 135/135**

SEATTLE SEAHAWKS

1. Steve Niehaus, Notre Dame, DT, 36/39
2. **Sammy Green, Florida, LB, 60/62**
2. **Steve Raible, Georgia Tech, WR, 84/84**
2. **Sherman Smith, Miami (OH), RB, 82/95**
3. Don Bitterlich, Temple, K, 3/3
3. Rick Engles, Tulsa, P, 15/22
3. Jeff Lloyd, West Texas A&M, DE, 0/25
4. Andy Bolton, Fisk, RB, 5/32
4. Randy Johnson, Georgia, G, 0/22
4. Steve Myer, New Mexico, QB, 12/12
5. **Don Dufek, Michigan, DB, 95/95**
5. Ernie Jones, Miami (FL), DB, 9/44
5. Larry Bates, Miami (FL), RB, 0/0
6. Al Darby, Florida, TE, 1/9
7. Lodie Dixon, Arkansas State, DT, 0/0
8. Larry Shipp, Louisiana State, WR, 0/0
9. Bob Bos, Iowa State, T, 0/0
10. Randy Coffield, Florida State, LB, 13/24
11. Keith Muehr, Southwestern Louisiana, P, 0/0
12. Ronnie Barnett, Texas-Arlington, WR, 0/0
13. Andy Reid, Georgia, RB, 0/1
14. Jarvis Blinks, Northwestern State (LA), DB, 0/0
15. Dan Smith, Washington State, T, 0/0

TAMPA BAY BUCCANEERS

1. **Lee Roy Selmon, Oklahoma, DE, 121/121**
2. Jimmy DuBose, Florida, RB, 33/33
2. **Dewey Selmon, Oklahoma, LB, 72/80**
3. Steve Young, Colorado, T, 13/27
3. Steve Maughan, Utah State, LB, 0/0
4. Everett Little, Houston, G, 10/10
4. Richard Appleby, Georgia, WR, 0/0
5. **Steve Wilson, Georgia, C, 125/125**
5. Mishael Kelson, West Texas State, DB, 0/0
6. **Curtis Jordan, Texas Tech, DB, 71/145**
7. Parnell Dickinson, Mississippi Valley State, QB, 8/8
9. Bruce Welch, Texas A&M, G, 0/0
10. Sid Smith, BYU, LB, 0/0
11. Melvin Washington, Colorado State, DB, 0/0
12. George Ragsdale, North Carolina A&T, RB, 39/39
13. Brad Jenkins, Nebraska, TE, 0/0
14. Carl Roaches, Texas A&M, WR, 0/76
15. Bob Dzierzak, Utah State, DT, 0/0

WASHINGTON REDSKINS

5. Mike Hughes, Baylor, G, 0/0
6. Tommy Marvaso, Cincinnati, DB, 0/14
8. Brian Fryer, Edmonton (Canada), WR, 4/4
9. Curtis Akins, Hawaii, G, 0/0
10. Paul Strohmeier, Washington, LB, 0/0
11. Dean Gissler, Nebraska, DE, 0/0
12. Walter Tullis, Delaware State, WR, 0/32
13. Waymon Britt, Michigan, DB, 0/0
14. Quinn Buckner, Indiana, DB, 0/0
15. John Monroe, Bluefield, RB, 0/0

1977 NFL

ATLANTA FALCONS

1. **Warren Bryant, Kentucky, T, 99/104**
1. **Wilson Faumuina, San Jose State, DT, 74/74**
2. **R.C. Thielemann, Arkansas, G, 114/157**
3. **Edgar Fields, Texas A&M, DT, 60/62**
4. Allan Leavitt, Georgia, K, 0/8
5. Shelton Diggs, USC, WR, 0/7
6. Keith Jenkins, Cincinnati, DB, 0/0
8. Walter Packer, Mississippi State, DB, 0/11
9. John Maxwell, Boston College, T, 0/0
9. Robert Speer, Arkansas State, DE, 0/0
10. Billy Ryckman, Louisiana Tech, WR, 44/44
11. Dave Farmer, USC, RB, 0/3
12. Don Parrish, Pittsburgh, NT, 0/71

BALTIMORE COLTS

1. **Randy Burke, Kentucky, WR, 57/57**
2. **Mike Ozdowski, Virginia, DE, 54/54**
6. Calvin O'Neal, Michigan, LB, 15/15
7. Blanchard Carter, UNLV, T, 0/13
8. Ken Helms, Georgia, T, 0/0
9. Glen Capriola, Boston College, RB, 0/0
10. Ron Baker, Oklahoma State, G, 32/155
11. Brian Ruff, Citadel, LB, 0/0
12. Bill Deutsch, North Dakota, RB, 0/0

BUFFALO BILLS

1. Phil Dokes, Oklahoma State, DT, 22/22
3. **Curtis Brown, Missouri, RB, 76/78**
3. John Kimbrough, St. Cloud State, WR, 14/14
4. Jimmy Dean, Texas A&M, DE, 0/3
5. Neil O'Donoghue, Auburn, K, 5/110
5. Fred Besana, California, QB, 0/0
6. Ron Pruitt, Nebraska, DE, 0/0
7. Mike Nelms, Baylor, DB, 0/68
8. Greg Morton, Michigan, DE, 9/9
11. Nate Jackson, Tennessee State, RB, 0/0
12. **Charles Romes, North Carolina Central, DB, 151/156**

CHICAGO BEARS

1. **Ted Albrecht, California, T, 77/77**
2. Mike Spivey, Colorado, DB, 46/77
3. **Robin Earl, Washington, TE, 84/84**
6. **Vince Evans, USC, QB, 56/100**
7. Gerald Butler, Nicholls State, WR, 0/0
9. Nick Buonamici, Ohio State, DT, 0/0
10. Dennis Breckner, Miami (FL), DE, 0/0
11. Connie Zelencik, Purdue, C, 0/14
12. Terry Irvin, Jackson State, DB, 0/0

CINCINNATI BENGALS

1. Mike Cobb, Michigan State, TE, 13/62
1. **Eddie Edwards, Miami (FL), DE, 170/170**
1. **Wilson Whitley, Houston, DT, 82/82**
2. **Pete Johnson, Ohio State, RB, 94/110**
3. Mike Voight, North Carolina, RB, 0/14
4. Jerry Anderson, Oklahoma, DB, 14/16
4. Rick Walker, UCLA, TE, 31/119
4. **Mike Wilson, Georgia, T, 114/174**
5. Ray Phillips, Nebraska, LB, 16/69
6. Tom Duniven, Texas Tech, QB, 0/1
7. **Louis Breeden, North Carolina Central, DB, 134/134**
7. Jim Corbett, Pittsburgh, TE, 44/44
8. Jose St. Victor, Syracuse, G, 0/0
9. Willie Zachary, Central State (OH), WR, 0/0
10. Bob Bialik, Hillsdale, P, 0/0
11. Carl Allen, Southern Mississippi, DB, 0/79
11. Joel Parrish, Georgia, G, 0/0
12. Alex Percival, Morehouse, WR, 0/0

CLEVELAND BROWNS

1. **Robert Jackson, Texas A&M, LB, 58/62**
2. Tom Skladany, Ohio State, P, 0/61
4. **Oliver Davis, Tennessee State, DB, 58/77**
4. Mickey Sims, South Carolina State, DT, 43/43
7. Bob Lingenfelter, Nebraska, T, 14/19
7. Blane Smith, Purdue, LB, 0/1
7. Kenny Randle, Southern Methodist, WR, 0/0
8. Bill Armstrong, Wake Forest, DB, 0/0
9. Daryl Brown, Tufts, DB, 0/0
10. Tom Burkett, North Carolina, T, 0/0
11. Charles Nash, Arizona, WR, 0/0
12. Leo Tierney, Georgia Tech, C, 2/7

DALLAS COWBOYS

1. **Tony Dorsett, Pittsburgh, RB, 157/173**
2. Glenn Carano, UNLV, QB, 36/36
3. **Tony Hill, Stanford, WR, 141/141**
3. Val Belcher, Houston, G, 0/0
4. **Guy Brown, Houston, LB, 85/85**
5. **Andy Frederick, New Mexico, T, 77/132**
6. **Jim Cooper, Temple, T, 133/133**
7. Dave Stalls, Northern Colorado, DE, 43/99
8. Al Cleveland, Pacific, DE, 0/0
8. Fred Williams, Arizona State, RB, 0/0
9. Mark Cantrell, North Carolina, C, 0/0
10. Steve DeBerg, San Jose State, QB, 0/206
11. Don Wardlow, Washington, TE, 0/0
12. Greg Peters, California, G, 0/0

DENVER BRONCOS

1. Steve Schindler, Boston College, G, 28/28
2. **Rob Lytle, Michigan, RB, 87/87**
4. **Bill Bryan, Duke, C, 153/153**
7. Larry Swider, Pittsburgh, P, 0/52
8. Calvin Culliver, Alabama, RB, 0/0
9. Charles Jackson, Washington, LB, 0/117
10. Oren Middlebrook, Arkansas State, WR, 0/16
11. Phil Heck, California, LB, 0/0
12. Scott Levenhagen, Western Illinois, TE, 0/0

DETROIT LIONS

2. **Walt Williams, New Mexico State, DB, 57/93**
3. **Rick Kane, San Jose State, RB, 113/125**
4. Luther Blue, Iowa State, WR, 39/42
5. Ron Crosby, Penn State, LB, 0/83
6. Reggie Pinkney, East Carolina, DB, 24/72
7. Tim Black, Baylor, LB, 0/4
8. Mark Griffin, North Carolina, T, 0/0
9. Steve Mathieson, Florida State, QB, 0/0
10. Gary Anderson, Stanford, G, 14/21
11. Tony Daykin, Georgia Tech, LB, 30/73
12. Dave Greenwood, Iowa State, G, 0/0

GREEN BAY PACKERS

1. **Mike Butler, Kansas, DE, 95/95**
1. **Ezra Johnson, Morris Brown, DE, 148/192**
2. **Greg Koch, Arkansas, T, 133/159**
3. Rick Scribner, Idaho State, G, 0/0
5. Nate Simpson, Tennessee State, RB, 43/43
6. Tim Moresco, Syracuse, DB, 14/52
7. **Derrel Gofourth, Oklahoma State, G, 85/116**
7. Rell Tipton, Baylor, G, 0/0
8. **David Whitehurst, Furman, QB, 54/54**
9. Joel Mullins, Arkansas State, T, 0/0
10. Jim Culbreath, Oklahoma, RB, 29/32
11. Terry Randolph, American International, DB, 14/14

HOUSTON OILERS

1. **Morris Towns, Missouri, T, 88/92**
2. George Reihner, Penn State, G, 27/27
3. **Rob Carpenter, Miami (OH), RB, 57/118**
3. Jimmie Giles, Alcorn State, TE, 14/188
3. **Tim Wilson, Maryland, FB, 83/101**
4. Warren Anderson, West Virginia State, WR, 8/10
6. **David Carter, Western Kentucky, C, 110/121**
6. Gary Woolford, Florida State, DB, 0/12
8. Eddie Foster, Houston, WR, 15/15
8. Steve Davis, Georgia, WR, 0/0
9. Bill Currier, South Carolina, DB, 44/111
10. Harvey Hull, Mississippi State, LB, 0/0
11. Al Romano, Pittsburgh, LB, 0/0
12. Ove Johansson, Abilene Christian, K, 0/2

KANSAS CITY CHIEFS

1. **Gary Green, Baylor, DB, 100/132**
2. **Tony Reed, Colorado, RB, 56/71**
3. **Tom Howard, Texas Tech, LB, 95/113**
4. Mark Bailey, Long Beach State, RB, 27/27
4. Eric Harris, Memphis, DB, 39/71
4. Darius Helton, North Carolina Central, G, 6/6
4. **Tony Samuels, Bethune-Cookman, TE, 50/56**
6. Rick Burleson, Texas, DE, 0/0
6. Andre Herrera, Southern Illinois, RB, 0/0
7. Chris Golub, Kansas, DB, 1/1
8. Waddell Smith, Kansas, WR, 0/2
8. Ron Olsonoski, St. Thomas (MN), LB, 0/0
9. Derrick Glanton, Bishop, DE, 0/0
9. Dave Green, New Mexico, T, 0/0
10. Mark Vitali, Purdue, QB, 0/0
11. Maurice Mitchell, Northern Michigan, WR, 0/0
12. Raymond Burks, UCLA, LB, 13/13

LOS ANGELES RAMS

1. **Bob Brudzinski, Ohio State, LB, 55/180**
2. **Nolan Cromwell, Kansas, DB, 161/161**
2. **Billy Waddy, Colorado, WR, 71/75**
3. Ed Fulton, Maryland, G, 4/9
3. **Wendell Tyler, UCLA, RB, 60/108**
4. **Vince Ferragamo, Nebraska, QB, 62/75**
4. Eary Jones, Memphis State, DE, 0/0
5. Donnie Hickman, USC, G, 0/10
5. Jeff Williams, Rhode Island, G, 1/56
6. Art Best, Kent State, RB, 0/31
8. Rod Bockwoldt, Weber State, DB, 0/0
10. Don Petersen, Boston College, TE, 0/0
11. Carson Long, Pittsburgh, K, 0/9
12. Barry Caudill, Southern Mississippi, C, 0/0

MIAMI DOLPHINS

1. **A.J. Duhe, LSU, LB, 108/108**
2. **Bob Baumhower, Alabama, NT, 130/130**
3. Mike Watson, Miami (OH), T, 0/0
5. Leroy Harris, Arkansas State, RB, 26/63
5. Mike Michel, Stanford, P, 13/23
7. Bruce Herron, New Mexico, LB, 0/71
8. Horace Perkins, Colorado, DB, 0/16
9. Robert Turner, Oklahoma State, RB, 0/4
10. Mark Carter, Eastern Michigan, T, 0/0
11. John Alexander, Rutgers, DE, 12/12
12. Terry Anderson, Bethune-Cookman, WR, 15/29

MINNESOTA VIKINGS

1. **Tommy Kramer, Rice, QB, 128/129**
2. **Dennis Swilley, North Texas, C, 139/139**
3. **Tom Hannon, Michigan State, DB, 117/117**
5. Ken Moore, Northern Illinois, TE, 0/6
8. Clint Strozier, Southern California, DB, 0/0
9. **Scott Studwell, Illinois, LB, 201/201**
10. Dan Beaver, Illinois, K, 0/0
11. Keith Hartwig, Arizona, WR, 0/4
12. Jim Kelleher, Colorado, RB, 0/0

NEW ENGLAND PATRIOTS

1. **Raymond Clayborn, Texas, DB, 191/208**
1. **Stanley Morgan, Tennessee, WR, 180/196**
2. **Don Hasselbeck, Colorado, TE, 86/123**
2. Horace Ivory, Oklahoma, RB, 46/58
3. Sidney Brown, Oklahoma, DB, 16/16
4. Gerald Skinner, Arkansas, T, 0/15
7. Ken Smith, Arkansas-Pine Bluff, WR, 0/0
8. Brad Benson, Penn State, T, 0/137
9. Jerry Vogele, Michigan, LB, 0/0
10. John Rasmussen, Wisconsin, T, 0/0
10. Giles Alexander, Tulsa, DE, 0/0
11. Ray Costict, Mississippi State, LB, 46/46
12. Dave Preston, Bowling Green State, RB, 0/76

NEW ORLEANS SAINTS

1. Joe Campbell, Maryland, DE, 45/65
2. Mike Fultz, Nebraska, DT, 49/58
3. Robert Watts, Boston College, LB, 0/2
5. Dave Hubbard, Brigham Young, T, 5/5
5. **Dave Lafary, Purdue, T, 109/109**
6. Cliff Parsley, Oklahoma State, P, 0/82
6. Tom Shick, Maryland, G, 0/0
7. Greg Boykin, Northwestern, RB, 14/30
8. Jimmy Stewart, Tulsa, DB, 9/14
9. Dave Knowles, Indiana, T, 0/0
10. Rafael Septien, Louisiana-Lafayette, K, 0/151
11. John Blain, San Jose State, T, 0/0
12. Oakley Dalton, Jackson State, DT, 1/1

NEW YORK GIANTS

1. **Gary Jeter, USC, DE, 75/168**
2. **Johnny Perkins, Abilene Christian, WR, 71/71**
4. Mike Vaughan, Oklahoma, T, 0/0
5. Randy Dean, Northwestern, QB, 23/23
6. Emery Moorehead, Colorado, TE, 36/158
6. Bob Jordan, Memphis State, T, 0/0
7. Al Dixon, Iowa State, TE, 28/79
8. Bill Rice, BYU, DT, 0/0
8. Otis Rodgers, Iowa State, LB, 0/0
9. Ken Mullins, Florida A&M, DE, 0/0
10. Mike Jones, Minnesota, WR, 0/0
11. Bill Helms, San Diego State, TE, 0/0
12. Elmo Simmons, Texas-Arlington, RB, 0/0

NEW YORK JETS

1. **Marvin Powell, USC, T, 124/133**
2. **Wesley Walker, California, WR, 154/154**
3. Tank Marshall, Texas A&M, DT, 5/5
4. **Scott Dierking, Purdue, RB, 102/110**
5. Perry Griggs, Troy State, WR, 0/1
5. Gary Gregory, Baylor, T, 0/0
6. **Joe Klecko, Temple, DT, 140/155**
7. Bob Grupp, Duke, P, 0/41
7. **Kevin Long, South Carolina, RB, 73/73**
7. Charlie White, Bethune-Cookman, RB, 13/20
8. **Dan Alexander, LSU, G, 192/192**
8. Ed Thompson, Ohio State, LB, 0/0
9. Matt Robinson, Georgia, QB, 35/69
10. John Hennessy, Michigan, LB, 46/46
11. Dave Butterfield, Nebraska, DB, 0/0
12. Phil Gargis, Auburn, RB, 0/0
12. Dave Conrad, Maryland, T, 0/0

OAKLAND RAIDERS

2. **Mike Davis, Colorado, DB, 107/115**
2. Ted McKnight, Minnesota-Duluth, RB, 0/68
4. **Mickey Marvin, Tennessee, G, 120/120**
5. **Jeff Barnes, California, LB, 157/157**
5. **Lester Hayes, Texas A&M, DB, 149/149**
7. Rich Martini, California-Davis, WR, 32/44
8. Terry Robiskie, LSU, RB, 24/33
12. Rolf Benirschke, California-Davis, K, 0/121
12. **Rod Martin, USC, LB, 165/165**

PHILADELPHIA EAGLES

5. Skip Sharp, Kansas, DB, 0/0
6. Mark Mitchell, Tulane, DB, 14/14
6. **Wilbert Montgomery, Abilene Christian, RB, 100/107**
6. Kevin Russell, Tennessee State, DB, 0/0
7. **Charlie Johnson, Colorado, NT, 76/117**
8. Cleveland Franklin, Baylor, RB, 30/61
9. T.J. Humphreys, Arkansas State, G, 0/0
10. John Mastronardo, Villanova, WR, 0/0
11. Rocco Moore, Western Michigan, G, 0/7
11. Mike Cordova, Stanford, QB, 0/0

PITTSBURGH STEELERS

1. **Robin Cole, New Mexico, LB, 150/166**
2. **Sidney Thornton, Northwestern State (LA), RB, 74/74**
3. **Tom Beasley, Virginia Tech, DE, 79/105**
3. **Jim Smith, Michigan, WR, 73/79**
4. Dan Audick, Hawaii, T, 0/76
4. **Ted Petersen, Eastern Illinois, T, 85/94**
4. Laverne Smith, Kansas, RB, 7/7
5. **Steve Courson, South Carolina, G, 73/103**
5. Cliff Stoudt, Youngstown State, QB, 30/66
5. **Dirt Winston, Arkansas, LB, 99/142**
6. Paul Harris, Alabama, LB, 0/20
7. Randy Frisch, Missouri, DT, 0/0
8. Phil August, Miami (FL), WR, 0/0
9. Roosevelt Kelly, Eastern Kentucky, TE, 0/0
10. Dave LaCrosse, Wake Forest, LB, 14/14
10. Alvin Cowans, Florida, DB, 0/0
11. Lou West, Cincinnati, DB, 0/0
12. Jimmy Stephens, Florida, TE, 0/0

SAN DIEGO CHARGERS

1. **Bob Rush, Memphis, C, 70/117**
3. **Linden King, Colorado State, LB, 108/164**
5. Cliff Olander, New Mexico State, QB, 15/15
5. **Clarence Williams, South Carolina, RB, 67/67**
6. Larry Barnes, Tennessee State, RB, 9/34

6. Dave Lindstrom, Boston University, DE, 0/118
6. **Pete Shaw, Northwestern, DB, 74/114**
7. Ron Bush, Southern California, DB, 0/0
9. Gene Washington, Georgia, WR, 0/2
10. Curtis Townsend, Arkansas, LB, 0/9
12. Jim Stansik, Eastern Michigan, TE, 0/0

SAN FRANCISCO 49ERS

3. Elmo Boyd, Eastern Kentucky, WR, 9/11
4. Stan Black, Mississippi State, DB, 13/13
6. Mike Burns, USC, DB, 14/29
6. Jim Harlan, Howard Payne, T, 0/14
7. Jim Van Wagner, Michigan Tech, RB, 0/5
9. David Posey, Florida, K, 0/11
11. Brian Billick, BYU, TE, 0/0
12. Scott Martin, North Dakota, G, 0/0

ST. LOUIS CARDINALS

1. Steve Pisarkiewicz, Missouri, QB, 9/10
2. George Franklin, Texas A&M-Kingsville, RB, 0/15
3. **Kurt Allerman, Penn State, LB, 86/125**
3. Terdell Middleton, Memphis, RB, 0/80
5. Andy Spiva, Tennessee, LB, 0/13
5. Ernest Lee, Texas, DT, 0/0
8. **Eric Williams, USC, LB, 70/97**
9. Johnny Jackson, Sourhern (LA), NT, 0/2
10. Jim LeJay, San Jose State, WR, 0/0
11. Greg Lee, Western Illinois, DB, 0/0
12. Rick Fenlaw, Texas, LB, 0/0

SEATTLE SEAHAWKS

1. **Steve August, Tulsa, T, 97/102**
2. **Terry Beeson, Kansas, LB, 77/82**
2. **Pete Cronan, Boston College, LB, 50/90**
2. **Tom Lynch, Boston College, G, 61/105**
3. **Dennis Boyd, Oregon State, DT, 59/59**

S4. **Al Hunter, Notre Dame, RB, 52/52**

4. **John Yarno, Idaho, C, 74/74**
4. Larry Seivers, Tennessee, WR, 0/0
6. Tony Benjamin, Duke, RB, 28/28
7. David Sims, Georgia Tech, RB, 29/29
9. George Adzick, Minnesota, DB, 0/0
10. Sam Adkins, Wichita State, QB, 11/11
11. Bill Westbeld, Dayton, T, 0/0
12. I.V. Wilson, Tulsa, DT, 0/0

TAMPA BAY BUCCANEERS

1. **Ricky Bell, USC, RB, 60/64**
2. **Dave Lewis, USC, LB, 75/97**
3. **Charley Hannah, Alabama, G, 77/148**
8. Randy Hedberg, Minot State, QB, 7/7
9. **Larry Mucker, Arizona State, WR, 53/53**
9. Byron Hemingway, Boston College, LB, 0/0
10. Robert Morgan, Florida, RB, 0/0
10. Aaron Ball, Cal State-Fullerton, LB, 0/0
11. Chuck Rodgers, North Dakota State, DB, 0/0
12. Chip Sheffield, Lenoir-Rhyne, WR, 0/0

WASHINGTON REDSKINS

4. Duncan McColl, Stanford, DE, 0/0
7. Reggie Haynes, UNLV, TE, 14/14
9. Mike Northington, Purdue, RB, 0/0
10. James Sykes, Rice, RB, 0/0
11. Don Harris, Rutgers, DB, 32/43
12. Curtis Kirkland, Missouri, DE, 0/0

1978 NFL

ATLANTA FALCONS

1. **Mike Kenn, Michigan, T, 251/251**
2. Steve Stewart, Minnesota, LB, 12/15
3. Stan Waldemore, Nebraska, G, 0/79
4. Brian Cabral, Colorado, LB, 3/70
5. Dennis Pearson, San Diego State, WR, 29/29
6. Rodney Parker, Tennessee State, WR, 0/19
7. **Alfred Jackson, Texas, WR, 88/88**
7. James Wright, TCU, TE, 15/79
8. David Adkins, Ohio State, LB, 0/0
8. David Williams, Tennessee-Martin, DB, 0/0
9. **Tom Pridemore, West Virginia, DB, 121/121**
10. Ricky Patton, Jackson State, RB, 20/52
10. **Ray Strong, UNLV, RB, 61/61**
11. Milton Reed, Baylor, DB, 0/0
12. Daria Butler, Oklahoma State, LB, 0/0

BALTIMORE COLTS

1. **Reese McCall, Auburn, TE, 69/117**
2. Mike Woods, Cincinnati, LB, 36/36
5. Frank Myers, Texas A&M, T, 0/26
6. Ben Garry, Southern Mississippi, RB, 14/14
7. Jeff Logan, Ohio State, RB, 0/0
8. Monte Anthony, Nebraska, RB, 0/0
9. Dave Studdard, Texas, T, 0/145
10. Dallas Owens, Kentucky, DB, 0/0
11. Henry Mason, Central Missouri, WR, 0/0
12. Bruce Allen, Richmond, P, 0/0

BUFFALO BILLS

1. Terry Miller, Oklahoma State, RB, 47/48
2. Dee Hardison, North Carolina, DE, 48/122
2. **Scott Hutchinson, Florida, DE, 53/69**
3. Danny Fulton, Nebaraska-Omaha, WR, 6/20
3. Dennis Johnson, Mississippi State, RB, 19/21
4. **Lucius Sanford, Georgia Tech, LB, 118/129**
5. Ken Spaeth, Nebraska, TE, 0/0
6. Eric Smith, Southern Mississippi, T, 0/0
7. Mario Celotto, USC, LB, 4/25
7. Steve Powell, Truman State, RB, 25/25
10. **Will Grant, Kentucky, C, 122/129**
11. Jerry Blanton, Kentucky, LB, 0/92
12. Richard Crump, Northeastern Oklahoma, RB, 0/0

CHICAGO BEARS

3. Brad Shearer, Texas, DT, 34/34
6. Mekeli Ieremia, Brigham Young, DT, 0/2
6. John Skibinski, Purdue, RB, 44/44
7. Herman Jones, Ohio State, WR, 0/0
8. George Freitas, California, TE, 0/0
9. Mike Martin, Kentucky, LB, 0/0
10. Ben Zambiasi, Georgia, LB, 0/0
11. Walt Underwood, Southern California, DE, 0/0
12. Lew Sibley, Louisiana State, LB, 0/0

CINCINNATI BENGALS

1. **Ross Browner, Notre Dame, DE, 127/138**
1. **Blair Bush, Washington, C, 68/246**
2. **Ray Griffin, Ohio State, DB, 88/88**
2. Deacon Turner, San Diego State, RB, 44/44
3. **Don Bass, Houston, WR, 52/55**
3. Ted Vincent, Wichita State, DT, 16/44
4. Dennis Law, East Tennessee State, WR, 14/14
5. **Tom Dinkel, Kansas, LB, 92/92**
5. Rob Hertel, USC, QB, 3/3
6. Steve Geise, Penn State, RB, 0/0
7. Joe Branson, Livingstone, DB, 0/0
7. Dan Bass, Elon, G, 0/0
8. Bill Miller, Western Illinois, T, 0/0
9. Ron Shumon, Wichita State, LB, 13/21
10. Tom DePaso, Penn State, LB, 12/12
11. Mark Donahue, Michigan, G, 31/31
11. Calvin Prince, Louisville, RB, 0/0
12. Kim Featsent, Kent State, WR, 0/0

CLEVELAND BROWNS

1. **Clay Matthews, USC, LB, 232/278**
1. **Ozzie Newsome, Alabama, TE, 198/198**
2. Johnny Evans, North Carolina State, P, 48/48
3. Larry Collins, Texas A&M-Kingsville, RB, 15/23
3. Mark Miller, Bowling Green State, QB, 10/10
4. Pete Pullara, Tennessee-Chattanooga, G, 0/0
5. Keith Wright, Memphis, WR, 33/33
6. Al Pitts, Michigan State, C, 0/0
8. Jesse Turnbow, Tennessee, DT, 16/16
9. Jon Kramer, Baylor, G, 0/0
10. Brent Watson, Tennessee, T, 0/0
11. Larry Gillard, Mississippi State, DT, 0/0
12. Leo Biedermann, California, T, 16/16

DALLAS COWBOYS

1. **Larry Bethea, Michigan State, DT, 81/81**
2. Todd Christensen, Brigham Young, TE, 0/137
3. Dave Hudgens, Oklahoma, DT, 0/0
4. Alois Blackwell, Houston, RB, 19/19
5. Rich Rosen, Syracuse, G, 0/0
6. Harold Randolph, East Carolina, LB, 0/0
7. Tom Randall, Iowa State, G, 11/24
8. Homer Butler, UCLA, WR, 0/0
9. Russ Williams, Tennessee, DB, 0/0
10. Barry Tomasetti, Iowa, G, 0/0
11. **Dennis Thurman, USC, DB, 121/137**
12. Lee Washburn, Montana State, G, 0/0

DENVER BRONCOS

1. **Don Latimer, Miami (FL), NT, 80/80**
2. William Gay, USC, DE, 0/151
8. Frank Smith, Alabama A&M, T, 0/0
10. Vince Kinney, Maryland, WR, 23/23
11. Lacy Brumley, Clemson, T, 0/0

DETROIT LIONS

1. **Luther Bradley, Notre Dame, DB, 56/56**
2. **Al Baker, Colorado State, DE, 67/181**
4. **Homer Elias, Tennessee State, G, 96/96**
4. Bill Fifer, West Texas A&M, T, 8/12
4. Larry Tearry, Wake Forest, C, 25/25
5. **Amos Fowler, Southern Mississippi, C, 97/97**
5. Dan Gray, Rutgers, DT, 14/14
6. Tony Ardizzone, Northwestern, C, 0/16
6. Dwight Hicks, Michigan, DB, 0/105
6. Jesse Thompson, California, WR, 22/22
7. Bruce Gibson, Pacific, RB, 0/0
8. Jim Breech, California, K, 0/197
10. Fred Arrington, Purdue, LB, 0/0
11. Richard Murray, Oklahoma, DT, 0/0
12. Mark Patterson, Washington State, DB, 0/0

GREEN BAY PACKERS

1. **John Anderson, Michigan, LB, 146/146**
1. **James Lofton, Stanford, WR, 136/233**
2. Mike Hunt, Minnesota, LB, 22/22
3. **Estus Hood, Illinois State, DB, 104/104**
5. **Mike Douglass, San Diego State, LB, 119/126**
5. Willie Wilder, Florida, RB, 0/0
6. **Leotis Harris, Arkansas, G, 74/74**
7. George Plasketes, Mississippi, LB, 0/0
8. Dennis Sproul, Arizona State, QB, 6/6
9. Keith Myers, Utah State, QB, 0/0
10. Larry Key, Florida State, RB, 0/0
10. Mark Totten, Florida, C, 0/0
11. **Terry Jones, Alabama, NT, 85/85**
12. Eason Ramson, Washington State, TE, 0/85

HOUSTON OILERS

1. **Earl Campbell, Texas, RB, 91/115**
3. **Gifford Nielsen, Brigham Young, QB, 55/55**
4. **Mike Renfro, TCU, WR, 75/133**
6. Conrad Rucker, Southern (LA), TE, 29/33
8. **J.C. Wilson, Pittsburgh, DB, 84/84**
9. Jim Mol, Morningside, DE, 0/0

S10. Johnnie Dirden, Sam Houston State, WR, 16/26

10. Steve Young, Wake Forest, TE, 0/0
11. Willie Thicklen, Alabama State, WR, 0/0
12. **John Schuhmacher, USC, G, 69/69**

KANSAS CITY CHIEFS

1. **Art Still, Kentucky, DE, 136/167**
2. Sylvester Hicks, Tennessee State, DE, 43/43
3. **Gary Spani, Kansas State, LB, 124/124**
4. Danny Johnson, Tennessee State, LB, 0/3
4. Pete Woods, Missouri, QB, 0/0
5. Jerrold McRae, Tennessee State, WR, 4/9
5. Robert Woods, Grambling State, WR, 0/4
5. Dwight Carey, Texas-Arlington, DT, 0/0
7. Bill Kellar, Stanford, WR, 5/5
7. Ricky Odom, USC, DB, 8/14
8. John Henry White, Louisiana Tech, RB, 0/0
9. Larry Brown, Miami (FL), T, 5/5
10. Earl Bryant, Jackson State, DE, 0/0
11. Ray Milo, New Mexico State, DB, 1/1
12. Willie Brock, Colorado, C, 0/4

LOS ANGELES RAMS

1. Elvis Peacock, Oklahoma, RB, 24/27
2. Stan Johnson, Tennessee State, NT, 0/10
2. Ron Smith, San Diego State, WR, 28/66
3. **Frank Corral, UCLA, K, 64/64**
3. Leon White, Colorado, C, 0/0
4. Mark Manges, Maryland, QB, 0/1
7. **Reggie Doss, Hampton, DE, 149/149**
9. Andre Anderson, New Mexico State, DE, 0/0
10. Charles Peal, Indiana, T, 0/0
11. Ron Hostetler, Penn State, LB, 0/0
12. Gus Coppens, UCLA, T, 0/9

MIAMI DOLPHINS

2. Guy Benjamin, Stanford, QB, 7/19
3. **Jimmy Cefalo, Penn State, WR, 90/90**
3. Lyman Smith, Duke, DT, 0/11
4. **Eric Laakso, Tulane, T, 86/86**
4. **Gerald Small, San Jose State, DB, 88/104**
5. Ted Burgmeier, Notre Dame, DB, 0/8
6. **Doug Betters, Nevada-Reno, DE, 146/146**
7. Karl Baldischwiler, Oklahoma, T, 0/118
7. Lloyd Henry, Northeast Missouri State, WR, 0/0
8. Sean Clancy, Amherst, LB, 16/26
9. **Bruce Hardy, Arizona State, TE, 151/151**
10. **Mark Dennard, Texas A&M, C, 59/91**
12. Bill Kenney, Northern Colorado, QB, 0/106
12. Mike Moore, Middle Tennessee, RB, 0/0

MINNESOTA VIKINGS

1. **Randy Holloway, Pittsburgh, DE, 97/103**
2. **John Turner, Miami (FL), DB, 101/116**
3. Whip Walton, San Diego State, LB, 0/2
4. **Jim Hough, Utah State, G, 111/111**
8. Mike Wood, Southeast Missouri State, K, 7/50
9. Mike Deutsch, Colorado State, P, 0/0
10. Hughie Shaw, Texas A&I, RB, 0/0
11. Ron Harris, Colorado State, RB, 0/0
12. Jeff Morrow, Minnesota, T, 0/0

NEW ENGLAND PATRIOTS

1. **Bob Cryder, Alabama, T, 75/107**
2. **Matt Cavanaugh, Pittsburgh, QB, 52/112**
3. Carlos Pennywell, Grambling State, WR, 38/38
4. **Dwight Wheeler, Tennessee State, T, 72/91**
5. Bill Matthews, South Dakota State, LB, 48/48
6. Kem Coleman, Mississippi, LB, 0/0
7. **Mike Hawkins, Texas A&M-Kingsville, LB, 59/62**
8. Terry Falcon, Montana, G, 18/31
8. **Mosi Tatupu, USC, RB, 194/199**
9. Tim Petersen, Arizona State, LB, 0/0
10. Bryan Ferguson, Miami (FL), DB, 0/0
11. Charlie Williams, Florida, LB, 0/0
12. John Gibney, Colgate, C, 0/0

NEW ORLEANS SAINTS

1. **Wes Chandler, Florida, WR, 52/150**
2. **J.T. Taylor, Missouri, T, 57/57**
3. **Barry Bennett, Concordia (MN), DT, 50/132**
4. Don Schwartz, Washington State, DB, 46/51
5. Eric Felton, Texas Tech, DB, 29/35
6. Frank Chesley, Wyoming, LB, 0/1
6. Mike Rieker, Lehigh, QB, 0/0
8. **Brooks Williams, North Carolina, TE, 51/78**
9. Richard Carter, North Carolina State, DB, 0/0
11. Nathan Besaint, Southern, DT, 0/0
11. Dave Riley, West Virginia, RB, 0/0
12. **Larry Hardy, Jackson State, TE, 101/101**

NEW YORK GIANTS

1. **Gordon King, Stanford, T, 84/97**
2. Odis McKinney, Colorado, DB, 29/119
4. Billy Taylor, Texas Tech, RB, 45/49
5. Brian DeRoo, Redlands, WR, 0/48
5. **Terry Jackson, San Diego State, DB, 75/107**
5. Jim Krahl, Texas Tech, DT, 16/21
6. Randy Pass, Georgia Tech, G, 0/0
7. Dan Doornink, Washington State, RB, 12/104
8. Jeff Grady, Florida A&M, LB, 0/0
9. Bill Swiacki, Amherst, TE, 0/0
10. Greg Jorgensen, Nebraska, G, 0/0
11. Dennis Heim, Southwest Missouri State, DT, 0/0
12. Greg Lawson, Western Illinois, RB, 0/0

NEW YORK JETS

1. **Chris Ward, Ohio State, T, 87/100**
2. Mark Merrill, Minnesota, LB, 22/68
3. **Mickey Shuler, Penn State, TE, 160/180**
4. Dodie Donnell, Nebraska, RB, 0/0
5. Randy Sidler, Penn State, LB, 0/0
6. **Bobby Jackson, Florida State, DB, 95/95**
6. Gregg Robinson, Dartmouth, DE, 16/16
7. Jim Earley, Michigan State, RB, 2/2
7. Levi Armstrong, UCLA, DB, 0/0
8. **Derrick Gaffney, Florida, WR, 100/100**
8. Mike Mock, Texas Tech, LB, 15/15
8. Roy Eppes, Clemson, DB, 0/0
9. Reggie Grant, Oregon, DB, 14/14
9. Neil Hutton, Penn State, DB, 0/0
10. Louis Richardson, Florida State, DE, 0/0
11. **Pat Ryan, Tennessee, QB, 141/145**
12. Alan Williams, Florida, P, 0/0

OAKLAND RAIDERS

2. **Dave Browning, Washington, DE, 65/77**
3. **Derrick Jensen, Texas-Arlington, RB, 106/106**
3. Lindsey Mason, Kansas, T, 43/57
4. Maurice Harvey, Ball State, DB, 0/86
4. Joe Stewart, Missouri, WR, 19/19
5. **Derrick Ramsey, Kentucky, TE, 75/122**
6. Mike Levenseller, Washington State, WR, 0/24
6. Tom Davis, Nebraska, C, 0/0
7. Earl Inmon, Bethune-Cookman, LB, 0/2
7. **Arthur Whittington, SMU, RB, 56/58**
8. Mark Nichols, Colorado State, LB, 0/15
11. Bob Glazebrook, Fresno State, DB, 0/78
11. Dean Jones, Fresno State, DB, 0/0
12. Joe Conron, Pacific, WR, 0/0

PHILADELPHIA EAGLES

3. **Reggie Wilkes, Georgia Tech, LB, 115/137**
4. **Dennis Harrison, Vanderbilt, DE, 97/136**
5. Norris Banks, Kansas, RB, 0/0

7. Greg Marshall, Oregon State, DT, 0/2
9. Charles Williams, Jackson State, DB, 7/7
11. **Billy Campfield, Kansas, RB, 69/73**
12. **Mark Slater, Minnesota, C, 73/82**

PITTSBURGH STEELERS
1. **Ron Johnson, Eastern Michigan, DB, 91/91**
2. Willie Fry, Notre Dame, DE, 0/0
3. **Craig Colquitt, Tennessee, P, 96/97**
4. **Larry Anderson, Louisiana Tech, DB, 52/82**
6. Randy Reutershan, Pittsburgh, WR, 11/11
7. Mark Dufresne, Nebraska, TE, 0/0
8. Rick Moser, Rhode Island, RB, 43/49
8. Andre Keys, Cal Poly-SLO, WR, 0/0
9. Lance Reynolds, BYU, T, 0/0
10. Doug Becker, Notre Dame, LB, 0/9
10. Tom Jurich, Northern Arizona, K, 0/1
11. Nat Terry, Florida State, DB, 6/10
11. Tom Brzoza, Pittsburgh, C, 0/0
12. Brad Carr, Maryland, LB, 0/0

SAN DIEGO CHARGERS
1. John Jefferson, Arizona State, WR, 45/102
2. Buddy Hardaway, Oklahoma State, T, 12/12
3. Rickey Anderson, South Carolina State, RB, 16/16
5. John Choma, Virginia, G, 0/27
7. Cliff Featherstone, Colorado State, DB, 0/0
8. Gavin Hedrick, Washington State, P, 0/0
9. Henry Bradley, Alcorn State, NT, 0/43
9. Blake Whitlatch, LSU, LB, 0/4
10. Charles Price, Cincinnati, TE, 0/0
12. Kevin Bell, Lamar, WR, 0/9

SAN FRANCISCO 49ERS
1. **Dan Bunz, Long Beach State, LB, 86/88**
1. Ken MacAfee, Notre Dame, TE, 29/29
2. **Walt Downing, Michigan, G, 83/83**
3. Ernie Hughes, Notre Dame, C, 18/45
4. Terry LeCount, Florida, WR, 5/72
5. **Archie Reese, Clemson, DE, 64/83**
5. Bruce Threadgill, Mississippi State, DB, 14/14
6. Elliott Walker, Pittsburgh, RB, 9/9
7. **Fred Quillan, Oregon, C, 143/143**
9. Dean Moore, Iowa, LB, 16/16
9. Herman Redden, Howard, DB, 0/0
9. Steve McDaniels, Notre Dame, T, 0/0
10. Mike Connell, Cincinnati, P, 16/48
11. Willie McCray, Troy State, DE, 16/16
12. Dan Irons, Texas Tech, T, 0/0

ST. LOUIS CARDINALS
1. **Ken Greene, Washington State, DB, 67/98**
1. Steve Little, Arkansas, K, 33/33
2. John Barefield, Texas A&M-Kingsville, LB, 30/30
3. Doug Greene, Texas A&M-Kingsville, DB, 15/38
4. Jimmy Childs, Cal Poly-San Luis Obispo, WR, 21/21
4. **George Collins, Georgia, T, 69/69**
5. Earl Carr, Florida, RB, 0/15
6. Jack Williams, Bowling Green, DE, 0/0
7. **Dave Stief, Portland State, WR, 68/71**
9. Joe Mosley, Central State (OH), TE, 0/0
10. Randy Gill, San Jose State, LB, 7/8
12. Anthony Clay, South Carolina State, LB, 0/0

SEATTLE SEAHAWKS
1. **Keith Simpson, Memphis, DB, 108/108**
2. **Keith Butler, Memphis, LB, 146/146**
3. Bob Jury, Pittsburgh, DB, 0/15
5. Louis Bullard, Jackson State, T, 35/35
6. Glenn Starks, Texas A&I, WR, 0/0
7. **John Harris, Arizona State, DB, 119/160**
9. Rich Grimmett, Illinois, T, 0/0
10. Rob Stewart, Lafayette, WR, 0/0
11. George Halas, Miami (FL), LB, 0/0
12. Jeff Bergeron, Lamar, RB, 0/0

TAMPA BAY BUCCANEERS
1. **Doug Williams, Grambling State, QB, 67/88**
2. Johnny Davis, Alabama, RB, 46/119
2. Brett Moritz, Nebraska, G, 6/6
6. Elijah Marshall, North Carolina State, WR, 0/0
8. John McGriff, Miami (FL), LB, 0/0
9. Willie Taylor, Pittsburgh, WR, 0/1
10. Aaron Brown, Ohio State, LB, 44/73
12. Kevin McLee, Georgia, RB, 0/0

WASHINGTON REDSKINS
6. Tony Green, Florida, RB, 16/31
8. Don Hover, Washington State, LB, 32/32
8. Walker Lee, North Carolina, WR, 0/0
9. John Hurley, Santa Clara, QB, 0/0
10. Scott Hertenstein, Azusa Pacific, DE, 0/0
11. Mike Williams, Texas A&M, DB, 0/0
12. Steve McCabe, Bowdoin, G, 0/0

1979 NFL

ATLANTA FALCONS
1. **Don Smith, Miami (FL), NT, 87/111**
2. Pat Howell, USC, G, 47/67
3. **William Andrews, Auburn, RB, 87/87**
3. James Mayberry, Colorado, RB, 48/48
4. **Lynn Cain, USC, RB, 82/89**
4. Charles Johnson, Grambling State, DB, 0/25
5. **Mike Zele, Kent State, NT, 52/52**
6. Mike Moroski, California-Davis, QB, 49/69
7. Roger Westlund, Washington, T, 0/0
8. Keith Miller, Northeastern Oklahoma, LB, 0/0
9. Dave Parkin, Utah State, DB, 0/9
10. Bruce Beekley, Oregon, LB, 0/15
11. Bill Leer, Colorado State, C, 0/0
12. Stuart Walker, Colorado, LB, 0/0

BALTIMORE COLTS
1. **Barry Krauss, Alabama, LB, 136/152**
3. **Kim Anderson, Arizona State, DB, 56/56**
5. Larry Braziel, USC, DB, 47/95
6. Jimmy Moore, Ohio State, G, 4/4
8. **Nesby Glasgow, Washington, DB, 126/203**
8. Steve Heimkreiter, Notre Dame, LB, 15/15
9. Russ Henderson, Virginia, P, 0/0
10. Steve Stephens, Oklahoma State, TE, 0/16
11. John Priestner, Western Ontario, LB, 0/0
12. Charlie Green, Kansas State, WR, 0/0

BUFFALO BILLS
1. **Jerry Butler, Clemson, WR, 88/88**
1. Tom Cousineau, Ohio State, LB, 0/66
2. **Jim Haslett, Indiana (PA), LB, 91/94**
2. **Fred Smerlas, Boston College, NT, 162/200**
3. **Jon Borchardt, Montana State, G, 89/130**
4. **Ken Johnson, Knoxville, DE, 74/76**
4. Jeff Nixon, Richmond, DB, 43/43
5. **Rod Kush, Nebraska-Omaha, DB, 50/66**
5. Dan Manucci, Kansas State, QB, 19/19
6. Mike Burrow, Auburn, G, 0/0
7. Tom Mullady, Rhodes, TE, 0/75
9. Kevin Baker, William Penn, DE, 0/0
10. David Marler, Mississippi State, QB, 0/0
11. Paul Lawler, Colgate, DB, 0/0
12. Mike Harris, Arizona State, RB, 0/0

CHICAGO BEARS
1. **Dan Hampton, Arkansas, DE, 157/157**
1. **Al Harris, Arizona State, DE, 117/149**
2. **Rickey Watts, Tulsa, WR, 56/56**
3. **Willie McClendon, Georgia, RB, 57/57**
6. John Sullivan, Illinois, LB, 0/28
7. Lee Kunz, Nebraska, LB, 48/48
8. Rick Moss, Purdue, DB, 0/0
9. Jerome Heavens, Notre Dame, RB, 0/0
10. Joe Restic, Notre Dame, DB, 0/0
11. Bob Wright, Cincinnati, T, 0/0
12. Dave Becker, Iowa, DB, 11/11

CINCINNATI BENGALS
1. **Charles Alexander, LSU, RB, 102/102**
1. Jack Thompson, Washington State, QB, 32/51
2. **Dan Ross, Northeastern, TE, 79/104**
3. Barney Cotton, Nebraska, G, 13/45
4. Vaughn Lusby, Arkansas, DB, 16/18
4. Mike White, Albany State (GA), DT, 31/51
5. Casey Merrill, California-Davis, DE, 0/97
6. **Steve Kreider, Lehigh, WR, 114/114**
7. **Max Montoya, UCLA, G, 157/223**
8. Howard Kurnick, Cincinnati, LB, 15/15
9. Scott Burk, Oklahoma State, DB, 16/16
10. Nathan Poole, Louisville, RB, 32/62
11. Ken Bungarda, Missouri, T, 0/15
12. Jim Browner, Notre Dame, DB, 18/18

CLEVELAND BROWNS
1. **Willis Adams, Houston, WR, 75/75**
2. Sam Claphan, Oklahoma, T, 0/87
2. **Lawrence Johnson, Wisconsin, DB, 64/96**
3. Jim Ramey, Kentucky, DE, 0/10
4. Matt Miller, Colorado, T, 41/41
5. Rich Dimler, USC, DT, 12/15
6. **Clinton Burrell, LSU, DB, 67/67**
6. Jim Ronan, Minnesota, DT, 0/0
7. **Cody Risien, Texas A&M, T, 146/146**
8. Kent Perkov, San Diego State, DE, 0/0
9. Carl McGee, Duke, LB, 0/6
9. **Curtis Weathers, Mississippi, LB, 94/94**
10. John Smith, Tennessee State, WR, 6/6
11. Randy Poeschl, Nebraska, DE, 0/0
12. Dewitt Methvin, Tulane, C, 0/0

DALLAS COWBOYS
1. Robert Shaw, Tennessee, C, 33/33
2. Aaron Mitchell, UNLV, DB, 31/44
3. **Doug Cosbie, Santa Clara, TE, 144/144**
4. Ralph DeLoach, California, DE, 0/1
5. Curtis Anderson, Central State (OH), DE, 0/6
5. **Ron Springs, Ohio State, RB, 88/112**
5. Bob Hukill, North Carolina, G, 0/0
6. Chris DeFrance, Arizona State, WR, 0/4
6. Tim Lavender, Southern California, DB, 0/0
6. Mike Salzano, North Carolina, G, 0/0
7. Greg Fitzpatrick, Youngstown State, LB, 0/0
8. Bruce Thornton, Illinois, DE, 41/47
9. Garry Cobb, USC, LB, 19/140
10. Mike Calhoun, Notre Dame, DT, 0/7
12. Quentin Lowry, Youngstown State, LB, 0/27

DENVER BRONCOS
1. Kelvin Clark, Nebraska, T, 45/88
3. Bruce Radford, Grambling State, NT, 16/37
4. Charles Jefferson, McNeese State, DB, 0/5
5. Rick Leach, Michigan, QB, 0/0
6. Jeff McIntyre, Arizona State, LB, 0/24
7. **Luke Prestridge, Baylor, P, 73/82**
9. Charlie Taylor, Rice, WR, 0/0
11. Zachary Dixon, Temple, RB, 5/67
12. Dave Jacobs, Syracuse, K, 0/12

DETROIT LIONS
1. **Keith Dorney, Penn State, T, 112/112**
2. **Ken Fantetti, Wyoming, LB, 95/95**
3. Bo Robinson, West Texas A&M, RB, 28/80
4. Jon Brooks, Clemson, LB, 15/20
4. **Ulysses Norris, Georgia, TE, 68/84**
5. Walt Brown, Pittsburgh, C, 0/0
8. John Mohring, C.W. Post, LB, 1/15
9. Jeff Komlo, Delaware, QB, 23/25
11. Eddie Cole, Mississippi, LB, 28/28
12. Bob Forster, Brown, C, 0/0
12. Bryan Sweeney, Texas A&I, WR, 0/0

GREEN BAY PACKERS
1. **Eddie Lee Ivery, Georgia Tech, RB, 72/72**
2. Steve Atkins, Maryland, RB, 19/20
3. Charles Johnson, Maryland, NT, 45/45
6. Dave Simmons, North Carolina, LB, 16/36
7. Henry Monroe, Mississippi State, DB, 3/6
7. **Rich Wingo, Alabama, LB, 69/69**
8. **Ron Cassidy, Utah State, WR, 60/60**
8. Rick Partridge, Utah, P, 0/32
9. John Thompson, Utah State, TE, 34/34
10. Frank Lockett, Nebraska, WR, 0/3
11. Mark Thorson, Ottawa, DB, 0/0
12. Bill Moats, South Dakota, P, 0/0

HOUSTON OILERS
2. **Jesse Baker, Jacksonville State, DE, 125/128**
2. **Mike Stensrud, Iowa State, NT, 95/139**
3. Kenny King, Oklahoma, RB, 12/97
6. **Daryl Hunt, Oklahoma, LB, 78/78**
6. Mike Murphy, Southwest Missouri State, LB, 3/3
7. Tim Ries, Southwest Missouri State, DB, 0/0
8. **Carter Hartwig, USC, DB, 86/86**
9. Rich Ellender, McNeese State, RB, 13/13
11. Mike Taylor, Georgia Tech, T, 0/0
12. Wayne Wilson, Shepherd, RB, 0/111

KANSAS CITY CHIEFS
1. **Mike Bell, Colorado State, DE, 135/135**
1. **Steve Fuller, Clemson, QB, 52/90**
4. Frank Manumaleuga, San Jose State, LB, 35/35
5. Earl Gant, Missouri, RB, 20/20
6. Robert Gaines, Washington, WR, 0/0
7. **Ken Kremer, Ball State, NT, 87/87**
8. Mike Williams, New Mexico, TE, 33/33
8. Robert Brewer, Temple, G, 0/0
9. James Folston, Cameron, TE, 0/0
9. Joe Robinson, Ohio State, T, 0/0
10. Gerald Jackson, Mississippi State, DB, 16/16
10. Mike DuPree, Florida, LB, 0/0
10. Larry Willis, Alcorn State, WR, 0/0
11. Stan Rome, Clemson, WR, 42/42
12. Michael Forrest, Arkansas, RB, 0/0

LOS ANGELES RAMS
1. **George Andrews, Nebraska, LB, 80/80**
1. **Kent Hill, Georgia Tech, G, 107/132**
2. Eddie Hill, Memphis, RB, 23/75
3. Jeff Moore, Tennessee, WR, 24/24
3. Mike Wellman, Kansas, C, 0/20
4. Jerry Wilkinson, Oregon State, DE, 16/29
4. Derwin Tucker, Illinois, DB, 0/0
5. Victor Hicks, Oklahoma, TE, 16/16
7. Jeff Delaney, Pittsburgh, DB, 16/42
9. Jeff Rutledge, Alabama, QB, 8/117
10. Grady Ebensberger, Houston, DT, 0/0
11. Jesse Deramus, Tennessee State, DT, 0/0
12. **Drew Hill, Georgia Tech, WR, 73/211**

MIAMI DOLPHINS
1. **Jon Giesler, Michigan, T, 126/126**
2. **Jeff Toews, Washington, G, 71/71**
3. Mel Land, Michigan State, LB, 16/19
3. **Ronnie Lee, Baylor, T, 138/186**
3. **Tony Nathan, Alabama, RB, 123/123**
4. Steve Howell, Baylor, FB, 42/42
5. Don Bessillieu, Georgia Tech, DB, 48/59
6. Steve Lindquist, Nebraska, G, 0/0
7. **Uwe von Schamann, Oklahoma, K, 89/89**
8. **Glenn Blackwood, Texas, DB, 118/118**
8. Jeff Groth, Bowling Green State, WR, 4/94
9. Jeff Weston, Notre Dame, T, 0/37
10. **Mike Kozlowski, Colorado, DB, 91/91**
10. Jerome Stanton, Michigan State, DB, 0/0
11. Mike Blanton, Georgia Tech, DE, 0/0
12. Larry Fortner, Miami (OH), QB, 0/0

MINNESOTA VIKINGS
1. **Ted Brown, North Carolina State, RB, 104/104**
2. **Dave Huffman, Notre Dame, G, 128/128**
4. Steve Dils, Stanford, QB, 47/106
5. Jerry Meter, Michigan, LB, 0/0
6. Joe Senser, West Chester, TE, 49/49
7. Bob Winkel, Kentucky, DT, 0/31
9. Billy Diggs, Winston-Salem State, WR, 0/0
11. Brian Nelson, Texas Tech, WR, 0/0
12. David Stephens, Kentucky, LB, 0/0

NEW ENGLAND PATRIOTS
1. **Rick Sanford, South Carolina, DB, 89/94**
2. Bob Golic, Notre Dame, NT, 33/187
4. Eddie Hare, Tulsa, P, 16/16
5. **John Zamberlin, Pacific Lutheran, LB, 56/78**
7. Judson Flint, California (PA), DB, 0/39
8. Randy Love, Houston, RB, 0/89
9. John Spagnola, Yale, TE, 0/133
10. Allan Clark, Northern Arizona, RB, 27/33
10. Martin Cox, Vanderbilt, WR, 0/0

NEW ORLEANS SAINTS
1. **Russell Erxleben, Texas, P, 58/59**
2. Reggie Mathis, Oklahoma, LB, 32/32
4. **Jim Kovach, Kentucky, LB, 83/87**
5. Harlan Huckleby, Michigan, RB, 0/84
6. Ricky Ray, Norfolk State, DB, 23/31
7. Stan Sytsma, Minnesota, LB, 0/2
8. Doug Panfil, Tulsa, G, 0/0
11. David Hall, Missouri-Rolla, WR, 0/0
12. Kelsey Finch, Tennessee, RB, 0/0

NEW YORK GIANTS
1. **Phil Simms, Morehead State, QB, 164/164**
2. **Earnest Gray, Memphis, WR, 85/90**
4. **Phil Tabor, Oklahoma, DE, 56/56**
5. Cleveland Jackson, UNLV, TE, 2/2
6. Eddie Hicks, East Carolina, RB, 17/17
6. Bob Torrey, Penn State, RB, 6/14
7. Steve Alvers, Miami (Fl), TE, 0/19
8. Roy Simmons, Georgia Tech, G, 48/58
8. D.K. Perry, Southern Methodist, DB, 0/0
9. Tom Rusk, Iowa, LB, 0/0
10. Dan Fowler, Kentucky, G, 1/1
11. Ken Johnson, Miami (FL), RB, 9/9
11. Mike Mince, Fresno State, DB, 0/0
12. Tim Gillespie, North Carolina State, G, 0/0

NEW YORK JETS
1. **Marty Lyons, Alabama, DE, 147/147**
2. **Mark Gastineau, East Central (OK), DE, 137/137**
3. Donald Dykes, Southeastern Louisiana, DB, 46/47
4. Eric Cunningham, Penn State, G, 17/17
4. **Johnny Lynn, UCLA, DB, 97/97**
5. **Stan Blinka, Sam Houston State, LB, 72/72**
5. Kelly Kirchbaum, Kentucky, LB, 0/4
6. Bill Dufek, Michigan, G, 0/0
7. Emmett King, Houston, RB, 0/0
7. Keith Brown, Minnesota, DB, 0/20
8. Marshall Harris, TCU, DE, 0/46
8. Willie Beamon, Boise State, LB, 0/0
9. Gordy Spratler, North Dakota State, RB, 0/0

10. Ed McGlasson, Youngstown State, C, 7/24
10. Steve Sybeldon, North Dakota, T, 0/0
11. Dan Sanders, Carson-Newman, QB, 0/0
12. Paul Darby, Southwest Texas State, WR, 23/23

OAKLAND RAIDERS
2. Willie Jones, Florida State, DE, 40/40
6. Ira Matthews, Wisconsin, RB, 37/37
6. Henry Williams, San Diego State, DB, 16/22
7. Jack Matia, Drake, T, 0/0
8. Robert Hawkins, Kentucky, RB, 0/0
9. Jim Rourke, Boston College, T, 0/77
10. Ricky Smith, Tulane, DB, 0/0
11. **Bruce Davis, UCLA, T, 121/160**
12. **Reggie Kinlaw, Oklahoma, NT, 68/98**
12. Dirk Abernathy, Bowling Green, DB, 0/0

PHILADELPHIA EAGLES
1. **Jerry Robinson, UCLA, LB, 87/184**
2. **Petey Perot, Northwestern State (LA), G, 67/74**
3. **Tony Franklin, Texas A&M, K, 73/140**
4. Ben Cowins, Arkansas, RB, 0/0
5. Scott Fitzkee, Penn State, WR, 22/36
7. Don Swafford, Florida, T, 0/0
7. Curtis Bunche, Albany State, DE, 0/0
8. Chuck Correal, Penn State, C, 0/16
8. **Max Runager, South Carolina, P, 72/144**
11. **Al Chesley, Pittsburgh, LB, 52/56**

PITTSBURGH STEELERS
1. **Greg Hawthorne, Baylor, RB, 59/105**
2. Zack Valentine, East Carolina, LB, 48/56
4. Russell Davis, Michigan, RB, 42/42
4. **Calvin Sweeney, USC, WR, 102/102**
5. Dwaine Board, North Carolina A&T, DE, 0/121
6. Matt Bahr, Penn State, K, 32/235
6. Bill Murrell, Winston-Salem State, TE, 0/12
6. **Dwayne Woodruff, Louisville, DB, 157/157**
7. Bruce Kimbal, Massachusetts, G, 0/25
8. Tom Graves, Michigan State, LB, 11/11
9. Richard Kirk, Denison, DE, 0/0
10. Tod Thompson, BYU, TE, 0/0
11. Charlie Moore, Wichita State, C, 0/0
12. Ed Smith, Vanderbilt, LB, 0/32
12. Mike Almond, Northwestern State (LA), WR, 0/0

SAN DIEGO CHARGERS
1. **Kellen Winslow, Missouri, TE, 109/109**
3. **Cliff Thrift, East Central (OK), LB, 69/97**
4. John Floyd, Louisiana-Monroe, WR, 23/27
8. Wilbert Haslip, Hawaii, RB, 0/5
9. Alvin Garrett, Angelo State (TX), WR, 0/55
10. Tony Petruccio, Penn State, DT, 0/0
10. Al Green, Louisiana State, DB, 0/0
11. Dave Rader, Tulsa, QB, 0/0
12. Frank Duncan, San Francisco State, DB, 26/26

SAN FRANCISCO 49ERS
2. James Owens, UCLA, RB, 30/70
3. **Joe Montana, Notre Dame, QB, 167/192**
5. Jerry Aldridge, Angelo State (TX), RB, 1/1
5. Tom Seabron, Michigan, LB, 16/18
6. Ruben Vaughan, Colorado, DT, 13/27
7. Phil Francis, Stanford, RB, 21/21
9. Steve Hamilton, Missouri, DT, 0/0
10. **Dwight Clark, Clemson, WR, 134/134**
10. Howard Ballage, Colorado, DB, 0/0
11. Billy McBride, Tennessee State, DB, 0/0

ST. LOUIS CARDINALS
1. **Ottis Anderson, Miami (FL), RB, 99/182**
2. Theotis Brown, UCLA, RB, 36/84
2. **Calvin Favron, Southeastern Louisiana, LB, 50/50**
3. **Joe Bostic, Clemson, G, 132/132**
4. **Roy Green, Henderson State, WR, 168/190**
5. Mark Bell, Colorado State, WR, 12/12
5. Steve Henry, Emporia State, DB, 8/15
6. Thomas Lott, Oklahoma, RB, 10/10
7. Kirk Gibson, Michigan State, WR, 0/0
8. Larry Miller, BYU, LB, 0/0
9. Bob Rozier, California, DE, 6/6
10. Jerry Holloway, Western Illinois, TE, 0/0
11. Nate Henderson, Florida State, T, 0/0
12. Ricky McBride, Georgia, LB, 0/0

SEATTLE SEAHAWKS
1. **Manu Tuiasosopo, UCLA, DT, 73/119**
2. **Joe Norman, Indiana, LB, 50/50**
3. **Michael Jackson, Washington, LB, 105/105**
4. Mark Bell, Colorado State, DE, 41/64
7. Larry Polowski, Boise State, LB, 14/14
9. Ezra Tate, Mississippi College, RB, 0/0
10. **Robert Hardy, Jackson State, DT, 54/54**
11. Jim Hinesly, Michigan State, G, 0/0
12. Jeff Moore, Jackson State, RB, 32/63

TAMPA BAY BUCCANEERS
2. **Gordon Jones, Pittsburgh, WR, 50/61**
2. Greg Roberts, Oklahoma, G, 45/45
3. Rick Berns, Nebraska, RB, 32/50
3. Jerry Eckwood, Arkansas, RB, 47/47
3. Reggie Lewis, North Texas, DE, 22/22
5. Chuck Fusina, Penn State, QB, 7/14
8. **Gene Sanders, Texas A&M, T, 77/77**
9. Henry Vereen, Nevada-Las Vegas, WR, 0/0
11. Bob Rippentrop, Fresno State, TE, 0/0
12. **David Logan, Pittsburgh, NT, 110/112**

WASHINGTON REDSKINS
4. **Don Warren, San Diego State, TE, 193/193**
7. **Rich Milot, Penn State, LB, 121/121**
9. Kris Haines, Notre Dame, WR, 1/21
11. **Monte Coleman, Central Arkansas, LB, 215/215**
11. Tony Hall, Knoxville, WR, 0/0

1980 NFL

ATLANTA FALCONS
1. **Junior Miller, Nebraska, TE, 56/71**
2. **Buddy Curry, North Carolina, LB, 109/109**
3. **Earl Jones, Norfolk State, DB, 57/57**
4. I.M. Hipp, Nebraska, RB, 0/1
4. Jim Laughlin, Ohio State, LB, 44/88
5. **Kenny Johnson, Mississippi State, DB, 85/127**
5. Brad Vassar, Pacific, LB, 0/0
6. Mike Davis, Colorado, DB, 0/0
7. Mike Smith, Grambling State, WR, 5/5
S7. Matthew Teague, Prairie View A&M, LB, 11/11
8. **Al Richardson, Georgia Tech, LB, 77/77**
9. Glen Keller, West Texas State, C, 0/0
10. Walt Bellamy, Virginia Military, DB, 0/0
11. Mike Babb, Oklahoma, DB, 0/0
12. Quinn Jones, Tulsa, RB, 0/0

BALTIMORE COLTS
1. **Curtis Dickey, Texas A&M, RB, 70/85**
1. Derrick Hatchett, Texas, DB, 48/49
2. **Ray Donaldson, Georgia, C, 184/244**
2. Tim Foley, Notre Dame, T, 6/6
4. **Ray Butler, USC, WR, 79/120**
6. Chris Foote, USC, C, 32/104
7. Wes Roberts, TCU, DE, 0/6
8. Ken Walter, Texas Tech, T, 0/0
9. Mark Bright, Temple, RB, 0/0
10. Larry Stewart, Maryland, T, 0/0
11. Eddy Whitley, Kansas State, TE, 0/0
12. Marvin Sims, Clemson, FB, 32/32
12. Randy Bielski, Towson State, K, 0/0

BUFFALO BILLS
1. **Jim Ritcher, North Carolina State, G, 203/218**
2. **Joe Cribbs, Auburn, RB, 64/102**
2. Gene Bradley, Arkansas State, QB, 0/0
3. **Mark Brammer, Michigan State, TE, 65/65**
3. John Schmeding, Boston College, G, 0/0
4. **Ervin Parker, South Carolina State, LB, 57/57**
5. Keith Lee, Colorado State, DB, 0/68
5. Jeff Pyburn, Georgia, DB, 0/0
8. Todd Krueger, Northern Michigan, QB, 0/0
9. Kent Davis, Southeast Missouri State, DB, 0/0
10. **Greg Cater, Tennessee-Chattanooga, P, 57/77**
11. Joe Gordon, Grambling, DT, 0/0
12. Roger Lapham, Maine, TE, 0/0

CHICAGO BEARS
1. **Otis Wilson, Louisville, LB, 109/110**
2. **Matt Suhey, Penn State, RB, 148/148**
4. Arland Thompson, Baylor, G, 0/17
5. Paul Tabor, Oklahoma, C, 16/16
6. Mike Guess, Ohio State, DB, 0/0
7. Emanuel Tolbert, Southern Methodist, WR, 0/0
8. Randy Clark, Northern Illinois, C, 0/94
9. Turk Schonert, Stanford, QB, 0/72
10. Willie Stephens, Texas Tech, DB, 0/0
11. Chris Judge, Texas Christian, DB, 0/0
12. Bob Fisher, SMU, TE, 22/22

CINCINNATI BENGALS
1. **Anthony Munoz, USC, T, 185/185**
2. Kirby Criswell, Kansas, LB, 0/6
3. Rod Horn, Nebraska, NT, 23/23
4. William Glass, Baylor, G, 15/15
5. Bryan Hicks, McNeese State, DB, 39/39
6. Jo Jo Heath, Pittsburgh, DB, 10/27
6. Andrew Melontree, Baylor, LB, 16/16
7. **Ron Simpkins, Michigan, LB, 84/91**
7. Gary Don Johnson, Baylor, DT, 0/0
8. Mark Lyles, Florida State, RB, 0/0
9. Greg Bright, Morehead State, DB, 20/20
10. Sandro Vitiello, Massachusetts, K, 2/2
11. Alton Alexis, Tulane, WR, 1/1
12. Mike Wright, Vanderbilt, QB, 0/0

CLEVELAND BROWNS
1. Charles White, USC, RB, 49/108
2. Cleveland Crosby, Arizona, DE, 0/9
3. Cliff Odom, Texas-Arlington, LB, 8/167
4. Ron Crews, UNLV, NT, 16/16
4. **Paul McDonald, USC, QB, 84/85**
5. **Elvis Franks, Morgan State, DE, 73/83**
8. Jeff Copeland, Texas Tech, LB, 0/0
9. Roy Dewalt, Texas-Arlington, RB, 0/0
10. Kevin Fidel, San Diego State, C, 0/0
11. Roland Sales, Arkansas, RB, 0/0
12. Marcus Jackson, Purdue, DE, 0/1

DALLAS COWBOYS
3. **James Jones, Mississippi State, RB, 62/62**
3. Bill Roe, Colorado, LB, 16/19
4. **Kurt Petersen, Missouri, G, 84/84**
5. Gary Hogeboom, Central Michigan, QB, 45/79
6. **Timmy Newsome, Winston-Salem State, RB, 121/121**
7. Lester Brown, Clemson, RB, 0/0
8. Larry Savage, Michigan State, LB, 0/0
9. Jackie Flowers, Florida State, WR, 0/0
11. Gary Padjen, Arizona State, LB, 0/41
12. Norm Wells, Northwestern, DT, 3/3

DENVER BRONCOS
2. **Rulon Jones, Utah State, DE, 129/129**
3. Larry Carter, Kentucky, DB, 0/0
4. Rick Parros, Utah State, RB, 46/51
5. **Mike Harden, Michigan, DB, 128/158**
5. Laval Short, Colorado, NT, 15/19
6. **Keith Bishop, Baylor, G, 129/129**
7. John Havekost, Nebraska, G, 0/0
8. Don Coleman, Oregon, WR, 0/0
9. Greg Bracelin, California, LB, 12/68
10. Virgil Seay, Troy State, WR, 0/52
11. Phil Farris, North Carolina, WR, 0/0

DETROIT LIONS
1. **Billy Sims, Oklahoma, RB, 60/60**
3. Mike Friede, Indiana, WR, 4/27
3. **Tom Turnure, Washington, C, 63/63**
4. **Eric Hipple, Utah State, QB, 102/102**
5. Tommie Ginn, Arkansas, C, 27/27
5. Mark Streeter, Arizona, DB, 0/0
6. **Chris Dieterich, North Carolina State, T, 105/105**
7. **Eddie Murray, Tulane, K, 174/250**
9. Tom Tuinei, Hawaii, DT, 12/12
9. DeWayne Jett, Hawaii, WR, 0/0
10. Donnie Henderson, Utah State, DB, 0/0
11. Wayne Smith, Purdue, DB, 37/108
12. Ray Williams, Washington State, RB, 6/6

GREEN BAY PACKERS
1. Bruce Clark, Penn State, DE, 0/113
1. **George Cumby, Oklahoma, LB, 80/92**
2. **Mark Lee, Washington, DB, 157/165**
3. Syd Kitson, Wake Forest, G, 49/50
4. Fred Nixon, Oklahoma, WR, 23/23
6. **Karl Swanke, Boston College, T, 84/84**
7. Buddy Aydelette, Alabama, T, 9/21
8. Tim Smith, Oregon State, DB, 0/0
9. Kelly Saalfeld, Nebraska, C, 0/7
10. Jafus White, Texas A&I, DB, 0/0
11. Ricky Skiles, Louisville, LB, 0/0
12. James Stewart, Memphis State, DB, 0/0

HOUSTON OILERS
2. Angelo Fields, Michigan State, T, 30/30
2. Daryle Skaugstad, California, NT, 25/37
3. **Tim Smith, Nebraska, WR, 90/90**
4. Chris Combs, New Mexico, TE, 0/32
5. John Corker, Oklahoma State, LB, 30/32
7. Craig Bradshaw, Utah State, QB, 2/2
8. Harold Bailey, Oklahoma State, WR, 20/20
9. Ed Harris, Bishop, RB, 0/0
11. Eddie Preston, Western Kentucky, WR, 0/0
12. Wiley Pitts, Temple, WR, 0/0

KANSAS CITY CHIEFS
1. **Brad Budde, USC, G, 92/92**
3. James Hadnot, Texas Tech, RB, 43/43
4. Dave Klug, Concordia (MN), LB, 26/26
5. **Carlos Carson, LSU, WR, 120/126**
5. Dan Pensick, Nebraska, DT, 0/0
6. Bubba Garcia, Texas-El Paso, WR, 6/6
6. Larry Heater, Arizona, RB, 0/29
8. Sam Stepney, Boston, LB, 0/0
9. Tom Donovan, Penn State, WR, 0/5
10. Rob Martinovich, Notre Dame, T, 0/0
11. Dale Markham, North Dakota, T, 0/3
12. Mike Brewington, East Carolina, LB, 0/0

LOS ANGELES RAMS
1. **Johnnie Johnson, Texas, DB, 121/124**
2. **Irv Pankey, Penn State, T, 144/150**
3. **LeRoy Irvin, Kansas, DB, 143/159**
3. Phil Murphy, South Carolina State, DT, 32/32
3. Jewerl Thomas, San Jose State, RB, 39/56
6. **Mike Guman, Penn State, RB, 106/106**
7. Kirk Collins, Baylor, DB, 29/29
7. Gerry Ellis, Missouri, RB, 0/103
8. Tom Pettigrew, Eastern Illinois, T, 0/0
9. George Farmer, Southern (LA), WR, 38/39
10. Bob Gruber, Pittsburgh, T, 0/1
11. Terry Greer, Alabama State, WR, 0/50
12. Kevin Scanlon, Arkansas, QB, 0/0

MIAMI DOLPHINS
1. **Don McNeal, Alabama, DB, 110/110**
2. **Dwight Stephenson, Alabama, C, 114/114**
3. **Bill Barnett, Nebraska, DE, 77/77**
4. Elmer Bailey, Minnesota, WR, 30/31
6. Eugene Byrd, Michigan State, WR, 0/0
7. **Joe Rose, California, TE, 82/83**
8. Jeff Allen, California-Davis, DB, 16/25
8. David Woodley, LSU, QB, 42/58
9. Mark Goodspeed, Nebraska, T, 0/3
10. Doug Lantz, Miami (OH), C, 0/0
10. Ben Long, South Dakota, LB, 0/0
11. Phil Driscoll, Mankato State, DE, 0/0
12. Chuck Stone, North Carolina State, G, 0/0

MINNESOTA VIKINGS
1. **Doug Martin, Washington, DE, 126/126**
2. **Willie Teal, LSU, DB, 79/80**
3. **Brent Boyd, UCLA, G, 59/59**
4. **Dennis Johnson, USC, LB, 77/85**
5. Doug Paschal, North Carolina, RB, 16/16
5. Paul Jones, California, RB, 0/0
6. Ray Yakavonis, East Stroudsburg, NT, 19/21
7. Henry Johnson, Georgia Tech, LB, 46/46
9. Dennis Mosley, Iowa, RB, 0/0
10. Kenny Brown, Nebraska, WR, 0/0
11. Sam Harrell, East Carolina, RB, 6/6
12. Thomas Lane, Florida A&M, DB, 0/0

NEW ENGLAND PATRIOTS
1. Vagas Ferguson, Notre Dame, RB, 31/33
1. **Roland James, Tennessee, DB, 145/145**
2. **Larry McGrew, USC, LB, 122/133**
3. Steve McMichael, Texas, DT, 6/213
5. Doug McDougald, Virginia Tech, DE, 8/8
6. Preston Brown, Vanderbilt, WR, 14/32
7. Tom Kearns, Kentucky, G, 0/0
8. Mike House, Pacific, TE, 0/0
9. Barry Burget, Oklahoma, LB, 0/0
10. Tom Daniel, Georgia Tech, C, 0/0
11. Mike Hubach, Kansas, P, 21/21
12. Jimmy Jordan, Florida State, QB, 0/0

NEW ORLEANS SAINTS
1. **Stan Brock, Colorado, T, 186/234**
2. **Dave Waymer, Notre Dame, DB, 149/197**
4. Mike Jolly, Michigan, DB, 0/35
6. Lester Boyd, Kentucky, LB, 0/0
7. Mike Morucci, Bloomsburg, RB, 0/0
8. Chuck Evans, Stanford, LB, 26/26
9. Frank Mordica, Vanderbilt, RB, 0/0
10. Tanya Webb, Michigan State, DE, 0/0
11. George Woodard, Texas A&M, RB, 0/0
12. Kiser Lewis, Florida A&M, LB, 0/0

NEW YORK GIANTS
1. **Mark Haynes, Colorado, DB, 75/127**
3. Myron Lapka, USC, NT, 10/16
4. Danny Pittman, Wyoming, WR, 35/49
5. Tony Blount, Virginia, DB, 3/3
6. **Scott Brunner, Delaware, QB, 57/73**
7. Bud Hebert, Oklahoma, DB, 10/10
7. Chris Linnin, Washington, DE, 10/10
8. Ken Harris, Alabama, RB, 0/0
9. Otis Wonsley, Alcorn State, RB, 0/72
10. Joe Sanford, Washington, T, 0/0
11. Steve Bernish, South Carolina, DE, 0/0
12. Mike Lansford, Washington, K, 0/124

NEW YORK JETS
1. **Lam Jones, Texas, WR, 61/61**
2. Ralph Clayton, Michigan, WR, 0/7
2. **Darrol Ray, Oklahoma, DB, 72/72**
3. **Lance Mehl, Penn State, LB, 97/97**
4. Jesse Johnson, Colorado, B, 45/45
5. Jim Zidd, Kansas, LB, 0/0
6. George Visger, Colorado, DT, 0/3
6. Tom Schremp, Wisconsin, DE, 0/0
7. Bobby Batton, UNLV, RB, 8/8

7. Bennie Leverett, Bethune-Cookman, RB, 0/0
8. Jeff Dziama, Boston College, LB, 0/0
9. Joe Peters, Arizona State, DT, 0/0
10. **Guy Bingham, Montana, C, 125/199**
11. James Zachery, Texas A&M, LB, 0/0
12. David Dumars, Northeast Louisiana, DB, 0/0

OAKLAND RAIDERS

1. **Marc Wilson, Brigham Young, QB, 96/126**
2. **Matt Millen, Penn State, LB, 133/180**
5. Kenny Lewis, Virginia Tech, RB, 0/19
5. John Adams, Louisiana State, LB, 0/0
5. William Bowens, North Alabama, LB, 0/0
7. **Malcolm Barnwell, Virginia Union, WR, 57/66**
8. Kenny Hill, Yale, DB, 34/110
10. Walter Carter, Florida State, DE, 0/2
11. Mike Massey, Arkansas, LB, 0/0
12. Calvin Muhammad, Texas Southern, WR, 23/47

PHILADELPHIA EAGLES

1. **Roynell Young, Alcorn State, DB, 117/117**
2. Perry Harrington, Jackson State, RB, 42/59
5. Nate Rivers, South Carolina State, RB, 0/3
6. Greg Murtha, Minnesota, T, 0/5
7. Terrell Ward, San Diego State, DB, 0/0
8. Mike Curcio, Temple, LB, 21/34
9. Bob Harris, Bowling Green, T, 0/0
11. Thomas Brown, Baylor, DE, 16/48
11. Lee Jukes, North Carolina State, WR, 0/0
12. Howard Fields, Baylor, DB, 0/0

PITTSBURGH STEELERS

1. **Mark Malone, Arizona State, QB, 60/73**
2. **John Goodman, Oklahoma, DE, 64/64**
2. **Bob Kohrs, Arizona State, DE, 55/55**
3. Ray Sydnor, Wisconsin, TE, 0/0
4. Bill Hurley, Syracuse, DB, 0/23
5. **Craig Wolfley, Syracuse, G, 129/153**
6. **Tunch Ilkin, Indiana State, T, 176/177**
7. Nate Johnson, Hillsdale, WR, 0/16
8. Ted Walton, Connecticut, DB, 0/0
9. Ron McCall, Arkansas-Pine Bluff, WR, 0/0
10. Woodrow Wilson, North Carolina State, DB, 0/0
10. Ken Fritz, Ohio State, G, 0/0
11. **Frank Pollard, Baylor, RB, 111/111**
12. Tyrone McGriff, Florida A&M, G, 36/36
12. Charles Vaclavik, Texas, DB, 0/0

SAN DIEGO CHARGERS

4. Bob Gregor, Washington State, DB, 30/30
4. **Ed Luther, San Jose State, QB, 61/61**
6. LaRue Harrington, Norfolk State, RB, 4/4
6. Wayne Hamilton, Alabama, LB, 0/0
7. Chuck Loewen, South Dakota State, T, 47/47
7. Stuart Dodds, Montana State, P, 0/0
8. Curtis Sirmones, North Alabama, RB, 0/0
9. Steve Whitman, Alabama, RB, 0/0
11. John Singleton, Texas-El Paso, DE, 0/0
12. Harry Price, McNeese State, WR, 0/0

SAN FRANCISCO 49ERS

1. **Earl Cooper, Rice, RB, 88/93**
1. **Jim Stuckey, Clemson, DE, 88/93**
2. **Keena Turner, Purdue, LB, 153/153**
3. Jim Miller, Mississippi, P, 41/45
3. Craig Puki, Tennessee, LB, 32/39
4. Ricky Churchman, Texas, DB, 19/19
4. David Hodge, Houston, LB, 0/0
5. Ken Times, Southern (LA), NT, 3/5
6. Herb Williams, Southern (LA), DB, 9/19
8. **Bobby Leopold, Notre Dame, LB, 54/66**
9. Dan Hartwig, California Lutheran, QB, 0/0

ST. LOUIS CARDINALS

1. **Curtis Greer, Michigan, DE, 94/94**
2. **Doug Marsh, Michigan, TE, 92/92**
3. **Charles Baker, New Mexico, LB, 109/109**
3. John Sinnott, Brown, T, 0/9
4. Rusty Lisch, Notre Dame, QB, 23/30
6. Bill Acker, Texas, NT, 24/55
7. Ben Apuna, Arizona State, LB, 0/10
8. Dupree Branch, Colorado State, DB, 0/0
8. Grant Hudson, Virginia, DT, 0/0
9. **Stafford Mays, Washington, DE, 104/119**
10. Rush Brown, Ball State, DT, 47/47
11. Delrick Brown, Houston, DB, 0/0
12. Tyrone Gray, Washington State, WR, 0/0

SEATTLE SEAHAWKS

1. **Jacob Green, Texas A&M, DE, 178/180**
2. Andre Hines, Stanford, T, 9/9
4. Terry Dion, Oregon, DE, 9/9
5. Joe Steele, Washington, RB, 0/0
5. Daniel Jacobs, Winston-Salem State, DE, 0/0
6. Mark McNeal, Idaho, DE, 0/0
8. Vic Minor, Louisiana-Monroe, DB, 20/20
8. Jack Cosgrove, Pacific, C, 0/0
9. Jim Swift, Iowa, T, 0/0
10. **Ron Essink, Grand Valley State, T, 83/83**
10. Billy Reaves, Morris Brown, WR, 0/0
11. Tali Ena, Washington State, RB, 0/0
12. Presnell Gilbert, U.S. International, DB, 0/0

TAMPA BAY BUCCANEERS

1. Ray Snell, Wisconsin, G, 45/65
2. **Kevin House, Southern Illinois, WR, 94/114**
3. **Scot Brantley, Florida, LB, 114/114**
4. Larry Flowers, Texas Tech, DB, 0/67
7. **Jim Leonard, Santa Clara, G, 56/87**
8. Derrick Goodard, Drake, DB, 0/0
9. **Gerald Carter, Texas A&M, WR, 100/103**
10. Andy Hawkins, Texas A&M-Kingsville, LB, 47/66
10. Brett Davis, Nevada-Las Vegas, RB, 0/0
11. Terry Jones, Central State (OK), DE, 0/0
12. Gene Coleman, Miami (FL), DB, 0/0

WASHINGTON REDSKINS

1. **Art Monk, Syracuse, WR, 205/224**
2. Mat Mendenhall, Brigham Young, DE, 23/23
6. Farley Bell, Cincinnati, LB, 0/0
7. Melvin Jones, Houston, G, 11/11
9. Lawrence McCullough, Illinois, WR, 0/0
10. Lewis Walker, Utah, RB, 0/0
11. Mike Matocha, Texas-Arlington, DE, 0/0
12. Marcene Emmett, North Alabama, DB, 0/0

1981 NFL

ATLANTA FALCONS

1. **Bobby Butler, Florida State, DB, 169/169**
2. Lyman White, LSU, LB, 18/18
3. Scott Woerner, Georgia, DB, 16/17
4. **John Scully, Notre Dame, G, 112/112**
5. **Eric Sanders, Nevada-Reno, T, 75/158**
6. Harry Stanback, North Carolina, DE, 0/2
8. Clifford Toney, Auburn, DB, 0/0
9. Calvin Fance, Rice, RB, 0/0
10. Robert Murphy, Ohio State, DB, 0/0
11. Keith Chappelle, Iowa, WR, 0/0
12. Mark McCants, Temple, DB, 0/0

BALTIMORE COLTS

1. **Randy McMillan, Pittsburgh, RB, 88/88**
1. **Donnell Thompson, North Carolina, DE, 147/147**
3. Randy Van Divier, Washington, T, 16/16
4. **Tim Sherwin, Boston College, TE, 79/82**
6. Bubba Green, North Carolina State, DT, 15/15
7. Obed Ariri, Clemson, K, 0/18
8. Hosea Taylor, Houston, DE, 20/20
8. Ken Sitton, Oklahoma, DB, 0/0
9. Tim Gooch, Kentucky, DT, 0/0
10. Trent Bryant, Arkansas, DB, 0/32
10. Gregg Gerken, Northern Arizona, LB, 0/0
11. Holden Smith, California, WR, 3/3
12. Eric Scoggins, USC, LB, 0/3

BUFFALO BILLS

1. **Booker Moore, Penn State, RB, 51/51**
2. Byron Franklin, Auburn, WR, 44/77
2. Chris Williams, LSU, DB, 21/21
3. Mike Mosley, Texas A&M, WR, 20/20
3. Robert Geathers, South Carolina State, DT, 0/0
5. Calvin Clark, Purdue, DE, 0/0
6. Robert Holt, Baylor, WR, 7/7
7. Steve Doolittle, Colorado, LB, 0/0
9. **Robb Riddick, Millersville, RB, 78/78**
10. Justin Cross, Western State (CO), T, 44/44
11. **Buster Barnett, Jackson State, TE, 56/56**
12. Keith Clark, Memphis State, LB, 0/0

CHICAGO BEARS

1. **Keith Van Horne, USC, T, 186/186**
2. **Mike Singletary, Baylor, LB, 179/179**
3. **Ken Margerum, Stanford, WR, 57/64**
4. **Todd Bell, Ohio State, DB, 83/103**
6. Reuben Henderson, San Diego State, DB, 20/46
7. Jeff Fisher, USC, DB, 49/49
8. Scott Zettek, Notre Dame, DT, 0/0
9. Frank Ditta, Baylor, G, 0/0
10. Tim Clifford, Indiana, QB, 0/0
11. Lonnie Johnson, Indiana, RB, 0/0
12. Bob Shupryt, New Mexico, LB, 0/0

CINCINNATI BENGALS

1. David Verser, Kansas, WR, 49/52
2. **Cris Collinsworth, Florida, WR, 107/107**
3. **John Simmons, SMU, DB, 64/72**
4. **Guy Frazier, Wyoming, LB, 51/74**
5. Benjie Pryor, Pittsburgh, TE, 0/0
6. Rex Robinson, Georgia, K, 0/3
7. **Jeff Schuh, Minnesota, LB, 73/87**
8. **Bobby Kemp, Cal State-Fullerton, DB, 83/95**
9. Jim Hannula, Northern Illinois, T, 15/15
9. Samoa Samoa, Washington State, RB, 0/0
10. Hubert Simpson, Tennessee, RB, 0/0
11. **Robert Jackson, Central Michigan, DB, 90/90**
12. Mark O'Connell, Ball State, QB, 0/0

CLEVELAND BROWNS

1. **Hanford Dixon, Southern Mississippi, DB, 131/131**
4. Mike Robinson, Arizona, DE, 18/18
5. Steve Cox, Arkansas, P, 48/89
6. Ron Simmons, Florida State, DT, 0/0
7. **Eddie Johnson, Louisville, LB, 148/148**
9. Randy Schleusener, Nebraska, G, 0/0
10. Dean Prater, Oklahoma State, DE, 0/77
11. Larry Friday, Mississippi State, DB, 0/1
12. Kevin McGill, Oregon, T, 0/0

DALLAS COWBOYS

1. **Howard Richards, Missouri, G, 67/69**
2. Doug Donley, Ohio State, WR, 43/43
3. **Glen Titensor, Brigham Young, G, 92/92**
4. Derrie Nelson, Nebraska, LB, 0/48
4. Scott Pelluer, Washington State, LB, 0/65
5. Danny Spradlin, Tennessee, LB, 25/63
6. Vince Skillings, Ohio State, DB, 0/0
7. **Ron Fellows, Missouri, DB, 86/112**
7. Ken Miller, Eastern Michigan, DB, 0/0
8. Paul Piurowski, Florida State, LB, 0/0
9. Mike Wilson, Washington State, WR, 0/136
10. Pat Graham, California, DT, 0/0
11. Tim Morrison, Georgia, G, 0/0
12. Nate Lundy, Indiana, WR, 0/0

DENVER BRONCOS

1. **Dennis Smith, USC, DB, 184/184**
2. Clay Brown, Brigham Young, TE, 3/4
4. Mark Herrmann, Purdue, QB, 2/40
5. **Ken Lanier, Florida State, T, 177/179**
6. Alvin Lewis, Colorado State, RB, 0/0
7. **Steve Busick, USC, LB, 73/78**
9. Rusty Olsen, Washington, DE, 0/0
11. Pat Walker, Miami (FL), WR, 0/0
12. John Hankerd, Notre Dame, LB, 0/0
12. Mandel Robinson, Wyoming, RB, 0/0

DETROIT LIONS

1. **Mark Nichols, San Jose State, WR, 76/76**
2. **Curtis Green, Alabama State, DE, 123/123**
3. Don Greco, Western Illinois, G, 45/45
4. Tracy Porter, LSU, WR, 20/52
5. **Larry Lee, UCLA, G, 62/96**
6. Sam Johnson, Maryland, DB, 0/0
7. Lee Spivey, Southern Methodist, T, 0/0
8. Bob Niziolek, Colorado, TE, 4/4
9. David Martin, Villanova, DB, 0/7
9. Hugh Jernigan, Arkansas, DB, 0/0
10. Andy Cannavino, Michigan, LB, 0/0
11. Willie Jackson, Mississippi State, DB, 0/0

GREEN BAY PACKERS

1. Rich Campbell, California, QB, 7/7
2. Gary Lewis, Texas-Arlington, TE, 44/44
3. Ray Stachowicz, Michigan State, P, 25/27
4. Richard Turner, Oklahoma, NT, 30/30
5. Byron Braggs, Alabama, DE, 41/55
7. Bill Whitaker, Missouri, DB, 25/39
8. Larry Werts, Jackson State, LB, 0/0
9. Tim Huffman, Notre Dame, G, 47/47
10. Nickie Hall, Tulane, QB, 0/0
11. Forrest Valora, Oklahoma, LB, 0/0
12. **Cliff Lewis, Southern Mississippi, LB, 57/57**

HOUSTON OILERS

3. **Mike Holston, Morgan State, WR, 60/64**
4. Nick Eyre, Brigham Young, T, 6/6
5. Delbert Fowler, West Virginia, LB, 0/0
6. Bill Kay, Purdue, DB, 41/56
7. Don Washington, Texas A&I, DB, 0/0
8. **Willie Tullis, Troy State, DB, 57/106**
9. **Avon Riley, UCLA, LB, 88/91**
10. Larry Jones, Colorado State, RB, 0/0
11. Claude Mathews, Auburn, G, 0/0
12. Bill Capece, Florida State, K, 0/37

KANSAS CITY CHIEFS

1. **Willie Scott, South Carolina, TE, 72/98**
2. Joe Delaney, Northwestern State (LA), RB, 23/23
3. **Lloyd Burruss, Maryland, DB, 145/145**
3. Marvin Harvey, Southern Mississippi, TE, 7/7
3. Roger Taylor, Oklahoma State, T, 13/13
4. Ron Washington, Arizona State, WR, 0/0
5. Todd Thomas, North Dakota, C, 15/15
6. Dock Luckie, Florida, DT, 0/0
7. **Billy Jackson, Alabama, RB, 57/57**
8. David Dorn, Rutgers, WR, 0/0
9. Anthony Vereen, Southeastern Louisiana, DB, 0/0
10. Les Studdard, Texas, C, 9/15
11. Frank Case, Penn State, DE, 7/7
12. Bob Gagliano, Utah State, QB, 2/32

LOS ANGELES RAMS

1. **Mel Owens, Michigan, LB, 122/122**
2. **Jim Collins, Syracuse, LB, 80/93**
3. Robert Cobb, Arizona, DE, 6/11
3. **Greg Meisner, Pittsburgh, NT, 103/135**
4. George Lilja, Michigan, G, 9/54
6. William Daniels, Alabama State, DT, 0/0
7. Ron Battle, North Texas, TE, 13/13
7. Mike Clark, Florida, DE, 0/14
8. Art Plunkett, UNLV, T, 0/71
9. Ron Seawell, Portland State, LB, 0/0
10. Robert Alexander, West Virginia, RB, 24/24
11. Marcellus Greene, Arizona, DB, 0/14
12. Jairo Penaranda, UCLA, RB, 16/20

MIAMI DOLPHINS

1. David Overstreet, Oklahoma, RB, 14/14
2. Andra Franklin, Nebraska, RB, 42/42
4. Sam Greene, Nevada-Las Vegas, WR, 0/0
4. Brad Wright, New Mexico, QB, 0/0
5. Ken Poole, Louisiana-Monroe, DE, 16/16
5. Tommy Vigorito, Virginia, RB, 35/35
6. Mack Moore, Texas A&M, DE, 23/26
6. **Fulton Walker, West Virginia, DB, 54/81**
7. Mike Daum, Cal Poly-SLO, T, 0/0
8. **William Judson, South Carolina State, DB, 115/115**
9. John Noonan, Nebraska, WR, 0/0
10. Steve Folsom, Utah, TE, 0/45
11. **Jim Jensen, Boston University, WR, 164/164**
12. John Alford, South Carolina State, DT, 0/0

MINNESOTA VIKINGS

2. Mardye McDole, Mississippi State, WR, 26/26
2. Jarvis Redwine, Nebraska, RB, 26/26
2. **Robin Sendlein, Texas, LB, 56/72**
3. **Tim Irwin, Tennessee, T, 188/201**
4. **John Swain, Miami (FL), DB, 50/77**
5. Wendell Ray, Missouri, DE, 0/0
7. Don Shaver, Kutztown, RB, 0/0
8. **Wade Wilson, Texas A&M-Commerce, QB, 76/125**
10. James Murphy, Utah State, WR, 0/10
11. Bill Stephanos, Boston College, T, 0/0
12. Brian Williams, Southern (LA), TE, 0/1

NEW ENGLAND PATRIOTS

1. **Brian Holloway, Stanford, T, 88/102**
2. **Tony Collins, East Carolina, RB, 102/103**
4. **Don Blackmon, Tulsa, LB, 89/89**
5. Steve Clark, Kansas State, DE, 7/7
6. **Ron Wooten, North Carolina, G, 98/98**
7. Ken Toler, Mississippi, WR, 25/25
8. **Lin Dawson, North Carolina State, TE, 105/105**
8. Ken Naber, Stanford, K, 0/0
S11. Chy Davidson, Rhode Island, WR, 0/4
11. Brian Buckley, Harvard, QB, 0/0
12. Cris Crissy, Princeton, DB, 0/1

NEW ORLEANS SAINTS

1. **George Rogers, South Carolina, RB, 51/92**
S1. **Dave Wilson, Illinois, QB, 53/53**
2. **Russell Gary, Nebraska, DB, 62/80**
2. **Rickey Jackson, Pittsburgh, LB, 195/227**
3. **Hoby Brenner, USC, TE, 175/175**
3. **Frank Warren, Auburn, DE, 189/189**
5. Jerry Boyarsky, Pittsburgh, NT, 11/98
5. Louis Oubre, Oklahoma, G, 37/40
6. Nat Hudson, Georgia, G, 16/18
6. **Johnnie Poe, Missouri, DB, 100/100**
6. **Glen Redd, Brigham Young, LB, 68/76**
7. Kevin Williams, USC, WR, 0/11
8. Gene Gladys, Penn State, LB, 0/0
8. Kevin Evans, Arkansas, DB, 0/0
9. Toussaint Tyler, Washington, RB, 18/18
10. Hokie Gajan, LSU, RB, 45/45

11. Lester Mickens, Kansas, WR, 0/0
12. **Jim Wilks, San Diego State, DE, 183/183**

NEW YORK GIANTS

1. **Lawrence Taylor, North Carolina, LB, 184/184**
2. Dave Young, Purdue, TE, 11/25
3. John Mistler, Arizona State, WR, 42/45
4. Cliff Chatman, Central Oklahoma, RB, 6/6
5. Bill Neill, Pittsburgh, NT, 24/40
6. Melvin Hoover, Arizona State, WR, 0/32
6. Edward O'Neal, Tuskegee, RB, 0/0
7. Louis Jackson, Cal Poly-San Luis Obispo, RB, 11/11
8. **Billy Ard, Wake Forest, G, 113/148**
8. Mark Reed, Moorhead State (MN), QB, 0/1
8. John Powers, Michigan, G, 0/0
9. **Byron Hunt, SMU, LB, 100/100**
10. Mike Barker, Grambling, DT, 0/0
12. Mike Maher, Western Illinois, TE, 0/0

NEW YORK JETS

1. **Freeman McNeil, UCLA, RB, 144/144**
2. **Marion Barber, Minnesota, RB, 85/85**
3. **Ben Rudolph, Long Beach State, DT, 88/88**
4. Al Washington, Ohio State, LB, 16/16
5. Tyrone Keys, Mississippi State, DE, 0/74
6. **John Woodring, Brown, LB, 52/52**
7. Kenny Neil, Iowa State, DE, 41/42
8. Lloyd Jones, BYU, WR, 0/0
8. J.C. Watts, Oklahoma, DB, 0/0
9. Admiral Dewey Larry, Nevada-Las Vegas, DB, 0/0
10. Marty Wetzel, Tulane, LB, 5/5
11. Ed Gall, Maryland, DT, 0/0
12. Mike Moeller, Drake, T, 0/0

OAKLAND RAIDERS

1. Curt Marsh, Washington, G, 45/45
1. **Ted Watts, Texas Tech, DB, 57/74**
2. **Howie Long, Villanova, DE, 179/179**
4. Johnny Robinson, Louisiana Tech, NT, 27/27
5. **James Davis, Southern (LA), DB, 83/83**
9. Curt Mohl, UCLA, T, 0/0
10. **Frank Hawkins, Nevada-Reno, RB, 88/88**
11. **Chester Willis, Auburn, RB, 52/52**
12. Phil Nelson, Delaware, TE, 0/0

PHILADELPHIA EAGLES

1. **Leonard Mitchell, Houston, T, 77/89**
2. Dean Miraldi, Utah, T, 30/50
3. Greg LaFleur, LSU, TE, 0/86
4. Calvin Murray, Ohio State, RB, 8/8
7. Doak Field, Baylor, LB, 0/7
7. Alan Duncan, Tennessee, K, 0/0
9. Chuck Commiskey, Mississippi, G, 0/34
10. Hubie Oliver, Arizona, RB, 46/52
11. Gail Davis, Virginia Union, T, 0/0
12. **Ray Ellis, Ohio State, DB, 73/100**

PITTSBURGH STEELERS

1. **Keith Gary, Oklahoma, DE, 86/86**
2. Anthony Washington, Fresno State, DB, 25/57
3. Rick Donnalley, North Carolina, C, 21/71
4. Robbie Martin, Cal Poly-San Luis Obispo, WR, 0/72
5. Ricky Martin, New Mexico, WR, 0/0
6. **Bryan Hinkle, Oregon, LB, 163/163**
7. **David Little, Florida, LB, 179/179**
8. Frank Wilson, Rice, TE, 1/1
9. James Hunter, USC, NT, 0/9
10. Mike Mayock, Boston College, DB, 0/9
11. Rick Trocano, Pittsburgh, DB, 0/8

SAN DIEGO CHARGERS

1. James Brooks, Auburn, RB, 38/162
3. Irvin Phillips, Arkansas Tech, DB, 15/20
4. Amos Lawrence, North Carolina, RB, 0/21
4. **Eric Sievers, Maryland, TE, 97/122**
5. **Keith Ferguson, Ohio State, DE, 67/134**
6. Bobby Duckworth, Arkansas, WR, 37/62
6. Andrew Gissinger, Syracuse, T, 41/41
7. **Pete Holohan, Notre Dame, TE, 90/163**
10. Robert Parham, Grambling, RB, 0/0
11. **Carlos Bradley, Wake Forest, LB, 51/54**
11. Matt Petrzelka, Iowa, T, 0/0
12. Stacy Charles, Bethune-Cookman, WR, 0/0

SAN FRANCISCO 49ERS

1. **Ronnie Lott, USC, DB, 129/192**
2. John Harty, Iowa, NT, 42/42
2. **Eric Wright, Missouri, DB, 110/110**
3. **Carlton Williamson, Pittsburgh, DB, 88/88**
5. Arrington Jones, Winston-Salem State, RB, 1/1
5. Lynn Thomas, Pittsburgh, DB, 24/24
6. **Pete Kugler, Penn State, NT, 81/81**
8. Garry White, Minnesota, RB, 0/0
11. Ronnie DeBose, UCLA, TE, 0/0
12. Major Ogilvie, Alabama, RB, 0/0
12. Joe Adams, Tennessee State, QB, 0/0

ST. LOUIS CARDINALS

1. **E.J. Junior, Alabama, LB, 111/170**
2. **Neil Lomax, Portland State, QB, 108/108**
3. Jeff Griffin, Utah, DB, 48/50
4. Steve Rhodes, Oklahoma, WR, 0/0
5. John Gillen, Illinois, LB, 20/28
6. **Dave Ahrens, Wisconsin, LB, 57/130**
7. Kevin Donnalley, North Dakota State, DB, 0/1
8. Mike Fisher, Baylor, WR, 2/2
9. **Stump Mitchell, The Citadel, RB, 116/116**
10. James Mallard, Alabama, WR, 0/0
10. Jim Joiner, Miami (FL), WR, 0/0
11. Mike Sherrod, Illinois, TE, 0/0
12. Joe Adams, Nebraska, G, 0/0

SEATTLE SEAHAWKS

1. **Kenny Easley, UCLA, DB, 89/89**
2. **David Hughes, Boise State, RB, 69/74**
3. Bill Dugan, Penn State, G, 40/44
4. Scott Phillips, BYU, WR, 0/0
5. **Edwin Bailey, South Carolina State, G, 139/139**
6. Steve Durham, Clemson, DE, 0/8
7. Ron Johnson, Long Beach State, WR, 0/47
7. Brad Scovill, Penn State, TE, 0/0
8. **Eric Lane, Brigham Young, RB, 97/97**
9. Jim Stone, Notre Dame, RB, 0/0
9. Jim Whatley, Washington State, WR, 0/0
10. Ken Dawson, Savannah State, RB, 0/0
11. Lance Olander, Colorado, RB, 0/0
12. Jeff Bednarek, Pacific, DT, 0/0

TAMPA BAY BUCCANEERS

1. **Hugh Green, Pittsburgh, LB, 54/136**
2. **James Wilder, Missouri, RB, 113/129**
4. **John Holt, West Texas A&M, DB, 72/109**
8. Denver Johnson, Tulsa, T, 0/0
9. Mike Ford, Southern Methodist, QB, 0/0
10. Ken McCune, Texas, DE, 0/0
11. Johnny Ray Smith, Lamar, DB, 25/26
12. Brad White, Tennessee, NT, 41/73

WASHINGTON REDSKINS

1. **Mark May, Pittsburgh, G, 123/159**
3. **Russ Grimm, Pittsburgh, G, 140/140**
4. Tom Flick, Washington, QB, 6/21
5. **Dexter Manley, Oklahoma State, DE, 125/143**
5. Gary Sayre, Cameron, G, 0/0
6. Larry Kubin, Penn State, LB, 37/43
8. Charlie Brown, South Carolina State, WR, 33/68
9. **Darryl Grant, Rice, DT, 139/141**
10. Allan Kennedy, Washington State, T, 0/33
10. Phil Kessel, Northern Michigan, QB, 0/0
11. Jerry Hill, North Alabama, WR, 0/0
12. **Clint Didier, Portland State, TE, 74/105**

1982 NFL

ATLANTA FALCONS

1. **Gerald Riggs, Arizona State, RB, 91/129**
2. Doug Rogers, Stanford, DE, 11/41
3. **Stacey Bailey, San Jose State, WR, 91/91**
4. Reggie Brown, Oregon, RB, 10/13
5. Von Mansfield, Wisconsin, DB, 0/10
6. Mike Kelley, Georgia Tech, QB, 0/3
7. David Toloumu, Hawaii, RB, 0/0
8. Ricky Eberhardt, Morris Brown, DB, 0/0
9. Mike Horan, Long Beach State, P, 0/205
10. Curtis Stowers, Mississippi State, LB, 0/0
11. Jeff Keller, Washington State, WR, 0/0
12. Dave Levenick, Wisconsin, LB, 24/24

BALTIMORE COLTS

1. **Johnie Cooks, Mississippi State, LB, 83/128**
1. Art Schlichter, Ohio State, QB, 13/13
2. **Rohn Stark, Florida State, P, 197/233**
3. Jim Burroughs, Michigan State, DB, 30/30
4. **Mike Pagel, Arizona State, QB, 51/132**
5. Terry Crouch, Oklahoma, G, 9/9
6. **Pat Beach, Washington State, TE, 129/160**
7. Fletcher Jenkins, Washington, DE, 9/9
8. Tony Loia, Arizona State, G, 0/0
9. Tony Berryhill, Clemson, C, 0/0
10. Tom Deery, Widener, DB, 0/0
11. Lamont Meacham, Western Kentucky, DB, 0/0
12. Johnnie Wright, South Carolina, RB, 7/7

BUFFALO BILLS

1. Perry Tuttle, Clemson, WR, 16/24
2. Matt Kofler, San Diego State, QB, 36/41
3. **Eugene Marve, Saginaw Valley State, LB, 76/156**
4. Van Williams, Carson-Newman, RB, 34/37
6. DeWayne Chivers, South Carolina, TE, 0/0
7. Gary Anderson, Syracuse, K, 0/353
8. Luc Tousignant, Fairmont State, QB, 0/0
9. Dennis Edwards, USC, DE, 0/3
10. Vic James, Colorado, DB, 0/0
11. Frank Kalil, Arizona, G, 0/0
12. Tony Suber, Gardner-Webb, DT, 0/0

CHICAGO BEARS

1. **Jim McMahon, Brigham Young, QB, 66/120**
3. Tim Wrightman, UCLA, TE, 32/32
4. **Dennis Gentry, Baylor, WR, 159/159**
5. Perry Hartnett, SMU, G, 11/12
5. Dennis Tabron, Duke, DB, 0/0
6. **Kurt Becker, Michigan, G, 92/94**
7. Henry Waechter, Nebraska, DE, 40/53
8. Jerry Doerger, Wisconsin, C, 2/10
9. Mike Hatchett, Texas, DB, 0/0
10. Joe Turner, Southern California, DB, 0/0
11. Guy Boliaux, Wisconsin, LB, 0/0
12. Ricky Young, Oklahoma State, LB, 0/0

CINCINNATI BENGALS

1. **Glen Collins, Mississippi State, DE, 55/58**
2. Emanuel Weaver, South Carolina State, NT, 5/7
3. **Rodney Holman, Tulane, TE, 165/212**
4. Rodney Tate, Texas, RB, 21/28
5. Paul Sorensen, Washington State, DB, 0/0
6. Arthur King, Grambling, DT, 0/0
7. Ben Needham, Michigan, LB, 0/0
8. Kari Yli-Renko, Cincinnati, T, 0/0
9. James Bennett, Northwestern State (LA), WR, 0/0
10. Larry Hogue, Utah State, DB, 0/0
11. Russell Davis, Idaho, RB, 0/0
12. Dan Feraday, Toronto, QB, 0/0

CLEVELAND BROWNS

1. **Chip Banks, USC, LB, 73/138**
2. **Keith Baldwin, Texas A&M, DE, 51/63**
4. Dwight Walker, Nicholls State, RB, 36/38
5. **Mike Baab, Texas, C, 114/147**
6. Mike Whitwell, Texas A&M, DB, 25/25
8. Bill Jackson, North Carolina, DB, 9/9
8. Mark Kafentzis, Hawaii, DB, 9/40
8. Van Heflin, Vanderbilt, TE, 0/0
9. Milton Baker, West Texas State, TE, 0/0
10. Ricky Floyd, Southern Mississippi, RB, 0/0
11. Steve Michuta, Grand Valley State, QB, 0/0
12. **Scott Nicolas, Miami (FL), LB, 73/85**

DALLAS COWBOYS

1. Rod Hill, Kentucky State, DB, 23/48
2. **Jeff Rohrer, Yale, LB, 83/83**
3. Jim Eliopulos, Wyoming, LB, 0/31
4. Brian Carpenter, Michigan, DB, 0/35
4. Monty Hunter, Salem, DB, 9/14
5. **Phil Pozderac, Notre Dame, T, 70/70**
6. Ken Hammond, Vanderbilt, G, 0/0
6. Charles Daum, Cal Poly-SLO, DT, 0/0
7. Bill Purifoy, Tulsa, DE, 0/0
8. George Peoples, Auburn, RB, 8/32
8. Dwight Sullivan, North Carolina State, RB, 0/0
9. Joe Gary, UCLA, DT, 0/0
10. Todd Eckerson, North Carolina State, T, 0/0
11. George Thompson, Albany State (GA), WR, 0/0
11. Mike Whiting, Florida State, RB, 0/0
12. Rich Burtness, Montana, G, 0/0

DENVER BRONCOS

1. **Gerald Willhite, San Jose State, RB, 78/78**
2. Orlando McDaniel, LSU, WR, 3/3
4. Dan Plater, BYU, WR, 0/0
5. **Sammy Winder, Southern Mississippi, RB, 127/127**
7. Alvin Ruben, Houston, DE, 0/0
9. Keith Uecker, Auburn, T, 21/85
10. **Ken Woodard, Tuskegee, LB, 73/104**
11. Stuart Yatsko, Oregon, G, 0/0
12. Brian Clark, Clemson, G, 0/0

DETROIT LIONS

1. **Jimmy Williams, Nebraska, LB, 107/152**
2. **Bobby Watkins, Southwest Texas State, DB, 83/83**
3. Steve Doig, New Hampshire, LB, 34/40
4. **Bruce McNorton, Georgetown (KY), DB, 116/116**
5. **William Graham, Texas, DB, 69/69**
6. Mike Machurek, Idaho State, QB, 4/4
7. Phil Bates, Nebraska, RB, 0/0
7. Victor Simmons, Oregon State, WR, 0/0
8. Martin Moss, UCLA, DE, 42/42
9. Danny Wagoner, Kansas, DB, 16/34
10. **Roosevelt Barnes, Purdue, LB, 57/57**
11. Edward Lee, South Carolina State, WR, 0/0
12. Ricky Porter, Slippery Rock, RB, 1/24
12. **Rob Rubick, Grand Valley State, TE, 88/88**

GREEN BAY PACKERS

1. **Ron Hallstrom, Iowa, G, 162/174**
3. Del Rodgers, Utah, RB, 23/31
4. **Robert Brown, Virginia Tech, DE, 164/164**
5. Mike Meade, Penn State, RB, 18/49
6. Chet Parlavecchio, Penn State, LB, 3/12
7. Joey Whitley, Texas-El Paso, DB, 0/0
8. Thomas Boyd, Alabama, LB, 0/4
9. Charles Riggins, Bethune-Cookman, DE, 0/3
10. Eddie Garcia, SMU, K, 19/19
11. John Macaulay, Stanford, C, 0/3
12. **Phil Epps, TCU, WR, 85/95**

HOUSTON OILERS

1. **Mike Munchak, Penn State, G, 159/159**
2. Oliver Luck, West Virginia, QB, 20/20
3. **Robert Abraham, North Carolina State, LB, 73/73**
3. **Stan Edwards, Michigan, RB, 53/56**
4. Steve Bryant, Purdue, WR, 41/42
5. Malcolm Taylor, Tennessee State, DE, 28/68
6. Gary Allen, Hawaii, RB, 8/30
9. Matt Bradley, Penn State, DB, 0/0
10. Ron Reeves, Texas Tech, QB, 0/0
11. Jim Campbell, Kentucky, TE, 0/0
12. Donnie Craft, Louisville, RB, 25/25

KANSAS CITY CHIEFS

1. **Anthony Hancock, Tennessee, WR, 59/59**
2. **Calvin Daniels, North Carolina, LB, 57/70**
4. Stuart Anderson, Virginia, LB, 0/40
4. Louis Haynes, North Texas, LB, 11/11
5. Del Thompson, Texas-El Paso, RB, 6/6
6. Durwood Roquemore, Texas A&M-Kingsville, DB, 24/29
7. Greg Smith, Kansas, DE, 0/16
8. Case deBruijn, Idaho State, P, 1/1
9. Lyndle Byford, Oklahoma, T, 0/0
10. Larry Brodsky, Miami (FL), WR, 0/0
11. Bob Carter, Arizona, WR, 0/0
12. Mike Miller, Southwest Texas State, DB, 0/0

LOS ANGELES RAIDERS

1. **Marcus Allen, USC, RB, 145/222**
2. Jim Romano, Penn State, C, 12/45
2. **Jack Squirek, Illinois, LB, 53/55**
2. Leo Wisniewski, Penn State, NT, 0/36
3. **Vann McElroy, Baylor, DB, 101/111**
4. Ed Muransky, Michigan, T, 24/24

LOS ANGELES RAMS

1. **Barry Redden, Richmond, RB, 67/108**
3. Bill Bechtold, Oklahoma, C, 0/0
4. Jeff Gaylord, Missouri, LB, 0/0
5. Doug Barnett, Azusa Pacific, DE, 25/37
5. Wally Kersten, Minnesota, T, 3/3
6. Kerry Locklin, New Mexico State, TE, 6/9
7. Joe Shearin, Texas, G, 31/42
8. A.J. Jones, Texas, RB, 29/37
8. Mike Reilly, Oklahoma, LB, 9/9
9. Bob Speight, Boston, T, 0/0
10. Miles McPherson, New Haven, DB, 0/35
11. Ricky Coffman, UCLA, WR, 0/0
12. Raymond Coley, Alabama A&M, DT, 0/0

MIAMI DOLPHINS

1. **Roy Foster, USC, G, 132/165**
2. **Mark Duper, Northwestern State (LA), WR, 146/146**
3. **Paul Lankford, Penn State, DB, 130/130**
4. Charles Bowser, Duke, LB, 42/42
5. Rich Diana, Yale, RB, 9/9
5. Bob Nelson, Miami (FL), NT, 0/62
6. Ron Hester, Florida State, LB, 9/9
6. Tom Tutson, South Carolina State, DB, 0/10
7. Larry Cowan, Jackson State, RB, 2/8
7. **Dan Johnson, Iowa State, TE, 66/66**
8. Tate Randle, Texas Tech, DB, 3/69
9. Mack Boatner, Southeastern Louisiana, RB, 0/7
9. Steve Clark, Utah, G, 41/41
10. Wayne Jones, Utah, G, 0/6
10. Robin Fisher, Florida, LB, 0/0
11. Gary Crum, Wyoming, T, 0/0
12. Mike Rodrique, Miami (FL), WR, 0/0

MINNESOTA VIKINGS

1. **Darrin Nelson, Stanford, RB, 129/152**
2. **Terry Tausch, Texas, G, 81/90**
4. Jim Fahnhorst, Minnesota, LB, 0/82
6. Greg Storr, Boston College, LB, 0/3

7. **Steve Jordan, Brown, TE, 176/176**
8. Kirk Harmon, Pacific, LB, 0/0
9. Bryan Howard, Tennessee State, DB, 2/2
10. Gerald Lucear, Temple, WR, 0/0
11. **Curtis Rouse, Tennessee-Chattanooga, G, 58/68**
12. Hobson Milner, Cincinnati, RB, 0/0

NEW ENGLAND PATRIOTS
1. **Kenneth Sims, Texas, DE, 74/74**
1. Lester Williams, Miami (FL), NT, 40/46
2. **Darryl Haley, Utah, T, 57/79**
2. **Andre Tippett, Iowa, LB, 151/151**
2. Robert Weathers, Arizona State, RB, 44/44
3. **Cedric Jones, Duke, WR, 120/120**
3. Clayton Weishuhn, Angelo State (TX), LB, 30/39
4. George Crump, East Carolina, DE, 9/9
4. Brian Ingram, Tennessee, LB, 39/40
5. **Fred Marion, Miami (FL), DB, 144/144**
6. Ricky Smith, Alabama State, DB, 26/49
7. Jeff Roberts, Tulane, LB, 0/0
8. Ken Collins, Washington State, LB, 0/0
9. Kelvin Murdock, Troy State, WR, 0/0
10. Brian Clark, Florida, K, 0/1
11. Steve Sandon, Northern Iowa, QB, 0/0
12. Greg Taylor, Virginia, RB, 1/1

NEW ORLEANS SAINTS
1. Lindsay Scott, Georgia, WR, 49/49
2. **Brad Edelman, Missouri, G, 90/90**
3. Kenny Duckett, Wake Forest, WR, 33/36
3. **Eugene Goodlow, Kansas State, WR, 54/54**
3. John Krimm, Notre Dame, DB, 9/9
3. Rodney Lewis, Nebraska, DB, 27/27
4. **Morten Andersen, Michigan State, K, 196/354**
5. **Tony Elliott, North Texas, NT, 84/84**
6. Marvin Lewis, Tulane, RB, 1/1
8. Chuck Slaughter, South Carolina, T, 1/1

NEW YORK GIANTS
1. Butch Woolfolk, Michigan, RB, 40/81
2. **Joe Morris, Syracuse, RB, 94/110**
4. Gerry Raymond, Boston College, G, 0/0
5. Rich Umphrey, Colorado, C, 34/45
6. Darrell Nicholson, North Carolina, LB, 0/0
7. Jeff Wiska, Michigan State, G, 0/4
8. Robert Hubble, Rice, TE, 0/0
9. John Higgins, Nevada-Las Vegas, DB, 0/0
10. Rich Baldinger, Wake Forest, G, 3/157
12. Mark Seale, Richmond, DT, 0/0

NEW YORK JETS
1. **Bob Crable, Notre Dame, LB, 66/66**
2. **Reggie McElroy, West Texas A&M, T, 92/165**
3. Dwayne Crutchfield, Iowa State, RB, 17/34
4. George Floyd, Eastern Kentucky, DB, 15/15
5. Mark Jerue, Washington, LB, 0/86
6. Lonell Phea, Houston, WR, 0/0
7. Tom Coombs, Idaho, TE, 15/15
8. Lawrence Texada, Henderson State, RB, 0/0
9. **Rocky Klever, Montana, TE, 65/65**
10. Darryl Hemphill, West Texas A&M, DB, 0/3
11. Perry Parmelee, Santa Clara, WR, 0/0
12. Tom Carlstrom, Nebraska, G, 0/0

OAKLAND RAIDERS
5. Ed Jackson, Louisiana Tech, LB, 0/0
7. Jeff Jackson, Toledo, DE, 0/0
10. Rich D'Amico, Penn State, LB, 0/0
11. Willie Turner, Louisiana State, WR, 0/0
12. Randy Smith, East Texas State, WR, 0/0

PHILADELPHIA EAGLES
1. **Mike Quick, North Carolina State, WR, 101/101**
2. Lawrence Sampleton, Texas, TE, 32/35
3. Vyto Kab, Penn State, TE, 40/58
4. **Anthony Griggs, Ohio State, LB, 57/90**
5. Dennis DeVaughn, Bishop, DB, 13/13
6. Curt Grieve, Yale, WR, 0/0
7. Harvey Armstrong, SMU, NT, 40/111
8. Jim Fritzsche, Purdue, T, 15/15
9. Tony Woodruff, Fresno State, WR, 23/23
11. Ron Ingram, Oklahoma State, WR, 0/0
12. Rob Taylor, Northwestern, T, 0/110

PITTSBURGH STEELERS
1. **Walter Abercrombie, Baylor, RB, 79/84**
2. John Meyer, Arizona State, T, 0/0
3. **Mike Merriweather, Pacific, LB, 85/149**
4. **Rick Woods, Boise State, DB, 66/71**
5. Ken Dallafior, Minnesota, G, 0/87
6. Craig Bingham, Syracuse, LB, 32/40
6. Mike Perko, Utah State, NT, 0/9
7. Emil Boures, Pittsburgh, T, 35/35
7. **Edmund Nelson, Auburn, DE, 72/84**
8. John Goodson, Texas, P, 9/9
9. Mike Hirn, Central Michigan, TE, 0/0
10. Sal Sunseri, Pittsburgh, LB, 0/0
11. Mikal Abdul Sorboor, Morgan State, G, 0/0
12. Al Hughes, Western Michigan, DE, 0/0

SAN DIEGO CHARGERS
7. Hollis Hall, Clemson, DB, 0/0
8. Maury Buford, Texas Tech, P, 41/136
9. Warren Lyles, Alabama, DT, 0/0
10. Andre Young, Louisiana Tech, DB, 36/36
11. Anthony Watson, New Mexico State, DB, 0/0

SAN FRANCISCO 49ERS
2. **Bubba Paris, Michigan, T, 117/130**
5. Newton Williams, Arizona State, RB, 6/22
6. Vince Williams, Oregon, RB, 3/3
7. **Ron Ferrari, Illinois, LB, 68/68**
9. Bryan Clark, Michigan State, QB, 0/1
10. **Dana McLemore, Hawaii, DB, 69/72**
10. Tim Barbian, Western Illinois, DT, 0/0
11. Gary Gibson, Arizona, LB, 0/0
12. Tim Washington, Fresno State, DB, 1/2

ST. LOUIS CARDINALS
1. **Luis Sharpe, UCLA, T, 189/189**
2. **David Galloway, Florida, DT, 89/99**
3. Rusty Guilbeau, McNeese State, LB, 0/57
3. Benny Perrin, Alabama, DB, 48/48
4. **Tootie Robbins, East Carolina, T, 132/159**
5. Vance Bedford, Texas, DB, 0/0
5. **Earl Ferrell, East Tennessee State, RB, 110/110**
6. Craig Shaffer, Indiana State, LB, 18/18
7. Bob Sebro, Colorado, C, 0/0
8. Chris Lindstrom, Boston University, DE, 0/19
9. Darnell Dailey, Maryland, LB, 0/0
10. Eddie McGill, Western Carolina, TE, 11/11
11. James Williams, North Carolina A&T, DE, 0/0
12. Bob Atha, Ohio State, K, 0/0

SEATTLE SEAHAWKS
1. **Jeff Bryant, Clemson, DE, 175/175**
2. **Bruce Scholtz, Texas, LB, 96/104**
3. Pete Metzelaars, Wabash, TE, 34/235
6. Jack Campbell, Utah, T, 1/1
7. Eugene Williams, Tulsa, LB, 13/13
8. Chester Cooper, Minnesota, WR, 0/0
9. David Jefferson, Miami (FL), LB, 0/0
10. Craig Austin, South Dakota, LB, 0/0
11. Sam Clancy, Pittsburgh, DE, 13/152
12. Frank Naylor, Rutgers, C, 0/0

TAMPA BAY BUCCANEERS
1. **Sean Farrell, Penn State, G, 64/123**
2. Booker Reese, Bethune-Cookman, DE, 24/35
3. **Jerry Bell, Arizona State, TE, 60/60**
3. **John Cannon, William & Mary, DE, 122/122**
4. Dave Barrett, Houston, RB, 7/7
5. **Jeff Davis, Clemson, LB, 83/83**
6. Andre Tyler, Stanford, WR, 14/14
7. Tom Morris, Michigan State, DB, 20/20
8. Kelvin Atkins, Illinois, LB, 0/13
9. Bob Lane, Northeast Louisiana, QB, 0/0
12. Michael Morton, UNLV, RB, 41/44

WASHINGTON REDSKINS
2. **Vernon Dean, San Diego State, DB, 85/101**
3. Carl Powell, Jackson State, WR, 0/0
4. Todd Liebenstein, UNLV, DE, 29/29
5. Mike Williams, Alabama A&M, TE, 14/14
6. Lamont Jeffers, Tennessee, LB, 0/0
7. John Schachtner, Northern Arizona, LB, 0/0
8. Ralph Warthen, Gardner-Webb, DT, 0/0
9. Ken Coffey, Southwest Texas State, DB, 41/41
9. Randy Trautman, Boise State, DT, 0/0
10. Harold Smith, Kentucky State, DE, 0/0
10. Terry Daniels, Tennessee, DB, 0/0
11. Bob Holly, Princeton, QB, 5/9
11. Dan Miller, Miami (FL), K, 0/5
12. Don Laster, Tennessee State, T, 8/22
12. Jeff Goff, Arkansas, LB, 0/0

1983 NFL

ATLANTA FALCONS
1. **Mike Pitts, Alabama, DT, 62/169**
2. **James Britt, LSU, DB, 60/60**
3. **Andrew Provence, South Carolina, DT, 69/69**
4. John Harper, Southern Illinois, LB, 13/13
5. **Brett Miller, Iowa, T, 68/118**
6. Anthony Allen, Washington, WR, 21/45
7. Jeff Turk, Boise State, DB, 0/0
8. **John Rade, Boise State, LB, 122/122**
10. Ralph Giacomarro, Penn State, P, 37/40
11. John Salley, Wyoming, DB, 0/0
12. Allama Matthews, Vanderbilt, TE, 37/37

BALTIMORE COLTS
1. John Elway, Stanford, QB, 0/234
2. Vernon Maxwell, Arizona State, LB, 32/77
3. George Achica, USC, DT, 4/4
4. Phil Smith, San Diego State, WR, 17/22
5. Sid Abramowitz, Tulsa, T, 17/22
6. Grant Feasel, Abilene Christian, C, 17/117
7. Alvin Moore, Arizona State, RB, 28/58
9. Jim Mills, Hawaii, T, 21/21
9. Chris Rose, Stanford, T, 0/0
10. Ronald Hopkins, Murray State, DB, 0/0
11. Jim Bob Taylor, Georgia Tech, QB, 8/8
12. Carl Williams, Texas Southern, WR, 0/0

BUFFALO BILLS
1. Tony Hunter, Notre Dame, TE, 24/47
1. **Jim Kelly, Miami (FL), QB, 160/160**
2. **Darryl Talley, West Virginia, LB, 188/216**
4. Trey Junkin, Louisiana Tech, TE, 18/281
4. Jimmy Payne, Georgia, DE, 0/0
5. Matt Vanden Boom, Wisconsin, DB, 0/0
7. Gurnest Brown, Maryland, DT, 0/0
8. James Durham, Houston, DB, 0/0
9. George Parker, Norfolk State, RB, 0/0
10. Richard Tharp, Louisville, DE, 3/3
11. Larry White, Jackson State, DE, 0/0
12. Julius Dawkins, Pittsburgh, WR, 27/27

CHICAGO BEARS
1. **Jimbo Covert, Pittsburgh, T, 111/111**
1. **Willie Gault, Tennessee, WR, 76/170**
2. **Mike Richardson, Arizona State, DB, 88/91**
3. **Dave Duerson, Notre Dame, DB, 102/160**
4. Pat Dunsmore, Drake, TE, 27/27
4. **Tom Thayer, Notre Dame, G, 123/126**
8. **Mark Bortz, Iowa, G, 171/171**
8. **Richard Dent, Tennessee State, DE, 170/203**
9. Rob Fada, Pittsburgh, G, 19/24
9. Mark Zavagnin, Notre Dame, LB, 0/0
10. Anthony Hutchison, Texas Tech, RB, 28/33
11. Gary Worthy, Wilmington, RB, 0/0
12. Oliver Williams, Illinois, WR, 0/14

CINCINNATI BENGALS
1. **Dave Rimington, Nebraska, C, 64/86**
2. **Ray Horton, Washington, DB, 89/147**
3. **Jimmy Turner, UCLA, DB, 56/64**
4. Steve Maidlow, Michigan State, LB, 32/50
5. Jeff Christensen, Eastern Illinois, QB, 1/4
6. Kiki DeAyala, Texas, LB, 28/28
6. **Larry Kinnebrew, Tennessee State, RB, 71/88**
7. James Griffin, Middle Tennessee State, DB, 48/108
8. **Mike Martin, Illinois, WR, 76/76**
9. Stanley Wilson, Oklahoma, RB, 36/36
10. **Tim Krumrie, Wisconsin, NT, 188/188**
11. Gary Williams, Ohio State, WR, 8/8
12. Andre Young, Bowling Green, LB, 0/0

CLEVELAND BROWNS
2. Ron Brown, Arizona State, WR, 0/100
3. **Reggie Camp, California, DE, 70/74**
5. Bill Contz, Penn State, T, 36/63
6. **Dave Puzzuoli, Pittsburgh, NT, 76/76**
6. Tim Stracka, Wisconsin, TE, 19/19
7. Rocky Belk, Miami (FL), WR, 10/10
8. Mike McClearn, Temple, G, 0/0
10. Thomas Hopkins, Alabama A&M, T, 2/2
11. Boyce Green, Carson-Newman, RB, 42/60
11. Howard McAdoo, Michigan State, LB, 0/0
12. **Paul Farren, Boston University, T, 132/132**

DALLAS COWBOYS
1. **Jim Jeffcoat, Arizona State, DE, 188/227**
2. Mike Walter, Oregon, LB, 15/149
3. Bryan Caldwell, Arizona State, DE, 0/8
4. Chris Faulkner, Florida, TE, 0/17
5. Chuck McSwain, Clemson, RB, 16/19
6. Reggie Collier, Southern Mississippi, QB, 4/6
7. Chris Schultz, Arizona, T, 21/21
8. Lawrence Ricks, Michigan, RB, 0/17
9. Al Gross, Arizona, DB, 0/58
10. Eric Moran, Washington, T, 0/37
11. Dan Taylor, Idaho State, T, 0/0
12. Lorenzo Bouier, Maine, RB, 0/0

DENVER BRONCOS
1. Chris Hinton, Northwestern, T, 0/177
2. **Mark Cooper, Miami (FL), G, 53/78**
3. **Clint Sampson, San Diego State, WR, 59/59**
5. George Harris, Houston, LB, 0/0
5. Bruce Baldwin, Harding, DB, 0/0
6. Victor Heflin, Delaware State, DB, 0/24
7. Myron Dupree, North Carolina Central, DB, 16/16
8. **Gary Kubiak, Texas A&M, QB, 119/119**
9. Brian Hawkins, San Jose State, DB, 0/0
10. **Walt Bowyer, Arizona State, DE, 61/61**
11. Don Bailey, Miami (FL), C, 0/20
12. **Karl Mecklenburg, Minnesota, LB, 180/180**

DETROIT LIONS
1. **James Jones, Florida, FB, 85/135**
2. Rich Strenger, Michigan, T, 49/49
3. **Mike Cofer, Tennessee, LB, 123/123**
4. August Curley, USC, LB, 38/38
5. **Demetrious Johnson, Missouri, DB, 62/65**
5. **Steve Mott, Alabama, C, 76/76**
6. Todd Brown, Nebraska, WR, 0/0
7. **Mike Black, Arizona State, P, 58/58**
8. Bill Stapleton, Washington, DB, 0/0
10. Dave Laube, Penn State, G, 0/0
11. Ben Tate, North Carolina Central, RB, 0/0
12. Jim Lane, Idaho State, C, 0/0

GREEN BAY PACKERS
1. **Tim Lewis, Pittsburgh, DB, 51/51**
2. Dave Drechsler, North Carolina, G, 32/32
4. Mike Miller, Tennessee, WR, 0/16
5. Bryan Thomas, Pittsburgh, RB, 0/0
6. Ron Sams, Pittsburgh, C, 3/15
7. **Jessie Clark, Louisiana Tech, RB, 60/88**
8. Carlton Briscoe, McNeese State, DB, 0/0
9. Robin Ham, West Texas State, C, 0/0
10. Byron Williams, Texas-Arlington, WR, 0/37
10. Jimmy Thomas, Indiana, DB, 0/0
11. Bucky Scribner, Kansas, P, 32/67
12. John Harvey, Southern California, DT, 0/0

HOUSTON OILERS
1. **Bruce Matthews, USC, G, 296/296**
2. **Keith Bostic, Michigan, DB, 92/96**
2. Harvey Salem, California, T, 47/126
3. **Steve Brown, Oregon, DB, 119/119**
3. **Chris Dressel, Stanford, TE, 64/111**
3. Tim Joiner, LSU, LB, 26/29
4. Greg Hill, Oklahoma State, DB, 14/79
4. Mike McCloskey, Penn State, TE, 47/48
5. Jerome Foster, Ohio State, DE, 25/44
5. **Larry Moriarty, Notre Dame, RB, 50/81**
6. Steve Haworth, Oklahoma, DB, 0/16
7. Herkie Walls, Texas, WR, 36/38
8. Robert Thompson, Michigan, LB, 0/22
9. Kevin Potter, Missouri, DB, 0/9

KANSAS CITY CHIEFS
1. Todd Blackledge, Penn State, QB, 40/46
2. **Dave Lutz, Georgia Tech, T, 139/187**
3. **Albert Lewis, Grambling State, DB, 150/225**
4. Ron Wetzel, Arizona State, TE, 16/16
5. Jim Arnold, Vanderbilt, P, 48/174
6. Ellis Gardner, Georgia Tech, T, 8/17
7. Ken Thomas, San Jose State, RB, 14/14
7. Daryl Posey, Mississippi College, RB, 0/0
8. **Irv Eatman, UCLA, T, 69/149**
9. **Adam Lingner, Illinois, C, 60/200**
10. Mark Shumate, Wisconsin, NT, 0/8
11. DeWayne Jackson, South Carolina State, DE, 0/0
12. Ken Jones, Tennessee, T, 0/0

LOS ANGELES RAIDERS
1. **Don Mosebar, USC, C, 173/173**
2. **Bill Pickel, Rutgers, NT, 121/174**
3. Tony Caldwell, Washington, LB, 35/36
4. **Greg Townsend, TCU, DE, 174/190**
5. **Dokie Williams, UCLA, WR, 74/74**
7. Jeff McCall, Clemson, RB, 0/0
8. Mike Dotterer, Stanford, RB, 0/0
9. Kent Jordan, St. Mary's (CA), TE, 0/0
10. **Mervyn Fernandez, San Jose State, WR, 86/86**
12. Scott Lindquist, Northern Arizona, QB, 0/0

LOS ANGELES RAMS
1. **Eric Dickerson, SMU, RB, 65/146**
2. **Henry Ellard, Fresno State, WR, 158/228**

2. **Mike Wilcher, North Carolina, LB, 122/124**
4. Chuck Nelson, Washington, K, 12/63
4. **Vince Newsome, Washington, DB, 110/141**
4. **Doug Reed, San Diego State, DE, 96/96**
5. Otis Grant, Michigan State, WR, 30/33
6. Gary Kowalski, Boston College, T, 15/58
7. Jeff Simmons, USC, WR, 3/3
8. Troy West, USC, DB, 0/3
9. Jack Belcher, Boston College, C, 0/0
11. Danny Triplett, Clemson, LB, 0/0
12. Clete Casper, Washington State, QB, 0/0

MIAMI DOLPHINS
1. **Dan Marino, Pittsburgh, QB, 242/242**
2. **Mike Charles, Syracuse, NT, 51/101**
3. Charles Benson, Baylor, DE, 24/28
6. **Reggie Roby, Iowa, P, 145/238**
7. Keith Woetzel, Rutgers, LB, 0/0
8. **Mark Clayton, Louisville, WR, 142/158**
9. **Mark Brown, Purdue, LB, 84/107**
10. Anthony Reed, South Carolina State, RB, 0/0
11. Joe Lukens, Ohio State, G, 0/0
12. Anthony Carter, Michigan, WR, 0/140

MINNESOTA VIKINGS
1. **Joey Browner, USC, DB, 138/145**
3. **Walker Lee Ashley, Penn State, LB, 78/94**
4. Mark Rush, Miami (FL), RB, 0/0
5. Mark Stewart, Washington, LB, 4/4
6. Mike Jones, Tennessee State, WR, 48/79
7. **Carl Lee, Marshall, DB, 169/181**
8. Norris Brown, Georgia, TE, 2/2
9. Rod Achter, Toledo, WR, 0/0
10. Melvin Brown, Mississippi, DB, 0/0
10. Walter Tate, Tennessee State, C, 0/0
11. Brian Butcher, Clemson, G, 0/0
12. Maurice Turner, Utah State, RB, 23/27

NEW ENGLAND PATRIOTS
1. **Tony Eason, Illinois, QB, 72/90**
2. Darryal Wilson, Tennessee, WR, 9/9
3. **Steve Moore, Tennessee State, T, 52/52**
3. **Stephen Starring, McNeese State, WR, 72/84**
4. **Johnny Rembert, Clemson, LB, 126/126**
5. Smiley Creswell, Michigan State, DE, 0/3
5. Darryl Lewis, Texas-Arlington, TE, 0/2
6. Mike Bass, Illinois, K, 0/0
7. **Craig James, SMU, RB, 52/52**
8. **Ronnie Lippett, Miami (FL), DB, 122/122**
9. Mark Keel, Arizona, TE, 0/10
9. Ricky Williams, Langston, RB, 0/3
10. Tom Ramsey, UCLA, QB, 21/28
10. **Toby Williams, Nebraska, NT, 80/80**
10. James Williams, Wyoming, TE, 0/0
11. Steve Parker, Abilene Christian, WR, 0/0
11. Calvin Eason, Houston, DB, 0/0
12. Andy Ekern, Missouri, TE, 0/2
12. Waddell Kelly, Arkansas State, RB, 0/0

NEW ORLEANS SAINTS
2. **Steve Korte, Arkansas, C, 83/83**
3. Cliff Austin, Clemson, RB, 11/58
3. **John Tice, Maryland, TE, 134/134**
4. Gary Lewis, Oklahoma State, NT, 6/6
8. David Greenwood, Wisconsin, DB, 0/27

NEW YORK GIANTS
1. **Terry Kinard, Clemson, DB, 105/121**
2. **Leonard Marshall, LSU, DE, 149/177**
3. **Karl Nelson, Iowa State, T, 57/57**
3. Jamie Williams, Nebraska, TE, 0/160
5. Malcolm Scott, LSU, TE, 16/19
6. Kevin Belcher, Texas-El Paso, C, 32/32
6. Darrell Patterson, Texas Christian, LB, 0/0
7. **Perry Williams, North Carolina State, DB, 146/146**
8. **Andy Headen, Clemson, LB, 74/74**
9. Ali Haji-Sheikh, Michigan, K, 34/51
11. Lee Jenkins, Tennessee, DB, 0/0
11. Clenzie Pierson, Rice, DT, 0/0
12. **Robbie Jones, Alabama, LB, 60/60**
12. John Tuggle, California, RB, 16/16
12. Frank Magwood, Clemson, WR, 0/0

NEW YORK JETS
1. **Ken O'Brien, California-Davis, QB, 124/129**
2. **Johnny Hector, Texas A&M, RB, 126/126**
3. **Jo-Jo Townsell, UCLA, WR, 83/83**
4. Wes Howell, California, TE, 0/0
5. John Walker, Nebraska-Omaha, NT, 0/3
6. Vincent White, Stanford, RB, 0/0
7. Darrin Newbold, Southwest Missouri State, LB, 0/0
8. Davlin Mullen, Western Kentucky, DB, 42/42
9. **Bobby Humphery, New Mexico State, DB, 88/104**
10. Dan Fike, Florida, G, 0/115
11. Mike Harmon, Mississippi, WR, 9/9
12. Stu Crum, Tulsa, K, 0/0

PHILADELPHIA EAGLES
1. **Michael Haddix, Mississippi State, RB, 88/120**
2. **Wes Hopkins, SMU, DB, 137/137**
2. Jody Schulz, East Carolina, LB, 44/44
3. Glen Young, Mississippi State, WR, 16/58
4. Michael Williams, Mississippi College, RB, 31/34
5. **Byron Darby, USC, DE, 58/87**
6. Victor Oatis, Northwestern State (LA), WR, 0/9
7. Anthony Edgar, Hawaii, RB, 0/0
7. Jon Schultheis, Princeton, G, 0/0
8. **Rich Kraynak, Pittsburgh, LB, 52/61**
9. Rich Pelzer, Rhode Island, T, 0/0
10. Thomas Strauthers, Jackson State, DE, 47/97
11. Steve Sebahar, Washington State, C, 0/0
12. David Mangrum, Baylor, QB, 0/0

PITTSBURGH STEELERS
1. Gabe Rivera, Texas Tech, NT, 6/6
2. Wayne Capers, Kansas, WR, 27/47
3. Todd Seabaugh, San Diego State, LB, 16/16
4. Bo Metcalf, Baylor, DB, 0/1
5. Gregg Garrity, Penn State, WR, 21/79
5. Paul Skansi, Washington, WR, 15/115
6. Eric Williams, North Carolina State, DB, 49/50
7. Mark Kirchner, Baylor, G, 3/32
8. Craig Dunaway, Michigan, TE, 11/11
8. Henry Odom, South Carolina State, RB, 16/16
9. Blake Wingle, UCLA, G, 34/39
10. Roosevelt Straughter, Northeast Louisiana, DB, 0/0
11. Mark Raugh, West Virginia, TE, 0/0
12. Roger Wiley, Sam Houston State, RB, 0/0

SAN DIEGO CHARGERS
1. **Gary Anderson, Arkansas, RB, 54/111**
1. **Gill Byrd, San Jose State, DB, 149/149**
1. **Billy Ray Smith, Arkansas, LB, 126/126**
4. **Danny Walters, Arkansas, DB, 54/54**
6. Trumaine Johnson, Grambling State, WR, 27/55
7. Bill Elko, LSU, NT, 26/29
8. Earnest Jackson, Texas A&M, RB, 28/81
9. Mike Green, Oklahoma State, LB, 47/47
10. Bruce Mathison, Nebraska, QB, 5/18
11. Tim Kearse, San Jose State, WR, 0/3
11. **Tim Spencer, Ohio State, RB, 78/78**
12. **Chuck Ehin, Brigham Young, NT, 65/65**
12. Billy Blaylock, Tennessee Tech, DB, 0/0

SAN FRANCISCO 49ERS
2. **Roger Craig, Nebraska, RB, 121/165**
3. Blanchard Montgomery, UCLA, LB, 27/27
4. **Tom Holmoe, Brigham Young, DB, 82/82**
5. **Riki Ellison, USC, LB, 80/124**
7. Gary Moten, SMU, LB, 6/7
9. Mike Mularkey, Florida, TE, 0/114
10. Jeff Merrell, Nebraska, DT, 0/0
11. **Jesse Sapolu, Hawaii, C, 183/183**

ST. LOUIS CARDINALS
1. **Leonard Smith, McNeese State, DB, 78/138**
2. **Cedric Mack, Baylor, DB, 117/140**
3. Ramsey Dardar, LSU, DT, 16/16
4. **Mark Duda, Maryland, DT, 55/55**
4. **Lionel Washington, Tulane, DB, 52/204**
5. Steve Bird, Eastern Kentucky, WR, 22/23
6. George Schmitt, Delaware, DB, 16/16
7. Carlos Scott, Texas-El Paso, C, 45/45
8. Bob Harris, Auburn, LB, 34/37
9. Otis Brown, Jackson State, RB, 0/0
10. Tim Lucas, California, LB, 0/75
11. Aaron Williams, Washington, WR, 0/0
12. James Lane, Alabama State, LB, 0/0

SEATTLE SEAHAWKS
1. **Curt Warner, Penn State, RB, 93/100**
5. Chris Castor, Duke, WR, 23/23
6. Reginald Gipson, Alabama A&M, RB, 0/0
7. **Sam Merriman, Idaho, LB, 71/71**
8. Matt Hernandez, Purdue, T, 8/21
9. Bob Clasby, Notre Dame, DT, 0/49
10. Pete Speros, Penn State, G, 0/0
11. Bob Mayberry, Clemson, G, 0/0
12. Don Dow, Washington, T, 0/0

TAMPA BAY BUCCANEERS
2. **Randy Grimes, Baylor, C, 118/118**
3. **Jeremiah Castille, Alabama, DB, 60/87**
4. Kelly Thomas, USC, T, 24/27
5. Tony Chickillo, Miami (FL), NT, 0/7
6. Gene Branton, Texas Southern, WR, 4/4
6. Ken Kaplan, New Hampshire, T, 32/35
7. Weldon Ledbetter, Oklahoma, RB, 0/0
8. John Samuelson, Azusa Pacific, LB, 0/0
9. Hasson Arbubakrr, Texas Tech, DE, 16/20
10. Darius Durham, San Diego State, WR, 0/0
11. Mark Witte, North Texas, TE, 48/51
12. John Higgenbotham, Northeastern Oklahoma, DT, 0/0

WASHINGTON REDSKINS
1. **Darrell Green, Texas A&M-Kingsville, DB, 295/295**
2. Richard Williams, Memphis, RB, 0/22
3. **Charles Mann, Nevada-Reno, DE, 163/177**
6. Babe Laufenberg, Indiana, QB, 0/16
6. Bob Winckler, Wisconsin, T, 0/0
7. Kelvin Bryant, North Carolina, RB, 46/46
8. Todd Hallstrom, Minnesota, T, 0/0
9. Marcus Gilbert, Texas Christian, RB, 0/0
10. Geff Gandy, Baylor, LB, 0/0

1984 NFL

ATLANTA FALCONS
1. **Rick Bryan, Oklahoma, DE, 109/109**
S1. Joey Jones, Alabama, WR, 11/11
2. Thomas Benson, Oklahoma, LB, 32/120
2. **Scott Case, Oklahoma, DB, 162/178**
3. Rod McSwain, Clemson, DB, 0/90
S3. Dennis Woodberry, Southern Arkansas, DB, 7/31
4. Rydell Malancon, LSU, LB, 7/10
5. Cliff Benson, Purdue, TE, 32/49
6. Ben Bennett, Duke, QB, 0/1
6. Dan Ralph, Oregon, DT, 0/6
7. Kirk Dodge, UNLV, LB, 0/23
8. Jeff Jackson, Auburn, LB, 27/52
9. Glen Howe, Southern Mississippi, T, 12/14
10. Derrick Franklin, Fresno State, DB, 0/0
11. Tommy Norman, Jackson State, WR, 0/0
12. Don Holmes, Mesa, WR, 0/60

BUFFALO BILLS
1. Greg Bell, Notre Dame, RB, 40/80
S1. **Dwight Drane, Oklahoma, DB, 82/82**
2. Eric Richardson, San Jose State, WR, 30/30
3. Rodney Bellinger, Miami (FL), DB, 42/42
3. **Sean McNanie, San Diego State, DE, 59/72**
3. Speedy Neal, Miami (FL), RB, 12/12
4. Mitchell Brookins, Illinois, WR, 21/21
5. **John Kidd, Northwestern, P, 92/215**
6. Tony Slaton, USC, C, 0/74
7. Stan David, Texas Tech, LB, 16/16
8. Stacy Rayfield, Texas-Arlington, DB, 0/0
9. Leroy Howell, Appalachian State, DE, 0/0
10. Joe Azelby, Harvard, LB, 14/14
11. Craig White, Missouri, WR, 14/14
12. Russell Davis, Maryland, WR, 0/0

CHICAGO BEARS
1. **Wilber Marshall, Florida, LB, 59/179**
2. **Ron Rivera, California, LB, 137/137**
3. Stefan Humphries, Michigan, G, 25/33
4. Tom Andrews, Louisville, T, 21/23
7. Nakita Robertson, Central Arkansas, RB, 0/0
8. Brad Anderson, Arizona, WR, 27/27
9. Mark Casale, Montclair State, QB, 0/0
10. **Shaun Gayle, Ohio State, DB, 144/160**
10. Kurt Vestman, Idaho, TE, 0/0
11. Mark Butkus, Illinois, DT, 0/0
12. Donald Jordan, Houston, RB, 13/13

CINCINNATI BENGALS
1. **Brian Blados, North Carolina, T, 98/107**
1. Ricky Hunley, Arizona, LB, 0/91
1. Pete Koch, Maryland, NT, 16/58
2. **Boomer Esiason, Maryland, QB, 134/187**
S2. Bill Johnson, Arkansas State, RB, 38/38
3. **Stanford Jennings, Furman, RB, 107/123**
4. John Farley, Sacramento State, RB, 13/13
5. **Barney Bussey, South Carolina State, DB, 104/144**
6. Don Kern, Arizona State, TE, 24/25
7. **Leo Barker, New Mexico State, LB, 122/122**
8. **Bruce Reimers, Iowa State, G, 108/135**
9. **Bruce Kozerski, Holy Cross, C, 172/172**
10. Aaron Jackson, North Carolina, LB, 0/0
10. Brent Ziegler, Syracuse, RB, 0/0
11. Steve McKeaver, Central State (OK), RB, 0/0
12. Steve Raquet, Holy Cross, LB, 0/0

CLEVELAND BROWNS
S1. **Mike Johnson, Virginia Tech, LB, 112/144**
S1. **Kevin Mack, Clemson, RB, 99/99**
1. Don Rogers, UCLA, DB, 31/31
2. Bruce Davis, Baylor, WR, 14/14
S2. **Gerald McNeil, Baylor, WR, 60/76**
S2. Tommy Robison, Texas A&M, LB, 0/12
2. **Chris Rockins, Oklahoma State, DB, 60/60**
4. **Rickey Bolden, SMU, T, 62/62**
4. **Brian Brennan, Boston College, WR, 117/132**
5. Dave Piepkorn, North Dakota State, T, 0/0
6. Terry Nugent, Colorado State, QB, 0/1
7. Jim Dumont, Rutgers, LB, 12/12
9. Don Jones, Texas A&M, WR, 0/0
10. **Earnest Byner, East Carolina, RB, 131/211**

DALLAS COWBOYS
1. Billy Jr. Cannon, Texas A&M, LB, 8/8
S1. **Todd Fowler, Stephen F. Austin State, TE, 52/52**
S2. Malcolm Moore, USC, WR, 0/3
2. Victor Scott, Colorado, DB, 45/45
3. Fred Cornwell, USC, TE, 30/30
S3. Jeff Spek, San Diego State, TE, 0/2
4. **Steve DeOssie, Boston College, LB, 75/175**
5. Norm Granger, Iowa, RB, 15/18
5. Steve Pelluer, Washington, QB, 47/65
6. **Eugene Lockhart, Houston, LB, 104/136**
6. Joe Levelis, Iowa, G, 0/0
7. Ed Martin, Indiana State, LB, 0/0
8. Mike Revell, Bethune-Cookman, RB, 0/0
9. John Hunt, Florida, T, 2/3
9. Neil Maune, Notre Dame, G, 0/0
10. Brian Salonen, Montana, LB, 32/32
11. Dowe Aughtman, Auburn, DT, 7/7
12. Carl Lewis, Houston, WR, 0/0

DENVER BRONCOS
S1. Freddie Gilbert, Georgia, DE, 35/37
S2. Rick Massie, Kentucky, WR, 13/13
2. **Andre Townsend, Mississippi, DE, 104/104**
3. **Tony Lilly, Florida, DB, 58/58**
S3. Reggie Smith, Kansas, T, 0/3
4. **Randy Robbins, Arizona, DB, 116/131**
6. Aaron Smith, Utah State, LB, 10/10
7. **Clarence Kay, Georgia, TE, 135/135**
8. Scott Garnett, Washington, NT, 16/27
8. Winford Hood, Georgia, G, 47/47
9. Chris Brewer, Arizona, RB, 13/16
10. Bobby Micho, Texas, TE, 20/26
11. **Gene Lang, LSU, RB, 55/89**
12. Murray Jarmin, Clemson, WR, 0/0

DETROIT LIONS
1. David Lewis, California, TE, 42/47
S1. Al Williams, Nevada-Reno, WR, 0/3
S2. **George Jamison, Cincinnati, LB, 130/162**
2. **Pete Mandley, Northern Arizona, WR, 74/92**
3. **Steve Baack, Oregon, NT, 55/55**
S3. Doug Hollie, SMU, DE, 0/5
3. **Eric Williams, Washington State, DE, 83/121**
3. Ernest Anderson, Oklahoma State, RB, 0/0
4. Dave D'Addio, Maryland, RB, 16/16
6. John Witkowski, Columbia, QB, 5/5
7. Jimmie Carter, New Mexico, LB, 0/1
7. Renwick Atkins, Kansas, T, 0/0
8. David Jones, Texas, G, 19/27
9. Rich Hollins, West Virginia, WR, 0/0
10. William Frizzell, North Carolina Central, DB, 24/134
10. James Thaxton, Louisiana Tech, DB, 0/0
11. Mike Saxon, San Diego State, P, 0/172
12. Glenn Streno, Tennessee, C, 0/0

GREEN BAY PACKERS
1. **Alphonso Carreker, Florida State, DE, 72/94**
S1. Buford Jordan, McNeese State, RB, 0/75
S2. Chuck Clanton, Auburn, DB, 3/3
3. Donnie Humphrey, Auburn, NT, 48/48
S3. John Sullivan, California, DB, 6/16
4. **John Dorsey, Connecticut, LB, 76/76**
5. Tom Flynn, Pittsburgh, DB, 38/68
6. Randy Wright, Wisconsin, QB, 46/46
7. Daryll Jones, Georgia, DB, 24/25
10. Gary Hoffman, Santa Clara, T, 1/4
11. **Mark Cannon, Texas-Arlington, C, 68/83**
12. Lenny Taylor, Tennessee, WR, 2/5
12. Mark Emans, Bowling Green, LB, 0/0

HOUSTON OILERS
S1. **Mike Rozier, Nebraska, RB, 68/92**
1. **Dean Steinkuhler, Nebraska, T, 100/100**
2. Bo Eason, California-Davis, DB, 38/38
S2. **Don Maggs, Tulane, T, 94/110**
2. **Doug Smith, Auburn, NT, 101/101**
S3. Lynn Madsen, Washington, DT, 15/15

3. **Johnny Meads, Nicholls State, LB, 117/119**
4. **Patrick Allen, Utah State, DB, 106/106**
4. Mark Studaway, Tennessee, DE, 6/14
5. **Robert Lyles, TCU, LB, 82/109**
6. **John Grimsley, Kentucky, LB, 106/133**
6. Eric Mullins, Stanford, WR, 13/13
7. Willie Joyner, Maryland, RB, 10/10
8. Kevin Baugh, Penn State, WR, 0/0
9. **Jeff Donaldson, Colorado, DB, 90/151**
9. Mike Johnson, Illinois, DE, 16/16
9. Mike Russell, Toledo, LB, 0/0

INDIANAPOLIS COLTS

1. Leonard Coleman, Vanderbilt, DB, 32/49
1. **Ron Solt, Maryland, G, 72/116**

S2. **Albert Bentley, Miami (FL), RB, 88/90**

2. Blaise Winter, Syracuse, DE, 16/102
2. Chris Scott, Purdue, DE, 33/33

S3. Byron Smith, California, DE, 19/19

4. Craig Curry, Texas, DB, 3/40
4. **George Wonsley, Mississippi State, RB, 73/78**
5. **Kevin Call, Colorado State, T, 130/130**
5. Golden Tate, Tennessee State, WR, 0/0
6. Dwight Beverly, Illinois, RB, 0/3
8. **Eugene Daniel, LSU, DB, 198/207**
11. Bob Stowe, Illinois, T, 0/0
12. Steve Hathaway, West Virginia, LB, 6/6

KANSAS CITY CHIEFS

S1. **Mark Adickes, Baylor, G, 53/77**

1. **John Alt, Iowa, T, 179/179**
1. **Bill Maas, Pittsburgh, NT, 116/130**
2. Scott Radecic, Penn State, LB, 48/182

S2. Lupe Sanchez, UCLA, DB, 0/39

3. **Herman Heard, Southern Colorado, RB, 87/87**

S3. Garcia Lane, Ohio State, DB, 17/17

4. Mark Robinson, Penn State, DB, 48/88
5. **Eric Holle, Texas, NT, 56/56**
5. Jeff Paine, Texas A&M, LB, 26/29
6. Rufus Stevens, Grambling, WR, 0/0
7. **Kevin Ross, Temple, DB, 156/204**
8. Randy Clark, Florida, DB, 0/2
9. Scott Auer, Michigan State, G, 23/23
9. Dave Hestera, Colorado, TE, 0/0
10. Al Wenglikowski, Pittsburgh, LB, 0/6
11. Bobby Johnson, San Jose State, RB, 0/0
12. Mark Lang, Texas, LB, 0/0

LOS ANGELES RAIDERS

S1. Chris Woods, Auburn, WR, 11/12

2. **Sean Jones, Northeastern, DE, 59/201**
3. Joe McCall, Pittsburgh, RB, 3/3
5. **Andy Parker, Utah, TE, 71/81**
6. **Stacey Toran, Notre Dame, DB, 72/72**
7. Mitch Willis, SMU, NT, 38/51
8. **Sam Seale, Western State (CO), DB, 61/121**
11. Gardner Williams, St. Mary's (CA), DB, 0/3
12. Randy Essington, Colorado, QB, 0/0

LOS ANGELES RAMS

S1. William Fuller, North Carolina, DE, 0/194

5. Hal Stephens, East Carolina, DE, 0/2
7. George Radachowsky, Boston College, DB, 0/52
8. Ed Brady, Illinois, LB, 32/188
9. George Reynolds, Penn State, P, 0/0
10. **Norwood Vann, East Carolina, LB, 51/52**
10. Joe Dooley, Ohio State, C, 0/0
11. Michael Harper, USC, WR, 0/35
11. Dwayne Love, Houston, RB, 0/0
12. Rod Fisher, Oklahoma State, DB, 0/0
12. Moe Bias, Illinois, LB, 0/0

MIAMI DOLPHINS

1. **Jackie Shipp, Oklahoma, LB, 71/74**
2. Jay Brophy, Miami (FL), LB, 31/34
4. Joe Carter, Alabama, RB, 30/30
5. Dean May, Louisville, QB, 0/5
6. Rowland Tatum, Ohio State, LB, 0/0
7. Bernard Carvalho, Hawaii, G, 0/0
8. Ronnie Landry, McNeese State, RB, 0/0
9. Jim Boyle, Tulane, T, 0/9
10. John Chesley, Oklahoma State, TE, 1/1
11. **Bud Brown, Southern Mississippi, DB, 73/73**
12. William Devane, Clemson, DT, 0/0
12. Mike Weingrad, Illinois, LB, 0/0

MINNESOTA VIKINGS

1. **Keith Millard, Washington State, DT, 75/93**

S2. Robert Smith, Grambling State, DE, 16/16

3. **Alfred Anderson, Baylor, RB, 108/108**

S3. **David Howard, Long Beach State, LB, 61/120**

5. **Allen Rice, Baylor, RB, 89/95**
6. Dwight Collins, Pittsburgh, WR, 16/16
7. John Haines, Texas, NT, 8/19
7. Loyd Lewis, Texas A&I, G, 0/0
8. Paul Sverchek, Cal Poly-San Luis Obispo, NT, 3/3
9. Keith Kidd, Arkansas, WR, 1/1
10. James Spencer, Oklahoma State, LB, 0/0
11. Edgar Pickett, Clemson, LB, 0/0
11. Lawrence Thompson, Miami (FL), WR, 0/0
12. Mike Jones, North Carolina A&T, RB, 0/0

NEW ENGLAND PATRIOTS

1. **Irving Fryar, Nebraska, WR, 129/255**

S1. Ricky Sanders, Southwest Texas State, WR, 0/134

2. **Ed Williams, Texas, LB, 62/62**
3. Jon Williams, Penn State, RB, 9/9
5. **Paul Fairchild, Kansas, G, 83/83**
6. **Ernest Gibson, Furman, DB, 67/72**
7. Derwin Williams, New Mexico, WR, 42/42
7. Bruce Kallmeyer, Kansas, K, 0/0
8. James Keyton, Arizona State, T, 0/0
9. Dave Windham, Jackson State, LB, 0/3
9. Scott Bolzan, Northern Illinois, T, 0/0
11. Charlie Flager, Washington State, G, 0/0
12. Harper Howell, UCLA, TE, 0/0

NEW ORLEANS SAINTS

S1. **Vaughan Johnson, North Carolina State, LB, 120/124**

2. **Jumpy Geathers, Wichita State, DE, 80/183**

S2. Mel Gray, Purdue, RB, 42/169

3. Tyrone Anthony, North Carolina, RB, 31/31
3. Terry Hoage, Georgia, DB, 30/142
4. **Joel Hilgenberg, Iowa, C, 142/142**
5. Jitter Fields, Texas, DB, 13/19
6. Don Thorp, Illinois, NT, 5/14
8. Clemon Terrell, Southern Mississippi, RB, 0/0
9. **Brian Hansen, Sioux Falls, P, 76/212**
10. Paul Gray, Western Kentucky, LB, 0/2
11. Michel Bourgeau, Boise State, DE, 0/0
12. Byron Nelson, Arizona, T, 0/0

NEW YORK GIANTS

1. **Carl Banks, Michigan State, LB, 126/173**
1. **William Roberts, Ohio State, G, 151/195**

S1. Gary Zimmerman, Oregon, T, 0/184

3. **Jeff Hostetler, West Virginia, QB, 91/152**
4. Conrad Goode, Missouri, T, 24/35
4. **Gary Reasons, Northwestern State (LA), LB, 122/134**
5. Clint Harris, East Carolina, DB, 0/0
6. Jim Scott, Clemson, DE, 0/0
7. **Lionel Manuel, Pacific, WR, 90/90**
10. David Jordan, Auburn, G, 30/33
10. Heyward Golden, South Carolina State, DB, 0/0
11. Frank Cephous, UCLA, RB, 16/16
12. Lawrence Green, Tennessee-Chattanooga, LB, 0/0

NEW YORK JETS

1. Russell Carter, SMU, DB, 40/64
1. Ron Faurot, Arkansas, DE, 20/20
2. Glenn Dennison, Miami (FL), TE, 16/18
2. **Jim Sweeney, Pittsburgh, C, 166/228**
3. **Kyle Clifton, TCU, LB, 204/204**
4. Bobby Bell, Missouri, LB, 15/18
5. Tron Armstrong, Eastern Kentucky, WR, 0/0
6. Tony Paige, Virginia Tech, RB, 48/130
7. Harry Hamilton, Penn State, DB, 46/98
8. **Billy Griggs, Virginia, TE, 64/64**
8. Brett Wright, Southeastern Louisiana, P, 0/0
9. **Tom Baldwin, Tulsa, NT, 64/64**
10. Ronny Cone, Georgia Tech, RB, 0/0
11. Dan Martin, Iowa State, T, 0/0
12. David Roberson, Houston, WR, 0/0

PHILADELPHIA EAGLES

1. **Kenny Jackson, Penn State, WR, 92/102**

S1. **Reggie White, Tennessee, DE, 121/237**

S2. Darryl Goodlow, Oklahoma, LB, 0/2

3. Rusty Russell, South Carolina, T, 1/1
4. **Evan Cooper, Michigan, DB, 60/85**
5. Andre Hardy, St. Mary's (CA), RB, 6/10
6. Scott Raridon, Nebraska, T, 0/0
7. Joe Hayes, Central Oklahoma, RB, 12/12
8. Manny Matsakis, Capital, K, 0/0
10. John Thomas, Texas Christian, DB, 0/0
11. John Robertson, East Carolina, T, 0/0
12. **Paul McFadden, Youngstown State, K, 60/79**

PITTSBURGH STEELERS

1. **Louis Lipps, Southern Mississippi, WR, 108/110**
2. Chris Kolodziejski, Wyoming, TE, 7/7
4. **Terry Long, East Carolina, G, 105/105**
4. **Weegie Thompson, Florida State, WR, 92/92**
5. Van Hughes, Southwest Texas State, DE, 0/8
6. Chris Brown, Notre Dame, DB, 22/22
7. Scott Campbell, Purdue, QB, 24/45
8. Randy Rasmussen, Minnesota, C, 31/43
9. Rich Erenberg, Colgate, RB, 46/46
10. Kirk McJunkin, Texas, T, 0/0
11. Elton Veals, Tulane, RB, 15/15
12. Scoop Gillespie, William Jewell, RB, 14/14

SAN DIEGO CHARGERS

1. Mossy Cade, Texas, DB, 0/30

S1. **Lee Williams, Bethune-Cookman, DE, 100/140**

2. Mike Guendling, Northwestern, LB, 9/9

S3. Clarence Collins, Illinois State, WR, 0/1

5. **Lionel James, Auburn, RB, 67/67**
6. Keith Guthrie, Texas A&M, NT, 11/11
7. Jesse Bendross, Alabama, WR, 32/35
8. Ray Woodard, Texas, DE, 0/9
8. Bob Craighead, Northeast Louisiana, RB, 0/0
9. Zack Barnes, Alabama State, DT, 0/0
11. Buford McGee, Mississippi, RB, 36/107
12. Maurice Harper, La Verne, WR, 0/0

SAN FRANCISCO 49ERS

S1. Derrick Crawford, Memphis, WR, 10/10

1. Todd Shell, Brigham Young, LB, 38/38

S2. Joe Conwell, North Carolina, T, 0/28

2. **John Frank, Ohio State, TE, 66/66**
3. **Guy McIntyre, Georgia, G, 145/186**
5. **Michael Carter, SMU, NT, 121/121**
5. **Jeff Fuller, Texas A&M, DB, 71/71**
9. Derrick Harmon, Cornell, RB, 39/39
9. Lee Miller, Cal State-Fullerton, DB, 0/0
10. Dave Moritz, Iowa, WR, 0/0
11. Kirk Pendleton, BYU, WR, 0/0

ST. LOUIS CARDINALS

1. Clyde Duncan, Tennessee, WR, 19/19

S1. Mike Ruether, Texas, G, 22/103

2. Doug Dawson, Texas, G, 32/106

S2. **Derek Kennard, Nevada-Reno, G, 73/133**

3. Rick McIvor, Texas, QB, 6/6

S3. Tim Riordan, Temple, QB, 0/1

4. Martin Bayless, Bowling Green State, DB, 3/193
5. John Goode, Youngstown State, TE, 16/30
5. Jeff Leiding, Texas, LB, 0/21
6. Rod Clark, Southwest Texas State, LB, 0/0
7. Quentin Walker, Virginia, RB, 3/3
8. **Niko Noga, Hawaii, LB, 76/122**
8. Bob Paulling, Clemson, K, 0/0
9. John Walker, Texas, RB, 0/0
10. Mark Smythe, Indiana, DT, 0/0
11. Kyle Mackey, Texas A&M-Commerce, QB, 0/7
12. Paul Parker, Oklahoma, G, 0/0

SEATTLE SEAHAWKS

S1. Gordon Hudson, Brigham Young, TE, 16/16

1. **Terry Taylor, Southern Illinois, DB, 79/149**

S2. Alvin Powell, Winston-Salem State, G, 18/20

2. **Daryl Turner, Michigan State, WR, 59/59**

S3. Frank Seurer, Kansas, QB, 0/9

3. **Fredd Young, New Mexico State, LB, 60/101**
4. Rickey Hagood, South Carolina, NT, 0/2
6. John Kaiser, Arizona, LB, 48/60
7. Sam Slater, Weber State, T, 0/0
8. John Puzar, Long Beach State, C, 0/0
9. Adam Schreiber, Texas, G, 6/201
10. **Randall Morris, Tennessee, RB, 61/64**
11. Steve Gemza, UCLA, T, 0/0
12. Theodis Windham, Utah State, DB, 0/0

TAMPA BAY BUCCANEERS

S1. Steve Young, Brigham Young, QB, 19/169

2. Keith Browner, USC, LB, 47/65
3. Fred Acorn, Texas, DB, 16/16
4. Michael Gunter, Tulsa, RB, 0/4
4. **Ron Heller, Penn State, T, 58/172**
6. **Chris Washington, Iowa State, LB, 76/84**
7. Jay Carroll, Minnesota, TE, 16/31
8. Fred Robinson, Miami (FL), LB, 0/46
9. **Rick Mallory, Washington, G, 57/57**
10. Jim Gallery, Minnesota, K, 0/19
11. Blair Kiel, Notre Dame, QB, 10/25
12. Thad Jemison, Ohio State, WR, 0/0

WASHINGTON REDSKINS

S1. Tony Zendejas, Nevada-Reno, K, 0/149

S2. **Gary Clark, James Madison, WR, 122/167**

2. Steve Hamilton, East Carolina, DE, 46/46
2. Bob Slater, Oklahoma, DT, 0/0
3. Jay Schroeder, UCLA, QB, 36/118

S3. Clarence Verdin, Louisiana-Lafayette, WR, 11/118

4. Jimmy Smith, Elon, RB, 1/9
5. Jeff Pegues, East Carolina, LB, 0/0
6. Curt Singer, Tennessee, T, 0/33
7. Mark Smith, North Carolina, WR, 0/0
8. Jeff Smith, Missouri, DB, 0/0
10. **Keith Griffin, Miami (FL), RB, 65/65**
11. **Anthony Jones, Wichita State, TE, 57/61**
12. Curtland Thomas, Missouri, WR, 0/2

1985 NFL

ATLANTA FALCONS

1. **Bill Fralic, Pittsburgh, G, 116/132**
2. **Mike Gann, Notre Dame, DE, 118/118**
4. Emile Harry, Stanford, WR, 0/83
6. Reggie Pleasant, Clemson, DB, 3/3
8. Ronnie Washington, Louisiana-Monroe, LB, 16/20
8. Ashley Lee, Virginia Tech, DB, 0/0
9. Micah Moon, North Carolina, LB, 0/0
10. Brent Martin, Stanford, C, 0/0
11. John Ayres, Illinois, DB, 0/0
12. **Ken Whisenhunt, Georgia Tech, TE, 55/74**

BUFFALO BILLS

1. **Derrick Burroughs, Memphis, DB, 58/58**
1. **Bruce Smith, Virginia Tech, DE, 217/279**
2. **Chris Burkett, Jackson State, WR, 55/131**
2. Mark Traynowicz, Nebraska, G, 45/52
3. **Hal Garner, Utah State, LB, 67/67**
3. **Frank Reich, Maryland, QB, 93/119**
4. Dale Hellestrae, SMU, T, 28/205
4. **Andre Reed, Kutztown State, WR, 221/234**
5. Jimmy Teal, Texas A&M, WR, 8/14
6. Mike Hamby, Utah State, DE, 16/16
7. Ron Pitts, UCLA, DB, 22/66
8. Jacque Robinson, Washington, FB, 0/3
9. Glenn Jones, Norfolk State, DB, 0/0
10. Chris Babyar, Illinois, G, 0/0
11. James Seawright, South Carolina, LB, 0/0
12. Paul Woodside, West Virginia, K, 0/0

CHICAGO BEARS

1. **William Perry, Clemson, DT, 114/138**
2. Reggie Phillips, SMU, DB, 44/60
3. James Maness, TCU, WR, 8/8
4. **Kevin Butler, Georgia, K, 171/184**
7. Charles Bennett, Louisiana-Lafayette, DE, 0/3
8. Steve Buxton, Indiana State, T, 0/0
9. **Thomas Sanders, Texas A&M, RB, 75/90**
10. Pat Coryatt, Baylor, DT, 0/0
11. **Jim Morrissey, Michigan State, LB, 108/114**

CINCINNATI BENGALS

1. **Eddie Brown, Miami (FL), WR, 102/102**
1. **Emanuel King, Alabama, LB, 51/67**
2. **Carl Zander, Tennessee, LB, 106/106**
3. Sean Thomas, TCU, DB, 5/11
4. Anthony Tuggle, Nicholls State, DB, 0/4
5. Lee Davis, Mississippi, DB, 7/10
5. Tony Degrate, Texas, NT, 0/1
6. Keith Lester, Murray State, TE, 0/1
6. Eric Stokes, Northeastern, C, 0/1
7. **Joe Walter, Texas Tech, T, 166/166**
7. Kim Locklin, New Mexico State, RB, 0/0
8. Dave Strobel, Iowa, LB, 0/0
9. Keith Cruise, Northwestern, DE, 0/0
10. Bernard King, Syracuse, LB, 0/0
11. Harold Stanfield, Mississippi College, TE, 0/0
12. Louis Garza, New Mexico State, T, 0/0

CLEVELAND BROWNS

S1. **Bernie Kosar, Miami (FL), QB, 108/126**

2. Greg Allen, Florida State, RB, 7/9
6. Mark Krerowicz, Ohio State, G, 3/3
7. **Reggie Langhorne, Elizabeth City State, WR, 102/134**
8. Fred Banks, Liberty, WR, 10/80
10. Larry Williams, Notre Dame, G, 42/61
11. Travis Tucker, Southern Connecticut State, TE, 36/36
12. Shane Swanson, Nebraska, WR, 0/3

DALLAS COWBOYS

1. Kevin Brooks, Michigan, DT, 48/69
2. Jesse Penn, Virginia Tech, LB, 42/42
3. **Crawford Ker, Florida, G, 80/92**
4. Robert Lavette, Georgia Tech, RB, 32/33
5. **Herschel Walker, Georgia, RB, 81/187**
6. Kurt Ploeger, Gustavus Adolphus, DE, 3/5
6. Matt Moran, Stanford, G, 0/0
7. Karl Powe, Alabama State, WR, 16/16

7. Jim Herrmann, BYU, DE, 0/0
8. Leon Gonzalez, Bethune-Cookman, WR, 11/13
9. Scott Strasburger, Nebraska, LB, 0/0
10. Joe Jones, Virginia Tech, TE, 0/3
11. Neal Dellocono, UCLA, LB, 0/0
12. Karl Jordan, Vanderbilt, LB, 0/0

DENVER BRONCOS

1. **Steve Sewell, Oklahoma, RB, 94/94**
2. **Simon Fletcher, Houston, LB, 172/172**
2. **Vance Johnson, Arizona, WR, 128/128**
4. Keli McGregor, Colorado State, TE, 2/8
5. Billy Hinson, Florida, G, 0/0
7. Dallas Cameron, Miami (FL), DT, 0/0
8. Eric Riley, Florida State, DB, 0/0
9. Daryl Smith, North Alabama, DB, 0/15
10. Buddy Funck, New Mexico, QB, 0/0
10. Ron Anderson, Southern Methodist, LB, 0/0
11. Gary Rolle, Florida, WR, 0/0
12. Dan Lynch, Washington State, G, 0/0

DETROIT LIONS

1. **Lomas Brown, Florida, T, 164/263**
2. **Kevin Glover, Maryland, C, 177/191**
3. James Johnson, San Diego State, LB, 11/13
4. Kevin Hancock, Baylor, LB, 0/1
5. Joe McIntosh, North Carolina State, RB, 0/2
6. Stan Short, Penn State, G, 0/0
7. Tony Staten, Angelo State, DB, 0/0
8. Scott Caldwell, Texas-Arlington, RB, 0/3
9. June James, Texas, LB, 16/27
10. Clayton Beauford, Auburn, WR, 0/1
11. Kevin Harris, Georgia, DB, 0/0
12. Mike Weaver, Georgia, G, 0/0

GREEN BAY PACKERS

1. **Ken Ruettgers, USC, T, 156/156**
3. **Rich Moran, San Diego State, G, 108/108**
4. Walter Stanley, Mesa, WR, 48/85
5. **Brian Noble, Arizona State, LB, 117/117**
6. Mark Lewis, Texas A&M, TE, 18/30
7. Gary Ellerson, Wisconsin, RB, 31/39
7. Eric Wilson, Maryland, LB, 0/17
8. **Ken Stills, Wisconsin, DB, 65/77**
9. Morris Johnson, Alabama A&M, G, 0/0
10. Ronnie Burgess, Wake Forest, DB, 7/7
11. Joe Shield, Trinity (CT), QB, 3/3
12. Jim Meyer, Arizona State, P, 0/0

HOUSTON OILERS

1. **Ray Childress, Texas A&M, DT, 160/163**
1. **Richard Johnson, Wisconsin, DB, 98/98**
2. **Richard Byrd, Southern Mississippi, DE, 75/75**
3. Mike Kelley, Notre Dame, C, 17/17
4. Tom Briehl, Stanford, LB, 19/19
5. Frank Bush, North Carolina State, LB, 19/19
5. Lee Johnson, Brigham Young, P, 41/259
6. Joe Krakoski, Washington, LB, 0/8
7. Mike Akiu, Hawaii, WR, 20/20
8. Chuck Thomas, Oklahoma, C, 0/73
9. Steve Tasker, Northwestern, WR, 9/169
10. Mike Golic, Notre Dame, DT, 18/115
11. **Willie Drewrey, West Virginia, WR, 71/128**
12. Mark Vonder Haar, Minnesota, DT, 0/0

INDIANAPOLIS COLTS

1. **Duane Bickett, USC, LB, 137/173**
2. Don Anderson, Purdue, DB, 5/16
3. Anthony Young, Temple, DB, 14/14
4. Willie Broughton, Miami (FL), DT, 30/111
5. Roger Caron, Harvard, T, 10/10
7. James Harbour, Mississippi, WR, 9/9
8. Ricky Nichols, East Carolina, WR, 3/3
9. **Mark Boyer, USC, TE, 71/114**
10. Andre Pinesett, Cal State-Fullerton, DT, 0/0
12. Dave Burnette, Arkansas, T, 0/1

KANSAS CITY CHIEFS

1. Ethan Horton, North Carolina, TE, 16/116
2. **Jonathan Hayes, Iowa, TE, 136/184**
4. Bob Olderman, Virginia, G, 16/16
5. Bruce King, Purdue, RB, 20/28
6. John Bostic, Bethune-Cookman, DB, 0/29
7. Dave Heffernan, Miami (FL), G, 0/2
7. Vince Thomson, Missouri Western, DE, 0/0
8. Ira Hillary, South Carolina, WR, 0/46
9. Mike Armentrout, Southwest Missouri State, DB, 0/0
10. Jeff Smith, Nebraska, RB, 28/56
11. Chris Jackson, Southern Methodist, C, 0/0
12. Harper LeBel, Colorado State, TE, 0/136

LOS ANGELES RAIDERS

1. Jessie Hester, Florida State, WR, 39/147
3. **Stefon Adams, East Carolina, DB, 53/65**
3. Tim Moffett, Mississippi, WR, 29/32
4. Jamie Kimmel, Syracuse, LB, 31/31
5. Dan Reeder, Delaware, RB, 0/13
6. Rusty Hilger, Oklahoma State, QB, 11/23
7. Kevin Belcher, Wisconsin, T, 4/5
7. Bret Clark, Nebraska, DB, 0/29
7. Nick Haden, Penn State, G, 0/8
7. Mark Pattison, Washington, WR, 2/18
8. Leonard Wingate, South Carolina State, DT, 0/1
9. Chris Sydnor, Penn State, DB, 0/0
10. **Reggie McKenzie, Tennessee, LB, 58/60**
10. Albert Myres, Tulsa, DB, 0/0
11. **Steve Strachan, Boston College, RB, 63/63**
12. Raymond Polk, Oklahoma State, DB, 0/0

LOS ANGELES RAMS

1. **Jerry Gray, Texas, DB, 104/134**
2. Chuck Scott, Vanderbilt, WR, 9/11
3. **Dale Hatcher, Clemson, P, 83/99**
5. **Kevin Greene, Auburn, LB, 119/228**
6. **Damone Johnson, Cal Poly-San Luis Obispo, TE, 82/82**
6. **Mike Young, UCLA, WR, 51/114**
7. Danny Bradley, Oklahoma, RB, 0/3
8. Marlon McIntyre, Pittsburgh, RB, 0/0
9. Gary Swanson, Cal Poly-SLO, LB, 0/0
10. **Duval Love, UCLA, G, 94/167**
11. Doug Flutie, Boston College, QB, 0/92
11. Kevin Brown, Northwestern, DB, 0/0

MIAMI DOLPHINS

1. **Lorenzo Hampton, Florida, RB, 70/70**
3. George Little, Iowa, DE, 39/39
3. Alex Moyer, Northwestern, LB, 13/13
4. **Jeff Dellenbach, Wisconsin, C, 145/211**
4. Mike Smith, Texas-El Paso, DB, 29/29
6. **Ron Davenport, Louisville, RB, 67/67**
6. George Shorthose, Missouri, WR, 0/3
7. **Fuad Reveiz, Tennessee, K, 54/147**
8. Dan Sharp, TCU, TE, 0/9
9. Adam Hinds, Oklahoma State, DB, 0/0
10. Mike Pendleton, Indiana, DB, 0/0
11. Mike Jones, Tulane, RB, 0/0
12. Ray Noble, California, DB, 0/0

MINNESOTA VIKINGS

1. **Chris Doleman, Pittsburgh, DE, 154/232**
2. **Issiac Holt, Alcorn State, DB, 58/113**
3. Tim Long, Memphis, C, 0/2
3. **Kirk Lowdermilk, Ohio State, C, 114/178**
3. Tim Meamber, Washington, LB, 4/4
4. Kyle Morrell, Brigham Young, DB, 5/5
4. Buster Rhymes, Oklahoma, WR, 20/20
5. Mark MacDonald, Boston College, G, 43/44
6. Steve Bono, UCLA, QB, 2/88
6. **Tim Newton, Florida, DT, 62/108**
8. Nikita Blair, Texas-El Paso, LB, 0/0
9. Jaime Covington, Syracuse, RB, 0/2
10. Juan Johnson, Langston, WR, 0/0
11. Tim Williams, North Carolina A&T, DB, 0/0
12. Byron Jones, Tulsa, DT, 0/0

NEW ENGLAND PATRIOTS

1. Trevor Matich, Brigham Young, C, 26/148
2. **Jim Bowman, Central Michigan, DB, 73/73**
2. Ben Thomas, Auburn, DE, 19/54
2. **Garin Veris, Stanford, DE, 78/88**
3. Audray McMillian, Houston, DB, 0/123
4. Tom Toth, Western Michigan, G, 0/51
4. Gerard Phelan, Boston College, WR, 0/0
8. Milford Hodge, Washington State, DE, 49/50
11. Paul Lewis, Boston, RB, 0/0
12. Tony Mumford, Penn State, RB, 0/2

NEW ORLEANS SAINTS

1. **Alvin Toles, Tennessee, LB, 55/55**
2. Daren Gilbert, Cal State-Fullerton, T, 42/42
3. Jack Del Rio, USC, LB, 32/160
4. Billy Allen, Florida State, DB, 0/0
7. **Eric Martin, LSU, WR, 143/153**
8. **Joe Kohlbrand, Miami (FL), LB, 72/72**
9. Earl Johnson, South Carolina, DB, 2/5
12. Treg Songy, Tulane, DB, 0/2

NEW YORK GIANTS

1. **George Adams, Kentucky, RB, 58/76**
2. Stacy Robinson, North Dakota State, WR, 43/43
3. Tyrone Davis, Clemson, DB, 7/7
3. Brian Johnston, North Carolina, C, 9/9
4. **Mark Bavaro, Notre Dame, TE, 82/126**
5. Tracy Henderson, Iowa State, WR, 0/0
6. Jack Oliver, Memphis, T, 0/3
6. Mark Pembrook, Cal State-Fullerton, DB, 0/0
8. **Lee Rouson, Colorado, RB, 76/92**
9. Frank Wright, South Carolina, DT, 0/0
10. Gregg Dubroc, Louisiana State, LB, 0/0
11. Allen Young, Virginia Tech, DB, 0/0
12. Herb Welch, UCLA, DB, 44/79

NEW YORK JETS

1. **Al Toon, Wisconsin, WR, 107/107**
2. Lester Lyles, Virginia, DB, 26/63
3. Donnie Elder, Memphis, DB, 10/82
4. Doug Allen, Arizona State, WR, 0/0
5. **Troy Benson, Pittsburgh, LB, 58/58**
5. Brian Luft, Southern California, DT, 0/0
5. Tony Smith, San Jose State, WR, 0/0
6. **Rich Miano, Hawaii, DB, 60/135**
6. Jeff Deaton, Stanford, G, 0/0
8. Matt Monger, Oklahoma State, LB, 43/56
9. Mike Waters, San Diego State, TE, 0/10
10. Kerry Glenn, Minnesota, DB, 39/74
11. Brad White, Texas Tech, DE, 0/0
12. Bill Wallace, Pittsburgh, WR, 0/0

PHILADELPHIA EAGLES

1. Kevin Allen, Indiana, T, 16/16
2. **Randall Cunningham, UNLV, QB, 122/161**
4. Greg Naron, North Carolina, G, 0/0
5. **Dwayne Jiles, Texas Tech, LB, 52/61**
6. **Ken Reeves, Texas A&M, T, 69/85**
8. Tom Polley, UNLV, LB, 2/4
9. Joe Drake, Arizona, NT, 16/19
9. Dave Toub, Texas-El Paso, C, 0/0
10. Mark Kelso, William & Mary, DB, 0/99
11. Herman Hunter, Tennessee State, RB, 16/35
12. Todd Russell, Boston College, DB, 0/0

PITTSBURGH STEELERS

1. Darryl Sims, Wisconsin, DE, 32/58
2. Mark Behning, Nebraska, T, 16/16
3. Liffort Hobley, LSU, DB, 0/84
4. Dan Turk, Wisconsin, C, 17/218
5. Cam Jacobs, Kentucky, LB, 0/3
6. **Gregg Carr, Auburn, LB, 57/57**
7. Alan Andrews, Rutgers, TE, 0/0
8. **Harry Newsome, Wake Forest, P, 76/140**
9. Fred Small, Washington, LB, 16/16
9. Andre Harris, Minnesota, DB, 0/0
10. Oliver White, Kentucky, TE, 0/0
11. Terry Matichak, Missouri, DB, 0/0
12. Jeff Sanchez, Georgia, DB, 0/0

SAN DIEGO CHARGERS

1. Jim Lachey, Ohio State, T, 44/131
2. Jeffery Dale, LSU, DB, 42/42
2. Wayne Davis, Indiana State, DB, 32/73
3. John Hendy, Long Beach State, DB, 16/16
4. **Ralf Mojsiejenko, Michigan State, P, 60/93**
6. Terry Lewis, Michigan State, DB, 10/10
7. Mark Fellows, Montana State, LB, 3/3
8. Curtis Adams, Central Michigan, RB, 27/27
9. Dan Remsberg, Abilene Christian, T, 0/21
9. Paul Berner, Pacific, QB, 0/0
10. David King, Auburn, DB, 1/4
11. Jeff Smith, Kentucky, DT, 0/0
12. Tony Simmons, Tennessee, DE, 16/16
12. Bret Pearson, Wisconsin, TE, 0/0

SAN FRANCISCO 49ERS

1. **Jerry Rice, Mississippi Valley State, WR, 238/303**
3. Ricky Moore, Alabama, RB, 0/22
5. **Bruce Collie, Texas-Arlington, G, 74/91**
6. Scott Barry, Cal-Davis, QB, 0/0
11. David Wood, Arizona, DE, 0/0
12. Donald Chumley, Georgia, DT, 0/0

ST. LOUIS CARDINALS

1. **Freddie Joe Nunn, Mississippi, DE, 131/157**
2. Scott Bergold, Wisconsin, T, 16/16
3. **Lance Smith, LSU, G, 140/182**
4. **Ron Wolfley, West Virginia, RB, 105/145**
5. K.D. Dunn, Clemson, TE, 0/33
5. Louis Wong, BYU, G, 0/0
6. **Jay Novacek, Wyoming, TE, 63/158**
8. Rob Monaco, Vanderbilt, C, 6/6
9. Scott Williams, Georgia, RB, 0/32
10. Dennis Williams, Furman, RB, 0/0
11. Ricky Anderson, Vanderbilt, K, 0/0
12. **Lonnie Young, Michigan State, DB, 79/147**

SEATTLE SEAHAWKS

2. Owen Gill, Iowa, RB, 0/32
3. Danny Greene, Washington, WR, 4/4
4. Tony Davis, Missouri, TE, 0/0
5. Arnold Brown, North Carolina Central, DB, 2/9
5. Mark Napolitan, Michigan State, C, 0/0
5. Johnnie Jones, Tennessee, RB, 0/0
7. **Ron Mattes, Virginia, T, 75/95**
8. Judious Lewis, Arkansas State, WR, 0/0
9. Bob Otto, Idaho State, DE, 0/7
10. John Conner, Arizona, QB, 0/0
10. James Bowers, Memphis State, DB, 0/0
11. Louis Cooper, Western Carolina, LB, 0/102

TAMPA BAY BUCCANEERS

1. **Ron Holmes, Washington, DE, 50/102**
3. **Ervin Randle, Baylor, LB, 85/105**
4. Mike Heaven, Illinois, DB, 0/0
7. Mike Prior, Illinois State, DB, 16/198
8. Phil Freeman, Arizona, WR, 37/37
9. Steve Calabria, Colgate, QB, 0/0
10. **Donald Igwebuike, Clemson, K, 72/80**
11. James Williams, Memphis State, RB, 0/0
12. Jim Melka, Wisconsin, LB, 0/1
12. Jim Rockford, Oklahoma, DB, 0/1

WASHINGTON REDSKINS

2. Tory Nixon, San Diego State, DB, 0/50
5. Raphel Cherry, Hawaii, DB, 16/42
6. Danzell Lee, Lamar, TE, 0/18
7. Lionel Vital, Nicholls State, RB, 3/3
7. Jamie Harris, Oklahoma State, KR, 0/0
8. **Barry Wilburn, Mississippi, DB, 62/91**
9. Mitch Geier, Troy State, G, 0/0
10. **Terry Orr, Texas, TE, 96/105**
11. Garry Kimble, Sam Houston State, DB, 3/3
11. **Raleigh McKenzie, Tennessee, G, 144/226**
12. **Dean Hamel, Tulsa, DT, 60/88**
12. Bryant Winn, Houston, LB, 0/3

1986 NFL

ATLANTA FALCONS

1. **Tony Casillas, Oklahoma, DT, 66/167**
1. **Tim Green, Syracuse, LB, 99/99**
6. **Floyd Dixon, Stephen F. Austin State, WR, 84/91**
6. Keith Williams, Southwest Missouri State, WR, 12/12
8. Kevin Hudgens, Idaho State, DE, 0/0
9. Kevin Starks, Minnesota, TE, 0/0
10. Tony Baker, East Carolina, RB, 2/18
11. Chris Hegg, Northeast Missouri State, QB, 0/0
12. Steve Griffin, Purdue, WR, 2/2

BUFFALO BILLS

1. **Ronnie Harmon, Iowa, RB, 57/181**
1. **Will Wolford, Vanderbilt, T, 102/191**
3. **Leonard Burton, South Carolina, C, 58/60**
5. Carl Byrum, Mississippi Valley State, RB, 41/41
7. **Mark Pike, Georgia Tech, DE, 173/173**
7. **Butch Rolle, Michigan State, TE, 92/124**
7. Bob Williams, Penn State, TE, 0/0
8. Tony Furjanic, Notre Dame, LB, 22/28
9. Reggie Bynum, Oregon State, WR, 1/1
10. Guy Teafatiller, Illinois, DT, 0/3
11. Tony Garbarczyk, Wake Forest, DE, 0/2
11. Billy Witt, North Alabama, DE, 2/2
12. Brian McClure, Bowling Green State, QB, 1/1
12. Derek Christian, West Virginia, LB, 0/0

CHICAGO BEARS

1. **Neal Anderson, Florida, RB, 116/116**
2. **Vestee Jackson, Washington, DB, 76/119**
3. David Williams, Illinois, WR, 0/18
4. Paul Blair, Oklahoma State, T, 24/26
5. Lew Barnes, Oregon, WR, 16/31
6. Jeff Powell, Tennessee, RB, 0/1
7. Bruce Jones, North Alabama, DB, 0/2
8. **Maurice Douglass, Kentucky, DB, 116/139**
9. John Teltschik, Texas, P, 0/54
10. Barton Hundley, Kansas State, DB, 0/0
11. **Glen Kozlowski, Brigham Young, WR, 66/66**

CINCINNATI BENGALS

1. **Joe Kelly, Washington, LB, 58/156**
1. **Tim McGee, Tennessee, WR, 121/134**
2. **Lewis Billups, North Alabama, DB, 83/88**
3. **David Fulcher, Arizona State, DB, 100/103**
3. **Mike Hammerstein, Michigan, DE, 56/56**
3. **Jim Skow, Nebraska, DE, 55/83**
4. Doug Gaynor, Long Beach State, QB, 1/1
4. **Eric Kattus, Michigan, TE, 79/83**
5. **Leon White, Brigham Young, LB, 92/119**
6. Gary Hunt, Memphis, DB, 3/3
7. Pat Franklin, Houston, RB, 2/10
8. David Douglas, Tennessee, C, 40/56
9. Cary Whittingham, Brigham Young, LB, 0/3
10. Jeff Shaw, Salem (WV), DT, 0/0
11. Tom Flaherty, Northwestern, LB, 3/3

11. Tim Stone, Kansas State, T, 0/0
12. Steve Bradley, Indiana, QB, 0/1

CLEVELAND BROWNS
2. **Webster Slaughter, San Diego State, WR, 84/162**
5. Nick Miller, Arkansas, LB, 9/9
7. Jim Meyer, Illinois State, T, 0/2
7. Mike Norseth, Kansas, QB, 0/1
9. Danny Taylor, Texas-El Paso, DB, 0/0
10. Willie Smith, Miami (FL), TE, 0/3
11. Randy Dausin, Texas A&M, G, 0/0
12. King Simmons, Texas Tech, DB, 0/3

DALLAS COWBOYS
1. Mike Sherrard, UCLA, WR, 16/105
2. **Darryl Clack, Arizona State, RB, 51/51**
3. Mark Walen, UCLA, DT, 24/24
4. Max Zendejas, Arizona, K, 0/27
6. Thornton Chandler, Alabama, TE, 49/49
6. Stan Gelbaugh, Maryland, QB, 0/21
6. Lloyd Yancey, Temple, G, 0/0
7. Johnny Holloway, Kansas, DB, 16/19
8. Topper Clemons, Wake Forest, RB, 0/3
9. John Ionata, Florida State, G, 0/0
10. Bryan Chester, Texas, G, 0/0
11. Garth Jax, Florida State, LB, 35/143
12. Chris Duliban, Texas, LB, 3/3
12. Tony Flack, Georgia, DB, 0/0

DENVER BRONCOS
4. Jim Juriga, Illinois, G, 44/44
5. Tony Colorito, USC, NT, 15/15
6. **Mark Jackson, Purdue, WR, 100/130**
6. **Orson Mobley, Salem, TE, 61/61**
7. Ray Phillips, North Carolina State, LB, 0/4
8. Bruce Klosterman, South Dakota State, LB, 37/42
9. Joe Thomas, Mississippi Valley State, WR, 0/1
10. Victor Hall, Jackson State, TE, 0/0
11. Thomas Dendy, South Carolina, RB, 0/0

DETROIT LIONS
1. Chuck Long, Iowa, QB, 23/27
2. Garry James, LSU, RB, 40/40
3. Joe Milinchik, North Carolina State, G, 41/96
4. Devon Mitchell, Iowa, DB, 26/26
5. Oscar Smith, Nicholls State, RB, 2/2
8. Allyn Griffin, Wyoming, WR, 0/0
9. Lyle Pickens, Colorado, DB, 0/1
10. Tracy Johnson, Morningside, LB, 0/0
11. Leland Melvin, Richmond, WR, 0/0
12. Allan Durden, Arizona, DB, 0/0

GREEN BAY PACKERS
2. Kenneth Davis, TCU, RB, 35/131
3. Robbie Bosco, BYU, QB, 0/0
4. **Tim Harris, Memphis, LB, 76/122**
4. Dan Knight, San Diego State, T, 0/0
5. Matt Koart, USC, DE, 6/6
6. **Burnell Dent, Tulane, LB, 95/95**
7. Ed Berry, Utah State, DB, 16/18
8. Michael Cline, Arkansas State, DT, 0/0
9. Brent Moore, USC, LB, 4/4
10. Gary Spann, TCU, LB, 0/2

HOUSTON OILERS
1. Jim Everett, Purdue, QB, 0/158
2. **Ernest Givins, Louisville, WR, 138/147**
3. **Allen Pinkett, Notre Dame, RB, 87/87**
5. Jeff Parks, Auburn, TE, 12/15
6. Ray Wallace, Purdue, RB, 20/29
8. Larry Griffin, North Carolina, DB, 3/89
9. Bob Sebring, Illinois, LB, 0/0
10. Don Sommer, Texas-El Paso, T, 0/3
11. Mark Cochran, Baylor, T, 0/3
12. Chuck Banks, West Virginia Tech, RB, 13/16

INDIANAPOLIS COLTS
1. **Jon Hand, Alabama, DE, 121/121**
2. **Jack Trudeau, Illinois, QB, 61/67**
4. **Bill Brooks, Boston University, WR, 106/169**
5. Scott Kellar, Northern Illinois, NT, 17/17
5. Gary Walker, Boston University, C, 0/1
7. Tommy Sims, Tennessee, DB, 1/1
7. Steve O'Malley, Northern Illinois, DT, 0/0
7. Chris White, Illinois, K, 0/0
8. Trell Hooper, Memphis, DB, 0/3
9. Bob Brotzki, Syracuse, T, 14/18
10. Pete Anderson, Georgia, G, 0/0
12. Steve Wade, Vanderbilt, DT, 0/0
12. Isaac Williams, Florida State, DT, 0/0

KANSAS CITY CHIEFS
1. Brian Jozwiak, West Virginia, G, 28/28
2. **Dino Hackett, Appalachian State, LB, 85/88**
3. **Leonard Griffin, Grambling State, DE, 103/103**
4. Tom Baugh, Southern Illinois, C, 29/45
4. Chas Fox, Furman, WR, 0/4
6. Kent Hagood, South Carolina, RB, 0/0
8. Lewis Colbert, Auburn, P, 18/20
9. Gary Baldinger, Wake Forest, DE, 23/44
10. Ike Readon, Hampton, NT, 0/3
11. Aaron Pearson, Mississippi State, LB, 43/43

LOS ANGELES RAIDERS
1. Bob Buczkowski, Pittsburgh, DE, 2/21
3. Brad Cochran, Michigan, DB, 0/0
4. **Napoleon McCallum, Navy, RB, 74/74**
4. **Vance Mueller, Occidental, RB, 73/73**
4. **Mike Wise, California-Davis, DE, 50/53**
6. Doug Marrone, Syracuse, G, 0/5
7. Bill Lewis, Nebraska, C, 26/71
8. Joe Mauntel, Eastern Kentucky, LB, 0/0
9. Zeph Lee, USC, DB, 23/24
10. Jeff Reinke, Mankato State, DE, 0/1
11. Randell Webster, Southwestern Oklahoma, LB, 0/0
12. Larry Shepherd, Houston, WR, 0/0

LOS ANGELES RAMS
1. Mike Schad, Queens (Canada), G, 7/62
2. **Tom Newberry, Wisconsin-LaCrosse, G, 131/147**
3. Hugh Millen, Washington, QB, 1/40
6. **Robert Jenkins, UCLA, T, 82/117**
6. Lynn Williams, Kansas, RB, 0/0
8. Hank Goebel, Cal State-Fullerton, T, 3/3
8. Steve Jarecki, UCLA, LB, 0/0
9. Elbert Watts, USC, DB, 0/9
10. Garrett Breeland, Southern California, LB, 0/0
11. Chul Schwanke, South Dakota, RB, 0/0
12. Marcus DuPree, Southern Mississippi, RB, 15/15

MIAMI DOLPHINS
2. **John Offerdahl, Western Michigan, LB, 89/89**
3. **T.J. Turner, Houston, DE, 101/101**
4. **James Pruitt, Cal State-Fullerton, WR, 50/67**
5. Kevin Wyatt, Arkansas, DB, 0/18
6. Brent Sowell, Alabama, DT, 0/0
7. Larry Kolic, Ohio State, LB, 16/16
8. John Stuart, Texas, T, 0/0
9. Reyna Thompson, Baylor, DB, 41/116
10. Jeff Wickersham, Louisiana State, QB, 0/0
11. Arnold Franklin, North Carolina, TE, 0/3
12. Rickey Isom, North Carolina State, RB, 3/3

MINNESOTA VIKINGS
1. Gerald Robinson, Auburn, DE, 16/89
4. Joe Phillips, SMU, NT, 32/200
5. **Hassan Jones, Florida State, WR, 100/108**
6. Thomas Rooks, Illinois, RB, 0/0
7. Carl Hilton, Houston, TE, 36/36
8. Gary Schippang, West Chester, T, 0/0
9. Mike Slaton, South Dakota, DB, 1/1
10. Joe Cormier, USC, LB, 0/2
11. John Armstrong, Richmond, DB, 0/3
12. Jesse Solomon, Florida State, LB, 45/116

NEW ENGLAND PATRIOTS
1. Reggie Dupard, SMU, RB, 37/51
2. Vencie Glenn, Indiana State, DB, 4/153
2. Mike Ruth, Boston College, NT, 7/7
4. Scott Gieselman, Boston College, TE, 0/0
5. Greg Robinson, Sacramento State, T, 3/6
7. **Brent Williams, Toledo, DE, 121/147**
7. Ray McDonald, Florida, WR, 0/0
8. Greg Baty, Stanford, TE, 21/102
9. George Colton, Maryland, G, 3/3
10. Cletis Jones, Florida State, RB, 0/0
11. Gene Thomas, Pacific, WR, 0/0
12. Don McAulay, Syracuse, K, 0/0

NEW ORLEANS SAINTS
1. **Jim Dombrowski, Virginia, G, 151/151**
2. **Dalton Hilliard, LSU, RB, 108/108**
3. **Rueben Mayes, Washington State, RB, 59/76**
3. **Pat Swilling, Georgia Tech, LB, 107/185**
3. Barry Word, Virginia, RB, 14/72
4. Kelvin Edwards, Liberty, WR, 14/35
5. Reggie Sutton, Miami (FL), DB, 26/26
6. Bob Thompson, Youngstown State, WR, 0/2
7. Gill Fenerty, Holy Cross, RB, 31/31
8. Filipo Mokofisi, Utah, LB, 0/0
9. Merlon Jones, Florida A&M, LB, 0/0
10. Jon Dumbauld, Kentucky, DE, 10/17
11. Pat Swoopes, Mississippi State, NT, 24/31
12. Sebastian Brown, Bethune-Cookman, WR, 0/0

NEW YORK GIANTS
1. **Eric Dorsey, Notre Dame, DE, 89/89**
2. **Mark Collins, Cal State-Fullerton, DB, 112/168**
2. **Erik Howard, Washington State, NT, 122/139**
2. **Pepper Johnson, Ohio State, LB, 106/193**
2. Greg Lasker, Arkansas, DB, 31/33
3. **John Washington, Oklahoma State, DE, 100/119**
5. Vince Warren, San Diego State, WR, 4/4
6. Ron Brown, Colorado, WR, 0/3
6. Solomon Miller, Utah State, WR, 16/24
7. Jon Francis, Boise State, RB, 0/9
8. Steve Cisowski, Santa Clara, T, 0/3
9. Jim Luebbers, Iowa State, DE, 0/0
10. Jerry Kimmel, Syracuse, LB, 2/2
11. Len Lynch, Maryland, G, 0/0

NEW YORK JETS
1. **Mike Haight, Iowa, G, 56/63**
2. Doug Williams, Texas A&M, T, 0/23
3. Tim Crawford, Texas Tech, LB, 0/3
4. Rogers Alexander, Penn State, LB, 1/4
5. Ron Hadley, Washington, LB, 0/6
7. Bob White, Rhode Island, C, 0/24
8. Robert Ducksworth, Southern Mississippi, DB, 2/2
9. Nuu Faaola, Hawaii, RB, 42/52
10. Carl Carr, North Carolina, LB, 0/3
11. Vince Amoia, Arizona State, RB, 0/0
12. Sal Cesario, Cal Poly-San Luis Obispo, T, 0/3

PHILADELPHIA EAGLES
1. **Keith Byars, Ohio State, RB, 105/189**
2. Alonzo Johnson, Florida, LB, 18/18
3. **Anthony Toney, Texas A&M, RB, 67/67**
4. **Matt Darwin, Texas A&M, T, 61/61**
5. Ray Criswell, Florida, P, 0/19
5. Dan McMillen, Colorado, DE, 1/2
6. Bob Landsee, Wisconsin, C, 9/9

S7. Charles Crawford, Oklahoma State, RB, 18/18

7. Byron Lee, Ohio State, LB, 6/6
7. Corn Redick, Cal State-Fullerton, WR, 0/1
8. **Seth Joyner, Texas-El Paso, LB, 120/195**
9. **Clyde Simmons, Western Carolina, DE, 124/236**
10. Junior Tautalatasi, Washington State, RB, 38/51
11. Steve Bogdalek, Michigan State, G, 0/0
12. Bobby Howard, Indiana, RB, 0/20
12. **Reggie Singletary, North Carolina State, G, 61/61**

PITTSBURGH STEELERS
1. John Rienstra, Temple, G, 42/65
2. **Gerald Williams, Auburn, NT, 120/161**
3. **Bubby Brister, Louisiana-Monroe, QB, 61/99**
4. Bill Callahan, Pittsburgh, DB, 0/1
5. Brent Jones, Santa Clara, TE, 0/143
5. Erroll Tucker, Utah, DB, 0/18
6. Domingo Bryant, Texas A&M, DB, 0/27
7. Rodney Carter, Purdue, RB, 40/40
8. Cap Boso, Illinois, TE, 0/55
9. Anthony Henton, Troy State, LB, 32/32
10. Warren Seitz, Missouri, TE, 16/18
11. Larry Station, Iowa, LB, 6/6
12. Mike Williams, Tulsa, LB, 0/0

SAN DIEGO CHARGERS
1. James FitzPatrick, USC, T, 38/65
1. **Leslie O'Neal, Oklahoma State, DE, 133/196**
3. Terry Unrein, Colorado State, NT, 21/21
3. Jeff Walker, Memphis, T, 16/30
4. Ty Allert, Texas, LB, 19/51
4. Tommy Taylor, UCLA, LB, 0/0
5. Donald Brown, Maryland, DB, 13/18
5. Doug Landry, Louisiana Tech, LB, 0/0
5. Matt Johnson, Southern California, DB, 0/0
6. Curt Pardridge, Northern Illinois, WR, 0/3
7. Fred Smalls, West Virginia, LB, 0/3
8. Mike Perrino, Notre Dame, T, 0/3
9. Mike Zordich, Penn State, DB, 0/185
11. Chuck Sanders, Slippery Rock, RB, 0/19
11. Drew Smetana, Oregon, T, 0/0
12. Jeff Sprowls, BYU, DB, 0/0
12. Mike Travis, Georgia Tech, DB, 0/0

SAN FRANCISCO 49ERS
2. **Larry Roberts, Alabama, DE, 89/89**
3. **Tim McKyer, Texas-Arlington, DB, 51/170**
3. **Tom Rathman, Nebraska, RB, 115/131**
3. **John Taylor, Delaware State, WR, 121/121**
4. **Kevin Fagan, Miami (FL), DE, 83/83**
4. **Charles Haley, James Madison, DE, 106/169**
4. **Steve Wallace, Auburn, T, 166/176**
5. Pat Miller, Florida, LB, 0/9
6. **Don Griffin, Middle Tennessee State, DB, 114/161**
8. Jim Popp, Vanderbilt, TE, 0/0
9. Tony Cherry, Oregon, RB, 6/6
10. Elliston Stinson, Rice, WR, 0/0
10. Harold Hallman, Auburn, LB, 0/0

ST. LOUIS CARDINALS
1. **Anthony Bell, Michigan State, LB, 76/102**
2. John Lee, UCLA, K, 11/11
3. Gene Chilton, Texas, C, 27/79
4. **Carl Carter, Texas Tech, DB, 57/90**
5. Jeff Tupper, Oklahoma, DE, 0/7
7. Eric Swanson, Tennessee, WR, 9/9
8. Ray Brown, Arkansas State, G, 33/262
9. Kent Kafentzis, Hawaii, DB, 0/0
10. **Vai Sikahema, Brigham Young, RB, 75/118**
10. Wes Smith, Texas A&M-Commerce, WR, 0/1
11. Wayne Dillard, Alcorn State, LB, 0/0
12. Kent Austin, Mississippi, QB, 16/16

SEATTLE SEAHAWKS
1. **John Williams, Florida, FB, 123/149**
3. **Patrick Hunter, Nevada-Reno, DB, 120/125**
5. Bobby Joe Edmonds, Arkansas, RB, 42/65
6. Eddie Anderson, Fort Valley State, DB, 5/159
7. Paul Miles, Nebraska, RB, 0/0
8. Alonzo Mitz, Florida, DE, 40/71
9. Mike Black, Sacramento State, T, 0/3
10. Don Fairbanks, Colorado, DE, 3/3
11. David Norrie, UCLA, QB, 0/2
12. John McVeigh, Kentucky, LB, 3/3

TAMPA BAY BUCCANEERS
1. **Rod Jones, SMU, DB, 57/146**
2. **Kevin Murphy, Oklahoma, LB, 88/116**
2. **Jackie Walker, Jackson State, LB, 57/57**
4. Craig Swoope, Illinois, DB, 16/30
5. J.D. Maarleveld, Maryland, T, 25/25
6. Kevin Walker, East Carolina, DB, 7/7
9. Tommy Barnhardt, North Carolina, P, 38/186
10. Ben Reed, Mississippi, DE, 0/3
11. Mark Drenth, Purdue, T, 0/0
12. Mike Crawford, Arizona State, RB, 0/3
12. Clay Miller, Michigan, T, 0/3

WASHINGTON REDSKINS
2. **Markus Koch, Boise State, DE, 68/68**
2. Walter Murray, Hawaii, WR, 0/19
3. **Alvin Walton, Kansas, DB, 77/77**
5. **Ravin Caldwell, Arkansas, LB, 79/79**
6. Jim Huddleston, Virginia, G, 0/1
6. **Mark Rypien, Washington State, QB, 77/104**
7. Rick Badanjek, Maryland, RB, 6/14
8. **Kurt Gouveia, Brigham Young, LB, 130/183**
9. Wayne Asberry, Texas A&M, DB, 0/0
11. Kenny Fells, Henderson State, RB, 0/0
12. Eric Yarber, Idaho, WR, 14/14

1987 NFL

ATLANTA FALCONS
1. **Chris Miller, Oregon, QB, 69/98**
2. Kenny Flowers, Clemson, RB, 16/16
4. Ralph Van Dyke, Southern Illinois, T, 0/2
5. Mark Mraz, Utah State, DE, 11/22
6. Paul Kiser, Wake Forest, G, 0/1
7. **Michael Reid, Wisconsin, LB, 67/67**
8. Curtis Taliaferro, Virginia Tech, LB, 0/0
9. Terrence Anthony, Iowa State, DB, 0/1
10. Jerry Reese, Illinois, TE, 0/0
11. **Elbert Shelley, Arkansas State, DB, 119/119**
12. Larry Emery, Wisconsin, RB, 5/5

BUFFALO BILLS
1. **Shane Conlan, Penn State, LB, 80/120**
2. Roland Mitchell, Texas Tech, DB, 14/89
2. **Nate Odomes, Wisconsin, DB, 108/115**
3. David Brandon, Memphis, LB, 0/122
3. **Jamie Mueller, Benedictine, RB, 57/57**
4. **Leon Seals, Jackson State, DE, 77/82**
7. Kerry Porter, Washington State, RB, 6/35
8. Bruce Mesner, Maryland, NT, 11/11
9. **Keith McKeller, Jacksonville State, TE, 80/80**
11. **Howard Ballard, Alabama A&M, T, 96/170**
12. Joe McGrail, Delaware, NT, 2/2

CHICAGO BEARS
1. **Jim Harbaugh, Michigan, QB, 89/177**
2. **Ron Morris, SMU, WR, 66/66**
4. Sean Smith, Grambling State, DE, 19/26
5. Steve Bryan, Oklahoma, DE, 0/12
5. Will Johnson, Louisiana-Monroe, LB, 11/11
6. John Adickes, Baylor, C, 22/23
7. Archie Harris, William & Mary, T, 0/3
8. Paul Migliazzo, Oklahoma, LB, 3/3
9. Lakei Heimuli, Brigham Young, RB, 3/3
10. Dick Chapura, Missouri, DT, 33/43
11. Tim Jessie, Auburn, RB, 0/3
12. Eric Jeffries, Texas, DB, 2/2

CINCINNATI BENGALS
1. **Jason Buck, Brigham Young, DE, 60/97**
2. **Eric Thomas, Tulane, DB, 80/111**
3. Len Bell, Indiana, DB, 1/1
3. **Skip McClendon, Arizona State, DE, 64/92**
4. **Jim Riggs, Clemson, TE, 79/82**
5. Greg Horne, Arkansas, P, 4/25
5. Marc Logan, Kentucky, RB, 12/139
6. Sonny Gordon, Ohio State, DB, 0/7
7. Chris Thatcher, Lafayette, G, 0/0
8. **Solomon Wilcots, Colorado, DB, 60/92**
9. Craig Raddatz, Wisconsin, LB, 0/0
10. David McCluskey, Georgia, RB, 3/3
11. Jim Warne, Arizona State, T, 0/3
12. John Holifield, West Virginia, RB, 3/3

CLEVELAND BROWNS
1. Mike Junkin, Duke, LB, 15/20
2. **Gregg Rakoczy, Miami (FL), C, 60/81**
3. Jeff Jaeger, Washington, K, 10/165
3. Tim Manoa, Penn State, RB, 44/53
6. **Stephen Braggs, Texas, DB, 66/83**
8. Steve Bullitt, Texas A&M, LB, 0/0
10. Frank Winters, Western Illinois, C, 28/231
11. Larry Brewton, Temple, DB, 0/0

DALLAS COWBOYS
1. **Danny Noonan, Nebraska, DT, 67/73**
2. **Ron Francis, Baylor, DB, 54/54**
3. Jeff Zimmerman, Florida, G, 34/34
4. **Kelvin Martin, Boston College, WR, 98/139**
5. Everett Gay, Texas, WR, 16/16
6. Joe Onosai, Hawaii, G, 0/0
7. Kevin Sweeney, Fresno State, QB, 6/6
8. **Kevin Gogan, Washington, G, 103/213**
9. Alvin Blount, Maryland, RB, 2/2
10. Dale Jones, Tennessee, LB, 3/3
11. Jeff Ward, Texas, K, 0/0
12. Scott Armstrong, Florida, LB, 0/0

DENVER BRONCOS
1. **Ricky Nattiel, Florida, WR, 70/70**
3. **Michael Brooks, LSU, LB, 89/138**
4. Marc Munford, Nebraska, LB, 48/48
6. Warren Marshall, James Madison, RB, 1/1
7. Wilbur Strozier, Georgia, TE, 0/18
8. Dan Morgan, Penn State, G, 0/2
9. Bruce Plummer, Mississippi State, DB, 26/52
10. Rafe Wilkinson, Richmond, LB, 0/0
11. Steve Roberts, Washington, DE, 0/0
11. Tommy Neal, Maryland, RB, 0/0
12. **Tyrone Braxton, North Dakota State, DB, 165/181**

DETROIT LIONS
1. Reggie Rogers, Washington, DE, 11/15
3. **Jerry Ball, SMU, NT, 84/191**
4. Garland Rivers, Michigan, DB, 0/2
6. Danny Lockett, Arizona, LB, 29/29
7. Dan Saleaumua, Arizona State, DT, 25/177
8. **Dennis Gibson, Iowa State, LB, 92/121**
9. Rick Calhoun, Cal State-Fullerton, RB, 0/3
10. Ray Brown, South Carolina, WR, 0/1
11. Brian Siverling, Penn State, TE, 0/0
12. Gary Lee, Georgia Tech, WR, 26/26

GREEN BAY PACKERS
1. Brent Fullwood, Auburn, RB, 45/46
2. **Johnny Holland, Texas A&M, LB, 103/103**
3. Dave Croston, Iowa, T, 16/16
3. Frankie Neal, Fort Hays State, WR, 12/12
3. **Scott Stephen, Arizona State, LB, 72/88**
4. Lorenzo Freeman, Pittsburgh, NT, 0/62
6. Willie Marshall, Temple, WR, 0/0
7. Tony Leiker, Stanford, DE, 1/1
7. Bill Smith, Mississippi, P, 0/0
8. Jeff Drost, Iowa, DT, 2/2
9. Gregg Harris, Wake Forest, G, 0/0
10. **Don Majkowski, Virginia, QB, 68/93**
11. Patrick Scott, Grambling State, WR, 24/24
12. Norman Jefferson, LSU, DB, 14/14

HOUSTON OILERS
1. Alonzo Highsmith, Miami (FL), RB, 40/65
1. **Haywood Jeffires, North Carolina State, WR, 123/132**
2. Walter Johnson, Louisiana Tech, LB, 26/41
3. Cody Carlson, Baylor, QB, 45/45
4. Mark Dusbabek, Minnesota, LB, 0/31
5. **Spencer Tillman, Oklahoma, RB, 68/115**
6. Toby Caston, LSU, LB, 22/90
6. **Al Smith, Utah State, LB, 125/125**
7. Robert Banks, Notre Dame, DE, 14/44
8. Michel James, Washington State, WR, 0/0
9. Wes Neighbors, Alabama, C, 0/0
10. **Curtis Duncan, Northwestern, WR, 102/102**
11. John Davis, Georgia Tech, G, 19/104
12. Ira Valentine, Texas A&M, RB, 7/7

INDIANAPOLIS COLTS
1. Cornelius Bennett, Alabama, LB, 32/206
3. Chris Gambol, Iowa, G, 1/34
4. **Randy Dixon, Pittsburgh, G, 118/118**
5. Roy Banks, Eastern Illinois, WR, 15/15
6. Freddie Robinson, Alabama, DB, 22/22
7. Mark Bellini, Brigham Young, WR, 25/25
8. Chuckie Miller, UCLA, DB, 3/3
9. Bob Ontko, Penn State, LB, 3/3
10. **Chris Goode, Alabama, DB, 96/96**
11. Jim Reynosa, Arizona State, DE, 0/0
12. David Adams, Arizona, RB, 0/3

KANSAS CITY CHIEFS
1. Paul Palmer, Temple, RB, 27/41
2. **Christian Okoye, Azusa Pacific, RB, 79/79**
3. Todd Howard, Texas A&M, LB, 19/19
5. Kitrick Taylor, Washington State, WR, 16/47
7. Doug Hudson, Nicholls State, QB, 1/1
8. Michael Clemons, William & Mary, RB, 8/8
9. Randy Watts, Catwaba, DE, 0/5
10. James Evans, Southern (LA), RB, 2/2
11. Craig Richardson, Eastern Washington, WR, 0/0
12. Bruce Holmes, Minnesota, LB, 3/4

LOS ANGELES RAIDERS
1. John Clay, Missouri, T, 10/12
2. **Bruce Wilkerson, Tennessee, T, 107/147**
3. **Steve Smith, Penn State, RB, 103/128**
4. Steve Beuerlein, Notre Dame, QB, 20/147
7. Bo Jackson, Auburn, RB, 38/38
9. Scott Eccles, Eastern New Mexico, TE, 0/1
10. Jim Ellis, Boise State, LB, 3/3
10. John Gesek, Sacramento State, G, 31/123
10. Rob Harrison, Sacramento State, DB, 2/2
11. Chris McLemore, Arizona, RB, 10/12
11. Mario Perry, Mississippi, TE, 3/3

LOS ANGELES RAMS
2. Donald Evans, Winston-Salem State, DE, 1/90
3. Cliff Hicks, Oregon, DB, 34/98
4. Doug Bartlett, Northern Illinois, DT, 0/10
4. **Larry Kelm, Texas A&M, LB, 78/88**
5. Scott Mersereau, Southern Connecticut State, DT, 0/102
6. Jon Embree, Colorado, TE, 13/13
8. **Michael Stewart, Fresno State, DB, 103/144**
9. Tracy Ham, Georgia Southern, RB, 0/0
10. David Smith, Northern Arizona, LB, 0/0
12. **Fred Stokes, Georgia Southern, DE, 60/133**
12. Alonzo Williams, Mesa, RB, 3/3

MIAMI DOLPHINS
1. John Bosa, Boston College, DE, 31/31
2. Rick Graf, Wisconsin, LB, 40/73
2. Scott Schwedes, Syracuse, WR, 41/46
4. Troy Stradford, Boston College, RB, 48/66
5. Chris Conlin, Penn State, G, 3/27
6. Lance Sellers, Boise State, LB, 0/3
7. Tom Brown, Pittsburgh, RB, 10/10
8. **Mark Dennis, Illinois, T, 90/125**
8. Joel Williams, Notre Dame, TE, 3/3
9. Tim Pidgeon, Syracuse, LB, 3/3
10. Bobby Taylor, Wisconsin, DB, 0/0
11. Terence Mann, Southern Methodist, DT, 0/0
12. Jim Karsatos, Ohio State, QB, 0/0

MINNESOTA VIKINGS
1. D.J. Dozier, Penn State, RB, 37/43
2. **Ray Berry, Baylor, LB, 82/89**
3. **Henry Thomas, LSU, DT, 118/213**
4. **Najee Mustafaa, Georgia Tech, DB, 68/97**
6. Greg Richardson, Alabama, WR, 2/4
8. **Rick Fenney, Washington, RB, 63/63**
9. Leonard Jones, Texas Tech, DB, 0/2
10. Bob Riley, Indiana, T, 0/3
11. Brent Pease, Montana, QB, 0/20
12. Keith Williams, Florida, DT, 0/0

NEW ENGLAND PATRIOTS
1. **Bruce Armstrong, Louisville, T, 212/212**
3. Bob Perryman, Michigan, RB, 49/68
4. Rich Gannon, Delaware, QB, 0/157
4. Tim Jordan, Wisconsin, LB, 30/30
4. Derrick Beasley, Winston-Salem, DB, 0/0
5. Tom Gibson, Northern Arizona, DE, 0/33
5. **Danny Villa, Arizona State, T, 75/157**
6. Gene Taylor, Fresno State, WR, 1/13
11. Carlos Reveiz, Tennessee, K, 0/0
12. Elgin Davis, Central Florida, RB, 9/9

NEW ORLEANS SAINTS
1. Shawn Knight, Brigham Young, DE, 10/31
2. **Lonzell Hill, Washington, WR, 55/55**
3. Michael Adams, Arkansas State, DB, 12/15
4. **Steve Trapilo, Boston College, G, 57/57**
5. **Milton Mack, Alcorn State, DB, 67/111**
6. Thomas Henley, Stanford, WR, 0/1
7. **Gene Atkins, Florida A&M, DB, 107/143**
8. **Toi Cook, Stanford, DB, 101/150**
9. Scott Leach, Ohio State, LB, 3/3
10. Robert Clark, North Carolina Central, WR, 18/67
11. Arthur Wells, Grambling State, TE, 0/2
12. Tyrone Sorrells, Georgia Tech, G, 0/0

NEW YORK GIANTS
1. **Mark Ingram, Michigan State, WR, 76/128**
2. **Adrian White, Florida, DB, 50/70**
3. **Stephen Baker, Fresno State, WR, 90/90**
4. Odessa Turner, Northwestern State (LA), WR, 44/67
5. Paul O'Connor, Miami (FL), G, 0/2
6. **Doug Riesenberg, California, T, 135/145**
6. Tim Richardson, Pacific, RB, 0/0
8. Rod Jones, Washington, TE, 0/9
9. Dana Wright, Findlay, RB, 0/5
9. Stan Parker, Nebraska, G, 0/0
10. Chuck Faucette, Maryland, LB, 0/10
11. Dave Walter, Michigan Tech, QB, 0/3
12. Bill Berthusen, Iowa State, NT, 1/4
12. Chad Stark, North Dakota State, RB, 0/2

NEW YORK JETS
1. Roger Vick, Texas A&M, RB, 44/58
2. Alex Gordon, Cincinnati, LB, 41/96
3. Onzy Elam, Tennessee State, LB, 9/10
5. Kirby Jackson, Mississippi State, DB, 0/70
6. Tracy Martin, North Dakota, WR, 12/12
7. **Gerald Nichols, Florida State, DT, 60/85**
8. Eddie Hunter, Virginia Tech, RB, 3/6
8. Mike Rice, Montana, P, 0/0
9. Ron McLean, Cal State-Fullerton, NT, 0/9
10. Sid Lewis, Penn State, DB, 2/2
11. Kirk Timmer, Montana State, LB, 0/1
12. Bill Ransdell, Kentucky, QB, 0/0

PHILADELPHIA EAGLES
1. **Jerome Brown, Miami (FL), DT, 76/76**
3. **Ben Tamburello, Auburn, G, 50/50**

S4. Cris Carter, Ohio State, WR, 41/234

4. **Byron Evans, Arizona, LB, 113/113**
5. **David Alexander, Tulsa, C, 124/131**
6. Chris Pike, Tulsa, DT, 0/32
6. Ron Moten, Florida, LB, 0/0
7. Brian Williams, Central Michigan, T, 0/0
9. Ken Lambiotte, William & Mary, QB, 0/0
10. Paul Carberry, Oregon State, DT, 0/0
12. Bobby Morse, Michigan State, RB, 11/38

PITTSBURGH STEELERS
1. **Rod Woodson, Purdue, DB, 134/238**
2. **Delton Hall, Clemson, DB, 60/76**
3. Charles Lockett, Long Beach State, WR, 27/27
4. **Thomas Everett, Baylor, DB, 73/128**
5. **Hardy Nickerson, California, LB, 84/225**
6. Tim Johnson, Penn State, DT, 41/146
6. **Greg Lloyd, Fort Valley State, LB, 131/147**
7. Chris Kelley, Akron, TE, 0/2
8. Charles Buchanan, Tennessee State, DE, 0/9
9. Joey Clinkscales, Tennessee, WR, 11/14
10. **Merril Hoge, Idaho State, RB, 109/114**
11. Paul Oswald, Kansas, C, 2/6
12. Theo Young, Arkansas, TE, 12/12

SAN DIEGO CHARGERS
1. **Rod Bernstine, Texas A&M, RB, 63/84**
2. Lou Brock, USC, DB, 1/4
3. Karl Wilson, LSU, DE, 20/103
4. Mark Vlasic, Iowa, QB, 9/15
5. Nelson Jones, North Carolina State, DB, 0/0
7. Jamie Holland, Ohio State, WR, 44/80
8. Ron Brown, USC, LB, 0/19
8. Joe MacEsker, Texas-El Paso, T, 0/0
9. Thomas Wilcher, Michigan, RB, 0/0
10. Anthony Anderson, Grambling State, DB, 3/3
11. Joe Goebel, UCLA, C, 2/2
12. Marcus Greenwood, UCLA, RB, 0/0

SAN FRANCISCO 49ERS
1. **Harris Barton, North Carolina, T, 138/138**
1. Terrence Flagler, Clemson, RB, 21/41
2. Jeff Bregel, USC, G, 21/21
5. Paul Jokisch, Michigan, WR, 0/0
6. Bob White, Penn State, LB, 0/0
7. Steve DeLine, Colorado State, K, 0/8
8. David Grayson, Fresno State, LB, 0/54
9. Jonathan Shelley, Mississippi, DB, 1/1
10. John Paye, Stanford, QB, 0/0
11. Calvin Nicholas, Grambling State, WR, 7/7

ST. LOUIS CARDINALS
1. Kelly Stouffer, Colorado State, QB, 0/22
2. **Tim McDonald, USC, DB, 80/191**
3. Robert Awalt, San Diego State, TE, 44/95
3. Colin Scotts, Hawaii, DT, 7/7
4. **Rod Saddler, Texas A&M, DT, 63/65**
5. John Bruno, Penn State, P, 0/3
5. Ilia Jarostchuk, New Hampshire, LB, 28/46
5. George Swarn, Miami (OH), RB, 0/1
6. Mark Garalczyk, Western Michigan, DT, 17/24
7. William Harris, Bishop, TE, 10/30
7. Tim Peoples, Washington, DB, 0/0
8. Steve Alvord, Washington, DT, 27/27
9. Wayne Davis, Alabama, LB, 28/28
10. Charles Wright, Tulsa, DB, 3/8
11. Todd Peat, Northern Illinois, G, 31/79

SEATTLE SEAHAWKS
S1. Brian Bosworth, Oklahoma, LB, 24/24

1. **Tony Woods, Pittsburgh, DE, 89/147**
2. **David Wyman, Stanford, LB, 61/92**
4. Mark Moore, Oklahoma State, DB, 5/5
5. Tommie Agee, Auburn, RB, 16/100
5. Ruben Rodriguez, Arizona, P, 44/53
7. Roland Barbay, LSU, NT, 5/5
7. Derek Tennell, UCLA, TE, 0/75
8. Sammy Garza, Texas-El Paso, QB, 0/2
9. M.L. Johnson, Hawaii, LB, 37/37
10. **Louis Clark, Mississippi State, WR, 55/55**
11. Darryl Oliver, Miami (FL), RB, 0/2
12. Tony Burse, Middle Tennessee State, RB, 12/12
12. Wes Dove, Syracuse, DE, 2/2

TAMPA BAY BUCCANEERS
1. **Vinny Testaverde, Miami (FL), QB, 76/223**
2. **Winston Moss, Miami (FL), LB, 60/169**
2. **Ricky Reynolds, Washington State, DB, 105/148**
2. Don Smith, Mississippi State, RB, 21/37
3. **Mark Carrier, Nicholls State, WR, 88/177**

S3. Dan Sileo, Miami (FL), DT, 10/10

4. Don Graham, Penn State, LB, 2/13
4. **Ron Hall, Hawaii, TE, 100/119**
4. **Bruce Hill, Arizona State, WR, 57/57**
5. Tony Mayes, Kentucky, DB, 0/3
5. Henry Rolling, Nevada-Reno, LB, 21/88
6. Steve Bartalo, Colorado State, RB, 9/9
7. Curt Jarvis, Alabama, NT, 38/38
7. Harry Swayne, Rutgers, T, 44/186
8. Stan Mataele, Arizona, NT, 0/2
9. Greg Davis, The Citadel, K, 0/169
9. Joe Armentrout, Wisconsin, RB, 0/0
10. Mike Simmonds, Indiana State, G, 5/5
11. Reggie Taylor, Cincinnati, RB, 0/0
12. Scott Cooper, Kearney State, DT, 0/0
12. Mike Shula, Alabama, QB, 0/0

WASHINGTON REDSKINS
2. Brian Davis, Nebraska, DB, 38/87
2. Wally Kleine, Notre Dame, T, 0/0
5. Timmy Smith, Texas Tech, RB, 21/22
6. Steve Gage, Tulsa, DB, 20/20
6. **Ed Simmons, Eastern Washington, T, 142/142**
7. **Johnny Thomas, Baylor, DB, 56/94**
8. Clarence Vaughn, Northern Illinois, DB, 48/48
9. Alfred Jenkins, Arizona, RB, 0/0
10. Ted Wilson, Central Florida, WR, 3/3
11. Laron Brown, Texas, WR, 0/3
12. Ray Hitchcock, Minnesota, C, 5/5

1988 NFL

ATLANTA FALCONS
1. **Aundray Bruce, Auburn, LB, 62/151**
2. Marcus Cotton, USC, LB, 34/44
3. Alex Higdon, Ohio State, TE, 3/3
5. Charles Dimry, UNLV, DB, 48/183
6. **Houston Hoover, Jackson State, G, 79/98**
6. George Thomas, UNLV, WR, 46/51
7. **Michael Haynes, Northern Arizona, WR, 99/147**
8. Phillip Brown, Alabama, LB, 0/0
9. James Primus, UCLA, RB, 21/21
10. Stan Clayton, Penn State, G, 15/26
11. James Milling, Maryland, WR, 24/24
12. Carter Wiley, Virginia Tech, DB, 0/0

BUFFALO BILLS
2. **Thurman Thomas, Oklahoma State, RB, 173/182**
3. Bernard Ford, Central Florida, WR, 0/24
5. Ezekial Gadson, Pittsburgh, DB, 0/0
5. Kirk Roach, Western Carolina, K, 0/0
6. Dan Murray, East Stroudsburg, LB, 0/4
7. Tim Borcky, Memphis State, T, 0/0
7. Bo Wright, Alabama, RB, 0/0
8. John Hagy, Texas, DB, 28/28
8. **Jeff Wright, Central Missouri State, NT, 98/98**
9. **Carlton Bailey, North Carolina, LB, 70/142**
10. Martin Mayhew, Florida State, DB, 0/118
11. Pete Curkendall, Penn State, DT, 0/0
12. Tom Erlandson, Washington, LB, 4/4
12. John Driscoll, New Hampshire, T, 0/0

CHICAGO BEARS
1. **Wendell Davis, LSU, WR, 81/81**
1. **Brad Muster, Stanford, RB, 75/95**
2. **Dante Jones, Oklahoma, LB, 87/92**
3. Ralph Jarvis, Temple, DE, 0/8
4. **James Thornton, Cal State-Fullerton, TE, 64/96**
5. Troy Johnson, Oklahoma, LB, 23/64
6. **Lemuel Stinson, Texas Tech, DB, 69/69**
7. Caesar Rentie, Oklahoma, T, 5/5
8. **David Tate, Colorado, DB, 78/142**
8. Harvey Reed, Howard, RB, 0/0
9. Rogie Magee, Louisiana State, WR, 0/0
10. Joel Porter, Baylor, G, 0/0
11. Steve Forch, Nebraska, LB, 0/0
12. Greg Clark, Arizona State, LB, 15/70

CINCINNATI BENGALS
1. **Rickey Dixon, Oklahoma, DB, 73/82**
2. Ickey Woods, UNLV, RB, 37/37
3. Kevin Walker, Maryland, LB, 44/44
4. **David Grant, West Virginia, DE, 61/70**
5. Herb Wester, Iowa, T, 0/0
6. Paul Jetton, Texas, G, 28/30
7. Rich Romer, Union (NY), LB, 9/9
8. Curtis Maxey, Grambling State, DE, 3/5
9. Brandy Wells, Notre Dame, DB, 0/0
10. Ellis Dillahunt, East Carolina, DB, 8/8
11. Paul Hickert, Murray State, K, 0/0
12. Carl Parker, Vanderbilt, WR, 6/6

CLEVELAND BROWNS
1. Clifford Charlton, Florida, LB, 31/31
2. **Michael Dean Perry, Clemson, DT, 109/148**
3. **Van Waiters, Indiana, LB, 64/80**
4. Anthony Blaylock, Winston-Salem State, DB, 49/71
7. Thane Gash, East Tennessee State, DB, 48/64
8. J.J. Birden, Oregon, WR, 0/93
9. Danny Copeland, Eastern Kentucky, DB, 0/73
10. Brian Washington, Nebraska, DB, 16/124
11. Hendley Hawkins, Nebraska, WR, 0/0
12. Steve Slayden, Duke, QB, 0/0

DALLAS COWBOYS
1. **Michael Irvin, Miami (FL), WR, 159/159**
2. **Ken Norton, UCLA, LB, 79/191**
3. Mark Hutson, Oklahoma, G, 0/0
4. Dave Widell, Boston College, C, 29/156
6. Scott Secules, Virginia, QB, 0/57
7. Owen Hooven, Oregon State, T, 0/0
8. Mark Higgs, Kentucky, RB, 5/90
9. Brian Bedford, California, WR, 0/0
10. Billy Owens, Pittsburgh, DB, 16/16
11. **Chad Hennings, Air Force, DT, 119/119**
12. Ben Hummel, UCLA, LB, 0/0

DENVER BRONCOS
1. Ted Gregory, Syracuse, NT, 0/3
2. Gerald Perry, Southern (LA), T, 40/97
3. Kevin Guidry, LSU, DB, 14/17
5. Corris Ervin, Central Florida, DB, 0/0
7. Pat Kelly, Syracuse, TE, 32/41
7. Garry Frank, Mississippi State, G, 0/0
9. Mel Farr, UCLA, RB, 0/1
10. Channing Williams, Arizona State, RB, 0/0
11. Richard Calvin, Washington State, RB, 0/0
12. Johnny Carter, Grambling, DT, 0/0

DETROIT LIONS
1. **Bennie Blades, Miami (FL), DB, 126/136**
2. Pat Carter, Florida State, TE, 15/154
2. **Chris Spielman, Ohio State, LB, 124/148**
3. Ray Roundtree, Penn State, WR, 4/4
4. **William White, Ohio State, DB, 95/170**
5. **Eric Andolsek, LSU, G, 61/61**
6. Carl Painter, Hampton, RB, 27/27
7. Jeff James, Stanford, WR, 0/0
8. Gary Hadd, Minnesota, DT, 5/15
9. Kip Corrington, Texas A&M, DB, 0/32
9. Todd Irvin, Mississippi, T, 0/0
10. Paco Craig, UCLA, WR, 8/8
11. Danny McCoin, Cincinnati, QB, 0/0

GREEN BAY PACKERS
1. **Sterling Sharpe, South Carolina, WR, 112/112**
2. Shawn Patterson, Arizona State, DE, 48/48
3. **Keith Woodside, Texas A&M, RB, 64/64**
4. **Chuck Cecil, Arizona, DB, 66/95**
4. Rollin Putzier, Oregon, DT, 0/16
5. Darrell Reed, Oklahoma, LB, 0/0
6. Nate Hill, Auburn, DE, 3/4
7. Gary Richard, Pittsburgh, DB, 10/10
8. Patrick Collins, Oklahoma, RB, 5/5
9. Neal Wilkinson, James Madison, TE, 0/0
10. Bud Keyes, Wisconsin, QB, 0/0
12. Scott Bolton, Auburn, WR, 4/4

HOUSTON OILERS
1. **Lorenzo White, Michigan State, RB, 95/107**
2. Quintin Jones, Pittsburgh, DB, 5/5
3. **Greg Montgomery, Michigan State, P, 94/142**
5. **Cris Dishman, Purdue, DB, 140/199**
5. Chris Verhulst, Cal State-Chico, TE, 17/28
6. Kurt Crain, Auburn, LB, 0/0
7. Tracey Eaton, Portland State, DB, 17/60
8. David Viaene, Minnesota-Duluth, C, 0/21
9. David Spradlin, Texas Christian, LB, 0/0
10. Marco Johnson, Hawaii, WR, 0/0
11. Jethro Franklin, Fresno State, DE, 0/7
12. John Brantley, Georgia, LB, 8/20

INDIANAPOLIS COLTS
3. Chris Chandler, Washington, QB, 18/180
4. **Michael Ball, Southern (LA), DB, 84/84**
5. **John Baylor, Southern Mississippi, DB, 74/74**
9. **Jeff Herrod, Mississippi, LB, 143/153**
10. O'Brien Alston, Maryland, LB, 19/19
11. Donnie Dee, Tulsa, TE, 14/17
12. Aatron Kenney, Wisconsin-Stevens Point, WR, 0/0
12. Tim Vesling, Syracuse, K, 0/0

KANSAS CITY CHIEFS
1. **Neil Smith, Nebraska, DE, 138/191**
3. **Kevin Porter, Auburn, DB, 76/78**
4. J.R. Ambrose, Mississippi, WR, 0/0
6. **James Saxon, San Jose State, FB, 54/111**
7. Troy Stedman, Washburn, LB, 5/5
8. Alfredo Roberts, Miami (FL), TE, 48/80
9. Azizuddin Abdur-Ra'oof, Maryland, WR, 0/0
10. Kenny Gamble, Colgate, RB, 19/19
11. Danny McManus, Florida State, QB, 0/0

LOS ANGELES RAIDERS
1. **Tim Brown, Notre Dame, WR, 240/255**
1. **Scott Davis, Illinois, DE, 75/75**
1. **Terry McDaniel, Tennessee, DB, 143/152**
4. Tim Rother, Nebraska, DT, 20/20
5. Dennis Price, UCLA, DB, 17/31
6. Erwin Grabisna, Case Western, LB, 0/0
7. Derrick Crudup, Oklahoma, DB, 20/20
8. Mike Alexander, Penn State, WR, 16/19
9. Reggie Ware, Auburn, RB, 0/0
9. Scott Tabor, California, P, 0/0
10. Newt Harrell, West Texas State, T, 0/0
11. David Weber, Carroll (WI), QB, 0/0
12. Greg Kunkel, Kentucky, G, 0/0

LOS ANGELES RAMS
1. **Aaron Cox, Arizona State, WR, 71/82**
1. Gaston Green, UCLA, RB, 31/58
2. **Flipper Anderson, UCLA, WR, 106/114**
2. **Anthony Newman, Oregon, DB, 111/178**
2. **Fred Strickland, Purdue, LB, 63/161**
3. **Mike Piel, Illinois, DE, 50/50**
5. **Robert Delpino, Missouri, RB, 72/88**
5. James Washington, UCLA, DB, 25/114
6. Keith Jones, Nebraska, RB, 0/16
6. Jeff Knapton, Wyoming, DT, 0/0
8. Darryl Franklin, Washington, WR, 0/0
9. Pat Foster, Montana, DT, 0/0
10. R.C. Mullin, Southwest Louisiana, T, 0/0
12. Jeff Beathard, Southern Oregon, WR, 0/0

MIAMI DOLPHINS
1. Eric Kumerow, Ohio State, DE, 42/42
2. **Jarvis Williams, Florida, DB, 91/104**
3. **Ferrell Edmunds, Maryland, TE, 66/89**
4. Greg Johnson, Oklahoma, T, 1/1
5. Rodney Thomas, Brigham Young, DB, 43/46
6. George Cooper, Ohio State, RB, 0/0
7. Kerwin Bell, Florida, QB, 0/2
8. Louis Cheek, Texas A&M, T, 28/45
8. **Harry Galbreath, Tennessee, G, 78/141**
9. **Jeff Cross, Missouri, DE, 125/125**
10. Artis Jackson, Texas Tech, DT, 0/0
11. Tom Kelleher, Holy Cross, RB, 0/0
12. Brian Kinchen, LSU, TE, 36/193

MINNESOTA VIKINGS
1. **Randall McDaniel, Arizona State, G, 190/222**
2. Brad Edwards, South Carolina, DB, 25/122
3. **Al Noga, Hawaii, DE, 73/93**
4. **Todd Kalis, Arizona State, G, 77/103**
5. Darrell Fullington, Miami (FL), DB, 47/79
6. Derrick White, Oklahoma, DB, 0/0
7. Brad Beckman, Nebraska-Omaha, TE, 0/24
8. Joe Cain, Oregon Tech, LB, 0/131
9. Paul McGowan, Florida State, LB, 0/0
10. **Brian Habib, Washington, G, 64/174**
11. Norman Floyd, South Carolina, DB, 0/0

NEW ENGLAND PATRIOTS
1. **John Stephens, Northwestern State (LA), RB, 76/88**
2. **Vincent Brown, Mississippi Valley State, LB, 123/123**
3. Tom Rehder, Notre Dame, T, 32/40
4. Teddy Garcia, Louisiana-Monroe, K, 16/28
4. **Tim Goad, North Carolina, NT, 109/141**
4. Sammy Martin, LSU, WR, 40/48
5. Troy Wolkow, Minnesota, G, 0/0
6. Steve Johnson, Virginia Tech, TE, 14/14
7. Darryl Usher, Illinois, WR, 0/13
9. Neil Galbraith, Central State, DB, 0/0
10. Rodney Lossow, Wisconsin, C, 0/0
11. Marvin Allen, Tulane, RB, 37/37
12. Dave Nugent, Boston College, DT, 0/0

NEW ORLEANS SAINTS
1. **Craig Heyward, Pittsburgh, RB, 66/149**
2. Brett Perriman, Miami (FL), WR, 46/153
3. Tony Stephens, Clemson, DT, 0/0
4. Lydell Carr, Oklahoma, RB, 0/5
5. Greg Scales, Wake Forest, TE, 44/44
5. Keith Taylor, Illinois, DB, 32/103
6. Bob Sims, Florida, G, 0/0
7. **Brian Forde, Washington State, LB, 64/64**
8. Glenn Derby, Wisconsin, T, 7/7
9. Clarence Nunn, San Diego State, DB, 0/0
10. Todd Santos, San Diego State, QB, 0/0
10. Vincent Fizer, Southern, LB, 0/0
11. Gary Couch, Minnesota, WR, 0/0
12. Paul Jurgensen, Georgia Tech, DE, 0/0

NEW YORK GIANTS
1. **Eric Moore, Indiana, G, 75/84**
2. **Jumbo Elliott, Michigan, T, 112/196**
3. Sheldon White, Miami (OH), DB, 32/72
4. Ricky Shaw, Oklahoma State, LB, 21/37
5. Jon Carter, Pittsburgh, DT, 0/13
6. David Houle, Michigan State, G, 0/0
7. Danta Whitaker, Mississippi Valley State, TE, 0/27
7. Mike Perez, San Jose State, QB, 0/0
8. Sammy Lilly, Georgia Tech, DB, 0/50
10. Eric Hickerson, Indiana, DB, 0/0
10. Steve Wilkes, Appalachian State, TE, 0/0
11. Greg Harris, Troy State, WR, 0/0
12. David Futrell, Brigham Young, DT, 0/0
12. Brendan McCormack, South Carolina, DT, 0/0

NEW YORK JETS
1. **Dave Cadigan, USC, G, 69/82**
2. Terry Williams, Bethune-Cookman, DB, 11/11
3. **James Hasty, Washington State, DB, 111/206**
3. **Erik McMillan, Missouri, DB, 76/86**
5. Mike Withycombe, Fresno State, G, 11/30
6. **Paul Frase, Syracuse, DE, 96/139**
7. Gary Patton, Eastern Michigan, RB, 0/0
8. Keith Neubert, Nebraska, TE, 17/17
9. Ralph Tamm, West Chester, G, 0/121
10. John Booty, TCU, DB, 38/102
11. John Galvin, Boston College, LB, 41/52
12. Albert Goss, Jackson State, DT, 0/0

PHILADELPHIA EAGLES
1. **Keith Jackson, Oklahoma, TE, 60/129**
2. **Eric Allen, Arizona State, DB, 111/217**
3. Matt Patchan, Miami (FL), T, 0/0
5. Eric Everett, Texas Tech, DB, 32/75
6. Don McPherson, Syracuse, QB, 0/0
6. Rob Sterling, Maine, DB, 0/0
7. Todd White, Cal State-Fullerton, WR, 0/0
8. David Smith, Western Kentucky, RB, 0/0
10. Joe Schuster, Iowa, DT, 0/0
11. **Izel Jenkins, North Carolina State, DB, 77/86**
12. Steve Kaufusi, Brigham Young, DE, 32/32

PHOENIX CARDINALS
1. **Ken Harvey, California, LB, 90/164**
2. Tony Jeffery, TCU, RB, 3/3
3. Tom Tupa, Ohio State, QB, 42/220
4. Michael Brim, Virginia Union, DB, 4/94
5. Chris Gaines, Vanderbilt, LB, 0/4
5. Tony Jordan, Kansas State, RB, 22/22
6. Jon Phillips, Oklahoma, G, 0/0
7. **Ernie Jones, Indiana, WR, 73/83**
8. Tim Moore, Michigan State, LB, 0/0
9. Scott Dill, Memphis, T, 29/110
10. Andy Schillinger, Miami (OH), WR, 3/3
11. Keith McCoy, Fresno State, DB, 0/0
12. Chris Carrier, Louisiana State, DB, 0/0

PITTSBURGH STEELERS
1. **Aaron Jones, Eastern Kentucky, DE, 67/112**
2. **Dermontti Dawson, Kentucky, C, 184/184**
3. Chuck Lanza, Notre Dame, C, 27/27
5. Darin Jordan, Northeastern, LB, 15/59
5. Jerry Reese, Kentucky, DE, 15/15
6. **Warren Williams, Miami (FL), RB, 66/71**
7. Marc Zeno, Tulane, WR, 0/0
8. Mike Hinnant, Temple, TE, 21/36
8. Mark Nichols, Michigan State, DT, 0/0
9. Gordie Lockbaum, Holy Cross, RB, 0/0
10. **John Jackson, Eastern Kentucky, T, 153/203**
11. Bobby Dawson, Illinois, DB, 0/0
12. James Earle, Clemson, LB, 0/0

SAN DIEGO CHARGERS
1. **Anthony Miller, Tennessee, WR, 93/155**
3. Quinn Early, Iowa, WR, 36/179
4. Joe Campbell, New Mexico State, DE, 25/25
4. **David Richards, UCLA, G, 80/135**
4. Stacy Searels, Auburn, T, 0/0
6. Cedric Figaro, Notre Dame, LB, 38/98
9. Joey Howard, Tennessee, T, 9/9
11. George Hinkle, Arizona, DE, 46/68
11. Ed Miller, Pittsburgh, C, 0/0
12. Wendell Phillips, North Alabama, DB, 0/0

SAN FRANCISCO 49ERS
2. **Pierce Holt, Angelo State (TX), DE, 70/109**
2. Danny Stubbs, Miami (FL), DE, 32/134
3. **Bill Romanowski, Boston College, LB, 96/243**
4. Barry Helton, Colorado, P, 47/50
7. Kevin Bryant, Delaware State, LB, 0/0
8. Larry Clarkson, Montana, T, 0/0
9. Brian Bonner, Minnesota, LB, 0/6
10. Tim Foley, Georgia Southern, K, 0/0
11. Chet Brooks, Texas A&M, DB, 33/33
12. George Jr. Mira, Miami (FL), LB, 0/0

SEATTLE SEAHAWKS
2. **Brian Blades, Miami (FL), WR, 156/156**
3. **Tommy Kane, Syracuse, WR, 57/57**
4. Kevin Harmon, Iowa, RB, 9/9
6. Roy Hart, South Carolina, NT, 16/17
7. Ray Jackson, Ohio State, DB, 0/0
8. Robert Tyler, South Carolina State, TE, 9/9
9. Deatrich Wise, Jackson State, DT, 0/0
10. Derwin Jones, Miami (FL), DE, 0/0
11. **Dwayne Harper, South Carolina State, DB, 94/148**
11. Rick McLeod, Washington, T, 0/0
12. Dave Des Rochers, San Diego State, T, 0/0

TAMPA BAY BUCCANEERS
1. **Paul Gruber, Wisconsin, T, 183/183**
2. Lars Tate, Georgia, RB, 30/33
4. John Bruhin, Tennessee, G, 49/49
4. Robert Goff, Auburn, DE, 28/121
4. Monte Robbins, Michigan, P, 0/0
5. William Howard, Tennessee, RB, 31/31
6. Shawn Lee, North Alabama, DT, 30/148
7. Kerry Goode, Alabama, RB, 14/15

8. Anthony Simpson, East Carolina, RB, 0/0
9. **Reuben Davis, North Carolina, DE, 65/139**
11. Frank Pillow, Tennessee State, WR, 34/34
12. Victor Jones, Virginia Tech, LB, 8/93

WASHINGTON REDSKINS

2. **Chip Lohmiller, Minnesota, K, 112/135**
3. Mike Oliphant, Puget Sound, RB, 8/26
4. Jamie Morris, Michigan, RB, 28/33
5. Carl Mims, Sam Houston State, DB, 0/0
6. Stan Humphries, Louisiana-Monroe, QB, 9/88
7. Harold Hicks, San Diego State, DB, 0/0
8. Darryl McGill, Wake Forest, RB, 0/0
9. Blake Peterson, Mesa (CO), LB, 0/0
10. Henry Brown, Ohio State, T, 0/0
11. Curt Koch, Colorado, DE, 0/0
12. Wayne Ross, San Diego State, P, 0/0

1989 NFL

ATLANTA FALCONS

1. Shawn Collins, Northern Arizona, WR, 36/49
1. **Deion Sanders, Florida State, DB, 70/188**
2. Ralph Norwood, LSU, T, 11/11
3. **Keith Jones, Illinois, RB, 50/50**
6. Troy Sadowski, Georgia, TE, 13/100
7. Undra Johnson, West Virginia, RB, 1/6
8. Paul Singer, Western Illinois, QB, 0/0
9. Chris Dunn, Cal Poly-San Luis Obispo, LB, 0/0
11. Greg Paterra, Slippery Rock, RB, 10/10
12. Tony Bowick, Tennessee-Chattanooga, NT, 12/12

BUFFALO BILLS

3. **Don Beebe, Chadron State, WR, 76/116**
4. John Kolesar, Michigan, WR, 0/0
5. Michael Andrews, Alcorn State, DB, 0/0
6. Sean Doctor, Marshall, RB, 0/0
7. Chris Hale, USC, DB, 43/43
7. Brian Jordan, Richmond, DB, 0/36
9. Pat Rabold, Wyoming, DT, 0/0
10. Carlo Cheattom, Auburn, DB, 0/0
11. Richard Harvey, Tulane, LB, 27/142
12. Derrell Marshall, Southern California, T, 0/0

CHICAGO BEARS

1. **Trace Armstrong, Florida, DE, 88/211**
1. **Donnell Woolford, Clemson, DB, 111/126**
2. **John Roper, Texas A&M, LB, 62/68**
2. Dave Zawatson, California, G, 4/22
3. **Jerry Fontenot, Texas A&M, C, 128/239**
4. **Markus Paul, Syracuse, DB, 70/71**
5. **Mark Green, Notre Dame, RB, 53/53**
5. Greg Gilbert, Alabama, LB, 0/0
7. Richard Brothers, Arkansas, DB, 0/0
7. Brent Snyder, Utah State, QB, 0/0
8. Chris Dyko, Washington State, T, 8/8
8. Tony Woods, Oklahoma, DT, 15/15
9. LaSalle Harper, Arkansas, LB, 3/4
9. Byron Sanders, Northwestern, RB, 0/0
10. Todd Millikan, Nebraska, TE, 0/0
10. John Simpson, Baylor, WR, 0/0
11. George Streeter, Notre Dame, DB, 4/8
11. Joe Nelms, California, DT, 0/0
12. Freddy Weygand, Auburn, WR, 0/0
12. Anthony Phillips, Oklahoma, G, 0/0

CINCINNATI BENGALS

2. **Eric Ball, UCLA, RB, 81/97**
2. Freddie Childress, Arkansas, G, 0/31
3. Erik Wilhelm, Oregon State, QB, 22/22
4. Rob Woods, Arizona, T, 0/2
4. Kerry Owens, Arkansas, LB, 0/0
5. Natu Tuatagaloa, California, DE, 46/76
6. Craig Taylor, West Virginia, RB, 36/36
7. Kendal Smith, Utah State, WR, 20/20
8. Chris Chenault, Kentucky, LB, 0/0
9. Richard Stephens, Tulsa, G, 0/29
10. Cornell Holloway, Pittsburgh, DB, 0/32
10. Bob Jean, New Hampshire, QB, 0/0
11. Dana Wells, Arizona, NT, 1/1
12. Scott Jones, Washington, T, 17/22

CLEVELAND BROWNS

1. **Eric Metcalf, Texas, RB, 88/179**
2. Lawyer Tillman, Auburn, WR, 32/37
4. Andrew Stewart, Cincinnati, DE, 16/16
5. Vernon Joines, Maryland, WR, 20/20
5. Kyle Kramer, Bowling Green State, DB, 14/14
6. Gary Wilkerson, Penn State, DB, 0/0
7. Mike Graybill, Boston University, T, 6/6
8. Rick Aeilts, Southeastern Missouri, TE, 0/0
10. John Buddenberg, Akron, T, 0/0
11. Dan Plocki, Maryland, K, 0/0
12. Marlon Brown, Memphis State, LB, 0/0

DALLAS COWBOYS

1. **Troy Aikman, UCLA, QB, 165/165**
S1. Steve Walsh, Miami (FL), QB, 9/80
2. **Daryl Johnston, Syracuse, RB, 151/151**
2. Steve Wisniewski, Penn State, G, 0/206
3. **Mark Stepnoski, Pittsburgh, C, 133/194**
3. Rhondy Weston, Florida, DE, 0/12
4. **Tony Tolbert, Texas-El Paso, DE, 144/144**
5. Willis Crockett, Georgia Tech, LB, 13/13
5. Keith Jennings, Clemson, TE, 10/92
5. Jeff Roth, Florida, DT, 0/0
7. Kevin Peterson, Northwestern, LB, 0/0
8. Charvez Foger, Nevada-Reno, RB, 0/0
9. Tim Jackson, Nebraska, DB, 1/1
10. Rod Carter, Miami (FL), LB, 0/0
11. Randy Shannon, Miami (FL), LB, 17/17
12. Scott Ankrom, TCU, WR, 10/10

DENVER BRONCOS

1. **Steve Atwater, Arkansas, DB, 155/167**
S1. Bobby Humphrey, Alabama, RB, 35/51
2. Warren Powers, Maryland, DE, 44/51
2. **Doug Widell, Boston College, G, 64/139**
3. Darrell Hamilton, North Carolina, T, 21/21
4. Jack McCullough, Clemson, DE, 16/16
5. Darren Carrington, Northern Arizona, DB, 16/113
6. Anthony Stafford, Oklahoma, WR, 0/0
7. Mel Bratton, Miami (FL), RB, 32/32
8. Paul Green, USC, TE, 0/49
9. Monte Smith, North Dakota, G, 14/14
9. Wayne Williams, Florida, RB, 0/0
10. Anthony Butts, Mississippi State, DT, 0/0
11. Richard Shelton, Liberty, DB, 3/44
12. John Javis, Howard, WR, 0/0

DETROIT LIONS

1. **Barry Sanders, Oklahoma State, RB, 153/153**
2. John Ford, Virginia, WR, 7/7
3. Mike Utley, Washington State, G, 32/32
4. **Ray Crockett, Baylor, DB, 79/214**
5. **Lawrence Pete, Nebraska, NT, 61/61**
6. Rodney Peete, USC, QB, 47/104
7. Jerry Woods, Northern Michigan, DB, 2/18
8. Chris Parker, West Virginia, DT, 0/0
9. Derek MacCready, Ohio State, DE, 0/0
10. Jason Phillips, Houston, WR, 29/58
11. Keith Karpinski, Penn State, LB, 16/16
12. James Cribbs, Memphis, DE, 7/7

GREEN BAY PACKERS

1. Tony Mandarich, Michigan State, T, 45/86
3. **Matt Brock, Oregon, DE, 76/108**
3. Anthony Dilweg, Duke, QB, 10/10
4. Jeff Graham, Long Beach State, QB, 0/0
5. Jeff Query, Millikin, WR, 48/86
5. **Vince Workman, Ohio State, RB, 56/106**
6. **Chris Jacke, Texas-El Paso, K, 126/147**
7. Mark Hall, Louisiana-Lafayette, DE, 10/10
8. Thomas King, Southwestern Louisiana, DB, 0/0
8. Brian Shulman, Auburn, P, 0/0
9. Scott Kirby, Arizona State, T, 0/0
10. Ben Jessie, Southwest Texas State, DB, 0/0
11. Cedric Stallworth, Georgia Tech, DB, 0/0
12. Stan Shiver, Florida State, DB, 0/0

HOUSTON OILERS

1. **David Williams, Florida, T, 102/128**
2. **Scott Kozak, Oregon, LB, 80/80**
3. **Bubba McDowell, Miami (FL), DB, 86/102**
4. Rod Harris, Texas A&M, WR, 0/38
5. **Glenn Montgomery, Houston, DT, 107/114**
6. **Bo Orlando, West Virginia, DB, 70/129**
7. Tracy Rogers, Fresno State, LB, 0/75
8. Alvoid Mays, West Virginia, DB, 0/74
9. Bob Mrosko, Penn State, TE, 15/42
10. Tracy Johnson, Clemson, RB, 16/121
11. Brian Smider, West Virginia, T, 0/0
12. Chuck Hartlieb, Iowa, QB, 0/0

INDIANAPOLIS COLTS

1. Andre Rison, Michigan State, WR, 16/186
3. Mitchell Benson, TCU, NT, 25/41
4. Pat Tomberlin, Florida State, G, 16/18
6. Quintus McDonald, Penn State, LB, 40/40
7. Ivy Joe Hunter, Kentucky, RB, 32/45
7. Charles Washington, Cameron, DB, 16/74
8. Kurt Larson, Michigan State, LB, 29/42
9. William Mackall, Tennessee-Martin, WR, 0/0
10. Jim Thompson, Auburn, T, 0/0
11. Wayne Johnson, Georgia, QB, 0/0
12. William DuBose, South Carolina State, RB, 0/0
12. Steve Taylor, Nebraska, QB, 0/0

KANSAS CITY CHIEFS

1. **Derrick Thomas, Alabama, LB, 169/169**
2. Mike Elkins, Wake Forest, QB, 1/1
3. Naz Worthen, North Carolina State, WR, 19/19
4. Stan Petry, TCU, DB, 34/36
6. Robb Thomas, Oregon State, WR, 39/136
7. Ron Sancho, Louisiana State, LB, 0/0
8. **Todd McNair, Temple, RB, 90/121**
8. Bryan Tobey, Grambling, RB, 0/0
9. Jack Phillips, Alcorn State, DB, 0/0
10. Rob McGovern, Holy Cross, LB, 27/46
11. Marcus Turner, UCLA, DB, 0/86
12. Bill Jones, Southwest Texas State, RB, 38/38

LOS ANGELES RAIDERS

6. Jeff Francis, Tennessee, QB, 0/1
6. Doug Lloyd, North Dakota State, RB, 1/1
8. Derrick Gainer, Florida A&M, RB, 2/34
9. Gary Gooden, Indiana, DB, 0/0
10. Charles Jackson, Jackson State, DT, 0/0

LOS ANGELES RAMS

1. **Cleveland Gary, Miami (FL), RB, 66/68**
1. Bill Hawkins, Miami (FL), DE, 42/42
2. **Darryl Henley, UCLA, DB, 76/76**
2. Brian Smith, Auburn, LB, 19/19
2. Frank Stams, Notre Dame, LB, 35/82
3. Kevin Robbins, Michigan State, T, 1/8
4. Jeff Carlson, Weber State, QB, 0/7
5. Alfred Jackson, San Diego State, WR, 12/45
6. Thom Kaumeyer, Oregon, DB, 0/8
6. Mark Messner, Michigan, LB, 4/4
7. George Bethune, Alabama, LB, 32/32
8. Warren Wheat, Brigham Young, G, 0/16
9. Vernon Kirk, Pittsburgh, TE, 0/0
10. Mike Williams, Northeastern, WR, 0/59

MIAMI DOLPHINS

1. **Louis Oliver, Florida, DB, 105/117**
1. Sammie Smith, Florida State, RB, 41/44
4. David Holmes, Syracuse, DB, 0/0
5. **Jeff Uhlenhake, Ohio State, C, 63/119**
6. Wes Pritchett, Notre Dame, LB, 0/3
7. Jim Zdelar, Youngstown, T, 0/0
8. **Pete Stoyanovich, Indiana, K, 110/182**
9. Dana Batiste, Texas A&M, LB, 0/0
10. Deval Glover, Syracuse, WR, 0/0
10. Greg Ross, Memphis State, DT, 0/0
11. **Bert Weidner, Kent State, G, 81/81**
12. **J.B. Brown, Maryland, DB, 122/166**

MINNESOTA VIKINGS

2. David Braxton, Wake Forest, LB, 4/71
3. John Hunter, Brigham Young, T, 0/26
4. Darryl Ingram, California, TE, 16/36
6. Jeff Mickel, Eastern Washington, T, 0/1
7. Benji Roland, Auburn, DE, 0/3
8. Alex Stewart, Cal State-Fullerton, DE, 0/0
11. Brad Baxter, Alabama State, RB, 0/94
12. Shawn Woodson, James Madison, LB, 0/0
12. Everett Ross, Ohio State, WR, 0/0

NEW ENGLAND PATRIOTS

1. Hart Lee Dykes, Oklahoma State, WR, 26/26
2. Eric Coleman, Wyoming, DB, 15/15
3. **Marv Cook, Iowa, TE, 80/112**
3. Chris Gannon, Louisiana-Lafayette, DE, 30/40
4. **Maurice Hurst, Southern (LA), DB, 105/105**
4. **Michael Timpson, Penn State, WR, 70/116**
6. Eric Mitchel, Oklahoma, RB, 0/0
7. Eric Lindstrom, Boston College, LB, 0/0
8. Rodney Rice, Brigham Young, DB, 10/26
8. Tony Zackery, Washington, DB, 18/19
9. Darron Norris, Texas, RB, 0/0
9. Curtis Wilson, Missouri, C, 0/0
10. Emanuel McNeil, Tennessee-Martin, NT, 1/3
11. Tony Hinz, Harvard, RB, 0/0
12. Aaron Chubb, Georgia, LB, 0/0

NEW ORLEANS SAINTS

1. **Wayne Martin, Arkansas, DE, 171/171**
2. Robert Massey, North Carolina Central, DB, 32/133
3. Kim Phillips, North Texas, DB, 5/6
4. Michael Mayes, LSU, DB, 2/27
5. Kevin Haverdink, Western Michigan, T, 41/41
6. **Floyd Turner, Northwestern State (LA), WR, 57/114**
7. David Griggs, Virginia, LB, 0/78
8. Fred Hadley, Mississippi State, WR, 0/0
9. Jerry Leggett, Cal State-Fullerton, LB, 0/0
10. Joe Henderson, Iowa State, RB, 0/0
11. Calvin Nicholson, Oregon State, DB, 9/9
12. Mike Cadore, Eastern Kentucky, WR, 0/0

NEW YORK GIANTS

1. **Brian Williams, Minnesota, C, 129/129**
3. **Greg Jackson, LSU, DB, 75/168**
3. **Bob Kratch, Iowa, G, 65/105**
4. Brad Henke, Arizona, DE, 0/2
4. **Lewis Tillman, Jackson State, RB, 80/109**
5. **Dave Meggett, Towson State, RB, 96/146**
6. **Howard Cross, Alabama, TE, 207/207**
7. Dave Popp, Eastern Illinois, T, 0/0
8. **Myron Guyton, Eastern Kentucky, DB, 68/98**
9. A.J. Greene, Wake Forest, DB, 2/2
10. Rodney Lowe, Mississippi, DE, 0/0
11. Jerome Rinehart, Tennessee-Martin, LB, 0/0
12. Eric Smith, UCLA, LB, 0/0

NEW YORK JETS

1. **Jeff Lageman, Virginia, DE, 82/122**
2. **Dennis Byrd, Tulsa, DT, 57/57**
3. Joe Mott, Iowa, LB, 32/34
4. Ron Stallworth, Auburn, DE, 32/32
5. Tony Martin, Mesa, WR, 0/177
6. Titus Dixon, Troy State, WR, 3/4
6. **Marvin Washington, Idaho, DE, 124/155**
7. Stevon Moore, Mississippi, DB, 0/121
8. A.B. Brown, West Virginia, RB, 33/33
9. Pat Marlatt, West Virginia, DT, 0/0
10. Adam Bob, Texas A&M, LB, 5/5
11. Artie Holmes, Washington State, DB, 0/0
12. Willie Snead, Florida, WR, 0/0

PHILADELPHIA EAGLES

2. Jessie Small, Eastern Kentucky, LB, 47/53
3. Robert Drummond, Syracuse, RB, 36/36
3. **Britt Hager, Texas, LB, 90/121**
6. **Heath Sherman, Texas A&M-Kingsville, RB, 76/76**

PHOENIX CARDINALS

1. **Eric Hill, LSU, LB, 133/160**
S1. Timm Rosenbach, Washington State, QB, 26/26
1. **Joe Wolf, Boston College, T, 94/94**
2. **Walter Reeves, Auburn, TE, 79/98**
3. Mike Zandofsky, Washington, G, 15/116
4. Jim Wahler, UCLA, NT, 49/62
5. Richard Tardits, Georgia, LB, 0/27
5. David Edeen, Wyoming, DE, 0/0
6. Jay Taylor, San Jose State, DB, 48/79
7. Ricky Royal, Sam Houston State, DB, 0/1
8. John Burch, Tennessee-Martin, RB, 0/0
9. Kendall Trainor, Arkansas, K, 0/0
10. Chris Becker, Texas Christian, P, 0/0
11. Jeff Hunter, Albany State (GA), DE, 0/43
12. Todd Nelson, Wisconsin, G, 0/0

PITTSBURGH STEELERS

1. Tom Ricketts, Pittsburgh, G, 42/53
1. Tim Worley, Georgia, RB, 33/48
2. **Carnell Lake, UCLA, DB, 154/185**
3. Derek Hill, Arizona, WR, 32/32
4. **Jerrol Williams, Purdue, LB, 64/85**
5. David Arnold, Michigan, DB, 15/15
6. Mark Stock, VMI, WR, 8/25
7. **D.J. Johnson, Kentucky, DB, 79/118**
8. Chris Asbeck, Cincinnati, DT, 0/0
9. A.J. Jenkins, Cal State-Fullerton, LB, 21/21
10. **Jerry Olsavsky, Pittsburgh, LB, 108/117**
11. Brian Slater, Washington, WR, 0/0
12. **Carlton Haselrig, Pittsburgh-Johnstown, G, 57/68**

SAN DIEGO CHARGERS

1. **Burt Grossman, Pittsburgh, DE, 72/86**
2. **Courtney Hall, Rice, C, 118/118**
2. Billy Joe Tolliver, Texas Tech, QB, 20/79
5. Elliot Smith, Alcorn State, DB, 2/11
7. **Marion Butts, Florida State, RB, 76/104**
7. Terrence Jones, Tulane, QB, 0/0
8. Dana Brinson, Nebraska, WR, 10/10
9. Pat Davis, Syracuse, TE, 0/0
10. Ricky Andrews, Washington, LB, 0/15
11. Victor Floyd, Florida State, RB, 6/6

SAN FRANCISCO 49ERS

1. **Keith DeLong, Tennessee, LB, 64/64**
2. **Wesley Walls, Mississippi, TE, 53/196**
3. Keith Henderson, Georgia, RB, 24/37
4. Michael Barber, Marshall, WR, 8/41
5. **Johnnie Jackson, Houston, DB, 53/55**
6. Steve Hendrickson, California, LB, 11/100
9. Rudy Harmon, Louisiana State, LB, 0/0
10. Andy Sinclair, Stanford, C, 0/0

11. Jim Bell, Boston College, RB, 0/0
11. Norm McGee, North Dakota, WR, 0/0
12. **Antonio Goss, North Carolina, LB, 84/92**

SEATTLE SEAHAWKS

1. **Andy Heck, Notre Dame, T, 77/185**
2. Joe Tofflemire, Arizona, C, 33/33
3. Elroy Harris, Eastern Kentucky, RB, 14/14
4. Travis McNeal, Tennessee-Chattanooga, TE, 48/76
4. James Henry, South Mississippi, DB, 0/0
7. Mike Nettles, Memphis State, DB, 0/0
8. Martin Williams, Western Illinois, DE, 0/0
9. David Franks, Connecticut, G, 0/0
10. Derrick Fenner, North Carolina, RB, 32/120
11. Mike Baum, Northwestern, DE, 0/0
12. R.J. Kors, Long Beach State, DB, 0/37

TAMPA BAY BUCCANEERS

1. **Broderick Thomas, Nebraska, LB, 80/144**
2. Danny Peebles, North Carolina State, WR, 23/30
4. Anthony Florence, Bethune-Cookman, DB, 0/6
5. Jamie Lawson, Nicholls State, RB, 11/12
6. Chris Mohr, Alabama, P, 16/239
6. Derrick Little, South Carolina, LB, 0/0
8. Carl Bax, Missouri, G, 15/15
9. Patrick Egu, Nevada-Reno, RB, 0/7
10. Ty Granger, Clemson, T, 0/0
11. Rod Mounts, Texas A&I, G, 0/0
11. Willie Griffin, Nebraska, DE, 0/0
11. Herb Duncan, Northern Arizona, WR, 0/0
12. Terry Young, Georgia Southern, DB, 0/0

WASHINGTON REDSKINS

3. Tracy Rocker, Auburn, DT, 24/24
4. Erik Affholter, USC, WR, 0/4
5. Lybrant Robinson, Delaware State, DE, 5/5
5. Tim Smiley, Arkansas State, DB, 0/0
6. **A.J. Johnson, Southwest Texas State, DB, 70/71**
6. A.J. Johnson, Southwest Texas State, DB, 0/0
7. Kevin Hendrix, South Carolina, LB, 0/0
9. Charles Darrington, Kentucky, TE, 0/0
10. **Mark Schlereth, Idaho, G, 75/156**
12. Jimmie Johnson, Howard, TE, 38/118
12. Joe Mickles, Mississippi, RB, 9/10

1990 NFL

ATLANTA FALCONS

1. **Steve Broussard, Washington State, RB, 50/121**
2. **Darion Conner, Jackson State, LB, 61/114**
3. Oliver Barnett, Kentucky, DE, 46/85
5. Reggie Redding, Cal State-Fullerton, G, 13/27
6. Mike Pringle, Cal State-Fullerton, RB, 3/3
8. **Tory Epps, Memphis, NT, 50/70**
9. Darrell Jordan, Northern Arizona, LB, 0/0
10. Donnie Salum, Arizona, LB, 0/0
11. Chris Ellison, Houston, DB, 0/0
12. Shawn McCarthy, Purdue, P, 0/29

BUFFALO BILLS

1. **James Williams, Fresno State, DB, 54/70**
2. **Carwell Gardner, Louisville, FB, 83/101**
3. **Glenn Parker, Arizona, G, 104/174**
4. Eddie Fuller, LSU, RB, 20/20
6. John Nies, Arizona, P, 4/4
7. Fred DeRiggi, Syracuse, NT, 0/2
7. Brent Griffith, Minnesota-Duluth, G, 0/0
7. Brent Collins, Carson-Newman, LB, 0/0
8. **Marvcus Patton, UCLA, LB, 80/208**
9. Clarkston Hines, Duke, WR, 0/0
10. **Mike Lodish, UCLA, NT, 74/166**
11. Al Edwards, Northwestern State (LA), WR, 37/37

CHICAGO BEARS

1. **Mark Carrier, USC, DB, 109/168**
2. **Ron Cox, Fresno State, LB, 97/113**
2. Fred Washington, TCU, DT, 11/11
3. **Tim Ryan, USC, DE, 58/58**
3. Peter Tom Willis, Florida State, QB, 21/21
4. Tony Moss, Louisiana State, WR, 0/0
5. Pat Chaffey, Oregon State, RB, 0/31
6. **John Mangum, Alabama, DB, 105/105**
7. Bill Anderson, Iowa, C, 0/0
8. James Rouse, Arkansas, RB, 30/30
9. Johnny Bailey, Texas A&M-Kingsville, RB, 30/81
10. Terry Price, Texas A&M, DE, 2/2
11. Brent White, Michigan, DE, 0/0
11. Roman Matusz, Pittsburgh, T, 0/0
12. Anthony Cooney, Arkansas, DB, 0/0

CINCINNATI BENGALS

1. **James Francis, Baylor, LB, 133/143**
2. **Harold Green, South Carolina, RB, 86/124**
3. Bernard Clark, Miami (FL), LB, 26/28
4. Mike Brennan, Notre Dame, T, 19/19
5. Lynn James, Arizona State, WR, 21/25
6. Don Odegard, UNLV, DB, 0/30
7. Craig Ogletree, Auburn, LB, 11/11
8. Doug Wellsandt, Washington State, TE, 0/16
9. Mitchell Price, Tulane, DB, 34/41
10. Eric Crigler, Murray State, T, 0/0
11. Tim O'Connor, Virginia, T, 0/0
12. Andre Riley, Washington, WR, 0/0

CLEVELAND BROWNS

2. **Leroy Hoard, Michigan, RB, 92/144**
3. **Anthony Pleasant, Tennessee State, DE, 106/202**
4. Harlon Barnett, Michigan State, DB, 38/99
5. **Rob Burnett, Syracuse, DE, 175/202**
6. **Randy Hilliard, Northwestern State (LA), DB, 57/120**
7. Scott Galbraith, USC, TE, 46/117
8. Jock Jones, Virginia Tech, LB, 20/46
9. Eugene Rowell, Southern Mississippi, WR, 3/3
10. Michael Wallace, Jackson State, DB, 0/0
11. Clemente Gordon, Grambling, QB, 0/0
12. Kerry Simien, Texas A&I, WR, 0/0

DALLAS COWBOYS

1. **Emmitt Smith, Florida, RB, 201/226**
2. Alexander Wright, Auburn, WR, 34/86
3. **Jimmie Jones, Miami (FL), DT, 63/121**
5. Stan Smagala, Notre Dame, DB, 11/11
9. **Kenneth Gant, Albany State (GA), DB, 72/113**
11. Dave Harper, Humboldt State, LB, 6/6

DENVER BRONCOS

2. Alton Montgomery, Houston, DB, 43/68
4. Jeroy Robinson, Texas A&M, LB, 3/6
5. Jeff Davidson, Ohio State, G, 44/44
5. **Le-Lo Lang, Washington, DB, 54/54**
6. Ronnie Haliburton, LSU, TE, 17/17
7. **Shannon Sharpe, Savannah State, TE, 172/204**
8. Brad Leggett, USC, C, 0/4
9. Todd Ellis, South Carolina, QB, 0/0
10. Jim Szymanski, Michigan State, DE, 7/7
10. Anthony Thompson, East Carolina, LB, 10/10

DETROIT LIONS

1. Andre Ware, Houston, QB, 14/14
2. **Dan Owens, USC, DE, 114/145**
3. **Marc Spindler, Pittsburgh, DE, 82/107**
4. Chris Oldham, Oregon, DB, 16/155
4. Rob Hinckley, Stanford, LB, 0/0
5. **Jeff Campbell, Colorado, WR, 52/68**
6. Maurice Henry, Kansas State, LB, 0/7
7. **Tracy Hayworth, Tennessee, LB, 72/72**
8. Roman Fortin, San Diego State, C, 16/147
8. Willie Green, Mississippi, WR, 47/114
9. Jack Linn, West Virginia, T, 7/11
10. Bill Miller, Illinois State, WR, 0/0
11. Reginald Warnsley, Southern Mississippi, RB, 0/0
12. Robert Claiborne, San Diego State, WR, 0/14

GREEN BAY PACKERS

1. **Tony Bennett, Mississippi, DE, 56/108**
1. **Darrell Thompson, Minnesota, RB, 60/60**
2. **LeRoy Butler, Florida State, DB, 181/181**
3. Bobby Houston, North Carolina State, LB, 1/109
4. **Jackie Harris, Louisiana-Monroe, TE, 60/167**
5. Charles Wilson, Memphis, WR, 30/76
6. **Bryce Paup, Northern Iowa, LB, 64/148**
7. Lester Archambeau, Stanford, DE, 36/147
8. Roger Brown, Virginia Tech, DB, 0/37
9. Kirk Baumgartner, Wisconsin-Stevens Point, QB, 0/0
10. Jerome Martin, Western Kentucky, DB, 0/0
11. Harry Jackson, St. Cloud (MN), RB, 0/0
12. Kirk Maggio, UCLA, P, 0/0

HOUSTON OILERS

1. **Lamar Lathon, Houston, LB, 67/115**
2. Jeff Alm, Notre Dame, DT, 44/44
3. Willis Peguese, Miami (FL), DE, 10/35
4. Eric Still, Tennessee, G, 0/0
5. Richard Newbill, Miami (FL), LB, 0/11
6. Tony Jones, Texas, WR, 33/43
7. Andy Murray, Kentucky, RB, 0/0
8. Brett Tucker, Northern Illinois, DB, 0/0
9. **Pat Coleman, Mississippi, WR, 51/52**
10. Dee Thomas, Nicholls State, DB, 6/6
11. Joey Banes, Houston, T, 0/1
12. Reggie Slack, Auburn, QB, 0/0

INDIANAPOLIS COLTS

1. **Jeff George, Illinois, QB, 52/131**
2. **Anthony Johnson, Notre Dame, RB, 53/159**
4. Rick Cunningham, Texas A&M, T, 2/80
4. Alan Grant, Stanford, DB, 32/72
4. William Schultz, USC, G, 46/56
4. Stacey Simmons, Florida, WR, 14/14
6. Tony Walker, Southeast Missouri State, LB, 43/43
7. James Singletary, East Carolina, LB, 0/0
8. Ken Clark, Nebraska, TE, 34/34
8. Harvey Wilson, Southern, DB, 0/0
9. Darvell Huffman, Boston University, WR, 3/3
11. Carnel Smith, Pittsburgh, DE, 0/0
12. Gene Benhart, Western Illinois, QB, 0/0
12. Dean Brown, Notre Dame, G, 0/0

KANSAS CITY CHIEFS

1. Percy Snow, Michigan State, LB, 30/40
2. **Tim Grunhard, Notre Dame, C, 169/169**
4. Fred Jones, Grambling State, WR, 41/41
5. **Derrick Graham, Appalachian State, G, 51/99**
5. Ken Hackemack, Texas, T, 0/0
6. Tom Sims, Pittsburgh, DT, 26/47
7. **Dave Szott, Penn State, G, 142/177**
9. Michael Owens, Syracuse, RB, 0/0
10. Craig Hudson, Wisconsin, TE, 0/0
11. Ernest Thompson, Georgia Southern, RB, 0/0
12. Tony Jeffery, San Jose State, WR, 0/0

LOS ANGELES RAIDERS

1. **Anthony Smith, Arizona, DE, 98/98**
2. **Aaron Wallace, Texas A&M, LB, 102/102**
4. **Torin Dorn, North Carolina, DB, 62/84**
6. Marcus Wilson, Virginia, RB, 1/49
7. Garry Lewis, Alcorn State, DB, 28/45
8. A.J. Jimerson, Norfolk State, LB, 17/17
9. Leon Perry, Oklahoma, RB, 0/0
11. Ron Lewis, Jackson State, WR, 0/0
11. Myron Jones, Fresno State, DB, 0/0
12. Major Harris, West Virginia, QB, 0/0
12. Demetrius Davis, Nevada-Reno, TE, 0/0

LOS ANGELES RAMS

1. **Bern Brostek, Washington, C, 106/106**
2. **Pat Terrell, Notre Dame, DB, 59/139**
3. Latin Berry, Oregon, DB, 16/32
6. Tim Stallworth, Washington State, WR, 0/1
7. Kent Elmore, Tennessee, P, 0/0
8. Elbert Crawford, Arkansas, G, 0/30
8. Ray Savage, Virginia, LB, 0/0
9. Tony Lomack, Florida, WR, 3/4
10. Steve Bates, James Madison, DE, 0/0
11. Bill Goldberg, Georgia, NT, 0/14
12. **David Lang, Northern Arizona, RB, 51/67**

MIAMI DOLPHINS

1. **Richmond Webb, Texas A&M, T, 164/184**
2. **Keith Sims, Iowa State, G, 113/142**
3. Alfred Oglesby, Houston, NT, 31/59
4. Scott Mitchell, Utah, QB, 31/99
5. Leroy Holt, Southern California, RB, 0/0
6. Sean Vanhorse, Howard, DB, 0/70
8. Thomas Woods, Tennessee, WR, 0/0
9. Phil Ross, Oregon State, TE, 0/0
12. Bobby Harden, Miami (FL), DB, 29/29

MINNESOTA VIKINGS

3. Marion Hobby, Tennessee, DE, 0/42
3. Mike Jones, Texas A&M, TE, 27/31
4. Alonzo Hampton, Pittsburgh, DB, 10/25
5. Cedric Smith, Florida, FB, 15/72
5. Reggie Thornton, Bowling Green State, WR, 0/6
7. John Levelis, C.W. Post, LB, 0/0
8. Craig Schlichting, Wyoming, DE, 0/0
9. Terry Allen, Clemson, RB, 47/130
10. Pat Newman, Utah State, WR, 0/34
10. Donald Smith, Liberty, DB, 0/3
12. Ron Goetz, Minnesota, LB, 0/0

NEW ENGLAND PATRIOTS

1. **Ray Agnew, North Carolina State, DT, 66/157**
1. Chris Singleton, Arizona, LB, 41/91
3. Tom Hodson, LSU, QB, 32/36
3. **Greg McMurtry, Michigan, WR, 58/67**
5. Jon Melander, Minnesota, G, 10/54
5. Junior Robinson, East Carolina, DB, 16/26
5. James Gray, Texas Tech, RB, 0/0
9. Shawn Bouwens, Nebraska Wesleyan, G, 0/73
10. Anthony Landry, Stephen F. Austin State, RB, 0/0
11. Sean Smith, Georgia Tech, DE, 17/17
12. Ventson Donelson, Michigan State, DB, 0/0
12. Blaine Rose, Maryland, G, 0/0

NEW ORLEANS SAINTS

1. **Renaldo Turnbull, West Virginia, DE, 104/120**
2. **Vince Buck, Central State (OH), DB, 84/84**
3. **Joel Smeenge, Western Michigan, DE, 72/156**
4. **DeMond Winston, Vanderbilt, LB, 51/51**
5. Charles Arbuckle, UCLA, TE, 0/42
6. Mike Buck, Maine, QB, 8/12
6. **James E. Williams, Mississippi State, LB, 78/137**
7. Scott Hough, Maine, G, 0/0
8. Gerry Gdowski, Nebraska, QB, 0/0
8. Derrick Carr, Bowling Green, DE, 0/0
9. Broderick Graves, Winston-Salem State, RB, 0/0
9. Lonnie Brockman, West Virginia, LB, 0/0
10. Ernest Spears, USC, DB, 16/16
10. Gary Cooper, Clemson, WR, 0/0
11. Webbie Burnett, Western Kentucky, DT, 0/0
12. **Chris Port, Duke, G, 69/69**

NEW YORK GIANTS

1. **Rodney Hampton, Georgia, RB, 104/104**
2. **Mike Fox, West Virginia, DE, 79/133**
3. Greg Mark, Miami (FL), DE, 0/6
4. Dave Whitmore, Stephen F. Austin State, DB, 16/64
5. Craig Kupp, Pacific Lutheran, QB, 0/1
7. Aaron Emanuel, Southern California, RB, 0/0
8. Barry Voorhees, Cal State-Northridge, T, 0/0
9. Clint James, Louisiana State, DE, 0/0
10. Otis Moore, Clemson, DT, 0/0
11. Tim Downing, Washington State, DE, 0/0
12. Matt Stover, Louisiana Tech, K, 0/239

NEW YORK JETS

S1. **Rob Moore, Syracuse, WR, 76/153**
1. **Blair Thomas, Penn State, RB, 51/64**
2. Reggie Rembert, West Virginia, WR, 0/28
3. Tony Stargell, Tennessee State, DB, 32/94
4. Troy Taylor, California, QB, 7/7
5. Tony Savage, Washington State, NT, 0/5
5. Robert McWright, Texas Christian, DB, 0/0
6. **Terance Mathis, New Mexico, WR, 64/206**
7. **Dwayne White, Alcorn State, G, 74/105**
7. Basil Proctor, West Virginia, LB, 0/0
8. **Roger Duffy, Penn State, G, 123/175**
9. Dale Dawkins, Miami (FL), WR, 36/36
10. Brad Quast, Iowa, LB, 0/0
11. Derrick Kelson, Purdue, DB, 0/0
12. Darrell Davis, TCU, DE, 28/28

PHILADELPHIA EAGLES

1. Ben Smith, Georgia, DB, 39/57
2. Mike Bellamy, Illinois, WR, 6/6
3. **Fred Barnett, Arkansas State, WR, 81/96**
5. **Calvin Williams, Purdue, WR, 93/100**
6. Kevin Thompson, Oklahoma, DB, 0/0
7. Terry Strouf, Wisconsin-LaCrosse, T, 0/0
8. Curt Dykes, Oregon, T, 0/0
9. Cecil Gray, North Carolina, DE, 14/45
10. Orlando Adams, Jacksonville State, DT, 0/0
11. **John Hudson, Auburn, G, 67/139**
11. Tyrone Watson, Tennessee State, WR, 0/0
12. Judd Garrett, Princeton, RB, 0/0

PHOENIX CARDINALS

2. Anthony Thompson, Indiana, RB, 30/37
3. **Ricky Proehl, Wake Forest, WR, 80/242**
4. Travis Davis, Michigan State, NT, 0/18
5. **Larry Centers, Stephen F. Austin State, FB, 126/198**
6. Tyrone Shavers, Lamar, WR, 0/1
7. Johnny Johnson, San Jose State, RB, 41/72
8. Mickey Washington, Texas A&M, DB, 0/108
9. David Bavaro, Syracuse, LB, 14/42
S9. Willie Williams, LSU, T, 16/32
10. Dave Elle, South Dakota, TE, 0/0
11. Dempsey Norman, St. Francis (IL), WR, 0/0
12. Donnie Riley, Central Michigan, RB, 0/0
12. Ken McMichel, Oklahoma, DB, 0/0

PITTSBURGH STEELERS

1. **Eric Green, Liberty, TE, 62/120**
2. **Kenny Davidson, LSU, DE, 59/93**
3. **Neil O'Donnell, Maryland, QB, 66/124**
3. Craig Veasey, Houston, DT, 23/69
4. Chris Calloway, Michigan, WR, 28/158
5. **Barry Foster, Arkansas, RB, 62/62**
6. Ronald Heard, Bowling Green, WR, 0/0
7. Dan Grayson, Washington State, LB, 0/0
8. Karl Dunbar, LSU, DE, 0/21
9. **Gary Jones, Texas A&M, DB, 52/78**
10. Eddie Miles, Minnesota, LB, 1/1
11. **Justin Strzelczyk, Maine, T, 133/133**
12. Richard Bell, Nebraska, RB, 8/8

SAN DIEGO CHARGERS

1. **Junior Seau, USC, LB, 200/230**
3. Leo Goeas, Hawaii, G, 40/111
3. Jeff Mills, Nebraska, LB, 5/46
3. Walter Wilson, East Carolina, TE, 14/14
6. Frank Cornish, UCLA, C, 32/69
6. John Friesz, Idaho, QB, 29/69
6. David Pool, Carson-Newman, DB, 0/43
6. **Derrick Walker, Michigan, TE, 60/129**
7. **Nate Lewis, Oregon Tech, WR, 58/82**
7. Jeff Novak, Southwest Texas State, G, 0/40
7. Joe Staysniak, Ohio State, G, 0/63
7. Keith Collins, Appalachian State, DB, 0/0
8. J.J. Flannigan, Colorado, RB, 0/0
9. Chris Goetz, Pittsburgh, G, 0/0
10. Kenny Berry, Miami (FL), DB, 0/0
11. Tommie Stowers, Missouri, TE, 0/17
12. Elliott Searcy, Southern, WR, 0/0

SAN FRANCISCO 49ERS

1. **Dexter Carter, Florida State, RB, 90/100**
2. **Dennis Brown, Washington, DE, 109/109**
2. **Eric Davis, Jacksonville State, DB, 81/188**
3. Ron Lewis, Florida State, WR, 13/34
4. Dean Caliguire, Pittsburgh, G, 2/9
6. **Frank Pollack, Northern Arizona, T, 89/89**
8. Dwight Pickens, Fresno State, WR, 0/0
9. Odell Haggins, Florida State, NT, 0/5
10. Martin Harrison, Washington, DE, 29/81
11. Anthony Shelton, Tennessee State, DB, 0/25

SEATTLE SEAHAWKS

1. **Cortez Kennedy, Miami (FL), DT, 167/167**
2. **Robert Blackmon, Baylor, DB, 106/135**
2. **Terry Wooden, Syracuse, LB, 89/120**
4. **Chris Warren, Ferrum, RB, 123/162**
5. Eric Hayes, Florida State, DT, 21/24
6. Ned Bolcar, Notre Dame, LB, 5/13
7. Bob Kula, Michigan State, T, 0/0
8. **Bill Hitchcock, Purdue, T, 51/51**
10. Robert Morris, Valdosta State, DE, 0/0
11. Daryl Reed, Oregon, DB, 0/0
12. John Gromos, Vanderbilt, QB, 0/0

TAMPA BAY BUCCANEERS

1. Keith McCants, Alabama, DE, 47/88
2. **Reggie Cobb, Tennessee, RB, 60/92**
4. Jesse Anderson, Mississippi State, TE, 32/35
4. **Tony Mayberry, Wake Forest, C, 160/160**
5. **Ian Beckles, Indiana, G, 102/127**
6. Derrick Douglas, Louisiana Tech, RB, 0/2
7. Donnie Gardner, Kentucky, DE, 0/10
9. Terry Cook, Fresno State, DE, 0/0
10. Mike Busch, Iowa State, TE, 0/0
11. Terry Anthony, Florida State, WR, 10/10
12. Todd Hammel, Stephen F. Austin, QB, 0/0

WASHINGTON REDSKINS

2. **Andre Collins, Penn State, LB, 75/144**
3. Mohammed Elewonibi, Brigham Young, T, 20/26
4. Cary Conklin, Washington, QB, 3/7
4. Rico Labbe, Boston College, DB, 0/0
5. **Brian Mitchell, Louisiana-Lafayette, RB, 159/223**
6. Kent Wells, Nebraska, DT, 0/6
9. Tim Moxley, Ohio State, G, 0/0
10. Thomas Rayam, Alabama, G, 0/20
10. D'Juan Francisco, Notre Dame, DB, 0/0
11. Jon Leverenz, Minnesota, LB, 0/0

1991 NFL

ATLANTA FALCONS

1. Bruce Pickens, Nebraska, DB, 27/48
1. Mike Pritchard, Colorado, WR, 47/127
2. Brett Favre, Southern Mississippi, QB, 2/225
4. **Moe Gardner, Illinois, DT, 90/90**
5. James Goode, Oklahoma, LB, 0/0
6. **Erric Pegram, North Texas, RB, 61/103**
7. Brian Mitchell, Brigham Young, DB, 36/36
7. Mark Tucker, USC, G, 0/16
8. Randy Austin, UCLA, TE, 0/0
9. Ernie Logan, East Carolina, NT, 8/119
10. Walter Sutton, Southwest Minnesota, WR, 0/0
10. Pete Lucas, Wisconsin-Stevens Point, T, 0/0
11. Joe Sims, Nebraska, T, 6/53
12. **Bob Christian, Northwestern, RB, 93/135**

BUFFALO BILLS

1. **Henry Jones, Illinois, DB, 144/158**
2. **Phil Hansen, North Dakota State, DE, 156/156**
3. Darryl Wren, Pittsburg State, DB, 0/20
5. Shawn Wilbourn, Long Beach State, DB, 0/0
6. Millard Hamilton, Clark, WR, 0/0
7. Amir Rasul, Florida A&M, RB, 0/0
8. Brad Lamb, Anderson (IN), WR, 8/8
9. **Mark Maddox, Northern Michigan, LB, 67/111**
10. Tony De Lorenzo, New Mexico State, G, 0/0
11. Dean Kirkland, Washington, G, 0/0
12. Stephen Clark, Texas, TE, 0/0

CHICAGO BEARS

1. Stan Thomas, Texas, T, 26/56
2. **Chris Zorich, Notre Dame, DT, 79/84**
3. **Chris Gardocki, Clemson, P, 52/228**
4. Joe Johnson, North Carolina State, DB, 0/0
5. Anthony Morgan, Tennessee, WR, 27/64
6. Darren Lewis, Texas A&M, RB, 33/33
7. Paul Justin, Arizona State, QB, 0/34
8. Larry Horton, Texas A&M, DB, 0/0
9. Mike Stonebreaker, Notre Dame, LB, 16/18
10. Tom Backes, Oklahoma, DE, 0/0
11. Stacy Long, Clemson, G, 0/0
12. John Cook, Washington, DT, 0/0

CINCINNATI BENGALS

1. **Alfred Williams, Colorado, DE, 63/128**
2. Lamar Rogers, Auburn, DE, 26/26
3. Bob Dahl, Notre Dame, G, 0/82
4. Rob Carpenter, Syracuse, WR, 0/60
4. Donald Hollas, Rice, QB, 20/32
5. Mike Arthur, Texas A&M, C, 23/64
6. Richard Fain, Florida, DB, 6/24
7. **Fernandus Vinson, North Carolina State, DB, 58/58**
8. Mike Dingle, South Carolina, RB, 8/8
9. Shane Garrett, Texas A&M, WR, 4/4
10. Jim Lavin, Georgia Tech, G, 0/0
11. Chris Smith, Brigham Young, TE, 0/0
12. Antoine Bennett, Florida A&M, DB, 14/14

CLEVELAND BROWNS

1. **Eric Turner, UCLA, DB, 77/109**
2. Ed King, Auburn, G, 38/57
3. **James Jones, Northern Iowa, DT, 112/160**
4. **Pio Sagapolutele, San Diego State, DT, 63/92**
6. **Michael Jackson, Southern Mississippi, WR, 114/114**
8. Frank Conover, Syracuse, DT, 4/4
9. Raymond Irvin, Central Florida, DB, 0/0
9. Shawn Wiggins, Wyoming, WR, 0/0
10. Brian Greenfield, Pittsburgh, P, 0/0
11. Todd Jones, Henderson State, T, 0/4
12. Elijah Austin, North Carolina State, DT, 0/0

DALLAS COWBOYS

1. **Alvin Harper, Tennessee, WR, 65/102**
1. **Russell Maryland, Miami (FL), DT, 75/154**
1. Kelvin Pritchett, Mississippi, DT, 0/208
2. **Dixon Edwards, Michigan State, LB, 75/120**
3. **Godfrey Myles, Florida, LB, 76/76**
3. **Erik Williams, Central State (OH), T, 141/146**
3. James Richards, California, G, 0/0
4. Tony Hill, Tennessee-Chattanooga, DE, 13/13
4. Bill Musgrave, Oregon, QB, 0/12
4. Curvin Richards, Pittsburgh, RB, 11/12
4. Kevin Harris, Texas Southern, DE, 0/0
5. Darrick Brownlow, Illinois, LB, 32/95
6. Mike Sullivan, Miami (FL), G, 0/48
7. **Leon Lett, Emporia State, DT, 109/121**
9. Damon Mays, Missouri, WR, 0/2
10. Sean Love, Penn State, G, 0/19
11. Tony Boles, Michigan, RB, 0/0
12. **Larry Brown, TCU, DB, 83/95**

DENVER BRONCOS

1. **Mike Croel, Nebraska, LB, 58/102**
2. Reggie Johnson, Florida State, TE, 44/77
3. **Keith Traylor, Central Oklahoma, DT, 94/200**
4. **Derek Russell, Arkansas, WR, 50/88**
5. Greg Lewis, Washington, RB, 32/32
6. Nick Subis, San Diego State, T, 16/16
8. Kenny Walker, Nebraska, DE, 31/31
9. Don Gibson, Southern California, DT, 0/0
10. Curtis Mayfield, Oklahoma State, WR, 0/0
11. Shawn Moore, Virginia, QB, 3/3

DETROIT LIONS

1. **Herman Moore, Virginia, WR, 145/146**
3. Reggie Barrett, Texas-El Paso, WR, 10/10
4. Kevin Scott, Stanford, DB, 44/44
5. **Scott Conover, Purdue, T, 67/67**
6. Richie Andrews, Florida State, K, 0/0
7. Franklin Thomas, Grambling, TE, 0/0
8. Cedric Jackson, TCU, RB, 8/8
9. Darryl Milburn, Grambling State, DE, 2/2
11. Slip Watkins, Louisiana State, KR, 0/0
12. Zeno Alexander, Arizona, LB, 0/0

GREEN BAY PACKERS

1. Vinnie Clark, Ohio State, DB, 32/83
2. Esera Tuaolo, Oregon State, NT, 20/111
3. **Don Davey, Wisconsin, DT, 50/92**
3. Chuck Webb, Tennessee, FB, 2/2
5. Jeff Fite, Memphis State, P, 0/0
6. Walter Dean, Grambling State, RB, 9/9
6. Joe Garten, Colorado, C, 0/0
7. Reggie Burnette, Houston, LB, 3/23
7. Frank Blevins, Oklahoma, LB, 0/0
8. Johnny Walker, Texas, WR, 0/0
9. Dean Witkowski, North Dakota, LB, 0/0
10. Rapier Porter, Arkansas-Pine Bluff, TE, 0/0
11. J.J. Wierenga, Central Michigan, DE, 0/0
12. Linzy Collins, Missouri, WR, 0/0

HOUSTON OILERS

2. Mike Dumas, Indiana, DB, 29/102
2. John Flannery, Syracuse, G, 47/80
2. **Darryll Lewis, Arizona, DB, 113/141**
3. **Kevin Donnalley, North Carolina, G, 109/193**
3. **Steve Jackson, Purdue, DB, 118/118**
4. **Marcus Robertson, Iowa State, DB, 135/162**
4. David Rocker, Auburn, DT, 0/34
5. Gary Wellman, USC, WR, 28/28
7. Kyle Freeman, Angelo State, LB, 0/0
8. **Gary Brown, Penn State, RB, 65/99**
9. Shawn Jefferson, Central Florida, WR, 0/195
10. Curtis Moore, Kansas, LB, 0/0
11. James Smith, Richmond, DB, 0/0
12. Alex Johnson, Miami (FL), WR, 5/5

INDIANAPOLIS COLTS

2. Shane Curry, Miami (FL), DE, 9/9
3. Dave McCloughan, Colorado, DB, 15/48
4. Mark Vander Poel, Colorado, T, 23/23
5. **Kerry Cash, Texas, TE, 52/71**
6. Mel Agee, Illinois, DE, 17/54
7. James Bradley, Michigan State, WR, 0/0
8. Tim Bruton, Missouri, TE, 0/0
9. Howard Griffith, Illinois, RB, 0/121
10. Frank Giannetti, Penn State, NT, 3/3
11. Jerry Crafts, Louisville, T, 0/54
12. Rob Luedeke, Penn State, C, 0/0

KANSAS CITY CHIEFS

1. Harvey Williams, LSU, RB, 35/110
2. **Joe Valerio, Pennsylvania, C, 61/62**
3. Tim Barnett, Jackson State, WR, 44/44
5. Charles Mincy, Washington, DB, 48/114
6. Darrell Malone, Jacksonville State, DB, 4/29
7. Bernard Ellison, Nevada-Reno, DB, 0/0
8. Tom Dohring, Michigan, T, 3/3
9. Robbie Keen, California, K, 0/0
10. Eric Ramsey, Auburn, DB, 0/0
11. Bobby Olive, Ohio State, WR, 0/2
12. Ron Shipley, New Mexico, G, 0/0

LOS ANGELES RAIDERS

1. Todd Marinovich, USC, QB, 8/8
2. Nick Bell, Iowa, RB, 35/35
4. Rocket Ismail, Notre Dame, WR, 45/126
6. **Nolan Harrison, Indiana, DE, 82/128**
6. Brian Jones, Texas, LB, 0/44
8. Todd Woulard, Alabama A&M, LB, 0/0
9. Tahaun Lewis, Nebraska, DB, 0/9
10. **Andrew Glover, Grambling State, TE, 93/154**
12. Dennis Johnson, Winston-Salem State, WR, 0/0

LOS ANGELES RAMS

1. **Todd Lyght, Notre Dame, DB, 143/175**
2. **Roman Phifer, UCLA, LB, 120/213**
4. Robert Bailey, Miami (FL), DB, 47/146
5. **Robert Young, Mississippi State, DE, 63/78**
6. Neal Fort, Brigham Young, T, 0/0
7. Tyrone Shelton, William & Mary, RB, 0/0
8. Pat Tyrance, Nebraska, LB, 0/0
9. Jeff Fields, Arkansas State, DT, 0/2
11. Terry Crews, Western Michigan, LB, 6/32
12. Jeff Pahukoa, Washington, G, 39/59
12. Ernie Thompson, Indiana, RB, 4/20

MIAMI DOLPHINS

1. Randal Hill, Miami (FL), WR, 27/103
3. Aaron Craver, Fresno State, RB, 28/103
5. **Bryan Cox, Western Illinois, LB, 77/165**
5. Gene Williams, Iowa State, G, 15/114
7. **Chris Green, Illinois, DB, 50/66**
8. Roland Smith, Miami (FL), DB, 0/0
9. **Scott Miller, UCLA, WR, 55/55**
10. Michael Titley, Iowa, TE, 0/0
11. Ernie Rogers, California, G, 0/0
12. Joe Brunson, Tennessee-Chattanooga, DT, 0/0

MINNESOTA VIKINGS

3. **Carlos Jenkins, Michigan State, LB, 51/80**
3. **Jake Reed, Grambling State, WR, 134/155**
4. Randy Baldwin, Mississippi, RB, 4/65
5. Chris Thome, Minnesota, C, 0/11
6. **Todd Scott, Louisiana-Lafayette, DB, 61/84**
7. Tripp Welborne, Michigan, DB, 2/2
7. Scotty Reagan, Humboldt State, DT, 0/0
8. Reggie Johnson, Arizona, DE, 0/0
9. Gerald Hudson, Oklahoma State, RB, 0/0
10. Brady Pierce, Wisconsin, T, 0/0
11. Ivan Caesar, Boston College, LB, 14/14
12. Darren Hughes, Carson-Newman, WR, 0/0

NEW ENGLAND PATRIOTS

1. **Pat Harlow, USC, T, 74/105**
1. Leonard Russell, Arizona State, RB, 43/85
2. Jerome Henderson, Clemson, DB, 40/98
3. Calvin Stephens, South Carolina, G, 13/13
4. **Scott Zolak, Maryland, QB, 54/55**
5. **Ben Coates, Livingstone, TE, 142/158**
5. Jon Vaughn, Michigan, RB, 32/60
6. David Key, Michigan, DB, 3/3
7. Blake Miller, LSU, C, 0/14
8. Harry Colon, Missouri, DB, 16/87
9. O'Neil Glenn, Maryland, G, 0/0
10. Randy Bethel, Miami (FL), TE, 0/0
11. Vince Moore, Tennessee, WR, 0/0
11. Paul Alsbury, Southwest Texas State, P, 0/0
12. Tim Edwards, Delta State, DT, 14/14

NEW ORLEANS SAINTS

2. Wesley Carroll, Miami (FL), WR, 28/40
5. Reggie Jones, Memphis, DB, 41/41
6. **Fred McAfee, Mississippi College, RB, 118/190**
7. Hayward Haynes, Florida State, G, 0/0
8. Frank Wainright, Northern Colorado, TE, 43/121
9. Anthony Wallace, California, RB, 0/0
11. Scott Ross, USC, LB, 4/4
12. Mark Drabczak, Minnesota, G, 0/0

NEW YORK GIANTS

1. Jarrod Bunch, Michigan, FB, 45/48
2. Kanavis McGhee, Colorado, LB, 40/50
3. Ed McCaffrey, Stanford, WR, 48/185
4. Clarence Jones, Maryland, T, 10/111
5. Anthony Moss, Florida State, LB, 0/0
6. **Corey Miller, South Carolina, LB, 105/110**
7. Simmie Carter, Southern Mississippi, DB, 0/0
8. Lamar McGriggs, Western Illinois, DB, 32/57
9. Jerry Bouldin, Mississippi State, WR, 0/0
10. Luis Cristobal, Miami (FL), G, 0/0
11. Ted Popson, Portland State, TE, 0/68
12. Larry Wanke, John Carroll, QB, 0/0

NEW YORK JETS

2. Browning Nagle, Louisville, QB, 18/24
3. **Mo Lewis, Georgia, LB, 200/200**
4. **Mark Gunn, Pittsburgh, DT, 54/69**
6. Blaise Bryant, Iowa State, RB, 0/0
6. Mike Riley, Tulane, DB, 0/0

7. Doug Parrish, San Francisco State, DB, 0/0
8. Tim James, Colorado, DB, 0/0
9. Paul Glonek, Arizona, DT, 0/0
10. Al Baker, Kentucky, RB, 0/0
11. Rocen Keeton, UCLA, LB, 0/0
12. Mark Hayes, Arizona State, T, 0/0

PHILADELPHIA EAGLES

1. **Antone Davis, Tennessee, T, 78/97**
2. Jesse Campbell, North Carolina State, DB, 0/92
3. Rob Selby, Auburn, G, 32/62
4. **William Thomas, Texas A&M, LB, 140/172**
6. **Andy Harmon, Kent State, DT, 86/86**
7. **James Joseph, Auburn, RB, 62/78**
8. Scott Kowalkowski, Notre Dame, LB, 32/158
9. Chuck Weatherspoon, Houston, RB, 0/4
10. Eric Harmon, Clemson, G, 0/0
11. **Mike Flores, Louisville, DE, 50/61**
12. Darrell Beavers, Morehead State, DB, 0/0

PHOENIX CARDINALS

1. **Eric Swann, none, DT, 111/127**
2. Mike Jones, North Carolina State, DE, 47/135
3. **Aeneas Williams, Southern (LA), DB, 160/211**
4. Dexter Davis, Clemson, DB, 33/59
5. Vance Hammond, Clemson, DT, 0/0
6. Eduardo Vega, Memphis State, T, 0/0
7. Ivory Lee Brown, Arkansas-Pine Bluff, RB, 7/7
8. Jerry Evans, Toledo, TE, 0/43
8. Scott Evans, Oklahoma, DE, 1/1
8. Greg Amsler, Tennessee, RB, 0/0
10. Herbie Anderson, Texas A&M-Kingsville, DB, 0/1
11. Nathan LaDuke, Arizona State, DB, 0/0
12. Jeff Bridewell, Cal-Davis, QB, 0/0

PITTSBURGH STEELERS

1. Huey Richardson, Florida, LB, 5/16
2. Jeff Graham, Ohio State, WR, 42/160
3. **Ernie Mills, Florida, WR, 86/118**
4. Adrian Cooper, Oklahoma, TE, 46/77
5. Sammy Walker, Texas Tech, DB, 18/24
6. Leroy Thompson, Penn State, RB, 43/80
7. Andre Jones, Notre Dame, LB, 0/6
8. Dean Dingman, Michigan, G, 0/0
9. Bruce McGonnigal, Virginia, TE, 0/2
10. Ariel Solomon, Colorado, C, 45/61
11. Efrum Thomas, Alabama, DB, 0/0
12. Jeff Brady, Kentucky, LB, 16/115

SAN DIEGO CHARGERS

1. **Stanley Richard, Texas, DB, 61/124**
2. **Eric Bieniemy, Colorado, RB, 62/142**
2. **Eric Moten, Michigan State, G, 67/67**
2. George Thornton, Alabama, DT, 32/37
4. Yancey Thigpen, Winston-Salem State, WR, 4/112
5. Floyd Fields, Arizona State, DB, 30/30
5. **Duane Young, Michigan State, TE, 69/73**
6. Jimmy Laister, Oregon Tech, T, 0/0
7. David Jones, Delaware State, TE, 0/16
7. Terry Beauford, Florida A&M, G, 0/0
9. Andy Katoa, Southern Oregon, LB, 0/0
10. Ronald Poles, Tennessee, RB, 0/0
10. Mike Heldt, Notre Dame, C, 0/0
11. Joachim Weinberg, Johnson C. Smith, WR, 0/0
12. Chris Samuels, Texas, RB, 3/3

SAN FRANCISCO 49ERS

1. Ted Washington, Louisville, NT, 44/215
2. John Johnson, Clemson, LB, 40/46
3. Ricky Watters, Notre Dame, RB, 43/144
4. Mitch Donahue, Wyoming, LB, 15/31
5. Harry Boatswain, New Haven, G, 45/74
5. **Merton Hanks, Iowa, DB, 125/137**
6. Scott Bowles, North Texas State, T, 0/0
7. Sheldon Canley, San Jose State, RB, 0/1
8. Tony Hargain, Oregon, WR, 0/12
9. Louis Riddick, Pittsburgh, DB, 0/94
10. Byron Holdbrooks, Alabama, DT, 0/0
11. Bobby Slaughter, Louisiana Tech, WR, 0/0
12. Cliff Confer, Michigan State, DE, 0/0

SEATTLE SEAHAWKS

1. Dan McGwire, San Diego State, QB, 12/13
2. Doug Thomas, Clemson, WR, 39/39
3. David Daniels, Penn State, WR, 29/29
4. **John Kasay, Georgia, K, 64/205**
5. Harlan Davis, Tennessee, DB, 0/0
6. **Michael Sinclair, Eastern New Mexico, DE, 144/148**
10. Erik Ringoen, Hofstra, LB, 0/0
11. Tony Stewart, Iowa, RB, 0/0
12. Ike Harris, South Carolina, G, 0/0

TAMPA BAY BUCCANEERS

1. **Charles McRae, Tennessee, T, 71/83**
3. **Lawrence Dawsey, Florida State, WR, 57/83**
3. Robert Wilson, Texas A&M, RB, 16/51
4. Tony Covington, Virginia, DB, 31/42
5. Tim Ryan, Notre Dame, G, 37/37
5. Terry Bagsby, East Texas State, LB, 0/0
6. Rhett Hall, California, DT, 21/68
7. Calvin Tiggle, Georgia Tech, LB, 24/24
8. **Marty Carter, Middle Tennessee State, DB, 62/161**
9. Treamelle Taylor, Nevada-Reno, WR, 0/0
10. Pat O'Hara, Southern California, QB, 0/0
10. Hyland Hickson, Michigan State, RB, 0/0
11. Mike Sunvold, Minnesota, DT, 0/0
12. Al Chamblee, Virginia Tech, LB, 22/22

WASHINGTON REDSKINS

1. Bobby Wilson, Michigan State, DT, 42/42
3. **Ricky Ervins, USC, RB, 62/76**
6. Dennis Ransom, Texas A&M, TE, 0/0
7. Keith Cash, Texas, TE, 0/64
8. Jimmy Spencer, Florida, DB, 0/177
9. Charles Bell, Baylor, DB, 0/0
10. Cris Shale, Bowling Green, P, 0/0
11. David Gulledge, Jacksonville State, DB, 4/4
12. Keenan McCardell, UNLV, WR, 0/185

1992 NFL

ATLANTA FALCONS

1. Tony Smith, Southern Mississippi, RB, 33/33
1. **Bob Whitfield, Stanford, T, 178/204**
2. **Chuck Smith, Tennessee, DE, 123/125**
3. Howard Dinkins, Florida State, LB, 3/3
4. Frankie Smith, Baylor, DB, 0/103
6. Terry Ray, Oklahoma, DB, 10/73
7. Tim Paulk, Florida, LB, 0/0
8. Derrick Moore, Northeastern State (OK), RB, 0/42
8. Reggie Dwight, Troy State, TE, 0/0
9. Keith Alex, Texas A&M, G, 14/14
10. Darryl Hardy, Tennessee, LB, 0/23
11. Robin Jones, Baylor, DE, 0/0

BUFFALO BILLS

1. **John Fina, Arizona, T, 148/155**
2. James Patton, Texas, NT, 13/13
3. Keith Goganious, Penn State, LB, 45/74
4. Frank Kmet, Purdue, DE, 0/0
5. **Matt Darby, UCLA, DB, 55/81**
6. Nate Turner, Nebraska, TE, 26/28
7. **Kurt Schulz, Eastern Washington, DB, 107/129**
8. Leonard Humphries, Penn State, DB, 0/13
9. Chris Walsh, Stanford, WR, 5/139
10. Barry Rose, Wisconsin-Stevens Point, WR, 0/3
11. Vince Marrow, Toledo, TE, 10/10
12. Matt Rodgers, Iowa, QB, 0/0

CHICAGO BEARS

1. **Alonzo Spellman, Ohio State, DE, 86/123**
2. Troy Auzenne, California, T, 49/61
3. Jeremy Lincoln, Tennessee, DB, 47/107
4. Will Furrer, Virginia Tech, QB, 2/9
5. Todd Harrison, North Carolina State, TE, 0/1
6. Mark Berry, Texas, DB, 0/0
7. John Brown, Houston, WR, 0/0
9. Mirko Jurkovic, Notre Dame, G, 0/0
10. Nikki Fisher, Virginia, RB, 0/0
11. Louis Age, Louisiana-Lafayette, T, 6/6
12. Chris Wilson, Oklahoma, LB, 0/0

CINCINNATI BENGALS

1. David Klingler, Houston, QB, 31/33
1. **Darryl Williams, Miami (FL), DB, 95/156**
2. **Carl Pickens, Tennessee, WR, 120/129**
3. **Leonard Wheeler, Troy State, DB, 61/92**
4. **Ricardo McDonald, Pittsburgh, LB, 88/119**
5. Craig Thompson, North Carolina A&T, TE, 29/29
6. Chris Burns, Middle Tennessee State, DT, 0/0
7. Lance Olberding, Iowa, T, 0/0
8. Roosevelt Nix, Central State (OH), DE, 16/18
9. Ostell Miles, Houston, RB, 26/26
10. Horace Smith, Oregon Tech, DB, 0/0
11. John Earle, Western Illinois, T, 0/0
12. Eric Shaw, Louisiana Tech, LB, 28/28

CLEVELAND BROWNS

1. Tommy Vardell, Stanford, RB, 40/87
2. Patrick Rowe, San Diego State, WR, 5/5
3. Gerald Dixon, South Carolina, LB, 43/136
3. Bill Johnson, Michigan State, DT, 39/98
6. Rico Smith, Colorado, WR, 29/29
6. George Williams, Notre Dame, DT, 0/0
7. Selwyn Jones, Colorado State, DB, 11/47
9. Tim Hill, Kansas, DB, 0/0
10. Marcus Lowe, Baylor, DT, 0/0
11. Augustin Olobia, Washington State, WR, 0/0
12. Tim Simpson, Illinois, G, 0/4
12. Keithen McCant, Nebraska, QB, 0/0

DALLAS COWBOYS

1. **Robert Jones, East Carolina, LB, 56/151**
1. **Kevin Smith, Texas A&M, DB, 103/103**
2. Jimmy Smith, Jackson State, WR, 7/178
2. **Darren Woodson, Arizona State, DB, 178/178**
3. James Brown, Virginia State, T, 0/114
3. Clayton Holmes, Carson-Newman, DB, 39/39
4. Tom Myslinski, Tennessee, G, 10/57
5. Gregg Briggs, Texas Southern, DB, 11/39
5. Rod Milstead, Delaware State, G, 0/56
6. Fallon Wacasey, Tulsa, TE, 0/0
9. Chris Hall, East Carolina, DB, 1/1
9. Nate Kirtman, Pomona-Pitzer, DB, 0/0
10. John Terry, Livingstone, G, 0/0
11. Tim Daniel, Florida A&M, WR, 0/0
12. Don Harris, Texas Tech, DB, 0/0

DENVER BRONCOS

1. Tommy Maddox, UCLA, QB, 29/93
2. **Shane Dronett, Texas, DT, 61/139**
4. Chuck Johnson, Texas, T, 16/16
5. Frank Robinson, Boise State, DB, 28/31
7. Ron Geater, Iowa, DE, 3/3
7. Jim Johnson, Michigan State, T, 0/0
7. Jon Bostick, Nebraska, WR, 0/0
8. Dietrich Lockridge, Jackson State, G, 0/0
9. Muhammad Oliver, Oregon, DB, 3/21
10. Bob Meeks, Auburn, C, 8/8
11. Cedric Tillman, Alcorn State, WR, 39/52
12. John Granby, Virginia Tech, WR, 4/4

DETROIT LIONS

1. **Robert Porcher, South Carolina State, DE, 187/187**
2. **Jason Hanson, Washington State, K, 223/223**
2. **Tracy Scroggins, Tulsa, DE, 142/142**
3. Thomas McLemore, Southern (LA), TE, 11/18
6. Larry Tharpe, Tennessee State, T, 48/76
8. **Willie Clay, Georgia Tech, DB, 54/118**
11. Ed Tillison, Northwest Missouri State, FB, 6/6

GREEN BAY PACKERS

1. Terrell Buckley, Florida State, DB, 46/209
2. Mark D'Onofrio, Penn State, LB, 2/2
3. **Robert Brooks, South Carolina, WR, 96/100**
4. **Edgar Bennett, Florida State, RB, 80/112**
5. Dexter McNabb, Florida, FB, 32/33
5. Orlando McKay, Washington, WR, 0/0
6. **Mark Chmura, Boston College, TE, 89/89**
7. Christopher Holder, Tuskegee, WR, 0/0
9. Ty Detmer, Brigham Young, QB, 7/54
9. Shazzon Bradley, Tennessee, DT, 0/0
10. Andrew Oberg, North Carolina, T, 0/0
11. Gabe Mokwuah, American International, LB, 0/0
12. Brett Collins, Washington, LB, 15/27

HOUSTON OILERS

2. **Eddie Robinson, Alabama State, LB, 127/175**
3. Corey Harris, Vanderbilt, DB, 5/183
4. Mike Mooney, Georgia Tech, T, 0/1
5. **Joe Bowden, Oklahoma, LB, 123/139**
5. Tony Brown, Fresno State, DB, 28/57
5. Tim Roberts, Southern Mississippi, DE, 24/37
6. Mario Bailey, Washington, WR, 0/0
7. Elbert Turner, Illinois, WR, 0/0
8. Bucky Richardson, Texas A&M, QB, 16/16
9. Bernard Dafney, Tennessee, G, 0/60
10. Dion Johnson, East Carolina, WR, 0/0
11. Anthony Davis, Utah, LB, 0/106
12. Joe Wood, Air Force, K, 0/0

INDIANAPOLIS COLTS

1. **Quentin Coryatt, Texas A&M, LB, 78/82**
1. Steve Emtman, Washington, DE, 18/50
2. **Ashley Ambrose, Mississippi Valley State, DB, 56/192**
4. Rodney Culver, Notre Dame, RB, 32/43
4. **Tony McCoy, Florida, DT, 108/114**
5. Maury Toy, UCLA, RB, 0/0
6. Shoun Habersham, Tennessee-Chattanooga, WR, 0/0
7. Derek Steele, Maryland, DE, 0/0
8. **Jason Belser, Oklahoma, DB, 141/173**
8. Ronald Humphrey, Mississippi Valley State, RB, 26/26
9. Eddie Miller, South Carolina, WR, 15/15
10. **Steve Grant, West Virginia, LB, 83/83**
12. Michael Brandon, Florida, DE, 15/31

KANSAS CITY CHIEFS

1. **Dale Carter, Tennessee, DB, 104/156**
2. Matt Blundin, Virginia, QB, 2/3
S2. Darren Mickell, Florida, DE, 45/89
4. Mike Evans, Michigan, DT, 12/12
6. Tony Smith, Notre Dame, WR, 0/0
7. Erick Anderson, Michigan, LB, 8/10
8. Jim Jennings, San Diego State, G, 0/0
9. Jay Leeuwenburg, Colorado, G, 0/137
10. Jerry Ostroski, Tulsa, G, 0/106
11. Doug Rigby, Wyoming, DE, 0/0
12. Corey Williams, Oklahoma State, DB, 0/0

LOS ANGELES RAIDERS

1. **Chester McGlockton, Clemson, DT, 90/179**
2. Greg Skrepenak, Michigan, T, 36/68
5. **Derrick Hoskins, Southern Mississippi, DB, 60/61**
6. Tony Rowell, Florida, C, 0/0
7. Kevin Smith, UCLA, TE, 14/15
7. Curtis Cotton, Nebraska, DB, 0/0
10. Alberto White, Texas Southern, DE, 8/13
12. Tom Roth, Southern Illinois, G, 0/0

LOS ANGELES RAMS

1. **Sean Gilbert, Pittsburgh, DT, 60/146**
2. Steve Israel, Pittsburgh, DB, 42/102
3. Marc Boutte, LSU, DT, 32/102
3. Todd Kinchen, LSU, WR, 49/83
4. Shawn Harper, Indiana, T, 0/9
5. Chris Crooms, Texas A&M, DB, 16/16
6. Joe Campbell, Middle Tennessee State, RB, 0/0
7. Darryl Ashmore, Northwestern, T, 42/119
8. Ricky Jones, Alabama State, QB, 0/0
9. T.J. Rubley, Tulsa, QB, 9/10
10. Tim Lester, Eastern Kentucky, RB, 41/93
11. Brian Townsend, Michigan, LB, 0/3
11. Brian Thomas, Southern, WR, 0/0
12. Kelvin Harris, Miami (FL), C, 0/0

MIAMI DOLPHINS

1. **Marco Coleman, Georgia Tech, DE, 63/207**
1. **Troy Vincent, Wisconsin, DB, 57/198**
2. Eddie Blake, Auburn, DT, 0/0
3. Larry Webster, Maryland, DT, 45/137
4. **Dwight Hollier, North Carolina, LB, 122/138**
5. Christopher Perez, Kansas, T, 0/0
6. Roosevelt Collins, TCU, LB, 10/10
7. Dave Moore, Pittsburgh, TE, 1/207
8. Andre Powell, Penn State, LB, 0/16
9. Tony Tellington, Youngstown, DB, 0/0
10. Raoul Spears, Southern California, RB, 0/0
11. Lee Miles, Baylor, WR, 0/0
11. Mark Barsotti, Fresno State, QB, 0/0
12. Milton Biggins, Western Kentucky, TE, 0/0
12. Kameno Bell, Illinois, RB, 0/0

MINNESOTA VIKINGS

2. Robert Harris, Southern (LA), DT, 34/97
4. **Roy Barker, North Carolina, DE, 60/118**
5. **Ed McDaniel, Clemson, LB, 125/125**
6. Mike Gaddis, Oklahoma, RB, 0/0
7. David Wilson, California, DB, 3/4
8. Luke Fisher, East Carolina, TE, 0/0
9. **Brad Johnson, Florida State, QB, 53/130**
9. Ronnie West, Pittsburg State, WR, 12/12
10. Brad Culpepper, Florida, DT, 26/131
11. **Charles Evans, Clark Atlanta, RB, 81/98**
12. Joe Randolph, Elon, WR, 0/0

NEW ENGLAND PATRIOTS

1. Eugene Chung, Virginia Tech, G, 34/55
2. Rod Smith, Notre Dame, DB, 48/102
3. **Todd Collins, Carson-Newman, LB, 76/106**
3. Kevin Turner, Alabama, FB, 48/106
4. Darren Anderson, Toledo, DB, 1/74
4. Dion Lambert, UCLA, DB, 30/31
5. **Dwayne Sabb, New Hampshire, LB, 74/74**
6. Tracy Boyd, Elizabeth City State, G, 0/0
7. Wayne Hawkins, Southwest Minnesota, WR, 0/0
7. Jim Gray, West Virginia, DT, 0/0
8. **Sam Gash, Penn State, FB, 88/177**
8. Scott Lockwood, USC, RB, 6/6
9. David Dixon, Arizona State, G, 0/152
10. Steve Gordon, California, C, 0/13

10. Turner Baur, Stanford, TE, 0/0
11. Mike Petko, Nebraska, LB, 0/0
12. Freeman Baysinger, Humboldt State, WR, 0/0

NEW ORLEANS SAINTS

1. Vaughn Dunbar, Indiana, RB, 25/39
3. **Tyrone Legette, Nebraska, DB, 53/91**
4. **Sean Lumpkin, Minnesota, DB, 67/67**
4. Gene McGuire, Notre Dame, C, 0/17
5. **Torrance Small, Alcorn State, WR, 72/133**
6. Kary Vincent, Texas A&M, DB, 0/0
8. Robert Stewart, Alabama, DT, 0/0
9. Don Jones, Washington, LB, 0/8
10. Marcus Dowdell, Tennessee State, WR, 13/41
11. Mike Gisler, Houston, C, 0/105
12. Scott Adell, North Carolina State, T, 0/0

NEW YORK GIANTS

S1. **Dave Brown, Duke, QB, 57/73**
1. Derek Brown, Notre Dame, TE, 45/105
2. **Phillippi Sparks, Arizona State, DB, 99/115**
3. **Aaron Pierce, Washington, TE, 72/82**
4. **Keith Hamilton, Pittsburgh, DT, 173/173**
5. Michael Wright, Washington State, DB, 0/0
6. **Stacey Dillard, Oklahoma, NT, 59/59**
7. **Corey Widmer, Montana State, LB, 114/114**
8. Kent Graham, Ohio State, QB, 48/83
9. Anthony Prior, Washington State, DB, 0/59
10. George Rooks, Syracuse, DT, 0/0
11. Nate Singleton, Grambling State, WR, 0/44
12. Charles Swann, Indiana State, WR, 0/13

NEW YORK JETS

1. **Johnny Mitchell, Nebraska, TE, 53/57**
2. **Kurt Barber, USC, LB, 50/50**
3. **Siupeli Malamala, Washington, T, 62/62**
4. Keo Coleman, Mississippi State, LB, 6/18
5. **Cal Dixon, Florida, C, 55/66**
6. Jeff Blake, East Carolina, QB, 3/120
6. Glenn Cadrez, Houston, LB, 49/167
8. Vincent Brownlee, Mississippi, WR, 0/0
10. Mario Johnson, Missouri, DT, 14/20
11. Eric Boles, Central Washington, WR, 0/0

PHILADELPHIA EAGLES

2. Siran Stacy, Alabama, RB, 16/16
3. Tommy Jeter, Texas, DT, 36/37
3. Tony Brooks, Notre Dame, RB, 5/5
4. Casey Weldon, Florida State, QB, 0/26
5. Corey Barlow, Auburn, DB, 10/10
6. Jeff Sydner, Hawaii, WR, 35/41
7. William Boatwright, Virginia Tech, G, 0/0
8. Chuck Bullough, Michigan State, LB, 0/4
9. Ephesians Bartley, Florida, LB, 6/6
10. **Mark McMillian, Alabama, DB, 64/127**
11. Pumpy Tudors, Tennessee-Chattanooga, P, 0/0
12. Brandon Houston, Oklahoma, T, 0/0

PHOENIX CARDINALS

2. Tony Sacca, Penn State, QB, 2/2
3. **Ed Cunningham, Washington, C, 50/61**
4. **Michael Bankston, Sam Houston State, DE, 96/144**
4. Jeff Christy, Pittsburgh, C, 0/148
6. Brian Brauninger, Oklahoma, T, 0/0
7. Derek Ware, Central Oklahoma, TE, 46/58
8. Eric Blount, North Carolina, WR, 10/10
9. Tyrone Williams, Western Ontario (Canada), WR, 0/5
9. David Henson, Central Arkansas, DT, 0/0
10. Reggie Yarbrough, Cal State-Fullerton, RB, 0/0
11. Rob Baxley, Iowa, T, 6/6
12. Lance Wilson, Texas, DT, 0/0

PITTSBURGH STEELERS

1. **Leon Searcy, Miami (FL), T, 63/126**
2. **Levon Kirkland, Clemson, LB, 144/176**
3. **Joel Steed, Colorado, NT, 115/115**
4. Charles Davenport, North Carolina State, WR, 38/38
5. Alan Haller, Michigan State, DB, 7/12
7. Russ Campbell, Kansas State, TE, 7/7
7. Scottie Graham, Ohio State, RB, 0/57
8. **Darren Perry, Penn State, DB, 110/126**
8. Hesham Ismail, Florida, G, 0/0
9. Nate Williams, Mississippi State, DT, 0/0
9. Elnardo Webster, Rutgers, LB, 3/3
10. Mike Saunders, Iowa, RB, 0/0
11. **Kendall Gammon, Pittsburg State, C, 64/218**
12. Cornelius Benton, Connecticut, QB, 0/0

SAN DIEGO CHARGERS

1. **Chris Mims, Tennessee, DE, 93/104**
2. Marquez Pope, Fresno State, DB, 23/129
3. Ray Ethridge, Pasadena City College (JC), WR, 0/16
5. Eric Jonasen, Bloomsburg, T, 32/32
5. Curtis Whitley, Clemson, C, 30/72
5. Kevin Little, North Carolina A&T, LB, 0/0
6. Reggie White, North Carolina A&T, NT, 22/38
7. **Deems May, North Carolina, TE, 57/104**
8. James Fuller, Portland State, DB, 10/23
9. Johnnie Barnes, Hampton, WR, 26/29
10. Arthur Paul, Arizona State, DT, 0/0
11. Keith McAfee, Texas A&M, RB, 0/0
12. Carlos Huerta, Miami (FL), K, 0/4

SAN FRANCISCO 49ERS

1. Dana Hall, Washington, DB, 44/91
2. Amp Lee, Florida State, RB, 31/116
3. Brian Bollinger, North Carolina, G, 39/39
4. Mark Thomas, North Carolina State, DE, 20/113
6. Damien Russell, Virginia Tech, DB, 16/16
9. Darian Hagan, Colorado, QB, 0/0
10. Corey Mayfield, Oklahoma, DT, 0/27
11. Tom Covington, Georgia Tech, TE, 0/0
12. Matt LaBounty, Oregon, DE, 6/84

SEATTLE SEAHAWKS

1. **Ray Roberts, Virginia, T, 57/127**
3. Bob Spitulski, Central Florida, LB, 26/26
5. Gary Dandridge, Appalachian State, DB, 0/0
6. Michael Bates, Arizona, RB, 31/145
7. Mike Frier, Appalachian State, DE, 3/35
8. Muhammad Shamsid-Deen, Tennessee-Chattanooga, RB, 0/0
9. Larry Stayner, Boise State, TE, 0/0
10. Anthony Hamlet, Miami (FL), DE, 0/0
11. Kris Rongen, Washington, G, 0/0
12. Chico Fraley, Washington, LB, 0/0
12. John MacNeill, Michigan State, DE, 0/0

TAMPA BAY BUCCANEERS

2. **Courtney Hawkins, Michigan State, WR, 77/131**
3. **Tyji Armstrong, Mississippi, TE, 59/87**
3. **Mark Wheeler, Texas A&M, DT, 55/108**
4. Craig Erickson, Miami (FL), QB, 37/52
5. **Santana Dotson, Baylor, DT, 64/152**
5. Rogerick Green, Kansas State, DB, 12/26
6. James Malone, UCLA, LB, 0/0
7. Ken Swilling, Georgia Tech, DB, 0/0
8. Anthony McDowell, Texas Tech, RB, 30/30
8. Mike Pawlawski, California, QB, 0/0
10. Elijah Alexander, Kansas State, LB, 12/123
11. Mazio Royster, USC, RB, 33/33
12. Klaus Wilmsmeyer, Louisville, P, 0/94

WASHINGTON REDSKINS

1. Desmond Howard, Michigan, WR, 48/156
2. Shane Collins, Arizona State, DE, 30/30
3. Paul Siever, Penn State, G, 0/0
4. Chris Hakel, William & Mary, QB, 0/0
6. Ray Rowe, San Diego State, TE, 4/4
7. Calvin Holmes, Southern California, DB, 0/0
8. Darryl Moore, Texas-El Paso, G, 2/2
9. Boone Powell, Texas, LB, 0/0
10. Tony Barker, Rice, LB, 8/8
11. Terry Smith, Penn State, WR, 0/0
12. Matt Elliott, Michigan, G, 16/63

1993 NFL

ATLANTA FALCONS

1. Lincoln Kennedy, Washington, T, 48/169
2. Roger Harper, Ohio State, DB, 42/56
3. Harold Alexander, Appalachian State, P, 31/31
5. **Ron George, Stanford, LB, 60/124**
6. **Mitch Lyons, Michigan State, TE, 51/90**
7. **Darnell Walker, Oklahoma, DB, 62/119**
8. Shannon Baker, Florida State, WR, 0/4

BUFFALO BILLS

1. **Thomas Smith, North Carolina, DB, 110/137**
2. John Parrella, Nebraska, DT, 10/172
4. **Russell Copeland, Memphis, WR, 58/72**
5. Mike Devlin, Iowa, C, 44/101
5. Sebastian Savage, North Carolina State, DB, 0/3
6. **Corbin Lacina, Augustana (SD), G, 55/129**
7. Willie Harris, Mississippi State, WR, 0/0
8. Chris Luneberg, West Chester, T, 0/0

CHICAGO BEARS

1. **Curtis Conway, USC, WR, 92/167**
2. **Carl Simpson, Florida State, DT, 74/87**
3. Chris Gedney, Syracuse, TE, 28/73
4. Myron Baker, Louisiana Tech, LB, 48/66
4. **Albert Fontenot, Baylor, DE, 61/130**
4. **Todd Perry, Kentucky, G, 118/165**
6. Dave Hoffmann, Washington, LB, 0/1
7. Keshon Johnson, Arizona, DB, 33/40

CINCINNATI BENGALS

1. **John Copeland, Alabama, DE, 107/107**
2. **Tony McGee, Michigan, TE, 136/159**
3. Ty Parten, Arizona, DE, 26/62
3. **Steve Tovar, Ohio State, LB, 73/121**
4. Marcello Simmons, SMU, DB, 16/16
5. Forey Duckett, Nevada-Reno, DB, 2/7
6. Tom Scott, East Carolina, T, 13/13
7. Lance Gunn, Texas, DB, 8/8
8. **Doug Pelfrey, Kentucky, K, 111/111**

CLEVELAND BROWNS

1. **Steve Everitt, Michigan, C, 54/103**
2. **Dan Footman, Florida State, DE, 50/69**
3. **Mike Caldwell, Middle Tennessee State, LB, 56/159**
5. **Herman Arvie, Grambling State, T, 61/61**
6. Rich McKenzie, Penn State, LB, 8/8
7. Travis Hill, Nebraska, LB, 18/21

DALLAS COWBOYS

2. **Darrin Smith, Miami (FL), LB, 57/156**
2. **Kevin Williams, Miami (FL), WR, 57/121**
3. Mike Middleton, Indiana, DB, 0/0
4. Derrick Lassic, Alabama, RB, 10/10
4. Ron Stone, Boston College, G, 32/173
6. Barry Minter, Tulsa, LB, 0/111
7. **Brock Marion, Nevada-Reno, DB, 71/182**
8. Reggie Givens, Penn State, LB, 0/41
8. Dave Thomas, Tennessee, DB, 28/130

DENVER BRONCOS

1. Dan Williams, Toledo, DE, 46/87
2. Glyn Milburn, Stanford, RB, 48/138
3. **Jason Elam, Hawaii, K, 204/204**
3. **Rondell Jones, North Carolina, DB, 62/76**
4. **Jeff Robinson, Idaho, TE, 64/181**
5. Kevin Williams, UCLA, RB, 0/3
6. Melvin Bonner, Baylor, WR, 3/3
7. Tony Kimbrough, Jackson State, WR, 27/27
7. Clarence Williams, Washington State, TE, 0/7
8. Brian Stablein, Ohio State, WR, 0/87

DETROIT LIONS

2. **Ryan McNeil, Miami (FL), DB, 62/161**
3. **Mike Compton, West Virginia, G, 104/151**
3. **Antonio London, Alabama, LB, 75/76**
6. **Greg Jeffries, Virginia, DB, 83/110**
7. Ty Hallock, Michigan State, RB, 31/86
8. Kevin Miniefield, Arizona State, DB, 0/51

GREEN BAY PACKERS

1. **Wayne Simmons, Clemson, LB, 64/90**
1. George Teague, Alabama, DB, 47/133
3. **Earl Dotson, Texas A&M-Kingsville, T, 120/120**
5. Mark Brunell, Washington, QB, 2/147
5. James Willis, Auburn, LB, 25/93
6. **Doug Evans, Louisiana Tech, DB, 79/162**
6. Paul Hutchins, Western Michigan, T, 17/17
6. Tim Watson, Howard, DB, 0/13
7. Bob Kuberski, Navy, DT, 37/42

HOUSTON OILERS

1. **Brad Hopkins, Illinois, T, 194/194**
2. **Michael Barrow, Miami (FL), LB, 61/173**
4. Travis Hannah, USC, WR, 37/37
5. **John Henry Mills, Wake Forest, LB, 64/100**
6. Chuck Bradley, Kentucky, T, 0/1
7. Patrick Robinson, Tennessee State, WR, 0/30
8. **Blaine Bishop, Ball State, DB, 126/138**

INDIANAPOLIS COLTS

1. **Sean Dawkins, California, WR, 77/140**
2. Roosevelt Potts, Louisiana-Monroe, RB, 49/71
3. **Ray Buchanan, Louisville, DB, 61/184**
4. **Derwin Gray, Brigham Young, DB, 64/67**
4. Devon McDonald, Notre Dame, LB, 47/63
6. Carlos Etheredge, Miami (FL), TE, 9/9
7. Lance Lewis, Nebraska, RB, 0/0
8. Marquise Thomas, Mississippi, LB, 0/0

KANSAS CITY CHIEFS

3. **Will Shields, Nebraska, G, 208/208**
4. Jaime Fields, Washington, LB, 17/17
5. Lindsay Knapp, Notre Dame, G, 1/10
6. Darius Turner, Washington, RB, 0/0
7. **Danan Hughes, Iowa, WR, 85/85**

LOS ANGELES RAIDERS

1. Patrick Bates, Texas A&M, DB, 29/44
3. Billy Joe Hobert, Washington, QB, 12/29
3. **James Trapp, Clemson, DB, 88/149**
5. Olanda Truitt, Mississipi State, WR, 24/46
7. **Greg Biekert, Colorado, LB, 144/176**
8. Greg Robinson, Louisiana-Monroe, RB, 12/29

LOS ANGELES RAMS

1. Jerome Bettis, Notre Dame, RB, 47/192
2. **Troy Drayton, Penn State, TE, 51/122**
3. Russell White, California, RB, 5/5
5. Chuck Belin, Wisconsin, G, 22/22
5. Sean LaChapelle, UCLA, WR, 10/22
6. Deral Boykin, Louisville, DB, 16/43
7. Brad Fichtel, Eastern Illinois, C, 1/1
8. Maa Tanuvasa, Hawaii, DE, 0/82
8. Jeff Buffaloe, Memphis State, P, 0/0

MIAMI DOLPHINS

1. **O.J. McDuffie, Penn State, WR, 116/116**
3. Terry Kirby, Virginia, RB, 36/110
4. Ronnie Bradford, Colorado, DB, 0/133
5. Chris Gray, Auburn, G, 42/177
6. Robert O'Neal, Clemson, DB, 0/2
7. David Merritt, North Carolina State, LB, 4/38
8. Dwayne Gordon, New Hampshire, LB, 0/113

MINNESOTA VIKINGS

1. **Robert Smith, Ohio State, RB, 98/98**
2. **Qadry Ismail, Syracuse, WR, 63/137**
3. Gilbert Brown, Kansas, DT, 0/125
3. John Gerak, Penn State, G, 46/62
4. Ashley Sheppard, Clemson, LB, 17/21
5. **Everett Lindsay, Mississippi, T, 104/136**
7. Gino Torretta, Miami (FL), QB, 1/2

NEW ENGLAND PATRIOTS

1. **Drew Bledsoe, Washington State, QB, 124/188**
2. **Vincent Brisby, Louisiana-Monroe, WR, 83/86**
2. **Todd Rucci, Penn State, G, 85/85**
2. **Chris Slade, Virginia, LB, 127/142**
4. **Corwin Brown, Michigan, DB, 61/120**
4. Kevin Johnson, Texas Southern, DT, 0/38
5. Rich Griffith, Arizona, TE, 3/90
5. Scott Sisson, Georgia Tech, K, 13/29
6. Lawrence Hatch, Florida, DB, 0/0
8. **Troy Brown, Marshall, WR, 175/175**

NEW ORLEANS SAINTS

1. **Willie Roaf, Louisiana Tech, T, 131/189**
1. **Irv Smith, Notre Dame, TE, 66/95**
2. Reggie Freeman, Florida State, LB, 10/10
4. **Derek Brown, Nebraska, RB, 56/56**
4. **Lorenzo Neal, Fresno State, FB, 50/194**
5. **Tyrone Hughes, Nebraska, DB, 63/81**
6. Ronnie Dixon, Cincinnati, DT, 2/43
7. Othello Henderson, UCLA, DB, 21/21
8. Jon Kirksey, Sacramento State, DT, 0/11

NEW YORK GIANTS

2. **Michael Strahan, Texas Southern, DE, 191/191**
3. **Marcus Buckley, Texas A&M, LB, 101/101**
4. **Greg Bishop, Pacific, G, 88/101**
5. Tommy Thigpen, North Carolina, LB, 0/0
6. Scott Davis, Iowa, G, 19/21
7. Todd Peterson, Georgia, K, 0/159
8. **Jessie Armstead, Miami (FL), LB, 144/176**

NEW YORK JETS

1. **Marvin Jones, Florida State, LB, 142/142**
2. Coleman Rudolph, Georgia Tech, DE, 4/48
4. David Ware, Virginia, T, 0/0
5. **Fred Baxter, Auburn, TE, 102/134**
5. **Adrian Murrell, West Virginia, RB, 73/122**
5. Kenny Shedd, Northern Iowa, WR, 0/60
6. **Richie Anderson, Penn State, FB, 134/161**
7. Alec Millen, Georgia, T, 0/0
8. Craig Hentrich, Notre Dame, P, 0/192

PHILADELPHIA EAGLES

1. Lester Holmes, Jackson State, G, 46/102
1. Leonard Renfro, Colorado, DT, 23/23
2. Victor Bailey, Missouri, WR, 32/34
3. Derrick Frazier, Texas A&M, DB, 19/25
3. Mike Reid, North Carolina State, DB, 12/12
6. Derrick Oden, Alabama, LB, 35/35
7. Joey Mickey, Oklahoma, TE, 0/5
8. Doug Skene, Michigan, G, 0/6

PHOENIX CARDINALS
1. Ernest Dye, South Carolina, T, 37/50
1. Garrison Hearst, Georgia, RB, 30/126
2. Ben Coleman, Wake Forest, G, 30/135
4. Ronald Moore, Pittsburg State, RB, 38/77
6. Brett Wallerstedt, Arizona State, LB, 7/30
7. Will White, Florida, DB, 0/0
8. Stevie Anderson, Grambling State, WR, 14/24
8. Chad Brown, Mississippi, DE, 18/18

PITTSBURGH STEELERS
1. **Deon Figures, Colorado, DB, 61/93**
2. **Chad Brown, Colorado, LB, 56/178**
3. **Andre Hastings, Georgia, WR, 54/104**
4. **Kevin Henry, Mississippi State, DE, 116/116**
5. Lonnie Palelei, UNLV, G, 4/44
5. Marc Woodard, Mississippi State, LB, 0/48
6. **Willie Williams, Western Carolina, DB, 83/188**
7. Craig Keith, Lenoir-Rhyne, TE, 17/28
7. Jeff Zgonina, Purdue, DT, 21/157
8. Alex Van Pelt, Pittsburgh, QB, 0/31

SAN DIEGO CHARGERS
1. Darrien Gordon, Stanford, DB, 48/138
2. **Natrone Means, North Carolina, RB, 59/88**
3. **Joe Cocozzo, Michigan, G, 77/77**
4. **Lewis Bush, Washington State, LB, 104/141**
4. **Raylee Johnson, Arkansas, DE, 145/159**
5. Walter Dunson, Middle Tennessee State, WR, 0/0
6. **Eric Castle, Oregon, DB, 53/53**
7. Doug Miller, South Dakota State, LB, 23/23
8. Trent Green, Indiana, QB, 0/104

SAN FRANCISCO 49ERS
1. Todd Kelly, Tennessee, LB, 25/46
1. **Dana Stubblefield, Kansas, DT, 108/154**
2. Adrian Hardy, Northwestern State (LA), DB, 12/36
5. Artie Smith, Louisiana Tech, DE, 18/73
6. **Chris Dalman, Stanford, C, 105/105**
7. Troy Wilson, Pittsburg State, DE, 21/61
8. Elvis Grbac, Michigan, QB, 43/106

SEATTLE SEAHAWKS
1. **Rick Mirer, Notre Dame, QB, 55/80**
2. **Carlton Gray, UCLA, DB, 53/102**
4. **Dean Wells, Kentucky, LB, 84/129**
5. Terrence Warren, Hampton, WR, 16/17
7. **Michael McCrary, Wake Forest, DE, 58/136**
8. Jeff Blackshear, Louisiana-Monroe, G, 47/128
8. **Antonio Edwards, Valdosta State, DE, 50/82**

TAMPA BAY BUCCANEERS
1. **Eric Curry, Alabama, DE, 59/75**
2. **Demetrious DuBose, Notre Dame, LB, 60/60**
3. **John Lynch, Stanford, DB, 164/195**
3. Lamar Thomas, Miami (FL), WR, 36/73
4. **Horace Copeland, Miami (FL), WR, 58/60**
4. Rudy Harris, Clemson, RB, 18/18
6. **Chidi Ahanotu, California, DE, 121/174**
7. Tyree Davis, Central Arkansas, WR, 1/14
8. Darrick Branch, Hawaii, WR, 0/0
8. Daron Alcorn, Akron, K, 0/0

WASHINGTON REDSKINS
1. **Tom Carter, Notre Dame, DB, 62/118**
2. Reggie Brooks, Notre Dame, RB, 29/40
3. Rick Hamilton, Central Florida, LB, 17/34
3. Ed Bunn, Texas-El Paso, P, 0/0
4. Sterling Palmer, Florida State, DE, 49/49
5. Greg Huntington, Penn State, C, 9/18
6. Darryl Morrison, Arizona, DB, 48/48
6. Frank Wycheck, Maryland, TE, 18/155
8. Lamont Hollinquest, USC, LB, 30/76

1994 NFL

ARIZONA CARDINALS
1. **Jamir Miller, UCLA, LB, 74/121**
2. Chuck Levy, Arizona, RB, 11/37
3. Rich Braham, West Virginia, C, 0/144
3. Eric England, Texas A&M, DE, 37/37
4. Perry Carter, Southern Mississippi, DB, 0/28
4. **Terry Irving, McNeese State, LB, 70/70**
4. John Reece, Nebraska, DB, 0/5
5. **Anthony Redmon, Auburn, G, 50/79**
6. Terry Samuels, Kentucky, TE, 20/20
7. Frank Harvey, Georgia, RB, 2/2

ATLANTA FALCONS
2. **Bert Emanuel, Rice, WR, 62/103**
3. Anthony Phillips, Texas A&M-Kingsville, DB, 18/20
3. Alai Kalaniuvalu, Oregon State, G, 0/0
4. Perry Klein, C.W. Post, QB, 2/2
4. Mitch Davis, Georgia, LB, 0/0
5. Harrison Houston, Florida, WR, 0/0
7. **Jamal Anderson, Utah, RB, 88/88**

BUFFALO BILLS
1. **Jeff Burris, Notre Dame, DB, 54/144**
2. Bucky Brooks, North Carolina, DB, 3/32
2. **Lonnie Johnson, Florida State, TE, 74/88**
2. **Sam Rogers, Colorado, LB, 101/133**
3. Corey Louchiey, South Carolina, T, 44/44
3. **Marlo Perry, Jackson State, LB, 76/76**
4. Sean Crocker, North Carolina, DB, 0/0
5. A.J. Ofodile, Missouri, TE, 0/24
6. Kevin Knox, Florida State, WR, 0/2
6. Anthony Abrams, Clark (GA), DE, 0/0
7. Filmel Johnson, Illinois, DB, 2/2

CHICAGO BEARS
1. **John Thierry, Alcorn State, DE, 73/131**
2. Marcus Spears, Northwestern State (LA), T, 9/103
3. **Jim Flanigan, Notre Dame, DT, 108/145**
4. Raymont Harris, Ohio State, RB, 42/54
6. Lloyd Hill, Texas Tech, WR, 0/0
7. Dennis Collier, Colorado, DB, 0/0

CINCINNATI BENGALS
1. **Dan Wilkinson, Ohio State, DT, 61/185**
2. **Darnay Scott, San Diego State, WR, 109/124**
3. Jeff Cothran, Ohio State, FB, 39/39
3. Steve Shine, Northwestern, LB, 0/0
4. **Corey Sawyer, Florida State, DB, 60/65**
5. Trent Pollard, Eastern Washington, T, 17/17
6. Jerry Reynolds, UNLV, T, 0/25
6. **Kimo von Oelhoffen, Boise State, DE, 79/174**
7. Ramondo Stallings, San Diego State, DE, 37/37

CLEVELAND BROWNS
1. **Derrick Alexander, Michigan, WR, 58/126**
1. **Antonio Langham, Alabama, DB, 63/102**
3. Romeo Bandison, Oregon, DT, 0/14
5. Issac Booth, California, DB, 36/36
6. Robert Strait, Baylor, RB, 0/0
7. Andre Hewitt, Clemson, T, 0/0

DALLAS COWBOYS
1. **Shante Carver, Arizona State, DE, 52/52**
2. **Larry Allen, Sonoma State, G, 176/176**
3. George Hegamin, North Carolina State, T, 31/64
4. DeWayne Dotson, Mississippi, LB, 0/25
4. Willie Jackson, Florida, WR, 0/113

S5. John Davis, Emporia State, TE, 0/81

6. Darren Studstill, West Virginia, DB, 1/16
7. Toddrick McIntosh, Florida State, DE, 0/15

DENVER BRONCOS
2. **Allen Aldridge, Houston, LB, 64/128**
4. Randy Fuller, Tennessee State, DB, 10/64
7. **Keith Burns, Oklahoma State, LB, 151/182**
7. Butler By'Not'e, Ohio State, RB, 9/16
7. **Tom Nalen, Boston College, C, 173/173**

DETROIT LIONS
1. **Johnnie Morton, USC, WR, 126/182**
2. **Van Malone, Texas, DB, 55/55**
3. **Shane Bonham, Tennessee, DT, 62/76**
4. Vaughn Bryant, Stanford, DB, 0/0
5. **Tony Semple, Memphis, G, 112/112**
6. Jocelyn Borgella, Cincinnati, DB, 15/15
7. Tom Beer, Wayne State (MI), LB, 41/41

GREEN BAY PACKERS
1. Aaron Taylor, Notre Dame, G, 46/75
3. LeShon Johnson, Northern Illinois, RB, 14/62
4. **Gabe Wilkins, Gardner-Webb, DE, 60/84**
5. **Dorsey Levens, Georgia Tech, RB, 102/144**
5. Terry Mickens, Florida A&M, WR, 47/79
6. Ruffin Hamilton, Tulane, LB, 5/44
6. **Bill Schroeder, Wisconsin-LaCrosse, WR, 74/111**
6. Jay Kearney, West Virginia, WR, 0/0
6. Paul Duckworth, Connecticut, LB, 0/0

HOUSTON OILERS
1. **Henry Ford, Arkansas, DT, 129/133**
2. Jeremy Nunley, Alabama, DE, 12/12
3. Malcolm Floyd, Fresno State, WR, 45/49
3. Mike Davis, Cincinnati, DB, 16/19
4. Sean Jackson, Florida State, RB, 0/0
5. Roderick Lewis, Arizona, TE, 45/45
5. Jim Reid, Virginia, T, 6/6
6. **Barron Wortham, Texas-El Paso, LB, 92/108**
6. Lee Gissendaner, Northwestern, WR, 0/0
7. Lemanski Hall, Alabama, LB, 31/101

INDIANAPOLIS COLTS
1. Trev Alberts, Nebraska, LB, 29/29
1. **Marshall Faulk, San Diego State, RB, 77/176**
2. Eric Mahlum, California, G, 36/36
3. **Jason Mathews, Texas A&M, T, 58/142**
4. **Bradford Banta, USC, TE, 92/156**
5. John Covington, Notre Dame, DB, 3/3
6. **Lamont Warren, Colorado, RB, 61/96**
7. Lance Teichelman, Texas A&M, DE, 1/1

KANSAS CITY CHIEFS
1. **Greg Hill, Texas A&M, RB, 63/79**
2. **Donnell Bennett, Miami (FL), RB, 86/102**
3. Lake Dawson, Notre Dame, WR, 43/43
3. Chris Penn, Tulsa, WR, 26/70
4. **Bracy Walker, North Carolina, DB, 56/167**
5. James Burton, Fresno State, DB, 0/45
5. Rob Waldrop, Arizona, DT, 3/3
6. Anthony Daigle, Fresno State, RB, 0/1
7. Tracy Greene, Grambling State, TE, 7/23
7. Steve Matthews, Memphis, QB, 0/3

LOS ANGELES RAIDERS
1. **Rob Fredrickson, Michigan State, LB, 58/128**
2. **James Folston, Louisiana-Monroe, LB, 66/85**
3. Calvin Jones, Nebraska, RB, 16/17
4. Austin Robbins, North Carolina, DT, 21/80
5. Roosevelt Patterson, Alabama, G, 0/0
7. **Rob Holmberg, Penn State, LB, 61/112**

LOS ANGELES RAMS
1. **Wayne Gandy, Auburn, T, 80/191**
2. **Isaac Bruce, Memphis, WR, 167/167**
2. Brad Ottis, Wayne State (NE), DE, 25/81
2. **Toby Wright, Nebraska, DB, 58/59**
3. James Bostic, Auburn, RB, 0/11
3. Ernest Jones, Oregon, DT, 0/29
3. **Keith Lyle, Virginia, DB, 105/136**
4. Chris Brantley, Rutgers, WR, 13/22
6. Rickey Brady, Oklahoma, TE, 1/1
6. Ronald Edwards, North Carolina A&T, T, 0/0

MIAMI DOLPHINS
1. **Tim Bowens, Mississippi, DT, 157/157**
2. Aubrey Beavers, Oklahoma, LB, 32/39
2. **Tim Ruddy, Notre Dame, C, 156/156**
4. Ronnie Woolfork, Colorado, LB, 0/0
5. William Gaines, Florida, DT, 8/52
6. Brant Boyer, Arizona, LB, 14/130
7. Sean Hill, Montana State, DB, 44/44

MINNESOTA VIKINGS
1. **Todd Steussie, California, T, 111/190**
1. **Dewayne Washington, North Carolina State, DB, 63/191**
2. **David Palmer, Alabama, WR, 84/84**
2. Fernando Smith, Jackson State, DE, 48/79
4. Mike Wells, Iowa, DT, 0/115
5. Shelly Hammonds, Penn State, DB, 1/1
6. **Andrew Jordan, Western Carolina, TE, 87/92**
7. **Pete Bercich, Notre Dame, LB, 57/57**

NEW ENGLAND PATRIOTS
1. **Willie McGinest, USC, DE, 171/171**
2. Kevin Lee, Alabama, WR, 7/9
3. Ervin Collier, Florida A&M, DT, 0/0
3. Joe Burch, Texas Southern, C, 0/0
4. John Burke, Virginia Tech, TE, 43/60
5. Pat O'Neill, Syracuse, P, 24/25
6. Steve Hawkins, Western Michigan, WR, 7/7
6. **Max Lane, Navy, T, 100/100**
7. **Marty Moore, Kentucky, LB, 96/112**
7. Jay Walker, Howard, QB, 0/1

NEW ORLEANS SAINTS
1. **Joe Johnson, Louisville, DE, 106/117**
2. **Mario Bates, Arizona State, RB, 53/98**
3. **Winfred Tubbs, Texas, LB, 52/98**
4. Doug Nussmeier, Idaho, QB, 8/8
5. Herman Carroll, Mississippi State, DE, 4/4
5. Craig Novitsky, UCLA, G, 41/41
6. Derrell Mitchell, Texas Tech, WR, 14/14
7. Lance Lundberg, Nebraska, T, 0/0

NEW YORK GIANTS
1. Thomas Lewis, Indiana, WR, 34/34
2. **Thomas Randolph, Kansas State, DB, 64/95**
2. **Jason Sehorn, USC, DB, 107/117**
3. Gary Downs, North Carolina State, RB, 20/69
4. Chris Maumalanga, Kansas, DT, 7/14

S4. **Tito Wooten, Louisiana-Monroe, DB, 75/83**

5. **Chad Bratzke, Eastern Kentucky, DE, 50/129**
6. Jason Winrow, Ohio State, G, 0/0

NEW YORK JETS
1. **Aaron Glenn, Texas A&M, DB, 121/180**
2. Ryan Yarborough, Wyoming, WR, 29/51
3. Lou Benfatti, Penn State, DT, 19/19
4. Orlando Parker, Troy State, WR, 2/2
5. Horace Morris, Tennessee, LB, 0/0
6. Fred Lester, Alabama A&M, RB, 0/0
7. Glenn Foley, Boston College, QB, 18/21

PHILADELPHIA EAGLES
1. Bernard Williams, Georgia, T, 16/16
2. **Charlie Garner, Tennessee, RB, 66/147**
2. Bruce Walker, UCLA, NT, 0/11
3. **Joe Panos, Wisconsin, G, 54/83**
3. Eric Zomalt, California, DB, 30/40
5. Marvin Goodwin, UCLA, DB, 0/0
6. Mitch Berger, Colorado, P, 5/159
6. Ryan McCoy, Houston, LB, 0/0
7. Mark Montgomery, Wisconsin, RB, 0/0

PITTSBURGH STEELERS
1. **Charles Johnson, Colorado, WR, 76/133**
2. Brentson Buckner, Clemson, DT, 44/174
3. **Jason Gildon, Oklahoma State, LB, 158/167**
3. Bam Morris, Texas Tech, RB, 28/74
4. Ta'ase Faumui, Hawaii, DE, 8/8
5. **Myron Bell, Michigan State, DB, 80/112**
5. Gary Brown, Georgia Tech, T, 0/25
6. Jim Miller, Michigan State, QB, 5/37
6. Eric Ravotti, Penn State, LB, 23/23
7. Brice Abrams, Michigan State, RB, 0/0

SAN DIEGO CHARGERS
2. **Isaac Davis, Arkansas, G, 55/58**
2. **Vaughn Parker, UCLA, T, 121/122**
3. Willie Clark, Notre Dame, DB, 43/59
3. Andre Coleman, Kansas State, WR, 44/58
5. **Rodney Harrison, Western Illinois, DB, 123/158**
5. Aaron Laing, New Mexico State, TE, 5/32
5. Tony Vinson, Towson State, RB, 0/16
5. Darren Krein, Miami (FL), DE, 0/0
7. Zane Beehn, Kentucky, LB, 0/0

SAN FRANCISCO 49ERS
1. William Floyd, Florida State, FB, 48/90
1. **Bryant Young, Notre Dame, DT, 176/176**
2. **Tyronne Drakeford, Virginia Tech, DB, 62/97**
2. **Kevin Mitchell, Syracuse, LB, 59/144**
3. Doug Brien, California, K, 22/154
3. Cory Fleming, Tennessee, WR, 0/18
5. **Tony Peterson, Notre Dame, LB, 71/87**
6. **Lee Woodall, West Chester, LB, 94/124**

SEATTLE SEAHAWKS
1. **Sam Adams, Texas A&M, DT, 89/179**
2. **Kevin Mawae, LSU, C, 62/180**
3. Lamar Smith, Houston, RB, 43/116
4. Larry Whigham, Louisiana-Monroe, DB, 0/136
7. **Carlester Crumpler, East Carolina, TE, 67/78**

TAMPA BAY BUCCANEERS
1. **Trent Dilfer, Fresno State, QB, 79/123**
2. **Errict Rhett, Florida, RB, 52/86**
3. Harold Bishop, LSU, TE, 6/34
5. **Pete Pierson, Washington, T, 100/101**
6. Bernard Carter, East Carolina, LB, 0/5
7. Jim Pyne, Virginia Tech, G, 42/81

WASHINGTON REDSKINS
1. Heath Shuler, Tennessee, QB, 19/29
2. **Tre' Johnson, Temple, G, 90/93**
3. **Joe Patton, Alabama A&M, T, 61/61**
3. Tydus Winans, Fresno State, WR, 23/25
4. Kurt Haws, Utah, TE, 6/6
6. Dexter Nottage, Florida A&M, DE, 47/48
7. **Gus Frerotte, Tulsa, QB, 52/127**

1995 NFL

ARIZONA CARDINALS
2. **Frank Sanders, Auburn, WR, 123/136**
3. Stoney Case, New Mexico, QB, 5/20
5. Tito Paul, Ohio State, DB, 31/67
5. Lance Scott, Utah, C, 0/32
5. Cedric Davis, Tennessee State, DB, 0/0
6. Anthony Bridges, North Texas, DB, 0/0
7. Chad Eaton, Washington State, DT, 0/103

7. Wesley Leasy, Mississippi State, LB, 28/28
7. Billy Williams, Tennessee, WR, 0/1

ATLANTA FALCONS
1. **Devin Bush, Florida State, DB, 56/116**
2. Ron Davis, Tennessee, DB, 12/12
3. Lorenzo Styles, Ohio State, LB, 28/70
5. Roell Preston, Mississippi, WR, 29/53
6. **Travis Hall, Brigham Young, DT, 134/150**
7. **John Burrough, Wyoming, DE, 64/89**

BUFFALO BILLS
1. **Ruben Brown, Pittsburgh, G, 136/157**
2. Todd Collins, Michigan, QB, 28/41
3. Damien Covington, North Carolina State, LB, 29/29
3. Marlon Kerner, Ohio State, DB, 43/43
4. Justin Armour, Stanford, WR, 15/39
4. Tony Cline, Stanford, TE, 42/52
4. **Ken Irvin, Memphis, DB, 108/147**
5. **John Holecek, Illinois, LB, 58/81**
6. Shannon Clavelle, Colorado, DE, 0/16
7. Darick Holmes, Portland State, RB, 48/60
7. Tom Nutten, Western Michigan, G, 1/77

CAROLINA PANTHERS
1. **Blake Brockermeyer, Texas, T, 58/136**
1. Kerry Collins, Penn State, QB, 45/152
1. Tyrone Poole, Fort Valley State (GA), DB, 47/130
2. Shawn King, Louisiana-Monroe, DE, 38/47
4. **Frank Garcia, Washington, C, 91/125**
5. Andrew Peterson, Washington, T, 4/4
5. Michael Senters, Northwestern, DB, 0/0
6. Steve Strahan, Baylor, DT, 0/0
6. Jerry Colquitt, Tennessee, QB, 0/0
7. Chad Cota, Oregon, DB, 48/125
7. Michael Reed, Boston College, DB, 3/3

CHICAGO BEARS
1. Rashaan Salaam, Colorado, RB, 31/33
2. Pat Riley, Miami (FL), DE, 1/1
2. **Todd Sauerbrun, West Virginia, P, 66/162**
3. **Sean Harris, Arizona, LB, 82/83**
3. Evan Pilgrim, Brigham Young, G, 19/31
4. Jack Jackson, Florida, WR, 12/12
6. Carl Reeves, North Carolina State, DE, 31/31
6. Kenny Gales, Wisconsin, DB, 0/0
7. Jamal Cox, Georgia Tech, LB, 0/0

CINCINNATI BENGALS
1. Ki-Jana Carter, Penn State, RB, 35/59
3. Melvin Tuten, Syracuse, T, 32/66
4. **Sam Shade, Alabama, DB, 60/117**
5. David Dunn, Fresno State, WR, 47/89
6. Ryan Grigson, Purdue, T, 0/0
7. John Walsh, Brigham Young, QB, 0/0

CLEVELAND BROWNS
1. Craig Powell, Ohio State, LB, 12/14
3. **Mike Frederick, Virginia, DE, 58/71**
3. Eric Zeier, Georgia, QB, 23/28
5. Tau Pupua, Weber State, DT, 0/0
5. Mike Miller, Notre Dame, WR, 0/0
7. A.C. Tellison, Miami (FL), WR, 0/0

DALLAS COWBOYS
2. Kendell Watkins, Mississippi State, TE, 16/16
2. **Sherman Williams, Alabama, RB, 60/60**
2. Shane Hannah, Michigan State, G, 0/0
S3. Darren Benson, Trinity Valley CC (TX), DT, 12/12
3. **Charlie Williams, Bowling Green State, DB, 81/81**
4. **Eric Bjornson, Washington, TE, 74/82**
4. Alundis Brice, Mississippi, DB, 25/25
4. Linc Harden, Oklahoma State, LB, 0/0
5. Dana Howard, Illinois, LB, 0/19
5. Edward Hervey, Southern California, WR, 0/0
7. Oscar Sturgis, North Carolina, DE, 1/1

DENVER BRONCOS
4. Jamie Brown, Florida A&M, T, 29/38
4. Ken Brown, Virginia Tech, LB, 2/2
5. Phil Yeboah-Kodie, Penn State, LB, 0/2
6. **Terrell Davis, Georgia, RB, 78/78**
6. Fritz Fequiere, Iowa, G, 0/0
7. **Byron Chamberlain, Wayne State (NE), TE, 73/106**
7. Steve Russ, Air Force, LB, 24/24

DETROIT LIONS
1. **Luther Elliss, Utah, DT, 126/134**
3. **David Sloan, New Mexico, TE, 90/110**
5. **Stephen Boyd, Boston College, LB, 86/86**
5. Kez McCorvey, Florida State, WR, 10/10
5. Ronald Cherry, McNeese State, T, 0/0
6. Kevin Hickman, Navy, TE, 13/13
6. **Cory Schlesinger, Nebraska, FB, 167/167**
7. Hessley Hempstead, Kansas, G, 32/32

GREEN BAY PACKERS
1. Craig Newsome, Arizona State, DB, 46/53
3. **Antonio Freeman, Virginia Tech, WR, 116/132**
3. **William Henderson, North Carolina, FB, 174/174**
3. Darius Holland, Colorado, DT, 42/111
3. **Brian Williams, USC, LB, 72/81**
4. Jeff Miller, Mississippi, T, 0/0
5. **Travis Jervey, The Citadel, RB, 56/109**
5. Jay Barker, Alabama, QB, 0/0
6. Charlie Simmons, Georgia Tech, WR, 0/0
7. **Adam Timmerman, South Dakota State, G, 61/173**

HOUSTON OILERS
1. **Steve McNair, Alcorn State, QB, 139/139**
2. **Anthony Cook, South Carolina State, DE, 51/67**
3. Torey Hunter, Washington State, DB, 12/12
3. **Chris Sanders, Ohio State, WR, 97/97**
3. **Rodney Thomas, Texas A&M, RB, 91/103**
4. **Michael Roan, Wisconsin, TE, 62/62**
5. **Gary Walker, Auburn, DT, 62/155**
6. Hicham El-Mashtoub, Arizona, C, 3/3
7. C.J. Richardson, Miami (FL), DB, 0/15

INDIANAPOLIS COLTS
1. **Ellis Johnson, Florida, DT, 104/149**
2. **Ken Dilger, Illinois, TE, 109/156**
3. Zack Crockett, Florida State, FB, 39/158
4. **Ray McElroy, Eastern Illinois, DB, 64/81**
5. Derek West, Colorado, T, 5/5
6. Brian Gelzheiser, Penn State, LB, 0/0
7. Jessie Cox, Texas Southern, LB, 0/0

JACKSONVILLE JAGUARS
1. **Tony Boselli, USC, T, 91/91**
1. **James Stewart, Tennessee, RB, 60/101**
2. **Brian DeMarco, Michigan State, G, 56/63**
2. **Bryan Schwartz, Augustana (SD), LB, 55/55**
3. Chris Hudson, Colorado, DB, 46/77
4. Rob Johnson, USC, QB, 8/48
4. Mike Thompson, Wisconsin, DT, 2/33
5. Ryan Christopherson, Wyoming, RB, 13/19
6. Marcus Price, LSU, T, 0/77
7. Curtis Marsh, Utah, WR, 10/15

KANSAS CITY CHIEFS
1. Trezelle Jenkins, Michigan, T, 9/9
3. Troy Dumas, Nebraska, LB, 13/15
3. **Tamarick Vanover, Florida State, WR, 70/77**
4. Steve Stenstrom, Stanford, QB, 0/17
5. Jerrott Willard, California, LB, 1/1
5. Mike Pelton, Auburn, DT, 0/0
6. **Tom Barndt, Pittsburgh, DT, 61/81**
6. Bryan Proby, Arizona State, DT, 3/3

MIAMI DOLPHINS
1. Billy Milner, Houston, T, 20/29
2. Andrew Greene, Indiana, G, 6/10
4. Pete Mitchell, Boston College, TE, 0/114
5. Norman Hand, Mississippi, DT, 9/115
6. Jeff Kopp, USC, LB, 16/63
7. Corey Swinson, Hampton, DT, 0/0
7. Shannon Myers, Lenoir-Rhyne, WR, 0/0

MINNESOTA VIKINGS
1. **Derrick Alexander, Florida State, DE, 57/73**
1. **Korey Stringer, Ohio State, T, 93/93**
2. **Corey Fuller, Florida State, DB, 64/152**
2. **Orlando Thomas, Louisiana-Lafayette, DB, 98/98**
4. Chad May, Kansas State, QB, 0/0
5. James Stewart, Miami (FL), RB, 4/4
6. John Solomon, Sam Houston State, LB, 0/0
7. **Jason Fisk, Stanford, DT, 56/166**
7. Jose White, Howard, DT, 0/18

NEW ENGLAND PATRIOTS
1. **Ty Law, Michigan, DB, 141/157**
2. **Ted Johnson, Colorado, LB, 125/125**
3. Jimmy Hitchcock, North Carolina, DB, 37/101
3. Curtis Martin, Pittsburgh, RB, 45/168
4. **Dave Wohlabaugh, Syracuse, C, 57/128**
6. Dino Philyaw, Oregon, RB, 0/23
7. Carlos Yancy, Georgia, DB, 4/4

NEW ORLEANS SAINTS
1. **Mark Fields, Washington State, LB, 93/136**
2. Ray Zellars, Notre Dame, RB, 48/48
3. Mike Verstegen, Wisconsin, G, 22/22
4. Dameian Jeffries, Alabama, DE, 2/2
5. William Strong, North Carolina State, DB, 9/9
6. Lee DeRamus, Wisconsin, WR, 23/23
7. Travis Davis, Notre Dame, DB, 0/73

NEW YORK GIANTS
1. Tyrone Wheatley, Michigan, RB, 46/124
2. **Scott Gragg, Montana, T, 77/171**
3. Rodney Young, LSU, DB, 33/33
4. Ben Talley, Tennessee, LB, 4/12
4. Rob Zatechka, Nebraska, G, 47/47
5. Roderick Mullen, Grambling State, DB, 0/53
6. Jamal Duff, San Diego State, DE, 15/41
6. **Charles Way, Virginia, RB, 75/75**
7. Bryne Diehl, Alabama, P, 0/0

NEW YORK JETS
1. **Kyle Brady, Penn State, TE, 63/167**
1. Hugh Douglas, Central State (OH), DE, 40/138
2. **Matt O'Dwyer, Northwestern, G, 60/122**
4. Tyrone Davis, Virginia, TE, 6/75
4. Melvin Hayes, Mississippi State, T, 4/4
5. Carl Greenwood, UCLA, DB, 24/24
6. Eddie Mason, North Carolina, LB, 15/80
7. Curtis Ceaser, Grambling State, WR, 4/4

OAKLAND RAIDERS
1. **Napoleon Kaufman, Washington, RB, 91/91**
2. **Barret Robbins, TCU, C, 121/121**
3. Joe Aska, Central Oklahoma, RB, 23/23
4. **Mike Morton, North Carolina, LB, 55/103**
5. Matt Dyson, Michigan, LB, 4/4
5. Jeff Kysar, Arizona State, T, 1/1
6. Eli Herring, Brigham Young, T, 0/0

PHILADELPHIA EAGLES
1. **Mike Mamula, Boston College, DE, 77/77**
2. **Barrett Brooks, Kansas State, T, 64/118**
2. **Bobby Taylor, Notre Dame, DB, 119/129**
3. **Greg Jefferson, Central Florida, DE, 57/57**
3. Chris Jones, Miami (FL), WR, 32/32
4. Dave Barr, California, QB, 0/2
6. Fred McCrary, Mississippi State, FB, 13/107
7. Kevin Bouie, Mississippi State, RB, 0/6
7. Howard Smothers, Bethune-Cookman, T, 0/0

PITTSBURGH STEELERS
1. **Mark Bruener, Washington, TE, 125/157**
2. **Kordell Stewart, Colorado, QB, 114/126**
3. **Brendan Stai, Nebraska, G, 68/105**
4. **Oliver Gibson, Notre Dame, DT, 60/133**
4. **Donta Jones, Nebraska, LB, 63/91**
5. Lance Brown, Indiana, DB, 32/58
5. **Lee Flowers, Georgia Tech, DB, 112/112**
6. Barron Miles, Nebraska, DB, 0/0
7. Henry Bailey, UNLV, WR, 0/8
7. Cole Ford, USC, K, 0/38

SAN DIEGO CHARGERS
2. **Terrell Fletcher, Wisconsin, RB, 111/111**
2. **Terrance Shaw, Stephen F. Austin State, DB, 69/140**
2. Jimmy Oliver, Texas Christian, WR, 0/0
3. Don Sasa, Washington State, DT, 9/14
3. Preston Harrison, Ohio State, LB, 0/0
4. Aaron Hayden, Tennessee, RB, 18/33
4. Chris Cowart, Florida State, LB, 0/0
5. 'Omar Ellison, Florida State, WR, 12/12
6. Tony Berti, Colorado, T, 33/33
6. Troy Sienkiewicz, New Mexico State, G, 28/28
6. Craig Whelihan, Pacific, QB, 19/19
6. Brandon Harrison, Howard Payne, WR, 0/0
7. Mark Montreuil, Concordia (QB), DB, 35/35

SAN FRANCISCO 49ERS
1. **J.J. Stokes, UCLA, WR, 111/118**
4. Tim Hanshaw, Brigham Young, G, 30/30
6. Antonio Armstrong, Texas A&M, LB, 0/4
7. Herbert Coleman, Trinity (IL), DE, 0/0

ST. LOUIS RAMS
1. **Kevin Carter, Florida, DE, 96/176**
2. Jesse James, Mississippi State, C, 3/3
2. Zach Wiegert, Nebraska, G, 49/136
3. Steve McLaughlin, Arizona, K, 8/8
4. Lovell Pinkney, Texas, TE, 8/8
5. **Mike Scurlock, Arizona, DB, 51/65**
7. Gerald McBurrows, Kansas, DB, 48/122
7. Bronzell Miller, Utah, DE, 0/3
7. Herman O'Berry, Oregon, DB, 9/9
7. **J.T. Thomas, Arizona State, WR, 51/51**

SEATTLE SEAHAWKS
1. **Joey Galloway, Ohio State, WR, 71/145**
2. **Christian Fauria, Colorado, TE, 103/167**
4. Jason Kyle, Arizona State, LB, 48/130
6. Henry McMillian, Florida, DT, 3/3
6. Eddie Goines, North Carolina State, WR, 0/0
7. Keif Bryant, Rutgers, DE, 0/0

TAMPA BAY BUCCANEERS
1. **Derrick Brooks, Florida State, LB, 176/176**
1. **Warren Sapp, Miami (FL), DT, 140/166**
2. Melvin Johnson, Kentucky, DB, 43/50
4. Jerry Wilson, Southern (LA), DB, 0/120
5. Clifton Abraham, Florida State, DB, 6/9
6. Wardell Rouse, Clemson, LB, 16/16
7. Steve Ingram, Maryland, T, 2/8
7. Jeff Rodgers, Texas A&M-Kingsville, DE, 0/0

WASHINGTON REDSKINS
1. **Michael Westbrook, Colorado, WR, 80/89**
2. **Cory Raymer, Wisconsin, C, 80/98**
3. **Darryl Pounds, Nicholls State, DB, 69/78**
4. Larry Jones, Miami (FL), RB, 0/0
5. Jamie Asher, Louisville, TE, 48/48
5. Rich Owens, Lehigh, DE, 42/97
6. Brian Thure, California, T, 4/4
7. Scott Turner, Illinois, DB, 41/101

1996 NFL

ARIZONA CARDINALS
1. **Simeon Rice, Illinois, DE, 79/158**
2. Leeland McElroy, Texas A&M, RB, 30/30
3. **Johnny McWilliams, USC, TE, 59/74**
4. **Aaron Graham, Nebraska, C, 62/92**
5. James Dexter, South Carolina, T, 40/49
5. Dell McGee, Auburn, DB, 3/3
5. Harry Stamps, Oklahoma, T, 0/0
6. Mike Foley, New Hampshire, DT, 0/0
7. Jarius Hayes, North Alabama, TE, 20/20

ATLANTA FALCONS
3. Shannon Brown, Alabama, DT, 0/0
4. Juran Bolden, Mississippi Delta C.C., DB, 48/93
4. Richard Huntley, Winston-Salem State, RB, 1/63
5. Gary Bandy, Baylor, DE, 0/0
6. **Craig Sauer, Minnesota, LB, 64/73**
7. Ethan Brooks, Williams, T, 2/76

BALTIMORE RAVENS
1. **Ray Lewis, Miami (FL), LB, 134/134**
1. **Jonathan Ogden, UCLA, T, 152/152**
2. **DeRon Jenkins, Tennessee, DB, 63/93**
5. **Jermaine Lewis, Maryland, WR, 88/111**
6. Dexter Daniels, Florida, LB, 4/4
6. James Roe, Norfolk State, WR, 23/23
7. Jon Stark, Trinity (IL), QB, 0/0

BUFFALO BILLS
1. **Eric Moulds, Mississippi State, WR, 154/154**
2. **Gabe Northern, LSU, LB, 64/73**
3. Matt Stevens, Appalachian State, DB, 13/108
4. **Sean Moran, Colorado State, LB, 57/120**
5. Raymond Jackson, Colorado State, DB, 35/73
6. Leon Neal, Washington, RB, 0/1
6. Dusty Zeigler, Notre Dame, C, 46/80
7. Dan Brandenburg, Indiana State, LB, 42/42
7. **Jay Riemersma, Michigan, TE, 90/112**
7. Eric Smedley, Indiana, DB, 35/42

CAROLINA PANTHERS
1. **Tim Biakabutuka, Michigan, RB, 50/50**
2. **Muhsin Muhammad, Michigan State, WR, 125/140**
3. Winslow Oliver, New Mexico, RB, 38/64
3. J.C. Price, Virginia Tech, DT, 0/0
4. **Norbert Davidds-Garrido, USC, T, 59/68**
4. Emmanuel McDaniel, East Carolina, DB, 18/75
5. Marquette Smith, Central Florida, RB, 0/0
6. Scott Greene, Michigan State, RB, 24/34
7. Kerry Hicks, Colorado, DE, 0/2
7. Donnell Baker, Southern, WR, 0/0

CHICAGO BEARS
1. **Walt Harris, Mississippi State, DB, 87/147**
2. **Bobby Engram, Penn State, WR, 62/135**
4. Paul Grasmanis, Notre Dame, DT, 45/104
5. **Chris Villarrial, Indiana (PA), G, 116/147**
6. Jon Clark, Temple, T, 2/10
7. Michael Hicks, South Carolina State, RB, 7/7
7. Marcus Keyes, North Alabama, DT, 2/2

CINCINNATI BENGALS
1. **Willie Anderson, Auburn, T, 158/158**
2. **Marco Battaglia, Rutgers, TE, 88/96**
3. Ken Blackman, Illinois, G, 35/35
4. **Jevon Langford, Oklahoma State, DE, 66/66**

5. **Greg Myers, Colorado State, DB, 58/64**
6. Tom Tumulty, Pittsburgh, LB, 31/31
7. **Rod Jones, Kansas, T, 57/63**

DALLAS COWBOYS

2. **Randall Godfrey, Georgia, LB, 64/146**
2. **Kavika Pittman, McNeese State, DE, 61/108**
3. Clay Shiver, Florida State, C, 44/44
3. Mike Ulufale, Brigham Young, DT, 3/3
3. Stepfret Williams, Louisiana-Monroe, WR, 21/26
5. Alan Campos, Louisville, LB, 15/15
5. Kenneth McDaniel, Norfolk State, T, 0/0
6. Wendell Davis, Oklahoma, DB, 34/34
7. Ryan Wood, Arizona State, RB, 0/0

DENVER BRONCOS

1. **John Mobley, Kutztown State, LB, 105/105**
2. Tory James, LSU, DB, 48/142
3. Mark Campbell, Florida, DT, 0/5
3. **Detron Smith, Texas A&M, RB, 91/113**
4. **Darrius Johnson, Oklahoma, DB, 61/63**
4. Jeff Lewis, Northern Arizona, QB, 5/12
5. Patrick Jeffers, Virginia, WR, 14/46
6. Tony Veland, Nebraska, DB, 12/27
7. Chris Banks, Kansas, G, 20/28
7. Leslie Ratliffe, Tennessee, T, 0/0
7. L.T. Levine, Kansas, RB, 0/0
7. Brian Gragert, Wyoming, P, 0/0

DETROIT LIONS

1. Reggie Brown, Texas A&M, LB, 26/26
1. **Jeff Hartings, Penn State, C, 72/149**
3. Ryan Stewart, Georgia Tech, DB, 41/41
4. Brad Ford, Alabama, DB, 14/14
5. Kerwin Waldroup, Central State (OH), DE, 40/40

GREEN BAY PACKERS

1. John Michels, USC, T, 24/24
2. Derrick Mayes, Notre Dame, WR, 29/58
3. **Mike Flanagan, UCLA, C, 98/98**
3. **Tyrone Williams, Nebraska, DB, 111/120**
4. Chris Darkins, Minnesota, DB, 14/14
6. **Marco Rivera, Penn State, G, 125/139**
7. **Keith McKenzie, Ball State, DE, 62/95**
7. Kyle Wachholtz, Southern California, QB, 0/0

HOUSTON OILERS

1. **Eddie George, Ohio State, RB, 128/141**
2. **Jason Layman, Tennessee, G, 61/61**
2. Bryant Mix, Alcorn State, DE, 7/7
3. **Terry Killens, Penn State, LB, 78/97**
4. Kendrick Burton, Alabama, DE, 4/4
4. **Jon Runyan, Michigan, T, 58/154**
5. Rayna Stewart, Northern Arizona, DB, 31/71
6. **Anthony Dorsett, Pittsburgh, DB, 56/118**
7. Mike Archie, Penn State, RB, 23/23

INDIANAPOLIS COLTS

1. **Marvin Harrison, Syracuse, WR, 154/154**
2. Dedric Mathis, Houston, DB, 29/29
3. Scott Slutzker, Iowa, TE, 27/41
4. Brian Milne, Penn State, RB, 0/63
5. Steve Martin, Missouri, DT, 30/127
6. Keith Conlin, Penn State, T, 0/0
6. Mike Cawley, James Madison, QB, 0/0
7. Adrian Robinson, Baylor, DB, 0/0

JACKSONVILLE JAGUARS

1. **Kevin Hardy, Illinois, LB, 86/134**
2. **Tony Brackens, Texas, DE, 107/107**
2. Michael Cheever, Georgia Tech, C, 17/17
3. **Aaron Beasley, West Virginia, DB, 76/121**
4. **Reggie Barlow, Alabama State, WR, 69/82**
5. Jimmy Herndon, Houston, T, 0/54
6. Chris Doering, Florida, WR, 0/40
6. John Fisher, Missouri Western, DB, 0/0
7. Clarence Jones, Tennessee State, WR, 0/0
7. Gregory Spann, Jackson State, WR, 0/0

KANSAS CITY CHIEFS

1. **Jerome Woods, Memphis, DB, 128/128**
2. **Reggie Tongue, Oregon State, DB, 63/145**
3. **John Browning, West Virginia, DT, 121/121**
4. **Donnie Edwards, UCLA, LB, 94/158**
5. Joe Horn, Itawamba J.C., WR, 49/141
6. Dietrich Jells, Pittsburgh, WR, 0/41
7. Ben Lynch, California, C, 0/52
7. Jeff Smith, Tennessee, C, 29/59
7. Darrell Williams, Tennessee State, DB, 0/0

MIAMI DOLPHINS

1. **Daryl Gardener, Baylor, DT, 82/102**
3. **Karim Abdul-Jabbar, UCLA, RB, 50/61**
3. Dorian Brew, Kansas, DB, 0/16
4. LaCurtis Jones, Baylor, LB, 0/10
4. **Stanley Pritchett, South Carolina, FB, 52/121**
4. Kirk Pointer, Austin Peay, DB, 0/0
5. Shane Burton, Tennessee, DE, 47/125
5. Jerris McPhail, East Carolina, RB, 23/26
5. **Zach Thomas, Texas Tech, LB, 147/147**
6. **Shawn Wooden, Notre Dame, DB, 93/104**
7. Jeff Buckey, Stanford, G, 38/45
7. Brice Hunter, Georgia, WR, 0/13

MINNESOTA VIKINGS

1. **Duane Clemons, California, DE, 58/142**
2. James Manley, Vanderbilt, DT, 0/0
3. **Moe Williams, Kentucky, RB, 117/132**
4. **Hunter Goodwin, Texas A&M, TE, 72/119**
5. Sean Boyd, North Carolina, DB, 0/2
7. Jon Merrill, Duke, G, 0/0

NEW ENGLAND PATRIOTS

1. **Terry Glenn, Ohio State, WR, 68/121**
2. **Lawyer Milloy, Washington, DB, 112/155**
3. **Tedy Bruschi, Arizona, LB, 145/145**
4. Kantroy Barber, West Virginia, RB, 0/2
4. Heath Irwin, Colorado, G, 44/87
4. **Chris Sullivan, Boston College, DE, 63/78**
5. Christian Peter, Nebraska, DT, 0/81
5. John Elmore, Texas, G, 0/0
6. Marrio Grier, Tennessee-Chattanooga, RB, 32/32
6. Devin Wyman, Kentucky State, DT, 15/15
6. Chris Griffin, New Mexico, TE, 0/0
7. J.R. Conrad, Oklahoma, G, 0/12
7. Lovett Purnell, West Virginia, TE, 34/36

NEW ORLEANS SAINTS

1. **Alex Molden, Oregon, DB, 74/98**
2. **Je'Rod Cherry, California, DB, 59/127**
3. **Brady Smith, Colorado State, DE, 62/143**
4. Ricky Whittle, Oregon, RB, 10/10
5. **Tom Ackerman, Eastern Washington, G, 78/105**
5. Terry Guess, Gardner-Webb, WR, 3/3
5. Mercury Hayes, Michigan, WR, 11/13
6. Keno Hills, Louisiana-Lafayette, G, 22/22
6. Toderick Malone, Alabama, WR, 0/0
7. Henry Lusk, Utah, TE, 16/19

NEW YORK GIANTS

1. **Cedric Jones, Oklahoma, DE, 73/73**
2. **Amani Toomer, Michigan, WR, 150/150**
3. **Roman Oben, Louisville, T, 50/137**
4. Danny Kanell, Florida State, QB, 30/43
6. Doug Colman, Nebraska, LB, 43/64
6. **Scott Galyon, Tennessee, LB, 58/95**
7. Conrad Hamilton, Eastern New Mexico, DB, 48/54

NEW YORK JETS

1. **Keyshawn Johnson, USC, WR, 62/151**
2. Alex Van Dyke, Nevada-Reno, WR, 36/42
3. **Ray Mickens, Texas A&M, DB, 126/142**
5. **Marcus Coleman, Texas Tech, DB, 91/149**
6. Hugh Hunter, Hampton, DE, 0/0
7. **Chris Hayes, Washington State, DB, 78/84**

OAKLAND RAIDERS

1. **Rickey Dudley, Ohio State, TE, 80/108**
2. **Lance Johnstone, Temple, DE, 76/155**
5. La'Roi Glover, San Diego State, DT, 2/145
6. Tim Hall, Robert Morris, RB, 18/18
7. Sedric Clark, Tulsa, LB, 0/6
7. Darius Smith, Sam Houston State, C, 0/0
7. Joey Wylie, Stephen F. Austin, G, 0/0

PHILADELPHIA EAGLES

1. **Jermane Mayberry, Texas A&M-Kingsville, G, 112/123**
2. **Brian Dawkins, Clemson, DB, 141/141**
2. Jason Dunn, Eastern Kentucky, TE, 41/129
3. Bobby Hoying, Ohio State, QB, 16/22
4. Ray Farmer, Duke, LB, 32/32
5. Whit Marshall, Georgia, LB, 1/16
6. Tony Johnson, Alabama, TE, 0/27
6. Phillip Riley, Florida State, WR, 0/1
6. Steve White, Tennessee, DE, 0/94

PITTSBURGH STEELERS

1. Jamain Stephens, North Carolina A&T, T, 18/39
3. Steve Conley, Arkansas, LB, 20/21
3. **Jon Witman, Penn State, RB, 85/85**
4. Jahine Arnold, Fresno State, WR, 12/13
4. **Earl Holmes, Florida A&M, LB, 81/140**
5. Israel Raybon, North Alabama, DE, 3/12
6. **Orpheus Roye, Florida State, DT, 61/152**
6. Spence Fischer, Duke, QB, 0/0
7. **Carlos Emmons, Arkansas State, LB, 51/135**

SAN DIEGO CHARGERS

2. Patrick Sapp, Clemson, LB, 32/63
2. Bryan Still, Virginia Tech, WR, 49/52
3. Brian Roche, San Jose State, TE, 18/22
4. **Charlie Jones, Fresno State, WR, 54/54**
5. Junior Soli, Arkansas, DT, 0/0
6. Jim Mills, Idaho, G, 2/2
6. Bryan Stoltenberg, Colorado, C, 9/50
7. Freddie Bradley, Sonoma State, RB, 10/10

SAN FRANCISCO 49ERS

2. Israel Ifeanyi, USC, DE, 3/3
3. **Terrell Owens, Tennessee-Chattanooga, WR, 121/142**
4. Daryl Price, Colorado, DE, 18/18
5. Iheanyi Uwaezuoke, California, WR, 35/60
6. Stephen Pitts, Penn State, RB, 0/0
7. Sean Manuel, New Mexico State, TE, 11/11
7. Sam Manuel, New Mexico State, LB, 0/0

ST. LOUIS RAMS

1. Eddie Kennison, LSU, WR, 45/152
1. Lawrence Phillips, Nebraska, RB, 25/35
2. Tony Banks, Michigan State, QB, 44/97
2. **Ernie Conwell, Washington, TE, 84/119**
3. Jerald Moore, Oklahoma, RB, 31/42
4. Percell Gaskins, Kansas State, LB, 15/27
5. **Fred Miller, Baylor, T, 60/155**
6. Hayward Clay, Texas A&M, TE, 11/14
6. Derrick Harris, Miami (FL), RB, 28/44
7. Chuck Osborne, Arizona, DT, 15/37

SEATTLE SEAHAWKS

1. **Pete Kendall, Boston College, G, 76/143**
2. Fred Thomas, Tennessee-Martin, DB, 47/136
3. **Reggie D. 2 Brown, Fresno State, RB, 61/61**
3. Robert Barr, Rutgers, T, 0/0
4. **Phillip Daniels, Georgia, DE, 60/140**
4. Eric Unverzagt, Wisconsin, LB, 9/9
6. T.J. Cunningham, Colorado, DB, 9/9
6. Reggie Green, Florida, G, 0/0
7. Johnie Church, Florida, DE, 0/0

TAMPA BAY BUCCANEERS

1. **Marcus Jones, North Carolina, DE, 85/85**
1. Regan Upshaw, California, DE, 48/110
2. **Mike Alstott, Purdue, RB, 142/142**
3. **Donnie Abraham, East Tennessee State, DB, 92/132**
4. Eric Austin, Jackson State, DB, 2/2
4. Jason Odom, Florida, T, 46/46
5. Jason Maniecki, Wisconsin, DT, 18/18
6. Nilo Silvan, Tennessee, WR, 7/7
7. Reggie Rusk, Kentucky, DB, 5/23

WASHINGTON REDSKINS

1. Andre Johnson, Penn State, T, 0/3
4. **Stephen Davis, Auburn, RB, 99/128**
5. **Leomont Evans, Clemson, DB, 59/59**
6. Kelvin Kinney, Virginia State, DE, 18/18
7. Jeremy Asher, Oregon, LB, 0/0
7. DeAndre Maxwell, San Diego State, WR, 0/0

1997 NFL

ARIZONA CARDINALS

1. **Tom Knight, Iowa, DB, 63/73**
2. **Jake Plummer, Arizona State, QB, 84/127**
3. Ty Howard, Ohio State, DB, 24/37
4. **Chris Dishman, Nebraska, G, 91/98**
5. Chad Carpenter, Washington State, WR, 0/0
6. Tony McCombs, Eastern Kentucky, LB, 26/26
6. Rod Brown, North Carolina State, RB, 0/0
7. Mark Smith, Auburn, DT, 46/67

ATLANTA FALCONS

1. Michael Booker, Nebraska, DB, 42/73
2. Nathan Davis, Indiana, DE, 2/6
2. Byron Hanspard, Texas Tech, RB, 28/28
3. O.J. Santiago, Kent State, TE, 41/78
4. **Henri Crockett, Florida State, LB, 73/103**
5. Marcus Wimberly, Miami (FL), DB, 6/6
6. **Calvin Collins, Texas A&M, G, 61/68**
7. Chris Bayne, Fresno State, DB, 23/23
7. Tony Graziani, Oregon, QB, 18/18

BALTIMORE RAVENS

1. **Peter Boulware, Florida State, LB, 126/126**
2. **Kim Herring, Penn State, DB, 54/98**
2. **Jamie Sharper, Virginia, LB, 80/136**
3. Jay Graham, Tennessee, RB, 22/36
4. Tyrus McCloud, Louisville, LB, 23/23
5. Jeff Mitchell, Florida, C, 41/119
6. **Cornell Brown, Virginia Tech, LB, 108/108**
6. Steve Lee, Indiana, RB, 0/0
7. Wally Richardson, Penn State, QB, 1/1
7. Ralph Staten, Alabama, DB, 25/25
7. Leland Taylor, Louisville, DT, 1/1
7. Chris Ward, Kentucky, DE, 5/5

BUFFALO BILLS

1. **Antowain Smith, Houston, RB, 57/131**
2. **Marcellus Wiley, Columbia, DE, 64/135**
4. Jamie Nails, Florida A&M, G, 49/78
5. Sean Woodson, Jackson State, DB, 0/0
6. Marcus Spriggs, Houston, T, 30/49
7. Pat Fitzgerald, Texas, TE, 0/0

CAROLINA PANTHERS

1. Rae Carruth, Colorado, WR, 22/22
2. **Mike Minter, Nebraska, DB, 132/132**
3. Kinnon Tatum, Notre Dame, LB, 31/31
4. Tarek Saleh, Wisconsin, LB, 14/59
6. Mike Finkes, Ohio State, DE, 0/8
7. **Kris Mangum, Mississippi, TE, 111/111**

CHICAGO BEARS

2. John Allred, USC, TE, 40/53
3. Bob Sapp, Washington, G, 0/1
4. Darnell Autry, Northwestern, RB, 13/24
4. **Marcus Robinson, South Carolina, WR, 51/97**
5. Van Hiles, Kentucky, DB, 16/16
6. Ricky Parker, San Diego State, DB, 0/12
6. Shawn Swayda, Arizona State, DE, 0/35
6. Richard Hogans, Memphis, LB, 0/0
7. Marvin Thomas, Memphis, DE, 0/4
7. Mike Miano, Southwest Missouri State, DT, 0/0

CINCINNATI BENGALS

1. **Reinard Wilson, Florida State, LB, 93/93**
2. **Corey Dillon, Washington, RB, 107/134**
3. Rod Payne, Michigan, C, 6/6
4. Tremain Mack, Miami (FL), DB, 44/44
5. Andre Purvis, North Carolina, DT, 21/21
6. **Canute Curtis, West Virginia, LB, 70/70**
7. William Carr, Michigan, DT, 0/0

DALLAS COWBOYS

1. **David LaFleur, LSU, TE, 60/60**
3. **Dexter Coakley, Appalachian State, LB, 127/139**
3. Steve Scifres, Wyoming, G, 6/7
3. Kenny Wheaton, Oregon, DB, 22/22
4. Antonio Anderson, Syracuse, DT, 21/21
4. Nicky Sualua, Ohio State, RB, 26/26
4. Macey Brooks, James Madison, WR, 0/0
6. Lee Vaughn, Wyoming, DB, 0/0
7. Omar Stoutmire, Fresno State, DB, 32/119

DENVER BRONCOS

1. **Trevor Pryce, Clemson, DT, 121/121**
3. **Dan Neil, Texas, G, 108/108**
4. Cory Gilliard, Ball State, DB, 0/1
4. Corey Gilliard, Ball State, DB, 0/0

DETROIT LIONS

1. **Bryant Westbrook, Texas, DB, 64/71**
2. Kevin Abrams, Syracuse, DB, 32/32
2. Juan Roque, Arizona State, T, 17/17
4. Matt Russell, Colorado, LB, 14/14
5. Pete Chryplewicz, Notre Dame, TE, 37/37
5. Duane Ashman, Virginia, DE, 0/0
6. Tony Ramirez, Northern Colorado, T, 30/30
7. Richard Jordan, Missouri Southern State, LB, 36/36
7. Terry Battle, Arizona State, RB, 0/0
7. Marcus Harris, Wyoming, WR, 0/0

GREEN BAY PACKERS

1. **Ross Verba, Iowa, T, 59/106**
2. **Darren Sharper, William & Mary, DB, 121/135**
3. Brett Conway, Penn State, K, 0/51
4. Jermaine Smith, Georgia, DT, 19/19
5. Anthony Hicks, Arkansas, LB, 0/0
7. Jerald Sowell, Tulane, FB, 0/137
7. Chris Miller, Southern California, WR, 0/0
7. Ron McAda, Army, QB, 0/0

INDIANAPOLIS COLTS

1. **Tarik Glenn, California, T, 138/138**
2. **Adam Meadows, Georgia, T, 103/103**
3. Bertrand Berry, Notre Dame, DE, 42/112
4. Monty Montgomery, Houston, DB, 35/59
5. Nate Jacquet, San Diego State, WR, 5/55
5. Carl Powell, Louisville, DE, 11/81
6. Scott Von der Ahe, Arizona State, LB, 9/9
7. Clarence Thompson, Knoxville, DB, 0/0

JACKSONVILLE JAGUARS

1. **Renaldo Wynn, Notre Dame, DE, 73/137**
2. Mike Logan, West Virginia, DB, 43/104
4. James Hamilton, North Carolina, LB, 16/16
4. **Seth Payne, Cornell, DT, 66/116**

5. **Damon Jones, Southern Illinois, TE, 50/50**
6. **Daimon Shelton, Sacramento State, FB, 59/119**
7. Jon Hesse, Nebraska, LB, 0/5

KANSAS CITY CHIEFS

1. **Tony Gonzalez, California, TE, 143/143**
2. **Kevin Lockett, Kansas State, WR, 54/86**
4. Pat Barnes, California, QB, 0/0
5. June Henley, Kansas, RB, 0/11
6. Isaac Byrd, Kansas, WR, 0/61
7. Nathan Parks, Stanford, T, 0/2

MIAMI DOLPHINS

1. Yatil Green, Miami (FL), WR, 8/8
2. **Sam Madison, Louisville, DB, 138/138**
3. **Derrick Rodgers, Arizona State, LB, 93/116**
3. Brent Smith, Mississippi State, G, 37/57
3. **Jason Taylor, Akron, DE, 140/140**
3. Ronnie Ward, Kansas, LB, 4/4
4. Jerome Daniels, Northeastern, G, 0/8
5. Barron Tanner, Oklahoma, DT, 29/78
5. Nicholas Lopez, Texas Southern, DE, 0/0
6. Mike Crawford, UNLV, LB, 7/7
6. John Fiala, Washington, LB, 0/75
6. Brian Manning, Stanford, WR, 7/10
6. **Ed Perry, James Madison, TE, 103/109**
7. Hudhaifa Ismaeli, Northwestern, DB, 0/0

MINNESOTA VIKINGS

1. **Dwayne Rudd, Alabama, LB, 61/109**
2. Torrian Gray, Virginia Tech, DB, 25/25
3. Stalin Colinet, Boston College, DT, 35/68
4. Antonio Banks, Virginia Tech, DB, 24/24
5. **Tony Williams, Memphis, DT, 52/103**
6. **Robert Tate, Cincinnati, DB, 67/107**
7. Matthew Hatchette, Langston, WR, 48/65
7. Artie Ulmer, Valdosta State, LB, 0/90

NEW ENGLAND PATRIOTS

1. Chris Canty, Kansas State, DB, 32/61
2. **Brandon Mitchell, Texas A&M, DE, 61/95**
3. Chris Carter, Texas, DB, 47/92
3. Sedrick Shaw, Iowa, RB, 14/18
4. Damon Denson, Michigan, G, 14/14
4. Ed Ellis, Buffalo, T, 9/54
5. Vernon Crawford, Florida State, LB, 41/41
6. Tony Gaiter, Miami (FL), WR, 1/6
7. Scott Rehberg, Central Michigan, G, 8/79

NEW ORLEANS SAINTS

1. **Chris Naeole, Colorado, G, 67/130**
2. **Rob Kelly, Ohio State, DB, 60/60**
2. **Jared Tomich, Nebraska, DE, 54/56**
3. Troy Davis, Iowa State, RB, 46/46
4. Keith Poole, Arizona State, WR, 48/54
4. Danny Wuerffel, Florida, QB, 16/25
6. Nick Savoie, LSU, TE, 1/1

NEW YORK GIANTS

1. **Ike Hilliard, Florida, WR, 98/114**
2. **Tiki Barber, Virginia, RB, 138/138**
3. **Brad Maynard, Ball State, P, 64/144**
3. **Ryan Phillips, Idaho, LB, 58/71**
4. Pete Monty, Wisconsin, LB, 46/52
5. **Sam Garnes, Cincinnati, DB, 74/106**
6. Mike Cherry, Murray State, QB, 2/2
7. Matt Keneley, USC, DT, 0/7

NEW YORK JETS

1. **James Farrior, Virginia, LB, 76/136**
2. Rick Terry, North Carolina, DT, 14/29
3. **Dedric Ward, Northern Iowa, WR, 59/103**
4. Terry Day, Mississippi State, DE, 1/1
4. Leon Johnson, North Carolina, RB, 32/74
5. Raymond Austin, Tennessee, DB, 16/43
5. Lamont Burns, East Carolina, G, 4/4
6. Chuck Clements, Houston, QB, 1/1
6. Tim Scharf, Northwestern, LB, 0/0
7. **Jason Ferguson, Georgia, DT, 101/117**
7. Steve Rosga, Colorado, DB, 0/0

OAKLAND RAIDERS

1. **Darrell Russell, USC, DT, 75/83**
3. **Adam Treu, Nebraska, C, 144/144**
3. Tim Kohn, Iowa State, T, 0/0
4. Chad Levitt, Cornell, RB, 10/10
6. **Calvin Branch, Colorado State, DB, 60/60**
6. **Grady Jackson, Knoxville, DT, 67/123**

PHILADELPHIA EAGLES

1. Jon Harris, Virginia, DE, 24/24
2. **James Darling, Washington State, LB, 59/136**
3. **Duce Staley, South Carolina, RB, 98/113**
4. Damien Robinson, Iowa, DB, 0/83
5. Luther Broughton, Furman, TE, 31/62
5. **N.D. Kalu, Rice, DE, 64/104**
6. Ed Jasper, Texas A&M, DT, 17/118
6. Antwuan Wyatt, Bethune-Cookman, WR, 1/1
7. DeAuntae Brown, Central State (OH), DB, 1/1
7. **Koy Detmer, Colorado, QB, 103/103**
7. Byron Capers, Florida State, DB, 0/0

PITTSBURGH STEELERS

1. **Chad Scott, Maryland, DB, 91/94**
2. Will Blackwell, San Diego State, WR, 47/47
3. **Mike Vrabel, Ohio State, LB, 51/128**
3. Paul Wiggins, Oregon, T, 1/2
5. George Jones, San Diego State, RB, 16/34
6. Rod Manuel, Oklahoma, DE, 3/3
6. Daryl Porter, Boston College, DB, 0/55
7. Mike Adams, Texas, WR, 6/6

SAN DIEGO CHARGERS

2. **Freddie Jones, North Carolina, TE, 75/123**
3. Michael Hamilton, North Carolina A&T, LB, 33/37
4. **Raleigh Roundtree, South Carolina State, G, 62/72**
5. Paul Bradford, Portland State, DB, 15/15
5. **Kenny Bynum, South Carolina State, RB, 53/53**
6. Daniel Palmer, Air Force, C, 0/0
7. Toran James, North Carolina A&T, LB, 14/14
7. Tony Corbin, Cal State-Sacramento, QB, 0/0

SAN FRANCISCO 49ERS

1. Jim Druckenmiller, Virginia Tech, QB, 6/6
2. Marc Edwards, Notre Dame, FB, 31/132
3. **Greg Clark, Stanford, TE, 55/55**

ST. LOUIS RAMS

1. **Orlando Pace, Ohio State, T, 135/135**
2. **Dexter McCleon, Clemson, DB, 91/131**
4. **Ryan Tucker, TCU, T, 59/112**
5. **Taje Allen, Texas, DB, 57/79**
6. Muadianvita Kazadi, Tulsa, LB, 12/12
7. Cedric White, North Carolina A&T, DE, 0/0

SEATTLE SEAHAWKS

1. **Walter Jones, Florida State, T, 137/137**
1. **Shawn Springs, Ohio State, DB, 93/123**
5. Eric Stokes, Nebraska, DB, 11/11
6. **Itula Mili, Brigham Young, TE, 104/104**
7. Carlos Jones, Miami (FL), DB, 0/0

TAMPA BAY BUCCANEERS

1. **Reidel Anthony, Florida, WR, 73/73**
1. **Warrick Dunn, Florida State, RB, 76/134**
2. **Jerry Wunsch, Wisconsin, T, 80/112**
3. **Ronde Barber, Virginia, DB, 129/129**
3. **Frank Middleton, Arizona, G, 63/109**
4. **Alshermond Singleton, Temple, LB, 87/124**
5. **Patrick Hape, Alabama, TE, 61/124**
6. Al Harris, Texas A&M-Kingsville, DB, 0/128
6. Nigea Carter, Michigan State, WR, 0/0
7. Anthony DeGrate, Stephen F. Austin, DT, 0/0

TENNESSEE TITANS

1. **Kenny Holmes, Miami (FL), DE, 58/98**
2. Joey Kent, Tennessee, WR, 30/30
3. Scott Sanderson, Washington State, T, 38/45
3. **Denard Walker, LSU, DB, 61/134**
4. Pratt Lyons, Troy State, DE, 32/32
4. **Derrick Mason, Michigan State, WR, 122/138**
5. George McCullough, Baylor, DB, 24/39
6. Dennis Stallings, Illinois, LB, 28/28
7. Armon Williams, Arizona, DB, 6/6

WASHINGTON REDSKINS

1. **Kenard Lang, Miami (FL), DE, 75/137**
2. **Greg Jones, Colorado, LB, 63/82**
3. **Derek Smith, Arizona State, LB, 64/140**
4. **Albert Connell, Texas A&M, WR, 50/61**
5. Brad Badger, Stanford, G, 42/126
5. Twan Russell, Miami (FL), LB, 27/78
5. Keith Thibodeaux, Northwestern State (LA), DB, 15/54
5. Jamel Williams, Nebraska, DB, 35/35

1998 NFL

ARIZONA CARDINALS

1. Andre Wadsworth, Florida State, DE, 36/36
2. **Corey Chavous, Vanderbilt, DB, 61/125**
2. **Anthony Clement, Louisiana-Lafayette, T, 82/96**
4. **Michael Pittman, Fresno State, RB, 56/117**
5. Terry Hardy, Southern Mississippi, TE, 49/49
6. Zack Walz, Dartmouth, LB, 46/46
7. **Pat Tillman, Arizona State, DB, 60/60**
7. Phil Savoy, Colorado, WR, 0/0
7. Jomo Cousins, Florida A&M, DE, 0/0
7. Ron Janes, Missouri, RB, 0/0

ATLANTA FALCONS

1. **Keith Brooking, Georgia Tech, LB, 113/113**
2. **Bob Hallen, Kent State, G, 59/86**
3. Jammi German, Miami (FL), WR, 29/35
4. Omar Brown, North Carolina, DB, 15/15
4. Tim Dwight, Iowa, WR, 38/101
6. **Elijah Williams, Florida, E, 50/50**
7. Ken Oxendine, Virginia Tech, RB, 21/21
7. **Ephraim Salaam, San Diego State, T, 60/110**
7. Henry Slay, West Virginia, DT, 0/3

BALTIMORE RAVENS

1. **Duane Starks, Miami (FL), DB, 62/94**
2. Patrick Johnson, Oregon, WR, 45/70
5. Martin Chase, Oklahoma, DT, 3/55
5. Ryan Sutter, Colorado, DB, 0/1
6. Sammy Williams, Oklahoma, T, 16/29
6. Ron Rogers, Georgia Tech, LB, 0/0
7. Cam Quayle, Weber State, TE, 0/0

BUFFALO BILLS

2. Sam Cowart, Florida State, LB, 45/100
3. Robert Hicks, Mississippi State, T, 37/37
5. Jonathan Linton, North Carolina, RB, 44/44
6. Fred Coleman, Washington, WR, 0/9
7. Kamil Loud, Cal Poly-San Luis Obispo, WR, 12/12
7. Victor Allotey, Indiana, G, 0/0

CAROLINA PANTHERS

1. Jason Peter, Nebraska, DE, 38/38
3. Chuck Wiley, LSU, DE, 16/79
3. Mitch Marrow, Pennsylvania, DE, 0/0
4. **Donald Hayes, Wisconsin, WR, 51/63**
5. Jerry Jensen, Washington, LB, 10/10
6. **Damien Richardson, Arizona State, DB, 77/77**
7. Viliami Maumau, Colorado, DT, 1/1
7. Jim Turner, Syracuse, WR, 0/0

CHICAGO BEARS

1. Curtis Enis, Penn State, RB, 36/36
2. **Tony Parrish, Washington, DB, 64/121**
3. **Olin Kreutz, Washington, C, 111/111**
4. Alonzo Mayes, Oklahoma State, TE, 37/37
6. Chris Draft, Stanford, LB, 1/95
6. **Patrick Mannelly, Duke, T, 125/125**
7. Moses Moreno, Colorado State, QB, 2/9
7. Chad Overhauser, UCLA, T, 0/3

CINCINNATI BENGALS

1. **Brian Simmons, North Carolina, LB, 110/110**
1. **Takeo Spikes, Auburn, LB, 79/114**
2. **Artrell Hawkins, Cincinnati, DB, 89/108**
3. **Steve Foley, Louisiana-Monroe, LB, 54/96**
3. **Mike Goff, Iowa, G, 85/117**
4. **Glen Steele, Michigan, DT, 90/90**
6. Jason Tucker, TCU, WR, 0/31
7. Marcus Parker, Virginia Tech, RB, 0/0
7. Damian Vaughn, Miami (OH), TE, 0/0

DALLAS COWBOYS

1. **Greg Ellis, North Carolina, DE, 124/124**
2. **Flozell Adams, Michigan State, T, 118/118**
4. **Michael Myers, Alabama, DT, 68/107**
5. **Darren Hambrick, South Carolina, LB, 51/76**
5. Oliver Ross, Iowa State, T, 2/78
6. **Izell Reese, Alabama-Birmingham, DB, 56/93**
7. Rodrick Monroe, Cincinnati, TE, 0/9
7. Tarik Smith, California, RB, 0/0
7. Antonio Fleming, Georgia, G, 0/0

DENVER BRONCOS

1. Marcus Nash, Tennessee, WR, 10/11
2. **Eric Brown, Mississippi State, DB, 53/97**
3. **Brian Griese, Michigan, QB, 53/75**
4. Curtis Alexander, Alabama, RB, 0/0
5. Chris Howard, Michigan, RB, 0/22
7. Trey Teague, Tennessee, C, 34/94
7. Nate Wayne, Mississippi, LB, 16/90

DETROIT LIONS

1. **Terry Fair, Tennessee, DB, 52/60**
2. Charlie Batch, Eastern Michigan, QB, 48/56
2. **Germane Crowell, Virginia, WR, 54/54**
6. Jamaal Alexander, Southern Mississippi, DB, 0/0
7. Chris Liwienski, Indiana, G, 0/94

GREEN BAY PACKERS

1. **Vonnie Holliday, North Carolina, DE, 66/107**

S2. **Mike Wahle, Navy, G, 97/113**

3. Jonathan Brown, Tennessee, DE, 4/7
4. Roosevelt Blackmon, Morris Brown, DB, 3/20
5. Corey Bradford, Jackson State, WR, 42/105
6. Matt Hasselbeck, Boston College, QB, 32/107
6. Scott McGarrahan, New Mexico, DB, 44/108
7. Eddie Watson, Purdue, RB, 0/6

INDIANAPOLIS COLTS

1. **Peyton Manning, Tennessee, QB, 128/128**
2. Jerome Pathon, Washington, WR, 46/99
3. E.G. Green, Florida State, WR, 29/29
4. **Steve McKinney, Texas A&M, C, 60/124**
5. Antony Jordan, Vanderbilt, LB, 15/27
7. Aaron Taylor, Nebraska, G, 0/0
7. Corey Gaines, Tennessee, DB, 0/0

JACKSONVILLE JAGUARS

1. **Donovin Darius, Syracuse, DB, 105/105**
1. **Fred Taylor, Florida, RB, 97/97**
2. Cordell Taylor, Hampton, DB, 11/13
3. Jonathan Quinn, Middle Tennessee State, QB, 11/17
4. Tavian Banks, Iowa, RB, 14/14
4. Harry Deligianis, Youngstown State, DT, 0/0
5. **John Wade, Marshall, C, 54/94**
6. Kevin McLeod, Auburn, FB, 0/8
6. Lamanzer Williams, Minnesota, DE, 2/2
7. **Alvis Whitted, North Carolina State, WR, 57/108**
7. Brandon Tolbert, Georgia, LB, 0/0

KANSAS CITY CHIEFS

1. **Victor Riley, Auburn, T, 55/111**
3. Rashaan Shehee, Washington, RB, 25/25
4. Greg Favors, Mississippi State, LB, 16/101
5. Robert Williams, North Carolina, DB, 17/18
6. **Derrick Ransom, Cincinnati, DT, 56/71**
7. **Eric Warfield, Nebraska, DB, 115/115**
7. Ernest Blackwell, Missouri, RB, 0/0

MIAMI DOLPHINS

1. John Avery, Mississippi, RB, 17/28
2. **Kenny Mixon, LSU, DE, 59/105**
2. **Patrick Surtain, Southern Mississippi, DB, 108/123**
3. Brad Jackson, Cincinnati, LB, 0/50
3. Larry Shannon, East Carolina, WR, 2/2
4. **Lorenzo Bromell, Clemson, DE, 53/77**
5. Scott Shaw, Michigan State, G, 0/2
6. Nathan Strikwerda, Northwestern, C, 0/0
6. John Dutton, Nevada, QB, 0/0
7. Jim Bundren, Clemson, G, 0/0

MINNESOTA VIKINGS

1. **Randy Moss, Marshall, WR, 109/125**
2. **Kailee Wong, Stanford, LB, 60/113**
3. Ramos McDonald, New Mexico, DB, 20/32
4. Kivuusama Mays, North Carolina, LB, 27/30
5. Kerry Cooks, Iowa, DB, 0/9
6. **Matt Birk, Harvard, C, 98/98**
7. Chester Burnett, Arizona, LB, 0/12
7. Tony Darden, Texas Tech, DB, 0/16

NEW ENGLAND PATRIOTS

1. Robert Edwards, Georgia, RB, 16/28
1. **Tebucky Jones, Syracuse, DB, 72/109**
2. **Rod Rutledge, Alabama, TE, 63/70**
2. Tony Simmons, Wisconsin, WR, 38/48
3. Chris Floyd, Michigan, RB, 40/42
3. Greg Spires, Florida State, DE, 42/121
4. Leonta Rheams, Houston, DT, 6/6
5. Ron Merkerson, Colorado, LB, 0/0
6. Harold Shaw, Southern Mississippi, RB, 35/35
7. Jason Andersen, Brigham Young, G, 16/19

NEW ORLEANS SAINTS

1. **Kyle Turley, San Diego State, T, 79/95**
2. Cam Cleeland, Washington, TE, 36/89
4. Julian Pittman, Florida State, DE, 2/2
4. **Fred Weary, Florida, DB, 56/87**
5. Wilmont Perry, Livingstone, RB, 13/13
6. Chris Bordano, SMU, LB, 31/33
7. Andy McCullough, Tennessee, WR, 0/2
7. Ron Warner, Kansas, DE, 1/24

NEW YORK GIANTS

1. **Shaun Williams, UCLA, DB, 92/92**
2. **Joe Jurevicius, Penn State, WR, 58/104**
3. Brian Alford, Purdue, WR, 4/4
5. Toby Myles, Jackson State, T, 8/11
6. Todd Pollack, Boston College, TE, 0/0
7. Ben Fricke, Houston, C, 0/16

NEW YORK JETS
2. Dorian Boose, Washington State, DE, 33/43
3. Scott Frost, Nebraska, DB, 43/59
3. Kevin Williams, Oklahoma State, DB, 28/43
4. Jason Fabini, Cincinnati, T, 114/114
5. Casey Dailey, Northwestern, LB, 6/6
5. Blake Spence, Oregon, TE, 15/18
5. Doug Karczewski, Virginia, G, 0/0
5. Eric Bateman, Brigham Young, T, 0/0
6. Dustin Johnson, Brigham Young, FB, 0/1
6. Eric Ogbogu, Maryland, DE, 41/90
6. Chris Brazzell, Angelo State, WR, 0/0
7. Lawrence Hart, Southern (LA), TE, 0/1

OAKLAND RAIDERS
1. Mo Collins, Florida, G, 71/71
1. Charles Woodson, Michigan, DB, 106/106
2. Leon Bender, Washington State, DT, 0/0
3. Jon Ritchie, Stanford, FB, 75/94
4. Gennaro DiNapoli, Virginia Tech, C, 11/39
5. Jeremy Brigham, Washington, TE, 47/47
5. Travian Smith, Oklahoma, LB, 84/84
7. Vincent Amey, Arizona State, DE, 4/4
7. David Sanders, Arkansas, DE, 0/0

PHILADELPHIA EAGLES
1. Tra Thomas, Florida State, T, 119/119
3. Allen Rossum, Notre Dame, DB, 31/109
3. Jeremiah Trotter, Stephen F. Austin State, LB, 87/115
4. Clarence Love, Toledo, DB, 6/31
4. Brandon Whiting, California, DE, 88/93
5. Ike Reese, Michigan State, LB, 112/128
7. Chris Akins, Texas, DT, 0/0
7. Melvin Thomas, Colorado, G, 0/0

PITTSBURGH STEELERS
1. Alan Faneca, LSU, G, 126/126
2. Jeremy Staat, Arizona State, DE, 28/30
3. Chris Conrad, Fresno State, T, 17/17
3. Hines Ward, Georgia, WR, 127/127
4. Carlos King, North Carolina State, RB, 1/1
4. Deshea Townsend, Alabama, DB, 123/123
5. Jason Simmons, Arizona State, DB, 49/104
6. Chris Fuamatu-Ma'afala, Utah, RB, 53/73
6. Ryan Olson, Colorado, LB, 0/0
7. Angel Rubio, Southeast Missouri State, DE, 0/2

SAN DIEGO CHARGERS
1. Ryan Leaf, Washington State, QB, 21/25
2. Mikhael Ricks, Stephen F. Austin State, TE, 35/82
S2. Jamal Williams, Oklahoma State, DT, 102/102
5. Cedric Harden, Florida A&M, DE, 5/5
6. Clifford Ivory, Troy State, DB, 0/0
7. Jon Haskins, Stanford, LB, 2/2
7. Kio Sanford, Kentucky, WR, 0/0

SAN FRANCISCO 49ERS
1. R.W. McQuarters, Oklahoma State, DB, 27/115
2. Jeremy Newberry, California, C, 90/90
3. Chris Ruhman, Texas A&M, T, 6/11
4. Lance Schulters, Hofstra, DB, 56/107
5. Phil Ostroski, Penn State, G, 28/28
6. Fred Beasley, Auburn, FB, 114/114
7. Ryan Thelwell, Minnesota, WR, 0/6

ST. LOUIS RAMS
1. Grant Wistrom, Nebraska, DE, 91/116
2. Robert Holcombe, Illinois, RB, 58/97
3. Leonard Little, Tennessee, DE, 97/97
4. Az-Zahir Hakim, San Diego State, WR, 56/104
4. Roland Williams, Syracuse, TE, 49/94
5. Raymond Priester, Clemson, RB, 0/0
6. Glenn Rountree, Clemson, G, 0/0
7. Jason Chorak, Washington, DE, 0/8

SEATTLE SEAHAWKS
1. Anthony Simmons, Clemson, LB, 87/87
2. Todd Weiner, Kansas State, T, 49/112
3. Ahman Green, Nebraska, RB, 30/112
4. DeShone Myles, Nevada-Reno, LB, 17/18
6. Carl Hansen, Stanford, DE, 0/5
6. Bobby Shaw, California, WR, 0/90
7. Jason McEndoo, Washington State, C, 1/1

TAMPA BAY BUCCANEERS
2. Jacquez Green, Florida, WR, 56/66
2. Brian Kelly, USC, DB, 117/117
3. Jamie Duncan, Vanderbilt, LB, 60/96
4. Todd Washington, Virginia Tech, G, 51/97
6. James Cannida, Nevada-Reno, DT, 40/50
6. Shevin Smith, Florida State, DB, 19/19
7. Chance McCarty, Texas Christian, DE, 0/0

TENNESSEE TITANS
1. Kevin Dyson, Utah, WR, 58/59
2. Samari Rolle, Florida State, DB, 101/117
3. Dainon Sidney, Alabama-Birmingham, DB, 48/50
4. Joe Salave'a, Arizona, DT, 49/87
5. Benji Olson, Washington, G, 124/124
6. Lee Wiggins, South Carolina, DB, 0/0
7. Kevin Long, Florida State, C, 63/63
7. Jimmy Sprotte, Arizona, LB, 0/9

WASHINGTON REDSKINS
2. Stephen Alexander, Oklahoma, TE, 53/102
3. Skip Hicks, UCLA, RB, 29/38
4. Shawn Barber, Richmond, LB, 49/92
5. Mark Fischer, Purdue, C, 22/22
6. Patrick Palmer, Northwestern State (LA), WR, 0/0
7. Antwaune Ponds, Syracuse, LB, 3/3
7. David Terrell, Texas-El Paso, DB, 61/77

1999 NFL

ARIZONA CARDINALS
1. David Boston, Ohio State, WR, 56/75
1. L.J. Shelton, Eastern Michigan, T, 82/98
2. Johnny Rutledge, Florida, LB, 40/46
3. Tom Burke, Wisconsin, DE, 36/36
4. Joel Makovicka, Nebraska, FB, 58/58
5. Yusuf Scott, Arizona, G, 24/24
5. Paris Johnson, Miami (OH), DB, 0/0
6. Melvin Bradley, Arkansas, LB, 1/1
6. Dennis McKinley, Mississippi State, FB, 58/58
6. Coby Rhinehart, SMU, DB, 61/61
7. Chris Greisen, Northwest Missouri State, QB, 5/5

ATLANTA FALCONS
1. Patrick Kerney, Virginia, DE, 112/112
2. Reggie Kelly, Mississippi State, TE, 62/105
3. Jeff Paulk, Arizona State, FB, 1/2
4. Johndale Carty, Utah State, DB, 61/61
5. Eugene Baker, Kent State, WR, 4/8
6. Jeff Kelly, Kansas State, LB, 29/29
6. Eric Thigpen, Iowa, DB, 0/0
7. Todd McClure, LSU, C, 89/89
7. Rondel Menendez, Eastern Kentucky, WR, 0/0

BALTIMORE RAVENS
1. Chris McAlister, Arizona, DB, 105/105
4. Edwin Mulitalo, Arizona, G, 102/102
4. Brandon Stokley, Louisiana-Lafayette, WR, 33/70
7. Anthony Poindexter, Virginia, DB, 12/12

BUFFALO BILLS
1. Antoine Winfield, Ohio State, DB, 72/102
2. Peerless Price, Tennessee, WR, 64/103
3. Shawn Bryson, Tennessee, RB, 37/85
4. Bobby Collins, North Alabama, TE, 26/30
4. Keith Newman, North Carolina, LB, 51/91
5. Jay Foreman, Nebraska, LB, 38/82
6. Armon Hatcher, Oregon State, DB, 0/4
7. Bryce Fisher, Air Force, DE, 13/65
7. Sheldon Jackson, Nebraska, TE, 45/45

CAROLINA PANTHERS
2. Mike Rucker, Nebraska, DE, 109/109
2. Chris Terry, Georgia, T, 57/82
4. Hannibal Navies, Colorado, LB, 39/85
6. Robert Daniel, Northwestern State (LA), DE, 0/0
7. Tony Booth, James Madison, DB, 0/0

CHICAGO BEARS
1. Cade McNown, UCLA, QB, 25/25
2. Russell Davis, North Carolina, DT, 11/91
3. D'Wayne Bates, Northwestern, WR, 23/47
3. Marty Booker, Louisiana-Monroe, WR, 69/99
3. Rex Tucker, Texas A&M, G, 35/43
4. Rosevelt Colvin, Purdue, LB, 56/90
4. Warrick Holdman, Texas A&M, LB, 59/89
5. Jerry Azumah, New Hampshire, DB, 105/105
5. Khari Samuel, Massachusetts, LB, 30/39
5. Jerry Wisne, Notre Dame, T, 7/9
6. Rashard Cook, USC, DB, 0/47
7. Jim Finn, Pennsylvania, FB, 0/90
7. Sulecio Sanford, Middle Tennessee, WR, 0/0

CINCINNATI BENGALS
1. Akili Smith, Oregon, QB, 22/22
2. Charles Fisher, West Virginia, DB, 1/1
3. Cory Hall, Fresno State, DB, 62/87
4. Craig Yeast, Kentucky, WR, 24/35
5. Nick Luchey, Miami (FL), FB, 48/75
5. Nick Williams, Miami (FL), RB, 0/0
6. Kelly Gregg, Oklahoma, NT, 0/73
7. Scott Covington, Miami (FL), QB, 3/4
7. Tony Coats, Washington, G, 0/0
7. Donald Broomfield, Clemson, DT, 0/0

CLEVELAND BROWNS
1. Tim Couch, Kentucky, QB, 62/62
2. Rahim Abdullah, Clemson, LB, 29/29
2. Kevin Johnson, Syracuse, WR, 73/101
3. Daylon McCutcheon, USC, DB, 103/103
3. Marquis Smith, California, DB, 46/46
4. Wali Rainer, Virginia, LB, 46/110
5. Darrin Chiaverini, Colorado, WR, 26/49
6. James Dearth, Tarleton State, TE, 2/82
6. Kendall Ogle, Maryland, LB, 2/2
6. Marcus Spriggs, Troy State, DT, 18/18
7. Madre Hill, Arkansas, RB, 5/7

DALLAS COWBOYS
1. Ebenezer Ekuban, North Carolina, DE, 60/92
2. Solomon Page, West Virginia, G, 59/67
3. Dat Nguyen, Texas A&M, LB, 90/90
4. Wane McGarity, Texas, WR, 22/31
4. Peppi Zellner, Fort Valley State (GA), DE, 57/89
6. MarTay Jenkins, Nebraska-Omaha, WR, 0/40
7. Kelvin Garmon, Baylor, G, 21/52
7. Mike Lucky, Arizona, TE, 46/46

DENVER BRONCOS
1. Al Wilson, Tennessee, LB, 110/110
2. Lennie Friedman, Duke, G, 33/65
2. Montae Reagor, Texas Tech, DT, 45/87
3. Travis McGriff, Florida, WR, 34/34
3. Chris Watson, Eastern Illinois, DB, 14/58
4. Olandis Gary, Georgia, RB, 35/48
5. David Bowens, Western Illinois, DE, 16/88
5. Darwin Brown, Texas Tech, DB, 0/0
6. Desmond Clark, Wake Forest, TE, 41/98
6. Chad Plummer, Cincinnati, WR, 0/4
7. Billy Miller, USC, TE, 22/73
7. Justin Swift, Kansas State, TE, 0/49

DETROIT LIONS
1. Chris Claiborne, USC, LB, 63/101
1. Aaron Gibson, Wisconsin, T, 16/38
3. Jared DeVries, Iowa, DE, 82/82
4. Sedrick Irvin, Michigan State, RB, 20/20
5. Tyree Talton, Northern Iowa, DB, 12/12
6. Clint Kriewaldt, Wisconsin-Stevens Point, LB, 49/95
7. Mike Pringley, North Carolina, DE, 9/12

GREEN BAY PACKERS
1. Antuan Edwards, Clemson, DB, 53/71
2. Fred Vinson, Vanderbilt, DB, 16/16
3. Cletidus Hunt, Kentucky State, DT, 85/85
3. Mike McKenzie, Memphis, DB, 70/95
4. Josh Bidwell, Oregon, P, 64/96
4. Aaron Brooks, Virginia, QB, 0/85
5. Craig Heimburger, Missouri, G, 2/13
5. De'Mond Parker, Oklahoma, RB, 19/19
6. Scott Curry, Montana, T, 5/5
6. Dee Miller, Ohio State, WR, 0/0
7. Chris Akins, Arkansas-Pine Bluff, DB, 13/61
7. Donald Driver, Alcorn State, WR, 98/98

INDIANAPOLIS COLTS
1. Edgerrin James, Miami (FL), RB, 96/96
2. Mike Peterson, Florida, LB, 57/105
3. Brandon Burlsworth, Arkansas, G, 0/0
4. Paul Miranda, Central Florida, DB, 5/16
5. Brad Scioli, Penn State, DE, 80/80
7. Hunter Smith, Notre Dame, P, 112/112
7. Corey Terry, Tennessee, LB, 0/15

JACKSONVILLE JAGUARS
1. Fernando Bryant, Alabama, DB, 72/84
2. Larry Smith, Florida State, DT, 51/64
3. Anthony Cesario, Colorado State, G, 0/0
4. Kevin Landolt, West Virginia, DT, 1/1
5. Jason Craft, Colorado State, DB, 70/100
6. Emarlos Leroy, Georgia, DT, 22/22
7. Chris White, Southern (LA), DE, 0/5
7. Dee Moronkola, Washington State, DB, 0/0

KANSAS CITY CHIEFS
1. John Tait, Brigham Young, T, 75/103
2. Mike Cloud, Boston College, RB, 56/78
3. Larry Atkins, UCLA, LB, 46/49
3. Gary Stills, West Virginia, DE, 88/88
4. Larry Parker, USC, WR, 38/38
7. Eric King, Richmond, G, 0/0

MIAMI DOLPHINS
2. J.J. Johnson, Mississippi State, RB, 36/36
2. Rob Konrad, Syracuse, FB, 82/82
3. Grey Ruegamer, Arizona State, C, 0/76
5. Cecil Collins, McNeese State, RB, 8/8
5. Bryan Jones, Oregon State, LB, 0/0
6. Brent Bartholomew, Ohio State, P, 2/9
7. Jermaine Haley, Butte J.C. (CA), DT, 43/62
7. Joe Wong, Brigham Young, G, 0/2

MINNESOTA VIKINGS
1. Daunte Culpepper, Central Florida, QB, 81/81
1. Dimitrius Underwood, Michigan State, DT, 0/19
2. Jim Kleinsasser, North Dakota, TE, 85/85
4. Kenny Wright, Northwestern State (LA), DB, 47/110
4. Jay Humphrey, Texas, T, 0/0
5. Chris Jones, Clemson, LB, 0/0
6. Antico Dalton, Hampton, LB, 2/5
6. Talance Sawyer, UNLV, DE, 39/39
7. Noel Scarlett, Langston, DT, 0/1

NEW ENGLAND PATRIOTS
1. Andy Katzenmoyer, Ohio State, LB, 24/24
1. Damien Woody, Boston College, C, 78/110
2. Kevin Faulk, LSU, RB, 91/91
3. Tony George, Florida, DB, 31/31
5. Derrick Fletcher, Baylor, T, 2/20
6. Marcus Washington, Colorado, DB, 0/0
7. Michael Bishop, Kansas State, QB, 8/8
7. Sean Morey, Brown, WR, 2/49

NEW ORLEANS SAINTS
1. Ricky Williams, Texas, RB, 38/82

NEW YORK GIANTS
1. Luke Petitgout, Notre Dame, T, 105/105
2. Joe Montgomery, Ohio State, RB, 10/13
3. Daniel Campbell, Texas A&M, TE, 60/95
4. Sean Bennett, Northwestern, RB, 16/16
5. Mike Rosenthal, Notre Dame, T, 40/74
6. Andre Weathers, Michigan, DB, 10/10
6. Lyle West, San Jose State, DB, 22/51
7. O.J. Childress, Clemson, LB, 4/4
7. Ryan Hale, Arkansas, DT, 25/25

NEW YORK JETS
2. Randy Thomas, Mississippi State, G, 61/106
3. David Loverne, San Jose State, G, 32/63
4. Jason Wiltz, Nebraska, DT, 27/27
5. Jermaine Jones, Northwestern State (LA), DB, 1/3
6. J.P. Machado, Illinois, G, 69/69
6. Marc Megna, Richmond, LB, 0/6
7. J.J. Syvrud, Jamestown, LB, 1/1
7. Ryan Young, Kansas State, T, 47/68

OAKLAND RAIDERS
1. Matt Stinchcomb, Georgia, G, 50/66
2. Tony Bryant, Florida State, DE, 50/82
4. Dameane Douglas, California, WR, 0/52
5. Eric Barton, Maryland, LB, 68/88
5. Roderick Coleman, East Carolina, DT, 60/89
6. Daren Yancy, Brigham Young, DT, 0/0
7. JoJuan Armour, Miami (OH), DB, 0/38

PHILADELPHIA EAGLES
1. Donovan McNabb, Syracuse, QB, 94/94
2. Barry Gardner, Northwestern, LB, 64/110
3. Doug Brzezinski, Boston College, G, 64/73
4. Na Brown, North Carolina, WR, 42/42
4. Damon Moore, Ohio State, DB, 48/54
4. John Welbourn, California, G, 56/78
6. Cecil Martin, Wisconsin, FB, 60/61
6. Troy Smith, East Carolina, WR, 1/1
7. Pernell Davis, Alabama-Birmingham, DT, 2/2
7. Jed Weaver, Oregon, TE, 16/90

PITTSBURGH STEELERS
1. Troy Edwards, Louisiana Tech, WR, 46/92
2. Scott Shields, Weber State, DB, 26/26
3. Kris Farris, UCLA, T, 0/3
3. Joey Porter, Colorado State, LB, 108/108
3. Amos Zereoue, West Virginia, RB, 66/84
4. Aaron Smith, Northern Colorado, DE, 102/102
5. Malcolm Johnson, Notre Dame, WR, 10/11
5. Jerame Tuman, Michigan, TE, 99/99
7. Kris Brown, Nebraska, K, 48/112
7. Antonio Dingle, Virginia, DT, 0/9
7. Chad Kelsay, Nebraska, LB, 6/6

SAN DIEGO CHARGERS
2. Jermaine Fazande, Oklahoma, RB, 20/20
3. Steve Heiden, South Dakota State, TE, 42/95
4. Jason Perry, North Carolina State, DB, 31/36
5. **Adrian Dingle, Clemson, DE, 70/70**
5. Reggie Nelson, McNeese State, T, 2/3
6. Tyrone Bell, North Alabama, DB, 0/1

SAN FRANCISCO 49ERS
1. Reggie McGrew, Florida, DT, 22/24
3. **Chike Okeafor, Purdue, DE, 57/105**
4. Anthony Parker, Weber State, DB, 21/21
4. Pierson Prioleau, Virginia Tech, DB, 28/97
5. Tyrone Hopson, Eastern Kentucky, G, 4/23
5. **Terry Jackson, Florida, FB, 100/100**
6. **Tai Streets, Michigan, WR, 65/78**
7. Kory Minor, Notre Dame, LB, 0/30

ST. LOUIS RAMS
1. **Torry Holt, North Carolina State, WR, 110/110**
2. **Dre' Bly, North Carolina, DB, 64/103**
3. **Rich Coady, Texas A&M, DB, 69/83**
4. Joe Germaine, Ohio State, QB, 3/3
5. Cameron Spikes, Texas A&M, G, 19/63
6. Lionel Barnes, Louisiana-Monroe, DE, 4/27
7. Rodney Williams, Georgia Tech, P, 0/15

SEATTLE SEAHAWKS
1. **Lamar King, Saginaw Valley State (MI), DE, 57/57**
3. Karsten Bailey, Auburn, WR, 11/19
3. Brock Huard, Washington, QB, 6/8
4. **Antonio Cochran, Georgia, DE, 82/85**
5. Charlie Rogers, Georgia Tech, RB, 40/67
5. Floyd Wedderburn, Penn State, G, 46/46
6. Steve Johnson, Tennessee, DB, 0/0

TAMPA BAY BUCCANEERS
1. **Anthony McFarland, LSU, DT, 93/93**
2. Shaun King, Tulane, QB, 31/34
3. **Martin Gramatica, Kansas State, K, 89/93**
4. **Dexter Jackson, Florida State, DB, 73/89**
5. John McLaughlin, California, DE, 18/18
6. Lamarr Glenn, Florida State, RB, 0/0
7. Autry Denson, Notre Dame, RB, 0/34
7. Darnell McDonald, Kansas State, WR, 9/9
7. Robert Hunt, Virginia, G, 0/0

TENNESSEE TITANS
1. **Jevon Kearse, Florida, DE, 66/95**
2. **John Thornton, West Virginia, DT, 51/99**
3. **Zach Piller, Florida, G, 84/84**
4. Donald Mitchell, SMU, DB, 44/44
4. Brad Ware, Auburn, DB, 0/0
5. Kevin Daft, California-Davis, QB, 0/0
6. Darran Hall, Colorado State, WR, 0/0
7. Phil Glover, Utah, LB, 1/10

WASHINGTON REDSKINS
1. **Champ Bailey, Georgia, DB, 80/110**
2. **Jon Jansen, Michigan, T, 96/96**
4. Nate Stimson, Georgia Tech, LB, 0/0
5. Derek Smith, Virginia Tech, T, 0/0
6. Jeff Hall, Tennessee, K, 0/3
7. Tim Alexander, Oregon State, WR, 0/0

2000 NFL

ARIZONA CARDINALS
1. Thomas Jones, Virginia, RB, 39/84
2. **Raynoch Thompson, Tennessee, LB, 64/64**
3. Darwin Walker, Tennessee, DT, 1/72
4. **David Barrett, Arkansas, DB, 62/91**
5. Jay Tant, Northwestern, TE, 5/5
5. Mao Tosi, Idaho, DT, 26/26
6. Jabari Issa, Washington, DE, 24/24
7. Sekou Sanyika, California, LB, 32/32

ATLANTA FALCONS
2. **Travis Claridge, USC, G, 52/52**
3. Mark Simoneau, Kansas State, LB, 45/91
4. Michael Thompson, Tennessee State, T, 12/12
5. Anthony Midget, Virginia Tech, DB, 0/0
6. Mareno Philyaw, Troy State, WR, 1/1
7. Darrick Vaughn, Southwest Texas State, DB, 32/48

BALTIMORE RAVENS
1. **Jamal Lewis, Tennessee, RB, 75/75**
1. **Travis Taylor, Florida, WR, 67/83**
3. Chris Redman, Louisville, QB, 10/10
5. Richard Mercier, Miami (FL), G, 0/0
6. **Adalius Thomas, Southern Mississippi, LB, 80/80**
6. Cedric Woodard, Texas, DT, 0/60

BUFFALO BILLS
1. Erik Flowers, Arizona State, DE, 31/58
2. Travares Tillman, Georgia Tech, DB, 28/56
3. Corey Moore, Virginia Tech, LB, 9/10
4. Avion Black, Tennessee State, WR, 16/27
5. **Sammy Morris, Texas Tech, RB, 53/82**
6. Leif Larsen, Texas-El Paso, DT, 16/16
7. Drew Haddad, Buffalo, WR, 1/2
7. **DaShon Polk, Arizona, LB, 53/85**

CAROLINA PANTHERS
1. Rashard Anderson, Jackson State, DB, 27/27
2. Deon Grant, Tennessee, DB, 48/80
3. Leander Jordan, Indiana (PA), T, 13/37
4. Alvin McKinley, Mississippi State, DE, 7/68
5. Gillis Wilson, Southern (LA), DE, 5/5
6. **Jeno James, Auburn, G, 55/85**
7. **Lester Towns, Washington, LB, 55/61**

CHICAGO BEARS
1. **Brian Urlacher, New Mexico, LB, 89/89**
2. **Mike Brown, Nebraska, DB, 78/78**
3. **Dustin Lyman, Wake Forest, TE, 55/55**
3. **Dez White, Georgia Tech, WR, 60/82**
4. Reggie Austin, Wake Forest, DB, 18/18
6. **Paul Edinger, Michigan State, K, 80/96**
6. Frank Murphy, Kansas State, WR, 0/20
7. **Michael Green, Northwestern State (LA), DB, 81/81**
7. James Cotton, Ohio State, LB, 0/0

CINCINNATI BENGALS
1. **Peter Warrick, Florida State, WR, 66/79**
2. **Mark Roman, LSU, DB, 50/82**
3. Ron Dugans, Florida State, WR, 46/46
4. Curtis Keaton, James Madison, RB, 19/25
5. Robert Bean, Mississippi State, DB, 27/32
6. Neil Rackers, Illinois, K, 48/86
7. **Brad St. Louis, Southwest Missouri State, TE, 91/91**

CLEVELAND BROWNS
1. Courtney Brown, Penn State, DE, 47/61
2. **Dennis Northcutt, Arizona, WR, 86/86**
3. JaJuan Dawson, Tulane, WR, 16/30
3. Travis Prentice, Miami (OH), RB, 16/30
4. **Lewis Sanders, Maryland, DB, 52/64**
4. **Aaron Shea, Michigan, TE, 65/65**
5. Lamar Chapman, Kansas State, DB, 8/8
5. Anthony Malbrough, Texas Tech, DB, 9/9
6. Brad Bedell, Colorado, T, 27/31
6. Spergon Wynn, Southwest Texas State, QB, 7/10
7. Rashidi Barnes, Colorado, DB, 14/14
7. Manuia Savea, Arizona, G, 0/0
7. Eric Chandler, Jackson State, DE, 0/0

DALLAS COWBOYS
2. Dwayne Goodrich, Tennessee, DB, 16/16
4. Kareem Larrimore, West Texas A&M, DB, 19/19
5. Michael Wiley, Ohio State, RB, 42/42
6. **Mario Edwards, Florida State, DB, 58/73**
7. Orantes Grant, Georgia, LB, 23/26

DENVER BRONCOS
1. **Deltha O'Neal, California, DB, 61/88**
2. **Ian Gold, Michigan, LB, 70/86**
2. **Kenoy Kennedy, Arkansas, DB, 73/89**
3. Chris Cole, Texas A&M, WR, 35/35
4. **Cooper Carlisle, Florida, G, 79/79**
4. Jerry Johnson, Florida State, DT, 9/9
5. Muneer Moore, Richmond, WR, 0/0
6. **Mike Anderson, Utah, RB, 74/74**
7. Jarious Jackson, Notre Dame, QB, 5/5
7. Leroy Fields, Jackson State, WR, 0/0

DETROIT LIONS
1. **Stockar McDougle, Oklahoma, T, 61/69**
2. **Barrett Green, West Virginia, LB, 54/65**
3. Reuben Droughns, Oregon, RB, 9/72
5. Todd Franz, Tulsa, DB, 0/46
6. Quinton Reese, Auburn, DE, 0/0
7. Alfonso Boone, Mt.San Antonio J.C., DT, 0/71

GREEN BAY PACKERS
1. **Bubba Franks, Miami (FL), TE, 90/90**
2. **Chad Clifton, Tennessee, T, 85/85**
3. Steve Warren, Nebraska, DT, 25/25
4. Gary Berry, Ohio State, DB, 4/4
4. **Na'il Diggs, Ohio State, LB, 84/84**
4. Anthony Lucas, Arkansas, WR, 0/0
5. **Kabeer Gbaja-Biamila, San Diego State, DE, 86/86**
5. Joey Jamison, Texas Southern, WR, 0/0
7. Charles Lee, Central Florida, WR, 22/44

7. Eugene McCaslin, Florida, LB, 1/1
7. Rondell Mealey, LSU, RB, 14/14
7. Ron Moore, Northwestern Oklahoma State, DT, 0/1
7. **Mark Tauscher, Wisconsin, T, 82/82**

INDIANAPOLIS COLTS
1. **Rob Morris, Brigham Young, LB, 82/82**
2. **Marcus Washington, Auburn, LB, 63/95**
3. **David Macklin, Penn State, DB, 64/96**
4. **Josh Williams, Michigan, DT, 73/73**
5. Matt Johnson, Brigham Young, G, 0/0
7. Rodregis Brooks, Alabama-Birmingham, DB, 5/5
7. Rob Renes, Michigan, DT, 0/0

JACKSONVILLE JAGUARS
1. R. Jay Soward, USC, WR, 13/13
2. **Brad Meester, Northern Iowa, C, 92/92**
3. T.J. Slaughter, Southern Mississippi, LB, 42/68
4. Joey Chustz, Louisiana Tech, T, 0/0
5. **Kiwaukee Thomas, Georgia Southern, DB, 75/85**
6. Emanuel Smith, Arkansas, WR, 1/1
7. **Danny Clark, Illinois, LB, 61/93**
7. **Rob Meier, Washington State, DE, 91/91**
7. Erik Olson, Colorado State, DB, 14/14
7. Shyrone Stith, Virginia Tech, RB, 14/15
7. Mark Baniewicz, Syracuse, T, 0/0

KANSAS CITY CHIEFS
1. Sylvester Morris, Jackson State, WR, 15/15
2. **William Bartee, Oklahoma, DB, 87/87**
3. **Greg Wesley, Arkansas-Pine Bluff, DB, 89/89**
4. Frank Moreau, Louisville, RB, 11/15
5. Pat Dennis, Louisiana-Monroe, DB, 16/41
5. **Dante Hall, Texas A&M, WR, 82/82**
6. Darnell Alford, Boston College, G, 3/3
7. Desmond Kitchings, Furman, WR, 0/0

MIAMI DOLPHINS
2. **Todd Wade, Mississippi, T, 63/86**
3. Ben Kelly, Colorado, DB, 4/13
4. Deon Dyer, North Carolina, FB, 45/45
5. **Arturo Freeman, South Carolina, DB, 72/74**
6. Ernest Grant, Arkansas-Pine Bluff, DT, 13/24
7. Jeff Harris, Georgia, DB, 0/0

MINNESOTA VIKINGS
1. **Chris Hovan, Boston College, DT, 77/93**
2. **Fred Robbins, Wake Forest, DT, 56/87**
2. Michael Boireau, Miami (FL), DE, 0/0
3. Doug Chapman, Marshall, RB, 26/26
4. Tyrone Carter, Minnesota, DB, 46/87
4. Antonio Wilson, Texas A&M-Commerce, LB, 16/16
5. Troy Walters, Stanford, WR, 18/70
7. Lewis Kelly, South Carolina State, T, 17/18
7. Mike Malano, San Diego State, C, 0/0
7. Giles Cole, Texas A&M-Kingsville, TE, 0/0

NEW ENGLAND PATRIOTS
2. Adrian Klemm, Hawaii, G, 26/42
3. J.R. Redmond, Arizona State, RB, 33/50
4. Greg Randall, Michigan State, T, 35/51
4. Greg Robinson-Randall, Michigan State, T, 0/0
5. Dave Stachelski, Boise State, TE, 0/9
5. Jeff Marriott, Missouri, DT, 0/0
6. **Tom Brady, Michigan, QB, 80/80**
6. **Antwan Harris, Virginia, DB, 52/52**
6. David Nugent, Purdue, DE, 15/24
7. **Patrick Pass, Georgia, FB, 75/75**
7. Casey Tisdale, New Mexico, LB, 0/0

NEW ORLEANS SAINTS
2. **Darren Howard, Kansas State, DE, 81/81**
4. **Terrelle Smith, Arizona State, FB, 59/91**
5. Chad Morton, USC, RB, 16/78
5. Tutan Reyes, Mississippi, G, 1/31
5. Austin Wheatley, Iowa, TE, 4/4
6. Marc Bulger, West Virginia, QB, 0/44
6. Michael Hawthorne, Purdue, DB, 28/63
6. Sherrod Gideon, Southern Mississippi, WR, 0/0
7. **Kevin Houser, Ohio State, C, 96/96**

NEW YORK GIANTS
1. **Ron Dayne, Wisconsin, RB, 62/72**
2. **Cornelius Griffin, Alabama, DT, 60/88**
3. Ron Dixon, Lambuth, WR, 37/37
4. **Brandon Short, Penn State, LB, 59/91**
5. Ralph Brown, Nebraska, DB, 37/65
6. Dhani Jones, Michigan, LB, 47/79
7. Jeremiah Parker, California, DE, 4/4

NEW YORK JETS
1. **John Abraham, South Carolina, DE, 73/73**
1. **Anthony Becht, West Virginia, TE, 78/94**
1. **Shaun Ellis, Tennessee, DE, 92/92**
1. Chad Pennington, Marshall, QB, 44/44
3. **Laveranues Coles, Florida State, WR, 61/93**
5. Windrell Hayes, USC, WR, 9/9
6. Tony Scott, North Carolina State, DB, 23/23
7. Richard Seals, Utah, DT, 0/0

OAKLAND RAIDERS
1. **Sebastian Janikowski, Florida State, K, 93/93**
2. **Jerry Porter, West Virginia, WR, 85/85**
4. Junior Ioane, Arizona State, DT, 9/36
5. **Shane Lechler, Texas A&M, P, 94/94**
7. Mondriel Fulcher, Miami (FL), TE, 25/25
7. Clifton Black, Southwest Texas State, DB, 0/0

PHILADELPHIA EAGLES
1. **Corey Simon, Florida State, DT, 78/91**
2. **Todd Pinkston, Southern Mississippi, WR, 78/78**
2. Bobbie Williams, Arkansas, G, 33/65
4. Gari Scott, Michigan State, WR, 3/3
6. Thomas Hamner, Minnesota, RB, 0/0
6. John Frank, Utah, DE, 0/0
6. John Romero, California, C, 0/0

PITTSBURGH STEELERS
1. **Plaxico Burress, Michigan State, WR, 71/87**
2. **Marvel Smith, Arizona State, T, 79/79**
3. **Kendrick Clancy, Mississippi, DT, 52/68**
3. Hank Poteat, Pittsburgh, DB, 41/52
4. Danny Farmer, UCLA, WR, 0/33
5. **Clark Haggans, Colorado State, LB, 76/76**
5. Tee Martin, Tennessee, QB, 1/3
6. Chris Combs, Duke, DE, 8/10
6. Jason Gavadza, Kent State, TE, 0/0

SAN DIEGO CHARGERS
2. Rogers Beckett, Marshall, DB, 48/71
3. Damion McIntosh, Kansas State, T, 41/71
4. Leonardo Carson, Auburn, DT, 41/64
4. Trevor Gaylor, Miami (OH), WR, 21/34
6. Shannon Taylor, Virginia, LB, 11/40
6. Damen Wheeler, Colorado, DB, 0/5
6. JaJuan Seider, Florida A&M, QB, 0/0
7. Jason Thomas, Hampton, G, 0/14

SAN FRANCISCO 49ERS
1. **Julian Peterson, Michigan State, LB, 79/79**
1. **Ahmed Plummer, Ohio State, DB, 70/70**
2. **John Engelberger, Virginia Tech, DE, 78/92**
2. **Jason Webster, Texas A&M, DB, 53/78**
3. **Jeff Ulbrich, Hawaii, LB, 68/68**
3. Giovanni Carmazzi, Hofstra, QB, 0/0
4. John Keith, Furman, DB, 23/23
5. John Milem, Lenoir-Rhyne, DE, 18/20
5. Paul Smith, Texas-El Paso, RB, 36/55
7. **Brian Jennings, Arizona State, TE, 95/95**
7. Tim Rattay, Louisiana Tech, QB, 32/32

ST. LOUIS RAMS
1. Trung Canidate, Arizona, RB, 35/46
2. Jacoby Shepherd, Oklahoma State, DB, 22/30
3. John St. Clair, Virginia, T, 32/59
4. Kaulana Noa, Hawaii, T, 0/0
5. **Brian Young, Texas-El Paso, DT, 59/90**
6. Matt Bowen, Iowa, DB, 17/72
7. Andrew Kline, San Diego State, G, 0/0

SEATTLE SEAHAWKS
1. **Shaun Alexander, Alabama, RB, 96/96**
1. Chris McIntosh, Wisconsin, T, 24/24
2. Ike Charlton, Virginia Tech, DB, 31/53
3. **Darrell Jackson, Florida, WR, 83/83**
4. Marcus Bell, Arizona, LB, 45/45
4. **Isaiah Kacyvenski, Harvard, LB, 87/87**
6. John Hilliard, Mississippi State, DE, 27/27
6. James Williams, Marshall, WR, 29/30
6. Tim Watson, Rowan, DT, 0/0

TAMPA BAY BUCCANEERS
2. **Cosey Coleman, Tennessee, G, 71/85**
3. **Nate Webster, Miami (FL), LB, 63/67**
5. James Whalen, Kentucky, TE, 0/26
6. David Gibson, USC, DB, 34/47
7. Joe Hamilton, Georgia Tech, QB, 1/1

TENNESSEE TITANS
1. **Keith Bulluck, Syracuse, LB, 95/95**
3. Byron Frisch, Brigham Young, DE, 0/23
3. **Erron Kinney, Florida, TE, 83/83**
4. Bobby Myers, Wisconsin, DB, 17/17
4. **Peter Sirmon, Oregon, LB, 65/65**

5. Frank Chamberlin, Boston College, LB, 43/57
5. Aric Morris, Michigan State, DB, 47/51
6. **Robaire Smith, Michigan State, DE, 50/82**
7. Mike Green, Houston, RB, 32/32
7. Wes Shivers, Mississippi State, T, 0/3

WASHINGTON REDSKINS

1. **LaVar Arrington, Penn State, LB, 78/78**
1. **Chris Samuels, Alabama, T, 92/92**
3. Lloyd Harrison, North Carolina State, DB, 2/16
4. Michael Moore, Troy State, G, 5/8
5. Quincy Sanders, UNLV, DB, 0/0
6. Todd Husak, Stanford, QB, 1/1
7. Delbert Cowsette, Maryland, DT, 32/32
7. Ethan Howell, Oklahoma State, WR, 0/0

2001 NFL

ARIZONA CARDINALS

1. **Leonard Davis, Texas, T, 75/75**
2. Michael Stone, Memphis, DB, 37/50
2. Kyle Vanden Bosch, Nebraska, DE, 35/51
3. **Adrian Wilson, North Carolina State, DB, 78/78**
4. Marcus Bell, Memphis, DT, 42/73
4. Bill Gramatica, South Florida, K, 33/34
5. Mario Fatafehi, Kansas State, DT, 7/45
6. Bobby Newcombe, Nebraska, WR, 0/0
7. **Renaldo Hill, Michigan State, DB, 55/71**
7. Tevita Ofahengaue, Brigham Young, TE, 0/0

ATLANTA FALCONS

1. **Michael Vick, Virginia Tech, QB, 58/58**
2. **Alge Crumpler, North Carolina, TE, 78/78**
4. **Roberto Garza, Texas A&M-Kingsville, G, 52/68**
4. **Matt Stewart, Vanderbilt, LB, 63/77**
5. Vinny Sutherland, Purdue, WR, 0/16
6. Randy Garner, Arkansas, DE, 0/0
7. Ronald Flemons, Texas A&M, DE, 5/6
7. **Kynan Forney, Hawaii, G, 74/74**
7. Corey Hall, Appalachian State, DB, 3/3
7. Quentin McCord, Kentucky, WR, 25/25

BALTIMORE RAVENS

1. **Todd Heap, Arizona State, TE, 66/66**
2. **Gary Baxter, Baylor, DB, 54/59**
3. Casey Rabach, Wisconsin, C, 42/58
4. **Ed Hartwell, Western Illinois, LB, 64/69**
5. Chris Barnes, New Mexico State, RB, 0/0
6. **Joe Maese, New Mexico, C, 62/65**
7. Dwayne Missouri, Northwestern, DE, 0/3

BUFFALO BILLS

1. **Nate Clements, Ohio State, DB, 80/80**
2. **Travis Henry, Tennessee, RB, 54/63**
2. **Aaron Schobel, TCU, DE, 80/80**
3. Ron Edwards, Texas A&M, DT, 48/48
3. **Jonas Jennings, Georgia, T, 52/55**
4. Brandon Spoon, North Carolina, LB, 14/14
5. Marques Sullivan, Illinois, G, 32/32
6. Tony Driver, Notre Dame, DB, 11/11
6. Dan O'Leary, Notre Dame, TE, 8/17
6. Jimmy Williams, Vanderbilt, DB, 0/64
7. Reggie Germany, Ohio State, WR, 16/16
7. Tyrone Robertson, Georgia, DT, 12/12

CAROLINA PANTHERS

1. **Dan Morgan, Miami (FL), LB, 55/55**
2. **Kris Jenkins, Maryland, DT, 53/53**
3. **Steve Smith, Utah, WR, 63/63**
4. Chris Weinke, Florida State, QB, 24/24
5. Jarrod Cooper, Kansas State, DB, 40/65
6. Dee Brown, Syracuse, RB, 14/28
7. Mike Roberg, Idaho, TE, 0/13
7. Louis Williams, LSU, C, 2/2

CHICAGO BEARS

1. **David Terrell, Michigan, WR, 53/54**
2. **Anthony Thomas, Michigan, RB, 51/61**
3. Mike Gandy, Notre Dame, T, 32/48
4. Karon Riley, Minnesota, LB, 5/25
5. Bernard Robertson, Tulane, T, 15/15
7. John Capel, Florida, WR, 0/0

CINCINNATI BENGALS

1. **Justin Smith, Missouri, DE, 79/79**
2. **Chad Johnson, Oregon State, WR, 76/76**
3. Sean Brewer, San Jose State, TE, 3/12
4. **Rudi Johnson, Auburn, RB, 54/54**
5. Victor Leyva, Arizona State, G, 10/10
6. Riall Johnson, Stanford, LB, 32/32
7. **T.J. Houshmandzadeh, Oregon State, WR, 60/60**

CLEVELAND BROWNS

1. **Gerard Warren, Florida, DT, 60/76**
2. **Quincy Morgan, Kansas State, WR, 54/79**
3. James Jackson, Miami (FL), RB, 43/52
4. **Anthony Henry, South Florida, DB, 61/73**
5. Jeremiah Pharms, Washington, LB, 0/0
6. Michael Jameson, Texas A&M, DB, 42/42
7. Andre King, Miami (FL), WR, 42/42
7. Paul Zukauskas, Boston College, G, 43/43

DALLAS COWBOYS

2. Quincy Carter, Georgia, QB, 31/38
2. **Tony Dixon, Alabama, DB, 56/56**
3. Willie Blade, Mississippi State, DT, 15/20
4. Markus Steele, USC, LB, 42/42
5. Matt Lehr, Virginia Tech, C, 43/58
6. Daleroy Stewart, Southern Mississippi, DT, 16/26
7. Char-ron Dorsey, Florida State, T, 9/11
7. John Nix, Southern Mississippi, DT, 30/31
7. Colston Weatherington, Central Missouri State, DE, 3/3

DENVER BRONCOS

1. **Willie Middlebrooks, Minnesota, DB, 51/56**
2. Paul Toviessi, Marshall, DE, 0/0
3. Reggie Hayward, Iowa State, DE, 47/62
4. **Ben Hamilton, Minnesota, G, 64/64**
4. Nick Harris, California, P, 0/79
6. Kevin Kasper, Iowa, WR, 14/38

DETROIT LIONS

1. **Jeff Backus, Michigan, T, 80/80**
2. **Dominic Raiola, Nebraska, C, 80/80**
2. **Shaun Rogers, Texas, DT, 76/76**
5. Scotty Anderson, Grambling State, WR, 34/34
5. Mike McMahon, Rutgers, QB, 20/29
6. Jason Glenn, Texas A&M, LB, 0/71

GREEN BAY PACKERS

1. Jamal Reynolds, Florida State, DE, 18/18
2. **Robert Ferguson, Texas A&M, WR, 56/56**
3. **Bhawoh Jue, Penn State, DB, 51/65**
3. **Torrance Marshall, Oklahoma, LB, 51/51**
4. Bill Ferrario, Wisconsin, G, 16/16
6. **David Martin, Tennessee, TE, 59/59**

INDIANAPOLIS COLTS

1. **Reggie Wayne, Miami (FL), WR, 77/77**
2. **Idrees Bashir, Memphis, DB, 51/62**
3. Cory Bird, Virginia Tech, DB, 45/45
4. **Ryan Diem, Northern Illinois, T, 74/74**
5. Raymond Walls, Southern Mississippi, DB, 4/41
6. Jason Doering, Wisconsin, DB, 47/53
7. Rick DeMulling, Idaho, G, 48/61

JACKSONVILLE JAGUARS

1. **Marcus Stroud, Georgia, DT, 80/80**
2. **Maurice Williams, Michigan, T, 69/69**
3. James Boyd, Penn State, DB, 26/26
3. Eric Westmoreland, Tennessee, LB, 28/44
5. David Leaverton, Tennessee, P, 0/0
6. Chad Ward, Washington, G, 0/0
7. Randy Chevrier, McGill, DT, 0/13
7. Anthony Denman, Notre Dame, LB, 0/27
7. Marlon McCree, Kentucky, DB, 31/76
7. Richmond Flowers, Chattanooga, WR, 0/0

KANSAS CITY CHIEFS

3. Eric Downing, Syracuse, DT, 42/45
3. Snoop Minnis, Florida State, WR, 15/15
4. **Monty Beisel, Kansas State, LB, 55/70**
4. George Layne, TCU, RB, 0/11
5. Bill Baber, Virginia, TE, 29/30
5. Derrick Blaylock, Stephen F. Austin State, RB, 40/47
6. Alex Sulfsted, Miami (OH), T, 0/17
7. **Shaunard Harts, Boise State, DB, 51/51**
7. Terdell Sands, Tennessee-Chattanooga, DT, 0/28

MIAMI DOLPHINS

1. Jamar Fletcher, Wisconsin, DB, 41/71
2. **Chris Chambers, Wisconsin, WR, 78/78**
3. **Morlon Greenwood, Syracuse, LB, 62/78**
3. **Travis Minor, Florida State, RB, 75/75**
5. Shawn Draper, Alabama, T, 0/0
6. Otis Leverette, Alabama-Birmingham, DE, 0/17
6. Brandon Winey, LSU, T, 0/24
6. Josh Heupel, Oklahoma, QB, 0/0
6. Rick Crowell, Colorado State, LB, 0/0

MINNESOTA VIKINGS

1. **Michael Bennett, Wisconsin, RB, 64/64**
2. Willie Howard, Stanford, DE, 8/8
3. Eric Kelly, Kentucky, DB, 48/48
4. Cedric James, TCU, WR, 5/5
4. Shawn Worthen, TCU, DT, 4/4
5. Patrick Chukwurah, Wyoming, LB, 27/55
6. Carey Scott, Kentucky State, DB, 1/7
7. Brian Crawford, Western Oregon, T, 0/0

NEW ENGLAND PATRIOTS

1. **Richard Seymour, Georgia, DE, 71/71**
2. **Matt Light, Purdue, T, 65/65**
3. Brock Williams, Notre Dame, DB, 0/12
4. Jabari Holloway, Notre Dame, TE, 0/26
4. Kenyatta Jones, South Florida, T, 18/21
5. Hakim Akbar, San Diego State, LB, 6/10
6. Leonard Myers, Miami (FL), DB, 15/17
6. Arther Love, South Carolina State, TE, 0/0
7. Owen Pochman, Brigham Young, K, 0/16
7. T.J. Turner, Michigan State, LB, 2/2

NEW ORLEANS SAINTS

1. **Deuce McAllister, Mississippi, RB, 66/66**
3. **Sedrick Hodge, North Carolina, LB, 63/63**
3. Kenny Smith, Alabama, DT, 30/30
4. Moran Norris, Kansas, FB, 5/62
5. Onomo Ojo, California-Davis, WR, 0/0
6. Mitch White, Oregon State, T, 0/0
7. Ennis Davis, Southern California, DT, 0/0

NEW YORK GIANTS

1. **Will Allen, Syracuse, DB, 72/72**
3. **Will Peterson, Western Illinois, DB, 51/51**
4. Jesse Palmer, Florida, QB, 8/8
4. Cedric Scott, Southern Mississippi, DE, 9/13
5. Jonathan Carter, Troy State, WR, 3/25
5. John Markham, Vanderbilt, K, 0/0
7. Ross Kolodziej, Wisconsin, DT, 10/39

NEW YORK JETS

1. **Santana Moss, Miami (FL), WR, 51/67**
2. **LaMont Jordan, Maryland, RB, 62/76**
3. **Kareem McKenzie, Penn State, T, 56/70**
4. Jamie Henderson, Georgia, DB, 32/32
7. Tupe Peko, Michigan State, G, 0/27
7. **James Reed, Iowa State, DT, 80/80**

OAKLAND RAIDERS

1. **Derrick Gibson, Florida State, DB, 53/53**
2. Marques Tuiasosopo, Washington, QB, 9/9
3. DeLawrence Grant, Oregon State, DE, 49/49
5. Ray Perryman, Northern Arizona, DB, 0/10
6. Chris Cooper, Nebraska-Omaha, DT, 44/54
7. Derek Combs, Ohio State, DB, 4/12
7. Ken-Yon Rambo, Ohio State, WR, 0/29

PHILADELPHIA EAGLES

1. **Freddie Mitchell, UCLA, WR, 63/63**
2. Quinton Caver, Arkansas, LB, 16/53
3. Derrick Burgess, Mississippi, DE, 29/45
4. Correll Buckhalter, Nebraska, RB, 30/30
5. A.J. Feeley, Oregon, QB, 7/18
5. Tony Stewart, Penn State, TE, 3/52

PITTSBURGH STEELERS

1. **Casey Hampton, Texas, NT, 70/70**
2. Kendrell Bell, Georgia, LB, 47/63
4. Mathias Nkwenti, Temple, T, 2/2
5. **Chukky Okobi, Purdue, C, 62/62**
6. Rodney Bailey, Ohio State, DE, 48/56
6. Roger Knight, Wisconsin, LB, 0/48
7. Chris Taylor, Texas A&M, WR, 0/0

SAN DIEGO CHARGERS

1. **LaDainian Tomlinson, TCU, RB, 79/79**
2. **Drew Brees, Purdue, QB, 59/59**
3. Tay Cody, Florida State, DB, 19/19
4. Carlos Polk, Nebraska, LB, 38/38
5. **Zeke Moreno, USC, LB, 57/61**
5. Elliot Silvers, Washington, T, 0/0
7. Robert Carswell, Clemson, DB, 18/18
7. Brandon Gorin, Purdue, T, 0/32

SAN FRANCISCO 49ERS

1. **Andre Carter, California, DE, 69/69**
2. Jamie Winborn, Vanderbilt, LB, 43/48
3. **Kevan Barlow, Pittsburgh, RB, 72/72**
6. Rashad Holman, Louisville, DB, 46/46
6. **Cedrick Wilson, Tennessee, WR, 53/69**
6. Menson Holloway, Texas-El Paso, DE, 0/0
7. Eric Johnson, Yale, TE, 44/44
7. Alex Lincoln, Auburn, LB, 0/0

ST. LOUIS RAMS

1. **Adam Archuleta, Arizona State, DB, 72/72**
1. **Damione Lewis, Miami (FL), DT, 69/69**
1. **Ryan Pickett, Ohio State, DT, 75/75**
2. **Tommy Polley, Florida State, LB, 57/73**
3. Brian Allen, Florida State, LB, 3/47
4. **Brandon Manumaleuna, Arizona, TE, 78/78**
4. Milton Wynn, Washington State, WR, 0/4
5. **Jerametrius Butler, Kansas State, DB, 57/57**
6. Francis St. Paul, Northern Arizona, WR, 0/0

SEATTLE SEAHAWKS

1. **Steve Hutchinson, Michigan, G, 68/68**
1. **Koren Robinson, North Carolina State, WR, 57/71**
2. **Ken Lucas, Mississippi, DB, 62/77**
3. **Heath Evans, Auburn, FB, 61/73**
4. Curtis Fuller, TCU, DB, 26/42
4. **Orlando Huff, Fresno State, LB, 55/71**
4. **Floyd Womack, Mississippi State, T, 53/53**
5. **Alex Bannister, Eastern Kentucky, WR, 57/57**
6. Josh Booty, Louisiana State, QB, 0/0
7. Harold Blackmon, Northwestern, DB, 9/9
7. Kris Kocurek, Texas Tech, DT, 0/1
7. Dennis Norman, Princeton, C, 1/17

TAMPA BAY BUCCANEERS

1. **Kenyatta Walker, Florida, T, 72/72**
3. **Dwight Smith, Akron, DB, 63/78**
4. **John Howell, Colorado State, DB, 54/64**
5. Russ Hochstein, Nebraska, C, 1/48
6. **Jameel Cook, Illinois, FB, 72/72**
6. **Ellis Wyms, Mississippi State, DE, 53/53**
7. Than Merril, Yale, DB, 0/15
7. Joe Tafoya, Arizona, DE, 0/50
7. Dauntae' Finger, North Carolina, TE, 0/0

TENNESSEE TITANS

2. **Andre Dyson, Utah, DB, 62/72**
3. **Shad Meier, Kansas State, TE, 52/53**
4. Justin McCareins, Northern Illinois, WR, 36/68
5. **Eddie Berlin, Northern Iowa, WR, 57/62**
6. Dan Alexander, Nebraska, RB, 7/11
6. Adam Haayer, Minnesota, T, 0/20
7. Keith Adams, Clemson, LB, 0/67

WASHINGTON REDSKINS

1. **Rod Gardner, Clemson, WR, 64/76**
2. **Fred Smoot, Mississippi State, DB, 60/71**
4. Sage Rosenfels, Iowa State, QB, 0/13
5. Darnerien McCants, Delaware State, WR, 29/41
6. Mario Monds, Cincinnati, DT, 0/7

2002 NFL

ARIZONA CARDINALS

1. Wendell Bryant, Wisconsin, DT, 29/29
2. Levar Fisher, North Carolina State, LB, 23/23
3. Dennis Johnson, Kentucky, DE, 28/29
3. Josh McCown, Sam Houston State, QB, 35/35
4. Nate Dwyer, Kansas, DT, 0/0
5. Jason McAddley, Alabama, WR, 11/34
6. Josh Scobey, Kansas State, RB, 27/43
7. Mike Banks, Iowa State, TE, 18/18

ATLANTA FALCONS

1. **T.J. Duckett, Michigan State, RB, 54/54**
3. Will Overstreet, Tennessee, LB, 6/6
4. Martin Bibla, Miami (FL), G, 31/31
5. Kurt Kittner, Illinois, QB, 7/7
5. **Kevin McCadam, Colorado State, DB, 55/55**
6. Kahlil Hill, Iowa, WR, 1/1
7. **Kevin Shaffer, Tulsa, T, 53/53**
7. Michael Coleman, Widener, WR, 0/0

BALTIMORE RAVENS

1. **Ed Reed, Miami (FL), DB, 58/58**
2. **Anthony Weaver, Notre Dame, DE, 57/57**
4. Ron Johnson, Minnesota, WR, 22/22
4. **Dave Zastudil, Ohio University, P, 61/61**
5. Terry Jones, Alabama, TE, 46/53
6. Lamont Brightful, Eastern Washington, DB, 28/30
6. Javin Hunter, Notre Dame, WR, 12/12
6. **Chester Taylor, Toledo, RB, 62/62**
6. **Chad Williams, Southern Mississippi, DB, 64/64**
7. Wes Pate, Stephen F. Austin, QB, 0/0

BUFFALO BILLS

1. **Mike Williams, Texas, T, 51/51**
2. **Ryan Denney, Brigham Young, DE, 56/56**
2. **Josh Reed, LSU, WR, 60/60**
3. **Coy Wire, Stanford, DB, 58/58**
5. **Justin Bannan, Colorado, DT, 55/55**
6. Kevin Thomas, UNLV, DB, 38/38
7. Mike Pucillo, Auburn, G, 15/25
7. Dominique Stevenson, Tennessee, LB, 20/21
7. Rodney Wright, Fresno State, WR, 0/0
7. Jarrett Ferguson, Virginia Tech, RB, 0/0

CAROLINA PANTHERS

1. **Julius Peppers, North Carolina, DE, 60/60**
2. DeShaun Foster, UCLA, RB, 33/33

3. **Will Witherspoon, Georgia, LB, 62/62**
4. **Dante Wesley, Arkansas-Pine Bluff, DB, 58/58**
5. Randy Fasani, Stanford, QB, 4/4
5. Kyle Johnson, Syracuse, RB, 0/30
6. Keith Heinrich, Sam Houston State, TE, 4/18
7. Brad Franklin, Louisiana-Lafayette, DB, 0/4
7. Pete Campion, North Dakota State, G, 0/0

CHICAGO BEARS

1. Marc Colombo, Boston College, T, 19/23
3. Terrence Metcalf, Mississippi, G, 40/40
3. Roosevelt Williams, Tuskegee, DB, 13/20
4. **Alex Brown, Florida, DE, 63/63**
5. Bobby Gray, Louisiana Tech, DB, 29/29
5. Bryan Knight, Pittsburgh, LB, 31/31
6. Jamin Elliott, Delaware, WR, 1/1
6. Bryan Fletcher, UCLA, TE, 0/16
6. Adrian Peterson, Georgia Southern, RB, 45/45

CINCINNATI BENGALS

1. **Levi Jones, Arizona State, T, 63/63**
2. Lamont Thompson, Washington State, DB, 13/61
3. **Matt Schobel, TCU, TE, 63/63**
4. Travis Dorsch, Purdue, P, 1/1
6. Marquand Manuel, Florida, DB, 28/59
7. Joey Evans, North Carolina, DE, 0/0

CLEVELAND BROWNS

1. William Green, Boston College, RB, 46/46
2. Andre' Davis, Virginia Tech, WR, 39/48
3. Melvin Fowler, Maryland, C, 30/41
4. Kevin Bentley, Northwestern, LB, 44/59
4. Darnell Sanders, Ohio State, TE, 26/28
4. Ben Taylor, Virginia Tech, LB, 39/39
5. **Andra Davis, Florida, LB, 59/59**
7. Joaquin Gonzalez, Miami (FL), T, 41/46

DALLAS COWBOYS

1. **Roy Williams, Oklahoma, DB, 64/64**
2. Antonio Bryant, Pittsburgh, WR, 37/63
2. **Andre Gurode, Colorado, G, 60/60**
3. Derek Ross, Ohio State, DB, 22/33
4. Jamar Martin, Ohio State, FB, 14/23
5. Pete Hunter, Virginia Union, DB, 30/34
6. Tyson Walter, Ohio State, C, 39/39
6. DeVeren Johnson, Sacred Heart, WR, 0/0
6. Bob Slowikowski, Virginia Tech, TE, 0/0

DENVER BRONCOS

1. **Ashley Lelie, Hawaii, WR, 64/64**
2. Clinton Portis, Miami (FL), RB, 29/60
3. Dorsett Davis, Mississippi State, DE, 14/14
4. **Sam Brandon, UNLV, DB, 55/55**
5. Herb Haygood, Michigan State, WR, 4/4
6. Jeb Putzier, Boise State, TE, 39/39
7. Monsanto Pope, Virginia, DT, 48/48
7. Chris Young, Georgia Tech, DB, 21/21

DETROIT LIONS

1. **Joey Harrington, Oregon, QB, 59/59**
2. **Kalimba Edwards, South Carolina, DE, 63/63**
3. Andre' Goodman, South Carolina, DB, 43/43
4. John Taylor, Montana State, LB, 0/0
5. John Owens, Notre Dame, TE, 22/24
6. Chris Cash, USC, DB, 27/30
7. Matt Murphy, Maryland, TE, 3/24
7. Victor Rogers, Colorado, T, 1/1
7. Luke Staley, Brigham Young, RB, 0/0

GREEN BAY PACKERS

1. Javon Walker, Florida State, WR, 48/48
3. Marques Anderson, UCLA, DB, 30/54
4. Najeh Davenport, Miami (FL), RB, 39/39
5. **Aaron Kampman, Iowa, DE, 56/56**
5. Craig Nall, Northwestern State (LA), QB, 6/6
6. Mike Houghton, San Diego State, G, 0/1

HOUSTON TEXANS

1. **David Carr, Fresno State, QB, 60/60**
2. **Jabar Gaffney, Florida, WR, 64/64**
2. **Chester Pitts, San Diego State, T, 64/64**
3. Charles Hill, Maryland, DT, 16/16
3. Fred Weary, Tennessee, G, 32/32
4. **Jonathan Wells, Ohio State, RB, 60/60**
5. Jarrod Baxter, New Mexico, FB, 24/32
5. Ramon Walker, Pittsburgh, DB, 35/35

S6. Milford Brown, Florida State, G, 18/18

6. Demarcus Faggins, Kansas State, DB, 39/39
6. Howard Green, LSU, DT, 0/19
7. Greg White, Minnesota, DE, 0/0
7. Ahmad Miller, UNLV, DT, 0/0

INDIANAPOLIS COLTS

1. **Dwight Freeney, Syracuse, DE, 63/63**
2. **Larry Tripplett, Washington, DT, 60/60**
3. Joe Jefferson, Western Kentucky, DB, 27/27
4. **David Thornton, North Carolina, LB, 63/63**
6. Brian Allen, Stanford, RB, 4/4
6. David Pugh, Virginia Tech, DT, 4/4
6. James Lewis, Miami (FL), DB, 0/0
7. Josh Mallard, Georgia, DE, 13/13

JACKSONVILLE JAGUARS

1. **John Henderson, Tennessee, DT, 64/64**
2. Mike Pearson, Florida, T, 40/40
3. **Akin Ayodele, Purdue, LB, 64/64**
4. David Garrard, East Carolina, QB, 17/17
4. Chris Luzar, Virginia, TE, 23/23
6. Clenton Ballard, Southwest Texas State, DT, 0/0
7. Hayden Epstein, Michigan, K, 6/15
7. Kendall Newson, Middle Tennessee State, WR, 0/6
7. Steve Smith, Oregon, DB, 4/4

KANSAS CITY CHIEFS

1. Ryan Sims, North Carolina, DT, 43/43
2. Eddie Freeman, Alabama-Birmingham, DE, 20/20
4. Omar Easy, Penn State, FB, 37/53
5. Scott Fujita, California, LB, 48/64
7. Maurice Rodriguez, Fresno State, LB, 0/0

MIAMI DOLPHINS

3. **Seth McKinney, Texas A&M, C, 61/61**
4. **Randy McMichael, Georgia, TE, 64/64**
5. Omare Lowe, Washington, DB, 1/22
5. Sam Simmons, Northwestern, WR, 11/11
7. Leonard Henry, East Carolina, RB, 6/6

MINNESOTA VIKINGS

1. **Bryant McKinnie, Miami (FL), T, 56/56**
2. Raonall Smith, Washington State, LB, 30/30
3. Willie Offord, South Carolina, DB, 47/47
4. **Brian Williams, North Carolina State, DB, 62/62**
4. Edward Ta'amu, Utah, G, 0/0
6. Nick Rogers, Georgia Tech, LB, 32/46
7. Chad Beasley, Virginia Tech, T, 0/8

NEW ENGLAND PATRIOTS

1. **Daniel Graham, Colorado, TE, 51/51**
2. **Deion Branch, Louisville, WR, 53/53**
4. Rohan Davey, LSU, QB, 7/7
4. **Jarvis Green, LSU, DE, 62/62**
7. **David Givens, Notre Dame, WR, 53/53**
7. Antwoine Womack, Virginia, RB, 0/0

NEW ORLEANS SAINTS

1. **Charles Grant, Georgia, DE, 64/64**
1. **Donte Stallworth, Tennessee, WR, 56/56**
2. **LeCharles Bentley, Ohio State, G, 57/57**
3. James Allen, Oregon State, LB, 48/48
4. Keyuo Craver, Nebraska, DB, 22/22
5. Mel Mitchell, Western Kentucky, DB, 44/44
6. John Gilmore, Penn State, TE, 0/55
6. J.T. O'Sullivan, California-Davis, QB, 0/1
7. Derrius Monroe, Virginia Tech, DE, 0/0

NEW YORK GIANTS

1. **Jeremy Shockey, Miami (FL), TE, 54/54**
2. Tim Carter, Auburn, WR, 37/37
3. Jeff Hatch, Pennsylvania, T, 4/4
5. **Nick Greisen, Wisconsin, LB, 54/54**
6. Wesly Mallard, Oregon, LB, 34/43
7. Daryl Jones, Miami (FL), WR, 13/15
7. Quincy Monk, North Carolina, LB, 13/15

NEW YORK JETS

1. **Bryan Thomas, Alabama-Birmingham, DE, 61/61**
2. Jon McGraw, Kansas State, DB, 33/41
3. **Chris Baker, Michigan State, TE, 52/52**
4. Alan Harper, Fresno State, DT, 11/11
5. **Jonathan Goodwin, Michigan, G, 58/58**

OAKLAND RAIDERS

1. Phillip Buchanon, Miami (FL), DB, 36/46
1. Napoleon Harris, Northwestern, LB, 45/60
2. Doug Jolley, Brigham Young, TE, 47/63
2. **Langston Walker, California, T, 50/50**
5. Kenyon Coleman, UCLA, DE, 1/41
6. Keyon Nash, Albany State (GA), DB, 2/2
6. Larry Ned, San Diego State, RB, 0/19
7. Ronald Curry, North Carolina, WR, 31/31

PHILADELPHIA EAGLES

1. **Lito Sheppard, Florida, DB, 53/53**
2. **Sheldon Brown, South Carolina, DB, 64/64**
2. **Michael Lewis, Colorado, DB, 62/62**
3. **Brian Westbrook, Villanova, RB, 55/55**
4. Scott Peters, Arizona State, C, 0/7
5. Freddie Milons, Alabama, WR, 0/0
6. Tyreo Harrison, Notre Dame, LB, 14/14
7. Raheem Brock, Temple, DE, 0/61

PITTSBURGH STEELERS

1. Kendall Simmons, Auburn, G, 46/46
2. **Antwaan Randle El, Indiana, WR, 64/64**
3. **Chris Hope, Florida State, DB, 62/62**
4. **Larry Foote, Michigan, LB, 62/62**
5. **Verron Haynes, Georgia, RB, 53/53**
6. Lee Mays, Texas-El Paso, WR, 48/48
7. LaVar Glover, Cincinnati, DB, 0/2
7. Brett Keisel, Brigham Young, DE, 34/34

SAN DIEGO CHARGERS

1. **Quentin Jammer, Texas, DB, 62/62**
2. Reche Caldwell, Florida, WR, 47/47
2. Toniu Fonoti, Nebraska, G, 33/34
3. **Ben Leber, Kansas State, LB, 57/57**
4. **Justin Peelle, Oregon, TE, 62/62**
5. Terry Charles, Portland State, WR, 0/0
6. Matt Anderle, Minnesota, T, 0/0
7. Seth Burford, Cal Poly-San Luis Obispo, QB, 0/0

SAN FRANCISCO 49ERS

1. Mike Rumph, Miami (FL), DB, 36/36
3. Saleem Rasheed, Alabama, LB, 45/45
4. Jeff Chandler, Florida, K, 8/13
4. Kevin Curtis, Texas Tech, DB, 0/0
5. Josh Shaw, Michigan State, DT, 3/8
5. Brandon Doman, Brigham Young, QB, 0/0
6. Mark Anelli, Wisconsin, TE, 2/2
7. **Eric Heitmann, Stanford, G, 57/57**
7. Kyle Kosier, Arizona State, G, 47/63
7. Teddy Gaines, Tennessee, DB, 0/0

ST. LOUIS RAMS

1. Robert Thomas, UCLA, LB, 42/52
2. Travis Fisher, Central Florida, DB, 47/47
3. Lamar Gordon, North Dakota State, RB, 23/40
3. Eric Crouch, Nebraska, WR, 0/0
4. Travis Scott, Arizona State, G, 0/0
5. Courtland Bullard, Ohio State, LB, 20/20
6. Steve Bellisari, Ohio State, QB, 0/0
7. **Chris Massey, Marshall, RB, 64/64**

SEATTLE SEAHAWKS

1. **Jerramy Stevens, Washington, TE, 60/60**
2. **Maurice Morris, Oregon, RB, 58/58**
2. Anton Palepoi, UNLV, DE, 21/35
3. Kris Richard, USC, DB, 38/39
4. Terreal Bierria, Georgia, DB, 29/29
5. **Rocky Bernard, Texas A&M, DT, 58/58**
5. **Ryan Hannam, Northern Iowa, TE, 52/52**
5. Matt Hill, Boise State, T, 26/26
6. Craig Jarrett, Michigan State, P, 0/4
7. Jeff Kelly, Southern Mississippi, QB, 1/1

TAMPA BAY BUCCANEERS

3. Marquis Walker, Michigan, WR, 0/0
4. Travis Stephens, Tennessee, RB, 1/1
5. **Jermaine Phillips, Georgia, DB, 52/52**
6. John Stamper, South Carolina, DE, 0/4
7. Tim Wansley, Georgia, DB, 13/13
7. Tracey Wistrom, Nebraska, TE, 0/0
7. Aaron Lockett, Kansas State, WR, 0/0
7. Zack Quaccia, Stanford, C, 0/0

TENNESSEE TITANS

1. **Albert Haynesworth, Tennessee, DT, 52/52**
2. **Tank Williams, Stanford, DB, 57/57**
3. Rocky Calmus, Oklahoma, LB, 27/27
4. **Tony Beckham, Wisconsin-Stout, DB, 50/50**
4. **Rocky Boiman, Notre Dame, LB, 54/54**
4. Mike Echols, Wisconsin, DB, 9/9
5. Jake Schifino, Akron, WR, 14/14
6. **Justin Hartwig, Kansas, C, 50/50**
7. Carlos Hall, Arkansas, DE, 45/59
7. Darrell Hill, Northern Illinois, WR, 33/33

WASHINGTON REDSKINS

1. Patrick Ramsey, Tulane, QB, 34/34
2. Ladell Betts, Iowa, RB, 48/48
3. Rashad Bauman, Oregon, DB, 28/43
3. Cliff Russell, Utah, WR, 3/18
5. Andre Lott, Tennessee, DB, 31/31
5. Robert Royal, LSU, TE, 35/35
6. Reggie Coleman, Tennessee, T, 0/0
7. **Rock Cartwright, Kansas State, FB, 60/60**
7. Jeff Grau, UCLA, C, 0/27
7. Greg Scott, Hampton, DE, 3/4

2003 NFL

ARIZONA CARDINALS

1. Bryant Johnson, Penn State, WR, 45/45
1. Calvin Pace, Wake Forest, DE, 35/35
2. Anquan Boldin, Florida State, WR, 40/40
3. Gerald Hayes, Pittsburgh, LB, 28/28
5. Kenny King, Alabama, DE, 11/11
6. Tony Gilbert, Georgia, LB, 0/40
6. Reggie Wells, Clarion, G, 40/40

ATLANTA FALCONS

2. Bryan Scott, Penn State, DB, 47/47
4. Justin Griffith, Mississippi State, FB, 44/44
5. Jon Olinger, Cincinnati, WR, 0/0
6. Waine Bacon, Alabama, DB, 0/11
6. LaTarence Dunbar, TCU, WR, 5/5
7. Demetrin Veal, Tennessee, DE, 3/18

BALTIMORE RAVENS

1. Kyle Boller, California, QB, 36/36
1. Terrell Suggs, Arizona State, LB, 48/48
3. Musa Smith, Georgia, RB, 21/21
4. Jarret Johnson, Alabama, DE, 47/47
4. Ovie Mughelli, Wake Forest, FB, 22/22
5. Aubrayo Franklin, Tennessee, DT, 22/22
5. Tony Pashos, Illinois, T, 22/22
6. Gerome Sapp, Notre Dame, DB, 14/43
7. Trent Smith, Oklahoma, TE, 0/5
7. Mike Mabry, Central Florida, C, 0/0
7. Antwoine Sanders, Utah, DB, 0/0

BUFFALO BILLS

1. Willis McGahee, Miami (FL), RB, 32/32
2. Chris Kelsay, Nebraska, DE, 48/48
3. Angelo Crowell, Virginia, LB, 37/37
4. Sam Aiken, North Carolina, WR, 37/37
4. Terrence McGee, Northwestern State (LA), DB, 45/45
5. Ben Sobieski, Iowa, T, 1/1
6. Lauvale Sape, Utah, DT, 11/11
7. Mario Haggan, Mississippi State, LB, 33/33

CAROLINA PANTHERS

1. Jordan Gross, Utah, T, 48/48
2. Bruce Nelson, Iowa, G, 14/14
3. Ricky Manning, UCLA, DB, 48/48
3. Mike Seidman, UCLA, TE, 40/40
4. Colin Branch, Stanford, DB, 32/32
5. Kindal Moorehead, Alabama, DT, 43/43
7. Walter Young, Illinois, WR, 7/7
7. Casey Moore, Stanford, RB, 0/0

CHICAGO BEARS

1. Rex Grossman, Florida, QB, 8/8
1. Michael Haynes, Penn State, DE, 42/42
2. Charles Tillman, Louisiana-Lafayette, DB, 39/39
3. Lance Briggs, Arizona, LB, 48/48
4. Todd Johnson, Florida, DB, 30/30
4. Ian Scott, Florida, DT, 34/34
5. Justin Gage, Missouri, WR, 41/41
5. Tron LaFavor, Florida, DT, 4/4
5. Bobby Wade, Arizona, WR, 40/42
6. Brock Forsey, Boise State, RB, 9/16
6. Joe Odom, Purdue, LB, 28/28
7. Bryan Anderson, Pittsburgh, G, 4/4

CINCINNATI BENGALS

1. Carson Palmer, USC, QB, 29/29
2. Eric Steinbach, Iowa, G, 47/47
3. Kelley Washington, Tennessee, WR, 39/39
4. Jeremi Johnson, Western Kentucky, FB, 48/48
4. Dennis Weathersby, Oregon State, DB, 4/4
5. Khalid Abdullah, Mars Hill, LB, 16/16
6. Langston Moore, South Carolina, DT, 15/23
7. Scott Kooistra, North Carolina State, T, 39/39
7. Elton Patterson, Central Florida, DE, 2/8

CLEVELAND BROWNS

1. Jeff Faine, Notre Dame, C, 36/36
2. Chaun Thompson, West Texas A&M, LB, 48/48
3. Chris Crocker, Marshall, DB, 44/44
4. Lee Suggs, Virginia Tech, RB, 25/25
5. Michael Lehan, Minnesota, DB, 32/32
5. Ryan Pontbriand, Rice, C, 43/43
6. Antonio Garay, Boston College, DE, 4/4

DALLAS COWBOYS

1. Terence Newman, Kansas State, DB, 48/48
2. Al Johnson, Wisconsin, C, 32/32
3. Jason Witten, Tennessee, TE, 47/47
4. Bradie James, LSU, LB, 46/46
6. Zuriel Smith, Hampton, WR, 9/9
6. B.J. Tucker, Wisconsin, DB, 0/6
7. Justin Bates, Colorado, G, 0/0

DENVER BRONCOS

1. George Foster, Georgia, T, 33/33
2. Terry Pierce, Kansas State, LB, 18/18
4. Nick Eason, Clemson, DT, 0/17
4. Quentin Griffin, Oklahoma, RB, 16/16
4. Bryant McNeal, Clemson, DE, 0/0
5. Ben Claxton, Mississippi, G, 0/2

5. Adrian Madise, TCU, WR, 11/11
6. Aaron Hunt, Texas Tech, DE, 0/0
7. Clint Mitchell, Florida, DE, 0/0
7. Ahmaad Galloway, Alabama, RB, 0/0

DETROIT LIONS

1. Charles Rogers, Michigan State, WR, 15/15
2. Boss Bailey, Georgia, LB, 27/27
3. Cory Redding, Texas, DE, 41/41
4. Artose Pinner, Kentucky, RB, 28/28
5. James Davis, West Virginia, LB, 40/40
5. Terrence Holt, North Carolina State, DB, 37/37
6. David Kircus, Grand Valley State, WR, 12/12
7. Blue Adams, Cincinnati, DB, 0/21
7. Ben Johnson, Wisconsin, T, 0/0
7. Brandon Drumm, Colorado, RB, 0/0
7. Travis Anglin, Memphis, WR, 0/0

GREEN BAY PACKERS

1. Nick Barnett, Oregon State, LB, 47/47
3. Kenny Peterson, Ohio State, DT, 34/34
5. Hunter Hillenmeyer, Vanderbilt, LB, 0/42
5. James Lee, Oregon State, DT, 9/9
6. Brennan Curtin, Notre Dame, T, 0/0
7. Chris Johnson, Louisville, DB, 0/14
7. Steve Josue, Carson-Newman, LB, 4/4
7. DeAndrew Rubin, South Florida, WR, 0/0
7. Carl Ford, Toledo, WR, 0/0

HOUSTON TEXANS

1. Andre Johnson, Miami (FL), WR, 45/45
S2. Tony Hollings, Georgia Tech, RB, 23/23
2. Ben Joppru, Michigan, TE, 0/0
3. Antwan Peek, Cincinnati, LB, 40/40
3. Dave Ragone, Louisville, QB, 2/2
3. Seth Wand, Northwest Missouri State, T, 45/45
4. Domanick Davis, LSU, RB, 40/40
6. Drew Henson, Michigan, QB, 0/7
6. Keith Wright, Missouri, DT, 0/0
7. Curry Burns, Louisville, DB, 1/9
7. Chance Pearce, Texas A&M, C, 0/0

INDIANAPOLIS COLTS

1. Dallas Clark, Iowa, TE, 40/40
2. Mike Doss, Ohio State, DB, 40/40
3. Donald Strickland, Colorado, DB, 16/19
4. Steve Sciullo, Marshall, G, 13/28
5. Robert Mathis, Alabama A&M, DE, 45/45
5. Keyon Whiteside, Tennessee, LB, 12/12
6. Makoa Freitas, Arizona, T, 28/28
6. Cato June, Michigan, LB, 40/40

JACKSONVILLE JAGUARS

1. Byron Leftwich, Marshall, QB, 40/40
2. Rashean Mathis, Bethune-Cookman, DB, 48/48
3. Vince Manuwai, Hawaii, G, 47/47
4. LaBrandon Toefield, LSU, RB, 39/39
4. George Wrighster, Oregon, TE, 35/35
6. Brandon Green, Rice, DE, 3/19
6. David Young, Georgia Southern, DB, 0/5
6. Marques Ogden, Howard, T, 0/0
7. Malaefou MacKenzie, USC, FB, 1/1

KANSAS CITY CHIEFS

1. Larry Johnson, Penn State, RB, 32/32
2. Kawika Mitchell, South Florida, LB, 43/43
3. Julian Battle, Tennessee, DB, 26/26
4. Brett Williams, Florida State, T, 5/5
5. Jordan Black, Notre Dame, T, 32/32
6. Jimmy Wilkerson, Oklahoma, DE, 43/43
7. Willie Pile, Virginia Tech, DB, 16/32
7. Montique Sharpe, Wake Forest, DT, 5/5

MIAMI DOLPHINS

2. Eddie Moore, Tennessee, LB, 18/18
3. Wade Smith, Memphis, T, 22/22
3. Taylor Whitley, Texas A&M, G, 16/18
5. Donald Lee, Mississippi State, TE, 32/47
5. J.R. Tolver, San Diego State, WR, 0/0
6. Yeremiah Bell, Eastern Kentucky, DB, 29/29
6. Corey Jenkins, South Carolina, LB, 19/23
6. Tim Provost, San Jose State, T, 0/0
7. Davern Williams, Troy State, DT, 0/3

MINNESOTA VIKINGS

1. Kevin Williams, Oklahoma State, DT, 46/46
2. E.J. Henderson, Maryland, LB, 45/45
3. Nate Burleson, Nevada-Reno, WR, 44/44
4. Onterrio Smith, Oregon, RB, 26/26
6. Eddie Johnson, Idaho State, P, 14/14
6. Mike Nattiel, Florida, LB, 32/32
7. Keenan Howry, Oregon, WR, 23/23

NEW ENGLAND PATRIOTS

1. Ty Warren, Texas A&M, DE, 48/48
2. Bethel Johnson, Texas A&M, WR, 39/39
2. Eugene Wilson, Illinois, DB, 47/47
4. Dan Klecko, Temple, DT, 30/30
4. Asante Samuel, Central Florida, DB, 44/44
5. Dan Koppen, Boston College, C, 41/41
6. Kliff Kingsbury, Texas Tech, QB, 0/1
7. Tully Banta-Cain, California, LB, 38/38
7. Ethan Kelley, Baylor, DT, 1/11
7. Spencer Nead, Brigham Young, FB, 0/10

NEW ORLEANS SAINTS

1. Johnathan Sullivan, Georgia, DT, 36/36
2. Jon Stinchcomb, Georgia, T, 10/10
3. Cie Grant, Ohio State, LB, 7/7
4. Montrae Holland, Florida State, G, 44/44
5. Melvin Williams, Kansas State, DE, 14/17
6. Kareem Kelly, Southern California, WR, 0/0
7. Talman Gardner, Florida State, WR, 21/21

NEW YORK GIANTS

1. William Joseph, Miami (FL), DT, 39/39
2. Osi Umenyiora, Troy State, DE, 45/45
3. Visanthe Shiancoe, Morgan State, TE, 48/48
4. Roderick Babers, Texas, DB, 0/7
5. David Diehl, Illinois, G, 48/48
6. Willie Ponder, Southeast Missouri State, WR, 26/26
6. David Tyree, Syracuse, WR, 45/45
6. Frank Walker, Tuskegee, DB, 30/30
7. Wayne Lucier, Colorado, G, 27/27
7. Kevin Walter, Eastern Michigan, WR, 0/43
7. Charles Drake, Michigan, DB, 0/0

NEW YORK JETS

1. Dewayne Robertson, Kentucky, DT, 45/45
2. Victor Hobson, Michigan, LB, 44/44
3. B.J. Askew, Michigan, FB, 42/42
5. Derek Pagel, Iowa, DB, 19/19
5. Matt Walters, Miami (FL), DE, 11/11
6. Brooks Bollinger, Wisconsin, QB, 12/12
7. Dave Yovanovits, Temple, G, 4/6

OAKLAND RAIDERS

1. Nnamdi Asomugha, California, DB, 47/47
1. Tyler Brayton, Colorado, DE, 47/47
2. Teyo Johnson, Stanford, TE, 24/31
3. Justin Fargas, USC, FB, 36/36
3. Sam Williams, Fresno State, DE, 10/10
4. Shurron Pierson, South Florida, DE, 6/12
5. Doug Gabriel, Central Florida, WR, 42/42
6. Dustin Rykert, Brigham Young, T, 0/0
7. Siddeeq Shabazz, New Mexico State, DB, 4/28
7. Ryan Hoag, Gustavus Adolphus, WR, 0/0

PHILADELPHIA EAGLES

1. Jerome McDougle, Miami (FL), DE, 19/19
2. L.J. Smith, Rutgers, TE, 47/47
3. Billy McMullen, Virginia, WR, 29/29
4. Jamaal Green, Miami (FL), DE, 8/8
6. Jeremy Bridges, Southern Mississippi, G, 0/21
7. Norman LeJeune, LSU, DB, 0/5
7. Norman LeJeune, Louisiana State, DB, 0/0

PITTSBURGH STEELERS

1. Troy Polamalu, USC, DB, 48/48
2. Alonzo Jackson, Florida State, LB, 9/18
4. Ike Taylor, Louisiana-Lafayette, DB, 45/45
5. Brian St. Pierre, Boston College, QB, 1/1
7. J.T. Wall, Georgia, RB, 0/0

SAN DIEGO CHARGERS

1. Sammy Davis, Texas A&M, DB, 44/44
2. Drayton Florence, Tuskegee, DB, 42/42
2. Terrence Kiel, Texas A&M, DB, 44/44
3. Courtney Van Buren, Arkansas-Pine Bluff, T, 9/9
4. Matt Wilhelm, Ohio State, LB, 25/25
5. Mike Scifres, Western Illinois, P, 38/38
6. Hanik Milligan, Houston, DB, 30/30
7. Andrew Pinnock, South Carolina, FB, 28/28

SAN FRANCISCO 49ERS

1. Kwame Harris, Stanford, T, 44/44
2. Anthony Adams, Penn State, DT, 44/44
3. Andrew Williams, Miami (FL), DE, 9/9
4. Brandon Lloyd, Illinois, WR, 45/45
5. Aaron Walker, Florida, TE, 32/32
6. Arnaz Battle, Notre Dame, WR, 32/32
7. Ken Dorsey, Miami (FL), QB, 12/12

ST. LOUIS RAMS

1. Jimmy Kennedy, Penn State, DT, 37/37
2. Pisa Tinoisamoa, Hawaii, LB, 48/48
3. Kevin Curtis, Utah State, WR, 35/35
4. DeJuan Groce, Nebraska, DB, 42/42
4. Shaun McDonald, Arizona State, WR, 40/40
5. Dan Curley, Eastern Washington, FB, 1/1
5. Kevin Garrett, SMU, DB, 23/23
5. Shane Walton, Notre Dame, DB, 4/4
6. Scott Tercero, California, G, 8/8
7. Richard Angulo, Western New Mexico, TE, 5/7
7. Scott Shanle, Nebraska, LB, 5/36

SEATTLE SEAHAWKS

1. Marcus Trufant, Washington State, DB, 47/47
2. Ken Hamlin, Arkansas, DB, 38/38
3. Wayne Hunter, Hawaii, T, 2/2
4. Solomon Bates, Arizona State, LB, 17/17
4. Seneca Wallace, Iowa State, QB, 7/7
5. Chris Davis, Syracuse, FB, 1/1
6. Rashad Moore, Tennessee, DT, 29/29
7. Josh Brown, Nebraska, K, 48/48
7. Taco Wallace, Kansas State, WR, 3/4

TAMPA BAY BUCCANEERS

2. Dewayne White, Louisville, DE, 44/44
3. Chris Simms, Texas, QB, 16/16
4. Austin King, Northwestern, C, 0/20
4. Lance Nimmo, West Virginia, T, 0/0
5. Sean Mahan, Notre Dame, G, 41/41
6. Torrie Cox, Pittsburgh, DB, 25/25

TENNESSEE TITANS

1. Andre Woolfolk, Oklahoma, DB, 29/29
2. Tyrone Calico, Middle Tennessee State, WR, 27/27
3. Chris Brown, Colorado, RB, 37/37
4. Rien Long, Washington State, DT, 39/39
5. Donnie Nickey, Ohio State, DB, 43/43
7. Todd Williams, Florida State, G, 7/7

WASHINGTON REDSKINS

2. Taylor Jacobs, Florida, WR, 38/38
3. Derrick Dockery, Texas, G, 48/48
7. Gibran Hamdan, Indiana, QB, 1/1

2004 NFL

ARIZONA CARDINALS

1. Larry Fitzgerald, Pittsburgh, WR, 32/32
2. Karlos Dansby, Auburn, LB, 30/30
3. Darnell Dockett, Florida State, DT, 32/32
4. Alex Stepanovich, Ohio State, C, 25/25
5. Antonio Smith, Oklahoma State, DE, 13/13
6. Nick Leckey, Kansas State, C, 30/30
7. John Navarre, Michigan, QB, 2/2

ATLANTA FALCONS

1. DeAngelo Hall, Virginia Tech, DB, 25/25
1. Michael Jenkins, Ohio State, WR, 30/30
3. Matt Schaub, Virginia, QB, 22/22
4. Demorrio Williams, Nebraska, LB, 32/32
5. Chad Lavalais, LSU, DT, 30/30
6. Etric Pruitt, Southern Mississippi, DB, 3/9
7. Quincy Wilson, West Virginia, RB, 0/0

BALTIMORE RAVENS

2. Dwan Edwards, Oregon State, DT, 16/16
3. Devard Darling, Washington State, WR, 13/13
5. Roderick Green, Central Missouri State, LB, 25/25
6. Clarence Moore, Northern Arizona, WR, 19/19
6. Josh Harris, Bowling Green, QB, 0/0
7. Brian Rimpf, East Carolina, G, 16/16
7. Derek Abney, Kentucky, WR, 0/0

BUFFALO BILLS

1. Lee Evans, Wisconsin, WR, 32/32
1. J.P. Losman, Tulane, QB, 13/13
3. Tim Anderson, Ohio State, DT, 19/19
4. Tim Euhus, Oregon State, TE, 23/23
7. Dylan McFarland, Montana, T, 3/3
7. Jonathan Smith, Georgia Tech, WR, 16/16

CAROLINA PANTHERS

1. Chris Gamble, Ohio State, DB, 31/31
2. Keary Colbert, USC, WR, 31/31
3. Travelle Wharton, South Carolina, T, 27/27
5. Drew Carter, Ohio State, WR, 3/3
6. Sean Tufts, Colorado, LB, 15/15
7. Michael Gaines, Central Florida, TE, 26/26

CHICAGO BEARS

1. Tommie Harris, Oklahoma, DT, 32/32
2. Tank Johnson, Washington, DT, 32/32
3. Bernard Berrian, Fresno State, WR, 27/27
4. Leon Joe, Maryland, LB, 15/19
4. Nathan Vasher, Texas, DB, 32/32
5. Craig Krenzel, Ohio State, QB, 6/6
5. Claude Harriott, Pittsburgh, DE, 0/0
7. Alfonso Marshall, Miami (FL), DB, 7/7

CINCINNATI BENGALS

1. Chris Perry, Michigan, RB, 16/16
2. Keiwan Ratliff, Florida, DB, 32/32
2. Madieu Williams, Maryland, DB, 20/20
3. Landon Johnson, Purdue, LB, 32/32
3. Caleb Miller, Arkansas, LB, 20/20
4. Stacy Andrews, Mississippi, T, 15/15
4. Matthias Askew, Michigan State, DT, 6/6
4. Robert Geathers, Georgia, DE, 30/30
5. Maurice Mann, Nevada, WR, 0/0
6. Greg Brooks, Southern Mississippi, DB, 11/11
7. Casey Bramlet, Wyoming, QB, 0/0

CLEVELAND BROWNS

1. Kellen Jr. Winslow, Miami (FL), TE, 2/2
2. Sean Jones, Georgia, DB, 16/16
4. Luke McCown, Louisiana Tech, QB, 5/5
5. Amon Gordon, Stanford, DT, 6/6
6. Kirk Chambers, Stanford, T, 21/21
7. Adimchinobe Echemandu, California, RB, 4/6

DALLAS COWBOYS

2. Julius Jones, Notre Dame, RB, 21/21
2. Jacob Rogers, USC, T, 2/2
3. Stephen Peterman, LSU, G, 3/3
4. Bruce Thornton, Georgia, DB, 1/13
5. Sean Ryan, Boston College, TE, 9/9
7. Patrick Crayton, Northwestern Oklahoma State, WR, 19/19
7. Nate Jones, Rutgers, DB, 32/32
7. Jacques Reeves, Purdue, DB, 31/31

DENVER BRONCOS

1. D.J. Williams, Miami (FL), LB, 32/32
2. Tatum Bell, Oklahoma State, RB, 29/29
2. Darius Watts, Marshall, WR, 22/22
3. Jeremy LeSueur, Michigan, DB, 0/3
5. Jeff Shoate, San Diego State, DB, 7/7
6. Triandos Luke, Alabama, WR, 10/10
6. Josh Sewell, Nebraska, C, 0/0
7. Matt Mauck, LSU, QB, 0/3
7. Bradlee Van Pelt, Colorado, QB, 3/3
7. Brandon Miree, Pittsburgh, RB, 0/0

DETROIT LIONS

1. Kevin Jones, Virginia Tech, RB, 28/28
1. Roy Williams, Texas, WR, 27/27
2. Teddy Lehman, Oklahoma, LB, 21/21
3. Keith Smith, McNeese State, DB, 30/30
5. Alex Lewis, Wisconsin, LB, 16/16
6. Kelly Butler, Purdue, T, 16/16

GREEN BAY PACKERS

1. Ahmad Carroll, Arkansas, DB, 30/30
3. B.J. Sander, Ohio State, P, 14/14
3. Joey Thomas, Montana State, DB, 20/25
3. Donnell Washington, Clemson, DT, 0/0
4. Carl Ford, Toledo, WR, 0/10
6. Corey Williams, Arkansas State, DT, 24/24
7. Scott Wells, Tennessee, G, 21/21

HOUSTON TEXANS

1. Jason Babin, Western Michigan, LB, 28/28
1. Dunta Robinson, South Carolina, DB, 32/32
4. Glenn Earl, Notre Dame, DB, 22/22
6. Charlie Anderson, Mississippi, LB, 31/31
6. Jammal Lord, Nebraska, DB, 1/1
6. Vontez Duff, Notre Dame, DB, 0/0
7. Raheem Orr, Rutgers, LB, 0/2
7. Sloan Thomas, Texas, WR, 0/1
7. B.J. Symons, Texas Tech, QB, 0/0

INDIANAPOLIS COLTS

2. Bob Sanders, Iowa, DB, 20/20
3. Gilbert Gardner, Purdue, LB, 22/22
3. Ben Hartsock, Ohio State, TE, 23/23
4. Jason David, Washington State, DB, 32/32
4. Kendyll Pope, Florida State, LB, 2/2
5. Jake Scott, Idaho, G, 28/28
6. Von Hutchins, Mississippi, DB, 19/19
6. Jim Sorgi, Wisconsin, QB, 9/9
7. David Kimball, Penn State, K, 0/0

JACKSONVILLE JAGUARS
1. Reggie Williams, Washington, WR, 32/32
2. Greg Jones, Florida State, RB, 30/30
2. Daryl Smith, Georgia Tech, LB, 31/31
3. Jorge Cordova, Nevada, LB, 0/0
4. Anthony Maddox, Delta State, DT, 7/7
4. Ernest Wilford, Virginia Tech, WR, 31/31
5. Josh Scobee, Louisiana Tech, K, 32/32
5. Chris Thompson, Nicholls State, DB, 0/12
5. Sean Bubin, Illinois, T, 0/0
7. Bobby McCray, Florida, DE, 32/32

KANSAS CITY CHIEFS
2. Junior Siavii, Oregon, DT, 26/26
2. Kris Wilson, Pittsburgh, TE, 17/17
3. Keyaron Fox, Georgia Tech, LB, 14/14
4. Jared Allen, Idaho State, DE, 31/31
4. Samie Parker, Oregon, WR, 16/16
6. Jeris McIntyre, Auburn, WR, 0/0
7. Kevin Sampson, Syracuse, T, 10/10

MIAMI DOLPHINS
1. Vernon Carey, Miami (FL), T, 30/30
4. Will Poole, USC, DB, 15/15
5. Tony Bua, Arkansas, LB, 7/7
6. Rex Hadnot, Houston, G, 30/30
7. Derrick Pope, Alabama, LB, 28/28
7. Tony Pape, Michigan, G, 0/0

MINNESOTA VIKINGS
1. Kenechi Udeze, USC, DE, 19/19
2. Dontarrious Thomas, Auburn, LB, 30/30
3. Darrion Scott, Ohio State, DE, 28/28
4. Nat Dorsey, Georgia Tech, T, 13/22
4. Mewelde Moore, Tulane, RB, 26/26
5. Rod Davis, Southern Mississippi, LB, 30/30
6. Deandre Eiland, South Carolina, DB, 0/0
7. Jeff Dugan, Maryland, TE, 15/15

NEW ENGLAND PATRIOTS
1. Ben Watson, Georgia, TE, 16/16
1. Vince Wilfork, Miami (FL), NT, 32/32
2. Marquise Hill, LSU, DE, 9/9
3. Guss Scott, Florida, DB, 5/5
4. Cedric Cobbs, Arkansas, RB, 3/3
4. Dexter Reid, North Carolina, DB, 13/29
5. P.K. Sam, Florida State, WR, 2/2
7. Christian Morton, Illinois, DB, 0/7

NEW ORLEANS SAINTS
1. Will Smith, Ohio State, DE, 32/32
2. Devery Henderson, LSU, WR, 15/15
2. Courtney Watson, Notre Dame, LB, 21/21
5. Mike Karney, Arizona State, FB, 32/32
5. Rodney Leisle, UCLA, DT, 3/3
7. Colby Bockwoldt, Brigham Young, LB, 32/32

NEW YORK GIANTS
1. Philip Rivers, North Carolina State, QB, 0/4
2. Chris Snee, Boston College, G, 27/27
4. Reggie Torbor, Auburn, LB, 30/30
5. Gibril Wilson, Tennessee, DB, 24/24
6. Jamaar Taylor, Texas A&M, WR, 13/13
7. Drew Strojny, Duke, T, 0/0
7. Isaac Hilton, Hampton, DE, 0/0

NEW YORK JETS
1. Jonathan Vilma, Miami (FL), LB, 32/32
3. Derrick Strait, Oklahoma, DB, 21/21
4. Jerricho Cotchery, North Carolina State, WR, 28/28
4. Adrian Jones, Kansas, T, 28/28
5. Erik Coleman, Washington State, DB, 32/32
6. Marko Cavka, Sacramento State, T, 0/0
7. Trevor Johnson, Nebraska, DE, 25/25
7. Darrell McClover, Miami (FL), LB, 16/16
7. Derrick Ward, Ottawa (KS), RB, 0/19
7. Rashad Washington, Kansas State, DB, 22/22

OAKLAND RAIDERS
1. Robert Gallery, Iowa, T, 32/32
2. Jake Grove, Virginia Tech, C, 19/19
3. Stuart Schweigert, Purdue, DB, 32/32
4. Carlos Francis, Texas Tech, WR, 5/5
5. Johnnie Morant, Syracuse, WR, 5/5
6. Cody Spencer, North Texas, LB, 0/23
6. Shawn Johnson, Delaware, DE, 0/0
7. Courtney Anderson, San Jose State, TE, 23/23
7. Andre Sommersell, Colorado State, LB, 0/0

PHILADELPHIA EAGLES
1. Shawn Andrews, Arkansas, G, 17/17
3. Matt Ware, UCLA, DB, 28/28
4. Trey Darilek, Texas-El Paso, G, 18/18
4. J.R. Reed, South Florida, DB, 14/14
5. Thomas Tapeh, Minnesota, FB, 7/7
6. Andy Hall, Delaware, QB, 1/1
6. Dexter Wynn, Colorado State, DB, 22/22
7. Adrien Clarke, Ohio State, G, 13/13
7. Bruce Perry, Maryland, RB, 2/2
7. Dominic Furio, Nevada-Las Vegas, C, 0/0

PITTSBURGH STEELERS
1. Ben Roethlisberger, Miami (OH), QB, 26/26
2. Ricardo Colclough, Tusculum, DB, 30/30
3. Max Starks, Florida, T, 26/26
5. Nathaniel Adibi, Virginia Tech, DE, 0/0
6. Matt Kranchick, Penn State, TE, 6/8
6. Bo Lacy, Arkansas, T, 0/0
6. Drew Caylor, Stanford, C, 0/0
7. Eric Taylor, Memphis, DT, 0/1

SAN DIEGO CHARGERS
1. Eli Manning, Mississippi, QB, 0/25
2. Igor Olshansky, Oregon, DE, 30/30
3. Nick Hardwick, Purdue, C, 27/27
3. Nate Kaeding, Iowa, K, 32/32
4. Shaun Phillips, Purdue, DE, 31/31
5. Dave Ball, UCLA, DE, 8/11
5. Michael Turner, Northern Illinois, RB, 30/30
6. Ryan Krause, Nebraska-Omaha, TE, 4/4
7. Ryon Bingham, Nebraska, DT, 1/1
7. Shane Olivea, Ohio State, T, 31/31
7. Carlos Joseph, Miami (FL), T, 0/0

SAN FRANCISCO 49ERS
1. Rashaun Woods, Oklahoma State, WR, 14/14
2. Justin Smiley, Alabama, G, 32/32
2. Shawntae Spencer, Pittsburgh, DB, 31/31
3. Derrick Hamilton, Clemson, WR, 2/2
4. Richard Seigler, Oregon State, LB, 7/7
4. Isaac Sopoaga, Hawaii, DT, 16/16
6. Andy Lee, Pittsburgh, P, 32/32
6. Keith Lewis, Oregon, DB, 32/32
7. Cody Pickett, Washington, QB, 7/7
7. Christian Ferrara, Syracuse, DT, 0/0

ST. LOUIS RAMS
1. Steven Jackson, Oregon State, RB, 29/29
3. Anthony Hargrove, Georgia Tech, DE, 31/31
4. Brandon Chillar, UCLA, LB, 32/32
5. Jason Shivers, Arizona State, DB, 0/1
6. Jeff Smoker, Michigan State, QB, 0/0
7. Larry Turner, Eastern Kentucky, C, 20/20
7. Erik Jensen, Iowa, TE, 0/0

SEATTLE SEAHAWKS
1. Marcus Tubbs, Texas, DT, 24/24
2. Michael Boulware, Florida State, DB, 32/32
3. Sean Locklear, North Carolina State, T, 32/32
4. Niko Koutouvides, Purdue, LB, 28/28
5. D.J. Hackett, Colorado, WR, 13/13
6. Craig Terrill, Purdue, DT, 20/20
7. Donnie Jones, LSU, P, 7/23

TAMPA BAY BUCCANEERS
1. Michael Clayton, LSU, WR, 30/30
3. Marquis Cooper, Washington, LB, 26/26
4. Will Allen, Ohio State, DB, 29/29
5. Jeb Terry, North Carolina, G, 20/20
6. Nate Lawrie, Yale, TE, 7/7
7. Casey Cramer, Dartmouth, RB, 0/7
7. Mark Jones, Tennessee, WR, 16/30
7. Lenny Williams, Southern, DB, 0/0

TENNESSEE TITANS
2. Travis LaBoy, Hawaii, DE, 28/28
2. Antwan Odom, Alabama, DE, 32/32
2. Ben Troupe, Florida, TE, 29/29
3. Rich Gardner, Penn State, DB, 28/28
3. Randy Starks, Maryland, DT, 30/30
4. Bo Schobel, TCU, DE, 13/13
4. Michael Waddell, North Carolina, DB, 32/32
5. Jacob Bell, Miami (OH), G, 24/24
5. Robert Reynolds, Ohio State, LB, 29/29
6. Troy Fleming, Tennessee, RB, 29/29
7. Eugene Amano, Southeast Missouri State, C, 31/31
7. Jared Clauss, Iowa, DT, 29/29
7. Sean McHugh, Penn State, FB, 0/4

WASHINGTON REDSKINS
1. Sean Taylor, Miami (FL), DB, 30/30
3. Chris Cooley, Utah State, TE, 32/32
5. Mark Wilson, California, TE, 2/2
6. Jim Molinaro, Notre Dame, T, 14/14

2005 NFL

ARIZONA CARDINALS
1. Antrel Rolle, Miami (FL), DB, 5/5
2. J.J. Arrington, California, RB, 15/15
3. Darryl Blackstock, Virginia, LB, 14/14
3. Eric Green, Virginia Tech, DB, 12/12
4. Elton Brown, Virginia, G, 9/9
5. Lance Mitchell, Oklahoma, LB, 12/12
7. LeRon McCoy, Indiana (PA), WR, 10/10

ATLANTA FALCONS
1. Roddy White, Alabama-Birmingham, WR, 16/16
2. Jonathan Babineaux, Iowa, DE, 16/16
3. Jordan Beck, Cal Poly, LB, 0/0
4. Chauncey Davis, Florida State, DE, 16/16
5. Michael Boley, Southern Mississippi, LB, 16/16
5. Frank Omiyale, Tennessee Tech, T, 0/0
6. DeAndra Cobb, Michigan State, RB, 3/3
7. Darrell Shropshire, South Carolina, DT, 10/10

BALTIMORE RAVENS
1. Mark Clayton, Oklahoma, WR, 14/14
2. Adam Terry, Syracuse, T, 7/7
2. Dan Cody, Oklahoma, DE, 0/0
4. Jason Brown, North Carolina, C, 6/6
5. Justin Green, Montana, FB, 12/12
6. Derek Anderson, Oregon State, QB, 0/0
7. Mike Smith, Texas Tech, LB, 6/6

BUFFALO BILLS
2. Roscoe Parrish, Miami (FL), WR, 10/10
3. Kevin Everett, Miami (FL), TE, 0/0
4. Duke Preston, Illinois, C, 15/15
5. Eric King, Wake Forest, DB, 16/16
6. Justin Geisinger, Vanderbilt, G, 0/0
7. Chris Roberson, Eastern Michigan, DB, 0/6
7. Lionel Gates, Louisville, RB, 0/0

CAROLINA PANTHERS
1. Thomas Davis, Georgia, LB, 16/16
2. Eric Shelton, Louisville, RB, 0/0
3. Evan Mathis, Alabama, G, 9/9
3. Atiyyah Ellison, Missouri, DT, 0/0
4. Stefan Lefors, Louisville, QB, 0/0
5. Ben Emanuel, UCLA, DB, 0/11
5. Geoff Hangartner, Texas A&M, C, 4/4
5. Adam Seward, Nevada-Las Vegas, LB, 4/4
6. Joe Berger, Michigan Tech, T, 0/3
6. Jovan Haye, Vanderbilt, DE, 2/2

CHICAGO BEARS
1. Cedric Benson, Texas, RB, 9/9
2. Mark Bradley, Oklahoma, WR, 7/7
4. Kyle Orton, Purdue, QB, 15/15
5. Airese Currie, Clemson, WR, 0/0
6. Chris Harris, Louisiana-Monroe, DB, 14/14
7. Rodriques Wilson, South Carolina, DB, 0/0

CINCINNATI BENGALS
1. David Pollack, Georgia, LB, 14/14
2. Odell Thurman, Georgia, LB, 16/16
3. Chris Henry, West Virginia, WR, 14/14
4. Eric Ghiaciuc, Central Michigan, C, 5/5
5. Adam Kieft, Central Michigan, T, 0/0
6. Tab Perry, UCLA, WR, 16/16
7. Jonathan Fanene, Utah, DE, 3/3

CLEVELAND BROWNS
1. Braylon Edwards, Michigan, WR, 10/10
2. Brodney Pool, Oklahoma, DB, 13/13
3. Charlie Frye, Akron, QB, 7/7
4. Antonio Perkins, Oklahoma, DB, 1/1
5. David McMillan, Kansas, DE, 4/4
6. Nick Speegle, New Mexico, LB, 14/14
6. Andrew Hoffman, Virginia, DT, 0/0
7. Jon Dunn, Virginia Tech, T, 0/0

DALLAS COWBOYS
1. Marcus Spears, LSU, DE, 16/16
1. Demarcus Ware, Troy, LB, 16/16
2. Kevin Burnett, Tennessee, LB, 13/13
4. Marion Barber, Minnesota, RB, 13/13
4. Chris Canty, Virginia, DE, 16/16
6. Rob Petitti, Pittsburgh, T, 16/16
6. Justin Beriault, Ball State, DB, 0/0
7. Jay Ratliff, Auburn, DE, 4/4

DENVER BRONCOS
2. Darrent Williams, Oklahoma State, DB, 12/12
3. Domonique Foxworth, Maryland, DB, 16/16
3. Karl Paymah, Washington State, DB, 13/13
3. Maurice Clarett, Ohio State, RB, 0/0
6. Chris Myers, Miami (FL), G, 9/9
7. Paul Ernster, Northern Arizona, K, 1/1

DETROIT LIONS
1. Mike Williams, USC, WR, 14/14
2. Shaun Cody, USC, DT, 16/16
3. Stanley Wilson, Stanford, DB, 9/9
5. Dan Orlovsky, Connecticut, QB, 2/2
6. Jonathan Goddard, Marshall, DE, 0/1
6. Bill Swancutt, Oregon State, DE, 8/8

GREEN BAY PACKERS
1. Aaron Rodgers, California, QB, 3/3
2. Nick Collins, Bethune-Cookman, DB, 16/16
2. Terrence Murphy, Texas A&M, WR, 3/3
4. Brady Poppinga, Brigham Young, LB, 12/12
4. Marviel Underwood, San Diego State, DB, 16/16
5. Michael Hawkins, Oklahoma, DB, 11/11
5. Junius Coston, North Carolina A&T, C, 0/0
6. Mike Montgomery, Texas A&M, DT, 12/12
6. Craig Bragg, UCLA, WR, 0/0
7. Will Whitticker, Michigan State, G, 15/15
7. Kurt Campbell, Albany (NY), DB, 0/0

HOUSTON TEXANS
1. Travis Johnson, Florida State, DT, 15/15
3. Vernand Morency, Oklahoma State, RB, 13/13
4. Jerome Mathis, Hampton, WR, 12/12
5. Drew Hodgdon, Arizona State, C, 4/4
6. C.C. Brown, Louisiana-Lafayette, DB, 16/16
7. Kenneth Pettway, Grambling State, LB, 0/0

INDIANAPOLIS COLTS
1. Marlin Jackson, Michigan, DB, 15/15
2. Kelvin Hayden, Illinois, DB, 16/16
3. Vincent Burns, Kentucky, DE, 0/0
4. Dylan Gandy, Texas Tech, G, 16/16
4. Matt Giordano, California, DB, 15/15
5. Jonathan Welsh, Wisconsin, DE, 6/6
5. Robert Hunt, North Dakota State, C, 0/0
5. Tyjuan Hagler, Cincinnati, LB, 0/0
6. Dave Rayner, Michigan State, K, 14/14
7. Anthony Davis, Wisconsin, RB, 0/0

JACKSONVILLE JAGUARS
1. Matt Jones, Arkansas, WR, 16/16
2. Khalif Barnes, Washington, T, 13/13
3. Scott Starks, Wisconsin, DB, 16/16
4. Alvin Pearman, Virginia, RB, 16/16
5. Gerald Sensabaugh, North Carolina, DB, 16/16
6. Chad Owens, Hawaii, WR, 1/1
6. Pat Thomas, North Carolina State, LB, 9/9
7. Chris Roberson, Eastern Michigan, DB, 0/0

KANSAS CITY CHIEFS
1. Derrick Johnson, Texas, LB, 16/16
3. Dustin Colquitt, Tennessee, P, 16/16
4. Craphonso Thorpe, Florida State, WR, 0/0
5. Boomer Grigsby, Illinois State, LB, 16/16
5. Alphonso Hodge, Miami (OH), DB, 0/0
6. Khari Long, Baylor, DE, 1/1
6. Will Svitek, Stanford, T, 1/1
7. James Kilian, Tulsa, QB, 0/0
7. Jeremy Parquet, Southern Mississippi, T, 0/0

MIAMI DOLPHINS
1. Ronnie Brown, Auburn, RB, 15/15
2. Matt Roth, Iowa, DE, 16/16
3. Channing Crowder, Florida, LB, 16/16
4. Travis Daniels, LSU, DB, 16/16
5. Manuel Wright, Southern California, DT, 0/0
5. Anthony Alabi, Texas Christian, T, 0/0
7. Kevin Vickerson, Michigan State, DT, 0/0

MINNESOTA VIKINGS
1. Erasmus James, Wisconsin, DE, 15/15
1. Troy Williamson, South Carolina, WR, 14/14
2. Marcus Johnson, Mississippi, G, 14/14
3. Dustin Fox, Ohio State, DB, 0/0
4. Ciatrick Fason, Florida, RB, 13/13
6. C.J. Mosley, Missouri, DT, 12/12
7. Adrian Ward, Texas-El Paso, DB, 0/0

NEW ENGLAND PATRIOTS
1. Logan Mankins, Fresno State, G, 16/16
3. Ellis Hobbs, Iowa State, DB, 16/16
3. Nick Kaczur, Toledo, T, 14/14
4. James Sanders, Fresno State, DB, 10/10
5. Ryan Claridge, Nevada-Las Vegas, LB, 0/0

7. Matt Cassel, Southern California, QB, 2/2
7. Andy Stokes, William Penn, TE, 0/0

NEW ORLEANS SAINTS
1. Jammal Brown, Oklahoma, T, 13/13
2. Josh Bullocks, Nebraska, DB, 16/16
3. Alfred Fincher, Connecticut, LB, 11/11
4. Chase Lyman, California, WR, 0/0
5. Adrian McPherson, Florida State, QB, 0/0
6. Jason Jefferson, Wisconsin, DT, 0/5
7. Jimmy Verdon, Arizona State, DT, 4/4

NEW YORK GIANTS
2. Corey Webster, LSU, DB, 15/15
3. Justin Tuck, Notre Dame, DE, 14/14
3. Brandon Jacobs, Southern Illinois, RB, 16/16
6. Eric Moore, Florida State, DE, 8/8

NEW YORK JETS
2. Justin Miller, Clemson, DB, 16/16
2. Mike Nugent, Ohio State, K, 16/16
2. Sione Pouha, Utah, DT, 14/14
4. Kerry Rhodes, Louisville, DB, 16/16
5. Andre Maddox, North Carolina State, DB, 0/0
5. Joel Dreessen, Colorado State, TE, 14/14
6. Cedric Houston, Tennessee, RB, 12/12
7. Harry Jr. Williams, Tuskegee, WR, 1/1

OAKLAND RAIDERS
1. Fabien Washington, Washington, DB, 16/16
2. Stanford Routt, Houston, DB, 14/14
3. Kirk Morrison, San Diego State, LB, 16/16
3. Andrew Walter, Arizona State, QB, 0/0
6. Anttaj Hawthorne, Wisconsin, DT, 2/2
7. Ryan Riddle, California, DE, 12/12
6. Pete McMahon, Iowa, T, 0/0

PHILADELPHIA EAGLES
1. Mike Patterson, USC, DT, 16/16
2. Reggie Brown, Georgia, WR, 16/16
3. Matt McCoy, San Diego State, LB, 4/4
3. Ryan Moats, Louisiana Tech, RB, 7/7
4. Sean Considine, Iowa, DB, 6/6
4. Todd Herremans, Saginaw Valley State, T, 4/4
5. Trent Cole, Cincinnati, DE, 15/15
5. Scott Young, Brigham Young, G, 0/0
6. Calvin Armstrong, Washington State, T, 0/0
7. Keyonta Marshall, Grand Valley State, DT, 1/1
7. David Bergeron, Stanford, LB, 0/0

PITTSBURGH STEELERS
1. Heath Miller, Virginia, TE, 16/16
2. Bryant McFadden, Florida State, DB, 12/12
3. Trai Essex, Northwestern, T, 6/6
4. Fred Gibson, Georgia, WR, 0/0
4. Rian Wallace, Temple, LB, 4/4
6. Chris Kemoeatu, Utah, G, 0/0
7. Noah Herron, Northwestern, RB, 2/7
7. Shaun Nua, Brigham Young, DE, 0/0

SAN DIEGO CHARGERS
1. Luis Castillo, Northwestern, DE, 16/16
1. Shawne Merriman, Maryland, LB, 15/15
2. Vincent Jackson, Northern Colorado, WR, 7/7
4. Darren Sproles, Kansas State, RB, 15/15
5. Wesley Britt, Alabama, T, 0/0
5. Wes Sims, Oklahoma, G, 2/2
7. Scott Mruczkowski, Bowling Green, C, 6/6

SAN FRANCISCO 49ERS
1. Alex Smith, Utah, QB, 9/9
2. David Baas, Michigan, G, 13/13
3. Frank Gore, Miami (FL), RB, 14/14
3. Adam Snyder, Oregon, T, 16/16
4. Ronald Fields, Mississippi State, DT, 4/4
5. Rasheed Marshall, West Virginia, WR, 12/12
6. Derrick Johnson, Washington, DB, 14/14
6. Billy Bajema, Oklahoma State, TE, 15/15
7. Patrick Estes, Virginia, TE, 7/7
7. Daven Holly, Cincinnati, DB, 0/3
7. Marcus Maxwell, Oregon, WR, 4/4

ST. LOUIS RAMS
1. Alex Barron, Florida State, T, 12/12
2. Ronald Bartell, Howard, DB, 10/10
3. O.J. Atogwe, Stanford, DB, 12/12
3. Richie Incognito, Nebraska, C, 0/0
4. Jerome Carter, Florida State, DB, 14/14
4. Claude Terrell, New Mexico, G, 14/14
5. Jerome Collins, Notre Dame, TE, 3/3
5. Reggie Hodges, Ball State, P, 5/8
6. Dante Ridgeway, Ball State, WR, 0/7
7. Ryan Fitzpatrick, Harvard, QB, 4/4
7. Madison Hedgecock, North Carolina, FB, 16/16

SEATTLE SEAHAWKS
1. Chris Spencer, Mississippi, C, 8/8
2. Lofa Tatupu, USC, LB, 16/16
3. LeRoy Hill, Clemson, LB, 15/15
3. David Greene, Georgia, QB, 0/0
4. Ray Willis, Florida State, T, 6/6
5. Jeb Huckeba, Arkansas, LB, 0/0
6. Tony Jackson, Iowa, TE, 0/0
7. Doug Nienhuis, Oregon State, T, 0/7
7. Cornelius Wortham, Alabama, LB, 8/8

TAMPA BAY BUCCANEERS
1. Cadillac Williams, Auburn, RB, 14/14
2. Barrett Ruud, Nebraska, LB, 16/16
3. Alex Smith, Stanford, TE, 16/16
3. Chris Colmer, North Carolina State, T, 0/0
4. Dan Buenning, Wisconsin, G, 16/16
5. Donte Nicholson, Oklahoma, DB, 9/9
5. Larry Brackins, Pearl River C.C., WR, 0/0
6. Anthony Bryant, Alabama, DT, 4/4
7. Hamza Abdullah, Washington State, DB, 0/1
7. Rick Razzano, Mississippi, RB, 0/0
7. Paris Warren, Utah, WR, 0/0
7. J.R. Russell, Louisville, WR, 0/0

TENNESSEE TITANS
1. Pacman Jones, West Virginia, DB, 15/15
2. Michael Roos, Eastern Washington, T, 16/16
3. Brandon Jones, Oklahoma, WR, 10/10
3. Courtney Roby, Indiana, WR, 13/13
4. Vincent Fuller, Virginia Tech, DB, 2/2
4. Roydell Williams, Tulane, WR, 11/11
4. David Stewart, Mississippi State, T, 0/0
5. Damien Nash, Missouri, RB, 3/3
5. Daniel Loper, Texas Tech, T, 0/0
6. Bo Scaife, Texas, TE, 16/16
7. Reynaldo Hill, Florida, DB, 15/15

WASHINGTON REDSKINS
1. Carlos Rogers, Auburn, DB, 12/12
1. Jason Campbell, Auburn, QB, 0/0
4. Manuel White, UCLA, RB, 0/0
5. Robert McCune, Louisville, LB, 5/5
6. Jared Newberry, Stanford, LB, 0/0
7. Nehemiah Broughton, The Citadel, FB, 4/4

2006 NFL

ARIZONA CARDINALS
1. Matt Leinart, USC, QB, 0/0
2. Deuce Lutui, USC, G, 0/0
3. Leonard Pope, Georgia, TE, 0/0
4. Gabe Watson, Michigan, DT, 0/0
5. Brandon Johnson, Louisville, LB, 0/0
6. Jon Lewis, Virginia Tech, DT, 0/0

ATLANTA FALCONS
2. Jimmy Williams, Virginia Tech, DB, 0/0
3. Jerious Norwood, Mississippi State, RB, 0/0
5. Quinn Ojennaka, Syracuse, G, 0/0
6. Adam Jennings, Fresno State, WR, 0/0
7. Todd Watkins, Brigham Young, WR, 0/0
7. D.J. Shockley, Georgia, QB, 0/0

BALTIMORE RAVENS
1. Haloti Ngata, Oregon, DT, 0/0
2. Chris Chester, Oklahoma, G, 0/0
3. David Pittman, Northwestern State, DB, 0/0
4. Demetrius Williams, Oregon, WR, 0/0
4. P.J. Daniels, Georgia Tech, RB, 0/0
5. Dawan Landry, Georgia Tech, DB, 0/0
5. Quinn Sypniewski, Colorado, TE, 0/0
6. Sam Koch, Nebraska, P, 0/0

[ST. LOUIS RAMS continued]
6. Derrick Martin, Wyoming, DB, 0/0
7. Ryan LaCasse, Syracuse, LB, 0/0

BUFFALO BILLS
1. Donte Whitner, Ohio State, DB, 0/0
1. John McCargo, North Carolina State, DT, 0/0
3. Ashton Youboty, Ohio State, DB, 0/0
4. Ko Simpson, South Carolina, DB, 0/0
5. Kyle Williams, LSU, DT, 0/0
5. Brad Butler, Virginia, T, 0/0
7. Keith Ellison, Oregon State, LB, 0/0
7. Terrance Pennington, New Mexico, T, 0/0
7. Aaron Merz, California, G, 0/0

CAROLINA PANTHERS
1. DeAngelo Williams, Memphis, RB, 0/0
2. Richard Marshall, Fresno State, DB, 0/0
3. James Anderson, Virginia Tech, LB, 0/0
3. Rashad Butler, Miami (FL), T, 0/0
4. Nate Salley, Ohio State, DB, 0/0
5. Jeff King, Virginia Tech, TE, 0/0
7. Will Montgomery, Virginia Tech, G, 0/0
7. Stanley McClover, Auburn, DE, 0/0

CHICAGO BEARS
2. Danieal Manning, Abilene Christian, DB, 0/0
2. Devin Hester, Miami (FL), DB, 0/0
3. Dusty Dvoracek, Oklahoma, DT, 0/0
4. Jamar Williams, Arizona State, LB, 0/0
5. Mark Anderson, Alabama, DE, 0/0
6. J.D. Runnels, Oklahoma, RB, 0/0
6. Tyler Reed, Penn State, G, 0/0

CINCINNATI BENGALS
1. Johnathan Joseph, South Carolina, DB, 0/0
2. Andrew Whitworth, LSU, T, 0/0
3. Frostee Rucker, USC, DE, 0/0
4. Domata Peko, Michigan State, DT, 0/0
5. A.J. Nicholson, Florida State, LB, 0/0
6. Reggie McNeal, Texas A&M, QB, 0/0
7. Ethan Kilmer, Penn State, WR, 0/0
7. Bennie Brazell, LSU, WR, 0/0

CLEVELAND BROWNS
1. Kamerion Wimbley, Florida State, DE, 0/0
2. D'Qwell Jackson, Maryland, LB, 0/0
3. Travis Wilson, Oklahoma, WR, 0/0
4. Leon Williams, Miami (FL), LB, 0/0
5. Jerome Harrison, Washington State, RB, 0/0
5. DeMario Minter, Georgia, DB, 0/0
6. Lawrence Vickers, Colorado, FB, 0/0
6. Babatunde Oshinowo, Stanford, DT, 0/0
7. Justin Hamilton, Virginia Tech, DB, 0/0

DALLAS COWBOYS
1. Bobby Carpenter, Ohio State, LB, 0/0
2. Anthony Fasano, Notre Dame, TE, 0/0
3. Jason Hatcher, Grambling State, DE, 0/0
4. Skyler Green, LSU, WR, 0/0
5. Pat Watkins, Florida State, DB, 0/0
6. Montavious Stanley, Louisville, DT, 0/0
7. Pat McQuistan, Weber State, T, 0/0
7. E.J. Whitley, Texas Tech, C, 0/0

DENVER BRONCOS
1. Jay Cutler, Vanderbilt, QB, 0/0
2. Tony Scheffler, Western Michigan, TE, 0/0
4. Brandon Marshall, Central Florida, WR, 0/0
4. Elvis Dumervile, Louisville, DE, 0/0
4. Domenik Hixon, Akron, WR, 0/0
5. Chris Kuper, North Dakota, G, 0/0
6. Greg Eslinger, Minnesota, C, 0/0

DETROIT LIONS
1. Ernie Sims, Florida State, LB, 0/0
2. Daniel Bullocks, Nebraska, DB, 0/0
3. Brian Calhoun, Wisconsin, RB, 0/0
3. Jonathan Scott, Texas, T, 0/0
6. Dee McCann, West Virginia, DB, 0/0
7. Fred Matua, USC, G, 0/0
7. Anthony Cannon, Tulane, LB, 0/0

GREEN BAY PACKERS
1. A.J. Hawk, Ohio State, LB, 0/0
2. Daryn Colledge, Boise State, T, 0/0
2. Greg Jennings, Western Michigan, WR, 0/0
3. Abdul Hodge, Iowa, LB, 0/0
3. Jason Spitz, Louisville, G, 0/0

HOUSTON TEXANS
1. Mario Williams, North Carolina State, DE, 0/0
2. DeMeco Ryans, Alabama, LB, 0/0
3. Charles Spencer, Pittsburgh, G, 0/0
3. Eric Winston, Miami(FL), T, 0/0
4. Owen Daniels, Wisconsin, TE, 0/0
7. Wali Lundy, Virginia, RB, 0/0
7. David Anderson, Colorado State, WR, 0/0

INDIANAPOLIS COLTS
1. Joseph Addai, LSU, RB, 0/0
2. Tim Jennings, Georgia, DB, 0/0
3. Freddie Keiaho, San Diego State, LB, 0/0
3. Michael Toudouze, TCU, G, 0/0
6. Charlie Johnson, Oklahoma State, T, 0/0
6. Antoine Bethea, Howard, DB, 0/0
7. T.J. Rushing, Stanford, DB, 0/0

JACKSONVILLE JAGUARS
1. Mercedes Lewis, UCLA, TE, 0/0
2. Maurice Drew, UCLA, RB, 0/0
3. Clint Ingram, Oklahoma, LB, 0/0
5. Brent Hawkins, Illinois State, DE, 0/0
7. James Wyche, Syracuse, DE, 0/0
7. Dee Webb, Florida, DB, 0/0

KANSAS CITY CHIEFS
1. Tamba Hali, Penn State, DE, 0/0
2. Bernard Pollard, Purdue, DB, 0/0
3. Brodie Croyle, Alabama, QB, 0/0
5. Marcus Maxey, Miami (FL), DB, 0/0
6. Tre' Stallings, Mississippi State, G, 0/0
6. Jeff Webb, San Diego State, WR, 0/0
7. Jarrad Page, UCLA, DB, 0/0

MIAMI DOLPHINS
1. Jason Allen, Tennessee, DB, 0/0
3. Derek Hagan, Arizona State, WR, 0/0
7. Fred Evans, Texas State, DT, 0/0
7. Rodrique Wright, Texas, DT, 0/0
7. Devin Aromashodu, Auburn, WR, 0/0

MINNESOTA VIKINGS
1. Chad Greenway, Iowa, LB, 0/0
2. Cedric Griffin, Texas, DB, 0/0
2. Ryan Cook, New Mexico, C, 0/0
4. Ray Edwards, Purdue, DE, 0/0
5. Greg Blue, Georgia, DB, 0/0
6. Tyrone Culver, Fresno State, DB, 0/0

NEW ENGLAND PATRIOTS
1. Laurence Maroney, Minnesota, RB, 0/0
2. Chad Jackson, Florida, WR, 0/0
3. David Thomas, Texas, TE, 0/0
4. Garrett Mills, Tulsa, FB, 0/0
4. Stephen Gostkowski, Memphis, K, 0/0
5. Ryan O'Callaghan, California, T, 0/0
6. Jeremy Mincey, Florida, DE, 0/0
6. Dan Stevenson, Notre Dame, G, 0/0
6. LeKevin Smith, Nebraska, DT, 0/0
7. Willie Andrews, Baylor, DB, 0/0

NEW ORLEANS SAINTS
1. Reggie Bush, USC, RB, 0/0
2. Roman Harper, Alabama, DB, 0/0
4. Jahri Evans, Bloomsburg, T, 0/0
5. Rob Ninkovich, Purdue, DE, 0/0
6. Mike Hass, Oregon State, WR, 0/0
6. Josh Lay, Pittsburgh, DB, 0/0
7. Zach Strief, Northwestern, G, 0/0
7. Marques Colston, Hofstra, WR, 0/0

NEW YORK GIANTS
1. Mathias Kiwanuka, Boston College, DE, 0/0
2. Sinorice Moss, Miami (FL), WR, 0/0
3. Gerris Wilkinson, Georgia Tech, LB, 0/0
4. Barry Cofield, Northwestern, DT, 0/0
4. Guy Whimper, East Carolina, DE, 0/0
7. Charlie Peprah, Alabama, DB, 0/0
7. Gerrick McPhearson, Maryland, DB, 0/0

NEW YORK JETS
1. D'Brickashaw Ferguson, Virginia, T, 0/0
1. Nick Mangold, Ohio State, C, 0/0

2. Kellen Clemens, Oregon, QB, 0/0
3. Anthony Schlegel, Ohio State, LB, 0/0
3. Eric Smith, Michigan State, DB, 0/0
4. Brad Smith, Missouri, QB, 0/0
4. Leon Washington, Florida State, RB, 0/0
5. Jason Pociask, Wisconsin, TE, 0/0
6. Drew Coleman, TCU, DB, 0/0
7. Titus Adams, Nebraska, DT, 0/0

OAKLAND RAIDERS
1. Michael Huff, Texas, DB, 0/0
2. Thomas Howard, Texas-El Paso, LB, 0/0
3. Paul McQuistan, Weber State, T, 0/0
4. Darnell Bing, USC, DB, 0/0
6. Kevin Boothe, Cornell, T, 0/0
7. Chris Morris, Michigan State, C, 0/0
7. Kevin McMahan, Maine, WR, 0/0

PHILADELPHIA EAGLES
1. Brodrick Bunkley, Florida State, DT, 0/0
2. Winston Justice, USC, T, 0/0
3. Chris Gocong, Cal Poly, DE, 0/0
4. Max Jean-Gilles, Georgia, G, 0/0
4. Jason Avant, Michigan, WR, 0/0
5. Jeremy Bloom, Colorado, DB, 0/0
5. Omar Gaither, Tennessee, LB, 0/0
6. LaJuan Ramsey, USC, DT, 0/0

PITTSBURGH STEELERS
1. Santonio Holmes, Ohio State, FB, 0/0
2. Tarvaris Jackson, Alabama State, QB, 0/0

3. Anthony Smith, Syracuse, DB, 0/0
3. Willie Reid, Florida State, WR, 0/0
4. Willie Colon, Hofstra, G, 0/0
4. Orien Harris, Miami (FL), DT, 0/0
5. Omar Jacobs, Bowling Green, QB, 0/0
5. Charles Davis, Purdue, TE, 0/0
6. Marvin Philip, California, C, 0/0
7. Cedric Humes, Virginia Tech, RB, 0/0

SAN DIEGO CHARGERS
1. Antonio Cromartie, Florida State, DB, 0/0
2. Marcus McNeill, Auburn, T, 0/0
3. Charlie Whitehurst, Clemson, QB, 0/0
5. Tim Dobbins, Iowa State, LB, 0/0
6. Jeromey Clary, Kansas State, T, 0/0
6. Kurt Smith, Virginia, K, 0/0
7. Chase Page, North Carolina, DT, 0/0
7. Jimmy Martin, Virginia Tech, C, 0/0

SAN FRANCISCO 49ERS
1. Vernon Davis, Maryland, TE, 0/0
1. Manny Lawson, North Carolina State, DE, 0/0
3. Brandon Williams, Wisconsin, WR, 0/0
4. Michael Robinson, Penn State, WR, 0/0
5. Parys Haralson, Tennessee, DE, 0/0
6. Delanie Walker, Central Missouri State, WR, 0/0
6. Marcus Hudson, North Carolina State, DB, 0/0

6. Melvin Oliver, LSU, DE, 0/0
7. Vickiel Vaughn, Arkansas, DB, 0/0

ST. LOUIS RAMS
1. Tye Hill, Clemson, DB, 0/0
2. Joe Klopfenstein, Colorado, TE, 0/0
3. Claude Wroten, LSU, DT, 0/0
3. Jon Alston, Stanford, LB, 0/0
3. Dominique Byrd, USC, TE, 0/0
4. Victor Adeyanju, Indiana, DE, 0/0
5. Marques Hagans, Virginia, WR, 0/0
7. Tim McGarigle, Northwestern, LB, 0/0
7. Mark Setterstrom, Minnesota, G, 0/0
7. Tony Palmer, Missouri, G, 0/0

SEATTLE SEAHAWKS
1. Kelly Jennings, Miami (FL), DB, 0/0
2. Darryl Tapp, Virginia Tech, DE, 0/0
4. Rob Sims, Ohio State, G, 0/0
5. David Kirtman, USC, RB, 0/0
7. Ryan Plackemeier, Wake Forest, P, 0/0
7. Ben Obomanu, Auburn, WR, 0/0

TAMPA BAY BUCCANEERS
1. Davin Joseph, Oklahoma, G, 0/0
2. Jeremy Trueblood, Boston College, T, 0/0
3. Maurice Stovall, Notre Dame, WR, 0/0
4. Alan Zemaitis, Penn State, DB, 0/0
5. Julian Jenkins, Stanford, DE, 0/0
6. Bruce Gradkowski, Toldeo, QB, 0/0

6. T.J. Williams, North Carolina State, TE, 0/0
7. Justin Phinisee, Oregon, DB, 0/0
7. Charles Bennett, Clemson, LB, 0/0
7. Tim Massaquoi, Michigan, TE, 0/0

TENNESSEE TITANS
1. Vince Young, Texas, QB, 0/0
2. Lendale White, USC, RB, 0/0
4. Calvin Lowry, Penn State, DB, 0/0
4. Joe Toledo, Washington, T, 0/0
4. Stephen Tulloch, North Carolina State, LB, 0/0
5. Terna Nande, Miami (OH), LB, 0/0
5. Jesse Mahelona, Tennessee, DT, 0/0
6. Jonathan Orr, Wisconsin, WR, 0/0
7. Cortland Finnegan, Samford, DB, 0/0
7. Spencer Toone, Utah, LB, 0/0
7. Quinton Ganther, Utah, RB, 0/0

WASHINGTON REDSKINS
2. Rocky McIntosh, Miami (FL), LB, 0/0
5. Anthony Montgomery, Minnesota, NT, 0/0
6. Reed Doughty, Colorado, DB, 0/0
6. Kedric Golston, Georgia, DT, 0/0
7. Kili Lefotu, Arizona, G, 0/0
7. Kevin Simon, Tennessee, LB, 0/0

THE STADIUMS

There are no books in libraries or bookstores filled with essays and photographs of National Football League stadiums. Tourists do not generally visit NFL stadiums just to take tours. The actual fields themselves look almost exactly the same, aside from the logos and the difference between turf and grass. Fans attend football games to watch the game itself alongside thousands of other fans; they do not go to soak in the atmosphere of the stadium. Football fans rarely wax nostalgic about old football stadiums the way baseball fans lament the loss of Tiger Stadium, hockey fans nostalgically yearn for the Montreal Forum, or basketball fans grieve for about the old Boston Garden. In some ways, football stadiums today are just as utilitarian as they've always been. NFL owners know that their games are the main event, and that their stadiums are there to make it comfortable for fans to watch the game.

Even the league's two remaining great gray ladies, Lambeau Field in Green Bay and Soldier Field in Chicago, have undergone major renovations in the past five years. They are today much closer to the new palaces built in the past decade than they are to the stadiums that housed teams touched by Curly Lambeau or George Halas.

And yet, the way NFL teams and fans look at stadiums has changed significantly over the NFL's history. When the league first started in the 1920s, the NFL expected little more from its stadiums than 100 yards to play on and some seats to which they could sell tickets. Some early teams didn't even have their own home fields and spent entire seasons on the road. Other teams had fields that they called home but played most of their schedule on the road anyway for financial or scheduling reasons. And many home fields were hardly suitable for a professional football team and its fans. During the second decade of the 20th century, most major league baseball teams had constructed ballparks that were considered palaces for their fans. The NFL, however, would not make stadiums that high a priority for another half a century. It was not unusual during the league's first two decades for NFL teams to play games on high school fields.

Many NFL teams used baseball parks as their home fields, but those NFL teams would have to fit their home games in by working around the baseball schedule, and the shape of many baseball stadiums was also less than ideal for football teams. Almost any of these NFL teams would consider themselves fortunate to be able to use the stadium of a major college football program. College football was far more popular in those days than the professional game, and college football powers almost always had better facilities than the professional teams. (Even today, college football stadiums resonate with their teams' fans significantly more than the stadiums of professional teams do with their fans; the few books in print devoted to football venues.)

The popularity of professional football increased sharply in the 1950s and 1960s, and that increase had a profound effect on the NFL's stadium situations. NFL teams were no longer satisfied with just finding someplace acceptable to play. Neutral site games were mostly a thing of the past. Teams wanted stadiums they could call home. And American cities were ready to pay attention. Football was no longer just an afterthought to baseball as far as stadium planning was concerned.

This situation gave rise to the multipurpose stadium. The first multipurpose stadium to open was DC Stadium, which would later be renamed for Robert F. Kennedy. While the baseball Washington Senators would be DC Stadium's primary tenant, the stadium was constructed in a way so that it could easily host football. The Washington Redskins played their first game there on October 1, 1961, and long outlived the relocated Senators in the venue. Many other cities followed Washington's lead and multipurpose stadiums soon sprouted up all over the country. Baseball teams would later regret their move into these stadiums, but at the time they were perfectly happy to move to shiny new modern ballparks. But it would

be pro football teams that would benefit the most from this trend, because these stadiums were a definite step up for the now vibrant league. In seven and eight home games per year, NFL teams could fill the huge amount of seats that ringed two- and three-deck behemoths, but baseball teams, playing far more games, were lucky to sell all 55,000-plus seats a few days per year.

The most important of the new multipurpose stadiums would be the Astrodome. The ability to play indoors was an appealing idea to many NFL teams in extreme climates. And while artificial turf was only installed in the Astrodome as a last resort, many football teams would find the turf to have many benefits. Players didn't like the harder and hotter artificial turf, but in colder climates the grass would shrivel away by the end of the year anyway. A playoff game at many northern stadiums on natural grass was often played on dirt spray-painted green.

The era of the multipurpose stadium would come to a sudden halt in the 1990s. The huge success of Baltimore's Camden Yards led most major league teams to decide that baseball-only stadiums were the way to go. The NFL, which by now was clearly the most successful pro sports league in the country by far, was ready for the divorce. Over the next decade, more than half the teams in the league would start building or planning lavish new stadiums with luxury boxes galore. Several older stadiums underwent football-related changes, notably in San Diego and Oakland, despite repercussions for baseball teams still playing there at the time.

Most cities were more than accommodating to the NFL's needs, though stadium battles were far from rare. Some teams would find themselves behind in the stadium race because their state was willing to spend hundreds of millions of dollars on a new pro football stadium. Commissioner Paul Tagliabue promised new stadiums built in warmer climates or in domes would be on the short list to host a Super Bowl, where prestige and tourism dollars would be pumped into the economy at a traditionally slow time of year.

The expansion Houston Texans became the first team to open a retractable roof stadium in 2002. The Arizona Cardinals completed the second such facility in 2006, but the Cards upped the ante with the first field that retracts to get more sunshine on the grass. The New York Jets and the New York Giants agreed to build a new stadium together, the only shared stadium in the same sport in either the major leagues or the NFL.

It has been a long trip for the NFL. Utility has given way to luxury. The owners have turned the facilities into cash cows that milk out millions in naming fees, license fees, and all manner of in-stadium signage. Fans have happily absorbed the extra costs. Some teams have waiting lists for season tickets for which people may wait decades. In places like Green Bay, fans often sign up their children onto the waiting list at birth despite the knowledge that the estimated time on the list may extend so long that the newborn may be an octogenarian when the name finally comes up on the list. Attempts by some teams to charge to be on such waiting lists have caused even bigger uproars than increases in seat licenses or ticket prices.

Almost every team in the NFL today is inextricably linked with its stadium. The idea of willingly giving up a home game to play at a neutral site is almost unimaginable for an NFL team. The Cardinals did it in 2005 to host the first-ever NFL game in Mexico, but the franchise did so with the knowledge that their impending state-of-the-art stadium could do something neither Sun Devil Stadium nor any of the other dozen places they've played in have ever done on a regular basis: Bring them sellouts. With sellouts comes the lifting of blackouts, so that those without seats can watch on television. And those who watch will want to see for themselves the inside of the newest NFL palace. Curly Lambeau and George Halas couldn't have drawn it up any better themselves.

ACTIVE TEAMS

STADIUM	CITY	NOTE	YEARS	SURFACE	CAPACITY
ARIZONA CARDINALS / PHOENIX CARDINALS / ST. LOUIS CARDINALS / CHICAGO CARDINALS / RACINE CARDINALS					
Normal Park	Chicago, IL	selected games 1922–25	1920–28	Grass	
Comiskey Park (I)	Chicago, IL	capacity was 32,000 in the early twenties, 52,000 at end of decade	1922–25, 1929–30, 1938, 1940–58	Grass	74,000
Wrigley Field	Chicago, IL	two games in 1920; one in 1958	1920, 1931–37, 1939, 1958	Grass	38,000
Forbes Field	Pittsburgh, PA	selected games 1944 while merged with Steelers as Card–Pitt	1944	Grass	35,000
Buffalo Civic Stadium	Buffalo, NY	aka War Memorial Stadium; one game each season	1938, 1940, 1942, 1943, 1958	Grass	45,748
Wisconsin State Fair Park	Milwaukee, WI	one game	1945	Grass	
Soldier Field (I)	Chicago, IL	—	1959	Grass	74,000
Metropolitan Stadium	Bloomington, MN	two games	1959	Grass	45,919
Busch Stadium (I)	St. Louis, MO	—	1960–65	Grass	34,000
Busch Stadium (II)	St. Louis, MO	aka Busch Memorial Stadium 1966–83	1966–87	Grass 1966–69, Turf 1970–87	60,000
Sun Devil Stadium	Tempe, AZ		1988–2005	Grass	73,014
Estadio Azteca	Mexico City, Mexico	home team for first game in Mexico	2005	Grass	114,465
Cardinals Stadium	Glendale, AZ	retractable dome, field	2006–	Grass	63,000
ATLANTA FALCONS					
Atlanta Fulton County Stadium	Atlanta, GA	aka Atlanta Stadium 1966–74	1966–91	Grass	60,700
Georgia Dome	Atlanta, GA	—	1992–	Turf	71,228
BALTIMORE RAVENS					
Memorial Stadium	Baltimore, MD	—	1996–97	Grass	65,000
M&T Bank Stadium	Baltimore, MD	aka Ravens Stadium 1998, 2002; PSINet Stadium 1999–2001 1998–2003; Turf 2004– 69,084	1998–	Grass	
BUFFALO BILLS					
War Memorial Stadium	Buffalo, NY	—	1960–72	Grass	46,201
Ralph Wilson Stadium	Buffalo, NY	aka Rich Stadium 1973–97	1973–	Turf	73,967
CAROLINA PANTHERS					
Clemson Memorial Stadium	Clemson, SC	—	1995	Grass	86,400
Bank of America Stadium	Charlotte, NC	aka Ericsson Stadium 1996–2003	1996–	Grass	73,298
CHICAGO BEARS / CHICAGO STALEYS / DECATUR STALEYS					
Staley Field	Decatur, IL	—	1920	Grass	—
Wrigley Field	Chicago, IL	aka Cubs Park 1921–26	1921–70	Grass	38,000
Chicago Stadium	Chicago, IL	special tiebreaking game moved inside due to blizzard	1932	—	17,317
Soldier Field (I)	Chicago, IL		1971–2001	Grass 1971–77, 1988–2001; Turf 1978–87	66,944
Memorial Stadium	Champaign, IL	—	2002	Turf	70,904
Soldier Field (II)	Chicago, IL	—	2003–	Grass	61,500
CLEVELAND BROWNS					
Cleveland Stadium	Cleveland, OH	aka Cleveland Municipal Stadium	1946–95	Grass	78,512
Cleveland Browns Stadium	Cleveland, OH	—	1999–	Grass	73,300
CINCINNATI BENGALS					
Nippert Stadium	Cincinnati, OH	—	1968–69	Grass	24,000
Cinergy Field	Cincinnati, OH	aka Riverfront Stadium 1970–96	1970–99	Turf	60,400
Paul Brown Stadium	Cincinnati, OH	—	2000–	Grass 2000–03; Turf 2004–	65,326
DALLAS COWBOYS					
Cotton Bowl	Dallas, TX	—	1960–70	Grass	68,252
Texas Stadium	Irving, TX	partial dome: stands mostly covered, not field	1971–	Turf	65,529
DENVER BRONCOS					
Mile High Stadium	Denver, CO	—	1960–2000	Grass	80,227
INVESCO Field at Mile High	Denver, CO	—	2001–	Grass	76,125
DETROIT LIONS / PORTSMOUTH SPARTANS					
Universal Stadium	Portsmouth, OH	aka Spartan Municipal Stadium	1930–33	Grass	—
Titan Stadium	Detroit, MI	one game in 1938 and two games in 1939	1934–39	Grass	—
Tiger Stadium	Detroit, MI	aka Briggs Stadium 1938–60	1938–74	Grass	52,416
Pontiac Silverdome	Pontiac, MI	dome	1975–2001	Turf	80,311
Ford Field	Detroit, MI	dome	2002–	Turf	64,500
GREEN BAY PACKERS					
Hagemeister Park	Green Bay, WI	—	1921–22	Grass	—
Bellevue Field	Green Bay, WI	—	1923–24	Grass	—
City Stadium	Green Bay, WI	aka Packer Stadium from 1925–30	1925–56	Grass	15,000
Borchert Field	Milwaukee, WI	one game	1933	Grass	
Wisconsin State Fair Park	Milwaukee, WI	selected games	1934–51	Grass	—
Marquette Stadium	Milwaukee, WI	selected games	1952	Grass	15,000
Milwaukee County Stadium	Milwaukee, WI	aka Milwaukee Stadium 1953; selected games	1953–94	Grass	53,192
Lambeau Field	Green Bay, WI	aka City Stadium 1957–64	1957–	Grass	72,601
HOUSTON TEXANS					
Reliant Stadium	Houston, TX	retractable roof	2002–	Grass	71,054
INDIANAPOLIS COLTS / BALTIMORE COLTS					
Memorial Stadium	Baltimore, MD	—	1953–83	Grass	65,000
RCA Dome	Indianapolis, IN	dome, aka Hoosier Dome 1984–93	1984–	Turf	55,506
JACKSONVILLE JAGUARS					
Alltel Stadium	Jacksonville, FL	aka ALLTEL Stadium 1998–2004; aka Jacksonville Municipal Stadium 1995–97	1995–	Grass	67,164
KANSAS CITY CHIEFS / DALLAS TEXANS					
Cotton Bowl	Dallas, TX	—	1960–62	Grass	68,252
Kansas City Municipal Stadium	Kansas City, MO	—	1963–71	Grass	49,002
Arrowhead Stadium	Kansas City, MO	—	1972–	Turf 1972–93; Grass 1994–	79,451
MIAMI DOLPHINS					
Orange Bowl	Miami, FL	—	1966–86	Grass	72,319
Tampa Stadium	Tampa, FL	one game	1969	Grass	40,000
Dolphin Stadium	Miami, FL	aka Joe Robbie Stadium 1987–95; Pro Player Park 1996, Pro Player Stadium 1996–2004, Dolphins Stadium 2005	1987–	Grass	75,192

ACTIVE TEAMS (CONT.)

STADIUM	CITY	NOTE	YEARS	SURFACE	CAPACITY
MINNESOTA VIKINGS					
Metropolitan Stadium	Bloomington, MN	—	1961–81	Grass	45,919
Hubert H. Humphrey Metrodome	Minneapolis, MN	dome	1982–	Turf	64,121
NEW ENGLAND PATRIOTS / BOSTON PATRIOTS					
Nickerson Field	Boston, MA	—	1960–62	Grass	15,000
Fenway Park	Boston, MA	—	1963–68	Grass	33,375
Legion Field	Birmingham, AL	one game	1968	Grass	83,000
Alumni Stadium	Newton, MA	—	1969	Grass	44,500
Harvard Stadium	Cambridge, MA	—	1970	Grass	30,898
Foxboro Stadium	Foxboro, MA	aka Schaeffer Stadium 1971–82; Sullivan Stadium 1983–89	1971–2001	Grass	60,292
Gillette Stadium	Foxboro, MA	aka CMGI Field 2002 prior to Patriots' first game	2002–	Grass	68,756
NEW ORLEANS SAINTS					
Tulane Stadium	New Orleans, LA	aka The Sugar Bowl	1967–74	Grass	80,985
Louisiana Superdome	New Orleans, LA	dome	1975–2004, 2006–	Turf	64,900
Tiger Stadium	Baton Rouge, LA	four games in 2005	2005	Grass	91,027
Giants Stadium	East Rutherford, NJ	one game in 2005	2005	Grass	78,741
Alamodome	San Antonio, TX	dome, three games in 2005	2005	Turf	59,000
NEW YORK JETS					
Polo Grounds	New York, NY	—	1960–63	Grass	55,000
Shea Stadium	New York, NY	—	1964–83	Grass	64,000
Meadowlands	East Rutherford, NJ	aka Giants Stadium (one game there in 1977)	1984–	Turf 1976–97, 2002–; Grass 1998–2001	79,466
NEW YORK GIANTS					
Polo Grounds	New York, NY	—	1925–55	Grass	55,000
Yankee Stadium	New York, NY	one home game in 1973	1956–73	Grass	67,000
Yale Bowl	New Haven, CT	—	1973–74	Grass	64,269
Shea Stadium	New York, NY	—	1975	Grass	64,000
Giants Stadium	East Rutherford, NJ	aka Meadowlands	1976–	Turf 1976–97, 2002–; Grass 1998–2001	80,242
OAKLAND RAIDERS / LOS ANGELES RAIDERS					
Kezar Stadium	San Francisco, CA	—	1960	Grass	59,942
Candlestick Park	San Francisco, CA	aka Monster Park	1961	Grass	69,843
Frank Youell Field	Oakland, CA	—	1962–65	Grass	22,000
Oakland–Alameda County Coliseum	Oakland, CA	—	1966–81	Grass	63,026
Los Angeles Memorial Coliseum	Los Angeles, CA	—	1982–94	Grass	92,000
McAfee Coliseum	Oakland, CA	aka Oakland–Alameda County Coliseum 1966–98; Network Associates Coliseum 1999–2004	1995–	Grass	63,192
PHILADELPHIA EAGLES					
Baker Bowl	Philadelphia, PA	aka National League Park	1933–35	Grass	22,000
Philadelphia Municipal Stadium	Philadelphia, PA	aka John F. Kennedy Stadium	1936–39	Grass	75,000
Temple Stadium	Philadelphia, PA	one game each season	1934–35	Grass	30,000
Point Stadium	Youngstown, OH	one game	1936	Grass	10,000
Connie Mack Stadium	Philadelphia, PA	aka Shibe Park 1940–52	1940–57	Grass	33,000
Erie Stadium	Erie, PA	one game; high school field	1938	Grass	
Buffalo Civic Stadium	Buffalo, NY	aka War Memorial Stadium; one game	1942	Grass	45,748
Forbes Field	Pittsburgh, PA	selected games 1943 while team merged with Steelers as "Steagles"	1943	Grass	35,000
Franklin Field	Philadelphia, PA	—	1958–70	Grass	52,593
Veterans Stadium	Philadelphia, PA	—	1971–2002	Turf	65,352
Lincoln Financial Field	Philadelphia, PA	—	2003–	Grass	68,400
PITTSBURGH STEELERS / PITTSBURGH PIRATES					
Forbes Field	Pittsburgh, PA	—	1933–63	Grass	35,000
Laidley Field	Charleston, WV	one game; high school field	1938	Grass	
Tulane Stadium	New Orleans, LA	one game	1938	Grass	35,000
Shibe Park	Philadelphia, PA	selected games 1943 while team merged with Eagles as "Steagles"	1943	Grass	33,000
Comiskey Park (I)	Chicago, IL	selected games 1944 while team merged with Cardinals as Card–Pitt	1944	Grass	74,000
Pitt Stadium	Pittsburgh, PA	selected games 1958–63	1958–69	Grass	56,150
Three Rivers Stadium	Pittsburgh, PA	—	1970–2000	Turf	65,900
Heinz Field	Pittsburgh, PA	—	2001–	Grass	64,350
ST. LOUIS RAMS / LOS ANGELES RAMS / CLEVELAND RAMS					
League Park	Cleveland, OH	—	1937, 1942–43, 1945	Grass	—
Shaw Stadium	Cleveland, OH	—	1938	Grass	—
Municipal Stadium	Cleveland, OH	aka Cleveland Municipal Stadium	1939–41	Grass	78,512
Broadmoor Stadium	Colorado Springs, CO	—	1939	Grass	
Rubber Bowl	Akron, OH	one game both years	1941–42	Grass	—
Los Angeles Memorial Coliseum	Los Angeles, CA	—	1946–79	Grass	92,000
Anaheim Stadium	Anaheim, CA	—	1980–94	Grass	70,500
Busch Stadium (II)	St. Louis, MO	three games before new stadium was completed	1995	Turf	50,345
Edward Jones Dome	St. Louis, MO	dome, aka Trans World Dome 1995–2001; Dome at America's Center 2002	1995–	Turf	66,000
SAN DIEGO CHARGERS / LOS ANGELES CHARGERS					
Los Angeles Memorial Coliseum	Los Angeles, CA	—	1960	Grass	92,000
Balboa Stadium	San Diego, CA	—	1961–66	Grass	34,500
Qualcomm Stadium	San Diego, CA	aka San Diego Stadium 1967–80; Jack Murphy Stadium 1981–96	1967–	Grass	70,000
Sun Devil Stadium	Tempe, AZ	one game in 2003	2003	Grass	69,732
SAN FRANCISCO 49ERS					
Kezar Stadium	San Francisco, CA	—	1946–70	Grass	59,942
Monster Park	San Francisco, CA	aka Candlestick Park 1971–94, 3Com Park 1995–2001; San Francisco Stadium at Candlestick Point 2002–04	1971–	Turf 1971–78; Grass 1979–	69,843
Stanford Stadium	Stanford, CA	one game in 1989	1989	Grass	85,500
SEATTLE SEAHAWKS					
Kingdome	Seattle, WA	dome	1976–98	Turf	66,000
Husky Stadium	Seattle, WA	—	1994, 2000–01	Turf	72,500

Active Teams (cont.)

STADIUM	CITY	NOTE	YEARS	SURFACE	CAPACITY
Qwest Field	Seattle, WA	partial dome: stands mostly covered, not field; aka Seahawks Stadium 2002–03	2002–	Turf	67,000

Tampa Bay Buccaneers

Houlihan Stadium	Tampa, FL	aka Tampa Stadium 1976–94	1976–97	Grass	74,300
Raymond James Stadium	Tampa, FL	—	1998–	Grass	65,657

Tennessee Titans / Tennessee Oilers / Houston Oilers

Jeppesen Stadium	Houston, TX	—	1960–64	Grass	33,000
Rice Stadium	Houston, TX	—	1965–67	Grass	71,882
Astrodome	Houston, TX	aka Harris County Domed Stadium in 1965	1968–96	Turf	60,000
Liberty Bowl	Memphis, TN	—	1997	Grass	62,380
Vanderbilt Stadium	Nashville, TN	—	1998	Grass	41,203
The Coliseum	Nashville, TN	aka Adelphia Coliseum 1999–2001	1999–	Grass	68,809

Washington Redskins / Boston Redskins / Boston Braves

Braves Field	Boston, MA	—	1932	Grass	40,000
Fenway Park	Boston, MA	—	1933–36	Grass	33,375
Griffith Stadium	Washington, DC	—	1937–60	Grass	36,034
Robert F. Kennedy Memorial Stadium	Washington, DC	aka D.C. Stadium 1961–68	1961–96	Grass	56,454
FedEx Field	Hyattsville, MD	aka Jack Kent Cooke Stadium 1997–99	1997–	Grass	91,665

Defunct Teams

STADIUM	CITY	NOTE	YEARS	SURFACE	CAPACITY

Akron Pros / Akron Indians

League Park	Akron, OH	—	1920–21	Grass	—
Elk's Field	Akron, OH	—	1922	Grass	—
Wooster Avenue Stadium	Akron, OH	—	1923	Grass	—
General Tire Field	Akron, OH	—	1924–25	Grass	—
Rubber Bowl	Akron, OH	—	1926	Grass	—

Baltimore Colts AAFC–NFL / Miami Seahawks AAFC

Orange Bowl	Miami, FL	—	1946	Grass	72,319
Babe Ruth Stadium	Baltimore, MD	aka Municipal Stadium	1947–49	Grass	20,000
Memorial Stadium	Baltimore, MD	team spent this one year in NFL	1950	Grass	65,000

Boston Bulldogs

Braves Field	Boston, MA	—	1929	Grass	40,000

Boston Yanks

Fenway Park	Boston, MA	—	1944–48	Grass	33,375
Yankee Stadium	New York, NY	one game in 1945 as result of merger with Brooklyn Dodgers	1945	Grass	67,000

Brooklyn Lions

Ebbets Field	Brooklyn, NY	—	1926	Grass	32,000

Brooklyn Tigers / Brooklyn Dodgers / Dayton Triangles

Triangle Park	Dayton, OH	—	1920–29	Grass	—
Ebbets Field	Brooklyn, NY	team merged with Boston Yanks in 1945	1930–44	Grass	32,000

Brooklyn Dodgers AAFC

Ebbets Field	Brooklyn, NY	merged with AAFC New York Yankees in 1949	1946–49	Grass	32,000

Buffalo All-Americans / Buffalo Bisons / Buffalo Rangers

Canisius Villa	Buffalo, NY	—	1920–21	Grass	—
Buffalo Baseball Park	Buffalo, NY	—	1922–23	Grass	—
Bison Stadium	Buffalo, NY	—	1924–27, 1929	Grass	—

Buffalo Bisons / Buffalo Bills AAFC

War Memorial Stadium	Buffalo, NY	aka Buffalo Civic Stadium	1946–49	Grass	45,748

Canton Bulldogs

Lakeside Park	Canton, OH	aka League Park 1920; team merged with Cleveland for 1924 season	1920–23, 1925–26	Grass	—

Chicago Rockets / Chicago Hornets AAFC

Soldier Field (I)	Chicago, IL	—	1946–49	Grass	74,000

Chicago Tigers

Cubs Park	Chicago, IL	aka Wrigley Field	1920	Grass	38,000

Cincinnati Celts

Redland Field	Cincinnati, OH	aka Crosley Field	1921	Grass	25,000

Cincinnati Reds

Crosley Field	Cincinnati, OH	aka Redland Field in 1933, only one home game in 1934	1933–34	Grass	30,000

Cleveland Bulldogs / Cleveland Indians

League Park	Cleveland, OH	aka Dunn Field	1923–25	Grass	—
Luna Bowl	Cleveland, OH	—	1927	Grass	—

Cleveland Indians

Municipal Stadium	Cleveland, OH	aka Cleveland Municipal Stadium	1931	Grass	78,512

Cleveland Tigers / Cleveland Indians

League Park	Cleveland, OH	aka Dunn Field	1920–21	Grass	—

Columbus Panhandles / Columbus Tigers

Neil Park	Columbus, OH	no home games in 1920	1920–23	Grass	—
Westside Athletic Park	Columbus, OH	—	1924–26	Grass	—

Dallas Texans / New York Yanks / New York Bulldogs

Polo Grounds	New York, NY	—	1949	Grass	55,000
Yankee Stadium	New York, NY	—	1950–51	Grass	67,000
Cotton Bowl	Dallas, TX	—	1952	Grass	68,252
Rubber Bowl	Akron, OH	one game	1952	Grass	—

Detroit Heralds

Navin Field	Detroit, MI	aka Tiger Stadium	1920	Grass	23,000

Detroit Tigers

Navin Field	Detroit, MI	aka Tiger Stadium	1921	Grass	23,000

DEFUNCT TEAMS (CONT.)

STADIUM	CITY	NOTE	YEARS	SURFACE	CAPACITY
DETROIT TIGERS / DETROIT PANTHERS					
Navin Field	Detroit, MI	aka Tiger Stadium	1925–26	Grass	30,000
Detroit Wolverines					
TITAN STADIUM	**DETROIT, MI**	—	**1928**	**GRASS**	—
DULUTH KELLEYS / DULUTH ESKIMOS / ORANGE TORNADOES / NEWARK TORNADOES					
Athletic Park	Duluth, MN	—	1923–27	Grass	—
Knights of Columbus Field	Orange, NJ	aka Bell Stadium	1929	Grass	—
Newark Schools Stadium	Newark, NJ	—	1930	Grass	—
EVANSVILLE CRIMSON GIANTS					
Evansville Field	Evansville, IN	no home games in 1922	1921–22	Grass	
FRANKFORD YELLOW JACKETS					
Frankford Stadium	Frankford, PA		1924–30	Grass	—
Baker Bowl	Philadelphia, PA	aka National League Park	1931	Grass	18,800
HAMMOND PROS					
Gleason Field	Hammond, IN	no home games 1920–22 or 1924–25	1920–26	Grass	
HARTFORD BLUES					
East Hartford Velodrome	Hartford, CT	—	1926	Grass	
KANSAS CITY COWBOYS / KANSAS CITY BLUES					
Muehlebach Field	Kansas City, MO	aka Municipal Stadium	1924–26	Grass	49,002
KENOSHA MAROONS					
Nash Field	Kenosha, WI	—	1924	Grass	
LOS ANGELES BUCCANEERS					
—		team played only road games	1926	—	
LOS ANGELES DONS AAFC					
Los Angeles Memorial Coliseum	Los Angeles, CA		1946–49	Grass	92,000
LOUISVILLE BRECKS / LOUISVILLE COLONELS					
Eclipse Park	Louisville, KY	—	1921	Grass	—
Kentucky Fairgrounds	Louisville, KY	one game	1922	Grass	—
Parkway Field	Louisville, KY	—	1923	Grass	—
—	—	team played only road games	1926	—	—
MILWAUKEE BADGERS					
Athletic Park	Milwaukee, WI	aka Borchert Field	1922–26	Grass	
MINNEAPOLIS MARINES / MINNEAPOLIS RED JACKETS					
Nicollet Park	Minneapolis, MN	—	1921–24, 1929–30	Grass	—
MUNCIE FLYERS					
Walnut Street Stadium	Muncie, IN	no home games in 1920	1920–21	Grass	
NEW YORK BRICKLEY GIANTS					
Polo Grounds	New York, NY	—	1921	Grass	34,000
NEW YORK YANKEES					
Yankee Stadium	New York, NY		1927–28	Grass	67,000
NEW YORK YANKEES AAFC					
Yankee Stadium	New York, NY		1946–49	Grass	67,000
OORANG INDIANS					
Lincoln Park	Marion, OH	Indians played just one home game in 1922; no home game in 1923	1922–23	Grass	—
POTTSVILLE MAROONS / BOSTON BULLDOGS					
Minersville Park	Minersville, PA	—	1925–28	Grass	—
Braves Field	Boston, MA	—	1929	Grass	40,000
PROVIDENCE STEAM ROLLER					
Providence Cycledrome	Providence, RI	—	1925–31	Grass	—
RACINE LEGION / RACINE TORNADOES					
Racine Baseball Association Field	Racine, WI	—	1922–24, 1926	Grass	—
ROCHESTER JEFFERSONS					
Bay Street Park	Rochester, NY	no home games in 1920	1920–21	Grass	—
Edgerton Park	Rochester, NY	no home games in 1923 or 1925	1922–25	Grass	—
ROCK ISLAND INDEPENDENTS					
Douglas Park	Rock Island, IL	—	1920–25	Grass	—
ST. LOUIS ALL-STARS					
Sportsman's Park	St. Louis, MO	aka Busch Stadium (I)	1923	Grass	34,000
ST. LOUIS GUNNERS					
Sportsman's Park	St. Louis, MO	aka Busch Stadium (I)	1934	Grass	34,000
STATEN ISLAND STAPLETONS					
Thompson's Stadium	New York, NY	—	1929–32	Grass	—
TOLEDO MAROONS					
Swayne Field	Toledo, OH	—	1922	Grass	—
Armory Park	Toledo, OH	—	1923	Grass	—
TONAWANDA KARDEX					
—		team played only one game (on road) and folded	1921	—	—
WASHINGTON SENATORS					
National Park	Washington, DC	aka Griffith Stadium	1921	Grass	32,000
NEUTRAL SITE STADIUMS (POSTSEASON AND EXHIBITION)					
Rose Bowl Stadium	Pasadena, CA	Super Bowl	1976, 1979, 1982, 1986, 1992	Grass	93,000
Gator Bowl Stadium	Jacksonville, FL	AFL All–Star Game	1967–68	Grass	42,000
Gilmore Stadium	Los Angeles, CA	NFL All–Star Game	1939–40	Grass	18,000
Wrigley Field	Los Angeles, CA	NFL All–Star Game	1938	Grass	22,000
Aloha Stadium	Honolulu, HI	Pro Bowl	1980–	Turf	50,000

HOW THIS ENCYCLOPEDIA WAS BORN

Mini-biographies of the editors and contributors to this imposing work are fine, but they don't tell the whole story. The roots of this encyclopedia literally go back decades to a lifelong fascination with pro football statistics that formed in the mind of a young football fan. Here are the personal recollections of the two people without whom this encyclopedia would never have been born.

Ken Pullis. My interest in pro football statistics dates back to the late 1950s when I came across an early edition of Roger Treat's *Official Encyclopedia of Football* in my school library. It didn't have a lot of player statistics, but it did list league leaders, record holders, and 1,000-yard rushers. I was hooked. Unfortunately, in those days the only source for pro football stats that I knew about was in the pro football preview magazines that would be published each summer; they listed most of the previous year's individual statistics.

Because of the lack of available information, I began keeping my own list of 1,000-yard rushers as well as other career data when I could find it—which wasn't often. *The Sporting News* made significant contributions to football researchers in 1967 when it published its first annual *Football Register,* with season-by-season statistics for the careers of active players. These early registers also included statistics for selected retired players. However, it wasn't until 1974 when David Neft and Richard Cohen published their first *Encyclopedia of Pro Football* that I was able to obtain single-season and career statistics for everyone who played since 1932, when the NFL began keeping track of official statistics. I purchased many editions of their annual paperback book over the years, and their hardcover 1991 *The Football Encyclopedia* maintains a place of honor in my bookshelf today.

In 1967, *The Sporting News* began publishing box scores that enabled me to track game-by-game data for prominent players. In 1977, I switched to *Pro Football Weekly* because it published more information. I began keeping track of a variety of statistics but didn't begin any original research until the late 1980s. That's when I started compiling a list of 100-yard receivers, quickly expanding it to include 100-yard rushers and receivers and 300-yard passers. It was this work that brought me into contact with Pete Palmer, who has unselfishly aided my efforts in countless ways.

Palmer's interest was mainly in team data, but we found combining our efforts helped us both. Over the past 15 years we have exchanged thousands of e-mails; although we have met only once, we have become friends. Working on this project introduced me to the tremendous research resources available at the Pro Football Hall of Fame in Canton. The late 1990s brought the MacMillan *Pro Football Encyclopedia* and two editions of *Total Football*. Both showed year-by-year statistics for all players, which had not been published previously.

Along with Palmer, several other individuals have contributed to my work. Foremost among them are Pete Fierle and his great staff at the Hall of Fame research library. Others include Bob Carroll, Eric Goska, Tod Maher, Terry Musolf, and T.J. Troup. Joe Cronin provided access to out-of-print record books, media guides and other publications.

In the early 1980s, I purchased a Commodore 64 computer to help me do my work more efficiently. The time it saved allowed me to expand my interests to include much of the data in this book and to later compile nearly complete game-by-game stats for players going back to 1960. I'm now on my fifth computer. I'm eternally grateful to my friend Steve Supanich, who convinced me in the late 1990s that the Internet would be a valuable resource. It has become the primary source for game-by-game and other data, as well as a way to communicate with fellow researchers.

Pete Palmer. I got started on my work in football by editing several editions in the 1970s of the old Barnes *Official Encyclopedia of Football*, which had been originated by Roger Treat. I was given the job based on my work with their baseball encyclopedia. As a result of my research for that book, I was invited to join the stat crew of the Patriots, where I have been now for 32 years. We collect the official stats for the league at all home games. It was originally all done by hand except for the typewritten play-by-play record, but has since been completely computerized.

I became interested in team game stats, which began being published in newspapers around 1939, trying to get them entered into the computer and then to get them to add up to the official data as published in the annual football guides. In those years, there were usually several hundred changes made to the stats after games, many of which did not even make it into the box scores published after the season in the league guides or team media guides. So it became quite a job to try to track these down.

Around this time, Bob Carroll founded the Professional Football Researchers Association. Through this group, I made contact with Ken Pullis, who had started his own research on individual game stats, with the goal of compiling an accurate list of all 100-yard rushers and receivers and 300-yard passers. With the help of Joe Horrigan and several trips to the archives of the Pro Football Hall of Fame in Canton, I was able to get weekly league stat sheets for many years, which helped considerably. I had copies of *Pro Football Weekly* dating back to the start of my subscription in 1978. Later, I made copies of all the game stats from 1967–77 from the Hall of Fame microfilm, obtaining most of the games not on the film with the help of Rick Korch at *PFW*.

Pullis and I began work on getting individual game stats for all categories back to 1960. We ran into the same problem while doing that as with corrections made after the game, and probably have now made 10,000 changes to the original game-by-game stats over this period. After all these changes, we now have virtually complete agreement with the official end-of-season figures.

The major problem in compiling this database has been plays where the player involved was changed—therefore, the team totals remained unchanged—and the player was not among the league leaders. Currently, we have only about 40 of these minor discrepancies left in 46 years of data. The other problem was getting individual return data for the NFL from 1960–66, when newspaper box scores did not show return data for players. We were able to get initial data on returns from 1967 to date from the complete *Pro Football Weekly* box scores, and we were able to compile 1960–66 AFL return data with the help of a good collection of game stats from the Hall of Fame.

ABOUT THE AUTHORS

Executive editor **Gary Gillette** is the co-editor of the *ESPN Baseball Encyclopedia* with Pete Palmer, his longtime collaborator, and a contributor to the *Baseball Prospectus 2006*. Gillette is the president of 24–7 Baseball, L.L.C. and of Luna di Domani, Inc. He was co-author of an extensive article entitled "The Changing Game" in the seventh and eighth editions of *Total Baseball* and the author of a groundbreaking article on the history of the home run in the sixth edition of *Total Baseball*. Gillette was a co-founder and vice president of Total Sports, Inc., an Internet and print sports information publisher headquartered in Raleigh, North Carolina, from 1997 to 1999. Aside from baseball-related consulting work, his current projects include editing a new history of big-league ballparks.

As a baseball columnist for ESPN.com and the author or editor of numerous baseball books, articles, and publications—not to mention a reformed Lions fan—Gillette has never understood why pro football lacked the extensive oeuvre of reference books that baseball fans have enjoyed over the years. Therefore, his goal in planning and laying out this work was to see that the uncounted millions of pro football fans finally got an up-to-date, affordable yet comprehensive encyclopedia worthy of their passion for the game. Gary lives in Detroit's historic Indian Village with his beloved wife Vicki and their two children, Karolina and Kamil.

Pete Palmer is a retired defense-industry computer programmer and a veritable oracle of American professional sports history. Palmer has been breaking new ground in baseball and football research for more than 30 years. His recent collaboration with Ken Pullis has resulted in a comprehensive database of game-by-game pro football statistics that dates back to the origins of the game and that forms the basis of this encyclopedia. Palmer was the co-author of the *Hidden Game of Football* (1988 and 1998) with Bob Carroll and John Thorn and edited the Barnes *Official Encyclopedia of Football* (originated by Roger Treat) during the 1970s. He has been a member of the New England Patriots stat crew since 1975 and is a member of PFRA (Pro Football Researchers Association) and SABR (Society for American Baseball Research).

Palmer's extensive baseball credits include the seminal 1984 book *The Hidden Game of Baseball* (with John Thorn), the first seven editions of *Total Baseball* (with John Thorn), and the *ESPN Baseball Encyclopedia* (with Gary Gillette). Along with his wife Beth and their three children, Palmer splits his time between Hollis in southern New Hampshire and Highland Beach in South Florida.

Ken Pullis is a retired air traffic controller and former military and civilian pilot. Although his professional experience has been in aviation, he has enjoyed a lifelong passion for pro football, especially statistics. He started his research on pro football in 1988 by compiling a list of every 100-yard rusher and receiver as well as every 300-yard passer. This avocation grew into a desire to compile game-by-game statistics for every NFL player in history, starting with the major categories of rushing, receiving, and passing. With Pete Palmer's help, that project grew even more massive, encompassing game-by-game scoring, punting, interceptions, sacks, and punt and kickoff returns; the work is now virtually complete going back to 1960. Pullis has been published by the Professional Football Researchers Association (PFRA) and was their 2002 Ralph E. Hay Award winner for career achievement in pro football research and historiography. He and his wife Jennifer have two grown children and split their time between Lorain, Ohio, and the Space Coast of Florida in Satellite Beach.

Managing editor **Matthew Silverman** was previously the managing editor for the second edition of *Total Football*—the last official encyclopedia of the NFL—as well as seven offshoot books in the series, including *Total Packers*, *Total Steelers*, *Total Cowboys*, *Total 49ers*, and *Total Super Bowl*. As a professional writer and editor

for more than two decades, Silverman was associate publisher at Total Sports Publishing and the principal editor for *Baseball: The Biographical Encyclopedia*. He was also an associate editor for the first three editions of *The ESPN Baseball Encyclopedia* and the managing editor of the sixth and seventh editions of *Total Baseball*, the editor for Ted Williams's 2001 autobiography, *Ted Williams: My Life in Pictures,* and co-editor of *Total Mets*. Silverman also contributed to *Total Baseball Daily* in the late 1990s and the *Total Baseball Companions* series in 2000. A former newspaper editor, he resides in the Hudson Valley in High Falls, N.Y., with his wife Debbie, his daughter Jan, and his son Tyler.

Sean Lahman has authored and edited several books on sports history, including the forthcoming *Historical Football Abstract*. Since 2003, he has covered professional football as a columnist for the *New York Sun*. Lahman was a contributor to the last three editions of the *ESPN Baseball Encyclopedia* and *Total Baseball* and developed statistical content for groundbreaking tennis and basketball encyclopedias. Lahman created the annual *Pro Football Prospectus* and, in 1998, founded the Football Project, an organization of researchers dedicated to collecting and digitizing play-by-play accounts of pro football games. Over the past ten years, he has led the effort to make sports statistics available to the general public, developing and contributing to a number of pioneering Websites. Lahman lives in Rochester in upstate New York with his wife, Heather, and their children Audrey, Henry, and Hannah.

Christina Kahrl may be better known as a co-founder, editor, and major contributor to the *Baseball Prospectus* but, from her earliest youth, she's always relished the game on the gridiron. For five years, she was responsible for building the progressive sports list at Brassey's Sports, publishing cutting-edge sports history and analysis about football, baseball, basketball, tennis, motor sports, and more. In the absence of a good history of the Oakland Raiders or of the game and its innovations in the 1970s and 1980s, she leapt at the invitation to contribute to the *ESPN Pro Football Encyclopedia*. A freelance writer and editor who has contributed articles to ESPN.com, Salon, Slate, *Playboy,* and the *New York Sun* in addition to her regular work at BaseballProspectus.com, she lives in the Washington, D.C., area in Fairfax, Virginia.

Greg Spira is a writer, editor, and researcher who lives in the Hudson Valley in Kingston, N.Y. He has served as an associate editor for all three editions of *The ESPN Baseball Encyclopedia* as well as an associate editor of the seventh edition of *Total Baseball* while working as an editor for Total Sports Publishing. Spira has contributed to sports book such as *Baseball: The Biographical Encyclopedia*, *Total Basketball,* and the *Baseball Prospectus*. A member of the Society for American Baseball Research for more than 15 years and an Internet denizen since the early 1990s, Spira has contributed to many sports Websites, both editorially and conceptually. Baseballbooks.net, a Website he maintains, focuses on sports books.

Tod Maher is an award-winning researcher and writer who lives in Monterey, California with his wife Marilyn. He is the three-time winner of the Nelson Ross Awarded (awarded annually for outstanding research by the Professional Football Researchers Association). He is also the 2001 winner of PFRA's Ralph Hay Award for career achievement in pro football research. He is also co-author of *The Pro Football Encyclopedia*, published by MacMillan in 1999, the *World Football League Encyclopedia,* and *Minor League Football: 1960-1985*. He is also a contributor to *The Football Encyclopedia; The Sports Encyclopedia Pro Football, The Early Years; The Hidden Game of Football: The Next Edition; and 23 Ways to Get to First Base: The ESPN Sports Uncyclopedia.*